THE AUTHORITY SINCE 1868

THE WORLD ALMANAC®

AND BOOK OF FACTS

1994

WORLD ALMANAC
AN IMPRINT OF FUNK & WAGNALLS CORPORATION

THE WORLD ALMANAC®
AND BOOK OF FACTS
1994

Editor: Robert Famighetti
Senior Editor: June Foley
Senior Editor: Thomas McGuire
Associate Editor: Christina Cheddar
Assistant Editor: Michael Northrop
Chronology Editor: Donald Young
Index: Aris Georgiadis

Funk & Wagnalls
Editorial Director: Leon L. Bram
Director of Manufacturing: Sally McCravey
Director of Editorial Production: Andrea J. Pitluk
Copy Editor: Matthew Friedlander
Keyboard Input: Melissa Humbert

World Almanac Books
Publisher: Richard W. Eiger
Sales Manager: James R. Keenley
Publicity Manager: Joyce H. Stein

The editors acknowledge with thanks the many letters of helpful comment and criticism from readers of THE WORLD ALMANAC. Because of the volume of mail directed to the editorial offices, it is not possible to reply to each letter writer. However, every communication is read by the editors and all comments and suggestions receive careful attention.

THE WORLD ALMANAC does not decide wagers.

The first edition of THE WORLD ALMANAC, a 120-page volume with 12 pages of advertising, was published by the New York World in 1868. Annual publication was suspended in 1876. Joseph Pulitzer, publisher of the New York World, revived THE WORLD ALMANAC in 1886 with the goal of making it a "compendium of universal knowledge." It has been published annually since then.

THE WORLD ALMANAC and BOOK OF FACTS 1994

Library of Congress Catalog Card Number 4-3781
International Standard Serial Number (ISSN) 0084-1382
ISBN (softcover) 0-88687-745-8
ISBN (hardcover) 0-88687-746-6
Microform Edition since 1868: University Microfilms Intl.
Printed in the United States of America
The softcover and hardcover editions are distributed to the trade in the United States by St. Martin's Press.

WORLD ALMANAC
An Imprint of Funk & Wagnalls
One International Boulevard, Suite 444
Mahwah, New Jersey 07495-0017

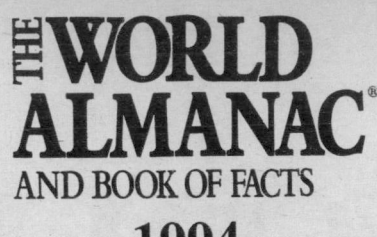

1994 HIGHLIGHTS

GENERAL INDEX

—H—

— J —

— K —

—X—

—Y—

—Z—

The World Almanac

and Book of Facts 1994

The Top 10 News Stories

Bill Clinton was inaugurated as the 42d U.S. president on January 20; he brought to the presidency a lengthy agenda of domestic policy initiatives.

Clinton proposed to Congress in September a complex and controversial plan to provide health insurance to all Americans and hold down health-care costs; the plan was largely the work of a task force headed by First Lady Hillary Rodham Clinton.

By the narrowest of margins, Clinton won congressional passage in August of a bill designed to reduce federal budget deficits by $496 billion over five years, through federal spending cuts and new taxes.

Although many issues remained unresolved, dramatic steps were taken in September to end 45 years of conflict in the Middle East, when Israel and the Palestine Liberation Organization exchanged letters of recognition and signed an agreement on Palestinian autonomy in Israeli-occupied territories.

Russian President Boris Yeltsin continued to press for economic and political reforms and, after a bloody confrontation in October, succeeded in dissolving a legislature dominated by hard-line opponents of his program.

During the year, negotiators repeatedly attempted to devise an acceptable partition plan to end the slaughter in Bosnia and Herzegovina.

The "Great Flood of 1993" left at least 50 dead, over 70,000 homeless, and some $12 billion in property damage in 9 midwestern states in the summer.

Clearing the way for black majority rule, South Africa announced that elections open to all races would be held in 1994.

Massive starvation in Somalia had ended by May; however, a deadly confrontation then developed between U.N. and U.S. peacekeeping forces and a fugitive Somali warlord.

A terrorist bomb exploded in New York City's World Trade Center in February, killing 6, and just a few months later, another bombing and assassination plot was uncovered.

America's Role in the Post-Cold War World

By Arthur M. Schlesinger, Jr.

The Cold War is history. Those grim days of Soviet-American confrontation, once so frightening, now seem remote, even improbable. Who today remembers bomb shelters, and teachers drilling schoolchildren to hide under desks, and loyalty oaths, and the blacklisting of movie stars, and SAC planes on 24-hour alert, and academics moving to Australia to flee nuclear war? The Great Fear is finally over. Communism is an extinct ideology, the Soviet Union a fading memory. A historical epoch has come to an end.

But the end of the epoch leaves American foreign policy all dressed up and nowhere to go. For the half-century of the Cold War, the United States had a supreme objective in the world: to stop Soviet expansionism. Containment, the diplomat George Kennan predicted in 1947, would lead to "the break-up or the gradual mellowing of Soviet power." In the end, it led to both, and the Western democracies under creative American leadership, expressed in such initiatives as the Marshall Plan, were victorious. Today, mission accomplished, the next question arises: Where do we go from here? What is America's role in the post-Cold War world?

"We have slain a large dragon," James Woolsey, President Bill Clinton's director of the Central Intelligence Agency, told Congress, "but we live now in a jungle filled with a bewildering variety of poisonous snakes. And in many ways, the dragon was easier to keep track of."

The zoological metaphor is catchy. Still, it would be a mistake to look back on the Cold War with nostalgia. For in those dark times nuclear war threatened civilization with total extinction. We lived for forty years on the edge of apocalypse. Poisonous snakes may do local harm, but they do not menace the future of humanity—or even the national security of the United States. Let us rejoice that the Cold War is behind us.

Mr. Woolsey launched his metaphor to strengthen the argument that, even though the Cold War is over, the republic must maintain national security spending at more or less Cold War levels. Such a reaction is predictable. The Cold War conferred power and money on the national security establishment—the intelligence community and the Pentagon. Giant bureaucracies in any case prefer to keep on doing what they have been doing. Cold War habits are bound to persist until we think through the role of the United States in the post-Cold War world and replace the containment of Soviet power with a new strategic objective.

Does America Need an Enemy?

Some say that Americans need an enemy to give focus and coherence to foreign policy. Americans had Germany as the enemy in two world wars, then the Soviet Union as the enemy in the Cold War. Who will be the designated enemy now? Some nominate Japan; some nominate Islamic fundamentalism; in due course other potential enemies will no doubt be proclaimed.

But this needing-an-enemy hypothesis is a demeaning idea for a great nation, especially one founded, like the American republic, on lofty ideals. Self-preservation must be the mainspring of a country's foreign policy, but no mature country wants an enemy to define its world role. Surely the republic of Jefferson and Lincoln and Wilson has something affirmative to offer suffering humanity. Moreover, history shows that the United States got along quite comfortably without an obsessive enemy in the century from 1815, the end of America's last war with Great Britain, to 1917, the year of America's entry into the First World War. Who needs an enemy now?

No, the search for a new enemy cannot save Americans from the much harder job of rethinking the U.S. role in the new era. The task is to construct a strategic design consistent with the perils and possibilities of the epoch into which the world is now moving.

Ethnic and National Hostility

The 20th century was an epoch defined above all by the warfare of ideologies. The liberal democratic idea was under siege by two mortal foes: fascism in the first half of the century, Communism in the second. Democracy finally succeeded in defeating both totalitarian creeds: fascism perishing with a bang, Communism with a whimper.

But the end of the warfare of ideologies does not mean, as some sages have optimistically forecast, the "end of history." One set of hatreds replaces another. Lifting the iron grip of ideological repression in Eastern Europe and the ex-Soviet Union releases pent-up ethnic, nationalist, religious, and linguistic antagonisms deeply rooted in history and in memory. The evaporation of the Cold War removes superpower restraints on national and tribal conflicts in the Third World.

At the same time, the collapse of Communism, the bankruptcy of Marxism-Leninism, have left behind, in the words of President Vaclav Havel of the Czech Republic, "a great unsettling void that had to be filled at any cost." It is a void of belief, a void of belonging—and the void is rendered the more acute by the spread of a world market, in which peoples, at the mercy of economic developments beyond their control, feel beleaguered and vulnerable and seek the reassurance of identity. It is this void that ethnicity and nationalism rush to fill. Tribal instincts are surging back, and the hostility of one tribe for another is a primordial human reaction. The tragedy of Yugoslavia is only the most murderous portent of the century to come.

The situation is intensified by the increase in mass migrations across national frontiers. As the 20th century staggers to a close, a number of factors—not just the end of the Cold War but, more fundamentally, the development of swifter modes of communication and transport, the growth of population, the breakdown of traditional structures, the flight from chaos, from tyranny, from poverty, from ethnic cleansing, from ecological disaster—drive people as never before from one country to another in the quest for a better life. Already 100 million people around the world today live outside the countries in which they were born.

What happens when people of different ethnic origins, speaking different languages, professing different religions, settle in the same geographical locality and live under the same political sovereignty? Unless a common purpose binds them together, tribal fears and enmities will drive them apart. On every side the potent mix of nationalism and ethnicity is tearing nations into pieces. Look around the globe. From India to Ireland, from Sri Lanka to Sudan, from Angola to Zaire, you will find growing ethnic and racial tensions. During the summer of 1993 in what used to be the Soviet Union, seven separate wars were going on in the Transcaucasus region. Even nations as stable as Canada and Britain and France, Belgium and Spain and Germany and Italy, face internal threats of secession. "The virus of tribalism," in the words of the British magazine *The Economist*, ". . .risks becoming the AIDS of international politics—lying dormant for years, then flaring up to destroy nations." If the 20th century has been the century of the warfare of ideologies, the 21st century begins as the century of the warfare of ethnicities.

A Parade of International Imperatives

And other troubles loom ahead: economic stagnation; overpopulation; environmental degradation; proliferation of nuclear, biological, and chemical weapons; terrorism; drugs; AIDS. The 21st century presents humankind with a formidable agenda.

The priority, indeed the condition for tackling nearly everything else, must be peace among nations. This means most urgently the completion of the task of bringing weapons of mass destruction under control. No one can rest happily at the thought of nuclear bombs in the hands of leaders like Saddam Hussein of Iraq and Kim Il Sung of North Korea. It means too the development of international means to prevent future Somalias and future Bosnias. The ultimate aim must be the evolution from a world of war to a world of law.

There follows a parade of international imperatives. There is the need to promote the spread of human rights. There is the need to protect the planet against toxic wastes, acid rain, ozone depletion, global warming, and other environmental scourges. There is the need for a global energy policy that will ensure both efficient use in rich countries and adequate supply in poor countries. There is the need to check the population explosion and to restrain mass migrations. There is the need to stop the sale of arms to unstable governments around the world—an area in which the United States has been a particular offender. There is the need to regulate the swarm of global corporations that float across frontiers and are unaccountable to national governments. There is the need to end terrorism and the international drug traffic.

Where Does America Fit In?

Where does the United States fit in? What should be the American objective? The goal of any country's foreign policy is to protect and advance its own national interest. Now the phrase "national interest" worries some goodhearted people, who fear that it implies egoistic concern with one's own country at the expense of other countries and thereby nourishes a nation's baser self. Yet national interest properly construed implies concern with the long-term international environment—and it implies respect for the national interests of other countries. Without the compass of national interest, moreover, there would be no order or predictability in international affairs. As George Washington said, "No nation is to be trusted farther than it is bound by its interest."

National interest is not, however, a self-executing formula. Historically, the United States has always had bedrock strategic interests—ensuring balances of power in Europe and Asia, guaranteeing the freedom of the seas, preventing extracontinental aggression in the western hemisphere. In recent times, it has developed economic and political interests—a freely trading world to be made safe for democracy and human rights. Though Americans argue endlessly over the best way to pursue those goals, a relationship to the national interest is necessary in a democracy to win public support for a sustainable foreign policy.

Some people these days propose that America, as the only remaining superpower, king of the hill, should simply impose a *pax Americana* on the fractious world. It is true that the United States is the world's only *military* superpower, but military power will not suffice without economic power behind it. The United States achieved a swift military victory in the Persian Gulf War of 1991, but it had to pass a begging bowl among its allies to meet the economic costs. Superpowers that cannot pay for their own wars won't stay in the superpower business very long.

Even if it should have the money, one wonders whether America has the power or the wisdom to rule the world. "We must face the fact," President John F.

Kennedy said a third of a century ago, "that the United States is neither omnipotent nor omniscient—that we are only 6 percent of the world's population—that we cannot impose our will upon the other 94 percent of mankind—that we cannot right every wrong or reverse each adversity—and that therefore there cannot be an American solution to every world problem."

What was true thirty years ago when the United States was at the height of its power is even more true today when a vast literature has arisen to chart America's relative decline. It seems essential for the new strategic conception to recognize the limits of American capacity to regenerate a corrupt world. How can the United States hope to disarm Somalia when it cannot disarm Los Angeles or Washington, D.C.? Nor do the American people have the inclination to be the world's policeman, rushing to arrest or occupy other countries every time the alarm bell rings. The notion of a world to be ordered unilaterally by the United States is fantasy.

A Need for Collective Action

If none of the parade of international imperatives is susceptible to solution by a single nation, the key to the future is collective action through the building of international institutions. Of course every nation will continue to advance its own interests, but nations will increasingly discover that joint action may be the best way to safeguard those interests. The end of the Cold War at last liberates the United Nations to do what its founders intended it should do: to get countries of the world to work together in keeping the peace, extending the rule of law, and promoting economic growth, human rights, environmental protection, and cultural dignity.

The world ahead will be turbulent, chaotic, and dangerous for a long time to come—a world of inconceivable poverty, exploding population, desperate inequalities, mass migrations, fanatic ethnic and religious animosities, artificial frontiers, continuing arms flows, angry competition for resources, disintegration of traditional structures, and instantaneous communication of hopes and grievances. In such a world, as the respected international civil servant Sir Brian Urquhart has said, "No one nation, or even a partnership of two or three powerful nations, is going to be able to assume the role of world arbitrator and policeman, even if we suppose the other nations would accept it, which they are most unlikely to do. The United Nations, therefore, must be brought to maturity to take that role."

This is not to suggest that the UN is capable of providing solutions to every world problem. At the moment it is an imperfect organization, underfunded, incompetently staffed, and overbureaucratized. Nor is it to suggest that the control of U.S. foreign policy be handed over to the UN. The existence of the UN does not abolish the basic dynamics of international politics—national interest and the search for a balance of power. The United States, and other nations, must retain the freedom to protect vital interests. But the UN and regional organizations like the European Community, the Organization of American States, and the Organization of African Unity supply arenas where clashes of interest and power can be contained, refined, and harmonized. International organization offers the means by which the collective wisdom and force of humankind might be brought to bear on the problems that assail all humanity.

Yet collective action is not easy. The impotence of the European Community in the face of the torment of Yugoslavia illustrates the difficulty of getting countries to act in unison, especially when the situation calls for sending ground forces into battle in countries that do not present a direct threat to the vital interests of one's own country.

While the UN Charter affirms the inherent right of unilateral self-defense against armed attack, military intervention for other purposes is more likely to be acceptable if it is multilateral in character. Still, even if the UN gets the stand-by military force requested by Boutros Boutros-Ghali, the UN Secretary-General, in his 1992 "Agenda for Peace," or the UN volunteer foreign legion proposed by Brian Urquhart, questions will remain about the timing, duration, and utility of military action. Hit-and-run raids rarely change conditions abroad; sustained military occupation is unpopular both in foreign lands and at home.

The Third World in particular is periodically convulsed by what the novelist V. S. Naipaul calls "movements of rage" directed against Western styles of modernity. Collective intervention by Western powers may only intensify resentments without solving problems: consider the case of Somalia. Moreover, most post-Cold War problems are simply not amenable to military solutions.

The persistence of economic stagnation, for example, makes all global troubles worse. Poverty feeds the movements of rage, embitters the competition for scarce resources, impedes the development of democratic institutions in ex-Communist countries, and reduces the freedom of maneuver in democratic countries. Never in history has global economic interdependence been so inclusive; never has a growing world economy been so vital for humanity's future.

The agenda for the 21st century is formidable. Surely the role of American leadership is to mobilize international institutions for the challenges ahead. Nor is such leadership alien to American traditions. It is rather the fulfillment of an American hope. Despite the republic's isolationist past, the vision of a new world order had its first great prophet in Woodrow Wilson after the First World War and its first great architects in the men who organized the Marshall Plan after the Second World War.

It is now time for American foreign policy once again to come in from the cold.

Arthur M. Schlesinger, Jr., the Pulitzer Prize-winning historian and writer, is Albert Schweitzer Professor in the Humanities at the City University of New York. He served as Special Assistant to the President in the Kennedy Administration.

The Great Flood of 1993

By Donald Young

The United States experienced a number of frightful natural calamities in the late 1980s and early 1990s: droughts, blizzards, several of the hottest summers on record, an earthquake in central California, and hurricanes in the Southeast. During the winter of 1992-1993, along the East Coast, 2 onslaughts of wind and precipitation had each been proclaimed the storm of the century.

As tragic and destructive as these events were, none could quite compare with the Great Flood of 1993 along the Mississippi and Missouri rivers and their tributaries. The flood did not rank first, among recent disasters, in the number of deaths or in the total amount of property damage. Compared with the other misfortunes, however, the flood disrupted more lives and put more stress on human spirit and endurance and gave promise of setting back agricultural production for a longer time.

Stated just in bloodless numbers, the deluge was impressive. Eight million acres were flooded and 12 million more were too wet to produce crops. Damage was put at $12 billion, with $8 billion of that suffered by farmers. Fifty people died. Almost 70,000 were left homeless. In 9 states—Illinois, Iowa, Kansas, Minnesota, Missouri, Nebraska, North Dakota, South Dakota, and Wisconsin—a total of 421 counties were declared federal disaster areas.

In human terms, the cost was nearly incalculable. Thousands lost all their possessions, fleeing to higher ground when levees collapsed, often without warning. Children were reported to be especially traumatized by their experiences. With whole towns underwater, often for weeks, many workers lost their sources of income as well as their homes. In Hardin, Mo., the ferocious waters tore away most of a cemetery and dropped 900 caskets into the maelstrom.

Endless Rainfall

The Midwestern flood appears to have had its origin, in part at least, in El Niño, the pool of warm water that develops every few years in the eastern Pacific Ocean off South America. El Niño spawned a strong subtropical jet stream that brought heavy winter 1992-1993 rains to the upper Mississippi Valley, saturating the ground. The cool summer of 1992 had resulted in less evaporation, so the land could hardly absorb more water. The mild summer, in turn, was attributed to the sun-blocking haze caused by fallout from the volcanic eruption of Mt. Pinatubo in the Philippines.

Another apparent villain in this story was a high pressure system that formed over the eastern United States in the spring and summer of 1993. The high pressure produced dry conditions throughout the East—including drought in the Southeast—and intense heat in the Northeast during the summer.

A strong jet stream, moving from west to east in typical fashion, and causing cooler and wetter weather, bumped into the high pressure system and was diverted to the north. The moisture it created, beginning in April, almost all came down in the upper Midwest.

The rain not only seemed to fall almost steadily for weeks, it also came down in often prodigious amounts. A foot of rain fell in southern Minnesota, beginning June 11, and 4 days later 11 more inches were recorded. Morris, Minn., reported 5.9 inches on the night of July 3-4. In Iowa, on July 9, 5 to 8 inches of rain were reported at a number of locations. Not until late July did the stubborn weather pattern in the Midwest and East begin to break up.

Dams and Levees

The Mississippi River and its tributaries drain one-third of the United States, 1.25 million square miles, covering all or parts of 31 states. Native Americans called the Mississippi the Father of Waters, and the river's historical and contemporary importance to the agriculture and commerce of the nation can hardly be overstated.

In 1927, 214 people died in a flood that also caused extensive damage in the lower Mississippi Valley. In the next year Congress passed the Mississippi River flood control act, directing the U.S. Army Corps of Engineers to confine the river to a prescribed channel. Some 300 dams were built on the river's tributaries. The government also constructed levees and flood walls along the major rivers of the system. Cities and towns put up their own levees. In 1993 levees, some rising to 50 feet or more, lined almost 3,600 miles of Mississippi River system riverbanks—the world's most extensive flood-control program.

Controlling the Mississippi and its tributaries proved, however, to be a most challenging task. Flooding is a recurring phenomenon, and the river has always responded to floods by widening its channel and eroding its banks to make room for the heavier volume of water to be transported south to the Gulf of Mexico. It has often changed its channel here and there, sometimes adding loops and cutting off others.

Throughout the years, the rich alluvial soil left by receding floodwaters proved irresistible to farmers. Elsewhere, settlements—some of which grew into major cities—occupied the banks of the Mississippi and its tributaries, which had become major arteries of transportation by the mid-19th century.

While dams could be built to control the flow of water downstream, the construction of levees on floodplains to shelter humans and farmlands proved to be a mixed blessing. By denying the river its ability to expand in many places, the engineers simply guaranteed that floodwaters would climb higher and would move more swiftly and with more force. Where levees were breached or nonexistent, the impact could be even more severe. Record crests of the rivers, reported in many places in 1993, would not have been set if they could have spread out into the floodplains. Furthermore, because sediments being transported downriver could not be deposited in floodplains, they tended to settle in the main channels, thus raising the rivers more.

The Corps of Engineers asserts that the investment of billions of dollars in flood control has been well worthwhile, and that the amount of damage averted since the 1920s far outweighs the cost of construction. In 1937, Cairo, Ill., which is situated on the Mississippi River where the channel narrows between high bluffs, was spared during a flood because a floodway had been constructed that redirected much of the water several miles to the west before returning it to the main channel.

The avalanche of 1993, however, could fairly be described as a "100-year flood," that is, one that was of a magnitude that would likely be seen only once in a century. The result was unfortunate: of about 1,400 levees along the paths of the raging waters, some 800 were breached, damaged, or demolished outright.

Most Corps levees, and most levees in larger cities, were concrete, and relatively few of these gave way. On the other hand, earthen levees built to protect many small towns and farmlands fared less well. Typically, they became saturated and ultimately succumbed to the pressures of the water.

Sandbags were another element in the line of defense against the roiling waters. The National Guard, prisoners, and countless volunteers filled—by one estimate—75 million sandbags during the flood. The bags fortified the levees and raised them higher where needed.

Course of the Flood

In 1992, Hurricane Andrew had swept through the Caribbean, Florida, and Louisiana in about 72 hours. But the Great Flood of 1993 (apparently it has not occurred to anyone to give human names to floods) rolled on and on for about 2 months, affording the prudent a chance to evacuate, but also leaving muck-filled streets and houses that required additional weeks to clean up.

Photographs taken from boats and aircraft illustrated the depth of the water. The rounded domes of grain silos barely broke above the water, and farm animals were seen crowding onto the sloped roofs of farm buildings.

Satellite photos, however, provided some of the most dramatic testimony to the scope of the flood. Rivers shown in older photos to be one-fourth to one-half of a mile in width had now spread out to a width of several miles. East of Kansas City, Mo., the width of the Missouri River was estimated to be as much as 10 miles. And beyond the rivers, patches of low ground had disappeared. After studying satellite photographs, Vice Pres. Al Gore observed, "It's as if another Great Lake has been added to the map of the United States."

At each town and city along the rivers, people asked similar questions. On what day would the river reach its crest here? What would be the height of the crest? How does that compare with the height of our levees? They also sought to estimate the flood stage, or the number of feet the river would rise above its banks.

On the Mississippi, the most destructive flooding occurred on the stretch of river from Davenport, in northeastern Iowa, down to the confluence with the Ohio River. On the Missouri River, the most devastation occurred from the region of Omaha, Neb., to the river's confluence with the Mississippi north of St. Louis. On July 19, the Mississippi was flooded for 464 miles (from McGregor, Iowa, to St. Louis) and the Missouri for 616 miles (from Omaha to St. Louis).

The drama played itself out in each city and community, but with variations on the main theme.

The story in Davenport, Iowa (population 96,000), was that the city had decided not to build any flood-control system. Davenport had missed the opportunity for full federal financing in the 1970s, and thereafter residents were reluctant to accept high construction costs. Furthermore, they didn't want to lose their excellent view of the river. In 1993, Davenport suffered extensive urban flooding.

Des Moines, Iowa, the state capital, suffered great disruption. Situated at the confluence of the Raccoon River with the Des Moines River, which flows southeast to the Mississippi, the city had levees, but one of them broke on July 11. The water treatment plant that provides the city's water was flooded. Pumps and generators were under 9 feet of water, and the filtration and purification system was contaminated. As a result, 250,000 people had to turn to outside sources for drinking water for almost 3 weeks. With no water available from hydrants, the danger of catastrophic fire was high.

Hannibal, Mo., on the Mississippi, had been the boyhood home of Mark Twain, whose writing reflected his fascination with the big river. He once wrote, "Except for the fact that the streets are quiet of kids and drays, there's really nothing good to say about a flood." In 1993, on the July 4 weekend, Hannibal went defiantly ahead with its National Tom Sawyer Days, featuring the usual frog races, picket-fence painting, and mud volleyball tournament. Hannibal had calculated that once every 500 years the river would crest at 30 feet, so it had built a levee of 31 feet. As the waters rose in July, 3 feet of sandbags were added to the top of the levee. The sandbags proved to be the difference . . . the river crested at 32 feet.

Jefferson City, Missouri's capital, on the Missouri River in the middle of the state, suffered its biggest blows on July 29. Flooding knocked out the city's sewage treatment plant, and the city began pumping raw sewage into the river. Route 54, the principal access route to the capital from the north, was closed when water overrode the sandbag walls along the road.

The Mississippi and Missouri rivers unite about 20 miles north of downtown St. Louis. Before the confluence, for about 20 miles, they run parallel to each other, just a few miles apart, as they arc around the city's northern suburbs. The peninsula of land between these 2 mighty tides of water, which contains a dozen villages and hundreds of farms, virtually vanished. Indeed, the rivers met 20 miles above their usual point of confluence. All of the peninsula's residents were evacuated.

As the largest city in harm's way, and the first to witness the combined flow of the Missouri and Mississippi, St. Louis was a center of attention. Predictions as to the ultimate crest there were revised upward frequently. More than 400 million gallons of water per minute swept past the graceful Gateway Arch on the St. Louis waterfront. In South St. Louis, a levee along the River des Peres, a drainage channel, collapsed, July 20. Water in the vicinity floated 51 propane gas tanks off their concrete moorings, and city officials, fearing a fiery explosion, evacuated a 40-square-block area. Divers sought to anchor the tanks. At the airport, planes were pushed about by the water until they wedged against trees. The Mississippi crested at St. Louis, Aug. 1, at 49.4 feet, a record, and the city's 11-mile concrete floodwall held firm.

Downriver, the historic towns of St. Genevieve, Mo., and Prairie du Rocher, Ill., across the divide, braced for the crest. Both had been founded by the French in the 18th century. St. Genevieve, with its houses built with logs stuck together with clay, animal hair, and straw, contained the nation's best examples of French colonial architecture. It had no government-issue, Corps of Engineers levee, however, because the town's 4,500 people couldn't afford their share of the cost, $10 million. Makeshift barriers were unable to prevent some flooding. After the town's plight was reported in the media, help began to arrive from afar. A busload of people came from Memphis, Tenn. Others traveled even greater distances. In 90-degree heat, volunteers filled 750,000 sandbags and backed them up with 100,000 tons of rock. Water lapped at the base of the 1789 Green Tree Inn, but the historic buildings were saved.

Prairie du Rocher, population 700, founded by the French in 1722, was saved by a bold gamble. The Army Corps of Engineers punched a 400-foot hole in a levee north of town in order to divert some of the water into farmland and ease the pressure on the town itself. On their own, at 4 A.M., town officials dynamited the levee in 2 more places, then put out a call for help on the main levee, to which hundreds of people responded. They raised the levee by another 18 inches, and the river was turned back.

At Cairo, at the southern tip of Illinois, the Ohio River joins the Mississippi. From Cairo south, the river opens up dramatically. Because the Ohio was low in 1993, the broad lower river easily absorbed the massive contribution from the upper Mississippi, and the South was spared the Midwest's agony.

It seemed almost a miracle that only 50 people perished in the flood. Most of the deaths were by drowning, and there were several electrocutions. In the most tragic accident, 4 boys and 2 adult counselors drowned in a cave in Missouri when water from a thunderstorm poured into its mouth.

The Damage and the Cleanup

For 2 months, the flood trapped 3,000 of the 25,000 barges that carry corn, wheat, soybeans, petroleum, and coal downriver. Many bridges, roads, and rail lines were knocked out. Most affected farmers lost their crops for 1993. But further east, in Indiana and Ohio, ideal weather was producing bumper crops. Initial government estimates of the trend in food prices and of the size of national crop harvests suggested that changes would be minimal. In fact, some analysts saw the flood and Southeastern drought, taken together, contributing only a 1 percent increase to the price of food.

Amid the devastation, some animal life benefited. Plants fertilized by river sediment flourished and provided abundant food for ducks and other waterfowl. Fish occupied new ground, so to speak, and eagles and hawks who search them out had new targets of opportunity.

Long after the national television crews had packed up, citizens went about the physically and emotionally stressful task of cleaning out homes and neighborhoods. Violet Merrigan, postmaster of Pattonsburg, Mo., told the *New York Times*: "There's the diarrhea and the nausea and the mold, which kind of makes you lightheaded.... There's the stench of hundreds of dead night-crawlers, and other dead animals all over the sidewalks."

No one could know all of the chemical pollutants the river water might have picked up, not to mention oil; the presence of human sewage meant that anyone working in the water had to get a tetanus shot. Potential damage to electrical systems and to roadbeds represented accidents waiting to happen and had to be investigated carefully.

Pres. Bill Clinton visited the flood area 4 times. One citizen of Des Moines who shook his hand said later, "We need some divine intervention. He has a lot of power, but he doesn't have that kind of power. He can't make the rain end."

The organizations most active in flood relief were the Federal Emergency Management Agency (FEMA), the Salvation Army, and the Red Cross. FEMA, stung by criticism of its slow response to Hurricane Andrew, got high marks in 1993, at least at first, for its well-organized relief effort. In locations declared to be disaster areas, residents could receive rental payments for temporary housing and unemployment payments for lost jobs. In addition, low-interest loans were made available for farmers and businesses. FEMA did come under some criticism, however, because of its tight regulations and overwhelming paperwork. The U.S. Small Business Administration was also on the scene, offering loans of up to $100,000 for homeowners and up to $500,000 for businesses. (Private insurance companies do not offer flood insurance, and while the federal government does offer flood insurance, only about 20 percent of eligible persons buy it.)

Congress approved $6.2 billion in flood relief. Clinton signed the bill in St. Louis, Aug. 12. The principal payouts would be to farmers who had lost crops and to people who had lost property, as well as for the restoration of public buildings.

Mike Espy, the secretary of agriculture, started a debate about the future when he recommended that some towns be moved to higher ground. Levees would then be dismantled so that the Mississippi River could reclaim its original floodplain. The extent to which that might happen—or to which breached and broken levees would be rebuilt—was not immediately clear.

Reflecting the stubborn optimism of Americans, developers in Davenport announced, while the waters were still rising, that a block that was then partially underwater would be the site of a new 220-room hotel.

Donald Young is a writer and editor specializing in current affairs and environmental issues.

The Clinton Presidency

By Bruce Drake

Bill Clinton came to the White House with an ambitious domestic agenda. The sheer volume of proposals and policy initiatives he set in motion stood in sharp contrast to the previous eight years of relative inactivity on the domestic front under the Bush administration and the second term of Ronald Reagan.

The two most important issues Clinton had promised to tackle —the economy and health-care reform—by themselves would have required of any new administration an enormous investment of political will and energy. But Clinton also chose to press ahead quickly on a wide range of issues: lifting the ban on gays in the military, seeking passage of a highly controversial U.S.-Mexico-Canada free trade agreement, pressing campaign finance reform and welfare reform, enacting a national service program to let young people repay federal education loans through community service, proposing an anticrime program, devising a timber policy for the Northwest that balanced economic and environmental interests, and launching a program to streamline government—or what Vice President Al Gore, put in charge of the effort by Clinton, called "reinventing government."

It was not surprising, therefore, that Clinton had a difficult first year in office. He was elected with a less than overwhelming mandate for so sweeping an agenda, having won only 43 percent of the vote in a three-way race against incumbent George Bush and maverick billionaire Ross Perot. And, to carry out his program, he first had to take control of the government—no small challenge after 12 years in which Republicans were in charge of the executive branch.

Ultimately, Clinton won a hard-fought victory on his initial top priority, a deficit-reduction package. But the narrowness of that victory, and the fact that it inspired little enthusiasm among many Americans, raised questions about the strength of his presidency.

On foreign affairs, Clinton was confronted with a more complicated geopolitical map than his predecessors. The competition with the Soviet Union and the Communist world, which had been the central focus of American policymaking for more than four decades, had given way to less clear-cut questions about what role the U.S. should play in restoring order or keeping the peace in countries like Bosnia and Herzegovina or Somalia.

First Days in Office

William Jefferson Clinton took the oath of office as the nation's 42d president on January 20, 1993. At 46, the former Arkansas governor represented a generational shift in the White House, having been born after World War II and having come of age during the turbulent era of the civil rights battles and Vietnam.

Clinton used his brief inaugural address and his first days in office to set a new tone now that the Democrats had control of both the White House and Congress. He promised "an end to the era of deadlock and drift and a new season of American renewal."

He underlined the break with recent Republican administrations by signing a series of executive orders. One imposed higher ethical standards on top officials of the executive branch. Another overturned five restrictions on abortions that had been imposed under the previous Republican administrations.

The first legislation he signed as president was a bill providing workers up to 12 weeks of unpaid leave in order to tend to family needs and crises. The signing of the family leave bill on February 5 was a symbolic moment for Clinton and fellow Democrats because the legislation was a key part of their agenda that had been stymied under the previous Republican administration.

Clinton had promised to be ready with an economic package and health-care reform plan within his first 100 days, but it was immediately clear that the magnitude of the economic and political challenges facing his new administration would force Clinton to alter some of his economic goals and force him to delay for several months tackling the health-care issue.

Battle of the Budget

A series of reports before he took office pointed to a steadily worsening federal budget deficit. The deficit threat increasingly drove Clinton's decision-making because, as he later told the nation's governors in August, "unless we did something about it, we would not have the capacity to deal with a whole range of other issues" during his term in office. One casualty of his rising concern about the deficit was his campaign promise to enact a middle-class tax cut—a promise that had helped his cause during the Democratic presidential primaries.

Speaking to a joint session of Congress on Feb. 17, Clinton outlined a package of tax hikes and spending reductions totaling $493 billion. Key elements were higher tax rates for corporations and those individuals in the highest income brackets, but there was also a broad-based energy tax based on the heat content of fuels as measured in British thermal units (Btu's), which would have meant increased costs for all Americans.

As he did during the campaign, Clinton also called for new government spending to make up for what he called the "investment" deficit in America. Mostly through a $16.3 billion economic stimulus bill, Clinton proposed government spending that he said would create jobs, fund public works projects, aid education, and increase important social welfare services.

Clinton said his program represented "a new direction" and an end to Republican economic policies under Reagan and Bush. Clinton did, in fact, turn the nation away from the low-tax policies of the Reagan-Bush years. But in putting the emphasis on deficit reduction, he set in motion the political forces that removed much of the "new Democrat" imprint he sought to put on the economic package, such as his domestic "investment" initiatives.

The first casualty was his economic stimulus bill. Republicans, despite their minority status, found new strength in their use of the filibuster in the Senate and succeeded in killing Clinton's economic stimulus package. The GOP critics skewered the bill as one that would worsen the deficit and do little to spur the economy. Senate Democrats tried and failed four times to muster the 60 votes necessary to break the filibuster and gave up on April 21.

Emboldened by their victory over the economic stimulus bill, Republicans turned to Clinton's deficit-reduction package and assailed Democrats for once again pursuing policies that resulted in more taxes on Americans. Another persistent source of criticism was Perot, the independent presidential candidate who had received 18.9 percent of the vote in the 1992 election. Perot began a new round of public appearances and advertising in late January, criticizing the proposed tax increases and what he saw as inadequate spending cuts. He also reincarnated his former campaign organization, United We Stand, America, as a citizen's advocacy group in order to actively raise funds and sponsor membership drives without being subjected to laws governing campaign organizations.

All in all Perot and the Republicans appeared to have been more successful than Clinton and the Democrats in putting their spin on the deficit-reduction plan. A *Washington Post* poll in August showed that two out of three Americans agreed with the charge that the package was too tax heavy, and many congressional Democrats feared they would pay the price in the next elections if the economy failed to show new strength.

Ultimately, Republicans voted as a block against the plan in both the House and the Senate, and Clinton had to struggle to hold the support of enough Democrats to win passage. He faced revolts from liberal and conservative wings of the party. In the House, conservative Democrats wanted more spending cuts, tighter caps on entitlement programs like Medicare, and fewer taxes, and in the Senate, Democrats like Oklahoma's David Boren not only wanted to steer the plan away from tax increases to spending cuts, but opposed the broad-based Btu tax. Liberals exerted counterpressure on Clinton as members of the increasingly influential Congressional Black Caucus and others decried the move toward more domestic cutbacks.

The final package was put together after painstaking negotiations and compromises. It kept to Clinton's original target of almost $500 billion in deficit reduction, relying on $255 billion in spending cuts and $241 billion in tax increases. But Clinton's Btu tax, which he had proposed as the fairest approach, gave way to a much more modest 4.3-cents-a-gallon gasoline tax; his "investment"proposals were cut roughly by half; a tax break aimed at encouraging business investment in new equipment was greatly whittled down; and increases he had sought in social spending were cut back.

In the final votes in early August the House approved the plan by the bare margin of 218-216, and, in the Senate, Vice President Gore had to cast a tie-breaking vote to get a 51-to-50 victory.

In assessing why the budget battle turned into such a cliffhanger, critics said Clinton made several mistakes that indicated he had lessons to learn as a new president. They said he failed to mount an effective public campaign for the package, letting the Republicans and Perot instead define it as a Democratic tax hike; that important elements of the original plan, like the Btu tax, were lost because Clinton was seen as too willing to bargain away parts of the package for votes; and that Clinton had erred by believing he could prevail with Democratic votes alone, rather than bolstering his support by courting moderate Republicans earlier in the process.

Taking on Health-Care Reform

Health care, with all the competing interests involved, promised to be another tough political battle for an administration that had already gone through the political wringer on the budget. However, supporters hoped that different dynamics would be at work, in part because the immediate benefit of reform would be more apparent to Americans than the results of the deficit-reduction plan and in part because the Clinton administration had learned the hard way about the importance of laying the political groundwork early with Congress.

The plan, to be fully in place by 1997, was aimed at providing a standard package of health benefits for all U.S. citizens and legal aliens, including the estimated 37 million Americans who currently had no insurance. The benefits were designed to be comparable to the kind of coverage that employees of big corporations commonly received. In general, insurance coverage would be provided through state-controlled regional insurance purchasing groups (health alliances)—creating a "managed competition" system intended to hold down costs.

Under the Clinton proposal, the Medicare and Medicaid programs would continue; however, there would be changes. Medicare recipients would see their premiums rise, but would receive coverage for prescription drugs and long-term home- and community-based care. While some Medicaid recipients would remain in the program, others would be privately insured through the health alliances.

Having realized during the deficit-reduction fight the extent to which new taxes were anathema to lawmakers and the public, administration officials tried to avoid measures that would be seen as tax increases. However, the initial package did contain higher levies on tobacco and a surtax on large corporations electing to become their own insurance provider. The major share of the cost would be borne largely by requiring all employers to pick up 80 percent of their full-time workers' health-care premiums and a portion of their part-time workers' premiums (which some Republicans said was tantamount to a tax) and from cost savings in Medicare and Medicaid. In addition, the plan depended on other measures to sharply curb the steady increase in health-care costs, including reduced paperwork and curbs on medical malpractice suits and health insurance fraud. The price of prescription drugs would also be investigated and monitored.

Employees would generally pay 20 percent of their health-insurance costs, and individuals not insured through an employer would have to pay for all or part of their own health insurance. The plan included subsidies for low-income people, as well as for small businesses.

Clinton unveiled the program in a nationally televised address before a joint session of Congress on September 22, but because it was presented so late in the year and the draft legislation was not available for some weeks following Clinton's speech, significant congressional action on the plan was not expected until 1994.

North American Free Trade

Clinton began another major fight in the fall—attempting to secure passage of the North American Free Trade Agreement (NAFTA) originally negotiated with Mexico and Canada during the Bush administration. The pact would erase tariffs and other barriers to trade among the three nations.

Clinton's support for the agreement was one of the ways he separated himself during the campaign from traditional Democrats, many of whom sided with organized labor, which feared a loss of jobs to Mexico, in opposing NAFTA. Clinton sought to make the pact more palatable to fellow Democrats by negotiating side agreements aimed at ensuring tighter enforcement of each nation's labor and environmental standards, but a number of important Democrats still refused to back him. With the lack of support from within his own party—and more vocal criticism from Perot, who released an anti-NAFTA book in September—the Clinton administration's political skills were put to the test.

Gays in the Military

Faced with these major battles, the new administration could ill afford to get sidetracked by protracted controversies or political miscues, but Clinton and his aides proved during the administration's opening months in office to be less surefooted than they had been during the presidential campaign.

The president's political judgment was questioned by many in Washington when he turned almost immediately after his inauguration to the issue of gays in the military. Clinton announced his intention to lift the ban despite intense opposition from the Joint Chiefs of Staff and many on Capitol Hill, including the influential chairman of the Senate Armed Services Committee, Democrat Sam Nunn of Georgia.

The firestorm over the issue distracted public attention from the focus Clinton wanted to put on the economy. In order to get it off the front burner, Clinton announced at the end of January an interim plan under which he would wait six months while Congress held hearings and a compromise could be reached.

In mid-July, after difficult negotiations with the Joint Chiefs and on Capitol Hill, Clinton announced what he called "an honorable compromise" that allowed homosexuals to serve as long as they were discreet about their orientation. The compromise, dubbed "don't ask, don't tell, don't pursue," permitted gays to serve in the military as long as they kept their orientation to themselves. Applicants for military service would no longer be asked to reveal their sexual orientation. The compromise also prohibited commanders from investigating military personnel on suspicion or hearsay of homosexual activity, but did allow them to discharge gay soldiers if such behavior were proved.

Controversial Nominations

At about the same time that the issue of gays in the military erupted, Clinton was faced with an a uproar over his first choice for attorney general—an insurance company executive named Zoe Baird—who had employed an illegal alien couple at her Connecticut home in violation of a 1986 immigration law. Baird withdrew as a nominee, only to give way to another embarrassing controversy when Clinton's next choice, U.S. District Court Judge Kimba Wood, was reported to have employed an illegal alien as a babysitter (although, unlike Baird, she had done so at a time when it was not illegal). The White House decided not to formally nominate her. (In the end, Clinton's choice of Janet Reno, who had been the Florida state chief prosecutor in Miami, proved to be a popular one.)

Clinton ran into even more serious trouble over his nomination of University of Pennsylvania law professor Lani Guinier to be assistant attorney general in charge of civil rights enforcement. Conservatives launched a well-honed campaign to publicize articles in which Guinier discussed ways of strengthening minority influence under the Voting Rights Act both in elections and in legislatures. Critics dubbed her a "quota queen," saying her views were antidemocratic and a rejection of the concept of one-person, one-vote. Guinier and supporters said her writings were being distorted.

As Democratic senators began to waver, Guinier was left in limbo while the White House wrestled with whether to stand by her. Clinton was caught between two political crosscurrents: the desire to maintain his image as a "new" centrist Democrat and the angry warnings of blacks, particularly important members of the Congressional Black Caucus, against dropping her. Clinton abandoned the nomination on June 3, saying he had not previously read her writings but now that he had, he found them "difficult to defend."

After several nomination mishaps, Clinton was eager to strike the right note when a resignation gave him the opportunity to name a Supreme Court justice, the first such nomination by a Democratic president in 26 years. In mid-June, Clinton announced his choice, Judge Ruth Bader Ginsburg of the U.S. Court of Appeals for the District of Columbia. Ginsburg, considered a judicial moderate, easily won confirmation by the Senate, 96-3, in August.

Political Miscues

There were a number of other miscues that undermined Clinton's image and distracted from important issues at hand. In May, press reports that Clinton got a $200 haircut from Christophe of Beverly Hills while Air Force One sat on a runway and delayed flights at Los Angeles International Airport dominated media coverage of his administration for days and gave the president a huge public relations black eye.

White House staffers also triggered an unnecessary controversy in May when they moved to dismiss the staff of the White House Travel Office, whose most visible job was arranging charters for journalists who accompanied Clinton on trips. The firings prompted charges that the ouster came at the behest of friends and relatives of Clinton who either wanted a share of the travel business or jobs in the office. There were also accusations that the FBI had been misused by Clinton aides to support its case against the fired staffers. The White House backed down and ultimately issued a report in July saying its own staff had acted inappropriately.

While Clinton often expressed irritation with press focus on his administration's difficulties, he and other aides conceded by late spring that the White House needed "tighter coordination." Clinton bolstered his staff by bringing in as counselor David Gergen, a former adviser to Republican presidents who was reputed to have great skills in helping his bosses get their message across. The addition of Gergen and other changes in key staff positions added up to a far more extensive shake-up of the White House staff than usually took place so early in an administration.

Foreign Policy Challenges

Foreign challenges also presented difficulties for Clinton in his first year. He was criticized by some for failing to develop a coherent foreign policy framework. Whether or not the criticism was valid, Clinton did come to the presidency less versed in foreign policy than many of his predecessors. He was also determined to keep his focus on domestic affairs and make U.S. economic security a priority in foreign policy considerations.

Clinton's most consistent policy effort was his determination to help Russia through its transition to political and economic democracy. He firmly supported Russian President Boris Yeltsin, with whom he met in Vancouver on April 3 and 4, and helped engineer increased economic aid to Russia on the part of the U.S. and its allies.

The U.S. did not play a pivotal role in the breakthrough that resulted in a peace agreement between Israel and the Palestine Liberation Organization in September. But Clinton presided at the September 13 White House signing ceremony for the framework accord and indicated the U.S. would play a more active role in assisting the two parties in working out a final agreement. Clinton also promised that the U.S. would do everything possible to make the pact politically viable in the Mideast.

His most visible foreign policy problems during the first year were precisely the kind of post-Cold War situations that proved so vexing for American policymakers—namely, the bloody war in Bosnia and the effort to restore order in Somalia. Both of these were areas where there was little public enthusiasm for major U.S. commitments and where administration officials were confronted by an array of unappetizing choices.

During the presidential campaign, Clinton had freely criticized President Bush for not taking a more aggressive American role in stopping the bloodshed in Bosnia, where the republic's Serbs had made huge territorial gains at the expense of the outgunned Muslim population. But after Clinton took office, the administration's policy wavered several times between threatening possible U.S. military action against the Serbs and following the European Community's lead in seeking to bring about a negotiated solution to the conflict.

In September, after yielding to European resistance to military measures, Clinton made clear to Bosnian President Alija Izetbegovic that the U.S. was unlikely to use force and indicated that the Bosnian Muslims should try to get the best deal they could through negotiations even though their bargaining position had greatly worsened since the beginning of the year.

Clinton took more assertive action on Somalia, as the humanitarian mission there to safeguard the supply line of food increasingly took on the form of a police action to put down powerful warlords as a step toward enabling the country to reconstitute itself. When the United Nations peacekeeping contingent found itself unable to cope with Mohammed Farah Aidid, the most powerful warlord, Clinton approved the use of U.S. forces to break Aidid's power. Administration officials found themselves caught between the belief that the U.N. mission might collapse if the U.S. withdrew and the fact that there was not the same kind of public support for an American commitment to restore order as there was earlier for the largely humanitarian mission that ensured the supply of food. Defense Secretary Les Aspin said in September the U.S. would remain until there was order in Somalia, but many on Capitol Hill openly questioned the extent of U.S. involvement and appeared ready to challenge the legality of Clinton's unilaterally committing American troops, especially as U.S. casualties mounted in bloody clashes with Aidid's forces. On October 7, after more than a dozen Americans had been killed in a single firefight, Clinton ordered that the number of U.S. troops in the region be doubled. But he also appointed a special envoy to pursue a political settlement in Somalia and promised to have all U.S. forces out of the country by March 31, 1994.

The Public Verdict

The public verdict on the first act of the Clinton presidency seemed to indicate that Clinton had not yet accomplished one of the most important political tasks before him—significantly broadening his base of support from the 43 percent of Americans who elected him. A *Washington Post*/ABC News poll in August found his overall approval rating after roughly 200 days in office to be 51 percent negative and 45 percent positive, generally in line with other major polls. His biggest triumph to that point—the budget victory—did not improve these standings because Americans were so evenly divided about whether they supported or opposed the economic plan. However, with many of his programs still untested and the effects of his economic program—whether good or bad—yet to be seen, there was time for public opinion to sway in many directions.

Bruce Drake is Managing Editor of National Public Radio in Washington, D.C.

CHRONOLOGY OF THE YEAR'S EVENTS

Reported Month by Month in 3 Categories: National, International, and General
Nov. 1, 1992 to Oct. 15, 1993

NOVEMBER

National

Clinton Elected 42d President — Gov. Bill Clinton of Arkansas was elected 42d president of the U.S. on **Nov. 3**. His running mate on the Democratic ticket, Sen. Al Gore, Jr., of Tennessee, was elected vice president. Clinton and Gore carried 32 states and the District of Columbia and thereby won 370 electoral votes. Pres. George Bush, the Republican candidate, and his running mate, Vice Pres. Dan Quayle, carried 18 states for a total of 168 electoral votes. In the nationwide popular vote, the official tally gave Clinton 44,908,254 (43 percent), Bush 39,102,343 (37.4 percent), independent candidate H. Ross Perot 19,741,065 (18.9 percent), and all other candidates 666,744 (0.7 percent). Communist governments had collapsed in many countries during the Bush years, and the president had enjoyed great popularity after the Persian Gulf War. But many voters felt that Bush had not responded aggressively enough to an economic recession that triggered a big increase in the ranks of the unemployed. Clinton, who took moderate positions on economic and social issues, was the biggest beneficiary of the desire for change, but Perot, a Texas billionaire with a folksy manner, won a large following with his pledge to eliminate the large annual federal budget deficits in just 5 years. The Democrats held control of both houses of Congress. After a final Senate seat was determined in a runoff election on **Nov. 24**, Democrats retained the 57-43 margin they had held prior to the **Nov. 3** election. In the House, the Republicans gained 10 seats, but the Democrats still held a 258-176 majority, with 1 independent. Altogether, there would be 110 new faces in the House, representing the biggest turnover since 1948. The new House would contain record numbers of women (47), blacks (38), and Hispanics (17). Reapportionment after the 1990 census accounted, in part, for the upheaval, but voters were in a mood for change and voted out a number of representatives in both parties during the primaries and general election. The new Senate would have a record number of women members, 6. Two women Democrats won Senate elections in California, and Carol Moseley Braun of Illinois would become the first black woman to serve in the Senate. The Democrats picked up 2 governorships, for a 30-18 margin over the Republicans. Independents held 2 state houses. Nationwide, Republicans gained ground in voting for state legislators. Fourteen states approved term limits for members of Congress, and 13 of these states also set limits of service for members of their state legislatures.

Court Rejects 'Gag Rule' on Abortions — A panel of the U.S. Circuit Court of Appeals for the District of Columbia rejected, **Nov. 3**, a regulation issued by the Bush administration that forbade anyone at federally funded family-planning clinics, except doctors, from discussing abortion with patients. In May, U.S. District Court Judge Charles Richey had ruled in favor of family-planning groups that had challenged the regulation. In upholding Richey, the appeals court panel held that the administration had improperly bypassed federal provisions requiring that proposed regulations be published in the Federal Register and that the public be allowed to comment on them for up to 90 days.

Decline Reported in Economic Indicators — The Commerce Dept. reported, **Nov. 3**, that the index of leading economic indicators, a gauge of future economic activity, had declined 0.3 percent in September. The Federal Reserve Board said, **Nov. 4**, that the economy was improving at a slow and uneven rate nationwide. The Labor Dept. reported, **Nov. 6**, that the unemployment rate had edged downward to 7.4 percent from 7.5 percent in October. The department said, **Nov. 10**, that prices charged by producers for finished goods had risen by 0.1 percent in October. On **Nov. 13**, the department said that consumer prices had risen 0.4 percent in October.

Court Reinstates Homosexual Sailor — A U.S. District Court judge reinstated a homosexual Naval officer who had been discharged because of his sexual orientation. In May, Petty Officer 1st Class Keith Meinhold, who had served in the Navy for 12 years, had stated on a television program that he was a homosexual. In August, in accord with a policy barring gay men and lesbians from military services, he received an honorable discharge. Meinhold sued for reinstatement, and on **Nov. 6**, Judge Terry Hatter, Jr., ordered the Navy to reinstate Meinhold until the case was resolved. On **Nov. 12**, the Navy swore Meinhold back into service. He became the first homosexual to be reinstated in the military as the result of a court challenge.

Clinton Prepares to Assume Presidency — Pres.-elect Bill Clinton announced, **Nov. 6**, that his transition team would be headed by Vernon Jordan, a Washington, D.C., attorney and former president of the National Urban League, and by Warren Christopher, a deputy secretary of state under Pres. Jimmy Carter. On **Nov. 12**, Clinton named 48 people to conduct the transition. Their principal task would be to help Clinton assemble his cabinet.

Report Issued on Search of Passport Files — The State Dept. issued a report on the search of passport files in the presidential campaign. *The Washington Post*, which had reported in October that the files of Democratic presidential candidate Bill Clinton and his mother had been searched, also reported, **Nov. 9**, that State Dept. officials had searched the files of independent presidential candidate H. Ross Perot. On **Nov. 10**, Elizabeth Tamposi was dismissed as assistant secretary of state for consular affairs. In his report of **Nov. 18**, Sherman Funk, inspector general for the State Dept., said that department personnel had searched the files of the Clintons and Perot in September in an effort to get politically damaging information. Funk placed primary responsibility on Tamposi and Steven Berry, acting assistant secretary of state for legislative affairs. Lawrence Eagleburger, the acting secretary of state, deplored the searches, **Nov. 18**, and said the department should never be in the political arena.

10 Women Accuse Senator of Harassment — It was reported, **Nov. 22**, that 10 women had accused Sen. Robert Packwood (R, Ore.) of sexual harassment. Packwood, who had been reelected to the Senate, was a strong supporter of issues of concern to women's rights groups. (By February, 23 women had made allegations against him.) Most of the women had been employed by Packwood or had worked with him. Packwood said he was sorry if anything he had done had caused anyone discomfort or embarrassment. On **Nov. 27**, he suggested that an alcohol problem might have been related to his conduct, and he entered an alcohol-treatment program.

Auditor of S&Ls Pays $400 Million U.S. Claim — Ernst & Young, the firm that had audited at least 300 thrifts that ultimately went bankrupt, reached a costly settlement with federal regulators. The regulators charged that the auditing firm had committed mistakes and was careless in many audits, and failed to identify weaknesses in real-estate portfolios that led to bankruptcies. On **Nov. 23**, Ernst & Young agreed to pay $400 million to settle the government's claims.

Senators Report on 'October Surprise' — A Senate subcommittee reported, **Nov. 23**, that it had found no evidence that the Reagan-for-president campaign in 1980 had sought to delay release of U.S. hostages in Iran until after the election. Reagan campaign managers had feared that then-Pres. Jimmy Carter would succeed in arranging for the release of the hostages just before the election—an "October surprise." Rumors had circulated for years that Reagan supporters had sought to make a deal with Iran not to free the captives until after the election, by promising to provide weapons if Ronald Reagan were elected. In its report, the Senate Foreign Relations subcommittee on Near Eastern and South Asian affairs found no evidence of any meetings or other actions in support of such a scheme. However, it did say members of the Reagan campaign had operated "on the outer limits of propriety."

International

U.N. Authorizes Blockade of Yugoslavia — The U.N. Security Council authorized a naval blockade as a means of enforcing its economic sanctions against Yugoslavia. On **Nov. 9**, the ethnic Serb leader in Bosnia and Herzegovina proposed a partition of Bosnia along ethnic lines. Much of Bosnia's territory had already been divided up by Serbs and Croats, and the Serb leader, Radovan Karadzic, recommended that the permanent partition be based on how the territory was then controlled. The U.N. Council adopted its blockade resolution, **Nov. 16**, by a 13-0 vote with 2 abstentions. Ships of all nations were empowered to halt and inspect vessels entering or leaving Yugoslav waters. The Council, however, did not act on an appeal from Muslim states that Bosnia be exempted from an arms embargo imposed in 1991 on Yugoslavia and all former Yugoslav republics.

Germany Confronts Neo-Nazis — Neo-Nazi violence, which had been on the rise in Germany, claimed more victims in November. Extreme right-wing organizations had focused their anger on a provision in Germany's constitution that guaranteed that any refugee could seek political asylum in Germany. Although most applicants were ultimately rejected, they were allowed to remain in Germany and receive extensive benefits while their status was being considered. Some 1,800 acts of violence against those seeking asylum had been reported in 1992. In Berlin, **Nov. 8**, 350,000 persons demonstrated against right-wing violence, and a similar protest drew 100,000 in Bonn, **Nov. 14**. Police in Halbe, south of Berlin, blocked an attempted march by neo-Nazis, **Nov. 15**. A Turkish woman and 2 Turkish girls, members of a family of "guest workers" who had lived in Germany for 2 decades, were killed in Moelln, **Nov. 23**, by a firebomb. Their deaths brought to 16 the number of people killed in right-wing attacks in 1992. Under a provision of the constitution, the government announced, **Nov. 27**, that it was banning the Nationalist Front, a neo-Nazi group.

Ex-Communists Win Lithuanian Election — On **Nov. 15**, in the second round of Lithuania's parliamentary elections, former communists of the Democratic Labor Party secured a majority in the Supreme Council. The DLP won at least 79 of the 141 seats to 35 for the Sajudis nationalist movement, which had run the government.

Czechs, Slovaks Move Toward Separation — The Czech and Slovak regional parliaments adopted a joint resolution, **Nov. 17**, authorizing the separation of Czechoslovakia into 2 separate, independent republics. The Czechoslovak Federal Assembly (parliament) approved a constitutional amendment, **Nov. 25**, permitting the dissolution without a national referendum.

Senators in Vietnam for MIA Inquiry — Three U.S. senators and a general traveled to Southeast Asia to seek information on 2,265 American servicemen who were missing in action during the Vietnam war. The delegation, headed by Sen. John Kerry (D, Mass.), met with Vietnamese Pres. Le Duc Anh in Hanoi, **Nov. 18**, and visited Laos, **Nov. 19**. Members of the delegation also traveled to the Mekong River Delta and Danang province, **Nov. 20**, to investigate reports of American MIAs living there. The Vietnamese gave their visitors personal effects of dead or captured Americans, including photographs, letters, diaries, wallets, and uniforms.

U.S., Europe Reach Compromise on Trade — Negotiators from the U.S. and the European Community achieved a breakthrough in trade talks, **Nov. 20**. For years, the U.S. had pressed European countries to reduce their subsidies on farm products. Subsidies for oilseed products had been a particular sticking point. Oilseed trade was relatively insignificant, but farm lobbies from France and the U.S. had prevented agreement. In the compromise, the U.S. accepted more modest limits on subsidies than it had sought, and the Europeans agreed to across-the-board limits. French negotiators, however, objected strongly to the agreement.

Nations Act Again on Ozone Threat — Delegates from 87 nations met in Copenhagen and agreed to accelerate their schedules for phasing out chemicals that damaged the Earth's ozone layer. Under the agreement of **Nov. 25**, some chemicals would be regulated for the first time. Chlorofluorocarbons (CFCs), chemicals thought to be most harmful to the ozone, would be phased out by 1996 rather than 2000.

U.S. Offers to Intervene In Somalia — The U.S. moved toward a humanitarian intervention in Somalia, where thieves had seized most of the food and other supplies being shipped from other countries to starving people. Lawrence Eagleburger, the acting U.S. secretary of state, meeting with U.N. Secretary General Boutros Boutros-Ghali in New York, **Nov. 26**, offered the use of as many as 30,000 American troops. The U.N. force in Somalia consisted of 500 Pakistani peacekeepers, and 3,000 from other countries were due to arrive soon. On **Nov. 30**, Boutros-Ghali endorsed immediate military action in Somalia.

Another Coup Thwarted in Venezuela — For the second time in less than a year, military rebels sought to overthrow the government of Venezuela. On **Nov. 27**, the rebels, aided by some civilians, seized a television station and 2 air bases. Planes bombed the presidential palace and other sites in Caracas, the capital. The insurgents denounced Pres. Carlos Andres Perez for his alleged disregard for poor people, and they pledged to install a "real democracy." Forces supporting the government overcame the rebellion by the afternoon of **Nov. 27**. The death toll from the brief conflict was reported to be at least 169.

General

Magic Johnson Retires a Second Time — Just 5 weeks after he said he would resume his career in the National Basketball Association, Earvin (Magic) Johnson of the Los Angeles Lakers issued a statement,

Nov. 2, that he was retiring for good. Johnson had retired the first time in 1991 as he announced that he had contracted the virus that causes AIDS. In his latest statement, Johnson noted that "various controversies" had surrounded his comeback. Some players had said they feared they might contract the virus from minor skin cuts that could occur during a game.

Fischer Defeats Spassky in Chess — Former world chess champion Bobby Fischer, playing in public for the first time in 2 decades, defeated Boris Spassky, from whom he had won the title in 1972, in a match in Yugoslavia. Their contest, sponsored by a Yugoslav businessman, ended, **Nov. 5**. Fischer, as the winner, received $3.35 million, and Spassky received $1.65 million. On **Dec. 15**, Fischer was indicted by a federal grand jury in Washington, D.C., on a charge that he had violated sanctions against Yugoslavia by playing there.

Catholic Church Issues New Catechism — A new universal catechism of the Roman Catholic Church was issued, **Nov. 16**, by a commission that had devoted 6 years to the task of revising the 400-year-old text. The compilation of teachings embraced many modern-day issues. For example, the catechism warned drivers against alcohol and "an immoderate taste for speed" that put themselves and others in danger. Economic sins cited for the first time included embezzlement, tax fraud, and forgery. The catechism remained conservative on social issues, declaring, for example, "Human life must be totally respected and protected from the moment of conception." It asserted that homosexuals "do not choose their homosexual condition" and urged that they be "treated with respect, compassion and sensitivity," but it also called on gays to remain chaste. The document declared that "Jews were not collectively responsible for the death of Jesus . . . All sinners were responsible for Christ's Passion."

DECEMBER

National

Economic Recovery Appears Underway — The index of leading economic indicators rose 0.4 percent in October, the Commerce Dept. reported, **Dec. 1.** The Labor Dept. said, **Dec. 4**, that the unemployment rate had declined by 0.2 of a point to 7.2 percent in November. The Federal Reserve Board reported, **Dec. 9**, "a slight to moderate pickup in some or all sectors of the economy." Prices charged by producers for finished goods declined by 0.2 percent in November, the Labor Dept. said, **Dec. 10**. The department reported, **Dec. 11**, that consumer prices had risen 0.2 percent in November. The Commerce Dept. reported, **Dec. 17**, that the merchandise trade deficit had shrunk substantially in October to $7.03 billion. In a final revision issued **Dec. 22**, the department said third-quarter gross domestic product had grown at a 3.4 percent annual rate. This was the 6th consecutive quarterly increase. The department reported, **Dec. 30**, that the leading economic indicators had jumped 0.8 percent in November. On Wall Street, the Dow Jones Industrial average closed, **Dec. 31**, at 3301.11, an increase of 4.2 percent for the year.

Clinton Selects His Cabinet — Pres.-elect Bill Clinton chose the members of his cabinet in December. They would be subject to approval by the Senate. On **Dec. 10**, Clinton named Sen. Lloyd Bentsen (D, Tex.), a fiscal conservative who had been the 1988 Democratic nominee for vice president, as secretary of the Treasury. He chose Rep. Leon Panetta (D, Cal.) to head the Office of Management and Budget. On **Dec. 11**, Clinton chose Robert Reich, a Harvard lecturer and adviser to Clinton, as secretary of Labor, and Laura D'Andrea Tyson, an economist at the Univ. of California at Berkeley, as head of the Council of Economic Advisers. He also named Donna Shalala, chancellor of the Univ. of Wisconsin, to be secretary of Health and Human Services, and Carol Browner, head of Florida's Dept. of Environmental Regulation, to be administrator of the Environmental Protection Agency. Thomas McLarty, a friend of Clinton since childhood, was named, **Dec. 12**, as his White House chief of staff, and Ron Brown, a Washington, D.C., lobbyist and chairman of the Democratic National Committee, was chosen as secretary of Commerce. On **Dec. 17**, Clinton named Henry Cisneros, former mayor of San Antonio, to be secretary of Housing and Urban Development, and Jesse Brown, director of the Disabled Veterans of America, as head of the Veterans Affairs Dept. On **Dec. 21**, Clinton chose Hazel O'Leary, a Minnesota power company executive, and Richard Riley, former governor of South Carolina, as secretary of Energy and secretary of Education, respectively. Warren Christopher, a lawyer and diplomat, was tapped, **Dec. 22**, to be secretary of State. Rep. Les Aspin (D, Wis.) was named secretary of Defense. Also on **Dec. 22**, Clinton named W. Anthony Lake as his national security adviser, R. James Woolsey as director of the CIA, and Madeleine Albright as ambassador to the U.N. On **Dec. 24**, Clinton chose Zoe Baird, a corporate lawyer who had worked in the Justice Dept. under Pres. Jimmy Carter, as attorney general. She was the first woman nominated to head the Justice Dept. (Baird withdrew on **Jan. 22**, after it became known that she and her husband had employed illegal aliens in their household.) Clinton rounded out his team, **Dec. 24**, by naming Rep. Mike Espy (D, Miss.) as secretary of Agriculture, former Denver Mayor Federico Pena as secretary of Transportation, former Arizona Gov. Bruce Babbitt as secretary of the Interior, Mickey Kantor as U.S. trade representative, and Joycelyn Elders as surgeon general.

Bush Pardons 6 in Iran-Contra Case — Pres. George Bush pardoned 6 former public officials involved in the Iran-contra case. In the final judicial action prior to the pardons, former CIA Director of Operations Clair George was convicted, **Dec. 9**, on 2 felony counts for giving false testimony to congressional committees. Acting under authority granted by the U.S. Constitution, Bush announced his pardons, **Dec. 24**. He said that the 6 men, "whether their actions were right or wrong," had been motivated by patriotism rather than by personal gain. He said that their prosecution represented an attempt to resolve "policy differences" through criminal trials. Former Defense Sec. Caspar Weinberger was the most prominent figure to receive a pardon. He had been facing a trial in January 1993 on charges relating to a diary he had withheld from prosecutors after having been asked to provide any notes he had taken on the arms-for-hostages deal with Iran. Three former CIA officials were pardoned: George, who had just been convicted; Duane Clarridge, who was awaiting trial in March 1993; and Alan Fiers, who had pleaded guilty to misdemeanor charges of withholding information from Congress. Robert McFarlane, a former national security adviser, and Elliott Abrams, a former assistant secretary of state, who had also pleaded guilty to withholding information, were also pardoned. Lawrence Walsh, the independent counsel who had conducted the prosecutions, denounced the pardons, **Dec. 24**. He said Bush was a "subject" of the investigation and that he was guilty of "misconduct" for withholding notes relevant to the Iran-contra investigation. Bush, **Dec. 30**, retained former Attorney Gen. Griffin Bell to represent him in the ongoing inquiry.

Inquiry Into Iraq Loans Rejected — Attorney Gen. William Barr said, **Dec. 9**, that he would not request appointment of an independent counsel to pursue allegations that the Bush administration had mishandled a bank fraud case involving loans to Iraq. The loans to Iraq, prior to the Gulf War, had been made by the Atlanta branch of Italy's Banca Nazionale del Lavaro. Barr's own investigator, retired Federal Judge Frederick Lacey said, **Dec. 9**, he had found no evidence that the U.S. government had sought to obstruct prosecution of the BNL case, and was certain that Italian bank officials were unaware of the illegal loans.

Independent Counsel Named in Passport Case — Attorney Gen. William Barr requested that an independent counsel be appointed to investigate a search, during the campaign, of the passport files of Pres.-elect Bill Clinton, his mother, and H. Ross Perot. A 3-judge panel, responded by naming Joseph di Genova, a former U.S. attorney, as independent counsel on **Dec. 14.**

Facing Losses, IBM to Cut 25,000 Jobs — (IBM) said that it would reduce its work force again. Still the world's largest computer manufacturer, IBM had once dominated the industry but had fallen behind in the development of personal computers. The company had cut 40,000 jobs in 1992 through voluntary retirements. IBM said, **Dec. 15**, that it would eliminate 25,000 jobs in 1993, through dismissals if necessary. The company also projected a $5.25 billion net loss for the 4th quarter. The value of IBM's shares plunged sharply on this news, and by **Dec. 16** its stock had declined by nearly 50 percent in 5 months.

International

Yeltsin Accepts a New Premier — Russian Pres. Boris Yeltsin, **Dec. 1**, appealed for an extension of his emergency powers, which would allow him to choose the government and control economic policy. A motion by conservative deputies to impeach Yeltsin, **Dec. 1**, received fewer than 400 votes in the 1,041-member Congress of People's Deputies. Yeltsin's opponents failed, **Dec. 5**, to pass constitutional amendments that would have put the cabinet under parliamentary control. The conservatives were more successful, **Dec. 9**, narrowly rejecting the confirmation as premier of Yegor Gaidar, Yeltsin's choice, who had served as acting premier since June. Gaidar had designed Yeltsin's economic-reform program, which had not yet produced many positive results. After vowing, **Dec. 10**, that he would keep Gaidar as acting premier, Yeltsin, **Dec. 14**, joined with the Congress in supporting the confirmation of Deputy Premier Viktor Chernomyrdin as the new premier. Yeltsin, **Dec. 19**, cut short a visit to China when he heard Chernomyrdin was being pressured to choose a conservative cabinet. However, the cabinet list, approved by Yeltsin, **Dec. 23**, contained mostly economic reformers who had served under Gaidar.

German Parties Agree to Curb Refugees — A German prosecutor said, **Dec. 1**, that 2 young men had admitted to a fire-bombing in Moelln in November that had killed a Turkish woman and 2 Turkish girls. They had been among the victims of violent neo-Nazi protests against the law allowing any foreigner to seek refuge or asylum in Germany. On **Dec. 6**, Germany's 2 major parties, the Christian Democratic Union and the Social Democrats, reached an agreement to modify the law, under which 400,000 had entered Germany in 1992. Would-be refugees would now be turned back if they were citizens of countries deemed by Parliament to be free of political persecution. The government, **Dec. 10**, banned a 2d right-wing party for inciting racial hatred.

U.S.-Led Force Enters Somalia — A U.N.-sanctioned military force, led by American troops, arrived in Somalia to ensure the delivery of food to starving people. The U.N. Security Council, voting unanimously, **Dec. 3**, authorized the intervening forces to use "all necessary means" to deliver the food, and the Council also called on warring factions to cease fighting. Some 1,800 Marines entered the capital, Mogadishu, **Dec. 9**, and began to restore the airport runway so that it could receive planes carrying food and supplies. Armed Somalis had fled elsewhere. On **Dec. 10**, Marines and French Legionnaires killed 2 Somalis in a van that was speeding toward a roadblock. The nation's 2 principal warlords signed a peace agreement, **Dec. 11**, in Mogadishu. U.S. and French troops entered Baidoa, a city hard-hit by famine, **Dec. 16**. Marines, **Dec. 20**, occupied the southern coastal city of Kismayu, following a massacre of more than 100 of its citizens by the forces of the local warlord. A civilian employee of the U.S. Army was killed, **Dec. 23**, when his truck struck a mine. Within the next few days, U.S., French, and Italian troops occupied other towns that needed food. Pres. Bush arrived in Somalia, **Dec. 31**, visited the U.S. Embassy in Mogadishu, and toured a schoolhouse where he greeted children recovering from hunger and illness.

Razing of Mosque Ignites Violence in India — Hindus in India destroyed a Muslim mosque and provoked new sectarian conflict. The mosque, built in 1528 in the northern Indian city of Ayodhya, stood on a site that Hindus said was the birthplace of the Hindu diety Ram. They wanted to build a temple there in his honor. On **Dec. 6**, militant Hindus tore down the mosque, using sledgehammers and bare hands. Violent clashes followed. On **Dec. 13**, the government said 1,210 people had been killed and 4,600 wounded.

Israel Deports 415 Palestinians — An Israeli border policeman was kidnapped, **Dec. 13**, by Hamas, a fundamentalist Muslim organization, and his body was found **Dec. 15**. The Israeli cabinet voted unanimously, **Dec. 16**, to expel 415 Palestinians who were Hamas sympathizers. They were rounded up and taken to the Lebanese border, **Dec. 17**, and, after the Israeli Supreme Court declined to block the expulsion, they were sent into Lebanese territory controlled by Israel. The Bush administration, **Dec. 17**, deplored the expulsions, which were illegal under international law. Lebanon barred the Palestinians from proceeding beyond the border area, forcing them to camp without food and supplies. The U.N. Security Council, **Dec. 18**, unanimously condemned the expulsion.

Ex-Dissident Wins Korean Presidency — Kim Young Sam, a longtime opponent of Korean governments, won the presidency of South Korea, **Dec. 18**, as the candidate of the ruling Democratic Liberal Party. He won with 42 percent in a large field. His principal challenger, Kim Dae Jung, was also a prominent dissident. Kim Young Sam would succeed Pres. Roh Tae Woo in February.

President of Serbia Reelected — Pres. Slobodan Milosevic of Serbia was reelected, **Dec. 20**. Official results, reported **Dec. 23**, gave him 56 percent of the vote to 35 percent for his principal challenger, Premier Milan Panic. Panic had blamed Milosevic for the civil war with Bosnia. U.S. Sec. of State Lawrence Eagleburger had charged that Milosevic bore some of the responsibility for Serbian atrocities committed in Bosnia. One of Milosevic's political allies charged in parliament, **Dec. 29**, that Panic was a foreign agent. Panic had come from California in 1992 to assume the premiership. In a no-confidence vote, **Dec. 29**, parliament ousted Panic as premier.

U.S. Downs Iraqi Plane in 'No-Fly Zone' — An Iraqi warplane was shot down, **Dec. 27**, by a U.S. fighter plane after it entered the so-called no-fly zone in southern Iraq. The U.S., Britain, and France had created the zone in August to help protect Shiite Muslims in the area from Iraqi attack.

U.S., Russia Agree on Nuclear Arms Treaty — The U.S. and Russia announced an agreement, **Dec. 29**, on the terms of a treaty that would reduce their strategic nuclear arms by two thirds. The details of the agreement, the second Strategic Arms Reduction Treaty (START), were worked out by Sec. of State Lawrence Eagleburger and Foreign Minister Andrei Kozyrev. The broad outlines of the treaty had been determined at a summit meeting of presidents George Bush and Boris Yeltsin in June.

President of Brazil Resigns — Pres. Fernando Collor de Mello of Brazil resigned in December. Vice Pres. Itamar Franco had been serving as acting president since October, pending outcome of a Senate trial of Collor on corruption charges. Collor resigned, **Dec. 29**, within hours after the Senate convened an impeachment trial. Franco was sworn in as president. At the trial, witnesses testified that they had had to pay large bribes to win government contracts. The Senate voted, **Dec. 30**, 76-3 to convict Collor. Collor and some of his relatives also faced criminal charges that they had received millions of dollars illegally.

General

Guidelines Announced for Food Labels — Implementation of the Nutrition Labeling and Education Act of 1990 advanced, **Dec. 2**, when the Bush administration announced guidelines for the manufacturers of packaged foods. The rules, to be fully in effect by May 1994, required that the amount of fat, sodium, protein, cholesterol, and carbohydrates be printed on the packaging for every product. A number of terms used in advertising, such as "light" and "low fat," could only be used if certain criteria were met.

Letterman Accepts $16 Million From CBS — David Letterman, host of NBC's popular "Late Night With David Letterman" show, announced, **Dec. 8**, he would leave NBC to accept an offer from CBS to host a show beginning at 11:30 P.M. Eastern time each week night and would receive an annual salary of $16 million. He also said he would give NBC until Jan. 15 to make another offer; however, NBC, **Jan. 14**, announced that Letterman would not return next season.

Prince, Princess of Wales Separate — Prince Charles, heir to the British throne, and his wife, Diana, separated in December. In making the announcement to Parliament, **Dec. 9**, Prime Minister John Major said the couple had no plans to divorce, would both participate fully in the upbringing of their 2 sons, and would continue their schedule of public appearances. On **Dec. 12**, Charles's sister, Princess Anne, married Timothy Laurence, a naval commander. She had been divorced from Capt. Mark Phillips in April.

JANUARY

National

Transition to New Leadership Continues — The 103d Congress convened, **Jan. 5**. The Senate and House contained 123 new faces, an unusually high number. Congress, **Jan. 6**, formally counted the votes cast by the members of the Electoral College, and Bill Clinton and Al Gore were declared elected as president and vice president. The Senate, **Jan. 6**, began confirmation hearings for those chosen by Clinton for cabinet positions and other top jobs in his administration. Clinton, **Jan. 8**, met in Austin, Tex., with Pres. Carlos Salinas de Gortari of Mexico. Clinton said he supported the North American Free Trade Agreement but would not press for its ratification by the Senate until Mexico gave assurances on matters of concern to U.S. labor leaders and environmentalists.

Economic Data Issued — The Office of Management and Budget, **Jan. 6**, issued projections for immense budget deficits through the next 6 years. The deficit for 1993 was put at $327.3 billion, and the shortfalls for 1994 through 1998 were foreseen as nearly as large. The Labor Dept. reported, **Jan. 8**, that the unemployment rate had held steady at 7.3 percent in December. The Commerce Dept. reported, **Jan. 14**, that a strong Christmas buying season had helped retail sales post a 5.1 percent increase in 1992. The department said, **Jan. 15**, that the merchandise trade deficit had widened in November 1992 to $7.59 billion. The Labor Dept. reported, **Jan. 15**, that consumer prices had risen 2.9 percent in 1992, the lowest annual inflation rate since 1986. Food and clothing costs had held nearly steady, but medical expenses had jumped 6.6 percent. The Commerce Dept. said, **Jan. 28**, that the gross national product had grown 2.1 percent in 1992, following a 1.2 percent decline in 1991. The growth rate had been accelerating toward the end of 1992.

Keating Guilty on More S&L Charges — Charles H. Keating, Jr., former chairman of the parent company of the failed Lincoln Savings & Loan Association, was convicted on more charges. On **Jan. 6**, a federal jury in Los Angeles found him guilty on 73 counts of fraud and racketeering. His son, Charles H. Keating, 3d, was found guilty on 64 counts. Prosecutors had accused the Keatings of defrauding investors and regulators and of diverting Lincoln's profits for their own use. The elder Keating, **July 8**, was sentenced to 12 years and 7 months in prison. He was currently serving a previous sentence for violations of California security laws.

Senators Report on POW-MIA Inquiry — The Senate Select Committee on POW-MIA Affairs reported, **Jan. 13**, that it had found "no compelling evidence" that any U.S. service personnel were being held in Indochina (although the committee determined that 305 POWs might have survived for a while in captivity after the peace agreement was signed in 1973). The committee rejected any suggestion that U.S. government officials had sought to conceal evidence that Americans were being held long after the war.

Attorney-General Rebukes FBI Director — Attorney-Gen. William Barr, **Jan. 15**, wrote to William Sessions, director of the FBI, and accused him of "a pattern of abuse." A report released by the FBI's Office of Professional Responsibility on **Jan. 19**, charged that Sessions had failed to pay income tax on his government limousine, used government funds for personal travel, assigned his security personnel to non-FBI work, and billed the government $10,000 for a fence around his house. Sessions, **Jan. 19**, denied the allegations. Barr left office with the installation of a new administration, but Sessions continued to serve.

Clinton Becomes 42d President — Bill Clinton (officially William Jefferson Clinton) was inaugurated in January as the 42d president of the U.S. The president-elect and Vice President-elect Al Gore began the celebration with a visit, **Jan. 17**, to the home of Pres. Thomas Jefferson in Charlottesville, Va. Clinton and Gore then traveled by bus to the capital, following the approximate route Jefferson had taken to his inaugural in 1801. They joined some 300,000 spectators at a musical program at the Lincoln Memorial that afternoon, then led a procession across the Potomac River to ring a replica of the Liberty Bell. Clinton addressed the diplomatic corps at Georgetown University, **Jan. 18**, then attended a service at Howard University in honor of the Rev. Martin Luther King, Jr. On **Jan. 19**, Clinton visited the gravesite of former Pres. John Kennedy and attended a Celebration for Children at the Kennedy Center and the Presidential Gala at the Capital Centre. On the morning of Inauguration Day, **Jan. 20**, Clinton and his wife and daughter attended an interfaith church service and were welcomed to the White House by Pres. George Bush and Barbara Bush. The two first families then traveled to the Capitol. Before a large throng of dignitaries and citizens, Gore and then Clinton took the oath for their respective offices. In his inaugural address, Clinton said, "This ceremony is held in the depth of winter, but by the words we speak and the faces we show the world, we force the spring." He asserted, "There is nothing wrong with America that cannot be cured by what is right with America." George and Barbara Bush left Washington immediately for Houston, where they were renting a home. The Clintons led the inaugural parade down Pennsylvania Avenue to the White House, walking the last 2 blocks. That evening, the president, vice president, and their wives attended 11 inaugural balls. On **Jan. 21**, the Clintons held an open house at the White House for 3,000 visitors. The White House announced, **Jan. 21**, that First Lady Hillary Clinton would have an office in the West Wing of the White House, the section usually reserved for high government officials. Meanwhile, the Senate, acting quickly, confirmed on **Jan. 20** and **21** most of Clinton's nominees for administration offices.

Large Corporations Face Turmoil — January was a difficult month for some major U.S. corporations. IBM, **Jan. 19**, announced that it had lost $4.97 billion in 1992, the largest one-year loss ever for any U.S. corporation. McDonnell Douglas, the largest U.S. defense contractor, announced, **Jan. 25**, that it would cut 8,700 jobs. Sears, Roebuck & Co., the nation's 3d largest retailer, said, **Jan. 25**, that it would eliminate 50,000 jobs, close 113 of 859 stores, and cease publication of its catalog, a marketing tool since 1896. Boeing, the world's largest airplane manufacturer, **Jan. 26**, announced production cutbacks that appeared likely to trigger 20,000 dismissals. The Pratt & Whitney unit of United Technologies said, **Jan. 26**, that it would eliminate 6,700 jobs.

Clinton Reverses Restrictions on Abortion — Pres. Bill Clinton, **Jan. 22**, issued executive orders overturning restrictions on abortion imposed during the administrations of Ronald Reagan and George Bush. Clinton canceled the rule barring anyone (except doctors) at federally funded family-planning clinics from discussing abortion; lifted the ban on fetal tissue use in federally funded medical research; ordered a review of the prohibition on RU-486, a French-made abortion pill; killed the policy barring U.S. aid to foreign family-planning programs that included abortion counseling; and ended a ban on abortions in U.S. military hospitals overseas if they were paid for by private funds.

Ban on Gays in Military Debated — During his presidential campaign, Bill Clinton had said he would end the policy of the armed forces that barred homosexuals from enlisting and that required the discharge of any service personnel found to be gay. At a meeting, **Jan. 25**, with Pres. Clinton, Gen. Colin Powell, chairman of the Joint Chiefs of Staff, and the other chiefs made clear their opposition to lifting the ban. The chiefs and others who supported the ban acknowledged that many homosexuals were serving secretly in the armed forces. But they contended that if gays could make their sexual orientation publicly known, the services would see a decline in morale and recruitment. Supporters of homosexual rights contended that the ban was a violation of gays' civil rights and that only actual misconduct should be the basis of disciplinary action or dismissal. On **Jan. 28**, U.S. District Judge Terry Hatter, ruling in the case of Petty Officer 1st Class Keith Meinhold, held that the ban on homosexuals was unconstitutional. An appeal was later filed. Clinton, **Jan. 29**, announced a 6-month interim policy: The armed forces would no longer ask recruits about their sexual orientation, and openly gay personnel would be placed on standby reserve status rather than receive a discharge.

Hillary Rodham Clinton to Head Health Task Force — On **Jan. 25**, Pres. Bill Clinton appointed his wife, Hillary Rodham Clinton, as head of the Task Force on National Health Care Reform. The task force would seek to find ways to provide medical coverage for all Americans and to control the costs of medical care. No other first lady had ever assumed such a major public responsibility.

Republicans Elect New Leader — The Republican National Committee, **Jan. 29**, elected Haley Barbour of Mississippi as its new chairman. Barbour, a lawyer and lobbyist, had once made an unsuccessful bid for a U.S. Senate seat. In a speech to the committee the retiring chairman, Rich Bond, warned that social conservatives in the GOP were driving away voters by making opposition to abortion a leading issue.

International

Czech, Slovak States Established — On **Jan. 1**, 2 independent states—the Czech Republic and Slovakia—were founded as a result of the division of Czechoslovakia. Slovaks generally celebrated, but Czechs were reported to have mixed feelings about the amicable divorce. Vaclav Havel, a former president of Czechoslovakia, was elected president of the Czech Republic, **Jan. 26**. Michal Kovac, an economist, was elected president of Slovakia, **Feb. 15**.

U.N. Forces in Somalia — Pres. George Bush concluded his trip to Somalia, **Jan. 1**, with a visit to an orphanage in Baidoa. After snipers fired on U.S. Marines in Mogadishu, the Marines, **Jan. 7**, raided the compound of one of the Somali warlords. No Americans were injured in the exchange of fire, but many Somalis fled or were killed or captured. Representatives of 14 Somali factions, meeting in Addis Ababa, the capital of Ethiopia, **Jan. 15**, signed a nationwide cease-fire. They agreed to relinquish their heavy artillery to the U.S.-led forces until a government was established. Militias were to be disarmed. On **Jan. 19**, planes flew 556 Marines from Somalia to their base in California. They were the first American service personnel to leave Somalia. U.S. and Belgian troops, **Jan. 25**, enforced the cease-fire by routing Somali guerrillas advancing on the city of Kismayu. A U.S. Marine, shot on patrol in Mogadishu, **Jan. 25**, became the 3d American to be killed in the U.S.-led relief operation.

Division of Bosnia Proposed — Talks aimed at ending the devastating civil war in Bosnia and Herzegovina opened in Geneva, **Jan. 2**. The conference cochairmen, Cyrus Vance and Lord Owen, representing the U.N. and the European Community, respectively, proposed to split Bosnia into 10 semiautonomous provinces. Pres. Alija Izetbegovic of Bosnia visited the U.S., **Jan. 7** and **8**, seeking Western military aid. A European Community investigation found, **Jan. 8**, that Bosnian Serbs had raped up to 20,000 Muslim women and girls. Deputy Premier Hakija Turajlic of Bosnia was assassinated, **Jan. 8**, by Serbian militiamen even though he was traveling under U.N. protection. The Croatian army, **Jan. 22**, attacked a Serbian-held enclave on the Adriatic Sea; the Serbians launched a counterattack, **Jan. 27**.

Bush, Yeltsin Sign Arms Treaty — Pres. George Bush and Russian Pres. Boris Yeltsin signed the 2d Strategic Arms Reduction Treaty (START II) in Moscow, **Jan. 3**. It required the signatories to cut their long-range nuclear arsenals by about two-thirds from existing levels. Land-based multiple-warhead missiles would be eliminated entirely. START II would not be implemented until the other signatories to START I —Ukraine, Belarus, and Kazakhstan—honored the terms of that treaty. Ukraine and Belarus had yet to ratify START I.

Allies Launch Air Attacks in Iraq — U.S., French, and British warplanes attacked missile batteries and radar stations in Iraq, **Jan. 13**. The White House said, **Jan. 13**, that Iraq had attempted to position anti-aircraft surface-to-air missiles in the southern no-fly zone created to protect Shiite Muslims from Iraqi attack. Pres. George Bush also sent 1,250 Army troops to Kuwait to guard against Iraqi incursions. In the northern no-fly zone, established to protect the Kurdish population, a U.S. fighter plane, **Jan. 17**, downed an Iraqi fighter. The Iraqi government said, **Jan. 19**, after more Allied attacks, that it would no longer harass Allied planes patrolling the no-fly zones and that it would guarantee the safety of U.N. arms experts conducting inspections in Iraq. The ruling council said its action was a gesture of goodwill toward the incoming Clinton administration. U.S. planes again attacked air-defense installations, **Jan. 22** and **23**.

Israel Drops Ban on Contacts With PLO — The Israeli parliament, **Jan. 19**, overturned the law barring Israelis from contact with members of the Palestine Liberation Organization. Although the government of Prime Minister Yitzhak Rabin remained opposed to direct contacts with the PLO, the law's repeal represented an attempt to revive the Middle East peace negotiations. Israel's deportation in December of more than 400 Palestinians remained a source of controversy. U.N. Secretary-Gen. Boutros Boutros-Ghali urged the Security Council, **Jan. 26**, to do whatever was necessary to force Israel to take back the deportees. The Israeli Supreme Court ruled, **Jan. 28**, that the expulsions were legal.

General

Nations Sign Chemical-Weapons Ban — After 24 years of negotiations, more than 120 countries began to sign, at a ceremony in Paris, **Jan. 13**, a treaty that would forbid the manufacture, stockpiling, and use of chemical weapons. Twenty-nine toxic chemicals and 14 "families" of compounds would be banned outright or controlled tightly if they had both military and civilian uses. Countries were given 10 years to destroy any existing stockpiles of chemical weapons. The U.S., Russia, and Iraq openly possessed chemical weapons, but 20 other nations were suspected to have them as well. Although the U.S. and Russia agreed to sign the treaty, Iraq did not.

EPA Issues Warning on Second-Hand Smoke — A U.S. Environmental Protection Agency report, **Jan. 7**, said that nonsmokers were at risk when they inhaled the smoke from other people's tobacco products. The EPA said that so-called passive smoking caused 3,000 cases of lung cancer in nonsmokers annually, up to 300,000 cases of bronchitis and other respiratory infections in small children, and a higher frequency of asthma attacks in up to 1 million children. Tobacco industry representatives said that studies on second-hand smoke were scientifically unsound.

Subway Opens in Los Angeles — Los Angeles, long notorious for its maze of highways and glut of private cars, got its first subway service, **Jan. 30**. The only route available linked 5 stations, from Union Station to MacArthur Park. The 4.4-mile route could be covered in 7 minutes. A 22.7-mile system, connecting 20 stations, was projected by 2001.

Cowboys Win Super Bowl — Before 98,374 fans at the Rose Bowl in Pasadena, Calif., **Jan. 31**, the Dallas Cowboys trounced the Buffalo Bills, 52-17, in Super Bowl XXVII. The victory gave the Cowboys their first championship in 15 years, while the Bills suffered their 3d straight Super Bowl loss, a new record. Dallas quarterback Troy Aikman, who completed 22 of 30 passes for 273 yards and 4 touchdowns, was voted the game's most valuable player.

FEBRUARY

National

Data Suggest Improving Economy — The index of leading economic indicators rose 1.9 percent in December, the Commerce Dept. reported, **Feb. 2**. That was the largest monthly increase in almost 10 years. The Labor Dept. reported, **Feb. 5**, that the unemployment rate had fallen from 7.3 percent to 7.1 percent in January. On Wall Street, **Feb. 5**, the Dow Jones industrial average closed at 3,442.14, an all-time high. The Labor Dept. reported, **Feb. 12**, that the prices charged by producers for finished goods had risen 0.2 percent in January. Concern among investors over Pres. Bill Clinton's economic program caused the Dow Jones average to tumble 82.94 points, **Feb. 16**, to 3,309.49, but stock prices soon resumed an upward trend. Consumer prices jumped 0.5 percent in January, the Labor Dept. reported, **Feb. 18**. The Commerce Dept. reported, **Feb. 18**, that the deficit in merchandise trade had been $84.34 billion for all of 1992, a 29 percent jump over 1991. In New York trading, **Feb. 22**, the Japanese yen closed at 116.40 to the U.S. dollar, a record high for the yen since World War II.

Reno Nominated for Attorney General — Pres. Bill Clinton in February nominated Janet Reno, a Florida state attorney, for the office of attorney general in his cabinet. Clinton's first announced choice for the position, Zoe Baird, had withdrawn her name from consideration in January, after it became known that she and her husband had hired illegal aliens when it was not legal to do so, and had also failed to pay Social Security taxes on their wages. White House officials reportedly learned, **Feb. 4**, that U.S. District Judge Kimba Wood of New York City, who was then thought to be in line for the appointment, had also employed an illegal alien as a babysitter, although at a time when such employment was not illegal. Wood, **Feb. 5**, withdrew her name from consideration. On **Feb. 11**, Clinton nominated Reno, who had been the chief state prosecutor in Miami since 1978.

GM's Pickup Truck, Financial Woes — A state-court jury in Atlanta, **Feb. 4**, found General Motors negligent and ordered the company to pay $105.2 million in damages to the parents of Shannon Moseley, 17, who had been killed in 1989 when his GM pickup truck burst into flames after being struck by another vehicle. The plaintiffs had argued that the placement of dual fuel tanks outside the truck's steel internal frame had increased the likelihood of a fire after a collision. One witness had testified that GM knew the design was flawed. GM charged, **Feb. 8**, that in November of

1992, NBC had shown rigged crash tests of GM pickup trucks on television. GM said NBC had ordered the company that had conducted the crash tests to place toy rocket engines under a truck to ensure that it caught fire when struck. NBC agreed, **Feb. 9**, to issue a televised apology that night and to pay GM $2 million, the cost of GM's investigation into the crash tests. GM, **Feb. 11**, reported a loss of $23.5 billion in 1992, by far the largest one-year loss in the U.S. corporate history, although most of the deficit was the result of a one-time charge to cover future costs of retirees' health benefits.

Family-Leave Act 1st Victory for Clinton — Pres. Bill Clinton claimed his first legislative victory when the Senate and House, **Feb. 4**, both passed the Family and Medical Leave Act. Clinton, who strongly supported the measure, signed it into law, **Feb. 5**. The bill, which applied to government workers and to employees of companies having 50 or more workers, permitted anyone employed at least one year to take up to 12 weeks of unpaid leave a year to deal with the birth or adoption of a child or with an illness suffered by the employee or another family member. Employers would be required to provide health-care benefits during the leave and to guarantee that employees on leave could reclaim their jobs. Pres. George Bush had vetoed similar bills twice.

Weinberger's Diaries Made Public — Lawrence Walsh, the independent prosecutor in the Iran-contra case, released excerpts from the diaries of Caspar Weinberger, **Feb. 8**. Walsh said that the diaries, which Weinberger had kept while serving as secretary of defense, showed that he had been involved in a cover-up of the scandal. Pres. George Bush had pardoned Weinberger in December, just before he was to go on trial. Walsh said that a Weinberger trial would have brought new evidence to light that members of the Reagan administration had sought to conceal facts from Congress and the public. In his interim report, Walsh suggested that Bush had pardoned Weinberger to avoid being called as a witness at the trial.

Clinton Announces Economic Program — Pres. Bill Clinton presented his economic program to Congress and the American people in February. The plan sought to add impetus to the economic recovery and at the same time cut deeply into the size of the annual federal budget deficits. In his first step to create a climate of shared sacrifice, Clinton announced, **Feb. 9**, that the White House staff would be reduced by 25 percent, with the elimination of 350 positions. He issued executive orders, **Feb. 10**, to phase out 100,000 federal jobs in 4 years and to reduce federal administrative expenses by 14 percent. The president unveiled the broad outlines of his program in a nationally televised address to a joint session of Congress, **Feb. 17**. The program, if enacted, was expected to reduce the aggregate budget deficit by $325 billion over 4 years. Clinton proposed to increase the personal income tax rate to 36 percent from 31 percent for those couples with taxable incomes of $140,000 or more and individuals with taxable incomes of $115,000 or more. He would also add a 10 percent surtax on family income above $250,000. For couples with total income of more than $32,000 receiving Social Security benefits, the portion of benefits subject to taxation would rise from 50 percent to 85 percent. The top corporate income-tax rate would rise from 34 percent to 36 percent, and the deductible portion of business meals and entertainment would be reduced from 80 percent to 50 percent. Taxes on gasoline and other forms of energy would be imposed, possibly increasing a family's annual fuel bill by $100 to $150. In an effort to cut federal spending under Clinton's plan, federal workers would forgo one annual raise; the Defense Dept. would cut expenditures on new weapons and reduce troop levels; and spending on over 150 civil projects, including a space station and the superconducting supercollider, would be slashed. Also, new limits would be imposed on Medicare payments to doctors, hospitals, and laboratories. On the other hand, Clinton endorsed a short-term economic stimulus plan with increased spending on education, mass transit, highway construction, and summer jobs.

Explosion Shuts Down World Trade Center — A powerful bomb exploded in an underground parking garage beneath the World Trade Center in New York City, **Feb. 26**, killing 6 people and forcing the temporary closing of the complex. The twin towers of the World Trade Center are the world's second and third tallest buildings. The lower Manhattan complex also includes a hotel, a building housing commodity exchanges, and a shopping arcade. The explosion, at 12:18 P.M. on a Friday, left a crater 200 feet wide and several stories deep within the garage. The Port Authority of New York and New Jersey operates the complex, including an underground train station where many people were trapped for awhile under rubble. Four Port Authority employees were killed as they ate lunch in their underground office. A 5th victim died of a heart attack after the explosion. The 6th victim's body was not recovered until **Mar. 15**. About 50,000 people evacuated the buildings. Most of the occupants of the 110-story towers had to walk down stairwells through dense smoke. More than 1,000 suffered injuries, mostly smoke inhalation.

Four Agents Die in Shootout With Cult — Four federal agents were killed, **Feb. 28**, during an unsuccessful raid on the compound of a religious cult near Waco, Tex. At least 2 cultists were killed and 16 agents were wounded. The Branch Davidians, a Christian group, had broken away from the Davidians, who in turn had left the Seventh-Day Adventist church. The leader of the Branch Davidians, David Koresh, had said that he was the messiah and that he believed the apocalypse would occur soon. Koresh claimed more than 100 people lived in the compound, named Mount Carmel, including Koresh's many wives and children. After an investigation, 100 agents of the U.S. Bureau of Alcohol, Tobacco, and Firearms attempted to approach the compound by surprise, **Feb. 28**, carrying warrants to search the premises for illegal guns and explosives and to arrest Koresh. But Koresh had apparently been warned of the ATF's plans, and the exchange of fire occurred. ATF agents were allowed to retrieve their comrades who had been hit. Then, ATF personnel, joined by hundreds of officers from federal, state, and local agencies, surrounded and laid siege to the compound.

International

Israel Offers Compromise on Deportees — Israeli Prime Minister Yitzhak Rabin made a proposal, **Feb. 1**, to defuse the controversy over some 400 Palestinians it had deported. Israel would allow 100 of the deportees to return right away, though most of them would be imprisoned, and the remaining exiles could return home in a year. But the deportees declared, **Feb. 2**, that they would all remain in no-man's land between Israel and Lebanon until all could return to Israel.

Fighting Resumes in Somalia — Sec. of State Warren Christopher reported, **Feb. 1**, that he and U.N. Secretary Gen. Boutros Boutros-Ghali had agreed that U.S. soldiers in Somalia should soon be replaced by a U.N. peace-keeping force. The American withdrawal from the southern port city of Kismayu was delayed, **Feb. 22**, by fighting between Somali factions. Rioting and demonstrations against foreigners erupted in Mogadishu, the capital, **Feb. 24**. Protesters fired on U.N. offices, the U.S. diplomatic mission, and hotels where foreigners stayed. Four Americans were wounded. An attacking clan leader was warned to pull out of Kismayu and on **Feb. 26**, 71 of his soldiers surrendered to international forces.

President, Premier Clash in Zaire; 1,000 Killed — Fighting erupted in Zaire in late January and early February after soldiers and shopkeepers protested the introduction of new high-denomination banknotes. Soldiers loyal to Pres. Mobutu Sese Seko fought with rebel soldiers, and about 1,000 people were killed. Premier Etienne Tshisekedi declared the new paper money to be worthless, and on **Feb. 4** he called for foreign military intervention to restore order. Mobutu, **Feb. 5**, rejected appeals from foreign diplomats that he step down as president, and he dismissed Tshisekedi, who refused to leave office. On **Feb. 24**, soldiers and tanks surrounded the legislature in the capital, Kinshasa, and Mobutu insisted that the lawmakers accept the banknotes. The legislators agreed, **Feb. 26**, to cooperate with Mobutu.

U.S. Drops Food, Medicine Over Bosnia — The United States began parachuting food and medical supplies into Muslim-held areas of Bosnia and Herzegovina in February. On **Feb. 10**, Sec. of State Warren Christopher said that the Clinton administration would actively engage in the Vance-Owen negotiations and would "tighten the enforcement of economic sanctions, increase political pressure on Serbia and deter Serbia from widening the war." By a unanimous vote, the U.N. Security Council, **Feb. 22**, approved creation of an international court to prosecute war crimes in the former Yugoslavia. Operating under the 1949 Geneva Convention, the court would be the first of its kind since those who judged accused war criminals after World War II. In a statement issued **Feb. 25**, Pres. Bill Clinton said he had ordered air drops over Bosnia to proceed, "strictly for humanitarian purposes." The action represented the first unilateral U.S. military involvement in the Yugoslav conflict. The supplies were to be dropped by unarmed transport flying at high altitude without fighter escorts. The first mission, to aid the besieged Muslims of Cerska, took place **Feb. 28**.

South African Transition Approved — The government of South Africa and the African National Congress reached agreement, **Feb. 12**, on a plan that would lead to black-majority rule in 1999. In the first step, South Africans of all races would elect a 400-seat assembly in 1994. The assembly would serve as a parliament until 1999 and would write a new constitution. A new president, chosen from the most successful party, would need cabinet approval for all major decisions. Not all blacks welcomed the plan. Mangosuthu Gatsha Buthelezi, president of the Inkatha Freedom Party, objected vigorously, **Feb. 13**, and he appeared to support greater regional autonomy. The left-wing Pan African Congress also protested, **Feb. 15**. The ANC, **Feb. 18**, approved the transition plan, although some ANC leaders said the transition period was too long.

Mulroney Steps Down in Canada — Prime Minister Brian Mulroney of Canada announced, **Feb. 24**, he would resign as leader of the Progressive Conservative Party and as prime minister when a successor was chosen. Given Mulroney's popularity rating of only 17 percent, his resignation was seen as likely to enhance the chances of his party in the national election that would take place in late 1993. Canada's economy was in a deep recession, and the 7 percent value-added tax adopted by the government in 1991 was unpopular. Mulroney's tenure of 8½ years had been noteworthy for the establishment of free trade with the U.S. and for his failure to resolve conflicts between Canadians of English and French descent.

General

Owner of Baseball Team Suspended — Marge Schott, the only woman who owned a major league baseball team, was suspended for one year, **Feb. 3**, by baseball's executive council. Schott, owner of the Cincinnati Reds, had been accused of making racist and anti-Semitic remarks. She was fined $25,000 and barred from the team's day-to-day operations for one year. She would continue as general partner of the Reds.

Impact of AIDS on Society Studied — In a report issued **Feb. 4**, the National Research Council said that AIDS had little impact on most Americans because the epidemic had struck mostly "marginalized" groups—homosexuals, drug users, the poor, and the undereducated. As a result, the report said, AIDS "may be ignored by the general population and by public policy."

MARCH

National

Standoff With Texas Cult Continues — The armed confrontation between federal authorities and the Branch Davidian religious cult continued in March. Many Davidians remained inside their compound near Waco, Tex; however, more than 30 people, mostly children, left or were freed from the compound by the cult leader, David Koresh. Fewer than 100, including at least 17 children, remained. Koresh said, **Mar. 2**, that he and his followers would surrender if his 58-minute taped monologue were broadcast on the radio. Although several stations played the tape, Koresh then said that God had told him to wait. Agents cut off the compound's electricity, **Mar. 12**, and concentrated floodlights on the compound at night, beginning **Mar. 14**. Two cultists came out, **Mar. 15**, to meet with federal officials, but negotiations made no headway. Three cult members who had left the compound earlier were indicted, **Mar. 30**, for conspiracy to murder federal officers. Four agents had been killed in an unsuccessful assault on the compound in February.

Data Suggest Inflationary Pressures — Statistics released in March suggested that inflation might become a problem for the U.S. economy. The Commerce Dept. reported, **Mar. 2**, that the index of leading economic indicators had risen 0.1 percent in January. The Labor Dept. said, **Mar. 5**, that the unemployment rate in February had edged downward from 7.1 percent to 7.0 percent and that 365,000 new jobs had been created. On Wall Street, the Dow Jones industrial average closed, **Mar. 10**, at 3478.34, a new all-time high. The Labor Dept. reported, **Mar. 12**, that prices charged by producers for finished goods had jumped 0.4 percent in February. The department said, **Mar. 17**, that consumer prices had risen 0.3 percent in February. The Federal Reserve Board said, **Mar. 17**, that the output of the nation's factories, mines, and utilities had risen 0.4 percent in February. The U.S. merchandise trade deficit had widened in January, to $7.3 billion, the Commerce Dept. reported, **Mar. 18**. The department said, **Mar. 26**, that after-tax profits of U.S. corporations had risen by 10 percent, to $231.8 billion, in 1992. On **Mar. 31**, the department reported that the index of leading economic indicators had jumped 0.5 percent in February.

Aid to Jobless Extended — The Senate, **Mar. 3**, and the House, **Mar. 4**, approved a bill extending through

October a program giving unemployed workers who had exhausted their benefits up to 6 months in additional aid. In a provision reflecting Pres. Bill Clinton's call for federal employees to forgo salary increases, the bill also froze the pay of members of Congress. On **Mar. 4,** Clinton signed the bill.

Suspects Held in New York Bombing — Five men were arrested in March in connection with the February bombing at the World Trade Center in New York City. In Jersey City, N.J., **Mar. 4,** FBI agents arrested Mohammed Salameh, a Jordanian-born Palestinian who lived in Jersey City. According to authorities, Salameh was a follower of Sheikh Omar Abdel Rahman, described as a spiritual leader of radical Islamic groups. Investigators had found fragments of a yellow Ford van at the site of the explosion and believed it had carried the bomb. They traced its vehicle identification number to a van rented by Salameh in Jersey City 3 days before the explosion. Salameh had notified the Ryder truck-rental agency that the van had been stolen, and when he returned to the agency to get a refund on a $400 deposit, he was arrested. The FBI said that his apartment contained evidence that he had been involved in making a bomb. A 2d man, Ibrahim Elgabrowny, was arrested, **Mar. 4,** in Brooklyn, N.Y. after resisting authorities as they searched his apartment in connection with the investigation. A chemical engineer, Nidal Ayyad, was arrested, **Mar. 10,** at his Maplewood, N.J. apartment. The FBI said he had had contacts with Salameh and had the expertise to make explosives. The 3 suspects were indicted in New York City, **Mar. 17.** Abdel Rahman denied, **Mar. 18,** that he had been involved in the bombing. While repair work continued, some tenants returned to the World Trade Center, **Mar. 18.** Mahmud Abouhalima was turned over to U.S. authorities by the Egyptian government and arrested on the plane, **Mar. 24,** upon arrival in the U.S. Abouhalima was reported to have been seen with Salameh the morning of the bombing. A fifth suspect, Bilal Alkaisi, was arrested on **Mar. 25,** the day after he turned himself in at FBI offices in Newark, N.J. Allegedly, Alkaisi was sighted at a N.J. storage shed containing materials to make explosives. Later, a timing mechanism was found in Alkaisi's apartment. A sixth man, Ramzi Ahmed Yousef, was indicted, **Mar. 31,** in connection with the bombing. Yousef, who shared an apartment with Salameh, was at large, and it was not known whether he was still in the U.S.

First Woman Attorney General Confirmed — In March, Janet Reno became the first woman to serve as attorney general of the U.S. Reno, a Florida state attorney, had been nominated for the office by Pres. Bill Clinton in February. At her confirmation hearings before the Senate Judiciary Committee, **Mar. 9** and **10,** Reno said that she would resist political pressures on the Justice Dept. and act forcefully against violent crime and drug trafficking. The committee, **Mar. 10,** and the full Senate, **Mar. 11,** approved her nomination unanimously. Reno took the oath of office **Mar. 12.**

Health Task Force Hears Many Opinions — The Task Force on National Health Care Reform, established by Pres. Bill Clinton and headed by First Lady Hillary Rodham Clinton, conducted its first public meeting in March. A U.S. District Court judge held, **Mar. 10,** that any hearing in which the task force gathered information must be open to the public, since the Federal Advisory Committee Act required that federal advisory bodies conduct open meetings. During a 13-hour public meeting, **Mar. 29,** the task force heard from more than 60 witnesses, including doctors, nurses, social workers, and representatives from insurance companies, small businesses, and nursing homes.

Doctor Killed by Opponent of Abortion — A doctor was shot dead, **Mar. 10,** outside an abortion clinic in Pensacola, Fla. The gunman, Michael Griffin, surrendered to police and accepted responsibility for the shooting. The victim, David Gunn, had performed many abortions in Pensacola and elsewhere. Demonstrations, sometimes becoming violent, had become commonplace at abortion clinics across the United States. Griffin was a member of Rescue America, an antiabortion organization. Don Teshman, national director of Rescue America, said, **Mar. 10,** that Dr. Gunn's death was unfortunate but that "it's also true that quite a number of babies' lives will be saved."

Clinton Economic Program Advances — Congress approved a budget resolution supporting Pres. Bill Clinton's plan to reduce the federal budget deficits. The budget resolution sets broad guidelines, which need to be fleshed out later in more specific implementing legislation before they can take effect. The House first passed its version, **Mar. 18,** providing for spending cuts and tax increases designed to achieve a net deficit reduction of $496 billion over 5 years. The House, **Mar. 19,** also approved the president's short-term economic-stimulus package, which included benefits for the long-term unemployed and outlays for highway construction, small business loans, community development, college loans, and summer jobs for youths. The Senate passed its version of the budget resolution, **Mar. 25,** which projected deficit reductions totaling $502 billion over 5 years. In conference committee, **Mar. 30,** Senate and House negotiators agreed to a budget reduction over 5 years. To secure the support of Senate and House Democrats from western states, the compromise conference resolution omitted cuts in crop subsidies and also eliminated increased fees on mining, grazing, and logging on public lands. The House, **Mar. 31,** and the Senate, **Apr. 1,** gave final approval to budget resolution.

Justice White Announces Retirement — Associate Justice Byron White announced, **Mar. 19,** that he would retire from the U.S. Supreme Court at the conclusion of the court's 1992-1993 term. Appointed by Pres. John Kennedy in 1962, White had served longer than any other justice currently on the court and had been the only sitting justice nominated by a Democratic president. White's voting record on the court generally placed him with the advocates of judicial restraint. At a press conference, **Mar. 23,** Pres. Bill Clinton was asked if the abortion issue would be considered in the search for a successor to White. Clinton said he would not seek to ascertain a candidate's views on a specific case but that he would seek someone who supported "the constitutional rights to privacy."

International

Search for Peace in Bosnia Stalls — Efforts to bring peace to Bosnia and Herzegovina enjoyed only limited success in March. Peace talks resumed, **Mar. 1,** at U.N. headquarters in New York. U.S. officials said, **Mar. 1,** that Pres. Bill Clinton had warned Pres. Slobodan Milosevic of Serbia that the U.S. would take military action if Serbia permitted civil war to spread to its Kosovo region, which was populated mostly by Muslim ethnic Albanians. In the first days of March the U.S. continued to airdrop food and supplies into Bosnia. In a letter released **Mar. 2,** the Bosnian Serb leader, Radovan Karadzic, warned that the "ill-advised American humanitarian" effort could cause the local conflict to expand even to a world war. Reports from Bosnia indicated that the Serbs were continuing to advance and to block U.N. truck convoys seeking to provide humanitarian aid. Gen. Philippe Morillon, the

U.N. commander in Bosnia, went to the besieged Muslim town of Srebrenica, **Mar. 12**, and residents persuaded him to stay to protect them from massacre at the hands of the Serbs. A U.N. effort to airlift sick and wounded Muslims from Srebrenica was suspended, **Mar. 24**, when Serbs shelled the landing zone. In New York, **Mar. 25**, Bosnian Muslims joined Croat leaders in endorsing the Vance-Owen plan to divide Bosnia into 10 semi-autonomous provinces, but Karadzic rejected the plan because most natural and industrial resources would remain in Muslim and Croat control. A U.N. truck convoy reached Srebrenica, **Mar. 28**, and the trucks took out several thousand refugees, **Mar. 29-31**.

U.N. Peace Force Approved for Somalia — U.N. Secretary-Gen. Boutros Boutros-Ghali proposed, **Mar. 3**, that a U.N. peacekeeping force replace the U.S.-led coalition forces in Somalia. The U.N. Security Council, **Mar. 26**, approved unanimously a resolution to send 28,000 soldiers and 2,800 civilians to Somalia. The troops would come from about 24 countries, and the civilians would run Somalia, which currently lacked a government. U.N.-sponsored talks in Ethiopia resulted in agreement, **Mar. 27**, by Somali leaders to the creation of a transitional government. Under the plan, a council of 74 representatives would lead the country until a national government could be formed.

Yeltsin Struggles to Keep His Powers — For several weeks during March, Russian Pres. Boris Yeltsin resisted attempts by his adversaries in the Congress of People's Deputies to curtail his powers. The congress, elected in 1989, was dominated by former Communists. On **Mar. 12**, the congress repudiated an agreement of December 1992 extending the president's powers to rule by decree. It also canceled an April referendum in which the people were to vote on the relative powers of congress and the president. While most of Russia was undergoing a painful adjustment to a market economy, the congress, **Mar. 13**, called for a slower transition to a market system. At a press conference in Moscow, **Mar. 16**, with French Pres. François Mitterrand, Yeltsin said a serious threat hung over democracy and reforms in Russia. Mitterrand said the West would continue to support the reform process in Russia. Yeltsin announced, **Mar. 20**, that he had signed a decree asserting "special powers" and that there would be a referendum **Apr. 25** on his presidency as well as a vote on a new constitution. Yeltsin's major cabinet ministers rallied behind him, **Mar. 21**, but the vice president, Gen. Aleksandr Rutskoi, said Yeltsin's decree was unconstitutional. On **Mar. 21** the Supreme Soviet, Russia's smaller standing parliament, asked the Constitutional Court to rule on Yeltsin's assumption of special powers. On **Mar. 23**, the court found, by a 10-3 vote, that Yeltsin had violated 9 provisions of the constitution. The court said Yeltsin could not ask the public to choose between presidential and parliamentary control. Ruslan Khasbulatov, chairman of the Congress of People's Deputies, called **Mar. 23**, for Yeltsin's impeachment. Pres. Bill Clinton, **Mar. 23**, publicly backed Yeltsin and "the historic movement toward democratic political reform in Russia." Yeltsin's decree was published, **Mar. 24**, with softer language containing no reference to special powers. Yeltsin and other leaders then sought to avoid further confrontation. On **Mar. 26**, the chairman of the Constitutional Court, Valery Zorkin, offered a compromise plan for government, and Yeltsin acknowledged that mistakes had been made in his economic reform program. But congress deputies responded negatively to a comprise plan between Yeltsin and Khasbulatov, and on **Mar. 28** a vote to impeach Yeltsin fell just 72 votes short—689 were needed. On **Mar. 29**, the Congress of People's Deputies approved an **Apr. 25** referendum but also terminated Yeltsin's powers to rule by decree.

North Korea to Exit From Nuclear Treaty — North Korea announced its withdrawal, **Mar. 12**, from the Nuclear Nonproliferation Treaty. More than 150 countries had signed the treaty, which sought to restrict the spread of nuclear-weapons technology and sales. North Korea gave, as reasons for its withdrawal, joint military exercises by U.S. and South Korean forces in South Korea as well as "unjust acts" by the International Atomic Energy Agency. The agency had asked to inspect suspicious sites in North Korea. South Korea's Foreign Ministry states, **Mar. 12**, that North Korea's withdrawal "heightens the suspicion that it is developing nuclear arms."

Bombs Kill 300 in India — Bombs that exploded in Bombay and Calcutta in March killed more than 300 people and left 1,100 injured. An explosion at the Bombay Stock Exchange, **Mar. 12**, killed about 50 people, and within 90 minutes 10 more bombs had claimed additional lives at banks, government offices, hotels, an airline office, and a shopping complex. Bombay police charged 2 men in the bombings, **Mar. 15**. At least 80 people were killed in Calcutta, **Mar. 17**, when an explosion destroyed 2 apartment buildings. Another bomb exploded in a Calcutta train station, **Mar. 19**. Bombay police said, **Mar. 19**, that a Muslim family in Bombay with links to organized crime had played a role in that city's bombings.

China's Parliament Elects New President — The National People's Congress, the parliament of China, convened **Mar. 15**. Major actions taken by the 2,977 delegates reflected decisions already made by Deng Xiaoping, China's paramount ruler, and other leaders. Premier Li Peng, **Mar. 15**, called for continued economic reform under the leadership of the Communist party. Jiang Zemin, the general secretary of the party, was elected president, **Mar. 27**. Li was reelected as premier, **Mar. 28**, but in something of a surprise more than 10 percent of the delegates voted against him or abstained. On **Mar. 29**, the delegates approved a new constitution that used the phrase "socialist market economy" to characterize the regime's capitalist-style reforms.

Salvadoran Army Blamed in Atrocities — A U.N. commission reported, **Mar. 15**, that it had concluded that most of the human-rights abuses during El Salvador's civil war had been committed by the U.S.-supported Salvadoran army. The commission had interviewed almost 20,000 Salvadorans. The commission linked some leaders of the Nationalist Republican Alliance (ARENA) party, which now ruled El Salvador, to death squads that operated during the 12-year-long war, which ended in 1992. The commission declared that no current members of the country's Supreme Court were capable of fairness in dealing with those accused of human-rights abuses. Defense Minister Gen. René Emilio Ponce, linked by the commission to the killing in 1989 of 6 Jesuit priests and 2 women, had already offered to resign. The report by the commission also said that the late Roberto D'Aubuisson, founder of ARENA, had probably ordered the slaying of Archbishop Oscar Arnulfo Romero in 1980. The report blamed the left-wing Farabundo Martí National Liberation Front for the assassination of many public officials. On **Mar. 20**, ARENA and other right-wing factions successfully supported approval by the National Assembly of an amnesty for those who had committed atrocities during the war, ending any prospects for prosecutions for human-rights abuses.

Clinton Meets Exiled President of Haiti — The Rev. Jean-Bertrand Aristide, who had been elected president of Haiti and then ousted in a military coup, met with Pres. Bill Clinton in Washington, **Mar. 16**. Clinton said he would seek to restore Aristide to power and that the U.S. would not support "continuation of an illegal government in Haiti."

Conservatives Win French Election — Conservative parties won an overwhelming majority of the seats in the French National Assembly in elections held in March. A trend toward the right was apparent in the first round of voting, **Mar. 21**, and after the runoff elections, **Mar. 28**, the conservatives had won 484 of the 577 seats. Scandals and an unemployment rate of 10.5 percent had turned many voters against the governing Socialist party. The results meant that Premier Pierre Beregovoy would have to step down. On **Mar. 29**, Pres. François Mitterrand, a Socialist, named as premier Edouard Balladur, a member of the neo-Gaullist Rally for the Republic party.

Israel's Likud Bloc Names New Leader — The Likud bloc, the principal opposition party in Israel, elected a new leader in March. After Likud was defeated by the Labor party in the 1992 election, the outgoing prime minister, Yitzhak Shamir, announced that he would step down as party leader. On **Mar. 25**, Likud members chose Benjamin Netanyahu, a former deputy foreign minister, as their new leader in a nationwide primary. At age 43, he was a generation younger than most prominent Israeli political leaders.

General

Gene Linked to Lou Gehrig's Disease — The British journal *Nature* reported, **Mar. 4**, that the gene whose mutation caused amyotrophic lateral sclerosis (ALS) had been identified. The disorder, also known as Lou Gehrig's disease for the baseball player who was one of its most prominent victims, causes muscles to waste away and leads to death for most patients within 5 years. Dr. Robert Horovitz of the Massachusetts Institute of Technology, one of the authors of the report, called the discovery "a major breakthrough," but he added, "at this point we do not have a therapy."

Eastern U.S. Storm Claims 200 Lives — A massive storm swept through the Southeast and up the East Coast, **Mar. 13** and **14**. Described by the National Weather Service as one of the worst storms of the century, the onslaught left 13 inches of snow in Birmingham, Ala., and 36 inches in Syracuse, N.Y. Dozens of tornadoes were reported in the South. Power was cut off to millions of homes, thousands of families fled coastal flooding, and most forms of transportation were brought to a near-halt in many states. More than 200 deaths were attributed to the storm.

Huntington's Disease Gene Identified — In a report published in the journal *Cell*, **Mar. 26**, scientists from the U.S., England, and Wales said that they had identified the gene responsible for Huntington's disease. The disease, which afflicts about 30,000 Americans every year, involves degeneration of the basal ganglia, 2 nerve clusters in the brain. Symptoms include rapid and involuntary motion, dementia, personality changes, and memory loss. Huntington's is incurable and is usually fatal within 20 years. Researchers said that although the discovery was a major breakthrough, no treatment for the disease was imminent.

APRIL

National

Texas Cult's Compound Burns, 72 Die— The confrontation between the Branch Davidians and law-enforcement officials ended tragically in April when the religious cult's compound near Waco, Tex., burned to the ground. At least 72 died in the inferno. A lawyer, Dick DeGuerin, visited the compound, **Mar. 29-Apr. 1**, to meet with his client, David Koresh, the leader of the cult. DeGuerin said that Koresh had been wounded in the initial federal assault on the compound in February and appeared to need medical treatment. Hopes, sometimes based on assurances by Koresh, that he would lead his followers out of the compound peacefully were repeatedly dashed. On **Apr. 14**, he said they would come out after he had completed a manuscript on the seven seals mentioned in the Book of Revelations in the Bible. On the morning of **Apr. 19**, the 51st day of the siege, Koresh said that there were 95 people in the compound. A total of 37 others had left since the confrontation began. On that day, the FBI decided to make a move. Bob Ricks, a senior FBI agent, said that an aide to Koresh had been told that the FBI intended to pump tear gas into the compound. Shortly after 6 a.m., armored vehicles moved forward, knocked holes in the walls of the compound, and released tear gas inside. The FBI said that those inside responded with gunfire. Shortly after 12 p.m., flames appeared at a window. The fire spread rapidly, and the compound was leveled within 30 minutes. Nine persons fled from the compound during the fire. When the site cooled, no one else was found alive. Two cultists who had escaped claimed that there had been no plans for a mass suicide and that the fire had been started when one of the armored vehicles had knocked over a container of fuel. Attorney Gen. Janet Reno said, **Apr. 19**, that she made the decision to move on the compound because agents surrounding it lacked adequate replacements, negotiations with Koresh had proved frustrating, and the FBI reported that babies in the compound were being beaten. Pres. Bill Clinton said, **Apr. 19**, that he stood by Reno's decision, and he said, **Apr. 20**, that he bore "full responsibility" for the result. Arson investigators concluded, **Apr. 26**, that the fire had been deliberately set by those inside the compound. Authorities said, **Apr. 29**, that 72 had died in the fire based on remains that had been found. They said it was possible other bodies had been completely incinerated. It was believed that 17 of the victims were children. The remains of 5 cultists killed in the February assault on the compound were also found.

Clinton Stimulus Plan Fails in Senate — Pres. Bill Clinton's $16.3 billion economic stimulus package was defeated by a filibuster by Senate Republicans in April. Republicans complained that the package, part of the president's economic-recovery program, emphasized low-priority projects, including aid to cities, summer jobs, and highway construction, without providing financing. Clinton charged, **Apr. 2**, that the Republican Senate minority was perpetuating gridlock. By **Apr. 6**, when the Senate began a recess, the Democrats had failed 3 times to end the filibuster. Clinton, **Apr. 8**, submitted to Congress a $1.52 trillion budget for the 1994 fiscal year (Oct. 1, 1993-Sept. 30, 1994) that reflected proposals in his February address to Congress. His budget projected a deficit of $264.1 billion in 1994, down from a likely deficit of $322 billion in 1993. The budget called for additional revenue of $296.2 billion over 5 years, mostly from increased income taxes on wealthy individuals and on corporations and an energy tax. Military spending would be reduced. Senate Democrats, **Apr. 21**, gave up their efforts to cut off the Republican filibuster on the stimulus package. However, the Senate did then give its approval, by voice vote, to one part of the plan, which provided $4 billion in extended jobless benefits for the long-term unemployed. The House also approved the benefits, **Apr. 22**.

Economic Growth Rate Slows — A report issued in late April suggested that the economic recovery was losing momentum. The Labor Dept. reported, **Apr. 2**, that the unemployed rate in March was 7 percent for the second consecutive month. The department said, **Apr. 8**, that the prices charged by producers for finished goods had risen 0.4 percent in March. Consumer prices rose only 0.1 percent in March, the department reported, **Apr. 9**. The Commerce Dept. said, **Apr. 16**, that the U.S. trade deficit had been $7.2 billion in February. The Japanese yen, which had appreciated by 12 percent in relation to the U.S. dollar since January, reached a record high, **Apr. 22**, when it stood at 109.95 to the dollar. The weaker dollar had the potential advantage of making U.S. products more attractive to Japanese buyers. To prevent the dollar from tumbling further, however, the Federal Reserve Bank of New York reportedly sold yen for dollars, **Apr. 27**, and brought the yen's surge to a halt, at least temporarily.

Clinton Attends Summit on Forests — Pres. Bill Clinton convened a meeting in Portland, Ore., **Apr. 2**, that sought to determine what should be done with the remaining old-growth forests occupying portions of Washington, Oregon, and northern California. In 1991, a federal court decided in favor of environmentalists, in a suit against the Interior Dept. The court held that the government had failed to protect the habitat of the northern spotted owl, an endangered species, and thus ordered a halt to all logging in the area. Loggers and their families, appearing at the summit in Portland, pleaded with Clinton, Vice Pres. Al Gore, and 4 cabinet secretaries who were present to devise a plan to permit cutting of the forests to resume. Representatives of environmental organizations argued that the loggers would soon run out of the old trees and that what was left should be saved. Spokespeople for the salmon industry said that logging had caused so much environmental damage to streams that their livelihood was also at risk. Clinton said he would seek a balanced solution to the controversy.

Ten Die at Ohio Prison — Nine inmates and a hostage died in April during an outbreak of violence at the Southern Ohio Correctional Facility near Lucasville, Ohio's only maximum security prison. On **Apr. 11**, 8 guards were taken hostage after they sought to break up a fight among inmates in the prison's recreational yard. Prison officials, police, and the National Guard began an 11-day siege of 450 barricaded prisoners, who demanded improvements in conditions within the prison. On **Apr. 12**, the prisoners released the bodies of 6 inmates who appeared to have been fatally beaten by other inmates. Another inmate was found dead the following day in an adjoining cell block. On **Apr. 14**, the prisoners warned they would kill a hostage if their demands were ignored, and the body of a slain guard was left outside the cell block, **Apr. 15**. In an agreement signed **Apr. 21**, Warden Arthur Tate promised to review inmate complaints. The prisoners then surrendered. The bodies of 2 more inmates were found inside the prison.

Gay-Rights Advocates March in Capital — A gay-rights march and rally in Washington, D.C., in April drew at least several hundred thousand demonstrators. Earlier, on **Apr. 16**, Pres. Bill Clinton met with gay and lesbian leaders in the White House in the first meeting of its kind involving an incumbent president. Clinton reportedly reaffirmed his commitment to lifting the ban on service by homosexuals in the U.S. military. Attendance at the **Apr. 25** march in Washington was put at 300,000 to 1 million. Participants called for an end to the military ban, more money to fight AIDS, and a civil-rights bill for gays.

L.A. Calm After Verdicts in King Case — Los Angeles remained quiet in April after a federal jury found 2 police officers guilty and two others not guilty of violating the civil rights of Rodney King, a black motorist whom they had arrested and beaten in 1991. In April 1992 the 4 Los Angeles policemen, all white, had been acquitted of all but one of the state charges brought as a result of the beating of King. That verdict had been followed by widespread urban rioting that left 52 dead and caused $1 billion in property damages. In the second trial, prosecutors had to prove that the accused had intended to deny King his constitutional rights. As in 1992, the principal evidence was an 81-second videotape, made by a man who lived near the site of the incident, which showed that the policemen struck King with their batons more than 50 times and kicked him as he lay on the ground. The defense contended that the blows were appropriate because King was putting up resistance. King testified, **Mar. 9**, that an officer had threatened to kill him and that in resisting, "I was just trying to stay alive, sir." Sgt. Stacey Koon, one of the defendants, testified, **Mar. 24**, that every blow struck had complied with police department policy. The jury, which included 2 blacks and 1 Hispanic, returned its verdict **Apr. 17**. They found Officer Laurence Powell, who had delivered most of the blows, guilty of violating King's right to be free from an arrest made with unreasonable force. Koon, the ranking officer present, was convicted of allowing the violation to occur. The other defendants, Theodore Briseno and Timothy Wind, were acquitted. After the verdict was reached, but before it was announced, 6,500 police officers, supported by National Guard troops, were mobilized throughout Los Angeles. They were not needed, however, and it appeared that most people accepted the split verdict.

Alabama Governor Convicted — Gov. Guy Hunt of Alabama, a Republican, was convicted, **Apr. 22**, of diverting money from an inaugural fund to his personal use, a felony. A circuit court jury in Montgomery delivered the verdict. The case involved $200,000 from Hunt's nonprofit inaugural fund that he had transferred to personal bank accounts and then spent. Hunt denied wrongdoing, and his lawyers planned an appeal based on the vagueness of the law; however, it was unlikely that the Alabama Court of Criminal Appeals would rule on the case before Hunt's term expires in January 1995. Required by state law to resign after his conviction, Hunt did so, **Apr. 22**, and he was succeeded as governor by Lt. Gov. Jim Folsom, Jr., a Democrat. Hunt was sentenced, **May 7**, to pay $211,000 in fines and restitution and perform 1,000 hours of community service.

Tailhook Report Says 90 Were Assaulted — A report released by the Defense Dept., **Apr. 23**, said that 83 women and 7 men were assaulted during the 1991 Tailhook Association convention at the Las Vegas Hilton. (The association's members are present and former Navy fliers.) The 300-page report, prepared by acting Pentagon Deputy Inspector General Derek Vander Schaaf, was based on more than 2,900 interviews. Up to 175 officers could face disciplinary action as a result of their conduct. The report said that victims were "groped, pinched, fondled" and "bitten" by their assailants and that oral sex and sexual intercourse performed in front of others contributed to a "general atmosphere of debauchery." In its latest report on the scandal, the Pentagon said that "Tailhook '91 is the culmination of a long-term failure of leadership in naval aviation."

Women Eligible for Aerial Combat — Women became eligible in April to pilot combat aircraft and to serve on fighter and bomber crews in all 4 branches of the U.S. armed forces. On **Apr. 28**, Defense Sec. Les Aspin, rejecting recommendations by a presidential panel in 1992 that a ban be continued, removed restrictions on aerial combat roles by women in the Air Force, Army, Marines, and Navy. He said he would also recommend that Congress lift a prohibition on participation in combat by women on most ships in the Navy.

International

Foreign Aid, Russian Voters Give Yeltsin a Lift — Russia's beleaguered president, Boris Yeltsin, strengthened his hand in April by obtaining promises of international financial assistance and by getting a vote of confidence in a national referendum. Pres. Bill Clinton said, **Apr. 1**, that support for the Yeltsin government was related to continued domestic U.S. economic growth. Yeltsin was embroiled in a power struggle with conservatives sympathetic with the former communist regime. Great Britain, **Apr. 1**, and Canada, **Apr. 2**, announced packages of financial aid to Russia. Representatives of Russia and its creditor nations agreed in Paris, **Apr. 2**, to reschedule about 75 percent of the $20 billion Russia owed in principal and interest in 1993. Clinton and Yeltsin met at a summit in Vancouver, Canada, **Apr. 3** and **4**. Clinton pledged $1.6 billion in aid. Of this, $894 million consisted of credits and grants for food. Other large sums would help Russia launch investment initiatives and dismantle and store elements of its nuclear arsenal. The Group of 7 nations—the world's leading industrial democracies—announced a $28.4 billion package of aid at a meeting in Tokyo, **Apr. 15**. In their communiqué, the G7 nations stated that continued democratic reform in Russia was "essential to world peace." The U.S. and Japan also announced separate commitments of $1.8 billion, the U.S. pledge being in addition to Clinton's previous promise of support. In the **Apr. 25** referendum, 58 percent of the voters declared that they had confidence in Yeltsin, and 53 percent said they approved of his social and economic policies. A court had held that a simple majority of those voters actually participating in the referendum would be sufficient to decide those 2 questions. Proposals for early parliamentary and presidential elections failed. Yeltsin, **Apr. 29**, proposed a new constitution that would abolish the Congress of People's Deputies and create a 2-chamber parliament. Under Yeltsin's draft, the president would have the power to disband parliament and call new elections in certain circumstances.

Macedonia Joins U.N. — On **Apr. 8**, Macedonia became a member of the U.N. under the formal, but temporary, designation as The Former Yugoslav Republic of Macedonia. A permanent name would be the subject of negotiations with Greece, which had expressed concerns that the use of the name "Macedonia" indicated that the new country was eyeing the territory of the Greek province of Macedonia.

U.S. Planes Bomb Iraqi Positions — Four U.S. planes patrolling the no-fly zone in northern Iraq, **Apr. 9**, were fired on by Iraqi antiaircraft guns, U.S. officials reported. The U.S. planes then bombed the Iraqi positions. Iraq denied initiating the exchange. No U.S. planes were damaged.

Black South African Leader Assassinated — Chris Hani, a secretary general of the South African Communist Party and a leader of the African National Congress, was shot fatally in the driveway of his home in a Johannesburg suburb, **Apr. 10**. Januzu Walus, a Pole who had become a South African citizen, was seized by police, and a pistol in his possession was identified as the weapon used in the assassination. On **Apr. 14**, designated as a day of mourning for Hani, as many as 8 people were killed and hundreds injured as demonstrations turned violent. Clive Derby-Lewis, a leader of the Conservative Party, was arrested, **Apr. 17**, in connection with Hani's death. More than 80,000 attended Hani's funeral, **Apr. 19**, and 4 million black workers went on strike for the day. On **Apr. 21**, 5 more people were held in connection with the assassination. Two were questioned and released.

Bosnian Serbs Reject Peace Plan — The self-proclaimed Bosnian Serb parliament in Bijeljina rejected in late April the U.N.-supported peace plan that would divide Bosnia and Herzegovina into regions based on ethnic makeup. The military situation in Bosnia had grown more complex, **Apr. 16**, when an alliance between Muslims and Croats broke down and they began to fight each other. The U.N. Security Council, **Apr. 17**, reaffirmed sanctions against the Yugoslav Federation—Serbia and Montenegro—for its support of the Bosnian Serb forces. A ceasefire agreement signed, **Apr. 18**, by Serbs and the Muslim defenders of Srebrenica provided that the town become a "safe area" for civilians under U.N. auspices. Yugoslav leaders, **Apr. 26**, urged the Bosnian Serbs to endorse the U.N. peace plan, but the Bosnian Serb parliament voted unanimously that day not to approve it. Pres. Bill Clinton, **Apr. 26**, committed the U.S. to the support of the U.N. sanctions, which went into effect **Apr. 27**. The sanctions froze Yugoslav assets abroad and banned shipment in or out of Yugoslavia, by land or water, of most products. The Serbian parliament in Belgrade, **Apr. 28**, endorsed the U.N. peace plan.

Clinton, Miyazawa Disagree on Trade — Pres. Bill Clinton and Japanese Prime Minister Kiichi Miyazawa failed to see eye to eye on trade issues when they met at the White House, **Apr. 16**. Clinton supported a policy of managed trade, in which market-share goals would be established in the Japanese market for products from the U.S. and other countries. Miyazawa rejected this concept and said later at a news conference that free trade "cannot be realized with managed trade . . . " Clinton had also asserted during their meeting that Japan did not have an open market and that hidden barriers turned away exports to Japan.

Italians Vote for Government Reforms — Allegations of corruption involving many leading Italian politicians produced a backlash in April. In a referendum held **Apr. 18** and **19**, 82 percent of voters endorsed an end to strict proportional representation in the Senate, the upper parliamentary chamber. Proportionality meant that even very small parties could gain representation. Weak and unstable coalition governments were the result. Legislation would be required to end proportional representation in the Chamber of Deputies, the lower parliamentary body. In other referendum results, voters also supported, overwhelmingly, an end to state financing for political parties. Premier Giuliano Amato, a Socialist, submitted his resignation, **Apr. 22**. Seven of his ministers had been touched by scandal. Pres. Oscar Luigi Scalfaro, **Apr. 26**, chose Carlo Azeglio Ciampi, the central bank governor and a political independent, as Amato's successor. Ciampi's broad-based government took office **Apr. 29**. Ciampi's government was immediately threatened when the Chamber of Deputies resisted lifting the immunity of former Socialist Premier Bettino Craxi, so he could be charged in 6 separate corruption cases. The Chamber eventually relented and lifted immunity for the least serious of the allegations.

IRA Bomb Rocks London Financial District — The Irish Republican Army claimed responsibility for a bomb that exploded, **Apr. 24**, in the financial district of London. One man was killed and 45 other people were injured. A 500-year-old church was destroyed, and many buildings were damaged. Despite the displacement of over 20,000 workers, the financial markets reopened Monday, **Apr. 26**. Later that day the police announced that more than 10 people had been arrested in connection with the bombing.

General

Doubt Cast on Value of AIDS Drug — A report published **Apr. 3** called into question the value of the drug AZT in combatting the onset of AIDS symptoms. The U.S. government had recommended the use of AZT by persons infected with the AIDS virus who had not yet developed any symptoms. But the new study showed that the drug did not slow the rate of progression to AIDS or death, when groups who did and did not take AZT were compared. The survey was sponsored by the Medical Research Council of Britain and the National AIDS Research Agency of France.

Parasite Blamed for Illnesses in Milwaukee — Many thousands of people became ill in Milwaukee in March and April, and city health officials said, **Apr. 7**, that a parasite was apparently the culprit. They believed that the parasite, cryptosporidium, had contaminated the city's water supply. It appeared that the protozoan was contained in animal feces washed into Lake Michigan, the city's reservoir. City residents were advised to boil drinking water. Symptoms, including nausea and diarrhea, usually lasted 7 to 10 days, but 6 deaths were attributed to the parasite. Estimates of those who became ill ran as high as 281,000.

Queen Opens Palace to Tourists — Queen Elizabeth II announced, **Apr. 29**, that for 8 weeks beginning in Aug. tourists would be able to enter parts of Buckingham Palace, her residence in London. Admission fees would help pay the cost—put as high as $62 million—of repairing Windsor Castle, which had been damaged by a fire in 1992.

MAY

National

Body of Cult Leader Identified — Investigators said, **May 2**, that they had identified the body of David Koresh, leader of the Branch Davidian cult who had died with scores of his followers when a fire destroyed their compound near Waco, Tex., in April. Aside from being badly burned, the body had a bullet wound in the middle of the forehead. It appeared that Koresh was fatally shot prior to the fire's destruction of the compound. A team of therapists reported, **May 3**, on their interviews with 19 of the 21 children who had left the compound during the 7 weeks it was under siege. (Two children, ages 7 months and 3 years, were too young to be interviewed.) The therapists said that the children had been beaten and deprived of food as a means of discipline. Children said Koresh had "wives" as young as 11. Investigators of the fire reported, **May 4**, at least 24 of the victims' bodies had bullet wounds.

Gay Issues Remain in Public Focus — Issues involving homosexuality remained prominent in May. On **May 3**, Airman Apprentice Terry Helvey pleaded guilty to murder with intent to do great bodily harm in the death, in October 1992, of a shipmate, Allen Schindler. At that time, both were serving on the *Belleau Wood*. Schindler had made it known that he was gay, and he was due to be discharged. While the ship was anchored in Sasebo, Japan, Helvey and another shipmate, Charles Vins, encountered Schindler in a public toilet, and Schindler was beaten to death. Vins pleaded guilty to reduced charges and testified against Helvey. Gay-rights leaders denounced the death of Schindler as a bias crime and charged that the Navy was trying to cover up the incident. Helvey gave different accounts of his motivation. His trial was held at the Yokosuko Naval Base near Tokyo. Meanwhile, Sen. Sam Nunn (D, Ga.), chairman of the Armed Services Committee, was conducting hearings on Pres. Bill Clinton's proposal to lift the ban on homosexuals serving in the U.S. military. He and other senators visited the Norfolk Naval Base, **May 10**, and Nunn said that the close quarters in which sailors had to live on ships would cause tense situations between heterosexuals and homosexuals. On **May 24** the Senate approved, 58-31, Clinton's appointment of Roberta Achtenberg as assistant secretary for fair housing and equal opportunity in the Dept. of Housing and Urban Development. She was the first open homosexual to be appointed to a position requiring Senate approval. Helvey, **May 27**, was sentenced to life in prison.

Data Raise Concerns on Inflation — Government statistics released in May helped revise concerns about inflation. The Commerce Dept. reported, **May 4**, that the index of leading economic indicators had declined by 1 percent in March, the sharpest drop since November 1990. The Labor Dept. said, **May 7**, that the unemployment rate had remained at an even 7 percent in April, for the 3d straight month. The department reported, **May 12**, that prices charged by producers for finished goods had jumped 0.6 percent in April. This increase, the largest for any month since October 1990, was attributed in part to the inclement weather that had driven up the cost of fruit and vegetables. The Labor Dept. announced, **May 13**, that consumer prices had risen 0.4 percent in April. On Wall Street, the Dow Jones industrial average broke through a new barrier and closed, **May 19**, at an all-time high of 3500.03. By **May 27** the average stood at 3554.83.

Congress Approves 'Motor-Voter' Bill — The House, **May 5**, and the Senate, **May 11**, approved a bill establishing new opportunities for citizens to register to vote. Under the bill, often called the "motor-voter" bill, citizens would be able, in any state, to register to vote when applying for a driver's license. They could also register at welfare and disability benefits offices, and could obtain registration forms at military recruitment stations. Registration by mail would be allowed in any state. Clinton signed the bill **May 20**.

7th Man Charged in Trade Center Bombing — A 7th man was charged, **May 6**, in connection with the bombing in February at the World Trade Center in New York City. Authorities said that the latest suspect, Mohammad Ahmad Ajaj, had arrived in the U.S. in September 1992 carrying instructions on how to construct a bomb like the one used in New York. Five other suspects linked to the bombing were also in custody, and one remained at large.

'Star Wars' Defense Plan Abandoned — Defense Sec. Les Aspin announced, **May 13**, that research on the Strategic Defense Initiative—better known as Star Wars—would be discontinued. Pres. Ronald Reagan had proposed SDI in 1983. The program envisioned creation of a defensive shield against incoming missiles, and $30 billion had been spent on research over 10 years. Aspin said that the study of ground-based defenses against missiles would continue under a scaled-down Ballistic Missile Defense Organization.

Ex-Reagan Aide to Advise Clinton — Pres. Bill Clinton in May appointed David Gergen, who was once an assistant to Pres. Ronald Reagan, to an advisory position in the White House. Clinton had found it difficult to keep public attention focused on his economic and other major policy initiatives, while peripheral controversies seemed to dominate news out of his administration. The dismissal of 7 staff members in the White House travel office had proved to be embarrassing. On **May 18**, Clinton received a haircut, which reportedly cost $200, while Air Force One sat on a runway at the Los Angeles International Airport for an hour, tying up other planes. The president's approval ratings had declined sharply. On **May 29**, Clinton announced that Gergen would serve as an adviser with the title of counselor to the president. Gergen had served as Reagan's communications director in the early 1980s and was, at the time of his appointment, an editor for *U.S. News and World Report* and a television commentator. Gergen was registered as an independent and had known Clinton for some time. Clinton also announced that George Stephanopoulos would step aside as his communications director and concentrate on development of policy.

White House Travel Office Center of Furor — The White House announced, **May 19**, that the 7 staff members of the White House travel office had been dismissed. Dee Dee Myers, White House press secretary, said that an accounting firm had found evidence of "gross mismanagement" in the office and that the FBI was investigating. The White House said, **May 19**, that a distant cousin of Pres. Bill Clinton, Catherine Cornelius, would assume temporary control of the office. The White House acknowledged, **May 21**, that Cornelius had sought in February to have herself put in charge of the travel office. It was also acknowledged that a partner of Harry Thomason, a television producer and a friend of the president, had sought without success to get White House business for a charter airplane consulting firm. On **May 21**, the White House also announced that World Wide Travel Inc., a company based in Little Rock, had voluntarily withdrawn as coordinator of operations at the travel office. Three executives of the company, which had been brought in after the dismissals, had contributed to Clinton's 1992 campaign. It was learned, **May 24**, that members of the White House staff had asked the FBI to rewrite a report on the travel office to make it supportive of the firings. The White House announced, **May 25**, that 5 of those dismissed would be placed on paid leave pending completion of the investigation.

House OKs Deficit-Reduction Package — The U.S. House of Representatives gave a boost to Pres. Bill Clinton's deficit-reduction program in May, passing the so-called budget reconciliation bill. The legislation, which projected a total reduction in the federal government's anticipated budget deficits of about $500 billion by 1998, was debated intensely throughout the month. Many Democrats insisted on strict controls on spending entitlement programs and a mechanism was incorporated into the bill requiring Congress and the president to act if entitlement spending significantly exceeded targets set in annual budget resolutions. The text of the bill did not specify some of the spending cuts that would be made in order for the deficit-reduction goals to be met. A key feature of the bill was an energy tax, which would be levied on all fuels based on their energy content in British thermal units (Btu's). A group of senators from both parties, led by David Boren (D, Okla.), signaled that the bill would face difficulty in the Senate when they insisted, **May 20**, on deeper spending cuts and fewer tax increases. Boren also opposed the Btu tax. With vigorous lobbying by Clinton and his aides, the bill barely got approval in the House, **May 27**, by a vote of 219 to 213; 38 Democrats and all voting Republicans opposed it. Ross Perot, an independent candidate for president in 1992, also opposed what he called Clinton's "tax and spend" program, and on **May 30** he also ran a 30-minute commercial on television denouncing the North American Free Trade Agreement, which Clinton supported. Perot said if NAFTA was approved, millions of U.S. jobs would be lost to Mexico.

Ex-Policeman Acquitted in Deaths of 2 Blacks — A former Miami police officer was acquitted in Orlando, Fla., **May 28**, on 2 manslaughter counts in the deaths of 2 men in 1989. The policeman, William Lozano, was Hispanic, and the 2 men who were killed were black. The victims were on a motorcycle being chased by a police car. Lozano shot and killed the driver, and the passenger was injured fatally in the subsequent crash of the cycle. The deaths had triggered serious rioting in Miami. Lozano was convicted of manslaughter in 1989, but an appeals court overturned the result in 1991, contending that the jury might have feared that more rioting would have followed an acquittal. At the second trial, the defense contended that Lozano had acted in self-defense. The acquittal in Orlando resulted in only sporadic violence in Miami; 5 people were reported injured, and more than 60 were arrested.

International

President of Sri Lanka Assassinated — Pres. Ranasinghe Premadasa of Sri Lanka was assassinated in May. Earlier, on **Apr. 23**, opposition leader Lalith Athulathmudali had also been assassinated, during a campaign rally. The gunman fled, but police, **Apr. 24**, produced the body of a man they said was the killer. On May Day, **May 1**, during a parade in Colombo, the capital, a suicide bomber riding a bicycle set off explosives strapped to his body that killed a total of 24 people, including the president and the bomber. Within hours, Prime Minister Dingiri Banda Wijetunge was sworn in as president. Although the Liberation Tigers of Tamil Eelam denied responsibility, the government blamed the Tamil separatist organization.

Bosnian Serb Voters Defiant in Referendum — The Bosnian Serb parliament—for the 3d time—and Bosnian Serb voters, in a referendum, rejected a U.N. peace plan for Bosnia and Herzegovina in May. Radovan Karadzic, leader of the Bosnian Serbs, signed the Vance-Owen peace plan, **May 2**, but said his assent was subject to the approval of the self-proclaimed Bosnian Serb parliament. The parliament turned down the plan, **May 6**, but voted to submit it to a referendum of all Bosnian Serbs. Pres. Slobodan Milosevic of Serbia, **May 6**, ordered a halt to the delivery of arms and fuel to the Bosnian Serbs. The U.N. Security Council, **May 6**, declared Sarajevo, the Bosnian capital, and 5 other cities that were Muslim strongholds to be "safe areas" where noncombatants could seek safety from Serb forces. The Council voted to send 50 military monitors to each city. European foreign ministers, meeting in Brussels, **May 10**, turned down Pres. Bill Clinton's proposal to increase pressure on the Bosnian Serbs, including air strikes on Serb positions and the rearming of the Muslims. Milosevic, **May 11**, urged cancellation of the forthcoming referendum and attempted to call a meeting of legislators from all the Serbian populated areas of the Balkans. In the **May 15-16** referendum, 96 percent of the 1.1 million Bosnian Serbs polled voted against the peace plan and, according to the announced results, the same percentage favored the creation of an independent Serb state within Bosnia. Karadzic, **May 16**, declared the peace plan to be dead and declared that he now represented Republic Srpska—the new Serb state. On **May 18**, however, Muslims and Croats in Bosnia agreed to a cease-fire and to some of the terms of the peace plan. On **May 22**, France, Great Britain, Russia, Spain, and the U.S. approved a joint policy calling for a negotiated settlement of the war. Alija Izetbegovic, the Muslim president of Bosnia, rejected negotiations, **May 23**. The U.N. Security Council, **May 25**, voted unanimously to establish a war-crimes tribunal, capable of imposing prison terms, to deal with atrocities in the war.

U.S. Gives U.N. Control in Somalia — **May 4** saw the conclusion of the first phase of the relief mission in Somalia. Lieut. Gen. Robert Johnston of the U.S. Marine Corps handed authority to Lieut. Gen. Cevik Bir of Turkey, the U.N. military commander. This was the first time U.S. troops served under U.N. leadership. The U.S.-led mission, begun in December, had essentially cleared the streets of the cities of weapons, and the distribution of food had brought an end to mass starvation. Clan warfare, starvation, and disease had claimed 350,000 lives in Somalia in 1992. The U.N.-controlled force was projected to reach 28,000 troops, including 5,000 Americans.

State-Owned Enterprises Privatized in Poland — The Polish parliament completed action, **May 7**, on legislation to transfer control of 600 state-owned enterprises to investment funds. Shares in the funds would be distributed to adult Poles at a nominal charge. At the insistence of former Communist deputies and some members of the right-wing National Christian Union, distribution would be free to pensioners and to civil servants who had not gotten pay increases in 1991. Financiers from Western countries would manage the funds. With the legislation's approval, the World Bank authorized $750 million in new loans to Poland.

Denmark Approves European Union Treaty — Danish citizens, voting in a referendum **May 18**, reversed a position they had taken a year earlier and ratified, by a 57 percent majority, the Maastricht treaty on greater European unity. The Danish government had won concessions from its partners in the European Community, allowing Denmark to opt out of closer cooperation on defense and monetary matters. The treaty, previously given final ratification by 9 other of the EC's 12 members, still awaited final approval in Great Britain and faced potential legal challenges in Germany.

Venezuelan President Faces Corruption Trial — The Supreme Court of Venezuela ruled, **May 20**, that grounds existed to try Pres. Carlos Andrés Pérez for misappropriating $17 million in government funds. The Senate, **May 21**, authorized the Court to try Pérez, who was suspended from office. The president of the Senate, Octavio Lepage, became acting president. The Venezuelan Congress had 30 days to elect a president to serve until Feb. 2, 1994, the end of Pérez's term.

Cardinal Shot to Death in Mexico — Cardinal Juan Jesús Posadas Ocampo, the archbishop of Guadalajara, Mex., was shot to death at Guadalajara's international airport, **May 24**. He had been driven to the airport in a limousine, and was to welcome a representative from the Vatican. His car was caught in a shootout between members of 2 drug cartels, and he may have been mistaken for a leader of a cartel. Six other people were killed. Police detained 2 suspects, but most of the gunmen got away.

Bomb Kills 5 at Museum in Florence — A car bomb exploded, **May 27**, near the renowned Uffizi Gallery in Florence, Italy, one of Europe's greatest art museums. Five people were killed and about two dozen injured. Three paintings by relatively minor artists were destroyed and about 30 were damaged. Masterpieces by Botticelli and Michelangelo survived behind shatterproof glass. Authorities believed that the Florence explosion and other recent terrorist acts were the work of the Mafia, which might be signaling that it had not been crippled by the recent roundup of hundreds of alleged mobsters.

British Leader Shakes Up Cabinet — British Prime Minister John Major made changes in his cabinet, **May 27**, in the face of continued national economic stress. More than 10 percent of the work force was unemployed, and Major's popularity ratings were low. The prime minister replaced Chancellor of the Exchequer Norman Lamont with Kenneth Clarke, the former home secretary. Michael Howard, former secretary of state for the environment, would succeed Clarke at the Home Office. Major announced several other changes among his ministers.

Germany Tightens Asylum Policy — Germany's parliament completed action, **May 28**, on constitutional changes that would restrict access to persons seeking asylum in Germany. More than 1 million persons seeking asylum had entered Germany in the past 4 years, and about 1.8 million Turks had been admitted as "guest workers." Under the changed policy, Germany would rebuff would-be immigrants from nations that Germany deemed free of persecution, and asylum-seekers crossing Germany's land borders would be turned back. On **May 29**, 5 members of a Turkish family in Solingen were killed when their home was firebombed. Attacks on foreigners in Germany were reportedly up sharply in 1993.

Clinton Compromises on China Trade — Pres. Bill Clinton, **May 28**, extended most-favored-nation trading status for China for one year. Most U.S. trading partners are granted MFN, which provides relatively low tariffs for imports into the U.S. In a compromise that sought to mollify both U.S. business interests and human-rights advocates, Clinton conditioned MFN on improvement in China's human rights record, including the release of political prisoners and better treatment for prisoners. China's trading status would be reviewed again in 1994.

General

Man Convicted in Assault With Condom — In a decision that advocates of women's rights hailed as a victory, a Texas man was found guilty of aggravated sexual assault, **May 13**, despite his claims that a woman had consented, in effect, to having sex when she gave him 2 condoms. The defendant, Joel Rene Valdez, admitted that he entered her bedroom without permission and that he was carrying a knife. He testified that he had consumed a case of beer. The woman testified that there was little that she could do to prevent an attack and that she asked him to use a condom because she feared for her life and feared that she might contract the virus that causes AIDS. The trial was held in Travis County Court in Austin.

Defender of Home Freed in Killing — A Louisiana man who said he was defending his home against someone he perceived to be an intruder was acquitted, **May 23**, by a jury in Baton Rouge in the shooting death of a 16-year-old Japanese exchange student. The youth, Yoshihiro Hattori, and his American host had come to the home of Rodney Peairs, seeking the location of a party, and had rung the doorbell. Peairs answered the door armed with a gun, and when Hattori, who spoke little English, failed to respond to Peairs' command to freeze, Peairs shot him. Peairs' lawyer contended that his client had the "absolute right" to answer a door holding a gun. The verdict provoked anger in Japan, where shootings were rare.

Mystery Illness Fatal to 10 in Southwest — An unidentified illness with no known cause had taken 10 lives on or near the Navajo Reservation by **May 29**. Victims lived in Arizona, Colorado, and New Mexico. Eight of those who had died were Navajo. Twenty-three persons were being treated at hospitals in New Mexico. Symptoms were flulike and progressed quickly to a severe respiratory ailment. Four who became ill recovered after treatment with antibiotics.

JUNE

National

Economic Data 'Flat' in June — Statistics released by the government in June showed little improvement in the economy. The Commerce Dept. said, **June 2**, that the index of leading economic indicators had risen 0.1 percent in April. The Labor Dept., **June 4**, put the unemployment rate at 6.9 percent in May, a decline of 0.1 percent. The department said, **June 11**, that prices charged by producers for finished goods remained unchanged in May. More encouraging news on inflation came, **June 15**, when the department said that consumer prices had risen only 0.1 percent in May. The Commerce Dept. said, **June 17**, that the merchandise trade deficit in April had been $10.49 billion, a 4-year high. Further discouraging news came with the department's announcement, **June 23**, of the final revision to the growth rate of the gross domestic product for the 1st quarter of 1993. The revision placed GDP growth at an annual rate of 0.7 percent, substantially lower than had been reported in April. Also, the department reported, **June 29**, that the index of leading economic indicators had dipped by 0.3 percent in May.

Clinton Drops Justice Dept. Nominee — On **June 3**, Pres. Bill Clinton withdrew his nomination of Lani Guinier to head the civil rights division of the Justice Dept. Guinier, whose father was black and whose mother was Jewish, was a professor of law at the Univ. of Pennsylvania and a friend of Bill and Hillary Rodham Clinton. After she had been nominated, conservatives had criticized her past discussion of means by which black voters could increase their influence in elections. In announcing his withdrawal of the nomination, **June 3**, Clinton said he had just read Guinier's articles and found them "difficult to defend." Guinier expressed frustration, **June 4**, at not being able to defend herself before the Senate. Black civil rights leaders sharply criticized Clinton's decision.

Republicans Win 2 Key Elections — Republicans took 2 major offices from the Democrats in June. On **June 5**, Texas state Treasurer Kay Bailey Hutchison was elected to the U.S. Senate. She defeated the incumbent Democrat, Bob Krueger, who had been appointed to the Senate by Gov. Ann Richards after Lloyd Bentsen resigned to become secretary of the Treasury. Hutchison, who won by a 2-1 margin, campaigned against Pres. Bill Clinton's economic program, particularly his proposed tax increases. On **June 8**, Richard Riordan, a businessman, defeated Michael Woo, a Democrat, and became the first Republican mayor of Los Angeles since 1961. Riordan, who spent $6 million of his own money in the campaign, ran as a tough opponent of crime. He would succeed Tom Bradley, a Democrat, who was retiring after 20 years as mayor.

Clinton and Press Exchange Salvos — Pres. Bill Clinton responded forcefully to tough questions from the press in June. On **June 7**, the White House announced that Mark Gearan, Clinton's deputy chief of staff, would become communications director. As part of an effort to mend fences with the press, which had given heavy coverage to administration misfortunes, the Clintons entertained 300 political journalists at a picnic at the White House, **June 13**. On **June 14**, Clinton rebuked a reporter who raised the issue of why it had taken so long for Clinton to fill a Supreme Court vacancy. During a **June 15** press conference, Clinton was asked if he could be accused of "wavering" on important policies, and he called his presidency "the most decisive . . . you've had in a very long time on all the big issues."

Judge Ginsburg Nominated for Supreme Court — Pres. Bill Clinton announced, **June 14**, that he was nominating Judge Ruth Bader Ginsburg of the U.S. Court of Appeals for the District of Columbia for a seat on the U.S. Supreme Court. If approved by the Senate, Ginsburg would succeed Justice Byron White, who had announced in March that he would retire at the end of the current court term. Since March, Clinton had reportedly come close to making other choices, and the selection of Ginsburg came as something of a surprise. A graduate of Columbia Law School, she had served as director of the Women's Rights Project of the American Civil Liberties Union. Ginsburg had won 5 of 6 gender-equality cases that she had argued before the Supreme Court. Pres. Jimmy Carter nominated her for the Court of Appeals in 1980. As a judge, she had taken generally moderate positions. On confirmation by the Senate, Ginsburg would become the high court's second woman justice and the first Jewish justice in 24 years.

Senate Approves Clinton Budget Bill — The Senate in June narrowly approved the budget bill that incorporated Pres. Bill Clinton's deficit-reduction program. The Democratic members of the Senate Finance Committee, **June 16**, abandoned the broad-based energy tax, the Btu tax, which Clinton had supported and which had been included in the bill approved by the House. The committee Democrats substituted a 4.3-cents-per-gallon tax increase on transportation fuels, which would yield far less revenue than the Btu tax. On **June 25** the Senate divided, 49-49, on the bill, with 2 Senators absent. All voting Republicans opposed it, and they were joined by 6 Democrats. The bill passed on the tie-breaking vote cast by Vice Pres. Al Gore. A conference committee would reconcile differences between the Senate and House versions of the bill.

FBI Arrests 9 in 2d New York Bomb Plot — On **June 24** the FBI arrested 8 men who, it was alleged, were plotting to bomb several sites in New York City and to assassinate the secretary general of the U.N., among others. The men were charged, **June 24**, with conspiracy in federal court in Manhattan, and 5 of them were charged with attempted bombing. Five of the men had come to the U.S. carrying Sudanese passports, and 6 worshipped at the mosque of Sheikh Omar Abdel Rahman. The sheikh had ties with several of the suspects charged in the bombing of the World Trade Center in February. Emad Salem, who had been a translator and bodyguard for the sheikh, was identified, **June 25**, as an informer who had secretly taped conversations among the alleged plotters. A 9th suspect was arrested and charged with conspiracy to transport explosives on **June 30**.

More Military Bases Face Closure — Concluding 5 days of deliberations, the Defense Base Closure and Realignment Commission recommended, **June 27**, that 33 major military installations be closed. Nearly 100 smaller bases would also be closed, and 45 others would be reduced in scale. The Defense Dept. estimated that the proposed closings and cutbacks would cause the loss of 120,000 jobs. Pres. Bill Clinton, **July 2**, approved the recommendations and proposed to spend $5 billion to assist communities affected by the commission's recommendations. Congressional approval was still needed.

Judge's Ruling Delays Trade Pact — U.S. Federal District Court Judge Charles Richey ruled, **June 30**, that the U.S. government must submit an environmental impact statement for the North American Free Trade Agreement. NAFTA, which had been ratified by Canada in early June, was to take effect in January 1994, assuming approval by the U.S. Congress and Mexican legislature, but the judge's ruling, if upheld on appeal, was expected to delay the approval process by several months. Many organizations opposed NAFTA because of concern about the loss of jobs in the U.S. and because of potential negative impacts on natural resources and human health.

International

Military Ousts Guatemala President — Pres. Jorge Serrano Elías was forced from office in June. On **May 25**, he had instituted executive rule and imprisoned opponents to "purge the state of . . . corruption." International criticism followed, and Guatemala's business, labor, and academic communities united in opposition to the president's move. On **June 1**, the constitutional court urged implementation of its earlier ruling that the action by the president was unconstitutional. Later on **June 1**, Defense Minister Jose Domingo Garcia Samayoa announced that the armed forces, acting in response to appeals from the judiciary and the public, had forced Serrano out. On **June 2**, Serrano flew to El Salvador. On the night of **June 5-6**, Congress elected as president the nation's human rights ombudsman, Ramiro de Leon Carpio. On **June 7** he dismissed the defense minister and reassigned several military commanders in an apparent effort to confirm civilian authority over the armed forces. Meanwhile, Serrano sought, and received, asylum in Panama.

Moderate Yugoslav President Ousted — Pres. Dobrica Cosic of Yugoslavia was voted out of office by Parliament, **June 1**. Pres. Slobodan Milosevic of Serbia, the principal component of what was left of Yugoslavia, was a leader in the move to remove Cosic, who had angered Serbian hard-liners by urging Bosnian Serbs to accept an international peace plan. Eight U.S. military officers arrived, **June 18**, in The Former Yugoslav Republic of Macedonia to help plan the deployment of a U.N. force that would seek to prevent the Bosnian conflict from spreading into Macedonia. Representatives of the 3 factions in Bosnia and Herzegovina met in Geneva, **June 23**, to consider a Serb-Croat plan to divide the country into 3 autonomous areas based on ethnicity.

Cambodia Parties to Share Power — Two Cambodian parties that had received the most support in a U.N.-sponsored election agreed in June to share power. The election was the key element in the 1991 peace accord, under which the nation's 4 leading factions agreed to end their 14-year civil war. The voting for a constituent assembly was completed on **May 28**, and by early June tabulations showed that Funcinpec, the French acronym for the royalist party, had received more than 45 percent of the vote. The incumbent Cambodian People's Party (CPP) had 39 percent. On **June 3**, Prince Norodom Sihanouk, the nation's dominant political figure and former monarch, installed himself as prime minister and sought to form a coalition government between Funcinpec and the Vietnamese-installed CPP. Sihanouk named his son, Prince Norodom Ranariddh, the Funcinpec leader, and Hun Sen, the CPP leader, as co-equal deputy premiers. His son, however, balked at the arrangement in a message made public **June 4**, in which he said he could not work with those who, he charged, had assassinated members of the royalist party. The new constituent assembly, **June 14**, granted Prince Sihanouk the powers he deemed necessary to "save our nation." Ranariddh said, **June 14**, that the Khmer Rouge, a Communist faction that had imposed brutal rule on Cambodia in the past, was willing to give up the territory it controlled and drop its demand for a place in the government. On **June 18**, Ranariddh and Hun Sen agreed to serve as co-presidents and to divide up cabinet posts.

U.S. Attacks Iraq Because of Plot to Kill Bush — The U.S. fired missiles at Iraq's intelligence headquarters in Baghdad in June in retaliation for an Iraqi plot to kill former Pres. George Bush. Fourteen men charged in the plot went on trial in Kuwait, **June 5**. One testified, **June 5**, that Iraqi intelligence had trained them and ordered them to kill Bush during his visit to Kuwait in April. On **June 26**, in a televised speech, Pres. Bill Clinton said, "The Iraqi attack against President Bush was an attack against our country," and he announced that the U.S. had launched an attack on Iraq's intelligence complex. Early on **June 27**, Iraq time, 23 Tomahawk missiles had been fired from 2 U.S. ships in the Persian Gulf. The main headquarters building was badly damaged. Iraq said, **June 27**, that 8 people had been killed in the attack and a dozen wounded, and it denied the existence of a plot. On **June 29**, a U.S. plane fired on an Iraqi antiaircraft battery in the southern no-fly zone after it reportedly locked its radar on a U.S. squadron.

U.S., Allies Attack Somali Warlord — The level of conflict between U.N. peacekeeping forces and a Somali warlord escalated rapidly in June. On **June 5**, 23 Pakistani members of the peacekeeping force were killed in a series of attacks in Mogadishu, the capital, after the U.N. troops had inspected munitions depots controlled by Gen. Mohammed Farah Aidid. Aidid was the strongest of the warlords in the city and a key figure in the Somali civil war. Americans came to the rescue of the Pakistanis, and 3 were wounded. Although Aidid denied responsibility for the deaths of the peacekeepers, U.S. helicopters bombed 3 of his arms caches. The U.N. Security Council, **June 6**, condemned the attacks on the peacekeepers and demanded that those responsible be punished. On **June 12**, U.S. helicopters and gunships destroyed 4 of Aidid's arms depots. Ground troops from several countries then moved in to seize heavy weapons, ammunition, and 200 of Aidid's men. U.S. planes, **June 13**, attacked a compound owned by a financial supporter of Aidid. These actions were overshadowed, **June 13**, when Pakistanis fired into a crowd of demonstrators protesting the attacks on Aidid, killing 20 and wounding 50. On **June 14** and **16**, U.S. planes attacked other targets linked to Aidid, and on **June 17**, U.N. troops stormed his headquarters, but Aidid was not present.

North Korea Reverses Itself on Nuclear Treaty — North Korea announced in June that it would suspend its withdrawal from the Nuclear Nonproliferation Treaty. Although North Korea and the U.S. did not have diplomatic relations, delegations from the 2 nations met at the U.N. in early June. In a joint statement, issued **June 11**, they said that North Korea had decided to suspend its withdrawal. North Korea, however, did not agree to allow inspection of its nuclear-energy facilities, as mandated by the treaty. The statement said the 2 nations had pledged not to threaten or use force against each other and had promised not to interfere in each other's internal affairs.

Woman Becomes Canada's Prime Minister — Kim Campbell became Canada's 19th prime minister in June, and she also became the first woman to hold the office. Prime Minister Brian Mulroney had announced his retirement, and on **June 13** his Progressive Conservative Party, which held a majority in Parliament, voted on a successor as party leader at a convention in Ottawa. The leading contenders were Campbell, 46, the defense minister, and Jean Charest, 34, the environment minister. Campbell defeated Charest, 53 percent to 47 percent, on the second ballot. Campbell, who was from British Columbia, was sworn in as prime minister **June 25**. She reduced the number of ministers in her cabinet from 39 to 25 and the number of government departments from 32 to 23. Charest was named deputy prime minister.

U.N. Imposes Oil Ban on Haiti — The U.N. Security Council, **June 16**, voted to impose a worldwide ban on oil shipments to Haiti and also voted to ban arms shipments and freeze Haitian assets abroad. The object was to force Haitian military leaders to accept the return of the Rev. Jean-Bertrand Aristide, Haiti's elected president. The sanctions became effective **June 23**. Talks sponsored by the U.N. opened in New York, **June 27**, between Aristide and Lt. Gen. Raoul Cedras, representing Haiti's military government.

Japan's Government Falls — Premier Kiichi Miyazawa lost a no-confidence vote in the Japanese parliament, **June 18**. The vote was 255-220, with 39 members of his own Liberal Democratic Party (LDP) voting against the government. Miyazawa had served as premier since 1991, a period of serious economic recession. He had been criticized for failing to move forcefully against widespread corruption in Japanese politics. As a result of the vote in parliament, new elections would be held on July 18th. On **June 22**, more than 40 LDP dissidents resigned from the party and on **June 23** they announced they had formed a new party, the Renaissance Party.

Kurdish Militants Attack Turks in Europe — Kurdish militants, seeking to call attention to their 9-year struggle to establish an independent Kurdish state, attacked Turkish diplomatic missions and businesses in more than two dozen European cities, **June 24**. Twenty people were taken hostage, then released, at the Turkish consulate in Munich. Hostages were also taken in Marseille. One Kurdish demonstrator was shot to death in Bern.

General

Pessimism Voiced at AIDS Conference — More than 14,000 people attended the 9th International Conference on AIDS, which opened in Berlin, **June 7**. Reports indicated that the number of people infected with the AIDS virus continued to rise worldwide, with especially sharp increases in Africa and Southeast Asia. Confirming a report first published in April, scientists said, **June 8**, that the antiviral drug AZT provided no long-term benefit in delaying the onset of symptoms and the death of AIDS patients. A research team headed by Dr. Jonas Salk said, **June 9**, that use of an experimental AIDS vaccine, on which much hope had been focused, had not slowed the course of the disease or lessened its severity. On **June 25**, Pres. Bill Clinton appointed the first AIDS-policy coordinator for the federal government. She was Kristine Gebbie, who had chaired the Centers for Disease Control and Prevention committee on HIV infection. In a final report before disbanding, **June 28**, the White House's National Commission on AIDS criticized the Bush administration's response to the epidemic as inadequate and challenged Pres. Clinton to do more to halt the spread of the disease.

Japan's Crown Prince Marries — Crown Prince Naruhito of Japan and Masako Owada were married, **June 9**, in a traditional Shinto ceremony at the Imperial Palace in Tokyo. The bride had been educated at Harvard and Oxford universities and had been a trade negotiator in the Japanese foreign service. She was the first woman with a career to join the royal family.

Mystery Illness Blamed on Rodents — Health officials concluded in early June that a mysterious illness in the Southwest was caused by microbes belonging to a family of viruses called hantaviruses that are found in the urine and droppings of rodents. On **June 9**, New Mexico state health officials began trapping rodents in an attempt to identify the virus. By late June at least 19 deaths had been linked to the disease.

'Jurassic Park' Stomps Box-Office Records — Universal Studios' long-awaited film "Jurassic Park," directed by Steven Spielberg, opened on **June 11**, setting a record for the largest opening day box-office earnings with $18.2 million in first-day gross ticket sales. Based on a novel by Michael Crichton, the movie tells the story of a former sideshow owner who exploits scientific technology to clone dinosaurs and develops a theme park to show off his creations. Spielberg spent over 2 years in preproduction creating the movie. In addition to using traditional clay models and stop-action photography, Spielberg utilized the groundbreaking computer-generated images of Industrial Light and Magic in more than half of the dinosaur scenes. The movie, which cost over $60 million to make, quickly went on to set records for the largest 3-day gross box-office earnings ($50.2 million) and the largest full-week gross earnings ($81.7 million). "Jurassic Park" had passed the $100 million and $200 million marks faster than any previous film.

Chicago Wins 3d Straight NBA Title — The Chicago Bulls won their 3d straight National Basketball Association championship, **June 20**, when they defeated the Phoenix Suns, 99-98, to take the final series, 4 games to 2. In the last seconds of the game the Bulls were down by 2 points, but John Paxson scored a 3-point basket, the final points of the game, with 3.9 seconds to play. For the 3d straight year, Michael Jordan of the Bulls was named the most valuable player in the finals. In the 6 games with the Suns, he averaged 41 points per game, a record for the final series. No team had won 3 straight titles since the Boston Celtics won their 8th straight championship in 1966.

JULY

National

Congress OKs Reduced Stimulus Program — Congress, **July 1**, completed action on an economic-stimulus package that fell far short of what Pres. Bill Clinton had wanted. In April, a Republican filibuster in the Senate had killed a bill that would have provided $16.3 billion for short-term economic assistance. The bill adopted by Congress provided only $3.5 billion, for summer jobs, expanded Small Business Administration loans, and the employment of police officers by communities. In signing the bill, **July 3**, Clinton expressed disappointment.

Clinton Offers Plan on Northwest Logging — Pres. Bill Clinton, **July 1**, presented a plan for logging on federal old-growth forests in the Northwest and for the protection of the northern spotted owl, an endangered species. A federal court had suspended logging in the Northwest in 1991 until the government devised a plan to protect the owl. At a forest summit in April 1993, Clinton had heard presentations from timber companies, environmentalists, and others on what to do. Clinton's plan would limit logging to 1.2 billion board feet per year in the U.S. forests of the Pacific Northwest, about one-fourth what the government had allowed in the 1980s. Reserves for the owl would be established. It was estimated that 6,000 jobs, mostly in Oregon, would be lost under the plan, and Clinton proposed to spend $1.2 billion over 5 years to aid the region economically, retrain workers, and restore rivers damaged by logging. The plan was subject to the court's approval.

U.S. Detains Radical Muslim Sheikh — Sheikh Omar Abdel Rahman, whose Muslim followers had been linked to 2 bombing plots, was taken into federal custody, **July 2**. Abdel Rahman had entered the U.S. in 1990. His residency status had been revoked in March 1992, and an immigration judge had held in March 1993 that he could be deported. The sheikh had appealed that ruling and had been free pending the outcome of the case.

White House Travel Office Report Issued — The White House issued a report, **July 2**, on the controversy involving the White House Travel Office. Chief of Staff Thomas McLarty and Budget Dir. Leon Panetta were the authors of the report. The report reprimanded 4 officials, but McLarty assumed ultimate responsibility. Those reprimanded included Catherine Cornelius, a distant cousin of Pres. Bill Clinton who had been appointed head of the travel office, and David Watkins, the White House director of administration. Cornelius was reprimanded for attempting to find evidence of wrongdoing by the travel staff, and the report said that she and Watkins had reported rumors of wrongdoing to the FBI to help prompt an investigation of the staff. The report confirmed that Harry Thomason, a friend of the Clintons, had pressed the White House to investigate the office. He had sought without success to bid for White House travel business. McLarty said 5 former travel office employees who had been cleared of wrongdoing would be given other government jobs.

Economic Indicators, Layoffs Announced — The Labor Dept., **July 2**, put the unemployment rate at 7.0 percent for June, an increase of 0.1 percent over May. The department said, **July 13**, that an index of prices charged by producers for finished goods had declined 0.3 percent in June. It reported, **July 14**, that the consumer price index was unchanged in June. Procter & Gamble Co., **July 15**, announced that it would close 30 factories and cut 13,000 jobs. The Commerce Dept. reported, **July 16**, that the merchandise trade deficit in May was $8.37 billion. Federal Reserve Board Chairman Alan Greenspan told a House subcommittee, **July 20**, that the rate of inflation had not eased as much as expected, and he testified, **July 22**, that "at some point" interest rates "are going to have to move up." IBM announced, **July 27**, that 35,000 jobs would be eliminated as part of a restructuring program.

Flood Devastates Parts of Midwest — A flood that was worse than anyone in the Midwest could remember surged down the Mississippi River and its tributaries in the summer of 1993. Fifty people died, and the lives of tens of thousands of others were disrupted. Heavy rains in the winter, spring, and summer left the ground saturated, and the excess water formed lakes. Ultimately, all of the overflow found its way downstream. Many record flood crests were set, and hundreds of levees collapsed or were overrun. All of Iowa and large portions of 8 other states were declared federal disaster areas. Pres. Bill Clinton, **July 4**, visited Davenport, Iowa, in the first of 4 trips to the impacted region. The Mississippi River, a major commercial artery for the Midwest, was closed to barge traffic, **July 6**, from Sioux City, Iowa, to St. Louis. The collapse of a levee, **July 11**, flooded Des Moines' water treatment plant and left 250,000 people without any drinking water from their taps. In St. Louis, **July 14**, Clinton said he would ask Congress to provide funds for flood relief. On **July 16**, the rising Missouri and Mississippi rivers converged near St. Charles, Mo., 20 miles upstream from their normal confluence. The flood, **July 17**, knocked out the Bayview Bridge, connecting Quincy, Ill., and West Quincy, Mo., the only crossing on the Mississippi for about 200 miles. Clinton, Vice Pres. Al Gore, 8 governors, and other officials met in Arnold, Mo., **July 17**, to map strategy to overcome the disaster. Tap water became available in Des Moines, **July 22**, but was not yet safe to drink. By **July 26**, disaster areas had been declared in Illinois, Iowa, Kansas, Minnesota, Missouri, Nebraska, North Dakota, South Dakota, and Wisconsin. In Kansas City, Mo., **July 28**, the Missouri River crested at 48.9 feet, 17 feet above flood stage. In Des Moines, **July 30**, tap water was declared safe to drink.

Clinton Dismisses FBI Director — Pres. Bill Clinton dismissed FBI Dir. William Sessions in July. Sessions, a former federal judge, had been appointed FBI director by Pres. Ronald Reagan in 1987. In January 1993 the Justice Dept.'s Office of Professional Responsibility sharply criticized Sessions and his wife for various alleged abuses, including failure to pay taxes for perquisites provided by the government. Sessions denied any wrongdoing and resisted pressure from Attorney Gen. Janet Reno that he resign. He rejected her July 17 demand that he resign or be fired. Clinton dismissed Sessions, **July 19**, and on **July 20** he nominated U.S. District Judge Louis J. Freeh of New York City to succeed him. Freeh had served in the FBI and had been a U.S. attorney. He had gained plaudits for his prosecution of the "pizza connection" drug-smuggling ring in 1987. The Senate, **Aug. 6**, confirmed Freeh's nomination unanimously.

Ex-House Postmaster Pleads Guilty — Robert Rota, former postmaster for the U.S. House, pleaded guilty, **July 19**, to one count of conspiring to embezzle public funds and 2 counts of helping embezzlement by House members. Rota had resigned in 1992 during an investigation into alleged irregularities at the House Post Office. In his plea agreement, in U.S. District Court in Washington, D.C., Rota was said to have given lawmakers cash, directly or indirectly, in transactions ostensibly involving stamps. Rota admitted giving $30,000 to 2 unidentified House members. Press reports said that the 2 beneficiaries in the transactions were Rep. Dan Rostenkowski (D, Ill.) and former Rep. Joe Kolter (D, Pa.). Prosecutors said Rota had not profited personally from the transactions.

Policy on Gays in the Military Announced — Pres. Bill Clinton, **July 19**, announced the circumstances under which homosexual men and women could serve in the U.S. military. The directive issued by Defense Sec. Les Aspin endorsed the "don't ask, don't tell, don't pursue" approach. Clinton had once promised to repeal outright the 50-year-old ban on homosexuals in the military, and the members of the joint chiefs of staff had initially opposed any modification in it. The administration's policy provided that enlistees would not be asked about their sexual orientation. Once in the service, they could visit bars or read publications that catered to homosexuals, and they could attend rallies in behalf of homosexual rights if they wore civilian clothes. Commission of homosexual acts, however, would be the basis for dismissal from the service. Commanding officers could not initiate investigations on the basis of rumors or hearsay, but only if there was credible information. The order would take effect in October. The joint chiefs supported the policy, but some gay rights leaders said Clinton had reneged on his earlier commitment.

Aide to Clinton Found Dead — Vincent Foster, the deputy White House counsel, was found shot to death in a park in northern Virginia, **July 20**. Foster had been a friend of Pres. Bill Clinton and Thomas McLarty, the White House chief of staff, since childhood. The White House counsel's office had come under criticism for the handling of presidential nominations and the White House travel office controversy. Investigators believed that Foster had taken his own life.

Committee Approves Court Nominee — Judge Ruth Bader Ginsburg appeared before the Senate Judiciary Committee, **July 20-23**, as it considered her nomination to serve on the U.S. Supreme Court. She said she believed that the courts had a role to play on social issues when the political process faltered. Ginsburg said a woman's right to an abortion was based on the equal protection clause of the 14th Amendment. On **July 29**, the committee unanimously approved her nomination, which then went to the full Senate.

International

Date Set for Open South Africa Election — Negotiators announced, **July 2**, in Johannesburg that South Africa's first election open to all races would be held on Apr. 27, 1994. The announcement was also made in Washington, D.C., by Pres. F. W. de Klerk and Nelson Mandela, president of the African National Congress. Pres. Bill Clinton met separately at the White House, **July 2**, with de Klerk and Mandela. While in the U.S., de Klerk and Mandela criticized each other's policies, but both promoted South Africa as a stable country worthy of foreign investment.

Haitian Leader to Return to Power — The Rev. Jean-Bertrand Aristide, the deposed president of Haiti, and Lt. Gen. Raoul Cedras, who led the coup in 1991 that ousted him, reached an agreement, **July 3**, that would put Aristide back in power by October. The agreement, brokered by the U.N. and signed in New York City, provided for an end to embargoes that the U.N. and the Organization of American States had imposed on Haiti. Pres. Bill Clinton, **July 4**, backed the agreement and pledged financial support to Haiti.

Leaders of 'G7' Nations Attend Summit — The heads of government of the world's 7 leading industrial nations, the so-called Group of 7, met in Tokyo in July. The 7 nations are the U.S., Canada, France, Germany, Great Britain, Italy, and Japan. On **July 7**, the opening date of the summit, trade ministers from the U.S., Canada, Japan, and the European Community announced an agreement that, if implemented, would eliminate tariffs on a wide range of manufactured products, including construction equipment, furniture, farm equipment, and pharmaceuticals. The leaders, **July 8**, declared their commitment to "the territorial integrity" of Bosnia and Herzegovina and said they could not accept a settlement dictated by Serbs and Croats at the expense of Bosnian Muslims. Pres. Boris Yeltsin of Russia joined the meeting, **July 8**, and on **July 9** the G7 nations announced a $3 billion loan package for Russia. The leaders declared, **July 9**, that their highest priority was the conclusion of trade talks being conducted under auspices of the General Agreement on Tariffs and Trade. Pres. Bill Clinton and Premier Kiichi Miyazawa announced a bilateral trade agreement, **July 10**. Japan said it would take steps to reduce its large trade surplus with the U.S.; however, the U.S. agreed not to insist on Japan's acceptance of numerical market-share goals for foreign products.

Clinton Visits South Korea — Pres. Bill Clinton visited South Korea in July. He addressed the parliament, **July 10**, and on **July 11** visited U.S. military personnel guarding the demilitarized zone between North and South Korea. Clinton warned North Korea that any use of nuclear weapons would mean the end of their country, and he said he would support tougher sanctions against North Korea if it did not open its nuclear-energy sites to international inspection. He said the U.S. would not remove any of its 36,000 troops from South Korea.

Bosnian Factions Support Federation — Ethnic leaders in Bosnia and Herzegovina agreed in July to support creation of a loose federation in the embattled state. Seven of the 10 members of Bosnia's collective presidency, meeting in Zagreb, Croatia, **July 11**, said that they had agreed that Bosnia's government "should be along the lines of a federal state" in which Muslims, Croats, and Serbs would have equal rights as citizens. Serb, Croat, and Muslim leaders met in Geneva in late July under the cloud of increased fighting around the capital city of Sarajevo. On **July 30** they agreed to the establishment of ethnically based republics in a loose federation. The central government would be responsible only for trade and external relations. Each republic would have its own currency and armed forces. The Serbs would get 60 percent of Bosnia's territory even though they constituted only about 31 percent of the prewar population. The Muslims, who made up 44 percent of the prewar population, would receive 25 to 30 percent of Bosnia's land area. The remaining 10 to 15 percent would become Croat-controlled. The Croats composed 17 percent of the prewar population.

U.N. Removes Italian General in Somalia — Four journalists were killed in Mogadishu, **July 12**, by Somalis when they went to the scene of an attack by an American helicopter on a stronghold of Somali warlord Mohammed Farah Aidid. On **July 14**, the U.N. announced the removal of Gen. Bruno Loi, commander of the Italian force participating in the Somali operation, because he had refused to engage his troops in the conflict with Aidid.

Voters Desert Japan's Ruling Party — Japan's voters went to the polls, **July 18**, to elect members of the lower house of the Diet (parliament), and no political party emerged with a majority of the seats. The Liberal Democratic Party had held a majority in the Diet since the party's founding in 1955, but many of its leaders had been implicated in corrupt activities in recent years, and the party had seemed unable or unwilling to institute political reform. The LDP had won 275 of the 511 seats in the 1990 election, but in July it took only 223 seats. The strength of the Social Democratic Party also declined, from 136 to 70 seats. Three centrist parties recently organized by LDP defectors captured 103 seats with their reform platforms. Prime Minister Kiichi Miyazawa resigned as LDP leader, **July 22**. On **July 28**, 7 parties formed a coalition that excluded the LDP, and on **July 29** they chose as their candidate for prime minister Morihiro Hosokawa, who had bolted the LDP in 1992 and formed the Japan New Party.

Britain Ratifies European Union Treaty — Britain in July completed ratification of the so-called Maastricht Treaty on greater European unity. Prime Minister John Major as well as the treaty, which he supported, suffered a defeat, **July 22**, on a key vote in the House of Commons when 23 members of his Conservative Party deserted him. In a tactical maneuver, they opposed Major's desire to "opt out" of the treaty's "social chapter," which would subject British industry to European Community regulation of labor relations and working conditions. In a shrewd, but politically risky move, Major called for a vote of confidence on his government's handling of the treaty, **July 23**. Tory rebels returned to the fold to uphold the government in the two-step confidence motion that cleared the way for ratification, pending court approval. First, the Tories defeated the Labor Party amendment to accept the "social chapter," with the vote falling along party lines, 339 to 301. The second vote, 339 to 299, supported Major's government. Had the government lost, the Conservatives would have had to face the electorate at a time when its standing in opinion polls was low. Britain's High Court, **July 30**, rejected a court challenge to the treaty. After an announcement, **Aug. 2**, that there would be no appeal, Britain notified the EC of its ratification of Maastricht. Eleven of the EC's 12 member countries had now completed ratification. In Germany, the treaty faced a court challenge.

Israeli Attacks Kill 130 in Lebanon — Two guerrilla groups, Hizballah and the Popular Front for the Liberation of Palestine, launched attacks on Israeli soldiers in the Israeli "security zone" in southern Lebanon in July. By late July, 7 Israelis had been killed. Beginning **July 25**, Israeli forces struck back at guerrilla bases and towns in southern Lebanon with air raids and artillery. Hizballah guerrillas, **July 25**, then shelled towns in northern Israel, causing 2 fatalities. A cease-fire went into effect, **July 31**, after Lebanon and Syria reportedly said they would take steps to stop the guerrilla attacks. The Israeli bombardment of 70 villages had killed about 130, mostly civilians, wounded approximately 500, destroyed up to 10,000 homes, and driven as many as 300,000 people from their homes.

Court Overturns War Crimes Conviction — The Supreme Court of Israel, **July 29**, overturned the conviction and death sentence of John Demjanjuk. Born in Ukraine, he had served in the Soviet army and claimed that he had been captured by the Germans in World War II. After the war, he moved to the U.S. He was stripped of his U.S. citizenship in 1986 when the government concluded he had lied about his Nazi past. In 1986 he was extradited to Israel and in 1988 found guilty of brutal mistreatment of Jews at the Nazi death camp at Treblinka. Evidence showed that he had been trained by his Nazi captors as a death-camp guard, and survivors of the camp identified him as a guard known as Ivan the Terrible. Subsequently, evidence from the Soviet KGB files indicated that the notorious Ivan was another Ukrainian, Ivan Marchenko. The KGB files also indicated that Demjanjuk had been a guard at 2 other camps, but the Israeli Supreme Court threw out the conviction because he had been tried as Ivan the Terrible, not for crimes committed elsewhere. The court also said it would be unreasonable to initiate new charges against Demjanjuk.

Mystery Illness Afflicts 46,000 Cubans — An illness of unknown origin had afflicted 46,000 Cubans by early July. The illness became apparent during the winter, and by spring as many as 4,000 new cases were being reported each week. Two patterns of symptoms had emerged. One involved impairment of vision, though not blindness. The second affected the nerves and was characterized by a tingling sensation in the hands and feet, muscle cramps, and weakness in the legs. Some of those with nerve damage suffered hearing loss and difficulty swallowing, speaking, and urinating. Delegations of scientists had come to Cuba to study the problem. Possible causes included nutritional deficiency, viral infection, cyanide poisoning, and an unidentified toxin. Dr. Jorge Antelo, Cuba's deputy health minister, said, **July 1**, that the number of reported cases had declined soon after the government had begun to distribute multivitamin pills to the national population. He said 25,000 people had been hospitalized, usually for up to 20 days, and that "much evidence points to a new disease."

Biological Parents Win Custody Fight — The biological parents of a 2-year-old girl won legal custody in July after a protracted dispute with adoptive parents. After the girl's birth in 1991 her mother, Cara Clausen, gave her up for adoption. She named as the father a man who in fact was not the baby's father, and he signed consent forms for adoption. Clausen lived in Iowa. The girl was adopted by Jan and Roberta DeBoer, who lived in Michigan. They named the girl Jessica. Clausen and the girl's natural father, Daniel Schmidt, later decided to fight for custody and subsequently married. They argued that the adoption was not final because Clausen had named the wrong father. An Iowa court supported them. The Michigan Supreme Court, **July 2**, decided, 6-1, to defer to the Iowa ruling. It ordered the DeBoers to surrender the child to the Schmidts by Aug. 2. Justice John Paul Stevens of the U.S. Supreme Court, **July 26**, refused the DeBoers' appeal to block the order. The full court, **July 30**, did the same, 7-2. As an attorney carried the girl from the DeBoers' Ann Arbor, Mich., home, **Aug. 2**, she cried and screamed "Mommy!"

AUGUST

National

'Great Flood' Leaves Heavy Damage — "The Great Flood of 1993," as it was now being called, receded in August, leaving considerable damage in 9 states. In St. Louis, the Mississippi River finally crested at a record 49.4 feet, **Aug. 1**, about 2.5 feet below the top of the flood wall. Although portions of South St. Louis were flooded, the central city was spared. In Alton, Ill., **Aug. 1**, 60,000 people lost their drinking water when floodwaters crashed into the city's water-treatment plant. On **Aug. 2**, the U.S. Army Corps of Engineers deliberately opened a levee outside the historic town of Prairie du Rocher, Ill., in order to channel floodwaters into farmlands and ease pressure on the levees at the town. Town officials dynamited the levee again, **Aug. 4**, and the strategy worked. On **Aug. 6**, Congress completed action on a $6.2 billion flood-relief package. It was reported, **Aug. 9**, that Agriculture Sec. Mike Espy had estimated that 8 million acres had been flooded and 12 million more acres were too wet to grow crops. State and federal officials put total damage estimates at $12 billion, with nearly $8 billion of this suffered by farmers. The final death toll appeared to be 50, and nearly 70,000 people were made homeless. In St. Louis, **Aug. 12**, Clinton signed the flood-relief bill.

Ginsburg Sworn In as Justice — The Senate, **Aug. 3**, approved the nomination of Judge Ruth Bader Ginsburg for the U.S. Supreme Court, by a vote of 96-3. She was sworn in, **Aug. 10**, as the court's 107th justice.

Unemployment Rate Declines — The Commerce Dept. reported, **Aug. 3**, that the index of leading economic indicators had risen by 0.1 percent in June. The Labor Dept. said, **Aug. 6**, that the unemployment rate in July stood at 6.8 percent, a drop of 0.2 percentage point from June. This was the lowest monthly rate since October 1991. The department said, **Aug. 12**, that the index of prices charged by producers for finished goods fell 0.2 percent in July, and it reported, **Aug. 15**, that the consumer price index rose 0.1 percent in July. June's deficit in merchandise trade, $12.06 billion, was the widest since February 1988, the Commerce Dept. announced **Aug. 19**. On Wall Street, the Dow Jones Industrial Average closed, **Aug. 25**, at an all-time high of 3652.09.

Two in Rodney King Case Sentenced — Federal Judge John Davies, **Aug. 4**, sentenced 2 police officers to 2½ years in prison for violating Rodney King's civil rights. The 1992 state court acquittal of the 2 officers and 2 other policemen in the beating of King had resulted in widespread protests and violence in Los Angeles and elsewhere that had taken more than 50 lives. In 1993, Stacey Koon and Laurence Powell were tried in federal court, and they were convicted in April. Although many in the black community in Los Angeles objected to the relatively lenient sentences, the city remained calm.

Congress Passes Bill to Reduce Deficits — After a long and acrimonious debate, Congress in August narrowly approved a bill, supported by Pres. Bill Clinton, that was designed to reduce federal budget deficits by $496 billion over 5 years. The bill, the centerpiece in Clinton's economic-recovery program, was modified many times during the spring and summer as supporters sought to pick up votes for it. The Senate and House had approved different versions of the bill in June, and conferees from both houses had spent weeks reconciling the differences. The votes in August were on the conference committee's final version. This final bill raised taxes on taxable incomes above $115,000 for individuals and $140,000 for couples from 31 percent to 36 percent. All taxable incomes over $250,000 would be subject to an additional tax of 3.6 percent. All salary income would be subject to a 2.9 percent Medicare tax. The federal tax on all transportation fuels would be increased by 4.3-cents-per-gallon. For individuals earning more than $34,000 (couples, $44,000), the portion of Social Security benefits subject to income tax would rise from 50 percent to 85 percent. On the spending side, total discretionary federal spending would be frozen at 1993 levels, with details of the cuts to be determined each year. Payments to health care providers under Medicare and Medicaid would be subject to new formulas and limits, with total savings of $63 billion anticipated. In the principal spending increase under the bill, the earned income tax credit for the working poor would be extended to families earning up to $27,000 a year. Public-opinion surveys showed Americans about equally divided on the bill. Republican leaders denounced the tax increases and called the spending cuts inadequate, and all Republicans in both houses voted against the bill. The House, **Aug. 5**, approved the bill by a bare 218-216 margin. The Senate, **Aug. 6**, divided 50-50, and the legislation passed with the tie-breaking vote of Vice Pres. Al Gore. Clinton signed the bill on **Aug. 10**.

White House Suicide Left Bitter Note — Investigators said, **Aug. 5**, that an autopsy indicated that Vincent Foster, the deputy White House counsel who had been found shot to death in July, had committed suicide. On **Aug. 10**, the Justice Dept. made public the contents of a note Foster wrote before his death. He said he was not meant for "the spotlight of public life in Washington. Here ruining people is considered sport."

Grazing Fees Raised on Public Lands — The Clinton administration announced, **Aug. 9**, that it was more than doubling the fees the federal government charges ranchers who graze their animals on public lands. Fees would still be lower than those generally charged on private lands. Pres. Bill Clinton had included a fee increase in his deficit-reduction plan but had dropped it to avoid defections in Congress. The administration also announced stricter environmental controls on grazing practices.

Clinton Announces Anticrime Measures — Pres. Bill Clinton, **Aug. 11**, endorsed legislation aimed at combating crime. He backed the so-called Brady bill, which would require a 5-day waiting period for the purchase of handguns. He proposed to spend $3.4 billion over 5 years to hire 50,000 more police officers. Clinton also favored extending the federal death penalty to almost 50 crimes. Clinton issued executive orders, **Aug. 11**, that required stricter licensing of gun dealers and that banned the import of semiautomatic assault-style handguns.

Polish-Born General to Head Joint Chiefs — Pres. Bill Clinton, **Aug. 11**, named an Army general, John Shalikashvili, to be the next chairman of the Joint Chiefs of Staff. He would succeed Gen. Colin Powell on the latter's retirement at the end of September. The appointment was subject to Senate approval. Born in Poland of Georgian descent, Shalikashvili came to the U.S. at age 16. Drafted into the Army, he served in Vietnam and Korea, rising rapidly in rank. He commanded the international relief effort for the Iraqi Kurds in 1991 and, at the time of his appointment by Clinton, he was supreme allied commander, Europe, NATO's top military officer.

Altman Acquitted in BCCI Case — Robert Altman, a Washington, D.C., lawyer, was acquitted in August on 4 charges related to the notorious Bank of Credit and Commerce International. Altman and his mentor, Clark Clifford, a prominent figure for many years in Democratic politics, had been indicted in both federal and New York state courts. Federal charges were later dropped, and Clifford was deemed unable to face trial in New York because of illness. The case involved the relationship between BCCI and First American Bancshares Inc., a Washington, D.C., bank in which Clifford and Altman were officers. Five of 9 state charges against Altman had also been dropped, and on **Aug. 14** he was found not guilty of misleading bank regulators and filing false documents.

Wetlands Policy Announced by Clinton — In a package of legislative and administrative measures announced **Aug. 24**, the Clinton administration made a commitment to "no net loss" of wetlands. The Bush administration had made a similar commitment, but environmentalists pointed out that wetlands acreage throughout the U.S. continued to disappear under farmland and development. Under the Clinton plan, a Bush administration proposal to open 1.7 million acres of wetlands in Alaska to development would be dropped. Also, owners allowed to develop wetlands would pay a fee to help protect or create wetlands elsewhere. Drainage projects would be subject to more stringent federal review. However, 53 million acres that had been drained and converted to farmland since 1985 would be exempted from new regulations.

Muslim Cleric Indicted in Bomb Plots — Sheikh Omar Abdel Rahman was indicted by a federal grand jury in New York City, **Aug. 25**, on conspiracy charges in connection with a number of terrorist activities. These included the February bombing of the World Trade Center, a foiled plot to bomb other targets in New York City, and the 1990 assassination of Rabbi Meir Kahane. The indictment said that Abdel Rahman had instructed and advised other conspirators. In all, 15 men were named in the indictment. Evidence included 150 hours of taped conversations recorded by a government informer. One of those indicted was El Sayyid Nosair, who had been acquitted in a New York state court of killing Kahane but now faced a federal charge of committing a murder to promote a larger conspiracy.

International

Demjanjuk Remains in Israeli Custody — Although John Demjanjuk's conviction in the "Ivan the Terrible" case was overturned in July, he remained in detention in Israel in August. On **Aug. 1**, an Israeli Supreme Court panel issued a restraining order keeping him in custody until prosecutors decided whether to try him for other alleged concentration camp activities during World War II. The 6th U.S. Circuit Court of Appeals held, **Aug. 3**, that he should be allowed to return to the U.S. while other charges were under review. Israel's Supreme Court, **Aug. 18**, ordered that Demjanjuk be set free, but then heard arguments that the decision be delayed.

Israel, Palestinians Near Agreement — A tense month in Middle East negotiations took a dramatically encouraging turn at the end of August, and it appeared that a plan for limited Palestinian self-rule might soon be approved. Yasir Arafat, chairman of the Palestine Liberation Organization, caused a rift in his ranks, **Aug. 3**, when he asked his negotiation delegation to offer more concessions to Israel than they were prepared to accept. For one thing, Arafat was willing to postpone discussion of the status of Jerusalem. The Palestinian delegates rejected Arafat's terms and presented their own proposal to U.S. Sec. of State Warren Christopher. The PLO announced, **Aug. 5**, that Arafat had ordered a restructuring of the PLO bureaucracy in order to overcome serious financial problems. Israeli and Palestinian officials reported, **Aug. 5**, that an Israeli cabinet minister and a senior adviser to Arafat had met, an historic initial contact between the old enemies. In January 1993, the Israeli Knesset (parliament) had repealed a law prohibiting contacts between Israeli citizens and PLO members. Two Palestinian delegates to the peace talks had reportedly decided, **Aug. 7**, to resign in protest over Arafat's direct intervention in the negotiations. But then, a compromise was announced, **Aug. 12**. Seven delegates were made a formal part of the PLO decision-making process and were appointed to the PLO committee that directed peace-talk strategy. Foreign Minister Shimon Peres of Israel announced, **Aug. 13**, that even though the delegates representing the Palestinians were now officially part of the PLO, Israel would continue to negotiate with them. Never before had Israel publicly been willing to negotiate in any manner with the PLO. Deploring this shift, former Israeli Prime Minister Yitzhak Shamir called the PLO a "murderous organization." On **Aug. 15**, about 400 Palestinian men who had been deported from Israel to southern Lebanon in 1992 agreed to Israel's terms for their return. Some would be returned to prison. Norway's Foreign Minister Johan Joergan Holst confirmed, **Aug. 30**, reports that he had mediated talks between the PLO and the Israeli government, beginning in April, that were separate from the publicly known peace talks. Most of the meetings had taken place in Norway. While much of the world rejoiced at the news, hard-liners on both sides were outraged as details of a tentative agreement came out, and one radical Palestinian leader appeared to call for Arafat's assassination. Peres told the Knesset, **Aug. 30**, "This is the beginning of the end" of Israel's dispute with the Palestinians. The Israeli government, **Aug. 31**, approved in principle a plan for interim Palestinian self-rule. Self-rule would be established in the Gaza Strip and in the historic biblical town of Jericho on the West Bank within a few months. Later, self-rule would be extended to the rest of the West Bank, excepting the Israeli settlements. Internationally supervised elections would be held in the occupied territories. Negotiations on the status of Jerusalem would begin within 2 years. In areas obtaining self-rule, Israel would control overall security and border crossings, but the Palestinians would control taxation, education, health, welfare, and the police.

Italy Reforms Electoral System — Reacting to public outrage over widespread political scandals, Italy's parliament gave final approval, **Aug. 4**, to a new means for electing its members. Previously, seats had been allocated according to proportional representation. With many parties winning seats, it had proved difficult to form stable coalition governments. Under the new electoral system, 75 percent of the seats in both parliamentary houses would be awarded to the candidate in each district who received the most votes. The remaining 25 percent of the seats would be distributed according to proportional representation.

Reformer Becomes Premier of Japan — Morihiro Hosokawa, who had left the ruling Liberal Democratic Party (LDP) in 1992, was elected premier of Japan in August as head of a coalition of reform-minded parties. The July election for seats in the lower house of the Diet (parliament) had proved inconclusive, and Hosokawa became the candidate of 7 parties for premier. In the 511-member house, **Aug. 6**, Hosokawa received a majority, 262 votes, to 224 for the new LDP leader, Yohei Kono. Hosokawa, at 55, was much younger than most recent Japanese premiers. He had quit the LDP to protest political and bureaucratic corruption. With Hosokawa's help, **Aug. 6**, Takako Doi, former head of the Socialist Party, became the first woman elected speaker of the lower house. In addition, Hosokawa's cabinet, announced **Aug. 9**, included 3 women, the most ever in a Japanese cabinet. Hosokawa said he would seek quick enactment of political-reform laws. He pledged, **Aug. 10**, to take steps to reduce Japan's large trade surplus with the U.S. and other nations. He also stated that World War II was, for Japan, "a war of aggression, a war that was wrong." His acknowledgment of Japanese guilt went beyond that made by any previous government official.

Four U.S. Soldiers Killed in Somalia — Four U.S. soldiers were killed, **Aug. 8**, in Mogadishu, the capital of Somalia, when a land mine exploded under their jeep. The soldiers were part of the U.N. peacekeeping force. In all, 12 U.S. troops had been killed in combat in Somalia since December.

Fed Acts to Halt Rise in Value of Yen — The U.S. dollar, **Aug. 17**, fell in value to 100.40 Japanese yen in trading in New York City. At the beginning of 1993, the dollar had been worth about 125 yen, but it was now at a post-World War II low against the Japanese currency. The dollar rebounded, **Aug. 19**, to 105.85 yen after the U.S. Federal Reserve Board intervened in world currency markets in an effort to reverse the trend.

U.S. Labels Sudan a Terrorist Supporter — The U.S. State Dept. informed the government of Sudan, **Aug. 18**, that the country would be added to the list of nations that the U.S. regarded as supporters of international terrorism, making the nation ineligible for all U.S. aid, except humanitarian relief. The department had concluded that Sudan had trained Islamic militants who had committed terrorist acts and acted as a "safe harbor" for alleged terrorists.

Political Hostages Freed in Nicaragua — Two rival political groups seized hostages in Nicaragua in August, but all of them were freed without harm. On **Aug. 19**, a band of rearmed former contra rebels seized a 38-member government delegation visiting their mountain camp. They demanded that Gen. Humberto Ortega Saavedra, a Marxist Sandinista, be ousted as defense minister. In retaliation, former Sandinista soldiers, **Aug. 20**, seized 34 conservative political leaders in Managua, the capital. The vice president and the president of the national assembly were among the captives. Some of the original hostages were released by both sides, **Aug. 21** and **22**, but then, on **Aug. 22**, leftists seized 9 journalists who had been covering the story. On **Aug. 25**, all of the remaining hostages were released.

General

Pope Attends Youth Festival in Colorado — Pope John Paul II visited the U.S. in August to participate in a Roman Catholic youth festival. Before his arrival, he visited Mexico, **Aug. 11**. During one speech in

1993 IN PICTURES

President Clinton and the First Lady in the inaugural parade along Pennsylvania Avenue, January 20.

RICK MAIMAN/SYGMA

THE NEW ADMINISTRATION

AP/WIDE WORLD PHOTOS

President Clinton signs the family-leave bill, his first legislative victory, in a February Rose Garden ceremony.

Hillary Rodham Clinton, head of the administration's health care reform task force, visits a Philadelphia hospital.

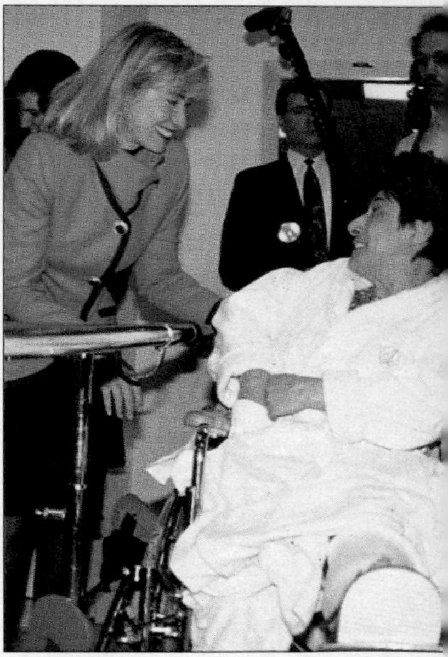

AP/WIDE WORLD PHOTOS

In May, ex-Reagan aide David Gergen is hired to help refocus Clinton's message.

REUTERS/BETTMANN

Clinton stresses U.S.-Japanese trade issues during a July economic summit in Tokyo.

The commander in chief at Ft. McNair July 19, after announcing his policy on gays in the military.

AP/WIDE WORLD PHOTOS

AP/WIDE WORLD PHOTOS

Ruth Bader Ginsburg, Clinton's first Supreme Court nominee, is sworn in August 10; to her right, her husband and Chief Justice William Rehnquist.

ROBERT GIROUX/AFP

President Clinton discusses his deficit reduction bill with Illinois congressman Dan Rostenkowski.

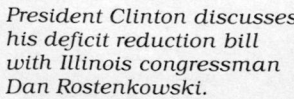

On the World Scene

LES STONE/SYGMA

Both friendship (left) and brutal hostility greeted U.S. troops on a peacekeeping mission in Somalia. Below: Cambodians vote in May elections aimed at ending civil war.

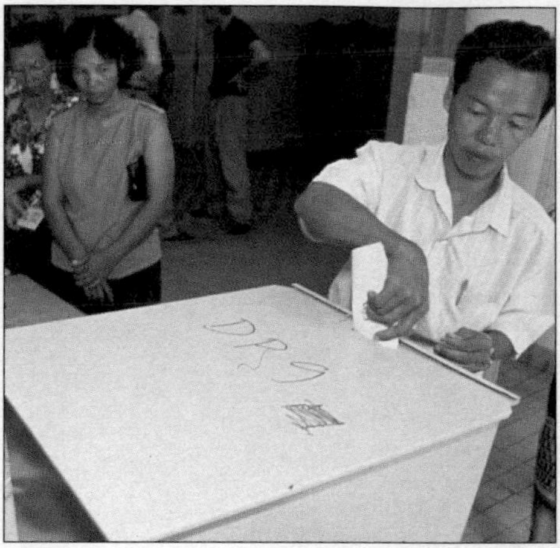

JASON BLEIBTREU/SYGMA

Russian President Boris Yeltsin campaigning for support during another turbulent year in the former Soviet republics.

MALCOLM LINTON/BLACK STAR

AP/WIDE WORLD PHOTOS

Historic handshake: Israeli leader Yitzhak Rabin and Palestine Liberation Organization head Yasir Arafat at the September 13 signing of a peace accord in Washington.

CHRIS MORRIS/BLACK STAR

A mass burial of Muslims April 28 attests to the continued horrors of ethnic warfare in Bosnia.

AP/WIDE WORLD PHOTOS

Nelson Mandela, president of South Africa's African National Congress, visits the Liberty Bell July 3.

AP/WIDE WORLD PHOTOS

Opposition leader Tsutomu Hata celebrates, in a traditional way, big gains by his party in July 18 Japanese elections.

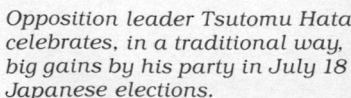

Confrontation in Waco

KWTX-TV/SYGMA

Four federal agents are killed in a February shoot-out with Branch Davidians in Waco, Texas (above). A two-month standoff ends April 19 as the compound goes up in flames (below); inset: the cult's leader, David Koresh.

AP/WIDE WORLD PHOTOS; INSET ROD AYDELOTTE/WACO TRIBUNE HERALD/SYGMA

MIDWEST UNDER WATER

Davenport, Iowa, was one of many places hit hard by massive floods in the Midwest in the summer.

CHRIS STEWART/BLACK STAR

AP/WIDE WORLD PHOTOS

In St. Joseph, Missouri, a boat is used to help wade through chest-high waters.

LES STONE/SYGMA

A message of determination, written with sandbags, tops a St. Charles County, Missouri, home.

TERRORISTS STRIKE

AP/WIDE WORLD PHOTOS

A woman is helped from the scene after a bombing at New York City's World Trade Center February 26.

Mahmud Abouhalima, turned over by Egypt, is taken into custody in connection with the bombing.

ABC NEWS/SYGMA

ALLAN TANNENBAUM/SYGMA

New York police search for evidence in the underground garage where the blast occurred.

Yucatan, the Pontiff condemned the mistreatment of native peoples. Pres. Bill Clinton welcomed the Pope to Denver, **Aug. 12**. The Pope addressed 90,000 young people in Denver's stadium, **Aug. 12**. In an address, **Aug. 14**, he deplored sexual abuse of children by priests, which had become a subject of great concern in the U.S. On **Aug. 15**, in the main event of the World Youth Day festival, the Pope conducted a mass south of Denver for up to 400,000 people.

Spacecraft Falls Silent Near Mars — The *Mars Observer* spacecraft ceased communicating from space in August as it approached Mars, its destination. The *Observer*, which cost $980 million, had been launched in September 1992. Contact with ground controllers was lost **Aug. 21**, 3 days before the spacecraft was to orbit the red planet and map the surface of Mars to obtain information on its geology in anticipation of a possible visit by a crewed spacecraft.

SEPTEMBER

National

Jobless Rate Down Again — The unemployment rate continued to edge downward in August, to 6.7 percent, the Labor Dept. reported, **Sept. 3**. The Commerce Dept. said, **Sept. 3**, that the index of indicators of future economic trends fell by 0.1 percent in July. Good news on inflation came, **Sept. 10**, when the Labor Dept. reported that prices charged by producers for finished goods declined 0.6 percent in August. This was the biggest monthly decline since February 1991, and the trend, based on revised data, had now been downward for 4 months. The Commerce Dept. reported, **Sept. 16**, that the U.S. trade deficit had fallen to $10.34 billion in August.

Clinton Seeks to 'Reinvent Government' — Pres. Bill Clinton and Vice Pres. Al Gore announced a broad program, **Sept. 7**, that had as its goal the streamlining of the federal government to make it leaner, more efficient, and more responsive. The program to "reinvent government," which included more than 800 recommendations, had been put together under Gore's leadership. Projected savings under the plan, if implemented, were put at $108 billion over 5 years. Under the plan, budgets and appropriations would be made for a 2-year period. Agencies could carry unspent funds into the next fiscal year. It would be easier to dismiss employees, and the number of government reports would be reduced. Mid-level managers would have more decision-making control. The federal work force would be cut by 252,000. Many regional offices of federal departments would be closed. Similar sweeping proposals had been offered during previous administrations, but with little effect. Many of the recommendations would require congressional approval.

National-Service Bill Approved — The Senate, **Sept. 8**, approved, 57-40, the national-service bill supported by Pres. Bill Clinton. Participants in the program would receive grants for up to 2 years, for as much as $4,725 a year, by performing community service administered at the state level through nonprofit organizations, state and federal agencies, colleges, and other groups. Grants would be applied toward study at a college, university, or technical school. Twenty thousand students would be funded the first year, and over 3 years the program would cost $1.5 billion. The House had already approved the bill in early August. On **Sept. 21**, nearly 1,000 people gathered at a White House ceremony to watch Clinton sign the bill.

Clinton Signs NAFTA Side Agreements — On **Sept. 14**, Pres. Bill Clinton signed 3 supplemental agreements to the North American Free Trade Agreement. Negotiators from Canada, Mexico, and the U.S. had concluded the side agreements as a means of firming up labor and environmental standards and to guard against the negative impact of a sudden flood of imports. Former Presidents Gerald Ford, Jimmy Carter, and George Bush joined Clinton at the White House signing ceremony and endorsed NAFTA. (Separately, the heads of government of Canada and Mexico also signed the side agreements on **Sept. 13** and **14**, respectively.) Richard Gephardt (D, Mo.), the House Majority Leader, announced his opposition to NAFTA, **Sept. 21**. Overruling a district court decision, a federal appeals court held, **Sept. 24**, that the administration could submit NAFTA to Congress without an environmental impact statement.

Vietnam War-Era Radical Surrenders — Katherine Ann Power, an opponent of the Vietnam War who had been sought for more than 20 years in the death of a police officer, surrendered in September. She had driven a getaway car in 1970 following a bank robbery in Boston in which a police officer was killed. She later moved to Oregon and had married. Deciding to abandon her life as a fugitive, Power appeared in State Superior Court in Boston, **Sept. 15**, and pleaded guilty to armed robbery and manslaughter. On **Sept. 24**, she pleaded guilty to an earlier burglary at a National Guard armory. She was sentenced, **Oct. 7**, to 8 to 12 years in a Massachusetts prison for the 1970 bank robbery.

Over 130 Military Bases to Close — Congress made little effort to overturn the recommendations of the Base Closure and Realignment Commission in September. The commission's recommendations were announced in June and approved by Pres. Bill Clinton in July, but they were subject to congressional veto. Subsequently, no measure was introduced in the House to overturn the decision to close 130 domestic military bases and scale down 45 others. On **Sept. 20**, the Senate, 83-12, rejected a motion to disapprove the commission's work, and the commission's recommendations became final.

Clinton Announces Health-Care Program — Pres. Bill Clinton announced his health-care reform package in September. For months, the president's health-care task force, headed by First Lady Hillary Rodham Clinton, had listened to recommendations for change from health-care professionals, insurers, and citizens. The particulars of the president's sweeping reforms had been openly debated for months, but his appearance before a joint session of Congress, **Sept. 22**, was nonetheless awaited with great anticipation. In his address, Clinton noted the immense cost of health care and the fact that millions of Americans had inadequate insurance or no insurance at all. Under his reform plan, all American citizens and legal immigrants would receive health-care coverage. Under the concept of "managed competition", regional alliances, each representing thousands of consumers, would negotiate with insurance companies (or possibly directly with networks of health-care providers) for lower-cost premiums. All employers would be required to cover at least 80 percent of the health-insurance costs of all their full-time employees (with small businesses being eligible for subsidies). All consumers would get an ID card establishing their eligibility for a standard package of benefits. Medicare would still cover senior citizens, but they would have the option to turn to the regional alliances. To reduce bureaucracy and paperwork, all health plans would use the same standard claim form. The reform program was projected to cost the federal government $350 billion over 7 years, to be funded largely out of savings from Medicare, Medicaid, and other health programs and by a tax on tobacco. Clinton projected that his plan would reduce the federal deficit by $91 billion over 7 years (the figure was later revised). The scope and complexity of the plan suggested that its progress through Congress would be slow. Appearing before congressional committees, **Sept. 28**, Hillary Clinton was the administration's lead witness in behalf of the health-care program. The American Medical Association, **Sept. 29**, declared its opposition to federal regulation of health insurance premiums and cuts in Medicare and Medicaid.

Newly Elected Senator Indicted — Kay Bailey Hutchison, who had been elected to a U.S. Senate seat from Texas earlier in 1993, was indicted, **Sept. 27**, on charges that she had used state workers, computers, and supplies for her "personal benefit" during her Senate campaign. Hutchison had been State Treasurer before her election to the Senate. Two of her aides were also charged. Hutchison denied that she had done anything wrong.

Report Rebukes Agency on Its Attack on Cult — The U.S. Treasury Dept. issued a report, **Sept. 30**, that sharply criticized top officials of its Bureau of Alcohol, Tobacco, and Firearms for their handling of the February raid on the Branch Davidian complex near Waco, Tex. In this initial raid, 4 agents and 6 cultists were killed. The report contended that ATF officials had subsequently deceived investigators and Congress and had sought to blame the failure of the raid on an undercover agent, who in fact had warned that the raid should be called off because the element of surprise had been lost. Treasury Sec. Lloyd Bentsen announced that he had replaced the head of the agency, Stephen Higgins, and had suspended 5 other ATF officials. Higgins had announced his resignation on Sept. 27.

International

Bosnian Diplomatic Deadlock Continues — Bosnian Muslims refused, **Sept. 1**, to accept a draft U.N. peace agreement unless Serbs and Croats ceded them more land. Leaders of the 3 factions broke off their negotiations, **Sept. 20**, aboard a British aircraft carrier in the Adriatic Sea. In an address and press conference, **Sept. 27**, during a visit to the U.N., Pres. Bill Clinton said that the U.S. would no longer support U.N. peacekeeping operations unless the U.N. became more selective in the tasks it undertook, defined missions more clearly, and reduced American dues. Clinton said that if there was to be a U.S. commitment to Bosnia, he would want "a clear political strategy along with a military strategy," and he would want to know "exactly what our financial responsibilities were." Bosnia's Muslim-dominated parliament joined, **Sept. 29**, in rejecting the U.N. peace plan.

Power Struggle in Russia Intensifies — The confrontation between Pres. Boris Yeltsin and the Russian parliament became more intense in September. On **Sept. 1**, Yeltsin suspended from office Vice Pres. Aleksandr Rutskoi, one of his adversaries, and First Deputy Premier Vladimir Shumeiko, a Yeltsin ally. A presidential spokesman said they had been suspended because of "reciprocal accusations of corruption." The Supreme Soviet (the standing legislature), **Sept. 3**, rejected Yeltsin's suspension of Rutskoi and referred the question to the Constitutional Court. Rutskoi, elected on the same ticket as Yeltsin in 1991, was the president's automatic successor. On **Sept. 18**, Yeltsin named former Premier Yegor Gaidar, the architect of Russia's market liberalizations who had been forced out of office by parliamentary opposition in 1992, as first deputy premier for economic affairs. Yeltsin, **Sept. 21**, suspended parliament and announced parliamentary elections for December. Rutskoi called this step a coup d'etat, and his supporters in the Supreme Soviet voted to depose Yeltsin and elected Rutskoi acting president. The Constitutional Court, **Sept. 22**, held that Yeltsin had violated the constitution and could be impeached. Yeltsin, **Sept. 23**, announced presidential elections for June 1994. On **Sept. 24**, the Congress of People's Deputies (the country's highest legislative body, from which the Supreme Soviet members are drawn) voted to hold simultaneous parliamentary and presidential elections by March 1994. Moscow authorities cut off electricity, phone service, and hot water to the parliament building, **Sept. 25**. Yeltsin, **Sept. 27**, ruled out simultaneous elections. The Interior Ministry moved, **Sept. 28**, to seal off the parliament building. Barricades and wire were put around the building.

Israel, PLO Sign Accord in Washington — In a dramatic ceremony at the White House in September, representatives of Israel and the Palestine Liberation Organization signed a declaration of principles for interim Palestinian self-rule. The broad outlines of the agreement had become known in August. PLO Chairman Yasir Arafat, **Sept. 4**, obtained the endorsement of the accord by Fatah, the PLO's largest and most moderate faction. During early September, a number of moderate Arab regimes endorsed the accord, but Iraq, Libya, Sudan, and Iran opposed it. Syria appeared cautious, while seeking to make its own peace with Israel. The PLO Executive Committee, though not unanimously, endorsed the accord, **Sept. 9**. In a letter to Israeli Prime Minister Yitzhak Rabin, Arafat declared, **Sept. 9**, "The PLO recognizes the right of the State of Israel to exist in peace and security." He renounced terrorism and other acts of violence. In reply, **Sept. 9**, Rabin stated, "The Government of Israel has decided to recognize the PLO as the representative of the Palestinian people." Some 3,000 invited guests attended the signing of the interim accord on the lawn of the White House, **Sept. 13**. Foreign Minister Shimon Peres signed for Israel and Mahmoud Abbas, a negotiator in the secret talks leading to the agreement, signed for the PLO. Rabin and Arafat made generous and conciliatory statements. The prime minister said, "Enough of blood and tears. Enough." Those present applauded as Rabin and Arafat shook hands, with some coaxing from Pres. Bill Clinton. The accord said the parties would strive to "achieve a just, lasting and comprehensive peace settlement." Demonstrations for and against the agreement occurred in Israel and the occupied territories. Benjamin Netanyahu, Israel's opposition leader, deplored the agreement. On **Sept. 14**, in Washington, representatives of Israel and Jordan signed an "agenda for peace," but Jordanian officials said a formal agreement awaited normalization of relations between Israel and other countries. Rabin met with King Hassan of Morocco, **Sept. 14**, in Morocco, the first official visit by an Israeli prime minister to any Arab country other than Egypt. On **Sept. 23**, the Israeli parliament approved the peace agreement, 61-50.

Shift of Power in South Africa Nears — South Africa's ruling National Party agreed, **Sept. 7**, to share power with a multiparty council that would be established within 2 months. The Transitional Executive Council, which would consist of a member from each of South Africa's two dozen political parties, would oversee preparations for the nation's first universal-suffrage election, to be held in April 1994. The council would organize a multiracial peacekeeping force. In an address at the U.N., **Sept. 24**, Nelson Mandela, leader of the African National Congress, said that the "countdown to democracy" had begun in South Africa, and he called for the lifting of remaining international economic sanctions.

Casualties Rise in Somalia — As many as 100 Somalis were killed, **Sept. 9**, in a clash with U.N. peacekeepers in Mogadishu. Somali soldiers had fired on the U.N. forces. The response included attacks from Pakistani tanks and 2 U.S. helicopters. Somali victims included women and children, who either joined in the attack or were used as shields. Three U.S. soldiers were killed, **Sept. 25**, when their helicopter was shot down.

Sihanouk Restored to Cambodian Throne — On **Sept. 17**, Cambodia's 2 leading political parties resolved the question of who should lead the nation. They agreed that Prince Norodom Sihanouk would be restored as king. Sihanouk had reigned, 1941-1955, and then had served as Cambodia's civilian leader, until ousted in a coup in 1970. The parties also agreed that Prince Norodom Ranariddh, a son of Sihanouk, would serve as First Prime Minister, and Hun Sen, leader of the opposition party who had been co-president with Ranariddh since June, would serve as Second Prime Minister. Sihanouk was installed as king on **Sept. 24**.

Georgian Rebels Take Provincial Capital — Rebels in the breakaway province of Abkhazia gained ground in September in their fight against the government of Georgia. In mid-September they began a siege of the provincial capital of Sukhumi. Pres. Eduard Shevardnadze of Georgia went to Sukhumi and, on **Sept. 17**, appealed to civilians with arms to join government troops in its defense. On **Sept. 27**, the rebels captured the city, with Shevardnadze fleeing at the last minute.

Demjanjuk Returns to U.S. — John Demjanjuk returned to the U.S. in September, nearly 2 months after his conviction for war crimes was overturned in Israel. An Israeli Supreme Court justice, **Sept. 19**, rejected appeals that he be tried on other charges relating to his conduct during World War II. He left Israel **Sept. 22**.

General

China's Bid for Olympics Rebuffed — The International Olympic Committee met in Monte Carlo, **Sept. 23**, to choose the site for the Summer Olympics to be held in the year 2000. China had vigorously promoted Beijing as the site, but many argued that a country with such a poor human rights record should not be chosen. Five cities competed for the honor. On the 4th ballot, Sydney, Australia, in an upset, edged out Beijing by a vote of 45-43.

Participants Complete 2 Years in Biosphere — Four men and 4 women emerged, **Sept. 26**, from the 3.15-acre, glass-enclosed "Biosphere 2" in the desert near Tucson. For 2 years, they shared their space with more than 3,800 species of plants and animals in recreated ecosystems that included a rain forest, a marsh, and a desert. Air and drinking water were recycled, although air had to be pumped in when the oxygen level fell. Most food was grown inside the biosphere.

OCTOBER

National

Tailhook Nearly Sinks Top Admiral — It was reported, **Oct. 1**, that Navy Secretary John Dalton had recommended that Adm. Frank Kelso be removed as Chief of Naval Operations. Kelso, the Navy's top officer, was one of 35 admirals and Marine Corps generals who had attended the Tailhook Association convention in Las Vegas in 1991 during which scores of women had been subjected to abuse and indignities by junior officers, and he had been nearby when such behavior was occurring. On **Oct. 4**, Defense Sec. Les Aspin decided to keep Kelso as CNO. A Pentagon spokesman said that Aspin did not agree with Dalton's view that Kelso should be judged by a higher or different standard than would be applied to other top officers. The Pentagon, **Oct. 15**, censured 3 admirals who had organized the 1991 convention. One of them had retired, and it was believed that the censure would effectively end the careers of the other 2. Twenty-nine other admirals, including Kelso, and one Marine general received letters of caution, which were not placed in their files.

Economic Indicators Rise Sharply — The Commerce Dept. reported, **Oct. 1**, that the index of leading economic indicators had risen 1 percent in August, the biggest advance of the year. The Census Bureau said, **Oct. 4**, that, despite the end of the recession, the number of poor people in the U.S. had risen in 1992 by 1.2 million, to 36.9 million. This total represented 14.5 percent of the population. The Labor Dept. reported, **Oct. 8**, that the unemployment rate remained at 6.7 percent in September.

Ex-House Official Admits Guilt — In a plea agreement with the federal government, made public **Oct. 5**, Jack Russ, former House sergeant-at-arms, admitted committing 3 felonies. Russ's plea came after 2 years of an ongoing Justice Dept. investigation into practices at the House bank. Russ agreed to plead guilty to embezzlement by a custodian of public funds, wire fraud, and making a false statement on his financial disclosure form. Russ agreed to cooperate with prosecutors.

Justice Dept. Issues Report on Waco Cult — The U.S. Justice Dept., **Oct. 8**, released a report on its handling of the 51-day siege of the Branch Davidian compound near Waco, Tex. At least 75 cult members died when federal agents attacked the compound in April. The report concluded that the department and Attorney Gen. Janet Reno had made no mistakes and that the cult bore the blame for the climactic fire that destroyed the compound. Investigators, however, found no evidence of child abuse by cultists, which Reno had cited as one reason for the assault on the compound. The report said nothing about Reno's assertion that the attack went forward because agents were exhausted and there was no one to replace them. According to the report, once tear gas had been fired into the buildings the cultists not only set the compound afire, but also killed children with knives, guns, and clubs.

Social Security Payment Increase Announced — The U.S. government announced, **Oct. 15**, that, based on the rate of increase in consumer prices, Social Security and other federal benefit recipients would receive a cost-of-living increase of 2.6 percent for 1994. The increase was the second-smallest annual rise since benefit payments were linked to inflation in 1975.

International

Yeltsin Routs Foes in Bloody Confrontation — Russian Pres. Boris Yeltsin delivered a crushing blow to adversaries in parliament in October, but not without a considerable loss of life. On **Oct. 1**, the Interior Ministry estimated that 600 fighting men with a large cache of arms had joined Yeltsin's political opponents in the parliament building, called the White House. On **Oct. 2**, anti-Yeltsin demonstrators built street barricades in Moscow. Ousted Vice Pres. Aleksandr Rutskoi called for people to take to the streets against Yeltsin's "dictatorship." On the afternoon of **Oct. 3**, armed opponents of Yeltsin marched to the White House, overrunning government forces. Yeltsin declared a state of emergency in Moscow. With some people already dead on the streets below, Rutskoi appeared on the White House balcony and urged the crowd to seize the mayor's office and television center. The mayor's office was taken, but the rebels, advancing under both Soviet and Czarist flags, were met at the TV complex by Interior Ministry units. In the ensuing fight, the stations went off the air and 62 people were killed. Before midnight, Interior forces had turned back the attackers. Meanwhile, thousands of Yeltsin supporters also demonstrated in the streets. By sunrise, **Oct. 5**, army armored personnel carriers were surrounding the parliament building. Fighting broke out on the streets nearby and, after an appeal to occupants of the building to surrender went unheeded, tanks fired into the building, portions of which began to burn. Troops entered the White House and began to occupy it, floor by floor. By mid-afternoon, organized resistance dwindled to occasional sniper's fire. Many in the building, including Rutskoi and the speaker of parliament, Ruslan Khasbulatov, surrendered and were taken away in buses. Yeltsin, **Oct. 5**, banned opposition parties and newspapers, notably those of Communist or extreme nationalist views. He also dismissed regional officials who had opposed his moves against the parliament. In an address to the nation, **Oct. 6**, Yeltsin called for a purge of regional councils and new local elections. Police said, **Oct. 8**, that 187 had died in the conflict and 437 had been wounded. Yeltsin decreed, **Oct. 12**, that both houses of parliament would be elected in December. On **Oct. 15**, he ordered that a popular referendum be held in December on a new constitution. Rutskoi and Khasbulatov were charged, **Oct. 15**, with organizing mass disorders.

Clinton Beefs Up U.S. Force in Somalia — Responding to more U.S. combat deaths, Pres. Bill Clinton in October moved to build up American military forces in Somalia. On **Oct. 3**, 3 U.S. marines were killed when a mine blew up their vehicle in Mogadishu, the capital. Later that day a U.N. force, principally American, launched an air and ground attack on a crowded market area in south Mogadishu, where aides to Somali warlord Gen. Mohammed Farah Aidid were hiding. About 20 Somalis were seized, but Aidid's forces counterattacked. A total of 18 Americans, 2 Pakistanis, and a Malaysian were killed in the fighting and rescue effort. Somali casualties were unknown, but they were believed to be high and to include civilians. The Pentagon reported that some 75 Americans were wounded. Television coverage showed Somalis interrogating a wounded U.S. Army officer, Michael Durant, and other Somalis dragging 2 dead Americans through the streets. The U.S. role in Somalia was hotly debated in Congress and across the country. Clinton, **Oct. 4**, ordered several hundred new troops to Somalia, as well as tanks, helicopters, and gunships. Clinton, **Oct. 7**, announced that U.S. forces in Somalia and offshore would be increased from the present 4,700 to about 20,000. He indicated that the Americans would operate more independently from the U.N. command. Robert Oakley, a former State Department official, was appointed as a special envoy to Somalia. The president said all U.S. forces would be out of Somalia by March 31, 1994. On **Oct. 14**, Aidid freed Durant.

U.S. Confronts Haiti's Military — The international effort to restore democratic government to Haiti faltered in October. It was reported, **Oct. 4**, that Col. Joseph Michel François, commander of Haiti's military policy, would defy an internationally brokered agreement that called for him to step down. The agreement also provided that, in return for the ending of the international oil embargo of Haiti, the ousted elected president, the Rev. Jean-Bertrand Aristide, would return from exile by the end of October and be restored to power. The settlement provided as well for creation of a 1,300-member international force that would separate the military from the police. On **Oct. 11**, however, armed demonstrators prevented U.S. and Canadian troops from landing at Port-au-Prince, the capital. A U.S. ship carrying the Americans and Canadians withdrew from Haitian waters, **Oct. 12**, and Pres. Bill Clinton said the U.S. soldiers would not return until Haitian authorities guaranteed their safety and that of Father Aristide. The U.N. Security Council voted, **Oct. 13**, to reimpose an oil and arms embargo on Haiti. On **Oct. 14**, gunmen in Port-au-Prince shot and killed the justice minister, Guy Malary, and 2 of his aides. Six weeks earlier, Aristide had appointed Malary and other members of a transitional cabinet. Clinton, **Oct. 15**, ordered 6 U.S. warships into the waters off Haiti, where they were to stop any ship that appeared to be violating the embargo. Leaders of Haiti's military and police did not step down as scheduled **Oct. 15**.

China Breaks Nuclear Moratorium — China exploded a nuclear weapon beneath its western desert, **Oct. 5**, breaking an informal moratorium on testing. Pres. Bill Clinton, **Oct. 5**, ordered preparations for a resumption of American tests.

Bhutto Returns as Pakistan's Prime Minister — In Pakistan's parliamentary election, **Oct. 6**, former Prime Minister Benazir Bhutto's Pakistan People's Party captured the largest bloc of seats, 86 of 217. The Pakistan Muslim League, headed by another former prime minister, Nawaz Sharif, won 72 seats. The new parliament chose Bhutto as prime minister, **Oct. 19**.

Greek Voters Restore Former Leader — In a national election held **Oct. 10**, Greeks returned former Prime Minister Andreas Papandreou and his Pan-Hellenic Socialist Movement to power. Papandreou had fallen from power in 1989 as a result of political scandals and accusations of inept management. Since then, however, voters had apparently grown tired of the economic austerity program of Prime Minister Constantine Mitsotakis.

Death Toll Announced for Indian Quake — Government officials, **Oct. 12**, announced an official death toll from September's earthquake in southern India. Chief Minister Sharad Pawar of the Maharashtra state government said 9,748 people died in the disaster, based upon the number of bodies that Army units leading the relief effort had removed from the rubble.

German Court Rejects Appeal to Block European Unity Treaty — The last obstacle blocking final ratification of the European Community's so-called Maastricht Treaty on greater economic and political unity was removed in October. In Germany, the only EC country that had not completed its ratification, the constitutional court rejected, **Oct. 12**, a legal challenge contending that the treaty would surrender national power in violation of the German constitution.

General

Superstar Michael Jordan Retires — Michael Jordan, acclaimed by many as the greatest basketball player ever, announced his retirement, **Oct. 6**. After leading North Carolina to the NCAA championship in 1982, Jordan had starred for 9 years with the Chicago Bulls of the NBA. Jordan said he had nothing more to accomplish in basketball. He said his decision was not based on the murder of his father, to whom he was greatly devoted, during the summer.

Phone-Cable Merger Valued at $33 Billion — The Bell Atlantic Corporation and Tele-Communications Inc. announced plans for a merger, **Oct. 13**, that was seen as a $33 billion deal. Bell Atlantic would buy Tele-Communications, the nation's largest cable operator, and the Liberty Media Corporation, its cable programming company, for $23 billion and assume $10 billion in debt. The new company would be well positioned to develop and deliver a variety of new programming to American homes. The merger was subject to federal approval.

Notable Decisions of the U.S. Supreme Court, 1992-1993 Term

The Supreme Court's 1992-1993 term began Oct. 5, 1992, and ended June 28, 1993. The Court issued 107 decisions, the same number as in the previous term, but a decrease from the average of 150 rulings per term during the mid-1980s. Forty percent of the decisions were unanimous, far more than in recent years, yet the Court remained divided in such important areas as civil rights and religion. The triad of Chief Justice William H. Rehnquist, Justice Anthony M. Kennedy, and Justice Antonin Scalia was in the majority more than 90 percent of the time, the highest figure among the justices. The most frequent dissenter was Justice David H. Souter. Among the major decisions were:

Abortion: The Court declined to hear a challenge by abortion-rights advocates to a Mississippi law requiring a 24-hour waiting period, a provision similar to one in Pennsylvania that had been upheld by the Court during the previous term (Dec. 7). The Court also declined to hear appeals from Louisiana and Guam, where laws banning abortions, except to save a woman's life or in some cases of rape or incest, had been declared unconstitutional by lower federal courts (Mar. 8). The Court ruled, 6-3, that federal courts could not prohibit antiabortion protesters from blocking access to abortion clinics by invoking the Civil Rights Act of 1871, which had been designed to protect former slaves from conspiracies to deprive them of their civil rights (Jan. 13).

Animal Sacrifice: The Court ruled unanimously that a ban imposed by the city of Hialeah, Florida, on ritual animal sacrifice was unconstitutional. The Court held that, because the ban was clearly directed only at members of the Santeria faith, a Caribbean religion combining Yoruba African traditions with Roman Catholicism, it violated the First Amendment guarantee of the free exercise of religion (June 11).

Employee Bias Suits: Shifting the burden of proof to the employee, the Court ruled, 5-4, that workers must provide explicit evidence that they had been discriminated against on the basis of race, religion, or other status in order to qualify for protection under civil rights legislation (June 25).

Hate Crimes: The Court ruled unanimously that states could impose harsher sentences on defendants convicted of so-called hate crimes—those motivated by religious, racial, or other biases—because those crimes could inflict great harm on victims and society in general. More than 20 states and the District of Columbia, as well as federal sentencing guidelines, permitted stricter sentencing for bias-motivated crimes (June 11).

"Minority-Majority" Voting Districts: The Court ruled, 5-4, that states that designed voting districts to increase black representation to compensate for past discrimination could not violate the constitutional rights of white voters to equal protection under the law. The shape of the North Carolina district in question was "bizarre," the Court said, resembling "the most egregious racial gerrymanders of the past," and the state must demonstrate a "compelling interest" for such design over one with compact and contiguous districts (June 28).

Refugees: The Court ruled, 8-1, that a U.S. policy in which boats carrying Haitian refugees were intercepted on the high seas and the refugees returned to Haiti without receiving asylum hearings did not violate U.S. law. The Court held that U.S. refugee law applied only when aliens were in U.S. territory (June 21).

Religion and Schools: The Court ruled unanimously that schools must allow church groups the same after-hours access to their facilities as secular community organizations were given (June 7). The Court ruled, 5-4, that local governments could comply with a federal law requiring equal educational opportunities for disabled children by paying for special services in parochial schools (June 18).

Rights of Suspects, Defendants, and Prisoners: In a unanimous decision the Court expanded the "plain view" doctrine, under which police do not need a warrant to seize narcotics or other illegal objects that are clearly visible. If such items are recognized by "plain feel" while a suspect is frisked for concealed weapons, the Court said, no warrant is needed for their seizure (June 7). The Court ruled unanimously that the government holds only limited power under the Constitution to seize the assets of convicted criminals by using civil forfeiture law. Such a seizure could be considered an "excessive fine" under the Eighth Amendment, applicable to both criminal and civil penalties (June 28). The Court ruled, 7-2, that confining a nonsmoking prisoner in a cell with a chain-smoking cellmate could constitute "cruel and unusual punishment" under the Eighth Amendment (June 18). The Court ruled, 5-4, that federal courts should refuse to grant habeas corpus review of violations of a defendant's rights during a trial unless the violation had a "substantial and injurious effect or influence in determining the jury's verdict" (April 21). The Court ruled, 7-2, that the conclusions of an expert witness need not be "generally accepted" within the scientific community, but the "methods and procedures" involved in reaching such conclusions must be valid (June 28).

Tax Deductions for Home Offices: The Court ruled, 8-1, that self-employed people maintaining offices in their homes could claim housing costs as business deductions only if their home office was their "primary" place of business, not if they did their most important work or most of their work elsewhere (Jan. 12).

The 1993 Nobel Prizes

Each of the 1993 Nobel Prizes, awarded in October, consisted of a large solid gold medal and a cash award of more than $800,000.

Chemistry: Kary B. Mullis, an American, and Michael Smith, a British-born Canadian, shared the award. Dr. Mullis invented a method to "amplify" (or copy) DNA; Dr. Smith designed one to splice foreign components into genetic material.

Memorial Prize in Economic Science: Robert W. Fogel and Douglass C. North, both Americans, shared the prize, the first ever awarded for work in economic history.

Literature: Toni Morrison, an American novelist and essayist whose works include *Song of Solomon*, *Beloved*, and *Jazz*, won the award. She was the first African-American to do so.

Peace: Frederik W. de Klerk, president of South Africa, and Nelson Mandela, leader of the African National Congress, shared the prize, for their efforts to end apartheid and to institute majority rule in South Africa.

Physics: Two Americans, Joseph H. Taylor and Russell A. Hulse, shared the prize for discovering the first known binary pulsar.

Physiology or Medicine: Philip A. Sharp and Richard J. Roberts shared the prize for their independent discovery of "split genes." Dr. Sharp is an American; Dr. Roberts, born in Britain, works in the U.S.

Notable Quotes in 1993

"I pray that I may be all that she would have been had she lived in an age when women could aspire and achieve, and daughters are cherished as much as sons."
Supreme Court Justice *Ruth Bader Ginsburg*, invoking the memory of her mother

"Vast sections of society are confused about what is right and what is wrong."
Pope John Paul II

"I love the game, but I don't need that kind of turmoil."
George Bush, on whether he had any interest in being commissioner of baseball

"To forget would mean to kill the victims a second time. We could not prevent their first death; we must not allow them to be killed again."
Elie Wiesel, at the dedication of the Holocaust Memorial Museum in Washington, D.C.

"We want a guy who's amiable and doesn't cause any trouble."
Rolling Stone *Mick Jagger*, on what the aging band was looking for in a replacement for retiring bass player Bill Wyman

"He ate everything but the drapes. . . . He's a man who does like to put it down."
NBC's *Tom Brokaw*, on a lunch held by President Bill Clinton with network news anchors

"That's the president of the United States you're talking about, pinhead."
Vice President *Al Gore* to David Letterman after Letterman joked: "What does (Clinton) love to hear all the time? 'Would you like fries with that?' "

"I don't think you're going to see a great, great uproar in this country about the Republican committee trying to bug the Democratic headquarters."
Richard Nixon, four days after the 1972 Watergate burglary, as recorded on a White House tape released in 1993

"If Thomas Jefferson was alive today, I would appoint him secretary of state, and then suggest to [Vice President Al] Gore that we both resign so he could become president."
President Bill Clinton, asked if Jefferson would merit a job in his administration

"I was not meant for the job or the spotlight of public life in Washington. Here ruining people is considered sport."
Note left by White House lawyer *Vincent Foster*, an apparent suicide

"I love Charles [Oakley]. . . . He'll push me, shove me, scratch me, hit me, bite me, but never an elbow."
Horace Grant, Chicago Bulls forward

"Fifty guys standing around in their little posing trunks with oil slapped on their body. Showing off and posing in front of 5,000 people. It's a joke."
Arnold Schwarzenegger on bodybuilding competitions

"It's just like Pepsi-Cola!"
Georgia's President *Eduard Shevardnadze*, after sampling Coca-Cola at the opening of a new Coke bottling plant in Tbilisi

"If that happens, I'll just buy a new audience."
David Letterman on whether his $14 million salary and new time slot might alienate his audience

"If he wants me as a character witness, I'll be there."
Senator *Bob Packwood*, while under an ethics committee investigation of sexual misconduct, referring to Representative Dan Rostenkowski, who was implicated in the House post office scandal

"If he starts sleeping through cabinet meetings, you'll know the transformation is complete."
Marlin Fitzwater, former press secretary to George Bush, on ex-Reagan aide David Gergen's efforts to reshape Bill Clinton's image

"Left to their own devices, the three networks would televise live executions. Except Fox—they'd televise live naked executions."
TV producer *Gary David Goldberg*

"Now she knows how most women in America feel every day. She's got an impossible job, she's underpaid and every night her boss wants to sleep with her."
Jay Leno on Hillary Rodham Clinton's appointment as head of the Clinton administration's health care task force

"Well, they look so much alike I get them confused."
Barry Manilow, after referring to the wedding of Lyle Lovett and Julia Child, rather than Julia Roberts

"There's a lot to be said for superficiality."
TV producer *Linda Bloodworth-Thomason*, calling Washington a more trivial town than Hollywood

"When I started doing screenplays, I described it as work for idiots, but it's really work for strong, passionate idiots."
Author *Stephen King*

"They're failures. Well, that's a little strong. But if $120,000 a year is the best job you've ever had, you haven't really done much."
Author *Tom Clancy*, on what's wrong with Congress

"You don't need to be 'straight' to fight and die for your country. You just need to shoot straight."
Barry Goldwater, on whether gays should be allowed to serve in the military

"What is so important about having Chicago schools open on a specific date? . . . We just add it on to the end of the school year, another 10 days or two weeks. I don't see anything wrong with that. Half the kids aren't going to graduate anyway"
James (Pate) Philip, president of the Illinois Senate

"We who have fought against you, the Palestinians, we say to you today in a loud and a clear voice: 'Enough of blood and tears. Enough!' "
Israeli Prime Minister *Yitzhak Rabin*, speaking at the White House signing of a peace accord with the Palestine Liberation Organization

"Although not a lawyer, Mr. Burr strove for such authenticity . . . that we regard his passing as though we lost one of our own."
R. William Ide III, president of the American Bar Association, on the death of actor Raymond Burr, who portrayed TV lawyer Perry Mason

"I can't really say I ever sat around and fantasized about how I would have liked to have ended my career. But I think if I had, it certainly would have been with a strong performance in a pennant race. I guess by striking out the last hitter."
Pitcher *Nolan Ryan*, whose career ended in Sept. 1993 when he tore a ligament in his right elbow.

Historical Anniversaries

1894—100 Years Ago

Economic depression continued in the U.S.

The U.S. Treasury offered a $50 million bond issue to restore the declining gold reserve, **Jan. 17,** but public response was poor; a 2nd issue was offered **Nov. 13.**

Labor unrest was widespread all year, with strikes for higher wages, shorter hours, and safer conditions involving some 750,000 U.S. workers, including 136,000 coal miners in Columbus, Oh. and 12,000 garment workers in New York City. The strike by workers of the Pullman Palace Car Co. was joined by Eugene Debs's American Railway Union. U.S. troops sent to Chicago to enforce a federal injunction against the strikers opened fire, killing two men and injuring several; mob violence brought extensive damage. A federal grand jury sentenced Debs to 6 months in prison, but he was successfully defended by Clarence Darrow, who resigned his position as a railroad counsel to do so.

A Chinese Exclusion Treaty, by which China agreed to keep its laborers from the U.S., was signed **Mar. 17.**

Coxey's Army, some 400 unemployed men led by Jacob S. Coxey, marched from Ohio to Washington, D.C. to protest unemployment and demand public work programs. Coxey and 2 other leaders were arrested for trespassing at the Capitol, **Apr. 30.**

The Democratic Silver Convention was held in Omaha, Neb. **June 21,** and William Jennings Bryan came to national prominence for his eloquence in leading 1,000 delegates to the adoption of a free-coinage plank on a silver-to-gold ratio of 16 to 1.

Congress made Labor Day a legal holiday, **June 28.**

Following controversy surrounding the overthrow of Hawaii's Queen Liliuokalani by proannexation sugar interests headed by Sanford B. Dole and aided by the U.S. Minister, the Republic of Hawaii was proclaimed **July 4.** Dole became president and a progressive constitution was adopted. U.S. recognition came **Aug. 7.**

The Bureau of Immigration was created by an Act of Congress **Aug. 18.**

The Carey Act, adopted **Aug. 18,** promised each state up to a million acres of public lands, if the state would agree to irrigate.

The controversial Wilson-Gorman Tariff Act, which became law **Aug. 27,** without Pres. Grover Cleveland's signature, reduced U.S. tariff duties and levied the first graduated tax on incomes over $4,000. One senator termed the income tax "socialism, communism, devilism," and in 1895 the Supreme Court would declare it unconstitutional.

The U.S. and Japan signed a commercial treaty, **Nov. 22.**

Radcliffe College for Women, affiliated with Harvard Univ., opened at Cambridge, Mass. Elizabeth Cary Agassiz, influential in its founding, became its first president.

William Ramsay and John Rayleigh discovered the inert gas they named argon.

Literature: *Pudd'nhead Wilson* by Mark Twain; *Trilby,* featuring the hypnotic "Svengali," by George du Maurier; *The Memoirs of Sherlock Holmes* by Arthur Conan Doyle; *The Jungle Book* by Rudyard Kipling.

Journalism: *Wealth Against Commonwealth,* a study of the Standard Oil Co. by Henry Demarest Lloyd, one of the first "muckrakers"; *The Yellow Book,* a London periodical, which gained fame through art director Aubrey Beardsley's provocative drawings.

Art: Edgar Degas's "Femme à sa toilette" and American artist Mary Cassatt's "La toilette" were exhibited at Paris. Louis Comfort Tiffany invented and trademarked a process for staining glass to achieve radiantly iridescent colors, which he used to create "art nouveau" style lamps, vases, jewelry, and windows.

Theater: *Arms and the Man* by George Bernard Shaw, in London.

Ballet: *Afternoon of a Faun,* with music by French composer Claude Debussy, in Paris.

Popular songs: "Humoresque" by Anton Dvorák; "The Sidewalks of New York" by Charles B. Lawlor and James W. Blake; "I've Been Working on the Railroad," published as "Levee Song."

Sports: The first U.S. Open golf tournament was held at St. Andrew Golf Club in Yonkers, N.Y. The first Penn Relays were held in Philadelphia.

Miscellaneous: Pêche Melba—a scoop of vanilla ice cream on a cooked peach half with a purée of raspberries topped by almond slivers—was created by Auguste Escoffier at London's Savoy Hotel. The dessert honored Nellie Melba, the Australian diva. The Hershey Bar was introduced by Milton S. Hershey, whose family would found Hershey, Pa., to be populated mainly by company employees, in 1903.

1944—50 Years Ago

On D-Day, **June 6,** some 176,000 Allied troops landed at 5 beachheads along a 50-mile Normandy coastline under the command of Gen. Dwight D. Eisenhower. The date marked the start of the reconquest of France, and the beginning of the end for the Axis forces in World War II. The Battle of the Bulge in the Ardennes Forest of Belgium, **Dec. 16–27,** was the last major counteroffensive.

In the Pacific, Japanese forces were retreating. U.S. forces headed by Gen. Douglas MacArthur returned to the Philippines, **Oct. 20,** and 4 separate operations of a 6-day naval battle in Leyte Gulf marked the effective end of the Japanese fleet. The kamikaze, or suicide plane, was first used during the Leyte campaign.

The Supreme Court ruled, **April 3,** that an American could not be denied the right to vote because of race.

Jacob Coxey, age 90, stood on the Capitol steps, **May 1,** and delivered the speech he had attempted to make 50 years earlier. (See *1894—100 Years Ago.*)

Meat rationing was ended **May 3,** except for steak and choice cuts of beef.

The Servicemen's Readjustment Act, or "G.I. Bill of Rights," was passed by Congress **June 22,** and would finance college educations and low-interest, no-down-payment home loans for millions of veterans.

The United Nations Monetary and Financial Conference took place at Bretton Woods, New Hampshire, **July 1–22.** Forty-four countries attended to develop plans for mutual assistance, including the establishment of the International Monetary Fund for currency stabilization.

Representatives of the U.S., Britain, China, and the USSR met at Dumbarton Oaks, Washington, D.C. to discuss postwar world organization, **Aug. 21–Oct. 7.** Proposals would become the basis for the United Nations charter.

Pres. Franklin D. Roosevelt was reelected to a 4th term, **Nov. 7,** and would be the only U.S. president to do so. Votes included several million absentee ballots sent by members of the armed forces. FDR won 36 states with 432 electoral votes, while New York governor Thomas E. Dewey won only 12 states with 99 electoral votes, failing to carry his home state. Vice Pres. Henry A. Wallace had been replaced on the Democratic ticket by Harry S. Truman, U.S. senator from Missouri.

A Federal Highway Act was passed by Congress, **Nov. 29,** creating a new U.S. national system of interstate highways, covering 40,000 miles.

Congress created, **Dec. 15,** the rank of General of the Army—"5-star general"—for Dwight D. Eisenhower, Douglas MacArthur, George C. Marshall, and Henry Arnold.

The first large-scale automatic digital computer was built by the IBM Corporation at Harvard Univ. to the specifications of Harvard prof. Howard H. Aiken. The Harvard-IBM Automatic Sequence Controlled Calculator, or Mark I, had more than 750,000 parts, was 51 feet long, and weighed 5 tons. It performed a multiplication in about 6 seconds.

Literature: *Winter Tales* by Isak Dinesen; *Dangling Man* by Saul Bellow; *A Bell for Adano* by John Hersey; *Strange Fruit* by Lillian Smith; *The Lost Weekend* by Charles Jackson; *The Razor's Edge* by W. Somerset Maugham.

Art: "Three Studies for Figures at the Base of a Crucifix" by Francis Bacon; "Effervescence" by Hans Hoffman; "Plantation Road" by Thomas Hart Benton; "Pelvis III" by Georgia O'Keeffe.

Theater: *Antigone* by Jean Anouilh, and *No Exit* by Jean-Paul Sartre, both in Paris; *Harvey* by Mary Coyle; *I Remember Mama* by John Van Druten—with young Marlon Brando.

Musicals: *On the Town,* with Betty Comden, Adolph Green, and Nancy Walker; music by Leonard Bernstein, lyrics by Comden and Green; dances derived from the ballet *Fancy Free* by Jerome Robbins.

Movies: *Henvy V,* with Laurence Olivier; *Thirty Seconds Over Tokyo,* with Clark Gable, Walter Pidgeon; Sergei Eisenstein's *Ivan the Terrible,* Part I; Alfred Hitchcock's *Lifeboat,* with Tallulah Bankhead, William Bendix, John Hodiak, Canada Lee; Preston Sturges's *Hail the Conquering Hero,* with Eddie Bracken, Ella Raines; Otto Preminger's *Laura,* with Clifton Webb, Gene Tierney, Dana Andrews; Billy Wilder's *Double Indemnity,* with Barbara Stanwyck, Fred MacMurray, Edward G. Robinson; George Cukor's *Gaslight,* with Ingrid Bergman, Charles Boyer; Howard Hawks's *To Have and Have Not,* with Humphrey Bogart, Lauren Bacall; *National Velvet,* with Mickey Rooney and 12-year-old Elizabeth Taylor.

Musicals: Vincente Minelli's *Meet Me in St. Louis,* with Judy Garland, songs including "The Trolley Song" and "The Boy Next Door"; Leo McCarey's *Going My Way,* with Bing Crosby, Barry Fitzgerald, songs including "Would You Like to Swing on a Star?"; Charles Vidor's *Cover Girl,* with Rita Hayworth, Gene Kelly, songs including "Long Ago (and Far Away)".

Pop Songs: "I'll Walk Alone"; "Don't Fence Me In"; "Nancy (with the Laughing Face)"; "Rum and Coca-Cola"; "You're Nobody Till Somebody Loves You"; "You Always Hurt the One You Love".

Sports: The St. Louis Cardinals won the World Series over the St. Louis Braves, 4 games to 2.

Miscellaneous: Chiquita Banana was introduced by the United Fruit Company.

1969—25 Years Ago

A human walked on the moon for the first time, **July 20,** when U.S. astronaut Neil A. Armstrong left the lunar module of Apollo 11. He announced, "That's one small step for man, one giant leap for mankind." Armstrong was joined by Edwin E. "Buzz" Aldrin Jr.; the two astronauts deposited a lunar capsule and an American flag on the moon.

Richard M. Nixon was inaugurated as the 37th U.S. president, Spiro T. Agnew as vice president, **Jan. 20.**

U.S. combat deaths in Vietnam since Jan. 1, 1961 topped those of the Korean War, reaching 33,641 **Apr. 1.**

The world's first entirely artificial heart, made of Dacron and plastic, was implanted into a human, **Apr. 4,** by Dr. Denton A. Cooley in Houston, Tex., and the patient lived until Apr. 8.

The Supreme Court ruled unanimously, **Apr. 7,** that laws prohibiting the reading or viewing of obscene material in the privacy of a home were unconstitutional.

Several hundred students, mostly members of the militant Students for a Democratic Society (SDS), occupied Harvard Univ.'s administration building, **Apr. 9;** student protests followed at many other institutions.

U.S. B-52s dropped almost 3,000 tons of bombs on enemy positions near the Cambodian border, **Apr. 24,** the heaviest bombing raid in the war.

Pres. Nixon met with South Vietnam Pres. Nguyen Van Thieu, **June 8,** and announced the start of U.S. troop withdrawal and a "Vietnamization" policy.

Chief Justice Earl Warren retired from the Supreme Court, **June 23,** after swearing in Warren Burger as his successor.

The body of 28-year-old Mary Jo Kopechne was retrieved, **July 19,** from a car that had plunged off Chappaquiddick Island, near Martha's Vineyard, Mass. Sen. Edward M. Kennedy had been driving the car, and had failed to report the accident to police for 10 hours.

Actress Sharon Tate and 4 others were found murdered, **Aug. 9,** in Los Angeles; Charles Manson and several members of his cult were arrested.

The Woodstock Music and Art Fair at Bethel, New York brought an estimated 300,000–400,000 young people for 4 days in **mid-Aug.** Performers included Jimi Hendrix, Richie Havens, Joan Baez, the Jefferson Airplane, the Who, and the Grateful Dead. Despite traffic jams, inadequate food, water, and medical supplies, heavy rains and heavy drug use, the general atmosphere was one of peaceful celebration.

North Vietnamese leader Ho Chi Minh died, **Sept. 3,** at age 79 after 15 years as president.

The Concorde supersonic jet made its first supersonic flight, **Oct. 1.**

The first Vietnam Moratorium Day took place, **Oct. 15,** millions wearing black armbands, many meeting or marching to protest the war. Huge peace demonstrations took place in several major cities in Oct. and Nov., the largest involving 250,000 people in Wash., D.C., **Nov. 15.**

Pres. Nixon appealed for the first time, **Nov. 3,** to "the great Silent Majority."

News reports, **Nov. 16,** charged a U.S. infantry unit with the massacre at My Lai, a village in South Vietnam on Mar. 16, 1968; said to have been slain were more than 450 villagers, including women and children.

Public Television's "Sesame Street" began in **Nov.** to teach preschool children letters and numbers using the same techniques as commercial TV. The stars that were born included Bert and Ernie, Cookie Monster, Oscar the Grouch, and Big Bird.

The federal government announced the relaxation of trade restrictions with China, **Dec. 19.**

A far-reaching tax reform bill was signed by Pres. Nixon, **Dec. 30.** It reduced individual tax rates and removed some 9 million poor from federal tax rolls, but was criticized as mainly benefiting the rich.

Literature: *Ada* by Vladimir Nabokov; *Portnoy's Complaint* by Philip Roth; *Slaughterhouse Five* by Kurt Vonnegut Jr.; *Bullet Park* by John Cheever; *The Godfather* by Mario Puzo.

Art: "The Finn" by Andrew Wyeth; "Orange Yellow Orange" by Mark Rothko.

Theater: *To Be Young, Gifted and Black* by Lorraine Hansberry, adapted by Robert Nemiroff; *Ceremonies in Dark Old Men* by Lonnie Elder III; *No Place to Be Somebody* by Charles Gordone; *Last of the Red Hot Lovers* by Neil Simon.

Movies: Dennis Hopper's *Easy Rider,* with Hopper, Peter Fonda, Jack Nicholson; John Schlesinger's *Midnight Cowboy,* with Dustin Hoffman, Jon Voight; Sam Peckinpah's *The Wild Bunch,* with William Holden, Robert Ryan, Ernest Borgnine; George Roy Hill's *Butch Cassidy and the Sundance Kid,* with Paul Newman, Robert Redford, Katharine Ross; Karel Reisz's *The Loves of Isadora Duncan,* with Vanessa Redgrave; Sidney Pollack's *They Shoot Horses, Don't They?* with Jane Fonda; Henry Hathaway's *True Grit,* with John Wayne; Woody Allen's *Take the Money and Run.*

Sports: On the 100th anniversary of major league baseball, the Natl. League added San Diego and Montreal; the American League, Kansas City and Seattle. Each league was split into divisions, playoffs for league pennants began; changes were also made in ballpark outfields, strike zones, and pitchers' mounds. Willie Mays hit his 600th home run, Sept. 22, the San Francisco Giants outfielder joining Babe Ruth as the only players to do so. Outfielder Mickey Mantle retired after 18 years with the New York Yankees. The New York Mets won their first World Series. Rod Laver won the Grand Slam of tennis—Australian, French, Wimbledon and U.S. singles titles—for the second time. The NCAA basketball championship was won by UCLA, whose center Lew Alcindor was the first player to win the tournament's MVP award 3 successive years.

Miscellaneous: *The Saturday Evening Post* ended publication after 148 years. *Penthouse,* a more explicit competitor of Hugh Hefner's *Playboy,* began publication.

UNITED STATES GOVERNMENT

LEGISLATIVE BRANCH

CONGRESS

Senate House

Architect of the Capitol
U.S. Botanic Garden
General Accounting Office
Government Printing Office
Library of Congress
Office of Technology Assessment
Congressional Budget Office
Copyright Royalty Tribunal
U.S. Tax Court

EXECUTIVE BRANCH

PRESIDENT

Vice President Cabinet

Executive Office of the President

White House Office
Office of Management and Budget
Council of Economic Advisers
National Economic Council
National Security Council
Office of Policy Development
Office of the U.S. Trade Representative
Council on Environmental Quality
Office of Science and Technology Policy
Office of Administration
Office of National Drug Control Policy
National Critical Materials Council
National Space Council

JUDICIAL BRANCH

Supreme Court of the United States

Courts of Appeals
District Courts
Claims Court
Court of Appeals for the Federal Circuit
Court of International Trade
Territorial Courts
Court of Military Appeals
Court of Veterans Appeals
Administrative Office of the Courts
Federal Judicial Center

The Clinton Administration

As of mid-1993

Terms of office of the president and vice president: Jan. 20, 1993, to Jan. 20, 1997. No person may be elected president of the United States for more than two 4-year terms.

President — Bill Clinton of Arkansas receives salary of $200,000 a year taxable; in addition an expense allowance of $50,000 to assist in defraying expenses resulting from his official duties. Also there may be expended not exceeding $100,000, nontaxable, a year for travel expenses and $20,000 for official entertainment available for allocation within the Executive Office of the President.

Vice President — Albert Gore, Jr., of Tennessee receives salary of $171,500 a year and $10,000 for expenses, all of which is taxable.

The Cabinet

(Salary: $148,400 per annum)

Secretary of State — Warren M. Christopher.
Secretary of Treasury — Lloyd Bentsen.
Secretary of Defense — Les Aspin.
Attorney General — Janet Reno.
Secretary of Interior — Bruce Babbitt.
Secretary of Agriculture — Mike Espy.
Secretary of Commerce — Ronald H. Brown.
Secretary of Labor — Robert B. Reich.
Secretary of Health and Human Services — Donna E. Shalala.
Secretary of Housing and Urban Development — Henry G. Cisneros.
Secretary of Transportation — Federico F. Pena.
Secretary of Energy — Hazel R. O'Leary.
Secretary of Education — Richard W. Riley.
Secretary of Veterans Affairs — Jesse Brown.

The White House Staff

1600 Pennsylvania Ave. NW 20500

Chief of Staff — Thomas F. McLarty 3d.
Asst. to the President & Deputy Chief of Staff — Roy Neel.
Counselor to the President — David Gergen.
Adviser on Policy and Strategy — George Stephanopoulos.
Assistants to the President:
Counsel to the President — Bernard W. Nussbaum.
Counsel to the President on Domestic Policy — Carol Rasco.
Presidential Personnel — Bruce Lindsay.
Public Events & Initiatives — Marcia Hale.
Science & Technology — Dr. John H. Gibbons.
Press Secretary — Dee Dee Myers.
Legislative Affairs — Howard Paster.
Communications — Mark Gearan.
Economic & Domestic Affairs — Robert Rubin.
Management & Admin. — David Watkins.
Cabinet Secy. — Christine A. Varney.
National Security — W. Anthony Lake.
Staff Secretary — John Podesta.
National Service — Eli Segal.
Media Affairs — Jeff Eller.
AIDS Policy Coordinator — Kristine M. Gebbie.

Executive Agencies

Council of Economic Advisers — Laura D'Andrea Tyson, chmn.
National Economic Council — Robert Rubin, dir.
Central Intelligence Agency — R. James Woolsey, dir.
Office of National Drug Control Policy — Lee P. Brown.
Office of Management and Budget — Leon E. Panetta, dir.
U.S. Trade Representative — Michael Kantor.
Council on Environmental Quality — vacant.

Department of State

2201 C St. NW 20520

Secretary of State — Warren M. Christopher.
Deputy Secretary — Clifton R. Wharton, Jr.
Under Sec. for Political Affairs — Peter Tarnoff.
Under Sec. for International Security Affairs — Lynn Davis.
Under Secretary for Management — Richard Moose.
Under Sec. for Global Affairs — Timothy Wirth.
Legal Advisor — Sherman M. Funk.
Assistant Secretaries for:
Administration — Patrick F. Kennedy.
African Affairs — George E. Moose.
Consular Affairs — Mary A. Ryan.
Diplomatic Security — Tony Quainton.
East Asian & Pacific Affairs — Winston Lord.
Economic & Business Affairs — Daniel Tarullo.
European & Canadian Affairs — Stephen Oxman.
Human Rights & Humanitarian Affairs — John H. F. Shattuck.
Intelligence & Research — Tobi Gati.
Inter-American Affairs — Alexander Watson.
International Narcotics Matters — vacant.

International Organization Affairs — Douglas J. Bennett, Jr.
Legislative Affairs — Wendy R. Sherman.
Near-Eastern & S. Asian Affairs — Edward Djerejian.
Oceans, International Environmental & Scientific Affairs — Elinor G. Constable.
Politico-Military Affairs — Robert L. Galucci.
Public Affairs — Thomas Dinilon.
South Asian Affairs — Robin Raphel.

Department of the Treasury

1500 Pennsylvania Ave. NW 20220

Secretary of the Treasury — Lloyd Bentsen.
Deputy Sec. of the Treasury — Roger Altman.
Under Sec. for Domestic Finance — Frank N. Newman.
Under Sec. for International Affairs — Lawrence Summers.
General Counsel — Jean Hanson.
Assistant Secretaries for:
Economic Policy — Alicia Hancock Munnell.
Enforcement — Ronald K. Noble.
Fiscal Affairs — vacant.
International Affairs — Jeffrey Shafer.
Legislative Affairs — Mary B. Levy.
Policy Management — vacant.
Public Affairs & Public Liaison — Jack R. DeVore.
Tax Policy — Leslie B. Samueis.
Bureaus:
Alcohol, Tobacco & Firearms — vacant.
Comptroller of the Currency — Eugene A. Ludwig.
Customs — George J. Weise, comm.
Engraving & Printing — Peter H. Daley, dir.
Federal Law Enforcement Training Center — Charles F. Rinkevich, dir.
Financial Management Service — vacant.
Internal Revenue Service — Margaret Richardson, comm.
Mint — David Ryder, dir.
Public Debt — Richard L. Gregg, comm.
Treasurer of the U.S. — vacant.
U.S. Savings Bond Division — vacant.
U.S. Secret Service — Guy Caputo, act.

Department of Defense

The Pentagon 20301

Secretary of Defense — Les Aspin.
Deputy Secretary — William Perry.
Under Secy. for Acquisition — John Deutch.
Under Secy. for Policy — Frank Wisner.
Asst. Secretaries for:
Command, Control, Communications & Intelligence — vacant.
Force Management & Personnel — vacant.
Health Affairs — vacant.
International Security Policy — vacant.
Legislative Affairs — vacant.
Policy & Plans — Graham T. Allison.
Products & Logistics — vacant.
Program Analysis & Evaluation — vacant.
Public Affairs — Kathleen DeLaski.
Reserve Affairs — Deborah Lee.
Special Operations & Low Intensity Conflict— vacant.
Comptroller— John Hamre.
General Counsel — Jamie Gorelick.
Administration — Ann Reese, dir.
Operational Test & Evaluation — vacant.
Chairman, Joint Chiefs of Staff — Gen. John Shalikashvili.
Secretary of the Army — Togo West.
Secretary of the Navy — John Dalton.
Secretary of the Air Force — Sheila Widnall.

Department of Justice

Constitution Ave. & 10th St. NW 20530

Attorney General — Janet Reno.
Deputy Attorney General — Philip B. Heymann.
Associate Attorney General — Webster L. Hubbell.
Solicitor General — Drew Days 3d.
Intelligence Policy & Review — vacant.
Professional Responsibility —vacant.
Assistants:
Antitrust Division — Anne Bingaman.
Civil Division — Frank Hunger.
Civil Rights Division — James Turner, act.
Criminal Division — vacant.
Environment & Natural Resources Division — Gerald Torres.
Justice Management Division — vacant.
Legal Counsel — Walter Dellinger.
Legal Policy — Eleanor Acheson.
Legislative Affairs — Sheila Foster.
Policy & Communications — vacant.
Tax Division — vacant.
Fed. Bureau of Investigation — Louis J. Freeh, dir.
Exec. Off. for Immigration Review — vacant.
Bureau of Prisons — Kathleen M. Hawk, dir.
Comm. Relations Service — Jeffrey Weiss, act. dir.
Office of Inspector General — vacant.
Office of Justice Programs — vacant.
Drug Enforcement Adm. — Robert C. Bonner.
Office of Special Counsel for Immigration-Related Unfair Employment Practices — vacant.
Exec. Off. for U.S. Trustees — John Logan, dir.
Exec. Off. for U.S. Attorneys — Anthony C. Moscato, dir.
Immigration and Naturalization Service — Gene McNary.
Pardon Attorney — Margaret Love.
U.S. Parole Commission — Edward F. Reilly, Jr., chmn.
U.S. Marshals Service — Eduardo Gonzalez, dir.
U.S. Natl. Central Bureau of Interpol — Shelley G. Altenstadtero, chief.

Department of the Interior

C St. between 18th & 19th Sts. NW 20240

Secretary of the Interior — Bruce Babbitt.
Deputy Secretary — Robert Hattoy, act.
Assistant Secretaries for:
Fish, Wildlife, and Parks — George T. Framton, Jr.
Indian Affairs — Ada Deer.
Land & Minerals — Robert Armstrong.
Policy, Budget, and Management — Bonnie R. Cohen.
Territorial & Intl. Affairs — Leslie Turner.
Water & Science — Elizabeth A. Reike.
Bureau of Land Management — Jim Baca, dir.
Bureau of Mines — Herman Enzer, act. dir.
Bureau of Reclamation — Daniel T. Beard, comm.
Fish & Wildlife Service — Mollie Beattie, dir.
Geological Survey — Robert Hirsch, act. dir.
National Park Service — Roger Kennedy, dir.
Public Affairs — Kevin Sweeney, dir.
Office of Congressional and Legislative Affairs — Stephanie Solien.
Solicitor — John D. Leshy.

Department of Agriculture

The Mall, 12th & 14th Sts. 20250

Secretary of Agriculture — Mike Espy.
Deputy Secretary — vacant.
Assistant Secretaries for:
Administration — Wardell Townsend, Jr.
Congressional Relations — Robin Rorapaugh.
Economics — Keith Collins, act.
Food & Consumer Services — Ellen Haas.
Internatl. Affairs & Commodity Programs — Eugene Moos.
Marketing & Inspection Services — Eugene Branstool.
Natural Resources & Environment — James Lyons.
Science & Education — R. D. Plowman, act.
General Counsel — James Gilliland.
Inspector General — Charles Gillum, act.
Public Affairs — Ali Webb.
Press Secretary — Steve Kinsella.

Department of Commerce

14th St. between Constitution & E St. NW 20230

Secretary of Commerce — Ronald H. Brown.
Deputy Secretary — vacant.
Chief of Staff — Carole Timble.
General Counsel — vacant.
Assistant Secretaries for:
Chief Financial Officer & Asst. for Administration — vacant.
Economic Development Adm. — vacant.
Export Enforcement — Douglas Lavin.
Import Administration — Loretta Dunn.
Intl. Economic Policy — vacant.
Legislative Affairs — vacant.
Natl. Telecommunications Information Adm. — vacant.
Oceans & Atmosphere — Douglas K. Hall.
Patent & Trademark Office & Act. Asst. Comm. — vacant.
Trade Development — vacant.
Bureau of the Census — vacant.
Bureau of Economic Analysis — Carol Carson, dir.
Under Secy. for International Trade — Jeffrey Garten.
Under Secy. for Econ. Affairs — Everett Ehrlich.
Under Secy. for Technology — Mary Lowe Good.
Natl. Technical Info. Service — vacant.
Natl. Institute for Standards & Technology — Arati Prabhakar, dir.
Minority Business Development Agency — Joe Lira.
Public Affairs — Eric Ruff, dir.

Department of Labor

200 Constitution Ave. NW 20210

Secretary of Labor — Robert B. Reich.
Deputy Secretary — Thomas P. Glynn.
Chief of Staff — Kathryn Higgins.
Assistant Secretaries for:
Administration and Management — vacant.
Congressional & Intergovernmental Affairs — Geri Palast.
Employment & Training — Doug Ross.
Employment Standards — vacant.
Labor-Management Standards — vacant.
Occupational Safety & Health — Joseph Dear.
Pension & Welfare Benefits — Olena Berg.
Policy — John Donahue.
Public Affairs — Anne Lewis.
Solicitor of Labor — Thomas S. Williamson.
Bureau of International Affairs — vacant.
Dep. Under Secy. for Labor-Management Relations & Cooperative Programs — vacant.
Women's Bureau — Karen Nussbaum, dir.
Inspector General — vacant.
Bureau of Labor Statistics — Katharine Abraham.

Department of Health and Human Services

200 Independence Ave. SW 20201

Secretary of HHS — Donna E. Shalala.
Under Secretary — vacant.
Assistant Secretaries for:
Children & Families — Mary Jo Bane.
Health — James Mason, M.D.
Legislation — Jerry D. Klepner.
Management & Budget — Kenneth Apfel.
Personnel Administration — Thomas McFee.
Planning & Evaluation — David T. Ellwood.
Public Affairs — Avis LaVelle.
General Counsel — Harriet Rabb.
Inspector General — June Gibbs Brown.
Office of Civil Rights — vacant.
Surgeon General — Joycelyn Elders.
Social Security Adm. — Shirley Sears Chater.
Office of Consumer Affairs — vacant.
Health Care Financing Adm. — vacant.

Department of Housing and Urban Development

451 7th St. SW 20410

Secretary of Housing & Urban Development — Henry G. Cisneros.
Deputy Secretary — Terrence Duvernay.
Assistant Secretaries for:
Administration — vacant.
Community Planning & Development — Andrew Cuomo.
Fair Housing & Equal Opportunity — Robert A. Achtenberg.
Field Mgt. — Frank Wing.
Housing & Federal Housing Commissioner — Nicolas P. Retsinas.
Labor Relations — Joseph A. Scudero.
Congressional & Intergovernmental Relations — William J. Gilmartin.
Policy Development & Research — Michael Stegman.
Public Affairs — Jean Nolan.
Public & Indian Housing — Joseph Shuldiner.
General Counsel — Nelson Diaz.
Inspector General — Susan Gaffney.

Department of Transportation

400 7th St. SW 20590

Secretary of Transportation — Federico F. Pena.
Deputy Secretary — Mortimer L. Downey.
Assistant Secretaries for:
Administration — Jon H. Seymour.
Budget & Programs — Louise Stoll.
Governmental Affairs — vacant.
Policy & International Affairs — vacant.
Public Affairs — Richard I. Mintz.
U. S. Coast Guard Commandant — Adm. J. W. Kime.
Federal Aviation Admin. — David Hinson.
Federal Highway Admin. — Rodney Slater.
Federal Railroad Admin. — Jolene Molitoris.
Maritime Admin. — Albert Herberger.
Federal Transit Admin. — Gordon J. Linton.
Research & Special Programs Admin. — vacant.
Saint Lawrence Seaway Development Corp. — Stan E. Parris.

Department of Energy

1000 Independence Ave. SW 20585

Secretary of Energy — Hazel R. O'Leary.
Deputy Secy. — William H. White.
Under Secretary — vacant.
General Counsel — Robert Nordhaus.
Inspector General — John C. Layton.
Assistant Secretaries for:
Congressional & Intergovernmental Affairs — William Taylor.
Conservation & Renewable Energy — vacant.
Defense Programs — Victor Reis.
Domesic & International Energy Policy — Susan Tierney.
Environment, Safety & Health — Tara Jeanne O'Toole.
Fossil Energy — vacant.
Nuclear Energy — vacant.
Energy Information Adm. — Jay Hakes, adm.
Economic Regulatory Adm. — Jay Thompson, act. adm.
Federal Energy Regulatory Comm. — Elizabeth Moler, chair.
Hearings & Appeals — vacant.
Energy Research — Martha Krebs.
Civilian Radioactive Waste Management — vacant.
Minority Economic Impact — vacant.
Board of Contract Appeals — vacant.
Public Affairs — vacant.

Department of Education

400 Maryland Ave. SW 20202

Secretary of Education — Richard W. Riley.
Under Secretary — Marshall S. Smith.

Deputy Secretary — Madeleine Kunin.
Chief of Staff — Polly Gault.
Inspector General — James B. Thomas, Jr.
General Counsel — Judith Winston.
Assistant Secretaries for:
- **Adult & Vocational Education** — Augusta Kappner.
- **Bilingual & Minority Language Affairs** — vacant.
- **Civil Rights** — Norma V. Cantu.
- **Educational Research and Improvement** — Porter Robinson.
- **Elementary and Secondary Education** — Thomas W. Payzant.
- **Human Resources & Administration** — vacant.
- **Intergovernmental & Interagency Affairs** — vacant.
- **Legislation & Congressional Affairs** — Kay Casstevens.
- **Management & Budget** — vacant.
- **Postsecondary Education** — David Longanecker.
- **Special Education and Rehabilitative Services** — Judith Heumann.

Department of Veterans Affairs

810 Vermont Ave. NW 20420

Secretary of Veterans Affairs — Jesse Brown.
Deputy — Hershel W. Gober.
Assistant Secretaries for:
- **Acquisition & Facilities** — Gary Krump, act.
- **Congressional Affairs** — Edward P. Scott.
- **Finance & Information Resources Mgmt.** — D. Mark Catlett.
- **Human Resources & Adm.** — Eugene Brickhouse.
- **Policy & Planning** — Victor P. Raymond.
- **Public & Intergovernmental Affairs** — Kathy E. Jurado.

Inspector General — Stephen Trodden.
Under Secy. for Benefits — vacant.
Under Secy. for Health — vacant.
National Cemetery System — Jerry W. Bowen, dir.
General Counsel — Mary Lou Keener.
Board of Veterans Appeals — Charles L. Cragin, chmn.

Judiciary of the U.S.

Data as of mid-1993

Justices of the United States Supreme Court

The Supreme Court comprises the chief justice of the United States and 8 associate justices, all appointed by the president with advice and consent of the Senate. Salaries: chief justice $171,500 annually, associate justice $164,100. The Supreme Court is located at the U.S. Supreme Court Bldg., 1 First St. NE, Wash., DC 20543.

Members of the Supreme Court at the start of the 1993–1994 term (Oct. 4, 1993): *Chief justice:* William H. Rehnquist; *associate justices:* Harry A. Blackmun, Ruth Bader Ginsburg, Anthony M. Kennedy, Sandra Day O'Connor, Antonin Scalia, David H. Souter, John Paul Stevens, Clarence Thomas.

Name; apptd from *Chief Justices in italics*	Service Term	 Yrs.	Born	Died
John Jay, N. Y.	1789-1795	5	1745	1829
John Rutledge, S. C.	1789-1791	1	1739	1800
William Cushing, Mass.	1789-1810	20	1732	1810
James Wilson, Pa.	1789-1798	8	1742	1798
John Blair, Va.	1789-1796	6	1732	1800
James Iredell, N. C.	1790-1799	9	1751	1799
Thomas Johnson, Md.	1791-1793	1	1732	1819
William Paterson, N. J.	1793-1806	13	1745	1806
John Rutledge, S.C.	1795(a)	—	1739	1800
Samuel Chase, Md.	1796-1811	15	1741	1811
Oliver Ellsworth, Conn.	1796-1800	4	1745	1807
Bushrod Washington, Va.	1798-1829	31	1762	1829
Alfred Moore, N. C.	1799-1804	4	1755	1810
John Marshall, Va.	1801-1835	34	1755	1835
William Johnson, S. C.	1804-1834	30	1771	1834
Henry B. Livingston, N. Y.	1806-1823	16	1757	1823
Thomas Todd, Ky.	1807-1826	18	1765	1826
Joseph Story, Mass.	1811-1845	33	1779	1845
Gabriel Duval, Md.	1811-1835	22	1752	1844
Smith Thompson, N. Y.	1823-1843	20	1768	1843
Robert Trimble, Ky.	1826-1828	2	1777	1828
John McLean, Oh.	1829-1861	32	1785	1861
Henry Baldwin, Pa.	1830-1844	14	1780	1844
James M. Wayne, Ga.	1835-1867	32	1790	1867
Roger B. Taney, Md.	1836-1864	28	1777	1864
Philip P. Barbour, Va.	1836-1841	4	1783	1841
John Catron, Tenn.	1837-1865	28	1786	1865
John McKinley, Ala.	1837-1852	15	1780	1852
Peter V. Daniel, Va.	1841-1860	19	1784	1860
Samuel Nelson, N. Y.	1845-1872	27	1792	1873
Levi Woodbury, N. H.	1845-1851	5	1789	1851
Robert C. Grier, Pa.	1846-1870	23	1794	1870
Benjamin R. Curtis, Mass.	1851-1857	6	1809	1874
John A. Campbell, Ala.	1853-1861	8	1811	1889
Nathan Clifford, Me.	1858-1881	23	1803	1881
Noah H. Swayne, Oh.	1862-1881	18	1804	1884
Samuel F. Miller, Ia.	1862-1890	28	1816	1890
David Davis, Ill.	1862-1877	14	1815	1886
Stephen J. Field, Cal.	1863-1897	34	1816	1899
Salmon P. Chase, Oh.	1864-1873	8	1808	1873
William Strong, Pa.	1870-1880	10	1808	1895
Joseph P. Bradley, N. J.	1870-1892	21	1813	1892
Ward Hunt, N. Y.	1872-1882	9	1810	1886

Name; apptd from *Chief Justices in italics*	Service Term	 Yrs.	Born	Died
Morrison R. Waite, Oh.	1874-1888	14	1816	1888
John M. Harlan, Ky.	1877-1911	34	1833	1911
William B. Woods, Ga.	1880-1887	6	1824	1887
Stanley Matthews, Oh.	1881-1889	7	1824	1889
Horace Gray, Mass.	1881-1902	20	1828	1902
Samuel Blatchford, N. Y.	1882-1893	11	1820	1893
Lucius Q. C. Lamar, Miss.	1888-1893	5	1825	1893
Melville W. Fuller, Ill.	1888-1910	21	1833	1910
David J. Brewer, Kan.	1889-1910	20	1837	1910
Henry B. Brown, Mich.	1890-1906	15	1836	1913
George Shiras Jr., Pa.	1892-1903	10	1832	1924
Howell E. Jackson, Tenn.	1893-1895	2	1832	1895
Edward D. White, La.	1894-1910	16	1845	1921
Rufus W. Peckham, N. Y.	1895-1909	13	1838	1909
Joseph McKenna, Cal.	1898-1925	26	1843	1926
Oliver W. Holmes, Mass.	1902-1932	29	1841	1935
William R. Day, Oh.	1903-1922	19	1849	1923
William H. Moody, Mass.	1906-1910	3	1853	1917
Horace H. Lurton, Tenn.	1909-1914	4	1844	1914
Charles E. Hughes, N. Y.	1910-1916	5	1862	1948
Willis Van Devanter, Wy.	1910-1937	26	1859	1941
Joseph R. Lamar, Ga.	1910-1916	5	1857	1916
Edward D. White, La.	1910-1921	10	1845	1921
Mahlon Pitney, N. J.	1912-1922	10	1858	1924
James C. McReynolds, Tenn.	1914-1941	26	1862	1946
Louis D. Brandeis, Mass.	1916-1939	22	1856	1941
John H. Clarke, Oh.	1916-1922	5	1857	1945
William H. Taft, Conn.	1921-1930	8	1857	1930
George Sutherland, Ut.	1922-1938	15	1862	1942
Pierce Butler, Minn.	1922-1939	16	1866	1939
Edward T. Sanford, Tenn.	1923-1930	7	1865	1930
Harlan F. Stone, N. Y.	1925-1941	16	1872	1946
Charles E. Hughes, N. Y.	1930-1941	11	1862	1948
Owen J. Roberts, Pa.	1930-1945	15	1875	1955
Benjamin N. Cardozo, N.Y.	1932-1938	6	1870	1938
Hugo L. Black, Ala.	1937-1971	34	1886	1971
Stanley F. Reed, Ky.	1938-1957	19	1884	1980
Felix Frankfurter, Mass.	1939-1962	23	1882	1965
William O. Douglas, Conn.	1939-1975	36	1898	1980
Frank Murphy, Mich.	1940-1949	9	1890	1949
Harlan F. Stone, N. Y.	1941-1946	5	1872	1946

Name; apptd from *Chief Justices in italics*	Service Term	Yrs.	Born	Died
James F. Byrnes, S. C.	1941-1942	1	1879	1972
Robert H. Jackson, N. Y.	1941-1954	12	1892	1954
Wiley B. Rutledge, Ia.	1943-1949	6	1894	1949
Harold H. Burton, Oh.	1945-1958	13	1888	1964
Fred M. Vinson, Ky.	1946-1953	7	1890	1953
Tom C. Clark, Tex.	1949-1967	18	1899	1977
Sherman Minton, Ind.	1949-1956	7	1890	1965
Earl Warren, Cal.	1953-1969	16	1891	1974
John Marshall Harlan, N. Y.	1955-1971	16	1899	1971
William J. Brennan Jr., N. J.	1956-1990	33	1906	—
Charles E. Whittaker, Mo.	1957-1962	5	1901	1973
Potter Stewart, Oh.	1958-1981	23	1915	1985
Byron R. White, Col.	1962-1993	31	1917	—
Arthur J. Goldberg, Ill.	1962-1965	3	1908	1990
Abe Fortas, Tenn.	1965-1969	4	1910	1982
Thurgood Marshall, N.Y.	1967-1991	24	1908	1993
Warren E. Burger, Va.	1969-1986	17	1907	—
Harry A. Blackmun, Minn.	1970 —	—	1908	—
Lewis F. Powell Jr., Va.	1972-1987	15	1907	—
William H. Rehnquist, Ariz.	1972-1986	14	1924	—
John Paul Stevens, Ill.	1975 —	—	1920	—
Sandra Day O'Connor, Ariz.	1981 —	—	1930	—
William H. Rehnquist, Ariz.	1986 —	—	1924	—
Antonin Scalia, Va.	1986 —	—	1936	—
Anthony M. Kennedy, Cal.	1988 —	—	1936	—
David H. Souter, N.H.	1990 —	—	1939	—
Clarence Thomas, Va.	1991 —	—	1948	—
Ruth Bader Ginsburg, D.C.	1993 —	—	1933	—

(a) Rejected Dec. 15, 1795.

U.S. Court of International Trade

New York, NY 10007 (Salaries, $133,600)

Chief Judge — Dominick L. DeCarlo.

Judges — Jane A. Restani, Gregory W. Carmen, Thomas J. Aquilino Jr., Nicholas Tsoucalas, R. Kenton Musgrave, Richard W. Goldberg.

U.S. Claims Court

Washington, D.C. 20005 (Salaries, $133,600)

Chief Judge — Loren A. Smith.

Judges — James F. Merow, John P. Wiese, Robert J. Yock, Reginald W. Gibson, Lawrence S. Margolis, Christine C. Nettesheim, Moody R. Tidwell 3d, Marian Blank Horn, Eric G. Bruggink, Bohdan A. Futey, Wilkes C. Robinson, Roger B. Andewelt, James T. Turner, Robert H. Hodges Jr., Diane G. Weinstein.

U.S. Tax Court

Washington DC 20217 (Salaries, $133,600)

Chief Judge — Lapsley W. Hamblen Jr.

Judges — Renato Beghe, Herbert L. Chabot, Edna G. Parker, Mary Ann Cohen, John O. Colvin, Perry Shields, Charles E. Clapp 2d, Joel Gerber, Julien I. Jacobs, Carolyn Miller Parr, Robert P. Ruwe, James S. Halpern, Carolyn P. Chiechi.

U.S. Courts of Appeals

(Salaries, $141,700. CJ means Chief Judge)

Federal Circuit — Helen W. Nies, CJ; Giles S. Rich, Pauline Newman, Glenn L. Archer Jr., H. Robert Mayer, Paul R. Michel, S. Jay Plager; Alan D. Lourie, Raymond C. Clevenger 3d, Randall F. Rader, Alvin A. Schall; Clerk's Office, Washington, DC 20439.

District of Columbia — Abner J. Mikva, CJ; Patricia M. Wald, Harry T. Edwards, Laurence H. Silberman; James L. Buckley, Stephen F. Williams, Douglas Ginsburg, David B. Sentelle; Karen LeCraft Henderson, A. Raymond Randolph; Clerk's Office, Washington, DC 20001.

First Circuit (Me., Mass., N.H., R.I., Puerto Rico) — Stephen Breyer, CJ; Juan R. Torruella, Bruce M. Selya, Conrad K. Cyr, Michael Boudin, Norman H. Stahl; Clerk's Office, Boston, MA 02109.

Second Circuit (Conn., N.Y., Vt.) — Thomas J. Meskill, CJ; James L. Oakes, Jon O. Newman, Amalya Lyle Kearse, Richard J. Cardamone, Ralph K. Winter Jr., George C. Pratt, Roger J. Miner, Frank X. Altimari, J. Daniel Mahoney, John M. Walker; Joseph M. McLaughlin, Dennis G. Jacobs; Clerk's Office, New York, NY 10007.

Third Circuit (Del., N.J., Pa., Virgin Is.) — Dolores K. Sloviter, CJ; Edward R. Becker, Carol Los Mansmann, Walter K. Stapleton, Morton I. Greenberg, Anthony J. Scirica, William D. Hutchinson, Robert E. Cowen, Richard L. Nygaard, Samuel A. Alito Jr., Jane R. Roth, Timothy K. Lewis; Clerk's Office, Philadelphia, PA 19106.

Fourth Circuit (Md., N.C., S.C., Va., W.Va.) — Sam J. Ervin 3d, CJ; Kenneth K. Hall, Donald Stuart Russell, H. Emory Widener Jr., James D. Phillips Jr., Francis D. Murnaghan Jr., J. Harvie Wilkinson 3d, William W. Wilkins Jr., Paul V. Niemeyer, Clyde H. Hamilton, J. Michael Luttig, Karen J. Williams; Clerk's Office, Richmond, VA 23219.

Fifth Circuit (La., Miss., Tex.) — Henry A. Politz, CJ; Carolyn D. King, Will Garwood, E. Grady Jolly, Patrick E. Higginbotham, W. Eugene Davis, Jerry E. Smith, Edith Hollan Jones, John M. Duhe Jr., Rhesa A. Barksdale, Jacques L. Wiener Jr., Emilio M. Garza, Harold R. DeMoss Jr.; Clerk's Office, New Orleans, LA 70130.

Sixth Circuit (Ky., Mich., Ohio, Tenn.) — Gilbert S. Merritt, CJ; Damon J. Keith, Boyce F. Martin Jr., Nathaniel R. Jones, Cornelia G. Kennedy, H. Ted Milburn, Ralph B. Guy Jr., David A. Nelson, James L. Ryan, Danny J. Boggs, Alan E. Norris, Richard H. Suhrheinrich, Eugene E. Siler Jr., Alice M. Batchelder; Clerk's Office, Cincinnati, OH 45202.

Seventh Circuit (Ill., Ind., Wis.) — William J. Bauer, CJ; Walter J. Cummings, Richard D. Cudahy, Richard A. Posner, John L. Coffey, Joel M. Flaum, Frank H. Easterbrook, Kenneth F. Ripple, Daniel A. Manion, Michael S. Kanne, Ilana D. Rovner; Clerk's Office, Chicago, IL 60604.

Eighth Circuit (Ark., Ia., Minn., Mo., Neb., N.D., S.D.) — Richard S. Arnold, CJ; Theodore McMillian, John R. Gibson, George C. Fagg, Pasco M. Bowman 2d, Roger L. Wollman, Frank J. Magill, C. Arlen Beam, James B. Loken, David R. Hanson, Morris S. Arnold; Clerk's Office, St. Louis, MO 63101.

Ninth Circuit (Alaska, Ariz., Cal., Ha., Ida., Mont., Nev., Ore., Wash., Guam, N. Mariana Islands) — J. Clifford Wallace, CJ; James R. Browning, Procter Hug Jr., Thomas Tang, Jerome Farris, Betty B. Fletcher, Mary M. Schroeder, Harry Pregerson, Cecil F. Poole, Dorothy W. Nelson, William C. Canby Jr., William A. Norris, Stephen Reinhardt, Robert R. Beezer, Cynthia M. Hall, Charles E. Wiggins, Melvin Brunetti, Alex Kozinski, David R. Thompson, John T. Noonan, Diarmuid F. O'Scannlain, Edward Leavy, Stephen S. Trott, Ferdinand F. Fernandez, Pamela Ann Rymer, Thomas G. Nelson, Andrew J. Kleinfeld; Clerk's Office, San Francisco, CA 94119.

Tenth Circuit (Col., Kan., N.M., Okla., Ut., Wy.) — Monroe G. McKay, CJ; James K. Logan, Stephanie K. Seymour, John P. Moore, Stephen H. Anderson, Deanell R. Tacha, Bobby R. Baldock, Wade Brorby, David M. Ebel, Paul J. Kelly Jr.; Clerk's Office, Denver, CO 80294.

Eleventh Circuit (Ala. Fla., Ga.)— Gerald B. Tjoflat, CJ; Peter T. Fay, Phyllis A. Kravitch, Joseph W. Hatchett, R. Lanier Anderson 3d, J.L. Edmondson, Emmett R. Cox, Stanley F. Birch Jr., Joel F. Dubina, Susan H. Black, Edward E. Carnes; Clerk's Office, Atlanta GA 30303.

Temporary Emergency Court of Appeals — Reynaldo G. Garza, CJ; Robert A. Grant, Charles M. Metzner, John W. Peck, Frederick A. Daugherty, Wesley E. Brown, Stanley A. Weigel; Clerk's Office, Washington, DC 20001.

U.S. District Courts

(Salaries, $133,600. CJ means Chief Judge)

Alabama — Northern: Sam C. Pointer Jr., CJ; James Hughes Hancock, Robert B. Propst, U. W. Clemon, William M. Acker Jr., Edwin L. Nelson, Sharon Lovelace Blackburn; Clerk's Office, Birmingham 35203. **Middle:** Myron H. Thompson, CJ; William H. Albritton, Ira Dement; Clerk's Office, Montgomery 36101. **Southern:** Alex T. Howard Jr., CJ; Charles R. Butler Jr., Richard W. Vollmer Jr.; Clerk's Office, Mobile 36602.

Alaska — H. Russel Holland, CJ; John K. Singleton, John W. Sedwick; Clerk's Office, Anchorage 99513.

Arizona — William D. Browning, CJ; Richard M. Bilby, Earl H. Carroll, Paul G. Rosenblat, Robert C. Bloomfield, Roger G. Strand, Stephen M. McNamee, John M. Roll; Clerk's Office, Phoenix 85025.

Arkansas — Eastern: Samuel M. Reasoner, CJ; Henry Woods, George Howard Jr., Susan Weber Wright; Clerk's Office, Little Rock 72203. **Western:** H. Franklin Waters, CJ; George Howard Jr., Jimm Larry Hendren; Clerk's Office, Fort Smith 72902.

California — Northern: Thelton E. Henderson, CJ; Robert P. Aguilar, Marilyn H. Patel, Eugene F. Lynch, John P. Vukasin Jr, Charles A. Legge, D. Lowell Jensen, Fern M. Smith, Vaughn R. Walker, James Ware, Susan B. Armstrong, Barbara A. Caulfield, Ronald J. Whyte; Clerk's Office, San Francisco 94102. **Eastern:** Robert E. Coyle, CJ; Lawrence K. Karlton, Edward J. Garcia, William B. Shubb, David F. Levi, Oliver W. Wanger, Garland E. Burrell Jr.; Clerk's Office, Sacramento 95814. **Central:** Manuel L. Real, CJ; Wm. Matthew Byrne Jr., Robert M. Takasugi, Mariana R. Pfaelzer, Terry J. Hatter Jr., A. Wallace Tashima, Consuelo Bland Marshall, David V. Kenyon, Richard A. Gadbois, Edward Rafeedie, Harry L. Hupp, Alicemarie H. Stotler, James M. Ideman, William J. Rea, William D. Keller, Stephen V. Wilson, J. Spencer Letts, Dickran M. Tevrizian Jr., John G. Davies, Ronald S.W. Lew, Gary L. Taylor, Linda Hodge McLaughlin, Lourdes G. Baird; Clerk's Office, Los Angeles 90012. **Southern:** Judith N. Keep, CJ; Gordon Thompson Jr., Earl B. Gilliam, Rudi M. Brewster, John S. Rhoades Sr., Marilyn L. Huff, Irma E. Gonzalez; Clerk's Office, San Diego 92101.

Colorado — Sherman G. Finesilver, CJ; Richard P. Matsch, Jim R. Carrigan, Zita L. Weinshienk, Lewis T. Babcock, Edward W. Nottingham, Daniel B. Sparr; Clerk's Office, Denver 80294.

Connecticut — Jose A. Cabranes, CJ; T.F. Gilroy Daly, Peter C. Dorsey, Alan H. Nevas, Alfred V. Covello; Clerk's Office, New Haven 06510.

Delaware — Joseph J. Longobardi, CJ; Joseph J. Farnan Jr., Sue L. Robinson, Roderick R. McKelvie; Clerk's Office, Wilmington 19801.

District of Columbia — John Garrett Penn, CJ; Charles R. Richey, Harold H. Greene, Joyce Hens Green, Norma H. Johnson, Thomas P. Jackson, Thomas F. Hogan, Stanley S. Harris, George H. Revercomb, Stanley Sporkin, Royce C. Lamberth; Clerk's Office, Washington DC 20001.

Florida — Northern: Maurice M. Paul, CJ; C. Roger Vinson, Lacey A. Collier, William H. Stafford; Clerk's Office, Tallahassee 32301. **Middle:** John H. Moore 2d, CJ; William Terrell Hodges, Elizabeth A. Kovachevich, George K. Sharp, Patricia C. Fawsett, Harvey E. Schlesinger, Ralph W. Nimmons Jr., Anne C. Conway, Steven D. Merry Day; Clerk's Office, Jacksonville 32201. **Southern:** Norman C. Roettger Jr., CJ; Jose A. Gonzalez Jr., Edward B. Davis, Lenore C. Nesbitt, Stanley Marcus, William J. Zloch, Kenneth L. Ryskamp, Federico A. Moreno, Shelby Highsmith, Donald L. Graham, K. Kenneth Moore, Ursula Ungaro-Benages; Clerk's Office, Miami 33128.

Georgia — Northern: William C. O'Kelley, CJ; Harold L. Murphy, G. Ernest Tidwell, Orinda Dale Evans, Robert L. Vining Jr., Harold T. Ward, J. Owen Forrester, Jack T. Camp, Julie E. Carnes; Clerk's Office, Atlanta 30335. **Middle:** Wilbur D. Owens Jr., CJ; J. Robert Elliott, Duross Fitzpatrick; Clerk's Office, Macon 31202. **Southern:** B. Avant Edenfield, CJ; Dudley H. Bowen Jr.; Clerk's Office, Savannah 31412.

Hawaii — Alan C. Kay, CJ; Harold M. Fong, David A. Ezra; Clerk's Office, Honolulu 96850.

Idaho — Edward J. Lodge, CJ; Clerk's Office, Boise 83724.

Illinois — Northern: James B. Moran, CJ; John F. Grady, Marvin E. Aspen, Milton I. Shadur, Charles P. Kocoras, John A. Nordberg, William T. Hart, Paul E. Plunkett, Charles R. Norgle Sr., James F. Holderman Jr., Ann C. Williams, Brian Barnett Duff, Harry D. Lienenweber, James B. Zagel, James H. Alesia, Suzanne B. Conlon, George M. Marovich, George W. Lindberg, Wayne R. Anderson, Philip G. Reinhard; Clerk's Office, Chicago 60604. **Central:** Michael M. Mihm, CJ; Harold Albert Baker, Richard Mills, Joe Billy McDade; Clerk's Office, Springfield 62705. **Southern:** William D. Stiehl, CJ; J. Phil Gilbert; Clerk's Office, E. St. Louis 62202.

Indiana — Northern: Allen Sharp, CJ; William C. Lee, James T. Moody, Robert L. Miller Jr., Rudy Lozano; Clerk's Office, South Bend 46601. **Southern:** Gene E. Brooks, CJ; S. Hugh Dillin, Sarah E. Barker, Larry J. McKinney, John D. Tinder; Clerk's Office, Indianapolis 46204.

Iowa — Northern: Michael J. Melloy, CJ; Clerk's Office, Cedar Rapids 52401. **Southern:** Charles R. Wolle, CJ; Harold D. Vietor, R. E. Longstaff; Clerk's Office, Des Moines 50309.

Kansas — Patrick F. Kelly, CJ; Sam A. Crow, C. Thomas Van Bebber, John W. Lungstrum, Monti L. Belot, Kathryn H. Vratil; Clerk's Office, Wichita 67202.

Kentucky — Eastern: William Bertelsman, CJ; Henry R. Wilhoit Jr., Karl S. Forester, Joseph M. Hood; Clerk's Office, Lexington 40586. **Western:** Ronald E. Meredith, CJ; Charles R. Simpson 3d, Edward H. Johnstone, John G. Heyburn 3d; Clerk's Office, Louisville 40202.

Louisiana — Eastern: Morley L. Sear, CJ; Adrian A. Duplantier, Robert F. Collins, George Arceneaux Jr., Veronica D. Wicker, Peter Beer, A J. McNamara, Martin L. C. Feldman, Marcel Livaudais Jr., Edith Brown Clement; Clerk's Office, New Orleans 70130. **Middle:** John V. Parker, CJ; Frank J. Polozola; Clerk's Office, Baton Rouge 70821. **Western:** John M. Shaw, CJ; F. A. Little Jr., Donald E. Walter, Richard Haiks, James T. Trimble, Rebecca F. Doherty; Clerk's Office, Shreveport 71101.

Maine — Gene Carter, CJ; D. Brock Hornby, Martin A. Brody; Clerk's Office, Portland 04112.

Maryland — William E. Black Jr., CJ; John R. Hargrove, J. Frederick Motz, Frederic N. Smalkin, William M. Nickerson, Marvin J. Garbis, Benson Everett Legg; Clerk's Office, Baltimore 21201.

Massachusetts — Joseph L. Tauro, CJ; A. David Mazzone, Robert E. Keeton, Rya W. Zobel, William G. Young, Mark L. Wolf, Douglas P. Woodlock, Edward F. Harrington; Clerk's Office, Boston 02109.

Michigan — Eastern: Julian A. Cook Jr., CJ; Stewart A. Newblatt, Avern Cohn, Anna Diggs Taylor, George E. Woods, George La Plata, Barbara K. Hackett, Lawrence P. Zatkoff, Patrick J. Duggan, Bernard A. Friedman, Paul V. Gadola, Gerald E. Rosen, Robert H. Cleland, Nancy G. Edmunds; Clerk's Office, Detroit 48226. **Western:** Benjamin F. Gibson, CJ; Richard A. Enslen, Robert H. Bell, David W. McKeague; Clerk's Office, Grand Rapids 49503.

Minnesota — Diana E. Murphy, CJ; Paul A. Magnuson, James M. Rosenbaum, David S. Doty, Richard H. Kyle; Clerk's Office, St. Paul 55101.

Mississippi — Northern: L. T. Senter Jr., CJ; Neal Biggers, Glen H. Davidson; Clerk's Office, Oxford 38655. **Southern:** William H. Barbour Jr., CJ; Harry T. Wingate, Tom S. Lee, Walter J. Gex 3d, Charles W. Pickering Sr., David Bramlette; Clerk's Office, Jackson 39201.

Missouri — Eastern: Edward D. Filippine, CJ; Stephen N. Limbaugh, George F. Gunn Jr., Jean Hamilton, Donald J. Stohr, Carol E. Jackson; Clerk's Office, St. Louis 63101. **Western:** Joseph E. Stevens Jr., CJ; D. Brook Bartlett, Dean Whipple, Fernando J. Gaitan Jr.; Clerk's Office, Kansas City 64106.

Montana — Paul G. Hatfield, CJ; Charles C. Lovell, Jack D. Shanstrom; Clerk's Office, Billings 59101.

Nebraska — Lyle E. Strom, CJ; William G. Cambridge, Richard G. Kopf; Clerk's Office, Omaha 68101.

Nevada — Lloyd D. George, CJ; Howard D. McKibben, Philip M. Pro; Clerk's Office, Las Vegas 89101.

New Hampshire — Joseph A. DiClerico, CJ; Paul J. Barbadaro, Steven J. McAuliffe; Clerk's Office, Concord 03301.

New Jersey — John F. Gerry, CJ; Anne E. Thompson, Dickinson R. Debevoise, H. Lee Sarokin, Harold A. Ackerman, John W. Bissell, Maryanne Trump Barry, Joseph H. Rodriguez, Garrett E. Brown Jr., Alfred J. Lechner Jr., Nicholas H. Politan, Alfred M. Wolin, John C. Lifland, William G. Bassler, Mary Little Parell, Jerome E. Simandle, Joseph E. Irenas; Clerk's Office, Newark 07102.

New Mexico — Juan G. Burciaga, CJ; John E. Conway, James A. Parker, C. Leroy Hansen; Clerk's Office, Albuquerque 87103.

New York — Northern: Thomas J. McAvoy, CJ; Con G. Cholakis, Frederick J. Scullin Jr.; Clerk's Office, Albany 12201. **Eastern:** Thomas C. Platt Jr., CJ; Charles P. Sifton, Eugene H. Nickerson, Israel Leo Glasser, Raymond J. Dearie, Leonard D. Wexler, Edward R. Korman, Reena Raggi; Arthur D. Spatt, Carol Bagley Amon, Sterling Johnson Jr., Denis R. Hurley; Clerk's Office, Brooklyn 11201. **Southern:** Thomas P. Criesa, CJ; David N. Edelstein, Charles L. Brieant, Kevin Thomas Duffy, Leonard B. Sand, Gerard L. Goettel, Charles S. Haight Jr., Pierre N. Leval, John E. Sprizzo, Shirley Wohl Kram, John F. Keenan, Peter K. Leisure, Louis L. Stanton, Miriam G. Cedarbaum, Michael B. Mukasey, Kenneth Conboy, Kimba Wood, Robert P. Patterson Jr., Lawrence McKenna, John S. Martin Jr., Loretta A. Preska, Sonia Sotomayer; Clerk's Office N. Y. City 10007. **Western:** Michael A. Telesca, CJ; Richard J. Arcara, David G. Larimer, William M. Skretny; Clerk's Office, Buffalo 14202.

North Carolina — Eastern: James C. Fox, CJ; W. Earl Britt, Terrence W. Boyle, Malcolm J. Howard; Clerk's Office, Raleigh 27611. **Middle:** Frank W. Bullock, CJ; N. Carlton Tilley Jr., William L. Osteen Sr.; Clerk's Office, Greensboro 27402. **Western:** Richard L. Voorhees, CJ; Robert D. Potter, Graham C. Mullen; Clerk's Office, Asheville 28801.

North Dakota — Rodney S. Webb, CJ; Patrick A. Conmy; Clerk's Office, Bismarck 58502.

Ohio — Northern: Thomas D. Lambros, CJ; Frank J. Battisti, George W. White, Ann Aldrich, David D. Dowd Jr., Sam H. Bell, Paul R. Matia; Clerk's Office, Cleveland 44114. **Southern:** John D. Holschuh, CJ; Carl B. Rubin, Walter H. Rice, S. Arthur Spiegel, Herman J. Weber, James L. Graham, George C. Smith, Sandra S. Beckwith; Clerk's Office, Columbus 43215.

Oklahoma — Northern: James O. Ellison, CJ; Thomas R. Brett; Clerk's Office, Tulsa 74103. **Eastern:** Frank H. Shey, CJ; Clerk's Office, Muskogee 74401. **Western:** Ralph G. Thompson, CJ; Wayne Alley, Lee R. West, David L. Russell, Robin Cauthron, Timothy D. Leonard; Clerk's Office, Oklahoma City 73102.

Oregon — James A. Redden, CJ; Helen J. Frye, Malcolm F. Marsh, Robert E. Jones, Michael R. Hogan; Clerk's Office, Portland 97205.

Pennsylvania — Eastern: Louis Charles Bechtle, CJ; Edward N. Cahn, Norma L. Shapiro, James T. Giles, James McGirr Kelly, Thomas N. O'Neill Jr., Marvin Katz, Edmund V. Ludwig, Robert F. Kelly, Franklin S. Van Antwerpen, Robert S. Gawthrop, Lowell A. Reed Jr., Jan E. Dubois, Herbert J. Hutton, Jay C. Waldman, Ronald L. Buckwalter, Stewart Dalzell, William H. Yohn Jr., Harvey Battle 3d, John R. Padova, J. Curtis Joyner, Eduardo C. Robreno; Clerk's Office, Philadelphia 19106. **Middle:** Sylvia H. Rambo, CJ; William W. Caldwell, Edward M. Kosik, James F. McClure Jr.; Clerk's Office, Scranton 18501. **Western:** Maurice B. Cohill Jr., CJ; Gustave Diamond, Donald E. Ziegler, Alan N. Bloch, Glenn E. Mencer, William L. Standish, D. Brooks Smith, Donald J. Lee; Clerk's Office, Pittsburgh 15230.

Rhode Island — Ronald R. Lagueux, CJ; Ernest C. Torres; Clerk's Office, Providence 02903.

South Carolina — Falcon B. Hawkins, CJ; C. Weston Houck, Matthew J. Perry Jr., George R. Anderson Jr., Joseph F. Anderson Jr., David C. Norton, Dennis W. Shedd, Henry M. Herlong Jr., William B. Traxler; Clerk's Office, Columbia 29202.

South Dakota — John Baily Jones, CJ; Richard H. Battey; Clerk's Office, Sioux Falls 57102.

Tennessee — Eastern: James H. Jarvis, CJ; Thomas G. Hill, R. Allan Edgar, Leon Jordan; Clerk's Office, Knoxville 37901. **Middle:** John T. Nixon, CJ; Thomas A. Wiseman Jr., Thomas A. Higgins, Robert L. Echols; Clerk's Office, Nashville 37203. **Western:** Odell Horton, CJ; Julia S. Gibbons, James D. Todd, Jerome Turner, John Phipps McCalla; Clerk's Office, Memphis 38103.

Texas — Northern: Barefoot Sanders, CJ; Mary Lou Robinson, Jerry Buchmeyer, A. Joe Fish, Robert B. Maloney, Sidney A. Fitzwater, Samuel R. Cummings, John H. McBryde, Jorge A. Solis, Terry Means, Joe Kendall; Clerk's Office, Dallas 75242. **Southern:** Norman W. Black, CJ; George P. Kazen, Filemon B. Vela, Hayden W. Head Jr., Ricardo H. Hinojosa, Lynn N. Hughes, David Hittner, Kenneth M. Hoyt, Simeon T. Lake 3d, Melinda Harmon, John Rainey, Samuel B. Kent, Ewing Werlein Jr., Lee H. Rosenthal; Clerk's Office, Houston 77208. **Eastern:** Robert M. Parker, CJ; William Wayne Justice, Howell Cobb, Sam B. Hall Jr., Paul N. Brown, Richard A. Schell; Clerk's Office, Tyler 75702. **Western:** Harry Lee Hudspeth, CJ; Hipolito F. Garcia, James R. Nowlin, Edward C. Prado, Walter S. Smith Jr., Sam Sparks; Clerk's Office, San Antonio 78206.

Utah — Bruce S. Jenkins, CJ; J. Thomas Greene, David Sam, David K. Winder, Dee V. Benson; Clerk's Office, Salt Lake City 84101.

Vermont — Fred I. Parker, CJ; Franklin S. Billings Jr.; Clerk's Office, Burlington 05402.

Virginia — Eastern: James C. Cacheris, CJ; Robert G. Doumar, Claude M. Hilton, James R. Spencer, Thomas S. Ellis 3d, Rebecca Beach Smith, Henry Coke Morgan Jr., Robert E. Payne; Clerk's Office, Alexandria 22320. **Western:** James C. Turk, CJ; James H. Michael Jr., Jackson L. Kiser, Samuel G. Wilson; Clerk's Office, Roanoke 24006.

Washington — Eastern: Justin L. Quackenbush, CJ; Alan A. McDonald; Fred Van Sickle, W. Fremming Nielsen; Clerk's Office, Spokane 99210. **Western:** Barbara J. Rothstein, CJ; John C. Coughenour, Carolyn R. Dimmick, Robert J. Bryan, William L. Dwyer, Thomas Zilly; Clerk's Office, Seattle 98104.

West Virginia — Northern: Robert Earl Maxwell, CJ; Frederick P. Stamp Jr., Irene M. Keeley; Clerk's Office, Elkins 26241. **Southern:** Charles H. Haden 2d, CJ; Robert J. Staker, John T. Copenhaver Jr., Elizabeth V. Hallanan, David A. Faber; Clerk's Office, Charleston 25329.

Wisconsin — Eastern: Terence T. Evans, CJ; Thomas J. Curran, J.P. Stadtmueller, Rudolph T. Randa; Clerk's Office, Milwaukee 53202. **Western:** Barbara B. Crabb, CJ; John C. Shabaz; Clerk's Office, Madison 53701.

Wyoming — Alan B. Johnson, CJ; Clarence A. Brimmer; Clerk's Office, Cheyenne 82001.

U.S. Territorial District Courts

Guam — John S. Unpingco; Clerk's Office, Agana 96910.
Puerto Rico — Gilberto Gierbolini, CJ; Juan M. Perez-Gimenez, Carmen Consuelo Cerezo, Jaime Pieras Jr., Raymond L. Acosta, Hector M. Laffitte, Jose Antonio Fuste; Clerk's Office, San Juan 00904.
Virgin Islands — Thomas K. Moore, CJ; Clerk's Office, Charlotte Amalie, St. Thomas 00801.

U.S. Court of Veterans Appeals

Washington, D.C. 20004 (Salaries, $133,600)
Chief Judge — Frank Q. Nebeker.
Judges — Kenneth B. Kramer, John J. Farley 3d, Hart T. Mankin, Ronald M. Holdaway, Donald L. Ivers, Jonathan R. Steinberg.

U.S. Government Independent Agencies

Source: National Archives & Records Administration Address: Washington, DC. Location and ZIP codes of agencies in parentheses; as of mid-1993.

ACTION — John Seal, act. dir. (1100 Vermont Ave., NW, 20525).
Administrative Conference of the United States — Brian C. Griffin, chmn. (Suite 500, 2120 L St. NW, 20037).
African Development Foundation — Gregory Robeson Smith, pres. (1400 Eye St. NW, 20005).
Central Intelligence Agency — R. James Woolsey, dir. (Wash., DC 20505).
Commission on Civil Rights — Arthur A. Fletcher, chmn. (624 9th St. NW, 20425).
Commodity Futures Trading Commission — William P. Albrecht, act. chmn. (2033 K St. NW, 20581).
Consumer Product Safety Commission — Jacqueline Jones-Smith, chmn. (East West Towers, 4340 East West Hwy., Bethesda, MD 20814).
Environmental Protection Agency — Carol M. Browner, adm. (401 M St., SW, 20460).
Equal Employment Opportunity Commission — Tony E. Gallegos, act. chmn. (1801 L St. NW., 20507).
Export-Import Bank of the United States — Kenneth D. Brody, pres. and chmn. (811 Vermont Ave. NW 20571).
Farm Credit Administration — Harold B. Steele, chmn., Farm Credit Administration Board (1501 Farm Credit Drive, McLean, VA 22102).
Federal Communications Commission — James H. Quello, chmn. (1919 M St. NW, 20554).
Federal Deposit Insurance Corporation — Andrew C. Hove Jr., chmn. (550 17th St. NW, 20429).
Federal Election Commission — Scott E. Thomas, chmn. (999 E St. NW, 20463).
Federal Emergency Management Agency — James Lee Witt, dir. (500 C St. SW, 20472).
Federal Housing Finance Board — Daniel F. Evans Jr., chmn. (1777 F St. NW., 20006).
Federal Labor Relations Authority — Jean McKee, chmn. (607 14th St. NW, 20424).
Federal Maritime Commission — William D. Hathaway, chmn. (800 N. Capitol St. NW, 20573).
Federal Mediation and Conciliation Service — Bernard E. DeLury, dir. (2100 K St. NW, 20427).
Federal Mine Safety & Health Review Commission — Arlene Holen, chmn. (1730 K St. NW, 20006).

Federal Reserve System — Chairman, board of governors: Alan Greenspan. (20th St. & Constitution Ave. NW, 20551).

Federal Retirement Thrift Investment Board — Roger W. Mehle, chmn. (1250 H St. NW, 20005).

Federal Trade Commission — Janet D. Steiger, chmn. (Pennsylvania Ave. at 6th St. NW, 20580).

General Accounting Office — Comptroller General of the U.S.; Charles A. Bowsher (441 G St. NW, 20548).

General Services Administration — Roger W. Johnson, adm. (18th & F Sts. NW, 20405).

Government Printing Office — Public printer: Michael F. DiMario, act. (North Capitol and H Sts. NW, 20401).

Inter-American Foundation — Frank D. Yturria, chmn. (901 N. Stuart St., Arlington, VA 22203).

Interstate Commerce Commission — Gail C. McDonald, chmn. (12th St. & Constitution Ave. NW, 20423).

Library of Congress — James H. Billington, librarian of Congress (101 Independence Ave. SE, 20540).

Merit Systems Protection Board — Benjamin L. Erdreich, chmn. (1120 Vermont Ave. NW, 20419).

National Aeronautics and Space Administration — Daniel S. Goldin, adm. (300 E St. SW, 20546).

National Archives & Records Administration — Trudy H. Peterson, act. archivist (7th St. & Pennsylvania Ave. NW, 20408).

National Credit Union Administration — Roger W. Jepsen, chmn. (1776 G St. NW, 20456).

National Foundation on the Arts and the Humanities — Jane Alexander, chmn. (arts) 1100 Pennsylvania Ave. NW, 20506; Donald Gibson, act. chmn. (humanities) same address. Institute of Museum Services: Linda Bell, act. dir., same address.

National Labor Relations Board — James M. Stephens, chmn. (1099 14th St. NW, 20570).

National Mediation Board — Kimberly A. Madigan, chmn. (Suite 250 East, 1301 K St. NW, 20572).

National Railroad Passenger Corporation (Amtrak) — W. Graham Claytor Jr., chmn. (60 Massachusetts Ave. NE, 20002).

National Science Foundation — James J. Duderstadt, chmn., National Science Board (1800 G St. NW, 20550).

National Transportation Safety Board — Carl W. Vogt, chmn. (490 L'Enfant Plaza SW, 20594).

Nuclear Regulatory Commission — Ivan Selin, chmn. (1717 H St. NW, 20555).

Occupational Safety and Health Review Commission — Edwin G. Foulke Jr., chmn. (1120 20th St. NW, 20036).

Office of Personnel Management — James B. King, dir. (1900 E St. NW, 20415).

Peace Corps — Carol Bellamy, dir. (1990 K St. NW, 20526).

Postal Rate Commission — George W. Haley, chmn. (1333 H St. NW, 20268-0001).

Railroad Retirement Board — Glen L. Bower, chmn. (Suite 558, 2000 L St. NW, 20036), Main Office (844 N. Rush St., Chicago, IL 60611).

Securities and Exchange Commission — Richard C. Breeden, chmn. (450 5th St. NW, 20549).

Selective Service System — Robert W. Gambino, dir. (National Headquarters, 20435).

Small Business Administration — Erskine B. Bowles, adm. (409 Third St. SW, 20416).

Smithsonian Institution — Robert McC. Adams, secy. (1000 Jefferson Dr. SW, 20560).

Tennessee Valley Authority — Chairman, board of directors: Craven Crowell (400 W. Summit Hill Dr., Knoxville, TN 37902 and Room 300, 412 1st St. SE, Washington, DC 20444).

United States Arms Control & Disarmament Agency — Thomas Graham, Jr., dir. (320 21st St. NW 20451).

United States Information Agency — Joseph D. Duffey, dir. (301 4th St. SW, 20547).

United States International Development Cooperation Agency — James H. Michel, act. dir. (320 21st St. NW, 20523).

United States International Trade Commission — Don E. Newquist, chmn. (500 E St. SW, 20436).

United States Postal Service — Marvin Runyon, postmaster general (475 L'Enfant Plaza SW, 20260).

Other Notable U.S. Agencies

Agency	Cabinet Department
Bureau of Alcohol, Tobacco, and Firearms	Treasury
Federal Aviation Administration	Transportation
Bureau of the Census	Commerce
U.S. Coast Guard	Transportation
Office of Consumer Affairs	Health & Human Services
U.S. Customs Service	Treasury
Centers for Disease Control & Prevention	Health & Human Services
Bureau of Economic Analysis	Commerce
Federal Bureau of Investigation	Justice
Fish & Wildlife Service	Interior
Food & Drug Administration	Health & Human Services
Foreign Service	State
Forest Service	Agriculture
National Institutes of Health	Health & Human Services
Federal Highway Administration	Transportation
Immigration & Naturalization Service	Justice
Bureau of Indian Affairs	Interior
U.S. Mint	Treasury
National Oceanic & Atmospheric Administration	Commerce
National Park Service	Interior
Bureau of Prisons	Justice
Internal Revenue Service	Treasury
U.S. Secret Service	Treasury
Social Security Administration	Health & Human Services
Surgeon General	Health & Human Services

Governors of States and Possessions

(as of mid-1993)

State	Capital, Zip Code	Governor	Party	Term years	Term expires	Annual salary
Alabama	Montgomery 36130	Jim Folsom Jr.	Dem.	4	Jan. 1995	$87,913
Alaska	Juneau 99811	Walter Hickel	Ind.	4	Dec. 1994	81,648
Arizona	Phoenix 85007	Fife Symington	Rep.	4	Jan. 1995	75,000
Arkansas	Little Rock 72201	Jim Guy Tucker	Dem.	4	Jan. 1995	60,000
California	Sacramento 95814	Pete Wilson	Rep.	4	Jan. 1995	120,000
Colorado	Denver 80203	Roy Romer	Dem.	4	Jan. 1995	70,000
Connecticut	Hartford 06106	Lowell Weicker	Ind.	4	Jan. 1995	78,000
Delaware	Dover 19901	Thomas R. Carper	Dem.	4	Jan. 1997	95,000
Florida	Tallahassee 32399	Lawton Chiles	Dem.	4	Jan. 1995	95,000
Georgia	Atlanta 30334	Zell Miller	Dem.	4	Jan. 1995	91,092
Hawaii	Honolulu 96813	John Waihee	Dem.	4	Dec. 1994	94,780
Idaho	Boise 83720	Cecil D. Andrus	Dem.	4	Jan. 1995	75,000
Illinois	Springfield 62706	Jim Edgar	Rep.	4	Jan. 1995	100,681
Indiana	Indianapolis 46204	Evan Bayh	Dem.	4	Jan. 1997	77,200
Iowa	Des Moines 50319	Terry E. Branstad	Rep.	4	Jan. 1995	76,900
Kansas	Topeka 66612	Joan Finney	Dem.	4	Jan. 1995	74,235
Kentucky	Frankfort 40601	Brereton C. Jones	Dem.	4	Dec. 1995	79,255
Louisiana	Baton Rouge 70804	Edwin W. Edwards	Dem.	4	May 1996	73,440
Maine	Augusta 04333	John McKernan Jr.	Rep.	4	Jan. 1995	70,000
Maryland	Annapolis 21401	William Donald Schaefer	Dem.	4	Jan. 1995	120,000
Massachusetts	Boston 02113	William Weld	Rep.	4	Jan. 1995	75,000
Michigan	Lansing 48913	John Engler	Rep.	4	Jan. 1995	106,700

State	Capital, Zip Code	Governor	Party	Term years	Term expires	Annual salary
Minnesota	St. Paul 55155	Arne Carlson	Rep.	4	Jan. 1995	109,053
Mississippi	Jackson 39205	Kirk Fordice	Rep.	4	Jan. 1996	75,600
Missouri	Jefferson City 65101	Mel Carnahan	Dem.	4	Jan. 1997	90,312
Montana	Helena 59620	Marc Racicot	Rep.	4	Jan. 1997	55,502
Nebraska	Lincoln 68509	Ben Nelson	Dem.	4	Jan. 1995	65,000
Nevada	Carson City 89710	Robert Miller	Dem.	4	Jan. 1995	90,000
New Hampshire	Concord 03301	Stephen Merrill	Rep.	2	Jan. 1995	71,587
New Jersey	Trenton 08625	James Florio	Dem.	4	Jan. 1994	85,000
New Mexico	Santa Fe 07503	Bruce King	Dem.	4	Jan. 1995	90,000
New York	Albany 12224	Mario M. Cuomo	Dem.	4	Jan. 1995	130,000
North Carolina	Raleigh 27603	James B. Hunt Jr.	Dem.	4	Jan. 1997	123,300
North Dakota	Bismarck 58505	Edward T. Schafer	Rep.	4	Jan. 1997	68,280
Ohio	Columbus 43215	George Voinovich	Rep.	4	Jan. 1995	110,250
Oklahoma	Oklahoma City 73105	David Walters	Dem.	4	Jan. 1995	70,000
Oregon	Salem 97310	Barbara Roberts	Dem.	4	Jan. 1995	80,000
Pennsylvania	Harrisburg 17120	Robert Casey	Dem.	4	Jan. 1995	105,000
Rhode Island	Providence 02903	Bruce Sundlun	Dem.	4	Jan. 1995	69,000
South Carolina	Columbia 29201	Carroll A. Campbell Jr.	Rep.	4	Jan. 1995	101,959
South Dakota	Pierre 57501	Walter Dale Miller	Rep.	4	Jan. 1995	65,761
Tennessee	Nashville 37219	Ned Ray McWherter	Dem.	4	Jan. 1995	85,000
Texas	Austin 78711	Ann Richards	Dem.	4	Jan. 1995	93,432
Utah	Salt Lake City 84114	Michael O. Leavitt	Rep.	4	Jan. 1997	70,000
Vermont	Montpelier 05602	Howard Dean	Dem.	2	Jan. 1995	85,977
Virginia	Richmond 23219	L. Douglas Wilder	Dem.	4	Jan. 1994	108,000
Washington	Olympia 98504	Mike Lowry	Dem.	4	Jan. 1997	121,000
West Virginia	Charleston 25305	Gaston Caperton	Dem.	4	Jan. 1997	72,000
Wisconsin	Madison 53703	Tommy G. Thompson	Rep.	4	Jan. 1995	92,283
Wyoming	Cheyenne 82002	Mike Sullivan	Dem.	4	Jan. 1995	70,000
Puerto Rico	San Juan 00936	Pedro J. Rosselló	—	4	Jan. 1995	—

State Officials, Salaries, Party Membership

As of mid-1993; † Ind. or other party.

Alabama

Governor — Jim Folsom Jr., D., $87,913.
Lt. Gov. — vacant.
Sec. of State — Billy Joe Camp, D., $57,203.
Atty. Gen. — Jimmy Evans, D., $90,474.
Treasurer — George Wallace Jr., D., $57,203.
Legislature: meets annually the 3d Tuesday in Apr. (first year of term of office), first Tuesday in Feb. (2d and 3d years), 2d Tuesday in Jan. (4th year) at Montgomery. Members receive $60 a day salary, plus $2,280 per month expenses and mileage of 10¢ per mile.
Senate — Dem., 26; Rep., 8; 1 vac. Total, 35.
House — Dem., 82; Rep., 23. Total, 105.

Alaska

Governor — Walter Hickel, †, $81,648.
Lt. Gov. — John B. Coghill, †, $76,188.
Atty. General — Charles Cole, R., $79,860.
Legislature: meets annually in January at Juneau, for 120 days with a 10-day extension possible upon 2/3 vote. First session in odd years. Members receive $22,872 per year plus $80 a day per diem.
Senate — Dem., 10; Rep., 10. Total, 20.
House — Dem., 20; Rep., 18; 2 other. Total, 40.

Arizona

Governor — Fife Symington, R., $75,000.
Sec. of State — Richard Mahoney, D., $54,600.
Atty. Gen. — Grant Woods, R., $76,440.
Treasurer — Tony West, R., $54,600.
Legislature: meets annually in January at Phoenix. Each member receives an annual salary of $15,000.
Senate — Dem., 12; Rep., 18. Total, 30.
House — Dem., 25; Rep., 35. Total, 60.

Arkansas

Governor — Jim Guy Tucker, D., $60,000.
Lt. Gov. — vacant.
Sec. of State — W. J. "Bill" McCuen, D., $37,000.
Atty. Gen. — Winston Bryant, D., $50,000.
Treasurer — Jimmie Lou Fisher Lumpkin, D., $37,000.
Auditor — Julia Hughes Jones, D., $37,000.
General Assembly: meets odd years in January at Little Rock. Members receive $12,500 per year, $77 a day while in regular session, plus travel expenses.
Senate — Dem., 30; Rep., 5. Total, 35.
House — Dem., 89; Rep. 10; 1 ind. Total, 100.

California

Governor — Pete Wilson, R., $120,000.
Lt. Gov. — Leo T. McCarthy, D., $90,000.
Sec. of State — March Fong Eu, D., $90,000.
Controller — Gray Davis, D., $90,000.
Atty. Gen. — Dan Lungren, R., $102,000.
Legislature: meets at Sacramento; regular sessions commence on the first Monday in Dec. of every even-numbered year; each session lasts 2 years. Members receive $52,500 per year plus mileage and $100 per diem.
Senate — Dem., 23; Rep., 14, 2 ind., 1 vac.; Total, 40.
Assembly — Dem., 48; Rep. 32; Total, 80.

Colorado

Governor — Roy Romer, D., $70,000.
Lt. Gov. — Mike Callihan, D., $48,500.
Secy. of State — Natalie Meyer, R., $48,500.
Atty. Gen. — Gale Norton, R., $60,000.
Treasurer — Gail Schoettler, D., $48,500.
General Assembly: meets annually in January at Denver. Members receive $17,500 annually.
Senate — Dem., 16; Rep., 19. Total, 35.
House — Dem., 31; Rep., 34. Total, 65.

Connecticut

Governor — Lowell Weicker, †, $78,000.
Lt. Gov. — Eunice S. Groark, †, $55,000.
Sec. of State — Pauline R. Kezer, R., $50,000.
Treasurer — Francisco Borges, D., $50,000.
Comptroller — William E. Curry Jr., D., $50,000.
Atty. Gen. — Richard Blumenthal, D., $60,000.
General Assembly: meets annually odd years in January and even years in February at Hartford. Salary $15,200 per year plus $4,500 (senator), $3,500 (representative) per year for expenses, plus travel allowance.
Senate — Dem., 19; Rep., 16; 1 vac. Total, 36.
House — Dem., 86; Rep., 64; 1 vac. Total, 151.

Delaware

Governor — Thomas R. Carper, D., $95,000.
Lt. Gov. — Ruth Ann Minner, D., $36,500.
Sec. of State — William P. Quillen, D., $73,700.
Atty. Gen. — Charles Oberly 3d, D., $84,700.
Treasurer — Janet C. Rzewnicki, R., $68,200.
General Assembly: 55 day session beginning the 2d Tuesday in January until June 30. Members receive $24,213 base salary, plus $5,500 expense account.

Senate — Dem., 15; Rep., 6. Total, 21.
House — Dem., 18; Rep., 23. Total, 41.

Florida

Governor — Lawton Chiles, D., $95,000.
Lt. Gov. — Buddy McKay, D., $91,000.
Sec. of State — Jim Smith, R., $94,040.
Comptroller — Gerald Lewis, D., $94,040.
Atty. Gen. — Robert Butterworth, D., $94,040.
Treasurer — Tom Gallagher, R., $94,040.
Legislature: meets annually at Tallahassee. Members receive $22,560 per year plus expense allowance while on official business.
Senate — Dem., 20; Rep., 20. Total, 40.
House — Dem., 71; Rep., 49. Total, 120.

Georgia

Governor — Zell Miller, D., $91,092.
Lt. Gov. — Pierre Howard, D., $59,145.
Sec. of State — Max Cleland, D., $72,966.
Insurance Comm. — Tim Ryles, D., $72,954.
Atty. Gen. — Michael J. Bowers, $74,645.
General Assembly: meets annually at Atlanta. Members receive $10,509 per year, $59 per diem, and $4,800 expense reimbursement. During session $59 per day for expenses.
Senate — Dem., 45; Rep., 11. Total, 56.
House — Dem., 145; Rep., 35. Total, 180.

Hawaii

Governor — John Waihee, D., $94,780.
Lt. Gov. — Benjamin Cayetano, D., $90,041.
Atty. Gen. — Robert Marks, $85,302.
Comptroller — Robert Takushi, $85,302.
Dir. of Budget & Finance — Yukio Takemoto, $85,302.
Legislature: meets annually on 3d Wednesday in January at Honolulu. Members receive $27,000 per year plus expenses.
Senate — Dem., 22. Rep., 3. Total, 25.
House — Dem., 47. Rep., 4. Total, 51.

Idaho

Governor — Cecil D. Andrus, D., $75,000.
Lt. Gov. — C. L. "Butch" Otter, R., $20,000.
Sec. of State — Pete T. Cenarrusa, R., $62,500.
Treasurer — Lydia Justice Edwards, R., $62,500.
Atty. Gen. — Larry EchoHawk, D., $67,500.
Legislature: meets annually the Monday on or nearest the 9th of January at Boise. Members receive $12,000 per year plus $70 per day during session if required to maintain a 2d residence; $40 if no 2d residence, plus $50.00 per day when engaged in legislative business when legislature is not in session.
Senate — Dem., 12; Rep., 23. Total, 35.
House — Dem., 20; Rep., 50. Total, 70.

Illinois

Governor — Jim Edgar, R., $100,681.
Lt. Gov. — Bob Kustra, R., $71,069.
Sec. of State — George H. Ryan, R., $88,836.
Comptroller — Dawn Clark Netsch, D., $76,991.
Atty. Gen. — Roland W. Burris, D., $88,836.
Treasurer — Patrick Quinn, D., $76,991.
General Assembly: meets annually in January at Springfield. Members receive $38,496 per annum.
Senate — Dem., 27; Rep., 32. Total, 59.
House — Dem., 67; Rep., 51. Total, 118.

Indiana

Governor — Evan Bayh, D., $77,200 plus discretionary expenses.
Lt. Gov. — Frank O'Bannon, D., $64,000 plus discretionary expenses.
Sec. of State — Joseph Hogsett, D., $46,000.
Atty. Gen. — Pamela Carter, D., $59,200.
Treasurer — Marjorie H. O'Laughlin, R., $46,000.
Auditor — Ann G. DeVore, R., $46,000.
General Assembly: meets annually in January. Members receive $11,600 per year plus $92 per day while in session, $25 per day while not in session.
Senate — Dem., 22; Rep., 28. Total, 50.
House — Dem., 55; Rep., 45. Total, 100.

Iowa

Governor — Terry E. Branstad, R., $76,900.
Lt. Gov. — Joy Corning, R., $60,000.
Sec. of State — Elaine Baxter, D., $60,000.
Atty. Gen. — Bonnie Campbell, D., $73,600.
Treasurer — Michael L. Fitzgerald, D., $60,000.
Auditor — Richard D. Johnson, R., $60,000.
Secy. of Agriculture — Dale M. Cochran, D., $60,000.
General Assembly: meets annually in January at Des Moines. Members receive $18,100 annually plus maximum expense allowance of $50 per day for first 110 days of first session, and first 100 days of 2d session (except for Polk Co. legislators); mileage expenses at 21¢ a mile.
Senate — Dem., 27; Rep., 23. Total, 50.
House — Dem., 49; Rep., 51. Total, 100.

Kansas

Governor — Joan Finney, D., $74,235.
Lt. Gov. — James Francisco, D., $20,998.
Sec. of State — Bill Graves, R., $57,668.
Atty. Gen. — Robert T. Stephan, R., $66,324.
Treasurer — Sally Thompson, D., $57,668.
Legislature: meets annually in January at Topeka. Members receive $60 a day plus $70 a day expenses while in session, plus $600 per month while not in session.
Senate — Dem., 18; Rep., 22. Total, 40.
House — Dem., 63; Rep., 62. Total, 125.

Kentucky

Governor — Brereton C. Jones, D., $79,255.
Lt. Gov. — Paul Patton, D., $67,378.
Sec. of State — Bob Babbage, D., $67,378.
Atty. Gen. — Chris Gorman, D., $67,378.
Treasurer — Francis J. Mills, D., $67,378.
Auditor — Ben Chandler, D., $67,378.
General Assembly: meets even years in January at Frankfort. Members receive $100 per day and $75 per day during session and $950 per month for expenses for interim.
Senate — Dem., 27; Rep., 11. Total, 38.
House — Dem., 68; Rep., 32. Total, 100.

Louisiana

Governor — Edwin W. Edwards, D., $73,440.
Lt. Gov. — Melinda Schwegmann, D., $63,367.
Sec. of State — Fox McKeithen, R., $60,169.
Atty. Gen. — Richard Ieyoub, D., $60,169.
Treasurer — Mary Landrieu, D., $60,169.
Legislature: meets annually for 60 legislative days commencing on the last Monday in March. Members receive $75 per day and mileage plus annual salary of $16,800.
Senate — Dem., 33; Rep., 6. Total, 39.
House — Dem., 88; Rep., 16, 1 ind. Total, 105.

Maine

Governor — John R. McKernan Jr., R., $70,000.
Sec. of State — G. William Diamond, D., $48,152.
Atty. Gen. — Michael E. Carpenter, D., $61,152.
Treasurer — Samuel Shapiro, D., $61,200.
Legislature: meets annually the first Wednesday in December at Augusta, and the Wednesday after the first Tuesday in Jan. in even numbered years. Members receive $10,500 for first regular sessions, $7,500 for second regular session plus expenses; presiding officers receive 50% more.
Senate — Dem., 20; Rep., 15. Total, 35.
House — Dem., 90; Rep., 61. Total, 151.

Maryland

Governor — William Donald Schaefer, D., $120,000.
Lt. Gov. — Melvin Steinberg, D., $100,000.
Comptroller — Louis L. Goldstein, D., $100,000.
Atty. Gen. — J. Joseph Curran Jr., D., $100,000.
Sec. of State — Winfield M. Kelly Jr., D., $70,000.
Treasurer — Lucille Maurer, D., $100,000.
General Assembly: meets 90 consecutive days annually beginning on the 2d Wednesday in January at Annapolis. Members receive $27,000 per year plus expenses.
Senate — Dem., 38; Rep., 9. Total, 47.
House — Dem., 117; Rep., 24. Total, 141.

Massachusetts

Governor — William Weld, R., $75,000.
Lt. Gov. — A. Paul Cellucci, R., $60,000.
Sec. of State — Michael Joseph Connolly, D., $60,000.
Atty. Gen. — L. Scott Harshbarger, D., $65,000.
Treasurer — Joseph Malone, R., $60,000.
Auditor — A. Joseph DeNucci, D., $60,000.
General Court (Legislature): meets each January in Boston. Salaries $30,000 per annum.
Senate — Dem., 31; Rep., 9. Total, 40.
House — Dem., 124; Rep., 35; ind., 1. Total, 160.

Michigan

Governor — John Engler, R., $106,700.
Lt. Gov. — Connie Binsfeld, R., $80,300.
Sec. of State — Richard H. Austin, D., $109,000.
Atty. Gen. — Frank J. Kelley, D., $109,000.
Treasurer — Doug Roberts, N-P, $83,100.
Legislature: meets annually in January at Lansing. Members receive $45,450 per year, plus $8,500 expense allowance.

Senate — Dem., 16; Rep., 20; 2 vac. Total, 38.
House — Dem., 55; Rep., 55. Total, 110.

Minnesota

Governor — Arne Carlson, R., $109,053.
Lt. Gov. — Joanell Dyrstad, IR, $59,981.
Sec. of State — Joan Anderson Growe, DFL., $59,981.
Atty. Gen. — Hubert H. Humphrey 3d, DFL., $85,194.
Treasurer — Michael McGrath, DFL., $59,981.
Auditor — Mark Dayton, IR, $65,437.
Legislature: meets for a total of 120 days within every 2 years at St. Paul. Members receive $27,979 per year, plus expense allowance during session.
Senate — DFL., 45; IR, 22. Total, 67.
House — DFL., 86; IR, 48. Total, 134.
(DFL means Democratic-Farmer-Labor. IR means Independent Republican.)

Mississippi

Governor — Kirk Fordice, R., $75,600.
Lt. Gov. — Eddie Briggs, R., $40,800.
Sec. of State — Dick Molpus, D., $54,000.
Atty. Gen. — Mike Moore, D., $61,200.
Treasurer — Marshall Bennett, D., $54,000.
Legislature: meets annually in January at Jackson. Members receive $10,100 per regular session plus travel allowance, and $500 per month while not in session.
Senate — Dem., 39; Rep., 13. Total, 52.
House — Dem., 93; Rep., 27, 2 ind. Total, 122.

Missouri

Governor — Mel Carnahan, D., $90,312.
Lt. Gov. — Roger Wilson, D., $54,343.
Sec. of State — Judith Moriarty, D., $72,327.
Atty. Gen. — Jeremiah W. Nixon, D., $78,322.
Treasurer — Bob Holden, D., $72,327.
State Auditor — Margaret Kelly, R., $72,327.
General Assembly: meets annually in Jefferson City on the first Wednesday after first Monday in January. Members receive $22,862 annually.
Senate — Dem., 18; Rep., 14, 2 vac. Total, 34.
House — Dem., 101; Rep., 61, 1 vac. Total, 163.

Montana

Governor — Marc Racicot, R., $55,502.
Lt. Gov. — Dennis Rehberg, R., $40,466.
Sec. of State — Mike Cooney, D., $37,526.
Atty. Gen. — Joe Mazurek, D., $50,841.
Legislative Assembly: meets odd years in January at Helena. Members receive $55.50 per legislative day plus $50 per day for expenses while in session.
Senate — Dem., 30; Rep., 20. Total, 50.
House — Dem., 53; Rep., 47. Total, 100.

Nebraska

Governor — Ben Nelson, D., $65,000.
Lt. Gov. — Maxine Moul, D., $47,000.
Sec. of State — Allen J. Beermann, R., $52,000.
Atty. Gen. — Don Stenberg, R., $64,500.
Treasurer — Dawn Rockey, D., $49,500.
Legislature: meets annually in January at Lincoln. Members receive salary of $12,000 annually plus expenses.
Unicameral body composed of 49 members who are elected on a nonpartisan ballot and are called senators.

Nevada

Governor — Robert Miller, D., $90,000.
Lt. Gov. — Sue Wagner, R., $20,000.
Sec. of State — Cheryl Lau, R., $62,500.
Comptroller — Darrel Daines, R., $62,500.
Atty. Gen. — Frankie Sue Del Papa, D., $85,000.
Treasurer — Bob Seale, R., $62,500.
Legislature: meets odd years in January at Carson City. Members receive $130 per day for 60 days (20 days for special sessions).
Senate — Dem., 10; Rep., 11. Total, 21.
Assembly — Dem., 29; Rep., 13. Total, 42.

New Hampshire

Governor — Stephen Merrill, R., $71,587.
Sec. of State — William M. Gardner, D., $63,430.
Atty. Gen. — Jeffrey Howard, R., $71,007.
Treasurer — Georgie A. Thomas, R., $63,430.
General Court (Legislature): meets every year in January at Concord. Members receive $200; presiding officers $250.
Senate — Dem., 11; Rep., 13. Total, 24.
House — Rep., 257; Dem., 137, ind. & other 5, vac. 1. Total, 400.

New Jersey

Governor — James J. Florio, D., $85,000.
Sec. of State — Daniel Dalton, D., $100,225.
Atty. Gen. — Robert J. Dei Tufo, D., $100,225.
Treasurer — Samuel Crane, D., $100,225.
Legislature: meets throughout the year at Trenton. Members receive $25,000 per year, except president of Senate and speaker of Assembly who receive 1/3 more.
Senate — Dem., 13; Rep., 27. Total, 40.
Assembly — Dem., 22; Rep. 58. Total, 80.

New Mexico

Governor — Bruce King, D., $90,000.
Lt. Gov. — Casey Luna, D., $65,000.
Sec. of State — Stephanie Gonzales, D., $65,000.
Atty. Gen. — Tom Udall, D., $72,500.
Treasurer — David King, D., $65,000.
Legislature: meets on the 3d Tuesday in January at Santa Fe; odd years for 60 days, even years for 30 days. Members receive $75 per day while in session.
Senate — Dem., 26; Rep., 16. Total, 42.
House — Dem., 45; Rep., 25. Total, 70.

New York

Governor — Mario M. Cuomo, D., $130,000.
Lt. Gov. — Stan Lundine, D., $110,000.
Sec. of State — Gail S. Shaffer, D., $87,338.
Comptroller — Edward V. Regan, R., $110,000.
Atty. Gen. — Robert Abrams, D., $110,000.
Legislature: meets annually in January at Albany. Members receive $57,500 per year.
Senate — Dem., 26; Rep., 35. Total, 61.
Assembly — Dem., 101; Rep., 48; 1 vac. Total, 150.

North Carolina

Governor — James B. Hunt Jr., D., $123,300 plus $11,500 per year expenses.
Lt. Gov. — Dennis Wicker, D., $75,774 plus expenses.
Sec. of State — Rufus L. Edmisten, D., $75,252.
Atty. Gen. — Michael Easley, D., $75,252.
Treasurer — Harlan E. Boyles, D., $75,252.
General Assembly: meets odd years in January at Raleigh. Members receive $12,504 annual salary and $6,624 annual expense allowance, plus $81 per diem subsistence and travel allowance while in session.
Senate — Dem., 39; Rep., 11. Total, 50.
House — Dem., 78; Rep., 42. Total, 120.

North Dakota

Governor — Edward T. Schafer, R., $68,280.
Lt. Gov. — Rosemarie Myrdal, R., $56,112.
Sec. of State — Alvin A. Jaeger, R., $51,752.
Atty. Gen. — Heidi Heitkamp, D., $57,936.
Treasurer — Kathi Gilmore, D., $51,744.
Legislative Assembly: meets odd years in January at Bismarck. Members receive $90 per day expenses during session and $180 per month.
Senate — Dem., 25; Rep., 24. Total, 49.
House — Dem., 33; Rep., 65. Total, 98.

Ohio

Governor — George Voinovich, R., $110,250.
Lt. Gov. — Michael DeWine, R., $57,011.
Sec. of State — Bob Taft, R., $81,444.
Atty. Gen. — Lee Fisher, D., $81,444.
Treasurer — Mary Ellen Withrow, D., $81,444.
Auditor — Thomas E. Ferguson, D., $81,444.
General Assembly: meets odd years at Columbus on first Monday in January; no limit on session. Members receive $43,833 per annum.
Senate — Dem., 13; Rep., 20. Total, 33.
House — Dem., 54; Rep., 45. Total, 99.

Oklahoma

Governor — David Walters, D., $70,000.
Lt. Gov. — Jack Mildren, D., $40,000.
Sec. of State — John Kennedy, D., $42,500.
Atty. Gen. — Susan Loving, D., $55,000.
Treasurer — Claudette Henry, R., $50,000.
Auditor— Clifton Scott, D., $50,000.
Legislature: meets annually the first Monday in Feb. at Oklahoma City. Members receive $32,000 annually.
Senate — Dem., 37; Rep., 11. Total, 48.
House — Dem., 68; Rep., 33. Total, 101.

Oregon

Governor — Barbara Roberts, D., $80,000.
Sec. of State — Phil Keisling, D., $61,500.
Atty. Gen. — Ted Kulongosk, D., $66,000.

Treasurer — Jim Hill, D., $61,500.
Legislative Assembly: meets odd years in January at Salem. Members receive $1,029 monthly and $73 expenses per day both during & out of session.
Senate — Dem., 16; Rep., 14. Total, 30.
House — Dem., 32; Rep., 28. Total, 60.

Pennsylvania

Governor — Robert Casey, D., $105,000.
Lt. Gov. — Mark S. Singel, D., $83,000.
Sec. of the Commonwealth — Brenda K. Mitchell, D., $72,000.
Atty. Gen. — Ernest R. Preate, R., $84,000.
Treasurer — Catherine Baker Knoll, D., $84,000.
General Assembly — convenes annually in January at Harrisburg. Members receive $47,000 per year plus expenses.
Senate — Dem., 25; Rep., 24; 1 vacancy. Total, 50.
House — Dem., 105; Rep., 98. Total, 203.

Rhode Island

Governor — Bruce Sundlun, D., $69,000.
Lt. Gov. — Robert A. Weygand, D., $52,000.
Sec. of State — Barbara M. Leonard, R., $52,000.
Atty. Gen. — Jeffrey B. Pine, R., $55,000.
Treasurer — Nancy J. Mayer, R., $52,000.
General Assembly: meets annually in January at Providence. Members receive $5 per day for 60 days, and travel allowance of 8¢ per mile.
Senate — Dem., 39; Rep., 11. Total, 50.
House — Dem., 85; Rep., 15. Total, 100.

South Carolina

Governor — Carroll A. Campbell Jr., R., $101,959.
Lt. Gov. — Nick Theodore, D., $44,737.
Sec. of State — Jim Miles, R., $88,434.
Comptroller Gen. — Earle E. Morris Jr., D., $88,434.
Atty. Gen. — T.T. Medlock, D., $88,434.
Treasurer — G.L. Patterson Jr., D., $85,000.
General Assembly: meets annually in January at Columbia. Members receive $10,400 per year and expense allowance of $79 per day, plus travel and postage allowance.
Senate — Dem., 30; Rep., 16. Total, 46.
House — Dem. 73; Rep., 50; 1 ind. Total, 124.

South Dakota

Governor — Walter Dale Miller, R., $65,761.
Lt. Gov. — vacant.
Sec. of State — Joyce Hazeltine, R., $44,681.
Treasurer — G. Homer Harding, R., $44,681.
Atty. Gen. — Mark Barnett, R., $55,853.
Auditor — Vernon Larson, R., $44,681.
Legislature: meets annually in January at Pierre. Members receive $4,267 for 40-day session in odd-numbered years, and $3,733 for 35-day session in even-numbered years, plus $75 per legislative day.
Senate — Dem., 20; Rep., 15. Total, 35.
House — Dem., 29; Rep., 41. Total, 70.

Tennessee

Governor — Ned Ray McWherter, D., $85,000.
Lt. Gov. — John S. Wilder, D., $49,500.
Sec. of State — Riley C. Darnell, D., $76,068.
Comptroller — William Snodgrass, D., $76,068.
Atty. Gen. — Charles W. Burson, D., $93,540.
General Assembly: meets annually in January at Nashville. Members receive $16,500 yearly plus $78.00 per diem plus office expenses.
Senate — Dem., 19; Rep., 14. Total, 33.
House — Dem., 63; Rep., 36. Total, 99.

Texas

Governor — Ann Richards, D., $99,122.
Lt. Gov. — Bob Bullock, D., $7,200.
Sec. of State — John Hannah, D., $76,966.
Comptroller — John Sharp, D., $79,246.
Atty. Gen. — Dan Morales, D., $79,246.
Treasurer — Martha Whitehead, D., $79,246.
Legislature: meets odd years in January at Austin. Members receive annual salary not exceeding $7,200, per diem while in session, and travel allowance.
Senate — Dem., 18; Rep., 13. Total, 31.
House — Dem., 92; Rep., 58. Total, 150.

Utah

Governor — Michael O. Leavitt, R., $70,000.
Lt. Gov. — Olene S. Walker, R., $52,500.
Atty. Gen. — Jan Graham, D., $56,000.
Treasurer — Edward T. Alter, R., $53,000.
Legislature: convenes for 45 days on 2d Monday in January each year; members receive $25 per day, $15 daily expenses, and mileage.
Senate — Dem., 11; Rep., 18. Total, 29.
House — Dem., 26; Rep., 49. Total, 75.

Vermont

Governor — Howard Dean, D., $85,977.
Lt. Gov. — Barbara W. Snelling, R., $35,842.
Sec. of State — Dennis M. Hooper, D., $54,102.
Atty. Gen. — Jeffrey Amestoy, R., $64,991.
Treasurer — Paul W. Ruse Jr., D., $54,102.
Auditor of Accounts — Edward S. Flanagan, D., $54,102.
General Assembly: meets odd years in January at Montpelier. Members receive $510 per week while in session plus $100 per day for special session, plus specified expenses.
Senate — Dem., 14; Rep., 16. Total, 30.
House — Dem., 87; Rep., 59., ind. 2, Prog. Coalition 2. Total, 150.

Virginia

Governor — L. Douglas Wilder, D., $108,000.
Lt. Gov. — Donald S. Beyer Jr., D., $29,550.
Atty. Gen. — Mary Sue Terry, D., $95,000.
Sec. of the Commonwealth — Pamela Womack, D., $57,735.
Treasurer — Eddie N. Moore Jr., $85,881.
General Assembly: meets annually in January at Richmond. Members receive $18,000 annually plus expense and mileage allowances.
Senate — Dem., 22; Rep., 18. Total, 40.
House — Dem., 58; Rep., 41; ind., 1. Total, 100.

Washington

Governor — Mike Lowry, D., $121,000.
Lt. Gov. — Joel Pritchard, R., $62,700.
Sec. of State — Ralph Munro, R., $64,300.
Atty. Gen. — Christine Gregoire, D., $92,000.
Treasurer — Daniel K. Grimm, D., $79,500.
Legislature: meets annually in January at Olympia. Members receive $25,900 annually plus $66 per diem and 28¢ per mile while in session, and $66 per diem for attending meetings during interim.
Senate — Dem., 28; Rep., 21. Total, 49.
House — Dem., 65; Rep., 33. Total, 98.

West Virginia

Governor — Gaston Caperton, D., $72,000.
Sec. of State — Ken Hechler, D., $43,200.
Atty. Gen. — Darrell McGraw, D., $50,400.
Treasurer — Larrie Bailey, D., $50,400.
Comm. of Agric. — Gus Douglass, D., $46,800.
Auditor — Glen B. Gainer 3d, D., $46,800.
Legislature: meets annually in January at Charleston. Members receive $6,500.
Senate — Dem., 32; Rep., 2. Total, 34.
House — Dem., 79; Rep., 21. Total, 100.

Wisconsin

Governor — Tommy G. Thompson, R., $92,283.
Lt. Gov. — Scott McCallum, R., $49,673.
Sec. of State — Douglas La Follette, D., $45,088.
Treasurer — Cathy S. Zeuske, R., $45,088.
Atty. Gen. — James E. Doyle, D., $82,706.
Superintendent of Public Instruction — Herbert J. Grover, $72,337.
Legislature: meets in January at Madison. Members receive $35,070 annually plus $64 per day expenses.
Senate — Dem., 15; Rep., 15, 3 vac. Total, 33.
Assembly — Dem., 52; Rep., 47. Total, 99.

Wyoming

Governor — Mike Sullivan, D., $70,000.
Sec. of State — Kathy Karpan, D., $52,500.
Atty. Gen. — Joseph Meyer, $52,500.
Treasurer — Stan Smith, R., $52,500.
Auditor — Dave Ferrari, R., $52,500.
Legislature: meets odd years in January, even years in February, at Cheyenne. Members receive $75 per day while in session, plus $60 per day for expenses.
Senate — Dem., 10; Rep., 20. Total, 30.
House — Dem., 19; Rep. 45. Total, 64.

Puerto Rico

Governor — Pedro J. Rosselló.
Legislature: composed of a Senate of 27 members and a House of Representatives of 53 members. Majority of the members of both chambers belongs to the New Progressive Party. They meet annually on the 2d Monday in January in San Juan.

CABINETS OF THE U. S.

Secretaries of State

The Department of Foreign Affairs was created by act of Congress July 27, 1789, and the name changed to Department of State on Sept. 15.

President	Secretary	Home	Apptd.
Washington	Thomas Jefferson	Va.	1789
"	Edmund Randolph	"	1794
"	Timothy Pickering	Pa.	1795
Adams, J.	Timothy Pickering	Pa.	1797
"	John Marshall	Va.	1800
Jefferson	James Madison	"	1801
Madison	Robert Smith	Md.	1809
"	James Monroe	Va.	1811
Monroe	John Quincy Adams	Mass.	1817
Adams, J.Q.	Henry Clay	Ky.	1825
Jackson	Martin Van Buren	N.Y.	1829
"	Edward Livingston	La.	1831
"	Louis McLane	Del.	1833
"	John Forsyth	Ga.	1834
Van Buren	John Forsyth	Ga.	1837
Harrison, W.H.	Daniel Webster	Mass.	1841
Tyler	Daniel Webster	Mass.	1841
"	Abel P. Upshur	Va.	1843
"	John C. Calhoun	S.C.	1844
Polk	John C. Calhoun	S.C.	1845
"	James Buchanan	Pa.	1845
Taylor	James Buchanan	Pa.	1849
"	John M. Clayton	Del.	1849
Fillmore	John M. Clayton	Del.	1850
"	Daniel Webster	Mass.	1850
"	Edward Everett	"	1852
Pierce	William L. Marcy	N.Y.	1853
Buchanan	William L. Marcy	N.Y.	1857
"	Lewis Cass	Mich.	1857
"	Jeremiah S. Black	Pa.	1860
Lincoln	Jeremiah S. Black	Pa.	1861
"	William H. Seward	N.Y.	1861
Johnson, A.	William H. Seward	N.Y.	1865
Grant	Elihu B. Washburne	Ill.	1869
"	Hamilton Fish	N.Y.	1869
Hayes	Hamilton Fish	N.Y.	1877
"	William M. Evarts	N.Y.	1877
Garfield	William M. Evarts	N.Y.	1881
"	James G. Blaine	Me.	1881
Arthur	James G. Blaine	Me.	1881
"	F.T. Frelinghuysen	N.J.	1881
Cleveland	F.T. Frelinghuysen	N.J.	1885
"	Thomas F. Bayard	Del.	1885
Harrison, B.	Thomas F. Bayard	Del.	1889
"	James G. Blaine	Me.	1889
"	John W. Foster	Ind.	1892
Cleveland	Walter Q. Gresham	Ind.	1893
"	Richard Olney	Mass.	1895
McKinley	Richard Olney	Mass.	1897
"	John Sherman	Oh.	1897
"	William R. Day	Oh.	1898
"	John Hay	D.C.	1898
Roosevelt, T.	John Hay	D.C.	1901
"	Elihu Root	N.Y.	1905
"	Robert Bacon	N.Y.	1909
Taft	Robert Bacon	N.Y.	1909
"	Philander C. Knox	Pa.	1909
Wilson	Philander C. Knox	Pa.	1913
"	William J. Bryan	Neb.	1913
"	Robert Lansing	N.Y.	1915
"	Bainbridge Colby	N.Y.	1920
Harding	Charles E. Hughes	N.Y.	1921
Coolidge	Charles E. Hughes	N.Y.	1923
"	Frank B. Kellogg	Minn.	1925
Hoover	Frank B. Kellogg	Minn.	1929
"	Henry L. Stimson	N.Y.	1929
Roosevelt, F.D.	Cordell Hull	Tenn.	1933
"	E.R. Stettinius Jr.	Va.	1944
Truman	E.R. Stettinius Jr.	Va.	1945
"	James F. Byrnes	S.C.	1945
"	George C. Marshall	Pa.	1947
"	Dean G. Acheson	Conn.	1949
Eisenhower	John Foster Dulles	N.Y.	1953
"	Christian A. Herter	Mass.	1959
Kennedy	Dean Rusk	N.Y.	1961
Johnson, L.B.	Dean Rusk	N.Y.	1963
Nixon	William P. Rogers	N.Y.	1969
"	Henry A. Kissinger	D.C.	1973
Ford	Henry A. Kissinger	D.C.	1974
Carter	Cyrus R. Vance	N.Y.	1977
"	Edmund S. Muskie	Me.	1980
Reagan	Alexander M. Haig Jr.	Conn.	1981
"	George P. Shultz	Cal.	1982
Bush	James A. Baker 3d	Tex.	1989
"	Lawrence S. Eagleburger	Mich.	1992
Clinton	Warren M. Christopher	Cal.	1993

Secretaries of the Treasury

The Treasury Department was organized by act of Congress Sept. 2, 1789.

President	Secretary	Home	Apptd.
Washington	Alexander Hamilton	N.Y.	1789
"	Oliver Wolcott	Conn.	1795
Adams, J.	Oliver Wolcott	Conn.	1797
"	Samuel Dexter	Mass.	1801
Jefferson	Samuel Dexter	Mass.	1801
"	Albert Gallatin	Pa.	1801
Madison	Albert Gallatin	Pa.	1809
"	George W. Campbell	Tenn.	1814
"	Alexander J. Dallas	Pa.	1814
"	William H. Crawford	Ga.	1816
Monroe	William H. Crawford	Ga.	1817
Adams, J.Q.	Richard Rush	Pa.	1825
Jackson	Samuel D. Ingham	Pa.	1829
"	Louis McLane	Del.	1831
"	William J. Duane	Pa.	1833
"	Roger B. Taney	Md.	1833
"	Levi Woodbury	N.H.	1834
Van Buren	Levi Woodbury	N.H.	1837
Harrison, W.H.	Thomas Ewing	Oh.	1841
Tyler	Thomas Ewing	Oh.	1841
"	Walter Forward	Pa.	1841
"	John C. Spencer	N.Y.	1843
"	George M. Bibb	Ky.	1844
Polk	Robert J. Walker	Miss.	1845
Taylor	William M. Meredith	Pa.	1849
Fillmore	Thomas Corwin	Oh.	1850
Pierce	James Guthrie	Ky.	1853
Buchanan	Howell Cobb	Ga.	1857
"	Phillip F. Thomas	Md.	1860
"	John A. Dix	N.Y.	1861
Lincoln	Salmon P. Chase	Oh.	1861
"	William P. Fessenden	Me.	1864
Lincoln	Hugh McCulloch	Ind.	1865
Johnson, A.	Hugh McCulloch	Ind.	1865
Grant	George S. Boutwell	Mass.	1869
"	William A. Richardson	Mass.	1873
"	Benjamin H. Bristow	Ky.	1874
"	Lot M. Morrill	Me.	1876
Hayes	John Sherman	Oh.	1877
Garfield	William Windom	Minn.	1881
Arthur	Charles J. Folger	N.Y.	1881
"	Walter Q. Gresham	Ind.	1884
"	Hugh McCulloch	Ind.	1884
Cleveland	Daniel Manning	N.Y.	1885
"	Charles S. Fairchild	N.Y.	1887
Harrison, B.	William Windom	Minn.	1889
"	Charles Foster	Oh.	1891
Cleveland	John G. Carlisle	Ky.	1893
McKinley	Lyman J. Gage	Ill.	1897
Roosevelt, T.	Lyman J. Gage	Ill.	1901
"	Leslie M. Shaw	Ia.	1902
"	George B. Cortelyou	N.Y.	1907
Taft	Franklin MacVeagh	Ill.	1909
Wilson	William G. McAdoo	N.Y.	1913
"	Carter Glass	Va.	1918
"	David F. Houston	Mo.	1920
Harding	Andrew W. Mellon	Pa.	1921
Coolidge	Andrew W. Mellon	Pa.	1923
Hoover	Andrew W. Mellon	Pa.	1929
"	Ogden L. Mills	N.Y.	1932
Roosevelt, F.D.	William H. Woodin	N.Y.	1933
"	Henry Morgenthau, Jr.	N.Y.	1934
Truman	Fred M. Vinson	Ky.	1945
"	John W. Snyder	Mo.	1946

President	Secretary	Home	Apptd.
Eisenhower	George M. Humphrey	Oh.	1953
"	Robert B. Anderson	Conn.	1957
Kennedy	C. Douglas Dillon	N.J.	1961
Johnson, L.B.	C. Douglas Dillon	N.J.	1963
"	Henry H. Fowler	Va.	1965
"	Joseph W. Barr	Ind.	1968
Nixon	David M. Kennedy	Ill.	1969
"	John B. Connally	Tex.	1971
"	George P. Shultz	Ill.	1972

President	Secretary	Home	Apptd.
Nixon	William E. Simon	N.J.	1974
Ford	William E. Simon	N.J.	1974
Carter	W. Michael Blumenthal	Mich.	1977
"	G. William Miller	R.I.	1979
Reagan	Donald T. Regan	N.Y.	1981
"	James A. Baker 3d	Tex.	1985
"	Nicholas F. Brady	N.J.	1988
Bush	Nicholas F. Brady	N.J.	1989
Clinton	Lloyd Bentsen	Tex.	1993

Secretaries of Defense

The Department of Defense, originally designated the National Military Establishment, was created Sept. 18, 1947. It is headed by the secretary of defense, who is a member of the president's cabinet.

The departments of the army, of the navy, and of the air force function within the Department of Defense, and since 1947 their respective secretaries are not members of the president's cabinet.

President	Secretary	Home	Apptd.
Truman	James V. Forrestal	N.Y.	1947
"	Louis A. Johnson	W.Va.	1949
"	George C. Marshall	Pa.	1950
"	Robert A. Lovett	N.Y.	1951
Eisenhower	Charles E. Wilson	Mich.	1953
"	Neil H. McElroy	Oh.	1957
"	Thomas S. Gates Jr.	Pa.	1959
Kennedy	Robert S. McNamara	Mich.	1961
Johnson, L.B.	Robert S. McNamara	Mich.	1963
"	Clark M. Clifford	Md.	1968

President	Secretary	Home	Apptd.
Nixon	Melvin R. Laird	Wis.	1969
"	Elliot L. Richardson	Mass.	1973
"	James R. Schlesinger	Va.	1973
Ford	James R. Schlesinger	Va.	1974
"	Donald H. Rumsfeld	Ill.	1975
Carter	Harold Brown	Cal.	1977
Reagan	Caspar W. Weinberger	Cal.	1981
"	Frank C. Carlucci	Pa.	1987
Bush	Richard B. Cheney	Wyo.	1989
Clinton	Les Aspin	Wis.	1993

Secretaries of War

The War Department (which included jurisdiction over the navy until 1798) was created by act of Congress Aug. 7, 1789, and Gen. Henry Knox was commissioned secretary of war under that act Sept. 12, 1789.

President	Secretary	Home	Apptd.
Washington	Henry Knox	Mass.	1789
"	Timothy Pickering	Pa.	1795
"	James McHenry	Md.	1796
Adams, J.	James McHenry	Md.	1797
"	Samuel Dexter	Mass.	1800
Jefferson	Henry Dearborn	Mass.	1801
Madison	William Eustis	Mass.	1809
"	John Armstrong	N.Y.	1813
"	James Monroe	Va.	1814
"	William H. Crawford	Ga.	1815
Monroe	John C. Calhoun	S.C.	1817
Adams, J.Q.	James Barbour	Va.	1825
"	Peter B. Porter	N.Y.	1828
Jackson	John H. Eaton	Tenn.	1829
"	Lewis Cass	Mich.	1831
"	Benjamin F. Butler	N.Y.	1837
Van Buren	Joel R. Poinsett	S.C.	1837
Harrison, W.H.	John Bell	Tenn.	1841
Tyler	John Bell	Tenn	1841
"	John C. Spencer	N.Y.	1841
"	James M. Porter	Pa.	1843
"	William Wilkins	Pa.	1844
Polk	William L. Marcy	N.Y.	1845
Taylor	George W. Crawford	Ga.	1849
Fillmore	Charles M. Conrad	La.	1850
Pierce	Jefferson Davis	Miss.	1853
Buchanan	John B. Floyd	Va.	1857
"	Joseph Holt	Ky.	1861
Lincoln	Simon Cameron	Pa.	1861
"	Edwin M. Stanton	Pa.	1862
Johnson, A.	Edwin M. Stanton	Pa.	1865
"	John M. Schofield	Ill.	1868

President	Secretary	Home	Apptd.
Grant	John A. Rawlins	Ill.	1869
"	William T. Sherman	Oh.	1869
"	William W. Belknap	Ia.	1869
"	Alphonso Taft	Oh.	1876
"	James D. Cameron	Pa.	1876
Hayes	George W. McCrary	Ia.	1877
"	Alexander Ramsey	Minn.	1879
Garfield	Robert T. Lincoln	Ill.	1881
Arthur	Robert T. Lincoln	Ill.	1881
Cleveland	William C. Endicott	Mass.	1885
Harrison, B.	Redfield Proctor	Vt.	1889
"	Stephen B. Elkins	W.Va.	1891
Cleveland	Daniel S. Lamont	N.Y.	1893
McKinley	Russel A. Alger	Mich.	1897
"	Elihu Root	N.Y.	1899
Roosevelt, T.	Elihu Root	N.Y.	1901
"	William H. Taft	Oh.	1904
"	Luke E. Wright	Tenn.	1908
Taft	Jacob M. Dickinson	Tenn.	1909
"	Henry L. Stimson	N.Y.	1911
Wilson	Lindley M. Garrison	N.J.	1913
"	Newton D. Baker	Oh.	1916
Harding	John W. Weeks	Mass.	1921
Coolidge	John W. Weeks	Mass.	1923
"	Dwight F. Davis	Mo.	1925
Hoover	James W. Good	Ill.	1929
"	Patrick J. Hurley	Okla.	1929
Roosevelt, F.D.	George H. Dern	Ut.	1933
"	Harry H. Woodring	Kan.	1937
"	Henry L. Stimson	N.Y.	1940
Truman	Robert P. Patterson	N.Y.	1945
"	*Kenneth C. Royall	N.C.	1947

Secretaries of the Navy

The Navy Department was created by act of Congress Apr. 30, 1798.

President	Secretary	Home	Apptd.
Adams, J.	Benjamin Stoddert	Md.	1798
Jefferson	Benjamin Stoddert	Md.	1801
"	Robert Smith	Md.	1801
Madison	Paul Hamilton	S.C.	1809
"	William Jones	Pa.	1813
"	Benjamin W. Crowninshield	Mass.	1814
Monroe	Benjamin W. Crowninshield	Mass.	1817
"	Smith Thompson	N.Y.	1818
"	Samuel L. Southard	N.J.	1823
Adams, J.Q.	Samuel L. Southard	N.J.	1825
Jackson	John Branch	N.C.	1829
"	Levi Woodbury	N.H.	1831
"	Mahlon Dickerson	N.J.	1834
Van Buren	Mahlon Dickerson	N.J.	1837
"	James K. Paulding	N.Y.	1838
Harrison, W.H.	George E. Badger	N.C.	1841
Tyler	George E. Badger	N.C.	1841

President	Secretary	Home	Apptd.
Tyler	Abel P. Upshur	Va.	1841
"	David Henshaw	Mass.	1843
"	Thomas W. Gilmer	Va.	1844
"	John Y. Mason	Va.	1844
Polk	George Bancroft	Mass.	1845
"	John Y. Mason	Va.	1846
Taylor	William B. Preston	Va.	1849
Fillmore	William A. Graham	N.C.	1850
"	John P. Kennedy	Md.	1852
Pierce	James C. Dobbin	N.C.	1853
Buchanan	Isaac Toucey	Conn.	1857
Lincoln	Gideon Welles	Conn.	1861
Johnson, A.	Gideon Welles	Conn.	1865
Grant	Adolph E. Borie	Pa.	1869
"	George M. Robeson	N.J.	1869
Hayes	Richard W. Thompson	Ind.	1877
"	Nathan Goff Jr.	W.Va.	1881

President	Secretary	Home	Apptd.
Garfield	William H. Hunt	La.	1881
Arthur	William E. Chandler	N.H.	1882
Cleveland	William C. Whitney	N.Y.	1885
Harrison, B.	Benjamin F. Tracy	N.Y.	1889
Cleveland	Hilary A. Herbert	Ala.	1893
McKinley	John D. Long	Mass.	1897
Roosevelt, T.	John D. Long	Mass.	1901
"	William H. Moody	Mass.	1902
"	Paul Morton	Ill.	1904
"	Charles J. Bonaparte	Md.	1905
"	Victor H. Metcalf	Cal.	1906
"	Truman H. Newberry	Mich.	1908

President	Secretary	Home	Apptd.
Taft	George von L. Meyer	Mass.	1909
Wilson	Josephus Daniels	N.C.	1913
Harding	Edwin Denby	Mich.	1921
Coolidge	Edwin Denby	Mich.	1923
"	Curtis D. Wilbur	Cal.	1924
Hoover	Charles Francis Adams	Mass.	1929
Roosevelt, F.D.	Claude A. Swanson	Va.	1933
"	Charles Edison	N.J.	1940
"	Frank Knox	Ill.	1940
"	James V. Forrestal	N.Y.	1944
Truman	*James V. Forrestal	N.Y.	1945

* Last members of Cabinet. The War Department became the Department of the Army and it and the Navy Department became branches of the Department of Defense, created Sept. 18, 1947.

Attorneys General

The office of attorney general was organized by act of Congress Sept. 24, 1789. The Department of Justice was created June 22, 1870.

President	Attorney General	Home	Apptd.
Washington	Edmund Randolph	Va.	1789
"	William Bradford	Pa.	1794
"	Charles Lee	Va.	1795
Adams, J.	Charles Lee	Va.	1797
Jefferson	Levi Lincoln	Mass.	1801
"	John Breckenridge	Ky.	1805
"	Caesar A. Rodney	Del.	1807
Madison	Caesar A. Rodney	Del.	1797
"	William Pinkney	Md.	1811
"	Richard Rush	Pa.	1814
Monroe	Richard Rush	Pa.	1817
"	William Wirt	Va.	1817
Adams, J.Q.	William Wirt	Va.	1825
Jackson	John M. Berrien	Ga.	1829
"	Roger B. Taney	Md.	1831
"	Benjamin F. Butler	N.Y.	1833
Van Buren	Benjamin F. Butler	N.Y.	1837
"	Felix Grundy	Tenn.	1838
"	Henry D. Gilpin	Pa.	1840
Harrison, W.H.	John J. Crittenden	Ky.	1841
Tyler	John J. Crittenden	Ky.	1841
"	Hugh S. Legare	S.C.	1841
"	John Nelson	Md.	1843
Polk	John Y. Mason	Va.	1845
"	Nathan Clifford	Me.	1846
"	Isaac Toucey	Conn.	1848
Taylor	Reverdy Johnson	Md.	1849
Fillmore	John J. Crittenden	Ky.	1850
Pierce	Caleb Cushing	Mass.	1853
Buchanan	Jeremiah S. Black	Pa.	1857
"	Edwin M. Stanton	Pa.	1860
Lincoln	Edward Bates	Mo.	1861
"	James Speed	Ky.	1864
Johnson, A.	James Speed	Ky.	1865
"	Henry Stanbery	Oh.	1866
"	William M. Evarts	N.Y.	1868
Grant	Ebenezer R. Hoar	Mass.	1869
"	Amos T. Akerman	Ga.	1870
"	George H. Williams	Ore.	1871
"	Edwards Pierrepont	N.Y.	1875
"	Alphonso Taft	Oh.	1876
Hayes	Charles Devens	Mass.	1877
Garfield	Wayne MacVeagh	Pa.	1881
Arthur	Benjamin H. Brewster	"	1881
Cleveland	Augustus Garland	Ark.	1885

President	Attorney General	Home	Apptd.
Harrison, B.	William H. H. Miller	Ind.	1889
Cleveland	Richard Olney	Mass.	1893
"	Judson Harmon	Oh.	1895
McKinley	Joseph McKenna	Cal.	1897
"	John W. Griggs	N.J.	1898
"	Philander C. Knox	Pa.	1901
Roosevelt, T.	Philander C. Knox	Pa.	1901
"	William H. Moody	Mass.	1904
"	Charles J. Bonaparte	Md.	1906
Taft	George W. Wickersham	N.Y.	1909
Wilson	J.C. McReynolds	Tenn.	1913
"	Thomas W. Gregory	Tex.	1914
"	A. Mitchell Palmer	Pa.	1919
Harding	Harry M. Daugherty	Oh.	1921
Coolidge	Harry M. Daugherty	Oh.	1923
"	Harlan F. Stone	N.Y.	1924
"	John G. Sargent	Vt.	1925
Hoover	William D. Mitchell	Minn.	1929
Roosevelt, F.D.	Homer S. Cummings	Conn.	1933
"	Frank Murphy	Mich.	1939
"	Robert H. Jackson	N.Y.	1940
"	Francis Biddle	Pa.	1941
Truman	Thomas C. Clark	Tex.	1945
"	J. Howard McGrath	R.I.	1949
"	J.P. McGranery	Pa.	1952
Eisenhower	Herbert Brownell Jr.	N.Y.	1953
"	William P. Rogers	Md.	1957
Kennedy	Robert F. Kennedy	Mass.	1961
Johnson, L.B.	Robert F. Kennedy	Mass.	1963
"	N. de B. Katzenbach	Ill.	1964
"	Ramsey Clark	Tex.	1967
Nixon	John N. Mitchell	N.Y.	1969
"	Richard G. Kleindienst	Ariz.	1972
"	Elliot L. Richardson	Mass.	1973
"	William B. Saxbe	Oh.	1974
Ford	William B. Saxbe	Oh.	1974
"	Edward H. Levi	Ill.	1975
Carter	Griffin B. Bell	Ga.	1977
"	Benjamin R. Civiletti	Md.	1979
Reagan	William French Smith	Cal.	1981
"	Edwin Meese 3d	Cal.	1985
"	Richard Thornburgh	Pa	1988
Bush	Richard Thornburgh	Pa.	1989
"	William P. Barr	N.Y.	1991
Clinton	Janet Reno	Fla.	1993

Secretaries of the Interior

The Department of the Interior was created by act of Congress Mar. 3, 1849.

President	Secretary	Home	Apptd.
Taylor	Thomas Ewing	Oh.	1849
Fillmore	Thomas M. T. McKennan	Pa.	1850
"	Alex H. H. Stuart	Va.	1850
Pierce	Robert McClelland	Mich.	1853
Buchanan	Jacob Thompson	Miss.	1857
Lincoln	Caleb B. Smith	Ind.	1861
"	John P. Usher	Ind.	1863
Johnson, A.	John P. Usher	Ind.	1865
"	James Harlan	Ia.	1865
"	Orville H. Browning	Ill.	1866

President	Secretary	Home	Apptd.
Grant	Jacob D. Cox	Oh.	1869
"	Columbus Delano	Oh.	1870
"	Zachariah Chandler	Mich.	1875
Hayes	Carl Schurz	Mo.	1877
Garfield	Samuel J. Kirkwood	Ia.	1881
Arthur	Henry M. Teller	Col.	1882
Cleveland	Lucius Q.C. Lamar	Miss.	1885
"	William F. Vilas	Wis.	1888
Harrison, B.	John W. Noble	Mo.	1889
Cleveland	Hoke Smith	Ga.	1893

President	Secretary	Home	Apptd.
Cleveland	David R. Francis	Mo.	1896
McKinley	Cornelius N. Bliss	N.Y.	1897
"	Ethan A. Hitchcock	Mo.	1898
Roosevelt, T.	Ethan A. Hitchcock	Mo.	1901
"	James R. Garfield	Oh.	1907
Taft	Richard A. Ballinger	Wash.	1909
"	Walter L. Fisher	Ill.	1911
Wilson	Franklin K. Lane	Cal.	1913
"	John B. Payne	Ill.	1920
Harding	Albert B. Fall	N.M.	1921
"	Hubert Work	Col.	1923
Coolidge	Hubert Work	Col.	1923
"	Roy O. West	Ill.	1929
Hoover	Ray Lyman Wilbur	Cal.	1929
Roosevelt, F.D.	Harold L. Ickes	Ill.	1933
Truman	Harold L. Ickes	Ill.	1945
"	Julius A. Krug	Wis.	1946
Truman	Oscar L. Chapman	Col.	1949
Eisenhower	Douglas McKay	Ore.	1953
"	Fred A Seaton	Neb.	1956
Kennedy	Stewart L. Udall	Ariz.	1961
Johnson, L.B.	Stewart L. Udall	Ariz.	1963
Nixon	Walter J. Hickel	Alas.	1969
"	Rogers C.B. Morton	Md.	1971
Ford	Rogers C.B. Morton	Md.	1971
"	Stanley K. Hathaway	Wyo.	1975
"	Thomas S. Kleppe	N.D.	1975
Carter	Cecil D. Andrus	Ida.	1977
Reagan	James G. Watt	Col.	1981
"	William P. Clark	Cal.	1983
"	Donald P. Hodel	Ore.	1985
Bush	Manuel Lujan	N.M.	1989
Clinton	Bruce Babbitt	Ariz.	1993

Secretaries of Agriculture

The Department of Agriculture was created by act of Congress May 15, 1862. On Feb. 8, 1889, its commissioner was renamed secretary of agriculture and became a member of the cabinet.

President	Secretary	Home	Apptd.
Cleveland	Norman J. Colman	Mo.	1889
Harrison, B.	Jeremiah M. Rusk	Wis.	1889
Cleveland	J. Sterling Morton	Neb.	1893
McKinley	James Wilson	Ia.	1897
Roosevelt, T.	James Wilson	Ia.	1901
Taft	James Wilson	Ia.	1909
Wilson	David F. Houston	Mo.	1913
"	Edwin T. Meredith	Ia.	1920
Harding	Henry C. Wallace	Ia.	1921
Coolidge	Henry C. Wallace	Ia.	1923
"	Howard M. Gore	W.Va.	1924
"	William M. Jardine	Kan.	1925
Hoover	Arthur M. Hyde	Mo.	1929
Roosevelt, F.D.	Henry A. Wallace	Ia.	1933
"	Claude R. Wickard	Ind.	1940
Truman	Clinton P. Anderson	N.M.	1945
"	Charles F. Brannan	Col.	1948
Eisenhower	Ezra Taft Benson	Ut.	1953
Kennedy	Orville L. Freeman	Minn.	1961
Johnson, L.B.	Orville L. Freeman	Minn.	1963
Nixon	Clifford M. Hardin	Ind.	1969
"	Earl L. Butz	Ind.	1971
Ford	Earl L. Butz	Ind.	1974
"	John A. Knebel	Va.	1976
Carter	Bob Bergland	Minn.	1977
Reagan	John R. Block	Ill.	1981
"	Richard E. Lyng	Cal.	1986
Bush	Clayton K. Yeutter	Neb.	1989
"	Edward Madigan	Ill.	1991
Clinton	Mike Espy	Miss.	1993

Secretaries of Commerce and Labor

The Department of Commerce and Labor, created by Congress Feb. 14, 1903, was divided by Congress Mar. 4, 1913, into separate departments of Commerce and Labor. The secretary of each was made a cabinet member.

President	Secretary	Home	Apptd.
	Secretaries of Commerce and Labor		
Roosevelt, T.	George B. Cortelyou	N.Y.	1903
"	Victor H. Metcalf	Cal.	1904
"	Oscar S. Straus	N.Y.	1906
Taft	Charles Nagel	Mo.	1909
	Secretaries of Labor		
Wilson	William B. Wilson	Pa.	1913
Harding	James J. Davis	Pa.	1921
Coolidge	James J. Davis	Pa.	1923
Hoover	James J. Davis	Pa.	1929
"	William N. Doak	Va.	1930
Roosevelt, F.D.	Frances Perkins	N.Y.	1933
Truman	L.B. Schwellenbach	Wash.	1945
"	Maurice J. Tobin	Mass.	1949
Eisenhower	Martin P. Durkin	Ill.	1953
"	James P. Mitchell	N.J.	1953
Kennedy	Arthur J. Goldberg	Ill.	1961
"	W. Willard Wirtz	Ill.	1962
Johnson, L.B.	W. Willard Wirtz	Ill.	1963
Nixon	George P. Shultz	Ill.	1969
"	James D. Hodgson	Cal.	1970
"	Peter J. Brennan	N.Y.	1973
Ford	Peter J. Brennan	N.Y.	1974
"	John T. Dunlop	Cal.	1975
"	W.J. Usery Jr.	Ga.	1976
Carter	F. Ray Marshall	Tex.	1977
Reagan	Raymond J. Donovan	N.J.	1981
"	William E. Brock	Tenn.	1985
"	Ann D. McLaughlin	D.C.	1987
Bush	Elizabeth Hanford Dole	N.C.	1989
"	Lynn Martin	Ill.	1991
Clinton	Robert B. Reich	Mass.	1993
	Secretaries of Commerce		
Wilson	William C. Redfield	N.Y.	1913
"	Joshua W. Alexander	Mo.	1919
Harding	Herbert C. Hoover	Cal.	1921
Coolidge	Herbert C. Hoover	Cal.	1923
"	William F. Whiting	Mass.	1928
Hoover	Robert P. Lamont	Ill.	1929
"	Roy D. Chapin	Mich.	1932
Roosevelt, F.D.	Daniel C. Roper	S.C.	1933
"	Harry L. Hopkins	N.Y.	1939
"	Jesse Jones	Tex.	1940
"	Henry A. Wallace	Ia.	1945
Truman	Henry A. Wallace	Ia.	1945
"	W. Averell Harriman	N.Y.	1947
"	Charles Sawyer	Oh.	1948
Eisenhower	Sinclair Weeks	Mass.	1953
"	Lewis L. Strauss	N.Y.	1958
"	Frederick H. Mueller	Mich.	1959
Kennedy	Luther H. Hodges	N.C.	1961
Johnson, L.B.	Luther H. Hodges	N.C.	1963
"	John T. Connor	N.J.	1965
"	Alex B. Trowbridge	N.J.	1967
"	Cyrus R. Smith	N.Y.	1968
Nixon	Maurice H. Stans	Minn.	1969
"	Peter G. Peterson	Ill.	1972
"	Frederick B. Dent	S.C.	1973
Ford	Frederick B. Dent	S.C.	1974
"	Rogers C.B. Morton	Md.	1975
"	Elliot L. Richardson	Mass.	1975
Carter	Juanita M. Kreps	N.C.	1977
"	Philip M. Klutznick	Ill.	1979
Reagan	Malcolm Baldrige	Conn.	1981
"	C. William Verity Jr.	Oh.	1987
Bush	Robert A. Mosbacher	Tex.	1989
"	Barbara H. Franklin	Pa.	1992
Clinton	Ronald H. Brown	D.C.	1993

Secretaries of Housing and Urban Development

The Department of Housing and Urban Development was created by act of Congress Sept. 9, 1965.

President	Secretary	Home	Apptd.
Johnson, L.B.	Robert C. Weaver	Wash.	1966
"	Robert C. Wood	Mass.	1969
Nixon	George W. Romney	Mich.	1969
"	James T. Lynn	Oh.	1973
Ford	James T. Lynn	Oh.	1974
Ford	Carla Anderson Hills	Cal.	1975
Carter	Patricia Roberts Harris	D.C.	1977
"	Moon Landrieu	La.	1979
Reagan	Samuel R. Pierce Jr.	N.Y.	1981
Bush	Jack F. Kemp	N.Y.	1989
Clinton	Henry G. Cisneros	Tex.	1993

Secretaries of Transportation

The Department of Transportation was created by act of Congress Oct. 15, 1966.

President	Secretary	Home	Apptd.
Johnson, L.B.	Alan S. Boyd	Fla.	1966
Nixon	John A. Volpe	Mass.	1969
"	Claude S. Brinegar	Cal.	1973
Ford	Claude S. Brinegar	Cal.	1974
"	William T. Coleman Jr.	Pa.	1975
Carter	Brock Adams	Wash.	1977
"	Neil E. Goldschmidt	Ore.	1979
Reagan	Andrew L. Lewis Jr.	Pa.	1981
"	Elizabeth Hanford Dole	N.C.	1983
"	James H. Burnley	N.C.	1987
Bush	Samuel K. Skinner	Ill.	1989
"	Andrew H. Card Jr.	Mass.	1992
Clinton	Federico F. Pena	Col.	1993

Secretaries of Energy

The Department of Energy was created by federal law Aug. 4, 1977.

President	Secretary	Home	Apptd.
Carter	James R. Schlesinger	Va.	1977
"	Charles Duncan Jr.	Wyo.	1979
Reagan	James B. Edwards	S.C.	1981
Reagan	Donald P. Hodel	Ore.	1982
"	John S. Herrington	Cal.	1985
Bush	James D. Watkins	Cal.	1989
Clinton	Hazel R. O'Leary	Minn.	1993

Secretaries of Health, Education, and Welfare

The Department of Health, Education, and Welfare, created by Congress Apr. 11, 1953, was divided by Congress Sept. 27, 1979, into separate departments of Education and of Health and Human Services. The secretary of each is a cabinet member.

President	Secretary	Home	Apptd.
Eisenhower	Oveta Culp Hobby	Tex.	1953
"	Marion B. Folsom	N.Y.	1955
"	Arthur S. Flemming	Oh.	1958
Kennedy	Abraham A. Ribicoff	Conn.	1961
"	Anthony J. Celebrezze	Oh.	1962
Johnson, L.B.	Anthony J. Celebrezze	Oh.	1963
"	John W. Gardner	N.Y.	1965
"	Wilbur J. Cohen	Mich.	1968
Nixon	Robert H. Finch	Cal.	1969
"	Elliot L. Richardson	Mass.	1970
"	Caspar W. Weinberger	Cal.	1973
Ford	Caspar W. Weinberger	Cal.	1974
"	Forrest D. Mathews	Ala.	1975
Carter	Joseph A. Califano, Jr.	D.C.	1977
"	Patricia Roberts Harris	D.C.	1979

Secretaries of Health and Human Services

President	Secretary	Home	Apptd.
Carter	Patricia Roberts Harris	D.C.	1979
Reagan	Richard S. Schweiker	Pa.	1981
"	Margaret M. Heckler	Mass.	1983
Reagan	Otis R. Bowen	Ind.	1985
Bush	Louis W. Sullivan	Ga.	1989
Clinton	Donna E. Shalala	Wis.	1993

Secretaries of Education

President	Secretary	Home	Apptd.
Carter	Shirley Hufstedler	Cal.	1979
Reagan	Terrel Bell	Ut.	1981
"	William J. Bennett	N.Y.	1985
"	Lauro F. Cavazos	Tex.	1988
Bush	Lauro F. Cavazos	Tex.	1989
"	Lamar Alexander	Tenn.	1991
Clinton	Richard W. Riley	S.C.	1993

Secretaries of Veterans Affairs

The Department of Veterans Affairs was created Oct. 25, 1988, when Pres. Reagan signed a bill that made the Veterans Administration into a cabinet post as of Mar. 15, 1989.

President	Secretary	Home	Apptd.
Bush	Edward J. Derwinski	Ill.	1989
Clinton	Jesse Brown	Ill.	1993

Role of the Cabinet

The Cabinet as a governmental institution is not provided for in the U.S. Constitution. It developed as an advisory body out of the desire of presidents to consult the heads of the executive departments on policy issues and problems. Aside from its role as a consultative and advisory body, the cabinet has no function and wields no executive authority. The president may or may not consult the cabinet and is not bound by its advice. Most presidents also consult numerous advisers outside the cabinet. A group of regular informal advisers to the president has been known in American history as a "kitchen cabinet." The formal cabinet meets at times set by the president, often once a week.

Speakers of the House of Representatives

Party designations: A, American; D, Democratic; DR, Democratic-Republican; F, Federalist; R, Republican; W, Whig.

Name	Party	State	Tenure
Frederick Muhlenberg	F	Pa.	1789-1791
Jonathan Trumbull	F	Conn.	1791-1793
Frederick Muhlenberg	F	Pa.	1793-1795
Jonathan Dayton	F	N.J.	1795-1799
Theodore Sedgwick	F	Mass.	1799-1801
Nathaniel Macon	DR	N.C.	1801-1807
Joseph B. Varnum	DR	Mass.	1807-1811
Henry Clay	DR	Ky.	1811-1814
Langdon Cheves	DR	S.C.	1814-1815
Henry Clay	DR	Ky.	1815-1820
John W. Taylor	DR	N.Y.	1820-1821
Philip P. Barbour	DR	Va.	1821-1823
Henry Clay	DR	Ky.	1823-1825
John W. Taylor	D	N.Y.	1825-1827
Andrew Stevenson	D	Va.	1827-1834
John Bell	D	Tenn.	1834-1835
James K. Polk	D	Tenn.	1835-1839
Robert M. T. Hunter	D	Va.	1839-1841
John White	W	Ky.	1841-1843
John W. Jones	D	Va.	1843-1845
John W. Davis	D	Ind.	1845-1847
Robert C. Winthrop	W	Mass.	1847-1849
Howell Cobb	D	Ga.	1849-1851
Linn Boyd	D	Ky.	1851-1855
Nathaniel P. Banks	A	Mass.	1856-1857
James L. Orr	D	S.C.	1857-1859
William Pennington	R	N.J.	1860-1861
Galusha A. Grow	R	Pa.	1861-1863
Schuyler Colfax	R	Ind.	1863-1869
Theodore M. Pomeroy	R	N.Y.	1869-1869
James G. Blaine	R	Me.	1869-1875
Michael C. Kerr	D	Ind.	1875-1876
Samuel J. Randall	D	Pa.	1876-1881
Joseph W. Keifer	R	Oh.	1881-1883
John G. Carlisle	D	Ky.	1883-1889
Thomas B. Reed	R	Me.	1889-1891
Charles F. Crisp	D	Ga.	1891-1895
Thomas B. Reed	R	Me.	1895-1899
David B. Henderson	R	Ia.	1899-1903
Joseph G. Cannon	R	Ill.	1903-1911
Champ Clark	D	Mo.	1911-1919
Frederick H. Gillett	R	Mass.	1919-1925
Nicholas Longworth	R	Oh.	1925-1931
John N. Garner	D	Tex.	1931-1933
Henry T. Rainey	D	Ill.	1933-1935
Joseph W. Byrns	D	Tenn.	1935-1936
William B. Bankhead	D	Ala.	1936-1940
Sam Rayburn	D	Tex.	1940-1947
Joseph W. Martin Jr.	R	Mass.	1947-1949
Sam Rayburn	D	Tex.	1949-1953
Joseph W. Martin Jr.	R	Mass.	1953-1955
Sam Rayburn	D	Tex.	1955-1961
John W. McCormack	D	Mass.	1962-1971
Carl Albert	D	Okla.	1971-1977
Thomas P. O'Neill Jr.	D	Mass.	1977-1987
James Wright	D	Tex.	1987-1989
Thomas S. Foley	D	Wash.	1989-

Floor Leaders in the U.S. Senate

Majority Leaders

Name	Party	State	Tenure
Charles Curtis	R	Kan.	1925-1929
James E. Watson	R	Ind.	1929-1933
Joseph T. Robinson	D	Ark.	1933-1937
Alben W. Barkley	D	Ky.	1937-1947
Wallace H. White	R	Me.	1947-1949
Scott W. Lucas	D	Ill.	1949-1951
Ernest W. McFarland	D	Ariz.	1951-1953
Robert A. Taft	R	Oh.	1953
William F. Knowland	R	Cal.	1953-1955
Lyndon B. Johnson	D	Tex	1955-1961
Mike Mansfield	D	Mont.	1961-1977
Robert C. Byrd	D	W.Va.	1977-1981
Howard H. Baker Jr.	R	Tenn.	1981-1985
Robert J. Dole	R	Kan.	1985-1987
Robert C. Byrd	D	W.Va.	1987-1989
George J. Mitchell	D	Me.	1989-

Minority Leaders

Name	Party	State	Tenure
Oscar W. Underwood	D	Ala	1920-1923
Joseph T. Robinson	D	Ark.	1923-1933
Charles L. McNary	R	Ore.	1933-1944
Wallace H. White	R	Me.	1944-1947
Alben W. Barkley	D	Ky.	1947-1949
Kenneth S. Wherry	R	Neb.	1949-1951
Henry Styles Bridges	R	N.H.	1952-1953
Lyndon B. Johnson	D	Tex.	1953-1955
William F. Knowland	R	Cal.	1955-1959
Everett M. Dirksen	R	Ill.	1959-1969
Hugh D. Scott	R	Penn.	1969-1977
Howard H. Baker Jr.	R	Tenn.	1977-1981
Robert C. Byrd	D	W.Va.	1981-1987
Robert J. Dole	R	Kan.	1987-

Federal Bureau of Investigation

The Federal Bureau of Investigation was created July 26, 1908, and was referred to as Office of Chief Examiner. It became the Bureau of Investigation (Mar. 26, 1909), United States Bureau of Investigation (July 1, 1932), Division of Investigation (Aug. 10, 1933), and Federal Bureau of Investigation (July 1, 1935).

Director	Assumed office
Stanley W. Finch	July 26, 1908
A(lexander) Bruce Bielaski	Apr. 30, 1912
William E. Allen, act.	Feb. 10, 1919
William J. Flynn	July 1, 1919
William J. Burns	Aug. 22, 1921
J. Edgar Hoover, act.	May 10, 1924
J. Edgar Hoover	Dec. 10, 1924
L. Patrick Gray, act.	May 3, 1972
William D. Ruckelshaus, act.	Apr. 27, 1973
Clarence M. Kelley	July 9, 1973
William H. Webster	Feb. 23, 1978
John E. Otto, act.	May 26, 1987
William S. Sessions	Nov. 2, 1987
Floyd I. Clarke, act.	July 19, 1993
Louis J. Freeh	Sept. 1, 1993

Central Intelligence Agency

On June 13, 1942, President Roosevelt established the Office of Strategic Services (OSS) and named William J. Donovan as its director. The OSS was disbanded Oct. 1, 1945, and its functions absorbed by the State and War departments. President Truman, Jan. 22, 1946, established the Central Intelligence Agency Group (CIG) to operate under the direction of the National Intelligence Authority (NIA). The National Security Act of 1947 replaced the NIA with the National Security Council and the CIG with the Central Intelligence Agency.

Director	Served	Appointed by President
Adm. Sidney W. Souers	1946	Truman
Gen. Hoyt S. Vandenberg	1946-1947	Truman
Adm. Roscoe H. Hillenkoetter	1947-1950	Truman
Gen. Walter Bedell Smith	1950-1953	Truman
Allen W. Dulles	1953-1961	Eisenhower
John A. McCone	1961-1965	Kennedy
Adm. William F. Raborn Jr.	1965-1966	Johnson
Richard Helms	1966-1973	Johnson
James R. Schlesinger	1973	Nixon
William E. Colby	1973-1976	Nixon
George Bush	1976-1977	Ford
Adm. Stansfield Turner	1977-1981	Carter
William J. Casey	1981-1987	Reagan
William H. Webster	1987-1991	Reagan
Robert M. Gates	1991-1993	Bush
R. James Woolsey	1993-	Clinton

U.S. Budget Receipts and Outlays—1989-1992

Source: Financial Management Service, U.S. Dept. of the Treasury
(Fiscal year ends Sept. 30)
(millions of dollars; some figures may not add due to independent rounding)
(outlays incl. selected departments and agencies)

Classification	Fiscal 1989	Fiscal 1990	Fiscal 1991	Fiscal 1992
Net Receipts				
Individual income taxes	$445,690	$466,884	$467,827	$476,465
Corporation income taxes	103,291	93,507	98,086	100,270
Social insurance taxes and contributions:				
Federal old-age and survivors insurance	240,595	255,031	265,503	273,137
Federal disability insurance	23,071	26,625	28,382	29,289
Federal hospital insurance	65,396	68,556	72,842	79,109
Railroad retirement fund	3,798	3,679	3,799	3,957
Total employment taxes and contributions	**332,859**	**353,891**	**370,526**	**385,491**
Other insurance and retirement:				
Unemployment	22,011	21,635	20,922	23,410
Federal employees retirement	4,428	4,405	4,459	4,683
Non-federal employees	119	117	108	105
Total social insurance taxes and contributions	**359,416**	**380,047**	**396,016**	**413,689**
Excise taxes	34,386	35,345	42,402	45,570
Estate and gift taxes	8,745	11,500	11,138	11,143
Customs duties	16,334	16,607	15,949	17,359
Deposits of earnings-Federal Reserve Banks	19,604	24,319	19,158	22,920
All other miscellaneous receipts	3,235	2,997	3,688	4,275
Net Budget Receipts	**$990,701**	**$1,031,308**	**$1,054,265**	**$1,091,692**
Net Outlays				
Legislative Branch	$2,095	$2,244	$2,296	$2,677
The Judiciary	1,492	1,641	1,989	2,295
Executive Office of the President:				
The White House Office	27	30	32	36
Office of Management and Budget	42	44	53	54
Total Executive Office	**124**	**157**	**193**	**190**
Funds appropriated to the President:				
International security assistance	1,012	8,352	9,531	7,203
Multinational assistance	1,492	1,695	1,520	1,717
Agency for International Development	1,215	1,773	1,835	2,142
International Development Assistance	2,780	3,528	3,444	4,029
Total funds appropriated to the President	**4,257**	**10,086**	**11,724**	**11,108**
Agriculture Department:				
Food stamp program	13,725	15,923	19,649	22,800
Farmer's Home Admin.	7,608	6,713	6,629	4,455
Forest service	2,944	2,934	3,001	3,293
Total Agriculture Department	**48,316**	**46,012**	**54,119**	**56,436**
Commerce Department				
Total Commerce Department	**2,571**	**3,734**	**2,585**	**2,567**
Bureau of the Census	557	1,575	451	302
Defense Department:				
Military personnel	80,676	75,622	83,439	81,171
Operation and maintenance	87,001	88,340	101,769	92,042
Procurement	81,620	80,972	82,028	74,881
Research, development, test, evaluation	37,002	37,458	34,589	34,632
Military construction	5,275	5,080	3,497	4,262
Total Defense Department (military)	**294,881**	**289,755**	**261,925**	**286,632**
Defense Department (civil)	23,450	24,975	26,543	28,265
Education Department	21,608	23,109	25,339	26,047
Energy Department	11,387	12,023	12,459	15,439
Health and Human Services Department:				
Food and Drug Administration	510	553	648	752
National Institutes of Health	6,992	7,492	7,677	8,376
Public Health Service	12,250	14,007	15,348	17,447
Health Care Financing Adm.	163,028	184,893	205,776	239,366
Total Health and Human Services Dept.	**172,301**	**193,679**	**217,969**	**257,961**
Social Security (Off Budget)	227,473	244,998	266,395	281,418
Housing and Urban Development Department	19,680	20,167	22,751	24,470
Interior Department	5,308	5,795	6,096	6,555
Justice Department:				
Federal Bureau of Investigation	1,528	1,473	1,695	1,832
Total Justice Department	**6,232**	**6,507**	**8,244**	**9,826**
Labor Department:				
Unemployment Trust Fund	18,730	20,250	28,434	41,294
Total Labor Department	**22,657**	**25,316**	**34,040**	**47,193**
State Department	3,722	3,979	4,252	5,007
Transportation Department				
Federal Aviation Adm	5,740	6,391	7,241	8,155
Total Transportation Department	**26,607**	**28,637**	**30,503**	**32,560**
Treasury Department:				
Internal Revenue Service	11,049	12,053	13,689	17,904
Interest on the public debt	240,863	264,853	285,472	292,330
Total Treasury Department	**230,566**	**255,264**	**276,352**	**293,428**
Veterans Affairs Department	30,041	28,998	31,214	33,737
Environmental Protection Agency	4,906	5,108	5,770	5,932
General Services Administration	−462	−123	487	469
National Aeronautics and Space Administration	11,036	12,429	13,878	13,961

(continued)

Classification	Fiscal 1989	Fiscal 1990	Fiscal 1991	Fiscal 1992
Office of Personnel Management	$29,073	$31,949	$34,808	$35,596
Small Business Administration	85	692	613	394
Selected independent agencies:				
Action	163	169	192	194
Board for International Broadcasting	199	208	228	210
Corporation for Public Broadcasting	228	229	299	327
District of Columbia	538	578	671	691
Equal Employment Opportunity Commission	182	181	192	209
Export-Import Bank of the United States	47	357	−88	−119
Federal Communications Commission	49	79	66	78
Federal Deposit Insurance Corporation	2,847	6,429	7,363	3,666
Federal Trade Commission	65	57	60	71
Interstate Commerce Comm.	44	43	45	40
Legal Services Corporation	309	291	344	329
National Archives & Record Adm.	71	157	172	226
National Foundation on the Arts and Humanities	309	307	325	331
National Labor Relations Board	136	141	143	155
National Science Foundation	1,752	1,838	2,081	2,249
Nuclear Regulatory Commission	189	221	−1	50
Railroad Retirement Board	4,315	4,477	4,358	4,843
Securities and Exchange Commission	140	129	143	117
Smithsonian Institution	288	302	340	378
Tennessee Valley Authority	348	−312	740	1,469
U.S. Information Agency	888	888	1,001	1,050
Total independent agencies	**33,770**	**73,666**	**81,217**	**18,876**
Undistributed offsetting receipts	−89,155	−99,025	−110,005	−117,118
Net Budget Outlays	**1,144,020**	**1,251,776**	**1,323,757**	**1,381,895**
Less net receipts	990,701	1,031,308	1,054,265	1,091,692
Deficit	**$−153,319**	**$−220,469**	**$−269,492**	**$−290,204**

Summary of Receipts, Outlays, and Surpluses or Deficits, 1936-1988

Source: Financial Management Service, U.S. Dept. of the Treasury

(millions of dollars)

Year	Receipts	Total Outlays	Surplus or Deficit (−)	Year	Receipts	Total Outlays	Surplus or Deficit (−)
1936	$3,923	$8,228	$−4,304	1963	$106,560	$111,316	$−4,756
1937	5,387	7,580	−2,193	1964	112,613	118,528	−5,915
1938	6,751	6,840	−89	1965	116,817	118,228	−1,411
1939	6,295	9,141	−2,846	1966	130,835	134,532	−3,698
1940	6,548	9,468	−2,920	1967	148,822	157,464	−8,643
1941	8,712	13,653	−4,941	1968	152,973	178,134	−25,161
1942	14,634	35,137	−20,503	1969	186,882	183,640	3,242
1943	24,001	78,555	−54,554	1970	192,807	195,649	−2,842
1944	43,747	91,304	−47,557	1971	187,139	210,172	−23,033
1945	45,159	92,712	−47,553	1972	207,309	230,681	−23,373
1946	39,296	55,232	−15,936	1973	230,799	245,707	−14,908
1947	38,514	34,496	4,018	1974	263,224	269,359	−6,135
1948	41,560	29,764	11,796	1975	279,090	332,332	−53,242
1949	39,415	38,835	580	1976	298,060	371,779	−73,719
1950	39,443	42,562	−3,119	Transition quarter[1]	81,232	95,973	−14,741
1951	51,616	45,514	6,102	1977	355,559	409,203	−53,644
1952	66,167	67,686	−1,519	1978	399,561	458,729	−59,168
1953	69,608	76,101	−6,493	1979	463,302	503,464	−40,162
1954	69,701	70,855	−1,154	1980	517,112	590,920	−73,808
1955	65,451	68,444	−2,993	1981	599,272	678,209	−78,936
1956	74,587	70,640	3,947	1982	617,766	745,706	−127,940
1957	79,990	76,578	3,412	1983	600,562	808,327	−207,764
1958	79,636	82,405	−2,769	1984	666,457	851,781	−185,324
1959	79,249	92,098	−12,849	1985	734,057	946,316	−212,260
1960	92,492	92,191	301	1986	769,091	990,231	−221,140
1961	94,388	97,723	−3,335	1987	854,143	1,003,804	−149,661
1962	99,676	106,821	−7,146	1988	908,166	1,063,318	−155,151

(1) Effective fiscal year 1977, fiscal year is reckoned Oct. 1-Sept. 30; Transition Quarter covers July 1, 1976-Sept. 30, 1976.

Net Receipts and Outlays, 1789-1935

Source: U.S. Dept. of the Treasury; annual statements for year ending June 30

(thousands of dollars)

Yearly average	Receipts	Outlays	Yearly average	Receipts	Outlays	Yearly average	Receipts	Outlays
1789-1800[1]	$5,717	$5,776	1866-1870	$447,301	$377,642	1901-1905	$559,481	$535,559
1801-1810[2]	13,056	9,086	1871-1875	336,830	287,460	1906-1910	628,507	639,178
1811-1820[2]	21,032	23,943	1876-1880	288,124	255,598	1911-1915	710,227	720,252
1821-1830[2]	21,928	16,162	1881-1885	366,961	257,691	1916-1920	3,483,652	8,065,333
1831-1840[2]	30,461	24,495	1886-1890	375,448	279,134	1921-1925	4,306,673	3,578,989
1841-1850[2]	28,545	34,097	1891-1895	352,891	363,599	1926-1930	4,069,138	3,182,807
1851-1860	60,237	60,163	1896-1900	434,877	457,451	1931-1935	2,770,973	5,214,874
1861-1865	160,907	683,785						

(1) Average for period March 4, 1789, to Dec. 31, 1800. (2) Years ended Dec. 31, 1801 to 1842; average for 1841-1850 is for the period Jan. 1, 1841, to June 30, 1850.

The Federal Budget Process

Source: Executive Office of the President, Office of Management and Budget.

CBO = Congressional Budget Office; GRH = Gramm-Rudman-Hollings (*Balanced Budget and Emergency Deficit Control Act of 1985*); OMB = Office of Management and Budget.

Executive budget process	Timing	Congressional budget process
Agencies subject to executive branch review submit initial budget request materials.	Sept. 1	
Fiscal year begins. President's initial GRH sequester order takes effect (amounts are withheld from obligation pending issuance of final order).	Oct. 1	Fiscal year begins.
	Oct. 10	CBO issues revised GRH report to OMB and Congress.
OMB reports on changes in initial GRH estimates and determinations resulting from legislation enacted and regulations promulgated after its initial report to Congress. President issues final GRH sequester order, effective immediately, and transmits message to Congress within 15 days of final order. Agencies not subject to executive branch review submit budget request materials.	Oct. 15	
	Nov. 15	Comptroller General issues GRH compliance report.
Legislative branch and the judiciary submit budget request materials.	Nov.-Dec.	
President transmits budget to Congress.	1st Mon. after Jan. 3	Congress receives the President's budget.
OMB sends allowance letters to agencies.	Jan.-Feb.	
	Feb. 15	CBO reports to the Budget Committees on the President's budget.
	Feb. 25	Committees submit views and estimates to Budget Committee in their own house.
OMB and the President conduct reviews to establish presidential policy to guide agencies in developing the next budget.	Apr.-June	
	Apr. 1	Senate Budget Committee reports concurrent resoluion on the budget.
	Apr. 15	Congress completes action on concurrent resolution.
	May 15	House may consider appropriations bills in the absence of a concurrent resolution on the budget.
	June 10	House Appropriations Committee reports last appropriations bill.
	June 15	Congress completes action on reconciliation legislation.
	June 30	House completes action on annual appropriations bills.
President transmits the mid-session review, updating the budget estimates.	July 15	Congress receives mid-session review of the budget.
OMB provides agencies with policy guidance for the upcoming budget.	July-Aug.	
Date of "snapshot" of projected deficits for the upcoming fiscal year for initial OMB and CBO GRH reports.	Aug. 15	
	Aug. 20	CBO issues its initial GRH report to OMB and Congress.
OMB issues its initial GRH report providing estimates and determinations to the President and Congress. President issues initial GRH sequester order and sends message to Congress within 15 days.	Aug. 25	

Public Debt of the U.S.

Source: Bureau of Public Debt, U.S. Dept. of the Treasury

Fiscal year	Debt (billions)	Per. cap. (dollars)	Interest paid (billions)	% of federal outlays	Fiscal year	Debt (billions)	Per. cap. (dollars)	Interest paid (billions)	% of federal outlays
1870	$2.4	$61.06	—	—	1977	$698.8	$3,170	$41.9	10.2
1880	2.0	41.60	—	—	1978	771.5	3,463	48.7	10.6
1890	1.1	17.80	—	—	1979	826.5	3,669	59.8	11.9
1900	1.2	16.60	—	—	1980	907.7	3,985	74.9	12.7
1910	1.1	12.41	—	—	1981	997.9	4,338	95.6	14.1
1920	24.2	228	—	—	1982	1,142.0	4,913	117.4	15.7
1930	16.1	131	—	—	1983	1,377.2	5,870	128.8	15.9
1940	43.0	325	$1.0	10.5	1984	1,572.3	6,640	153.8	18.1
1945	258.7	1,849	3.8	4.1	1985	1,823.1	7,598	178.9	18.9
1950	256.1	1,688	5.7	13.4	1986	2,125.3	8,774	190.2	19.2
1955	272.8	1,651	6.4	9.4	1987	2,350.3	9,615	195.4	19.5
1960	284.1	1,572	9.2	10.0	1988	2,602.3	10,534	214.1	20.1
1965	313.8	1,613	11.3	9.6	1989	2,857.4	11,545	240.9	21.0
1970	370.1	1,814	19.3	9.9	1990	3,233.3	13,000	264.8	21.1
1975	533.2	2,475	32.7	9.8	1991	3,665.3	14,436	285.4	21.5
1976	620.4	2,852	37.1	10.0	1992	4,064.6	15,846	292.3	21.1

Note: Through 1976 the fiscal year ended June 30. From 1977 on, fiscal year ends Sept. 30.

Consumer Price Index

The Consumer Price Index (CPI) is a measure of the average change in prices over time of basic consumer goods and services. From Jan. 1978, the Bureau of Labor Statistics began publishing CPI's for two population groups: (1) a CPI for all urban consumers (CPI-U), which covers about 80% of the total population; and (2) a CPI for urban wage earners and clerical workers (CPI-W), which covers about 32% of the total population. The CPI-U includes, in addition to wage earners and clerical workers, groups such as professional, managerial, and technical workers, the self-employed, short-term workers, the unemployed, retirees, and others not in the labor force.

The CPI is based on prices of food, clothing, shelter, and fuels, transportation fares, charges for doctors' and dentists' services, drugs, and prices of the other goods and services bought for day-to-day living. The index measures price changes from a designated reference period, 1982-84, which equals 100.0.

Use of this reference period began in January 1988.

Consumer Price Indexes, 1993

Source: Bureau of Labor Statistics, U.S. Dept. of Labor

	CPI-U			Seasonally adjusted percent change	CPI-W			Seasonally adjusted percent change
	Unadjusted indexes	Unadjusted percent change to July 1993 from-			Unadjusted indexes	Unadjusted percent change to July 1993 from-		
(1982-84=100)	July 1993	July 1992	June 1993	from- June to July	July 1993	July 1992	June 1993	from- June to July
Food, beverages	141.1	2.2	0	0	140.8	2.2	0	0.1
Housing	141.9	2.6	0.3	0	139.1	2.5	0.2	0
Apparel, upkeep	129.4	0.2	−1.9	0	128.4	0.2	−1.8	0
Transportation	130.3	2.4	0	0.2	129.4	2.1	−0.1	0.2
Medical care	202.2	6.0	0.5	0.4	201.7	6.0	0.5	0.4
Entertainment	145.3	2.0	−1	0	143.7	1.9	−0.1	−0.1
Other goods, services	193.7	6.3	0.3	0.4	193.8	6.1	0.3	0.3
Services	158.4	3.9	0.4	0.2	156.0	3.7	0.3	0.1
Special Indexes								
All items less food	145.2	2.9	0.1	0.4	142.4	2.7	0	0.1
Commodities less food	125.5	1.0	−0.6	0	125.5	1.2	−0.5	0
Nondurables	134.2	1.3	−0.6	−0.6	134.1	1.3	−0.5	−0.5
Energy	105.8	−0.2	−0.7	0	105.2	−0.4	−0.8	−0.1
All items less energy	149.7	3.0	0.1	0.1	147.3	2.9	0.1	0.1

Consumer Price Indexes for Selected Items and Groups

Source: Bureau of Labor Statistics, U.S. Dept. of Labor

(all urban consumers = CPI-U)

(1982-84 = 100. Annual averages of monthly figures)

	1970	1975	1980	1985	1989	1990	1991	1992
All Items	**38.8**	**53.8**	**82.4**	**107.6**	**124.0**	**130.7**	**136.2**	**140.3**
Food and beverages	**40.1**	**60.2**	**86.7**	**105.6**	**124.9**	**132.1**	**136.8**	**138.7**
Food	39.2	59.8	86.8	105.6	125.1	132.4	136.3	137.9
Food at home	39.9	61.8	88.4	104.3	124.2	132.3	135.8	136.8
Cereals, bakery prods.	37.1	62.9	83.9	107.9	132.4	140.0	145.8	151.5
Meats, poultry, fish, eggs	44.6	67.0	92.0	100.1	121.3	130.0	132.6	130.9
Dairy prods.	44.7	62.6	90.9	103.2	115.6	126.5	125.1	128.5
Fruits, vegetables	37.8	56.9	82.1	106.4	138.0	149.0	155.8	155.4
Sugar, sweets	30.5	65.3	90.5	105.8	119.4	124.7	129.3	133.1
Fats, oils	39.2	73.5	89.3	106.9	121.2	126.3	131.7	129.8
Nonalcoholic beverages	27.1	41.3	91.4	104.3	111.3	113.5	114.1	114.3
Other prepared foods	39.6	58.9	83.6	106.4	125.5	131.2	137.1	140.1
Food away from home	37.5	54.5	83.4	108.3	127.4	133.4	137.9	140.7
Alcoholic beverages	52.1	65.9	86.4	106.4	123.5	129.3	142.8	147.3
Housing	**36.4**	**50.7**	**81.1**	**107.7**	**123.0**	**128.5**	**133.6**	**137.5**
Shelter	35.5	48.8	81.0	109.8	132.8	140.0	146.3	151.2
Rent	46.5	58.0	80.9	111.8	132.8	146.7	155.6	160.9
Maintenance, repairs	35.8	54.1	82.4	106.5	118.0	122.2	126.3	128.6
Fuel, other utilities	29.1	45.4	75.4	106.5	107.8	111.6	115.3	117.8
Energy services	31.8	50.0	75.8	106.9	114.7	117.4	112.6	114.8
Household furnishings & operation	46.8	63.4	86.3	103.8	111.2	113.3	116.0	118.0
House furnishings	55.5	69.8	88.5	101.7	105.5	106.7	107.5	109.0
Apparel & upkeep	**59.2**	**72.5**	**90.9**	**105.0**	**118.6**	**124.1**	**128.7**	**131.9**
Apparel commodities	63.3	76.7	92.9	104.0	116.7	122.0	126.4	129.4
Men's & boys'	62.2	75.5	89.4	105.0	117.0	120.4	124.2	126.5
Women's & girls'	71.8	85.5	96.0	104.9	116.4	122.6	127.6	130.4
Footwear	56.8	69.6	91.8	102.3	114.4	117.4	120.9	125.0
Transportation	**37.5**	**50.1**	**83.1**	**106.4**	**114.1**	**120.5**	**123.8**	**126.5**
Private	37.5	50.6	84.2	106.2	112.9	118.8	121.9	124.6
New cars	53.0	62.9	88.4	106.1	119.2	121.4	126.0	128.4
Used cars	31.2	43.8	62.3	113.7	120.4	117.6	118.1	123.2
Gasoline	27.9	45.1	97.5	98.6	88.5	101.0	99.2	99.0
Public	35.2	43.5	69.0	110.5	129.5	142.6	148.9	151.4
Medical care	**34.0**	**47.5**	**74.9**	**113.5**	**149.3**	**162.8**	**177.0**	**190.1**
Entertainment	**47.5**	**62.0**	**83.6**	**107.9**	**126.5**	**132.4**	**138.4**	**142.3**
Other goods & services	**40.9**	**53.9**	**75.2**	**114.5**	**147.7**	**159.0**	**171.6**	**183.3**
Tobacco products	43.1	54.7	72.0	116.7	164.4	181.5	202.7	219.8
Personal care	43.5	57.9	81.9	106.3	125.0	130.4	134.9	138.3
Toilet goods	42.7	58.0	79.6	107.6	123.2	128.2	132.8	136.5
Personal care services	44.2	57.7	83.7	108.9	126.8	132.8	137.0	140.0
Personal, educational expenses	35.5	48.7	70.9	119.1	158.1	170.2	183.7	197.4

Consumer Price Indexes[1] Annual Percent Change

Source: Bureau of Labor Statistics, U.S. Dept. of Labor

	1981[2]	1982	1983	1984	1985	1986	1987	1988	1989	1990	1991	1992
All items	10.3	6.2	3.2	4.3	3.6	1.9	3.6	4.1	4.8	5.4	4.2	3.0
Food	7.8	4.1	2.1	3.8	2.3	3.2	4.1	4.1	5.8	5.8	2.9	1.2
Shelter	11.7	7.1	2.3	4.9	5.6	5.5	4.7	4.8	4.5	5.4	4.5	3.3
Rent, residential	8.7	7.6	5.8	5.2	6.2	5.8	4.1	3.8	3.9	5.6	6.1	2.5
Fuel & other utilities	14.6	9.8	5.6	4.6	1.6	−2.3	−1.1	−1.4	3.3	3.5	3.3	2.2
Apparel and upkeep	4.8	2.6	2.5	1.9	2.8	0.9	4.4	4.3	2.8	4.6	3.7	2.5
Private transportation	11.4	3.5	2.3	4.3	2.5	−4.7	−3.0	3.3	4.9	5.2	2.6	2.2
New cars	6.0	3.9	2.6	2.9	3.2	4.2	3.6	2.0	2.0	1.8	3.8	2.5
Gasoline	11.3	−5.3	−3.3	−1.6	.8	−21.9	−4.0	0.9	9.5	14.1	−1.8	−0.2
Public transportation	24.1	10.9	4.8	6.2	4.5	5.9	3.5	1.8	5.0	10.1	4.4	1.7
Medical care	10.7	11.6	8.8	6.2	6.3	7.5	6.6	6.5	7.7	9.0	8.7	7.4
Entertainment	7.8	6.5	4.3	3.7	3.9	3.4	3.3	4.3	5.2	4.7	4.5	2.8
Commodities	8.4	4.1	2.9	3.4	2.1	−0.9	3.2	3.5	4.7	5.2	4.2	2.0

(1) The Consumer Price Index (CPI-U) measures the average change in prices of goods and services purchased by all urban consumers. (2) Change from 1980.

Consumer Price Index by Region and Selected Cities

Source: Bureau of Labor Statistics, U.S. Dept. of Labor

Area (1982-84 = 100)	CPI-U Indexes May 1993	CPI-U Indexes June 1993	CPI-U Indexes July 1993	Percent change: July 1992–July 1993	CPI-W Indexes May 1993	CPI-W Indexes June 1993	CPI-W Indexes July 1993	Percent change: July 1992–July 1993
U.S. city average	**144.2**	**144.4**	**144.4**	**2.8**	**141.9**	**142.0**	**142.1**	**2.7**
Northeast urban	**150.8**	**151.2**	**151.4**	**2.6**	**148.7**	**149.0**	**149.1**	**2.5**
More than 1,200,000	151.2	151.7	151.9	2.7	148.0	148.5	148.6	2.6
500,000 to 1,200,000	150.3	150.3	150.4	2.0	148.3	148.4	148.4	2.0
50,000 to 500,000	149.2	149.5	149.7	2.8	151.0	151.2	151.2	2.7
North Central urban	**139.8**	**140.0**	**140.0**	**2.7**	**137.2**	**137.3**	**137.2**	**2.6**
More than 1,200,000	141.0	141.1	141.3	2.8	137.5	137.6	137.8	2.8
360,000 to 1,200,000	137.8	138.6	138.2	3.0	134.7	135.5	135.0	2.8
50,000 to 360,000	141.9	141.4	141.1	2.4	139.9	139.3	138.9	2.2
Less than 50,000	134.4	134.9	134.9	2.5	133.5	133.8	133.9	2.1
South urban	**140.7**	**140.8**	**140.9**	**3.0**	**139.3**	**139.6**	**139.6**	**2.9**
More than 1,200,000	141.1	141.0	141.0	2.5	139.4	139.6	139.5	2.4
450,000 to 1,200,000	142.1	142.6	142.7	3.2	138.9	139.4	139.5	3.2
50,000 to 450,000	140.0	140.2	140.1	3.0	140.1	140.2	140.2	2.9
Less than 50,000	138.7	138.8	139.0	3.7	138.8	138.9	139.2	3.5
West urban	**146.0**	**146.0**	**146.0**	**2.9**	**143.5**	**143.4**	**143.4**	**2.6**
More than 1,250,000	148.1	147.8	147.7	2.6	143.9	143.7	143.6	2.5
50,000 to 330,000	143.6	144.0	144.9	4.2	141.8	142.1	142.8	3.8
Selected areas								
Chicago, Ill.–Gary-Lake County, Ill., Ind., Wis.	145.7	145.6	145.5	2.9	141.4	141.2	141.1	3.0
L.A.–Anaheim, Riverside, Cal.	150.1	149.7	149.8	2.1	145.1	144.8	144.8	1.8
New York, N.Y.–Northern N.J., Long Island, N.Y.	153.8	154.2	154.3	2.9	150.4	150.7	150.7	2.8
Philadelphia, Wilmington, Trenton, Pa., Del., N.J., Md.	149.4	150.5	150.7	2.3	149.3	150.4	150.6	2.2
San Francisco–Oakland, San Jose, Cal.	146.9	146.1	146.1	2.7	144.8	144.0	144.1	2.6
Baltimore, Md.	142.8	—	143.7	2.2	142.1	—	143.0	2.0
Boston, Lawrence, Salem, Mass., N.H.	151.8	—	152.4	2.4	151.2	—	151.5	2.2
Cleveland, Akron, Lorain, Oh.	139.6	—	140.9	2.8	132.7	—	133.9	2.6
Miami, Ft. Lauderdale, Fla.	139.0	—	139.0	3.9	137.2	—	137.2	3.9
St. Louis, E. St. Louis, Mo., Ill.	136.8	—	138.8	2.3	136.4	—	138.3	2.1
Washington, D.C.–Md.—Va.	149.2	—	149.2	3.0	147.0	—	147.0	2.6
Dallas–Fort Worth, Tex.	—	136.2	—	—	—	136.5	—	—
Detroit, Ann Arbor, Mich.	—	139.1	—	—	—	135.1	—	—
Houston, Galveston, Brazoria, Tex.	—	132.9	—	—	—	132.4	—	—
Pittsburgh, Beaver Valley, Pa.	—	139.5	—	—	—	133.7	—	—

Percent Change in Consumer Prices in Selected Countries

Source: International Monetary Fund

Country	1975-1980, avg.	1980-1985, avg.	1987-1988, avg.	1988-1989, avg.	1989-1990, avg.	1990-1991, avg.	1991-1992, avg.
Canada	8.7	7.4	4.0	5.0	4.8	5.6	1.5
France	10.5	9.6	2.7	3.5	3.4	3.1	2.4
Germany	4.1	3.9	1.3	2.8	2.7	3.5	4.0
Italy	16.3	13.7	5.1	6.3	6.5	6.4	5.6
Japan	6.5	2.7	0.7	2.3	3.1	3.3	1.7
Spain	18.6	12.2	4.8	6.8	6.7	5.9	5.8
Sweden	10.5	9.0	5.8	6.4	10.5	9.3	2.3
Switzerland	2.3	4.3	1.9	3.2	5.4	5.8	4.0
United Kingdom	14.4	7.2	4.9	7.8	9.5	5.9	3.7
United States	8.9	5.5	4.0	4.8	5.4	4.2	3.0

Index of Leading Economic Indicators

Source: Bureau of Economic Analysis, U.S. Dept. of Commerce

The index of leading economic indicators is used to project the U.S. economy's performance six months or a year ahead. The index is made up of 11 measurements of economic activity that tend to change direction long before the overall economy does.

Components
- Average work week of production workers in manufacturing
- Average weekly claims for state unemployment insurance
- New orders for consumer goods and materials, adjusted for inflation
- Vendor performance (companies receiving slower deliveries from suppliers)
- Contracts and orders for plant and equipment, adjusted for inflation

Components
- New building permits issued
- Change in manufacturers unfilled orders, durable goods
- Change in sensitive materials prices
- Index of stock prices
- Money supply: M-2, adjusted for inflation
- Index of consumer expectations

Gross Domestic Product, Gross National Product, Net National Product, National Income, and Personal Income

Source: Bureau of Economic Analysis, U.S. Dept. of Commerce

(billions of dollars)

	1960	1970	1980	1990	1991	1992
Gross domestic product	—	—	—	$5,513.8	$5,677.5	$5,950.7
Gross national product	$515.3	$1,015.5	$2,732.0	$5,524.5	5,694.9	5,961.9
Less: Capital consumption allowances	46.4	88.8	303.8	594.8	626.1	653.4
Equals: Net national product	468.9	926.6	2,428.1	4,929.8	5,068.8	5,308.5
Less: Indirect business tax and nontax liability	45.3	94.0	213.3	439.2	475.2	504.2
Business transfer payments	2.0	4.1	12.1	27.7	28.1	29.7
Statistical discrepancy	−2.8	−1.1	4.9	8.1	21.9	34.1
Plus: Subsidies less current surplus of government enterprises	.4	2.9	5.7	4.8	0.5	2.9
Equals: National income	424.9	832.6	2,203.5	4,459.6	4,544.2	4,743.4
Less: Corporate profits with inventory valuation and capital consumption adjustment	49.5	74.7	177.2	319.0	346.3	393.8
Net interest	11.3	41.2	200.9	490.1	449.5	415.2
Contributions for social insurance	21.9	62.2	216.5	501.7	528.8	553.5
Wage accruals less disbursement	.0	.0	.0	−0.1	−0.1	−1.5
Plus: Government transfer payment to persons	27.5	81.8	312.6	661.7	748.3	841.6
Personal interest income	24.9	69.3	271.9	721.3	700.6	670.2
Personal dividend income	12.9	22.2	52.9	124.8	137.0	139.3
Business transfer payments	2.0	4.1	12.1	23.2	22.8	24.5
Equals: Personal income	409.4	831.8	2,258.5	4,679.8	4,828.3	5,058.1

Gross Domestic Product

Source: Bureau of Economic Analysis, U.S. Dept. of Commerce

(billions of dollars)

	1991	1992	1993 (1st Quarter)
Gross domestic product	5,677.5	5,950.7	6,145.8
Personal consumption expenditures	3,887.7	4,095.8	4,234.7
Durable goods	446.1	480.4	498.8
Nondurable goods	1,251.5	1,290.7	1,320.8
Services	2,190.1	2,324.7	2,415.1
Gross private domestic investment	721.1	770.4	844.0
Fixed investment	731.3	766.0	809.0
Nonresidential	541.1	548.2	573.8
Structures	180.1	168.4	168.0
Producers' durable equipment	390.9	379.9	405.8
Residential	190.3	217.7	235.2
Change in business inventories	−10.2	4.4	34.9
Nonfarm	−10.3	2.2	32.6
Farm	0	2.2	2.3
Net exports of goods and services	−21.8	−30.4	−49.4
Exports	598.2	636.3	649.4
Imports	620.0	666.7	698.9
Government purchases	1,090.5	1,114.9	1,116.6
Federal	447.3	449.1	441.1
National defense	323.8	315.8	304.2
Nondefense	123.6	133.4	136.9
State and local	643.2	665.8	675.4

Notable Bankruptcy Filings Since 1970

Year	Company
1970	Penn Central
1982	Manville
1983	Baldwin-United
1985	Wheeling-Pittsburgh Steel
1986	LTV Corp.
1987	Texaco
1988	Financial Corp. of America
1989	MCorp
1989	Southmark
1989	Lomas Financial
1989	American Continental
1990	Drexel Burnham Lambert
1990	Allied/Federal
1990	Ames Department Stores
1990	Continental Airlines
1990	Pan Am
1991	America West Airlines
1991	Orion Pictures
1991	Maxwell Communications
1991	Carter Hawley Hale
1992	R.H. Macy
1992	Zale Corp.
1992	T.W.A.

Chapter 11

Chapter 11 refers to the provisions in the Federal Bankruptcy Act for court-supervised reorganization of debtor companies. A company files for Chapter 11 protection when it can no longer pay its creditors or when it expects future liabilities it cannot hope to pay, like product liability damage awards. In 1991, the U.S. Supreme Court ruled that the provision of Federal bankruptcy law that permits corporations to reorganize while continuing to operate was also available for use by individuals.

Process

1. Judge issues automatic stay
- Creditors cannot press suits for repayment.
- Debts are frozen.
- Company's day-to-day operations continue.
- Significant spending must have judge's approval.
- Secured creditors can ask court for hardship exemption from debt freeze.

2. Unsecured creditors form a committee
- Representatives are chosen to deal with the company.
- Creditors can ask the court to appoint an examiner to investigate possible fraud or mismanagement.
- Court can name a trustee to run the company.

3. The committee and company negotiate a reorganization plan.
- Parties negotiate a repayment plan for frozen debts. This step can take months or years.

4. Creditors approve the plan
- Must have assent of majority of creditors as well as creditors who are owed two-thirds of the debt.

5. Judge approves the plan

Reorganized Company Emerges

- It must meet the terms of the agreed repayment plan.
- It operates as a normal company.

State Finances

Revenue, Expenditures, Debt, and Taxes

Source: Census Bureau, U.S. Dept. of Commerce (fiscal year 1992)

State	Revenue (millions)	Expenditures (millions)	Debt (millions)	Per cap.[1] debt	Per cap.[1] taxes	Per cap.[1] expenditures
Alabama	$10,536	$9,651	$4,129	$998	$1,019	$2,333
Alaska	6,327	5,255	4,942	8,418	2,730	8,952
Arizona	9,551	9,096	2,849	743	1,259	2,373
Arkansas	5,864	5,478	1,942	809	1,145	2,283
California	100,154	97,079	37,824	1,225	1,494	3,145
Colorado	9,079	7,492	2,977	857	1,018	2,159
Connecticut	11,784	11,627	11,957	3,644	1,846	3,543
Delaware	2,848	2,504	3,542	5,140	1,944	3,634
Florida	28,311	27,089	12,295	911	1,068	2,008
Georgia	14,761	14,054	4,471	662	1,076	2,081
Hawaii	5,299	5,301	4,687	4,040	2,335	4,570
Idaho	2,902	2,604	1,292	1,210	1,303	2,440
Illinois	27,865	26,832	18,742	1,611	1,157	2,306
Indiana	13,490	12,341	5,172	913	1,143	2,179
Iowa	7,520	7,227	1,884	669	1,280	2,569
Kansas	5,794	5,484	486	192	1,110	2,173
Kentucky	10,640	10,154	6,619	1,762	1,353	2,704
Louisiana	11,842	11,750	9,994	2,331	991	2,740
Maine	3,755	3,722	2,637	2,135	1,347	3,013
Maryland	13,730	13,004	8,335	1,698	1,324	2,649
Massachusetts	20,456	20,368	24,008	4,002	1,651	3,395
Michigan	26,298	25,509	10,357	1,097	1,195	2,703
Minnesota	15,090	13,526	4,143	924	1,662	3,019
Mississippi	6,177	5,762	1,626	621	954	2,204
Missouri	11,619	10,446	6,301	1,213	988	2,011
Montana	2,661	2,460	1,868	2,266	1,153	2,984
Nebraska	3,751	3,624	1,754	1,092	1,176	2,256
Nevada	3,948	3,826	1,934	1,457	1,369	2,883
New Hampshire	2,727	2,871	4,313	3,882	770	2,584
New Jersey	28,922	29,316	19,786	2,540	1,643	3,763
New Mexico	5,582	4,972	1,605	1,015	1,415	3,144
New York	74,931	73,153	55,868	3,083	1,661	4,037
North Carolina	17,664	16,046	3,819	558	1,316	2,344
North Dakota	2,072	2,001	1,027	1,615	1,186	3,145
Ohio	35,590	30,425	12,193	1,106	1,099	2,761
Oklahoma	8,379	8,183	3,657	1,138	1,206	2,547
Oregon	10,025	7,979	6,295	2,114	1,113	2,680
Pennsylvania	36,699	33,622	12,962	1,079	1,354	2,799
Rhode Island	3,609	3,968	5,151	5,125	1,270	3,948
South Carolina	9,897	9,428	4,685	1,300	1,092	2,616
South Dakota	1,756	1,565	1,889	2,657	794	2,200
Tennessee	11,126	10,406	2,806	558	900	2,071
Texas	36,763	33,894	8,001	453	964	1,919
Utah	4,917	4,481	2,153	1,187	1,096	2,471
Vermont	1,898	1,841	1,543	2,706	1,339	3,230
Virginia	15,292	13,921	7,403	1,160	1,101	2,182
Washington	17,366	17,316	7,192	1,400	1,648	3,371
West Virginia	5,452	5,262	2,594	1,431	1,297	2,903
Wisconsin	17,131	13,596	7,299	1,457	1,380	2,715
Wyoming	2,007	1,925	895	1,920	1,386	4,131
United States	**$741,857**	**$699,432**	**$371,901**	**$1,461**	**$1,288**	**$2,748**

(1) Per capita amounts are based on population figures of the resident U.S. population (excluding the District of Columbia) as of July 1, 1992.

State and Local Government Receipts and Expenditures

Source: Bureau of Economic Analysis, U.S. Dept. of Commerce

(billions of dollars)

	1991	1992	First Quarter 1993[1]
Receipts	$777.9	$837.7	$863.3
Personal tax and nontax receipts	145.4	153.2	156.9
Income taxes	110.3	115.8	118.1
Nontaxes	16.7	17.9	18.6
Other	18.4	19.5	20.2
Corporate profits tax accruals	21.5	25.2	26.8
Indirect business tax and nontax accruals	397.0	422.7	435.9
Sales taxes	189.0	200.8	207.1
Property taxes	167.7	180.5	188.0
Other	40.4	41.4	40.9
Contributions for social insurance	60.6	63.7	65.4
Federal grants-in-aid	153.3	173.0	178.2
Expenditures	760.7	822.3	853.2
Purchases	643.2	665.8	675.4
Compensation of employees	435.6	454.9	467.8
Other	$207.6	$210.8	$207.6
Transfer payments to persons	198.0	233.6	253.5
Net interest paid	−48.4	−43.8	−41.3
Interest paid	63.7	66.5	68.1
Less: Interest received by government	112.1	110.3	109.5
Less: Dividends received by government	9.5	10.0	10.4
Subsidies less current surplus of government enterprises	−22.6	−23.3	−24.1
Subsidies	.4	.4	.4
Less: Current surplus of government enterprises	23.0	23.7	24.5
Less: Wage accruals less disbursements	0	0	0
Surplus or deficit (−), national income and product accounts	17.1	15.5	10.1

(1) Seasonally adjusted at annual rates

Federal Grants to State and Local Governments

Source: Office of Management and Budget

(millions of dollars)

	1980	1985	1990	1991	1992
National defense	$93	$157	$241	$185	$318
Energy	499	529	461	457	448
Natural resources and environment	5,363	4,069	3,745	4,040	3,929
Agriculture	569	2,420	1,285	1,220	1,142
Commerce and housing credit	3	2	0	0	11
Transportation	13,087	17,055	19,225	19,878	20,608
Community and regional development	6,486	5,221	4,965	4,273	4,539
Education, employment, training, and social services	21,862	17,817	23,359	26,566	28,795
Health	15,758	24,451	43,890	55,783	71,416
Income security	18,495	27,153	35,189	38,864	43,486
Veterans benefits and services	90	91	134	141	164
Administration of justice	529	95	574	940	987
General government[1]	8,616	6,838	2,309	2,224	2,274
Total	**$91,451**	**$105,897**	**$135,377**	**$154,570**	**$178,117**

(1) Includes general purpose fiscal assistance.

All Banks in U.S.—Number, Deposits

Source: Federal Reserve System

Comprises all national banks in the United States and all state commercial banks, trust companies, mutual stock savings banks, private and industrial banks, and special types of institutions that are treated as banks by the federal bank supervisory agencies. Data as of June 30 prior to 1975.

Year	Number of banks						Total deposits (millions of dollars)					
		F.R.S. members			Nonmembers			F.R.S. members			Nonmembers	
	Total all banks	Total	Nat'l	State	Mutual savings	Other	Total all banks	Total	Nat'l	State	Mutual savings	Other
1925	**26,479**	9,538	8,066	1,472	621	18,320	**$51,641**	$32,457	$19,912	$12,546	$7,089	$12,095
1930	**23,855**	8,315	7,247	1,068	604	14,936	**59,828**	38,069	23,235	14,834	9,117	12,642
1935	**16,047**	6,410	5,425	985	569	9,068	**51,149**	34,938	22,477	12,461	9,830	6,381
1940	**14,955**	6,398	5,164	1,234	551	8,008	**70,770**	51,729	33,014	18,715	10,631	8,410
1945	**14,542**	6,840	5,015	1,825	539	7,163	**151,033**	118,378	76,534	41,844	14,413	18,242
1950	**14,674**	6,885	4,971	1,914	527	7,262	**163,770**	122,707	82,430	40,277	19,927	21,137
1955	**14,309**	6,611	4,744	1,867	525	7,173	**208,850**	154,670	98,636	56,034	27,310	26,870
1960	**14,006**	6,217	4,542	1,675	513	7,276	**249,163**	179,519	116,178	63,341	35,316	34,328
1965	**14,295**	6,235	4,803	1,432	504	7,556	**362,611**	259,743	171,528	88,215	50,980	51,889
1970	**14,167**	5,805	4,638	1,167	496	7,866	**502,542**	346,289	254,322	91,967	69,285	86,968
1975	**15,108**	5,787	4,741	1,046	475	8,846	**896,879**	590,999	447,590	143,409	110.569	195,311
1980	**15,145**	5,422	4,425	997	460	9,263	**1,333,399**	843,030	651,848	191,182	150,000	340,369
1985	**14,713**	6,044	4,964	1,080	344	8,325	**1,973,816**	1,285.562	1,033,631	251,931	137,535	500,179
1990	**12,736**	5,034	4,012	1,022	361	7,341	**2,522,492**	1,679,654	1,374,004	305,650	183,522	659,316
1991	**12,312**	4,808	3,823	985	358	7,146	**2,546.753**	1,694,124	1,380,379	313,745	178,231	674,398
1992	**11,927**	4,598	3,631	967	428	6,901	**2,573,682**	1,721,979	1,370,564	351,415	177,832	673,871

Largest U.S. Commercial Banks

Source: *American Banker* (as of Dec. 31, 1992)

Bank	Assets (millions)
Citicorp, New York	$213,701.0
BankAmerica Corp., San Francisco	180,646.0
Chemical Banking Corp., New York	139,655.0
Nationsbank Corp., Charlotte, N.C.	118,059.3
J.P. Morgan & Co., New York	102,941.0
Chase Manhattan Corp., New York	95,862.0
Bankers Trust New York Corp., New York	72,448.0
Banc One Corp., Columbus, Oh.	61,417.4
Wells Fargo & Co., San Francisco	52,537.0
PNC Bank Corp., Pittsburgh	51,379.9
First Union Corp., Charlotte, N.C.	51,326.7
First Interstate Bancorp, Los Angeles	50,863.1
First Chicago Corp., Chicago	49,281.0
Fleet Financial Group, Providence	46,938.5
Norwest Corp., Minneapolis	44,557.1
NBD Bancorp, Detroit	40,937.2
Bank of New York Co., New York	40,909.0
Barnett Banks, Jacksonville, Fla.	39,464.8
Republic New York Corp., New York	37,146.4
Suntrust Banks, Atlanta	36,648.6
Wachovia Corp., Winston-Salem, N.C.	33,366.5
Bank of Boston Corp., Boston	32,346.1
Mellon Bank Corp., Pittsburgh	31,574.0
First Fidelity Bancorp, Lawrenceville, N.J.	31,480.3
Keycorp, Albany, N.Y.	30,114.1
National City Corp., Cleveland	$28,963.5
Comerica, Detroit	26,586.8
Shawmut National Corp., Hartford	25,288.3
Society Corp., Cleveland	24,978.3
Corestates Financial Corp., Philadelphia	23,699.1
First Bank System, Minneapolis	23,527.0
Boatmen's Bancshares, St. Louis	23,386.7
National Westminster Bancorp, Jersey City, N.J.	22,714.6
Continental Bank Corp., Chicago	22,467.0
U.S. Bancorp, Portland, Ore.	20,741.1
First of America Bank Corp., Kalamazoo, Mich.	20,146.8
Marine Midland Banks, Buffalo	17,109.2
MNC Financial, Baltimore	16,985.5
Union Bank, San Francisco	16,843.5
State Street Boston Corp., Boston	16,489.8
Northern Trust Corp., Chicago	14,959.6
Midlantic Corp., Edison, N.J.	14,421.8
Huntington Bancshares, Columbus, Oh.	13,894.9
UJB Financial, Princeton, N.J.	13,770.9
Firstar Corp., Milwaukee	13,168.9
Harris Bankcorp, Chicago	12,729.2
Southtrust Corp., Birmingham, Ala.	12,714.4
Bancorp Hawaii, Honolulu	12,713.1
Crestar Financial Corp., Richmond	12,674.7
Meridian Bancorp, Reading, Pa.	12,208.3

Bank Failures

Source: Federal Deposit Insurance Corp.

Year	Closed or Assisted
1934	61
1935	32
1936	72
1937	84
1938	81
1939	72
1940	48
1955	5
1959	3
1960	2
1961	9
1963	2
1964	8
1965	9
1966	8
1967	4
1969	9
1970	8
1971	6
1972	3
1973	6
1975	14
1976	17
1978	7
1979	10
1980	10
1981	10
1982	42
1983	48
1984	72
1985	120
1986	145
1987	184
1988	221
1989	207
1990	169
1991	127
1992	122

Federal Deposit Insurance Corporation (FDIC)

The primary purpose of the Federal Deposit Insurance Corporation (FDIC) is to insure deposits in all banks approved for insurance coverage benefits under the Federal Deposit Insurance Act. The major functions of the FDIC are to protect depositors of insured banks, to act as receiver for all national banks placed in receivership and for state banks placed in receivership when appointed receiver by state authorities, and to ensure the continuance or development of safe and sound banking practices. The FDIC's income consists of assessments on insured banks and income from investments; it receives no appropriations from Congress. It may borrow from the U.S. Treasury not to exceed $30 billion outstanding, but has made no such borrowings since it was organized in 1933. The FDIC deficit (Deposit Insurance Fund) as of Mar. 31, 1993, was $1.2 billion.

The Savings and Loan Crisis

As of September 1993, the Congressional Budget Office estimated that handling losses in failed savings and loan institutions would cost $120 billion from 1990 through 1998. This does not include $60 billion spent before 1989.

Federal Reserve Board Discount Rate

The discount rate is the rate of interest set by the Federal Reserve that member banks are charged when borrowing money through the Federal Reserve System.

Year	Effective Date	Rate
1980:	Feb. 15	13
	May 30	12
	June 13	11
	July 28	10
	Sept. 26	11
	Nov. 17	12
	Dec. 5	13
1981:	May 5	14
	Nov. 2	13
	Dec. 4	12
1982:	July 20	11½
	Aug. 2	11
	Aug. 16	10½
	Aug. 27	10
	Oct. 12	9½
	Nov. 22	9
	Dec. 15	8½
1984:	April 9	9
	Nov. 21	8½
	Dec. 24	8
1985:	May 20	7½
1986:	March 7	7
	April 21	6½
	July 11	6
	Aug. 21	5½
1987:	Sept. 4	6
1988:	Aug. 9	6½
1989:	Feb. 24	7
1990:	Dec. 18	6½
1991:	Feb. 1	6
1991:	Apr. 30	5½
	Sept. 13	5
	Nov. 6	4½
	Dec. 20	3½
1992:	July 3	3

Federal Reserve System

(as of Aug. 1993)

The Federal Reserve System is the central bank for the United States. The system was established on December 23, 1913, originally to give the country an elastic currency, to provide facilities for discounting commercial paper, and to improve the supervision of banking. Since then, the System's responsibilities have been broadened. Over the years, stability and growth of the economy, a high level of employment, stability in the purchasing power of the dollar, and reasonable balance in transactions with foreign countries have come to be recognized as primary objectives of governmental economic policy.

The Federal Reserve System consists of the Board of Governors, the 12 District Reserve Banks and their branch offices, and the Federal Open Market Committee. Several advisory councils help the Board meet its varied responsibilities.

The hub of the System is the seven member Board of Governors in Washington. The members of the Board are appointed by the President and confirmed by the Senate, to serve 14-year terms. The President also appoints the Chairman and Vice-Chairman of the Board from among the Board members for 4-year terms that may be renewed. Currently, the board members are: Alan Greenspan, Chairman; David W. Mullins Jr., Vice Chairman; Edward W. Kelley Jr.; Wayne D. Angell; John P. La Ware; Lawrence B. Lindsey; Susan M. Phillips.

The Board is the policy-making body. In addition to its policy-making responsibilities, it supervises the budget and operations of the Reserve Banks, approves the appointments of their presidents, and appoints 3 of each District Bank's directors, including the chairman and vice chairman of each Reserve Bank's board.

The 12 Reserve Banks and their branch offices serve as the decentralized portion of the System, carrying out day-to-day operations such as circulating currency and coin, providing fiscal agency functions and payments mechanism services. The District Banks are located in Boston, New York, Philadelphia, Cleveland, Richmond, Atlanta, Chicago, St. Louis, Minneapolis, Kansas City, Dallas, and San Francisco.

The System's principal function is monetary policy, which it controls using three tools: reserve requirements, the discount rate, and open market operations. Uniform reserve requirements, set by the Board, are applied to the transaction accounts and nonpersonal time deposits of all depository institutions. Responsibility for setting the discount rate (the interest rate at which depository institutions can borrow money from the Reserve Banks) is shared by the Board of Governors and the Reserve Banks. Changes in the discount rate are recommended by the individual Boards of Directors of the Reserve Banks and are subject to approval by the Board of Governors. The most important tool of monetary policy is open market operations (the purchase and sale of government securities). Responsibility for influencing the cost and availability of money and credit through the purchase and sale of government securities lies with the Federal Open Market Committee (FOMC). This committee is composed of the 7 members of the Board of Governors, the president of the Federal Reserve Bank of New York, and 4 other Federal Reserve Bank presidents, who serve one-year terms on a rotating basis. The committee bases its decisions on current economic and financial developments and outlook, setting yearly growth objectives for key measures of money supply and credit. The decisions of the committee are carried out by the Domestic Trading Desk of the Federal Reserve Bank of New York.

The Federal Reserve Act prescribes a Federal Advisory Council, consisting of one member from each Federal Reserve District, elected annually by the Board of Directors of each of the 12 Federal Reserve Banks. They meet with the Federal Reserve Board four times a year to discuss business and financial conditions and to make advisory recommendations.

The Consumer Advisory Council is a statutory body, including both consumer and creditor representatives, which advises the Board of Governors on its implementation of consumer regulations and other consumer-related matters.

Following the passage of the Monetary Control Act of 1980, the Board of Governors established the Thrift Institutions Advisory Council to provide information and views on the special needs and problems of thrift institutions. The group is comprised of representatives of mutual savings banks, savings and loan associations, and credit unions.

U.S. Corporate Profits by Industry

Source: Bureau of Economic Analysis, U.S. Dept. of Commerce

(billions of dollars)

	1991	1992	First[1] Quarter 1993
Corporate profits with inventory valuation and capital consumption adjustments	**346.3**	**393.8**	**424.2**
Domestic industries	**279.8**	**329.8**	**357.0**
Financial	49.9	46.8	54.5
Nonfinancial	229.9	283.0	302.6
Rest of the world	**66.5**	**64.0**	**67.2**
Receipts from the rest of the world	62.5	66.4	73.4
Less: Payments to the rest of the world	−4.0	2.5	6.2
Corporate profits with inventory valuation adjustment	**337.8**	**364.2**	**383.6**
Domestic industries	**271.3**	**300.2**	**316.4**
Financial	60.9	56.8	64.1
Federal Reserve banks	20.2	17.8	16.6
Other	40.7	38.9	47.5
Nonfinancial	210.4	243.5	252.3

(1) Seasonally adjusted at annual rates.

	1991	1992	First[1] Quarter 1993
Manufacturing	89.3	113.8	110.7
Durable goods	25.8	41.0	40.7
Primary metal industries	1.1	.4	−.8
Fabricated metal prods.	5.4	7.1	4.7
Industrial machinery and equip.	8.9	9.4	7.3
Electronic and other electric equip.	6.6	9.3	10.6
Motor vehicles and equip.	−6.9	3.1	4.7
Other	10.8	11.7	14.3
Nondurable goods	63.5	72.9	70.0
Food and kindred prods.	16.6	16.6	15.7
Chemicals and allied prods.	16.1	18.1	19.6
Petroleum and coal prods.	7.7	9.4	8.9
Other	23.1	28.7	25.8
Transportation and public utilities	46.1	44.4	47.0
Wholesale and retail trade	44.0	47.7	51.9
Other	31.1	37.5	42.7
Rest of the world	**66.5**	**64.0**	**67.2**

United States Mint

Source: United States Mint, U.S. Dept. of the Treasury

The United States Mint was created by an act of Congress on April 2, 1792, which established the U.S. national coinage system. Supervision of the Mint was a function of the Secretary of State, but in 1799, the Mint became an independent agency reporting directly to the President. The Mint was made a statutory bureau of the Treasury Department in 1873, with a director appointed by the President to oversee its operations.

The Mint manufactures and ships all U.S. coins for circulation to the Federal Reserve banks and branches, which issue coins to the public and the business community through depository institutions. The Mint also safeguards the Treasury Department's stored gold and silver and other monetary assets.

The composition of dimes, quarters, and half dollars, traditionally produced from silver, was changed by the Coinage Act of 1965, which mandated that these coins be minted from a cupronickel-clad alloy and reduced the silver content of the half dollar to 40 percent. In 1970, legislative action mandated that the half dollar, and a dollar coin, be minted from the same cupronickel-clad alloy.

The Eisenhower dollar was minted from 1971 through 1978, when legislation called for the minting of the smaller Susan B. Anthony dollar coin. The Anthony dollar, which was minted from 1979 through 1981, marked the first time that a woman, other than a mythical figure, appeared on a U.S. circulating coin.

Mint headquarters is located in Washington, D.C. Mint production facilities are located in Philadelphia, PA; Denver, CO; San Francisco, CA; and West Point, NY. In addition, the Mint is responsible for the U.S. Bullion Depository at Fort Knox, KY.

Proof coin sets, silver proof coin sets, and uncirculated coin sets are available annually from the Mint. The Mint also produces ongoing series of national and historic medals in honor of outstanding persons or events and sites of special meaning to the American people.

Since 1982, the Mint has produced the following congressionally authorized commemorative coins: the 1982 George Washington commemorative half dollar; 1984 U.S. Olympic coins; 1986 U.S. Statue of Liberty coins; 1987 bicentennial of the U.S. Constitution coins; 1988 U.S. Olympic coins; 1989 U.S. Congress coins; 1990 Eisenhower centennial coin; 1991 United Services Organization 50th anniversary coin; 1991 Korean War Memorial coin; 1991 Mount Rushmore anniversary coins; 1992 U.S. Olympic coins; 1992 White House 200th anniversary coin; and 1992 Christopher Columbus quincentenary coins.

The Mint in 1993 offered the Bill of Rights commemorative coins in gold and silver. Surcharges from sales of these coins support teaching and graduate study of the Constitution of the United States. The World War II 50th anniversary coins also were available in gold, silver, and clad. Surcharges from sales of these coins help fund the creation of World War II memorials in the United States and France.

Designs for clad, silver, and gold 1994 World Cup coins have been selected, with sales of these coins to help fund scholarships and staging of the 1994 World Cup in the United States. In addition, the 1996 Atlanta centennial Olympic Games commemorative coins, scheduled to go on sale in 1995 and 1996, will help support the staging of the 1996 Olympic Games in Atlanta, GA.

The congressionally authorized American eagle gold and silver bullion coins produced by the Mint are available through dealers worldwide. The gold eagles are sold in one-ounce, half-ounce, quarter-ounce, and one-tenth-ounce sizes; the price of the coins fluctuates with the daily market value of gold. The American eagle silver bullion coin contains one troy ounce of .999 fine silver and is priced according to the daily market value of silver. These coins also are available in proof condition, separately priced.

The Mint offers free public tours and operates sales centers at the U.S. Mints in Denver and Philadelphia. The Mint also operates a museum and sales center at the Old Mint in San Francisco and a sales center at Union Station in Washington, D.C.

Information about Mint programs and products is available from the United States Mint, Customer Service Center, 10001 Aerospace Road, Lanham, MD 20706. Telephone: (301) 436-7400.

Portraits on U.S. Treasury Bills, Bonds, Notes, and Savings Bonds

Denomination	Savings bonds	Treas. bills	Treas. bonds	Treas. notes
50	Washington		Jefferson	
75	Adams			
100	Jefferson		Jackson	
200	Madison			
500	Hamilton		Washington	
1,000	Franklin	H. McCulloch	Lincoln	Lincoln
5,000	Revere	J.G. Carlisle	Monroe	Monroe
10,000	J. Wilson	J. Sherman	Cleveland	Cleveland
50,000		C. Glass		
100,000		A. Gallatin	Grant	Grant
1,000,000		O. Wolcott	T. Roosevelt	T. Roosevelt
100,000,000				Madison
500,000,000				McKinley

Large Denominations of U.S. Currency Discontinued

The largest denomination of United States currency now being issued is the $100 bill. Issuance of currency in denominations larger than $100 was discontinued in 1969.

As large denomination bills reach the Federal Reserve Bank they are removed from circulation.

Because some of the discontinued currency is expected to be in the hands of holders for many years, the description of the various denominations below is continued:

Amt.	Portrait	Embellishment on back
$ 1	Washington	Great Seal of U.S.
2	Jefferson	Signers of Declaration
5	Lincoln	Lincoln Memorial
10	Hamilton	U.S. Treasury
20	Jackson	White House
50	Grant	U.S. Capitol
100	Franklin	Independence Hall

Amt.	Portrait	Embellishment on back
$ 500	McKinley	Ornate denominational marking
1,000	Cleveland	Ornate denominational marking
5,000	Madison	Ornate denominational marking
10,000	Chase	Ornate denominational marking
100,000*	W. Wilson	Ornate denominational marking

* For use only in transactions between Federal Reserve System and Treasury Department.

U.S. Currency and Coin

Source: Financial Management Service, U.S. Dept. of the Treasury (Mar. 31, 1993)

Amounts Outstanding and in Circulation

	Total currency and coin	Total currency	Federal Reserve notes[1]	U.S. notes	Currency no longer issued
Currency					
Amounts outstanding	$395,458,605,364	$374,471,288,466	$373,886,055,293	$322,539,016	$262,694,157
Less amounts held by:					
Treasury	509,126,491	41,848,106	4,530,288	37,112,039	205,779
Federal Reserve banks	62,126,759,101	61,623,603,315	61,623,599,799	300	3,216
Amounts in circulation	**$332,822,719,772**	**$312,805,837,045**	**$312,257,925,206**	**$285,426,677**	**$262,485,162**

	Total	Dollars[3]	Fractional coin
Coin[2]			
Amounts outstanding	$20,987,316,898	$2,024,703,898	$18,962,613,000
Less amounts held by:			
Treasury	467,278,385	305,182,245	162,096,140
Federal Reserve banks	503,155,786	118,873,015	384,282,771
Amounts in circulation	**$20,016,882,727**	**$1,600,648,638**	**$18,416,234,089**

Currency in Circulation by Denominations

Denomination	Total currency in circulation	Federal Reserve notes[1]	U.S. notes	Currency no longer issued
1 Dollar	$5,304,356,907	$5,154,336,328	$143,481	$149,877,098
2 Dollars	917,111,492	784,359,718	132,738,966	12,808
5 Dollars	6,332,792,210	6,186,740,170	111,285,810	34,766,230
10 Dollars	12,133,540,290	12,109,938,660	5,950	23,595,680
20 Dollars	70,202,720,044	70,182,595,780	3,380	20,120,884
50 Dollars	37,661,467,850	37,649,949,450	—	11,518,400
100 Dollars	179,932,145,750	179,868,854,100	41,249,000	22,042,650
500 Dollars	146,619,900	146,431,000	—	188,900
1,000 Dollars	169,852,000	169,645,000	—	207,000
5,000 Dollars	1,780,000	1,725,000	—	55,000
10,000 Dollars	3,450,000	3,350,000	—	100,000
Fractional parts	487	—	—	487
Partial notes[4]	115	—	90	25
Total currency	**$312,805,837,045**	**$312,257,925,206**	**$285,426,677**	**$262,485,162**

Comparative Totals of Money in Circulation — Selected Dates

Date	Dollars (in millions)	Per capita[5]	Date	Dollars (in millions)	Per capita[5]	Date	Dollars (in millions)	Per capita[5]
Mar. 31, 1993	332,822.7	1,293.58	June 30, 1975	81,196.4	380.08	June 30, 1940	7,847.5	59.40
Mar. 31, 1992	303,215.0	1,219.15	June 30, 1970	54,351.0	265.39	June 30, 1935	5,567.1	43.75
Mar. 31, 1991	286,675.0	1,138.62	June 30, 1965	39,719.8	204.14	June 30, 1930	4,522.0	36.74
Mar. 31, 1990	257,664.4	1,028.71	June 30, 1960	32,064.6	177.47	June 30, 1925	4,815.2	41.56
June 30, 1989	249,182.7	1,002.54	June 30, 1955	30,229.3	182.90	June 30, 1920	5,467.6	51.36
June 30, 1985	185,890.7	778.58	June 30, 1950	27,156.3	179.03	June 30, 1915	3,319.6	33.01
June 30, 1980	127,097.2	558.28	June 30, 1945	26,746.4	191.14	June 30, 1910	3,148.7	34.07

(1) Issued on and after July 1, 1929. (2) Excludes coin sold to collectors at premium prices. (3) Includes $481,781,898 in standard silver dollars. (4) Represents value of certain partial denominations not presented for redemption. (5) Based on Bureau of the Census estimates of population.

The requirement for a gold reserve against U.S. notes was repealed by Public Law 90-269 approved Mar. 18, 1968. Silver certificates issued on and after July 1, 1929, became redeemable from the general fund on June 24, 1968. The amount of security after those dates has been reduced accordingly.

Consumer Credit Outstanding, 1970 to 1992

Source: Federal Reserve System

(billions of dollars)

Estimated amounts of credit outstanding as of end of year. Not seasonally adjusted (unless noted).

Type of Credit	1970	1975	1980	1985	1988	1989	1990	1991	1992
Credit outstanding	**133.8**	**207.5**	**355.4**	**601.6**	**742.1**	**799.5**	**813.0**	**799.9**	**809.2**
Ratio to disposable personal income[1] (percent)	18.5	18.0	18.2	20.4	20.9	20.6	19.5	18.5	17.8
Installment	**105.5**	**168.7**	**302.1**	**526.2**	**673.5**	**736.3**	**752.9**	**749.0**	**756.9**
Automobile paper	36.3	57.2	111.9	210.4	285.4	292.4	284.9	261.2	260.0
Revolving	5.1	15.0	58.5	128.9	184.0	209.4	234.8	256.9	267.9
All other loans[2]	64.1	99.7	131.6	213.8	181.3	239.2	238.4	236.5	229.0
Commercial banks	48.7	82.9	147.0	245.1	324.8	342.8	347.1	340.7	331.9
Finance companies	27.6	32.7	62.3	111.7	144.7	138.9	133.3	121.9	117.1
Credit unions	13.0	25.7	44.0	72.7	88.3	93.1	93.1	92.7	97.6
Retailers[3]	13.9	18.2	28.7	43.0	48.4	44.2	43.5	39.8	42.1
Other[4]	2.3	9.2	20.1	53.8	67.1	67.2	57.0	50.3	47.8
Noninstallment	**28.3**	**38.8**	**53.3**	**75.3**	**68.7**	**63.2**	**60.1**	**50.9**	**52.3**

(1) Based on fourth quarter seasonally adjusted disposable personal income at annual rates as published by the U.S. Bureau of Economic Analysis. (2) Comprises mobile home loans and all other installment loans not incl. in automobile or revolving credit, such as loans for education, boats, trailers, or vacations. (3) Excludes 30-day charge credit held by travel and entertainment companies. (4) Comprises savings institutions and gasoline companies.

Leading U.S. Businesses in 1992

Source: FORTUNE Magazine; World Almanac Research

(millions of dollars in sales, unless otherwise noted)

Aerospace

Boeing	$30,184
United Technologies	22,032
McDonnell-Douglas	17,513
Allied-Signal	12,089
Lockheed	10,138
General Dynamics	8,731
Textron	8,348
Martin Marietta	5,970
Northrop	5,550
Grumman	3,504

Apparel

Levi Strauss	$5,570
VF	3,865
Fruit of the Loom	1,855
Hartmarx	1,054
Kellwood	917
Russell	899
Gitano Group	826
Leslie Fay	777
Crystal Brands	736
Warnaco Group	627

Beverages

Pepsico	$22,084
Coca-Cola	13,238
Anheuser-Busch	11,401
Coca-Cola Enterprises	5,127
J.E. Seagram	4,130
Whitman	2,397
Adolph Coors	1,806
Brown-Forman	1,264
Dr Pepper/Seven-Up	663
Coca-Cola Bottling Cons.	656

Building Materials

American Standard	$3,801
Corning	3,744
Owens-Illinois	3,718
Owens-Corning	2,878
Armstrong World Ind.	2,550
USG	1,777
Lafarge	1,511
Anchor Glass	1,163
Holnam	946

Chemicals

E.I. Du Pont De Nemours	$37,643
Dow Chemical	19,177
Occidental Petroleum	8,940
Monsanto	8,485
Hoechst Celanese	7,044
Miles	6,499
W.R. Grace	6,330
Union Carbide	6,167
PPG Industries	5,858
BASF	5,042

Computers, Office Equip.

IBM	$65,096
Hewlett-Packard	16,427
Digital Equipment	14,027
Unisys	8,422
Apple Computer	7,087
Compaq Computer	4,132
Sun Microsystems	3,628
Pitney Bowes	3,460
Seagate Technology	2,889
Amdahl	2,554

Electronics, Electrical Equip.

General Electric	$62,202
Motorola	13,341
Westinghouse Electric	12,100
Rockwell International	10,995
Raytheon	9,119
Emerson Electric	7,706
Texas Instruments	7,470
Whirlpool	7,309
Cooper Industries	6,159
North American Philips	6,138

Food

Philip Morris	$50,157
Conagra	21,219
Sara Lee	13,321
IBP	11,130
Archer Daniels	9,344
General Mills	7,796
Ralston Purina	7,768
Borden	7,143
H.J. Heinz	6,628
CPC International	6,599

Forest Products

International Paper	$13,600
Georgia-Pacific	11,847
Weyerhaeuser	9,260
Kimberly-Clark	7,091
Stone Container	5,533
Champion International	4,950
Scott Paper	4,886
James River	4,748
Mead	4,703
Boise Cascade	3,732

Furniture

Interco	$1,472
Leggett & Platt	1,170
Herman Miller	810
Hon Industries	712
Sealy	654
Kimball International	624
La-Z-Boy Chair	621

Industrial and Farm Equip.

Tenneco	$13,606
Caterpillar	10,194
Deere	6,961
Black & Decker	4,790
Dresser Industries	4,283
Ingersoll-Rand	3,784
Cummins Engine	3,749
Baker Hughes	2,545
Parker Hannifin	2,382
Dover	2,291

Life Insurance[1]

Prudential of America	$154,780
Metropolitan Life	118,178
Teachers Insurance & Annuity	61,778
Aetna Life	50,897
New York Life	46,925
Equitable Life Assurance	46,624
Connecticut General Life	44,076
Northwestern Mutual Life	39,666
John Hancock Mutual Life	39,146
Principal Mutual Life	35,125

Metal Products

Gillette	$5,190
Crown Cork & Seal	3,781
Masco	3,554
Tyco Laboratories	3,066
Illinois Tool Works	2,821
Ball	2,446
McDermott	2,373
Stanley Works	2,218
Masco Industries	1,678
Harsco	1,633

Metals

Aluminum Co. of America	$9,588
Reynolds Metals	5,620
LTV	5,425
Bethlehem Steel	4,013
Amax	3,703
Inland Steel Ind.	3,494
Phelps Dodge	2,594
National Steel	2,373
Maxxam	2,254
Armco	2,084

Motor Vehicles and Parts

General Motors	$132,775
Ford Motor	100,786
Chrysler	36,897
TRW	8,311
Dana	5,036
Eaton	4,109
Navistar International	3,892
Varity	3,186
Paccar	2,761
Arvin Industries	1,893

Petroleum Refining

Exxon	$103,547
Mobil	57,389
Chevron	37,464
Texaco	37,130
Amoco	25,543
Shell Oil	21,702
Atlantic Richfield	18,061
USX	16,186
Phillips Petroleum	11,933
Coastal	10,063

Pharmaceuticals

Johnson & Johnson	$13,846
Bristol-Myers Squibb	11,805
Merck	9,801
Abbott Laboratories	7,894
American Home Products	7,874
Pfizer	7,415
Eli Lilly	6,282
Warner-Lambert	5,598
American Cyanamid	5,348
Rhône-Poulenc Rorer	4,096

Publishing & Printing

R.R. Donnelley	$4,193
Times Mirror	3,702
Gannett	3,469
Berkshire Hathaway	3,029
Reader's Digest	2,667
Knight-Ridder	2,335
Tribune	2,109
McGraw-Hill	2,050
Dow Jones	1,825
New York Times	1,774

Retailing[2]

Sears Roebuck	$59,101
Wal-Mart Stores	55,484
K Mart	37,724
Kroger	22,145
J.C. Penney	19,085
American Stores	19,051
Dayton Hudson	17,927
Safeway	15,152
Great Atlantic & Pacific Tea	11,593
May Department Stores	11,170

Rubber and Plastic Prods.

Goodyear Tire	$11,924
Premark International	2,954
Rubbermaid	1,810
M.A. Hanna	1,338
Cooper Tire & Rubber	1,176
Mark IV Industries	1,146
A. Schulman	739
Insilco	725
Standard Products	658
Bandag	602

Scientific and Photographic Equip.

Eastman Kodak	$20,577
Xerox	18,261
Minnesota Mining	13,883
Baxter International	8,471
Honeywell	6,254
Johnson Controls	5,165
EG&G	2,789
Becton Dickinson	2,365
Polaroid	2,168
Bausch & Lomb	1,722

Soaps, Cosmetics

Procter & Gamble	$29,890
Unilever U.S.	9,217
Colgate-Palmolive	7,035
Avon Products	3,848
Clorox	1,717
International Flavors	1,126
Alberto-Culver	1,091
Helene Curtis	1,023
Safety-Kleen	796
Stanhome	744

Textiles

Collins & Aikman Group	$2,227
Burlington Ind. Equity	2,066
Springs Industries	1,976

Shaw Industries	1,751
West Point-Pepperell	1,500
DWG	1,279
Amoskeag	1,248
Unifi	1,091
JPS Textile Group	852
Cone Mills	770
Tobacco	
RJR Nabisco Holdings	$15,734
American Brands	8,840
Universal	2,989
Standard Commercial	1,185
Dibrell Brothers	1,085
UST	1,013
Brooke Group	929
Toys, Sporting Goods	
Hasbro	$2,541
Mattel	1,880
Tyco Toys	769
Fisher-Price	696
Transportation Equip.	
Brunswick	$2,228
Coltec Industries	1,369
Trinity Industries	1,194
Harley-Davidson	1,106
Huffy	704
Avondale Industries	592
Transportation[3]	
United Parcel Service	$16,541
AMR	14,495
UAL	12,890
Delta Air Lines	10,837
CSX	8,734
Northwest Airlines	7,964
Federal Express	7,550
Union Pacific	7,294
USAir Group	6,696
Continental Airlines	5,575
Utilities[1]	
GTE	$42,144
BellSouth	31,463
Bell Atlantic	28,100
US West	27,964
NYNEX	27,714
Pacific Gas & Electric	24,188
Southwestern Bell	23,810
Ameritech	22,818
Pacific Telesis Group	22,516
Southern	20,038

(1) Millions of dollars of assets as of Dec. 31, 1992. (2) Incl. revenue from nonretailing activities. (3) Incl. revenue from nontransportation activities.

U.S. Industrial Corporations with Largest Sales in 1992

Source: FORTUNE Magazine

(millions of dollars)

Company, headquarters	Sales
General Motors, Detroit, Mich.	$132,775
Exxon, Irving, Tex.	103,547
Ford Motor, Dearborn, Mich.	100,786
IBM, Armonk, N.Y.	65,096
General Electric, Fairfield, Conn.	62,202
Mobil, Fairfax, Va.	57,389
Philip Morris, New York, N.Y.	50,157
E.I. du Pont de Nemours, Wilmington, Del.	37,643
Chevron, San Francisco, Cal.	37,464
Texaco, White Plains, N.Y.	37,130
Chrysler, Highland Park, Mich.	$36,897
Boeing, Seattle, Wash.	30,184
Procter & Gamble, Cincinnati, Oh.	29,890
Amoco, Chicago, Ill.	25,543
Pepsico, Purchase, N.Y.	22,084
United Technologies, Hartford, Conn.	22,032
Shell Oil, Houston, Tex.	21,702
Conagra, Omaha, Neb.	21,219
Eastman Kodak, Rochester, N.Y.	20,577
Dow Chemical, Midland, Mich.	19,177

Largest Corporate Mergers or Acquisitions in U.S.

(as of mid-1993)

Company	Acquirer	Dollars	Year
Tele-Communications Inc., Liberty Media[1 2]	Bell Atlantic	$33.0 bln.	1993
RJR Nabisco	Kohlberg Kravis Roberts	24.9 bln.	1988
Warner Communications	Time	13.9 bln.	1989
Gulf Oil	Chevron	13.3 bln.	1984
Kraft	Philip Morris	13.1 bln.	1988
McCaw Cellular[1]	AT&T	12.6 bln.	1993
Squibb	Bristol-Myers	11.5 bln.	1989
Getty Oil	Texaco	10.1 bln.	1984
Conoco	DuPont	8.0 bln.	1981
Standard Oil	British Petroleum	7.9 bln.*	1987
Federated Dept. Stores	Campeau	7.4 bln.	1988
NCR	AT&T	7.4 bln.	1991
MCA	Matsushita	6.5 bln.	1990
Marathon Oil	U.S. Steel	6.5 bln.	1981
Contel	GTE	6.2 bln.	1990
Beatrice	Kohlberg Kravis Roberts	6.2 bln.	1986
RCA	General Electric	6.2 bln.	1986
Medco	Merck	6.0 bln.	1993
Superior Oil	Mobil Oil	5.7 bln.	1984
Pillsbury	Grand Metropolitan	5.7 bln.	1988
General Foods	Philip Morris	5.6 bln.	1986
Safeway Stores	Kohlberg Kravis Roberts	5.3 bln.	1986
Farmers Group	B.A.T. Industries	5.2 bln.	1988
Southern Pacific	Santa Fe Railroad	5.2 bln.	1983
Southland	J.T. Acquisition	5.1 bln.	1987
Hughes Aircraft	General Motors	5.0 bln.	1985
Nabisco	R.J. Reynolds	4.9 bln.	1985
Signal Cos.	Allied Corp.	4.9 bln.	1986
Sperry	Burroughs	4.8 bln.	1986
Connecticut General	INA	4.3 bln.	1981
Borg-Warner	AV Holdings	4.2 bln.	1987
Texasgulf	Elf Aquitaine	4.2 bln.	1981
Cities Service	Occidental Petroleum	4.0 bln.	1982
Security Pacific	BankAmerica	4.0 bln.	1991
Travelers[1]	Primerica	4.0 bln.[4]	1993
Dome Petroleum	Amoco	3.8 bln.	1987
R.H. Macy	various investors	3.7 bln.	1986
American Hospital	Baxter Travenol	3.7 bln.	1986
Owens-Illinois	Kohlberg Kravis Roberts	3.6 bln.	1987
Belridge Oil	Shell Oil	3.6 bln.	1979
NWA	Checchi Group	3.6 bln.	1988
Allied Stores	Campeau	3.5 bln.	1986
Fort Howard Paper	Morgan Stanley Group	3.5 bln.	1988
ABC Broadcasting	Capital Cities Comm.	3.5 bln.	1985
Columbia Pictures	Sony	3.4 bln.	1989
Viacom	National Amusements	3.4 bln.	1987
LIN Broadcasting	McCaw Cellular	3.3 bln.[3]	1989
Panhandle Eastern	Texas Eastern	3.2 bln.	1989
Chesebrough-Ponds	Unilever N.V.	3.1 bln.	1987
MidCon	Occidental Petroleum	3.0 bln.	1986
American Medical Intl.	IMA Holdings	3.0 bln.	1989
Texas Oil and Gas	USX Corp.	3.0 bln.	1986
Emhart	Black & Decker	2.8 bln.	1989
Carnation	Nestle	2.8 bln.	1984
Celanese	American Hoechst	2.7 bln.	1987
Esmark	Beatrice Foods	2.7 bln.	1984
G.D. Searle	Monsanto	2.7 bln.	1986
Continental Group	Kiewit-Murdock	2.7 bln.	1984
St. Joe Minerals	Fluor	2.6 bln.	1981
Electronic Data Systems	General Motors	2.6 bln.	1984
Firestone Tire	Bridgestone	2.6 bln.	1988
Macmillan	Maxwell Comm.	2.6 bln.	1988
Associated Dry Goods	May Dept. Stores	2.5 bln.	1986

* For the 45% of Standard Oil that British Petroleum did not already own. (1) Proposed. (2) Includes $10 billion in assumed debt. (3) For about 42% of LIN's shares. (4) For the 73% of Travelers that Primerica did not already own.

Fastest Growing Franchises in 1992[1]

Source: *Entrepreneur* magazine

Company	Business	Minimum start-up cost[2]
Subway	submarine sandwiches	$38,000
7-Eleven Convenience Stores	convenience stores	12,500
Jani-King	commercial cleaning	1,500
Burger King Corp.	hamburgers	274,400
Dunkin' Donuts	donuts	175,000
McDonald's	hamburgers	varies
Coverall North America Inc.	commercial cleaning	350
CleanNet	commercial cleaning	0
Little Caesars Pizza	pizza	170,000
Mail Boxes Etc.	packaging, mailing, and shipping services	27,700
Chem-Dry	carpet, upholstery, and drapery services	6,600
Domino's Pizza Inc.	pizza	76,500
O.P.E.N. Cleaning Systems	commercial cleaning	500
Miracle Ear	health-care equipment	35,000
Choice Hotels Int'l.	hotels and motels	1,500,000
MicroAge Computer Centers Inc.	misc. computer-related products and services	56,000
Blockbuster Video	videocassette rentals	365,000
Jazzercise Inc.	fitness centers	$2,000
Worldwide Refinishing Systems Inc.	porcelain, marble restoration	6,500
Travelodge	hotels and motels	500,000
Merry Maids	residential cleaning	7,500
Futurekids Inc.	computer learning centers	19,600
GNC Franchising Inc.	health food, vitamin stores	37,700
Play It Again Sports	sports equipment and apparel	68,000
H & R Block	income tax services	5,000
Howard Johnson Franchise Sys. Inc.	hotels and motels	varies
Decorating Den	miscellaneous decorative products and services	8,600
Re/Max Int'l. Inc.	real estate services	50,000
Valet Park	miscellaneous services	3,750
Super 8 Motels Inc.	hotels and motels	150,000

(1) Based on the number of new franchise units added. (2) Not including franchise fee, which varies.

Largest U.S. Black-Owned Companies in 1992

Source: *Black Enterprise* Magazine

Company (Business)	Location	Sales (millions)
TLC Beatrice International Holdings (food distributor and processor, primarily in Europe)	New York, N.Y.	$1,665.0
Johnson Publishing Co. (Ebony, Jet)	Chicago, Ill.	274.2
Philadelphia Coca-Cola Bottling Co.	Philadelphia, Pa.	266.0
Trainer Oldsmobile-Cadillac-Pontiac-GM Truck	Warner Robins, Ga.	254.6
Shack-Woods and Associates (Ford and Volkswagen)	Long Beach, Cal.	228.3
Pavilion Lincoln-Mercury	Austin, Tex.	$223.8
H. J. Russell and Co. (construction)	Altanta, Ga.	145.6
Mel Farr Automotive Group (Ford and Toyota)	Oak Park, Mich.	118.0
S and J Enterprises (Ford and Subaru)	Charlotte, N.C.	112.2
Anderson-Dubose Co. (food distributor)	Solon, Ohio	110.0

Capital Gains Tax

Source: U.S. Chamber of Commerce

The following shows how the top effective tax rate on capital gains has changed since 1960.

Year	Effective rate (percent)	Year	Effective rate (percent)	Year	Effective rate (percent)	Year	Effective rate (percent)
1960	25.0	1971	34.4	1979	28.0	1988	33.0
1968	26.9	1972	45.5	1981	20.0	1991	28.0
1969	27.5	1976	49.1	1987	28.0		
1970	32.2						

Global Stock Markets

Source: Morgan Stanley Capital International Perspective

(in local currencies)

Index[1]	Aug. 26, 1993	52-week Range
The World	**456.7**	**456.9- 367.3**
E.A.F.E.[2]	566.3	570.2- 427.6
Australia	400.3	400.3- 289.8
Austria	427.1	427.1- 315.6
Belgium	458.0	469.5- 358.1
Canada	421.5	422.7- 355.5
Denmark	768.8	795.7- 556.5
Finland	109.0	114.0- 37.5
France	638.2	638.2- 471.0
Germany	281.1	285.1- 213.1
Hong Kong	5,172.1	5,294.1- 3,589.8
Ireland	178.8	181.0- 104.4
Italy	533.0	533.0- 266.0
Japan	962.5	982.3- 719.1
Malaysia	289.9	289.9- 181.8
Netherlands	418.6	422.2- 318.4
New Zealand	99.2	100.8- 62.3
Norway	748.5	782.3- 461.4
Singapore	974.7	974.7- 718.3
Spain	264.8	264.8- 144.9
Sweden	1,640.6	1,763.0- 787.2
Switzerland	311.5	314.1- 216.1
United Kingdom	934.2	934.8- 677.1
United States	431.7	431.7- 376.7

(1) Base: Jan. 1, 1970 = 100. (2) Europe, Australia, Far East Index.

Foreign Exchange Rates: 1970 to 1992

Source: International Monetary Fund

(National currency units per dollar except as indicated; data are annual averages)

Year	Australia[1] (dollar)	Austria (schilling)	Belgium (franc)	Canada (dollar)	Denmark (krone)	France (franc)	Germany[2] (deutsche mark)	Greece (drachma)
1970	1.1136	25.880	49.680	1.0103	7.489	5.5200	3.6480	30.00
1975	1.3077	17.443	36.799	1.0175	5.748	4.2876	2.4613	32.29
1980	1.1400	12.945	29.237	1.1693	5.634	4.2250	1.8175	42.62
1984	.8794	20.009	57.784	1.2951	10.357	8.7391	2.8454	112.73
1985	.7003	20.690	59.378	1.3655	10.596	8.9852	2.9440	138.12
1987	.7009	12.643	37.334	1.3260	6.840	6.0107	1.7974	135.43
1988	.7842	12.243	36.768	1.2307	6.732	5.9569	1.7562	141.89
1989	.7925	13.231	39.404	1.1840	7.310	6.3801	1.8800	162.42
1990	.7813	11.370	33.418	1.1668	6.189	5.4453	1.6157	158.51
1991	.7791	11.676	34.148	1.1457	6.396	5.6421	1.6595	182.27
1992	.7353	10.989	32.150	1.2087	6.036	5.2938	1.5617	190.62

Year	India (rupee)	Ireland[1] (pound)	Italy (lira)	Japan (yen)	Malaysia (ringgit)	Netherlands (guilder)	Norway (kroner)	Portugal (escudo)
1970	7.576	2.3959	623	357.60	3.0900	3.5970	7.1400	28.75
1975	8.409	2.2216	653	296.78	2.4030	2.5293	5.2282	25.51
1980	7.887	2.0577	856	226.63	2.1767	1.9875	4.9381	50.08
1984	11.363	1.0871	1,756	237.52	2.3436	3.2087	8.1615	146.39
1985	12.369	1.0656	1,909	238.54	2.4830	3.3214	8.5972	170.39
1987	12.962	1.4881	1,296	144.64	2.5196	2.0257	6.7375	140.88
1988	13.917	1.5261	1,301	128.15	2.6188	1.9766	6.5170	143.95
1989	16.226	1.4190	1,372	137.96	2.7088	2.1207	6.9045	157.46
1990	17.504	1.6585	1,198	144.79	2.7048	1.8209	6.2597	142.55
1991	22.742	1.6155	1,240	134.71	2.7501	1.8697	6.4829	144.48
1992	25.918	1.7053	1,232	126.65	2.5474	1.7885	6.2145	135.00

Year	Singapore (dollar)	South Korea (won)	Spain (peseta)	Sweden (krona)	Switzerland (franc)	Thailand (baht)	United Kingdom[1] (pound)
1970	3.0800	310.57	69.72	5.1700	4.3160	21.000	2.3959
1975	2.3713	484.00	57.43	4.1530	2.5839	20.379	2.2216
1980	2.1412	607.43	71.76	4.2309	1.6772	20.476	2.3243
1984	2.1331	805.69	160.78	8.2718	2.3497	23.639	1.3366
1985	2.2002	870.02	170.04	8.6039	2.4571	27.159	1.2963
1987	2.1059	822.57	123.48	6.3404	1.4912	25.723	1.6389
1988	2.0124	731.57	116.49	6.1272	1.4633	25.294	1.7813
1989	1.9508	671.46	118.38	6.4469	1.6359	25.702	1.6897
1990	1.8125	707.76	101.93	5.9188	1.3892	25.585	1.7847
1991	1.7276	733.35	103.91	6.0475	1.4340	25.517	1.7694
1992	1.6290	780.65	102.38	5.8238	1.4062	25.400	1.7655

(1) Value of one unit of foreign currency in dollars. (2) W. Germany prior to 1991.

Foreign Direct Investment[1] in the U.S. by Selected Countries

Source: Bureau of Economic Analysis; U.S. Dept. of Commerce

(millions of dollars)

	1991	1992
All countries[2]	**$414,358**	**$419,526**
Canada	37,301	38,997
Europe[2]	251,248	248,461
Austria	488	387
Belgium	3,089	4,066
Denmark	1,301	1,308
Finland	1,305	1,385
France	24,155	23,808
Germany	28,618	29,205
Ireland	1,823	2,273
Italy	2,705	571
Netherlands	59,355	61,341
Spain	1,155	1,290
Sweden	5,684	6,923
Switzerland	19,189	19,562
United Kingdom	100,386	94,718
South and Central America[2]	7,020	7,378
Brazil	478	502
Mexico	$708	$1,184
Panama	4,841	4,732
Venezuela	538	502
Other Western Hemisphere[2]	10,646	11,518
Bahamas	1,194	989
Bermuda	1,261	1,577
Middle East[2]	4,771	4,813
Israel	1,147	1,131
Kuwait	1,891	1,893
Saudi Arabia	1,598	1,642
United Arab Emirates	99	121
Asia and Pacific[2]	102,730	107,725
Australia	6,083	7,140
Hong Kong	1,763	1,714
Japan	92,896	96,743
Singapore	870	847
Taiwan	1,142	1,154

(1) The book value of foreign direct investors' equity in, and net outstanding loans to, their U.S. affiliates. A U.S. affiliate is a U.S. business enterprise in which a single foreign direct investor owns at least 10 percent of the voting securities or the equivalent. (2) Totals include countries not shown.

U.S. International Transactions

Source: Bureau of Economic Analysis, U.S. Dept. of Commerce

(millions of dollars)

	1965	1970	1975	1980	1985	1990	1991	1992
Exports of goods, services, and income[1]	**$42,722**	**$68,387**	**$157,936**	**$344,440**	**$380,051**	**$680,890**	**$708,489**	**$730,460**
Merchandise, adjusted, excluding military[2]	26,461	42,469	107,088	224,250	215,915	388,705	416,937	440,138
Services	8,824	14,171	25,497	47,584	73,026	148,638	164,260	179,710
Income receipts on U.S. assets abroad:	7,437	11,748	25,351	71,388	82,282	143,547	127,292	110,612
Imports of goods, services, and income	**-32,708**	**-59,901**	**-33,745**	**-333,774**	**-473,998**	**-738,401**	**-723,388**	**-763,965**
Merchandise, adjusted, excluding military[2]	-21,510	-39,866	-98,185	-249,750	-338,088	-497,558	-490,739	-536,276
Services	-9,111	-14,520	-4,795	-21,996	-41,491	-116,583	-118,378	-123,299
Income payments on foreign assets in the U.S.	-2,088	-5,515	-12,564	-45,532	-67,875	-124,261	-114,272	-104,391
Unilateral transfers, net	**-4,583**	**-6,156**	**-7,075**	**-8,349**	**-22,950**	**-32,916**	**6,575**	**-32,895**
U.S. assets abroad, net (increase/capital outflow [-])	**-5,716**	**-9,337**	**-39,703**	**-86,967**	**-34,069**	**-56,321**	**-59,974**	**-50,961**
U.S. official reserve assets, net	1,225	2,481	-849	-8,155	-3,858	-2,158	5,763	3,901
U.S. Government assets, other than official reserve assets, net	-1,605	-1,589	-3,474	-5,162	-2,821	-2,304	2,905	-1,609
U.S. private assets, net	-5,336	-10,229	-35,380	-73,651	-27,391	-56,467	-68,643	-53,253
Foreign assets in U.S., net (increase/capital inflow [+])	742	6,359	15,670	58,112	130,012	99,379	83,439	129,579
Statistical discrepancy (sum of above items with sign reversed)	-457	-219	5,917	25,386	24,825	47,370	-15,140	-12,216
Memorandum:								
Balance on current account	5,431	2,331	18,116	2,317	-121,721	-90,428	-8,324	-66,400

(1) Excludes transfers of goods and services under U.S. military grant programs. (2) Excludes exports of goods under U.S. military agency sales contracts identified in Census export documents, excludes imports of goods under direct defense expenditures identified in Census import documents, and reflects various other adjustments.

North American Free Trade Agreement

The United States, Canada, and Mexico announced a comprehensive plan for free trade across North America on Aug. 12, 1992, and portrayed it as an opportunity for greater economic growth for all three nations. The North American Free Trade Agreement (NAFTA) was greeted enthusiastically by business groups generally, but U.S. labor unions, long opposed to opening the southern border, contended that the accord would send jobs to Mexico, where labor costs were lower and environmental regulations laxer than in the United States.

The three countries attempted to satisfy some of the NAFTA opposition by concluding side agreements, announced on Aug. 13, 1993. These additional agreements called for the establishment of a 5-step procedure to enforce existing labor and environmental laws in the U.S., Canada, and Mexico. Secretariats to process, investigate, and enforce this procedure would be established, one in Canada to handle environmental complaints and the other in Washington to deal with labor issues. Failure to comply with a decision of a secretariat could result in fines of up to $20 million on national governments and limited trade sanctions. The side agreements were signed (separately) by Canada on Sept. 13, 1993, and by the U.S. and Mexico on Sept. 14, 1993.

NAFTA would bring together 360 million consumers in a $6.6 trillion market and would create the world's richest and largest trading bloc. The agreement must be ratified by the legislatures of the three nations. Canada ratified the agreement June 23, 1993. The Clinton administration said, after conclusion of the side agreements, that it would submit NAFTA to Congress for approval.

Key Provisions

Agriculture—Tariffs on all farm products would be eliminated over 15 years. All three countries agreed to allow domestic price-support systems, provided that they did not distort trade.

Automobiles—After eight years, at least 62.5% of an automobile's value must have been produced in North America for it to qualify for duty-free status. Tariffs would be phased out over 10 years.

Banking—U.S. and Canadian banks would be allowed to acquire Mexican banks accounting for as much as 8 percent of the industry's capital. All limits on bank ownership would end Jan. 1, 2000.

Disputes—Special judges would be empaneled to resolve disagreements.

Energy—Mexico would not alter its constitution, which prohibited foreign ownership of its oil fields, but after 10 years U.S. and Canadian companies would be allowed to bid on all contracts offered by Mexican oil and electricity monopolies.

Environment—The agreement could not be used to overrule national and state environmental, health or safety laws.

Immigration—All three countries would ease restrictions on the movement of business executives and professionals.

Jobs—Visa restrictions would be reduced for business executives and professionals. Current barriers designed to limit Mexican migration to the U.S. would remain in force.

Patent and Copyright protection—Mexico would strengthen its laws providing protection to intellectual property. It would honor foreign patents for pharmaceuticals for 20 years.

Textiles—A strict "rule of origin" provision would require garments to be made from yarn and fabric also produced in North America. Tariffs would be phased out over five years.

Tariffs—Tariffs on 10,000 customs goods would be eliminated over 15 years. One-half of U.S. exports to Mexico would be considered duty-free within five years.

Trucking—Trucks would be allowed free access on cross-border routes and throughout the three countries by the end of 1999.

National Income by Industry

Source: Bureau of Economic Analysis, U.S. Dept. of Commerce

(billions of dollars)

	1960	1970	1975	1980	1990	1991	1992
National income without capital consumption adjustment	**$428.6**	**$835.1**	**$1,315.0**	**$2,263.9**	**$4,497.5**	**$4,587.5**	**$4,769.0**
Domestic industries	**425.1**	**827.8**	**1,297.4**	**2,216.3**	**4,486.7**	**4,570.1**	**4,757.7**
Private industries	**371.6**	**695.4**	**1,088.3**	**1,894.5**	**3,828.9**	**3,870.6**	**4,029.3**
Agriculture, forestry, fisheries	17.8	25.9	46.5	61.4	97.1	90.9	95.6
Mining	5.6	8.4	21.2	43.8	38.1	36.7	36.1
Construction	22.5	47.4	69.9	126.6	234.4	210.1	219.6
Manufacturing	125.3	215.6	317.5	532.1	846.9	841.0	873.8
Durable goods	73.4	127.7	185.0	313.7	484.3	464.2	480.5
Nondurable goods	52.0	87.9	132.5	218.4	362.6	376.7	393.5
Transportation, public utilities	35.8	64.4	101.1	177.3	328.7	335.2	337.2
Transportation	18.5	31.5	48.0	85.8	139.4	140.8	144.8
Communications	8.2	17.6	26.8	48.1	96.4	95.3	98.6
Electric, gas, and sanitary services	9.1	86.8	90.2	43.4	92.9	99.0	93.9
Wholesale trade	25.0	47.5	83.0	143.3	263.6	266.0	272.9
Retail trade	41.3	79.9	123.1	189.4	392.1	403.3	418.3
Finance, insurance, and real estate	51.3	96.4	143.9	279.5	679.8	685.0	703.2
Services	46.9	109.8	182.1	341.0	948.3	1,002.4	1,072.5
Government	**53.5**	**132.4**	**209.1**	**321.8**	**657.9**	**699.4**	**728.4**

National Income by Type of Income

Source: Bureau of Economic Analysis, U.S. Dept. of Commerce

(billions of dollars)

	1960	1970	1975	1980	1990	1991	1992
National income[1]	**$424.9**	**$832.6**	**$1,289.1**	**$2,203.5**	**$4,459.6**	**$4,544.2**	**$4,743.4**
Compensation of employees	**296.7**	**618.3**	**948.7**	**1,638.2**	**3,290.3**	**3,390.8**	**3,525.2**
Wages and salaries	272.8	551.5	814.7	1,372.0	2,738.9	2,812.2	2,916.6
Government	49.2	117.1	176.1	260.1	514.0	543.5	562.5
Other	223.7	434.3	638.6	1,111.8	2,224.9	2,268.7	2,354.1
Supplements to wages, salary	23.8	66.8	134.0	266.3	551.4	578.7	608.6
Employer contrib. for social ins.	12.6	34.3	68.0	127.9	277.3	290.4	302.9
Other labor income	11.2	32.5	65.9	138.4	274.0	288.3	305.7
Proprietors' income	**52.1**	**80.2**	**125.4**	**180.7**	**373.2**	**368.0**	**404.5**
Farm	11.6	14.7	25.4	20.5	42.5	35.8	39.5
Nonfarm	40.5	65.4	100.0	160.1	330.7	332.2	364.9
Rental income of persons with capital consump. adjust.	**15.3**	**18.2**	**13.5**	**6.6**	**−12.9**	**−10.4**	**4.7**
Corp. profits with inventory adjustment	**49.8**	**69.5**	**123.9**	**194.0**	**319.0**	**346.3**	**393.8**
Corp. profits before tax	49.9	76.0	134.8	237.1	332.3	334.7	371.6
Corp. profits tax liability	22.7	34.4	50.9	84.8	135.3	124.0	140.2
Corp. profits after tax	27.2	41.7	83.9	152.3	197.0	210.7	231.4
Dividends	12.9	22.5	29.6	54.7	133.7	146.5	149.3
Undistributed profits	14.3	19.2	54.3	97.6	63.3	64.2	82.1
Inventory valuation adjustment	−.2	−6.6	−11.0	−43.1	−14.2	3.1	−7.4
Net interest	**11.3**	**41.2**	**83.8**	**200.9**	**490.1**	**449.5**	**415.2**

(1) National income is the aggregate of labor and property earnings that arises in the current production of goods and services. It is the sum of employee compensation, proprietors' income, rental income, corporate profits, and net interest. It measures the total factor costs of the goods and services produced by the economy. Income is measured before deduction of taxes on income.

Distribution of Total Personal Income[1]

Source: Bureau of Economic Analysis; U.S. Dept. of Commerce

(billions of dollars)

Year	Personal income	Personal taxes	Disposable Personal income	Personal outlays	Personal Savings: Amount	Personal Savings: As pct. of disposable income
1960	$ 402.3	$ 50.4	$ 352.0	$ 332.3	$ 19.7	5.6%
1965	540.7	64.9	475.8	442.1	33.7	7.1
1970	811.1	115.8	695.3	639.5	55.8	8.0
1975	1,265.0	168.9	1,096.1	1,001.8	94.3	8.6
1980	2,165.3	336.5	1,828.9	1,718.7	110.2	6.0
1981	2,429.5	387.7	2,041.7	1,904.3	137.4	6.7
1982	2,584.6	404.1	2,180.5	2,044.5	136.0	6.2
1983	2,838.6	410.5	2,428.1	2,297.4	130.6	5.4
1984	3,108.7	440.2	2,668.6	2,504.5	164.1	6.1
1985	3,325.3	486.6	2,838.7	2,713.3	125.4	4.4
1986	3,526.2	512.9	3,013.3	2,888.5	124.9	4.1
1987	3,776.6	571.7	3,205.9	3,104.1	101.8	3.2
1988	4,070.8	591.6	3,479.2	3,333.6	145.6	4.2
1989	4,384.3	658.8	3,725.5	3,553.7	171.8	4.6
1990	4,679.8	621.0	4,058.8	3,853.1	205.8	5.1
1991	4,828.4	618.7	4,209.6	4,009.9	199.6	4.7
1992	5,058.1	627.3	4,430.6	4,218.1	212.6	4.8

(1) Figures may not add because of rounding.

U.S. Direct Investment[1] Abroad in Selected Countries

Source: Bureau of Economic Analysis, U.S. Dept. of Commerce

(millions of dollars)

	1990	1991	1992
All countries	$424,096	$460,955	$486,670
Africa			
Egypt	1,465	1,239	922
Nigeria	161	611	274
S. Africa	956	857	871
Asia and Pacific (excl. Japan)			
China	—	431	469
Hong Kong	6,187	6,516	8,544
India	513	410	479
Indonesia	3,226	3,783	4,278
Malaysia	1,384	1,711	1,714
Philippines	1,629	1,377	1,565
Singapore	3,385	5,294	6,631
South Korea	2,178	2,862	2,779
Taiwan	2,014	2,626	2,870
Thailand	1,585	2,038	2,459
Australia	14,846	15,795	16,697
Bermuda	21,737	23,059	25,799
Canada	67,033	68,853	68,432
European Communities			
Belgium	9,050	10,607	10,771
Denmark	1,597	1,813	1,707
France	18,874	20,798	23,257
Germany	27,259	34,027	35,393
Greece	288	363	429
Ireland	6,880	6,634	7,229
Italy	13,117	14,775	13,605
Luxembourg	1,390	1,782	1,863
Netherlands	22,658	19,772	19,114
Portugal	598	1,026	1,160
Spain	7,704	7,992	8,165
United Kingdom	68,224	78,072	77,842
Other Europe			
Austria	889	1,258	1,365
Finland	551	359	322
Norway	3,815	4,349	4,047
Sweden	1,600	2,242	2,033
Switzerland	25,199	25,604	28,662
Turkey	494	529	705
Japan	20,997	24,938	26,213
South America			
Argentina	2,956	2,767	3,353
Brazil	14,918	14,882	16,114
Chile	1,368	1,916	2,446
Colombia	1,728	1,627	2,077
Ecuador	387	296	310
Peru	410	522	466
Venezuela	1,490	1,424	1,725
Central America			
Mexico	9,398	12,257	13,330
Panama	7,409	10,427	11,457
Middle East			
Israel	756	1,014	1,543
Saudi Arabia	1,981	2,163	2,503
United Arab Emirates	519	466	480

(1) The book value of U.S. direct investors' equity in, and net outstanding loans to, their foreign affiliates. A foreign affiliate is a foreign business enterprise in which a single U.S. investor owns at least 10% of the voting securities or the equivalent.

Gold Reserves of Central Banks and Governments

Source: IMF, *International Financial Statistics;* million fine troy ounces

Year end	All countries[1]	United States	Canada	Japan	Belgium	France	Germany	Italy	Netherlands	Switzerland	United Kingdom
1975	1,018.71	274.71	21.95	21.11	42.17	100.93	117.61	82.48	54.33	83.20	21.03
1976	1,014.23	274.68	21.62	21.11	42.17	101.02	117.61	82.48	54.33	83.28	21.03
1977	1,029.19	277.55	22.01	21.62	42.45	101.67	118.30	82.91	54.63	83.28	22.23
1978	1,036.82	276.41	22.13	23.97	42.59	101.99	118.64	83.12	54.78	83.28	22.83
1979	944.44	264.60	22.18	24.23	34.21	81.92	95.25	66.71	43.97	83.28	18.25
1980	952.99	264.32	20.98	24.23	34.18	81.85	95.18	66.67	43.94	83.28	18.84
1981	953.72	264.11	20.46	24.23	34.18	81.85	95.18	66.67	43.94	83.28	19.03
1982	949.16	264.03	20.26	24.23	34.18	81.85	95.18	66.67	43.94	83.28	19.01
1983	947.84	263.39	20.17	24.23	34.18	81.85	95.18	66.67	43.94	83.28	19.01
1984	946.79	262.79	20.14	24.23	34.18	81.85	95.18	66.67	43.94	83.28	19.03
1985	949.39	262.65	20.11	24.33	34.18	81.85	95.18	66.67	43.94	83.28	19.03
1986	949.11	262.04	19.72	24.23	34.18	81.85	95.18	66.67	43.94	83.28	19.01
1987	944.49	262.38	18.52	24.23	33.63	81.85	95.18	66.67	43.94	83.28	19.01
1988	944.92	261.87	17.14	24.23	33.67	81.85	95.18	66.67	43.94	83.28	19.00
1989	938.95	261.93	16.10	24.23	30.23	81.85	95.18	66.67	43.94	83.28	18.99
1990	940.29	261.91	14.76	24.23	30.23	81.85	95.18	66.67	43.94	83.28	18.94
1991	939.58	261.91	12.96	24.23	30.23	81.85	95.18	66.67	43.94	83.28	18.89
1992	930.30	261.91	9.94	24.23	25.04	81.85	95.18	66.67	43.94	83.28	18.61

(1) Covers IMF members with reported gold holdings. For countries not listed above, see *International Financial Statistics,* a monthly publication of the International Monetary Fund.

Industrial Production Indexes,[1] by Industry Groups

Source: Bureau of Economic Analysis, U.S. Dept. of Commerce; billions of dollars

Industry Groups	1991	1992	May 1993
Mining	**100.4**	**97.6**	**96.9**
Metal mining	156.7	161.8	163.8
Coal	109.3	105.5	106.0
Oil and gas extraction	96.0	92.6	91.4
Crude oil	89.1	85.7	82.6
Natural gas	107.0	106.7	.....
Stone and earth minerals	94.2	93.8	94.6
Utilities	**111.9**	**111.9**	**113.4**
Electric	112.7	111.6	112.7
Gas	109.0	112.9	116.2
Manufacturing	**103.7**	**106.9**	**111.4**
Durable	103.9	108.2	114.8
Lumber and products	90.5	96.4	98.1
Furniture and fixtures	94.0	98.9	106.9
Clay, glass, and stone products	92.6	95.9	99.5
Primary metals	98.5	101.2	106.5
Iron and steel	100.7	104.8	112.0
Nonferrous	95.5	96.2	98.9
Fabricated metal products	95.0	96.8	100.1
Machinery and computer equipment	113.8	124.9	143.4
Electrical machinery	112.8	120.0	129.4
Transportation equipment	102.0	102.7	105.7
Motor vehicles and parts	94.8	105.0	119.0
Instruments	105.4	104.3	102.2
Nondurable	103.5	105.4	107.3
Foods	105.3	106.0	106.4
Tobacco products	96.7	99.6	100.9
Textile mill products	96.9	104.7	105.8
Apparel products	91.8	92.6	91.9
Paper and products	106.2	108.2	112.9
Printing and publishing	96.8	95.0	95.0
Chemicals and products	111.3	115.0	119.0
Petroleum products	101.6	102.0	105.9
Rubber and plastics products	104.5	109.7	112.6
Leather and products	87.9	92.5	98.4

(1) 1987 = 100.

Average Yields of Long-Term Treasury, Corporate, and Municipal Bonds

Source: Office of Market Finance, U.S. Dept. of the Treasury

Period	Treasury 30-Year Bonds	New Aa Corporate Bonds[1]	New Aa Municipal Bonds[2]
1982			
June	13.92	15.96	12.14
Dec.	10.54	12.15	9.84
1983			
June	10.93	11.90	9.08
Dec.	11.88	12.87	9.77
1984			
June	13.44	14.49	10.44
Dec.	11.52	12.47	9.65
1985			
June	10.45	11.33	8.46
Dec.	9.54	10.42	8.44
1986			
June	7.57	9.39	7.75
Dec.	7.37	8.87	6.70
1987			
June	8.57	9.64	7.69
Dec.	9.12	10.22	7.83
1988			
June	9.00	10.08	7.67
Dec.	9.01	10.05	7.40
1989			
June	8.27	9.24	6.94
Dec.	7.90	9.23	6.76
1990			
June	8.46	9.69	6.98
Dec.	8.24	9.55	6.85
1991			
Jan.	8.27	9.60	7.00
Apr.	8.21	9.07	6.81
Sept. . . .	7.95	8.79	6.58
Dec.	7.70	8.55	6.43
1992			
Jan.	7.58	8.36	6.29
Feb.	7.85	8.63	6.42
Mar.	7.97	8.62	6.59
Apr.	7.96	8.59	6.54
May	7.89	8.57	6.39
June	7.84	8.45	6.32
July	7.60	8.19	5.90
Aug.	7.39	7.96	5.81
Sept. . . .	7.34	7.99	6.05
Oct.	7.53	8.17	6.18
Nov.	7.61	8.25	6.22
Dec.	7.44	8.12	6.02
1993			
Jan.	7.34	7.91	6.05
Feb.	7.09	7.73	5.74
Mar.	6.82	7.39	5.54

(1) Treasury series based on 3-week moving average of reoffering yields of new corporate bonds rated Aa by Moody's Investors Service with an original maturity of at least 20 years. (2) Index of new reoffering yields on 20-year general obligations rated Aa by Moody's Investors Service. Source: U.S. Treasury, 1982-1990; Moody's, 1991-1993.

Top Mutual Funds in 1992

Source: Lipper Analytical Services Inc.

Fund	Total Return
Fidelity Sel. Saving & Loan	57.8%
Harris Oakmark	48.9
Fidelity Sel. Reg. Banks	48.5
J. Hancock Reg. Bank; B	47.4
Fidelity Sel. Financial	42.8
Heartland: Value	42.5
Skyline Special Equities	42.4
Fidelity Sel. Automotive	41.6
PaineWebber Reg. Fin.; A	38.7
PaineWebber Reg. Fin.; B	37.8%
Parnassus	36.8
Fidelity Sel. Software	35.5
Sife Trust Fund	33.9
Ret. Plan Amer.: Global Value	33.8
Crabbe Huson Growth	33.4
Regis: ICM Small Company	32.3
GT Global America	31.7
Main Street: Income & Growth	31.1%
J. Hancock Spec. Equities	30.4
Thomson Opportunity; A	29.6
Royce Fund: OTC	29.4
Pioneer Capital Growth	29.0
Fidelity Low-Priced Stock	29.0
Capstone PBHG Growth	28.5
Thomson Opportunity; B	28.5

Performance of Mutual Funds by Type

Source: Lipper Analytical Services Inc.

	1992 Results				Five-Year Results			
Fund type	No. of funds	Best	Return Average	Worst	No. of funds	Best	Return Average	Worst
Capital Appreciation	122	+29.57	+8.28	−19.94	101	+26.23	+14.67	−9.38
Growth	305	+48.90	+7.79	−25.36	204	+26.56	+14.86	−8.08
Small Company Growth	119	+42.48	+12.54	−11.08	70	+34.24	+17.24	+2.54
Growth and Income	252	+31.08	+8.61	−8.22	168	+32.14	+13.88	+6.73
Equity Income	69	+21.10	+9.46	−2.86	40	+17.99	+12.68	+6.07
Health/Biotechnology	10	+18.36	−8.28	−22.88	7	+31.01	+24.78	+18.01
Natural Resources	19	+13.34	+1.95	−13.23	14	+13.57	+7.23	−1.65
Environmental	7	+4.92	−6.18	−18.72	1	+13.70	+13.70	+13.70
Science and Technology	18	+35.54	+13.54	−4.03	16	+25.91	+16.29	+8.34
Specialty/Miscellaneous	27	+41.57	+11.52	−11.54	22	+28.50	+14.12	−12.91
Utility	28	+21.00	+9.16	+0.43	13	+16.85	+14.52	+13.12
Financial Services	12	+57.83	+35.18	+5.12	10	+26.85	+21.52	+16.77
Real Estate	6	+21.04	+12.83	+4.15	2	+13.78	+12.44	+11.09
Option Income	5	+14.13	+10.05	+4.97	5	+13.54	+10.73	+8.64
Gold Oriented	32	+2.90	−14.58	−60.71	22	+6.70	−7.65	−29.95
Global	43	+9.01	−0.27	−14.20	20	+13.52	+7.63	+1.11
Global Small Company	8	+11.44	+1.49	−5.58	2	+13.12	+10.32	+7.52
International	86	+5.85	−5.05	−26.63	39	+15.57	+5.90	+0.60
European Region	27	+7.53	−8.02	−33.60	7	+6.66	+4.65	−1.55
Pacific Region	19	+26.42	+0.40	−18.17	7	+13.43	+5.95	−1.41
Japanese	5	−13.40	−21.33	−28.88	3	+1.27	−0.10	−0.88
Latin American	3	+2.15	+0.39	−2.32	0	N/A	N/A	N/A
Canadian	3	−2.87	−6.55	−9.21	3	+10.39	+2.96	−4.63
Flexible-Portfolio	54	+21.09	+7.51	−15.36	18	+17.75	+10.88	+4.60
Global Flexible Portfolio	14	+12.19	+2.86	−6.18	5	+11.13	+6.74	+2.79
Balanced	69	+19.99	+7.17	−6.06	43	+17.78	+12.63	+8.70
Balanced Target Maturity	7	+9.54	+5.31	+1.91	1	+12.41	+12.41	+12.41
Convertible Securities	25	+31.17	+13.56	+3.79	17	+19.19	+12.85	+7.55
Income	13	+21.76	+8.77	+2.27	11	+14.26	+11.76	+9.04

Dow Jones Industrial Average Since 1961

High		Year	Low		High		Year	Low	
Dec. 13	734.91	**1961**	Jan. 3	610.25	Sept. 8	907.74	**1978**	Feb. 28	742.12
Jan. 3	726.01	**1962**	June 26	535.76	Oct. 5	897.61	**1979**	Nov. 7	796.67
Dec. 18	767.21	**1963**	Jan. 2	646.79	Nov. 20	1000.17	**1980**	Apr. 21	759.13
Nov. 18	891.71	**1964**	Jan. 2	766.08	Apr. 27	1024.05	**1981**	Sept. 25	824.01
Dec. 31	969.26	**1965**	June 28	840.59	Dec. 27	1070.55	**1982**	Aug. 12	776.92
Feb. 9	995.15	**1966**	Oct. 7	744.32	Nov. 29	1287.20	**1983**	Jan. 3	1027.04
Sept. 25	943.08	**1967**	Jan. 3	786.41	Jan. 6	1286.64	**1984**	July 24	1086.57
Dec. 3	985.21	**1968**	Mar. 21	825.13	Dec. 16	1553.10	**1985**	Jan. 4	1184.96
May 14	968.85	**1969**	Dec. 17	769.93	Dec. 2	1955.57	**1986**	Jan. 22	1502.29
Dec. 29	842.00	**1970**	May 6	631.16	Aug. 25	2722.42	**1987**	Oct. 19	1738.74
Apr. 28	950.82	**1971**	Nov. 23	797.97	Oct. 21	2183.50	**1988**	Jan. 20	1879.14
Dec. 11	1036.27	**1972**	Jan. 26	889.15	Oct. 9	2791.41	**1989**	Jan. 3	2144.64
Jan. 11	1051.70	**1973**	Dec. 5	788.31	July 16	2999.75	**1990**	Oct. 11	2365.10
Mar. 13	891.66	**1974**	Dec. 6	577.60	Dec. 31	3168.83	**1991**	Jan. 9	2470.30
July 15	881.81	**1975**	Jan. 2	632.04	June 1	3413.21	**1992**	Oct. 9	3136.58
Sept. 21	1014.79	**1976**	Jan. 2	858.71	Aug. 26	3652.37	**1993***	Jan. 20	3241.95
Jan. 3	999.75	**1977**	Nov. 2	800.85				*As of	Oct.1

Components of Dow Jones Industrial Average

Allied-Signal
Aluminum Co. of Amer.
American Express
AT&T
Bethlehem Steel
Boeing
Caterpillar
Chevron
Coca-Cola
Disney (Walt)
DuPont
Eastman Kodak
Exxon
General Electric
General Motors
Goodyear
IBM
International Paper
McDonald's
Merck
Minn. Mining & Manuf.
Morgan (J.P.)
Philip Morris
Procter & Gamble
Sears
Texaco
Union Carbide
United Technologies
Westinghouse
Woolworth

Components of Dow Jones Transportation Average

AMR Corp.
Airborne Freight
Alaska Air
American President
Burlington Northern
CSX
Carolina Freight
Consolidated Freightways
Consolidated Rail
Delta Air Lines
Federal Express
Norfolk Southern
Roadway Services
Ryder System
Santa Fe Pacific
Southwest Air Lines
UAL
Union Pacific
USAir Group
XTRA Corp

Components of Dow Jones Utility Average

American Electric Power
Arkla
Centerior Energy
Commonwealth Edison
Consolidated Edison
Consolidated Natural Gas
Detroit Edison
Houston Industries
Niagara Mohawk Power
Pacific Gas & Electric
Panhandle Eastern
Peoples Energy
Philadelphia Electric
Public Service Enterprises
SCE

Milestones of the Dow Jones Industrial Average

First close over...	
100	Jan. 12, 1906
500	March 12, 1956
1,000	Nov. 14, 1972
1,500	Dec. 11, 1985
2,000	Jan. 8, 1987
2,500	July 17, 1987
3,000	April 17, 1991
3,400	June 1, 1992
3,500	May 19, 1993
3,600	Aug. 18, 1993

Most Active Common Stocks in 1992

New York Exchange	Volume (millions of shares)	American Exchange	Volume (millions of shares)	NASDAQ	Volume (millions of shares)
Glaxo	569.39	Chambers Devel. "A"	105.82	Intel	553.72
RJR Nabisco	543.23	Amdahl	102.89	Tele-Commun. "A"	443.85
General Motors	537.62	U.S. Bioscience	81.66	Novell	434.32
IBM	512.98	Echo Bay Mines Ltd.	72.33	Microsoft	402.46
Philip Morris	472.41	Sulcus Computer	71.97	Seagate Technology	390.22
Téléfonos de México	464.88	Exploration Co. of La.	68.77	Sun Microsystems	384.36
Citicorp	453.48	Hillhaven	66.60	Apple Computer	367.89
AT & T	428.89	Ivax	66.28	Oracle Systems	343.86
Chrysler	427.79	Fruit of the Loom	62.49	Téléfonos de México	339.40
Merck	406.01	Interdigital Communic.	51.04	Amgen	329.46
Ford Motor	395.74	Hasbro	47.71	Medco Containment	305.99
Unisys	346.20	Energy Service Co.	37.99	MCI Communications	299.99
Bristol-Myers Squibb	334.12	Nabors Industries	36.01	Comverse Technol.	290.44
Coca-Cola	331.88	American Exploration	33.36	Costco Wholesale	277.82
American Express	324.73	New York Times Co.	32.13	Dell Computer	268.54

Who Owns Stocks?

Source: Federal Reserve

(as of Mar. 31, 1993)

Stockholder	Percent	Stockholder	Percent	Stockholder	Percent
Households	45.8	State, Local Govt. Retirement Funds	9.3	Other Insurance Cos.	2.6
Private Pension Funds	22.0	Foreign	6.6	Brokers & Dealers	0.3
Mutual Funds	10.3	Life Insurance Cos.	2.7	Mutual Savings Banks	0.2
				Commercial Banks	0.1

Selected Personal Consumption Expenditures in the U.S.

Source: Bureau of Economic Analysis, U.S. Dept. of Commerce

(billions of dollars)

	1986	1987	1988	1989	1990	1991	1992
Personal consumption expenditures	**$2,797.4**	**$3,009.4**	**$3,296.1**	**$3.523.1**	**$3,761.2**	**$3,906.4**	**$4,139.9**
Food & Tobacco	**533.7**	**566.4**	**569.8**	**605.6**	**648.2**	**666.8**	**684.5**
Food purchased for off-premise consumption	339.1	353.7	351.7	373.7	400.2	411.1	418.0
Purchased meals and beverages	151.6	165.5	171.7	180.6	193.1	198.5	203.5
Tobacco products	33.6	35.6	36.2	40.5	43.4	45.4	50.9
Clothing, accessories, jewelry	**207.5**	**222.3**	**231.8**	**248.7**	**259.3**	**264.3**	**282.4**
Shoes	24.3	25.9	27.4	30.1	31.4	31.3	32.3
Clothing and accessories less shoes	142.4	152.5	158.9	170.1	175.7	181.6	195.7
Jewelry and watches	22.8	24.7	28.8	29.7	31.3	31.6	34.0
Personal care	**41.4**	**44.4**	**51.4**	**55.8**	**59.2**	**60.9**	**63.2**
Toilet articles, preparations	24.6	26.3	31.8	34.1	36.8	38.2	39.3
Barbershops, beauty parlors, baths, health clubs	16.8	18.2	19.6	21.6	22.4	22.6	23.9
Housing	**434.2**	**468.9**	**484.2**	**514.4**	**547.5**	**574.4**	**600.0**
Owner-occupied nonfarm dwellings space rent	293.7	316.9	334.1	355.8	379.5	399.1	417.8
Tenant-occupied nonfarm dwellings rent	114.3	123.6	125.3	132.6	141.1	147.7	153.8
Rental value of farm dwellings	9.7	10.3	4.9	5.0	5.2	5.3	5.3
Household operation	**347.5**	**363.3**	**398.9**	**422.6**	**437.3**	**452.7**	**475.2**
Furniture, incl. bedding	30.4	31.8	34.0	36.9	36.7	36.8	40.0
Kitchen, other household appliances	25.5	26.7	24.1	25.7	26.4	27.1	29.2
China, glassware, tableware, utensils	14.3	15.3	16.4	17.9	18.7	19.4	21.0
Other durable house furnishings	30.6	33.5	37.7	40.2	42.0	41.9	45.2
Semidurable house furnishings	15.2	16.0	19.4	20.4	21.2	21.9	23.6
Household utilities	122.4	125.8	127.3	134.1	136.7	145.3	149.9
Telephone, telegraph	42.7	44.1	50.2	51.7	53.8	56.2	58.7
Medical care	**357.6**	**399.0**	**487.7**	**536.4**	**597.8**	**651.7**	**704.6**
Drug preparations, sundries	30.2	32.3	50.8	55.0	60.6	64.4	65.9
Physicians	80.6	94.0	110.6	121.6	133.8	144.0	153.1
Dentists	22.8	25.0	27.9	30.0	31.6	32.9	36.4
Hospitals and nursing homes	152.4	166.3	190.9	209.5	231.3	255.3	279.6
Health insurance	22.4	25.3	26.4	31.2	36.6	40.0	45.9
Personal business	**192.5**	**215.4**	**255.0**	**272.2**	**296.0**	**323.4**	**356.0**
Brokerage charges, investment counseling	19.7	20.5	19.3	21.6	22.0	24.3	28.5
Bank service charges, trust services, safe deposit box	13.0	14.6	19.8	22.0	23.7	25.2	27.6
Legal services	30.9	35.0	41.7	45.5	49.2	49.9	54.0
Funeral, burial expenses	6.6	7.0	7.8	7.9	8.5	9.0	9.6
Transportation	**366.3**	**379.7**	**413.2**	**437.3**	**453.9**	**434.6**	**463.1**
User-operated transportation	335.9	346.3	376.9	399.6	414.0	395.5	423.9
New autos	101.3	93.5	101.0	99.9	96.6	79.5	87.3
Used autos	33.6	38.5	30.5	32.5	33.1	36.7	39.5
Repair, greasing, washing, parking, storage, rental, leasing	52.0	55.9	73.5	79.1	82.6	82.4	89.5
Gasoline and oil	73.5	75.3	86.9	96.2	108.4	102.9	103.4
Tolls	1.7	1.9	1.8	2.1	2.0	2.0	2.1
Insurance premiums less claims paid	12.6	15.4	16.8	16.8	18.1	22.7	24.6
Purchased local transportation	7.8	8.2	8.3	8.1	8.9	9.1	9.2
Mass transit systems	3.8	4.0	5.4	5.3	5.7	5.7	5.9
Taxicab	3.3	3.5	2.9	2.8	3.2	3.4	3.3
Purchased intercity transportation	22.6	25.5	28.0	29.5	30.9	30.0	30.0
Railway (excl. commutation)	.7	.7	.6	.7	.7	.7	.7
Bus	1.1	1.4	2.2	1.7	1.4	1.5	1.5
Airline	18.8	20.8	23.0	24.7	26.4	25.6	25.7
Recreation	**201.2**	**223.2**	**246.8**	**266.0**	**285.7**	**299.4**	**318.8**
Books, maps	8.6	9.5	14.6	15.8	17.5	18.3	20.2
Magazines, newspapers, sheet music	13.9	15.4	20.8	22.0	23.8	24.7	25.4
Nondurable toys and sport supplies	23.1	26.2	27.5	30.0	32.1	33.5	35.2
Wheel goods, durable toys, sports equipment, boats, pleasure aircraft	29.7	33.2	30.0	31.0	31.3	31.4	34.0
Video & audio prods., computers, musical instruments	—	—	44.5	47.3	50.4	55.4	59.1
Flowers, seeds, potted plants	5.8	7.0	9.3	10.1	10.3	10.4	11.0
Admissions to specified spectator amusements	10.2	11.3	11.1	12.1	14.0	14.9	16.1
Motion picture theaters	3.9	4.2	3.6	3.9	4.7	5.0	5.5
Legitimate theater, opera	3.3	4.0	3.6	3.9	4.5	4.7	5.1
Spectator sports	2.9	3.0	3.9	4.3	4.9	5.2	5.5
Clubs, fraternal organizations	5.0	5.5	7.6	8.0	8.4	8.6	9.0
Commerical participant amusements	16.0	17.1	19.1	20.5	23.1	23.8	25.7
Education & Research	**46.6**	**50.9**	**71.6**	**79.4**	**86.2**	**91.8**	**98.2**
Higher education	16.9	17.7	36.7	40.3	44.0	47.3	50.8
Nursery, elementary and secondary schools	14.5	15.5	17.1	19.2	19.8	20.6	21.6
Religious and welfare activities	**62.9**	**68.1**	**86.0**	**92.7**	**101.6**	**105.7**	**116.2**

AGRICULTURE

The U.S. Farm Population

Source: Bureau of the Census, U.S. Dept. of Commerce

The total estimated number of persons living on U.S. farms in 1991 was 4,632,000, about the same as in 1990. As late as 1950, there were 23 million farm residents in the U.S. The farm population peaked at about 32 million in the 1910-1920 period. When the first reports of farm population were published in 1945, 20 percent of Americans were farm residents. In 1991, only about 2 percent of Americans were farm residents. In 1991, farm residence was no longer a reliable indication of whether someone was involved in farming: 32 percent of farm managers were not farm residents and 86 percent of farm workers lived elsewhere. The Midwest was home to a larger proportion of the nation's farm population—49.3 percent—than any other region of the country in 1991. Whites comprised most of the U.S. farm population (97 percent). Approximately 29 percent of men living on farms had some college education, compared with 43 percent of men who did not live on farms.

Persons in Farm Occupations, 1820-1991

Source: Economic Research Service, U.S. Dept. of Agriculture; Bureau of the Census, U.S. Dept. of Commerce

(in thousands)

Year	Total workers[1]	Farm occupations Number	Farm occupations % of total
1820	2,881	2,069	71.8
1850	7,697	4,902	63.7
1870	12,925	6,850	53.0
1900	29,030	10,888	37.5
1920	42,206	11,390	27.0
1930	48,686	10,321	21.2
1940	51,742	8,995	17.4
1950	59,230	6,858	11.6
1960	67,990	4,132	6.1
1970	79,802	2,881	3.6
1980	104,058	2,818	2.7
1985 (March)	106,214	2,949	2.8
1990 (March)	117,491	2,864	2.4
1991 (March)	116,000	2,848	2.5

(1) Total workers for 1985 to 1991 are employed workers 15 years and over; total workers for 1970 and 1980 are members of the experienced civilian labor force 16 years and over; total workers for 1900 to 1960 are members of the experienced civilian labor force 14 years and over; and total workers for 1820 to 1890 are gainfully employed workers 10 years and over.

Farms—Number and Acreage by State, 1980 & 1992

Source: Natl. Agricultural Statistics Service, U.S. Dept. of Agriculture

State	Farms (1,000) 1980	Farms (1,000) 1992	Acreage (mil.) 1980	Acreage (mil.) 1992	Acreage per Farm 1980	Acreage per Farm 1992
U.S.	**2,437**	**2,094**	**1,039**	**980**	**426**	**468**
Alabama	59	46	12	10	207	213
Alaska	(z)	1	2	1	3,378	1,778
Arizona	7	8	38	36	5,080	4,500
Arkansas	58	46	17	16	280	337
California	79	80	34	30	417	373
Colorado	26	26	36	33	1,358	1,286
Connecticut	4	4	(z)	(z)	117	103
Delaware	4	3	1	1	186	207
Florida	38	39	13	11	344	269
Georgia	59	46	15	12	254	263
Hawaii	4	5	2	2	458	380
Idaho	24	21	15	14	623	643
Illinois	108	81	29	28	269	351
Indiana	88	65	17	16	193	246
Iowa	121	102	34	33	284	327
Kansas	75	67	48	48	644	713
Kentucky	103	91	15	14	143	155
Louisiana	37	30	10	9	273	290
Maine	8	7	2	1	195	200
Maryland	17	16	3	2	157	141
Massachusetts	6	7	1	1	116	99
Michigan	66	54	11	11	175	200
Minnesota	104	88	30	30	291	339
Mississippi	56	38	15	13	265	337
Missouri	121	107	31	30	261	283
Montana	24	25	62	60	2,601	2,439
Nebraska	65	56	48	47	734	841
Nevada	3	3	9	9	3,100	3,560
New Hampshire	3	3	1	(z)	160	162
New Jersey	10	9	1	1	109	104
New Mexico	13	14	47	44	3,467	3,274
New York	48	38	9	8	200	216
North Carolina	92	60	12	10	126	158
North Dakota	41	33	42	40	1,043	1,224
Ohio	96	78	16	15	171	197
Oklahoma	72	71	35	34	481	479
Oregon	34	38	18	18	517	467
Pennsylvania	61	52	9	8	145	154
Rhode Island	1	1	(z)	(z)	87	90
South Carolina	35	25	6	5	188	212
South Dakota	39	35	45	44	1,169	1,263
Tennessee	96	88	14	13	142	143
Texas	192	183	138	130	715	710
Utah	13	13	12	11	919	856
Vermont	7	7	2	2	226	219
Virginia	59	44	10	9	169	198
Washington	37	37	16	16	429	432
West Virginia	20	20	4	4	191	185
Wisconsin	94	79	19	17	200	219
Wyoming	9	9	35	35	3,846	3,783

(z) Less than 500 farms or 500,000 acres

Livestock on Farms in the U.S.

Source: Natl. Agricultural Statistics Service, U.S. Dept. of Agriculture (in thousands)

Year (On Jan. 1)	All cattle	Milk cows	Sheep	Hogs[3]
1890	60,014	15,000	44,518	48,130
1900	59,739	16,544	48,105	51,055
1910	58,993	19,450	50,239	48,072
1920	70,400	21,455	40,743	60,159
1925	63,373	22,575	38,543	55,770
1930	61,003	23,032	51,565	55,705
1935	68,846	26,082	51,808	39,066
1940	68,309	24,940	52,107	61,165
1945	85,573	27,770	46,520	59,373
1950	77,963	23,853	29,826	58,937
1955	96,592	23,462	31,582	50,474
1960	96,236	19,527	33,170	59,026
1965	109,000	16,981[2]	25,127	56,106
1970	112,369	12,091	20,423	57,046
1980	111,242	10,758	12,699	67,318
1985	109,582	10,777	10,716	54,073
1990	98,162	10,153	11,363	53,821
1991	98,896	10,156	11,200	54,477
1992	99,559	9,913	10,750	57,684
1993[1]	100,892	9,844	10,174	59,016

(1) Total estimated value on farms as of Jan. 1, 1993, was (avg. value per head in parentheses): cattle & calves $65,481,884 ($649.00) sheep & lambs $715,834 ($70.20); hogs & pigs $4,281,213 ($71.60). (2) From 1965, milk cows and heifers that have calved. (3) As of Dec. 1 of preceding year.

U.S. Farms, 1940-1992

Source: U.S. Dept. of Agriculture

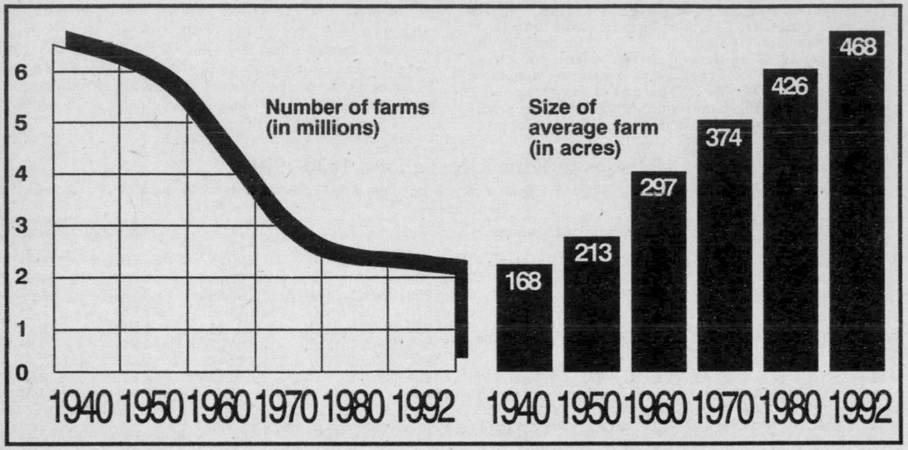

Eggs: U.S. Production, Price, and Value, 1991-92[1]

Source: Economic Research Service, U.S. Dept. of Agriculture

State	Eggs Produced[2] 1991 (million)	Eggs Produced[2] 1992 (million)	Price Per Dozen 1991 (cents)	Price Per Dozen 1992 (cents)	Value of Production 1991 (1,000 dollars)	Value of Production 1992 (1,000 dollars)
AL	2,417	2,512	91.4	81.3	184,095	170,188
AK	0.7	0.5	149.0	169.0	87	70
AZ	85	85	56.0	49.7	3,967	3,520
AR	3,737	3,601	91.8	88.3	285,881	264,974
CA	7,444	7,007	58.4	47.6	362,275	277,944
CO	873	837	73.0	61.4	53,108	42,827
CT	947	940	104.0	96.9	82,073	75,905
DE	165	164	113.0	107.0	15,538	14,623
FL	2,537	2,341	57.2	46.7	120.903	91.104
GA	4,301	4,326	80.8	74.8	289,601	269.654
HI	224.5	222.4	85.5	85.5	15,996	15,846
ID	203	214	72.9	62.6	12,332	11,164
IL	809	801	70.5	48.0	47,529	32,040
IN	5,290	5,207	60.1	48.8	264,941	211,751
IA	2,247	2,902	53.0	39.4	99,243	95,282
KS	389	355	47.8	38.3	15,495	11,330
KY	507	578	73.5	61.7	31,054	29,719
LA	254	316	115.0	97.0	24,342	25,543
ME	1,070	1,078	97.0	89.5	86,492	80,401
MD	903	855	75.4	62.2	56,739	44,318
MA	237	213	102.0	97.0	20,145	17,218
MI	1,396	1,398	53.8	40.4	62,587	47,066
MN	2,697	2,805	54.0	41.0	121,365	95,838
MS	1,478	1,408	86.7	82.1	106,786	96,331
MO	1,622	1,575	51.5	41.0	69,611	53,813
MT	164	160	66.0	49.0	9,020	6,533
NE	1,400	1,777	48.9	36.0	57,050	53,310
NV	1.8	1.5	52.7	38.8	79	49
NH	52	63	104.0	104.0	4,507	5,460
NJ	491	515	83.0	70.0	33,961	30,042
NM	302	303	70.0	58.0	17,617	14,645
NY	987	1,040	64.0	53.9	52,640	46,713
NC	3,045	3,026	78.7	71.4	199,701	180,047
ND	45	41	48.0	41.0	1,800	1,401
OH	4,637	5,021	54.7	40.7	211,370	170,296
OK	830	873	100.0	96.0	69,167	69,840
OR	686	686	74.6	76.6	42,646	43,790
PA	5,130	5,513	52.0	42.9	222,300	197,090
RI	50	57	99.0	91.0	4,125	4,323
SC	1,420	1,447	65.9	57.3	77,982	69,094
SD	602	690	45.8	32.5	22,976	18,688
TN	279	262	80.7	72.8	18,763	15,895
TX	3,356	3,462	72.6	63.0	203,038	181,755
UT	486	493	59.0	53.0	23,895	21,774
VT	30	31	102.0	98.0	2,550	2,532
VA	988	1,008	81.2	75.3	66,855	63,252
WA	1,313	1,305	71.5	63.4	78,233	68,948
WV	174	180	109.0	104.0	15,805	15,600
WI	896	831	54.0	42.5	40,320	29,431
WY	1.7	1.7	83.0	65.5	118	93
U.S.	**69,196**	**70,528**	**67.8**	**57.7**	**3,908,730**	**3,389,070**

(1) Estimates cover the 12 month period from Dec. 1, of the previous year through Nov. 30. (2) States may not add to U.S. total due to rounding.

U.S. Meat Production and Consumption

Source: Economic Research Service, U.S. Dept. of Agriculture; in millions of pounds

Year	Beef Production	Beef Consumption[1]	Veal Production	Veal Consumption[1]	Lamb and mutton Production	Lamb and mutton Consumption[1]	Pork (exclud. lard) Production	Pork (exclud. lard) Consumption[1]	All meats[3] Production	All meats[3] Consumption[1]	Lard Production	Lard Consumption[2]
1940	7,175	7,257	981	981	876	873	10,044	9,701	19,076	18,812	2,288	1,901
1950	9,534	9,529	1,230	1,206	597	596	10,714	10,390	22,075	21,721	2,631	1,891
1960	14,728	15,465	1,109	1,118	769	857	13,905	14,057	30,511	31,497	2,562	1,358
1970	21,684	23,451	588	613	551	669	14,699	14,957	37,522	39,689	1,913	939
1980	21,643	23,560	400	420	318	351	16,617	16,838	38,978	41,701	1,207	588
1990	22,743	24,031	327	325	363	397	15,354	16,030	38,787	40,784	(4)	(4)
1991	22,917	24,113	306	305	363	396	15,999	16,399	39,585	41,214	(4)	(4)
1992	23,086	24,261	310	312	348	388	17,234	17,475	40,978	42,436	(4)	(4)

(1) Includes shipments. (2) Direct use. Excludes lard used in such products as table spreads and shortenings. (3) Meats may not add to total. (4) Data collection discontinued.

Government Agricultural Payments by State, 1992[1]

Source: Economic Research Service, U.S. Dept. of Agriculture; in thousands of dollars

State	Feed Grain	Wheat	Rice	Cotton	Wool Act	Conservation[2]	Miscellaneous[3]	Total
Alabama	$4,086	$4,165	$0	$28,731	$101	$29,144	$52,905	$119,132
Alaska	118	0	0	0	10	1,095	471	1,694
Arizona	2,330	4,813	0	46,592	2,074	1,481	18,290	75,580
Arkansas	6,969	25,758	198,861	45,173	303	17,658	115,304	410,026
California	10,643	23,134	103,570	91,232	10,794	13,479	177,530	430,382
Colorado	36,381	54,185	0	0	7,625	84,998	20,045	203,234
Connecticut	438	0	0	0	41	582	1,156	2,217
Delaware	1,819	237	0	0	7	537	376	2,976
Florida	2,327	560	273	2,457	15	14,569	32,884	53,085
Georgia	14,791	13,197	0	25,525	41	32,954	95,792	182,300
Hawaii	0	0	0	0	15	731	1,076	1,822
Idaho	16,101	50,781	0	0	4,752	42,514	23,247	137,395
Illinois	345,505	23,974	0	0	670	62,406	48,096	480,651
Indiana	157,033	10,982	0	0	336	35,245	28,922	232,518
Iowa	449,568	319	0	0	2,816	175,822	33,753	662,278
Kansas	123,952	249,608	0	39	2,272	157,719	58,555	592,145
Kentucky	28,989	6,209	0	0	192	29,615	7,120	72,125
Louisiana	4,070	4,339	78,784	60,908	27	10,389	112,318	270,835
Maine	503	1	0	0	97	4,635	5,017	10,253
Maryland	7,549	1,054	0	0	130	2,864	4,470	16,067
Massachusetts	145	0	0	0	72	836	3,708	4,761
Michigan	74,688	14,569	0	0	890	20,733	31,629	142,509
Minnesota	208,034	63,480	0	0	2,180	106,692	41,637	422,023
Mississippi	3,568	6,649	40,763	103,746	9	39,696	85,473	279,904
Missouri	67,963	31,481	15,027	14,174	1,306	100,132	53,562	293,645
Montana	34,840	105,910	0	0	11,541	108,749	37,733	298,773
Nebraska	305,462	53,412	0	0	1,620	83,662	34,573	478,729
Nevada	237	603	0	0	1,118	837	8,449	11,244
New Hampshire	125	0	0	0	57	798	570	1,550
New Jersey	2,020	360	0	0	44	671	7,600	10,695
New Mexico	7,854	7,372	0	4,224	8,173	21,106	11,538	60,267
New York	21,096	3,018	0	0	407	7,487	15,864	47,872
North Carolina	21,048	5,400	0	9,964	85	10,809	27,499	74,805
North Dakota	75,561	202,923	0	0	2,933	109,955	51,784	443,156
Ohio	96,457	19,087	0	0	1,331	28,335	20,912	166,122
Oklahoma	8,063	126,992	187	18,202	2,648	54,841	37,389	248,322
Oregon	4,677	30,395	0	0	3,919	29,882	18,601	87,474
Pennsylvania	13,335	968	0	0	568	10,008	23,886	48,765
Rhode Island	1	0	0	0	5	121	181	308
South Carolina	10,892	6,792	0	11,717	5	13,859	29,323	72,588
South Dakota	88,340	58,450	0	0	10,348	73,891	40,870	271,899
Tennessee	12,221	6,728	92	28,911	92	27,603	40,219	115,866
Texas	107,439	89,920	74,743	259,358	81,655	179,671	369,253	1,162,039
Utah	2,344	4,016	0	0	7,820	11,212	10,580	35,972
Vermont	413	1	0	0	168	2,057	2,911	5,550
Virginia	9,525	2,971	0	224	755	7,331	8,266	29,072
Washington	17,636	82,019	0	0	799	56,594	31,695	188,743
West Virginia	1,254	75	0	0	408	2,100	3,025	6,862
Wisconsin	88,977	1,742	0	0	541	48,774	25,993	166,027
Wyoming	1,886	4,039	0	0	14,267	12,542	3,929	36,663
United States	**$2,499,273**	**$1,402,688**	**$512,300**	**$751,177**	**$188,082**	**$1,899,421**	**$1,915,979**	**$9,168,920**

(1) Includes both cash payments and payment-in-kind (PIK). (2) Includes amount paid under agriculture and conservation programs (Conservation Reserve, Agriculture Conservation, Emergency Conservation, and Great Plains Program). (3) The programs included are Rural Clean Water, Forest Incentive, Water Bank, Dairy Indemnity, Dairy Termination, Extended Warehouse Storage, Extended Farm Storage, Colorado River Salinity, Livestock Emergency Assistance, Interest Penalty Payments, Disaster, Loan Deficiency, Market Gains, Naval Stores Conservation, Milk Marketing Fee, Animal Waste Management, and interest.

Federal Food Assistance Programs[1]

Source: Food and Nutrition Service, U.S. Dept. of Agriculture; in millions of dollars

Program	1983	1984	1985	1986	1987	1988	1989	1990	1991	1992
Food Stamps[2]	$11,847	$11,579	$11,703	$11,638	$11,605	$12,317	$12,932	$15,491	$18,769	$22,460
P.R. Nutr. Asst.[3]	825	825	825	820	853	879	908	937	963	1,002
Natl. School Lunch[4]	3,203	3,335	3,380	3,537	3,685	3,730	3,770	3,834	4,215	4,566
School Breakfast	344	364	379	406	447	482	513	596	685	787
WIC[5]	1,126	1,388	1,489	1,583	1,680	1,798	1,911	2,122	2,301	2,597
Summer Food Svc.[4]	93	96	112	115	129	133	146	164	176	204
Child/Adult Care[4]	356	407	452	496	548	628	703	820	950	1,099
Special Milk	17	16	16	16	15	19	18	19	20	20
Nutrition for the Elderly[4]	120	127	134	137	139	146	146	142	140	145
Food Distrib. to Indian Reserv.	44	51	60	60	63	62	65	66	65	62
Commodity Supp. Food[4,6]	42	48	48	48	56	62	73	85	93	105
Food Dist.—Charitable Instit.[7]	154	190	170	240	158	159	136	104	90	115
Emergency Food Assistance	998	1,075	1,026	895	895	645	276	257	256	236
Soup Kitchens/Food Banks	0	0	0	0	0	0	34	70	44	35
Other Costs[8]	53	52	56	60	62	58	66	76	72	88
Total[9]	**$19,222**	**$19,552**	**$19,851**	**$20,051**	**$20,335**	**$21,118**	**$21,696**	**$24,782**	**$28,841**	**$33,520**

(1) Data are for fiscal (not calendar) years. (2) Includes the federal share of state administrative expenses and other federal costs. (3) Puerto Rico participated in the Food Stamp Program from FY 1975 until July 1982, when it initiated a separate grant program. (4) Includes the value of commodities (entitlement, bonus, and cash in lieu). (5) Special Supplemental Pgm. for Women, Infants, and Children includes program studies and farmers market demonstration projects. (6) Includes elderly feeding projects. (7) Includes summer camps. (8) Includes child nutrition state admin. expenses, nutrition studies, nutrition education and training, and nutrition assistance to the Northern Marianas. (9) Excludes food program administration (FPA) costs.

Farm Marketings by State, 1991 and 1992

Source: Economic Research Service, U.S. Dept. of Agriculture; in thousands of dollars

State/Rank	1991 Farm marketings Total	1991 Crops	1991 Livestock and products	1992 Farm marketings Total	1992 Crops	1992 Livestock and products
Alabama (25)	$3,006,747	$769,639	$2,237,108	$2,830,062	$767,503	$2,062,559
Alaska (50)	26,559	20,173	6,386	25,478	19,631	5,847
Arizona (32)	1,867,235	1,081,013	786,222	1,835,250	942,787	892,463
Arkansas (11)	4,241,502	1,577,632	2,663,870	4,602,230	1,900,501	2,701,729
California (1)	17,776,785	12,522,600	5,254,185	18,234,014	13,179,284	5,054,730
Colorado (17)	3,762,245	1,098,989	2,663,256	4,038,389	1,083,185	2,955,204
Connecticut (44)	472,178	263,957	208,221	488,746	249,113	239,633
Delaware (40)	621,954	183,784	438,170	635,762	184,436	451,326
Florida (8)	6,124,957	4,953,331	1,171,626	6,144,508	4,984,913	1,159,595
Georgia (16)	3,933,768	1,772,025	2,161,743	4,073,125	1,763,842	2,309,283
Hawaii (41)	561,873	474,272	87,601	564,151	475,722	88,429
Idaho (26)	2,651,430	1,586,238	1,065,192	2,815,512	1,642,545	1,172,967
Illinois (5)	7,534,410	5,181,365	2,353,045	7,633,692	5,431,346	2,202,346
Indiana (12)	4,500,353	2,583,245	1,917,108	4,505,292	2,683,849	1,821,443
Iowa (3)	10,249,590	4,529,154	5,720,436	10,329,712	4,715,624	5,614,088
Kansas (7)	7,076,365	2,275,897	4,800,468	7,000,307	2,442,242	4,558,065
Kentucky (22)	3,196,220	1,490,870	1,705,350	3,221,305	1,580,236	1,641,069
Louisiana (31)	1,728,110	1,091,798	636,312	1,846,181	1,258,928	587,253
Maine (42)	483,586	192,052	291,534	513,187	212,686	300,501
Maryland (35)	1,352,025	563,821	788,204	1,390,765	586,792	803,973
Massachusetts (43)	485,376	356,021	129,355	491,234	356,298	134,936
Michigan (20)	3,209,894	1,922,219	1,287,675	3,286,329	1,961,720	1,324,609
Minnesota (6)	7,378,091	3,785,567	3,592,524	7,082,069	3,459,768	3,622,301
Mississippi (27)	2,383,299	1,107,762	1,275,537	2,601,966	1,246,850	1,355,116
Missouri (15)	3,910,867	1,642,464	2,268,403	4,123,300	1,934,931	2,188,369
Montana (33)	1,514,382	704,411	809,971	1,742,408	821,096	921,312
Nebraska (4)	9,044,459	3,111,126	5,933,333	8,782,653	3,109,062	5,673,591
Nevada (47)	296,946	88,220	208,726	272,795	71,147	201,648
New Hampshire (48)	142,474	79,135	63,339	143,983	78,975	65,008
New Jersey (39)	658,186	465,203	192,983	656,888	464,505	192,383
New Mexico (34)	1,452,294	474,405	977,889	1,530,425	490,324	1,040,101
New York (24)	2,873,699	1,081,117	1,792,582	2,946,039	1,031,986	1,914,053
North Carolina (10)	4,955,786	2,338,602	2,617,184	5,181,017	2,386,168	2,794,849
North Dakota (23)	2,546,552	1,876,863	669,689	3,093,612	2,338,761	754,851
Ohio (14)	4,164,857	2,483,541	1,681,316	4,167,316	2,587,323	1,579,993
Oklahoma (18)	3,856,406	1,068,129	2,788,277	3,634,931	1,137,254	2,497,677
Oregon (28)	2,524,544	1,699,026	825,518	2,489,821	1,694,516	795,305
Pennsylvania (19)	3,401,890	996,834	2,405,056	3,618,490	1,064,239	2,554,251
Rhode Island (49)	69,293	56,904	12,389	72,218	59,527	12,691
South Carolina (36)	1,226,129	677,414	548,715	1,176,746	631,500	545,246
South Dakota (21)	3,313,596	1,188,465	2,125,131	3,229,480	1,263,112	1,966,368
Tennessee (30)	1,936,439	892,657	1,043,782	2,103,471	1,042,225	1,061,246
Texas (2)	12,216,963	4,336,062	7,880,901	11,619,842	4,096,754	7,523,088
Utah (38)	720,860	171,254	549,606	738,338	181,976	556,362
Vermont (45)	434,044	64,437	369,607	451,898	63,396	388,502
Virginia (29)	2,115,662	752,685	1,362,977	2,134,353	781,438	1,352,915
Washington (13)	4,143,238	2,844,292	1,298,946	4,454,223	2,922,152	1,532,071
West Virginia (46)	323,901	70,787	253,114	342,548	75,476	267,072
Wisconsin (9)	5,416,533	1,225,460	4,191,073	5,499,038	1,185,676	4,313,362
Wyoming (37)	836,923	168,850	668,073	773,312	167,127	606,185
United States	**$168,721,475**	**$81,941,767**	**$86,779,708**	**$171,168,411**	**$84,810,447**	**$86,357,964**

Value of U.S. Agricultural Exports and Imports, 1970-1990

Source: Economic Research Service, U.S. Dept. of Agriculture; in billions of dollars, except percent

Year	Trade balance	Exports, domestic products	Percent of all exports	Imports for consumption	Percent of all imports	Year	Trade balance	Exports, domestic products	Percent of all exports	Imports for consumption	Percent of all imports
1970 . . .	$1.5	$7.3	17	$5.8	15	1981 . . .	26.6	43.3	18	16.8	6
1972 . . .	2.9	9.4	19	6.5	12	1982 . . .	21.2	36.6	17	15.4	6
1973 . . .	9.3	17.7	25	8.4	12	1983 . . .	19.5	36.1	18	16.6	7
1974 . . .	11.7	21.9	23	10.2	10	1984 . . .	18.5	37.8	17	19.3	6
1975 . . .	12.6	21.9	21	9.3	10	1985 . . .	9.1	29.0	13	20.0	6
1976 . . .	12.0	23.0	20	11.0	9	1986 . . .	4.8	26.2	13	21.5	6
1977 . . .	10.2	23.6	20	13.4	9	1987 . . .	8.3	28.7	12	20.4	5
1978 . . .	14.6	29.4	21	14.8	9	1988 . . .	16.1	37.1	12	21.0	5
1979 . . .	18.0	34.7	19	16.7	8	1989 . . .	18.2	39.9	11	21.7	5
1980 . . .	23.9	41.2	18	17.4	7	1990 . . .	16.6	39.3	10	22.8	5

Farm Real Estate Debt Outstanding by Lender Groups[1]

Source: Economic Research Service, U.S. Dept. of Agriculture; in thousands of dollars

Dec. 31	Total farm real estate debt[2]	Amounts held by principal lender groups: Federal land banks[2]	Farmers Home Administration[3]	Life insurance companies[4]	All commercial banks	Other[5]
1960	$12,867,524	$2,539,000	$723,000	$2,975,000	$1,592,000	$5,039,000
1970	30,492,357	7,145,363	2,440,043	5,610,300	3,772,377	11,524,000
1980	97,486,996	36,196,103	8,163,270	12,927,800	8,563,457	31,636,000
1985	105,739,201	44,583,842	10,426,971	11,830,400	11,384,920	27,507,000
1986	95,879,799	37,757,626	10,348,597	10,940,200	12,710,650	24,123,000
1987	87,717,601	32,637,687	10,083,239	9,895,800	14,455,162	20,646,000
1988	82,952,518	30,326,707	9,606,796	9,581,700	15,416,700	18,020,000
1989	80,476,478	28,501,000	8,719,822	9,597,900	16,646,179	17,011,577
1990	78,398,009	26,885,056	8,092,982	10,186,300	17,227,171	16,006,500
1991	79,133,192	26,700,747	7,462,411	10,029,300	18,436,918	16,503,786
1992	79,759,547	26,907,316	6,779,546	9,208,000	19,862,622	17,001,963

(1) Includes operator households. (2) Includes data for joint stock land banks and real estate loans by Agricultural Credit Assn. (3) Includes loans made directly by FmHA for farm ownership, soil and water loans to individuals, Indian tribe land acquisition, grazing associations, and half of economic emergency loans. Also includes loans for rural housing on farm tracts and labor housing. (4) American Council of Life Insurance. (5) Estimated by ERS, USDA. Includes Commodity Credit Corporation storage and drying facility loans.

Grain, Hay, Potato, Cotton, Soybean, Tobacco Production, by State, 1992

Source: Economic Research Service, U.S. Dept. of Agriculture

1992 State	Barley (1,000 bushels)	Corn, grain (1,000 bushels)	Cotton lint (1,000 bales)	All Hay (1,000 tons)	Oats (1,000 bushels)	Potatoes (1,000 cwt.)	Soybeans (1,000 bushels)	Tobacco (1,000 pounds)	All Wheat (1,000 bushels)
Alabama	—	30,080	621	1,491	1,500	1,733	7,830	—	4,180
Alaska	—	—	—	—	—	—	—	—	—
Arizona	2,205	1,870	863	1,224	—	1,800	—	—	7,700
Arkansas	—	12,350	1,681	2,796	1,600	—	104,280	—	39,100
California	11,160	23,925	3,111	7,755	2,800	15,592	—	—	46,365
Colorado	9,000	123,580	—	3,961	2,100	24,120	—	—	72,619
Connecticut	—	—	—	194	—	—	—	2,320	—
Delaware	2,590	19,159	—	52	—	1,380	6,880	—	4,060
Florida	—	8,250	72	875	—	9,370	1,350	19,575	840
Georgia	—	69,000	744	1,624	3,685	—	18,560	100,980	16,100
Hawaii	—	—	—	—	—	—	—	—	—
Idaho	54,000	4,290	—	3,655	1,440	127,050	—	—	100,000
Illinois	—	1,646,450	—	3,316	7,930	1,320	405,490	—	62,100
Indiana	—	877,590	—	1,971	2,800	989	194,360	18,900	22,500
Iowa	—	1,903,650	—	6,615	25,125	280	363,880	—	1,560
Kansas	680	259,500	0	6,670	7,840	—	68,450	—	363,800
Kentucky	1,188	171,600	—	4,935	—	—	44,080	524,378	23,100
Louisiana	—	37,080	1,299	644	—	—	35,100	—	6,120
Maine	—	—	—	417	1,650	24,300	—	—	—
Maryland	4,672	58,280	—	648	594	320	17,985	11,931	12,760
Massachusetts	—	—	—	248	—	825	—	678	—
Michigan	1,736	241,500	—	4,640	8,400	13,920	47,520	—	35,280
Minnesota	50,625	741,000	—	6,550	35,000	18,388	172,800	—	139,860
Mississippi	—	27,000	2,131	2,025	—	—	59,500	—	10,500
Missouri	—	324,000	541	7,030	2,430	1,764	161,500	3,298	64,800
Montana	52,800	2,750	—	4,650	3,920	2,465	—	—	139,581
Nebraska	1,500	1,066,500	—	8,023	15,400	3,298	103,320	—	55,500
Nevada	550	—	—	1,062	—	2,925	—	—	800
New Hampshire	—	—	—	181	—	—	—	—	—
New Jersey	448	9,840	—	333	—	840	4,224	—	1,400
New Mexico	—	11,360	67	1,401	—	3,247	—	—	11,220
New York	—	61,640	—	3,590	7,700	7,808	—	—	6,160
North Carolina	1,980	98,800	468	1,234	3,000	3,614	36,450	609,873	27,750
North Dakota	172,250	36,540	—	3,515	37,400	27,690	17,250	—	469,850
Ohio	—	507,650	—	4,550	12,070	1,440	147,200	21,840	59,095
Oklahoma	396	17,550	210	4,940	2,250	—	5,940	—	171,100
Oregon	9,450	2,250	—	2,440	4,230	21,075	—	—	47,800
Pennsylvania	6,390	118,800	—	4,900	13,735	4,940	11,115	21,030	10,175
Rhode Island	—	—	—	18	—	377	—	—	—
South Carolina	558	30,800	226	450	2,205	—	14,740	112,320	12,925
South Dakota	20,520	277,200	—	7,020	42,900	1,500	63,000	—	119,590
Tennessee	—	79,360	834	3,465	—	—	33,250	146,556	13,440
Texas	270	202,500	3,322	9,800	5,720	2,459	12,870	—	129,200
Utah	8,970	3,240	—	2,240	1,050	1,650	—	—	6,256
Vermont	—	—	—	835	—	—	—	—	—
Virginia	7,110	40,020	28	2,905	—	1,980	15,500	111,459	15,105
Washington	19,800	15,840	—	2,962	1,800	69,300	—	—	119,640
West Virginia	—	5,400	—	1,070	360	—	—	3,623	539
Wisconsin	4,160	306,800	—	6,090	34,410	25,160	22,080	12,837	2,640
Wyoming	11,340	3,920	—	2,131	1,560	448	—	—	5,720
United States	**456,348**	**9,478,914**	**16,219**	**149,141**	**294,604**	**425,367**	**2,196,504**	**1,721,598**	**2,458,830**

Production of Chief U.S. Crops

Source: National Agricultural Statistics Service: U.S. Dept. of Agriculture

Year	Corn for grain (1,000 bushels)	Oats (1,000 bushels)	Barley (1,000 bushels)	Sorghum for grain (1,000 bushels)	All Wheat (1,000 bushels)	Rye (1,000 bushels)	Flax-seed (1,000 bushels)	Cotton lint (1,000 bales)	Cotton seed (1,000 tons)
1970 . .	4,152,243	915,236	416,091	683,179	1,351,558	36,840	29,416	10,192	4,068
1975 . .	5,828,961	638,960	379,162	754,354	2,126,927	15,924	15,553	8,302	3,218
1980 . .	6,639,396	458,792	361,135	579,343	2,380,934	15,958	7,728	11,122	4,470
1982 . .	8,235,101	592,630	515,935	835,083	2,764,967	19,533	10,278	11,963	4,744
1985 . .	8,875,453	518,490	590,213	1,120,271	2,424,115	20,373	8,293	13,432	5,279
1986 . .	8,225,764	384,996	608,532	938,869	2,090,570	19,067	11,538	9,731	3,801
1987 . .	7,131,300	373,713	521,499	730,809	2,107,685	19,526	7,444	14,760	5,769
1988 . .	4,928,681	217,600	289,994	576,686	1,812,201	14,689	1,615	15,412	6,062
1989 . .	7,525,493	373,587	404,203	615,420	2,036,618	13,647	1,215	12,196	4,677
1990 . .	7,934,028	357,524	422,196	573,303	2,736,428	10,176	3,812	15,505	5,969
1991 . .	7,475,480	243,451	464,326	584,860	1,981,139	9,761	6,200	17,614	6,926
1992 . .	9,478,914	294,604	456,348	884,010	2,458,830	11,952	3,288	16,260	6,265

Year	Tobacco (1,000 lbs.)	All Hay (1,000 tons)	Beans dry edible (1,000 cwt.)	Peas dry edible (1,000 cwt.)	Peanuts (1,000 lbs.)	Soy-beans (1,000 bushels)	Pota-toes (1,000 cwt.)	Sweet pota-toes (1,000 cwt.)
1970	1,906,453	126,969	17,399	3,315	2,983,121	1,127,100	325,716	13,164
1975	2,182,304	132,397	17,442	2,731	3,846,722	1,548,344	321,978	12,891
1980	1,786,225	130,740	26,729	3,285	2,302,762	1,797,543	303,905	10,953
1982	1,994,494	149,241	25,563	NA	3,440,255	2,190,297	355,131	14,833
1985	1,511,638	148,719	22,298	NA	4,122,787	2,099,056	407,109	14,573
1986	1,161,940	155,385	22,960	3,196	3,697,085	1,942,558	361,511	12,368
1987	1,188,868	147,319	26,031	3,385	3,616,010	1,938,087	385,774	11,611
1988	1,369,500	126,010	19,253	3,868	3,980,917	1,548,841	356,438	10,945
1989	1,367,188	145,512	23,729	3,883	3,989,995	1,923,666	370,444	11,358
1990	1,626,380	146,820	32,379	2,372	3,602,770	1,925,947	402,110	12,594
1991	1,664,372	153,325	33,765	3,715	4,926,570	1,986,539	417,622	11,203
1992	1,683,831	149,140	22,047	2,535	4,284,390	2,196,504	411,636	11,760

Year	Rice (1,000 cwt.)	Sugar-cane (1,000 tons)	Sugar beets (1,000 tons)	Pecans (1,000 tons)	Al-monds (1,000 tons)	Wal-nuts (1,000 tons)	Hazel-nuts[1] (1,000 tons)	Oranges[2] (1,000 boxes)	Grape-fruit[2] (1,000 boxes)
1970	NA	23,996	26,378	NA	NA	111.8	9.3	185,770	53,910
1975	NA	28,344	29,704	NA	NA	199.3	12.1	237,810	61,610
1980	146,150	26,963	23,502	91.8	264.4	197.0	15.4	273,630	73,200
1982	153,637	29,770	20,894	109.3	283.5	234.0	18.8	176,690	70,550
1985	134,913	28,213	22,529	122.2	375.6	219.0	24.6	158,350	56,150
1986	133,356	30,311	25,150	136.4	201.3	180.0	15.1	175,440	57,870
1987	129,603	29,218	28,072	131.1	519.0	247.0	21.8	181,175	63,775
1988	159,897	29,904	24,810	154.1	451.9	209.0	16.5	200,250	68,700
1989	154,487	29,426	25,131	125.3	394.7	229.0	13.0	209,050	69,500
1990	156,088	28,136	27,513	102.5	519.7	227.0	21.7	186,075	48,600
1991	157,457	30,252	28,203	149.5	385.8	259.0	25.5	178,950	55,500
1992	179,088	30,852	28,848	88.0	451.9	200.0	27.5	209,610	55,265

NA = Not available. (1) Formerly called filberts. (2) Crop year ending in year cited.

Principal U.S. Crops: Area Planted and Harvested, 1990-92

Source: Natl. Agricultural Statistics Service, U.S. Dept. of Agriculture; in thousand acres

State	Area Planted[1] 1990	Area Planted[1] 1991	Area Planted[1] 1992	Area Harvested[2] 1990	Area Harvested[2] 1991	Area Harvested[2] 1992	State	Area Planted[1] 1990	Area Planted[1] 1991	Area Planted[1] 1992	Area Harvested[2] 1990	Area Harvested[2] 1991	Area Harvested[2] 1992
AL	2,516	2,354	2,246	2,338	2,229	2,130	NE	18,732	19,009	19,276	18,044	18,366	18,330
AZ	809	778	744	802	770	736	NV	525	502	407	520	495	403
AR	8,320	8,180	8,310	8,080	7,863	8,110	NH	93	94	105	91	92	103
CA	5,289	4,872	4,899	4,789	4,396	4,433	NJ	419	431	446	361	380	391
CO	6,131	6,023	5,867	5,862	5,591	5,394	NM	1,200	1,287	1,302	880	1,042	1,053
CT	133	132	134	129	125	128	NY	3,630	3,541	3,325	3,538	3,443	3,185
DE	506	568	531	496	556	515	NC	4,618	4,666	4,757	4,336	4,397	4,519
FL	1,115	1,104	1,152	1,076	1,048	1,093	ND	22,119	21,338	21,732	21,014	20,655	21,011
GA	4,405	4,185	4,039	3,788	3,777	3,690	OH	10,348	10,229	10,479	10,132	9,972	10,137
HI	79	74	71	79	74	71	OK	11,067	11,185	11,112	9,688	8,518	9,397
ID	4,273	4,311	4,177	4,175	4,079	4,006	OR	2,375	2,367	2,233	2,290	2,260	2,145
IL	23,608	23,695	23,940	22,759	22,906	23,237	PA	4,203	4,182	4,176	4,094	4,067	4,065
IN	11,731	11,813	12,219	11,485	11,527	11,709	RI	10	10	11	10	10	11
IA	24,182	23,877	24,372	23,276	23,356	23,816	SC	2,225	1,945	1,989	2,046	1,824	1,887
KS	21,937	21,901	21,903	20,978	20,712	20,255	SD	16,359	16,328	17,047	15,528	15,606	15,858
KY	5,748	5,770	5,643	5,505	5,495	5,415	TN	4,639	4,567	4,517	4,477	4,379	4,324
LA	4,485	4,010	4,150	4,346	3,665	4,029	TX	23,002	23,501	23,872	18,544	17,714	18,772
ME	379	369	385	361	351	374	UT	1,042	1,040	1,050	992	973	990
MD	1,626	1,626	1,680	1,551	1,562	1,620	VT	451	442	473	441	434	463
MA	142	141	140	135	136	135	VA	2,897	2,833	2,858	2,725	2,656	2,705
MI	6,756	6,918	7,044	6,510	6,733	6,797	WA	4,171	5,469	4,226	3,999	3,861	3,950
MN	19,488	19,294	19,905	18,765	18,692	19,301	WV	677	630	652	668	615	639
MS	4,991	4,716	4,990	4,719	4,478	4,855	WI	8,885	8,830	8,668	8,550	8,449	8,096
MO	12,989	13,204	13,201	12,685	12,900	12,904	WY	1,789	1,960	1,777	1,735	1,899	1,706
MT	9,798	9,680	9,320	8,926	8,687	8,369	**U.S.[3]**	**326,913**	**326,032**	**327,612**	**308,318**	**303,864**	**307,314**

(1) Crops included in area planted are corn, sorghum, oats, barley, winter wheat, rye, durum wheat, other spring wheat, rice, soybeans, peanuts, sunflower, cotton, dry edible beans, potatoes, and sugarbeets. The harvested acreage is used for all hay, tobacco, and sugarcane in computing total area planted. (2) Crops included in area harvested are listed in footnote 1. (3) State figures do not add to U.S. totals due to sunflower and sugarbeet unallocated acreage.

Average Prices Received by U.S. Farmers

Source: Natl. Agricultural Statistics Service, U.S. Dept. of Agriculture

The figures represent dollars per 100 lbs. for hogs, beef cattle, veal calves, sheep, lamb, and milk (wholesale); dollars per head for milk cows; cents per lb. for chickens, broilers, turkeys, and wool; cents per dozen for eggs.

Weighted calendar year prices for livestock and livestock products other than wool. For 1943 through 1963, wool prices are weighted on marketing year basis. The marketing year was changed in 1964 from a calendar year to a Dec.-Nov. basis for hogs, chickens, broilers, and eggs.

Year	Hogs	Cattle (beef)	Calves (veal)	Sheep	Lambs	Milk cows	Milk	Chickens (excl. broilers)	Broilers	Turkeys	Eggs	Wool
1930	8.84	7.71	9.68	4.74	7.76	74	2.21	...	...	20.2	23.7	19.5
1940	5.39	7.56	8.83	3.95	8.10	61	1.82	13.0	17.3	15.2	18.0	28.4
1950	18.00	23.30	26.30	11.60	25.10	198	3.89	22.2	27.4	32.8	36.3	62.1
1960	15.30	20.40	22.90	5.61	17.90	223	4.21	12.2	16.9	25.4	36.1	42.0
1970	22.70	27.10	34.50	7.51	26.40	332	5.71	9.1	13.6	22.6	39.1	35.4
1975	46.10	32.20	27.20	11.30	42.10	412	8.75	9.9	26.3	34.8	54.5	44.8
1979	41.80	66.10	88.80	26.30	66.70	1,040	12.00	14.4	25.9	41.3	58.3	86.3
1980	38.00	62.40	76.80	21.30	63.60	1,190	13.05	11.0	27.7	41.3	56.3	88.1
1984	47.10	57.30	59.90	16.40	60.10	895	13.46	15.9	33.7	48.9	72.3	79.5
1985	44.00	53.70	62.10	23.90	67.70	860	12.76	14.8	30.1	49.1	57.1	63.3
1986	49.30	52.60	61.10	25.60	69.00	820	12.51	12.5	34.5	47.1	61.6	66.8
1987	51.20	61.10	78.50	29.50	77.60	920	12.54	11.0	28.7	34.8	54.9	91.7
1988	42.30	66.60	89.20	25.60	69.10	990	12.26	9.2	33.1	38.6	52.8	1.38
1989	42.50	69.50	90.80	24.40	66.10	1,030	13.56	14.9	36.6	40.9	68.9	1.24
1990	53.70	74.60	95.60	23.20	55.50	1,160	13.74	9.3	32.6	39.4	70.9	80.0
1991	49.10	72.70	98.00	19.70	52.20	1,100	12.27	7.1	30.8	38.4	67.6	55.0
1992	41.60	71.30	89.00	25.80	59.50	1,130	13.15	8.6	31.8	37.7	57.7	74.0

The figures represent cents per lb. for cotton, apples, and peanuts; dollars per bushel for oats, wheat, corn, barley, and soybeans; dollars per 100 lbs. for rice, sorghum, and potatoes; dollars per ton for cottonseed and baled hay.

Weighted crop year prices. Crop years are as follows: apples, June-May; wheat, oats, barley, hay, and potatoes, July-June; cotton, rice, peanuts, and cottonseed, August-July; soybeans, September-August; and corn and sorghum grain, October-September.

Year	Corn	Wheat	Upland cotton[1]	Oats	Barley	Rice	Soybeans	Sorghum	Peanuts	Cottonseed	Hay	Potatoes	Apples
1930	.598	.663	9.46	0.311	.420	1.74	1.34	1.02	5.01	22.00	11.00	1.47	...
1940	.618	.674	9.83	0.298	.393	1.80	.892	.873	3.72	21.70	9.78	.850	...
1950	1.52	2.00	39.90	0.788	1.19	5.09	2.47	1.88	10.9	86.60	21.10	1.50	...
1960	1.00	1.74	30.08	0.599	.840	4.55	2.13	1.49	10.0	42.50	21.70	2.00	2.72
1970	1.33	1.33	21.86	0.623	.973	5.17	2.85	2.04	12.8	56.40	26.10	2.21	6.52
1975	2.54	3.55	51.10	1.45	2.42	8.35	4.92	4.21	19.6	97.00	52.10	4.48	8.80
1979	2.52	3.78	62.3	1.36	2.29	10.50	6.28	4.18	20.6	121.00	59.50	3.43	15.40
1980	3.11	3.91	74.4	1.79	2.86	12.80	7.57	5.25	25.1	129.00	71.00	6.55	12.1
1984	2.63	3.39	58.7	1.67	2.29	8.04	5.84	4.15	27.9	99.50	72.70	5.69	15.5
1985	2.23	3.08	56.8	1.23	1.98	6.53	5.05	3.45	24.4	66.00	67.60	3.92	17.3
1986	1.50	2.42	51.5	1.21	1.61	3.75	4.78	2.45	29.2	80.00	59.70	5.03	19.1
1987	1.94	2.57	63.7	1.56	1.81	7.27	5.88	3.04	28.0	82.50	65.00	4.38	12.7
1988	2.54	3.72	55.6	2.61	2.79	6.83	7.42	4.05	28.0	118.00	85.20	6.02	17.4
1989	2.36	3.72	63.6	1.49	2.42	7.35	5.69	3.75	28.0	105.00	85.40	7.36	13.9
1990	2.28	2.61	67.1	1.14	2.14	6.70	5.74	2.12	34.7	121.00	80.60	6.08	20.9
1991	2.37	3.00	56.8	1.21	2.10	7.58	5.58	2.25	28.3	71.00	71.20	4.96	25.1
1992	2.05	3.25	53.1	1.30	2.05	6.20	5.40	1.90	3.00	97.00	72.10	5.28	19.2

(1) Beginning in 1964, 480 lb. net weight bales.

Grain Storage Capacity at Principal U.S. Grain Centers

Source: Chicago Board of Trade Market Information Department, Aug. 1993

(bushels)

Cities	Capacity
Atlantic Coast	**16,000,000**
Great Lakes	
Toledo	63,100,000
Buffalo	15,200,000
Chicago	52,400,000
Milwaukee	6,600,000
Duluth	58,200,000
River Points	
Minneapolis	82,300,000
Peoria	3,300,000
St. Louis	17,700,000
Sioux City	3,800,000
Omaha-Council Bluffs	7,800,000
Atchison	16,900,000
St. Joseph	22,300,000
Kansas City, Mo.	95,200,000

Cities	Capacity
Southwest	
Fort Worth	68,000,000
Texas High Plains	72,700,000
Enid	79,700,000
Gulf Points	
South Mississippi	47,300,000
Texas Gulf	45,800,000
Plains	
Wichita	37,400,000
Topeka	55,500,000
Salina	49,500,000
Hutchinson	42,000,000
Hastings-Grand Island	25,100,000
Lincoln	33,700,000
Pacific N.W.	
Puget Sound (incl. Portland)	35,100,000
California Ports	NA

Atlantic Coast — Albany, N.Y., Philadelphia, Pa., Baltimore, Md., Norfolk, Va. **Gulf Points** — New Orleans, Baton Rouge, Ama, Belle Chasse, La., Mobile, Ala. **Texas Gulf** — Houston, Galveston, Beaumont, Port Arthur, Corpus Christi, Brownsville. **Pacific N.W.** — Seattle, Tacoma, Wash., Portland, Ore., Columbia River. **Texas High Plains** — Amarillo, Lubbock, Hereford, Plainview. NA = not available.

World Wheat, Rice, and Corn Production, 1990

Source: U.N. Food and Agriculture Organization

(thousands of metric tons)

Country	Wheat	Rice	Corn
World, total	**595,149**	**518,508**	**475,429**
Afghanistan	1,925	430	800
Argentina	10,800	467	5,049
Australia	15,712	923	202
Austria	1,370	—	1,400
Bangladesh	890	28,140	3
Belgium-Lux.	1,527	—	60
Brazil	3,140	7,425	21,298
Bulgaria	5,095	23	1,241
Burma (Myanmar)	124	13,965	186
Cambodia	—	2,400	55
Canada	31,798	—	7,033
Chile	1,718	136	823
China	96,004	188,403	87,345
Colombia	105	2,117	1,213
Cuba	—	500	95
Czechoslovakia	6,707	—	468
Denmark	4,101	—	—
Ecuador	22	760	400
Egypt	4,267	2,800	4,400
Ethiopia	870	—	2,000
Finland	627	—	—
France	33,363	109	8,996
Germany	15,787	—	1,546
Greece	1,580	100	1,700
Hungary	6,159	35	4,500
India	49,652	112,500	9,500
Indonesia	—	44,490	6,741
Iran	7,000	1,400	7
Iraq	805	200	110
Ireland	603	—	—
Israel	160	—	22
Italy	8,109	1,282	5,864
Japan	952	13,124	1
Korea, North	220	5,500	4,400
Korean, South	1	7,786	2
Laos	—	1,491	67
Madagascar	1	2,400	170
Malaysia	—	1,650	35
Mexico	3,899	—	—
Nepal	855	3,300	950
Netherlands	1,076	—	5
New Zealand	220	—	160
Pakistan	14,315	4,713	1,279
Panama	—	—	115
Peru	95	966	621
Philippines	—	9,319	4,854
Poland	9,026	—	290
Portugal	268	153	643
Romania	7,320	67	6,810
South Africa	1,794	—	9,442
Soviet Union	108,000	2,473	16,000
Spain	4,760	569	3,051
Sri Lanka	—	2,200	36
Sweden	2,173	—	—
Switzerland	572	—	231
Syria	2,069	—	132
Thailand	—	19,000	3,675
Turkey	20,000	235	2,000
United Kingdom	13,900	—	—
United States	74,534	7,027	201,509
Uruguay	420	517	101
Venezuela	—	400	1,150
Vietnam	—	18,400	850
Yugoslavia	6,359	40	6,270

Note: Some figures are FAO estimates. Where production is small or nonexistent, — is indicated.

Wheat, Rice, and Corn—Exports and Imports of 10 Leading Countries

Source: U.N. Food and Agriculture Organization

(thousands of metric tons)

Leading Exporters	Exports[1]			Leading Importers	Imports[1]		
Wheat	**1980**	**1990**	**1991p**	**Wheat**	**1980**	**1990**	**1991p**
U.S.	41,199	29,064	34,869	Soviet Union	16,000	15,650	21,000
Canada	16,262	21,731	24,500	China	13,789	9,500	15,500
France	13,423	18,600	18,000	Italy	3,028	5,500	7,300
Australia	9,577	11,760	7,600	Egypt	5,423	5,668	6,000
Turkey	530	544	5,000	Japan	5,840	5,622	5,750
Argentina	3,845	5,592	4,600	Brazil	3,910	4,444	4,672
United Kingdom	1,100	4,165	4,600	South Korea	2,095	4,200	4,396
Germany, Fed. Rep.[2]	1,502	3,295	4,400	Algeria	2,294	4,600	4,000
Italy	1,620	2,700	3,600	Iran	1,896	4,000	2,500
Saudi Arabia	27	1,661	2,425	Indonesia	1,474	2,300	2,300
Rice	**1980**	**1990**	**1991p**	**Rice**	**1980**	**1990**	**1991p**
Thailand	3,049	3,993	4,600	Iran	583	565	800
U.S.	3,028	2,317	2,123	Soviet Union	1,283	400	800
Pakistan	1,163	1,320	1,200	Saudi Arabia	356	525	550
Vietnam	5	1,000	1,200	Senegal	340	430	400
China	580	689	750	Hong Kong	362	368	400
Australia	468	443	600	Malaysia	167	355	400
Italy	475	580	593	South Africa	126	346	375
India	900	500	450	Brazil	0	800	350
Uruguay	184	270	334	Turkey	32	161	350
Spain	45	210	210	Ivory Coast	275	310	325
Corn	**1980**	**1990**	**1991p**	**Corn**	**1980**	**1990**	**1991p**
United States	60,737	43,807	40,007	Japan	13,989	16,042	16,200
China	125	6,571	10,000	Soviet Union	11,800	8,720	12,200
Argentina	9,098	4,000	6,400	South Korea	2,355	5,571	6,800
France	2,380	5,300	5,700	Taiwan	2,703	5,250	5,700
Hungary	300	500	1,400	South Africa	0	375	5,000
Canada	1,056	142	1,000	Netherlands	2,638	1,869	1,800
Thailand	2,142	1,193	800	Zimbabwe	0	100	1,800
Greece	0	400	700	Malaysia	717	1,490	1,750
Yugoslavia	300	21	600	Spain	4,251	1,523	1,600
Belgium-Luxembourg	1,742	16	200	United Kingdom	2,349	1,250	1,575

(1) Marketing years. (2) Data for total Germany not available. p = preliminary.

EMPLOYMENT

U.S. Labor Force, Employment and Unemployment

Source: Bureau of Labor Statistics, U.S. Dept. of Labor; seasonally adjusted

Selected Unemployment Indicators

Category Characteristic	1990 II	1990 III	1990 IV	1991 I	1991 II	1991 III	1991 IV	1992 I	1992 II	1992 III	1992 IV	1993 I	1993 II
Total (all civilian workers)	**5.3**	**5.6**	**6.0**	**6.5**	**6.7**	**6.8**	**6.9**	**7.2**	**7.5**	**7.5**	**7.3**	**7.0**	**7.0**
Men, 20 years and over	4.7	5.0	5.5	6.1	6.4	6.5	6.5	6.9	7.2	7.2	7.0	6.5	6.5
Women, 20 years and over	4.6	4.9	5.1	5.4	5.7	5.6	6.0	6.0	6.2	6.4	6.3	6.0	5.9
Both sexes, 16 to 19 years	14.9	15.9	16.6	18.0	18.7	19.0	19.0	19.6	21.0	20.3	19.4	19.6	20.1
White	4.6	4.8	5.1	5.8	6.0	6.1	6.2	6.4	6.5	6.6	6.4	6.1	6.1
Black and other	9.4	10.5	10.9	10.9	11.2	11.0	11.4	12.4	13.0	12.8	12.7	12.3	12.1
Black	10.5	11.7	12.1	12.1	12.7	12.2	12.6	13.9	14.5	14.2	14.1	13.6	13.3
Hispanic origin	7.7	8.1	8.7	9.6	9.6	10.1	10.1	11.5	11.2	11.6	11.8	11.4	10.1
Married men, spouse present	3.2	3.5	3.7	4.2	4.4	4.4	4.5	4.9	5.0	5.3	4.9	4.6	4.5
Married women, spouse present	3.6	3.8	4.1	4.3	4.5	4.5	4.7	4.8	5.1	5.1	5.0	4.5	4.7
Women who maintain families	7.7	8.5	8.7	9.1	9.3	9.0	9.2	9.5	10.1	9.9	10.0	9.9	9.8
Full-time workers	4.9	5.3	5.7	6.2	6.5	6.5	6.6	7.0	7.2	7.3	7.0	6.7	6.6
Part-time workers	7.3	7.6	7.4	8.0	8.5	8.3	8.5	9.0	9.2	9.2	9.4	9.1	9.0
Unemployed 15 weeks and over[1]	1.1	1.3	1.4	1.6	1.8	1.9	2.1	2.5	2.6	2.8	2.8	2.5	2.3
Labor force time lost[2]	6.0	6.3	6.8	7.4	7.6	7.7	7.9	8.2	8.3	8.4	8.2	7.9	7.8
Industry													
Nonagricultural private wage and salary workers	5.4	5.7	6.2	6.8	7.1	7.0	7.2	7.6	7.8	7.9	7.6	7.2	7.2
Goods-producing industries	6.5	6.9	7.9	8.7	9.1	9.0	9.2	9.5	9.9	10.1	9.4	8.8	9.0
Mining	4.2	4.3	5.2	6.5	7.7	8.7	8.6	7.6	8.2	9.2	6.4	6.8	8.8
Construction	10.6	11.2	13.5	14.6	15.1	15.8	16.2	17.3	17.1	17.1	15.4	14.4	15.1
Manufacturing	5.4	5.8	6.4	7.1	7.5	7.1	7.2	7.3	7.8	8.1	7.8	7.2	7.2
Durable goods	5.3	5.9	6.6	7.6	7.9	7.2	7.2	7.4	7.8	8.4	8.3	7.1	7.2
Nondurable goods	5.5	5.6	6.0	6.4	6.9	6.9	7.2	7.2	7.9	7.7	7.2	7.5	7.2
Service-producing industries	5.0	5.2	5.5	5.9	6.2	6.2	6.4	6.8	6.9	7.0	6.9	6.6	6.5
Transportation and public utilities	3.5	3.9	4.3	5.0	5.3	5.1	5.9	5.5	5.0	5.6	5.9	4.8	5.0
Wholesale and retail trade	6.2	6.3	6.8	7.4	7.5	7.8	7.7	8.3	8.5	8.7	8.0	7.9	8.1
Finance and service industries	4.4	4.6	4.8	5.1	5.4	5.4	5.7	6.0	6.2	6.0	6.3	6.0	5.6
Government workers	2.5	2.8	2.8	3.2	3.1	3.2	3.5	3.9	3.5	3.4	3.5	3.6	3.3
Agricultural wage and salary workers	9.6	9.7	10.2	12.0	11.2	11.5	11.9	10.7	12.4	13.2	12.8	12.3	11.1

(1) Unemployment as a percent of the civilian labor force. (2) Aggregate hours lost by the unemployed and persons on part time for economic reasons as a percent of potentially available labor force hours.

Employed Persons by Occupation, Sex, and Age

Source: Bureau of Labor Statistics, U.S. Dept. of Labor

(in thousands)

Occupation	Total 16 years and over 1991	Total 16 years and over 1992	Men 16 years and over 1991	Men 16 years and over 1992	Women 16 years and over 1991	Women 16 years and over 1992
Total	**116,877**	**117,598**	**63,593**	**63,805**	**53,284**	**53,793**
Managerial and professional specialty	31,012	31,153	16,656	16,416	14,356	14,736
Executive, administrative, and managerial	14,954	14,767	8,890	8,641	6,064	6,126
Officials and administrators, public administration	591	619	336	361	255	258
Other executive, administrative, and managerial	10,412	10,187	6,611	6,384	3,801	3,802
Management-related occupations	3,951	3,961	1,943	1,896	2,008	2,065
Professional specialty	16,058	16,386	7,767	7,775	8,292	8,611
Engineers	1,846	1,751	1,694	1,603	152	148
Mathematical and computer scientists	923	935	583	622	339	313
Natural scientists	438	459	324	334	114	125
Health diagnosing occupations	849	914	696	747	153	167
Health assessment and treating occupations	2,376	2,517	328	332	2,048	2,184
Teachers, college and university	773	737	457	435	316	302
Teachers, except college and university	4,029	4,216	1,038	1,062	2,992	3,154
Lawyers and judges	772	788	626	620	146	167
Other professional specialty occupations	4,051	4,068	2,020	2,018	2,031	2,050
Technical, sales, and administrative support	36,086	36,808	12,734	13,269	23,352	23,539
Technicians and related support	3,794	4,253	1,921	2,169	1,873	2,084
Sales occupations	13,958	13,919	7,142	7,252	6,816	6,667
Administrative support, including clerical	18,334	18,636	3,671	3,848	14,663	14,788
Service occupations	15,986	16,096	6,429	6,494	9,557	9,602
Precision production, craft, and repair	13,162	13,128	12,030	12,000	1,132	1,128
Mechanics and repairers	4,427	4,441	4,264	4,293	163	147
Construction trades	4,808	4,790	4,721	4,702	88	89
Other precision production, craft, and repair	3,927	3,897	3,045	3,005	881	892
Operators, fabricators, and laborers	17,172	16,957	12,842	12,720	4,330	4,237
Machine operators, assemblers, and inspectors	7,696	7,524	4,610	4,535	3,086	2,989
Transportation and material moving occupations	4,878	4,878	4,441	4,451	437	427
Handlers, equipment cleaners, helpers, and laborers	4,597	4,556	3,791	3,734	806	821
Farming, forestry, and fishing	3,459	3,456	2,903	2,905	557	551

Note: Data for 1992 are not fully comparable with data for prior years because of the introduction of the occupational classification system used in the 1990 census.

Selected Unemployment Insurance Data by State

Calendar year 1992, state programs only

Source: Employment and Training Admin., U.S. Dept. of Labor

State	Insured Claimants	First Payments	Final Payments	Initial Claims	Benefits Paid	Average Weekly Benefit Amount	Employers Subject to State Law
AK	46,940	44,094	23,502	96,387	$117,356,159	$169.92	13,595
AL.	179,501	157,084	40,255	357,722	208,562,138	120.95	77,517
AR	144,378	99,922	36,484	240,416	185,383,263	150.63	51,070
AZ	124,770	90,486	38,791	197,204	211,218,020	146.75	81,011
CA	1,398,923	1,443,782	657,585	3,718,795	3,851,818,253	152.07	772,499
CO	115,076	79,360	35,629	161,297	178,798,392	177.54	93,169
CT	157,275	157,319	70,569	320,842	587,162,128	210.78	93,387
DC	32,423	20,031	18,358	43,789	127,890,580	227.72	21,087
DE	33,445	28,787	7,868	62,734	72,263,852	181.02	19,697
FL.	427,156	339,288	191,037	627,518	860,664,948	158.01	318,565
GA	310,731	231,957	97,785	455,754	381,474,993	148.17	145,515
HI	50,159	39,381	10,980	81,903	137,717,882	239.80	26,990
IA	103,379	88,604	27,502	158,477	194,800,426	170.38	63,360
ID	51,716	46,156	16,010	111,601	83,533,355	156.22	27,793
IL	472,014	390,904	175,163	883,168	1,338,706,871	183.21	250,759
IN	217,854	149,845	45,226	356,070	216,750,547	125.98	110,146
KS	84,746	70,823	27,518	146,014	188,709,911	179.06	58,780
KY	142,470	127,034	30,142	310,284	227,500,554	144.43	72,650
LA.	132,700	109,968	36,948	243,626	209,629,877	118.06	81,730
MA	309,384	249,341	131,636	485,500	1,035,951,213	226.31	146,851
MD	200,277	144,628	32,250	305,466	460,716,268	180.25	113,289
ME	67,322	58,640	25,826	136,741	145,515,586	166.73	33,827
MI.	672,589	487,246	159,494	1,197,825	1,287,583,689	211.29	187,666
MN	140,221	133,506	47,410	237,288	409,170,477	198.09	102,972
MO	243,793	184,467	73,148	517,986	380,203,456	146.07	128,605
MS	109,982	79,145	26,353	208,404	128,545,059	122.62	45,820
MT	30,238	25,147	9,507	56,115	44,845,680	134.62	24,607
NC	349,452	243,700	58,903	780,541	378,479,337	158.50	136,775
ND	17,936	14,936	6,147	31,965	29,707,904	146.22	17,865
NE	43,507	33,436	10,433	71,638	50,394,676	132.95	39,391
NH	52,832	39,915	6,875	67,353	61,112,771	135.55	31,400
NJ.	375,463	339,837	201,575	631,750	1,428,882,933	224.88	200,420
NM	39,398	31,702	12,681	68,619	72,762,929	138.28	34,336
NV	97,078	60,268	24,916	123,522	154,800,311	167.89	29,708
NY	726,608	673,398	365,156	1,353,373	2,634,623,256	197.42	431,276
OH	417,429	357,397	120,629	823,073	971,732,545	179.87	211,093
OK	81,277	65,969	28,834	159,409	147,771,561	159.50	66,189
OR	150,441	141,756	52,363	358,642	382,072,229	171.81	80,110
PA	610,759	517,810	194,509	1,251,135	1,751,434,187	200.92	233,178
PR	118,619	112,984	67,601	248,073	179,349,935	83.50	50,006
RI	65,195	60,746	30,009	137,756	196,453,246	206.09	31,646
SC	186,655	125,030	39,721	375,209	215,450,616	142.89	72,060
SD	10,965	8,868	1,119	22,479	12,040,598	127.84	19,262
TN	246,856	189,667	68,157	475,802	288,504,996	123.85	95,338
TX.	569,160	429,726	220,997	888,525	1,181,146,078	176.11	331,008
UT	47,823	37,685	13,000	67,330	82,164,098	174.49	34,899
VA	219,104	137,598	50,060	369,577	288,440,500	164.15	132,219
VI	3,604	2,660	1,083	4,873	6,306,143	160.58	2,899
VT.	28,342	26,477	7,650	47,483	65,877,963	155.31	19,027
WA	248,165	219,217	73,267	545,753	661,184,886	175.62	141,151
WI.	235,061	215,669	49,764	478,927	462,783,556	175.46	105,933
WV	68,483	60,922	18,621	105,070	147,535,478	162.74	35,715
WY	16,927	12,222	4,042	32,491	29,332,631	163.42	15,628
U.S.	**11,026,601**	**9,243,338**	**3,821,088**	**21,239,294**	**25,152,817,940**	**165.14**	**5,761,484**

Employment and Unemployment in the U.S.

Source: Bureau of Labor Statistics, U.S. Dept. of Labor

Civilian labor force, persons 16 years of age and over (in thousands)

Year*	Employed	Unemployed	Unemployment Rate	Year*	Employed	Unemployed	Unemployment Rate
1940[1]	47,520	8,120	14.6%	1984	105,005	8,539	7.5
1950	58,918	3,288	5.0	1985	107,150	8,312	7.2
1960	65,778	3,852	5.5	1986[2]	109,597	8,237	7.0
1970	78,678	4,093	4.9	1987	112,440	7,425	6.2
1975	85,846	7,929	8.5	1988	114,968	6,701	5.5
1980	99,303	7,637	7.1	1989	117,342	6,528	5.3
1981	100,397	8,273	7.6	1990	117,914	6,874	5.5
1982	99,526	10,678	9.7	1991	116,877	8,426	6.7
1983	100,834	10,717	9.6	1992	117,598	9,384	7.4

(1) Persons 14 years of age and over; (2) Not strictly comparable with prior years.

* **Early unemployment rates:** 1915, 9.7; 1916, 4.8; 1917, 4.8; 1918, 1.4; 1919, 2.3; 1920, 4.0; 1921, 11.9; 1922, 7.6; 1923, 3.2; 1924, 5.5; 1925, 4.0; 1926, 1.9; 1927, 4.1; 1928, 4.4; 1929, 3.2; 1930, 8.7; 1931, 15.9; 1932, 23.6; 1933, 24.9; 1934, 21.7; 1935, 20.1; 1936, 16.9; 1937, 14.3; 1938, 19.0; 1939, 17.2.

Employment and Training Services and Unemployment Insurance

Source: Employment and Training Administration, U.S. Dept. of Labor; September 1993.

Employment Service

The Federal-State Employment Service consists of the United States Employment Service and affiliated state employment services that make up the nation's public employment service system. From July 1, 1991, to June 30, 1992, the public employment service listed 5.6 million job openings and placed more than 2.6 million people in jobs.

The employment service refers employable applicants to job openings that use their highest skills and helps the unemployed obtain services or training to make them employable. It also provides special attention to handicapped workers, migrants and seasonal farmworkers, workers who lose their jobs because of foreign trade competition, and other worker groups. Veterans receive priority services including referral to jobs and training. During program year 1991, 382,000 veterans were placed in jobs.

Job Training

The Job Training Partnership Act (JTPA), which became fully operational on October 1, 1983, provides job training and employment services for economically disadvantaged youths and adults, dislocated workers, and others who face significant employment barriers. The goal of the Act is to move as many jobless workers as possible into permanent, unsubsidized, self-sustaining employment.

As of the end of program year 1991, JTPA had provided approximately 8 million Americans with training and employment services since its inception. Its placement rate is almost 69 percent, making it one of the most successful job and training efforts ever undertaken.

Title I of the Act's five titles basically establishes an administrative structure for the delivery of job and training services. Generally, state governors receive bloc grants from the Labor Department, and the funds are then distributed to Service Delivery Areas — areas of 200,000 population or more where local elected officials work with Private Industry Councils to plan and conduct local training projects.

Title II is in two parts, with Title II-A spelling out the Act's provision of employment and training projects for the economically disadvantaged. In program year 1991 (July 1, 1991, to Sept. 30, 1992), these projects served more than 1 million people.

Title II-B outlines a summer youth program offering basic and remedial education, institutional and on-the-job training, work experience, and supportive services. This program had nearly 550,000 participants in program year 1990. Beginning July 1, 1993, a new Title II-C provided for a year-round youth training program.

Title III, Economic Dislocation and Worker Adjustment Assistance, provides for job and training help for dislocated workers — workers who lose jobs and are unlikely to return to their previous industries or occupations. This includes workers who lose their jobs because of plant closings or mass layoffs; long-term unemployed persons with limited local opportunities for jobs in their fields; farmers, ranchers, and other self-employed persons who become jobless due to general economic conditions or natural disasters; and, under certain circumstances, displaced homemakers. Such assistance benefitted 330,643 workers in program year 1991.

Title IV authorizes programs to address the employment and training needs of specific groups facing significant barriers to productive employment, including Native Americans, migrant and seasonal farmworkers, and the disabled. In program year 1991, these programs served 11,310 Native Americans; 10,123 migrant and seasonal farmworkers; and more than 2,000 disabled persons.

In addition, Title IV includes the Job Corps, which each year enrolls approximately 100,000 young people between the ages of 16 and 21 in 107 residential job training centers throughout the United States; the National Commission for Employment Policy; and nationally administered programs for technical assistance, labor market information, research and evaluation, and pilots and demonstrations.

With recent amendments to JTPA, Title V is now the Jobs for Employable Dependent Individuals (JEDI) Incentive Bonus Program. Title VI provides for new State human resources investment councils, and Title VII covers transition provisions and technical conforming amendments.

Trade Adjustment Assistance for Workers

The Trade Adjustment Assistance (TAA) is available to workers who lose their jobs or whose hours of work and wages are reduced as a result of increased imports. TAA includes a variety of benefits and reemployment services to help unemployed workers prepare for and obtain suitable employment. Workers may be eligible for training, job search, relocation, and other reemployment services. Additionally, weekly trade readjustment allowances (TRA) may be payable to eligible workers following their exhaustion of unemployment insurance benefits. In fiscal year 1992, about 8,727 workers received $42.7 million in TRA payments; 18,582 workers entered training; 594 workers were involved in job search visits; and 751 workers relocated in order to obtain long term jobs.

The TAA program is administered by the Employment and Training Administration's Office of Trade Adjustment Assistance. State employment security agencies serve as agents of the U.S., under an agreement with the Secretary of Labor, for administering the TAA benefit provisions in the Trade Act of 1974, as amended.

Unemployment Insurance

Unlike old-age and survivors insurance, entirely a federal program, the unemployment insurance program is a Federal-State system that provides insured wage earners with partial replacement of wages lost during involuntary unemployment. The program protects most workers. During calendar year 1992, an estimated 105 million workers in commerce, industry, agriculture, and government, including the armed forces, were covered under the Federal-State system.

Each state, as well as the District of Columbia, Puerto Rico, and the Virgin Islands, has its own law and operates its own program. The amount and duration of the weekly benefits are determined by state laws, based on prior wages and length of employment. States are required to extend the duration of benefits when unemployment rises to and remains above specified state levels; costs of extended benefits are shared by the state and federal governments.

Under the Federal Unemployment Tax Act, as amended in 1985, the tax rate is 6.2% on the first $7,000 paid to each employee of employers with one or more employees in 20 weeks of the year or a quarterly payroll of $1,500. A credit of up to 5.4% is allowed for taxes paid under state unemployment insurance laws that meet certain criteria, leaving the federal share at 0.8% of taxable wages.

Social Security Requirement

The Social Security Act requires, as a condition of such grants, prompt payment of due benefits. The Federal Unemployment Tax Act provides safeguards for workers' right to benefits if they refuse jobs that fail to meet certain labor standards. Through the Unemployment Insurance Service of the Employment and Training Administration, the Secretary of Labor determines whether states qualify for grants and for tax offset credit from employers.

Benefits are financed solely by employer contributions, except in Alaska, Pennsylvania, and New Jersey where employees also contribute. Benefits are paid through the states' public employment offices, at which unemployed workers must register for work and to which they must report regularly for referral to a possible job during the time when they are drawing weekly benefit payments. During the fiscal year 1992, $25.61 billion in benefits was paid under state unemployment insurance programs to 9.6 million beneficiaries. They received an average weekly payment of $172.77 for total unemployment for an average of 15.9 weeks.

10 Facts About Women Workers

Source: Women's Bureau, U.S. Dept. of Labor

1. Of the 100 million women 16 and older in the U.S., 58 million were labor force participants (working or looking for work) during 1992. Women accounted for 60 percent of labor force growth between 1982 and 1992.
2. Women represented 45 percent of all persons in the civilian labor force in 1992. Women are projected to comprise 47 percent of the labor force by the year 2005.
3. Teenage women (16-19 years old) are not as active in the labor force as adult women (20 years of age and over). Only 49 percent were in the labor force, compared with 58 percent of adult women. In addition, teenage women's unemployment rate was three times as high as that of adult women—18.5 percent and 6.3 percent, respectively.
4. The unemployment rate for all women in the labor force was 6.9 percent in 1992. Teenage black and Hispanic women continued to experience very high unemployment rates —37.2 percent and 26.4 percent, respectively.
5. Of the 54 million employed women in the United States in 1992, 40 million worked full time (35 or more hours per week); nearly 14 million, or 25 percent of all women workers, held part-time jobs. Two-thirds (66 percent) of all part-time workers were women.
6. Women have made substantial progress in obtaining jobs in virtually all managerial and professional specialty occupations. In 1983 they held 40 percent (9.7 million) of these high-paying jobs; in 1992 they held 47 percent (14.7 million). Women employed in managerial and professional specialty occupations had 1992 median weekly earnings between $357 and $917.
7. Women are still overrepresented in low-paying jobs. Almost half (44 percent) of employed women work in technical, sales, and administrative support jobs—23.5 million women. Even though the earnings gap between men and women is slowly closing, women earn only 75 cents for every dollar earned by men when comparing 1992 median weekly earnings of full-time workers ($381 for women and $505 for men). The five most lucrative occupations for women are lawyer, physician, pharmacist, engineer, and computer systems analyst and scientist. (This list excludes any occupation at which fewer than 50,000 females are employed.)
8. Median earnings for female high school graduates (with no college) working year-round, full time in 1991 were less than those of fully employed men who were high school dropouts—$18,042 and $20,944, respectively. In addition, men with an associate's degree working year-round, full time earned nearly the same as similarly employed women with a master's degree—$32,221 and $33,122, respectively.
9. Of the approximately 67 million families in the United States in 1992, 12 million (18 percent) were maintained by women. In black families, women maintained 47 percent; in Hispanic families, 24 percent; and in white families, 14 percent. The median weekly earnings of families maintained by women in 1992 was $385, compared with $779 for married-couple families and $519 for families maintained by men.
10. In 1991 women represented 63 percent of all persons 18 years old and over who were living below the poverty level. The poverty rate for families maintained by women with no husband present was six times as high as for married-couple families—35.6 percent and 6.0 percent, respectively. Women maintained 54 percent of all poor families in 1991. Women maintained 78 percent of poor black families, about 46 percent of poor Hispanic families, and 44 percent of poor white families.

The Family and Medical Leave Act of 1993

Source: Women's Bureau, U.S. Dept. of Labor; effective Aug. 5, 1993.

Employee Rights

- Public and private sector employees who have been employed by the employer for one year and worked at least 1,250 hours can take up to 12 weeks of unpaid leave in any 12-month period for the birth or adoption of a child; acquiring a foster child; the serious illness of a child, spouse, or parent; or the serious illness of the employee.
- The right to take leave applies equally to male and female workers who are employed at or within 75 miles of the work place by an employer of 50 or more workers.
- Leave can be taken intermittently or on a schedule that reduces the usual number of hours per workday or workweek to care for an ill child, spouse, or parent or because of the employee's illness. Intermittent or reduced leave schedules because of the birth of a child, adoption, or foster care are subject to employer approval. Such a reduced or intermittent leave schedule does not reduce the total amount of leave to which the employee is entitled.
- An employee may elect or an employer may require the employee to substitute categories of paid leave for any part of the 12-week period.
- The employee maintains any preexisting health insurance for the duration of the leave and at the level and under the same conditions coverage was provided prior to commencement of the leave.
- At the end of the leave, the employee must be restored to the original or an equivalent position with equivalent benefits, pay, and all other terms of employment.

Other Requirements

- When husband and wife work for the same employer, the total amount of leave that they may take is limited to 12 weeks if they are taking leave for the birth or adoption of a child or to care for a sick parent.
- An employer may require certification from a health care provider to support a claim for leave.
- When the need for leave is foreseeable, an employee is required to provide at least 30 days advance notice.
- A new Commission on Leave will conduct a comprehensive study of existing and proposed leave policies, including the potential costs, benefits, and impact on productivity, and report its findings to Congress within 2 years of its first meeting.

Exclusions

- The law excludes any person employed at a worksite with fewer than 50 total employees at the worksite and employed by the employer within 75 miles of the worksite. Where employees have no fixed worksite, as is the case for many construction workers, transportation workers, and salespersons, such employees' "worksite" should be construed to mean the single site of employment to which they are assigned as their home base.
- An employer may deny job restoration to salaried employees who are among the highest paid 10 percent of the persons employed by the employer within 75 miles of the facility at which the employee works, if such denial is necessary to prevent substantial and grievous economic injury to the employer's operation.

Relationship to State Laws and Employer Policies

The Act does not supersede any state or local law, collective bargaining agreement, or employment benefit plan providing greater employee family leave rights, nor does it diminish the capacity to adopt more generous family leave policies.

Median Weekly Earnings of Full-Time Wage and Salary Workers by Age, Sex, and Union Affiliation

Source: Bureau of Labor Statistics, U.S. Dept. of Labor

	1991				1992			
Sex and Age	Total	Members of unions[1]	Represented by unions[2]	Non-union	Total	Members of unions[1]	Represented by unions[2]	Non-union
Total, 16 years and over	$430	$526	$522	$404	$445	$547	$541	$413
16 to 24 years	278	356	347	272	277	352	346	272
25 years and over	468	539	535	436	480	559	554	450
25 to 34 years	417	496	491	403	424	506	499	410
35 to 44 years	499	557	555	479	504	576	572	484
45 to 54 years	507	581	580	480	523	601	601	496
55 to 64 years	469	534	529	427	483	552	549	447
65 years and over	381	522	526	348	378	495	493	354
Men, 16 years and over	497	568	567	473	505	589	586	480
16 to 24 years	286	377	368	279	285	374	367	279
25 years and over	525	579	579	508	539	597	596	515
25 to 34 years	462	520	518	440	470	535	528	449
35 to 44 years	578	591	592	567	584	609	608	570
45 to 54 years	614	613	615	612	636	636	638	633
55 to 64 years	562	579	580	543	578	597	598	557
65 years and over	465	601	607	404	421	571	557	400
Women, 16 years and over	368	467	462	348	381	484	481	361
16 to 24 years	267	321	317	263	267	319	322	263
25 years and over	388	477	473	369	400	491	489	383
25 to 34 years	372	440	432	360	383	451	445	374
35 to 44 years	408	491	490	389	419	504	503	399
45 to 54 years	398	499	497	375	417	519	518	391
55 to 64 years	363	448	445	337	376	461	460	355
65 years and over	319	388	392	306	328	409	419	310

(1) Data refer to members of a labor union or an employee association similar to a union. (2) Data refer to members of a labor union or an employee association similar to a union as well as workers who report no union affiliation but whose jobs are covered by a union or an employee association contract. **Note:** Data refer to the sole or principal job of full-time workers. Excluded are self-employed workers whose businesses are incorporated although they technically qualify as wage and salary workers. Detail for the above race and Hispanic-origin groups will not sum to totals because data for the "other races" group are not presented and Hispanics are included in both the white and black population groups.

Employment Status of Persons in Families by Family Relationship, 1992

Source: Bureau of Labor Statistics, U.S. Dept. of Labor; in thousands

	Civilian Labor Force					Not in Labor Force				
Family Relationship	Total	Percent of Population	Employed	Unemployed Number	Unemployed Percent	Total	Home-makers	Students	Unable to Work	Other Reasons
Total, 16 years and over[1]	**101,215**	**66.8**	**93,754**	**7,461**	**7.4**	**50,388**	**20,292**	**6,998**	**2,643**	**20,455**
Husbands	40,193	77.5	38,274	1,918	4.8	11,641	212	175	990	10,264
With employed wife	26,813	91.5	25,656	1,157	4.3	2,500	101	103	408	1,889
With unemployed wife	1,328	90.6	1,147	181	13.6	137	5	5	26	101
With wife not in labor force	12,052	57.2	11,471	580	4.8	9,004	107	68	556	8,274
Wives	30,778	59.4	29,313	1,465	4.8	21,056	15,460	366	449	4,781
With employed husband	26,803	70.0	25,656	1,147	4.3	11,471	9,757	305	165	1,244
With unemployed husband	1,338	69.7	1,157	181	13.5	580	478	18	22	63
With husband not in labor force	2,637	22.7	2,500	137	5.2	9,004	5,225	44	262	3,473
Relatives in married-couple families	12,833	63.1	11,075	1,758	13.7	7,493	729	4,419	360	1,984
16 to 19 years	4,358	51.6	3,621	738	16.9	4,084	128	3,256	10	689
20 to 24 years	4,747	75.7	4,197	550	11.6	1,527	148	1,025	44	311
25 years and over	3,727	66.4	3,257	470	12.6	1,882	453	138	306	984
Women who maintain families	7,303	62.3	6,582	721	9.9	4,423	2,744	231	291	1,156
Relatives in families maintained by women	5,689	59.0	4,598	1,092	19.2	3,947	771	1,478	364	1,335
16 to 19 years	1,240	44.6	859	381	30.7	1,541	95	1,126	12	309
20 to 24 years	1,602	72.1	1,302	300	18.7	620	142	267	27	185
25 years and over	2,848	61.5	2,437	411	14.4	1,786	534	85	325	841
Men who maintain families	2,514	77.9	2,288	226	9.0	711	44	40	92	535
Relatives in families maintained by men	1,905	63.0	1,624	281	14.7	1,117	332	289	97	399
16 to 19 years	288	51.4	218	70	24.3	272	22	193	1	56
20 to 24 years	479	77.0	412	68	14.1	143	31	69	6	37
25 years and over	1,137	61.8	994	143	12.6	702	279	27	90	306

(1) Excludes persons living alone or with nonrelatives, persons in married-couple families where the husband or wife is in the Armed Forces, and persons in unrelated subfamilies. **Note:** Estimates shown in this table for husbands, wives, and women who maintain families are somewhat different from marital status estimates shown in other tables in this publication because of differences in definitions and weighting patterns used in aggregating the data.

Work Stoppages (Strikes) in the U.S., 1955-1992

Source: Bureau of Labor Statistics, U.S. Dept. of Labor

(involving 1,000 workers or more)

	Number stoppages[1]	Workers involved[1] (thousands)	Work days idle[1] (thousands)		Number stoppages[1]	Workers involved[1] (thousands)	Work days idle[1] (thousands)
1955	363	2,055	21,100	1978	219	1,006	23,774
1960	222	896	13,260	1979	235	1,021	20,409
1965	268	999	15,140	1980	187	795	20,844
1966	321	1,300	16,000	1981	145	729	16,908
1967	381	2,192	31,320	1982	96	656	9,061
1968	392	1,855	35,567	1983	81	909	17,461
1969	412	1,576	29,397	1984	62	376	8,499
1970	381	2,468	52,761	1985	54	324	7,079
1971	298	2,516	35,538	1986	69	533	11,861
1972	250	975	16,764	1987	46	174	4,481
1973	317	1,400	16,260	1988	40	118	4,364
1974	424	1,796	31,809	1989	51	452	16,996
1975	235	965	17,563	1990	44	185	5,926
1976	231	1,519	23,962	1991	40	392	4,584
1977	298	1,212	21,258	1992	35	364	3,989

(1) The number of stoppages and workers relate to stoppages that began in the year. Days of idleness include all stoppages in effect. Workers are counted more than once if they were involved in more than one stoppage during the year.

Work Stoppages Involving 5,000 Workers or More Beginning in 1992

Source: Bureau of Labor Statistics, U.S. Labor Dept.

Employer, location, and union	Began	Ended	Workers involved[1]	Estimated days idle in 1992[1]
Kroger Co., Michigan, Food and Commercial Workers	4/13	6/19	7,800	388,200
Railroad industry, interstate, various unions	6/24	6/25	230,000	460,000
General Motors, Lordstown, OH, Automobile Workers	8/27	9/5	45,100	217,600
Board of Education, Detroit, MI, teachers (AFT)	8/31	9/26	10,500	199,500
General Motors, Lansing, MI, Automobile Workers	9/25	9/28	7,200	14,400
USAir, interstate, Machinists	10/5	10/10	8,300	41,500

(1) Workers and days idle are rounded to the nearest 100.

Unemployed Jobseekers, 1992

Source: Bureau of Labor Statistics, U.S. Dept. of Labor

	Thousands of Persons		Methods Used as a Percent of Total Jobseekers						
Sex, Age, and Race	Total Unemployed	Total Jobseekers	Public Employment Agency	Private Employment Agency	Employer Directly	Placed or Answered Ads	Friends or Relatives	Other	Average Number of Methods Used
Total, 16 years and over	**9,384**	**8,027**	**22.6**	**9.3**	**74.3**	**41.7**	**23.7**	**5.3**	**1.77**
16 to 19 years	1,352	1,283	11.6	4.0	81.5	27.5	18.1	3.5	1.46
20 to 24 years	1,546	1,365	21.8	8.7	74.8	42.1	22.2	3.8	1.73
25 to 34 years	2,662	2,258	26.2	9.9	73.2	45.6	24.4	4.5	1.84
35 to 44 years	1,941	1,602	25.9	11.4	72.9	45.0	25.7	6.6	1.87
45 to 54 years	1,145	933	25.3	12.4	71.7	44.8	26.6	8.2	1.89
55 to 64 years	603	473	22.4	10.2	70.7	43.9	26.4	7.4	1.81
65 years and over	135	112	15.2	6.9	68.6	37.6	24.0	7.4	1.60
Men, 16 years and over	**5,380**	**4,444**	**24.7**	**9.8**	**74.8**	**40.4**	**26.6**	**6.2**	**1.82**
16 to 19 years	761	720	12.3	3.8	81.7	26.1	20.0	3.4	1.47
20 to 24 years	884	759	23.3	9.0	75.3	41.5	25.7	4.2	1.79
25 to 34 years	1,508	1,217	29.1	10.5	74.1	44.8	28.7	5.0	1.92
35 to 44 years	1,095	857	28.9	12.4	72.9	43.9	28.8	8.2	1.95
45 to 54 years	675	535	27.6	12.9	71.2	42.2	28.2	10.8	1.93
55 to 64 years	387	299	23.7	11.3	72.2	42.2	27.7	8.8	1.86
65 years and over	69	57	15.0	6.0	72.0	31.1	24.3	6.9	1.55
Women, 16 years and over	**4,005**	**3,582**	**20.0**	**8.7**	**73.8**	**43.3**	**20.0**	**4.1**	**1.70**
16 to 19 years	591	563	10.8	4.2	81.2	29.4	15.7	3.5	1.45
20 to 24 years	662	606	19.9	8.3	74.1	42.9	17.7	3.3	1.66
25 to 34 years	1,154	1,041	22.8	9.3	72.1	46.6	19.4	3.9	1.74
35 to 44 years	845	744	22.3	10.3	72.9	46.2	22.2	4.8	1.79
45 to 54 years	470	398	22.1	11.7	72.3	48.2	24.4	4.7	1.83
55 to 64 years	216	174	20.2	8.4	68.2	46.8	24.2	5.1	1.73
65 years and over	66	55	15.4	7.8	65.2	44.4	23.7	7.8	1.64
White, 16 years and over	**7,047**	**5,896**	**21.9**	**9.0**	**74.8**	**43.3**	**23.9**	**5.7**	**1.79**
Men	4,121	3,320	24.4	9.6	75.3	41.6	26.8	6.8	1.84
Women	2,926	2,576	18.8	8.2	74.1	45.5	20.3	4.3	1.71
Black, 16 years and over	**1,958**	**1,787**	**25.0**	**10.3**	**73.9**	**35.4**	**21.5**	**4.0**	**1.70**
Men	1,046	933	26.2	10.3	74.2	34.9	24.9	4.3	1.75
Women	912	854	23.6	10.3	73.4	35.9	17.8	3.7	1.65

Note: The jobseekers total is less than the total unemployed because it does not include persons on layoff or waiting to begin a new job within 30 days, groups for whom jobseeking information is not collected. The percent using each method will always total more than 100 because many jobseekers use more than one method.

Absences from Work of Employed, Full-Time Wage and Salary Workers, 1992

Source: Bureau of Labor Statistics, U.S. Dept. of Labor
(in thousands)

Industry	Total Employed	Absence Rate[1] Total	Absence Rate[1] Illness	Absence Rate[1] Other Reasons	Lost Worktime Rate[2] Total	Lost Worktime Rate[2] Illness	Lost Worktime Rate[2] Other Reasons
Agricultural wage and salary workers	1,200	3.8	1.9	2.0	2.8	1.6	1.2
Private nonagricultural wage and salary workers	67,570	4.7	2.6	2.1	2.7	1.6	1.2
Mining	605	4.7	2.4	2.3	3.7	1.5	2.2
Construction	4,081	5.0	2.6	2.4	3.4	1.8	1.6
Manufacturing	18,197	4.6	2.9	1.7	2.7	1.8	.9
Durable goods	10,608	4.6	3.0	1.6	2.8	1.8	.9
Nondurable goods	7,589	4.7	2.8	1.9	2.7	1.7	1.0
Transportation and public utilities	5,658	4.5	2.7	1.8	3.1	1.8	1.3
Transportation	3,033	4.7	2.6	2.1	3.7	2.0	1.7
Communications and other public utilities	2,625	4.2	2.7	1.5	2.4	1.6	.8
Wholesale and retail trade	14,346	4.3	2.2	2.2	2.4	1.3	1.1
Wholesale trade	3,781	3.8	2.1	1.7	2.2	1.3	.9
Retail trade	10,565	4.5	2.2	2.3	2.4	1.3	1.2
Finance, insurance, and real estate	5,850	3.8	2.1	1.7	2.0	1.1	.9
Services	18,832	5.2	2.7	2.5	2.8	1.5	1.3
Government workers	15,373	5.5	2.9	2.7	3.2	1.7	1.5

(1) Absences refer to work missed due to illnesses or other personal reasons. Excluded is work missed due to vacation, holiday, labor-management dispute, or bad weather resulting in an employer temporarily curtailing business activity. The absence rate is the ratio of workers with absences to total full-time employment. To be counted as having had an absence, a person who usually works 35 hours or more per week must have been at work fewer than 35 hours or have not been at work at all during the survey reference week. (2) Hours absent as a percent of total hours usually worked. **Note:** Data for 1992 are not fully comparable with data for prior years because of the introduction of the occupational and industrial classification systems used in the 1990 census.

Federal Minimum Hourly Wage Rates Since 1950

Source: U.S. Dept. of Labor

The Fair Labor Standards Act of 1938 and subsequent amendments provide for minimum wage coverage applicable to specified nonsupervisory employment categories. Exempt from coverage are executives and administrators or professionals.

Effective date	Minimum Rates for Nonfarm Workers: Laws prior to 1966[1]	Minimum Rates for Nonfarm Workers: Percent, avg earnings[2]	Minimum Rates for Nonfarm Workers: 1966 and later[3]	Minimum rates for farm workers[4]
Jan. 25, 1950	$.75	54	(X)	(X)
Mar. 1, 1956	1.00	52	(X)	(X)
Sept. 3, 1961	1.15	50	(X)	(X)
Sept. 3, 1963	1.25	51	(X)	(X)
Feb. 1, 1967	1.40	50	$1.00	$1.00
Feb. 1, 1968	1.60	54	1.15	1.15
Feb. 1, 1969	(5)	(5)	1.30	1.30
Feb. 1, 1970	(5)	(5)	1.45	(5)
Feb. 1, 1971	(5)	(5)	1.60	(5)
May 1, 1974	2.00	46	1.90	1.60
Jan. 1, 1975	2.10	45	2.00	1.80
Jan. 1, 1976	2.30	46	2.20	2.00
Jan. 1, 1977	(5)	(5)	2.30	2.20
Jan. 1, 1978	2.65	44	2.65	2.65
Jan. 1, 1979	2.90	45	2.90	2.90
Jan. 1, 1980	3.10	43	3.10	3.10
Jan. 1, 1981	3.35	42	3.35	3.35
Apr. 1, 1990	3.80[6]	35	3.80[6]	3.80[6]
Apr. 1, 1991	4.25[6]	38	4.25[6]	4.25[6]

(X) Not applicable. (1) Applies to workers covered prior to 1961 Amendments and, after Sept. 1965, to workers covered by 1961 Amendments. Rates set by 1961 Amendments were: Sept. 1961, $1.00; Sept. 1964, $1.15; and Sept. 1965, $1.25. (2) Percent of gross average hourly earnings of production workers in manufacturing. (3) Applies to workers newly covered by Amendments of 1966, 1974, and 1977, and Title IX of Education Amendments of 1972. (4) Included in coverage as of 1966, 1974, and 1977 Amendments. (5) No change in rate. (6) Training wage for workers age 16-19 in first six months of first job: 1990, $3.35; 1991, $3.62 and from Apr. 1, 1991 additional requirements re subsequent employment by a different employer for an additional 90 days. The training wage expired Mar. 31, 1993.

Part-Time Workers, 1992

Source: Bureau of Labor Statistics, U.S. Dept. of Labor
(in thousands)

Reason for Working Less Than 35 Hours	All industries: Total	All industries: Usually Work Full-Time	All industries: Usually Work Part-Time	Nonagricultural industries: Total	Nonagricultural industries: Usually Work Full-Time	Nonagricultural industries: Usually Work Part-Time
Total, 16 years and over	**30,147**	**11,029**	**19,118**	**29,245**	**10,710**	**18,535**
Economic reasons	**6,385**	**2,026**	**4,359**	**6,116**	**1,910**	**4,206**
Slack work	3,220	1,728	1,492	3,037	1,623	1,414
Material shortages or repairs to plant and equipment	39	39	—	38	38	—
New job started during week	188	188	—	180	180	—
Job terminated during week	71	71	—	69	69	—
Could find only part-time work	2,867	—	2,867	2,792	—	2,792
Other reasons	**23,762**	**9,003**	**14,759**	**23,129**	**8,800**	**14,329**
Does not want, or unavailable for, full-time work	12,054	—	12,054	11,732	—	11,732
Vacation	1,716	1,716	—	1,696	1,696	—
Illness	1,500	1,326	174	1,473	1,310	163
Bad weather	557	557	—	462	462	—
Industrial dispute	10	10	—	10	10	—
Legal or religious holiday	3,856	3,856	—	3,837	3,837	—
Full time for this job	1,650	—	1,650	1,613	—	1,613
All other reasons	2,419	1,538	881	2,306	1,485	821
Average hours:						
Economic reasons	22.2	24.4	21.2	22.3	24.5	21.3
Other reasons	22.7	27.8	19.5	22.7	27.9	19.6
Worked 30 to 34 hours:						
Economic reasons	2,065	924	1,141	1,994	883	1,111
Other reasons	8,905	6,001	2,904	8,750	5,914	2,836

Distribution of Wage and Salary Workers Paid Hourly Rates

Source: Bureau of Labor Statistics, U.S. Dept. of Labor; unpublished tabulations from Current Population Survey, 1992.

(in thousands)

	Total paid hourly rates	$4.25* or less	Less than $10.00	$10.00 or more
Sex and age				
Total, 16 years and over	62,683	4,762	41,295	21,388
16 to 24 years	14,173	2,479	13,090	1,083
20 to 24 years	9,300	1,065	8,293	1,007
25 years and over	48,511	2,283	28,207	20,304
25 to 54 years	42,054	1,854	24,073	17,981
25 to 34 years	17,835	912	11,411	6,424
35 to 44 years	15,005	602	7,801	7,124
45 to 54 years	9,215	340	4,782	4,433
55 years and over	6,456	429	4,114	2,324
55 to 64 years	5,076	252	3,018	2,058
65 years and over	1,380	177	1,114	266
Men, 16 years and over	31,510	1,792	17,849	13,661
16 to 24 years	7,399	1,093	6,695	704
20 to 24 years	4,909	444	4,259	650
25 years and over	24,111	699	11,155	12,956
Women, 16 years and over	31,173	2,970	23,446	7,727
16 to 24 years	6,773	1,386	6,394	379
20 to 24 years	4,397	621	4,041	356
25 years and over	24,400	1,584	17,053	7,347
Family relationship				
Husbands	16,400	310	N/A	N/A
Wives	15,701	895	N/A	N/A
Women who maintain families	4,061	386	N/A	N/A
Men who maintain families	1,289	52	N/A	N/A
Race and Hispanic origin				
White				
Total, 16 years and over	52,452	3,872	33,960	18,492
Men	26,508	1,431	14,538	11,970
Women	25,944	2,442	19,423	6,521
Black				
Total, 16 years and over	8,054	719	5,859	2,195
Men	3,926	288	2,640	1,286
Women	4,129	432	3,220	909
Hispanic origin				
Total, 16 years and over	5,984	590	4,528	1,456
Men	3,638	298	2,580	1,058
Women	2,346	292	1,946	400
Full- and part-time status and sex				
Full-time workers				
Total, 16 years and over	46,645	1,742	27,579	19,066
Men	26,426	731	13,331	13,095
Women	20,219	1,011	14,249	5,970
Part-time workers				
Total, 16 years and over	16,037	3,020	13,715	2,322
Men	5,084	1,061	4,520	564
Women	10,953	1,959	9,198	1,755

Note: Data exclude the incorporated self-employed. * $4.25 = minimum wage from April 1, 1991. N/A = Not available.

Average Hours and Earnings of Production Workers, 1964-1992

Source: Bureau of Labor Statistics, U.S. Dept. of Labor

(annual averages)

	Weekly hours	Total private[1] Hourly earnings	Weekly earnings		Weekly hours	Total private[1] Hourly earnings	Weekly earnings
1964	38.7	$2.36	$91.33	1979	35.7	6.16	219.91
1965	38.8	2.46	95.45	1980	35.3	6.66	235.10
1966	38.6	2.56	98.82	1981	35.2	7.25	255.20
1967	38.0	2.68	101.84	1982	34.8	7.68	267.26
1968	37.8	2.85	107.73	1983	35.0	8.02	280.70
1969	37.7	3.04	114.61	1984	35.2	8.32	292.86
1970	37.1	3.23	119.83	1985	34.9	8.57	299.09
1971	36.9	3.45	127.31	1986	34.8	8.76	304.85
1972	37.0	3.70	136.90	1987	34.8	8.98	312.50
1973	36.9	3.94	145.39	1988	34.7	9.28	322.02
1974	36.5	4.24	154.76	1989	34.6	9.66	334.24
1975	36.1	4.53	163.53	1990	34.5	10.01	345.35
1976	36.1	4.86	175.45	1991	34.3	10.32	353.98
1977	36.0	5.25	189.00	1992	34.4	10.58	363.95
1978	35.8	5.69	203.70				

(1) Data relate to production workers in mining and manufacturing; construction workers in construction; and nonsupervisory workers in transportation and public utilities; wholesale and retail trade; finance, insurance, and real estate; and services.

Workers Paid Hourly Rates, 1979-1992

Source: Bureau of Labor Statistics, U.S. Dept. of Labor; unpublished tabulations from the Current Population Survey.

(in thousands)

Year	Total Wage and Salary Workers	Workers paid hourly rates: Total	Percent of Wage and Salary Workers	Paid Below Prevailing Minimum Wage	Paid at Prevailing Minimum Wage
Both sexes					
1979	85,773	50,637	59.0	2,846	3,907
1980	85,780	50,210	58.5	3,017	4,581
1981 (end 1970 weights)	86,651	50,770	58.6	3,440	4,201
1981 (begin 1980 weights)	88,516	51,869	58.6	3,513	4,311
1982	87,368	50,846	58.2	2,348	4,148
1983	88,290	51,820	58.7	2,077	4,261
1984	92,194	54,143	58.7	1,838	4,125
1985	94,521	55,762	59.0	1,639	3,899
1986	96,903	57,529	59.4	1,599	3,461
1987	99,303	59,552	60.0	1,468	3,229
1988	101,407	60,878	60.0	1,319	2,608
1989	103,480	62,389	60.3	1,372	1,790
1990 (2nd quarter - 1st quarter 1991)*	103,587	62,112	60.0	2,221	968
1991 (2nd quarter - 1st quarter 1992)	102,872	61,782	60.1	2,351	3,365
1992	103,688	62,683	60.5	1,896	2,866
Men					
1979	48,389	27,771	57.4	820	1,318
1980	47,641	27,075	56.8	957	1,654
1981 (end 1970 weights)	47,769	26,936	56.4	1,090	1,489
1981 (begin 1980 weights)	48,844	27,576	56.5	1,119	1,533
1982	47,591	26,481	55.6	697	1,587
1983	47,856	26,831	56.1	585	1,658
1984	50,022	28,140	56.3	490	1,626
1985	51,015	28,893	56.6	440	1,544
1986	51,942	29,666	57.1	408	1,336
1987	52,938	30,474	57.6	364	1,283
1988	53,912	31,058	57.6	311	1,066
1989	54,789	31,687	57.8	379	733
1990 (2nd quarter - 1st quarter 1991)	54,573	31,355	57.5	732	318
1991 (2nd quarter - 1st quarter 1992)	53,879	31,010	57.6	781	1,301
1992	54,135	31,510	58.2	628	1,164
Women					
1979	37,384	22,866	61.2	2,026	2,589
1980	38,140	23,135	60.7	2,060	2,927
1981 (end 1970 weights)	38,882	23,834	61.3	2,350	2,711
1981 (begin 1980 weights)	39,672	24,294	61.2	2,394	2,778
1982	39,777	24,365	61.3	1,651	2,561
1983	40,433	24,989	61.8	1,492	2,603
1984	42,172	26,003	61.7	1,348	2,499
1985	43,506	26,869	61.8	1,198	2,356
1986	44,961	27,863	62.0	1,192	2,125
1987	46,365	29,078	62.7	1,105	1,946
1988	47,495	29,820	62.8	1,008	1,542
1989	48,691	30,702	63.1	994	1,056
1990 (2nd quarter - 1st quarter 1991)	49,014	30,757	62.8	1,489	650
1991 (2nd quarter - 1st quarter 1992)	48,993	30,771	62.8	1,570	2,064
1992	49,554	31,173	62.9	1,268	1,702

* The prevailing federal minimum wage was $2.90 in 1979, $3.10 in 1980, and $3.35 in 1981-89. The minimum wage rose to $3.80 in April 1990, and to $4.25 in April 1991. **NOTE:** Data exclude the incorporated self-employed. Estimates based on sample weights applicable to 1970 census population controls are not strictly comparable to those weights applicable to 1980 controls. Data for 1981 are shown both ways. Although the new weights caused the number of wage and salary workers to rise by 1.9 million, hourly paid workers to rise by 1.1 million, and those at or below the minimum wage to rise by 183,000, percentages and medians changed very little or not at all.

Employment Status of the Civilian Noninstitutional Population in Poverty and Nonpoverty Areas, 1992

Source: Bureau of Labor Statistics, U.S. Dept. of Labor

(in thousands)

	Total U.S.		Metropolitan Areas		Nonmetropolitan Areas	
	Poverty Areas	Nonpoverty Areas	Poverty Areas	Nonpoverty Areas	Poverty Areas	Nonpoverty Areas
Civilian noninstitutional population	26,797	164,778	17,122	131,998	9,676	32,780
Civilian labor force	15,364	111,618	9,666	90,393	5,698	21,226
Percent of population	57.3	67.7	56.5	68.5	58.9	64.8
Employed	13,520	104,078	8,313	84,283	5,207	19,795
Unemployed	1,844	7,540	1,353	6,110	491	1,431
Unemployment rate	12.0	6.8	14.0	6.8	8.6	6.7
Men, 20 years and over	11.2	6.5	13.2	6.5	7.8	6.3
Women, 20 years and over	10.5	5.7	12.2	5.7	7.6	5.6
Both sexes, 16 to 19 years	30.5	18.4	34.7	18.7	23.4	17.5
Men	30.6	20.0	35.4	20.5	23.2	18.3
Women	30.3	16.7	33.9	16.7	23.7	16.7
Not in labor force	11,434	53,160	7,456	41,605	3,977	11,555

Employer-Provided Pension Plans

Source: Bureau of the Census, Economics and Statistics Administration, U.S. Dept. of Commerce; April 1993

- **Coverage rates rise slightly.** In 1991, 68 percent of workers were covered by employer-provided pension plans, up from 66 percent in 1987 but not significantly different from 1984. These plans may include 401(k) plans. Covered workers are those whose employer offered a retirement plan for any employees. However, not every covered worker was a participant. In 1991, 53 percent of all workers participated in pension plans, the same as in 1987 but lower than the 55 percent who did so in 1984. Covered workers did not participate in 1991 for the following reasons: 33 percent had not worked for the firm long enough; 23 percent chose not to participate; 22 percent did not work sufficient hours per year; 11 percent were in an ineligible job category; and 11 percent started the job too close to retirement age or had another, unspecified reason.
- **Who is covered?** Many factors affect coverage rates. *Size of company:* Employees of larger firms have a much higher pension coverage rate than those in smaller firms. Coverage rates in 1991 ranged from 90 percent in firms with more than 1,000 employees to 23 percent in those with fewer than 25 employees. *Level of earnings:* Highly paid workers were more likely to be covered by pension plans. Coverage rates ranged from 82 percent for those with monthly earnings of $2,000 or more to 43 percent for those who earned less than $500 per month. Employees covered by employer-sponsored plans had much higher median monthly earnings than those not covered: $2,003 versus $1,253. *Union status:* Union members had a higher coverage rate than nonmembers (89 versus 62 percent). By industry, pension coverage ranged from 100 percent in the armed forces and 92 percent in public administration to 37 percent in personal services and 34 percent in agriculture, forestry, and fisheries.
- **More workers are vested.** In 1991, 47 percent of all workers were vested in a pension plan, an increase from the 1984 and 1987 rates of 45 percent. These workers were eligible to receive a lump-sum distribution at retirement or continuing payments during retirement. Since vesting is usually linked to the length of service on the job, young workers are less likely to be vested than older workers. Vesting rates ranged from 33 percent of workers under age 30 to 55 percent of those 50 to 59 years of age.
- **IRA ownership down, 401(k) plan participation up.** Individual Retirement Accounts (IRA's) were established in 1974 as a means of building savings for retirement for workers not covered by an employer-provided pension plan. In 1982, eligibility was extended to all workers. IRA's thus became a popular way to supplement pension income: 77 percent of workers who had IRA's in 1991 were also covered by employer-sponsored pension plans, about the same as in 1987 and 1984. However, ownership of IRA's, which had increased from 21 to 24 percent of all workers between 1984 and 1987, fell to 20 percent in 1991. This drop probably reflects both the effect of the Tax Reform Act of 1986, which limited the tax deductibility of IRA contributions, and the growing popularity of 401(k) and other types of thrift savings plans. The percentage of workers participating in employer-sponsored thrift plans, known as 401(k)'s, tripled between 1984 and 1991, from 6 to 19 percent. Larger firms were likelier to offer 401(k)'s: participation in 1991 ranged from 3 percent at firms employing fewer than 25 people to 28 percent at those employing 1,000 or more. Increasing numbers of workers are both IRA and 401(k) plan participants: 6 percent in 1991, up from 4 percent in 1987 and 2 percent in 1984.

Employer Costs for Employee Compensation, March 1993

Source: Bureau of Labor Statistics, U.S. Dept. of Labor; dollar figures are costs per hour worked.

			Benefit Costs					
	Total Compensation	Wages and Salaries	Total[1]	Paid Leave	Supplemental Pay	Insurance	Retirement and Savings	Legally Required Benefits
Civilian workers	**$17.88**	**$12.68**	**$5.20**	**$1.22**	**$0.39**	**$1.32**	**$0.70**	**$1.53**
Occupational group:								
White-collar occupations	21.23	15.38	5.86	1.55	0.38	1.48	0.87	1.54
Professional specialty and technical	29.33	21.41	7.92	2.05	0.42	1.94	1.51	1.96
Executive, administrative, and managerial	30.48	21.98	8.50	2.65	0.67	1.76	1.19	2.13
Administrative support including clerical	14.36	10.05	4.31	1.08	0.25	1.35	0.50	1.12
Blue-collar occupations	16.58	11.08	5.50	1.02	0.55	1.42	0.61	1.84
Service occupations	10.04	7.25	2.79	0.58	0.17	0.69	0.35	1.00
Industry group:								
Services	18.91	13.80	5.11	1.26	0.27	1.29	0.83	1.43
Health services	17.55	12.66	4.88	1.36	0.44	1.16	0.49	1.42
Hospitals	19.74	13.83	5.91	1.69	0.60	1.54	0.56	1.51
Educational services	26.87	19.56	7.32	1.63	0.08	2.09	1.95	1.53
Elementary and secondary education	27.24	19.78	7.46	1.54	0.08	2.25	2.09	1.47
Higher education	27.39	20.02	7.37	1.86	0.10	1.91	1.81	1.68
			Percent of Total Compensation					
Civilian workers	**100.0**	**70.9**	**29.1**	**6.8**	**2.2**	**7.4**	**3.9**	**8.6**
Occupational group:								
White-collar occupations	100.0	72.4	27.6	7.3	1.8	7.0	4.1	7.3
Professional specialty and technical	100.0	73.0	27.0	7.0	1.4	6.6	5.1	6.7
Executive, administrative, and managerial	100.0	72.1	27.9	8.7	2.2	5.8	3.9	7.0
Administrative support including clerical	100.0	70.0	30.0	7.5	1.7	9.4	3.4	7.8
Blue-collar occupations	100.0	66.8	33.2	6.1	3.3	8.6	3.7	11.1
Service occupations	100.0	72.2	27.8	5.8	1.7	6.8	3.5	10.0
Industry group:								
Services	100.0	73.0	27.0	6.7	1.4	6.8	4.4	7.6
Health services	100.0	72.2	27.8	7.8	2.5	6.6	2.8	8.1
Hospitals	100.0	70.0	30.0	8.6	3.0	7.8	2.8	7.7
Educational services	100.0	72.8	27.2	6.1	0.3	7.8	7.3	5.7
Elementary and secondary education	100.0	72.6	27.4	5.7	0.3	8.3	7.7	5.4
Higher education	100.0	73.1	26.9	6.8	0.4	7.0	6.6	6.2

(1) Includes severance pay and supplemental unemployment benefits.

Civilian Employment of the Federal Government in May 1993

Source: Workforce Analysis and Statistics Division, U.S. Office of Personnel Management
(Payroll in thousands of dollars, for the month of May, 1993)

Agency	All Areas Employment	All Areas Payroll	United States Employment	United States Payroll	Wash., D.C. MSA Employment	Wash., D.C. MSA Payroll	Overseas Employment	Overseas Payroll
Total, all agencies[1]	**3,033,215**	**$10,323,268**	**2,918,308**	**$9,917,094**	**380,442**	**$1,717,767**	**114,907**	**$406,174**
Legislative Branch	**38,779**	**157,762**	**38,721**	**157,390**	**36,508**	**145,240**	**58**	**372**
Congress	20,695	66,417	20,695	66,417	20,695	66,417	—	—
U.S. Senate	7,723	24,698	7,723	24,698	7,723	24,698	—	—
House of Rep Summary	12,954	41,633	12,954	41,633	12,954	41,633	—	—
Comm. on Scty & Coop in Eur	18	86	18	86	18	86	—	—
Architect of the Capitol	2,334	9,238	2,334	9,238	2,334	9,238	—	—
Botanic Garden	51	216	51	216	51	216	—	—
Competit Policy Council	6	28	6	28	6	28	—	—
Congressional Budget Ofc	239	1,631	239	1,631	239	1,631	—	—
Copyright Royalty Tribunal	8	65	8	65	8	65	—	—
General Accounting Ofc	5,109	31,747	5,058	31,445	3,349	21,166	51	302
Government Printing Ofc	4,775	22,350	4,775	22,350	4,302	20,585	—	—
John C Stennis Ctr Pub Dev	6	16	6	16	—	—	—	—
Library of Congress	4,999	23,358	4,992	23,288	4,973	23,220	7	70
Nat Comm on AIDS Syndrome	11	44	11	44	11	44	—	—
Nat Comm Prev Infant Mort	10	27	10	27	10	27	—	—
Ofc Technology Assessment	217	1,301	217	1,301	217	1,301	—	—
U.S. Tax Court	319	1,324	319	1,324	313	1,302	—	—
Judicial Branch	**28,075**	**133,183**	**27,769**	**131,727**	**2,070**	**11,006**	**306**	**1,456**
Supreme Court	371	1,094	371	1,094	371	1,094	—	—
U.S. Courts	27,618	131,639	27,312	130,183	1,613	9,462	306	1,456
U.S. Court of Vets Appeals	86	450	86	450	86	450	—	—
Executive Branch	**2,966,361**	**10,032,323**	**2,851,818**	**9,627,977**	**341,864**	**1,561,521**	**114,543**	**404,346**
Exec Ofc of the President	1,991	7,598	1,983	7,557	1,983	7,557	8	41
White House Office	559	1,798	559	1,798	559	1,798	—	—
Ofc of Vice President	23	105	23	105	23	105	—	—
Ofc of Mgt & Budget	564	2,456	564	2,456	564	2,456	—	—
Office of Administration	241	715	241	715	241	715	—	—
Council Economic Advisors	33	133	33	133	33	133	—	—
Council on Environ Qual	23	83	23	83	23	83	—	—
Ofc of Policy Development	52	190	52	190	52	190	—	—
Exec Residence at WH	93	581	93	581	93	581	—	—
Natl Crit Materials Coun	2	8	2	8	2	8	—	—
National Security Council	65	240	65	240	65	240	—	—
National Space Council	7	5	7	5	7	5	—	—
Ofc of Natl Drug Control	90	351	90	351	90	351	—	—
Ofc of Sci and Tech Policy	39	110	39	110	39	110	—	—
Ofc of U.S. Trade Rep	200	823	192	782	192	782	8	41
Executive Departments	**2,001,621**	**6,968,252**	**1,906,940**	**6,629,080**	**259,118**	**1,157,252**	**94,681**	**339,172**
State	26,220	153,086	9,852	54,772	8,852	48,150	16,368	98,314
Treasury	165,530	743,467	164,373	736,703	24,523	138,892	1,157	6,764
Defense, Total	941,608	2,731,443	873,639	2,532,490	89,692	282,341	67,969	198,953
Dept of the Army	306,562	827,905	276,610	742,534	26,493	56,125	29,952	85,371
Army, Mil Func Total	275,857	751,411	245,996	666,321	25,314	52,599	29,861	85,090
Army, Civil Func Total	30,705	76,494	30,614	76,213	1,179	3,526	91	281
Corps of Engineers	30,565	76,170	30,474	75,889	1,039	3,202	91	281
Cemeterial Expenses	140	324	140	324	140	324	—	—
Dept of the Navy	285,079	898,000	273,357	863,786	37,394	124,463	11,722	34,214
Dept of the Air Force	196,074	557,131	186,662	532,198	5,892	20,795	9,412	24,933
Defense Log Agcy	64,120	178,758	63,603	177,237	2,993	12,281	517	1,521
Other Defense Activities	89,773	269,649	73,407	216,735	16,920	68,677	16,366	52,914
Justice	98,022	463,622	96,105	453,637	21,981	101,927	1,917	9,985
Interior	84,736	335,269	84,341	333,498	9,780	48,816	395	1,771
Agriculture	123,057	464,622	121,550	459,343	13,467	68,851	1,507	5,279
Commerce	38,651	177,589	37,734	172,925	20,479	106,950	917	4,664
Labor	17,609	88,358	17,567	88,102	6,170	32,860	42	256
Health and Human Services	132,406	585,517	131,706	582,495	31,443	161,902	700	3,022
Housing & Urban Dev	13,208	65,684	13,095	65,104	3,404	20,202	113	580
Transportation	69,922	302,919	69,349	300,318	10,776	47,158	573	2,601
Energy	20,637	124,146	20,633	124,109	7,298	50,722	4	37
Education	5,001	26,508	4,996	26,480	3,451	19,050	5	28
Veterans Affairs	265,014	706,022	262,000	699,104	7,802	29,431	3,014	6,918
Independent Agencies[1]	**962,749**	**3,056,473**	**942,895**	**2,991,340**	**80,763**	**396,712**	**19,854**	**65,133**
Action	418	2,196	416	2,182	159	939	2	14
Environmtl Protect Agcy	18,478	98,110	18,457	97,994	6,050	35,857	21	116
Equal Employ Opp Comm	2,938	14,475	2,938	14,475	765	4,253	—	—
Federal Deposit Ins Corp.	21,889	123,339	21,880	123,280	3,802	26,359	9	59
Fed Emergency Mgmt Agcy	4,117	18,265	4,025	17,941	1,556	8,266	92	324
General Svcs Admin	20,780	95,503	20,677	95,031	6,795	37,554	103	472
Natl Archives & Recds Admin.	3,133	9,270	3,133	9,270	1,298	5,080	—	—
Natl Aero Space Admin	25,149	148,159	25,141	148,097	5,754	36,474	8	62
Nuclear Regulatory Comm	3,542	17,195	3,542	17,195	2,356	11,815	—	—
Office of Personnel Mgmt	6,842	24,985	6,818	24,928	2,913	13,415	24	57
Panama Canal Commission	8,495	27,934	19	115	7	66	8,476	27,819
Securities & Exchnge Comm	2,697	16,381	2,697	16,381	1,762	10,589	—	—
Small Business Admin	5,363	25,461	5,251	25,016	988	5,614	112	445
Smithsonian, Summary	5,491	22,862	5,320	22,233	4,923	20,498	171	629
Tennessee Valley Auth	19,145	75,470	19,145	75,470	9	39	—	—
U.S. Information Agency	8,298	33,960	4,335	24,638	4,072	22,504	3,963	9,322
U.S. Intnatl Dev Coop Agcy	4,385	26,413	2,292	13,990	2,285	13,951	2,093	12,423
U.S. Postal Service	779,606	2,166,456	775,817	2,155,088	21,115	67,329	3,789	11,368

(1) Included in total are other independent agencies with fewer than 2,500 employees.

Labor Union Directory

Source: Bureau of Labor Statistics, U.S. Dept. of Labor; World Almanac questionnaire

(*) Independent union; all others affiliated with AFL-CIO.

American Federation of Labor & Congress of Industrial Organizations (AFL-CIO), 815 16th St. NW, Washington, DC 20006; founded 1955; Lane Kirkland, Pres. (since 1979); 14 mln. members.

Actors and Artistes of America, Associated (AAAA), 165 W. 46th St., New York, NY 10036; founded 1919; Theodore Bikel, Pres.; no individual members, 7 National Performing Arts Unions are affiliates; approx. 220,000 combined membership.

Actors' Equity Association, 165 W. 46th St., New York, NY 10036; founded 1913; Ron Silver, Pres.; 36,000 active members.

Air Line Pilots Association, 1625 Massachusetts Ave. NW, Washington, DC 20036; J. Randolph Babbitt, Pres.; 43,000 members.

Aluminum, Brick & Glass Workers International Union (ABGWIU), 3362 Hollenberg Drive, Bridgeton, MO 63044; founded 1953; Ernie Labaff, Pres. (since 1985); 45,000 members, 390 locals.

Automobile, Aerospace & Agricultural Implement Workers of America, International Union, United (UAW), 8000 E. Jefferson Ave., Detroit, MI 48214; founded 1935; Owen Bieber, Pres. (since 1983); 1,000,000 members, 1,194 locals.

Bakery, Confectionery & Tobacco Workers International Union (BC&T), 10401 Connecticut Ave., Kensington, MD 20895; founded 1886; Frank Hurt, Pres. (since 1992); 125,000 members.

Boilermakers, Iron Ship Builders, Blacksmiths, Forgers and Helpers, International Brotherhood of (IBBISB/BF&H), 570 New Brotherhood Bldg., 753 State Ave., Kansas City, KS 66101; founded 1880; Charles W. Jones, Pres. (since 1983); 80,000 members.

Bricklayers and Allied Craftsmen, International Union of, 815 15th St. NW, Washington, DC 20005; John T. Joyce, Pres.; 100,000 members, 430 locals.

Carpenters and Joiners of America, United Brotherhood of, 101 Constitution Ave. NW, Washington, DC 20001; founded 1881; Sigurd Lucassen, Gen. Pres. (since 1988); 500,000 members, 1,500 locals.

Chemical Workers Union, International (ICWU), 1655 West Market St., Akron, OH 44313; founded 1944; Frank D. Martino, Pres. (since 1975); 50,000 members, 350 locals.

Clothing and Textile Workers Union, Amalgamated (ACTWU), 15 Union Square, New York, NY 10003; founded 1976 (by merger of 2 unions); Jack Sheinkman, Pres. (since 1987); 234,000 members, 1,400 locals.

Communications Workers of America, 501 3rd St. NW, Washington, DC 20001-2797; Morton Bahr, Pres.; 700,000 members, 1,200 locals.

Distillery, Wine & Allied Workers International Union (DWU), 66 Grand Ave., Englewood, NJ 07631; founded 1940; George J. Orlando, Pres. (since 1984); 15,500 members, 57 locals.

***Education Association, National,** 1201 16th St. NW, Washington, DC 20036; Keith Geiger, Pres. (since 1989); 2,000,000 members, 12,000 affiliates.

Electrical Workers, International Brotherhood of (IBEW), 1125 15th St. NW, Washington, DC 20005; founded 1891; J.J. Barry, Int'l Pres. (since 1986); 750,000 members.

Electronic, Electrical, Salaried, Machine and Furniture Workers, International Union of (IUE), 1126 16th St. NW, Washington, DC 20036; founded 1949; William H. Bywater, Pres. (since 1982); 150,000 members, 500 locals.

Farm Workers of America, United (UFW), P.O. Box 62, Keene, CA 93531; founded 1962; Arturo Rodriguez, Pres. (since 1993); 20,000 members.

***Federal Employees, National Federation of (NFFE),** 1016 16th St. NW, Washington, DC 20036; founded 1917; Sheila K. Velazco, Pres.; 60,000+ members, 487 locals.

Fire Fighters, International Association of, 1750 New York Ave. NW, Washington, DC 20006; founded 1918; Alfred K. Whitehead, Pres. (since 1988); 195,000 members, 1,943 locals.

Firemen and Oilers, International Brotherhood of, 1100 Circle 75 Parkway, Suite 350, Atlanta, GA 30339; Jimmy L. Walker, Pres.; 25,000 members.

Food and Commercial Workers International Union, United (UFCW), 1775 K St. NW, Washington, DC 20006; founded 1979 following merger; William H. Wynn, Int'l Pres. (since 1979); 1,224,840 members, 600 locals.

Garment Workers of America, United (UGWA), 4207 Lebanon Rd., Hermitage, TN 37076; founded 1891; Dave Johnson, Gen. Pres. (since 1991); 20,000 members, 120 locals.

Glass, Molders, Pottery, Plastics & Allied Workers Intl. Union (GMP), 608 E. Baltimore Pike, P.O. Box 607, Media, PA 19063; founded 1842; James E. Hatfield, Int'l Pres. (since 1977); 90,000 members, 435 locals.

Government Employees, American Federation of (AFGE), 80 F St. NW, Washington, DC 20001; founded 1932; John N. Sturdivant, Natl. Pres. (since 1988); 200,000 members, 1,300 locals.

Grain Millers, American Federation of (AFGM), 4949 Olson Memorial Hwy., Minneapolis, MN 55422; founded 1936; Larry R. Jackson, Gen. Pres. (since 1991); 28,000 members, 210 locals.

Graphic Communications International Union (GCIU), 1900 L St., NW, Washington, DC 20036; founded 1983; James J. Norton, Pres. (since 1985); 182,706 members, 520 locals.

Hotel Employees and Restaurant Employees International Union, 1219 28th St. NW, Washington, DC 20007; Edward T. Henley, Gen. Pres.; 330,000 members, 190 locals.

Industrial Workers of America, International Union, Allied (AIW), 3520 W. Oklahoma Ave., Milwaukee, WI 53215; founded 1935; Dominick D'Ambrosio, Intl. Pres. (since 1975); 61,000 members, 330 locals.

Iron Workers, International Association of Bridge, Structural and Ornamental, 1750 New York Ave. NW, Washington, DC 20006; founded 1896; Jake West, Gen. Pres. (since 1989); 140,000 members, 300 locals.

Laborers' International Union of North America (LIUNA), 905 16th St. NW, Washington, DC 20006; founded 1903; Arthur A. Coia, Gen. Pres. (since 1993); 700,000 members.

Ladies Garment Workers Union, International (ILGWU), 1710 Broadway, New York, NY 10019; founded 1900; Jay Mazur, Pres. (since 1986); 150,000 members, 340 locals.

Leather Goods, Plastic and Novelty Workers' Union, International, 265 W. 14th St., New York, NY 10011; Andrew McKenzie, Gen. Pres.; 20,000 members, 85 locals.

Letter Carriers, National Association of (NALC), 100 Indiana Ave. NW, Washington, DC 20001; founded 1889; Vincent R. Sombrotto, Pres. (since 1978); 311,202 members, 3,466 locals.

***Locomotive Engineers, Brotherhood of (BLE),** The Standard Bldg., 1370 Ontario Ave., Cleveland, OH 44113-1702; founded 1863; Ronald P. McLaughlin, Pres. (since 1991); 55,000 members, 650 divisions.

Longshoremen's Association, International, 17 Battery Pl., New York, NY 10004; John Bowers, Pres.; 76,579 members, 331 locals.

***Longshoremen's & Warehousemen's Union, International (ILWU),** 1188 Franklin St., San Francisco, CA 94109; founded 1937; David Arian, Pres. (since 1991); 55,000 members, 58 locals.

Machinists and Aerospace Workers, International Association of (IAM), 9000 Machinist Pl., Upper Marlboro, MD 20772-2687; founded 1888; George J. Kourpias, Int'l Pres.; 826,875 members, 1,700 locals.

Maintenance of Way Employees, Brotherhood of (BMWE), 12050 Woodward Ave., Detroit, MI 48203; founded 1887; Mac. A. Fleming, Pres.; 75,000 members, 827 locals.

Marine & Shipbuilding Workers of America, Industrial Union of (IUMSWA), 5101 River Rd., #110, Bethesda, MD 20816; founded 1934 (merged with Machinists and Aerospace Workers, Dec. 1, 1990).

Marine Engineer Beneficial Assn./National Maritime Union (MEBA/NMU), 444 N. Capitol St. NW, Suite 800, Washington, DC 20001; C.E. DeFries, Pres.; 50,000 members.

***Mine Workers of America, United (UMWA),** 900 15th St. NW, Washington, DC 20005; founded 1890; Richard Trumka, Int'l Pres. (since 1982); 186,000 members, 800 locals.

Musicians of the United States and Canada, American Federation of (AF of M), 1501 Broadway, Suite 600, New York, NY 10036; founded 1896; Mark Tully Massagli, Pres.; 160,000 members.

Newspaper Guild, The (TNG), 8611 Second Ave., Silver Spring, MD 20910; founded 1933; Charles Dale, Pres. (since 1987); 33,000 members, 80 locals.

Novelty & Production Workers, Intl. Union of Allied, 1815 Franklin Ave., Valley Stream, NY 11581; Julius Isaacson, Pres.; 30,000 members, 18 locals.

*Nurses Association, American, 600 Maryland Ave. SW, Washington, DC 20024-2571; Virginia Trotter Betts, J.D., R.N., Pres.; 53 constituent state assns.

Office and Professional Employees International Union (OPEIU), 265 W. 14th St., New York, NY 10011; founded 1945 (AFL Charter); John Kelly, Int'l Pres. (since 1979); 135,000 members, 300 locals.

Oil, Chemical and Atomic Workers International Union (OCAW), PO Box 2812, Denver, CO 80201; Robert E. Wages, Pres.; 100,000 members, 400 locals.

Operating Engineers, International Union of (IUOE), 1125 17th St. NW, Washington, DC 20036; founded 1896; Frank Hanley, Gen. Pres.; 375,000 members, 200 locals.

Painters and Allied Trades, International Brotherhood of (IBPAT), 1750 New York Ave. NW, Washington, DC 20006; founded 1887; A. L. "Mike" Monroe, Gen. Pres.; 149,177 members, 626 locals.

Paperworkers International Union, United (UPIU), 3340 Perimeter Hill Dr., Nashville, TN 37211; founded 1884; Wayne E. Glenn, Pres. (since 1978); 229,000 members, 1,100 locals.

***Plant Guard Workers of America, International Union, United (UPGWA),** 25510 Kelly Rd., Roseville, MI 48066; founded 1948; Gene McConville, Pres.; 28,000 members, 176 locals.

Plasterers' and Cement Mason's International Association of the United States & Canada; Operative, 1125 17th St. NW, Washington, DC 20036; Dominic A. Martell, Gen. Pres.; 65,000 members, 365 locals.

Plumbing and Pipe Fitting Industry of the United States and Canada, United Association of Journeymen and Apprentices of the, 901 Massachusetts Ave. NW, Washington, DC 20001; founded 1889; Marvin J. Boede, Pres. (since 1982); 303,000 members.

***Police, Fraternal Order of,** 2100 Gardiner Lane, Louisville, KY 40205; Dewey R. Stokes, Natl. Pres. and Charles R. Orms, Natl. Secy.; 225,000 members, 1,860 affiliates.

***Postal Supervisors, National Association of,** 490 L'Enfant Plaza SW, Suite 3200, Washington, DC 20024-2120; Rubin Handolman, Pres.; 44,000 members, 443 locals.

Postal Workers Union, American (APWU), 1300 L St. NW, Washington, DC 20005; founded 1971; Moe Biller, Pres. (since 1980); 330,000 members, 2,000 locals.

Railway Carmen Division of Transportation Communications Int'l. Union (BRC Division/TCU), 3 Research Pl., Rockville, MD 20850; founded 1888; R. P. Wojtowicz, Gen. Pres. (since 1992); 50,000 members, 310 locals.

Retail, Wholesale and Department Store Union, 30 E. 29th St., New York, NY 10016; Lenore Miller, Pres.; 200,000 members, 250 locals.

Roofers, Waterproofers & Allied Workers, United Union of, 1125 17th St. NW, Washington, DC 20036; Earl J. Kruse, Pres.; 27,000 members, 138 locals.

Rubber, Cork, Linoleum and Plastic Workers of America, United (URW), 570 White Pond Dr., Akron, OH 44320-1156; founded 1935; Kenneth L. Coss, Int'l Pres.; 100,000 members, 400 locals.

***Rural Letter Carriers' Association, National,** 4th floor, 1630 Duke St., Alexandria, VA 22314; founded 1903; Vernon H. Meier, Pres. (since 1989); 80,000 members; 47 state organizations.

Seafarers International Union of North America (SIUNA), 5201 Auth Way, Camp Springs, MD 20746; founded 1938; Michael Sacco, Pres.; 85,000 members.

Service Employees International Union (SEIU), 1313 L St. NW, Washington, DC 20005; founded 1921; John J. Sweeney, Pres. (since 1980); 950,000 members, 300 locals.

Sheet Metal Workers' International Association (SMWIA), 1750 New York Ave. NW, Washington, DC 20006; founded 1888; Edward J. Carlough, Gen. Pres. (since 1970); 150,000 members, 245 locals.

State, County and Municipal Employees, American Federation of, 1625 L St. NW, Washington, DC 20036; Gerald McEntee, Pres.; 1.2 mln. members, 2,991 locals.

Steelworkers of America, United (USWA), 5 Gateway Center, Pittsburgh, PA 15222; founded 1936; Lynn Williams, Int'l Pres. (since 1984); 750,000 members, 3,500 locals.

Teachers, American Federation of (AFT), 555 New Jersey Ave. NW, Washington, DC 20001; founded 1916; Albert Shanker, Pres. (since 1974); 850,000 members.

Teamsters, Chauffeurs, Warehousemen and Helpers of America, International Brotherhood of (IBT), 25 Louisiana Ave. NW, Washington, DC 20001; founded 1903; Ronald R. Carey, Pres. (since 1992); 1.5 mln. members, 700 locals.

Television and Radio Artists, American Federation of, 260 Madison Ave., New York, NY 10016; founded 1937; Reed Farrell, Pres.; 67,000 members, 38 locals.

Textile Workers of America, United (UTWA), 2 Echelon Plaza, Laurel Rd., P.O. Box 749, Voorhees, NJ 08043-0749; founded 1901; Ron Myslowka, Intl. Pres. (since 1992); 20,000 members, 180 locals.

Theatrical Stage Employees, International Alliance of, 1515 Broadway, New York, NY 10036; founded 1893; Alfred W. Di Tolla, Pres. (since 1986); 70,000 members, 750 locals.

Transit Union, Amalgamated (ATU), 5025 Wisconsin Ave. NW, Washington, DC 20016; founded 1892; James La Sala, Intl. Pres. (since 1986); 160,000 members, 275 locals.

Transport Workers Union of America, 80 West End Ave., New York, NY 10023; founded 1934; George Leitz, Int'l Pres. (since 1985); 100,000 members, 94 locals.

Transportation Communications International Union (TCU), 3 Research Place, Rockville, MD 20850; founded 1899; Robert A. Scardelletti, Int'l Pres. (since 1991); 127,725 members, 750 locals.

***Transportation Union, United (UTU),** 14600 Detroit Ave., Cleveland, OH 44107; founded 1969; G. Thomas DuBose, Pres. (since 1979); 100,000 members, 769 locals.

***Treasury Employees Union, National (NTEU),** 901 E. St. NW Suite 600, Washington, DC 20004; founded 1938; Robert M. Tobias, Natl. Pres. (since 1983); 140,000 represented, 250 chapters.

***University Professors, American Association of (AAUP),** 1012-14th St., Washington, DC 20005; founded 1915; Carol Simpson Stern, Pres.; 40,000 members, 600 chapters.

Upholstery Division - United Steelworkers of America, 25 N. 4th St., Philadelphia, PA 19106; founded 1882; Ernest F. Shock, dir.; approx. 18,000 members, 91 locals.

Utility Workers Union of America (UWUA), 815 16th St. NW, Washington, DC 20006; founded 1938; Marshall M. Hicks, Natl. Pres. (since 1991); 55,000 members, 220 locals.

International Woodworkers of America —U.S. (IWA—U.S.), 25 Cornell Ave., Gladstone, OR 97027; founded 1937; Wilson J. Hubbell, Natl. Pres.; 20,000 members.

U.S. Union Membership, 1930-1992

Source: Bureau of Labor Statistics, U.S. Dept. of Labor

Year	Labor[1] force (thousands)	Union[2] members (thousands)	Percent
1930	29,424	3,401	11.6
1935	27,053	3,584	13.2
1940	32,376	8,717	26.9
1945	40,394	14,322	35.5
1950	45,222	14,267	31.5
1955	50,675	16,802	33.2
1960	54,234	17,049	31.4
1965	60,815	17,299	28.4
1970	70,920	19,381	27.3
1975	76,945	19,611	25.5
1980	90,564	19,843	21.9
1983	88,290	17,717	20.1
1984	92,194	17,340	18.8
1985	94,521	16,996	18.0
1986	96,903	16,975	17.5
1987	99,303	16,913	17.0
1988	101,407	17,002	16.8
1989	103,480	16,960	16.4
1990	103,905	16,740	16.1
1991	102,786	16,568	16.1
1992	103,688	16,390	15.8

(1) Does not include agricultural employment; from 1983 data do not include self-employed or unemployed persons. (2) From 1930 to 1980 data are the number of dues-paying members of traditional trade unions with members counted regardless of employment status; from 1983 members include employee associations that engage in collective bargaining with employers.

TAXES

Federal Income Tax

Source: George W. Smith III, CPA, Nationally Syndicated Tax Author and Columnist

On August 10, President Bill Clinton signed the Omnibus Budget Reconciliation Act of 1993, legislation intended—through a combination of $241 billion in tax increases and $255 billion in spending cuts—to reduce the federal government's budget deficits by a total of $496 billion over five years. Many of the tax provisions of the act were retroactive to January 1, 1993, and therefore will affect some Americans when they file their 1993 income tax returns. Other portions of the legislation will take effect in 1994 or later.

Tax Highlights of the Omnibus Budget Reconciliation Act of 1993

Individual Income Taxes. The act increases the top tax rate to 36% for joint filers with taxable income over $140,000, heads of households with taxable income over $127,500, and singles with taxable income of more than $115,000. Congress also added a 10% surtax on taxable income of more than $250,000 ($125,000 for married individuals filing separately). This provision creates a marginal top tax rate of 39.6% and is retroactive to January 1, 1993.

Social Security Benefits. Effective January 1, 1994, retirees whose incomes, including half their Social Security benefits, exceed $34,000 for singles or $44,000 for married couples filing jointly will pay income tax on up to 85% of their benefits. The current law, taxing up to 50% of Social Security benefits, will continue to apply for retirees whose incomes, including half their Social Security benefits, exceed $25,000 for singles or $32,000 for married taxpayers filing jointly.

Estate and Gift Taxes. The act reinstates the 1992 top tax rate of 53% on estates between $2.5 million and $3 million, and 55% on estates of more than $3 million. On taxable estates between $10 million and $21.04 million, an additional tax of 5% of the transfer above $10 million will continue to be imposed as well. The effective date is retroactive to January 1, 1993.

Corporate Tax Rates. The act increases the top tax rate for corporations with taxable income over $10 million per year from 34% to 35%. The tax rate for qualified personal service corporations also increases from 34% to 35%. The effective date is January 1, 1993.

Moving Expense Deductions. For expenses incurred after 1993, moving expense deductions associated with a new job will be limited. Deductions for meals while traveling, living expenses in temporary quarters, pre-move house-hunting trips, and the costs of selling an old residence or buying or renting a new residence will no longer be deductible. In addition, the job distance test to qualify for a deduction has been increased to 50 miles from 35 miles. A taxpayer will no longer need to itemize deductions to take a qualified moving expense deduction.

Business Meals and Entertainment. The act reduces the proportion of qualified business meals and entertainment costs that can be deducted as business expenses to 50% starting in 1994. For 1993, the deduction remains at 80%. Also beginning in 1994, Congress eliminated the deduction as a business expense of dues in business, social, athletic, luncheon, sporting, and country clubs, including airport and hotel clubs.

Lobbying Expenses. The act eliminates the business deduction for lobbying Congress and federal, state, and local government agencies, beginning in 1994.

Energy Tax. The act imposes a 4.3-cents-per-gallon tax on transportation fuels, including gasoline and diesel fuel. Commercial airline fuel is exempt for 2 years. The effective date is October 1, 1993.

Medicare Tax. Effective in 1994, Congress repealed the $135,000 limit on earned income subject to the payroll tax for Medicare. Therefore, *all* wages will be subject to the Medicare tax of 1.45% for both employers and employees. Self-employed individuals will pay a 2.9% Medicare tax on their net self-employed income.

Earned Income Tax Credit. The tax credit rate increases for low-income working taxpayers starting in 1994. Also new is a credit of up to $300 that is extended to childless low-income workers over age 25 and below age 65. The Young Child Care Credit and Supplemental Health Insurance Credit are repealed as of 1994.

Rental Passive Losses. The act allows certain real estate professionals to use losses from rental real estate to offset other nonpassive income, such as wages and self-employment profits. The effective date is January 1, 1994.

Charitable Contributions. Effective January 1, 1994, taxpayers deducting charitable contributions of $250 or more will have to obtain written substantiation from the charity before filing a tax return.

Equipment Write-off. Congress elected to allow small businesses to deduct as an expense up to $17,500 of the cost of new equipment. Previously, the maximum was $10,000. The change is effective for property placed in service for tax years beginning in 1993.

Retirement Plans. The new law reduces from $235,840 to $150,000 the level of compensation for which tax-deferred contributions can be made to retirement plans. The effective date is January 1, 1994.

Nonresidential Real Estate. For property placed in service on or after May 13, 1993, the depreciation recovery period has been increased to 39 years. Under prior law it was 31.5 years.

Alternative Minimum Tax (AMT). Retroactive to January 1, 1993, the 24% AMT rate has been replaced with a two-tier tax rate of 26% and 28%.

Estates and Trusts. Retroactive to January 1, 1993, the tax rates for the taxable income of estates and trusts increased as follows:

Taxable Income Amount	Tax Rate
0 to $1,500	15%
$1,501 to $3,500	28%
$3,501 to $5,500	31%
$5,501 to $7,500	36%

In addition, there is a 10% surtax on taxable income over $7,500. This provision creates a marginal top rate of 39.6%.

Other Tax Law Changes and Recent Tax Developments

- The highest income tax rate for individuals, estates, and trusts was changed for 1993. There are currently four tax rates: 15%, 28%, 31%, and 36%. In addition, for individuals there is a 10% surtax on taxable incomes over $250,000 ($125,000 for married individuals filing separately). For estates and trusts, the surtax starts at $7,500. This provision creates a marginal top tax rate of 39.6% for individuals, estates, and trusts.
- The maximum income tax rate on capital gains for individuals, estates, and trusts remains at 28%.
- Effective January 1, 1993, the limitation on elective deferrals to 401(k) plans is increased to $8,994 from $8,728.
- An individual may not claim an exemption for a dependent child in 1993 who qualifies as a full time student and is over age 23 at the end of the year unless the child's gross income is less than $2,350.
- Interest earned on Series EE bonds issued in 1990 or later may be exempt from federal income tax if used to pay tuition and fees for a taxpayer, spouse, or dependents to attend a college, university, or qualified technical school during the year the bonds are redeemed. This exclusion is subject to an income phase-out in 1993 starting when adjusted gross income exceeds $45,500 for a single taxpayer; $68,250 for taxpayers filing jointly. The full phase-out occurs at $60,500 for a single taxpayer and $98,250 for taxpayers filing jointly.
- Parents may elect to include on their income tax return the unearned income of a dependent child under age 14

whose unearned income is more than $500 but less than $5,000. The income must consist solely of interest and dividends. Form 8814, Parent's Election to Report Child's Interest and Dividends, is required to report this income. This election is not available if estimated tax payments were made in the child's name.

- For individuals age 55 or over, the 3 out of 5 year home use rule for the sale of a principal residence has been expanded. Certain incapacitated individuals who reside in state-licensed facilities may exclude from gross income up to $125,000 of gain resulting from the sale of their home if the house was used as their principal residence for at least one year out of the last five years. This is a once-in-a-lifetime exclusion.
- Interest on Veterans Affairs (VA) dividends left on deposit with the Department of Veterans Affairs is not taxable.
- Face-lifts, tummy tucks, liposuction, and many other elective cosmetic surgeries are no longer a deductible medical expense.
- Starting in 1993, the Unemployment Compensation Amendment Act of 1992 made three important changes to the treatment of distributions from qualified pension plans and annuities:
  (1) It made all pension plan distributions eligible for rollovers except certain periodic payments, minimum distributions, and amounts not excluded from gross income.
  (2) It required plans to permit direct rollovers.
  (3) It imposed a mandatory 20 percent income tax withholding on distributions that are not directly rolled over.
- For a taxpayer to be eligible for the child and dependent care credit, the dependent must be under age 13. The taxpayer must also report the name, address, and identification number of the child care provider on his or her income tax return or the taxpayer will not be entitled to the credit.
- A taxpayer must list the Social Security number of any dependent claimed on his or her income tax return who is at least 1 year old by the end of the tax year. The penalty for noncompliance can be $50 per omitted number.
- A business deduction is not allowed for the base rate charged on the first telephone line into a personal residence. This disallowance does not affect the deductibility of long distance calls or optional services such as call waiting, call forwarding, three-way calling, or extra directory listings as long as they are business related.
- For 1993, the Social Security tax base (the maximum amount of earnings on which the Social Security tax can apply) increased to $57,600. The Medicare tax base increased to $135,000. For Social Security, the tax rate is 6.2% for employees and the same for employers. For Medicare, the rate is 1.45% for both employees and employers. Thus, the maximum an employee and an employer each will pay is 6.2% of $57,605 plus 1.45% of $135,000, or $5,528.70 each. Starting in 1994, the $135,000 maximum tax base for Medicare has been eliminated. Consequently, all wages will be subject to the Medicare tax.
- IRA investments are allowed for certain gold and silver coins issued by the U.S. government. Investments also may include certain coins issued by a state government.
- Jury duty pay returned by an employee to an employer in exchange for his or her normal salary is deductible as an adjustment to income.
- The business use of a cellular phone must be for the convenience of the employer and a condition of employment to be an allowable business deduction for employees. All phone calls must be substantiated and business related.
- Self-employed persons are entitled to an income tax adjustment of one-half of their Social Security self-employment tax liability. The self-employment tax rate for 1993 is 15.3%. The maximum Social Security tax a self-employed individual will pay in 1993 is $11,057.40.
- To be deductible, points paid for the purchase of a taxpayer's principal residence must meet the following requirements:
  (1) The purchase must be for the taxpayer's *principal* residence.
  (2) The amount paid must be clearly designated as "points," "loan origination fees," "loan discount," or "discount points."
  (3) Points must be computed as a percentage of the taxpayer's stated principal loan amount.
  (4) The payment of points must be an established business practice in the area.
  (5) The points must be paid from the taxpayer's own funds. The points may not be borrowed.
  (6) FHA and VA loan origination fees paid by a home buyer may be treated as "points".
- A sole proprietor claiming a home office deduction on Schedule C, Profit or Loss From Business, must file Form 8829, Expenses for Business Use of Your Home, with his or her income tax return.
- For 1993, the standard mileage rate for business use of an automobile remains at 28 cents per mile. This rate applies to all business miles driven. U.S. Postal Service employees who collect or deliver mail on a rural route can use a special standard mileage rate of 42 cents per mile.
- Travel expenses reimbursed to employees that include an additional Saturday night's lodging and meals in order to take advantage of lower air fares for roundtrip tickets are deductible by the company and excludable from employees' gross income. The reimbursements are not subject to employment taxes and withholding.
- The maximum earned income that retirees under the age of 65 can receive in 1993 without losing all or part of their Social Security benefits is $7,680. For individuals age 65 through age 69, the maximum amount is $10,560. Individuals receiving Social Security benefits who are age 70 or over can receive full benefits regardless of earnings.

1993 Individual Tax Rates

There are four tax rates for 1993: 15%, 28%, 31%, and 36%. The dollar bracket amounts are adjusted each year for inflation.

Single

Tax Rates	Taxable Income
15%	$0 to $22,100
28%	$22,101 to $53,500
31%	$53,501 to $115,000
36%	$115,001 to $250,000

Married Filing Jointly or Qualifying Widow(er)

Tax Rates	Taxable Income
15%	$0 to $36,900
28%	$36,901 to $89,150
31%	$89,151 to $140,000
36%	$140,001 to $250,000

Married Filing Separately

Tax Rate	Taxable Income
15%	$0 to $18,450
28%	$18,451 to $44,575
31%	$44,576 to $70,000
36%	$70,001 to $125,000

Head of Household

Tax Rate	Taxable Income
15%	$0 to $29,600
28%	$29,601 to $76,400
31%	$76,401 to $127,500
36%	$127,501 to $250,000

Please note, however, there is also a 10% surtax on taxable incomes over $250,000 ($125,000 for married individuals filing separately). This provision creates a marginal top tax rate of 39.6%.

The maximum tax rate on net capital gains for an individual, estate, or trust is 28%.

The alternative minimum tax rate for noncorporate taxpayers is 26% for alternative minimum taxable income less the exemption amount up to $175,000 ($87,500 for married individuals filing separately). Above that dollar level, a 28% rate applies.

Standard Deduction

The standard deduction is a flat dollar amount that is subtracted from the adjusted gross income of taxpayers who do not itemize their deductions. The amount of the basic standard deduction depends upon the taxpayer's filing status and is adjusted annually for inflation. The standard deductions for 1993 are as follows:

1993 Basic Standard Deduction

Single	$3,700
Married filing jointly or qualifying widow(er)	$6,200
Married filing separately	$3,100
Head of household	$5,450

Taxpayers with itemized deductions such as medical expenses, property taxes, investment and home mortgage interest, charitable contributions, moving expenses, and gambling losses totaling more than the standard deduction amount should not use the standard deduction. Instead, they should itemize their deductions.

An individual claimed as a dependent on another person's income tax return may claim on his or her own tax return only the larger of $600 or the amount of earned income up to the amount of the basic standard deduction that the taxpayer would normally be allowed. Earned income includes wages, salaries, commissions, and tips. It also includes net profit from self-employment received as compensation for personal services rendered. Any part of a scholarship or fellowship grant that must be included in gross income is also earned income.

Example 1: During 1993, a dependent parent, age 60, had unearned income (interest and dividends) of $1,700. She had no earned income. Her basic standard deduction would be $600. She would have taxable income of $1,100. A dependent cannot claim his or her own personal exemption.

Example 2: A dependent son had $10,000 of unearned income and $100 of earned income. He is entitled to a $600 standard deduction. He is limited to this amount because he is a dependent and his earned income is less than $600. The taxpayer would, therefore, have $9,500 in taxable income.

Example 3: A dependent daughter with $4,000 of earned income and $600 of unearned income would claim a maximum $3,700 standard deduction because her earned income of $4,000 is greater than the standard deduction. She would have taxable income of $900.

Additional Standard Deduction for Age and Blindness

Elderly or blind taxpayers may claim an additional standard deduction in addition to the basic standard deduction. Taxpayers who are age 65 or over or blind at the end of 1993 qualify. Individuals who claim the additional standard deduction because of blindness must attach a doctor's statement to their income tax return.

1993 Additional Standard Deduction

Single or head of household, age 65 or over OR blind	$ 900
Single or head of household, age 65 or over AND blind	$1,800
Married filing jointly or qualifying widow(er), age 65 or over OR blind (per person)	$ 700
Married filing jointly or qualifying widow(er), age 65 or over AND blind (per person)	$1,400
Married filing separately, age 65 or over OR blind	$ 700
Married filing separately, age 65 or over AND blind	$1,400

Example 1: A single, sixty-five-year-old individual would have a standard deduction of $4,600 computed as follows:

Basic standard deduction for a single person	$3,700
Additional standard deduction for age	900
Total	$4,600

Example 2: A seventy-year-old husband and a fifty-eight-year old blind wife filing jointly would be entitled to a standard deduction totaling $7,600 computed as follows:

Basic standard deduction for married filing jointly	$6,200
Additional standard deduction for (husband's) age	700
Additional standard deduction for (wife's) blindness	700
Total	$7,600

The additional and basic standard deductions are adjusted each year for inflation. However, the additional standard deduction for 1993 remains the same as 1992. Taxpayers who itemize their deductions cannot claim the additional or basic standard deductions.

Dependent and Personal Exemptions

The exemption amount for 1993 has been increased to $2,350. This amount is adjusted each year for inflation.

The deduction for exemptions is phased out for certain higher income taxpayers. The exemption amount is reduced by 2% for each $2,500 ($1,250 for married filing separately) or a fraction thereof by which the adjusted gross income exceeds the threshold amount.

The 1993 threshold amount for the phase-out of the personal exemption begins as follows:

Married filing jointly	$162,700
Qualifying widow(er)	$162,700
Head of household	$135,600
Single	$108,450
Married filing separately	$ 81,350

The exemption amount is fully phased out when adjusted gross income is more than $122,500 ($61,250 for married filing separately) over the threshold amount.

Adjustments to Income

Individual Retirement Accounts (IRAs)

Taxpayers who are not covered by a qualified employer retirement plan may take an IRA deduction up to the lesser of $2,000, or the amount of their earned income, regardless of their total income. Income earned from IRAs will remain tax-free until the taxpayer withdraws it.

Taxpayers may still make contributions to their IRAs even if they are covered by a qualified retirement plan of their employer. However, there are limits as to the amount that can be deducted on their income tax return if they are covered by a qualified retirement plan. If either husband or wife participates in a qualified plan, *both* spouses are subject to these limitations.

For 1993, married taxpayers filing jointly with adjusted gross income of $40,000 or less may take an IRA deduction whether or not either one is an active participant in a qualified retirement plan. Single taxpayers in a qualified retirement plan may also deduct IRA contributions if their adjusted gross income is $25,000 or less.

The IRA deduction is phased out over the next $10,000 of adjusted gross income if taxpayers are active participants in a qualified retirement plan. Consequently, married couples filing jointly with adjusted gross income of $50,000 or more, or single filers with adjusted gross income of $35,000 or more, may not deduct any contributions to their IRAs.

A qualified retirement plan generally includes: (1) a qualified pension, profit-sharing, or stock bonus plan; (2) a qualified annuity plan; (3) a simplified employee pension plan; or (4) a plan established for its employees by federal, state, or local government or by an agency of these entities.

Itemized Deductions

- Many elective cosmetic surgeries, including hair transplants and other similar procedures, are no longer a deductible medical expense. Only cosmetic surgery for congenital abnormality, personal injury resulting from an accident or trauma, or a disfiguring disease is allowed as a medical deduction. In general, medical expenses are deductible, but only the amount that exceeds 7.5 percent of the taxpayer's adjusted gross income.

- Consumer interest, such as finance charges on personal credit cards and installment interest paid on personal automobile loans, is no longer deductible.
- Investment interest is deductible only to the extent of net investment income. Any excess is carried over to future years.
- Most mortgage interest on a taxpayer's first and second home remains fully deductible; however, there are limitations.
- Interest on home equity loans is deductible, but only up to the first $100,000 in equity debt.
- State and local income taxes, real estate taxes, and personal property taxes remain fully deductible. Sales taxes are not deductible.
- Casualty and theft losses are deductible subject to the $100 limitation rule and the 10% of adjusted gross income provision.
- Miscellaneous deductions, such as union and professional dues, tax preparation fees, safe deposit box rental expense, and employee business expenses, are deductible, but only the amount that exceeds 2 percent of the taxpayer's adjusted gross income.
- An individual can deduct gambling losses such as the cost of lottery tickets, but only up to the amount of the winnings reported on page 1, Form 1040.

Moving Expenses

Taxpayers who change jobs during the year can usually deduct part of their moving expenses. These expenses include the cost of moving household goods, travel to the new home, house-hunting trips, temporary living quarters, and other related expenses. To qualify, the move must be job-related and it must meet several other requirements, including distance and time tests. The expenses for moving household goods and traveling to a new home have some limitations. All other deductible moving expenses, such as house-hunting trips or temporary living quarters, are subject to a $3,000 ceiling. Meal expenses are only 80% deductible. Moving expenses are deductible only if the taxpayer itemizes deductions on Schedule A of Form 1040. Moves within the U.S. are reported on Form 3903, Moving Expenses.

Effective January 1, 1994, the new 1993 tax law makes 4 modifications:

(1) The distance test is extended from 35 to 50 miles.
(2) Pre-move house-hunting trips, temporary living expenses, and the closing costs of selling the old home and buying a new one are nondeductible. Meals while traveling to the new location are not deductible.
(3) Moving expenses paid or reimbursed by the taxpayer's employer are excludable from gross income.
(4) Moving expenses are deductible as an adjustment to income and not as an itemized deduction on Schedule A.

Employee Business Expenses

All employee business expenses including travel, automobile, telephone, gifts, and entertainment are deductible only as itemized miscellaneous deductions. Only 80% (50% for 1994) of the cost of customer meals and entertainment is deductible. These expenses are then subject to the 2% of the taxpayer's adjusted gross income limitation for miscellaneous deductions. Beginning in 1994, country club dues will no longer be deductible.

Itemized Deduction Reduction

Many itemized deductions otherwise allowed are reduced by the lesser of 3% of a taxpayer's adjusted gross income in excess of $108,450 ($54,225 for married taxpayers filing separately) or 80% of the amount of these itemized deductions otherwise allowable for the year. These amounts are adjusted each year for inflation. This provision does not affect medical expenses, investment interest expense, casualty losses, or gambling losses to the extent of gambling gains.

Earned Income Credit, Young Child Credit, and Health Insurance Credit

Low income workers who have dependent children and maintain a household are eligible for a refundable earned income credit. The credit for 1993 is calculated on earned income such as wages and tips. For a taxpayer with one qualifying child, the maximum credit is $1,434. For a taxpayer with two or more qualifying children, it is $1,511. The credit begins to be phased out when the taxpayer's adjusted gross income is more than $12,200.

In addition to the basic earned income credit, a supplemental young child care credit is also available to low income workers with a qualifying child who has not attained the age of one by the close of the calendar year. The maximum credit is $388. If this supplemental credit is claimed, the dependent care credit may not be claimed. This credit is repealed effective in 1994.

A supplemental credit for health insurance premium costs that cover one or more qualifying children is also available. The maximum credit for 1993 is $465. If medical expenses are itemized on Schedule A, these amounts must be reduced dollar for dollar by the amount of the allowable supplemental health insurance credit. This credit is also repealed for 1994.

If an individual qualifies, these credits are refundable even if the taxpayer is not required to file an income tax return. However, a tax return must be filed in order to receive these credits. Taxpayers must fill out Schedule EIC and attach it to their tax return to receive these credits. To assist individuals, the IRS publishes a table showing the earned income credit at various levels of income. This chart is available free at any IRS office. The IRS will also assist individuals with the preparation of this form.

Effective for years beginning after 1993, the earned income tax credit (EITC) has been increased and extended to include low-income childless workers over age 25 and below age 65.

Taxing Children's Income

A child who may be claimed as a dependent by another taxpayer may not claim his or her own personal exemption on a tax return. Children under age 14 with at least one living parent may use up to $600 of their standard deduction against unearned income. Unearned income includes dividend and interest income. If the child's unearned income is more than $1,200, that income will be taxed at the child's tax rate or the parent's rate, whichever is higher.

Parents have the option of including a child's unearned income on their tax return. However, when this income is included on the parents' tax return, all the income over $1,000 is subject to the higher tax rate. Therefore, if the child includes the unearned income on his or her tax return, the child could receive the benefit of a lower tax rate on an additional $200 of unearned income.

When to File

U.S. individual income tax returns for 1993 are required to be filed with the Internal Revenue Service no later than Friday, April 15, 1994.

What if you can't file on time? File Form 4868, Application for Automatic Extension of Time to File U.S. Individual Income Tax Return. This gives the taxpayer an automatic four-month extension of time to file, until Monday, August 15, 1994. However, this is not an extension of time to pay the tax. Any federal income tax owed must be paid to the Internal Revenue Service by midnight April 15, 1994; otherwise, penalties and interest may be assessed for any income tax balance not paid. Form 4868 provides space for you to estimate your tax obligation, if any.

Who Must File

Whether a U.S. citizen or resident alien living in the U.S. must file an income tax return depends on the person's gross income, filing status, and age.

Generally, a U.S. citizen or resident alien will have to file an income tax return if the person's gross income for the year is at least as much as the amount shown in the following table.

Filing Status	1993 Gross Income
Single	
• Under 65	$ 6,050
• 65 or older	6,950
Married filing jointly	
• Both spouses under 65	10,900
• One spouse 65 or older	11,600
• Both spouses 65 or older	12,300
Married filing separately	2,350
Head of household	
• Under 65	7,800
• 65 or older	8,700
Qualifying widow(er)	
• Under 65	8,500
• 65 or older	9,250

Example 1: John and Mary Smith intend to file a joint return for 1993. John's income is entirely from wages. Mary receives no income subject to tax. Neither John nor Mary is blind. John is 67 years old, but Mary will not be 65 until next year. For 1993, their combined gross income subject to tax will be $11,900. They will have to file a tax return because their gross income will be at least $11,600.

If Mary were age 65, they would not have to file a 1993 tax return because their gross income would be less than $12,300 as shown in the table.

Some Exceptions to Filing Requirements. A tax return must be filed if:

- Net earnings from self-employment for the year are $400 or more.
- Advance earned income credit payments were received during the year from an employer.
- Taxpayers file for the earned income credit, young child credit, or health insurance credit.
- A taxpayer wishes to receive an income tax refund.
- Gross income is less than the filing requirement amount, but additional taxes are owed for:
  - Social security tax on unreported tips.
  - Alternative minimum tax.
  - Recapture of investment credit.
  - Tax attributable to qualified retirement distributions (including IRAs), annuities, and modified endowment contracts.

Which Form to File

Use either Form 1040EZ or Form 1040A unless the filing of Form 1040 allows you to pay a lower tax, or the rules say you must file Form 1040. The 1040EZ and 1040A are generally easier to complete than the longer Form 1040.

You may be able to use the short Form 1040EZ if:

- You are single and do not claim any dependents. In 1993 married couples filing jointly with no dependents may also use Form 1040EZ.
- You are not 65 or older or blind.
- You have income only from wages, salaries, tips, taxable scholarships or fellowships, and not more than $400 of interest income.
- Your taxable income is less than $50,000.
- You do not itemize deductions, claim any adjustments to income, or have tax credits.
- You did not receive any advanced earned income credit payments.
- You did not make estimated tax payments.
- You file on or before April 15th. You cannot use Form 1040EZ if you apply for an extension.

You may be able to use Form 1040A if:

- You have income from wages, salaries, tips, taxable scholarships or fellowships, interest, and dividends.
- You have income from Individual Retirement Account (IRA) distributions, pensions, annuities, unemployment compensation, and Social Security or railroad retirement benefits.
- Your taxable income is less than $50,000.
- You do not itemize deductions.
- You claim a deduction for qualified contributions to an IRA.
- You claim a credit for child and dependent care expenses, credit for the elderly or the disabled, earned income credit, supplemental young child credit, or the health insurance credit.
- You have made estimated tax payments.
- You filed for an extension of time to file.

Even if you do meet the above tests, you will have to file the longer Form 1040 if any of the following situations apply:

- Your taxable income is $50,000 or more.
- You itemize deductions.
- You receive any nontaxable dividends or capital gain distributions.
- You have foreign bank accounts and/or foreign trusts.
- You have taxable refunds of state or local income taxes.
- You have business, farm, or rental income.
- You have miscellaneous income not allowed on Form 1040EZ or 1040A such as alimony or lottery winnings.
- You have other adjustments to income such as alimony paid.
- You can claim a foreign tax credit or certain other credits to which you are entitled.
- You have other taxes such as self-employment tax or the alternative minimum tax.
- You file any additional required forms, such as:

  Form 2555, Foreign Earned Income.

  Form 3903, Moving Expenses.

  Form 4972, Tax on Lump-Sum Distributions.

  Form 5329, Return for Additional Taxes Attributable to Qualified Retirement Plans (including IRAs), Annuities, and Modified Endowment Contracts.

  Form 8814, Parent's Election to Report Child's Interest and Dividends.

1993 Corporate Tax Rates

Taxable Income Amount	Tax Rate
Not over $50,000	15%
$50,001 to $75,000	25%
$75,001 to $10,000,000	34%
over $10,000,000	35%

An additional 5% tax, up to $11,750, applies to corporate taxable income over $100,000 and up to $335,000. There is an additional 3% tax, up to $100,000, that applies to corporate taxable income over $15 million and up to $18,333,333. Corporations with taxable income over $18,333,333, and personal service corporations (used by professional individuals such as attorneys and doctors), pay a flat rate of 35%.

Internal Revenue Service Audit

Although fewer than one out of every hundred individual tax returns will probably be audited this year, the IRS is good at selecting returns for audit that will yield additional income taxes.

If your return is audited and you feel you are not being treated fairly, or that proper attention is not being paid to your statements, you have a right to ask for a hearing at the IRS appellate level. If you are still dissatisfied, you can take your case to the United States Tax Court. If the total amount in question is less than $10,000, your case can be handled under the Small Tax Case procedures. If you are still dissatisfied, your next move would be the United States Circuit Court of Appeals.

Your Rights As a Taxpayer

Congress responded to complaints that taxpayers were not being treated fairly by the IRS and passed a comprehensive law to force the IRS to explain, in easy to understand language, the actions it proposes to take against a taxpayer and to relax some of its audit and collection procedures. This law is called, "The Taxpayer Bill of Rights."

You can learn more about this law by obtaining a free copy of IRS Publication 1, "Your Rights As a Taxpayer." Call 1-800-TAX-FORM for a copy.

Some Frequently Used Federal Tax Forms

706
U.S. Estate (and Generation-Skipping Transfer) Tax Return
Used for the estate of a deceased U.S. resident or citizen.

709-A
U.S. Short Form Gift Tax Return
Used by married couples to report nontaxable gifts of more than $10,000 but less than $20,000.

1040
U.S. Individual Income Tax Return
Used by citizens and residents of the U.S. to report their income tax. Certain taxpayers may also use the shorter 1040A or 1040EZ.

1040-ES
Estimated Tax for Individuals
Used to make estimated income tax payments that may be required during the year (including self-employment tax and the alternative minimum tax).

1040NR
U.S. Nonresident Alien Income Tax Return
Used by all nonresident alien individuals who file a U.S. tax return, whether or not engaged in a trade or business within the U.S. Also used when required for filing nonresident alien fiduciary (estate and trust) returns.

1040X
Amended U.S. Individual Income Tax Return
Used to correct errors, omissions, and other adjustments on Forms 1040, 1040A, or 1040EZ tax returns that have already been filed.

1041
U.S. Fiduciary Income Tax Return
Used by a fiduciary for a domestic estate or domestic trust.

1065
U.S. Partnership Return of Income
Used by partnerships as an information return.

1116
Foreign Tax Credit—Individual, Fiduciary, or Nonresident Alien Individual
Used to figure and support the foreign tax credit claimed for the amount of any income, war profits, and excess profits taxes paid or accrued during the tax year to any foreign country or U.S. possession.

1120
U.S. Corporation Income Tax Return
Used by a corporation to report their income, deductions, and payment of taxes.

1120S
U.S. Income Tax Return for an S Corporation
Used by S corporations to report income and deductions under Subchapter S of the IRS code. Stockholders' share of taxable income is reported on their individual 1040.

1139
Corporation Application for Tentative Refund
Used by corporations that have certain loss and credit carrybacks and desire a quick refund of taxes.

1310
Statement of Person Claiming Refund Due a Deceased Taxpayer
Used by a claimant to secure payment of refund on behalf of a deceased taxpayer.

2106
Employee Business Expenses
For use by employees and outside salespersons to support deductions from income for travel, transportation, and other business expenses.

2119
Sale of Your Home
For use by individuals who sold their principal residence. Also used by those individuals age 55 or older who elect to exclude gain on the sale of their principal residence.

2120
Multiple Support Declaration
Used as a statement to disclaim as an income tax exemption an individual to whose support the taxpayer and others have jointly contributed.

2441
Child and Dependent Care Expenses
Used to figure the credit for child and dependent care expenses.

2848
Power of Attorney and Declaration of Representative
Used as an authorization for one person to act for another in any tax matter (except alcohol and tobacco taxes and firearms activities).

3903
Moving Expenses
For optional use to support deductions from income for expenses of travel, transportation (including meals and lodging), and certain expenses of selling an old residence and buying a new residence for employees or self-employed individuals moving to a new job location in the U.S. or its possessions.

4562
Depreciation and Amortization
For use by individuals, estates and trusts, partnerships, and corporations claiming depreciation, amortization, and section 179 expense deduction. Also used to provide required information for automobiles and all other "listed property."

4684
Casualties and Thefts
For use by all taxpayers for reporting gains and losses from casualties and thefts.

4868
Application for Automatic Extension of Time to File U.S. Individual Income Tax Return
Used to apply for an automatic 4-month extension of time to file Form 1040 or 1040A.

5329
Return for Additional Taxes Attributable to Qualified Retirement Plans (including IRAs), Annuities, and Modified Endowment Contracts
Used to report tax on excess contributions, premature distributions, excess distributions, and excess accumulations.

5500EZ
Annual Return of One-Participant (Owners and Their Spouses) Pension Benefit Plan
Used to report on a pension, profit-sharing, etc., plan covering an individual, partner, or an individual and spouse, or partners and spouses who wholly own a business.

6251
Alternative Minimum Tax—Individuals
Used by individuals to report tax preference items and to figure their alternative minimum tax liability.

7004
Application for Automatic Extension of Time to File Corporation Income Tax Return
Used by corporations and certain exempt organizations to request an automatic extension of 6 months to file their returns.

8283
Noncash Charitable Contributions
Used by taxpayers to report noncash contributions of property in which the total claimed fair market value of all property contributed exceeds $500.

8582
Passive Activity Loss Limitations
Used to determine limitations on passive activity losses.

8606
Nondeductible IRA Contributions, IRA Basis, and Nontaxable IRA Distributions
Used to report the nondeductible amount of IRA contributions and distributions. It is also used to determine IRA basis.

8615
Tax for Children Under Age 14 Who Have Investment Income of More Than $1,200
Used to figure the tax on unearned income of more than $1,200 belonging to a child under age 14.

8815
Exclusion of Interest from Series EE U.S. Savings Bonds Issued After 1989.
Used to figure the amount of interest on post-1989 Series EE U.S. Savings Bonds that can be excluded from income when the bonds are cashed and qualified higher education expenses are paid.

State Government Individual Income Taxes

Source: U.S. Advisory Commission on Intergovernmental Relations

As of November 1992. Only basic rates, brackets, and exemptions are shown. Local income tax rates, even those mandated by the state, are not included. Taxable income rates and brackets listed below apply to single taxpayers and married taxpayers filing "combined separate" returns in states where this is permitted.

		Taxable Income Brackets		Personal Exemptions			Standard Deduction[a]			
State	Tax Rates (range in percent)	Lowest: Amount Under	Highest: Amount Over	Single	Married-Joint Return	Dependents	Percent	Single	Married-Joint Return	Federal Income Tax Deductible[b]
AL·*	2.0-5.0%	$500	$3,000	$1,500	$3,000	$300	20%	$2,000	$4,000	yes
AK				No state income tax						
AZ[c]	0.8-7.0	10,000	150,000	2,100	4,200	2,100	NA	3,500	7,000	no
AR*	1.0-7.0	3,000	25,000	20[d]	40[d]	20[d]	10	1,000	1,000	no
CA[c]*	1.0-11.0	4,552	207,200	62[d]	124[d]	62[d]	NA	2,343	4,686	no
CO				5 percent of federal taxable income						no
CT*	4.5	Flat rate		12,000	24,000	0	NA	NA	NA	NA
DE·*	3.2-7.7	2,000	40,000	1,250	2,500	1,250	NA	1,300	1,600	no
DC	6.0-9.5	10,000	20,000	1,370	2,740	1,370	NA	2,000	2,000	no
FL				No state income tax						
GA	1.0-6.0	750	7,000	1,500	3,000	1,500	NA	2,300	3,000	no
HI*	2.0-10.0	1,500	20,500	1,040	2,080	1,040	NA	1,000	1,700	no
ID*	2.0-8.2	1,000	20,000			Same as federal				no
IL*	3.0	Flat rate		1,000	2,000	1,000	NA	NA	NA	no
IN·	3.4	Flat rate		1,000	2,000	1,000	NA	NA	NA	no
IA[c]*	0.4-9.98	1,060	47,700	20[d]	40[d]	15[d]	NA	1,310	3,220	yes
KS*	4.5-7.75	20,000	30,000	2,000	4,000	2,000	NA	3,000	5,000	no
KY·*	2.0-6.0	3,000	8,000	20[d]	40[d]	20[d]	NA	650	650	no
LA	2.0-6.0	10,000	50,000	4,500	9,000	1,000	Combined with exemptions			yes
ME[c]*	2.1-9.89	4,150	37,500	2,100	4,200	2,100	NA	3,600	6,000	no
MD·*	2.0-6.0	1,000	100,000	1,200	2,400	1,200	15	2,000	4,000	no
MA*	5.95-12.0	Flat rate		2,200	4,400	1,000	NA	NA	NA	no
MI·*	4.6	Flat rate		2,100	4,200	2,100	NA	NA	NA	no
MN	6.0-8.5	14,340	47,110			Same as federal				no
MS	3.0-5.0	5,000	10,000	6,000	9,500	1,500	NA	2,300	3,400	no
MO·*	1.5-6.0	1,000	9,000	1,200	2,400	400	NA	Same as federal		yes
MT[c]*	2.0-11.0	1,700	59,400	1,360	2,720	1,360	20	2,540	5,080	yes
NE[c]*	2.37-6.92	1,800	27,000	1,360	2,720	1,360	NA	Same as federal		no
NV				No state income tax						
NH*				Limited income tax						
NJ*	2.0-7.0	20,000	75,000	1,000	2,000	1,500	NA	NA	NA	no
NM	1.8-8.5	5,200	41,600	Same as federal			NA	Same as federal		no
NY·*	4.0-7.875	5,500	13,000	0	0	1,000	NA	6,000	9,500	no
NC*	6.0-7.75	12,750	60,000	2,000	4,000	2,000	NA	3,000	5,000	no
ND*				14 percent of federal income tax liability						yes
OH·*	0.743-6.9	5,000	100,000	650	1,300	650	NA	NA	NA	no
OK*	0.5-7.0	1,000	9,950	1,000	2,000	1,000	15	2,000	2,000	yes
OR[c]*	5.0-9.0	2,000	5,000	109	218	109	NA	1,800	3,000	yes
PA·*	2.95	Flat rate		NA	NA	NA	NA	NA	NA	no
RI*				27.5 percent of federal income tax liability						no
SC[c]	2.5-7.0	2,120	10,600	2,300	4,600	2,300		Same as federal		no
SD				No state income tax						
TN*				Limited income tax						
TX				No state income tax						
UT*	2.55-7.2	750	3,750	1,725	3,450	1,725		Same as federal		partial
VT*				28-34 percent of federal income tax liability						no
VA	2.0-5.75	3,000	17,000	800	1,600	800	NA	3,000	5,000	no
WA				No state income tax						
WV	3.0-6.5	10,000	60,000	2,000	4,000	2,000	NA	NA	NA	no
WI*	4.9-6.93	7,500	15,000	0	0	50[d]	NA	5,200	8,900	no
WY				No state income tax						

Notes: (NA) = not applicable. (+) = states in which one or more local governments levy a local income tax. (a) The lesser of (1) the percentage indicated, multiplied by adjusted gross income (AGI), or (2) the dollar value listed. In some states, when a standard deduction computed using a percentage of AGI is less than the fixed amount shown above, a minimum dollar deduction is allowed. Maryland and Utah have a minimum deduction as well. (b) A state provision that allows the taxpayer to deduct fully the federal income tax reduces the effective marginal tax rate for persons in the highest state and federal tax brackets by approximately 30% of the nominal tax rate—the deduction is of a lesser benefit to other taxpayers with lower federal and state top tax brackets. (c) Elements of income tax are indexed by an inflation factor. (d) Exemption is a tax credit.

***State Notes:**

Alabama: Social Security taxes are included in itemized deductions. Taxable income brackets for married filing joint over $6,000, taxed at highest rate.

Arkansas: Tax credit per dependent. Taxpayers 65 or older, or blind or deaf, receive a $20 credit. No tax is imposed on (1) a single taxpayer whose gross income is less than $5,000; (2) a married couple with gross income less than $10,000; and (3) a head of household with gross income less than $7,150.

California: Taxpayers 65 and older receive an additional $62 credit.

Connecticut: Personal exemption amount is reduced by $1,000 for each $1,000, or fraction thereof, by which the taxpayer's Connecticut AGI exceeds $24,000 (single, married filing separately), $38,000 (head of household), $48,000 (married filing jointly).

Delaware: Lowest personal income tax rate (3.2%) applies to income in the $2,000-5,000 bracket. Taxable income under $2,000 is not subject to tax and is referred to as the "zero bracket" amount.

Hawaii: A refundable food/excise tax credit of at least $55 per exemption is granted; a refundable medical services excise tax credit of 4% of qualified medical expenses, subject to limitation, is granted.

Idaho: Idaho allows a refundable $15 per exemption credit.

Illinois: Effective 1/1/90, an additional $1,000 exemption for taxpayer or spouse 65 years of age or older. An additional $1,000 exemption for taxpayer or spouse who is blind.

Indiana: Additional $1,000 exemption if taxpayer or spouse is over 65 or blind.

Iowa: Tax may not reduce after-tax income of taxpayer below $7,500 (single) or $11,500 (married filing jointly, head of household, surviving spouse). Only limitation for the standard deduction is that the deduction otherwise allowable of $1,310 or $3,220 may not exceed the amount of income remaining after the federal tax deduction. Additional $20 personal exemption is allowed for each blind taxpayer age 65 years and older. Voters within a school district may approve a school district income surtax, which is computed as a percentage of regular state tax liability before refundable credits.

Kansas: A child care credit equal to 25% of the federal child care credit is allowed to taxpayers claiming the federal credit.

Kentucky: Tax credit per dependent. Taxpayers 65 or older receive a $60 credit.

Maine: Rates include a variable surcharge that is imposed for tax years 1991 and 1992. A 5% surcharge will be imposed on tax liabilities arising from the first $75,000 of taxable income for married taxpayers filing a joint return ($37,500 for single filers or married filing separately and $56,250 for head of household filers). Any taxpayer with taxable income in excess of these amounts will pay a top marginal rate of 8.6% and a 15% surcharge.

Maryland: For tax years 1992-1994 only, the state's income tax rate is 6% for taxable income $100,000 or over for single, married filing separately, and dependent taxpayers; $150,000 for all others. All counties have a local income tax surcharge of at least 20% of the state tax liability; most counties have a surcharge of 50%. The maximum local income tax rate is 60% (50% for income taxed at the 6% state rate). Single taxpayers have a minimum standard deduction of $1,500; married taxpayers a minimum standard deduction of $3,000. Blind and elderly get an additional exemption of $1,000. An additional $1,200 exemption is allowed for elderly dependents.

Massachusetts: 12% (flat rate) imposed on net capital gains, interest, and dividends of residents, and Massachusetts business income of nonresidents. All other net income taxed at 5.95%. No tax is imposed on a single person whose gross income is $8,000 or less ($12,000 married). Social Security taxes are deducted from taxable income up to $2,000 per taxpayer.

Michigan: Persons who can be claimed as a dependent on someone else's return get an exception of $1,000. If their AGI is $1,500 or less, they owe no tax.

Missouri: For taxpayers itemizing deductions, Social Security taxes are deductible.

Montana: Standard deductions are 20% of the taxpayer's AGI. Maximum amounts are given.

Nebraska: Taxable income brackets will vary by filing status. Married individuals filing separate returns: lowest amount under $1,500; highest amount over $22,500.

New Hampshire: There is a 5% tax on taxable interest and dividends in excess of $1,200 ($2,400 married). There is no filing requirement for an individual whose total interest and dividend income, after deducting all interest from U.S. obligations, New Hampshire and Vermont banks or credit unions, and dividends from New Hampshire non-holding company bonds, is less than $1,200 ($2,400 for joint filers) for a taxable period.

New Jersey: No taxpayer is subject to tax if gross income is $3,000 or less ($1,500 married, filing separately).

New York: A supplemental tax is imposed on taxpayers with New York adjusted gross income in excess of $100,000. Taxpayers must add back the benefit of the lower tax brackets (i.e., 4%, 5%, 6%, and 7%). Taxpayers with New York AGI in excess of $150,000 are taxed at a flat rate of 7.875%.

North Carolina: Breaking points for higher marginal tax rates vary according to filing status. Taxable income brackets shown are for single taxpayers. North Carolina taxable income reflects federal reductions of personal exemptions and itemized deductions for higher income brackets.

North Dakota: Information in table applies to the short-form method, which is used by 95% of taxpayers. As an alternative, taxpayers may use the long-form method with tax ranging from 2.67% to 12.0% applied to income brackets ranging from $3,000 to over $50,000.

Ohio: Taxpayers take a $20 tax credit per exemption.

Oklahoma: These rates and brackets apply to single persons not deducting federal income tax. For individuals deducting the tax, rates range from 0.5% of the first $1,000 to 10% on income over $16,000 (single rate).

Oregon: Federal tax deduction limited to $3,000 ($1,500 if married filing separately).

Pennsylvania: There are eight classes of income: (1) compensation; (2) net profits; (3) interest; (4) dividends; (5) sale or exchange of property; (6) rents, royalties, patents, and copyrights; (7) income derived through estates or trusts; and (8) gambling and lottery winnings in excess of $1,250 ($2,500 married).

Rhode Island: For 1992, if a taxpayer's federal income tax liability is greater than $15,000, the effective tax rate is 29.75% of federal income tax liability in excess of $15,000. For 1993, the effective tax rate on federal income tax liability in excess of $15,000 is 32%. For the period 1/1/94 and thereafter, the tax rate is equal to 27.5% of the taxpayer's federal income tax liability.

Tennessee: Interest and dividends taxed at 6%. Persons over 65 having total annual gross income derived from any and all sources of $9,000 or less are exempt. Blindness is a basis for total exemption.

Utah: One-half of federal tax liability is deductible. In determining Utah taxable income, 25% of federal personal exemptions are added back. Exemptions reflect this add-back.

Vermont: Refundable state earned income tax credit (28% of federal credit, maximum $619). Three percent surtax of liability between $3,400 and $13,100 and 6% liability over $13,100 are reflected in rates.

Wisconsin: The standard deduction is gradually phased out as income increases; deduction is completely phased out at $50,830 of AGI for single filers and $55,000 of AGI for joint filers. Taxpayers age 65 and older receive additional $25 exemption.

ENERGY

World Energy Production and Consumption Trends

Source: Energy Information Administration, U.S. Dept. of Energy, *International Energy Annual 1991*

Since 1982, the world's total output of primary energy—petroleum, natural gas, coal, hydroelectricity, and nuclear electricity—has increased steadily at an average annual rate of 2.4 percent. World production increased from 279 quadrillion Btu in 1982 to 346 quadrillion Btu in 1991. In 1991 world production of petroleum was more than 66 million barrels per day, or 136 quadrillion Btu. Over the past 10 years, petroleum has been the world's most heavily used source of energy. Between 1982 and 1991, petroleum production increased by more than 8 million barrels per day. In that period, production by OPEC (Organization of Petroleum Exporting Countries) increased by 5.4 million barrels per day.

In 1991 three countries—the U.S., the former U.S.S.R., and China—were the leading producers and consumers of energy. These three countries produced 47 percent and consumed 48 percent of the world totals. The former U.S.S.R. and the U.S. were the world's largest producers of energy in 1991, supplying 39 percent of the world total. The United States accounted for 23 percent of the world's total energy consumption—more than any other country. The U.S. consumed 20 percent more than it produced—an imbalance of 13.6 quadrillion Btu.

U.S. Energy Summary

Source: Energy Information Administration, U.S. Dept. of Energy, *Annual Energy Review 1992*

In 1992 a gradually reviving domestic economy, low energy prices, and mild weather had the combined effect of producing modest growth in U.S. total energy consumption, which rose to a record 82 quadrillion Btu. The increase, which was the first since 1989, came as a result of increases in the consumption of petroleum, natural gas, coal, and nuclear electric power. Total sales of electricity, however, declined—for only the second time in 44 years. This decline was probably the result of a combination of factors: mild summer weather that held down residential and commercial demand for electricity for air conditioning; the growing prevalence of electric utilities' demand-side management practices, which attempt to reduce electricity use, particularly during periods of peak demand; and increasing electricity generation by nonutility power producers, which may have counteracted, to some extent, an increase in industrial demand attributable to gradually improving economy. Electricity sales of 2.8 trillion kilowatt-hours were 0.2 percent below 1991 sales.

Energy consumption per dollar of gross domestic product (GDP) declined slightly in 1992. About 17,000 Btu of energy were consumed for each dollar in 1992, compared with 23,000 Btu per dollar in the early 1970s (1987 dollars used throughout). However, energy consumption per capita rose from 322 million Btu in 1991 to 323 million Btu in 1992.

U.S. total energy production declined in 1992 for the second consecutive year, down 1.2 percent to 67 quadrillion Btu. Essentially all of the decline was attributed to lower crude oil production, which fell 0.5 quadrillion Btu from the 1991 level to 15 quadrillion Btu, and lower hydroelectric power production, which fell 0.4 quadrillion Btu to 2.5 quadrillion Btu. Crude oil production dropped to 7.2 million barrels per day, down 3.6 percent from the level in 1991. Hydroelectric power production fell 13 percent to 239 billion kilowatt-hours, the lowest level since 1988. The decline was attributable to persistent drought in western states.

U.S. net imports of energy rose to 14 quadrillion Btu in 1992, an increase of 7.9 percent from the 1991 level and the highest net import volume since 1979. Petroleum net imports rose 4.6 percent to 15 quadrillion Btu, natural gas net imports rose 10 percent to 1.8 quadrillion Btu, and coal net exports declined 0.5 percent to 2.6 quadrillion Btu. U.S. net imports of petroleum totaled 6.9 million barrels per day in 1992. Members of OPEC supplied 4.1 million barrels per day, well over half the total. Despite a decline from the 1991 level, coal remained the primary U.S. energy export. Coal exports totaled 103 million short tons in 1992.

U.S. Energy Overview, 1960-1992

Source: Energy Information Administration, U.S. Dept. of Energy; *Annual Energy Review 1992;* in quadrillion Btu

Activity and Energy Source	1960	1965	1970	1975	1980	1985	1990	1991	1992P
Production	**41.49**	**49.34**	**62.07**	**59.86**	**64.76**	**64.87R**	**67.85**	**67.54R**	**66.72**
Coal	10.82	13.06	14.61	14.99	18.60	19.33	22.46	21.59R	21.56
Natural Gas (Dry)	12.66	15.78	21.67	19.64	19.91	16.98	18.36	18.28R	18.27
Crude Oil[1]	14.93	16.52	20.40	17.73	18.25	18.99	15.57	15.70R	15.19
Natural Gas Plant Liquids	1.46	1.88	2.51	2.37	2.25	2.24	2.17	2.31R	2.36
Nuclear Electric Power	0.01	0.04	0.24	1.90	2.74	4.15	6.16	6.58R	6.65
Hydroelectric Power[2]	1.61	2.06	2.63	3.15	2.90	2.97R	2.93	2.88	2.51
Other[3]	(4)	0.01	0.02	0.07	0.11	0.21	0.20	0.19	0.19
Imports	**4.23**	**5.92**	**8.39**	**14.11**	**15.97**	**12.10**	**18.99**	**18.58R**	**19.45**
Natural Gas	0.16	0.47	0.85	0.98	1.01	0.95	1.55	1.80R	2.09
Crude Oil[5]	2.20	2.65	2.81	8.72	11.19	6.81	12.77	12.55	13.19
Petroleum Products[6]	1.80	2.75	4.66	4.23	3.46	3.80	4.35	3.79R	3.68
Other[7]	0.07	0.04	0.07	0.19	0.31	0.54	0.32	0.43R	0.49
Exports	**1.48**	**1.85**	**2.66**	**2.36**	**3.72**	**4.23**	**4.91**	**5.22R**	**5.03**
Coal	1.02	1.38	1.94	1.76	2.42	2.44	2.77	2.85	2.68
Crude Oil	0.43	0.39	0.55	0.44	1.16	1.66	1.82	2.13	2.01
Other[8]	0.03	0.09	0.18	0.16	0.14	0.14	0.31	0.24R	0.34
Adjustments[9]	**-0.43**	**-0.72**	**-1.37**	**-1.07**	**-1.05**	**1.24**	**-0.67R**	**0.24R**	**1.21**
Consumption	**43.80**	**52.68**	**66.43**	**70.55**	**75.96**	**73.98R**	**81.26R**	**81.14R**	**82.36**
Coal	9.84	11.58	12.26	12.66	15.42	17.48	19.10R	18.77R	18.92
Natural Gas[10]	12.39	15.77	21.79	19.95	20.39	17.83	19.30	19.63R	20.32
Petroleum[11]	19.92	23.25	29.52	32.73	34.20	30.92	33.55	32.85R	33.47
Nuclear Electric Power	0.01	0.04	0.24	1.90	2.74	4.15	6.16	6.58R	6.65
Hydroelectric Power[12]	1.66	2.06	2.65	3.22	3.12	3.40R	2.95	3.12R	2.79
Other[13]	(4)	-0.01	-0.04	0.09	0.08	0.20	0.21	0.20	0.22

(1) Includes lease condensate. (2) Electric utility and industrial generation. (3) "Other" production is electricity generated for distribution from wood, waste, geothermal, wind, photovoltaic, and solar thermal energy. (4) Less than 0.005 quadrillion Btu. (5) Includes imports of crude oil for the Strategic Petroleum Reserve, which began in 1977. (6) Includes imports of unfinished oils and natural gas plant liquids. (7) "Other" imports are coal, electricity, and coal coke. (8) "Other" exports are natural gas, petroleum products, electricity, and coal coke. (9) A balancing item. Includes stock changes, losses, gains, miscellaneous blending components, and unaccounted for supply. (10) Includes supplemental gaseous fuels. (11) Petroleum products supplied, including natural gas plant liquids and crude oil burned as fuel. (12) Electric utility and industrial generation, and net imports of electricity. (13) "Other" consumption is net imports of coal coke and electricity generated for distribution from wood, waste, geothermal, wind, photovoltaic, and solar thermal energy. R = Revised data. P = Preliminary data. **Notes:** Due to a lack of consistent historical data, some renewable energy sources are not included. For 1991 consumption, 3.3 quadrillion Btu of renewable energy consumed by U.S. electric utilities to generate electricity for distribution is included, but an estimated 3.4 quadrillion Btu of renewable energy used by other sectors in the United States is not included. Sum of components may not equal total due to independent rounding.

World's Major Producers of Primary Energy, 1991

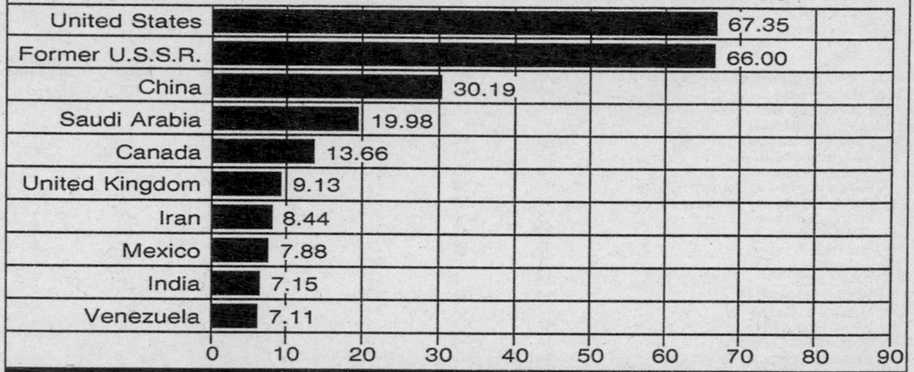

SOURCE: Energy Information Administration; International Energy Annual 1991; Quadrillion Btu

World's Major Consumers of Primary Energy, 1991

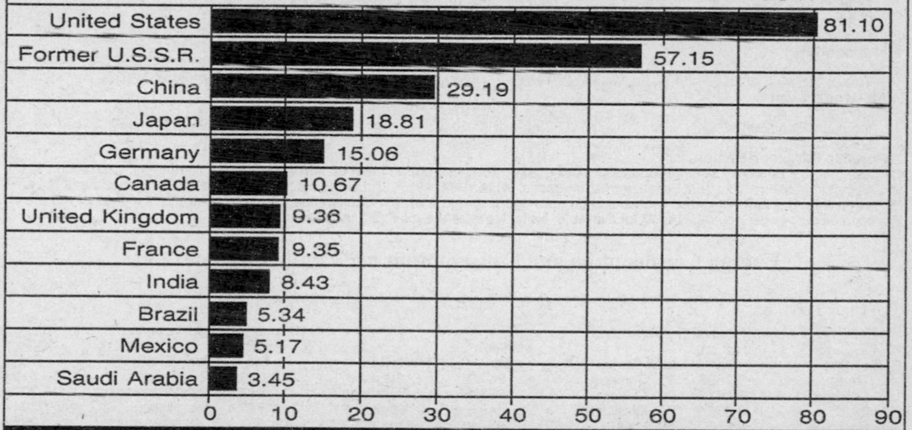

SOURCE: Energy Information Administration; International Energy Annual 1991; Quadrillion Btu

U.S. Net Imports of Petroleum, 1973-1992

Source: Energy Information Administration, U.S. Dept. of Energy, *Monthly Energy Review*, June 1993; thousand barrels per day

Average Annual Rate	Net Imports[1]			Petroleum Products Supplied
	From Arab OPEC[2]	From OPEC[3]	From All Countries	
1973	914	2,991	6,025	17,308
1974	752	3,277	5,892	16,653
1975	1,382	3,599	5,846	16,322
1976	2,423	5,063	7,090	17,461
1977	3,184	6,190	8,565	18,431
1978	2,962	5,747	8,002	18,847
1979	3,054	5,633	7,985	18,513
1980	2,549	4,293	6,365	17,056
1981	1,844	3,315	5,401	16,058
1982	852	2,136	4,298	15,296
1983	630	1,843	4,312	15,231
1984	817	2,037	4,715	15,726
1985	470	1,821	4,286	15,726
1986	1,160	2,828	5,439	16,281
1987	1,272	3,053	5,914	16,665
1988	1,837	3,513	6,587	17,283
1989	2,128	4,124	7,202	17,325
1990	2,243	4,285	7,161	16,988
1991	2,057R	4,064R	6,626R	16,714R
1992	1,972R	4,071R	6,938R	17,033R

R = Revised. (1) Net Imports is imports minus exports. Imports from members of the Organization of Petroleum Exporting Countries (OPEC) exclude indirect imports, which are petroleum products primarily from Caribbean and West European areas and refined from crude oil produced by OPEC. (2) The Arab members of OPEC are Algeria, Iraq, Kuwait, Libya, Qatar, Saudi Arabia, and the United Arab Emirates. Net imports from the Neutral Zone between Kuwait and Saudi Arabia are included in net imports from Arab OPEC. (3) OPEC currently consists of Gabon, Indonesia, Iran, Nigeria, and Venezuela, as well as the Arab members; prior to 1993, it also included Ecuador. **Notes:** Beginning in October 1977, Strategic Petroleum Reserves are included. Geographic coverage is the 50 States and the District of Columbia. Annual averages may not equal average of quarters due to independent rounding.

Appliance Use in U.S. Households, 1978-1990

Source: Energy Information Administration, U.S. Dept. of Energy, *Annual Energy Review 1992*

(percent of households)

Appliance	1978	1980	1982	1984	1987	1990	Change 1980-1990
Total Households	100	100	100	100	100	100	—
Type of Appliances							
Electric Appliances							
Television Set (Color)	NA	82	85	88	93	96	14
Television Set (B/W)	NA	51	47	43	36	31	−20
Clothes Washer	75	75	72	74	76	76	1
Range (Stove-Top Burner)	53	54	53	54	57	58	4
Oven, Regular or Microwave	54	59	59	63	79	88	29
Oven, Microwave	8	14	21	34	61	79	65
Clothes Dryer	45	47	45	46	51	53	6
Separate Freezer	35	38	37	37	34	35	−3
Dishwasher	35	37	36	38	43	45	8
Dehumidifier	NA	9	9	9	10	12	3
Waterbed Heaters	NA	NA	NA	10	14	15	NA
Window or Ceiling Fan	NA	NA	28	35	46	51	NA
Whole House Fan	NA	NA	8	8	9	10	NA
Evaporative Cooler	NA	4	4	4	3	4	(1)
Personal Computer	NA	NA	NA	NA	NA	16	NA
Pump for Well Water	NA	NA	NA	NA	NA	15	NA
Swimming-Pool Pump[2]	NA	4	3	NA	NA	5	1
Gas Appliances[3]							
Range (Stove-Top Burner)	48	46	47	45	43	42	−4
Oven	47	42	42	42	41	41	−1
Clothes Dryer	14	14	15	16	15	16	2
Outdoor Gas Grill	NA	9	11	13	20	26	17
Outdoor Gas Light	2	2	2	1	1	1	−1
Swimming Pool Heater[4]	NA	NA	NA	1	1	2	NA
Refrigerators[5]							
One	86	86	86	88	86	84	−2
Two or More	14	14	13	12	14	15	1
Air Conditioning							
Central[6]	23	27	28	30	36	39	12
Individual Room Units[6]	33	30	30	30	30	29	−1
None	44	43	42	40	36	32	−11
Portable Kerosene Heaters	(1)	(1)	3	6	6	5	5

(1) Less than 0.5 percent. (2) All reported swimming pools were assumed to have an electric pump for filtering and circulating the water. (3) Includes natural gas or liquefied petroleum gases. (4) In 1984, 1987, and 1990, also includes heaters for jacuzzis and hot tubs. (5) Fewer than 0.5 percent of the households do not have a refrigerator. (6) Households with both central and individual room units are counted only under central. NA = Not available. **Note:** No data are available for years not shown.

Energy Consumption and Consumption per Capita by State, 1991

Source: Energy Information Administration, U.S. Dept. of Energy, *Annual Energy Review 1992*

Consumption

Rank State	Trillion Btu	Rank State	Trillion Btu
1. Texas	9,785.1	27. Colorado	964.2
2. California	7,161.9	28. Oregon	953.4
3. Ohio	3,686.9	29. Mississippi	949.6
4. New York	3,558.5	30. Iowa	937.4
5. Illinois	3,513.0	31. Arizona	923.6
6. Pennsylvania	3,491.6	32. West Virginia	782.9
7. Louisiana	3,468.9	33. Arkansas	769.6
8. Florida	3,021.9	34. Connecticut	732.0
9. Michigan	2,753.9	35. New Mexico	588.0
10. Indiana	2,421.0	36. Alaska	587.6
11. New Jersey	2,299.7	37. Utah	566.3
12. Georgia	2,057.0	38. Nebraska	522.0
13. Washington	1,965.1	39. Nevada	400.2
14. North Carolina	1,961.6	40. Wyoming	390.8
15. Virginia	1,848.4	41. Idaho	387.7
16. Tennessee	1,746.5	42. Maine	362.3
17. Alabama	1,590.7	43. Montana	342.1
18. Missouri	1,512.6	44. North Dakota	320.3
19. Kentucky	1,476.5	45. Hawaii	271.6
20. Wisconsin	1,411.7	46. New Hampshire	238.7
21. Minnesota	1,363.7	47. Delaware	236.6
22. Massachusetts	1,313.1	48. Rhode Island	214.5
23. Oklahoma	1,283.0	49. South Dakota	205.0
24. Maryland	1,215.3	50. District of Columbia	175.1
25. South Carolina	1,209.3	51. Vermont	132.5
26. Kansas	1,038.9	**Total United States**	**81,119.0**

Consumption per Capita

Rank State	Million Btu	Rank State	Million Btu
1. Alaska	1,030.9	27. Georgia	310.6
2. Wyoming	849.5	28. Minnesota	307.7
3. Louisiana	815.4	29. Illinois	304.4
4. Texas	564.0	30. New Jersey	296.6
5. North Dakota	504.4	31. Virginia	294.3
6. West Virginia	434.2	32. District of Columbia	294.3
7. Indiana	431.5	33. Maine	293.6
8. Montana	422.9	34. Michigan	293.6
9. Kansas	416.4	35. Missouri	293.3
10. Oklahoma	404.1	36. Pennsylvania	292.0
11. Kentucky	397.7	37. North Carolina	291.2
12. Washington	392.1	38. South Dakota	291.2
13. Alabama	388.8	39. Colorado	285.4
14. New Mexico	379.6	40. Wisconsin	284.8
15. Idaho	372.7	41. Maryland	250.1
16. Mississippi	366.2	42. Arizona	246.4
17. Tennessee	352.6	43. Hawaii	238.9
18. Delaware	347.9	44. California	235.7
19. South Carolina	339.7	45. Vermont	233.7
20. Ohio	337.0	46. Florida	227.8
21. Iowa	335.4	47. Connecticut	222.6
22. Nebraska	327.7	48. Massachusetts	219.0
23. Oregon	326.3	49. New Hampshire	216.2
24. Arkansas	324.3	50. Rhode Island	213.4
25. Utah	320.0	51. New York	197.1
26. Nevada	311.9	**Total United States**	**321.7**

World's Largest Capacity Hydro Plants

Source: U.S. Committee on Large Dams of the Intl. Commission on Large Dams, Sept. 1993

Rank order	Name	Country	Rated capacity now (MW)	Rated capacity planned (MW)
1	Turukhansk (Lower Tunguska)*	former USSR		20,000
2	Itaipu	Brazil/Paraguay	7,400	13,320
3	Grand Coulee	USA	6,495	10,830
4	Guri (Raúl Leoni)	Venezuela	10,300	10,300
5	Tucurui	Brazil	2,640	7,260
6	Sayano Shushensk*	former USSR	6,400	6,400
7=	Corpus Posadas	Argentina/Paraguay	4,700	6,000
7=	Krasnoyarsk	former USSR	6,000	6,000
9	La Grande 2	Canada	5,328	5,328
10	Churchill Falls	Canada	5,225	5,225
11	Xingo	Brazil	3,012	5,020
12	Tarbela	Pakistan	1,750	4,678
13=	Bratsk	former USSR	4,500	4,500
13=	Ust-Ilim	former USSR	3,675	4,500
15	Cabora Bassa	Mozambique	2,425	4,150
16	Boguchany	former USSR		4,000
17=	Rogun*	former USSR		3,600
17=	Oak Creek	USA	3,600	3,600
19	Paulo Afonso I	Brazil	1,524	3,409
20	Pati*	Argentina		3,300
21=	Ilha Solteira	Brazil	3,200	3,200
21=	Brumley Gap*	USA	3,200	3,200
23	Chapetón*	Argentina		3,000
24	Gezhouba	China	2,715	2,715
25	John Day	USA	2,160	2,700
25	Nurek	former USSR	900	2,700
25=	Yacireta*	Argentina/Paraguay		2,700

* Planned or under construction.

Major Dams of the World

Source: U.S. Committee on Large Dams of the Intl. Commission of Large Dams, Sept. 1993

World's Highest Dams

Rank order	Name	Country	Height above lowest formation (m)
1	Rogun*	former USSR	335
2	Nurek	former USSR	300
3	Grand Dixence	Switzerland	285
4	Inguri	former USSR	272
5	Chicoasén	Mexico	261
6	Tehri*	India	261
7	Kishau*	India	253
8=	Ertan	China	245
9=	Sayano-Shushensk*	former USSR	245
10	Guavio*	Colombia	243
11	Mica	Canada	242
12	Mauvoisin	Switzerland	237
13	Chivor	Colombia	237
14	El Cajón	Honduras	234
15	Chirkei	former USSR	233
16	Oroville	USA	230
17	Bhakra	India	226
18	Hoover	USA	221
19	Contra	Switzerland	220
20	Mratinje	Yugoslavia	220

* Under construction.

World's Largest Volume Embankment Dams

Rank order	Name	Country	Volume cubic meters × 1000
1	Tarbela	Pakistan	148,500
2	Fort Peck	USA	96,050
3	Tucurui	Brazil	85,200
4	Ataturk*	Turkey	85,000
5	Yacireta*	Argentina	81,000
6	Rogun*	former USSR	75,500
7	Oahe	USA	70,339
8	Guri	Venezuela	70,000
9	Parambikulam	India	69,165
10	High Island West	Hong Kong	67,000
11	Gardiner	Canada	65,000
12	Afsluitdijk	Netherlands	63,400
13	Mangla	Pakistan	63,379
14	Oroville	USA	59,635
15	San Luis	USA	59,559
16	Nurek	former USSR	58,000
17	Tanda	Pakistan	57,250
18	Garrison	USA	50,843
19	Chochiti	USA	50,228
20	Oosterschelde	Netherlands	50,000

* Under construction.

World's Largest Capacity Manmade Reservoirs

Rank order	Name	Country	Capacity cubic meters × 1000
1	Owen Falls	Uganda	204,800
2	Bratsk	former USSR	169,000
3	Aswan (High)	Egypt	162,000
4	Kariba	Zimbabwe/Zambia	160,368
5	Akosombo	Ghana	147,960
6	Daniel Johnson	Canada	141,851
7	Guri	Venezuela	135,000
8	Krasnoyarsk	former USSR	73,300
9	W A C Bennett (Portage Mt.)	Canada	70,309
10	Zeya	former USSR	68,400
11	Cabora Bassa	Mozambique	63,000
12	La Grande 2	Canada	61,715
13	La Grande 3	Canada	60,020
14	Ust-Ilim	former USSR	59,300
15	Boguchany*	former USSR	58,200
16	Kuibyshev	former USSR	58,000
17	Serra de Mesa	Brazil	54,400
18	Caniapiscau Barrage KA 3	Canada	53,790
19	Bukhtarma	former USSR	49,800
20	Ataturk	Turkey	48,700

* Under construction

Major U.S. Dams and Reservoirs

Source: Committee on Register of Dams, Corps of Engineers, U.S. Army, Sept. 1993

Highest Dams

Order	Dam Name	River	State	Type	Height Feet	Height Meters	Year Complete
1	Oroville	Feather	California	E	754	230	1968
2	Hoover	Colorado	Nevada	A	725	221	1936
3	Dworshak	N Fork Clearwater	Idaho	G	718	219	1973
4	Glen Canyon	Colorado	Arizona	A	708	216	1966
5	New Bullards Bar	North Yuba	California	A	636	194	1970
6	New Melones	Stanislaus	California	R	626	191	1979
7	Swift	Lewis	Washington	E	610	186	1958
8	Mossyrock	Cowlitz	Washington	A	607	185	1968
9	Shasta	Sacramento	California	G	600	183	1945
10	Hungry Horse	S Fork Flathead	Montana	A	564	172	1953
11	Grand Coulee	Columbia	Washington	G	551	168	1942
12	Ross	Skagit	Washington	A	541	165	1949

E = Embankment, Earthfill; R = Embankment, Rockfill; G = Gravity; A = Arch.

Largest Embankment Dams

Order	Dam Name	River	State	Type	Volume Cubic yards X 1000	Volume Cubic Meters X 1000	Year Complete
1	Fort Peck	Missouri	Montana	E	125,624	96,050	1937
2	Oahe	Missouri	South Dakota	E	91,996	70,339	1958
3	Oroville	Feather	California	E	77,997	59,635	1968
4	San Luis	San Luis Creek	California E		77,897	59,559	1967
5	Garrison	Missouri	North Dakota	E	66,498	50,843	1953
6	Cochiti	Rio Grande	New Mexico	E	65,693	50,228	1975
7	Earthquake Lake	Madison	Montana	E-G	49,998	38,228	1959
8	Fort Randall	Missouri	South Dakota	E	49,962	38,200	1952
9	Castaic	Castaic Creek	California	E	43,998	33,640	1973
10	Ludington P/S	Lake Michigan	Michigan	E	37,699	28,824	1973
11	Kingsley	N. Platte	Nebraska	E	31,999	24,466	1941
12	Warm Springs	Dry Creek	California	E	29,977	22,920	1982

E = Embankment, Earthfill; G = Gravity.

Largest Man-Made Reservoirs

Order	Dam Name	Reservoir	Location	Reservoir Capacity Acre-Feet	Reservoir Capacity Cubic Meters x 1000	Year Completed
1	Hoover	Lake Mead	Nevada	28,253,000	34,850,000	1936
2	Glen Canyon	Lake Powell	Arizona	26,997,000	33,300,000	1966
3	Garrison	Lake Sakakawea	North Dakota	22,635,000	27,920,000	1953
4	Oahe	Lake Oahe	South Dakota	22,238,000	27,430,000	1958
5	Fort Peck	Fort Peck Lake	Montana	17,933,000	22,120,000	1937
6	Grand Coulee	F D Roosevelt Lake	Washington	9,558,000	11,790,000	1942
7	Libby	Lake Koocanusa	Montana	5,813,000	7,170,000	1973
8	Fort Randall	Lake Francis Case	South Dakota	4,621,000	5,700,000	1952
9	Shasta	Lake Shasta	California	4,548,000	5,610,000	1945
10	Toledo Bend	Toledo Bend Lake	Louisiana	4,475,000	5,520,000	1968
11	Wolf Creek	Cumberland Lake	Kentucky	3,997,000	4,930,000	1951
12	Flaming Gorge	Flaming Gorge Reservoir	Utah	3,786,000	4,670,000	1964

1 acre foot = 1 acre of water, 1 foot deep

Gasoline Retail Prices, U.S. City Average, 1973-1992

Source: Energy Information Administration, U.S. Dept. of Energy, *Monthly Energy Review*, June 1993

(cents per gallon, including taxes)

Average	Leaded Regular	Unleaded Regular	Unleaded Premium	All Types[1]	Average	Leaded Regular	Unleaded Regular	Unleaded Premium	All Types[1]
1973 . .	38.8	NA	NA	NA	1983 . .	115.7	124.1	138.3	122.5
1974 . .	53.2	NA	NA	NA	1984 . .	112.9	121.2	136.6	119.8
1975 . .	56.7	NA	NA	NA	1985 . .	111.5	120.2	134.0	119.6
1976 . .	59.0	61.4	NA	NA	1986 . .	85.7	92.7	108.5	93.1
1977 . .	62.2	65.6	NA	NA	1987 . .	89.7	94.8	109.3	95.7
1978 . .	62.6	67.0	NA	65.2	1988 . .	89.9	94.6	110.7	96.3
1979 . .	85.7	90.3	NA	88.2	1989 . .	99.8	102.1	119.7	106.0
1980 . .	119.1	124.5	NA	122.1	1990 . .	114.9	116.4	134.9	121.7
1981 . .	131.1	137.8	147.0[3]	135.3	1991 . .	NA	114.0	132.1	119.6
1982 . .	122.2	129.6	141.5	128.1	1992 . .	NA	112.7	131.6	119.0

(1) Also includes types of motor gasoline not shown separately. (2) In Sept. 1981, the Bureau of Labor Statistics changed the weights used in the calculation of average motor gasoline prices. From Sept. 1981 forward, gasohol is included in the average for all types, and unleaded premium is weighted more heavily. (3) Based on Sept. through Dec. data only. **Notes:** Geographic coverage for 1973-1977 is 56 urban areas; for 1978 forward, 85 urban areas. NA = Not available.

World Crude Oil and Natural Gas Reserves, January 1, 1992

Source: Energy Information Administration, U.S. Dept. of Energy, *Annual Energy Review 1992*

Region and Country	Crude Oil (billion barrels) *Oil and Gas Journal*	Crude Oil (billion barrels) *World Oil*	Natural Gas (trillion cubic feet) *Oil and Gas Journal*	Natural Gas (trillion cubic feet) *World Oil*
North America	**81.6**	**81.7**	**335.3**	**334.0**
Canada	5.6	6.1	96.7	96.0
Mexico	51.3	50.9	71.5	71.0
United States	24.7	24.7	167.1	167.1
Central and South America	**68.5**	**73.1**	**167.0**	**186.9**
Argentina	1.6	1.5	20.4	22.7
Bolivia	0.1	0.1	4.5	4.1
Brazil	2.8	3.0	4.0	4.4
Colombia	1.9	1.7	3.9	3.6
Ecuador	1.6	1.7	3.9	3.9
Trinidad and Tobago	0.5	0.6	8.9	8.7
Venezuela	59.1	62.7	110.0	128.5
Other	0.9	1.8	11.4	11.0
Western Europe	**14.7**	**22.2**	**181.4**	**215.5**
Denmark	0.8	0.7	4.1	4.0
Germany	0.4	0.3	8.8	8.2
Italy	0.7	0.7	11.4	11.4
Netherlands	0.1	0.1	69.6	68.9
Norway	7.6	15.3	60.7	96.7
United Kingdom	4.0	4.1	19.2	19.2
Other	1.1	1.0	7.6	7.1
Eastern Europe and Former U.S.S.R.	**58.5**	**61.8**	**1,763.5**	**1,871.3**
Former U.S.S.R.	57.0	59.9	1,750.0	1,853.4
Other[1]	1.5	1.9	13.5	17.9
Middle East	**661.6**	**596.6**	**1,319.1**	**1,344.9**
Bahrain	0.1	0.1	6.0	5.9
Iran	92.9	62.5	600.4	600.0
Iraq	100.0	100.0	95.0	109.4
Kuwait	96.5	95.2	48.5	51.8
Oman	4.3	4.4	9.9	13.0
Qatar	3.7	2.9	162.0	162.0
Saudi Arabia	260.3	261.9	184.5	184.5
United Arab Emirates	98.1	65.8	199.3	195.7
Other	5.7	3.8	13.5	22.6
Africa	**60.5**	**75.5**	**310.2**	**334.0**
Algeria	9.2	9.9	116.5	128.1
Cameroon	0.4	0.4	3.9	3.9
Egypt	4.5	3.5	12.4	12.0
Libya	22.8	38.4	43.0	43.5
Nigeria	17.9	17.9	104.7	120.1
Tunisia	1.7	1.8	3.0	3.2
Other	4.0	3.6	26.7	23.2
Far East and Oceania	**44.1**	**56.4**	**299.3**	**389.3**
Australia	1.5	2.1	15.1	75.4
Brunei	1.3	1.1	11.2	11.9
China	24.0	30.0	35.4	35.0
India	6.1	6.1	25.8	25.8
Indonesia	6.6	11.8	64.8	104.3
Malaysia	3.0	3.6	59.1	59.1
New Zealand	0.2	0.2	3.4	3.4
Pakistan	0.2	0.4	22.6	26.7
Thailand	0.3	0.3	13.6	14.7
Other	0.9	0.8	48.3	33.0
World	**989.4**	**967.1**	**4,375.8**	**4,675.9**

(1) Albania, Bulgaria, Czechoslovakia, Hungary, Poland, and Romania. **Notes:** Data for Kuwait and Saudi Arabia include one-half of the reserves in the Neutral Zone between Kuwait and Saudi Arabia. All reserve figures except those for the former U.S.S.R. and natural gas reserves in Canada are proved reserves recoverable with present technology and prices. Former U.S.S.R. figures are "explored reserves," which include proved, probable, and some possible. The Canadian natural gas figure includes proved and some probable. The latest Energy Information Administration data for the United States are for December 31, 1991. Sum of components may not equal total due to rounding.

Nuclear Electricity Gross Generation by Selected Country, March 1993

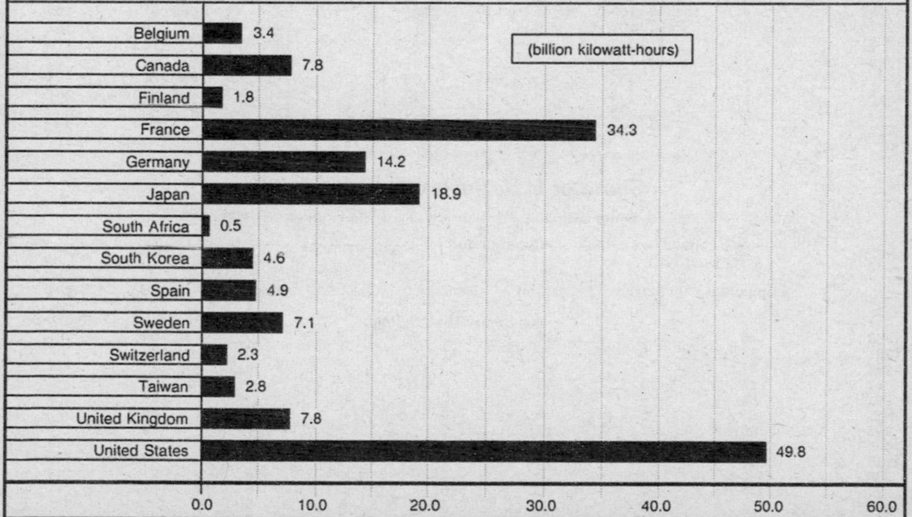

SOURCE: Energy Information Administration, U.S. Dept. of Energy; Monthly Energy Review, June 1993

World Nuclear Power

Source: International Atomic Energy Agency, Dec. 31, 1992

Country	Reactors in Operation No. of Units	Reactors in Operation Total MW(e)[1]	Reactors under Construction No. of Units	Reactors under Construction Total MW(e)[1]	Nuclear Electricity Supplied in 1992 TW(e) .h	Nuclear Electricity Supplied in 1992 % of Total	Total Operating Experience to 31 December 1992 Years	Total Operating Experience to 31 December 1992 Months
Argentina	2	935	1	692	6.6	14.4	28	7
Belgium	7	5,484	—	—	40.9	59.9	114	7
Brazil	1	626	1	1,245	1.8	0.7	10	9
Bulgaria	6	3,538	—	—	11.6	32.5	65	6
Canada	21	14,874	1	881	76.0	15.2	283	2
China	1	288	2	1,812	0.5	0.1	1	1
Cuba	—	—	2	816	—	—	—	—
Czechoslovakia	4	1,632	2	1,784	12.3	20.7	26	8
Finland	4	2,310	—	—	18.2	33.2	55	4
France	56	57,688	5	7,125	321.7	72.9	709	10
Germany	21	22,559	—	—	150.0	30.1	448	0
Hungary	4	1,729	—	—	13.1	48.4	30	2
India	9	1,593	5	1,010	5.6	3.3	101	3
Iran	—	—	2	2,392	—	—	—	—
Italy	—	—	—	—	—	—	81	0
Japan	44	34,238	9	8,129	217.0	27.7	556	11
Kazakhstan	1	135	—	—	0.5	0.6	19	6
Korea, South	9	7,220	3	2,550	58.5	43.2	72	1
Lithuania	2	2,760	1	1,380	15.6*	80.0*	14	6
Mexico	1	654	1	654	3.0	3.2	3	4
Netherlands	2	504	—	—	3.8	4.9	43	9
Pakistan	1	125	—	—	0.5	1.2	21	3
Romania	—	—	5	3,155	—	—	—	—
Russia	28	18,893	18	14,175	119.6	11.8	439	9
S. Africa	2	1,842	—	—	9.3	6.0	16	2
Spain	9	7,101	—	—	53.4	36.4	119	8
Sweden	12	10,002	—	—	60.8	43.2	183	2
Switzerland	5	2,952	—	—	22.1	39.6	88	10
Ukraine	15	13,020	6	5,700	71.0*	25.0*	128	11
United Kingdom	37	12,066	1	1,188	69.1	23.2	962	10
United States	109	98,729	3	3,480	618.8	22.3	1,702	4
Total[2]	**424**	**330,651**	**72**	**59,720**	**2,027.4**	—	**6,479**	**9**

(1) 1 terawatt-hour (TW(e).h) = 10^6 megawatt-hour (MW(e).h). For an average power plant, 1 TW(e).h = 0.39 megatonnes of coal equivalent (input) and 0.23 megatonnes of oil equivalent (input). (2) Includes Taiwan data. * IAEA estimate.

U.S. Nuclear Power Plant Operations

Source: Energy Information Administration, *Monthly Energy Review*, June 1993

Year	Operable Reactors Number	Nuclear-Based Electricity Generation Million Net Kilowatthours	Nuclear Portion of Domestic Electricity Generation Percent	Year	Operable Reactors Number	Nuclear-Based Electricity Generation Million Net Kilowatthours	Nuclear Portion of Domestic Electricity Generation Percent
1976	61	191,104	9.4	1985	95	383,691	15.5
1977	65	250,883	11.8	1986	100	414,038	16.6
1978	70	276,403	12.5	1987	107	455,270	17.7
1979	68	255,155	11.4	1988	108	526,973	19.5
1980	70	251,116	11.0	1989	110	529,355	19.0
1981	74	272,674	11.9	1990	111	576,862R	20.5R
1982	77	282,773	12.6	1991	111	612,565R	21.7
1983	80	293,677	12.7	1992	109	618,776	22.1
1984	86	327,634	13.6				

R = Revised

Status of U.S. Nuclear Reactor Units

Source: Energy Information Administration, *Monthly Energy Review*, June 1993

	Licensed for Operation		Construction Permits					
	Operable	In Startup	Granted	Pending	On Order	Announced	Total	Total Design Capacity Million Net Kilowatts
	Number of Reactor Units							
1980	70	2	82	12	3	0	169	163
1981	74	0	75	11	3	0	163	157
1982	77	2	60	3	2	0	144	135
1983	80	3	53	0	2	0	138	129
1984	86	6	38	0	2	0	132	123
1985	95	3	30	0	2	0	130	121
1986	100	7	19	0	2	0	128	119
1987	107	4	14	0	2	0	127	119
1988	108	3	12	0	0	0	123	115
1989	110	1	10	0	0	0	121	113
1990	111	0	8R	0	0	0	119R	111R
1991	111	0	8	0	0	0	119	111
1992	109	0	8	0	0	0	117	111

R = Revised

SCIENCE AND TECHNOLOGY

Computer Glossary

Source: *Electronic Computer Glossary* by Alan Freedman, The Computer Language Co. Inc., 1992

access: to store data on and retrieve data from a disk or other device connected to the computer.
analog: of or relating to the representation of an object that resembles the original. For example, the telephone system converts sound waves into electrical impulses.
arithmetic logic unit (ALU): a part of the *central processing unit (CPU)* that performs arithmetic operations and logical comparisons.
artificial intelligence (AI): a broad range of computer applications that resemble human intelligence and behavior, such as understanding speech, making judgments, and learning.
ASCII: an acronym for American Standard Code for Information Interchange; a widely-used binary code for storing data, often used to transfer data from one system to an incompatible system.
assembly language: a low-level, machine-oriented language, specific to a CPU, using mnemonics to represent each machine-language instruction.
authorization code: an identification number or password used to gain access to a computer system.
back up: to make a copy of important data to be used if the current file is destroyed.
BASIC: an acronym for Beginner's All-purpose Symbolic Instruction Code; a computer language used by many small and personal computer systems.
baud rate: the number of changes in an electrical line per second. Often used as measurement of printer or modem speed.
binary code: a representation of the base-2 number system in which the only allowable digits are 0 and 1.
bit: short for binary digit; a single binary digit (0 or 1) or the smallest unit of information stored in a computer, such as a memory cell.
board: short for printed circuit board; a flat board that holds chips and other electronic components connected by electronically conductive pathways.
boot: to start the computer.
buffer: a temporary place to put information for processing when it is being transferred between devices.
bug: a mistake that occurs in a program within a computer or in the unit's electrical system.
bus: a common channel, or pathway, between hardware devices.
byte: an 8-bit sequence of binary digits. Each byte corresponds to 1 character of data, representing a single letter, number, or symbol.
C: a high-level programming language often used to write commercial products due to its transportability to many different computer systems.
C++: an object-oriented version of C.
cache: a memory unit between the main memory and the CPU that accelerates retrieval of data.
CAD/CAM: abbreviation for computer-aided design/computer-aided manufacturing.
cathode ray tube (CRT): a vacuum tube used as a display screen in a terminal or TV. Term usually used to refer to the entire terminal.
CD-ROM: an acronym for Compact Disk-Read Only Memory; general term applied to a variety of storage formats by which audio, text, and graphics are retrieved by a laser beam that scans tracks of microscopic holes in a rotating compact disk. The disk can store over 600 million characters, but the user cannot store new information or alter the existing information.
central processing unit (CPU): the part within the computer that interprets and executes the instructions the user gives the system. It is composed of an arithmetic logic unit, a control unit, and some memory.
chip: short for integrated circuit chip, a collection of interconnected microminiature electronic components.
COBOL: an acronym for Common Business Oriented Language; widely used programming language.
code: a set of machine symbols that represents data or instructions; also to write a program.
computer: a programmable machine that accepts, processes, and displays data.
connect time: the time a user at a workstation is logged-on to a computer system.
cursor: the movable symbol on the computer monitor that marks the place where the operator is working.
cybernetics: the comparative study of human and machine processes in order to understand the similarities and differences.
database: a large amount of data stored in a well-organized format and managed by a program that allows access to the information.
Data Encryption Standard (DES): the U.S. National Institute of Standards and Technology system for encryption of commercial data.
data glove: a glove used to report the position of a user's hand in *virtual reality* systems.
debug: to eliminate a mistake within a computer program or in the unit's electrical system.
desktop publishing: the use of a personal computer to produce high-quality output (camera-ready hard copy or digital files) ready for commercial printing.
digital: of or relating to the representation, manipulation, or transmission of data by discrete signals.
disk: a revolving magnetized plate on which information and programs are stored. See also *floppy disk*.
disk drive: a peripheral machine that rotates a storage disk in order to read or record information.
DOS: stands for disk operating system; a single-user operating system used on IBM-compatible PCs.
download: to transmit data from a central to a remote computer, from a file server to a workstation, or from a computer to a floppy disk.
dump: a printout of the contents of memory or a file.
electronic mail: transmission of memos and messages over a *network*. Also called e-mail.
encryption: the encoding of data for security purposes.
field: the physical unit of data in a record.
file: any collection data treated as a single unit.
file server: a computer that stores data and programs that are shared by many users in a network.
floppy disk: a small, inexpensive removable disk used to record and store information.
font: a set of type characters of a particular design.
format: the arrangement by which data are stored or displayed.
FORTRAN: an acronym for Formula Translator; a high-level computer language widely used for scientific, engineering, or mathematical purposes.
global memory: the shared central memory of a multiple-processor system.
groupware: interactive software designed for several users working together on one project.
hard copy: printed computer output.
hard disk: a metal disk covered with a magnetic recording surface. Hard disks are often installed inside PCs for increased storage capacity.

hardware: the physical apparatus that makes up a computer: chips, transformers, boards, and wires. Also used to describe various pieces of equipment including the CPU, printer, modem, and CRT.

hexadecimal: refers to the base-16 number system, which is used to condense binary-based codes, such as bytes, for more efficient computer processing.

integrated circuit (IC): the formal name for a *chip*.

interface: a connection and interaction between hardware, software, and the user.

Internet: a network of computer networks involving millions of scientists and other users.

joystick: a hand-held lever that can be tilted in different directions to control the movement of the cursor on the terminal screen.

K: abbreviation for kilobyte, used to denote 1,024 units of stored matter.

keyboard: a set of input keys; also used as a verb meaning to type data into a computer for processing.

language: any set of related commands or instructions that are understandable to a computer.

light pen: an input device in which directions are given to the computer by touching the terminal screen with a light-sensitive stylus.

load: the actual operation of putting information and data into the computer or memory.

local area network (LAN): a computer system that links computers, printers, and other peripheral devices in a network for transmitting data between users situated near one another.

machine language: a set of binary-code instructions capable of being directly understood by a computer.

machine readable: any paper form or storage medium that can be automatically read by the computer.

mainframe computer: the largest type of computer, usually capable of processing data quickly and able to serve many users simultaneously.

memory: the computer's internal storage capacity.

menu: programs, functions, or other choices displayed on the monitor for user selection.

microcomputer: a computer that uses a microprocessor for its CPU. Personal computers are microcomputers.

microprocessor: a complete CPU on a single chip.

minicomputer: an intermediate computer system sized between the very small microcomputer and the large mainframe computer.

modem: an acronym for modulator-demodulator; a device that enables data to be transmitted between computers, generally over telephone lines, but sometimes via fiber-optic cable or wireless radio frequency.

monitor: a high-resolution screen used to display the output of a computer.

mouse: a hand-held object that when rolled across a flat surface is used as an input device.

multitasking: the ability to run more than one program on one computer at the same time.

network: in communications, terminals and computers linked together with the ability to interact with each other. In database management, a database design.

nibble: half a byte, or four bits.

noise: extraneous, random disturbances that degrade or disrupt data communications.

object-oriented programming: a programming method with formalized rules for developing self-contained software routines that can be reused in other program applications, allowing greater programming flexibility.

on-line: immediately accessible by a computer's CPU.

operating system: a master control program that runs the computer and acts as a scheduler and traffic cop.

optical character reader (OCR): a device capable of recognizing characters in a special typeface.

optical fiber: an ultrathin strand of glass with the ability to carry billions of bits of encoded data per second when pulses of laser light are beamed through it.

optoelectronics: a technology that joins light and electricity. OCRs, laser printers, and CD-ROMs are examples of optoelectronic devices.

Pascal: a popular high-level programming language.

PC: an abbreviation for personal computer; a microcomputer that serves one user.

peripheral: any hardware device connected to a computer, such as keyboards, printers, or joy sticks.

pixel: an acronym for picture element; the smallest display element on a video display screen.

printer: a device that converts computer output into printed images.

program: a sequence of detailed, coded instructions telling a computer how to perform a specific function.

RAM: an abbreviation for Random Access Memory; same as *memory*. Contents of RAM may be retrieved and altered by the user.

random access: the ability to retrieve records in a file directly without reading any previous records.

record: a group of related fields that are used to store data about a subject.

ROM: an abbreviation for Read Only Memory; a permanent memory.

sector: a defined portion of concentric track on a disk.

software: the programs, or sets of instructions, that tell the computer what to do.

supercomputer: a term applied to the fastest, most powerful computers at a given time; typically used to manipulate large amounts of data.

telecommuting: working at home and communicating via computer with the office.

teleconferencing: to communicate with a number of people simultaneously via telephone lines with audio, video, or computer connections.

terminal: a keyboard and display unit (usually a CRT) that allows a person to communicate with a computer.

timesharing: the simultaneous use of a computer by more than one person, as in a *local area network*.

track: a concentric band on a magnetic disk that contains a specified amount of data.

user-friendly: easy to learn and use.

UNIX: a multi-user operating system that runs on a wide variety of computers.

virtual memory: the use of hard disk storage to expand effective memory capability.

virtual reality: interaction with a computer to create an artificial reality that projects the user into a 3- dimensional space.

virus: a destructive program that is secretly attached to an existing program, once run it alters or deletes data, or causes other computer system malfunctions, whenever the preexisting program is run.

window: a separate viewing area on a display screen.

word: a computer's basic storage unit; a sequence of bits—8 to 32—occupying a single storage location and processed as a unit by the computer.

word processor: a text creation and editing program or system that allows electronic writing and correcting of documents.

workstation: a high-performance, single-user microcomputer or minicomputer; or in a *local area network*, a PC that serves a single user.

worm: a destructive program that reproduces itself and deletes data from a computer's memory.

write-access: authorization to record or alter data stored in a computer.

The Internet

The Internet links people together via computer terminals and telephone lines (and in some cases wireless radio connections) in a web of networks and shared software, allowing users in one area to reach other users anywhere in the "net." Among the services available through the Internet are telnet, granting users access to more powerful computers; usenet newsgroups, allowing open discussion between users; archives with access to scientific and government research; and electronic mail. Originally created by the Pentagon, the Internet is now subsidized by the National Science Foundation, which controls the Internet's core computer network. It is thought that 15 million people in the U.S. and 25 million worldwide access the Internet regularly. Despite the increasing accessibility through some public libraries, computer bulletin boards, and software packages, the primary users remain government officials, scientists, and corporate researchers.

Inventions and Discoveries

Invention	Date	Inventor	Nation.
Adding machine	1642	Pascal	French
Adding machine	1885	Burroughs	U.S.
Aerosol spray	1926	Rotheim	Norwegian
Air brake	1868	Westinghouse	U.S.
Air conditioning	1911	Carrier	U.S.
Air pump	1654	Guericke	German
Airplane, automatic pilot	1912	Sperry	U.S.
Airplane, experimental	1896	Langley	U.S.
Airplane jet engine	1939	Ohain	German
Airplane with motor	1903	Wright bros.	U.S.
Airplane, hydro	1911	Curtiss	U.S.
Airship	1852	Giffard	French
Airship, rigid dirigible	1900	Zeppelin	German
Arc welder	1919	Thomson	U.S.
Aspartame	1965	Schlatter	U.S.
Autogyro	1920	de la Cierva	Spanish
Automobile, differential gear	1885	Benz	German
Automobile, electric	1892	Morrison	U.S.
Automobile, exp'mtl	1864	Marcus	Austrian
Automobile, gasoline	1889	Daimler	German
Automobile, gasoline	1892	Duryea	U.S.
Automobile magneto	1897	Bosch	German
Automobile muffler	...	Maxim, H.P.	U.S.
Automobile self-starter	1911	Kettering	U.S.
Babbitt metal	1839	Babbitt	U.S.
Bakelite	1907	Baekeland	Belg., U.S.
Balloon	1783	Montgolfier	French
Barometer	1643	Torricelli	Italian
Bicycle, modern	1885	Starley	English
Bifocal lens	1780	Franklin	U.S.
Block signals, railway	1867	Hall	U.S.
Bomb, depth	1916	Tait	U.S.
Bottle machine	1895	Owens	U.S.
Braille printing	1829	Braille	French
Burner, gas	1855	Bunsen	German
Calculating machine	1833	Babbage	English
Calculator, electronic pocket	1972	Merryman, Van Tassel	U.S.
Camera, Kodak	1888	Eastman, Walker	U.S.
Camera, Polaroid Land	1948	Land	U.S.
Car coupler	1873	Janney	U.S.
Carburetor, gasoline	1893	Maybach	German
Card time recorder	1894	Cooper	U.S.
Carding machine	1797	Whittemore	U.S.
Carpet sweeper	1876	Bissell	U.S.
Cassette, audio	1963	Philips Co.	Dutch
Cassette, videotape	1969	Sony	Japanese
Cash register	1879	Ritty	U.S.
Cathode ray oscilloscope	1897	Braun	German
Cathode ray tube	1878	Crookes	English
CAT, or CT, scan (computerized tomography)	1973	Hounsfield	English
Cellophane	1908	Brandenberger	Swiss
Celluloid	1870	Hyatt	U.S.
Cement, Portland	1824	Aspdin	English
Chronometer	1761	Harrison	English
Circuit breaker	1925	Hilliard	U.S.
Circuit, integrated	1959	Kilby, Noyce, Texas Instr.	U.S.
Clock, pendulum	1657	Huygens	Dutch
Coaxial cable system	1929	Affel, Espensched	U.S.
Coke oven	1893	Hoffman	Austrian
Compressed air rock drill	1871	Ingersoll	U.S.
Comptometer	1887	Felt	U.S.
Computer, automatic sequence	1944	Aiken, et al.	U.S.
Computer, mini	1960	Digital Corp.	U.S.
Condenser microphone (telephone)	1916	Wente	U.S.
Contraceptive, oral	1954	Pincus, Rock	U.S.
Corn, hybrid	1917	Jones	U.S.
Cotton gin	1793	Whitney	U.S.
Cream separator	1878	DeLaval	Swedish
Cultivator, disc	1878	Mallon	U.S.
Cystoscope	1878	Nitze	German
Diesel engine	1895	Diesel	German
Disk, compact	1972	RCA	U.S.
Disk, floppy	1970	IBM	U.S.
Disk player, compact	1979	Sony, Philips Co.	Japan., Dutch
Disk, video	1972	Philips Co.	Dutch
Dynamite	1866	Nobel	Swedish
Dynamo, continuous current	1871	Gramme	Belgian
Dynamo, hydrogen cooled	1915	Schuler	U.S.
Electric battery	1800	Volta	Italian
Electric fan	1882	Wheeler	U.S.
Electrocardiograph	1903	Einthoven	Dutch
Electroencephalograph	1929	Berger	German
Electromagnet	1824	Sturgeon	English
Electron spectrometer	1944	Deutsch, Elliott, Evans	U.S.
Electron tube multigrid	1913	Langmuir	U.S.
Electroplating	1805	Brugnatelli	Italian
Electrostatic generator	1929	Van de Graaff	U.S.
Elevator brake	1852	Otis	U.S.
Elevator, push button	1922	Larson	U.S.
Engine, automatic transmission	1910	Fottinger	German
Engine, coal-gas 4-cycle	1876	Otto	German
Engine, compression ignition	1883	Daimler	German
Engine, electric ignition	1883	Benz	German
Engine, gas, compound	1926	Eickemeyer	U.S.
Engine, gasoline	1872	Brayton, Geo.	U.S.
Engine, gasoline	1889	Daimler	German
Engine, jet	1930	Whittle	English
Engine, steam, piston	1705	Newcomen	English
Engine, steam, piston	1769	Watt	Scottish
Engraving, half-tone	1852	Talbot	U.S.
Fiberglass	1938	Owens-Corning	U.S.
Fiber optics	1955	Kapany	English
Filament, tungsten	1913	Coolidge	U.S.
Flanged rail	1831	Stevens	U.S.
Flatiron, electric	1882	Seely	U.S.
Food, frozen	1924	Birdseye	U.S.
Freon (low-boiling fluorine compounds)	1930	Midgley, et al.	U.S.
Furnace (for steel)	1858	Siemens	German
Galvanometer	1820	Sweigger	German
Gas discharge tube	1922	Hull	U.S.
Gas lighting	1792	Murdoch	Scottish
Gas mantle	1885	Welsbach	Austrian
Gasoline (lead ethyl)	1922	Midgley	U.S.
Gasoline, cracked	1913	Burton	U.S.
Gasoline, high octane	1930	Ipatieff	Russian
Geiger counter	1913	Geiger	German
Glass, laminated safety	1909	Benedictus	French
Glider	1853	Cayley	English
Gun, breechloader	1811	Thornton	U.S.
Gun, Browning	1897	Browning	U.S.
Gun, magazine	1875	Hotchkiss	U.S.
Gun, silencer	1908	Maxim, H.P.	U.S.
Guncotton	1847	Schoenbein	German
Gyrocompass	1911	Sperry	U.S.
Gyroscope	1852	Foucault	French
Harvester-thresher	1818	Lane	U.S.
Heart, artificial	1982	Jarvik	U.S.
Helicopter	1939	Sikorsky	U.S.
Hydrometer	1768	Baume	French

(continued)

Invention	Date	Inventor	Nation.
Hydrogen bomb	1952	U.S. government scientists	U.S.
Ice-making machine	1851	Gorrie	U.S.
Iron lung	1928	Drinker, Slaw	U.S.
Kaleidoscope	1817	Brewster	Scottish
Kinetoscope	1889	Edison	U.S.
Lacquer, nitrocellulose	1921	Flaherty	U.S.
Lamp, arc	1847	Staite	English
Lamp, flourescent	1938	General Electric, Westinghouse	U.S.
Lamp, incandescent	1879	Edison	U.S.
Lamp, incand., frosted	1924	Pipkin	U.S.
Lamp, incand., gas	1913	Langmuir	U.S.
Lamp, Klieg	1911	Kliegl, A.&J.	U.S.
Lamp, mercury vapor	1912	Hewitt	U.S.
Lamp, miner's safety	1816	Davy	English
Lamp, neon	1909	Claude	French
Lathe, turret	1845	Fitch	U.S.
Launderette	1934	Cantrell	U.S.
Lens, achromatic	1758	Dollond	English
Lens, fused bifocal	1908	Borsch	U.S.
Leyden jar (condenser)	1745	von Kleist	German
Lightning rod	1752	Franklin	U.S.
Linoleum	1860	Walton	English
Linotype	1884	Mergenthaler	U.S.
Lock, cylinder	1851	Yale	U.S.
Locomotive, electric	1851	Vail	U.S.
Locomotive, exp'mtl	1802	Trevithick	English
Locomotive, exp'mtl	1812	Fenton et al.	English
Locomotive, exp'mtl	1813	Hedley	English
Locomotive, exp'mtl	1814	Stephenson	English
Locomotive practical	1829	Stephenson	English
Locomotive, 1st U.S.	1830	Cooper, P.	U.S.
Loom, power	1785	Cartwright	English
Loudspeaker, dynamic	1924	Rice, Kellogg	U.S.
Machine gun	1861	Gatling	U.S.
Machine gun, improved	1872	Hotchkiss	U.S.
Machine gun (Maxim)	1883	Maxim, H.S.	U.S., Eng.
Magnet, electro	1828	Henry	U.S.
Mantle, gas	1885	Welsbach	Austrian
Mason jar	1858	Mason, J.	U.S.
Match, friction	1827	John Walker	English
Mercerized textiles	1843	Mercer, J.	English
Meter, induction	1888	Shallenberg	U.S.
Metronome	1816	Malezel	German
Microcomputer	1973	Truong, et al.	French
Micrometer	1636	Gascoigne	English
Microphone	1877	Berliner	U.S.
Microprocessor	1971	Intel Corp.	U.S.
Microscope, compound	1590	Janssen	Dutch
Microscope, electronic	1931	Knoll, Ruska	German
Microscope, field ion	1951	Mueller	German
Monitor, warship	1861	Ericsson	U.S.
Monotype	1887	Lanston	U.S.
Motor, AC	1892	Tesla	U.S.
Motor, DC	1837	Davenport	U.S.
Motor, induction	1887	Tesla	U.S.
Motorcycle	1885	Daimler	German
Movie machine	1894	Jenkins	U.S.
Movie, panoramic	1952	Waller	U.S.
Movie, talking	1927	Warner Bros.	U.S.
Mower, lawn	1831	Budding, Ferrabee	English
Mowing machine	1822	Bailey	U.S.
Neoprene	1930	Carothers	U.S.
Nylon synthetic	1930	Carothers	U.S.
Nylon	1937	Du Pont lab.	U.S.
Oil cracking furnace	1891	Gavrilov	Russian
Oil filled power cable	1921	Emanueli	Italian
Oleomargarine	1869	Mege-Mouries	French
Ophthalmoscope	1851	Helmholtz	German
Paper	105	Lun	Chinese
Paper machine	1809	Dickinson	U.S.
Parachute	1785	Blanchard	French
Pen, ballpoint	1938	Biro	Hungarian
Pen, fountain	1884	Waterman	U.S.
Pen, steel	1780	Harrison	English
Pendulum	1583	Galileo	Italian
Percussion cap	1807	Forsythe	Scottish
Phonograph	1877	Edison	U.S.
Photo, color	1892	Ives	U.S.
Photo film, celluloid	1893	Reichenbach	U.S.
Photo film, transparent	1884	Eastman, Goodwin	U.S.
Photoelectric cell	1895	Elster	German
Photographic paper	1835	Talbot	U.S.
Photography	1835	Talbot	English
Photography	1835	Daguerre	French
Photography	1816	Niepce	French
Photophone	1880	Bell	U.S.-Scot.
Phototelegraphy	1925	Bell Labs	U.S.
Piano	1709	Cristofori	Italian
Piano, player	1863	Fourneaux	French
Pin, safety	1849	Hunt	U.S.
Pistol (revolver)	1836	Colt	U.S.
Plow, cast iron	1785	Ransome	English
Plow, disc	1896	Hardy	U.S.
Pneumatic hammer	1890	King	U.S.
Powder, smokeless	1884	Vieille	French
Printing press, rotary	1845	Hoe	U.S.
Printing press, web	1865	Bullock	U.S.
Propeller, screw	1804	Stevens	U.S.
Propeller, screw	1837	Ericsson	Swedish
Pulsars	1967	Bell	English
Punch card accounting	1889	Hollerith	U.S.
Quasars	1963	Schmidt	U.S.
Radar	1940	Watson-Watt	Scottish
Radio amplifier	1906	De Forest	U.S.
Radio beacon	1928	Donovan	U.S.
Radio crystal oscillator	1918	Nicolson	U.S.
Radio receiver, cascade tuning	1913	Alexanderson	U.S.
Radio receiver, heterodyne	1913	Fessenden	U.S.
Radio transmitter triode modulation	1914	Alexanderson	U.S.
Radio tube-diode	1905	Fleming	English
Radio tube oscillator	1915	De Forest	U.S.
Radio tube triode	1906	De Forest	U.S.
Radio, signals	1895	Marconi	Italian
Radio, magnetic detector	1902	Marconi	Italian
Radio FM 2-path	1933	Armstrong	U.S.
Rayon (acetate)	1895	Cross	English
Rayon (cuprammonium)	1890	Despeissis	French
Rayon (nitrocellulose)	1884	Chardonnet	French
Razor, electric	1917	Schick	U.S.
Razor, safety	1895	Gillette	U.S.
Reaper	1834	McCormick	U.S.
Record, cylinder	1887	Bell, Tainter	U.S.
Record, disc	1887	Berliner	U.S.
Record, long playing	1947	Goldmark	U.S.
Record, wax cylinder	1888	Edison	U.S.
Refrigerator car	1868	David	U.S.
Resin, synthetic	1931	Hill	English
Richter scale	1935	Richter	U.S.
Rifle, repeating	1860	Spencer	U.S.
Rocket engine	1926	Goddard	U.S.
Rubber, vulcanized	1839	Goodyear	U.S.
Saccharin	1879	Remsen, Fahlberg	U.S.
Saw, band	1808	Newberry	English
Saw, circular	1777	Miller	English
Sewing machine	1846	Howe	U.S.
Shoe-sewing machine	1860	McKay	U.S.
Shrapnel shell	1784	Shrapnel	English
Shuttle, flying	1733	Kay	English
Sleeping-car	1865	Pullman	U.S.
Slide rule	1620	Oughtred	English
Soap, hardwater	1928	Bertsch	German
Spectroscope	1859	Kirchoff, Bunsen	German
Spectroscope (mass)	1918	Dempster	U.S.
Spinning jenny	1767	Hargreaves	English
Spinning mule	1779	Crompton	English
Steamboat, exp'mtl	1778	Jouffroy	French
Steamboat, exp'mtl	1785	Fitch	U.S.
Steamboat, exp'mtl	1787	Rumsey	U.S.
Steamboat, exp'mtl	1788	Miller	Scottish
Steamboat, exp'mtl	1803	Fulton	U.S.
Steamboat, exp'mtl	1804	Stevens	U.S.
Steamboat, practical	1802	Symington	Scottish
Steamboat, practical	1807	Fulton	U.S.
Steam car	1770	Cugnot	French
Steam turbine	1884	Parsons	English
Steel (converter)	1856	Bessemer	English
Steel alloy	1891	Harvey	U.S.
Steel alloy, high-speed	1901	Taylor, White	U.S.
Steel, electric	1900	Heroult	French
Steel, manganese	1884	Hadfield	English
Steel, stainless	1916	Brearley	English
Stereoscope	1838	Wheatstone	English
Stethoscope	1819	Laennec	French
Stethoscope, binaural	1840	Cammann	U.S.
Stock ticker	1870	Edison	U.S.
Storage battery, rechargeable	1859	Plante	French
Stove, electric	1896	Hadaway	U.S.
Submarine	1891	Holland	U.S.
Submarine, even keel	1894	Lake	U.S.
Submarine, torpedo	1776	Bushnell	U.S.

(continued)

Invention	Date	Inventor	Nation.
Superconductivity (BCS theory)	1957	Bardeen, Cooper, Schreiffer	U.S.
Tank, military	1914	Swinton	English
Tape recorder, magnetic	1899	Poulsen	Danish
Teflon	1938	Du Pont	U.S.
Telegraph, magnetic	1837	Morse	U.S.
Telegraph, quadruplex	1864	Edison	U.S.
Telegraph, railroad	1887	Woods	U.S.
Telegraph, wireless high frequency	1895	Marconi	Italian
Telephone	1876	Bell	U.S.-Scot.
Telephone amplifier	1912	De Forest	U.S.
Telephone, automatic	1891	Stowger	U.S.
Telephone, radio	1900	Poulsen, Fessenden	Danish
Telephone, radio	1906	De Forest	U.S.
Telephone, radio, l. d.	1915	AT&T	U.S.
Telephone, recording	1898	Poulsen	Danish
Telephone, wireless	1899	Collins	U.S.
Telescope	1608	Lippershey	Neth.
Telescope	1609	Galileo	Italian
Telescope, astronomical	1611	Kepler	German
Teletype	1928	Morkrum, Kleinschmidt	U.S.
Television, iconoscope	1923	Zworykin	U.S.
Television, electronic	1927	Farnsworth	U.S.
Television, mech. scanner	1923	Baird	Scottish
Thermometer	1593	Galileo	Italian
Thermometer	1730	Reaumur	French
Thermometer, mercury	1714	Fahrenheit	German
Time recorder	1890	Bundy	U.S.
Time, self-regulator	1918	Bryce	U.S.
Tire, double-tube	1845	Thomson	Scottish
Tire, pneumatic	1888	Dunlop	Scottish
Toaster, automatic	1918	Strite	U.S.
Tool, pneumatic	1865	Law	English
Torpedo, marine	1804	Fulton	U.S.
Tractor, crawler	1904	Holt	U.S.
Transformer AC.	1885	Stanley	U.S.
Transistor	1947	Shockley, Brattain, Bardeen	U.S.
Trolley car, electric	1884-87	Van DePoele, Sprague	U.S.
Tungsten, ductile	1912	Coolidge	U.S.
Tupperware	1945	Tupper	U.S.
Turbine, gas	1849	Bourdin	French
Turbine, hydraulic	1849	Francis	U.S.
Turbine, steam	1884	Parsons	English
Type, movable	1447	Gutenberg	German
Typewriter	1867	Sholes, Soule, Glidden	U.S.
Vacuum cleaner, electric	1907	Spangler	U.S.
Velcro	1948	de Mestral	Swiss
Video game ("Pong")	1972	Buschnel	U.S.
Video home system (VHS)	1975	Matsushita, JVC	Japanese
Washer, electric	1901	Fisher	U.S.
Welding, atomic hydrogen	1924	Langmuir, Palmer	U.S.
Welding, electric	1877	Thomson	U.S.
Wind tunnel	1912	Eiffel	French
Wire, barbed	1874	Glidden	U.S.
Wire, barbed	1875	Haisn	U.S.
Wrench, double-acting	1913	Owen	U.S.
X-ray tube	1913	Coolidge	U.S.
Zipper	1891	Judson	U.S.

Discoveries and Innovations: Chemistry, Physics, Biology, Medicine

	Date	Discoverer	Nation.
Acetylene gas	1862	Berthelot	French
ACTH	1927	Evans, Long	U.S.
Adrenalin	1901	Takamine	Japanese
Aluminum, electrolytic process	1886	Hall	U.S.
Aluminum, isolated	1825	Oersted	Danish
Anesthesia, ether	1842	Long	U.S.
Anesthesia, local	1885	Koller	Austrian
Anesthesia, spinal	1898	Bier	German
Aniline dye	1856	Perkin	English
Anti-rabies	1885	Pasteur	French
Antiseptic surgery	1867	Lister	English
Antitoxin, diphtheria	1891	Von Behring	German
Argyrol	1897	Bayer	German
Arsphenamine	1910	Ehrlich	German
Aspirin	1889	Dresser	German
Atabrine	...	Mietzsch, et al.	German
Atomic numbers	1913	Moseley	English
Atomic theory	1803	Dalton	English
Atomic time clock	1947	Libby	U.S.
Atom-smashing theory	1919	Rutherford	English
Bacitracin	1945	Johnson, et al.	U.S.
Bacteria (described)	1676	Leeuwenhoek	Dutch
Barbital	1903	Fischer	German
Bleaching powder	1798	Tennant	English
Blood, circulation	1628	Harvey	English
Bordeaux mixture	1885	Millardet	French
Bromine from sea	1924	Edgar Kramer	U.S.
Calcium carbide	1888	Wilson	U.S.
Calculus	1670	Newton	English
Camphor synthetic	1896	Haller	French
Canning (food)	1804	Appert	French
Carbomycin	1952	Tanner	U.S.
Carbon oxides	1925	Fisher	German
Chloamphenicol	1947	Burkholder	U.S.
Chlorine	1774	Scheele	Swedish
Chloroform	1831	Guthrie, S.	U.S.
Chlortetracycline	1948	Duggen	U.S.
Classification of plants and animals	1735	Linnaeus	Swedish
Cocaine	1860	Niermann	German
Combustion explained	1777	Lavoisier	French
Conditioned reflex	1914	Pavlov	Russian
Cortisone	1936	Kendall	U.S.
Cortisone, synthesis	1946	Sarett	U.S.
Cosmic rays	1910	Gockel	Swiss
Cyanamide	1905	Frank, Caro	German
Cyclotron	1930	Lawrence	U.S.
DDT (not applied as insecticide until 1939)	1874	Zeidler	German
Deuterium	1932	Urey, Brickwedde, Murphy	U.S.
DNA (structure)	1951	Crick Watson Wilkins	English U.S. English
Electric resistance (law)	1827	Ohm	German
Electric waves	1888	Hertz	German
Electrolysis	1852	Faraday	English
Electromagnetism	1819	Oersted	Danish
Electron	1897	Thomson, J.	English
Electron diffraction	1936	Thomson, G. Davisson	English U.S.
Electroshock treatment	1938	Cerletti, Bini	Italian
Erythromycin	1952	McGuire	U.S.
Evolution, natural selection	1858	Darwin	English
Falling bodies, law	1590	Galileo	Italian
Gases, law of combining volumes	1808	Gay-Lussac	French
Geometry, analytic	1619	Descartes	French
Gold (cyanide process for extraction)	1887	MacArthur, Forest	British
Gravitation, law	1687	Newton	English
Holograph	1948	Gabor	British
Human heart transplant	1967	Barnard	S. African
Human immunodeficiency virus identified	1984	Montagnier, Gallo	French, U.S.
Indigo, synthesis of	1880	Baeyer	German
Induction, electric	1830	Henry	U.S.
Insulin	1922	Banting, Best, Macleod	Canadian, Scottish
Intelligence testing	1905	Binet, Simon	French
In vitro fertilization	1978	Steptoe, Edwards	English
Isoniazid	1952	Hoffman-La-Roche Domagk	U.S. German
Isotopes, theory	1912	Soddy	English
Laser (light amplification by stimulated emission of radiation)	1958	Townes, Schawlow	U.S.
Light, velocity	1675	Roemer	Danish
Light, wave theory	1690	Huygens	Dutch

(continued)

	Date	Discoverer	Nation.
Lithography	1796	Senefelder	Bohemian
Lobotomy	1935	Egas Moniz	Portuguese
LSD-25	1943	Hoffman	Swiss
Mendelian laws	1866	Mendel	Austrian
Mercator projection (map)	1568	Mercator (Kremer)	Flemish
Methanol	1661	Boyle	Irish
Milk condensation	1853	Borden	U.S.
Molecular hypothesis	1811	Avogadro	Italian
Motion, laws of	1687	Newton	English
Neomycin	1949	Waksman, Lechevalier	U.S.
Neutron	1932	Chadwick	English
Nitric acid	1648	Glauber	German
Nitric oxide	1772	Priestley	English
Nitroglycerin	1846	Sobrero	Italian
Oil cracking process	1891	Dewar	U.S.
Oxygen	1774	Priestley	English
Oxytetracycline	1950	Finlay, et al.	U.S.
Ozone	1840	Schonbein	German
Paper, sulfite process	1867	Tilghman	U.S.
Paper, wood pulp, sulfate process	1884	Dahl	German
Penicillin	1929	Fleming	Scottish
practical use	1941	Florey, Chain	English
Periodic law and table of elements	1869	Mendeleyev	Russian
Planetary motion, laws	1609	Kepler	German
Plutonium fission	1940	Kennedy, Wahl, Seaborg, Segre	U.S.
Polymyxin	1947	Ainsworth	English
Positron	1932	Anderson	U.S.
Proton	1919	Rutherford	N. Zealand
Psychoanalysis	1900	Freud	Austrian
Quantum theory	1900	Planck	German
Quasars	1963	Matthews, Sandage	U.S.
Quinine synthetic	1946	Woodward, Doering	U.S.
Radioactivity	1896	Becquerel	French
Radium	1898	Curie, Pierre	French
		Curie, Marie	Pol.-Fr.
Relativity theory	1905	Einstein	German
Reserpine	1949	Jal Vaikl	Indian
Schick test	1913	Schick	U.S.
Silicon	1823	Berzelius	Swedish
Smallpox eradication	1979	World Health Organization	United Nations
Streptomycin	1945	Waksman	U.S.
Sulfadiazine	1940	Roblin	U.S.
Sulfanilamide	1935	Bovet, Trefouel	French
Sulfanilamide theory	1908	Gelmo	German
Sulfapyridine	1938	Ewins, Phelps	English
Sulfathiazole	...	Fosbinder, Walter	U.S.
Sulfuric acid	1831	Phillips	English
Sulfuric acid, lead	1746	Roebuck	English
Thiacetazone	1950	Behnisch, Mietzsch, Domagk	German
Tuberculin	1890	Koch	German
Uranium fission (theory)	1939	Hahn, Meitner, Strassmann	German
		Bohr	Danish
		Fermi	Italian
		Einstein, Pegram, Wheeler	U.S.
Uranium fission, atomic reactor	1942	Fermi, Szilard	U.S.
Vaccine, measles	1954	Enders, Peebles	U.S.
Vaccine, meningitis (first conjugate)	1987	Gordon, et. al., Connaught Lab., Inc.	U.S.
Vaccine, polio	1955	Salk	U.S.
Vaccine, polio, oral	1955	Sabin	U.S.
Vaccine, rabies	1885	Pasteur	French
Vaccine, smallpox	1796	Jenner	English
Vaccine, typhus	1909	Nicolle	French
Van Allen belts, radiation	1958	Van Allen	U.S.
Vitamin A	1913	McCollum, Davis	U.S.
Vitamin B	1916	McCollum	U.S.
Vitamin C	1928	Szent-Gyorgyi, King	U.S.
Vitamin D	1922	McCollum	U.S.
Wassermann test	1906	Wassermann	German
Xerography	1938	Carlson	U.S.
X-ray	1895	Roentgen	German

Chemical Elements, Atomic Weights, Discoverers

Atomic weights, based on the exact number 12 as the assigned atomic mass of the principal isotope of carbon, carbon 12, are provided through the courtesy of the International Union of Pure and Applied Chemistry and Butterworth Scientific Publications.

For the radioactive elements, with the exception of uranium and thorium, the mass number of either the isotope of longest half-life (*) or the better known isotope (**) is given.

Chemical element	Symbol	Atomic number	Atomic weight	Year discov.	Discoverer
Actinium	Ac	89	227*	1899	Debierne
Aluminum	Al	13	26.9815	1825	Oersted
Americium	Am	95	243*	1944	Seaborg, et al.
Antimony	Sb	51	121.75	1450	Valentine
Argon	Ar	18	39.948	1894	Rayleigh, Ramsay
Arsenic	As	33	74.9216	13th c.	Albertus Magnus
Astatine	At	85	210*	1940	Corson, et al.
Barium	Ba	56	137.34	1808	Davy
Berkelium	Bk	97	249**	1949	Thompson, Ghiorso, Seaborg
Beryllium	Be	4	9.0122	1798	Vauquelin
Bismuth	Bi	83	208.980	15th c.	Valentine
Boron	B	5	10.811a	1808	Gay-Lussac, Thenard
Bromine	Br	35	79.904b	1826	Balard
Cadmium	Cd	48	112.40	1817	Stromeyer
Calcium	Ca	20	40.08	1808	Davy
Californium	Cf	98	251*	1950	Thompson, et al.
Carbon	C	6	12.01115a	B.C.	unknown
Cerium	Ce	58	140.12	1803	Klaproth
Cesium	Cs	55	132.905	1860	Bunsen, Kirchhoff
Chlorine	Cl	17	35.453b	1774	Scheele
Chromium	Cr	24	51.996b	1797	Vauquelin
Cobalt	Co	27	58.9332	1735	Brandt
Copper	Cu	29	63.546b	B.C.	unknown
Curium	Cm	96	247*	1944	Seaborg, James, Ghiorso
Dysprosium	Dy	66	162.50	1886	Boisbaudran
Einsteinium	Es	99	254*	1952	Ghiorso, et al.
Erbium	Er	68	167.26	1843	Mosander
Europium	Eu	63	151.96	1901	Demarcay

Chemical element	Symbol	Atomic number	Atomic weight	Year discov.	Discoverer
Fluorine	F	9	18.9984	1771	Scheele
Francium	Fr	87	223*	1939	Perey
Gadolinium	Gd	64	157.25	1886	Marignac
Gallium	Ga	31	69.72	1875	Boisbaudran
Germanium	Ge	32	72.59	1886	Winkler
Gold	Au	79	196.967	B.C.	unknown
Hafnium	Hf	72	178.49	1923	Coster, Hevesy
Hahnium	Ha	105	262*	1970	Ghiorso, et al.
Hassium	Hs	108	265*	1984	Münzenberg, et al.
Helium	He	2	4.0026	1868	Janssen, Lockyer
Holmium	Ho	67	164.930	1878	Soret, Delafontaine
Hydrogen	H	1	1.00797a	1766	Cavendish
Indium	In	49	114.82	1863	Reich, Richter
Iodine	I	53	126.9044	1811	Courtois
Iridium	Ir	77	192.2	1804	Tennant
Iron	Fe	26	55.847b	B.C.	unknown
Krypton	Kr	36	83.80	1898	Ramsay, Travers
Lanthanum	La	57	138.91	1839	Mosander
Lawrencium	Lr	103	262*	1961	Ghiorso, T. Sikkeland, A.E. Larsh, and R.M. Latimer
Lead	Pb	82	207.19	B.C.	unknown
Lithium	Li	3	6.939	1817	Arfvedson
Lutetium	Lu	71	174.97	1907	Welsbach, Urbain
Magnesium	Mg	12	24.312	1829	Bussy
Manganese	Mn	25	54.9380	1774	Gahn
Meitnerium	Mt	109	266*	1982	Münzenberg, et al.
Mendelevium	Md	101	258*	1955	Ghiorso, et al.
Mercury	Hg	80	200.59	B.C.	unknown
Molybdenum	Mo	42	95.94	1782	Hjelm
Neodymium	Nd	60	144.24	1885	Welsbach
Neon	Ne	10	20.183	1898	Ramsay, Travers
Neptunium	Np	93	237*	1940	McMillan, Abelson
Nickel	Ni	28	58.71	1751	Cronstedt
Nielsbohrium	Ns	107	262*	1981	Münzenberg, et al.
Niobium[1]	Nb	41	92.906	1801	Hatchett
Nitrogen	N	7	14.0067	1772	Rutherford
Nobelium	No	102	259*	1958	Ghiorso, et al.
Osmium	Os	76	190.2	1804	Tennant
Oxygen	O	8	15.9994a	1774	Priestley, Scheele
Palladium	Pd	46	106.4	1803	Wollaston
Phosphorus	P	15	30.9738	1669	Brand
Platinum	Pt	78	195.09	1735	Ulloa
Plutonium	Pu	94	242**	1940	Seaborg, et al.
Polonium	Po	84	210**	1898	P. and M. Curie
Potassium	K	19	39.102	1807	Davy
Praseodymium	Pr	59	140.907	1885	Welsbach
Promethium	Pm	61	147**	1945	Glendenin, Marinsky, Coryell
Protactinium	Pa	91	231*	1917	Hahn, Meitner
Radium	Ra	88	226*	1898	P. & M. Curie, Bemont
Radon	Rn	86	222*	1900	Dorn
Rhenium	Re	75	186.2	1925	Noddack, Tacke, Berg
Rhodium	Rh	45	102.905	1803	Wollaston
Rubidium	Rb	37	85.47	1861	Bunsen, Kirchhoff
Ruthenium	Ru	44	101.07	1845	Klaus
Rutherfordium	Rf	104	261*	1969	Ghiorso, et al.
Samarium	Sm	62	150.35	1879	Boisbaudran
Scandium	Sc	21	44.956	1879	Nilson
Selenium	Se	34	78.96	1817	Berzelius
Silicon	Si	14	28.086a	1823	Berzelius
Silver	Ag	47	107.868b	B.C.	unknown
Sodium	Na	11	22.9898	1807	Davy
Strontium	Sr	38	87.62	1790	Crawford
Sulfur	S	16	32.064 a	B.C.	unknown
Tantalum	Ta	73	180.948	1802	Ekeberg
Technetium	Tc	43	99**	1937	Perrier and Segre
Tellurium	Te	52	127.60	1782	Von Reichenstein
Terbium	Tb	65	158.924	1843	Mosander
Thallium	Tl	81	204.37	1861	Crookes
Thorium	Th	90	232.038	1828	Berzelius
Thulium	Tm	69	168.934	1879	Cleve
Tin	Sn	50	118.69	B.C.	unknown
Titanium	Ti	22	47.90	1791	Gregor
Tungsten (Wolfram)	W	74	183.85	1783	d'Elhujar
Uranium	U	92	238.03	1789	Klaproth
Vanadium	V	23	50.942	1830	Sefstrom
Xenon	Xe	54	131.30	1898	Ramsay, Travers
Ytterbium	Yb	70	173.04	1878	Marignac
Yttrium	Y	39	88.905	1794	Gadolin
Zinc	Zn	30	65.37	B.C.	unknown
Zirconium	Zr	40	91.22	1789	Klaproth

(1) Formerly Columbium. (a) Atomic weights so designated are known to be variable because of natural variations in isotopic composition. The observed ranges are: hydrogen ±0.0001; boron ±0.003; carbon ±0.005; oxygen ±0.0001; silicon ±0.001; sulfur ±0.003. (b) Atomic weights so designated are believed to have the following experimental uncertainties: chlorine ±0.001; chromium ±0.001; iron ±0.003; bromine ±0.001; silver ±0.001; copper ±0.001.

METEOROLOGY

National Weather Service Watches and Warnings

Source: National Weather Service, NOAA, U.S. Dept. of Commerce; *Glossary of Meteorology*, American Meteorological Society

National Weather Service forecasters issue a Severe Thunderstorm or Tornado Watch for a specific area where threatening weather is most likely to occur during the valid time of the watch. A Severe Thunderstorm Watch is issued for a specific area where severe thunderstorms are most likely. A Tornado Watch is issued when severe thunderstorms that produce tornados are likely to occur in a specific area. A Watch alerts people to check for threatening weather, make plans for action, and listen for a Tornado Warning. A Tornado Warning means that a tornado has been sighted or indicated by radar, and that safety precautions should be taken at once. A Hurricane Watch means that an existing hurricane poses a threat to coastal and inland communities, within 24-36 hours, in the area specified by the Watch. A Hurricane Warning means hurricane force winds and/or dangerously high water and exceptionally high waves are expected in a specified coastal area within 24 hours.

Tornado—A violent rotating column of air in contact with the ground and pendant from a thundercloud, usually recognized as a funnel-shaped vortex accompanied by a loud roar. With rotating winds est. up to 300 mph., on a local scale, it is the most destructive storm. Tornado paths have varied in length from a few feet to nearly 300 miles (avg. 5 mi.); diameter from a few feet to over a mile (average 220 yards); average forward speed, 30 mph.

Cyclone—An atmospheric circulation of winds rotating counterclockwise in the northern hemisphere and clockwise in the southern hemisphere. Tornadoes, hurricanes, and the lows shown on weather maps are all examples of cyclones having various sizes and intensities. Cyclones are usually accompanied by precipitation or stormy weather.

Hurricane—A severe cyclone originating over tropical ocean waters and having winds 74 miles an hour or higher. (In the western Pacific, such storms are known as typhoons.) The area of strong winds takes the form of a circle or an oval, sometimes as much as 500 miles in diameter. In the lower latitudes hurricanes usually move toward the west or northwest at 10 to 15 mph. When the center approaches 25° to 30° North Latitude, direction of motion often changes to northeast, with increased forward speed.

Blizzard—A severe weather condition characterized by strong winds bearing a great amount of snow. The National Weather Service specifies winds of 35-miles an hour or higher, and sufficient falling and/or blowing snow to frequently reduce visibility to less than 1/4 mile for a duration of at least three hours.

Severe Thunderstorm—A thunderstorm with winds of 58 mph. or greater and/or hail three-fourths of an inch or larger in diameter.

Flood—The condition that occurs when water overflows the natural or artificial confines of a stream or other body of water, or accumulates by drainage over low-lying areas.

National Weather Service Marine Warnings and Advisories

Small Craft Advisory: A Small Craft Advisory alerts mariners to sustained (exceeding two hours) weather and/or sea conditions either present or forecast, potentially hazardous to small boats. Although there is no definition of a small craft, hazardous conditions generally include winds of 18 to 33 knots and/or dangerous wave conditions. It is the responsibility of the mariner, based on his experience, location and size or type of boat, to determine if the conditions are hazardous. When a mariner becomes aware of a Small Craft Advisory, he should immediately obtain the latest marine forecast to determine the reason for the Advisory.

Gale Warning indicates that winds within the range 34 to 47 knots, not directly associated with a tropical storm, are forecast for the area.

Tropical Storm Warning indicates that winds of 34 to 63 knots are forecast in a specified coastal area in 24 hours or less. Only issued for winds of tropical weather systems.

Storm Warning indicates that winds 48 knots and above, no matter how high the speed, not directly associated with a tropical storm, are forecast for the area.

Hurricane Warning indicates that winds 64 knots or greater are forecast for the area. Only issued for winds produced by tropical weather systems.

Special Marine Warning: A warning for potentially hazardous weather conditions, usually of short duration (2 hours or less) and producing wind speeds of 34 knots or more, not adequately covered by existing marine warnings.

Primary sources of dissemination are commercial radio, TV, U.S. Coast Guard radio stations, and NOAA VHF-FM broadcasts. These broadcasts on 162.40 to 162.55 MHz can usually be received 20-40 miles from the transmitting antenna site, depending on terrain and quality of the receiver used. Where transmitting antennas are on high ground, the range may be somewhat greater, reaching 60 miles or more.

Speed of Winds in the U.S.

Source: National Climatic Data Center, NESDIS, NOAA, U.S. Dept. of Commerce

Miles per hour — average through 1991. High through 1991. Wind velocities in true values.

Station	Avg.	High	Station	Avg.	High	Station	Avg.	High
Albuquerque, N.M.	9.1	(b)90	Helena, Mont.	7.8	73	Mt. Washington, N.H.	35.3	231
Anchorage, Alas.	7.0	75	Honolulu, Ha.	11.4	(b)67	New Orleans, La.	8.2	(b)98
Atlanta, Ga.	9.1	60	Houston, Tex.	7.9	51	New York, N.Y.(c)	9.4	(b)70
Baltimore, Md.	9.2	80	Indianapolis, Ind.	9.6	46	Omaha, Neb.	10.6	(b)109
Bismarck, N.D.	10.2	(b)72	Jacksonville, Fla.	8.0	(b)82	Philadelphia, Pa.	9.5	73
Boston, Mass.	12.5	(b)61	Kansas City, Mo.	10.8	(b)70	Phoenix, Ariz.	6.3	(b)86
Buffalo, N.Y.	12.0	91	Lexington, Ky.	9.2	46	Pittsburgh, Pa.	9.1	58
Cape Hatteras, N.C.	11.1	(b)110	Little Rock, Ark.	7.8	65	Portland, Ore.	7.9	88
Casper, Wyo.	12.9	81	Los Angeles, Cal.	6.2	49	St. Louis, Mo.	9.7	(b)60
Chicago, Ill.	10.4	58	Louisville, Ky.	8.4	(b)61	Salt Lake City, Ut.	8.8	71
Cleveland, Oh.	10.6	(b)74	Memphis, Tenn.	8.9	46	San Diego, Cal.	6.9	56
Dallas, Tex.	10.8	73	Miami, Fla.	9.3	(a)74	San Francisco, Cal.	8.7	47
Denver, Col.	8.7	(b)56	Milwaukee, Wis.	11.6	54	Seattle, Wash.	9.0	66
Detroit, Mich.	10.4	48	Minneapolis, Minn.	10.6	(b)92	Spokane, Wash.	8.9	59
Galveston, Tex.	11.0	(d)100	Mobile, Ala.	9.0	63	Washington, D.C.	9.3	(b)78

(a) Highest velocity ever recorded in Miami area was 132 mph, at former station in Miami Beach in September 1926. (b) Previous location. (c) Data for Central Park; Battery Place data through 1960, avg. 14.5, high 113. (d) Recorded before anemometer blew away. Estimated high 120.

Monthly Normal Temperature and Precipitation

Source: National Climatic Data Center, NESDIS, NOAA, U.S. Dept. of Commerce

The normal temperatures below are based on records for the 30-year period 1951 to 1980 inclusive. For stations that did not have continuous records from the same instrument site for the entire 30 years, the means have been adjusted to the record at the present site.

Airport station; *city office stations. T, temperature in Fahrenheit; P, precipitation in inches; L, less than .05 inch.

Station	Jan. T.	Jan. P.	Feb. T.	Feb. P.	Mar. T.	Mar. P.	Apr. T.	Apr. P.	May T.	May P.	June T.	June P.	July T.	July P.	Aug. T.	Aug. P.	Sept. T.	Sept. P.	Oct. T.	Oct. P.	Nov. T.	Nov. P.	Dec. T.	Dec. P.
Albany, N.Y.	21	2.4	23	2.3	34	3.0	47	2.9	58	3.3	67	3.3	71	3.0	69	3.3	61	3.2	51	2.9	39	3.0	26	3.0
Albuquerque, N.M.	35	0.4	39	0.4	46	0.5	55	0.4	64	0.5	75	0.5	79	1.3	76	1.5	69	0.9	57	0.9	44	0.4	36	0.5
Anchorage, Alas.	13	0.8	18	0.9	24	0.7	35	0.7	46	0.6	54	1.1	58	2.0	56	2.1	48	2.5	35	1.7	22	1.1	14	1.1
Asheville, N.C.	37	3.5	39	3.6	46	5.1	56	3.8	63	4.2	70	4.2	73	4.4	73	4.8	70	4.0	56	3.3	46	3.3	39	3.5
Atlanta, Ga.	42	4.9	45	4.4	53	5.9	62	4.4	69	4.0	76	3.4	79	4.7	78	3.4	73	3.2	62	2.5	52	3.4	45	4.2
Atlantic City, N.J.	34	3.3	35	3.2	42	3.7	51	3.1	60	2.9	68	2.9	74	3.9	74	4.5	68	2.7	58	2.8	48	3.5	38	3.5
Baltimore, Md.	33	3.0	35	3.0	43	3.7	54	3.4	63	3.4	72	3.8	77	3.9	76	4.6	69	3.5	57	3.1	46	3.1	37	3.4
Barrow, Alas.	-14	0.2	-20	0.2	-16	0.2	-2	0.2	19	0.2	33	0.4	39	0.9	38	1.0	31	0.6	14	0.6	-1	0.3	-13	0.2
Birmingham, Ala.	42	5.2	46	4.7	54	6.6	63	5.0	70	4.5	77	3.7	80	5.4	80	3.9	74	4.3	62	2.7	52	3.6	45	5.0
Bismarck, N.D.	7	0.5	15	0.5	26	0.7	43	1.5	55	2.2	64	3.0	70	2.0	69	1.7	57	1.4	46	0.8	29	0.5	15	0.5
Boise, Ida.	30	1.6	36	1.1	41	1.0	49	1.2	57	1.2	66	1.0	75	0.3	72	0.4	63	0.6	52	0.8	40	1.3	32	1.3
Boston, Mass.	30	4.0	31	3.7	38	4.1	49	3.7	59	3.5	68	2.9	74	2.7	72	3.7	65	3.4	55	3.4	45	4.2	34	4.9
Buffalo, N.Y.	24	3.0	25	2.4	33	3.0	45	3.0	56	2.9	66	2.7	71	3.0	69	4.2	62	3.4	52	2.9	40	3.6	29	3.4
Burlington, Vt.	17	1.9	18	1.7	29	2.2	43	2.8	55	3.0	65	3.6	70	3.4	67	3.9	59	3.2	48	2.8	37	2.8	23	2.4
Caribou, Me.	11	2.4	13	2.1	24	2.4	37	2.6	50	2.9	60	3.2	65	4.0	63	4.0	54	3.5	43	3.1	31	3.2	16	3.1
Charleston, S.C.	49	3.3	51	3.4	57	4.4	66	2.6	73	4.4	79	6.5	82	7.3	81	6.5	77	4.9	68	2.9	59	2.2	52	3.1
Chicago, Ill.	21	1.6	26	1.3	36	2.6	49	3.7	59	3.2	69	4.1	73	3.6	72	3.5	65	3.4	54	2.3	40	2.1	28	2.1
Cleveland, Oh.	26	2.5	27	2.2	37	3.0	48	3.3	58	3.3	68	3.5	72	3.4	70	3.4	64	2.9	53	2.5	42	2.8	31	2.8
Columbus, Oh.	27	2.8	30	2.2	40	3.2	51	3.4	61	3.8	70	4.0	74	4.0	72	3.7	66	2.8	54	1.9	42	2.6	32	2.6
Dallas-Ft. Worth, Tex.	44	1.7	49	1.9	56	2.4	66	3.6	74	4.3	82	2.6	86	2.0	86	1.8	79	3.3	68	2.5	56	1.8	48	1.7
Denver, Col.	30	0.5	34	0.7	38	1.2	47	1.8	57	2.5	67	1.6	73	1.9	71	1.5	63	1.2	52	1.0	39	0.8	33	0.6
Des Moines, Ia.	19	1.0	25	1.1	35	2.2	51	3.2	62	4.0	72	4.2	76	3.2	74	4.1	65	3.1	54	2.2	39	1.5	26	1.5
Detroit, Mich.	23	1.9	26	1.7	35	2.5	47	3.2	58	2.8	68	3.4	72	3.1	71	3.2	63	2.3	52	2.1	40	2.3	29	2.5
Dodge City, Kan.	30	0.5	35	0.5	42	1.5	54	1.8	64	3.3	75	3.0	80	3.1	78	2.5	69	1.9	58	1.3	43	0.8	34	0.5
Duluth, Minn.	6	1.2	12	0.9	23	1.8	38	2.2	50	3.2	59	4.0	65	4.0	63	4.1	54	3.3	44	2.2	28	1.7	14	1.3
Eureka, Cal.*	47	7.0	49	5.2	48	5.1	49	2.9	52	1.6	55	0.6	56	0.1	57	0.4	57	0.9	54	2.7	51	5.9	48	6.2
Fairbanks, Alas.	-13	0.5	-4	0.5	9	0.4	30	0.3	48	0.6	59	1.3	62	1.8	57	1.9	45	1.1	25	0.7	4	0.7	-10	0.7
Fresno, Cal.	46	2.0	51	1.9	54	1.6	60	1.2	68	0.3	75	0.1	81	L	79	L	74	0.2	65	0.4	53	1.2	45	1.6
Galveston, Tex.*	54	3.0	56	2.3	62	2.1	69	2.6	76	3.3	81	3.5	83	3.8	83	4.4	80	5.8	73	2.6	63	3.2	57	3.6
Grand Junction, Col.	26	0.6	34	0.5	42	0.8	52	0.7	62	0.8	72	0.4	79	0.5	76	0.9	67	0.7	55	0.9	40	0.6	28	0.6
Gr. Rapids, Mich.	22	1.9	24	1.5	33	2.5	46	3.6	58	3.0	67	3.9	71	3.0	70	3.5	62	3.1	51	2.9	39	2.9	27	2.6
Hartford, Conn.	25	3.5	28	3.2	37	4.2	49	4.0	59	3.4	69	3.4	73	3.1	71	4.0	63	3.9	52	3.5	42	4.1	29	4.2
Helena, Mon.	18	0.7	26	0.4	32	0.7	42	1.0	52	1.7	60	2.0	68	1.0	66	1.2	56	0.8	45	0.7	31	0.5	23	0.6
Honolulu, Ha.	73	3.8	73	2.7	74	3.5	76	1.5	78	1.2	79	0.5	80	0.6	81	0.6	81	0.6	80	1.9	77	3.2	74	3.4
Houston, Tex.	51	3.2	55	3.3	61	2.7	69	4.2	75	4.7	81	4.0	83	3.3	83	3.7	78	4.9	70	3.7	60	3.4	54	3.7
Huron, S.D.	11	0.4	18	0.8	29	1.2	46	2.0	57	2.7	68	3.3	74	2.3	72	2.0	61	1.4	49	1.4	32	0.7	19	0.5
Indianapolis, Ind.	26	2.7	30	2.5	40	3.6	52	3.7	63	3.7	72	4.0	75	4.3	73	3.5	67	2.7	55	2.5	42	3.0	32	3.0
Jackson, Miss.	46	5.0	49	4.9	56	5.9	65	5.9	73	4.8	79	2.9	82	4.4	81	3.7	76	3.6	65	2.6	55	4.2	49	5.4
Jacksonville, Fla.	53	3.1	55	3.5	61	3.7	68	3.3	74	4.9	79	5.4	81	6.5	81	7.2	78	7.3	70	3.4	61	1.9	55	2.6
Juneau, Alas.	22	3.7	28	3.7	31	3.3	39	2.9	46	3.4	53	3.0	56	4.1	55	5.0	49	6.4	42	7.7	33	5.2	27	4.7
Kansas City, Mo.	26	1.0	32	1.0	42	2.1	55	2.7	65	3.4	76	4.1	79	3.5	77	3.2	68	3.3	58	2.5	43	1.2	32	1.1
Knoxville, Tenn.	38	4.7	42	4.2	50	5.5	60	3.9	67	3.7	74	4.0	78	4.3	77	3.0	72	3.0	60	2.7	49	3.8	41	4.6
Lander, Wyo.	20	0.5	26	0.6	32	1.1	42	2.2	53	2.7	62	1.5	71	0.7	69	0.5	58	0.9	47	1.2	31	0.8	23	0.5
Lexington, Ky.	32	3.6	35	3.3	44	4.8	55	4.0	64	4.2	72	4.3	76	5.0	75	4.0	69	3.3	57	2.3	45	3.3	36	3.8
Little Rock, Ark.	40	3.9	44	3.8	52	4.7	62	5.4	71	5.3	79	3.7	82	3.6	81	3.1	74	4.3	63	2.8	51	4.4	43	4.2
Los Angeles, Cal.*	57	3.7	59	3.0	60	2.4	62	1.2	65	0.2	69	L	74	L	75	0.1	73	0.3	69	0.2	63	1.9	58	2.0
Louisville, Ky.	33	3.4	36	3.2	45	4.7	57	4.1	65	4.2	74	3.6	78	4.1	76	3.3	70	3.6	58	2.6	46	3.5	37	3.5
Marquette, Mich.*	12	2.0	14	1.9	23	2.8	37	3.6	50	4.0	60	3.9	65	3.2	63	3.3	54	3.9	44	3.3	30	2.9	18	2.4
Memphis, Tenn.	40	4.6	44	4.3	52	5.4	63	5.8	71	5.1	79	3.6	82	4.0	81	3.7	74	3.6	63	2.4	51	4.2	43	4.9
Miami, Fla.	67	2.1	68	2.1	72	1.9	75	3.1	79	6.5	81	9.2	83	6.0	83	7.0	82	8.1	78	7.1	73	2.7	69	1.9
Milwaukee, Wis.	19	1.6	23	1.3	32	2.6	45	3.4	55	2.6	65	3.6	71	3.5	69	3.1	62	2.9	51	2.3	37	2.0	25	2.0
Minneapolis, Minn.	11	0.8	18	0.9	29	1.7	46	2.1	59	3.2	68	4.1	73	3.5	71	3.6	61	2.5	50	1.9	33	1.3	19	0.9
Mobile, Ala.	51	4.6	54	4.9	60	6.5	68	5.4	75	5.5	81	5.1	82	7.7	82	6.8	78	6.6	69	2.6	59	3.7	53	5.4
Moline, Ill.	20	1.6	25	1.3	36	2.8	50	4.0	61	4.2	71	4.3	75	4.9	73	3.8	65	3.7	54	2.7	39	2.0	26	1.9
Nashville, Tenn.	37	4.5	40	4.0	49	5.6	60	4.8	68	4.6	76	3.7	79	3.8	78	3.4	72	3.7	60	2.6	49	3.5	41	4.6
Newark, N.J.	31	3.1	33	3.1	41	4.2	52	3.6	62	3.6	72	2.9	77	3.9	76	4.3	68	3.7	57	3.1	47	3.6	36	3.4
New Orleans, La.	52	5.0	55	5.2	61	4.7	69	4.5	75	5.1	80	4.6	82	6.7	82	6.0	79	5.9	69	2.7	60	4.1	55	5.3
New York, N.Y.*	32	3.2	33	3.1	41	4.2	53	3.8	62	3.8	71	3.2	77	3.8	75	4.0	68	3.7	58	3.4	47	4.1	36	3.8
Nome, Alas.	9	0.8	3	0.5	7	0.6	18	0.6	36	0.5	45	1.2	51	2.2	50	3.1	42	2.3	28	1.3	16	0.9	4	0.7
Norfolk, Va.	40	3.7	41	3.3	49	3.9	58	2.9	67	3.8	76	3.5	78	5.2	78	5.3	72	4.4	61	3.4	52	2.9	44	3.2
Okla. City, Okla.	36	1.0	41	1.3	49	2.1	60	2.9	68	5.5	77	3.9	82	3.0	81	2.4	73	3.4	62	2.7	49	1.5	40	1.2
Omaha, Neb.	19	0.8	25	0.9	35	1.9	50	2.9	62	4.3	71	4.1	76	3.6	74	4.1	64	2.5	54	2.1	38	1.3	26	0.8
Pago Pago, Amer. Samoa.	81	13	81	13	81	11	81	11	80	11	80	8.6	79	6.5	79	7.1	79	6.7	80	11	80	11	81	14
Philadelphia, Pa.	31	3.2	33	2.8	42	3.9	53	3.5	63	3.2	72	3.9	77	3.9	75	4.1	68	3.4	57	2.8	46	3.3	36	3.5
Phoenix, Ariz.	52	0.7	56	0.6	61	0.8	68	0.3	77	0.1	87	0.2	92	0.7	90	1.0	85	0.6	73	0.6	61	0.5	53	0.8
Pittsburgh, Pa.	27	2.9	29	2.4	39	3.6	50	3.3	60	3.5	68	3.3	72	3.8	71	3.3	64	2.8	53	2.5	42	2.3	31	2.6
Portland, Me.	22	3.8	23	3.6	32	4.0	43	3.9	53	3.3	62	3.1	68	2.8	67	2.8	59	3.3	49	3.8	38	4.7	26	4.5
Portland, Ore.	39	6.2	43	3.9	46	3.6	50	2.3	57	2.1	63	1.5	68	0.5	67	1.1	63	1.6	54	3.1	46	5.2	41	6.4
Providence, R.I.	28	4.1	29	3.7	37	4.3	48	4.0	58	3.5	67	2.8	73	3.0	71	4.0	64	3.5	53	3.8	43	4.2	32	4.5
Raleigh, N.C.	40	3.6	42	3.4	49	3.7	59	2.9	67	3.7	74	3.7	78	4.4	77	4.4	71	3.3	60	2.7	50	2.9	42	3.1
Rapid City, S.D.	21	0.4	26	0.6	33	1.0	45	2.0	56	2.6	65	3.3	73	2.1	71	1.4	61	1.0	50	0.8	35	0.5	26	0.5
Reno, Nev.	32	1.2	37	1.0	41	0.7	46	0.5	55	0.7	62	0.3	70	0.3	67	0.3	60	0.3	50	0.3	40	0.6	33	1.2
Richmond, Va.	37	3.2	39	3.1	47	3.6	58	2.9	66	3.6	74	3.6	78	5.1	77	5.0	70	3.5	59	3.7	49	3.3	40	3.4
St. Louis, Mo.	29	1.7	34	2.1	43	3.3	56	3.6	66	3.5	75	3.7	79	3.6	77	2.6	70	2.7	58	2.3	45	2.5	34	2.2
Salt Lake City, Ut.	29	1.4	34	1.3	41	1.7	49	2.2	59	1.5	68	1.0	78	0.7	75	0.9	65	0.9	53	1.1	40	1.2	30	1.4
San Antonio, Tex.	50	1.6	54	1.9	62	1.3	70	2.7	76	3.7	82	3.0	85	1.9	84	2.7	79	3.8	70	2.9	60	2.3	53	1.4
San Diego, Cal.	57	2.1	58	1.4	59	1.6	61	0.8	63	0.2	66	0.1	70	L	72	0.1	71	0.2	68	0.3	62	1.1	57	1.4
San Francisco, Cal.	49	4.7	52	3.2	53	2.6	55	1.5	58	0.3	61	0.1	62	L	63	0.1	64	0.2	61	1.1	55	2.4	49	3.6
San Juan, P.R.	77	3.0	77	2.0	78	2.3	80	3.6	79	5.6	80	4.7	82	4.9	82	5.9	82	6.0	81	5.9	80	5.6	78	4.7
Sault Ste. Marie, Mich.*	13	2.2	14	1.7	24	2.0	38	2.4	50	2.9	58	3.3	64	3.0	63	3.5	55	3.9	45	2.9	33	3.2	20	2.6
Savannah, Ga.	49	3.1	52	3.2	58	3.8	66	3.2	73	4.6	79	5.7	81	7.4	81	6.7	77	5.2	67	2.3	58	1.9	51	2.8
Seattle, Wash.	39	6.0	43	4.2	44	3.6	49	2.4	55	1.6	60	1.4	65	0.7	64	1.3	60	2.0	52	3.4	45	5.6	41	6.3
Spokane, Wash.	26	2.5	32	1.6	38	1.4	46	1.1	54	1.4	62	1.2	70	0.5	68	0.7	60	0.7	48	1.1	35	2.1	29	2.5
Springfield, Mo.	32	1.6	36	2.1	45	3.4	56	4.0	65	4.3	73	4.7	78	3.6	77	2.8	70	4.2	58	3.2	45	2.9	36	2.6
Syracuse, N.Y.	23	2.6	24	2.7	33	3.1	46	3.3	57	3.2	66	3.6	71	3.8	69	3.8	62	3.3	51	3.1	41	3.5	28	3.2
Tampa, Fla.	60	2.2	61	3.0	66	3.5	72	1.8	77	3.4	81	5.3	82	7.4	82	7.6	81	6.2	74	2.3	67	1.9	61	2.1
Washington, D.C.	31	2.8	34	2.6	42	3.4	53	3.1	62	3.6	71	4.2	76	3.8	74	4.2	67	3.3	55	3.0	45	3.0	35	3.3
Wilmington, Del.	31	3.1	33	3.0	42	3.9	52	3.4	62	3.2	71	3.5	76	3.9	75	4.0	68	3.6	56	2.9	46	3.3	36	3.5

Normal Temperatures, Highs, Lows, Precipitation

Source: National Climatic Data Center, NESDIS, NOAA, U.S. Dept. of Commerce

The normal temperatures below are based on records for the thirty-year period 1951-1980. The extreme temperatures (through 1990) are listed for the stations shown and may not agree with the states records shown on pages 168-169.

Airport stations; * designates city office stations. The minus (−) sign indicates temperatures below zero. Fahrenheit thermometer registration.

State	Station	Normal temperature January Max.	January Min.	July Max.	July Min.	Extreme temperature Highest	Extreme temperature Lowest	Normal annual precipitation (inches)
Alabama	Mobile	61	41	91	73	104	3	64.64
Alabama	Montgomery	57	36	92	72	105	0	49.16
Alaska	Juneau	27	16	64	47	90	−22	53.15
Arizona	Phoenix	65	39	105	80	118	17	7.11
Arkansas	Little Rock	50	30	93	71	112	−5	49.20
California	Los Angeles*	67	48	84	64	110	28	14.85
California	San Francisco	55.	42	71	53	106	20	19.71
Colorado	Denver	43	16	88	59	104	−30	15.31
Connecticut	Hartford	34	17	85	62	102	−26	44.39
Delaware	Wilmington	39	23	86	66	102	−14	41.38
Dist. of Col.	Washington	43	28	88	70	104	−5	39.00
Florida	Jacksonville	65	42	91	72	105	7	52.76
Florida	Key West	72	66	89	80	95	41	39.42
Florida	Miami	75	59	89	76	98	30	57.55
Georgia	Atlanta	51	33	88	09	105	−8	48.61
Hawaii	Honolulu	80	65	87	73	94	53	23.47
Idaho	Boise	37	23	91	59	111	−23	11.71
Illinois	Chicago	29	14	83	63	104	−27	33.34
Indiana	Indianapolis	34	18	85	65	104	−23	39.12
Iowa	Des Moines	27	10	86	66	108	−24	30.83
Iowa	Dubuque	24	7	82	62	101	−28	38.59
Kansas	Wichita	40	19	93	70	113	−21	28.61
Kentucky	Louisville	41	24	88	68	105	−20	43.56
Louisiana	New Orleans	62	43	91	74	102	11	59.74
Maine	Portland	31	12	79	57	103	−39	43.52
Maryland	Baltimore	41	24	87	67	105	−7	41.84
Massachusetts	Boston	36	23	82	65	102	−12	43.84
Michigan	Detroit	31	16	83	61	104	−21	30.97
Michigan	Sault Ste. Marie*	21	5	75	52	98	−36	33.48
Minnesota	Minn.-St. Paul	20	2	83	63	105	−34	26.36
Mississippi	Jackson	57	35	93	68	106	2	52.82
Missouri	St. Louis	38	20	89	69	107	−18	33.91
Montana	Helena	28	8	84	52	105	−42	11.37
Nebraska	Omaha	30	10	89	67	114	−23	30.34
Nevada	Las Vegas	55	33	105	76	116	8	4.19
New Hampshire	Concord	31	9	83	56	102	−37	36.53
New Jersey	Atlantic City	41	23	84	65	106	−11	41.93
New Mexico	Albuquerque	47	22	93	65	105	−17	8.12
New Mexico	Roswell	55	27	94	69	109	−9	9.70
New York	Albany	30	12	83	60	100	−28	35.74
New York	New York-La Guardia	37	26	84	69	107	−3	42.82
No. Carolina	Charlotte	50	31	88	69	104	−5	43.16
No. Carolina	Raleigh	50	29	88	67	105	−9	41.76
No. Dakota	Bismarck	18	−4	84	56	109	−44	15.36
Ohio	Cincinnati-Greater	37	20	86	65	102	−25	40.14
Ohio	Cleveland	33	19	82	61	104	−19	35.40
Oklahoma	Oklahoma City	47	25	94	71	110	−8	30.89
Oregon	Portland	44	34	80	56	107	−3	37.39
Pennsylvania	Harrisburg	37	22	86	65	107	−9	39.09
Pennsylvania	Philadelphia	39	24	86	67	104	−7	41.42
Rhode Island	Block Island	37	25	76	64	92	−4	41.91
So. Carolina	Charleston	59	37	89	72	104	6	51.59
So. Dakota	Huron	22	0	87	61	112	−39	18.66
So. Dakota	Rapid City	32	9	87	59	110	−29	16.27
Tennessee	Nashville	46	28	90	69	107	−17	48.49
Texas	Amarillo	49	22	91	66	108	−14	19.10
Texas	Galveston*	59	48	87	79	101	8	40.24
Texas	Houston	62	41	94	73	107	7	44.76
Utah	Salt Lake City	37	20	93	62	107	−30	15.31
Vermont	Burlington	25	8	81	59	101	−30	33.69
Virginia	Norfolk	48	32	90	70	104	−3	45.22
Washington	Seattle-Tacoma	44	34	75	54	99	0	38.60
Washington	Spokane	31	20	84	55	108	−25	16.71
West Virginia	Huntington	41	25	86	65	102	−16	40.74
Wisconsin	Madison	25	7	83	58	104	−37	30.84
Wisconsin	Milwaukee	26	11	80	61	103	−26	30.94
Wyoming	Cheyenne	37	15	83	55	100	−34	13.31
Puerto Rico	San Juan	83	70	88	76	98	60	53.99

Mean Annual Snowfall (inches) based on record through 1980: Boston, Mass., 42; Sault Ste. Marie, Mich., 113; Albany, N.Y., 65.2; Rochester, N.Y., 89.2; Burlington, Vt., 78.6; Cheyenne, Wyo., 53.3; Juneau, Alas., 105.8.

Wettest Spot: Mount Waialeale, Ha., on the island of Kauai, is the rainiest place in the world, according to the National Geographic Society, with an average annual rainfall of 460 inches.

Highest Temperature: A temperature of 136° F. observed at Azizia, Tripolitania in northern Africa on Sept. 13, 1922, is generally accepted as the world's highest temperature recorded under standard conditions.

The record high in the United States was 134° F. in Death Valley, Cal., July 10, 1913.

Lowest Temperature: A record low temperature of −128.6° F. was recorded at the Soviet Antarctica station Vostok on July 21, 1983.

The record low in the United States was −80° F. at Prospect Creek, Alas., Jan. 23, 1971.

The lowest official temperature on the North American continent was recorded at −81° F. in February 1947, at a lonely airport in the Yukon called Snag.

These are the meteorological champions—the official temperature extremes—but there are plenty of other claimants to thermometer fame. However, sun readings are unofficial records, since meteorological data to qualify officially must be taken on instruments in a sheltered and ventilated location.

Annual Climatological Data

Source: National Climatic Data Center, NESDIS, NOAA, U.S. Dept. of Commerce

1992 Station	Elev. ft.	Temperature °F Highest	Date	Lowest	Date	Precipitation[1] Total (in.)	Greatest in 24 hours	Date	Sleet or snow Total (in.)	Greatest in 24 hours	Date	Fastest[2] Wind MPH	Date	No. of days Clear*	Cloudy*	Prec. .01 in. or more	Snow, sleet 1 in. or more
Albany, N.Y.	275	90	8/27	−3	2/10	31.38	1.47	5/30	31.9	5.6	12/11	38	12/24	67	190	145	12
Albuquerque, N.M.	5311	100	7/6	10	12/17	12.08	0.84	8/11	20.1	4.8	11/20	40	12/4	144	120	88	9
Anchorage, Alas.	114	74	7/1	−16	3/5	14.44	1.16	9/5	79.8	11.1	10/26	32	10/22	64	238	113	21
Asheville, N.C.	2140	92	7/13	11	1/17	54.04	2.47	5/7	0.5	0.4	3/11	35	12/11	92	165	136	0
Atlanta, Ga.	1010	96	7/12	18	1/16	60.11	5.87	9/4	5.0	5.0	1/18	39	7/5	110	156	130	1
Atlantic City, N.J.	11	94	7/14	13	1/19	37.49	2.12	12/10	—	—	—	45	12/11	—	—	123	—
Baltimore, Md.	148	98	7/14	9	1/19	38.93	2.62	9/25	5.6	2.2	1/25	35	4/24	87	174	128	3
Barrow, Alas.	31	62	8/29	−44	1/31	2.70	0.20	8/7	43.3	2.7	9/12	46	12/3	117	196	87	10
Birmingham, Ala.	678	95	8/10	17	1/16	55.60	2.71	8/20	4.4	4.4	1/18	—	—	—	—	130	1
Bismarck, N.D.	1647	99	8/8	−23	12/31	12.70	1.38	6/14	48.6	5.1	3/20	45	12/24	90	161	89	19
Boise, Ida.	2838	106	7/31	0	12/6	7.67	0.62	6/12	9.6	2.0	11/27	40	4/8	111	153	73	3
Boston, Mass.	15	92	5/23	7	2/10	43.72	5.14	12/11	26.5	9.3	12/12	51	12/12	90	179	132	7
Buffalo, N.Y.	705	90	6/17	−6	2/12	47.56	2.30	7/14	84.0	15.1	3/11	51	11/12	58	209	190	22
Burlington, Vt.	332	91	5/23	−17	2/10	30.85	2.36	9/22	67.6	8.0	2/4	35	5/17	68	207	161	23
Caribou, Me.	624	93	5/22	−21	3/1	36.27	2.21	8/27	86.6	14.0	2/28	32	12/24	—	—	163	26
Charleston, S.C.	40	98	7/11	25	1/17	53.87	3.44	10/3	0.0	0.0	—	30	3/27	89	177	128	0
Chicago, Ill.	658	93	8/9	−12	1/16	30.12	1.82	11/1	25.8	8.8	3/21	41	7/2	81	197	125	7
Cleveland, Oh.	777	91	8/10	−2	1/16	48.53	2.81	12/30	67.0	8.3	1/15	37	6/18	58	224	167	23
Columbus, Oh.	812	91	8/10	−3	1/19	39.60	5.16	7/12	22.1	4.5	1/25	39	11/12	57	231	151	6
Dallas-Ft. Worth, Tex.	551	100	8/10	17	1/16	42.19	2.66	12/13	T	T	12/15	44	10/15	118	154	92	0
Denver, Co.	5283	99	7/6	−5	1/15	15.68	1.99	8/23	71.14	14.5	1/7	40	3/8	113	135	90	18
Des Moines, Ia.	938	92	7/7	−7	1/15	33.51	2.58	7/12	20.4	9.3	11/25	40	7/2	92	169	123	6
Detroit, Mich.	633	92	6/17	−3	1/19	37.33	1.86	9/9	39.0	11.1	1/14	35	11/12	66	205	149	9
Dodge City, Kan.	2582	102	7/7	5	12/20	21.66	1.90	6/27	—	—	—	—	—	—	—	85	—
Duluth, Minn.	1428	86	8/8	−23	2/12	28.67	2.11	7/1	80.3	8.6	11/2	32	12/25	75	196	135	21
Fairbanks, Alas.	436	91	6/29	−45	12/26	12.73	0.95	7/6	146.2	9.4	5/12	31	5/15	78	212	121	41
Fresno, Cal.	328	108	8/18	29	12/19	14.08	1.76	10/29	T	T	2/15	28	6/12	170	116	38	0
Galveston, Tex.	7	95	8/26	31	1/16	52.63	4.04	2/3	T	T	4/19	37	1/13	—	—	97	0
Grand Rapids, Mich.	784	95	6/17	1	2/12	42.36	3.38	6/8	55.0	10.0	3/21	39	6/17	64	223	153	16
Hartford, Conn.	169	96	5/22	2	2/13	41.98	3.48	6/5	23.6	4.6	3/19	39	12/24	93	177	134	8
Helena, Mont.	3828	98	8/14	−21	12/31	9.33	0.67	10/3	36.3	6.2	8/22	54	8/19	94	153	83	12
Honolulu, Ha.	7	92	9/10	58	2/9	19.00	2.90	12/25	0.0	0.0	—	38	9/11	108	74	98	0
Houston, Tex.	96	97	8/26	27	11/28	52.33	4.56	3/4	T	T	5/28	48	8/31	76	164	109	0
Huron, S.D.	1281	95	4/30	−13	1/15	22.49	1.62	6/30	31.0	6.5	2/11	64	7/7	101	164	93	9
Indianapolis, Ind.	792	91	6/17	−8	1/16	44.18	2.72	7/8	16.7	3.9	1/14	37	6/18	67	222	150	7
Jackson, Miss.	291	97	8/10	20	1/16	48.41	4.79	8/26	0.2	0.2	1/18	35	6/29	98	144	111	0
Jacksonville, Fla.	26	98	7/12	24	1/17	63.18	7.90	10/3	T	T	3/30	46	4/25	62	174	126	0
Kansas City, Mo.	1014	93	8/8	4	1/15	50.63	3.79	7/9	10.2	2.8	4/20	38	10/7	105	158	119	3
Knoxville, Tenn.	979	93	7/13	9	1/16	44.23	2.03	8/6	0.3	0.3	12/25	30	3/10	87	174	135	0
Lander, Wyo.	5557	95	8/9	−20	12/5	13.22	0.90	7/1	76.4	15.4	11/22	40	5/19	117	133	67	16
Lexington, Ky.	966	90	8/9	2	1/16	49.09	4.99	6/18	7.3	1.9	12/25	38	6/18	69	198	145	2
Little Rock, Ark.	257	97	8/10	16	1/16	41.91	2.38	3/9	T	T	12/5	—	—	—	—	119	0
Los Angeles, Cal.	97	92	7/8	40	12/20	16.59	2.31	12/6	0.0	0.0	—	—	—	154	112	43	0
Louisville, Ky.	477	94	7/13	5	1/16	40.79	3.13	8/7	4.5	0.9	12/25	29	10/8	76	198	140	0
Marquette, Mich.	1415	88	6/12	−17	2/12	31.27	2.46	7/1	190.1	17.2	2/7	—	—	—	—	168	54
Memphis, Tenn.	258	95	7/13	14	1/16	47.15	3.86	3/9	T	T	12/25	32	11/12	100	160	111	0
Miami, Fla.	7	97	7/5	46	1/16	57.82	8.01	11/17	0.0	0.0	—	86	8/24	79	109	128	0
Milwaukee, Wis.	672	90	8/25	−5	1/16	33.95	1.82	11/1	31.5	6.6	3/21	35	11/1	77	201	139	8
Minneapolis, Minn.	834	92	6/12	−14	1/15	29.67	3.39	9/15	45.0	6.5	11/1	35	6/17	78	192	113	17
Mobile, Ala.	211	99	7/8	25	1/20	70.46	3.79	11/11	T	T	7/8	60	7/8	92	157	127	0
Moline, Ill.	582	93	8/9	−9	1/19	39.94	2.43	9/9	18.0	6.1	12/9	46	4/10	97	189	126	5
Nashville, Tenn.	590	96	8/9	9	1/16	39.84	4.32	7/2	1.3	1.0	3/12	35	11/12	88	161	119	1
Newark, N.J.	7	98	5/22	10	1/19	36.74	2.97	6/5	13.9	7.3	3/18	39	12/11	84	188	126	3
New Orleans, La.	4	97	7/11	27	1/21	81.87	4.96	8/25	T	T	3/25	39	8/26	83	162	134	0
New York, N.Y.	132	93	7/14	11	1/19	43.35	2.90	6/5	12.3	6.2	3/18	39	12/11	—	—	128	4
Norfolk, Va.	24	102	7/10	19	1/20	47.28	3.14	1/3	T	T	4/5	37	3/27	83	170	118	0
Oklahoma City, Okla.	1285	98	7/2	14	1/16	39.85	2.31	9/5	—	—	—	43	10/7	—	—	103	—
Omaha, Neb.	997	92	7/1	−4	1/15	34.69	1.92	10/7	21.5	9.9	4/20	37	12/23	79	192	118	5
Philadelphia, Pa.	5	97	7/14	11	1/19	30.41	3.03	12/10	4.7	2.1	3/22	44	12/11	86	176	119	1
Phoenix, Ariz.	1110	113	8/17	36	12/20	14.24	1.80	7/23	T	T	10/24	35	5/23	187	80	61	0
Pittsburgh, Pa.	1137	89	7/14	−1	1/19	36.65	2.31	8/27	45.6	8.4	12/10	36	11/12	55	217	147	15
Portland, Me.	43	90	5/22	−7	2/13	38.51	2.40	6/5	41.0	11.4	3/20	36	1/23	89	180	133	11
Portland, Ore.	21	101	8/11	27	12/18	29.50	1.63	11/20	4.6	2.5	12/31	35	12/16	73	189	126	2
Providence, R.I.	51	94	5/22	5	1/17	47.48	3.02	12/11	21.1	4.8	3/19	39	3/27	90	187	133	7
Raleigh, N.C.	434	96	7/13	19	12/25	43.18	3.78	8/12	T	T	12/27	35	3/11	93	167	120	0
Rapid City, S.D.	3162	103	8/8	−13	12/31	13.50	1.01	7/20	36.4	7.3	12/12	51	4/19	123	130	94	12
Reno, Nev.	4404	102	8/11	5	12/5	5.36	0.95	12/28	16.0	11.3	12/28	41	12/10	134	114	45	4
Richmond, Va.	164	98	7/14	16	1/20	41.55	3.43	3/6	0.8	0.8	2/8	40	7/31	83	179	127	0
Scottsbluff, Neb.	3957	98	8/8	−13	12/5	15.83	1.03	5/21	40.2	6.8	1/7	46	6/3	115	133	86	14
St. Louis, Mo.	535	97	7/2	8	1/16	33.49	2.88	8/26	9.9	3.5	1/13	37	9/9	69	202	113	3
Salt Lake City, Ut.	4221	103	8/2	1	1/20	12.07	1.10	11/1	48.6	7.5	11/19	54	11/22	114	134	84	13
San Antonio, Tex.	788	100	8/26	24	11/27	46.49	3.59	3/3	T	T	11/4	32	6/11	91	152	102	0
San Diego, Cal.	13	91	9/23	38	12/20	12.81	2.04	3/2	0.0	0.0	—	29	3/26	150	123	49	0
San Francisco, Cal.	8	92	10/6	35	12/18	20.69	1.76	12/28	T	T	12/29	38	6/14	143	104	63	0
Sault Ste. Marie, Mich.	721	86	5/22	−17	2/9	35.81	1.46	4/21	125.7	9..9	12/25	33	12/25	69	213	158	37
Savannah, Ga.	46	100	7/10	25	1/17	58.36	3.82	6/25	0.0	0.0	—	35	7/1	100	164	110	0
Seattle, Wash.	400	92	6/24	25	1/7	32.78	1.80	1/27	6.7	2.8	12/10	32	4/16	67	192	141	3
Spokane, Wash.	2356	101	8/14	3	12/6	14.52	1.01	6/12	61.7	10.9	12/19	38	4/17	82	192	105	21
Springfield, Mo.	1268	93	8/10	4	1/15	48.04	2.89	7/4	8.6	4.6	1/13	46	7/2	103	178	120	2
Syracuse, N.Y.	410	88	8/26	−8	2/12	43.61	1.97	5/30	154.8	21.5	1/18	35	1/18	66	211	197	46
Tampa, Fla.	19	96	7/9	36	1/17	34.98	3.68	8/28	0.0	0.0	—	29	6/25	93	111	93	0
Washington, D.C.	10	99	7/14	14	1/19	36.38	1.84	1/4	7.6	3.8	1/25	38	12/11	70	188	122	3
Wilmington, Del.	74	97	7/14	10	1/19	37.04	2.33	12/10	3.4	1.4	1/25	39	12/24	86	179	115	0

* To get partly cloudy days deduct the total of clear and cloudy days from 365 (1 yr.). T—trace. (1) Date shown is the starting date of the storm (in some cases it lasted more than one day). (2) Sustained for at least 1 minute, not peak gust.

Record Temperatures by States Through 1992

Source: National Climatic Data Center, NESDIS, NOAA, U.S. Dept. of Commerce

State	Lowest °F	Highest	Latest date	Station	Approximate elevation in feet
Alabama	−27		Jan. 30, 1966	New Market	760
		112	Sept. 5, 1925	Centerville	345
Alaska	−80		Jan. 23, 1971	Prospect Creek Camp	1,100
		100	June 27, 1915	Fort Yukon	420
Arizona	−40		Jan. 7, 1971	Hawley Lake	8,180
		127	July 7, 1905 [1]	Parker	345
Arkansas	−29		Feb. 13, 1905	Pond	1,250
		120	Aug. 10, 1936	Ozark	396
California	−45		Jan. 20, 1937	Boca	5,532
		134	July 10, 1913	Greenland Ranch	−178
Colorado	−61		Feb. 1, 1985	Maybell	5,920
		118	July 11, 1888	Bennett	5,484
Connecticut	−32		Feb. 16, 1943	Falls Village	585
		105	July 21, 1991 [1]	Danbury	450
Delaware	−17		Jan. 17, 1893	Millsboro	20
		110	July 21, 1930	Millsboro	20
Dist. of Col.	−15		Feb. 11, 1899	Washington	112
		106	July 20, 1930	Washington	112
Florida	−2		Feb. 13, 1899	Tallahassee	193
		109	June 29, 1931	Monticello	207
Georgia	−17		Jan. 27, 1940	CCC Camp F-16	1,000
		112	Jul. 24, 1952	Louisville	132
Hawaii	12		May 17, 1979	Mauna Kea	13,770
		100	Apr. 27, 1931	Pahala	850
Idaho	−60		Jan. 18, 1943	Island Park Dam	6,285
		118	July 28, 1934	Orofino	1,027
Illinois	−35		Jan. 22, 1930	Mount Carroll	817
		117	July 14, 1954	E. St. Louis	410
Indiana	−35		Feb. 2, 1951	Greensburg	954
		116	July 14, 1936	Collegeville	672
Iowa	−47		Jan. 12, 1912	Washta	1,157
		118	July 20, 1934	Keokuk	614
Kansas	−40		Feb. 13, 1905	Lebanon	1,812
		121	July 24, 1936 [1]	Alton (near)	1,651
Kentucky	−34		Jan. 28, 1963	Cynthiana	684
		114	July 28, 1930	Greensburg	581
Louisiana	−16		Feb. 13, 1899	Minden	194
		114	Aug. 10, 1936	Plain Dealing	268
Maine	−48		Jan. 19, 1925	Van Buren	510
		105	July 10, 1911 [1]	North Bridgton	450
Maryland	−40		Jan. 13, 1912	Oakland	2,461
		109	July 10, 1936 [1]	Cumberland and Frederick	623; 325
Massachusetts	−35		Jan. 12, 1981	Chester	640
		107	Aug. 2, 1975	Chester and New Bedford	120; 640
Michigan	−51		Feb. 9, 1934	Vanderbilt	785
		112	July 13, 1936	Mio	963
Minnesota	−59		Feb. 16, 1903 [1]	Pokegama Dam	1,280
		114	July 6, 1936 [1]	Moorhead	904
Mississippi	−19		Jan. 30, 1966	Corinth	420
		115	July 29, 1930	Holly Springs	600
Missouri	−40		Feb. 13, 1905	Warsaw	700
		118	July 14, 1954 [1]	Warsaw and Union	687; 560
Montana	−70		Jan. 20, 1954	Rogers Pass	5,470
		117	July 5, 1937	Medicine Lake	1,950
Nebraska	−47		Feb. 12, 1899	Camp Clarke	3,700
		118	July 24, 1936 [1]	Minden	2,169
Nevada	−50		Jan. 8, 1937	San Jacinto	5,200
		122	June 26, 1990 [1]	Laughlin	680
New Hampshire	−46		Jan. 28 1925	Pittsburgh	1,575
		106	July 4, 1911	Nashua	125
New Jersey	−34		Jan. 5, 1904	River Vale	70
		110	July 10, 1936	Runyon	18
New Mexico	−50		Feb. 1, 1951	Gavilan	7,350
		116	July 14, 1934 [1]	Orogrande	4,171
New York	−52		Feb. 18, 1979	Old Forge	1,720
		108	July 22, 1926	Troy	35
North Carolina	−34		Jan. 21, 1985	Mt. Mitchell	6,525
		110	Aug. 21, 1983	Fayetteville	213
North Dakota	−60		Feb. 15, 1936	Parshall	1,929
		121	July 6, 1936	Steele	1,857
Ohio	−39		Feb. 10, 1899	Milligan	800
		113	July 21, 1934 [1]	Gallipolis (near)	673
Oklahoma	−27		Jan. 18, 1930	Watts	958
		120	July 26, 1943 [1]	Tishmomingo	670
Oregon	−54		Feb. 10, 1933 [1]	Seneca	4,700
		119	Aug. 10, 1898	Pendleton	1,074
Pennsylvania	−42		Jan. 5, 1904	Smethport	1,500
		111	July 10, 1936 [1]	Phoenixville	100
Rhode Island	−23		Jan. 11, 1942	Kingston	100
		104	Aug. 2, 1975	Providence	51
South Carolina	−19		Jan. 21, 1985	Caesar's Head	3,100
		111	June 28, 1954 [1]	Camden	170
South Dakota	−58		Feb. 17, 1936	McIntosh	2,277
		120	July 5, 1936	Gannvalley	1,750

State	Lowest °F	Highest	Latest date	Station	Approximate elevation in feet
Tennessee	−32		Dec. 30, 1917	Mountain City	2,471
		113	*Aug. 9, 1930* [1]	*Perryville*	*377*
Texas	−23		Feb. 8, 1933	Seminole	3,275
		120	*Aug. 12, 1936*	*Seymour*	*1,291*
Utah	−69		Feb. 1, 1985	Peter's Sink	8,092
		117	*Jul. 5, 1985*	*Saint George*	*2,880*
Vermont	−50		Dec. 30, 1933	Bloomfield	915
		105	*July 4, 1911*	*Vernon*	*310*
Virginia	−30		Jan. 22, 1985	Mountain Lake Bio. Station	3,870
		110	*July 15, 1954*	*Balcony Falls*	*725*
Washington	−48		Dec. 30, 1968	Mazama and Winthrop	2,120; 1,765
		118	*Aug. 5, 1961* [1]	*Ice Harbor Dam*	*475*
West Virginia	−37		Dec. 30, 1917	Lewisburg	2,200
		112	*July 10, 1936* [1]	*Martinsburg*	*435*
Wisconsin	−54		Jan. 24, 1922	Danbury	908
		114	*July 13, 1936*	*Wisconsin Dells*	*900*
Wyoming	−63		Feb. 9, 1933	Moran	6,770
		114	*July 12, 1900*	*Basin*	*3,500*

(1) Also on earlier dates at the same or other places.

International Temperature and Precipitation

Source: Environmental Data Service, U.S. Dept. of Commerce

A standard period of 30 years has been used to obtain the average daily maximum and minimum temperatures and precipitation. The length of record of extreme maximum and minimum temperatures includes all available years of data for a given location and is usually for a longer period.

		Temperature F°						Average annual precipitation
		Average Daily				Extreme		
	Elev.	January		July				
Station	Feet	Max.	Min.	Max.	Min.	Max.	Min.	(inches)
Addis Ababa, Ethiopia	8,038	75	43	69	50	94	32	48.7
Algiers, Algeria	194	59	49	83	70	107	32	30.0
Amsterdam, Netherlands	5	40	34	69	59	95	3	25.6
Athens, Greece	351	54	42	90	72	109	20	15.8
Auckland, New Zealand	23	73	60	56	40	00	33	49.1
Bangkok, Thailand	53	89	67	90	76	104	50	57.8
Beirut, Lebanon	111	62	51	87	73	107	30	35.1
Berlin, Germany	187	35	26	74	55	96	−15	23.1
Bogotá, Colombia	8,355	67	48	64	50	75	30	41.8
Bombay, India	27	88	62	88	75	110	46	71.2
Bucharest, Romania	269	33	20	86	61	105	−18	22.8
Budapest, Hungary	394	35	26	82	61	103	−10	24.2
Buenos Aires, Argentina	89	85	63	57	42	104	22	37.4
Cairo, Egypt	381	65	47	96	70	117	34	1.1
Capetown, South Africa	56	78	60	63	45	103	28	20.0
Caracas, Venezuela	3,418	75	56	78	61	91	45	32.9
Casablanca, Morocco	164	63	45	79	65	110	31	15.9
Copenhagen, Denmark	43	36	29	72	55	91	−3	23.3
Damascus, Syria	2,362	53	36	96	64	113	21	8.6
Dublin, Ireland	155	47	35	67	51	86	8	29.7
Geneva, Switzerland	1,329	3y	29	77	58	101	−1	33.9
Havana, Cuba	80	79	65	89	75	104	43	48.2
Hong Kong	109	64	56	87	78	97	32	85.1
Istanbul, Turkey	59	45	36	81	65	100	17	31.5
Jerusalem, Israel	2,654	55	41	87	63	107	26	19.7
Lagos, Nigeria	10	88	74	83	74	104	60	72.3
La Paz, Bolivia	12,001	63	43	62	33	80	26	22.6
Lima, Peru	394	82	66	67	57	93	49	1.6
London, England	149	44	35	73	55	99	9	22.9
Madrid, Spain	2,188	47	33	87	62	102	14	16.5
Manila, Philippines	49	86	69	88	75	101	58	82.0
Mexico City, Mexico	7,340	66	42	74	54	92	24	23.0
Montreal, Canada	187	21	6	78	61	97	−35	40.8
Moscow, Russia	505	21	9	76	55	96	−27	24.8
Nairobi, Kenya	5,971	77	54	69	51	87	41	37.7
Oslo, Norway	308	30	20	73	56	93	−21	26.9
Paris, France	164	42	32	76	55	105	1	22.3
Prague, Czech Republic	662	34	25	74	58	98	−16	19.3
Reykjavik, Iceland	92	36	28	58	48	74	4	33.9
Rome, Italy	377	54	39	88	64	104	20	29.5
San Salvador, El Salvador	2,238	90	60	89	65	105	45	70.0
Santiago, Chile	1,706	85	53	59	37	99	24	14.2
Sao Paolo, Brazil	2,628	77	63	66	53	100	32	57.3
Shanghai, China	16	47	32	91	75	104	10	45.0
Singapore	33	86	73	88	75	97	66	95.0
Stockholm, Sweden	146	31	23	70	55	97	−26	22.4
Sydney, Australia	62	78	65	60	46	114	35	46.5
Teheran, Iran	3,937	45	27	99	72	109	−5	9.7
Tokyo, Japan	19	47	29	83	70	101	17	61.6
Toronto, Canada	379	30	16	79	59	105	−26	32.2
Tripoli, Libya	72	61	47	85	71	114	33	15.1
Vienna, Austria	664	34	26	75	59	98	−14	25.6
Warsaw, Poland	294	30	21	75	56	98	−22	22.0

Tides and Their Causes

Source: U.S. Dept. of Commerce, (NOAA) Natl. Oceanic & Atmospheric Admin., (NOS) Natl. Ocean Service

The tides are a natural phenomenon involving the alternating rise and fall in the large fluid bodies of the earth caused by the combined gravitational attraction of the sun and moon. The combination of these two variable force influences produces the complex recurrent cycle of the tides. Tides may occur in both oceans and seas, to a limited extent in large lakes, the atmosphere, and, to a very minute degree, in the earth itself. The period between succeeding tides varies as the result of many factors and force influences.

The tide-generating force represents the difference between (1) the centrifugal force produced by the revolution of the earth around the common center-of-gravity of the earth-moon system and (2) the gravitational attraction of the moon acting upon the earth's overlying waters. Since, on the average, the moon is only 238,852 miles from the earth compared with the sun's much greater distance of 92,956,000 miles, this closer distance outranks the much smaller mass of the moon compared with that of the sun, and the moon's tide-raising force is, accordingly, $2\frac{1}{5}$ times that of the sun.

The effect of the tide-generating forces of the moon and sun acting tangentially to the earth's surface (the so-called "tractive force") tends to cause a maximum accumulation of the waters of the oceans at two diametrically opposite positions on the surface of the earth and to withdraw compensating amounts of water from all points 90° removed from the positions of these tidal bulges. As the earth rotates beneath the maxima and minima of these tide-generating forces, a sequence of two high tides, separated by two low tides, ideally is produced each day (semidiurnal tide).

Twice in each lunar month, when the sun, moon, and earth are directly aligned, with the moon between the earth and the sun (at new moon) or on the opposite side of the earth from the sun (at full moon), the sun and the moon exert their gravitational force in a mutual or additive fashion. The highest high tides and lowest low tides are produced. These are called *spring* tides. At two positions 90° in between, the gravitational forces of the moon and sun — imposed at right angles—tend to counteract each other to the greatest extent, and the range between high and low tides is reduced. These are called *neap* tides. This semi-monthly variation between the spring and neap tides is called the *phase inequality*.

The inclination of the moon's monthly orbit to the equator and the inclination of the sun during the earth's yearly orbit to the equator produce a difference in the height of succeeding high tides and in the extent of depression of succeeding low tides that is known as the diurnal inequality. In most cases, this produces a type of tide called a mixed tide. In extreme cases, these phenomena can result in only one high tide and one low each tide (diurnal tide). There are also other monthly and yearly variations in the tide due to the elliptical shape of the orbits themselves.

The datum for Charting and Predictions is (MLLW) Mean Lower Low Water. This became effective January 1989 according to the convention of 1980 which prescribed that datums on all United States coastlines would be the same. Namely (MHHW) Mean Higher High Water, (MHW) Mean High Water, (MTL) Mean Tide Level, (MSL) Mean Sea Level, (MLW) Mean Low Water, (MLLW) Mean Lower Low Water. Diurnal range of tide is the difference in height between mean higher high water and mean lower low water. Mean range of tide is the difference in height between mean high water and mean low water.

The actual range of tide in the waters of the open oceans may amount to only one to three feet. However, as the ocean tide approaches shoal waters and its effects are augmented the tidal range may be greatly increased. In Nova Scotia along the narrow channel of the Bay of Fundy, the range of tides, or difference between high and low waters, may reach 43 1/2 feet or more (under spring tide conditions) due to resonant amplification.

At New Orleans, the periodic rise and fall of the diurnal tide is affected by the seasonal stages of the Mississippi River, being about 10 inches at low stage and zero at high. The Canadian Tide Tables for 1972 gave a maximum range of nearly 50 feet at Leaf Basin, Ungava Bay, Quebec.

In every case, actual high or low tide can vary considerably from the average, due to weather conditions such as strong winds, abrupt barometric pressure changes, or prolonged periods of extreme high or low pressure.

The Average Rise and Fall of Tides[1]

Places	Ft.	In.	Places	Ft.	In.	Places	Ft.	In.
Baltimore, Md.	1	8	Mobile, Ala.	1	6	San Diego, Cal.	5	9
Boston, Mass.	10	4	New London, Conn.	3	1	Sandy Hook, N.J.	5	2
Charleston, S.C.	5	10	Newport, R.I.	3	11	San Francisco, Cal.	5	10
Cristobal, Panama	1	1	New York, N.Y.	5	1	Savannah, Ga.	8	3
Eastport, Me.	19	4	Old Pt. Comfort, Va.	3	0	Seattle, Wash.	11	4
Galveston, Tex.	1	5	Philadelphia, Pa.	6	9	Tampa, Fla.	2	10
Halifax, N.S.	4	5[2]	Portland, Me.	9	11	Vancouver, B.C.	10	6
Key West, Fla.	1	10	St. John's, Nfld.	2	7[2]	Washington, D.C.	3	2

(1) Diurnal range. (2) Mean range.

Hurricane Names in 1994

Names assigned to Atlantic hurricanes, 1994 — Alberto, Beryl, Chris, Debby, Ernesto, Florence, Gordon, Helene, Isaac, Joyce, Keith, Leslie, Michael, Nadine, Oscar, Patty, Rafael, Sandy, Tony, Valerie, William.

Names assigned to Eastern Pacific hurricanes, 1994 — Aletta, Bud, Carlotta, Daniel, Emilia, Fabio, Gilma, Hector, Ileana, John, Kristy, Lane, Miriam, Norman, Olivia, Paul, Rosa, Sergio, Tara, Vicente, Willa, Xavier, Yolanda, Zeke.

Historic Floods of the Mississippi River Region

Source: U.S. Army Corps of Engineers, Vicksburg, Miss.

Year	Location	Volume (cu. ft./sec.)	Damage (1993 dollars)
1844	upper Mississippi	1.3 million	NA
1913	lower Mississippi	1.97 million	NA
1927	upper and lower Mississippi	2.3 million	$4.4 billion
1937	lower Mississippi and Ohio valleys	2.0 million	$150 million
1945	upper and lower Mississippi	1.9 million	NA
1950	lower Mississippi	1.96 million	NA
1973	upper and lower Mississippi	1.9 million	$11.54 billion
1983	upper and lower Mississippi	1.8 million	$1.15 billion
1993	upper Mississippi	1.0 million	$12 billion*

* Preliminary figure based on World Almanac research. NA = not available.

Glossary of Inland Flood Terms

Source: U.S. Army Corps of Engineers

Crest: The highest level that a river reaches. National Weather Service river gauges, automatic measuring devices stationed every few miles along large rivers, record not only the water level every six hours but also the precise time and height at which the river crests at that gauge. Mathematical formulas based on the historical record then predict how long the crest will take to reach the next gauge. The crest is measured from the river's deepest point.

Cubic Feet per Second (cfs): Engineers measure the flow of water past a given point as the volume per second, in cubic feet. This figure is essentially calculated by multiplying the width of the stream or river by the average depth and then by the speed of the water. For example, if a stream is 10 feet wide, has an average depth of 1 foot, and has a speed of 5 feet per second, then the stream is flowing at 50 cubic feet per second (10 times 1 times 5). One cubic foot of water equals about 7.5 gallons and weighs 62 pounds.

Flood Stage: The height of a river above which damage begins to occur, typically because the river begins to overflow its banks.

100-Year Flood: More accurately referred to as a "1 percent chance flood," a flood that, based on the historical record, has 1 chance in 100 of occurring in any given year. Of course, if a location has a 100-year flood, that does not mean that it is safe from another such flood for 99 years.

Levee: A structure of earth, stone, or concrete built parallel to a river to protect land from flooding.

Saturation: A soil condition in which all the spaces between soil particles are filled with water. The soil is therefore unable to absorb any additional rainfall or snow melt. Earthen levees may weaken if they become saturated.

Spillway: A feature in a dam that allows the release of large volumes of excess water from the reservoir to prevent water from flowing over the top of the dam. The spillway is usually a gap in the top of a dam that the water reaches only during floods.

Stage: The height of a river above a given level or the river bottom, as measured by a gauge.

Wind Chill Table

Source: National Weather Service, NOAA, U.S. Dept. of Commerce

Both temperature and wind cause heat loss from body surfaces. A combination of cold and wind makes a body feel colder than the actual temperature. The table shows, for example, that a temperature of 20 degrees Fahrenheit, plus a wind of 20 miles per hour, causes a body heat loss equal to that in minus 10 degrees with no wind. In other words, the wind makes 20 degrees feel like minus 10.

Top line of figures shows actual temperatures in degrees Fahrenheit. Column at left shows wind speeds.

MPH	35	30	25	20	15	10	5	0	−5	−10	−15	−20	−25	−30	−35	−40	−45
5	33	27	21	16	12	7	0	−5	−10	−15	−21	−26	−31	−36	−42	−47	−52
10	22	16	10	3	−3	−9	−15	−22	−27	−34	−40	−46	−52	−58	−64	−71	−77
15	16	9	2	−5	−11	−18	−25	−31	−38	−45	−51	−58	−65	−72	−78	−85	−92
20	12	4	−3	−10	−17	−24	−31	−39	−46	−53	−60	−67	−74	−81	−88	−95	−103
25	8	1	−7	−15	−22	−29	−36	−44	−51	−59	−66	−74	−81	−88	−96	−103	−110
30	6	−2	−10	−18	−25	−33	−41	−49	−56	−64	−71	−79	−86	−93	−101	−109	−116
35	4	−4	−12	−20	−27	−35	−43	−52	−58	−67	−74	−82	−89	−97	−105	−113	−120
40	3	−5	−13	−21	−29	−37	−45	−53	−60	−69	−76	−84	−92	−100	−107	−115	−123
45	2	−6	−14	−22	−30	−38	−46	−54	−62	−70	−78	−85	−93	−102	−109	−117	−125

(Wind speeds greater than 45 mph have little additional chilling effect.)

Heat Index

The index is a measure of the contribution that high humidity makes with abnormally high temperatures in reducing the body's ability to cool itself. For example, the index shows that for an actual air temperature of 100 degrees Fahrenheit and a relative humidity of 50 percent, the effect on the human body would be same as 120 degrees. Sunstroke and heat exhaustion are likely when the heat index reaches 105. This index is a measure of what hot weather "feels like" to the average person for various temperatures and relative humidities.

Relative Humidity	Air Temperature* 70	75	80	85	90	95	100	105	110	115	120
	Apparent Temperature*										
0%	64	69	73	78	83	87	91	95	99	103	107
10%	65	70	75	80	85	90	95	100	105	111	116
20%	66	72	77	82	87	93	99	105	112	120	130
30%	67	73	78	84	90	96	104	113	123	135	148
40%	68	74	79	86	93	101	110	123	137	151	
50%	69	75	81	88	96	107	120	135	150		
60%	70	76	82	90	100	114	132	149			
70%	70	77	85	93	106	124	144				
80%	71	78	86	97	113	136					
90%	71	79	88	102	122						
100%	72	80	91	108							

*Degrees Fahrenheit.

ENVIRONMENT

U.S. Environmental Quality Index, 1992

Source: Feb.-Mar. 1993 issue of *National Wildlife* magazine; World Almanac research.

In 1993, *National Wildlife* magazine published the twenty-fifth in its series of annual reports on the environment. According to the report, conflict continued to increase in 1992 over whether economic or ecological concerns should be of primary importance in the allocation of America's natural resources. The continued sluggishness of the U.S. economy rendered this debate increasingly political, as the environment once again became a theme in the presidential election.

Wildlife: The Endangered Species Act expired in 1992 and, while it would continue to be enforced, the controversy surrounding reauthorizing the law centered on a few publicized conflicts between economic development and species survival. One example was provided by a controversy in the Southeast over the use of turtle excluder devices (TEDs), which allow endangered sea turtles to escape from shrimping nets. In December, the National Marine Fisheries Service extended mandatory use of TEDs to year round, despite industry fears that the devices might reduce catches. Meanwhile, the decline in duck populations, a traditional indicator of the health of North America's ecosystems, was the worst recorded since the 1930s. This decline prompted calls for increased protection, that is to say decreased development, of wetlands, which play roles in the life cycles of ducks and many other endangered and threatened animals.

Air: In mid-1992, a change in the regulations of the Clean Air Act was made that allowed large companies, citing a change in production methods, to increase pollutant emissions by up to 245 tons a year. The presidential council recommending this change contended that obtaining permits for such "minor" changes would be a costly process, while critics charged that the move would gut the Clean Air Act. The Clean Air Act also authorized the trading of pollution credits and debits, in an attempt to use market incentives to lower pollution. The first sales of credits for unused pollution capacity were made by Wisconsin Power and Light in 1992. The purchaser, the Tennessee Valley Authority, paid $2.5–4 million for the credits, which would allow it to discharge as many as 25,000 tons of sulfur dioxide. Meanwhile, the California Air Resources Board reported continued declines in hazardous air pollution for locations in the California basin, though current levels remained unhealthy. Smog levels in Southern California were the lowest ever recorded. Reductions in pollution were reported elsewhere in the U.S. as well. The Environmental Protection Agency (EPA) announced stricter testing for some cities and metropolitan areas, as a way to further reduce air pollution, but carbon dioxide emissions remained high in 1992.

Water: As congress began considering the rewrite of the Clean Water Act, an EPA study reported that U.S. water pollution had decreased in the two decades since the law's original passage. The study noted that two-thirds of surface water meets water-quality standards, despite continued problems with contaminated runoff from farms, streets, and lawns. Agricultural runoff figured prominently in an EPA analysis that found nearly half of more than 500,000 miles of rivers tested to be too polluted for their intended uses. There was also bad news concerning U.S. coastal waters, where pollution had closed a third of all shellfish fisheries, and where there were more than 2,000 beach closings because of sewage contamination in 1991. The beach closings were spread among 14 states; another 10 coastal states did not regularly test for contamination. A Florida study found that, rather than dispersing, wastewater can concentrate in coastal waters into something resembling "underwater smog."

Energy: A federal energy bill passed in 1992 set new standards for such things as lighting and electric motors, imposed safeguards for fish and other wildlife at hydroelectric plants, and established incentives for producers of renewable energies, such as solar and wind. Meanwhile, states and electric utilities appeared to be making some progress with conservation efforts. One example of this was the increased emphasis electric utilities placed on "demand-side management," an approach that attempts to reduce demand for electricity by such methods as giving away high-efficiency light bulbs and helping customers weatherize their homes. With the cooperation of regulators, utilities can potentially make more money by encouraging conservation than they can by continuing to build generating capacity. While the energy bill stated that the federal government should try to stay out of the way of such efforts by utilities and states, federal authorities drew the line at fuel efficiency standards, with the National Highway Traffic Safety Administration preempting a Maryland law giving sales-tax rebates for more fuel-efficient cars, on the grounds that allowing states to set their own standards would unduly burden U.S. automakers. Meanwhile, with one quarter of the nation's electricity going to lighting, the EPA began a program to encourage corporations and government agencies to use high-efficiency light bulbs.

Forests: In 1992, U.S. courts continued to halt logging of Pacific Northwest old-growth forests, the habitat of the endangered northern spotted owl. The situation was complicated, though, by the third meeting in 14 years of a committee made up mainly of high-ranking federal officials and empowered to overrule the Endangered Species Act for extremely compelling economic reasons. Their ruling to open up approximately 1,700 acres of public old-growth forests had no immediate effect, however, because of court challenges. Meanwhile, the logging industry appeared to be moving from the Northwest to the South, where a longer growing season and cheaper land offered incentives unrelated to wildlife protection. The U.S. Forest Service formalized its approach of ecosystem management, implying an increased emphasis on recreational and wildlife uses of public forests.

Soil: In a highly significant change in farming practices, an increasing number of farmers were using conservation tillage, or "no-till," methods. A survey found that in 1991 the technique, which involves avoiding plowing and leaving at least a third of a field's plant residues intact, was used in more than 28 percent of the 281 million planted acres in the U.S. Conservation tillage was developed as a way to control erosion and is required in some cases by the 1990 U.S. farm bill; it has demonstrated other potential benefits, such as lowering the cost of some crop yields and reducing the need for pesticides and fertilizers. A study by the World Resources Institute acknowledged that the U.S. soil conservation program was among the world's best but cited continued problems, especially in such areas as the Central Valley of California and the watersheds of the Mississippi and Missouri rivers. The topic of grazing cattle on public rangelands in the West was again contentious in 1992. Supporters of a failed bill to raise grazing fees on these lands charged that U.S. taxpayers were subsidizing overgrazing.

Hazardous Waste Sites

Source: Environmental Protection Agency, *Natl. Priorities List Fact Book, Feb. 1992*

State/Territory	Final General	Federal	Total*
Alabama	10	2	12
Alaska	2	4	6
Arizona	7	3	10
Arkansas	10	0	12
California	67	20	95
Colorado	13	3	17
Connecticut	14	1	15
Delaware	19	1	20
District of Columbia	0	0	0
Florida	47	4	55
Georgia	11	2	13
Hawaii	0	1	2
Idaho	7	2	9
Illinois	32	4	37
Indiana	32	0	33
Iowa	19	1	20
Kansas	9	1	11
Kentucky	17	0	19
Louisiana	10	1	12
Maine	7	2	9
Maryland	8	2	10
Massachusetts	22	3	26
Michigan	77	0	77
Minnesota	39	2	41
Mississippi	2	0	2
Missouri	19	3	23
Montana	8	0	8
Nebraska	5	1	8
Nevada	1	0	1
New Hampshire	15	1	17
New Jersey	102	6	108
New Mexico	8	2	10
New York	79	4	84
North Carolina	21	1	23
North Dakota	2	0	2
Ohio	30	3	33
Oklahoma	9	1	10
Oregon	7	1	9
Pennsylvania	90	4	100
Rhode Island	9	2	12
South Carolina	22	1	24
South Dakota	2	1	4
Tennessee	12	2	15
Texas	25	3	29
Utah	7	4	13
Vermont	8	0	8
Virginia	19	1	22
Washington	31	14	49
West Virginia	5	0	5
Wisconsin	39	0	40
Wyoming	2	1	3
American Samoa	0	0	0
Guam	1	0	2
Northern Marianas	0	0	0
Palau	0	0	0
Puerto Rico	8	1	9
Virgin Islands	0	0	1
Total	**1067**	**116**	**1235***

* Includes previously proposed sites

Toxics Release Inventory, 1991

Source: Environmental Protection Agency

Pollutants discharged into the nation's air, water, and land and injected underground by major manufacturing facilities (excluding power plants and mining facilities) continued to decrease nationally in 1991, according to the EPA's Toxics Release Inventory (TRI). The pollutants reported released in 1991 represented a decrease of 9% from the 1990 figure and a decrease of 31% from the figure in 1988, the baseline year. In addition, new data became available in 1991, as required by the Pollution Prevention Act of 1990: major manufacturing facilities reported that some 38 billion pounds of wastes were "managed," that is, sent to treatment facilities or recycled.

1991 pollutant releases	3,385 million pounds
Air releases	2,010 million pounds
Water releases	244 million pounds
Underground injection	710 million pounds
Land releases	421 million pounds
1991 pollutant transfers	3,865 million pounds
To publicly owned treatment works	412 million pounds
To treatment/disposal/other	661 million pounds
To recycling	2,354 million pounds
To energy recovery	438 million pounds
Top states, total releases (air, water, land, and underground injection):	
Louisiana	459 million pounds
Texas	411 million pounds
Tennessee	215 million pounds
Ohio	171 million pounds
Indiana	136 million pounds
Top industries, total releases	
Chemicals	1,550 million pounds
Primary metals	433 million pounds
Paper	242 million pounds
Plastics	152 million pounds
Transportation equipment	149 million pounds
Top chemicals, total releases	
Ammonia	485 million pounds
Hydrochloric acid	288 million pounds
Methanol	252 million pounds
Toluene	200 million pounds
Acetone	165 million pounds

Releases of Toxic Substances, 1988-1991

Source: Environmental Protection Agency

	Percent Change 1990-1991	Percent Change 1988-1991
Total releases	−9	−31
Air releases	−13	−26
Water releases*	+24	−22
Underground injection	−5	−47
Land releases	−9	−20
Transfers for treatment/disposal	−19	−34
To publicly owned treatment works	−12	−28
To other treatment facilities	−6	−28
To disposal facilities	−32	−39

* The net increase in water releases from 1990 to 1991 is largely attributable to increased runoff from four fertilizer facilities in Louisiana. Excluding those increases, reported water releases would have decreased about 7% from 1990 to 1991.

"Urban Air": Soot in Selected Cities, 1990

Source: Environmental Protection Agency

(Micrograms per cubic meter of air of suspended particles that are 10 microns or less in diameter)

Area	High*	Average
Anaheim-Santa Ana, Calif.	108	48
Atlanta, Ga.	110	51
Chicago	149	45
Detroit	114	35
Los Angeles-Long Beach	132	55
Minneapolis-St. Paul, Minn.-Wis.	140	34
New York	103	37
Oakland, Calif.	118	33
Pittsburgh	191	43
Riverside-San Bernardino, Calif.	278	80
St. Louis	164	82

* The EPA treats the reading from the highest day as a statistical anomaly and reports the reading for the second highest day of the year. Note: Figures are for metropolitan areas.

Some Endangered Species

Source: Fish and Wildlife Service, U.S. Dept. of Interior; as of June 3, 1993. For a complete list of threatened and endangered species, write to: Publications Unit, U.S. Fish and Wildlife Service (110 WEBB), Washington, DC 20240.

Common name	Scientific name	Range
Mammals		
Asian wild ass	Equus hemianus	Southwestern & Central Asia
Point Arena mountain beaver	Aplodontia rufa nigra	U.S. (Cal.)
Bobcat	Felis rufus escuinapae	Central Mexico
Ozark big-eared bat	Plecotus townsendii ingens	U.S. (Mo., Okla., Ariz.)
Brown or grizzly bear	Ursus arctos horribilis	U.S. (48 conterminous states)
Cheetah	Acinonyx jubatus	Africa to India
Eastern cougar	Felis concolor cougar	Eastern N.A.
Columbian white-tailed deer	Odocoileus virginianus leucurus	U.S. (Wash., Ore.)
Chinese river dolphin	Lipotes vexillifer	China
Asian elephant	Elephas maximus	Southcentral, Southeast Asia
San Joaquin kit fox	Vulpes macrotis mutica	U.S. (Cal.)
Gorilla	Gorilla gorilla	Central & W. Africa
Leopard	Panthera pardus	Africa, Asia
Asiatic lion	Panthera leo persica	Turkey to India
Howler monkey	Alouatta pigra	Mexico to S. America
Southeastern beach mouse	Peromyscus polionotus phasma	U.S. (Fla.)
Ocelot	Felis pardalis	U.S. (Tex., Ariz.)
Southern sea otter	Enhydra lutris hereis	U.S. (Wash., Ore., Cal.)
Giant panda	Ailuropoda melanoleuca	China
Florida panther	Felis concolor coryi	U.S. (La., Ark. east to S.C., Fla.)
Utah prairie dog	Cynomys parvidens	U.S. (Ut.)
Morro Bay kangaroo rat	Dipodomys heermanni morroensis	U.S. (Cal.)
Black rhinoceros	Diceros bicornis	Sub-Saharan Africa
Carolina northern flying squirrel	Glaucomys sabrinus coloratus	U.S. (N.C., Tenn.)
Tiger	Panthera tigris	Asia
Hualapai Mexican vole	Microtus mexicanus hualpaiensis	U.S. (Ariz.)
Gray whale	Eschrichtius robustus	N. Pacific Ocean
Wild yak	Bos grunniens	China (Tibet), India
Mountain zebra	Equus zebra zebra	South Africa
Red wolf	Canis rufus	U.S. (Southeast to central Tex.)
Birds		
Masked bobwhite (quail)	Colinus virginianus ridgwayi	U.S. (Ariz.)
California condor	Gymnogyps californianus	U.S. (Ore., Cal.)
Hooded crane	Grus monacha	Japan, USSR
White-necked crow	Corvus leucognaphalus	U.S. (P.R.), Dominican Rep., Haiti
Eskimo curlew	Numenius borealis	Alaska and N. Canada
Bald eagle	Haliaeetus leucocephalus	U.S. (most states), Canada
American peregrine falcon	Falco peregrinus anatum	Canada to Mexico
Hawaiian hawk	Buteo solitarius	U.S. (Hi.)
Indigo macaw	Anodorhynchus leari	Brazil
West African ostrich	Struthio camelus spatzi	Spanish Sahara
Golden parakeet	Aratinga guarouba	Brazil
Australian parrot	Geopsittacus occidentalis	Australia
Attwater's greater prairie-chicken	Tympanuchus cupido attwateri	U.S. (Tex.)
Bachman's warbler (wood)	Vermivora bachmanii	U.S. (Southeast), Cuba
Kirtland's warbler (wood)	Dendroica kirtlandii	U.S., Canada, Bahama Is.
Ivory-billed woodpecker	Campephilus principalis	U.S. (Southcentral and Southeast), Cuba
Reptiles		
American alligator	Alligator mississippiensis	U.S (Southeastern)
American crocodile	Crocodylus acutus	U.S. (Fla.)
Atlantic salt marsh snake	Nerodia fasciatia taeniata	U.S. (Fla.)
Plymouth red-bellied turtle	Pseudemys rubiventris bangsi	U.S. (Mass.)
Fishes		
Bonytail chub	Gila elegans	U.S. (Ariz., Cal., Col., Nev., Ut., Wyo.)
Cave crayfish	Cambarus aculabrum	U.S. (Ariz.)
Gila trout	Salmo gilae	U.S. (Ariz., N.M.)
Plants		
Florida golden aster	Chrysopsis floridana	U.S. (Fla.)
Autumn buttercup	Ranunculus acriformis	U.S. (Ut.)
Bakersfield cactus	Opuntia treleasei	U.S. (Cal.)
Santa Cruz cypress	Cypressus abramsiana	U.S. (Cal.)
Maguire daisy	Erigeron maguireivar masguirei	U.S. (Ut.)
Short's goldenrod	Solidago shortii	U.S. (Ky.)
Tennessee yellow-eyed grass	Xyris tennesseensis	U.S. (Ala., Ga., Tenn.)
Mountain golden heather	Hudsonia montana	U.S. (N.C.)
Cooley's meadowrue	Thalictrum cooleyi	U.S. (N.C., Fla.)
Wheeler's peperomia	Peperomia wheeleri	U.S. (P.R.)
Chapman rhododendron	Rhododendron chapmanii	U.S. (Fla.)
Texas wild-rice	Zizania texana	U.S. (Tex.)

U.S. List of Endangered and Threatened Species

Source: Fish and Wildlife Service, U.S. Dept. of Interior; as of June 3, 1993.

	Endangered			Threatened			
Group	U.S. Only	U.S. & Foreign	Foreign Only	U.S. Only	U.S. & Foreign	Foreign Only	Total Listed Species
Mammals	37	19	249	6	3	22	336
Birds	57	16	153	8	9	0	243
Reptiles	8	8	64	14	4	14	112
Amphibians	6	0	8	4	1	0	19
Fishes	55	3	11	31	6	0	106
Snails	12	0	1	7	0	0	20
Clams	50	0	2	5	0	0	57
Crustaceans	10	0	0	2	0	0	12
Insects	13	2	4	9	0	0	28
Arachnids	3	0	0	0	0	0	3
Animals, Total	**251**	**48**	**492**	**86**	**23**	**36**	**936**
Plants	**301**	**7**	**1**	**67**	**9**	**2**	**387**
Total	**552**	**55**	**493**	**153**	**32**	**38**	**1323**

Note: When separate populations of a species are listed as endangered and as threatened, those species are tallied twice. The 10 species so counted are chimpanzee, grizzly bear, leopard, gray wolf, bald eagle, piping plover, roseate tern, Nile crocodile, green sea turtle, and olive ridley sea turtle. In addition, 9 species of lemurs; 9 of gibbons; 2 each of musk deer, sifakas, and uakaris; and 29 to 41 of Oahu tree snails are each counted as 1 species above.

Gestation, Longevity, and Incubation of Animals

Average longevity figures were supplied by Ronald T. Reuther. They refer to animals in captivity; the potential life span of animals is rarely attained in nature. Maximum longevity figures are from the Biology Data Book, 1972. Figures on gestation and incubation are averages based on estimates by leading authorities.

Animal	Gestation (days)	Average longevity (years)	Maximum longevity (yrs., mos.)
Ass	365	12	35-10
Baboon	187	20	35-7
Bear: Black	219	18	36-10
Grizzly	225	25	—
Polar	240	20	34-8
Beaver	122	5	20-6
Bison	278	15	—
Camel (Bactrian)	406	12	29-5
Cat (domestic)	63	12	28
Chimpanzee	231	20	44-6
Chipmunk	31	6	8
Cow	284	15	30
Deer (white-tailed)	201	8	17-6
Dog (domestic)	61	12	20
Elephant (African)	—	35	60
Elephant (Asian)	645	40	70
Elk	250	15	26-6
Fox (red)	52	7	14
Giraffe	425	10	33-7
Goat (domestic)	151	8	18
Gorilla	257	20	39-4
Guinea pig	68	4	7-6
Hippopotamus	238	25	—
Horse	330	20	46
Kangaroo	42	7	—
Leopard	98	12	19-4
Lion	100	15	25-1
Monkey (rhesus)	164	15	—
Moose	240	12	—
Mouse (meadow)	21	3	—
Mouse (dom. white)	19	3	3-6
Opossum (American)	14-17	1	—
Pig (domestic)	112	10	27
Puma	90	12	19
Rabbit (domestic)	31	5	13
Rhinoceros (black)	450	15	—
Rhinoceros (white)	—	20	—
Sea lion (California)	350	12	28
Sheep (domestic)	154	12	20
Squirrel (gray)	44	10	—
Tiger	105	16	26-3
Wolf (maned)	63	5	—
Zebra (Grant's)	365	15	—

Incubation time (days)

Chicken	21
Duck	30
Goose	30
Pigeon	18
Turkey	26

Speeds of Animals

Source: Natural History magazine, March 1974. Copyright © The American Museum of Natural History, 1974.

Animal	Mph	Animal	Mph	Animal	Mph
Cheetah	70	Mongolian wild ass	40	Human	27.89
Pronghorn antelope	61	Greyhound	39.35	Elephant	25
Wildebeest	50	Whippet	35.50	Black mamba snake	20
Lion	50	Rabbit (domestic)	35	Six-lined race runner	18
Thomson's gazelle	50	Mule deer	35	Wild turkey	15
Quarterhorse	47.5	Jackal	35	Squirrel	12
Elk	45	Reindeer	32	Pig (domestic)	11
Cape hunting dog	45	Giraffe	32	Chicken	9
Coyote	43	White-tailed deer	30	Spider (Tegenaria atrica)	1.17
Gray fox	42	Wart hog	30	Giant tortoise	0.17
Hyena	40	Grizzly bear	30	Three-toed sloth	0.15
Zebra	40	Cat (domestic)	30	Garden snail	0.03

Most of these measurements are for maximum speeds over approximate quarter-mile distances. Exceptions are the lion and elephant, whose speeds were clocked in the act of charging; the whippet, which was timed over a 200-yard course; the cheetah, timed over a 100-yard distance; the human, timed for a 15-yard segment of a 100-yard run (of 13.6 seconds); and the black mamba, six-lined race runner, spider, giant tortoise, three-toed sloth, and garden snail, which were measured over various small distances.

Major Venomous Animals

Snakes

Coral snake - 2 to 4 ft. long, in Americas south of Canada; bite is nearly painless; very slow onset of paralysis, difficulty breathing; mortality high without antivenin.

Rattlesnake - 2 to 8 ft. long, throughout W. Hemisphere. Rapid onset of symptoms of severe pain, swelling; mortality low, but amputation of affected limb is sometimes necessary; antivenin. Probably higher mortality rate for Mojave rattler.

Cottonmouth water moccasin - up to 5 ft. long, wetlands of southern U.S. from Virginia to Texas. Rapid onset of symptoms of severe pain, swelling; mortality low, but tissue destruction can be extensive; antivenin.

Copperhead - less than 4 ft. long, from New England to Texas; pain and swelling; very seldom fatal; antivenin seldom needed.

Bushmaster - up to 12 ft. long, wet tropical forests of C. and S. America; few bites occur, but mortality rate is high.

Barba Amarilla or **Fer-de-lance** - up to 7 ft. long, from tropical Mexico to Brazil; severe tissue damage common; moderate mortality; antivenin.

Asian pit vipers - from 2 to 5 ft. long throughout Asia; reactions and mortality vary but most bites cause tissue damage and mortality is generally low.

Sharp-nosed pit viper or **One Hundred Pace Snake** - up to 5 ft. long, in southern Vietnam and Taiwan, China; the most toxic of Asian pit vipers; very rapid onset of swelling and tissue damage, internal bleeding; moderate mortality; antivenin.

Boomslang - under 6 ft. long, in African savannahs; rapid onset of nausea and dizziness, often followed by slight recovery and then sudden death from internal hemorrhaging; bites rare, mortality high; antivenin.

European vipers - from 1 to 3 ft. long; bleeding and tissue damage; mortality low; antivenins.

Puff adder - up to 5 ft. long, fat; south of the Sahara and throughout the Middle East; rapid large swelling, great pain, dizziness; moderate mortality often from internal bleeding; antivenin.

Gaboon viper - over 6 ft. long, fat; 2-inch fangs; south of the Sahara; massive tissue damage, internal bleeding; few recorded bites.

Saw-scaled or carpet viper - up to 2 ft. long, in dry areas from India to Africa; severe bleeding, fever; high mortality, causes more human fatalities than any other snake; antivenin.

Desert horned viper - in dry areas of Africa and western Asia; swelling and tissue damage; low mortality; antivenin.

Russell's viper or **tic-polonga** - over 5 ft. long, throughout Asia; internal bleeding; moderate mortality rate; bite reports common; antivenin.

Black mamba - up to 14 ft. long, fast-moving; S. and C. Africa; rapid onset of dizziness, difficulty breathing, erratic heart-beat; mortality high, nears 100% without antivenin.

Kraits - in S. Asia; rapid onset of sleepiness; numbness; up to 50% mortality even with antivenin treatment.

Common or Asian cobra - 4 to 8 ft. long, throughout S. Asia; considerable tissue damage, sometimes paralysis; mortality probably not more than 10%; antivenin.

King cobra - up to 16 ft. long, throughout S. Asia; rapid swelling, dizziness, loss of consciousness, difficulty breathing, erratic heart-beat; mortality varies sharply with amount of venom involved, most bites involve non-fatal amounts; antivenin.

Yellow or Cape cobra - 7 ft. long, in southern Africa; most toxic venom of any cobra; rapid onset of swelling, breathing and cardiac difficulties; mortality high without treatment; antivenin.

Ringhals, or spitting, cobra - 5 ft. and 7 ft. long; southern Africa; squirt venom through holes in front of fangs as a defense; venom is severely irritating and can cause blindness.

Australian brown snakes - very slow onset of symptoms of cardiac or respiratory distress; moderate mortality; antivenin.

Tiger snake - 2 to 6 ft. long, S. Australia; pain, numbness, mental disturbances with rapid onset of paralysis; may be the most deadly of all land snakes though antivenin is quite effective.

Death adder - less than 3 ft. long, Australia; rapid onset of faintness, cardiac and respiratory distress; at least 50% mortality without antivenin.

Taipan - up to 11 ft. long, in Australia and New Guinea; rapid paralysis with severe breathing difficulty; mortality nears 100% without antivenin.

Sea snakes - throughout Pacific, Indian oceans except NE Pacific; almost painless bite, variety of muscle pain, paralysis; mortality rate low, many bites are not envenomed; some antivenins.

Notes: Not all snake bites by venomous snakes are actually envenomed. Any animal bite, however, carries the danger of tetanus and anyone suffering a venomous snake bite should seek medical attention. Antivenins are not certain cures; they are only an aid in the treatment of bites. Mortality rates above are for envenomed bites; low mortality, up to 2% result in death; moderate, 2–5%; high, 5–15%. Even when the victim recovers fully, prolonged hospitalization and extensive medical procedures are usually required.

Lizards

Gila monster - up to 24 inches long with heavy body and tail, in high desert in southwest U.S. and N. Mexico; immediate severe pain followed by vomiting, thirst, difficulty swallowing, weakness approaching paralysis; no recent mortality.

Mexican beaded lizard - similar to Gila monster, Mexican westcoast; reaction and mortality rate similar to Gila monster.

Insects

Ants, bees, wasps, hornets, etc. Global distribution. Usual reaction is piercing pain in area of sting. Not directly fatal, except in cases of massive multiple stings. Many people suffer allergic reactions - swelling, rashes, partial paralysis - and a few may die within minutes from severe sensitivity to the venom (anaphylactic shock).

Spiders, scorpions

Black widow - small, round-bodied with hour-glass marking; the widow and its relatives are found around the world in tropical and temperate zones; sharp pain, weakness, clammy skin, muscular rigidity, breathing difficulty and, in small children, convulsions; low mortality; antivenin.

Recluse or fiddleback and brown spiders - small, oblong body; throughout U.S.; pain with later ulceration at place of bite; in severe cases fever, nausea, and stomach cramps; ulceration may last months; very low mortality.

Atrax spiders - several varieties, often large, in Australia; slow onset of breathing, circulation difficulties; low mortality.

Tarantulas - large, hairy spiders found around the world; American tarantulas, and probably all others, are **harmless,** though their bite may cause some pain and swelling.

Scorpions - crab-like body with stinger in tail, various sizes, many varieties throughout tropical and subtropical areas; various symptoms may include severe pain spreading from the wound, numbness, severe emotional agitation, cramps; severe reactions include vomiting, diarrhea, respiratory failure; low mortality, usually in children; antivenins.

Sea Life

Sea wasps - jellyfish, with tentacles up to 30 ft. long, in the S. Pacific; very rapid onset of circulatory problems; high mortality largely because of speed of toxic reaction; antivenin.

Portuguese man-of-war - jellyfish-like, with tentacles up to 70 ft. long, in most warm water areas; immediate severe pain; not fatal, though shock may cause death in a rare case.

Octopi - global distribution, usually in warm waters; all varieties produce venom but only a few can cause death; rapid onset of paralysis with breathing difficulty.

Stingrays - several varieties of differing sizes, found in tropical and temperate seas and some fresh water; severe pain, rapid onset of nausea, vomiting, breathing difficulties; wound area may ulcerate, gangrene may appear; seldom fatal.

Stonefish - brownish fish that lies motionless as a rock on bottom in shallow water; throughout S. Pacific and Indian oceans; extraordinary pain, rapid paralysis; low mortality.

Cone-shells - molluscs in small, beautiful shells in the S. Pacific and Indian oceans; shoot barbs into victims; paralysis; low mortality.

How Much Water Is Used . . .?

Source: American Water Works Assn.

1. In the average residence during a year? **107,000 gallons**
2. By an average person daily? **168 gallons**
3. To flush a toilet? **5-7 gallons**
4. To take a shower? **25-50 gallons**
5. To brush your teeth (water running)? **2 gallons**
6. To shave (water running)? **10-15 gallons**
7. To wash dishes by hand? **20 gallons**
8. To run a dishwasher? **10 gallons**

Mammals: Orders and Major Families

Subclass Theria
Infraclass Placentalia

Family	Suborder / Infraorder / Superfamily	Order
Canidae: wolf, dog, jackal, fox	Canoidea; Fissipedia (toe-footed)	Carnivora
Ursidae: bear, giant panda	Canoidea; Fissipedia (toe-footed)	Carnivora
Procyonidae: coati, racoon, lesser panda	Canoidea; Fissipedia (toe-footed)	Carnivora
Mustelidae: badger, weasel, skunk, otter	Canoidea; Fissipedia (toe-footed)	Carnivora
Felidae: cat, leopard, lion, tiger, cheetah	Feloidea; Fissipedia (toe-footed)	Carnivora
Hyaenidae: hyena, aardwolf	Feloidea; Fissipedia (toe-footed)	Carnivora
Viverridae: mongoose, civet	Feloidea; Fissipedia (toe-footed)	Carnivora
Otariidae: eared seals, sea lion	Pinnipedia (fin-footed)	Carnivora
Odobenidae: walrus	Pinnipedia (fin-footed)	Carnivora
Phocidae: earless seals	Pinnipedia (fin-footed)	Carnivora
Suidae: pig	Suina; Suiformes	Artiodactyla
Tayassuidae: peccary	Suina; Suiformes	Artiodactyla
Hippopotamidae: hippopotamus	Ancodonta; Suiformes	Artiodactyla
Camelidae: camel, llama	Tylopoda	Artiodactyla
Giraffidae: giraffe, okapi	Ruminantia	Artiodactyla
Cervidae: deer, moose, reindeer, wapiti (elk)	Ruminantia	Artiodactyla
Antilocapridae: pronghorn	Bovoidea; Ruminantia	Artiodactyla
Subfamily (**Family** Bovidae)		
Bovinae: cattle, eland, kudu, bison, yak	Bovoidea; Ruminantia	Artiodactyla
Hippotraginae: sable, oryx, waterbuck	Bovoidea; Ruminantia	Artiodactyla
Acelaphinae: hartebeest, wildebeest (gnu)	Bovoidea; Ruminantia	Artiodactyla
Antilopinae: gazelle, springbok, saiga	Bovoidea; Ruminantia	Artiodactyla
Caprinae: sheep, goat, musk ox	Bovoidea; Ruminantia	Artiodactyla
Family		
Equidae: horse, donkey zebra	Hippomorpha	Perissodactyla
Tapiridae: tapir	Ceratomorpha	Perissodactyla
Rhinocerotidae: rhinoceros	Ceratomorpha	Perissodactyla
Aplodontidae: mountain beaver	Sciuromorpha	Rodentia
Sciuridae: chipmunk, squirrel, marmot	Sciuromorpha	Rodentia
Cricetidae: field mice, lemming, muskrat, hamster, gerbil	Myomorpha	Rodentia
Muridae: rat, Old World mice	Myomorpha	Rodentia
Heteromyidae: New World mice	Myomorpha	Rodentia
Geomyidae: gopher	Myomorpha	Rodentia
Dipodidae: jerboa	Myomorpha	Rodentia
Chinchillidae: chinchilla	Caviomorpha	Rodentia
Dasyproctidae: agouti, paca	Caviomorpha	Rodentia
Erethizontidae: New World porcupine	Caviomorpha	Rodentia
Hystricidae: Old World porcupine		Rodentia
Castoridae: beaver		Rodentia
Bats - various familes		Chiroptera

Canoids have long snouts and unretractable claws.

Feloids have retractable claws.

Most carnivora also eat some plants and insects.

The artiodactyla have an even number of toes.

All ruminants have 4-chamber stomachs and chew cuds.

The perissodactyla have an odd number of toes.

Rodents are the most numerous of all mammals.

Rodent suborders are distinguished by the placement of a major jaw muscle.

Subclass Theria
Infraclass Placentalia

Family	Suborder / Infraorder / Superfamily	Order
Leporidae: rabbit, hare		Lagomorpha
Ochotonidae: pika		Lagomorpha
Manidae: pangolin		Pholidata
Erinaceidae: hedgehog		Insectivora
Talpidae: mole		Insectivora
Saricidae: some shrews		Insectivora
Dasypodidae: armadillo	Loricata	Edentate (toothless)
Bradypodidae: sloth	Pilosa	Edentate (toothless)
Myrmecophagidae: hairy anteater	Vermilingua	Edentate (toothless)
Physeteridae: sperm whale	Odontoceti (toothed)	Cetacea
Monodontidae: narwhal, beluga	Odontoceti (toothed)	Cetacea
Phocoenidae: porpoise	Odontoceti (toothed)	Cetacea
Delphinidae: dolphin, killer whale	Odontoceti (toothed)	Cetacea
Eschrichtiidae: gray whale	Mysticeti (baleen)	Cetacea
Balaenidae: right whale	Mysticeti (baleen)	Cetacea
Balaenopteridae: humpback whale	Mysticeti (baleen)	Cetacea
Manatee, dugong		Sirenea
Elephantidae: elephant		Proboscidea
Tupaiidae: tree shrew	Prosimii	Primates
Lemuridae: lemur	Prosimii	Primates
Daubentoniidae: aye-aye	Prosimii	Primates
Lorisidae: loris, potto	Prosimii	Primates
Tarsiidae: tarsier	Prosimii	Primates
Callitrichidae: marmoset	Anthropoidea	Primates
Cebidae: New World monkeys (flat-nosed)	Anthropoidea	Primates
Cercopithecidae: baboon, Old World monkeys (long-nosed, bare buttocks)	Anthropoidea	Primates
Hylobatidae: gibbon	Anthropoidea	Primates
Pongidae (great apes): gorilla, chimpanzee, orangutan	Anthropoidea	Primates
Hominidae: human	Anthropoidea	Primates

The prosimians usually have longer snouts than anthropoids.

Most primates have opposable thumbs; all but man have opposable big toes.

Infraclass Marsupialia

Family	Superfamily	Order
Dasyuridae: mouse- and ratlike, Tasmanian devil	Dasyuroidea	Marsupicanivora
Notoryctidae: molelike	Dasyuroidea	Marsupicanivora
Thylacinidae: wolflike	Dasyuroidea	Marsupicanivora
Didelphidae: American opossums	Didelphoidea	Marsupicanivora
Caenolestidae: ratlike So. America only		Paucituberculata
Peramelidae: bandicoot		Peramalina
Burramyidae: mouse- and squirrellike	Phalangeroidea	Diprodonta
Macropodidae: kangaroo, wallaby	Phalangeroidea	Diprodonta
Petauridae: squirrellike, some Australian possums	Phalangeroidea	Diprodonta
Phalangeridae: cuscus, some Australian possums	Phalangeroidea	Diprodonta
Tarsipedidae: honey possum	Tarsipedoidea	Diprodonta
Vombatidae: wombat	Vombatoidea	Diprodonta
Phascolarctidae: koala	Vombatoidea	Diprodonta

Subclass Prototheria

Family		Order
Ornithorhynchidae: duck-billed platypus		Monotremata
Tachyglossidae: echidna (spiny anteater)		Monotremata

Major U.S. Public Zoological Parks

Source: World Almanac questionnaire, 1993; budget and attendance in millions. (*) park has not provided up-to-date data.

Zoo	Budget	Attendance	Acres	Species	Major attractions
Arizona-Sonora Desert Museum (Tucson)	$4.3	0.6	198	200	"Living" museum, 90% outdoors, hummingbird aviary
Audubon (New Orleans)	7.8	0.9	58	500	White alligators, Louisiana Swamp, Reptile Encounter
Bronx (N.Y.C.)	24.6	2.1	265	670	Himalayan Highlands, African Plains, Wild Asia, MouseHouse, endangered species
Buffalo	4.0	0.5+	23	206	Habicat, Gorilla Habitat, Children's Zoo
Chicago (Brookfield)	27.0	2.0	215	400+	7 Seas Seascape, Tropic World, Africa!
Cincinnati	12.0	1.3	67	761	Gorilla World, white bengal tigers, Jungle Trails
Cleveland	2.9	0.9	165	563	Rain Forest—600 animals, 10,000 plants
Dallas	6.0	0.5	70	329	25-acre Wilds of Africa with monorail, nature trail, Gorilla Conservation Center
Denver	6.8	1.3	76	310	Tropical Discovery, Northern Shores
Detroit	8.8	1.0	125	413	Penguinarium, Chimps of Harambee
Houston	5.7	1.5	50	596	Bird Garden, white tigers, African lion pride
Lincoln Park (Chicago)	14.0	4.0	35	339	Great Ape House, Bird House, Lion House, Farm-in-Zoo
Los Angeles	7.2	1.8	113	500+	Adventure Island, World of Birds, Tiger Falls
Louisville	4.5	0.6	133	395	American wildcat, polar bears, Black-footed ferret
Memphis	5.7	0.7	70	445	Cat Country, Primate World, The Forest
Miami Metrozoo	7.0	0.8	290	281	Koalas, Aviary, cageless exhibits, Asian River Life
Milwaukee*	12.0	1.4	200	350	Sea Lion Exhibit, Predator Prey, new Aviary
Minnesota	12.0	1.2	485	311	Malayan sun bear, Siberian tigers, World of Birds
National (Wash. D.C.)*	13.0	3.0	163	509	Giant pandas, Komodo dragon lizards, gorillas
Oklahoma City	12.0	0.6	110	500+	Aquaticus dolphin & sea lion shows, Great EscApe, Children's Discovery
Omaha/Henry Doorly Zoo	4.5	1.3	110	475	Indoor rainforest, free-flight aviary, cat complex
Philadelphia	16.0	1.2	42	560	World of Primates, Treehouse, Rare Animal House, African Plains, female white lion
Phoenix	8.0	1.0	125	324	African Veldt, Arizona Trail, 200 endangered animals
Gladys Porter (Brownsville, Tex.)	2.0	0.4	31	450	Free-flight aviary, Herpetarium, 4 geographic areas
Rio Grande (Albuquerque)*	3.2	0.5	60	292	Ape Country, Free-flying bird show, rainforest
Riverbanks (Columbia, S.C.)	3.9	0.9	39	483	Aquarium Reptile Complex, Riverbanks Farm
St. Louis	14.7	2.7	83	665	Living World, Bear Pits, Jungle of the Apes
San Antonio	7.3	1.0	40	700	Australian Walkabout, Amazonia, Aquarium
San Diego*	40.0	3.5	100	800	Tiger River, Southeast Asian exhibit, koalas
San Diego (Wild Animal Park)*	15.0	1.4	2,200	450	Mixed-species enclosures; exotic species, monorail with 50-minute, narrated tour
San Francisco	11.0	1.0	140	270	Primate Discovery Center, Koala Crossing, Gorilla World, Penguin Island, Children's Zoo
Toledo*	7.8	0.8	30	400	Hippoquarium, African savanna, Children's Zoo
Washington Pk (Portland)	15.0	1.1	64	166	Alaska Tundra, Penguinarium, Africa exhibit
Woodland Pk (Seattle)*	7.5	0.9	92	300	African savanna, gorillas, Asian Elephant Forest

Top 50 American Kennel Club Registrations

Source: American Kennel Club, New York, N.Y.; dogs registered Jan. 1, 1992, to Dec. 31, 1992.

Breed	Rank	Number Registered 1992	Rank	Number Registered 1991	Breed	Rank	Number Registered 1992	Rank	Number Registered 1991
Labrador Retrievers	1	120,879	1	105,876	Collies	26	17,081	24	18,129
Rottweilers	2	95,445	4	76,889	Pugs	27	16,008	27	15,387
Cocker Spaniels	3	91,925	2	98,937	Brittanys	28	14,901	28	14,282
Chinese Shar-Pei	*	90,081	—	—	German Shorthaired Pointers	29	13,737	31	12,158
German Shepherd Dogs	4	76,941	5	68,844	Miniature Pinschers	30	13,353	33	10,772
Poodles	5	73,449	3	77,709	Bichons Frises	31	12,172	29	12,245
Golden Retrievers	6	69,850	6	67,284	Bulldogs	32	12,046	30	12,186
Beagles	7	60,661	7	56,956	Akitas	33	11,383	35	9,949
Dachshunds	8	50,046	8	48,713	Great Danes	34	11,067	34	10,159
Shetland Sheepdogs	9	43,449	10	44,106	West Highland White Terriers	35	10,015	32	11,128
Chow Chows	10	42,670	9	45,131	Scottish Terriers	36	7,914	36	8,724
Shih Tzu	11	42,561	12	41,367	Samoyeds	37	7,267	37	7,649
Pomeranians	12	42,488	13	41,034	Pembroke Welsh Corgis	38	6,501	40	6,039
Miniature Schnauzers	13	41,058	11	42,404	Keeshonden	39	6,177	38	7,017
Yorkshire Terriers	14	39,904	14	39,772	Cairn Terriers	40	6,141	39	6,911
Dalmatians	15	38,927	15	30,225	Alaskan Malamutes	41	5,644	41	5,631
Chihuahuas	16	31,301	16	29,860	Chesapeake Bay Retrievers	42	5,295	42	4,738
Boxers	17	30,123	17	26,722	Saint Bernards	43	4,863	43	4,637
Siberian Huskies	18	26,057	19	23,436	Weimaraners	44	4,758	45	4,136
English Springer Spaniels	19	22,183	20	22,448	Airedale Terriers	45	4,236	44	4,328
Doberman Pinschers	20	22,113	21	20,734	Great Pyrenees	46	3,776	48	3,269
Basset Hounds	21	21,137	22	20,497	Schipperkes	47	3,752	46	3,705
Lhasa Apsos	22	20,616	18	23,543	Mastiffs	48	3,294	54	2,886
Pekingese	23	18,218	23	18,843	Old English Sheepdogs	49	3,178	47	3,417
Maltese	24	17,615	25	17,502	Newfoundlands	50	3,153	50	3,180
Boston Terriers	25	17,271	26	17,075					

* Breed recognized by AKC only as of 1992; will not be officially ranked for first time until 1993.

Cat Breeds

Source: Cat Fanciers' Assn., Manasquan, N.J.

Only a small percentage of house cats in the U.S. are pedigreed, or registered with one of the official registering bodies, the largest of which is the Cat Fanciers' Assn., sponsor of more than 600 clubs. The Cat Fanciers' Assn. recognized 40 breeds as of mid-1993 (in order of registration totals): Persian (Traditional, Pointed Pattern, and Colorpoint Carrier), Maine Coon Cat, Siamese, Abyssinian, Exotic Shorthair, Scottish Fold Shorthair, Scottish Fold Longhair, Oriental Shorthair, Birman, Burmese, Ocicat, Tonkinese, Cornish Rex, Somali, Colorpoint Shorthair, Devon Rex, Manx, Russian Blue, Balinese, British Shorthair, Egyptian Mau, Japanese Bobtail Shorthair, Japanese Bobtail Longhair, Javanese, Norwegian Forest Cat, Cartreux, American Curl, Highland Fold, Cymric, Korat, Turkish Angora, Bombay, Singapura, Turkish Van, Havana Brown, Selkirk Rex, American Wirehair, and Oriental Longhair.

Giant Trees of the U.S.

Source: The American Forestry Assn., Washington, D.C.

Approximately 850 native and naturalized species of trees are grown in the U.S. The oldest living thing on earth is believed to be a bristlecone pine tree in California named Methusalah, estimated to be 4,700 years old. The world's largest living thing, the General Sherman giant sequoia in California, weighs more than 1,400 tons—as much as 9 blue whales or 360 elephants.

Recognition as the National Champion of each species is determined by total mass of each tree, based on this formula: the circumference in inches as measured at a point 4½ feet above the ground plus the total height of the tree in feet plus ¼ of the average crown spread in feet. Trees within 5 points of each other are declared co-champions. Of all the trees nominated at the beginning of AFA's Big Tree program in 1940, only 4 trees have never lost their title—the giant sequoia (Sequoia Natl. Park, Cal.), white oak (Wye Mills State Park, Md.), western juniper (Stanislaus Natl. Forest, Cal.), and Rocky Mountain juniper (Cache Natl. Forest, Ut.). The coast redwood Dyerville Giant (Dyerville, Cal.) was also one of the original champs until it fell in March 1991. Florida has more national champs (113) than any other state. No champions have been identified for nearly 200 species, including white fir, papaya, eucalyptus, California sycamore, and saguaro.

Anyone can nominate candidates for the National Register of Big Trees. For information, write to American Forestry Assn., P.O. Box 2000, Washington, DC 20013. The following is a small selection of the trees registered.

(Figure in parentheses is year of most recent measurement; * = co-champion)

Species	Height (ft.)	Location
Alder, Hazel (1989)	35	Norfolk, Va.
Allthorn (1989)*	13	Midland, Tex.
Anacahuite (1992)	25	Mercedes, Tex.
Anise, Florida (1991)	29	Perry County, Ala.
Apple, Common (1986)	70	East End, Va.
Ash, Carolina (1988)	48	Chesapeake, Va.
Ash, Texas (1989)	66	Lost Maples State Natl. Area, Tex.
Ash, Velvet (1991)	81	Modesto, Cal.
Aspen, Bigtooth (1989)*	66	Caroline Co., Md.
Avocado (1991)	60	Whittier, Cal.
Bald Cypress, Montezuma (1991)	45	Hidalgo Co., Tex.
Basswood, White (1986)	75	Henderson Co., N.C.
Beech, American (1984)	130	Ashtabula Co., Oh.
Birch, Gray (1989)	77	Somers, Ct.
Birch, River (1988)*	90	Appleton Comm., Tenn.
Birch, Water (1973)	53	Wallowa Co., Ore.
Blackbead, Ebony (1986)	40	Hidalgo Co., Tex.
Bladdernut, Sierra (1986)	28	Fresno, Co., Cal.
Bluewood (1989)	30	San Juan, Tex.
Box elder (1991)*	98	Livingston Co., Mich.
Buckeye, Bottlebrush (1989)	20	Cashiers, N.C.
Buffaloberry, Silver (1975)	22	Malheur Co., Ore.
Bumelia, Tough (1987)	41	Amelia Is., Fla.
Butternut (1989)*	88	Eugene, Ore.
California Laurel (1978)	88	Siskiyou Natl. For., Ore.
Camphor-Tree (1977)	72	Hardee Co., Fla.
Catalpa, Southern (1981)	80	Henderson Co., Ill.
Catclaw, Wright (1986)	36	Uvalde Co., Tex.
Cedar, Atlantic white (1985)	88	Escambia Co., Ala.
Cherry, Bitter (1985)	104	Vashon Is., Wash.
Chestnut, American (1992)	110	Grand Traverse, Mich.
Coconut, Palm (1979)	92	Hilo, Hi.
Crab Apple, Southern (1992)	36	Swannanoa, N.C.
Cranberrybush, American (1989)*	25	Trenton, Mich.
Cypress, Monterey (1991)*	93	Mendocino Co., Cal.
Dahoon, Myrtle (1972)	46	Lawtey, Fla.
Devilwood (1989)	36	Perry, Fla.
Dogwood, Blackfruit (1986)	18	Shasta Co., Cal.
Dogwood, Swamp (1989)*	23	Chesapeake, Va.
Douglas-Fir, Coast (1991)	329	Coos Co., Ore.
Elder, American (1987)	16	Jefferson Natl. For., Va.
Elder, Pacific Red (1989)	30	Lincoln Co., Ore.
Elm, American (1991)	100	Louisville, Kan.
Elm, Siberian (1991)	146	Detroit, Mich.
Fiddlewood, Florida (1988)	39	Dade Co., Fla.
Fig, Shortleaf (1986)	41	Monroe Co., Fla.
Fir, Grand (1987)	251	Olympic Natl. Park, Wash.
Fringetree (1989)*	32	Fairfax Co., Va.
Geiger Tree (1988)	25	Lee Co., Fla.
Guajillo (1989)	15	Starr Co., Tex.
Guiana Plum (1976)	31	Coral Gables, Fla.
Gumbo-Limbo (1984)*	36	Miami Shores, Fla.
Hackberry, Common (1989)	111	Rock Co., Wis.
Haw, May (1989)	12	Williamsburg, Va.
Hawthorne, Fleshy (1988)	8	Kirkwood, Mo.
Hazel, California (1984)	47	Seattle, Wash.
Hemlock, Western (1991)*	227	Olympic Natl. Park, Wash.
Hickory, Mockernut (1985)*	125	Monroe Co., Ala.
Hickory, Shellbark (1986)	105	Rixeyville, Va.
Holly, Carolina (1986)	25	Jacksonville, Fla.
Honeylocust (1972)	115	Wayne Co., Mich.
Huisache (1989)	33	Big Bend Natl. Park, Tex.
Jerusalem-thorn (1969)	36	Florence, Ariz.
Jujube, Common (1989)	43	Fort Worth, Tex.
Juniper, Western (1945)	86	Stanislaus Natl. Forest, Cal.
Larch, European (1989)	83	Greenwich, Ct.
Laurelcherry, English (1987)	32	Seattle, Wash.
Lidflower, Pale (1991)	33	Monroe Co., Fla.
Loblolly Bay (1963)	94	Ocala Natl. Forest, Fla.
Locust, Black (1974)	96	Dansville, N.Y.
Magnolia, Umbrella (1969)	50	Bucks Co., Pa.
Mahogany, W. Indies (1988)	70	Lee Co., Fla.
Mango (1991)	40	Pompano Beach, Fla.
Manzanita, Common (1989)	22	Guerneville, Cal.
Maple, Black (1976)	118	Allegan Co., Mich.
Maple, Douglas (1985)*	65	Ahsahka, Ida.
Mesquite, Honey (1984)	52	Real County, Tex.
Mountain Laurel (1991)	25	Asheville, N.C.
Mulberry, Black (1971)	68	Westminster, Md.
Nannyberry (1989)	40	Oakland Co., Mich.
Oak, Bluejack (1985)	64	Cherokee Co., Tex.
Oak, Cherrybark (1991)	124	Sussex Co., Va.
Oak, Harvard (1986)	30	Yoakum Co., Tex.
Oysterwood (1986)	24	Monroe Co., Fla.
Palm, Texas Sabal (1989)	45	Hidalgo Co., Tex.
Palmetto, Cabbage (1991)	62	Brunswick, Ga.
Paper-Mulberry (1989)	34	Yorktown, Va.
Pawpaw, Common (1986)	60	Newton Co., Miss.
Peach (1986)	18	Morrisville, Va.
Pear, Common (1991)	59	Waitsburg, Wash.
Pecan (1980)	143	Cocke Co., Tenn.
Persimmon, Texas (1965)	26	Uvalde Co., Tex.
Pine, Bishop (1986)	112	Mendocino Co., Cal.
Pine, Digger (1991)*	114	Bar 71 Ranch, Cal.
Pine, Virginia (1989)	120	Chambers Co., Ala.
Pistache, Texas (1976)	39	Val Verde Co., Tex.
Plum, Chicasaw (1988)	32	Henderson Co., N.C.
Plum, Wildgoose (1989)	26	New Salem Village, Ill.
Poison-Sumac (1972)	16	Robins Is., N.Y.
Poplar, Balsam (1984)	138	Marquette, Mich.
Portiatree (1968)	42	Kekaha, Ha.
Privet, California (1989)*	28	Yorktown, Va.
Redbud, Eastern (1989)	36	Nashville, Tenn.
Redwood, Coast (1972)	362	Humboldt Redwoods State Park, Cal.
Ribbonbush (1977)	23	No. Warner Springs, Cal.
Russian-Olive (1982)	58	Cortez, Col.
Saffron-Plum (1987)	31	Santa Ana, Tex.
Sassafras (1954)	76	Owensboro, Ky.
Sequoia, Giant (1976)	275	Sequoia Natl. Park, Cal.
Serviceberry, Downy (1986)	60	Burkes Garden, Va.
Silktree, Mimosa (1986)*	54	Webster Parish, La.
Sophora, Mescalbean (1983)	27	Comal Co., Tex.
Spruce, Norway (1989)	94	Susquehanna City, Pa.
Stewartia, Virginia (1987)	15	Chesapeake, Va.
Sparkleberry Tree (1991)*	29	Evergreen, Ala.
Sweetgum, American (1986)	136	Craven Co., N.C.
Sycamore, Arizona (1981)	114	Sierra Co., N.M.
Tamarisk (1981)	34	Columbus, N.M.
Thatchpalm, Florida (1986)	23	Monroe Co., Fla.
Walnut, Arizona (1987)	85	Mimbres Valley, N.M.
Walnut, Black (1991)	105	Southhampton Co., Va.
Willow, Sitka (1988)	34	Coupeville, Wash.
Willow, Weeping (1982)*	114	Asheville, N.C.
Yew, Florida (1986)	20	Torreya State Park, Fla.
Yucca, Mojave (1987)	24	Needles Res. Area, Cal.
Yucca, Torrey (1987)	23	Lincoln Natl. Forest, N.M.

Minerals

Source: Bureau of Mines, U.S. Dept. of the Interior, as of mid-1993.

Aluminum: the second most abundant metal element in the Earth's crust. Bauxite is the main source of aluminum; convert to aluminum equivalent by multiplying by 0.211. Guinea and Australia have 49 percent of the world's reserves. Aluminum is used in the U.S. principally in packaging (35%), transportation (20%), and building (17%).

Chromium: some two-thirds of the world's chromite production is in Kazakhstan and South Africa. The chemical and metallurgical industries use about 80% of the chromite consumed in the world.

Cobalt: used in superalloys for jet engines; chemicals (paint driers, catalysts, magnetic coatings); permanent magnets; and cemented carbides for cutting tools. Principal cobalt-producing countries include Zaire, Zambia, and the former USSR. The U.S. uses about one-third of total world consumption. Although its resources are relatively large, the U.S. has produced no cobalt since 1971; most cobalt resources are low grade, and production from these deposits is not economically feasible.

Columbium: used mostly as an additive in steelmaking and in superalloys. Brazil and Canada are the world's leading producers. There is no U.S. columbium mining industry.

Copper: main uses of copper in the U.S. are in building construction (41%), electrical and electronic products (24%), industrial machinery and equipment (13%), transportation (12%), and consumer and general products (10%). The leading producer is Chile, followed by the U.S., Poland, Russia, Peru, Kazakhstan, Australia, and China. Principal mining states are Arizona, New Mexico, and Utah.

Gold: used in the U.S. in jewelry and the arts (70%), the electronics and other industries (23%), and in dentistry (7%). South Africa has about half of the world's resources; significant quantities are also present in the U.S., Canada, the former USSR, and Brazil. Gold mining in the U.S. takes place in nearly all of the western states and Alaska.

Iron ore: the source of primary iron for the world's iron and steel industries. Major iron ore producers include the former USSR, Brazil, Australia, and China.

Lead: the U.S., Australia, China, and the former USSR are the world's largest producers of lead. Transportation accounted for the major end use in the U.S., with 75% used in batteries, gasoline additives, and other applications. Other uses include emergency power supply batteries, construction sheeting, sporting ammunition, and TV tubes. The U.S. produces and consumes more than 20% of the world's lead metal.

Manganese: essential to iron and steel production. The U.S., Japan, and Western Europe are all nearly deficient in economically minable manganese. South Africa and the former USSR have over 80% of the world's reserves.

Nickel: vital to the stainless steel industry and played a key role in the development of the chemical and aerospace industries. Leading producers include the former USSR, Canada, Australia, and New Caledonia.

Platinum-Group Metals: the platinum group comprises 6 closely related metals: platinum, palladium, rhodium, ruthenium, iridium, and osmium. They commonly occur together in nature and are among the scarcest of the metallic elements. They are consumed in the U.S. by the following industries: automotive (38%), electrical and electronic (29%), dental (9%), and other (24%). The former USSR and South Africa have nearly all the world's reserves.

Silver: used in the following U.S. industries: photography; electrical and electronic products; sterlingware, electroplated ware, and jewelry. Silver is mined in more than 60 countries. Nevada produces over 34% of U.S. silver, Idaho 14%.

Tantalum: a refractory metal with unique electrical, chemical, and physical properties; it is used in the U.S. mostly to produce electronic components, mainly tantalum capacitors. Australia, Brazil, Canada, and Thailand are the leading producers. There is no U.S. tantalum mining industry.

Titanium: a metal that is mostly used in jet engines, airframes, and space and missile applications. It is produced in Ukraine, Russia, Kazakhstan, Japan, the western and central U.S., the United Kingdom, and China.

Vanadium: used as an alloying element in steel, as an alloying agent in aerospace titanium alloys, and as a catalyst in the production of sulfuric acid and maleic anhydride. The former USSR and South Africa are the world's largest producers.

Zinc: used as a protective coating on steel, as diecastings, as an alloying metal with copper to make brass, and as a component of chemical compounds in rubber and paints. It is mined in over 50 countries, with Canada the leading producer, followed by Australia, the former USSR, Peru, China, and the U.S. In the U.S., mine production comes mostly from Tennessee, Missouri, New York, and Alaska.

World Mineral Reserve Base

Source: Bureau of Mines, U.S. Dept. of the Interior, as of mid-1993.

Mineral	Reserve Base[1]
Aluminum	28,000 mln. metric tons[2]
Chromium	6,800 mln. metric tons
Cobalt	8,800 thou. metric tons
Columbium	4,200 kilograms
Copper	590 mln. metric tons
Gold	51,000 metric tons
Iron	230,000 mln. metric tons[3]
Lead	125 mln. metric tons
Manganese	4,800,000 thousand metric tons
Nickel	110,000 thousand metric tons
Platinum—Group Metals	66 mln. kilograms
Silver	420,000 metric tons
Tantalum	35 mln. kilograms
Titanium	595 mln. metric tons
Vanadium	27,000 thousand metric tons
Zinc	325 mln. metric tons

(1) Includes demonstrated resources that are currently economic (reserves), marginally economic (marginal reserves), and some of those that are currently subeconomic. (2) Bauxite. (3) Crude ore.

U.S. Nonfuel Mineral Production—10 Leading States in 1991

Source: Bureau of Mines, U.S. Dept. of the Interior

Rank/State	Value (millions)	Percent of U.S. total	Principal minerals
1. California	$3,017	9.80	Cement, boron minerals, sand & gravel (construction), stone (crushed)
2. Arizona	3,791	9.06	Copper, gold, sand and gravel
3. Nevada	2,510	8.15	Gold, sand & gravel (construction), silver
4. Florida	1,422	4.62	Stone (crushed), cement, phosphate rock
5. Michigan	1,398	4.54	Iron ore, cement, sand & gravel, stone
6. Georgia	1,392	4.52	Clays, stone (crushed)
7. Minnesota	1,389	4.51	Iron ore, sand & gravel (construction), stone (crushed)
8. Texas	1,379	4.48	Cement, stone (crushed), sand & gravel (construction), salt
9. Utah	1,182	3.84	Cement, lime, sand & gravel (construction), salt, copper
10. New Mexico	976	3.17	Potassium salts, copper

U.S. Nonfuel Mineral Production

Source: Bureau of Mines, U.S. Dept. of the Interior

Production as measured by mine shipments, sales, or marketable production (including consumption by producers)

		1987	1988	1989	1990	1991[1]	1992[1]
Antimony (ore and concentrate)		—	W	W	W	W	W
Bauxite	thousand metric tons, dried equivalent	576	588	W	W	W	W
Beryllium (metal equivalent)	metric tons	220	212	184	182	174	193
Copper (recoverable content of ores, etc.)	thousand metric tons	1,244	1,417	1,498	1,588	1,631	1,720[E]
Gold (recoverable content of ores, etc.)	metric tons	153.9	200.9	265.7	294.3	289.9	320.0[E]
Iron ore, usable (includes byproduct material)	million metric tons	47.6	57.5	59.0	56.4	56.8	56.7[E]
Lead (in concentrate)	thousand metric tons	319	394	420	495	477	410[E]
Magnesium metal (primary)	thousand metric tons	124	142	152	139	131	135[E]
Molybdenum (content of ore and concentrate)	metric tons	34,073	43,051	63,105	61,611	53,364	45,400[E]
Nickel (content of ore and concentrate)	metric tons	—	—	—	330	5,523	6,671
Silver (recoverable content of ores, etc.)	metric tons	1,241	1,661	2,007	2,125	1,848	1,800[E]
Tungsten (content of ore and concentrate)	metric tons	34	W	W	W	W	W
Zinc (recoverable content of ores, etc.)	thousand metric tons	216	244	276	515	518	520[E]
Asbestos	thousand metric tons	51	18	17	W	20	16
Barite	thousand metric tons	406	404	290	430	448	326
Boron minerals	thousand metric tons	625	578	562	608	626	521[E]
Bromine	million kilograms	152	163	175	177	170	166[E]
Cement: (portland, masonry, etc.)	thousand short tons	78,198	76,867	77,189	77,111	71,300	76,484[E]
Clays	thousand metric tons	43,234	44,515	42,254	42,904	41,017	40,712
Diatomite	thousand metric tons	596	629	617	631	610	595
Feldspar	thousand metric tons	655	650	655	630	580	725
Fluorspar	thousand metric tons	64	64	66	64	58	50[E]
Garnet (industrial)	metric tons	38,353	42,506	42,605	47,009	50,860	54,304[E]
Gem stones	million dollars	21.4	43.5	42.9	52.9	84.4	51.2
Gypsum	thousand short tons	15,612	16,390	17,624	16,406	15,456	16,300[E]
Helium (extracted from natural gas)	million cubic meters	54.6	63.3	66.3	64.6	86.4	88.2[E]
Helium (Grade A)	million cubic meters	61.9	71.4	79.9	84.8	88.1	90.7[E]
Iodine	thousand kilograms	W	1,015	1,508	1,973	1,999	1,995
Lime	thousand short tons	15,577	17,052	17,152	17,452	17,270	18,000[E]
Mica (scrap & flake)	thousand metric tons	146	130	119	109	103	93[E]
Peat	thousand short tons	955	844	761	763	697	719
Perlite (sold and used by producers)	thousand metric tons	484	523	545	576	514	541
Phosphate rock (marketable product)	thousand metric tons	40,954	45,389	49,817	46,343	48,096	46,965
Pumice and pumicite	thousand metric tons	356	353	424	443	401	481
Salt	thousand short tons	36,943	39,170	39,278	40,558	40,031	39,800[E]
Sand and gravel (construction)	thousand short tons	895,200[E]	923,400	897,300[E]	910,600	780,300[E]	805,700[E]
Sand and gravel (industrial)	thousand short tons	28,010	28,480	29,205	28,406	25,600	26,967
Sodium sulfate (natural)	thousand metric tons	346	361	340	349	354	350[E]
Stone (crushed)	million short tons	1,200	1,248[E]	1,213	1,222[E]	1,103	1,162
Stone (dimension)[1]	thousand short tons	1,179	1,159[E]	1,238	1,186	1,139	1,086[E]
Sulfur	thousand metric tons	10,539	10,746	11,592	11,560	10,820	10,600[E]
Talc and pyrophyllite	thousand metric tons	1,163	1,234	1,253	1,267	1,037*	997*
Vermiculite	thousand metric tons	275	276	249	209[E]	168	170[E]

(E) Estimated. (W) Withheld to avoid disclosing company proprietary data. (—) No production. * Talc only. (1) 1991 and 1992 production includes Puerto Rico.

U.S. Reliance on Foreign Supplies of Minerals

Source: Bureau of Mines, U.S. Dept. of the Interior

Mineral	Percent imported in 1992	Major sources (1988-91)	Major uses
Columbium	100%	Brazil, Canada, Germany	Steelmaking and aerospace alloys
Graphite	100	Mexico, China, Brazil, Madagascar	Metallurgical processes
Manganese	100	S. Africa, France, Gabon	Steelmaking
Mica (sheet)	100	India, Belgium, Brazil, Japan	Electronic and electrical equipment
Strontium (celestite)	100	Mexico, Spain, Germany	Television picture tubes, pyrotechnics
Bauxite and alumina	100	Australia, Guinea, Jamaica, Brazil	Aluminum production
Diamonds (industrial)	98	Ireland, Zaire, Britain, South Africa	Machinery for grinding and cutting
Fluorspar	87	Mexico, South Africa, China, Canada	Raw material for metallurgical and chemical industries
Platinum group	94	South Africa, Britain, USSR and former USSR	Catalytic converters for autos, electrical and electronic equipment
Cobalt	76	Zaire, Zambia, Canada, Norway	Aerospace alloys, magnets, cutting tools, chemicals
Tantalum	87	Germany, Thailand, Australia	Electronic components
Nickel	64	Canada, Norway, Australia, Dominican Rep.	Stainless steel and other alloys
Chromium	74	South Africa, Turkey, Zimbabwe, Yugoslavia	Stainless steel
Tin	73	Brazil, Bolivia, China, Indonesia, Malaysia	Cans, electrical construction
Tungsten	85	China, Bolivia, Germany, Peru	Lamp filaments
Barite	53	China, India, Mexico, Morocco	Oil drilling fluids
Potash	67	Canada, Israel, USSR and former USSR, Germany	Fertilizer
Cadmium	49	Canada, Mexico, Australia, Germany	Batteries, plating and coating of metals
Silver	NA	Mexico, Canada, Britain, Peru	Photography, electrical and electronic prods.

U.S. Copper, Lead, and Zinc Production, 1950-1992

Source: Bureau of Mines, U.S. Dept. of the Interior

Year	Copper Quantity (metric tons)	Copper Value ($1,000)	Lead Quantity (metric tons)	Lead Value ($1,000)	Zinc Quantity (metric tons)	Zinc Value ($1,000)
1950	827	379,122	390,839	113,078	565,516	167,000
1960	1,037	733,706	223,774	57,722	395,013	112,365
1965	1,226	957,028	273,196	93,959	554,429	178,284
1970	1,560	1,984,484	518,698	178,609	484,560	163,650
1975	1,282	1,814,763	563,783	267,230	425,792	366,097
1980	1,181	2,666,931	550,366	515,189	317,103	261,671
1985	1,105	1,631,000	413,955	174,008	226,545	201,607
1987	1,244	2,262,000	311,381	246,720	216,281	200,529
1988	1,417	3,764,000	384,983	315,222	244,314	324,249
1989	1,497	4,323,000	410,915	356,476	275,883	499,103
1990	1,586	4,310,000	483,704	490,750	515,355	847,485
1991	1,631	3,931,000	465,931	343,907	517,804	602,426
1992	1,705	4,180,000	397,923	307,922	523,430	673,800

U.S. Pig Iron and Raw Steel Output, 1940-1992

Source: American Iron and Steel Institute (net tons)

Year	Total pig iron	Raw steel
1940	46,071,666	66,982,686
1945	53,223,169	79,701,648
1950	64,586,907	96,836,075
1955	76,857,417	117,036,085
1960	66,480,648	99,281,601
1965	88,184,901	131,461,601
1970	91,435,000	131,514,000
1975	101,208,000	116,642,000
1980	68,721,000	111,835,000
1985	50,446,000	88,259,000
1986	43,952,000	81,606,000
1987	48,410,000	89,151,000
1988	55,745,000	99,924,000
1989	55,873,000	97,943,000
1990	54,750,000	98,906,000
1991	48,637,000	87,896,000
1992	52,224,000	92,949,000

Steel figures include only that portion of the capacity and production of steel for castings used by foundries that were operated by companies producing steel ingots.

World Gold Production, 1972-1992

Source: Bureau of Mines, U.S. Dept. of the Interior

(Troy Ounces)

		Africa			North and South America				Other			
Year	World prod.	South Africa	Ghana	Zaire[r]	United States	Canada	Mexico	Colombia	Australia	China	Philippines	USSR
1972	44,843,374	29,245,273	724,051	80,377	1,449,943	2,078,567	146,061	188,137	754,866	NA	606,730	NA
1975	38,476,371	22,937,820	523,889	115,743	1,052,252	1,653,611	144,710	308,864	526,821	NA	502,577	NA
1977	38,906,145	22,501,886	480,884	96,452	1,100,347	1,733,609	212,709	257,070	624,270	NA	558,554	NA
1978	38,983,019	22,648,558	402,034	32,151	998,832	1,735,077	202,003	246,446	647,579	NA	586,531	NA
1979	38,768,978	22,617,179	362,000	73,947	964,390	1,644,265	190,364	269,369	596,910	NA	535,166	NA
1980	39,197,315	21,669,468	353,000	96,452	969,782	1,627,477	195,991	510,439	547,591	NA	753,452	8,425,000
1982	43,082,814	21,355,111	331,000	135,033	1,465,686	2,081,230	214,349	472,674	866,815	1,800,000	834,439	8,550,000
1984	46,929,444	21,860,933	287,000	321,507	2,084,615	2,682,786	270,998	730,670	1,295,963	1,900,000	827,149	8,650,000
1985	49,283,691	21,565,230	299,363	257,206	2,427,232	2,815,118	265,693	1,142,385	1,881,491	1,950,000	1,062,997	8,700,000
1986	51,534,056	20,513,665	287,127	257,206	3,739,015	3,364,700	250,615	1,285,878	2,413,842	2,100,000	1,296,400	8,850,000
1987	53,033,614	19,176,500	327,598	385,809	4,947,040	3,724,000	256,822	853,600	3,558,954	2,300,000	1,048,081	8,850,000
1988	60,308,973	19,965,611	355,620	401,884	6,459,534	4,334,338	292,508	932,822	5,046,059	2,507,758	980,019	8,925,046
1989	65,335,998	19,530,290	429,470	340,798	8,543,449	5,127,850	276,914	948,640	6,544,702	2,893,567	964,265	9,773,826
1990	68,632,896	19,454,414	541,419	299,002	9,458,395	5,381,166	268,073	943,689	7,849,186	3,215,074	790,619	9,709,524
1991	69,083,682	19,323,014	845,886	282,927	9,542,501	5,676,278	287,331	1,120,260	7,530,283	3,858,089	801,775	8,359,193
1992	72,269,724	19,737,341	997,670	257,206	10,581,581	5,081,393	321,507	1,189,578	7,716,178	4,501,104	771,618	8,101,987*

NA = not available. r = revised to reflect improved data. * = USSR as constituted prior to Dec. 1991.

U.S. and World Silver Production, 1930-1992

Source: Bureau of Mines, U.S. Dept. of the Interior

(metric tons)

Largest production of silver in the United States in 1915—2,332 metric tons.

Year	United States	World
1930	1,578	7,736
1935	1,428	6,865
1940	2,164	8,565
1945	904	5,039
1950	1,347	6,323
1955	1,134	6,967
1960	1,120	7,505
1965	1,238	8,007
1970	1,400	9,670
1975	1,087	9,428
1980	1,006	10,556
1985	1,227	13,051
1986	1,074	12,970
1987	1,241	14,019
1988	1,661	15,484
1989	2,008	16,041
1990	2,121	16,216
1991	1,855	15,692
1992	1,804	15,345

Aluminum Summary, 1980 to 1992

Source: Bureau of Mines, U.S. Dept. of the Interior

Item	Unit	1980	1985	1988	1989	1990	1991	1992
U.S. production	1,000 metric ton	5,914	5,262	6,066	6,084	6,441	6,407	6,799
Primary aluminum	1,000 metric ton	4,654	3,500	3,944	4,030	4,048	4,121	4,042
Secondary aluminum[1]	1,000 metric ton	1,260	1,762	2,122	2,054	2,393	2,286	2,757
Primary aluminum value	Bil. dol	7.3	6.3	9.5	7.8	6.6	5.4	5.1
Price (Primary alum.)[2]	Cents/lb	71.6	81.0	110.1	87.8	74.0	59.5	57.5
Imports for consumption[3]	1,000 metric ton	647	1,420	1,620	1,470	1,514	1,490	1,725
Exports[3]	1,000 metric ton	1,346	908	1,247	1,613	1,659	1,762	1,453
World production	1,000 metric ton	15,383	15,398	18,495	19,104	19,292	19,528	19,219

(1) Recoverable metal content from purchased scrap, old and new; (2) Average prices for primary aluminum, quoted by *Metals Week;* (3) Crude and semicrude (including metal and alloys, plates, bars, etc., and scrap).

TRADE AND TRANSPORTATION

U.S. Foreign Trade with Leading Countries and Areas, 1992

Source: Office of Trade and Economic Analysis, U.S. Dept. of Commerce

(millions of dollars, not seasonally adjusted)

Country/Area	Trade Balance	Rank	Exports	Rank	Imports	Rank
Total	$-84,501.2	(X)	$488,163.6	(X)	$532,664.8	(X)
Japan	-49,600.9	1	47,812.8	2	97,413.8	2
China	-18,309.2	2	7,418.4	15	25,727.6	5
Taiwan	-9,345.7	3	15,250.3	6	24,596.0	6
Canada	-8,035.7	4	90,594.3	1	98,630.0	1
Germany	-7,571.8	5	21,248.6	5	28,820.4	4
Nigeria	-4,101.4	6	1,001.1	49	5,102.5	20
Malaysia	-3,931.2	7	4,362.9	21	8,294.1	14
Italy	-3,593.0	8	8,721.3	14	12,314.4	10
Thailand	-3,539.7	9	3,989.2	23	7,528.9	17
Saudi Arabia	-3,204.5	10	7,166.8	16	10,371.3	12
Venezuela	-2,737.4	11	5,443.7	19	8,181.1	15
Angola	-2,145.1	12	157.7	91	2,302.8	31
South Korea	-2,043.4	13	14,638.8	7	16,682.2	8
Sweden	-1,871.2	14	2,844.9	28	4,716.2	21
India	-1,862.7	15	1,917.1	36	3,779.8	26
Brazil	-1,858.2	16	5,751.1	17	7,609.3	16
Indonesia	-1,750.0	17	2,779.5	29	4,529.5	22
Singapore	-1,686.8	18	9,625.8	11	11,312.6	11
Philippines	-1,596.4	19	2,758.5	30	4,354.9	24
Switzerland	-1,104.5	20	4,540.2	20	5,644.7	18
Algeria	-898.2	21	687.9	59	1,586.1	36
Gabon	-866.2	22	54.7	120	920.9	46
Hong Kong	-715.9	23	9,077.1	12	9,793.1	13
Macao	-701.5	24	19.6	151	721.2	54
Norway	-689.7	25	1,278.9	42	1,968.6	33
North America	-2,654.7	(X)	131,186.5	(X)	133,841.2	(X)
Western Europe	6,373.6	(X)	117,100.3	(X)	110,726.7	(X)
European Community (EC)	8,964.9	(X)	102,958.1	(X)	93,993.2	(X)
European Free Trade Association	-4,184.9	(X)	10,836.5	(X)	15,021.4	(X)
Eastern Europe	2,517.8	(X)	4,069.2	(X)	1,551.4	(X)
Former Soviet Republics	2,105.3	(X)	2,763.5	(X)	658.2	(X)
Organization for Economic Cooperation & Development (OECD) in Europe	6,399.3	(X)	116,536.5	(X)	110,137.2	(X)
Pacific Rim Countries	-83,972.3	(X)	124,451.3	(X)	208,423.6	(X)
Asia—Near East	1,146.7	(X)	16,872.8	(X)	15,726.1	(X)
Asia—(NICS)	-13,791.9	(X)	48,592.0	(X)	62,383.9	(X)
Asia—South	-3,169.0	(X)	3,172.3	(X)	6,341.2	(X)
Assn. of Southeast Asian Nations (ASEAN)	-12,080.6	(X)	23,968.9	(X)	36,049.5	(X)
South/Central America	1,673.1	(X)	35,204.0	(X)	33,530.9	(X)
Twenty Latin American Republics	5,857.7	(X)	71,346.8	(X)	65,489.0	(X)
Central American Common Market	572.4	(X)	4,299.8	(X)	3,727.3	(X)
Latin American Free Trade Association (LAFTA)	4,605.2	(X)	63,633.4	(X)	59,028.3	(X)
North Atlantic Treaty Organization (NATO)	1,219.4	(X)	194,823.7	(X)	193,604.3	(X)
Organization of Petroleum Exporting Countries (OPEC)	-11,240.2	(X)	21,959.6	(X)	33,199.8	(X)
Unidentified[1]	300.9	(X)	300.9	(X)	(X)	(X)

Definitions of Areas:

North America - Canada, Mexico.

Western Europe - Andorra, Austria, Belgium, Bosnia and Herzegovina, Croatia, Cyprus, Denmark, Faroe Islands, Fed. Rep. of Yugoslavia, Finland, France, Germany, Gibraltar, Greece, Iceland, Ireland, Italy, Liechtenstein, Luxembourg, Malta and Gozo, Macedonia, Monaco, Netherlands, Norway, Portugal, San Marino, Slovenia, Spain, Svalbard, Jan Mayen Island, Sweden, Switzerland, Turkey, United Kingdom, Vatican City.

European Community - Belgium, Denmark, France, Germany, Greece, Ireland, Italy, Luxembourg, Netherlands, Portugal, Spain, United Kingdom.

European Free Trade Association - Austria, Finland, Iceland, Liechtenstein, Norway, Sweden, Switzerland.

Eastern Europe - Albania, Armenia, Azerbaijan, Belarus, Bulgaria, Czech Republic, Estonia, Georgia, Hungary, Kazakhstan, Kyrgyzstan, Latvia, Lithuania, Moldova, Poland, Romania, Russia, Slovakia, Tajikistan, Turkmenistan, Ukraine, Uzbekistan.

Former Soviet Republics - Armenia, Azerbaijan, Belarus, Estonia, Georgia, Kazakhstan, Kyrgyzstan, Latvia, Lithuania, Moldova, Russia, Tajikistan, Turkmenistan, Ukraine, Uzbekistan.

OECD - Austria, Belgium, Denmark, Finland, France, Germany, Greece, Iceland, Ireland, Italy, Liechtenstein, Luxembourg, Monaco, Netherlands, Norway, Portugal, San Marino, Spain, Svalbard, Jan Mayen Island, Sweden, Switzerland, Turkey, United Kingdom.

Pacific Rim Countries - Australia, Brunei, China, Hong Kong, Indonesia, Japan, South Korea, Macao, Malaysia, New Zealand, Papua New Guinea, Philippines, Singapore, Taiwan.

Asia Near East - Bahrain, Iran, Iraq, Israel, Jordan, Kuwait, Lebanon, Oman, Qatar, Saudi Arabia, Syria, United Arab Emirates, Yemen.

Asia NICS - Hong Kong, South Korea, Singapore, Taiwan.

Asia South - Afghanistan, Bangladesh, India, Nepal, Pakistan, Sri Lanka.

ASEAN - Brunei, Indonesia, Malaysia, Philippines, Singapore, Thailand.

South/Central America - Anguilla, Antigua and Barbuda, Argentina, Aruba, Bahamas, Barbados, Belize, Bermuda, Bolivia, Brazil, British Virgin Islands, Cayman Islands, Chile, Colombia, Costa Rica, Cuba, Dominica, Dominican Republic, Ecuador, El Salvador, Falkland Islands, French Guiana, Grenada, Guadeloupe, Guatemala, Guyana, Haiti, Honduras, Jamaica, Martinique, Montserrat, Netherlands Antilles, Nicaragua, Panama, Paraguay, Peru, St. Kitts and Nevis, St. Lucia, St. Vincent and the Grenadines, Suriname, Trinidad and Tobago, Turks and Caicos Islands, Uruguay, Venezuela.

Twenty Latin American Republics - Argentina, Bolivia, Brazil, Chile, Colombia, Costa Rica, Cuba, Dominican Republic, Ecuador, El Salvador, Guatemala, Haiti, Honduras, Mexico, Nicaragua, Panama, Paraguay, Peru, Uruguay, Venezuela.

Central American Common Market - Costa Rica, El Salvador, Guatemala, Honduras, Nicaragua.

LAFTA - Argentina, Bolivia, Brazil, Chile, Colombia, Ecuador, Mexico, Paraguay, Peru, Uruguay, Venezuela.

NATO - Belgium, Canada, Denmark, France, Germany, Greece, Iceland, Italy, Luxembourg, Netherlands, Norway, Portugal, Spain, Turkey, United Kingdom.

OPEC - Algeria, Ecuador, Gabon, Indonesia, Iran, Iraq, Kuwait, Libya, Nigeria, Qatar, Saudi Arabia, United Arab Emirates, Venezuela.

(1) The export totals reflect shipments of certain grains, oilseeds, and satellites that are not included in the country/area totals.
(X) Not applicable. **Note:** Details may not equal totals due to rounding.

U.S. Exports and Imports by Principal Commodity Groupings, 1992

Source: Office of Trade and Economic Analysis, U.S. Dept. of Commerce

(millions of dollars, not seasonally adjusted, current dollar basis)

Item	Exports	Imports
Total	**$448,163.6**	**$532,664.8**
Agricultural commodities	**42,237.7**	**23,374.9**
Animal feeds	3,550.2	337.0
Bulbs	111.8	200.8
Cereal flour	924.4	723.9
Cocoa	30.6	774.4
Coffee	17.7	1,562.8
Corn	4,965.8	68.5
Cotton, raw and linters	2,014.6	11.4
Dairy products; eggs	710.5	506.3
Fur skins, raw	95.4	61.3
Grains, unmilled	893.6	121.6
Hides and skins	1,252.8	124.0
Live animals	608.6	1,437.3
Meat and preparations	4,207.9	2,711.5
Oils/fats, animal	496.8	17.5
Oils/fats, vegetable	725.0	954.5
Plants	135.3	102.4
Rice	725.8	91.6
Seeds	302.4	152.8
Soybeans	4,462.8	15.8
Sugar	5.6	662.0
Tobacco, unmanufactured	1,649.1	950.8
Vegetables and fruit	5,736.3	5,697.6
Wheat	4,503.2	191.1
Other agricultural	4,111.6	5,897.9
Manufactured goods	**347,493.7**	**434,348.8**
ADP equipment; office mach.	26,999.9	36,377.1
Airplanes	26,285.7	3,859.8
Airplane parts	9,366.4	3,358.1
Aluminum	2,666.5	2,539.6
Artwork/antiques	1,075.8	2,086.9
Basketware, etc.	1,522.0	2,188.8
Chemicals - cosmetics	2,631.5	1,711.4
Chemicals - dyeing	1,871.2	1,623.4
Chemicals - fertilizers	2,371.3	951.5
Chemicals - inorganic	4,122.8	3,305.0
Chemicals - medicinal	5,357.3	3,809.8
Chemicals - organic	10,992.6	9,408.1
Chemicals - plastics	10,257.9	4,292.0
Chemicals - other	6,264.6	2,622.4
Clothing	4,091.5	31,226.5
Copper	1,171.9	1,641.7
Electrical machinery	32,172.4	39,710.4
Footwear	603.4	10,163.4
Furniture and parts	2,553.0	5,502.5
Gem diamonds	368.7	4,147.8
General industrial mach.	18,479.6	15,519.7
Glass	1,213.1	849.7
Glassware	495.5	1,015.4
Gold, nonmonetary	4,109.4	1,898.7
Iron and steel mill products	3,606.1	8,327.7
Lighting, plumbing	976.7	1,546.9
Metal manufactures	$5,513.1	$6,727.0
Metalworking machinery	3,033.9	3,187.0
Motorcycles, bicycles	1,439.2	1,912.9
Nickel	195.6	797.0
Optical goods	766.4	1,645.1
Paper and paperboard	6,347.8	7,998.2
Photographic equipment	2,950.1	3,843.5
Plastic articles	2,776.9	3,571.9
Platinum	291.5	1,428.6
Pottery	103.4	1,404.2
Power generating mach.	17,994.7	15,888.1
Printed materials	3,803.3	1,875.3
Records/magnetic media	4,846.1	3,105.7
Rubber articles	621.8	877.7
Rubber tires and tubes	1,409.0	2,511.7
Scientific instruments	14,374.5	7,602.0
Ships, boats	1,421.0	319.4
Silver and bullion	209.4	449.2
Spacecraft	269.6	91.8
Specialized ind. mach.	16,688.6	11,814.4
Telecommunications equip.	11,247.8	25,802.8
Textile yarn, fabric	5,776.0	7,843.9
Toys/games/sporting goods	2,437.2	10,749.0
Travel goods	193.9	2,508.6
Vehicles/new cars - Canada	5,930.5	13,890.4
Vehicles/new cars - Japan	694.1	20,801.1
Vehicles/new cars - other	5,095.3	11,561.3
Vehicles/trucks	3,706.1	9,771.9
Vehicles/chassis/bodies	309.7	338.1
Vehicles/parts	16,753.1	15,838.3
Watches/clocks/parts	207.6	2,320.1
Wood manufactures	1,389.4	2,409.7
Zinc	37.8	854.7
Other manufactured goods	27,030.7	32,923.9
Mineral fuel	**11,254.1**	**55,255.6**
Coal	4,427.0	419.1
Crude oil	32.4	38,553.1
Petroleum preparations	4,011.3	11,277.1
Liquefied propane/butane	257.2	707.1
Natural gas	352.5	3,030.0
Electricity	62.9	589.8
Other mineral fuels	2,110.8	679.5
Selected commodities:		
Fish and preparations	3,382.9	5,657.3
Cork, wood, lumber	5,314.1	3,970.0
Pulp and waste paper	3,859.2	2,129.4
Metal ores; scrap	3,470.4	3,339.8
Crude fertilizers	1,387.8	894.0
Cigarettes	4,192.5	270.8
Alcoholic bev., distilled	343.9	1,827.4
All other	**2,800.6**	**1,596.9**

Note: Details may not equal totals due to rounding.

U.S. Exports, Imports, and Merchandise Trade Balance, 1950-1992

Source: Office of Trade and Economic Analysis, U.S. Dept. of Commerce

(millions of dollars)

	Principal Census trade totals					Other Census totals		
Year	U.S. exports and reexports excluding military grant-aid	U.S. general imports f.a.s. transaction values[1]	U.S. merchandise balance f.a.s.[1]	U.S. general imports c.i.f.	U.S. balance exports f.a.s. imports c.i.f.	Military grant-aid shipments	Exports of domestic merchandise	Re-exports
1950	$9,997	$8,954	$1,043	$ —	$ —	$282	$10,146	$133
1955	14,298	11,566	2,732	—	—	1,256	15,426	128
1960	19,659	15,073	4,586	—	—	949	20,408	201
1965	26,742	21,520	5,222	—	—	779	27,178	343
1970	42,681	40,356	2,325	42,833	−152	565	42,612	634
1975	107,652	98,503	9,149	105,935	1,716	461	106,622	1,490
1980	220,626	244,871	−24,245	256,984	−36,358	156	216,668	4,115
1985	213,133	345,276[2]	−132,143	361,626	−148,493	13	206,925	6,221
1990	394,030	495,042[2]	−101,012	516,987	−122,957	15	375,606	18,439
1991	421,730	485,453[2]	−66,723	508,363	−86,633	NA	401,109	20,621
1992	448,164	532,665[2]	−84,501	554,023	−105,859	NA	425,737	22,427

Note: Export values include both commercially financed shipments and shipments under government-financed programs such as AID and PL-480. (1) Prior to 1974, imports are customs values, i.e., generally at prices in principal foreign markets. (2) In 1981 import value changes back to customs value. NA = Not available.

New Passenger Cars Imported into the U.S., by Country of Origin,[1] 1964-1990

Source: Bureau of the Census, U.S. Dept. of Commerce

	Japan	West Germany	Italy	United Kingdom	Sweden	France	South Korea	Mexico	Canada	Total[2]
1964...	16,023	364,683	10,843	77,548	18,562	39,532	N.A.	N.A.	9,201	536,725
1965...	25,538	376,950	9,509	66,565	26,010	24,941	N.A.	N.A.	33,378	563,673
1966...	56,050	527,137	14,110	81,870	34,632	33,122	N.A.	N.A.	152,333	899,895
1967...	70,304	472,360	16,928	67,928	43,371	25,454	N.A.	N.A.	323,638	1,020,618
1968...	169,849	707,972	33,843	96,787	52,515	39,551	N.A.	N.A.	500,881	1,620,452
1969...	260,005	642,157	41,569	104,050	41,008	24,457	N.A.	N.A.	691,146	1,846,717
1970...	381,338	674,945	42,523	76,257	57,844	37,114	N.A.	N.A.	692,783	2,013,420
1971...	703,672	770,807	51,469	106,710	61,925	23,316	N.A.	0	802,281	2,587,484
1972...	697,788	676,967	64,614	72,038	64,541	14,713	N.A.	9	842,300	2,485,901
1973...	624,805	677,465	56,102	64,140	58,626	8,219	N.A.	4,469	871,557	2,437,345
1974...	791,791	619,757	107,071	72,512	60,817	21,331	N.A.	3,914	817,559	2,572,557
1975...	695,573	370,012	102,344	67,106	51,993	15,647	N.A.	0	733,766	2,074,653
1976...	1,128,936	349,804	82,500	77,190	37,466	21,916	N.A.	0	825,590	2,536,749
1977...	1,341,530	423,492	55,437	56,889	39,370	19,215	N.A.	N.A.	849,814	2,790,144
1978...	1,563,047	416,231	69,689	54,478	56,140	28,502	N.A.	6	833,061	3,024,982
1979...	1,617,328	495,565	72,456	46,911	65,907	27,887	N.A.	4	677,008	3,005,523
1980...	1,991,502	338,711	46,899	32,517	61,496	47,386	N.A.	1	594,770	3,116,448
1981...	1,911,525	234,052	21,635	12,728	68,042	42,477	N.A.	1	563,943	2,856,286
1982...	1,801,185	259,385	9,402	13,023	89,231	50,032	N.A.	27	702,495	2,926,407
1983...	1,871,192	239,807	5,442	17,261	114,726	40,823	N.A.	2	835,665	3,133,836
1984...	1,948,714	335,032	8,582	19,833	114,854	37,788	N.A.	N.A.	1,073,425	3,559,427
1985...	2,527,467	473,110	8,689	24,474	142,640	42,882	N.A.	13,647	1,144,805	4,397,679
1986...	2,618,711	451,699	11,829	27,506	148,700	10,869	169,309	41,983	1,162,226	4,691,297
1987...	2,417,509	377,542	8,648	50,059	138,565	26,707	399,856	126,266	926,927	4,589,010
1988...	2,123,051	264,249	6,053	31,636	108,006	15,990	455,741	148,065	1,191,357	4,450,213
1989...	2,051,525	216,881	9,319	29,378	101,571	4,885	270,609	133,049	1,151,122	4,042,728
1990...	1,867,794	245,286	11,045	27,271	93,084	1,976	201,475	215,986	1,220,221	3,944,602

(1) Excludes passenger cars assembled in U.S. foreign trade zones. (2) Includes countries not shown separately.

50 Busiest United States Ports, 1991

Source: Corps of Engineers, Dept. of the Army, U.S. Dept. of Defense

(ports ranked by tonnage handled, all figures in tons)

Rank	Port	Total	Domestic	Foreign	Imports	Exports
1	South Louisiana, LA, Port of	189,374,451	100,252,774	89,121,677	25,859,022	63,262,655
2	Houston, TX	131,233,876	62,943,241	68,290,635	41,065,418	27,225,217
3	New York, NY	126,860,940	83,082,893	43,778,047	36,076,481	7,701,566
4	Valdez, AK	99,616,158	99,576,371	39,787	23,986	15,801
5	Baton Rouge, LA	87,630,227	49,341,472	38,288,755	19,891,036	18,397,719
6	New Orleans, LA	60,897,696	31,784,891	29,112,805	13,190,037	15,922,768
7	Corpus Christi, TX	59,052,232	22,886,556	36,165,676	30,545,740	5,619,936
8	Plaquemine, LA, Port of	53,781,692	37,163,309	16,618,383	2,888,779	13,729,604
9	Norfolk Harbor, VA	53,472,834	9,514,842	43,957,992	4,749,565	39,208,427
10	Long Beach, CA	52,890,856	26,775,954	26,114,902	10,852,590	15,262,312
11	Tampa, FL	49,548,191	28,185,229	21,362,962	5,699,268	15,663,694
12	Los Angeles, CA	47,007,818	21,766,328	25,241,490	13,104,955	12,136,535
13	Texas City, TX	43,289,659	19,260,752	24,028,907	20,894,862	3,134,045
14	Mobile, AL	41,260,410	20,638,650	20,621,760	7,041,682	13,580,078
15	Lake Charles, LA	41,241,080	17,506,750	23,734,330	17,826,283	5,908,047
16	Baltimore, MD	37,744,610	14,394,950	23,349,660	8,905,761	14,443,899
17	Duluth-Superior, MN	37,715,527	31,516,232	6,199,295	720,502	5,478,793
18	Philadelphia, PA	37,256,505	13,798,731	23,457,774	22,269,992	1,187,782
19	Pittsburgh, PA	31,277,381	31,277,381	0	0	0
20	Port Arthur, TX	29,835,115	9,322,861	20,512,254	17,540,467	2,971,787
21	Pascagoula, MS	29,567,012	10,152,815	19,414,197	16,015,036	3,399,161
22	Portland, OR	29,299,132	12,487,795	16,811,337	2,957,439	13,853,898
23	St. Louis, Metro., MO	29,262,653	29,262,653	0	0	0
24	Newport News, VA	29,168,022	3,352,965	25,815,057	1,166,447	24,648,610
25	Paulsboro, NJ	23,712,833	10,868,539	12,844,294	12,651,940	192,354
26	Beaumont, TX	22,383,039	16,023,672	6,359,367	4,415,802	1,943,565
27	Marcus Hook, PA	22,337,153	13,560,809	8,776,344	8,493,382	282,962
28	Chicago, IL	21,767,354	19,975,150	1,792,204	1,529,071	263,133
29	Seattle, WA	20,897,097	6,972,843	13,924,254	6,129,956	7,794,298
30	Richmond, CA	19,919,081	14,501,561	5,417,520	2,123,441	3,294,079
31	Tacoma, WA	19,544,196	5,091,025	14,453,171	4,896,733	9,556,438
32	Boston, MA	18,562,490	9,144,085	9,418,405	8,772,215	646,190
33	Huntington, WV	18,042,588	18,042,588	0	0	0
34	Jacksonville, FL	15,780,263	8,226,322	7,553,941	4,866,254	2,687,687
35	Freeport, TX	15,665,993	7,966,433	7,699,560	6,522,710	1,176,850
36	Port Everglades, FL	14,498,908	9,966,821	4,532,087	3,481,434	1,050,653
37	Anacortes, WA	14,480,734	12,858,072	1,622,662	404,258	1,218,404
38	Detroit, MI	14,320,909	11,938,978	2,381,931	1,886,256	495,675
39	San Juan, PR	14,163,380	8,762,131	5,401,249	4,761,348	639,901
40	Indiana Harbor, IN	13,767,044	13,709,364	57,680	38,224	19,456
41	Lorain, OH	13,631,998	13,523,439	108,559	105,270	3,289
42	Cleveland, OH	13,405,999	10,609,015	2,796,984	2,716,169	80,815
43	Savannah, GA	13,325,692	2,427,463	10,898,229	4,921,284	5,976,945
44	Toledo, OH	12,537,683	6,417,750	6,119,933	783,926	5,336,007
45	Two Harbors, MN	12,500,967	12,500,967	0	0	0
46	Memphis, TN	12,297,780	12,297,757	23	0	23
47	Cincinnati, OH	11,717,298	11,717,298	0	0	0
48	Ashtabula, OH	11,276,068	6,808,618	4,467,450	398,424	4,069,026
49	Honolulu, HI	11,208,056	10,603,204	604,852	422,602	182,250
50	Galveston, TX	10,858,221	3,326,998	7,531,223	3,621,711	3,909,512

Commerce on U.S. Inland Waterways

Source: Corps of Engineers, Dept. of the Army, U.S. Dept. of Defense, 1991

Mississippi River System and Gulf Intracoastal Waterway

Waterway	Tons
Mississippi River, Minneapolis to the Gulf	462,735,996
Mississippi River, Minneapolis to St. Louis	79,356,272
Mississippi River, St. Louis to Cairo	101,799,998
Mississippi River, Cairo to Baton Rouge	181,802,058
Mississippi River, Baton Rouge to New Orleans	331,655,147
Mississippi River, New Orleans to the Gulf	281,225,303
Gulf Intracoastal Waterway	112,739,177
Mississippi River System	626,384,122

Ton-Mileage of Freight Carried on Inland Waterways

System	Ton-miles
Atlantic Coast Waterways	28,204,948
Gulf Coast Waterways	42,545,820
Pacific Coast Waterways	23,999,523
Mississippi River System, including Ohio River and tributaries	268,089,639
Great Lakes System, U.S. commerce only	85,847,239
Total:	**448,687,169**

Note: Tons are for calendar year 1989; all tons are in U.S. short tons (2,000 lbs. per ton); ton-miles(000) have been omitted.

Important Waterways and Canals

The St. Lawrence & Great Lakes Waterway, the largest inland navigation system on the North American continent, extends from the Atlantic Ocean to Duluth at the western end of Lake Superior, a distance of 2,342 miles. With the deepening of channels and locks to 27 ft., ocean carriers are able to penetrate to ports in the Canadian interior and the American midwest.

The major canals are those of the St. Lawrence Great Lakes waterway — the 3 canals of the St. Lawrence Seaway, with their 7 locks, providing navigation for vessels of 26-foot draft from Montreal to Lake Ontario; the Welland Ship Canal, with its 8 locks, by-passing the Niagara River between Lake Ontario and Lake Erie; and the Sault Ste. Marie Canal and lock between Lake Huron and Lake Superior. These 16 locks overcome a drop of 580 ft. from the head of the lakes to Montreal. From Montreal to Lake Ontario the former bottleneck of narrow, shallow canals and of slow passage through 22 locks has been overcome, giving faster and safer movement for larger vessels. The current locks and linking channels now accommodate all but the largest ocean-going vessels and the upper St. Lawrence and Great Lakes are open to 80% of the world's saltwater fleet.

Subsidiary Canadian canals or branches include the St. Peters Canal between Bras d'Or Lakes and the Atlantic Ocean in Nova Scotia; the St. Ours and Chambly Canals on the Richelieu River, Quebec; the Ste. Anne and Carillon Canals on the Ottawa River; the Rideau Canal between the Ottawa River and Lake Ontario; the Trent and Murrary Canals between Lake Ontario and Georgian Bay in Ontario; and the St. Andrew's Canal on the Red River. The commercial value of these canals is not great but they are maintained to control water levels and permit the passage of small vessels and pleasure craft. The Canso Canal permits shipping to pass through the causeway connecting Cape Breton Island with the Nova Scotia mainland.

The Welland Canal overcomes the 326-ft. drop of Niagara Falls and the rapids of the Niagara River. It has 8 locks, each 859 ft. long, 80 ft. wide, and 30 ft. deep. Regulations permit ships of 730-ft. length and 75-ft. beam to transit.

Shortest Navigable Distances Between Ports

Source: *Distances Between Ports* (Pub. 151, 7th Edition, 1993), Defense Mapping Agency Hydrographic/Topographic Center

Distances shown are in nautical miles (1,852 meters or about 6,076.115 feet). For statute miles, multiply by 1.15.

From	To	Distance
New York, New York	Barcelona, Spain	3,714
"	Cape Town, South Africa	6,786
"	Cherbourg, France	3,134
"	Copenhagen, Denmark	3,826
"	Galveston, Texas	1,935
"	Glasgow, Scotland	3,210
"	Hamburg, Germany	3,654
"	Havana, Cuba	1,186
"	Helsinki, Finland	4,289
"	Oslo, Norway	3,704
"	Piraeus, Greece	4,688
"	Southampton, England	3,169
Montreal, Canada	Algiers, Algeria	3,842
"	Barcelona, Spain	3,959
"	Cape Town, South Africa	7,118
"	Gibraltar[3]	3,429
"	Halifax, Nova Scotia	895
"	Havana, Cuba	2,528
"	Istanbul, Turkey	5,226
"	Kingston, Jamaica	3,269
"	Lagos, Nigeria	5,170
"	Marseille, France	4,116
"	Naples, Italy	4,406
"	Oslo, Norway	3,165
"	Piraeus, Greece	4,856
"	Port Said, Egypt	5,348
"	Southampton, England	2,913
Colón,[1] Panama	Buenos Aires, Argentina	5,385
"	Copenhagen, Denmark	5,233
"	Galveston, Texas	1,508
"	Gibraltar[3]	4,332
"	Hamburg, Germany	5,061
"	Helsinki, Finland	5,696
"	Lagos, Nigeria	5,049
"	Lisbon, Portugal	4,152
"	Oslo, Norway	5,053
"	Piraeus, Greece	5,759
"	Port Said, Egypt	6,251
"	St. John's, Newfoundland	2,695
"	Southampton, England	4,576
San Francisco, Calif.	Bombay, India	9,794
"	Calcutta, India	9,384
"	Colón, Panama	3,264
Vancouver, Canada	Calcutta, India	8,727
"	Melbourne, Australia	7,365
Panama, Panama	Jakarta, Indonesia	10,603
Port Said, Egypt	Ho Chi Minh City, Vietnam	5,684
"	Hong Kong	6,489
"	Manila, Philippines	6,365
"	Melbourne, Australia	7,886
"	Singapore	5,035
"	Yokohama, Japan	7,024
Cape Town,[2] South Africa	Jakarta, Indonesia	5,276
"	Melbourne, Australia	5,719
"	Singapore	5,614
Singapore	Jakarta, Indonesia	525

(1) Colón on the Atlantic is 44 nautical miles from Panamá (port) on the Pacific; (2) Cape Town is 35 nautical miles northwest of the Cape of Good Hope. (3) Gibraltar (port) is 24 nautical miles east of the Strait of Gibraltar.

Major Merchant Fleets of the World

Source: Maritime Administration, U.S. Dept. of Commerce (tonnage in thousands)

Fleets of oceangoing steam and motor ships totaling 1 million gross tons or over as of Jan. 1, 1993. Excludes ships operating exclusively on the Great Lakes and inland waterways and special types such as channel ships, icebreakers, cable ships, and merchant ships owned by any military force. Gross tonnage is a volume measurement; each cargo gross ton represents 100 cubic ft. of enclosed space. Deadweight tonnage is the carrying capacity of a ship in long tons (2,240 lbs.). Tonnage figures may not add, due to rounding.

	Total			Type of Vessel: Freighters			Bulk Carriers			Tankers		
	No. of Ships	Gross Tons	Dwt. Tons	No. of Ships	Gross Tons	Dwt. Tons	No. of Ships	Gross Tons	Dwt. Tons	No. of Ships	Gross Tons	Dwt. Tons
All Countries[1]	23,753	402,217	656,591	12,339	101,635	123,179	5,420	138,712	246,983	5,642	156,683	285,009
United States[2]	603	15,406	22,500	349	6,824	7,232	23	574	991	220	7,825	14,180
Privately owned[3]	384	12,611	18,774	167	4,648	4,498	21	536	929	193	7,349	13,320
Government owned	219	2,795	3,726	182	2,176	2,734	2	38	62	27	476	860
Australia	74	2,313	3,495	21	241	271	30	1,007	1,685	23	1,065	1,539
Bahamas	818	19,412	32,173	380	4,003	5,213	147	4,343	7,690	242	10,062	19,034
Bermuda	62	3,150	5,369	18	177	200	9	204	347	35	2,769	4,822
Brazil	220	5,131	8,783	59	543	698	77	2,434	4,250	83	2,153	3,834
*Bulgaria	117	1,266	1,880	59	371	463	37	603	949	19	290	468
*China	1,231	12,631	19,388	752	5,364	7,438	285	5,433	9,181	170	1,661	2,685
Cyprus	1,251	20,050	35,630	616	4,085	5,996	488	10,858	19,840	140	5,046	9,766
Denmark	281	4,335	6,309	189	2,294	2,563	14	555	1,029	78	1,486	2,717
France	106	3,020	4,742	45	1,003	1,084	6	103	153	48	1,853	3,485
Germany	419	4,462	5,672	351	3,475	4,263	22	522	853	39	327	513
Greece	904	24,431	46,101	193	1,540	2,258	458	11,834	22,134	231	10,898	21,639
Hong Kong	200	7,085	11,981	64	1,135	1,286	104	4,821	8,839	31	1,039	1,853
India	296	6,029	10,036	97	914	1,339	119	2,928	4,994	77	2,162	3,693
Indonesia	365	1,588	2,514	247	842	1,310	19	181	268	92	549	922
Iran	124	4,421	8,228	38	385	533	50	1,058	1,757	36	2,978	5,938
Isle of Man	68	1,498	2,583	28	275	314	12	311	543	28	912	1,726
Italy	468	6,411	9,737	172	1,346	1,355	60	2,317	4,208	217	2,473	4,110
Japan	913	21,109	32,562	351	3,849	3,077	251	8,653	15,992	296	8,407	13,437
Korea, South	422	6,383	10,238	225	1,996	2,307	130	3,869	7,013	67	518	918
Kuwait	43	2,208	3,792	13	281	370	0	0	0	30	1,927	3,422
Latvia	118	1,023	1,316	75	431	425	0	0	0	43	592	891
Liberia	1,568	55,139	97,173	367	5,911	6,363	540	17,333	32,001	639	31,143	58,679
Luxembourg	51	1,609	2,605	16	199	225	17	881	1,630	17	496	745
Malaysia	185	1,865	2,779	107	666	926	24	468	842	54	731	1,011
Malta	752	10,569	17,971	343	2,286	3,313	255	5,209	9,163	147	3,002	5,468
Marshall Islands	31	2,031	4,002	4	86	102	18	625	1,163	9	1,320	2,737
Netherlands	367	3,240	4,265	285	1,950	2,403	19	393	638	58	766	1,206
Norway	737	20,230	35,371	193	1,860	2,049	219	6,114	11,079	311	11,866	22,173
Panama	3,171	49,589	79,414	1,719	13,966	16,325	717	17,115	29,587	704	18,169	33,375
Philippines	534	7,979	13,420	239	1,382	1,833	251	6,202	10,871	39	360	699
Poland	212	2,780	4,046	119	980	1,111	85	1,671	2,740	5	109	185
Romania	255	2,701	4,135	193	1,147	1,535	50	1,110	1,820	12	444	780
Russia	1,363	10,036	13,370	1,006	5,509	6,369	135	2,092	3,209	211	2,378	3,781
Saint Vincent	431	4,344	7,114	285	1,625	2,313	97	1,881	3,286	47	823	1,503
Singapore	493	9,525	15,377	227	2,706	3,168	82	2,514	4,480	184	4,305	7,729
Spain	222	2,116	3,904	130	350	558	30	530	959	61	1,234	2,384
Sweden	172	2,467	3,157	90	1,079	1,035	10	220	374	67	1,011	1,723
Taiwan	215	5,955	9,146	134	2,444	2,852	60	2,537	4,622	21	974	1,672
Turkey	339	3,817	6,583	189	715	1,039	93	2,239	3,987	54	849	1,551
United Kingdom	154	2,749	3,081	58	1,062	1,032	19	139	209	59	1,159	1,731
Vanuatu	119	2,018	3,021	55	644	599	52	1,115	1,948	11	253	472

(1) Includes combination passenger & cargo ships. (2) Excludes nonmerchant type and/or Navy-owned vessels that are currently in the National Reserve Fleet. (3) Includes 18 integrated tug/barge vessels of 637,000 deadweight tons. (*) = Source material limited.

Fastest Scheduled Passenger Train Runs in the U.S. and Canada

Source: Darrell J. Smith, Natl. Railroad Passenger Corp.; 1993 timetables

Railroad	Train	From	To	Mi.	Min.	MPH
Amtrak	Eight Metroliner Service trains	Wilmington	Baltimore	68.4	42	97.7
Amtrak	16 Metroliner Service trains	Baltimore	Wilmington	68.4	43	95.0
Amtrak	Express Metroliner Service train 203	Metropark	Baltimore	160.0	103	93.0
Amtrak	Express Metroliner Service train 202	New Carrollton	New York City	216.0	141	91.9
Amtrak	Express Metroliner Service train 220	Washington	Philadelphia	135.0	88	91.8
Amtrak	Express Metroliner Service train 223	New York	Baltimore	185.0	123	90.2
Amtrak	Two Metroliner Service trains	Newark	Philadelphia	80.7	55	87.7
Amtrak	Nine Metroliner Service trains	Newark	Philadelphia	80.7	56	86.8
VIA	Renaissance	Dorval	Kingston	165.0	117	84.6
VIA	York	Kingston	Cornwall	108.0	77	84.4
Amtrak	Three Metroliner Service trains	Philadelphia	Newark	80.7	58	83.2
VIA	York	Cornwall	Kingston	108.0	78	83.1
VIA	Renaissance	Kingston	Dorval	165.0	120	82.5

Notes: The fastest scheduled passenger train runs in the world are those of France's TGV Atlantique, between Paris and various cities in western France, at 186.4 mph. On Dec. 12, 1992, Amtrak operated the Swedish X-2000 train at 155 mph, and on July 18, 1993, operated the German ICE train at 162 mph, both on a portion (in northern New Jersey) of the Northeast Corridor. The runs were part of Amtrak's program to test high-speed equipment for use on the Washington-Boston Northeast Corridor.

Top 50 U.S. Industrial Exporters

Source: FORTUNE magazine; June 14, 1993.

Rank 1992	Rank 1991	Company	Export sales 1992 $ millions	% change from 1991	As % of total sales %	As % of total sales Rank
1	1	Boeing	$17,486.0	−2.1	57.5	1
2	2	General Motors	14,045.1[1]	−6.8	10.6	35
3	3	General Electric	8,200.0	−4.8	13.2	27
4	4	IBM	7,524.0	−1.9	11.6	31
5	5	Ford	7,220.0[2]	−1.6	7.2	45
6	6	Chrysler	7,051.8	14.3	19.1	14
7	7	McDonnell Douglas	4,983.0	−19.1	28.5	6
8	12	Philip Morris	3,797.0	24.0	7.6	42
9	11	Hewlett-Packard	3,720.0	15.4	22.6	10
10	8	du Pont	3,509.0	−7.9	9.4	38
11	14	Motorola	3,460.0	18.2	25.9	8
12	10	United Technologies	3,451.0	−3.8	15.7	17
13	9	Caterpillar	3,341.0	−9.9	32.8	4
14	13	Eastman Kodak	3,220.0	6.6	15.6	18
15	15	Archer Daniels Midland	2,700.0	3.8	28.9	5
16	17	Intel	2,339.0	21.3	39.1	3
17	16	Digital Equipment	1,900.0	−13.6	13.5	24
18	18	Allied-Signal	1,810.0	4.7	15.0	21
19	20	Unisys	1,795.8	12.4	21.3	11
20	19	Sun Microsystems	1,783.6	11.1	49.2	2
21	21	Raytheon	1,760.0	13.1	19.3	13
22	22	Weyerhaeuser	1,500.0	−3.2	16.2	16
23	25	Merck	1,489.8	11.0	15.2	20
24	26	Minnesota Mining & Mfg.	1,433.0	12.4	10.3	36
25	31	Westinghouse Electric	1,360.0	19.2	11.2	32
26	*	IBP	1,300.0	30.3	11.7	30
27	33	Xerox	1,292.0	24.2	7.1	46
28	23	Dow Chemical	1,247.0	−9.4	6.5	47
29	29	Textron	1,244.0	6.2	14.9	22
30	27	International Paper	1,200.0[2]	—	8.8	40
31	*	RJR Nabisco	1,171.0	16.9	7.4	43
32	28	Union Carbide	1,125.0	−6.3	18.2	15
33	37	Compaq Computer	1,104.0[3]	16.2	26.7	7
34	30	Hoechst Celanese	1,072.0	−7.4	15.2	19
35	38	FMC	997.7	9.3	25.0	9
36	35	Abbott Laboratories	996.7	4.1	12.6	29
37	39	Miles	956.0[4]	9.0	14.7	23
38	*	Apple Computer	934.7	20.8	13.2	26
39	32	Monsanto	927.0	−17.8	10.9	34
40	43	Bristol-Myers Squibb	915.0[1]	13.4	7.8	41
41	45	Exxon	906.0	21.8	0.9	50
42	34	Aluminum Co. of America	886.0	−8.4	9.2	39
43	*	Georgia Pacific	859.0	30.0	7.3	44
44	44	Lockheed	831.0	24.8	10.0	37
45	42	Honeywell	830.0	2.7	13.3	25
46	40	Cooper Industries	805.0	−3.6	13.1	28
47	*	Cummins Engine	781.0	48.5	20.8	12
48	46	Deere	778.0	9.1	11.2	33
49	48	Tenneco	702.0	1.4	5.2	49
50	41	Rockwell Intl.	701.0	−15.3	6.4	48
		Total	$135,440.2			

* Not on last year's list. [1] FORTUNE estimate. [2] Excludes some U.S. exports. [3] Exports from U.S. and Canada. [4] Owned by Bayer AG, Germany.

Passenger Car Production, U.S. Plants

Source: American Automobile Manufacturers Assn.

	1991	1992
Chrysler Corp.		
Horizon	—	—
Acclaim	82,358	70,768
Sundance	61,605	64,953
Total Plymouth	**143,963**	**135,721**
Concorde	—	—
LeBaron	—	9,755
LeBaron J	29,388	45,235
Fifth Avenue (Y)	36,706	40,436
Imperial	9,335	6,635
New Yorker (C)	15,142	21,339
Total Chrysler-Plymouth	**234,534**	**259,121**
Shadow	69,463	93,920
Daytona	11,492	14,544
Spirit	80,216	68,068
Dynasty	114,439	86,697
Viper	3	310
Total Dodge	**275,613**	**263,539**
Total Chrysler Corp.	**510,147**	**522,660**
Ford Motor Co.		
Thunderbird	71,395	97,822
Taurus	317,810	427,621
Tempo	112,105	129,334
Escort	188,450	179,143
Mustang	81,594	88,568
Total Ford	**771,354**	**922,488**
Cougar	52,157	61,042
Sable	110,619	123,531
Topaz	49,493	57,961
Town Car	126,354	117,789
Mark	9,297	11,468
Continental	52,406	39,299
Total Lincoln-Mercury	**400,326**	**411,090**
Total Ford Motor Co.	**1,171,680**	**1,333,578**
General Motors Corp.		
Caprice	124,224	103,594
Corvette	21,082	20,839
Beretta-Corsica	240,745	187,441
Camaro	52,177	47,757
Cavalier	252,857	212,117
Geo Prizm	94,927	75,479
Total Chevrolet	**786,012**	**647,227**
Grand Prix	114,718	110,485
6000	19,603	—
Grand Am	147,467	251,822
Firebird	20,322	14,786
Bonneville H.	88,355	98,748
Sunbird	118,615	86,119
Total Pontiac	**509,080**	**561,940**
Custom Cruiser	7,811	1,984
Delta 88	93,051	66,620
Oldsmobile 98	75,362	26,154
Toronado	5,934	3,553
Calais	34,616	296
Achieva	6,199	87,372
Cutless Supreme	105,151	76,855
Ciera	111,628	133,140
Total Oldsmobile	**439,752**	**359,974**
LeSabre	111,232	157,790
Roadmaster	60,259	50,566
Park Avenue	93,700	58,587
Riviera	10,314	11,801
Century	98,670	88,820
Skylark	61,537	60,351
Reatta	1,210	—
Total Buick	**436,922**	**427,915**
DeVille	160,223	122,844
Fleetwood	—	17,384
Brougham	22,234	2,170
Eldorado	16,276	29,866
Seville	26,786	46,440
Allante	2,900	2,408
Total Cadillac	**228,419**	**221,112**
Saturn	95,821	212,122
Total General Motors Corp.	**2,496,006**	**2,466,290**
Diamond Star		
Mitsubishi Eclipse	57,926	72,367
Mitsubishi Mirage	24,192	10,140
Plymouth Laser	27,778	21,993
Eagle Talon	34,923	31,802
Eagle Summit	9,117	3,481
Total Diamond Star	**153,936**	**139,783**
Honda		
Accord	366,231	356,382
Civic	84,968	101,872
Total Honda	**451,199**	**458,254**
Mazda	**165,314**	**167,940**
Nissan		
Altima	—	52,166
Sentra	133,505	119,238
Total Nissan	**133,505**	**171,404**
Subaru Legacy	**57,945**	**57,623**
Toyota		
Corolla	111,139	105,370
Camry	187,708	240,382
Total Toyota	**298,847**	**345,752**
Total Passenger Cars	**5,438,579**	**5,663,284**

Selected Motor Vehicle Statistics

Source: Federal Highway Administration; U.S. Dept. of Transportation; Insurance Institute for Highway Safety; 1991 figures unless otherwise specified.

State	Driver's age Jan. 1, 1993 (1) Regular	(2) Juvenile	State gas tax cents/gal. (Oct.1, 1992)	Safety belt use law[3] (Aug. 1, 1993)	Licensed drivers per 1,000 resident population	Registered motor vehicles per 1,000 resident population	Licensed drivers per registered motor vehicle	Gallons of fuel used per vehicle	Miles per gallon	Annual miles driven per vehicle	Vehicle miles per licensed driver
Alabama. . . .	16	—	18	S	673	905	0.74	704	16.48	11,605	15,594
Alaska	16	—	8	S	551	826	0.67	509	16.78	8,539	12,794
Arizona	16	—	18	S	638	760	0.84	695	17.64	12,262	14,599
Arkansas . . .	16	—	18.7	S	726	624	1.16	1,068	13.89	14,824	12,737
California . . .	16/18	14	16	P	653	732	0.89	638	18.18	11,593	12,999
Colorado . . .	18	16	22	S	605	902	0.67	554	16.45	9,111	13,580
Connecticut . .	16/18	—	26	P	673	787	0.86	570	18.04	10,286	12,026
Delaware . . .	16/18	—	19	S	713	785	0.91	697	18.07	12,596	13,863
Dist. of Col. . .	18	16	20	S	689	412	1.67	764	18.23	13,921	8,319
Florida	16	—	11.6	S	695	752	0.92	656	17.33	11,371	12,293
Georgia	16	—	7.5	S*	676	863	0.78	757	16.88	12,776	16,302
Hawaii	15	—	16	P	597	692	0.86	505	20.53	10,373	12,017
Idaho	17	15	21	S	678	1,016	0.67	551	17.75	9,777	14,652
Illinois	16/18	—	19	S	632	710	0.89	639	16.33	10,428	11,711
Indiana	16/18	—	15	S	642	787	0.82	756	16.27	12,295	15,068
Iowa	16/18	—	20	P	670	955	0.70	604	14.28	8,627	12,294
Kansas	16	14	18	S	687	753	0.91	760	16.23	12,337	13,523
Kentucky . . .	16	—	15.4	No	647	798	0.81	749	15.88	11,885	14,662
Louisiana . . .	15/17	15	20	S	606	716	0.85	686	16.60	11,396	13,477
Maine	16/17	16	19	No	718	793	0.91	695	17.41	12,105	13,358
Maryland . . .	16/18	16	23.5	S	692	747	0.93	639	17.83	11,390	12,299
Massachusetts	17/18	16½	21	No	705	611	1.15	683	18.60	12,702	11.003
Michigan . . .	16/18	14	15	S	687	773	0.89	649	17.42	11,309	12,722
Minnesota . .	16/18	15	20	S	571	739	0.77	708	16.95	11,993	15,522
Mississippi . .	15	—	18.2	P	727	728	1.00	819	16.10	13,191	13,211
Missouri	16	—	13.03	S	715	766	0.93	823	15.68	12,906	13,823
Montana . . .	15/16	13	21.4	S	747	948	0.79	687	15.80	10,857	13,774
Nebraska . . .	16	14	24.3	S	683	882	0.78	664	15.12	10,036	12,947
Nevada	16	14	24	S	659	686	0.96	887	13.45	11,926	12,417
New Hampshire .	16/18	16	18.6	No	763	820	0.93	611	17.95	10,960	11,779
New Jersey .	17	16	10.5	S	720	711	1.01	670	16.04	10,743	10,616
New Mexico .	15/16	—	17	P	694	853	0.81	769	16.53	12,702	15,620
New York . . .	17/18	16	22.89	P	568	541	1.05	650	16.96	11,018	10,499
North Carolina	16/18	—	21.9	P	675	774	0.87	724	17.18	12,439	14,258
North Dakota .	16	14	17	No**	669	990	0.68	654	14.47	9,466	14,006
Ohio	16/18	14	21	S	679	794	0.86	630	17.00	10,709	12,521
Oklahoma . .	16	—	17	S	717	841	0.85	727	17.65	12,827	15,034
Oregon	16	14	22	P	757	858	0.88	662	15.53	10,276	11,649
Pennsylvania .	17/18	16	22.4	S	660	672	0.98	672	16.15	10,859	11,050
Rhode Island .	16/18	—	26	S	668	626	1.07	623	18.26	11,381	10,664
South Carolina	16	15	16	S	667	694	0.96	837	16.66	13,943	14,521
South Dakota	16	14	18	No	700	999	0.70	661	14.46	9,560	13,630
Tennessee . .	16	14	20	S	673	917	0.73	638	16.30	10,407	14,175
Texas	16/18	15	20	P	642	732	0.88	763	16.38	12,504	14,255
Utah	16/18	—	19	S	591	695	0.85	720	17.37	12,516	14,713
Vermont . . .	18	16	16	S***	726	788	0.92	734	17.91	13,137	14,250
Virginia	16/19	—	17.5	S	698	799	0.87	693	17.55	12,166	13,922
Washington . .	16/18	—	23	S	673	878	0.77	591	17.85	10,548	13,756
West Virginia .	16/18	16	20.35	S***	713	707	1.01	765	16.44	12,585	12,484
Wisconsin . . .	16/18	14	22.2	S	672	744	0.90	673	18.32	12,336	13,660
Wyoming . . .	16	14	9	S	725	1,019	0.71	938	13.65	12,801	17,983
Average . . .					**662**	**747**	**0.89**	**683**	**16.89**	**11,532**	**13,006**

(1) Unrestricted operation of private passenger car. When 2 ages are shown, license is issued at lower age upon completion of approved driver education course. (2) Juvenile license issued with consent of parent or guardian. (3) P = an officer may stop a vehicle for a violation (primary); S = an officer may only issue a seat belt citation when the vehicle is stopped for another moving violation (secondary); *Although the Georgia law is secondary, for persons 4-18 years of age it is enforced primarily. **North Dakota enacted a seat belt law to be enforced secondarily; however, the law may not go into effect depending on the outcome of a referendum in the June 1994 election. ***The Vermont law is effective 1/1/94; the West Virginia law is effective 9/1/93.

U.S. Car Sales by Vehicle Size and Type, 1983-1992

Source: American Automobile Manufacturers Assn.

Year	Small	Midsize	Large	Luxury	Total
1992	32.9%	44.5%	9.2%	13.4%	100.0%
1991	35.7	42.6	8.3	13.4	100.0
1990	35.2	42.8	9.5	12.5	100.0
1989	38.6	41.9	9.9	11.8	100.0
1988	37.6	42.5	10.0	9.9	100.0
1987	38.4	42.3	9.1	10.2	100.0
1986	37.6	42.5	9.8	10.1	100.0
1985	37.9	42.1	9.8	10.2	100.0
1984	39.1	39.6	11.6	9.7	100.0
1983	38.8	40.6	10.7	9.9	100.0

U.S. Car Sales by Type of Buyer, 1980-1992

Source: American Automobile Manufacturers Assn.

Year	Sales in Thousands: Consumer	Business	Government	Total	% of Total Sales: Consumer	Business
1992	4,569	3,679	104	8,352	54.7%	44.0%
1991	4,538	3,752	97	8,387	54.1	44.8
1990	5,768	3,567	149	9,484	60.8	37.6
1989	6,375	3,402	136	9,913	64.3	34.3
1988	6,802	3,699	138	10,639	63.9	34.8
1987	6,748	3,395	135	10,278	65.7	33.0
1986	7,658	3,666	127	11,450	66.9	32.0
1985	7,083	3,822	134	11,039	64.2	34.6
1984	6,590	3,669	135	10,394	63.4	35.3
1983	6,054	3,006	119	9,179	66.0	32.7
1982	5,285	2,593	102	7,980	66.2	32.5
1981	5,623	2,787	116	8,535	66.0	32.7
1980	6,062	2,791	126	8,979	67.5	31.1

Domestic and Imported Retail Car Sales in the U.S., 1980-1992

Source: American Automobile Manufacturers Assn.

Calendar Year	Domestic	Imports: From Japan	From Germany	Other Countries	Total Imports	Total U.S. Sales	Import Percent Total	Japan	U.S. Sponsored Imports
1980	6,581,307	1,905,968	305,219	186,700	2,397,887	8,979,194	26.7	21.2	223,310
1981	6,208,760	1,858,896	282,881	185,502	2,327,279	8,536,039	27.3	21.8	174,665
1982	5,758,586	1,801,969	247,080	174,508	2,223,557	7,982,143	27.9	22.6	139,767
1983	6,795,295	1,915,621	279,748	191,403	2,386,772	9,182,067	26.0	20.9	138,798
1984	7,951,523	1,906,206	344,416	188,220	2,438,842	10,390,365	23.5	18.3	116,965
1985	8,204,542	2,217,837	423,983	195,925	2,837,745	11,042,287	25.7	20.1	206,252
1986	8,214,897	2,382,614	443,721	418,286	3,244,621	11,459,518	28.3	20.8	314,358
1987	7,080,858	2,190,405	347,881	657,465	3,195,751	10,276,609	31.1	21.3	348,154
1988	7,526,038	2,022,602	280,099	700,991	3,003,692	10,529,730	28.5	19.2	393,412
1989	7,072,902	1,897,143	248,561	553,660	2,699,364	9,772,266	27.6	19.4	340,425
1990	6,896,888	1,719,384	265,116	418,823	2,403,323	9,300,211	25.8	18.5	296,778
1991	6,136,757	1,500,309	192,776	344,814	2,037,899	8,174,656	24.9	18.4	254,572
1992	6,276,557	1,452,737	200,851	283,939	1,937,527	8,214,084	23.6	17.7	228,927

World Motor Vehicle Production, 1950-1992

Source: American Automobile Manufacturers Assn.

(in thousands)

Year	United States	Canada	Europe	Japan	Other	World Total	U.S. % of World Total
1992	9,702	1,968	17,244	12,499	5,964	47,377	20.5
1991	8,811	1,873	17,527	13,245	5,040	46,496	19.0
1990	9,783	1,928	18,651	13,487	4,496	48,345	20.2
1989	10,874	2,002	18,979	13,026	4,220	49,101	22.1
1988	11,214	1,949	18,234	12,700	4,113	48,210	23.3
1987	10,925	1,635	17,548	12,249	3,546	45,903	23.8
1986	11,335	1,854	16,727	12,260	3,121	45,297	25.0
1985	11,653	1,933	16,015	12,271	2,939	44,811	26.0
1984	10,925	1,829	15,290	11,465	2,549	42,058	26.0
1983	9,225	1,525	15,706	11,112	2,187	39,755	23.2
1982	6,986	1,276	14,808	10,732	2,311	36,113	19.3
1981	7,943	1,289	14,439	11,180	2,379	37,230	21.3
1980	8,010	1,324	15,445	11,043	2,692	38,514	20.8
1970	8,284	1,160	13,033	5,289	1,637	29,403	28.2
1960	7,905	398	6,837	482	866	16,488	47.9
1950	8,006	388	1,991	32	160	10,577	75.7

Note: As far as can be determined, production refers to vehicles locally manufactured.

World Motor Vehicle Production, 1992

Source: American Automobile Manufacturers Assn.

Country	Passenger Cars	Commercial Vehicles	Total
Argentina	220,498	41,445	261,943
Australia	279,550	4,858	284,408
Austria	23,479	4,491	27,970
Belgium	222,680	75,392	298,072
Brazil	814,423	257,141	1,071,564
Canada	1,024,739	943,758	1,968,497
China	180,000	900,000	1,080,000
Commonwealth of Independent States	930,000	600,000	1,530,000
Czechoslovakia	202,450	26,608	229,058
France	3,329,490	438,310	3,767,800
Germany	4,863,721	330,221	5,193,942
Hungary	12,000	6,000	18,000
India	153,867	170,518	324,385
Italy	1,476,627	209,860	1,686,487
Japan	9,378,694	3,120,590	12,499,284
Korea, South	1,306,752	422,944	1,729,696
Malaysia	117,773	11,414	129,187
Mexico	778,413	304,678	1,083,091
Netherlands	94,019	23,973	117,992
Poland	200,000	30,000	230,000
Spain	1,790,615	331,272	2,121,887
Sweden	293,499	63,096	356,595
United Kingdom	1,291,880	248,453	1,540,333
United States	5,663,284	4,038,218	9,701,502
Yugoslavia	116,391	9,250	125,641
Total	**34,764,844**	**12,612,490**	**47,377,334**

Note: As far as can be determined, production in this table refers to vehicles locally manufactured.

Top Selling Passenger Cars in the U.S. by Calendar Year, 1989-1992 (Domestic and Import)

Source: American Automobile Manufacturers Assn.

1992

Rank	Car	Sales
1.	Ford Taurus	409,751
2.	Honda Accord	393,477
3.	Toyota Camry	286,602
4.	Ford Escort	236,622
5.	Honda Civic/CRX	219,228
6.	Chevrolet Lumina	218,114
7.	Chevrolet Cavalier	212,374
8.	Pontiac Grand Am	210,332
9.	Ford Tempo	207,173
10.	Saturn	196,126
11.	Toyota Corolla	196,118
12.	Chevrolet Corsica/Beretta	166,625
13.	Nissan Sentra	158,909
14.	Buick LeSabre	138,409
15.	Cadillac DeVille/Fleetwood	127,766
16.	Oldsmobile Ciera	117,292
17.	Mercury Sable	116,623
18.	Lincoln Town Car	115,075
19.	Buick Century	114,273
20.	Pontiac Grand Prix	103,517

1991

Rank	Car	Sales
1.	Honda Accord	399,297
2.	Ford Taurus	299,659
3.	Toyota Camry	263,818
4.	Chevrolet Cavalier	259,385
5.	Ford Escort	247,864
6.	Chevrolet Corsica/Beretta	231,227
7.	Chevrolet Lumina	217,555
8.	Honda Civic	205,715
9.	Toyota Corolla	199,083
10.	Ford Tempo	189,457

1990

Rank	Car	Sales
1.	Honda Accord	417,179
2.	Ford Taurus	313,274
3.	Chevrolet Cavalier	295,123
4.	Ford Escort	288,727
5.	Toyota Camry	284,595
6.	Chevrolet Corsica/Beretta	277,176
7.	Toyota Corolla	228,211
8.	Honda Civic	220,852
9.	Chevrolet Lumina	218,288
10.	Ford Tempo	215,290

1989

Rank	Car	Sales
1.	Honda Accord	362,707
2.	Ford Taurus	348,081
3.	Ford Escort	333,535
4.	Chevrolet Corsica/Beretta	328,006
5.	Chevrolet Cavalier	295,715
6.	Toyota Camry	257,466
7.	Ford Tempo	228,426
8.	Nissan Sentra	221,292
9.	Pontiac Grand Am	202,185
10.	Toyota Corolla	199,975

Licensed Drivers, by Age

Source: Federal Highway Administration, U.S. Dept. of Transportation

Age	1991 Male	1991 Female	1991 Total	1991 Percent male	Estimated 1992 Male (1,000)	Estimated 1992 Female (1,000)	Estimated 1992 Total (1,000)	Percent change total drivers 1981-1991
Under 16	34,738	30,372	65,110	53.35	35,335	30,750	66,085	−36.79
16	738,889	654,916	1,393,806	53.01	751,593	663,057	1,414,650	−18.30
17	1,098,120	970,474	2,068,595	53.09	1,117,000	982,538	2,099,538	−23.81
18	1,310,554	1,155,524	2,466,078	53.14	1,333,086	1,169,888	2,502,974	−22.74
19	1,490,071	1,330,268	2,820,339	52.83	1,515,689	1,346,804	2,862,493	−19.42
(19 and under)	4,672,373	4,141,555	8,813,928	53.01	4,752,703	4,193,037	8,945,740	−21.42
20	1,658,907	1,510,566	3,169,472	52.34	1,687,427	1,529,343	3,216,770	−12.54
21	1,749,527	1,604,432	3,353,959	52.16	1,779,606	1,624,376	3,403,982	−10.66
22	1,739,128	1,602,800	3,341,927	52.04	1,769,028	1,622,724	3,391,752	−12.68
23	1,770,181	1,625,316	3,395,497	52.13	1,800,615	1,645,521	3,446,136	−12.85
24	1,799,897	1,654,267	3,454,164	52.11	1,830,841	1,674,831	3,505,672	−12.64
(20-24)	8,717,640	7,997,380	16,715,020	52.15	8,867,517	8,096,795	16,964,312	−12.28
25-29	10,077,882	9,474,395	19,552,277	51.54	10,251,144	9,592,169	19,843,313	1.76
30-34	10,602,820	10,166,862	20,769,681	51.05	10,785,108	10,293,245	21,078,353	17.88
35-39	9,909,582	9,598,466	19,508,047	50.80	10,079,951	9,717,783	19,797,734	35.68
40-44	8,853,965	8,625,425	17,479,390	50.65	9,006,186	8,732,646	17,738,832	53.01
45-49	6,984,470	6,712,628	13,697,098	50.99	7,104,550	6,796,072	13,900,622	35.27
50-54	5,533,913	5,282,952	10,816,865	51.16	5,629,055	5,348,624	10,977,679	7.99
55-59	4,873,679	4,628,134	9,501,813	51.29	4,957,469	4,685,666	9,643,135	−2.54
60-64	4,710,051	4,492,971	9,203,022	51.18	4,791,028	4,548,823	9,339,851	8.74
65-69	4,294,243	4,166,932	8,461,175	50.75	4,368,071	4,218,731	8,586,802	25.89
70 and over	7,434,760	7,041,999	14,476,759	51.36	7,562,581	7,129,537	14,692,118	59.21
Total	86,665,378	82,329,699	168,995,077	51.28	88,155,363	83,353,128	171,508,491	14.90

Some Countries with Safety Belt Use Laws

Source: American Automobile Manufacturers Assn.

Country	Effective Date
Australia	1/72
Austria	7/76
Belgium	6/75
Brazil	6/72
Bulgaria	1976
Canadian Provinces	
Alberta	7/87
British Columbia	10/77
Manitoba	4/84
Newfoundland	7/82
New Brunswick	11/83
Nova Scotia	1/85
Ontario	1/76
Prince Edward Island	1/88
Quebec	7/76
Saskatchewan	7/77
Denmark	1/76
Finland	7/75
France	10/79
Greece	12/79
Hong Kong	10/83
Hungary	7/77
Iceland	10/81
Ireland	2/79
Israel	7/75
Ivory Coast	1970
Japan	12/71
Jordan	12/83
Luxembourg	6/75
Malaysia	4/79
Netherlands	6/75
New Zealand	6/72
Norway	9/75
Poland	1/84
Portugal	1/78
Singapore	7/81
South Africa	12/77
Spain	10/74
Sweden	1/75
Switzerland	1/76
Turkey	10/84

Tips for Fuel-Efficient Driving

Source: U.S. Environmental Protection Agency

When Buying a New Vehicle

- **Buy the type of vehicle that best suits your needs.** Check the federal *Gas Mileage Guide*, available free at all auto dealerships, to compare the fuel economy of similar models. In general, *larger displacement engines and higher horsepower ratings will result in lower fuel economy.* The additional power and torque may be useful for mountain driving or trailer towing situations, but your fuel economy will suffer during almost all types of driving. *Avoid unnecessary optional equipment* (especially heavy options such as four-wheel drive and options such as air conditioning that tax the engine). Extra equipment adds weight and decreases fuel economy. Beware of "sport" packages, which often include fuel-guzzling features (such as energy robbing tires) not reflected by *Guide* mileage values.

Conserving Fuel with Your Current Vehicle:

- **Drive your vehicle wisely.** *Avoid idles* of more than one minute (turn off your engine in traffic jams, limit vehicle warm-ups in winter, park and go in instead of using drive up lanes at restaurants and banks). *Go easy on the brakes and gas pedal* (anticipate stops and avoid "jack-rabbit" starts). Pay attention to speed. *You can improve your fuel economy about 15 percent by driving 55 mph rather than 65 mph.* Put your vehicle's transmission into overdrive or a "fuel economy" position when cruising on the highway. If you have manual transmission, follow recommended shift guidelines or heed your shift indicator light. *Do not carry unneeded items* that add weight. Reduce drag by placing items inside the vehicle or trunk rather than on roof racks. *Use air conditioning only when necessary.*
- **Maintain your vehicle regularly.** *Periodic tune-ups improve vehicle fuel economy and performance.* Dragging brakes, low transmission fluid levels, out of tune engines, and old plugged fuel or air filters all hurt fuel economy. *Inflate tires* to maximum recommended pressure and perform periodic *wheel alignments. Use energy conserving oils* which increase fuel economy by reducing internal engine friction (the best are labeled "Energy Conserving II").
- **Keep track of your vehicle's fuel economy.** A marked increase in the amount of fuel you use could indicate the need for a tune-up or for necessary repairs.
- **Use your vehicle effectively.** *Use your vehicle only when necessary.* Combine errands into one trip. If you have access to more than one vehicle, drive the one that's most fuel efficient whenever possible. Consider carpooling, bicycling, walking, or public transportation.

How Americans Get to Work[1]

Source: Bureau of the Census, U.S. Dept. of Commerce

Means of Transportation	1990 Number	1990 Percent	1980 Number	1980 Percent
Workers 16 years and over	115,070,274	100.0	96,617,296	100.0
Car, truck, or van	99,592,932	86.5	81,258,496	84.1
Drove alone	84,215,298	73.2	62,193,449	64.4
Carpool	15,377,634	13.4	19,065,047	19.7
Public transportation	6,069,589	5.3	6,175,061	6.4
Bus or trolley bus[2]	3,445,000	3.0	3,924,787	4.1
Streetcar or trolley car[2]	78,130	0.1	—	—
Subway or elevated	1,755,476	1.5	1,528,852	1.6
Railroad	574,052	0.5	554,089	0.6
Ferryboat	37,497	0.0	—	—
Taxicab	179,434	0.2	167,133	0.2
Motorcycle	237,404	0.2	419,007	0.4
Bicycle	466,856	0.4	468,348	0.5
Walked	4,488,886	3.9	5,413,248	5.6
Other means	808,582	0.7	703,273	0.7
Worked at home	3,406,025	3.0	2,179,863	2.3

(1) Means of transportation used to commute to and from work. (2) This category was "Bus or streetcar" in 1980.

Personal Consumption Expenditures for Transportation

Source: American Automobile Manufacturers Assn.; Bureau of Economic Analysis, U.S. Dept. of Commerce; in millions of dollars

	1980	1982	1984	1986	1988	1990	1991	1992
User-Operated Transportation								
New Autos	$46,395	$53,336	$77,560	$100,328	$101,041	$96,692	$79,500	$85,374
Net Purchases of Used Autos	10,848	13,551	21,152	25,356	30,532	33,663	35,782	38,464
Other Motor Vehicles[1]	11,489	15,605	28,589	40,818	45,577	49,586	47,155	55,923
Tires, Tubes, and Accessories and Parts	14,889	15,230	17,302	18,353	20,685	22,483	23,006	23,948
Repair, Greasing, Washing, Parking, Storage, and Rental	33,662	37,903	49,723	60,695	73,531	82,538	83,678	87,511
Gasoline and Oil	86,689	94,125	94,532	79,699	86,899	108,471	105,459	105,446
Bridge, Tunnel, Ferry, and Road Tolls	1,104	1,306	1,387	1,794	1,774	2,024	2,021	2,115
Insurance Premiums, Less Claims Paid	9,443	9,150	10,099	12,724	16,842	18,066	21,826	25,200
Total User-Operated Transportation	**$214,879**	**$240,205**	**$300,344**	**$339,767**	**$376,881**	**$413,523**	**$398,427**	**$423,979**
Purchased Local Transportation								
Transit Systems	$2,927	$3,839	$4,244	$4,913	$5,377	$5,707	$5,707	$5,696
Taxicabs	1,866	1,513	2,498	2,998	2,935	3,209	3,358	3,394
Total Purchased Local Transportation	**$4,793**	**$5,352**	**$6,742**	**$7,911**	**$8,312**	**$8,916**	**$9,065**	**$9,090**
Purchased Intercity Transportation								
Railway Excluding Commutation	$300	$317	$415	$472	$588	$708	$722	$699
Bus	1,403	1,665	1,632	1,469	2,181	1,396	1,521	1,378
Airline	13,454	14,708	17,721	18,993	22,993	26,467	25,842	25,867
Other	910	1,173	1,380	1,737	2,229	2,644	2,651	2,672
Total Purchased Intercity Transportation	**$15,057**	**$17,861**	**$21,128**	**$22,671**	**$27,991**	**$31,215**	**$30,736**	**$30,616**
Total Transportation	**$235,739**	**$263,416**	**$328,214**	**$370,349**	**$413,184**	**$453,654**	**$438,228**	**$463,685**
Total Personal Consumption Expenditures	**$1,748,077**	**$2,059,179**	**$2,460,288**	**$2,850,553**	**$3,296,126**	**$3,748,417**	**$3,887,689**	**$4,095,823**

(1) New and used trucks, recreation vehicles, etc.

Road Mileage Between Selected U.S. Cities

	Atlanta	Boston	Chicago	Cincinnati	Cleveland	Dallas	Denver	Des Moines	Detroit	Houston
Atlanta, Ga.	...	1,037	674	440	672	795	1,398	870	699	789
Boston, Mass.	1,037	...	963	840	628	1,748	1,949	1,280	695	1,804
Chicago, Ill.	674	963	...	287	335	917	996	327	266	1,067
Cincinnati, Oh.	440	840	287	...	244	920	1,164	571	259	1,029
Cleveland, Oh.	672	628	335	244	...	1,159	1,321	652	170	1,273
Dallas Tex.	795	1,748	917	920	1,159	...	781	684	1,143	243
Denver, Col.	1,398	1,949	996	1,164	1,321	781	...	669	1,253	1,019
Detroit, Mich.	699	695	266	259	170	1,143	1,253	584	...	1,265
Houston, Tex.	789	1,804	1,067	1,029	1,273	243	1,019	905	1,265	...
Indianapolis, Ind.	493	906	181	106	294	865	1,058	465	278	987
Kansas City, Mo.	798	1,391	499	591	779	489	600	195	743	710
Los Angeles, Cal.	2,182	2,979	2,054	2,179	2,367	1,387	1,059	1,727	2,311	1,538
Memphis, Tenn.	371	1,296	530	468	712	452	1,040	599	713	561
Milwaukee, Wis.	761	1,050	87	374	422	991	1,029	361	353	1,142
Minneapolis, Minn.	1,068	1,368	405	692	740	936	841	252	671	1,157
New Orleans, La.	479	1,507	912	786	1,030	496	1,273	978	1,045	356
New York, N.Y.	841	206	802	647	473	1,552	1,771	1,119	637	1,608
Omaha, Neb.	986	1,412	459	693	784	644	537	132	716	865
Philadelphia, Pa.	741	296	738	567	413	1,452	1,691	1,051	573	1,508
Pittsburgh, Pa.	687	561	452	287	129	1,204	1,411	763	287	1,313
Portland Ore.	2,601	3,046	2,083	2,333	2,418	2,009	1,238	1,786	2,349	2,205
St. Louis, Mo.	541	1,141	289	340	529	630	857	333	513	779
San Francisco	2,496	3,095	2,142	2,362	2,467	1,753	1,235	1,815	2,399	1,912
Seattle, Wash.	2,618	2,976	2,013	2,300	2,348	2,078	1,307	1,749	2,279	2,274
Tulsa, Okla.	772	1,537	683	736	925	257	681	443	909	478
Wash., D.C.	608	429	671	481	346	1,319	1,616	984	506	1,375

	Indianapolis	Kansas City	Los Angeles	Louisville	Memphis	Milwaukee	Minneapolis	New Orleans	New York	Omaha
Atlanta, Ga.	493	798	2,182	382	371	761	1,068	479	841	986
Boston, Mass.	906	1,391	2,979	941	1,296	1,050	1,368	1,507	206	1,412
Chicago, Ill.	181	499	2,054	292	530	87	405	912	802	459
Cincinnati, Oh.	106	591	2,179	101	468	374	692	786	647	693
Cleveland Oh.	294	779	2,367	345	712	422	740	1,030	473	784
Dallas, Tex.	865	489	1,387	819	452	991	936	496	1,552	644
Denver, Col.	1,058	600	1,059	1,120	1,040	1,029	841	1,273	1,771	537
Detroit, Mich.	278	743	2,311	360	713	353	671	1,045	637	716
Houston, Tex.	987	710	1,538	928	561	1,142	1,157	356	1,608	865
Indianapolis, Ind.	...	485	2,073	111	435	268	586	796	713	587
Kansas City, Mo.	485	...	1,589	520	451	537	447	806	1,198	201
Los Angeles, Cal.	2,073	1,589	...	2,108	1,817	2,087	1,889	1,883	2,786	1,595
Memphis, Tenn.	435	451	1,817	367	...	612	826	390	1,100	652
Milwaukee, Wis.	268	537	2,087	379	612	...	332	994	889	493
Minneapolis, Minn.	586	447	1,889	697	826	332	...	1,214	1,207	357
New Orleans, La.	796	806	1,883	685	390	994	1,214	...	1,311	1,007
New York, N.Y.	713	1,198	2,786	748	1,100	889	1,207	1,311	...	1,251
Omaha, Neb.	587	201	1,595	687	652	493	357	1,007	1,251	...
Philadelphia, Pa.	633	1,118	2,706	668	1,000	825	1,143	1,211	100	1,183
Pittsburgh, Pa.	353	838	2,426	388	752	539	857	1,070	368	895
Portland, Ore.	1,227	1,809	959	2,320	2,259	2,010	1,678	2,505	2,885	1,654
St. Louis, Mo.	235	257	1,845	263	285	363	552	673	948	449
San Francisco	2,256	1,835	379	2,349	2,125	2,175	1,940	2,249	2,934	1,683
Seattle, Wash.	2,194	1,839	1,131	2,305	2,290	1,940	1,608	2,574	2,815	1,638
Tulsa, Okla.	631	248	1,452	659	401	757	695	647	1,344	387
Washington, D.C.	558	1,043	2,631	582	867	758	1,076	1,078	233	1,116

	Philadelphia	Pittsburgh	Portland	St. Louis	Salt Lake City	San Francisco	Seattle	Toledo	Tulsa	Wash., D.C.
Atlanta, Ga.	741	687	2,601	541	1,878	2,496	2,618	640	772	608
Boston, Mass.	296	561	3,046	1,141	2,343	3,095	2,976	739	1,537	429
Chicago, Ill.	738	452	2,083	289	1,390	2,142	2,013	232	683	671
Cincinnati, Oh.	567	287	2,333	340	1,610	2,362	2,300	200	736	481
Cleveland Oh.	413	129	2,418	529	1,715	2,467	2,348	111	925	346
Dallas, Tex.	1,452	1,204	2,009	630	1,242	1,753	2,078	1,084	257	1,319
Denver, Col.	1,691	1,411	1,238	857	504	1,235	1,307	1,218	681	1,616
Detroit, Mich.	576	287	2,349	513	1,647	2,399	2,279	59	909	506
Houston, Tex.	1,508	1,313	2,205	779	1,438	1,912	2,274	1,206	478	1,375
Indianapolis, Ind.	633	353	2,227	235	1,504	2,256	2,194	219	631	558
Kansas City, Mo.	1,118	838	1,809	257	1,086	1,835	1,839	687	248	1,043
Los Angeles, Cal.	2,706	2,426	959	1,845	715	379	1,131	2,276	1,452	2,631
Memphis, Tenn.	1,000	752	2,259	285	1,535	2,125	2,290	654	401	867
Milwaukee, Wis.	825	539	2,010	363	1,423	2,175	1,940	319	757	758
Minneapolis, Minn.	1,143	857	1,678	552	1,186	1,940	1,608	637	695	1,076
New Orleans, La.	1,211	1,070	2,505	673	1,738	2,249	2,574	986	647	1,078
New York, N.Y.	100	368	2,885	948	2,182	2,934	2,815	578	1,344	233
Omaha, Neb.	1,183	895	1,654	449	931	1,683	1,638	681	387	1,116
Philadelphia, Pa.	...	288	2,821	868	2,114	2,866	2,751	514	1,264	133
Pittsburgh, Pa.	288	...	2,535	588	1,826	2,578	2,465	228	984	221
Portland, Ore.	2,821	2,535	...	2,060	767	636	172	2,315	1,913	2,754
St. Louis, Mo.	868	588	2,060	...	1,337	2,089	2,081	454	396	793
San Francisco	2,866	2,578	636	2,089	752	...	808	2,364	1,760	2,799
Seattle, Wash.	2,751	2,465	172	2,081	836	808	...	2,245	1,982	2,684
Tulsa, Okla.	1,264	984	1,913	396	1,172	1,760	1,982	850	...	1,189
Washington, D.C.	133	221	2,754	793	2,047	2,799	2,684	447	1,189	...

Air Distances Between Selected World Cities in Statute Miles

Point-to-point measurements are usually from City Hall.

	Bangkok	Beijing	Berlin	Cairo	Cape Town	Caracas	Chicago	Hong Kong	Honolulu	Lima
Bangkok	...	2,046	5,352	4,523	6,300	10,555	8,570	1,077	6,609	12,244
Beijing	2,046	...	4,584	4,698	8,044	8,950	6,604	1,217	5,077	10,349
Berlin	5,352	4,584	...	1,797	5,961	5,238	4,414	5,443	7,320	6,896
Cairo	4,523	4,698	1,797	...	4,480	6,342	6,141	5,066	8,848	7,726
Cape Town	6,300	8,044	5,961	4,480	...	6,366	8,491	7,376	11,535	6,072
Caracas	10,555	8,950	5,238	6,342	6,366	...	2,495	10,165	6,021	1,707
Chicago	8,570	6,604	4,414	6,141	8,491	2,495	...	7,797	4,256	3,775
Hong Kong	1,077	1,217	5,443	5,066	7,376	10,165	7,797	...	5,556	11,418
Honolulu	6,609	5,077	7,320	8,848	11,535	6,021	4,256	5,556	...	5,947
London	5,944	5,074	583	2,185	5,989	4,655	3,958	5,990	7,240	6,316
Los Angeles	7,637	6,250	5,782	7,520	9,969	3,632	1,745	7,240	2,557	4,171
Madrid	6,337	5,745	1,165	2,087	5,308	4,346	4,189	6,558	7,872	5,907
Melbourne	4,568	5,643	9,918	8,675	6,425	9,717	9,673	4,595	5,505	8,059
Mexico City	9,793	7,753	6,056	7,700	8,519	2,234	1,690	8,788	3,789	2,639
Montreal	8,338	6,519	3,740	5,427	7,922	2,438	745	7,736	4,918	3,970
Moscow	4,389	3,607	1,006	1,803	6,279	6,177	4,987	4,437	7,047	7,862
New York	8,669	6,844	3,979	5,619	7,803	2,120	714	8,060	4,969	3,639
Paris	5,877	5,120	548	1,998	5,786	4,732	4,143	5,990	7,449	6,370
Rio de Janeiro	9,994	10,768	6,209	6,143	3,781	2,804	5,282	11,009	8,288	2,342
Rome	5,494	5,063	737	1,326	5,231	5,195	4,824	5,774	8,040	6,750
San Francisco	7,931	5,918	5,672	7,466	10,248	3,902	1,859	6,905	2,398	4,518
Singapore	883	2,771	6,164	5,137	6,008	11,402	9,372	1,605	6,726	11,689
Stockholm	5,089	4,133	528	2,096	6,423	5,471	4,331	5,063	6,875	7,166
Tokyo	2,865	1,307	5,557	5,958	9,154	8,808	6,314	1,791	3,859	9,631
Warsaw	5,033	4,325	322	1,619	5,935	5,559	4,679	5,147	7,366	7,215
Washington, D.C.	8,807	6,942	4,181	5,822	7,895	2,047	596	8,155	4,838	3,509

	London	Los Angeles	Madrid	Melbourne	Mexico City	Montreal	Moscow	New Delhi	New York	Paris
Bangkok	5,944	7,637	6,337	4,568	9,793	8,338	4,389	1,813	8,669	5,877
Beijing	5,074	6,250	5,745	5,643	7,753	6,519	3,607	2,353	6,844	5,120
Berlin	583	5,782	1,165	9,918	6,056	3,740	1,006	3,598	3,979	548
Cairo	2,185	7,520	2,087	8,675	7,700	5,427	1,803	2,758	5,619	1,998
Cape Town	5,989	9,969	5,308	6,425	8,519	7,922	6,279	5,769	7,803	5,786
Caracas	4,655	3,632	4,346	9,717	2,234	2,438	6,177	8,833	2,120	4,732
Chicago	3,958	1,745	4,189	9,673	1,690	745	4,987	7,486	714	4,143
Hong Kong	5,990	7,240	6,558	4,595	8,788	7,736	4,437	2,339	8,060	5,990
Honolulu	7,240	2,557	7,872	5,505	3,789	4,918	7,047	7,412	4,969	7,449
London	...	5,439	785	10,500	5,558	3,254	1,564	4,181	3,469	214
Los Angeles	5,439	...	5,848	7,931	1,542	2,427	6,068	7,011	2,451	5,601
Madrid	785	5,848	...	10,758	5,643	3,448	2,147	4,530	3,593	655
Melbourne	10,500	7,931	10,758	...	8,426	10,395	8,950	6,329	10,359	10,430
Mexico City	5,558	1,542	5,643	8,426	...	2,317	6,676	9,120	2,090	5,725
Montreal	3,254	2,427	3,448	10,395	2,317	...	4,401	7,012	331	3,432
Moscow	1,564	6,068	2,147	8,950	6,676	4,401	...	2,698	4,683	1,554
New York	3,469	2,451	3,593	10,359	2,090	331	4,683	7,318	...	3,636
Paris	214	5,601	655	10,430	5,725	3,432	1,554	4,102	3,636	...
Rio de Janeiro	5,750	6,330	5,045	8,226	4,764	5,078	7,170	8,753	4,801	5,684
Rome	895	6,326	851	9,929	6,377	4,104	1,483	3,684	4,293	690
San Francisco	5,367	347	5,803	7,856	1,887	2,543	5,885	7,691	2,572	5,577
Singapore	6,747	8,767	7,080	3,759	10,327	9,203	5,228	2,571	9,534	6,673
Stockholm	942	5,454	1,653	9,630	6,012	3,714	716	3,414	3,986	1,003
Tokyo	5,959	5,470	6,706	5,062	7,035	6,471	4,660	3,638	6,757	6,053
Warsaw	905	5,922	1,427	9,598	6,337	4,022	721	3,277	4,270	852
Washington, D.C.	3,674	2,300	3,792	10,180	1,885	489	4,876	7,500	205	3,840

	Rio de Janiero	Rome	San Francisco	Singapore	Stockholm	Teheran	Tokyo	Vienna	Warsaw	Wash., D.C.
Bangkok	9,994	5,494	7,931	883	5,089	3,391	2,865	5,252	5,033	8,807
Beijing	10,768	5,063	5,918	2,771	4,133	3,490	1,307	4,648	4,325	6,942
Berlin	6,209	737	5,672	6,164	528	2,185	5,557	326	322	4,181
Cairo	6,143	1,326	7,466	5,137	2,096	1,234	5,958	1,481	1,619	5,822
Cape Town	3,781	5,231	10,248	6,008	6,423	5,241	9,154	5,656	5,935	7,895
Caracas	2,804	5,195	3,902	11,402	5,471	7,320	8,808	5,372	5,559	2,047
Chicago	5,282	4,824	1,859	9,372	4,331	6,502	6,314	4,698	4,679	596
Hong Kong	11,009	5,774	6,905	1,605	5,063	3,843	1,791	5,431	5,147	8,155
Honolulu	8,288	8,040	2,398	6,726	6,875	8,070	3,859	7,632	7,366	4,838
London	5,750	895	5,367	6,747	942	2,743	5,959	771	905	3,674
Los Angeles	6,330	6,326	347	8,767	5,454	7,682	5,470	6,108	5,922	2,300
Madrid	5,045	851	5,803	7,080	1,653	2,978	6,706	1,128	1,427	3,792
Melbourne	8,226	9,929	7,856	3,759	9,630	7,826	5,062	9,790	9,598	10,180
Mexico City	4,764	6,377	1,887	10,327	6,012	8,184	7,035	6,320	6,337	1,885
Montreal	5,078	4,104	2,543	9,203	3,714	5,880	6,471	4,009	4,022	489
Moscow	7,170	1,483	5,885	5,228	716	1,532	4,660	1,043	721	4,876
New York	4,801	4,293	2,572	9,534	3,986	6,141	6,757	4,234	4,270	205
Paris	5,684	690	5,577	6,673	1,003	2,625	6,053	645	852	3,840
Rio de Janeiro	...	5,707	6,613	9,785	6,683	7,374	11,532	6,127	6,455	4,779
Rome	5,707	...	6,259	6,229	1,245	2,127	6,142	477	820	4,497
San Francisco	6,613	6,259	...	8,448	5,399	7,362	5,150	5,994	5,854	2,441
Singapore	9,785	6,229	8,448	...	5,936	4,103	3,300	6,035	5,843	9,662
Stockholm	6,683	1,245	5,399	5,936	...	2,173	5,053	780	494	4,183
Tokyo	11,532	6,142	5,150	3,300	5,053	4,775	...	5,689	5,347	6,791
Warsaw	6,455	820	5,854	5,843	494	1,879	5,689	347	...	4,472
Washington, D.C.	4,779	4,497	2,441	9,662	4,183	6,341	6,791	4,438	4,472	...

EDUCATION

Historical Summary of Public Elementary and Secondary Schools

Source: National Center for Education Statistics, U.S. Dept. of Education

Pupils and teachers (thousands)	1909-10	1919-20	1929-30	1939-40	1949-50	1959-60[1]	1969-70[1]	1979-80	1989-90	1990-91
Total U.S. population	90,492	104,512	121,770	130,880	148,665	179,323	203,212	224,567	246,819	249,415
Population 5-17 years of age	24,009	27,556	31,417	30,150	30,168	43,881	52,490	48,041	44,949	45,311
Percent aged 5-17 years	26.5	26.4	25.8	23.0	20.3	24.5	25.8	21.4	18.2	18.2
Enrollment (thousands)										
Elementary and secondary	17,814	21,578	25,678	25,434	25,111	36,087	45,619	41,645	40,543	41,217
Percent pop. 5-17 enrolled	74.2	78.3	81.7	84.4	83.2	82.2	86.9	86.7	90.2	91.0
Percent in high schools	5.1	10.2	17.1	26.0	22.7	23.5	28.5	32.9	28.1	27.5
High school graduates (thousands)	111	231	592	1,143	1,063	1,627	2,589	2,748	2,320	2,237
Average school term (in days)	157.5	161.9	172.7	175.0	177.9	178.0	178.9	178.5	—	179.8
Total instructional staff	—	678	880	912	962	1,464	2,253	2,441	—	—
Teachers, librarians: Men	110	93	140	195	195	402	691	782	—	—
Women	413	565	703	681	719	985	1,440	1,518	—	—
Percent men	21.1	14.1	16.6	22.2	21.3	29.0	33.4	34.0	—	—
Revenue & expenditures (millions)										
Total revenue	$433	$970	$2,088	$2,260	$5,437	$14,746	$40,267	$96,881	$207,753	$222,823
Total expenditures	426	1,036	2,316	2,344	5,837	15,613	40,683	95,962	212,100	228,933
Current elem. and secondary	356	861	1,843	1,941	4,687	12,239	34,218	86,984	187,558	201,550
Capital outlay	69	153	370	257	1,014	2,661	4,659	6,506	17,788	19,771
Interest on school debt	—	18	92	130	100	489	1,171	1,874	3,770	4,314
Other	—	3	9	13	35	132	636	598	2,985	3,298
Salaries and pupil cost					(Data in unadjusted dollars)					
Average annual teacher salary[2]	$485	$871	$1,420	$1,441	$3,010	$5,174	$8,840	$16,715	$32,723	$34,385
Expenditure per capita total pop.	4.71	9.91	19.03	17.91	39	87	200	427	859	918
Current expenditure per pupil ADA[3]	27.85	53.32	86.70	88.09	209	375	816	2,272	4,962	5,245

(1) Because of a modification of the scope, "current expenditures for elementary and secondary schools" data for 1959-60 and later years are not entirely comparable with data for prior years. (2) Includes supervisors, principals, teachers and other non-supervisory instructional staff. (3) "ADA" means average daily attendance in elementary and secondary day schools.

1992 High School Graduates, 1991-1992 High School Drop-Outs

Source: Bureau of the Census, U.S. Dept. of Commerce; numbers in table in thousands

The proportion of the most recent high school graduates who had enrolled in colleges or universities was at an all-time high of 63 percent in the fall of 1992. In 1980 about half the most recent high school graduates had enrolled in college by the fall. Young women continued to be more likely than young men to enter colleges and universities—65 versus 60 percent. There also continued to be wide gaps in the college enrollment rates by race and ethnic group. Whereas 64 percent of the white high school graduates entered college, the enrollment rates for black and Hispanic youths were much lower—49 and 47 percent, respectively. The majority of the 1992 college freshmen (63 percent) were enrolled in 4-year institutions. Among these students, about two-fifths were combining school with some labor force activity. Among the youths enrolled in 2-year colleges, the proportion in the labor force was much higher—two-thirds. The labor force participation rate was still higher—78 percent—among the high school graduates who had not enrolled in college. The unemployment rate for this group, at 19.4 percent, was well below the jobless rate for 1991 graduates, at 25.3 percent the group's highest in 8 years. As for school dropouts, of the 400,000 youths who had dropped out of high school between October 1991 and October 1992, only about 60 percent were in the labor force. Their unemployment rate of 39.1 percent was double the rate for the year's high school graduates.

		Civilian Labor Force						
				Employed		Unemployed		
Characteristic	Civilian Non-institutional Population	Number	Participation Rate	Number	Percent of Population	Number	Percent of Labor Force	Not in Labor Force
Total 1992 high school graduates	**2,461**	**1,475**	**60.0**	**1,225**	**49.8**	**251**	**17.0**	**986**
Men	1,240	785	63.3	656	52.9	129	16.5	455
Women	1,221	690	56.5	569	46.6	121	17.6	531
White	1,954	1,220	62.4	1,060	54.3	159	13.1	734
Black	359	172	47.8	104	28.9	68	39.6	188
Hispanic origin	210	133	63.6	97	46.1	37	27.4	76
Enrolled in college	1,542	761	49.3	649	42.1	112	14.7	781
Enrolled in 2-year college	571	384	67.2	333	58.3	51	13.2	188
Enrolled in 4-year college	971	377	38.8	315	32.5	61	16.3	594
Full-time students	1,429	665	46.6	567	39.7	98	14.8	763
Part-time students	113	95	84.1	82	71.9	14	14.5	18
Men	749	367	49.0	317	42.4	49	13.5	382
Women	793	394	49.7	331	41.8	63	15.9	399
White	1,258	646	51.4	573	45.6	73	11.3	612
Black	175	58	32.8	35	20.1	22	(1)	118
Hispanic origin	120	69	57.4	48	40.2	21	(1)	51
Not enrolled in college	919	714	77.8	576	62.7	138	19.4	204
Men	491	418	85.2	339	69.0	80	19.1	73
Women	428	296	69.2	237	55.5	59	19.8	132
White	696	574	82.5	487	70.0	86	15.1	122
Black	184	114	62.0	69	37.2	46	40.0	70
Hispanic origin	90	64	71.8	48	54.1	16	(1)	25
Total 1991-1992 high school dropouts[2]	406	242	59.6	147	36.3	95	39.1	164
Men	189	130	69.1	85	45.2	45	34.7	58
Women	218	112	51.4	62	28.6	50	44.3	106
White	319	190	59.7	128	40.3	62	32.5	129
Black	66	35	52.5	7	(1)	28	(1)	31
Hispanic origin	80	40	49.9	23	28.4	17	(1)	40

(1) Data not shown where base is less than 75,000. (2) Data refer to persons who dropped out of school between October 1991 and October 1992. Note: Detail for the above race and Hispanic-origin groups will not sum to totals because data for the "other races" group are not presented and Hispanics are included in both the white and black population groups. Because of rounding, sum of individual items may not equal totals.

Fall Enrollment and Teachers in Full-time Day Schools
Elementary and Secondary Day Schools, Fall 1991

Source: National Center for Education Statistics, U.S. Dept. of Education; National Education Assn.

	Local school districts	Classroom teachers	Total enrollment	Pupils per teacher	Teacher's average pay (1991-1992)	Instructional aides	Expenditure per pupil
United States	**15,173**	**2,431,622**	**42,000,343**	**17.3**	**$34,098**	**410,498**	**$5,245**
Alabama	129	40,480	722,004	17.8	26,951	3,543	3,627
Alaska	56	7,118	118,680	16.7	44,718	1,626	8,330
Arizona	229	33,978	656,980	19.3	31,176	5,489	4,309
Arkansas	325	25,785	438,518	17.0	27,070	4,511	3,700
California	1,005	224,000	5,107,145	22.8	40,192	55,290	4,491
Colorado	176	33,093	593,030	17.9	33,072	4,441	5,064
Connecticut	166	34,383	481,050	14.0	46,971	5,547	7,602
Delaware	19	6,095	102,196	16.8	34,548	732	5,865
District of Columbia	1	6,087	80,618	13.2	38,798	308	9,259
Florida	69	109,939	1,932,131	17.6	31,070	21,384	5,276
Georgia	183	63,816	1,177,569	18.5	29,509	17,534	4,466
Hawaii	1	9,451	174,747	18.5	34,528	1,049	5,166
Idaho	114	11,626	225,680	19.4	26,334	1,402	3,386
Illinois	942	110,143	1,848,166	16.8	36,461	15,607	5,520
Indiana	296	54,546	956,994	17.5	34,809	11,912	4,930
Iowa	435	31,395	491,363	15.7	29,202	4,536	4,679
Kansas	304	29,324	445,390	15.2	30,731	3,150	4,874
Kentucky	176	37,571	646,024	17.2	30,870	7,652	4,354
Louisiana	66	46,118	765,589	16.6	25,948	8,433	4,146
Maine	283	15,416	216,400	14.0	30,097	3,386	5,458
Maryland	24	43,616	736,238	16.9	38,728	6,231	6,566
Massachusetts	352	55,963	846,155	15.1	37,256	9,009	6,366
Michigan	561	82,967	1,591,120	19.2	41,149	12,969	5,883
Minnesota	434	44,903	773,571	17.2	34,451	7,888	5,239
Mississippi	150	28,111	504,127	17.9	24,367	9,788	3,187
Missouri	543	52,306	827,404	15.8	28,895	5,009	4,754
Montana	539	9,883	155,779	15.8	27,590	1,373	5,204
Nebraska	777	19,069	279,552	14.7	27,231	3,065	5,038
Nevada	17	11,409	211,810	18.6	33,857	—	4,653
New Hampshire	174	11,464	177,138	15.5	33,170	2,253	5,672
New Jersey	608	80,515	1,109,796	13.8	41,027	10,000	8,645
New Mexico	88	17,498	308,667	17.6	26,389	4,080	3,895
New York	717	171,914	2,643,993	15.4	43,335	24,110	8,565
North Carolina	133	65,326	1,097,598	16.8	28,791	19,407	4,488
North Dakota	276	7,733	118,376	15.3	24,495	1,135	4,199
Ohio	613	103,372	1,783,767	17.3	33,243	9,229	5,245
Oklahoma	593	37,650	588,263	15.6	25,339	5,746	3,791
Oregon	296	26,745	498,614	18.6	34,100	4,746	5,683
Pennsylvania	503	100,475	1,692,797	16.8	38,715	11,316	6,541
Rhode Island	37	9,709	142,144	14.6	36,417	1,217	6,343
South Carolina	95	37,115	627,470	16.9	28,068	6,597	4,351
South Dakota	189	8,868	131,576	14.8	23,291	1,205	3,965
Tennessee	140	43,062	833,651	19.4	28,621	7,963	3,782
Texas	1,051	219,192	3,464,371	15.8	29,041	33,976	4,438
Utah	40	18,305	456,430	24.9	26,339	3,812	2,960
Vermont	279	7,031	97,137	13.8	33,646	2,052	6,738
Virginia	141	64,537	1,016,204	15.7	31,657	10,283	4,836
Washington	296	42,931	869,327	20.2	34,823	6,797	5,000
West Virginia	55	20,997	320,249	15.3	27,366	2,748	4,911
Wisconsin	428	52,028	814,671	15.7	35,227	7,741	5,871
Wyoming	49	6,564	102,074	15.6	30,425	1,221	5,723

Programs for the Disabled

Source: Office of Special Educ. and Rehabilitative Services, U.S. Dept. of Education

Number of children 0 to 21 years old served annually in educational programs for the disabled; in thousands.

Type of Disability	1982-83	1983-84	1984-85	1985-86	1986-87	1987-88	1988-89	1989-90	1990-91
All disabilities	**4,255**	**4,298**	**4,315**	**4,317**	**4,374**	**4,446**	**4,544**	**4,641**	**4,771**
Learning disabilities	1,741	1,806	1,832	1,862	1,914	1,928	1,987	2,050	2,130
Speech impairments	1,131	1,128	1,126	1,125	1,136	953	967	973	987
Mental retardation	757	727	694	660	643	582	564	548	536
Serious emotional disturbance	352	361	372	375	383	373	376	381	391
Hearing impairments	73	72	69	66	65	56	56	57	58
Orthopedic impairments	57	56	56	57	57	47	47	48	49
Visual impairments	28	29	28	27	26	22	23	22	23
Deaf-blindness	2	2	2	2	2	12	2	2	1

Note: Counts are based on reports from the 50 States, District of Columbia and Puerto Rico (i.e., figures from U.S. territories are not included). Details may not add to totals because of rounding.

Microcomputer Use by Public Elementary and Secondary Schools, 1981 to 1990[1]

Source: Digest of Education Statistics 1992, National Center for Education Statistics, U.S. Dept. of Education; in percent.

	All Schools	Elementary	Junior High	Senior High	K-12	Other
1981	18.2	11.1	25.6	42.7	—	—
1982	30.0	20.2	39.8	57.8	—	—
1983	68.4	62.4	80.5	86.1	—	—
1984	85.1	82.2	93.1	94.6	—	—
1985	92.2	91.0	97.3	97.4	—	—
1986	95.6	94.9	98.5	98.7	—	—
1987	96.4	96.0	98.6	99.0	—	—
1988	97.1	96.8	98.8	99.1	—	—
1989	97.0	96.8	98.5	99.1	—	—
1990	97.2	97.3	98.4	98.8	98.7	86.4

Notes: (1) Schools were surveyed in the Fall. — Data not available. Some data have been revised from previously published figures.

Preprimary School Enrollment: 1970 to 1992

Source: Bureau of the Census, U.S. Dept. of Commerce

As of October. Civilian noninstitutional population. Includes public and nonpublic nursery school and kindergarten programs. Excludes 5 year olds enrolled in elementary school.

Item	1970	1975	1980	1985	1986	1987	1988	1989	1990	1991	1992
Number of Children (1,000)											
Population, 3 to 5 years old	**10,949**	**10,183**	**9,284**	**10,733**	**10,866**	**10,872**	**10,894**	**11,038**	**11,207**	**11,370**	**11,544**
Total Enrolled[1]	**4,104**	**4,954**	**4,878**	**5,865**	**5,971**	**5,932**	**5,977**	**6,026**	**6,659**	**6,334**	**6,403**
Nursery school	1,094	1,745	1,981	2,477	2,545	2,555	2,621	2,825	3,378	2,824	2,857
Public	332	570	628	848	829	819	852	930	1,202	996	1,074
Private	762	1,174	1,353	1,631	1,715	1,736	1,770	1,894	2,177	1,827	1,784
Kindergarten	3,010	3,211	2,897	3,388	3,426	3,377	3,356	3,201	3,281	3,510	3,546
Public	2,498	2,682	2,438	2,847	2,859	2,842	2,875	2,704	2,767	2,968	2,996
Private	511	528	459	541	567	535	481	496	513	543	550
White	3,443	4,105	3,994	4,757	4,851	4,748	4,891	4,911	5,389	5,104	5,137
Black	586	731	725	919	892	893	814	872	964	928	966
Hispanic[2]	(NA)	(NA)	370	496	593	587	544	520	642	675	728
3 years old	454	683	857	1,035	1,041	1,022	1,028	1,005	1,205	1,075	1,081
4 years old	1,007	1,418	1,423	1,765	1,772	1,717	1,768	1,882	2,086	1,993	1,982
5 years old	2,643	2,852	2,598	3,065	3,157	3,192	3,183	3,139	3,367	3,266	3,340
Enrollment Rate											
Total enrolled[1]	**37.5**	**48.6**	**52.5**	**54.6**	**55.0**	**54.6**	**54.4**	**54.6**	**59.4**	**55.7**	**55.5**
White	37.8	48.6	52.7	54.7	55.2	54.1	55.4	55.0	59.7	56.2	55.8
Black	34.9	48.1	51.8	55.8	54.1	54.2	48.2	54.2	57.8	53.1	55.1
Hispanic[2]	(NA)	(NA)	43.3	43.3	47.8	45.5	44.2	41.6	49.0	46.4	48.4
3 years old	12.9	21.5	27.3	28.8	28.9	28.6	27.6	27.1	32.6	28.2	27.7
4 years old	27.8	40.5	46.3	49.1	49.0	47.7	49.1	51.0	56.0	53.0	52.1
5 years old	69.3	81.3	84.7	86.5	86.7	86.1	86.6	86.4	88.8	86.0	87.2

(NA) Not available. (1) Includes races not shown separately. (2) Persons of Hispanic origin may be of any race. The method of identifying Hispanic children was changed in 1980 from allocation based on status of mother to status reported for each child. Using the new method, the number of Hispanic children is larger.

Number of Private Schools and Their Enrollment in Grades K Through 12, 1990-1991

Source: National Center for Education Statistics, U.S. Dept. of Education

Selected Characteristics	Number of Schools				Kindergarten through 12th grade enrollment[1]			
	Total	Catholic	Other religious	Non-sectarian	Total	Catholic	Other religious	Non-sectarian
Total	**24,690**	**8,731**	**11,476**	**4,483**	**4,673,878**	**2,555,930**	**1,468,534**	**649,414**
School enrollment								
Less than 150	13,072	1,703	8,217	3,152	824,438	175,995	461,852	186,591
150 to 299	7,027	4,148	2,082	797	1,499,516	904,563	430,038	164,915
300 to 499	2,923	1,824	775	324	1,112,661	692,766	291,324	128,571
500 to 749	1,122	700	301	121	682,309	420,341	184,861	77,107
750 or more	546	357	101	88	554,956	362,266	100,460	92,230
Minority status								
Less than 5%	9,885	3,343	5,620	922	1,680,489	871,541	659,317	149,631
5-19%	7,115	2,474	2,962	1,679	1,492,350	757,822	462,148	272,380
20-49%	4,176	1,355	1,708	1,113	824,003	456,891	207,049	160,063
50% or more	3,515	1,559	1,187	769	677,035	469,677	140,019	67,339
Community								
Urban/central city	9,411	4,027	3,610	1,774	2,299,025	1,402,887	623,994	272,144
Suburban fringe	7,694	3,001	3,209	1,484	1,553,338	842,895	493,451	216,992
Small city/rural	7,585	1,703	4,657	1,225	821,516	310,150	351,088	160,278

(1) Includes only prekindergarten and kindergarten pupils who attend schools that offer first grade. **Note:** Details may not add to totals due to rounding.

Education and Income, 1993

Source: Bureau of the Census, U.S. Dept. of Commerce

Mean monthly income was notably different at all levels of educational attainment between whites and blacks, with whites earning more at all levels. Note: at the master's degree level, because of the sample size, the difference in mean monthly income levels was not statistically significant. Between men and women, mean monthly income was significantly different at all educational levels, with men earning more than women. The figures in the following table are based upon a sample population survey that includes a representative sample of all people, including those without a monthly income.

Level of Education	Mean Monthly Income				
	White	Black	Hispanic[1]	Male	Female
Doctorate	$4,679	N.A.[2]	N.A.[2]	$4,915	$3,162
Master's degree	3,248	$2,786	$2,840	3,748	2,614
Bachelor's degree	2,552	2,002	1,895	3,235	1,698
Some college	1,595	1,204	1,298	2,002	1,115
High school graduate	1,405	1,009	1,092	1,853	943
Some high school	909	652	760	1,116	579

N.A.= Not available. [1] Hispanic people may be of any race. [2] There were too few black and Hispanic recipients of doctoral degrees to determine monthly income.

Percent of Public School Teachers Who Are Men, 1991-1992

Source: National Education Association

Rank/State	Pct. Men
1. Massachusetts	37.9
2. Minnesota	36.8*
3. Pennsylvania	36.4
4. Oregon	36.2
5. Montana	35.4
6. Wyoming	35.3
7. Washington	34.6
8. Vermont	32.5*
9. Iowa	32.2
9. Alaska	32.2
11. North Dakota	31.6
12. Utah	31.4
12. Maine	31.4
14. New York	31.0
15. Idaho	30.8
16. California	30.3
17. Colorado	30.1
18. Illinois	30.0
18. Indiana	30.0*
20. Wisconsin	29.9
21. Kansas	29.8*
22. Connecticut	29.7
23. Nebraska	29.4
24. Ohio	29.3
25. Arizona	28.8*
26. Rhode Island	28.4
26. South Dakota	28.4
28. New Jersey	28.0
29. New Hampshire	27.7
30. New Mexico	27.2
31. Nevada	27.1
32. West Virginia	26.8
33. Delaware	26.7
34. Oklahoma	25.2
35. Michigan	24.3*
36. Maryland	23.8
37. Missouri	23.7
38. Florida	23.1
39. Arkansas	22.0
39. Tennessee	22.0
41. Texas	21.7
42. Dist. of Col.	21.6
43. Hawaii	21.5
44. Kentucky	21.2
45. Alabama	20.5
46. North Carolina	19.0
47. Louisiana	18.9*
47. Virginia	18.9*
49. Mississippi	18.4
50. South Carolina	17.0
51. Georgia	16.9
U.S. Average	**27.1**

* Estimated

Public High School Graduation Rates, 1991

Source: National Center for Education Statistics, U.S. Dept. of Education

	Graduation Rate	Rank
U.S.	**71.2%**	
Alabama	65.6	(44)
Alaska	72.3	(33)
Arizona	72.4	(32)
Arkansas	76.6	(21)
California	67.7	(42)
Colorado	74.5	(26)
Connecticut	78.6	(16)
Delaware	68.0	(40)
D.C.	59.5	(50)
Florida	61.2	(48)
Georgia	64.0	(46)
Hawaii	76.1	(23)
Idaho	79.7	(12)
Illinois	77.5	(18)
Indiana	75.3	(25)
Iowa	85.9	(4)
Kansas	81.1	(10)
Kentucky	70.0	(36)
Louisiana	54.3	(51)
Maine	79.0	(14)
Maryland	73.1	(29)
Massachusetts	79.7	(12)
Michigan	69.9	(37)
Minnesota	89.5	(1)
Mississippi	61.7	(47)
Missouri	72.5	(31)
Montana	84.9	(5)
Nebraska	86.3	(3)
Nevada	77.4	(20)
New Hampshire	76.2	(22)
New Jersey	82.1	(8)
New Mexico	69.5	(38)
New York	64.4	(45)
North Carolina	68.4	(39)
North Dakota	86.7	(2)
Ohio	72.3	(33)
Oklahoma	75.5	(24)
Oregon	71.6	(35)
Pennsylvania	78.5	(17)
Rhode Island	73.6	(27)
South Carolina	61.2	(48)
South Dakota	84.2	(6)
Tennessee	67.8	(41)
Texas	65.9	(43)
Utah	79.0	(14)
Vermont[1]	80.9	(11)
Virginia	73.6	(27)
Washington	73.1	(29)
West Virginia	77.5	(18)
Wisconsin	82.5	(7)
Wyoming	81.7	(9)

Scholastic Aptitude Test (SAT) Mean Scores and Characteristics of College Bound Seniors: 1970 to 1993

Source: College Entrance Examination Board

(For school year ending in year shown)

Type of Test and Characteristic	Unit	1970	1975	1980	1985	1987	1988	1989	1990	1991	1992	1993
Test Scores[1]												
Verbal, total[1]	Point	460	434	424	431	430	428	427	424	422	423	424
Male	Point	459	437	428	437	435	435	434	429	426	428	428
Female	Point	461	431	420	425	425	422	421	419	418	419	420
Math, total[2]	Point	488	472	466	475	476	476	476	476	474	476	478
Male	Point	509	495	491	499	500	498	500	499	497	499	502
Female	Point	465	449	443	452	453	455	454	455	453	456	457
Participants (thousands)												
Total		996	992	989	1,080	1,134	1,088	1,025	1,033	NA	1,034	1,109
Male	Percent	NA	49.9	48.2	48.3	48.0	48.0	48.0	48	48	48	47
White	Percent	NA	86.0	82.1	80.0	78.0	77.0	75.0	73	72	71	70
Black	Percent	NA	7.9	9.1	8.9	9.0	9.0	10.0	10	10	10	11
Obtaining scores[1] of—600 or above:												
Verbal	Percent	NA	7.9	7.2	7.0	8.0	7.0	7.8	7	7	7	7
Math	Percent	NA	15.6	15.1	17.0	18.0	17.0	18.0	18	17	18	19
Below 400:												
Verbal	Percent	NA	37.8	41.8	40.0	40.0	42.0	40.5	41	43	42	42
Math	Percent	NA	28.5	30.2	28.0	29.0	27.0	28.0	28	29	27	28

(NA) Not available. (1) Minimum score, 200; maximum score, 800. (2) 1970 is an estimate based on total number of persons taking SAT.

American College Testing (ACT) Program Mean Scores and Characteristics of College-Bound Students: 1970 to 1992

Source: The American College Testing Program

Data for academic year ending in year shown.

Type of Test and Mean Test Scores[1]	Unit	1970	1975	1980	1985	1986	1987*	1988*	1989*	1990*	1991*	1992*
Composite	Point	19.9	18.6	18.5	18.6	20.8	20.8	20.8	20.6	20.6	20.6	20.6
Male	Point	20.3	19.5	19.3	19.4	19.6	19.5	19.6	19.3	21.0	20.9	20.9
Female	Point	19.4	17.8	17.9	17.9	18.1	18.1	18.1	18.0	20.3	20.4	20.5
English	Point	18.5	17.7	17.9	18.1	18.5	18.4	18.5	18.4	20.5	20.3	20.2
Male	Point	17.6	17.1	17.3	17.6	17.9	17.9	18.0	17.8	20.1	19.8	19.8
Female	Point	19.4	18.3	18.3	18.6	18.9	18.9	19.0	18.9	20.9	20.7	20.6
Math	Point	20.0	17.6	17.4	17.2	17.3	17.2	17.2	17.1	19.9	20.0	20.0
Male	Point	21.1	19.3	18.9	18.6	18.8	18.6	18.4	18.3	20.7	20.6	20.7
Female	Point	18.8	16.2	16.2	16.0	16.0	16.1	16.1	16.1	19.3	19.4	19.5
Participants												
Total	1,000	788	714	822	739	730	777	842	855	817	796	832
Male	Percent	52	46	45	46	46	46	46	46	46	45	45
White	Percent	(NA)	77	83	82	82	81	81	80	79	79	79
Black	Percent	4	7	8	8	8	8	9	9	9	9	9
Obtaining composite scores of—												
27 or above	Percent	14	14	13	14	14	14	14	14	12	11	12
18 or below	Percent	21	33	33	32	31	31	31	32	35	35	35

* Beginning with the October 1989 test (1990 scores), an entirely new ACT Assessment was introduced. The Enhanced ACT Assessment increases the emphasis on rhetorical skills in the measurement of writing proficiency, increases the number of advanced math items, and includes a new reading test which features inferential and reasoning skills and a test designed to measure science reasoning. The Enhanced ACT also provides subscores in English, Mathematics, and Reading. The "Composite" scores for 1986-1989 have been converted to provide a basis of comparison; all 1990, 1991, and 1992 scores are for the Enhanced ACT. It is not possible to make direct comparisons between these data and data from earlier years.

(NA) Not available. Minimum score, 1; maximum score, 36. Test scores and characteristics of college-bound students based on a 10% sample prior to 1985. Beginning in 1985, these data are based on the performance of all ACT-tested students who graduated in the spring of a given school year and who took the ACT Assessment during junior or senior year of high school.

SAT Mean Scores by State 1983-1993

Source: College Entrance Examination Board

	1983		1990		1991		1992		1993		% Graduates Taking SAT*
	Verbal	Math	Verbal	Math	Verbal	Math	Verbal	Math	Verbal	Math	
Alabama	466	508	470	514	476	515	476	520	480	526	9
Alaska	437	468	438	476	439	481	433	475	438	477	42
Arizona	465	505	445	497	442	490	440	493	444	497	28
Arkansas	482	518	470	511	482	523	474	516	478	519	6
California	421	474	419	484	415	482	416	484	415	484	47
Colorado	469	520	456	513	453	506	453	507	454	509	28
Connecticut	433	465	430	471	429	468	430	470	430	474	88
Delaware	433	467	433	470	428	464	432	463	429	465	68
Dist. of Columbia	399	427	409	441	405	435	405	437	405	441	76
Florida	423	464	418	466	416	466	416	468	416	466	52
Georgia	390	428	401	443	400	444	398	444	399	445	65
Hawaii	393	471	404	481	405	478	401	477	401	478	56
Idaho	479	513	466	502	463	505	460	503	465	507	18
Illinois	462	517	466	528	471	535	473	537	475	541	15
Indiana	410	454	408	459	408	457	409	459	409	460	61
Iowa	520	573	511	577	515	578	512	584	520	583	5
Kansas	498	540	492	548	493	546	487	546	494	548	9
Kentucky	475	513	473	521	473	520	470	518	476	522	11
Louisiana	469	502	476	517	476	518	471	520	481	527	9
Maine	427	464	423	463	421	458	422	460	422	463	69
Maryland	427	466	430	478	429	475	431	476	431	478	66
Massachusetts	427	463	427	473	426	470	428	474	427	476	81
Michigan	458	511	454	514	461	519	464	523	469	528	11
Minnesota	482	538	477	542	480	543	492	561	489	556	10
Mississippi	474	507	477	519	477	520	478	526	481	521	4
Missouri	466	510	473	522	476	526	475	529	481	532	11
Montana	480	535	464	523	464	518	465	523	459	516	24
Nebraska	494	546	484	546	481	543	478	540	479	544	10
Nevada	441	480	434	487	435	484	434	488	432	488	28
New Hampshire	444	481	442	486	440	481	440	483	442	487	78
New Jersey	418	455	418	473	417	469	420	471	419	473	76
New Mexico	484	519	480	527	474	522	475	521	478	525	11
New York	422	466	412	470	413	468	416	466	416	471	74
North Carolina	394	431	401	440	400	444	405	450	406	453	60
North Dakota	505	560	505	564	502	571	501	567	518	583	6
Ohio	458	504	450	499	450	496	450	501	454	505	22
Oklahoma	489	521	478	523	476	521	480	527	482	530	9

	1983 Verbal	1983 Math	1990 Verbal	1990 Math	1991 Verbal	1991 Math	1992 Verbal	1992 Math	1993 Verbal	1993 Math	% Graduates Taking SAT*
Oregon	432	469	439	484	439	483	439	486	441	492	56
Pennsylvania	425	461	420	463	417	459	418	459	418	460	70
Rhode Island	422	459	422	461	421	459	421	460	419	464	71
South Carolina	383	415	397	437	395	437	394	437	396	442	61
South Dakota	517	560	506	555	496	551	490	550	502	558	6
Tennessee	483	519	483	525	487	528	484	529	486	531	13
Texas	412	453	413	461	411	463	410	466	413	472	45
Utah	508	545	492	539	494	537	496	545	500	549	4
Vermont	434	472	431	466	424	466	429	468	426	467	68
Virginia	427	463	425	470	424	466	425	468	425	469	63
Washington	463	510	437	486	433	480	432	484	435	486	52
West Virginia	466	512	443	490	441	485	440	484	439	485	17
Wisconsin	473	533	476	543	481	542	481	548	485	551	10
Wyoming	492	530	458	519	466	514	462	516	463	507	13
National Average	**425**	**468**	**424**	**476**	**422**	**474**	**423**	**476**	**424**	**478**	**43**

* Based on number of high school graduates in 1993 as projected by the Western Interstate Commission for Higher Education, and number of students in the Class of 1993 who took the SAT. **Note:** Making comparison of states, or ranking them, on the basis of SAT scores alone is invalid and strongly discouraged by the College Board.

Tuition and College Costs 1993-1994

Based on the *Peterson's Guides* Annual Survey of Undergraduate Institutions, the average cost of tuition, mandatory fees, and college room and board at four-year private colleges is $14,176. The average cost at four-year public colleges is $6,083 for state residents and $9,961 for nonresidents. Two-year public colleges are the least expensive group of institutions; tuition and fees average $1,679 for state residents and $3,938 for nonresidents. Tuition and fees at two-year private colleges average $5,813.

The most expensive four-year institutions, including tuition, mandatory fees, and college room and board, are Sarah Lawrence College ($25,900); Brandeis University ($25,655); Barnard College ($25,492); Bard College ($25,184); Yale University ($25,110); Tufts University ($24,962); Hampshire College ($24,930); Bennington College ($24,850); Tulane University ($24,830); Massachusetts Institute of Technology ($24,800). The least expensive four-year undergraduate institutions are the United States service academies, which are all free.

Institutions of Higher Education—Charges: 1970 to 1992

Source: National Center for Education Statistics, U.S. Dept. of Education

Data are for the entire academic year ending in year shown. Figures for 1970 are average charges for full-time resident degree-credit students; figures for later years are average charges per full-time equivalent student. Room and board are based on full-time students.

Academic Control and Year	Tuition and Required Fees: All institutions	Tuition and Required Fees: 2-yr. colleges	Tuition and Required Fees: 4-yr. universities	Board Rates: All institutions	Board Rates: 2-yr. colleges	Board Rates: 4-yr. universities	Dormitory Charges: All institutions	Dormitory Charges: 2-yr. colleges	Dormitory Charges: 4-yr. universities
Public:									
1970	$323	$178	$427	$511	$465	$540	$369	$308	$395
1980	583	355	840	867	894	898	715	572	749
1990	1,356	756	2,035	1,635	1,581	1,728	1,513	962	1,561
1991	1,454	824	2,159	1,691	1,594	1,767	1,612	1,050	1,658
1992	1,624	937	2,410	1,780	1,612	1,852	1,731	1,074	1,789
Private:									
1970	1,533	1,034	1,809	561	546	608	436	413	503
1980	3,130	2,062	3,811	955	924	1,078	827	769	999
1990	8,147	5,196	10,348	1,948	1,811	2,339	1,923	1,663	2,411
1991	8,772	5,570	11,379	2,074	1,989	2,470	2,063	1,744	2,654
1992	9,434	5,752	12,192	2,252	2,090	2,727	2,221	1,789	2,860

Colleges and Universities Offering Remedial Instruction or Tutoring

Source: National Center for Education Statistics, U.S. Dept. of Education.

Type of institution	Percent of Colleges Offering Remedial Instruction or Tutoring: 1980-81	1984-85	1988-89	1989-90	1990-91	1991-92	Change in Percentage Points: 1980-81 to 1984-85	1984-85 to 1988-89	1988-89 to 1990-91	1990-91 to 1991-92
All 4-year colleges	78.9	85.8	89.0	90.2	89.0	88.6	6.9	3.2	0.0	−0.5
All 2-year colleges	83.8	93.4	93.8	94.9	94.1	90.9	9.6	0.4	0.3	−3.2
Public institutions										
4-year colleges	89.8	92.9	94.7	99.5	95.5	95.0	3.1	1.8	0.8	−0.5
2-year colleges	89.6	97.2	98.9	99.0	98.8	96.0	7.6	1.7	−0.1	−2.8
Private institutions										
4-year colleges	73.8	82.5	86.3	85.9	86.0	85.6	8.7	3.8	−0.3	−0.4
2-year colleges	61.9	78.9	77.8	79.8	79.8	76.1	17.0	−1.1	2.0	−3.6

Salaries of College Professors, 1992-1993

Source: American Association of University Professors

Type of Institution (by highest degree offered)	Public	Private/ Independent	Church-Related
Doctoral Degrees			
Professor	$63,250	$80,280	$70,770
Associate Professor	45,840	53,860	50,640
Assistant Professor	38,880	45,510	42,090
Master's Degrees			
Professor	$54,240	$57,060	$55,970
Associate Professor	43,430	44,020	44,800
Assistant Professor	36,160	35,360	37,090
Four-Year Liberal Arts Degrees			
Professor	$48,600	$54,620	$43,210
Associate Professor	40,180	41,710	36,220
Assistant Professor	33,430	34,400	30,500
Two-Year Degrees			
Professor	$47,820	$36,710	$32,010
Associate Professor	39,760	31,800	29,290
Assistant Professor	34,300	27,100	24,850

Public Libraries

Source: World Almanac questionnaire (1992)

City	No. bound Volumes	Circulation	Annual Acquisitions Expend.
Akron, Oh. (17)	1,498,836	3,191,088	$1,900,000
Albuquerque, N.M. (12)	810,871	2,830,979	1,150,000
Anaheim, Cal. (5)	393,231	1,550,000	450,000
Anchorage, Alas.[a] (5)	395,700	1,099,780	662,790
Arlington, Tex. (5)	246,125	1,211,662	260,533
Atlanta, Ga.[a] (33)	1,678,750	2,303,681	3,011,362
Baltimore, Md. (28)	2,217,508	1,673,310	1,904,681
Baton Rouge, La. (10)	815,467	2,276,247	1,146,850
Birmingham, Ala. (19)	889,000	2,000,000	1,200,000
Boston, Mass. (26)	6,000,000	1,600,000	2,000,000
Buffalo, N.Y. (53)	2,494,000	7,587,811	2,629,489
Charlotte, N.C.[a] (19)	1,200,000	2,700,000	1,400,000
Chicago, Ill. (Main)	1,700,000	950,000	3,600,000
Branches (82)	4,600,000	8,400,000	4,600,000
Cincinnati, Oh. (42)	4,261,202	10,413,286	5,561,019
Cleveland, Oh. (28)	2,734,894	5,624,099	6,098,471
Colorado Springs, Col. (13)	867,906	2,470,986	1,998,445
Columbus, Oh. (20)	1,928,603	8,341,885	5,178,015
Corpus Christi, Tex. (4)	362,433	1,153,718	520,756
Dallas, Tex.[a] (19)	2,409,864	4,364,027	17,201,527
Dayton, Oh. (20)	1,555,475	6,224,061	2,316,854
Denver, Col.[a] (21)	2,239,106	3,396,268	1,856,485
Des Moines, Ia. (5)	549,544	1,241,800	267,050
Detroit, Mich. (25)	2,763,442	1,494,160	1,932,650
District of Columbia[a] (25)	1,507,556	1,843,098	1,530,000
El Paso, Tex.[a] (10)	600,000	1,300,000	3,500,000
Fairfax, Va.[a] (22)	1,761,264	8,454,714	3,387,721
Ft. Worth, Tex. (10)	1,693,975	2,238,871	1,266,213
Fresno, Cal. (36)	1,192,409	2,003,511	500,000
Honolulu, Ha. (49)	2,389,153	6,290,173	3,579,085
Houston, Tex. (34)	3,982,539	6,342,340	4,038,166
Indianapolis, Ind.[a] (21)	1,500,000	5,376,388	2,170,167
Jersey City, N.J. (11)	792,423	285,549	139,412
Kansas City, Mo. (8)	1,817,937	2,032,835	1,589,306
Los Angeles, Cal.[a] (62)	5,663,240	10,382,321	4,469,364
Louisville, Ky. (14)	700,000	2,603,723	1,575,340
Memphis, Tenn.[a] (23)	1,700,000	2,700,000	3,228,007
Mesa, Ariz. (2)	556,416	2,064,658	$768,638
Miami, Fla.[a] (28)	2,386,204	4,200,000	2,200,000
Milwaukee, Wis. (12)	2,306,006	3,057,442	1,788,125
Minneapolis, Minn. (14)	1,977,573	3,065,032	2,026,182
Mobile, Ala. (6)	415,000	1,323,318	700,000
Nashville, Tenn. (16)	665,249	1,849,973	820,310
New Orleans, La. (15)	928,871	1,251,366	892,728
New York, N.Y. (research)	10,700,000	—	9,400,000
Branches (82)	4,000,000	9,908,640	6,650,000
Brooklyn[a] (58)	4,637,167	8,610,459	5,133,434
Queens[a] (61)	5,500,000	11,320,000	5,500,000
Norfolk, Va. (11)	901,775	767,110	500,626
Oklahoma City, Okla.[a] (11)	933,241	4,184,437	1,346,726
Oakland, Cal. (16)	1,300,000	1,580,000	762,000
Omaha, Neb. (9)	613,472	1,985,822	933,050
Philadelphia, Pa.[a] (53)	3,458,700	4,800,000	6,200,000
Phoenix, Az. (11)	1,783,410	5,962,000	2,200,000
Pittsburgh, Pa. (19)	1,934,390	2,925,154	1,300,000
Portland, Ore.[a] (15)	4,000,000	2,000,000	1,400,000
Richmond, Va. (8)	785,023	842,143	427,734
Rochester, N.Y. (11)	1,542,038	1,597,407	1,029,258
Sacramento, Cal.[a] (24)	1,663,893	3,977,515	2,045,262
St. Louis, Mo. (12)	1,400,000	1,830,302	1,670,000
St. Paul, Minn. (12)	599,048	2,628,951	894,113
San Diego, Cal. (32)	2,030,185	5,364,276	2,480,597
San Francisco, Cal. (27)	2,000,000	3,300,000	1,015,855
Shreveport, La. (19)	475,685	1,081,232	400,000
Syracuse, N.Y. (8)	650,080	1,911,930	1,281,088
Tampa, Fla.[a] (17)	1,100,600	3,200,000	1,800,000
Toledo, Oh. (18)	1,793,735	5,849,356	2,968,076
Tucson, Ariz. (17)	1,200,000	5,100,000	1,355,000
Tulsa, Okla. (20)	874,272	3,344,153	1,550,000
Wichita, Kan. (11)	875,558	1,718,806	464,630
Yonkers, N.Y.[a] (3)	233,532	865,901	481,286

(a) Has not provided up-to-date information. Figure in parentheses denotes number of branches.

Funding of Public Libraries, 1991

Source: National Center for Education Statistics, U.S. Dept. of Education; per capita spending

United States	$17.83
Alabama	$9.88
Alaska	$28.64
Arizona	$16.16
Arkansas	$6.75
California	$17.54
Colorado	$20.51
Connecticut	$27.20
Delaware	$9.48
District of Columbia	$35.62
Florida	$15.09
Georgia	$11.62
Hawaii	$19.39
Idaho	$13.62
Illinois	$22.72
Indiana	$22.80
Iowa	$14.67
Kansas	$17.41
Kentucky	$9.16
Louisiana	$12.62
Maine	$15.40
Maryland	$25.52
Massachusetts	$21.36
Michigan	$15.51
Minnesota	$20.58
Mississippi	$7.62
Missouri	$15.50
Montana	$9.02
Nebraska	$15.38
Nevada	$16.41
New Hampshire	$17.40
New Jersey	$27.40
New Mexico	$10.71
New York	$30.36
North Carolina	$12.01
North Dakota	$8.70
Ohio	$28.34
Oklahoma	$12.37
Oregon	$17.86
Pennsylvania	$12.92
Rhode Island	$18.63
South Carolina	$9.67
South Dakota	$13.59
Tennessee	$7.44
Texas	$9.53
Utah	$15.71
Vermont	$13.24
Virginia	$18.79
Washington	$23.79
West Virginia	$8.38
Wisconsin	$19.10
Wyoming	$22.40

American Colleges and Universities

General Information for the 1992-93 Academic Year

Source: Peterson's Guides

These listings include all accredited undergraduate degree-granting institutions in the United States and U.S. territories that have a total institutional enrollment of 1,000 or more. Four-year colleges (those that award a bachelor's as their highest undergraduate degree) are listed first, followed by two-year colleges (those that award an associate as their highest or primary undergraduate degree).

All institutions are coeducational except those where the zip code is directly followed by: (1)–men only, (2)–primarily men, (3)–women only, (4)–primarily women.

Year is that of founding.

Governing official is the chief executive officer.

Institutional control: 1–independent (nonprofit), 2–independent-religious, 3–proprietary (profit making), 4–federal, 5–state, 7–commonwealth (Puerto Rico), 8–territory (U.S. territories), 9–county, 10–district, 11–city, 12–state and local, 13–state related.

Highest degree offered: B–bachelor's, M–master's, F–first professional, D–doctorate.

Enrollment is the total number of matriculated undergraduate and (if applicable) graduate students.

Faculty is the total number of faculty members teaching undergraduate courses and (if available) graduate courses.

Any data not reported are indicated as NR.

Four-Year Colleges

Name, address	Year	Governing official, control, and highest degree offered		Enrollment	Faculty
Abilene Christian U, Abilene, TX 79699	1906	Dr. Royce Money	2-M	4,055	227
Acad of Art Coll, San Francisco, CA 94105	1929	Dr. Andrew Jameson	3-M	2,318	140
Adams State Coll, Alamosa, CO 81102	1921	Dr. William M. Fulkerson, Jr.	5-M	2,482	120
Adelphi U, Garden City, NY 11530	1896	Dr. Peter Diamandopoulos	1-D	8,261	663
Adrian Coll, Adrian, MI 49221	1859	Dr. Stanley P. Caine	2-B	1,145	134
Alabama A&M U, Normal, AL 35762	1875	Dr. David B. Henson	5-D	5,069	337
Alabama State U, Montgomery, AL 36101	1874	Dr. C. C. Baker	5-M	5,800	270
Albany State Coll, Albany, GA 31705	1903	Dr. Billy C. Black	5-M	3,106	150
Albertson Coll, Caldwell, ID 83605	1891	Mr. Robert L. Hendren, Jr.	1-M	1,062	118
Albion Coll, Albion, MI 49224	1835	Dr. Melvin L. Vulgamore	2-B	1,677	131
Albright Coll, Reading, PA 19612	1856	Dr. Ellen S. Hurwitz	2-B	1,260	112
Alfred U, Alfred, NY 14802	1836	Dr. Edward G. Coll, Jr.	1-D	2,258	197
Allegheny Coll, Meadville, PA 16335	1815	Dr. Daniel F. Sullivan	2-B	1,783	202
Allentown Coll of St Francis de Sales, Center Valley, PA 18034-9568	1962	Rev. Daniel Gambet, OSFS	2-M	2,100	98
Alma Coll, Alma, MI 48801-1599	1886	Dr. Alan J. Stone	2-B	1,295	110
Alvernia Coll, Reading, PA 19607-1799	1958	Dr. Daniel N. DeLucca	2-B	1,332	106
Alverno Coll, Milwaukee, WI 53234-3922 (3)	1887	Sr. Joel Read	2-B	2,514	208
Amber U, Garland, TX 75041	1971	Dr. Douglas W. Warner	1-M	1,610	65
American International Coll, Springfield, MA 01109-3189	1885	Dr. Harry J. Courniotes	1-M	1,815	122
American Tech Inst, Brunswick, TN 38014 (2)	1985	NR	1-B	1,500	8
American U, Washington, DC 20016	1893	Mr. Elliott Milstein	2-D	10,153	1,335
Amherst Coll, Amherst, MA 01002	1821	Dr. Peter R. Pouncey	1-B	1,575	191
Anderson Coll, Anderson, SC 29621	1911	Dr. Mark L. Hopkins	2-B	1,172	73
Anderson U, Anderson, IN 46012	1917	Dr. James L. Edwards	2-M	2,249	184
Andrews U, Berrien Springs, MI 49104	1874	Dr. W. Richard Lesher	2-D	2,979	329
Angelo State U, San Angelo, TX 76909	1928	Dr. Lloyd Drexell Vincent	5-M	6,102	240
Anna Maria Coll, Paxton, MA 01612	1946	Sr. Bernadette Madore	2-M	1,486	92
Appalachian State U, Boone, NC 28608	1899	Dr. John E. Thomas	5-D	11,650	688
Aquinas Coll, Grand Rapids, MI 49506-1799	1886	Mr. R. Paul Nelson	2-M	2,544	197
Arizona State U, Tempe, AZ 85287	1885	Dr. Lattie F. Coor	5-D	43,635	1,822
Arkansas State U, State University, AR 72467	1909	Dr. John N. Mangieri	5-D	10,177	449
Arkansas Tech U, Russellville, AR 72801-2222	1909	Dr. Robert C. Brown	5-M	4,790	230
Armstrong State Coll, Savannah, GA 31419	1935	Dr. Robert A. Burnett	5-B	4,839	179
Art Ctr Coll of Design, Pasadena, CA 91103	1930	Mr. David R. Brown	1-M	1,275	310
Asbury Coll, Wilmore, KY 40390-1198	1890	Dr. David J. Gyertson	2-B	1,129	102
Ashland U, Ashland, OH 44805	1878	Mr. G. William Benz	2-M	5,652	202
Assumption Coll, Worcester, MA 01615-0005	1904	Dr. Joseph H. Hagan	2-M	2,896	189
Athens State Coll, Athens, AL 35611	1822	Dr. Jerry F. Bartlett	5-B	3,234	182
Atlantic Union Coll, South Lancaster, MA 01561	1882	Dr. Lawrence T. Geraty	2-M	1,273	87
Auburn U, Auburn University, AL 36849	1856	Dr. William V. Muse	5-D	21,551	1,181
Auburn U at Montgomery, Montgomery, AL 36117-3596	1967	Dr. James O. Williams	5-M	6,386	383
Audrey Cohen Coll, New York, NY 10014	1964	Dr. Audrey C. Cohen	1-M	1,096	66
Augsburg Coll, Minneapolis, MN 55454	1869	Dr. Charles S. Anderson	2-M	2,924	189
Augusta Coll, Augusta, GA 30904-2200	1925	Dr. Martha Farmer	5-M	5,579	237
Augustana Coll, Rock Island, IL 61201	1860	Dr. Thomas Tredway	2-B	2,080	173
Augustana Coll, Sioux Falls, SD 57197	1860	Dr. Ralph H. Wagoner	2-M	1,929	156
Aurora U, Aurora, IL 60506	1893	Dr. Thomas H. Zarle	1-M	2,025	240
Austin Coll, Sherman, TX 75091	1849	Dr. Harry E. Smith	2-M	1,174	96
Austin Peay State U, Clarksville, TN 37044	1927	Dr. Oscar Page	5-M	7,670	469
Averett Coll, Danville, VA 24541	1859	Dr. Frank R. Campbell	2-M	1,674	63
Avila Coll, Kansas City, MO 64145	1916	Dr. Larry Kramer	2-M	1,409	135
Azusa Pacific U, Azusa, CA 91702	1899	Dr. Richard E. Felix	2-M	3,651	319
Babson Coll, Babson Park, MA 02157-0310	1919	Mr. William F. Glavin	1-M	3,157	168
Baker Coll of Flint, Flint, MI 48507	1911	Mr. Edward J. Kurtz	1-B	4,179	127
Baker Coll of Muskegon, Muskegon, MI 49442	1888	Mr. Robert D. Jewell	1-B	1,860	60
Baker Coll of Owosso, Owosso, MI 48867	1984	NR	1-B	1,274	67
Baker U, Baldwin City, KS 66006	1858	Dr. Daniel M. Lambert	2-M	1,840	74
Baldwin-Wallace Coll, Berea, OH 44017	1845	Dr. Neal Malicky	2-M	4,736	374
Ball State U, Muncie, IN 47306	1918	Dr. John E. Worthen	5-D	20,333	1,123
Bard Coll, Annandale-on-Hudson, NY 12504	1860	Dr. Leon Botstein	1-M	1,178	135
Barnard Coll, New York, NY 10027-6598 (3)	1889	Ms. Ellen V. Futter	1-B	2,190	249
Barry U, Miami Shores, FL 33161	1940	Sr. Jeanne O'Laughlin, OP	2-D	6,466	376
Barton Coll, Wilson, NC 27893	1902	Dr. James B. Hemby	2-B	1,720	106

Name, address	Year	Governing official, control, and highest degree offered	Enrollment	Faculty
Baruch Coll of the City U of New York, New York, NY 10010	1919	Dr. Matthew Goldstein 12-D	15,030	820
Bates Coll, Lewiston, ME 04240	1855	Dr. Donald W. Harward 1-B	1,515	176
Bayamón Central U, Bayamón, PR 00960-1725	1970	Rev. Vincent A. M. Van Rooij, OP 2-M	2,921	112
Baylor U, Waco, TX 76798	1845	Dr. Herbert H. Reynolds 2-D	12,185	636
Beaver Coll, Glenside, PA 19038-3295	1853	Dr. Bette E. Landman 2-M	2,220	184
Belhaven Coll, Jackson, MS 39202-1789	1883	Dr. Newton Wilson 2-B	1,056	73
Bellarmine Coll, Louisville, KY 40205-0671	1950	Dr. Joseph J. McGowan, Jr. 2-M	2,326	175
Bellevue Coll, Bellevue, NE 68005-3039	1965	Dr. John B. Muller 1-M	2,157	83
Belmont Abbey Coll, Belmont, NC 28012	1876	Dr. Joseph Brosnan 2-B	1,016	84
Belmont U, Nashville, TN 37212	1951	Dr. William E. Troutt 2-M	2,866	298
Beloit Coll, Beloit, WI 53511	1846	Mr. Victor E. Ferrall, Jr. 1-M	1,187	136
Bemidji State U, Bemidji, MN 56601	1919	Dr. Linda Baer 5-M	4,816	220
Benedict Coll, Columbia, SC 29204	1870	Dr. Ruby W. Watts 2-B	1,207	100
Benedictine Coll, Atchison, KS 66002	1859	Dr. Thomas O. James 2-M	1,130	91
Bentley Coll, Waltham, MA 02154-4705	1917	Dr. Joseph M. Cronin 1-M	5,577	374
Berea Coll, Berea, KY 40404	1855	Dr. John B. Stephenson 1-B	1,563	128
Berklee Coll of Music, Boston, MA 02215	1945	Dr. Lee Eliot Berk 1-B	2,555	263
Berry Coll, Mount Berry, GA 30149-0159	1902	Dr. Gloria M. Shatto 1-M	1,745	126
Bethel Coll, St Paul, MN 55112	1871	Dr. George K. Brushaber 2-M	1,963	177
Bethune-Cookman Coll, Daytona Beach, FL 32115	1904	Dr. Oswald P. Bronson, Sr. 2-B	2,301	199
Biola U, La Mirada, CA 90639	1908	Dr. Clyde Cook 2-D	2,883	216
Birmingham-Southern Coll, Birmingham, AL 35254	1856	Dr. Neal R. Berte 2-M	1,763	141
Black Hills State U, Spearfish, SD 57799-9501	1883	Dr. Clifford M. Trump 5-M	2,814	103
Bloomfield Coll, Bloomfield, NJ 07003	1868	Dr. John F. Noonan 2-B	2,036	180
Bloomsburg U of Pennsylvania, Bloomsburg, PA 17815	1839	Dr. Harry Ausprich 5-M	7,551	398
Bluefield State Coll, Bluefield, WV 24701	1895	Dr. Leonard C. Nelson 5-B	2,931	178
Boise State U, Boise, ID 83725	1932	Dr. Charles Ruch 5-M	13,231	878
Boricua Coll, New York, NY 10032	1974	Dr. Victor G. Alicea 1-B	1,146	128
Boston Coll, Chestnut Hill, MA 02167	1863	Rev. J. Donald Monan, SJ 2-D	14,455	957
Boston U, Boston, MA 02215	1839	Dr. John Silber 1-D	28,364	2,556
Bowdoin Coll, Brunswick, ME 04011	1794	Mr. Robert H. Edwards 1-B	1,445	132
Bowie State U, Bowie, MD 20715	1865	Dr. Nathanael Pollard, Jr. 5-M	4,437	234
Bowling Green State U, Bowling Green, OH 43403	1910	Dr. Paul J. Olscamp 5-D	17,502	852
Bradley U, Peoria, IL 61625	1897	Dr. John R. Brazil 1-M	6,191	428
Brandeis U, Waltham, MA 02254-9110	1948	Dr. Samuel O. Thier 1-D	3,829	468
Brenau U, Gainesville, GA 30501-3697 (4)	1878	Dr. John S. Burd 1-M	1,987	159
Brewton-Parker Coll, Mt Vernon, GA 30445	1904	Dr. Y. Lynn Holmes 2-B	1,974	229
Briar Cliff Coll, Sioux City, IA 51104	1930	Sr. Margaret Wick 2-B	1,144	72
Bridgewater State Coll, Bridgewater, MA 02325	1840	Dr. Adrian Tinsley 5-M	8,350	334
Brigham Young U, Provo, UT 84602	1875	Dr. Rex E. Lee 2-D	31,108	1,652
Brigham Young U–Hawaii Cmps, Laie, Oahu, HI 96762	1955	Dr. Alton L. Wade 2-B	2,064	149
Brooklyn Coll of the City U of New York, Brooklyn, NY 11210	1930	Dr. Vernon E. Lattin 12-M	17,218	850
Brown U, Providence, RI 02912	1764	Dr. Vartan Gregorian 1-D	7,593	663
Bryant Coll, Smithfield, RI 02917	1863	Dr. William E. Trueheart 1-M	4,598	216
Bryn Mawr Coll, Bryn Mawr, PA 19010 (4)	1885	Dr. Mary Patterson McPherson 1-D	1,847	209
Bucknell U, Lewisburg, PA 17837	1846	Dr. Gary A. Sojka 1-M	3,603	268
Butler U, Indianapolis, IN 46208	1855	Dr. Geoffrey Bannister 1-M	3,825	368
Cabrini Coll, Radnor, PA 19087-3699	1957	Dr. Antoinette Iadarola 2-M	1,760	141
Caldwell Coll, Caldwell, NJ 07006-6195	1939	Sr. Vivien Jennings 2-M	1,339	89
California Coll for Health Sciences, National City, CA 91950	1977	NR 3-M	4,200	9
California Coll of Arts and Crafts, Oakland, CA 94618	1907	Mr. Neil J. Hoffman 1-M	1,146	167
California Inst of Tech, Pasadena, CA 91125	1891	Dr. Thomas E. Everhart 1-D	2,009	270
California Lutheran U, Thousand Oaks, CA 91360	1959	Dr. Luther S. Luedtke 2-M	2,970	261
California Polytechnic State U, San Luis Obispo, San Luis Obispo, CA 93407	1901	Dr. Warren J. Baker 5-M	16,377	953
California State Polytechnic U, Pomona, Pomona, CA 91768	1938	Dr. Bob Suzuki 5-M	18,297	916
California State U, Bakersfield, Bakersfield, CA 93311	1970	Dr. Tomas A. Arciniega 5-M	5,422	337
California State U, Chico, Chico, CA 95929-0720	1887	Dr. Manuel Esteban 5-M	15,172	873
California State U, Dominguez Hills, Carson, CA 90747	1960	Dr. Robert Detweiler 5-M	10,477	401
California State U, Fresno, Fresno, CA 93740	1911	Dr. John D. Welty 5-D	18,902	1,220
California State U, Fullerton, Fullerton, CA 92634-9480	1957	Dr. Milton A. Gordon 5-M	24,411	1,245
California State U, Hayward, Hayward, CA 94542	1957	Dr. Norma Rees 5-M	12,986	578
California State U, Long Beach, Long Beach, CA 90840-0119	1949	Dr. Karl W. E. Anatol 5-M	30,071	1,441
California State U, Northridge, Northridge, CA 91330	1958	Dr. Blenda J. Wilson 5-M	29,084	1,292
California State U, Sacramento, Sacramento, CA 95819-6048	1947	Dr. Donald R. Gerth 5-M	24,468	1,171
California State U, San Bernardino, San Bernardino, CA 92407	1965	Dr. Anthony H. Evans 5-M	12,483	626
California State U, San Marcos, San Marcos, CA 92096	1990	NR 5-M	1,904	121
California State U, Stanislaus, Turlock, CA 95380	1957	Dr. John W. Moore 5-M	5,907	335
California U of Pennsylvania, California, PA 15419-1394	1852	Dr. John Pierce Watkins 5-M	6,484	375
Calumet Coll of Saint Joseph, Whiting, IN 46394	1951	Dr. Dennis C. Rittenmeyer 2-B	1,086	110
Calvin Coll, Grand Rapids, MI 49546	1876	Dr. Anthony J. Diekema 2-M	3,725	282
Cameron U, Lawton, OK 73505	1908	Dr. Don Davis 5-M	5,988	306
Campbellsville Coll, Campbellsville, KY 42718-2799	1906	Dr. Kenneth W. Winters 2-B	1,042	72
Campbell U, Buies Creek, NC 27506	1887	Dr. Norman A. Wiggins 2-F	5,806	261
Canisius Coll, Buffalo, NY 14208	1870	Rev. James M. Demske, SJ 2-M	4,859	361
Capital U, Columbus, OH 43209-2394	1830	NR 2-F	3,680	161
Cardinal Stritch Coll, Milwaukee, WI 53217-3985	1937	Sr. Mary Lea Schneider 2-M	5,150	518
Carleton Coll, Northfield, MN 55057	1866	Dr. Stephen R. Lewis, Jr. 1-B	1,662	163
Carlow Coll, Pittsburgh, PA 15213 (4)	1929	Dr. Grace Ann Geibel, RSM 2-M	1,668	200
Carnegie Mellon U, Pittsburgh, PA 15213	1900	Dr. Robert Mehrabian 1-D	7,131	722
Carroll Coll, Helena, MT 59625	1909	Dr. Matthew Quinn 2-B	1,382	114
Carroll Coll, Waukesha, WI 53186	1846	Dr. Frank Falcone 2-M	2,108	117
Carson-Newman Coll, Jefferson City, TN 37760	1851	Dr. J. Cordell Maddox 2-M	2,022	182
Carthage Coll, Kenosha, WI 53140	1847	Dr. F. Gregory Campbell 2-M	2,092	151
Case Western Reserve U, Cleveland, OH 44106	1826	Dr. Agnar Pytte 1-D	9,156	1,742
Castleton State Coll, Castleton, VT 05735	1787	Dr. Lyle A. Gray 5-M	2,028	165
Catholic U of America, Washington, DC 20064	1887	Br. F. Patrick Ellis 2-D	6,464	694
Cedar Crest Coll, Allentown, PA 18104 (4)	1867	Dr. Dorothy G. Blaney 2-B	1,342	137

Name, address	Year	Governing official, control, and highest degree offered		Enroll-ment	Faculty
Cedarville Coll, Cedarville, OH 45314	1887	Dr. Paul H. Dixon	2-B	2,172	163
Centenary Coll of Louisiana, Shreveport, LA 71134	1825	Dr. Kenneth L. Schwab	2-M	1,048	95
Central Connecticut State U, New Britain, CT 06050-4010	1849	Dr. John W. Shumaker	5-M	10,655	774
Central Michigan U, Mount Pleasant, MI 48859	1892	Dr. Leonard E. Plachta	5-D	16,349	858
Central Missouri State U, Warrensburg, MO 64093	1871	Dr. Ed Elliott	5-M	11,631	524
Central State U, Wilberforce, OH 45384	1887	Dr. Arthur E. Thomas	5-M	3,279	147
Central U of Iowa, Pella, IA 50219	1853	Dr. William M. Wiebenga	2-B	1,520	135
Central Washington U, Ellensburg, WA 98926	1891	Dr. Ivory V. Nelson	5-M	7,697	344
Central Wesleyan Coll, Central, SC 29630-1020	1906	Dr. John M. Newby	2-M	1,091	132
Chadron State Coll, Chadron, NE 69337	1911	Dr. Samuel H. Rankin	5-M	3,693	137
Chapman U, Orange, CA 92666	1861	Dr. James Doti	2-M	2,568	220
Charleston Southern U, Charleston, SC 29411	1964	Dr. Jairy C. Hunter, Jr.	2-M	2,491	131
Charter Oak State Coll, Farmington, CT 06032-1934	1973	Dr. Merle W. Harris	5-B	1,145	NR
Chestnut Hill Coll, Philadelphia, PA 19118-2695 (3)	1924	Dr. Carol J. Vale, SSJ	2-M	1,351	120
Cheyney U of Pennsylvania, Cheyney, PA 19319	1837	Dr. Douglas Covington	5-M	1,550	91
Chicago State U, Chicago, IL 60628	1867	Dr. Dolores Cross	5-M	8,675	397
Christian Brothers U, Memphis, TN 38104-5581	1871	Br. Stanislaus Sobczyk, FSC	2-M	1,736	149
Christopher Newport U, Newport News, VA 23606	1961	Dr. Anthony Santoro	5-M	4,880	279
The Citadel, The Military Coll of South Carolina, Charleston, SC 29409 (1)	1842	Lt. Gen. Claudius E. Watts, III	5-M	3,600	166
City Coll of the City U of New York, New York, NY 10031	1847	Dr. Augusta Sousa Kappner	12-D	14,783	1,140
City U, Bellevue, WA 98004	1973	Dr. Michael A. Pastore	1-M	3,520	811
Clarion U of Pennsylvania, Clarion, PA 16214	1867	Dr. Diane L. Reinhard	5-M	6,159	373
Clark Atlanta U, Atlanta, GA 30314	1869	NR	2-D	4,480	321
Clarkson U, Potsdam, NY 13699	1896	Dr. Richard H. Gallagher	1-D	2,978	203
Clark U, Worcester, MA 01610-1477	1887	Dr. Richard P. Traina	1-D	2,866	NR
Clayton State Coll, Morrow, GA 30260	1969	NR	5-B	4,861	191
Cleary Coll, Ypsilanti, MI 48197	1883	Mr. Thomas Sullivan	1-B	1,100	67
Clemson U, Clemson, SC 29634	1889	Dr. Max Lennon	5-D	17,666	1,266
Cleveland State U, Cleveland, OH 44115	1964	Dr. Claire A. Van Ummersen	5-D	18,199	686
Clinch Valley Coll of the U of Virginia, Wise, VA 24293	1954	Dr. L. Jay Lemons	5-B	1,729	90
Coastal Carolina U, Myrtle Beach, SC 29578	1954	Dr. Ronald R. Ingle	5-B	4,023	253
Coe Coll, Cedar Rapids, IA 52402	1851	Dr. John E. Brown	2-B	1,285	109
Colby Coll, Waterville, ME 04901	1813	Dr. William R. Cotter	1-B	1,716	172
Colgate U, Hamilton, NY 13346	1819	Dr. Neil R. Grabois	1-M	2,691	273
Coll Misericordia, Dallas, PA 18612-1098	1924	Dr. Carol A. Jobe	2-M	1,689	120
Coll of Aeronautics, Flushing, NY 11371 (2)	1932	Dr. Richard B. Goetze, Jr.	1-B	1,230	88
Coll of Charleston, Charleston, SC 29424	1770	Dr. Alexander M. Sanders, Jr.	5-M	9,660	538
Coll of Great Falls, Great Falls, MT 59405	1932	Dr. Frederick W. Gilliard	2-M	1,328	139
Coll of Insurance, New York, NY 10007	1962	Dr. Ellen Thrower	1-M	2,379	93
Coll of Mount St Joseph, Cincinnati, OH 45233-1670	1920	Ms. Francis Marie Thrailkill, OSU	2-M	2,592	218
Coll of Mount Saint Vincent, Riverdale, NY 10471	1911	Dr. Mary C. Stuart	1-M	1,060	95
Coll of New Rochelle, New Rochelle, NY 10805-2308 (4)	1904	Sr. Dorothy A. Kelly, OSU	1-M	2,445	92
Coll of New Rochelle, New Resources Division, New Rochelle, NY 10805-2308	1972	NR	1-B	3,242	468
Coll of Notre Dame, Belmont, CA 94002	1851	Sr. Veronica Skillin	2-M	1,497	147
Coll of Notre Dame of Maryland, Baltimore, MD 21210 (3)	1873	Sr. Rosemarie Nassif	2-M	1,019	81
Coll of Saint Benedict, Saint Joseph, MN 56374 (3)	1887	Sr. Colman O'Connell, OSB	2-B	1,787	147
Coll of St Catherine, St Paul, MN 55105 (3)	1905	Dr. Anita Pampusch	2-M	2,638	231
Coll of Saint Elizabeth, Morristown, NJ 07960-6989 (4)	1899	Sr. Jacqueline Burns	2-B	1,298	129
Coll of St Francis, Joliet, IL 60435	1920	Dr. John C. Orr	2-M	1,888	124
Coll of Saint Mary, Omaha, NE 68124 (4)	1923	Dr. Kenneth Nielsen	2-B	1,322	134
Coll of Saint Rose, Albany, NY 12203	1920	Dr. Louis C. Vaccaro	1-M	3,715	241
Coll of St Scholastica, Duluth, MN 55811	1912	Dr. Daniel H. Pilon	2-M	1,988	122
Coll of Santa Fe, Santa Fe, NM 87501	1947	Dr. James A. Fries	1-M	1,472	129
Coll of Staten Island of the City U of New York, Staten Island, NY 10314-6600	1955	Dr. Edmond L. Volpe	12-M	12,123	734
Coll of the Holy Cross, Worcester, MA 01610	1843	Rev. John E. Brooks, SJ	2-B	2,742	265
Coll of the Ozarks, Point Lookout, MO 65726	1906	Dr. Jerry C. Davis	2-B	1,524	109
The Coll of West Virginia, Beckley, WV 25802	1933	Dr. Charles Polk	1-B	1,847	115
Coll of William and Mary, Williamsburg, VA 23187-8795	1693	Mr. Timothy J. Sullivan	5-D	7,732	656
The Coll of Wooster, Wooster, OH 44691	1866	Dr. Henry J. Copeland	2-B	1,686	155
Colorado Christian U, Lakewood, CO 80226	1914	Dr. Ronald Schmidt	2-M	1,000	81
The Colorado Coll, Colorado Springs, CO 80903	1874	Dr. Kathryn Mohrman	1-M	1,945	199
Colorado Sch of Mines, Golden, CO 80401	1874	Dr. George S. Ansell	5-D	2,957	200
Colorado State U, Fort Collins, CO 80523	1862	Dr. Albert C. Yates	5-D	21,210	1,021
Colorado Tech Coll, Colorado Springs, CO 80907	1965	Mr. David D. O'Donnell	3-M	1,540	80
Columbia Coll, Chicago, IL 60605	1890	Mr. John B. Duff	1-M	7,133	791
Columbia Coll, New York, NY 10027	1754	Mr. Steven Marcus	1-B	3,422	475
Columbia Coll, Columbia, SC 29203 (3)	1854	Dr. Peter T. Mitchell	2-M	1,228	77
Columbia Union Coll, Takoma Park, MD 20912	1904	Dr. Charles Scriven	2-B	1,121	56
Columbia U, Sch of Engineering & Applied Sci, New York, NY 10027	1864	Mr. David H. Auston	1-D	1,832	101
Columbia U, Sch of General Studies, New York, NY 10027	1754	Ms. Caroline W. Bynum	1-M	1,196	450
Columbia U, Sch of Nursing, New York, NY 10032 (4)	1892	NR	1-M	498	40
Columbus Coll, Columbus, GA 31907-2079	1958	Dr. Frank D. Brown	5-M	5,009	228
Columbus Coll of Art and Design, Columbus, OH 43215-1758	1879	Mr. Joseph V. Canzani	1-B	1,667	108
Concord Coll, Athens, WV 24712	1872	Dr. Jerry L. Beasley	5-B	2,960	145
Concordia Coll, Moorhead, MN 56562	1891	Dr. Paul J. Dovre	2-B	2,942	253
Concordia Coll, St Paul, MN 55104	1893	Dr. Robert Holst	2-M	1,265	116
Concordia Coll, Portland, OR 97211	1905	Dr. Charles E. Schlimpert	2-B	1,066	83
Concordia U, River Forest, IL 60305-1499	1864	Dr. Eugene L. Krentz	2-M	1,726	157
Concordia U Wisconsin, Mequon, WI 53092-7699	1881	Dr. R. John Buuck	2-M	2,370	135
Connecticut Coll, New London, CT 06320	1911	Ms. Claire L. Gaudiani	1-M	1,838	180
Converse Coll, Spartanburg, SC 29302 (3)	1889	Dr. Ellen Wood Hall	1-M	1,120	100
Cooper Union for the Advancement of Science & Art, New York, NY 10003	1859	Mr. John Jay Iselin	1-M	1,062	167
Coppin State Coll, Baltimore, MD 21216	1900	Dr. Calvin W. Burnett	5-M	2,816	153
Cornell Coll, Mount Vernon, IA 52314-1098	1853	Dr. David G. Marker	2-B	1,162	125
Cornell U, Ithaca, NY 14853	1865	Dr. Frank H. T. Rhodes	1-D	18,450	1,593
Creighton U, Omaha, NE 68178	1878	Rev. Michael G. Morrison, SJ	2-D	5,600	1,261
Culver-Stockton Coll, Canton, MO 63435-1299	1853	Dr. Edwin B. Strong, Jr.	2-B	1,145	66
Cumberland Coll, Williamsburg, KY 40769-1372	1889	Dr. James Taylor	2-M	1,498	100
Curry Coll, Milton, MA 02186	1879	Dr. Catherine W. Ingold	1-M	1,143	178

Name, address	Year	Governing official, control, and highest degree offered		Enroll-ment	Faculty
Daemen Coll, Amherst, NY 14226	1947	Dr. Robert S. Marshall	1-M	1,625	152
Dakota State U, Madison, SD 57042	1881	Dr. Jerald Tunheim	5-B	1,504	68
Dallas Baptist U, Dallas, TX 75211-9288	1965	Dr. Gary R. Cook	2-M	2,712	175
Dartmouth Coll, Hanover, NH 03755	1769	Mr. James O. Freedman	1-D	5,475	468
Davenport Coll of Business, Grand Rapids, MI 49503	1866	Mr. Donald W. Maine	1-B	4,500	188
Davenport Coll of Business, Kalamazoo Cmps, Kalamazoo, MI 49006 (4)	1866	Mr. C. Dexter Rohm	1-B	1,942	106
Davenport Coll of Business, Lansing Cmps, Lansing, MI 48933	1979	Mr. Don Colizzi	1-B	1,512	86
David Lipscomb U, Nashville, TN 37204	1891	Dr. Harold Hazelip	2-M	2,272	178
Davidson Coll, Davidson, NC 28036	1837	Dr. John W. Kuykendall	2-B	1,550	127
Delaware State Coll, Dover, DE 19901	1891	Dr. William B. DeLauder	5-M	2,935	182
Delaware Valley Coll, Doylestown, PA 18901-2697	1896	Mr. George F. West	1-B	1,286	106
Delta State U, Cleveland, MS 38733	1925	Dr. F. Kent Wyatt	5-D	3,665	225
Denison U, Granville, OH 43023	1831	Dr. Michele Tolela Myers	1-B	2,003	162
DePaul U, Chicago, IL 60604	1898	Rev. John T. Richardson, CM	2-D	16,499	1,170
DePauw U, Greencastle, IN 46135	1837	Dr. Robert G. Bottoms	2-B	2,058	217
Detroit Coll of Business, Dearborn, MI 48126	1962	Dr. James Mendola	1-B	2,872	142
Detroit Coll of Business, Warren Cmps, Warren, MI 48092	1975	Ms. Janet Guggenheim	1-B	1,397	106
DeVry Inst of Tech, Phoenix, AZ 85021	1967	Mr. James A. Dugan	3-B	2,563	86
DeVry Inst of Tech, Pomona, CA 91768-2642	1983	Mr. David G. Moore	3-B	2,112	71
DeVry Inst of Tech, Decatur, GA 30030	1969	Dr. Ronald Bush	3-B	2,801	81
DeVry Inst of Tech, Addison, IL 60101-6106	1982	Mr. Jerry R. Dill	3-B	2,687	102
DeVry Inst of Tech, Chicago, IL 60618	1931	Dr. E. Arthur Stunnard	3-B	3,192	112
DeVry Inst of Tech, Kansas City, MO 64131	1931	Mr. Charles R. Levalley	3-B	1,781	76
DeVry Inst of Tech, Columbus, OH 43209-2705	1952	Mr. Richard A. Czerniak	3-B	2,752	91
DeVry Inst of Tech, Irving, TX 75038-2440	1969	Dr. Francis V. Cannon	3-B	2,141	99
Dickinson Coll, Carlisle, PA 17013-2896	1773	Dr. A. Lee Fritschler	1-B	2,047	188
Dickinson State U, Dickinson, ND 58601-4896	1918	Dr. Albert A. Watrel	5-B	1,605	98
Dillard U, New Orleans, LA 70122	1869	Dr. Samuel DuBois Cook	2-B	1,625	124
Dominican Coll of Blauvelt, Orangeburg, NY 10962	1952	Sr. Kathleen Sullivan	1-B	1,500	162
Dordt Coll, Sioux Center, IA 51250-1697	1955	Dr. John B. Hulst	2-B	1,077	90
Dowling Coll, Oakdale, NY 11769	1955	Dr. Victor P. Meskill	1-M	5,146	387
Drake U, Des Moines, IA 50311	1881	Dr. Michael R. Ferrari	1-D	6,333	278
Drew U, Madison, NJ 07940	1867	Mr. Thomas H. Kean	2-D	2,045	220
Drexel U, Philadelphia, PA 19104-2875	1891	Dr. Richard D. Breslin	1-D	11,038	841
Drury Coll, Springfield, MO 65802	1873	Dr. John E. Moore, Jr.	2-M	1,406	129
Duke U, Durham, NC 27708-0586	1838	Dr. Nanneri O. Keohane	2-D	11,426	2,304
Duquesne U, Pittsburgh, PA 15282	1878	Dr. John E. Murray, Jr.	2-D	8,359	638
Dyke Coll, Cleveland, OH 44115	1848	Dr. John C. Corfias	1-B	1,426	92
D'Youville Coll, Buffalo, NY 14201	1908	Dr. Denise A. Roche, GNSH	1-M	1,660	128
Earlham Coll, Richmond, IN 47374	1847	Dr. Richard J. Wood	2-M	1,106	108
East Carolina U, Greenville, NC 27858-4353	1907	Dr. Richard Eakin	5-D	17,757	1,188
East Central U, Ada, OK 74820	1909	Dr. Bill S. Cole	5-M	4,388	200
Eastern Coll, St Davids, PA 19087-3696	1932	Dr. Roberta Hestenes	2-M	1,745	141
Eastern Connecticut State U, Willimantic, CT 06226	1889	Mr. David G. Carter	5-M	4,328	195
Eastern Illinois U, Charleston, IL 61920-3099	1895	Mr. David L. Jorns	5-M	11,411	676
Eastern Kentucky U, Richmond, KY 40475	1906	Dr. Hanly Funderburk	5-M	16,866	829
Eastern Mennonite Coll, Harrisonburg, VA 22801	1917	Dr. Joseph L. Lapp	2-M	1,070	104
Eastern Michigan U, Ypsilanti, MI 48197	1849	Dr. William E. Shelton	5-D	25,620	1,081
Eastern Montana Coll, Billings, MT 59101	1927	Dr. Bruce H. Carpenter	5-M	3,761	192
Eastern Nazarene Coll, Quincy, MA 02170-2999	1918	Dr. Kent R. Hill	2-M	1,283	66
Eastern New Mexico U, Portales, NM 88130	1934	Dr. Everett L. Frost	5-M	3,916	224
Eastern Oregon State Coll, La Grande, OR 97850	1929	Mr. David E. Gilbert	5-M	2,171	145
Eastern Washington U, Cheney, WA 99004-2496	1882	Dr. Marshall Drummond	5-M	8,363	423
East Stroudsburg U of Pennsylvania, East Stroudsburg, PA 18301-2999	1893	Dr. James Gilbert	5-M	5,352	273
East Tennessee State U, Johnson City, TN 37614	1911	Dr. Roy S. Nicks	5-D	12,055	629
East Texas Baptist U, Marshall, TX 75670-1498	1912	Dr. Bob E. Riley	2-M	1,187	75
East Texas State U, Commerce, TX 75429-3011	1889	Dr. Jerry D. Morris	5-D	8,344	360
East Texas State U at Texarkana, Texarkana, TX 75505-0518	1971	Dr. John F. Moss	5-M	1,399	59
Eckerd Coll, St Petersburg, FL 33733	1958	Dr. Peter H. Armacost	2-B	1,368	113
Edgewood Coll, Madison, WI 53711	1927	Dr. James A. Ebben	2-M	1,692	111
Edinboro U of Pennsylvania, Edinboro, PA 16444	1857	Mr. Foster F. Diebold	5-M	8,202	417
Elizabeth City State U, Elizabeth City, NC 27909	1891	Dr. Jimmy R. Jenkins	5-B	2,100	133
Elizabethtown Coll, Elizabethtown, PA 17022-2298	1899	Dr. Gerhard E. Spiegler	2-B	1,864	157
Elmhurst Coll, Elmhurst, IL 60126-3296	1871	Dr. Ivan E. Frick	2-B	2,725	140
Elmira Coll, Elmira, NY 14901	1855	Dr. Thomas K. Meier	1-M	1,076	75
Elms Coll, Chicopee, MA 01013 (3)	1928	Sr. Mary A. Dooley	2-M	1,150	94
Elon Coll, Elon College, NC 27244	1889	Dr. J. Fred Young	2-M	3,227	238
Embry-Riddle Aeronautical U, Daytona Beach, FL 32114-3900	1926	Dr. Steven M. Sliwa	1-M	4,508	232
Embry-Riddle Aeronautical U, Coll of Continuing Ed, Daytona Beach, FL 32114	1970	NR	1-M	4,707	1,782
Embry-Riddle Aeronautical U, Western Cmps, Prescott, AZ 86301	1978	Mr. Paul S. Daly	1-B	1,661	86
Emerson Coll, Boston, MA 02116	1880	Dr. Jacqueline W. Liebergott	1-D	2,776	246
Emmanuel Coll, Boston, MA 02115 (3)	1919	Sr. Janet Eisner, SND	2-M	1,393	100
Emory U, Atlanta, GA 30322	1836	Dr. James T. Laney	2-D	9,958	1,929
Emporia State U, Emporia, KS 66801-5087	1863	Dr. Robert E. Glennen	5-M	6,006	244
Eugene Lang Coll, New Sch for Social Research, New York, NY 10011	1985	Dr. Beatrice Banu	1-B	320	60
Evangel Coll, Springfield, MO 65802	1955	Dr. Robert H. Spence	2-B	1,420	115
Evergreen State Coll, Olympia, WA 98505	1967	Dr. Jane Jervis	5-M	3,410	179
Fairfield U, Fairfield, CT 06430	1942	Rev. Aloysius P. Kelley, SJ	2-M	4,873	319
Fairleigh Dickinson U, Madison, NJ 07940	1942	Dr. Francis J. Mertz	1-D	8,451	606
Fairmont State Coll, Fairmont, WV 26554	1865	Dr. Robert J. Dillman	5-B	6,615	349
Fashion Inst of Tech, New York, NY 10001-5992	1944	Mr. Allan F. Hershfield	12-M	12,121	820
Faulkner U, Montgomery, AL 36109-3398	1942	Dr. Billy D. Hilyer	2-D	1,990	125
Fayetteville State U, Fayetteville, NC 28301	1867	Dr. Lloyd V. Hackley	5-M	3,902	220
Felician Coll, Lodi, NJ 07644	1942	Sr. Theresa Martin	2-B	1,002	99
Ferris State U, Big Rapids, MI 49307	1884	Dr. Helen Popovich	5-M	12,461	751
Ferrum Coll, Ferrum, VA 24088	1913	Dr. Jerry M. Boone	2-B	1,234	102
Fitchburg State Coll, Fitchburg, MA 01420-2697	1894	Dr. Vincent J. Mara	5-M	5,317	243
Flagler Coll, St Augustine, FL 32085	1968	Dr. William L. Proctor	1-B	1,275	112

Name, address	Year	Governing official, control, and highest degree offered		Enrollment	Faculty
Florida A&M U, Tallahassee, FL 32307	1887	Dr. Frederick Humphries	5-D	9,508	670
Florida Atlantic U, Boca Raton, FL 33431	1961	Dr. Anthony James Catanese	5-D	14,778	563
Florida Inst of Tech, Melbourne, FL 32901-6988	1958	Dr. Lynn E. Weaver	1-D	5,826	459
Florida International U, Miami, FL 33199	1965	Dr. Modesto A. Maidique	5-D	19,142	1,143
Florida Memorial Coll, Miami, FL 33054	1879	Dr. Albert E. Smith	2-B	1,489	NR
Florida Southern Coll, Lakeland, FL 33801	1885	Dr. Robert A. Davis	2-M	2,604	120
Florida State U, Tallahassee, FL 32306	1857	Dr. Dale W. Lick	5-D	28,512	1,526
Fontbonne Coll, St Louis, MO 63105	1917	Dr. Meneve Dunham	2-M	1,989	131
Fordham U, New York, NY 10458	1841	Rev. Joseph A. O'Hare, SJ	2-D	14,612	759
Fort Hays State U, Hays, KS 67601	1902	Dr. Edward H. Hammond	5-M	5,603	265
Fort Lauderdale Coll, Fort Lauderdale, FL 33304	1940	Mr. William P. Bedard	3-M	1,120	34
Fort Lewis Coll, Durango, CO 81301-3999	1911	Mr. Joel M. Jones	5-B	4,096	230
Fort Valley State Coll, Fort Valley, GA 31030	1895	Dr. Oscar L. Prater	5-M	2,368	154
Framingham State Coll, Framingham, MA 01701	1839	Dr. Paul F. Weller	5-M	5,146	220
Franciscan U of Steubenville, Steubenville, OH 43952	1946	Rev. Michael Scanlan, TOR	2-M	1,812	128
Francis Marion U, Florence, SC 29501-0547	1970	Dr. Thomas C. Stanton	5-M	3,975	209
Franklin and Marshall Coll, Lancaster, PA 17604-3003	1787	Dr. A. Richard Kneedler	1-B	1,800	197
Franklin Pierce Coll, Rindge, NH 03461-0060	1962	Dr. Walter Peterson	1-B	1,235	106
Franklin U, Columbus, OH 43215	1902	Dr. Paul J. Otte	1-B	3,852	196
Freed-Hardeman U, Henderson, TN 38340	1869	Dr. Milton R. Sewell	2-M	1,236	91
Fresno Pacific Coll, Fresno, CA 93702	1944	Dr. Richard Kriegbaum	2-M	1,530	157
Friends U, Wichita, KS 67213	1898	Dr. Biff Green	2-M	1,540	88
Frostburg State U, Frostburg, MD 21532	1898	Dr. Catherine R. Gira	5-M	5,295	305
Furman U, Greenville, SC 29613	1826	Dr. John E. Johns	1-M	2,936	204
Gallaudet U, Washington, DC 20002-3625	1856	Dr. I. King Jordan	1-M	2,287	330
Gannon U, Erie, PA 16541	1925	Msgr. David Rubino, PhD	2-M	4,384	331
Gardner-Webb U, Boiling Springs, NC 28017	1905	Dr. M. Christopher White	2-M	2,053	163
Geneva Coll, Beaver Falls, PA 15010	1848	Dr. John H. White	2-M	1,438	102
George Fox Coll, Newberg, OR 97132	1891	Dr. Edward F. Stevens	2-D	1,439	133
George Mason U, Fairfax, VA 22030	1957	Dr. George W. Johnson	5-D	20,829	1,114
Georgetown Coll, Georgetown, KY 40324-1696	1829	Dr. William H. Crouch, Jr.	2-M	1,476	94
Georgetown U, Washington, DC 20057	1789	Rev. Leo J. O'Donovan, SJ	2-D	12,084	1,740
George Washington U, Washington, DC 20052	1821	Mr. Stephen J. Trachtenberg	1-D	16,293	2,308
Georgia Coll, Milledgeville, GA 31061	1889	Dr. Edwin G. Speir	5-M	5,501	264
Georgia Inst of Tech, Atlanta, GA 30332	1885	Dr. John P. Crecine	5-D	12,891	658
Georgian Court Coll, Lakewood, NJ 08701-2697 (4)	1908	Sr. Barbara Williams	2-M	2,503	182
Georgia Southern U, Statesboro, GA 30460	1906	Dr. Nicholas Henry	5-M	13,411	615
Georgia Southwestern Coll, Americus, GA 31709	1906	Dr. William H. Capitan	5-M	2,533	155
Georgia State U, Atlanta, GA 30303	1913	Dr. Carl V. Patton	5-D	24,101	1,221
Gettysburg Coll, Gettysburg, PA 17325	1832	Dr. Gordon A. Haaland	2-B	1,950	174
Glenville State Coll, Glenville, WV 26351	1872	Dr. William K. Simmons	5-B	2,358	152
GMI Engineering & Management Inst, Flint, MI 48504-4898	1919	Dr. James E. A. John	1-M	3,141	130
Golden Gate U, San Francisco, CA 94105	1901	Dr. Thomas M. Stauffer	1-D	7,490	826
Goldey-Beacom Coll, Wilmington, DE 19808	1886	Mr. William R. Baldt	1-M	1,757	70
Gonzaga U, Spokane, WA 99258	1887	Rev. Bernard J. Coughlin, SJ	2-D	5,214	230
Gordon Coll, Wenham, MA 01984	1889	Dr. R. Judson Carlberg	2-B	1,234	101
Governors State U, University Park, IL 60466	1969	Dr. Paula Wolff	5-M	5,194	307
Graceland Coll, Lamoni, IA 50140	1895	Dr. William T. Higdon	2-B	1,058	77
Grambling State U, Grambling, LA 71245	1901	Dr. Harold Lundy	5-M	7,533	224
Grand Canyon U, Phoenix, AZ 85017	1949	Dr. Bill Williams	2-M	1,747	164
Grand Valley State U, Allendale, MI 49401	1960	Mr. Arend D. Lubbers	5-M	12,867	599
Grand View Coll, Des Moines, IA 50316-1599	1896	Dr. Arthur E. Puotinen	2-B	1,478	120
Greensboro Coll, Greensboro, NC 27401	1838	Dr. Craven E. Williams	2-B	1,000	81
Grinnell Coll, Grinnell, IA 50112	1846	Dr. Pamela A. Ferguson	1-B	1,240	151
Grove City Coll, Grove City, PA 16127-2104	1876	Dr. Jerry H. Combee	2-B	2,217	141
Guilford Coll, Greensboro, NC 27410	1837	Dr. William R. Rogers	2-B	1,202	111
Gustavus Adolphus Coll, St Peter, MN 56082	1862	Dr. Axel D. Steuer	2-B	2,275	217
Gwynedd-Mercy Coll, Gwynedd Valley, PA 19437	1948	Sr. Isabelle Keiss, RSM	2-M	1,653	173
Hahnemann U, Philadelphia, PA 19102	1848	Mr. Iqbal F. Paroo	1-D	1,551	430
Hamilton Coll, Clinton, NY 13323	1812	Dr. Harry C. Payne	1-B	1,710	192
Hamline U, St Paul, MN 55104	1854	Dr. Larry G. Osnes	2-F	2,465	230
Hampshire Coll, Amherst, MA 01002	1965	Dr. Gregory S. Prince, Jr.	1-B	1,173	99
Hampton U, Hampton, VA 23668	1868	Dr. William R. Harvey	1-D	5,704	390
Hanover Coll, Hanover, IN 47243	1827	Dr. Russell L. Nichols	2-B	1,071	103
Harding U, Searcy, AR 72149	1924	Dr. David B. Burks, Jr.	2-M	3,463	201
Hardin-Simmons U, Abilene, TX 79698-0001	1891	Dr. Lanny Hall	2-M	1,950	30
Harris-Stowe State Coll, St Louis, MO 63103	1857	Dr. Henry Givens, Jr.	5-B	1,945	99
Hartwick Coll, Oneonta, NY 13820	1797	Dr. Richard A. Detweiler	1-B	1,470	139
Harvard U, Cambridge, MA 02138	1636	Dr. Neil Rudenstine	1-D	18,273	2,278
Hastings Coll, Hastings, NE 68902	1882	Dr. Thomas J. Reeves	2-M	1,016	86
Haverford Coll, Haverford, PA 19041-1392	1833	Dr. Tom G. Kessinger	1-B	1,138	107
Hawaii Pacific U, Honolulu, HI 96813	1965	Mr. Chatt Wright	1-M	6,976	381
Heidelberg Coll, Tiffin, OH 44883	1850	Dr. William C. Cassell	2-M	1,182	113
Henderson State U, Arkadelphia, AR 71999-0001	1890	Dr. Charles D. Dunn	5-M	3,742	173
High Point U, High Point, NC 27262-3598	1924	Dr. Jacob C. Martinson, Jr.	2-B	2,326	108
Hillsdale Coll, Hillsdale, MI 49242	1844	Dr. George C. Roche, III	1-B	1,080	108
Hobart Coll, Geneva, NY 14456 (1)	1822	Dr. Richard H. Hersh	2-B	1,061	177
Hofstra U, Hempstead, NY 11550	1935	Dr. James M. Shuart	1-D	11,998	984
Holy Family Coll, Philadelphia, PA 19114-2094	1954	Sr. Francesca Onley	2-M	2,465	224
Hood Coll, Frederick, MD 21701-8575 (4)	1893	Dr. Martha E. Church	2-M	2,005	94
Hope Coll, Holland, MI 49422-9000	1862	Dr. John H. Jacobson, Jr.	2-B	2,755	233
Houghton Coll, Houghton, NY 14744	1883	Dr. Daniel R. Chamberlain	2-B	1,140	100
Houston Baptist U, Houston, TX 77074	1960	Dr. E. Douglas Hodo	2-M	2,200	145
Howard Payne U, Brownwood, TX 76801	1889	Dr. Don Newbury	2-B	1,427	108
Howard U, Washington, DC 20059	1867	Dr. Franklyn G. Jenifer	1-D	11,941	780
Humboldt State U, Arcata, CA 95521-8299	1913	Dr. Alistair W. McCrone	5-M	7,851	551
Hunter Coll of the City U of New York, New York, NY 10021	1870	Dr. Paul Le Clerc	12-M	18,390	696
Huron U, Huron, SD 57350	1883	NR	3-M	1,076	78
Husson Coll, Bangor, ME 04401	1898	Dr. William H. Beardsley	1-M	2,080	67
Idaho State U, Pocatello, ID 83209	1901	Dr. Richard Bowen	5-D	10,755	601
Illinois Benedictine Coll, Lisle, IL 60532-0900	1887	Dr. Richard C. Becker	2-M	2,982	245
Illinois Inst of Tech, Chicago, IL 60616	1890	Mr. Lewis Collens	1-D	6,693	498
Illinois State U, Normal, IL 61761	1857	Dr. Thomas P. Wallace	5-D	21,765	947
Illinois Wesleyan U, Bloomington, IL 61702	1850	Dr. Minor Myers, Jr.	2-B	1,822	180

Name, address	Year	Governing official, control, and highest degree offered		Enrollment	Faculty
Immaculata Coll, Immaculata, PA 19345-0900 (4)	1920	Sr. Marie Roseanne Bonfini	2-M	2,522	167
Incarnate Word Coll, San Antonio, TX 78209	1881	Dr. Louis J. Agnese, Jr.	2-M	2,801	196
Indiana Inst of Tech, Fort Wayne, IN 46803	1930	Mr. Donald J. Andorfer	1-B	1,150	42
Indiana State U, Terre Haute, IN 47809	1865	Dr. John W. Moore	5-D	12,271	718
Indiana U at South Bend, South Bend, IN 46634	1922	Dr. H. Daniel Cohen	5-M	7,801	557
Indiana U Bloomington, Bloomington, IN 47405	1820	Dr. Kenneth R. R. Gros Louis	5-D	36,076	1,575
Indiana U East, Richmond, IN 47374	1971	Dr. Charlie Nelms	5-B	2,411	179
Indiana U Kokomo, Kokomo, IN 46904	1945	Dr. Emita B. Hill	5-M	3,522	195
Indiana U Northwest, Gary, IN 46408	1959	Dr. Hilda Richards	5-M	5,963	372
Indiana U of Pennsylvania, Indiana, PA 15705	1875	Dr. Lawrence K. Pettit	5-D	14,357	758
Indiana U–Purdue U at Fort Wayne, Fort Wayne, IN 46805-1499	1917	Dr. Joanne B. Lantz	5-M	12,090	667
Indiana U–Purdue U at Indianapolis, Indianapolis, IN 46202-2896	1969	Mr. Gerald L. Bepko	5-D	28,345	2,065
Indiana U Southeast, New Albany, IN 47150	1941	Dr. Leon Rand	5-M	5,942	335
Indiana Wesleyan U, Marion, IN 46953	1920	Dr. James Barnes	2-M	3,450	105
Inter American U of PR, Arecibo Cmps, Arecibo, PR 00613	1957	Dr. Zaida Vega	1-B	4,509	231
Inter Amer U of PR, Barranquitas Regional Coll, Barranquitas, PR 00618	1957	Mr. Vidal Rivera Garcia	1-B	1,424	75
Inter American U of PR, San Germán Cmps, San Germán, PR 00683	1912	Prof. Agnes Mojica	1-M	5,553	277
International Correspondence Inst, Irving, TX 75063	1967	NR	2-B	11,800	NR
Iona Coll, New Rochelle, NY 10801	1940	Br. John G. Driscoll, CFC	1-M	7,397	511
Iowa State U of Science and Tech, Ames, IA 50011	1858	Dr. Martin C. Jischke	5-D	25,263	1,759
Ithaca Coll, Ithaca, NY 14850	1892	Dr. James J. Whalen	1-M	6,058	597
ITT Tech Inst, Indianapolis, IN 46268	1966	Mr. Larry L. Graphman	3-B	1,035	44
Jackson State U, Jackson, MS 39217	1877	Dr. James E. Lyons, Sr.	5-D	6,203	380
Jacksonville State U, Jacksonville, AL 36265-9982	1883	Dr. Harold J. McGee	5-M	8,022	349
Jacksonville U, Jacksonville, FL 32211	1934	Dr. James J. Brady	1-M	2,567	245
James Madison U, Harrisonburg, VA 22807	1908	Dr. Ronald E. Carrier	5-M	11,203	777
Jamestown Coll, Jamestown, ND 58405	1883	Dr. James Walker	2-B	1,083	68
Jersey City State Coll, Jersey City, NJ 07305	1927	Dr. Carlos Hernandez	5-M	7,193	434
John Brown U, Siloam Springs, AR 72761	1919	Dr. John E. Brown, III	2-B	1,018	88
John Carroll U, University Heights, OH 44118	1886	Rev. Michael J. Lavelle, SJ	2-M	4,488	333
John F Kennedy U, Orinda, CA 94563	1964	Mr. Charles E. Glasser	1-F	1,753	86
John Jay Coll of Criminal Justice of City U of NY, New York, NY 10019	1964	Dr. Gerald Lynch	12-M	8,500	496
Johns Hopkins U, Baltimore, MD 21218	1876	Dr. William C. Richardson	1-D	4,613	473
Johnson & Wales U, Providence, RI 02903	1914	Dr. John A. Yena	1-M	7,920	312
Johnson C Smith U, Charlotte, NC 28216	1867	Dr. Robert L. Albright	1-B	1,256	96
Johnson State Coll, Johnson, VT 05656	1828	Dr. Robert Hahn	5-M	1,758	140
Jones Coll, Jacksonville, FL 32211	1918	Mrs. Dorothy D. Jones	1-B	1,000	57
Juniata Coll, Huntingdon, PA 16652-2119	1876	Dr. Robert W. Neff	1-B	1,050	104
Kalamazoo Coll, Kalamazoo, MI 49006	1833	Dr. Lawrence Bryan	1-B	1,245	109
Kansas Newman Coll, Wichita, KS 67213	1933	Sr. Tarcisia Roths	2-B	1,618	170
Kansas State U, Manhattan, KS 66506	1863	Dr. Jon Wefald	5-D	21,224	1,083
Kean Coll of New Jersey, Union, NJ 07083	1855	Dr. Elsa Gomez	5-M	12,497	824
Keene State Coll, Keene, NH 03431	1909	Dr. Judith A. Sturnick	5-M	3,987	350
Kennesaw State Coll, Marietta, GA 30061	1963	Dr. Betty L. Siegel	5-M	11,670	449
Kent State U, Kent, OH 44242-0001	1910	Dr. Carol A. Cartwright	5-D	24,100	1,340
Kentucky State U, Frankfort, KY 40601	1886	Dr. Mary L. Smith	13-M	2,545	158
Kenyon Coll, Gambier, OH 43022-9623	1824	Dr. Philip H. Jordan, Jr.	1-B	1,488	164
King's Coll, Wilkes-Barre, PA 18711-0801	1946	Rev. James Lackenmier, CSC	2-M	2,356	162
Kutztown U of Pennsylvania, Kutztown, PA 19530	1866	Dr. David E. McFarland	5-M	7,791	400
Lafayette Coll, Easton, PA 18042	1826	Dr. Robert I. Rotberg	2-B	2,225	228
Lakeland Coll, Sheboygan, WI 53082-0359	1862	Dr. David R. Black	2-M	2,656	165
Lake Superior State U, Sault Sainte Marie, MI 49783	1946	Dr. Robert D. Arbuckle	5-M	3,384	179
Lamar U–Beaumont, Beaumont, TX 77705	1923	Dr. Rex Cottle	5-D	11,295	725
Lambuth U, Jackson, TN 38301	1843	Dr. Thomas F. Boyd	2-B	1,153	87
Lander U, Greenwood, SC 29649-2099	1872	Dr. William C. Moran	5-M	2,521	162
La Roche Coll, Pittsburgh, PA 15237	1963	Msgr. William Kerr	2-M	1,763	123
La Salle U, Philadelphia, PA 19141	1863	Br. Joseph Burke	2-M	5,900	324
La Sierra U, Riverside, CA 92515	1922	Dr. Fritz Guy	2-D	1,524	102
Lawrence Tech U, Southfield, MI 48075	1932	Dr. Richard E. Marburger	1-M	4,886	307
Lawrence U, Appleton, WI 54912	1847	Dr. Richard Warch	1-B	1,202	136
Lebanon Valley Coll, Annville, PA 17003	1866	Mr. John A. Synodinos	2-M	1,535	89
Lee Coll, Cleveland, TN 37311	1918	Dr. Paul Conn	2-B	1,922	157
Lehigh U, Bethlehem, PA 18015-3094	1865	Dr. Peter Likins	1-D	6,550	484
Lehman Coll of the City U of New York, Bronx, NY 10468	1931	Dr. Ricardo R. Fernandez	12-M	9,956	NR
Le Moyne Coll, Syracuse, NY 13214	1946	Rev. Kevin G. O'Connell, SJ	2-B	2,403	205
LeMoyne-Owen Coll, Memphis, TN 38126	1862	Dr. Doris W. Weathers	2-M	1,200	100
Lenoir-Rhyne Coll, Hickory, NC 28603	1891	Dr. John E. Trainer, Jr.	2-M	1,522	120
Lesley Coll, Cambridge, MA 02138 (3)	1909	Ms. Margaret A. McKenna	1-D	5,129	39
LeTourneau U, Longview, TX 75607-7001	1946	Dr. Alvin O. Austin	2-M	1,600	119
Lewis & Clark Coll, Portland, OR 97219	1867	Dr. Michael J. Mooney	1-F	3,453	302
Lewis-Clark State Coll, Lewiston, ID 83501	1894	Dr. Lee A. Vickers	5-B	3,029	120
Lewis U, Romeoville, IL 60441	1932	Br. James Gaffney, FSC	2-M	4,102	160
Liberty U, Lynchburg, VA 24506-8001	1971	Dr. A. Pierre Guillermin	2-D	3,834	216
Lincoln Memorial U, Harrogate, TN 37752	1897	Dr. Scott D. Miller	1-M	1,860	139
Lincoln U, Jefferson City, MO 65102	1866	Dr. Wendell G. Rayburn, Sr.	5-M	4,031	246
Lincoln U, Lincoln University, PA 19352	1854	Dr. Niara Sudarkasa	13-M	1,477	138
Lindenwood Coll, St Charles, MO 63301	1827	Dr. Dennis Spellmann	2-M	2,825	162
Lindsey Wilson Coll, Columbia, KY 42728	1903	Dr. John B. Begley	2-B	1,099	55
Linfield Coll, McMinnville, OR 97128	1849	Dr. Vivian A. Bull	2-M	1,528	150
Livingston U, Livingston, AL 35470	1835	Dr. Asa N. Green	5-M	1,977	110
Lock Haven U of Pennsylvania, Lock Haven, PA 17745-2390	1870	Dr. Craig Dean Willis	5-M	3,895	226
Long Island U, Brooklyn Cmps, Brooklyn, NY 11201	1926	Dr. David J. Steinberg	1-F	6,838	507
Long Island U, C W Post Cmps, Brookville, NY 11548	1954	NR	1-D	8,220	722
Long Island U, Southampton Cmps, Southampton, NY 11968	1963	Dr. David J. Steinberg	1-M	1,458	120
Longwood Coll, Farmville, VA 23909	1839	Dr. William F. Dorrill	5-M	3,202	211
Loras Coll, Dubuque, IA 52004	1839	Rev. Msgr. James Barta	2-M	1,776	133
Louisiana Coll, Pineville, LA 71359	1906	Dr. Robert L. Lynn	2-B	1,026	77

Name, address	Year	Governing official, control, and highest degree offered		Enroll-ment	Faculty
Louisiana State U and A&M Coll, Baton Rouge, LA 70803	1860	Dr. William E. Davis	5-D	26,607	1,340
Louisiana State U in Shreveport, Shreveport, LA 71115-2399	1965	Dr. John R. Darling, Jr.	5-M	4,665	234
Louisiana State U Medical Ctr, New Orleans, LA 70112	1931	Dr. Perry G. Rigby	5-D	2,908	NR
Louisiana Tech U, Ruston, LA 71272	1894	Dr. Daniel D. Reneau	5-D	10,263	482
Lourdes Coll, Sylvania, OH 43560	1958	Sr. Ann Francis Klimkowski, OSF	2-B	1,469	119
Loyola Coll, Baltimore, MD 21210-2699	1852	NR	2-M	6,221	406
Loyola Marymount U, Los Angeles, CA 90045-2699	1911	Rev. Thomas P. O'Malley, SJ	2-F	6,397	438
Loyola U Chicago, Chicago, IL 60611	1870	Rev. Raymond C. Baumhart, SJ	2-D	15,298	876
Loyola U, New Orleans, New Orleans, LA 70118	1912	Rev. James C. Carter, SJ	2-M	5,582	391
Lubbock Christian U, Lubbock, TX 79407	1957	Dr. Ken Jones	2-M	1,141	97
Luther Coll, Decorah, IA 52101	1861	Dr. H. George Anderson	2-B	2,327	193
Lycoming Coll, Williamsport, PA 17701	1812	Dr. James E. Douthat	2-B	1,478	125
Lynchburg Coll, Lynchburg, VA 24501-3199	1903	Dr. Charles O. Warren, Jr.	2-M	2,379	186
Lyndon State Coll, Lyndonville, VT 05851	1911	Dr. Margaret R. Williams	5-M	1,195	111
Lynn U, Boca Raton, FL 33431	1962	Dr. Donald E. Ross	1-M	1,200	75
Macalester Coll, St Paul, MN 55105-1899	1874	Dr. Robert M. Gavin, Jr.	2-B	1,838	187
Madonna U, Livonia, MI 48150-1173	1947	Sr. Mary Francilene	2-M	4,419	241
Malone Coll, Canton, OH 44709	1892	Dr. E. Arthur Self	2-M	1,801	125
Manchester Coll, North Manchester, IN 46962	1889	Dr. Edgar C. Butterbaugh	2-M	1,080	102
Manhattan Coll, Riverdale, NY 10471	1853	Br. Thomas J. Scanlan	2-M	3,616	276
Manhattanville Coll, Purchase, NY 10577	1841	Dr. Marcia A. Savage	1-M	1,502	207
Mankato State U, Mankato, MN 56002-8400	1867	Dr. Richard R. Rush	5-M	13,925	552
Mannes Coll of Music, New Sch for Social Research, New York, NY 10024	1916	Dr. Charles Kaufman	1-M	230	216
Mansfield U of Pennsylvania, Mansfield, PA 16933	1857	Mr. Rod C. Kelchner	5-M	3,223	188
Marian Coll, Indianapolis, IN 46222	1851	Dr. Daniel A. Felicetti	2-B	1,288	138
Marian Coll of Fond du Lac, Fond du Lac, WI 54935	1936	Mr. Matthew G. Flanigan	2-M	2,271	103
Marietta Coll, Marietta, OH 45750	1835	Dr. Patrick D. McDonough	1-M	1,379	110
Marist Coll, Poughkeepsie, NY 12601	1929	Dr. Dennis J. Murray	1-M	4,294	352
Marquette U, Milwaukee, WI 53233	1881	Rev. Albert J. DiUlio, SJ	2-D	11,017	975
Marshall U, Huntington, WV 25755	1837	Dr. J. Wade Gilley	5-D	12,744	589
Mars Hill Coll, Mars Hill, NC 28754	1856	Dr. Fred B. Bentley	2-B	1,070	122
Marygrove Coll, Detroit, MI 48221-2599	1910	Dr. John E. Shay, Jr.	2-M	1,300	60
Marylhurst Coll, Marylhurst, OR 97036	1893	Ms. Nancy A. Wilgenbusch	2-M	1,238	223
Marymount Coll, Tarrytown, NY 10591-3796 (4)	1907	Dr. Brigid Driscoll, RSHM	1-B	1,142	129
Marymount Manhattan Coll, New York, NY 10021 (4)	1936	Dr. Regina Peruggi	1-B	1,600	155
Marymount U, Arlington, VA 22207	1950	Sr. M. Majella Berg, RSHM	2-M	3,839	333
Maryville U of St Louis, St Louis, MO 63141	1872	Dr. Keith Lovin	1-M	3,722	280
Mary Washington Coll, Fredericksburg, VA 22401	1908	Dr. William M. Anderson, Jr.	5-M	3,432	228
Marywood Coll, Scranton, PA 18509	1915	Sr. Mary Reap, IHM	2-M	2,902	216
Massachusetts Coll of Art, Boston, MA 02115	1873	Dr. William F. O'Neil	5-M	1,206	92
Mass Coll of Pharmacy and Allied Health Sciences, Boston, MA 02115	1823	Dr. Louis P. Jeffrey	1-D	1,325	122
Massachusetts Inst of Tech, Cambridge, MA 02139	1861	Dr. Charles M. Vest	1-D	9,798	975
McKendree Coll, Lebanon, IL 62254	1828	Dr. Gerrit J. TenBrink	2-B	1,450	74
McMurry U, Abilene, TX 79697	1923	Dr. Robert E. Shimp	2-B	1,518	121
McNeese State U, Lake Charles, LA 70609	1939	Dr. Robert D. Hebert	5-M	8,474	342
Medaille Coll, Buffalo, NY 14214	1875	Mr. Kevin I. Sullivan	1-B	1,215	88
Medgar Evers Coll of the City U of New York, Brooklyn, NY 11225	1969	Dr. Edison O. Jackson	12-B	5,000	272
Medical Coll of Georgia, Augusta, GA 30912	1828	Dr. Francis J. Tedesco	5-D	2,058	751
Medical U of South Carolina, Charleston, SC 29425	1824	Dr. James B. Edwards	5-D	2,290	2,435
Memphis State U, Memphis, TN 38152	1912	Dr. V. Lane Rawlins	5-D	20,578	1,120
Mercer U, Macon, GA 31207	1833	Dr. R. Kirby Godsey	2-F	6,348	670
Mercer U, Cecil B Day Cmps, Atlanta, GA 30341	1968	Dr. R. Kirby Godsey	2-M	1,599	44
Mercy Coll, Dobbs Ferry, NY 10522	1951	Dr. Jay Sexter	1-M	6,211	480
Mercyhurst Coll, Erie, PA 16546	1926	Dr. William P. Garvey	2-M	2,308	145
Meredith Coll, Raleigh, NC 27607-5298 (3)	1891	Dr. John E. Weems	2-M	2,049	200
Merrimack Coll, North Andover, MA 01845	1947	Rev. John E. Deegan, OSA	2-B	2,952	169
Messiah Coll, Grantham, PA 17027	1909	Dr. D. Ray Hostetter	2-B	2,263	182
Methodist Coll, Fayetteville, NC 28311	1956	Dr. M. Elton Hendricks	2-B	1,508	85
Metropolitan State Coll of Denver, Denver, CO 80217	1963	Dr. Sheila Kaplan	5-B	17,570	908
Metropolitan State U, St Paul, MN 55106-5000	1971	Mr. Richard Green	5-M	5,390	522
Miami U, Oxford, OH 45056	1809	Dr. Paul G. Risser	5-D	16,104	1,027
Michigan State U, East Lansing, MI 48824	1855	Dr. Gordon Guyer	5-D	40,047	4,006
Michigan Tech U, Houghton, MI 49931	1885	Dr. Curtis J. Tompkins	5-D	6,961	365
MidAmerica Nazarene Coll, Olathe, KS 66062-1899	1966	Dr. Richard Spindle	2-M	1,446	105
Middlebury Coll, Middlebury, VT 05753	1800	Dr. John McCardell	1-M	1,960	220
Middle Tennessee State U, Murfreesboro, TN 37132	1911	Dr. James E. Walker	5-D	16,780	877
Midwestern State U, Wichita Falls, TX 76308	1922	Dr. Louis J. Rodriguez	5-M	5,764	213
Millersville U of Pennsylvania, Millersville, PA 17551-0302	1854	Dr. Joseph A. Caputo	5-M	6,545	398
Millikin U, Decatur, IL 62522	1901	Dr. Curtis L. McCray	2-B	1,892	187
Millsaps Coll, Jackson, MS 39210	1890	Dr. George M. Harmon	2-M	1,329	106
Mills Coll, Oakland, CA 94613 (3)	1852	Dr. Janet H. McKay	1-M	1,083	143
Milwaukee Sch of Engineering, Milwaukee, WI 53202-3109	1903	Dr. Hermann Viets	1-M	3,166	253
Minot State U, Minot, ND 58707	1913	Dr. H. Erik Shaar	5-M	3,797	192
Mississippi Coll, Clinton, MS 39058	1826	Dr. Lewis Nobles	2-M	3,771	234
Mississippi State U, Mississippi State, MS 39762	1878	Dr. Donald W. Zacharias	5-D	14,619	824
Mississippi U for Women, Columbus, MS 39701 (4)	1884	Dr. Clyda S. Rent	5-M	2,652	160
Mississippi Valley State U, Itta Bena, MS 38941	1946	Dr. William W. Sutton	5-M	2,222	137
Missouri Baptist Coll, St Louis, MO 63141	1968	Dr. Thomas S. Field	2-B	1,429	79
Missouri Southern State Coll, Joplin, MO 64801-1595	1937	Dr. Julio Leon	5-B	5,640	278
Missouri Valley Coll, Marshall, MO 65340	1889	Dr. Earl J. Reeves	2-B	1,153	68
Missouri Western State Coll, St Joseph, MO 64507-2294	1915	Dr. Janet Gorman Murphy	5-B	5,093	296
Molloy Coll, Rockville Centre, NY 11570-1199	1955	Dr. Janet A. Fitzgerald, OP	1-M	1,549	188
Monmouth Coll, West Long Branch, NJ 07764-1898	1933	Dr. Rebecca Stafford	1-M	4,201	321
Montana Coll of Mineral Science and Tech, Butte, MT 59701-8997	1895	Dr. Lindsay D. Norman, Jr.	5-M	1,975	139
Montana State U, Bozeman, MT 59717	1893	Dr. Michael P. Malone	5-D	10,540	663
Montclair State Coll, Upper Montclair, NJ 07043-1624	1908	Dr. Irvin D. Reid	5-M	13,657	816
Moody Bible Inst, Chicago, IL 60610	1886	Dr. Joseph M. Stowell, III	2-M	1,495	78
Moorhead State U, Moorhead, MN 56563	1885	Dr. Roland Dille	5-M	8,723	435
Moravian Coll, Bethlehem, PA 18018-6650	1742	Dr. Roger Harry Martin	2-M	1,332	129
Morehead State U, Morehead, KY 40351	1922	Dr. Ronald Eaglin	5-M	9,169	391

Name, address	Year	Governing official, control, and highest degree offered		Enroll-ment	Faculty
Morehouse Coll, Atlanta, GA 30314 (1)	1867	Dr. Leroy Keith, Jr.	1-B	2,990	178
Morgan State U, Baltimore, MD 21239	1867	Dr. Earl Richardson	5-D	5,307	297
Morningside Coll, Sioux City, IA 51106-1751	1894	Dr. Jerry Israel	2-M	1,288	100
Mount Aloysius Coll, Cresson, PA 16630	1939	Dr. Edward F. Pierce	2-B	1,045	88
Mount Holyoke Coll, South Hadley, MA 01075 (3)	1837	Mrs. Elizabeth T. Kennan	1-M	1,932	240
Mount Marty Coll, Yankton, SD 57078-3724	1936	Sr. Jacquelyn Ernster	2-M	1,104	81
Mount Mary Coll, Milwaukee, WI 53222 (3)	1913	Sr. Ruth Hollenbach	2-M	1,526	155
Mount Mercy Coll, Cedar Rapids, IA 52402	1928	Dr. Thomas R. Feld	2-B	1,398	110
Mount Saint Mary Coll, Newburgh, NY 12550	1960	Sr. Ann Sakac	1-M	1,721	149
Mount St Mary's Coll, Los Angeles, CA 90049 (4)	1925	Sr. Karen Kennelly	2-M	1,491	177
Mount Saint Mary's Coll, Emmitsburg, MD 21727	1808	Rev. James N. Loughran, SJ	2-M	1,723	165
Mount Union Coll, Alliance, OH 44601	1846	Dr. Harold M. Kolenbrander	2-B	1,410	96
Mount Vernon Nazarene Coll, Mount Vernon, OH 43050	1964	Dr. E. LeBron Fairbanks	2-M	1,126	69
Muhlenberg Coll, Allentown, PA 18104	1848	Mr. Arthur R. Taylor	2-B	1,641	161
Murray State U, Murray, KY 42071	1922	Dr. Ronald J. Kurth	5-M	8,190	371
Muskingum Coll, New Concord, OH 43762	1837	Dr. Samuel W. Speck, Jr.	2-M	1,135	102
National-Louis U, Evanston, IL 60201	1886	NR	1-D	7,600	243
National U, San Diego, CA 92108	1971	Dr. Jerry C. Lee	1-M	8,972	1,281
Nazareth Coll of Rochester, Rochester, NY 14618-3790	1924	Dr. Rose Marie Beston	1-M	2,673	185
Nebraska Wesleyan U, Lincoln, NE 68504	1887	Dr. John W. White, Jr.	2-B	1,694	151
Neumann Coll, Aston, PA 19014	1965	Dr. Nan B. Hechenberger	2-M	1,214	111
New Hampshire Coll, Manchester, NH 03106-1045	1932	Dr. Richard A. Gustafson	1-M	2,513	179
New Jersey Inst of Tech, Newark, NJ 07102	1881	Dr. Saul K. Fenster	13-D	7,697	452
New Mexico Highlands U, Las Vegas, NM 87701	1893	Dr. Gilbert Sanchez	5-M	2,807	134
New Mexico Inst of Mining and Tech, Socorro, NM 87801	1889	Dr. Laurence H. Lattman	5-D	1,592	101
New Mexico State U, Las Cruces, NM 88003	1888	Dr. James E. Halligan	5-D	15,500	794
New Sch Bach of Arts, New Sch for Social Research, New York, NY 10011	1919	NR	1-B	233	545
New York Inst of Tech, Old Westbury, NY 11568-8000	1955	Dr. Matthew Schure	1-F	10,221	1,253
New York U, New York, NY 10011	1831	Dr. L. Jay Oliva	1-D	33,973	4,110
Niagara U, Niagara University, NY 14109	1856	Rev. Brian J. O'Connell, CM	1-M	3,002	214
Nicholls State U, Thibodaux, LA 70310	1948	Dr. Donald J. Ayo	5-M	7,605	265
Nichols Coll, Dudley, MA 01571	1815	Dr. Lowell C. Smith	1-M	1,865	49
Norfolk State U, Norfolk, VA 23504	1935	Dr. Harrison B. Wilson	5-M	8,624	526
North Adams State Coll, North Adams, MA 01247	1894	Dr. Thomas D. Aceto	5-M	1,694	127
North Carolina Ag and Tech State U, Greensboro, NC 27411	1891	Dr. Edward B. Fort	5-M	7,580	424
North Carolina Central U, Durham, NC 27707	1910	Mr. Julius L. Chambers	5-F	5,385	376
North Carolina State U, Raleigh, NC 27695	1887	Dr. Larry K. Monteith	5-D	27,156	1,431
North Central Bible Coll, Minneapolis, MN 55404	1930	Dr. Don H. Argue	2-B	1,042	66
North Central Coll, Naperville, IL 60566-7063	1861	Dr. Harold R. Wilde	2-M	2,535	178
North Dakota State U, Fargo, ND 58105	1890	Dr. Jim Ozbun	5-D	9,307	536
Northeastern Illinois U, Chicago, IL 60625-4699	1961	Dr. Gordon Lamb	5-M	10,820	496
Northeastern State U, Tahlequah, OK 74464-2399	1846	Dr. W. Roger Webb	5-D	9,023	329
Northeastern U, Boston, MA 02115	1898	Mr. John A. Curry	1-D	27,619	2,206
Northeast Louisiana U, Monroe, LA 71209	1931	Mr. Lawson L. Swearingen, Jr.	5-M	11,732	527
Northeast Missouri State U, Kirksville, MO 63501	1867	Dr. Russell G. Warren	5-M	5,941	470
Northern Arizona U, Flagstaff, AZ 86011	1899	Dr. Patsy Reed	5-D	18,491	722
Northern Illinois U, De Kalb, IL 60115-2864	1895	Dr. John E. LaTourette	5-D	24,052	1,233
Northern Kentucky U, Highland Heights, KY 41099	1968	Dr. Leon E. Boothe	5-F	11,218	609
Northern Michigan U, Marquette, MI 49855	1899	Dr. William E. Vandament	5-M	8,897	359
Northern Montana Coll, Havre, MT 59501	1929	Dr. William Daehling	5-M	1,742	113
Northern State U, Aberdeen, SD 57401	1901	Dr. John Hutchinson	5-M	2,867	121
North Georgia Coll, Dahlonega, GA 30597	1873	Dr. Delmas J. Allen	5-M	2,794	147
North Park Coll, Chicago, IL 60625	1891	Dr. David G. Horner	2-M	1,107	80
Northwestern Coll, Orange City, IA 51041-1996	1882	Dr. James E. Bultman	2-M	1,055	84
Northwestern Coll, St Paul, MN 55113-1598	1902	Dr. Donald Ericksen	2-B	1,244	110
Northwestern Oklahoma State U, Alva, OK 73717-9898	1897	Dr. Joe J. Struckle	5-M	2,106	121
Northwestern State U of Louisiana, Natchitoches, LA 71497	1884	Dr. Robert A. Alost	5-M	8,412	200
Northwestern U, Evanston, IL 60208	1851	Dr. Arnold R. Weber	1-D	12,032	1,079
Northwest Missouri State U, Maryville, MO 64468-6001	1905	Dr. Dean L. Hubbard	5-M	5,865	274
Northwest Nazarene Coll, Nampa, ID 83686	1913	Dr. Gilbert Ford	2-M	1,248	101
Northwood U, Midland, MI 48640	1959	Dr. David E. Fry	1-M	1,701	62
Norwich U, Northfield, VT 05663	1819	Dr. Richard Schneider	1-M	2,620	194
Notre Dame Coll, Manchester, NH 03104	1950	Dr. Carol J. Descoteaux, CSC	2-M	1,300	98
Nova U, Fort Lauderdale, FL 33314	1964	Dr. Stephen Feldman	1-D	10,879	435
Oakland U, Rochester, MI 48309	1957	Dr. Sandra Packard	5-D	13,068	616
Oakwood Coll, Huntsville, AL 35896	1896	Dr. Benjamin F. Reaves	2-B	1,225	110
Oberlin Coll, Oberlin, OH 44074	1833	Mr. S. Frederick Starr	1-M	2,902	232
Occidental Coll, Los Angeles, CA 90041	1887	Dr. John B. Slaughter	1-M	1,649	184
Oglethorpe U, Atlanta, GA 30319	1835	Dr. Donald S. Stanton	1-M	1,195	102
Ohio Dominican Coll, Columbus, OH 43219	1911	Sr. Mary Andrew Matesich	2-B	1,510	99
Ohio Northern U, Ada, OH 45810	1871	Dr. DeBow Freed	2-F	2,872	227
Ohio State U, Columbus, OH 43210	1870	Dr. E. Gordon Gee	5-D	52,183	3,823
Ohio State U-Lima Cmps, Lima, OH 45804	1960	Dr. Violet I. Meek	5-B	1,410	74
Ohio State U-Mansfield Cmps, Mansfield, OH 44906	1958	Dr. John O. Riedl, Jr.	5-B	1,465	75
Ohio State U-Marion Cmps, Marion, OH 43302	1957	Dr. Dominic Dottavio	5-B	1,066	86
Ohio State U-Newark Cmps, Newark, OH 43055	1957	Dr. Julius S. Greenstein	5-B	1,732	93
Ohio U, Athens, OH 45701	1804	Dr. Charles J. Ping	5-D	18,248	920
Ohio U-Chillicothe, Chillicothe, OH 45601	1946	Dr. Delbert Meyer	5-B	1,738	81
Ohio U-Lancaster, Lancaster, OH 43130	1968	Dr. Raymond Wilkes	5-M	1,554	127
Ohio U-Zanesville, Zanesville, OH 43701	1946	Dr. Craig D. Laubenthal	5-M	1,232	49
Ohio Wesleyan U, Delaware, OH 43015	1842	Dr. David L. Warren	2-B	2,037	179
Oklahoma Baptist U, Shawnee, OK 74801	1910	Dr. Bob R. Agee	2-B	2,260	155
Oklahoma Christian U of Science and Arts, Oklahoma City, OK 73136	1950	Dr. J. Terry Johnson	2-M	1,636	124
Oklahoma City U, Oklahoma City, OK 73106	1904	Dr. Jerald C. Walker	2-F	4,450	263
Oklahoma Panhandle State U, Goodwell, OK 73939	1909	Dr. Ray Brown	5-B	1,209	83
Oklahoma State U, Stillwater, OK 74078	1890	Dr. John Campbell	5-D	19,477	896
Old Dominion U, Norfolk, VA 23529	1930	Dr. James V. Koch	5-D	16,561	1,040
Olivet Nazarene U, Kankakee, IL 60901	1907	Dr. John C. Bowling	2-M	1,996	115
Oral Roberts U, Tulsa, OK 74171	1963	Mr. Richard Roberts	2-D	4,054	211
Oregon Health Sciences U, Portland, OR 97201	1974	Dr. Peter O. Kohler	5-D	1,388	76
Oregon Inst of Tech, Klamath Falls, OR 97601-8801	1947	Dr. Lawrence J. Wolf	5-B	2,757	182

Name, address	Year	Governing official, control, and highest degree offered		Enroll-ment	Faculty
Oregon State U, Corvallis, OR 97331	1868	Dr. John V. Byrne	5-D	14,336	2,285
Orlando Coll, Orlando, FL 32810	1918	Mrs. Ouida B. Kirby	3-M	2,127	106
Otterbein Coll, Westerville, OH 43081	1847	Dr. C. Brent DeVore	2-M	2,531	186
Ouachita Baptist U, Arkadelphia, AR 71998	1886	Dr. Ben M. Elrod	2-B	1,296	103
Our Lady of Holy Cross Coll, New Orleans, LA 70131	1916	Rev. Thomas E. Chambers, CSC	2-M	1,145	63
Our Lady of the Lake U of San Antonio, San Antonio, TX 78207-4689	1911	Sr. Elizabeth Anne Sueltenfuss	2-M	2,947	171
Pace U, New York, NY 10038	1906	Dr. Patricia Ewers	1-D	13,567	1,053
Pacific Lutheran U, Tacoma, WA 98447	1890	Dr. Loren J. Anderson	2-M	3,451	320
Pacific Union Coll, Angwin, CA 94508	1882	Dr. D. Malcolm Maxwell	2-M	1,512	134
Pacific U, Forest Grove, OR 97116	1849	Dr. Robert F. Duvall	1-F	1,575	199
Palm Beach Atlantic Coll, West Palm Beach, FL 33416-4708	1968	Dr. Paul R. Corts	2-M	1,715	121
Palmer Coll of Chiropractic, Davenport, IA 52803	1895	Dr. Donald P. Kern	1-F	1,700	129
Parks Coll of Saint Louis U, Cahokia, IL 62206	1927	Dr. Margaret J. Baty	2-B	1,070	109
Parsons Sch of Design, New Sch for Social Research, New York, NY 10011	1896	Mr. Charles S. Olton	1-M	1,777	332
Pembroke State U, Pembroke, NC 28372	1887	Dr. Joseph Oxendine	5-M	3,041	193
Pennsylvania Coll of Optometry, Philadelphia, PA 19141	1919	Dr. Thomas L. Lewis	1-F	5,913	75
Penn State U at Erie, The Behrend Coll, Erie, PA 16563	1948	Dr. John M. Lilley	13-M	3,159	140
Penn State U at Harrisburg—The Capital Coll, Middletown, PA 17057-4898	1966	Dr. Ruth Leventhal	13-D	3,646	203
Penn State U Univ Park Cmps, University Park, PA 16802	1855	Dr. Joab L. Thomas	13-D	38,446	2,108
Pepperdine U, Malibu, CA 90263	1937	Dr. David Davenport	2-D	7,011	297
Peru State Coll, Peru, NE 68421	1867	Dr. Robert L. Burns	5-M	1,592	77
Philadelphia Coll of Pharmacy and Science, Philadelphia, PA 19104-4495	1821	Dr. Allen Misher	1-D	1,786	198
Philadelphia Coll of Textiles and Science, Philadelphia, PA 19144	1884	Dr. James P. Gallagher	1-M	3,357	113
Pittsburg State U, Pittsburg, KS 66762	1903	Dr. Donald W. Wilson	5-M	6,515	289
Plymouth State Coll of the U System of NH, Plymouth, NH 03264	1871	Dr. Theodora J. Kalikow	5-M	4,000	263
Point Loma Nazarene Coll, San Diego, CA 92106	1902	Dr. Jim L. Bond	2-M	2,450	138
Point Park Coll, Pittsburgh, PA 15222	1960	Dr. J. Matthew Simon	1-M	2,834	194
Polytechnic U, Brooklyn Cmps, Brooklyn, NY 11201-2999	1854	Dr. George Bugliarello	1-D	2,173	393
Pomona Coll, Claremont, CA 91711	1887	Dr. Peter W. Stanley	1-B	1,389	188
Pontifical Catholic U of Puerto Rico, Ponce, PR 00732	1948	Rev. F. Tosello Giangiacomo	2-M	12,366	577
Prairie View A&M U, Prairie View, TX 77446	1878	Lt. Gen. Julius W. Becton, Jr.	5-M	5,660	303
Pratt Inst, Brooklyn, NY 11205	1887	Dr. Warren F. Ilchman	1-M	2,898	447
Presbyterian Coll, Clinton, SC 29325	1880	Dr. Kenneth B. Orr	2-B	1,167	109
Princeton U, Princeton, NJ 08544	1746	Mr. Harold T. Shapiro	1-D	6,438	935
Providence Coll, Providence, RI 02918	1917	Rev. John F. Cunningham, OP	2-D	6,387	303
Purdue U, West Lafayette, IN 47907	1869	Dr. Steven C. Beering	5-D	36,163	2,269
Purdue U Calumet, Hammond, IN 46323-2094	1951	Dr. James Yackel	5-M	8,285	457
Purdue U North Central, Westville, IN 46391	1967	Dr. Dale W. Alspaugh	5-M	3,588	218
Queens Coll, Charlotte, NC 28274	1857	Dr. Billy O. Wireman	2-M	1,602	115
Queens Coll of the City U of New York, Flushing, NY 11367-1597	1937	Dr. Shirley Strum Kenny	12-M	17,921	1,274
Quincy U, Quincy, IL 62301	1860	Rev. James Toal, OFM	2-M	1,223	98
Quinnipiac Coll, Hamden, CT 06518	1929	Dr. John L. Lahey	1-F	4,658	333
Radford U, Radford, VA 24142	1910	Dr. Donald N. Dedmon	5-M	9,432	392
Ramapo Coll of New Jersey, Mahwah, NJ 07430	1969	Dr. Robert A. Scott	5-B	4,636	309
Randolph-Macon Coll, Ashland, VA 23005-5505	1830	Dr. Ladell Payne	2-B	1,118	142
Reed Coll, Portland, OR 97202-8199	1909	Dr. Steven Koblik	1-M	1,230	133
Regis Coll, Weston, MA 02193 (3)	1927	Sr. Sheila Megley, RSM	2-M	1,121	104
Regis U, Denver, CO 80221	1877	Rev. Michael J. Sheeran, SJ	2-M	6,471	87
Rensselaer Polytechnic Inst, Troy, NY 12180	1824	Dr. R. Byron Pipes	1-D	6,839	465
Rhode Island Coll, Providence, RI 02908	1854	Dr. John Nazarian	5-M	9,838	502
Rhode Island Sch of Design, Providence, RI 02903-2784	1877	Mr. Louis A. Fazzano	1-M	1,986	286
Rhodes Coll, Memphis, TN 38112	1848	Dr. James H. Daughdrill, Jr.	2-M	1,414	154
Rice U, Houston, TX 77251	1912	Dr. Malcolm Gillis	1-D	4,033	542
Rider Coll, Lawrenceville, NJ 08648	1865	Dr. J. Barton Luedeke	1-M	5,484	448
Rivier Coll, Nashua, NH 03060	1933	Sr. Jeanne Perreault	2-M	2,765	202
Roanoke Coll, Salem, VA 24153	1842	Dr. David M. Gring	2-B	1,677	150
Robert Morris Coll, Coraopolis, PA 15108	1921	Dr. Edward A. Nicholson	1-M	5,566	238
Rochester Inst of Tech, Rochester, NY 14623-0887	1829	Dr. Albert J. Simone	1-D	13,004	1,087
Rockford Coll, Rockford, IL 61108-2393	1847	Dr. Bill Shields	1-M	1,491	123
Rockhurst Coll, Kansas City, MO 64110	1910	Rev. Thomas J. Savage, SJ	2-M	2,702	203
Roger Williams U, Bristol, RI 02809	1948	Dr. Malcolm H. Forbes	1-B	2,111	229
Rollins Coll, Winter Park, FL 32789-4499	1885	Dr. Rita Bornstein	1-M	2,093	284
Roosevelt U, Chicago, IL 60605	1945	Dr. Theodore L. Gross	1-M	6,444	508
Rosary Coll, River Forest, IL 60305	1901	Dr. Jean Murray, OP	2-M	1,766	116
Rose-Hulman Inst of Tech, Terre Haute, IN 47803 (1)	1874	Dr. Samuel F. Hulbert	1-M	1,420	97
Rowan Coll of New Jersey, Glassboro, NJ 08028	1923	Dr. Herman D. James	5-M	7,983	323
Rush U, Chicago, IL 60612	1969	Dr. Leo M. Henikoff	1-M	1,301	170
Rust Coll, Holly Springs, MS 38635	1866	Dr. David L. Beckley	2-B	1,129	61
Rutgers, State U of NJ, Camden Coll of Arts & Scis, Camden, NJ 08102	1927	NR	5-B	2,672	NR
Rutgers, State U of NJ, Coll of Engineering, Piscataway, NJ 08855-0909	1864	Dr. Ellis H. Dill	5-B	2,454	NR
Rutgers, State U of NJ, Coll of Nursing, Newark, NJ 07102	1956	Ms. Dorothy J. DeMaio	5-D	391	NR
Rutgers, State U of NJ, Coll of Pharmacy, New Brunswick, NJ 08903-2101	1927	Dr. John Louis Colaizzi	5-D	858	NR
Rutgers, State U of NJ, Cook Coll, New Brunswick, NJ 08903-2101	1921	Mr. Daryl B. Lund	5-B	2,908	NR
Rutgers, State U of NJ, Douglass Coll, New Brunswick, NJ 08903-0270 (3)	1918	Dr. Mary S. Hartman	5-B	3,181	NR
Rutgers, State U of NJ, Livingston Coll, New Brunswick, NJ 08903-2101	1969	NR	5-B	3,645	NR
Rutgers, State U of NJ, Mason Gross Sch of Arts, New Brunswick, NJ 08903-2101	1976	Dr. Marilyn F. Somville	5-M	630	NR

Name, address	Year	Governing official, control, and highest degree offered		Enroll-ment	Faculty
Rutgers, State U of NJ, Newark Coll of Arts & Scis, Newark, NJ 07102	1946	Dr. David Hosford	5-B	3,782	NR
Rutgers, State U of NJ, Rutgers Coll, New Brunswick, NJ 08903-2101	1766	Dr. James W. Reed	5-B	8,550	NR
Rutgers, State U of NJ, U Coll–Camden, Camden, NJ 08102	1950	Dr. Robert A. Catlin	5-B	851	NR
Rutgers, State U of NJ, U Coll–Newark, Newark, NJ 07102-1896	1934	NR	5-B	2,000	NR
Rutgers, State U of NJ, U Coll–New Brunswick, New Brunswick, NJ 08903	1934	NR	5-B	3,249	NR
Sacred Heart U, Fairfield, CT 06432	1963	Dr. Anthony J. Cernera	2-M	5,185	303
The Sage Colleges, Troy, NY 12180-4115 (3)	1916	Dr. Sara Chapman	1-M	1,250	212
Saginaw Valley State U, University Center, MI 48710	1963	Dr. Eric R. Gilbertson	5-M	6,869	386
St Ambrose U, Davenport, IA 52803	1882	Dr. Edward J. Rogalski	2-M	2,417	197
Saint Anselm Coll, Manchester, NH 03102	1889	Rev. Jonathan DeFelice, OSB	2-B	1,857	160
Saint Augustine's Coll, Raleigh, NC 27610-2298	1867	Dr. Prezell R. Robinson	2-B	1,918	92
St Bonaventure U, St Bonaventure, NY 14778-2284	1858	Sr. Alice Gallin, OSU	2-M	2,797	231
St Cloud State U, St Cloud, MN 56301-4498	1869	Dr. Robert Bess	5-M	16,047	761
St Edward's U, Austin, TX 78704	1885	Dr. Patricia Hayes	2-M	3,047	211
St Francis Coll, Brooklyn Heights, NY 11201	1884	Br. Donald Sullivan, OSF	1-B	2,099	132
Saint Francis Coll, Loretto, PA 15940	1847	Rev. Christian R. Oravec	2-M	1,508	93
St John Fisher Coll, Rochester, NY 14618	1948	Dr. William L. Pickett	2-M	2,401	213
Saint John's U, Collegeville, MN 56321 (1)	1857	Br. Dietrich Reinhart, OSB	2-M	1,902	165
St John's U, Jamaica, NY 11439	1870	Rev. Donald J. Harrington, CM	2-D	18,813	1,037
Saint Joseph Coll, West Hartford, CT 06117 (3)	1932	Ms. Winifred E. Coleman	2-M	2,007	155
Saint Joseph's Coll, Rensselaer, IN 47978	1889	Dr. Albert J. Shannon	2-M	1,000	87
St Joseph's Coll, Brooklyn, NY 11205-3688	1916	Sr. George Aquin O'Connor	1-B	1,004	98
St Joseph's Coll, Suffolk Cmps, Patchogue, NY 11772	1916	Sr. George Aquin O'Connor	1-B	1,933	168
Saint Joseph's U, Philadelphia, PA 19131	1851	Rev. Nicholas S. Rashford, SJ	2-M	6,909	350
St Lawrence U, Canton, NY 13617	1856	Dr. Patti McGill Peterson	1-M	2,137	185
Saint Louis U, St Louis, MO 63103	1818	Rev. Lawrence Biondi, SJ	2-D	11,747	2,868
Saint Mary Coll, Leavenworth, KS 66048-5082	1923	Dr. Peter Clifford, FSC	2-B	1,023	108
Saint Mary-of-the-Woods Coll, Saint Mary-of-the-Woods, IN 47876 (3)	1840	Dr. Barbara Doherty, SP	2-M	1,258	55
Saint Mary's Coll, Notre Dame, IN 46556 (3)	1844	Dr. William A. Hickey	2-B	1,576	196
Saint Mary's Coll of California, Moraga, CA 94556	1863	Br. Mel Anderson, FSC	2-M	4,112	167
St Mary's Coll of Maryland, St Mary's City, MD 20686	1840	Dr. Edward T. Lewis	5-B	1,301	146
Saint Mary's Coll of Minnesota, Winona, MN 55987-1399	1912	Br. Louis DeThomasis, FSC	2-M	6,186	288
St Mary's U of San Antonio, San Antonio, TX 78228-8507	1852	Rev. John Moder, SM	2-D	4,007	281
Saint Michael's Coll, Colchester, VT 05439	1904	Dr. Paul J. Reiss	2-M	2,555	168
St Norbert Coll, De Pere, WI 54115	1898	Dr. Thomas A. Manion	2-M	1,981	143
St Olaf Coll, Northfield, MN 55057-1098	1874	Dr. Melvin George	2-B	3,015	329
Saint Peter's Coll, Jersey City, NJ 07306	1872	NR	2-M	3,567	420
St Thomas Aquinas Coll, Sparkill, NY 10976	1958	Dr. Donald T. McNelis	1-M	1,454	115
St Thomas U, Miami, FL 33054	1961	Rev. Edward McCarthy, OSA	2-F	2,703	149
Saint Vincent Coll, Latrobe, PA 15650	1846	Rev. John F. Murtha, OSB	2-B	1,248	103
Saint Xavier U, Chicago, IL 60655	1847	Dr. Ronald Champagne	2-M	3,850	226
Salem State Coll, Salem, MA 01970	1854	Dr. Nancy D. Harrington	5-M	10,132	300
Salisbury State U, Salisbury, MD 21801-6837	1925	Dr. Thomas E. Bellavance	5-M	6,022	323
Salve Regina U, Newport, RI 02840-4192	1934	Dr. M. Lucille McKillop, RSM	2-M	2,314	212
Samford U, Birmingham, AL 35229	1841	Dr. Thomas E. Corts	2-F	4,248	323
Sam Houston State U, Huntsville, TX 77341	1879	Dr. Martin J. Anisman	5-D	12,412	498
San Diego State U, San Diego, CA 92182	1897	Dr. Thomas B. Day	5-D	30,369	2,139
San Francisco State U, San Francisco, CA 94132	1899	Dr. Robert A. Corrigan	5-D	26,530	1,429
Sangamon State U, Springfield, IL 62794-9243	1969	Dr. Naomi B. Lynn	5-M	4,536	236
San Jose State U, San Jose, CA 95192	1857	Mr. J. Handel Evans	5-M	29,626	1,522
Santa Clara U, Santa Clara, CA 95053	1851	Rev. Paul L. Locatelli, SJ	2-D	7,802	577
Sarah Lawrence Coll, Bronxville, NY 10708	1926	Dr. Alice Stone Ilchman	1-M	1,255	211
Savannah Coll of Art and Design, Savannah, GA 31402-3146	1978	Mr. Richard G. Rowan	1-M	2,330	127
Savannah State Coll, Savannah, GA 31404	1890	NR	5-B	3,100	149
Sch of the Art Inst of Chicago, Chicago, IL 60603	1866	Mr. Peter Brown	1-M	1,729	304
Sch of Visual Arts, New York, NY 10010	1947	Mr. David Rhodes	3-M	2,571	599
Seattle Pacific U, Seattle, WA 98119	1891	NR	2-M	3,531	244
Seattle U, Seattle, WA 98122	1891	Rev. William J. Sullivan, SJ	2-D	4,864	451
Seton Hall U, South Orange, NJ 07079	1856	Rev. Thomas R. Peterson, OP	2-D	9,970	640
Seton Hill Coll, Greensburg, PA 15601 (4)	1883	Ms. JoAnne W. Boyle	2-B	1,027	113
Shawnee State U, Portsmouth, OH 45662	1986	NR	5-B	3,636	266
Shaw U, Raleigh, NC 27601	1865	Dr. Talbert O. Shaw	2-B	2,491	242
Shenandoah U, Winchester, VA 22601	1875	Dr. James A. Davis	2-M	1,467	180
Shepherd Coll, Shepherdstown, WV 25443	1871	Dr. Michael P. Riccards	5-B	3,559	246
Shippensburg U of Pennsylvania, Shippensburg, PA 17257	1871	Dr. Anthony F. Ceddia	5-M	6,688	359
Siena Coll, Loudonville, NY 12211-1462	1937	Fr. William McConville, OFM	2-B	3,492	260
Siena Heights Coll, Adrian, MI 49221-1796	1919	Sr. Cathleen Real, CHM	2-M	1,141	110
Simmons Coll, Boston, MA 02115 (3)	1899	Dr. Jean A. Dowdall	1-D	3,079	337
Simpson Coll, Indianola, IA 50125	1860	Dr. Stephen G. Jennings	2-B	1,690	146
Skidmore Coll, Saratoga Springs, NY 12866	1903	Dr. David H. Porter	1-M	2,158	211
Slippery Rock U of Pennsylvania, Slippery Rock, PA 16057	1889	Dr. Robert Aebersold	5-M	7,777	408
Smith Coll, Northampton, MA 01063 (3)	1871	Ms. Mary Maples Dunn	1-D	2,879	276
Sonoma State U, Rohnert Park, CA 94928	1961	Dr. Ruben Arminana	5-M	7,405	422
South Carolina State U, Orangeburg, SC 29117	1896	Dr. Barbara R. Hatton	5-D	5,024	241
South Dakota Sch of Mines and Tech, Rapid City, SD 57701-3995	1885	Dr. Richard J. Gowen	5-D	2,444	131
South Dakota State U, Brookings, SD 57007	1881	Dr. Robert T. Wagner	5-D	8,550	500
Southeastern Coll of the Assemblies of God, Lakeland, FL 33801	1935	Dr. James Hennesy	2-B	1,209	79
Southeastern Louisiana U, Hammond, LA 70402	1925	Dr. G. Warren Smith	5-M	12,847	425
Southeastern Oklahoma State U, Durant, OK 74701	1909	Dr. Larry Williams	5-M	4,109	193
Southeastern U of the Health Sciences, North Miami Beach, FL 33162		Dr. Morton Terry	1-F	1,343	NR
Southeast Missouri State U, Cape Girardeau, MO 63701	1873	Dr. Kala M. Stroup	5-M	8,704	436
Southern Arkansas U, Magnolia, AR 71753	1909	Dr. Steven G. Gamble	5-M	2,742	130

Name, address	Year	Governing official, control, and highest degree offered	Enroll-ment	Faculty
Southern Coll of Seventh-day Adventists, Collegedale, TN 37315	1892	Dr. Donald R. Sahly 2-B	1,494	99
Southern Coll of Tech, Marietta, GA 30060-2896	1948	Dr. Stephen R. Cheshier 5-M	3,922	199
Southern Connecticut State U, New Haven, CT 06515	1893	Mr. Michael J. Adanti 5-M	12,420	747
Southern Illinois U at Carbondale, Carbondale, IL 62901	1869	Dr. John C. Guyon 5-D	24,766	1,399
Southern Illinois U at Edwardsville, Edwardsville, IL 62026	1957	Dr. Earl E. Lazerson 5-D	11,670	724
Southern Methodist U, Dallas, TX 75275	1911	Mr. A. Kenneth Pye 2-D	8,538	643
Southern Nazarene U, Bethany, OK 73008	1899	Dr. Loren P. Gresham 2-M	1,591	103
Southern Oregon State Coll, Ashland, OR 97520	1926	Dr. Joseph Cox 5-M	4,478	300
Southern U and A&M Coll, Baton Rouge, LA 70813	1880	Dr. Marvin L. Yates 5-D	10,000	603
Southern U at New Orleans, New Orleans, LA 70126	1959	Dr. Robert B. Gex 5-M	4,556	235
Southern Utah U, Cedar City, UT 84720	1897	Mr. Gerald R. Sherratt 5-M	4,434	155
Southwest Baptist U, Bolivar, MO 65613	1878	Dr. Roy Blunt 2-M	3,087	208
Southwestern Baptist Theological Sem, Fort Worth, TX 76122-0150	1908	Dr. Russell H. Dilday 2-D	3,364	183
Southwestern Oklahoma State U, Weatherford, OK 73096	1901	Dr. Joe Anna Hibler 5-M	4,953	223
Southwestern U, Georgetown, TX 78626	1840	Dr. Roy B. Shilling, Jr. 2-B	1,204	133
Southwest Missouri State U, Springfield, MO 65804	1905	Dr. John H. Keiser 5-M	19,002	844
Southwest State U, Marshall, MN 56258	1963	Dr. Oliver Ford, III 5-B	2,742	131
Southwest Texas State U, San Marcos, TX 78666	1899	Dr. Jerome Supple 5-M	25,249	874
Spalding U, Louisville, KY 40203	1814	Dr. Eileen M. Egan 2-D	1,141	112
Spelman Coll, Atlanta, GA 30314 (3)	1881	Dr. Johnnetta B. Cole 1-B	2,026	174
Springfield Coll, Springfield, MA 01109	1885	Dr. Randolph W. Bromery 1-D	3,468	232
Spring Hill Coll, Mobile, AL 36608	1830	Rev. William J. Rewak, SJ 2-M	1,273	84
Stanford U, Stanford, CA 94305	1891	Mr. Gerhard Casper 1-D	13,893	1,408
State U of NY at Binghamton, Binghamton, NY 13902-6000	1946	Dr. Lois B. DeFleur 5-D	11,966	687
State U of NY at Buffalo, Buffalo, NY 14260	1846	Mr. William R. Greiner 5-D	23,470	1,915
State U of NY at Stony Brook, Stony Brook, NY 11794	1957	Dr. John H. Marburger, III 5-D	17,233	1,577
State U of NY Coll at Brockport, Brockport, NY 14420	1867	Dr. John E. Van de Wetering 5-M	7,994	530
State U of NY Coll at Buffalo, Buffalo, NY 14222	1867	Dr. F. C. Richardson 5-M	11,211	577
State U of NY Coll at Fredonia, Fredonia, NY 14063	1826	Dr. Donald A. MacPhee 5-M	4,889	271
State U of NY Coll at Geneseo, Geneseo, NY 14454	1867	Dr. Carol C. Harter 5-M	5,578	323
State U of NY Coll at New Paltz, New Paltz, NY 12561-2449	1828	Dr. Alice Chandler 5-M	8,141	504
State U of NY Coll at Old Westbury, Old Westbury, NY 11568	1965	Dr. L. Eudora Pettigrew 5-B	4,200	259
State U of NY Coll at Oneonta, Oneonta, NY 13820	1889	Dr. Alan B. Donovan 5-M	5,963	306
State U of NY Coll at Oswego, Oswego, NY 13126	1861	Dr. Stephen Weber 5-M	8,235	388
State U of NY Coll at Plattsburgh, Plattsburgh, NY 12901	1889	Dr. Charles Warren 5-M	6,161	388
State U of NY Coll at Potsdam, Potsdam, NY 13676	1816	Dr. William Merwin 5-M	4,579	273
State U of NY Coll at Purchase, Purchase, NY 10577	1967	Dr. Sheldon Grebstein 5-M	2,494	298
State U of NY Coll of Environ Sci and Forestry, Syracuse, NY 13210-2779	1911	Dr. Ross S. Whaley 5-D	1,844	122
State U of NY Empire State Coll, Saratoga Springs, NY 12866-4391	1971	Dr. James W. Hall 5-M	10,000	360
State U of NY Health Science Ctr at Brooklyn, Brooklyn, NY 11203	1858	Dr. Donald J. Scherl 5-D	1,641	156
State U of NY Health Science Ctr at Syracuse, Syracuse, NY 13210	1950	Dr. Gregory L. Eastwood 5-D	1,100	45
State U of NY Inst of Tech at Utica/Rome, Utica, NY 13504	1966	Dr. Peter J. Cayan 5-M	2,550	138
Stephen F Austin State U, Nacogdoches, TX 75962	1923	Dr. Daniel D. Angel 5-D	12,721	667
Stephens Coll, Columbia, MO 65215 (3)	1833	Dr. Patsy H. Sampson 1-B	1,045	95
Stetson U, DeLand, FL 32720	1883	Dr. H. Douglas Lee 2-F	3,069	188
Stevens Inst of Tech, Hoboken, NJ 07030	1870	Dr. Harold J. Raveche 1-D	3,240	250
Stockton State Coll, Pomona, NJ 08240-9988	1971	Dr. Vera King Farris 5-B	5,054	293
Stonehill Coll, North Easton, MA 02357	1948	Rev. Bartley MacPhaidin, CSC 2-B	1,925	179
Strayer Coll, Washington, DC 20005	1892	Mr. Ron K. Bailey 3-M	5,566	178
Suffolk U, Boston, MA 02108	1906	Mr. David J. Sargent 1-F	6,076	378
Sullivan Coll, Louisville, KY 40232	1864	NR 3-B	1,990	68
Sul Ross State U, Alpine, TX 79832	1920	Dr. R. Vic Morgan 5-M	2,706	165
Susquehanna U, Selinsgrove, PA 17870	1858	Dr. Joel L. Cunningham 2-B	1,447	136
Swarthmore Coll, Swarthmore, PA 19081	1864	Dr. Alfred H. Bloom 1-B	1,267	171
Syracuse U, Syracuse, NY 13244	1870	Dr. Kenneth A. Shaw 1-D	15,421	1,568
Tampa Coll, Tampa, FL 33614	1890	Mr. David Zorn 3-M	1,527	57
Tarleton State U, Stephenville, TX 76402	1899	Dr. Dennis P. McCabe 5-M	6,425	223
Taylor U, Upland, IN 46989-1001	1846	Dr. Jay L. Kesler 1-B	1,817	139
Teikyo Marycrest U, Davenport, IA 52804-4096	1939	Dr. Joseph D. Olander 1-M	1,264	83
Teikyo Post U, Waterbury, CT 06723-2540	1890	Dr. Norman L. Stewart 1-B	1,964	166
Temple U, Philadelphia, PA 19122	1884	Mr. Peter J. Liacouras 13-D	27,736	2,374
Tennessee State U, Nashville, TN 37209-1561	1912	Dr. James A. Hefner 5-M	7,591	430
Tennessee Tech U, Cookeville, TN 38505	1915	Dr. Angelo A. Volpe 5-D	8,244	393
Texas A&I U, Kingsville, TX 78363	1925	Dr. Manuel L. Ibanez 5-D	6,414	324
Texas A&M International U, Laredo, TX 78040	1969	Dr. Leo Sayavedra 5-M	1,573	57
Texas A&M U, College Station, TX 77843	1876	Dr. William H. Mobley 5-D	41,710	2,424
Texas A&M U at Galveston, Galveston, TX 77553	1962	Dr. David J. Schmidly 5-B	1,278	86
Texas A&M U–Corpus Christi, Corpus Christi, TX 78412	1971	Dr. Robert R. Furgason 5-D	3,557	279
Texas Christian U, Fort Worth, TX 76129	1873	Dr. William E. Tucker 2-D	6,728	375
Texas Lutheran Coll, Seguin, TX 78155	1891	Dr. Charles H. Oestreich 2-B	1,072	90
Texas Southern U, Houston, TX 77004	1947	Dr. William H. Harris 5-D	10,800	400
Texas Tech U, Lubbock, TX 79409	1923	Dr. Robert W. Lawless 5-D	24,215	944
Texas Wesleyan U, Fort Worth, TX 76105	1890	Dr. Jake B. Schrum 2-M	1,772	120
Texas Woman's U, Denton, TX 76204-1925 (4)	1901	Dr. Shirley Sears Chater 5-D	9,636	538
Thomas Edison State Coll, Trenton, NJ 08608-1176	1972	Dr. George A. Pruitt 5-B	8,612	NR
Thomas Jefferson U, Philadelphia, PA 19107	1824	Dr. Paul C. Brucker 1-M	1,560	83
Thomas More Coll, Crestview Hills, KY 41017	1921	Rev. William F. Cleves 2-B	1,308	110
Tiffin U, Tiffin, OH 44883	1888	Dr. George Kidd, Jr. 1-M	1,014	70
Tougaloo Coll, Tougaloo, MS 39174	1869	Dr. Adib A. Shakir 2-B	1,131	91
Touro Coll, New York, NY 10010	1971	NR 1-F	8,942	894
Towson State U, Towson, MD 21204-7097	1866	Dr. Hoke L. Smith 5-M	15,232	903
Trenton State Coll, Trenton, NJ 08650-4700	1855	Dr. Harold Eickhoff 5-M	6,170	526
Trevecca Nazarene Coll, Nashville, TN 37210	1901	Dr. Millard Reed 2-M	1,386	131
Trinity Coll, Hartford, CT 06106	1823	Mr. Tom Gerety, Jr. 1-M	2,027	214
Trinity Coll, Washington, DC 20017-1094 (3)	1897	NR 2-M	1,164	110
Trinity Coll of Vermont, Burlington, VT 05401 (4)	1925	Sr. Janice Ryan 2-M	1,115	103
Trinity U, San Antonio, TX 78212	1869	Dr. Ronald K. Calgaard 2-M	2,518	261

Name, address	Year	Governing official, control, and highest degree offered		Enroll-ment	Faculty
Tri-State U, Angola, IN 46703	1884	Dr. R. John Reynolds	1-B	1,051	92
Troy State U, Troy, AL 36082	1887	Dr. Jack Hawkins, Jr.	5-M	4,750	205
Troy State U at Dothan, Dothan, AL 36304	1961	Dr. Thomas Harrison	5-M	2,319	62
Troy State U in Montgomery, Montgomery, AL 36103-4419	1957	Dr. Glenda S. McGaha	5-M	3,331	168
Tufts U, Medford, MA 02155	1852	Dr. John A. DiBiaggio	1-D	7,642	1,660
Tulane U, New Orleans, LA 70118	1834	Dr. Eamon M. Kelly	1-D	11,345	717
Tusculum Coll, Greeneville, TN 37743	1794	Dr. Robert E. Knott	2-M	1,040	88
Tuskegee U, Tuskegee, AL 36088	1881	Dr. Benjamin F. Payton	1-M	3,598	267
Union Coll, Schenectady, NY 12308	1795	Dr. Roger H. Hull	1-M	2,309	194
Union Inst, Cincinnati, OH 45206	1964	Mr. Robert T. Conley	1-D	1,440	739
Union U, Jackson, TN 38305	1823	Dr. Hyran E. Barefoot	2-M	2,009	120
United States Air Force Acad, USAF Academy, CO 80840-5025	1954	Lt. Gen. Bradley C. Hosmer	4-B	4,000	517
United States International U, San Diego, CA 92131-1799	1952	Dr. Garry D. Hays	1-D	3,489	84
United States Merchant Marine Acad, Kings Point, NY 11024	1943	Rear Adm. P. L. Krinsky, USMS	4-B	1,001	80
United States Military Acad, West Point, NY 10996	1802	Lt. Gen. Howard D. Graves	4-B	4,340	491
United States Naval Acad, Annapolis, MD 21402 (2)	1845	Rear Adm. Thomas Lynch	4-B	4,265	650
Universidad del Turabo, Gurabo, PR 00798	1972	Dr. Dennis Alicea	1-M	7,796	363
Universidad Politécnica de Puerto Rico, Hato Rey, PR 00919	1966	Mr. Ernesto Vazquez-Barquet	1-B	4,720	186
U at Albany, State U of NY, Albany, NY 12222	1844	Dr. H. Patrick Swygert	5-D	15,168	902
U of Akron, Akron, OH 44325-0001	1870	Dr. Peggy Gordon Elliott	5-D	27,079	1,722
U of Alabama, Tuscaloosa, AL 35487-0132	1831	Dr. E. Roger Sayers	5-D	18,784	995
U of Alabama at Birmingham, Birmingham, AL 35294	1969	Dr. Charles A. McCallum	5-D	16,658	1,830
U of Alabama in Huntsville, Huntsville, AL 35899	1950	Dr. Frank Franz	5-D	8,026	441
U of Alaska Anchorage, Anchorage, AK 99508	1954	Dr. Donald F. Behrend	5-M	17,126	1,162
U of Alaska Fairbanks, Fairbanks, AK 99775-0660	1917	Dr. Joan K. Wadlow	5-D	5,072	717
U of Arizona, Tucson, AZ 85721	1885	Dr. Manuel T. Pacheco	5-D	35,129	1,652
U of Arkansas, Fayetteville, AR 72701	1871	Dr. Daniel E. Ferritor	5-D	14,582	837
U of Arkansas at Little Rock, Little Rock, AR 72204	1927	Dr. Charles E. Hathaway	5-D	12,419	786
U of Arkansas at Pine Bluff, Pine Bluff, AR 71601-2799	1873	Dr. Lawrence A. Davis, Jr.	5-M	3,709	193
U of Arkansas for Medical Sciences, Little Rock, AR 72205	1879	Dr. Harry P. Ward	5-D	1,734	NR
U of Baltimore, Baltimore, MD 21201	1925	Dr. H. Mebane Turner	5-F	5,844	275
U of Bridgeport, Bridgeport, CT 06601	1927	Dr. Edwin G. Eigel, Jr.	1-M	1,500	150
U of California at Berkeley, Berkeley, CA 94720	1868	Dr. Chang-Lin Tien	5-D	30,622	1,512
U of California, Davis, Davis, CA 95616	1906	Dr. Theodore L. Hullar	5-D	22,889	1,612
U of California, Irvine, Irvine, CA 92717	1965	Ms. Laurel L. Wilkening	5-D	17,189	785
U of California, Los Angeles, Los Angeles, CA 90024	1919	Dr. Charles E. Young	5-D	35,407	3,280
U of California, Riverside, Riverside, CA 92521	1954	Dr. Raymond L. Orbach	5-D	8,805	739
U of California, San Diego, La Jolla, CA 92093	1959	Dr. Richard C. Atkinson	5-D	18,241	1,384
U of California, Santa Barbara, Santa Barbara, CA 93106	1891	Dr. Barbara S. Uehling	5-D	18,655	853
U of California, Santa Cruz, Santa Cruz, CA 95064	1965	Dr. Karl S. Pister	5-D	10,256	559
U of Central Arkansas, Conway, AR 72035	1907	Dr. Winfred L. Thompson	5-M	9,473	566
U of Central Florida, Orlando, FL 32816	1963	Dr. John C. Hitt	5-D	21,590	910
U of Central Oklahoma, Edmond, OK 73034-0172	1890	Mr. George Nigh	5-M	15,839	640
U of Charleston, Charleston, WV 25304	1888	Dr. Edwin H. Welch	1-M	1,479	238
U of Chicago, Chicago, IL 60637	1891	Mr. Hugo F. Sonneschein	1-D	10,231	1,843
U of Cincinnati, Cincinnati, OH 45221	1819	Dr. Joseph A. Steger	5-D	17,931	968
U of Colorado at Boulder, Boulder, CO 80309	1876	NR	5-D	25,089	1,193
U of Colorado at Colorado Springs, Colorado Springs, CO 80933-7150	1965	Dr. Linda Bunnell Jones	5-D	5,751	361
U of Colorado at Denver, Denver, CO 80217	1912	Mr. John Buechner	5-D	11,188	516
U of Colorado Health Sciences Ctr, Denver, CO 80262	1883	Dr. Vincent A. Fulginiti	5-D	2,167	NR
U of Connecticut, Storrs, CT 06269	1881	Dr. Harry J. Hartley	5-D	18,399	1,250
U of Connecticut at Hartford, West Hartford, CT 06117	1946	Dr. Russell F. Farnen	5-B	1,183	91
U of Connecticut at Stamford, Stamford, CT 06903	1951	NR	5-M	1,600	93
U of Dallas, Irving, TX 75062-4799	1956	Dr. Robert F. Sasseen	2-D	2,869	136
U of Dayton, Dayton, OH 45469-1611	1850	Br. Raymond L. Fitz, SM	2-D	10,658	794
U of Delaware, Newark, DE 19716	1743	Dr. David P. Roselle	13-D	17,489	954
U of Denver, Denver, CO 80208	1864	Mr. Daniel Ritchie	1-D	8,213	392
U of Detroit Mercy, Detroit, MI 48221	1877	Sr. Maureen A. Fay, OP	2-D	7,774	495
U of Dubuque, Dubuque, IA 52001	1852	Dr. John J. Agria	2-M	1,264	86
U of Evansville, Evansville, IN 47722	1854	Dr. James S. Vinson	2-M	2,928	165
The U of Findlay, Findlay, OH 45840	1882	Dr. Kenneth E. Zirkle	2-M	3,136	235
U of Florida, Gainesville, FL 32611-2073	1853	Dr. John V. Lombardi	5-D	34,361	2,660
U of Georgia, Athens, GA 30602	1785	Dr. Charles B. Knapp	5-D	28,493	2,538
U of Hartford, West Hartford, CT 06117	1877	Dr. Humphrey Tonkin	1-D	7,340	730
U of Hawaii at Hilo, Hilo, HI 96720	1970	Dr. Edward J. Kormondy	5-B	2,675	235
U of Hawaii at Manoa, Honolulu, HI 96822	1907	Dr. Kenneth P. Mortimer	5-D	19,810	1,526
U of Health Sciences/Chicago Medical Sch, North Chicago, IL 60064	1912	Mr. Herman M. Finch	1-D	1,070	18
U of Houston–Clear Lake, Houston, TX 77058	1971	Dr. Glenn A. Goerke	5-M	7,281	374
U of Houston–Downtown, Houston, TX 77002	1974	Dr. George Magner	5-B	8,702	361
U of Houston–Victoria, Victoria, TX 77901	1973	Dr. Lesta Van Der Wert Turchen	5-M	1,223	74
U of Idaho, Moscow, ID 83843-4140	1889	Dr. Elisabeth Zinser	5-D	10,790	570
U of Illinois at Chicago, Chicago, IL 60680	1965	Dr. James J. Stukel	5-D	24,985	2,529
U of Illinois at Urbana-Champaign, Champaign, IL 61820	1867	Dr. Michael J. Aiken	5-D	35,815	2,203
U of Indianapolis, Indianapolis, IN 46227-3697	1902	Dr. G. Benjamin Lantz, Jr.	2-M	3,729	276
The U of Iowa, Iowa City, IA 52242	1847	Dr. Hunter R. Rawlings, III	5-D	27,463	1,729
U of Kansas, Lawrence, KS 66045	1866	Dr. Gene A. Budig	5-D	29,161	2,002
U of Kentucky, Lexington, KY 40506-0032	1865	Dr. Charles T. Wethington, Jr.	5-D	24,197	2,081
U of La Verne, La Verne, CA 91750	1891	Dr. Stephen Morgan	1-D	7,047	840
U of Louisville, Louisville, KY 40292	1798	Dr. Donald C. Swain	5-D	22,633	1,191
U of Maine, Orono, ME 04469	1865	Dr. Frederick E. Hutchinson	5-D	12,313	781
U of Maine at Farmington, Farmington, ME 04938	1864	Dr. Michael J. Orendulf	5-B	2,267	148
U of Maine at Presque Isle, Presque Isle, ME 04769	1903	Dr. W. Michael Easton	5-B	1,577	105
U of Mary, Bismarck, ND 58504	1959	Sr. Thomas Welder	2-M	1,851	100
U of Mary Hardin-Baylor, Belton, TX 76513	1845	Dr. Jerry G. Bawcom	2-M	1,904	113
U of Maryland Baltimore County, Baltimore, MD 21228-5398	1966	Dr. Freeman A. Hrabowski	5-D	10,654	623
U of Maryland Coll Park, College Park, MD 20742	1856	Dr. William E. Kirwan	5-D	32,858	1,803
U of Maryland Eastern Shore, Princess Anne, MD 21853	1886	Dr. William P. Hytche	5-D	2,430	154
U of Maryland U Coll, College Park, MD 20742-1628	1947	Dr. T. Benjamin Massey	5-M	38,567	1,641

Name, address	Year	Governing official, control, and highest degree offered		Enroll-ment	Faculty
U of Massachusetts at Amherst, Amherst, MA 01003	1863	Dr. David K. Scott	5-D	21,834	1,254
U of Massachusetts at Boston, Boston, MA 02125-3393	1964	Dr. Sherry H. Penney	5-D	10,590	820
U of Massachusetts Dartmouth, North Dartmouth, MA 02747	1895	Dr. Peter H. Cressy	5-M	5,525	413
U of Massachusetts Lowell, Lowell, MA 01854	1894	Dr. William T. Hogan	5-D	13,618	604
U of Miami, Coral Gables, FL 33124	1925	Mr. Edward T. Foote, II	1-D	13,857	1,615
U of Michigan, Ann Arbor, MI 48109	1817	Dr. James J. Duderstadt	5-D	36,626	3,374
U of Michigan–Dearborn, Dearborn, MI 48128	1959	Dr. James C. Renick	5-M	7,318	385
U of Michigan–Flint, Flint, MI 48502-2186	1956	Dr. Clinton B. Jones	5-M	6,652	211
U of Minnesota, Duluth, Duluth, MN 55812	1947	Dr. Lawrence A. Ianni	5-M	7,680	510
U of Minnesota, Morris, Morris, MN 56267	1959	Dr. David C. Johnson	5-B	1,923	142
U of Minnesota, Twin Cities Cmps, Minneapolis, MN 55455-0213	1851	Dr. Nils Hasselmo	5-D	38,019	2,953
U of Mississippi, University, MS 38677	1844	Dr. R. Gerald Turner	5-D	10,704	461
U of Mississippi Medical Ctr, Jackson, MS 39216	1955	Dr. Norman Crooks Nelson	5-D	1,631	617
U of Missouri–Columbia, Columbia, MO 65211	1839	Dr. Charles A. Kiesler	5-D	23,346	1,517
U of Missouri–Kansas City, Kansas City, MO 64110	1929	Dr. Eleanor B. Schwartz	5-D	10,489	540
U of Missouri–Rolla, Rolla, MO 65401	1870	Dr. John T. Park	5-D	5,657	345
U of Missouri–St Louis, St Louis, MO 63121-4499	1963	Dr. Blanche M. Touhill	5-D	11,774	635
U of Mobile, Mobile, AL 36663-0220	1961	Dr. Michael A. Magnoli	2-M	1,703	106
U of Montana, Missoula, MT 59812	1893	Dr. George M. Dennison	5-D	10,614	520
U of Montevallo, Montevallo, Al 35115	1896	Dr. Robert M. McChesney	5-M	3,254	172
U of Nebraska at Kearney, Kearney, NE 68849	1903	Dr. William R. Nester	5-M	8,775	415
U of Nebraska at Omaha, Omaha, NE 68182	1908	Dr. Del D. Weber	5-M	17,045	750
U of Nebraska–Lincoln, Lincoln, NE 68588	1869	Dr. Graham B. Spanier	5-D	24,573	1,516
U of Nebraska Medical Ctr, Omaha, NE 68198	1869	Dr. Carol A. Aschenbrener	5-D	2,757	489
U of Nevada, Las Vegas, Las Vegas, NV 89154	1957	Dr. Robert Maxson	5-D	19,504	1,001
U of Nevada, Reno, Reno, NV 89557	1874	Dr. Joseph N. Crowley	5-D	11,909	545
U of New England, Biddeford, ME 04005-9526	1939	Dr. Thomas Hedley Reynolds	1-F	1,287	154
U of New Hampshire, Durham, NH 03824	1866	Dr. Dale F. Nitzschke	5-D	12,257	900
U of New Haven, West Haven, CT 06516	1920	Dr. Lawrence J. DeNardis	1-D	5,916	401
U of New Mexico, Albuquerque, NM 87131-2039	1889	Dr. Richard E. Peck	5-D	25,009	1,315
U of New Orleans, New Orleans, LA 70148	1958	Dr. Gregory M. O'Brien	5-D	16,308	819
U of North Alabama, Florence, AL 35632-0001	1872	Mr. Robert L. Potts	5-M	5,523	239
U of North Carolina at Asheville, Asheville, NC 28804	1927	Dr. Samuel Schuman	5-M	3,277	235
U of North Carolina at Chapel Hill, Chapel Hill, NC 27599	1795	Mr. Paul Hardin, III	5-D	23,944	2,430
U of North Carolina at Charlotte, Charlotte, NC 28223	1946	Dr. James H. Woodward, Jr.	5-M	15,363	872
U of North Carolina at Greensboro, Greensboro, NC 27412	1891	Dr. William E. Moran	5-D	12,117	724
U of North Carolina at Wilmington, Wilmington, NC 28403	1947	Dr. James R. Leutze	5-M	7,898	419
U of North Dakota, Grand Forks, ND 58202	1883	Dr. Kendall Baker	5-D	12,438	752
U of Northern Colorado, Greeley, CO 80639	1890	Dr. Herman D. Lujan	5-D	10,328	548
U of Northern Iowa, Cedar Falls, IA 50614	1876	Dr. Constantine W. Curris	5-D	13,045	810
U of North Florida, Jacksonville, FL 32224	1965	Dr. Adam W. Herbert	5-D	9,073	214
U of North Texas, Denton, TX 76203	1890	Dr. Alfred F. Hurley	5-D	26,433	1,088
U of Notre Dame, Notre Dame, IN 46556	1842	Rev. Edward A. Malloy, CSC	2-D	10,000	820
U of Oklahoma, Norman, OK 73019	1890	Dr. Richard L. Van Horn	5-D	20,015	957
U of Oklahoma Health Sciences Ctr, Oklahoma City, OK 73190	1890	Dr. Jay H. Stein	5-D	3,016	838
U of Oregon, Eugene, OR 97403	1872	Dr. Myles Brand	5-D	16,719	1,464
U of Osteopathic Medicine and Health Sciences, Des Moines, IA 50312	1898	Dr. J. Leonard Azneer	1-F	1,090	108
U of Pennsylvania, Philadelphia, PA 19104	1740	Dr. Claire Fagin	1-D	22,418	3,916
U of Phoenix, Phoenix, AZ 85072-9382	1976	Mr. William Gibbs	3-M	15,341	1,500
U of Pittsburgh, Pittsburgh, PA 15260	1787	Dr. J. Dennis O'Connor	13-D	27,852	3,312
U of Pittsburgh at Bradford, Bradford, PA 16701	1963	Dr. Richard E. McDowell	13-B	1,309	95
U of Pittsburgh at Greensburg, Greensburg, PA 15601	1963	Dr. George F. Chambers	13-B	1,465	89
U of Pittsburgh at Johnstown, Johnstown, PA 15904	1927	Dr. Frank H. Blackington, III	13-B	3,243	192
U of Portland, Portland, OR 97203	1901	Rev. David T. Tyson, CSC	2-M	2,716	200
U of Puerto Rico at Ponce, Ponce, PR 00732	1970	Mr. Pedro E. Laboy	7-B	2,263	124
U of Puerto Rico, Cayey U Coll, Cayey, PR 00737	1967	Dr. Margarita Benitez	7-B	3,236	182
U of Puerto Rico, Humacao U Coll, Humacao, PR 00791	1962	Dr. Felix Castrodad	7-B	3,884	243
U of Puerto Rico Medical Sciences Cmps, San Juan, PR 00936-5067	1950	Dr. Francisco H. Oquendo	7-D	2,981	719
U of Puget Sound, Tacoma, WA 98416	1888	Dr. Susan Resneck Pierce	2-M	3,162	230
U of Redlands, Redlands, CA 92373-0999	1907	Dr. James R. Appleton	1-M	3,950	156
U of Rhode Island, Kingston, RI 02881	1892	Dr. Robert L. Carothers	5-D	12,360	750
U of Richmond, Richmond, VA 23173	1830	Dr. Richard L. Morrill	2-F	4,579	360
U of Rio Grande, Rio Grande, OH 45674	1876	Dr. Barry M. Dorsey	1-M	2,072	114
U of Rochester, Rochester, NY 14627-0001	1850	Mr. G. Dennis O'Brien	1-D	9,539	1,376
U of St Thomas, St Paul, MN 55105	1885	Rev. Dennis Dease	2-F	10,423	636
U of St Thomas, Houston, TX 77006	1947	Mr. Joseph M. McFadden	2-D	2,079	172
U of San Diego, San Diego, CA 92110-2492	1949	Dr. Author E. Hughes	2-F	6,083	466
U of San Francisco, San Francisco, CA 94117-1080	1855	Rev. John P. Schlegel, SJ	2-D	7,328	713
U of Science and Arts of Oklahoma, Chickasha, OK 73018-0001	1908	Dr. Roy Troutt	5-B	1,619	75
U of Scranton, Scranton, PA 18510-4501	1888	Rev. J. A. Panuska, SJ	2-M	5,061	387
U of South Alabama, Mobile, AL 36688	1963	Dr. Frederick P. Whiddon	5-D	12,311	802
U of South Carolina, Columbia, SC 29208	1801	Dr. John M. Palms	5-D	26,138	1,466
U of South Carolina–Aiken, Aiken, SC 29801	1961	Dr. Robert E. Alexander	5-B	3,208	232
U of South Carolina at Spartanburg, Spartanburg, SC 29303	1967	Dr. Olin B. Sansbury, Jr.	5-B	3,536	237
U of South Dakota, Vermillion, SD 57069-2390	1862	Dr. Betty Turner Asher	5-D	7,591	354
U of Southern California, Los Angeles, CA 90089	1880	Dr. Steven B. Sample	1-D	27,353	3,086
U of Southern Colorado, Pueblo, CO 81001	1933	Dr. Robert Shirley	5-M	4,488	278
U of Southern Indiana, Evansville, IN 47712	1965	Dr. David L. Rice	5-M	7,430	359
U of Southern Maine, Portland, ME 04103	1878	Dr. Richard L. Pattenaude	5-M	10,077	574
U of Southern Mississippi, Hattiesburg, MS 39406	1910	Dr. Aubrey K. Lucas	5-D	11,680	646
U of South Florida, Tampa, FL 33620	1956	Dr. Francis T. Borkowski	5-D	34,161	1,504
U of Southwestern Louisiana, Lafayette, LA 70504	1898	Dr. Ray P. Authement	5-D	15,677	631
U of Tampa, Tampa, FL 33606	1931	Dr. David G. Ruffer	1-M	2,506	182
U of Tennessee at Chattanooga, Chattanooga, TN 37403	1886	Dr. Frederick W. Obear	5-M	8,147	495
U of Tennessee at Martin, Martin, TN 38238	1927	Dr. Margaret N. Perry	5-M	5,660	283
U of Tennessee, Knoxville, Knoxville, TN 37996	1794	Dr. William T. Snyder	5-D	25,998	1,155
U of Tennessee, Memphis, Memphis, TN 38163	1911	NR	5-D	2,001	992
U of Texas at Arlington, Arlington, TX 76019	1895	Dr. Ryan C. Amacher	5-D	24,727	863
U of Texas at Austin, Austin, TX 78712	1883	Mr. Robert M. Berdahl	5-D	49,253	2,358
The U of Texas at Brownsville, Brownsville, TX 78520-4991	1973	NR	5-M	1,675	390
U of Texas at Dallas, Richardson, TX 75083-0688	1969	Dr. Robert H. Rutford	5-D	8,993	NR

Name, address	Year	Governing official, control, and highest degree offered		Enroll-ment	Faculty
U of Texas at El Paso, El Paso, TX 79968	1913	Dr. Diana Natalicio	5-D	17,209	724
U of Texas at San Antonio, San Antonio, TX 78249	1969	Dr. Samuel A. Kirkpatrick	5-D	16,767	660
U of Texas at Tyler, Tyler, TX 75701	1971	Dr. George F. Hamm	5-M	3,988	219
U of Texas Health Science Ctr at Houston, Houston, TX 77225	1943	Dr. M. David Low	5-D	3,204	200
U of Texas Health Science Ctr at San Antonio, San Antonio, TX 78284	1976	Dr. John P. Howe, III	5-D	2,573	1,213
U of Texas Medical Branch at Galveston, Galveston, TX 77555	1891	Dr. Thomas N. James	5-D	2,112	118
U of Texas of the Permian Basin, Odessa, TX 79762-0001	1969	Dr. Charles A. Sorber	5-M	2,224	78
U of Texas–Pan American, Edinburg, TX 78539	1927	Dr. Miguel A. Nevarez	5-M	13,298	478
U of Texas Southwestern Medical Ctr at Dallas, Dallas, TX 75235-9096	1943	Dr. C. Kern Wildenthal	5-D	1,582	272
U of the Arts, Philadelphia, PA 19102	1870	NR	1-M	1,420	294
U of the District of Columbia, Washington, DC 20008	1976	Dr. Tilden J. LeMelle	10-M	11,578	612
U of the Pacific, Stockton, CA 95211	1851	Dr. Bill L. Atchley	1-D	5,694	309
U of the Sacred Heart, Santurce, PR 00914	1935	Dr. Jose Jaime Rivera	2-M	5,030	366
U of the South, Sewanee, TN 37375-1000	1857	Dr. Samuel R. Williamson	2-D	1,214	141
U of the State of NY, Regents Coll, Albany, NY 12203	1970	Mr. C. Wayne Williams	1-B	14,464	NR
U of the Virgin Islands, Charlotte Amalie, St Thomas, VI 00802	1962	Dr. Orville Kean	8-M	2,924	266
U of Toledo, Toledo, OH 43606-3398	1872	Mr. Frank E. Horton	5-D	24,541	1,391
U of Tulsa, Tulsa, OK 74104	1894	Dr. Robert H. Donaldson	2-D	4,922	439
U of Utah, Salt Lake City, UT 84112	1850	Dr. Arthur K. Smith	5-D	25,549	1,343
U of Vermont, Burlington, VT 05405	1791	Mr. Thomas P. Salmon	5-D	9,532	1,014
U of Virginia, Charlottesville, VA 22906	1819	Mr. John T. Casteen, III	5-D	17,604	1,887
U of Washington, Seattle, WA 98195	1861	Mr. William P. Gerberding	5-D	34,598	4,067
U of West Florida, Pensacola, FL 32514-5750	1963	Dr. Morris L. Marx	5-M	7,941	255
U of Wisconsin–Eau Claire, Eau Claire, WI 54702-4004	1916	Dr. Larry Schnack	5-M	10,431	572
U of Wisconsin–Green Bay, Green Bay, WI 54311-7001	1968	Dr. David L. Outcalt	5-M	4,801	241
U of Wisconsin–La Crosse, La Crosse, WI 54601	1909	Dr. Judith L. Kuipers	5-M	8,362	450
U of Wisconsin–Madison, Madison, WI 53706	1848	Dr. David Ward	5-D	43,196	2,325
U of Wisconsin–Milwaukee, Milwaukee, WI 53201	1956	Dr. John H. Schroeder, Jr.	5-D	24,341	1,302
U of Wisconsin–Oshkosh, Oshkosh, WI 54901	1871	Dr. John E. Kerrigan	5-M	11,039	524
U of Wisconsin–Parkside, Kenosha, WI 53141	1968	Dr. Sheila Kaplan	5-M	4,993	293
U of Wisconsin–Platteville, Platteville, WI 53818	1866	Dr. Lee A. Halgren	5-M	5,225	280
U of Wisconsin–River Falls, River Falls, WI 54022	1874	Dr. Gary A. Thibodeau	5-M	5,440	295
U of Wisconsin–Stevens Point, Stevens Point, WI 54481	1894	Dr. Keith R. Sanders	5-M	8,545	462
U of Wisconsin–Stout, Menomonie, WI 54751	1891	Dr. Charles Sorensen	5-M	7,343	415
U of Wisconsin–Superior, Superior, WI 54880	1893	Dr. Betty J. Youngblood	5-M	2,891	162
U of Wisconsin–Whitewater, Whitewater, WI 53190	1868	Dr. H. Gaylon Greenhill	5-M	10,512	475
U of Wyoming, Laramie, WY 82071	1886	Dr. Terry P. Roark	5-D	12,052	754
Upper Iowa U, Fayette, IA 52142	1857	Dr. James R. Rocheleau	1-B	2,641	230
Upsala Coll, East Orange, NJ 07019-1186	1893	Dr. Robert E. Karsten	2-M	1,163	116
Ursinus Coll, Collegeville, PA 19426	1869	Dr. Richard P. Richter	2-B	1,113	120
Ursuline Coll, Pepper Pike, OH 44124 (4)	1871	Sr. Anne Marie Diederich, OSU, PhD	2-M	1,600	135
Utah State U, Logan, UT 84322	1888	Dr. George H. Emert	5-D	15,425	784
Utica Coll of Syracuse U, Utica, NY 13502-4892	1946	Dr. Michael K. Simpson	1-B	1,707	141
Valdosta State Coll, Valdosta, GA 31698	1906	Dr. Hugh C. Bailey	5-M	7,898	390
Valley City State U, Valley City, ND 58072	1890	Dr. Charles B. House, Jr.	5-B	1,003	68
Valparaiso U, Valparaiso, IN 46383	1859	Dr. Alan F. Harre	2-F	3,757	346
Vanderbilt U, Nashville, TN 37240	1873	Mr. Joe B. Wyatt	1-D	9,724	1,861
Vassar Coll, Poughkeepsie, NY 12601	1861	Dr. Frances D. Fergusson	1-M	2,272	234
Villanova U, Villanova, PA 19085	1842	Rev. Edmund J. Dobbin, OSA	2-D	11,413	886
Virginia Commonwealth U, Richmond, VA 23284	1838	Dr. Eugene P. Trani	5-D	21,939	2,401
Virginia Military Inst, Lexington, VA 24450 (1)	1839	Maj. Gen. John W. Knapp	5-B	1,265	111
Virginia Polytechnic Inst and State U, Blacksburg, VA 24061-0202	1872	Dr. James D. McComas	5-D	23,637	1,909
Virginia State U, Petersburg, VA 23806	1882	Mr. Eddie N. Moore, Jr.	5-M	4,435	224
Virginia Union U, Richmond, VA 23220	1865	Dr. S. Dallas Simmons	2-M	1,511	122
Virginia Wesleyan Coll, Norfolk, VA 23502-5599	1961	Dr. William T. Greer, Jr.	2-B	1,513	91
Viterbo Coll, La Crosse, WI 54601	1890	Dr. William J. Medland	2-M	1,392	107
Wagner Coll, Staten Island, NY 10301	1883	Dr. Norman R. Smith	1-M	1,501	155
Wake Forest U, Winston-Salem, NC 27109	1834	Dr. Thomas K. Hearn, Jr.	1-D	5,624	1,507
Walla Walla Coll, College Place, WA 99324	1892	Dr. Niels-Erik Andreasen	1-M	1,789	169
Walsh Coll of Accountancy and Business Admin, Troy, MI 48007-7006	1922	Mr. David A. Spencer	1-M	3,578	102
Walsh U, North Canton, OH 44720	1958	Rev. Richard Mucowski	2-M	1,550	113
Wartburg Coll, Waverly, IA 50677	1852	Dr. Robert Vogel	2-B	1,445	136
Washburn U of Topeka, Topeka, KS 66621	1865	Dr. Hugh Thompson	11-F	6,630	400
Washington and Jefferson Coll, Washington, PA 15301	1781	Dr. Howard J. Burnett	1-B	1,144	110
Washington and Lee U, Lexington, VA 24450	1749	Dr. John D. Wilson	1-D	1,985	167
Washington State U, Pullman, WA 99164	1890	Dr. Samuel H. Smith	5-D	17,882	1,112
Washington U, St Louis, MO 63130	1853	Dr. William H. Danforth	1-D	9,429	3,284
Waynesburg Coll, Waynesburg, PA 15370	1849	Mr. Timothy R. Thyreen	2-M	1,351	99
Wayne State Coll, Wayne, NE 68787	1910	Dr. Donald J. Mash	5-M	3,761	209
Wayne State U, Detroit, MI 48202	1868	Mr. David Adamany	5-D	34,945	2,533
Weber State U, Ogden, UT 84408	1889	Dr. Paul H. Thompson	5-M	14,993	457
Webster U, St Louis, MO 63119	1915	Dr. Daniel H. Perlman	1-D	9,699	1,149
Wellesley Coll, Wellesley, MA 02181 (3)	1870	Dr. Luella G. Goldberg	1-B	2,340	313
Wentworth Inst of Tech, Boston, MA 02115	1904	Dr. John F. Van Domelen	1-B	2,601	231
Wesleyan U, Middletown, CT 06459	1831	Mr. William M. Chace	1-D	3,331	321
Wesley Coll, Dover, DE 19901	1873	Dr. Reed M. Stewart	2-B	1,294	103
West Chester U of Pennsylvania, West Chester, PA 19383	1871	Dr. Madeleine Wing Adler	5-M	11,806	659
West Coast U, Los Angeles, CA 90020-1765	1909	Dr. Robert M. L. Baker, Jr.	1-M	1,600	250
Western Carolina U, Cullowhee, NC 28723	1889	Dr. Myron L. Coulter	5-M	6,576	430
Western Illinois U, Macomb, IL 61455	1899	Dr. Ralph H. Wagoner	5-M	13,377	703
Western International U, Phoenix, AZ 85021	1978	Dr. Robert S. Webber	1-M	1,552	80
Western Kentucky U, Bowling Green, KY 42101-3576	1906	Dr. Thomas C. Meredith	5-M	15,750	768
Western Maryland Coll, Westminster, MD 21157-4390	1867	Dr. Robert H. Chambers	1-M	2,143	194
Western Michigan U, Kalamazoo, MI 49008	1903	Dr. Diether H. Haenicke	5-D	27,282	1,115
Western New England Coll, Springfield, MA 01119	1919	Dr. Beverly W. Miller	1-F	4,242	259
Western New Mexico U, Silver City, NM 88061	1893	Dr. Jerry L. Gallentine	5-M	2,240	113
Western Oregon State Coll, Monmouth, OR 97361	1856	Dr. Richard S. Meyers	5-M	3,936	282
Western State Coll of Colorado, Gunnison, CO 81231	1911	Dr. Kaye Howe	5-B	2,668	143

Name, address	Year	Governing official, control, and highest degree offered		Enroll-ment	Faculty
Western State U Coll of Law of Orange County, Fullerton, CA 92631	1966	NR	3-F	1,804	78
Western Washington U, Bellingham, WA 98225	1893	Dr. Roland L. DeLorme	5-M	10,150	525
Westfield State Coll, Westfield, MA 01086	1838	Dr. Ronald L. Applbaum	5-M	5,103	365
West Georgia Coll, Carrollton, GA 30118	1933	Dr. Maurice K. Townsend	5-M	7,717	309
West Liberty State Coll, West Liberty, WV 26074	1837	Dr. Clyde D. Campbell	5-B	2,377	153
Westminster Coll, New Wilmington, PA 16172-0001	1852	Dr. Oscar E. Remick	2-M	1,554	140
Westminster Coll of Salt Lake City, Salt Lake City, UT 84105	1875	Dr. Charles H. Dick	1-M	2,141	201
Westmont Coll, Santa Barbara, CA 93108	1940	Dr. David K. Winter	2-B	1,317	110
West Texas A&M U, Canyon, TX 79016-0001	1909	Dr. Barry B. Thompson	5-M	6,405	312
West Virginia Inst of Tech, Montgomery, WV 25136	1895	Dr. John P. Carrier	5-M	3,051	214
West Virginia State Coll, Institute, WV 25112	1891	NR	5-B	4,896	233
West Virginia U, Morgantown, WV 26506	1867	Dr. Neil S. Bucklew	5-D	22,712	1,543
West Virginia Wesleyan Coll, Buckhannon, WV 26201	1890	Dr. Thomas B. Courtice	2-M	1,655	126
Wheaton Coll, Wheaton, IL 60187	1860	Dr. A. Duane Litfin	2-M	2,606	259
Wheaton Coll, Norton, MA 02766	1834	Dr. Dale Rogers Marshall	1-B	1,319	110
Wheeling Jesuit Coll, Wheeling, WV 26003-6233	1954	Fr. Thomas S. Acker, SJ	2-M	1,438	80
Wheelock Coll, Boston, MA 02215 (4)	1888	Dr. Gerald N. Tirozzi	1-M	1,343	203
Whitman Coll, Walla Walla, WA 99362	1859	Mr. Charles Anderson	1-B	1,198	129
Whittier Coll, Whittier, CA 90608	1887	Dr. James L. Ash, Jr.	1-F	1,957	101
Whitworth Coll, Spokane, WA 99251	1890	Dr. William P. Robinson	2-M	1,676	95
Wichita State U, Wichita, KS 67260	1895	Dr. Eugene Morgan Hughes	5-D	15,120	488
Widener U, Chester, PA 19013	1821	Dr. Robert J. Bruce	1-D	8,938	312
Wilkes U, Wilkes-Barre, PA 18766	1933	Dr. Christopher N. Breiseth	1-M	3,200	228
Willamette U, Salem, OR 97301	1842	Dr. Jerry E. Hudson	2-F	2,332	247
William Carey Coll, Hattiesburg, MS 39401	1906	Dr. James W. Edwards	2-M	2,032	156
William Jewell Coll, Liberty, MO 64068	1849	Dr. J. Gordon Kingsley	2-B	1,384	146
William Paterson Coll of New Jersey, Wayne, NJ 07470	1855	Dr. Arnold Speert	5-M	9,391	320
Williams Coll, Williamstown, MA 01267	1793	Dr. Francis C. Oakley	1-M	2,064	267
Wilmington Coll, New Castle, DE 19720	1967	Dr. Audrey K. Doberstein	1-D	2,500	253
Wingate Coll, Wingate, NC 28174	1895	Dr. Jerry E. McGee	2-M	1,434	97
Winona State U, Winona, MN 55987	1858	Dr. Darrell Krueger	5-M	7,500	400
Winston-Salem State U, Winston-Salem, NC 27110	1892	Dr. Cleon F. Thompson, Jr.	5-B	2,655	179
Winthrop U, Rock Hill, SC 29733	1886	Dr. Anthony DiGiorgio	5-M	5,025	420
Wittenberg U, Springfield, OH 45501	1845	Dr. William A. Kinnison	2-B	2,250	182
Wofford Coll, Spartanburg, SC 29303-3663	1854	Dr. Joab M. Lesesne	2-B	1,127	94
Woodbury U, Burbank, CA 91510	1884	Dr. Paul E. Sago	1-M	1,106	125
Worcester Polytechnic Inst, Worcester, MA 01609	1865	Dr. Jon C. Strauss	1-D	3,171	345
Worcester State Coll, Worcester, MA 01602	1874	Dr. Kalyan K. Ghosh	5-M	4,418	194
Wright State U, Dayton, OH 45435	1964	Dr. Paige E. Mulhollan	5-D	17,657	950
Xavier U, Cincinnati, OH 45207-5311	1831	Rev. James E. Hoff, SJ	2-M	6,383	411
Xavier U of Louisiana, New Orleans, LA 70125	1925	Dr. Norman C. Francis	2-F	3,330	253
Yale U, New Haven, CT 06520	1701	Mr. Richard C. Levin	1-D	11,129	712
Yeshiva U, New York, NY 10033-3201	1886	Dr. Norman Lamm	1-D	4,899	1,092
York Coll of Pennsylvania, York, PA 17405-7199	1787	Dr. George W. Waldner	1-M	4,942	286
York Coll of the City U of New York, Jamaica, NY 11451	1967	Dr. Josephine D. Davis	12-B	6,480	200
Youngstown State U, Youngstown, OH 44555	1908	Dr. Leslie H. Cochran	5-D	14,806	889

Two-Year Colleges

The highest undergraduate degree offered for all two-year colleges is the associate degree.

Abraham Baldwin Ag Coll, Tifton, GA 31794-2601	1933	Dr. Harold J. Loyd	5	2,851	135
Adirondack Comm Coll, Queensbury, NY 12804	1960	Dr. Roger Andersen	12	3,778	224
Aiken Tech Coll, Aiken, SC 29802	1972	Dr. Paul L. Blowers	12	2,373	124
Aims Comm Coll, Greeley, CO 80632	1967	Dr. George R. Conger	10	9,035	434
Alabama Southern Comm Coll, Monroeville, AL 36460	1965	Dr. John A. Johnson	5	1,898	107
Alabama Southern Comm Coll, Thomasville, AL 36784	1965	Dr. Hoyt Jones	5	1,225	119
Alamance Comm Coll, Graham, NC 27253	1959	Dr. W. Ronald McCarter	5	3,775	145
Albuquerque Tech Vocational Inst, Albuquerque, NM 87106	1965	NR	5	12,806	746
Allan Hancock Coll, Santa Maria, CA 93454	1920	Dr. Ann F. Stephenson	12	8,221	417
Allegany Comm Coll, Cumberland, MD 21502	1961	Dr. Donald L. Alexander	12	2,915	210
Allen County Comm Coll, Iola, KS 66749	1923	Mr. John Masterson	12	1,717	125
Alpena Comm Coll, Alpena, MI 49707	1952	Dr. Donald L. Newport	12	2,118	128
Alvin Comm Coll, Alvin, TX 77511-4898	1949	Dr. A. Rodney Allbright	12	4,085	141
Amarillo Coll, Amarillo, TX 79178	1929	Dr. Luther Bud Joyner	12	6,547	374
American Inst of Business, Des Moines, IA 50321	1921	Mr. Keith Fenton	1	1,040	55
American River Coll, Sacramento, CA 95841	1955	Dr. Queen F. Randall	10	20,824	700
Angelina Coll, Lufkin, TX 75902	1968	Dr. Larry M. Phillips	12	3,398	151
Anne Arundel Comm Coll, Arnold, MD 21012	1961	Dr. Thomas E. Florestano	12	11,749	590
Anoka-Ramsey Comm Coll, Coon Rapids, MN 55433	1965	Dr. Patrick M. Johns	5	6,250	228
Antelope Valley Coll, Lancaster, CA 93536	1929	Dr. Allan W. Kurki	12	10,751	400
Arapahoe Comm Coll, Littleton, CO 80160-9002	1965	Dr. James F. Weber	5	7,165	298
Arizona Western Coll, Yuma, AZ 85366-0929	1962	Dr. James R. Carruthers	12	5,400	334
Arkansas State U–Beebe Branch, Beebe, AR 72012	1927	Mr. William H. Owen, Jr.	5	1,872	79
Art Inst of Atlanta, Atlanta, GA 30326	1949	Mr. Hal R. Griffith	3	1,386	106
Art Inst of Dallas, Dallas, TX 75231	1978	Dr. Pat DeCoursey	3	1,000	84
Art Inst of Fort Lauderdale, Fort Lauderdale, FL 33316	1968	Mr. David P. Higley	3	2,100	150
The Art Inst of Houston, Houston, TX 77056	1978	NR	3	1,083	91
The Art Inst of Philadelphia, Philadelphia, PA 19103-5198	1966	Dr. Max R. Tudor	3	1,200	90
Art Inst of Pittsburgh, Pittsburgh, PA 15222	1921	Ms. Saundra M. Van Dyke	3	2,500	106
Art Inst of Seattle, Seattle, WA 98121	1982	Mr. David J. Pauldine	3	1,605	101
Asnuntuck Comm Coll, Enfield, CT 06082	1972	Dr. Harvey S. Irlen	5	2,122	79
Atlanta Metropolitan Coll, Atlanta, GA 30310	1974	Dr. Edwin A. Thompson	5	1,700	100
Atlantic Comm Coll, Mays Landing, NJ 08330	1966	Dr. John May	9	5,687	215
Austin Comm Coll, Austin, MN 55912	1940	Dr. Vicky R. Smith	5	1,373	73
Austin Comm Coll, Austin, TX 78752	1972	Mr. Roland K. Smith	10	25,275	1,388
Bainbridge Coll, Bainbridge, GA 31717	1972	Dr. Edward D. Mobley	5	1,023	39
Bakersfield Coll, Bakersfield, CA 93305	1913	Dr. Richard Wright	12	12,267	496
Baltimore City Comm Coll, Baltimore, MD 21215	1947	Dr. James D. Tschichtelin	5	6,856	493
Barstow Coll, Barstow, CA 92311	1959	Dr. Joseph A. Clark, Jr.	12	3,569	128
Barton County Comm Coll, Great Bend, KS 67530	1969	Dr. Jimmie L. Downing	12	4,460	205
Bay de Noc Comm Coll, Escanaba, MI 49829	1963	Dr. Dwight E. Link	9	2,238	143

Name, address	Year	Governing official, control		Enroll-ment	Faculty
Beaufort County Comm Coll, Washington, NC 27889	1967	Dr. Ron Champion	5	1,281	95
Bee County Coll, Beeville, TX 78102	1965	Dr. Norman Wallace	9	2,520	116
Belleville Area Coll, Belleville, IL 62221	1946	Dr. Joseph Cipfl	10	15,440	842
Bellevue Comm Coll, Bellevue, WA 98007-6484	1966	Dr. B. Jean Floten	5	10,543	670
Belmont Tech Coll, St Clairsville, OH 43950	1971	Dr. Wesley R. Channell	5	1,750	133
Bergen Comm Coll, Paramus, NJ 07652	1965	Dr. Jose Lopez-Isa	9	8,659	613
Berkeley Coll of Business, West Paterson, NJ 07424	1931	Mr. Kevin L. Luing	3	1,608	110
Berkshire Comm Coll, Pittsfield, MA 01201	1960	Dr. Cathryn L. Addy	5	2,641	126
Bessemer State Tech Coll, Bessemer, AL 35021	1966	Dr. W. Michael Bailey	5	1,868	102
Bevill State Comm Coll, Fayette, AL 35555	1969	Dr. Wayland DeWitt	5	1,145	63
Big Bend Comm Coll, Moses Lake, WA 98837-3299	1962	Dr. Greg Fitch	5	1,850	147
Bishop State Comm Coll, Mobile, AL 36603	1965	NR	5	2,757	90
Bismarck State Coll, Bismarck, ND 58501	1939	Dr. Kermit Lidstrom	5	2,472	117
Black Hawk Coll, Moline, IL 61265	1946	Dr. Charles E. Laws	12	5,881	305
Blackhawk Tech Coll, Janesville, WI 53547	1968	Dr. James C. Catania	10	2,700	293
Blinn Coll, Brenham, TX 77833	1883	Mr. Walter C. Schwartz	12	8,105	326
Blue Mountain Comm Coll, Pendleton, OR 97801	1962	Mr. Ronald L. Daniels	12	5,588	189
Blue Ridge Comm Coll, Flat Rock, NC 28731	1969	Dr. David W. Sink	12	1,514	98
Blue Ridge Comm Coll, Weyers Cave, VA 24486	1965	Dr. James R. Perkins	5	2,950	141
Borough of Manhattan Comm Coll of City U of NY, New York, NY 10007	1963	Dr. Steven M. Curtis	12	15,677	995
Bossier Parish Comm Coll, Bossier City, LA 71111	1967	Mr. James M. Conerly	12	4,356	134
Bowling Green State U–Firelands Coll, Huron, OH 44839	1968	Dr. R. Darby Williams	5	1,451	75
Brainerd Comm Coll, Brainerd, MN 56401	1938	Ms. Sally Jane Ihne	5	1,856	97
Bramson ORT Tech Inst, Forest Hills, NY 11375	1977	Dr. Howard J. Friedman	1	1,360	57
Brazosport Coll, Lake Jackson, TX 77566	1948	Dr. John R. Grable	12	3,346	157
Brevard Comm Coll, Cocoa, FL 32922	1960	Dr. Maxwell C. King	5	14,083	976
Briarcliffe–The Coll for Bus/Data Systems Inst, Woodbury, NY 11797	1966	Mr. Richard Turan	3	1,400	114
Bristol Comm Coll, Fall River, MA 02720	1965	Ms. Eileen Farley	5	3,143	183
Brookdale Comm Coll, Lincroft, NJ 07738	1967	Dr. Peter Burnham	9	12,809	443
Brookhaven Coll, Farmers Branch, TX 75244	1978	Dr. Walter G. Bumphus	9	9,060	525
Broome Comm Coll, Binghamton, NY 13902	1946	Dr. Donald A. Dellow	12	5,685	451
Broward Comm Coll, Fort Lauderdale, FL 33301	1960	Dr. Willis N. Holcombe	5	28,433	775
Brunswick Coll, Brunswick, GA 31523	1961	Dr. Dorothy L. Lord	5	1,841	75
Bryant and Stratton Business Inst, Buffalo, NY 14202	1854	Mr. William Schatt	3	1,009	26
Bucks County Comm Coll, Newtown, PA 18940	1964	Dr. James J. Linksz	9	11,348	375
Bunker Hill Comm Coll, Boston, MA 02129	1973	NR	5	6,120	145
Burlington County Coll, Pemberton, NJ 08068	1966	Dr. Robert Messina	9	7,085	150
Butler County Comm Coll, El Dorado, KS 67042	1927	Dr. Rodney V. Cox, Jr	12	6,627	473
Butler County Comm Coll, Butler, PA 16003	1965	Dr. Thaddeus H. Penar	9	3,290	135
Camden County Coll, Blackwood, NJ 08012	1967	Dr. Bob Barringer	12	15,713	385
Cañada Coll, Redwood City, CA 94061	1968	NR	10	6,936	263
Cape Cod Comm Coll, West Barnstable, MA 02668	1961	NR	5	4,009	258
Cape Fear Comm Coll, Wilmington, NC 28401	1959	Dr. Richard C. Conrath	5	3,150	153
Capital Comm Tech Coll, Hartford, CT 06105	1946	NR	5	3,773	130
Carl Albert State Coll, Poteau, OK 74953	1934	NR	5	1,979	160
Carl Sandburg Coll, Galesburg, IL 61401	1967	NR	12	3,397	234
Carteret Comm Coll, Morehead City, NC 28557	1963	Dr. Donald W. Bryant	5	1,602	93
Casper Coll, Casper, WY 82601	1945	Dr. LeRoy Strausner	10	2,400	185
Catawba Valley Comm Coll, Hickory, NC 28602-9699	1960	Dr. Cuyler A. Dunbar	12	3,566	175
Catonsville Comm Coll, Catonsville, MD 21228	1957	Dr. Frederick J. Walsh	9	10,731	534
Cayuga County Comm Coll, Auburn, NY 13021-3099	1953	Dr. Lawrence H. Poole	12	2,924	212
Cazenovia Coll, Cazenovia, NY 13035	1824	Dr. Stephen M. Schneeweiss	1	1,042	145
Cecil Comm Coll, North East, MD 21901	1968	Dr. Robert L. Gell	9	1,033	108
Cedar Valley Coll, Lancaster, TX 75134	1977	Dr. Carol J. Spencer	5	3,281	130
Central Alabama Comm Coll, Alexander City, AL 35010	1965	Dr. James H. Cornell	5	2,092	139
Central Arizona Coll, Coolidge, AZ 85228	1961	Dr. John J. Klein	9	14,724	NR
Central Carolina Comm Coll, Sanford, NC 27330	1962	Dr. Marvin R. Joyner	12	3,050	189
Central Carolina Tech Coll, Sumter, SC 29150	1963	Dr. Herbert C. Robbins	5	2,232	144
Central Comm Coll–Grand Island Cmps, Grand Island, NE 68802	1976	Dr. William Giddings	12	2,510	198
Central Comm Coll–Hastings Cmps, Hastings, NE 68902	1966	Dr. Judy Dresser	12	3,063	144
Central Comm Coll–Platte Cmps, Columbus, NE 68602	1968	Dr. Peter Rush	12	2,524	118
Central Florida Comm Coll, Ocala, FL 34478	1957	NR	12	5,616	178
Central Ohio Tech Coll, Newark, OH 43055	1971	Dr. Julius S. Greenstein	5	1,860	99
Central Oregon Comm Coll, Bend, OR 97701	1949	Dr. Robert L. Barber	10	3,138	184
Central Piedmont Comm Coll, Charlotte, NC 28235	1963	Mr. Paul A. Zeiss	12	15,871	1,220
Central Texas Coll, Killeen, TX 76540	1967	Dr. James R. Anderson	12	6,825	300
Central Virginia Comm Coll, Lynchburg, VA 24502-4907	1966	Dr. Belle S. Wheelan	5	4,105	120
Central Wyoming Coll, Riverton, WY 82501	1966	Dr. JoAnne McFarland	12	1,607	147
Cerritos Coll, Norwalk, CA 90650	1956	Dr. Ernest Martinez	12	21,067	683
Cerro Coso Comm Coll, Ridgecrest, CA 93555	1973	Dr. Raymond A. McCue	5	4,118	282
Chabot Coll, Hayward, CA 94545	1961	Dr. Raul J. Cardoza	5	15,290	957
Chaffey Coll, Rancho Cucamonga, CA 91737-3002	1883	Dr. Jerry W. Young	10	15,000	540
Champlain Coll, Burlington, VT 05401	1878	Dr. Roger H. Perry	1	1,966	117
Charles County Comm Coll, La Plata, MD 20646	1958	Dr. John Sine	12	5,769	247
Charles Stewart Mott Comm Coll, Flint, MI 48503	1923	Dr. Charles R. Donnelly	10	11,222	454
Chattahoochee Valley State Comm Coll, Phenix City, AL 36869	1974	Mr. Bob Boothe	5	1,763	77
Chattanooga State Tech Comm Coll, Chattanooga, TN 37406	1965	Dr. James L. Catanzaro	5	8,943	358
Chemeketa Comm Coll, Salem, OR 97309	1955	Dr. Gerard Berger	12	10,757	881
Chesapeake Coll, Wye Mills, MD 21679	1965	Dr. John R. Kotula	12	2,131	95
Chipola Jr Coll, Marianna, FL 32446	1947	Dr. Jerry W. Kandzer	5	2,949	142
Chippewa Valley Tech Coll, Eau Claire, WI 54701	1912	Mr. Norbert K. Wurtzel	10	3,800	400
Cincinnati Tech Coll, Cincinnati, OH 45223	1966	Dr. James P. Long	5	5,562	317
Cisco Jr Coll, Cisco, TX 76437	1940	Dr. Roger C. Schustereit	12	2,559	98
City Coll of San Francisco, San Francisco, CA 94112	1935	Dr. Evans S. Dobelle	12	34,000	1,117
City Colls of Chicago, Harold Washington Coll, Chicago, IL 60601	1962	Dr. Wayne Watson	12	6,804	197
City Colls of Chicago, Harry S Truman Coll, Chicago, IL 60640	1956	Dr. Wallace B. Appelson	12	5,078	160
City Colls of Chicago, Kennedy-King Coll, Chicago, IL 60621	1935	Dr. Harold Pates	12	2,680	106
City Colls of Chicago, Malcolm X Coll, Chicago, IL 60612	1911	Ms. Zerrie D. Campbell	12	2,670	142
City Colls of Chicago, Olive-Harvey Coll, Chicago, IL 60628	1970	Mr. Homer D. Franklin	12	3,698	123

Name, address	Year	Governing official, control		Enrollment	Faculty
City Colls of Chicago, Richard J Daley Coll, Chicago, IL 60652	1960	Mr. William P. Conway	12	5,557	NR
City Colls of Chicago, Wilbur Wright Coll, Chicago, IL 60634	1934	Mr. Raymond F. LeFevour	12	6,188	161
Clackamas Comm Coll, Oregon City, OR 97045	1966	Dr. John S. Keyser	9	6,621	512
Clark Coll, Vancouver, WA 98663	1933	Dr. Earl P. Johnson	5	9,100	320
Clark State Comm Coll, Springfield, OH 45501	1962	Mr. Albert A. Salerno	5	3,113	131
Clatsop Comm Coll, Astoria, OR 97103	1958	Dr. John W. Wubben	9	2,265	165
Cleveland Inst of Electronics, Cleveland, OH 44114 (2)	1934	Mr. John R. Drinko	3	2,700	6
Cleveland State Comm Coll, Cleveland, TN 37320-3570	1967	Dr. James W. Ford	5	3,596	184
Clinton Comm Coll, Clinton, IA 52732	1946	Dr. Desna L. Wallin	5	1,274	75
Clinton Comm Coll, Plattsburgh, NY 12901	1969	Dr. Jay L. Fennell	12	2,080	156
Cloud County Comm Coll, Concordia, KS 66901-1002	1965	Dr. James P. Ihrig	12	3,018	225
Clovis Comm Coll, Clovis, NM 88101	1971	Dr. Jay Gurley	5	3,328	NR
Coastal Carolina Comm Coll, Jacksonville, NC 28546-6877	1964	Dr. Ronald K. Lingle, Jr.	12	3,590	192
Coastline Comm Coll, Fountain Valley, CA 92708	1976	Dr. William M. Vega	12	15,562	505
Cochise Coll, Douglas, AZ 85607	1962	Dr. Walter S. Patton	12	4,938	342
Coffeyville Comm Coll, Coffeyville, KS 67337	1923	Dr. Dan Kinney	12	2,300	86
Colby Comm Coll, Colby, KS 67701	1964	Dr. Mikel Ary	12	1,023	80
Coll of Alameda, Alameda, CA 94501	1970	Dr. Marie B. Smith	12	5,962	NR
Coll of DuPage, Glen Ellyn, IL 60137	1967	Dr. Harold D. McAninch	12	31,625	1,808
Coll of Eastern Utah, Price, UT 84501	1937	Dr. Michael A. Petersen	5	2,746	96
Coll of Lake County, Grayslake, IL 60030-1198	1967	Dr. Daniel J. La Vista	10	15,644	677
Coll of Marin, Kentfield, CA 94904	1926	Dr. John D. Randall	12	9,604	464
Coll of Southern Idaho, Twin Falls, ID 83303-1238	1964	Mr. Gerald R. Meyerhoeffer	12	3,804	244
Coll of The Albemarle, Elizabeth City, NC 27906-2327	1960	Dr. Larry R. Donnithorne	5	2,038	117
Coll of the Canyons, Santa Clarita, CA 91355	1969	Dr. Dianne G. Van Hook	12	6,250	229
Coll of the Desert, Palm Desert, CA 92260	1959	Dr. David A. George	12	10,975	419
Coll of the Mainland, Texas City, TX 77591	1967	Mr. Larry L. Stanley	12	3,883	180
Coll of the Redwoods, Eureka, CA 95501	1964	Dr. Cedric A. Sampson	12	7,222	379
Coll of the Sequoias, Visalia, CA 93277	1925	Dr. Robert A. Lombardi	12	9,499	479
Coll of the Siskiyous, Weed, CA 96094	1957	Dr. Martha Romero	12	2,441	146
Collin County Comm Coll, McKinney, TX 75070	1985	NR	12	9,590	528
Colorado Inst of Art, Denver, CO 80203	1952	Dr. W. C. Bottoms	3	1,328	77
Columbia Coll, Columbia, CA 95310	1968	Dr. Kenneth White	12	3,618	119
Columbia-Greene Comm Coll, Hudson, NY 12534	1969	Dr. Terry A. Cline	12	1,778	115
Columbia State Comm Coll, Columbia, TN 38401	1966	Dr. Paul Sands	5	3,721	197
Columbus State Comm Coll, Columbus, OH 43216	1963	Dr. Harold M. Nestor	5	16,510	842
Comm Coll of Allegheny County Allegheny Cmps, Pittsburgh, PA 15212	1966	Dr. J. David Griffin	9	13,831	274
Comm Coll of Allegheny County Boyce Cmps, Monroeville, PA 15146	1966	Dr. Carl A. Di Sibio	9	4,635	190
Comm Coll of Allegheny County, North Cmps, Pittsburgh, PA 15237	1972	Dr. Fred F. Bartok	9	4,336	1,398
Comm Coll of Allegheny County South Cmps, West Mifflin, PA 15122	1967	Dr. Thomas A. Juravich	9	5,688	760
Comm Coll of Aurora, Aurora, CO 80011-9036	1983	Dr. Larry Carter	5	4,695	197
Comm Coll of Beaver County, Monaca, PA 15061	1966	Ms. Margaret Williams-Betlyn	5	2,800	150
Comm Coll of Denver, Denver, CO 80217-3363	1970	Dr. Byron McClenney	5	7,021	271
Comm Coll of Philadelphia, Philadelphia, PA 19130	1964	Dr. Bob Barringer	12	19,476	1,170
Comm Coll of Rhode Island, Warwick, RI 02886-1807	1964	Mr. Edward Liston	5	12,365	720
Comm Coll of Southern Nevada, North Las Vegas, NV 89030	1971	Dr. Paul E. Meacham	5	17,747	730
Comm Coll of the Air Force, Maxwell Air Force Base, AL 36112-6655	1972	Col. Paul A. Reid	4	478,245	11,000
Comm Coll of Vermont, Waterbury, VT 05676	1970	Dr. Michael Holland	5	2,358	591
Compton Comm Coll, Compton, CA 90221-5393	1927	Dr. Warren A. Washington	12	5,700	347
Connors State Coll, Warner, OK 74469	1908	Dr. Carl O. Westbrook	5	2,379	110
Contra Costa Coll, San Pablo, CA 94806	1948	Dr. D. Candy Rose	12	8,242	244
Cooke County Coll, Gainesville, TX 76240	1924	Dr. Luther Bud Joyner	9	4,068	175
Copiah-Lincoln Comm Coll, Wesson, MS 39191	1928	Dr. Billy B. Thames	12	1,531	116
Corning Comm Coll, Corning, NY 14830	1956	Dr. Donald H. Hangen	12	3,512	147
Cosumnes River Coll, Sacramento, CA 95823	1970	Dr. Marc E. Hall	10	11,525	398
County Coll of Morris, Randolph, NJ 07869	1966	Dr. Edward J. Yaw	9	10,568	553
Cowley County Comm Coll and Voc-Tech Sch, Arkansas City, KS 67005	1922	Dr. Patrick J. McAtee	12	3,059	184
Crafton Hills Coll, Yucaipa, CA 92399	1972	Dr. Luis S. Gomez	12	5,136	190
Crowder Coll, Neosho, MO 64850	1963	Dr. Kent A. Farnsworth	12	1,895	147
Cuesta Coll, San Luis Obispo, CA 93403-8106	1964	Dr. Grace N. Mitchell	10	8,004	298
Culinary Inst of America, Hyde Park, NY 12538-1499	1946	Mr. Ferdinand E. Metz	1	1,923	101
Cumberland County Coll, Vineland, NJ 08360	1963	Dr. Roland J. Chapdelaine	12	2,783	118
Cuyahoga Comm Coll, Eastern Cmps, Highland Hills, OH 44122	1971	Mr. Paul E. Shumaker	12	5,858	225
Cuyahoga Comm Coll, Metropolitan Cmps, Cleveland, OH 44115	1963	Dr. Ronald R. Zambetti	12	7,004	474
Cuyahoga Comm Coll, Western Cmps, Parma, OH 44130	1966	Mr. Ronald M. Sobel	12	12,961	596
Cuyamaca Coll, El Cajon, CA 92019	1978	Dr. Samuel M. Ciccati	5	4,945	NR
Cypress Coll, Cypress, CA 90630	1966	Dr. Kirk Avery	12	14,672	434
Dabney S Lancaster Comm Coll, Clifton Forge, VA 24422	1964	Dr. John F. Backels	5	1,653	NR
Dalton Coll, Dalton, GA 30720	1963	Dr. Derrell C. Roberts	5	2,884	108
Danville Area Comm Coll, Danville, IL 61832	1946	Dr. Harry J. Braun	12	3,429	143
Danville Comm Coll, Danville, VA 24541	1967	Dr. B. Carlyle Ramsey	5	4,045	152
Darton Coll, Albany, GA 31707	1965	Dr. Peter J. Sireno	5	2,633	136
Davidson County Comm Coll, Lexington, NC 27293	1958	Dr. J. Bryan Brooks	12	2,252	149
Daytona Beach Comm Coll, Daytona Beach, FL 32120-2811	1958	NR	5	10,807	704
Dean Jr Coll, Franklin, MA 02038	1865	Mr. John A. Dunn	1	1,000	126
DeKalb Coll, Decatur, GA 30034	1964	Dr. Marvin M. Cole	5	15,976	1,010
Delaware County Comm Coll, Media, PA 19063-1094	1967	Dr. Richard D. De Cosmo	12	10,269	486
Delaware Tech & Comm Coll, Southern Cmps, Georgetown, DE 19947	1967	Mr. Jack F. Owens	5	3,563	159
Delaware Tech & Comm Coll, Stanton/Wilmington Cmps, Newark, DE 19702	1968	Dr. Orlando J. George, Jr.	5	6,273	348
Delaware Tech & Comm Coll, Terry Cmps, Dover, DE 19901	1972	Mr. Wayne N. Dabson	5	1,997	105
Delgado Comm Coll, New Orleans, LA 70119	1921	Dr. Ione Elioff	5	15,115	1,029
Del Mar Coll, Corpus Christi, TX 78404	1935	Mr. B. R. Venters	12	11,659	480

Name, address	Year	Governing official, control		Enrollment	Faculty
Delta Coll, University Center, MI 48710	1961	Dr. Peter D. Boyse	10	11,228	508
Des Moines Area Comm Coll, Ankeny, IA 50021	1966	Dr. Joseph Borgen	12	11,040	NR
DeVry Inst of Tech, Woodbridge, NJ 07095	1969	NR	3	2,202	75
Diablo Valley Coll, Pleasant Hill, CA 94523	1949	Dr. Phyllis L. Peterson	12	23,000	800
Dixie Coll, St George, UT 84770	1911	Dr. Douglas Alder	5	2,347	107
Dodge City Comm Coll, Dodge City, KS 67801	1935	Dr. Thomas E. Gamble	12	2,601	161
Doña Ana Branch Comm Coll, Las Cruces, NM 88003-0001	1973	NR	12	3,615	158
Dundalk Comm Coll, Baltimore, MD 21222	1970	Dr. Martha A. Smith	9	3,383	237
Durham Tech Comm Coll, Durham, NC 27703	1961	Dr. Phail Wynn, Jr.	5	5,003	271
Dutchess Comm Coll, Poughkeepsie, NY 12601	1957	Dr. D. David Conklin	12	7,693	415
Dyersburg State Comm Coll, Dyersburg, TN 38025-0648	1969	Dr. Karen A. Bowyer	5	2,100	132
East Arkansas Comm Coll, Forrest City, AR 72335	1974	Dr. Tom Spencer	5	1,804	89
East Central Coll, Union, MO 63084	1968	Dr. Dale Gibson	10	3,216	155
East Central Comm Coll, Decatur, MS 39327	1928	Dr. Eddie M. Smith	12	1,402	56
Eastern Arizona Coll, Thatcher, AZ 85552-0769	1888	Mr. Gherald L. Hoopes, Jr.	12	1,819	268
Eastern New Mexico U–Roswell, Roswell, NM 88202	1958	Dr. Loyd R. Hughes	5	2,085	140
Eastern Oklahoma State Coll, Wilburton, OK 74578	1907	NR	5	2,474	54
Eastern Wyoming Coll, Torrington, WY 82240	1948	Dr. Roy Mason	12	2,024	136
Eastfield Coll, Mesquite, TX 75150	1970	Dr. Robert Aguero	12	9,526	399
East Los Angeles Coll, Monterey Park, CA 91754	1945	Dr. Omero Suarez	12	13,423	450
East Mississippi Comm Coll, Scooba, MS 39358	1927	Dr. Thomas L. Davis	12	1,381	175
Edgecombe Comm Coll, Tarboro, NC 27886	1968	Mr. Charles B. McIntyre	12	2,018	168
Edison Comm Coll, Fort Myers, FL 33906-6210	1962	Dr. Kenneth Walker	12	9,120	724
Edison State Comm Coll, Piqua, OH 45356	1973	Dr. Kenneth A. Yowell	5	3,297	183
Edmonds Comm Coll, Lynnwood, WA 98036	1967	Mr. Thomas C. Nielsen	12	8,140	381
Elaine P Nunez Comm Coll, Chalmette, LA 70043	1967	Dr. Carol S. Hopson	12	1,887	47
El Centro Coll, Dallas, TX 75202	1966	Dr. Wright L. Lassiter, Jr.	9	6,328	331
Elgin Comm Coll, Elgin, IL 60123	1949	Dr. Paul Heath	12	9,031	400
El Paso Comm Coll, El Paso, TX 79998	1969	Dr. Leonardo de la Garza	9	18,474	1,539
Enterprise State Jr Coll, Enterprise, AL 36331	1965	Dr. Joseph D. Talmadge	5	2,285	125
Erie Comm Coll, City Cmps, Buffalo, NY 14203-2601	1971	Dr. Louis M. Ricci	12	4,034	256
Erie Comm Coll, North Cmps, Williamsville, NY 14221-7095	1946	Dr. Louis M. Ricci	12	7,131	391
Erie Comm Coll, South Cmps, Orchard Park, NY 14127-2199	1974	Dr. Louis M. Ricci	12	3,545	282
Essex Comm Coll, Baltimore, MD 21237	1957	Dr. Donald J. Slowinski	12	10,767	599
Essex County Coll, Newark, NJ 07102	1966	Dr. Zachary Yamba	9	8,500	270
Everett Comm Coll, Everett, WA 98201	1941	Ms. Susan C. Carroll	5	7,726	252
Evergreen Valley Coll, San Jose, CA 95135	1975	NR	12	11,255	275
Fairleigh Dickinson U, Edward Williams Coll, Hackensack, NJ 07601	1964	Mr. Kenneth T. Vehrkens	1	1,158	62
Fashion Inst of Design & Merchandising, LA Cmps, Los Angeles, CA 90015	1969	Ms. Tonian Hohberg	3	2,934	180
Fayetteville Tech Comm Coll, Fayetteville, NC 28303-0236	1961	Dr. Craig Allen	5	6,975	317
Feather River Comm Coll District, Quincy, CA 95971	1968	Dr. Donald Donato	12	1,300	92
Fergus Falls Comm Coll, Fergus Falls, MN 56537	1960	Mr. Dan F. True	5	1,300	60
Finger Lakes Comm Coll, Canandaigua, NY 14424-8395	1965	Dr. Daniel T. Hayes	12	4,002	234
Fiorello H LaGuardia Comm Coll of City U of NY, Long Island City, NY 11101	1970	Dr. Raymond C. Bowen	12	9,702	585
Flathead Valley Comm Coll, Kalispell, MT 59901	1967	Dr. Howard L. Fryett	12	1,719	105
Florence-Darlington Tech Coll, Florence, SC 29501-0548	1963	Dr. Michael B. McCall	5	2,039	201
Florida Comm Coll at Jacksonville, Jacksonville, FL 32202	1963	Dr. Charles C. Spence	5	19,734	1,575
Florida Keys Comm Coll, Key West, FL 33040	1965	Dr. William A. Seeker	5	2,200	94
Floyd Coll, Rome, GA 30162	1970	Dr. H. Lynn Cundiff	5	2,825	66
Foothill Coll, Los Altos Hills, CA 94022	1958	Dr. Thomas H. Clements	12	17,162	578
Forsyth Tech Comm Coll, Winston-Salem, NC 27103	1964	Dr. Bob H. Greene	5	5,175	574
Fort Scott Comm Coll, Fort Scott, KS 66701	1919	Dr. Laura Meeks	12	1,815	141
Fox Valley Tech Coll, Appleton, WI 54913	1967	Dr. H. Victor Baldi	12	6,500	1,241
Frederick Comm Coll, Frederick, MD 21702	1957	Dr. Lee J. Betts	12	4,336	267
Fresno City Coll, Fresno, CA 93741	1910	Dr. Brice W. Harris	10	18,598	832
Front Range Comm Coll, Westminster, CO 80030	1968	Dr. Thomas Gonzales	5	11,547	450
Fullerton Coll, Fullerton, CA 92632	1913	Dr. Philip W. Borst	12	21,211	678
Fulton-Montgomery Comm Coll, Johnstown, NY 12095	1964	Dr. Jacqueline D. Taylor	12	1,953	122
Gadsden State Comm Coll, Gadsden, AL 35902-0227	1985	NR	5	6,210	303
Gainesville Coll, Gainesville, GA 30503	1964	Dr. J. Foster Watkins	5	2,942	118
Galveston Coll, Galveston, TX 77550	1967	Dr. Marc A. Nigliazzo	12	2,331	122
Garden City Comm Coll, Garden City, KS 67846	1919	Dr. James H. Tangeman	10	2,111	101
Garland County Comm Coll, Hot Springs, AR 71913	1973	NR	12	2,313	111
Gaston Coll, Dallas, NC 28034	1963	Dr. W. Wayne Scott	12	4,047	309
Gateway Comm Coll, Phoenix, AZ 85034	1968	Dr. Phil Randolph	12	6,617	253
Gateway Comm-Tech Coll, New Haven, CT 06511	1968	Dr. Antonio Perez	5	5,207	259
Gateway Tech Coll, Kenosha, WI 53144	1911	Mr. William P. Nickolai	12	12,741	755
Gavilan Coll, Gilroy, CA 95020	1919	Dr. Glenn E. Mayle	12	4,029	164
Genesee Comm Coll, Batavia, NY 14020-9704	1966	Dr. Stuart Steiner	12	3,648	214
George Corley Wallace State Comm Coll, Selma, AL 36702	1966	Dr. Julius Ray Brown	5	1,800	78
George C Wallace State Comm Coll, Dothan, AL 36303	1949	Dr. Larry Beaty	5	4,060	180
Georgia Military Coll, Milledgeville, GA 31061	1879	NR	12	2,549	179
Germanna Comm Coll, Locust Grove, VA 22508	1970	Dr. Francis S. Turnage	5	2,500	83
Glendale Comm Coll, Glendale, AZ 85302	1965	Dr. John R. Waltrip	12	17,936	680
Glendale Comm Coll, Glendale, CA 91208	1927	Dr. John A. Davitt	12	15,337	345
Glen Oaks Comm Coll, Centreville, MI 49032	1965	Dr. Philip G. Ward	12	1,387	89
Gloucester County Coll, Sewell, NJ 08080	1967	Dr. Richard H. Jones	9	5,266	264
Gogebic Comm Coll, Ironwood, MI 49938	1932	Dr. James R. Grote	12	1,376	91
Golden West Coll, Huntington Beach, CA 92647-0592	1966	NR	12	15,295	462
Gordon Coll, Barnesville, GA 30204	1852	Dr. Jerry M. Williamson	5	1,913	105
Grand Rapids Comm Coll, Grand Rapids, MI 49503	1914	Mr. Richard Calkins	11	14,200	535
Grays Harbor Coll, Aberdeen, WA 98520	1930	Dr. Jewell Manspeaker	5	2,815	140
Grayson County Coll, Denison, TX 75020	1964	Dr. Jim M. Williams	12	3,400	176
Great Lakes Jr Coll of Business, Saginaw, MI 48607	1907	NR	1	2,097	150
Greenfield Comm Coll, Greenfield, MA 01301	1962	Dr. Katherine H. Sloan	5	1,954	124
Green River Comm Coll, Auburn, WA 98002	1965	Mr. Richard A. Rutkowski	5	7,955	253
Greenville Tech Coll, Greenville, SC 29606	1962	Dr. Thomas E. Barton, Jr.	5	8,814	480
Grossmont Coll, El Cajon, CA 92020-1799	1961	Dr. Richard M. Sanchez	12	15,004	572
Gulf Coast Comm Coll, Panama City, FL 32401	1957	Dr. Robert L. McSpadden	5	8,053	338

Name, address	Year	Governing official, control		Enroll-ment	Faculty
Hagerstown Jr Coll, Hagerstown, MD 21742-6590	1946	Dr. Norman P. Shea	9	3,109	180
Harford Comm Coll, Bel Air, MD 21015	1957	Dr. Richard J. Pappas	12	5,508	364
Harrisburg Area Comm Coll, Harrisburg, PA 17110	1964	Dr. Mary L. Fifield	12	11,561	485
Hartnell Coll, Salinas, CA 93901	1920	Dr. James R. Hardt	10	7,772	356
Hawkeye Comm Coll, Waterloo, IA 50704	1967	Dr. Phillip O. Barry	12	2,467	151
Haywood Comm Coll, Clyde, NC 28721	1964	Dr. Dan W. Moore	12	1,255	126
Henry Ford Comm Coll, Dearborn, MI 48128	1938	Dr. Andrew A. Mazzara	10	14,975	1,005
Herkimer County Comm Coll, Herkimer, NY 13350	1966	Dr. Ronald F. Williams	12	2,391	109
Hesser Coll, Manchester, NH 03103	1900	Mr. Linwood W. Galeucia	3	3,000	60
Hibbing Comm Coll, Hibbing, MN 55746	1916	Dr. Anthony Kuznik	5	1,115	65
Highland Comm Coll, Freeport, IL 61032	1962	Dr. Ruth Mercedes Smith	12	3,181	159
Highland Comm Coll, Highland, KS 66035	1858	Dr. Eric M. Priest	12	2,160	102
Highline Comm Coll, Des Moines, WA 98198	1961	Dr. Edward M. Command	5	10,300	432
Hill Coll of the Hill Jr Coll District, Hillsboro, TX 76645	1923	Dr. W. R. Auvenshine	10	2,000	80
Hillsborough Comm Coll, Tampa, FL 33631-3127	1968	Dr. Andreas A. Paloumpis	5	20,838	343
Hinds Comm Coll, Raymond, MS 39154	1917	NR	12	9,288	725
Hocking Tech Coll, Nelsonville, OH 45764	1968	Dr. John J. Light	5	5,948	252
Holmes Comm Coll, Goodman, MS 39079	1928	NR	12	2,317	125
Holyoke Comm Coll, Holyoke, MA 01040	1946	Dr. David M. Bartley	5	3,646	222
Horry-Georgetown Tech Coll, Conway, SC 29526	1965	Dr. D. Kent Sharples	12	2,404	113
Housatonic Comm-Tech Coll, Bridgeport, CT 06608	1966	Dr. Vincent S. Darnowski	5	2,658	105
Houston Comm Coll System, Houston, TX 77270	1971	Dr. Charles Green	12	37,410	2,277
Howard Coll, Big Spring, TX 79720	1945	Dr. Cheryl T. Sparks	12	2,399	147
Howard Comm Coll, Columbia, MD 21044	1966	Dr. Dwight A. Burrill	12	4,961	312
Hudson County Comm Coll, Jersey City, NJ 07306	1974	NR	12	3,076	198
Hudson Valley Comm Coll, Troy, NY 12180	1953	Dr. Joseph J. Bulmer	12	10,647	514
Hutchinson Comm Coll, Hutchinson, KS 67501	1928	Dr. Edward E. Berger	12	3,888	264
ICS Ctr for Degree Studies, Scranton, PA 18515	1975	Mr. Gary Keisling	3	20,363	5
Illinois Central Coll, East Peoria, IL 61635	1967	Dr. Thomas K. Thomas	12	13,632	626
Illinois Eastern Comm Colls, Frontier Comm Coll, Fairfield, IL 62837	1976	Mr. Richard Mason	12	1,907	148
Illinois Eastern Comm Colls, Lincoln Trail Coll, Robinson, IL 62454	1969	Dr. Donald E. Donnay	12	1,085	67
Illinois Eastern Comm Colls, Olney Central Coll, Olney, IL 62450	1962	Dr. Judith M. Hansen	12	1,550	92
Illinois Eastern Comm Colls, Wabash Valley Coll, Mount Carmel, IL 62863	1960	Dr. Harry K. Benson	12	2,562	94
Illinois Valley Comm Coll, Oglesby, IL 61348	1924	Dr. Alfred E. Wisgoski	10	4,497	176
Imperial Valley Coll, Imperial, CA 92251-2663	1922	Dr. John A. DePaoli	12	5,226	290
Independence Comm Coll, Independence, KS 67301	1925	Dr. Don Schoening	10	1,605	153
Indiana Business Coll, Indianapolis, IN 46204	1902	Mr. Kenneth J. Konesco	3	1,700	70
Indiana Vocational Tech Coll–Central Indiana, Indianapolis, IN 46206	1963	Dr. Meredith L. Carter	5	5,767	363
Indiana Vocational Tech Coll–Columbus, Columbus, IN 47203	1963	NR	5	2,612	198
Indiana Vocational Tech Coll–Eastcentral, Muncie, IN 47302	1968	Dr. Luanne G. Pruens	5	2,315	169
Indiana Vocational Tech Coll–Kokomo, Kokomo, IN 46901	1968	Dr. Shanon Christiansen	5	1,739	125
Indiana Vocational Tech Coll–Lafayette, Lafayette, IN 47903	1968	Dr. Elizabeth J. Doversberger	5	1,830	128
Indiana Vocational Tech Coll–Northcentral, South Bend, IN 46619	1968	Dr. Carl F. Lutz	5	2,686	219
Indiana Vocational Tech Coll–Northeast, Fort Wayne, IN 46805	1969	Mr. Jon L. Rupright	5	4,197	290
Indiana Vocational Tech Coll–Northwest, Gary, IN 46409	1963	Dr. Rob Jeffs	5	2,503	213
Indiana Vocational Tech Coll–Southcentral, Sellersburg, IN 47172	1968	Mr. Jonathan W. Thomas	5	2,092	124
Indiana Vocational Tech Coll–Southwest, Evansville, IN 47710	1963	Dr. H. Victor Baldi	5	2,092	185
Indiana Vocational Tech Coll–Wabash Valley, Terre Haute, IN 47802	1966	Dr. Sam E. Borden	5	2,310	181
Indiana Vocational Tech Coll–Whitewater, Richmond, IN 47374	1963	Mr. James Steck	5	1,186	108
Indian Hills Comm Coll, Ottumwa, IA 52501	1966	Dr. Lyle A. Hellyer	12	3,279	137
Indian River Comm Coll, Fort Pierce, FL 34981-5599	1960	Dr. Edwin R. Massey	5	13,156	821
Inver Hills Comm Coll, Inver Grove Heights, MN 55076	1969	Dr. Steve Wallace	5	5,383	237
Iowa Central Comm Coll, Fort Dodge, IA 50501	1966	Dr. Jack L. Bottenfield	12	2,500	155
Iowa Lakes Comm Coll, Estherville, IA 51334	1967	Mr. Richard H. Blacker	12	1,574	40
Iowa Western Comm Coll, Council Bluffs, IA 51502	1966	Dr. Carl L. Heinrich	10	3,623	152
Irvine Valley Coll, Irvine, CA 92720	1979	Dr. Anna L. McFarlin	12	10,007	223
Itasca Comm Coll, Grand Rapids, MN 55744	1922	Dr. Lawrence N. Dukes	5	1,169	75
Itawamba Comm Coll, Fulton, MS 38843	1947	Dr. David Cole	12	3,500	102
ITT Tech Inst, Fort Wayne, IN 46825	1967	Mr. Jack B. Cozad	3	1,114	34
Jackson Comm Coll, Jackson, MI 49201	1928	Dr. Clyde LeTarte	9	8,100	435
Jackson State Comm Coll, Jackson, TN 38301	1967	Dr. Walter L. Nelms	5	3,461	177
James H Faulkner State Jr Coll, Bay Minette, AL 36507	1965	Dr. Gary L. Branch	5	3,496	173
James Sprunt Comm Coll, Kenansville, NC 28349	1964	Dr. Donald L. Reichard	5	1,051	71
Jamestown Comm Coll, Jamestown, NY 14701	1950	Dr. Timothy G. Davies	12	4,664	316
Jefferson Coll, Hillsboro, MO 63050-2441	1963	Dr. Gery Hochanadel	12	4,220	199
Jefferson Comm Coll, Watertown, NY 13601	1961	Dr. John W. Deans	12	2,100	180
Jefferson Davis Comm Coll, Brewton, AL 36427	1965	NR	5	1,832	44
Jefferson State Comm Coll, Birmingham, AL 35215	1965	Dr. Judy M. Merritt	5	7,440	301
Jefferson Tech Coll, Steubenville, OH 43952	1966	Dr. Edward L. Florak	12	1,691	98
John A Logan Coll, Carterville, IL 62918	1967	Dr. Ray Hancock	12	4,971	193
John C Calhoun State Comm Coll, Decatur, AL 35609	1965	Dr. Richard Carpenter	5	8,070	404
Johnston Comm Coll, Smithfield, NC 27577	1969	Dr. John L. Tart	5	2,850	235
John Tyler Comm Coll, Chester, VA 23831	1967	Dr. Marshall W. Smith	5	5,562	226
John Wood Comm Coll, Quincy, IL 62301	1974	Dr. Robert C. Keys	10	3,950	143
Joliet Jr Coll, Joliet, IL 60436	1901	Dr. Raymond A. Pietak	12	10,427	591
Jones County Jr Coll, Ellisville, MS 39437	1928	Dr. T. Terrell Tisdale	12	4,400	153
Jordan Coll, Cedar Springs, MI 49319	1967	Dr. Lexie K. Coxon	2	2,118	176
J Sargeant Reynolds Comm Coll, Richmond, VA 23285-5622	1972	Dr. S. A. Burnette	5	12,739	580
Kalamazoo Valley Comm Coll, Kalamazoo, MI 49009	1966	Dr. Marilyn J. Schlack	12	9,637	406
Kankakee Comm Coll, Kankakee, IL 60901	1966	Dr. Larry D. Huffman	12	4,000	213
Kansas City Kansas Comm Coll, Kansas City, KS 66112	1923	Dr. Thomas R. Burke	9	5,876	367
Kaskaskia Coll, Centralia, IL 62801	1966	Mr. Raymond D. Woods	12	3,498	192

Name, address	Year	Governing official	control	Enrollment	Faculty
Kellogg Comm Coll, Battle Creek, MI 49017	1956	Dr. Paul R. Ohm	12	7,662	268
Kelsey Jenney Coll, San Diego, CA 92101	1863	NR	1	1,000	50
Kent State U, Ashtabula Cmps, Ashtabula, OH 44004	1958	Dr. John K. Mahan	5	1,025	69
Kent State U, Salem Cmps, Salem, OH 44460	1966	Dr. James F. Cooney	5	1,010	62
Kent State U, Stark Cmps, Canton, OH 44720	1967	Dr. William G. Bittle	5	2,531	124
Kent State U, Trumbull Cmps, Warren, OH 44483	1954	Dr. David A. Allen, Jr.	5	1,869	95
Kent State U, Tuscarawas Cmps, New Philadelphia, OH 44663	1962	NR	5	1,246	83
Keystone Jr Coll, La Plume, PA 18440	1868	Dr. Robert E. Mooney, Jr.	1	1,008	88
Kilgore Coll, Kilgore, TX 75662	1935	NR	12	4,540	240
Kings River Comm Coll, Reedley, CA 93654	1926	Mr. Richard J. Giese	12	6,722	221
Kirkwood Comm Coll, Cedar Rapids, IA 52406	1966	Dr. Norm Nielsen	12	9,612	450
Kirtland Comm Coll, Roscommon, MI 48653	1966	Dr. Dorothy N. Franke	10	1,309	95
Kishwaukee Coll, Malta, IL 60150	1967	Dr. Norman L. Jenkins	12	3,388	NR
Labette Comm Coll, Parsons, KS 67357	1923	Mr. Joseph C. Birmingham	12	2,598	261
Lake City Comm Coll, Lake City, FL 32055	1962	Dr. Muriel Kay Heimer	5	2,551	186
Lake Land Coll, Mattoon, IL 61938	1966	Dr. Robert K. Luther	12	4,543	361
Lakeland Comm Coll, Mentor, OH 44060	1967	Dr. Ralph R. Doty	12	9,174	434
Lake Michigan Coll, Benton Harbor, MI 49022	1946	Dr. Anne E. Mulder	10	3,816	240
Lakeshore Tech Coll, Cleveland, WI 53015	1967	Dr. Dennis Ladwig	12	2,678	344
Lake-Sumter Comm Coll, Leesburg, FL 34788	1962	Dr. Robert Westrick	12	2,394	117
Lake Tahoe Comm Coll, South Lake Tahoe, CA 96151	1975	Dr. Guy F. Lease	12	3,000	121
Lakewood Comm Coll, White Bear Lake, MN 55110	1967	Dr. Neil Christenson	5	6,414	215
Lamar U–Orange, Orange, TX 77630	1969	Dr. Steve Maradian	5	1,550	63
Lamar U–Port Arthur, Port Arthur, TX 77641	1909	Dr. Sam Monroe	5	2,109	109
Lane Comm Coll, Eugene, OR 97405-0640	1964	Dr. Jerry Moskus	12	9,350	553
Lansing Comm Coll, Lansing, MI 48901	1957	Dr. Abel B. Sykes, Jr.	12	21,828	1,236
Laramie County Comm Coll, Cheyenne, WY 82007	1968	Dr. Charles Bohlen	9	4,300	220
Laredo Jr Coll, Laredo, TX 78040	1946	Dr. Roger L. Worsley	12	5,944	297
Las Positas Coll, Livermore, CA 94550	1988	NR	5	5,722	NR
Lassen Coll, Susanville, CA 96130	1925	Dr. Larry J. Blake	12	2,825	204
Lawson State Comm Coll, Birmingham, AL 35221	1965	Dr. Perry W. Ward	5	2,044	89
Lee Coll, Baytown, TX 77522-0818	1934	Dr. Jackson N. Sasser	10	5,481	236
Lehigh County Comm Coll, Schnecksville, PA 18078-2598	1967	Mr. James R. Davis	12	5,200	155
Lewis and Clark Comm Coll, Godfrey, IL 62035	1970	NR	10	5,853	305
Lima Tech Coll, Lima, OH 45804	1971	Dr. James J. Countryman	5	2,750	167
Lincoln Land Comm Coll, Springfield, IL 62794-9256	1967	Dr. Norman Stephens, Jr.	10	10,012	401
Linn-Benton Comm Coll, Albany, OR 97321	1966	Mr. Jon Carnahan	12	6,357	479
Long Beach City Coll, Long Beach, CA 90808	1927	Miss Barbara A. Adams	5	27,000	850
Longview Comm Coll, Lee's Summit, MO 64081	1969	Mr. Aldo W. Leker	12	9,414	385
Lorain County Comm Coll, Elyria, OH 44035	1963	Dr. Roy Church	12	7,681	333
Lord Fairfax Comm Coll, Middletown, VA 22645	1969	Dr. Marilyn C. Beck	5	3,200	158
Los Angeles City Coll, Los Angeles, CA 90029	1929	Mr. Jose Robledo	10	17,500	614
Los Angeles Harbor Coll, Wilmington, CA 90744	1949	Mr. James L. Heinselman	12	9,200	350
Los Angeles Mission Coll, Sylmar, CA 91342-3244	1974	Dr. Jack Fujimoto	12	7,380	115
Los Angeles Pierce Coll, Woodland Hills, CA 91371	1947	Mr. Lowell J. Erickson	12	18,314	519
Los Angeles Southwest Coll, Los Angeles, CA 90047	1967	Dr. Carolyn G. Williams	12	6,557	250
Los Angeles Trade-Tech Coll, Los Angeles, CA 90015	1925	Mr. Thomas L. Stevens	12	13,713	259
Los Angeles Valley Coll, Van Nuys, CA 91401	1949	Dr. Mary E. Lee	12	17,768	482
Los Medanos Coll, Pittsburg, CA 94565	1974	Mr. Stanley H. Chin	10	7,493	223
Louisiana State U at Alexandria, Alexandria, LA 71302	1960	Dr. Ben F. Martin	5	2,771	91
Louisiana State U at Eunice, Eunice, LA 70535	1967	Dr. Michael Smith	5	2,861	120
Lurleen B Wallace State Jr Coll, Andalusia, AL 36420	1969	Dr. Seth Hammett	5	1,263	39
Luzerne County Comm Coll, Nanticoke, PA 18634-9804	1966	Mr. Donald R. Bronsard	9	7,285	406
Macomb Comm Coll, Warren, MI 48093	1954	Dr. Albert L. Lorenzo	10	28,165	841
Macon Coll, Macon, GA 31297	1968	Dr. S. Aaron Hyatt	5	5,080	129
Madison Area Tech Coll, Madison, WI 53704	1911	Dr. Beverly S. Simone	10	11,622	1,960
Manatee Comm Coll, Bradenton, FL 34206	1957	Dr. Stephen J. Korcheck	5	8,726	314
Manchester Comm-Tech Coll, Manchester, CT 06040	1963	Dr. Jonathan M. Daube	5	6,686	205
Maple Woods Comm Coll, Kansas City, MO 64156	1969	Dr. Stephen R. Brainard	12	5,167	186
Marion Tech Coll, Marion, OH 43302-5694	1971	Dr. John Richard Bryson	13	1,697	105
Marshalltown Comm Coll, Marshalltown, IA 50158	1927	Dr. William Simpson	10	1,245	100
Marymount Coll, Palos Verdes, California, Rancho Palos Verdes, CA 90274-6299	1932	Dr. Thomas M. McFadden	2	1,074	91
Massachusetts Bay Comm Coll, Wellesley Hills, MA 02181	1961	Mr. Roger A. Van Winkle	5	5,233	278
Massasoit Comm Coll, Brockton, MA 02402	1966	Dr. Gerard F. Burke	5	6,502	427
McCook Comm Coll, McCook, NE 69001	1926	Dr. Robert G. Smallfoot	12	1,100	64
McLennan Comm Coll, Waco, TX 76708	1965	Dr. Dennis F. Michaelis	9	6,006	259
Mendocino Coll, Ukiah, CA 95482	1973	Dr. Carl J. Ehmann	12	4,810	169
Merced Coll, Merced, CA 95348	1962	Dr. E. Jan Moser	12	7,803	421
Mercer County Comm Coll, Trenton, NJ 08690	1966	Dr. Thomas Sepe	12	9,053	356
Meridian Comm Coll, Meridian, MS 39307	1937	Dr. William F. Scaggs	12	3,081	236
Mesa Comm Coll, Mesa, AZ 85202	1965	Dr. Larry K. Christiansen	12	19,879	736
Metropolitan Comm Coll, Omaha, NE 68103-0777	1974	Dr. J. Richard Gilliland	12	10,301	373
Miami-Dade Comm Coll, Miami, FL 33132	1960	Dr. Robert H. McCabe	12	53,824	2,189
Miami U–Hamilton Cmps, Hamilton, OH 45011	1968	Dr. Harriet V. Taylor	5	2,182	160
Miami U–Middletown Cmps, Middletown, OH 45042	1966	Dr. Michael P. Governanti	5	2,329	165
Middle Georgia Coll, Cochran, GA 31014	1884	Dr. Joe Ben Welch	5	1,878	82
Middlesex Comm Coll, Middletown, CT 06457	1966	Dr. Leila Gonzalez Sullivan	5	3,230	130
Middlesex Comm Coll, Bedford, MA 01730	1970	Dr. Carole A. Cowan	5	7,190	295
Middlesex County Coll, Edison, NJ 08818	1964	Dr. Flora M. Edwards	9	12,500	287
Midland Coll, Midland, TX 79705	1969	Dr. David E. Daniel	12	3,789	192
Midlands Tech Coll, Columbia, SC 29202	1974	Dr. James L. Hudgins	12	8,729	655
Mid Michigan Comm Coll, Harrison, MI 48625-9447	1965	Dr. Charles J. Corrigan	12	2,134	199
Mid-Plains Comm Coll, North Platte, NE 69101	1965	Dr. William A. Griffin, Jr.	10	1,947	87
Mid-State Tech Coll, Wisconsin Rapids, WI 54494	1917	Dr. M. H. Schneeberg	12	2,808	86
Mineral Area Coll, Flat River, MO 63601	1922	Dr. Dixie A. Kohn	10	3,064	128
Minneapolis Comm Coll, Minneapolis, MN 55403-1779	1965	Dr. Jacquelyn Belcher	5	4,310	189
MiraCosta Coll, Oceanside, CA 92056	1934	Dr. H. Deon Holt	5	8,389	376
Mississippi County Comm Coll, Blytheville, AR 72316-1109	1975	Dr. John P. Sullins	5	1,745	128
Mississippi Delta Comm Coll, Moorhead, MS 38761	1926	Dr. Bobby Garvin	10	2,472	128
Mississippi Gulf Coast Comm Coll, Perkinston, MS 39573	1911	Dr. Richard Miller	10	8,827	527
Mitchell Comm Coll, Statesville, NC 28677	1852	Dr. Douglas O. Eason	5	1,526	90
Moberly Area Comm Coll, Moberly, MO 65270	1927	Dr. Andrew Komar, Jr.	12	1,846	95
Modesto Jr Coll, Modesto, CA 95350	1921	Dr. Stanley L. Hodges	12	8,300	454
Mohave Comm Coll, Kingman, AZ 86401	1971	Dr. Charles W. Hall	5	5,329	241

Name, address	Year	Governing official, control		Enroll-ment	Faculty
Mohawk Valley Comm Coll, Utica, NY 13501	1946	Dr. Michael I. Schafer	12	6,500	340
Monroe Coll, Bronx, NY 10468	1933	Mr. Stephen J. Jerome	3	2,400	100
Monroe Comm Coll, Rochester, NY 14623	1961	Dr. Peter A. Spina	12	13,312	660
Monroe County Comm Coll, Monroe, MI 48161	1964	Mr. Gerald D. Welch	9	3,924	178
Montcalm Comm Coll, Sidney, MI 48885-0300	1965	Dr. Donald C. Burns	12	1,693	112
Monterey Peninsula Coll, Monterey, CA 93940-4799	1947	Dr. David W. Hopkins, Jr.	5	8,500	390
Montgomery Coll–Germantown Cmps, Germantown, MD 20874	1975	Dr. Robert E. Parilla	12	3,930	176
Montgomery Coll–Rockville Cmps, Rockville, MD 20850	1965	Dr. Robert E. Parilla	12	14,355	705
Montgomery Coll–Takoma Park Cmps, Takoma Park, MD 20912	1946	Dr. Robert E. Parilla	12	4,830	219
Montgomery County Comm Coll, Blue Bell, PA 19422	1964	Dr. Edward M. Sweitzer	9	9,411	412
Moorpark Coll, Moorpark, CA 93021	1967	Dr. James W. Walker	9	12,078	450
Moraine Park Tech Coll, Fond du Lac, WI 54936	1967	Dr. John J. Shanahan	12	6,074	290
Moraine Valley Comm Coll, Palos Hills, IL 60465	1967	Dr. Vernon O. Crawley	12	14,074	636
Morgan Comm Coll, Fort Morgan, CO 80701	1967	Dr. Richard Bond	5	1,002	132
Morton Coll, Cicero, IL 60650	1924	Mr. Charles P. Ferro	12	4,695	275
Motlow State Comm Coll, Tullahoma, TN 37388	1969	Dr. A. Frank Glass	5	3,211	245
Mountain Empire Comm Coll, Big Stone Gap, VA 24219	1972	Dr. Robert H. Sandel	5	2,641	133
Mountain View Coll, Dallas, TX 75211-6599	1970	Dr. Rodger A. Pool	9	6,600	268
Mt Hood Comm Coll, Gresham, OR 97030	1966	Dr. Paul Kreider	12	7,960	501
Mount Ida Coll, Newton Centre, MA 02159	1899	Dr. Bryan E. Carlson	1	1,750	177
Mt San Antonio Coll, Walnut, CA 91789	1946	Dr. William H. Feddersen	10	23,294	821
Mt San Jacinto Coll, San Jacinto, CA 92583	1963	Dr. Richard H. Lowe	12	7,010	181
Mount Wachusett Comm Coll, Gardner, MA 01440	1963	Dr. Daniel M. Asquino	5	2,200	112
Murray State Coll, Tishomingo, OK 73460-3130	1908	Dr. Clyde R. Kindell	5	1,674	69
Muscatine Comm Coll, Muscatine, IA 52761	1929	Dr. Victor G. McAvoy	5	1,203	68
Muskegon Comm Coll, Muskegon, MI 49442	1926	Dr. James L. Stevenson	12	5,169	150
Muskingum Area Tech Coll, Zanesville, OH 43701-2694	1969	Dr. Lynn H. Willett	12	2,701	104
Napa Valley Coll, Napa, CA 94558	1942	Dr. Diane E. Carey	12	7,102	297
Nash Comm Coll, Rocky Mount, NC 27804	1967	Dr. J. Reid Parrott, Jr.	5	1,911	175
Nashville State Tech Inst, Nashville, TN 37209	1970	Dr. George H. Van Allen	5	6,082	294
Nassau Comm Coll, Garden City, NY 11530	1959	Dr. Sean A. Fanelli	12	18,641	1,440
National Ed Ctr–Bauder Coll Cmps, Fort Lauderdale, FL 33334	1964	NR	3	1,000	41
National Ed Ctr–Brown Inst Cmps, Minneapolis, MN 55407	1946	Mr. Steve Marks	3	1,197	79
National Ed Ctr–Spartan Sch of Aeronautics Cmps, Tulsa, OK 74158-2833 (2)	1928	Mr. Ross L. Alloway	3	1,773	150
Navajo Comm Coll, Tsaile, AZ 86556	1968	Dr. Tommy Lewis, Jr.	4	1,804	155
Navarro Coll, Corsicana, TX 75110	1946	Dr. Gerald Burson	12	3,202	198
Neosho County Comm Coll, Chanute, KS 66720	1936	Mr. Jim Stringer	12	1,920	117
Newbury Coll, Brookline, MA 02146	1962	Mr. Edward J. Tassinari	1	1,001	81
The New England Banking Inst, Boston, MA 02111	1909	NR	1	1,046	360
New England Inst of Tech, Warwick, RI 02886	1940	Dr. Richard I. Gouse	1	1,950	134
New Hampshire Tech Inst, Concord, NH 03302-2039	1964	Dr. David E. Larrabee, Sr.	5	1,522	145
New Mexico Jr Coll, Hobbs, NM 88240	1965	Dr. Charles D. Hays	12	2,438	109
New Mexico State U–Carlsbad, Carlsbad, NM 88220	1950	Dr. Shelton W. Marlow	5	1,214	72
New Orleans Baptist Theological Sem, New Orleans, LA 70126	1917	Dr. Landrum P. Leavell, II	2	1,917	18
New River Comm Coll, Dublin, VA 24084	1969	Dr. Edwin L. Barnes	5	2,003	200
Niagara County Comm Coll, Sanborn, NY 14132	1962	Mr. Gerald L. Miller	12	5,610	455
Nicolet Area Tech Coll, Rhinelander, WI 54501	1968	Dr. Adrian Lorbetske	12	1,700	84
Normandale Comm Coll, Bloomington, MN 55431	1968	Dr. Thomas J. Horak	5	9,221	300
Northampton County Area Comm Coll, Bethlehem, PA 18017	1967	Dr. Robert J. Kopecek	12	6,725	372
North Arkansas Comm/Tech Coll, Harrison, AR 72601	1974	Dr. Bill Baker	12	1,415	84
North Central Michigan Coll, Petoskey, MI 49770	1958	Mr. Robert B. Graham	9	2,230	102
North Central Missouri Coll, Trenton, MO 64683	1925	Dr. James Selby	10	1,050	70
North Central Tech Coll, Mansfield, OH 44901	1961	Dr. Byron E. Kee	5	2,971	181
Northcentral Tech Coll, Wausau, WI 54401	1912	Mr. Dean Dietrich	10	4,881	211
North Country Comm Coll, Saranac Lake, NY 12983	1967	Dr. Gail Rogers Rice	12	1,823	140
North Dakota State Coll of Science, Wahpeton, ND 58076	1903	Dr. Jerry Olson	5	2,147	146
Northeast Alabama State Jr Coll, Rainsville, AL 35986	1963	Dr. Charles M. Pendley	5	1,787	53
Northeast Comm Coll, Norfolk, NE 68702	1973	Dr. Robert P. Cox	12	3,257	122
Northeastern Jr Coll, Sterling, CO 80751	1941	Dr. Henry M. Milander	12	1,743	79
Northeastern Oklahoma A&M Coll, Miami, OK 74354	1919	Dr. Jerry D. Carroll	5	2,600	133
Northeast Iowa Comm Coll, Peosta Cmps, Peosta, IA 52068	1970	Ms. Karla Berns	12	1,450	66
Northeast Mississippi Comm Coll, Booneville, MS 38829	1948	Mr. Joe M. Childers	10	2,775	NR
Northeast State Tech Comm Coll, Blountville, TN 37617	1966	Dr. R. Wade Powers	5	3,464	166
Northeast Texas Comm Coll, Mount Pleasant, TX 75456-1307	1985	NR	12	2,024	85
Northeast Wisconsin Tech Coll, Green Bay, WI 54307	1913	Dr. Gerald D. Prindiville	12	7,614	310
Northern Essex Comm Coll, Haverhill, MA 01830	1960	Dr. John R. Dimitry	5	6,609	457
Northern Nevada Comm Coll, Elko, NV 89801	1967	Dr. Ronald K. Remington	5	2,500	188
Northern New Mexico Comm Coll, Española, NM 87532	1909	Ms. Connie A. Valdez	5	1,832	163
Northern Oklahoma Coll, Tonkawa, OK 74653-0310	1901	Dr. Joe Kinzer	5	2,100	80
Northern Virginia Comm Coll, Annandale, VA 22003	1965	Dr. Richard J. Ernst	5	39,250	1,314
North Florida Jr Coll, Madison, FL 32340	1958	Dr. William H. McCoy	5	1,050	30
North Harris Montgomery Comm Coll District, Houston, TX 77060	1972	Dr. John E. Pickelman	12	3,080	196
North Idaho Coll, Coeur d'Alene, ID 83814	1933	Dr. Carl R. Bennett	12	3,068	168
North Iowa Area Comm Coll, Mason City, IA 50401	1918	Dr. David Buettner	12	3,074	107
North Lake Coll, Irving, TX 75038	1977	Dr. James F. Horton, Jr.	9	6,835	280
Northland Pioneer Coll, Holbrook, AZ 86025	1974	Dr. John H. Anderson	12	4,350	400
North Seattle Comm Coll, Seattle, WA 98103	1970	Dr. Peter Ku	5	8,990	290
Northwest Alabama Comm Coll, Phil Campbell, AL 35581	1961	NR	5	2,049	83
NorthWest Arkansas Comm Coll, Bentonville, AR 72712	1989	NR	12	1,889	124
Northwest Coll, Powell, WY 82435	1946	Dr. John P. Hanna	12	1,930	173
Northwestern Coll, Lima, OH 45805	1920	Mr. Loren R. Jarvis	1	1,400	59
Northwestern Connecticut Comm Coll, Winsted, CT 06098	1965	Dr. Booker T. DeVaughn	5	2,053	87
Northwestern Michigan Coll, Traverse City, MI 49684	1951	Dr. Timothy G. Quinn	12	4,275	231
Northwest Mississippi Comm Coll, Senatobia, MS 38668	1927	Dr. David M. Haraway	12	4,000	180
Northwest Tech Coll, Archbold, OH 43502	1968	Dr. Larry G. McDougle	5	2,054	121
Norwalk Comm-Tech Coll, Norwalk, CT 06854	1961	Dr. William H. Schwab	5	4,943	135
Oakland Comm Coll, Bloomfield Hills, MI 48304	1964	Dr. Patsy J. Fulton	12	29,333	788

Name, address	Year	Governing official, control		Enrollment	Faculty
Oakton Comm Coll, Des Plaines, IL 60016	1969	Dr. Thomas TenHoeve	10	11,253	495
Ocean County Coll, Toms River, NJ 08754-2001	1964	Dr. Milton Shaw	9	8,353	375
Odessa Coll, Odessa, TX 79764	1946	Dr. Philip T. Speegle	12	4,800	255
Ohio U–Southern Cmps, Ironton, OH 45638	1956	Dr. Bill Dingus	5	2,358	122
Ohlone Coll, Fremont, CA 94539	1967	Dr. Peter Blomerley	12	9,827	434
Okaloosa-Walton Comm Coll, Niceville, FL 32578	1963	Dr. James R. Richburg	12	5,820	265
Oklahoma City Comm Coll, Oklahoma City, OK 73159	1969	Dr. Bobby Gaines	5	10,875	340
Oklahoma State U, Oklahoma City, Oklahoma City, OK 73107	1961	Dr. James Hooper	5	4,357	205
Oklahoma State U, Tech Branch, Okmulgee, Okmulgee, OK 74447	1946	Dr. Robert Klabenes	5	2,300	138
Olympic Coll, Bremerton, WA 98310-1699	1946	Dr. Wallace A. Simpson	5	6,605	415
Onondaga Comm Coll, Syracuse, NY 13215	1962	Dr. Bruce H. Leslie	12	8,517	494
Orangeburg-Calhoun Tech Coll, Orangeburg, SC 29115	1968	Mr. M. Rudolph Groomes	12	1,848	120
Orange Coast Coll, Costa Mesa, CA 92628-5005	1947	Mr. David A. Grant	12	27,960	880
Orange County Comm Coll, Middletown, NY 10940	1950	Dr. William F. Messner	12	6,027	349
Owensboro Comm Coll, Owensboro, KY 42303	1986	NR	5	2,980	124
Owens Tech Coll, Toledo, OH 43699-1947	1966	NR	5	8,860	370
Owens Tech Coll, Findlay Cmps, Findlay, OH 45840	1983	NR	5	1,299	83
Oxnard Coll, Oxnard, CA 93033	1975	Dr. Elise D. Schneider	9	6,500	288
Palm Beach Comm Coll, Lake Worth, FL 33461	1933	Dr. Edward M. Eissey	5	16,543	656
Palo Alto Coll, San Antonio, TX 78224	1987	NR	12	6,666	317
Palomar Coll, San Marcos, CA 92069	1946	Dr. George R. Boggs	12	24,335	1,097
Palo Verde Coll, Blythe, CA 92225	1947	Dr. Wilford J. Beumel	12	1,200	69
Panola Coll, Carthage, TX 75633	1947	Dr. W. F. Edmondson	12	1,381	62
Paradise Valley Comm Coll, Phoenix, AZ 85032	1985	NR	12	5,313	222
Paris Jr Coll, Paris, TX 75460	1924	Mr. Bobby R. Walters	12	2,389	117
Parkland Coll, Champaign, IL 61821	1967	Dr. Zelema M. Harris	10	9,343	549
Pasadena City Coll, Pasadena, CA 91106	1924	Dr. Jack A. Scott	10	24,209	946
Pasco-Hernando Comm Coll, Dade City, FL 33525-7599	1972	Dr. Milton O. Jones	5	4,954	204
Passaic County Comm Coll, Paterson, NJ 07505-1179	1968	Mr. Elliott Collins	9	3,776	225
Patrick Henry Comm Coll, Martinsville, VA 24115	1962	NR	5	2,570	88
Paul D Camp Comm Coll, Franklin, VA 23851-0737	1971	Mr. Jerome J. Friga	5	1,464	59
Pearl River Comm Coll, Poplarville, MS 39470	1909	Dr. Ted J. Alexander	12	2,786	160
Pellissippi State Tech Comm Coll, Knoxville, TN 37933-0990	1974	Dr. Fred Martin	5	7,838	428
Peninsula Coll, Port Angeles, WA 98362-2779	1961	Ms. Joyce M. Helens	5	2,904	149
Pennsylvania Coll of Tech, Williamsport, PA 17701	1965	Dr. Robert Breuder	13	4,781	330
Penn State U Altoona Cmps, Altoona, PA 16601-3760	1929	Dr. Kjell Meling	13	2,502	134
Penn State U Berks Cmps, Reading, PA 19610-6009	1924	Dr. Frederick H. Gaige	13	1,773	103
Penn State U Delaware County Cmps, Media, PA 19063-5596	1966	Dr. Edward S. J. Tomezsko	13	1,565	91
Penn State U DuBois Cmps, DuBois, PA 15801-3199	1935	Dr. Donald T. Hartman	13	1,047	55
Penn State U Hazleton Cmps, Hazleton, PA 18201-1291	1934	Dr. James J. Staudenmeier	13	1,248	78
Penn State U McKeesport Cmps, McKeesport, PA 15132-7698	1947	Dr. Joanne E. Burley	13	1,015	79
Penn State U New Kensington Cmps, New Kensington, PA 15068-1798	1958	Dr. Roy Myers	13	1,095	83
Penn State U Ogontz Cmps, Abington, PA 19001	1950	Dr. Anthony Fusaro	13	3,455	168
Penn State U Schuylkill Cmps, Schuylkill Haven, PA 17972-2208	1934	Dr. Wayne Lammie	13	1,140	65
Penn State U Shenango Cmps, Sharon, PA 16146-1537	1965	Dr. Albert N. Skomra	13	1,118	79
Penn State U Worthington Scranton Cmps, Dunmore, PA 18512-1699	1923	Dr. James D. Gallagher	13	1,270	89
Penn State U York Cmps, York, PA 17403-3298	1926	Dr. John J. Romano	13	2,052	132
Penn Valley Comm Coll, Kansas City, MO 64111	1969	Dr. E. Paul Williams	12	5,822	311
Pensacola Jr Coll, Pensacola, FL 32504-8998	1948	Dr. Horace E. Hartsell	5	13,000	950
Phillips Jr Coll, New Orleans, LA 70123	1970	NR	3	1,100	NR
Phillips Jr Coll, Condie Cmps, Campbell, CA 95008	1968	Ms. Sylvia Karp	3	1,000	45
Piedmont Tech Coll, Greenwood, SC 29648	1966	Dr. Lex D. Walters	5	2,747	127
Piedmont Virginia Comm Coll, Charlottesville, VA 22902	1972	Dr. Deborah M. DiCroce	5	4,316	262
Pierce Coll, Tacoma, WA 98498	1967	Dr. Frank Brouillet	5	9,340	499
Pikes Peak Comm Coll, Colorado Springs, CO 80906-5498	1969	Dr. Marijane Axtell Paulsen	5	6,841	430
Pima Comm Coll, Tucson, AZ 85702-3010	1966	Dr. Johnas F. Hockaday	5	30,172	1,632
Pitt Comm Coll, Greenville, NC 27835-7007	1961	Dr. Charles E. Russell	12	4,501	233
Polk Comm Coll, Winter Haven, FL 33881-4299	1964	Dr. Maryly VanLeer Peck	5	6,100	260
Porterville Coll, Porterville, CA 93257	1927	Dr. John McCuen	5	2,886	128
Portland Comm Coll, Portland, OR 97219	1961	Dr. Daniel F. Moriarty	12	34,028	1,215
Potomac State Coll of West Virginia U, Keyser, WV 26726	1901	Dr. Joseph M. Gratto	5	1,205	83
Prairie State Coll, Chicago Heights, IL 60411	1958	Dr. T. Lightfield	12	5,834	289
Prince George's Comm Coll, Largo, MD 20772	1958	Dr. Robert I. Bickford	9	13,318	600
Pueblo Comm Coll, Pueblo, CO 81004	1979	Dr. Joe May	5	3,200	396
Queensborough Comm Coll of City U of NY, Bayside, NY 11364	1958	Dr. Kurt R. Schmeller	12	12,300	563
Quincy Coll, Quincy, MA 02169	1958	Dr. O. Clayton Johnson	11	2,280	69
Quinebaug Valley Comm-Tech Coll, Danielson, CT 06239	1971	Ms. Dianne E. Williams	5	1,178	55
Quinsigamond Comm Coll, Worcester, MA 01606	1963	Dr. Clifford S. Peterson	5	5,044	239
Randolph Comm Coll, Asheboro, NC 27204	1962	Dr. Larry K. Linker	5	1,548	80
Rappahannock Comm Coll, Glenns, VA 23149	1970	Dr. John H. Upton	12	2,089	129
Raritan Valley Comm Coll, Somerville, NJ 08876	1965	Dr. S. Charles Irace	9	5,882	276
Reading Area Comm Coll, Reading, PA 19603	1971	Dr. Gust Zogas	9	3,418	159
Redlands Comm Coll, El Reno, OK 73036	1938	Dr. Larry F. Devane	5	1,908	101
Red Rocks Comm Coll, Lakewood, CO 80401	1969	Dr. Dorothy A. Horrell	5	6,831	276
Rend Lake Coll, Ina, IL 62846	1967	Mr. Mark S. Kern	5	4,322	201
Richard Bland Coll of the Coll of William and Mary, Petersburg, VA 23805	1961	Dr. Clarence Maze, Jr.	5	1,264	49
Richland Coll, Dallas, TX 75243-2199	1972	Dr. Stephen Mittelstet	12	13,391	665
Richland Comm Coll, Decatur, IL 62521	1971	Dr. Charles R. Novak	10	4,000	194
Richmond Comm Coll, Hamlet, NC 28345	1964	Mr. Joseph W. Grimsley	5	1,092	100
Ricks Coll, Rexburg, ID 83460	1888	Dr. Steven D. Bennion	2	7,943	384
Rio Hondo Coll, Whittier, CA 90608	1960	Dr. Alex A. Sanchez	12	14,500	710
Rio Salado Comm Coll, Phoenix, AZ 85003	1978	Dr. Linda Thor	12	8,931	467
Riverside Comm Coll, Riverside, CA 92506	1916	Dr. Salvatore Rotella	12	23,000	480
Roane State Comm Coll, Harriman, TN 37748	1971	Dr. Sherry L. Hoppe	5	5,840	333
Robert Morris Coll, Chicago Cmps, Chicago, IL 60601	1913	Mr. Richard D. Pickett	1	1,733	95

Name, address	Year	Governing official, control		Enrollment	Faculty
Rochester Comm Coll, Rochester, MN 55904	1915	Dr. Karen E. Nagle	5	4,001	186
Rockingham Comm Coll, Wentworth, NC 27375	1964	Dr. N. J. Owens, Jr.	5	2,020	111
Rockland Comm Coll, Suffern, NY 10901	1959	Dr. Neal A. Raisman	12	8,044	792
Rock Valley Coll, Rockford, IL 61114-5699	1964	Dr. Karl J. Jacobs	10	7,960	226
Rogers State Coll, Claremore, OK 74017-2099	1909	Dr. Richard H. Mosier	5	3,875	270
Rogue Comm Coll, Grants Pass, OR 97527	1970	Dr. Harvey Bennett	12	2,785	334
Rose State Coll, Midwest City, OK 73110-2799	1971	Dr. Larry Nutter	12	9,800	341
Rowan-Cabarrus Comm Coll, Salisbury, NC 28145	1963	Dr. Richard L. Brownell	5	3,500	130
Roxbury Comm Coll, Roxbury Crossing, MA 02120	1973	Dr. Grace C. Brown	5	2,500	NR
Sacramento City Coll, Sacramento, CA 95822	1916	Dr. Robert M. Harris	12	16,403	420
Saddleback Coll, Mission Viejo, CA 92692	1967	NR	12	19,274	651
Saint Augustine Coll, Chicago, IL 60640	1980	Fr. Carlos A. Plazas	1	1,341	150
Saint Charles County Comm Coll, St Peters, MO 63376	1986	NR	5	4,631	201
St Clair County Comm Coll, Port Huron, MI 48061	1923	Dr. R. Ernest Dear	9	4,914	241
St Cloud Tech Coll, St Cloud, MN 56303-1240	1948	NR	12	1,977	100
St Johns River Comm Coll, Palatka, FL 32177	1958	Dr. R. L. McLendon, Jr.	5	3,391	157
St Louis Comm Coll at Florissant Valley, St Louis, MO 63135-1499	1963	Dr. Michael T. Murphy	10	9,923	416
St Louis Comm Coll at Forest Park, St Louis, MO 63110	1962	Dr. Henry D. Shannon	10	7,521	368
St Louis Comm Coll at Meramec, Kirkwood, MO 63122	1963	Mr. Richard A. Black	10	14,764	577
St Mary's Cmps of the Coll of St Catherine, Minneapolis, MN 55454	1964	Dr. Anita M. Pampusch	2	1,057	88
St Paul Tech Coll, St Paul, MN 55102	1922	Dr. Donovan Schwichtenberg	12	3,570	565
St Petersburg Jr Coll, St Petersburg, FL 33733-3489	1927	Dr. Carl M. Kuttler, Jr.	12	23,488	569
Salem Comm Coll, Carneys Point, NJ 08069-2799	1971	Ms. Linda C. Jolly	9	1,553	74
Salt Lake Comm Coll, Salt Lake City, UT 84130	1948	Dr. Frank W. Budd	5	17,029	849
Sampson Comm Coll, Clinton, NC 28328	1965	Dr. Clifton W. Paderick	12	1,049	99
San Antonio Coll, San Antonio, TX 78212-4299	1925	Dr. Ruth Burgos-Sasscer	12	19,908	847
Sandhills Comm Coll, Pinehurst, NC 28374	1963	Dr. John Dempsey	12	2,301	130
San Diego City Coll, San Diego, CA 92101	1914	Dr. Jerome Hunter	12	13,200	250
San Diego Mesa Coll, San Diego, CA 92111-4998	1962	Dr. Constance Carroll	10	24,460	768
San Diego Miramar Coll, San Diego, CA 92126-2999	1969	Dr. Jerome Hunter	12	6,998	180
San Jacinto Coll–Central Cmps, Pasadena, TX 77501-2007	1961	Dr. Monte Blue	12	10,562	539
San Jacinto Coll–North Cmps, Houston, TX 77049	1974	Dr. Edwin E. Lehr	12	4,291	212
San Jacinto Coll–South Cmps, Houston, TX 77089	1979	Dr. Parker Williams	12	5,635	213
San Joaquin Delta Coll, Stockton, CA 95207	1935	Dr. L. H. Horton, Jr.	10	17,199	579
San Jose City Coll, San Jose, CA 95128	1921	Ms. Del M. Anderson	10	10,856	390
San Juan Coll, Farmington, NM 87402-4699	1958	Dr. James C. Henderson	9	3,963	165
Santa Barbara City Coll, Santa Barbara, CA 93109	1908	Dr. Peter R. MacDougall	10	11,481	500
Santa Fe Comm Coll, Gainesville, FL 32606	1966	Dr. Larry W. Tyree	12	11,813	539
Santa Fe Comm Coll, Santa Fe, NM 87502	1983	Dr. Bill J. Priest	12	3,296	294
Santa Monica Coll, Santa Monica, CA 90405	1929	Dr. Richard L. Moore	12	23,203	664
Santa Rosa Jr Coll, Santa Rosa, CA 95401	1918	Dr. Robert F. Agrella	12	28,223	1,387
Sauk Valley Comm Coll, Dixon, IL 61021	1965	Dr. Richard L. Behrendt	10	2,870	185
Schenectady County Comm Coll, Schenectady, NY 12305	1968	Dr. Gabriel J. Basil	12	3,824	239
Schoolcraft Coll, Livonia, MI 48152	1961	Dr. Richard W. McDowell	10	10,057	446
Scott Comm Coll, Bettendorf, IA 52722-6804	1966	Dr. Lenny E. Stone	12	3,850	185
Seattle Central Comm Coll, Seattle, WA 98122	1966	Dr. Charles H. Mitchell	5	9,673	388
Seminole Comm Coll, Sanford, FL 32773	1966	Dr. Earl S. Weldon	12	6,404	512
Seminole Jr Coll, Seminole, OK 74818-0351	1931	Dr. James J. Cook	5	1,844	76
Seward County Comm Coll, Liberal, KS 67905-1137	1969	Mr. Donald E. Guild	12	1,609	147
Shasta Coll, Redding, CA 96049	1948	Mr. George C. Kutras	12	12,820	397
Shawnee Comm Coll, Ullin, IL 62992	1967	NR	12	2,500	194
Shelby State Comm Coll, Memphis, TN 38174-0568	1970	Dr. Lawrence M. Cox	5	6,988	354
Shelton State Comm Coll, Tuscaloosa, AL 35405	1979	Dr. Tom Umphrey	5	7,000	NR
Sheridan Coll, Sheridan, WY 82801	1948	Dr. Stephen Maier	12	2,998	156
Shoreline Comm Coll, Seattle, WA 98133	1964	Dr. Ronald E. Bell	5	8,092	253
Sierra Coll, Rocklin, CA 95677	1936	Dr. Kevin M. Ramirez	5	15,057	503
Sinclair Comm Coll, Dayton, OH 45402	1887	Dr. David H. Ponitz	12	20,800	933
Skyline Coll, San Bruno, CA 94066-1698	1969	Ms. Linda Graef Salter	9	9,144	268
Snead State Jr Coll, Boaz, AL 35957	1935	Dr. William H. Osborn	5	1,715	78
Snow Coll, Ephraim, UT 84627	1888	Dr. Gerald Day	5	2,344	93
Solano Comm Coll, Suisun City, CA 94585	1945	Dr. Virginia L. Holton	9	11,370	402
South Arkansas Comm Coll, El Dorado, AR 71731-7010	1975	Dr. Ben Whitfield	5	1,200	81
Southeast Comm Coll, Lincoln Cmps, Lincoln, NE 68520	1973	NR	10	4,168	538
Southeastern Comm Coll, Whiteville, NC 28472	1964	Dr. Stephen C. Scott	5	1,750	145
Southeastern Comm Coll, North Cmps, West Burlington, IA 52655-0605	1968	Dr. R. Gene Gardner	12	2,166	94
Southeastern Illinois Coll, Harrisburg, IL 62946	1960	Dr. Harry W. Abell	5	3,763	152
Southern Arkansas U Tech, Camden, AR 71701	1968	Dr. George J. Brown	5	1,197	114
Southern Maine Tech Coll, South Portland, ME 04106	1946	Dr. Wayne H. Ross	5	1,359	148
Southern State Comm Coll, Hillsboro, OH 45133	1975	Dr. George R. McCormick	5	1,654	114
Southern Union State Jr Coll, Wadley, AL 36276	1922	Dr. Richard J. Federinko	5	3,334	167
Southern U, Shreveport–Bossier City Cmps, Shreveport, LA 71107	1964	Dr. Robert H. Smith	5	1,054	75
Southern West Virginia Comm Coll, Logan, WV 25601	1971	Dr. Harry J. Boyer	5	3,115	198
South Florida Comm Coll, Avon Park, FL 33825	1965	Dr. Catherine P. Cornelius	5	1,500	266
South Georgia Coll, Douglas, GA 31533-5098	1906	Dr. Edward D. Jackson, Jr.	5	1,495	57
South Mountain Comm Coll, Phoenix, AZ 85040	1979	Dr. John A. Cordova	12	3,061	173
South Plains Coll, Levelland, TX 79336	1958	Dr. Marvin L. Baker	12	5,960	339
South Puget Sound Comm Coll, Olympia, WA 98512-6218	1970	Dr. Kenneth Minnaert	5	5,200	201
South Seattle Comm Coll, Seattle, WA 98106-1499	1970	Mr. Jerry M. Brockey	5	3,421	292
Southside Virginia Comm Coll, Alberta, VA 23821	1970	Dr. John J. Cavan	5	1,996	169
South Suburban Coll, South Holland, IL 60473	1927	Dr. Richard Fonte	12	7,583	323
Southwestern Coll, Chula Vista, CA 91910-7299	1961	Mr. Joseph M. Conte	12	17,222	672
Southwestern Comm Coll, Creston, IA 50801	1966	NR	5	1,372	65
Southwestern Comm Coll, Sylva, NC 28779	1964	Dr. Barry W. Russell	5	1,544	197
Southwestern Michigan Coll, Dowagiac, MI 49047	1964	Mr. David C. Briegel	12	2,873	182
Southwestern Oregon Comm Coll, Coos Bay, OR 97420	1961	Dr. Stephen J. Kridelbaugh	12	1,924	161
Southwest Mississippi Comm Coll, Summit, MS 39666	1918	NR	10	1,520	89
Southwest State Tech Coll, Mobile, AL 36605	1954	Dr. Thomas A. McLeod	5	1,039	98
Southwest Texas Jr Coll, Uvalde, TX 78801	1946	Mr. Billy Word	12	2,859	147
Southwest Virginia Comm Coll, Richlands, VA 24641	1968	Dr. Charles R. King	5	4,896	235
Southwest Wisconsin Tech Coll, Fennimore, WI 53809	1967	Dr. Richard A. Rogers	12	1,550	101
Spartanburg Methodist Coll, Spartanburg, SC 29301	1911	Dr. George D. Fields	2	1,050	32
Spartanburg Tech Coll, Spartanburg, SC 29305	1961	Dr. Jack A. Powers	5	2,500	NR
Spokane Comm Coll, Spokane, WA 99207	1963	Dr. Joseph Rich	5	8,000	481

Name, address	Year	Governing official, control		Enrollment	Faculty
Spokane Falls Comm Coll, Spokane, WA 99204	1967	Dr. Vern Loland	5	6,431	656
Spoon River Coll, Canton, IL 61520	1959	Dr. Felix T. Haynes	5	2,300	133
Springfield Tech Comm Coll, Springfield, MA 01105	1967	Mr. Andrew M. Scibelli	5	3,810	234
Stark Tech Coll, Canton, OH 44720	1970	Dr. John J. McGrath	12	4,537	188
State Comm Coll of East St Louis, East St Louis, IL 62201	1969	NR	5	1,268	83
State Fair Comm Coll, Sedalia, MO 65301	1966	Dr. Marvin Fielding	10	2,369	98
State Tech Inst at Memphis, Memphis, TN 38134	1967	Dr. Charles Temple	5	10,519	527
State U of NY Coll of A&T at Cobleskill, Cobleskill, NY 12043	1916	Dr. Kenneth E. Wing	5	2,797	164
State U of NY Coll of A&T at Morrisville, Morrisville, NY 13408	1908	Dr. Frederick W. Woodward	5	3,449	171
State U of NY Coll of Tech at Alfred, Alfred, NY 14802	1908	Dr. William Rezak	5	3,518	176
State U of NY Coll of Tech at Canton, Canton, NY 13617	1906	Dr. Joseph L. Kennedy	5	2,278	107
State U of NY Coll of Tech at Farmingdale, Farmingdale, NY 11735	1912	Dr. Frank A. Cipriani	5	8,800	393
Suffolk County Comm Coll–Ammerman Cmps, Selden, NY 11784	1962	Dr. John F. Cooper	12	13,154	782
Suffolk County Comm Coll–Eastern Cmps, Riverhead, NY 11901	1977	Mr. Steven T. Kenny	12	2,680	216
Suffolk County Comm Coll–Western Cmps, Brentwood, NY 11717	1974	Mr. Salvatore J. LaLima	12	6,097	349
Sullivan County Comm Coll, Loch Sheldrake, NY 12759-4002	1962	Dr. Jeffrey B. Willens	12	2,093	167
Surry Comm Coll, Dobson, NC 27017	1965	Dr. Swanson Richards	5	3,036	98
Tacoma Comm Coll, Tacoma, WA 98465	1965	Dr. Raymond Needham	5	5,012	284
Tallahassee Comm Coll, Tallahassee, FL 32304-2895	1966	Dr. James H. Hinson, Jr.	12	9,800	370
Tarrant County Jr Coll, Fort Worth, TX 76102	1967	Mr. C. A. Roberson	9	28,515	1,019
Tech Coll of the Lowcountry, Beaufort, SC 29901-1288	1972	Dr. Anne S. McNutt	5	1,424	66
Temple Jr Coll, Temple, TX 76504-7435	1926	Dr. Marvin R. Felder	10	2,363	122
Terra Tech Coll, Fremont, OH 43420-9670	1968	Dr. Charlotte J. Lee	5	2,940	148
Texarkana Coll, Texarkana, TX 75599	1927	Dr. Carl M. Nelson	12	4,099	188
Texas Southmost Coll, Brownsville, TX 78520-4991	1926	Dr. Juliet V. Garcia	10	6,429	390
Texas State Tech Coll–Harlingen Cmps, Harlingen, TX 78550-3697	1967	Dr. J. Gilbert Leal	5	3,236	195
Texas State Tech Coll–Waco Cmps, Waco, TX 76705	1965	Mr. Don E. Goodwin	5	3,108	332
Thomas Nelson Comm Coll, Hampton, VA 23670	1968	Dr. Robert G. Templin, Jr.	5	7,815	318
Three Rivers Comm Coll, Poplar Bluff, MO 63901	1966	Dr. Stephen M. Poort	5	3,061	67
Three Rivers Comm-Tech Coll, Norwich, CT 06360	1969	Dr. Booker T. DeVaughn	5	4,275	128
Tidewater Comm Coll, Portsmouth, VA 23703	1968	Dr. Larry Whitworth	5	16,943	708
Tomball Coll, Tomball, TX 77375-4036	1988	NR	12	3,604	187
Tompkins Cortland Comm Coll, Dryden, NY 13053	1968	Dr. Eduardo J. Marti	12	2,899	190
Treasure Valley Comm Coll, Ontario, OR 97914	1962	NR	12	2,231	117
Tri-County Tech Coll, Pendleton, SC 29670	1962	Dr. Don C. Garrison	5	3,155	250
Trident Tech Coll, Charleston, SC 29411	1964	Dr. Mary Dellamura Thornley	12	9,120	375
Trinidad State Jr Coll, Trinidad, CO 81082	1925	Dr. Harold Deselms	5	2,392	111
Trinity Valley Comm Coll, Athens, TX 75751	1946	Mr. Ron Baugh	12	4,786	224
Triton Coll, River Grove, IL 60171	1964	Dr. George Jorndt	5	12,968	835
Trocaire Coll, Buffalo, NY 14220	1958	Ms. Barbara Ciarico, RSM	1	1,123	101
Truckee Meadows Comm Coll, Reno, NV 89512	1971	Dr. John Gwaltney	5	9,551	489
Tulsa Jr Coll, Tulsa, OK 74135	1968	Dr. Dean P. VanTrease	5	22,702	700
Tunxis Comm Coll, Farmington, CT 06032	1969	Ms. Marilyn Menack	5	2,465	175
Tyler Jr Coll, Tyler, TX 75711	1926	Dr. Raymond M. Hawkins	12	7,984	364
Ulster County Comm Coll, Stone Ridge, NY 12484	1961	Mr. Robert T. Brown	12	2,319	194
Umpqua Comm Coll, Roseburg, OR 97470	1964	Dr. James Kraby	12	2,112	120
Union County Coll, Cranford, NJ 07016	1933	Dr. Thomas H. Brown	12	10,476	424
U of Akron–Wayne Coll, Orrville, OH 44667	1972	Dr. Peggy Gordon Elliott	5	1,461	109
U of Alaska Anchorage, Kenai Peninsula Coll, Soldotna, AK 99669	1964	NR	5	1,673	85
U of Alaska Anchorage, Matanuska-Susitna Coll, Palmer, AK 99645	1958	Mr. Ted Berry	5	1,689	114
U of Alaska Southeast, Sitka Cmps, Sitka, AK 99835	1962	Ms. Elaine Sunde	5	1,200	91
U of Cincinnati Clermont Coll, Batavia, OH 45103	1972	Dr. Roger J. Barry	5	1,651	106
U of Cincinnati Raymond Walters Coll, Cincinnati, OH 45236	1967	Dr. Roger J. Barry	5	4,300	195
U of Hawaii–Kapiolani Comm Coll, Honolulu, HI 96816	1957	Mr. John F. Morton	5	7,116	239
U of Hawaii–Kauai Comm Coll, Lihue, HI 96766	1965	Mr. David Iha	5	1,563	84
U of Kentucky, Ashland Comm Coll, Ashland, KY 41101-3683	1937	Mr. Charles Dassance	5	3,267	142
U of Kentucky, Elizabethtown Comm Coll, Elizabethtown, KY 42701	1964	Dr. Charles E. Stebbins	5	4,297	136
U of Kentucky, Hazard Comm Coll, Hazard, KY 41701	1968	Dr. G. Edward Hughes	5	1,695	85
U of Kentucky, Henderson Comm Coll, Henderson, KY 42420	1963	Dr. Patrick R. Lake	5	1,479	96
U of Kentucky, Hopkinsville Comm Coll, Hopkinsville, KY 42241-2100	1965	Dr. Jim Kerley	5	3,000	113
U of Kentucky, Jefferson Comm Coll, Louisville, KY 40202	1968	Dr. Ronald J. Horvath	5	11,861	365
U of Kentucky, Lexington Comm Coll, Lexington, KY 40506	1965	Dr. Allen G. Edwards	5	4,862	302
U of Kentucky, Madisonville Comm Coll, Madisonville, KY 42431	1968	Dr. Arthur D. Stumpf	5	2,312	127
U of Kentucky, Maysville Comm Coll, Maysville, KY 41056	1967	Dr. James C. Shires	5	1,325	111
U of Kentucky, Paducah Comm Coll, Paducah, KY 42002	1932	Dr. Leonard O'Hara	5	3,133	102
U of Kentucky, Prestonsburg Comm Coll, Prestonsburg, KY 41653	1964	Dr. Deborah Lee Floyd	5	2,887	124
U of Kentucky, Somerset Comm Coll, Somerset, KY 42501	1965	Dr. Rollin J. Watson	5	2,528	153
U of Kentucky, Southeast Comm Coll, Cumberland, KY 40823-1099	1960	Dr. W. Bruce Ayers	5	2,453	107
U of Maine at Augusta, Augusta, ME 04330	1965	Dr. George P. Connick	5	4,972	172
U of Minnesota, Crookston, Crookston, MN 56716	1966	Dr. Donald G. Sargeant	5	1,352	71
U of New Mexico–Gallup Branch, Gallup, NM 87301	1968	Dr. John M. Phillips	5	2,650	117
U of New Mexico–Valencia Cmps, Los Lunas, NM 87031	1981	Dr. Ralph Sigala	5	1,367	93
U of Puerto Rico, Carolina Regional Coll, Carolina, PR 00984-4800	1974	Prof. Marta Arroyo	7	1,751	87
U of South Carolina at Beaufort, Beaufort, SC 29902	1959	Dr. Chris P. Plyler	5	1,070	64
U of South Carolina at Salkehatchie, Allendale, SC 29810	1965	Dr. Carl A. Clayton	5	1,006	40
U of South Carolina at Sumter, Sumter, SC 29150	1966	Mr. J. C. Anderson, Jr.	5	1,627	98
U of Wisconsin Ctr–Fox Valley, Menasha, WI 54952	1933	Dr. James W. Perry	5	1,447	55

Name, address	Year	Governing official, control	Enrollment	Faculty
U of Wisconsin Ctr–Waukesha County, Waukesha, WI 53188	1966	Dr. Mary S. Knudten, 5	2,140	86
Utah Valley Comm Coll, Orem, UT 84058	1941	Dr. Kerry D. Romesburg, 5	9,623	425
Valencia Comm Coll, Orlando, FL 32802	1967	Dr. Paul C. Gianini, Jr., 5	22,094	893
Vance-Granville Comm Coll, Henderson, NC 27536	1969	Dr. Ben F. Currin, 5	2,670	153
Ventura Coll, Ventura, CA 93003	1925	Dr. Jesus Carreon, 12	12,158	541
Vernon Regional Jr Coll, Vernon, TX 76384-4092	1972	Dr. Wade Kirk, 12	1,780	115
Victoria Coll, Victoria, TX 77901	1925	Dr. Jimmy Goodson, 9	3,411	120
Victor Valley Coll, Victorville, CA 92392-9699	1961	Dr. Edward O. Gould, 5	8,000	325
Vincennes U, Vincennes, IN 47591	1801	Dr. Phillip M. Summers, 5	7,211	400
Vincennes U–Jasper Ctr, Jasper, IN 47546	1970	NR, 5	1,274	62
Virginia Western Comm Coll, Roanoke, VA 24038	1966	Dr. Charles L. Downs, 5	6,895	202
Volunteer State Comm Coll, Gallatin, TN 37066	1970	Dr. Hal R. Ramer, 5	5,218	276
Wake Tech Comm Coll, Raleigh, NC 27603	1958	Dr. Bruce I. Howell, 12	6,850	325
Wallace State Comm Coll, Hanceville, AL 35077-2000	1966	Dr. James C. Bailey, 5	5,953	266
Walla Walla Comm Coll, Walla Walla, WA 99362	1967	Dr. Steven L. VanAusdle, 5	5,674	278
Walters State Comm Coll, Morristown, TN 37813	1970	Dr. Jack E. Campbell, 5	5,427	253
Washington State Comm Coll, Marietta, OH 45750	1971	Dr. Carson K. Miller, 5	2,138	122
Washtenaw Comm Coll, Ann Arbor, MI 48106	1965	Dr. Gunder A. Myran, 12	10,954	757
Waubonsee Comm Coll, Sugar Grove, IL 60554	1966	Dr. John J. Swalec, 10	7,550	542
Waukesha County Tech Coll, Pewaukee, WI 53072	1923	Dr. Richard T. Anderson, 12	4,700	520
Wayne Comm Coll, Goldsboro, NC 27533-8002	1957	Dr. Edward H. Wilson, Jr., 12	2,752	153
Wayne County Comm Coll, Detroit, MI 48226	1967	Dr. Rafael L. Cortada, 12	9,577	417
Weatherford Coll, Weatherford, TX 76086	1869	Dr. Jim Boyd, 5	2,277	94
Wenatchee Valley Coll, Wenatchee, WA 98801	1939	Dr. Arnie Heuchert, 12	3,419	168
Westark Comm Coll, Fort Smith, AR 72913	1928	Mr. Joel R. Stubblefield, 12	5,472	234
Westchester Comm Coll, Valhalla, NY 10595-1698	1946	Dr. Joseph N. Hankin, 12	11,870	574
Western Iowa Tech Comm Coll, Sioux City, IA 51102-0265	1966	Dr. Robert E. Dunker, 5	2,575	157
Western Nebraska Comm Coll–Scottsbluff Cmps, Scottsbluff, NE 69361	1926	Dr. John N. Harms, 12	1,656	56
Western Nevada Comm Coll, Carson City, NV 89703	1971	Dr. Anthony D. Calabro, 5	4,847	358
Western Oklahoma State Coll, Altus, OK 73521	1926	Dr. Stephen R. Hensley, 5	1,803	78
Western Texas Coll, Snyder, TX 79549	1969	Dr. Harry L. Krenek, 12	1,095	55
Western Wisconsin Tech Coll, La Crosse, WI 54602	1911	Dr. James Lee Rasch, 10	4,006	185
Western Wyoming Comm Coll, Rock Springs, WY 82902	1959	Dr. T. L. Boggs, 12	2,572	112
West Hills Coll, Coalinga, CA 93210	1932	Dr. Lincoln H. Hall, 5	3,500	160
West Los Angeles Coll, Culver City, CA 90230-3500	1969	Dr. Evelyn C. Wong, 12	8,958	320
Westmoreland County Comm Coll, Youngwood, PA 15697	1970	Dr. Daniel C. Krezenski, 9	6,845	390
West Shore Comm Coll, Scottville, MI 49454	1967	Dr. William M. Anderson, 10	1,430	71
West Valley Coll, Saratoga, CA 95070	1963	Dr. Leo Chavez, 12	14,224	560
West Virginia Northern Comm Coll, Wheeling, WV 26003	1972	Dr. Ron Hutkin, 5	2,991	165
Wharton County Jr Coll, Wharton, TX 77488	1946	Dr. Elbert C. Hutchins, 12	3,361	161
Whatcom Comm Coll, Bellingham, WA 98226	1970	Dr. Harold G. Heiner, 5	2,234	104
Wilkes Comm Coll, Wilkesboro, NC 28697	1965	Dr. James R. Randolph, 5	1,962	102
William Rainey Harper Coll, Palatine, IL 60067-7398	1965	Dr. Paul N. Thompson, 12	15,842	1,004
Willmar Comm Coll, Willmar, MN 56201	1961	Mr. Harold G. Conradi, 5	1,383	61
Willmar Tech Coll, Willmar, MN 56201	1961	NR, 12	1,275	91
Wilson Tech Comm Coll, Wilson, NC 27893	1958	Dr. Frank L. Eagles, 5	1,292	89
Wisconsin Indianhead Tech Coll, New Richmond Cmps, New Richmond, WI 54017	1972	Ms. Marilyn McCarty, 10	1,102	65
Wisconsin Indianhead Tech Coll, Rice Lake Cmps, Rice Lake, WI 54868	1941	Ms. Mary Ellen Filkins, 10	1,136	79
Wood Coll, Mathiston, MS 39752	1886	Dr. Doyce W. Gunter, 2	1,500	35
Wor-Wic Tech Comm Coll, Salisbury, MD 21801	1976	NR, 12	1,834	94
Wytheville Comm Coll, Wytheville, VA 24382	1967	Dr. William F. Snyder, 5	2,460	137
Yakima Valley Comm Coll, Yakima, WA 98907	1928	Dr. V. Philip Tullar, 5	5,500	410
Yavapai Coll, Prescott, AZ 86301	1966	Dr. Doreen Dailey, 12	5,739	364
York Tech Coll, Rock Hill, SC 29730	1961	Mr. Dennis F. Merrell, 5	3,187	218
Yuba Coll, Marysville, CA 95901	1927	Dr. Patricia L. Wirth, 12	12,373	267

College Freshman Attitudes

The 27th annual survey of college freshmen conducted by the American Council on Education and the Univ. of California at Los Angeles reported an increased interest in activism, racial understanding, and social change. A record two out of every five freshmen participated in organized demonstrations in 1992 (40.5 percent, up from 39.0 percent in 1991, and more than double the levels recorded during the late 1960s); a record percentage of students said "helping to promote racial understanding" was an "essential" or "very important" goal (42.0 percent, up from 33.7 percent in 1991), and a record percentage of students said that "influencing social values" was an "essential" or "very important" goal (43.3 percent, up from 39.6 percent in 1991).

The trend of strong interest in careers in the health professions continued, with the percentage of new college freshmen indicating an interest in majoring in that area reaching a new high in 1992 (15.6 percent, up from 12.9 percent in 1991). This trend began five years earlier, and the latest figure represented a doubling of interest since 1987. In contrast, the percentage of students planning business careers continued to decline; the figure, 14.3 percent in 1992, decreased by almost one-half in just five years.

Economic constraints continued to affect students, with record numbers of freshmen indicating that they selected their college on the basis of low tuition (30.0 percent, up from 27.7 in 1991), because of the offer of financial assistance (28.3 percent, up from 27.8 in 1991), or because they wanted to live near home (23.6 percent, up from 21.3 percent in 1991). A record one in six freshmen (17.4 percent, compared with 13.1 percent in 1989) indicated a "major concern" about their ability to finance college, while the percentage who said they decided to attend college because they "could not find a job" reached an all-time high (8.2 percent, up from 7.3 percent in 1991). A record 3.3 percent reported their father's occupation as "unemployed."

Regarding life goals, the commitment of freshmen to "being very well off financially" dropped for the fifth straight year (from 75.6 percent in 1987 to 73.0 percent in 1992), while the percentage of students who wanted to "develop a meaningful philosophy of life" increased for the fifth straight year (to 45.6 percent).

ASTRONOMY AND CALENDAR

Edited by Dr. Kenneth L. Franklin, Astronomer Emeritus
American Museum of Natural History-Hayden Planetarium

Celestial Events Summary, 1994

(Greenwich Mean Time, or GMT)

This year begins with 3 of the planets conjoined with the sun, and on January 11, the moon is new. Thus 4 of the naked eye planetary bodies are invisible, leaving only Jupiter in the morning and Saturn in the evening for us to view. In March, Saturn has 2 close encounters, once with Mars, the other, Mercury. In April, Mars and Mercury brush each other. Venus gives a fine evening show from mid-spring to mid-autumn. From late spring to the end of the year, first Jupiter then Saturn liven our nights, and Mars increasingly dominates the morning sky from late summer to year's end. In early October, Venus and Jupiter give us a bit of a show in the southwest twilight, but never get much closer than about 7°.

For North America, The Event is the annular solar eclipse of May 10. The entire continent will see at least a bite taken from the solar disk by the moon. In a narrow band starting from Scammon's Lagoon in Baja California, Mexico, through El Paso, central Missouri, Lakes Erie and Ontario, central NY state, almost all of Vermont and New Hampshire, southern Maine, and most of Nova Scotia, observers will see a ring, or an annulus, of the sun surrounding the dark obscuring disk of the moon. In a total solar eclipse all of the bright photosphere of the sun is hidden by the moon. During totality, the sun's corona may be safely observed with the naked eye and even with powerful binoculars or telescopes with no danger to the eye. Not so in an annular eclipse, however. The ring of the sun still unhidden provides a strong danger to the eye, even without use of a light collector. For this reason, the viewer is strongly advised to use adequate eye protection at all times while observing this eclipse. It is not the eclipse, itself, but the exposed solar surface that the source of danger to the eye. Of course, that surface, and the danger, is exposed to view every clear day. We don't usually have a need or desire to stare at the sun, but an eclipse offers the opportunity for a prolonged gaze, thus the danger during an eclipse. The next central eclipse whose path crosses the United States will be total, August 21, 2017.

Watchers of meteor showers will again stay up late for the Perseid shower, which usually peaks about August 11-12. The swift streaks of light crossing the sky are caused by chunks—meteoroids—of comet Swift-Tuttle as they crash into our upper atmosphere. That comet passed our way in 1992 after an absence from our neighborhood of 130 years, so the region behind it should be much more cluttered with debris than the region in front of it. Avid observers will watch the skies all week surrounding this date, because the cloud of meteoroids is somewhat stretched out along the comet's path and beside it, thus giving us a protracted viewing period, perhaps even greater than this shower's usual 4-5 day duration.

Whenever notice is given in the following listing of some celestial object passing close to another, we may not see the actual event, but regard the notice that the evenings before and after that time will be good times to see the relative movements in our ever-changing, dramatic sky.

Celestial Events Highlights, 1994

(GMT, or as indicated)

January

Mercury begins this year lost in the sun's glare, passing superior conjunction, beyond the sun, on the 3rd.

Venus follows Mercury to superior conjunction on the 17th, also lost in the sun's light, coming to easy view in mid-spring in evening twilight.

Mars, in conjunction last December 27, is mingling with the inferior planets at this time, but will be visible in the morning sky in early March.

Jupiter, the brightest planet to be seen until mid-spring, can be seen these mornings in Libra, becoming an evening object after passing opposition April 30.

Saturn looks like a first magnitude star low in the evening twilight all this month.

Moon passes Jupiter on the 6th, Saturn on the 15th, the other planets too close to the sun to observe the moon's passage.

Jan. 2—Earth at perihelion, 91.4 million miles from the sun.

Jan. 3—Mercury at superior conjunction entering the evening sky, nearly 134 million miles from us, beyond the sun.

Jan. 4—Quadrantid meteor shower.

Jan. 6—Moon passes 3° south of Jupiter.

Jan. 11—Neptune in conjunction with the sun, about 2,900 million miles away.

Jan. 12—Uranus in conjunction with the sun, over 1,900 million miles away.

Jan. 15—Moon passes 7° north of Saturn.

Jan. 17—Venus in superior conjunction beyond the sun, 159 million miles from us, entering the evening sky.

Jan. 19—Sun enters Capricornus.

February

Mercury may be briefly visible in the southwest evening twilight early this month, passing very close to Saturn on the evening of the 1st.

Venus, while technically in the evening sky, is too deep in the evening twilight to be seen.

Mars is similarly invisible, until late in the month, but in the morning sky.

Jupiter is stationary on the 28th, thus beginning its retrograde motion, westward among the stars, prior to opposition April 30.

Saturn may be visible for the first few days of the month, perhaps pointing out Mercury on the evening of the 1st, but soon thereafter enters the evening twilight to be lost to view until mid-March.

Moon passes Jupiter on the 3rd, Neptune and Uranus on the 8th.

Feb. 2—Mercury passes 1.3° north of Saturn, seen close the evening of the 1st.

Feb. 3—Moon passes 3° south of Jupiter.

Feb. 4—Mercury at greatest elongation, 18° east of the sun.

Feb. 8—Moon passes 3° north of Neptune and 5° north of Uranus.

Feb. 10—Mercury stationary, beginning its retrograde motion, westward against the background stars, prior to inferior conjunction.

Feb. 16—Sun enters Aquarius.

Feb. 20—Mercury in inferior conjunction, between the earth and the sun, less than 60 million miles away, entering the morning sky.

Feb. 21—Saturn in conjunction with the sun, beyond it, to enter our morning sky, 999 million miles away.

Feb. 27—Mercury passes 4° north of Mars.

Feb. 28—Jupiter stationary, beginning its retrograde, westward, motion.

March

Mercury rises southeast of the sun all month, passing just 0.3° south of Saturn about 3 AM EST, on the morning of the 24th.

Venus may become visible very low in the evening twilight after mid-month.

Mars, looking like a star a bit fainter than 1st magnitude in Aquarius for most of this year, passes only 0.4° north of slightly brighter Saturn in the dawn sky of the 14th, about 5 AM EST.

Jupiter, in Libra, is 2° north of the moon on the 2nd and the 29th.

Saturn has close encounters this month with Mars on the 14th, and Mercury on the 24th, its passing of the moon on the 11th being a distant 7°.

Moon passes Jupiter on the 2nd, Neptune and Uranus on the 7th, Mercury and Mars on the 10th, Saturn on the 11th, Venus on the 13th, and Jupiter on the 29th.

Mar. 2—Moon passes 2° south of Jupiter.

Mar. 4—Pluto stationary, beginning retrograde, westward, motion; Mercury stationary, resuming direct, eastward, motion.

Mar. 7—Moon passes 4° south of Uranus and 5° south of Neptune.

Mar. 10—Moon passes 5° south of Mercury and 7° south of Mars.

Mar. 11—Moon passes 7° south of Saturn; sun enters Pisces.

Mar. 13—Moon passes 5° south of Venus.

Mar. 14—Mars passes 0.4° north of Saturn.

Mar. 19—Mercury at greatest elongation, 28° west of the sun.

Mar. 20—Vernal equinox; spring begins in the northern hemisphere at 20:28 GMT, 3:28 PM EST.

Mar. 24—Mercury 0.3° south of Saturn.

Mar. 29—Moon passes 2° south of Jupiter.

April

Mercury, nearly 1.5 magnitudes brighter, passes close to Mars on the 4th, but soon moves into the morning twilight, thus lost to view.

Venus is becoming more prominent in the western evening sky, so close to the thin crescent moon on the evening of the 12th as to be occulted, its shadow passing across our Arctic regions, a good photo opportunity.

Mars, in Pisces after the 1st week, passes close to Mercury on the 4th.

Jupiter, at magnitude minus 2.5, coming to opposition on the 30th, still dominates the night sky, but evenings belong to Venus at magnitude minus 3.9.

Saturn continues to take over the morning sky in Aquarius, about as bright as Mars.

Moon passes Neptune on the 3rd, Uranus on the 4th, Saturn on the 7th, Mars and Mercury on the 9th, occults Venus on the 12th, and passes Jupiter on the 26th.

Apr. 3—Moon passes 4° north of Neptune.

Apr. 4—Mercury passes 1.5° south of Mars; moon passes 5° north of Uranus.

Apr. 9—Moon passes 6° north of Mars and 7° north of Mercury.

Apr. 12—Moon passes 1° north of Venus, occulting it for viewers in the Arctic regions.

Apr. 18—Sun enters Aries.

Apr. 25—Neptune stationary, beginning its retrograde motion.

Apr. 26—Moon passes 3° south of Jupiter.

Apr. 30—Jupiter at opposition, 411 million miles away; Mercury in superior conjunction, 123 million miles away.

May

Mercury, by the 20th, may become easily visible in the northwest twilight after sunset, lower and fainter than brilliant Venus, which sets over an hour later.

Venus, in Taurus, may be seen north of Aldebaran on the 4th, and is north of the thin crescent moon on the evening of the 12th.

Mars continues to linger in the low morning sky, as it slides across constellations, in Aries before the end of the month.

Jupiter, now in the sky all night, is the brightest object continuously visible, surpassed only by the fleeting moon, and by Venus, who leaves the sky early for her beauty sleep.

Saturn is slowly brightening, heading for its late summer opposition when its turn to patrol the sky all night comes around the 1st of September.

Moon passes Neptune and Uranus on the 1st, Saturn on the 5th, Mars on the 8th, eclipses the sun on the 10th, passes Venus on the 13th, Jupiter on the 23rd, partially enters the earth's shadow on the 25th, and on the 28th, again passes Uranus and Neptune.

May 1—Uranus stationary; moon passes 4° north of Neptune; moon passes 5° north of Uranus.

May 5—Venus passes 6° north of Aldebaran; moon passes 6° south of Saturn.

May 8—Moon passes 4° north of Mars.

May 10—Annular eclipse of the sun.

May 13—Moon passes 4° south of Venus; sun enters Taurus.

May 15—Mercury passes 8° north of Aldebaran.

May 17—Pluto at opposition, 2,723 million miles from us.

May 23—Moon passes 3° south of Jupiter.

May 25—Partial eclipse of the moon.

May 28—Moon passes 4° north of Neptune and 5° north of Uranus.

May 30—Mercury at greatest elongation, 23° east of the sun.

June

Mercury, although fairly well placed for viewing, is turning its dark side toward us as it heads for inferior conjunction on the 25th, thus becoming fainter in our sky.

Venus, passing Pollux and the moon this month at unspectacular distances, is becoming more spectacular by just being in our western evening sky well after sunset.

Mars' most exciting adventure this month, other than entering Taurus about the 22nd, is being about 2° from the thin crescent moon in the dawn sky of the 6th.

Jupiter, in Virgo, is brighter and yellower than Spica to its west.

Saturn is a bright 1st magnitude object in Aquarius, not known for bright objects.

Moon passes Saturn on the 1st, Mars on the 6th, Mercury on the 11th, Venus on the 12th, Jupiter on the 19th, Neptune on the 24th, Uranus on the 25th, and Saturn, again, on the 28th.

June 1—Moon passes 7° north of Saturn.

June 6—Moon passes 2° north of Mars.

June 10—Venus passes 5° south of Pollux.

June 11—Moon passes 3° south of Mercury.

June 12—Mercury stationary, beginning its retrograde motion; moon passes 7° south of Venus.

June 19—Moon passes 3° south of Jupiter.

June 20—Sun enters Gemini.

June 21—Summer solstice at 14:48 GMT (9:48 EST); summer begins in the northern hemisphere.

June 24—Saturn stationary, beginning its retrograde motion; moon passes 4° north of Neptune.

June 25—Moon passes 5° north of Uranus; Mercury at inferior conjunction, 51.7 million miles away.

June 28—Moon passes 7° north of Saturn.

July

Mercury is in the morning sky virtually the entire month, but not easy to see.

Venus passes Regulus, the bright star of Leo, by a little over 2 moon diameters on the 10th.

Mars, in Taurus all month, is occulted by the moon on the 5th, but for us in North America we see them only close together that morning.

Jupiter is stationary on the 2nd, resuming its direct motion, again heading for Libra.

Saturn continues to lurk in Aquarius, passed only by the moon on the 26th.

Moon occults Mars on the 5th, passes Mercury on the 7th, Venus on the 12th, Jupiter on the 16th, Neptune and Uranus on the 22nd, and Saturn on the 26th.

July 2—Jupiter stationary, resuming its direct motion.

July 5—Moon occults Mars; earth at aphelion, 94.4 million miles from the sun.

July 6—Mercury stationary, resuming its direct motion.

July 7—Moon passes 1.3° south of Mars, occulting it.

July 10—Venus passes 1.1° north of Regulus.

July 12—Moon passes 7° south of Venus.

July 14—Neptune at opposition, 2,710 million miles away.

July 16—Moon passes 3° south of Jupiter.

July 17—Uranus at opposition, almost 1,734 million miles away; Mercury at greatest elongation, 21° west of the sun.

July 18—Mars passes 5° north of Aldebaran.

July 20—Sun enters Cancer.

July 22—Moon passes 4° north of Neptune, and 5° north of Uranus.

July 26—Moon passes 7° north of Saturn.

July 30—Mercury 3° north of Pollux.

August

Mercury is lost in the sun all month.

Venus is at greatest elongation, 46° east of the sun on the 24th, appearing like a half moon in telescopes.

Mars continues its dogged round of the sky all month, moving into Gemini about the 15th.

Jupiter decreases its distance from Venus, fading slightly as Venus grows still brighter.

Saturn attains its greatest brilliancy this year, but never getting brighter than 0.5 magnitude.

Moon passes Mars on the 3rd, Venus on the 10th, Jupiter on the 13th, Neptune and Uranus on the 18th, and Saturn on the 22nd.

Aug. 3—Moon passes 3° south of Mars.

Aug. 9—Pluto stationary.

Aug. 10—Moon passes 3° south of Venus; sun enters Leo.

Aug. 11—Watch for Perseid meteor shower tonight and tomorrow night.

Aug. 13—Mercury in superior conjunction, over 125 million miles away; moon passes 2° south of Jupiter.

Aug. 18—Moon passes 4° north of Neptune and 5° north of Uranus.

Aug. 22—Moon passes 7° north of Saturn.

Aug. 24—Venus at greatest elongation, 46° east of the sun.

Aug. 31—Venus 0.7° south of Spica.

September

Mercury is in the evening sky all month and half of October, appearing as a zero magnitude star to the left of the set sun in the evening twilight, passing 0.1° south of Spica on the 21st, a binocular and telescope photo opportunity.

Venus achieves greatest brilliancy on the 28th, minus 4.6 magnitude, putting nearby Jupiter in his place, after a pleasant encounter with the crescent moon on the evening of the 8th.

Mars begins to brighten almost imperceptibly in preparation for its show at the end of the year, sneaking into Cancer just as the month ends.

Jupiter closes in on Venus, just to lose the spectacle to the traditional evening star, but providing a pleasant supporting role to the passing moon on the evenings of the 9th and 10th.

Saturn, at opposition on the 1st, has the whole night to itself, after the evening show in the west, and before the challenging Mars to the east.

Moon passes Mars on the 1st, Mercury on the 7th, Venus and Jupiter on the 9th, Neptune and Uranus on the 14th, Saturn on the 18th, and Mars, again, on the 29th.

Sep. 1—Moon passes 4° south of Mars; Saturn at opposition, about 808 million miles from us.

Sep. 7—Moon passes 3° south of Mercury.

Sep. 9—Moon passes 2° north of Venus, and 1.4° south of Jupiter.

Sep. 14—Moon passes 4° north of Neptune and 5° north of Uranus.

Sep. 16—Sun enters Virgo.

Sep. 18—Moon passes 7° north of Saturn.

Sep. 21—Mercury passes 0.1° south of Spica.

Sep. 23—Autumnal equinox; autumn begins in the northern hemisphere at 6:19 GMT (1:19 AM EST).

Sep. 24—Mars passes 6° south of Pollux.

Sep. 26—Mercury at greatest elongation, 26° east of the sun.

Sep. 28—Venus at greatest brilliancy.

Sep. 29—Moon passes 6° south of Mars.

October

Mercury, except for the 1st week, and then only for very dedicated observers, is lost to view in the solar glare.

Venus and **Jupiter** are about 7° apart in the N-S direction, Venus considerably more to the left in the evening twilight, and it will plunge into the brighter parts of the twilight before Jupiter.

Mars, in Cancer all month, continues to brighten during the rest of the year.

Jupiter plays with a standoffish Venus for the rest of the month, but remains visible with some difficulty into November.

Saturn takes over the night sky as Venus and Jupiter leave, but Mars is becoming a serious contender.

Moon passes Mercury on the 6th, Venus and Jupiter on the 7th, occulting Jupiter, passes Neptune and Uranus on the 12th, Saturn on the 15th, and Mars on the 28th.

Oct. 2—Uranus and Neptune stationary, resuming their direct motions.

Oct. 6—Moon passes 3° north of Mercury.

Oct. 7—Moon passes 7° north of Venus, 0.7° south of Jupiter, occulting it; Venus is 34 million miles away, Jupiter, over 578 million miles.

Oct. 9—Mercury stationary, beginning its retrograde motion.

Oct. 12—Moon passes 4° north of Neptune, 5° north of Uranus; Venus stationary, beginning its retrograde motion.

Oct. 15—Moon passes 7° north of Saturn.

Oct. 21—Mercury at inferior conjunction, 62 million miles from us; Orionid meteor shower.

Oct. 28—Moon passes 7° south of Mars.

Oct. 29—Mercury stationary, resuming its direct motion.

Oct. 30—Sun enters Libra.

November

Mercury is a morning object early in the month, passing Venus on the 12th.

Venus emerges into the morning sky, taking charge by mid-November, passing Mercury on the 12th.

Mars leaves Cancer for Leo on the 6th, brightening by half a magnitude this month.

Jupiter is lost to view all month, passing through conjunction on the 17th.

Saturn is alone in the evening sky, still faithful to Aquarius.

Moon passes Mercury on the 2nd, totally eclipses the sun on the 3rd, passes Neptune and Uranus on the 8th, Saturn on the 11th, has a penumbral eclipse on the 18th, passes Mars on the 25th, and Venus on the 30th.

Nov. 2—Moon passes 4° south of Mercury; Venus in inferior conjunction.

Nov. 3—Mercury passes 4° north of Spica; total solar eclipse.

Nov. 6—Mercury at greatest elongation, 10° west of the sun.

Nov. 8—Moon passes 4° north of Neptune and 6° north of Uranus.

Nov. 9—Saturn stationary, resuming its direct motion.

Nov. 11—Moon passes 7° north of Saturn.

Nov. 12—Mercury 5° north of Venus.

Nov. 17—Jupiter in conjunction with the sun, 593 million miles away; Leonid meteor shower.

Nov. 18—Moon in penumbral eclipse.

Nov. 20—Pluto in conjunction with the sun, nearly 2,851 million miles from earth.

Nov. 22—Sun enters Scorpius.

Nov. 25—Moon passes 8° south of Mars.

Nov. 29—Sun enters Ophiuchus.

Nov. 30—Moon passes 2° south of Venus.

December

Mercury is lost to view all month, passing superior conjunction on the 14th.

Venus is at greatest brilliancy in the dawn sky on the 9th.

Mars stays in Leo, slowing its direct motion, passing 2° north of Regulus on the 8th, and brightening over a half magnitude during the month.

Jupiter emerges from the dawn solar glare early in the month, quickly moving into Scorpius from Libra, where it has spent the year.

Saturn, prominent in our western sky after sunset, remains in Aquarius.

Moon passes Neptune on the 5th, Uranus on the 6th, Saturn on the 9th, Mars on the 23rd, Venus on the 29th, and occults Jupiter on the 30th.

Dec. 5—Moon passes 4° north of Neptune.

Dec. 6—Moon passes 6° north of Uranus.

Dec. 8—Mars passes 2° north of Regulus.

Dec. 9—Moon passes 7° north of Saturn; Venus at greatest brilliancy.

Dec. 13—Geminid meteor shower.

Dec. 14—Mercury in superior conjunction, nearly 135 million miles away.

Dec. 16—Sun enters Sagittarius.

Dec. 22—Winter solstice; winter begins in the northern hemisphere at 2:23 GMT (10:23 PM EST, Dec. 21).

Dec. 23—Moon passes 9° south of Mars.

Dec. 29—Moon passes 3° south of Venus.

Dec. 30—Moon occults Jupiter.

Planets and the Sun

The planets of the solar system, in order of their mean distance from the sun, are Mercury, Venus, the earth, Mars, Jupiter, Saturn, Uranus, Neptune and Pluto. Both Uranus and Neptune are visible through good field glasses, but Pluto is so distant and so small that only large telescopes or long exposure photographs can make it visible.

Since Mercury and Venus are nearer to the sun than is the earth, their motions about the sun are seen from the earth as wide swings first to one side of the sun and then to the other, although they are both passing continuously around the sun in orbits that are almost circular. When their passage takes them either between the earth and the sun, or beyond the sun as seen from the earth, they are invisible to us. Because of the laws that govern the motions of planets about the sun, both Mercury and Venus require much less time to pass between the earth and the sun than around the far side of the sun, so their periods of visibility and invisibility are unequal.

The planets that lie farther from the sun than does the earth may be seen for longer periods of time and are invisible only when they are so located in our sky that they rise and set about the same time as the sun when, of course, they are overwhelmed by the sun's great brilliance. None of the planets has any light of its own but each shines only by reflecting sunlight from its surface. Mercury and Venus, because they are between the earth and the sun, show phases very much as the moon does. The planets farther from the sun are always seen as full, although Mars does occasionally present a slightly gibbous phase — like the moon when not quite full.

The planets move rapidly among the stars because they are very much nearer to us. The stars are also in motion, some of them at tremendous speeds, but they are so far away that their motion does not change their apparent positions in the heavens sufficiently for anyone to perceive that change in a single lifetime. The very nearest star is about 7,000 times as far away as the most distant planet.

Planets of the Solar System

Mercury

Mercury, nearest planet to the sun, is the second smallest of the nine planets known to be orbiting the sun. Its diameter is 3,100 miles and its mean distance from the sun is 36,000,000 miles.

Mercury moves with great speed in its journey about the sun, averaging about 30 miles a second to complete its circuit in 88 of our days. Mercury rotates upon its axis over a period of nearly 59 days, thus exposing all of its surface periodically to the sun. It is believed that the surface passing before the sun may have a temperature of about 800° F., while the temperature on the side turned temporarily away from the sun does not fall as low as might be expected. This night temperature has been described by Russian astronomers as "room temperature" — possibly about 70° F. This would contradict the former belief that Mercury did not possess an atmosphere, for some sort of atmosphere would be needed to retain the fierce solar radiation that strikes Mercury. A shallow but dense layer of carbon dioxide would produce the "greenhouse" effect, in which heat accumulated during exposure to the sun would not completely escape at night. The actual presence of a carbon dioxide atmosphere is in dispute. Other research, however, has indicated a nighttime temperature approaching −300° F.

This uncertainty about conditions upon Mercury and its motion arise from its shorter angular distance from the sun as seen from the earth, for Mercury is always too much in line with the sun to be observed against a dark sky, but is always seen during either morning or evening twilight.

Mariner 10 made 3 passes by Mercury in 1974 and 1975. A large fraction of the surface was photographed from varying distances, revealing a degree of cratering similar to that of the moon. An atmosphere of hydrogen and helium may be made up of gases of the solar wind temporarily concentrated by the presence of Mercury. The discovery of a weak but permanent magnetic field was a surprise. It has been held that both a fluid core and rapid rotation were necessary for the generation of a planetary magnetic field. Mercury may demonstrate these conditions to be unnecessary, or the field may reveal something about the history of Mercury.

Venus

Venus, slightly smaller than the earth, moves about the sun at a mean distance of 67,000,000 miles in 225 of our days. Its synodical revolution — its return to the same relationship with the earth and the sun, which is a result of the combination of its own motion and that of the earth — is 584 days. Every 19 months, then, Venus will be nearer to the earth than any other planet of the solar system. The planet is covered with a dense, white, cloudy atmosphere that conceals whatever is below it. This same cloud reflects sunlight efficiently so that when Venus is favorably situated, it is the third brightest object in the sky, exceeded only by the sun and the moon.

Spectral analysis of sunlight reflected from Venus' cloud tops has shown features that can best be explained by identifying the material of the clouds as sulphuric acid (oil of vitriol). Infrared spectroscopy from a balloon-borne telescope nearly 20 miles above the earth's surface gave indications of a small amount of water vapor present in the same region of the atmosphere of Venus. In 1956, radio astronomers at the Naval Research Laboratories in Washington, D.C., found a temperature for Venus of about 600° F., in marked contrast to minus 125° F., previously found at the cloud tops. Subsequent radio work confirmed a high temperature and produced evidence for this temperature to be associated with the solid body of Venus. With this peculiarity in mind, space scientists devised experiments for the U.S. space probe Mariner 2 to perform when it flew by in 1962. Mariner 2 confirmed the high temperature and the fact that it pertained to the ground rather than to some special activity of the atmosphere. In addition, Mariner 2 was unable to detect any radiation belts similar to the earth's so-called Van Allen belts. Nor was it able to detect the existence of a magnetic field even as weak as 1/100,000 of that of the earth.

In 1967, a Russian space probe, Venera 4, and the American Mariner 5 arrived at Venus within a few hours of each other. Venera 4 was designed to allow an instrument package to land gently on the planet's surface via parachute. It ceased transmission of information in about 75 minutes when the temperature it read went above 500° F. After considerable controversy, it was agreed that it still had 20 miles to go to reach the surface. The U.S. probe, Mariner 5, went around the dark side of Venus at a distance of about 6,000 miles. Again, it detected no significant magnetic field but its radio signals passed to earth through Venus' atmosphere twice — once on the night side and once on the day side. The results are startling. Venus' atmosphere is nearly all carbon dioxide and must exert a pressure at the planet's surface of up to 100 times the earth's normal sea-level pressure of one atmosphere. Since the earth and Venus are about the same size, and were presumably formed at the same time by the same general process from the same mixture of chemical elements, one is faced with the question: Which is the planet with the unusual history — earth or Venus?

Radar astronomers using powerful transmitters as well as sensitive receivers and computers have succeeded in determining the rotation period of Venus. It turns out to be 243 days clockwise — in other words, contrary to the spin of most of the other planets and to its own motion around the sun. If it were exactly 243.16 days, Venus would always present the same face toward the earth at every inferior conjunction. This rate and sense of rotation allows a "day" on Venus of 117.4 earth days. Any part of Venus will receive sunlight on its clouds for over 58 days and will be in darkness for 58 days. Recent radar observations have shown surface features below the clouds. Large craters, continent-sized highlands, and extensive, dry "ocean" basins have been identified.

Mariner 10 passed Venus before traveling on to Mercury in 1974. The carbon dioxide molecule found in such abundance in the atmosphere is rather opaque to certain ultraviolet wavelengths, enabling sensitive television cameras to take pictures of the Venusian cloud cover. Photos radioed to earth show a spiral pattern in the clouds from equator to the poles.

In December, 1978, two U.S. Pioneer probes arrived at Venus. One went into orbit about Venus, the other split into 5 separate probes targeted for widely spaced entry points to sample different conditions. The instrumentation ensemble was selected on the basis of previous missions that had shown the range of conditions to be studied. The probes confirmed expected high surface temperatures and high winds aloft. Winds of about 200 miles per hour, there, may account for the transfer of heat into the night side in spite of the low rotation speed of the planet. Surface winds were light at the time, however. Atmosphere and cloud chemistries were examined in detail, providing much data for continued analysis. The probes detected 4 layers of clouds and more light on the surface than expected solely from sunlight. This light allowed Russian scientists to obtain at least two photos showing rocks on the surface. Sulphur seems to play a large role in the chemistry of Venus, and reactions involving sulphur may be responsible for the glow. To learn more about the weather and atmospheric circulation on Venus, the orbiter takes daily photos of the daylight side cloud cover. It confirms the cloud pattern and its circulation shown by Mariner 10. The ionosphere shows large variability. The orbiter's radar operates in 2 modes: one for ground elevation variability, and the second for ground reflectivity in 2 dimensions, thus "imaging" the surface. Radar maps of the entire planet that show the features mentioned above have been produced.

The Venus orbiter Magellan was launched May 5, 1989. It was equipped to observe Venus by a side-scanning radar system, together with one to gather data on variations in elevations directly beneath the craft. Magellan has mapped all but a small fraction of the planet. The side-looking radar illuminates the surface and its features with radio waves and records the strength and distance of returning echoes. Computer processing produces what seems to be a view of the landscape as if seen through a clear atmosphere from above, near sunset, with a resolution better than about a mile on Venus.

Craters over 20 miles wide are believed to have been caused by impacting bodies. One 150-mile-wide crater, the largest found to date, has been named for Margaret Mead. Smaller craters are probably due to volcanic action. The largest such caldera has been named Sakajawea. Many lava flows have been seen, and some old craters and plains seem to be filled with lava.

Most of the surface is believed to be younger than 1000 to 500 million years old. Modifications of previously existing surface features have been due to tectonic actions such as faulting, and to weathering. Tectonic actions in general are distinctly different from such actions on earth. The intense heat at the surface of Venus can prevent the surface materials from cooling to the same brittle condition as on earth. The same actions on earth, thus, may produce somewhat different results on Venus. Although there are deep regions, somewhat similar to our ocean basins, there is no water to fill them. There seems to be no activity on Venus similar to our moving tectonic plates, but there may be local stretching and compressing that produce rift valleys and higher plains and mountains. Although there is no weathering due to water on Venus, the action of winds is in evidence. Extensive sand dunes have been seen, and windblown deposits indicate stable wind patterns for very long periods of time.

Despite deterioration in the physical condition of the orbiter, Magellan continues to function in adapted capacities.

Mars

Mars is the first planet beyond the earth, away from the sun. Mars' diameter is about 4,200 miles, although a determination of the radius and mass of Mars by the space-probe Mariner 4, which flew by Mars on July 14, 1965, at a distance of less than 6,000 miles, indicated that these dimensions were slightly larger than had been previously estimated. While Mars' orbit is also nearly circular, it is somewhat more eccentric than the orbits of many of the other planets, and Mars is more than 30 million miles farther from the sun in some parts of its year than it is at others. Mars takes 687 of our days to make one circuit of the sun, traveling at about 15 miles a second. Mars rotates upon its axis in almost the same period of time that the earth does — 24 hours and 37 minutes. Mars' mean distance from the sun is 141 million miles, so that the temperature on Mars would be lower than that on the earth even if Mars' atmosphere were about the same as ours. The atmosphere is not, however, for Mariner 4 reported that atmospheric pressure on Mars is between 1% and 2% of the earth's atmospheric pressure. This thin atmosphere appears to be largely carbon dioxide. No evidence of free water was found.

There appears to be no magnetic field about Mars. This would eliminate the previous conception of a dangerous radiation belt around Mars. The same lack of a magnetic field would expose the surface of Mars to an influx of cosmic radiation about 100 times as intense as that on earth.

Deductions from years of telescopic observation indicate that 5/8ths of the surface of Mars is a desert of reddish rock, sand, and soil. The rest of Mars is covered by irregular patches that appear generally green in hues that change through the Martian year. These were formerly held to be some sort of primitive vegetation, but with the findings of Mariner 4 of a complete lack of water and oxygen, such growth does not appear possible. The nature of the green areas is now unknown. They may be regions covered with volcanic salts whose color changes with changing temperatures and atmospheric conditions, or they may be gray, rather than green. When large gray areas are placed beside large red areas, the gray areas will appear green to the eye.

Mars' axis of rotation is inclined from a vertical to the plane of its orbit about the sun by about 25° and therefore Mars has seasons as does the earth, except that the Martian seasons are longer because Mars' year is longer. White caps form about the winter pole of Mars, growing through the winter and shrinking in summer. These polar caps are now believed to be both water ice and carbon dioxide ice. It is the carbon dioxide that is seen to come and go with the seasons. The water ice is apparently in many layers with dust between them, indicating climatic cycles.

The canals of Mars have become more of a mystery than they were before the voyage of Mariner 4. Markings forming a network of fine lines crossing much of the surface of Mars have been seen there by men who have devoted much time to the study of the planet, but no canals have shown clearly enough in previous photographs to be universally accepted. A few of the 21 photographs sent back to earth by Mariner 4 covered areas crossed by canals. The pictures show faint, ill-defined, broad, dark markings, but no positive identification of the nature of the markings.

Mariners 6 & 7 in 1969 sent back many more photographs of higher quality than those of the pioneering Mariner 4. These pictures showed cratering similar to the earlier views, but in addition showed 2 other types of terrain. Some regions seemed featureless for many square miles, but others were chaotic, showing high relief without apparent organization into mountain chains or craters.

Mariner 9, the first artificial body to be placed in an orbit about Mars, has transmitted over 10,000 photographs covering 100% of the planet's surface. Preliminary study of these photos and other data shows that Mars resembles no other planet we know. Using terrestrial terms, however, scientists describe features that seem to be clearly of volcanic origin. One of these features is Nix Olympica (now called Olympus Mons), apparently a shield volcano whose caldera is over 50 miles wide, whose outer slopes are over 300 miles in diameter, and which stands about 90,000 feet above the surrounding plain. Some features may have been produced by cracking (faulting) of the surface and the sliding of one region over or past another. Many craters seem to have been produced by impacting bodies such as may have come from the nearby asteroid belt. Features near the south pole may have been produced by glaciers that are no longer present. Flowing water, nonexistent on Mars at the present time, probably carved canyons, one 10 times longer and 3 times deeper than the Grand Canyon.

Although the Russians landed a probe on the Martian surface, it transmitted for only 20 seconds. In 1976, the U.S. landed 2 Viking spacecraft on the Martian surface. The landers had devices aboard to perform chemical analyses of the soil in search of evidence of life. The results have been inconclusive. The 2 Viking orbiters have returned the best pictures yet of Martian topographic features. Many features can be explained only if Mars once had large quantities of flowing water.

Mars' position in its orbit and its speed around that orbit in relation to the earth's position and speed bring Mars fairly close to the earth on occasions about two years apart and then move Mars and the earth too far apart for accurate observation and photography. Every 15-17 years, the close approaches are especially favorable to close observation.

Mars has 2 satellites, discovered in 1877 by Asaph Hall. The outer satellite, Deimos, revolves around Mars in about 31 hours. The inner satellite, Phobos, whips around Mars in a little more than 7 hours, making 3 trips around the planet each Martian day. Mariner and Viking photos show these bodies to be irregularly shaped and pitted with numerous craters. Phobos also shows a system of linear grooves, each about 1/3-mile across and roughly parallel. Phobos measures about 8 by 12 miles and Deimos about 5 by 7.5 miles in size.

Jupiter

Jupiter is the largest of the planets. Its equatorial diameter is 88,000 miles, 11 times the diameter of the earth. Its polar diameter is about 6,000 miles shorter. This is an equilibrium condition resulting from the liquidity of the planet and its extremely rapid rate of rotation: a Jupiter day is only 10 earth hours long. For a planet this size, this rotational speed is amazing, and it moves a point on Jupiter's equator at a speed of 22,000 miles an hour, as compared with 1,000 miles an hour for a point on the earth's equator. Jupiter is at an average distance of 480 million miles from the sun and takes almost 12 of our years to make one complete circuit of the sun.

The only directly observable chemical constituents of Jupiter's atmosphere are methane (CH_4) and ammonia (NH_3), but it is reasonable to assume the same mixture of elements available to make Jupiter as to make the sun. This would mean a large fraction of hydrogen and helium must be present also, as well as water (H_2O). The temperature at the tops of the clouds may be about minus 260° F. The clouds are probably ammonia ice crystals, becoming ammonia droplets lower down. There may be a space before water ice crystals show up as clouds: in turn, these become water droplets near the bottom of the entire cloud layer. The total atmosphere may be only a few hundred miles in depth, pulled down by the surface gravity (= 2.64 times earth's) to a relatively thin layer. Of course, the gases become denser with depth until they may turn into a slush or a slurry. Perhaps there is no surface — no real interface between the gaseous atmosphere and the body of Jupiter. Pioneers 10 and 11 provided evidence for considering Jupiter to be almost entirely liquid hydrogen. Long before a rocky core about the size of the earth is reached, hydrogen mixed with helium becomes a liquid metal at very high temperature and pressure. Jupiter's cloudy atmosphere is a fairly good reflector of sunlight and makes it appear far brighter than any of the stars.

Fourteen of Jupiter's 17 or more satellites have been found through earth-based observations. Four of the moons are large and bright, rivaling our own moon and the planet Mercury in diameter, and may be seen through a field glass. They move rapidly around Jupiter and their change of position from night to night is extremely interesting to watch. The other satellites are much smaller and in all but one instance much farther from Jupiter and cannot be seen except through powerful telescopes. The 4 outermost satellites are revolving around Jupiter clockwise as seen from the north, contrary to the motions of the great majority of the satellites in the solar system and to the direction of revolution of the planets around the sun. The reason for this retrograde motion is not known, but one theory is that Jupiter's tremendous gravitational power may have captured 4 of the minor planets or asteroids that move about the sun between Mars and Jupiter, and that these would necessarily revolve backward. At the great distance of these bodies from Jupiter — some 14 million miles — direct motion would result in decay of the orbits, while retrograde orbits would be stable. Jupiter's mass is more than twice the mass of all the other planets put together, and accounts for Jupiter's tremendous gravitational field and so, probably, for its numerous satellites and its dense atmosphere.

In December 1973, Pioneer 10 passed about 80,000 miles from the equator of Jupiter and was whipped into a path that would take it beyond the system of planets on June 13, 1983, and out of our solar system in about 50 years. In December 1974, Pioneer 11 passed within 30,000 miles of Jupiter, moving roughly from south to north, over the poles.

Photographs from both encounters were useful at the time but were far surpassed by those of Voyagers I and II. Thousands of high resolution multi-color pictures show rapid variations of features both large and small. The Great Red Spot exhibits internal counterclockwise rotation. Much turbulence is seen in adjacent material passing north or south of it. The satellites Amalthea, Io, Europa, Ganymede, and Callisto were photographed, some in great detail. Each is individual and unique, with no similarities to other known planets or satellites. Io has active volcanoes that probably have ejected material into a doughnut-shaped ring enveloping its orbit about Jupiter. This is not to be confused with the thin flat disk-like ring closer to Jupiter's surface. Now that such a ring has been seen by the Voyagers, older uncertain observations from earth can be reinterpreted as early sightings of this structure.

Saturn

Saturn, last of the planets visible to the unaided eye, is almost twice as far from the sun as Jupiter, almost

900 million miles. It is second in size to Jupiter but its mass is much smaller. Saturn's specific gravity is less than that of water. Its diameter is about 71,000 miles at the equator; its rotational speed spins it completely around in a little more than 10 hours, and its atmosphere is much like that of Jupiter, except that its temperature at the top of its cloud layer is at least 100° F. lower. At about 300° F. below zero, the ammonia would be frozen out of Saturn's clouds. The theoretical construction of Saturn resembles that of Jupiter; it is either all gas, or it has a small dense center surrounded by a layer of liquid and a deep atmosphere.

Until Pioneer 11 passed Saturn in September 1979 only 10 satellites of the planet were known. Data retrieved since that time have confused scientists. Added to data interpretations from the fly-by are earth-based observations using techniques employed while the rings were edge-on and virtually invisible. It was hoped that the Voyager I and II fly-bys would help scientists sort out the satellite system, but it is still not entirely understood. It is now believed that Saturn has at least 22 satellites, some sharing orbits.

Saturn's ring system begins about 7,000 miles above the visible disk of Saturn, lying above its equator and extending about 35,000 miles into space. The diameter of the ring system visible from earth is about 170,000 miles; the rings are estimated to be no thicker than 10 miles. In 1973, radar observation showed the ring particles to be large chunks of material averaging a meter on a side.

Voyager I and II observations showed the rings to be considerably more complex than had been believed, so much so that interpretation will take much time. To the untrained eye, the Voyager photographs could be mistaken for pictures of a colorful phonograph record.

Uranus

Voyager II, after passing Saturn in August 1981, headed for a rendezvous with Uranus culminating in a fly-by January 24, 1986. This encounter answered many questions, and raised others.

Uranus, discovered by Sir William Herschel on Mar. 13, 1781, lies at a distance of 1.8 billion miles from the sun, taking 84 years to make its circuit around our star. Uranus has a diameter of about 32,000 miles and spins once in some 16.8 hours, according to fly-by data. One of the most fascinating features of Uranus is how far it is tipped over. Its north pole lies 98° from being directly up and down to its orbit plane. Thus, its seasons are extreme. When the sun rises at the north pole, it stays up for 42 years; then it sets and the north pole will be in darkness (and winter) for 42 years.

The satellite system of Uranus consists of at least 15 moons (the 5 largest having been known before the fly-by), which have orbits lying in the plane of the planet's equator. In that plane there is also a complex of rings, 9 of which were discovered in 1978. Invisible from earth, the 9 original rings were found by observers watching Uranus pass before a star. As they waited, they saw their photoelectric equipment register several short eclipses of the star. Then the planet occulted the star as expected. After the star came out from behind Uranus, the star winked out several more times. Subsequent observations and analyses indicated the 9 narrow, nearly opaque rings circling Uranus. Evidence from the Voyager II fly-by has shown the ring particles to be predominantly a yard or so in diameter.

In addition to the 10 new, very small satellites, Voyager II returned detailed photos of the 5 large satellites. As in the case of other satellites newly observed in the Voyager program, these bodies proved to be entirely different from each other and any others. Miranda has grooved markings, reminiscent of Jupiter's Ganymede, but often arranged in a chevron pattern. Ariel shows rifts and channels. Umbriel is extremely dark, prompting some observers to regard its surface as among the oldest in the system. Titania has rifts and fractures, but not the evidence of flow found on Ariel. Oberon's main feature is its surface saturated with craters, unrelieved by other formations.

The structure of Uranus is subject to some debate. Basically, however, it may have a rocky core surrounded by a thick icy mantle on top of which is a crust of hydrogen and helium that gradually becomes an atmosphere. Perhaps continued analysis of the wealth of data returned by Voyager II will shed some light on this problem.

Neptune

Neptune, currently the most distant planet from the sun (until 1999), lies at an average distance of 2.8 billion miles. It was the last planet visited in Voyager II's epic 12 year trek from earth. While much new information was immediately perceived, much more must await further analysis of the tremendous amount of data returned from the spacecraft.

As with the other giant planets, there may be no solid surface to give real meaning to a measure of a diameter. However, a mean value of 30,600 miles may be assigned to a diameter between atmosphere levels where the pressure is about the same as sea level on earth, as determined by radio experimenters. A different radio observational technique gave evidence of a rotation period for the bulk of Neptune of 16.1 hours, a shorter value than the 18.2 hours given by the clouds seen in the blue atmosphere. Neptune orbits the sun in 164 years in nearly a circular orbit.

Voyager II, which passed 3000 miles from Neptune's north pole, found a magnetic field that is considerably asymmetric to the planet's structure, similar, but not so extreme, to that found at Uranus.

Neptune's atmosphere was seen to be quite blue, with quickly changing white clouds often suspended high above an apparent surface. In that apparent surface were found features, one of which was reminiscent of the Great Red Spot of Jupiter, even to the counterclockwise rotation expected in a high-pressure system in the southern hemisphere. Atmospheric constituents are mostly hydrocarbon compounds. Although lightning and auroras have been found on other giant planets, only the aurora phenomenon has been seen on Neptune.

Six new satellites were discerned around Neptune, one confirming a 1981 sighting that was then difficult to recover for proper identification. Five of these satellites orbit Neptune in a half day or less. Of the eight satellites of Neptune, the largest, Triton, is in a retrograde orbit suggesting that it was captured rather than being coeval with Neptune. Triton's large size, sufficient to raise significant tides on Neptune, will one day, say 100 million years from now, cause Triton to come close enough to Neptune for it to be torn apart. Nereid was found in 1949, and is in a long looping orbit suggesting it, too, was captured. Each of the satellites that has been photographed by the two Voyagers in the planetary encounters has been different from any of the other satellites, and certainly from any of the planets. Only about half of Triton has been observed, but its terrain shows cratering and a strange regional feature described as resembling the skin of a cantaloupe. Triton has a tenuous atmosphere of nitrogen with a trace of hydrocarbons, and evidence of active geysers injecting material into it. At minus 238 degrees Celsius, Triton is one of the coldest objects in the solar system observed by Voyager II.

In addition to the satellite system, Voyager II confirmed the existence of at least three rings composed of very fine particles. There may some clumpiness in their structure, but the known satellites may not contribute to the formation or maintenance of the rings, as they have in other systems.

As with the other giant planets, Neptune is emitting more energy than it receives from the sun, Voyager finding the excess to be 2.7 times the solar contribution. These excesses are thought to be cooling from internal heat sources and from the heat of formation of the planets.

Pluto

Although Pluto on the average stays about 3.6 billion miles from the sun, its orbit is so eccentric that its minimum distance of 2.7 billion miles is less than the current distance of Neptune. Thus Pluto, until 1999, is temporarily planet number 8 from the sun. At its mean distance, Pluto takes 247.7 years to circumnavigate the sun, a 3/2 resonance with Neptune. Until recently that was about all that was known of Pluto.

About a century ago, a hypothetical planet was believed to lie beyond Neptune and Uranus because neither planet followed the paths predicted by astronomers even when all known gravitational influences were considered. Little more than a guess, a mass of one earth was assigned to the mysterious body and mathematical searches were begun. Amid some controversy about the validity of the predictive process, Pluto was found nearly where it was predicted to be. It was found by Clyde Tombaugh at the Lowell Observatory in Flagstaff, Ariz., in 1930.

At the U.S. Naval Observatory, also in Flagstaff, on July 2, 1978, James Christy obtained a photograph of Pluto that was distinctly elongated. Repeated observations of this shape and its variation were convincing evidence of the discovery of a satellite of Pluto, now named Charon. Subsequent observations show it to be 750 miles across, at a distance of over 12,000 miles from Pluto, and taking 6.4 days to move around Pluto. In this same length of time Pluto and Charon each rotate once around their individual axes. The Pluto-Charon system thus appears to rotate as virtually a ridged body. Gravitational laws allow these interactions to give us the mass of Pluto as 0.0020 of the earth. This mass, together with a new diameter for Pluto of 1,430 miles makes the density about twice that of water. Theorists predict a rocky core for Pluto surrounded by a thick mantle of ice.

It is now clear that Pluto, the body found by Tombaugh, could not have influenced Neptune and Uranus to go astray. Theorists are again at work looking for a new planet X.

Because the rotational axis of the system is tipped from the reference plane of the solar system by about 98°.3, similar to that of Uranus, there is only a short interval every half solar period when Pluto and Charon alternately eclipse each other. Analysis of the variations in light in and out of the recent eclipses has led to the diameters quoted above, and to interesting knowledge of other aspects of the system. Each component is approximately spherical, but they are otherwise different. Pluto is red, Charon grey. Charon has a surface identified as water ice; Pluto's surface is frozen methane. There are large regions on Pluto that are dark, others light; Pluto has spots, and, perhaps, polar caps. Although extremely cold, Pluto's methane surface produces a tenuous atmosphere that may be slowly escaping into space, perhaps going to Charon. When Pluto occulted a star, the star's light faded in such a way as to have passed through a haze layer lying above the planet's surface, indicating an inversion of temperatures, 110°K above, and 50°K below, suggesting Pluto has primitive weather.

There are tentative plans for a spacecraft reconnaissance of the Pluto system, thus completing direct, close-up observation of each of the planets of the solar system.

Greenwich Sidereal Time for 0^h GMT, 1994

(Add 12 hours to obtain Right Ascension of Mean Sun)

Date		h	m	Date		h	m	Date		h	m	Date		h	m
Jan.	1	06	41.7	Apr.	1	12	36.5	July	10	19	10.8	Oct.	8	01	05.6
	11	07	21.1		11	13	15.9		20	19	50.2		18	01	45.0
	21	08	0.5		21	13	55.4		30	20	29.6		28	02	24.4
	31	08	40.0	May	1	14	34.8	Aug.	9	21	09.0	Nov.	7	03	03.9
Feb.	10	09	19.4		11	15	14.2		19	21	48.5		17	03	43.3
	20	09	58.8		21	15	53.6		29	22	27.9		27	04	22.7
Mar.	2	10	38.2		31	16	33.1	Sept.	8	23	07.3	Dec.	7	05	02.1
	12	11	17.7	June	10	17	12.5		18	23	46.7		17	05	41.6
	22	11	57.1		20	17	51.9		28	00	26.2		27	06	21.0
					30	18	31.3								

Astronomical Signs and Symbols

☉	The Sun	⊕	The Earth	♅	Uranus	□	Quadrature
☽	The Moon	♂	Mars	♆	Neptune	☍	Opposition
☿	Mercury	♃	Jupiter	♇	Pluto	☊	Ascending Node
♀	Venus	♄	Saturn	☌	Conjunction	☋	Descending Node

Two heavenly bodies are in "conjunction" (☌) when they are due north and south of each other, either in Right Ascension (with respect to the north celestial pole) or in Celestial Longitude (with respect to the north ecliptic pole). If the bodies are seen near each other, they will rise and set at nearly the same time. They are in "opposition" (☍) when their Right Ascensions differ by exactly 12 hours, or their Celestial Longitudes differ by 180°. One of the two objects in opposition will rise while the other is setting. "Quadrature" (□) refers to the arrangement when the coordinates of two bodies differ by exactly 90°. These terms may refer to the relative positions of any two bodies as seen from the earth, but one of the bodies is so frequently the sun that mention of the sun is omitted; otherwise both bodies are named. The geocentric angular separation between sun and object is termed "elongation." Elongation is limited only for Mercury and Venus; the "greatest elongation" for each of these bodies is noted in the appropriate tables and is approximately the time for longest observation. When a planet is in its "ascending" (☊) or "descending" (☋) node, it is passing northward or southward, respectively, through the plane of the earth's orbit, across the celestial circle called the ecliptic. The term "perihelion" means nearest to the sun, and "aphelion," farthest from the sun. An "occultation" of a planet or star is an eclipse of it by some other body, usually the moon.

Planetary Configurations, 1994

Greenwich Mean Time (0 designates midnight; 12 designates noon; * = star; ☽ = moon)

Mo.	d. h. m.		
Jan.	2 06	-	⊕ closest to ☉; Perihelion
	3 20	- ☌ ☿ ☉	Superior Conj.
	6 22	- ☌ ♃ ☽	♃ 3° N
	11 08	- ☌ ♆ ☉	
	12 17	- ☌ ♅ ☉	
	15 00	- ☌ ♄ ☽	♄ 7° S
	17 02	- ☌ ♀ ☉	
Feb.	2 04	- ☌ ☿ ♄	☿ 1°.3 N
	3 08	- ☌ ♃ ☽	♃ 3° N
	4 21	-	☿ Gr Elong; 18° E of ☉
	8 08	- ☌ ♆ ☽	♆ 3° S
	8 12	- ☌ ♅ ☽	♅ 5° S
	10 18	-	☿ Stationary
	20 08	- ☌ ☿ ☉	Inferior Conj.
	21 17	- ☌ ♄ ☉	
	27 01	- ☌ ☿ ♂	☿ 4° N
	28 21	-	♃ Stationary
Mar.	2 16	- ☌ ♃ ☽	♃ 2° N
	4 01	-	♇ Stationary
	4 12	-	☿ Stationary
	7 16	- ☌ ♆ ☽	♆ 4° S
	7 21	- ☌ ♅ ☽	♅ 5° S
	10 04	- ☌ ☿ ☽	☿ 5° S
	10 23	- ☌ ♂ ☽	♂ 7° S
	11 04	- ☌ ♄ ☽	♄ 7° S
	13 17	- ☌ ♀ ☽	♀ 5° S
	14 10	- ☌ ♂ ♄	♂ 0°.4 N
	19 02	-	☿ Gr Elong; 28° W of ☉
	20 28	-	Vernal Equinox; Spring begins in Northern Hemisphere
	24 08	- ☌ ☿ ♄	☿ 0°.3 S
	29 23	- ☌ ♃ ☽	♃ 2° N
Apr.	3 22	- ☌ ♆ ☽	♆ 4° S
	4 02	- ☌ ☿ ♂	☿ 1°.5 S
	4 04	- ☌ ♅ ☽	♅ 5° S
	7 16	- ☌ ♄ ☽	♄ 7° S
	9 02	- ☌ ♂ ☽	♂ 6° S
	9 11	- ☌ ☿ ☽	☿ 7° S
	12 23	- ☌ ♀ ☽	♀ 1°.0 S; Occultation
	25 09	-	♆ Stationary
	26 05	- ☌ ♃ ☽	♃ 3° N
	30 09	- ☍ ♃ ☉	
	30 10	- ☌ ☿ ☉	Superior Conj.
May	1 01	-	♅ Stationary
	1 06	- ☌ ♆ ☽	♆ 4° S
	1 12	- ☌ ♅ ☽	♅ 5° S
	5 00	- ☌ ♀ *	♀ 6° N of Aldebaran
	5 03	- ☌ ♄ ☽	♄ 7° S
	8 04	- ☌ ♂ ☽	♂ 4° S
	10 17	- ☌ ☽ ☉	Annular Solar Eclipse
	13 06	- ☌ ♀ ☽	♀ 4° N
	15 11	- ☌ ☿ *	☿ 8° N of Aldebaran
	17 20	- ☍ ♇ ☉	
	23 11	- ☌ ♄ ☽	♃ 3° N
	25 04	- ☍ ☽ ☉	Partial Lunar Eclipse
	28 14	- ☌ ♆ ☽	♆ 4° S
	28 20	- ☌ ♅ ☽	♅ 5° S
	30 07	-	☿ Gr Elong; 23° E of ☉
June	1 12	- ☌ ♄ ☽	♄ 7° S
	6 05	- ☌ ♂ ☽	♂ 2° S
	10 05	- ☌ ♀ *	♀ 5° S of Pollux
	11 00	- ☌ ☿ ☽	☿ 3° N
	12 12	-	☿ Stationary
	12 13	- ☌ ♀ ☽	♀ 7° N
	19 16	- ☌ ♃ ☽	♃ 3° N
	21 14 48		Summer Solstice; Summer begins in Northern Hemisphere
	24 04	-	♄ Stationary
	24 23	- ☌ ♆ ☽	♆ 4° S
	25 05	- ☌ ♅ ☽	♅ 5° S
	25 10	- ☌ ☿ ☉	Inferior Conj.
	28 21	- ☌ ♄ ☽	♄ 7° S
July	2 16	-	♃ Stationary
	5 05	- ☌ ♂ ☽	♂ 0°.3 N; Occultation
	5 19	-	⊕ farthest from ☉; Aphelion
	6 20	-	☿ Stationary
	7 13	- ☌ ☿ ☽	☿ 1°.3 S
	10 17	- ☌ ♀ *	♀ 1°.1 N of Regulus
	12 12	- ☌ ♀ ☽	♀ 7° N
	14 16	- ☍ ♆ ☉	
	16 23	- ☌ ♃ ☽	♃ 3° N
	17 04	- ☍ ♅ ☉	
	17 14	-	☿ Gr Elong; 21° W of ☉
	18 21	- ☌ ♂ *	♂ 5° N of Aldebaran
	22 07	- ☌ ♆ ☽	♆ 4° S
	22 12	- ☌ ♅ ☽	♅ 5° S
	26 04	- ☌ ♄ ☽	♄ 7° S
	31 07	- ☌ ☿ *	☿ 6° S of Pollux
Aug.	3 04	- ☌ ♂ ☽	♂ 3° N
	9 14	-	♇ Stationary
	10 23	- ☌ ♀ ☽	♀ 3° N
	13 01	- ☌ ☿ ☉	Superior Conj.
	13 07	- ☌ ♃ ☽	♃ 2° N
	18 14	- ☌ ♆ ☽	♆ 4° S
	18 18	- ☌ ♅ ☽	♅ 5° S
	22 10	- ☌ ♄ ☽	♄ 7° S
	24 23	-	♀ Gr Elong; 46° E of ☉
	31 21	- ☌ ♀ *	♀ 0°.7 S of Spica
Sept.	1 03	- ☌ ♂ ☽	♂ 4° N
	1 17	- ☍ ♄ ☉	
	7 09	- ☌ ☿ ☽	☿ 3° N
	9 01	- ☌ ♀ ☽	♀ 2° S
	9 20	- ☌ ♃ ☽	♃ 1°.4 N
	14 19	- ☌ ♆ ☽	♆ 4° S
	14 23	- ☌ ♅ ☽	♅ 5° S
	18 13	- ☌ ♄ ☽	♄ 7° S
	21 13	- ☌ ☿ *	☿ 0°.1 S of Spica
	23 06 19		Autumnal Equinox; Autumn begins in Northern Hemisphere
	24 15	- ☌ ♂ *	♂ 6° S of Pollux
	26 16	-	☿ Gr Elong; 26° E of ☉
	28 22	-	♀ Gr Brilliancy
	29 22	- ☌ ♂ ☽	♂ 6° N
Oct.	2 03	-	♅ Stationary
	2 14	-	♆ Stationary
	6 18	- ☌ ☿ ☽	☿ 3° S
	7 10	- ☌ ♀ ☽	♀ 7° S
	7 12	- ☌ ♃ ☽	♃ 0°.7 N; Occultation
	9 09	-	☿ Stationary
	12 01	- ☌ ♆ ☽	♆ 4° S
	12 04	- ☌ ♅ ☽	♅ 5° S
	12 23	-	♀ Stationary
	15 16	- ☌ ♄ ☽	♄ 7° S
	21 05	- ☌ ☿ ☉	Inferior Conj.
	28 13	- ☌ ♂ ☽	♂ 7° N
	29 17	-	☿ Stationary
Nov.	2 10	- ☌ ☿ ☽	☿ 4° N
	2 23	- ☌ ♀ ☉	Inferior Conj.
	3 01	- ☌ ☿ *	☿ 4° N of Spica
	3 14	- ☌ ☽ ☉	Total Solar Eclipse
	6 01	-	☿ Gr Elong; 19° W of ☉
	8 08	- ☌ ♆ ☽	♆ 4° S
	8 12	- ☌ ♅ ☽	♅ 6° S
	9 21	-	♄ Stationary
	11 21	- ☌ ♄ ☽	♄ 7° S
	12 18	- ☌ ☿ ♀	☿ 5° N
	17 20	- ☌ ♃ ☉	
	18 07	- ☍ ☽ ☉	Penumbral Lunar Eclipse
	20 13	- ☌ ♇ ☉	
	25 20	- ☌ ♂ ☽	♂ 8° N
	30 14	- ☌ ♀ ☽	♀ 2° N
Dec.	5 19	- ☌ ♆ ☽	♆ 4° S
	6 00	- ☌ ♅ ☽	♅ 6° S
	8 08	- ☌ ♂ *	♂ 2° N of Regulus
	9 05	- ☌ ♄ ☽	♄ 7° S
	9 11	-	♀ Gr Brilliancy
	14 03	- ☌ ☿ ☉	Superior Conj.
	22 02 23		Winter Solstice; Winter begins in Northern Hemisphere
	23 15	- ☌ ♂ ☽	♂ 9° N
	29 05	- ☌ ♀ ☽	♀ 3° N
	30 00	- ☌ ♃ ☽	♃ 1°.1 S; Occultation

Rising and Setting of Planets, 1994

Greenwich Mean Time (0 designates midnight)

Venus, 1994

		20° N. Latitude Rise	Set	30° N. Latitude Rise	Set	40° N. Latitude Rise	Set	50° N. Latitude Rise	Set	60° N. Latitude Rise	Set
Jan.	1	6:21	17:14	6:43	16:52	7:10	16:25	7:48	15:47	8:57	14:38
	11	6:35	17:31	6:56	17:10	7:21	16:44	7:58	16:08	9:02	15:04
	21	6:46	17:48	7:04	17:30	7:27	17:07	8:00	16:35	8:54	15:40
	31	6:53	18:05	7:08	17:50	7:28	17:31	7:54	17:05	8:37	16:22
Feb.	10	6:57	18:22	7:09	18:10	7:23	17:55	7:43	17:36	8:14	17:05
	20	6:58	18:37	7:06	18:29	7:16	18:20	7:28	18:07	7:48	17:48
Mar.	2	6:58	18:51	7:01	18:47	7:06	18:43	7:11	18:38	7:20	18:30
	12	6:56	19:04	6:56	19:05	6:55	19:07	6:53	19:08	6:50	19:12
	22	6:55	19:18	6:50	19:23	6:43	19:30	6:34	19:39	6:21	19:53
Apr.	1	6:54	19:31	6:45	19:41	6:33	19:53	6:17	20:10	5:51	20:36
	11	6:55	19:46	6:41	20:00	6:24	20:17	6:01	20:41	5:23	21:20
	21	6:58	20:02	6:41	20:19	6:19	20:41	5:48	21:12	4:57	22:05
May	1	7:04	20:18	6:43	20:39	6:18	21:05	5:41	21:42	4:35	22:48
	11	7:13	20:34	6:50	20:57	6:21	21:26	5:40	22:08	4:22	23:26
	21	7:25	20:49	7:01	21:13	6:31	21:43	5:47	22:27	4:23	23:51
	31	7:39	21:01	7:15	21:25	6:46	21:54	6:02	22:37	4:40	23:59
June	10	7:53	21:11	7:32	21:32	7:04	22:00	6:24	22:39	5:12	23:50
	20	8:08	21:16	7:49	21:35	7:25	21:59	6:50	22:33	5:51	23:30
	30	8:21	21:18	8:05	21:34	7:45	21:53	7:18	22:20	6:33	23:04
July	10	8:32	21:16	8:20	21:28	8:06	21:42	7:45	22:02	7:13	22:34
	20	8:42	21:12	8:34	21:19	8:24	21:29	8:11	21:41	7:50	22:01
	30	8:49	21:05	8:46	21:08	8:41	21:12	8:35	21:18	8:26	21:27
Aug.	9	8:55	20:56	8:56	20:55	8:56	20:54	8:57	20:53	8:59	20:51
	19	8:59	20:45	9:04	20:40	9:10	20:34	9:18	20:26	9:30	20:13
	29	9:01	20:33	9:10	20:24	9:21	20:13	9:36	19:57	9:59	19:34
Sept.	8	9:00	20:19	9:13	20:06	9:29	19:50	9:51	19:28	10:25	18:53
	18	8:55	20:02	9:11	19:45	9:32	19:25	10:00	18:56	10:47	18:09
	28	8:42	19:40	9:02	19:20	9:26	18:56	10:00	18:22	10:59	17:23
Oct.	8	8:19	19:10	8:40	18:48	9:07	18:21	9:45	17:43	10:53	16:35
	18	7:40	18:29	8:01	18:07	8:28	17:40	9:07	17:01	10:16	15:52
	28	6:42	17:37	7:02	17:18	7:27	16:53	8:01	16:19	9:01	15:19
Nov.	7	5:36	16:43	5:52	16:27	6:12	16:08	6:39	15:40	7:24	14:56
	17	4:37	15:57	4:49	15:44	5:04	15:29	5:25	15:09	5:58	14:36
	27	3:55	15:22	4:05	15:12	4:18	15:00	4:35	14:42	5:01	14:16
Dec.	7	3:29	14:58	3:39	14:48	3:51	14:36	4:07	14:20	4:32	13:55
	17	3:15	14:42	3:26	14:31	3:39	14:18	3:56	14:00	4:24	13:32
	27	3:09	14:32	3:22	14:19	3:37	14:04	3:57	13:43	4:30	13:11

Mars, 1994

		20° N. Latitude Rise	Set	30° N. Latitude Rise	Set	40° N. Latitude Rise	Set	50° N. Latitude Rise	Set	60° N. Latitude Rise	Set
Jan.	1	6:32	17:23	6:54	17:01	7:22	16:34	8:01	15:55	9:11	14:44
	11	6:25	17:18	6:46	16:57	7:13	16:31	7:50	15:53	8:57	14:47
	21	6:17	17:14	6:37	16:54	7:02	16:29	7:37	15:54	8:38	14:53
	31	6:08	17:10	6:26	16:51	6:49	16:28	7:21	15:57	8:15	15:03
Feb.	10	5:57	17:06	6:14	16:49	6:34	16:29	7:02	16:01	7:49	15:14
	20	5:46	17:01	6:00	16:47	6:18	16:29	6:42	16:05	7:21	15:26
Mar.	2	5:33	16:57	5:45	16:45	6:00	16:30	6:20	16:10	6:51	15:39
	12	5:20	16:51	5:29	16:42	5:41	16:31	5:56	16:15	6:21	15:51
	22	5:06	16:46	5:12	16:39	5:21	16:31	5:32	16:20	5:49	16:03
Apr.	1	4:51	16:40	4:55	16:36	5:00	16:31	5:07	16:24	5:17	16:14
	11	4:35	16:34	4:37	16:32	4:39	16:31	4:41	16:29	4:45	16:25
	21	4:20	16:27	4:19	16:29	4:17	16:30	4:15	16:33	4:12	16:36
May	1	4:04	16:21	4:01	16:25	3:56	16:30	3:50	16:36	3:40	16:47
	11	3:49	16:14	3:43	16:21	3:35	16:29	3:24	16:40	3:07	16:57
	21	3:34	16:07	3:25	16:16	3:14	16:27	2:59	16:43	2:35	17:07
	31	3:19	16:01	3:07	16:12	2:53	16:26	2:34	16:46	2:04	17:17
June	10	3:04	15:54	2:51	16:07	2:34	16:24	2:11	16:48	1:33	17:26
	20	2:50	15:47	2:35	16:03	2:15	16:22	1:48	16:50	1:03	17:35
	30	2:37	15:40	2:20	15:57	1:58	16:19	1:27	16:50	0:35	17:43
July	10	2:24	15:32	2:05	15:52	1:41	16:16	1:07	16:50	0:09	17:49
	20	2:12	15:25	1:52	15:45	1:26	16:11	0:50	16:48	23:43	17:53
	30	2:01	15:16	1:39	15:37	1:12	16:05	0:34	16:43	23:22	17:53
Aug.	9	1:49	15:07	1:28	15:29	1:00	15:57	0:20	16:37	23:05	17:50
	19	1:38	14:56	1:16	15:19	0:48	15:47	0:07	16:27	22:52	17:42
	29	1:27	14:45	1:05	15:07	0:37	15:35	23:56	16:15	22:42	17:30
Sept.	8	1:16	14:32	0:54	14:54	0:27	15:21	23:46	16:01	22:34	17:13
	18	1:04	14:18	0:43	14:39	0:16	15:06	23:37	15:44	22:29	16:52
	28	0:51	14:02	0:31	14:22	0:06	14:48	23:28	15:24	22:25	16:28
Oct.	8	0:38	13:45	0:18	14:04	23:53	14:28	23:19	15:02	22:21	16:01
	18	0:23	13:27	0:05	13:45	23:41	14:07	23:09	14:39	22:15	15:33
	28	0:06	13:06	23:48	13:23	23:27	13:44	22:58	14:13	22:09	15:03
Nov.	7	23:47	12:44	23:31	13:00	23:12	13:19	22:44	13:47	22:00	14:31
	17	23:26	12:21	23:12	12:35	22:54	12:53	22:29	13:18	21:48	13:59
	27	23:04	11:55	22:50	12:09	22:33	12:25	22:10	12:49	21:32	13:27
Dec.	7	22:38	11:27	22:25	11:40	22:09	11:56	21:47	12:18	21:12	12:53
	17	22:09	10:56	21:56	11:09	21:41	11:24	21:20	11:45	20:46	12:19
	27	21:35	10:22	21:23	10:35	21:08	10:50	20:47	11:11	20:13	11:44

Jupiter, 1994

		20° N. Latitude Rise	20° N. Latitude Set	30° N. Latitude Rise	30° N. Latitude Set	40° N. Latitude Rise	40° N. Latitude Set	50° N. Latitude Rise	50° N. Latitude Set	60° N. Latitude Rise	60° N. Latitude Set
Jan.	1	2:07	13:30	2:18	13:18	2:33	13:03	2:52	12:44	3:23	12:13
	11	1:34	12:55	1:46	12:43	2:01	12:28	2:21	12:08	2:53	11:36
	21	1:00	12:20	1:12	12:08	1:27	11:52	1:48	11:32	2:21	10:59
	31	0:25	11:44	0:37	11:32	0:53	11:16	1:14	10:55	1:48	10:21
Feb.	10	23:45	11:07	*0:01	10:55	0:17	10:39	0:39	10:17	1:13	9:43
	20	23:07	10:30	23:20	10:17	23:36	10:01	*0:02	9:39	0:36	9:04
Mar.	2	22:28	9:51	22:41	9:38	22:57	9:22	23:19	9:00	23:53	8:26
	12	21:48	9:11	22:01	8:58	22:17	8:42	22:38	8:20	23:12	7:46
	22	21:06	8:30	21:19	8:17	21:34	8:01	21:56	7:40	22:29	7:06
Apr.	1	20:23	7:48	20:36	7:35	20:51	7:20	21:12	6:59	21:45	6:26
	11	19:40	7:05	19:52	6:53	20:07	6:38	20:27	6:17	20:59	5:45
	21	18:55	6:21	19:07	6:10	19:21	5:55	19:41	5:35	20:12	5:04
May	1	18:10	5:38	18:22	5:26	18:36	5:12	18:55	4:53	19:25	4:23
	11	17:25	4:54	17:37	4:43	17:50	4:29	18:09	4:11	18:38	3:42
	21	16:41	4:11	16:52	4:00	17:05	3:47	17:23	3:29	17:51	3:01
	31	15:57	3:28	16:08	3:18	16:21	3:05	16:38	2:47	17:06	2:20
June	10	15:15	2:46	15:25	2:36	15:38	2:23	15:55	2:06	16:22	1:39
	20	14:33	2:05	14:44	1:55	14:56	1:42	15:13	1:25	15:39	0:59
	30	13:53	1:25	14:03	1:15	14:16	1:02	14:33	0:45	14:59	0:19
July	10	13:14	0:46	13:25	0:35	13:37	0:23	13:54	0:06	14:21	23:35
	20	12:37	0:08	12:47	23:53	13:00	23:41	13:17	23:23	13:44	22:56
	30	12:00	23:27	12:11	23:16	12:24	23:03	12:42	22:45	13:09	22:17
Aug.	9	11:25	22:50	11:36	22:39	11:50	22:26	12:08	22:08	12:36	21:39
	19	10:51	22:15	11:02	22:04	11:16	21:50	11:35	21:31	12:05	21:01
	29	10:18	21:40	10:29	21:28	10:44	21:14	11:04	20:54	11:35	20:23
Sept.	8	9:45	21:06	9:57	20:54	10:12	20:39	10:33	20:18	11:05	19:46
	18	9:13	20:33	9:26	20:20	9:42	20:04	10:03	19:43	10:37	19:09
	28	8:42	20:00	8:56	19:47	9:12	19:30	9:34	19:08	10:10	18:32
Oct.	8	8:12	19:27	8:26	19:14	8:43	18:56	9:06	18:33	9:44	17:55
	18	7:42	18:55	7:56	18:41	8:14	18:23	8:38	17:59	9:18	17:19
	28	7:12	18:24	7:27	18:09	7:45	17:50	8:11	17:25	8:52	16:43
Nov.	7	6:42	17:52	6:58	17:37	7:17	17:17	7:43	16:51	8:26	16:08
	17	6:13	17:21	6:29	17:05	6:49	16:45	7:16	16:17	8:01	15:32
	27	5:43	16:50	6:00	16:33	6:20	16:13	6:49	15:44	7:36	14:57
Dec.	7	5:14	16:19	5:31	16:02	5:52	15:40	6:21	15:11	7:10	14:22
	17	4:44	15:48	5:01	15:30	5:23	15:08	5:54	14:38	6:44	13:48
	27	4:14	15:16	4:32	14:58	4:54	14:36	5:25	14:05	6:17	13:13
				*2nd Rise 23:58				*2nd Set 23:58			

Saturn, 1994

		20° N. Latitude Rise	20° N. Latitude Set	30° N. Latitude Rise	30° N. Latitude Set	40° N. Latitude Rise	40° N. Latitude Set	50° N. Latitude Rise	50° N. Latitude Set	60° N. Latitude Rise	60° N. Latitude Set
Jan.	1	9:34	20:56	9:46	20:44	10:00	20:30	10:20	20:10	10:51	19:39
	11	8:58	20:21	9:09	20:10	9:24	19:55	9:43	19:36	10:13	19:06
	21	8:22	19:47	8:33	19:35	8:47	19:22	9:06	19:03	9:35	18:34
	31	7:47	19:12	7:57	19:01	8:11	18:48	8:29	18:30	8:57	18:02
Feb.	10	7:11	18:38	7:22	18:28	7:34	18:15	7:52	17:58	8:19	17:30
	20	6:36	18:04	6:46	17:54	6:58	17:42	7:15	17:25	7:41	16:59
Mar.	2	6:00	17:30	6:10	17:20	6:22	17:08	6:38	16:53	7:03	16:28
	12	5:25	16:56	5:34	16:47	5:46	16:35	6:01	16:20	6:25	15:56
	22	4:49	16:22	4:58	16:13	5:09	16:02	5:24	15:47	5:47	15:24
Apr.	1	4:14	15:47	4:22	15:38	4:33	15:28	4:47	15:14	5:09	14:52
	11	3:38	15:12	3:46	15:04	3:56	14:54	4:10	14:40	4:31	14:19
	21	3:02	14:37	3:10	14:29	3:19	14:19	3:32	14:06	3:53	13:46
May	1	2:25	14:01	2:33	13:54	2:42	13:44	2:55	13:32	3:14	13:12
	11	1:48	13:25	1:56	13:18	2:05	13:08	2:17	12:56	2:36	12:37
	21	1:11	12:48	1:18	12:41	1:27	12:32	1:39	12:20	1:58	12:02
	31	0:33	12:11	0:40	12:04	0:49	11:55	1:01	11:43	1:19	11:25
June	10	23:51	11:33	*0:02	11:26	0:11	11:17	0:22	11:05	0:40	10:47
	20	23:12	10:54	23:19	10:47	23:28	10:38	23:40	10:27	*0:01	10:09
	30	22:33	10:15	22:40	10:07	22:49	9:59	23:00	9:47	23:18	9:29
July	10	21:53	9:34	22:00	9:27	22:09	9:18	22:21	9:06	22:39	8:48
	20	21:13	8:54	21:20	8:46	21:29	8:37	21:41	8:25	22:00	8:06
	30	20:32	8:12	20:39	8:05	20:49	7:55	21:01	7:43	21:20	7:24
Aug.	9	19:51	7:30	19:58	7:22	20:08	7:13	20:21	7:00	20:41	6:40
	19	19:09	6:48	19:17	6:40	19:27	6:30	19:40	6:17	20:01	5:56
	29	18:28	6:05	18:36	5:57	18:46	5:47	19:00	5:33	19:21	5:12
Sept.	8	17:46	5:23	17:54	5:14	18:05	5:04	18:19	4:50	18:41	4:28
	18	17:04	4:40	17:13	4:31	17:24	4:21	17:38	4:06	18:01	3:44
	28	16:23	3:58	16:32	3:49	16:43	3:38	16:58	3:23	17:21	3:00
Oct.	8	15:42	3:16	15:51	3:07	16:02	2:56	16:17	2:41	16:41	2:17
	18	15:01	2:35	15:10	2:26	15:22	2:14	15:37	1:59	16:01	1:35
	28	14:20	1:55	14:30	1:45	14:42	1:33	14:57	1:18	15:21	0:54
Nov.	7	13:41	1:15	13:50	1:05	14:02	0:54	14:17	0:38	14:42	0:14
	17	13:02	0:36	13:11	0:26	13:23	0:15	13:38	23:55	14:02	23:31
	27	12:23	23:53	12:32	23:44	12:44	23:33	12:59	23:17	13:23	22:53
Dec.	7	11:45	23:16	11:54	23:07	12:05	22:55	12:20	22:40	12:44	22:17
	17	11:07	22:39	11:16	22:30	11:27	22:19	11:42	22:04	12:05	21:41
	27	10:30	22:03	10:39	21:54	10:50	21:43	11:04	21:29	11:26	21:07
				*2nd Rise 23:58						*2nd Rise 23:57	

Calculation of Risetimes

The *Daily Calendar* pages contain rise and set times for the sun and moon for the Greenwich Meridian at north latitudes 20°, 30°, 40°, 50°, and 60°. You probably live somewhere west of the Greenwich meridian, 0° longitude, and within the range of latitudes in the table. Notice that from day to day, the values for the sun at any particular latitude do not change very much. This slow variation for the sun means that no important correction needs to be made from one day to the next, once a proper correction for your latitude has been made. Thus, whenever it rises or sets at the 0° meridian, that will also be the time of that phenomenon at your Standard Time meridian. Any correction necessary for you to be able to observe that phenomenon from your location will be to account for your distance from the Standard Time meridian, and for your latitude.

The moon, however, moves its own diameter, about a half degree, in an hour, or about 12°.5 in one complete turn of the earth—one day. Most of this is eastward against the background stars of the sky, but some is also north or south of the equator. If there is little change on the same day of the times over the range of latitudes, the moon is near the celestial equator. All of this motion considerably affects the times of rise or set, as you can see from the adjacent entries in the table. Thus, it is necessary also to take your longitude into account in addition to your latitude. If you have no need for total accuracy, simply note that the time will be between the four values you find surrounding your location and the dates of interest.

The process of finding more accurate corrections is called interpolation. In the example, linear interpolation involving simple differences is used. In extreme cases, higher order interpolation should be used. If such cases are important to you, it is suggested that you make a plot of the times, draw smooth curves through the plots, and interpolate by eye between the relevant curves. Some people find this exercise fun.

Let's find the time of the June Full Moon in Brandon, Manitoba.

First, where is Brandon? Find Brandon's latitude and longitude on page 262.

I. Brandon, Manitoba 49° 51′ 00″ N
99° 57′ 00″ W

IA. Convert these values to decimals:
51 / 60 = 0°.85
49 + .85 = 49°.85
57 / 60 = 0°.95
99 + .95 = 99°.95

IB. Fraction Brandon lies between 50° and 60°:
49°.85 − 40° = 9.85; 9.85 / 10 = .985

IC. Fraction world must turn between Greenwich and Brandon:
99.95 / 360 = .278

ID. The CST meridian is 90°, thus 99°.95 is 99.95 − 90 = 9.95 degrees west of the CST. In 24 hours, there are 24 × 60 = 1440 minutes; 1440 / 360 = 4 minutes for every degree around the earth. So events happen
4 × 9.95 = 40
minutes later for Brandon than on the CST meridian of 90°.

IE. The values IB and IC are interpolates for Brandon; ID is the time correction from local to Standard time for Brandon. These values need never be calculated for Brandon again.

IIA. We need the Greenwich times for moonrise at latitudes 50° and 60°, and for June 23 and 24, the day of Full Moon and the next day.

	50°	Diff.	60°
June 23	20:04	55	20:59
June 24	20:48	45	21:33

IIB. We want IB and the June 23 time difference:
.985 × 55 = 54
Add this to the June 23 time:
20:04 + 54 = 20:58
And for June 24:
.985 × 45 = 44
Add this to the June 24 rise time:
20:48 + 44 = 21:32
These two times are for the latitude of Brandon, but for the Greenwich meridian.

IIC. To get the time for Brandon, take the difference in the times just determined,
21:32 − 20:58 = 34
and find what fraction of this one day difference occurred while the earth turned from Greenwich to Brandon, .278:
.278 × 34 = 9.4 minutes after 20:58
Thus, 20:58 + 9 = 21:07, the time the moon will rise at the 90° CST meridian, at the latitude of Brandon.

IID. Events happen at Brandon 40 later than at the 90° meridian, therefore
21:07 + 40 = 21:47 CST at Brandon on June 23. However, the date is in the Daylight Time period, so we must add a 1 hour correction. Finally, Brandon's moonrise is 22:47 CDT on June 23, 1994.

Star Tables

These tables include stars of visual magnitude 2.5 and brighter. Coordinates are for mid-1994. Where no parallax figures are given, the trigonometric parallax figure is smaller than the margin for error and the distance given is obtained by indirect methods. Stars of variable magnitude designated by v.

To find the time when the star is on meridian, subtract Right Ascension of Mean Sun from the sidereal time table on page 235 from the star's right ascension, first adding 24h to the latter, if necessary. Mark this result P.M., if less than 12h; but if greater than 12, subtract 12h and mark the remainder A.M.

Star	Magnitude	Parallax ″	Light yrs.	Right ascen. h. m.	Declination ° ′
α Andromedae (Alpheratz)	2.06	0.02	90	0 08.1	29 04
β Cassiopeiae	2.27v	0.07	45	0 08.9	59 07
α Phoenicis	2.39	0.04	93	0 26.0	−42 20

Star	Magnitude	Parallax ″	Light yrs.	Right ascen. h. m.	Declination ° ′
α Cassiopeiae (Schedir)	2.23	0.01	150	0 40.2	56 30
β Ceti	2.04	0.06	57	0 43.3	−18 01
γ Cassiopeiae	2.47v	0.03	96	0 56.4	60 41
β Andromedae	2.06	0.04	76	1 09.4	35 35
α Eridani (Achernar)	0.46	0.02	118	1 37.5	−57 16
γ Andromedae	2.26		260	2 03.5	42 18
α Arietis	2.00	0.04	76	2 06.9	23 28
o Ceti	2.00v	0.01	103	2 19.1	−3 00
α Ursae Min. (Pole Star)	2.02v		680	2 25.8	89 14
β Persei (Algol)	2.12v	0.03	105	3 07.8	40 56
α Persei	1.80	0.03	570	3 23.9	49 51
α Tauri (Aldebaran)	0.85v	0.05	68	4 35.6	16 30
β Orionis (Rigel)	0.12v		900	5 14.3	−8 12
α Aurigae (Capella)	0.08	0.07	45	5 16.3	46 00
γ Orionis (Bellatrix)	1.64	0.03	470	5 24.8	6 21
β Tauri (El Nath)	1.65	0.02	300	5 25.9	28 36
δ Orionis	2.23v		1500	5 31.7	−0 18
ε Orionis	1.70		1600	5 36.0	−1 12
ζ Orionis	2.05	0.02	1600	5 40.5	−1 57
κ Orionis	2.06	0.01	2100	5 47.5	−9 40
α Orionis (Betelgeuse)	0.50v		520	5 54.9	7 24
β Aurigae	1.90	0.04	88	5 59.1	44 57
β Canis Majoris	1.98	0.01	750	6 22.5	−17 57
α Carinae (Canopus)	−0.72	0.02	98	6 23.8	−52 42
γ Geminorum	1.93	0.03	105	6 37.4	16 24
α Canis Majoris (Sirius)	−1.46	0.38	8.7	6 44.9	−16 42
ε Canis Majoris	1.50		680	6 58.4	−28 58
δ Canis Majoris	1.86		2100	7 08.2	−26 23
η Canis Majoris	2.44		2700	7 23.9	−29 18
α Geminorum (Castor)	1.99	0.07	45	7 34.2	31 54
α Canis Minoris (Procyon)	0.38	0.29	11.3	7 39.0	5 14
β Geminorum (Pollux)	1.14	0.09	35	7 45.0	28 02
ζ Puppis	2.25		2400	8 03.4	−39 59
γ Velorum	1.82		520	8 09.4	−47 19
ε Carinae	1.86		340	8 22.4	−59 30
δ Velorum	1.96	0.04	76	8 44.6	−54 41
λ Velorum	2.21	0.02	750	9 07.8	−43 25
β Carinae	1.68	0.04	86	9 13.1	−69 42
ι Carinae	2.25		750	9 16.9	−59 15
κ Velorum	2.50	0.01	470	9 21.9	−54 59
α Hydrae	1.98	0.02	94	9 27.3	−8 38
α Leonis (Regulus)	1.35	0.04	84	10 08.1	12 00
γ Leonis	1.90	0.02	90	10 19.7	19 55
β Ursae Majoris (Merak)	2.37	0.04	78	11 01.5	56 25

Star	Magnitude	Parallax ″	Light yrs.	Right ascen. h. m.	Declination ° ′
α Ursae Majoris (Dubhe)	1.70	0.03	105	11 03.4	61 47
β Leonis (Denebola)	2.14	0.08	43	11 48.8	14 36
γ Ursae Majoris (Phecda)	2.44	0.02	90	11 53.5	53 44
α Crucis	1.58		370	12 26.3	−63 04
γ Crucis	1.63		220	12 30.9	−57 05
γ Centauri	2.17		160	12 41.2	−48 56
β Crucis	1.25v		490	12 47.4	−59 40
ε Ursae Majoris (Alioth)	1.77v	0.01	68	12 53.8	55 59
ζ Ursae Majoris (Mizar)	2.05	0.04	88	13 23.7	54 57
α Virginis (Spica)	0.97v	0.02	220	13 24.9	−11 08
ε Centauri	2.30v		570	13 39.5	−53 26
η Ursae Majoris (Alkaid)	1.86		210	13 47.3	49 20
β Centauri	0.61v	0.02	490	14 03.4	−60 21
θ Centauri	2.06	0.06	55	14 06.4	−36 21
α Bootis (Arcturus)	−0.04	0.09	36	14 15.4	19 13
η Centauri	2.31v		390	14 35.2	−42 08
α Centauri	−0.01	0.75	4.3	14 39.2	−60 49
α Lupi	2.30v		430	14 41.6	−47 22
ε Bootis	2.40	0.01	103	14 44.7	27 06
β Ursae Minoris	2.08	0.03	105	14 50.7	74 11
α Coronae Borealis	2.23v	0.04	76	15 34.5	26 44
δ Scorpii	2.32		590	16 00.0	−22 36
α Scorpii (Antares)	0.96v	0.02	520	16 29.1	−26 25
α Trianguli Australis	1.92	0.02	82	16 48.1	−69 01
ε Scorpii	2.29	0.05	66	16 49.8	−34 17
η Ophiuchi	2.43	0.05	69	17 10.1	−15 43
λ Scorpii	1.63v		310	17 33.2	−37 06
α Ophiuchi	2.08	0.06	58	17 34.7	12 34
θ Scorpii	1.87	0.02	650	17 36.9	−43 00
κ Scorpii	2.41v		470	17 42.1	−39 02
γ Draconis	2.23	0.02	108	17 56.5	51 29
ε Sagittarii	1.85	0.02	124	18 23.8	−34 23
α Lyrae (Vega)	0.03	0.12	26.5	18 36.8	38 47
σ Sagittarii	2.02		300	18 54.9	−26 18
α Aquilae (Altair)	0.77	0.20	16.5	19 50.5	8 51
γ Cygni	2.20		750	20 22.0	40 14
α Pavonis	1.94		310	20 25.2	−56 45
α Cygni (Deneb)	1.25		1600	20 41.2	45 16
ε Cygni	2.46	0.04	74	20 46.0	33 57
α Cephei	2.44	0.06	52	21 18.4	62 34
ε Pegasi	2.39		780	21 43.9	9 51
α Gruis	1.74	0.05	64	22 07.9	−46 59
β Gruis	2.11v		280	22 42.3	−46 55
α Piscis Austrinis (Fomalhaut)	1.16	0.14	22.6	22 57.3	−29 39
β Pegasi	2.42v	0.02	210	23 03.5	28 03
α Pegasi	2.49	0.03	109	23 04.5	15 11

Astronomical Constants; Speed of Light

The following were adopted in 1968, in accordance with the resolutions and recommendations of the International Astronomical Union (Hamburg 1964): Speed of light, 299,792.5 kilometers per second, or about 186,282.3976 statute miles per second; solar parallax, 8″.794; constant of nutation, 9″.210; and constant of aberration, 20″.496.

Constellations

Culturally, constellations are imagined patterns among the stars that, in some cases, have been recognized through millenia of tradition. In the early days of astronomy, knowledge of the constellations was necessary in order to function as an astronomer. For today's astronomers, constellations are simply areas on the entire sky in which interesting objects await observation and interpretation.

Because western culture has prevailed in establishing modern science, equally viable and interesting constellations and celestial traditions of other cultures (of Asia or Africa, for example) are not well known outside of their regions of origin. Even the patterns with which we are most familiar today have undergone considerable change over the centuries, because the western heritage embraces teachings of cultures disparate in time as well as place.

Today, students of the sky the world over recognize 88 constellations that cover the entire celestial sphere. Many of these have their origins in ancient days; many are "modern," contrived out of unformed stars by astronomers a few centuries ago. Unformed stars were those usually too faint or inconveniently placed to be included in depicting the more prominent constellations. When astronomers began to travel to South Africa in the 16th and 17th centuries, they found a sky that itself was unformed, and showing numerous brilliant stars. Thus, we find constellations in the southern hemisphere like the "air pump," the "microscope," the "furnace," and other technological marvels of the time, as well as some arguably traditional forms, such as the "fly."

Many of the commonly recognized constellations had their origins in ancient Asia Minor—Syria, Babylon, etc. These were adopted by the Greeks and Romans who translated their names and stories into their own languages, some details being modified in the process. After the declines of these cultures, most such knowledge entered oral tradition, or remained hidden in monastic libraries. Beginning in the 8th century, the Moslem explosion spread through the Mediterranean world. Wherever possible, everything was translated into Arabic to be taught in the universities the Moslems established all over their new-found world.

In the 13th century, Alphonsus XX of Spain, an avid student of astronomy, succeeded in having Claudius Ptolemy's *Almagest*, as its Arabian title was known, translated into Latin. It thus became widely available to European scholars. In the process, the constellation names were translated, but the star names were retained in their Arabic forms. Transliterating Arabic into the Roman alphabet has never been an exact art, so many of the star names we use today only "seem" Arabic to all but scholars.

Names of stars often indicated what parts of the traditional figures they represented: Deneb, the tail of the swan; Betelgeuse, the armpit of the giant. Thus, the names were an indication of the position in the sky of a particular star, provided one recognized the traditional form of the mythic figure.

In English, usage of the Latin names for the constellations couples often inconceivable creatures, represented in unimaginable configurations, with names that often seem unintelligible. Avoiding traditional names, astronomers may designate the brighter stars in a constellation with Greek letters, usually in order of brightness. Thus, the "alpha star" is often the brightest star of that constellation. The "of" implies possession, so the genetive (possessive) form of the constellation name is used, as in Alpha Orionis, the first star of Orion (Betelgeuse). Astronomers usually use a 3-letter form for the constellation name, understanding it to be read as either the nominative or genitive case of the name.

Until the 1920's, astronomers used curved boundaries for the constellation areas. As these were rather arbitrary at best, the International Astronomical Union adopted boundaries that ran due north-south and east-west, filling the sky much as the contiguous states fill up the area of the "lower 48" United States.

Within these boundaries, and occasionally crossing them, popular "asterisms" are recognized: the Big Dipper is a small part of Ursa Major, the big bear; the Sickle is the traditional head and mane of Leo, the lion; one of the horntips of Taurus, the bull, properly belongs to Auriga, the charioteer; the northeast star of the Great Square of Pegasus is Alpha Andromedae.

It is unlikely that further change will occur in the realm of the celestial constellations.

Name	Genitive	Abbreviation	Meaning
Andromeda	Andromedae	And	Chained Maiden
Antlia	Antliae	Ant	Air Pump
Apus	Apodis	Aps	Bird of Paradise
Aquarius	Aquarii	Aqr	Water Bearer
Aquila	Aquilae	Aql	Eagle
Ara	Arae	Ara	Altar
Aries	Arietis	Ari	Ram
Auriga	Aurigae	Aur	Charioteer
Bootes	Bootis	Boo	Herdsmen
Caelum	Caeli	Cae	Chisel
Camelopardalis	Camelopardalis	Cam	Giraffe
Cancer	Cancri	Cnc	Crab
Canes Venatici	Canum Venaticorum	CVn	Hunting Dogs
Canis Major	Canis Majoris	CMa	Great Dog
Canis Minor	Canis Minoris	CMi	Little Dog
Capricornus	Capricorni	Cap	Sea-goat
Carina	Carinae	Car	Keel
Cassiopeia	Cassiopeiae	Cas	Queen
Centaurus	Centauri	Cen	Centaur
Cepheus	Cephei	Cep	King
Cetus	Ceti	Cet	Whale
Chamaeleon	Chamaeleontis	Cha	Chameleon
Circinus	Circini	Cir	Compasses (art)
Columba	Columbae	Col	Dove
Coma Berenices	Comae Berenices	Com	Berenice's Hair
Corona Australis	Coronae Australis	CrA	Southern Crown
Corona Borealis	Coronae Borealis	CrB	Northern Crown
Corvus	Corvi	Crv	Crow
Crater	Crateris	Crt	Cup
Crux	Crucis	Cru	Cross (southern)
Cygnus	Cygni	Cyg	Swan
Delphinus	Delphini	Del	Dolphin
Dorado	Doradus	Dor	Goldfish
Draco	Draconis	Dra	Dragon
Equuleus	Equulei	Equ	Little Horse
Eridanus	Eridani	Eri	River
Fornax	Fornacis	For	Furnace
Gemini	Geminorum	Gem	Twins
Grus	Gruis	Gru	Crane (bird)
Hercules	Herculis	Her	Hercules
Horologium	Horologii	Hor	Clock
Hydra	Hydrae	Hya	Water Snake (female)
Hydrus	Hydri	Hyi	Water Snake (male)
Indus	Indi	Ind	Indian
Lacerta	Lacertae	Lac	Lizard
Leo	Leonis	Leo	Lion
Leo Minor	Leonis Minoris	LMi	Little Lion
Lepus	Leporis	Lep	Hare
Libra	Librae	Lib	Balance
Lupus	Lupi	Lup	Wolf
Lynx	Lyncis	Lyn	Lynx
Lyra	Lyrae	Lyr	Lyre
Mensa	Mensae	Men	Table Mountain
Microscopium	Microscopii	Mic	Microscope
Monoceros	Monocerotis	Mon	Unicorn
Musca	Muscae	Mus	Fly
Norma	Normae	Nor	Square (rule)
Octans	Octantis	Oct	Octant
Ophiuchus	Ophiuchi	Oph	Serpent Bearer
Orion	Orionis	Ori	Hunter
Pavo	Pavonis	Pav	Peacock
Pegasus	Pegasi	Peg	Flying Horse
Perseus	Persei	Per	Hero
Phoenix	Phoenicis	Phe	Phoenix
Pictor	Pictoris	Pic	Painter
Pisces	Piscium	Psc	Fishes
Piscis Austrinius	Piscis Austrini	PsA	Southern Fish
Puppis	Puppis	Pup	Stern (deck)
Pyxis	Pyxidis	Pyx	Compass (sea)
Reticulum	Reticuli	Ret	Reticle
Sagitta	Sagittae	Sge	Arrow
Sagittarius	Sagittarii	Sgr	Archer
Scorpius	Scorpii	Sco	Scorpion
Sculptor	Sculptoris	Scl	Sculptor
Scutum	Scuti	Sct	Shield
Serpens	Serpentis	Ser	Serpent
Sextans	Sextantis	Sex	Sextant
Taurus	Tauri	Tau	Bull
Telescopium	Telescopii	Tel	Telescope
Triangulum	Trianguli	Tri	Triangle
Triangulum Australe	Trianguli Australis	TrA	Southern Triangle
Tucana	Tucanae	Tuc	Toucan
Ursa Major	Ursae Majoris	UMa	Great Bear
Ursa Minor	Ursae Minoris	UMi	Little Bear
Vela	Velorum	Vel	Sail
Virgo	Virginis	Vir	Maiden
Volans	Volantis	Vol	Flying Fish
Vulpecula	Vulpeculae	Vul	Fox

Aurora Borealis and Aurora Australis

The Aurora Borealis, also called the Northern Lights, is a broad display of rather faint light in the northern skies at night. The Aurora Australis, a similar phenomenon, appears at the same time in southern skies. The aurora appears in a wide variety of forms. Sometimes it is seen as a quiet glow, almost foglike in character; sometimes as vertical streamers in which there may be considerable motion; sometimes as a series of luminous expanding arcs. There are many colors, with white, yellow, and red predominating.

The auroras are most vivid and most frequently seen at about 20 degrees from the magnetic poles, along the northern coast of the North American continent and the eastern part of the northern coast of Europe. They have been seen as far south as Key West and as far north as Australia and New Zealand, but rarely.

While the cause of the auroras is not known beyond question, there does seem to be a definite correlation between auroral displays and sun-spot activity. It is thought that atomic particles expelled from the sun by the forces that cause solar flares speed through space at velocities of 400 to 600 miles per second. These particles are entrapped by the earth's magnetic field, forming what are termed the Van Allen belts. The encounter of these clouds of the solar wind with the earth's magnetic field weakens the field so that previously trapped particles are allowed to impact the upper atmosphere. The collisions between solar and terrestrial atoms result in the glow in the upper atmosphere called the aurora. The glow may be vivid where the lines of magnetic force converge near the magnetic poles.

The auroral displays appear at heights ranging from 50 to about 600 miles and have given us a means of estimating the extent of the earth's atmosphere.

The auroras are often accompanied by magnetic storms whose forces, also guided by the lines of force of the earth's magnetic field, disrupt electrical communication.

Eclipses, 1994

There are four eclipses, two of the sun and two of the moon.

I. Annular eclipse of the sun, May 10.

The partial phases of this eclipse are visible throughout North America, from south of Panama to beyond the North Pole, including far eastern Siberia, Bering Strait, Greenland, Iceland, the Scandinavian Peninsula, and as a sunset phenomenon in parts of western Europe and western Africa; the Hawaiian Islands experience a partial phase at sunrise.

The path of annularity begins in the eastern Pacific Ocean, southeast of Hawaii, passes over the middle of the Baja Peninsula, enters the United States at El Paso, passes through central Missouri, over Lakes Erie and Ontario, central New York state, portions of New England, and portions of the Canadian Maritime Provinces.

Circumstances of the Eclipse

Event	Date		h	m
Eclipse begins	May	10	14	12.2
Central Eclipse begins		10	15	23.3
Central Eclipse at local noon		10	17	19.8
Central Eclipse ends		10	18	59.5
Eclipse ends		10	20	10.6

Maximum Duration: 6 min 08.5 sec.

II. Partial eclipse of the moon, May 25.

The beginning of the umbral phase is generally visible in the United States (except for the far west, Alaska, and Hawaii), southeastern and central Canada, Mexico, Central America, South America, the southern tip of Greenland, Iceland, most of Antarctica, most of Africa, most of Europe, the southeastern North Pacific Ocean, the eastern South Pacific Ocean, the Atlantic Ocean, and the southwestern Indian Ocean. The end of the umbral phase is generally visible in the United States (except Alaska and Hawaii), Canada (except for the northwest), Mexico, Central America, South America, the southern tip of Greenland, most of Antarctica, southern and western Africa, the southern United Kingdom, southern and western France, the Iberian Peninsula, the southeastern North Pacific Ocean, the eastern South Pacific Ocean, and the Atlantic Ocean.

Circumstances of the Eclipse

Event	Date		h	m
Moon enters penumbra	May	25	1	17.9
Moon enters umbra		25	2	37.3
Middle of eclipse		25	3	30.3
Moon leaves umbra		25	4	23.3
Moon leaves penumbra		25	5	42.7

Magnitude of the eclipse: 0.249

III. Total eclipse of the sun, November 3.

The partial phases are visible in South America, parts of Antarctica including the Palmer Peninsula, and parts of southern Africa.

The path of totality begins in the eastern Pacific Ocean, enters South America in southern Peru, crosses northern Chile, parts of Argentina, Paraguay, and southern Brazil, and the South Atlantic Ocean. The path of totality ends south of Madagascar.

Circumstances of the Eclipse

Event	Date		h	m
Eclipse begins	Nov.	3	11	05.0
Central Eclipse begins		3	12	02.7
Central Eclipse at local noon		3	13	47.1
Central Eclipse ends		3	15	15.4
Eclipse ends		3	16	13.1

Maximum duration: 4 min 27.6 sec.

IV. Penumbral eclipse of the moon, November 18.

The beginning of the penumbral phases generally visible in North America, Greenland, Iceland, the Arctic regions, Central America, South America, Hawaii, western Africa, Europe, extreme western Asia, the Palmer Peninsula of Antarctica, the eastern Pacific Ocean, and most of the Atlantic Ocean. The end is generally visible in North America, Greenland, Iceland, the Arctic regions, Central America, western South America, Hawaii, northeastern Asia, eastern Australia, New Zealand, the Pacific Ocean, and the western North Atlantic Ocean.

Circumstances of the Eclipse

Event	Date		h	m
Moon enters penumbra	Nov.	18	4	25.7
Middle of eclipse		18	6	43.9
Moon leaves penumbra		18	9	02.1

Penumbral magnitude of the eclipse: 0.908.

Transit of Mercury, 1993

A transit of Mercury over the face of the sun will occur on November 6.

The beginning of the transit will be generally visible in the Hawaiian Islands, the Aleutians Islands except the eastern end, Siberia except the northeastern tip, western Pacific Ocean, New Zealand, Australia, the Indian Ocean, Asia, Antarctica except the Palmer Peninsula, the southeastern Arabian Peninsula, and extreme eastern Africa. The end is generally visible in Asia, Siberia except the eastern end, the western Pacific Ocean, New Zealand, Australia, Antarctica except the Palmer Peninsula, the Indian Ocean, Africa east of the South Atlantic coast, Turkey, and the southern former USSR from the western Black Sea.

Geocentric Circumstances of the Transit

Event	Date		h	m
Ingress, exterior contact	Nov.	6	3	05.9
Ingress, interior contact		6	3	11.8
Least angular distance from Sun's center		6	3	56.6
Egress, interior contact		6	4	41.4
Egress, exterior contact		6	4	47.2

Least angular distance: 15′16″.7

The Planets and the Solar System

Planet	Mean daily motion ″	Orbital velocity miles per sec.	Sidereal revolution days	Synodical revolution days	Dist. from sun in millions of mi. Max.	Min.	Dist. from Earth in millions of mi. Max.	Min.	Light at[1] perihelion	aphelion
Mercury . .	14732	29.75	88.0	115.9	43.4	28.6	136	50	10.58	4.59
Venus . . .	5768	21.76	224.7	583.9	67.7	66.8	161	25	1.94	1.89
Earth	3548	18.51	365.3	—	94.6	91.4	—	—	1.03	0.97
Mars	1886	14.99	687.0	779.9	155.0	128.5	248	35	0.524	0.360
Jupiter . . .	299	8.12	4331.8	398.9	507.0	460.6	600	368	0.0408	0.0336
Saturn . . .	120	5.99	10760.0	378.1	937.5	838.4	1031	745	0.01230	0.00984
Uranus . . .	42	4.23	30684.0	369.7	1859.7	1669.3	1953	1606	0.00300	0.00250
Neptune . .	21	3.38	60188.3	367.5	2821.7	2760.4	2915	2667	0.00114	0.00109
Pluto	14	2.95	90466.8	366.7	4551.4	2756.4	4644	2663	0.00114	0.00042

1. Light at perihelion and aphelion is solar illumination in units of mean illumination at Earth.

Planet	Mean longitude of:* ascending node °	′	″	perihelion °	′	″	Inclination* of orbit to ecliptic °	′	″	Mean* distance**	Eccentricity* of orbit	Mean longitude at the epoch* °	′	″
Mercury. . . .	48	16	4	77	22	24	7	0	18	.387098	.205307	214	37	25
Venus.	76	37	55	131	29	21	3	23	41	.732333	.006774	306	33	46
Earth	0	0	0	102	50	45	0	0	0	1.000001	.016711	343	52	31
Mars	49	31	1	335	57	44	1	50	59	1.523679	.093396	56	22	37
Jupiter	100	24	36	14	14	44	1	18	13	5.202603	.048486	232	42	23
Saturn	113	37	8	92	57	8	2	29	21	9.554910	.055527	344	56	27
Uranus	73	58	42	172	55	34	0	46	23	19.218450	.046297	291	10	12
Neptune . . .	131	43	31	48	2	52	1	46	14	30.110390	.008988	292	38	33
Pluto*** . . .	110	13	37	224	0	32	17	8	9	39.810100	.254949	229	37	8

* Consistent for the standard Epoch: 1994 September 5 Ephemeris Time. ** Astronomical units *** Consistent for the standard Epoch: 1993 August 1 Ephemeris Time.

Sun and planets	Semi-diameter at unit distance ′ ″	Semi-diameter at mean least dist. ′ ″	Semi-diameter in miles mean s.d.	Volume ⊕=1.	Mass. ⊕=1.	Density ⊕=1.	Sidereal period of rotation d.	h.	m.	s.	Gravity at surface ⊕=1.	Reflecting power Pct.	Probable temperature °F.
Sun.	959.62	____	432449	1299370	332946	0.26	24	16	48		27.9	____	+10,000
Mercury . . .	3.37	5.5	1515	0.0559	0.0553	1.00	58	15	30		0.37	0.11	+ 620
Venus	8.34	30.1	3760	0.8541	0.8150	0.97	243	R			0.88	0.65	+ 900
Earth	____	____	3963	1.000	1.000	1.00		23	56	6.7	1.00	0.37	+ 72
Moon.	2.40	932.4	1080	0.020	0.0123	0.62	27	7	43		0.17	0.12	− 10
Mars	4.69	8.95	2108.5	0.1506	0.1074	0.73		24	37	26	0.38	0.15	− 10
Jupiter	98.35	23.4	44419	1403	317.89	0.25		9	3	30	2.64	0.52	− 240
Saturn	82.83	9.7	37448	832	95.18	0.13		10	39	22	1.15	0.47	− 300
Uranus	35.4	1.9	15881	63	14.54	0.23		17	14	R	1.15	0.40	− 340
Neptune . . .	33.4	1.2	15387	55	17.15	0.30		16	6		1.12	0.35	− 370
Pluto	1.9	0.05	714	0.006	0.0020	0.37	6	9	17		0.04	0.5	? ?

(R) retrograde of Venus and Uranus.

The Sun

The sun, the controlling body of our solar system, is a star whose dimensions cause it to be classified among stars as average in size, temperature, and brightness. Its proximity to the earth makes it appear to us as tremendously large and bright. A series of thermo-nuclear reactions involving the atoms of the elements of which it is composed produces the heat and light that make life possible on earth.

The sun has a diameter of 864,000 miles and is distant, on the average, 92,900,000 miles from the earth. It is 1.41 times as dense as water. The light of the sun reaches the earth in 499.012 seconds or slightly more than 8 minutes. The average solar surface temperature has been measured by several indirect methods that agree closely on a value of 6,000° Kelvin or about 10,000° F. The interior temperature of the sun is about 35,000,000° F.

When sunlight is analyzed with a spectroscope, it is found to consist of a continuous spectrum composed of all the colors of the rainbow in order, crossed by many dark lines. The "absorption lines" are produced by gaseous materials in the atmosphere of the sun. More than 60 of the natural terrestrial elements have been identified in the sun, all in gaseous form because of the intense heat of the sun.

Spheres and Corona

The radiating surface of the sun is called the **photosphere,** and just above it is the **chromosphere.** The chromosphere is visible to the naked eye only at times of total solar eclipses, appearing then to be a pinkish-violet layer with occasional great prominences projecting above its general level. With proper instruments the chromosphere can be seen or photographed whenever the sun is visible without waiting for a total eclipse. Above the chromosphere is the **corona,** also visible to the naked eye only at times of total eclipse. Instruments also permit the brighter portions of the corona to be studied whenever conditions are favorable. The pearly light of the corona surges millions of miles from the sun. Iron, nickel, and calcium are believed to be principal contributors to the composition of the corona, all in a state of extreme attenuation and high ionization that indicates temperatures on the order of a million degrees Fahrenheit.

Sunspots

There is an intimate connection between sunspots and the corona. At times of low sunspot activity, the fine streamers of the corona will be much longer above the sun's equator than over the polar regions of the sun, while during high sunspot activity, the corona extends fairly evenly outward from all regions of the sun, but to a much greater distance in space. Sunspots are dark, irregularly-shaped regions whose diameters may reach tens of thousands of miles. The average life of a sunspot group is from two to three weeks, but there have been groups that have lasted for more than a year, being carried repeatedly around as the sun rotated upon its axis. The record for the duration of a sunspot is 18 months. Sunspots reach a low point every 11.3 years, with a peak of activity occurring irregularly between two successive minima.

The sun is 400,000 times as bright as the full moon and gives the earth 6 million times as much light as do all the other stars put together. Actually, most of the stars that can be easily seen on any clear night are brighter than the sun.

The Zodiac

The sun's apparent yearly path among the stars is known as the **ecliptic.** The zone, 16° wide, 8° on each side of the ecliptic, is known as the **zodiac.** Inside of this zone are the apparent paths of the sun, moon, earth, and major planets. Beginning at the point on the ecliptic that marks the position of the sun at the vernal equinox, and thence proceeding eastward, the zodiac is divided into twelve signs of 30° each, as shown herewith.

These signs are named from the twelve constellations of the zodiac with which the signs coincided in the time of the astronomer Hipparchus, about 2,000 years ago. Owing to the precession of the equinoxes, that is to say, to the retrograde motion of the equinoxes along the ecliptic, each sign in the zodiac has, in the course of 2,000 years, moved backward 30° into the constellation west of it; so that the sign Aries is now in the constellation Pisces, and so on. The vernal equinox will move from Pisces into Aquarius about the middle of the 26th century. The signs of the zodiac with their Latin and English names are as follows:

Spring	1.	♈ Aries.	The Ram.
	2.	♉ Taurus.	The Bull.
	3.	♊ Gemini.	The Twins.
Summer	4.	♋ Cancer.	The Crab.
	5.	♌ Leo.	The Lion.
	6.	♍ Virgo.	The Virgin.
Autumn	7.	♎ Libra.	The Balance.
	8.	♏ Scorpius.	The Scorpion.
	9.	♐ Sagittarius.	The Archer.
Winter	10.	♑ Capricorn.	The Goat.
	11.	♒ Aquarius.	The Water Bearer.
	12.	♓ Pisces.	The Fishes.

Twilight

Twilight is that evening period of waning light from the time of sunset to dark, often termed dusk. Morning twilight, a time of increasing light, is called dawn. The source of this light is the sun shining on the atmosphere above the observer. Twilight is a time of very slowly changing sky illumination with no abrupt variations. Nevertheless, there are three commonly accepted divisions in this smooth continuum defined by the distance the sun lies below the astronomical horizon: civil twilight, nautical twilight, and astronomical twilight. The astronomical horizon is that great circle lying 90° from the zenith, the point directly over the observer's head. Twilight ends in the evening or begins in the morning at a particular time. Nominally, evening events are repeated in reverse order in the morning.

Civil twilight is the time between the moment of sunset, when the sun's apparent upper edge is just at the horizon until the center of the sun is 6° directly below the horizon. In many states, this is the time in the evening when automobile headlights must be turned on, not to see better, but to be seen by other drivers. After this time, a newspaper becomes increasingly difficult to read.

Nautical twilight ends when the sun's center is 12° below the horizon. By this time in the evening, the bright stars used by navigators have appeared and the horizon may still be seen. After this time, the horizon is more difficult to perceive, preventing navigators from making star sights.

Astronomical twilight ends in the evening when the sun is 18° below the horizon, and the sky is dark enough, at least away from the sun's location, to allow astronomical work to proceed. Sunlight, however, is still shining on the higher levels of the atmosphere from the observer's zenith to the horizon toward the sun. Although not named as a period of twilight, when the sun is 24° below the horizon, no part of the observer's atmosphere, even toward the sun, receives any sunlight.

In the tropics, the sun moves nearly vertically accomplishing its 6°, 12°, or 18° depression very quickly. In the polar regions, the sun's diurnal motion may actually be nearly along the horizon, prolonging the twilight period, or even not permitting darkness to fall at all. In mid-latitudes, civil twilight may last about a half hour, nautical, an hour, and astronomers can go to work in about 90 minutes.

The twilight tables given in The World Almanac are for astronomical twilight, and presented for reference only. Although the instant of the sun's horizontal depression may be calculated precisely, the phenomena associated with the event are sufficiently imprecise that the table is not recalculated each year.

Moon's Perigee and Apogee, 1994

Perigee						Apogee					
Month	Day	h	Month	Day	h	Month	Day	h	Month	Day	h
Jan.. . .	6	1	July	18	18	Jan.	19	5	July	30	23
Jan.. . .	31	4	Aug..	12	23	Feb.	16	2	Aug..	27	18
Feb.. . .	27	22	Sept.	8	14	Mar.	15	17	Sept.	24	12
Mar. . .	28	6	Oct.	6	14	Apr.	12	0	Oct.	22	2
Apr.. . .	25	17	Nov..	4	0	May	9	2	Nov..	18	5
May. . .	24	3	Dec..	2	12	June.	5	13	Dec..	15	8
June . .	21	7	Dec..	30	23	July	3	5			
Perihelion						Aphelion					
Jan.	2	6				July	5	16			

Moon Phases, 1994

Greenwich Mean Time

New Moon				First Q				Full Moon				Last Q			
Month	Day	h	m	Month	Day	h	m	Month	Day	h	m	Month	Day	h	m
												Jan.	5	00	00
Jan.	11	23	10	Jan.	19	20	27	Jan.	27	13	23	Feb.	3	08	06
Feb.	10	14	30	Feb.	18	17	47	Feb.	26	01	15	Mar.	4	16	53
Mar.	12	07	05	Mar.	20	12	14	Mar.	27	11	09	Apr.	3	02	55
Apr.	11	00	17	Apr.	19	02	34	Apr.	25	19	45	May	2	14	32
May	10	17	07	May	18	12	50	May	25	03	39	June	1	04	02
June	9	08	26	June	16	19	56	June	23	11	33	June	30	19	31
July	8	21	37	July	16	01	12	July	22	22	16	July	30	12	40
Aug.	7	08	45	Aug.	14	05	57	Aug.	21	06	47	Aug.	29	06	41
Sept.	5	18	33	Sept.	12	11	34	Sept.	19	20	00	Sept.	28	00	23
Oct.	5	03	55	Oct.	11	19	17	Oct.	19	12	18	Nov.	27	16	44
Nov.	3	13	35	Nov.	10	06	14	Nov.	18	06	57	Nov.	26	07	04
Dec.	2	23	54	Dec.	9	21	06	Dec.	18	02	17	Dec.	25	19	06

The Moon

The moon completes a circuit around the earth in a period whose mean or average duration is 27 days 7 hours 43.2 minutes. This is the moon's sidereal period. Because of the motion of the moon in common with the earth around the sun, the mean duration of the lunar month — the period from one new moon to the next new moon — is 29 days 12 hours 44.05 minutes. This is the moon's synodical period.

The mean distance of the moon from the earth according to the American Ephemeris is 238,857 miles. Because the orbit of the moon about the earth is not circular but elliptical, however, the maximum distance from the earth that the moon may reach is 252,710 miles and the least distance is 221,463 miles. All distances are from the center of one object to the center of the other.

The moon's diameter is 2,160 miles. If we deduct the radius of the moon, 1,080 miles, and the radius of the earth, 3,963 miles from the minimum distance or perigee, given above, we shall have for the nearest approach of the bodies' surfaces 216,420 miles.

The moon rotates on its axis in a period of time exactly equal to its sidereal revolution about the earth — 27.321666 days. The moon's revolution about the earth is irregular because of its elliptical orbit. The moon's rotation, however, is regular and this, together with the irregular revolution, produces what is called "libration in longitude," which permits us to see first farther around the east side and then farther around the west side of the moon. The moon's variation north or south of the ecliptic permits us to see farther over first one pole and then the other of the moon; this is called "libration in latitude." These two libration effects permit us to see a total of about 60% of the moon's surface over a period of time. The hidden side of the moon was photographed in 1959 by the Soviet space vehicle Lunik III. Since then many excellent pictures of nearly all of the moon's surface have been transmitted to earth by Lunar Orbiters launched by the U.S.

The tides are caused mainly by the moon, because of its proximity to the earth. The ratio of the tide-raising power of the moon to that of the sun is 11 to 5.

Harvest Moon and Hunter's Moon

The Harvest Moon, the full moon nearest the Autumnal Equinox, ushers in a period of several successive days when the moon rises soon after sunset. This phenomenon gives farmers in temperate latitudes extra hours of light in which to harvest their crops before frost and winter come. The 1993 Harvest Moon falls on Sept. 19 GMT. Harvest Moon in the south temperate latitudes falls on Mar. 27.

The next full moon after Harvest Moon is called the Hunter's Moon, accompanied by a similar phenomenon but less marked; — Oct. 19, northern hemisphere; May 25, southern hemisphere.

The Earth: Size, Computation of Time, Seasons

Size and Dimensions

The earth is the fifth largest planet and the third from the sun. Its mass is 6 sextillion, 588 quintillion short tons. Using the parameters of an ellipsoid adopted by the International Astronomical Union in 1964 and recognized by the International Union of Geodesy and Geophysics in 1967, the length of the equator is 24,901.55 miles, the length of a meridian is 24,859.82 miles, the equatorial diameter is 7,926.41 miles, and the area of this reference ellipsoid is approximately 196,938,800 square miles.

The earth is considered a solid, rigid mass with a dense core of magnetic, probably metallic material. The outer part of the core is probably liquid. Around the core is a thick shell or mantle of heavy crystalline rock that in turn is covered by a thin crust forming the solid granite and basalt base of the continents and ocean basins. Over broad areas of the earth's surface the crust has a thin cover of sedimentary rock such as sandstone, shale, and limestone formed by weathering of the earth's surface and deposition of sands, clays, and plant and animal remains.

The temperature in the earth increases about 1° F. with every 100 to 200 feet in depth, in the upper 100 kilometers of the earth, and the temperature near the core is believed to be near the melting point of the core materials under the conditions at that depth. The heat of the earth is believed to be derived from radioactivity in the rocks, pressures developed within the earth, and original heat (if the earth in fact was formed at high temperatures).

Atmosphere of the Earth

The earth's atmosphere is a blanket composed of nitrogen, oxygen, and argon, in amounts of about 78%, 21%, and 1% by volume. Also present in minute quantities are carbon dioxide, hydrogen, neon, helium, krypton, and xenon.

Water vapor displaces other gases and varies from nearly zero to about 4% by volume. The height of the **ozone** layer varies from approximately 12 to 21 miles above the earth. Traces exist as low as 6 miles and as high as 35 miles. Traces of methane have been found.

The atmosphere rests on the earth's surface with the weight equivalent to a layer of water 34 ft. deep. For about 300,000 ft. upward the gases remain in the proportions stated. Gravity holds the gases to the earth. The weight of the air compresses it at the bottom, so that the greatest density is at the earth's surface. Pressure, as well as density, decreases as height increases because the weight pressing upon any layer is always less than that pressing upon the layers below.

The temperature of the air drops with increased height until the **tropopause** is reached. This may vary from 25,000 to 60,000 ft. The atmosphere below the tropopause is the **troposphere;** the atmosphere for about twenty miles above the tropopause is the **stratosphere,** where the temperature generally increases with height except at high latitudes in winter. A temperature maximum near the 30-mile level is called the **stratopause.** Above this boundary is the **mesosphere,** where the temperature decreases with height to a minimum, the **mesopause,** at a height of 50 miles. Extending above the mesosphere to the outer fringes of the atmosphere is the **thermosphere,** a region where temperature increases with height to a value measured in thousands of degrees Fahrenheit. The lower portion of this region, extending from 50 to about 400 miles in altitude, is characterized by a high ion density, and is thus called the **ionosphere.** The outer region is called **exosphere;** this is the region where gas molecules traveling at high speed may escape into outer space, above 600 miles.

Latitude, Longitude

Position on the globe is measured by means of meridians and parallels. Meridians, which are imaginary lines drawn around the earth through the poles, determine **longitude.** The meridian running through Greenwich, England, is the **prime meridian of longitude,** and all others are either east or west. Parallels, which are imaginary circles parallel with the equator, determine **latitude.** The length of a degree of longitude varies as the cosine of the latitude. At the equator a degree is 69.171 statute miles; this is gradually reduced toward the poles. Value of a longitude degree at the poles is zero.

Latitude is reckoned by the number of degrees north or south of the equator, an imaginary circle on the earth's surface everywhere equidistant between the two poles. According to the International Astronomical Union ellipsoid of 1964, the length of a degree of latitude is 68.708 statute miles at the equator and varies slightly north and south because of the oblate form of the globe; at the poles it is 69.403 statute miles.

Definitions of Time

The earth rotates on its axis and follows an elliptical orbit around the sun. The rotation makes the sun appear to move across the sky from East to West. It determines day and night and the complete rotation, in relation to the sun, is called the **apparent** or **true solar day.** This varies but an average determines the **mean solar day** of 24 hours.

The mean solar day is in universal use for civil purposes. It may be obtained from apparent solar time by correcting observations of the sun for the equation of time, but when high precision is required, the mean solar time is calculated from its relation to sidereal time. These relations are extremely complicated, but for most practical uses, they may be considered as follows:

Sidereal time is the measure of time defined by the diurnal motion of the vernal equinox, and is determined from observation of the meridian transits of stars. One complete rotation of the earth relative to the equinox is called the **sidereal day.** The **mean sidereal day** is 23 hours, 56 minutes, 4.091 seconds of mean solar time.

The **Calendar Year** begins at 12 o'clock midnight precisely local clock time, on the night of Dec. 31-Jan. 1. The day and the calendar month also begin at midnight by the clock. The interval required for the earth to make one absolute revolution around the sun is a **sidereal year;** it consisted of 365 days, 6 hours, 9 minutes, and 9.5 seconds of mean solar time (approximately 24 hours per day) in 1900, and is increasing at the rate of 0.0001-second annually.

The **Tropical Year,** on which the return of the seasons depends, is the interval between two consecutive returns of the sun to the vernal equinox. The tropical year consisted of 365 days, 5 hours, 48 minutes, and 46 seconds in 1900. It is decreasing at the rate of 0.530 seconds per century.

In 1956 the unit of time interval was defined to be identical with the second of **Ephemeris Time,** 1/31,556,925.9747 of the tropical year for 1900 January Od 12th hour E.T. A physical definition of the second based on a quantum transition of cesium (atomic second) was adopted in 1964. The atomic second is equal to 9,192,631,770 cycles of the emitted radiation. In 1967 this atomic second was adopted as the unit of time interval for the Intern'l System of Units.

The Zones and Seasons

The five zones of the earth's surface are Torrid, lying between the Tropics of Cancer and Capricorn; North Temperate, between Cancer and the Arctic Circle; South Temperate, between Capricorn and the Antarctic Circle; the Frigid Zones, between the polar Circles and the Poles.

The inclination or tilt of the earth's axis with respect to the sun determines the seasons. These are commonly marked in the North Temperate Zone, where spring begins at the vernal equinox, summer at the summer solstice, autumn at the autumnal equinox and winter at the winter solstice.

In the South Temperate Zone, the seasons are reversed. Spring begins at the autumnal equinox, summer at the winter solstice, etc.

If the earth's axis were perpendicular to the plane of the earth's orbit around the sun there would be no change of seasons. Day and night would be of nearly constant length and there would be equable conditions of temperature. But the axis is tilted 23° 27′ away from a perpendicular to the orbit and only in March and September is the axis at right angles to the sun.

The points at which the sun crosses the equator are the equinoxes, when day and night are most nearly equal. The points at which the sun is at a maximum distance from the equator are the solstices. Days and nights are then most unequal.

In June the North Pole is tilted 23° 27′ toward the sun and the days in the northern hemisphere are longer than the nights, while the days in the southern hemisphere are shorter than the nights. In December the North Pole is tilted 23° 27′ away from the sun and the situation is reversed.

The Seasons in 1994

In 1994 the 4 seasons will begin as follows: add one hour to EST for Atlantic Time; subtract one hour for Central, two hours for Mountain, 3 hours for Pacific, 4 hours for Yukon, 5 hours for Alaska-Hawaii and six hours for Bering Time. Also shown in Greenwich Mean Time.

		Date	GMT	EST
Vernal Equinox	**Spring**	Mar. 20	20:28	15:28
Summer Solstice	**Summer**	June 21	14:48	9:48
Autumnal Equinox	**Autumn**	Sept. 23	6:19	1:19
Winter Solstice	**Winter**	Dec. 21	2:23	21:23*

* Previous Day

Poles of the Earth

The geographic (rotation) poles, or points where the earth's axis of rotation cuts the surface, are not absolutely fixed in the body of the earth. The pole of rotation describes an irregular curve about its mean position.

Two periods have been detected in this motion: (1) an annual period due to seasonal changes in barometric pressure, load of ice and snow on the surface and to other phenomena of seasonal character; (2) a period of about 14 months due to the shape and constitution of the earth.

In addition there are small but as yet unpredictable irregularities. The whole motion is so small that the actual pole at any time remains within a circle of 30 or 40 feet in radius centered at the mean position of the pole.

The pole of rotation for the time being is of course the pole having a latitude of 90° and an indeterminate longitude.

Magnetic Poles

The **north magnetic pole** of the earth is that region where the magnetic force is vertically downward and the **south magnetic pole** that region where the magnetic force is vertically upward. A compass placed at the magnetic poles experiences no directive force in azimuth.

There are slow changes in the distribution of the earth's magnetic field. These changes were at one time attributed in part to a periodic movement of the magnetic poles around the geographical poles, but later evidence refutes this theory and points, rather, to a slow migration of "disturbance" foci over the earth.

There appear shifts in position of the magnetic poles due to the changes in the earth's magnetic field. The center of the area designated as the north magnetic pole was estimated to be in about latitude 70.5° N and longitude 96° W in 1905; from recent nearby measurements and studies of the secular changes, the position in 1970 is estimated as latitude 76.2° N and longitude 101° W. Improved data rather than actual motion account for at least part of the change.

The position of the south magnetic pole in 1912 was near 71° S and longitude 150° E; the position in 1970 is estimated at latitude 66° S and longitude 139.1° E.

The direction of the horizontal components of the magnetic field at any point is known as magnetic north at that point, and the angle by which it deviates east or west of true north is known as the magnetic declination, or in the mariner's terminology, the **variation of the compass.**

A compass without error points in the direction of magnetic north. (In general this is *not* the direction of the magnetic north pole.) If one follows the direction indicated by the north end of the compass, he will travel along a rather irregular curve that eventually reaches the north magnetic pole (though not usually by a great-circle route). However, the action of the compass should not be thought of as due to any influence of the distant pole, but simply as an indication of the distribution of the earth's magnetism at the place of observation.

Rotation of the Earth

The speed of rotation of the earth about its axis has been found to be slightly variable. The variations may be classified as:

(A) **Secular.** Tidal friction acts as a brake on the rotation and causes a slow secular increase in the length of the day, about 1 millisecond per century.

(B) **Irregular.** The speed of rotation may increase for a number of years, about 5 to 10, and then start decreasing. The maximum difference from the mean in the length of the day during a century is about 5 milliseconds. The accumulated difference in time has amounted to approximately 44 seconds since 1900. The cause is probably motion in the interior of the earth.

(C) **Periodic.** Seasonal variations exist with periods of one year and six months. The cumulative effect is such that each year the earth is late about 30 milliseconds near June 1 and is ahead about 30 milliseconds near Oct. 1. The maximum seasonal variation in the length of the day is about 0.5 millisecond. It is believed that the principal cause of the annual variation is the seasonal change in the wind patterns of the northern and southern hemispheres. The semiannual variation is due chiefly to tidal action of the sun, which distorts the shape of the earth slightly.

The secular and irregular variations were discovered by comparing time based on the rotation of the earth with time based on the orbital motion of the moon about the earth and of the planets about the sun. The periodic variation was determined largely with the aid of quartz-crystal clocks. The introduction of the cesium-beam atomic clock in 1955 made it possible to determine in greater detail than before the nature of the irregular and periodic variations.

Morning and Evening Stars, 1994

(GMT)

	Morning	Evening
Jan.	Mercury, Jan. 1 to 3	Mercury, from Jan. 3
	Venus, Jan. 1 to Jan. 17	Venus, from Jan. 17
	Mars, Jan. 1	Saturn, Jan. 1
	Jupiter, Jan. 1	Uranus, Jan. 1 to Jan. 12
	Uranus, from Jan. 12	Neptune, Jan. 1 to Jan. 11
	Neptune, from Jan. 11	
	Pluto, Jan. 1	
Feb.	Mercury, from Feb. 20	Mercury, to Feb. 20
	Mars	Venus
	Jupiter	Saturn, to Feb. 21
	Saturn, from Feb. 21	
	Uranus	
	Neptune	
	Pluto	
Mar.	Mercury	Venus
	Mars	
	Jupiter	
	Saturn	
	Uranus	
	Neptune	
	Pluto	
Apr.	Mercury, to Apr. 30	Mercury, from Apr. 30
	Mars	Venus
	Jupiter, to Apr. 30	Jupiter, from Apr. 30
	Saturn	
	Uranus	
	Neptune	
	Pluto	
May	Mars	Mercury
	Saturn	Venus
	Uranus	Jupiter
	Neptune	Pluto, from May 17
	Pluto, to May 17	
June	Mercury, from Jun. 25	Mercury, to Jun. 25
	Mars	Venus
	Saturn	Jupiter
	Uranus	Pluto
	Neptune	
July	Mercury	Venus
	Mars	Jupiter
	Saturn	Uranus, from July 17
	Uranus, to July 17	Neptune, from July 14
	Neptune, to July 14	Pluto
Aug.	Mercury, to Aug. 13	Mercury, from Aug. 13
	Mars	Jupiter
	Saturn	Uranus
		Neptune
		Pluto
Sept.	Mars	Mercury
	Saturn, to Sept. 1	Venus
		Jupiter
		Saturn, from Sept. 1
		Uranus
		Neptune
		Pluto
Oct.	Mercury, from Oct. 21	Mercury, to Oct. 21
	Mars	Venus
		Jupiter
		Saturn
		Uranus
		Neptune
		Pluto
Nov.	Mercury	Venus, to Nov. 2
	Venus, from Nov. 2	Jupiter, to Nov. 17
	Mars	Saturn
	Jupiter, from Nov. 17	Uranus
	Pluto, from Nov. 20	Neptune
		Pluto, to Nov. 20
Dec.	Mercury, to Dec. 14	Mercury, from Dec. 14
	Venus	Saturn
	Jupiter	Uranus
	Pluto	Neptune

Chronological Eras, 1994

The year 1994 of the Christian Era comprises the latter part of the 218th and the beginning of the 219th year of the independence of the United States of America.

Era	Year	Begins in 1994	
Byzantine	7503	Sept.	14
Jewish	5755	Sept.	5 (sunset)
Roman (Ab Urbe Condita)	2747	Jan.	14
Nabonassar (Babylonian)	2743	Apr.	25
Japanese	2654	Jan.	1
Grecian (Seleucidae)	2306	Sept. or Oct.	14 14
Diocletian	1711	Sept.	11
Indian (Saka)	1916	Mar.	22
Mohammedan (Hegira)	1415	June	9

Chronological Cycles, 1994

Dominical Letter	B	Golden Number (Lunar Cycle)	XIX	Roman Indiction	2
Epact	17	Solar Cycle	15	Julian Period (year of)	6707

Astronomical Twilight—Meridian of Greenwich

Date 1993[1]	20° Begin	20° End	30° Begin	30° End	40° Begin	40° End	50° Begin	50° End	60° Begin	60° End
	h m	h m	h m	h m	h m	h m	h m	h m	h m	h m
Jan. 1	5 16	6 50	5 30	6 35	5 45	6 21	6 00	6 07	6 18	5 49
11	5 19	6 56	5 33	6 43	5 46	6 30	6 00	6 17	6 15	6 01
21	5 21	7 01	5 32	6 51	5 43	6 40	5 55	6 30	6 06	6 18

Date 1993[1]	20° Begin	20° End	30° Begin	30° End	40° Begin	40° End	50° Begin	50° End	60° Begin	60° End
	h m	h m	h m	h m	h m	h m	h m	h m	h m	h m
Feb. 1	5 21	7 07	5 29	6 58	5 38	6 51	5 45	6 44	5 51	6 38
11	5 18	7 11	5 24	7 05	5 29	7 01	5 32	6 59	5 32	7 01
21	5 13	7 15	5 17	7 12	5 17	7 12	5 16	7 14	5 09	7 23
Mar. 1	5 08	7 18	5 08	7 19	5 06	7 21	4 59	7 29	4 44	7 45
11	5 00	7 21	4 58	7 24	4 50	7 32	4 38	7 46	4 12	8 12
21	4 52	7 24	4 45	7 32	4 33	7 44	4 14	8 04	3 37	8 43
Apr. 1	4 42	7 28	4 31	7 39	4 14	7 57	3 47	8 25	2 53	9 21
11	4 32	7 32	4 18	7 47	3 56	8 09	3 20	8 47	2 03	10 10
21	4 23	7 36	4 04	7 54	3 37	8 23	2 52	9 11	0 37	11 47
May 1	4 14	7 41	3 52	8 04	3 19	8 37	2 22	9 39		
11	4 08	7 46	3 41	8 13	3 03	8 53	1 49	10 09		
21	4 02	7 52	3 32	8 22	2 48	9 07	1 13	10 46		
June 1	3 58	7 58	3 26	8 30	2 36	9 20	0 21	11 52		
11	3 56	8 03	3 22	8 36	2 29	9 30				
21	3 57	8 06	3 22	8 40	2 28	9 35				
July 1	3 59	8 07	3 25	8 41	2 30	9 35				
11	4 03	8 06	3 30	8 39	2 40	9 30				
21	4 08	8 03	3 39	8 33	2 52	9 18	1 12	11 23		
Aug. 1	4 15	7 56	3 48	8 23	3 09	9 01	1 49	10 20		
11	4 20	7 50	3 56	8 13	3 22	8 46	2 21	9 46		
21	4 24	7 41	4 05	8 01	3 34	8 27	2 47	9 15		
Sept. 1	4 29	7 31	4 14	7 46	3 51	8 08	3 13	8 43	1 40	10 02
11	4 32	7 20	4 20	7 33	4 02	7 50	3 33	8 16	2 36	9 12
21	4 35	7 11	4 26	7 19	4 14	7 31	3 52	7 52	3 11	8 31
Oct. 1	4 38	7 02	4 33	7 05	4 25	7 13	4 10	7 28	3 41	7 54
11	4 40	6 53	4 40	6 53	4 35	6 58	4 26	7 05	4 07	7 23
21	4 43	6 47	4 45	6 44	4 45	6 43	4 41	6 46	4 32	6 55
Nov. 1	4 46	6 41	4 52	6 34	4 56	6 30	4 58	6 27	4 56	6 27
11	4 50	6 38	4 59	6 28	5 06	6 21	5 13	6 14	5 17	6 08
21	4 55	6 36	5 06	6 25	5 16	6 15	5 26	6 04	5 37	5 52
Dec. 1	5 00	6 37	5 13	6 24	5 25	6 11	5 38	5 58	5 53	5 42
11	5 06	6 40	5 20	6 26	5 34	6 12	5 48	5 57	6 06	5 38
21	5 11	6 45	5 25	6 30	5 39	6 16	5 55	6 00	6 15	5 40
31	5 15	6 50	5 30	6 35	5 44	6 21	6 00	6 06	6 18	5 48

(1) Although the instant of the sun's horizontal depression may be calculated precisely, the phenomena associated with astronomical twilight are sufficiently imprecise that the table is not recalculated each year.

Total Eclipses, 1940-2000

Date	Duration m	Duration s	Width miles	Path of Totality
1940 Oct. 1	5	35	135	Colombia, Brazil, Atlantic Ocean, S. Africa
1941 Sept. 21	3	21	88	Soviet Union, China, Pacific Ocean
1943 Feb. 4	2	39	142	Japan, Pacific Ocean, Alaska
1944 Jan. 25	4	08	90	Peru, Brazil, W. Africa
1945 July 9	1	15	57	US, Canada, Greenland, Scandinavia, USSR
1947 May 20	5	13	121	S. America, Atlantic Ocean, Africa
1948 Nov. 1	1	55	52	Africa, Indian Ocean
1950 Sept. 12	1	13	83	Arctic Ocean, Siberia, Pacific Ocean
1952 Feb. 25	3	09	85	Africa, Middle East, Soviet Union
1954 June 30	2	35	95	US, Canada, Iceland, Europe, Middle East
1955 June 20	7	07	157	SE Asia, Philippines, Pacific Ocean
1956 June 8	4	44	266	South Pacific Ocean
1958 Oct. 12	5	10	129	Pacific Ocean, Chile, Argentina
1959 Oct. 2	3	01	75	New England, Atlantic Ocean, Africa
1961 Feb. 15	2	45	160	Europe, Soviet Union
1962 Feb. 5	4	08	91	Borneo, New Guinea, Pacific Ocean
1963 July 20	1	39	63	Pacific Ocean, Alaska, Canada, Maine
1965 May 30	5	15	123	New Zealand, Pacific Ocean
1966 Nov. 12	1	57	52	Pacific Ocean, S. America, Atlantic Ocean
1968 Sept. 22	0	39	64	Soviet Union, China
1970 Mar. 7	3	27	95	Pacific Ocean, Mexico, Eastern US, Canada
1972 July 10	2	35	109	Siberia, Alaska, Canada
1973 June 30	7	03	159	Atlantic Ocean, Central Africa, Indian Ocean
1974 June 20	5	08	214	Indian Ocean, Australia
1976 Oct. 23	4	46	123	Africa, Indian Ocean, Australia
1977 Oct. 12	2	37	61	Pacific Ocean, Colombia, Venezuela
1979 Feb. 26	2	49	185	NW US, Canada, Greenland
1980 Feb. 16	4	08	92	Africa, Indian Ocean, India, Burma, China
1981 July 31	2	02	67	Soviet Union, Pacific Ocean
1983 June 11	5	10	123	Indian Ocean, Indonesia, New Guinea
1984 Nov. 22	1	59	53	New Guinea, Pacific Ocean
1985 Nov. 12	1	58	430	Antarctica
1986 Oct. 3h[1]	0	01	1	North Atlantic Ocean
1987 Mar. 29h	0	07	3	South Atlantic Ocean, Africa
1988 Mar. 18	3	46	104	Sumatra, Borneo, Philippines, Pacific Ocean
1990 July 22	2	32	125	Finland, Soviet Union, Aleutian Islands
1991 July 11	6	53	160	Hawaii, Mexico, C. America, Colombia, Brazil
1992 June 30	5	20	182	South Atlantic Ocean
1994 Nov. 3	4	23	117	Peru, Bolivia, Paraguay, Brazil
1995 Oct. 24	2	09	48	Iran, India, SE Asia
1997 Mar. 9	2	50	221	Mongolia, Siberia
1998 Feb. 26	4	08	94	Galapagos Islands, Panama, Colombia, Venezuela
1999 Aug. 11	2	22	69	Europe, Middle East, India

(1) "h" indicates annular-total hybrid eclipse.

1st Month January 1994 31 days

Greenwich Mean Time

NOTE: Light numbers indicate Sun. **Dark** numbers indicate **Moon.** *Degrees are North Latitude.*

FM = full moon; LQ = last quarter; NM = new moon; FQ = first quarter.

CAUTION: Must be converted to local time. For instructions see page 239.

Day of month week year	Sun on Meridian Moon phase	Sun's Declination	20° Rise Sun Moon	20° Set Sun Moon	30° Rise Sun Moon	30° Set Sun Moon	40° Rise Sun Moon	40° Set Sun Moon	50° Rise Sun Moon	50° Set Sun Moon	60° Rise Sun Moon	60° Set Sun Moon
	h m s	° ′	h m	h m	h m	h m	h m	h m	h m	h m	h m	h m
1 Sa	12 3 32	−23 2	6 35	17 32	6 56	17 11	7 22	16 45	7 59	16 09	9 02	15 05
1			21 09	9 06	21 03	9 14	20 56	9 23	20 47	9 36	20 32	9 55
2 Su	12 4 00	−22 57	6 35	17 33	6 56	17 12	7 22	16 46	7 59	16 10	9 02	15 06
2			22 07	9 48	22 06	9 52	22 05	9 56	22 03	10 01	22 01	10 09
3 Mo	12 4 28	−22 52	6 36	17 33	6 56	17 13	7 22	16 47	7 58	16 11	9 01	15 08
3			23 05	10 30	23 09	10 29	23 13	10 27	23 20	10 25	23 30	10 22
4 Tu	12 4 56	−22 46	6 36	17 34	6 57	17 13	7 22	16 48	7 58	16 12	9 01	15 10
4			– –	11 13	– –	11 07	– –	11 00	– –	10 50	– –	10 35
5 We	12 5 23	−22 40	6 36	17 35	6 57	17 14	7 22	16 49	7 58	16 13	9 00	15 11
5	00 00 LQ		0 04	11 57	0 12	11 47	0 23	11 34	0 37	11 17	1 00	10 50
6 Th	12 5 49	−22 33	6 37	17 35	6 57	17 15	7 22	16 50	7 58	16 14	8 59	15 13
6			1 04	12 44	1 17	12 30	1 33	12 12	1 55	11 48	2 30	11 09
7 Fr	12 6 15	−22 26	6 37	17 36	6 57	17 16	7 22	16 51	7 57	16 15	8 58	15 15
7			2 05	13 35	2 22	13 17	2 42	12 55	3 11	12 25	3 59	11 34
8 Sa	12 6 41	−22 18	6 37	17 36	6 57	17 17	7 22	16 52	7 57	16 17	8 57	15 17
8			3 07	14 29	3 26	14 09	3 50	13 44	4 24	13 10	5 22	12 10
9 Su	12 7 06	−22 10	6 37	17 37	6 57	17 17	7 22	16 53	7 57	16 18	8 56	15 19
9			4 07	15 26	4 27	15 06	4 53	14 40	5 29	14 04	6 32	13 01
10 Mo	12 7 31	−22 1	6 37	17 38	6 57	17 18	7 22	16 54	7 56	16 19	8 55	15 21
10			5 05	16 25	5 25	16 06	5 50	15 41	6 26	15 06	7 27	14 06
11 Tu	12 7 55	−21 52	6 37	17 38	6 57	17 19	7 21	16 55	7 56	16 21	8 54	15 23
11	23 10 NM		5 59	17 24	6 17	17 07	6 40	16 45	7 12	16 15	8 05	15 23
12 We	12 8 18	−21 43	6 38	17 39	6 57	17 20	7 21	16 56	7 55	16 22	8 52	15 25
12			6 48	18 22	7 03	18 08	7 22	17 50	7 49	17 26	8 32	16 45
13 Th	12 8 41	−21 33	6 38	17 40	6 57	17 21	7 21	16 57	7 54	16 23	8 51	15 27
13			7 32	19 17	7 44	19 07	7 59	18 54	8 19	18 36	8 51	18 08
14 Fr	12 9 03	−21 23	6 38	17 40	6 57	17 21	7 21	16 58	7 54	16 25	8 50	15 29
14			8 13	20 10	8 21	20 04	8 31	19 56	8 45	19 45	9 06	19 28
15 Sa	12 9 25	−21 12	6 38	17 41	6 57	17 22	7 20	16 59	7 53	16 26	8 48	15 31
15			8 51	21 01	8 55	20 59	9 01	20 56	9 07	20 53	9 18	20 47
16 Su	12 9 46	−21 01	6 38	17 42	6 57	17 23	7 20	17 00	7 52	16 28	8 46	15 34
16			9 28	21 51	9 28	21 53	9 28	21 55	9 28	21 58	9 29	22 03
17 Mo	12 10 06	−20 50	6 38	17 42	6 56	17 24	7 19	17 01	7 51	16 29	8 45	15 36
17			10 03	22 40	9 59	22 45	9 55	22 53	9 49	23 02	9 39	23 17
18 Tu	12 10 25	−20 38	6 38	17 43	6 56	17 25	7 19	17 02	7 50	16 31	8 43	15 38
18			10 39	23 28	10 31	23 38	10 22	23 50	10 10	– –	9 51	– –
19 We	12 10 44	−20 25	6 38	17 44	6 56	17 26	7 18	17 03	7 50	16 32	8 41	15 41
19	20 27 FQ		11 16	– –	11 04	– –	10 51	– –	10 32	0 06	10 04	0 32
20 Th	12 11 02	−20 13	6 38	17 44	6 56	17 27	7 18	17 05	7 49	16 34	8 40	15 43
20			11 55	0 18	11 40	0 31	11 23	0 47	10 58	1 09	10 20	1 45
21 Fr	12 11 19	−19 60	6 38	17 45	6 55	17 27	7 17	17 06	7 48	16 36	8 38	15 45
21			12 36	1 08	12 19	1 24	11 58	1 44	11 29	2 12	10 41	2 58
22 Sa	12 11 35	−19 46	6 38	17 46	6 55	17 28	7 17	17 07	7 47	16 37	8 36	15 48
22			13 22	2 00	13 03	2 18	12 39	2 41	12 06	3 14	11 10	4 08
23 Su	12 11 51	−19 33	6 38	17 46	6 55	17 29	7 16	17 08	7 45	16 39	8 34	15 50
23			14 11	2 52	13 51	3 12	13 26	3 37	12 50	4 12	11 50	5 12
24 Mo	12 12 06	−19 19	6 37	17 47	6 54	17 30	7 15	17 09	7 44	16 40	8 32	15 53
24			15 04	3 44	14 45	4 04	14 20	4 30	13 44	5 05	12 44	6 06
25 Tu	12 12 20	−19 4	6 37	17 48	6 54	17 31	7 15	17 10	7 43	16 42	8 30	15 55
25			16 01	4 36	15 42	4 55	15 19	5 19	14 47	5 52	13 52	6 49
26 We	12 12 33	−18 49	6 37	17 48	6 54	17 32	7 14	17 12	7 42	16 44	8 28	15 58
26			16 59	5 26	16 44	5 43	16 24	6 04	15 57	6 33	15 12	7 20
27 Th	12 12 45	−18 34	6 37	17 49	6 53	17 33	7 13	17 13	7 41	16 45	8 26	16 01
27	13 23 FM		17 59	6 14	17 47	6 28	17 32	6 45	17 12	7 08	16 39	7 44
28 Fr	12 12 57	−18 19	6 37	17 49	6 53	17 34	7 12	17 14	7 39	16 47	8 23	16 03
28			18 59	7 01	18 51	7 10	18 42	7 22	18 29	7 38	18 09	8 02
29 Sa	12 13 08	−18 3	6 36	17 50	6 52	17 34	7 12	17 15	7 38	16 49	8 21	16 06
29			19 58	7 45	19 55	7 50	19 52	7 56	19 47	8 05	19 40	8 17
30 Su	12 13 18	−17 47	6 36	17 51	6 52	17 35	7 11	17 16	7 37	16 50	8 19	16 08
30			20 58	8 29	21 00	8 29	21 03	8 29	21 06	8 30	21 11	8 31
31 Mo	12 13 27	−17 30	6 36	17 51	6 51	17 36	7 10	17 18	7 35	16 52	8 17	16 11
31			21 58	9 12	22 05	9 08	22 13	9 02	22 25	8 55	22 43	8 45

2nd Month — February 1994 — 28 days

Greenwich Mean Time

NOTE: Light numbers indicate Sun. **Dark** numbers indicate **Moon.** *Degrees are North Latitude.*

FM = full moon; LQ = last quarter; NM = new moon; FQ = first quarter.

CAUTION: Must be converted to local time. For instructions see page 239.

Day of month / week / year	Sun on Meridian / Moon phase (h m s)	Sun's Declination (° ′)	20° Rise Sun/Moon (h m)	20° Set Sun/Moon (h m)	30° Rise Sun/Moon (h m)	30° Set Sun/Moon (h m)	40° Rise Sun/Moon (h m)	40° Set Sun/Moon (h m)	50° Rise Sun/Moon (h m)	50° Set Sun/Moon (h m)	60° Rise Sun/Moon (h m)	60° Set Sun/Moon (h m)
1 Tu	12 13 35	−17 13	6 36	17 52	6 51	17 37	7 09	17 19	7 34	16 54	8 14	16 14
32			22 59	9 57	23 10	9 48	23 24	9 37	23 43	9 22	– –	9 00
2 We	12 13 43	−16 56	6 35	17 52	6 50	17 38	7 08	17 20	7 33	16 56	8 12	16 16
33			23 59	10 43	– –	10 30	– –	10 14	– –	9 52	0 14	9 17
3 Th	12 13 50	−16 39	6 35	17 53	6 49	17 39	7 07	17 21	7 31	16 57	8 10	16 19
34	8 6 LQ		– –	11 32	0 15	11 16	0 34	10 55	1 00	10 27	1 44	9 41
4 Fr	12 13 56	−16 21	6 35	17 53	6 49	17 40	7 06	17 22	7 30	16 59	8 07	16 21
35			1 00	12 25	1 19	12 06	1 41	11 42	2 14	11 09	3 08	10 13
5 Sa	12 14 01	−16 3	6 34	17 54	6 48	17 40	7 05	17 24	7 28	17 01	8 05	16 24
36			2 00	13 20	2 20	13 00	2 45	12 34	3 21	11 59	4 22	10 57
6 Su	12 14 05	−15 45	6 34	17 55	6 47	17 41	7 04	17 25	7 26	17 02	8 02	16 27
37			2 58	14 17	3 18	13 57	3 43	13 32	4 19	12 57	5 21	11 56
7 Mo	12 14 09	−15 27	6 33	17 55	6 47	17 42	7 03	17 26	7 25	17 04	8 00	16 29
38			3 51	15 15	4 10	14 57	4 34	14 34	5 08	14 01	6 04	13 07
8 Tu	12 14 12	−15 8	6 33	17 56	6 46	17 43	7 02	17 27	7 23	17 06	7 57	16 32
39			4 41	16 12	4 58	15 56	5 19	15 37	5 47	15 10	6 34	14 25
9 We	12 14 14	−14 49	6 32	17 56	6 45	17 44	7 01	17 28	7 22	17 08	7 55	16 35
40			5 27	17 07	5 40	16 55	5 57	16 40	6 20	16 19	6 56	15 46
10 Th	12 14 15	−14 29	6 32	17 57	6 44	17 45	6 59	17 30	7 20	17 09	7 52	16 37
41	14 30 NM		6 09	18 01	6 19	17 52	6 31	17 42	6 47	17 29	7 13	17 07
11 Fr	12 14 15	−14 10	6 32	17 57	6 44	17 45	6 58	17 31	7 18	17 11	7 50	16 40
42			6 48	18 52	6 54	18 48	7 01	18 43	7 11	18 36	7 26	18 25
12 Sa	12 14 15	−13 50	6 31	17 58	6 43	17 46	6 57	17 32	7 16	17 13	7 47	16 43
43			7 25	19 42	7 27	19 43	7 29	19 43	7 33	19 42	7 38	19 42
13 Su	12 14 14	−13 30	6 30	17 58	6 42	17 47	6 56	17 33	7 15	17 15	7 44	16 45
44			8 01	20 32	7 59	20 36	7 57	20 41	7 53	20 47	7 49	20 58
14 Mo	12 14 12	−13 10	6 30	17 59	6 41	17 48	6 55	17 34	7 13	17 16	7 42	16 48
45			8 37	21 21	8 31	21 29	8 24	21 38	8 14	21 52	8 00	22 12
15 Tu	12 14 10	−12 50	6 29	17 59	6 40	17 49	6 53	17 36	7 11	17 18	7 39	16 51
46			9 13	22 10	9 04	22 21	8 52	22 36	8 37	22 55	8 13	23 26
16 We	12 14 06	−12 29	6 29	18 00	6 39	17 49	6 52	17 37	7 09	17 20	7 36	16 53
47			9 51	23 00	9 39	23 14	9 23	23 32	9 01	23 58	8 27	– –
17 Th	12 14 02	−12 8	6 28	18 00	6 38	17 50	6 51	17 38	7 07	17 21	7 33	16 56
48			10 32	23 50	10 16	– –	9 56	– –	9 30	– –	8 46	0 39
18 Fr	12 13 58	−11 47	6 28	18 01	6 37	17 51	6 49	17 39	7 06	17 23	7 31	16 58
49	17 47 FQ		11 15	– –	10 57	0 07	10 34	0 29	10 03	0 59	9 11	1 49
19 Sa	12 13 52	−11 26	6 27	18 01	6 37	17 52	6 48	17 40	7 04	17 25	7 28	17 01
50			12 02	0 41	11 42	1 00	11 18	1 24	10 43	1 58	9 45	2 55
20 Su	12 13 46	−11 5	6 26	18 01	6 36	17 52	6 47	17 41	7 02	17 27	7 25	17 04
51			12 52	1 32	12 32	1 52	12 07	2 17	11 32	2 52	10 32	3 53
21 Mo	12 13 39	−10 43	6 26	18 02	6 35	17 53	6 45	17 42	7 00	17 28	7 22	17 06
52			13 46	2 24	13 27	2 43	13 03	3 07	12 29	3 42	11 32	4 40
22 Tu	12 13 32	−10 21	6 25	18 02	6 34	17 54	6 44	17 44	6 58	17 30	7 19	17 09
53			14 42	3 14	14 25	3 32	14 04	3 54	13 34	4 25	12 45	5 16
23 We	12 13 24	− 9 59	6 24	18 03	6 33	17 55	6 43	17 45	6 56	17 32	7 17	17 11
54			15 41	4 02	15 27	4 18	15 10	4 36	14 46	5 02	14 08	5 44
24 Th	12 13 15	− 9 37	6 24	18 03	6 32	17 55	6 41	17 46	6 54	17 33	7 14	17 14
55			16 41	4 50	16 31	5 01	16 19	5 15	16 02	5 35	15 36	6 05
25 Fr	12 13 06	− 9 15	6 23	18 03	6 31	17 56	6 40	17 47	6 52	17 35	7 11	17 16
56			17 42	5 35	17 36	5 43	17 30	5 52	17 21	6 04	17 08	6 22
26 Sa	12 12 56	− 8 53	6 22	18 04	6 30	17 57	6 38	17 48	6 50	17 37	7 08	17 19
57	1 15 FM		18 43	6 20	18 43	6 23	18 42	6 26	18 42	6 31	18 41	6 37
27 Su	12 12 46	− 8 31	6 22	18 04	6 28	17 57	6 37	17 49	6 48	17 38	7 05	17 22
58			19 45	7 05	19 50	7 03	19 55	7 01	20 03	6 57	20 16	6 52
28 Mo	12 12 35	− 8 8	6 21	18 05	6 27	17 58	6 35	17 50	6 46	17 40	7 02	17 24
59			20 47	7 51	20 57	7 44	21 09	7 36	21 25	7 24	21 51	7 07

3rd Month — March 1994 — 31 days

Greenwich Mean Time

NOTE: Light numbers indicate Sun. **Dark** numbers indicate **Moon.** *Degrees are North Latitude.*

FM = full moon; LQ = last quarter; NM = new moon; FQ = first quarter.

CAUTION: Must be converted to local time. For instructions see page 239.

Day of month week year	Sun on Meridian **Moon phase** h m s	Sun's Declination ° ′	20° Rise Sun **Moon** h m	20° Set Sun **Moon** h m	30° Rise Sun **Moon** h m	30° Set Sun **Moon** h m	40° Rise Sun **Moon** h m	40° Set Sun **Moon** h m	50° Rise Sun **Moon** h m	50° Set Sun **Moon** h m	60° Rise Sun **Moon** h m	60° Set Sun **Moon** h m
1 Tu	12 12 23	– 7 45	6 20	18 05	6 26	17 59	6 34	17 51	6 44	17 42	6 59	17 27
60			**21 50**	**8 39**	**22 04**	**8 27**	**22 21**	**8 13**	**22 45**	**7 54**	**23 24**	**7 25**
2 We	12 12 11	– 7 23	6 19	18 05	6 25	18 00	6 32	17 53	6 42	17 43	6 56	17 29
61			**22 53**	**9 29**	**23 10**	**9 13**	**23 32**	**8 55**	**– –**	**8 29**	**– –**	**7 47**
3 Th	12 11 59	– 6 60	6 19	18 06	6 24	18 00	6 31	17 54	6 40	17 45	6 53	17 32
62			**23 54**	**10 21**	**– –**	**10 03**	**– –**	**9 41**	**0 02**	**9 09**	**0 52**	**8 17**
4 Fr	12 11 46	– 6 37	6 18	18 06	6 23	18 01	6 29	17 55	6 38	17 47	6 51	17 34
63	**16 53 LQ**		**– –**	**11 16**	**0 14**	**10 57**	**0 38**	**10 32**	**1 12**	**9 57**	**2 11**	**8 58**
5 Sa	12 11 32	– 6 14	6 17	18 06	6 22	18 02	6 28	17 56	6 36	17 48	6 48	17 37
64			**0 53**	**12 13**	**1 13**	**11 53**	**1 38**	**11 28**	**2 14**	**10 53**	**3 15**	**9 52**
6 Su	12 11 19	– 5 50	6 16	18 07	6 21	18 02	6 26	17 57	6 34	17 50	6 45	17 39
65			**1 48**	**13 10**	**2 07**	**12 52**	**2 31**	**12 28**	**3 05**	**11 55**	**4 02**	**10 59**
7 Mo	12 11 05	– 5 27	6 15	18 07	6 20	18 03	6 25	17 58	6 32	17 52	6 42	17 42
66			**2 38**	**14 07**	**2 56**	**13 50**	**3 17**	**13 30**	**3 47**	**13 02**	**4 36**	**12 14**
8 Tu	12 10 50	– 5 4	6 15	18 07	6 19	18 04	6 23	17 59	6 29	17 53	6 39	17 44
67			**3 25**	**15 02**	**3 39**	**14 49**	**3 57**	**14 32**	**4 22**	**14 10**	**5 01**	**13 33**
9 We	12 10 35	– 4 40	6 14	18 08	6 17	18 04	6 22	18 00	6 27	17 55	6 36	17 47
68			**4 07**	**15 55**	**4 18**	**15 45**	**4 32**	**15 34**	**4 50**	**15 18**	**5 19**	**14 52**
10 Th	12 10 20	– 4 17	6 13	18 08	6 16	18 05	6 20	18 01	6 25	17 56	6 33	17 49
69			**4 47**	**16 46**	**4 54**	**16 41**	**5 03**	**16 34**	**5 15**	**16 25**	**5 34**	**16 10**
11 Fr	12 10 04	– 3 53	6 12	18 08	6 15	18 06	6 19	18 02	6 23	17 58	6 30	17 52
70			**5 24**	**17 37**	**5 28**	**17 35**	**5 32**	**17 33**	**5 37**	**17 31**	**5 46**	**17 27**
12 Sa	12 9 49	– 3 30	6 11	18 09	6 14	18 06	6 17	18 03	6 21	18 00	6 27	17 54
71	**7 5 NM**		**6 00**	**18 26**	**6 00**	**18 28**	**5 59**	**18 31**	**5 59**	**18 36**	**5 57**	**18 42**
13 Su	12 9 32	– 3 6	6 10	18 09	6 13	18 07	6 15	18 04	6 19	18 01	6 24	17 57
72			**6 36**	**19 15**	**6 32**	**19 21**	**6 27**	**19 29**	**6 20**	**19 40**	**6 09**	**19 56**
14 Mo	12 9 16	– 2 42	6 10	18 09	6 12	18 07	6 14	18 05	6 17	18 03	6 21	17 59
73			**7 12**	**20 04**	**7 04**	**20 14**	**6 55**	**20 26**	**6 41**	**20 43**	**6 21**	**21 10**
15 Tu	12 8 59	– 2 19	6 09	18 10	6 10	18 08	6 12	18 06	6 14	18 04	6 18	18 02
74			**7 50**	**20 53**	**7 39**	**21 07**	**7 24**	**21 23**	**7 05**	**21 46**	**6 36**	**22 23**
16 We	12 8 42	– 1 55	6 08	18 10	6 09	18 09	6 11	18 08	6 12	18 06	6 15	18 04
75			**8 29**	**21 43**	**8 15**	**22 00**	**7 57**	**22 20**	**7 32**	**22 48**	**6 53**	**23 34**
17 Th	12 8 25	– 1 31	6 07	18 10	6 08	18 09	6 09	18 09	6 10	18 08	6 12	18 07
76			**9 11**	**22 34**	**8 54**	**22 52**	**8 33**	**23 15**	**8 04**	**23 47**	**7 16**	**– –**
18 Fr	12 8 08	– 1 8	6 06	18 10	6 07	18 10	6 07	18 10	6 08	18 09	6 09	18 09
77			**9 56**	**23 24**	**9 37**	**23 44**	**9 14**	**– –**	**8 41**	**– –**	**7 46**	**0 41**
19 Sa	12 7 50	– 0 44	6 05	18 11	6 06	18 11	6 06	18 11	6 06	18 11	6 06	18 11
78			**10 44**	**– –**	**10 24**	**– –**	**10 00**	**0 08**	**9 25**	**0 42**	**8 27**	**1 41**
20 Su	12 7 33	– 0 20	6 04	18 11	6 04	18 11	6 04	18 12	6 04	18 12	6 03	18 14
79	**12 14 FQ**		**11 35**	**0 14**	**11 16**	**0 34**	**10 52**	**0 58**	**10 18**	**1 33**	**9 20**	**2 31**
21 Mo	12 7 15	0 3	6 04	18 11	6 03	18 12	6 02	18 13	6 01	18 14	6 00	18 16
80			**12 29**	**1 03**	**12 11**	**1 22**	**11 49**	**1 45**	**11 18**	**2 17**	**10 25**	**3 11**
22 Tu	12 6 57	0 27	6 03	18 12	6 02	18 12	6 01	18 14	5 59	18 16	5 57	18 19
81			**13 25**	**1 51**	**13 10**	**2 08**	**12 51**	**2 28**	**12 24**	**2 56**	**11 41**	**3 42**
23 We	12 6 39	0 51	6 02	18 12	6 01	18 13	5 59	18 15	5 57	18 17	5 54	18 21
82			**14 23**	**2 38**	**14 11**	**2 51**	**13 56**	**3 08**	**13 36**	**3 30**	**13 04**	**4 05**
24 Th	12 6 21	1 14	6 01	18 12	5 59	18 14	5 58	18 16	5 55	18 19	5 50	18 24
83			**15 22**	**3 24**	**15 14**	**3 33**	**15 05**	**3 45**	**14 52**	**4 00**	**14 32**	**4 24**
25 Fr	12 6 02	1 38	6 00	18 12	5 58	18 14	5 56	18 17	5 53	18 20	5 47	18 26
84			**16 22**	**4 08**	**16 19**	**4 13**	**16 16**	**4 20**	**16 11**	**4 28**	**16 04**	**4 40**
26 Sa	12 5 44	2 2	5 59	18 13	5 57	18 15	5 54	18 18	5 50	18 22	5 44	18 28
85			**17 24**	**4 53**	**17 26**	**4 54**	**17 29**	**4 54**	**17 32**	**4 55**	**17 38**	**4 55**
27 Su	12 5 26	2 25	5 58	18 13	5 56	18 15	5 53	18 19	5 48	18 24	5 41	18 31
86	**11 9 FM**		**18 28**	**5 39**	**18 35**	**5 35**	**18 43**	**5 29**	**18 55**	**5 22**	**19 14**	**5 11**
28 Mo	12 5 08	2 49	5 57	18 13	5 55	18 16	5 51	18 20	5 46	18 25	5 38	18 33
87			**19 32**	**6 27**	**19 44**	**6 18**	**19 59**	**6 07**	**20 19**	**5 52**	**20 51**	**5 28**
29 Tu	12 4 49	3 12	5 57	18 13	5 53	18 17	5 49	18 21	5 44	18 27	5 35	18 36
88			**20 38**	**7 18**	**20 53**	**7 04**	**21 13**	**6 48**	**21 40**	**6 25**	**22 25**	**5 49**
30 We	12 4 31	3 35	5 56	18 14	5 52	18 17	5 48	18 22	5 42	18 28	5 32	18 38
89			**21 42**	**8 11**	**22 00**	**7 54**	**22 24**	**7 33**	**22 56**	**7 04**	**23 51**	**6 17**
31 Th	12 4 13	3 59	5 55	18 14	5 51	18 18	5 46	18 23	5 40	18 30	5 29	18 41
90			**22 44**	**9 08**	**23 04**	**8 49**	**23 29**	**8 25**	**– –**	**7 51**	**– –**	**6 55**

4th Month — April 1994 — 30 days

Greenwich Mean Time

NOTE: Light numbers indicate Sun. **Dark** numbers indicate **Moon.** *Degrees are North Latitude.*

FM = full moon; LQ = last quarter; NM = new moon; FQ = first quarter.

CAUTION: Must be converted to local time. For instructions see page 239.

Day of month week year	Sun on Meridian **Moon phase** h m s	Sun's Declination ° ′	20° Rise Sun **Moon** h m	20° Set Sun **Moon** h m	30° Rise Sun **Moon** h m	30° Set Sun **Moon** h m	40° Rise Sun **Moon** h m	40° Set Sun **Moon** h m	50° Rise Sun **Moon** h m	50° Set Sun **Moon** h m	60° Rise Sun **Moon** h m	60° Set Sun **Moon** h m
1 Fr	12 3 55	4 22	5 54	18 14	5 50	18 18	5 45	18 24	5 37	18 31	5 26	18 43
91			**23 42**	**10 06**	**– –**	**9 46**	**– –**	**9 21**	**0 03**	**8 46**	**1 03**	**7 46**
2 Sa	12 3 37	4 45	5 53	18 14	5 49	18 19	5 43	18 25	5 35	18 33	5 23	18 46
92			**– –**	**11 05**	**0 01**	**10 46**	**0 26**	**10 22**	**1 00**	**9 48**	**1 58**	**8 51**
3 Su	12 3 20	5 8	5 52	18 15	5 47	18 20	5 41	18 26	5 33	18 35	5 20	18 48
93	**2 55 LQ**		**0 35**	**12 02**	**0 53**	**11 45**	**1 15**	**11 24**	**1 46**	**10 54**	**2 37**	**10 05**
4 Mo	12 3 02	5 31	5 51	18 15	5 46	18 20	5 40	18 27	5 31	18 36	5 17	18 50
94			**1 23**	**12 58**	**1 38**	**12 44**	**1 57**	**12 27**	**2 23**	**12 02**	**3 05**	**11 23**
5 Tu	12 2 45	5 54	5 50	18 15	5 45	18 21	5 38	18 28	5 29	18 38	5 14	18 53
95			**2 07**	**13 52**	**2 19**	**13 41**	**2 34**	**13 28**	**2 54**	**13 10**	**3 25**	**12 42**
6 We	12 2 27	6 17	5 50	18 16	5 44	18 22	5 37	18 29	5 27	18 39	5 11	18 55
96			**2 47**	**14 43**	**2 55**	**14 37**	**3 06**	**14 28**	**3 19**	**14 17**	**3 41**	**13 59**
7 Th	12 2 11	6 39	5 49	18 16	5 43	18 22	5 35	18 30	5 25	18 41	5 08	18 58
97			**3 25**	**15 33**	**3 29**	**15 31**	**3 35**	**15 27**	**3 42**	**15 23**	**3 54**	**15 15**
8 Fr	12 1 54	7 2	5 48	18 16	5 42	18 23	5 34	18 31	5 22	18 42	5 05	19 00
98			**4 01**	**16 22**	**4 02**	**16 24**	**4 03**	**16 25**	**4 04**	**16 27**	**4 06**	**16 30**
9 Sa	12 1 37	7 24	5 47	18 16	5 40	18 23	5 32	18 32	5 20	18 44	5 02	19 03
99			**4 37**	**17 11**	**4 34**	**17 16**	**4 30**	**17 22**	**4 25**	**17 31**	**4 17**	**17 44**
10 Su	12 1 21	7 47	5 46	18 17	5 39	18 24	5 30	18 33	5 18	18 45	4 59	19 05
100			**5 13**	**18 00**	**5 06**	**18 09**	**4 58**	**18 20**	**4 47**	**18 34**	**4 30**	**18 58**
11 Mo	12 1 05	8 9	5 45	18 17	5 38	18 25	5 29	18 34	5 16	18 47	4 56	19 08
101	**0 17 NM**		**5 50**	**18 49**	**5 39**	**19 01**	**5 27**	**19 16**	**5 10**	**19 37**	**4 43**	**20 10**
12 Tu	12 0 50	8 31	5 45	18 17	5 37	18 25	5 27	18 35	5 14	18 49	4 53	19 10
102			**6 29**	**19 39**	**6 15**	**19 54**	**5 58**	**20 13**	**5 36**	**20 39**	**5 00**	**21 22**
13 We	12 0 34	8 53	5 44	18 18	5 36	18 26	5 26	18 36	5 12	18 50	4 50	19 12
103			**7 10**	**20 29**	**6 54**	**20 47**	**6 33**	**21 08**	**6 06**	**21 39**	**5 21**	**22 30**
14 Th	12 0 19	9 15	5 43	18 18	5 35	18 26	5 24	18 37	5 10	18 52	4 47	19 15
104			**7 53**	**21 19**	**7 35**	**21 38**	**7 13**	**22 02**	**6 41**	**22 36**	**5 49**	**23 32**
15 Fr	12 0 05	9 36	5 42	18 18	5 34	18 27	5 23	18 38	5 08	18 53	4 44	19 17
105			**8 40**	**22 09**	**8 21**	**22 29**	**7 57**	**22 53**	**7 23**	**23 27**	**6 26**	**– –**
16 Sa	11 59 50	9 58	5 42	18 18	5 33	18 28	5 21	18 39	5 06	18 55	4 41	19 20
106			**9 30**	**22 58**	**9 10**	**23 17**	**8 46**	**23 40**	**8 12**	**– –**	**7 14**	**0 26**
17 Su	11 59 36	10 19	5 41	18 19	5 31	18 28	5 20	18 40	5 04	18 56	4 38	19 22
107			**10 21**	**23 45**	**10 03**	**– –**	**9 40**	**– –**	**9 08**	**0 13**	**8 14**	**1 08**
18 Mo	11 59 23	10 40	5 40	18 19	5 30	18 29	5 18	18 41	5 02	18 58	4 36	19 25
108			**11 15**	**– –**	**10 59**	**0 03**	**10 39**	**0 24**	**10 11**	**0 53**	**9 24**	**1 42**
19 Tu	11 59 09	11 1	5 39	18 19	5 29	18 29	5 17	18 42	5 00	19 00	4 33	19 27
109	**2 34 FQ**		**12 10**	**0 31**	**11 57**	**0 46**	**11 41**	**1 04**	**11 18**	**1 28**	**10 42**	**2 07**
20 We	11 58 56	11 22	5 38	18 20	5 28	18 30	5 15	18 43	4 58	19 01	4 30	19 30
110			**13 07**	**1 15**	**12 57**	**1 27**	**12 46**	**1 40**	**12 30**	**1 59**	**12 05**	**2 27**
21 Th	11 58 44	11 42	5 38	18 20	5 27	18 31	5 14	18 44	4 56	19 03	4 27	19 32
111			**14 05**	**1 59**	**14 00**	**2 06**	**13 53**	**2 15**	**13 45**	**2 26**	**13 32**	**2 44**
22 Fr	11 58 32	12 3	5 37	18 20	5 26	18 31	5 13	18 45	4 54	19 04	4 24	19 35
112			**15 04**	**2 42**	**15 04**	**2 45**	**15 03**	**2 48**	**15 03**	**2 53**	**15 02**	**2 59**
23 Sa	11 58 20	12 23	5 36	18 21	5 25	18 32	5 11	18 46	4 52	19 06	4 21	19 37
113			**16 05**	**3 27**	**16 10**	**3 25**	**16 15**	**3 22**	**16 23**	**3 19**	**16 35**	**3 14**
24 Su	11 58 09	12 43	5 36	18 21	5 24	18 33	5 10	18 47	4 50	19 07	4 18	19 40
114			**17 09**	**4 13**	**17 18**	**4 06**	**17 30**	**3 58**	**17 46**	**3 47**	**18 11**	**3 30**
25 Mo	11 57 58	13 3	5 35	18 21	5 23	18 33	5 08	18 48	4 48	19 09	4 15	19 42
115	**19 45 FM**		**18 15**	**5 02**	**18 28**	**4 51**	**18 45**	**4 37**	**19 09**	**4 18**	**19 47**	**3 49**
26 Tu	11 57 48	13 22	5 34	18 22	5 22	18 34	5 07	18 49	4 46	19 10	4 13	19 45
116			**19 21**	**5 55**	**19 38**	**5 39**	**19 59**	**5 21**	**20 30**	**4 55**	**21 20**	**4 13**
27 We	11 57 39	13 41	5 34	18 22	5 21	18 35	5 06	18 50	4 44	19 12	4 10	19 47
117			**20 26**	**6 51**	**20 46**	**6 33**	**21 10**	**6 10**	**21 44**	**5 39**	**22 42**	**4 47**
28 Th	11 57 29	14 0	5 33	18 22	5 20	18 35	5 04	18 51	4 42	19 14	4 07	19 50
118			**21 29**	**7 51**	**21 48**	**7 31**	**22 13**	**7 07**	**22 48**	**6 32**	**23 47**	**5 33**
29 Fr	11 57 21	14 19	5 32	18 23	5 19	18 36	5 03	18 52	4 41	19 15	4 04	19 52
119			**22 26**	**8 52**	**22 44**	**8 32**	**23 08**	**8 08**	**23 40**	**7 33**	**– –**	**6 35**
30 Sa	11 57 13	14 38	5 32	18 23	5 18	18 36	5 02	18 53	4 39	19 17	4 02	19 55
120			**23 18**	**9 52**	**23 34**	**9 34**	**23 54**	**9 12**	**– –**	**8 41**	**0 34**	**7 48**

5th Month May 1994 31 days

Greenwich Mean Time

NOTE: Light numbers indicate Sun. **Dark** numbers indicate **Moon.** *Degrees are North Latitude.*

FM = full moon; LQ = last quarter; NM = new moon; FQ = first quarter.

CAUTION: Must be converted to local time. For instructions see page 239.

Day of month week year	Sun on Meridian **Moon phase** h m s	Sun's Declination ° ′	20° Rise Sun **Moon** h m	20° Set Sun **Moon** h m	30° Rise Sun **Moon** h m	30° Set Sun **Moon** h m	40° Rise Sun **Moon** h m	40° Set Sun **Moon** h m	50° Rise Sun **Moon** h m	50° Set Sun **Moon** h m	60° Rise Sun **Moon** h m	60° Set Sun **Moon** h m
1 Su	11 57 05	14 56	5 31	18 23	5 17	18 37	5 01	18 54	4 37	19 18	3 59	19 57
121			**– –**	**10 50**	**– –**	**10 35**	**– –**	**10 17**	**0 22**	**9 50**	**1 07**	**9 08**
2 Mo	11 56 58	15 14	5 30	18 24	5 17	18 38	4 59	18 55	4 35	19 20	3 56	20 00
122	**14 32 LQ**		**0 04**	**11 46**	**0 17**	**11 34**	**0 33**	**11 20**	**0 55**	**11 00**	**1 30**	**10 28**
3 Tu	11 56 51	15 32	5 30	18 24	5 16	18 38	4 58	18 56	4 33	19 21	3 53	20 02
123			**0 46**	**12 39**	**0 56**	**12 31**	**1 07**	**12 22**	**1 23**	**12 08**	**1 48**	**11 47**
4 We	11 56 46	15 50	5 29	18 24	5 15	18 39	4 57	18 57	4 32	19 23	3 51	20 05
124			**1 25**	**13 30**	**1 31**	**13 26**	**1 38**	**13 21**	**1 47**	**13 15**	**2 02**	**13 04**
5 Th	11 56 40	16 7	5 29	18 25	5 14	18 40	4 56	18 58	4 30	19 24	3 48	20 07
125			**2 02**	**14 19**	**2 04**	**14 19**	**2 06**	**14 19**	**2 09**	**14 19**	**2 14**	**14 19**
6 Fr	11 56 35	16 24	5 28	18 25	5 13	18 40	4 55	18 59	4 28	19 26	3 45	20 09
126			**2 38**	**15 08**	**2 36**	**15 12**	**2 33**	**15 17**	**2 30**	**15 23**	**2 26**	**15 33**
7 Sa	11 56 31	16 41	5 28	18 26	5 12	18 41	4 53	19 00	4 27	19 27	3 43	20 12
127			**3 14**	**15 57**	**3 08**	**16 04**	**3 01**	**16 14**	**2 52**	**16 27**	**2 38**	**16 47**
8 Su	11 56 28	16 58	5 27	18 26	5 12	18 42	4 52	19 01	4 25	19 29	3 40	20 14
128			**3 50**	**16 46**	**3 41**	**16 57**	**3 30**	**17 11**	**3 14**	**17 29**	**2 51**	**17 59**
9 Mo	11 56 25	17 14	5 27	18 26	5 11	18 42	4 51	19 02	4 24	19 30	3 38	20 17
129			**4 28**	**17 35**	**4 16**	**17 49**	**4 00**	**18 07**	**3 39**	**18 32**	**3 07**	**19 11**
10 Tu	11 56 22	17 30	5 26	18 27	5 10	18 43	4 50	19 03	4 22	19 32	3 35	20 19
130	**17 7 NM**		**5 09**	**18 25**	**4 53**	**18 42**	**4 34**	**19 03**	**4 08**	**19 32**	**3 26**	**20 21**
11 We	11 56 20	17 46	5 26	18 27	5 09	18 44	4 49	19 04	4 20	19 33	3 33	20 22
131			**5 52**	**19 16**	**5 34**	**19 34**	**5 12**	**19 58**	**4 42**	**20 30**	**3 52**	**21 26**
12 Th	11 56 19	18 1	5 25	18 28	5 09	18 44	4 48	19 05	4 19	19 35	3 30	20 24
132			**6 38**	**20 06**	**6 19**	**20 26**	**5 55**	**20 50**	**5 22**	**21 24**	**4 26**	**22 22**
13 Fr	11 56 18	18 16	5 25	18 28	5 08	18 45	4 47	19 06	4 17	19 36	3 28	20 26
133			**7 26**	**20 55**	**7 07**	**21 14**	**6 43**	**21 38**	**6 09**	**22 12**	**5 10**	**23 08**
14 Sa	11 56 18	18 31	5 24	18 28	5 07	18 46	4 46	19 07	4 16	19 38	3 25	20 29
134			**8 17**	**21 43**	**7 59**	**22 01**	**7 35**	**22 23**	**7 02**	**22 53**	**6 07**	**23 44**
15 Su	11 56 18	18 45	5 24	18 29	5 07	18 46	4 45	19 08	4 15	19 39	3 23	20 31
135			**9 10**	**22 29**	**8 53**	**22 44**	**8 32**	**23 03**	**8 03**	**23 29**	**7 14**	**– –**
16 Mo	11 56 19	18 60	5 24	18 29	5 06	18 47	4 44	19 09	4 13	19 40	3 21	20 34
136			**10 04**	**23 13**	**9 50**	**23 25**	**9 32**	**23 40**	**9 08**	**– –**	**8 28**	**0 11**
17 Tu	11 56 21	19 13	5 23	18 30	5 06	18 47	4 43	19 10	4 12	19 42	3 18	20 36
137			**10 59**	**23 55**	**10 48**	**– –**	**10 35**	**– –**	**10 17**	**0 01**	**9 48**	**0 33**
18 We	11 56 23	19 27	5 23	18 30	5 05	18 48	4 42	19 11	4 11	19 43	3 16	20 38
138	**12 50 FQ**		**11 55**	**– –**	**11 48**	**0 04**	**11 40**	**0 14**	**11 28**	**0 29**	**11 11**	**0 50**
19 Th	11 56 25	19 40	5 23	18 30	5 04	18 49	4 42	19 12	4 09	19 44	3 14	20 40
139			**12 51**	**0 37**	**12 49**	**0 42**	**12 46**	**0 47**	**12 42**	**0 54**	**12 36**	**1 05**
20 Fr	11 56 29	19 53	5 22	18 31	5 04	18 49	4 41	19 13	4 08	19 46	3 12	20 43
140			**13 50**	**1 19**	**13 52**	**1 19**	**13 55**	**1 19**	**13 58**	**1 20**	**14 05**	**1 19**
21 Sa	11 56 32	20 5	5 22	18 31	5 03	18 50	4 40	19 14	4 07	19 47	3 10	20 45
141			**14 50**	**2 03**	**14 57**	**1 58**	**15 06**	**1 53**	**15 17**	**1 45**	**15 36**	**1 34**
22 Su	11 56 36	20 18	5 22	18 32	5 03	18 51	4 39	19 14	4 06	19 48	3 08	20 47
142			**15 53**	**2 49**	**16 04**	**2 40**	**16 18**	**2 29**	**16 38**	**2 14**	**17 10**	**1 51**
23 Mo	11 56 41	20 29	5 22	18 32	5 03	18 51	4 39	19 15	4 04	19 50	3 06	20 49
143			**16 58**	**3 39**	**17 13**	**3 25**	**17 32**	**3 09**	**17 59**	**2 47**	**18 44**	**2 12**
24 Tu	11 56 46	20 41	5 21	18 32	5 02	18 52	4 38	19 16	4 03	19 51	3 04	20 51
144			**18 04**	**4 33**	**18 22**	**4 16**	**18 45**	**3 55**	**19 17**	**3 26**	**20 12**	**2 40**
25 We	11 56 52	20 52	5 21	18 33	5 02	18 52	4 37	19 17	4 02	19 52	3 02	20 54
145	**3 39 FM**		**19 08**	**5 31**	**19 28**	**5 12**	**19 53**	**4 48**	**20 28**	**4 15**	**21 27**	**3 19**
26 Th	11 56 58	21 3	5 21	18 33	5 01	18 53	4 37	19 18	4 01	19 53	3 00	20 56
146			**20 10**	**6 32**	**20 29**	**6 12**	**20 53**	**5 48**	**21 27**	**5 13**	**22 24**	**4 13**
27 Fr	11 57 04	21 13	5 21	18 34	5 01	18 53	4 36	19 19	4 00	19 55	2 58	20 58
147			**21 06**	**7 34**	**21 23**	**7 16**	**21 45**	**6 52**	**22 15**	**6 19**	**23 05**	**5 23**
28 Sa	11 57 11	21 23	5 20	18 34	5 01	18 54	4 35	19 19	3 59	19 56	2 56	21 00
148			**21 56**	**8 36**	**22 11**	**8 19**	**22 29**	**7 59**	**22 53**	**7 30**	**23 33**	**6 42**
29 Su	11 57 19	21 33	5 20	18 34	5 00	18 55	4 35	19 20	3 58	19 57	2 55	21 01
149			**22 42**	**9 35**	**22 53**	**9 21**	**23 06**	**9 05**	**23 25**	**8 42**	**23 53**	**8 06**
30 Mo	11 57 27	21 42	5 20	18 35	5 00	18 55	4 34	19 21	3 58	19 58	2 53	21 03
150			**23 23**	**10 30**	**23 30**	**10 21**	**23 39**	**10 09**	**23 51**	**9 53**	**– –**	**9 28**
31 Tu	11 57 36	21 51	5 20	18 35	5 00	18 56	4 34	19 22	3 57	19 59	2 51	21 05
151			**– –**	**11 23**	**– –**	**11 18**	**– –**	**11 11**	**– –**	**11 02**	**0 09**	**10 48**

6th Month — June 1994 — 30 days

Greenwich Mean Time

NOTE: Light numbers indicate Sun. **Dark** numbers indicate **Moon.** *Degrees are North Latitude.*

FM = full moon; LQ = last quarter; NM = new moon; FQ = first quarter.

CAUTION: Must be converted to local time. For instructions see page 239.

Day of month week year	Sun on Meridian **Moon phase** h m s	Sun's Declination ° ′	20° Rise Sun **Moon** h m	20° Set Sun **Moon** h m	30° Rise Sun **Moon** h m	30° Set Sun **Moon** h m	40° Rise Sun **Moon** h m	40° Set Sun **Moon** h m	50° Rise Sun **Moon** h m	50° Set Sun **Moon** h m	60° Rise Sun **Moon** h m	60° Set Sun **Moon** h m
1 We	11 57 44	21 59	5 20	18 36	4 59	18 56	4 33	19 22	3 56	20 00	2 50	21 07
152	4 2 LQ		0 01	12 14	0 04	12 13	0 08	12 11	0 14	12 09	0 22	12 05
2 Th	11 57 54	22 8	5 20	18 36	4 59	18 57	4 33	19 23	3 55	20 01	2 48	21 09
153			0 38	13 04	0 37	13 06	0 36	13 09	0 36	13 14	0 34	13 20
3 Fr	11 58 04	22 15	5 20	18 36	4 59	18 57	4 33	19 24	3 55	20 02	2 47	21 10
154			1 14	13 53	1 09	13 59	1 04	14 07	0 57	14 17	0 46	14 34
4 Sa	11 58 14	22 23	5 20	18 37	4 59	18 58	4 32	19 25	3 54	20 03	2 46	21 12
155			1 50	14 41	1 42	14 51	1 32	15 04	1 19	15 20	0 59	15 47
5 Su	11 58 24	22 30	5 20	18 37	4 59	18 58	4 32	19 25	3 53	20 04	2 44	21 13
156			2 27	15 31	2 16	15 44	2 02	16 00	1 43	16 23	1 13	16 59
6 Mo	11 58 35	22 36	5 20	18 37	4 59	18 59	4 32	19 26	3 53	20 05	2 43	21 15
157			3 07	16 21	2 53	16 37	2 35	16 57	2 10	17 24	1 31	18 10
7 Tu	11 58 46	22 42	5 20	18 38	4 58	18 59	4 31	19 26	3 52	20 05	2 42	21 16
158			3 49	17 11	3 32	17 29	3 11	17 52	2 42	18 24	1 55	19 17
8 We	11 58 57	22 48	5 20	18 38	4 58	19 00	4 31	19 27	3 52	20 06	2 41	21 18
159			4 34	18 02	4 16	18 21	3 52	18 45	3 20	19 19	2 26	20 17
9 Th	11 59 09	22 54	5 20	18 39	4 58	19 00	4 31	19 28	3 52	20 07	2 40	21 19
160	8 26 NM		5 23	18 52	5 03	19 11	4 39	19 36	4 05	20 10	3 07	21 07
10 Fr	11 59 21	22 58	5 20	18 39	4 58	19 01	4 31	19 28	3 51	20 08	2 39	21 20
161			6 13	19 41	5 54	19 59	5 30	20 22	4 57	20 54	4 00	21 47
11 Sa	11 59 33	23 3	5 20	18 39	4 58	19 01	4 31	19 29	3 51	20 08	2 39	21 21
162			7 06	20 28	6 49	20 44	6 27	21 04	5 56	21 32	5 04	22 17
12 Su	11 59 46	23 7	5 20	18 40	4 58	19 01	4 31	19 29	3 51	20 09	2 38	21 22
163			8 00	21 12	7 45	21 26	7 26	21 42	7 00	22 05	6 17	22 40
13 Mo	11 59 58	23 11	5 20	18 40	4 58	19 02	4 31	19 30	3 51	20 10	2 37	21 23
164			8 55	21 55	8 43	22 05	8 28	22 17	8 08	22 33	7 35	22 58
14 Tu	12 0 11	23 14	5 20	18 40	4 58	19 02	4 31	19 30	3 50	20 10	2 37	21 24
165			9 50	22 37	9 42	22 43	9 32	22 50	9 18	22 59	8 57	23 14
15 We	12 0 24	23 17	5 20	18 40	4 58	19 02	4 31	19 30	3 50	20 11	2 36	21 25
166			10 45	23 18	10 42	23 20	10 37	23 22	10 30	23 24	10 20	23 28
16 Th	12 0 36	23 20	5 21	18 41	4 59	19 03	4 31	19 31	3 50	20 11	2 36	21 26
167	19 56 FQ		11 42	24 00	11 42	23 57	11 43	23 54	11 44	23 49	11 46	23 42
17 Fr	12 0 49	23 22	5 21	18 41	4 59	19 03	4 31	19 31	3 50	20 12	2 36	21 26
168			12 40	– –	12 45	– –	12 51	– –	13 00	– –	13 13	23 57
18 Sa	12 1 02	23 24	5 21	18 41	4 59	19 03	4 31	19 31	3 50	20 12	2 36	21 27
169			13 39	0 43	13 49	0 36	14 01	0 27	14 17	0 15	14 43	– –
19 Su	12 1 15	23 25	5 21	18 41	4 59	19 04	4 31	19 32	3 50	20 12	2 36	21 27
170			14 41	1 30	14 55	1 18	15 12	1 04	15 36	0 45	16 14	0 15
20 Mo	12 1 28	23 26	5 21	18 42	4 59	19 04	4 31	19 32	3 50	20 13	2 36	21 27
171			15 45	2 20	16 02	2 05	16 23	1 46	16 53	1 20	17 43	0 39
21 Tu	12 1 41	23 26	5 21	18 42	4 59	19 04	4 31	19 32	3 51	20 13	2 36	21 28
172			16 49	3 14	17 08	2 56	17 32	2 34	18 06	2 03	19 04	1 11
22 We	12 1 54	23 26	5 22	18 42	5 00	19 04	4 31	19 32	3 51	20 13	2 36	21 28
173			17 51	4 13	18 11	3 54	18 36	3 29	19 10	2 55	20 10	1 56
23 Th	12 2 07	23 26	5 22	18 42	5 00	19 04	4 32	19 33	3 51	20 13	2 36	21 28
174	11 33 FM		18 50	5 15	19 09	4 55	19 32	4 31	20 04	3 56	20 59	2 57
24 Fr	12 2 20	23 25	5 22	18 43	5 00	19 05	4 32	19 33	3 51	20 13	2 37	21 28
175			19 44	6 17	20 00	5 59	20 20	5 37	20 48	5 06	21 33	4 13
25 Sa	12 2 33	23 24	5 22	18 43	5 00	19 05	4 32	19 33	3 52	20 13	2 37	21 28
176			20 33	7 18	20 46	7 03	21 01	6 45	21 23	6 19	21 57	5 36
26 Su	12 2 45	23 22	5 23	18 43	5 01	19 05	4 33	19 33	3 52	20 13	2 38	21 27
177			21 17	8 17	21 26	8 05	21 37	7 51	21 52	7 32	22 15	7 01
27 Mo	12 2 58	23 20	5 23	18 43	5 01	19 05	4 33	19 33	3 53	20 13	2 38	21 27
178			21 57	9 12	22 02	9 05	22 09	8 56	22 17	8 44	22 30	8 24
28 Tu	12 3 10	23 18	5 23	18 43	5 01	19 05	4 33	19 33	3 53	20 13	2 39	21 27
179			22 36	10 05	22 37	10 02	22 38	9 58	22 40	9 53	22 43	9 44
29 We	12 3 22	23 15	5 23	18 43	5 02	19 05	4 34	19 33	3 54	20 13	2 40	21 26
180			23 12	10 56	23 10	10 57	23 06	10 58	23 02	11 00	22 55	11 02
30 Th	12 3 34	23 12	5 24	18 43	5 02	19 05	4 34	19 33	3 54	20 13	2 41	21 26
181	19 31 LQ		23 49	11 46	23 42	11 51	23 34	11 57	23 24	12 05	23 07	12 17

7th Month July 1994 31 days

Greenwich Mean Time

NOTE: Light numbers indicate Sun. **Dark** numbers indicate **Moon.** *Degrees are North Latitude.*

FM = full moon; LQ = last quarter; NM = new moon; FQ = first quarter.

CAUTION: Must be converted to local time. For instructions see page 239.

Day of month week year	Sun on Meridian **Moon phase** h m s	Sun's Declination ° '	20° Rise Sun **Moon** h m	20° Set Sun **Moon** h m	30° Rise Sun **Moon** h m	30° Set Sun **Moon** h m	40° Rise Sun **Moon** h m	40° Set Sun **Moon** h m	50° Rise Sun **Moon** h m	50° Set Sun **Moon** h m	60° Rise Sun **Moon** h m	60° Set Sun **Moon** h m
1 Fr	12 3 46	23 8	5 24	18 43	5 02	19 05	4 35	19 33	3 55	20 12	2 42	21 25
182			**– –**	**12 35**	**– –**	**12 44**	**– –**	**12 54**	**23 47**	**13 09**	**23 21**	**13 31**
2 Sa	12 3 57	23 4	5 24	18 43	5 03	19 05	4 35	19 33	3 55	20 12	2 43	21 24
183			**0 26**	**13 25**	**0 16**	**13 37**	**0 04**	**13 51**	**– –**	**14 12**	**23 38**	**14 44**
3 Su	12 4 09	23 0	5 25	18 43	5 03	19 05	4 36	19 32	3 56	20 12	2 44	21 23
184			**1 05**	**14 14**	**0 51**	**14 29**	**0 35**	**14 48**	**0 13**	**15 14**	**23 59**	**15 56**
4 Mo	12 4 20	22 55	5 25	18 44	5 04	19 05	4 36	19 32	3 57	20 11	2 45	21 22
185			**1 46**	**15 05**	**1 30**	**15 22**	**1 10**	**15 44**	**0 43**	**16 14**	**– –**	**17 04**
5 Tu	12 4 30	22 50	5 25	18 44	5 04	19 05	4 37	19 32	3 58	20 11	2 47	21 21
186			**2 30**	**15 55**	**2 12**	**16 14**	**1 49**	**16 38**	**1 18**	**17 11**	**0 26**	**18 07**
6 We	12 4 40	22 44	5 26	18 44	5 04	19 05	4 37	19 32	3 58	20 10	2 48	21 20
187			**3 17**	**16 46**	**2 58**	**17 05**	**2 34**	**17 30**	**2 00**	**18 04**	**1 03**	**19 02**
7 Th	12 4 50	22 38	5 26	18 44	5 05	19 05	4 38	19 31	3 59	20 10	2 49	21 19
188			**4 07**	**17 36**	**3 48**	**17 55**	**3 23**	**18 18**	**2 49**	**18 51**	**1 51**	**19 46**
8 Fr	12 5 00	22 31	5 26	18 43	5 05	19 04	4 39	19 31	4 00	20 09	2 51	21 18
189	**21 37 NM**		**5 00**	**18 24**	**4 41**	**18 41**	**4 18**	**19 02**	**3 46**	**19 32**	**2 52**	**20 20**
9 Sa	12 5 09	22 25	5 27	18 43	5 06	19 04	4 39	19 31	4 01	20 09	2 52	21 17
190			**5 54**	**19 10**	**5 38**	**19 25**	**5 18**	**19 43**	**4 49**	**20 07**	**4 03**	**20 46**
10 Su	12 5 18	22 17	5 27	18 43	5 06	19 04	4 40	19 30	4 02	20 08	2 54	21 15
191			**6 49**	**19 55**	**6 36**	**20 06**	**6 20**	**20 19**	**5 57**	**20 38**	**5 21**	**21 06**
11 Mo	12 5 26	22 10	5 28	18 43	5 07	19 04	4 41	19 30	4 03	20 07	2 56	21 14
192			**7 45**	**20 37**	**7 36**	**20 44**	**7 24**	**20 53**	**7 08**	**21 05**	**6 43**	**21 23**
12 Tu	12 5 34	22 2	5 28	18 43	5 07	19 04	4 41	19 29	4 04	20 07	2 58	21 12
193			**8 41**	**21 19**	**8 36**	**21 22**	**8 29**	**21 26**	**8 21**	**21 30**	**8 07**	**21 38**
13 We	12 5 42	21 53	5 28	18 43	5 08	19 03	4 42	19 29	4 05	20 06	2 59	21 11
194			**9 38**	**22 00**	**9 37**	**21 59**	**9 36**	**21 57**	**9 34**	**21 55**	**9 32**	**21 52**
14 Th	12 5 49	21 45	5 29	18 43	5 08	19 03	4 43	19 28	4 06	20 05	3 01	21 09
195			**10 35**	**22 43**	**10 38**	**22 37**	**10 43**	**22 30**	**10 49**	**22 21**	**10 58**	**22 07**
15 Fr	12 5 55	21 36	5 29	18 43	5 09	19 03	4 43	19 28	4 07	20 04	3 03	21 07
196			**11 33**	**23 27**	**11 41**	**23 17**	**11 51**	**23 05**	**12 05**	**22 49**	**12 26**	**22 23**
16 Sa	12 6 01	21 26	5 29	18 43	5 09	19 02	4 44	19 27	4 08	20 03	3 05	21 06
197	**1 12 FQ**		**12 33**	**– –**	**12 45**	**– –**	**13 00**	**23 44**	**13 21**	**23 21**	**13 55**	**22 44**
17 Su	12 6 06	21 16	5 30	18 42	5 10	19 02	4 45	19 27	4 09	20 02	3 07	21 04
198			**13 34**	**0 15**	**13 50**	**0 01**	**14 09**	**– –**	**14 37**	**23 59**	**15 22**	**23 11**
18 Mo	12 6 11	21 6	5 30	18 42	5 11	19 02	4 46	19 26	4 11	20 01	3 09	21 02
199			**14 36**	**1 06**	**14 54**	**0 49**	**15 17**	**0 28**	**15 50**	**– –**	**16 44**	**23 50**
19 Tu	12 6 15	20 56	5 30	18 42	5 11	19 01	4 47	19 25	4 12	20 00	3 11	21 00
200			**15 37**	**2 01**	**15 57**	**1 42**	**16 21**	**1 19**	**16 56**	**0 46**	**17 55**	**– –**
20 We	12 6 19	20 45	5 31	18 42	5 12	19 01	4 47	19 25	4 13	19 59	3 13	20 58
201			**16 36**	**3 00**	**16 56**	**2 41**	**17 20**	**2 16**	**17 53**	**1 41**	**18 50**	**0 42**
21 Th	12 6 22	20 33	5 31	18 41	5 12	19 00	4 48	19 24	4 14	19 58	3 15	20 56
202			**17 32**	**4 01**	**17 49**	**3 42**	**18 11**	**3 19**	**18 41**	**2 46**	**19 31**	**1 50**
22 Fr	12 6 24	20 22	5 32	18 41	5 13	19 00	4 49	19 23	4 15	19 57	3 17	20 54
203	**20 16 FM**		**18 23**	**5 02**	**18 37**	**4 45**	**18 55**	**4 25**	**19 20**	**3 56**	**19 59**	**3 09**
23 Sa	12 6 26	20 10	5 32	18 41	5 13	18 59	4 50	19 22	4 17	19 55	3 19	20 52
204			**19 09**	**6 01**	**19 20**	**5 48**	**19 33**	**5 32**	**19 52**	**5 09**	**20 20**	**4 33**
24 Su	12 6 28	19 58	5 32	18 40	5 14	18 59	4 51	19 22	4 18	19 54	3 22	20 50
205			**19 52**	**6 59**	**19 59**	**6 49**	**20 07**	**6 38**	**20 19**	**6 22**	**20 37**	**5 57**
25 Mo	12 6 29	19 45	5 33	18 40	5 15	18 58	4 52	19 21	4 19	19 53	3 24	20 47
206			**20 31**	**7 53**	**20 34**	**7 48**	**20 38**	**7 42**	**20 43**	**7 33**	**20 51**	**7 19**
26 Tu	12 6 29	19 32	5 33	18 40	5 15	18 57	4 53	19 20	4 21	19 51	3 26	20 45
207			**21 09**	**8 46**	**21 08**	**8 45**	**21 07**	**8 44**	**21 06**	**8 42**	**21 03**	**8 39**
27 We	12 6 28	19 19	5 33	18 39	5 16	18 57	4 53	19 19	4 22	19 50	3 28	20 43
208			**21 46**	**9 37**	**21 42**	**9 40**	**21 36**	**9 44**	**21 28**	**9 49**	**21 16**	**9 56**
28 Th	12 6 27	19 5	5 34	18 39	5 16	18 56	4 54	19 18	4 23	19 49	3 31	20 41
209			**22 24**	**10 27**	**22 15**	**10 34**	**22 05**	**10 43**	**21 51**	**10 54**	**21 29**	**11 12**
29 Fr	12 6 26	18 51	5 34	18 38	5 17	18 56	4 55	19 17	4 25	19 47	3 33	20 38
210			**23 02**	**11 17**	**22 50**	**11 27**	**22 36**	**11 40**	**22 16**	**11 58**	**21 45**	**12 26**
30 Sa	12 6 24	18 37	5 35	18 38	5 18	18 55	4 56	19 16	4 26	19 46	3 35	20 36
211	**12 40 LQ**		**23 42**	**12 07**	**23 27**	**12 20**	**23 09**	**12 37**	**22 44**	**13 00**	**22 04**	**13 38**
31 Su	12 6 21	18 23	5 35	18 38	5 18	18 54	4 57	19 15	4 27	19 44	3 38	20 33
212			**– –**	**12 57**	**– –**	**13 13**	**23 46**	**13 33**	**23 17**	**14 01**	**22 29**	**14 48**

8th Month — August 1994 — 31 days

Greenwich Mean Time

NOTE: Light numbers indicate Sun. **Dark** numbers indicate **Moon.** *Degrees are North Latitude.*

FM = full moon; LQ = last quarter; NM = new moon; FQ = first quarter.

CAUTION: Must be converted to local time. For instructions see page 239.

Day of month week year	Sun on Meridian **Moon phase** h m s	Sun's Declination ° ′	20° Rise Sun **Moon** h m	20° Set Sun **Moon** h m	30° Rise Sun **Moon** h m	30° Set Sun **Moon** h m	40° Rise Sun **Moon** h m	40° Set Sun **Moon** h m	50° Rise Sun **Moon** h m	50° Set Sun **Moon** h m	60° Rise Sun **Moon** h m	60° Set Sun **Moon** h m
1 Mo	12 6 18	18 8	5 35	18 37	5 19	18 53	4 58	19 14	4 29	19 43	3 40	20 31
213			**0 25**	**13 47**	**0 07**	**14 05**	**– –**	**14 28**	**23 55**	**15 00**	**23 01**	**15 53**
2 Tu	12 6 14	17 53	5 36	18 37	5 19	18 53	4 59	19 13	4 30	19 41	3 42	20 28
214			**1 10**	**14 38**	**0 51**	**14 57**	**0 28**	**15 21**	**– –**	**15 54**	**23 44**	**16 52**
3 We	12 6 09	17 37	5 36	18 36	5 20	18 52	5 00	19 12	4 32	19 40	3 45	20 26
215			**1 59**	**15 27**	**1 39**	**15 47**	**1 15**	**16 10**	**0 41**	**16 44**	**– –**	**17 40**
4 Th	12 6 04	17 22	5 36	18 36	5 21	18 51	5 01	19 11	4 33	19 38	3 47	20 23
216			**2 50**	**16 16**	**2 31**	**16 34**	**2 08**	**16 57**	**1 35**	**17 28**	**0 39**	**18 19**
5 Fr	12 5 59	17 6	5 37	18 35	5 21	18 50	5 02	19 10	4 34	19 36	3 49	20 21
217			**3 44**	**17 04**	**3 27**	**17 20**	**3 05**	**17 39**	**2 36**	**18 06**	**1 46**	**18 48**
6 Sa	12 5 52	16 49	5 37	18 34	5 22	18 50	5 03	19 08	4 36	19 35	3 52	20 18
218			**4 39**	**17 50**	**4 25**	**18 02**	**4 07**	**18 18**	**3 42**	**18 39**	**3 01**	**19 11**
7 Su	12 5 45	16 33	5 37	18 34	5 22	18 49	5 04	19 07	4 37	19 33	3 54	20 16
219	**8 45 NM**		**5 36**	**18 34**	**5 25**	**18 43**	**5 11**	**18 53**	**4 53**	**19 08**	**4 23**	**19 30**
8 Mo	12 5 38	16 16	5 38	18 33	5 23	18 48	5 05	19 06	4 39	19 31	3 57	20 13
220			**6 33**	**19 17**	**6 26**	**19 22**	**6 18**	**19 27**	**6 06**	**19 35**	**5 48**	**19 46**
9 Tu	12 5 30	15 59	5 38	18 33	5 24	18 47	5 06	19 05	4 40	19 30	3 59	20 10
221			**7 31**	**19 59**	**7 28**	**20 00**	**7 25**	**20 00**	**7 21**	**20 00**	**7 14**	**20 01**
10 We	12 5 21	15 42	5 38	18 32	5 24	18 46	5 06	19 04	4 42	19 28	4 01	20 08
222			**8 29**	**20 43**	**8 31**	**20 38**	**8 33**	**20 33**	**8 37**	**20 26**	**8 42**	**20 16**
11 Th	12 5 12	15 24	5 39	18 31	5 25	18 45	5 07	19 02	4 43	19 26	4 04	20 05
223			**9 27**	**21 27**	**9 34**	**21 18**	**9 42**	**21 08**	**9 53**	**20 54**	**10 11**	**20 32**
12 Fr	12 5 02	15 6	5 39	18 31	5 25	18 44	5 08	19 01	4 45	19 24	4 06	20 02
224			**10 27**	**22 14**	**10 38**	**22 01**	**10 51**	**21 46**	**11 10**	**21 25**	**11 40**	**20 52**
13 Sa	12 4 52	14 48	5 39	18 30	5 26	18 43	5 09	19 00	4 46	19 23	4 09	19 59
225			**11 28**	**23 04**	**11 43**	**22 48**	**12 01**	**22 28**	**12 26**	**22 01**	**13 07**	**21 17**
14 Su	12 4 41	14 30	5 40	18 30	5 27	18 42	5 10	18 58	4 48	19 21	4 11	19 57
226	**5 57 FQ**		**12 29**	**23 57**	**12 47**	**23 39**	**13 09**	**23 16**	**13 39**	**22 44**	**14 30**	**21 51**
15 Mo	12 4 30	14 11	5 40	18 29	5 27	18 41	5 11	18 57	4 49	19 19	4 13	19 54
227			**13 30**	**– –**	**13 49**	**– –**	**14 13**	**– –**	**14 47**	**23 36**	**15 44**	**22 38**
16 Tu	12 4 17	13 53	5 40	18 28	5 28	18 40	5 12	18 56	4 51	19 17	4 16	19 51
228			**14 28**	**0 53**	**14 48**	**0 34**	**15 12**	**0 10**	**15 46**	**– –**	**16 44**	**23 38**
17 We	12 4 05	13 34	5 40	18 27	5 28	18 39	5 13	18 54	4 52	19 15	4 18	19 48
229			**15 24**	**1 52**	**15 42**	**1 33**	**16 04**	**1 09**	**16 36**	**0 35**	**17 28**	**– –**
18 Th	12 3 52	13 15	5 41	18 27	5 29	18 38	5 14	18 53	4 54	19 13	4 21	19 45
230			**16 15**	**2 51**	**16 31**	**2 34**	**16 50**	**2 12**	**17 17**	**1 42**	**18 00**	**0 51**
19 Fr	12 3 38	12 55	5 41	18 26	5 29	18 37	5 15	18 52	4 55	19 11	4 23	19 42
231			**17 02**	**3 50**	**17 15**	**3 35**	**17 30**	**3 17**	**17 51**	**2 52**	**18 24**	**2 11**
20 Sa	12 3 24	12 36	5 41	18 25	5 30	18 36	5 16	18 50	4 57	19 09	4 25	19 40
232			**17 46**	**4 47**	**17 55**	**4 36**	**18 06**	**4 23**	**18 20**	**4 04**	**18 43**	**3 34**
21 Su	12 3 09	12 16	5 42	18 24	5 31	18 35	5 17	18 49	4 58	19 07	4 28	19 37
233	**6 47 FM**		**18 27**	**5 42**	**18 32**	**5 35**	**18 38**	**5 27**	**18 46**	**5 15**	**18 58**	**4 56**
22 Mo	12 2 54	11 56	5 42	18 24	5 31	18 34	5 18	18 47	5 00	19 05	4 30	19 34
234			**19 06**	**6 36**	**19 06**	**6 33**	**19 08**	**6 29**	**19 09**	**6 24**	**19 11**	**6 17**
23 Tu	12 2 39	11 36	5 42	18 23	5 32	18 33	5 19	18 46	5 01	19 03	4 33	19 31
235			**19 43**	**7 28**	**19 40**	**7 29**	**19 37**	**7 30**	**19 32**	**7 32**	**19 24**	**7 35**
24 We	12 2 23	11 15	5 42	18 22	5 32	18 32	5 20	18 44	5 03	19 01	4 35	19 28
236			**20 21**	**8 18**	**20 14**	**8 24**	**20 06**	**8 30**	**19 55**	**8 38**	**19 38**	**8 51**
25 Th	12 2 07	10 55	5 43	18 21	5 33	18 31	5 21	18 43	5 04	18 59	4 37	19 25
237			**20 59**	**9 09**	**20 49**	**9 17**	**20 36**	**9 28**	**20 19**	**9 43**	**19 53**	**10 06**
26 Fr	12 1 50	10 34	5 43	18 21	5 33	18 30	5 22	18 41	5 06	18 57	4 40	19 22
238			**21 38**	**9 59**	**21 25**	**10 11**	**21 09**	**10 26**	**20 46**	**10 46**	**20 10**	**11 20**
27 Sa	12 1 33	10 13	5 43	18 20	5 34	18 29	5 23	18 40	5 07	18 55	4 42	19 19
239			**22 20**	**10 49**	**22 04**	**11 04**	**21 44**	**11 22**	**21 17**	**11 48**	**20 33**	**12 30**
28 Su	12 1 15	9 52	5 43	18 19	5 35	18 27	5 24	18 38	5 08	18 53	4 45	19 16
240			**23 04**	**11 39**	**22 46**	**11 56**	**22 24**	**12 17**	**21 53**	**12 47**	**21 01**	**13 37**
29 Mo	12 0 57	9 31	5 44	18 18	5 35	18 26	5 25	18 37	5 10	18 51	4 47	19 13
241	**6 41 LQ**		**23 50**	**12 29**	**23 32**	**12 47**	**23 08**	**13 10**	**22 35**	**13 43**	**21 39**	**14 38**
30 Tu	12 0 39	9 10	5 44	18 17	5 36	18 25	5 25	18 35	5 11	18 49	4 49	19 10
242			**– –**	**13 18**	**– –**	**13 37**	**23 58**	**14 01**	**23 24**	**14 34**	**22 28**	**15 31**
31 We	12 0 21	8 48	5 44	18 16	5 36	18 24	5 26	18 34	5 13	18 47	4 52	19 07
243			**0 40**	**14 07**	**0 21**	**14 25**	**– –**	**14 48**	**– –**	**15 20**	**23 29**	**16 13**

9th Month — September 1994 — 30 days

Greenwich Mean Time

NOTE: Light numbers indicate Sun. **Dark** numbers indicate **Moon.** *Degrees are North Latitude.*

FM = full moon; LQ = last quarter; NM = new moon; FQ = first quarter.

CAUTION: Must be converted to local time. For instructions see page 239.

Day of month week year	Sun on Meridian **Moon phase** h m s	Sun's Declination ° ′	20° Rise Sun **Moon** h m	20° Set Sun **Moon** h m	30° Rise Sun **Moon** h m	30° Set Sun **Moon** h m	40° Rise Sun **Moon** h m	40° Set Sun **Moon** h m	50° Rise Sun **Moon** h m	50° Set Sun **Moon** h m	60° Rise Sun **Moon** h m	60° Set Sun **Moon** h m
1 Th	12 0 02	8 27	5 44	18 15	5 37	18 23	5 27	18 32	5 14	18 45	4 54	19 04
244			**1 32**	**14 55**	**1 14**	**15 11**	**0 52**	**15 32**	**0 21**	**16 00**	**– –**	**16 47**
2 Fr	11 59 43	8 5	5 45	18 15	5 37	18 22	5 28	18 30	5 16	18 42	4 56	19 01
245			**2 26**	**15 41**	**2 11**	**15 55**	**1 51**	**16 12**	**1 24**	**16 35**	**0 40**	**17 13**
3 Sa	11 59 24	7 43	5 45	18 14	5 38	18 20	5 29	18 29	5 17	18 40	4 59	18 58
246			**3 22**	**16 26**	**3 10**	**16 36**	**2 54**	**16 49**	**2 33**	**17 07**	**1 58**	**17 34**
4 Su	11 59 04	7 21	5 45	18 13	5 38	18 19	5 30	18 27	5 19	18 38	5 01	18 55
247			**4 19**	**17 10**	**4 11**	**17 16**	**4 00**	**17 24**	**3 45**	**17 35**	**3 22**	**17 51**
5 Mo	11 58 44	6 59	5 46	18 12	5 39	18 18	5 31	18 26	5 20	18 36	5 04	18 52
248	**18 33 NM**		**5 17**	**17 53**	**5 13**	**17 56**	**5 07**	**17 58**	**5 00**	**18 02**	**4 48**	**18 07**
6 Tu	11 58 24	6 36	5 45	18 11	5 39	18 17	5 32	18 24	5 22	18 34	5 06	18 49
249			**6 17**	**18 37**	**6 17**	**18 35**	**6 17**	**18 32**	**6 17**	**18 29**	**6 17**	**18 23**
7 We	11 58 04	6 14	5 46	18 10	5 40	18 16	5 33	18 22	5 23	18 32	5 08	18 46
250			**7 17**	**19 23**	**7 21**	**19 16**	**7 27**	**19 08**	**7 35**	**18 57**	**7 47**	**18 39**
8 Th	11 57 43	5 52	5 46	18 09	5 41	18 14	5 34	18 21	5 25	18 30	5 11	18 43
251			**8 18**	**20 10**	**8 27**	**19 59**	**8 38**	**19 46**	**8 54**	**19 27**	**9 19**	**18 59**
9 Fr	11 57 23	5 29	5 46	18 08	5 41	18 13	5 35	18 19	5 26	18 27	5 13	18 40
252			**9 20**	**21 00**	**9 33**	**20 46**	**9 50**	**20 27**	**10 12**	**20 03**	**10 49**	**19 23**
10 Sa	11 57 02	5 6	5 46	18 08	5 42	18 12	5 36	18 18	5 28	18 25	5 15	18 37
253			**10 23**	**21 53**	**10 39**	**21 36**	**10 59**	**21 14**	**11 28**	**20 44**	**12 16**	**19 55**
11 Su	11 56 41	4 44	5 46	18 07	5 42	18 11	5 37	18 16	5 29	18 23	5 18	18 34
254			**11 24**	**22 49**	**11 43**	**22 30**	**12 06**	**22 07**	**12 38**	**21 34**	**13 34**	**20 38**
12 Mo	11 56 20	4 21	5 47	18 06	5 43	18 09	5 38	18 14	5 31	18 21	5 20	18 31
255	**11 34 FQ**		**12 24**	**23 47**	**12 43**	**23 28**	**13 07**	**23 04**	**13 40**	**22 31**	**14 38**	**21 34**
13 Tu	11 55 59	3 58	5 47	18 05	5 43	18 08	5 39	18 13	5 32	18 19	5 22	18 28
256			**13 20**	**– –**	**13 38**	**– –**	**14 01**	**– –**	**14 33**	**23 35**	**15 26**	**22 42**
14 We	11 55 38	3 35	5 47	18 04	5 44	18 07	5 40	18 11	5 34	18 16	5 25	18 25
257			**14 11**	**0 46**	**14 28**	**0 28**	**14 48**	**0 06**	**15 16**	**– –**	**16 02**	**23 59**
15 Th	11 55 16	3 12	5 47	18 03	5 44	18 06	5 41	18 09	5 35	18 14	5 27	18 22
258			**14 59**	**1 44**	**15 13**	**1 28**	**15 29**	**1 09**	**15 52**	**0 43**	**16 28**	**– –**
16 Fr	11 54 55	2 49	5 48	18 02	5 45	18 04	5 42	18 08	5 37	18 12	5 29	18 19
259			**15 43**	**2 40**	**15 53**	**2 28**	**16 06**	**2 13**	**16 22**	**1 53**	**16 48**	**1 19**
17 Sa	11 54 33	2 26	5 48	18 01	5 45	18 03	5 42	18 06	5 38	18 10	5 32	18 16
260			**16 24**	**3 35**	**16 31**	**3 27**	**16 38**	**3 16**	**16 49**	**3 02**	**17 04**	**2 40**
18 Su	11 54 12	2 3	5 48	18 00	5 46	18 02	5 43	18 04	5 40	18 08	5 34	18 13
261			**17 03**	**4 28**	**17 06**	**4 24**	**17 09**	**4 18**	**17 12**	**4 11**	**17 18**	**3 59**
19 Mo	11 53 50	1 39	5 48	17 59	5 46	18 01	5 44	18 03	5 41	18 05	5 36	18 10
262	**20 0 FM**		**17 41**	**5 20**	**17 40**	**5 20**	**17 38**	**5 19**	**17 35**	**5 18**	**17 32**	**5 17**
20 Tu	11 53 29	1 16	5 48	17 58	5 47	17 59	5 45	18 01	5 43	18 03	5 39	18 07
263			**18 19**	**6 11**	**18 13**	**6 15**	**18 07**	**6 19**	**17 58**	**6 25**	**17 45**	**6 34**
21 We	11 53 08	0 53	5 49	17 57	5 48	17 58	5 46	17 59	5 44	18 01	5 41	18 04
264			**18 57**	**7 01**	**18 48**	**7 09**	**18 37**	**7 18**	**18 22**	**7 30**	**18 00**	**7 49**
22 Th	11 52 46	0 30	5 49	17 57	5 48	17 57	5 47	17 58	5 46	17 59	5 43	18 01
265			**19 36**	**7 51**	**19 24**	**8 02**	**19 09**	**8 15**	**18 48**	**8 34**	**18 17**	**9 03**
23 Fr	11 52 25	0 6	5 49	17 56	5 49	17 56	5 48	17 56	5 47	17 57	5 46	17 58
266			**20 16**	**8 41**	**20 01**	**8 55**	**19 43**	**9 12**	**18 18**	**9 36**	**18 37**	**10 14**
24 Sa	11 52 04	– 0 17	5 49	17 55	5 49	17 54	5 49	17 54	5 49	17 54	5 48	17 55
267			**20 59**	**9 31**	**20 42**	**9 48**	**20 21**	**10 08**	**19 52**	**10 36**	**19 04**	**11 23**
25 Su	11 51 44	– 0 41	5 49	17 54	5 50	17 53	5 50	17 53	5 50	17 52	5 51	17 52
268			**21 44**	**10 21**	**21 26**	**10 39**	**21 03**	**11 02**	**20 31**	**11 33**	**19 38**	**12 26**
26 Mo	11 51 23	– 1 4	5 50	17 53	5 50	17 52	5 51	17 51	5 52	17 50	5 53	17 49
269			**22 32**	**11 10**	**22 13**	**11 29**	**21 50**	**11 53**	**21 17**	**12 25**	**20 22**	**13 21**
27 Tu	11 51 02	– 1 27	5 50	17 52	5 51	17 51	5 52	17 49	5 53	17 48	5 55	17 46
270			**23 22**	**11 59**	**23 04**	**12 17**	**22 42**	**12 40**	**22 10**	**13 13**	**21 16**	**14 07**
28 We	11 50 42	– 1 51	5 50	17 51	5 51	17 50	5 53	17 48	5 55	17 46	5 58	17 42
271	**00 23 LQ**		**– –**	**12 46**	**23 58**	**13 03**	**23 37**	**13 25**	**23 09**	**13 54**	**22 21**	**14 43**
29 Th	11 50 22	– 2 14	5 50	17 50	5 52	17 48	5 54	17 46	5 56	17 43	6 00	17 39
272			**0 14**	**13 32**	**– –**	**13 47**	**– –**	**14 05**	**– –**	**14 31**	**23 35**	**15 12**
30 Fr	11 50 02	– 2 37	5 51	17 49	5 53	17 47	5 55	17 45	5 58	17 41	6 02	17 36
273			**1 08**	**14 16**	**0 54**	**14 28**	**0 37**	**14 43**	**0 13**	**15 03**	**– –**	**15 35**

10th Month **October 1994** 31 days

Greenwich Mean Time

NOTE: Light numbers indicate Sun. **Dark** numbers indicate **Moon.** *Degrees are North Latitude.*

FM = full moon; LQ = last quarter; NM = new moon; FQ = first quarter.

CAUTION: Must be converted to local time. For instructions see page 239.

Day of month week year	Sun on Meridian **Moon phase**	Sun's Declination	20° Rise Sun **Moon**	20° Set Sun **Moon**	30° Rise Sun **Moon**	30° Set Sun **Moon**	40° Rise Sun **Moon**	40° Set Sun **Moon**	50° Rise Sun **Moon**	50° Set Sun **Moon**	60° Rise Sun **Moon**	60° Set Sun **Moon**
	h m s	° ′	h m	h m	h m	h m	h m	h m	h m	h m	h m	h m
1 Sa	11 49 43	− 3 1	5 51	17 48	5 53	17 46	5 56	17 43	5 59	17 39	6 05	17 33
274			**2 04**	**15 00**	**1 53**	**15 08**	**1 40**	**15 19**	**1 22**	**15 33**	**0 54**	**15 54**
2 Su	11 49 24	− 3 24	5 51	17 47	5 54	17 45	5 57	17 41	6 01	17 37	6 07	17 30
275			**3 00**	**15 43**	**2 54**	**15 48**	**2 46**	**15 53**	**2 35**	**16 00**	**2 17**	**16 11**
3 Mo	11 49 05	− 3 47	5 51	17 47	5 54	17 43	5 58	17 40	6 03	17 35	6 09	17 27
276			**3 59**	**16 27**	**3 57**	**16 27**	**3 54**	**16 27**	**3 50**	**16 27**	**3 45**	**16 27**
4 Tu	11 48 47	− 4 10	5 52	17 46	5 55	17 42	5 59	17 38	6 04	17 33	6 12	17 24
277			**4 59**	**17 12**	**5 01**	**17 08**	**5 04**	**17 02**	**5 08**	**16 55**	**5 15**	**16 43**
5 We	11 48 29	− 4 34	5 52	17 45	5 55	17 41	6 00	17 36	6 06	17 30	6 14	17 21
278	**3 55 NM**		**6 01**	**18 00**	**6 08**	**17 51**	**6 16**	**17 40**	**6 28**	**17 25**	**6 47**	**17 02**
6 Th	11 48 11	− 4 57	5 52	17 44	5 56	17 40	6 01	17 35	6 07	17 28	6 17	17 18
279			**7 04**	**18 50**	**7 16**	**18 37**	**7 30**	**18 21**	**7 49**	**17 59**	**8 21**	**17 25**
7 Fr	11 47 53	− 5 20	5 52	17 43	5 57	17 39	6 02	17 33	6 09	17 26	6 19	17 15
280			**8 09**	**19 44**	**8 24**	**19 28**	**8 43**	**19 08**	**9 09**	**18 40**	**9 52**	**17 54**
8 Sa	11 47 36	− 5 43	5 53	17 42	5 57	17 38	6 03	17 32	6 10	17 24	6 22	17 12
281			**9 13**	**20 41**	**9 31**	**20 23**	**9 53**	**20 00**	**10 24**	**19 28**	**11 16**	**18 34**
9 Su	11 47 20	− 6 5	5 53	17 42	5 58	17 36	6 04	17 30	6 12	17 22	6 24	17 10
282			**10 15**	**21 40**	**10 34**	**21 21**	**10 58**	**20 58**	**11 31**	**20 24**	**12 28**	**19 28**
10 Mo	11 47 04	− 6 28	5 53	17 41	5 58	17 35	6 05	17 29	6 13	17 20	6 26	17 07
283			**11 14**	**22 40**	**11 33**	**22 22**	**11 56**	**21 59**	**12 28**	**21 27**	**13 23**	**20 34**
11 Tu	11 46 48	− 6 51	5 53	17 40	5 59	17 34	6 06	17 27	6 15	17 18	6 29	17 04
284	**19 17 FQ**		**12 08**	**23 39**	**12 25**	**23 23**	**12 46**	**23 03**	**13 15**	**22 35**	**14 03**	**21 49**
12 We	11 46 33	− 7 14	5 54	17 39	6 00	17 33	6 07	17 26	6 17	17 16	6 31	17 01
285			**12 57**	**– –**	**13 12**	**– –**	**13 29**	**– –**	**13 54**	**23 45**	**14 32**	**23 09**
13 Th	11 46 18	− 7 36	5 54	17 38	6 00	17 32	6 08	17 24	6 18	17 14	6 34	16 58
286			**13 42**	**0 36**	**13 53**	**0 23**	**14 07**	**0 07**	**14 25**	**– –**	**14 54**	**– –**
14 Fr	11 46 04	− 7 59	5 54	17 37	6 01	17 31	6 09	17 22	6 20	17 12	6 36	16 55
287			**14 24**	**1 31**	**14 31**	**1 22**	**14 40**	**1 10**	**14 52**	**0 54**	**15 11**	**0 29**
15 Sa	11 45 50	− 8 21	5 55	17 37	6 02	17 30	6 10	17 21	6 21	17 10	6 39	16 52
288			**15 03**	**2 24**	**15 07**	**2 19**	**15 11**	**2 12**	**15 17**	**2 02**	**15 26**	**1 48**
16 Su	11 45 37	− 8 43	5 55	17 36	6 02	17 29	6 11	17 20	6 23	17 07	6 41	16 49
289			**15 41**	**3 16**	**15 41**	**3 14**	**15 40**	**3 12**	**15 40**	**3 09**	**15 39**	**3 05**
17 Mo	11 45 25	− 9 5	5 55	17 35	6 03	17 27	6 12	17 18	6 25	17 05	6 44	16 46
290			**16 18**	**4 06**	**16 14**	**4 09**	**16 09**	**4 11**	**16 03**	**4 15**	**15 53**	**4 21**
18 Tu	11 45 13	− 9 27	5 56	17 34	6 04	17 26	6 13	17 17	6 26	17 03	6 46	16 43
291			**16 56**	**4 56**	**16 48**	**5 02**	**16 39**	**5 10**	**16 26**	**5 20**	**16 07**	**5 35**
19 We	11 45 01	− 9 49	5 56	17 34	6 04	17 25	6 14	17 15	6 28	17 01	6 49	16 40
292	**12 18 FM**		**17 34**	**5 46**	**17 23**	**5 56**	**17 10**	**6 07**	**16 51**	**6 23**	**16 23**	**6 49**
20 Th	11 44 50	−10 11	5 56	17 33	6 05	17 24	6 15	17 14	6 29	16 59	6 51	16 38
293			**18 14**	**6 36**	**18 00**	**6 49**	**17 43**	**7 03**	**17 20**	**7 26**	**16 42**	**8 01**
21 Fr	11 44 40	−10 32	5 57	17 32	6 06	17 23	6 16	17 12	6 31	16 58	6 54	16 35
294			**18 56**	**7 26**	**18 40**	**7 41**	**18 20**	**8 00**	**17 52**	**8 27**	**17 07**	**9 11**
22 Sa	11 44 31	−10 53	5 57	17 32	6 06	17 22	6 18	17 11	6 33	16 56	6 56	16 32
295			**19 41**	**8 16**	**19 23**	**8 33**	**19 01**	**8 55**	**18 30**	**9 25**	**17 38**	**10 16**
23 Su	11 44 22	−11 15	5 58	17 31	6 07	17 21	6 19	17 10	6 34	16 54	6 59	16 29
296			**20 27**	**9 05**	**20 09**	**9 24**	**19 46**	**9 47**	**19 13**	**10 19**	**18 18**	**11 13**
24 Mo	11 44 14	−11 36	5 58	17 30	6 08	17 20	6 20	17 08	6 36	16 52	7 01	16 26
297			**21 16**	**9 54**	**20 58**	**10 12**	**20 35**	**10 35**	**20 03**	**11 08**	**19 09**	**12 02**
25 Tu	11 44 07	−11 56	5 58	17 30	6 08	17 19	6 21	17 07	6 38	16 50	7 04	16 24
298			**22 07**	**10 40**	**21 50**	**10 58**	**21 28**	**11 20**	**20 58**	**11 51**	**20 09**	**12 42**
26 We	11 44 00	−12 17	5 59	17 29	6 09	17 18	6 22	17 06	6 39	16 48	7 06	16 21
299			**22 59**	**11 26**	**22 44**	**11 42**	**22 25**	**12 02**	**21 59**	**12 29**	**21 17**	**13 13**
27 Th	11 43 54	−12 38	5 59	17 28	6 10	17 18	6 23	17 04	6 41	16 46	7 09	16 18
300			**23 52**	**12 10**	**23 40**	**12 23**	**23 25**	**12 39**	**23 05**	**13 02**	**22 32**	**13 37**
28 Fr	11 43 49	−12 58	6 00	17 28	6 11	17 17	6 24	17 03	6 43	16 44	7 11	16 15
301			**– –**	**12 52**	**– –**	**13 02**	**– –**	**13 15**	**– –**	**13 31**	**23 51**	**13 57**
29 Sa	11 43 45	−13 18	6 00	17 27	6 11	17 16	6 25	17 02	6 44	16 43	7 14	16 13
302			**0 46**	**13 34**	**0 38**	**13 41**	**0 27**	**13 48**	**0 13**	**13 59**	**– –**	**14 14**
30 Su	11 43 41	−13 38	6 00	17 27	6 12	17 15	6 26	17 00	6 46	16 41	7 16	16 10
303			**1 42**	**14 17**	**1 38**	**14 19**	**1 32**	**14 21**	**1 25**	**14 25**	**1 14**	**14 30**
31 Mo	11 43 38	−13 58	6 01	17 26	6 13	17 14	6 28	16 59	6 47	16 39	7 19	16 07
304			**2 39**	**15 00**	**2 40**	**14 58**	**2 40**	**14 55**	**2 40**	**14 52**	**2 40**	**14 46**

11th Month — November 1994 — 30 days

Greenwich Mean Time

NOTE: Light numbers indicate Sun. **Dark** numbers indicate **Moon.** *Degrees are North Latitude.*

FM = full moon; LQ = last quarter; NM = new moon; FQ = first quarter.

CAUTION: Must be converted to local time. For instructions see page 239.

Day of month week year	Sun on Meridian **Moon phase** h m s	Sun's Declination ° ′	20° Rise Sun **Moon** h m	20° Set Sun **Moon** h m	30° Rise Sun **Moon** h m	30° Set Sun **Moon** h m	40° Rise Sun **Moon** h m	40° Set Sun **Moon** h m	50° Rise Sun **Moon** h m	50° Set Sun **Moon** h m	60° Rise Sun **Moon** h m	60° Set Sun **Moon** h m
1 Tu	11 43 37	−14 17	6 01	17 26	6 14	17 13	6 29	16 58	6 49	16 37	7 21	16 05
305			**3 39**	**15 46**	**3 44**	**15 39**	**3 50**	**15 31**	**3 57**	**15 20**	**4 10**	**15 03**
2 We	11 43 35	−14 36	6 02	17 25	6 14	17 12	6 30	16 57	6 51	16 36	7 24	16 02
306			**4 42**	**16 35**	**4 51**	**16 24**	**5 02**	**16 10**	**5 18**	**15 52**	**5 42**	**15 23**
3 Th	11 43 35	−14 55	6 02	17 25	6 15	17 12	6 31	16 56	6 52	16 34	7 27	16 00
307	**13 35 NM**		**5 46**	**17 28**	**6 00**	**17 13**	**6 16**	**16 55**	**6 39**	**16 30**	**7 16**	**15 50**
4 Fr	11 43 36	−15 14	6 03	17 24	6 16	17 11	6 32	16 55	6 54	16 32	7 29	15 57
308			**6 53**	**18 25**	**7 09**	**18 07**	**7 30**	**17 45**	**7 59**	**17 15**	**8 47**	**16 25**
5 Sa	11 43 37	−15 32	6 03	17 24	6 17	17 10	6 33	16 53	6 56	16 31	7 32	15 55
309			**7 58**	**19 25**	**8 17**	**19 06**	**8 40**	**18 43**	**9 13**	**18 10**	**10 08**	**17 14**
6 Su	11 43 39	−15 51	6 04	17 23	6 18	17 09	6 34	16 52	6 57	16 29	7 34	15 52
310			**9 01**	**20 27**	**9 20**	**20 09**	**9 44**	**19 45**	**10 17**	**19 13**	**11 13**	**18 17**
7 Mo	11 43 42	−16 9	6 04	17 23	6 18	17 09	6 36	16 51	6 59	16 28	7 37	15 50
311			**9 59**	**21 29**	**10 17**	**21 12**	**10 39**	**20 51**	**11 10**	**20 21**	**12 01**	**19 32**
8 Tu	11 43 46	−16 26	6 05	17 23	6 19	17 08	6 37	16 50	7 01	16 26	7 39	15 47
312			**10 52**	**22 29**	**11 08**	**22 15**	**11 27**	**21 57**	**11 53**	**21 33**	**12 35**	**20 53**
9 We	11 43 50	−16 44	6 05	17 22	6 20	17 07	6 38	16 49	7 02	16 25	7 42	15 45
313			**11 40**	**23 26**	**11 52**	**23 15**	**12 07**	**23 02**	**12 27**	**22 44**	**12 59**	**22 15**
10 Th	11 43 56	−17 1	6 06	17 22	6 21	17 07	6 39	16 48	7 04	16 23	7 45	15 42
314	**6 14 FQ**		**12 23**	**– –**	**12 32**	**– –**	**12 42**	**– –**	**12 56**	**23 54**	**13 18**	**23 36**
11 Fr	11 44 02	−17 18	6 06	17 21	6 22	17 06	6 40	16 47	7 06	16 22	7 47	15 40
315			**13 04**	**0 20**	**13 08**	**0 13**	**13 14**	**0 05**	**13 22**	**– –**	**13 34**	**– –**
12 Sa	11 44 09	−17 34	6 07	17 21	6 22	17 06	6 41	16 47	7 07	16 20	7 50	15 38
316			**13 42**	**1 12**	**13 43**	**1 10**	**13 44**	**1 06**	**13 45**	**1 01**	**13 47**	**0 54**
13 Su	11 44 17	−17 50	6 08	17 21	6 23	17 05	6 42	16 46	7 09	16 19	7 52	15 36
317			**14 19**	**2 03**	**14 16**	**2 04**	**14 12**	**2 05**	**14 08**	**2 07**	**14 01**	**2 10**
14 Mo	11 44 26	−18 6	6 08	17 21	6 24	17 05	6 44	16 45	7 11	16 18	7 55	15 33
318			**14 56**	**2 53**	**14 49**	**2 58**	**14 41**	**3 04**	**14 31**	**3 12**	**14 15**	**3 24**
15 Tu	11 44 35	−18 22	6 09	17 20	6 25	17 04	6 45	16 44	7 12	16 16	7 57	15 31
319			**15 34**	**3 42**	**15 24**	**3 51**	**15 12**	**4 01**	**14 55**	**4 15**	**14 30**	**4 38**
16 We	11 44 46	−18 37	6 09	17 20	6 26	17 04	6 46	16 43	7 14	16 15	8 00	15 29
320			**16 13**	**4 32**	**16 00**	**4 44**	**15 44**	**4 58**	**15 22**	**5 18**	**14 48**	**5 50**
17 Th	11 44 57	−18 52	6 10	17 20	6 26	17 03	6 47	16 42	7 16	16 14	8 02	15 27
321			**16 54**	**5 22**	**16 39**	**5 36**	**16 20**	**5 54**	**15 53**	**6 20**	**15 10**	**7 00**
18 Fr	11 45 09	−19 7	6 10	17 20	6 27	17 03	6 48	16 42	7 17	16 13	8 05	15 25
322	**6 57 FM**		**17 38**	**6 12**	**17 21**	**6 28**	**16 59**	**6 49**	**16 29**	**7 19**	**15 39**	**8 07**
19 Sa	11 45 22	−19 21	6 11	17 20	6 28	17 02	6 49	16 41	7 19	16 12	8 07	15 23
323			**18 24**	**7 01**	**18 06**	**7 20**	**17 43**	**7 42**	**17 10**	**8 14**	**16 16**	**9 08**
20 Su	11 45 36	−19 35	6 12	17 19	6 29	17 02	6 50	16 40	7 20	16 10	8 10	15 21
324			**19 12**	**7 50**	**18 54**	**8 09**	**18 31**	**8 32**	**17 58**	**9 05**	**17 03**	**10 00**
21 Mo	11 45 50	−19 49	6 12	17 19	6 30	17 02	6 52	16 40	7 22	16 09	8 12	15 19
325			**20 02**	**8 38**	**19 45**	**8 56**	**19 23**	**9 18**	**18 52**	**9 50**	**18 00**	**10 42**
22 Tu	11 46 06	−20 2	6 13	17 19	6 31	17 01	6 53	16 39	7 23	16 08	8 14	15 17
326			**20 54**	**9 24**	**20 38**	**9 40**	**20 18**	**10 01**	**19 51**	**10 29**	**19 06**	**11 16**
23 We	11 46 22	−20 15	6 13	17 19	6 31	17 01	6 54	16 39	7 25	16 07	8 17	15 15
327			**21 46**	**10 07**	**21 32**	**10 22**	**21 16**	**10 39**	**20 54**	**11 04**	**20 18**	**11 42**
24 Th	11 46 39	−20 27	6 14	17 19	6 32	17 01	6 55	16 38	7 26	16 06	8 19	15 14
328			**22 38**	**10 50**	**22 28**	**11 01**	**22 16**	**11 15**	**22 00**	**11 34**	**21 34**	**12 03**
25 Fr	11 46 57	−20 39	6 15	17 19	6 33	17 01	6 56	16 38	7 28	16 06	8 21	15 12
329			**23 32**	**11 31**	**23 26**	**11 39**	**23 18**	**11 48**	**23 08**	**12 01**	**22 53**	**12 20**
26 Sa	11 47 15	−20 51	6 15	17 19	6 34	17 00	6 57	16 37	7 29	16 05	8 24	15 10
330	**7 4 LQ**		**– –**	**12 11**	**– –**	**12 15**	**– –**	**12 20**	**– –**	**12 26**	**– –**	**12 36**
27 Su	11 47 35	−21 2	6 16	17 19	6 35	17 00	6 58	16 37	7 31	16 04	8 26	15 09
331			**0 26**	**12 53**	**0 24**	**12 52**	**0 22**	**12 52**	**0 19**	**12 52**	**0 14**	**12 51**
28 Mo	11 47 55	−21 13	6 17	17 19	6 36	17 00	6 59	16 36	7 32	16 03	8 28	15 07
332			**1 23**	**13 35**	**1 25**	**13 31**	**1 28**	**13 25**	**1 32**	**13 18**	**1 39**	**13 07**
29 Tu	11 48 15	−21 24	6 17	17 19	6 36	17 00	7 00	16 36	7 34	16 03	8 30	15 06
333			**2 22**	**14 21**	**2 29**	**14 12**	**2 37**	**14 01**	**2 49**	**13 47**	**3 07**	**13 24**
30 We	11 48 37	−21 34	6 18	17 19	6 37	17 00	7 01	16 36	7 35	16 02	8 32	15 04
334			**3 23**	**15 10**	**3 35**	**14 58**	**3 48**	**14 42**	**4 07**	**14 20**	**4 38**	**13 47**

12th Month December 1994 31 days

Greenwich Mean Time

NOTE: Light numbers indicate Sun. **Dark** numbers indicate **Moon.** *Degrees are North Latitude.*

FM = full moon; LQ = last quarter; NM = new moon; FQ = first quarter.

CAUTION: Must be converted to local time. For instructions see page 239.

Day of month week year	Sun on Meridian Moon phase	Sun's Declination	20° Rise Sun Moon	20° Set Sun Moon	30° Rise Sun Moon	30° Set Sun Moon	40° Rise Sun Moon	40° Set Sun Moon	50° Rise Sun Moon	50° Set Sun Moon	60° Rise Sun Moon	60° Set Sun Moon
	h m s	° ′	h m	h m	h m	h m	h m	h m	h m	h m	h m	h m
1 Th	11 48 59	−21 44	6 18	17 19	6 38	17 00	7 02	16 35	7 36	16 01	8 34	15 03
335			4 28	16 04	4 43	15 48	5 01	15 28	5 27	15 01	6 09	14 16
2 Fr	11 49 22	−21 53	6 19	17 20	6 39	17 00	7 03	16 35	7 38	16 01	8 36	15 02
336	23 54 NM		5 34	17 03	5 51	16 45	6 13	16 22	6 44	15 50	7 36	14 57
3 Sa	11 49 45	−22 2	6 20	17 20	6 40	17 00	7 04	16 35	7 39	16 00	8 38	15 01
337			6 39	18 06	6 58	17 47	7 22	17 23	7 55	16 49	8 52	15 53
4 Su	11 50 09	−22 10	6 20	17 20	6 40	17 00	7 05	16 35	7 40	16 00	8 40	15 00
338			7 42	19 10	8 00	18 52	8 23	18 29	8 56	17 57	9 50	17 04
5 Mo	11 50 34	−22 18	6 21	17 20	6 41	17 00	7 06	16 35	7 41	15 59	8 42	14 59
339			8 39	20 13	8 56	19 57	9 17	19 38	9 45	19 11	10 32	18 26
6 Tu	11 50 59	−22 26	6 22	17 20	6 42	17 00	7 07	16 35	7 43	15 59	8 44	14 58
340			9 31	21 13	9 45	21 01	10 02	20 46	10 25	20 25	11 02	19 51
7 We	11 51 25	−22 33	6 22	17 20	6 43	17 00	7 08	16 35	7 44	15 59	8 46	14 57
341			10 18	22 11	10 28	22 03	10 41	21 52	10 58	21 38	11 24	21 16
8 Th	11 51 51	−22 40	6 23	17 21	6 43	17 00	7 09	16 35	7 45	15 59	8 47	14 56
342			11 01	23 06	11 07	23 01	11 15	22 56	11 25	22 49	11 41	22 37
9 Fr	11 52 17	−22 46	6 23	17 21	6 44	17 00	7 10	16 35	7 46	15 58	8 49	14 55
343	21 6 FQ		11 41	23 58	11 43	23 58	11 46	23 57	11 50	23 56	11 56	23 55
10 Sa	11 52 44	−22 52	6 24	17 21	6 45	17 01	7 11	16 35	7 47	15 58	8 50	14 55
344			12 19	– –	12 17	– –	12 16	– –	12 13	– –	12 09	– –
11 Su	11 53 12	−22 57	6 25	17 22	6 45	17 01	7 11	16 35	7 48	15 58	8 52	14 54
345			12 56	0 49	12 51	0 52	12 45	0 57	12 36	1 02	12 23	1 11
12 Mo	11 53 40	−23 2	6 25	17 22	6 46	17 01	7 12	16 35	7 49	15 58	8 53	14 54
346			13 34	1 38	13 25	1 46	13 14	1 55	13 00	2 07	12 38	2 25
13 Tu	11 54 08	−23 7	6 26	17 22	6 47	17 01	7 13	16 35	7 50	15 58	8 55	14 54
347			14 12	2 28	14 01	2 39	13 46	2 52	13 26	3 10	12 55	3 38
14 We	11 54 36	−23 11	6 26	17 23	6 47	17 02	7 14	16 35	7 51	15 58	8 56	14 53
348			14 53	3 18	14 38	3 31	14 20	3 48	13 55	4 11	13 15	4 49
15 Th	11 55 05	−23 14	6 27	17 23	6 48	17 02	7 14	16 36	7 52	15 58	8 57	14 53
349			15 36	4 07	15 19	4 23	14 58	4 43	14 29	5 11	13 41	5 57
16 Fr	11 55 34	−23 18	6 28	17 23	6 49	17 02	7 15	16 36	7 53	15 59	8 58	14 53
350			16 21	4 57	16 03	5 15	15 40	5 37	15 08	6 08	14 15	7 01
17 Sa	11 56 03	−23 20	6 28	17 24	6 49	17 03	7 16	16 36	7 53	15 59	8 59	14 53
351			17 09	5 47	16 50	6 05	16 27	6 29	15 54	7 01	14 59	7 56
18 Su	11 56 32	−23 22	6 29	17 24	6 50	17 03	7 16	16 37	7 54	15 59	9 00	14 53
352	2 17 FM		17 59	6 35	17 40	6 53	17 18	7 16	16 46	7 49	15 53	8 43
19 Mo	11 57 02	−23 24	6 29	17 25	6 50	17 04	7 17	16 37	7 55	15 59	9 01	14 53
353			18 50	7 22	18 33	7 39	18 13	8 01	17 44	8 30	16 56	9 19
20 Tu	11 57 31	−23 25	6 30	17 25	6 51	17 04	7 18	16 37	7 55	16 00	9 01	14 54
354			19 42	8 07	19 28	8 22	19 10	8 41	18 46	9 07	18 07	9 48
21 We	11 58 01	−23 26	6 30	17 26	6 52	17 04	7 18	16 38	7 56	16 00	9 02	14 54
355			20 34	8 50	20 23	9 02	20 10	9 17	19 51	9 38	19 21	10 11
22 Th	11 58 31	−23 26	6 31	17 26	6 52	17 05	7 19	16 38	7 56	16 01	9 02	14 55
356			21 27	9 31	21 20	9 40	21 11	9 51	20 58	10 06	20 39	10 29
23 Fr	11 59 01	−23 26	6 31	17 27	6 53	17 06	7 19	16 39	7 57	16 01	9 03	14 55
357			22 21	10 11	22 17	10 17	22 13	10 23	22 07	10 32	21 59	10 45
24 Sa	11 59 31	−23 25	6 32	17 27	6 53	17 06	7 20	16 39	7 57	16 02	9 03	14 56
358			23 15	10 52	23 16	10 53	23 17	10 54	23 18	10 57	23 20	11 00
25 Su	12 0 00	−23 24	6 32	17 28	6 53	17 07	7 20	16 40	7 58	16 03	9 03	14 57
359	19 6 LQ		– –	11 32	– –	11 30	– –	11 26	– –	11 22	– –	11 15
26 Mo	12 0 30	−23 23	6 33	17 28	6 54	17 07	7 20	16 41	7 58	16 03	9 04	14 58
360			0 11	12 15	0 16	12 08	0 22	12 00	0 31	11 48	0 44	11 31
27 Tu	12 0 60	−23 21	6 33	17 29	6 54	17 08	7 21	16 41	7 58	16 04	9 04	14 59
361			1 09	13 01	1 18	12 50	1 30	12 36	1 45	12 18	2 10	11 50
28 We	12 1 29	−23 18	6 34	17 30	6 55	17 08	7 21	16 42	7 58	16 05	9 04	15 00
362			2 10	13 50	2 23	13 36	2 39	13 18	3 02	12 53	3 38	12 14
29 Th	12 1 59	−23 15	6 34	17 30	6 55	17 09	7 21	16 43	7 58	16 06	9 03	15 01
363			3 13	14 45	3 29	14 27	3 49	14 06	4 18	13 36	5 05	12 47
30 Fr	12 2 28	−23 12	6 34	17 31	6 55	17 10	7 22	16 44	7 59	16 07	9 03	15 02
364			4 17	15 44	4 35	15 25	4 58	15 02	5 31	14 29	6 25	13 33
31 Sa	12 2 57	−23 8	6 35	17 31	6 56	17 10	7 22	16 44	7 59	16 07	9 03	15 03
365			5 20	16 46	5 39	16 28	6 03	16 04	6 36	15 31	7 32	14 35

Latitude, Longitude, and Altitude of U.S. and Canadian Cities

Source for U.S. geographic positions: National Oceanic and Atmospheric Administration, U.S. Dept. of Commerce.

Source for Canadian cities: Geodetic Survey of Canada, Dept. of Energy, Mines, and Resources.

Source for altitudes: U.S. Geological Survey and World Almanac research.

* Approx. altitude at downtown business area U.S.; in Canada at city hall except where (a), in which case altitude is at tower of major airport.

City	Lat. N °	'	"	Long. W °	'	"	Alt.* feet
Abilene, Tex.	32	27	05	99	43	51	1710
Akron, Oh.	41	05	00	81	30	44	874
Albany, N.Y.	42	39	01	73	45	01	20
Albuquerque, N.M.	35	05	01	106	39	05	4,945
Allentown, Pa.	40	36	11	75	28	06	255
Alert, N.W.T.	82	29	50	62	21	15	95
Amarillo, Tex.	35	12	27	101	50	04	3,685
Anchorage, Alas.	61	10	00	149	59	00	118
Ann Arbor, Mich.	42	16	59	83	44	52	880
Asheville, N.C.	35	35	42	82	33	26	1,985
Ashland, Ky.	38	28	36	82	38	23	536
Atlanta, Ga.	33	45	10	84	23	37	1,050
Atlantic City, N.J.	39	21	32	74	25	53	10
Augusta, Ga.	33	28	20	81	58	00	143
Augusta, Me.	44	18	53	69	46	29	45
Austin, Tex.	30	16	09	97	44	37	505
Bakersfield, Cal.	35	22	31	119	01	18	400
Baltimore, Md.	39	17	26	76	36	45	20
Bangor, Me.	44	48	13	68	46	18	20
Baton Rouge, La.	30	26	58	91	11	00	57
Battle Creek, Mich.	42	18	58	85	10	48	820
Bay City, Mich.	43	36	04	83	53	15	595
Beaumont, Tex.	30	05	20	94	06	09	20
Belleville, Ont.	44	09	42	77	23	11	257
Bellingham, Wash.	48	45	34	122	28	36	60
Berkeley, Cal.	37	52	10	122	16	17	40
Billings, Mon.	45	47	00	108	30	04	3,120
Biloxi, Miss.	30	23	48	88	53	00	20
Binghamton, N.Y.	42	06	03	75	54	47	865
Birmingham, Ala.	33	31	01	86	48	36	600
Bismarck, N.D.	46	48	23	100	47	17	1,674
Bloomington, Ill.	40	28	58	88	59	36	800
Boise, Ida.	43	37	07	116	11	58	2,704
Boston, Mass.	42	21	24	71	03	25	21
Bowling Green, Ky.	36	59	41	86	26	33	510
Brandon, Man.	49	51	00	99	57	00	1,265(a)
Brantford, Ont.	43	08	34	80	15	39	705(a)
Brattleboro, Vt.	42	51	06	72	33	48	300
Bridgeport, Conn.	41	10	49	73	11	22	10
Brockton, Mass.	42	05	02	71	01	25	130
Brownsville, Tex.	25	54	07	97	29	58	35
Buffalo, N.Y.	42	52	52	78	52	21	585
Burlington, Ont.	43	19	33	79	47	57	284
Burlington, Vt.	44	28	34	73	12	46	110
Butte, Mon.	46	01	06	112	32	11	5,765
Calgary, Alta.	51	02	46	114	03	24	3,427
Cambridge, Mass.	42	22	01	71	06	22	20
Canton, Oh.	40	47	50	81	22	37	1,030
Carson City, Nev.	39	10	00	119	46	00	4,680
Cedar Rapids, Ia.	41	58	01	91	39	53	730
Central Islip, N.Y.	40	47	24	73	12	00	80
Champaign, Ill.	40	07	05	88	14	48	740
Charleston, S.C.	32	46	35	79	55	53	9
Charleston, W.Va.	38	21	01	81	37	52	601
Charlotte, N.C.	35	13	44	80	50	45	720
Charlottetown, P.E.I.	46	14	07	63	07	49	31
Chattanooga, Tenn.	35	02	41	85	18	32	675
Cheyenne, Wy.	41	08	09	104	49	07	6,100
Chicago, Ill.	41	52	28	87	38	22	595
Churchill, Man.	58	45	15	94	10	00	94(a)
Cincinnati, Oh.	39	06	07	84	30	35	550
Cleveland, Oh.	41	29	51	81	41	50	660
Colorado Springs	38	50	07	104	49	16	5,980
Columbia, Mo.	38	57	03	92	19	46	730
Columbia, S.C.	34	00	02	81	02	00	190
Columbus, Ga.	32	28	07	84	59	24	265
Columbus, Oh.	39	57	47	83	00	17	780
Concord, N.H.	43	12	22	71	32	25	290
Corpus Christi, Tex.	27	47	51	97	23	45	35
Dallas, Tex.	32	47	09	96	47	37	435
Dartmouth, N.S.	44	39	50	63	34	08	24
Dawson, Yukon	64	03	30	139	26	00	1,211(a)
Dayton, Oh.	39	45	32	84	11	43	574
Daytona Beach, Fla.	29	12	44	81	01	10	7
Decatur, Ill.	39	50	42	88	56	47	682
Denver, Col.	39	44	58	104	59	22	5,280
Des Moines, Ia.	41	35	14	93	37	00	803
Detroit, Mich.	42	19	48	83	02	57	585
Dodge City, Kan.	37	45	17	100	01	09	2,480
Dubuque, Ia.	42	29	55	90	40	08	620
Duluth, Minn.	46	46	56	92	06	24	610
Durham, N.C.	36	00	00	78	54	45	405
Eau Claire, Wis.	44	48	31	91	29	49	790
Edmonton, Alta.	53	32	43	113	29	21	2,186
El Paso, Tex.	31	45	36	106	29	11	3,695
Elizabeth, N.J.	40	39	43	74	12	59	21
Enid, Okla.	36	23	40	97	52	35	1,240
Erie, Pa.	42	07	15	80	04	57	685
Eugene, Ore.	44	03	16	123	05	30	422
Eureka, Cal.	40	48	08	124	09	46	45
Evansville, Ind.	37	58	20	87	34	21	385
Fairbanks, Alas.	64	48	00	147	51	00	448
Fall River, Mass.	41	42	06	71	09	18	40
Fargo, N.D.	46	52	30	96	47	18	900
Flagstaff, Ariz.	35	11	36	111	39	06	6,900
Flint, Mich.	43	00	50	83	41	33	750
Ft. Smith, Ark.	35	23	10	94	25	36	440
Ft. Wayne, Ind.	41	04	21	85	08	26	790
Ft. Worth, Tex.	32	44	55	97	19	44	670
Fredericton, N.B.	45	57	47	66	38	38	29
Fresno, Cal.	36	44	12	119	47	11	285
Gadsden, Ala.	34	00	57	86	00	41	555
Gainesville, Fla.	29	38	56	82	19	19	175
Gallup, N.M.	35	31	30	108	44	30	6,540
Galveston, Tex.	29	18	10	94	47	43	5
Gary, Ind.	41	36	12	87	20	19	590
Grand Junction, Col.	39	04	06	108	33	54	4,590
Grand Rapids, Mich.	42	58	03	85	40	13	610
Great Falls, Mon.	47	29	33	111	18	23	3,340
Green Bay, Wis.	44	30	48	88	00	50	590
Greensboro, N.C.	36	04	17	79	47	25	839
Greenville, S.C.	34	50	50	82	24	01	966
Guelph, Ont.	43	32	35	80	14	54	1,065
Gulfport, Miss.	30	22	04	89	05	36	20
Halifax, N.S.	44	38	54	63	34	30	60
Hamilton, Ont.	43	15	20	79	52	30	329
Hamilton, Oh.	39	23	59	84	33	47	600
Harrisburg, Pa.	40	15	43	76	52	59	365
Hartford, Conn.	41	46	12	72	40	49	40
Helena, Mon.	46	35	33	112	02	24	4,155
Hilo, Ha.	19	43	30	155	05	24	40
Honolulu, Ha.	21	18	22	157	51	35	21
Houston, Tex.	29	45	26	95	21	37	40
Hull, Que.	45	25	42	75	42	41	185
Huntsville, Ala.	34	44	18	86	35	19	640
Indianapolis, Ind.	39	46	07	86	09	46	710
Iowa City, Ia.	41	39	37	91	31	53	685
Jackson, Mich.	42	14	43	84	24	22	940
Jackson, Miss.	32	17	56	90	11	06	298
Jacksonville, Fla.	30	19	44	81	39	42	20
Jersey City, N.J.	40	43	50	74	03	56	20
Johnstown, Pa.	40	19	35	78	55	03	1,185
Joplin, Mo.	37	05	26	94	30	00	990
Juneau, Alas.	58	18	12	134	24	30	50
Kalamazoo, Mich.	42	17	29	85	35	14	755
Kansas City, Kan.	39	07	04	94	38	24	750
Kansas City, Mo.	39	04	56	94	35	20	750
Kenosha, Wis.	42	35	43	87	50	11	610
Key West, Fla.	24	33	30	81	48	12	5
Kingston, Ont.	44	13	53	76	28	48	264
Kitchener, Ont.	43	26	58	80	29	12	1,100
Knoxville, Tenn.	35	57	39	83	55	07	890
Lafayette, Ind.	40	25	11	86	53	39	550
Lancaster, Pa.	40	02	25	76	18	29	355
Lansing, Mich.	42	44	01	84	33	15	830
Laredo, Tex.	27	30	22	99	30	30	440
La Salle, Que.	45	25	30	73	39	30	110
Las Vegas, Nev.	36	10	20	115	08	37	2,030
Laval, Que.	45	33	05	73	44	42	142
Lawrence, Mass.	42	42	16	71	10	08	65
Lethbridge, Alta.	49	41	38	112	49	58	2,985
Lexington, Ky.	38	02	50	84	29	46	955
Lihue, Ha.	21	58	48	159	22	30	210
Lima, Oh.	40	44	35	84	06	20	865
Lincoln, Neb.	40	48	59	96	42	15	1,150
Little Rock, Ark.	34	44	42	92	16	37	286
London, Ont.	42	59	17	81	14	03	822
Long Beach, Cal.	33	46	14	118	11	18	35
Los Angeles, Cal.	34	03	15	118	14	28	340
Louisville, Ky.	38	14	47	85	45	49	450
Lowell, Mass.	42	38	25	71	19	14	100
Lubbock, Tex.	33	35	05	101	50	33	3,195
Macon, Ga.	32	50	12	83	37	36	335
Madison, Wis.	43	04	23	89	22	55	860
Manchester, N.H.	42	59	28	71	27	41	175
Marshall, Tex.	32	33	00	94	23	00	410
Memphis, Tenn.	35	08	46	90	03	13	275
Meriden, Conn.	41	32	06	72	47	30	190
Miami, Fla.	25	46	37	80	11	32	10
Milwaukee, Wis.	43	02	19	87	54	15	635

City	Lat. N °	'	"	Long. W °	'	"	Alt.* feet
Minneapolis, Minn.	44	58	57	93	15	43	815
Minot, N.D.	48	14	09	101	17	38	1,550
Mississauga, Ont.	43	33	00	79	35	00	260(a)
Mobile, Ala.	30	41	36	88	02	33	5
Moncton, N.B.	46	05	18	64	46	41	38
Montgomery, Ala.	32	22	33	86	18	31	160
Montpelier, Vt.	44	15	36	72	34	41	485
Montréal, Que.	45	30	33	73	33	14	90
Moose Jaw, Sask.	50	23	34	105	32	04	1,784
Muncie, Ind.	40	11	28	85	23	16	950
Nashville, Tenn.	36	09	33	86	46	55	450
Natchez, Miss.	31	33	48	91	23	30	210
Newark, N.J.	40	44	14	74	10	19	55
New Britain, Conn.	41	40	08	72	46	59	200
New Haven, Conn.	41	18	25	72	55	30	40
New Orleans, La.	29	56	53	90	04	10	5
New York, N.Y.	40	45	06	73	59	39	55
Niagara Falls, N.Y.	43	05	34	79	03	26	570
Niagara Falls, Ont.	43	06	22	79	03	51	590
Nome, Alas.	64	30	00	165	25	00	25
Norfolk, Va.	36	51	10	76	17	21	10
North Bay, Ont.	46	18	35	79	27	45	670
Oakland, Cal.	37	48	03	122	15	54	25
Ogden, Ut.	41	13	31	111	58	21	4,295
Oklahoma City	35	28	26	97	31	04	1,195
Omaha, Neb.	41	15	42	95	56	14	1,040
Orlando, Fla.	28	32	42	81	22	38	70
Ottawa, Ont.	45	26	24	75	41	42	185
Paducah, Ky.	37	05	13	88	35	56	345
Pasadena, Cal.	34	08	44	118	08	41	830
Paterson, N.J.	40	55	01	74	10	21	100
Pensacola, Fla.	30	24	51	87	12	56	15
Peoria, Ill.	40	41	42	89	35	33	470
Peterborough, Ont.	44	18	32	78	19	13	673
Philadelphia, Pa.	39	56	58	75	09	21	100
Phoenix, Ariz.	33	27	12	112	04	28	1,080
Pierre, S.D.	44	22	18	100	20	54	1,480
Pittsburgh, Pa.	40	26	19	80	00	00	745
Pittsfield, Mass.	42	26	53	73	15	14	1,015
Pocatello, Ida.	42	51	38	112	27	01	4,460
Pt. Arthur, Tex.	29	52	30	93	56	15	10
Portland, Me.	43	39	33	70	15	19	25
Portland, Ore.	45	31	06	122	40	35	77
Portsmouth, N.H.	43	04	30	70	45	24	20
Portsmouth, Va.	36	50	07	76	18	14	10
Prince Rupert, B.C.	54	19	00	130	19	00	125(a)
Providence, R.I.	41	49	32	71	24	41	80
Provo, Ut.	40	14	06	111	39	24	4,550
Pueblo, Col.	38	16	17	104	36	33	4,690
Québec City, Que.	46	48	51	71	12	30	163
Racine, Wis.	42	43	49	87	47	12	630
Rapid City, S.D.	44	04	52	103	13	11	3,230
Raleigh, N.C.	35	46	38	78	38	21	365
Reading, Pa.	40	20	09	75	55	40	265
Regina, Sask.	50	26	55	104	36	50	1,894(a)
Reno, Nev.	39	31	27	119	48	40	4,490
Richmond, Va.	37	32	15	77	26	09	160
Roanoke, Va.	37	16	13	79	56	44	905
Rochester, Minn.	44	01	21	92	28	03	990
Rochester, N.Y.	43	09	41	77	36	21	515
Rockford, Ill.	42	16	07	89	05	48	715
Sacramento, Cal.	38	34	57	121	29	41	30
Saginaw, Mich.	43	25	52	83	56	05	595
St. Catharines, Ont.	43	09	33	79	14	50	362(a)
St. Cloud, Minn.	45	34	00	94	10	24	1,040
St. John, N.B.	45	16	22	66	03	48	27
St. John's, Nfld.	47	33	42	52	42	48	200(a)
St. Joseph, Mo.	39	45	57	94	51	02	850
St. Louis, Mo.	38	37	45	90	12	22	455
St. Paul, Minn.	44	57	19	93	06	07	780
St. Petersburg, Fla.	27	46	18	82	38	19	20
Salem, Ore.	44	56	24	123	01	59	155
Salina, Kan.	38	50	36	97	36	46	1,229
Salt Lake City, Ut.	40	45	23	111	53	26	4,390
San Antonio, Tex.	29	25	37	98	29	06	650
San Bernardino, Cal.	34	06	30	117	17	28	1,080
San Diego, Cal.	32	42	53	117	09	21	20
San Francisco, Cal.	37	46	39	122	24	40	65
San Jose, Cal.	37	20	16	121	53	24	90
San Juan, P.R.	18	27	00	66	04	15	35
Santa Barbara, Cal.	34	25	18	119	41	55	100
Santa Cruz, Cal.	36	58	18	122	01	18	20
Santa Fe, N.M.	35	41	11	105	56	10	6,950
Sarasota, Fla.	27	20	05	82	32	30	20
Saskatoon, Sask.	52	07	49	106	39	35	1,587
Sault Ste. Marie, Ont.	46	30	24	84	20	04	589
Savannah, Ga.	32	04	42	81	05	37	20
Schenectady, N.Y.	42	48	42	73	55	42	245
Seattle, Wash.	47	36	32	122	20	12	10
Sheboygan, Wis.	43	45	03	87	42	52	630
Sherbrooke, Que.	45	24	27	71	51	07	535(a)
Sheridan, Wy.	44	47	55	106	57	10	3,740
Shreveport, La.	32	30	46	93	44	58	204
Sioux City, Ia.	42	29	46	96	24	30	1,110
Sioux Falls, S.D.	43	32	35	96	43	35	1,395
South Bend, Ind.	41	40	33	86	15	01	710
Spartanburg, S.C.	34	57	03	81	56	06	875
Spokane, Wash.	47	39	32	117	25	33	1,890
Springfield, Ill.	39	47	58	89	38	51	610
Springfield, Mass.	42	06	21	72	35	32	85
Springfield, Mo.	37	13	03	93	17	32	1,300
Springfield, Oh.	39	55	38	83	48	29	980
Stamford, Conn.	41	03	09	73	32	24	35
Steubenville, Oh.	40	21	42	80	36	53	660
Stockton, Cal.	37	57	30	121	17	16	20
Sudbury, Ont.	46	29	24	80	59	24	850(a)
Superior, Wis.	46	43	14	92	06	07	630
Sydney, N.S.	46	08	15	60	11	48	15
Syracuse, N.Y.	43	03	04	76	09	14	400
Tacoma, Wash.	47	14	59	122	26	15	110
Tallahassee, Fla.	30	26	30	84	16	56	150
Tampa, Fla.	27	56	58	82	27	25	15
Terre Haute, Ind.	39	28	03	87	24	26	496
Texarkana, Tex.	33	25	48	94	02	30	324
Thunder Bay, Ont.	48	22	54	89	14	42	616
Toledo, Oh.	41	39	14	83	32	39	585
Topeka, Kan.	39	03	16	95	40	23	930
Toronto, Ont.	43	39	10	79	23	00	300
Trenton, N.J.	40	13	14	74	46	13	35
Trois-Rivières, Que.	46	20	36	72	32	37	115(a)
Troy, N.Y.	42	43	45	73	40	58	35
Tucson, Ariz.	32	13	15	110	58	08	2,390
Tulsa, Okla.	36	09	12	95	59	34	804
Urbana, Ill.	40	06	42	88	12	06	725
Utica, N.Y.	43	06	12	75	13	33	415
Vancouver, B.C.	49	18	56	123	04	44	141
Victoria, B.C.	48	25	43	123	21	49	57
Waco, Tex.	31	33	12	97	08	00	405
Walla Walla, Wash.	46	04	08	118	20	24	936
Washington, D.C.	38	53	51	77	00	33	25
Waterloo, Ia.	42	29	40	92	20	20	850
West Palm Beach, Fla.	26	42	36	80	03	07	15
Wheeling, W. Va.	40	04	03	80	43	20	650
Whitehorse, Yukon	60	43	17	135	03	03	2,305(a)
White Plains, N.Y.	41	02	00	73	45	48	220
Wichita, Kan.	37	41	30	97	20	16	1,290
Wilkes-Barre, Pa.	41	14	32	75	53	17	640
Wilmington, Del.	39	44	46	75	32	51	135
Wilmington, N.C.	34	14	14	77	56	58	35
Windsor, Ont.	42	18	56	83	02	10	603
Winnipeg, Man.	49	53	56	97	08	23	762
Winston-Salem, N.C.	36	05	52	80	14	42	860
Worcester, Mass.	42	15	37	71	48	17	475
Yakima, Wash.	46	36	09	120	30	39	1,060
Yellowknife, N.W.T.	62	27	16	114	22	33	674(a)
Yonkers, N.Y.	40	55	55	73	53	54	10
Youngstown, Oh.	41	05	57	80	39	02	840
Yuma, Ariz.	32	42	54	114	37	24	160
Zanesville, Oh.	39	56	18	82	00	30	720

World Cities

Source: Defense Mapping Agency and World Almanac Research.

Athens, Greece	37	58	00N	23	44	00E	300
Beijing, China	39	54	00N	116	28	00E	600
Berlin, Germany	52	32	00N	13	25	00E	110
Bangkok, Thailand	13	45	00N	100	30	00E	0
Bogotá, Colombia	04	35	00N	74	05	00W	11,490
Buenos Aires, Argentina	34	36	00S	58	22	00W	0
Jerusalem, Israel	31	47	00N	35	13	00E	2,500
Johannesburg, So. Afr.	26	10	00S	28	02	00E	5,740
Kathmandu, Nepal	27	40	00N	86	30	00E	4,500
Kiev, Ukraine	50	26	00N	30	31	00E	0
London, UK (Greenwich)	51	30	00N	00	00	00	245
Manila, Philippines	14	35	00N	120	58	00E	0
Mecca, Saudi Arabia	21	25	00N	39	50	00E	6,562
Mexico City, Mexico	19	25	45	99	07	00	7,347
Moscow, Russia	55	45	00N	37	42	00E	394
New Delhi, India	28	38	00N	77	12	00E	770
Panama City, Panama	30	24	00N	87	13	00W	0
Paris, France	48	50	14N	02	20	14E	300
Rio de Janeiro, Brazil	22	53	43S	43	13	22W	30
Rome, Italy	41	53	00N	12	30	00E	95
Santiago, Chile	33	29	00S	70	38	00W	4,921
Syndey, Australia	33	52	00S	151	12	00E	25
Tokyo, Japan	35	45	00N	139	45	00E	30
Tripoli, Libya	32	54	00N	13	11	00E	0
Warsaw, Poland	52	15	00N	21	00	00E	360
Wellington, New Zealand	41	17	00S	174	47	00E	0

Perpetual Calendar

The number shown for each year indicates which Gregorian calendar to use. For 1583-1802, or for Julian calendar, see page 266. For years 1803-1820, use numbers for 1983-2000, respectively.

1821....2	1847....6	1873....4	1899....1	1925....5	1951....2	1977....7	2003....4	2029....2	2055....6
1822....3	1848...14	1874....5	1900....2	1926....6	1952...10	1978....1	2004...12	2030....3	2056...14
1823....4	1849....2	1875....6	1901....3	1927....7	1953....5	1979....2	2005....7	2031....4	2057....2
1824...12	1850....3	1876...14	1902....4	1928....8	1954....6	1980...10	2006....1	2032...12	2058....3
1825....7	1851....4	1877....2	1903....5	1929....3	1955....7	1981....5	2007....2	2033....7	2059....4
1826....1	1852...12	1878....3	1904...13	1930....4	1956....8	1982....6	2008...10	2034....1	2060..12
1827....2	1853....7	1879....4	1905....1	1931....5	1957....3	1983....7	2009....5	2035....2	2061..7
1828...10	1854....1	1880...12	1906....2	1932...13	1958....4	1984....8	2010....6	2036...10	2062..1
1829....5	1855....2	1881....7	1907....3	1933....1	1959....5	1985....3	2011....7	2037....5	2063..2
1830....6	1856...10	1882....1	1908...11	1934....2	1960...13	1986....4	2012....8	2038....6	2064..10
1831....7	1857....5	1883....2	1909....6	1935....3	1961....1	1987....5	2013....3	2039....7	2065..5
1832....8	1858....6	1884...10	1910....7	1936...11	1962....2	1988...13	2014....4	2040....8	2066..6
1833....3	1859....7	1885....5	1911....1	1937....6	1963....3	1989....1	2015....5	2041....3	2067..7
1834....4	1860....8	1886....6	1912....9	1938....7	1964...11	1990....2	2016...13	2042....4	2068..8
1835....5	1861....3	1887....7	1913....4	1939....1	1965....6	1991....3	2017....1	2043....5	2069..3
1836...13	1862....4	1888....8	1914....5	1940....9	1966....7	1992...11	2018....2	2044...13	2070..4
1837....1	1863....5	1889....3	1915....6	1941....4	1967....1	1993....6	2019....3	2045....1	2071..5
1838....2	1864...13	1890....4	1916...14	1942....5	1968....9	1994....7	2020...11	2046....2	2072..13
1839....3	1865....1	1891....5	1917....2	1943....6	1969....4	1995....1	2021....6	2047....3	2073..1
1840...11	1866....2	1892...13	1918....3	1944...14	1970....5	1996....9	2022....7	2048...11	2074..2
1841....6	1867....3	1893....1	1919....4	1945....2	1971....6	1997....4	2023....1	2049....6	2075..3
1842....7	1868...11	1894....2	1920...12	1946....3	1972...14	1998....5	2024....9	2050....7	2076..11
1843....1	1869....6	1895....3	1921....7	1947....4	1973....2	1999....6	2025....4	2051....1	2077..6
1844....9	1870....7	1896...11	1922....1	1948...12	1974....3	2000...14	2026....5	2052....9	2078..7
1845....4	1871....1	1897....6	1923....2	1949....7	1975....4	2001....2	2027....6	2053....4	2079..1
1846....5	1872....9	1898....7	1924...10	1950....1	1976...12	2002....3	2028...14	2054....5	2080..9

1 1995

JANUARY

S	M	T	W	T	F	S
1	2	3	4	5	6	7
8	9	10	11	12	13	14
15	16	17	18	19	20	21
22	23	24	25	26	27	28
29	30	31				

FEBRUARY

S	M	T	W	T	F	S
			1	2	3	4
5	6	7	8	9	10	11
12	13	14	15	16	17	18
19	20	21	22	23	24	25
26	27	28				

MARCH

S	M	T	W	T	F	S
			1	2	3	4
5	6	7	8	9	10	11
12	13	14	15	16	17	18
19	20	21	22	23	24	25
26	27	28	29	30	31	

APRIL

S	M	T	W	T	F	S
						1
2	3	4	5	6	7	8
9	10	11	12	13	14	15
16	17	18	19	20	21	22
23	24	25	26	27	28	29
30						

MAY

S	M	T	W	T	F	S
	1	2	3	4	5	6
7	8	9	10	11	12	13
14	15	16	17	18	19	20
21	22	23	24	25	26	27
28	29	30	31			

JUNE

S	M	T	W	T	F	S
				1	2	3
4	5	6	7	8	9	10
11	12	13	14	15	16	17
18	19	20	21	22	23	24
25	26	27	28	29	30	

JULY

S	M	T	W	T	F	S
						1
2	3	4	5	6	7	8
9	10	11	12	13	14	15
16	17	18	19	20	21	22
23	24	25	26	27	28	29
30	31					

AUGUST

S	M	T	W	T	F	S
		1	2	3	4	5
6	7	8	9	10	11	12
13	14	15	16	17	18	19
20	21	22	23	24	25	26
27	28	29	30	31		

SEPTEMBER

S	M	T	W	T	F	S
					1	2
3	4	5	6	7	8	9
10	11	12	13	14	15	16
17	18	19	20	21	22	23
24	25	26	27	28	29	30

OCTOBER

S	M	T	W	T	F	S
1	2	3	4	5	6	7
8	9	10	11	12	13	14
15	16	17	18	19	20	21
22	23	24	25	26	27	28
29	30	31				

NOVEMBER

S	M	T	W	T	F	S
			1	2	3	4
5	6	7	8	9	10	11
12	13	14	15	16	17	18
19	20	21	22	23	24	25
26	27	28	29	30		

DECEMBER

S	M	T	W	T	F	S
					1	2
3	4	5	6	7	8	9
10	11	12	13	14	15	16
17	18	19	20	21	22	23
24	25	26	27	28	29	30
31						

2

JANUARY

S	M	T	W	T	F	S
	1	2	3	4	5	6
7	8	9	10	11	12	13
14	15	16	17	18	19	20
21	22	23	24	25	26	27
28	29	30	31			

FEBRUARY

S	M	T	W	T	F	S
				1	2	3
4	5	6	7	8	9	10
11	12	13	14	15	16	17
18	19	20	21	22	23	24
25	26	27	28			

MARCH

S	M	T	W	T	F	S
				1	2	3
4	5	6	7	8	9	10
11	12	13	14	15	16	17
18	19	20	21	22	23	24
25	26	27	28	29	30	31

APRIL

S	M	T	W	T	F	S
1	2	3	4	5	6	7
8	9	10	11	12	13	14
15	16	17	18	19	20	21
22	23	24	25	26	27	28
29	30					

MAY

S	M	T	W	T	F	S
		1	2	3	4	5
6	7	8	9	10	11	12
13	14	15	16	17	18	19
20	21	22	23	24	25	26
27	28	29	30	31		

JUNE

S	M	T	W	T	F	S
					1	2
3	4	5	6	7	8	9
10	11	12	13	14	15	16
17	18	19	20	21	22	23
24	25	26	27	28	29	30

JULY

S	M	T	W	T	F	S
1	2	3	4	5	6	7
8	9	10	11	12	13	14
15	16	17	18	19	20	21
22	23	24	25	26	27	28
29	30	31				

AUGUST

S	M	T	W	T	F	S
			1	2	3	4
5	6	7	8	9	10	11
12	13	14	15	16	17	18
19	20	21	22	23	24	25
26	27	28	29	30	31	

SEPTEMBER

S	M	T	W	T	F	S
						1
2	3	4	5	6	7	8
9	10	11	12	13	14	15
16	17	18	19	20	21	22
23	24	25	26	27	28	29
30						

OCTOBER

S	M	T	W	T	F	S
	1	2	3	4	5	6
7	8	9	10	11	12	13
14	15	16	17	18	19	20
21	22	23	24	25	26	27
28	29	30	31			

NOVEMBER

S	M	T	W	T	F	S
				1	2	3
4	5	6	7	8	9	10
11	12	13	14	15	16	17
18	19	20	21	22	23	24
25	26	27	28	29	30	

DECEMBER

S	M	T	W	T	F	S
						1
2	3	4	5	6	7	8
9	10	11	12	13	14	15
16	17	18	19	20	21	22
23	24	25	26	27	28	29
30	31					

3

JANUARY

S	M	T	W	T	F	S
		1	2	3	4	5
6	7	8	9	10	11	12
13	14	15	16	17	18	19
20	21	22	23	24	25	26
27	28	29	30	31		

FEBRUARY

S	M	T	W	T	F	S
					1	2
3	4	5	6	7	8	9
10	11	12	13	14	15	16
17	18	19	20	21	22	23
24	25	26	27	28		

MARCH

S	M	T	W	T	F	S
					1	2
3	4	5	6	7	8	9
10	11	12	13	14	15	16
17	18	19	20	21	22	23
24	25	26	27	28	29	30
31						

APRIL

S	M	T	W	T	F	S
	1	2	3	4	5	6
7	8	9	10	11	12	13
14	15	16	17	18	19	20
21	22	23	24	25	26	27
28	29	30				

MAY

S	M	T	W	T	F	S
			1	2	3	4
5	6	7	8	9	10	11
12	13	14	15	16	17	18
19	20	21	22	23	24	25
26	27	28	29	30	31	

JUNE

S	M	T	W	T	F	S
						1
2	3	4	5	6	7	8
9	10	11	12	13	14	15
16	17	18	19	20	21	22
23	24	25	26	27	28	29
30						

JULY

S	M	T	W	T	F	S
	1	2	3	4	5	6
7	8	9	10	11	12	13
14	15	16	17	18	19	20
21	22	23	24	25	26	27
28	29	30	31			

AUGUST

S	M	T	W	T	F	S
				1	2	3
4	5	6	7	8	9	10
11	12	13	14	15	16	17
18	19	20	21	22	23	24
25	26	27	28	29	30	31

SEPTEMBER

S	M	T	W	T	F	S
1	2	3	4	5	6	7
8	9	10	11	12	13	14
15	16	17	18	19	20	21
22	23	24	25	26	27	28
29	30					

OCTOBER

S	M	T	W	T	F	S
		1	2	3	4	5
6	7	8	9	10	11	12
13	14	15	16	17	18	19
20	21	22	23	24	25	26
27	28	29	30	31		

NOVEMBER

S	M	T	W	T	F	S
					1	2
3	4	5	6	7	8	9
10	11	12	13	14	15	16
17	18	19	20	21	22	23
24	25	26	27	28	29	30

DECEMBER

S	M	T	W	T	F	S
1	2	3	4	5	6	7
8	9	10	11	12	13	14
15	16	17	18	19	20	21
22	23	24	25	26	27	28
29	30	31				

4

JANUARY

S	M	T	W	T	F	S
			1	2	3	4
5	6	7	8	9	10	11
12	13	14	15	16	17	18
19	20	21	22	23	24	25
26	27	28	29	30	31	

FEBRUARY

S	M	T	W	T	F	S
						1
2	3	4	5	6	7	8
9	10	11	12	13	14	15
16	17	18	19	20	21	22
23	24	25	26	27	28	

MARCH

S	M	T	W	T	F	S
						1
2	3	4	5	6	7	8
9	10	11	12	13	14	15
16	17	18	19	20	21	22
23	24	25	26	27	28	29
30	31					

APRIL

S	M	T	W	T	F	S
		1	2	3	4	5
6	7	8	9	10	11	12
13	14	15	16	17	18	19
20	21	22	23	24	25	26
27	28	29	30			

MAY

S	M	T	W	T	F	S
				1	2	3
4	5	6	7	8	9	10
11	12	13	14	15	16	17
18	19	20	21	22	23	24
25	26	27	28	29	30	31

JUNE

S	M	T	W	T	F	S
1	2	3	4	5	6	7
8	9	10	11	12	13	14
15	16	17	18	19	20	21
22	23	24	25	26	27	28
29	30					

JULY

S	M	T	W	T	F	S
		1	2	3	4	5
6	7	8	9	10	11	12
13	14	15	16	17	18	19
20	21	22	23	24	25	26
27	28	29	30	31		

AUGUST

S	M	T	W	T	F	S
					1	2
3	4	5	6	7	8	9
10	11	12	13	14	15	16
17	18	19	20	21	22	23
24	25	26	27	28	29	30
31						

SEPTEMBER

S	M	T	W	T	F	S
	1	2	3	4	5	6
7	8	9	10	11	12	13
14	15	16	17	18	19	20
21	22	23	24	25	26	27
28	29	30				

OCTOBER

S	M	T	W	T	F	S
			1	2	3	4
5	6	7	8	9	10	11
12	13	14	15	16	17	18
19	20	21	22	23	24	25
26	27	28	29	30	31	

NOVEMBER

S	M	T	W	T	F	S
						1
2	3	4	5	6	7	8
9	10	11	12	13	14	15
16	17	18	19	20	21	22
23	24	25	26	27	28	29
30						

DECEMBER

S	M	T	W	T	F	S
	1	2	3	4	5	6
7	8	9	10	11	12	13
14	15	16	17	18	19	20
21	22	23	24	25	26	27
28	29	30	31			

5

JANUARY

S	M	T	W	T	F	S
				1	2	3
4	5	6	7	8	9	10
11	12	13	14	15	16	17
18	19	20	21	22	23	24
25	26	27	28	29	30	31

FEBRUARY

S	M	T	W	T	F	S
1	2	3	4	5	6	7
8	9	10	11	12	13	14
15	16	17	18	19	20	21
22	23	24	25	26	27	28

MARCH

S	M	T	W	T	F	S
1	2	3	4	5	6	7
8	9	10	11	12	13	14
15	16	17	18	19	20	21
22	23	24	25	26	27	28
29	30	31				

APRIL

S	M	T	W	T	F	S
			1	2	3	4
5	6	7	8	9	10	11
12	13	14	15	16	17	18
19	20	21	22	23	24	25
26	27	28	29	30		

MAY

S	M	T	W	T	F	S
					1	2
3	4	5	6	7	8	9
10	11	12	13	14	15	16
17	18	19	20	21	22	23
24	25	26	27	28	29	30
31						

JUNE

S	M	T	W	T	F	S
	1	2	3	4	5	6
7	8	9	10	11	12	13
14	15	16	17	18	19	20
21	22	23	24	25	26	27
28	29	30				

JULY

S	M	T	W	T	F	S
			1	2	3	4
5	6	7	8	9	10	11
12	13	14	15	16	17	18
19	20	21	22	23	24	25
26	27	28	29	30	31	

AUGUST

S	M	T	W	T	F	S
						1
2	3	4	5	6	7	8
9	10	11	12	13	14	15
16	17	18	19	20	21	22
23	24	25	26	27	28	29
30	31					

SEPTEMBER

S	M	T	W	T	F	S
		1	2	3	4	5
6	7	8	9	10	11	12
13	14	15	16	17	18	19
20	21	22	23	24	25	26
27	28	29	30			

OCTOBER

S	M	T	W	T	F	S
				1	2	3
4	5	6	7	8	9	10
11	12	13	14	15	16	17
18	19	20	21	22	23	24
25	26	27	28	29	30	31

NOVEMBER

S	M	T	W	T	F	S
1	2	3	4	5	6	7
8	9	10	11	12	13	14
15	16	17	18	19	20	21
22	23	24	25	26	27	28
29	30					

DECEMBER

S	M	T	W	T	F	S
		1	2	3	4	5
6	7	8	9	10	11	12
13	14	15	16	17	18	19
20	21	22	23	24	25	26
27	28	29	30	31		

6 1993

JANUARY

S	M	T	W	T	F	S
					1	2
3	4	5	6	7	8	9
10	11	12	13	14	15	16
17	18	19	20	21	22	23
24	25	26	27	28	29	30
31						

FEBRUARY

S	M	T	W	T	F	S
	1	2	3	4	5	6
7	8	9	10	11	12	13
14	15	16	17	18	19	20
21	22	23	24	25	26	27
28						

MARCH

S	M	T	W	T	F	S
	1	2	3	4	5	6
7	8	9	10	11	12	13
14	15	16	17	18	19	20
21	22	23	24	25	26	27
28	29	30	31			

APRIL

S	M	T	W	T	F	S
				1	2	3
4	5	6	7	8	9	10
11	12	13	14	15	16	17
18	19	20	21	22	23	24
25	26	27	28	29	30	

MAY

S	M	T	W	T	F	S
						1
2	3	4	5	6	7	8
9	10	11	12	13	14	15
16	17	18	19	20	21	22
23	24	25	26	27	28	29
30	31					

JUNE

S	M	T	W	T	F	S
		1	2	3	4	5
6	7	8	9	10	11	12
13	14	15	16	17	18	19
20	21	22	23	24	25	26
27	28	29	30			

JULY

S	M	T	W	T	F	S
				1	2	3
4	5	6	7	8	9	10
11	12	13	14	15	16	17
18	19	20	21	22	23	24
25	26	27	28	29	30	31

AUGUST

S	M	T	W	T	F	S
1	2	3	4	5	6	7
8	9	10	11	12	13	14
15	16	17	18	19	20	21
22	23	24	25	26	27	28
29	30	31				

SEPTEMBER

S	M	T	W	T	F	S
			1	2	3	4
5	6	7	8	9	10	11
12	13	14	15	16	17	18
19	20	21	22	23	24	25
26	27	28	29	30		

OCTOBER

S	M	T	W	T	F	S
					1	2
3	4	5	6	7	8	9
10	11	12	13	14	15	16
17	18	19	20	21	22	23
24	25	26	27	28	29	30
31						

NOVEMBER

S	M	T	W	T	F	S
	1	2	3	4	5	6
7	8	9	10	11	12	13
14	15	16	17	18	19	20
21	22	23	24	25	26	27
28	29	30				

DECEMBER

S	M	T	W	T	F	S
			1	2	3	4
5	6	7	8	9	10	11
12	13	14	15	16	17	18
19	20	21	22	23	24	25
26	27	28	29	30	31	

7 — 1994

JANUARY

S	M	T	W	T	F	S
						1
2	3	4	5	6	7	8
9	10	11	12	13	14	15
16	17	18	19	20	21	22
23	24	25	26	27	28	29
30	31					

FEBRUARY

S	M	T	W	T	F	S
		1	2	3	4	5
6	7	8	9	10	11	12
13	14	15	16	17	18	19
20	21	22	23	24	25	26
27	28					

MARCH

S	M	T	W	T	F	S
		1	2	3	4	5
6	7	8	9	10	11	12
13	14	15	16	17	18	19
20	21	22	23	24	25	26
27	28	29	30	31		

APRIL

S	M	T	W	T	F	S
					1	2
3	4	5	6	7	8	9
10	11	12	13	14	15	16
17	18	19	20	21	22	23
24	25	26	27	28	29	30

MAY

S	M	T	W	T	F	S
1	2	3	4	5	6	7
8	9	10	11	12	13	14
15	16	17	18	19	20	21
22	23	24	25	26	27	28
29	30	31				

JUNE

S	M	T	W	T	F	S
			1	2	3	4
5	6	7	8	9	10	11
12	13	14	15	16	17	18
19	20	21	22	23	24	25
26	27	28	29	30		

JULY

S	M	T	W	T	F	S
					1	2
3	4	5	6	7	8	9
10	11	12	13	14	15	16
17	18	19	20	21	22	23
24	25	26	27	28	29	30
31						

AUGUST

S	M	T	W	T	F	S
	1	2	3	4	5	6
7	8	9	10	11	12	13
14	15	16	17	18	19	20
21	22	23	24	25	26	27
28	29	30	31			

SEPTEMBER

S	M	T	W	T	F	S
				1	2	3
4	5	6	7	8	9	10
11	12	13	14	15	16	17
18	19	20	21	22	23	24
25	26	27	28	29	30	

OCTOBER

S	M	T	W	T	F	S
						1
2	3	4	5	6	7	8
9	10	11	12	13	14	15
16	17	18	19	20	21	22
23	24	25	26	27	28	29
30	31					

NOVEMBER

S	M	T	W	T	F	S
		1	2	3	4	5
6	7	8	9	10	11	12
13	14	15	16	17	18	19
20	21	22	23	24	25	26
27	28	29	30			

DECEMBER

S	M	T	W	T	F	S
				1	2	3
4	5	6	7	8	9	10
11	12	13	14	15	16	17
18	19	20	21	22	23	24
25	26	27	28	29	30	31

8

JANUARY

S	M	T	W	T	F	S
1	2	3	4	5	6	7
8	9	10	11	12	13	14
15	16	17	18	19	20	21
22	23	24	25	26	27	28
29	30	31				

FEBRUARY

S	M	T	W	T	F	S
			1	2	3	4
5	6	7	8	9	10	11
12	13	14	15	16	17	18
19	20	21	22	23	24	25
26	27	28	29			

MARCH

S	M	T	W	T	F	S
				1	2	3
4	5	6	7	8	9	10
11	12	13	14	15	16	17
18	19	20	21	22	23	24
25	26	27	28	29	30	31

APRIL

S	M	T	W	T	F	S
1	2	3	4	5	6	7
8	9	10	11	12	13	14
15	16	17	18	19	20	21
22	23	24	25	26	27	28
29	30					

MAY

S	M	T	W	T	F	S
		1	2	3	4	5
6	7	8	9	10	11	12
13	14	15	16	17	18	19
20	21	22	23	24	25	26
27	28	29	30	31		

JUNE

S	M	T	W	T	F	S
					1	2
3	4	5	6	7	8	9
10	11	12	13	14	15	16
17	18	19	20	21	22	23
24	25	26	27	28	29	30

JULY

S	M	T	W	T	F	S
1	2	3	4	5	6	7
8	9	10	11	12	13	14
15	16	17	18	19	20	21
22	23	24	25	26	27	28
29	30	31				

AUGUST

S	M	T	W	T	F	S
			1	2	3	4
5	6	7	8	9	10	11
12	13	14	15	16	17	18
19	20	21	22	23	24	25
26	27	28	29	30	31	

SEPTEMBER

S	M	T	W	T	F	S
						1
2	3	4	5	6	7	8
9	10	11	12	13	14	15
16	17	18	19	20	21	22
23	24	25	26	27	28	29
30						

OCTOBER

S	M	T	W	T	F	S
	1	2	3	4	5	6
7	8	9	10	11	12	13
14	15	16	17	18	19	20
21	22	23	24	25	26	27
28	29	30	31			

NOVEMBER

S	M	T	W	T	F	S
				1	2	3
4	5	6	7	8	9	10
11	12	13	14	15	16	17
18	19	20	21	22	23	24
25	26	27	28	29	30	

DECEMBER

S	M	T	W	T	F	S
						1
2	3	4	5	6	7	8
9	10	11	12	13	14	15
16	17	18	19	20	21	22
23	24	25	26	27	28	29
30	31					

9

JANUARY

S	M	T	W	T	F	S
	1	2	3	4	5	6
7	8	9	10	11	12	13
14	15	16	17	18	19	20
21	22	23	24	25	26	27
28	29	30	31			

FEBRUARY

S	M	T	W	T	F	S
				1	2	3
4	5	6	7	8	9	10
11	12	13	14	15	16	17
18	19	20	21	22	23	24
25	26	27	28	29		

MARCH

S	M	T	W	T	F	S
					1	2
3	4	5	6	7	8	9
10	11	12	13	14	15	16
17	18	19	20	21	22	23
24	25	26	27	28	29	30
31						

APRIL

S	M	T	W	T	F	S
	1	2	3	4	5	6
7	8	9	10	11	12	13
14	15	16	17	18	19	20
21	22	23	24	25	26	27
28	29	30				

MAY

S	M	T	W	T	F	S
			1	2	3	4
5	6	7	8	9	10	11
12	13	14	15	16	17	18
19	20	21	22	23	24	25
26	27	28	29	30	31	

JUNE

S	M	T	W	T	F	S
						1
2	3	4	5	6	7	8
9	10	11	12	13	14	15
16	17	18	19	20	21	22
23	24	25	26	27	28	29
30						

JULY

S	M	T	W	T	F	S
	1	2	3	4	5	6
7	8	9	10	11	12	13
14	15	16	17	18	19	20
21	22	23	24	25	26	27
28	29	30	31			

AUGUST

S	M	T	W	T	F	S
				1	2	3
4	5	6	7	8	9	10
11	12	13	14	15	16	17
18	19	20	21	22	23	24
25	26	27	28	29	30	31

SEPTEMBER

S	M	T	W	T	F	S
1	2	3	4	5	6	7
8	9	10	11	12	13	14
15	16	17	18	19	20	21
22	23	24	25	26	27	28
29	30					

OCTOBER

S	M	T	W	T	F	S
		1	2	3	4	5
6	7	8	9	10	11	12
13	14	15	16	17	18	19
20	21	22	23	24	25	26
27	28	29	30	31		

NOVEMBER

S	M	T	W	T	F	S
					1	2
3	4	5	6	7	8	9
10	11	12	13	14	15	16
17	18	19	20	21	22	23
24	25	26	27	28	29	30

DECEMBER

S	M	T	W	T	F	S
1	2	3	4	5	6	7
8	9	10	11	12	13	14
15	16	17	18	19	20	21
22	23	24	25	26	27	28
29	30	31				

10

JANUARY

S	M	T	W	T	F	S
		1	2	3	4	5
6	7	8	9	10	11	12
13	14	15	16	17	18	19
20	21	22	23	24	25	26
27	28	29	30	31		

FEBRUARY

S	M	T	W	T	F	S
					1	2
3	4	5	6	7	8	9
10	11	12	13	14	15	16
17	18	19	20	21	22	23
24	25	26	27	28	29	

MARCH

S	M	T	W	T	F	S
						1
2	3	4	5	6	7	8
9	10	11	12	13	14	15
16	17	18	19	20	21	22
23	24	25	26	27	28	29
30	31					

APRIL

S	M	T	W	T	F	S
		1	2	3	4	5
6	7	8	9	10	11	12
13	14	15	16	17	18	19
20	21	22	23	24	25	26
27	28	29	30			

MAY

S	M	T	W	T	F	S
				1	2	3
4	5	6	7	8	9	10
11	12	13	14	15	16	17
18	19	20	21	22	23	24
25	26	27	28	29	30	31

JUNE

S	M	T	W	T	F	S
1	2	3	4	5	6	7
8	9	10	11	12	13	14
15	16	17	18	19	20	21
22	23	24	25	26	27	28
29	30					

JULY

S	M	T	W	T	F	S
		1	2	3	4	5
6	7	8	9	10	11	12
13	14	15	16	17	18	19
20	21	22	23	24	25	26
27	28	29	30	31		

AUGUST

S	M	T	W	T	F	S
					1	2
3	4	5	6	7	8	9
10	11	12	13	14	15	16
17	18	19	20	21	22	23
24	25	26	27	28	29	30
31						

SEPTEMBER

S	M	T	W	T	F	S
	1	2	3	4	5	6
7	8	9	10	11	12	13
14	15	16	17	18	19	20
21	22	23	24	25	26	27
28	29	30				

OCTOBER

S	M	T	W	T	F	S
			1	2	3	4
5	6	7	8	9	10	11
12	13	14	15	16	17	18
19	20	21	22	23	24	25
26	27	28	29	30	31	

NOVEMBER

S	M	T	W	T	F	S
						1
2	3	4	5	6	7	8
9	10	11	12	13	14	15
16	17	18	19	20	21	22
23	24	25	26	27	28	29
30						

DECEMBER

S	M	T	W	T	F	S
	1	2	3	4	5	6
7	8	9	10	11	12	13
14	15	16	17	18	19	20
21	22	23	24	25	26	27
28	29	30	31			

11

JANUARY

S	M	T	W	T	F	S
			1	2	3	4
5	6	7	8	9	10	11
12	13	14	15	16	17	18
19	20	21	22	23	24	25
26	27	28	29	30	31	

FEBRUARY

S	M	T	W	T	F	S
						1
2	3	4	5	6	7	8
9	10	11	12	13	14	15
16	17	18	19	20	21	22
23	24	25	26	27	28	29

MARCH

S	M	T	W	T	F	S
1	2	3	4	5	6	7
8	9	10	11	12	13	14
15	16	17	18	19	20	21
22	23	24	25	26	27	28
29	30	31				

APRIL

S	M	T	W	T	F	S
			1	2	3	4
5	6	7	8	9	10	11
12	13	14	15	16	17	18
19	20	21	22	23	24	25
26	27	28	29	30		

MAY

S	M	T	W	T	F	S
					1	2
3	4	5	6	7	8	9
10	11	12	13	14	15	16
17	18	19	20	21	22	23
24	25	26	27	28	29	30
31						

JUNE

S	M	T	W	T	F	S
	1	2	3	4	5	6
7	8	9	10	11	12	13
14	15	16	17	18	19	20
21	22	23	24	25	26	27
28	29	30				

JULY

S	M	T	W	T	F	S
			1	2	3	4
5	6	7	8	9	10	11
12	13	14	15	16	17	18
19	20	21	22	23	24	25
26	27	28	29	30	31	

AUGUST

S	M	T	W	T	F	S
						1
2	3	4	5	6	7	8
9	10	11	12	13	14	15
16	17	18	19	20	21	22
23	24	25	26	27	28	29
30	31					

SEPTEMBER

S	M	T	W	T	F	S
		1	2	3	4	5
6	7	8	9	10	11	12
13	14	15	16	17	18	19
20	21	22	23	24	25	26
27	28	29	30			

OCTOBER

S	M	T	W	T	F	S
				1	2	3
4	5	6	7	8	9	10
11	12	13	14	15	16	17
18	19	20	21	22	23	24
25	26	27	28	29	30	31

NOVEMBER

S	M	T	W	T	F	S
1	2	3	4	5	6	7
8	9	10	11	12	13	14
15	16	17	18	19	20	21
22	23	24	25	26	27	28
29	30					

DECEMBER

S	M	T	W	T	F	S
		1	2	3	4	5
6	7	8	9	10	11	12
13	14	15	16	17	18	19
20	21	22	23	24	25	26
27	28	29	30	31		

12

JANUARY

S	M	T	W	T	F	S
				1	2	3
4	5	6	7	8	9	10
11	12	13	14	15	16	17
18	19	20	21	22	23	24
25	26	27	28	29	30	31

FEBRUARY

S	M	T	W	T	F	S
1	2	3	4	5	6	7
8	9	10	11	12	13	14
15	16	17	18	19	20	21
22	23	24	25	26	27	28
29						

MARCH

S	M	T	W	T	F	S
	1	2	3	4	5	6
7	8	9	10	11	12	13
14	15	16	17	18	19	20
21	22	23	24	25	26	27
28	29	30	31			

APRIL

S	M	T	W	T	F	S
				1	2	3
4	5	6	7	8	9	10
11	12	13	14	15	16	17
18	19	20	21	22	23	24
25	26	27	28	29	30	

MAY

S	M	T	W	T	F	S
						1
2	3	4	5	6	7	8
9	10	11	12	13	14	15
16	17	18	19	20	21	22
23	24	25	26	27	28	29
30	31					

JUNE

S	M	T	W	T	F	S
		1	2	3	4	5
6	7	8	9	10	11	12
13	14	15	16	17	18	19
20	21	22	23	24	25	26
27	28	29	30			

JULY

S	M	T	W	T	F	S
				1	2	3
4	5	6	7	8	9	10
11	12	13	14	15	16	17
18	19	20	21	22	23	24
25	26	27	28	29	30	31

AUGUST

S	M	T	W	T	F	S
1	2	3	4	5	6	7
8	9	10	11	12	13	14
15	16	17	18	19	20	21
22	23	24	25	26	27	28
29	30	31				

SEPTEMBER

S	M	T	W	T	F	S
			1	2	3	4
5	6	7	8	9	10	11
12	13	14	15	16	17	18
19	20	21	22	23	24	25
26	27	28	29	30		

OCTOBER

S	M	T	W	T	F	S
					1	2
3	4	5	6	7	8	9
10	11	12	13	14	15	16
17	18	19	20	21	22	23
24	25	26	27	28	29	30
31						

NOVEMBER

S	M	T	W	T	F	S
	1	2	3	4	5	6
7	8	9	10	11	12	13
14	15	16	17	18	19	20
21	22	23	24	25	26	27
28	29	30				

DECEMBER

S	M	T	W	T	F	S
			1	2	3	4
5	6	7	8	9	10	11
12	13	14	15	16	17	18
19	20	21	22	23	24	25
26	27	28	29	30	31	

13

JANUARY

S	M	T	W	T	F	S
					1	2
3	4	5	6	7	8	9
10	11	12	13	14	15	16
17	18	19	20	21	22	23
24	25	26	27	28	29	30
31						

FEBRUARY

S	M	T	W	T	F	S
	1	2	3	4	5	6
7	8	9	10	11	12	13
14	15	16	17	18	19	20
21	22	23	24	25	26	27
28	29					

MARCH

S	M	T	W	T	F	S
		1	2	3	4	5
6	7	8	9	10	11	12
13	14	15	16	17	18	19
20	21	22	23	24	25	26
27	28	29	30	31		

APRIL

S	M	T	W	T	F	S
					1	2
3	4	5	6	7	8	9
10	11	12	13	14	15	16
17	18	19	20	21	22	23
24	25	26	27	28	29	30

MAY

S	M	T	W	T	F	S
1	2	3	4	5	6	7
8	9	10	11	12	13	14
15	16	17	18	19	20	21
22	23	24	25	26	27	28
29	30	31				

JUNE

S	M	T	W	T	F	S
			1	2	3	4
5	6	7	8	9	10	11
12	13	14	15	16	17	18
19	20	21	22	23	24	25
26	27	28	29	30		

JULY

S	M	T	W	T	F	S
					1	2
3	4	5	6	7	8	9
10	11	12	13	14	15	16
17	18	19	20	21	22	23
24	25	26	27	28	29	30
31						

AUGUST

S	M	T	W	T	F	S
	1	2	3	4	5	6
7	8	9	10	11	12	13
14	15	16	17	18	19	20
21	22	23	24	25	26	27
28	29	30	31			

SEPTEMBER

S	M	T	W	T	F	S
				1	2	3
4	5	6	7	8	9	10
11	12	13	14	15	16	17
18	19	20	21	22	23	24
25	26	27	28	29	30	

OCTOBER

S	M	T	W	T	F	S
						1
2	3	4	5	6	7	8
9	10	11	12	13	14	15
16	17	18	19	20	21	22
23	24	25	26	27	28	29
30	31					

NOVEMBER

S	M	T	W	T	F	S
		1	2	3	4	5
6	7	8	9	10	11	12
13	14	15	16	17	18	19
20	21	22	23	24	25	26
27	28	29	30			

DECEMBER

S	M	T	W	T	F	S
				1	2	3
4	5	6	7	8	9	10
11	12	13	14	15	16	17
18	19	20	21	22	23	24
25	26	27	28	29	30	31

14

JANUARY

S	M	T	W	T	F	S
						1
2	3	4	5	6	7	8
9	10	11	12	13	14	15
16	17	18	19	20	21	22
23	24	25	26	27	28	29
30	31					

FEBRUARY

S	M	T	W	T	F	S
		1	2	3	4	5
6	7	8	9	10	11	12
13	14	15	16	17	18	19
20	21	22	23	24	25	26
27	28	29				

MARCH

S	M	T	W	T	F	S
			1	2	3	4
5	6	7	8	9	10	11
12	13	14	15	16	17	18
19	20	21	22	23	24	25
26	27	28	29	30	31	

APRIL

S	M	T	W	T	F	S
						1
2	3	4	5	6	7	8
9	10	11	12	13	14	15
16	17	18	19	20	21	22
23	24	25	26	27	28	29
30						

MAY

S	M	T	W	T	F	S
	1	2	3	4	5	6
7	8	9	10	11	12	13
14	15	16	17	18	19	20
21	22	23	24	25	26	27
28	29	30	31			

JUNE

S	M	T	W	T	F	S
				1	2	3
4	5	6	7	8	9	10
11	12	13	14	15	16	17
18	19	20	21	22	23	24
25	26	27	28	29	30	

JULY

S	M	T	W	T	F	S
						1
2	3	4	5	6	7	8
9	10	11	12	13	14	15
16	17	18	19	20	21	22
23	24	25	26	27	28	29
30	31					

AUGUST

S	M	T	W	T	F	S
		1	2	3	4	5
6	7	8	9	10	11	12
13	14	15	16	17	18	19
20	21	22	23	24	25	26
27	28	29	30	31		

SEPTEMBER

S	M	T	W	T	F	S
					1	2
3	4	5	6	7	8	9
10	11	12	13	14	15	16
17	18	19	20	21	22	23
24	25	26	27	28	29	30

OCTOBER

S	M	T	W	T	F	S
1	2	3	4	5	6	7
8	9	10	11	12	13	14
15	16	17	18	19	20	21
22	23	24	25	26	27	28
29	30	31				

NOVEMBER

S	M	T	W	T	F	S
			1	2	3	4
5	6	7	8	9	10	11
12	13	14	15	16	17	18
19	20	21	22	23	24	25
26	27	28	29	30		

DECEMBER

S	M	T	W	T	F	S
					1	2
3	4	5	6	7	8	9
10	11	12	13	14	15	16
17	18	19	20	21	22	23
24	25	26	27	28	29	30
31						

Julian and Gregorian Calendars; Leap Year; Century

Calendars based on the movements of sun and moon have been used since ancient times, but none has been perfect. The Julian calendar, under which Western nations measured time until A.D. 1582, was authorized by Julius Caesar in 46 B.C., the year 709 of Rome. His expert was a Greek, Sosigenes. The Julian calendar, on the assumption that the true year was 365 1/4 days long, gave every fourth year 366 days. The Venerable Bede, an Anglo-Saxon monk, announced in A.D. 730 that the 365 1/4-day Julian year was 11 min., 14 sec. too long, making a cumulative error of about a day every 128 years, but nothing was done about it for over 800 years.

By 1582 the accumulated error was estimated to have amounted to 10 days. In that year Pope Gregory XIII decreed that the day following Oct. 4, 1582, should be called Oct. 15, thus dropping 10 days.

However, with common years 365 days and a 366-day leap year every fourth year, the error in the length of the year would have recurred at the rate of a little more than 3 days every 400 years. So 3 of every 4 centesimal years (ending in 00) were made common years, not leap years. Thus 1600 was a leap year, 1700, 1800 and 1900 were not, but 2000 will be. **Leap years** are those divisible by 4 except centesimal years, which are common unless divisible by 400.

The Gregorian calendar was adopted at once by France, Italy, Spain, Portugal and Luxembourg. Within 2 years most German Catholic states, Belgium and parts of Switzerland and the Netherlands were brought under the new calendar, and Hungary followed in 1587. The rest of the Netherlands, along with Denmark and the German Protestant states made the change in 1699-1700 (German Protestants retained the old reckoning of Easter until 1776).

The British government imposed the Gregorian calendar on all its possessions, including the American colonies, in 1752. The British decreed that the day following Sept. 2, 1752, should be called Sept. 14, a loss of 11 days. All dates preceding were marked O.S., for Old Style. In addition, New Year's Day was moved to Jan. 1 from Mar. 25 (e.g., under the old reckoning, Mar. 24, 1700, had been followed by Mar. 25, 1701). George Washington's birth date, which was Feb. 11, 1731, O.S., became Feb. 22, 1732, N.S. In 1753 Sweden too went Gregorian, retaining the old Easter rules until 1844.

In 1793 the French revolutionary government adopted a calendar of 12 months of 30 days each with 5 extra days in September of each common year and a 6th extra day every 4th year. Napoleon reinstated the Gregorian calendar in 1806.

The Gregorian system later spread to non-European regions, first in the European colonies, then in the independent countries, replacing traditional calendars at least for official purposes. Japan in 1873, Egypt in 1875, China in 1912 and Turkey in 1917 made the change, usually in conjunction with political upheavals. In China, the republican government began reckoning years from its 1911 founding — e.g., 1948 was designated the year 37. After 1949, the Communists adopted the Common, or Christian Era, year count, even for the traditional lunar calendar.

In 1918 the revolutionary government in Russia decreed that the day after Jan. 31, 1918, Old Style, would become Feb. 14, 1918, New Style. Greece followed in 1923. (In Russia the Orthodox Church has retained the Julian calendar, as have various Middle Eastern Christian sects.) For the first time in history, all major cultures have one calendar.

To change from the Julian to the Gregorian calendar, add 10 days to dates Oct. 5, 1582, through Feb. 28, 1700; after that date add 11 days through Feb. 28, 1800; 12 days through Feb. 28, 1900; and 13 days through Feb. 28, 2100.

A **century** consists of 100 consecutive calendar years. The 1st century A.D. consisted of the years 1 through 100. The 20th century consists of the years 1901 through 2000 and will end Dec. 31, 2000. The 21st century will begin Jan. 1, 2001.

Julian Calendar

To find which of the 14 calendars printed on pages 264-265 applies to any year, starting Jan. 1, under the Julian system, find the century for the desired year in the three left-hand columns below; read across. Then find the year in the four top rows; read down. The number in the intersection is the calendar designation for that year.

Year (last two figures of desired year)

				01	02	03	04	05	06	07	08	09	10	11	12	13	14	15	16	17	18	19	20	21	22	23	24	25	26	27	28
				29	30	31	32	33	34	35	36	37	38	39	40	41	42	43	44	45	46	47	48	49	50	51	52	53	54	55	56
				57	58	59	60	61	62	63	64	65	66	67	68	69	70	71	72	73	74	75	76	77	78	79	80	81	82	83	84
Century			00	85	86	87	88	89	90	91	92	93	94	95	96	97	98	99													
0	700	1400	12	7	1	2	10	5	6	7	8	3	4	5	13	1	2	3	11	6	7	1	9	4	5	6	14	2	3	4	12
100	800	1500	11	6	7	1	9	4	5	6	14	2	3	4	12	7	1	2	10	5	6	7	8	3	4	5	13	1	2	3	11
200	900	1600	10	5	6	7	8	3	4	5	13	1	2	3	11	6	7	1	9	4	5	6	14	2	3	4	12	7	1	2	10
300	1000	1700	9	4	5	6	14	2	3	4	12	7	1	2	10	5	6	7	8	3	4	5	13	1	2	3	11	6	7	1	9
400	1100	1800	8	3	4	5	13	1	2	3	11	6	7	1	9	4	5	6	14	2	3	4	12	7	1	2	10	5	6	7	8
500	1200	1900	14	2	3	4	12	7	1	2	10	5	6	7	8	3	4	5	13	1	2	3	11	6	7	1	9	4	5	6	14
600	1300	2000	13	1	2	3	11	6	7	1	9	4	5	6	14	2	3	4	12	7	1	2	10	5	6	7	8	3	4	5	13

Gregorian Calendar

Pick desired year from table below or on page 264 (for years 1803 to 2080). The number shown with each year shows which calendar to use for that year, as shown on pages 264-265. (The Gregorian calendar was inaugurated Oct. 15, 1582. From that date to Dec. 31, 1582, use calendar 6.)

1583-1802

1583. . 7	1603. . 4	1623. . 1	1643. . 5	1663. . 2	1683. . 6	1703. . 2	1723. . 6	1743. . 3	1763. . 7	1783. . 4
1584. . 8	1604. 12	1624. . 9	1644. 13	1664. 10	1684. 14	1704. 10	1724. 14	1744. 11	1764. . 8	1784. 12
1585. . 3	1605. . 7	1625. . 4	1645. . 1	1665. . 5	1685. . 2	1705. . 5	1725. . 2	1745. . 6	1765. . 3	1785. . 7
1586. . 4	1606. . 1	1626. . 5	1646. . 2	1666. . 6	1686. . 3	1706. . 6	1726. . 3	1746. . 7	1766. . 4	1786. . 1
1587. . 5	1607. . 2	1627. . 6	1647. . 3	1667. . 7	1687. . 4	1707. . 7	1727. . 4	1747. . 1	1767. . 5	1787. . 2
1588. 13	1608. 10	1628. 14	1648. 11	1668. . 8	1688. 12	1708. . 8	1728. 12	1748. . 9	1768. 13	1788. 10
1589. . 1	1609. . 5	1629. . 2	1649. . 6	1669. . 3	1689. . 7	1709. . 3	1729. . 7	1749. . 4	1769. . 1	1789. . 5
1590. . 2	1610. . 6	1630. . 3	1650. . 7	1670. . 4	1690. . 1	1710. . 4	1730. . 1	1750. . 5	1770. . 2	1790. . 6
1591. . 3	1611. . 7	1631. . 4	1651. . 1	1671. . 5	1691. . 2	1711. . 5	1731. . 2	1751. . 6	1771. . 3	1791. . 7
1592. 11	1612. . 8	1632. 12	1652. . 9	1672. 13	1692. 10	1712. 13	1732. 10	1752. 14	1772. 11	1792. . 8
1593. . 6	1613. . 3	1633. . 7	1653. . 4	1673. . 1	1693. . 5	1713. . 1	1733. . 5	1753. . 2	1773. . 6	1793. . 3
1594. . 7	1614. . 4	1634. . 1	1654. . 5	1674. . 2	1694. . 6	1714. . 2	1734. . 6	1754. . 3	1774. . 7	1794. . 4
1595. . 1	1615. . 5	1635. . 2	1655. . 6	1675. . 3	1695. . 7	1715. . 3	1735. . 7	1755. . 4	1775. . 1	1795. . 5
1596. . 9	1616. 13	1636. 10	1656. 14	1676. 11	1696. . 8	1716. 11	1736. . 8	1756. 12	1776. . 9	1796. 13
1597. . 4	1617. . 1	1637. . 5	1657. . 2	1677. . 6	1697. . 3	1717. . 6	1737. . 3	1757. . 7	1777. . 4	1797. . 1
1598. . 5	1618. . 2	1638. . 6	1658. . 3	1678. . 7	1698. . 4	1718. . 7	1738. . 4	1758. . 1	1778. . 5	1798. . 2
1599. . 6	1619. . 3	1639. . 7	1659. . 4	1679. . 1	1699. . 5	1719. . 1	1739. . 5	1759. . 2	1779. . 6	1799. . 3
1600. 14	1620. 11	1640. . 8	1660. 12	1680. . 9	1700. . 6	1720. . 9	1740. 13	1760. 10	1780. 14	1800. . 4
1601. . 2	1621. . 6	1641. . 3	1661. . 7	1681. . 4	1701. . 7	1721. . 4	1741. . 1	1761. . 5	1781. . 2	1801. . 5
1602. . 3	1622. . 7	1642. . 4	1662. . 1	1682. . 5	1702. . 1	1722. . 5	1742. . 2	1762. . 6	1782. . 3	1802. . 6

The Julian Period

How many days have you lived? To determine this, you must multiply your age by 365, add the number of days since your last birthday until today, and account for all leap years. Chances are your answer would be wrong. Astronomers, however, find it convenient to express dates and long time intervals in days rather than in years, months and days. This is done by placing events within the Julian period.

The Julian period was devised in 1582 by Joseph Scaliger and named after his father Julius (not after the Julian calendar). Scaliger had Julian Day (JD) #1 begin at noon, Jan. 1, 4713 B.C., the most recent time that three major chronological cycles began on the same day — 1) the 28-year solar cycle, after which dates in the Julian calendar (e.g., Feb. 11) return to the same days of the week (e.g., Monday); 2) the 19-year lunar cycle, after which the phases of the moon return to the same dates of the year; and 3) the 15-year indiction cycle, used in ancient Rome to regulate taxes. It will take 7980 years to complete the period, the product of 28, 19, and 15.

Noon of Dec. 31, 1993, marks the beginning of JD 2,449,353; that many days will have passed since the start of the Julian period. The JD at noon of any date in 1994 may be found by adding to this figure the day of the year for that date, which is given in the left hand column in the chart below. Simple JD conversion tables are used by astronomers.

Days Between Two Dates

Table covers period of two ordinary years. Example—Days between Feb. 10, 1989 and Dec. 15, 1990; subtract 41 from 714; answer is 673 days. For leap year, such as 1992, one day must be added: final answer is 674.

Date	Jan.	Feb.	Mar.	April	May	June	July	Aug.	Sept.	Oct.	Nov.	Dec.
1	1	32	60	91	121	152	182	213	244	274	305	335
2	2	33	61	92	122	153	183	214	245	275	306	336
3	3	34	62	93	123	154	184	215	246	276	307	337
4	4	35	63	94	124	155	185	216	247	277	308	338
5	5	36	64	95	125	156	186	217	248	278	309	339
6	6	37	65	96	126	157	187	218	249	279	310	340
7	7	38	66	97	127	158	188	219	250	280	311	341
8	8	39	67	98	128	159	189	220	251	281	312	342
9	9	40	68	99	129	160	190	221	252	282	313	343
10	10	41	69	100	130	161	191	222	253	283	314	344
11	11	42	70	101	131	162	192	223	254	284	315	345
12	12	43	71	102	132	163	193	224	255	285	316	346
13	13	44	72	103	133	164	194	225	256	286	317	347
14	14	45	73	104	134	165	195	226	257	287	318	348
15	15	46	74	105	135	166	196	227	258	288	319	349
16	16	47	75	106	136	167	197	228	259	289	320	350
17	17	48	76	107	137	168	198	229	260	290	321	351
18	18	49	77	108	138	169	199	230	261	291	322	352
19	19	50	78	109	139	170	200	231	262	292	323	353
20	20	51	79	110	140	171	201	232	263	293	324	354
21	21	52	80	111	141	172	202	233	264	294	325	355
22	22	53	81	112	142	173	203	234	265	295	326	356
23	23	54	82	113	143	174	204	235	266	296	327	357
24	24	55	83	114	144	175	205	236	267	297	328	358
25	25	56	84	115	145	176	206	237	268	298	329	359
26	26	57	85	116	146	177	207	238	269	299'	330	360
27	27	58	86	117	147	178	208	239	270	300	331	361
28	28	59	87	118	148	179	209	240	271	301	332	362
29	29	—	88	119	149	180	210	241	272	302	333	363
30	30	—	89	120	150	181	211	242	273	303	334	364
31	31	—	90	—	151	—	212	243	—	304	—	365

Date	Jan.	Feb.	Mar.	April	May	June	July	Aug.	Sept.	Oct.	Nov.	Dec.
1	366	397	425	456	486	517	547	578	609	639	670	700
2	367	398	426	457	487	518	548	579	610	640	671	701
3	368	399	427	458	488	519	549	580	611	641	672	702
4	369	400	428	459	489	520	550	581	612	642	673	703
5	370	401	429	460	490	521	551	582	613	643	674	704
6	371	402	430	461	491	522	552	583	614	644	675	705
7	372	403	431	462	492	523	553	584	615	645	676	706
8	373	404	432	463	493	524	554	585	616	646	677	707
9	374	405	433	464	494	525	555	586	617	647	678	708
10	375	406	434	465	495	526	556	587	618	648	679	709
11	376	407	435	466	496	527	557	588	619	649	680	710
12	377	408	436	467	497	528	558	589	620	650	681	711
13	378	409	437	468	498	529	559	590	621	651	682	712
14	379	410	438	469	499	530	560	591	622	652	683	713
15	380	411	439	470	500	531	561	592	623	653	684	714
16	381	412	440	471	501	532	562	593	624	654	685	715
17	382	413	441	472	502	533	563	594	625	655	686	716
18	383	414	442	473	503	534	564	595	626	656	687	717
19	384	415	443	474	504	535	565	596	627	657	688	718
20	385	416	444	475	505	536	566	597	628	658	689	719
21	386	417	445	476	506	537	567	598	629	659	690	720
22	387	418	446	477	507	538	568	599	630	660	691	721
23	388	419	447	478	508	539	569	600	631	661	692	722
24	389	420	448	479	509	540	570	601	632	662	693	723
25	390	421	449	480	510	541	571	602	633	663	694	724
26	301	422	450	481	511	542	572	603	634	664	695	725
27	392	423	451	482	512	543	573	604	635	665	696	726
28	393	424	452	483	513	544	574	605	636	666	697	727
29	394	—	453	484	514	545	575	606	637	667	698	728
30	395	—	454	485	515	546	576	607	638	668	699	729
31	396	—	455	—	516	—	577	608	—	669	—	730

Lunar Calendar, Chinese New Year, Vietnamese Tet

The ancient Chinese lunar calendar is divided into 12 months of either 29 or 30 days (compensating for the fact that the mean duration of the lunar month is 29 days, 12 hours, 44.05 minutes). The calendar is synchronized with the solar year by the addition of extra months at fixed intervals.

The Chinese calendar runs on a sexagenary cycle, i.e., 60 years. The cycles 1876-1935 and 1936-1995, with the years grouped under their twelve animal designations, are printed below. A new cycle will begin in 1996 and last until 2055. The Year 1994 (Lunar Year 4692) is found in the eleventh column, under Dog, and is known as a "Year of the Dog." Readers can find the animal name for the year of their birth, marriage, etc., in the same chart. (Note: the first 3-7 weeks of each of the Western years belong to the previous Chinese year and animal designation.)

Both the Western (Gregorian) and traditional lunar calendars are used publicly in China and North and South Korea, and two New Year's celebrations are held. On Taiwan, in overseas Chinese communities, and in Vietnam, the lunar calendar has been used only to set the dates for traditional festivals, with the Gregorian system in general use.

The four-day Chinese New Year, Hsin Nien, the three-day Vietnamese New Year festival, Tet, and the three-to-four-day Korean festival, Suhl, begin at the first new moon after the sun enters Aquarius. The day may fall, therefore, between Jan. 21 and Feb. 19 of the Gregorian calendar. Feb. 10, 1994 marks the start of the new Chinese year. The date is fixed according to the date of the new moon in the Far East. Since this is west of the International Date Line, the date may be one day later than that of the new moon in the United States.

Rat	Ox	Tiger	Hare (Rabbit)	Dragon	Snake	Horse	Sheep (Goat)	Monkey	Rooster	Dog	Pig
1876	1877	1878	1879	1880	1881	1882	1883	1884	1885	1886	1887
1888	1889	1890	1891	1892	1893	1894	1895	1896	1897	1898	1899
1900	1901	1902	1903	1904	1905	1906	1907	1908	1909	1910	1911
1912	1913	1914	1915	1916	1917	1918	1919	1920	1921	1922	1923
1924	1925	1926	1927	1928	1929	1930	1931	1932	1933	1934	1935
1936	1937	1938	1939	1940	1941	1942	1943	1944	1945	1946	1947
1948	1949	1950	1951	1952	1953	1954	1955	1956	1957	1958	1959
1960	1961	1962	1963	1964	1965	1966	1967	1968	1969	1970	1971
1972	1973	1974	1975	1976	1977	1978	1979	1980	1981	1982	1983
1984	1985	1986	1987	1988	1989	1990	1991	1992	1993	1994	1995
1996	1997	1998	1999	2000	2001	2002	2003	2004	2005	2006	2007

Standard Time, Daylight Saving Time, and Others

Source: Defense Mapping Agency Hydrographic/Topographic Center; U.S. Dept. of Transportation

Standard Time

Standard Time is reckoned from Greenwich, England, recognized as the Prime Meridian of Longitude. The world is divided into 24 zones, each 15° of arc, or one hour in time apart. The Greenwich meridian (0°) extends through the center of the initial zone, and the zones to the east are numbered from 1 to 12 with the prefix "minus" indicating the number of hours to be subtracted to obtain Greenwich Time. Each zone extends 7½° on either side of its central meridian.

Westward zones are similarly numbered, but prefixed "plus" showing the number of hours that must be added to get Greenwich Time. While these zones apply generally to sea areas, it should be noted that the Standard Time maintained in many countries does not coincide with zone time. A graphical representation of the zones is shown on the Standard Time Zone Chart of the World published by the Defense Mapping Agency, Attn: PR, 8613 Lee Highway, Fairfax, VA 22031-2137.

The United States and possessions are divided into eight Standard Time zones, as set forth by the Uniform Time Act of 1966, which also provides for the use of Daylight Saving Time therein. Each zone is approximately 15° of longitude in width. All places in each zone use, instead of their own local time, the time counted from the transit of the "mean sun" across the Standard Time meridian which passes near the middle of that zone.

These time zones are designated as Atlantic, Eastern, Central, Mountain, Pacific, Yukon, Alaska-Hawaii, and Bering (Samoa), and the time in these zones is basically reckoned from the 60th, 75th, 90th, 105th, 120th, 135th, 150th and 165th meridians west of Greenwich. The line wanders to conform to local geographical regions. The time in the various zones is earlier than Greenwich Time by 4, 5, 6, 7, 8, 9, 10, and 11 hours respectively.

24-Hour Time

24-hour time is widely used in scientific work throughout the world. In the United States it is used also in operations of the Armed Forces. In Europe it is frequently used by the transportation networks in preference to the 12-hour a.m. and p.m. system. With the 24-hour system the day begins at midnight and is designated 0000 through 2359.

International Date Line

The Date Line is a zig-zag line that approximately coincides with the 180th meridian, and it is where the calendar dates are separated. The date must be advanced one day when crossing in a westerly direction and set back one day when crossing in an easterly direction.

The line is deflected eastward through the Bering Strait and westward of the Aleutians to prevent separating these areas by date. The line is again deflected eastward of the Tonga and New Zealand Islands in the South Pacific for the same reason.

Daylight Saving Time

Daylight Saving Time is achieved by advancing the clock one hour. Under the Uniform Time Act, which became effective in 1967, all states, the District of Columbia, and U.S. possessions were to observe Daylight Saving Time beginning at 2 a.m. on the last Sunday in April and ending at 2 a.m. on the last Sunday in October. Any state could, by law, exempt itself; a 1972 amendment to the act authorized states split by time zones to take that into consideration in exempting themselves. Arizona, Hawaii, Puerto Rico, the Virgin Islands, American Samoa, and part of Indiana are now exempt. Some local zone boundaries in Kansas, Texas, Florida, Michigan, and Alaska have been modified by the Dept. of Transportation, which oversees the act. To conserve energy Congress put most of the nation on year-round Daylight Saving Time for two years effective Jan. 6, 1974 through Oct. 26, 1975, but another bill, signed in October 1974, restored Standard Time from the last Sunday in that month to the last Sunday in February 1975. At the end of 1975, Congress failed to renew this temporary legislation and the nation returned to the older end-of-April to end-of-October DST system.

On July 8, 1986, Pres. Ronald Reagan signed legislation moving up the start of Daylight Saving Time to the first Sunday in April. Daylight Saving Time, which used to start the last Sunday in April, still ends the last Sunday in October. The Transportation Dept. estimated that the earlier starting date would help save more than $28 million in traffic accident costs and prevent more than 1,500 injuries and 20 deaths annually. The law, opposed by some farm state lawmakers, took effect in 1987.

International

Adjusting clock time to be able to use the added daylight on summer evenings is common throughout the world.

Western Europe is on Daylight Saving Time generally from the last Sunday in March to the last Sunday in September; however, the United Kingdom continues until the last Sunday in October.

Russia, which lies over 11 time zones, maintains its Standard Time 1 hour fast of the zone designation. Additionally, it proclaims Daylight Saving Time as does Europe.

China, which lies across 5 time zones, has decreed that the entire country be placed on Greenwich Time plus 8 hours, with Daylight Saving Time from April 12 to September 12.

Many of the countries in the Southern Hemisphere maintain Daylight Saving Time generally from October to March; however, most countries near the equator do not deviate from Standard Time.

Standard Time Differences—World Cities

The time indicated in the table is fixed by law and is called the legal time, or, more generally, Standard Time. Use of Daylight Saving Time varies widely. * Indicates morning of the following day. At 12:00 noon, Eastern Standard Time, the Standard Time (in 24-hour time) in foreign cities is as follows:

Addis Ababa 20 00	Cape Town 19 00	Lima 12 00	Santiago (Chile) 13 00
Alexandria 19 00	Caracas 13 00	Lisbon 17 00	Seoul 2 00*
Amsterdam 18 00	Casablanca 17 00	Liverpool 17 00	Shanghai 1 00*
Athens 19 00	Copenhagen 18 00	London 17 00	Singapore 1 00*
Auckland 5 00*	Delhi 22 30	Madrid 18 00	Stockholm 18 00
Baghdad 20 00	Dhaka 23 00	Manila 1 00*	Sydney (Australia) 3 00*
Bangkok 0 00	Dublin 17 00	Mecca (Saudi Arabia) 20 00	Tashkent 23 00
Beijing 1 00*	Gdańsk 18 00	Melbourne 3 00*	Teheran 20 30
Belfast 17 00	Geneva 18 00	Mexico City 11 00	Tel Aviv 19 00
Berlin 18 00	Havana 12 00	Montevideo 14 00	Tokyo 2 00*
Bogotá 12 00	Helsinki 19 00	Moscow 20 00	Valparaiso 13 00
Bombay 22 30	Ho Chi Minh City 0 00	Nagasaki 2 00*	Vladivostok 3 00*
Bremen 18 00	Hong Kong 1 00*	Oslo 18 00	Vienna 18 00
Brussels 18 00	Istanbul 19 00	Paris 18 00	Warsaw 18 00
Bucharest 19 00	Jakarta 0 00	Prague 18 00	Wellington (N.Z.) 5 00*
Budapest 18 00	Jerusalem 19 00	Rio de Janeiro 14 00	Yangon (Rangoon) 23 30
Buenos Aires 14 00	Johannesburg 19 00	Rome 18 00	Yokohama 2 00*
Cairo 19 00	Karachi 22 00	St. Petersburg 20 00	Zürich 18 00
Calcutta 22 30	Le Havre 18 00		

Standard Time Differences — North American Cities

At 12 o'clock noon, Eastern Standard Time, the Standard Time in N.A. cities is as follows:

Akron, Oh.	12 00	Noon	Frankfort, Ky.	12 00	Noon	*Phoenix, Ariz.	10 00	A.M.
Albuquerque, N.M.	10 00	A.M.	Galveston, Tex.	11 00	A.M.	Pierre, S.D.	11 00	A.M.
Atlanta, Ga.	12 00	Noon	Grand Rapids, Mich.	12 00	Noon	Pittsburgh, Pa.	12 00	Noon
Austin, Tex.	11 00	A.M.	Halifax, N.S.	1 00	P.M.	Portland, Me.	12 00	Noon
Baltimore, Md.	12 00	Noon	Hartford, Conn.	12 00	Noon	Portland, Ore.	9 00	A.M.
Birmingham, Ala.	11 00	A.M.	Helena, Mon.	10 00	A.M.	Providence, R.I.	12 00	Noon
Bismarck, N.D.	11 00	A.M.	*Honolulu, Ha.	7 00	A.M.	*Regina, Sask.	11 00	A.M.
Boise, Ida.	10 00	A.M.	Houston, Tex.	11 00	A.M.	Reno, Nev.	9 00	A.M.
Boston, Mass.	12 00	Noon	*Indianapolis, Ind.	12 00	Noon	Richmond, Va.	12 00	Noon
Buffalo, N.Y.	12 00	Noon	Jacksonville, Fla.	12 00	Noon	Rochester, N.Y.	12 00	Noon
Butte, Mon.	10 00	A.M.	Juneau, Alas.	8 00	A.M.	Sacramento, Cal.	9 00	A.M.
Calgary, Alta.	10 00	A.M.	Kansas City, Mo.	11 00	A.M.	St. John's, Nfld.	1 30	P.M.
Charleston, S.C.	12 00	Noon	Knoxville, Tenn.	12 00	Noon	St. Louis, Mo.	11 00	A.M.
Charleston, W.Va.	12 00	Noon	Lexington, Ky.	12 00	Noon	St. Paul, Minn.	11 00	A.M.
Charlotte, N.C.	12 00	Noon	Lincoln, Neb.	11 00	A.M.	Salt Lake City, Ut.	10 00	A.M.
Charlottetown, P.E.I.	1 00	P.M.	Little Rock, Ark.	11 00	A.M.	San Antonio, Tex.	11 00	A.M.
Chattanooga, Tenn.	12 00	Noon	Los Angeles, Cal.	9 00	A.M.	San Diego, Cal.	9 00	A.M.
Cheyenne, Wy.	10 00	A.M.	Louisville, Ky.	12 00	Noon	San Francisco, Cal.	9 00	A.M.
Chicago, Ill.	11 00	A.M.	*Mexico City	11 00	A.M.	Santa Fe, N.M.	10 00	A.M.
Cleveland, Oh.	12 00	Noon	Memphis, Tenn.	11 00	A.M.	Savannah, Ga.	12 00	Noon
Colorado Spr., Col.	10 00	A.M.	Miami, Fla.	12 00	Noon	Seattle, Wash.	9 00	A.M.
Columbus, Oh.	12 00	Noon	Milwaukee, Wis.	11 00	A.M.	Shreveport, La.	11 00	A.M.
Dallas, Tex.	11 00	A.M.	Minneapolis, Minn.	11 00	AM.	Sioux Falls, S.D.	11 00	A.M.
*Dawson, Yuk.	9 00	A.M.	Mobile, Ala.	11 00	A.M.	Spokane, Wash.	9 00	A.M.
Dayton, Oh.	12 00	Noon	Montreal, Que.	12 00	Noon	Tampa, Fla.	12 00	Noon
Denver, Col.	10 00	A.M.	Nashville, Tenn.	11 00	A.M.	Toledo, Oh.	12 00	Noon
Des Moines, Ia.	11 00	A.M.	New Haven, Conn.	12 00	Noon	Topeka, Kan.	11 00	A.M.
Detroit, Mich.	12 00	Noon	New Orleans, La.	11 00	A.M.	Toronto, Ont.	12 00	Noon
Duluth, Minn.	11 00	A.M.	New York, N.Y.	12 00	Noon	*Tucson, Ariz.	10 00	A.M.
El Paso, Tex.	10 00	A.M.	Nome, Alas.	8 00	A.M.	Tulsa, Okla.	11 00	A.M.
Erie, Pa.	12 00	Noon	Norfolk, Va.	12 00	Noon	Vancouver, B.C.	9 00	A.M.
Evansville, Ind.	11 00	A.M.	Okla. City, Okla.	11 00	A.M.	Washington, D.C.	12 00	Noon
Fairbanks, Alas.	8 00	A.M.	Omaha, Neb.	11 00	A.M.	Wichita, Kan.	11 00	A.M.
Flint, Mich.	12 00	Noon	Peoria, Ill.	11 00	A.M.	Wilmington, Del.	12 00	Noon
*Fort Wayne, Ind.	12 00	Noon	Philadelphia, Pa.	12 00	Noon	Winnipeg, Man.	11 00	A.M.
Fort Worth, Tex.	11 00	A.M.						

* Cities with an asterisk do not observe Daylight Saving Time. During much of the year, it is necessary to add one hour to the cities which do observe Daylight Saving Time to get the proper time relation.

Legal or Public Holidays, 1994

Technically there are no national holidays in the United States; each state has jurisdiction over its holidays, which are designated by legislative enactment or executive proclamation. In practice, however, most states observe the federal legal public holidays, even though the President and Congress can legally designate holidays only for the District of Columbia and for federal employees. Federal legal public holidays are New Year's Day, Martin Luther King Day, Washington's Birthday, Memorial Day, Independence Day, Labor Day, Columbus Day, Veterans' Day, Thanksgiving, and Christmas.

Chief Legal or Public Holidays

When a holiday falls on a Sunday or a Saturday it is usually observed on the following Monday or the preceding Friday. For some holidays, government and business closing practices vary. In most states, the office of the Secretary of State can provide details for holiday closings. The following will be legal or public holidays in most states in 1994:

Jan. 1 (Sat.) — New Year's Day.

Jan. 17 (3d Mon. in Jan.) — Martin Luther King Day.

Feb. 12 (Sat.) — Lincoln's Birthday.

Feb. 21 (3d Mon. in Feb.) — Washington's Birthday, or Presidents' Day, or Washington-Lincoln Day.

May 30 (last Mon. in May) — Memorial Day, or Decoration Day.

July 4 (Mon.) — Independence Day.

Sept. 5 (1st Mon. in Sept.) — Labor Day.

Oct. 10 (2d Monday in Oct.) — Columbus Day, or Discoverers' Day, or Pioneers' Day.

Nov. 11 (Fri.) — Veterans' Day.

Nov. 24 (4th Thurs. in Nov.) — Thanksgiving Day.

Dec. 26 (Mon.) — Christmas Day, obsvd.

In some states, the following will be legal or public holidays in 1994:

Apr. 1 (Fri.) — Good Friday. In some states, observed for half or part of day.

Nov. 8 (1st Tues. after 1st Mon. in Nov.) — Election Day.

Selected Foreign Holidays

Jan. 2 — Ancestors Day, Haiti.
Jan. 6 — La Befana, Italy.
Jan. 31 — Australia Day obsvd., Australia.
Feb. 1 — Vinegrower's Day, Bulgaria.
Feb. 11 — National Foundation Day, Japan.
Mar. 8 — International Women's Day, UN nations.
Mar. 17 — St. Patrick's Day, Ireland.
Mar. 26 — Fiesta del Arbol (Arbor Day), Spain.
Apr. 7 — World Health Day, UN nations.
Apr. 8 — Buddha's Birthday, Korea, Japan.
Apr. 22 — Independence Day, Israel.
Apr. 26 — ANZAC Day, Australia, New Zealand, and Western Samoa.
May 5 — Cinco de Mayo, Mexico.
May 25 — African Freedom Day, Chad, Zambia.
July 1 — Canada Day, Canada.
July 14 — Bastille Day, France.
Aug. 2 — Picnic Day, Australia.
Aug. 10 — Independence Day, Ecuador.
Sept. 15 — Respect for the Aged Day, Japan.
Sept. 19 — St. Gennaro, Italy.
Oct. 2 — Mahatma Gandi's Birthday, India.
Oct. 10 — Thanksgiving Day, Canada.
Nov. 1-2 — Day of the Dead, Mexico.
Nov. 11 — Remembrance Day, Canada.
Dec. 26 — Boxing Day, Australia, Canada, United Kingdom.

AEROSPACE

Notable Crewed Space Flights

Sources: National Aeronautics and Space Administration and The World Almanac

The following table does not include aerospacecraft, such as the U.S. Space Shuttle.

Crew, date	Mission name	Orbits[1]	Duration	Remarks
Yuri A. Gagarin (4/12/61)	Vostok 1	1	1h 48m	1st manned orbital flight.
Alan B. Shepard Jr. (5/5/61)	Mercury-Redstone 3	(2)	15m 22s	1st American in space.
Virgil I. Grissom (7/21/61)	Mercury-Redstone 4	(2)	15m 37s	Spacecraft sank. Grissom rescued.
Gherman S. Titov (8/6-7/61)	Vostok 2	16	25h 18m	1st space flight of more than 24 hrs.
John H. Glenn Jr. (2/20/62)	Mercury-Atlas 6	3	4h 55m 23s	1st American in orbit.
M. Scott Carpenter (5/24/62)	Mercury-Atlas 7	3	4h 56m 05s	Manual retrofire error caused 250 mi. landing overshoot.
Andrian G. Nikolayev (8/11-15/62)	Vostok 3	64	94h 22m	Vostok 3 and 4 made first group flight.
Pavel R. Popovich (8/12-15/62)	Vostok 4	48	70h 57m	On 1st orbit it came within 3 miles of Vostok 3.
Walter M. Schirra Jr. (10/3/62)	Mercury-Atlas 8	6	9h 13m 11s	Then-closest splashdown to recovery vessel (9,000 yds.).
L. Gordon Cooper (5/15-16/63)	Mercury-Atlas 9	22	34h 19m 49s	1st U.S. evaluation of effects on man of one day in space.
Valery F. Bykovsky (6/14-19/63)	Vostok 5	81	119h 06m	Vostok 5 and 6 made 2d group flight.
Valentina V. Tereshkova (6/16-19/63)	Vostok 6	48	70h 50m	1st woman in space.
Vladimir M. Komarov, Konstantin P. Feoktistov, Boris B. Yegorov (10/12/64)	Voskhod 1	16	24h 17m	1st 3-man orbital flight, first without space suits.
Pavel I. Belyayev, Aleksei A. Leonov (3/18/65)	Voskhod 2	17	26h 02m	Leonov made 1st "space walk" (10 min.).
Virgil I. Grissom, John W. Young (3/23/65)	Gemini-Titan III	3	4h 53m 00s	1st manned spacecraft to change its orbital path.
James A. McDivitt, Edward H. White 2d, (6/3-7/65)	Gemini-Titan IV	62	97h 56m 11s	White was 1st American to "walk in space" (20 min.).
L. Gordon Cooper Jr., Charles Conrad Jr. (8/21-29/65)	Gemini-Titan V	120	190h 55m 14s	1st use of fuel cells for electric power; evaluated guidance and navigation system.
Frank Borman, James A. Lovell Jr. (12/4-18/65)	Gemini-Titan VII	206	330h 35m 31s	Longest duration Gemini flight.
Walter M. Schirra Jr., Thomas P. Stafford (12/15-16/65)	Gemini-Titan VI-A	16	25h 51m 24s	Completed world's first space rendezvous with Gemini VII.
Neil A. Armstrong, David R. Scott (3/16-17/66)	Gemini-Titan VIII	6.5	10h 41m 26s	1st docking of one space vehicle with another; mission aborted, control malfunction.
Thomas P. Stafford, Eugene A. Cernan (6/3-6/66)	Gemini-Titan IX-A	45	72h 21m	Closest splashdown to recovery vessel (769.9 yds.).
John W. Young, Michael Collins (7/18-21/66)	Gemini-Titan X	43	70h 46m 39s	1st use of Agena target vehicle's propulsion systems.
Charles Conrad Jr., Richard F. Gordon Jr. (9/12-15/66)	Gemini-Titan XI	44	71h 17m 08s	Docked, made 2 revolutions of earth tethered; set Gemini altitude record (739.2 mi.).
James A. Lovell Jr., Edwin E. Aldrin Jr. (11/11-15/66)	Gemini-Titan XII	59	94h 34m 31s	Final Gemini mission; record 5½ hrs. of extravehicular activity.
Vladimir M. Komarov (4/23/67)	Soyuz 1	17	26h 40m	Crashed after re-entry killing Komarov.
Walter M. Schirra Jr., Donn F. Eisele, R. Walter Cunningham (10/11-22/68)	Apollo-Saturn 7	163	260h 09m 03s	1st manned flight of Apollo spacecraft command-service module only.
Georgi T. Beregovoi (10/26-30/68)	Soyuz 3	64	94h 51m	Made rendezvous with unmanned Soyuz 2.
Frank Borman, James A. Lovell Jr., William A. Anders (12/21-27/68)	Apollo-Saturn 8	10[3]	147h 00m 42s	1st flight to moon (command-service module only); views of lunar surface televised to earth.
Vladimir A. Shatalov (1/14-17/69)	Soyuz 4	45	71h 14m	Docked with Soyuz 5.

Crew, date	Mission name	Orbits[1]	Duration	Remarks
Boris V. Volyanov, Aleksei S. Yeliseyev, Yevgeny V. Khrunov (1/15-18/69)	Soyuz 5	46	72h 46m	Docked with Soyuz 4; Yeliseyev and Khrunov transferred to Soyuz 4.
James A. McDivitt, David R. Scott, Russell L. Schweickart (3/3-13/69)	Apollo-Saturn 9	151	241h 00m 54s	1st manned flight of lunar module.
Thomas P. Stafford, Eugene A. Cernan, John W. Young (5/18-26/69)	Apollo-Saturn 10	31[4]	192h 03m 23s	1st lunar module orbit of moon.
Neil A. Armstrong, Edwin E. Aldrin Jr., Michael Collins (7/16-24/69)	Apollo-Saturn 11	30[3]	195h 18m 35s	1st lunar landing made by Armstrong and Aldrin; collected 48.5 lbs. of soil, rock samples; lunar stay time 21 h, 36m, 21 s.
Georgi S. Shonin, Valery N. Kubasov (10/11-16/69)	Soyuz 6	79	118h 42m	1st welding of metals in space.
Anatoly V. Filipchenko, Vladislav N. Volkov, Viktor V. Gorbatko (10/12-17/69)	Soyuz 7	79	118h 41m	Space lab construction tests made; Soyuz 6, 7 and 8 — 1st time 3 spacecraft 7 crew orbited earth at once.
Charles Conrad Jr., Richard F. Gordon, Alan L. Bean (11/14-24/69)	Apollo-Saturn 12	45[3]	244h 36m 25s	Conrad and Bean made 2d moon landing; collected 74.7 lbs. of samples, lunar stay time 31 h, 31 m.
James A. Lovell Jr., Fred W. Haise Jr., John L. Swigart Jr. (4/11-17/70)	Apollo-Saturn 13	...	142h 54m 41s	Aborted after service module oxygen tank ruptured; crew returned safely using lunar module oxygen and power.
Alan B. Shepard Jr., Stuart A. Roosa, Edgar D. Mitchell (1/31-2/9/71)	Apollo-Saturn 14	34[3]	216h 01m 57s	Shepard and Mitchell made 3d moon landing, collected 96 lbs. of lunar samples; lunar stay 33 h, 31 m.
Georgi T. Dobrovolsky, Vladislav N. Volkov, Viktor I. Patsayev (6/6-30/71)	Soyuz 11	360	569h 40m	Docked with Salyut space station; and orbited in Salyut for 23 days; crew died during re-entry from loss of pressurization.
David R. Scott, Alfred M. Worden, James B. Irwin (7/26-8/7/71)	Apollo-Saturn 15	74[3]	295h 11m 53s	Scott and Irwin made 4th moon landing; first lunar rover use; first deep space walk; 170 lbs. of samples; 66 h, 55 m, stay.
Charles M. Duke Jr., Thomas K. Mattingly, John W. Young (4/16-27/72)	Apollo-Saturn 16	64[3]	265h 51m 05s	Young and Duke made 5th moon landing; collected 213 lbs. of lunar samples; lunar stay line 71 h, 2 m.
Eugene A. Cernan, Ronald E. Evans, Harrison H. Schmitt (12/7-19/72)	Apollo-Saturn 17	75[3]	301h 51m 59s	Cernan and Schmitt made 6th manned lunar landing; collected 243 lbs. of samples; record lunar stay of 75 h.
Charles Conrad Jr., Joseph P. Kerwin, Paul J. Weitz (5/25-6/22/73)	Skylab 2	...	672h 49m 49s	1st American manned orbiting space station; made long-flights tests, crew repaired damage caused during boost.
Alan L. Bean, Jack R. Lousma, Owen K. Garriott (7/28-9/25/73)	Skylab 3	...	1,427h 09m 04s	Crew systems and operational tests, exceeded pre-mission plans for scientific activities; space walk total 13h, 44 m.
Gerald P. Carr, Edward G. Gibson, William Pogue (11/16/73-2/8/74)	Skylab 4	...	2,017h 15m 32s	Final Skylab mission; record space walk of 7 h, 1 m., record space walks total for a mission 22 h, 21 m.
Alexi Leonov, Valeri Kubasov (7/15-21/75)	Soyuz 19	96	143h 31m	U.S.-USSR joint flight. Crews linked-up in space, conducted experiments, shared meals, and held a joint news conference.
Vance Brand, Thomas P. Stafford, Donald K. Slayton (7/15-24/75)	Apollo 18	136	217h 28m 23s	
Leonid Kizim, Vladmir Solovyov, Oleg Atkov (2/8-10/2/84).	Soyuz T-10/Salyut 7	...	5,868h 50m	Set space endurance record (since broken).
Vladimir Titov, Muso Manarov, Anatoly Levchenko (12/21/87-12/21/88)	Soyuz TM-4/Mir	...	8,782h 39m 47s	Set space endurance record.

(1) The U.S. measures orbital flights in revolutions while the Soviets use "orbits." (2) Suborbital. (3) Moon orbits in command module. (4) Moon orbits.

Fire aboard spacecraft Apollo I on the ground at Cape Kennedy, Fla., killed Virgil I. Grissom, Edward H. White, and Roger B. Chaffee on Jan. 27, 1967. They were the only U.S. astronauts killed in space tests.

U.S. Space Shuttle Missions

Source: National Aeronautics and Space Administration and the World Almanac; as of Aug. 1993

Name, date	Crew
Columbia (4/12-14/81)	Robert L. Crippen, John W. Young.
Columbia (11/12-14/81)	Joe Engle, Richard Truly.
Columbia (3/22-30/82)	Jack Lousma, C. Gordon Fullerton.
Columbia (6/27-7/4/82)	Thomas Mattingly 2d, Henry Hartsfield Jr.
Columbia (11/11-16/82)	Vance Brand, Robert Overmyer, William Lenoir, Joseph Allen.
Challenger (4/4-9/83)	Paul Weitz, Karol Bobko, Story Musgrave, Donald Peterson.
Challenger (6/18-24/83)	Robert L. Crippen, Norman Thagard, John Fabian, Frederick Hauck, Sally K. Ride (first U.S. woman in space).
Challenger (8/30-9/5/83)	Richard Truly, Daniel Brandenstein, William Thornton, Guion Bluford (first U.S. black in space), Dale Gardner.
Columbia (11/28-12/8/83)	John Young, Brewster Shaw Jr., Robert Parker, Owen Garriott, Byron Lichtenberg, Ulf Merbold.
Challenger (2/3-11/84)	Vance Brand, Robert Gibson, Ronald McNair, Bruce McCandless, Robert Stewart.
Challenger (4/6-13/84)	Robert L. Crippen, Francis R. Scobee, George D. Nelson, Terry J. Hart, James D. Van Hoften.
Discovery (8/30-9/5/84)	Henry W. Hartsfield Jr., Michael L. Coats, Steven A. Hawley, Judith A. Resnik, Richard M. Mullane, Charles D. Walker.
Challenger (10/5-13/84)	Robert L. Crippen, Jon A. McBride, Kathryn D. Sullivan, Sally K. Ride, Marc Garneau (first Canadian), David C. Leestma, Paul D. Scully-Power.
Discovery (11/8-16/84)	Frederick H. Hauck, David M. Walker, Dr. Anna L. Fisher, Joseph P. Allen, Dale A. Gardner.
Discovery (1/24-27/85)	Thomas K. Mattingly, Loren J. Shriver, James F. Buchli, Ellison S. Onizuka, Gary E. Payton.
Discovery (4/12-19/85)	Karol J. Bobko, Donald E. Williams, Sen. Jake Garn, Charles D. Walker, Jeffrey A. Hoffman, S. David Griggs, M. Rhea Seddon.
Challenger (4/29-5/6/85)	Robert F. Overmyer, Frederick D. Gregory, Don L. Lind, Taylor G. Wang, Lodewijk van den Berg, Norman Thagard, William Thornton.
Discovery (6/17-24/85)	John O. Creighton, Shannon W. Lucid, Steven R. Nagel, Daniel C. Brandenstein, John W. Fabian, Prince Sultan Salman al-Saud (first Arab), Patrick Baudry.
Challenger (7/29-8/6/85)	Roy D. Bridges Jr., Anthony W. England, Karl G. Henize, F. Story Musgrave, C. Gordon Fullerton, Loren W. Acton, John-David F. Bartoe.
Discovery (8/27-9/3/85)	John M. Lounge, James D. van Hoften, William F. Fisher, Joe H. Engle, Richard O. Covey.
Atlantis (10/4-7/85)	Karol J. Bobko, Ronald J. Grabe, David C. Hilmers, William A. Pailes, Robert C. Stewart.
Challenger (10/30-11/6/85)	Henry W. Hartsfield Jr., Steven R. Nagel, Bonnie J. Dunbar, James F. Buchli, Guion S. Bluford Jr., Ernst Messerschmid, Reinhard Furrer, Wubbo J. Ockels.
Atlantis (11/26-12/3/85)	Brewster H. Shaw Jr., Bryan D. O'Connor, Charles Walker, Rodolfo Neri (first Mexican), Jerry L. Ross, Sherwood C. Spring, Mary L. Cleave.
Columbia (1/12-18/86)	Robert L. Gibson, Charles F. Bolden Jr., George D. Nelson, Rep. Bill Nelson (first congressperson), Franklin R. Chang-Diaz, Steven A. Hawley, Robert J. Cenker.
Challenger (1/28/86-exploded after takeoff)	Francis R. Scobee, Michael J. Smith, Ronald E. McNair, Ellison S. Onizuka, Judith A. Resnik, Gregory B. Jarvis, Sharon Christa McAuliffe.
Discovery (9/29-10/3/88)	Frederick H. Hauck, Richard O. Covey, David C. Hilmers, George D. Nelson, John M. Lounge.
Atlantis (12/3-6/88)	Robert L. Gibson, Guy S. Gardner, Richard M. Mullane, Jerry L. Ross, William M. Shepherd.
Discovery (3/13-18/89)	Michael L. Coats, John E. Blaha, James F. Buchli, Robert C. Springer, James P. Bagian.
Atlantis (5/4-8/89)	David M. Walker, Ronald J. Grabe, Mary L. Cleave, Norman E. Thagard, Mark C. Lee.
Columbia (8/8-13/89)	Brewster H. Shaw Jr., Richard N. Richards, David C. Leestma, James C. Adamson, Mark N. Brown.
Atlantis (10/18-23/89)	Donald E. Williams, Michael J. McCulley, Shannon W. Lucid, Ellen S. Baker, Franklin R. Chang-Diaz.
Discovery (11/22-27/89)	Frederick D. Gregory, John E. Blaha, Manley L. Carter, F. Story Musgrave, Katherine C. Thornton.
Columbia (1/9-20/90)	Daniel C. Brandenstein, Bonnie J. Dunbar, James D. Wetherbee, Marsha S. Ivins, G. David Low.
Atlantis (2/28-3/4/90)	John O. Creighton, John H. Casper, David C. Hilmers, Richard M. Mullane, Pierre J. Thuot.
Discovery (4/24-29/90)	Bruce McCandless 2d, Kathryn D. Sullivan, Loren J. Shriver, Charles F. Bolden Jr., Steven A. Hawley.
Discovery (10/6-10/90)	Richard N. Richards, Robert D. Cabana, Bruce E. Melnick, William M. Shepherd, Thomas D. Akers.
Atlantis (11/15-20/90)	Richard O. Covey, Frank L. Culbertson, Robert C. Springer, Carl J. Meade, Charles D. Gemar.
Columbia (12/2-10/90)	Vance D. Brand, Guy S. Gardner, Jeffrey A. Hoffman, John M. Lounge, Robert A.R. Parker, Samuel T. Durrance, Ronald A. Parise.
Atlantis (4/5-11/91)	Stephen R. Nagel, Kenneth D. Cameron, Linda M. Godwin, Jerry L. Ross, Jerome Apt.
Discovery (4/28-5/6/91)	Michael L. Coats, L. Blaine Hammond Jr., Guion S. Bluford Jr., Gregory J. Harbaugh, Richard J. Hieb, Donald R. McMonagle, Charles L. Veach.
Columbia (6/5-14/91)	Byron O. O'Connor, Sidney M. Gutierrez, James P. Bagian, Margaret Rhea Seddon, Francis A. Gaffney, Millie Hughes-Fulford, Tamara E. Jernigan.
Atlantis (8/2-11/91)	John E. Blaha, Michael A. Baker, Shannon W. Lucid, G. David Low, James C. Adamson.
Discovery (9/12-18/91)	John O. Creighton, Kenneth S. Reightler Jr., Charles D. Gemar, James F. Buchli, Mark N. Brown.
Atlantis (11/24-12/1/91)	Frederick D. Gregory, Terrence T. Hendricks, F. Story Musgrave, James S. Voss, Mario Runco Jr., Thomas J. Hennen.
Discovery (1/22-30/92)	Ronald J. Grabe, Stephen S. Oswald, Norman E. Thagard, William E. Readdy, David Hilmers, Roberta L. Bondar, Ulf Merbold.
Atlantis (3/24-4/2/92)	Charles F. Bolden Jr., Brian Duffy, Michael Foale, David C. Leestma, Kathryn D. Sullivan, Bryon K. Lichtenberg, Dirk D. Frimout.
Endeavour (5/7-16/92)	Daniel C. Brandenstein, Kevin C. Chilton, Thomas D. Akers, Richard J. Hieb, Kathryn C. Thornton, Bruce E. Melnick, Pierre J. Thout. *Set extravehicular duration in space record.*
Columbia (6/25-7/9/92)	Richard N. Richards, Kenneth D. Bowersox, Bonnie J. Dunbar, Ellen S. Baker, Lawrence J. DeLucas, Carl J. Meade, Eugene H. Trinh. *Set Duration Record for Shuttle Flight.*
Atlantis (7/31-8/8/92)	Jeffrey A. Hoffman, Loren J. Shriver, Franco Malerda, Franklin R. Chang-Diaz, Andrew M. Allen, Marsha S. Ivins, Claude Nicollier.
Endeavour (9/12-21/92)	Robert L. Gibson, Curtis L. Brown Jr., Jay Apt, N. Jan Davis, Mae Carol Jemison (first black woman), Mark C. Lee, Mamoru Mohri (first Japanese national).
Columbia (10/22-11/1/92)	James D. Wetherbee, Michael A. Baker, Charles L. Veach, William M. Shepherd, Tamara E. Jernigan, Steven G. MacLean.
Discovery (12/2-9/92)	David M. Walker, Robert D. Cabana, Guion S. Bluford Jr., James S. Voss, Michael R. Clifford.
Endeavour (1/13-19/93)	Gregory Harbaugh, Mario Runco Jr., John H. Casper, Donald R. McMonagle, Susan J. Helms.
Discovery (4/8-17/93)	Kenneth D. Cameron, Stephen S. Oswald, Michael Foale, Ellen Ochoa (first Hispanic woman), Kenneth D. Cockrell.
Columbia (4/26-5/6/93)	Stephen R. Nagel, Terrence T. Henricks, Jerry L. Ross, Bernard A. Harris Jr., Charles J. Precourt, Ulrich Walter, Hans William Schlegel.
Endeavour (6/21-7/1/93)	Ronald J. Grabe, Brian Duffy, G. David Low, Nancy J. Sherlock, Janice E. Voss, Peter J. K. Wisoff.

Notable U.S. Uncrewed and Planetary Missions

Source: National Aeronautics and Space Administration

Spacecraft	Launch date (GMT)	Mission	Remarks
Mariner 2	Aug. 27, 1962	Venus	Passed within 22,000 miles from Venus 12/14/62; contact lost 1/3/63 at 54 million miles
Ranger 7	July 28, 1964	Moon	Yielded over 4,000 photos
Mariner 4	Nov. 28, 1964	Mars	Passed behind Mars 7/14/65; took 22 photos from 6,000 miles
Ranger 8	Feb. 17, 1965	Moon	Yielded over 7,000 photos
Surveyor 3	Apr. 17, 1967	Moon	Scooped and tested lunar soil
Mariner 5	June 14, 1967	Venus	In solar orbit; closest Venus fly-by 10/19/67
Mariner 6	Feb. 24, 1969	Mars	Came within 2,000 miles of Mars 7/31/69; sent back data, photos
Mariner 7	Mar. 27, 1969	Mars	Came within 2,000 miles of Mars 8/5/69
Mariner 9	May 30, 1971	Mars	First craft to orbit Mars 11/13/71; sent back over 7,000 photos
Pioneer 10	Mar. 2, 1972	Jupiter	Passed Jupiter 12/3/73; exited the solar system 6/14/83; still operating in outer solar system
Mariner 10	Nov. 3, 1973	Venus, Mercury	Passed Venus 2/5/74; arrived Mercury 3/29/74. First time gravity of one planet (Venus) used to whip spacecraft toward another (Mercury)
Viking 1	Aug. 20, 1975	Mars	Landed on Mars 7/20/76; did scientific research, sent photos; functioned 6 1/2 years
Viking 2	Sept. 9, 1975	Mars	Landed on Mars 9/3/76; functioned 3 1/2 years
Voyager 1	Sept. 5, 1977	Jupiter, Saturn	Encountered Jupiter 3/5/79, provided evidence of Jupiter ring; passed near Saturn 11/12/80
Voyager 2	Aug. 20, 1977	Jupiter, Saturn, Uranus, Neptune	Encountered Jupiter 7/9/79; Saturn 8/26/81; Uranus 1/8 and 1/27/86; Neptune 8/24/89
Pioneer Venus 1	May 20, 1978	Venus	Entered Venus orbit 12/4/78; spent 14 years studying planet; ceased operating 10/19/92
Pioneer Venus 2	Aug. 8, 1978	Venus	Encountered Venus 12/9/78; probes impacted on surface
Magellan	May 4, 1989	Venus	Orbit and map Venus; monitoring geological activity on surface; still operating in outer solar system
Titan IV	June 14, 1989	Orbit Earth	First of 41 such rockets whose primary purpose is defense
Galileo	Oct. 18, 1989	Jupiter	Used Earth's gravity to propel it toward Jupiter; encountered Venus Feb. 1991

Notable Proposed U.S. Space Missions

Source: National Aeronautics and Space Administration

Year, Month	Mission	Purpose
1994 Feb.	Wind (a)	Will determine solar wind input to Earth's magnetosphere
1994	International Microgravity Laboratory - 2 (b)	Spacelab mission to study materials, fluid, and life sciences
1996	Mars Environmental Survey Pathfinder (a)	Technical demonstration of Mars Environmental Survey
1996	X-ray Timing Explorer (a)	Study temporal variability in compact x-ray emitting objects
1997	Cassini (a)	Study of Saturn's atmosphere, rings, magnetosphere and moons
1998	Earth Observing System (a)	Provide long-term data sets of interactions between Earth's land, atmosphere, water, and life
1998, 1999	Advanced X-ray Astrophysics Facility (2 spacecraft) (a)	Study of dark matter, stellar evolution, galactic clusters
TBD	Pluto Fast Flyby (a)	First fly-by of Pluto for photographic survey and other studies
2001	Space Infrared Telescope Facility (a)	High sensitivity observations of celestial sources

(a) Launched by expendable rocket. (b) Carried aboard Shuttle. TBD=To Be Determined.

Aircraft Operating Statistics, 1992

Source: Air Transport Association of America; figures are averages for most commonly used models

	Number of Seats	Speed Airborne	Flight Length	Fuel (Gallons Per Hour)	Aircraft Operating Cost Per Hour
B747-400	403	534	4,375	3,361	$7,098
B747-100	399	520	3,094	3,507	5,905
L-1011-100/200	293	495	1,519	2,362	4,072
DC-10-10	282	488	1,387	2,189	4,056
A300-600	266	474	1,206	1,686	3,917
DC-10-30	265	522	2,962	2,607	4,595
B767-300	224	489	2,087	1,485	3,384
B757-200	188	458	1,105	996	2,293
B767-200	187	483	2,064	1,434	2,956
A320-100/200	149	441	944	757	1,868
B727-200	148	430	689	1,242	2,263
B737-400	145	400	564	769	1,743
MD-80	142	419	662	889	1,842
B737-300	131	415	633	739	1,768
DC-9-50	122	387	453	890	1,640
B727-100	117	429	638	1,137	2,220
B737-100/200	112	387	444	793	1,735
DC-9-30	102	381	441	794	1,658
F-100	99	361	388	690	1,445
DC-9-10	77	361	359	727	1,439

Summary of Worldwide Payloads, 1986-1992

Source: National Aeronautics and Space Administration

(A payload is something carried into space by a rocket)

Year	Total[1]	USSR/CIS[2]	United States	Japan	European Space Agency	India	China
1986	132	114	9	3	0	—	3
1987	133	116	9	3	1	—	1
1988	136	107	15	2	2	2	3
1989	129	95	22	4	2	0	0
1990	100	96	31	7	1	1	5
1991	156	101	30	2	4	1	1
1992	128	77	27	3	1	2	2
Total	**4,300[3]**	**2,838**	**1,158**	**56**	**31**	**15**	**32**

(1) Incl. launches in countries not shown. (2) Figures for 1986-1991 are for the Soviet Union; 1992 figure is for the Commonwealth of Independent States. (3) Incl. launches in prior years not shown.

Traffic at U.S. Airports, 1992

Source: Air Transport Association of America

Airport	Passenger Arrivals and Departures	Airport	Passenger Arrivals and Departures
Chicago (O'Hare)	64,441,087	Minneapolis/St. Paul	22,907,490
Dallas/Ft. Worth	51,943,567	Detroit	22,840,643
Los Angeles	46,032,988	Honolulu	22,608,188
Atlanta	42,032,988	Phoenix	22,111,555
San Francisco	31,789,021	Orlando	21,147,888
Denver	30,877,180	St. Louis	20,984,782
New York (JFK)	27,760,912	Las Vegas	20,913,054
Miami	26,483,717	New York (La Guardia)	19,662,521
Newark	24,286,986	Houston	19,354,013
Boston	22,988,717	Pittsburgh	18,748,884

U.S. Scheduled Airline Traffic, 1990-1992

Source: Air Transport Association of America; in thousands

	1990	1991	1992
Passenger traffic			
Revenue passengers enplaned	465,560	452,301	473,305
Revenue passenger miles	457,926,286	447,954,829	478,081,118
Available seat miles	733,374,893	715,199,140	751,815,137
Revenue passenger load factor (%)	62.4	62.6	63.6
Cargo traffic (ton miles)	12,549,104	12,129,963	13,053,681
Revenue freight and express (ton miles)	10,546,329	10,225,199	10,989,344
Revenue U.S. Mail (ton miles)	2,002,775	1,904,764	2,064,337
Financial			
Passenger revenue	$58,453,215	$57,091,625	$59,747,693
Net profit	– $3,921,002	– $1,940,157	– $4,028,452

Leading Passenger Airlines, 1992

Source: Air Transport Association of America; in thousands

Airline	Passengers	Airline	Passengers	Airline	Passengers
American	85,955	Trans World	22,292	Simmons	2,341
Delta	82,911	America West	15,118	West Air	1,947
United	66,596	Alaska	6,167	USAir Shuttle	1,472
USAir	54,654	Aloha	4,662	Trans States	1,322
Northwest	43,443	Hawaiian	4,645	Executive Airlines	912
Continental	38,359	Air Wisconsin	2,864	Midwest Express	808
Southwest	31,023	Horizon Air	2,380		

U.S. Airline Safety, Scheduled Commercial Carriers

Source: National Transportation Safety Board

	Departures (millions)	Fatal accidents	Fatalities	Fatal accidents per 100,000 departures		Departures (millions)	Fatal accidents	Fatalities	Fatal accidents per 100,000 departures
1977	4.9	3	78	0.061	1985	5.8	4	197	0.069
1978	5.0	5	160	0.100	1986	6.4	2	5	0.016
1979	5.4	4	351	0.074	1987	6.6	4[1]	231	0.046[1]
1980	5.4	0	0	0.000	1988	6.7	3[1]	285	0.030[1]
1981	5.2	4	4	0.077	1989	6.6	11	278	0.166
1982	5.0	4	233	0.060	1990	6.9	6	39	0.087
1983	5.0	4	15	0.079	1991	6.8	4	62	0.059
1984	5.4	1	4	0.018	1992	6.9	4	33	0.058

(1) Sabotage-caused accidents are included in the number of fatal accidents, but not in the calculation of accident rates.

National Aviation Hall of Fame

The National Aviation Hall of Fame at Dayton, Oh., is dedicated to honoring the outstanding pioneers of air and space.

Allen, William M.
Andrews, Frank M.
Armstrong, Neil A.
Arnold, Henry H. "Hap"
Atwood, John Leland

Balchen, Bernt
Baldwin, Thomas S.
Beachey, Lincoln
Beech, Olive A.
Beech, Walter H.
Bell, Alexander Graham
Bell, Lawrence D.
Bellanca, Giuseppe Mario
Bendix, Vincent T.
Boeing, William E.
Bong, Richard I.
Borman, Frank
Boyd, Albert
Bradley, Mark E.
Brown, George "Scratchley"
Byrd, Richard E.

Cessna, Clyde V.
Chamberlin, Clarence D.
Chanute, Octave
Chennault, Claire L.
Cochran (Odlum), Jacqueline
Collins, Michael
Conrad Jr., Charles
Crawford, Frederick C.
Crossfield, A. Scott
Cunningham, Alfred A.
Curtiss, Glenn H.

deSeversky, Alexander P.
Doolittle, James H.
Douglas, Donald W.
Draper, Charles S.

Eaker, Ira C.
Earhart (Putnam), Amelia
Eielson, C. Benjamin
Ellyson, Theodore G.
Ely, Eugene B.
Everest, Frank K.

Fairchild, Sherman M.
Fleet, Reuben H.
Fokker, Anthony H.G.
Ford, Henry
Foss, Joseph
Foulois, Benjamin D.
Frye, Jack

Gabreski, Francis S.
Glenn Jr., John H.
Goddard, George W.
Goddard, Robert H.
Godfrey, Arthur
Goldwater, Barry M.
Grissom, Virgil I.
Gross, Robert E.
Grumman, Leroy R.
Guggenheim, Harry F.

Haughton, Daniel J.
Hegenberger, Albert F.
Heinemann, Edward H.
Hoover, Robert A.
Hughes, Howard R.

Ingalls, David S.

James Jr., Daniel "Chappie"
Jeppesen, Elrey B.
Johnson, Clarence L.
Johnston, Alvin M. "Tex"
Jones, Thomas V.

Kenney, George C.
Kettering, Charles F.
Kindelberger, James H.
Knabenshue, A. Roy
Knight, William J.

Lahm, Frank P.
Langley, Samuel P.
Lear Sr., William P.
LeMay, Curtis E.
LeVier, Anthony W.
Lindbergh, Anne M.
Lindbergh, Charles A.
Link, Edwin A.
Lockheed, Allan H.
Loening, Grover
Luke Jr., Frank

Macready, Carl B.
Macready, John A.
Martin, Glenn L.
McDonnell, James S.
Mitscher, Marc A.
Meyer, John C.
Mitchell, William "Billy"
Montgomery, John J.
Moorer, Thomas H.
Moss, Sanford A.

Neumann, Gerhard
Nichols, Ruth R.
Northrop, John K.

Patterson, William A.
Piper Sr., William T.
Post, Wiley H.

Read, Albert C.
Reeve, Robert C.
Rentschler, Frederick B.
Richardson, Holden C.
Rickenbacker, Edward V.
Rodgers, Calbraith P.
Rogers, Will
Rushworth, Robert A.
Ryan, T. Claude

Schirra, Walter M.
Schriever, Bernard A.
Selfridge, Thomas E.
Shepard Jr., Alan B.
Sikorsky, Igor I.
Six, Robert F.
Smith, C.R.
Spaatz, Carl A.
Sperry Sr., Elmer A.
Sperry Sr., Lawrence B.
Stanley, Robert M.
Stapp, John P.
Stearmam, Lloyd C.

Taylor, Charles E.
Thomas, Lowell
Towers, John H.
Trippe, Juan T.
Turner, Roscoe
Twining, Nathan F.

Vandenberg, Hoyt
von Braun, Wernher
von Karman, Theodore
von Ohain, Hans P.
Vought, Chance M.

Wade, Leigh
Walden, Henry W.
Wells, Edward
Wilson, Thornton A.
Wright, Orville
Wright, Wilbur

Yeager, Charles E.
Young, John W.

International Aviation and Space Records

The National Aeronautic Association of the USA, 1815 North Fort Myer Dr., Arlington, VA 22209, representative in the United States of the Fédération Aéronautique Internationale, is the certifying agency for world aviation and space records. The International Aeronautical Federation was formed in 1905 by representatives from Belgium, France, Germany, Great Britain, Spain, Italy, Switzerland, and the United States, with headquarters in Paris. Regulations for the control of official records were signed Oct. 14, 1905.

World absolute records are defined as maximum performance, regardless of class or type of aircraft used. Absolute records for space flight (Class K, spacecraft, and Class P, aerospacecraft) are kept separately. All other records, also international in scope, are termed "World Class" records and are divided into 17 classes, including: Class A, free balloons; Class B, airships; Class C-1, airplanes; Class C-2, seaplanes; Class C-3, amphibians; Class D, gliders; and Class E, rotorcrafts, such as helicopters. Classes are subdivided into four groups based on their power source: Group I—piston engine, Group II—turboprop, Group III—jet engine, Group IV—rocket engine. Sometimes there are also further divisions for weight subclasses, such as Class C-1d, which is a light airplane weighing 3,858 to 6,614 pounds. All FAI course records listed here were accomplished in Class C-1 landplanes. A partial listing of world records follows (records to Jan. 1, 1993):

World Absolute Records—Maximum Performance in Any Class

Speed over a straight course — 2,193.16 mph — Capt. Elden W. Joersz, USAF, U.S., Lockheed SR-71A; Beale AFB, Cal., July 28, 1976.

Speed over a closed circuit — 2,092.294 mph — Maj. Adolphus H. Bledsoe Jr., USAF, U.S.; Voyager; Edwards AFB, Cal., Dec. 14-23, 1986.

Altitude — 123,523.58 feet — Alexander Fedotov, USSR; MiG-25 E-266M; Pomoskovnoye, USSR, Aug. 31, 1977.

Altitude in horizontal flight — 85,068.997 ft. — Capt. Robert C. Helt, USAF, U.S.; Lockheed SR-71; Beale AFB, Cal., July 28, 1976.

Spacecraft (Class K)

Duration — 365 days, 22 hours, 39 minutes, 47 seconds — Vladimir B. Titov, Musa H. Manarov, USSR; Soyuz TM4; Dec. 21, 1987-Dec. 21, 1988.

Altitude — 234,672.5 mi. — Frank Borman, James A. Lovell Jr., William Anders, U.S.; Apollo 8; Dec. 21-27, 1968.

Greatest mass lifted — 282,197 lbs. — Frank Borman, James A. Lovell Jr., William Anders, U.S.; Apollo 8; Dec. 21-27, 1968.

Distance — 87,436,800 mi. — Anatoly N. Beresovoy, Valentin V. Lebedev, USSR; Salyut 7, Soyuz T-5, Soyuz T-7; May 13-Dec. 10, 1982.

"World Class" Records

Free Balloons-Class A

Altitude — 113,739.9 ft. — Cmdr. Malcolm D. Ross, USNR, U.S.; Lee Lewis Memorial Winzen Research Balloon; Gulf of Mexico, May 4, 1961.

Distance — 5,208.67 — Ben Abruzzo, Larry M. Newman, Rocky Aoki, Ron Clark, U.S.; Raven Experimental; Nagashima, Japan to Covello, Cal., Nov. 9-12, 1981.

Duration — 144 hrs. 16 min — Richard Abruzzo, Troy Bradley, U.S.; Cameron R-77; Bangor, Maine to Ben Slimane, Morocco, Sept. 16-22, 1992.

Airplanes (Class C-1, Group I)

Distance, closed circuit — 24,986.727 mi — Richard Rutan, Jeana Yeager, U.S.; Voyager; Edwards AFB, Cal., Dec. 14-23, 1986.

Speed for 100 kilometers (62.137 miles) without payload, closed circuit — 469.549 mph — Jacqueline Cochran, U.S.; North American P-51 Mustang; Coachella Valley, Cal., Dec. 10, 1947.

Speed for 1,000 kilometers (621.369 miles) without payload, closed circuit — 431.09 mph — Jacqueline Cochran, U.S.; North American P-51 Mustang; Santa Rosa Summit, Cal.-Santa Fe, N.Mex.-Flagstaff, Ariz. course, May 24, 1948.

Speed for 5,000 kilometers (3,106.849 miles) without payload, closed circuit — 338.39 mph — Capt. James Bauer, USAF, Boeing B-29 Superfortress; Dayton, Oh., June 28, 1946.

Speed around the world, eastbound — 203.64 mph — D.N. Dalton, Australia; Beechcraft Duke; Brisbane, Aust.; elapsed time: 5 days 2 hrs. 19 min. 57 sec., July 20-25, 1975.

Light Airplanes—(Class C-1d, Group I)

Great Circle distance without landing — 7,929.71 mi. — Peter Wilkins, Australia; Piper Malibu; Sydney, Aust. to Phoenix, Ariz., Mar. 30-Apr. 1, 1987.

Speed for 100 kilometers (62.137 miles) without payload, closed circuit — 322.780 mph — Ms. R. M. Sharpe, Great Britain; Vickers Supermarine Spitfire 5-B; Wolverhampton, Eng., June 17, 1950.

Airplanes (Class C-1, Group II)

Great Circle distance without landing — 8,732.09 mi. — Lt. Col. Edgar L. Allison, USAF, U.S.; Lockheed HC-130 Hercules; Ching-Chuan Kang, Taiwan to Scott AFB, Ill., Feb. 20, 1972.

Altitude — 51,014 ft. — Donald R. Wilson, U.S.; LTV L450F; Greenville, Tex., Mar. 27, 1972.

Speed for 1,000 kilometers (621.369 miles) without payload, closed circuit — 541.449 mph — Ivan Soukhomline, USSR; Tupolev Tu-114; Sternberg, USSR, Mar. 24, 1960.

Speed for 5,000 kilometers (3,106.849 miles) without payload, closed circuit — 545.072 mph — Ivan Soukhomline, USSR; Tupolev Tu-114; Sternberg, USSR, Apr. 9, 1960.

Speed around the world, eastbound — 304.80 mph — Joe Harnish, David B. Webster, U.S.; Gulfstream Commander 695A; Elkhart, Ind.; elapsed time: 75 hrs. 54 min. 25 sec., Mar. 21-24, 1983.

Airplanes (Class C-1, Group III)

Great Circle distance without landing — 12,532.28 mi. — Maj. Clyde P. Evely, USAF, U.S.; Boeing B- 52H; Kadena, Okinawa, Japan to Madrid, Spain, Jan. 10-11, 1962.

Distance, closed circuit — 12,521.78 mi. — Vladimir Tersky, Yuri Resnitsky, USSR; AN-124; Podmoskovnoye, USSR, May 6-7, 1987.

Altitude — 123,523.58 ft. — Alexander Fedotov, USSR; E-226M; Podmoskovnoye, USSR, Aug. 31, 1977.

Speed for 100 kilometers (62.137 miles) without payload, closed circuit — 1,618.7 mph — Alexander Fedotov, USSR; E-266, Apr. 8, 1973.

Speed for 500 kilometers (310.68 miles) without payload, closed circuit — 1,852.61 mph — Mikhail Komarov, USSR; E-266, Oct. 5, 1967.

Speed for 1,000 kilometers (621.369 miles) without payload, closed circuit — 2,092.294 mph — Maj. Adolphus H. Bledsoe, USAF, U.S.; Lockheed SR-71 Blackbird; Beale AFB, Cal., July 27, 1976.

Speed for 2,000 kilometers (1,242.7 miles) without payload, closed circuit — 1,250.42 mph — S. Agapov, B. Veremey, USSR; Aircraft "101"; Podmoskovnoye, USSR, July 20, 1983.

Speed around the world, eastbound — 637.71 mph — Allen E. Paulson, Robert K. Smyth, John Salamanaks, Jeff Bailey, U.S.; Gulfstream IV N400GA; Houston, Tex., Feb. 26-28, 1988.

Gliders (Class D-1—single seater)

Distance, straight line — 907.7 mi. — Hans Werner Grosse, West Germany; ASK12; Luebeck, W. Germany-Biarritz, France, Apr. 25, 1972.

Distance to a goal & return — 1,023.25 mi. — Thomas L. Knauff, U.S.; Nimbus II; Williamsport, Pa., Apr. 25, 1983.

Helicopters (Class E-I)

Great Circle distance without landing — 2,213.04 mi — Robert G. Ferry, U.S.; Hughes YOH-6A No. 24213; Culver City, Cal. to Ormond Beach, Fla., Apr. 6-7, 1966.

Speed around the world — 35.40 mph — H. Ross Perot Jr., J.W. Coburn, U.S.; Bell 206 L-II Long Ranger No. 3911Z; Dallas, Texas; elapsed time: 29 days 3 hrs. 8 min. 13 sec., Sept. 1-30, 1982.

FAI Course Records

Los Angeles to New York — 1,214.65 mph — Capt. Robert G. Sowers, USAF, U.S.; Convair B-58 Hustler; elapsed time: 2 hrs. 58.71 sec., Mar. 5, 1962.

New York to Los Angeles — 1,081.80 mph — Capt. Robert G. Sowers, USAF, U.S.; Convair B-58 Hustler; elapsed time: 2 hrs. 15 min. 50.08 sec., Mar. 5, 1962.

London to New York — 1,021.54 mph — Capt. Peter Horton, U.S.; British Airways Concorde G-BOAF; Mar. 14, 1990.

Baltimore to Moscow, USSR — 563.36 mph — Col. James B. Swindal, USAF, U.S.; Boeing VC-137 (707); elapsed time: 8 hrs. 33 min. 45.4 sec., May 19, 1963.

New York to London — 1,806.964 mph — Maj. James V. Sullivan, USAF, U.S.; Lockheed SR-71; elapsed time 1 hr. 54 min. 56.4 sec., Sept. 1, 1974.

London to Los Angeles — 1,435.587 mph — Capt. Harold B. Adams, USAF, U.S.; Lockheed SR-71; elapsed time: 3 hrs. 47 min. 39 sec., Sept. 13, 1974.

Notable Around the World and Intercontinental Trips

	From/To	Miles	Time	Date
Nellie Bly	New York/New York		72d 06h 11m	1889
George Francis Train	New York/New York		67d 12h 03m	1890
Charles Fitzmorris	Chicago/Chicago		60d 13h 29m	1901
J. W. Willis Sayre	Seattle/Seattle		54d 09h 42m	1903
J. Alcock-A.W. Brown[1]	Newfoundland/Ireland	1,960	16h 12m	June 14-15, 1919
Two U.S. Army airplanes	Seattle/Seattle	26,103	35d 01h 11m	1924
Richard E. Byrd[2]	Spitsbergen/N. Pole	1,545	15h 30m	May 9, 1926
Amundsen-Ellsworth-Nobile Expedition	Spitsbergen/Teller, Alaska		80h	May 11-14,1926
E.S. Evans and L. Wells (N.Y.World)[3]	New York/New York	18,410	28d 14h 36m 05s	June 16-July 14, 1926
Charles Lindbergh[4]	New York/Paris	3,610	33h 29m 30s	May 20-21, 1927
Amelia Earhart, W. Stultz, L. Gordon	Newfoundland/Wales		20h 40m	June 17-18, 1928
Graf Zeppelin	Friedrichshafen, Ger./Lakehurst, N.J.	6,630	4d 15h 46m	Oct. 11-15, 1928
Graf Zeppelin	Friedrichshafen, Ger./Lakehurst, N.J..	21,700	20d 04h	Aug. 14-Sept. 4, 1929
Wiley Post and Harold Gatty (Monoplane Winnie Mae)	New York/New York	15,474	8d 15h 51m	July 1, 1931
C. Pangborn-H. Herndon Jr.[5]	Misawa, Japan/Wenatchee, Wash.	4,458	41h 34m	Oct. 3-5, 1931
Amelia Earhart[6]	Newfoundland/Ireland	2,026	14h 56m	May 20-21, 1932
Wiley Post (Monoplane Winnie Mae)[7]	New York/New York	15,596	115h 36m 30s	July 15-22, 1933
Hindenburg Zeppelin	Lakehurst, N.J./Frankfort, Ger.		42h 53m	Aug. 9-11, 1936
H. R. Ekins (Scripps-Howard Newspapers in race) (Zeppelin Hindenburg to Germany, airplanes from Frankfurt)	Lakehurst, N.J./Lakehurst, N.J.	25,654	18d 11h 14m 33s	Sept, 30-Oct. 19, 1936
Howard Hughes and 4 assistants	New York/New York	14,824	3d 19h 08m 10s	July 10-13, 1938
Douglas Corrigan	New York/Dublin		28h 13m	July 17-18, 1938
Mrs. Clara Adams (Pan American Clipper)	Port Washington, N.Y./Newark, N.J.		16d 19h 04m	June 28-July 15, 1939
Globester, U.S. Air Transport Command	Wash., D.C./Wash., D.C.	23,279	149h 44m	Oct. 4, 1945
Capt. William P. Odom (A-26 Reynolds Bombshell)	New York/New York	20,000	78h 55m 12s	Apr. 12-16, 1947
America, Pan American 4-engine Lockheed Constellation[8]	New York/New York	22,219	101h 32m	June 17-30, 1947
Col. Edward Eagan	New York/New York	20,559	147h 15m	Dec. 13, 1948
USAF B-50 Lucky Lady II (Capt. James Gallagher)[9]	Ft. Worth, Tex./Ft. Worth, Tex.	23,452	94h 01m	Feb. 26-Mar. 2, 1949
Col. D. Schilling, USAF[10]	England/Limestone, Me.	3,300	10h 01m	Sept. 22, 1950
C.F. Blair Jr.	Norway/Alaska	3,300	10h 29m	May 29, 1951
Two U.S. S-55.	Massachusetts/Scotland	3,410	42h 30m	July 15-31, 1952
Canberra Bomber[11]	N. Ireland/Newfoundland	2,073	04h 34m	Aug. 26, 1952
	Newfoundland/N. Ireland	2,073	03h 25m	Aug. 26, 1952
Three USAF B-52 Stratofortresses[12]	Merced, Cal./Cal..	24,325	45h 19m	Jan. 15-18, 1957
Max Conrad	Chicago/Rome	5,000	34h 03m	Mar. 5-6, 1959
USSR TU-114[13]	Moscow/New York	5,092	11h 06m	June 28, 1959
Boeing 707-320	New York/Moscow	c.5090	08h 54m	July 23, 1959
Peter Gluckmann (solo)	San Francisco/San Francisco	22,800	29d	Aug. 22-Sept. 20, 1959
Sue Snyder	Chicago/Chicago	21,219	62h 59m	June 22-24, 1960
Max Conrad (solo)	Miami/Miami	25,946	8d 18h 35m 57s	Feb. 28-Mar. 8, 1961
Sam Miller & Louis Fodor	New York/New York		46h 28m	Aug. 3-4, 1963
Robert & Joan Wallick	Manila/Manila	23,129	5d 06h 17m 10s	June 2-7, 1966
Arthur Godfrey, Richard Merrill Fred Austin, Karl Keller	New York/New York	23,333	86h 9m 01s	June 4-7, 1966
Trevor K. Brougham	Darwin, Australia/Darwin	24,800	5d 05h 57m	Aug. 5-10, 1972
Walter H. Mullikin, Albert Frink, Lyman Watt, Frank Cassaniti, Edward Shields	New York/New York	23,137	1d 22h 50s	May 1-3,1976
David Kunst[14]	Waseca, Minn./Waseca, Minn.	14,500	4yrs 3mos 16d	June 10, 1970-Oct. 5, 1974
Arnold Palmer	Denver/Denver	22,985	57h 25m 42s	May 17-19, 1976
Boeing 747[15]	San Francisco/San Francisco	26,382	54h 7m 12s	Oct. 28-31, 1977
Concorde	London/Wash., D.C.	1,023 mph	03h 34m 48s	May 29, 1976
Concorde	Paris/New York	1,037.50 mph	03h 30m 11s	Aug. 22, 1978
Richard Rutan & Jeana Yeager[16]	Edwards AFB, Cal.	24,986	09d 03m 44s	Dec. 14-23, 1986

(1) Non-stop transatlantic flight. (2) Polar flight. (3) Mileage by train and auto, 4,110; by plane, 6,300; by steamship, 8,000. (4) Solo transatlantic flight in the Ryan monoplane the "Spirit of St. Louis". (5) Non-stop Pacific flight. (6) Women's transoceanic solo flight. (7) First to fly solo around northern circumference of the world, also first to fly twice around the world. (8) Inception of regular commercial global air service. (9) First non-stop round-the-world flight, refueled 4 times in flight. (10) Non-stop jet transatlantic flight. (11) Transatlantic round trip on same day. (12) First non-stop global flight by jet planes; refueled in flight by KC-97 aerial tankers; average speed approx. 525 mph. (13) Non-stop between Moscow and New York. (14) First to circle the earth on foot. (15) Speed record around the world over both the earth's poles. (16) Circled the earth non-stop without refueling.

WEIGHTS AND MEASURES

Source: National Institute of Standards and Technology, U.S. Dept. of Commerce

The International System of Units

Two systems of weights and measures exist side by side in the United States today, with roughly equal but separate legislative sanction: the U.S. Customary System and the International (Metric) System. Throughout U.S. history, the Customary System (inherited from, but now different from, the British Imperial System) has been, as its name implies, customarily used; a plethora of federal and state legislation has given it, through implication, standing as our primary weights and measures system. However, the Metric System (incorporated in the scientists' new SI or Systeme Internationale d'Unites) is the only system that has ever received specific legislative sanction by Congress. The "Law of 1866" reads:

> It shall be lawful throughout the United States of America to employ the weights and measures of the metric system; and no contract or dealing, or pleading in any court, shall be deemed invalid or liable to objection because the weights or measures expressed or referred to therein are weights or measures of the metric system.

Over the last 100 years, the Metric System has seen slow, steadily increasing use in the United States. In science and also in the pharmaceutical industry, the use of metrics has for many years been predominant; today, the manufacturing industry is steadily increasing its use of the metric system largely motivated by the automotive industry, which is now predominantly metric.

On Feb. 10, 1964, the National Bureau of Standards issued the following bulletin:

> Henceforth it shall be the policy of the National Bureau of Standards to use the units of the International System (SI), as adopted by the 11th General Conference on Weights and Measures (October 1960), except when the use of these units would obviously impair communication or reduce the usefulness of a report.

The Trade Act of 1988, and other legislation, calls for the federal government to adopt metric specifications and mandates the Commerce Dept. to oversee the program. The conversion process is currently underway.

What had been the Metric System became the International System (SI), a more complete scientific system.

Seven units have been adopted to serve as the base for the International System as follows: **length**—meter; **mass**—kilogram; **time**—second; **electric current**—ampere; **thermodynamic temperature**—kelvin; **amount of substance**—mole; and **luminous intensity**—candela.

Prefixes

The following prefixes, in combination with the basic unit names, provide the multiples and submultiples in the International System. For example, the unit name "meter," with the prefix "kilo" added, produces "kilometer," meaning "1,000 meters."

Prefix	Symbol	Multiples	Equivalent	Prefix	Symbol	Submultiples	Equivalent
exa	E	10^{18}	quintillionfold	deci	d	10^{-1}	tenth part
peta	P	10^{15}	quadrillionfold	centi	c	10^{-2}	hundredth part
tera	T	10^{12}	trillionfold	milli	m	10^{-3}	thousandth part
giga	G	10^{9}	billionfold	micro	μ	10^{-6}	millionth part
mega	M	10^{6}	millionfold	nano	n	10^{-9}	billionth part
kilo	k	10^{3}	thousandfold	pico	p	10^{-12}	trillionth part
hecto	h	10^{2}	hundredfold	femto	f	10^{-15}	quadrillionth part
deka	da	10	tenfold	atto	a	10^{-18}	quintillionth part

Tables of Metric Weights and Measures

Linear Measure

10 millimeters (mm)	= 1 centimeter (cm)
10 centimeters	= 1 decimeter (dm) = 100 millimeters
10 decimeters	= 1 meter (m) = 1,000 millimeters
10 meters	= 1 dekameter (dam)
10 dekameters	= 1 hectometer (hm) = 100 meters
10 hectometers	= 1 kilometer (km) = 1,000 meters

Area Measure

100 square millimeters (mm^2)	= 1 square centimeter (cm^2)
10,000 square centimeters	= 1 square meter (m^2) = 1,000,000 square millimeters
100 square meters	= 1 are (a)
100 ares	= 1 hectare (ha) = 10,000 square meters
100 hectares	= 1 square kilometer (km^2) = 1,000,000 square meters

Fluid Volume Measure

10 milliliters (mL)	= 1 centiliter (cL)
10 centiliters	= 1 deciliter (dL) = 100 milliliters
10 deciliters	= 1 liter (L) = 1,000 milliliters
10 liters	= 1 dekaliter (daL)
10 dekaliters	= 1 hectoliter (hL) = 100 liters
10 hectoliters	= 1 kiloliter (kL) = 1,000 liters

Cubic Measure

1,000 cubic millimeters (mm^3)	= 1 cubic centimeter (cm^3)
1,000 cubic centimeters	= 1 cubic decimeter (dm^3) = 1,000,000 cubic millimeters
1,000 cubic decimeters	= 1 cubic meter (m^3) = 1 stere = 1,000,000 cubic centimeters = 1,000,000,000 cubic millimeters

Weight

10 milligrams (mg)	= 1 centigram (cg)
10 centigrams	= 1 decigram (dg) = 100 milligrams
10 decigrams	= 1 gram (g) = 1,000 milligrams
10 grams	= 1 dekagram (dag)
10 dekagrams	= 1 hectogram (hg) = 100 grams
10 hectograms	= 1 kilogram (kg) = 1,000 grams
1,000 kilograms	= 1 metric ton (t)

Table of U.S. Customary Weights and Measures

Linear Measure

12 inches (in)	= 1 foot (ft)
3 feet	= 1 yard (yd)
5 1/2 yards	= 1 rod (rd), pole, or perch (16 1/2 feet)
40 rods	= 1 furlong (fur) = 220 yards = 660 feet
8 furlongs	= 1 statute mile (mi) = 1,760 yards = 5,280 feet
3 miles	= 1 league = 5,280 yards = 15,840 feet
6076.11549 feet	= 1 International Nautical Mile

Liquid Measure

When necessary to distinguish the liquid pint or quart from the dry pint or quart, the word "liquid" or the abbreviation "liq" should be used in combination with the name or abbreviation of the liquid unit.

4 gills	= 1 pint (pt) = 28.875 cubic inches
2 pints	= 1 quart (qt) = 57.75 cubic inches
4 quarts	= 1 gallon (gal) = 231 cubic inches = 8 pints = 32 gills

Area Measure

Squares and cubes of units are sometimes abbreviated by using "superior" figures. For example. ft^2 means square foot, and ft^3 means cubic foot.

144 square inches	= 1 square foot (ft^2)
9 square feet	= 1 square yard (yd^2) = 1,296 square inches
30 ¼ square yards	= 1 square rod (rd^2) = 272 ¼ square feet
160 square rods	= 1 acre = 4,840 square yards = 43,560 square feet
640 acres	= 1 square mile (mi^2)
1 mile square	= 1 section (of land)
6 miles square	= 1 township = 36 sections = 36 square miles

Cubic Measure

1 cubic foot (ft^3)	= 1,728 cubic inches (in^3)
27 cubic feet	= 1 cubic yard (yd^3)

Gunter's or Surveyors' Chain Measure

7.92 inches (in)	= 1 link
100 links	= 1 chain (ch) = 4 rods = 66 feet
80 chains	= 1 survey mile (mi) = 320 rods = 5,280 feet

Troy Weight

24 grains	= 1 pennyweight (dwt)
20 pennyweights	= 1 ounce troy (oz t) = 480 grains
12 ounces troy	= 1 pound troy (lb t) = 240 pennyweights = 5,760 grains

Dry Measure

When necessary to distinguish the dry pint or quart from the liquid pint or quart, the word "dry" should be used in combination with the name or abbreviation of the dry unit.

2 pints (pt)	= 1 quart (qt) = 67.2006 cubic inches
8 quarts	= 1 peck (pk) = 537.605 cubic inches = 16 pints
4 pecks	= 1 bushel (bu) = 2,150.42 cubic inches = 32 quarts

Avoirdupois Weight

When necessary to distinguish the avoirdupois ounce or pound from the troy ounce or pound, the word "avoirdupois" or the abbreviation "avdp" should be used in combination with the name or abbreviation of the avoirdupois unit.

(The "grain" is the same in avoirdupois and troy weight.)

27 11/32 grains	= 1 dram (dr)
16 drams	= 1 ounce (oz) = 437 ½ grains
16 ounces	= 1 pound (lb) = 256 drams = 7,000 grains
100 pounds	= 1 hundredweight (cwt)*
20 hundredweights	= 1 ton = 2,000 pounds*

In "gross" or "long" measure, the following values are recognized.

112 pounds	= 1 gross or long hundredweight*
20 gross or long hundredweights	= 1 gross or long ton = 2,240 pounds*

*When the terms "hundredweight" and "ton" are used unmodified, they are commonly understood to mean the 100-pound hundredweight and the 2,000-pound ton, respectively; these units may be designated "net" or "short" when necessary to distinguish them from the corresponding units in gross or long measure.

Tables of Equivalents

In this table it is necessary to distinguish between the "international" and the "survey" foot. The international foot, defined in 1959 as exactly equal to 0.3048 meter, is shorter than the old survey foot by exactly 2 parts in one million. The survey foot is still used in data expressed in feet in geodetic surveys within the U.S. In this table the survey foot is italicized.

When the name of a unit is enclosed in brackets thus, [1 hand], this indicates (1) that the unit is not in general current use in the United States, or (2) that the unit is believed to be based on "custom and usage" rather than on formal definition.

Equivalents involving decimals are, in most instances, rounded off to the third decimal place except where they are exact, in which cases these exact equivalents are so designated.

Lengths

1 angstrom (A)	0.1 nanometer (exactly) 0.000 1 micrometer (exactly) 0.000 000 1 millimeter (exactly) 0.000 000 004 inch
1 cable's length	120 fathoms (exactly) 720 *feet* (exactly) 219 meters
1 centimeter (cm)	0.3937 inch
1 chain (ch) (Gunter's or surveyors)	66 *feet* (exactly) 20.1168 meters
1 chain (engineers)	100 feet 30.48 meters (exactly)
1 decimeter (dm)	3.937 inches
1 degree (geographical)	364,566.929 feet 69.047 miles (avg.) 111.123 kilometers (avg.)
-of latitude	68.708 miles at equator 69.403 miles at poles
-of longitude	69.171 miles at equator
1 dekameter (dam)	32.808 feet
1 fathom	6 *feet* (exactly) 1.8288 meters (exactly)
1 foot (ft)	0.3048 meters (exactly)
1 furlong (fur)	10 chains (surveyors) (exactly) 660 *feet* (exactly) ⅛ statute mile (exactly) 201.168 meters
[1 hand] (height measure for horses from ground to top of shoulders)	4 inches
1 inch (in)	2.54 centimeters (exactly)
1 kilometer (km)	0.621 mile 3,281.5 feet
1 league (land)	3 survey miles (exactly) 4.828 kilometers
1 link (Gunter's or surveyors)	7.92 inches (exactly) 0.201 meter
1 link engineers	1 foot 0.305 meter
1 meter (m)	39.37 inches 1.094 yards
1 micrometer (μm) [the Greek letter mu]	0.001 millimeter (exactly) 0.000 039 37 inch
1 mil	0.001 inch (exactly) 0.025 4 millimeter (exactly)
1 mile (mi) (statute or land)	5,280 feet (exactly) 1.609 kilometers
1 international nautical mile (nmi)	1.852 kilometers (exactly) 1.150779 survey miles 6,076.11549 feet
1 millimeter (mm)	0.039 37 inch
1 nanometer (nm)	0.001 micrometer (exactly) 0.000 000 039 37 inch
1 pica (typography)	12 points
1 point (typography)	0.013 837 inch (exactly) 0.351 millimeter
1 rod (rd), pole, or perch	16 ½ *feet* (exactly) 5.029 meters
1 yard (yd)	0.9144 meter (exactly)

Areas or Surfaces

1 acre	43,560 square *feet* (exactly) 4,840 square yards 0.405 hectare
1 are (a)	119.599 square yards 0.025 acre

1 bolt (cloth measure):
  length . . . . 100 yards (on modern looms)
  width . . . . 42 inches (usually, for cotton); 60 inches (usually, for wool)
1 hectare (ha) . . . . 2.471 acres
[1 square (building)] . . . . 100 square feet
1 square centimeter (cm^2) . . . . 0.155 square inch
1 square decimeter (dm^2) . . . . 15.500 square inches
1 square foot (ft^2) . . . . 929.030 square centimeters
1 square inch (in^2) . . . . 6.4516 square centimeters (exactly)
1 square kilometer (km^2) . . . 247.104 acres; 0.386 square mile
1 square meter (m^2) . . . . . . 1.196 square yards; 10.764 square feet
1 square mile (mi^2) . . . . 258.999 hectares
1 square millimeter (mm^2) . . . . 0.002 square inch
1 square rod (rd^2) sq. pole, or sq. perch . . . . 25.293 square meters
1 square yard (yd^2) . . . . 0.836 square meter

Capacities or Volumes

1 barrel (bbl) liquid . . . . 31 to 42 gallons°

°There are a variety of "barrels," established by law or usage. For example: federal taxes on fermented liquors are based on a barrel of 31 gallons: many state laws fix the "barrel for liquids" as 31 ½ gallons; one state fixes a 36-gallon barrel for cistern measurement; federal law recognizes a 40-gallon barrel for "proof spirits"; by custom, 42 gallons comprise a barrel of crude oil or petroleum products for statistical purposes, and this equivalent is recognized "for liquids" by 4 states.

1 barrel (bbl), standard, for fruits, vegetables, and other dry commodities except dry cranberries . . . . 7,056 cubic inches; 105 dry quarts; 3.281 bushels, struck measure
1 barrel (bbl), standard, cranberry . . . 5,826 cubic inches; $86\frac{45}{64}$ dry quarts; 2.709 bushels, struck measure
1 board foot (lumber measure) . . a foot-square board 1 inch thick
1 bushel (bu) (U.S.) (struck measure) . . . 2,150.42 cubic inches (exactly); 35.239 liters
[1 bushel, heaped (U.S.)] . . . 2,747.715 cubic inches; 1.278 bushels, struck measure°

°Frequently recognized as 1¼ bushels, struck measure.

[1 bushel (bu) (British Imperial) (struck measure)] . . . 1.032 U.S. bushels struck measure; 2,219.36 cubic inches
1 cord (cd) firewood . . . . 128 cubic feet (exactly)
1 cubic centimeter (cm^3) . . . . 0.061 cubic inch
1 cubic decimeter (dm^3) . . . . 61.024 cubic inches
1 cubic inch (in^3) . . . . 0.554 fluid ounce; 4.433 fluid drams; 16.387 cubic centimeters
1 cubic foot (ft^3) . . . . 7.481 gallons; 28.317 cubic decimeters
1 cubic meter (m^3) . . . . 1.308 cubic yards
1 cubic yard (yd^3) . . . . 0.765 cubic meter
1 cup, measuring . . . . 8 fluid ounces (exactly); ½ liquid pint (exactly)
[1 dram, fluid (fl dr) (British)] . . . . 0.961 U.S. fluid dram; 0.217 cubic inch; 3.552 milliliters
1 dekaliter (daL) . . . . 2.642 gallons; 1.135 pecks
1 gallon (gal) (U.S.) . . . . . . 231 cubic inches (exactly); 3.785 liters; 0.833 British gallon; 128 U.S. fluid ounces (exactly)
[1 gallon (gal) British Imperial] . . . . . . 277.42 cubic inches; 1.201 U.S. gallons; 4.546 liters; 160 British fluid ounces (exactly)
1 gill (gi) . . . . 7.219 cubic inches; 4 fluid ounces (exactly); 0.118 liter
1 hectoliter (hL) . . . . 26.418 gallons; 2.838 bushels
1 liter (L) (1 cubic decimeter exactly) . . . . 1.057 liquid quarts; 0.908 dry quart; 61.025 cubic inches
1 milliliter (mL) (1 cu cm exactly) . . . . . . 0.271 fluid dram; 16.231 minims; 0.061 cubic inch
1 ounce, liquid (U.S.) . . . . 1.805 cubic inches; 29.573 milliliters; 1.041 British fluid ounces
[1 ounce, fluid (fl oz) (British)] . . . 0.961 U.S. fluid ounce; 1.734 cubic inches; 28.412 milliliters
1 peck (pk) . . . . 8.810 liters
1 pint (pt), dry . . . . 33.600 cubic inches; 0.551 liter
1 pint (pt), liquid . . . . 28.875 cubic inches (exactly); 0.473 liter
1 quart (qt) dry (U.S.) . . . . 67.201 cubic inches; 1.101 liters; 0.969 British quart
1 quart (qt) liquid (U.S.) . . . 57.75 cubic in (exactly); 0.946 liter; 0.833 British quart
[1 quart (qt) (British)] . . . . 69.354 cubic inches; 1.032 U.S. dry quarts; 1.201 U.S. liquid quarts
1 tablespoon . . . . 3 teaspoons°(exactly); 4 fluid drams; ½ fluid ounce (exactly)
1 teaspoon . . . . ⅓ tablespoon°(exactly); $1\frac{1}{3}$ fluid drams°

°The equivalent "1 teaspoon—$1\frac{1}{3}$ fluid drams" has been found by the bureau to correspond more closely with the actual capacities of "measuring" and silver teaspoons than the equivalent "1 teaspoon—1 fluid dram" which is given by many dictionaries.

Weights or Masses

1 assay ton°° (AT) . . . . 29.167 grams

°°Used in assaying. The assay ton bears the same relation to the milligram that a ton of 2,000 pounds avoirdupois bears to the ounce troy; hence the weight in milligrams of precious metal obtained from one assay ton of ore gives directly the number of troy ounces to the net ton.

1 bale (cotton measure) . . . . 500 pounds in U.S.; 750 pounds in Egypt
1 carat (c) . . . . 200 milligrams (exactly); 3.086 grains
1 dram avoirdupois (dr avdp) . . . $27\frac{11}{32}$ (=27.344) grains; 1.772 grams
gamma, see microgram
1 grain . . . . 64.799 milligrams
1 gram . . . . 15.432 grains; 0.035 ounce, avoirdupois
1 hundredweight, gross or long°°° (gross cwt) . . . . . 112 pounds (exactly); 50.802 kilograms
1 hundredweight, net or short (cwt. or net cwt.) . . . . 100 pounds (exactly); 45.359 kilograms
1 kilogram (kg) . . . . 2.205 pounds
1 microgram (μg [The Greek letter mu in combination with the letter g]) . . . . . 0.000001 gram (exactly)
1 milligram (mg) . . . . 0.015 grain
1 ounce, avoirdupois (oz avdp) . . . . 437.5 grains (exactly); 0.911 troy ounce; 28.350 grams
1 ounce, troy (oz t) . . . . . . 480 grains (exactly); 1.097 avoirdupois ounces; 31.103 grams
1 pennyweight (dwt) . . . . . 1.555 grams
1 pound, avoirdupois (lb avdp) . . . . 7,000 grains (exactly); 1.215 troy pounds; 453.592 37 grams (exactly)
1 pound, troy (lb t) . . . . . . 5,760 grains (exactly); 0.823 avoirdupois pound; 373.242 grams
1 ton, gross or long°°° (gross ton) . . . . 2,240 pounds (exactly); 1.12 net tons (exactly); 1.016 metric tons

°°°The gross or long ton and hundredweight are used commercially in the United States to only a limited extent, usually in restricted industrial fields. These units are the same as British "ton" and "hundredweight."

1 ton, metric (t) . . . . 2,204.623 pounds; 0.984 gross ton; 1.102 net tons
1 ton, net or short (sh ton) . . 2,000 pounds (exactly); 0.893 gross ton; 0.907 metric ton

Tables of Interrelation of Units of Measurement

Units of length and area of the international and survey measures are included in the following tables. Units unique to the survey measure are italicized. See p. 279, Tables of Equivalents, 1st para.

1 international foot = 0.999 998 survey foot (exactly)
1 survey foot = 1200/3937 meter (exactly)
1 international foot = 12 × 0.0254 meter (exactly)

Bold face type indicates exact values

Units of Length

Units	Inches	*Links*	Feet	Yards	*Rods*	*Chains*	Miles	cm	Meters
1 inch=	**1**	0.126 263	0.083 333	0.027 778	0.005 051	0.001 263	0.000 016	**2.54**	**0.025 4**
1 *link*=	**7.92**	**1**	**0.66**	**0.22**	**0.04**	**0.01**	**0.000 125**	20.117	0.201 168
1 foot=	**12**	1.515 152	**1**	0.333 333	0.060 606	0.015 152	0.000 189	**30.48**	**0.304 8**
1 yard=	**36**	4.545 45	**3**	**1**	0.181 818	0.045 455	0.000 568	**91.44**	**0.914 4**
1 *rod*=	**198**	**25**	**16.5**	**5.5**	**1**	**0.25**	**0.003 125**	502.92	5.029 2
1 *chain*=	**792**	**100**	**66**	**22**	**4**	**1**	**0.012 5**	2011.68	20.116 8
1 mile=	**63 360**	**8000**	**5280**	**1760**	**320**	**80**	**1**	**160 934.4**	**1609.344**
1 cm=	0.3937	0.049 710	0.032 808	0.010 936	0.001 988	0.000 497	0.000 006	**1**	**0.01**
1 meter=	39.37	4.970 960	3.280 840	1.093 613	0.198 838	0.049 710	0.000 621	**100**	**1**

Units of Area

Units	Sq. inches	*Sq. links*	Sq. feet	Sq. yards	*Sq. rods*	*Sq. chains*
1 sq. inch=	**1**	.015 942 3	0.006 944	0.000 771 605	0.000 025 5	0.000 001 594
1 sq. *link*=	62.726 4	**1**	**0.435 6**	**0.0484**	**0.0016**	**0.000 1**
1 sq. foot=	**144**	2.295 684	**1**	0.111 111 1	0.003 673 09	0.000 229 568
1 sq. yard=	**1296**	20.661 16	**9**	**1**	0.033 057 85	0.002 066 12
1 sq. *rod*=	**39 204**	**625**	**272.25**	**30.25**	**1**	**0.062 5**
1 sq. *chain*=	**627 264**	**10 000**	**4 356**	**484**	**16**	**1**
1 *acre*=	**6 272 640**	**100 000**	**43 560**	**4 840**	**160**	**10**
1 sq. mile=	**4 014 489 600**	**64 000 000**	**27 878 400**	**3 097 600**	**102 400**	**6400**
1 sq. cm=	0.155 000 3	0.002 471 05	0.001 076	0.000 119 599	0.000 003 954	0.000 000 247
1 sq. meter=	1550.003	24.710 44	10.763 91	1.195 990	0.039 536 70	0.002 471 044
1 *hectare*=	15 500 031	247 104	107 639.1	11 959.90	395.367 0	24.710 44

Units	*Acres*	Sq. miles	Sq. cm	Sq. meters	*Hectares*
1 sq. inch=	0.000 000 159 423	0.000 000 000 249 10	**6.451 6**	**0.000 645 16**	0.000 000 065
1 sq. *link*=	**0.000 01**	**0.000 000 015 625**	404.685 642 24	0.040 468 56	0.000 004 047
1 sq. foot=	0.000 022 956 84	0.000 000 035 870 06	929.034 1	0.092 903 41	0.000 009 290
1 sq. yard=	0.000 206 611 6	0.000 000 322 830 6	**8 361.273 6**	**0.836 127 36**	0.000 083 613
1 sq. *rod*=	**0.006 25**	**0.000 009 765 625**	252 929.5	25.292 95	0.002 529 295
1 sq. *chain*=	**0.1**	**0.000 156 25**	4 046 873	404.687 3	0.040 468 73
1 *acre*=	**1**	**0.001 562 5**	40 468 73	4 046.873	0.404 687 3
1 sq. mile=	**640**	**1**	25 899 881 103	2 589 988.11	258.998 811 034
1 sq. cm=	0.000 000 024 711	0.000 000 000 038 610	**1**	**0.000 1**	**0.000 000 01**
1 sq. meter=	0.000 247 104 4	0.000 000 386 102 2	**10 000**	**1**	**0.0001**
1 *hectare*=	2.471 044	0.003 861 006	**100 000 000**	**10 000**	**1**

Units of Mass Not Greater than Pounds and Kilograms

Units	Grains	Pennyweights	Avdp drams	Avdp ounces
1 grain=	**1**	0.041 666 67	0.036 571 43	0.002 285 71
1 pennyweight=	**24**	**1**	0.877 714 3	0.054 857 14
1 dram avdp=	**27.343 75**	1.139 323	**1**	**0.062 5**
1 ounce avdp=	**437.5**	18.229 17	**16**	**1**
1 ounce troy=	**480**	**20**	17.554 29	1.097 143
1 pound troy=	**5760**	**240**	210.651 4	13.165 71
1 pound avdp=	**7000**	291.666 7	**256**	**16**
1 milligram=	0.015 432	0.000 643 015	0.000 564 383	0.000 035 274
1 gram=	15.432 36	0.643 014 9	0.564 383 4	0.035 273 96
1 kilogram=	15 432.36	643.014 9	564.383 4	35.273 96

Units	Troy ounces	Troy pounds	Avdp pounds	Milligrams	Grams	Kilograms
1 grain=	0.002 083 33	0.000 173 611	0.000 142 857	**64.798 91**	**0.064 798 91**	0.000 064 799
1 pennyw't.=	**0.05**	0.004 166 667	0.003 428 571	**1555.173 84**	**1.555 173 84**	0.001 555 174
1 dram avdp=	0.056 966 15	0.004 747 179	0.003 906 25	1771.845 195	1.771 845 195	0.001 771 845
1 oz avdp=	0.911 458 3	0.075 954 86	**0.062 5**	**28 349.523 125**	**28.349 523 125**	0.028 349 52
1 oz troy=	**1**	0.083 333 333	0.068 571 43	**31 103.476 8**	**31.103 476 8**	0.031 103 48
1 lb troy=	**12**	**1**	0.822 857 1	**373 241.721 6**	**373.241 721 6**	0.373 241 722
1 lb avdp=	14.583 33	1.215 278	**1**	**453 592.37**	**453.592 37**	**0.453 592 37**
1 milligram=	0.000 032 151	0.000 002 679	0.000 002 205	**1**	**0.001**	**0.000 001**
1 gram=	0.032 150 75	0.002 679 229	0.002 204 623	**1000**	**1**	**0.001**
1 kilogram=	32.150 75	2.679 229	2.204 623	**1 000 000**	**1000**	**1**

Units of Mass Not Less than Avoirdupois Ounces

Units	Avdp oz	Avdp lb	Short cwt	Short tons	Long tons	Kilograms	Metric tons
1 oz av=	**1**	**0.0625**	**0.000 625**	**0.000 031 25**	0.000 027 902	0.028 349 523	0.000 028 350
1 lb av=	**16**	**1**	**0.01**	**0.000 5**	0.000 446 429	**0.453 592 37**	0.000 453 592
1 sh cwt=	**1 600**	**100**	**1**	**0.05**	0.044 642 86	**45.359 237**	**0.045 359 237**
1 sh ton=	**32 000**	**2000**	**20**	**1**	0.892 857 1	**907.184 74**	**0.907 184 74**
1 long ton=	**35 840**	**2240**	**22.4**	**1.12**	**1**	**1016.046 908 8**	1.016 046 909
1 kg=	35.273 96	2.204 623	0.022 046 23	0.001 102 311	0.000 984 207	**1**	**0.001**
1 metric ton=	35 273.96	2 204.623	22.046 23	1.102 311	0.984 206 5	**1000**	**1**

Units of Volume

Units	Cubic inches	Cubic feet	Cubic yards	Cubic cm	Cubic dm	Cubic meters
1 cubic inch=	1	0.000 578 704	0.000 021 433	16.387 064	0.016 387	0.000 016 387
1 cubic foot=	1728	1	0.037 037 04	28 316.846 592	28.316 847	0.028 316 847
1 cubic yard=	46 656	27	1	764 554.857 984	764.554 858	0.764 554 858
1 cubic cm=	0.061 023 74	0.000 035 315	0.000 001 308	1	0.001	0.000 001
1 cubic dm=	61.023 74	0.035 314 67	0.001 307 951	1 000	1	0.001
1 cubic meter	61 023.74	35.314 67	1.307 951	1 000 000	1000	1

Units of Capacity (Liquid Measure)

Units	Minims	Fluid drams	Fluid ounces	Gills	Liquid pt
1 minim=	1	0.016 666 7	0.002 083 33	0.000 520 833	0.000 130 208
1 fluid dram=	60	1	0.125	0.031 25	0.007 812 5
1 fluid ounce=	480	8	1	0.25	0.062 5
1 gill=	1920	32	4	1	0.25
1 liquid pint=	7680	128	16	4	1
1 liquid quart=	15 360	256	32	8	2
1 gallon=	61 440	1024	128	32	8
1 cubic inch=	265.974	4.432 900	0.554 112 6	0.138 528 1	0.034 632 03
1 cubic foot=	459 603.1	7 660.052	957.506 5	239.376 6	59.844 16
1 milliliter=	16.230 73	0.270 512 18	0.033 814 02	0.008 453 506	.002 113 376
1 liter=	16 230.73	270.512 18	33.814 02	8.453 506	2.113 376

Units	Liquid quarts	Gallons	Cubic inches	Cubic feet	Liters
1 minim=	0.000 065 104 17	0.000 016 276 04	0.003 759 766	0.000 002 175 790	0.000 061 611 52
1 flu. dram=	0.003 906 25	0.000 976 562 5	0.225 585 9	0.000 130 547 4	0.003 696 691
1 fluid oz=	0.031 25	0.007 812 5	1.804 687 5	0.001 044 379	0.029 573 53
1 gill=	0.125	0.031 25	7.218 75	0.004 177 517	0.118 294 118
1 liquid pt=	0.5	0.125	28.875	0.016 710 07	0.473 176 473
1 liquid qt=	1	0.25	57.75	0.033 420 14	0.946 352 946
1 gallon=	4	1	231	0.133 680 6	3.785 411 784
1 cubic in.=	0.017 316 02	0.004 329 004	1	0.000 578 703 7	0.016 387 064
1 cubic foot=	29.922 08	7.480 519	1728	1	28.316 846 592
1 liter=	1.056 688	0.264 172 05	61.023 74	0.035 314 67	1

Units of Capacity (Dry Measure)

Units	Dry pints	Dry quarts	Pecks	Bushels	Cubic in.	Liters
1 dry pint=	1	0.5	0.062 5	0.015 625	33.600 312 5	0.550 610 47
1 dry quart=	2	1	0.125	0.031 25	67.200 625	1.101 220 9
1 peck=	16	8	1	0.25	537.605	8.809 767 5
1 bushel=	64	32	4	1	2150.42	35.239 07
1 cubic inch=	0.029 761 6	0.014 880 8	0.001 860 10	0.000 465 025	1	0.016 387 06
1 liter=	1.816 166	0.908 083	0.113 510 37	0.028 377 59	61.023 74	1

Miscellaneous Measures

Caliber—the diameter of a gun bore. In the U.S., caliber is traditionally expressed in hundredths of inches, eg. .22 or .30. In Britain, caliber is often expressed in thousandths of inches, eg. .270 or .465. Now, it is commonly expressed in millimeters, eg. the 5.56 mm. M16 rifle. Heavier weapons' caliber has long been expressed in millimeters, eg. the 81 mm. mortar, the 105 mm. howitzer (light), the 155 mm. howitzer (medium or heavy).

Naval guns' caliber refers to the barrel length as a multiple of the bore diameter. A 5-inch, 50-caliber naval gun has a 5-inch bore and a barrel length of 250 inches.

Carat, karat—a measure of the amount of alloy per 24 parts in gold. Thus 24-carat gold is pure; 18-carat gold is one-fourth alloy.

Decibel (dB)—a measure of the relative loudness or intensity of sound. A 20-decibel sound is 10 times louder than a 10-decibel sound; 30 decibels is 100 times louder; 40 decibels is 1,000 times louder, etc. One decibel is the smallest difference between sounds detectable by the human ear. A 120-decibel sound is painful.

10 decibels	– a light whisper
20	– quiet conversation
30	– normal conversation
40	– light traffic
50	– typewriter, loud conversation
60	– noisy office
70	– normal traffic, quiet train
80	– rock music, subway
90	– heavy traffic, thunder
100	– jet plane at takeoff

Em—a printer's measure designating the square width of any given type size. Thus, an em of 10-point type is 10 points. An en is half an em.

Gauge—a measure of shotgun bore diameter. Gauge numbers originally referred to the number of lead balls of the gun barrel diameter in a pound. Thus, a 16 gauge shotgun's bore was smaller than a 12-gauge shotgun's. Today, an international agreement assigns millimeter measures to each gauge, eg:

Gauge	Bore diameter in mm
6	23.34
10	19.67
12	18.52
14	17.60
16	16.81
20	15.90

Horsepower—the power needed to lift 550 pounds one foot in one second, or to lift 33,000 pounds one foot in one minute. Equivalent to 746 watts or 2,546.0756 Btu/h.

Quire—25 sheets of paper

Ream—500 sheets of paper

Knot—a measure of the speed of ships. A knot equals 1 nautical mile per hour.

Electrical Units

The **watt** is the unit of power (electrical, mechanical, thermal, etc.). Electrical power is given by the product of the voltage and the current.

Energy is sold by the **joule**, but in common practice the billing of electrical energy is expressed in terms of the **kilowatt-hour**, which is 3,600,000 joules or 3.6 megajoules.

The **horsepower** is a non-metric unit sometimes used in mechanics. It is equal to 746 watts.

The **ohm** is the unit of electrical resistance and represents the physical property of a conductor that offers a resistance to the flow of electricity, permitting just 1 ampere to flow at 1 volt of pressure.

Compound Interest

Compounded Annually

Principal	Period	4%	5%	6%	7%	8%	9%	10%	12%	14%	16%
$100	1 day	0.011	0.014	0.016	0.019	0.022	0.025	0.027	0.033	0.038	0.044
	1 week	0.077	0.096	0.115	0.134	0.153	0.173	0.192	0.230	0.268	0.307
	6 mos.	2.00	2.50	3.00	3.50	4.00	4.50	5.00	6.00	7.00	8.00
	1 year	4.00	5.00	6.00	7.00	8.00	9.00	10.00	12.00	14.00	16.00
	2 years	8.16	10.25	12.36	14.49	16.64	18.81	21.00	25.44	29.96	34.56
	3 years	12.49	15.76	19.10	22.50	25.97	29.50	33.10	40.49	48.15	56.09
	4 years	16.99	21.55	26.25	31.08	36.05	41.16	46.41	57.35	68.90	81.06
	5 years	21.67	27.63	33.82	40.26	46.93	53.86	61.05	76.23	92.54	110.03
	6 years	26.53	34.01	41.85	50.07	58.69	67.71	77.16	97.38	119.50	143.64
	7 years	31.59	40.71	50.36	60.58	71.38	82.80	94.87	121.07	150.23	182.62
	8 years	36.86	47.75	59.38	71.82	85.09	99.26	114.36	147.60	185.26	227.84
	9 years	42.33	55.13	68.95	83.85	99.90	117.19	135.79	177.31	225.19	280.30
	10 years	48.02	62.89	79.08	96.72	115.89	136.74	159.37	210.58	270.72	341.14
	12 years	60.10	79.59	101.22	125.22	151.82	181.27	213.84	289.60	381.79	493.60
	15 years	80.09	107.89	139.66	175.90	217.22	264.25	317.72	447.36	613.79	826.55
	20 years	119.11	165.33	220.71	286.97	366.10	460.44	572.75	864.63	1,274.35	1,846.08

Ancient Measures

Biblical

Cubit	=	21.8 inches
Omer	=	0.45 peck
		3.964 liters
Ephah	=	10 omers
Shekel	=	0.497 ounce
		14.1 grams

Greek

Cubit	=	18.3 inches
Stadion	=	607.2 or 622 feet
Obolos	=	715.38 milligrams
Drachma	=	4.2923 grams
Mina	=	0.9463 pounds
Talent	=	60 mina

Roman

Cubit	=	17.5 inches
Stadium	=	202 yards
As, libra, pondus	=	325.971 grams, .71864 pounds

Weight of Water

1	cubic inch	.0360 pound
12	cubic inches	.433 pound
1	cubic foot	62.4 pounds
1	cubic foot	7.48052 U.S. gal
1.8	cubic feet	112.0 pounds
35.96	cubic feet	2240.0 pounds
1	imperial gallon	10.0 pounds
11.2	imperial gallons	112.0 pounds
224	imperial gallons	2240.0 pounds
1	U.S. gallon	8.33 pounds
13.45	U.S. gallons	112.0 pounds
269.0	U.S. gallons	2240.0 pounds

Density of Gases and Vapors

at 0°C and 760 mmHg

Source: National Institute of Standards and Technology (kilograms per cubic meter)

Gas	Wgt.
Acetylene	1.171
Air	1.293
Ammonia	.759
Argon	1.784
Arsine	3.48
Butane-iso	2.60
Butane-n	2.519
Carbon dioxide	1.977
Carbon monoxide	1.250
Carbon oxysulfide	2.72
Chlorine	3.214
Chlorine monoxide	3.89
Ethane	1.356
Ethylene	1.260
Fluorine	1.696
Helium	.178
Hydrogen	.090
Hydrogen bromide	3.50
Hydrogen chloride	1.639
Hydrogen iodide	5.724
Hydrogen selenide	3.66
Hydrogen sulfide	1.539
Krypton	3.745
Methane	.717
Methyl chloride	2.25
Methyl ether	2.091
Methyl fluoride	1.545
Mono methylamine	1.38
Neon	.900
Nitric oxide	1.341
Nitrogen	1.250
Nitrosyl chloride	2.99
Nitrous oxide	1.997
Oxygen	1.429
Phosphine	1.48
Propane	2.020
Silicon tetrafluoride	4.67
Sulfur dioxide	2.927
Xenon	5.897

Temperature Conversion Table

The numbers in **bold face type** refer to the temperature either in degrees Celsius or Fahrenheit which are to be converted. If converting from degrees Fahrenheit to Celsius, the equivalent will be found in the column on the left, while if converting from degrees Celsius to Fahrenheit the answer will be found in the column on the right.

For temperatures not shown. To convert Fahrenheit to Celsius subtract 32 degrees and multiply by 5, divide by 9; to convert Celsius to Fahrenheit, multiply by 9, divide by 5 and add 32 degrees.

Celsius		Fahrenheit
− 273.2	**− 459.7**	
− 184	**− 300**	
− 169	**− 273**	− 459.4
− 157	**− 250**	− 418
− 129	**− 200**	− 328
− 101	**− 150**	− 238
− 73.3	**− 100**	− 148
− 45.6	**− 50**	− 58
− 40.0	**− 40**	− 40
− 34.4	**− 30**	− 22
− 28.9	**− 20**	− 4
− 23.3	**− 10**	14
− 17.8	**0**	32
− 12.2	**10**	50
− 6.67	**20**	68
− 1.11	**30**	86
4.44	**40**	104
10.0	**50**	122
15.6	**60**	140
21.1	**70**	158
23.9	**75**	167
26.7	**80**	176
29.4	**85**	185
32.2	**90**	194
35.0	**95**	203
36.7	**98**	208.4
37.8	**100**	212
43	**110**	230
49	**120**	248
54	**130**	266
60	**140**	284
66	**150**	302
93	**200**	392
121	**250**	482
149	**300**	572

Boiling and Freezing Points of Water

Water boils at 212°F at sea level. For every 550 feet above sea level, boiling point of water is lower by about 1°F. Methyl alcohol boils at 148°F. Average human oral temperature, 98.6°F. Water freezes at 32°F. Although "Centigrade" is still frequently used, the International Committee on Weights and Measures and the National Institute of Standards have recommended since 1948 that this scale be called "Celsius."

Breaking the Sound Barrier; Speed of Sound

The prefix Mach is used to describe supersonic speed. It derives from Ernst Mach, a Czech-born German physicist, who contributed to the study of sound. When a plane moves at the speed of sound it is Mach 1. When twice the speed of sound it is Mach 2. When it is near but below the speed of sound its speed can be designated at less than Mach 1, for example, Mach .90. Mach is defined as "in jet propulsion, the ratio of the velocity of a rocket or a jet to the velocity of sound in the medium being considered."

When a plane passes the sound barrier—flying faster than sound travels—listeners in the area hear thunderclaps, but pilots do not hear them.

Sound is produced by vibrations of an object and is transmitted by alternate increase and decrease in pressures that radiate outward through a material media of molecules —somewhat like waves spreading out on a pond after a rock has been tossed into it.

The frequency of sound is determined by the number of times the vibrating waves undulate per second, and is measured in cycles per second. The slower the cycle of waves, the lower the frequency. As frequencies increase, the sound is higher in pitch.

Sound is audible to human beings only if the frequency falls within a certain range. The human ear is usually not sensitive to frequencies of less than 20 vibrations per second, or more than about 20,000 vibrations per second—although this range varies among individuals. Anything at a pitch higher than the human ear can hear is termed ultrasonic.

Intensity or loudness is the strength of the pressure of these radiating waves, and is measured in decibels. The human ear responds to intensity in a range from zero to 120 decibels. Any sound with pressure over 120 decibels is painful.

The speed of sound is generally placed at 1,088 feet per second at sea level at 32°F. It varies in other temperatures and in different media. Sound travels faster in water than in air, and even faster in iron and steel. If in air it travels a mile in 5 seconds, it does a mile under water in 1 second, and through iron in 1/3 of a second. It travels through ice cold vapor at approximately 4,708 feet per second; ice-cold water, 4,938; granite, 12,960; hardwood, 12,620; brick, 11,960; glass, 16,410 to 19,690; silver, 8,658; gold, 5,717.

Colors of the Spectrum

Color, an electromagnetic wave phenomenon, is a sensation produced through the excitation of the retina of the eye by rays of light. The colors of the spectrum may be produced by viewing a light beam refracted by passage through a prism, which breaks the light into its wave lengths.

Customarily, the primary colors of the spectrum are thought of as those 6 monochromatic colors that occupy relatively large areas of the spectrum: red, orange, yellow, green, blue, and violet. However, Sir Isaac Newton named a 7th, indigo, situated between blue and violet on the spectrum. Aubert estimated (1865) the solar spectrum to contain approximately 1,000 distinguishable hues of which according to Rood (1881) 2 million tints and shades can be distinguished; Luckiesh stated (1915) that 55 distinctly different hues have been seen in a single spectrum.

Many physicists recognize only 3 primary colors: red, yellow, and blue (Mayer, 1775); red, green, and violet (Thomas Young, 1801); red, green, and blue (Clerk Maxwell, 1860).

The color sensation of black is due to complete lack of stimulation of the retina, that of white to complete stimulation. The infra-red and ultra-violet rays, below the red (long) end of the spectrum and above the violet (short) end respectively, are invisible to the naked eye. Heat is the principal effect of the infrared rays and chemical action that of the ultraviolet rays.

Common Fractions Reduced to Decimals

8ths	16ths	32ds	64ths	
			1	.015625
		1	2	.03125
			3	.046875
	1	2	4	.0625
			5	.078125
		3	6	.09375
			7	.109375
1	2	4	8	.125
			9	.140625
		5	10	.15625
			11	.171875
	3	6	12	.1875
			13	.203125
		7	14	.21875
			15	.234375
2	4	8	16	.25
			17	.265625
		9	18	.28125
			19	.296875
	5	10	20	.3125
			21	.328125
		11	22	.34375

8ths	16ths	32ds	64ths	
			23	.359375
3	6	12	24	.375
			25	.390625
		13	26	.40625
			27	.421875
	7	14	28	.4375
			29	.453125
		15	30	.46875
			31	.484375
4	8	16	32	.5
			33	.515625
		17	34	.53125
			35	.546875
	9	18	36	.5625
			37	.578125
		19	38	.59375
			39	.609375
5	10	20	40	.625
			41	.640625
		21	42	.65625
			43	.671875
	11	22	44	.6875

8ths	16ths	32ds	64ths	
			45	.703125
		23	46	.71875
			47	.734375
6	12	24	48	.75
			49	.765625
		25	50	.78125
			51	.796875
	13	26	52	.8125
			53	.828125
		27	54	.84375
			55	.859375
7	14	28	56	.875
			57	.890625
		29	58	.90625
			59	.921875
	15	30	60	.9375
			61	.953125
		31	62	.96875
			63	.984375
8	16	32	64	1.

Spirits Measures

Pony	0.5 jigger
Shot	0.666 jigger 1.0 ounce
Jigger	1.5 shot
Pint	16 shots 0.625 fifth
Fifth	25.6 shots 1.6 pints 0.8 quart 0.75706 liter
Quart	32 shots 1.25 fifth
Magnum	2 quarts 2.49797 bottles (wine)

For champagne and brandy only:

Jeroboam	6.4 pints 1.6 magnum 0.8 gallon

For champagne only:

Rehoboam	3 magnums
Methuselah	4 magnums
Salmanazar	6 magnums
Balthazar	8 magnums
Nebuchadnezzar	10 magnums

Wine bottle (standard):

	0.800633 quart 0.7576778 liter

Mathematical Formulas

To find the CIRCUMFERENCE of a:

Circle — Multiply the diameter by 3.14159265 (usually 3.1416).

To find the AREA of a:

Circle — Multiply the square of the diameter by .785398 (usually .7854).

Rectangle — Multiply the length of the base by the height.

Sphere (surface) — Multiply the square of the radius by 3.1416 and multiply by 4.

Square — Square the length of one side.

Trapezoid — Add the two parallel sides, multiply by the height and divide by 2.

Triangle — Multiply the base by the height and divide by 2.

To find the VOLUME of a:

Cone — Multiply the square of the radius of the base by 3.1416, multiply by the height, and divide by 3.

Cube — Cube the length of one edge.

Cylinder — Multiply the square of the radius of the base by 3.1416 and multiply by the height.

Pyramid — Multiply the area of the base by the height and divide by 3.

Rectangular Prism — Multiply the length by the width by the height.

Sphere — Multiply the cube of the radius by 3.1416, multiply by 4 and divide by 3.

Playing Cards and Dice Chances

Poker Hands

Hand	Number possible	Odds against
Royal flush	4	649,739 to 1
Other straight flush	36	72,192 to 1
Four of a kind	624	4,164 to 1
Full house	3,744	693 to 1
Flush	5,108	508 to 1
Straight	10,200	254 to 1
Three of a kind	54,912	46 to 1
Two pairs	123,552	20 to 1
One pair	1,098,240	4 to 3 (1.37 to 1)
Nothing	1,302,540	1 to 1
Total	**2,598,960**	

Dice
(probabilities on 2 dice)

Total	Odds against (Single toss)	Total	Odds against (Single toss)
2	35 to 1	8	31 to 5
3	17 to 1	9	8 to 1
4	11 to 1	10	11 to 1
5	8 to 1	11	17 to 1
6	31 to 5	12	35 to 1
7	5 to 1		

Dice
(Probabilities of consecutive winning plays)

No. consecutive wins	By 7, 11, or point	No. consecutive wins	By 7, 11 or point
1	244 in 495	6	1 in 70
2	6 in 25	7	1 in 141
3	3 in 25	8	1 in 287
4	1 in 17	9	1 in 582
5	1 in 34		

Pinochle Auction
(Odds against finding in "widow" of 3 cards)

Open places	Odds against	Open places	Odds against
1	5 to 1	4	3 to 2 for
2	2 to 1	5	2 to 1 for
3	Even		

Bridge

The odds—against suit distribution in a hand of 4-4-3-2 are about 4 to 1, against 5-4-2-2 about 8 to 1, against 6-4-2-1 about 20 to 1, against 7-4-1-1 about 254 to 1, against 8-4-1-0 about 2,211 to 1, and against 13-0-0-0 about 158,753,389,899 to 1.

Measures of Force and Pressure

Dyne = force necessary to accelerate a 1-gram mass 1 centimeter per second squared = 0.000072 poundal

Poundal = force necessary to accelerate a 1-pound mass 1 foot per second squared = 13,825.5 dynes = 0.138255 newtons

Newton = force needed to accelerate a 1-kilogram mass 1 meter per second squared

Pascal (pressure) = 1 newton per square meter = 0.020885 pound per square foot

Atmosphere (air pressure at sea level) = 2,116.102 pounds per square foot = 14.6952 pounds per square inch = 1.0332 kilograms per square centimeter = 101,323 newtons per square meter.

Large Numbers

U.S.	Number of zeros	French British, German	U.S.	Number of zeros	French British, German
million	6	million	sextillion	21	1,000 trillion
billion	9	milliard	septillion	24	quadrillion
trillion	12	billion	octillion	27	1,000 quadrillion
quadrillion	15	1,000 billion	nonillion	30	quintillion
quintillion	18	trillion	decillion	33	1,000 quintillion

Roman Numerals

I	–	1	VI	–	6	XI	–	11	L	–	50	CD	–	400	$\overline{X}$	–	10,000
II	–	2	VII	–	7	XIX	–	19	LX	–	60	D	–	500	$\overline{L}$	–	50,000
III	–	3	VIII	–	8	XX	–	20	XC	–	90	CM	–	900	$\overline{C}$	–	100,000
IV	–	4	IX	–	9	XXX	–	30	C	–	100	M	–	1,000	$\overline{D}$	–	500,000
V	–	5	X	–	10	XL	–	40	CC	–	200	$\overline{V}$	–	5,000	$\overline{M}$	–	1,000,000

ARTS AND MEDIA

Notable Movies of the Year (Sept. 1992 to Aug. 1993)

Movie	Stars	Director
A Few Good Men	Tom Cruise, Jack Nicholson, Demi Moore, Kevin Bacon	Rob Reiner
Aladdin	Robin Williams, Jonathan Freeman, Gilbert Gottfried	John Musker, Ron Clements
Benny and Joon	Johnny Depp, Mary Stuart Masterson, Aiden Quinn	Jeremiah Chechik
Bob Roberts	Tim Robbins, Giancarlo Esposito, Gore Vidal	Tim Robbins
Bram Stoker's Dracula	Gary Oldman, Winona Ryder, Anthony Hopkins	Francis Ford Coppola
Chaplin	Robert Downey, Jr., Dan Aykroyd, Anthony Hopkins	Richard Attenborough
Cliffhanger	Sylvester Stallone, John Lithgow, Janine Turner	Renny Harlin
Dave	Kevin Kline, Sigourney Weaver	Ivan Reitman
Damage	Jeremy Irons, Juliette Binoche, Miranda Richardson	Louis Malle
Dennis the Menace	Walter Matthau, Mason Gamble, Christopher Lloyd	Nick Castle
Falling Down	Michael Douglas, Robert Duvall, Barbara Hershey	Joel Schumacher
Glengarry Glen Ross	Al Pacino, Jack Lemmon, Ed Harris, Alec Baldwin	James Foley
Groundhog Day	Bill Murray, Andie McDowell	Harold Ramis
Hero	Dustin Hoffman, Geena Davis, Andy Garcia	Stephen Frears
Hoffa	Jack Nicholson, Danny DeVito, Armand Assante	Danny DeVito
Home Alone 2	Macaulay Culkin, Joe Pesci, Daniel Stern	John Hughes
Honeymoon in Vegas	James Caan, Nicolas Cage, Sarah Jessica Parker	Andrew Bergman
Hot Shots! Part Deux	Charlie Sheen, Lloyd Bridges, Valeria Golina	Jim Abrahams
Husbands and Wives	Woody Allen, Mia Farrow, Judy Davis, Blythe Danner	Woody Allen
Indecent Proposal	Robert Redford, Demi Moore, Woody Harrelson	Adrian Lyne
In the Line of Fire	Clint Eastwood, John Malkovich, Rene Russo	Wolfgang Peterson
Jurassic Park	Sam Neill, Laura Dern, Jeff Goldblum	Steven Spielberg
Last Action Hero	Arnold Schwarzenegger, Austin O'Brien	John McTiernan
Lorenzo's Oil	Susan Sarandon, Nick Nolte	George Miller
Lost in Yonkers	Richard Dreyfuss, Mercedes Ruehl, Irene Worth	Martha Coolidge
Mad Dog and Glory	Robert De Niro, Uma Thurman, Bill Murray	John NcNaughton
Made in America	Whoopi Goldberg, Ted Danson	Richard Benjamin
Malcolm X	Denzel Washington, Angela Bassett, Al Freeman, Jr.	Spike Lee
Map of the Human Heart	Patrick Bergin, Ann Parillaud	Vincent Ward
Matinee	John Goodman, Cathy Moriarty	Joe Dante
Mr. Saturday Night	Billy Crystal, David Paymer	Billy Crystal
Much Ado About Nothing	Kenneth Branagh, Emma Thompson, Michael Keaton	Kenneth Branagh
Night and the City	Robert De Niro, Jessica Lange	Irwin Winkler
Of Mice and Men	Gary Sinise, John Malkovich, Sherilyn Fenn	Gary Sinise
Passion Fish	Mary McDonnell, Alfre Woodard	John Sayles
Point of No Return	Bridget Fonda, Gabriel Byrne, Harvey Keitel	John Badham
Posse	Mario Van Peebles, Charles Lane, Big Daddy Kane	Mario Van Peebles
Rising Sun	Sean Connery, Wesley Snipes	Philip Kaufman
Scent of a Woman	Al Pacino, Chris O'Donnell	Martin Brest
Sliver	Sharon Stone, William Baldwin, Tom Berenger	Phillip Noyce
Sniper	Tom Berenger, Billy Zane	Luis Llosa
Sleepless in Seattle	Tom Hanks, Meg Ryan	Nora Ephron
The Bodyguard	Kevin Costner, Whitney Houston	Mike Jackson
The Crying Game	Stephen Rea, Miranda Richardson, Jaye Davidson	Neil Jordan
The Firm	Tom Cruise, Ed Harris, Holly Hunter, Hal Holbrook	Sidney Pollack
The Fugitive	Harrison Ford, Tommy Lee Jones	Andrew Davis
The Last of the Mohicans	Daniel Day-Lewis, Madeleine Stowe	Michael Mann
Under Siege	Steven Seagal, Tommy Lee Jones, Gary Busey	Andrew Davis
Unforgiven	Clint Eastwood, Gene Hackman, Morgan Freeman	Clint Eastwood
What's Love Got to Do With It?	Angela Bassett, Laurence Fishburne	Brian Gibson

Notable New York Theater Openings, 1992-1993 Season

Ain't Broadway Grand, musical by Mitch Leigh and Lee Adams about showman Mike Todd; with Mike Burstyn.

Angels in America: Millennium Approaches, play by Tony Kushner; with Ron Leibman, Joe Mantello, and Stephen Spinella.

Anna Christie, revival of the 1922 Eugene O'Neill drama; with Natasha Richardson, Liam Neeson, Rip Torn, and Anne Meara.

Blood Brothers, musical by Willy Russell; with Stephanie Lawrence, Barbara Walsh, and Warwick Evans.

Camelot, revival of the Alan Jay Lerner and Frederick Loewe 1960 musical; with Robert Goulet.

Fool Moon, an evening of clowning with Bill Irwin and David Shiner.

Kiss of the Spider Woman, musical by John Kander and Fred Ebb based on Manuel Puig's novel; with Chita Rivera, Brent Carver, and Anthony Crivello.

Putting It Together, revue based on the music and lyrics of Stephen Sondheim; with Julie Andrews and Stephen Collins.

Redwood Curtain, play by Lanford Wilson; with Jeff Daniels, Sung Yun Cho, and Debra Monk.

Saint Joan, revival of the George Bernard Shaw classic; with Maryann Plunkett, Nicholas Kepros, and Remak Ramsay.

Shakespeare for My Father, reminiscences conceived and written by Lynn Redgrave; with Lynn Redgrave.

Someone to Watch Over Me, drama by Frank McGuinness; with Stephen Rea, Alec McCowen, and James McDaniel.

The Goodbye Girl, musical by Marvin Hamlisch and David Zippel based on Neil Simon's play; with Bernadette Peters and Martin Short.

The Last Yankee, play by Arthur Miller; with John Heard, Frances Conroy, and Tom Aldredge.

The Seagull, revival of the Chekhov classic; with Tyne Daly, Jon Voight, Tony Roberts, Ethan Hawke, and Maryann Plunkett.

The Show-Off, revival of George Kelly's 1924 play; with Sophie Hayden and Pat Carroll.

The Sisters Rosensweig, drama by Wendy Wasserstein; with Jane Alexander, Frances McDormand, Robert Klein, and Madeline Kahn.

The Song of Jacob Zula, play by Tug Yourgrau; with K. Todd Freeman, Danny Johnson, and Zakes Mokae.

Three Men on a Horse, revival of the John Cecil Holm and George Abbott comedy; with Tony Randall, Jack Klugman, Julie Hagerty, Jerry Stiller, and Ellen Greene.

Tommy, revival of the 1969 Peter Townsend rock opera; with Michael Cerveris, Marcia Mitzman, and Paul Kandel.

Wrong Turn at Lungfish, comedy by Garry Marshall; with George C. Scott, Jami Gertz, and Tony Danza.

Record Long Run Broadway Plays[1]

Source: *Variety*

Play	Performances
Chorus Line	6,137
Oh, Calcutta (revival)	5,959
*Cats	4,485
42d Street	3,486
Grease	3,388
Fiddler on the Roof	3,242
Life With Father	3,224
Tobacco Road	3,182
Hello Dolly	2,844
My Fair Lady	2,717
*Les Miserables	2,572
Annie	2,377
Man of La Mancha	2,328
Abie's Irish Rose	2,327
*Phantom of the Opera	2,271
Oklahoma!	2,212
Pippin	1,944
South Pacific	1,925
Magic Show	1,920
Deathtrap	1,792
Gemini	1,788
Harvey	1,775
Dancin'	1,774
La Cage aux Folles	1,761
Hair	1,750
The Wiz	1,672
Born Yesterday	1,642
Ain't Misbehavin'	1,604
Best Little Whorehouse in Texas	1,584
Mary, Mary	1,572
Evita	1,567
Voice of the Turtle	1,557
Barefoot in the Park	1,530
Dreamgirls	1,521
Mame	1,508
Same Time, Next Year	1,453
Arsenic and Old Lace	1,444
The Sound of Music	1,443
How To Succeed in Business Without Really Trying	1,417
Me and My Girl	1,412
Hellzapoppin	1,404
The Music Man	1,375
Funny Girl	1,348
Mumenschanz	1,326
Oh! Calcutta! (original)	1,314
Brighton Beach Memoirs	1,299
Angel Street	1,295
Lightnin'	1,291
Promises, Promises	1,281
The King and I	1,246
Cactus Flower	1,234
Sleuth	1,222
Torch Song Trilogy	1,222
"1776"	1,217
Equus	1,209
Sugar Babies	1,208
Guys and Dolls	1,200
Amadeus	1,181
Cabaret	1,165
Mister Roberts	1,157
Annie Get Your Gun	1,147
Seven Year Itch	1,141
Butterflies Are Free	1,128

(1) Number of performances through July 4, 1993. * Still running July 4, 1993.

All-Time Top 50 American Movies

Source: *Variety*, Jan. 1993

Rental figures are in absolute dollars, reflecting actual amounts received by the distributors (estimated for movies in current release). Ticket price inflation favors recent films, but older films have the advantage of numerous reissues.

Rank/Title/Date	Rentals (millions)
1. E.T. The Extra-Terrestrial (1982)	$228.6
2. Star Wars* (1977)	193.8
3. Return of the Jedi* (1983)	169.2
4. Batman (1989)	150.5
5. The Empire Strikes Back* (1980)	141.7
6. Home Alone* (1990)	140.1
7. Ghostbusters (1984)	132.7
8. Jaws (1975)	129.5
9. Raiders of the Lost Ark (1981)	115.6
10. Indiana Jones and the Last Crusade (1989)	115.5
11. Terminator 2* (1991)	112.0
12. Indiana Jones and the Temple Of Doom (1984)	109.0
13. Beverly Hills Cop (1984)	108.0
14. Back to the Future (1985)	105.5
15. **Home Alone 2** (1992)	102.0
16. **Batman Returns** (1992)	100.1
17. Ghost (1990)	98.2
18. Grease (1978)	96.3
19. Tootsie (1982)	$94.9
20. The Exorcist (1973)	89.0
21. Rain Man (1989)	86.8
22. The Godfather (1972)	86.3
23. Robin Hood: Prince of Thieves (1991)	86.0
24. Superman (1978)	82.8
24. Close Encounters of the Third Kind (1977/1980)	82.8
26. Pretty Woman* (1990)	81.9
27. Dances with Wolves (1990)	81.5
28. Three Men and a Baby (1987)	81.4
29. Who Framed Roger Rabbit (1988)	81.2
30. Beverly Hills Cop II (1987)	80.9
31. **Lethal Weapon 3** (1992)	80.0
32. The Sound of Music* (1965)	79.9
33. Gremlins (1984)	79.5
33. Lethal Weapon 2 (1989)	79.5
35. Top Gun (1986)	79.4
35. Gone With the Wind (1939)	$79.4
37. Rambo: First Blood Part II (1985)	78.9
38. The Sting (1973)	78.2
39. Rocky IV (1985)	76.0
40. Saturday Night Fever (1977)	74.1
41. Back to the Future, Part II (1989)	72.3
42. Honey, I Shrunk the Kids (1989)	72.0
43. National Lampoon's Animal House (1978)	70.8
44. Crocodile Dundee (1986)	70.2
45. Fatal Attraction (1987)	70.0
46. Platoon (1986)	69.9
47. **Beauty and the Beast** (1991)	69.4
48. Look Who's Talking (1989)	68.9
49. 101 Dalmatians (1961)	68.7
50. Teenage Mutant Ninja Turtles (1990)	67.7

Note: Boldface print = film new to list or significant improvement since previous year; * rentals adjusted since last report.

Top 50 Movies, 1992

Source: *Variety*, Jan. 1993

Figures represent U.S. and Canadian rentals accruing to distributors, not total ticket sales receipts taken in at theaters.

Rank/Title/Month Released	Rentals (millions)
1. Home Alone 2; Nov.	$102.0
2. Batman Returns; June	100.1
3. Lethal Weapon 3; May	80.0
4. Sister Act; May	62.4
5. Aladdin; Nov.	60.0
6. Wayne's World; Feb.	54.0
7. A League of Their Own; July	53.1
8. Basic Instinct; March	53.0
9. The Bodyguard; Nov.	52.9
10. A Few Good Men; Dec.	52.0
11. Bram Stoker's Dracula; Nov.	47.2
12. The Hand That Rocks the Cradle; Jan.	39.3
13. Patriot Games; June	37.5
14. Fried Green Tomatoes; Dec. 1991	37.4
15. Unforgiven; Aug.	36.0
16. White Men Can't Jump; March	34.1
17. Boomerang; July	34.0
18. Under Seige; Oct.	$33.0
19. Alien 3; May	31.8
20. The Last of the Mohicans; Sept.	31.5
21. Death Becomes Her; July	30.4
21. Beauty and the Beast; continuing	30.4
21. Housesitter; June	30.4
24. Far and Away; May	28.9
25. Honey, I Blew Up the Kid; July	27.4
26. Beethoven; April	26.5
27. Unlawful Entry; June	26.4
28. My Cousin Vinny; March	25.6
29. Malcolm X; Nov.	25.0
29. Hook; continuing	25.0
30. Father of the Bride; continuing	24.0
32. Sneakers; Sept.	23.4
33. Single White Female; Aug.	21.1
33. The Prince of Tides; continuing	21.1
35. Medicine Man; Feb.	$20.9
36. Forever Young; Dec.	20.0
36. The Mighty Ducks; Oct.	20.0
36. JFK; continuing	20.0
39. Mo' Money; July	19.2
40. The Distinguished Gentleman; Dec.	19.0
41. Passenger 57; Nov.	18.0
42. Encino Man; May	17.6
43. Honeymoon in Vegas; Aug.	16.1
44. Universal Soldier; July	16.0
45. A River Runs Through It; Oct.	15.6
46. Grand Canyon; Dec. 91.	15.1
47. The Lawnmower Man; March	13.6
48. Sleepwalkers; April	13.2
49. Final Analysis; Feb.	12.7
49. Stop! or My Mom Will Shoot; Feb.	12.7

National Film Registry

"Culturally, historically, or esthetically significant" films placed on the National Film Registry, Library of Congress.

Films Chosen in 1989
The Best Years of Our Lives (1946)
Casablanca (1942)
Citizen Kane (1941)
The Crowd (1928)
Dr. Strangelove (or, How I Learned to Stop Worrying and Love the Bomb) (1964)
The General (1927)
Gone With the Wind (1939)
The Grapes of Wrath (1940)
High Noon (1952)
Intolerance (1916)
The Learning Tree (1969)
The Maltese Falcon (1941)
Mr. Smith Goes to Washington (1939)
Modern Times (1936)
Nanook of the North (1921)
On the Waterfront (1954)
The Searchers (1956)
Singin' in the Rain (1952)
Snow White and the Seven Dwarfs (1937)
Some Like It Hot (1959)
Star Wars (1977)
Sunrise (1927)
Sunset Boulevard (1950)
Vertigo (1958)
The Wizard of Oz (1939)

Films Chosen in 1990
All About Eve (1950)
All Quiet on the Western Front (1930)
Bringing Up Baby (1938)
Dodsworth (1936)
Duck Soup (1933)
Fantasia (1940)
The Freshman (1925)
The Godfather (1972)
The Great Train Robbery (1903)
Harlan County, U. S. A. (1976)
How Green Was My Valley (1941)
It's a Wonderful Life (1946)
Killer of Sheep (1977)
Love Me Tonight (1932)
Meshes of the Afternoon (1943)
Ninotchka (1939)
Primary (1960)
Raging Bull (1980)
Rebel Without a Cause (1955)
Red River (1948)
The River (1937)
Sullivan's Travels (1941)
Top Hat (1935)
The Treasure of the Sierra Madre (1948)
A Woman under the Influence (1974)

Films Chosen in 1991
The Battle of San Pietro (1945)
The Blood of Jesus (1941)
Chinatown (1974)
City Lights (1931)
David Holzman's Diary (1968)
Frankenstein (1931)
Gertie the Dinosaur (1914)
Gigi (1958)
Greed (1924)
High School (1968)
I Am a Fugitive from a Chain Gang (1932)
The Italian (1915)
King Kong (1933)
Lawrence of Arabia (1962)
The Magnificent Ambersons (1942)
My Darling Clementine (1946)
Out of the Past (1947)
A Place in the Sun (1951)
The Poor Little Rich Girl (1917)
The Prisoner of Zenda (1937)
Shadow of a Doubt (1943)
Sherlock, Jr. (1924)
Tevya (1939)
Trouble in Paradise (1932)
2001: A Space Odyssey (1968)

Films Chosen in 1992
Adam's Rib (1949)
Annie Hall (1977)
The Bank Dick (1940)
Big Business (1929)
The Big Parade (1925)
The Birth of a Nation (1915)
Bonnie and Clyde (1967)
Carmen Jones (1954)
Castro Street (1966)
Detour (1946)
Dog Star Man (1964)
Double Indemnity (1944)
Footlight Parade (1933)
The Gold Rush (1925)
Letter from an Unknown Woman (1948)
Morocco (1930)
Nashville (1975)
The Night of the Hunter (1955)
Paths of Glory (1957)
Psycho (1960)
Ride the High Country (1962)
Salesman (1969)
Salt of the Earth (1954)
What's Opera, Doc? (1957)
Within Our Gates (1920)

Most Popular Movie Videos, 1992

Source: Alexander & Associates/Video Flash

Top 10 Rentals
1. Terminator 2
2. Home Alone
3. The Silence of the Lambs
4. The Boyz N the Hood
5. The Hand That Rocks the Cradle
6. City Slickers
7. Robin Hood: Prince of Thieves
8. Thelma and Louise
9. Cape Fear
10. 101 Dalmatians

Top 10 Sales
1. Beauty and the Beast
2. 101 Dalmatians
3. Dances with Wolves
4. Fantasia
5. Hook
6. Sister Act
7. Home Alone
8. Robin Hood: Prince of Thieves
9. The Great Mouse Detective
10. Rescuers Down Under

Notable Books of 1992

Source: American Library Association

Fiction

Leviathan, Paul Auster
Before and After, Rosellen Brown
A Good Scent from a Strange Mountain, Robert Olen Butler
The Brothers K., David James Duncan
Turtle Moon, Alice Hoffman
Let the Dead Bury Their Dead and Other Stories, Randall Kenan
Billie Dyer and Other Stories, William Maxwell
All the Pretty Horses, Cormac McCarthy
Small Spaces Between Emergencies, Alison Moore
Jazz, Toni Morrison
Bailey's Cafe, Gloria Naylor
The English Patient, Michael Ondaatje
The Patron Saint of Liars, Ann Patchett
A Thousand Acres, Jane Smiley

Poetry

Judeville: The Complete Poems, 1970-1990, David Budbill
Moon Crossing Bridge, Tess Gallagher

Nonfiction

Eleanor Roosevelt, Blanche Wiesen Cook
The Meadow, James Galvin
Who Will Tell the People, William B. Greider
Young Men and Fire, Norman MacLean
Truman, David McCullough
Talking to High Monks in the Snow, Lydia Yuri Minatoya
Becoming a Man, Paul Monette
Technopoly, Neil Postman
Down from Troy: Richard Selzer
Going Back to Bisbee, Richard Shelton
Lincoln at Gettysburg: Garry Wills

Bestselling Books of 1992

Source: *Publishers Weekly*, Mar. 1, 1993. Rankings are determined by sales figures provided by publishers; numbers generally reflect reports of copies "shipped and billed" in 1992 but not final net sales.

Hardcover Fiction

1. *Dolores Claiborne*, Stephen King
2. *The Pelican Brief*, John Grisham
3. *Gerald's Game*, Stephen King
4. *Mixed Blessings*, Danielle Steel
5. *Jewels*, Danielle Steel
6. *The Stars Shine Down*, Sidney Sheldon
7. *Tale of the Body Thief*, Anne Rice
8. *Mexico*, James A. Michener
9. *Waiting to Exhale*, Terry McMillan
10. *All Around the Town*, Mary Higgins Clark
11. *Scruples Two*, Judith Krantz
12. *Sahara*, Clive Cussler
13. *Hideaway*, Dean R. Koontz
14. *The Road to Omaha*, Robert Ludlum
15. *Star Wars: Dark Force Rising*, Timothy Zahn

Hardcover Nonfiction

1. *The Way Things Ought to Be*, Rush Limbaugh
2. *It Doesn't Take a Hero*, H. Norman Schwarzkopf
3. *How to Satisfy a Woman Every Time*, Naura Hayden
4. *Every Living Thing*, James Herriot
5. *A Return to Love*, Marianne Williamson
6. *Sam Walton*, Sam Walton
7. *Diana*, Andrew Morton
8. *Truman*, David McCullough
9. *Silent Passage*, Gail Sheehy
10. *Sex*, Madonna
11. *The Juiceman's Power of Juicing*, Ray Kordich
12. *Harvey Penick's Little Red Book*, Harvey Penick
13. *More Wealth Without Risk*, Charles Givens
14. *I Can't Believe I Said That*, Kathie Lee Gifford
15. *Creating Love*, John Bradshaw

Trade Paperback

1. *Life's Little Instruction Book*, H. Jackson Brown, Jr.
2. *Forever in Your Embrace*, Kathleen Woodiwiss
3. *Live and Learn and Pass It On*, H. Jackson Brown, Jr.
4. *The T-Factor Fat Gram Counter*, Dr. Martin Katahn and Jamie Pope-Cordle
5. *Attack of the Deranged Mutant Killer Monster Snow Goons*, Bill Watterson
6. *The Indispensable Calvin and Hobbes*, Bill Watterson
7. *Mrs. Fields Cookie Book*, Debbie Fields and the editors of Time-Life Books
8. *Cows of Our Planet*, Gary Larson
9. *Prophet*, Frank Peretti
10. *Juicing for Life*, Cherie Clabom and Maureen Keane
11. *The Complete & Up-to-Date Fat Book*, Karen J. Bellerson
12. *Daisy Faye and the Miracle Man*, Fannie Flagg
13. *You Just Don't Understand*, Deborah Tannen
14. *America: What Went Wrong*, Donald L. Barlett and James B. Steele
15. *Don't Know Much About History*, Kenneth Davis

Mass-Market Paperback

1. *The Firm*, John Grisham
2. *The Silence of the Lambs*, Thomas Harris
3. *A Time to Kill*, John Grisham
4. *Scarlett*, Alexandra Ripley
5. *Heartbeat*, Danielle Steel
6. *Message from Nam*, Danielle Steel
7. *The Sum of All Fears*, Tom Clancy
8. *Four Past Midnight*, Stephen King
9. *Needful Things*, Stephen King
10. *No Greater Love*, Danielle Steel
11. *Secrets of the Morning*, V. C. Andrews
12. *September*, Rosamunde Pilcher
13. *Jurassic Park*, Michael Crichton
14. *Stand*, Stephen King
15. *Loves Music, Loves to Dance*, Mary Higgins Clark

Almanacs, Atlases, and Annuals

1. *The World Almanac and Book of Facts, 1993*, ed. Mark Hoffman
2. *The World Almanac and Book of Facts, 1992*, ed. Mark Hoffman
3. *J.K. Lasser's Your Income Tax, 1993*
4. *1993 Information Please Almanac*, ed. Otto Johnson
5. *The Ernst & Young Tax Guide 1992*, ed. Peter Bernstein

Notable Children's Books of 1992

Source: American Library Association

All Ages

Red Dragonfly on My Shoulder, Sylvia Cassedy, illus. Molly Bang
The World in 1492; Jean Fritz and others, illus. Stefano Vitale
Gonna Sing My Head Off! ed. Kathleen Krull, illus. Allen Garns
I Saw Esau, ed. Iona Opie and Peter Opie, illus. Maurice Sendak
Charlie Parker Played Be Bop, Chris Raschka
An Angel for Solomon Singer, Cynthia Rylant, ed. Peter Catalanatto
The Stinky Cheese Man and Other Fairly Stupid Tales, Jon Scieszka, illus. Lane Smith
Talking with Artists, ed. Pat Cummings
The Widow's Broom, Chris Van Allsburg

Younger Readers

The Fortune-Tellers, Lloyd Alexander, illus. Trina Schart Hyman
Hugh Can Do, Jennifer Armstrong, illus. Kimberley Bulcken Root
Old Black Fly, Jim Aylesworth, illus. Stephen Gammell
Emily, Michael Bedard, illus. Barbara Cooney
Moon Rope, Lois Ehlert, trans. Amy Prince
Lunch, Denise Fleming
My Great-Aunt Arizona, Gloria Houston, illus. Susan Condie Lamb
Bently and Egg, William Joyce
Soap Soup and Other Verses, Karla Kuskin
The Moonbow of Mr. B. Bones, J. Patrick Lewis, illus. Dirk Zimmer
Mirette on the High Wire, Emily Arnold McCully
Martha Speaks, Susan Meddaugh
The Life and Times of the Apple, Charles Micucci
Back Home, Gloria Jean Pinkney, illus. Jerry Pinkney
Chicken Sunday, illus. Patricia Polacco
Don't You Know There's a War On? James Stevenson
Talking Like the Rain, ed. X. J. Kennedy and Dorothy M. Kennedy, illus. Jane Dyer
Farmer Duck, Martin Waddell, illus. Helen Oxenbury
June 29, 1999, Davis Wiesner
Working Cotton, Sherley Anne Williams, illus. Carole Byard
Letting a Swift River Go, Jane Yoken, illus. Barbara Cooney
Seven Blind Mice, Ed Young

Middle-Grade Readers

"Who Was That Masked Man, Anyway?", Avi
Wings Along the Waterway, Mary Barrett Brown
The Moon and I, Betsy Byars
Loop the Loop, Barbara Dugan, illus. James Stevenson
Who Shrank My Grandmother's House? Barbara Esbensen, illus. Eric Beddows
Li'l Sis and Uncle Willie, Gwen Everett
Jim Ugly, Sid Fleischman, illus. Jos. A. Smith
Love Flute, Paul Goble
Words of Stone, Kevin Henkes
Surtsey, Kathryn Lasky, photos Christopher C. Knight
Underrunners, Margaret Mahy
The Dark-Thirty, Patricia McKissack, illus. Brian Pinkney
The Amazing Potato, Milton Meltzer
All but Alice, Phyllis Reynolds Naylor
Life's a Funny Proposition, Horatio, Barbara Garland Polikoff
Antarctica, Laurence Pringle
Sukey and the Mermaid, Robert D. San Souci, illus. Brian Pinkney

Junior High School-Age Readers

Steal Away, Jennifer Armstrong
What's Your Story? Marion Dane Bauer
No Place to Be, Judith Berck
Ajeemah and His Son, James Berry
What Hearts, Bruce Brooks
An Indian Winter, Russell Freedman, illus. Karl Bodmer
A Twilight Struggle, Barbara Harrison and Daniel Terris
Letters from Rifka, Karen Hesse
Against the Storm, Gaye Hicyilmaz
The Harmony Arms, Ron Koertge
Letters from a Slave Girl, Mary E. Lyons
Sojourner Truth, Patricia McKissack and Frederick McKissack
Somewhere in the Darkness, Walter Dean Myers
The Beggar's Ride, Theresa Nelson
Rosa Parks, Rosa Parks and Jim Haskins
Missing May, Cynthia Rylant
Children of the Dust Bowl, Jerry Stanley
When the Road Ends, Jean Thesman
The Same Sky, ed. Naomi Shihab Nye
The Leaving, Budge Wilson
The Pigman and Me, Paul Zindel

Young Adults (Teenagers)—Fiction

Steal Away, Jennifer Armstrong
What You Don't Know Can Kill You, Fran Arrick
Blue Heron, Avi
Ajeemah and His Son, James Berry
Cherokee Bat and the Goat Guys, Francesca Lia Block
Lily, Cindy Bonner
What Hearts, Bruce Brooks
Two Moons in August, Martha Brooks
Jumping the Nail, Eve Bunting
The Place of Lions, Eric Campbell
My Father, the Nutcase, Judith Casely
Flight #116 Is Down, Caroline B. Cooney
The Sleep of Stone, Louise Cooper
Tunes for Bears to Dance To, Robert Cormier
Gone, Kit Craig
If Rock and Roll Were a Machine, Terry Davis
AK, Peter Dickinson
Dear Nobody, Berlie Doherty
Binge, Charles Ferry
Becca's Story, James D. Forman
Song of the Buffalo Boy, Sherry Garland
Jumper, Steven Gould
The Pelican Brief, John Grisham
Dinotopia: A Land Apart from Time, James Gurney
The Music of Summer, Rosa Guy
Fool's Hill, Barbara Hall
Letters from Rifka, Karen Hesse
The Big Wander, Will Hobbs
Turtle Moon, Alice Hoffman
Acquaintance with the Night, Sollace Holtze
One of the Boys, Scott Johnson
A Sudden Wild Magic, Diana Wynne Jones
Someone Else's Baby, Geraldine Kaye
Crossing Blood, Nanci Kincaid
The Harmony Arms, Ron Koertge
The Primrose Way, Jackie French Koller
Bardic Voices: The Lark and the Wren, Mercedes Lackey
Kiss the Dust, Elizabeth Laird
Letters from a Slave Girl, Mary E. Lyons
Not a Swan, Michelle Magorian
When the Broken Heart Still Beats, Carolyn Meyer
Way Past Cool, Jess Mowry
The Righteous Revenge of Artemis Bonner, Walter Dean Myers
Somewhere in the Darkness, Walter Dean Myers
The Beggar's Ride, Theresa Nelson
The Haymeadow, Gary Paulsen
Family of Strangers, Susan Beth Pfeffer
Is Kissing a Girl Who Smokes Like Licking an Ashtray? Randy Powell
A Little Bit Dead, Chap Reaver
Time Windows, Kathryn Reiss
The Last Pendragon, Robert Rice
A Break with Charity, Ann Rinaldi
Missing May, Cynthia Rylant
Blue Skin of the Sea, Graham Salisbury
The Stinky Cheese Man and Other Fairly Stupid Tales, Jon Scieszka
Child of Faerie, Child of Earth, Joseph Sherman
River Rats, Carolyn Stevermer
Crosses, Shelley Stoehr
The Weirdo, Theodore Taylor
When the Road Ends, Jean Thesman
Plague, Jean Ure
Stormsearch, Robert Westall
Yaxley's Cat, Robert Westall
Weeping Willow, Ruth White
Bad Boy, Diana Wieler
Crocodile Burning, Michael Williams
The Leaving, Budge Wilson
Lockie Leonard, Human Torpedo, Tim Winton
Maizon at Blue Gill, Jacqueline Woodson
Searching for Dragons, Patricia C. Wrede
Briar Rose, Jane Yolen
A Plague of Sorcerers, Mary Frances Zambreno

Top 100 Daily Newspapers in the U.S.

Source: *1993 Editor & Publisher International Yearbook*
(circulation as of Sept. 30, 1992; m=morning, e=evening)

In 1992, another year of sluggish economic growth brought the discontinuation or merging of 26 daily newspapers. The addition of 10 new dailies during the year brought the total number of daily newspapers published in the U.S. as of Feb. 1, 1993, to 1,570, a loss of 16 when compared with the same date in 1992. There was also a circulation drop of 522,626, when comparing the average daily circulation for the 6-month period ending Sept. 30, 1992, with the average for the same period in 1991, from 60,687,125 to 60,164,499. The trend toward morning distribution that began in the mid-1970s continued, 26 evening dailies switching to morning distribution, to bring the total number of morning papers up to 596 over 1991's count of 571, while the number of evening papers dropped from 1,042 to 996. Another trend continued: the number of daily newspapers publishing Sunday editions increased from 875 to 891; total Sunday circulation increased from 62,067,820 to 62,159,971.

	Newspaper		Circulation
1.	*Wall Street Journal* (New York, NY)	(m)	1,795,206
2.	*USA Today* (Arlington, VA)	(m)	1,506,708
3.	*Times* (Los Angeles, CA)	(m)	1,146,631
4.	*Times* (New York, NY)	(m)	1,145,890
5.	*Post* (Washington, DC)	(m)	802,057
6.	*Daily News* (New York, NY)	(m)	777,129
7.	*Newsday* (Long Island/New York, NY)	(all day)	758,358
8.	*Tribune* (Chicago, IL)	(m)	724,257
9.	*Free Press* (Detroit, MI)	(m)	580,372
10.	*Chronicle* (San Francisco, CA)	(m)	556,765
11.	*Sun-Times* (Chicago, IL)	(m)	528,324
12.	*Globe* (Boston, MA)	(m)	508,867
13.	*Inquirer* (Philadelphia, PA)	(m)	502,149
14.	*Star-Ledger* (Newark, NJ)	(m)	481,027
15.	*Morning News* (Dallas, TX)	(m)	479,215
16.	*Post* (New York, NY)	(m)	437,962
17.	*Chronical* (Houston, TX)	(all day)	419,759
18.	*Star Tribune* (Minneapolis, MN)	(m)	410,920
19.	*Plain Dealer* (Cleveland, OH)	(m)	410,237
20.	*Herald* (Miami, FL)	(m)	404,679
21.	*News* (Detroit, MI)	(e)	398,630
22.	*Union-Tribune* (San Diego, CA)	(all day)	373,453
23.	*Times* (St. Petersburg, FL)	(m)	358,051
24.	*Rocky Mountain News* (Denver, CO)	(m)	356,577
25.	*Arizona Republic* (Phoenix, AZ)	(m)	342,341
26.	*Post-Dispatch* (St. Louis, MO)	(m)	339,545
27.	*Oregonian* (Portland, OR)	(all day)	336,087
28.	*Register* (Orange County, CA)	(all day)	332,164
29.	*Herald* (Boston, MA)	(m)	330,614
30.	*News* (Buffalo, NY)	(all day)	305,482
31.	*Constitution* (Atlanta, GA)	(m)	302,616
32.	*Post* (Houston, TX)	(m)	300,121
33.	*Tribune* (Tampa, FL)	(m)	295,436
34.	*Star* (Kansas City, MO)	(m)	287,119
35.	*Sentinel* (Orlando, FL)	(all day)	285,172
36.	*Mercury News* (San Jose, CA)	(all day)	270,174
37.	*Times-Picayune* (New Orleans, LA)	(all day)	269,639
38.	*Post* (Denver, CO)	(m)	269,020
39.	*Dispatch* (Columbus, OH)	(m)	264,601
40.	*Bee* (Sacramento, CA)	(m)	264,259
41.	*Star-Telegram* (Fort Worth, TX)	(all day)	256,199
42.	*Sun-Sentinel* (Fort Lauderdale, FL)	(m)	252,158
43.	*Times* (Seattle, WA)	(e)	239,476
44.	*Journal* (Milwaukee, WI)	(e)	236,943
45.	*Courier-Journal* (Louisville, KY)	(m)	236,103
46.	*Observer* (Charlotte, NC)	(m)	231,027
47.	*Star* (Indianapolis, IN)	(m)	230,041
48.	*Courant* (Hartford, CT)	(m)	229,284
49.	*Sun* (Baltimore, MD)	(m)	227,706
50.	*Times-Dispatch* (Richmond, VA)	(m)	214,227
51.	*Pioneer Press* (St. Paul, MN)	(m)	212,057
52.	*Daily Oklahoman* (Oklahoma City, OK)	(m)	210,004
53.	*Daily News* (Los Angeles, CA)	(m)	207,421
54.	*Post-Intelligencer* (Seattle, WA)	(m)	207,299
55.	*Enquirer* (Cincinnati, OH)	(m)	199,257
56.	*Journal* (Providence, RI)	(all day)	194,880
57.	*Daily News* (Philadelphia, PA)	(m)	193,192
58.	*Register* (Des Moines, IA)	(m)	191,511
59.	*Times-Union* (Jacksonville, FL)	(m)	180,619
60.	*Daily News* (Dayton, OH)	(m)	179,405
61.	*Palm Beach Post* (West Palm Beach, FL)	(m)	178,412
62.	*Democrat-Gazette* (Little Rock, AR)	(m)	176,741
63.	*Commercial Appeal* (Memphis, TN)	(m)	176,411
64.	*Express-News* (San Antonio, TX)	(all day)	175,611
65.	*American-Statesman* (Austin, TX)	(m)	170,798
66.	*Sentinel* (Milwaukee, WI)	(m)	169,961
67.	*Press* (Asbury Park, NJ)	(e)	164,756
68.	*News* (Birmingham, AL)	(e)	163,380
69.	*Record* (Hackensack, NJ)	(m)	160,086
70.	*Beacon Journal* (Akron, OH)	(m)	158,605
71.	*Journal* (Atlanta, GA)	(e)	156,199
72.	*Virginian-Pilot* (Norfolk, VA)	(m)	155,362
73.	*Post-Gazette* (Pittsburgh, PA)	(m)	155,307
74.	*Press-Enterprise* (Riverside, CA)	(m)	154,790
75.	*Press* (Grand Rapids, MI)	(e)	150,702
76.	*Blade* (Toledo, OH)	(m)	146,334
77.	*Bee* (Fresno, CA)	(m)	146,183
78.	*News & Observer* (Raleigh, NC)	(m)	145,988
79.	*Tennessean* (Nashville, TN)	(m)	139,086
80.	*Democrat and Chronicle* (Rochester, NY)	(m)	137,556
81.	*Morning Call* (Allentown, PA)	(m)	137,108
82.	*The State* (Columbia, SC)	(m)	134,945
83.	*Examiner* (San Francisco, CA)	(e)	134,821
84.	*Review-Journal* (Las Vegas, NV)	(m)	131,769
85.	*World-Herald* (Omaha, NE)	(m)	129,259
86.	*World* (Tulsa, OK)	(m)	127,467
87.	*Morning News Tribune* (Tacoma, WA)	(m)	126,303
88.	*News-Sentinel* (Knoxville, TN)	(m)	125,965
89.	*News Journal* (Wilmington, DE)	(all day)	124,091
90.	*Herald-Leader* (Lexington, KY)	(m)	123,474
91.	*Press-Telegram* (Long Beach, CA)	(m)	122,716
92.	*Herald-Tribune* (Sarasota, FL)	(m)	121,438
93.	*Spokesman-Review* (Spokane, WA)	(m)	120,022
94.	*Daily Herald* (Chicago, IL)	(m)	119,878
95.	*Evening Sun* (Baltimore, MD)	(e)	119,302
96.	*Tribune* (Salt Lake City, UT)	(m)	117,858
97.	*Eagle* (Wichita, KS)	(m)	117,399
98.	*Telegram & Gazette* (Worcester, MA)	(m)	115,129
99.	*Journal* (Albuquerque, NM)	(m)	115,094
100.	*Times & World-News* (Roanoke, VA)	(m)	114,872

100 Bestselling U.S. Magazines

Source: Audit Bureau of Circulations, Schaumburg, Ill.

General magazines, exclusive of groups and comics; also exclusive of magazines that failed to file reports to ABC by press time. Based on total average paid circulation during the 6 months prior to Dec. 31, 1992.

Magazine	Circulation
1. Modern Maturity	22,879,886
2. NRTA/AARP Bulletin	22,746,026
3. Reader's Digest	16,258,476
4. TV Guide	14,498,341
5. National Geographic	9,708,254
6. Better Homes & Gardens	8,002,585
7. Family Circle	5,283,660
8. Good Housekeeping	5,139,355
9. Ladies Home Journal	5,041,143
10. Woman's Day	4,810,445
11. McCall's	4,704,772
12. Time	4,203,991
13. People	3,506,816
14. Sports Ilustrated	3,432,044
15. Playboy	3,402,630
16. National Enquirer	3,401,263
17. Redbook	3,395,029
18. Newsweek	3,240,131
19. Prevention	3,234,901
20. AAA World	3,107,468
21. American Legion	2,953,941
22. Star	2,931,305
23. Cosmopolitan	2,705,224
24. Southern Living	2,374,530
25. U.S. News & World Report	2,307,569
26. Smithsonian	2,211,552
27. Money	2,146,140
28. Glamour	2,083,849
29. Motorland	2,072,359
30. VFW	2,062,914
31. NEA Today	2,059,728
32. Field & Stream	2,007,234
33. Seventeen	1,915,426
34. Home & Away	1,912,160
35. Country Living	1,839,363
36. Popular Science	1,812,019
37. Ebony	1,791,536
38. Life	1,777,087
39. Parents	1,749,322
40. Popular Mechanics	1,642,081
41. Outdoor Life	1,502,542
42. American Rifleman	1,485,190
43. Sunset	1,452,086
44. Golf Digest	1,421,883
45. Self	1,408,975
46. Soap Opera Digest	1,396,346
47. Elks	1,383,318
48. YM	1,340,415
49. American Hunter	1,329,124
50. New Woman	1,313,181
51. Boys' Life	1,288,545
52. Vogue	1,284,193
53. First for Women	1,258,595
54. Penthouse	1,254,207
55. Bon Appetit	1,231,327
56. True Story Plus	1,225,347
57. Mademoiselle	1,219,159
58. Sesame Street	1,218,722
59. Rolling Stone	1,211,586
60. Woman's World	1,204,042
61. Teen	1,188,257
62. Golf	1,183,684
63. Kiplingers	1,166,539
64. Vanity Fair	1,151,887
65. Us	1,102,783
66. Globe	1,102,335
67. Country Home	1,095,721
68. Travel & Leisure	1,092,414
69. Family Handyman	1,047,679
70. Scouting	1,030,194
71. Cooking Light	1,025,511
72. Conde Nast Traveler	1,020,592
73. Car and Driver	1,019,630
74. Discover	1,014,152
75. Home Mechanix	1,013,963
76. Health	1,013,428
77. Home	1,013,182
78. Weight Watchers	1,006,397
79. PC Magazine	1,004,235
80. Consumer's Digest	1,003,558
81. House Beautiful	1,002,458
82. Michigan Living	983,194
83. Motor Trend	943,441
84. Gourmet	915,171
85. Jet	909,014
86. Essence	906,034
87. Elle	901,619
88. American Health	895,668
89. The Workbasket	890,006
90. Victoria	886,661
91. Business Week, NA.	886,229
92. Endless Vacation	885,604
93. Working Woman	866,816
94. Entertainment Weekly	866,431
95. Nation's Business	861,581
96. Hot Rod	856,774
97. Workbench	831,751
98. American Legion Auxiliary	828,855
99. Mature Outlook	824,559
100. Sport	816,990

Some Notable U.S. Dance Companies

Source: Dance/USA, July 1993

African-American Dance Ensemble, Durham, NC
Alvin Ailey American Dance Theater, New York, NY
Aman Folk Ensemble, Los Angeles, CA
American Ballet Theatre, New York, NY
American Repertory Ballet Company, Princeton, NJ
Atlanta Ballet, GA
Avaz International Dance Theatre, Los Angeles, CA
Ballet Arizona, Phoenix, AZ
Ballet Austin, Austin, TX
Ballet Chicago, IL
Ballet Florida, West Palm Beach, FL
Ballet Hispanico of New York, New York, NY
BalletMet, Columbus, OH
Ballet Omaha, NE
Ballet West, Salt Lake City, UT
Tandy Beal and Company, Santa Cruz, CA
Maria Benitez Teatro Flamenco, Santa Fe, NM
Boston Ballet, Boston, MA
Trisha Brown Company, New York, NY
Donald Byrd/The Group, New York, NY
Caribbean Dance Company, St. Croix, VI
Chen & Dancers, New York, NY
Lucinda Childs Dance Company, New York, NY
Cincinnati Ballet, Cincinnati, OH
Cleveland/San Jose Ballet, Cleveland, OH
Colorado Ballet, Denver, CO
Contraband, San Francisco, CA
Cunningham Dance Foundation, New York, NY
Dallas Black Dance Theatre, Dallas, TX
Dance Alloy, Pittsburgh, PA
Dance Exchange, Washington, DC
Dance Theatre of Harlem, New York, NY
DanceBrazil, New York, NY
Danceteller, Philadelphia, PA
Della Davidson Dance Company, San Francisco, CA
Dayton Ballet Association, Dayton, OH
Dayton Contemporary Dance Company, Dayton, OH
Laura Dean Musicians and Dancers, New York, NY
Douglas Dunn & Dancers, New York, NY
Eiko & Koma, New York, NY
Eugene Ballet Company, Eugene, OR
Garth Fagan's Dance, Rochester, NY
Feld Ballet, New York, NY
Fort Worth Ballet, Fort Worth, TX
Joe Goode Performance Group, San Francisco, CA
David Gordon Pick Up Co., New York, NY
Martha Graham Dance Co., New York, NY
Hartford Ballet, Hartford, CT
Erick Hawkins Dance Co., New York, NY
Joseph Holmes Dance Theater, Chicago, IL
Houston Ballet, Houston, TX
Hubbard Street Dance, Chicago, IL
Indianapolis Ballet Theatre, Indianapolis, IN
Isaacs, McCaleb & Dancers, San Diego, CA
Jazz Tap Ensemble, Los Angeles, CA
Margaret Jenkins Dance Company, San Francisco, CA
Joffrey Ballet, New York, NY
Bill T. Jones/Arnie Zane Company, New York, NY
Rebecca Kelly Dance Company, New York, NY
KHADRA International Folk Ballet, San Francisco, CA
Ko-Thi Dance Company, Bronx, NY
Lula Washington's L.A. Contemporary Dance Theatre, Los Angeles, CA
Ralph Lemon Company, New York, NY

Lewitzky Dance Company, Los Angeles, CA
Jose Limon Dance Company, New York, NY
LINES Contemporary Ballet, San Francisco, CA
Loretta Livingston & Dancers, Los Angeles, CA
Los Angeles Chamber Ballet, CA
Louisville Ballet, Louisville, KY
Lar Lubovitch Dance Company, New York, NY
Susan Marshall & Company, New York, NY
Miami City Ballet, Miami Beach, FL
Bebe Miller and Company, New York, NY
Milwaukee Ballet, Milwaukee, WI
Elisa Monte Dance Company, New York, NY
Montgomery Ballet, Montgomery, AL
Mordine & Company, Chicago, IL
Mark Morris Dance Group, New York, NY
Jennifer Muller/The Works, New York, NY
Muntu Dance Theater, Chicago, IL
New Dance, Minneapolis, MN
New York City Ballet, New York, NY
Rosalind Newman and Dancers, New York, NY
Nikolais and Louis Dance, New York, NY
North Carolina Dance Theatre, Winston-Salem, NC
Oakland Ballet, Oakland, CA
ODC/San Francisco, San Francisco, CA
Ohio Ballet, Akron, OH
Oregon Ballet Theater, Portland, OR
Pacific Northwest Ballet, Seattle, WA
Parsons Dance Company, New York, NY
Pennsylvania Ballet, Philadelphia, PA
Pepatian, Bronx, NY
Philadanco, Philadelphia, PA
Pilobolus Dance Theater, Washington, CT
Stuart Pimsler Dance & Theater, Columbus, OH
Pittsburgh Ballet Theatre, Pittsburgh, PA
Pittsburgh Dance Alloy, Pittsburgh, PA
Repertory Dance Theatre, Salt Lake City, UT
Richmond Ballet, Richmond, VA
Elizabeth Streb Ringside, New York, NY
Ririe-Woodbury Dance Company, Salt Lake City, UT
Cleo Parker Robinson Dance Theater, Denver, CO
Nicholas Rodriguez and DanceCompass, Montclair, NJ
San Francisco Ballet, San Francisco, CA
Carlota Santana Spanish Dance Arts Co., New York, NY
Sarasota Ballet, FL
Solomons Company/Dance, New York, NY
Southern Ballet Theater, Winter Park, FL
State Ballet of Missouri, Kansas City, MO
Paul Taylor Dance Company, New York, NY
Joyce Trisler Danscompany, New York, NY
Tulsa Ballet Theatre, Tulsa, OK
Urban Bush Women, New York, NY
Dan Wagoner and Dancers, New York, NY
Washington Ballet, Washington, DC
June Watanabe and Company, San Rafael, CA
Nina Wiener Dance Company, New York, NY
Zenon Dance Company, Minneapolis, MN
ZeroMoving Dance Company, Philadelphia, PA
Zivili Kolo Ensemble, Granville, OH

Symphony Orchestras of the U.S.

Source: American Symphony Orchestra League, 777 14th St., N.W., Washington, DC 20005
(All orchestras listed had budgets in excess of $1.05 million in fiscal 1992.)

Symphony Orchestra[1]	Music Director[2]
Alabama (Birmingham)	Paul Polivnick
Atlanta (Ga.)	Yoel Levi
Austin (Tex.)	Sung Kwak
Baltimore (Md.)	David Zinman
Boston (Mass.)	Seiji Ozawa
Brooklyn Philharmonic (N.Y.)	Dennis Russell Davies
Buffalo Philharmonic (N.Y.)	Maximiano Valdez
Cedar Rapids (Ia.)	Christian Tiemeyer
Charleston (S.C.)	David Stahl
Charlotte (N.C.)	Leo B. Driehuys
Chattanooga, & Opera Assn. (Tenn.)	Robert Bernhardt
Chicago (Ill.)	Daniel Barenboim
Cincinnati (Oh.)	Jesus Lopez-Cobos
Cleveland (Oh.)	Christoph von Dohnanyi
Colorado (Denver)	David T. Abosch
Colorado Springs (Col.)	Christopher P. Wilkins
Columbus (Oh.)	Alessandro Siciliani
Dallas (Tex.)	Andrew Litton
Dayton Philharmonic (Oh.)	Isaiah Jackson
Delaware (Wilmington)	Stephen Gunzenhauser
Detroit (Mich.)	Neeme Jarvi
Florida Philharmonic (Fort Lauderdale)	James Judd
The Florida Orchestra (Tampa)	Jahja Ling
Florida Symphonic Pops (Boca Raton)	Derek Stannard
Fort Wayne Philharmonic (Ind.)	Edward Chivzel
Fort Worth (Tex.)	John Giordano
Grand Rapids (Mich.)	Catherine Comet
Grant Park (Chicago, Ill.)	Catherine M. Cahill
Hartford (Conn.)	Michael Lankester
Honolulu (Ha.)	Donald Johanos
Houston (Tex.)	Christoph Eschenbach
Hudson Valley Philharmonic (Poughkeepsie, N.Y.)	Randall Craig Fleischer
Indianapolis (Ind.)	Raymond Leppard
Jacksonville (Fla.)	Roger Nierenberg
Kansas City (Mo.)	William McGlaughlin
Knoxville (Tenn.)	Kirk Trevor
Long Beach (Cal.)	JoAnn Falletta
Long Island Philharmonic (N.Y.)	Marin Alsop
Los Angeles Chamber Or. (Cal.)	Christof Perick
Los Angeles Philharmonic (Cal.)	Esa-Pekka Salonen
The Louisville Orchestra (Ky.)	Lawrence Leighton Smith
Memphis (Tenn.)	Alan Balter
Milwaukee (Wis.)	Zdenek Macal
The Minnesota Orchestra (Minneapolis)	Edo de Waart
Mississippi (Jackson)	Colman Pearce
Naples Philharmonic (Fla.)	Timothy W. Russell
The Nashville Symphony (Tenn.)	Kenneth S. Schermerhorn
National (Washington, D.C.)	Mstislav Rostropovich
New Haven (Conn.)	Michael Palmer
New Jersey (Newark)	Zdenek Macal
New Mexico (Albuquerque)	Neal H. Stulberg
New World Symphony (Miami Beach, Fla.)	Michael Tilson Thomas
New York Chamber Sym. of the 92nd St. Y (N.Y.C.)	Gerard Schwarz
New York Philharmonic (N.Y.C.)	Kurt Masur
North Carolina (Raleigh)	Gerhardt Zimmermann
Ohio Chamber Orchestra (Cleveland)	Vacant
Oklahoma City Philharmonic (Okla.)	Joel A. Levine
Omaha (Neb.)	Bruce B. Hangen
Oregon (Portland)	James DePreist
Pacific Symphony (Irvine, Cal.)	Carl St. Clair
The Philadelphia Orchestra (Pa.)	Wolfgang Sawallisch
Phoenix (Ariz.)	James L. Sedares
Pittsburgh (Pa.)	Lorin Maazel
Portland (Me.)	Toshiyuki Shimada
Puerto Rico (Santurce)	Roselin Pabon
Rhode Island Philharmonic Or. (Providence)	Zuohuang Chen
The Richmond Symphony (Va.)	George Manahan
Rochester Philharmonic Or. (N.Y.)	Mark Elder
Sacramento (Cal.)	Alasdair P. Neale
St. Louis (Mo.)	Leonard Slatkin
St. Paul Chamber Or. (Minn.)	Hugh Wolff
San Antonio (Tex.)	Christopher P. Wilkins
San Diego (Cal.)	Yoav Talmi
San Francisco (Cal.)	Herbert Blomstedt
San Jose (Cal.)	Leonid Grin
Savannah (Ga.)	Philip B. Greenberg

Symphony Orchestra[1]	Music Director[2]
Seattle (Wash.)	Gerard Schwarz
Shreveport (La)	Peter Leonard
Spokane (Wash.)	Vakhtang Jordania
Springfield (Mass.)	Raymond C. Harvey
Syracuse (N.Y.)	Kazuyoshi Akiyama
Toldeo (Oh.)	Andrew Massey
Tucson (Ariz.)	Robert E. Bernhardt
Tulsa Philharmonic Or. (Okla.)	Bernard Rubenstein
Utah (Salt Lake City)	Joseph Silverstein
The Virginia Symphony (Norfolk).	JoAnn Falletta
West Virginia (Charleston)	Thomas B. Conlin
Wichita (Kan.)	Zuohuang Chen
Winston-Salem Piedmont Triad Symphony (N.C.)	Peter J. Perret

(1) Orchestra name=place name + Symphony Orchestra, unless otherwise noted; (2) General title; listed is highest-ranking member of conducting personnel.

U.S. Opera Companies with Budgets of $500,000 or More

Source: OPERA America; July 1993

(Companies listed in state order.)

Anchorage Opera; Margaret Wood, gen. dir.
Arizona Opera Co. (Tucson); Glynn Ross, gen. dir.
Opera Theatre at Wildwood (Ariz.); Ann Chotard, art. dir.
Fullerton Civic Light Opera (Calif.); Griff Duncan, gen. mgr.
Long Beach Opera (Calif.); Michael Milenski, gen. dir.
Long Beach Civic Light Opera (Calif.); Pegge Logefeil, mng. dir.
Los Angeles Music Center Opera Assn.; Peter Hemmings, exec. dir.
Opera Pacific (Costa Mesa, Calif.); David DiChiera, gen. dir.
Sacramento Opera Assn. (Calif.); Marianne H. Oaks, gen. dir.
San Diego Civic Light Opera; C. E. Franks, exec. dir.
San Diego Opera Assn.; Ian Campbell, gen. dir.
San Francisco Opera; Lotfi Mansouri, gen. dir.
San Francisco Opera Center (inc. Western Opera Theater)
Opera San José (Calif.); Irene Dalis, art. dir.
San José Civic Light Opera (Calif.); Dianna Shuster, dir.
Central City Opera (Denver); Daniel Rule, gen. mgr.
Opera Colorado (Denver); Nathaniel Merrill, art. dir.
Connecticut Grand Opera & Stamford State Opera, Laurence Gilgore, art. dir.
Connecticut Opera (Hartford); George Osborne, gen. dir.
Goodspeed Opera House (E. Haddam, Conn.); Michael Price, exec. dir.
Washington Opera (D.C.); Martin Feinstein, gen. dir.
Fort Lauderdale Opera; William H. Martin, gen. mgr.
Greater Miami Opera Assn.; Robert Heuer, gen. mgr.
Orlando Opera Co. (Fla.); Robert Swedberg, gen. dir.
Palm Beach Opera; Herbert P. Benn, gen. mgr.
Sarasota Opera Assn. (Fla.); Deane Allyn, exec. dir.
The Atlanta Opera (Ga.); William Fred Scott, art. dir.; Alfred Kennedy, gen. mgr.
Augusta Opera (Ga.); Edward Bradberry, gen. dir.
Hawaii Opera Theatre; J. Mario Ramos, gen. dir.
Chicago Opera Theater; Alan Stone, art. dir.
Lyric Opera of Chicago; Ardis Krainik, gen. mgr.
Indianapolis Opera; Nando Scheller, gen. dir.
Des Moines Metro Opera (Indianola); Robert Larsen, art. dir.
Kentucky Opera Assn. (Louisville); Thomson Smillie, gen. dir.
New Orleans Opera Assn.; Arthur Cosenza, gen. dir.
Baltimore Opera Co.; Michael Harrison, gen. dir.
Opera Company of Boston; Sarah Caldwell, art. dir.
Boston Opera Theatre; Robert Canon, exec. dir.
Michigan Opera Theatre (Detroit); David DiChiera, gen. dir.
Opera Grand Rapids (Mich.); Robert Lyall, gen. dir.
Minnesota Opera Co. (St. Paul); Kevin Smith, gen. dir.
Lyric Opera of Kansas City (Missouri); Russell Patterson, gen. dir. & art. dir.
Opera Theatre of St. Louis (Missouri); Charles MacKay, gen. dir.
Opera/Omaha (Neb.); Mary Robert, gen. dir.
Nevada Opera (Reno); Ted Puffer, gen. dir.
Opera Festival of N.J. (Princeton Junction); Deborah S. Sandler, exec. dir.
Metro Lyric Opera (Allenhurst, N.J.); Era M. Tognoli, gen. & art. dir.
New Jersey State Opera (Newark); Alfredo Silipigni, gen. dir.
Albuquerque Civic Light Opera; Linda E. McVey, exec. dir.
Santa Fe Opera (New Mexico); John Crosby, gen. dir.
Tri-Cities Opera (Binghamton, N.Y.); Richard Hood, exec. dir.
St. Ann Center for Restoration and the Arts (Brooklyn, N.Y.); Susan Feldman, art. dir.
Greater Buffalo Opera (N.Y.); Judith Wolf, exec. dir.
Chautauqua Opera (N.Y.); Linda Jackson, gen. mgr.
Glimmerglass Opera (Cooperstown, N.Y.); Paul Kellogg, gen. mgr.
Lake George Opera Festival (N.Y.); John Balme, art. dir.; Susan T. Danis, exec. dir.
Syracuse Opera; Julie Richard, mng. dir.
Light Opera of Manhattan; Raymond Allen, Jerry Gotham, art. dir.
Metropolitan Opera Assn. (N.Y.C.); Joseph Volpe, gen. mgr.
Music-Theatre Group (N.Y. & Stockbridge, Mass.); Lyn Austin, prod. dir.
New York City Opera; Christopher Keene, gen. dir.
New York City Opera Natl. Co.; Nancy Kelly, adm. dir.
Opera Orchestra of N.Y. (N.Y.C.); Eve Queler, art dir.
Opera Carolina (Charlotte, N.C.); James Wright, gen. dir.
Cincinnati Opera Assn.; James deBlasis, art. dir.
Cleveland Opera; David Bamberger, gen. dir.
Lyric Opera Cleveland (Oh.); Michael McConnell, exec. dir.
Opera/Columbus (Oh.); John Gage, gen. dir.
Dayton Opera Assn. (Oh.); Jane Nelson, mng. dir.
Lyric Theatre of Oklahoma; Gayle Pearson, gen. mgr.
Tulsa Opera (Oklahoma); Myrna S. Ruffner, gen. mgr.
Portland Opera Assn. (Oregon); Robert Bailey, exec. dir.
American Music Theater Festival (Phila.); Marjorie Samoff, prod. dir.
Opera Company of Philadelphia; Robert B. Driver, gen. dir.
Pennsylvania Opera Theater (Phila.); Barbara Silverstein, art. dir. & gen. mgr.
Pittsburgh Civic Light Opera; Charles Gray, exec. dir.
Pittsburgh Opera; Tito Capobianco, gen. dir.
Knoxville Opera (Tenn.); Robert Lyall, gen. dir.
Nashville Opera (Tenn.); Kyle Rideout, gen. dir.
Opera Memphis (Tenn.); Michael Ching, art. dir.; Bert Adler Wolff, gen. dir.
Austin Lyric Opera (Tex.) Walter Ducloux, art. dir.
Dallas Opera; Plato Karayanis, gen. dir.
Lyric Opera of Dallas (Tex.); John Burrows, art. dir.
Fort Worth Opera; William Walker, gen. dir.
Houston Grand Opera Assn.; R. David Gockley, gen. dir.
Texas Opera Theater (Houston); James Ireland, gen. mgr.
Utah Opera (Salt Lake City); Anne Ewers, gen. dir.
Virginia Opera (Norfolk); Peter Mark, gen. dir.
Wolf Trap Opera (Vienna, Va.); Peter Russell, gen. dir.
Seattle Opera Assn.; Speight Jenkins, gen. dir.
Florentine Opera of Milwaukee; Dennis Hanthorn, gen. mgr.
Skylight Opera Theatre (Milwaukee); Chas Rader-Shieber, art. dir.

Top 20 Cable Video Networks

Source: *Cable Television Developments*, June 1993; Natl. Cable Television Assn. Ranked by number of subscribers.

Rank	Network[1]	Systems	Subscribers (millions)
1	ESPN (1979)	26,200[2]	61.6
2	CNN (1980)	11,325	61.0
3	USA Network (1980)	12,000[2]	60.1
4	TBS (1976)	14,954[2]	60.0
5	The Discovery Channel (1985)	9,300	59.0
6	Nickelodeon (1979)	9,171	59.0
	Nick At Nite (1985)	4,381	
7	C-Span (1979)	4,336	58.7
8	TNT (Turner Network Television) (1988)	8,731	58.4
9	The Family Channel (1977)	10,102	57.4
10	TNN: The Nashville Network (1983)	13,391	57.4
11	MTV: Music Television (1981)	8,096	57.3
12	Lifetime (1984)	5,800	57.0
13	Arts & Entertainment Network (1984)	8,000	56.0
14	The Weather Channel (1982)	4,925	53.4
15	Headline News (1982)	6,700	51.4
16	CNBC (1989)	4,000[2]	48.3
17	VH-1 (Video Hits One) (1985)	5,304	47.4
18	QVC Network (1986)	4,197	44.6
19	AMC (American Movie Classics) (1984)	4,100	44.5
20	WGN/UVI (1978)	14,354	38.1

(1) Date in parentheses is year service began. (2) Includes non-cable affiliates.

U.S. Households With Cable Television, 1975-1992

Source: *Cable Television Developments*, June 1993

Year	Basic Cable Subscribers	Percent of Households With TVs	Year	Basic Cable Subscribers	Percent of Households With TVs
1975	9,196,690	13.2	1984	37,290,870	43.7
1976	10,787,970	15.1	1985	39,872,520	46.2
1977	12,168,450	16.6	1986	42,237,140	48.1
1978	13,391,910	17.9	1987	44,970,880	50.5
1979	14,814,380	19.4	1988	48,636,520	53.8
1980	17,671,490	22.6	1989	52,564,470	57.1
1981	23,219,200	28.3	1990	54,871,330	59.0
1982	29,340,570	35.0	1991	55,786,390	60.6
1983	34,113,790	40.5	1992	57,211,600	61.5

Number of Cable TV Systems: 1970-1993

Source: *Cable Television Developments*, June 1993

Year	Systems	Year	Systems	Year	Systems	Year	Systems
1970	2,490	1976	3,681	1982	4,825	1988	8,500
1971	2,639	1977	3,832	1983	5,600	1989	9,050
1972	2,841	1978	3,875	1984	6,200	1990	9,575
1973	2,991	1979	4,150	1985	6,600	1991	10,704
1974	3,158	1980	4,225	1986	7,500	1992	11,075
1975	3,506	1981	4,375	1987	7,900	1993	11,385

TV Viewing Shares: Broadcast Years 1983/1984-1991/1992[1]

Source: *Cable Television Developments*, June 1993

Total Television Households

	'83/'84	'84/'85	'85/'86	'86/'87	'87/'88	'88/'89	'89/'90	'90/'91	'91/'92
Broadcast Network Affiliates	69	66	66	64	61	58	55	53	54
Independent TV Stations[2]	19	18	18	20	20	20	20	21	20
Public TV Stations	3	3	3	4	4	3	3	3	3
Basic Cable Networks[2]	9	11	11	13	15	17	21	24	24
Pay Cable Services	5	6	5	4	7	7	6	6	6

All Cable Households

	'83/'84	'84/'85	'85/'86	'86/'87	'87/'88	'88/'89	'89/'90	'90/'91	'91/'92
Broadcast Network Affiliates	58	56	56	53	52	49	46	46	47
Independent TV Stations[2]	17	17	17	17	17	16	16	17	16
Public TV Stations	3	3	3	3	3	3	3	2	3
Basic Cable Networks[2]	17	19	19	23	25	28	32	35	35
Pay Cable Services	11	11	10	10	11	11	10	9	8

Pay Cable Households

	'83/'84	'84/'85	'85/'86	'86/'87	'87/'88	'88/'89	'89/'90	'90/'91	'91/'92
Broadcast Network Affiliates	53	51	51	48	48	45	43	41	43
Independent TV Stations[2]	17	17	17	16	17	16	16	16	16
Public TV Stations	3	3	3	3	3	2	2	2	2
Basic Cable Networks[2]	17	19	19	23	24	27	30	34	33
Pay Cable Services	18	18	17	17	18	18	18	17	17

(1) For all television viewing Monday-Sunday, 24 hours/day. Due to multiset use and rounding off of numbers, totals are over 100. (2) For broadcast years 1983/1984-1985/1986, superstation shares are divided between independent stations and basic cable networks categories; for broadcast years 1986/1987-1991/1992, TBS has been counted in the basic cable networks category.

Average Television Viewing Time, 1993

Source: Nielsen Media Research, May 1993 (Hours:Minutes per week)

		Mon.-Fri. 10am-4:30pm	Mon.-Fri. 4:30pm-7:30pm	Mon.-Sun. 8-11pm	Sat. 7am-1pm	Mon.-Fri. 11:30pm-1am
Total Persons		3:58	3:19	7:58	:41	1:11
Total Women	18+	5:34	3:57	9:14	:36	1:26
	18-24	4:55	2:56	6:32	:32	1:12
	25-54	4:33	3:09	8:32	:34	1:24
	55+	7:48	5:55	11:46	:42	1:35
Total Men	18+	3:09	2:54	8:22	:34	1:24
	18-24	3:04	2:18	5:54	:29	1:20
	25-54	2:28	2:19	7:54	:35	1:28
	55+	4:50	4:38	10:49	:35	1:19
Total Teens	12-17	1:57	2:58	6:10	:44	:44
Children	2-5	4:47	2:52	4:19	1:11	:20
	6-11	1:40	2:56	4:58	1:06	:19

America's Favorite Prime-Time Television Programs, 1992-1993

Source: Nielsen Media Research

(Nielsen People Meter Average Audience Estimates)

Regularly Scheduled Network Programs (Sept. 21, 1992-Apr. 18, 1993)

Percent of TV households and persons in TV households

Rank	Program	TV Households	Women	Men	Teens	Children
1.	60 Minutes	21.9	16.5	16.1	2.8	2.9
2.	Roseanne	20.7	15.3	10.6	15.3	12.2
3.	Home Improvement	19.2	14.1	12.0	13.4	11.8
4.	Murphy Brown	17.9	14.7	9.6	6.6	4.9
5.	Murder, She Wrote	17.7	16.0	10.1	2.6	2.4
6.	Coach	17.5	13.1	10.7	10.4	8.4
7.	NFL Monday Night Football	16.7	7.6	15.3	7.5	4.1
8.	CBS Sunday Movie	16.1	14.3	8.4	3.9	2.6
8.	Cheers	16.1	11.6	10.4	7.0	5.1
10.	Full House	15.8	10.7	6.4	13.0	16.9
11.	Northern Exposure	15.2	11.8	9.0	3.9	2.0
12.	Rescue: 911	15.1	11.7	9.2	6.4	7.2
12.	20/20	15.1	11.6	9.0	4.6	4.8
14.	CBS Tuesday Movie	14.8	11.8	8.3	5.9	4.2
15.	Love and War	14.7	11.9	7.7	4.5	3.1
16.	Fresh Prince of Bel Air	14.6	9.5	6.6	17.1	12.4
16.	Hangin' With Mr. Cooper	14.6	9.9	6.1	13.2	14.0
16.	Jackie Thomas Show	14.6	10.5	7.8	10.3	7.0
19.	Evening Shade	14.5	12.4	8.2	3.6	3.7
20.	Hearts Afire	14.2	12.1	7.7	3.8	3.6
20.	Unsolved Mysteries	14.2	11.2	8.8	4.7	4.5
22.	Primetime Live	14.1	10.7	9.1	2.5	1.6
23.	NBC Monday Night Movies	13.9	11.2	6.4	7.6	4.6
24.	Dr. Quinn Medicine Woman	13.7	12.3	8.0	5.3	5.0
25.	Seinfeld	13.6	9.9	8.7	5.0	3.2
26.	Blossom	13.5	8.7	5.6	17.1	11.5
26.	48 Hours	13.5	10.2	8.4	3.0	2.0
28.	ABC Sunday Night Movie	13.3	10.2	8.2	6.9	4.9
29.	Matlock	13.2	11.6	7.8	2.5	2.2
30.	Simpsons	13.0	6.3	7.2	15.5	16.2
30.	Wings	13.0	9.5	8.1	5.3	4.0
32.	Family Matters	12.6	8.4	6.0	10.3	14.7
33.	NFL Post 1	12.4	6.3	10.7	4.9	4.1
34.	America's Funniest Home Videos	12.2	8.9	7.6	7.5	10.2
34.	Step By Step	12.2	8.0	5.5	10.9	16.1
36.	NBC Sunday Night Movie	12.1	8.9	8.2	5.6	3.6
37.	ABC Monday Night Movie	11.9	8.7	7.2	4.9	3.2
37.	In the Heat of the Night	11.9	9.9	7.4	2.5	2.5
39.	Getting By	11.8	7.7	4.9	10.7	15.0
39.	Laurie Hill	11.8	8.8	6.4	6.8	5.9
41.	L.A. Law	11.6	8.8	6.8	3.7	2.0
42.	America's Funniest People	11.5	8.0	7.1	8.7	10.6
42.	Knots Landing	11.5	10.2	4.9	3.6	2.7
44.	Married . . .With Children	11.4	6.0	7.7	12.0	6.9
45.	How'd They Do That?	11.2	8.2	7.5	4.0	3.8
46.	American Detective	11.1	7.7	8.1	3.0	2.9
46.	Martin	11.1	5.6	5.3	15.4	12.3
48.	Street Stories	11.0	8.4	6.9	2.6	2.5
49.	Dateline NBC	10.8	8.0	6.7	2.6	1.5
49.	Empty Nest	10.8	8.7	5.4	5.3	4.8

Favorite Syndicated Programs, 1992-1993

Source: Nielsen Media Research, Aug. 31, 1992-Apr. 18, 1993

(Ratings based on Designated Market Area coverage as reported by Nielsen's Cassandra Report)

Rank	Program	TV Households	Women	Men	Teens	Children
1.	Wheel of Fortune	13.9	11.8	8.0	3.3	3.4
2.	Jeopardy	12.0	9.9	6.9	3.0	2.3
2.	Star Trek	12.0	7.1	9.2	6.4	5.1
4.	Star Trek: Deep Space 9	10.9	6.5	8.2	5.8	4.8
5.	Oprah Winfrey	10.4	8.4	3.4	2.7	1.7
6.	Entertainment Tonight	8.7	6.4	5.0	2.1	1.9
7.	Magic II	8.2	4.9	4.7	4.6	5.8
8.	Married . . .With Children	7.8	4.1	4.5	6.8	4.7
9.	Wheel of Fortune-Wknd	7.6	6.3	4.5	1.7	1.6
10.	Current Affair	7.5	5.1	4.2	2.3	1.8
10.	Inside Edition	7.5	5.6	4.0	1.8	1.6
12.	Tri Star Showcase III	7.3	4.8	4.7	3.1	2.9
13.	Buena Vista I	7.0	4.4	4.1	3.4	3.8
14.	Warner Bros. Vol. 29	6.9	4.2	4.2	4.0	3.4
15.	Imagination I	6.8	4.1	3.2	4.6	7.4
15.	Roseanne	6.8	4.4	3.1	5.8	4.3
17.	Kung Fu	6.7	3.7	4.9	3.4	3.2
18.	Designing Women	6.3	4.3	2.7	3.4	2.2
18.	National Geographic on Assignment	6.3	3.3	4.6	2.1	2.2
18.	World Wrestling Fed.	6.3	2.5	4.0	5.2	5.6

All-Time Top Television Programs

Source: A.C. Nielsen estimates, Jan. 1961 through May 20, 1993, excluding unsponsored or joint network telecasts or programs under 30 minutes long. Ranked by rating (percent of average TV audience).

Rank	Program	Telecast Date	Network	Rating (%)	Households (000)
1.	M*A*S*H (last episode)	2/28/83	CBS	60.2	50,150
2.	Dallas (Who shot J.R.?)	11/21/80	CBS	53.3	41,470
3.	Roots-Pt. 8	1/30/77	ABC	51.1	36,380
4.	Super Bowl XVI	1/24/82	CBS	49.1	40,020
5.	Super Bowl XVII	1/30/83	NBC	48.6	40,480
6.	Super Bowl XX	1/26/86	NBC	48.3	41,490
7.	Gone With the Wind-Pt. 1	11/7/76	NBC	47.7	33,960
8.	Gone With the Wind-Pt. 2	11/8/76	NBC	47.4	33,750
9.	Super Bowl XII	1/15/78	CBS	47.2	34,410
10.	Super Bowl XIII	1/21/79	NBC	47.1	35,090
11.	Bob Hope Christmas Show	1/15/70	NBC	46.6	27,260
12.	Super Bowl XVIII	1/22/84	CBS	46.4	38,800
12.	Super Bowl XIX	1/20/85	ABC	46.4	39,390
14.	Super Bowl XIV	1/20/80	CBS	46.3	35,330
15.	ABC Theater (The Day After)	11/20/83	ABC	46.0	38,550
16.	Roots-Pt. 6	1/28/77	ABC	45.9	32,680
16.	The Fugitive	8/29/67	ABC	45.9	25,700
18.	Super Bowl XXI	1/25/87	CBS	45.8	40,030
19.	Roots-Pt. 5	1/27/77	ABC	45.7	32,540
20.	Cheers (last episode)	5/20/93	NBC	45.5	42,360
21.	Ed Sullivan	2/9/64	CBS	45.3	23,240
22.	Super Bowl XXVII	1/31/93	NBC	45.1	41,990
23.	Bob Hope Christmas Show	1/14/71	NBC	45.0	27,050
24.	Roots-Pt. 3	1/25/77	ABC	44.8	31,900
25.	Super Bowl XI	1/9/77	NBC	44.4	31,610
25.	Super Bowl XV	1/25/81	NBC	44.4	34,540
27.	Super Bowl VI	1/16/72	CBS	44.2	27,450
28.	Roots-Pt. 2	1/24/77	ABC	44.1	31,400
29.	Beverly Hillbillies	1/8/64	CBS	44.0	22,570
30.	Roots-Pt. 4	1/26/77	ABC	43.8	31,190
30.	Ed Sullivan	2/16/64	CBS	43.8	22,445
32.	Super Bowl XXIII	1/22/89	NBC	43.5	39,320
33.	Academy Awards	4/7/70	ABC	43.4	25,390
34.	Thorn Birds-Pt. 3	3/29/83	ABC	43.2	35,990
35.	Thorn Birds-Pt. 4	3/30/83	ABC	43.1	35,900
36.	CBS NFC Championship	1/10/82	CBS	42.9	34,960
37.	Beverly Hillbillies	1/15/64	CBS	42.8	21,960
38.	Super Bowl VII	1/14/73	NBC	42.7	27,670
39.	Thorn Birds-Pt. 2	3/28/83	ABC	42.5	35,400
40.	Super Bowl IX	1/12/75	NBC	42.4	29,040
40.	Beverly Hillbillies	2/26/64	CBS	42.4	21,750

Top-Rated TV Shows of the Past

Source: A.C. Nielsen

1950s

Program	Network	Rating*
1. A. Godfrey's Talent Scouts	CBS	32.9
2. I Love Lucy	CBS	31.6
3. You Bet Your Life	NBC	30.1
4. Dragnet	NBC	24.6
5. The Jack Benny Show	CBS	22.3
6. A. Godfrey and Friends	CBS	19.5
7. Gunsmoke	CBS	15.6
8. The Red Skelton Show	NBC	15.2
9. December Bride	CBS	13.8
10. I've Got a Secret	CBS	12.9
11. $64,000 Question	CBS	11.2
12. Disneyland	ABC	10.8
13. The Ed Sullivan Show	CBS	10.6
14. Have Gun—Will Travel	CBS	10.3
15. The Danny Thomas Show	CBS	9.9

1960s

Program	Network	Rating*
1. Bonanza	NBC	29.6
2. The Red Skelton Show	CBS	26.4
3. The Andy Griffith Show	CBS	22.4
4. The Beverly Hillbillies	CBS	21.9
5. The Ed Sullivan Show	CBS	21.7
6. The Lucy Show/Here's Lucy	CBS	21.3
7. The Jackie Gleason Show	CBS	16.5
8. Bewitched	ABC	14.8
9. Gomer Pyle	CBS	13.4
10. Candid Camera	CBS	11.2
11. The Dick Van Dyke Show	CBS	11.1
12. The Danny Thomas Show	CBS	10.7
13. Family Affair	CBS	9.8
14. Laugh-In	NBC	7.9
15. Rawhide	CBS	7.5

1970s

Program	Network	Rating*
1. All in the Family	CBS	23.1
2. M*A*S*H	CBS	17.6
3. Hawaii Five-O	CBS	16.5
4. Happy Days	ABC	15.9
5. The Waltons	CBS	14.0
6. The Mary Tyler Moore Show	CBS	13.7
7. Sanford & Son	NBC	13.4
8. One Day at a Time	CBS	11.4
9. Three's Company	ABC	10.8
10. 60 Minutes	CBS	10.0
11. Maude	CBS	9.8
12. Gunsmoke	CBS	9.7
13. Charlie's Angels	ABC	9.6
14. The Jeffersons	CBS	9.4
15. Laverne & Shirley	ABC	9.3

* Avg. rating over decade

U.S. Television Set Ownership

Source: A.C. Nielsen; Jan. 1, 1993

Total Households with TV: 93,100,000 (98% of U.S. households own at least one TV set)

Homes with:

Color TV sets	91,238,000	98%	2 or more sets	59,584,000	64%
B&W only	1,862,000	2%	One set	33,516,000	36%

Recordings & Music Videos

Gold & Platinum Awards Certification Levels

(Audio and Video)

Source: Recording Industry Assn. of America, *Inside the Recording Industry: A Statistical Overview*, 1992

	Gold	Platinum	Multi-Platinum
Single	500,000 units; EP counts as two units	1 million units; EP counts as two units	2 million units; EP counts as two units
Album	500,000 units; manufacturers' $ volume at least $1 million based at 33⅓% of list price	1 million units; manufacturers' $ volume at least $2 million based at 33⅓% of list price	2 million units; manufacturers' $ volume at least $4 million based at 33⅓% of list price
Short Form	250,000 units; max. running time of 30 minutes	500,000 units; max. running time of 30 minutes	1 million units; max. running time of 30 minutes
Multi-Box	250,000 units; min. running time of 120 minutes	500,000 units; min. running time of 120 minutes	1 million units; min. running time of 120 minutes
Video Single	25,000 units; max. running time of 15 minutes; two songs per title	50,000 units; max. running time of 15 minutes; two songs per title	100,000 units; max. running time of 15 minutes; two songs per title
Video Long Form	50,000 units	100,000 units	200,000 units
Video Multi-Box	50,000 units	100,000 units	200,000 units

Multi-Platinum and Platinum Awards

Awards in 1992 for albums and singles released in 1992, music videos released at any time.

Albums, Multi-Platinum

(Number in parentheses = millions sold)

Bryan Adams; Waking Up the Neighbours (2)
Michael Bolton; Timeless (The Classics) (3)
Garth Brooks; Beyond the Season (2)
Garth Brooks; The Chase (5)
Mariah Carey; MTV Unplugged EP (1)
Eric Clapton; Unplugged (3)
Billy Ray Cyrus; Some Gave All (5)
Def Leppard; Adrenalize (3)
En Vogue; Funky Divas (2)
Whitney Houston; I Will Always Love You (3)
Wynonna Judd; Wynonna (2)
Kriss Kross; Totally Krossed Out (3)
R.E.M.; Automatic for the People (2)
Soundtrack: Boomerang (2)
Randy Travis; Storms of Life (3)

Singles, Multi-Platinum

(Number in parentheses = millions sold)

Kriss Kross; Jump (2)
Sir Mix-a-Lot; Baby Got Back (2)

Albums, Platinum

AC/DC; Live
Alice in Chains; Dirt
John Anderson: Seminole Wind
Arrested Development; 3 Years, 5 Months and 2 Days in the Life of . . .
The Black Crowes; Southern Harmony and Musical Companion
Clint Black; The Hard Way
Mary J. Blige; What's the 411?
Bobby Brown; Bobby
Jimmy Buffett; Boats, Beaches, Bars & Ballads
The Cure; Wish
Peter Gabriel; Us
Vince Gill; I Still Believe in You
Amy Grant; Home for Christmas
House of Pain; House of Pain
Alan Jackson; A Lot about Livin'
Elton John; The One
Annie Lennox; Diva
Bob Marley; Songs of Freedom
MC Ren; Kizz My Black Azz
Megadeth; Coundown to Extinction
Nine Inch Nails; Broken
Prince & New Power Generation; Prince & New Power Generation
Queen; Classic Queen
Lionel Richie; Back to Front
Jon Secada; Jon Secada
Sir Mix-a-Lot; Mack Daddy
Soundtrack: Mo' Money
Soundtrack: Singles
Soundtrack: Wayne's World
Bruce Springsteen; Human Touch
Bruce Springsteen; Lucky Town
George Strait; Pure Country (Soundtrack)
TLC: Ooooooohhh . . . On the TLC Tip
Various; A Very Special Christmas 2
Wilson Phillips; Shadows and Light
ZZ Top; Greatest Hits

Singles, Platinum

Boyz II Men; End of the Road
Eric Clapton; Tears in Heaven
Billy Ray Cyrus; Achy Breaky Heart
House of Pain; Jump Around
Nirvana; Smells Like Teen Spirit
Shai; If I Ever Fall in Love
TLC; Ain't 2 Proud 2 Beg
TLC; Baby Baby Baby
Wreckx 'N' Effect; Rump Shaker

Music Videos, Multi-Platinum

(Number in parentheses = units sold)

Garth Brooks; Garth Brooks (400,000)
Garth Brooks; This Is Garth Brooks (400,000)
Carreras, Domingo, Pavarotti in Concert (400,000)
Billy Ray Cyrus; Billy Ray Cyrus (300,000)
Kidsongs; A Day with the Animals (300,000)
Kidsongs; A Day at the Circus (200,000)
Kidsongs; A Day at Old MacDonald's Farm (400,000)
Kidsongs; I'd Like to Teach the World to Sing (200,000)
Kidsongs; Cars, Boats, Trains and Planes (200,000)
Queensryche; Operation Livecrime (200,000)

Music Video Singles, Multi-Platinum

(Number in parentheses = units sold)

Kriss Kross; Jump (100,000)

100 Leading U.S. Advertisers, 1990-1991

Source: *Advertising Age*, Sept. 23, 1992 © Crain Communications Inc. 1992

Rank '91	'90	Advertiser	Ad spending 1991
1.	1.	Procter & Gamble	$2,149.0
2.	2.	Philip Morris	2,045.6
3.	4.	General Motors	1,442.1
4.	3.	Sears, Roebuck	1,179.4
5.	6.	PepsiCo	903.4
6.	5.	Grand Metropolitan	744.7
7.	12.	Johnson & Johnson	733.0
8.	8.	McDonald's	694.8
9.	16.	Ford	676.6
10.	11.	Eastman Kodak	661.4
11.	15.	Warner Lambert	656.5
12.	17.	Toyota	632.2
13.	7.	AT&T	617.3
14.	14.	Nestle SA	600.5
15.	19.	Unilever NV	593.7
16.	10.	Time Warner	587.5
17.	18.	Kellogg	577.7
18.	13.	RJR Nabisco	571.0
19.	20.	General Mills	555.6
20.	21.	Chrysler	531.1
21.	9.	Kmart	527.2
22.	22.	Anheuser-Busch	508.4
23.	23.	Walt Disney	489.1
24.	25.	American Home Products	447.1
25.	26.	Sony	438.6
26.	37.	H.J. Heinz	403.1
27.	31.	Ralston Purina	393.5
28.	29.	Coca-Cola	367.4
29.	28.	J.C. Penney	362.6
30.	24.	Bristol-Myers Squibb	352.5
31.	36.	Honda	333.1
32.	32.	Hershey Foods	298.9
33.	33.	Matsushita Electric Industrial	292.3
34.	43.	R.H. Macy	289.4
35.	30.	May Dept. Stores	277.3
36.	38.	Sara Lee	$273.0
37.	27.	Nissan	268.9
38.	42.	Mars	253.9
39.	39.	U.S. Government	253.0
40.	46.	ConAgra	249.7
41.	34.	Quaker Oats	237.7
42.	44.	Colgate-Palmolive	227.5
43.	35.	Dayton Hudson	226.5
44.	50.	American Express	226.4
45.	58.	Nike	223.3
46.	41.	Federated Dept. Stores	222.8
47.	49.	American Brands	217.5
48.	45.	Mazda	215.0
49.	69.	Circuit City Stores	213.7
50.	47.	Tandy	213.3
51.	55.	SmithKline Beecham	208.3
52.	53.	Adolph Coors	206.9
53.	52.	American Stores	201.6
54.	54.	Hasbro	201.4
55.	48.	General Electric	198.8
56.	91.	Schering-Plough	198.4
57.	70.	Wal-Mart	189.8
58.	63.	Clorox	182.6
59.	57.	Gillette	182.5
60.	64.	Paramount	179.4
61.	66.	S.C. Johnson & Son	174.0
62.	61.	U.S. dairy farmers	167.9
63.	89.	Delta Air Lines	164.6
64.	62.	Campbell Soup	164.1
65.	73.	Helene Curtis Industries	157.4
66.	67.	Carter Hawley Hale Stores	151.9
67.	75.	AMR	150.1
68.	83.	ITT	141.5
69.	78.	Marriott	$139.7
70.	*	MCI Comm.	139.5
71.	85.	Thompson Medical/Slim-Fast Food	137.5
72.	88.	News Corp.	135.8
73.	60.	Philips NV	133.1
74.	*	Dr. Pepper/Seven-Up	131.4
75.	80.	CPC International	131.4
76.	*	Sprint	131.4
77.	59.	Goodyear Tire & Rubber	130.7
78.	65.	Levi Strauss	129.4
79.	56.	Loews	129.0
80.	74.	Revlon	128.0
81.	84.	Bell Atlantic	127.5
82.	76.	Dow Chemical	127.1
83.	51.	Montgomery Ward	126.7
84.	*	Reebok International	126.5
85.	81.	Seagram	126.3
86.	87.	Wm. Wrigley Jr.	125.4
87.	96.	Wendy's International	124.1
88.	92.	Daimler-Benz AG	122.2
89.	72.	Hallmark Cards	121.8
90.	77.	Mobil	120.0
91.	82.	Hyundai	119.5
92.	99.	Upjohn	119.3
93.	93.	UAL	119.2
94.	97.	Canon	117.6
95.	*	Ciba-Geigy	115.4
96.	95.	U.S. Shoe	113.3
97.	*	B.A.T.	113.0
98.	*	Kimberley-Clark	107.7
99.	*	American Cyanamid	105.2
100.	100.	Monsanto	100.8

* Did not rank among 100 leading advertisers in 1990.

Total U.S. Ad Spending by Category and Medium, 1991

Source: *Advertising Age*, Sept. 23, 1992 © Crain Communications Inc. 1992

(in millions)

Category	Total ad spending	Magazine	Sunday magazines	Newspaper	Network TV	Spot TV	Syndicated TV	Cable TV	Network radio
Automotive	$5,259.1	$940.3	$38.3	$746.2	$1,559.5	$1,480.6	$120.7	$117.7	$72.2
Retail	5,125.9	197.1	93.0	2,491.9	351.7	1,528.0	40.1	42.9	92.1
Business, consumer svcs.	3,582.8	443.3	28.4	1,207.2	598.3	811.2	72.8	112.2	77.2
Food	3,551.9	433.4	29.1	36.5	1,443.8	974.0	346.1	141.0	41.9
Entertainment	2,913.2	58.5	35.7	387.3	802.3	1,196.0	196.1	83.0	15.6
Toiletries & cosmetics	2,249.3	631.8	21.9	6.8	958.6	293.3	215.3	92.5	8.2
Travel & hotels*	2,123.2	335.4	49.1	1,064.5	212.7	233.6	8.6	49.1	33.4
Drugs & remedies	1,807.9	164.8	19.5	78.2	851.6	341.4	171.3	80.2	56.3
Direct response cos.	1,192.9	555.7	302.3	65.1	39.7	76.6	33.6	53.2	62.1
Candy, snacks & soft drinks	1,146.2	55.2	2.4	13.5	434.3	318.3	185.1	72.2	20.5
Apparel, footwear	904.8	416.0	21.5	7.0	235.4	88.5	58.9	41.0	7.5
Beer & wine	839.6	51.6	5.4	12.8	347.0	209.2	60.1	43.5	1.5
Insurance & real estate	705.3	141.6	8.9	187.3	171.5	106.2	9.1	19.0	19.1
Publishing & media	700.4	195.7	11.8	194.1	40.3	137.7	12.1	19.1	21.9
Sporting goods, toys	688.1	146.0	2.3	4.6	159.7	204.5	115.6	51.1	0.8
Household equipment	610.3	113.1	10.6	20.8	272.0	96.1	58.5	28.7	6.9
Soaps & cleansers	599.0	71.5	2.6	3.0	269.9	161.8	56.8	25.5	0.9
Computers, office equip.	529.0	287.0	9.7	44.7	118.5	17.0	7.0	19.3	12.9
Cigarettes	494.7	265.7	29.0	12.7	0.0	0.2	0.0	0.1	2.1
Electronic entertainment	371.5	91.8	1.8	16.2	116.7	71.4	29.3	31.9	9.1
Jewelry, optical	345.9	156.9	11.5	6.0	103.9	23.4	21.2	16.5	2.3
Gasoline & lubricants	303.4	27.8	0.5	15.2	48.4	152.3	1.9	8.9	0.0
Building materials	299.0	79.7	7.1	36.0	71.7	63.7	5.3	21.6	0.5
Liquor	283.5	228.9	8.2	7.7	0.0	5.0	0.7	0.3	1.4
Household furnishings	240.2	116.8	11.0	28.3	41.2	35.3	2.9	2.8	0.0
Horticulture & farming	204.9	21.0	8.9	48.5	30.1	50.1	2.0	12.6	9.1
Pets & pet foods	197.9	39.0	4.5	5.4	82.0	28.4	19.0	14.6	2.9
Freight, courier svcs	152.2	42.8	0.2	6.6	61.7	34.3	0.0	4.1	0.2
Industrial materials	106.7	57.6	0.5	5.8	27.5	10.0	0.0	3.8	0.0
Business propositions	34.9	27.5	0.6	2.9	1.3	1.2	0.0	0.6	0.0
Airplanes, aviation	12.6	10.1	0.0	1.5	0.1	0.7	0.0	0.1	0.0
Miscellaneous	243.9	111.5	17.6	73.2	4.8	1.2	0.1	2.4	0.1
Total	**37,820.2**	**6,515.2**	**794.0**	**6,837.3**	**9,456.2**	**8,751.2**	**1,850.4**	**1,211.6**	**578.7**

* Includes airline travel.

AWARDS — MEDALS — PRIZES

The Alfred B. Nobel Prize Winners

Alfred B. Nobel (1833-1896), inventor of dynamite, bequeathed $9,000,000, the interest to be distributed yearly to those who had most benefited humankind in physics, chemistry, medicine-physiology, literature, and peace. Prizes in these five areas were first awarded in 1901. The first Nobel Memorial Prize in Economic Science was awarded in 1969, funded by the central bank of Sweden. No awards given for years omitted. In 1992, each prize was worth approximately $1.2 million.

Physics

1992 Georges Charpak, Pol.-Fr.
1991 Pierre-Giles de Gennes, French
1990 Richard E. Taylor, Can.; Jerome I. Friedman, Henry W. Kendall, both U.S.
1989 Norman F. Ramsey, U.S.; Hans G. Dehmelt, German-U.S. & Wolfgang Paul, German
1988 Leon M. Lederman, Melvin Schwartz, Jack Steinberger, all U.S.
1987 K. Alex Muller, Swiss; J. Georg Bednorz, W. German
1986 Ernest Ruska, German; Gerd Binnig, W. German; Heinrich Rohrer, Swiss
1985 Klaus von Klitzing, W. German
1984 Carlo Rubbia, Italian; Simon van der Meere, Dutch
1983 Subrahmanyan Chandrasekhar, William A. Fowler, both U.S.
1982 Kenneth G. Wilson, U.S.
1981 Nicolass Bloembergen, Arthur Schaalow, both U.S.; Kai M. Siegbahn, Swedish
1980 James W. Cronin, Val L. Fitch, U.S.
1979 Steven Weinberg, Sheldon L. Glashow, both U.S.; Abdus Salam, Pakistani
1978 Pyotr Kapitsa, USSR; Arno Penzias, Robert Wilson, both U.S.
1977 John H. Van Vleck, Philip W. Anderson, both U.S.; Nevill F. Mott, British
1976 Burton Richter, U.S.
Samuel C.C. Ting, U.S.
1975 James Rainwater, U.S.
Ben Mottelson, U.S.-Danish
Aage Bohr, Danish
1974 Martin Ryle, British
Antony Hewish, British
1973 Ivar Giaever, U.S.
Leo Esaki, Japanese
Brian D. Josephson, British
1972 John Bardeen, U.S.
Leon N. Cooper, U.S.
John R. Schrieffer, U.S.
1971 Dennis Gabor, British
1970 Louis Neel, French
Hannes Alfven, Swedish
1969 Murray Gell-Mann, U.S.
1968 Luis W. Alvarez, U.S.
1967 Hans A. Bethe, U.S.
1966 Alfred Kastler, French
1965 Richard P. Feynman, U.S.
Julian S. Schwinger, U.S.
Shinichiro Tomonaga, Japanese
1964 Nikolai G. Basov, USSR
Aleksander M. Prochorov, USSR
Charles H. Townes, U.S.
1963 Maria Goeppert-Mayer, U.S.
J. Hans D. Jensen, German
Eugene P. Wigner, U.S.
1962 Lev. D. Landau, USSR
1961 Robert Hofstadter, U.S.
Rudolf L. Mossbauer, German
1960 Donald A. Glaser, U.S.
1959 Owen Chamberlain, U.S.
Emilio G. Segre, U.S.
1958 Pavel Cherenkov, Ilya Frank, Igor Y. Tamm, all USSR
1957 Tsung-dao Lee, Chen Ning Yang, both U.S.
1956 John Bardeen, U.S.
Walter H. Brattain, U.S.
William Shockley, U.S.
1955 Polykarp Kusch, U.S.
Willis E. Lamb, U.S.
1954 Max Born, British
Walter Bothe, German
1953 Frits Zernike, Dutch
1952 Felix Bloch, U.S.
Edward M. Purcell, U.S.
1951 Sir John D. Cockroft, British
Ernest T. S. Walton, Irish
1950 Cecil F. Powell, British
1949 Hideki Yukawa, Japanese
1948 Patrick M. S. Blackett, British
1947 Sir Edward V. Appleton, British
1946 Percy Williams Bridgman, U.S.
1945 Wolfgang Pauli, U.S.
1944 Isidor Isaac Rabi, U.S.
1943 Otto Stern, U.S.
1939 Ernest O. Lawrence, U.S.
1938 Enrico Fermi, U.S.
1937 Clinton J. Davisson, U.S.
Sir George P. Thomson, British
1936 Carl D. Anderson, U.S.
Victor F. Hess, Austrian
1935 Sir James Chadwick, British
1933 Paul A. M. Dirac, British
Erwin Schrodinger, Austrian
1932 Werner Heisenberg, German
1930 Sir Chandrasekhara V. Raman, Indian
1929 Prince Louis-Victor de Broglie, French
1928 Owen W. Richardson, British
1927 Arthur H. Compton, U.S.
Charles T. R. Wilson, British
1926 Jean B. Perrin, French
1925 James Franck, Gustav Hertz, both German
1924 Karl M. G. Siegbahn, Swedish
1923 Robert A. Millikan, U.S.
1922 Niels Bohr, Danish
1921 Albert Einstein, Ger.-U.S.
1920 Charles E. Guillaume, French
1919 Johannes Stark, German
1918 Max K. E. L. Planck, German
1917 Charles G. Barkla, British
1915 Sir William H. Bragg, British
Sir William L. Bragg, British
1914 Max von Laue, German
1913 Heike Kamerlingh-Onnes, Dutch
1912 Nils G. Dalen, Swedish
1911 Wilhelm Wien, German
1910 Johannes D. van der Waals, Dutch
1909 Carl F. Braun, German
Guglielmo Marconi, Italian
1908 Gabriel Lippmann, French
1907 Albert A. Michelson, U.S.
1906 Sir Joseph J. Thomson, British
1905 Philipp E. A. von Lenard, Ger.
1904 John W. Strutt, Lord Rayleigh, British
1903 Antoine Henri Becquerel, French
Marie Curie, Polish-French
Pierre Curie, French
1902 Hendrik A. Lorentz, Pieter Zeeman, both Dutch
1901 Wilhelm C. Roentgen, German

Chemistry

1992 Rudolph A. Marcus, Can.-U.S.
1991 Richard R. Ernst, Swiss
1990 Elias James Corey, U.S.
1989 Thomas R. Cech, Sidney Altman, both U.S.
1988 Johann Deisenhofer, Robert Huber, Hartmut Michel, all W. German
1987 Donald J. Cram, Charles J. Pederson, both U.S.; Jean-Marie Lehn, French
1986 Dudley Herschbach, Yuan T. Lee, both U.S.; John C. Polanyi, Canadian
1985 Herbert A. Hauptman, Jerome Karle, both U.S.
1984 Bruce Merrifield, U.S.
1983 Henry Taube, Canadian
1982 Aaron Klug, S. African
1981 Kenichi Fukui, Japan., Roald Hoffmann, U.S.
1980 Paul Berg., U.S.;
Walter Gilbert, U.S.,
Frederick Sanger, U.K.
1979 Herbert C. Brown, U.S.
George Wittig, German
1978 Peter Mitchell, British
1977 Ilya Prigogine, Belgian
1976 William N. Lipscomb, U.S.
1975 John Cornforth, Austral.-Brit.
Vladimir Prelog, Yugo.-Swiss.
1974 Paul J. Flory, U.S.
1973 Ernst Otto Fischer, W. German
Geoffrey Wilkinson, British
1972 Christian B. Anfinsen, U.S.
Stanford Moore, U.S.
William H. Stein, U.S.
1971 Gerhard Herzberg, Canadian
1970 Luis F. Leloir, Arg.
1969 Derek H. R. Barton, British
Odd Hassel, Norwegian
1968 Lars Onsager, U.S.
1967 Manfred Eigen, German
Ronald G. W. Norrish, British
George Porter, British
1966 Robert S. Mulliken, U.S.
1965 Robert B. Woodward, U.S.
1964 Dorothy C. Hodgkin, British
1963 Giulio Natta, Italian
Karl Ziegler, German
1962 John C. Kendrew, British
Max F. Perutz, British
1961 Melvin Calvin, U.S.
1960 Willard F. Libby, U.S.
1959 Jaroslav Heyrovsky, Czech.
1958 Frederick Sanger, British
1957 Sir Alexander R. Todd, British
1956 Sir Cyril N. Hinshelwood, British
Nikolai N. Semenov, USSR
1955 Vincent du Vigneaud, U.S.
1954 Linus C. Pauling, U.S.
1953 Hermann Staudinger, German
1952 Archer J. P. Martin, British
Richard L. M. Synge, British
1951 Edwin M. McMillan, U.S.
Glenn T. Seaborg, U.S.
1950 Kurt Alder, German
Otto P. H. Diels, German
1949 William F. Giauque, U.S.
1948 Arne W. K. Tiselius, Swedish

1947 Sir Robert Robinson, British
1946 James B. Sumner, John H. Northrop, Wendell M. Stanley, U.S.
1945 Artturi I. Virtanen, Finnish
1944 Otto Hahn, German
1943 Georg de Hevesy, Hungarian
1939 Adolf F. J. Butenandt, German
Leopold Ruzicka, Swiss
1938 Richard Kuhn, German
1937 Walter N. Haworth, British
Paul Karrer, Swiss
1936 Peter J. W. Debye, Dutch
1935 Frederic Joliot-Curie, French
Irene Joliot-Curie, French
1934 Harold C. Urey, U.S.
1932 Irving Langmuir, U.S.
1931 Friedrich Bergius, German
Karl Bosch, German
1930 Hans Fischer, German
1929 Sir Arthur Harden, British
Hans von Euler-Chelpin, Swed.
1928 Adolf O. R. Windaus, German
1927 Heinrich O. Wieland, German
1926 Theodor Svedberg, Swedish
1925 Richard A. Zsigmondy, German
1923 Fritz Pregl, Austrian
1922 Francis W. Aston, British
1921 Frederick Soddy, British
1920 Walther H. Nernst, German
1918 Fritz Haber, German
1915 Richard M. Willstatter, German
1914 Theodore W. Richards, U.S.
1913 Alfred Werner, Swiss
1912 Victor Grignard, French
Paul Sabatier, French
1911 Marie Curie, Polish-French
1910 Otto Wallach, German
1909 Wilhelm Ostwald, German
1908 Ernest Rutherford, British
1907 Eduard Buchner, German
1906 Henri Moissan, French
1905 Adolf von Baeyer, German
1904 Sir William Ramsay, British
1903 Svante A. Arrhenius, Swedish
1902 Emil Fischer, German
1901 Jacobus H. van't Hoff, Dutch

Physiology or Medicine

1992 Edmond H. Fisher, Edwin G. Krebs, both U.S.
1991 Edwin Neher, Bert Sakmann, both German
1990 Joseph E. Murray, E. Donnall Thomas, both U.S.
1989 J. Michael Bishop, Harold E. Varmus, both U.S.
1988 Gertrude B. Elion, George H. Hitchings, both U.S; Sir James Black, Brit.
1987 Susumu Tonegawa, Japanese
1986 Rita Levi-Montalcini, It.-U.S., Stanley Cohen, U.S.
1985 Michael S. Brown, Joseph L. Goldstein, both U.S.
1984 Cesar Milstein, Brit.-Argentine; Georges J. F. Koehler, German; Niels K. Jerne, Brit.-Danish
1983 Barbara McClintock, U.S.
1982 Sune Bergstrom, Bengt Samuelsson, both Swedish; John R. Vane, British
1981 Roger W. Sperry, David H. Hubel, Tosten N. Wiesel, all U.S.
1980 Baruj Benacerraf, George Snell, both U.S.; Jean Dausset, France
1979 Allan M. Cormack, U.S.
Geoffrey N. Hounsfield, British
1978 Daniel Nathans, Hamilton O. Smith, both U.S.; Werner Arber, Swiss
1977 Rosalyn S. Yalow, Roger C.L. Guillemin, Andrew V. Schally, U.S.
1976 Baruch S. Blumberg, U.S.
Daniel Carleton Gajdusek, U.S.
1975 David Baltimore, Howard Temin, both U.S.; Renato Dulbecco, Ital.-U.S.
1974 Albert Claude, Lux.-U.S.; George Emil Palade, Rom.-U.S.; Christian Rene de Duve, Belg.
1973 Karl von Frisch, Ger.; Konrad Lorenz, Ger.-Austrian; Nikolaas Tinbergen, Brit.
1972 Gerald M. Edelman, U.S.
Rodney R. Porter, British
1971 Earl W. Sutherland Jr., U.S.
1970 Julius Axelrod, U.S.
Sir Bernard Katz, British
Ulf von Euler, Swedish
1969 Max Delbruck, Alfred D. Hershey, Salvador Luria, all U.S.
1968 Robert W. Holley, H. Gobind Khorana, Marshall W. Nirenberg, all U.S.
1967 Ragnar Granit, Swedish
Haldan Keffer Hartline, U.S.
George Wald, U.S.
1966 Charles B. Huggins, Francis Peyton Rous, both U.S.
1965 Francois Jacob, Andre Lwoff, Jacques Monod, all French
1964 Konrad E. Bloch, U.S.
Feodor Lynen, German
1963 Sir John C. Eccles, Australian
Alan L. Hodgkin, British
Andrew F. Huxley, British
1962 Francis H. C. Crick, British
James D. Watson, U.S.
Maurice H. F. Wilkins, British
1961 Georg von Bekesy, U.S.
1960 Sir F. MacFarlane Burnet, Australian
Peter B. Medawar, British
1959 Arthur Kornberg, U.S.
Severo Ochoa, U.S.
1958 George W. Beadle, U.S.
Edward L. Tatum, U.S.
Joshua Lederberg, U.S.
1957 Daniel Bovet, Italian
1956 Andre F. Cournand, U.S.
Werner Forssmann, German
Dickinson W. Richards Jr., U.S.
1955 Alex H. T. Theorell, Swedish
1954 John F. Enders, Frederick C. Robbins, Thomas H. Weller, all U.S.
1953 Hans A. Krebs, British
Fritz A. Lipmann, U.S.
1952 Selman A. Waksman, U.S.
1951 Max Theiler, U.S.
1950 Philip S. Hench, Edward C. Kendall, both U.S.
Tadeus Reichstein, Swiss
1949 Walter R. Hess, Swiss
Antonio Moniz, Portuguese
1948 Paul H. Müller, Swiss
1947 Carl F. Cori, Gerty T. Cori, both U.S.
Bernardo A. Houssay, Arg.
1946 Hermann J. Muller, U.S.
1945 Ernst B. Chain, British
Sir Alexander Fleming, British
Sir Howard W. Florey, British
1944 Joseph Erlanger, U.S.
Herbert S. Gasser, U.S.
1943 Henrik C. P. Dam, Danish
Edward A. Doisy, U.S.
1939 Gerhard Domagk, German
1938 Corneille J. F. Heymans, Belg.
1937 Albert Szent-Gyorgyi, Hung.-U.S.
1936 Sir Henry H. Dale, British
Otto Loewi, U.S.
1935 Hans Spemann, German
1934 George R. Minot, Wm. P. Murphy, G. H. Whipple, all U.S.
1933 Thomas H. Morgan, U.S.
1932 Edgar D. Adrian, British
Sir Charles S. Sherrington, Brit.
1931 Otto H. Warburg, German
1930 Karl Landsteiner, U.S.
1929 Christiaan Eijkman, Dutch
Sir Frederick G. Hopkins, British
1928 Charles J. H. Nicolle, French
1927 Julius Wagner-Jauregg, Austria
1926 Johannes A. G. Fibiger, Danish
1924 Willem Einthoven, Dutch
1923 Frederick G. Banting, Canadian
John J. R. Macleod, Scottish
1922 Archibald V. Hill, British
Otto F. Meyerhof, German
1920 Schack A. S. Krogh, Danish
1919 Jules Bordet, Belgian
1914 Robert Barany, Austrian
1913 Charles R. Richet, French
1912 Alexis Carrel, French
1911 Allvar Gullstrand, Swedish
1910 Albrecht Kossel, German
1909 Emil T. Kocher, Swiss
1908 Paul Ehrlich, German
Elie Metchnikoff, French
1907 Charles L. A. Laveran, French
1906 Camillo Golgi, Italian
Santiago Ramon y Cajal, Sp.
1905 Robert Koch, German
1904 Ivan P. Pavlov, Russian
1903 Niels R. Finsen, Danish
1902 Sir Ronald Ross, British
1901 Emil A. von Behring, German

Literature

1992 Derek Walcott, West Indian
1991 Nadine Gordimer, South African
1990 Octavio Paz, Mexican
1989 Camilo José Cela, Spanish
1988 Naguib Mahfouz, Egyptian
1987 Joseph Brodsky, USSR-U.S.
1986 Wole Soyinka, Nigerian
1985 Claude Simon, French
1984 Jaroslav Siefert, Czech.
1983 William Golding, British
1982 Gabriel Garcia Marquez, Colombian-Mex.
1981 Elias Canetti, Bulgarian-British
1980 Czeslaw Milosz, Polish-U.S.
1979 Odysseus Elytis, Greek
1978 Isaac Bashevis Singer, U.S. (Yiddish)
1977 Vicente Aleixandre, Spanish
1976 Saul Bellow, U.S.
1975 Eugenio Montale, Ital.
1974 Eyvind Johnson, Harry Edmund Martinson, both Swedish
1973 Patrick White, Australian
1972 Heinrich Boll, W. German
1971 Pablo Neruda, Chilean
1970 Aleksandr I. Solzhenitsyn, Russ.
1969 Samuel Beckett, Irish
1968 Yasunari Kawabata, Japanese
1967 Miguel Angel Asturias, Guate.
1966 Samuel Joseph Agnon, Israeli
Nelly Sachs, Swedish
1965 Mikhail Sholokhov, Russian
1964 Jean Paul Sartre, French (Prize declined)
1963 Giorgos Seferis, Greek
1962 John Steinbeck, U.S.
1961 Ivo Andric, Yugoslavian
1960 Saint-John Perse, French
1959 Salvatore Quasimodo, Italian
1958 Boris L. Pasternak, Russian (Prize declined)
1957 Albert Camus, French
1956 Juan Ramon Jimenez, Span.
1955 Halldor K. Laxness, Icelandic
1954 Ernest Hemingway, U.S.
1953 Sir Winston Churchill, British
1952 Francois Mauriac, French
1951 Par F. Lagerkvist, Swedish
1950 Bertrand Russell, British
1949 William Faulkner, U.S.

1948 T.S. Eliot, British
1947 Andre Gide, French
1946 Hermann Hesse, Swiss
1945 Gabriela Mistral, Chilean
1944 Johannes V. Jensen, Danish
1939 Frans E. Sillanpaa, Finnish
1938 Pearl S. Buck, U.S.
1937 Roger Martin du Gard, French
1936 Eugene O'Neill, U.S.
1934 Luigi Pirandello, Italian
1933 Ivan A. Bunin, Russian
1932 John Galsworthy, British
1931 Erik A. Karlfeldt, Swedish
1930 Sinclair Lewis, U.S.
1929 Thomas Mann, German
1928 Sigrid Undset, Norwegian
1927 Henri Bergson, French
1926 Grazia Deledda, Italian
1925 George Bernard Shaw, British
1924 Wladyslaw S. Reymont, Polish
1923 William Butler Yeats, Irish
1922 Jacinto Benavente, Spanish
1921 Anatole France, French
1920 Knut Hamsun, Norwegian
1919 Carl F. G. Spitteler, Swiss
1917 Karl A. Gjellerup, Danish
Henrik Pontoppidan, Danish
1916 Verner von Heidenstam, Swed.
1915 Romain Rolland, French
1913 Rabindranath Tagore, Indian
1912 Gerhart Hauptmann, German
1911 Maurice Maeterlinck, Belgian
1910 Paul J. L. Heyse, German
1909 Selma Lagerlof, Swedish
1908 Rudolf C. Eucken, German
1907 Rudyard Kipling, British
1906 Giosue Carducci, Italian
1905 Henryk Sienkiewicz, Polish
1904 Frederic Mistral, French
Jose Echegaray, Spanish
1903 Bjornsterne Bjornson, Norw.
1902 Theodor Mommsen, German
1901 Rene F. A Sully Prudhomme, French

Peace

1992 Rigoberta Menchú, Guatemalan
1991 Daw Aung San Suu Kyi, Myanmarese
1990 Mikhail S. Gorbachev, USSR
1989 Dalai Lama, Tibetan
1988 United Nations Peacekeeping Forces
1987 Oscar Arias Sanchez, Costa Rican
1986 Elie Wiesel, Romanian-U.S.
1985 Intl. Physicians for the Prevention of Nuclear War, U.S.
1984 Bishop Desmond Tutu, So. African
1983 Lech Walesa, Polish
1982 Alva Myrdal, Swedish; Alfonso Garcia Robles, Mexican
1981 Office of U.N. High Commissioner for Refugees
1980 Adolfo Perez Esquivel, Argentine
1979 Mother Teresa of Calcutta, Albanian-Indian
1978 Anwar Sadat, Egyptian
Menachem Begin, Israeli
1977 Amnesty International
1976 Mairead Corrigan, Betty Williams, N. Irish
1975 Andrei Sakharov, USSR
1974 Eisaku Sato, Japanese, Sean MacBride, Irish
1973 Henry Kissinger, U.S.
Le Duc Tho, N. Vietnamese (Tho declined)
1971 Willy Brandt, W. German
1970 Norman E. Borlaug, U.S.
1969 Intl. Labor Organization
1968 Rene Cassin, French
1965 U.N. Children's Fund (UNICEF)
1964 Martin Luther King Jr., U.S.
1963 International Red Cross, League of Red Cross Societies
1962 Linus C. Pauling, U.S.
1961 Dag Hammarskjold, Swedish
1960 Albert J. Luthuli, South African
1959 Philip J. Noel-Baker, British
1958 Georges Pire, Belgian
1957 Lester B. Pearson, Canadian
1954 Office of the UN High Commissioner for Refugees
1953 George C. Marshall, U.S.
1952 Albert Schweitzer, French
1951 Leon Jouhaux, French
1950 Ralph J. Bunche, U.S.
1949 Lord John Boyd Orr of Brechin Mearns, British
1947 Friends Service Council, Brit.
Amer. Friends Service Com.
1946 Emily G. Balch,
John R. Mott, both U.S.
1945 Cordell Hull, U.S.
1944 International Red Cross
1938 Nansen International Office for Refugees
1937 Viscount Cecil of Chelwood, Brit.
1936 Carlos de Saavedra Lamas, Arg.
1935 Carl von Ossietzky, German
1934 Arthur Henderson, British
1933 Sir Norman Angell, British
1931 Jane Addams, U.S.
Nicholas Murray Butler, U.S.
1930 Nathan Soderblom, Swedish
1929 Frank B. Kellogg, U.S.
1927 Ferdinand E. Buisson, French
Ludwig Quidde, German
1926 Aristide Briand, French
Gustav Stresemann, German
1925 Sir J. Austen Chamberlain, Brit.
Charles G. Dawes, U.S.
1922 Fridtjof Nansen, Norwegian
1921 Karl H. Branting, Swedish
Christian L. Lange, Norwegian
1920 Leon V.A. Bourgeois, French
1919 Woodrow Wilson, U.S.
1917 International Red Cross
1913 Henri La Fontaine, Belgian
1912 Elihu Root, U.S.
1911 Tobias M.C. Asser, Dutch
Alfred H. Fried, Austrian
1910 Permanent Intl. Peace Bureau
1909 Auguste M. F. Beernaert, Belg.
Paul H. B. B. d'Estournelles de Constant, French
1908 Klas P. Arnoldson, Swedish
Fredrik Bajer, Danish
1907 Ernesto T. Moneta, Italian
Louis Renault, French
1906 Theodore Roosevelt, U.S.
1905 Baroness Bertha von Suttner, Austrian
1904 Institute of International Law
1903 Sir William R. Cremer, British
1902 Elie Ducommun,
Charles A. Gobat, both Swiss
1901 Jean H. Dunant, Swiss
Frederic Passy, French

Nobel Memorial Prize in Economic Science

1992 Gary S. Becker, U.S.
1991 Ronald H. Coase, Br.-U.S.
1990 Harry M. Markowitz, William F. Sharpe, Merton H. Miller, all U.S.
1989 Trygve Haavelmo, Norwegian
1988 Maurice Allais, French
1987 Robert M. Solow, U.S.
1986 James M. Buchanan, U.S.
1985 Franco Modigliani, It.-U.S.
1984 Richard Stone, British
1983 Gerard Debreu, Fr.-U.S.
1982 George J. Stigler, U.S.
1981 James Tobin, U.S.
1980 Lawrence R. Klein, U.S.
1979 Theodore W. Schultz, U.S.
Sir Arthur Lewis, British
1978 Herbert A. Simon, U.S.
1977 Bertil Ohlin, Swedish
James E. Meade, British
1976 Milton Friedman, U.S.
1975 Tjalling Koopmans, Dutch-U.S.
Leonid Kantorovich, USSR
1974 Gunnar Myrdal, Swed.
Friedrich A. von Hayek, Austrian
1973 Wassily Leontief, U.S.
1972 Kenneth J. Arrow, U.S.
John R. Hicks, British
1971 Simon Kuznets, U.S.
1970 Paul A. Samuelson, U.S.
1969 Ragnar Frisch, Norwegian
Jan Tinbergen, Dutch

Pulitzer Prizes in Journalism, Letters, and Music

The Pulitzer Prizes were endowed by Joseph Pulitzer (1847-1911), publisher of the New York World, in a bequest to Columbia University and are awarded annually by the president of the university on recommendation of the Pulitzer Prize Board for work done during the preceding year. The administrator is Seymour Topping of Columbia Univ. All prizes are $3,000 (originally $500) in each category, except Meritorious Public Service for which a gold medal is given.

Journalism

Meritorious Public Service

For distinguished and meritorious public service by a United States newspaper.

1918—New York Times. Also special award to Minna Lewinson and Henry Beetle Hough.
1919—Milwaukee Journal.
1921—Boston Post.
1922—New York World.
1923—Memphis (Tenn.) Commercial Appeal.
1924—New York World.
1926—Enquirer-Sun, Columbus, Ga.
1927—Canton (Oh.) Daily News.
1928—Indianapolis Times.
1929—Evening World, New York.
1931—Atlanta (Ga.) Constitution.
1932—Indianapolis (Ind.) News.
1933—New York World-Telegram.
1934—Medford (Ore.) Mail-Tribune.
1935—Sacramento (Cal.) Bee.
1936—Cedar Rapids (Ia.) Gazette.
1937—St.Louis Post-Dispatch.

1938—Bismarck (N.D.) Tribune.
1939—Miami (Fla.) Daily News.
1940—Waterbury (Conn.) Republican and American.
1941—St.Louis Post-Dispatch.
1942—Los Angeles Times.
1943—Omaha World Herald.
1944—New York Times.
1945—Detroit Free Press.
1946—Scranton (Pa.) Times.
1947—Baltimore Sun.
1948—St. Louis Post-Dispatch.
1949—Nebraska State Journal.
1950—Chicago Daily News; St. Louis Post-Dispatch.
1951—Miami (Fla.) Herald and Brooklyn Eagle.
1952—St. Louis Post-Dispatch.
1953—Whiteville (N.C.) News Reporter; Tabor City (N.C.) Tribune.
1954—Newsday (Long Island, N.Y.)
1955—Columbus (Ga.) Ledger and Sunday Ledger-Enquirer.
1956—Watsonville (Cal.) Register-Pajaronian.
1957—Chicago Daily News.
1958—Arkansas Gazette, Little Rock.
1959—Utica (N.Y.) Observer-Dispatch and Utica Daily Press.
1960—Los Angeles Times.
1961—Amarillo (Tex.) Globe-Times.
1962—Panama City (Fla.) News-Herald.
1963—Chicago Daily News.
1964—St.Petersburg (Fla.) Times.
1965—Hutchinson (Kan.) News.
1966—Boston Globe.
1967—Louisville Courier-Journal; Milwaukee Journal.
1968—Riverside (Cal.) Press-Enterprise.
1969—Los Angeles Times.
1970—Newsday (Long Island, N.Y.).
1971—Winston Salem (N.C.) Journal & Sentinel.
1972—New York Times.
1973—Washington Post.
1974—Newsday (Long Island, N.Y.).
1975—Boston Globe.
1976—Anchorage Daily News.
1977—Lufkin (Tex.) News.
1978—Philadelphia Inquirer.
1979—Point Reyes (Cal.) Light.
1980—Gannett News Service.
1981—Charlotte (N.C.) Observer.
1982—Detroit News.
1983—Jackson (Miss.) Clarion-Ledger.
1984—Los Angeles Times.
1985—Ft. Worth (Tex.) Star-Telegram.
1986—Denver Post.
1987—Pittsburgh Press.
1988—Charlotte Observer.
1989—Anchorage Daily News.
1990—Philadelphia Inquirer, Gilbert M. Gaul; Washington (N.C.) Daily News.
1991—Des Moines Register, Jane Schorer.
1992—Sacramento Bee, Tom Knudson.
1993—Miami Herald.

Reporting

This category originally embraced all fields, local, national, and international. Later separate categories were created for national and international reporting.

1917—Herbert Bayard Swope, New York World.
1918—Harold A. Littledale, New York Evening Post.
1920—John J. Leary Jr., New York World.
1921—Louis Seibold, New York World.
1922—Kirke L. Simpson, Associated Press.
1923—Alva Johnston, New York Times.
1924—Magner White, San Diego Sun.
1925—James W. Mulroy and Alvin H. Goldstein, Chicago Daily News.
1926—William Burke Miller, Louisville Courier-Journal.
1927—John T. Rogers, St. Louis Post-Dispatch.
1929—Paul Y. Anderson, St. Louis Post-Dispatch.
1930—Russell D. Owens, New York Times. Also $500 to W.O. Dapping, Auburn (N.Y.) Citizen.
1931—A.B. MacDonald, Kansas City (Mo.) Star.
1932—W.C. Richards, D.D. Martin, J.S. Pooler, F.D. Webb, J.N.W. Sloan, Detroit Free Press.
1933—Francis A. Jamieson, Associated Press.
1934—Royce Brier, San Francisco Chronicle.
1935—William H. Taylor, New York Herald Tribune.
1936—Lauren D. Lyman, New York Times.
1937—John J. O'Neill, N.Y.Herald Tribune; William L. Laurence, N.Y Times; Howard W. Blakeslee, A.P.; Gobind Behari Lal, Universal Service; and David Dietz, Scripps-Howard Newspapers.
1938—Raymond Sprigle, Pittsburgh Post-Gazette.
1939—Thomas L. Stokes, Scripps-Howard Newspaper Alliance.
1940—S.Burton Heath, New York World-Telegram.
1941—Westbrook Pegler, New York World-Telegram.
1942—Stanton Delaplane, San Francisco Chronicle.
1943—George Weller, Chicago Daily News.
1944—Paul Schoenstein, New York Journal-American.
1945—Jack S. McDowell, San Francisco Call-Bulletin.
1946—William L. Laurence, New York Times.
1947—Frederick Woltman, New York World-Telegram.
1948—George E. Goodwin, Atlanta Journal.
1949—Malcolm Johnson, New York Sun.
1950—Meyer Berger, New York Times.
1951—Edward S. Montgomery, San Francisco Examiner.
1952—Geo. de Carvalho, San Francisco Chronicle.

(1) General or Spot; (2) Special or Investigative

1953—(1) Providence (R.I.) Journal and Evening Bulletin; (2) Edward J. Mowery, New York World-Telegram & Sun.
1954—(1) Vicksburg (Miss.) Sunday Post-Herald; (2) Alvin Scott McCoy, Kansas City (Mo.) Star.
1955—(1) Mrs. Caro Brown, Alice (Tex.) Daily Echo; (2) Roland K. Towery, Cuero (Tex.) Record.
1956—(1) Lee Hills, Detroit Free Press; (2) Arthur Daley, New York Times.
1957—(1) Salt Lake Tribune, Salt Lake City, Ut.; (2) Wallace Turner and William Lambert, Portland Oregonian.
1958—(1) Fargo, (N.D.) Forum; (2) George Beveridge, Evening Star, Washington, D.C.
1959—(1) Mary Lou Werner, Washington Evening Star; (2) John Harold Brislin, Scranton (Pa.) Tribune, and The Scrantonian.
1960—(1) Jack Nelson, Atlanta Constitution; (2) Miriam Ottenberg, Washington Evening Star.
1961—(1) Sanche de Gramont, New York Herald Tribune; (2) Edgar May, Buffalo Evening News.
1962—(1) Robert D.Mullins, Deseret News, Salt Lake City; (2) George Bliss, Chicago Tribune.
1963—(1) Shared by Sylvan Fox, William Longgood, and Anthony Shannon, New York World-Telegram & Sun; (2) Oscar Griffin Jr., Pecos (Tex.) Independent and Enterprise.
1964—(1) Norman C. Miller, Wall Street Journal; (2) Shared by James V. Magee, Albert V. Gaudiosi, and Frederick A. Meyer, Philadelphia Bulletin.
1965—(1) Melvin H. Ruder, Hungry Horse News (Columbia Falls, Mon.); (2) Gene Goltz, Houston Post.
1966—(1) Los Angeles Times Staff; (2) John A. Frasca, Tampa (Fla.) Tribune.
1967—(1) Robert V. Cox, Chambersburg (Pa.) Public Opinion; (2) Gene Miller, Miami Herald.
1968—Detroit Free Press Staff; (2) J. Anthony Lukas, New York Times.
1969—(1) John Fetterman, Louisville Courier-Journal and Times; (2) Albert L. Delugach, St. Louis Globe Democrat, and Denny Walsh, Life.
1970—(1) Thomas Fitzpatrick, Chicago Sun-Times; (2) Harold Eugene Martin, Montgomery Advertiser & Alabama Journal.
1971—(1) Akron Beacon Journal Staff, (2) William Hugh Jones, Chicago Tribune.
1972—(1) Richard Cooper and John Machacek, Rochester Times-Union; (2) Timothy Leland, Gerard M. O'Neill, Stephen A. Kurkjian and Anne De Santis, Boston Globe.
1973—(1) Chicago Tribune; (2) Sun Newspapers of Omaha.
1974—(1) Hugh F. Hough, Arthur M. Petacque, Chicago Sun-Times; (2) William Sherman, New York Daily News.
1975—(1) Xenia (Oh.) Daily Gazette; (2) Indianapolis Star.
1976—(1) Gene Miller, Miami Herald; (2) Chicago Tribune.
1977—(1) Margo Huston, Milwaukee Journal; (2) Acel Moore, Wendell Rawls Jr., Philadelphia Inquirer.
1978—(1) Richard Whitt, Louisville Courier-Journal; (2) Anthony R. Dolan, Stamford (Conn.) Advocate.
1979—(1) San Diego (Cal.) Evening Tribune; (2) Gilbert M. Gaul, Elliot G. Jaspin, Pottsville (Pa.) Republican.
1980—(1) Philadelphia Inquirer; (2) Stephen A. Kurkjian, Alexander B. Hawes Jr., Nils Bruzelius, Joan Vennochi, Robert M. Porterfield, Boston Globe.
1981—(1) Longview (Wash.) Daily News staff; (2) Clark Hallas and Robert B. Lowe, Arizona Daily Star.
1982—(1) Kansas City Star, Kansas City Times; (2) Paul Henderson, Seattle Times.
1983—(1) Fort Wayne (Ind.) News-Sentinel; (2) Loretta Tofani, Washington Post.
1984—(1) Newsday (N.Y.); (2) Boston Globe.
1985—(1) Thomas Turcol, Virginian-Pilot and Ledger-Star, Norfolk, Va.; (2) William K. Marimow, Philadelphia Inquirer; Lucy Morgan & Jack Reed, St. Petersburg (Fla.) Times.
1986—(1) Edna Buchanan, Miami Herald; (2) Jeffrey A. Marx & Michael M. York, Lexington (Ky.) Herald-Leader.
1987—(1) Akron Beacon Journal; (2) Daniel R. Biddle, H.G. Bissinger, Fredric N. Tulsky, Philadelphia Inquirer; John Woestendiek, Philadelphia Inquirer.

1988—(1) Alabama Journal; Lawrence (Mass.) Eagle-Tribune; (2) Walt Bogdanich, Wall Street Journal.
1989—(1) Louisville Courier-Journal; (2) Bill Dedman, Atlanta Journal and Constitution.
1990—(1) San Jose Mercury News; (2) Lon Kilzer, Chris Ison, Star Tribune, Minneapolis-St. Paul.
1991—(1) Miami Herald; (2) Joseph T. Hallinan, Susan M. Headden, Indianapolis Star.
1992—(1) New York Newsday; (2) Lorraine Adams, Dan Malone, Dallas Morning News.
1993—(1) Los Angeles Times; Jeff Brazil, Steve Berry, Orlando Sentinel.

Criticism or Commentary

(1) Criticism; (2) Commentary

1970—(1) Ada Louise Huxtable, New York Times; (2) Marquis W. Childs, St. Louis Post-Dispatch.
1971—(1) Harold C. Schonberg, New York Times; (2) William A. Caldwell, The Record, Hackensack, N.J.
1972—(1) Frank Peters Jr., St. Louis Post-Dispatch; (2) Mike Royko, Chicago Daily News.
1973—(1) Ronald Powers, Chicago Sun-Times; (2) David S. Broder, Washington Post.
1974—(1) Emily Genauer, Newsday, (N.Y.); (2) Edwin A. Roberts Jr., National Observer.
1975—(1) Roger Ebert, Chicago Sun Times; (2) Mary McGrory, Washington Star.
1976—(1) Alan M. Kriegsman, Washington Post; (2) Walter W. (Red) Smith, New York Times.
1977—(1) William McPherson, Washington Post; (2) George F. Will, Wash. Post Writers Group.
1978—(1) Walter Kerr, New York Times; (2) William Safire, New York Times.
1979—(1) Paul Gapp, Chicago Tribune; (2) Russell Baker, New York Times.
1980—(1) William A. Henry III, Boston Globe; (2) Ellen Goodman, Boston Globe.
1981—(1) Jonathan Yardley, Washington Star; (2) Dave Anderson, New York Times.
1982—(1) Martin Bernheimer, Los Angeles Times; (2) Art Buchwald, Los Angeles Times Syndicate.
1983—(1) Manuela Hoelterhoff, Wall St. Journal; (2) Claude Sitton, Raleigh (N.C.) News & Observer.
1984—Paul Goldberger, New York Times; (2) Vermont Royster, Wall St. Journal
1985—(1) Howard Rosenberg, Los Angeles Times; (2) Murray Kempton, Newsday (N.Y.).
1986—(1) Donal J. Henahan, New York Times; (2) Jimmy Breslin, New York Daily News.
1987—(1) Richard Eder, Los Angeles Times; (2) Charles Krauthammer, Washington Post.
1988—(1) Tom Shales, Washington Post; (2) Dave Barry, Miami Herald.
1989—(1) Michael Skube, News and Observer, Raleigh, N.C.; (2) Clarence Page, Chicago Tribune.
1990—(1) Allan Temko, San Francisco Chronicle; (2) Jim Murray, Los Angeles Times
1991—(1) David Shaw, Los Angeles Times; (2) Jim Hoagland, Washington Post.
1992—(1) No award; (2) Anna Quindlen, New York Times.
1993—(1) Michael Dirda, Washington Post; (2) Liz Balmaseda, Miami Herald.

National Reporting

1942—Louis Stark, New York Times.
1944—Dewey L. Fleming, Baltimore Sun.
1945—James B. Reston, New York Times.
1946—Edward A. Harris, St. Louis Post-Dispatch.
1947—Edward T. Folliard, Washington Post.
1948—Bert Andrews, New York Herald Tribune; Nat S. Finney, Minneapolis Tribune.
1949—Charles P. Trussell, New York Times.
1950—Edwin O. Guthman, Seattle Times.
1952—Anthony Leviero, New York Times.
1953—Don Whitehead, Associated Press.
1954—Richard Wilson, Des Moines Register.
1955—Anthony Lewis, Washington Daily News.
1956—Charles L. Bartlett, Chattanooga Times.
1957—James Reston, New York Times.
1958—Relman Morin, AP; Clark Mollenhoff, Des Moines Register & Tribune.
1959—Howard Van Smith, Miami (Fla.) News.
1960—Vance Trimble, Scripps-Howard, Washington, D.C.
1961—Edward R. Cony, Wall Street Journal.
1962—Nathan G. Caldwell and Gene S. Graham, Nashville Tennessean.
1963—Anthony Lewis, New York Times.
1964—Merriman Smith, UPI.
1965—Louis M. Kohlmeier, Wall Street Journal.
1966—Haynes Johnson, Washington Evening Star.
1967—Monroe Karmin and Stanley Penn, Wall Street Journal.
1968—Howard James, Christian Science Monitor; Nathan K. Kotz, Des Moines Register.
1969—Robert Cahn, Christian Science Monitor.
1970—William J. Eaton, Chicago Daily News.
1971—Lucinda Franks & Thomas Powers, UPI.
1972—Jack Anderson, United Feature Syndicate.
1973—Robert Boyd and Clark Hoyt, Knight Newspapers.
1974—James R. Polk, Washington Star-News; Jack White, Providence Journal-Bulletin.
1975—Donald L. Barlett and James B. Steele, Philadelphia Inquirer.
1976—James Risser, Des Moines Register.
1977—Walter Mears, Associated Press.
1978—Gaylord D. Shaw, Los Angeles Times.
1979—James Risser, Des Moines Register.
1980—Charles Stafford, Bette Swenson Orsini, St. Petersburg (Fla.) Times.
1981—John M. Crewdson, New York Times.
1982—Rick Atkinson, Kansas City Times.
1983—Boston Globe.
1984—John Noble Wilford, New York Times.
1985—Thomas J. Knudson, Des Moines (Ia.) Register.
1986—Craig Flournoy & George Rodrigue, Dallas Morning News; Arthur Howe, Philadelphia Inquirer.
1987—Miami Herald; New York Times.
1988—Tim Weiner, Philadelphia Inquirer.
1989—Donald L. Barlett & James B. Steele, Philadelphia Inquirer.
1990—Ross Anderson, Bill Dietrich, Mary Ann Gwinn, Eric Nalder, Seattle Times.
1991—Marjie Lundstrom, Rochelle Sharpe, Gannett News Service.
1992—Jeff Taylor, Mike McGraw, Kansas City Star.
1993—David Maraniss, Washington Post.

International Reporting

1942—Laurence Edmund Allen, Associated Press.
1943—Ira Wolfert, No. Am. Newspaper Alliance.
1944—Daniel DeLuce, Associated Press.
1945—Mark S. Watson, Baltimore Sun.
1946—Homer W. Bigart, New York Herald Tribune.
1947—Eddy Gilmore, Associated Press.
1948—Paul W. Ward, Baltimore Sun.
1949—Price Day, Baltimore Sun.
1950—Edmund Stevens, Christian Science Monitor.
1951—Keyes Beech and Fred Sparks, Chicago Daily News; Homer Bigart and Marguerite Higgins, New York Herald Tribune; Relman Morin and Don Whitehead, AP.
1952—John M. Hightower, Associated Press.
1953—Austin C. Wehrwein, Milwaukee Journal.
1954—Jim G. Lucas, Scripps-Howard Newspapers.
1955—Harrison Salisbury, New York Times.
1956—William Randolph Hearst Jr., Frank Conniff, Hearst Newspapers; Kingsbury Smith, INS.
1957—Russell Jones, United Press.
1958—New York Times.
1959—Joseph Martin and Philip Santora, New York Daily News.
1960—A.M. Rosenthal, New York Times.
1961—Lynn Heinzerling, Associated Press.
1962—Walter Lippmann, New York Herald Tribune Synd.
1963—Hal Hendrix, Miami (Fla.) News.
1964—Malcolm W. Browne, AP; David Halberstam, New York Times.
1965—J.A. Livingston, Philadelphia Bulletin.
1966—Peter Arnett, AP.
1967—R. John Hughes, Christian Science Monitor.
1968—Alfred Friendly, Washington Post.
1969—William Tuohy, Los Angeles Times.
1970—Seymour M. Hersh, Dispatch News Service.
1971—Jimmie Lee Hoagland, Washington Post.
1972—Peter R. Kann, Wall Street Journal.
1973—Max Frankel, New York Times.
1974—Hedrick Smith, New York Times.
1975—William Mullen and Ovie Carter, Chicago Tribune.
1976—Sydney H. Schanberg, New York Times.
1978—Henry Kamm, New York Times.
1979—Richard Ben Cramer, Philadelphia Inquirer.
1980—Joel Brinkley, Jay Mather, Louisville (Ky.) Courier-Journal.
1981—Shirley Christian, Miami Herald.
1982—John Darnton, New York Times.
1983—Thomas L. Friedman, New York Times; Loren Jenkins, Washington Post.
1984—Karen Elliot House, Wall St. Journal

1985—Josh Friedman, Dennis Bell, Ozier Muhammad, Newsday (N.Y.).
1986—Lewis M. Simons, Pete Carey, Katherine Ellison, San Jose (Calif.) Mercury News.
1987—Michael Parks, Los Angeles Times.
1988—Thomas L. Friedman, New York Times.
1989—Glenn Frankel, Washington Post; Bill Keller, New York Times.
1990—Nicholas D. Kirstof, Sheryl WuDunn, New York Times.
1991—Caryle Murphy, Washington Post; Serge Schmemann, New York Times.
1992—Patrick J. Sloyan, Newsday (N.Y.).
1993—John F. Burns, New York Times; Roy Gutman, Newsday (N.Y.)

Correspondence

For Washington or foreign correspondence. Category was merged with those in national and international reporting in 1948.
1929—Paul Scott Mowrer, Chicago Daily News.
1930—Leland Stowe, New York Herald Tribune.
1931—H.R. Knickerbocker, Philadelphia Public Ledger and New York Evening Post.
1932—Walter Duranty, New York Times, and Charles G. Ross, St. Louis Post-Dispatch.
1933—Edgar Ansel Mowrer, Chicago Daily News.
1934—Frederick T. Birchall, New York Times.
1935—Arthur Krock, New York Times.
1936—Wilfred C. Barber, Chicago Tribune.
1937—Anne O'Hare McCormick, New York Times.
1938—Arthur Krock, New York Times.
1939—Louis P. Lochner, Associated Press.
1940—Otto D. Tolischus, New York Times.
1941—Bronze plaque to commemorate work of American correspondents on war fronts.
1942—Carlos P. Romulo, Philippines Herald.
1943—Hanson W. Baldwin, New York Times.
1944—Ernest Taylor Pyle, Scripps-Howard Newspaper Alliance.
1945—Harold V. (Hal) Boyle, Associated Press.
1946—Arnaldo Cortesi, New York Times.
1947—Brooks Atkinson, New York Times.

Editorial Writing

1917—New York Tribune.
1918—Louisville (Ky.) Courier-Journal.
1920—Harvey E. Newbranch, Omaha Evening World-Herald.
1922—Frank M. O'Brien, New York Herald.
1923—William Allen White, Emporia Gazette.
1924—Frank Buxton, Boston Herald, Special Prize. Frank I. Cobb, New York World.
1925—Robert Lathan, Charleston (S.C.) News and Courier.
1926—Edward M. Kingsbury, New York Times.
1927—F. Lauriston Bullard, Boston Herald.
1928—Grover C. Hall, Montgomery Advertiser.
1929—Louis Isaac Jaffe, Norfolk Virginian-Pilot.
1931—Chas. Ryckman, Fremont (Neb.) Tribune.
1933—Kansas City (Mo.) Star.
1934—E. P. Chase, Atlantic (Ia.) News Telegraph.
1936—Felix Morley, Washington Post. George B. Parker, Scripps-Howard Newspapers.
1937—John W. Owens, Baltimore Sun.
1938—W.W. Waymack, Des Moines (Ia.) Register and Tribune.
1939—Ronald G. Callvert, Portland Oregonian.
1940—Bart Howard, St. Louis Post-Dispatch.
1941—Reuben Maury, Daily News, N.Y.
1942—Geoffrey Parsons, New York Herald Tribune.
1943—Forrest W. Seymour, Des Moines (Ia.) Register and Tribune.
1944—Henry J. Haskell, Kansas City (Mo.) Star.
1945—George W. Potter, Providence (R.I.) Journal-Bulletin.
1946—Hodding Carter, Greenville (Miss.) Delta Democrat-Times.
1947—William H. Grimes, Wall Street Journal.
1948—Virginius Dabney, Richmond (Va.) Times-Dispatch.
1949—John H. Crider, Boston (Mass.) Herald, Herbert Elliston, Washington Post.
1950—Carl M. Saunders, Jackson (Mich.) Citizen-Patriot.
1951—William H. Fitzpatrick, New Orleans States.
1952—Louis LaCoss, St. Louis Globe Democrat.
1953—Vermont C. Royster, Wall Street Journal.
1954—Don Murray, Boston Herald.
1955—Royce Howes, Detroit Free Press.
1956—Lauren K. Soth, Des Moines (Ia.) Register and Tribune.
1957—Buford Boone, Tuscaloosa (Ala.) News.
1958—Harry S. Ashmore, Arkansas Gazette.
1959—Ralph McGill, Atlanta Constitution.
1960—Lenoir Chambers, Norfolk Virginian-Pilot.
1961—William J. Dorvillier, San Juan (Puerto Rico) Star.
1962—Thomas M. Storke, Santa Barbara (Cal.) News-Press.
1963—Ira B. Harkey Jr., Pascagoula (Miss.) Chronicle.
1964—Hazel Brannon Smith, Lexington (Miss.) Advertiser.
1965—John R. Harrison, Gainesville (Fla.) Sun.
1966—Robert Lasch, St. Louis Post-Dispatch.
1967—Eugene C. Patterson, Atlanta Constitution.
1968—John S. Knight, Knight Newspapers.
1969—Paul Greenberg, Pine Bluff (Ark.) Commercial.
1970—Philip L. Geyelin, Washington Post.
1971—Horance G. Davis Jr., Gainesville (Fla.) Sun.
1972—John Strohmeyer, Bethlehem (Pa.) Globe-Times.
1973—Roger B. Linscott, Berkshire Eagle, Pittsfield, Mass.
1974—F. Gilman Spencer, Trenton (N.J.) Trentonian.
1975—John D. Maurice, Charleston (W.Va.) Daily Mail.
1976—Philip Kerby, Los Angeles Times.
1977—Warren L. Lerude, Foster Church, and Norman F. Cardoza, Reno (Nev.) Evening Gazette and Nevada State Journal.
1978—Meg Greenfield, Washington Post.
1979—Edwin M. Yoder, Washington Star.
1980—Robert L. Bartley, Wall Street Journal.
1982—Jack Rosenthal, New York Times.
1983—Editorial board, Miami Herald.
1984—Albert Scardino, Georgia Gazette.
1985—Richard Aregood, Philadelphia Daily News.
1986—Jack Fuller, Chicago Tribune.
1987—Jonathan Freedman, Tribune (San Diego).
1988—Jane Healy, Orlando Sentinel.
1989—Lois Wille, Chicago Tribune.
1990—Thomas J. Hylton, Pottstown (Pa.) Mercury.
1991—Ron Casey, Harold Jackson, Joey Kennedy, Birmingham (Ala.) News.
1992—Maria Henson, Lexington (Ky.) Herald-Leader.
1993—No award.

Editorial Cartooning

1922—Rollin Kirby, New York World.
1924—Jay N. Darling, Des Moines Register.
1925—Rollin Kirby, New York World.
1926—D. R. Fitzpatrick, St. Louis Post-Dispatch.
1927—Nelson Harding, Brooklyn Eagle.
1928—Nelson Harding, Brooklyn Eagle.
1929—Rollin Kirby, New York World.
1930—Charles Macauley, Brooklyn Eagle.
1931—Edmund Duffy, Baltimore Sun.
1932—John T. McCutcheon, Chicago Tribune.
1933—H. M. Talburt, Washington Daily News.
1934—Edmund Duffy, Baltimore Sun.
1935—Ross A. Lewis, Milwaukee Journal.
1937—C. D. Batchelor, New York Daily News.
1938—Vaughn Shoemaker, Chicago Daily News.
1939—Charles G. Werner, Daily Oklahoman.
1940—Edmund Duffy, Baltimore Sun.
1941—Jacob Burck, Chicago Times.
1942—Herbert L. Block, Newspaper Enterprise Assn.
1943—Jay N. Darling, Des Moines Register.
1944—Clifford K. Berryman, Washington Star.
1945—Bill Mauldin, United Feature Syndicate.
1946—Bruce Alexander Russell, Los Angeles Times.
1947—Vaughn Shoemaker, Chicago Daily News.
1948—Reuben L. (Rube) Goldberg, N. Y. Sun.
1949—Lute Pease, Newark (N.J.) Evening News.
1950—James T. Berryman, Washington Star.
1951—Reginald W. Manning, Arizona Republic.
1952—Fred L. Packer, New York Mirror.
1953—Edward D. Kuekes, Cleveland Plain Dealer.
1954—Herbert L. Block, Washington Post & Times-Herald.
1955—Daniel R. Fitzpatrick, St. Louis Post-Dispatch.
1956—Robert York, Louisville (Ky.) Times.
1957—Tom Little, Nashville Tennessean.
1958—Bruce M. Shanks, Buffalo Evening News.
1959—Bill Mauldin, St. Louis Post-Dispatch.
1961—Carey Orr, Chicago Tribune.
1962—Edmund S. Valtman, Hartford Times.
1963—Frank Miller, Des Moines Register.
1964—Paul Conrad, Denver Post.
1966—Don Wright, Miami News.
1967—Patrick B. Oliphant, Denver Post.
1968—Eugene Gray Payne, Charlotte Observer.
1969—John Fischetti, Chicago Daily News.
1970—Thomas F. Darcy, Newsday.
1971—Paul Conrad, L. A. Times.
1972—Jeffrey K. MacNelly, Richmond News-Leader.
1974—Paul Szep, Boston Globe.
1975—Garry Trudeau, Universal Press Syndicate.
1976—Tony Auth, Philadelphia Inquirer.
1977—Paul Szep, Boston Globe.
1978—Jeffrey K. MacNelly, Richmond News Leader.

1979—Herbert L. Block, Washington Post.
1980—Don Wright, Miami (Fla.) News.
1981—Mike Peters, Dayton (Oh.) Daily News.
1982—Ben Sargent, Austin American-Statesman.
1983—Richard Lochner, Chicago Tribune.
1984—Paul Conrad, Los Angeles Times.
1985—Jeffrey K. MacNelly, Chicago Tribune.
1986—Jules Feiffer, Village Voice (N.Y. City).
1987—Berke Breathed, Washington Post.
1988—Doug Marlette, Atlanta Constitution, Charlotte Observer.
1989—Jack Higgins, Chicago Sun-Times.
1990—Tom Toles, Buffalo News.
1991—Jim Borgman, Cincinnati Enquirer.
1992—Signe Wilkinson, Philadelphia Daily News.
1993—Stephen R. Benson, Arizona Republic.

Spot News Photography

1942—Milton Brooks, Detroit News.
1943—Frank Noel, Associated Press.
1944—Frank Filan, AP; Earl L. Bunker, Omaha World-Herald.
1945—Joe Rosenthal, Associated Press, for photograph of planting American flag on Iwo Jima.
1947—Arnold Hardy, amateur, Atlanta, Ga.
1948—Frank Cushing, Boston Traveler.
1949—Nathaniel Fein, New York Herald Tribune.
1950—Bill Crouch, Oakland (Cal.) Tribune.
1951—Max Desfor, Associated Press.
1952—John Robinson and Don Ultang, Des Moines Register and Tribune.
1953—William M. Gallagher, Flint (Mich.) Journal.
1954—Mrs. Walter M. Schau, amateur.
1955—John L. Gaunt Jr., Los Angeles Times.
1956—New York Daily News.
1957—Harry A. Trask, Boston Traveler.
1958—William C. Beall, Washington Daily News.
1959—William Seaman, Minneapolis Star.
1960—Andrew Lopez, UPI.
1961—Yasushi Nagao, Mainichi Newspapers, Tokyo.
1962—Paul Vathis, Associated Press.
1963—Hector Rondon, La Republica, Caracas, Venezuela.
1964—Robert H. Jackson, Dallas Times-Herald.
1965—Horst Faas, Associated Press.
1966—Kyoichi Sawada, UPI.
1967—Jack R. Thornell, Associated Press.
1968—Rocco Morabito, Jacksonville Journal.
1969—Edward Adams, AP.
1970—Steve Starr, AP.
1971—John Paul Filo, Valley Daily News & Daily Dispatch of Tarentum & New Kensington, Pa.
1972—Horst Faas and Michel Laurent, AP.
1973—Huynh Cong Ut, AP.
1974—Anthony K. Roberts, AP.
1975—Gerald H. Gay, Seattle Times.
1976—Stanley Forman, Boston Herald American.
1977—Neal Ulevich, Associated Press; Stanley Forman, Boston Herald American.
1978—John H. Blair, UPI.
1979—Thomas J. Kelly III, Pottstown (Pa.) Mercury.
1980—UPI.
1981—Larry C. Price, Ft. Worth (Tex.) Star-Telegram.
1982—Ron Edmonds, Associated Press.
1983—Bill Foley, AP.
1984—Stan Grossfeld, Boston Globe.
1985—The Register, Santa Ana, Calif.
1986—Carol Guzy & Michel duCille, Miami Herald.
1987—Kim Komenich, San Francisco Examiner.
1988—Scott Shaw, Odessa (Tex.) American.
1989—Ron Olshwanger, St. Louis Post-Dispatch.
1990—Oakland (Calif.) Tribune photo staff.
1991—Greg Marinovich, Associated Press.
1992—Associated Press staff.
1993—Ken Geiger, William Snyder, Dallas Morning News.

Feature Photography

1968—Toshio Sakai, UPI.
1969—Moneta Sleet Jr., Ebony.
1970—Dallas Kinney, Palm Beach Post.
1971—Jack Dykinga, Chicago Sun-Times.
1972—Dave Kennerly, UPI.
1973—Brian Lanker, Topeka Capitol-Journal.
1974—Slava Veder, AP.
1975—Matthew Lewis, Washington Post.
1976—Louisville Courier-Journal and Louisville Times.
1977—Robin Hood, Chattanooga News-Free Press.
1978—J. Ross Baughman, AP.
1979—Staff photographers, Boston Herald American.
1980—Erwin H. Hagler, Dallas Times-Herald.
1981—Taro M. Yamasaki, Detroit Free Press.
1982—John H. White, Chicago Sun-Times.
1983—James B. Dickman, Dallas Times-Herald.
1984—Anthony Suad, Denver Post.
1985—Stan Grossfeld, Boston Globe; Larry C. Price, Philadelphia Inquirer.
1986—Tom Gralish, Philadelphia Inquirer.
1987—David Peterson, Des Moines Register.
1988—Michel duCille, Miami Herald.
1989—Manny Crisostomo, Detroit Free Press.
1990—David C. Turnley, Detroit Free Press.
1991—William Snyder, Dallas Morning News.
1992—John Kaplan, Block Newspapers (Toledo, Oh.).
1993—Associated Press staff.

Special Citation

1938—Edmonton (Alberta) Journal, bronze plaque.
1941—New York Times.
1944—Byron Price and Mrs. William Allen White. Also to Richard Rodgers and Oscar Hammerstein 2d, for musical, Oklahoma!
1945—Press cartographers for war maps.
1947—(Pulitzer centennial year.) Columbia Univ. and the Graduate School of Journalism, and St. Louis Post-Dispatch.
1948—Dr. Frank Diehl Fackenthal.
1951—Cyrus L. Sulzberger, New York Times.
1952—Max Kase, New York Journal-American, Kansas City Star.
1953—New York Times; Lester Markel.
1957—Kenneth Roberts, for his historical novels.
1958—Walter Lippmann, New York Herald Tribune.
1960—Garrett Mattingly, for The Armada.
1961—American Heritage Picture History of the Civil War.
1964—Gannett Newspapers.
1973—James T. Flexner, for biography of George Washington.
1976—John Hohenberg, for services to American journalism.
1977—Alex Haley, for Roots.
1978—Richard Lee Strout, Christian Science Monitor and New Republic.
—E.B. White.
1984—Theodore Geisel ("Dr. Seuss").
1985—William Schuman, composer, educational leader.
1987—Joseph Pulitzer Jr.
1992—Art Spiegelman, Maus.

Feature Writing

1979—Jon D. Franklin, Baltimore Evening Sun.
1980—Madeleine Blais, Miami Herald Tropic Magazine.
Janet Cooke, Washington Post.
1981—Teresa Carpenter, Village Voice, New York City.
1982—Saul Pett, Associated Press.
1984—Peter M. Rinearson, Seattle Times.
1985—Alice Steinbach, Baltimore Sun.
1986—John Camp, St. Paul Pioneer Press & Dispatch.
1987—Steve Twomey, Philadephia Inquirer.
1988—Jacqui Banaszynski, St. Paul Pioneer Press Dispatch.
1989—David Zucchino, Philadelphia Inquirer.
1990—Dave Curtin, Colorado Springs Gazette Telegraph.
1991—Sheryl James, St. Petersburg Times.
1992—Howell Raines, New York Times.
1993—George Lardner Jr., Washington Post.

Explanatory Journalism

1985—Jon Franklin, Baltimore Evening Sun.
1986—New York Times staff.
1987—Jeff Lyon & Peter Gorner, Chicago Tribune.
1988—Daniel Hertzberg, James B. Stewart, Wall Street Journal.
1989—David Hanners, William Snyder, Karen Blessen, Dallas Morning News.
1990—David A. Vise, Steve Coll, Washington Post.
1991—Susan C. Faludi, Wall Street Journal.
1992—Robert S. Capers, Eric Lipton, Hartford (Conn.) Courant.
1993—Mike Toner, Atlanta Journal-Constitution.

Specialized Reporting

1985—Randall Savage, Jackie Crosby, Macon (Ga.) Telegraph and News.
1986—Andrew Schneider & Mary Pat Flaherty, Pittsburgh Press.
1987—Alex S. Jones, New York Times.
1988—Dean Baquet, William Gaines, Ann Marie Lipinski, Chicago Tribune.
1989—Edward Humes, Orange County (Calif.) Register.
1990—Tamar Stieber, Albuquerque Journal.
1991—Natalie Angier, New York Times.
1992—Deborah Blum, Sacramento Bee.
1993—Paul Ingrassia, Joseph B. White, Wall Street Journal.

Letters

Fiction

For fiction in book form by an American author, preferably dealing with American life.
1918—Ernest Poole, His Family.
1919—Booth Tarkington, The Magnificent Ambersons.
1921—Edith Wharton, The Age of Innocence.
1922—Booth Tarkington, Alice Adams.
1923—Willa Cather, One of Ours.
1924—Margaret Wilson, The Able McLaughlins.
1925—Edna Ferber, So Big.
1926—Sinclair Lewis, Arrowsmith. (Refused prize.)
1927—Louis Bromfield, Early Autumn.
1928—Thornton Wilder, Bridge of San Luis Rey.
1929—Julia M. Peterkin, Scarlet Sister Mary.
1930—Oliver LaFarge, Laughing Boy.
1931—Margaret Ayer Barnes, Years of Grace.
1932—Pearl S. Buck, The Good Earth.
1933—T. S. Stribling, The Store.
1934—Caroline Miller, Lamb in His Bosom.
1935—Josephine W. Johnson, Now in November.
1936—Harold L. Davis, Honey in the Horn.
1937—Margaret Mitchell, Gone with the Wind.
1938—John P. Marquand, The Late George Apley.
1939—Marjorie Kinnan Rawlings, The Yearling.
1940—John Steinbeck, The Grapes of Wrath.
1942—Ellen Glasgow, In This Our Life.
1943—Upton Sinclair, Dragon's Teeth.
1944—Martin Flavin, Journey in the Dark.
1945—John Hersey, A Bell for Adano.
1947—Robert Penn Warren, All the King's Men.
1948—James A. Michener, Tales of the South Pacific.
1949—James Gould Cozzens, Guard of Honor.
1950—A. B. Guthrie Jr., The Way West.
1951—Conrad Richter, The Town.
1952—Herman Wouk, The Caine Mutiny.
1953—Ernest Hemingway, The Old Man and the Sea.
1955—William Faulkner, A Fable.
1956—MacKinlay Kantor, Andersonville.
1958—James Agee, A Death in the Family.
1959—Robert Lewis Taylor, The Travels of Jaimie McPheeters.
1960—Allen Drury, Advise and Consent.
1961—Harper Lee, To Kill a Mockingbird.
1962—Edwin O'Connor, The Edge of Sadness.
1963—William Faulkner, The Reivers.
1965—Shirley Ann Grau, The Keepers of the House.
1966—Katherine Anne Porter, Collected Stories of Katherine Anne Porter.
1967—Bernard Malamud, The Fixer.
1968—William Styron, The Confessions of Nat Turner.
1969—N. Scott Momaday, House Made of Dawn.
1970—Jean Stafford, Collected Stories.
1972—Wallace Stegner, Angle of Repose.
1973—Eudora Welty, The Optimist's Daughter.
1975—Michael Shaara, The Killer Angels.
1976—Saul Bellow, Humboldt's Gift.
1978—James Alan McPherson, Elbow Room.
1979—John Cheever, The Stories of John Cheever.
1980—Norman Mailer, The Executioner's Song.
1981—John Kennedy Toole, A Confederacy of Dunces.
1982—John Updike, Rabbit Is Rich.
1983—Alice Walker, The Color Purple.
1984—William Kennedy, Ironweed.
1985—Alison Lurie, Foreign Affairs.
1986—Larry McMurtry, Lonesome Dove.
1987—Peter Taylor, A Summons to Memphis.
1988—Toni Morrison, Beloved.
1989—Anne Tyler, Breathing Lessons.
1990—Oscar Hijuelos, The Mambo Kings Play Songs of Love.
1991—John Updike, Rabbit at Rest.
1992—Jane Smiley, A Thousand Acres.
1993—Robert Olen Butler, A Good Scent from a Strange Mountain.

Drama

For an American play, preferably original and dealing with American life.
1918—Jesse Lynch Williams, Why Marry?
1920—Eugene O'Neill, Beyond the Horizon.
1921—Zona Gale, Miss Lulu Bett.
1922—Eugene O'Neill, Anna Christie.
1923—Owen Davis, Icebound.
1924—Hatcher Hughes, Hell-Bent for Heaven.
1925—Sidney Howard, They Knew What They Wanted.
1926—George Kelly, Craig's Wife.
1927—Paul Green, In Abraham's Bosom.
1928—Eugene O'Neill, Strange Interlude.
1929—Elmer Rice, Street Scene.
1930—Marc Connelly, The Green Pastures.
1931—Susan Glaspell, Alison's House.
1932—George S. Kaufman, Morrie Ryskind, and Ira Gershwin, Of Thee I Sing.
1933—Maxwell Anderson, Both Your Houses.
1934—Sidney Kingsley, Men in White.
1935—Zoe Akins, The Old Maid.
1936—Robert E. Sherwood, Idiot's Delight.
1937—George S. Kaufman and Moss Hart, You Can't Take It With You.
1938—Thornton Wilder, Our Town.
1939—Robert E. Sherwood, Abe Lincoln in Illinois.
1940—William Saroyan, The Time of Your Life.
1941—Robert E. Sherwood, There Shall Be No Night.
1943—Thornton Wilder, The Skin of Our Teeth.
1945—Mary Chase, Harvey.
1946—Russel Crouse and Howard Lindsay, State of the Union.
1948—Tennessee Williams, A Streetcar Named Desire.
1949—Arthur Miller, Death of a Salesman.
1950—Richard Rodgers, Oscar Hammerstein 2d, and Joshua Logan, South Pacific.
1952—Joseph Kramm, The Shrike.
1953—William Inge, Picnic.
1954—John Patrick, Teahouse of the August Moon.
1955—Tennessee Williams, Cat on a Hot Tin Roof.
1956—Frances Goodrich and Albert Hackett, The Diary of Anne Frank.
1957—Eugene O'Neill, Long Day's Journey Into Night.
1958—Ketti Frings, Look Homeward, Angel.
1959—Archibald MacLeish, J. B.
1960—George Abbott, Jerome Weidman, Sheldon Harnick, and Jerry Bock, Fiorello.
1961—Tad Mosel, All the Way Home.
1962—Frank Loesser and Abe Burrows, How To Succeed In Business Without Really Trying.
1965—Frank D. Gilroy, The Subject Was Roses.
1967—Edward Albee, A Delicate Balance.
1969—Howard Sackler, The Great White Hope.
1970—Charles Gordone, No Place to Be Somebody.
1971—Paul Zindel, The Effect of Gamma Rays on Man-in-the-Moon Marigolds.
1973—Jason Miller, That Championship Season.
1975—Edward Albee, Seascape.
1976—Michael Bennett, James Kirkwood, Nicholas Dante, Marvin Hamlisch and Edward Kleban, A Chorus Line.
1977—Michael Cristofer, The Shadow Box.
1978—Donald L. Coburn, The Gin Game.
1979—Sam Shepard, Buried Child.
1980—Lanford Wilson, Talley's Folly.
1981—Beth Henley, Crimes of the Heart.
1982—Charles Fuller, A Soldier's Play.
1983—Marsha Norman, 'night, Mother.
1984—David Mamet, Glengarry Glen Ross.
1985—Stephen Sondheim and James Lapine, Sunday in the Park with George.
1987—August Wilson, Fences.
1988—Alfred Uhry, Driving Miss Daisy.
1989—Wendy Wasserstein, The Heidi Chronicles.
1990—August Wilson, The Piano Lesson.
1991—Neil Simon, Lost in Yonkers.
1992—Robert Schenkkan, The Kentucky Cycle.
1993—Tony Kushner, Angels in America: Millennium Approaches.

History

For a book on the history of the United States.
1917—J. J. Jusserand, With Americans of Past and Present Days.
1918—James Ford Rhodes, History of the Civil War.
1920—Justin H. Smith, The War with Mexico.
1921—William Sowden Sims, The Victory at Sea.
1922—James Truslow Adams, The Founding of New England.
1923—Charles Warren, The Supreme Court in United States History.
1924—Charles Howard McIlwain, The American Revolution: A Constitutional Interpretation.
1925—Frederick L. Paxton, A History of the American Frontier.
1926—Edward Channing, A History of the U.S.

1927—Samuel Flagg Bemis, Pinckney's Treaty.
1928—Vernon Louis Parrington, Main Currents in American Thought.
1929—Fred A. Shannon, The Organization and Administration of the Union Army, 1861-65.
1930—Claude H. Van Tyne, The War of Independence.
1931—Bernadotte E. Schmitt, The Coming of the War, 1914.
1932—Gen. John J. Pershing, My Experiences in the World War.
1933—Frederick J. Turner, The Significance of Sections in American History.
1934—Herbert Agar, The People's Choice.
1935—Charles McLean Andrews, The Colonial Period of American History.
1936—Andrew C. McLaughlin, The Constitutional History of the United States.
1937—Van Wyck Brooks, The Flowering of New England.
1938—Paul Herman Buck, The Road to Reunion, 1865-1900.
1939—Frank Luther Mott, A History of American Magazines.
1940—Carl Sandburg, Abraham Lincoln: The War Years.
1941—Marcus Lee Hansen, The Atlantic Migration, 1607-1860.
1942—Margaret Leech, Reveille in Washington.
1943—Esther Forbes, Paul Revere and the World He Lived In.
1944—Merle Curti, The Growth of American Thought.
1945—Stephen Bonsal, Unfinished Business.
1946—Arthur M. Schlesinger Jr., The Age of Jackson.
1947—James Phinney Baxter 3d, Scientists Against Time.
1948—Bernard De Voto, Across the Wide Missouri.
1949—Roy F. Nichols, The Disruption of American Democracy.
1950—O. W. Larkin, Art and Life in America.
1951—R. Carlyle Buley, The Old Northwest: Pioneer Period 1815-1840.
1952—Oscar Handlin, The Uprooted.
1953—George Dangerfield, The Era of Good Feelings.
1954—Bruce Catton, A Stillness at Appomattox.
1955—Paul Horgan, Great River: The Rio Grande in North American History.
1956—Richard Hofstadter, The Age of Reform.
1957—George F. Kennan, Russia Leaves the War.
1958—Bray Hammond, Banks and Politics in America—From the Revolution to the Civil War.
1959—Leonard D. White and Jean Schneider, The Republican Era; 1869-1901.
1960—Margaret Leech, In the Days of McKinley.
1961—Herbert Feis, Between War and Peace: The Potsdam Conference.
1962—Lawrence H. Gibson, The Triumphant Empire: Thunder-clouds Gather in the West.
1963—Constance McLaughlin Green, Washington: Village and Capital, 1800-1878.
1964—Sumner Chilton Powell, Puritan Village: The Formation of A New England Town.
1965—Irwin Unger, The Greenback Era.
1966—Perry Miller, Life of the Mind in America.
1967—William H. Goetzmann, Exploration and Empire: the Explorer and Scientist in the Winning of the American West.
1968—Bernard Bailyn, The Ideological Origins of the American Revolution.
1969—Leonard W. Levy, Origin of the Fifth Amendment.
1970—Dean Acheson, Present at the Creation: My Years in the State Department.
1971—James McGregor Burns, Roosevelt: The Soldier of Freedom.
1972—Carl N. Degler, Neither Black Nor White.
1973—Michael Kammen, People of Paradox: An Inquiry Concerning the Origins of American Civilization.
1974—Daniel J. Boorstin, The Americans: The Democratic Experience.
1975—Dumas Malone, Jefferson and His Time.
1976—Paul Horgan, Lamy of Santa Fe.
1977—David M. Potter, The Impending Crisis.
1978—Alfred D. Chandler Jr., The Visible Hand: The Managerial Revolution in American Business.
1979—Don E. Fehrenbacher, The Dred Scott Case: Its Significance in American Law and Politics.
1980—Leon F. Litwack, Been in the Storm So Long.
1981—Lawrence A. Cremin, American Education: The National Experience, 1783-1876.
1982—C. Vann Woodward, ed., Mary Chestnut's Civil War.
1983—Rhys L. Issac, The Transformation of Virginia, 1740-1790.
1985—Thomas K. McCraw, Prophets of Regulation.
1986—Walter A. McDougall, . . . The Heavens and the Earth.
1987—Bernard Bailyn, Voyagers to the West.
1988—Robert V. Bruce, The Launching of Modern American Science 1846-1876.
1989—Taylor Branch, Parting the Waters: America in the King Years, 1954-63; and James M. McPherson, Battle Cry of Freedom: The Civil War Era.
1990—Stanley Karnow, In Our Image: America's Empire in the Philippines.
1991—Laurel Thatcher Ulrich, A Midwife's Tale: The Life of Martha Ballard, based on her diary, 1785-1812.
1992—Mark E. Neely Jr., The Fate of Liberty: Abraham Lincoln and Civil Liberties.
1993—Gordon S. Wood, The Radicalism of the American Revolution.

Biography or Autobiography

For a distinguished biography or autobiography by an American author.
1917—Laura E. Richards and Maude Howe Elliott, assisted by Florence Howe Hall, Julia Ward Howe.
1918—William Cabell Bruce, Benjamin Franklin, Self-Revealed.
1919—Henry Adams, The Education of Henry Adams.
1920—Albert J. Beveridge, The Life of John Marshall.
1921—Edward Bok, The Americanization of Edward Bok.
1922—Hamlin Garland, A Daughter of the Middle Border.
1923—Burton J. Hendrick, The Life and Letters of Walter H. Page.
1924—Michael Pupin, From Immigrant to Inventor.
1925—M. A. DeWolfe Howe, Barrett Wendell and His Letters.
1926—Harvey Cushing, Life of Sir William Osler.
1927—Emory Holloway, Whitman: An Interpretation in Narrative.
1928—Charles Edward Russell, The American Orchestra and Theodore Thomas.
1929—Burton J. Hendrick, The Training of an American: The Earlier Life and Letters of Walter H. Page.
1930—Marquis James, The Raven (Sam Houston).
1931—Henry James, Charles W. Eliot.
1932—Henry F. Pringle, Theodore Roosevelt.
1933—Allan Nevins, Grover Cleveland.
1934—Tyler Dennett, John Hay.
1935—Douglas Southall Freeman, R. E. Lee
1936—Ralph Barton Perry, The Thought and Character of William James.
1937—Allan Nevins, Hamilton Fish: The Inner History of the Grant Administration.
1938—Divided between Odell Shepard, Pedlar's Progress; Marquis James, Andrew Jackson.
1939—Carl Van Doren, Benjamin Franklin.
1940—Ray Stannard Baker, Woodrow Wilson, Life and Letters.
1941—Ola Elizabeth Winslow, Jonathan Edwards.
1942—Forrest Wilson, Crusader in Crinoline.
1943—Samuel Eliot Morison, Admiral of the Ocean Sea (Columbus).
1944—Carleton Mabee, The American Leonardo: The Life of Samuel F. B. Morse.
1945—Russell Blaine Nye, George Bancroft; Brahmin Rebel.
1946—Linny Marsh Wolfe, Son of the Wilderness.
1947—William Allen White, The Autobiography of William Allen White.
1948—Margaret Clapp, Forgotten First Citizen: John Bigelow.
1949—Robert E. Sherwood, Roosevelt and Hopkins.
1950—Samuel Flag Bemis, John Quincy Adams and the Foundations of American Foreign Policy.
1951—Margaret Louise Coit, John C. Calhoun: American Portrait.
1952—Merlo J. Pusey, Charles Evans Hughes.
1953—David J. Mays, Edmund Pendleton, 1721-1803.
1954—Charles A. Lindbergh, The Spirit of St. Louis.
1955—William S. White, The Taft Story.
1956—Talbot F. Hamlin, Benjamin Henry Latrobe.
1957—John F. Kennedy, Profiles in Courage.
1958—Douglas Southall Freeman (decd. 1953), George Washington, Vols. I-VI; John Alexander Carroll and Mary Wells Ashworth, Vol. VII.
1959—Arthur Walworth, Woodrow Wilson: American Prophet.
1960—Samuel Eliot Morison, John Paul Jones.
1961—David Donald, Charles Sumner and the Coming of the Civil War.
1963—Leon Edel, Henry James: Vol. II, The Conquest of London, 1870-1881; Vol. III, The Middle Years, 1881-1895.
1964—Walter Jackson Bate, John Keats.
1965—Ernest Samuels, Henry Adams.
1966—Arthur M. Schlesinger Jr., A Thousand Days.
1967—Justin Kaplan, Mr. Clemens and Mark Twain.
1968—George F. Kennan, Memoirs (1925-1950).
1969—B. L. Reid, The Man from New York: John Quinn and his Friends.
1970—T. Harry Williams, Huey Long.
1971—Lawrence Thompson, Robert Frost: The Years of Triumph, 1915-1938.
1972—Joseph P. Lash, Eleanor and Franklin.
1973—W. A. Swanberg, Luce and His Empire.
1974—Louis Sheaffer, O'Neill, Son and Artist.
1975—Robert A. Caro, The Power Broker: Robert Moses and the Fall of New York.
1976—R.W.B. Lewis, Edith Wharton: A Biography.

1977—John E. Mack, A Prince of Our Disorder: The Life of T.E. Lawrence.
1978—Walter Jackson Bate, Samuel Johnson.
1979—Leonard Baker, Days of Sorrow and Pain: Leo Baeck and the Berlin Jews.
1980—Edmund Morris, The Rise of Theodore Roosevelt.
1981—Robert K. Massie, Peter the Great: His Life and World.
1982—William S. McFeely, Grant: A Biography.
1983—Russell Baker, Growing Up.
1984—Louis R. Harlan, Booker T. Washington.
1985—Kenneth Silverman, The Life and Times of Cotton Mather.
1986—Elizabeth Frank, Louise Bogan: A Portrait.
1987—David J. Garrow, Bearing the Cross: Martin Luther King Jr. and the Southern Christian Leadership Conference.
1988—David Herbert Donald, Look Homeward: A Life of Thomas Wolfe.
1989—Richard Ellmann, Oscar Wilde.
1990—Sebastian de Grazia, Machiavelli in Hell.
1991—Steven Naifeh, and Gregory White Smith, Jackson Pollock: An American Saga.
1992—Lewis B. Puller Jr., Fortunate Son: The Healing of a Vietnam Vet.
1993—David McCullough, Truman.

American Poetry

Before this prize was established in 1922, awards were made from gifts provided by the Poetry Society: **1918**—Love Songs, by Sara Teasdale. **1919**—Old Road to Paradise, by Margaret Widemer; Corn Huskers, by Carl Sandburg.
1922—Edwin Arlington Robinson, Collected Poems.
1923—Edna St. Vincent Millay, The Ballad of the Harp-Weaver; A Few Figs from Thistles; Eight Sonnets in American Poetry, 1922; A Miscellany.
1924—Robert Frost, New Hampshire: A Poem with Notes and Grace Notes.
1925—Edwin Arlington Robinson, The Man Who Died Twice.
1926—Amy Lowell, What's O'Clock.
1927—Leonora Speyer, Fiddler's Farewell.
1928—Edwin Arlington Robinson, Tristram.
1929—Stephen Vincent Benet, John Brown's Body.
1930—Conrad Aiken, Selected Poems.
1931—Robert Frost, Collected Poems.
1932—George Dillon, The Flowering Stone.
1933—Archibald MacLeish, Conquistador.
1934—Robert Hillyer, Collected Verse.
1935—Audrey Wurdemann, Bright Ambush.
1936—Robert P. Tristram Coffin, Strange Holiness.
1937—Robert Frost, A Further Range.
1938—Marya Zaturenska, Cold Morning Sky.
1939—John Gould Fletcher, Selected Poems.
1940—Mark Van Doren, Collected Poems.
1941—Leonard Bacon, Sunderland Capture.
1942—William Rose Benet, The Dust Which Is God.
1943—Robert Frost, A Witness Tree.
1944—Stephen Vincent Benet, Western Star.
1945—Karl Shapiro, V-Letter and Other Poems.
1947—Robert Lowell, Lord Weary's Castle.
1948—W. H. Auden, The Age of Anxiety.
1949—Peter Viereck, Terror and Decorum.
1950—Gwendolyn Brooks, Annie Allen.
1951—Carl Sandburg, Complete Poems.
1952—Marianne Moore, Collected Poems.
1953—Archibald MacLeish, Collected Poems.
1954—Theodore Roethke, The Waking.
1955—Wallace Stevens, Collected Poems.
1956—Elizabeth Bishop, Poems, North and South.
1957—Richard Wilbur, Things of This World.
1958—Robert Penn Warren, Promises: Poems 1954-1956.
1959—Stanley Kunitz, Selected Poems 1928-1958.
1960—W. D. Snodgrass, Heart's Needle.
1961—Phyllis McGinley, Times Three: Selected Verse from Three Decades.
1962—Alan Dugan, Poems.
1963—William Carlos Williams, Pictures From Breughel.
1964—Louis Simpson, At the End of the Open Road.
1965—John Berryman, 77 Dream Songs.
1966—Richard Eberhart, Selected Poems.
1967—Anne Sexton, Live or Die.
1968—Anthony Hecht, The Hard Hours.
1969—George Oppen, Of Being Numerous.
1970—Richard Howard, Untitled Subjects.
1971—William S. Merwin, The Carrier of Ladders.
1972—James Wright, Collected Poems.
1973—Maxine Winokur Kumin, Up Country.
1975—Gary Snyder, Turtle Island.
1976—John Ashbery, Self-Portrait in a Convex Mirror.
1977—James Merrill, Divine Comedies.
1978—Howard Nemerov, Collected Poems.
1979—Robert Penn Warren, Now and Then: Poems 1976-1978.
1980—Donald Justice, Selected Poems.
1981—James Schuyler, The Morning of the Poem.
1982—Sylvia Plath, The Collected Poems.
1983—Galway Kinnell, Selected Poems.
1984—Mary Oliver, American Primitive.
1985—Carolyn Kizer, Yin.
1986—Henry Taylor, The Flying Change.
1987—Rita Dove, Thomas and Beulah.
1988—William Meredith, Partial Accounts: New and Selected Poems.
1989—Richard Wilbur, New and Collected Poems.
1990—Charles Simic, The World Doesn't End.
1991—Mona Van Duyn, Near Changes.
1992—James Tate, Selected Poems.
1993—Louise Glück, The Wild Iris.

General Non-Fiction

1962—Theodore H. White, The Making of the President 1960.
1963—Barbara W. Tuchman, The Guns of August.
1964—Richard Hofstadter, Anti-Intellectualism in American Life.
1965—Howard Mumford Jones, O Strange New World.
1966—Edwin Way Teale, Wandering Through Winter.
1967—David Brion Davis, The Problem of Slavery in Western Culture.
1968—Will and Ariel Durant, Rousseau and Revolution.
1969—Norman Mailer, The Armies of the Night; Rene Jules Dubos, So Human an Animal: How We Are Shaped by Surroundings and Events.
1970—Eric H. Erikson, Gandhi's Truth.
1971—John Toland, The Rising Sun.
1972—Barbara W. Tuchman, Stilwell and the American Experience in China, 1911-1945.
1973—Frances FitzGerald, Fire in the Lake: The Vietnamese and the Americans in Vietnam; Robert Coles, Children of Crisis, Volumes II & III.
1974—Ernest Becker, The Denial of Death.
1975—Annie Dillard, Pilgrim at Tinker Creek.
1976—Robert N. Butler, Why Survive? Being Old in America.
1977—William W. Warner, Beautiful Swimmers.
1978—Carl Sagan, The Dragons of Eden.
1979—Edward O. Wilson, On Human Nature.
1980—Douglas R. Hofstadter, Gödel, Escher, Bach: An Eternal Golden Braid.
1981 —Carl E. Schorske, Fin-de-Siecle Vienna: Politics and Culture.
1982—Tracy Kidder, The Soul of a New Machine.
1983—Susan Sheehan, Is There No Place on Earth for Me?
1984—Paul Starr, Social Transformation of American Medicine.
1985—Studs Terkel, The Good War.
1986—Joseph Lelyveld, Move Your Shadow; J. Anthony Lukas, Common Ground.
1987—David K. Shipler, Arab and Jew.
1988—Richard Rhodes, The Making of the Atomic Bomb.
1989—Neil Sheehan, A Bright Shining Lie: John Paul Vann and America in Vietnam.
1990—Dale Maharidge and Michael Williamson, And Their Children After Them.
1991—Bert Holldobler and Edward O. Wilson, The Ants.
1992—Daniel Yergin, The Prize: The Epic Quest for Oil.
1993—Garry Wills, Lincoln at Gettysburg.

Music

For composition by an American (before 1977, by a composer resident in the U.S.), in the larger forms of chamber, orchestra, or choral music or for an operatic work including ballet. A special posthumous award was granted in 1976 to Scott Joplin.
1943—William Schuman, Secular Cantata No. 2, A Free Song.
1944—Howard Hanson, Symphony No. 4, Op. 34.
1945—Aaron Copland, Appalachian Spring.
1946—Leo Sowerby, The Canticle of the Sun.
1947—Charles E. Ives, Symphony No. 3.
1948—Walter Piston, Symphony No. 3.
1949—Virgil Thomson, Louisiana Story.
1950—Gian-Carlo Menotti, The Consul.
1951—Douglas Moore, Giants in the Earth.
1952—Gail Kubik, Symphony Concertante.
1954—Quincy Porter, Concerto for Two Pianos and Orchestra.
1955—Gian-Carlo Menotti, The Saint of Bleecker Street.
1956—Ernest Toch, Symphony No. 3.
1957—Norman Dello Joio, Meditations on Ecclesiastes.
1958—Samuel Barber, Vanessa.
1959—John La Montaine, Concerto for Piano and Orchestra.
1960—Elliott Carter, Second String Quartet.
1961—Walter Piston, Symphony No. 7.

1962—Robert Ward, The Crucible.
1963—Samuel Barber, Piano Concerto No. 1.
1966—Leslie Bassett, Variations for Orchestra.
1967—Leon Kirchner, Quartet No. 3.
1968—George Crumb, Echoes of Time and The River.
1969—Karel Husa, String Quartet No. 3.
1970—Charles W. Wuorinen, Time's Encomium.
1971—Mario Davidovsky, Synchronisms No. 6.
1972—Jacob Druckman, Windows.
1973—Elliott Carter, String Quartet No. 3.
1974—Donald Martino, Notturno. (Special citation) Roger Sessions.
1975—Dominick Argento, From the Diary of Virginia Woolf.
1976—Ned Rorem, Air Music.
1977—Richard Wernick, Visions of Terror and Wonder.
1978—Michael Colgrass, Deja Vu for Percussion and Orchestra.
1979—Joseph Schwantner, Aftertones of Infinity.
1980—David Del Tredici, In Memory of a Summer Day.
1982—Roger Sessions, Concerto For Orchestra. (Special Citation) Milton Babbitt.
1983—Ellen T. Zwilich, Three Movements for Orchestra.
1984—Bernard Rands, Canti del Sole.
1985—Stephen Albert, Symphony, RiverRun.
1986—George Perle, Wind Quintet IV.
1987—John Harbison, The Flight Into Egypt.
1988—William Bolcom, 12 New Etudes for Piano.
1989—Roger Reynolds, Whispers Out of Time.
1990—Mel Powell, Duplicates: A Concerto For Two Pianos and Orchestra.
1991—Shulamit Ran, Symphony.
1992—Wayne Peterson, The Face of the Night, The Heart of the Dark.
1993—Christopher Rouse, Trombone Concerto.

Special Awards

Awarded in 1992 or 1993

Books

Academy of American Poets Awards: Fellowship for Distinguished Poetic Achievement, $20,000: Adrienne Rich; Lamont Poetry Selection, $1,000 and purchase of 2,000 copies of book: Kathryn Stripling Byer, *Wildwood Flower*; Lavan Younger Poet Awards, $1,000 each: Cyrus Cassells, Richard Lyons, Rosanna Warren.

Curtis Benjamin Award for Creative Publishing, by Assn. of American Publishers: Jason Epstein, Random House.

Bollingen Prize in Poetry, by Yale Library, for lifetime achievement, $10,000: Mark Strand.

Caldecott Medal, by American Library Assn., for most distinguished American picture book: Emily Arnold McCully, *Mirette on the High Wire*.

Christopher Awards, by The Christophers, for expression of highest values of human spirit, bronze medallion each: Joseph Iron Eye Dudley, *Choteau Creek: A Sioux Reminiscence*; Marian Wright Edelman, *The Measure of Our Success: A Letter to My Children and Yours*; Eric Silver, *The Book of the Just: The Unsung Heroes Who Rescued Jews from Hitler*; Robert Ellsberg, ed., *Fritz Eichenberg: Works of Mercy*; Judy Barron and Sean Barron, *There's a Boy in Here;* Katie Kelly, *A Year in Saigon*.

Golden Kite Awards, by Society of Children's Book Writers and Illustrators, statuette each: Mary E. Lyons, *Letters from a Slave Girl*; nonfiction: Jim Murphy, *The Long Road to Gettysburg*; illustration: Patricia Polacco, *Chicken Sunday*.

International Fiction Prize, by Irish Times and Aer Lingus, for work of fiction published in Ireland, U.K., or U.S., $45,000: Norman Rush, *Mating*.

Ruth Lilly Poetry Prize, by Modern Poetry Assn. and American Council for the Arts, for lifetime achievement, $75,000: Charles Wright.

Lincoln Prize, by Lincoln Soldiers Institute at Gettysburg College, for lifetime contribution to Civil War studies, $40,000 and bronze bust of Lincoln: Kenneth M. Stampp; best book on Civil War pub. 1992, $10,000: Albert Castel, *Decision in the West*.

National Book Awards, by National Book Foundation, $10,000 each: nonfiction: Paul Monette, *Becoming a Man*; poetry: Mary Oliver, *New and Selected Poems*; fiction: Cormac McCarthy, *All the Pretty Horses*; Medal for Distinguished Contribution to American Letters: James Laughlin, *New Directions*.

National Book Critics Circle Awards: fiction: Cormac McCarthy, *All the Pretty Horses*; nonfiction: Norman Maclean, *Young Men and Fire*; criticism: Garry Wills, *Lincoln at Gettysburg*; biography/autobiography: Carol Brightman, *Writing Dangerously: Mary McCarthy and Her World*; poetry: Hayden Carruth, *Collected Poems 1946-1991*.

Newbery Award, by American Library Assn., for most distinguished contribution to American literature for children: Cynthia Ryland, *Missing May*.

Francis Parkman Prize, by Society of American Historians, for scholarship combined with literary excellence, $1,000: David McCullough, *Truman*; James Fenimore Cooper Prize, for historical fiction, $1,000: Noah Gordon, *Shaman*; Allan Nevins Prize, for best-written dissertation in American history, $1,000: Amy J. Kinsel, "From These Honored Dead: Gettysburg in American Culture, 1863-1938."

PEN/Faulkner Award for Fiction, $15,000: E. Annie Proulx, *Postcards*.

Edgar Allan Poe Awards, by Mystery Writers of America, bust of Poe each: novel: Margaret Maron, *Bootlegger's Daughter*; grand master, for lifetime achievement: Donald E. Westlake; reader of the year: President Bill Clinton.

Rhea Award for the Short Story, by Dungannon Foundation, for lifetime achievement, $25,000: Grace Paley.

Whiting Writers' Awards, by Whiting Foundation, for achievement and promise alike, $30,000 each: Roger Fanning, Eva Hoffman, R. S. Jones, J. S. Marcus, James Mead, Suzan Lori-Parks, Katha Pollitt, Keith Reddin, Jose Rivera, Damien Wilkins.

Journalism

Helen B. Bernstein Award, by New York Public Library, $15,000: Samuel G. Freedman, *Upon This Rock: The Miracles of a Black Church* .

National Journalism Awards, by Scripps Howard Foundation, for print journalism, bronze plaques: Charles E. Scripps Award, for newspaper's service to literacy, $2,500: *Anderson* (S.C.) *Independent-Mail*; Pyle Award, for human interest writing, $2,500: Bill Harden, *Washington Post*; Stone Award, for editorial writing, $2,000: Robert Friedman, *St. Petersburg Times*; Meeman Award, for environmental reporting, $2,000 each: *Orlando* (Fla.) *Sentinel* and *National Law Journal*, New York, N.Y.; Howard Award, for public service reporting, $2,500 each: *San Francisco Examiner* and *Albuquerque* (N.M.) *Tribune*; E. W. Scripps Award, for service to First Amendment, $2,500: David Lawrence Jr., *Miami Herald*.

National Magazine Awards, by American Society of Magazine Editors and Columbia Univ. Graduate School of Journalism: general excellence, circulation over 1 million: *Newsweek*; under 1 million: *The Atlantic Monthly, American Photo, Lingua Franca*; single-topic issue: *Newsweek*, "How He Won: The Untold Story of Bill Clinton's Triumph"; feature writing: *The New Yorker*, "Whose Art Is It?" Jane Kramer; fiction: *The New Yorker*, "A Wilderness Station," Alice Munro; "Parachute Silk," Emily Carter; "Career Move," Martin Amis; design: *Harper's Bazaar*; photography: *Harper's Bazaar*; reporting: *IEEE Spectrum*, "Seeking Nuclear Safeguards"; personal service: *Good Housekeeping* and *Philadelphia*; public interest: *The Family Therapy Networker*; essays and criticism; *The American Lawyer*, "Maybe the Jury Was Right."

George Polk Awards, by Long Island Univ., for excellence in jornalism: national: Gregory Vistica, *San Diego Un-*

ion-Tribune; local: *Los Angeles Times*; social commentary: Henry Louis Gates, op-ed article, *New York Times*; career: Herbert Mitgang, *New York Times*, and Roy Gutman, *Newsday*; health: Seth Rosenfeld, *San Francisco Examiner*; legal: Marianne Lavelle, Marcia Coyle, Claudia MacLachlan, *National Law Journal*; environmental: John-Thor Dahlburg, *Los Angeles Times*; magazine: Lawrence Weschler, *New Yorker*; photography: Carlos Guerrero, *El Nuevo Herald*.

Reuben Awards, by National Cartoonists Society: cartoonist of the year: Cathy Guisewite, "Cathy"; editorial cartoon: Jim Morin; animation: Eric Goldberg; comic book: Todd McFarlane; newspaper comic strip: Wiley Miller; sports cartoon: Eddie Germano; gag cartoon: Arnie Levin; newspaper panel: Don Addis; advertising illustration: Daryl Cagle; greeting cards: Sandra Boynton; magazine and book illustration: Burne Hogarth.

Science in Society Print Journalism Awards, by Natl. Assn. of Science Writers, $1,000 each and certificate: newspapers: Jon Van, *Chicago Tribune*; magazines: Nancy Pappas, *Consumer Reports*; commendation: Rochelle Green, *Consumer Reports*.

Movie, TV, Radio, and Theater

Astaire Awards, for achievement in dance in Broadway theater, by Theater Development Fund: performance: Chita Rivera, *Kiss of the Spider Woman*; choreography: Wayne Cilento, *Tommy*.

Susan Smith Blackburn Awards, for female playwright, $5,000: Marlane Meyer, *Moe's Lucky Seven*, commissioned by South Coast Repertory Co., Costa Mesa, Cal.; 2d prize, $1,000: Jane Anderson, *Hotel Oubliette*, premiere at Williamstown Theater Festival, Mass.

Christopher Awards, by The Christophers: movies: *Enchanted April, Howards End, Lorenzo's Oil, Sarafina!*; TV specials: *Against Her Will, The Broken Cord, Father/Son, Miles from Nowhere, Jonathan: The Boy Nobody Wanted, Sr. Thea: Her Own Story, A Town Torn Apart*.

Directors Guild of America: movie director: Clint Eastwood, *Unforgiven*; D. W. Griffith Award, for lifetime achievement: Sidney Lumet; TV directors: comedy series: Tom Cherones, *Seinfeld*, "The Contest"; nighttime drama series: Rob Thompson, *Northern Exposure*, "Cicely"; daytime dramatic show: Helaine Head, *Wonderworks*, "You Must Remember This"; musical-variety show: Bobby Quinn, *The Tonight Show*; documentary: Joseph Berlinger and Bruce Sinofsky, *Brother's Keeper*; daytime serial: Susan Strickler, *Another World*; drama special: Ron Lagomarsino, *Picket Fences*, pilot episode; commercial: Leslie Dektor, Philips Electronics; Career Achievement Award: Harry Coyle, sports direction.

Drama Desk Awards, by New York theater critics writing for non-New York publications: play: Tony Kushner, *Angels in America*; musical: *Kiss of the Spider Woman*; actor: Ron Leibman, *Angels in America*; actress: Jane Alexander, *The Sisters Rosensweig*; director: George C. Wolfe, *Angels in America*; musical actor: Brent Carver, *Kiss of the Spider Woman*; musical actress: Chita Rivera, *Kiss of the Spider Woman*; musical director: Des McAnuff, *Tommy*; music: John Kander, *Kiss of the Spider Woman*.

Alfred I. Dupont-Columbia Univ. Awards, for broadcast journalism: gold baton: National Public Radio, for coverage of Los Angeles riots, for series including *Morning Edition, All Things Considered*, and *American Folklife*, and for reporting of Senate hearings on nomination of Clarence Thomas to Supreme Court.

Emmy Awards, by Academy of Television Arts and Sciences, for primetime programs, 1992-93: Dramatic series: *Picket Fences*, CBS; actor: Tom Skerritt, *Picket Fences*, CBS; actress: Kathy Baker, *Picket Fences*, CBS; supporting actor: Chad Lowe, *Life Goes On*, ABC; supporting actress: Mary Alice, *I'll Fly Away*, NBC; writing: Tom Fontana, *Homicide: Life on the Street*, NBC; directing: Barry Levinson, *Homicide: Life on the Street*, NBC. Comedy series: *Seinfeld*, NBC; actor: Ted Danson, *Cheers*, NBC; actress: Roseanne Arnold, *Roseanne*, ABC; supporting actor: Michael Richards, *Seinfeld*, NBC; supporting actress: Laurie Metcalf, *Roseanne*, ABC; writing: Larry David, *Seinfeld*, NBC; directing: Betty Thomas, *Dream On*, HBO. Variety, music, or comedy series: *Saturday Night Live*, NBC; performance: Dana Carvey, *Saturday Night Live's Presidential Bash*, NBC; writing: *The Ben Stiller Show*, Fox; directing: Walter C. Miller, *The 1992 Tony Awards*, CBS. Variety, music, or comedy special: *Bob Hope: The First 90 Years*, NBC. Made-for-TV movie (tie): *Barbarians at the Gate*, HBO, and *Stalin*, HBO. Miniseries: *Mystery!: Prime Suspect 2*, PBS; actor: Robert Morse, *Tru*, PBS; actress: Holly Hunter, *The Positively True Adventures of the Alleged Texas Cheerleader-Murdering Mom*, HBO; supporting actor: Beau Bridges, *The Positively True Adventures of the Alleged Texas Cheerleader-Murdering Mom*, HBO; supporting actress: Mary Tyler Moore, *Stolen Babies*, Lifetime; writing: Jane Anderson, *The Positively True Adventures of the Alleged Texas Cheerleader-Murdering Mom*, HBO; directing: James Sadwith, *Sinatra*, CBS.

National Society of Film Critics: film: *Unforgiven*; actor: Stephen Rea, *The Crying Game*; actress: Emma Thompson, *Howards End*; supporting actor: Gene Hackman, *Unforgiven*; supporting actress: Judy Davis, *Husbands and Wives*; screenplay: David Webb Peoples, *Unforgiven*; foreign film: *Raise the Red Lantern*; cinematography: *Raise the Red Lantern*; documentary: *American Dream*, Barbara Kopple; experimental: *Another Girl, Another Planet*, Michael Almereyda.

New York Drama Critics Circle, $1,000: play, Tony Kishner, *Angels in America*; foreign: Frank McGuiness, *Someone Who'll Watch Over Me*; musical: *Kiss of the Spider Woman*.

Tony (Antoinette Perry) Awards: play: Tony Kushner, *Angeles in America*; musical: *Kiss of the Spider Woman*; revival: *Anna Christie*; actor: Ron Leibman, *Angels in America*; actress: Madeline Kahn, *The Sisters Rosensweig*; actor, musical: Brent Carver, *Kiss of the Spider Woman*; actress, musical: Chita Rivera, *Kiss of the Spider Woman*; featured actor: Stephen Spinella, *Angeles in America*; featured actress: Debra Monk, *Redwood Curtain*; featured actor, musical: Anthony Crivello, *Kiss of the Spider Woman;* featured actress, musical: Andrea Martin, *My Favorite Year*; director: George C. Wolfe, *Angels in America*; director, musical: Des McAnuff, *Tommy*; book, musical: Terrence McNally, *Kiss of the Spider Woman*; original musical score: John Kander and Fred Ebb, *Kiss of the Spider Woman*, and Pete Townshend, *Tommy*; scenic design: John Arnone, *Tommy*; costume design: Forence Klotz, *Kiss of the Spider Woman*; lighting design: Chris Parry, *Tommy*; choreography: Wayne Cilento, *Tommy*; special award: *Oklahoma*, in recognition of 50th anniversary; regional theater; La Jolla Playhouse, Calif.

Miscellaneous

American Institute of Architects Gold Medal: Kevin Roche.

Breakthrough Awards, by Women and Media, for influencing change in gender stereotypes: Blanche Wisen Cook, for her biography *Eleanor Roosevelt*; AWRT Foundation and Capital Cities/ABC, for public service campaign; Barbara Reynolds, *USA Today* columnist; Jones Intercable, for funding Women in Cable; CNN.

Charles Frankel Prizes, by Natl. Endowment for the Humanities, for those who have increased public awareness of the humanities, $5,000 each: Eudora Welty, Shelby Foote, Allan Bloom, Richard Rodriguez, Harold K. Skramstad Jr.

Gavel Award, by American Bar Assn., for lifetime achievement: Fred Friendly, for PBS series on legal and social issues.

John F. Kennedy Center for the Performing Arts Awards, for contribution to U.S. cultural life: Lionel Hampton, Ginger Rogers, Mstislav Rostropovich, Paul Taylor, and Paul Newman and Joanne Woodward.

McGraw-Hill Prize in Education, for distinguished contribution to the advancement of education, $25,000 each: Shirley A. Hill, pres. of Natl. Council of Teachers of Mathematics; Thomas W. Payzant, superintendent of San Diego City Schools; Edward Zigler, co-founder of Head Start.

National Inventors Hall of Fame, inductees: John Ericsson, William P. Lear, John T. Parsons, Baruch S. Blumberg, Irving Millman.

National Medal of Arts, by White House, for outstanding contributions to cultural life in the U.S.: Marilyn Horne, Allan Houser, James Earl Jones, Minnie Pearl, Robert Saudek, Earl Scruggs, Robert Shaw, Billy Taylor, Robert Venturi, Denise Scott Brown, Robert Wise, AT&T Foundation, Lila Wallace-Reader's Digest Fund.

Rock-and-Roll Hall of Fame, inductees: Ruth Brown, Cream, Creedence Clearwater Revival, the Doors, Etta James, Frankie Lymon and the Teen-Agers, Van Morrison, Sly and the Family Stone; pre-rock: Dinah Washington; business: Milt Gabler, Dick Clark.

Samuel H. Scripps American Dance Festival Award, $25,000: Talley Beatty.

Templeton Prize for Progress in Religion, by Templeton Foundation, about $1 million: Charles W. Colson.

Van Cliburn International Piano Competition: gold medal, silver cup, $15,000: Simone Pedroni of Novara, Italy.

Westinghouse Talent Search: 1st prize, $40,000 scholarship: Elizabeth Michele Pine, Illinois Math & Science Academy, Aurora, Ill.

The Spingarn Medal

The Spingarn Medal has been awarded annually since 1914 by the National Association for the Advancement of Colored People for the highest achievement by a black American.

1946 Dr. Percy L. Julian
1947 Channing H. Tobias
1948 Ralph J. Bunche
1949 Charles Hamilton Houston
1950 Mabel Keaton Staupers
1951 Harry T. Moore
1952 Paul R. Williams
1953 Theodore K. Lawless
1954 Carl Murphy
1955 Jack Roosevelt Robinson
1956 Martin Luther King Jr.
1957 Mrs. Daisy Bates and the Little Rock Nine
1958 Edward Kennedy (Duke) Ellington
1959 Langston Hughes
1960 Kenneth B. Clark
1961 Robert C. Weaver
1962 Medgar Wiley Evers
1963 Roy Wilkins
1964 Leontyne Price
1965 John H. Johnson
1966 Edward W. Brooke
1967 Sammy Davis Jr.
1968 Clarence M. Mitchell Jr.
1969 Jacob Lawrence
1970 Leon Howard Sullivan
1971 Gordon Parks
1972 Wilson C. Riles
1973 Damon Keith
1974 Henry (Hank) Aaron
1975 Alvin Ailey
1976 Alex Haley
1977 Andrew Young
1978 Mrs. Rosa L. Parks
1979 Dr. Rayford W. Logan
1980 Coleman Young
1981 Dr. Benjamin Elijah Mays
1982 Lena Horne
1983 Thomas Bradley
1984 Bill Cosby
1985 Dr. Benjamin L. Hooks
1986 Percy E. Sutton
1987 Frederick Douglass Patterson
1988 Jesse Jackson
1989 L. Douglas Wilder
1990 Gen. Colin L. Powell
1991 Barbara Jordan
1992 Dorothy I. Height

Miss America Winners

1921 Margaret Gorman, Washington, D.C.
1922-23 Mary Campbell, Columbus, Ohio
1924 Ruth Malcolmson, Philadelphia, Pennsylvania
1925 Fay Lamphier, Oakland, California
1926 Norma Smallwood, Tulsa, Oklahoma
1927 Lois Delaner, Joliet, Illinois
1933 Marion Bergeron, West Haven, Connecticut
1935 Henrietta Leaver, Pittsburgh, Pennsylvania
1936 Rose Coyle, Philadelphia, Pennsylvania
1937 Bette Cooper, Bertrand Island, New Jersey
1938 Marilyn Meseke, Marion, Ohio
1939 Patricia Donnelly, Detroit, Michigan
1940 Frances Marie Burke, Philadelphia, Pennsylvania
1941 Rosemary LaPlanche, Los Angeles, California
1942 Jo-Caroll Dennison, Tyler, Texas
1943 Jean Bartel, Los Angeles, California
1944 Venus Ramey, Washington, D.C.
1945 Bess Myerson, New York City, N.Y.
1946 Marilyn Buferd, Los Angeles, California
1947 Barbara Walker, Memphis, Tennessee
1948 BeBe Shopp, Hopkins, Minnesota
1949 Jacque Mercer, Litchfield, Arizona
1951 Yolande Betbeze, Mobile, Alabama
1952 Coleen Kay Hutchins, Salt Lake City, Utah
1953 Neva Jane Langley, Macon, Georgia
1954 Evelyn Margaret Ay, Ephrata, Pennsylvania
1955 Lee Meriwether, San Francisco, California
1956 Sharon Ritchie, Denver, Colorado
1957 Marian McKnight, Manning, South Carolina
1958 Marilyn Van Derbur, Denver, Colorado
1959 Mary Ann Mobley, Brandon, Mississippi
1960 Lynda Lee Mead, Natchez, Mississippi
1961 Nancy Fleming, Montague, Michigan
1962 Maria Fletcher, Asheville, North Carolina
1963 Jacquelyn Mayer, Sandusky, Ohio
1964 Donna Axum, El Dorado, Arkansas
1965 Vonda Kay Van Dyke, Phoenix, Arizona
1966 Deborah Irene Bryant, Overland Park, Kansas
1967 Jane Anne Jayroe, Laverne, Oklahoma
1968 Debra Dene Barnes, Moran, Kansas
1969 Judith Anne Ford, Belvidere, Illinois
1970 Pamela Anne Eldred, Birmingham, Michigan
1971 Phyllis Ann George, Denton, Texas
1972 Laurie Lea Schaefer, Columbus, Ohio
1973 Terry Anne Meeuwsen, DePere, Wisconsin
1974 Rebecca Ann King, Denver, Colorado
1975 Shirley Cothran, Fort Worth, Texas
1976 Tawney Elaine Godin, Yonkers, N.Y.
1977 Dorothy Kathleen Benham, Edina, Minnesota
1978 Susan Perkins, Columbus, Ohio
1979 Kylene Barker, Galax, Virginia
1980 Cheryl Prewitt, Ackerman, Mississippi
1981 Susan Powell, Elk City, Oklahoma
1982 Elizabeth Ward, Russellville, Arkansas
1983 Debra Maffett, Anaheim, California
1984 Vanessa Williams, Milwood, New York*
Suzette Charles, Mays Landing, New Jersey
1985 Sharlene Wells, Salt Lake City, Utah
1986 Susan Akin, Meridian, Mississippi
1987 Kellye Cash, Memphis, Tennessee
1988 Kaye Lani Rae Rafko, Monroe, Michigan
1989 Gretchen Carlson, Anoka, Minnesota
1990 Debbye Turner, Columbia, Missouri
1991 Marjorie Vincent, Oak Park, Illinois
1992 Carolyn Suzanne Sapp, Honolulu, Hawaii
1993 Leanza Cornett, Jacksonville, Florida
1994 Kimberly Aiken, Columbia, South Carolina

* Resigned July 23, 1984.

Motion Picture Academy Awards (Oscars)

1927-28

Actor: Emil Jannings, *The Way of All Flesh.*
Actress: Janet Gaynor, *Seventh Heaven.*
Director: Frank Borzage, *Seventh Heaven;* Lewis Milestone, *Two Arabian Knights.*
Picture: *Wings,* Paramount.

1928-29
Actor: Warner Baxter, *In Old Arizona.*
Actress: Mary Pickford, *Coquette.*
Director: Frank Lloyd, *The Divine Lady.*
Picture: *Broadway Melody,* MGM.

1929-30
Actor: George Arliss, *Disraeli.*
Actress: Norma Shearer, *The Divorcee.*
Director: Lewis Milestone, *All Quiet on the Western Front.*
Picture: *All Quiet on the Western Front,* Univ.

1930-31
Actor: Lionel Barrymore, *Free Soul.*
Actress: Marie Dressler, *Min and Bill.*
Director: Norman Taurog, *Skippy.*
Picture: *Cimarron,* RKO.

1931-32
Actor: Fredric March, *Dr. Jekyll and Mr. Hyde;* Wallace Beery, *The Champ* (tie).
Actress: Helen Hayes, *Sin of Madelon Claudet.*
Director: Frank Borzage, *Bad Girl.*
Picture: *Grand Hotel,* MGM.
Special: Walt Disney, *Mickey Mouse.*

1932-33
Actor: Charles Laughton, *Private Life of Henry VIII.*
Actress: Katharine Hepburn, *Morning Glory.*
Director: Frank Lloyd, *Cavalcade.*
Picture: *Cavalcade,* Fox.

1934
Actor: Clark Gable, *It Happened One Night.*
Actress: Claudette Colbert, *It Happened One Night.*
Director: Frank Capra, *It Happened One Night.*
Picture: *It Happened One Night,* Columbia.

1935
Actor: Victor McLaglen, *The Informer.*
Actress: Bette Davis, *Dangerous.*
Director: John Ford, *The Informer.*
Picture: *Mutiny on the Bounty,* MGM.

1936
Actor: Paul Muni, *Story of Louis Pasteur.*
Actress: Luise Rainer, *The Great Ziegfeld.*
Sup. Actor: Walter Brennan, *Come and Get It.*
Sup. Actress: Gale Sondergaard, *Anthony Adverse.*
Director: Frank Capra, *Mr. Deeds Goes to Town.*
Picture: *The Great Ziegfeld,* MGM.

1937
Actor: Spencer Tracy, *Captains Courageous.*
Actress: Luise Rainer, *The Good Earth.*
Sup. Actor: Joseph Schildkraut, *Life of Emile Zola.*
Sup. Actress: Alice Brady, *In Old Chicago.*
Director: Leo McCarey, *The Awful Truth.*
Picture: *Life of Emile Zola,* Warner.

1938
Actor: Spencer Tracy, *Boys Town.*
Actress: Bette Davis, *Jezebel.*
Sup. Actor: Walter Brennan, *Kentucky.*
Sup. Actress: Fay Bainter, *Jezebel.*
Director: Frank Capra, *You Can't Take It With You.*
Picture: *You Can't Take It With You,* Columbia.

1939
Actor: Robert Donat, *Goodbye Mr. Chips.*
Actress: Vivien Leigh, *Gone With the Wind.*
Sup. Actor: Thomas Mitchell, *Stage Coach.*
Sup. Actress: Hattie McDaniel, *Gone With the Wind.*
Director: Victor Fleming, *Gone With the Wind.*
Picture: *Gone With the Wind,* Selznick International.

1940
Actor: James Stewart, *The Philadelphia Story.*
Actress: Ginger Rogers, *Kitty Foyle.*
Sup. Actor: Walter Brennan, *The Westerner.*
Sup. Actress: Jane Darwell, *The Grapes of Wrath.*
Director: John Ford, *The Grapes of Wrath.*
Picture: *Rebecca,* Selznick International.

1941
Actor: Gary Cooper, *Sergeant York.*
Actress: Joan Fontaine, *Suspicion.*
Sup. Actor: Donald Crisp, *How Green Was My Valley.*
Sup. Actress: Mary Astor, *The Great Lie.*
Director: John Ford, *How Green Was My Valley.*
Picture: *How Green Was My Valley,* 20th Cent.-Fox.

1942
Actor: James Cagney, *Yankee Doodle Dandy.*
Actress: Greer Garson, *Mrs. Miniver.*
Sup. Actor: Van Heflin, *Johnny Eager.*
Sup. Actress: Teresa Wright, *Mrs. Miniver.*
Director: William Wyler, *Mrs. Miniver.*
Picture: *Mrs. Miniver,* MGM.

1943
Actor: Paul Lukas, *Watch on the Rhine.*
Actress: Jennifer Jones, *The Song of Bernadette.*
Sup. Actor: Charles Coburn, *The More the Merrier.*
Sup. Actress: Katina Paxinou, *For Whom the Bell Tolls.*
Director: Michael Curtiz, *Casablanca.*
Picture: *Casablanca,* Warner.

1944
Actor: Bing Crosby, *Going My Way.*
Actress: Ingrid Bergman, *Gaslight.*
Sup. Actor: Barry Fitzgerald, *Going My Way.*
Sup. Actress: Ethel Barrymore, *None But the Lonely Heart.*
Director: Leo McCarey, *Going My Way.*
Picture: *Going My Way,* Paramount.

1945
Actor: Ray Milland, *The Lost Weekend.*
Actress: Joan Crawford, *Mildred Pierce.*
Sup. Actor: James Dunn, *A Tree Grows in Brooklyn.*
Sup. Actress: Anne Revere, *National Velvet.*
Director: Billy Wilder, *The Lost Weekend.*
Picture: *The Lost Weekend,* Paramount.

1946
Actor: Fredric March, *Best Years of Our Lives.*
Actress: Olivia de Havilland, *To Each His Own.*
Sup. Actor: Harold Russell, *The Best Years of Our Lives.*
Sup. Actress: Anne Baxter, *The Razor's Edge.*
Director: William Wyler, *The Best Years of Our Lives.*
Picture: *The Best Years of Our Lives,* Goldwyn, RKO.

1947
Actor: Ronald Colman, *A Double Life.*
Actress: Loretta Young, *The Farmer's Daughter.*
Sup. Actor: Edmund Gwenn, *Miracle on 34th Street.*
Sup. Actress: Celeste Holm, *Gentleman's Agreement.*
Director: Elia Kazan, *Gentleman's Agreement.*
Picture: *Gentleman's Agreement,* 20th Cent.-Fox.

1948
Actor: Laurence Olivier, *Hamlet.*
Actress: Jane Wyman, *Johnny Belinda.*
Sup. Actor: Walter Huston, *Treasure of Sierra Madre.*
Sup. Actress: Claire Trevor, *Key Largo.*
Director: John Huston, *Treasure of Sierra Madre.*
Picture: *Hamlet,* Two Cities Film, Universal International.

1949
Actor: Broderick Crawford, *All the King's Men.*
Actress: Olivia de Havilland, *The Heiress.*
Sup. Actor: Dean Jagger, *Twelve O'Clock High.*
Sup. Actress: Mercedes McCambridge, *All the King's Men.*
Director: Joseph L. Mankiewicz, *Letter to Three Wives.*
Picture: *All the King's Men,* Columbia.

1950
Actor: Jose Ferrer, *Cyrano de Bergerac.*
Actress: Judy Holliday, *Born Yesterday.*
Sup. Actor: George Sanders, *All About Eve.*
Sup. Actress: Josephine Hull, *Harvey.*
Director: Joseph L. Mankiewicz, *All About Eve.*
Picture: *All About Eve,* 20th Century-Fox.

1951
Actor: Humphrey Bogart, *The African Queen.*
Actress: Vivien Leigh, *A Streetcar Named Desire.*
Sup. Actor: Karl Malden, *A Streetcar Named Desire.*
Sup. Actress: Kim Hunter, *A Streetcar Named Desire.*
Director: George Stevens, *A Place in the Sun.*
Picture: *An American in Paris,* MGM.

1952
Actor: Gary Cooper, *High Noon.*
Actress: Shirley Booth, *Come Back, Little Sheba.*
Sup. Actor: Anthony Quinn, *Viva Zapata!*
Sup. Actress: Gloria Grahame, *The Bad and the Beautiful.*
Director: John Ford, *The Quiet Man.*
Picture: *Greatest Show on Earth,* C.B. DeMille, Paramount.

1953
Actor: William Holden, *Stalag 17.*
Actress: Audrey Hepburn, *Roman Holiday.*
Sup. Actor: Frank Sinatra, *From Here to Eternity.*
Sup. Actress: Donna Reed, *From Here to Eternity.*
Director: Fred Zinnemann, *From Here to Eternity.*
Picture: *From Here to Eternity,* Columbia.

1954
Actor: Marlon Brando, *On the Waterfront.*
Actress: Grace Kelly, *The Country Girl.*
Sup. Actor: Edmond O'Brien, *The Barefoot Contessa.*
Sup. Actress: Eva Marie Saint, *On the Waterfront.*
Director: Elia Kazan, *On the Waterfront.*
Picture: *On the Waterfront,* Horizon-American, Colum.

1955
Actor: Ernest Borgnine, *Marty.*
Actress: Anna Magnani, *The Rose Tattoo.*
Sup. Actor: Jack Lemmon, *Mister Roberts.*
Sup. Actress: Jo Van Fleet, *East of Eden.*
Director: Delbert Mann, *Marty.*
Picture: *Marty,* Hecht and Lancaster's Steven Prods., U.A.

1956
Actor: Yul Brynner, *The King and I.*
Actress: Ingrid Bergman, *Anastasia.*
Sup. Actor: Anthony Quinn, *Lust for Life.*
Sup. Actress: Dorothy Malone, *Written on the Wind.*
Director: George Stevens, *Giant.*
Picture: *Around the World in 80 Days,* Michael Todd, U.A.

1957
Actor: Alec Guinness, *The Bridge on the River Kwai.*
Actress: Joanne Woodward, *The Three Faces of Eve.*
Sup. Actor: Red Buttons, *Sayonara.*
Sup. Actress: Miyoshi Umeki, *Sayonara.*
Director: David Lean, *The Bridge on the River Kwai.*
Picture: *The Bridge on the River Kwai,* Columbia.

1958
Actor: David Niven, *Separate Tables.*
Actress: Susan Hayward, *I Want to Live.*
Sup. Actor: Burl Ives, *The Big Country.*
Sup. Actress: Wendy Hiller, *Separate Tables.*
Director: Vincente Minnelli, *Gigi.*
Picture: *Gigi,* Arthur Freed Production, MGM.

1959
Actor: Charlton Heston, *Ben-Hur.*
Actress: Simone Signoret, *Room at the Top.*
Sup. Actor: Hugh Griffith, *Ben-Hur.*
Sup. Actress: Shelley Winters, *Diary of Anne Frank.*
Director: William Wyler, *Ben-Hur.*
Picture: *Ben-Hur,* MGM.

1960
Actor: Burt Lancaster, *Elmer Gantry.*
Actress: Elizabeth Taylor, *Butterfield 8.*
Sup. Actor: Peter Ustinov, *Spartacus.*
Sup. Actress: Shirley Jones, *Elmer Gantry.*
Director: Billy Wilder, *The Apartment.*
Picture: *The Apartment,* Mirisch Co., U.A.

1961
Actor: Maximilian Schell, *Judgment at Nuremberg.*
Actress: Sophia Loren, *Two Women.*
Sup. Actor: George Chakiris, *West Side Story.*
Sup. Actress: Rita Moreno, *West Side Story.*
Director: Jerome Robbins, Robert Wise, *West Side Story.*
Picture: *West Side Story,* United Artists.

1962
Actor: Gregory Peck, *To Kill a Mockingbird.*
Actress: Anne Bancroft, *The Miracle Worker.*
Sup. Actor: Ed Begley, *Sweet Bird of Youth.*
Sup. Actress: Patty Duke, *The Miracle Worker.*
Director: David Lean, *Lawrence of Arabia.*
Picture: *Lawrence of Arabia,* Columbia.

1963
Actor: Sidney Poitier, *Lilies of the Field.*
Actress: Patricia Neal, *Hud.*
Sup. Actor: Melvyn Douglas, *Hud.*
Sup. Actress: Margaret Rutherford, *The V.I.P.s.*
Director: Tony Richardson, *Tom Jones.*
Picture: *Tom Jones.* Woodfall Prod., UA-Lopert Pictures.

1964
Actor: Rex Harrison, *My Fair Lady.*
Actress: Julie Andrews, *Mary Poppins.*
Sup. Actor: Peter Ustinov, *Topkapi.*
Sup. Actress: Lila Kedrova, *Zorba the Greek.*
Director: George Cukor, *My Fair Lady.*
Picture: *My Fair Lady,* Warner Bros.

1965
Actor: Lee Marvin, *Cat Ballou.*
Actress: Julie Christie, *Darling.*
Sup. Actor: Martin Balsam, *A Thousand Clowns.*
Sup. Actress: Shelley Winters, *A Patch of Blue.*
Director: Robert Wise, *The Sound of Music.*
Picture: *The Sound of Music,* 20th Century-Fox.

1966
Actor: Paul Scofield, *A Man for All Seasons.*
Actress: Elizabeth Taylor, *Who's Afraid of Virginia Woolf?*
Sup. Actor: Walter Matthau, *The Fortune Cookie.*
Sup. Actress: Sandy Dennis, *Who's Afraid of Virginia Woolf?*
Director: Fred Zinnemann, *A Man for All Seasons.*
Picture: *A Man for All Seasons,* Columbia.

1967
Actor: Rod Steiger, *In the Heat of the Night.*
Actress: Katharine Hepburn, *Guess Who's Coming to Dinner.*
Sup. Actor: George Kennedy, *Cool Hand Luke.*
Sup. Actress: Estelle Parsons, *Bonnie and Clyde.*
Director: Mike Nichols, *The Graduate.*
Picture: *In the Heat of the Night.*

1968
Actor: Cliff Robertson, *Charly.*
Actress: Katharine Hepburn, *The Lion in Winter;* Barbra Streisand, *Funny Girl* (tie).
Sup. Actor: Jack Albertson, *The Subject Was Roses.*
Sup. Actress: Ruth Gordon, *Rosemary's Baby.*
Director: Sir Carol Reed, *Oliver!*
Picture: *Oliver!*

1969
Actor: John Wayne, *True Grit.*
Actress: Maggie Smith, *The Prime of Miss Jean Brodie.*
Sup. Actor: Gig Young, *They Shoot Horses, Don't They?*
Sup. Actress: Goldie Hawn, *Cactus Flower.*
Director: John Schlesinger, *Midnight Cowboy.*
Picture: *Midnight Cowboy.*

1970
Actor: George C. Scott, *Patton* (refused).
Actress: Glenda Jackson, *Women in Love.*
Sup. Actor: John Mills, *Ryan's Daughter.*
Sup. Actress: Helen Hayes, *Airport.*
Director: Franklin Schaffner, *Patton.*
Picture: *Patton.*

1971
Actor: Gene Hackman, *The French Connection.*
Actress: Jane Fonda, *Klute.*
Sup. Actor: Ben Johnson, *The Last Picture Show.*
Sup. Actress: Cloris Leachman, *The Last Picture Show.*
Director: William Friedkin, *The French Connection.*
Picture: *The French Connection.*

1972
Actor: Marlon Brando, *The Godfather* (refused).
Actress: Liza Minnelli, *Cabaret.*
Sup. Actor: Joel Grey, *Cabaret.*
Sup. Actress: Eileen Heckart, *Butterflies are Free.*
Director: Bob Fosse, *Cabaret.*
Picture: *The Godfather.*

1973
Actor: Jack Lemmon, *Save the Tiger.*
Actress: Glenda Jackson, *A Touch of Class.*
Sup. Actor: John Houseman, *The Paper Chase.*
Sup. Actress: Tatum O'Neal, *Paper Moon.*
Director: George Roy Hill, *The Sting.*
Picture: *The Sting.*

1974
Actor: Art Carney, *Harry and Tonto.*
Actress: Ellen Burstyn, *Alice Doesn't Live Here Anymore.*
Sup. Actor: Robert DeNiro, *The Godfather, Part II.*
Sup. Actress: Ingrid Bergman, *Murder on the Orient Express.*
Director: Francis Ford Coppola, *The Godfather, Part II.*
Picture: *The Godfather, Part II.*

1975
Actor: Jack Nicholson, *One Flew Over the Cuckoo's Nest.*
Actress: Louise Fletcher, *One Flew Over the Cuckoo's Nest.*
Sup. Actor: George Burns, *The Sunshine Boys.*
Sup. Actress: Lee Grant, *Shampoo.*
Director: Milos Forman, *One Flew Over the Cuckoo's Nest.*
Picture: *One Flew Over the Cuckoo's Nest.*

1976
Actor: Peter Finch, *Network.*
Actress: Faye Dunaway, *Network.*
Sup. Actor: Jason Robards, *All the President's Men.*
Sup. Actress: Beatrice Straight, *Network.*
Director: John G. Avildsen, *Rocky.*
Picture: *Rocky.*

1977
Actor: Richard Dreyfuss, *The Goodbye Girl.*
Actress: Diane Keaton, *Annie Hall.*
Sup. Actor: Jason Robards, *Julia.*
Sup. Actress: Vanessa Redgrave, *Julia.*
Director: Woody Allen, *Annie Hall.*
Picture: *Annie Hall.*

1978
Actor: Jon Voight, *Coming Home.*
Actress: Jane Fonda, *Coming Home.*
Sup. Actor: Christopher Walken, *The Deer Hunter.*
Sup. Actress: Maggie Smith, *California Suite.*
Director: Michael Cimino, *The Deer Hunter.*
Picture: *The Deer Hunter.*

1979
Actor: Dustin Hoffman, *Kramer vs. Kramer.*
Actress: Sally Field, *Norma Rae.*
Sup. Actor: Melvyn Douglas, *Being There.*
Sup. Actress: Meryl Streep, *Kramer vs. Kramer.*
Director: Robert Benton, *Kramer vs. Kramer.*
Picture: *Kramer vs. Kramer.*

1980
Actor: Robert DeNiro, *Raging Bull.*
Actress: Sissy Spacek, *Coal Miner's Daughter.*
Sup. Actor: Timothy Hutton, *Ordinary People.*
Sup. Actress: Mary Steenburgen, *Melvin & Howard.*
Director: Robert Redford, *Ordinary People.*
Picture: *Ordinary People.*

1981
Actor: Henry Fonda, *On Golden Pond.*

Actress: Katharine Hepburn, *On Golden Pond.*
Sup. Actor: John Gielgud, *Arthur.*
Sup. Actress: Maureen Stapleton, *Reds.*
Director: Warren Beatty, *Reds.*
Picture: *Chariots of Fire.*

1982

Actor: Ben Kingsley, *Gandhi.*
Actress: Meryl Streep, *Sophie's Choice.*
Sup. Actor: Louis Gossett, Jr., *An Officer and a Gentleman.*
Sup. Actress: Jessica Lange, *Tootsie.*
Director: Richard Attenborough, *Gandhi.*
Picture: *Gandhi.*

1983

Actor: Robert Duvall, *Tender Mercies.*
Actress: Shirley MacLaine, *Terms of Endearment.*
Supporting Actor: Jack Nicholson, *Terms of Endearment.*
Supporting Actress: Linda Hunt, *The Year of Living Dangerously.*
Director: James L. Brooks, *Terms of Endearment.*
Picture: *Terms of Endearment.*

1984

Actor: F. Murray Abraham, *Amadeus.*
Actress: Sally Field, *Places in the Heart.*
Supporting Actor: Haing S. Ngor, *The Killing Fields.*
Supporting Actress: Peggy Ashcroft, *A Passage to India.*
Director: Milos Forman, *Amadeus.*
Picture: *Amadeus.*

1985

Actor: William Hurt, *Kiss of the Spider Woman.*
Actress: Geraldine Page, *The Trip to Bountiful.*
Supporting Actor: Don Ameche, *Cocoon.*
Supporting Actress: Anjelica Huston, *Prizzi's Honor.*
Director: Sydney Pollack, *Out of Africa.*
Picture: *Out of Africa.*

1986

Actor: Paul Newman, *The Color of Money.*
Actress: Marlee Matlin, *Children of a Lesser God.*
Supporting Actor: Michael Caine, *Hannah and Her Sisters.*
Supporting Actress: Dianne Wiest, *Hannah and Her Sisters.*
Director: Oliver Stone, *Platoon.*
Picture: *Platoon.*

1987

Actor: Michael Douglas, *Wall Street.*
Actress: Cher, *Moonstruck.*
Supporting Actor: Sean Connery, *The Untouchables.*
Supporting Actress: Olympia Dukakis, *Moonstruck.*
Director: Bernardo Bertolucci, *The Last Emperor.*
Picture: *The Last Emperor.*

1988

Actor: Dustin Hoffman, *Rain Man.*
Actress: Jodie Foster, *The Accused.*
Supporting Actor: Kevin Kline, *A Fish Called Wanda.*
Supporting Actress: Geena Davis, *The Accidental Tourist.*
Director: Barry Levinson, *Rain Man.*
Picture: *Rain Man.*

1989

Actor: Daniel Day-Lewis, *My Left Foot.*
Actress: Jessica Tandy, *Driving Miss Daisy.*
Supporting Actor: Denzel Washington, *Glory.*
Supporting Actress: Brenda Fricker, *My Left Foot.*
Director: Oliver Stone, *Born on the Fourth of July.*
Picture: *Driving Miss Daisy.*

1990

Actor: Jeremy Irons, *Reversal of Fortune.*
Actress: Kathy Bates, *Misery.*
Supporting Actor: Joe Pesci, *Goodfellas.*
Supporting Actress: Whoopi Goldberg, *Ghost.*
Director: Kevin Costner, *Dances With Wolves.*
Picture: *Dances With Wolves*

1991

Actor: Anthony Hopkins, *The Silence of the Lambs.*
Actress: Jodie Foster, *The Silence of the Lambs.*
Supporting Actor: Jack Palance, *City Slickers.*
Supporting Actress: Mercedes Ruehl, *The Fisher King.*
Director: Jonathan Demme, *The Silence of the Lambs.*
Picture: *The Silence of the Lambs.*

1992

Picture: *Unforgiven.*
Actor: Al Pacino, *Scent of a Woman.*
Actress: Emma Thompson, *Howards End.*
Supporting Actor: Gene Hackman, *Unforgiven.*
Supporting Actress: Marisa Tomei, *My Cousin Vinny.*
Director: Clint Eastwood, *Unforgiven.*
Foreign-Language Film: *Indochine*, France
Original Screenplay: Neil Jordan, *The Crying Game.*
Adapted Screenplay: Ruth Prawer Jhabvala, *Howards End.*
Cinematography: Philippe Rousselot, *A River Runs Through It.*
Editing: Joel Cox, *Unforgiven.*
Original Score: Alan Menken, *Aladdin.*
Original Song: "Whole New World," from *Aladdin*, Alan Menken, Tim Rice.
Art Direction: Luciana Arrighi, Ian Whittaker, *Howards End.*
Costume Design: Eiko Ishioka, *Bram Stoker's Dracula.*
Makeup: Greg Cannom, Michele Burke, Matthew W. Mungle, *Bram Stoker's Dracula.*
Visual Effects: Ken Ralston, Doug Chiang, Doug Smythe, Tom Woodruff Jr., *Death Becomes Her.*
Sound: Chris Jenkins, Doug Hemphill, Mark Smith, Simon Kaye, *The Last of the Mohicans.*
Documentary Feature: *The Panama Deception.*
Documentary Short Subject: *Educating Peter.*
Short Film, Live: *Omnibus.*
Short Film, Animated: *Mona Lisa Descending a Staircase.*
Honorary Award: Federico Fellini.
Jean Hersholt Humanitarian Awards: Audrey Hepburn, Elizabeth Taylor.
Academy Award of Merit: Chadwell O'Connor.
Gordon E. Sawyer Award: Erich Kaestner.

Grammy Awards

Source: National Academy of Recording Arts & Sciences

1958

Record: Domenico Modugno, *Nel Blu Dipinto Di Blu (Volare).*
Album: Henry Mancini, *The Music from Peter Gunn.*

1959

Record: Bobby Darin, *Mack the Knife.*
Album: Frank Sinatra, *Come Dance With Me.*

1960

Record: Percy Faith, *Theme From A Summer Place.*
Album: Bob Newhart, *Button Down Mind.*

1961

Record: Henry Mancini, *Moon River.*
Album: Judy Garland, *Judy At Carnegie Hall.*

1962

Record: Tony Bennett, *I Left My Heart in San Francisco.*
Album: Vaughn Meader, *The First Family.*

1963

Record: Henry Mancini, *The Days of Wine and Roses.*
Album: *The Barbra Streisand Album.*

1964

Record: Stan Getz and Astrud Gilberto, *The Girl From Ipanema.*
Album: *Getz/Gilberto.*

1965

Record: Herb Alpert, *A Taste Of Honey.*
Album: Frank Sinatra, *September of My Years.*

1966

Record: Frank Sinatra, *Strangers in the Night.*
Album: Frank Sinatra, *A Man and His Music.*

1967

Record: 5th Dimension, *Up, Up and Away.*
Album: The Beatles, *Sgt. Pepper's Lonely Hearts Club Band.*

1968

Record: Simon & Garfunkel, *Mrs. Robinson.*
Album: Glen Campbell, *By the Time I Get to Phoenix.*

1969

Record: 5th Dimension, *Aquarius/Let the Sunshine In.*
Album: *Blood, Sweat and Tears.*

1970

Record: Simon & Garfunkel, *Bridge Over Troubled Water.*
Album: *Bridge Over Troubled Water.*

1971

Record: Carole King, *It's Too Late.*
Album: Carole King, *Tapestry.*

1972

Record: Roberta Flack, *The First Time Ever I Saw Your Face.*
Album: *The Concert For Bangla Desh.*

1973

Record: Roberta Flack, *Killing Me Softly with His Song.*
Album: Stevie Wonder, *Innervisions.*

1974

Record: Olivia Newton-John, *I Honestly Love You.*
Album: Stevie Wonder, *Fulfullingness' First Finale.*

1975

Record: Captain & Tennille, *Love Will Keep Us Together.*
Album: Paul Simon, *Still Crazy After All These Years.*

1976

Record: George Benson, *This Masquerade.*
Album: Stevie Wonder, *Songs in the Key of Life.*

1977

Record: Eagles, *Hotel California.*
Album: Fleetwood Mac, *Rumours.*

1978

Record: Billy Joel, *Just the Way You Are.*
Album: Bee Gees, *Saturday Night Fever.*

1979

Record: The Doobie Brothers, *What a Fool Believes.*
Album: Billy Joel, *52nd Street.*

1980

Record: Christopher Cross, *Sailing.*
Album: Christopher Cross, *Christopher Cross.*

1981

Record: Kim Carnes, *Bette Davis Eyes.*
Album: John Lennon, Yoko Ono, *Double Fantasy.*

1982

Record: Toto, *Rosanna.*
Album: Toto, *Toto IV.*

1983

Record: Michael Jackson, *Beat It.*
Album: Michael Jackson, *Thriller.*

1984

Record: Tina Turner, *What's Love Got to Do With It.*
Album: Lionel Richie, *Can't Slow Down.*

1985

Record: USA for Africa, *We Are the World.*
Album: Phil Collins, *No Jacket Required.*

1986

Record: Steve Winwood, *Higher Love.*
Album: Paul Simon, *Graceland.*

1987

Record: Paul Simon, *Graceland.*
Album: U2, *The Joshua Tree.*

1988

Record: Bobby McFerrin, *Don't Worry, Be Happy.*
Album: George Michael, *Faith.*

1989

Record: Bette Midler, *Wind Beneath My Wings.*
Album: Bonnie Raitt, *Nick of Time.*

1990

Record: Phil Collins, *Another Day in Paradise.*
Album: Quincy Jones, *Back on the Block.*

1991

Record: Natalie Cole, with Nat "King" Cole, *Unforgettable.*
Album: Natalie Cole, with Nat "King" Cole, *Unforgettable.*

1992

Record: Eric Clapton, *Tears in Heaven.*
Album: Eric Clapton, *Unplugged.*
Song: *Tears in Heaven.*
New Artist: Arrested Development.
Female Pop Vocalist: K. D. Laing, *Constant Craving.*
Male Pop Vocalist: Eric Clapton, *Tears in Heaven.*
Duo or Group Pop Vocal: Celine Dion and Peabo Bryson, *Beauty and the Beast.*
Traditional Pop Vocalist: Tony Bennett, *Perfectly Frank.*
Pop-Musical Performance: *Beauty and the Beast,* Nuremberg Symphony Orchestra.
Female Rock Vocalist: Melissa Etheridge, *Ain't It Heavy.*
Male Rock Vocalist: Eric Clapton, *Unplugged.*
Rock Duo or Group: U2, *Achtung Baby.*
Hard Rock: Red Hot Chili Peppers, *Give It Away.*
Metal: Nine-Inch Nails, *Wish.*
Rock Instrumental Performance: Stevie Ray Vaughan and Double Trouble, *Little Wing.*
Rock Song: Eric Clapton and Jim Gordon, *Layla.*

Newbery Medal Books

The Newbery Medal is awarded annually by the Association for Library Service to Children, a division of the American Library Association, to the author of the most distinguished contribution to American literature for children.

Year Awarded	Book, Author
1922	*The Story of Mankind,* Hendrik Willem van Loon
1923	*The Voyages of Dr. Dolittle,* Hugh Lofting
1924	*The Dark Frigate,* Charles Boardman Hawes
1925	*Tales from Silver Lands,* Charles Joseph Finger
1926	*Shen of the Sea,* Arthur Bowie Chrisman
1927	*Smoky, the Cowhorse,* Will James
1928	*Gay-Neck,* Dhan Gopal Mukerji
1929	*The Trumpeter of Krakow,* Eric P. Kelly
1930	*Hitty, Her First Hundred Years,* Rachel Field
1931	*The Cat Who Went to Heaven,* Elizabeth Coatsworth
1932	*Waterless Mountain,* Laura Adams Armer
1933	*Young Fu of the Upper Yangtze,* Elizabeth Foreman Lewis
1934	*Invincible Louisa,* Cornelia Lynde Meigs
1935	*Dobry,* Monica Shannon
1936	*Caddie Woodlawn,* Carol Ryrie Brink
1937	*Roller Skates,* Ruth Sawyer
1938	*The White Stag,* Kate Seredy
1939	*Thimble Summer,* Elizabeth Enright
1940	*Daniel Boone,* James Daugherty
1941	*Call It Courage,* Armstrong Sperry
1942	*The Matchlock Gun,* Walter D. Edmonds
1943	*Adam of the Road,* Elizabeth Janet Gray
1944	*Johnny Tremain,* Esther Forbes
1945	*Rabbit Hill,* Robert Lawson
1946	*Strawberry Girl,* Lois Lenski
1947	*Miss Hickory,* Carolyn S. Bailey
1948	*Twenty-One Balloons,* William Pène Du Bois
1949	*King of the Wind,* Marguerite Henry
1950	*The Door in the Wall,* Marguerite de Angeli
1951	*Amos Fortune, Free Man,* Elizabeth Yates
1952	*Ginger Pye,* Eleanor Estes
1953	*Secret of the Andes,* Ann Nolan Clark
1954	*. . . And Now Miguel,* Joseph Krumgold
1955	*The Wheel on the School,* Meindert DeJong
1956	*Carry On, Mr. Bowditch,* Jean Lee Latham
1957	*Miracles on Maple Hill,* Virginia Sorensen
1958	*Rifles for Watie,* Harold Keith
1959	*The Witch of Blackbird Pond,* Elizabeth George Speare
1960	*Onion John,* Joseph Krumgold
1961	*Island of the Blue Dolphins,* Scott O'Dell
1962	*The Bronze Bow,* Elizabeth George Speare
1963	*A Wrinkle in Time,* Madeleine L'Engle
1964	*It's Like This, Cat,* Emily Cheney Neville
1965	*Shadow of a Bull,* Maja Wojciechowska
1966	*I, Juan de Pareja,* Elizabeth Borton de Trevino
1967	*Up a Road Slowly,* Irene Hunt
1968	*From the Mixed-Up Files of Mrs. Basil E. Frankweiler,* E. L. Konigsburg
1969	*The High King,* Lloyd Alexander
1970	*Sounder,* William H. Armstrong
1971	*The Summer of the Swans,* Betsy Byars
1972	*Mrs. Frisby and the Rats of NIMH,* Robert C. O'Brien
1973	*Julie of the Wolves,* Jean George
1974	*The Slave Dancer,* Paula Fox
1975	*M. C. Higgins the Great,* Virginia Hamilton
1976	*Grey King,* Susan Cooper
1977	*Roll of Thunder, Hear My Cry,* Mildred D. Taylor
1978	*Bridge to Terabithia,* Katherine Paterson
1979	*The Westing Game,* Ellen Raskin
1980	*A Gathering of Days,* Joan Blos
1981	*Jacob Have I Loved,* Katherine Paterson
1982	*A Visit to William Blake's Inn: Poems for Innocent and Experienced Travelers,* Nancy Willard
1983	*Dicey's Song,* Cynthia Voigt
1984	*Dear Mr. Henshaw,* Beverly Cleary
1985	*The Hero and the Crown,* Robin McKinley
1986	*Sarah, Plain and Tall,* Patricia MacLachlan
1987	*The Whipping Boy,* Sid Fleischman
1988	*Lincoln: A Photobiography,* Russell Freedman
1989	*Joyful Noise: Poems for Two Voices,* Paul Fleischman
1990	*Number the Stars,* Lois Lowry
1991	*Maniac Magee,* Jerry Spinelli
1992	*Shiloh,* Phyllis Reynolds Naylor
1993	*Missing May,* Cynthia Ryland

NOTED PERSONALITIES

Widely Known Americans of the Present

Statesmen, journalists, authors of nonfiction, and other prominent persons not listed in other categories; as of mid-1993.

Name (Birthplace)	Birthdate
Ailes, Roger (Knoxville, Tenn.)	7/3/40
Albright, Madeleine (Prague, Czech.)	5/15/37
Angelou, Maya (St. Louis, Mo.)	4/4/28
Arledge, Roone (Forest Hills, N.Y.)	7/8/31
Anderson, Jack (Long Beach, Cal.)	10/19/22
Annenberg, Walter H. (Milwaukee, Wis.)	1908
Armstrong, Neil (Wapakoneta, Oh.)	8/5/30
Ash, Mary Kay (Hot Wells, Tex.)	—
Aspin, Les (Milwaukee, Wis.)	7/21/38
Babbitt, Bruce (Los Angeles, Cal.)	6/27/38
Baker, James A. (Houston, Tex.)	4/28/30
Baker, Russell (Loudoun Co., Va.)	8/14/25
Barry, Dave (Armonk, N.Y.)	7/3/47
Barthelmy, Sidney K. (New Orleans, La.)	3/17/42
Bennett, William J. (Salem, Oh.)	5/4/44
Bentsen, Lloyd (Mission, Tex.)	2/11/21
Biden, Joseph R. Jr. (Scranton, Pa.)	11/20/42
Blackmun, Harry (Nashville, Ill.)	11/12/08
Blass, Bill (Ft. Wayne, Ind.)	6/22/22
Bloom, Harold (New York, N.Y.)	7/11/30
Bombeck, Erma (Dayton, Oh.)	2/21/27
Boorstin, Daniel (Atlanta, Ga.)	10/1/14
Boxer, Barbara (Brooklyn, N.Y.)	11/11/40
Bradlee, Ben (Boston, Mass.)	8/26/21
Bradley, Bill (Crystal City, Mo.)	7/28/43
Bradley, Ed (Philadelphia, Pa.)	6/22/41
Bradley, Thomas (Calvert, Tex.)	12/29/17
Braun, Carol Moseley (Chicago, Ill.)	8/16/47
Brennan, William J. (Newark, N.J.)	4/25/06
Breslin, Jimmy (Jamaica, N.Y.)	10/17/30
Brinkley, Christie (Monroe, Mich.)	2/2/53
Brinkley, David (Wilmington, N.C.)	7/10/20
Broder, David (Chicago Heights, Ill.)	9/11/29
Brody, Jane (Brooklyn, N.Y.)	5/19/41
Brokaw, Tom (Webster, S. Dak.)	2/6/40
Brothers, Joyce (New York, N.Y.)	9/20/28
Brown, Helen Gurley (Green Forest, Ark.)	2/18/22
Brown, Jerry (San Francisco, Cal.)	4/7/38
Brown, Ron (Washington, D.C.)	8/1/41
Buchanan, Pat (Washington, D.C.)	11/2/38
Buchwald, Art (Mt. Vernon, N.Y.)	10/20/25
Buckley, William F. (New York, N.Y.)	11/24/25
Buffet, Warren (Omaha, Neb.)	8/30/30
Bumpers, Dale (Charleston, Ark.)	8/12/25
Buscaglia, Leo (Los Angeles, Cal.)	3/31/24
Bush, Barbara (Rye, N.Y.)	6/8/25
Byrd, Robert (N. Wilkesboro, N.C.)	11/20/17
Canby, Vincent (Chicago, Ill.)	7/27/24
Carter, Jimmy (Plains, Ga.)	10/1/24
Carter, Rosalynn (Plains, Ga.)	8/18/27
Chancellor, John (Chicago, Ill.)	7/14/27
Child, Julia (Pasadena, Cal.)	8/15/12
Chisholm, Shirley (Brooklyn, N.Y.)	11/30/24
Christopher, Warren (Scranton, Pa.)	10/27/25
Chung, Connie (Washington, D.C.)	8/20/46
Claiborne, Craig (Sunflower, Miss.)	9/4/20
Claiborne, Liz (Brussels, Belg.)	3/31/29
Clinton, Bill (Hope, Ark.)	8/19/46
Clinton, Chelsea (Little Rock, Ark.)	2/27/80
Clinton, Hillary Rodham (Chicago, Ill.)	10/26/47
Collins, Martha (Shelby Cty, Ky.)	12/7/36
Commager, Henry Steele (Pittsburgh, Pa.)	10/25/02
Cooney, Joan Ganz (Phoenix, Ariz.)	10/30/29
Cosell, Howard (Winston-Salem, N.C.)	3/25/20
Couric, Katie (Washington, D.C.)	1/7/57
Crawford, Cindy (DeKalb, Ill.)	2/20/66
Crist, Judith (New York, N.Y.)	5/22/22
Cronkite, Walter (St. Joseph, Mo.)	11/4/16
Cuomo, Mario (Queens, N.Y.)	6/15/32
Daley, Richard M. (Chicago, Ill.)	4/24/42
D'Amato, Alfonse M. (Brooklyn, N.Y.)	8/1/37
Deford, Frank (Baltimore, Md.)	12/16/38
Dellums, Ronald (Oakland, Cal.)	11/24/35
Dershowitz, Alan (Brooklyn, N.Y.)	9/1/38
Dingell, John D. Jr. (Colorado Spngs., Col.)	7/8/26
Dinkins, David (Trenton, N.J.)	7/10/27
Dixon, Sharon Pratt (Washington, D.C.)	1/31/44
Dodd, Christopher (Willimantic, Conn.)	5/27/44
Dole, Elizabeth (Salisbury, N.C.)	7/29/36
Dole, Robert (Russell, Kan.)	7/22/23
Domenici, Pete (Albuquerque, N.M.)	5/7/32
Donaldson, Sam (El Paso, Tex.)	3/11/34

Name (Birthplace)	Birthdate
Drew, Elizabeth (Cincinnati, Oh.)	11/16/35
Dukakis, Michael S. (Boston, Mass.)	11/3/33
Edelman, Marian Wright (Bennetsville, S.C.)	6/6/39
Eisner, Michael (New York, N.Y.)	3/7/42
Ephron, Nora (New York, N.Y.)	5/19/41
Evangelista, Linda (St. Catherine's, Canada)	5/10/65
Falwell, Jerry (Lynchburg, Va.)	8/11/33
Feinstein, Dianne (San Francisco, Cal.)	6/22/33
Ferraro, Geraldine (Newburgh, N.Y.)	8/26/35
Florio, James J. (New York, N.Y.)	8/29/37
Foley, Thomas S. (Spokane, Wash.)	3/6/29
Foote, Shelby (Greenville, Miss.)	11/17/16
Ford, Betty (Chicago, Ill.)	4/8/18
Ford, Gerald R. (Omaha, Neb.)	7/14/13
Frank, Barney (Bayonne, N.J.)	3/31/40
Frankel, Max (Gera, Germany)	4/3/30
Friedan, Betty (Peoria, Ill.)	2/4/21
Friedman, Milton (Brooklyn, N.Y.)	7/31/12
Galbraith, John Kenneth (Ontario, Can.)	10/15/08
Gates, William (Seattle, Wash.)	10/28/55
Gephardt, Richard (St. Louis, Mo.)	1/31/41
Gergen, David R. (Durham, N.C.)	5/9/42
Gibson, Charles (Evanston, Ill.)	3/9/43
Gingrich, Newt (Harrisburg, Pa.)	6/17/43
Ginsberg, Allen (Paterson, N.J.)	6/3/21
Ginsburg, Ruth Bader (Brooklyn, N.Y.)	3/15/33
Glenn, John (Cambridge, Oh.)	7/18/21
Goldwater, Barry M. (Phoenix, Ariz.)	1/1/09
Goodman, Ellen (Newton, Mass.)	4/11/41
Gore, Al (Washington, D.C.)	3/31/48
Gore, Tipper (Washington, D.C.)	8/19/48
Gottlieb, Robert A. (New York)	4/9/31
Gould, Stephen Jay (New York, N.Y.)	9/10/41
Graham, Billy (Charlotte, N.C.)	11/7/18
Graham, Donald (Baltimore, Md.)	4/22/45
Graham, Katharine (New York, N.Y.)	6/16/17
Gramm, Phil (Ft. Bennington, Ga.)	7/8/42
Gray, William H. 3d (Baton Rouge, La.)	8/20/41
Greene, Bob (Columbus, Oh.)	5/10/47
Greenfield, Meg (Seattle, Wash.)	12/27/30
Greenspan, Alan (New York, N.Y.)	3/6/26
Gumbel, Bryant (New Orleans, La.)	9/29/48
Halberstam, David (New York, N.Y.)	4/10/34
Harkin, Tom (Cumming, Ia.)	11/19/39
Harvey, Paul (Tulsa, Okla.)	9/4/18
Hatfield, Mark O. (Dallas, Ore.)	7/12/22
Heflin, Howell (Poulan, Ga.)	6/19/21
Hefner, Hugh (Chicago, Ill.)	4/9/26
Helms, Jesse (Monroe, N.C.)	10/18/21
Helmsley, Leona (New York, N.Y.)	c.1920
Heloise (Waco, Tex.)	4/15/51
Hollings, Ernest (Charleston, S.C.)	1/1/22
Iacocca, Lee A. (Allentown, Pa.)	10/15/24
Iman (Somalia, Ethiopia)	7/25/55
Inouye, Daniel K. (Honolulu, Ha.)	9/7/24
Jackson, Jesse (Greenville, S.C.)	10/8/41
Jennings, Peter (Toronto, Ont.)	8/29/38
Johnson, Lady Bird (Karnack, Tex.)	12/22/12
Jordan, Barbara (Houston, Tex.)	2/21/36
Kael, Pauline (Petaluma, Calif.)	6/19/19
Karan, Donna (Forest Hills, N.Y.)	10/2/48
Kassebaum, Nancy (Topeka, Kan.)	7/29/32
Keillor, Garrison (Anoka, Minn.)	8/7/42
Kemp, Jack (Los Angeles, Cal.)	7/13/35
Kennedy, Anthony (Sacramento, Cal.)	7/23/36
Kennedy, Edward M. (Brookline, Mass.)	2/22/32
Kennedy, Rose (Boston, Mass.)	7/22/90
Kerr, Walter (Evanston, Ill.)	7/8/13
King, Coretta Scott (Marion, Ala.)	4/27/27
King, Don (Cleveland, Oh.)	12/6/32
King, Larry (Brooklyn, N.Y.)	11/19/34
Kinsley, Michael (Detroit, Mich.)	3/9/51
Kirkland, Lane (Camden, S.C.)	3/12/22
Kirkpatrick, Jeane (Duncan, Okla.)	11/19/26
Kissinger, Henry (Fuerth, Germany)	5/27/23
Klein, Calvin (New York, N.Y.)	11/19/42
Koch, Edward I. (New York, N.Y.)	12/12/24
Koop, C. Everett (Brooklyn, N.Y.)	10/14/16
Koppel, Ted (Lancashire, Eng.)	2/8/40
Kryzyzewski, Mike (Chicago, Ill.)	2/13/47
Kuhn, Maggie (Buffalo, N.Y.)	1905
Kunstler, William (New York, N.Y.)	7/7/19

Name (Birthplace)	Birthdate
Kuralt, Charles (Wilmington, N.C.)	9/10/34
Landers, Ann (Sioux City, Ia.)	7/4/18
Lauder, Estee (New York, N.Y.)	9/1/08
Lauren, Ralph (Bronx, N.Y.)	10/14/39
Leahy, Patrick (Montpelier, Vt.)	3/31/40
Lear, Frances (Hudson, N.Y.)	7/14/23
Lear, Norman (New Haven, Conn.)	7/27/22
Lehrer, Jim (Wichita, Kan.)	5/19/34
Lewis, Anthony (New York, N.Y.)	3/27/27
Limbaugh, Rush (Cape Girardeau, Mo.)	1/12/41
Lindbergh, Anne Morrow (Englewood, N.J.)	1906
Lorenzo, Frank (New York, N.Y.)	5/19/40
Lott, Trent (Grenada, Miss.)	10/9/41
Lugar, Richard G. (Indianapolis, Ind.)	4/4/32
Lukas, J. Anthony (New York, N.Y.)	4/25/33
Lunden, Joan (Sacramento, Calif.)	9/19/50
MacNeil, Robert (Montreal, Que.)	1/19/31
Manchester, William (Attleboro, Mass.)	4/1/22
Martin, Lynn (Evanston, Ill.)	12/26/39
Maslin, Janet (New York, N.Y.)	8/12/49
McClendon, Sarah (Tyler, Tex.)	7/8/10
McGovern, George (Avon, S.D.)	7/19/22
McNamara, Robert (San Francisco, Cal.)	6/9/16
Metzenbaum, Howard (Cleveland, Oh.)	6/4/17
Michel, Robert H. (Peoria, Ill.)	3/2/23
Mikulski, Barbara (Baltimore, Md.)	7/20/36
Mitchell, George (Waterville, Me.)	8/20/33
Mondale, Walter (Ceylon, Minn.)	1/5/28
Mosbacher, Robert (Mt. Vernon, N.Y.)	3/11/27
Moyers, Bill (Hugo, Okla.)	6/5/34
Moynihan, Daniel P. (Tulsa, Okla.)	3/16/27
Mudd, Roger (Washington, D.C.)	2/9/28
Murray, Patty (Seattle, Wash.)	10/11/50
Nader, Ralph (Winsted, Conn.)	2/27/34
Nidetch, Jean (Brooklyn, N.Y.)	10/12/23
Nixon, Richard (Yorba Linda, Cal.)	1/9/13
North, Oliver (San Antonio, Tex.)	10/7/43
Norton, Eleanor Holmes (Washington, D.C.)	6/13/37
Novak, Robert (Joliet, Ill.)	2/26/31
Novello, Antonia (Fajardo, P.R.)	8/23/44
Nunn, Sam (Perry, Ga.)	9/8/38
O'Connor, Cardinal John (Phila., Pa.)	1/15/20
O'Connor, Sandra Day (nr. Duncan, Ariz.)	3/26/30
Onassis, Jacqueline (Southampton, N.Y.)	7/28/29
O'Neill, Thomas P. (Cambridge, Mass.)	12/9/12
Osgood, Charles (New York, N.Y.)	1/8/33
Packwood, Bob (Portland, Ore.)	9/11/32
Paglia, Camille (Endicott, N.Y.)	—
Panetta, Leon F. (Monterey, Cal.)	6/28/38
Pauley, Jane (Indianapolis, Ind.)	10/31/50
Pauling, Linus (Portland, Ore.)	2/28/01
Perot, H. Ross (Texarkana, Tex.)	6/27/30
Phillips, Kevin (New York, N.Y.)	11/30/40
Pickens, T. Boone (Holdenville, Okla.)	5/22/28
Pickering, Thomas (Orange, N.J.)	11/5/31
Plimpton, George (New York, N.Y.)	3/18/27
Podhoretz, Norman (New York, N.Y.)	1/16/30
Poussaint, Alvin F. (New York, N.Y.)	5/15/34
Powell, Colin (New York, N.Y.)	4/5/37
Quayle, Dan (Indianapolis, Ind.)	2/4/47
Quinn, Jane Bryant (Niagara Falls, N.Y.)	2/5/39
Rangel, Charles (New York, N.Y.)	6/11/30
Rather, Dan (Wharton, Tex.)	10/31/31
Reagan, Nancy (New York, N.Y.)	7/6/23
Reagan, Ronald (Tampico, Ill.)	2/6/11
Rehnquist, William (Milwaukee, Wis.)	10/1/24
Reich, Robert B. (Scranton, Pa.)	6/24/46
Reno, Janet (Miami, Fla.)	7/21/38
Rich, Frank (Washington, D.C.)	6/2/49
Richards, Ann (Waco, Tex.)	9/3/33
Ride, Sally K. (Encino, Calif.)	1952
Roberts, Oral (nr. Ada, Okla.)	1/24/18
Robertson, Pat (Lexington, Va.)	3/22/30
Rockefeller, David (New York, N.Y.)	6/12/15
Rockefeller, John D. 4th "Jay" (New York, N.Y.)	6/18/37
Rockefeller, Laurance S. (New York, N.Y.)	5/26/10

Name (Birthplace)	Birthdate
Rooney, Andy (Albany, N.Y.)	1/14/19
Rostenkowski, Dan (Chicago, Ill.)	1/2/28
Rukeyser, Louis (New York, N.Y.)	1/30/33
Safer, Morley (Toronto, Ontario)	11/8/31
Safire, William (New York, N.Y.)	12/17/29
Sagan, Carl (New York, N.Y.)	11/9/34
Salk, Jonas (New York, N.Y.)	10/28/14
Sawyer, Diane (Glasgow, Ky.)	12/22/45
Scalia, Antonin (Trenton, N.J.)	3/11/36
Schlesinger, Arthur Jr. (Columbus, Oh.)	10/15/17
Schroeder, Patricia (Portland, Ore.)	7/30/40
Schuller, Robert (Alton, Ia.)	9/16/26
Schwarzkopf, H. Norman (Trenton, N.J.)	8/22/34
Scott, Willard (Alexandria, Va.)	3/7/34
Scowcroft, Brent (Ogden, Ut.)	3/19/25
Seaborg, Glenn T. (Ishpeming, Mich.)	4/19/12
Shalala, Donna E. (Cleveland, Oh.)	2/14/41
Shanker, Albert (New York, N.Y.)	9/14/28
Shaw, Bernard (Chicago, Ill.)	1940
Shriver, Maria (Chicago, Ill.)	11/6/55
Shultz, George P. (New York, N.Y.)	12/13/20
Silver, Joan Micklin (Omaha, Neb.)	5/25/35
Silverstein, Shel (Chicago, Ill.)	1932
Simmons, Richard (New Orleans, La.)	7/12/48
Simon, Paul (Eugene, Ore.)	11/29/28
Simpson, Alan K. (Cody, Wyo.)	9/2/31
Skinner, Samuel (Chicago, Ill.)	6/10/38
Smith, Hedrick (Kilmacolm, Scotland)	7/9/33
Smith, Liz (Ft. Worth, Tex.)	2/2/23
Souter, David H. (Melrose, Mass.)	9/17/39
Specter, J. Arlen (Wichita, Kans.)	2/12/30
Spock, Benjamin (New Haven, Conn.)	5/2/03
Stahl, Lesley (Lynn, Mass.)	12/16/41
Steinbrenner, George (Rocky River, Oh.)	7/4/30
Steinem, Gloria (Toledo, Oh.)	3/25/34
Stephanopolous, George (Fall River, Mass.)	2/10/61
Stern, David J. (New York, N.Y.)	9/22/42
Stevens, John Paul (Chicago, Ill.)	4/20/20
Sulzberger, Arthur Ochs (New York, N.Y.)	2/5/26
Sununu, John H. (Havana, Cuba)	7/2/39
Tagliabue, Paul (Jersey City, N.J.)	11/24/40
Tartikoff, Brandon (Long Island, N.Y.)	1949
Terkel, Studs (New York, N.Y.)	5/16/12
Thomas, Clarence (Savannah, Ga.)	6/23/48
Thurmond, J. Strom (Edgefield, S.C.)	12/5/02
Tiegs, Cheryl (Minnesota)	9/27/47
Tinker, Grant (Stamford, Conn.)	1/11/26
Tisch, Laurence (New York, N.Y.)	3/15/23
Toland, John (LaCrosse, Wis.)	6/29/12
Trillin, Calvin (Kansas City, Mo.)	12/5/35
Truman, Margaret (Independence, Mo.)	2/17/24
Trump, Donald (New York, N.Y.)	1946
Turner, Ted (Cincinnati, Oh.)	1938
Udall, Morris K. (St. Johns, Ariz.)	6/15/22
Ueberroth, Peter (Chicago, Ill.)	9/2/37
Valenti, Jack (Houston, Tex.)	9/5/21
Van Buren, Abigail (Sioux City, Ia.)	7/4/18
Wallace, George (Clio, Ala.)	8/25/19
Wallace, Mike (Brookline, Mass.)	5/9/18
Walters, Barbara (Boston, Mass.)	9/25/31
Wattleton, Faye (St. Louis, Mo.)	7/8/43
Weicker, Lowell (Paris, France)	5/16/31
Wenner, Jann (New York, N.Y.)	1/7/46
Westheimer, Ruth (Germany)	1928
White, Bill (Lakewood, Fla.)	1/28/34
White, Byron (Ft. Collins, Col.)	6/8/17
Wicker, Tom (Hamlet, N.C.)	6/18/26
Wiesel, Elie (Sighet, Transyl.)	9/30/28
Wilder, L. Douglas (Richmond, Va.)	1/17/31
Will, George (Champaign, Ill.)	1941
Wilson, Pete (Lake Forest, Ill.)	8/23/33
Yamaguchi, Kristi (Hayward, Cal.)	7/12/71
Yard, Molly (Shanghai, China)	c.1910
Young, Andrew (New Orleans, La.)	3/12/32
Young, Coleman (Tuscaloosa, Ala.)	5/24/18
Zahn, Paula (Omaha, Neb.)	2/24/56

Noted Black Americans

Names of black athletes and entertainers are not included here as they are listed elsewhere in The World Almanac.

The Rev. Dr. Ralph David Abernathy, 1926-1990, organizer, 1957, and president, 1968, of the Southern Christian Leadership Conference.

Maya Angelou, b. 1928, writer, read her poem "On the Pulse of Morning" at Pres. Bill Clinton's inauguration.

Crispus Attucks, c. 1723-1770, agitator who led group that precipitated the "Boston Massacre," Mar. 5, 1770.

James Baldwin, 1924-1987, author, playwright; *The Fire Next Time, Blues for Mister Charlie, Just Above My Head.*

Benjamin Banneker, 1731-1806, inventor, astronomer, mathematician, and gazetteer; served on commission that surveyed and laid out Washington, D. C.

Imamu Amiri Baraka, b. LeRoi Jones, 1934, poet, playwright.

James P. Beckwourth, 1798-c. 1867, western fur-trader, scout, after whom Beckwourth Pass in northern California is named.

Dr. Mary McCleod Bethune, 1875-1955, adviser to presidents Roosevelt, Truman; division administrator, Natl. Youth Administration, 1935; founder, pres. Bethune-Cookman College.
Henry Blair, 19th century, obtained patents (believed among first issued to a black) for a corn-planter, 1834, and for a cotton-planter, 1836.
Guion S. Bluford Jr., b. 1942, astronaut, first black Amer. to go into space, 1983.
Julian Bond, b. 1940, civil rights leader first elected to the Georgia state legislature, 1965; helped found Student Nonviolent Coordinating Committee.
Edward Bouchet, 1852-1918, first black to earn a Ph.D., Yale, 1876, at a U.S. university; first black elected to Phi Beta Kappa.
Thomas Bradley, b. 1917, mayor of Los Angeles, 1973-1993.
Andrew F. Brimmer, b. 1926, first black member, 1966, Federal Reserve Board.
Edward W. Brooke, b. 1919, attorney general, 1962, of Massachusetts; first black elected to U. S. Senate, 1967, since 19th century Reconstruction.
Gwendolyn Brooks, b. 1917, poet, novelist; first black to win a Pulitzer Prize, 1950, for *Annie Allen.*
Sterling A. Brown, 1901-1989, poet, literature professor; helped establish Afro-American literary criticism.
William Wells Brown, 1815-1884, novelist, dramatist; first American black to publish a novel.
Dr. Ralph Bunche, 1904-1971, first black to win the Nobel Peace Prize, 1950; undersecretary of the UN, 1950.
Sherian Grace Cadoria, b. 1940, brigadier general; highest ranking black woman in U.S. armed forces as of 1990.
Alexa Canady, b. 1950, first black woman neurosurgeon in U.S.
George E. Carruthers, b. 1940, physicist developed the Apollo 16 lunar surface ultraviolet camera/spectograph.
George Washington Carver, 1861-1943, botanist, chemurgist, and educator; his extensive experiments in soil building and plant diseases revolutionized the economy of the South.
Charles Waddell Chestnutt, 1858-1932, author known primarily for his short stories, including *The Conjure Woman.*
Shirley Chisholm, b. 1924, first black woman elected to House of Representatives, Brooklyn, N. Y., 1968.
Bishop Philip R. Cousin, b. 1933, Pres., Natl. Council of Churches of Christ in the USA, 1985-.
Countee Cullen, 1903-1946, poet, played a prominent role in the "Harlem Renaissance" of the 1920s; "Heritage," *The Black Christ.*
Lt. Gen. Benjamin O. Davis Jr. b. 1912, West Point, 1936, first black Air Force general, 1954.
Brig. Gen. Benjamin O. Davis Sr., 1877-1970, first black general, 1940, in U. S. Army.
William L. Dawson, 1886-1970, Illinois congressman, first black chairman of a major House of Representatives committee.
David Dinkins, b. 1927, first black mayor of New York City, 1990-.
Sharon Pratt Dixon, b. 1944, mayor of Washington, D.C., 1990-.
Aaron Douglas, 1900-1979, painter; called father of black American art.
Frederick Douglass, 1817-1895, author, editor, orator, diplomat; edited the abolitionist weekly, The North Star, in Rochester, N. Y.; U.S. minister and consul general to Haiti.
St. Clair Drake, 1911-1990, black studies pioneer, *Black Metropolis* (1945, with Horace R. Cayton); first permanent director, African and Afro-American Studies, Stanford Univ.
Dr. Charles Richard Drew, 1904-1950, pioneer in development of blood banks; director of American Red Cross blood donor project in World War II.
William Edward Burghardt Du Bois, 1868-1963, historian, sociologist; a founder of the National Association for the Advancement of Colored People (NAACP), 1909, and founder of its magazine The Crisis; author, *The Souls of Black Folk.*
Paul Laurence Dunbar, 1872-1906, poet, novelist; won fame with *Lyrics of Lowly Life,* 1896.
Jean Baptiste Point du Sable, c. 1750-1818, pioneer trader and first settler of Chicago, 1779.
Marian Wright Edelman, b. 1939, founder, pres. of Children's Defense Fund.
Joycelyn Elders, b. 1933, first black U.S. Surgeon General, confirmed 1993.
Ralph Ellison, b. 1914, novelist, essayist, *Invisible Man.*
Michael Espy, b. 1953, first black secretary of Agriculture.
James Farmer, b. 1920, a founder of the Congress of Racial Equality, 1942; asst. secretary, Dept. of HEW, 1969.
Henry O. Flipper, 1856-1940, first black to graduate, 1877, from West Point.
Charles Fuller, b. 1939, Pulitzer Prize-winning playwright; *A Soldier's Play.*
Mary Hatwood Futrell, b. 1940, president, Natl. Education Assn., 1983-.
Marcus Garvey, 1887-1940, founded Universal Negro Improvement Assn., 1911.
Kenneth Gibson, b. 1932, Newark, N.J., mayor, 1970-1986.
Charles Gordone, b. 1925, won 1970 Pulitzer Prize in Drama, with *No Place to Be Somebody.*
Vice Adm. Samuel L. Gravely Jr. b. 1922, first black admiral, 1971, served in World War II, Korea, and Vietnam; commander, Third Fleet.
William H. Gray 3d, b. 1941, U.S. representative from Pa., 1979—; chairman, Budget Committee, 1985-88; chairman, House Democratic Caucus, 1988-89; majority whip, 1989-.
Ewart Guinier, 1911-1990, trade unionist, first chairman of Harvard Univ.'s Department of Afro-American Studies.
Alex Haley, 1921-1992, Pulitzer Prize-winning author; *Roots, The Autobiography of Malcolm X.*
Jupiter Hammon, c. 1720-1800, poet; the first black American to have his works published, 1761.
Lorraine Hansberry, 1930-1965, playwright; won New York Drama Critics Circle Award, 1959, with *Raisin in the Sun.*
Barbara Harris, b. 1931, first woman Episcopal bishop.
Patricia Roberts Harris, 1924-1985, U. S. ambassador to Luxembourg, 1965-67; secretary, Dept. of HUD, 1977-1979, Dept. of HHS, 1979-1981.
William H. Hastie, 1904-1976 first black federal judge, appointed 1937; governor of Virgin Islands, 1946-49; judge, U.S. Circuit Court of Appeals, 1949.
Matthew A. Henson, 1866-1955, member of Peary's 1909 expedition to the North Pole; placed U.S. flag at the Pole.
Chester Himes, 1909-1984, novelist, *Cotton Comes to Harlem.*
Dr. William A. Hinton, 1883-1959, developed the Hinton and Davies-Hinton tests for detection of syphilis; first black professor, 1949, at Harvard Medical School.
Benjamin L. Hooks, b. 1925, first black member, 1972-1979, Federal Communications Comm.; exec. dir., NAACP, 1977—.
Nathan I. Huggins, 1927-1989, historian, scholar; Harvard professor from 1980, director of that university's Institute for Afro-American Research from 1981.
Langston Hughes, 1902-1967, poet; story, song lyric author, a major influence in the "Harlem Renaissance" of the 1920s; *The Weary Blues, Montage of a Dream Deferred.*
Charlayne Hunter-Gault, b. 1942, first black woman admitted to Univ. of Ga., 1961; ran *N.Y. Times* Harlem Bureau, 1968-1977; broadcast journalist, 1978—.
Nora Zeale Hurston, 1903-1960, novelist, folklorist; *Their Eyes Were Watching God; Mules and Men.*
Rev. Jesse Jackson, b. 1941, national director, Operation Bread Basket; campaigned for Democratic presidential nomination, 1984, 1988; pres., founder, Rainbow Coalition; "shadow senator" for District of Columbia, 1991-.
Maynard Jackson, b. 1938, mayor of Atlanta, 1973-1981; 1989-93.
Gen. Daniel James Jr. 1920-1978, first black 4-star general, 1975; Commander, North American Air Defense Command.
Mae C. Jemison, M.D., b. 1956, astronaut, first black woman launched into space, 1992.
Pvt. Henry Johnson, 1897-1929, the first American decorated by France in World War I with the Croix de Guerre.
James Weldon Johnson, 1871-1938, poet, lyricist, novelist; first black admitted to Florida bar; U.S. consul in Venezuela and Nicaragua.
John H. Johnson, b. 1918, publisher, editor of Ebony, Jet, Ebony Jr. magazines, from 1942.
Barbara Jordan, b. 1936, former congresswoman from Texas; member, House Judiciary Committee.
Vernon E. Jordan, b. 1935, executive director, National Urban League, 1972.
Ernest Everett Just, 1883-1941, marine biologist, studied egg development; author, *Biology of Cell Surfaces,* 1941.
Leontine T.C. Kelly, b. 1920, United Methodist bishop; first black woman bishop of a major American denomination, 1989.
The Rev. Dr. Martin Luther King Jr., 1929-1968, led 382-day Montgomery, Ala., boycott that brought 1956 U.S. Supreme Court decision holding segregation on buses unconstitutional; founder, president, Southern Christian Leadership Conference, 1957; won Nobel Peace Prize, 1964.
Lewis H. Latimer, 1848-1928, associate of Edison; supervised installation of first electric street lighting in N.Y.C.
Mickey Leland, 1944-1989, U.S. representative from Texas, 1978 until death; chairman of Congressional Black Caucus, House Select Committee on Hunger.
Malcolm X, 1925-1965, Black Muslim leader and black nationalist whose ideas and oratory contributed to the black pride and black power movements in the 1960s.
Thurgood Marshall, 1908-1993, first black U.S. solicitor general, 1965; first black justice of the U.S. Supreme Court, 1967-1991; as a lawyer led the legal battery that won the Supreme Court decision declaring racial segregation of public schools unconstitutional, 1954.

Jan Matzeliger, 1852-1889, invented lasting machine, patented 1883, which revolutionized the shoe industry.
Benjamin Mays, 1895-1984, educator, civil rights leader; headed Morehouse College, 1940-1967.
Wade H. McCree Jr., 1920-1987, solicitor general of the U.S., 1977-1981.
Donald E. McHenry, b. 1936, U.S. ambassador to the United Nations, 1979-1981.
Ronald McNair, 1950-1986, physicist, astronaut; killed in *Challenger* explosion.
Dorie Miller, 1919-1943, Navy hero of Pearl Harbor attack; awarded the Navy Cross.
Ernest N. Morial, b. 1929, elected first black mayor of New Orleans, 1977.
Toni Morrison, b. 1931, novelist; *Song of Solomon, Sula, Tar Baby;* won 1988 Pulitzer Prize for *Beloved.*
Willard Motley, 1912-1965, novelist; *Knock on Any Door.*
Elijah Muhammad, 1897-1975, founded Black Muslims, 1931.
Pedro Alonzo Nino, navigator of the Nina, one of Columbus' 3 ships on his first voyage of discovery to the New World, 1492.
Rosa Parks, b. 1913, Montgomery Ala. citizen arrested for refusing to move to the back of the bus, Dec. 1, 1955, bringing a 382-day bus boycott led by Martin Luther King Jr.
Frederick D. Patterson, 1901-1988, founder of United Negro College Fund, 1944; Tuskegee Institute's third pres., 1935-1953.
Harold R. Perry, 1916-1991, first black American made a Roman Catholic bishop in the 20th century, 1966; first black clergyman to deliver the opening prayer in Congress, 1964.
Adam Clayton Powell, 1908-1972, early civil rights leader, congressman, 1945-1969; chairman, House Committee on Education and Labor, 1960-1967.
Colin Powell, b. 1937, first black Natl. Security Advisor, 1987-88; first black chairman of Joint Chiefs of Staff, 1989-.
Joseph H. Rainey, 1832-1887, first black elected to House of Representatives, 1869, from South Carolina.
A. Philip Randolph, 1889-1979, organized the Brotherhood of Sleeping Car Porters, 1925; organizer of 1941 and 1963 March on Washington movements; vice president, AFL-CIO.
Charles Rangel, b. 1930, congressman from N.Y.C. from 1970; member, Ways and Means Committee; chairman, Select Committee on Narcotics Abuse & Control.
Hiram R. Revels, 1822-1901, first black U.S. senator, elected in Mississippi, served 1870-1871.
Lloyd Richards, b. 1922(?), first black to direct a Broadway play, 1959; dean, Yale Univ. School of Drama & artistic director of Yale Repertory Theatre, 1979-1991.
Wilson C. Riles, b. 1917, elected, 1970, California State Superintendent of Public Instruction.
Norbert Rillieux, 1806-1894; invented a vacuum pan evaporator, 1846, revolutionizing the sugar-refining industry.
Paul Robeson, 1898-1976, actor and concert singer, graduated 1st in class at Rutgers, 1918, Phi Beta Kappa; grad. Columbia Univ. law school, 1923; associated with communist causes.
Max Robinson, 1939-1988, TV journalist, first black to anchor network news, 1978.
Carl T. Rowan, b. 1925, prize-winning journalist; director of the U.S. Information Agency, 1964, the first black to sit on the National Security Council; U. S. ambassador to Finland, 1963.
John B. Russwurm, 1799-1851, with **Samuel E. Cornish,** 1793-1858, founded, 1827, the nation's first black newspaper, Freedom's Journal, in N.Y.C.
Bayard Rustin, 1910-1987, organizer of the 1963 March on Washington; executive director, A. Philip Randolph Institute.
Peter Salem, at the Battle of Bunker Hill, June 17, 1775, shot and killed British commander Maj. John Pitcairn.
Ntozake Shange, b. 1948, writer, *For Colored Girls Who Have Considered Suicide/When the Rainbow is Enuf.*
Bishop Stephen Spottswood, 1897-1974, board chairman of NAACP, 1961-1974.
The Rev. Leon H. Sullivan, b. 1922, economic development planner, first black on General Motors Bd. of Directors.
Willard Townsend, 1895-1957, organized the United Transport Service Employees, 1935 (redcaps, etc.); vice pres. AFL-CIO.
Sojourner Truth, 1797-1883, born Isabella Baumfree; preacher, abolitonist; raised funds for Union in Civil War; worked for black educational opportunities.
Harriet Tubman, 1823-1913, Underground Railroad conductor served as nurse and spy for Union Army in the Civil War.
Nat Turner, 1800-1831, led the most significant of over 200 slave revolts in U.S., in Southampton, Va.; hanged.
Alice Walker, b. 1944, novelist, essayist, *The Color Purple.*
Booker T. Washington, 1856-1915, founder, 1881, and first president of Tuskegee Institute; author, *Up From Slavery.*
Harold Washington, 1922-1987, first black mayor of Chicago, from 1983 until death.
Dr. Robert C. Weaver, b. 1907, first black member of the U.S. Cabinet, secretary, Dept. of HUD, 1966.
Ida B. Wells (Barnett), 1862-1931, journalist who waged antilynching crusade.
Clifton R. Wharton Jr., b. 1926, first black pres. of major U.S. univ.; chancellor, nation's largest univ. system, 8 yrs.; chairman & CEO, country's largest pension fund, 1987—.
Phillis Wheatley, c. 1753-1784, poet; 2d American woman and first black woman to have her works published, 1770.
Bill White, b. 1934, first black baseball league president; named Natl. League head, 1989.
Walter White, 1893-1955, exec. secretary, NAACP, 1931-1955.
L. Douglas Wilder, b. 1931, first black elected governor, became Virginia chief executive in 1989.
Roy Wilkins, 1901-1981, exec. director, NAACP, 1955-1977.
Dr. Daniel Hale Williams, 1858-1931, performed one of first 2 open-heart operations, 1893; founded Provident, Chicago's first Negro hospital; first black elected a fellow of the American College of Surgeons.
August Wilson, b. 1945, playwright, won 1987 Pulitzer Prize for *Fences,* 1990 Pulitzer for *The Piano Lesson.*
Granville T. Woods, 1856-1910, invented the third-rail system now used in subways, a complex railway telegraph device that helped reduce train accidents, and an automatic air brake.
Dr. Carter G. Woodson, 1875-1950, historian; founded Assn. for the Study of Negro Life and History, 1915, and Journal of Negro History, 1916.
Richard Wright, 1908-1960, novelist; *Native Son, Black Boy.*
Frank Yerby, 1916-1991, first best-selling American black novelist; *The Foxes of Harrow, Vixen.*
Andrew Young, b. 1932, civil rights leader, congressman from Georgia, U.S. ambassador to the United Nations, 1977-79; mayor of Atlanta, 1982-89.
Whitney M. Young Jr., 1921-1971, exec. director, 1961, National Urban League; author, lecturer, newspaper columnist.

About 5,000 blacks served in the Continental Army during the **American Revolution,** mostly in integrated units, some in all-black combat units. Some 200,000 blacks served in the Union Army during the **Civil War;** 38,000 gave their lives; 22 won the Medal of Honor, the nation's highest award. Of 367,000 blacks in the armed forces during **World War I,** 100,000 served in France. More than 1,000,000 blacks served in the armed forces during **World War II;** all-black fighter and bomber AAF units and infantry divisions gave distinguished service. In 1954 the policy of all-black units was finally abolished. Of 274,937 blacks who served in the armed forces during the **Vietnam War** (1965-1974), 5,681 were killed in combat. During the **Persian Gulf War** (1990-1991), 104,000 blacks served in the Kuwaiti theater—20 percent of U.S. soldiers, compared with 8.7% during World War II and 9.8% in Vietnam.

As of Jan. 1992, there were 338 black mayors, 2 black governors, 358 state representatives, and 26 U.S. representatives. There were then 7,552 blacks holding elected office in the U.S. and Virgin Islands, an increase of 1.0% over the previous year, according to a survey by the Joint Center for Political Studies, Washington, D.C. The number of black women elected to local, county, state, and congressional offices rose to 2,121, up by 68, or 3.3%, from the Jan. 1991 figure. From 1989 to Jan. 1992, male black elected officials increased by 19, while female black elected officials increased by 307. In Nov. 1992, Carol Moseley Braun of Illinois became the first black woman elected to the U.S. Senate.

Notable Living American Fiction Writers and Playwrights

Name (Birthplace)	Birthdate
Adams, Alice (Fredericksburg, Va.)	8/14/26
Albee, Edward (Washington, D.C.)	3/12/28
Auchincloss, Louis (Lawrence, N.Y.)	9/27/17
Barth, John (Cambridge, Md.)	5/27/30
Beattie, Ann (Washington, D.C.)	9/7/47
Bellow, Saul (Quebec, Canada)	7/10/15
Benchley, Peter (New York, N.Y.)	5/8/40
Berger, Thomas (Cincinnati, Oh.)	7/20/24
Blume, Judy (Elizabeth, N.J.)	2/12/38
Bradbury, Ray (Waukegan, Ill.)	8/22/20
Brooks, Gwendolyn (Topeka, Kan.)	6/7/17
Calisher, Hortense (New York, N.Y.)	12/20/11
Clancy, Tom (Baltimore, Md.)	1947
Clark, Mary Higgins (New York, N.Y.)	12/24/31

Name (Birthplace)	Birthdate
Clavell, James (England)	10/10/24
Cleary, Beverly (McMinnville, Ore.)	1916
Connell, Evan S. (Kansas City, Mo.)	8/17/24
Conroy, Pat (Atlanta, Ga.)	10/26/45
Crews, Harry (Alma, Ga.)	6/6/35
Crichton, Michael (Chicago, Ill.)	10/23/42
Dailey, Janet (Storm Lake, Ia.)	5/21/44
De Vries, Peter (Chicago, Ill.)	2/27/10
Didion, Joan (Sacramento, Cal.)	12/5/34
Doctorow, E. L. (New York, N.Y.)	1/6/31
Dunne, John Gregory (Hartford, Conn.)	5/25/32
Elkin, Stanley (New York, N.Y.)	5/11/30
Ellison, Ralph (Oklahoma City, Okla.)	3/1/14
Fast, Howard (New York, N.Y.)	11/11/14
Fox, Paula (New York, N.Y.)	4/22/23
French, Marilyn (New York, N.Y.)	11/21/29
Fuller, Charles (Philadelphia, Pa.)	3/5/39
Gaddis, William (New York, N.Y.)	1922
Gilroy, Frank (New York, N.Y.)	10/13/25
Godwin, Gail (Birmingham, Ala.)	6/18/37
Goldman, William (Chicago, Ill.)	8/12/31
Gordon, Mary (Long Island, N.Y.)	12/8/49
Grau, Shirley Ann (New Orleans, La.)	7/8/29
Grisham, John (Jonesboro, Ark.)	2/8/55
Guare, John (New York, N.Y.)	2/5/38
Hailey, Arthur (Luton, England)	4/5/20
Haley, Alex (Ithaca, N.Y.)	8/11/21
Hawkes, John (Stamford, Conn.)	8/17/25
Heller, Joseph (Brooklyn, N.Y.)	5/1/23
Helprin, Mark (New York, N.Y.)	6/28/47
Hersey, John (Tientsin, China)	6/17/14
Hinton, S.E. (Tulsa, Okla.)	1948
Irving, John (Exeter, N.H.)	3/2/42
Jong, Erica (New York, N.Y.)	3/26/42
Kennedy, William (Albany, N.Y.)	1/16/28
Kerr, Jean (Scranton, Pa.)	7/10/23
King, Stephen (Portland, Me.)	9/21/47
Kingston, Maxine Hong (Stockton, Cal.)	10/27/40
Knowles, John (Fairmont, W. Va.)	9/16/26
Krantz, Judith (New York, N.Y.)	1/9/28
LeGuin, Ursula (Berkeley, Cal.)	10/21/29
L'Engle, Madeleine (New York, N.Y.)	11/29/18
Leonard, Elmore (New Orleans, La.)	10/11/25
Levin, Ira (New York, N.Y.)	8/27/29
Ludlum, Robert (New York, N.Y.)	5/25/27
Lurie, Alison (Chicago, Ill.)	9/3/26
Mailer, Norman (Long Branch, N.J.)	1/31/23
Mamet, David (Chicago, Ill.)	11/30/47

Name (Birthplace)	Birthdate
McGuane, Thomas (Wyandotte, Mich.)	12/11/39
McMurtry, Larry (Wichita Falls, Tex.)	6/3/36
Michener, James A. (New York, N.Y.)	2/3/07
Miller, Arthur (New York, N.Y.)	10/17/15
Morris, Wright (Central City, Neb.)	1/6/10
Morrison, Toni (Lorain, Oh.)	2/18/31
Oates, Joyce Carol (Lockport, N.Y.)	6/16/38
Ozick, Cynthia (New York, N.Y.)	4/17/28
Paley, Grace (New York, N.Y.)	12/11/22
Piercy, Marge (Detroit, Mich.)	3/31/36
Potok, Chaim (New York, N.Y.)	2/17/29
Price, Reynolds (Macon, N.C.)	2/1/33
Puzo, Mario (New York, N.Y.)	10/15/20
Pynchon, Thomas (Glen Cove, N.Y.)	5/8/37
Rabe, David (Dubuque, Ia.)	3/10/40
Reed, Ishmael (Chattanooga, Tenn.)	2/22/38
Rice, Anne (New Orleans, La.)	10/14/41
Roth, Henry (Austria-Hungary)	2/8/06
Roth, Philip (Newark, N.J.)	3/19/33
Salinger, J. D. (New York, N.Y.)	1/1/19
Sanders, Lawrence (New York, N.Y.)	1920
Sendak, Maurice (New York, N.Y.)	6/10/28
Shepard, Sam (Ft. Sheridan, Ill.)	11/5/43
Simon, Neil (New York, N.Y.)	7/4/27
Spillane, Mickey (Brooklyn, N.Y.)	3/9/18
Stegner, Wallace (Lake Mills, Ia.)	2/18/09
Stern, Richard (New York, N.Y.)	2/25/28
Stone, Robert (Brooklyn, N.Y.)	8/21/37
Styron, William (Newport News, Va.)	6/11/25
Taylor, Peter (Trenton, Tenn.)	1/8/17
Theroux, Paul (Medford, Mass.)	4/10/41
Turow, Scott F. (Chicago, Ill.)	4/12/49
Tyler, Anne (Minneapolis, Minn.)	10/25/41
Updike, John (Shillington, Pa.)	3/18/32
Uris, Leon (Baltimore, Md.)	8/3/24
Vidal, Gore (West Point, N.Y.)	10/3/25
Vonnegut, Kurt Jr. (Indianapolis, Ind.)	11/11/22
Walker, Alice (Eatonton, Ga.)	2/9/44
Wambaugh, Joseph (East Pittsburgh, Pa.)	1/22/37
Wasserstein, Wendy (New York, N.Y.)	—
Welty, Eudora (Jackson, Miss.)	4/13/09
Wideman, John Edgar (Pittsburgh, Pa.)	6/14/41
Wilson, August (Pittsburgh, Pa.)	4/27/45
Wilson, Lanford (Lebanon, Mo.)	4/13/37
Wolfe, Tom (Richmond, Va.)	3/2/31
Wolff, Tobias (Birmingham, Ala.)	6/19/45
Wouk, Herman (New York, N.Y.)	5/27/15

American Architects and Some of Their Achievements

Max Abramovitz, b. 1908, Avery Fisher Hall, Lincoln Center, N.Y.C.

Henry Bacon, 1866-1924, Lincoln Memorial.

Pietro Belluschi, b. 1899, Juilliard School of Music, Lincoln Center, N.Y.C.

Marcel Breuer, 1902-1981, Whitney Museum of American Art, N.Y.C. (with Hamilton Smith).

Charles Bulfinch, 1763-1844, State House, Boston; Capitol, Wash. D.C., (part).

Gordon Bunshaft, 1909-1990, Lever House, Park Ave, N.Y.C.; Hirshhorn Museum, Wash., D.C.

Daniel H. Burnham, 1846-1912, Union Station, Wash. D.C.; Flatiron, N.Y.C.

Irwin Chanin, 1892-1988, New York City theaters, skyscrapers.

Ralph Adams Cram, 1863-1942, Cathedral of St. John the Divine, N.Y.C.; U.S. Military Academy (part).

R. Buckminster Fuller, 1895-1983, U.S. Pavilion, Expo 67, Montreal (geodesic domes).

Cass Gilbert, 1859-1934, Custom House, Woolworth Bldg., N.Y.C.; Supreme Court bldg., Wash., D.C.

Bertram G. Goodhue, 1869-1924, Capitol, Lincoln, Neb.; St. Thomas, St. Bartholomew, N.Y.C.

Walter Gropius, 1883-1969, Pan Am Building, N.Y.C. (with Pietro Belluschi).

Peter Harrison, 1716-1775, Touro Synagogue, Redwood Library, Newport, R.I.

Wallace K. Harrison, 1895-1981, Metropolitan Opera House, Lincoln Center, N.Y.C.

Thomas Hastings, 1860-1929, Public Library, Frick Mansion, N.Y.C.

James Hoban, 1762-1831, The White House.

Raymond Hood, 1881-1934, Rockefeller Center, N.Y.C. (part); Daily News, N.Y.C.; Tribune, Chicago.

Richard M. Hunt, 1827-1895, Metropolitan Museum, N.Y.C. (part); Natl. Observatory, Wash., D.C.

William Le Baron Jenney, 1832-1907, Home Insurance, Chicago (demolished 1931).

Philip C. Johnson, b. 1906, N.Y. State Theater, Lincoln Center, N.Y.C.

Albert Kahn, 1869-1942, Athletic Club Bldg., General Motors Bldg., Detroit.

Louis Kahn, 1901-1974, Salk Laboratory, La Jolla, Cal.; Yale Art Gallery.

Christopher Grant LaFarge, 1862-1938, Roman Catholic Chapel, West Point.

Benjamin H. Latrobe, 1764-1820, U.S. Capitol (part).

William Lescaze, 1896-1969, Philadelphia Savings Fund Society; Borg-Warner Bldg., Chicago.

Bernard R. Maybeck, 1862-1957, Hearst Hall, Chick House, Univ. of Cal., First Church of Christ Scientist, Berkeley.

Charles F. McKim, 1847-1909, Public Library, Boston, Columbia Univ., N.Y.C. (part).

Charles M. McKim, b. 1920, KUHT-TV Transmitter Building, Houston; Lutheran Church of the Redeemer, Houston.

Ludwig Mies van der Rohe, 1886-1969, Seagram Building, N.Y.C. (with Philip C. Johnson); National Gallery, Berlin.

Robert Mills, 1781-1855, Washington Monument.

Richard J. Neutra, 1892-1970, Mathematics Park, Princeton; Orange Co. Courthouse, Santa Ana, Cal.

Gyo Obata, b. 1923, Natl. Air & Space Mus., Smithsonian Institution; Dallas-Ft. Worth Airport.

Frederick L. Olmsted, 1822-1903, Central Park, N.Y.C.; Fairmount Park, Philadelphia.

I(eoh) M(ing) Pei, b. 1917, National Center for Atmospheric Research, Boulder, Col.; East Wing, Natl. Gallery of Art, Wash., D.C.; Pyramid, The Louvre, Paris.

William Pereira, 1909-1985, Cape Canaveral; Transamerica Bldg., San Francisco.
John Russell Pope, 1874-1937, National Gallery.
John Portman, b. 1924, Peachtree Center, Atlanta.
George Browne Post, 1837-1913, New York Stock Exchange, Wisconsin state capitol.
James Renwick Jr., 1818-1895, Grace Church, St. Patrick's Cathedral, N.Y.C.; Smithsonian, Corcoran Galleries, Wash., D.C.
Henry H. Richardson, 1838-1886, Trinity Church, Boston.
Kevin Roche, b. 1922, Oakland Cal. Museum; Fine Arts Center, U. of Mass.
James Gamble Rogers, 1867-1947, Columbia-Presbyterian Medical Center, N.Y.C.; Northwestern Univ., Chicago.
John Wellborn Root, 1887-1963, Palmolive Building, Chicago; Hotel Statler, Washington; Hotel Tamanaco, Caracas.
Paul Rudolph, b. 1918, Jewitt Art Center, Wellesley College; Art & Architecture Bldg., Yale.
Charles M. Russell, 1866-1926, Western life.
Eero Saarinen, 1910-1961, Gateway to the West Arch, St. Louis; Trans World Flight Center, N.Y.C.
Louis Skidmore, 1897-1962, AEC town site, Oak Ridge, Tenn.; Terrace Plaza Hotel, Cincinnati.
Clarence S. Stein, 1882-1975, Temple Emanu-El, N.Y.C.
Edward Durell Stone, 1902-1978, U.S. Embassy, New Delhi, India; (H. Hartford) Gallery of Modern Art, N.Y.C.
Louis H. Sullivan, 1856-1924, Auditorium, Chicago.
Richard Upjohn, 1802-1878, Trinity Church, N.Y.C.
Ralph T. Walker, 1889-1973, N.Y. Telephone Hdqrs., N.Y.C.; IBM Research Lab., Poughkeepsie, N.Y.
Roland A. Wank, 1898-1970, Cincinnati Union Terminal; head architect TVA, 1933-44.
Stanford White, 1853-1906, Washington Arch; first Madison Square Garden, N.Y.C.
Frank Lloyd Wright, 1867 (or 1869)-1959, Imperial Hotel, Tokyo; Guggenheim Museum, N.Y.C.; Unity Church, Oak Park, Ill; Robie House, Chicago; Taliesin, Wis.
William Wurster, 1895-1973, Ghirardelli Sq., San Francisco; Cowell College, U. Cal., Berkeley.
Minoru Yamasaki, 1912-1986, World Trade Center, N.Y.C.

Noted American Cartoonists

Charles Addams, 1912-1988, macabre cartoons.
Brad Anderson, b. 1924, Marmaduke.
Peter Arno, 1904-1968, *New Yorker* urban characterizations.
Tex Avery, 1908-1980, **Friz Freleng,** b. 1905?, **Chuck Jones,** b. 1912, animators of Bugs Bunny, Porky Pig, Daffy Duck.
George Baker, 1915-1975, The Sad Sack.
C. C. Beck, 1910-1989, Captain Marvel.
Jim Berry, b. 1932, Berry's World.
Herb Block (Herblock), b. 1909, leading political cartoonist.
George Booth, b. 1926, *New Yorker* cartoonist.
Berke Breathed, b. 1957, Bloom County.
Clare Briggs, 1875-1930, Mr. & Mrs.
Dik Browne, 1917-1989, Hi & Lois, Hagar the Horrible.
Marjorie Buell, 1904-1993, Little Lulu.
Ernie Bushmiller, 1905-1982, Nancy.
Milton Caniff, 1907-1988, Terry & the Pirates; Steve Canyon.
Al Capp, 1909-1979, Li'l Abner.
Roz Chast, b. 1954, *New Yorker* "bonfire of the banalities" cartoons.
Paul Conrad, 1924, political cartoonist.
Roy Crane, 1901-1977, Captain Easy; Buz Sawyer.
Robert Crumb, b. 1943, "Underground" cartoonist.
Jay N. Darling (Ding), 1876-1962, political cartoonist.
Jack Davis, b. 1926, *Mad* magazine.
Jim Davis, b. 1945, Garfield.
Billy DeBeck, 1890-1942, Barney Google.
Rudolph Dirks, 1877-1968, The Katzenjammer Kids.
Walt Disney, 1901-1966, producer of animated cartoons; created Mickey Mouse and Donald Duck.
Steve Ditko, b. 1927, Spider-Man.
Mort Drucker, b. 1929, *Mad* magazine.
Jules Feiffer, b. 1929, satirical *Village Voice* cartoonist.
Bud Fisher, 1884-1954, Mutt & Jeff.
Ham Fisher, 1900-1955, Joe Palooka.
James Montgomery Flagg, 1877-1960, illustrator; created the famous Uncle Sam recruiting poster during WWI.
Max Fleischer, 1883-1972, creator of Betty Boop, Popeye cartoons.
Hal Foster, 1892-1982, Tarzan; Prince Valiant.
Fontaine Fox, 1884-1964, Toonerville Folks.
Rube Goldberg, 1883-1970, Boob McNutt.
Chester Gould, 1900-1985, Dick Tracy.
Harold Gray, 1894-1968, Little Orphan Annie.
Matt Groening, b. 1954, Life is Hell, The Simpsons.
Cathy Guisewite, b. 1950, Cathy.
Bill Hanna, b. 1910, & **Joe Barbera,** b. 1911, animators of Tom & Jerry, Huckleberry Hound, Yogi Bear, Flintstones.
Johnny Hart, b. 1931, BC, Wizard of Id.
Jimmy Hatlo, 1898-1963, Little Iodine.
John Held Jr., 1889-1958, "Jazz Age" cartoonist.
George Herriman, 1881-1944, Krazy Kat.
Harry Hershfield, 1885-1974, Abie the Agent.
Al Hirschfeld, b. 1903, *N.Y. Times* theater caricaturist.
Burne Hogarth, b. 1911, Tarzan.
Helen Hokinson, 1900-1949, satirized clubwomen.
Nicole Hollander, b. 1939, Sylvia.
Lynn Johnston, b. 1947, For Better Or For Worse.
Bob Kane, b. 1916, Batman.
Bil Keane, b. 1922, The Family Circus.
Walt Kelly, 1913-1973, Pogo.
Hank Ketcham, b. 1920, Dennis the Menace.
Ted Key, b. 1912, Hazel.
Frank King, 1883-1969, Gasoline Alley.
Jack Kirby, b. 1917, Fantastic Four.
Rollin Kirby, 1875-1952, political cartoonist.
B(ernard) Kliban, 1935-1991, cat books.
Edward Koren, b. 1935, *New Yorker* woolly characters.
Harvey Kurtzman, 1921-1993, *Mad* magazine.
Walter Lantz, b. 1900, Woody Woodpecker.
Gary Larson, b. 1950, The Far Side.
Mell Lazarus, b. 1929, Momma, Miss Peach.
Stan Lee, b. 1922, Marvel Comics.
David Levine, b. 1926, *N.Y. Review of Books* caricatures.
Doug Marlette, b. 1949, editorial cartoonist; Kudzu.
Don Martin, b. 1931, *Mad* magazine.
Bill Mauldin, b. 1921, depicted squalid life of the G.I. in WWII.
Jeff MacNelly, b. 1947, political cartoonist, and strip Shoe.
Winsor McCay, 1872-1934, Little Nemo.
John T. McCutcheon, 1870-1949, midwestern rural life.
George McManus, 1884-1954, Bringing Up Father.
Dale Messick, b. 1906, Brenda Starr.
Norman Mingo, 1896-1980, Alfred E. Neuman.
Bob Montana, 1920-1975, Archie.
Dick Moores, 1909-1986, Gasoline Alley.
Willard Mullin, 1902-1978, sports cartoonist; created Dodgers "Bum" and Mets "Kid".
Russell Myers, b. 1938, Broom Hilda.
Thomas Nast, 1840-1902, political cartoonist; created the Democratic donkey and Republican elephant.
Pat Oliphant, b. 1935, political cartoonist.
Frederick Burr Opper, 1857-1937, Happy Hooligan.
Richard Outcault, 1863-1928, Yellow Kid; Buster Brown.
Mike Peters, b. 1943, editorial cartoons; Mother Goose & Grimm.
George Price, b. 1901, *New Yorker* lower-class life.
Alex Raymond, 1909-1956, Flash Gordon; Jungle Jim.
Art Sansom, 1920-1991, The Born Loser.
Charles Schulz, b. 1922, Peanuts.
Elzie C. Segar, 1894-1938, Popeye.
Jerry Siegel, b. 1914, & **Joe Shuster,** b. 1914, Superman.
Sydney Smith, 1887-1935, The Gumps.
Otto Soglow, 1900-1975, Little King; Canyon Kiddies.
Art Spiegelman, b. 1948, Raw; Maus.
William Steig, b. 1907, *New Yorker* cartoonist.
James Swinnerton, 1875-1974, Little Jimmy.
Paul Terry, 1887-1971, animator of Mighty Mouse.
Bob Thaves, b. 1924, Frank and Ernest.
James Thurber, 1894-1961, *New Yorker* cartoonist.
Garry Trudeau, b. 1948, Doonesbury.
Mort Walker, b. 1923, Beetle Bailey.
Bill Watterson, b. 1958, Calvin and Hobbes.
Russ Westover, 1887-1966, Tillie the Toiler.
Frank Willard, 1893-1958, Moon Mullins.
J. R. Williams, 1888-1957, The Willets Family; Out Our Way.
Gahan Wilson, b. 1930, cartoonist of the macabre.
Tom Wilson, b. 1931, Ziggy.
Art Young, 1866-1943, political radical and satirist.
Chic Young, 1901-1973, Blondie.

Noted Political Leaders of the Past

(U.S. presidents and vice presidents, Supreme Court justices, signers of Declaration of Independence, listed elsewhere.)

Abu Bakr, 573-634, Mohammedan leader, first caliph, chosen successor to Mohammed.
Dean Acheson, 1893-1971, (U.S.) secretary of state, chief architect of cold war foreign policy.

Samuel Adams, 1722-1803, (U.S.) patriot, Boston Tea Party firebrand.
Konrad Adenauer, 1876-1967, (G.) West German chancellor.
Emilio Aguinaldo, 1869-1964, (Philip.) revolutionary, fought against Spain and the U.S.
Akbar, 1542-1605, greatest Mogul emperor of India.
Salvador Allende Gossens, 1908-1973, (Chil.) president, advocate of democratic socialism.
Herbert H. Asquith, 1852-1928, (Br.) Liberal prime minister, instituted an advanced program of social reform.
Atahualpa, ?-1533, Inca (ruling chief) of Peru.
Kemal Atatürk, 1881-1938, (Turk.) founded modern Turkey.
Clement Attlee, 1883-1967, (Br.) Labour party leader, prime minister, enacted national health, nationalized many industries.
Stephen F. Austin, 1793-1836, (U.S.) led Texas colonization.
Mikhail Bakunin, 1814-1876, (R.) revolutionary, leading exponent of anarchism.
Arthur J. Balfour, 1848-1930, (Br.) as foreign secretary under Lloyd George issued Balfour Declaration expressing official British approval of Zionism.
Bernard M. Baruch, 1870-1965, (U.S.) financier, gvt. adviser.
Fulgencio Batista y Zaldivar, 1901-1973, (Cub.) ruler overthrown by Castro.
Lord Beaverbrook, 1879-1964, (Br.) financier, statesman, newspaper owner.
Menachem Begin, 1914-1992, (Isr.) Israeli prime minister, won 1978 Nobel Peace Prize.
Eduard Benes, 1884-1948, (Czech.) president during interwar and post-WW II eras.
David Ben-Gurion, 1886-1973, (Isr.) first premier of Israel.
Thomas Hart Benton, 1782-1858, (U.S.) Missouri senator, championed agrarian interests and westward expansion.
Lavrenti Beria, 1899-1953, (USSR) Communist leader prominent in political purges under Stalin.
Aneurin Bevan, 1897-1960, (Br.) Labour party leader.
Ernest Bevin, 1881-1951, (Br.) Labour party leader, foreign minister, helped lay foundation for NATO.
Otto von Bismarck, 1815-1898, (G.) statesman known as the Iron Chancellor, uniter of Germany, 1870.
James G. Blaine, 1830-1893, (U.S.) Republican politician, diplomat, influential in launching Pan-American movement.
Léon Blum, 1872-1950, (F.) socialist leader, writer, headed first Popular Front government.
Simón Bolívar, 1783-1830, (Venez.) South American revolutionary who liberated much of the continent from Spanish rule.
William E. Borah, 1865-1940, (U.S.) isolationist senator, instrumental in blocking U.S. membership in League of Nations and the World Court.
Cesare Borgia, 1476-1507, (It.) soldier, politician, an outstanding figure of the Italian Renaissance.
Leonid Brezhnev, 1906-1982, (USSR) leader of the Soviet Union, 1964-82.
Aristide Briand, 1862-1932, (F.) foreign minister, chief architect of Locarno Pact and anti-war Kellogg-Briand Pact.
William Jennings Bryan, 1860-1925, (U.S.) Democratic, populist leader, orator, 3 times lost race for presidency.
Nikolai Bukharin, 1888-1938, (USSR) communist leader.
William C. Bullitt, 1891-1967, (U.S.) diplomat, first ambassador to USSR, ambassador to France.
Ralph Bunche, 1904-1971, (U.S.) a founder and key diplomat of United Nations for more than 20 years.
John C. Calhoun, 1782-1850, (U.S.) political leader, champion of states' rights and a symbol of the Old South.
Robert Castlereagh, 1769-1822, (Br.) foreign secy, guided Grand Alliance against Napoleon.
Camillo Benso Cavour, 1810-1861, (It.) statesman, largely responsible for uniting Italy under the House of Savoy.
Nicolae Ceausescu, 1918-1989, Rumanian Communist leader, head of state from 1967-1989.
Austen Chamberlain, 1863-1937, (Br.) Conservative party leader, largely responsible for Locarno Pact of 1925.
Neville Chamberlain, 1869-1940, (Br.) Conservative prime minister whose appeasement of Hitler led to Munich Pact.
Salmon P. Chase, 1808-1873, (U.S.) public official, abolitionist, jurist, 6th Supreme Court chief justice.
Chiang Kai-shek, 1887-1975, (Chin.) Nationalist Chinese president whose govt. was driven from mainland to Taiwan.
Chou En-lai, 1898-1976, (Chin.) diplomat, prime minister, a leading figure of the Chinese Communist party.
Winston Churchill, 1874-1965, (Br.) prime minister, soldier, author, guided Britain through WW II.
Galeazzo Ciano, 1903-1944, (It.) fascist foreign minister, helped create Rome-Berlin Axis, executed by Mussolini.
Henry Clay, 1777-1852, (U.S.) "The Great Compromiser," one of most influential pre-Civil War political leaders.
Georges Clemenceau, 1841-1929, (F.) twice premier, Wilson's chief antagonist at Paris Peace Conference after WW I.
DeWitt Clinton, 1769-1828, (U.S.) political leader, responsible for promoting idea of the Erie Canal.
Robert Clive, 1725-1774, (Br.) first administrator of Bengal, laid foundation for British Empire in India.
Jean Baptiste Colbert, 1619-1683, (F.) statesman, influential under Louis XIV, created the French navy.
Oliver Cromwell, 1599-1658, (Br.) Lord Protector of England, led parliamentary forces during Civil War.
Curzon of Kedleston, 1859-1925, (Br.) viceroy of India, foreign secretary, major force in dealing with post-WW I problems in Europe and Far East.
Édouard Daladier, 1884-1970, (F.) radical socialist politician, arrested by Vichy, interned by Germans until liberation in 1945.
Georges Danton, 1759-1794, (F.) a leading figure in the French Revolution.
Jefferson Davis, 1808-1889, (U.S.) president of the Confederate States of America.
Charles G. Dawes, 1865-1951, (U.S.) statesman, banker, advanced Dawes Plan to stabilize post-WW I German finances.
Alcide De Gasperi, 1881-1954, (It.) premier, founder of the Christian Democratic party.
Charles DeGaulle, 1890-1970, (F.) general, statesman, and first president of the Fifth Republic.
Eamon De Valera, 1882-1975, (Ir.-U.S.) statesman, led fight for Irish independence.
Thomas E. Dewey, 1902-1971, (U.S.) New York governor, twice loser in try for presidency.
Ngo Dinh Diem, 1901-1963, (Viet.) South Vietnamese president, assassinated in government take-over.
Everett M. Dirksen, 1896-1969, (U.S.) Senate Republican minority leader, orator.
Benjamin Disraeli, 1804-1881, (Br.) prime minister, considered founder of modern Conservative party.
Engelbert Dollfuss, 1892-1934, (Aus.) chancellor, assassinated by Austrian Nazis.
Andrea Doria, 1466-1560, (It.) Genoese admiral, statesman, called "Father of Peace" and "Liberator of Genoa."
Stephen A. Douglas, 1813-1861, (U.S.) Democratic leader, orator, opposed Lincoln for the presidency.
Alexander Dubcek, 1921-1992, (Czech.) statesman whose attempted liberalization was crushed, 1968.
John Foster Dulles, 1888-1959, (U.S.) secretary of state under Eisenhower, cold war policy maker.
Friedrich Ebert, 1871-1925, (G.) Social Democratic movement leader, instrumental in bringing about Weimar constitution.
Sir Anthony Eden, 1897-1977, (Br.) foreign secretary, prime minister during Suez invasion of 1956.
Ludwig Erhard, 1897-1977, (G.) economist, West German chancellor, led nation's economic rise after WW II.
Hamilton Fish, 1808-1893, (U.S.) secretary of state, successfully mediated disputes with Great Britain, Latin America.
James V. Forrestal, 1892-1949, (U.S.) secretary of navy, first secretary of defense.
Francisco Franco, 1892-1975, (Sp.) leader of rebel forces during Spanish Civil War and dictator of Spain.
Benjamin Franklin, 1706-1790, (U.S.) printer, publisher, author, inventor, scientist, diplomat.
Louis de Frontenac, 1620-1698, (F.) governor of New France (Canada); encouraged explorations, fought Iroquois.
Hugh Gaitskell, 1906-1963, (Br.) Labour party leader, major force in reversing its stand for unilateral disarmament.
Albert Gallatin, 1761-1849, (U.S.) secretary of treasury who was instrumental in negotiating end of War of 1812.
Léon Gambetta, 1838-1882, (F.) statesman, politician, one of the founders of the Third Republic.
Indira Gandhi, 1917-1984, (Ind.) succeeded father, Jawaharlal Nehru, as prime minister, assassinated.
Mohandas K. Gandhi, 1869-1948, (Ind.) political leader, ascetic, led nationalist movement against British rule.
Giuseppe Garibaldi, 1807-1882, (It.) patriot, soldier, a leading figure in the Risorgimento, the Italian unification movement.
Genghis Khan, c. 1167-1227, Mongol conqueror, ruler of vast Asian empire.
William E. Gladstone, 1809-1898, (Br.) prime minister 4 times, dominant force of Liberal party from 1868 to 1894.
Paul Joseph Goebbels, 1897-1945, (G.) Nazi propagandist, master of mass psychology.
Klement Gottwald, 1896-1953, (Czech.) communist leader ushered communism into his country.
Che (Ernesto) Guevara, 1928-1967, (Arg.) guerilla leader, prominent in Cuban revolution, killed in Bolivia.
Haile Selassie, 1891-1975, (Eth.) emperor, maintained monarchy through invasion, occupation, internal resistance.
Alexander Hamilton, 1755-1804, (U.S.) first treasury secretary, champion of strong central government.
Dag Hammarskjold, 1905-1961, (Swed.) statesman, UN secretary general.
John Hancock, 1737-1793, (U.S.) revolutionary leader, first signer of Declaration of Independence.
John Hay, 1838-1905, (U.S.) secretary of state, primarily associated with Open Door Policy toward China.

Patrick Henry, 1736-1799, (U.S.) major revolutionary figure, remarkable orator.

Édouard Herriot, 1872-1957, (F.) Radical Socialist leader, twice premier, president of National Assembly.

Theodor Herzl, 1860-1904, (Aus.) founder of modern Zionism.

Heinrich Himmler, 1900-1945, (G.) chief of Nazi SS and Gestapo, primarily responsible for the Holocaust.

Paul von Hindenburg, 1847-1934, (G.) field marshal, president.

Hirohito, 1902-1989; emperor of Japan from 1926.

Adolf Hitler, 1889-1945, (G.) dictator, founder of National Socialism; wrote *Mein Kampf,* strategy for world domination.

Ho Chi Minh, 1890-1969, (Viet.) North Vietnamese president, Vietnamese Communist leader, national hero.

Harry L. Hopkins, 1890-1946, (U.S.) New Deal administrator, closest adviser to FDR during WW II.

Edward M. House, 1858-1938, (U.S.) diplomat, confidential adviser to Woodrow Wilson.

Samuel Houston, 1793-1863, (U.S.) leader of struggle to win control of Texas from Mexico.

Cordell Hull, 1871-1955, (U.S.) secretary of state, initiated reciprocal trade to lower tariffs, helped organize UN.

Hubert H. Humphrey, 1911-1978, (U.S.) Minnesota Democrat, senator, vice president, spent 32 years in public service.

Ibn Saud, c. 1888-1953, (S. Arab.) founder of Saudi Arabia and its first king.

Jacob Javits, 1904-1986 (U.S.) U.S. senator from New York for 24 years.

Jinnah, Muhammed Ali, 1876-1948, (Pak.) founder, first governor-general of Pakistan.

Benito Juarez, 1806-1872, (Mex.) rallied countrymen against foreign threats, sought to create democratic, federal republic.

Kamehameha I, c. 1758-1819, (Haw.) founder, first monarch of unified Hawaii.

Frank B. Kellogg, 1856-1937, (U.S.) secretary of state, negotiated Kellogg-Briand Pact to outlaw war.

Robert F. Kennedy, 1925-1968, (U.S.) attorney general, senator, assassinated while seeking presidential nomination.

Aleksandr Kerensky, 1881-1970, (R.) revolutionary, served as premier after Feb. 1917 revolution until Bolshevik overthrow.

Ruhollah Khomeini, 1900-1989, (Iran), religious leader with Islamic title "ayatollah," directed overthrow of shah, 1979, became source of political authority in succeeding governments.

Nikita Khrushchev, 1894-1971, (USSR) premier, first secretary of Communist party, initiated de-Stalinization.

Lajos Kossuth, 1802-1894, (Hung.) principal figure in 1848 Hungarian revolution.

Pyotr Kropotkin, 1842-1921, (R.) anarchist, championed the peasants but opposed Bolshevism.

Kublai Khan, c. 1215-1294, Mongol emperor, founder of Yüan dynasty in China.

Béla Kun, 1886-c.1939, (Hung.) communist, member of 3d International, tried to foment worldwide revolution.

Robert M. LaFollette, 1855-1925, (U.S.) Wisconsin public official, leader of progressive movement.

Pierre Laval, 1883-1945, (F.) politician, Vichy foreign minister, executed for treason.

Andrew Bonar Law, 1858-1923, (Br.) Conservative party politician, led opposition to Irish home rule.

Vladimir Ilyich Lenin (Ulyanov), 1870-1924, (USSR) revolutionary, founder of Bolshevism, Soviet leader 1917-1924.

Ferdinand de Lesseps, 1805-1894, (F.) diplomat, engineer, conceived idea of Suez Canal.

Rene Levesque, 1922-1987 (Can.) Premier of Quebec, 1976-85; led unsuccessful fight to separate from Canada.

Maxim Litvinov, 1876-1951, (USSR) revolutionary, commissar of foreign affairs, favored cooperation with Western powers.

Liu Shao-ch'i, c.1898-1974, (Chin.) communist leader, fell from grace during "cultural revolution."

David Lloyd George, 1863-1945, (Br.) Liberal party prime minister, laid foundations for modern welfare state.

Henry Cabot Lodge, 1850-1924, (U.S.) Republican senator, led opposition to participation in League of Nations.

Huey P. Long, 1893-1935, (U.S.) Louisiana political demagogue, governor, assassinated.

Rosa Luxemburg, 1871-1919, (G.) revolutionary, leader of the German Social Democratic party and Spartacus party.

J. Ramsay MacDonald, 1866-1937, (Br.) first Labour party prime minister of Great Britain.

Harold Macmillan, 1895-1987 (Br.) prime minister of Great Britain, 1957-63.

Joseph R. McCarthy, 1908-1957, (U.S.) senator notorious for his witch hunt for communists in the government.

Makarios III, 1913-1977, (Cypr.) Greek Orthodox archbishop, first president of Cyprus.

Malcolm X (Malcolm Little), 1925-1965, (U.S.) black separatist leader, assassinated.

Mao Tse-tung, 1893-1976, (Chin.) chief Chinese Marxist theorist, soldier, led Chinese revolution establishing his nation as an important communist state.

Jean Paul Marat, 1743-1793, (F.) revolutionary, politician, identified with radical Jacobins, assassinated.

José Martí, 1853-1895, (Cub.) patriot, poet, leader of Cuban struggle for independence.

Jan Masaryk, 1886-1948, (Czech.) foreign minister, died by mysterious suicide following communist coup.

Thomas G. Masaryk, 1850-1937, (Czech.) statesman, philosopher, first president of Czechoslovak Republic.

Jules Mazarin, 1602-1661, (F.) cardinal, statesman, prime minister under Louis XIII and queen regent Anne of Austria.

Giuseppe Mazzini, 1805-1872, (It.), reformer dedicated to the Risorgimento, 19th-century movement for the political and social renewal of Italy.

Tom Mboya, 1930-1969, (Kenyan) political leader, instrumental in securing independence for his country.

Cosimo I de' Medici, 1519-1574, (It.) Duke of Florence, grand duke of Tuscany.

Lorenzo de' Medici, the Magnificent, 1449-1492, (It.) merchant prince, a towering figure in Italian Renaissance.

Catherine de Medicis, 1519-1589, (F.) queen consort of Henry II, regent of France, influential in Catholic-Huguenot wars.

Golda Meir, 1898-1979, (Isr.) prime minister, 1969-74.

Klemens W.N.L. Metternich, 1773-1859, (Aus.) statesman, arbiter of post-Napoleonic Europe.

Anastas Mikoyan, 1895-1978, (USSR) prominent Soviet leader from 1917; president 1964-65.

Guy Mollet, 1905-1975, (F.) social politician, resistance leader.

Henry Morgenthau Jr., 1891-1967, (U.S.) secretary of treasury, raised funds to finance New Deal and U.S. WW II activities.

Gouverneur Morris, 1752-1816, (U.S.) statesman, diplomat, financial expert who helped plan decimal coinage system.

Wayne Morse, 1900-1974, (U.S.) senator, long-time critic of Vietnam War.

Muhammad Ali, 1769?-1849, (Egypt), pasha, founder of dynasty that encouraged emergence of modern Egyptian state.

Benito Mussolini, 1883-1945, (It.) dictator and leader of the Italian fascist state.

Imre Nagy, c. 1895-1958, (Hung.) communist premier, assassinated after Soviets crushed 1956 uprising.

Gamal Abdel Nasser, 1918-1970, (Egypt.) leader of Arab unification, second Egyptian president.

Jawaharlal Nehru, 1889-1964, (Ind.) prime minister, guided India through its early years of independence.

Kwame Nkrumah, 1909-1972, (Ghan.) dictatorial prime minister, deposed in 1966.

Frederick North, 1732-1792, (Br.) prime minister, his inept policies led to loss of American colonies.

Daniel O'Connell, 1775-1847, (Ir.) political leader, known as The Liberator.

Omar, c.581-644, Mohammedan leader, 2d caliph, led Islam to become an imperial power.

Ignace Paderewski, 1860-1941, (Pol.) statesman, pianist, composer, briefly prime minister, an ardent patriot.

Viscount Palmerston, 1784-1865, (Br.) Whig-Liberal prime minister, foreign minister, embodied British nationalism.

George Papandreou, 1888-1968, (Gk.) Republican politician, served three times as prime minister.

Franz von Papen, 1879-1969, (G.) politician, played major role in overthrow of Weimar Republic and rise of Hitler.

Charles Stewart Parnell, 1846-1891, (Ir.) nationalist leader, "uncrowned king of Ireland."

Lester Pearson, 1897-1972, (Can.) diplomat, Liberal party leader, prime minister.

Robert Peel, 1788-1850, (Br.) reformist prime minister, founder of Conservative party.

Juan Perón, 1895-1974, (Arg.) president, dictator.

Joseph Pilsudski, 1867-1935, (Pol.) statesman, instrumental in re-establishing Polish state in the 20th century.

Charles Pinckney, 1757-1824, (U.S.) founding father, his Pinckney plan was largely incorporated into constitution.

William Pitt, the Elder, 1708-1778, (Br.) statesman, called the "Great Commoner," transformed Britain into imperial power.

William Pitt, the Younger, 1759-1806, (Br.) prime minister during French Revolutionary wars.

Georgi Plekhanov, 1857-1918, (R.) revolutionary, social philosopher, called "father of Russian Marxism."

Raymond Poincaré, 1860-1934, (F.) 9th president of the Republic, advocated harsh punishment of Germany after WW I.

Georges Pompidou, 1911-1974, (F.) Gaullist political leader, president from 1969 to 1974.

Grigori Potemkin, 1739-1791, (R.) field marshal, favorite of Catherine II.

Edmund Randolph, 1753-1813, (U.S.) attorney, prominent in drafting, ratification of constitution.

John Randolph, 1773-1833, (U.S.) southern planter, strong advocate of states' rights.
Jeannette Rankin, 1880-1973, (U.S.) pacifist, first woman member of U.S. Congress.
Walter Rathenau, 1867-1922, (G.) industrialist, social theorist, statesman.
Sam Rayburn, 1882-1961, (U.S.) Democratic leader, representative for 47 years, House speaker for 17.
Paul Reynaud, 1878-1966, (F.) statesman, premier in 1940 at the time of France's defeat by Germany.
Syngman Rhee, 1875-1965, (Kor.) first president of the Republic of Korea.
Cecil Rhodes, 1853-1902, (Br.) imperialist, industrial magnate, established Rhodes scholarships in his will.
Cardinal de Richelieu, 1585-1642, (F.) statesman, known as "red eminence," chief minister to Louis XIII.
Maximilien Robespierre, 1758-1794, (F.) leading figure of French Revolution, responsible for much of Reign of Terror.
Nelson Rockefeller, 1908-1979, (U.S.) Republican gov. of N.Y., 1959-73; U.S. vice president, 1974-77.
Eleanor Roosevelt, 1884-1962, (U.S.) humanitarian, United Nations diplomat.
Elihu Root, 1845-1937, (U.S.) lawyer, statesman, diplomat, leading Republican supporter of the League of Nations.
John Russell, 1792-1878, (Br.) Liberal prime minister during the Irish potato famine.
Anwar el-Sadat, 1918-1981, (Egypt) president, 1970-1981, promoted peace with Israel; assassinated.
António de O. Salazar, 1899-1970, (Port.) statesman, longtime dictator.
José de San Martin, 1778-1850, South American revolutionary, protector of Peru.
Eisaku Sato, 1901-1975, (Jap.) prime minister, presided over Japan's post-WW II emergence as major world power.
Philipp Scheidemann, 1865-1939, (G.) Social Democratic leader, first chancellor of the German republic.
Robert Schuman, 1886-1963, (F.) statesman, founded European Coal and Steel Community.
Carl Schurz, 1829-1906, (U.S.) German-American political leader, journalist, orator, dedicated reformer.
Kurt Schuschnigg, 1897-1977, (Aus.) chancellor, unsuccessful in stopping his country's annexation by Germany.
William H. Seward, 1801-1872, (U.S.) anti-slavery activist, as Lincoln's secretary of state purchased Alaska.
Carlo Sforza, 1872-1952, (It.) foreign minister, anti-fascist.
Sitting Bull, c. 1831-1890, (Native Amer.) Sioux leader in Battle of Little Bighorn over George A. Custer, 1876; fostered Ghost Dance religion.
Alfred E. Smith, 1873-1944, (U.S.) New York Democratic governor, first Roman Catholic to run for presidency.
Jan C. Smuts, 1870-1950, (S.Af.) statesman, philosopher, soldier, prime minister.
Paul Henri Spaak, 1899-1972, (Belg.) statesman, socialist leader.
Joseph Stalin, 1879-1953, (USSR) Soviet dictator, 1924-53.
Edwin M. Stanton, 1814-1869, (U.S.) Lincoln's secretary of war during the Civil War.
Edward R. Stettinius Jr., 1900-1949, (U.S.) industrialist, secretary of state who coordinated aid to WW II allies.
Adlai E. Stevenson, 1900-1965, (U.S.) Democratic leader, diplomat, Illinois governor, presidential candidate.
Henry L. Stimson, 1867-1950, (U.S.) statesman, served in 5 administrations, influenced foreign policy in 1930s and 1940s.
Gustav Stresemann, 1878-1929, (G.) chancellor, foreign minister, dedicated to regaining friendship for post-WW I Germany.
Sukarno, 1901-1970, (Indon.) dictatorial first president of the Indonesian republic.
Sun Yat-sen, 1866-1925, (Chin.) revolutionary, leader of Kuomintang, regarded as the father of modern China.
Robert A. Taft, 1889-1953, (U.S.) conservative Senate leader, called "Mr. Republican."
Charles de Talleyrand, 1754-1838, (F.) statesman, diplomat, the major force of the Congress of Vienna of 1814-15.
U Thant, 1909-1974 (Bur.) statesman, UN secretary-general.
Norman M. Thomas, 1884-1968, (U.S.) social reformer, 6 times unsuccessful Socialist party presidential candidate.
Josip Broz Tito, 1892-1980, (Yug.) president of Yugoslavia from 1953, World War II guerrilla chief, postwar rival of Stalin, leader of 3d world movement.
Palmiro Togliatti, 1893-1964, (It.) major leader of Italian Communist party.
Hideki Tojo, 1885-1948, (Jap.) statesman, soldier, prime minister during most of WW II.
François Toussaint L'Ouverture, c. 1744-1803, (Hait.) patriot, martyr, thwarted French colonial aims.
Leon Trotsky, 1879-1940, (USSR) revolutionary, founded Red Army, expelled from party in conflict with Stalin.
Rafael L. Trujillo Molina, 1891-1961, (Dom.) absolute dictator, assassinated.
Moise K. Tshombe, 1919-1969, (Cong.) politician, president of secessionist Katanga, premier of Republic of Congo (Zaire).
William M. Tweed, 1823-1878, (U.S.) politician, absolute leader of Tammany Hall, NYC's Democratic political machine.
Walter Ulbricht, 1893-1973, (G.) communist leader of German Democratic Republic.
Arthur H. Vandenberg, 1884-1951, (U.S.) senator, proponent of anti-communist bipartisan foreign policy after WW II.
Eleutherios Venizelos, 1864-1936, (Gk.) most prominent Greek statesman in early 20th century; expanded territory.
Hendrik F. Verwoerd, 1901-1966, (S.Af.) prime minister, rigorously applied apartheid policy despite protest.
Robert Walpole, 1676-1745, (Br.) statesman, generally considered Britain's first prime minister.
Daniel Webster, 1782-1852, (U.S.) orator, politician, advocate of business interests during Jacksonian agrarianism.
Chaim Weizmann, 1874-1952, Zionist leader, scientist, first Israeli president.
Wendell L. Willkie, 1892-1944, (U.S.) Republican who tried to unseat FDR when he ran for his 3d term.
Emiliano Zapata, c. 1879-1919, (Mex.) revolutionary, major influence on modern Mexico.

Notable Military and Naval Leaders of the Past

Creighton Abrams, 1914-1974, (U.S.) commanded forces in Vietnam, 1968-72.
Harold Alexander, 1891-1969, (Br.) led Allied invasion of Italy, WW2, 1943.
Ethan Allen, 1738-1789, (U.S.) headed Green Mountain Boys; captured Ft. Ticonderoga, 1775, Amer. Revolutionary War.
Edmund Allenby, 1861-1936, (Br.) in Boer War, WW1; led Egyptian expeditionary force, 1917-18.
Benedict Arnold, 1741-1801, (U.S.) victorious at Saratoga; tried to betray West Point to British, Amer. Revolutionary War.
Henry "Hap" Arnold, 1886-1950, (U.S.) commanded Army Air Force in WW2.
John Barry, 1745-1803, (U.S.) won numerous sea battles during Amer. Revolutionary War.
Pierre Beauregard, 1818-1893, (U.S.) Confederate general ordered bombardment of Ft. Sumter that began the Civil War.
Gebhard v. Blücher, 1742-1819, (G.) helped defeat Napoleon at Waterloo.
Napoleon Bonaparte, 1769-1821, (F.) defeated Russia and Austria at Austerlitz, 1805; invaded Russia, 1812; defeated at Waterloo, 1815.
Edward Braddock, 1695-1755, (Br.) commanded forces in French and Indian War.
Omar N. Bradley, 1893-1981, (U.S.) headed U.S. ground troops in Normandy invasion, WW2, 1944.
John Burgoyne, 1722-1792, (Br.) defeated at Saratoga, Amer. Revolutionary War.
Claire Chennault, 1890-1958, (U.S.) headed Flying Tigers in WW2.
Mark Clark, 1896-1984, (U.S.) led forces in WW2 and Korean War.
Karl v. Clausewitz, 1780-1831, (G.) wrote books on military theory.
Lucius D. Clay, 1897-1978, (U.S.) led Berlin airlift, 1948-49.
Henry Clinton, 1738-1795, (Br.) commander of forces in American Revolutionary War, 1778-81.
Cochise, c. 1815-1874, (Native Amer.) Chief of Chiricahua band of Apache Indians in Arizona.
Charles Cornwallis, 1738-1805, (Br.) victorious at Brandywine, 1777; surrendered at Yorktown, Amer. Revolutionary War.
Crazy Horse, 1849-1877, (U.S.) Sioux war chief victorious at Little Big Horn.
George A. Custer, 1839-1876, (U.S.) defeated and killed at Little Big Horn.
Moshe Dayan, 1915-1981, (Isr.) directed campaigns in the 1967, 1973 Arab-Israeli wars.
Stephen Decatur, 1779-1820, (U.S.) naval hero of Barbary wars, War of 1812.
Anton Denikin, 1872-1947, (R.) led White forces in Russian civil war.
George Dewey, 1837-1917, (U.S.) destroyed Spanish fleet at Manila, 1898, Spanish-American War.
Hugh C. Dowding, 1883-1970, (Br.) headed RAF, WW2, 1936-40.
Jubal Early, 1816-1894, (U.S.) Confederate general led raid on Washington, Civil War, 1864.
Dwight D. Eisenhower, 1890-1969, (U.S.) commanded Allied forces in Europe, WW2.
David Farragut, 1801-1870, (U.S.) Union admiral captured New Orleans, Mobile Bay, Civil War.
Ferdinand Foch, 1851-1929, (F.) headed victorious Allied armies, WW1, 1918.

Nathan Bedford Forrest, 1821-1877, (U.S.) Confederate general led cavalry raids against Union supply lines, Civil War.
Frederick the Great, 1712-1786, (G.) led Prussia in The Seven Years War.
Horatio Gates, 1728-1806, (U.S.) commanded army at Saratoga, Amer. Revolutionary War.
Geronimo, 1829-1909 (Native Amer.) leader of Chiricahua band of Apache Indians.
Charles G. Gordon, 1833-1885, (Br.) led forces in China, Crimean War; killed at Khartoum.
Ulysses S. Grant, 1822-1885, (U.S.) headed Union army, Civil War, 1864-65; forced Lee's surrender, 1865.
Nathanael Greene, 1742-1786, (U.S.) defeated British in Southern campaign, 1780-81.
Heinz Guderian, 1888-1953, (G.) tank theorist, led panzer forces in Poland, France, Russia, WW2.
Douglas Haig, 1861-1928, (Br.) led British armies in France, WW1, 1915-18.
William F. Halsey, 1882-1959, (U.S.) defeated Japanese fleet at Leyte Gulf, WW2, 1944.
Sir Arthur Travers Harris, 1895-1984, (Br.) led Britain's WW2 bomber command.
Richard Howe, 1726-1799, (Br.) commanded navy in Amer. Revolutionary War, 1776-78; June 1 victory against French, 1794.
William Howe, 1729-1814, (Br.) commanded forces in American Revolutionary War, 1776-78.
Isaac Hull, 1773-1843, (U.S.) sunk British frigate *Guerriere*, War of 1812.
Thomas (Stonewall) Jackson, 1824-1863, (U.S.) Confederate general led Shenandoah Valley campaign, Civil War.
Joseph Joffre, 1852-1931, (F.) headed Allied armies, won Battle of the Marne, WW1, 1914.
John Paul Jones, 1747-1792, (U.S.) commanded *Bonhomme Richard* in victory over Serapis, Amer. Revolutionary War, 1779.
Stephen Kearny, 1794-1848, (U.S.) headed Army of the West in Mexican War.
Ernest J. King, 1878-1956, (U.S.) chief naval strategist in WW2.
Horatio H. Kitchener, 1850-1916, (Br.) led forces in Boer War; victorious at Khartoum; organized army in WW1.
Lavrenti Kornilov, 1870-1918, (R.) Commander-in-Chief, 1917; led counter-revolutionary march on Petrograd.
Thaddeus Kosciusko, 1746-1817, (P.) aided American cause in Amer. Revolutionary War.
Mikhail Kutuzov, 1745-1813, (R.) fought French at Borodino, Napoleonic Wars, 1812; abandoned Moscow; forced French retreat.
Marquis de Lafayette, 1757-1834, (F.) aided American cause in Amer. Revolutionary War.
T(homas) E. Lawrence (of Arabia), 1888-1935, (Br.) organized revolt of Arabs against Turks in WW1.
Henry (Light-Horse Harry) Lee, 1756-1818, (U.S.) cavalry officer in Amer. Revolutionary War.
Robert E. Lee, 1807-1870, (U.S.) Confederate general defeated at Gettysburg, Civil War; surrendered to Grant, 1865.
Lyman Lemnitzer, 1899-1988, (U.S.) WWII hero, later general, chairman of Joint Chiefs of Staff.
James Longstreet, 1821-1904, (U.S.) aided Lee at Gettysburg, Civil War.
Douglas MacArthur, 1880-1964, (U.S.) commanded forces in SW Pacific in WW2; headed occupation forces in Japan, 1945-51; UN commander in Korean War.
Francis Marion, 1733-1795, (U.S.) led guerrilla actions in S.C. during Amer. Revolutionary War.
Duke of Marlborough, 1650-1722, (Br.) led forces against Louis XIV in War of the Spanish Succession.
George C. Marshall, 1880-1959, (U.S.) chief of staff in WW2; authored Marshall Plan.
George B. McClellan, 1826-1885, (U.S.) Union general, commanded Army of the Potomac, Civil War, 1861-62.
George Meade, 1815-1872; (U.S.) commanded Union forces at Gettysburg, Civil War.
Billy Mitchell, 1879-1936, (U.S.) WW1 air-power advocate; court-martialed for insubordination, later vindicated.
Helmuth v. Moltke, 1800-1891; (G.) victorious in Austro-Prussian, Franco-Prussian wars.
Louis de Montcalm, 1712-1759, (F.) headed troops in Canada, French and Indian War; defeated at Quebec, 1759.
Bernard Law Montgomery, 1887-1976, (Br.) stopped German offensive at Alamein, WW2, 1942; helped plan Normandy invasion.
Daniel Morgan, 1736-1802, (U.S.) victorious at Cowpens, 1781, Amer. Revolutionary War.
Louis Mountbatten, 1900-1979, (Br.) Supreme Allied Commander of SE Asia, WW2, 1943-46.
Joachim Murat, 1767-1815, (F.) leader of cavalry at Marengo, 1800; Austerlitz, 1805; and Jena, 1806, Napoleonic Wars.
Horatio Nelson, 1758-1805, (Br.) naval commander destroyed French fleet at Trafalgar.
Michel Ney, 1769-1815, (F.) commanded forces in Switzerland, Austria, Russia, Napoleonic Wars; defeated at Waterloo.
Chester Nimitz, 1885-1966, (U.S.) commander of naval forces in Pacific in WW2.
George S. Patton, 1885-1945, (U.S.) led assault on Sicily, 1943, 3d Army invasion of German-occupied Europe, WW2.
Oliver Perry, 1785-1819, (U.S.) won Battle of Lake Erie in War of 1812.
John Pershing, 1860-1948, (U.S.) commanded Mexican border campaign, 1916; American expeditionary forces in WW1.
Henri Philippe Pétain, 1856-1951, (F.) defended Verdun, 1916; headed Vichy government in WW2.
George E. Pickett, 1825-1875, (U.S.) Confederate general famed for "charge" at Gettysburg, Civil War.
Hyman Rickover, 1900-1986 (U.S.) father of the nuclear navy.
Erwin Rommel, 1891-1944, (G.) headed Afrika Korps, WW2.
Karl v. Rundstedt, 1875-1953, (G.) supreme commander in West, WW2, 1943-45.
Aleksandr Samsonov, 1859-1914, (R.) led invasion of E. Prussia, WW1, defeated at Tannenberg, 1914.
Winfield Scott, 1786-1866, (U.S.) hero of War of 1812; headed forces in Mexican war, took Mexico City.
Philip Sheridan, 1831-1888, (U.S.) Union cavalry officer, headed Army of the Shenandoah, Civil War, 1864-65.
William T. Sherman, 1820-1891, (U.S.) Union general, sacked Atlanta during "march to the sea," Civil War, 1864.
Carl Spaatz, 1891-1974, (U.S.) directed strategic bombing against Germany, later Japan, in WW2.
Raymond Spruance, 1886-1969, (U.S.) victorious at Midway Island, WW2, 1942.
Joseph W. Stilwell, 1883-1946, (U.S.) headed forces in the China, Burma, India theater in WW2.
J.E.B. Stuart, 1833-1864, (U.S.) Confederate cavalry commander, Civil War.
George H. Thomas, 1816-1870, (U.S.) saved Union army at Chattanooga, 1863; victorious at Nashville, 1864, Civil War.
Semyon Timoshenko, 1895-1970, (USSR) defended Moscow, Stalingrad, WW2; led winter offensive, 1942-43.
Alfred v. Tirpitz, 1849-1930, (G.) responsible for submarine blockade in WW1.
Jonathan M. Wainwright, 1883-1953, (U.S.) forced to surrender on Corregidor, WW2, 1942.
George Washington, 1732-1799, (U.S.) led Continental army, Amer. Revolutionary War, 1775-83.
Archibald Wavell, 1883-1950, (Br.) commanded forces in N. and E. Africa, and SE Asia in WW2.
Anthony Wayne, 1745-1796, (U.S.) captured Stony Point, 1779, Amer. Revolutionary War; defeated Indians at Fallen Timbers, 1794.
Duke of Wellington, 1769-1852, (Br.) defeated Napoleon at Waterloo.
James Wolfe, 1727-1759, (Br.) captured Quebec from French, French and Indian War, 1759.
Georgi Zhukov, 1895-1974, (USSR) defended Moscow, 1941, led assault on Berlin, WW2.

Poets Laureate of England

There is no authentic record of the origin of the office of Poet Laureate of England. According to Warton, there was a Versificator Regis, or King's Poet, in the reign of Henry III (1216-1272), and he was paid 100 shillings a year. Geoffrey Chaucer (1340-1400) assumed the title of Poet Laureate, and in 1389 got a royal grant of a yearly allowance of wine. In the reign of Edward IV (1461-1483), John Kay held the post. Under Henry VII (1485-1509), Andrew Bernard was the Poet Laureate, and was succeeded under Henry VIII (1509-1547) by John Skelton. Next came Edmund Spenser, who died in 1599; then Samuel Daniel, appointed 1599, and then Ben Jonson, 1619. Sir William D'Avenant was appointed in 1637. He was a godson of William Shakespeare.

Others were John Dryden, 1670; Thomas Shadwell, 1688; Nahum Tate, 1692; Nicholas Rowe, 1715; the Rev. Laurence Eusden, 1718; Colley Cibber, 1730; William Whitehead, 1757, on the refusal of Gray; Rev. Thomas Warton, 1785, on the refusal of Mason; Henry J. Pye, 1790; Robert Southey, 1813, on the refusal of Sir Walter Scott; William Wordsworth, 1843; Alfred, Lord Tennyson, 1850; Alfred Austin, 1896; Robert Bridges, 1913; John Masefield, 1930; Cecil Day Lewis, 1967; Sir John Betjeman, 1972; Ted Hughes, 1984.

U.S. Poet Laureate

Robert Penn Warren, the poet, novelist, and essayist, was named the country's first official Poet Laureate on Feb. 26, 1986. The only writer to have won the Pulitzer Prize for fiction and poetry (twice), Warren was chosen by Daniel J. Boorstin, the Librarian of Congress. The appointment began in September, 1986. Other appointments, all beginning in September, are: 1987, Richard Wilbur; 1988, Howard Nemerov; 1990, Mark Strand; 1991, Joseph Brodsky; 1992, Mona Van Duyn, the first female poet laureate; 1993, Rita Dove, the first black poet laureate.

Noted Writers of the Past

George Ade, 1866-1944, (U.S.) humorist. *Fables in Slang.*

Conrad Aiken, 1889-1973, (U.S.) poet, critic. *Ushant.*

Louisa May Alcott, 1832-1888, (U.S.) novelist. *Little Women.*

Sholom Aleichem, 1859-1916. (R.) Yiddish writer. *Tevye's Daughter, Adventures of Mottel, The Old Country.*

Vicente Aleixandre, 1898-1984, (Sp.) poet. *La destrucción o el amor, Dialogolos del conocimiento.*

Horatio Alger, 1832-1899, (U.S.) "rags-to-riches" books.

Hans Christian Andersen, 1805-1875, (Den.) author of fairy tales. *The Princess and the Pea, The Ugly Duckling.*

Maxwell Anderson, 1888-1959, (U.S.) playwright. *What Price Glory?, High Tor, Winterset, Key Largo.*

Sherwood Anderson, 1876-1941, (U.S.) short-story writer, "Death in the Woods"; *Winesburg, Ohio* (collection).

Matthew Arnold, 1822-1888, (Br.) poet, critic. "Thrysis," "Dover Beach," "The Gypsy Scholar"; "Culture and Anarchy."

Jane Austen, 1775-1817, (Br.) novelist. *Pride and Prejudice, Sense and Sensibility, Emma, Mansfield Park, Persuasion.*

Isaac Babel, 1894-1941, (R.) short-story writer, playwright. *Odessa Tales, Red Cavalry.*

Honoré de Balzac, 1799-1850, (Fr.) novelist. *Le Père Goriot, Cousine Bette, Eugénie Grandet, The Human Comedy.*

James M. Barrie, 1860-1937, (Br.) playwright, novelist. *Peter Pan, Dear Brutus, What Every Woman Knows.*

Charles Baudelaire, 1821-1867, (Fr.) symbolist poet. *Les Fleurs du Mal.*

L. Frank Baum, 1856-1919, (U.S.) writer. Wizard of Oz series of children's books.

Simone de Beauvoir, 1908-1986, (Fr.) novelist, essayist. *The Second Sex, Memoirs of a Dutiful Daughter.*

Samuel Beckett, 1906-1989, (Ir.) novelist, playwright, in French and English. *Waiting for Godot, Endgame* (plays); *Murphy, Watt, Molloy* (novels).

Brendan Behan, 1923-1964, (Ir.) playwright. *The Quare Fellow, The Hostage, Borstal Boy.*

Robert Benchley, 1889-1945, (U.S.) humorist. *From Bed to Worse, My Ten Years in a Quandary.*

Stephen Vincent Benét, 1898-1943, (U.S.) poet, novelist. *John Brown's Body.*

John Berryman, 1914-1972, (U.S.) poet. *Homage to Mistress Bradstreet.*

Ambrose Bierce, 1842-1914, (U.S.) short-story writer, journalist. *In the Midst of Life, The Devil's Dictionary.*

William Blake, 1757-1827, (Br.) poet, artist. *Songs of Innocence, Songs of Experience, The Marriage of Heaven and Hell.*

Giovanni Boccaccio, 1313-1375, (It.) poet, storyteller. *Decameron, Filostrato.*

Jorge Luis Borges, 1900-1986 (Arg.) short-story writer, poet, essayist, *Labyrinths.*

James Boswell, 1740-1795, (Sc.) biographer. *The Life of Samuel Johnson, A Journal of a Tour of the Hebrides.*

Anne Bradstreet, c. 1612-1672, (U.S.) poet. *The Tenth Muse Lately Sprung Up in America.*

Bertolt Brecht, 1898-1956, (G.) dramatist, poet. *The Threepenny Opera, Mother Courage and Her Children.*

Charlotte Brontë, 1816-1855, (Br.) novelist. *Jane Eyre.*

Emily Brontë, 1818-1848, (Br.) novelist. *Wuthering Heights.*

Elizabeth Barrett Browning, 1806-1861, (Br.) poet. *Sonnets from the Portuguese, Aurora Leigh.*

Robert Browning, 1812-1889, (Br.) poet. "My Last Duchess," "Fra Lippo Lippi," *The Ring and The Book.*

Pearl Buck, 1892-1973, (U.S.) novelist. *The Good Earth.*

Mikhail Bulgakov, 1891-1940, (R.) novelist, playwright. *The Heart of a Dog, The Master and Margarita.*

John Bunyan, 1628-1688, (Br.) writer. *Pilgrim's Progress.*

Robert Burns, 1759-1796, (Sc.) poet. "Flow Gently, Sweet Afton," "My Heart's in the Highlands," "Auld Lang Syne."

Edgar Rice Burroughs, 1875-1950, (U.S.) novelist. *Tarzan of the Apes.*

George Gordon Lord Byron, 1788-1824, (Br.) poet. *Don Juan, Childe Harold, Manfred, Cain.*

Italo Calvino, 1923-1985 (It.) novelist, short story writer. *If on a Winter's Night a Traveler . . .*

Albert Camus, 1913-1960, (F.) novelist. *The Plague, The Stranger, Caligula, The Fall.*

Karel Capek, 1890-1938, (Czech.) playwright, novelist, essayist. *R.U.R. (Rossum's Universal Robots).*

Lewis Carroll, 1832-1898, (Br.) writer, mathematician. *Alice's Adventures in Wonderland, Through the Looking Glass.*

Giacomo Casanova, 1725-1798, (It.) adventurer, memoirist.

Willa Cather, 1876-1947, (U.S.) novelist, essayist. *O Pioneers!, My Ántonia, Death Comes for the Archbishop.*

Miguel de Cervantes Saavedra, 1547-1616, (Sp.) novelist, dramatist, poet. *Don Quixote de la Mancha.*

Raymond Chandler, 1888-1959, (U.S.) writer of detective fiction. Philip Marlowe series.

Geoffrey Chaucer, c. 1340-1400, (Br.) poet. *The Canterbury Tales, Troilus and Criseyde.*

John Cheever, 1912-1982, (U.S.) short story writer, novelist. *The Wapshot Scandal,* "The Country Husband."

Anton Chekhov, 1860-1904, (R.) short-story writer, dramatist. *Uncle Vanya, The Cherry Orchard, The Three Sisters.*

G.K. Chesterton, 1874-1936, (Br.) critic, novelist. Father Brown series of mysteries.

Kate Chopin, 1851-1904, (U.S.) novelist, short-story writer. *The Awakening.*

Agatha Christie, 1891-1976, (Br.) mystery writer. *And Then There Were None, Murder on the Orient Express.*

Jean Cocteau, 1889-1963, (F.) writer, visual artist, filmmaker. *The Beauty and the Beast, Enfants Terribles.*

Samuel Taylor Coleridge, 1772-1834, (Br.) poet, critic. "Kubla Khan," "The Rime of the Ancient Mariner," "Christabel."

(Sidonie) Colette, 1873-1954, (F.) novelist. *Claudine, Gigi.*

Joseph Conrad, 1857-1924, (Br.) novelist. *Lord Jim, Heart of Darkness, The Nigger of the Narcissus, Nostromo.*

James Fenimore Cooper, 1789-1851, (U.S.) novelist. *Leather-Stocking Tales.*

Pierre Corneille, 1606-1684, (F.) dramatist. *Medeé, Le Cid, Horace, Cinna, Polyeucte.*

Hart Crane, 1899-1932, (U.S.) poet. "The Bridge."

Stephen Crane, 1871-1900, (U.S.) novelist, short-story writer. *The Red Badge of Courage,* "The Open Boat."

e.e. cummings, 1894-1962, (U.S.) poet. *Tulips and Chimneys.*

Roald Dahl, (Br.) 1916-1990, (U.S.) writer. *Charlie and the Chocolate Factory.*

Gabriele D'Annunzio, 1863-1938, (It.) poet, novelist, dramatist. *The Child of Pleasure, The Intruder, The Victim.*

Dante Alighieri, 1265-1321, (It.) poet. *The Divine Comedy.*

Daniel Defoe, 1660-1731, (Br.) writer. *Robinson Crusoe, Moll Flanders, Journal of the Plague Year.*

Charles Dickens, 1812-1870, (Br.) novelist. *David Copperfield, Oliver Twist, Great Expectations, The Pickwick Papers.*

Emily Dickinson, 1830-1886, (U.S.) poet.

Isak Dinesen (Karen Blixen), 1885-1962, (Dan.) author. *Out of Africa, Seven Gothic Tales, Winter's Tales.*

John Donne, 1573-1631, (Br.) poet. *Songs and Sonnets.*

John Dos Passos, 1896-1970, (U.S.) novelist. *U.S.A.*

Fyodor Dostoyevsky, 1821-1881, (R.) novelist. *Crime and Punishment, The Brothers Karamazov, The Possessed.*

Arthur Conan Doyle, 1859-1930, (Br.) novelist, created Sherlock Holmes mystery series.

Theodore Dreiser, 1871-1945, (U.S.) novelist. *An American Tragedy, Sister Carrie.*

John Dryden, 1631-1700, (Br.) poet, dramatist, critic. *All for Love, Mac Flecknoe, Absalom and Achitopel.*

Alexandre Dumas, 1802-1870, (F.) novelist, dramatist. *The Three Musketeers, The Count of Monte Cristo.*

Alexandre Dumas (fils), 1824-1895, (F.) dramatist, novelist. *La Dame aux camélias, Le Demi-Monde.*

Ilya G. Ehrenburg, 1891-1967, (R.) writer. *The Thaw.*

George Eliot (Mary Ann Evans or Marian Evans), 1819-1880, (Br.) novelist. *Adam Bede, Silas Marner, Middlemarch, The Mill on the Floss, Daniel Deronda.*

T.S. Eliot, 1888-1965, (Br.) poet, critic. *The Waste Land,* "The Love Song of J. Alfred Prufrock," *Four Quartets.*

Ralph Waldo Emerson, 1803-1882, (U.S.) poet, essayist. "Brahma," "Nature," "The Over-Soul," "Self-Reliance."

James T. Farrell, 1904-1979, (U.S.) novelist. *Studs Lonigan.*

William Faulkner, 1897-1962, (U.S.) novelist. *Sanctuary, Light in August, The Sound and the Fury, Absalom, Absalom!*

Henry Fielding, 1707-1754, (Br.) novelist. *Tom Jones.*

F. Scott Fitzgerald, 1896-1940, (U.S.) short-story writer, novelist. *The Great Gatsby, Tender is the Night.*

Gustave Flaubert, 1821-1880, (F.) novelist. *Madame Bovary.*

C.S. Forester, 1899-1966, (Br.) novelist. Horatio Hornblower series.

E.M. Forster, 1879-1970, (Br.) novelist. *A Passage to India.*

Anatole France, 1844-1924, (F.) writer. *Penguin Island, My Friend's Book, Le Crime de Sylvestre Bonnard.*

Robert Frost, 1874-1963, (U.S.) poet. "Birches," "Fire and Ice," "Stopping by Woods on a Snowy Evening."

John Galsworthy, 1867-1933, (Br.) novelist, dramatist. *The Forsyte Saga, A Modern Comedy.*

Erle Stanley Gardner, 1889-1970, (U.S.) novelist. Perry Mason series of mysteries.

Jean Genet, 1911-1986, (Fr.) playwright, novelist. *The Blacks, The Maids, The Balcony.*

André Gide, 1869-1951, (F.) writer. *The Immoralist, The Pastoral Symphony, Strait is the Gate.*

Jean Giraudoux, 1882-1944, (F.) novelist, dramatist. *Electra, The Madwoman of Chaillot, Ondine, Tiger at the Gate.*

Johann W. von Goethe, 1749-1832, (G.) poet, dramatist, novelist. *Faust, The Sorrows of Young Werther.*

Nikolai Gogol, 1809-1852, (R.) short-story writer, dramatist, novelist. *Dead Souls, The Inspector General.*

Oliver Goldsmith, 1730?-1774, (Br.-Ir.) writer. *The Vicar of Wakefield, She Stoops to Conquer.*

Maxim Gorky, 1868-1936, (R.) writer. *The Lower Depths.*

Robert Graves, 1895-1985, (Br.) poet, classical scholar, novelist. *I, Claudius; The White Goddess.*

Thomas Gray, 1716-1771, (Br.) poet. "Elegy Written in a Country Churchyard," "The Progress of Poesy."

Graham Greene, 1904-1991, (Br.) novelist. *The Power and the Glory, The Heart of the Matter, The Ministry of Fear.*

Zane Grey, 1875-1939, (U.S.) writer of western stories.

Jakob Grimm, 1785-1863, (G.) philologist, folklorist. *German Methodology, Grimm's Fairy Tales.*

Wilhelm Grimm, 1786-1859, (G.) philologist, folklorist. *Grimm's Fairy Tales.*

Dashiell Hammett, 1894-1961, (U.S.) writer of detective fiction, created Sam Spade.

Knute Hamsun, 1859-1952 (Nor.) novelist. *Hunger.*

Thomas Hardy, 1840-1928, (Br.) novelist, poet. *The Return of the Native, Tess of the D'Urbervilles, Jude the Obscure.*

Joel Chandler Harris, 1848-1908, (U.S.) short-story writer. Uncle Remus series.

Moss Hart, 1904-1961, (U.S.) playwright. *Once in a Lifetime, You Can't Take It With You, The Man Who Came to Dinner.*

Bret Harte, 1836-1902, (U.S.) short-story writer, poet. *The Luck of Roaring Camp.*

Jaroslav Hasek, 1883-1923, (Czech.) writer. *The Good Soldier Schweik.*

Nathaniel Hawthorne, 1804-1864, (U.S.) novelist, short story writer. *The Scarlet Letter,* "The Artist of the Beautiful."

Heinrich Heine, 1797-1856, (G.) poet. *Book of Songs.*

Lillian Hellman, 1905-1984, (U.S.) playwright, author of memoirs, "The Little Foxes," *An Unfinished Woman, Pentimento.*

Ernest Hemingway, 1899-1961, (U.S.) novelist, short-story writer. *A Farewell to Arms, For Whom the Bell Tolls.*

O. Henry (W.S. Porter), 1862-1910, (U.S.) short-story writer. "The Gift of the Magi."

Hermann Hesse, 1877-1962, (G.) novelist, poet. *Death and the Lover, Steppenwolf, Siddhartha.*

Oliver Wendell Holmes, 1809-1894, (U.S.) poet, novelist. *The Autocrat of the Breakfast-Table.*

Alfred E. Housman, 1859-1936, (Br.) poet. *A Shropshire Lad.*

William Dean Howells, 1837-1920, (U.S.) novelist, critic. *The Rise of Silas Lapham.*

Langston Hughes, 1902-1967, (U.S.) poet, playwright. *The Weary Blues, One-Way Ticket, Shakespeare in Harlem.*

Victor Hugo, 1802-1885, (F.) poet, dramatist, novelist. *Notre Dame de Paris, Les Misérables.*

Nora Zeale Hurston, 1903-1960, novelist, folklorist. *Their Eyes Were Watching God, Mules and Men.*

Aldous Huxley 1894-1963, (Br.) writer. *Brave New World.*

Henrik Ibsen, 1828-1906, (Nor.) dramatist, poet. *A Doll's House, Ghosts, The Wild Duck, Hedda Gabler.*

Washington Irving, 1783-1859, (U.S.) writer. "Rip Van Winkle," "The Legend of Sleepy Hollow."

Shirley Jackson, 1919-1965, (U.S.) writer. "The Lottery."

Henry James, 1843-1916, (U.S.) novelist, short-story writer, critic. *The Portrait of a Lady, The American, Daisy Miller.*

Robinson Jeffers, 1887-1962, (U.S.) poet, dramatist. *Tamar and Other Poems, Medea.*

Samuel Johnson, 1709-1784, (Br.) author, scholar, critic. *Dictionary of the English Language.*

Ben Jonson, 1572-1637, (Br.) dramatist, poet. *Volpone.*

James Joyce, 1882-1941, (Ir.) writer. *Ulysses, Dubliners, A Portrait of the Artist as a Young Man, Finnegans Wake.*

Franz Kafka, 1883-1924, (G.) novelist, short-story writer. *The Trial, Amerika, The Castle, The Metamorphosis.*

George S. Kaufman, 1889-1961, (U.S.) playwright. *The Man Who Came to Dinner, You Can't Take It With You, Stage Door.*

Nikos Kazantzakis, 1883?-1957, (Gk.) novelist. *Zorba the Greek, A Greek Passion.*

John Keats, 1795-1821, (Br.) poet. "Ode on a Grecian Urn," "Ode to a Nightingale," "La Belle Dame Sans Merci."

Joyce Kilmer, 1886-1918, (U.S.) poet, "Trees."

Rudyard Kipling, 1865-1936, (Br.) author, poet. "The White Man's Burden," "Gunga Din," *The Jungle Book.*

Jean de la Fontaine, 1621-1695, (F.) poet. *Fables choisies.*

Pär Lagerkvist, 1891-1974, (Swed.) poet, dramatist, novelist. *Barabbas, The Sybil.*

Selma Lagerlöf, 1858-1940, (Swed.) novelist. *Jerusalem, The Ring of the Lowenskolds.*

Alphonse de Lamartine, 1790-1869, (F.) poet, novelist, statesman. *Méditations poétiques.*

Charles Lamb, 1775-1834, (Br.) essayist. *Specimens of English Dramatic Poets, Essays of Elia.*

Giuseppe di Lampedusa, 1896-1957, (It.) novelist. *The Leopard.*

Ring Lardner, 1885-1933, (U.S.) short story writer, humorist. *You Know Me, Al.*

D. H. Lawrence, 1885-1930, (Br.) novelist. *Sons and Lovers, Women in Love, Lady Chatterley's Lover.*

Mikhail Lermontov, 1814-1841, (R.) novelist, poet. "Demon," *Hero of Our Time.*

Alain-René Lesage, 1668-1747, (F.) novelist. *Gil Blas de Santillane.*

Gotthold Lessing, 1729-1781, (G.) dramatist, philosopher, critic. *Miss Sara Sampson, Minna von Barnhelm.*

Sinclair Lewis, 1885-1951, (U.S.) novelist. *Babbitt, Arrowsmith, Dodsworth, Main Street.*

Vachel Lindsay, 1879-1931, (U.S.) poet. *General William Booth Enters into Heaven, The Congo.*

Hugh Lofting, 1886-1947, (Br.) writer. Dr. Doolittle series of children's books.

Jack London, 1876-1916, (U.S.) novelist, journalist. *Call of the Wild, The Sea-Wolf.*

Henry Wadsworth Longfellow, 1807-1882, (U.S.) poet. *Evangeline, The Song of Hiawatha.*

Amy Lowell, 1874-1925, (U.S.) poet, critic. "Lilacs."

James Russell Lowell, 1819-1891, (U.S.) poet, editor. *Poems, The Biglow Papers.*

Robert Lowell, 1917-1977, (U.S.) poet. "Lord Weary's Castle," "For the Union Dead."

Niccolò Machiavelli, 1469-1527, (It.) writer, statesman. *The Prince, Discourses on Livy.*

Bernard Malamud, 1914-1986, (U.S.) short story writer, novelist. "The Magic Barrel," *The Assistant, The Fixer.*

Stéphane Mallarmé, 1842-1898, (F.) poet. *The Afternoon of a Faun.*

Thomas Malory, ?-1471, (Br.) writer. *Morte d'Arthur.*

Andre Malraux, 1901-1976, (F.) novelist. *Man's Fate.*

Osip Mandelstam, 1891-1938, (R.) poet. *Stone, Tristia.*

Thomas Mann, 1875-1955, (G.) novelist, essayist. *Buddenbrooks, Death in Venice, The Magic Mountain.*

Katherine Mansfield, 1888-1923, (Br.) short story writer. "Bliss," "The Garden Party."

Christopher Marlowe, 1564-1593, (Br.) dramatist, poet. *Tamburlaine the Great, Dr. Faustus, The Jew of Malta.*

John Masefield, 1878-1967, (Br.) poet. "Sea Fever," "Cargoes," *Salt Water Ballads.*

Edgar Lee Masters, 1869-1950, (U.S.) poet, biographer. *Spoon River Anthology.*

W. Somerset Maugham, 1874-1965, (Br.) author. *Of Human Bondage, The Razor's Edge, The Moon and Sixpence.*

Guy de Maupassant, 1850-1893, (F.) novelist, short-story writer. "A Life," "Bel-Ami," "The Necklace."

François Mauriac, 1885-1970, (F.) novelist, dramatist. *Viper's Tangle, The Kiss to the Leper.*

Vladimir Mayakovsky, 1893-1930, (R.) poet, dramatist. *The Cloud in Trousers.*

Mary McCarthy, 1912-1989, (U.S.) critic, novelist. *Memories of a Catholic Girlhood.*

Carson McCullers, 1917-1967, (U.S.) novelist. *The Heart is a Lonely Hunter, Member of the Wedding.*

Herman Melville, 1819-1891, (U.S.) novelist, poet. *Moby Dick, Typee, Billy Budd, Omoo.*

H.L. Mencken, 1880-1956, (U.S.) author, critic, editor. *Prejudices, The American Language.*

George Meredith, 1828-1909, (Br.) novelist, poet. *The Ordeal of Richard Feverel, The Egoist.*

Prosper Mérimée, 1803-1870, (F.) author. *Carmen.*

Edna St. Vincent Millay, 1892-1950, (U.S.) poet. *The Harp Weaver and Other Poems, A Few Figs from Thistles.*

A.A. Milne, 1882-1956, (Br.) author. *Winnie-the-Pooh.*

John Milton, 1608-1674, (Br.) poet. *Paradise Lost.*

Mishima Yukio (Hiraoka Kimitake), 1925-1970, (Jap.) writer. *Confessions of a Mask.*

Gabriela Mistral, 1889-1957, (Chil.) poet. *Sonnets of Death, Desolación, Tala, Lagar.*

Margaret Mitchell, 1900-1949, (U.S.) novelist. *Gone With the Wind.*

Jean Baptiste Molière, 1622-1673, (F.) dramatist. *Le Tartuffe, Le Misanthrope, Le Bourgeois Gentilhomme.*

Ferenc Molnár, 1878-1952, (Hung.) dramatist, novelist. *Liliom, The Guardsman, The Swan.*

Michel de Montaigne, 1533-1592, (F.) essayist. *Essais.*

Eugenio Montale, 1896-1981, (It.) poet.

Clement C. Moore, 1779-1863, (U.S.) poet, educator. "A Visit from Saint Nicholas."

Marianne Moore, 1887-1972, (U.S.) poet. *O to Be a Dragon.*

Thomas More, 1478-1535, (Br.) writer. *Utopia.*

H.H. Munro (Saki), 1870-1916, (Br.) writer. *Reginald, The Chronicles of Clovis, Beasts and Super-Beasts.*

Murasaki (Shikibu), Lady, c. 978-1031?, (Jap.) novelist. *The Tale of Genji.*

Alfred de Musset, 1810-1857, (F.) poet, dramatist. *Confession d'un enfant du siècle.*

Vladimir Nabokov, 1899-1977, (Rus.-U.S.) novelist. *Lolita.*

Ogden Nash, 1902-1971, (U.S.) poet. *Hard Lines, I'm a Stranger Here Myself, The Private Dining Room.*

Pablo Neruda, 1904-1973, (Chil.) poet. *Twenty Love Poems and One Song of Despair, Toward the Splendid City.*

Sean O'Casey, 1884-1964, (Ir.) dramatist. *Juno and the Paycock, The Plough and the Stars.*

Flannery O'Connor, 1925-1964, (U.S.) novelist, short story writer. *Wise Blood,* "A Good Man Is Hard to Find."

Clifford Odets, 1906-1963, (U.S.) playwright. *Waiting for Lefty, Awake and Sing, Golden Boy, The Country Girl.*

John O'Hara, 1905-1970, (U.S.) novelist, short-story writer. *From the Terrace, Appointment in Samarra, Pal Joey.*

Omar Khayyam, c. 1028-1122, (Per.) poet. *Rubaiyat.*

Eugene O'Neill, 1888-1953, (U.S.) playwright. *Emperor Jones, Anna Christie, Long Day's Journey into Night.*

George Orwell, 1903-1950, (Br.) novelist, essayist. *Animal Farm, Nineteen Eighty-Four.*

Thomas (Tom) Paine, 1737-1809, (U.S.) writer, political theorist. *Common Sense.*

Dorothy Parker, 1893-1967, (U.S.) poet, short-story writer. *Enough Rope, Laments for the Living.*

Boris Pasternak, 1890-1960, (R.) poet, novelist. *Doctor Zhivago, My Sister, Life.*

Samuel Pepys, 1633-1703, (Br.) public official, diarist.

S. J. Perelman, 1904-1979, (U.S.) humorist. *The Road to Miltown, Under the Spreading Atrophy.*

Francesco Petrarca, 1304-1374, (It.) poet. *Africa, Trionfi, Canzoniere, On Solitude.*

Luigi Pirandello, 1867-1936, (It.) novelist, dramatist. *Six Characters in Search of an Author.*

Edgar Allan Poe, 1809-1849, (U.S.) poet, short-story writer, critic. "Annabel Lee," "The Raven," "The Purloined Letter."

Alexander Pope, 1688-1744, (Br.) poet. *The Rape of the Lock, An Essay on Man.*

Katherine Anne Porter, 1890-1980, (U.S.) novelist, short story writer. *Ship of Fools.*

Ezra Pound, 1885-1972, (U.S.) poet. *Cantos.*

Marcel Proust, 1871-1922, (F.) novelist. *A la recherche du temps perdu (Remembrance of Things Past).*

Aleksandr Pushkin, 1799-1837, (R.) poet, prose writer. *Boris Godunov, Eugene Onegin, The Bronze Horseman.*

François Rabelais, 1495-1553, (F.) writer. *Gargantua, Pantagruel.*

Jean Racine, 1639-1699, (F.) dramatist. *Andromaque, Phèdre, Bérénice, Britannicus.*

Ayn Rand, 1905-1982 (Rus.-U.S.) novelist, philosopher. *The Fountainhead, Atlas Shrugged.*

Erich Maria Remarque, 1898-1970, (Ger.-U.S.) novelist. *All Quiet on the Western Front.*

Samuel Richardson, 1689-1761, (Br.) novelist. *Clarissa Harlowe, Pamela; or, Virtue Rewarded.*

Rainer Maria Rilke, 1875-1926, (G.) poet. *Life and Songs, Duino Elegies, Poems from the Book of Hours.*

Arthur Rimbaud, 1854-1891, (F.) poet. *A Season in Hell.*

Edwin Arlington Robinson, 1869-1935, (U.S.) poet. "Richard Cory," "Miniver Cheevy."

Theodore Roethke, 1908-1963, (U.S.) poet. *Open House, The Waking, The Far Field.*

Romain Rolland, 1866-1944, (F.) novelist, biographer. *Jean-Christophe.*

Pierre de Ronsard, 1524-1585, (F.) poet. *Sonnets pour Hélène, La Franciade.*

Edmond Rostand, 1868-1918, (F.) poet, dramatist. *Cyrano de Bergerac.*

Damon Runyon, 1880-1946, (U.S.) short-story writer, journalist. *Guys and Dolls, Blue Plate Special.*

John Ruskin, 1819-1900, (Br.) critic, social theorist. *Modern Painters, The Seven Lamps of Architecture.*

Antoine de Saint-Exupery, 1900-1944, (F.) writer. *Wind, Sand and Stars, Le Petit Prince.*

George Sand (Amandine Aurore Dupine), 1804-1876, (F.) novelist. *Consuelo, The Haunted Pool, The Master Bell-Ringer.*

Carl Sandburg, 1878-1967, (U.S.) poet. *The People, Yes; Chicago Poems, Smoke and Steel, Harvest Poems.*

George Santayana, 1863-1952, (U.S.) poet, essayist, philosopher. *The Sense of Beauty, The Realms of Being.*

William Saroyan, 1908-1981, (U.S.) playwright, novelist. *The Time of Your Life, The Human Comedy.*

Jean-Paul Sartre, 1905-1980, (Fr.) philosopher, novelist, playwright, *Nausea, No Exit, Being and Nothingness.*

Friedrich von Schiller, 1759-1805, (G.) dramatist, poet, historian. *Don Carlos, Maria Stuart, Wilhelm Tell.*

Sir Walter Scott, 1771-1832, (Sc.) novelist, poet. *Ivanhoe.*

Jaroslav Seifert, 1902-1986, (Cz.) poet.

Dr. Seuss (Theodor Seuss Geisel), 1904-1991, (U.S.) children's book author & illustrator. *The Cat in the Hat.*

William Shakespeare, 1564-1616, (Br.) dramatist, poet. *Romeo and Juliet, Hamlet, King Lear, Julius Caesar, The Merchant of Venice, Othello, Macbeth, The Tempest;* sonnets.

George Bernard Shaw, 1856-1950, (Ir.-Br.) playwright, critic. *St. Joan, Pygmalion, Major Barbara, Man and Superman.*

Mary Wollstonecraft Shelley, 1797-1851, (Br.) novelist. *Frankenstein.*

Percy Bysshe Shelley, 1792-1822, (Br.) poet. *Prometheus Unbound, Adonais,* "Ode to the West Wind," "To a Skylark."

Richard B. Sheridan, 1751-1816, (Br.) dramatist. *The Rivals, School for Scandal.*

Mikhail Sholokhov, 1906-1984 (U.S.S.R.) writer. *And Quiet Flows the Don.*

Upton Sinclair, 1878-1968, (U.S.) novelist. *The Jungle.*

Isaac Bashevis Singer, 1904-1991, (Pol.-U.S.) novelist, short-story writer, in Yiddish. *The Magician of Lubin.*

Edmund Spenser, 1552-1599, (Br.) poet. *The Faerie Queen.*

Christina Stead, 1903-1983 (Austral.) novelist, short-story writer. *The Man Who Loved Children.*

Richard Steele, 1672-1729, (Br.) essayist, playwright, began the Tatler and Spectator. *The Conscious Lovers.*

Lincoln Steffens, 1866-1936, (U.S.) editor, writer. *The Shame of the Cities.*

Gertrude Stein, 1874-1946, (U.S.) writer. *Three Lives.*

John Steinbeck, 1902-1968, (U.S.) novelist. *Grapes of Wrath, Of Mice and Men, Winter of Our Discontent.*

Stendhal (Marie Henri Beyle), 1783-1842, (F.) novelist. *The Red and the Black, The Charterhouse of Parma.*

Laurence Sterne, 1713-1768, (Br.) novelist. *Tristram Shandy.*

Wallace Stevens, 1879-1955, (U.S.) poet. *Harmonium, The Man With the Blue Guitar, Notes toward a Supreme Fiction.*

Robert Louis Stevenson, 1850-1894, (Br.) novelist, poet, essayist. *Treasure Island, A Child's Garden of Verses.*

Rex Stout, 1886-1975, (U.S.) novelist, created Nero Wolfe.

Harriet Beecher Stowe, 1811-1896, (U.S.) novelist. *Uncle Tom's Cabin.*

Lytton Strachey, 1880-1932, (Br.) biographer, critic. *Eminent Victorians, Queen Victoria, Elizabeth and Essex.*

August Strindberg, 1849-1912, (Swed.) dramatist, novelist. *The Father, Miss Julie, The Creditors.*

Jonathan Swift, 1667-1745, (Br.) writer. *Gulliver's Travels.*

Algernon C. Swinburne, 1837-1909, (Br.) poet, critic. Atalanta.

John M. Synge, 1871-1909, (Ir.) poet, dramatist. *Riders to the Sea, The Playboy of the Western World.*

Rabindranath Tagore, 1861-1941, (Ind.), author, poet. *Sadhana, The Realization of Life, Gitanjali.*

Booth Tarkington, 1869-1946, (U.S.) novelist. *Seventeen, Alice Adams, Penrod.*

Sara Teasdale, 1884-1933, (U.S.) poet. *Helen of Troy and Other Poems, Rivers to the Sea, Flame and Shadow.*

Alfred Lord Tennyson, 1809-1892, (Br.) poet. *Idylls of the King, In Memoriam,* "The Charge of the Light Brigade."

William Makepeace Thackeray, 1811-1863, (Br.) novelist. *Vanity Fair, Henry Esmond, Pendennis.*

Dylan Thomas, 1914-1953, (Welsh) poet. *Under Milk Wood, A Child's Christmas in Wales.*

Henry David Thoreau, 1817-1862, (U.S.) transcendentalist thinker, writer. *Walden.*

James Thurber, 1894-1961, (U.S.) humorist, cartoonist. "The Secret Life of Walter Mitty," *My Life and Hard Times.*

J.R.R. Tolkien, 1892-1973, (Br.) writer. *Lord of the Rings.*

Leo Tolstoy, 1828-1910, (R.) novelist, short-story writer. *War and Peace, Anna Karenina,* "The Death of Ivan Ilyich."

Anthony Trollope, 1815-1882, (Br.) novelist. *The Warden, Barchester Towers,* The Palliser novels.

Ivan Turgenev, 1818-1883, (R.) novelist, short-story writer. *Fathers and Sons, First Love, A Month in the Country.*

Mark Twain (Samuel Clemens), 1835-1910, (U.S.) novelist, humorist. *The Adventures of Huckleberry Finn, Tom Sawyer.*

Sigrid Undset, 1881-1949, (Nor.) novelist, poet. *Kristin Lavransdatter.*

Paul Valéry, 1871-1945, (F.) poet, critic. *La Jeune Parque, The Graveyard by the Sea.*

Jules Verne, 1828-1905, (F.) novelist. *Twenty Thousand Leagues Under the Sea.*

François Villon, 1431-1463?, (F.) poet. *Le petit et le Grand Testament.*

Evelyn Waugh, 1903-1966, (Br.) novelist. *The Loved One.*

H.G. Wells, 1866-1946, (Br.) novelist. *The Time Machine, The Invisible Man, The War of the Worlds.*

Rebecca West, 1893-1983 (Br.) critic. *Black Lamb and Grey Falcon.*

Edith Wharton, 1862-1937, (U.S.) novelist. *The Age of Innocence, The House of Mirth, Ethan Frome.*

E.B. White, 1899-1985 (U.S.), essayist, novelist. *Here is New York, Charlotte's Web, Stuart Little.*

T.H. White, 1906-1964, (Br.) author. *The Once and Future King, A Book of Beasts.*

Walt Whitman, 1819-1892, (U.S.) poet. *Leaves of Grass.*

John Greenleaf Whittier, 1807-1892, (U.S.) poet, journalist. *Snow-bound.*

Oscar Wilde, 1854-1900, (Ir.) playwright, story-writer. *The Picture of Dorian Gray, The Importance of Being Earnest.*

Laura Ingalls Wilder, 1867-1957, (U.S.) novelist. *Little House on the Prairie* series of children's books.

Thornton Wilder, 1897-1975, (U.S.) playwright. *Our Town, The Skin of Our Teeth, The Matchmaker.*

Tennessee Williams, 1912-1983 (U.S.) playwright. *A Streetcar Named Desire, Cat on a Hot Tin Roof, The Glass Menagerie.*

William Carlos Williams, 1883-1963, (U.S.) poet. *Tempers, Al Que Quiere!, Paterson.*

Edmund Wilson, 1895-1972, (U.S.) critic, novelist. *Axel's Castle, To the Finland Station.*

P.G. Wodehouse, 1881-1975, (U.S.) humorist. The "Jeeves" novels, *Anything Goes.*

Thomas Wolfe, 1900-1938, (U.S.) novelist. *Look Homeward, Angel, You Can't Go Home Again, Of Time and the River.*

Virginia Woolf, 1882-1941, (Br.) novelist, essayist. *Mrs. Dalloway, To the Lighthouse, The Waves, A Room of One's Own.*

William Wordsworth, 1770-1850, (Br.) poet. "Tintern Abbey," "Ode: Intimations of Immortality," *The Prelude.*

William Butler Yeats, 1865-1939, (Ir.) poet, playwright. *The Wild Swans at Coole, The Tower, Last Poems.*

Émile Zola, 1840-1902, (F.) novelist. *Nana, The Dram Shop.*

Noted Artists and Sculptors of the Past

Artists are painters unless otherwise indicated.

Washington Allston, 1779-1843, (U.S.) landscapist. Belshazzar's Feast.

Albrecht Altdorfer, 1480-1538, (Ger.) landscapist. Battle of Alexander.

Andrea del Sarto, 1486-1530, frescoes. Madonna of the Harpies.

Fra Angelico, c. 1400-1455, (It.) Renaissance muralist. Madonna of the Linen Drapers' Guild.

Alexsandr Archipenko, 1887-1964, (U.S.) sculptor. Boxing Match, Medranos.

John James Audubon, 1785-1851, (U.S.) Birds of America.

Hans Baldung Grien, 1484-1545, (Ger.) Todentanz.

Ernst Barlach, 1870-1938, (Ger.) Expressionist sculptor. Man Drawing a Sword.

Frederic-Auguste Bartholdi, 1834-1904, (Fr.) Liberty Enlightening the World, Lion of Belfort.

Fra Bartolommeo, 1472-1517, (It.) Vision of St. Bernard.

Aubrey Beardsley, 1872-1898, (Br.) illustrator. Salome, Lysistrata.

Max Beckmann, 1884-1950, (Ger.) Expressionist. The Descent from the Cross.

Gentile Bellini, 1426-1507, (It.) Renaissance. Procession in St. Mark's Square.

Giovanni Bellini, 1428-1516, (It.) St. Francis in Ecstasy.

Jacopo Bellini, 1400-1470, (It.) Crucifixion.

George Wesley Bellows, 1882-1925, (U.S.) sports artist. Stag at Sharkey's.

Thomas Hart Benton, 1889-1975, (U.S.) American regionalist. Threshing Wheat, Arts of the West.

Gianlorenzo Bernini, 1598-1680, (It.) Baroque sculpture. The Assumption.

Albert Bierstadt, 1830-1902, (U.S.) landscapist. The Rocky Mountains, Mount Corcoran.

George Caleb Bingham, 1811-1879, (U.S.) Fur Traders Descending the Missouri.

William Blake, 1752-1827, (Br.) engraver. Book of Job, Songs of Innocence, Songs of Experience.

Rosa Bonheur, 1822-1899, (Fr.) The Horse Fair.

Pierre Bonnard, 1867-1947, (Fr.) Intimist. The Breakfast Room.

Gutzon Borglum, 1871-1941, (U.S.) sculptor. Mt. Rushmore Memorial.

Hieronymus Bosch, 1450-1516, (Flem.) religious allegories. The Crowning with Thorns.

Sandro Botticelli, 1444-1510, (It.) Renaissance. Birth of Venus.

Constantin Brancusi, 1876-1957, (Rum.) Nonobjective sculptor. Flying Turtle, The Kiss.

Georges Braque, 1882-1963, (Fr.) Cubist. Violin and Palette.

Pieter Bruegel the Elder, c. 1525-1569, (Flem.) The Peasant Dance.

Pieter Bruegel the Younger, 1564-1638, (Flem.) Village Fair, The Crucifixion.

Edward Burne-Jones, 1833-1898, (Br.) Pre-Raphaelite artist-craftsman. The Mirror of Venus.

Alexander Calder, 1898-1976, (U.S.) sculptor. Lobster Trap and Fish Tail.

Michelangelo Merisi da Caravaggio, 1573-1610, (It.) Baroque. The Supper at Emmaus.

Emily Carr, 1871-1945, (Can.) landscapist. Blunden Harbour, Big Raven.

Carlo Carra, 1881-1966, (It.) Metaphysical school. Lot's Daughters.

Mary Cassatt, 1845-1926, (U.S.) Impressionist. Woman Bathing.

George Catlin, 1796-1872, (U.S.) American Indian life. Gallery of Indians.

Benvenuto Cellini, 1500-1571, (It.) Mannerist sculptor, goldsmith. Perseus.

Paul Cezanne, 1839-1906, (Fr.) Card Players, Mont-Sainte-Victoire with Large Pine Trees.

Marc Chagall, 1887-1985, (Rus.) Jewish life and folklore. I and the Village.

Jean Simeon Chardin, 1699-1779, (Fr.) still lifes. The Kiss, The Grace.

Frederic Church, 1826-1900, (U.S.) Hudson River school. Niagara, Andes of Ecuador.

Giovanni Cimabue, 1240-1302, (It.) Byzantine mosaicist. Madonna Enthroned with St. Francis.

Claude Lorrain, 1600-1682, (Fr.) ideal-landscapist. The Enchanted Castle.

Thomas Cole, 1801-1848, (U.S.) Hudson River school. The Ox-Bow.

John Constable, 1776-1837, (Br.) landscapist. Salisbury Cathedral from the Bishop's Grounds.

John Singleton Copley, 1738-1815, (U.S.) portraitist. Samuel Adams, Watson and the Shark.

Lovis Corinth, 1858-1925, (Ger.) Expressionist. Apocalypse.

Jean-Baptiste-Camille Corot, 1796-1875, (Fr.) landscapist. Souvenir de Mortefontaine, Pastorale.

Correggio, 1494-1534, (It.) Renaissance muralist. Mystic Marriages of St. Catherine.

Gustave Courbet, 1819-1877, (Fr.) Realist. The Artist's Studio.

Lucas Cranach the Elder, 1472-1553, (Ger.) Protestant Reformation portraitist. Luther.

Nathaniel Currier, 1813-1888, and **James M. Ives,** 1824-1895, (both U.S.) lithographers. A Midnight Race on the Mississippi.

John Steuart Curry, 1897-1946, (U.S.) Americana, murals. Baptism in Kansas.

Salvador Dali, 1904-1989, (Sp.) Surrealist. Persistence of Memory.

Honore Daumier, 1808-1879, (Fr.) caricaturist. The Third-Class Carriage.

Jacques-Louis David, 1748-1825, (Fr.) Neoclassicist. The Oath of the Horatii.

Arthur Davies, 1862-1928, (U.S.) Romantic landscapist. Unicorns.

Edgar Degas, 1834-1917, (Fr.) The Ballet Class.

Eugene Delacroix, 1789-1863, (Fr.) Romantic. Massacre at Chios.

Paul Delaroche, 1797-1856, (Fr.) historical themes. Children of Edward IV.

Luca Della Robbia, 1400-1482, (It.) Renaissance terracotta artist. Cantoria (singing gallery), Florence cathedral.

Donatello, 1386-1466, (It.) Renaissance sculptor. David, Gattamelata.

Jean Dubuffet, 1902-1985, (Fr.) painter, sculptor, printmaker. Group of Four Trees.

Marcel Duchamp, 1887-1968, (Fr.) Nude Descending a Staircase.

Raoul Dufy, 1877-1953, (Fr.) Fauvist. Chateau and Horses.

Asher Brown Durand, 1796-1886, (U.S.) Hudson River school. Kindred Spirits.
Albrecht Durer, 1471-1528, (Ger.) Renaissance engraver, woodcuts. St. Jerome in His Study, Melancholia I, Apocalypse.
Anthony van Dyck, 1599-1641, (Flem.) Baroque portraitist. Portrait of Charles I Hunting.
Thomas Eakins, 1844-1916, (U.S.) Realist. The Gross Clinic.
Jacob Epstein, 1880-1959, (Br.) religious and allegorical sculptor. Genesis, Ecce Homo.
Jan van Eyck, 1380-1441, (Flem.) naturalistic panels. Adoration of the Lamb.
Anselm Feuerbach, 1829-1880, (Ger.) Romantic Classicism. Judgement of Paris, Iphigenia.
John Bernard Flannagan, 1895-1942, (U.S.) animal sculptor. Triumph of the Egg.
Jean-Honore Fragonard, 1732-1806, (Fr.) Rococo. The Swing.
Daniel Chester French, 1850-1931, (U.S.) The Minute Man of Concord; seated Lincoln, Lincoln Memorial, Washington, D.C.
Caspar David Friedrich, 1774-1840, (Ger.) Romantic landscapes. Man and Woman Gazing at the Moon.
Thomas Gainsborough, 1727-1788, (Br.) portraitist. The Blue Boy.
Paul Gauguin, 1848-1903, (Fr.) Post-impressionist. The Tahitians.
Lorenzo Ghiberti, 1378-1455, (It.) Renaissance sculptor. Gates of Paradise baptistry doors, Florence.
Alberto Giacometti, 1901-1966, (It.) attenuated sculptures of solitary figures. Man Pointing.
Giorgione, c. 1477-1510, (It.) Renaissance. The Tempest.
Giotto di Bondone, 1267-1337, (It.) Renaissance. Presentation of Christ in the Temple.
Francois Girardon, 1628-1715, (Fr.) Baroque sculptor of classical themes. Apollo Tended by the Nymphs.
Vincent van Gogh, 1853-1890, (Dutch) The Starry Night, L'Arlesienne.
Arshile Gorky, 1905-1948, (U.S.) Surrealist. The Liver Is the Cock's Comb.
Francisco de Goya y Lucientes, 1746-1828, (Sp.) The Naked Maja, The Disasters of War (etchings).
El Greco, 1541-1614, View of Toledo.
Horatio Greenough, 1805-1852, (U.S.) Neo-classical sculptor. George Washington.
Matthias Grünewald, 1480-1528, (Ger.) mystical religious themes. The Resurrection.
Frans Hals, c. 1580-1666, (Dutch) portraitist. Laughing Cavalier, Gypsy Girl.
Childe Hassam, 1859-1935, (U.S.) Impressionist. Southwest Wind.
Edward Hicks, 1780-1849, (U.S.) folk painter. The Peaceable Kingdom.
Hans Hofmann, 1880-1966, (U.S.) early Abstract Expressionist. Spring, The Gate.
William Hogarth, 1697-1764, (Br.) caricaturist. The Rake's Progress.
Katsushika Hokusai, 1760-1849, (Jap.) printmaker. Crabs.
Hans Holbein the Elder, 1460-1524, (Ger.) late Gothic. Presentation of Christ in the Temple.
Hans Holbein the Younger, 1497-1543, (Ger.) portraitist. Henry VIII.
Winslow Homer, 1836-1910, (U.S.) marine themes. Marine Coast, High Cliff.
Edward Hopper, 1882-1967, (U.S.) realistic urban scenes. Sunlight in a Cafeteria.
Jean-Auguste-Dominique Ingres, 1780-1867, (Fr.) Classicist. Valpincon Bather.
George Inness, 1825-1894, (U.S.) luminous landscapist. Delaware Water Gap.
Vasily Kandinsky, 1866-1944, (Rus.) Abstractionist. Capricious Forms.
Paul Klee, 1879-1940, (Swiss) Abstractionist. Twittering Machine.
Oscar Kokoschka, 1886-1980, (Aus.) Expressionist. View of Prague.
Kathe Kollwitz, 1867-1945, (Ger.) printmaker, social justice themes. The Peasant War.
Gaston Lachaise, 1882-1935, (U.S.) figurative sculptor. Standing Woman.
John La Farge, 1835-1910, (U.S.) muralist. Red and White Peonies.
Fernand Leger, 1881-1955, (Fr.) machine art. The Cyclists.
Leonardo da Vinci, 1452-1519, (It.) Mona Lisa, Last Supper, The Annunciation.
Emanuel Leutze, 1816-1868, (U.S.) historical themes. Washington Crossing the Delaware.
Jacques Lipchitz, 1891-1973, (Fr.) Cubist sculptor. Harpist.
Filippino Lippi, 1457-1504, (It.) Renaissance. The Vision of St. Bernard.
Fra Filippo Lippi, 1406-1469, (It.) Renaissance. Coronation of the Virgin.
Morris Louis, 1912-1962, (U.S.) Abstract Expressionist. Signa, Stripes.
Aristide Maillol, 1861-1944, (Fr.) sculptor. The Mediterranean.
Edouard Manet, 1832-1883, (Fr.) forerunner of Impressionism. Luncheon on the Grass, Olympia.
Andrea Mantegna, 1431-1506, (It.) Renaissance frescoes. Triumph of Caesar.
Franz Marc, 1880-1916, (Ger.) Expressionist. Blue Horses.
John Marin, 1870-1953, (U.S.) expressionist seascapes. Maine Island.
Reginald Marsh, 1898-1954, (U.S.) satirical artist. Tattoo and Haircut.
Masaccio, 1401-1428, (It.) Renaissance. The Tribute Money.
Henri Matisse, 1869-1954, (Fr.) Fauvist. Woman with the Hat.
Michelangelo Buonarroti, 1475-1564, (It.) Pieta, David, Moses, The Last Judgment, Sistine Ceiling.
Jean-Francois Millet, 1814-1875, (Fr.) painter of peasant subjects. The Gleaners, The Man with a Hoe.
Joan Miró, 1893-1983, (Sp.) Exuberant colors, playful images. Catalan landscape, Dutch Interior.
Amedeo Modigliani, 1884-1920, (It.) Reclining Nude.
Piet Mondrian, 1872-1944, (Dutch) Abstractionist. Composition.
Claude Monet, 1840-1926, (Fr.) Impressionist. The Bridge at Argenteuil, Haystacks.
Henry Moore, 1898-1986, (Br.) sculptor of large-scale, abstract works. Reclining Figure (several).
Gustave Moreau, 1826-1898, (Fr.) Symbolist. The Apparition, Dance of Salome.
James Wilson Morrice, 1865-1924, (Can.) landscapist. The Ferry, Quebec, Venice, Looking Over the Lagoon.
Grandma Moses, 1860-1961, (U.S.) folk painter. Out for the Christmas Trees.
Edvard Munch, 1863-1944, (Nor.) Expressionist. The Cry.
Bartolome Murillo, 1618-1682, (Sp.) Baroque religious artist. Vision of St. Anthony. The Two Trinities.
Barnett Newman, 1905-1970, (U.S.) Abstract Expressionist. Stations of the Cross.
Isamu Noguchi, 1904-1988, (U.S.) trad. Japanese art, modern techniques.
Georgia O'Keeffe, 1887-1986, (U.S.) Southwest motifs. Cow's Skull.
Jose Clemente Orozco, 1883-1949, (Mex.) frescoes. House of Tears.
Charles Willson Peale, 1741-1827, (U.S.) American Revolutionary portraitist. Washington, Franklin, Jefferson, John Adams.
Rembrandt Peale, 1778-1860, (U.S.) portraitist. Thomas Jefferson.
Pietro Perugino, 1446-1523, (It.) Renaissance. Delivery of the Keys to St. Peter.
Pablo Picasso, 1881-1973, (Sp.) Guernica, Dove, Head of a Woman.
Piero della Francesca, c. 1415-1492, (It.) Renaissance. Duke of Urbino, Flagellation of Christ.
Camille Pissarro, 1830-1903, (Fr.) Impressionist. Morning Sunlight.
Jackson Pollock, 1912-1956, (U.S.) Abstract Expressionist. Autumn Rhythm.
Nicolas Poussin, 1594-1665, (Fr.) Baroque pictorial classicism. St. John on Patmos.
Maurice B. Prendergast, c. 1860-1924, (U.S.) Post-impressionist water colorist. Umbrellas in the Rain.
Pierre-Paul Prud'hon, 1758-1823, (Fr.) Romanticist. Crime pursued by Vengeance and Justice.
Pierre Cecile Puvis de Chavannes, 1824-1898, (Fr.) muralist. The Poor Fisherman.
Raphael Sanzio, 1483-1520, (It.) Renaissance. Disputa, School of Athens, Sistine Madonna.
Man Ray, 1890-1976, (U.S.) Dadaist. Observing Time, The Lovers.
Odilon Redon, 1840-1916, (Fr.) Symbolist lithographer. In the Dream.
Rembrandt van Rijn, 1606-1669, (Dutch) The Bridal Couple, The Night Watch.
Frederic Remington, 1861-1909, (U.S.) painter, sculptor, portrayer of the American West. Bronco Buster.
Pierre-Auguste Renoir, 1841-1919, (Fr.) Impressionist. The Luncheon of the Boating Party.
Joshua Reynolds, 1723-1792, (Br.) portraitist. Mrs. Siddons as the Tragic Muse.
Diego Rivera, 1886-1957, (Mex.) frescoes. The Fecund Earth.
Norman Rockwell, 1894-1978, (U.S.) illustrator. Saturday Evening Post covers.
Auguste Rodin, 1840-1917, (Fr.) sculptor. The Thinker, The Burghers of Calais.

Mark Rothko, 1903-1970, (U.S.) Abstract Expressionist. Light, Earth and Blue.

Georges Rouault, 1871-1958, (Fr.) Expressionist. The Old King.

Henri Rousseau, 1844-1910, (Fr.) primitive exotic themes. The Snake Charmer.

Theodore Rousseau, 1812-1867, (Swiss-Fr.) landscapist. Under the Birches, Evening.

Peter Paul Rubens, 1577-1640, (Flem.) Baroque. Mystic Marriage of St. Catherine.

Jacob van Ruisdael, c. 1628-1682, (Dutch) landscapist. Jewish Cemetery.

Salomon van Ruysdael, c. 1600-1670, (Dutch) landscapist. River with Ferry-Boat.

Albert Pinkham Ryder, 1847-1917, (U.S.) seascapes and allegories. Toilers of the Sea.

Augustus Saint-Gaudens, 1848-1907, (U.S.) memorial statues. Farragut, Mrs. Henry Adams (Grief).

Andrea Sansovino, 1460-1529, (It.) Renaissance sculptor. Baptism of Christ.

Jacopo Sansovino, 1486-1570, (It.) Renaissance sculptor. St. John the Baptist.

John Singer Sargent, 1856-1925, (U.S.) Edwardian society portraitist. The Wyndham Sisters, Madam X.

Georges Seurat, 1859-1891, (Fr.) Pointillist. Sunday Afternoon on the Island of Grande Jatte.

Gino Severini, 1883-1966, (It.) Futurist and Cubist. Dynamic Hieroglyph of the Bal Tabarin.

Ben Shahn, 1898-1969, (U.S.) social and political themes. Sacco and Vanzetti series, Seurat's Lunch, Handball.

Charles Sheeler, 1883-1965, (U.S.) Abstractionist. Upper Deck.

David Alfaro Siqueiros, 1896-1974, (Mex.) political muralist. March of Humanity.

John F. Sloan, 1871-1951, (U.S.) depictions of New York City. Wake of the Ferry.

David Smith, 1906-1965, (U.S.) welded metal sculpture. Hudson River Landscape, Zig, Cubi series.

Gilbert Stuart, 1755-1828, (U.S.) portraitist. George Washington.

Thomas Sully, 1783-1872, (U.S.) portraitist. Col. Thomas Handasyd Perkins, The Passage of the Delaware.

Yves Tanguy, 1900-1955, (Fr.) Surrealist. Rose of the Four Winds.

Giovanni Battista Tiepolo, 1696-1770, (It.) Rococo frescoes. The Crucifixion.

Jacopo Tintoretto, 1518-1594, (It.) Mannerist. The Last Supper.

Titian, c. 1485-1576, (It.) Renaissance. Venus and the Lute Player, The Bacchanal.

Henri de Toulouse-Lautrec, 1864-1901, (Fr.) At the Moulin Rouge.

John Trumbull, 1756-1843, (U.S.) historical themes. The Declaration of Independence.

J(oseph) M(allord) W(illiam) Turner, 1775-1851, (Br.) Romantic landscapist. Snow Storm.

Paolo Uccello, 1397-1475, (It.) Gothic-Renaissance. The Rout of San Romano.

Maurice Utrillo, 1883-1955, (Fr.) Impressionist. Sacre-Coeur de Montmartre.

John Vanderlyn, 1775-1852, (U.S.) Neo-classicist. Ariadne Asleep on the Island of Naxos.

Diego Velazquez, 1599-1660, (Sp.) Baroque. Las Meninas, Portrait of Juan de Pareja.

Jan Vermeer, 1632-1675, (Dutch) interior genre subjects. Young Woman with a Water Jug.

Paolo Veronese, 1528-1588, (It.) devotional themes, vastly peopled canvases. The Temptation of St. Anthony.

Andrea del Verrocchio, 1435-1488, (It.) Florentine sculptor. Colleoni.

Maurice de Vlaminck, 1876-1958, (Fr.) Fauvist landscapist. The Storm.

Andy Warhol, 1928-1987 (U.S.) Pop Art. Campbell's Soup Cans.

Antoine Watteau, 1684-1721, (Fr.) Rococo painter of "scenes of gallantry". The Embarkation for Cythera.

George Frederic Watts, 1817-1904, (Br.) painter and sculptor of grandiose allegorical themes. Hope, Physical Energy.

Benjamin West, 1738-1820, (U.S.) realistic historical themes. Death of General Wolfe.

James Abbott McNeill Whistler, 1834-1903, (U.S.) Arrangement in Grey and Black, No. 1: The Artist's Mother.

Archibald M. Willard, 1836-1918, (U.S.) The Spirit of '76.

Grant Wood, 1891-1942, (U.S.) Midwestern regionalist. American Gothic, Daughters of Revolution.

Ossip Zadkine, 1890-1967, (Rus.) School of Paris sculptor. The Destroyed City, Musicians, Christ.

Noted Philosophers and Religionists of the Past

Lyman Abbott, 1835-1922, (U.S.) clergyman, reformer; advocate of Christian Socialism.

Pierre Abelard, 1079-1142, (F.) philosopher, theologian, and teacher, used dialectic method to support Christian dogma.

Felix Adler, 1851-1933, (U.S.) German-born founder of the Ethical Culture Society.

Aristotle, 384-322 B.C., (Gr.) philosopher, emphasized direct observation of nature.

St. Augustine, 354-430, Latin bishop considered the founder of formalized Christian theology.

Averroes, 1126-1198, (Sp.) Islamic philosopher.

Roger Bacon, c.1214-1294, (Br.) philosopher and scientist.

Bahaullah (Mirza Husayn Ali), 1817-1892, (Pers.) founder of Bahai faith.

Karl Barth, 1886-1968, (Sw.) theologian, a leading force in 20th-century Protestantism.

St. Benedict, c.480-547, (It.) founded the Benedictines.

Jeremy Bentham, 1748-1832, (Br.) philosopher, reformer, founder of Utilitarianism.

Henri Bergson, 1859-1941, (F.) philosopher of evolution.

George Berkeley, 1685-1753, (Ir.) philosopher, churchman.

John Biddle, 1615-1662, (Br.) founder of English Unitarianism.

Jakob Boehme, 1575-1624, (G.) theosophist and mystic.

William Brewster, 1567-1644, (Br.) headed Pilgrims, signed Mayflower Compact.

Emil Brunner, 1889-1966, (Sw.) Protestant theologian.

Giordano Bruno, 1548-1600, (It.) philosopher, first to state the cosmic theory.

Martin Buber, 1878-1965, (G.) Jewish philosopher, theologian, wrote *I and Thou.*

Buddha (Siddhartha Gautama), c.563-c.483 BC, (Ind.) philosopher, founded Buddhism.

John Calvin, 1509-1564, (F.) theologian, a key figure in the Protestant Reformation.

Rudolph Carnap, 1891-1970, (U.S.) German-born philosopher, a founder of logical positivism.

William Ellery Channing, 1780-1842, (U.S.) clergyman, early spokesman for Unitarianism.

Auguste Comte, 1798-1857, (F.) philosopher, the founder of positivism.

Confucius, 551-479 BC, (Chin.) founder of Confucianism.

John Cotton, 1584-1652, (Br.) Puritan theologian.

Thomas Cranmer, 1489-1556, (Br.) churchman, wrote much of *Book of Common Prayer;* promoter of English Reformation.

René Descartes, 1596-1650, (F.) philosopher, mathematician, "father of modern philosophy."

John Dewey, 1859-1952, (U.S.) philosopher, educator; helped inaugurate the progressive education movement.

Denis Diderot, 1713-1784, (F.) philosopher, creator of first modern encyclopedia.

Mary Baker Eddy, 1821-1910, (U.S.) founder of Christian Science, wrote *Science and Health.*

Jonathan Edwards, 1703-1758, (U.S.) preacher, theologian.

(Desiderius) Erasmus, c.1466-1536, (Du.) Renaissance humanist, wrote *On the Freedom of the Will.*

Johann Fichte, 1762-1814, (G.) philosopher, the first of the Transcendental Idealists.

George Fox, 1624-1691, (Br.) founder of Society of Friends.

St. Francis of Assisi, 1182-1226, (It.) founded Franciscans.

al Ghazali, 1058-1111, Islamic philosopher.

Georg W. Hegel, 1770-1831, (G.) Idealist philosopher.

Martin Heidegger, 1889-1976, (G.) existentialist philosopher, affected fields ranging from physics to literary criticism.

Johann G. Herder, 1744-1803, (G.) philosopher, cultural historian; a founder of German Romanticism.

David Hume, 1711-1776, (Sc.) philosopher, historian.

Jan Hus, 1369-1415, (Czech.) religious reformer.

Edmund Husserl, 1859-1938, (G.) philosopher, founded the Phenomenological movement.

Thomas Huxley, 1825-1895, (Br.) philosopher, educator.

Ignatius of Loyola, 1491-1556, (Sp.) founder of the Jesuits.

William Inge, 1860-1954, (Br.) theologian, explored the mystic aspects of Christianity.

William James, 1842-1910, (U.S.) philosopher, psychologist; advanced theory of the pragmatic nature of truth.

Karl Jaspers, 1883-1969, (G.) existentialist philosopher.

Immanuel Kant, 1724-1804, (G.) metaphysician, preeminent founder of modern critical philosophy; *Critique of Pure Reason.*

Soren Kierkegaard, 1813-1855, (Den.) philosopher, considered the father of Existentialism.

John Knox, 1505-1572, (Sc.) leader of the Protestant Reformation in Scotland.

Lao-Tzu, 604-531 BC, (Chin.) philosopher, considered the founder of the Taoist religion.

Gottfried von Leibniz, 1646-1716, (G.) philosopher, mathematician, influenced German Enlightenment.
Martin Luther, 1483-1546, (G.) leader of the Protestant Reformation, founded Lutheran church.
Maimonides, 1135-1204, (Sp.) Jewish philosopher.
Jacques Maritain, 1882-1973, (F.) Neo-Thomist philosopher.
Cotton Mather, 1663-1728, (U.S.) defender of orthodox Puritanism; founded Yale, 1701.
Philipp Melanchthon, 1497-1560, (G.) theologian, humanist; an important voice in the Reformation.
Thomas Merton, 1915-1968, (U.S.) Trappist monk, spiritual writer; *The Seven Storey Mountain.*
John Stuart Mill, 1806-1873, (Br.) philosopher, economist; *Essay on Liberty.*
Mohammed, c.570-632, Arab prophet of the religion of Islam.
Dwight Moody, 1837-1899, (U.S.) evangelist.
George E. Moore, 1873-1958, (Br.) ethical theorist.
Elijah Muhammad, 1897-1975, (U.S.) leader of the Black Muslim sect.
Heinrich Muhlenberg, 1711-1787, (G.) organized the Lutheran Church in America.
John H. Newman, 1801-1890, (Br.) Roman Catholic cardinal, led Oxford Movement; *Apologia pro Vita Sua.*
Reinhold Niebuhr, 1892-1971, (U.S.) Protestant theologian, social and political critic.
Friedrich Nietzsche, 1844-1900, (G.) moral philosopher; *The Birth of Tragedy, Thus Spake Zarathustra.*
Blaise Pascal, 1623-1662, (F.) philosopher, mathematician.
St. Patrick, c.389-c.461, brought Christianity to Ireland.
St. Paul, ?-c.67, a founder of Christianity; his epistles are first Christian theological writing.
Charles S. Peirce, 1839-1914, (U.S.) philosopher, logician; originated concept of Pragmatism, 1878.
Plato, 427?-347? B.C., (Gr.) philosopher, argued for independent reality of ideas; *Republic.*
Josiah Royce 1855-1916, (U.S.) Idealist philosopher.
Charles T. Russell, 1852-1916, (U.S.) founder of Jehovah's Witnesses.
Fredrich von Schelling, 1775-1854, (G.) philosopher of romantic movement.
Friedrich Schleiermacher, 1768-1834, (G.) theologian, a founder of modern Protestant theology.
Arthur Schopenhauer, 1788-1860, (G.) philosopher.
Joseph Smith, 1805-1844, (U.S.) founded Latter Day Saints (Mormon) movement, 1830.
Socrates, 469-399 B.C., (Gr.) philosopher, refined dialectic method.
Herbert Spencer, 1820-1903, (Br.) philosopher of evolution.
Baruch Spinoza, 1632-1677, (Du.) rationalist philosopher.
Billy Sunday, 1862-1935, (U.S.) evangelist.
Daisetz Teitaro Suzuki, 1870-1966, (Jap.) Buddhist scholar.
Emanuel Swedenborg, 1688-1772, (Swed.) philosopher, mystic.
Thomas à Becket, 1118-1170, (Br.) archbishop of Canterbury, opposed Henry II.
Thomas à Kempis, c.1380-1471, (G.) theologian probably wrote *Imitation of Christ.*
Thomas Aquinas, 1225-1274, (It.) Roman Catholic saint, founder of system declared official Catholic philosophy; *Summa Theologica.*
Paul Tillich, 1886-1965, (U.S.) German-born philosopher and theologian; brought depth psychology to Protestantism.
John Wesley, 1703-1791, (Br.) theologian, evangelist; founded Methodism.
Alfred North Whitehead, 1861-1947, (Br.) philosopher, mathematician; *Principia Mathematica* (with Bertrand Russell).
William of Occam, c.1285-c.1349 (Br.) medieval scholastic philosopher.
Roger Williams, c.1603-1683, (U.S.) clergyman, championed religious freedom and separation of church and state.
Ludwig Wittgenstein, 1889-1951, (Aus.) philosopher, influenced language philosophy.
John Wycliffe, 1320-1384, (Br.) theologian, reformer.
Brigham Young, 1801-1877, (U.S.) Mormon leader after Smith's assassination, colonized Utah.
Huldrych Zwingli, 1484-1531, (Sw.) theologian, led Swiss Protestant Reformation.

Noted Social Reformers and Educators of the Past

Jane Addams, 1860-1935, (U.S.) co-founder of Hull House; won Nobel Peace Prize, 1931.
Susan B. Anthony, 1820-1906, (U.S.) a leader in temperance, anti-slavery, and women's suffrage movements.
Henry Barnard, 1811-1900, (U.S.) public school reformer.
Thomas Barnardo, 1845-1905, (Br.) social reformer, pioneered in the care of destitute children.
Clara Barton, 1821-1912, (U.S.) organizer of the American Red Cross.
Henry Ward Beecher, 1813-1887, (U.S.) clergyman, abolitionist.
Sarah G. Blanding, 1899-1985, (U.S.), head of Vassar College, 1946-64.
Amelia Bloomer, 1818-1894, (U.S.) social reformer, women's rights advocate.
William Booth, 1829-1912, (Br.) founded the Salvation Army.
John Brown, 1800-1859, (U.S.) abolitionist who led murder of 5 pro-slavery men, was hanged.
Nicholas Murray Butler, 1862-1947, (U.S.) educator headed Columbia Univ., 1902-45; won Nobel Peace Prize, 1931.
Frances X. (Mother) Cabrini, 1850-1917, (U.S.) Italian-born nun founded charitable institutions; first American canonized.
Carrie Chapman Catt, 1859-1947, (U.S.) suffragette, helped win passage of the 19th amendment.
Clarence Darrow, 1857-1938, (U.S.) lawyer, defender of "underdog," opponent of capital punishment.
Dorothy Day, 1897-1980, (U.S.) founder of Catholic Worker Movement.
Eugene V. Debs, 1855-1926, (U.S.) labor leader, led Pullman strike, 1894; 4-time Socialist presidential candidate.
Melvil Dewey, 1851-1931, (U.S.) devised decimal system of library-book classification.
Dorothea Dix, 1802-1887, (U.S.) crusader for humane care of mentally ill.
Frederick Douglass, 1817-1895, (U.S.) abolitionist.
W.E.B. DuBois, 1868-1963, (U.S.) Negro-rights leader, educator, and writer.
William Lloyd Garrison, 1805-1879, (U.S.) abolitionist, reformer.
Giovanni Gentile, 1875-1944, (It.) philosopher, educator; reformed Italian educational system.
Emma Goldman, 1869-1940, (Rus.-U.S.) published anarchist *Mother Earth,* birth control advocate.
Samuel Gompers, 1850-1924, (U.S.) labor leader; a founder and president of AFL.
William Green, 1873-1952, (U.S.) president of AFL, 1924-52.
Michael Harrington, 1928-1989, (U.S.) revealed poverty in affluent U.S. in *The Other America,* 1963.
Sidney Hillman, 1887-1946, (U.S.) labor leader, helped organize CIO.
John Holt, 1924-1985, (U.S.) educator and author, *How Children Fail.*
Samuel G. Howe, 1801-1876, (U.S.) social reformer, changed public attitudes toward the handicapped.
Helen Keller, 1880-1968, (U.S.) crusader for better treatment for the handicapped.
Martin Luther King Jr., 1929-1968, (U.S.) civil rights leader; won Nobel Peace Prize, 1964.
John L. Lewis, 1880-1969, (U.S.) labor leader, headed United Mine Workers, 1920-60.
Horace Mann, 1796-1859, (U.S.) pioneered modern public school system.
William H. McGuffey, 1800-1873, (U.S.) author of *Reader,* the mainstay of 19th century U.S. public education.
Alexander Meiklejohn, 1872-1964, (U.S.) British-born educator, championed academic freedom and experimental curricula.
Karl Menninger, 1893-1991, (U.S.) with brother William made Menninger Clinic, and Menninger Foundation in Topeka, Kans., the center of U.S. psychiatry.
Lucretia Mott, 1793-1880, (U.S.) reformer, pioneer feminist.
Philip Murray, 1886-1952, (U.S.) Scotch-born labor leader.
Florence Nightingale, 1820-1910, (Br.) founder of modern nursing.
Emmeline Pankhurst, 1858-1928, (Br.) woman suffragist.
Elizabeth P. Peabody, 1804-1894, (U.S.) education pioneer, founded 1st kindergarten in U.S., 1860.
Walter Reuther, 1907-1970, (U.S.) labor leader, headed UAW.
Jacob Riis, 1849-1914, (U.S.) crusader for urban reforms.
Margaret Sanger, 1883-1966, (U.S.) social reformer, pioneered the birth control movement.
Elizabeth Seton, 1774-1821, (U.S.) established parochial school education in U.S.
Earl of Shaftesbury (A.A. Cooper), 1801-1885, (Br.) social reformer.
Elizabeth Cady Stanton, 1815-1902, (U.S.) women's suffrage pioneer.
Lucy Stone, 1818-1893, (U.S.) feminist, abolitionist.
Harriet Tubman, c.1820-1913, (U.S.) abolitionist, ran Underground Railroad.
Booker T. Washington, 1856-1915, (U.S.) educator, reformer; championed vocational training for blacks.
Walter F. White, 1893-1955, (U.S.) headed NAACP, 1931-55.
William Wilberforce, 1759-1833, (Br.) social reformer, prominent in struggle to abolish the slave trade.

Emma Hart Willard, 1787-1870, (U.S.) pioneered higher education for women.

Frances E. Willard, 1839-1898, (U.S.) temperance, woman's rights leader.

Mary Wollstonecraft, 1759-1797 (Br.) wrote *Vindication of the Rights of Women.*

Whitney M. Young Jr., 1921-1971, (U.S.) civil rights leader, headed National Urban League, 1961-71.

Noted Historians, Economists, and Social Scientists of the Past

Brooks Adams, 1848-1927, (U.S.) historian, political theoretician; *The Law of Civilization and Decay.*

Henry Adams, 1838-1911, (U.S.) historian; *History of the United States of America, The Education of Henry Adams.*

Francis Bacon, 1561-1626, (Br.) philosopher, essayist, and statesman; applied scientific induction to philosophy.

George Bancroft, 1800-1891, (U.S.) historian, wrote 10-volume *History of the United States.*

Charles A. Beard, 1874-1948, (U.S.) historian; *The Economic Basis of Politics;* helped found New School for Social Research.

Bede (the Venerable), c.673-735, (Br.) scholar historian whose writings virtually comprise the learning of his time.

Ruth Benedict, 1887-1948, (U.S.) anthropologist, studied Indian tribes of the Southwest.

Bruno Bettleheim, 1903-1990, (Aust.-U.S.) psychoanalyst specializing in autistic children; *The Uses of Enchantment.*

Louis Blanc, 1811-1882, (F.) Socialist leader and historian whose ideas were a link between utopian and Marxist socialism.

Leonard Bloomfield, 1887-1949, (U.S.) linguist. *Language.*

Franz Boas, 1858-1942, (U.S.) German-born anthropologist, studied American Indians.

Van Wyck Brooks, 1886-1963, (U.S.) historian, critic of New England culture, esp. literature.

Edmund Burke, 1729-1797, (Ir.) British parliamentarian and political philosopher; influenced many Federalists.

Joseph Campbell, 1904-1987, (U.S.) wrote books on mythology, folklore.

Thomas Carlyle, 1795-1881, (Sc.) historian, critic; *Sartor Resartus, Past and Present, The French Revolution.*

Edward Channing, 1856-1931, (U.S.) historian, wrote 6-volume *A History of the United States.*

John R. Commons, 1862-1945, (U.S.) economist, labor historian; *Legal Foundations of Capitalism.*

Benedetto Croce, 1866-1952, (It.) philosopher, statesman, and historian; *Philosophy of the Spirit.*

Bernard A. De Voto, 1897-1955, (U.S.) historian; wrote trilogy on American West; edited Mark Twain manuscripts.

Ariel Durant, 1898-1981, (U.S.) historian, collaborated with husband on 11-volume *The Story of Civilization.*

Will Durant, 1885-1981, (U.S.) historian. *The Story of Civilization, The Story of Philosophy.*

Emile Durkheim, 1858-1917, (F.) a founder of modern sociology; *The Rules of Sociological Method.*

Friedrich Engels, 1820-1895, (G.) political writer, with Marx wrote the *Communist Manifesto.*

Irving Fisher, 1867-1947, (U.S.) economist, contributed to the development of modern monetary theory.

John Fiske, 1842-1901, (U.S.) historian and lecturer, popularized Darwinian theory of evolution.

Charles Fourier, 1772-1837, (F.) utopian socialist.

Henry George, 1839-1897, (U.S.) economist, reformer, led single-tax movement.

Edward Gibbon, 1737-1794, (Br.) historian, wrote *The History of the Decline and Fall of the Roman Empire.*

Francesco Guicciardini, 1483-1540, (It.) historian, wrote *Storia d'Italia,* principal historical work of the 16th-century.

Thomas Hobbes, 1588-1679, (Br.) political philosopher; *Leviathan.*

Richard Hofstadter, 1916-1970, (U.S.) historian; *The Age of Reform.*

John Maynard Keynes, 1883-1946, (Br.) economist, principal advocate of deficit spending.

Alfred L. Kroeber, 1876-1960, (U.S.) cultural anthropologist, studied Indians of North and South America.

James L. Laughlin, 1850-1933, (U.S.) economist, helped establish Federal Reserve System.

Lucien Lévy-Bruhl, 1857-1939, (F.) philosopher, studied the psychology of primitive societies; *Primitive Mentality.*

Kurt Lewin, 1890-1947, (U.S.) German-born psychologist, studied human motivation and group dynamics.

John Locke, 1632-1704, (Br.) philosopher; *Essay Concerning Human Understanding.*

Konrad Lorenz, 1904-1989, (Aus.) ethologist, pioneer in study of animal behavior.

Thomas B. Macauley, 1800-1859, (Br.) historian, statesman.

Bronislaw Malinowski, 1884-1942, (Pol.) considered the father of social anthropology.

Thomas R. Malthus, 1766-1834, (Br.) economist, famed for *Essay on the Principle of Population.*

Karl Mannheim, 1893-1947, (Hung.) sociologist, historian; *Ideology and Utopia.*

Karl Marx, 1818-1883, (G.) political philosopher, proponent of modern communism; *Communist Manifesto, Das Kapital.*

Giuseppe Mazzini, 1805-1872, (It.) political philosopher.

George H. Mead, 1863-1931, (U.S.) philosopher, social psychologist.

Margaret Mead, 1901-1978, (U.S.) cultural anthropologist, popularized field; *Coming of Age in Samoa.*

James Mill, 1773-1836, (Sc.) philosopher, historian, economist; a proponent of Utilitarianism.

John Stuart Mill, 1806-1873, (Br.) philosopher, political economist; *Essay on Liberty.*

Perry G. Miller, 1905-1963, (U.S.) historian, interpreted 17th-century New England.

Theodor Mommsen, 1817-1903, (G.) historian; *The History of Rome.*

Charles-Louis Montesquieu, 1689-1755, (F.) social philosopher; *The Spirit of Laws.*

Samuel Eliot Morison, 1887-1976, (U.S.) historian, chronicled voyages of early explorers.

Lewis Mumford, 1895-1990, (U.S.) sociologist, critic, *The Culture of Cities.*

Gunnar Myrdal, 1898-1987 (Swe.) economist, social scientist.

Allan Nevins, 1890-1971, (U.S.) historian, biographer; *The Ordeal of the Union.*

Jose Ortega y Gasset, 1883-1955, (Sp.) philosopher, advocated control by elite; *The Revolt of the Masses.*

Robert Owen, 1771-1858, (Br.) political philosopher, reformer; pioneer in cooperative movement.

Vilfredo Pareto, 1848-1923, (It.) economist, sociologist.

Francis Parkman, 1823-1893, (U.S.) historian; *France and England in North America, 1851-92.*

Marco Polo, c.1254-1324, (It.) narrated an account of his travels to China.

William Prescott, 1796-1859, (U.S.) early American historian; *The Conquest of Peru.*

Pierre Joseph Proudhon, 1809-1865, (F.) social theorist, the father of anarchism; *The Philosophy of Property.*

Francois Quesnay, 1694-1774, (F.) economic theorist, demonstrated circular flow of economic activity through society.

David Ricardo, 1772-1823, (Br.) economic theorist, advocated free international trade.

James H. Robinson, 1863-1936, (U.S.) historian, educator.

Carl Rogers, 1902-1987, (U.S.) psychotherapist, author.

Jean-Jacques Rousseau, 1712-1778, (F.) social philosopher, the father of romantic sensibility; *Confessions.*

Edward Sapir, 1884-1939 (Ger.-U.S.) anthropologist, studied ethnology and linguistics of some U.S. Indian groups.

Ferdinand de Saussure, 1857-1913, (Swiss) a founder of modern linguistics.

Hjalmar Schacht, 1877-1970, (G.) economist; Reichsbank president.

Joseph Schumpeter, 1883-1950, (U.S.) Czech.-born economist, championed big business, capitalism.

Albert Schweitzer, 1875-1965, (Alsatian) social philosopher, theologian, medical missionary.

George Simmel, 1858-1918, (G.) sociologist, philosopher; helped establish German sociology.

B.F. Skinner, 1904-1989, (U.S.) psychologist, championed behaviorism.

Adam Smith, 1723-1790, (Br.) economist, advocated laissez-faire economy and free trade.

Jared Sparks, 1789-1866, (U.S.) historian, educator, editor; *The Library of American Biography.*

Oswald Spengler, 1880-1936, (G.) philosopher and historian; *The Decline of the West.*

William G. Sumner, 1840-1910, (U.S.) social scientist, economist; championed laissez-faire economy, Social Darwinism.

Hippolyte Taine, 1828-1893, (F.) historian, basis of naturalistic school; *The Origins of Contemporary France.*

Frank W. Taussig, 1859-1940, (U.S.) economist, educator.

A(lan) J(ohn) P(ercivale) Taylor, 1906-1989, (Br.) historian, *The Origins of the Second World War.*

Nikolaas Tinbergen, 1907-1988, (Dutch-Br.) ethologist, pioneer in study of animal behavior.

Alexis de Tocqueville, 1805-1859, (F.) political scientist, historian; *Democracy in America.*

Francis E. Townsend, 1867-1960, (U.S.) led old-age pension movement, 1933.

Arnold Toynbee, 1889-1975, (Br.) historian; *A Study of History.*

Heinrich von Treitschke, 1834-1896, (G.) historian, political writer; *A History of Germany in the 19th Century.*

George Trevelyan, 1838-1928, (Br.) historian, statesman; favored "literary" over "scientific" history; *History of England.*

Barbara Tuchman, 1912-1989, (U.S.) author of popular history books, *The Guns of August, The March of Folly.*

Frederick J. Turner, 1861-1932, (U.S.) historian, educator; *The Frontier in American History.*

Thorstein B. Veblen, 1857-1929, (U.S.) economist, social philosopher; *The Theory of the Leisure Class.*

Giovanni Vico, 1668-1744, (It.) historian, philosopher; regarded by many as first modern historian. *New Science.*

Voltaire (F.M. Arouet), 1694-1778, (F.) philosopher, historian, writer of "philosophical romances," *Candide.*

Izaak Walton, 1593-1683, (Br.) wrote biographies, political-philosophical study of fishing, *The Compleat Angler.*

Sidney J., 1859-1947, and wife **Beatrice,** 1858-1943, **Webb** (Br.) leading figures in Fabian Society and British Labour Party.

Walter P. Webb, 1888-1963, (U.S.) historian of the West.

Max Weber, 1864-1920, (G.) sociologist. *The Protestant Ethic and the Spirit of Capitalism.*

Noted Scientists of the Past

Howard H. Aiken, 1900-1973, (U.S.) mathematician, credited with designing forerunner of digital computer.

Albertus Magnus, 1193-1280, (G.) theologian, philosopher, established medieval Christian study of natural science.

Andre-Marie Ampère, 1775-1836, (F.) scientist known for contributions to electrodynamics.

Amedeo Avogadro, 1776-1856, (It.) chemist, physicist, advanced important theories on properties of gases.

John Bardeen, 1908-1991, (U.S.) co-inventor of the transistor that led to modern electronics.

A.C. Becquerel, 1788-1878, (F.) physicist, pioneer in electrochemical science.

A.H. Becquerel, 1852-1908, (F.) physicist, discovered radioactivity in uranium.

Alexander Graham Bell, 1847-1922, (U.S.) inventor, first to patent and commercially exploit the telephone, 1876.

Daniel Bernoulli, 1700-1782, (Swiss) mathematician, advanced kinetic theory of gases and fluids.

Jöns Jakob Berzelius, 1779-1848, (Swed.) chemist, developed modern chemical symbols and formulas.

Henry Bessemer, 1813-1898, (Br.) engineer, invented Bessemer steel-making process.

Louis Blériot, 1872-1936, (F.) engineer, pioneer aviator, invented and constructed monoplanes.

Niels Bohr, 1885-1962, (Dan.) physicist, leading figure in the development of quantum theory.

Max Born, 1882-1970, (G.) physicist known for research in quantum mechanics.

Satyendranath Bose, 1894-1974, (In.) physicist, chemist, mathematician known for Bose statistics, forerunner of modern quantum theory.

Walter Brattain, 1902-1987, (U.S.) inventor, worked on invention of transistor.

Louis de Broglie, 1893-1987, (F.) physicist, best known for wave theory.

Robert Bunsen, 1811-1899, (G.) chemist, invented Bunsen burner.

Luther Burbank, 1849-1926, (U.S.) plant breeder whose work developed plant breeding into a modern science.

Vannevar Bush, 1890-1974, (U.S.) electrical engineer, developed differential analyzer, first electronic analogue computer.

Alexis Carrel, 1873-1944, (F.) surgeon, biologist, developed methods of suturing blood vessels and transplanting organs.

George Washington Carver, 1860?-1943, (U.S.) agricultural chemist at Tuskegee Institute, discovered hundreds of uses for peanut, sweet potato, soybean.

Henry Cavendish, 1731-1810, (Br.) chemist, physicist, discovered hydrogen.

James Chadwick, 1891-1974, (Br.) physicist, discovered the neutron.

Jean M. Charcot, 1825-1893, (F.) neurologist known for work on hysteria, hypnotism, sclerosis.

Albert Claude, 1899-1983, (Belg.) a founder of modern cell biology.

John D. Cockcroft, 1897-1967, (Br.) nuclear physicist, constructed first atomic particle accelerator with E.T.S. Walton.

Nicholas Copernicus, 1473-1543, (Pol.) astronomer who first described solar system, with earth as one of planets revolving around sun.

William Crookes, 1832-1919, (Br.) physicist, chemist, discovered thallium, invented a cathode-ray tube, radiometer.

Marie Curie, 1867-1934, (Pol.-F.) physical chemist known for work on radium and its compounds.

Pierre Curie, 1859-1906, (F.) physical chemist known for work with his wife on radioactivity.

Gottlieb Daimler, 1834-1900, (G.) engineer, inventor, pioneer automobile manufacturer.

John Dalton, 1766-1844, (Br.) chemist, physicist, formulated atomic theory, made first table of atomic weights.

Charles Darwin, 1809-1882, (Br.) naturalist, established theory of organic evolution; *Origin of Species.*

Humphry Davy, 1778-1829, (Br.) chemist, research in electrochemistry led to isolation of potassium, sodium, calcium, barium, boron, magnesium, and strontium.

Lee De Forest, 1873-1961, (U.S.) inventor, pioneer in development of wireless telegraphy, sound pictures, television.

Max Delbruck, 1907-1981, (U.S.) pioneer in modern molecular genetics.

Rudolf Diesel, 1858-1913, (G.) mechanical engineer, patented Diesel engine.

Thomas Dooley, 1927-1961, (U.S.) "jungle doctor," noted for efforts to supply medical aid to underdeveloped countries.

Christian Doppler, 1803-1853, (Aus.) physicist, demonstrated Doppler effect (change in energy wavelengths caused by motion).

Thomas A. Edison, 1847-1931, (U.S.) inventor, held over 1,000 patents, including incandescent electric lamp, phonograph.

Paul Ehrlich, 1854-1915, (G.) bacteriologist, pioneer in modern immunology and bacteriology.

Albert Einstein, 1879-1955, (Ger.-U.S.) theoretical physicist, known for formulation of relativity theory.

John F. Enders, 1897-1985, (U.S.) virologist who helped discover vaccines against polio, measles, and mumps.

Leonhard Euler, 1707-1783, (Swiss), mathematician, physicist, authored first calculus book.

Gabriel Fahrenheit, 1686-1736, (G.) physicist, introduced Fahrenheit scale for thermometers.

Michael Faraday, 1791-1867, (Br.) chemist, physicist, known for work in field of electricity.

Pierre de Fermat, 1601-1665, (F.) mathematician, discovered analytic geometry, founded modern theory of numbers and calculus of probabilities.

Enrico Fermi, 1901-1954, (It.) physicist, one of chief architects of the nuclear age.

Galileo Ferraris, 1847-1897, (It.) physicist, electrical engineer, discovered principle of rotary magnetic field.

Richard Feynman, 1918-1988, (U.S.) a leading theoretical physicist of the postwar generation.

Camille Flammarion, 1842-1925, (F.) astronomer, popularized study of astronomy.

Alexander Fleming, 1881-1955, (Scot.) bacteriologist, discovered penicillin.

Jean B.J. Fourier, 1768-1830, (F.) mathematician, discovered theorem governing periodic oscillation.

James Franck, 1882-1964, (G.) physicist, proved value of quantum theory.

Sigmund Freud, 1856-1939, (Aus.) psychiatrist, founder of psychoanalysis.

Galileo Galilei, 1564-1642, (It.) astronomer, physicist, a founder of the experimental method.

Luigi Galvani, 1737-1798, (It.) physician, physicist, known as founder of galvanism.

Carl Friedrich Gauss, 1777-1855, (G.) mathematician, astronomer, physicist, made important contributions to almost every field of physical science, founded a number of new fields.

Joseph Gay-Lussac, 1778-1850, (F.) chemist, physicist, investigated behavior of gases, discovered law of combining volumes.

Josiah W. Gibbs, 1839-1903, (U.S.) theoretical physicist, chemist, founded chemical thermodynamics.

Robert H. Goddard, 1882-1945 (U.S.) physicist, father of modern rocketry.

George W. Goethals, 1858-1928, (U.S.) army engineer, built the Panama Canal.

William C. Gorgas, 1854-1920, (U.S.) sanitarian, U.S. army surgeon-general, his work to prevent yellow fever, malaria helped insure construction of Panama Canal.

Ernest Haeckel, 1834-1919, (G.) zoologist, evolutionist, a strong proponent of Darwin.

Otto Hahn, 1879-1968, (G.) chemist, worked on atomic fission.

J.B.S. Haldane, 1892-1964, (Sc.) scientist, known for work as geneticist and application of mathematics to science.

James Hall, 1761-1832, (Br.) geologist, chemist, founded experimental geology, geochemistry.

Edmund Halley, 1656-1742, (Br.) astronomer, calculated the orbits of many planets.

William Harvey, 1578-1657, (Br.) physician, anatomist, discovered circulation of the blood.

Hermann v. Helmholtz, 1821-1894, (G.) physicist, anatomist, physiologist, made fundamental contributions to physiology, optics, electrodynamics, mathematics, meteorology.

William Herschel, 1738-1822, (Br.) astronomer, discovered Uranus.

Heinrich Hertz, 1857-1894, (G.) physicist, his discoveries led to wireless telegraphy.

David Hilbert, 1862-1943, (G.) mathematician, formulated first satisfactory set of axioms for modern Euclidean geometry.

Edwin P. Hubble, 1889-1953, (U.S.) astronomer, produced first observational evidence of expanding universe.

Alexander v. Humboldt, 1769-1859, (G.) explorer, naturalist, propagator of earth sciences, originated ecology, geophysics.

Julian Huxley, 1887-1975, (Br.) biologist, a gifted exponent and philosopher of science.

Edward Jenner, 1749-1823, (Br.) physician, discovered vaccination.

William Jenner, 1815-1898, (Br.) physician, pathological anatomist.

Frederic Joliot-Curie, 1900-1958, (F.) physicist, with his wife continued work of Curies on radioactivity.

Irene Joliot-Curie, 1897-1956, (F.) physicist, continued work of Curies in radioactivity.

James P. Joule, 1818-1889, (Br.) physicist, determined relationship between heat and mechanical energy (conservation of energy).

Carl Jung, 1875-1961, (Sw.) psychiatrist, founder of analytical psychology.

Wm. Thomson Kelvin, 1824-1907, (Br.) mathematician, physicist, known for work on heat and electricity.

Sister Elizabeth Kenny, 1886-1952, (Austral.) nurse, developed method of treatment for polio.

Johannes Kepler, 1571-1630, (G.) astronomer, discovered important laws of planetary motion.

Joseph Lagrange, 1736-1813, (F.) geometer, astronomer, worked in all fields of analysis, and number theory, and analytical and celestial mechanics.

Jean B. Lamarck, 1744-1829, (F.) naturalist, forerunner of Darwin in evolutionary theory.

Edwin Land, 1910-1991, (U.S.) invented Polaroid camera.

Irving Langmuir, 1881-1957, (U.S.) physical chemist, his studies of molecular films on solid and liquid surfaces opened new fields in colloid research and biochemistry.

Pierre S. Laplace, 1749-1827, (F.) astronomer, physicist, put forth nebular hypothesis of origin of solar system.

Antoine Lavoisier, 1743-1794, (F.) chemist, founder of modern chemistry.

Ernest O. Lawrence, 1901-1958, (U.S.) physicist, invented the cyclotron.

Louis Leakey, 1903-1972, (Br.) anthropologist, discovered important fossils, remains of early hominids.

Anton van Leeuwenhoek, 1632-1723, (Du.) microscopist, father of microbiology.

Gottfried Wilhelm Leibniz, 1646-1716, (G.) mathematician, developed theories of differential and integral calculus.

Justus von Liebig, 1803-1873, (G.) chemist, established quantitative organic chemical analysis.

Joseph Lister, 1827-1912, (Br.) pioneer of antiseptic surgery.

Percival Lowell, 1855-1916, (U.S.) astronomer, predicted the existence of Pluto.

Louis (1864-1984) and **Auguste Lumière,** 1862-1954, (Fr.) invented cinematograph, first mechanism to project moving pictures on screen.

Guglielmo Marconi, 1874-1937, (It.) physicist, known for his development of wireless telegraphy.

James Clerk Maxwell, 1831-1879, (Sc.) physicist, known especially for his work in electricity and magnetism.

Maria Goeppert Mayer, 1906-1972, (G.-U.S.) physicist, independently developed theory of structure of atomic nuclei.

Lise Meitner, 1878-1968, (Aus.) physicist whose work contributed to the development of the atomic bomb.

Gregor J. Mendel, 1822-1884, (Aus.) botanist, known for his experimental work on heredity.

Franz Mesmer, 1734-1815, (G.) physician, developed theory of animal magnetism.

Albert A. Michelson, 1852-1931, (U.S.) physicist, established speed of light as a fundamental constant.

Robert A. Millikan, 1868-1953, (U.S.) physicist, noted for study of elementary electronic charge and photoelectric effect.

Thomas Hunt Morgan, 1866-1945, (U.S.) geneticist, embryologist, established chromosome theory of heredity.

Isaac Newton, 1642-1727, (Br.) natural philosopher, mathematician, discovered law of gravitation, laws of motion.

Robert N. Noyce, 1927-1989, (U.S.) inventor of the microchip, which revolutionized the electronics industry.

J. Robert Oppenheimer, 1904-1967, (U.S.) physicist, director of Los Alamos during development of the atomic bomb.

Wilhelm Ostwald, 1853-1932, (G.) physical chemist, philosopher, chief founder of physical chemistry.

Robert Morris Page, 1903-1992, (U.S.) physicist, research director of U.S. Naval Research Laboratory, a leading figure in development of radar technology.

Louis Pasteur, 1822-1895, (F.) chemist, originated process of pasteurization.

Max Planck, 1858-1947, (G.) physicist, originated and developed quantum theory.

Henri Poincaré, 1854-1912, (F.) mathematician, physicist, influenced cosmology, relativity, and topology.

Joseph Priestley, 1733-1804, (Br.) chemist, one of the discoverers of oxygen.

Rabi, Isidor Isaac, 1899-1988 (U.S.) physicist, pioneered atom exploration.

Walter S. Reed, 1851-1902, (U.S.) army pathologist, bacteriologist, proved mosquitos transmit yellow fever.

Bernhard Riemann, 1826-1866, (G.) mathematician, contributed to development of calculus, complex variable theory, and mathematical physics.

Wilhelm Roentgen, 1845-1923, (G.) physicist, discovered X-rays.

Bertrand Russell, 1872-1970, (Br.) logician, philosopher, one of the founders of modern logic, wrote *Principia Mathematica.*

Ernest Rutherford, 1871-1937, (Br.) physicist, discovered the atomic nucleus.

Albert B. Sabin, 1906-1993, (Rus.-U.S.) In 1954, developed oral polio vaccine, which was licensed in 1961.

Giovanni Schiaparelli, 1835-1910, (It.) astronomer, hypothesized canals on the surface of Mars.

Angelo Secchi, 1818-1878, (It.) astronomer, pioneer in classifying stars by their spectra.

Harlow Shapley, 1885-1972, (U.S.) astronomer, noted for his studies of the galaxy.

Charles P. Steinmetz, 1865-1923, (G.-U.S.) electrical engineer, developed basic ideas on alternating current systems.

Leo Szilard, 1898-1964, (Hung.-U.S.) physicist, helped create first sustained nuclear reaction.

Nikola Tesla, 1856-1943, (Croatia-U.S.) electrical engineer, contributed to most developments in electronics.

Rudolf Virchow, 1821-1902, (G.) pathologist, a founder of cellular pathology.

Alessandro Volta, 1745-1827, (It.) physicist, pioneer in electricity.

Werner von Braun, 1912-1977 (G-U.S.) pioneered development of rockets for warfare and space exploration.

Alfred Russell Wallace, 1823-1913, (Br.) naturalist, proposed concept of evolution similar to Darwin.

August v. Wasserman, 1866-1925, (G.) bacteriologist, discovered reaction used as test for syphilis.

James E. Watt, 1736-1819, (Sc.) mechanical engineer, inventor, invented modern steam condensing engine.

Alfred L. Wegener, 1880-1930, (G.) meteorologist, geophysicist, postulated theory of continental drift.

Norbert Wiener, 1894-1964, (U.S.) mathematician, founder of the science of cybernetics.

Sewall Wright, 1889-1988 (U.S.) evolutionary theorist.

Ferdinand v. Zeppelin, 1838-1917 (G.) soldier, aeronaut, airship designer.

Noted Business Leaders, Industrialists, and Philanthropists of the Past

Elizabeth Arden (F.N. Graham), 1884-1966, (U.S.) Canadian-born founder of cosmetics empire.

Philip D. Armour, 1832-1901, (U.S.) industrialist, streamlined meat packing.

John Jacob Astor, 1763-1848, (U.S.) German-born fur trader, banker, real estate magnate; at death, richest in U.S.

Francis W. Ayer, 1848-1923, (U.S.) ad industry pioneer.

August Belmont, 1816-1890, (U.S.) German-born financier.

James B. (Diamond Jim) Brady, 1856-1917, (U.S.) financier, philanthropist, legendary bon vivant.

Adolphus Busch, 1839-1913, (U.S.) German-born businessman, established brewery empire.

Asa Candler, 1851-1929, (U.S.) founded Coca-Cola Co.

Andrew Carnegie, 1835-1919, (U.S.) Scots-born industrialist, founded U.S. Steel; financed over 2,800 libraries.

Tom Carvel, 1908-1989, (Gr.-U.S.) founded ice cream chain.

William Colgate, 1783-1857, (U.S.) British-born businessman, philanthropist; founded soap-making empire.

Jay Cooke, 1821-1905, (U.S.) financier, sold $1 billion in Union bonds during Civil War.

Peter Cooper, 1791-1883, (U.S.) industrialist, inventor, philanthropist.

Ezra Cornell, 1807-1874, (U.S.) businessman, philanthropist; headed Western Union, established univ.

Erastus Corning, 1794-1872, (U.S.) financier, headed N.Y. Central.

Charles Crocker, 1822-1888, (U.S.) railroad builder, financier.

Samuel Cunard, 1787-1865, (Can.) pioneered trans-Atlantic steam navigation.

Marcus Daly, 1841-1900, (U.S.) Irish-born copper magnate.

George T. Delacorte, 1893-1991, (U.S.) publisher; Central Park donations included Alice in Wonderland statue.

Walt Disney, 1901-1966, (U.S.) pioneer in cinema animation, built entertainment empire.
Herbert H. Dow, 1866-1930, (U.S.) Canadian-born founder of chemical co.
James Duke, 1856-1925, (U.S.) founded American Tobacco, Duke Univ.
Eleuthere I. du Pont, 1771-1834, (U.S.) French-born gunpowder manufacturer; founded one of world's largest business empires.
Thomas C. Durant, 1820-1885, (U.S.) railroad official, financier.
William C. Durant, 1861-1947, (U.S.) industrialist, formed General Motors.
George Eastman, 1854-1932, (U.S.) inventor, manufacturer of photographic equipment.
Marshall Field, 1834-1906, (U.S.) merchant, founded Chicago's largest department store.
Harvey Firestone, 1868-1938, (U.S.) industrialist, founded tire co.
Henry M. Flagler, 1830-1913, (U.S.) financier, helped form Standard Oil; developed Florida as resort state.
Malcolm Forbes, 1919-1990, (U.S.) *Forbes* magazine publisher.
Henry Ford, 1863-1947, (U.S.) auto maker, developed first popular low-priced car.
Henry Ford 2d, 1917-1987, (U.S.) headed auto company founded by grandfather.
Henry C. Frick, 1849-1919, (U.S.) industrialist, helped organize U.S. Steel.
Jakob Fugger (Jakob the Rich), 1459-1525, (G.) headed leading banking house, trading concern, in 16th-century Europe.
Alfred C. Fuller, 1885-1973, (U.S.) Canadian-born businessman, founded brush co.
Elbert H. Gary, 1846-1927, (U.S.) U.S. Steel head, 1903-27.
Jean Paul Getty, 1892-1976, (U.S.) founded oil empire.
Amadeo P. Giannini, 1870-1949, (U.S.) founded Bank of America.
Stephen Girard, 1750-1831, (U.S.) French-born financier, philanthropist; richest man in U.S. at his death.
Jay Gould, 1836-1892, (U.S.) railroad magnate, financier, speculator.
Hetty Green, 1834-1916, (U.S.) financier, the "witch of Wall St."; richest woman in U.S. in her day.
William Gregg, 1800-1867, (U.S.) launched textile industry in the South.
Meyer Guggenheim, 1828-1905, (U.S.) Swiss-born merchant, philanthropist; built merchandising, mining empires.
Armand Hammer, 1898-1990, (U.S.) headed Occidental Petroleum; promoted U.S.-Soviet ties.
Edward H. Harriman, 1848-1909, (U.S.) railroad financier, administrator; headed Union Pacific.
William Randolph Hearst, 1863-1951, (U.S.) a dominant figure in American journalism; built vast publishing empire.
Henry J. Heinz, 1844-1919, (U.S.) founded food empire.
James J. Hill, 1838-1916, (U.S.) Canadian-born railroad magnate, financier; founded Great Northern Railway.
Conrad N. Hilton, 1888-1979, (U.S.) intl. hotel chain founder.
Howard Hughes, 1905-1976, (U.S.) industrialist, financier, movie maker.
H.L. Hunt, 1889-1974, (U.S.) oil magnate.
Collis P. Huntington, 1821-1900, (U.S.) railroad magnate.
Henry E. Huntington, 1850-1927, (U.S.) railroad builder, philanthropist.
Walter L. Jacobs, 1898-1985, (U.S.) founder of the first rental car agency, which later became Hertz.
Howard Johnson, 1896-1972, (U.S.) founded restaurants.
Henry J. Kaiser, 1882-1967, (U.S.) industrialist, built empire in steel, aluminum.
Minor C. Keith, 1848-1929, (U.S.) railroad magnate; founded United Fruit Co.
Will K. Kellogg, 1860-1951, (U.S.) businessman, philanthropist, founded breakfast food co.
Richard King, 1825-1885, (U.S.) cattleman, founded half-million acre King Ranch in Texas.
William S. Knudsen, 1879-1948, (U.S.) Danish-born auto industry executive.
Samuel H. Kress, 1863-1955, (U.S.) businessman, art collector, philanthropist; founded "dime store" chain.
Ray A. Kroc, 1902-1984, (U.S.) builder of McDonald's fast food empire; owner, San Diego Padres baseball team.
Alfred Krupp, 1812-1887, (G.) armaments magnate.
Albert Lasker, 1880-1952, (U.S.) businessman, philanthropist.
Thomas Lipton, 1850-1931, (Scot.) merchant, built tea empire.
James McGill, 1744-1813, (Can.) Scots-born fur trader, founded univ.
Andrew W. Mellon, 1855-1937, (U.S.) financier, industrialist; benefactor of National Gallery of Art.
Charles E. Merrill, 1885-1956, (U.S.) financier, developed firm of Merrill Lynch.
John Pierpont Morgan, 1837-1913, (U.S.) most powerful figure in finance and industry at the turn-of-the-century.
Malcolm Muir, 1885-1979, (U.S.) created *Business Week* magazine; headed *Newsweek*, 1937-61.
Samuel Newhouse, 1895-1979, (U.S.) publishing and broadcasting magnate, built communications empire.
Aristotle Onassis, 1900-1975, (Gr.) shipping magnate.
William S. Paley, 1901-1989, (U.S.) built CBS communications empire.
George Peabody, 1795-1869, (U.S.) merchant, financier, philanthropist.
James C. Penney, 1875-1971, (U.S.) businessman, developed department store chain.
William C. Procter, 1862-1934, (U.S.) headed soap co.
John D. Rockefeller, 1839-1937, (U.S.) industrialist, established Standard Oil; became world's wealthiest person.
John D. Rockefeller Jr., 1874-1960, (U.S.) philanthropist, established foundation; provided land for United Nations.
Meyer A. Rothschild, 1743-1812, (G.) founded international banking house.
Thomas Fortune Ryan, 1851-1928, (U.S.) financier, dominated N.Y. City public transport; a founder of Amer. Tobacco.
Russell Sage, 1816-1906, (U.S.) financier.
David Sarnoff, 1891-1971, (U.S.) broadcasting pioneer, established first radio network, NBC.
Richard W. Sears, 1863-1914, (U.S.) founded mail-order co.
(Ernst) Werner von Siemens, 1816-1892, (G.) industrialist, inventor.
Alfred P. Sloan, 1875-1966, (U.S.) industrialist, philanthropist; headed General Motors.
A. Leland Stanford, 1824-1893, (U.S.) railroad official, philanthropist; founded univ.
Nathan Strauss, 1848-1931, (U.S.) German-born merchant, philanthropist; headed Macy's.
Levi Strauss, c.1829-1902, (U.S.) pants manufacturer.
Clement Studebaker, 1831-1901, (U.S.) wagon, carriage manufacturer.
Gustavus Swift, 1839-1903, (U.S.) pioneer meat-packer; promoted refrigerated railroad cars.
Gerard Swope, 1872-1957, (U.S.) industrialist, economist; headed General Electric.
James Walter Thompson, 1847-1928, (U.S.) ad executive.
Theodore N. Vail, 1845-1920, (U.S.) organized Bell Telephone system, headed ATT.
Cornelius Vanderbilt, 1794-1877, (U.S.) financier, established steamship, railroad empires.
Henry Villard, 1835-1900, (U.S.) German-born railroad executive, financier.
Charles R. Walgreen, 1873-1939, (U.S.) founded drugstore chain.
DeWitt Wallace, 1890-1981, (U.S.) and **Lila Wallace,** 1890-1984, (U.S.) co-founders of *Reader's Digest* magazine, philanthropists.
Sam Walton, 1918-1992, (U.S.) founder of Wal-Mart stores.
John Wanamaker, 1838-1922, (U.S.) pioneered department-store merchandising.
Aaron Montgomery Ward, 1843-1913, (U.S.) established first mail-order firm.
Thomas J. Watson, 1874-1956, (U.S.) headed IBM, 1924-49.
John Hay Whitney, 1905-1982, (U.S.) publisher, sportsman, philanthropist.
Charles E. Wilson, 1890-1961, (U.S.) auto industry executive; public official.
Frank W. Woolworth, 1852-1919, (U.S.) created 5 & 10 chain.
William Wrigley Jr., 1861-1932, (U.S.) founded chewing gum company.

Composers of the Western World

Carl Philipp Emanuel Bach, 1714-1788, (G.) Prussian and Wurtembergian Sonatas.
Johann Christian Bach, 1735-1782, (G.) Concertos; sonatas.
Johann Sebastian Bach, 1685-1750, (G.) St. Matthew Passion, The Well-Tempered Clavichord.
Samuel Barber, 1910-1981, (U.S.) Adagio for Strings, Vanessa.
Bela Bartok, 1881-1945, (Hung.) Concerto for Orchestra, The Miraculous Mandarin.
Ludwig Van Beethoven, 1770-1827, (G.) Concertos (Emperor); sonatas (Moonlight, Pastorale, Pathetique); symphonies (Eroica).
Vincenzo Bellini, 1801-1835, (It.) La Sonnambula, Norma, I Puritani.
Alban Berg, 1885-1935, (Aus.) Wozzeck, Lulu.

Hector Berlioz, 1803-1869, (F.) Damnation of Faust, Symphonie Fantastique, Requiem.
Leonard Bernstein, 1918-1990, (U.S.) Jeremiah Symphony, Chichester Psalms, Mass.
Georges Bizet, 1838-1875, (F.) Carmen, Pearl Fishers.
Ernest Bloch, 1880-1959, (Swiss-U.S.) Schelomo, Voice in the Wilderness, Sacred Service.
Luigi Boccherini, 1743-1805, (It.) Cello Concerto in B Flat, Symphony in C.
Alexander Borodin, 1833-1887, (R.) Prince Igor, In the Steppes of Central Asia.
Johannes Brahms, 1833-1897, (G.) Liebeslieder Waltzes, Rhapsody in E Flat Major, Opus 119 for Piano, Academic Festival Overture; symphonies; quartets.
Benjamin Britten, 1913-1976, (Br.) Peter Grimes, Turn of the Screw, Ceremony of Carols, War Requiem.
Anton Bruckner, 1824-1896, (Aus.) Symphonies (Romantic), Intermezzo for String Quintet.
Ferruccio Busoni, 1866-1924, (It.) Doctor Faust, Comedy Overture.
Dietrich Buxtehude, 1637-1707, (D.) Cantatas, trio sonatas.
William Byrd, 1543-1623, (Br.) Masses, sacred songs.
(Alexis-) Emmanuel Chabrier, 1841-1894, (Fr.) Le Roi Malgre Lui, Espana.
Gustave Charpentier, 1860-1956, (F.) Louise.
Frederic Chopin, 1810-1849, (P.) Polonaises, mazurkas, waltzes, etudes, nocturnes. Polonaise No. 6 in A Flat Major (Heroic); sonatas.
Aaron Copland, 1900-1990, (U.S.) Appalachian Spring.
(Achille-) Claude Debussy, 1862-1918, (F.) Pelleas et Melisande, La Mer, Prelude to the Afternoon of a Faun.
C.P. Leo Delibes, 1836-1891, (F.) Lakme, Coppelia, Sylvia.
Norman Dello Joio, b. 1913, (U.S.), Triumph of St. Joan, Psalm of David.
Gaetano Donizetti, 1797-1848, (It.) Elixir of Love, Lucia Di Lammermoor, Daughter of the Regiment.
Paul Dukas, 1865-1935, (Fr.) Sorcerer's Apprentice.
Antonin Dvorak, 1841-1904, (C.) Symphony in E Minor (From the New World).
Edward Elgar, 1857-1934, (Br.) Pomp and Circumstance.
Manuel de Falla, 1876-1946, (Sp.) La Vide Breve, El Amor Brujo.
Gabriel Faure, 1845-1924, (Fr.) Requiem, Ballade.
Friedrich von Flotow, 1812-1883, (G.) Martha.
Cesar Franck, 1822-1890, (Belg.) D Minor Symphony.
George Gershwin, 1898-1937, (U.S.) Rhapsody in Blue, American in Paris, Porgy and Bess.
Umberto Giordano, 1867-1948, (It.) Andrea Chenier.
Alexander K. Glazunoff, 1865-1936, (R.) Symphonies, Stenka Razin.
Mikhail Glinka, 1804-1857, (R.) Ruslan and Ludmilla.
Christoph W. Gluck, 1714-1787, (G.) Alceste, Iphigenie en Tauride.
Charles Gounod, 1818-1893, (F.) Faust, Romeo and Juliet.
Edvard Grieg, 1843-1907, (Nor.) Peer Gynt Suite, Concerto in A Minor.
George Frederick Handel, 1685-1759, (G., Br.) Messiah, Xerxes, Berenice.
Howard Hanson, 1896-1981, (U.S.) Symphonies No. 1 (Nordic) and 2 (Romantic).
Roy Harris, 1898-1979, (U.S.) Symphonies, Amer. Portraits.
Joseph Haydn, 1732-1809, (Aus.) Symphonies (Clock); oratorios; chamber music.
Paul Hindemith, 1895-1963, (U.S.) Mathis Der Maler.
Gustav Holst, 1874-1934, (Br.) The Planets.
Arthur Honegger, 1892-1955, (Swiss) Judith, Le Roi David, Pacific 231.
Alan Hovhaness, b. 1911, (U.S.) Symphonies, Magnificat.
Engelbert Humperdinck, 1854-1921, (G.) Hansel and Gretel.
Charles Ives, 1874-1954, (U.S.) Third Symphony.
Aram Khachaturian, 1903-1978, (Armen.) Gayane (ballet), symphonies.
Zoltan Kodaly, 1882-1967, (Hung.) Hary Janos, Psalmus Hungaricus.
Fritz Kreisler, 1875-1962, (Aus.) Caprice Viennois, Tambourin Chinois.
Rodolphe Kreutzer, 1766-1831, (F.) 40 etudes for violin.
Edouard V.A. Lalo, 1823-1892, (F.) Symphonie Espagnole.
Ruggiero Leoncavallo, 1857-1919, (It.) Pagliacci.
Franz Liszt, 1811-1886, (Hung.) 20 Hungarian rhapsodies; symphonic poems.
Edward MacDowell, 1861-1908, (U.S.) To a Wild Rose.
Gustav Mahler, 1860-1911, (Aus.) Lied von der Erde.
Pietro Mascagni, 1863-1945, (It.) Cavalleria Rusticana.
Jules Massenet, 1842-1912, (F.) Manon, Le Cid, Thais.
Felix Mendelssohn, 1809-1847, (G.) Midsummer Night's Dream, Songs Without Words.
Gian-Carlo Menotti, b. 1911, (It.-U.S.) The Medium, The Consul, Amahl and the Night Visitors.
Giacomo Meyerbeer, 1791-1864, (G.) Robert le Diable, Les Huguenots.
Claudio Monteverdi, 1567-1643, (It.) Opera; masses; madrigals.
Modest Moussorgsky, 1835-1881, (R.) Boris Godunov, Pictures at an Exhibition.
Wolfgang Amadeus Mozart, 1756-1791, (Aus.) Magic Flute, Marriage of Figaro; concertos; symphonies, etc.
Jacques Offenbach, 1819-1880, (F.) Tales of Hoffmann.
Carl Orff, 1895-1982, (G.) Carmina Burana.
Ignace Paderewski, 1860-1941, (P.) Minuet in G.
Niccolo Paganini, 1782-1840, (It.) Violinist, many bravura variations for violin.
Giovanni P. da Palestrina, c. 1525-1594, (It.) Masses; madrigals.
Amilcare Ponchielli, 1834-1886, (It.) La Gioconda.
Francis Poulenc, 1899-1963, (F.) Dialogues des Carmelites.
Serge Prokofiev, 1891-1953, (R.) Love for Three Oranges, Lt. Kije, Peter and the Wolf.
Giacomo Puccini, 1858-1924, (It.) La Boheme, Manon Lescaut, Tosca, Madame Butterfly.
Sergei Rachmaninov, 1873-1943, (R.) 24 preludes, 4 concerti, 4 symphonies. Prelude in C Sharp Minor.
Maurice Ravel, 1875-1937, (Fr.) Bolero, Daphnis et Chloe, Rapsodie Espagnole.
Nikolai Rimsky-Korsakov, 1844-1908, (R.) Golden Cockerel, Capriccio Espagnol, Scheherazade, Russian Easter Overture.
Gioacchino Rossini, 1792-1868, (It.) Barber of Seville, Semiramide, William Tell.
Chas. Camille Saint-Saens, 1835-1921, (F.) Samson and Delilah, Danse Macabre.
Alessandro Scarlatti, 1660-1725, (It.) Cantatas; concertos.
Domenico Scarlatti, 1685-1757, (It.) Harpsichord sonatas.
Arnold Schoenberg, 1874-1951, (Aus.) Pelleas and Melisande, Transfigured Night, De Profundis.
Franz Schubert, 1797-1828, (A.) Lieder; symphonies (Unfinished); overtures (Rosamunde).
William Schuman, b. 1910, (U.S.) Credendum, New England Triptych.
Robert Schumann, 1810-1856, (G.) Symphonies, songs.
Aleksandr Scriabin, 1872-1915, (R.) Prometheus.
Dimitri Shostakovich, 1906-1975, (R.) Symphonies, Lady Macbeth of Mzensk, The Nose.
Jean Sibelius, 1865-1957, (Finn.) Finlandia, Karelia.
Bedrich Smetana, 1824-1884, (Cz.). The Bartered Bride.
Karlheinz Stockhausen, b. 1928, (G.) Kontrapunkte, Kontakte.
Richard Strauss, 1864-1949, (G.) Salome, Elektra, Der Rosenkavalier, Thus Spake Zarathustra.
Igor F. Stravinsky, 1882-1971, (R.-U.S.) Oedipus Rex, Le Sacre du Printemps, Petrushka.
Peter I. Tchaikovsky, 1840-1893, (R.) Nutcracker Suite, Swan Lake, Eugene Onegin.
Ambroise Thomas, 1811-1896, (F.) Mignon.
Virgil Thomson, 1896-1989, (U.S.) Opera, ballet; Four Saints in Three Acts.
Ralph Vaughan Williams, 1872-1958, (Br.) Job, London Symphony, Symphony No. 7 (Antartica).
Giuseppe Verdi, 1813-1901, (It.) Aida, Rigoletto, Don Carlo, Il Trovatore, La Traviata, Falstaff, Macbeth.
Heitor Villa-Lobos, 1887-1959, (Brazil) Choros.
Antonio Vivaldi, 1678-1741, (It.) Concerti, The Four Seasons.
Richard Wagner, 1813-1883, (G.) Rienzi, Tannhauser, Lohengrin, Tristan und Isolde.
Carl Maria von Weber, 1786-1826, (G.) Der Freischutz.

Composers of Operettas, Musicals, and Popular Music

Richard Adler, b. 1921, (U.S.) *Pajama Game; Damn Yankees.*
Milton Ager, 1893-1979, (U.S.) I Wonder What's Become of Sally; Hard Hearted Hannah; Ain't She Sweet?
Leroy Anderson, 1908-1975, (U.S.) Syncopated Clock.
Paul Anka, b. 1941, (Can.) My Way; She's a Lady; Tonight Show theme.
Harold Arlen, 1905-1986, (U.S.) Stormy Weather; Over the Rainbow; Blues in the Night; That Old Black Magic.
Burt Bacharach, b. 1928, (U.S.) Raindrops Keep Fallin' on My Head; Walk on By; What the World Needs Now is Love.
Ernest Ball, 1878-1927, (U.S.) Mother Machree; When Irish Eyes Are Smiling.
Irving Berlin, 1888-1989 (U.S.) *This is the Army; Annie Get Your Gun; Call Me Madam;* God Bless America; White Christmas.
Leonard Bernstein, 1918-1990, (U.S.) *On the Town; Wonderful Town; Candide; West Side Story.*

Eubie Blake, 1883-1983, (U.S.) *Shuffle Along;* I'm Just Wild about Harry.
Jerry Bock, b. 1928, (U.S.) *Mr. Wonderful; Fiorello; Fiddler on the Roof; The Rothschilds.*
Carrie Jacobs Bond, 1862-1946, (U.S.) I Love You Truly.
Nacio Herb Brown, 1896-1964, (U.S.) Singing in the Rain; You Were Meant for Me; All I Do Is Dream of You.
Hoagy Carmichael, 1899-1981, (U.S.) Stardust; Georgia on My Mind; Old Buttermilk Sky.
George M. Cohan, 1878-1942, (U.S.) Give My Regards to Broadway; You're A Grand Old Flag; Over There.
Cy Coleman, b. 1929, (U.S.) *Sweet Charity;* Witchcraft.
Noel Coward, 1899-1973 (Br.) *Bitter Sweet;* Mad Dogs and Englishmen; Mad About the Boy.
Neil Diamond, b. 1941, (U.S.) I'm a Believer; Sweet Caroline.
Walter Donaldson, 1893-1947, (U.S.) My Buddy; Carolina in the Morning; You're Driving Me Crazy; Makin' Whoopee.
Vernon Duke, 1903-1969, (U.S.) April in Paris.
Bob Dylan, b. 1941, (U.S.) Blowin' in the Wind.
Gus Edwards, 1879-1945, (U.S.) School Days; By the Light of the Silvery Moon; In My Merry Oldsmobile.
Sherman Edwards, 1919-1981, (U.S.) See You in September; Wonderful! Wonderful!
Duke Ellington, 1899-1974, (U.S.) Sophisticated Lady; Satin Doll; It Don't Mean a Thing; Solitude.
Sammy Fain, 1902-1989, (U.S.) I'll Be Seeing You; Love Is a Many-Splendored Thing.
Fred Fisher, 1875-1942, (U.S.) Peg O' My Heart; Chicago.
Stephen Collins Foster, 1826-1864, (U.S.) My Old Kentucky Home; Old Folks At Home.
Rudolf Friml, 1879-1972, (naturalized U.S.) *The Firefly; Rose Marie; Vagabond King; Bird of Paradise.*
John Gay, 1685-1732, (Br.) *The Beggar's Opera.*
George Gershwin, 1898-1937, (U.S.) Someone to Watch Over Me; I've Got a Crush on You; Embraceable You.
Ferde Grofe, 1892-1972, (U.S.) Grand Canyon Suite.
Marvin Hamlisch, b. 1944, (U.S.) The Way We Were, Nobody Does It Better, *A Chorus Line.*
W. C. Handy, 1873-1958, (U.S.) St. Louis Blues.
Ray Henderson, 1896-1970, (U.S.) *George White's Scandals;* That Old Gang of Mine; Five Foot Two, Eyes of Blue.
Victor Herbert, 1859-1924, (Ir.-U.S.) *Mlle. Modiste; Babes in Toyland; The Red Mill; Naughty Marietta; Sweethearts.*
Jerry Herman, b. 1932, (U.S.) *Hello Dolly; Mame.*
Brian Holland, b. 1941, **Lamont Dozier,** b. 1941, **Eddie Holland,** b. 1939, (all U.S.) Heat Wave; Stop! In the Name of Love; Baby, I Need Your Loving.
Scott Joplin, 1868-1917, (U.S.) *Treemonisha.*
John Kander, b. 1927, (U.S.) *Cabaret; Chicago; Funny Lady.*
Jerome Kern, 1885-1945, (U.S.) *Sally; Sunny; Show Boat.*
Carole King, b. 1942, (U.S.) Will You Love Me Tomorrow?; Natural Woman; One Fine Day; Up on the Roof.
Burton Lane, b. 1912, (U.S.) *Finian's Rainbow.*
Franz Lehar, 1870-1948, (Hung.) *Merry Widow.*
Jerry Leiber, & Mike Stoller, both b. 1933, (both U.S.) Hound Dog; Searchin'; Yakety Yak; Love Me Tender.
Mitch Leigh, b. 1928, (U.S.) *Man of La Mancha.*
John Lennon, 1940-1980, & **Paul McCartney,** b. 1942, (both Br.) I Want to Hold Your Hand; She Loves You; Hard Day's Night; Can't Buy Me Love; And I Love Her.
Frank Loesser, 1910-1969, (U.S.) *Guys and Dolls; Where's Charley?; The Most Happy Fella; How to Succeed . . .*
Frederick Loewe, 1901-1988, (Aust.-U.S.) *The Day Before Spring; Brigadoon; Paint Your Wagon; My Fair Lady; Camelot.*
Henry Mancini, b. 1924, (U.S.) Moon River; Days of Wine and Roses; Pink Panther Theme.
Barry Mann, b. 1939, & **Cynthia Weil,** b. 1937, (both U.S.) You've Lost That Loving Feeling, Saturday Night at the Movies.
Jimmy McHugh, 1894-1969 (U.S.) Don't Blame Me; I'm in the Mood for Love; I Feel a Song Coming On.
Alan Menken, b. 1950, (U.S.) *Little Shop of Horrors.*
Joseph Meyer, 1894-1987, (U.S.) If You Knew Susie; California, Here I Come; Crazy Rhythm.
Chauncey Olcott, 1860-1932, (U.S.) Mother Machree.
Jerome "Doc" Pomus, 1925-1991, (U.S.) Save the Last Dance for Me, A Teenager in Love.
Cole Porter, 1893-1964, (U.S.) *Anything Goes; Kiss Me Kate; Can Can; Silk Stockings.*
Smokey Robinson, b. 1940, (U.S.) Shop Around; My Guy; My Girl; Get Ready.
Richard Rodgers, 1902-1979, (U.S.) *Connecticut Yankee; Oklahoma!; Carousel; South Pacific; The King and I; The Sound of Music.*
Sigmund Romberg, 1887-1951, (Hung.) *Maytime; The Student Prince; Desert Song; Blossom Time.*
Harold Rome, b. 1908, (U.S.) *Pins and Needles; Call Me Mister; Wish You Were Here; Fanny; Destry Rides Again.*
Vincent Rose, b. 1880-1944, (U.S.) Avalon; Whispering; Blueberry Hill.
Harry Ruby, 1895-1974, (U.S.) Three Little Words; Who's Sorry Now?
Arthur Schwartz, 1900-1984, (U.S.) *The Band Wagon;* Dancing in the Dark; By Myself; That's Entertainment.
Neil Sedaka, b. 1939, (U.S.) Breaking Up Is Hard to Do.
Paul Simon, b. 1942, (U.S.) Sounds of Silence; I Am a Rock; Mrs. Robinson; Bridge Over Troubled Waters.
Stephen Sondheim, b. 1930, (U.S.) *A Little Night Music; Company; Sweeney Todd; Sunday in the Park with George.*
John Philip Sousa. 1854-1932, (U.S.) *El Capitan;* Stars and Stripes Forever.
Oskar Straus, 1870-1954, (Aus.) *Chocolate Soldier.*
Johann Strauss, 1825-1899, (Aus.) *Gypsy Baron; Die Fledermaus;* waltzes: Blue Danube, Artist's Life.
Charles Strouse, b. 1928, (U.S.) *Bye Bye, Birdie; Annie.*
Jule Styne, b. 1905, (b. Br.-U.S.) *Gentlemen Prefer Blondes; Bells Are Ringing; Gypsy; Funny Girl.*
Arthur S. Sullivan, 1842-1900, (Br.) *H.M.S. Pinafore, Pirates of Penzance; The Mikado.*
Deems Taylor, 1885-1966, (U.S.) *Peter Ibbetson.*
Egbert van Alstyne, 1882-1951, (U.S.) In the Shade of the Old Apple Tree; Memories; Pretty Baby.
Jimmy Van Heusen, 1913-1990, (U.S.) Moonlight Becomes You; Swinging on a Star; All the Way; Love and Marriage.
Albert von Tilzer, 1878-1956, (U.S.) I'll Be With You in Apple Blossom Time; Take Me Out to the Ball Game.
Harry von Tilzer, 1872-1946, (U.S.) Only a Bird in a Gilded Cage; On a Sunday Afternoon.
Fats Waller, 1904-1943, (U.S.) Honeysuckle Rose; Ain't Misbehavin'.
Harry Warren, 1893-1981, (U.S.) You're My Everything; We're in the Money; I Only Have Eyes for You.
Jimmy Webb, b. 1946, (U.S.) Up, Up and Away; By the Time I Get to Phoenix; Didn't We?; Wichita Lineman.
Andrew Lloyd Webber, b. 1948, (Br.) *Jesus Christ Superstar, Evita, Cats, The Phantom of the Opera.*
Kurt Weill, 1900-1950, (G.-U.S.) *Threepenny Opera; Lady in the Dark; Knickerbocker Holiday; One Touch of Venus.*
Percy Wenrich, 1887-1952, (U.S.) When You Wore a Tulip; Moonlight Bay; Put On Your Old Gray Bonnet.
Richard A. Whiting, 1891-1938, (U.S.) Till We Meet Again; Sleepytime Gal; Beyond the Blue Horizon; My Ideal.
John Williams, b. 1932, (U.S.) *Jaws, E.T., Star Wars* series, *Raiders of the Lost Ark* series.
Meredith Willson, 1902-1984, (U.S.) *The Music Man.*
Stevie Wonder, b. 1950, (U.S.) You Are the Sunshine of My Life; Signed, Sealed, Delivered, I'm Yours.
Vincent Youmans, 1898-1946, (U.S.) *Two Little Girls in Blue; Wildflower; No, No, Nanette; Hit the Deck; Rainbow; Smiles.*

Lyricists

Howard Ashman, 1950-1991, (U.S.) *Little Shop of Horrors, The Little Mermaid.*
Johnny Burke, 1908-1984, (U.S.) What's New?; Misty; Imagination; Polka Dots and Moonbeams.
Sammy Cahn, 1913-1993, (U.S.) High Hopes; Love and Marriage; The Second Time Around; It's Magic.
Betty Comden, b. 1919 (U.S.) and **Adolph Green,** b. 1915 (U.S.) The Party's Over; Just in Time; New York, New York.
Hal David, b. 1921 (U.S.) What the World Needs Now Is Love; Close to You.
Buddy De Sylva, 1895-1950, (U.S.) When Day is Done; Look for the Silver Lining; April Showers.
Howard Dietz, 1896-1983, (U.S.) Dancing in the Dark; You and the Night and the Music; That's Entertainment.
Al Dubin, 1891-1945, (U.S.) Tiptoe Through the Tulips; Anniversary Waltz; Lullaby of Broadway.
Fred Ebb, b. 1936 (U.S.) *Cabaret, Zorba, Woman of the Year.*
Dorothy Fields, 1905-1974, (U.S.) On the Sunny Side of the Street; Don't Blame Me; The Way You Look Tonight.
Ira Gershwin, 1896-1983, (U.S.) The Man I Love; Fascinating Rhythm; S'Wonderful; Embraceable You.
William S. Gilbert, 1836-1911, (Br.) *The Mikado; H.M.S. Pinafore, Pirates of Penzance.*
Gerry Goffin, b. 1939, (U.S.) Will You Love Me Tomorrow, Take Good Care of My Baby, Up on the Roof, One Fine Day.
Mack Gordon, 1905-1959, (Pol.-U.S.) You'll Never Know; The More I See You; Chattanooga Choo-Choo.
Oscar Hammerstein II, 1895-1960, (U.S.) Ol' Man River; *Oklahoma; Carousel.*
E. Y. (Yip) Harburg, 1898-1981, (U.S.) Brother, Can You Spare a Dime; April in Paris; Over the Rainbow.
Lorenz Hart, 1895-1943, (U.S.) Isn't It Romantic; Blue Moon; Lover; Manhattan; My Funny Valentine; Mountain Greenery.

DuBose Heyward, 1885-1940, (U.S.) Summertime; A Woman Is A Sometime Thing.
Gus Kahn, 1886-1941, (U.S.) Memories; Ain't We Got Fun.
Alan J. Lerner, 1918-1986, (U.S.) *Brigadoon; My Fair Lady; Camelot; Gigi.; On a Clear Day You Can See Forever.*
Johnny Mercer, 1909-1976, (U.S.) Blues in the Night; Come Rain or Come Shine; Laura; That Old Black Magic.
Bob Merrill, b. 1921, (U.S.) People; Don't Rain on My Parade.
Jack Norworth, 1879-1959, (U.S.) Take Me Out to the Ball Game; Shine On Harvest Moon.
Mitchell Parish, 1901-1993, (U.S.) Stairway to the Stars; Stardust.
Andy Razaf, 1895-1973, (U.S.) Honeysuckle Rose, Ain't Misbehavin', S'posin'.
Leo Robin, 1900-1984, (U.S.) Thanks for the Memory; Hooray for Love; Diamonds are a Girl's Best Friend.
Paul Francis Webster, 1907-1984, (U.S.) I Got It Bad and That Ain't Good, Secret Love, The Shadow of Your Smile, Love Is a Many-Splendored Thing.
Jack Yellen, 1892-1991, (U.S.) Down by the O-Hi-O; Ain't She Sweet; Happy Days Are Here Again.

Noted Jazz Artists

Jazz has been called America's only completely unique contribution to Western culture. The following individuals have made major contributions in this field:

Julian "Cannonball" Adderley, 1928-1975: alto sax.
Louis "Satchmo" Armstrong, 1900-1971: trumpet, singer; originated the "scat" vocal.
Mildred Bailey, 1907-1951: blues singer.
Chet Baker, 1929-1988: trumpet.
Count Basie, 1904-1984: orchestra leader, piano.
Sidney Bechet, 1897-1959: early innovator, soprano sax.
Bix Beiderbecke, 1903-1931: cornet, piano, composer.
Bunny Berigan, 1909-1942: trumpet, singer.
Barney Bigard, 1906-1980: clarinet.
Art Blakey, 1919-1990: drums, leader.
Jimmy Blanton, 1921-1942: bass.
Charles "Buddy" Bolden, 1868-1931: cornet; formed the first jazz band in the 1890s.
Big Bill Broonzy, 1893-1958: blues singer, guitar.
Clifford Brown, 1930-1956: trumpet.
Ray Brown, b. 1926: bass.
Dave Brubeck, b. 1920: piano, combo leader.
Don Byas, 1912-1972: tenor sax.
Harry Carney, 1910-1974: baritone sax.
Benny Carter, b. 1907: alto sax, trumpet, clarinet.
Ron Carter, b. 1937: bass, cello.
Sidney Catlett, 1910-1951: drums.
Charlie Christian, 1919-1942: guitar.
Kenny Clarke, 1914-1985: pioneer of modern drums.
Buck Clayton, b. 1911: trumpet, arranger.
Al Cohn, 1925-1988: tenor sax, composer.
Cozy Cole, 1909-1981: drums.
Ornette Coleman, b. 1930: saxophone; unorthodox style.
John Coltrane, 1926-1967: tenor sax innovator.
Eddie Condon, 1904-1973: guitar, band leader; promoter of Dixieland.
Chick Corea, b. 1941: pianist, composer.
Tadd Dameron, 1917-1965: piano, composer.
Eddie "Lockjaw" Davis, 1921-1986: tenor sax.
Miles Davis, 1926-1991: trumpet; pioneer of cool jazz.
Wild Bill Davison, 1906-1989: cornet, leader; prominent in early Chicago jazz.
Buddy De Franco, b. 1933: clarinet.
Paul Desmond, 1924-1977: alto sax.
Vic Dickenson, 1906-1984: trombone, composer.
Warren "Baby" Dodds, 1898-1959: Dixieland drummer.
Johnny Dodds, 1892-1940: clarinet.
Eric Dolphy, 1928-1964: alto sax, composer.
Jimmy Dorsey, 1904-1957: clarinet, alto sax; band leader.
Tommy Dorsey, 1905-1956: trombone; band leader.
Roy Eldridge, 1911-1989: trumpet, drums, singer.
Duke Ellington, 1899-1974: piano, band leader, composer.
Bill Evans, 1929-1980: piano.
Gil Evans, 1912-1988: composer, arranger, piano.
Ella Fitzgerald, b. 1918: singer.
"Red" Garland, 1923-1984; piano.
Erroll Garner, 1921-1977: piano, composer, "Misty."
Stan Getz, 1927-1991: tenor sax.
Dizzy Gillespie, 1917-1993: trumpet, composer; bop developer.
Benny Goodman, 1909-1986: clarinet, band and combo leader.
Dexter Gordon, 1923-1990: tenor sax; bop-derived style.
Stephane Grappelli, b. 1908: violin.
Bobby Hackett, 1915-1976: trumpet, cornet.
Lionel Hampton, b. 1913: vibes, drums, piano, combo leader.
Herbie Hancock, b. 1940: piano, composer.
W. C. Handy, 1873-1958: composer, "St. Louis Blues."
Coleman Hawkins, 1904-1969: tenor sax; 1939 recording of "Body and Soul" a classic.
Roy Haynes, b. 1926: drums.
Fletcher Henderson, 1898-1952: orchestra leader, arranger; pioneered jazz and dance bands of the 30s.
Woody Herman, 1913-87: clarinet, alto sax, band leader.
Jay C. Higginbotham, 1906-1973: trombone.
Earl "Fatha" Hines, 1905-1983: piano, songwriter.
Johnny Hodges, 1906-1970: alto sax.
Billie Holiday, 1915-1959: blues singer, "Strange Fruit."
Sam "Lightnin' " Hopkins, 1912-1982: blues singer, guitar.
Mahalia Jackson, 1911-1972: gospel singer.
Milt Jackson, b. 1923: vibes, piano, guitar.
Illinois Jacquet, b. 1922: tenor sax.
Keith Jarrett, b. 1945: technically phenomenal pianist.
Blind Lemon Jefferson, 1897-1930: blues singer, guitar.
Bunk Johnson, 1879-1949: cornet, trumpet.
James P. Johnson, 1891-1955: piano, composer.
J. J. Johnson, b. 1924: trombone, composer.
Elvin Jones, b. 1927: drums.
Jo Jones, 1911-1985: drums.
Philly Joe Jones, 1923-1985: drums.
Quincy Jones, b. 1933: arranger.
Thad Jones, 1923-1986: trumpet, cornet.
Scott Joplin, 1868-1917: composer; "Maple Leaf Rag."
Stan Kenton, 1912-1979: orchestra leader, composer, piano.
Barney Kessel, b. 1923: guitar.
Lee Konitz, b. 1927: alto sax.
Gene Krupa, 1909-1973: drums, band and combo leader.
Scott LaFaro, 1936-1961: bass.
Huddie Ledbetter (Leadbelly), 1888-1949: blues singer, guitar.
John Lewis, b. 1920: composer, piano, combo leader.
Mel Lewis, 1929-1990: drummer, orchestra leader.
Jimmie Lunceford, 1902-1947: band leader, sax.
Herbie Mann, b. 1930: flute.
Wynton Marsalis, b. 1961: trumpet.
Jimmy McPartland, b. 1907: trumpet.
Marian McPartland, b. 1920: piano.
Glenn Miller, 1904-1944: trombone, dance band leader.
Charles Mingus, 1922-1979: bass, composer, combo leader.
Thelonious Monk, 1920-1982: piano, composer, combo leader; a developer of bop.
Wes Montgomery, 1925-1968: guitar.
"Jelly Roll" Morton, 1885-1941: composer, piano, singer.
Bennie Moten, 1894-1935: piano; an early organizer of large jazz orchestras.
Gerry Mulligan, b. 1927: baritone sax, arranger, leader.
Turk Murphy, 1915-1987: trombone, band leader.
Theodore "Fats" Navarro, 1923-1950: trumpet.
Red Nichols, 1905-1965: cornet, combo leader.
Red Norvo, b. 1908: vibes, band leader.
Anita O'Day, b. 1919: singer.
King Oliver, 1885-1938: cornet, band leader; teacher of Louis Armstrong.
Sy Oliver, 1910-1988: Swing Era arranger, composer, conductor.
Kid Ory, 1886-1973: trombone, "Muskrat Ramble".
Charlie "Bird" Parker, 1920-1955: alto sax, composer; rated by many as the greatest jazz improviser.
Art Pepper, 1925-1982: alto sax.
Oscar Peterson, b. 1925: piano, composer, combo leader.
Oscar Pettiford, 1922-1960: a leading bassist in the bop era.
Bud Powell, 1924-1966: piano; modern jazz pioneer.
Tito Puente, b. 1923: band leader.
Sun Ra, 1915?-1993: big band leader, pianist, composer.
Gertrude "Ma" Rainey, 1886-1939: blues singer.
Don Redman, 1900-1964: composer, arranger; pioneer in the evolution of the large orchestra.
Django Reinhardt, 1910-1953: guitar; Belgian gypsy, first European to influence American jazz.
Buddy Rich, 1917-1987: drums, band leader.
Max Roach, b. 1925: drums.
Sonny Rollins, b. 1929: tenor sax.
Frank Rosollino, 1926-1978: trombone.
Jimmy Rushing, 1903-1972: blues singer.
George Russell, b. 1923: composer, piano.
Pee Wee Russell, 1906-1969: clarinet.
Artie Shaw, b. 1910: clarinet, combo leader.
George Shearing, b. 1919: piano, composer.
Horace Silver, b. 1928: piano, combo leader.
Zoot Sims, 1925-1985: tenor, alto sax; clarinet.

Zutty Singleton, 1898-1975: Dixieland drummer.
Bessie Smith, 1894-1937: blues singer.
Clarence "Pinetop" Smith, 1904-1929: piano, singer; pioneer of boogie woogie.
Willie "The Lion" Smith, 1897-1973: stride style pianist.
Muggsy Spanier, 1906-1967: cornet, band leader.
Billy Strayhorn, 1915-67: composer, piano.
Sonny Stitt, 1924-1982: alto, tenor sax.
Art Tatum, 1910-1956: piano; technical virtuoso.
Billy Taylor, b. 1921: piano, composer.
Cecil Taylor, b. 1933: piano, composer.
Jack Teagarden, 1905-1964: trombone, singer.
Mel Torme, b. 1925: singer.
Dave Tough, 1908-1948: drums.
Lennie Tristano, 1919-1978: piano, composer.
Joe Turner, 1911-1985: blues singer.
McCoy Tyner, b. 1938: piano, composer.
Sarah Vaughan, 1924-1990: singer.
Joe Venuti, 1904-1978: first great jazz violinist.
Thomas "Fats" Waller, 1904-1943: piano, singer, composer. "Ain't Misbehavin' ".
Dinah Washington, 1924-1963: singer.
Chick Webb, 1902-1939: band leader, drums.
Ben Webster, 1909-1973: tenor sax.
Paul Whiteman, 1890-1967: orchestra leader; a major figure in the introduction of jazz to a large audience.
Charles "Cootie" Williams, 1908-1985: trumpet, band leader.
Mary Lou Williams, 1914-1981: piano, composer.
Teddy Wilson, 1912-1986: piano, composer.
Kai Winding, 1922-1983: trombone, composer.
Jimmy Yancey, 1894-1951: piano.
Lester "Pres" Young, 1909-1959: tenor sax, composer: a bop pioneer.

Rock & Roll Notables

For more than a quarter of a century, rock & roll has been an important force in American popular culture. The following individuals or groups have made a significant impact. Next to each is an associated single record or record album.

Paula Abdul: "Forever Your Girl"
Aerosmith: "Sweet Emotion"
The Allman Brothers Band: "Ramblin' Man"
The Animals: "House of the Rising Sun"
Paul Anka: "Lonely Boy"
The Association: "Cherish"
Frankie Avalon: "Venus"

The Band: "The Weight"
The Beach Boys: "Good Vibrations"
The Beatles: *Sergeant Pepper's Lonely-Hearts Club Band*
The Bee Gees: "Stayin' Alive"
Pat Benatar: "Hit Me With Your Best Shot"
Chuck Berry: "Johnny B. Goode"
The Big Bopper: "Chantilly Lace"
Black Sabbath: "Paranoid"
Blind Faith: "Can't Find My Way Home"
Blondie: "Heart of Glass"
Blood, Sweat and Tears: "Spinning Wheel"
Bon Jovi: *Slippery When Wet*
Gary "U.S." Bonds: "Quarter to Three"
Booker T. and the MGs: "Green Onions"
Earl Bostic: "Flamingo"
David Bowie: "Let's Dance"
James Brown: "Papa's Got a Brand New Bag"
Jackson Browne: "Doctor My Eyes"
Buffalo Springfield: "For What It's Worth"
The Byrds: "Turn! Turn! Turn!"

Canned Heat: "Going Up the Country"
The Cars: "Shake It Up"
Tracy Chapman: "Fast Car"
Ray Charles: "Georgia on My Mind"
Chubby Checker: "The Twist"
Chicago: "Saturday in the Park"
Eric Clapton: "Layla"
The Coasters: "Yakety Yak"
Eddie Cochran: "Summertime Blues"
Phil Collins: "Another Day in Paradise"
Sam Cooke: "You Send Me"
Alice Cooper: "School's Out"
Elvis Costello: "Alison"
Cream: "Sunshine of Your Love"
Credence Clearwater Revival: "Proud Mary"
Crosby, Stills, Nash and Young: "Suite: Judy Blue Eyes"
The Crystals: "Da Doo Ron Ron"

DJ Jazzy Jeff & the Fresh Prince: "Summertime"
Danny and the Juniors: "At the Hop"
Bobby Darin: "Splish Splash"
Spencer Davis Group: "Gimme Some Lovin' "
Bo Diddley: "Who Do You Love?"
Dion and the Belmonts: "A Teenager in Love"
Dire Straits: *Brothers in Arms*
Fats Domino: "Blueberry Hill"
The Doobie Brothers: "What a Fool Believes"
The Doors: "Light My Fire"
The Drifters: "Save the Last Dance for Me"
Bob Dylan: "Like a Rolling Stone"

The Eagles: "Hotel California"
Earth, Wind and Fire: "Shining Star"
Emerson, Lake and Palmer: "From the Beginning"
The Eurythmics: "Sweet Dreams (Are Made of This)"
Everly Brothers: "Wake Up Little Susie"

The Five Satins: "In the Still of the Night"
Fleetwood Mac: *Rumours*
The Four Seasons: "Sherry"
The Four Tops: "I Can't Help Myself"
Aretha Franklin: "Respect"

Marvin Gaye: "I Heard It through the Grapevine"
Grand Funk Railroad: "We're an American Band"
The Grateful Dead: "Truckin' "
Guns 'N Roses: *Appetite for Destruction*

Bill Haley and the Comets: "Rock Around the Clock"
M.C. Hammer: "U Can't Touch This"
Jimi Hendrix: *Are You Experienced?*
Buddy Holly and the Crickets: "That'll Be the Day"
Whitney Houston: "The Greatest Love"

The Isley Brothers: "It's Your Thing"

The Jackson 5/The Jacksons: "ABC"
Janet Jackson: *Rhythm Nation*
Michael Jackson: *Thriller*
Tommy James & The Shondells: "Crimson and Clover"
Jay and the Americans: "This Magic Moment"
The Jefferson Airplane/Jefferson Starship: "White Rabbit"
Jethro Tull: *Aqualung*
Joan Jett: "I Love Rock' n' Roll"
Billy Joel: "Piano Man"
Elton John: "Sad Songs"
Janis Joplin: "Me and Bobby McGee"

Chaka Khan: "I Feel for You"
B.B. King: "The Thrill Is Gone"
Carole King: *Tapestry*
The Kinks: "You Really Got Me"
Kiss: "Rock' n' Roll All Night"
Gladys Knight and the Pips: "Midnight Train to Georgia"

L.L. Cool J: "Mama Said Knock You Out"
Led Zeppelin: "Stairway to Heaven"
Brenda Lee: "I'm Sorry"
Jerry Lee Lewis: "Whole Lotta Shakin' Going On"
Little Anthony and the Imperials: "Tears on My Pillow"
Little Richard: "Tutti Frutti"
Lovin Spoonful: "Do You Believe in Magic?"
Frankie Lymon: "Why Do Fools Fall in Love?"
Lynyrd Skynyrd: "Freebird"

Madonna: "Material Girl"
The Mamas and the Papas: "Monday, Monday"
Bob Marley: "Jamming"
Martha and the Vandellas: "Dancin' in the Streets"
The Marvelettes: "Please Mr. Postman"
Clyde McPhatter: "Money Honey"
John Mellencamp: "Hurt So Good"
George Michael: *Faith*
Joni Mitchell: "Big Yellow Taxi"
The Monkees: "I'm a Believer"
Moody Blues: "Nights in White Satin"

Rick Nelson: "Hello Mary Lou"

Roy Orbison: "Oh Pretty Woman"

Carl Perkins: "Blue Suede Shoes"
Tom Petty and the Heartbreakers: "Refugee"
Pink Floyd: *The Wall*
Poco: *Deliverin'*
The Police: "Every Breath You Take"

Iggy Pop: "Lust for Life"
Elvis Presley: "Love Me Tender"
The Pretenders: *Learning to Crawl*
Lloyd Price: "Stagger Lee"
Prince: "Purple Rain"
Procul Harum: "A Whiter Shade of Pale"
Public Enemy: "Fight the Power"

Queen: "Bohemian Rhapsody"

R.E.M.: "Losing My Religion"
The Rascals: "Good Lovin' "
Otis Redding: "The Dock of the Bay"
Lou Reed: "Walk on the Wild Side"
Righteous Brothers: "You've Lost that Lovin' Feeling"
Johnny Rivers: "Poor Side of Town"
Smokey Robinson and the Miracles: "Ooh Baby Baby"
The Rolling Stones: "Satisfaction"
The Ronettes: "Be My Baby"
Linda Ronstadt: "You're No Good"
Run D.M.C.: "Raisin' Hell"

Sam and Dave: "Soul Man"
Santana: "Black Magic Woman"
Neil Sedaka: "Breaking Up is Hard to Do"
Del Shannon: "Runaway"
The Shirelles: "Soldier Boy"
Simon and Garfunkel: "Bridge Over Troubled Water"
Carly Simon: "You're So Vain"
Sly and the Family Stone: "Everyday People"
Patti Smith: "Because the Night"
Southside Johnny and the Asbury Jukes: *This Time*
Dusty Springfield: "You Don't Have to Say You Love Me"
Bruce Springsteen: "Born in the U.S.A."
Steely Dan: "Rikki Don't Lose That Number"
Steppenwolf: "Born to Be Wild"
Rod Stewart: "Maggie Mae"
Sting: "If You Love Somebody, Set Them Free"
Donna Summer: "She Works Hard for the Money"
The Supremes: "Stop! In the Name of Love"

Talking Heads: "Once in a Lifetime"
James Taylor: "You've Got a Friend"
The Temptations: "My Girl"
Three Dog Night: "Joy to the World"
Traffic: "Feelin' Alright"
Big Joe Turner: "Shake, Rattle & Roll"
Tina Turner: "What's Love Got to Do with It?"

U2: *Joshua Tree*

Van Halen: "Jump"

Dionne Warwick: "I'll Never Fall in Love Again"
Muddy Waters: "Rollin' Stone"
Mary Wells: "My Guy"
The Who: "My Generation"
Jackie Wilson: "That's Why"
Stevie Wonder: "You Are the Sunshine of My Life"

The Yardbirds: "For Your Love"
Yes: "Yours Is No Disgrace"

Frank Zappa/Mothers of Invention: *Sheik Yerbouti*

Entertainment Personalities — Where and When Born

Actors, Actresses, Dancers, Musicians, Producers, Directors, Radio-TV Performers, Singers
(As of mid-1993)

Name	Birthplace	Born
Abbado, Claudio	Milan, Italy	6/26/33
Abbott, George	Forestville, N.Y.	6/25/87
Abdul, Paula	San Fernando, Cal.	6/19/62
Abraham, F. Murray	Pittsburgh, Pa.	10/24/39
Adams, Bryan	Kingston, Ont.	11/5/59
Adams, Don	New York, N.Y.	4/19/26
Adams, Edie	Kingston, Pa.	4/16/29
Adams, Joey	New York, N.Y.	1/6/11
Adams, Mason	New York, N.Y.	2/26/19
Adjani, Isabelle	W. Germany	6/27/55
Agutter, Jenny	London, England	12/20/52
Aiello, Danny	New York, N.Y.	6/20/33
Aimee, Anouk	Paris, France	4/27/32
Akins, Claude	Nelson, Ga.	5/25/18
Albanese, Licia	Bari, Italy	7/22/13
Alberghetti, Anna Maria	Pesaro, Italy	5/15/36
Albert, Eddie	Rock Island, Ill.	4/22/08
Albert, Marv	New York, N.Y.	6/12/43
Alda, Alan	New York, N.Y.	1/28/36
Alexander, Jane	Boston, Mass.	10/28/39
Alexander, Jason	Newark, N.J.	9/23/59
Allen, Debbie	Houston, Tex.	1/16/50
Allen, Joan	Rochelle, Ill.	8/20/56
Allen, Karen	Carrollton, Ill.	10/5/51
Allen, Mel	Birmingham, Ala.	2/14/13
Allen, Nancy	New York, N.Y.	6/24/49
Allen, Steve	New York, N.Y.	12/26/21
Allen, Tim	Denver, Col.	6/13/-
Allen, Woody	Brooklyn, N.Y.	12/1/35
Alley, Kirstie	Wichita, Kan.	1/12/55
Allman, Gregg	Nashville, Tenn.	12/7/47
Allyson, June	New York, N.Y.	10/7/17
Alonso, Maria Conchita	Cuba	1957
Alpert, Herb	Los Angeles, Cal.	3/31/35
Altman, Robert	Kansas City, Mo.	2/20/25
Ameche, Don	Kenosha, Wis.	5/31/08
Ames, Ed	Boston, Mass.	7/9/27
Ames, Leon	Portland, Ind.	1/20/03
Amos, John	Newark, N.J.	12/27/42
Amsterdam, Morey	Chicago, Ill.	12/14/14
Anderson, Harry	Newport, R.I.	10/14/49
Anderson, Ian	Dunfermline, Scotland	8/10/47
Anderson, Kevin	Illinois	1/13/60
Anderson, Loni	St. Paul, Minn.	8/5/46
Anderson, Lynn	Grand Forks, N.D.	9/26/47
Anderson, Melissa Sue	Berkeley, Cal.	9/26/62
Anderson, Richard	Long Branch, N.J.	8/8/26
Anderson, Richard Dean	Minneapolis, Minn.	1/23/50
Andersson, Bibi	Stockholm, Sweden	11/11/35
Andress, Ursula	Bern, Switzerland	3/19/36
Andrews, Anthony	London, England	1/12/48
Andrews, Julie	Walton, England	10/1/35
Andrews, Maxene	Minneapolis, Minn.	1/3/18
Andrews, Patty	Minneapolis, Minn.	2/16/20
Anka, Paul	Ottawa, Ont.	7/30/41
Ann-Margret	Stockholm, Sweden	4/28/41
Anton, Susan	Oak Glen, Cal.	10/12/50
Applegate, Christina	Los Angeles, Cal.	11/25/72
Archer, Anne	Los Angeles, Cal.	8/25/50
Arkin, Alan	New York, N.Y.	3/26/34
Arnaz, Desi Jr.	Los Angeles, Cal.	1/19/53
Arnaz, Lucie	Hollywood, Cal.	7/17/51
Arness, James	Minneapolis, Minn.	5/26/23
Arnold, Eddy	Henderson, Tenn.	5/15/18
Arnold, Roseanne	Salt Lake City, Ut.	11/3/52
Arquette, Rosanna	New York, N.Y.	8/10/59
Arroyo, Martina	New York, N.Y.	2/2/37
Arthur, Beatrice	New York, N.Y.	5/13/26
Ashley, Elizabeth	Ocala, Fla.	8/30/41
Asner, Ed.	Kansas City, Mo.	11/15/29
Assante, Armand	New York, N.Y.	10/4/49
Astin, John	Baltimore, Md.	3/30/30
Atherton, William	New Haven, Conn.	7/30/47
Atkins, Chet	Luttrell, Tenn.	6/20/24
Attenborough, Richard	Cambridge, England	8/29/23
Auberjonois, Rene	New York, N.Y.	6/1/40
Aumont, Jean-Pierre	Paris, France	1/5/09
Austin, Patti	New York, N.Y.	8/10/48
Autry, Alan	Shreveport, La.	7/31/52
Autry, Gene	Tioga, Tex.	9/29/07
Avalon, Frankie	Philadelphia, Pa.	9/18/39
Ax, Emmanuel	Lvov, USSR	6/8/49
Axton, Hoyt	Duncan, Okla.	3/25/38
Aykroyd, Dan	Ottawa, Ont.	7/1/52
Ayres, Lew	Minneapolis, Minn.	12/28/08
Aznavour, Charles	Paris, France	5/22/24
Bacall, Lauren	New York, N.Y.	9/16/24
Bacon, Kevin	Philadelphia, Pa.	7/8/58
Baez, Joan	Staten Island, N.Y.	1/9/41
Bain, Conrad	Lethbridge, Alta.	2/4/23
Baio, Scott	Brooklyn, N.Y.	9/22/61
Baker, Anita	Toledo, Oh.	1/26/58
Baker, Carroll	Johnstown, Pa.	5/28/31
Baker, Joe Don	Groesbeck, Tex.	2/12/36
Bakula, Scott	St. Louis, Mo.	10/9/-
Baldwin, Alec	Massapequa, N.Y.	4/3/58
Baldwin, William	Massapequa, N.Y.	1963
Ballard, Kaye	Cleveland, Oh.	11/20/26

Name	Birthplace	Born
Balsam, Martin	New York, N.Y.	11/4/19
Bancroft, Anne	New York, N.Y.	9/17/31
Banks, Jonathan	Washington, D.C.	1/31/47
Bannon, Jack	Los Angeles, Cal.	6/14/40
Bardot, Brigitte	Paris, France	9/28/34
Barker, Bob	Darrington, Wash.	12/12/23
Barkin, Ellen	New York, N.Y.	4/16/55
Barrault, Jean-Louis	Vesinet, France	9/8/10
Barrie, Barbara	Chicago, Ill.	5/23/31
Barry, Gene	New York, N.Y.	6/14/19
Barty, Billy	Millsboro, Pa.	10/25/24
Barrymore, Drew	Los Angeles, Cal.	2/22/75
Baryshnikov, Mikhail	Riga, Latvia	1/28/48
Basinger, Kim	Athens, Ga.	12/8/53
Bassey, Shirley	Cardiff, Wales	1/8/37
Bateman, Jason	Rye, N.Y.	1/14/69
Bateman, Justine	Rye, N.Y.	2/19/66
Bates, Alan	Allestree, England	2/17/34
Bates, Kathy	Memphis, Tenn.	6/28/48
Battle, Kathleen	Portsmouth, Oh.	8/13/48
Baxter, Meredith	Los Angeles, Cal.	6/21/47
Beal, John	Joplin, Mo.	8/13/09
Beasley, Allyce	New York, N.Y.	7/6/54
Beatty, Ned	Louisville, Ky.	7/6/37
Beatty, Warren	Richmond, Va.	3/30/37
Beck, John	Chicago, Ill.	1/28/43
Bedelia, Bonnie	New York, N.Y.	3/25/48
Beery, Noah Jr.	New York, N.Y.	8/10/13
Begley, Ed Jr.	Los Angeles, Cal.	9/16/49
Belafonte, Harry	New York, N.Y.	3/1/27
Bel Geddes, Barbara	New York, N.Y.	10/31/22
Belmondo, Jean-Paul	Neuilly-sur-Seine, France	4/9/33
Belushi, Jim	Chicago, Ill.	6/15/54
Benatar, Pat	Brooklyn, N.Y.	1/10/53
Benedict, Dirk	Helena, Mont.	3/1/45
Bening, Annette	Topeka, Kan.	1958
Benjamin, Richard	New York, N.Y.	5/22/38
Bennett, Tony	New York, N.Y.	8/3/26
Benson, George	Pittsburgh, Pa.	3/22/43
Benson, Robby	Dallas, Tex.	1/21/55
Beradino, John	Los Angeles, Cal.	5/1/17
Berenger, Tom	Chicago, Ill.	5/31/50
Bergen, Candice	Beverly Hills, Cal.	5/9/46
Bergen, Polly	Knoxville, Tenn.	7/14/30
Bergerac, Jacques	Biarritz, France	5/26/27
Bergman, Ingmar	Uppsala, Sweden	7/14/18
Berle, Milton	New York, N.Y.	7/12/08
Berlinger, Warren	Brooklyn, N.Y.	8/31/37
Berman, Lazar	Leningrad, USSR	2/26/30
Berman, Shelley	Chicago, Ill.	2/3/26
Bernard, Crystal	Dallas, Tex.	9/30/64
Bernhard, Sandra	Flint, Mich.	6/6/55
Bernsen, Corbin	No. Hollywood, Cal.	9/7/55
Berry, Chuck	St. Louis, Mo.	10/18/26
Berry, Halle	Cleveland, Oh.	1969
Berry, Ken	Moline, Ill.	11/3/33
Bertinelli, Valerie	Wilmington, Del.	4/23/60
Bialik, Mayim	San Diego, Cal.	12/12/75
Bikel, Theodore	Vienna, Austria	5/2/24
Birney, David	Washington, D.C.	4/23/39
Bishop, Joey	Bronx, N.Y.	2/3/18
Bisoglio, Val	New York, N.Y.	5/7/26
Bisset, Jacqueline	Weybridge, England	9/13/44
Bixby, Bill	San Francisco, Cal.	1/22/34
Black, Clint	Katy, Tex.	1962
Black, Karen	Park Ridge, Ill.	7/1/42
Blackstone Jr., Harry	Three Rivers, Mich.	6/30/34
Blades, Ruben	Panama City, Panama	7/16/48
Blaine, Vivian	Newark, N.J.	11/21/21
Blair, Linda	St. Louis, Mo.	1/22/59
Blake, Robert	Nutley, N.J.	9/18/33
Bledsoe, Tempestt	Chicago, Ill.	8/1/73
Bloom, Claire	London, England	2/15/31
Blyth, Ann	Mt. Kisco, N.Y.	8/16/28
Bochco, Steven	New York, N.Y.	12/16/43
Bogarde, Dirk	London, England	3/28/20
Bogosian, Eric	Boston, Mass.	4/24/53
Bogdanovich, Peter	Kingston, N.Y.	7/30/39
Bolton, Michael	New Haven, Conn.	—
Bonham-Carter, Helena	London, England	5/26/66
Bon Jovi, Jon	Sayreville, N.J.	3/2/62
Bono, Sonny	Detroit, Mich.	2/16/35
Booke, Sorrell	Buffalo, N.Y.	1/4/30
Boone, Debby	Hackensack, N.J.	9/22/56
Boone, Pat	Jacksonville, Fla.	6/1/34
Borge, Victor	Copenhagen, Denmark	1/3/09
Borgnine, Ernest	Hamden, Conn.	1/24/17
Bosco, Philip	Jersey City, N.J.	9/26/30
Bosley, Tom	Chicago, Ill.	10/1/27
Bostwick, Barry	San Mateo, Cal.	2/24/46
Bottoms, Timothy	Santa Barbara, Cal.	8/30/51
Bowie, David	London, England	1/8/47
Boxleitner, Bruce	Elgin, Ill.	5/12/50
Boy George	London, England	6/14/61
Boyle, Peter	Philadelphia, Pa.	10/18/33
Bracco, Lorraine	New York, N.Y.	1955
Bracken, Eddie	New York, N.Y.	2/7/20
Branagh, Kenneth	Belfast, No. Ireland	12/10/60
Brando, Marlon	Omaha, Neb.	4/3/24
Brazzi, Rossano	Bologna, Italy	9/18/16
Brennan, Eileen	Los Angeles, Cal.	9/3/35
Brenner, David	Philadelphia, Pa.	2/4/45
Brewer, Teresa	Toledo, Oh.	5/7/31
Bridges, Beau	Hollywood, Cal.	12/9/41
Bridges, Jeff	Los Angeles, Cal.	12/4/49
Bridges, Lloyd	San Leandro, Cal.	1/15/13
Brimley, Wilford	Salt Lake City, Ut.	9/27/34
Broderick, Matthew	New York, N.Y.	3/21/62
Brolin, James	Los Angeles, Cal.	7/18/40
Bronson, Charles	Ehrenfeld, Pa.	11/3/22
Brooks, Albert	Beverly Hills, Cal.	7/22/47
Brooks, Avery	Evansville, Ind.	10/2/48
Brooks, Garth	Tulsa, Okla.	2/2/62
Brooks, Mel	New York, N.Y.	6/28/26
Brosnan, Pierce	Co. Meath, Ireland	5/15/53
Brown, Blair	Washington, D.C.	1948
Brown, Bryan	Sydney, Australia	1947
Brown, James	Pulaski, Tenn.	6/17/28
Brown, Jim	St. Simons Island, Ga.	2/17/36
Brown, Les	Reinerton, Pa.	3/14/12
Brown, Ray	Pittsburgh, Pa.	10/13/26
Browne, Roscoe Lee	Woodbury, N.J.	5/2/25
Buckley, Betty	Ft. Worth, Tex.	7/3/47
Bujold, Genevieve	Montreal, Que.	7/1/42
Bumbry, Grace	St. Louis, Mo.	1/4/37
Burghoff, Gary	Bristol, Conn.	5/24/40
Burke, Delta	Orlando, Fla.	7/30/56
Burnett, Carol	San Antonio, Tex.	4/26/33
Burns, George	New York, N.Y.	1/20/96
Burr, Raymond	New Westminster, B.C.	5/21/17
Burrows, Darren E.	Winfield, Kan.	9/12/66
Burstyn, Ellen	Detroit, Mich.	12/7/32
Burton, LeVar	Landstuhl, W. Germany	2/16/57
Busey, Gary	Goose Creek, Tex.	6/29/44
Busfield, Timothy	Lansing, Mich.	6/12/57
Butkus, Dick	Chicago, Ill.	12/9/42
Buttons, Red	New York, N.Y.	2/5/19
Buzzi, Ruth	Westerly, R.I.	7/24/36
Byrne, David	Dumbarton, Scotland	5/14/52
Caan, James	New York, N.Y.	3/26/39
Caballe, Montserrat	Barcelona, Spain	4/12/33
Caesar, Sid	Yonkers, N.Y.	9/8/22
Cage, Nicolas	Long Beach, Cal.	1/7/64
Caine, Michael	London, England	3/14/33
Caldwell, Sarah	Maryville, Mo.	3/6/24
Caldwell, Zoe	Melbourne, Australia	9/14/33
Calhoun, Rory	Los Angeles, Cal.	8/8/23
Calloway, Cab	Rochester, N.Y.	12/25/07
Cameron, Kirk	Panorama City, Cal.	10/12/70
Camp, Hamilton	London, England	10/30/34
Campanella, Joseph	New York, N.Y.	11/21/27
Campbell, Glen	Billstown, Ark.	4/22/36
Candy, John	Toronto, Ont.	10/31/50
Cannell, Stephen J.	Los Angeles, Cal.	2/5/42
Cannon, Dyan	Tacoma, Wash.	1/4/37
Cantrell, Lana	Sydney, Australia	8/7/43
Cara, Irene	New York, N.Y.	3/18/59
Carey, Macdonald	Sioux City, Ia.	3/15/13
Carey, Mariah	Huntington, N.Y.	1970
Cariou, Len	Winnipeg, Canada	9/30/39
Carlin, George	New York, N.Y.	5/12/37
Carlisle, Kitty	New Orleans, La.	9/3/15
Carmen, Eric	Cleveland, Oh.	8/11/49
Carmichael, Ian	Hull, England	6/18/20
Carney, Art	Mt. Vernon, N.Y.	11/4/18
Caron, Leslie	Boulogne, France	7/1/31
Carr, Vikki	El Paso, Tex.	7/19/41
Carradine, David	Hollywood, Cal.	10/8/36
Carradine, Keith	San Mateo, Cal.	8/8/49
Carreras, Jose	Barcelona, Spain	12/5/47
Carroll, Diahann	Bronx, N.Y.	7/17/35
Carroll, Pat	Shreveport, La.	5/5/27
Carson, Johnny	Corning, Ia.	10/23/25
Carter, Dixie	McLemoresville, Tenn.	5/25/39
Carter, Jack	New York, N.Y.	6/24/23
Carter, June	Maces Spring, Va.	6/23/29

Name	Birthplace	Born
Carter, Lynda	Phoenix, Ariz.	7/24/51
Carter, Nell	Birmingham, Ala.	9/13/48
Carvey, Dana	Missoula, Mont.	6/6/55
Casadesus, Gaby	Marseilles, France	8/9/01
Cash, Johnny	Kingsland, Ark.	2/26/32
Cash, Rosanne	Memphis, Tenn.	5/24/55
Cass, Peggy	Boston, Mass.	5/21/24
Cassidy, David	New York, N.Y.	4/12/50
Cavett, Dick	Gibbon, Neb.	11/19/36
Chamberlain, Richard	Beverly Hills, Cal.	3/31/35
Channing, Carol	Seattle, Wash.	1/31/23
Channing, Stockard	New York, N.Y.	2/13/44
Chaplin, Geraldine	Santa Monica, Cal.	7/31/44
Chapman, Tracy	Cleveland, Oh.	1964
Charisse, Cyd	Amarillo, Tex.	3/8/21
Charles, Ray	Albany, Ga.	9/23/30
Charo	Murcia, Spain	1/15/51
Chase, Chevy	New York, N.Y.	10/8/43
Checker, Chubby	Philadelphia, Pa.	10/3/41
Cher	El Centro, Cal.	5/20/46
Chiklis, Michael	Lowell, Mass.	8/30/63
Chong, Rae Dawn	California	1962
Chong, Thomas	Edmonton, Alta.	5/24/38
Christie, Julie	Assam, India	4/14/40
Christopher, William	Evanston, Ill.	10/20/32
Clapton, Eric	Surrey, England	3/30/45
Clark, Dane	New York, N.Y.	2/18/13
Clark, Dick	Mt. Vernon, N.Y.	11/30/29
Clark, Petula	Ewell, Surrey, England	11/15/32
Clark, Roy	Meherrin, Va.	4/15/33
Clark, Susan	Sarnia, Ont.	3/8/40
Clary, Robert	Paris, France	3/1/26
Clayburgh, Jill	New York, N.Y.	4/30/44
Cleese, John	England	10/27/39
Cliburn, Van	Shreveport, La.	7/12/34
Clooney, Rosemary	Maysville, Ky.	5/23/28
Close, Glenn	Greenwich, Conn.	3/19/47
Coburn, James	Laurel, Neb.	8/31/28
Coca, Imogene	Philadelphia, Pa.	11/18/08
Colbert, Claudette	Paris, France	9/13/03
Cole, Gary	Park Ridge, Ill.	9/20/57
Cole, Natalie	Los Angeles, Cal.	2/6/50
Cole, Olivia	Memphis, Tenn.	11/26/42
Coleman, Dabney	Austin, Tex.	1/3/32
Coleman, Gary	Zion, Ill.	2/8/68
Collins, Joan	London, England	5/23/33
Collins, Judy	Seattle, Wash.	5/1/39
Collins, Pauline	Exmouth, England	9/3/40
Collins, Phil	London, England	1/30/51
Comden, Betty	Brooklyn, N.Y.	5/3/19
Como, Perry	Canonsburg, Pa.	5/18/12
Conner, Nadine	Compton, Cal.	2/20/13
Connery, Sean	Edinburgh, Scotland	8/25/30
Connick Jr., Harry	New Orleans, La.	9/11/67
Conniff, Ray	Attleboro, Mass.	11/6/16
Connors, Mike	Fresno, Cal.	8/15/25
Conrad, Robert	Chicago, Ill.	3/1/35
Conrad, William	Louisville, Ky.	9/27/20
Constantine, Michael	Reading, Pa.	5/22/27
Conti, Tom	Paisley, Scotland	11/22/41
Conway, Tim	Willoughby, Oh.	12/15/33
Cook, Barbara	Atlanta, Ga.	10/25/27
Cook, Peter	Torquay, England	11/17/37
Cooke, Alistair	Manchester, England	11/20/08
Coolidge, Rita	Nashville, Tenn.	5/1/45
Cooper, Alice	Detroit, Mich.	2/4/48
Cooper, Jackie	Los Angeles, Cal.	9/15/21
Copperfield, David	Metuchen, N.J.	9/16/56
Coppola, Francis	Detroit, Mich.	4/7/39
Corbin, Barry	Lamesa, Tex.	10/16/40
Corby, Ellen	Racine, Wis.	6/3/13
Cord, Alex	New York, N.Y.	8/3/31
Corea, Chick	Chelsea, Mass.	6/12/41
Corelli, Franco	Ancona, Italy	4/8/23
Corey, Jeff	New York, N.Y.	8/10/14
Cosby, Bill	Philadelphia, Pa.	7/12/37
Costas, Bob	New York, N.Y.	3/22/52
Costello, Elvis	London, England	8/25/54
Costner, Kevin	Compton, Cal.	1/18/55
Cotten, Joseph	Petersburg, Va.	5/15/05
Cougar, John	Seymour, Ind.	10/7/51
Courtenay, Tom	Hull, England	2/25/37
Cox, Ronny	Cloudcroft, N.M.	8/23/38
Craddock, Crash	Greensboro, N.C.	6/16/40
Crain, Jeanne	Barstow, Cal.	5/25/25
Crawford, Michael	Salisbury, England	1/19/42
Crenna, Richard	Los Angeles, Cal.	11/30/26
Crespin, Regine	Marseilles, France	2/23/26
Cronyn, Hume	London, Ont.	7/18/11
Crosby, David	Los Angeles, Cal.	8/14/41
Cross, Ben	London, England	12/16/47
Crouse, Lindsay	New York, N.Y.	5/12/48
Crowell, Rodney	Houston, Tex.	8/17/50
Cruise, Tom	Syracuse, N.Y.	7/3/62
Crystal, Billy	Long Beach, N.Y.	3/14/47
Culkin, Macaulay	New York, N.Y.	8/26/80
Cullum, John	Knoxville, Tenn.	3/2/30
Culp, Robert	Oakland, Cal.	8/16/30
Cummings, Constance	Seattle, Wash.	5/15/10
Curry, Tim	Cheshire, England	4/19/46
Curtin, Jane	Cambridge, Mass.	9/6/47
Curtis, Jamie Lee	Los Angeles, Cal.	11/22/58
Curtis, Keene	Salt Lake City, Ut.	2/15/23
Curtis, Tony	New York, N.Y.	6/3/25
Cusack, Cyril	Durban, S. Africa	11/26/10
Cusack, Joan	Evanston, Ill.	10/11/62
Cusack, John	Evanston, Ill.	6/28/66
Cushing, Peter	Surrey, England	5/26/13
Cyrus, Billy Ray	Flatwoods, Ky.	1961
Dafoe, Willem	Appleton, Wis.	7/22/55
Dahl, Arlene	Minneapolis, Minn.	8/11/28
Dale, Jim	Rothwell, England	8/15/35
Dalton, Abby	Las Vegas, Nev.	8/15/32
Dalton, Timothy	Wales	3/21/44
Daltrey, Roger	London, England	3/1/44
Daly, Timothy	Suffern, N.J.	3/1/58
Daly, Tyne	Madison, Wis.	2/21/47
Damone, Vic	Brooklyn, N.Y.	6/12/28
D'Angelo, Beverly	Columbus, Oh.	11/15/54
Dangerfield, Rodney	Babylon, N.Y.	11/22/22
Daniels, Charlie	Wilmington, N.C.	10/28/36
Daniels, Jeff	Georgia	2/19/55
Daniels, William	Brooklyn, N.Y.	3/31/27
Danner, Blythe	Philadelphia, Pa.	2/3/44
Danson, Ted	San Diego, Cal.	12/29/47
Danza, Tony	New York, N.Y.	4/21/50
Darby, Kim	Hollywood, Cal.	7/8/48
D'Arby, Terence Trent	New York, N.Y.	3/15/62
Davidson, John	Pittsburgh, Pa.	12/13/41
Davis, Ann B.	Schenectady, N.Y.	5/5/26
Davis, Clifton	Chicago, Ill.	10/4/45
Davis, Geena	Wareham, Mass.	1/21/57
Davis, Judy	Perth, Australia	1956
Davis, Mac	Lubbock, Tex.	1/21/42
Davis, Ossie	Cogdell, Ga.	12/18/17
Dawber, Pam	Farmington Hills, Mich.	10/18/51
Dawson, Richard	Hampshire, England	11/20/32
Day, Doris	Cincinnati, Oh.	4/3/24
Day-Lewis, Daniel	London, England	4/29/57
Dean, Jimmy	Plainview, Tex.	8/10/28
De Camp, Rosemary	Prescott, Ariz.	11/14/10
DeCarlo, Yvonne	Vancouver, B.C.	9/1/22
Dee, Frances	Los Angeles, Cal.	11/26/07
Dee, Ruby	Cleveland, Oh.	10/27/23
Dee, Sandra	Bayonne, N.J.	4/23/42
Defore, Don	Cedar Rapids, Ia.	8/25/17
DeHaven, Gloria	Los Angeles, Cal.	7/23/25
De Havilland, Olivia	Tokyo, Japan	7/1/16
Delany, Dana	New York, N.Y.	3/13/57
Della Chiesa, Vivienne	Chicago, Ill.	10/9/20
Delon, Alain	Sceaux, France	11/8/35
DeLuise, Dom	Brooklyn, N.Y.	8/1/33
De Mille, Agnes	New York, N.Y.	9/18/05
Demme, Jonathan	Rockville Centre, N.Y.	2/22/44
De Mornay, Rebecca	Santa Rosa, Cal.	11/29/61
Deneuve, Catherine	Paris, France	10/22/43
De Niro, Robert	New York, N.Y.	8/17/43
Dennehy, Brian	Bridgeport, Conn.	7/9/38
Denver, Bob	New Rochelle, N.Y.	1/9/35
Denver, John	Roswell, N.M.	12/31/43
DePalma, Brian	Newark, N.J.	9/11/40
Depardieu, Gerard	Chateauroux, France	12/27/48
Depp, Johnny	Owensboro, Ky.	6/9/63
Derek, Bo	Long Beach, Cal.	11/20/56
Derek, John	Hollywood, Cal.	8/12/26
Dern, Bruce	Chicago, Ill.	6/4/36
Dern, Laura	Santa Monica, Cal.	2/1/67
Devane, William	Albany, N.Y.	9/5/37
DeVito, Danny	Neptune, N.J.	11/17/44
DeWitt, Joyce	Wheeling, W.Va.	4/23/49
Dey, Susan	Pekin, Ill.	12/10/52
Diamond, Neil	Brooklyn, N.Y.	1/24/41
Dickinson, Angie	Kulm, N.D.	9/30/31
Diddley, Bo	McComb, Miss.	12/20/28
Diller, Phyllis	Lima, Oh.	7/17/17
Dillman, Bradford	San Francisco, Cal.	4/14/30

Name	Birthplace	Born
Dillon, Matt	New Rochelle, N.Y.	2/18/64
Dobson, Kevin	New York, N.Y.	3/18/44
Domingo, Placido	Madrid, Spain	1/21/41
Domino, Fats	New Orleans, La.	2/26/28
Donahue, Phil	Cleveland, Oh.	12/21/35
Donahue, Troy	New York, N.Y.	1/27/36
Dotrice, Roy	Guernsey, England	5/26/23
Douglas, Kirk	Amsterdam, N.Y.	12/9/18
Douglas, Michael	New Brunswick, N.J.	9/25/44
Down, Leslie-Ann	London, England	3/17/54
Downey, Robert Jr.	New York, N.Y.	4/4/65
Downs, Hugh	Akron, Oh.	2/14/21
Drake, Larry	Tulsa, Okla.	2/21/-
Drew, Ellen	Kansas City, Mo.	11/23/15
Dryer, Fred	Hawthorne, Cal.	7/6/46
Dreyfuss, Richard	Brooklyn, N.Y.	10/29/47
Dru, Joanne	Logan, W.Va.	1/31/23
Duffy, Julia	Minneapolis, Minn.	6/27/51
Duffy, Patrick	Townsend, Mont.	3/17/49
Dufour, Val	New Orleans, La.	2/5/27
Dukakis, Olympia	Lowell, Mass.	6/20/31
Duke, Patty	New York, N.Y.	12/14/46
Dukes, David	San Francisco, Cal.	6/6/45
Dullea, Keir	Cleveland, Oh.	5/30/36
Dunaway, Faye	Bascom, Fla.	1/14/41
Duncan, Sandy	Henderson, Tex.	2/20/46
Dunham, Katherine	Joliet, Ill.	6/22/10
Dunne, Griffin	New York, N.Y.	6/8/55
Durbin, Deanna	Winnipeg, Man.	12/4/21
Durning, Charles	Highland Falls, N.Y.	2/28/23
Dussault, Nancy	Pensacola, Fla.	6/30/36
Dutton, Charles S.	Baltimore, Md.	1/30/51
Duvall, Robert	San Diego, Cal.	1/5/31
Duvall, Shelley	Houston, Tex.	7/7/49
Dylan, Bob	Duluth, Minn.	5/24/41
Dysart, Richard	Augusta, Me.	3/30/29
Dzundza, George	Rosenheim, Germany	7/19/45
Easton, Sheena	Bellshill, Scotland	4/27/59
Eastwood, Clint	San Francisco, Cal.	5/31/30
Ebert, Roger	Urbana, Ill.	6/18/42
Ebsen, Buddy	Belleville, Ill.	4/2/08
Edelman, Herb	Brooklyn, N.Y.	11/5/33
Eden, Barbara	Tucson, Ariz.	8/23/34
Edwards, Anthony	Santa Barbara, Cal.	1/19/62
Edwards, Blake	Tulsa, Okla.	7/26/22
Edwards, Ralph	Merino, Col.	6/13/13
Eichhorn, Lisa	Reading, Pa.	2/4/52
Eikenberry, Jill	New Haven, Conn.	1/21/47
Ekberg, Anita	Malmo, Sweden	9/29/31
Ekland, Britt	Stockholm, Sweden	10/6/42
Elam, Jack	Miami, Ariz.	11/13/16
Elizondo, Hector	New York, N.Y.	12/22/36
Elliott, Bob	Boston, Mass.	3/26/23
Elliott, Sam	Sacramento, Cal.	8/9/44
Englund, Robert	Hollywood, Cal.	6/6/48
Elvira (Cassandra Peterson)	Manhattan, Kan.	9/17/51
Estefan, Gloria	Havana, Cuba	9/1/58
Estevez, Emilio	New York, N.Y.	5/12/62
Estrada, Erik	New York, N.Y.	3/16/49
Evans, Dale	Uvalde, Tex.	10/31/12
Evans, Linda	Hartford, Conn.	11/18/42
Evans, Robert	New York, N.Y.	6/29/30
Everett, Chad	South Bend, Ind.	6/11/36
Everly, Don	Brownie, Ky.	2/1/37
Everly, Phil	Chicago, Ill.	1/19/38
Evigan, Greg	S. Amboy, N.J.	10/14/53
Ewell, Tom	Owensboro, Ky.	4/29/09
Fabares, Shelley	Santa Monica, Cal.	1/19/42
Fabian (Forte)	Philadelphia, Pa.	2/6/43
Fabray, Nanette	San Diego, Cal.	10/27/20
Fairbanks, Douglas Jr.	New York, N.Y.	12/9/09
Fairchild, Morgan	Dallas, Tex.	2/3/50
Falana, Lola	Philadelphia, Pa.	9/11/46
Falk, Peter	New York, N.Y.	9/16/27
Farentino, James	Brooklyn, N.Y.	2/24/38
Fargo, Donna	Mt. Airy, N.C.	11/10/45
Farr, Jamie	Toledo, Oh.	7/1/34
Farrell, Eileen	Willimantic, Conn.	2/13/20
Farrell, Mike	St. Paul, Minn.	2/6/39
Farrow, Mia	Los Angeles, Cal.	2/9/45
Faustino, David	California	3/3/74
Fawcett, Farrah	Corpus Christi, Tex.	2/2/47
Faye, Alice	New York, N.Y.	5/5/12
Feinstein, Michael	Columbus, Oh.	9/7/56
Feld, Fritz	Berlin, Germany	10/15/00
Feldon, Barbara	Pittsburgh, Pa.	3/12/41
Feliciano, Jose	Lares, Puerto Rico	9/10/45
Fell, Norman	Philadelphia, Pa.	3/24/24
Fellini, Federico	Rimini, Italy	1/20/20
Fenn, Sherilyn	Detroit, Mich.	1965
Ferrell, Conchata	Charleston, W. Va.	3/28/43
Ferrer, Mel	Elberon, N.J.	8/25/17
Fiedler, John	Platville, Wis.	2/3/25
Field, Sally	Pasadena, Cal.	11/6/46
Finney, Albert	Salford, England	5/9/36
Firkusny, Rudolf	Napajedla, Czechoslovakia	2/11/12
Firth, Peter	Yorkshire, England	10/27/53
Fischer-Dieskau, Dietrich	Berlin, Germany	5/28/25
Fishburne, Larry	Augusta, Ga.	7/30/61
Fisher, Carrie	Beverly Hills, Cal.	10/21/56
Fisher, Eddie	Philadelphia, Pa.	8/10/28
Fitzgerald, Ella	Newport News, Va.	4/25/18
Fitzgerald, Geraldine	Dublin, Ireland	11/24/13
Flack, Roberta	Black Mountain, N.C.	2/10/39
Flanagan, Fionnula	Dublin, Ireland	12/10/41
Flanders, Ed	Minneapolis, Minn.	12/29/34
Fleming, Rhonda	Hollywood, Cal.	8/10/23
Fletcher, Louise	Birmingham, Ala.	7/22/34
Foch, Nina	Leyden, Netherlands	4/20/24
Fogelberg, Dan	Peoria, Ill.	8/13/51
Fonda, Bridget	Los Angeles, Cal.	1964
Fonda, Jane	New York, N.Y.	12/21/37
Fonda, Peter	New York, N.Y.	2/23/39
Fontaine, Joan	Tokyo, Japan	10/22/17
Ford, Faith	Alexandria, La.	9/14/-
Ford, Glenn	Quebec, Canada	5/1/16
Ford, Harrison	Chicago, Ill.	7/13/42
Forrest, Steve	Huntsville, Tex.	9/29/24
Forsythe, John	Penns Grove, N.J.	1/29/18
Foster, Jodie	New York, N.Y.	11/19/62
Fox, James	London, England	5/19/39
Fox, Michael J.	Edmonton, Alta.	6/9/61
Foxworth, Robert	Houston, Tex.	11/1/41
Frampton, Peter	Kent, England	4/22/50
Franciosa, Anthony	New York, N.Y.	10/25/28
Francis, Anne	Ossining, N.Y.	9/16/30
Francis, Arlene	Boston, Mass.	10/20/08
Francis, Connie	Newark, N.J.	12/12/38
Frankenheimer, John	Malba, N.Y.	2/19/30
Franklin, Aretha	Memphis, Tenn.	3/25/42
Franklin, Bonnie	Santa Monica, Cal.	1/6/44
Franklin, Joe	New York, N.Y.	1929
Frann, Mary	St. Louis, Mo.	2/27/43
Franz, Dennis	Maywood, Ill.	10/28/44
Freeman Jr., Al	San Antonio, Tex.	3/21/34
Freeman, Morgan	Memphis, Tenn.	6/1/37
Friedkin, William	Chicago, Ill.	8/29/39
Frost, David	Tenterden, England	4/7/39
Funicello, Annette	Utica, N.Y.	10/22/42
Funt, Allen	New York, N.Y.	9/16/14
Gabor, Eva	Hungary	1921
Gabor, Zsa Zsa	Hungary	2/6/17
Gabriel, John	Niagara Falls, N.Y.	5/25/31
Gabriel, Peter	London, England	2/13/50
Gail, Max	Detroit, Mich.	4/5/43
Galway, James	Belfast, Ireland	12/8/39
Garagiola, Joe	St. Louis, Mo.	2/12/26
Garcia, Andy	Havana, Cuba	4/12/56
Garfunkel, Art	New York, N.Y.	11/5/41
Garland, Beverly	Santa Cruz, Cal.	10/17/26
Garner, James	Norman, Okla.	4/7/28
Garr, Teri	Lakewood, Oh.	12/11/45
Garrett, Betty	St. Joseph, Mo.	5/23/19
Garson, Greer	Co. Down, N. Ireland	9/29/08
Gatlin, Larry	Seminole, Tex.	5/2/48
Gayle, Crystal	Paintsville, Ky.	1/9/51
Gaynor, Mitzi	Chicago, Ill.	9/4/30
Gazzara, Ben	New York, N.Y.	8/28/30
Gedda, Nicolai	Stockholm, Sweden	7/11/25
Gere, Richard	Philadelphia, Pa.	8/31/49
Getty, Estelle	New York, N.Y.	7/25/24
Ghostley, Alice	Eve, Mo.	8/14/26
Giannini, Giancarlo	Spezia, Italy	8/1/42
Gibbs, Marla	Chicago, Ill.	6/14/31
Gibson, Debbie	New York, N.Y.	8/31/70
Gibson, Henry	Germantown, Pa.	9/21/35
Gibson, Mel	Peekskill, N.Y.	1/3/56
Gielgud, John	London, England	4/14/04
Gifford, Frank	Santa Monica, Cal.	8/16/30
Gilbert, Melissa	Los Angeles, Cal.	5/8/64
Gilberto, Astrud	Salvador, Brazil	3/30/40
Gillette, Anita	Baltimore, Md.	8/16/38
Gilley, Mickey	Natchez, Miss.	3/9/36
Ginty, Robert	New York, N.Y.	11/14/48

Name	Birthplace	Born
Givens, Robin	New York, N.Y.	11/27/64
Glaser, Paul Michael	Cambridge, Mass.	3/25/42
Glenn, Scott	Pittsburgh, Pa.	1/26/42
Gless, Sharon	Los Angeles, Cal.	5/31/43
Glover, Danny	San Francisco, Cal.	7/22/47
Godard, Jean Luc	Paris, France	12/3/30
Godunov, Alexander	Sakhalin Is., USSR	11/28/49
Goldberg, Whoopi	New York, N.Y.	11/13/50
Goldblum, Jeff	Pittsburgh, Pa.	10/22/52
Goldsboro, Bobby	Marianna, Fla.	1/18/42
Goldthwait, Bob	Syracuse, N.Y.	1962
Goodman, John	St. Louis, Mo.	6/20/53
Gordon, Gale	New York, N.Y.	2/2/06
Gorme, Eydie	Bronx, N.Y.	8/16/32
Gorshin, Frank	Pittsburgh, Pa.	4/5/34
Gossett Jr., Louis	Brooklyn, N.Y.	5/27/36
Gould, Elliott	Brooklyn, N.Y.	8/29/38
Gould, Harold	Schenectady, N.Y.	12/10/23
Gould, Morton	Richmond Hill, N.Y.	12/10/13
Goulet, Robert	Lawrence, Mass.	11/26/33
Gowdy, Curt	Green River, Wyo.	7/31/19
Graham, Virginia	Chicago, Ill.	7/4/12
Grammer, Kelsey	Virgin Islands	2/20/-
Granger, Farley	San Jose, Cal.	7/1/25
Granger, Stewart	London, England	5/6/13
Grant, Amy	Augusta, Ga.	12/25/60
Grant, Lee	New York, N.Y.	10/31/29
Graves, Peter	Minneapolis, Minn.	3/18/26
Gray, Linda	Santa Monica, Cal.	9/12/40
Grayson, Kathryn	Winston-Salem, N.C.	2/9/22
Greco, Jose	Abruzzi, Italy	12/23/18
Green, Adolph	New York, N.Y.	12/2/15
Green, Al	Forest City, Ark.	4/13/46
Greene, Michele	Las Vegas, Nev.	2/3/-
Greene, Shecky	Chicago, Ill.	4/8/26
Gregory, Cynthia	Los Angeles, Cal.	7/8/46
Gregory, Dick	St. Louis, Mo.	10/12/32
Gregory, James	Bronx, N.Y.	12/23/11
Grey, Jennifer	New York, N.Y.	3/22/60
Grey, Joel	Cleveland, Oh.	4/11/32
Grier, David Alan	Detroit, Mich.	6/30/55
Griffin, Merv	San Mateo, Cal.	7/6/25
Griffith, Andy	Mount Airy, N.C.	6/1/26
Griffith, Melanie	New York, N.Y.	8/9/57
Grimes, Tammy	Lynn, Mass.	1/30/34
Grizzard, George	Roanoke Rapids, N.C.	4/1/28
Grodin, Charles	Pittsburgh, Pa.	4/21/35
Groh, David	New York, N.Y.	5/21/41
Grosbard, Ulu	Antwerp, Belgium	1/19/29
Gross, Michael	Chicago, Ill.	6/21/47
Guardino, Harry	New York, N.Y.	12/23/25
Guillaume, Robert	St. Louis, Mo.	11/30/37
Guinness, Alec	London, England	4/2/14
Gumbel, Greg	New Orleans, La.	5/3/46
Guthrie, Arlo	New York, N.Y.	7/10/47
Guttenberg, Steve	New York, N.Y.	8/24/58
Guy, Jasmine	Boston, Mass.	3/10/64
Hackett, Buddy	Brooklyn, N.Y.	8/31/24
Hackman, Gene	San Bernardino, Cal.	1/30/30
Hagen, Uta	Gottingen, Germany	6/12/19
Haggard, Merle	Bakersfield, Cal.	4/6/37
Hagman, Larry	Weatherford, Tex.	9/21/31
Haid, Charles	San Francisco, Cal.	6/2/44
Hale, Barbara	DeKalb, Ill.	4/18/22
Hall, Arsenio	Cleveland, Oh.	2/12/55
Hall, Daryl	Pottstown, Pa.	10/11/48
Hall, Deidre	Milwaukee, Wis.	10/31/48
Hall, Huntz	New York, N.Y.	8/15/19
Hall, Monty	Winnipeg, Man.	8/25/25
Hall, Tom T.	Olive Hill, Ky.	5/25/36
Hamel, Veronica	Philadelphia, Pa.	11/20/43
Hamill, Mark	Oakland, Cal.	9/25/51
Hamilton, George	Memphis, Tenn.	8/12/39
Hamilton, Linda	Salisbury, Md.	9/26/56
Hamlin, Harry	Pasadena, Cal.	10/30/51
Hammer	Oakland, Cal.	1962
Hampton, Lionel	Birmingham, Ala.	4/12/13
Hancock, Herbie	Chicago, Ill.	4/12/40
Hanks, Tom	Oakland, Cal.	7/9/56
Hannah, Daryl	Chicago, Ill.	1961
Hardison, Kadeem	New York, N.Y.	7/24/-
Harewood, Dorian	Dayton, Oh.	8/6/51
Harmon, Mark	Burbank, Cal.	9/2/51
Harper, Jessica	Chicago, Ill.	10/10/49
Harper, Tess	Mammoth Springs, Ark.	8/15/50
Harper, Valerie	Suffern, N.Y.	8/22/40
Harrelson, Woody	Midland, Tex.	7/23/61
Harrington, Pat	New York, N.Y.	8/13/29
Harris, Barbara	Evanston, Ill.	7/25/35
Harris, Ed	Englewood, N.J.	11/28/50
Harris, Emmylou	Birmingham, Ala.	4/2/47
Harris, Julie	Grosse Pte. Park, Mich.	12/2/25
Harris, Neil Patrick	Albuquerque, N.M.	6/15/73
Harris, Phil	Linton, Ind.	6/24/04
Harris, Richard	Co. Limerick, Ireland	10/1/33
Harris, Rosemary	Ashby, England	9/19/30
Harrison, George	Liverpool, England	2/25/43
Harrison, Gregory	Avalon, Cal.	5/31/50
Harry, Deborah	Miami, Fla.	7/1/45
Hart, Mary	Madison, S.D.	11/8/51
Hartley, Mariette	New York, N.Y.	6/21/40
Hartman, David	Pawtucket, R.I.	5/19/35
Hartman, Lisa	Houston, Tex.	6/1/56
Hartman, Phil	Ontario, Canada	9/24/48
Hasselhoff, David	Baltimore, Md.	7/17/52
Hasso, Signe	Stockholm, Sweden	8/15/10
Hauer, Rutger	Netherlands	1/23/44
Haver, June	Rock Island, Ill.	6/10/26
Havoc, June	Seattle, Wash.	11/8/16
Hawn, Goldie	Washington, D.C.	11/21/45
Hayden, Melissa	Toronto, Ont.	4/25/23
Hayes, Isaac	Covington, Tenn.	8/20/42
Hays, Robert	Bethesda, Md.	7/24/47
Heard, John	Washington, D.C.	3/7/45
Hearn, George	Memphis, Tenn.	1935
Heckart, Eileen	Columbus, Oh.	3/29/19
Helmond, Katherine	Galveston, Tex.	7/5/34
Hemingway, Margaux	Portland, Ore.	2/19/55
Hemingway, Mariel	Mill Valley, Cal.	11/21/61
Hemmings, David	Guildford, England	11/18/41
Hemsley, Sherman	Philadelphia, Pa.	2/1/38
Henderson, Florence	Dale, Ind.	2/14/34
Henderson, Skitch	Halstad, Minn.	1/27/18
Henley, Don	Gilmer, Tex.	7/22/47
Henner, Marilu	Chicago, Ill.	4/6/52
Henning, Doug	Ft. Garry, Man.	5/3/47
Hepburn, Katharine	Hartford, Conn.	5/12/07
Herman, Pee-wee	Peekskill, N.Y.	8/27/52
Herrmann, Edward	Washington, D.C.	7/21/43
Hershey, Barbara	Los Angeles, Cal.	2/5/48
Hesseman, Howard	Lebanon, Ore.	2/27/40
Heston, Charlton	Evanston, Ill.	10/4/24
Hewett, Christopher	Sussex, England	4/5/-
Hildegarde	Adell, Wis.	2/1/06
Hill, Arthur	Melfort, Sask.	8/1/22
Hill, Steven	Seattle, Wash.	2/24/22
Hill, George Roy	Minneapolis, Minn.	12/20/22
Hiller, Wendy	Stockport, England	8/15/12
Hillerman, John	Denison, Tex.	12/30/32
Hines, Gregory	New York, N.Y.	2/14/46
Hines, Jerome	Hollywood, Cal.	11/8/21
Hingle, Pat	Miami, Fla.	7/19/24
Hirsch, Judd	New York, N.Y.	3/15/35
Hirt, Al	New Orleans, La.	11/7/22
Ho, Don	Kakaako, Oahu, Ha.	8/13/30
Hoffman, Dustin	Los Angeles, Cal.	8/8/37
Hogan, Paul	New South Wales, Australia	10/8/39
Holbrook, Hal	Cleveland, Oh.	2/17/25
Holder, Geoffrey	Trinidad	8/1/30
Holliman, Earl	Delhi, La.	9/11/28
Holm, Celeste	New York, N.Y.	4/29/19
Hooks, Jan	Decatur, Ga.	4/23/57
Hooks, Robert	Washington, D.C.	4/18/37
Hope, Bob	London, England	5/29/03
Hopkins, Anthony	Wales	12/31/37
Hopkins, Telma	Louisville, Ky.	10/28/48
Hopper, Dennis	Dodge City, Kan.	5/17/36
Horne, Lena	Brooklyn, N.Y.	6/30/17
Horne, Marilyn	Bradford, Pa.	1/16/34
Horsley, Lee	Muleshoe, Tex.	5/15/55
Hoskins, Bob	Suffolk, England	10/26/42
Houston, Whitney	E. Orange, N.J.	8/9/63
Howard, Ken	El Centro, Cal.	3/28/44
Howard, Ron	Duncan, Okla.	3/1/53
Howell, C. Thomas	Los Angeles, Cal.	12/7/66
Howes, Sally Ann	London, England	7/20/30
Hughes, Barnard	Bedford Hills, N.Y.	7/16/15
Hulce, Tom	Whitewater, Wis.	12/6/53
Humperdinck, Engelbert	Madras, India	5/3/36
Hunt, Helen	Los Angeles, Cal.	6/15/63
Hunt, Linda	Morristown, N.J.	4/2/45
Hunter, Holly	Conyers, Ga.	3/20/58
Hunter, Kim	Detroit, Mich.	11/12/22
Hunter, Ross	Cleveland, Oh.	5/6/21
Hunter, Tab	New York, N.Y.	7/11/31

Name	Birthplace	Born
Hurt, John	Chesterfield, England	1/22/40
Hurt, Mary Beth	Marshalltown, Ia.	9/26/46
Hurt, William	Washington, D.C.	3/20/50
Hussey, Ruth	Providence, R.I.	10/30/14
Huston, Anjelica	Ireland	7/8/51
Hutton, Betty	Battle Creek, Mich.	2/26/21
Hutton, Timothy	Malibu, Cal.	8/16/60
Hyman, Earle	Rocky Mount, N.C.	10/11/26
Ian, Janis	New York, N.Y.	4/7/51
Idol, Billy	London, England	11/30/55
Iglesias, Julio	Madrid, Spain	9/23/43
Ingram, James	Akron, Oh.	2/16/56
Irons, Jeremy	Cowes, England	9/19/48
Irving, Amy	Palo Alto, Cal.	9/10/53
Irving, George S.	Springfield, Mass.	11/1/22
Ives, Burl	Hunt Township, Ill.	6/14/09
Ivey, Judith	El Paso, Tex.	9/4/51
Ivory, James	Berkeley, Cal.	6/7/28
Jackee	Winston-Salem, N.C.	8/14/57
Jackson, Anne	Allegheny, Pa.	9/3/25
Jackson, Glenda	Liverpool, England	5/9/36
Jackson, Janet	Gary, Ind.	5/16/66
Jackson, Jermaine	Gary, Ind.	12/11/54
Jackson, La Toya	Gary, Ind.	5/29/56
Jackson, Kate	Birmingham, Ala.	10/29/48
Jackson, Michael	Gary, Ind.	8/29/58
Jacobi, Derek	London, England	10/22/38
Jaeckel, Richard	Long Beach, N.Y.	10/10/26
Jagger, Mick	Dartford, England	7/26/43
James, Dennis	Jersey City, N.J.	8/24/17
Janis, Conrad	New York, N.Y.	2/11/28
Jarreau, Al	Milwaukee, Wis.	3/12/40
Jeffreys, Anne	Goldsboro, N.C.	1/26/23
Jennings, Waylon	Littlefield, Tex.	6/15/37
Jeter, Michael	Lawrenceburg, Tenn.	8/20/52
Jett, Joan	Philadelphia, Pa.	9/22/60
Jewison, Norman	Toronto, Ont.	7/21/26
Jillian, Ann	Cambridge, Mass.	1/29/50
Joel, Billy	Bronx, N.Y.	5/9/49
John, Elton	Middlesex, England	3/25/47
Johns, Glynis	Durban, S. Africa	10/5/23
Johnson, Anne-Marie	Los Angeles, Cal.	7/18/-
Johnson, Arte	Benton Harbor, Mich.	1/20/29
Johnson, Ben	Foraker, Okla.	6/13/18
Johnson, Don	Flatt Creek, Mo.	12/15/49
Johnson, Van	Newport, R.I.	8/25/16
Jones, Charlie	Ft. Smith, Ark.	11/9/30
Jones, Dean	Morgan City, Ala.	1/25/35
Jones, George	Saratoga, Tex.	9/12/31
Jones, Grace	Spanishtown, Jamaica	5/19/52
Jones, Grandpa	Niagara, Ky.	10/20/13
Jones, Henry	Philadelphia, Pa.	8/1/12
Jones, Jack	Hollywood, Cal.	1/14/38
Jones, James Earl	Tate Co., Miss.	1/17/31
Jones, Jennifer	Tulsa, Okla.	3/2/19
Jones, Shirley	Smithton, Pa.	3/31/34
Jones, Tom	Pontypridd, Wales	6/7/40
Jones, Tommy Lee	San Saba, Tex.	9/15/46
Jordan, Richard	New York, N.Y.	7/19/38
Jourdan, Louis	Marseilles, France	6/19/19
Judd, Naomi	Ashland, Ky.	1/11/46
Judd, Wynonna	Ashland, Ky.	5/3/64
Julia, Raul	San Juan, P.R.	3/9/40
Jump, Gordon	Dayton, Oh.	4/1/32
Kahn, Madeline	Boston, Mass.	9/29/42
Kanaly, Steve	Burbank, Cal.	3/14/46
Kane, Carol	Cleveland, Oh.	6/18/52
Karlen, John	New York, N.Y.	5/28/33
Karras, Alex	Gary, Ind.	7/15/35
Kasem, Casey	Detroit, Mich.	1933
Kavner, Julie	Los Angeles, Cal.	9/7/51
Kazan, Elia	Istanbul, Turkey	9/7/09
Kazan, Lainie	New York, N.Y.	5/15/42
Keach, Stacy	Savannah, Ga.	6/2/41
Keaton, Diane	Santa Ana, Cal.	1/5/46
Keaton, Michael	Pittsburgh, Pa.	9/9/51
Keel, Howard	Gillespie, Ill.	4/13/17
Keeshan, Bob	Lynbrook, N.Y.	6/27/27
Keitel, Harvey	Brooklyn, N.Y.	—
Keith, Brian	Bayonne, N.J.	11/14/21
Keith, David	Knoxville, Tenn.	5/8/54
Kellerman, Sally	Long Beach, Cal.	6/2/37
Kelley, DeForest	Atlanta, Ga.	1/20/20
Kelly, Gene	Pittsburgh, Pa.	8/23/12
Kennedy, George	New York, N.Y.	2/18/25
Kennedy, Jayne	Washington, D.C.	11/27/51
Kent, Allegra	Los Angeles, Cal.	8/11/37

Name	Birthplace	Born
Kercheval, Ken	Wolcottville, Ind.	7/15/35
Kerns, Joanna	San Francisco, Cal.	2/12/53
Kerr, Deborah	Helensburgh, Scotland	9/30/21
Khan, Chaka	Great Lakes, Ill.	3/23/53
Kidder, Margot	Yellowknife, N.W.T.	10/17/48
Kidman, Nicole	Hawaii	1977
Kiley, Richard	Chicago, Ill.	3/31/22
Kilmer, Val	Los Angeles, Cal.	12/31/59
Kimbrough, Charles	St. Paul, Minn.	5/23/-
King, Alan	Brooklyn, N.Y.	12/26/27
King, B. B.	Itta Bena, Miss.	9/16/25
King, Carole	Brooklyn, N.Y.	2/9/42
King, Larry	New York, N.Y.	11/19/33
King, Perry	Alliance, Oh.	4/30/48
Kingsley, Ben	Yorkshire, England	12/31/43
Kinski, Nastassia	Berlin, W. Germany	1/24/60
Kirby, Bruno	New York, N.Y.	1949
Kirby, Durward	Covington, Ky.	8/24/12
Kirkland, Gelsey	Bethlehem, Pa.	12/29/53
Kitt, Eartha	North, S.C.	1/26/28
Klein, Robert	New York, N.Y.	2/8/42
Klemperer, Werner	Cologne, Germany	3/22/19
Kline, Kevin	St. Louis, Mo.	10/24/47
Klugman, Jack	Philadelphia, Pa.	4/27/22
Knight, Gladys	Atlanta, Ga.	5/28/44
Knotts, Don	Morgantown, W. Va.	7/21/24
Kopell, Bernie	New York, N.Y.	6/21/33
Korman, Harvey	Chicago, Ill.	2/15/27
Kotto, Yaphet	New York, N.Y.	11/15/37
Kramer, Stanley	New York, N.Y.	9/29/13
Kristofferson, Kris	Brownsville, Tex.	6/22/36
Kubelik, Rafael	Bychori, Czechoslovakia	6/29/14
Kubrick, Stanley	Bronx, N.Y.	7/26/28
Kurtz, Swoosie	Omaha, Neb.	9/6/44
LaBelle, Patti	Philadelphia, Pa.	10/4/44
Ladd, Cheryl	Huron, S.D.	7/12/51
Ladd, Diane	Meridian, Miss.	11/29/32
Lahti, Christine	Detroit, Mich.	4/5/50
Laine, Cleo	Middlesex, England	10/28/27
Laine, Frankie	Chicago, Ill.	3/30/13
Lamarr, Hedy	Vienna, Austria	11/9/13
Lamas, Lorenzo	Santa Monica, Cal.	1/20/58
Lamb, Gil	Minneapolis, Minn.	6/14/06
Lamour, Dorothy	New Orleans, La.	12/10/14
Lancaster, Burt	New York, N.Y.	11/2/13
Landau, Martin	New York, N.Y.	6/20/34
Landis, John	Chicago, Ill.	8/3/50
Lane, Diane	New York, N.Y.	1/22/63
Lane, Priscilla	Indianola, Ia.	6/12/17
Lang, K.D.	Consort, Alberta	11/2/61
Lang, Stephen	New York, N.Y.	7/11/52
Lange, Hope	Redding Ridge, Conn.	11/28/31
Lange, Jessica	Cloquet, Minn.	4/20/49
Langella, Frank	Bayonne, N.J.	1/1/40
Langford, Frances	Lakeland, Fla.	4/4/13
Lansbury, Angela	London, England	10/16/25
Lansing, Robert	San Diego, Cal.	6/5/28
Laredo, Ruth	Detroit, Mich.	11/20/37
Larroquette, John	New Orleans, La.	11/25/47
Lasser, Louise	New York, N.Y.	4/11/39
Lauper, Cyndi	New York, N.Y.	6/20/53
Laurie, Piper	Detroit, Mich.	1/22/32
Lauter, Ed	Long Beach, N.Y.	10/30/40
Lavin, Linda	Portland, Me.	10/15/37
Lawrence, Carol	Melrose Park, Ill.	9/5/34
Lawrence, Steve	Brooklyn, N.Y.	7/8/35
Lawrence, Vicki	Inglewood, Cal.	3/26/49
Leach, Robin	London, England	8/29/41
Leachman, Cloris	Des Moines, Ia.	4/4/26
Lear, Norman	New Haven, Conn.	7/27/22
Learned, Michael	Washington, D.C.	4/9/39
LeBon, Simon	Bushey, England	10/27/58
Lee, Brenda	Atlanta, Ga.	12/11/44
Lee, Christopher	London, England	5/27/22
Lee, Michele	Los Angeles, Cal.	6/24/42
Lee, Peggy	Jamestown, N.D.	5/26/20
Lee, Spike	Atlanta, Ga.	3/20/57
Legrand, Michel	Paris, France	2/24/32
Leibman, Ron	New York, N.Y.	10/11/37
Leifer, Carol	E. Williston, N.Y.	1956
Leigh, Janet	Merced, Cal.	7/6/27
Leigh, Jennifer Jason	Los Angeles, Cal.	2/5/62
Leinsdorf, Erich	Vienna, Austria	2/4/12
Leisure, David	San Diego, Cal.	11/16/-
Lemmon, Jack	Boston, Mass.	2/8/25
Leno, Jay	New Rochelle, N.Y.	4/28/50
Leonard, Sheldon	New York, N.Y.	2/22/07

Name	Birthplace	Born
Leontovich, Eugenie	Moscow, Russia	3/21/00
Leslie, Joan	Detroit, Mich.	1/26/25
Letterman, David	Indianapolis, Ind.	4/12/47
Levine, James	Cincinnati, Oh.	6/23/43
Levinson, Barry	Baltimore, Md.	6/2/32
Lewis, Dawnn	New York, N.Y.	8/13/60
Lewis, Huey	New York, N.Y.	7/5/51
Lewis, Jerry	Newark, N.J.	3/16/26
Lewis, Jerry Lee	Ferriday, La.	9/29/35
Lewis, Richard	New York, N.Y.	6/29/47
Lewis, Shari	New York, N.Y.	1/17/34
Light, Judith	Trenton, N.J.	2/9/50
Lightfoot, Gordon	Orillia, Ont.	11/17/38
Linden, Hal	New York, N.Y.	3/20/31
Lindfors, Viveca	Uppsala, Sweden	12/29/20
Linkletter, Art	Saskatchewan, Canada	7/17/12
Linn-Baker, Mark	St. Louis, Mo.	6/17/53
Liotta, Ray	Newark, N.J.	12/18/55
Lithgow, John	Rochester, N.Y.	10/19/45
Little, Rich	Ottawa, Ont.	11/26/38
Little Richard	Macon, Ga.	12/5/32
Lloyd, Christopher	Stamford, Conn.	10/22/38
Lloyd, Emily	England	9/29/70
Locke, Sondra	Shelbyville, Tenn.	5/28/47
Lockhart, June	New York, N.Y.	6/25/25
Locklear, Heather	Los Angeles, Cal.	9/25/61
Loggia, Robert	New York, N.Y.	1/3/30
Loggins, Kenny	Everett, Wash.	1/17/47
Lollobrigida, Gina	Subiaco, Italy	7/4/27
Lom, Herbert	Prague, Czechoslovakia	1/9/17
Long, Shelley	Ft. Wayne, Ind.	8/23/49
Lord, Jack	New York, N.Y.	12/30/22
Loren, Sophia	Rome, Italy	9/20/34
Loring, Gloria	New York, N.Y.	12/10/46
Loudon, Dorothy	Boston, Mass.	9/17/33
Louis-Dreyfus, Julia	New York, N.Y.	1/13/62
Lovitz, Jon	Tarzana, Cal.	7/21/57
Lowe, Rob	Charlottesville, Va.	3/17/64
Loy, Myrna	Helena, Mon.	8/2/05
Lucas, George	Modesto, Cal.	5/14/44
Lucci, Susan	Scarsdale, N.Y.	12/23/50
Luckinbill, Laurence	Ft. Smith, Ark.	11/21/34
Ludwig, Christa	Berlin, Germany	3/16/28
Lumet, Sidney	Philadelphia, Pa.	6/25/24
Lupino, Ida	London, England	2/4/14
LuPone, Patti	Northport, N.Y.	4/21/49
Lynch, David	Missoula, Mont.	1/20/46
Lynn, Jeffrey	Auburn, Mass.	2/16/09
Lynn, Loretta	Butcher Hollow, Ky.	4/14/35
Maazel, Lorin	Paris, France	3/6/30
MacArthur, James	Los Angeles, Cal.	12/8/37
MacCorkindale, Simon	Cambridge, England	2/12/52
MacDowell, Andie	Gaffney, S.C.	4/21/58
MacGraw, Ali	Pound Ridge, N.Y.	4/1/38
Mac Lachlan, Kyle	Yakima, Wash.	2/22/59
MacLaine, Shirley	Richmond, Va.	4/24/34
MacLeod, Gavin	Mt. Kisco, N.Y.	2/28/30
MacNee, Patrick	London, England	2/6/22
MacNeil, Cornell	Minneapolis, Minn.	9/24/22
Macchio, Ralph	Long Island, N.Y.	11/4/62
Macy, Bill	Revere, Mass.	5/18/22
Madden, John	Austin, Minn.	4/10/36
Madigan, Amy	Chicago, Ill.	9/11/51
Madonna (Ciccone)	Bay City, Mich.	8/16/58
Majors, Lee	Wyandotte, Mich.	4/23/40
Malbin, Elaine	New York, N.Y.	5/24/32
Malden, Karl	Chicago, Ill.	3/22/13
Malkovich, John	Christopher, Ill.	12/9/53
Malle, Louis	Thumeries, France	10/30/32
Malone, Dorothy	Chicago, Ill.	1/30/25
Manchester, Melissa	Bronx, N.Y.	2/15/51
Mancini, Henry	Cleveland, Oh.	4/16/24
Mandel, Howie	Toronto, Ont.	11/29/55
Mandrell, Barbara	Houston, Tex.	12/25/48
Mangione, Chuck	Rochester, N.Y.	11/29/40
Manilow, Barry	New York, N.Y.	6/17/46
Mann, Herbie	New York, N.Y.	4/16/30
Manoff, Dinah	New York, N.Y.	1/25/58
Mantegna, Joe	Chicago, Ill.	11/13/47
Marceau, Marcel	Strasbourg, France	3/22/23
Marchand, Nancy	Buffalo, N.Y.	6/19/28
Margolin, Janet	New York, N.Y.	7/25/43
Marin, Cheech	Los Angeles, Cal.	7/13/46
Markova, Alicia	London, England	12/1/10
Marriner, Neville	Lincoln, England	4/15/24
Marsalis, Branford	New Orleans, La.	8/26/60
Marsalis, Wynton	New Orleans, La.	10/18/61
Marsh, Jean	London, England	7/1/34
Marshall, E. G.	Owatonna, Minn.	6/18/10
Marshall, Penny	New York, N.Y.	10/15/43
Marshall, Peter	Huntington, W.Va.	3/30/27
Martin, Dean	Steubenville, Oh.	6/17/17
Martin, Dick	Detroit, Mich.	1/30/23
Martin, Steve	Waco, Tex.	4/14/45
Martin, Tony	San Francisco, Cal.	12/25/13
Martins, Peter	Copenhagen, Denmark	10/27/46
Mason, Jackie	Sheboygan, Wis.	6/9/31
Mason, Marsha	St. Louis, Mo.	4/3/42
Masterson, Mary Stuart	Los Angeles, Cal.	6/28/66
Mastrantonio, Mary Eliz.	Lombard, Ill.	11/17/58
Mastroianni, Marcello	Rome, Italy	9/28/23
Masur, Kurt	Brieg, Germany	7/18/27
Matheson, Tim	Glendale, Cal.	12/31/47
Mathis, Johnny	San Francisco, Cal.	9/30/35
Matlin, Marlee	Morton Grove, Ill.	8/24/65
Mattea, Kathy	Cross Lanes, W. Va.	—
Matthau, Walter	New York, N.Y.	10/1/20
Mature, Victor	Louisville, Ky.	1/29/16
May, Elaine	Philadelphia, Pa.	4/21/32
Mayfield, Curtis	Chicago, Ill.	6/3/42
Mayo, Virginia	St. Louis, Mo.	11/30/20
Mazursky, Paul	Brooklyn, N.Y.	4/25/30
McArdle, Andrea	Philadelphia, Pa.	11/5/63
McBride, Patricia	Teaneck, N.J.	8/23/42
McCallum, David	Glasgow, Scotland	9/19/33
McCambridge, Mercedes	Joliet, Ill.	3/17/18
McCarthy, Andrew	New York, N.Y.	1962
McCarthy, Kevin	Seattle, Wash.	2/15/14
McCartney, Paul	Liverpool, England	6/18/42
McCarver, Tim	Memphis, Tenn.	10/16/41
McClanahan, Rue	Healdton, Okla.	2/21/36
McClure, Doug	Glendale, Cal.	5/11/35
McClurg, Edie	Kansas City, Mo.	7/23/51
McCoo, Marilyn	Jersey City, N.J.	9/30/43
McDonnell, Mary	Ithaca, N.Y.	1953
McDowall, Roddy	London, England	9/28/28
McDowell, Malcolm	Leeds, England	6/13/43
McEntire, Reba	McAlester, Okla.	3/28/54
McFerrin, Bobby	New York, N.Y.	3/11/50
McGavin, Darren	Spokane, Wash.	5/7/22
McGoohan, Patrick	New York, N.Y.	3/19/28
McGovern, Elizabeth	Evanston, Ill.	7/18/61
McGovern, Maureen	Youngstown, Oh.	7/27/49
McGuire, Al	New York, N.Y.	9/7/31
McGuire, Dorothy	Omaha, Neb.	6/14/19
McKechnie, Donna	Pontiac, Mich.	11/16/42
McKee, Lonette	Detroit, Mich.	1954
McKellen, Ian	Burnley, England	5/25/39
McLerie, Allyn	Grand Mere, Que.	12/1/26
McMahon, Ed	Detroit, Mich.	3/6/23
McNichol, Kristy	Los Angeles, Cal.	9/11/62
McQueen, Butterfly	Tampa, Fla.	1/7/11
McRaney, Gerald	Collins, Miss.	8/19/48
Meadows, Audrey	Wu Chang, China	2/8/24
Meadows, Jayne	Wu Chang, China	9/27/20
Meara, Anne	New York, N.Y.	9/20/29
Mehta, Zubin	Bombay, India	4/29/36
Mendes, Sergio	Niteroi, Brazil	2/11/41
Menuhin, Yehudi	New York, N.Y.	4/22/16
Mercer, Marian	Akron, Oh.	11/26/35
Mercouri, Melina	Athens, Greece	10/18/25
Meredith, Burgess	Cleveland, Oh.	11/16/08
Merrick, David	Hong Kong	11/27/12
Merrill, Dina	New York, N.Y.	12/9/25
Merrill, Robert	Brooklyn, N.Y.	6/4/19
Messina, Jim	Maywood, Cal.	12/5/47
Metcalf, Laurie	Carbondale, Ill.	6/16/55
Meyers, Ari	San Juan, Puerto Rico	4/6/69
Michael, George	Watford, England	6/26/63
Michaels, Al	New York, N.Y.	11/12/44
Midler, Bette	Paterson, N.J.	12/1/45
Milano, Alyssa	New York, N.Y.	12/19/72
Miles, Sarah	Ingatestone, England	12/31/41
Miles, Vera	near Boise City, Okla.	8/23/29
Miller, Ann	Houston, Tex.	4/12/19
Miller, Dennis	Pittsburgh, Pa.	11/3/53
Miller, Mitch	Rochester, N.Y.	7/4/11
Miller, Penelope Ann	Log Angeles, Cal.	1/13/64
Mills, Donna	Chicago, Ill.	12/11/42
Mills, John	Suffolk, England	2/22/08
Milner, Martin	Detroit, Mich.	12/28/27
Milnes, Sherrill	Downers Grove, Ill.	1/10/35
Milsap, Ronnie	Robinsville, N.C.	1/16/44
Minnelli, Liza	Los Angeles, Cal.	3/12/46

Name	Birthplace	Born
Mitchell, Cameron	Dallastown, Pa.	4/11/18
Mitchell, James	Sacramento, Cal.	2/29/20
Mitchell, Joni	McLeod, Alta.	11/7/43
Mitchum, Robert	Bridgeport, Conn.	8/6/17
Modine, Matthew	Loma Linda, Cal.	3/22/59
Moffat, Donald	Plymouth, England	12/26/30
Moffo, Anna	Wayne, Pa.	6/27/27
Molinaro, Al.	Kenosha, Wis.	6/24/19
Moll, Richard	Pasadena, Cal.	1/13/43
Montalban, Ricardo	Mexico City, Mexico	11/25/20
Montgomery, Elizabeth	Hollywood, Cal.	4/15/33
Moody, Ron	London, England	1/8/24
Moore, Clayton	Chicago, Ill.	9/14/08
Moore, Demi	Roswell, N.M.	11/11/62
Moore, Dudley	London, England	4/19/35
Moore, Garry	Baltimore, Md.	1/31/15
Moore, Mary Tyler	Brooklyn, N.Y.	12/29/37
Moore, Melba	New York, N.Y.	10/29/45
Moore, Roger	London, England	10/14/27
Moore, Terry	Los Angeles, Cal.	1/1/29
Moranis, Rick	Toronto, Ont.	4/18/53
Moreno, Rita	Humacao, P.R.	12/11/31
Morgan, Dennis	Prentice, Wis.	12/10/10
Morgan, Harry	Detroit, Mich.	4/10/15
Morgan, Henry	New York, N.Y.	3/31/15
Moriarty, Michael	Detroit, Mich.	4/5/41
Morita, Pat	Isleton, Cal.	6/28/32
Morris, Howard	New York, N.Y.	9/4/25
Morrow, Rob	New Rochelle, N.Y.	9/21/62
Morse, Robert	Newton, Mass.	5/18/31
Morton, Joe	New York, N.Y.	10/18/47
Moses, William	Los Angeles, Cal.	11/17/59
Muldaur, Diana	New York, N.Y.	8/19/38
Mulgrew, Kate	Dubuque, Ia.	4/29/55
Mulhare, Edward	Ireland	4/8/23
Mull, Martin	Chicago, Ill.	8/18/43
Mulligan, Richard	New York, N.Y.	11/13/32
Munsel, Patrice	Spokane, Wash.	5/14/25
Murphy, Ben	Jonesboro, Ark.	3/6/42
Murphy, Eddie	Brooklyn, N.Y.	4/3/61
Murphy, Michael	Los Angeles, Cal.	5/5/38
Murray, Anne	Springhill, Nova Scotia	6/20/45
Murray, Bill	Evanston, Ill.	9/21/50
Murray, Don	Hollywood, Cal.	7/31/29
Musante, Tony	Bridgeport, Conn.	6/30/36
Musburger, Brent	Portland, Ore.	5/26/39
Muti, Riccardo	Naples, Italy	7/28/41
Myers, Mike	Toronto, Ont.	1962
Nabors, Jim	Sylacauga, Ala.	6/12/33
Nash, Graham	Blackpool, England	2/2/42
Natwick, Mildred	Baltimore, Md.	6/19/08
Naughton, James	Middletown, Conn.	7/6/46
Neal, Patricia	Packard, Ky.	1/20/26
Nealon, Kevin	Bridgeport, Conn.	11/18/53
Neeson, Liam	N. Ireland	6/7/52
Neill, Sam	New Zealand	1948
Nelligan, Kate	London, Ontario	3/16/51
Nelson, Craig T.	Spokane, Wash.	4/4/46
Nelson, Ed	New Orleans, La.	12/21/28
Nelson, Harriet (Hilliard)	Des Moines, Ia.	7/18/14
Nelson, Judd	Portland, Me.	11/28/59
Nelson, Tracy	Santa Monica, Cal.	10/25/63
Nelson, Willie	Abbott, Tex.	4/30/33
Nero, Peter	New York, N.Y.	5/22/34
Neuwirth, Bebe	Newark, N.J.	12/31/-
New Kids On The Block		
Knight, Jonathan	Worcester, Mass.	11/29/68
Knight, Jordan	Worcester, Mass.	5/17/70
McIntyre, Joe	Needham, Mass.	12/31/72
Wahlberg, Donnie	Boston, Mass.	8/17/69
Wood, Danny	Boston, Mass.	5/14/69
Newhart, Bob	Oak Park, Ill.	9/29/29
Newley, Anthony	Hackney, England	9/24/31
Newman, Paul	Cleveland, Oh.	1/26/25
Newman, Randy	Los Angeles, Cal.	11/28/43
Newton, Wayne	Norfolk, Va.	4/3/42
Newton-John, Olivia	Cambridge, England	9/26/47
Nicholas, Denise	Detroit, Mich.	7/12/44
Nicholas, Fayard	Philadelphia, Pa.	10/20/14
Nicholas, Harold	Philadelphia, Pa.	3/27/24
Nichols, Mike	Berlin, Germany	11/6/31
Nicholson, Jack	Neptune, N.J.	4/28/37
Nicks, Stevie	Phoenix, Ariz.	5/26/48
Nielsen, Leslie	Regina, Sask	2/11/26
Nilsson, Birgit	Karup, Sweden	5/17/18
Nimoy, Leonard	Boston, Mass.	3/26/31
Nolte, Nick	Omaha, Neb.	2/8/40
Norman, Jessye	Augusta, Ga.	9/15/45

Name	Birthplace	Born
Norris, Chuck	Ryan, Okla.	3/10/40
North, Sheree	Los Angeles, Cal.	1/17/33
Noth, Christopher	Madison, Wis.	11/13/-
Novak, Kim	Chicago, Ill.	2/13/33
Oates, John	New York, N.Y.	4/7/48
O'Brian, Hugh	Rochester, N.Y.	4/19/25
O'Brien, Conan	Brookline, Mass.	1963
O'Brien, Margaret	San Diego, Cal.	1/15/37
Ocean, Billy	Trinidad	1/21/50
O'Connell, Helen	Lima, Oh.	5/23/21
O'Connor, Carroll	New York, N.Y.	8/2/24
O'Connor, Donald	Chicago, Ill.	8/28/25
O'Connor, Sinead	Dublin, Ireland	12/8/67
Odetta	Birmingham, Ala.	12/31/30
O'Donnell, Chris	Winnetka, Ill.	1970
O'Hara, Maureen	Dublin, Ireland	8/17/20
O'Herlihy, Dan	Wexford, Ireland	5/1/19
Oldman, Gary	London, England	3/21/58
Olin, Ken	Chicago, Ill.	7/30/54
Olin, Lena	Sweden	3/22/55
Olmos, Edward James	E. Los Angeles, Cal.	2/24/47
Olsen, Merlin	Logan, Ut.	9/15/40
O'Neal, Patrick	Ocala, Fla.	9/26/27
O'Neal, Ryan	Los Angeles, Cal.	4/20/41
O'Neal, Tatum	Los Angeles, Cal.	11/5/63
O'Neill, Ed	Youngstown, Oh.	1946
Ontkean, Michael	Vancouver, B.C.	1/24/46
Orbach, Jerry	New York, N.Y.	10/20/35
Orlando, Tony	New York, N.Y.	4/3/44
Osbourne, Ozzy	Birmingham, England	12/3/46
O'Shea, Milo	Dublin, Ireland	6/2/26
Oslin, K.T.	Crossit, Ark.	1942
Osmond, Donny	Ogden, Ut.	12/9/57
Osmond, Marie	Ogden, Ut.	10/13/59
O'Sullivan, Maureen	Boyle, Ireland	5/17/11
O'Toole, Annette	Houston, Tex.	4/1/53
O'Toole, Peter	Connemara, Ireland	8/2/32
Owens, Buck	Sherman, Tex.	8/12/29
Oz, Frank	Herford, England	5/25/44
Ozawa, Seiji	Shenyang, China	9/1/35
Paar, Jack	Canton, Oh.	5/1/18
Pacino, Al	New York, N.Y.	4/25/40
Packer, Billy	Wellsville, N.Y.	2/25/40
Page, Patti	Claremore, Okla.	11/8/27
Paige, Janis	Tacoma, Wash.	9/16/22
Palance, Jack	Lattimer, Pa.	2/18/20
Palin, Michael	England	5/5/43
Palmer, Betsy	East Chicago, Ind.	11/1/29
Papas, Irene	Greece	3/9/26
Parker, Alan	London, England	2/14/44
Parker, Eleanor	Cedarville, Oh.	6/26/22
Parker, Fess	Ft. Worth, Tex.	8/16/25
Parker, Jameson	Baltimore, Md.	11/18/47
Parker, Jean	Deer Lodge, Mon.	8/11/12
Parker, Sarah Jessica	Nelsonville, Oh.	3/25/65
Parsons, Estelle	Lynn, Mass.	11/20/27
Parton, Dolly	Sevierville, Tenn.	1/19/46
Patinkin, Mandy	Chicago, Ill.	11/30/52
Pavarotti, Luciano	Modena, Italy	10/12/35
Paycheck, Johnny	Greenfield, Oh.	5/31/41
Pearl, Minnie	Centerville, Tenn.	10/25/12
Peck, Gregory	La Jolla, Cal.	4/5/16
Pendergrass, Teddy	Philadelphia, Pa.	3/26/50
Penn, Arthur	Philadelphia, Pa.	9/27/22
Penn, Sean	Burbank, Cal.	8/17/60
Penny, Joe	London, England	9/14/56
Peppard, George	Detroit, Mich.	10/1/28
Perkins, Elizabeth	New York, N.Y.	11/18/60
Perlman, Itzhak	Tel Aviv, Israel	8/31/45
Perlman, Rhea	Brooklyn, N.Y.	3/31/48
Perlman, Ron	New York, N.Y.	4/13/50
Perrine, Valerie	Galveston, Tex.	9/3/43
Perry, Luke	Fredericktown, Oh.	10/11/-
Persoff, Nehemiah	Jerusalem, Palestine	8/14/20
Pesci, Joe	Newark, N.J.	2/9/43
Peters, Bernadette	New York, N.Y.	2/28/48
Peters, Brock	New York, N.Y.	7/2/27
Peters, Roberta	New York, N.Y.	5/4/30
Petty, Tom	Gainesville, Fla.	10/20/53
Pfeiffer, Michelle	Santa Ana, Cal.	4/29/57
Phillips, Lou Diamond	Philippines	2/17/62
Phillips, Michelle	Long Beach, Cal.	6/4/44
Phoenix, River	Madras, Ore.	8/23/70
Pickett, Cindy	Norman, Okla.	4/18/47
Pinchot, Bronson	New York, N.Y.	5/20/59
Piscopo, Joe	Passaic, N.J.	6/17/51
Pitt, Brad	Missouri	12/18/65
Pleasence, Donald	Worksop, England	10/5/19

Name	Birthplace	Born
Pleshette, Suzanne	New York, N.Y.	1/31/37
Plowright, Joan	Brigg, England	10/28/29
Plummer, Amanda	New York, N.Y.	3/23/57
Plummer, Christopher	Toronto, Ont.	12/13/27
Poitier, Sidney	Miami, Fla.	2/20/27
Polanski, Roman	Paris, France	8/18/33
Pollack, Sydney	Lafayette, Ind.	7/1/34
Ponti, Carlo	Milan, Italy	12/11/13
Post, Markie	Palo Alto, Cal.	11/4/50
Poston, Tom	Columbus, Oh.	10/17/27
Potts, Annie	Nashville, Tenn.	10/28/52
Povich, Maury	Washington, D.C.	1/17/39
Powell, Jane	Portland, Ore.	4/1/28
Powers, Stefanie	Hollywood, Cal.	11/2/42
Prentiss, Paula	San Antonio, Tex.	3/4/39
Presley, Priscilla	New York, N.Y.	5/24/46
Preston, Billy	Houston, Tex.	9/9/46
Previn, Andre	Berlin, Germany	4/6/29
Price, Leontyne	Laurel, Miss.	2/10/27
Price, Ray	Perryville, Tex.	1/12/26
Price, Vincent	St. Louis, Mo.	5/27/11
Pride, Charlie	Sledge, Miss.	3/18/39
Priestley, Jason	Vancouver, B.C.	8/28/69
Prince	Minneapolis, Minn.	6/7/58
Principal, Victoria	Japan	—
Prosky, Robert	Philadelphia, Pa.	12/13/30
Pryce, Jonathan	Wales	6/1/47
Pryor, Richard	Peoria, Ill.	12/1/40
Pulliam, Keshia Knight	Newark, N.J.	4/9/79
Pyle, Denver	Bethune, Col.	5/11/20
Quaid, Dennis	Houston, Tex.	4/9/54
Quaid, Randy	Houston, Tex.	10/1/50
Quinn, Aidan	Chicago, Ill.	3/8/59
Quinn, Anthony	Chihuahua, Mexico	4/21/15
Quinn, Martha	Albany, N.Y.	5/11/59
Rabb, Ellis	Memphis, Tenn.	6/20/30
Rabbitt, Eddie	Brooklyn, N.Y.	11/27/41
Rachins, Alan	Cambridge, Mass.	10/10/47
Rae, Charlotte	Milwaukee, Wis.	4/22/26
Rainer, Luise	Vienna, Austria	1/12/09
Raitt, Bonnie	Burbank, Cal.	11/8/49
Ralston, Esther	Bar Harbor, Me.	9/17/02
Ramey, Samuel	Colby, Kan.	3/28/42
Rampal, Jean-Pierre	Marseilles, France	1/7/22
Randall, Tony	Tulsa, Okla.	2/26/20
Randolph, John	New York, N.Y.	6/1/15
Randolph, Joyce	Detroit, Mich.	10/21/25
Raphael, Sally Jessy	Easton, Pa.	2/25/43
Rashad, Phylicia	Houston, Tex.	6/17/48
Ratzenberger, John	Bridgeport, Conn.	4/6/47
Rawls, Lou	Chicago, Ill.	12/1/36
Raye, Martha	Butte, Mon.	8/27/16
Raymond, Gene	New York, N.Y.	8/13/08
Reddy, Helen	Melbourne, Australia	10/25/41
Redford, Robert	Santa Monica, Cal.	8/18/37
Redgrave, Lynn	London, England	3/8/43
Redgrave, Vanessa	London, England	1/30/37
Reed, Jerry	Atlanta, Ga.	3/20/37
Reed, Oliver	London, England	2/13/38
Reed, Rex	Ft. Worth, Tex.	10/2/38
Reed, Shanna	Kansas City, Kan.	10/30/-
Reese, Della	Detroit, Mich.	7/6/31
Reeve, Christopher	New York, N.Y.	9/25/52
Reeves, Keanu	Beirut, Lebanon	9/2/64
Regalbuto, Joe	New York, N.Y.	8/24/-
Reid, Tim	Norfolk, Va.	12/19/44
Reilly, Charles Nelson	New York, N.Y.	1/13/31
Reiner, Carl	Bronx, N.Y.	3/20/22
Reiner, Rob	Bronx, N.Y.	3/6/45
Reinhold, Judge	Wilmington, Del.	5/21/56
Reinking, Ann	Seattle, Wash.	11/10/50
Reiser, Paul	New York, N.Y.	3/30/57
Resnik, Regina	New York, N.Y.	8/30/24
Reynolds, Burt	Waycross, Ga.	2/11/36
Reynolds, Debbie	El Paso, Tex.	4/1/32
Rhue, Madlyn	Washington, D.C.	10/3/34
Rich, Charlie	Forest City, Ark.	12/14/32
Richards, Keith	Kent, England	12/18/43
Richards, Michael	Los Angeles, Cal.	—
Richardson, Miranda	Lancashire, England	1958
Richardson, Natasha	London, England	5/11/63
Richie, Lionel	Tuskegee, Ala.	6/20/50
Rickles, Don	New York, N.Y.	5/8/26
Rickman, Alan	London, England	1946
Riegert, Peter	New York, N.Y.	4/11/47
Rigg, Diana	Doncaster, England	7/20/38
Ringwald, Molly	Rosewood, Cal.	2/14/68
Ritter, John	Burbank, Cal.	9/17/48

Name	Birthplace	Born
Rivera, Chita	Washington, D.C.	1/23/33
Rivera, Geraldo	New York, N.Y.	7/4/43
Rivers, Joan	Brooklyn, N.Y.	6/8/37
Robards, Jason Jr.	Chicago, Ill.	7/26/22
Robbins, Jerome	New York, N.Y.	10/11/18
Robbins, Tim	W. Covina, Cal.	10/16/58
Roberts, Doris	St. Louis, Mo.	11/4/29
Roberts, Eric	Biloxi, Miss.	4/18/56
Roberts, Julia	Smyrna, Ga.	10/25/67
Roberts, Pernell	Waycross, Ga.	5/18/30
Roberts, Tony	New York, N.Y.	10/22/39
Robertson, Cliff	La Jolla, Cal.	9/9/25
Robertson, Dale	Harrah, Okla.	7/14/23
Robinson, Charles	Houston, Tex.	11/9/-
Robinson, Smokey	Detroit, Mich.	2/19/40
Roche, Eugene	Boston, Mass.	9/22/28
Rodgers, Jimmy	Camas, Wash.	9/18/33
Rodrigues, Percy	Montreal, Que.	6/13/24
Rodriquez, Johnny	Sabinal, Tex.	12/10/51
Rogers, Fred	Latrobe, Pa.	3/20/28
Rogers, Ginger	Independence, Mo.	7/16/11
Rogers, Kenny	Houston, Tex.	8/21/38
Rogers, Mimi	Coral Gables, Fla.	1/27/56
Rogers, Roy	Cincinnati, Oh.	11/5/12
Roland, Gilbert	Juarez, Mexico	12/11/05
Rolle, Esther	Pompano Beach, Fla.	11/8/33
Rollins, Howard	Baltimore, Md.	10/17/50
Romero, Cesar	New York, N.Y.	2/15/07
Ronstadt, Linda	Tucson, Ariz.	7/15/46
Rooney, Mickey	Brooklyn, N.Y.	9/23/20
Rose Marie	New York, N.Y.	8/15/25
Ross, Diana	Detroit, Mich.	3/26/44
Ross, Katharine	Hollywood, Cal.	1/29/42
Ross, Marion	Albert Lea, Minn.	10/25/28
Rossellini, Isabella	Rome, Italy	6/18/52
Rostropovich, Mstislav	Baku, USSR	3/12/27
Roth, David Lee	Bloomington, Ind.	10/10/55
Rourke, Mickey	Miami, Fla.	1953
Rowlands, Gena	Cambria, Wis.	6/19/34
Ruehl, Mercedes	New York, N.Y.	—
Rush, Barbara	Denver, Col.	1/4/30
Russell, Jane	Bemidji, Minn.	6/21/21
Russell, Ken	Southampton, England	7/3/27
Russell, Kurt	Springfield, Mass.	3/17/51
Russell, Mark	Buffalo, N.Y.	8/23/32
Russell, Nipsey	Atlanta, Ga.	10/13/24
Russell, Theresa	San Diego, Cal.	3/20/57
Rutherford, Ann	Toronto, Ont.	11/2/20
Ruttan, Susan	Oregon City, Ore.	9/16/50
Ryan, Meg	Fairfield, Conn.	11/19/63
Ryan, Peggy	Long Beach, Cal.	8/28/24
Ryan, Roz	Detroit, Mich.	7/7/51
Rydell, Bobby	Philadelphia, Pa.	4/26/42
Ryder, Winona	Winona, Minn.	10/29/71
Saget, Bob	Philadelphia, Pa.	5/17/56
Sahl, Mort	Montreal, Que.	5/11/27
Saint, Eva Marie	Newark, N.J.	7/4/24
St. James, Susan	Los Angeles, Cal.	8/14/46
St. John, Jill	Los Angeles, Cal.	8/19/40
Sajak, Pat	Chicago, Ill.	10/26/47
Saks, Gene	New York, N.Y.	11/8/21
Sales, Soupy	Franklinton, N.C.	1/8/26
Samms, Emma	London, England	8/28/60
Sanderson, William	Memphis, Tenn.	1/10/48
Sandy, Gary	Dayton, Oh.	12/25/45
Sanford, Isabel	New York, N.Y.	8/29/17
Sarandon, Susan	New York, N.Y.	10/4/46
Sarnoff, Dorothy	New York, N.Y.	5/25/17
Savage, Fred	Highland Park, Ill.	7/9/76
Savalas, Telly	Garden City, N.Y.	1/21/24
Saxon, John	Brooklyn, N.Y.	8/5/35
Sayles, John	Schenectady, N.Y.	9/28/50
Scaggs, Boz	Dallas, Tex.	6/8/44
Schallert, William	Los Angeles, Cal.	7/6/22
Scheider, Roy	Orange, N.J.	11/10/32
Schell, Maria	Vienna, Austria	1/15/26
Schell, Maximilian	Vienna, Austria	12/8/30
Schenkel, Chris	Bippus, Ind.	8/21/23
Schnabel, Stefan	Berlin, Germany	2/2/12
Schneider, John	Mt. Kisco, N.Y.	4/8/54
Schroder, Rick	Staten Island, N.Y.	4/3/70
Schwarzenegger, Arnold	Graz, Austria	7/30/47
Schwarzkopf, Elisabeth	Jarotschin, Poland	12/9/15
Sciorra, Annabella	New York, N.Y.	1964
Scofield, Paul	Hurst, Pierpont, England	1/21/22
Scolari, Peter	New Rochelle, Ill.	9/12/54
Scorsese, Martin	New York, N.Y.	11/17/42

Name	Birthplace	Born
Scott, George C.	Wise, Va.	10/18/27
Scott, Lizabeth.	Scranton, Pa.	9/29/22
Scott, Martha	Jamesport, Mo.	9/22/14
Scotto, Renata.	Savona, Italy	2/24/35
Scully, Vin	New York, N.Y.	11/29/27
Seagal, Steven	Lansing, Mich.	4/10/51
Sedaka, Neil	New York, N.Y.	3/13/39
Seeger, Pete.	New York, N.Y.	5/3/19
Segal, George	Great Neck, N.Y.	2/13/34
Segal, Vivienne	Philadelphia, Pa.	4/19/97
Seidelman, Susan.	Philadelphia, Pa.	12/11/52
Seinfeld, Jerry	New York, N.Y.	1954
Sellecca, Connie	New York, N.Y.	5/25/55
Selleck, Tom.	Detroit, Mich.	1/29/45
Severinsen, Doc.	Arlington, Ore.	7/7/27
Seymour, Jane	Middlesex, England.	2/15/51
Shackelford, Ted	Oklahoma City, Okla.	6/23/46
Shaffer, Paul.	Thunder Bay, Ont.	11/28/49
Shandling, Garry	Tucson, Ariz.	11/29/49
Shankar, Ravi	India	4/7/20
Sharif, Omar	Alexandria, Egypt.	4/10/32
Shatner, William	Montreal, Que.	3/22/31
Shea, John.	N. Conway, N.H.	4/14/49
Shearer, Moira.	Scotland	1/17/26
Sheedy, Ally	New York, N.Y.	6/12/62
Sheen, Charlie.	New York, N.Y.	9/3/65
Sheen, Martin	Dayton, Oh.	8/3/40
Shelley, Carole	London, England	8/16/39
Shepard, Sam	Ft. Sheridan, Ill.	11/5/43
Shepherd, Cybill.	Memphis, Tenn.	2/18/49
Shields, Brooke	New York, N.Y.	5/31/65
Shire, Talia.	New York, N.Y.	4/25/46
Shore, Dinah.	Winchester, Tenn.	3/1/17
Short, Bobby.	Danville, Ill.	9/15/24
Short, Martin	Hamilton, Ont.	3/26/50
Shull, Richard B.	Evanston, Ill.	2/24/29
Sidney, Sylvia	New York, N.Y.	8/8/10
Siepi, Cesare	Milan, Italy.	2/10/23
Sikking, James B.	Los Angeles, Cal.	3/5/34
Sills, Beverly.	Brooklyn, N.Y.	5/25/29
Silver, Ron	New York, N.Y.	7/2/46
Simmons, Gene	Haifa, Israel	8/25/49
Simmons, Jean	London, England	1/31/29
Simmons, Richard.	New Orleans, La.	7/12/48
Simon, Carly.	New York, N.Y.	6/25/45
Simon, Paul	Newark, N.J.	10/13/41
Simone, Nina.	Tyron, N.C.	2/21/33
Sinatra, Frank	Hoboken, N.J.	12/12/15
Sinbad	Benton Harbor, Mich.	11/10/-
Sinclair, Madge	Kingston, Jamaica	4/28/38
Siskel, Gene	Chicago, Ill.	1/26/46
Skelton, Red (Richard)	Vincennes, Ind.	7/18/13
Skerritt, Tom.	Detroit, Mich.	8/25/33
Slater, Christian	New York, N.Y.	8/19/69
Slater, Helen.	Massapequa, N.Y.	12/14/63
Slezak, Erika.	Hollywood, Cal.	8/5/46
Slick, Grace	Chicago, Ill.	10/30/39
Smirnoff, Yakov	Odessa, USSR	1/24/51
Smith, Allison	New York, N.Y.	12/9/69
Smith, Buffalo Bob	Buffalo, N.Y.	11/27/17
Smith, Jaclyn	Houston, Tex.	10/26/47
Smith, Keely	Norfolk, Va.	3/9/35
Smith, Maggie	Ilford, England.	12/28/34
Smith, Will	Philadelphia, Pa.	9/25/69
Smits, Jimmy	New York, N.Y.	7/9/55
Smothers, Dick	New York, N.Y.	11/20/39
Smothers, Tom	New York, N.Y.	2/2/37
Snipes, Wesley	Orlando, Fla.	7/31/63
Snow, Hank	Nova Scotia, Canada	5/9/14
Solti, Georg	Budapest, Hungary.	10/21/12
Somers, Suzanne	San Bruno, Cal.	10/16/46
Sommer, Elke	Berlin, Germany	11/5/41
Sorvino, Paul.	New York, N.Y.	1939
Sothern, Ann.	Valley City, N.D.	1/22/09
Soul, David.	Chicago, Ill.	8/28/43
Spacek, Sissy	Quitman, Tex.	12/25/49
Spacey, Kevin	S. Orange, N.J.	7/26/59
Spader, James	Boston, Mass.	2/7/60
Spelling, Aaron	Dallas, Tex.	4/22/28
Spencer, John	New Jersey	1946
Spielberg, Steven	Cincinnati, Oh.	12/18/47
Springfield, Dusty	London, England	4/16/39
Springfield, Rick	Sydney, Australia.	8/23/49
Springsteen, Bruce	Freehold, N.J.	9/23/49
Stack, Robert	Los Angeles, Cal.	1/13/19
Stafford, Jo	Coalinga, Cal.	11/12/18
Stahl, Richard	Detroit, Mich.	1/4/32
Stallone, Sylvester	New York, N.Y.	7/6/46
Stamos, John	Cypress, Cal.	8/19/63
Stamp, Terence	Stepney, England.	7/22/39
Stander, Lionel	New York, N.Y.	1/11/08
Stang, Arnold	New York, N.Y.	9/28/25
Stanley, Kim	Tularosa, N.M.	2/11/25
Stanton, Harry Dean	Kentucky	7/14/26
Stapleton, Jean	New York, N.Y.	1/19/23
Stapleton, Maureen	Troy, N.Y.	6/21/25
Starr, Ringo	Liverpool, England	7/7/40
Steenburgen, Mary	Newport, Ariz.	2/8/53
Steiger, Rod	W. Hampton, N.Y.	4/14/25
Stephens, James	Mt. Kisco, N.Y.	5/18/51
Stern, Daniel	Stamford, Conn.	5/28/57
Stern, Howard	New York, N.Y.	1/12/54
Stern, Isaac	Kreminiecz, Russia	7/21/20
Sternhagen, Frances	Washington, D.C.	1/13/30
Stevens, Andrew	Memphis, Tenn.	6/10/55
Stevens, Cat	London, England	7/21/48
Stevens, Connie	Brooklyn, N.Y.	8/8/38
Stevens, Rise	New York, N.Y.	6/11/13
Stevens, Stella	Yazoo City, Miss.	10/1/36
Stevenson, McLean	Normal, Ill.	11/14/29
Stevenson, Parker	Philadelphia, Pa.	6/4/52
Stewart, James	Indiana, Pa.	5/20/08
Stewart, Patrick	Mirfield, England	7/13/40
Stewart, Rod	London, England	1/10/45
Stickney, Dorothy	Dickinson, N.D.	6/21/00
Stiers, David Ogden	Peoria, Ill.	10/31/42
Stiller, Jerry	New York, N.Y.	6/8/29
Stills, Stephen	Dallas, Tex.	1/3/45
Sting (G. Sumner)	Newcastle, England	10/2/51
Stockwell, Dean	Hollywood, Cal.	3/5/36
Stoltz, Eric	American Samoa	1961
Stone, Oliver	New York, N.Y.	9/15/46
Stone, Sharon	Meadville, Pa.	1958
Stookey, Paul	Baltimore, Md.	12/30/37
Storch, Larry	New York, N.Y.	1/8/23
Storm, Gale	Bloomington, Tex.	4/5/22
Stowe, Madeleine	Los Angeles, Cal.	8/18/58
Straight, Beatrice	Old Westbury, N.Y.	8/2/18
Strait, George	Pearsall, Tex.	5/1/52
Strasser, Robin	New York, N.Y.	5/7/45
Stratas, Teresa	Toronto, Ont.	5/26/38
Strauss, Peter	New York, N.Y.	2/20/47
Streep, Meryl	Summit, N.J.	6/22/49
Streisand, Barbra	Brooklyn, N.Y.	4/24/42
Stritch, Elaine	Detroit, Mich.	2/2/26
Struthers, Sally	Portland, Ore.	7/28/48
Stuarti, Enzo	Rome, Italy	3/3/25
Sullivan, Barry	New York, N.Y.	8/29/12
Sullivan, Susan	New York, N.Y.	11/18/44
Sumac, Yma	Ichocan, Peru	9/10/27
Summer, Donna	Boston, Mass.	12/31/48
Sutherland, Donald	St. John, New Brunswick	7/17/34
Sutherland, Joan	Sydney, Australia.	11/7/26
Sutherland, Kiefer	London, England	12/20/66
Swayze, Patrick	Houston, Tex.	8/18/54
Swit, Loretta	Passaic, N.J.	11/4/37
Mr. T (Lawrence Tero)	Chicago, Ill.	5/21/52
Tallchief, Maria	Fairfax, Okla.	1/24/25
Tandy, Jessica.	London, England	6/7/09
Tarkenton, Fran	Richmond, Va.	2/3/40
Taylor, Elizabeth.	London, England	2/27/32
Taylor, James	Boston, Mass.	3/12/48
Taylor, Rip	Washington, D.C.	1/13/30
Taylor, Rod	Sydney, Australia.	1/11/29
Te Kanawa, Kiri	Gisborne, New Zealand	3/6/44
Tebaldi, Renata	Pesaro, Italy.	2/1/22
Temple, Shirley	Santa Monica, Cal.	4/23/28
Tennant, Victoria	London, England	9/30/50
Tennille, Toni.	Montgomery, Ala.	5/8/43
Tharp, Twyla.	Portland, Ind.	7/1/41
Thicke, Alan	Kirkland Lake, Ont.	3/1/47
Thomas, Jay	New Orleans, La.	7/12/48
Thomas, Marlo.	Detroit, Mich.	11/21/43
Thomas, Philip Michael	Columbus, Oh.	5/26/49
Thomas, Richard	New York, N.Y.	6/13/51
Thompson, Emma.	London, England	4/15/59
Thompson, Jack.	Sydney, Australia.	8/31/40
Thompson, Lea	Rochester, Minn.	5/31/61
Thompson, Sada	Des Moines, Ia.	9/27/29
Thulin, Ingrid	Sweden	1/27/29
Tiegs, Cheryl.	Minnesota	9/27/47
Tiffany	Norwalk, Cal.	10/2/71
Tillis, Mel	Tampa, Fla.	8/8/32
Tiny Tim	New York, N.Y.	4/12/23
Todd, Richard	Dublin, Ireland.	6/11/19

Name	Birthplace	Born
Tomei, Marisa	New York, N.Y.	12/4/64
Tomlin, Lily	Detroit, Mich.	9/1/39
Tomlinson, David	Scotland	5/7/17
Torme, Mel	Chicago, Ill.	9/13/25
Torn, Rip	Temple, Tex.	2/6/31
Townsend, Robert	Chicago, Ill.	2/6/57
Travanti, Daniel J.	Kenosha, Wis.	3/7/40
Travers, Mary	Louisville, Ky.	11/9/36
Travis, Nancy	New York, N.Y.	9/21/61
Travis, Randy	Marshville, N.C.	5/4/59
Travolta, John	Englewood, N.J.	2/18/54
Trebek, Alex	Sudbury, Ont.	7/22/40
Trevor, Claire	New York, N.Y.	3/8/09
Troyanos, Tatiana	New York, N.Y.	9/12/38
Tucker, Michael	Baltimore, Md.	2/6/44
Tucker, Tanya	Seminole, Tex.	10/10/58
Tune, Tommy	Wichita Falls, Tex.	2/28/39
Turner, Janine	Lincoln, Neb.	12/6/62
Turner, Kathleen	Springfield, Mo.	6/19/54
Turner, Lana	Wallace, Ida.	2/8/20
Turner, Tina	Nutbush, Tenn.	11/26/38
Turturro, John	New York, N.Y.	2/28/57
Twiggy (Leslie Hornby)	London, England	9/19/46
Tyson, Cicely	New York, N.Y.	12/19/33
Uecker, Bob	Milwaukee, Wis.	1/26/35
Uggams, Leslie	New York, N.Y.	5/25/43
Ullman, Tracey	Slough, England	12/30/59
Ullmann, Liv	Tokyo, Japan	12/16/38
Underwood, Blair	Tacoma, Wash.	8/25/64
Urich, Robert	Toronto, Oh.	12/19/46
Ustinov, Peter	London, England	4/16/21
Vaccaro, Brenda	Brooklyn, N.Y.	11/18/39
Vale, Jerry	New York, N.Y.	7/8/31
Valente, Caterina	Paris, France	1/14/31
Valli, Frankie	Newark, N.J.	5/3/37
Van Ark, Joan	New York, N.Y.	6/16/43
Vandross, Luther	New York, N.Y.	4/20/51
Van Dyke, Dick	West Plains, Mo.	12/13/25
Van Dyke, Jerry	Danville, Ill.	7/27/31
Van Fleet, Jo.	Oakland, Cal.	12/30/22
Van Halen, Eddie	Nijmegan, Netherlands	1/26/57
Van Pallandt, Nina	Copenhagen, Denmark	7/15/32
Van Patten, Dick	New York, N.Y.	12/9/28
Van Peebles, Mario	Mexico	1/15/57
Vaughn, Robert	New York, N.Y.	11/22/32
Venuta, Benay	San Francisco, Cal.	1/27/11
Verdon, Gwen	Los Angeles, Cal.	1/13/25
Vereen, Ben	Miami, Fla.	10/10/46
Verrett, Shirley	New Orleans, La.	5/31/31
Vickers, Jon	Prince Albert, Sask.	10/26/26
Vigoda, Abe	New York, N.Y.	2/24/21
Vincent, Jan-Michael	Denver, Col.	7/15/44
Vinson, Helen	Beaumont, Tex.	9/17/07
Vinton, Bobby	Canonsburg, Pa.	4/16/35
Vitale, Dick	E. Rutherford, N.J.	6/9/40
Voight, Jon	Yonkers, N.Y.	12/29/38
Von Stade, Frederica	Somerville, N.J.	6/1/45
Von Sydow, Max	Lund, Sweden	4/10/29
Wagner, Lindsay	Los Angeles, Cal.	6/22/49
Wagner, Robert	Detroit, Mich.	2/10/30
Wagoner, Porter	West Plains, Mo.	8/12/27
Wahl, Ken	Chicago, Ill.	2/14/56
Wain, Bea	Bronx, N.Y.	4/30/17
Waite, Ralph	White Plains, N.Y.	6/22/29
Walden, Robert	New York, N.Y.	9/25/43
Walken, Christopher	New York, N.Y.	3/31/43
Wallach, Eli	Brooklyn, N.Y.	12/7/15
Walston, Ray	Laurel, Miss.	11/2/24
Walter, Jessica	New York, N.Y.	1/31/44
Wanamaker, Sam	Chicago, Ill.	6/14/19
Ward, Fred	San Diego, Cal.	1943
Ward, Simon	London, England	10/19/41
Warden, Jack	Newark, N.J.	9/18/20
Warfield, William	W. Helena, Ark.	1/22/20
Warner, Malcolm-Jamal	Jersey City, N.J.	8/18/70
Warren, Lesley Ann	New York, N.Y.	8/16/46
Warrick, Ruth	St. Joseph, Mo.	6/29/16
Warwick, Dionne	E. Orange, N.J.	12/12/41
Washington, Denzel	Mt. Vernon, N.Y.	12/28/54
Waterston, Sam	Cambridge, Mass.	11/15/40
Watkins, Carlene	Hartford, Conn.	6/4/52
Watts, Andre	Nuremberg, Germany	6/20/46
Wayans, Damon	New York, N.Y.	1960
Wayans, Keenan Ivory	New York, N.Y.	6/8/58
Wayne, David	Traverse City, Mich.	1/30/14
Waxman, Al	Toronto, Ont.	3/2/35
Weaver, Dennis	Joplin, Mo.	6/4/24
Weaver, Fritz	Pittsburgh, Pa.	1/19/26
Weaver, Sigourney	New York, N.Y.	10/8/49
Weir, Peter	Sydney, Australia	8/8/44
Weitz, Bruce	Norwalk, Conn.	5/27/43
Welch, Raquel	Chicago, Ill.	9/5/40
Weld, Tuesday	New York, N.Y.	8/27/43
Wells, Kitty	Nashville, Tenn.	8/30/19
Wendt, George	Chicago, Ill.	10/17/48
Weston, Jack	Cleveland, Oh.	8/21/24
Wheaton, Wil	Burbank, Cal.	7/29/72
Whitaker, Forest	Longview, Tex.	7/15/61
White, Barry	Galveston, Tex.	9/12/44
White, Betty	Oak Park, Ill.	1/17/22
White, Jesse	Buffalo, N.Y.	1/3/19
White, Vanna	N. Myrtle Beach, S.C.	2/18/57
Whiting, Margaret	Detroit, Mich.	7/22/24
Whitmore, James	White Plains, N.Y.	10/1/21
Widmark, Richard	Sunrise, Minn.	12/26/14
Wiest, Dianne	Kansas City, Mo.	3/28/48
Wilder, Billy	Vienna, Austria	6/22/06
Wilder, Gene	Milwaukee, Wis.	6/11/35
Williams, Andy	Wall Lake, Ia.	12/3/30
Williams, Billy Dee	New York, N.Y.	4/6/37
Williams, Cindy	Van Nuys, Cal.	8/22/47
Williams, Esther	Los Angeles, Cal.	8/8/23
Williams, Hal	Columbus, Oh.	12/14/38
Williams Jr., Hank	Shreveport, La.	5/26/49
Williams, Joe	Cordele, Ga.	12/12/18
Williams, JoBeth	Houston, Tex.	1953
Williams, Paul	Omaha, Neb.	9/19/40
Williams, Robin	Chicago, Ill.	7/21/52
Williams, Treat	Rowayton, Conn.	12/1/51
Williams, Vanessa	New York, N.Y.	3/18/63
Williamson, Nicol	Hamilton, Scotland	9/14/38
Willis, Bruce	W. Germany	3/19/55
Wilson, Demond	Valdosta, Ga.	10/13/46
Wilson, Elizabeth	Grand Rapids, Mich.	4/4/25
Wilson, Flip	Jersey City, N.J.	12/8/33
Wilson, Nancy	Chillicothe, Oh.	2/20/37
Windom, William	New York, N.Y.	9/28/23
Winfield, Paul	Los Angeles, Cal.	5/22/41
Winfrey, Oprah	Kosciusko, Miss.	1/29/54
Winger, Debra	Cleveland, Oh.	5/16/55
Winkler, Henry	New York, N.Y.	10/30/45
Winningham, Mare	Phoenix, Ariz.	5/6/59
Winters, Jonathan	Dayton, Oh.	11/11/25
Winters, Shelley	St. Louis, Mo.	8/18/22
Winwood, Steve	Birmingham, England	5/12/48
Wiseman, Joseph	Montreal, Que.	5/15/18
Withers, Jane	Atlanta, Ga.	4/12/26
Wonder, Stevie	Saginaw, Mich.	5/13/50
Woodard, Alfre	Tulsa, Okla.	11/2/53
Woods, James	Vernal, N.J.	4/18/47
Woodward, Edward	Croyden, England	6/1/30
Woodward, Joanne	Thomasville, Ga.	2/27/30
Woolery, Chuck	Ashland, Ky.	3/16/-
Worth, Irene	Nebraska	6/23/16
Wray, Fay	Alberta, Canada	9/10/07
Wright, Martha	Seattle, Wash.	3/23/26
Wright, Max	Detroit, Mich.	8/2/-
Wright, Steven	New York, N.Y.	12/6/55
Wright, Teresa	New York, N.Y.	10/27/18
Wyatt, Jane	Campgaw, N.J.	8/10/11
Wyman, Jane	St. Joseph, Mo.	1/4/14
Wynette, Tammy	Red Bay, Ala.	5/5/42
Yarborough, Glenn	Milwaukee, Wis.	1/12/30
Yarrow, Peter	New York, N.Y.	5/31/38
York, Michael	Fulmer, England	3/27/42
York, Susannah	London, England	1/9/42
Young, Alan	Northumberland, England	11/19/19
Young, Burt	New York, N.Y.	4/30/40
Young, Loretta	Salt Lake City, Ut.	1/6/13
Young, Neil	Toronto, Ont.	11/12/45
Young, Robert	Chicago, Ill.	2/22/07
Young, Sean	Louisville, Ky.	11/20/59
Youngman, Henny	Liverpool, England	1/12/06
Zappa, Frank	Baltimore, Md.	12/21/40
Zeffirelli, Franco	Florence, Italy	2/12/23
Zerbe, Anthony	Long Beach, Cal.	5/20/36
Zimbalist, Efrem Jr.	New York, N.Y.	11/30/23
Zukerman, Pinchas	Tel Aviv, Israel	7/16/48

Entertainment Personalities of the Past

(as of mid-1993)

Born	Died	Name
1895	1974	Abbott, Bud
1903	1992	Acuff, Roy
1872	1953	Adams, Maude
1855	1926	Adler, Jacob P.
1903	1984	Adler, Luther
1898	1933	Adoree, Renee
1902	1986	Aherne, Brian
1931	1989	Ailey, Alvin
1909	1964	Albertson, Frank
1907	1981	Albertson, Jack
1894	1956	Allen, Fred
1906	1964	Allen, Gracie
1883	1950	Allgood, Sara
1902	1993	Anderson, Marian
1909	1992	Andrews, Dana
1913	1967	Andrews, Laverne
1887	1933	Arbuckle, Fatty (Roscoe)
1908	1990	Arden, Eve
1900	1976	Arlen, Richard
1868	1946	Arliss, George
1888	1945	Armetta, Henry
1900	1971	Armstrong, Louis
1917	1986	Arnaz, Desi
1890	1956	Arnold, Edward
1905	1974	Arquette, Cliff
1900	1991	Arthur, Jean
1899	1987	Astaire, Fred
1906	1987	Astor, Mary
1885	1946	Atwill, Lionel
1905	1967	Auer, Mischa
1900	1972	Austin, Gene
1913	1989	Backus, Jim
1918	1990	Bailey, Pearl
1892	1968	Bainter, Fay
1906	1975	Baker, Josephine
1904	1983	Balanchine, George
1911	1989	Ball, Lucille
1882	1956	Bancroft, George
1902	1968	Bankhead, Tallulah
1890	1952	Banks, Leslie
1890	1955	Bara, Theda
1810	1891	Barnum, Phineas T.
1879	1959	Barrymore, Ethel
1882	1942	Barrymore, John
1878	1954	Barrymore, Lionel
1848	1905	Barrymore, Maurice
1897	1963	Barthelmess, Richard
1914	1984	Basehart, Richard
1904	1984	Basie, Count
1923	1985	Baxter, Anne
1889	1951	Baxter, Warner
1904	1965	Beatty, Clyde
1902	1962	Beavers, Louise
1884	1946	Beery, Noah
1889	1949	Beery, Wallace
1901	1970	Begley, Ed
1904	1991	Bellamy, Ralph
1949	1982	Belushi, John
1906	1968	Benaderet, Bea
1906	1964	Bendix, William
1904	1965	Bennett, Constance
1910	1990	Bennett, Joan
1943	1987	Bennett, Michael
1894	1974	Benny, Jack
1924	1970	Benzell, Mimi
1899	1966	Berg, Gertrude
1903	1978	Bergen, Edgar
1915	1982	Bergman, Ingrid
1895	1976	Berkeley, Busby
1923	1986	Bernardi, Herschel
1844	1923	Bernhardt, Sarah
1893	1943	Bernie, Ben
1889	1967	Bickford, Charles
1911	1960	Bjoerling, Jussi
1895	1973	Blackmer, Sidney
1908	1989	Blanc, Mel
1928	1972	Blocker, Dan
1909	1979	Blondell, Joan
1888	1959	Blore, Eric
1901	1975	Blue, Ben
1899	1957	Bogart, Humphrey
1880	1965	Boland, Mary
1895	1969	Boles, John

Born	Died	Name
1904	1987	Bolger, Ray
1903	1960	Bond, Ward
1892	1981	Bondi, Beulah
1917	1981	Boone, Richard
1833	1893	Booth, Edwin
1796	1852	Booth, Junius Brutus
1907	1992	Booth, Shirley
1905	1965	Bow, Clara
1874	1946	Bowes, Maj. Edward
1928	1977	Boyd, Stephen
1898	1972	Boyd, William
1899	1978	Boyer, Charles
1893	1939	Brady, Alice
1894	1974	Brennan, Walter
1904	1979	Brent, George
1891	1951	Brice, Fanny
1891	1959	Broderick, Helen
1892	1973	Brown, Joe E.
1926	1966	Bruce, Lenny
1895	1953	Bruce, Nigel
1910	1982	Bruce, Virginia
1915	1985	Brynner, Yul
1903	1979	Buchanan, Edgar
1938	1982	Buono, Victor
1885	1970	Burke, Billie
1911	1967	Burnette, Smiley
1925	1984	Burton, Richard
1897	1946	Busch, Mae
1883	1966	Bushman, Francis X.
1896	1946	Butterworth, Charles
1893	1971	Byington, Spring
1904	1972	Cabot, Bruce
1918	1977	Cabot, Sebastian
1899	1986	Cagney, James
1895	1956	Calhern, Louis
1923	1977	Callas, Maria
1933	1976	Cambridge, Godfrey
1865	1940	Campbell, Mrs. Patrick
1892	1964	Cantor, Eddie
1897	1991	Capra, Frank
1878	1947	Carey, Harry
1950	1983	Carpenter, Karen
1906	1988	Carradine, John
1880	1961	Carrillo, Leo
1892	1972	Carroll, Leo G.
1905	1965	Carroll, Nancy
1910	1963	Carson, Jack
1873	1921	Caruso, Enrico
1876	1973	Casals, Pablo
1929	1989	Cassavetes, John
1893	1969	Castle, Irene
1887	1918	Castle, Vernon
1873	1938	Chaliapin, Feodor
1919	1980	Champion, Gower
1918	1961	Chandler, Jeff
1883	1930	Chaney, Lon
1905	1973	Chaney Jr., Lon
1942	1981	Chapin, Harry
1889	1977	Chaplin, Charles
1893	1961	Chatterton, Ruth
1888	1972	Chevalier, Maurice
1888	1960	Clark, Bobby
1914	1968	Clark, Fred
1920	1966	Clift, Montgomery
1932	1963	Cline, Patsy
1892	1967	Clyde, Andy
1911	1976	Cobb, Lee J.
1877	1961	Coburn, Charles
1878	1942	Cohan, George M.
1902	1986	Cohen, Myron
1919	1965	Cole, Nat (King)
1890	1965	Collins, Ray
1891	1958	Colman, Ronald
1908	1934	Columbo, Russ
1917	1982	Conried, Hans
1911	1975	Conte, Richard
1914	1984	Coogan, Jackie
1935	1964	Cooke, Sam
1901	1961	Cooper, Gary
1888	1971	Cooper, Gladys
1896	1973	Cooper, Melville
1914	1968	Corey, Wendell
1893	1974	Cornell, Katherine

Born	Died	Name
1890	1972	Correll, Charles (Andy)
1905	1979	Costello, Dolores
1906	1959	Costello, Lou
1899	1973	Coward, Noel
1924	1973	Cox, Wally
1908	1983	Crabbe, Buster
1928	1978	Crane, Bob
1911	1986	Crawford, Broderick
1908	1977	Crawford, Joan
1880	1942	Crews, Laura Hope
1880	1974	Crisp, Donald
1942	1973	Croce, Jim
1903	1977	Crosby, Bing
1910	1986	Crothers, Scatman
1908	1990	Cummings, Robert
1878	1968	Currie, Finlay
1914	1978	Dailey, Dan
1923	1965	Dandridge, Dorothy
1894	1963	Daniell, Henry
1901	1971	Daniels, Bebe
1936	1973	Darin, Bobby
1921	1965	Darnell, Linda
1879	1967	Darwell, Jane
1909	1986	Da Silva, Howard
1866	1949	Davenport, Harry
1908	1989	Davis, Bette
1907	1961	Davis, Joan
1925	1990	Davis Jr., Sammy
1931	1955	Dean, James
1905	1968	Dekker, Albert
1908	1983	Del Rio, Dolores
1892	1983	Demarest, William
1881	1959	DeMille, Cecil B.
1891	1967	Denny, Reginald
1901	1974	DeSica, Vittorio
1905	1977	Devine, Andy
1924	1991	Dewhurst, Colleen
1942	1972	De Wilde, Brandon
1907	1974	De Wolfe, Billy
1920	1985	Diamond, Selma
1901	1992	Dietrich, Marlene
1879	1947	Digges, Dudley
1901	1966	Disney, Walt
1894	1949	Dix, Richard
1905	1958	Donat, Robert
1889	1972	Donlevy, Brian
1901	1981	Douglas, Melvyn
1907	1959	Douglas, Paul
1889	1956	Draper, Ruth
1881	1965	Dresser, Louise
1869	1934	Dressler, Marie
1820	1897	Drew, Mrs. John
1909	1951	Duchin, Eddy
1890	1974	Dumbrille, Douglass
1889	1965	Dumont, Margaret
1878	1927	Duncan, Isadora
1905	1967	Dunn, James
1898	1990	Dunne, Irene
1893	1980	Durante, Jimmy
1907	1968	Duryea, Dan
1858	1924	Duse, Eleanora
1894	1929	Eagels, Jeanne
1914	1993	Eckstine, Billy
1901	1967	Eddy, Nelson
1897	1971	Edwards, Cliff
1879	1945	Edwards, Gus
1899	1974	Ellington, Duke
1941	1974	Elliot, Cass
1891	1967	Elman, Mischa
1881	1951	Errol, Leon
1888	1976	Evans, Edith
1901	1989	Evans, Maurice
1883	1939	Fairbanks, Douglas
1914	1970	Farmer, Frances
1870	1929	Farnum, Dustin
1876	1953	Farnum, William
1882	1967	Farrar, Geraldine
1904	1971	Farrell, Glenda
1897	1961	Fay, Frank
1895	1962	Fazenda, Louise
1933	1982	Feldman, Marty
1912	1992	Ferrer, Jose

Born	Died	Name
1898	1985	Fetchit, Stepin
1894	1979	Fiedler, Arthur
1918	1973	Field, Betty
1898	1979	Fields, Gracie
1879	1946	Fields, W.C.
1931	1978	Fields, Totie
1916	1977	Finch, Peter
1902	1975	Fine, Larry
1865	1932	Fiske, Minnie Maddern
1888	1961	Fitzgerald, Barry
1895	1962	Flagstad, Kirsten
1900	1971	Flippen, Jay C.
1909	1959	Flynn, Errol
1925	1974	Flynn, Joe
1910	1968	Foley, Red
1905	1982	Fonda, Henry
1920	1978	Fontaine, Frank
1887	1983	Fontanne, Lynn
1919	1991	Fonteyn, Margot
1895	1973	Ford, John
1901	1976	Ford, Paul
1919	1991	Ford, Tennessee Ernie
1899	1966	Ford, Wallace
1927	1987	Fosse, Bob
1901	1970	Foster, Preston
1922	1991	Foxx, Redd
1857	1928	Foy, Eddie
1903	1968	Francis, Kay
1887	1966	Frawley, William
1870	1955	Friganza, Trixie
1890	1958	Frisco, Joe
1901	1960	Gable, Clark
1905	1990	Garbo, Greta
1922	1990	Gardner, Ava
1913	1952	Garfield, John
1922	1969	Garland, Judy
1939	1984	Gaye, Marvin
1906	1984	Gaynor, Janet
1902	1978	Geer, Will
1900	1954	George, Gladys
1892	1962	Gibson, Hoot
1894	1971	Gilbert, Billy
1895	1936	Gilbert, John
1855	1937	Gillette, William
1897	1987	Gingold, Hermione
1898	1968	Gish, Dorothy
1893	1993	Gish, Lillian
1916	1987	Gleason, Jackie
1886	1959	Gleason, James
1884	1938	Gluck, Alma
1905	1990	Goddard, Paulette
1903	1983	Godfrey, Arthur
1882	1974	Goldwyn, Samuel
1909	1986	Goodman, Benny
1915	1969	Gorcey, Leo
1896	1985	Gordon, Ruth
1899	1982	Gosden, Freeman (Amos)
1869	1944	Gottschalk, Ferdinand
1829	1869	Gottschalk, Louis
1916	1973	Grable, Betty
1894	1991	Graham, Martha
1925	1981	Grahame, Gloria
1904	1986	Grant, Cary
1915	1987	Greene, Lorne
1879	1954	Greenstreet, Sydney
1874	1948	Griffith, David Wark
1912	1980	Griffith, Hugh
1912	1967	Guthrie, Woody
1875	1959	Gwenn, Edmund
1926	1993	Gwynne, Fred
1892	1950	Hale, Alan
1925	1981	Haley, Bill
1899	1979	Haley, Jack
1902	1985	Hamilton, Margaret
1847	1919	Hammerstein, Oscar
1893	1964	Hardwicke, Cedric
1892	1957	Hardy, Oliver
1911	1937	Harlow, Jean
1908	1990	Harrison, Rex
1870	1946	Hart, William S.
1928	1973	Harvey, Laurence
1910	1973	Hawkins, Jack
1890	1973	Hayakawa, Sessue
1885	1969	Hayes, Gabby
1900	1993	Hayes, Helen
1902	1971	Hayward, Leland
1917	1975	Hayward, Susan
1918	1987	Hayworth, Rita
1896	1937	Healy, Ted
1910	1971	Heflin, Van
1901	1987	Heifetz, Jascha
1873	1918	Held, Anna
1942	1970	Hendrix, Jimi
1912	1969	Henie, Sonja
1908	1992	Henreid, Paul
1936	1990	Henson, Jim
1929	1993	Hepburn, Audrey
1886	1956	Hersholt, Jean
1899	1980	Hitchcock, Alfred
1914	1955	Hodiak, John
1894	1973	Holden, Fay
1918	1981	Holden, William
1922	1965	Holliday, Judy
1936	1959	Holly, Buddy
1888	1951	Holt, Jack
1918	1973	Holt, Tim
1898	1978	Homolka, Oscar
1902	1972	Hopkins, Miriam
1858	1935	Hopper, DeWolf
1915	1970	Hopper, William
1904	1989	Horowitz, Vladimir
1886	1970	Horton, Edward Everett
1874	1926	Houdini, Harry
1902	1988	Houseman, John
1906	1952	Howard, Curly
1881	1965	Howard, Eugene
1867	1961	Howard, Joe
1890	1943	Howard, Leslie
1897	1975	Howard, Moe
1891	1955	Howard, Shemp
1885	1955	Howard, Tom
1916	1988	Howard, Trevor
1885	1949	Howard, Willie
1925	1985	Hudson, Rock
1890	1977	Hull, Henry
1886	1957	Hull, Josephine
1895	1958	Humphrey, Doris
1925	1969	Hunter, Jeffrey
1901	1962	Husing, Ted
1906	1987	Huston, John
1884	1950	Huston, Walter
1892	1950	Ingram, Rex
1895	1969	Ingram, Rex
1895	1980	Iturbi, Jose
1838	1905	Irving, Henry
1875	1942	Jackson, Joe
1911	1972	Jackson, Mahalia
1891	1984	Jaffe, Sam
1903	1991	Jagger, Dean
1916	1983	James, Harry
1889	1956	Janis, Elsie
1886	1950	Jannings, Emil
1930	1980	Janssen, David
1900	1974	Jenkins, Allen
1898	1981	Jessel, George
1892	1962	Johnson, Chic
1886	1950	Jolson, Al
1889	1942	Jones, Buck
1933	1983	Jones, Carolyn
1911	1965	Jones, Spike
1943	1970	Joplin, Janis
1902	1982	Jory, Victor
1905	1981	Joslyn, Allyn
1910	1966	Kane, Helen
1887	1969	Karloff, Boris
1893	1970	Karns, Roscoe
1913	1987	Kaye, Danny
1811	1868	Kean, Charles
1806	1880	Kean, Mrs. Charles
1787	1833	Kean, Edmund
1895	1966	Keaton, Buster
1910	1993	Keeler, Ruby
1894	1973	Kellaway, Cecil
1898	1979	Kelly, Emmett
1928	1982	Kelly, Grace
1910	1981	Kelly, Patsy
1907	1968	Kelton, Pert
1926	1959	Kendall, Kay
1914	1990	Kennedy, Arthur
1890	1948	Kennedy, Edgar
1886	1956	Kibbee, Guy
1888	1964	Kilbride, Percy
1923	1986	Knight, Ted
1901	1980	Kostelanetz, Andre
1919	1962	Kovacs, Ernie
1885	1974	Kruger, Otto
1921	1991	Kulp, Nancy
1913	1964	Ladd, Alan
1895	1967	Lahr, Bert
1919	1973	Lake, Veronica
1915	1982	Lamas, Fernando
1902	1986	Lanchester, Elsa
1919	1948	Landis, Carole
1904	1972	Landis, Jessie Royce
1936	1991	Landon, Michael
1884	1944	Langdon, Harry
1853	1929	Langtry, Lillie
1921	1959	Lanza, Mario
1870	1950	Lauder, Harry
1899	1962	Laughton, Charles
1890	1965	Laurel, Stan
1923	1984	Lawford, Peter
1898	1952	Lawrence, Gertrude
1908	1991	Lean, David
1940	1973	Lee, Bruce
1907	1952	Lee, Canada
1914	1970	Lee, Gypsy Rose
1888	1976	Lehmann, Lotte
1913	1967	Leigh, Vivien
1922	1976	Leighton, Margaret
1940	1980	Lennon, John
1898	1981	Lenya, Lotte
1870	1941	Leonard, Eddie
1900	1987	LeRoy, Mervyn
1906	1972	Levant, Oscar
1905	1980	Levene, Sam
1902	1971	Lewis, Joe E.
1892	1971	Lewis, Ted
1919	1987	Liberace
1820	1887	Lind, Jenny
1894	1989	Lillie, Beatrice
1893	1971	Lloyd, Harold
1870	1922	Lloyd, Marie
1891	1957	Lockhart, Gene
1913	1969	Logan, Ella
1909	1942	Lombard, Carole
1902	1977	Lombardo, Guy
1927	1974	Long, Richard
1895	1975	Lopez, Vincent
1888	1968	Lorne, Marion
1904	1964	Lorre, Peter
1912	1962	Lovejoy, Frank
1890	1971	Lowe, Edmund
1892	1947	Lubitsch, Ernst
1882	1956	Lugosi, Bela
1894	1971	Lukas, Paul
1892	1977	Lunt, Alfred
1926	1982	Lynde, Paul
1926	1971	Lynn, Diana
1903	1965	MacDonald, Jeanette
1902	1969	MacLane, Barton
1908	1991	MacMurray, Fred
1921	1986	MacRae, Gordon
1909	1973	Macready, George
1908	1973	Magnani, Anna
1890	1975	Main, Marjorie
1932	1967	Mansfield, Jayne
1905	1980	Mantovani, Annunzio
1897	1975	March, Fredric
1945	1981	Marley, Bob
1890	1966	Marshall, Herbert
1913	1990	Martin, Mary
1920	1981	Martin, Ross
1924	1987	Marvin, Lee
1888	1964	Marx, Arthur (Harpo)
1901	1979	Marx, Herbert (Zeppo)
1890	1977	Marx, Julius (Groucho)
1886	1961	Marx, Leonard (Chico)
1893	1977	Marx, Milton (Gummo)
1909	1984	Mason, James
1896	1983	Massey, Raymond
1885	1957	Mayer, Louis B.
1895	1973	Maynard, Ken
1884	1945	McCormack, John
1905	1990	McCrea, Joel
1895	1952	McDaniel, Hattie
1899	1981	McHugh, Frank
1907	1991	McIntire, John
1883	1959	McLaglen, Victor
1907	1971	McMahon, Horace
1930	1980	McQueen, Steve

Born	Died	Name
1920	1980	Medford, Kay
1880	1946	Meek, Donald
1861	1931	Melba, Nellie
1890	1973	Melchior, Lauritz
1890	1963	Menjou, Adolphe
1902	1966	Menken, Helen
1908	1984	Merman, Ethel
1905	1986	Milland, Ray
1904	1944	Miller, Glenn
1898	1936	Miller, Marilyn
1903	1955	Minnevitch, Borrah
1913	1955	Miranda, Carmen
1892	1962	Mitchell, Thomas
1880	1940	Mix, Tom
1926	1962	Monroe, Marilyn
1911	1973	Monroe, Vaughn
1917	1951	Montez, Maria
1904	1981	Montgomery, Robert
1901	1947	Moore, Grace
1876	1962	Moore, Victor
1906	1974	Moorehead, Agnes
1890	1949	Morgan, Frank
1900	1941	Morgan, Helen
1901	1970	Morris, Chester
1914	1959	Morris, Wayne
1943	1971	Morrison, Jim
1932	1982	Morrow, Vic
1915	1977	Mostel, Zero
1897	1969	Mowbray, Alan
1895	1967	Muni, Paul
1915	1970	Munshin, Jules
1924	1971	Murphy, Audie
1902	1992	Murphy, George
1885	1965	Murray, Mae
1896	1970	Nagel, Conrad
1900	1973	Naish, J. Carroll
1898	1961	Naldi, Nita
1906	1975	Nelson, Ozzie
1940	1985	Nelson, Rick
1885	1967	Nesbit, Evelyn
1909	1983	Niven, David
1890	1950	Nijinsky, Vaslav
1893	1974	Nilsson, Anna Q.
1902	1985	Nolan, Lloyd
1894	1930	Normand, Mabel
1899	1968	Novarro, Ramon
1938	1993	Nureyev, Rudolf
1903	1978	Oakie, Jack
1860	1926	Oakley, Annie
1928	1982	Oates, Warren
1911	1979	Oberon, Merle
1915	1985	O'Brien, Edmond
1899	1983	O'Brien, Pat
1908	1981	O'Connell, Arthur
1880	1959	O'Connor, Una
1908	1968	O'Keefe, Dennis
1880	1938	Oland, Warner
1860	1932	Olcott, Chauncey
1883	1942	Oliver, Edna May
1907	1989	Olivier, Laurence
1892	1963	Olsen, Ole
1849	1920	O'Neill, James
1936	1988	Orbison, Roy
1899	1985	Ormandy, Eugene
1876	1949	Ouspenskaya, Maria
1887	1972	Owen, Reginald
1860	1941	Paderewski, Ignace
1924	1987	Page, Geraldine
1889	1954	Pallette, Eugene
1914	1986	Palmer, Lilli
1894	1958	Pangborn, Franklin
1914	1992	Parks, Bert
1914	1975	Parks, Larry
1881	1940	Pasternack, Josef A.
1837	1908	Pastor, Tony
1843	1919	Patti, Adelina
1840	1889	Patti, Carlotta
1885	1931	Pavlova, Anna
1912	1989	Payne, John
1904	1984	Peerce, Jan
1899	1967	Pendleton, Nat
1905	1941	Penner, Joe
1932	1992	Perkins, Anthony
1915	1963	Piaf, Edith
1893	1979	Pickford, Mary
1897	1984	Pidgeon, Walter

Born	Died	Name
1892	1957	Pinza, Ezio
1898	1963	Pitts, Zasu
1904	1976	Pons, Lily
1897	1981	Ponselle, Rosa
1904	1963	Powell, Dick
1912	1982	Powell, Eleanor
1892	1984	Powell, William
1913	1958	Power, Tyrone
1905	1986	Preminger, Otto
1935	1977	Presley, Elvis
1918	1987	Preston, Robert
1911	1978	Prima, Louis
1954	1977	Prinze, Freddie
1946	1989	Radner, Gilda
1895	1980	Raft, George
1890	1967	Rains, Claude
1892	1967	Rathbone, Basil
1897	1960	Ratoff, Gregory
1941	1967	Redding, Otis
1908	1985	Redgrave, Michael
1921	1986	Reed, Donna
1932	1992	Reed, Robert
1914	1959	Reeves, George
1873	1943	Reinhardt, Max
1935	1991	Remick, Lee
1909	1971	Rennie, Michael
1902	1983	Richardson, Ralph
1921	1985	Riddle, Nelson
1898	1977	Ritchard, Cyril
1907	1974	Ritter, Tex
1905	1969	Ritter, Thelma
1901	1965	Ritz, Al
1906	1986	Ritz, Harry
1903	1985	Ritz, Jimmy
1925	1982	Robbins, Marty
1898	1976	Robeson, Paul
1878	1949	Robinson, Bill
1893	1973	Robinson, Edward G.
1905	1977	Rochester (E. Anderson)
1897	1933	Rodgers, Jimmie
1879	1935	Rogers, Will
1880	1962	Rooney, Pat
1899	1966	Rose, Billy
1922	1987	Rowan, Dan
1887	1982	Rubinstein, Artur
1886	1970	Ruggles, Charles
1924	1961	Russell, Gail
1861	1922	Russell, Lillian
1911	1976	Russell, Rosalind
1892	1972	Rutherford, Margaret
1903	1973	Ryan, Irene
1909	1973	Ryan, Robert
1877	1968	St. Denis, Ruth
1884	1955	Sakall, S.Z.
1885	1936	Sale (Chic), Charles
1906	1972	Sanders, George
1895	1964	Schildkraut, Joseph
1889	1965	Schipa, Tito
1882	1951	Schnabel, Artur
1920	1981	Scott, Hazel
1898	1987	Scott, Randolph
1914	1965	Scott, Zachary
1843	1896	Scott-Siddons, Mrs.
1938	1979	Seberg, Jean
1892	1974	Seeley, Blossom
1893	1987	Segovia, Andres
1925	1980	Sellers, Peter
1902	1965	Selznick, David O.
1884	1960	Sennett, Mack
1927	1978	Shaw, Robert
1891	1972	Shawn, Ted
1868	1949	Shean, Al
1902	1983	Shearer, Norma
1915	1967	Sheridan, Ann
1875	1953	Shubert, Lee
1755	1831	Siddons, Mrs. Sarah
1921	1985	Signoret, Simone
1912	1985	Silvers, Phil
1900	1976	Sim, Alastair
1858	1942	Skinner, Otis
1863	1948	Smith, C. Aubrey
1907	1986	Smith, Kate
1854	1932	Sousa, John Philip
1884	1957	Sparks, Ned
1907	1990	Stanwyck, Barbara
1934	1970	Stevens, Inger
1882	1977	Stokowski, Leopold

Born	Died	Name
1879	1953	Stone, Lewis
1904	1980	Stone, Milburn
1898	1959	Sturges, Preston
1911	1960	Sullavan, Margaret
1902	1974	Sullivan, Ed
1903	1956	Sullivan, Francis L.
1892	1946	Summerville, Slim
1899	1983	Swanson, Gloria
1904	1969	Swarthout, Gladys
1893	1957	Talmadge, Norma
1899	1972	Tamiroff, Akim
1878	1947	Tanguay, Eva
1885	1966	Taylor, Deems
1899	1958	Taylor, Estelle
1887	1946	Taylor, Laurette
1911	1969	Taylor, Robert
1847	1928	Terry, Ellen
1899	1936	Thalberg, Irving
1912	1991	Thomas, Danny
1882	1976	Thorndike, Sybil
1896	1960	Tibbett, Lawrence
1920	1991	Tierney, Gene
1909	1958	Todd, Michael
1903	1968	Tone, Franchot
1867	1957	Toscanini, Arturo
1898	1968	Tracy, Lee
1900	1967	Tracy, Spencer
1903	1972	Traubel, Helen
1894	1975	Treacher, Arthur
1853	1917	Tree, Herbert Beerbohm
1890	1973	Truex, Ernest
1932	1984	Truffaut, Francois
1919	1986	Tucker, Forrest
1915	1975	Tucker, Richard
1884	1966	Tucker, Sophie
1874	1940	Turpin, Ben
1908	1959	Twelvetrees, Helen
1933	1993	Twitty, Conway
1895	1926	Valentino, Rudolph
1901	1986	Vallee, Rudy
1911	1979	Vance, Vivian
1924	1990	Vaughan, Sarah
1893	1943	Veidt, Conrad
1926	1981	Vera-Ellen
1885	1957	Von Stroheim, Erich
1906	1981	Von Zell, Harry
1922	1992	Walker, Nancy
1914	1951	Walker, Robert
1887	1980	Walsh, Raoul
1876	1962	Walter, Bruno
1876	1958	Warner, H. B.
1924	1963	Washington, Dinah
1900	1977	Waters, Ethel
1907	1979	Wayne, John
1891	1966	Webb, Clifton
1920	1982	Webb, Jack
1903	1992	Welk, Lawrence
1915	1985	Welles, Orson
1896	1975	Wellman, William
1892	1980	West, Mae
1895	1968	Wheeler, Bert
1889	1938	White, Pearl
1891	1967	Whiteman, Paul
1865	1948	Whitty, May
1912	1979	Wilding, Michael
1877	1922	Williams, Bert
1923	1953	Williams, Hank
1905	1975	Wills, Bob
1903	1978	Wills, Chill
1917	1972	Wilson, Marie
1884	1969	Winninger, Charles
1904	1959	Withers, Grant
1907	1961	Wong, Anna May
1938	1981	Wood, Natalie
1892	1978	Wood, Peggy
1888	1963	Woolley, Monty
1902	1981	Wyler, William
1886	1966	Wynn, Ed
1916	1986	Wynn, Keenan
1890	1960	Young, Clara Kimball
1913	1978	Young, Gig
1887	1953	Young, Roland
1902	1979	Zanuck, Darryl F.
1869	1932	Ziegfeld, Florenz
1873	1976	Zukor, Adolph

Original Names of Selected Entertainers

Edie Adams: Elizabeth Edith Enke
Eddie Albert: Edward Albert Heimberger
Alan Alda: Alphonso D'Abruzzo
Jane Alexander: Jane Quigley
Fred Allen: John Sullivan
Woody Allen: Allen Konigsberg
Julie Andrews: Julia Wells
Eve Arden: Eunice Quedens
Beatrice Arthur: Bernice Frankel
Jean Arthur: Gladys Greene
Fred Astaire: Frederick Austerlitz
Alan Autry: Carlos Brown
Lauren Bacall: Betty Joan Perske
Anne Bancroft: Anna Maria Italiano
Brigitte Bardot: Camille Javal
Gene Barry: Eugene Klass
Orson Bean: Dallas Burrows
Bonnie Bedelia: Bonnie Culkin
Pat Benatar: Patricia Andrejewcki
Robbie Benson: Robert Segal
Tony Bennett: Anthony Benedetto
Busby Berkeley: William Berkeley Enos
Jack Benny: Benjamin Kubelsky
Joey Bishop: Joseph Gottlieb
Robert Blake: Michael Gubitosi
Victor Borge: Borge Rosenbaum
David Bowie: David Robert Jones
Boy George: George Alan O'Dowd
Fanny Brice: Fanny Borach
Charles Bronson: Charles Buchinski
Albert Brooks: Albert Einstein
Mel Brooks: Melvin Kaminsky
George Burns: Nathan Birnbaum
Ellen Burstyn: Edna Gilhooley
Richard Burton: Richard Jenkins
Red Buttons: Aaron Chwatt
Nicolas Cage: Nicholas Coppola
Michael Caine: Maurice Micklewhite
Maria Callas: Maria Kalogeropoulos
Vikki Carr: Florencia Casillas
Diahann Carroll: Carol Diahann Johnson
Cyd Charisse: Tula Finklea
Ray Charles: Ray Charles Robinson
Cher: Cherilyn Sarkisian
Patsy Cline: Virginia Patterson Hensley
Lee J. Cobb: Leo Jacoby
Claudette Colbert: Lily Chauchoin
Michael Connors: Kreker Ohanian
Robert Conrad: Conrad Robert Falk
Alice Cooper: Vincent Furnier
David Copperfield: David Kotkin
Howard Cosell: Howard Cohen
Elvis Costello: Declan Patrick McManus
Lou Costello: Louis Cristillo
Joan Crawford: Lucille Le Sueur
Michael Crawford: Michael Dumbell-Smith
Tom Cruise: Thomas Mapother
Tony Curtis: Bernard Schwartz
Vic Damone: Vito Farinola
Rodney Dangerfield: Jacob Cohen
Bobby Darin: Walden Robert Cassotto
Doris Day: Doris von Kappelhoff
Yvonne De Carlo: Peggy Middleton
Sandra Dee: Alexandra Zuck
John Denver: Henry John Deutschendorf Jr.
Bo Derek: Cathleen Collins
John Derek: Derek Harris
Danny DeVito: Daniel Michaeli
Susan Dey: Susan Smith
Angie Dickinson: Angeline Brown
Bo Diddley: Elias Bates
Phyllis Diller: Phyllis Driver
Diana Dors: Diana Fluck
Kirk Douglas: Issur Danielovitch
Melvyn Douglas: Melvyn Hesselberg
Bob Dylan: Robert Zimmerman
Sheena Easton: Sheena Shirley Orr
Barbara Eden: Barbara Huffman
Ron Ely: Ronald Pierce
Chad Everett: Raymond Cramton
Tom Ewell: S. Yewell Tompkins
Douglas Fairbanks: Douglas Ullman
Morgan Fairchild: Patsy McClenny
Alice Faye: Ann Leppert
Stepin Fetchit: Lincoln Perry
Sally Field: Sally Mahoney
W.C. Fields: William Claude Dukenfield
Peter Finch: William Mitchell
Barry Fitzgerald: William Joseph Shields
Joan Fontaine: Joan de Havilland
John Ford: Sean O'Fearna
John Forsythe: John Freund
Redd Foxx : John Sanford
Anthony Franciosa: Anthony Papaleo
Arlene Francis: Arlene Kazanjian
Connie Francis: Concetta Franconero
Greta Garbo: Greta Gustafsson
Vincent Gardenia: Vincent Scognamiglio
John Garfield: Julius Garfinkle
Judy Garland: Frances Gumm
James Garner: James Bumgarner
Crystal Gayle: Brenda Gayle Webb
Paulette Goddard: Marion Levy
Whoopi Goldberg: Caryn Johnson
Eydie Gorme: Edith Gormezano
Stewart Granger: James Stewart
Cary Grant: Archibald Leach
Lee Grant: Lyova Rosenthal
Joel Grey: Joe Katz
Robert Guillaume: Robert Williams
Buddy Hackett: Leonard Hacker
Hammer: Stanley Kirk Burrell
Jean Harlow: Harlean Carpentier
Rex Harrison: Reginald Carey
Laurence Harvey: Larushka Skikne
Helen Hayes: Helen Brown
Susan Hayward: Edythe Marriner
Rita Hayworth: Margarita Cansino
Pee-Wee Herman: Paul Rubenfeld
Barbara Hershey: Barbara Herzstine
William Holden: William Beedle
Judy Holliday: Judith Tuvim
Harry Houdini: Ehrich Weiss
Leslie Howard: Leslie Stainer
Moe Howard: Moses Horowitz
Rock Hudson: Roy Scherer Jr. (later Fitzgerald)
Engelbert Humperdinck: Arnold Dorsey
Kim Hunter: Janet Cole
Mary Beth Hurt: Mary Supinger
Betty Hutton: Betty Thornberg
David Janssen: David Meyer
Elton John: Reginald Dwight
Don Johnson: Donald Wayne
Jennifer Jones: Phyllis Isley
Tom Jones: Thomas Woodward
Louis Jourdan: Louis Gendre
Boris Karloff: William Henry Pratt
Danny Kaye: David Kaminsky
Diane Keaton: Diane Hall
Michael Keaton: Michael Douglas
Howard Keel: Harold Leek
Chaka Khan: Yvette Stevens
Carole King: Carole Klein
Larry King: Larry Zeigler
Ben Kingsley: Krishna Banji
Nastassja Kinski: Nastassja Naksyznyski
Ted Knight: Tadeus Wladyslaw Konopka
Cheryl Ladd: Cheryl Stoppelmoor
Veronica Lake: Constance Ockleman
Dorothy Lamour: Mary Kaumeyer
Michael Landon: Eugene Orowitz
Mario Lanza: Alfredo Cocozza
Stan Laurel: Arthur Jefferson
Steve Lawrence: Sidney Leibowitz
Brenda Lee: Brenda Mae Tarpley
Bruce Lee: Lee Yuen Kam
Gypsy Rose Lee: Rose Louise Hovick
Michelle Lee: Michelle Dusiak
Peggy Lee: Norma Egstrom
Janet Leigh: Jeanette Morrison
Vivien Leigh: Vivien Hartley
Huey Lewis: Hugh Cregg
Jerry Lewis: Joseph Levitch
Hal Linden: Harold Lipshitz
Carole Lombard: Jane Peters
Jack Lord: John Joseph Ryan
Sophia Loren: Sophia Scicoloni
Peter Lorre: Laszio Lowenstein
Myrna Loy: Myrna Williams
Bela Lugosi: Bela Ferenc Blasko
Moms Mabley: Loretta Mary Aitken
Shirley MacLaine: Shirley Beaty

Madonna: Madonna Louise Ciccone
Lee Majors: Harvey Lee Yeary 2d
Karl Malden: Malden Sekulovich
Jayne Mansfield: Vera Jane Palmer
Fredric March: Frederick Bickel
Peter Marshall: Pierre LaCock
Dean Martin: Dino Crocetti
Ethel Merman: Ethel Zimmerman
George Michael: Georgios Panayiotou
Ray Milland: Reginald Truscott-Jones
Ann Miller: Lucille Collier
Joni Mitchell: Roberta Joan Anderson
Marilyn Monroe: Norma Jean Mortenson, (later) Baker
Yves Montand: Ivo Levi
Ron Moody: Ronald Moodnick
Demi Moore: Demi Guynes
Garry Moore: Thomas Garrison Morfit
Rita Moreno: Rosita Alverio
Harry Morgan: Harry Bratsburg
Paul Muni: Muni Weisenfreund
Mike Nichols: Michael Igor Peschowsky
Chuck Norris: Carlos Ray
Sheree North: Dawn Bethel
Hugh O'Brian: Hugh Krampke
Maureen O'Hara: Maureen Fitzsimmons
Patti Page: Clara Ann Fowler
Jack Palance: Walter Palanuik
Bert Parks: Bert Jacobson
Minnie Pearl: Sarah Ophelia Cannon
Bernadette Peters: Bernadette Lazzaro
Edith Piaf: Edith Gassion
Slim Pickens: Louis Lindley
Mary Pickford: Gladys Smith
Stephanie Powers: Stefania Federkiewicz
Paula Prentiss: Paula Ragusa
Robert Preston: Robert Preston Meservey
Prince: Prince Rogers Nelson
Tony Randall: Leonard Rosenberg
Martha Raye: Margaret O'Reed
Donna Reed: Donna Belle Mullenger
Della Reese: Delloreese Patricia Early
Joan Rivers: Joan Sandra Molinsky
Edward G. Robinson: Emmanuel Goldenberg
Ginger Rogers: Virginia McMath
Roy Rogers: Leonard Slye
Mickey Rooney: Joe Yule Jr.
Lillian Russell: Helen Leonard
Theresa Russell: Theresa Paup
Winona Ryder: Winona Horowitz
Susan St. James: Susan Miller
Soupy Sales: Milton Hines
Susan Sarandon: Susan Tomaling
Randolph Scott: George Randolph Crane
Jane Seymour: Joyce Frankenberg
Omar Sharif: Michael Shalhoub
Martin Sheen: Ramon Estevez
Beverly Sills: Belle Silverman
Talia Shire: Talia Coppola
Phil Silvers: Philip Silversmith
Suzanne Somers: Suzanne Mahoney
Ann Sothern: Harriette Lake
Robert Stack: Robert Modini
Barbara Stanwyck: Ruby Stevens
Jean Stapleton: Jeanne Murray
Ringo Starr: Richard Starkey
Connie Stevens: Concetta Ingolia
Sting: Gordon Sumner
Donna Summer: La Donna Gaines
Rip Taylor: Charles Elmer Jr.
Robert Taylor: Spangler Arlington Brugh
Danny Thomas: Muzyad Yakhoob, later Amos Jacobs
Randy Travis: Randy Traywick
Sophie Tucker: Sophia Kalish
Tina Turner: Annie Mae Bullock
Conway Twitty: Harold Lloyd Jenkins
Rudolph Valentino: Rudolpho D'Antonguolla
Frankie Valli: Frank Castelluccio
David Wayne: Wayne McMeekan
John Wayne: Marion Morrison
Clifton Webb: Webb Parmalee Hollenbeck
Raquel Welch: Raquel Tejada
Gene Wilder: Jerome Silberman
Shelley Winters: Shirley Schrift
Stevie Wonder: Stevland Morris
Natalie Wood: Natasha Gurdin
Jane Wyman: Sarah Jane Fulks
Gig Young: Byron Barr

Selected International Figures of the Present

(Excluding heads of state, entertainers, and athletes; for heads of state, see individual nations)

Name (Birthplace)	Birthdate
Chinua Achebe (Ogidi, Nigeria)	11/16/30
Jorge Amado (Bahia, Brazil)	8/1/12
Martin Amis (Oxford, England)	8/25/49
Yasir Arafat (Jerusalem, Palestine)	1929
Moshe Arens (Kaumas, Lithuania)	12/27/25
Oscar Arias Sanchez (Heredia, Costa Rica)	9/13/41
Hanan Ashrawi (Ramallah, Palestine)	1946
Margaret Atwood (Ottawa, Ontario)	11/18/39
Benazir Bhutto (Karachi, Pakistan)	6/21/53
Boutros Boutros-Ghali (Cairo, Egypt)	11/14/22
British Royal Family	
Queen Elizabeth II (London, England)	4/21/26
Prince Philip (Corfu, Greece)	6/1/21
Prince Charles (London, England)	11/14/48
Princess Diana (Sandringham, England)	7/1/61
Prince William (London, England)	6/21/82
Prince Henry (London, England)	9/15/84
Princess Anne (London, England)	8/15/50
Prince Andrew (London, England)	2/19/60
Sarah Ferguson (London, England)	10/15/59
Princess Beatrice (London, England)	8/8/88
Princess Eugenie (London, England)	3/23/90
Prince Edward (London, England)	3/1/64
Princess Margaret (Glamis, Scotland)	8/21/30
Tina Brown (Maidenhead, England)	11/21/53
Gro Harlem Bruntland (Oslo, Norway)	4/2/39
Kim Campbell (Port Alberni, British Columbia	3/10/47
Elias Canetti (Ruschuk, Bulgaria)	7/25/05
Camilo Jose Cela (Ira Flavia, Spain)	5/11/16
Dalai Lama: Tenzin Gyatso (Kokonor, Tibet)	6/6/35
Robertson Davies (Thamesville, Ontario)	8/28/13
Jacques Derrida (El Biar, Algeria)	7/15/30
Takako Doi (Hyogo, Japan)	11/30/28
Margaret Drabble (Sheffield, England)	6/5/39
Valery Giscard d'Estaing (Koblenz, Germany)	2/2/26
Carlos Fuentes (Mexico City, Mexico)	11/11/28
Athol Fugard (Kanroo, South Africa)	1932
Gabriel Garcia Marquez (Aracata, Colombia)	3/6/28
Mikhail Gorbachev (Privalnaye, Stavropol, USSR)	3/21/31
Raisa Gorbachev (Rubtsovsk, USSR)	1934
Nadine Gordimer (Springs, South Africa)	11/2/23
Germaine Greer (Melbourne, Australia)	1/29/39
Stephen Hawking (Oxford, England)	1/8/42
Michael Heseltine (Swansea, Wales)	3/21/33
Morihiro Hosokawa (Kumamoto, Japan)	1/14/38
Ted Hughes (Mytholmroyd, England)	8/17/30
P.D. James (Oxford, England)	8/3/20
Milan Kundera (Brno, Czechoslovakia)	4/1/29
John le Carré (Poole, England)	10/19/31
Doris Lessing (Kermanshah, Persia)	10/22/19
Naguib Mahfouz (Cairo, Egypt)	12/11/11
Nelson Mandela (Transkei, South Africa)	1918
Winnie Mandela (Transkei, South Africa)	1934
Crown Princess Masako (Tokyo, Japan)	12/9/63
Czeslaw Milosz (Sateinial, Lithuania)	6/3/11
Monaco Royal Family	
Prince Ranier III (Monaco)	5/31/23
Prince Albert (Monte Carlo, Monaco)	3/14/58
Princess Caroline (Monte Carlo, Monaco)	1/23/57
Princess Stephanie (Monaco-Ville, Monaco)	2/1/65
Alice Munro (Wingham, Ontario)	7/10/31
Iris Murdoch (Dublin, Ireland)	7/15/19
Rupert Murdoch (Melbourne, Australia)	3/11/31
Crown Price Naruhito (Tokyo, Japan)	2/23/60
Edna O'Brien (Tuamgraney, Ireland)	12/15/31
Amoz Oz (Jerusalem, Palestine)	5/4/39
Andreas Papandreou (Chios, Greece)	2/5/19
Octavio Paz (Mexico City, Mexico)	3/31/14
Shimon Perez (Wolozyn, Poland)	8/16/23
Yitzak Rabin (Jerusalem, Palestine)	3/1/22
Mordecai Richler (Montreal, Quebec)	1/27/31
Mary Robinson (Ballina, Ireland)	5/21/44
Salman Rushdie (Bombay, India)	6/19/47
Yitzak Shamir (Kuzinoy, Poland)	11/3/14
Eduard Shevardnadze (Mamati, USSR)	1/25/28
Wole Soyinka (Abeokuta, Nigeria)	7/13/34
Muriel Spark (Edinburgh, Scotland)	2/1/18
Hanna Suchocka (Pleszewa, Poland)	4/3/46
Mother Teresa (Skopje, Macedonia)	8/27/10
Margaret Thatcher (Grantham, England)	10/13/25

UNITED STATES POPULATION

A Typical American as Seen Through the Eyes of the Census Bureau

by
Dr. Harry A. Scarr
Deputy Director, Bureau of the Census
U.S. Department of Commerce

I am often asked to describe a typical American: What do we do? Where do we live? How much money do we make? Based upon Census Bureau data, I see typical America as a patchwork of cultures, lifestyles, and economic groups.

Who We Are

Typical America contains many racial and ethnic groups. More than 23 million of us (9.3 percent) are of Hispanic origin, and 8 million of us (3.2 percent) identify ourselves as Asians or Pacific Islanders. Blacks number over 31 million, or 12.4 percent of the population, and the American Indian/Eskimo/Aleut populations make up about 2 million (0.8 percent). Nearly 190 million people (75.2 percent) consider themselves to be non-Hispanic white.

According to the 1990 Census, nearly 20 million of us were not born in America but call it home. In 1992, about 33 percent of our population growth came from net immigration.

This means America speaks many **languages:** over 31.8 million of us speak a language other than English at home; over half of this number speaks Spanish.

We are also aging: our **median age** has risen from 30.0 years in 1980 to 33.1 in 1991 (the median for blacks is 28.1, and the median for whites is 34.1). Nearly 26 percent of us are under 18 years of age, and over 12.6 percent are 65 and older.

Women outnumber men in America by 6.2 million; 51 percent of the total population is female.

There are 95.7 million **households** in our nation; 70 percent of them contain families. Of all households, 55 percent are maintained by married couples, but only 26 percent of all households with children under 18 include a married couple. About one-fourth of all households contain a person living alone.

What We Do

About 67 percent of Americans 16 years and over are in the labor force: almost 76 percent of men and nearly 58 percent of women. Over 8 million working-age Americans are prevented from working because of a disability.

Our top three **occupation groups** are administrative support, including clerical; professional specialty; and executive, administrative, and managerial. There are 19.6 million employed persons working in the retail sales industry.

Of the over 115 million employed workers, 73 percent drive to work alone and 13 percent are in carpools. About 76 percent of us work in the county in which we live, and our **commuting time** averages about 22 minutes.

Workers are well represented among mothers: almost 58 percent of mothers with children under 6, and 75.9 percent of mothers with children 6 to 17 are in the labor force.

The number of **women-owned businesses** (sole proprietorship, partnership, or subchapter S companies) increased by a dramatic 57 percent in the late 1980s. **Minority-owned firms** also dramatically increased in number: Asian-Pacific Islander by 89 percent, Hispanic by 81 percent, American Indian/Eskimo/Aleut by 58 percent, and black by 38 percent.

Most **state and local government employees** are in education-related activities: two-fifths of the 4.5 million state employees and over one-half of the 10.9 million local government workers.

Personal and business services grew 13 times faster than the population in the late 1980s.

Where We Live

Typical America, or at least half of it (55.6 percent), lives in the South and West regions of the country. Between 1980 and 1990, the West grew by 22.3 percent, and the South grew by 13.4 percent. This dramatic growth rate caused a shift of 19 seats in the House of Representatives. Eight states gained seats: California (+7), Florida (+4), Texas (+3), and Arizona, Georgia, North Carolina, Virginia, and Washington (+1 each). Thirteen states lost seats: New York (−3); Illinois, Michigan, Ohio, and Pennsylvania (−2 each); and Iowa, Kansas, Kentucky, Louisiana, Massachusetts, Montana, New Jersey, and West Virginia (−1 each).

Since 1990, the U.S. population has been increasing by about 3 million persons a year. Our five most populous states are California (30.9 million), New York (18.1 million), Texas (17.7 million), Florida (13.5 million), and Pennsylvania (12 million). The five states at the other end of the spectrum are Delaware (689,000), North Dakota (636,000), Alaska (587,000), Vermont (570,000), and Wyoming (466,000).

Most of us—79.5 percent—live in **metropolitan areas,** and over half of us (53.7) live in one of the 41 metropolitan areas with populations of at least 1 million.

Our five largest metropolitan areas are scattered across the map: New York/Northern New Jersey/Long Island (19.4 million), Los Angeles/Riverside/Orange County (14.8 million), Chicago/Gary/Kenosha Counties (8.3 million), Washington/Baltimore (6.8 million), and San Francisco/Oakland/San Jose (6.3 million). Although the New York area remains in first position, the Los Angeles area is growing at a much faster rate (2 versus 0.2 percent since 1990).

Within those metro areas are some big **cities.** Our five largest cities are New York (7.3 million), Los Angeles (3.5 million), Chicago (2.8 million), Houston (1.6 million), and Philadelphia (1.6 million).

Our five largest **counties** are Los Angeles, CA (9.0 million), Cook, IL (5.1 million), Harris, TX (2.9 million), San Diego, CA (2.5 million), and Orange, CA (2.4 million).

How We Live

Typical Americans live in a household with others. The average number of people living in a household in the United States was 2.62 in 1992.

We have a total of about 105 million **housing units** nationwide; nearly 93 million of them are occupied. The vast majority of housing units have public water and sewer service, and our top two house heating fuel sources are utility gas (51 million units) and electricity (27 million units). About 3 million units lack complete plumbing facilities, and 4 million lack complete kitchen facilities.

Almost two thirds (64 percent) of us are **homeowners.** Of the 60 million owner units, nearly 35 million have mortgages. The median monthly costs for all owner units is $455. The median for mortgage units is $761, while the median for non-mortgage units is $222. The median value of owner homes is $80,000.

If you live in one of the 33 million **renter-occupied housing units,** your housing costs are $462 per month.

Quality of Life

Education: America has a higher proportion of high school graduates than at any other time in U.S. history: more than 79 percent of all Americans age 25 and over. About 27 percent of these graduates have gone on to earn a bachelor's degree or higher.

Educational attainment has a direct impact on many aspects of life, but most directly on earnings. Average annual earnings for persons without a high school diploma are $14,078; with a diploma, $19,567; with a bachelor's degree, $32,728; with a doctorate, $53,705; and with a professional degree, $65,648. We spend an average of $4,700 annually per student in our public elementary and secondary schools.

Assets: Home ownership accounts for over 40 percent of Americans' net worth. Interest-earning assets account for almost 20 percent. About 20 percent of America's households hold about 44 percent of our nation's net worth.

Pensions: Two-thirds of the work force is covered by a pension of some type. Most of us (92 percent) are covered by Social Security. Nearly all government employees (92 percent) are covered by pensions, while only 36 percent of agricultural and personal service workers are covered by employer-sponsored pensions.

Health insurance: Nearly 86 percent of us have health insurance. Those most likely to be insured are the elderly, the employed, and those with at least a high school diploma.

Child care: Families with working mothers and preschool children spend about 8 percent of their combined income on child care for their children. Most of the care for preschoolers takes place in a home environment, such as with relatives or neighbors (67 percent); about 23 percent of child care for preschoolers is in organized facilities, such as nursery schools and day care centers; 9 percent are cared for by the mother while she works; and 1 percent are involved in a school-based activity.

Child support: Of the 5.7 million women awarded child support, 5.0 million were supposed to receive payments in 1989. Of the women due payments, about half received the full amount they were due. The average amount of child support received in 1989 was $2,995. The aggregate amount of child support received in 1989 was $11.2 billion, 69 percent of $16.3 billion due.

Assistance: About 4 percent of our adult population needs assistance with everyday activities. This need increases to 45 percent for persons 85 and over. Most caregivers are female relatives.

Voting: The 1992 presidential election was decided by 61.3 percent of our voting-age population. That was better than the 57 percent who determined the outcome of the 1988 presidential election. Voter registration increased for the 1992 election; about 68 percent of us who are old enough to vote registered to do so in 1992, up slightly from 67 percent in 1988.

Federal Aid: In fiscal year 1992, the federal government dispensed nearly $2 trillion to state and local governments and U.S. territories. California received $140 billion of these funds. On a per capita basis, Alaska received the most, with spending of over $6,800 per person.

Funds were divided this way: $612 billion in payments to individuals, such as Social Security; $162 billion in salaries to military and civilian employees; $200 billion in contracts; $178 billion in grants to state and local governments, for example: Medicaid, Aid to Families With Dependent Children, and highway construction; and $40 billion in other programs, including research grants and agricultural subsidies.

Lotteries: Thirty-two states operate lotteries, which produced $8.8 billion in net revenue in fiscal year 1991. During the same time, state general expenditures amounted to $554.6 billion. State expenditures for highways were up 6.3 percent in 1991 to $47 billion. Expenditures for hospitals rose 8.1 percent to $24.5 billion in 1991.

Estimated Population of American Colonies: 1630-1780

Source: Bureau of the Census (thousands)

Colony	1780	1770	1750	1740	1720	1700	1690	1670	1650	1630
Total	**2,780.4**	**2,148.1**	**1,170.8**	**905.6**	**466.2**	**250.9**	**210.4**	**111.9**	**50.4**	**4.6**
Maine (counties)[1]	49.1	31.3	...	...	...	...	...	...	1.0	0.4
New Hampshire[2]	87.8	62.4	27.5	23.3	9.4	5.0	4.2	1.8	1.3	0.5
Vermont[3]	47.6	10.0	...	...	...	...	...	...	...	...
Plymouth and Massachusetts[1,2,4]	268.6	235.3	188.0	151.6	91.0	55.9	56.9	35.3	15.6	0.9
Rhode Island[2]	52.9	58.2	33.2	25.3	11.7	5.9	4.2	2.2	0.8	...
Connecticut[2]	206.7	183.9	111.3	89.6	58.8	26.0	21.6	12.6	4.1	...
New York[2]	210.5	162.9	76.7	63.7	36.9	19.1	13.9	5.8	4.1	0.4
New Jersey[2]	139.6	117.4	71.4	51.4	29.8	14.0	8.0	1.0	...	...
Pennsylvania[2]	327.3	240.1	119.7	85.6	31.0	18.0	11.4	...	...	...
Delaware[2]	45.4	35.5	28.7	19.9	5.4	2.5	1.5	0.7	0.2	...
Maryland[2]	245.5	202.6	141.1	116.1	66.1	29.6	24.0	13.2	4.5	...
Virginia[2]	538.0	447.0	231.0	180.4	87.8	58.6	53.0	35.3	18.7	2.5
North Carolina[2]	270.1	197.2	73.0	51.8	21.3	10.7	7.6	3.8	...	...
South Carolina[2]	180.0	124.2	64.0	45.0	17.0	5.7	3.9	0.2	...	...
Georgia[2]	56.1	23.4	5.2	2.0	...	...	...	...	...	...
Kentucky[5]	45.0	15.7	...	...	...	...	...	...	...	...
Tennessee[6]	10.0	1.0	...	...	...	...	...	...	...	...

(1) For 1660-1750, Maine counties included with Massachusetts. Maine was a part of Massachusetts until it became a separate state in 1820. (2) One of the original 13 states. (3) Admitted to statehood in 1791. (4) Plymouth became a part of the Province of Massachusetts in 1691. (5) Admitted to statehood in 1792. (6) Admitted to statehood in 1796.

U.S. Population by Official

(Members of the Armed Forces overseas or

State	1790[1]	1800[1]	1810[1]	1820	1830	1840	1850	1860	1870	1880	1890
Ala. . .	......	1	9	127,901	309,527	590,756	771,623	964,201	996,992	1,262,505	1,513,401
Alas. .	......	......	......	......	......	......	......	......	......	33,426	32,052
Ariz. . .	......	......	......	......	......	......	......	......	9,658	40,440	88,243
Ark. . .	......	......	1	14,273	30,388	97,574	209,897	435,450	484,471	802,525	1,128,211
Cal. . .	......	......	......	......	......	......	92,597	379,994	560,247	864,694	1,213,398
Col. . .	......	......	......	......	......	......	......	34,277	39,864	194,327	413,249
Conn. .	238	251	262	275,248	297,675	309,978	370,792	460,147	537,454	622,700	746,258
Del. . .	59	64	73	72,749	76,748	78,085	91,532	112,216	125,015	146,608	168,493
D.C. . .	......	8	16	23,336	30,261	33,745	51,687	75,080	131,700	177,624	230,392
Fla. . .	......	......	......	......	34,730	54,477	87,445	140,424	187,748	269,493	391,422
Ga. . .	83	163	252	340,989	516,823	691,392	906,185	1,057,286	1,184,109	1,542,180	1,837,353
Ha. . .	......	......	......	......	......	......	......	......	......	......	......
Ida. . .	......	......	......	......	......	......	......	......	14,999	32,610	88,548
Ill. . . .	......	......	12	55,211	157,445	476,183	851,470	1,711,951	2,539,891	3,077,871	3,826,352
Ind. . .	......	6	25	147,178	343,031	685,866	988,416	1,350,428	1,680,637	1,978,301	2,192,404
Ia. . . .	......	......	......	......	......	43,112	192,214	674,913	1,194,020	1,624,615	1,912,297
Kan. . .	......	......	......	......	......	......	......	107,206	364,399	996,096	1,428,108
Ky. . .	74	221	407	564,317	687,917	779,828	982,405	1,155,684	1,321,011	1,648,690	1,858,635
La. . .	......	......	77	153,407	215,739	352,411	517,762	708,002	726,915	939,946	1,118,588
Me. . .	97	152	229	298,335	399,455	501,793	583,169	628,279	626,915	648,936	661,086
Md. . .	320	342	381	407,350	447,040	470,019	583,034	687,049	780,894	934,943	1,042,390
Mass. .	379	423	472	523,287	610,408	737,699	994,514	1,231,066	1,457,351	1,783,085	2,238,947
Mich. .	......	......	5	8,896	31,639	212,267	397,654	749,113	1,184,059	1,636,937	2,093,890
Minn. .	......	......	......	......	......	......	6,077	172,023	439,706	780,773	1,310,283
Miss. .	......	8	31	75,448	136,621	375,651	606,526	791,305	827,922	1,131,597	1,289,600
Mo. . .	......	......	20	66,586	140,455	383,702	682,044	1,182,012	1,721,295	2,168,380	2,679,185
Mon. . .	......	......	......	......	......	......	......	......	20,595	39,159	142,924
Neb. . .	......	......	......	......	......	......	......	28,841	122,993	452,402	1,062,656
Nev. . .	......	......	......	......	......	......	......	6,857	42,491	62,266	47,355
N.H. . .	142	184	214	244,161	269,328	284,574	317,976	326,073	318,300	346,991	376,530
N.J. . .	184	211	246	277,575	320,823	373,306	489,555	672,035	906,096	1,131,116	1,444,933
N.M. . .	......	......	......	......	......	......	61,547	93,516	91,874	119,565	160,282
N.Y. . .	340	589	959	1,372,812	1,918,608	2,428,921	3,097,394	3,880,735	4,382,759	5,082,871	6,003,174
N.C. . .	394	478	556	638,829	737,987	753,419	869,039	992,622	1,071,361	1,399,750	1,617,949
N.D. . .	......	......	......	......	......	......	......	......	2,405[2]	36,909	190,983
Oh. . .	......	45	231	581,434	937,903	1,519,467	1,980,329	2,339,511	2,665,260	3,198,062	3,672,329
Okla. .	......	......	......	......	......	......	......	......	......	......	258,657
Ore. . .	......	......	......	......	......	......	12,093	52,465	90,923	174,768	317,704
Pa. . .	434	602	810	1,049,458	1,348,233	1,724,033	2,311,786	2,906,215	3,521,951	4,282,891	5,258,113
R.I. . .	69	69	77	83,059	97,199	108,830	147,545	174,620	217,353	276,531	345,506
S.C. . .	249	346	415	502,741	581,185	594,398	668,507	703,708	705,606	995,577	1,151,149
S.D. . .	......	......	......	......	......	......	......	4,837[2]	11,776[2]	98,268	348,600
Tenn. .	36	106	262	422,823	681,904	829,210	1,002,717	1,109,801	1,258,520	1,542,359	1,767,518
Tex. . .	......	......	......	......	......	......	212,592	604,215	818,579	1,591,749	2,235,527
Ut. . .	......	......	......	......	......	......	11,380	40,273	86,786	143,963	210,779
Vt. . .	85	154	218	235,981	280,652	291,948	314,120	315,098	330,551	332,286	332,422
Va. . .	692	808	878	938,261	1,044,054	1,025,227	1,119,348	1,219,630	1,225,163	1,512,565	1,655,980
Wash. .	......	......	......	......	......	......	1,201	11,594	23,955	75,116	357,232
W. Va. .	56	79	105	136,808	176,924	224,537	302,313	376,688	442,014	618,457	762,794
Wis. . .	......	......	......	......	......	30,945	305,391	775,881	1,054,670	1,315,497	1,693,330
Wy. . .	......	......	......	......	......	......	......	......	9,118	20,789	62,555
U.S. . .	**3,929**	**5,308**	**7,240**	**9,638,453**	**12,860,702**	**17,063,353[3]**	**23,191,876**	**31,443,321[3]**	**38,558,371**	**50,189,209**	**62,979,766**

Note: Where possible, population shown is that of 1990 area of state.
(1) Totals for 1790, 1800, and 1810 are in thousands. (2) 1860 figure is for Dakota Territory; 1870 figures are for parts of Dakota Territory. (3) U.S. total includes persons (5,318 in 1830 and 6,100 in 1840) on public ships in the service of the United States not credited to any region, division, or state.

Congressional Apportionment

	1990	1980		1990	1980		1990	1980		1990	1980		1990	1980
AL . .	7	7	ID. . .	2	2	MN . .	8	8	ND . .	1	1	UT . .	3	3
AK . .	1	1	IL. . .	20	22	MS . .	5	5	OH . .	19	21	VT . .	1	1
AZ . .	6	5	IN. . .	10	10	MO . .	9	9	OK . .	6	6	VA . .	11	10
AR . .	4	4	IA. . .	5	6	MT . .	1	2	OR . .	5	5	WA . .	9	8
CA . .	52	45	KS . .	4	5	NE . .	3	3	PA . .	21	23	WV . .	3	4
CO . .	6	6	KY . .	6	7	NV . .	2	2	RI . .	2	2	WI . .	9	9
CT . .	6	6	LA . .	7	8	NH . .	2	2	SC . .	6	6	WY . .	1	1
DE . .	1	1	ME . .	2	2	NJ . .	13	14	SD . .	1	1			
FL . .	23	19	MD . .	8	8	NM . .	3	3	TN . .	9	9	**Totals**	**435**	**435**
GA . .	11	10	MA . .	10	11	NY . .	31	34	TX . .	30	27			
HI. . .	2	2	MI. . .	16	18	NC . .	12	11						

The primary reason the Constitution provided for a census of the population every 10 years was to give a basis for apportionment of representatives among the states. This apportionment largely determines the number of electoral votes allotted to each state.

The number of representatives of each state in Congress is determined by the state's population, but each state is entitled to one representative regardless of population. A Congressional apportionment has been made after each decennial census except that of 1920.

Under provisions of a law that became effective Nov. 15, 1941, apportionment of representatives is made by the method of equal proportions. In the application of this method, the apportionment is made so that the average population per representative has the least possible variation between one state and any other. The first House of Representatives, in 1789, had 65 members, as provided by the Constitution. As the population grew, the number of representatives was increased, but the total membership has been fixed at 435 since the apportionment based on the 1910 census.

Census from 1790 to 1990

other U.S. nationals overseas are not included.)

1900	1910	1920	1930	1940	1950	1960	1970	1980	1990
1,828,697	2,138,093	2,348,174	2,646,248	2,832,961	3,061,743	3,266,740	3,444,354	3,894,025	4,040,587
63,592	64,356	55,036	59,278	72,524	128,643	226,167	302,583	401,851	550,043
122,931	204,354	334,162	435,573	499,261	749,587	1,302,161	1,775,399	2,716,546	3,665,228
1,311,564	1,574,449	1,752,204	1,854,482	1,949,387	1,909,511	1,786,272	1,923,322	2,286,357	2,350,725
1,485,053	2,377,549	3,426,861	5,677,251	6,907,387	10,586,223	15,717,204	19,971,069	23,667,764	29,760,021
539,700	799,024	939,629	1,035,791	1,123,296	1,325,089	1,753,947	2,209,596	2,889,735	3,294,394
908,420	1,114,756	1,380,631	1,606,903	1,709,242	2,007,280	2,535,234	3,032,217	3,107,564	3,287,116
184,735	202,322	223,003	238,380	266,505	318,085	446,292	548,104	594,338	666,168
278,718	331,069	437,571	486,869	663,091	802,178	763,956	756,668	638,432	606,900
528,542	752,619	968,470	1,468,211	1,897,414	2,771,305	4,951,560	6,791,418	9,746,961	12,937,926
2,216,331	2,609,121	2,895,832	2,908,506	3,123,723	3,444,578	3,943,116	4,587,930	5,462,982	6,478,216
154,001	191,874	255,881	368,300	422,770	499,794	632,772	769,913	964,691	1,108,229
161,772	325,594	431,866	445,032	524,873	588,637	667,191	713,015	944,127	1,006,749
4,821,550	5,638,591	6,485,280	7,630,654	7,897,241	8,712,176	10,081,158	11,110,285	11,427,409	11,430,602
2,516,462	2,700,876	2,930,390	3,238,503	3,427,796	3,934,224	4,662,498	5,195,392	5,490,214	5,544,159
2,231,853	2,224,771	2,404,021	2,470,939	2,538,268	2,621,073	2,757,537	2,825,368	2,913,808	2,776,755
1,470,495	1,690,949	1,769,257	1,880,999	1,801,028	1,905,299	2,178,611	2,249,071	2,364,236	2,477,574
2,147,174	2,289,905	2,416,630	2,614,589	2,845,627	2,944,806	3,038,156	3,220,711	3,660,324	3,685,296
1,381,625	1,656,388	1,798,509	2,101,593	2,363,880	2,683,516	3,257,022	3,644,637	4,206,116	4,219,973
694,466	742,371	768,014	797,423	847,226	913,774	969,265	993,722	1,125,043	1,227,928
1,188,044	1,295,346	1,449,661	1,631,526	1,821,244	2,343,001	3,100,689	3,923,897	4,216,933	4,781,468
2,805,346	3,366,416	3,852,356	4,249,614	4,316,721	4,690,514	5,148,578	5,689,170	5,737,093	6,016,425
2,420,982	2,810,173	3,668,412	4,842,325	5,256,106	6,371,766	7,823,194	8,881,826	9,262,044	9,295,297
1,751,394	2,075,708	2,387,125	2,563,953	2,792,300	2,982,483	3,413,864	3,806,103	4,075,970	4,375,099
1,551,270	1,797,114	1,790,618	2,009,821	2,183,796	2,178,914	2,178,141	2,216,994	2,520,770	2,573,216
3,106,665	3,293,335	3,404,055	3,629,367	3,784,664	3,954,653	4,319,813	4,677,623	4,916,766	5,117,073
243,329	376,053	548,889	537,606	559,456	591,024	674,767	694,409	786,690	799,065
1,066,300	1,192,214	1,296,372	1,377,963	1,315,834	1,325,510	1,411,330	1,485,333	1,569,825	1,578,385
42,335	81,875	77,407	91,058	110,247	160,083	285,278	488,738	800,508	1,201,833
411,588	430,572	443,083	465,293	491,524	533,242	606,921	737,681	920,610	1,109,252
1,883,669	2,537,167	3,155,900	4,041,334	4,160,165	4,835,329	6,066,782	7,171,112	7,365,011	7,730,188
195,310	327,301	360,350	423,317	531,818	681,187	951,023	1,017,055	1,303,302	1,515,069
7,268,894	9,113,614	10,385,227	12,588,066	13,479,142	14,830,192	16,782,304	18,241,391	17,558,165	17,990,455
1,893,810	2,206,287	2,559,123	3,170,276	3,571,623	4,061,929	4,556,155	5,084,411	5,880,095	6,628,637
319,146	577,056	646,872	680,845	641,935	619,636	632,446	617,792	652,717	638,800
4,157,545	4,767,121	5,759,394	6,646,697	6,907,612	7,946,627	9,706,397	10,657,423	10,797,603	10,847,115
790,391	1,657,155	2,028,283	2,396,040	2,336,434	2,233,351	2,328,284	2,559,463	3,025,487	3,145,585
413,536	672,765	783,389	953,786	1,089,684	1,521,341	1,768,687	2,091,533	2,633,156	2,842,321
6,302,115	7,665,111	8,720,017	9,631,350	9,900,180	10,498,012	11,319,366	11,800,766	11,864,720	11,881,643
428,556	542,610	604,397	687,497	713,346	791,896	859,488	949,723	947,154	1,003,464
1,340,316	1,515,400	1,683,724	1,738,765	1,899,804	2,117,027	2,382,594	2,590,713	3,120,729	3,486,703
401,570	583,888	636,547	692,849	642,961	652,740	680,514	666,257	690,768	696,004
2,020,616	2,184,789	2,337,885	2,616,556	2,915,841	3,291,718	3,567,089	3,926,018	4,591,023	4,877,185
3,048,710	3,896,542	4,663,228	5,824,715	6,414,824	7,711,194	9,579,677	11,198,655	14,225,513	16,986,510
276,749	373,351	449,396	507,847	550,310	688,862	890,627	1,059,273	1,461,037	1,722,850
343,641	355,956	352,428	359,611	359,231	377,747	389,881	444,732	511,456	562,758
1,854,184	2,061,612	2,309,187	2,421,851	2,677,773	3,318,680	3,966,949	4,651,448	5,346,797	6,187,358
518,103	1,141,990	1,356,621	1,563,396	1,736,191	2,378,963	2,853,214	3,413,244	4,132,353	4,866,692
958,800	1,221,119	1,463,701	1,729,205	1,901,974	2,005,552	1,860,421	1,744,237	1,950,186	1,793,477
2,069,042	2,333,860	2,632,067	2,939,006	3,137,587	3,434,575	3,951,777	4,417,821	4,705,642	4,891,769
92,531	145,965	194,402	225,565	250,742	290,529	330,066	332,416	469,557	453,588
76,212,168	**92,228,496**	**106,021,537**	**123,202,624**	**132,164,569**	**151,325,798**	**179,323,175**	**203,302,031**	**226,542,203**	**248,709,873**

U.S. Center of Population, 1790-1990

Center of Population is that point which may be considered as center of population gravity of the U.S. or that point upon which the U.S. would balance if it were a rigid plane without weight and the population distributed thereon with each individual being assumed to have equal weight and to exert an influence on a central point proportional to his or her distance from that point. The 1990 center is 818.6 miles from the 1790 center of population, and 39.5 miles southwest of the 1980 center.

Year	N. Lat. °	′	″	W.Long. °	′	″	Approximate location
1790	39	16	30	76	11	12	23 miles east of Baltimore, Md.
1800	39	16	6	76	56	30	18 miles west of Baltimore, Md.
1810	39	11	30	77	37	12	40 miles northwest by west of Washington, D.C. (in Va.)
1820	39	5	42	78	33	0	16 miles east of Moorefield, W. Va.[1]
1830	38	57	54	79	16	54	19 miles west-southwest of Moorefield, W. Va.[1]
1840	39	2	0	80	18	0	16 miles south of Clarksburg, W. Va.[1]
1850	38	59	0	81	19	0	23 miles southeast of Parkersburg, W. Va.[1]
1860	39	0	24	82	48	48	20 miles south by east of Chillicothe, Oh.
1870	39	12	0	83	35	42	48 miles east by north of Cincinnati, Oh.
1880	39	4	8	84	39	40	8 miles west by south of Cincinnati, Oh. (in Ky.)
1890	39	11	56	85	32	53	20 miles east of Columbus, Ind.
1900	39	9	36	85	48	54	6 miles southeast of Columbus, Ind.
1910	39	10	12	86	32	20	In the city of Bloomington, Ind.
1920	39	10	21	86	43	15	8 miles south-southeast of Spencer, Owen County, Ind.
1930	39	3	45	87	8	6	3 miles northeast of Linton, Greene County, Ind.
1940	38	56	54	87	22	35	2 miles southeast by east of Carlisle, Haddon township, Sullivan Co., Ind.
1950 (Inc. Alaska & Hawaii)	38	48	15	88	22	8	3 miles northeast of Louisville, Clay County, Ill.
1960	38	35	58	89	12	35	6 1/2 miles northwest of Centralia, Clinton Co., Ill.
1970	38	27	47	89	42	22	5 miles east southeast of Mascoutah, St. Clair County, Ill.
1980	38	8	13	90	34	26	1/4 mile west of De Soto, Jefferson Co., Mo.
1990	37	52	20	91	12	55	9.7 miles northwest of Steelville, Mo.

(1) West Virginia was set off from Virginia Dec. 31, 1862, and admitted as a state June 20, 1863.

Race and Hispanic Origin for the United States: 1990 and 1980

Source: Bureau of the Census

	1990 Census		1980 Census		
	Number	Percent	Number	Percent	Percent change 1980-1990
Race					
All persons	248,709,873	100.0	226,545,805	100.0	9.8
White	199,686,070	80.3	188,371,622	83.1	6.0
Black	29,986,060	12.1	26,495,025	11.7	13.2
American Indian, Eskimo, or Aleut	1,959,234	0.8	1,420,400	0.6	37.9
American Indian	1,878,285	0.8	1,364,033	0.6	37.7
Eskimo	57,152	0.0	42,162	0.0	35.6
Aleut	23,797	0.0	14,205	0.0	67.5
Asian or Pacific Islander	7,273,662	2.9	3,500,439[1]	1.5	107.8
Chinese	1,645,472	0.7	806,040	0.4	104.1
Filipino	1,406,770	0.6	774,652	0.3	81.6
Japanese	847,562	0.3	700,974	0.3	20.9
Asian Indian	815,447	0.3	361,531	0.2	125.6
Korean	798,849	0.3	354,593	0.2	125.3
Vietnamese	614,547	0.2	261,729	0.1	134.8
Hawaiian	211,014	0.1	166,814	0.1	26.5
Samoan	62,964	0.0	41,948	0.0	50.1
Guamanian	49,345	0.0	32,158	0.0	53.4
Other Asian or Pacific Islander	821,692	0.3	(NA)	(NA)	(NA)
Other race	9,804,847	3.9	6,758,319	3.0	45.1
Hispanic Origin					
Hispanic origin[2]	22,354,059	9.0	14,608,673	6.4	53.0
Mexican	13,495,938	5.4	8,740,439	3.9	54.4
Puerto Rican	2,727,754	1.1	2,013,945	0.9	35.4
Cuban	1,043,932	0.4	803,226	0.4	30.0
Other Hispanic	5,086,435	2.0	3,051,063	1.3	66.7
Not of Hispanic origin	226,355,814	91.0	211,937,132	93.6	6.8

(NA) Not Available from 1980 100-percent tabulations. (1) The 1980 numbers for Asians or Pacific Islanders shown in this table are not entirely comparable with 1990 counts. The 1980 count of 3,500,439 Asians or Pacific Islanders based on 100-percent tabulations includes only the nine specific Asian or Pacific Islander groups listed separately in the 1980 race item. The 1980 total Asian or Pacific Islander population of 3,726,440 from sample tabulations is comparable to the 1990 count; these figures include groups not listed separately in the race item on the 1980 census form. (2) Persons of Hispanic origin may be of any race.

Definitions of Race and Hispanic Origin Groups

Source: Bureau of the Census

Race

The concept of race as used by the Census Bureau reflects self-identification. It does not denote any clear-cut scientific definition of biological stock. The data for race represent self-classification by people according to the race with which they most closely identify.

Persons identified their race by classifying themselves in one of the categories listed, i.e., White, Black, American Indian, Eskimo, Aleut, Chinese, Filipino, Japanese, Asian Indian, Korean, Vietnamese, Hawaiian, Samoan, Guamanian, Other API, or Other race. In cases where persons did not identify with any of the given race categories they were directed to identify as "Other API" ("API" means Asian or Pacific Islander) or "Other race" and write in the name of their race in the space provided. Thus, data for the Asian or Pacific Islander groups not listed on the census questionnaire but contained in Census Bureau tables—Cambodian, Hmong, Laotian, Thai, Bangladeshi, Burmese, Indonesian, Malayan, Okinawan, Pakistani, Sri Lankan, Tongan, Tahitian, Northern Mariana Islander, Palauan, and Fijian—were tabulated from write-in responses.

The "Other race" category includes persons not included in the race categories described above. Persons reporting in the "Other race" category and providing write-in entries such as a Spanish/Hispanic origin group (i.e., Mexican, Cuban, Puerto Rican) are included here.

Spanish/Hispanic origin

Persons of Spanish/Hispanic origin or descent are those who classify themselves in one of the specific Hispanic origin categories listed on the census questionnaire—for example, Mexican, Puerto Rican, or Cuban—as well as those who indicated that they were of other Spanish/Hispanic origin. Persons reporting "Other Spanish/Hispanic" are those whose origins are from other Spanish-speaking countries of the Caribbean, Central or South America, or from Spain, or persons identifying themselves generally as Spanish, Spanish-American, Hispano, Hispanic, Latino, etc.

Spanish origin and race are distinct; thus, persons of Spanish/Hispanic origin may be of any race.

The Census

On April 1, 1990, the Bureau of the Census began to take the 21st decennial census of the United States. The Census Bureau took the first census in 1790, when it counted 3.9 million people, and has conducted a census every 10 years over the past 200 years, as mandated by the U.S. Constitution, Article 1, Section 2. The primary purpose of the census was, and is, to provide population counts needed to apportion seats in the U.S. House of Representatives, and to subsequently determine state legislative district boundaries. In addition, the findings of the 1990 census are critical to many other federal, state, and local programs, including federal programs that determine compliances with the Voting Rights Act and amendments; allocate funds from federal grant programs; identify areas needing bilingual education; assess the need for equal employment opportunity programs; allocate funds and analyze programs for American Indians and Alaska Natives; identify areas needing energy assistance; develop programs to reduce unemployment; identify areas needing programs to stimulate economic growth; establish fair lending practices; assess the need for developing or expanding low-income housing programs; and identify areas requiring child assistance programs. For state and local government programs, the census results help develop social services programs, including programs for the elderly and handicapped; assess transportation systems and improve commuting patterns; identify areas for low-cost housing programs; establish occupational and vocational education programs; plan school district boundaries and school construction programs; and assess the need for state housing bonds for below-market interest rates on mortgages.

U.S. Population by Age, Sex and Household, 1990

Source: Bureau of the Census; 1990 Census

Total population	**248,709,873**
Sex	
Male	121,239,418
Female	127,470,455
Age	
Under 5 years	18,354,443
5 to 17 years	45,249,989
18 to 20 years	11,726,868
21 to 24 years	15,010,898
25 to 44 years	80,754,835
45 to 54 years	25,223,086
55 to 59 years	10,531,756
60 to 64 years	10,616,167
65 to 74 years	18,106,558
75 to 84 years	10,055,108
85 years and over	3,080,165
Median age	32.9
Under 18 years	63,604,432
Percent of total population	25.6
65 years and over	31,241,831
Percent of total population	12.6

Households by Type	
Total households	**91,947,410**
Family households (families)	64,517,947
Married-couple families	50,708,322
Percent of total households	55.1
Other family, male householder	3,143,582
Other family, female householder	10,666,043
Nonfamily households	27,429,463
Percent of total households	29.8
Householder living alone	22,580,420
Householder 65 years and over	8,824,845
Persons living in households	242,012,129
Persons per household	2.63
Group Quarters	
Persons living in group quarters	6,697,744
Institutionalized persons	3,334,018
Other persons in group quarters	3,363,726

Projections of Total Population by Race: 1994 to 2050

Source: Bureau of the Census; based upon 1990 Census

	Total Population (1,000)				By Race (middle series) Number (1,000)				Percent distribution			
Year	Lowest series	Middle series	Highest series	Zero migration	White	Black	American Indian[1]	Asian/ Pacific Islander	White	Black	American Indian[1]	Asian/ Pacific Islander
1994	258,932	260,202	261,399	257,484	215,948	32,662	2,215	9,377	82.9	12.6	0.9	3.6
1995	260,715	262,754	264,685	259,078	217,511	33,147	2,247	9,849	82.8	12.6	0.9	3.7
2000	268,108	274,815	281,306	265,984	224,594	35,525	2,409	12,287	81.7	12.9	0.9	4.5
2005	273,605	286,324	298,773	271,807	230,993	37,907	2,583	14,840	80.7	13.2	0.9	5.2
2010	278,078	298,109	317,895	277,497	237,412	40,429	2,772	17,496	79.6	13.6	0.9	5.9
2015	282,045	310,370	338,580	283,320	244,073	43,074	2,971	20,252	78.6	13.9	1.0	6.5
2020	285,200	322,602	360,123	288,752	250,587	45,743	3,175	23,096	77.7	14.2	1.0	7.2
2030	286,710	344,951	405,130	296,313	261,318	51,031	3,610	28,993	75.8	14.8	1.0	8.4
2040	282,286	364,349	453,687	299,606	268,778	56,445	4,099	35,027	73.8	15.5	1.1	9.6
2050	275,647	382,674	506,740	301,010	274,761	62,181	4,641	41,091	71.8	16.2	1.2	10.7

For the series shown, different assumptions were made regarding fertility rates (lifetime births per woman), life expectancy, and immigration in the coming decades. Yearly net immigration was assumed to be 350,000 for the lowest series; 880,000 for the middle series; and 1,370,000 for the highest series. Immigration is not a factor in the zero migration series. All figures shown are for July 1st of the given year.

[1]American Indian refers to American Indian, Eskimo, and Aleut.

U.S. Asian and Pacific Islander Population, Social and Economic Characteristics: 1991

Source: Bureau of the Census

(Figures are estimates from March 1, 1991, Sample Survey)

Characteristics	Total (in thousands)[1]	Percent Distribution[1]
Total persons	**7,023**	**100.0**
Under 5 years old	606	8.6
5 to 14 years old	1,170	16.7
15 to 44 years old	3,494	49.8
45 to 64 years old	1,240	17.6
65 years old and over	514	7.3
YEARS OF SCHOOL COMPLETED		
Characteristics		
Persons 25 years old and over	**4,158**	**100.0**
Elementary: 0 to 8 years	515	12.4
High School: 1 to 3 years	243	5.8
4 years	1,186	28.5
College: 1 to 3 years	591	14.2
4 years or more	1,623	39.0
LABOR FORCE STATUS		
Characteristics		
Civilians 16 years old and over	**5,121**	**100.0**
Civilian labor force	3,261	63.7
Employed	3,054	59.6
Unemployed	207	4.0
Unemployment rate[2]	6.3	(NA)
Not in labor force	1,860	36.3

	Total (in thousands)[1]	Percent Distribution[1]
FAMILY TYPE AND INCOME IN 1990		
Characteristics		
Total families	**1,536**	**100.0**
Married couple	1,230	80.1
Female householder, no spouse present	194	12.7
Male householder, no spouse present	112	7.3
Less than $5,000	60	3.9
$5,000 to $9,999	70	4.6
$10,000 to $14,999	88	5.7
$15,000 to $24,999	193	12.5
$25,000 to $34,999	197	12.8
$35,000 to $49,999	303	19.7
$50,000 and over	626	40.7
Median income ($)	42,245[3]	(NA)
POVERTY		
Characteristics		
Families below poverty level	169	11.0
Persons below poverty level	858	12.2
HOUSING TENURE		
Characteristics		
Total occupied units	**1,958**	**100.0**
Owner-occupied	995	50.8
Renter-occupied	947	48.4
No cash rent	15	0.8

(NA) = not applicable. [1]Due to rounding, figures may not equal totals. [2]Total unemployment as percent of civilian labor force. [3]Number not in thousands.

Population by State: 1990

Source: Bureau of the Census

State	1990 population	Percent change 1980-90	Minority population 1990	Minority percent change 1980-90	State	1990 population	Percent change 1980-90	Minority population 1990	Minority percent change 1980-90
U.S.	248,709,873	9.8%	60,581,577	30.9%	CO.	3,294,394	14.0	635,449	27.2
CA.	29,760,021	25.7	12,730,895	61.1	CT	3,287,116	5.8	532,932	43.2
NY	17,990,455	2.5	5,530,266	25.9	OK.	3,145,585	4.0	597,997	31.6
TX	16,986,510	19.4	6,694,830	37.2	OR.	2,842,321	7.9	262,589	48.3
FL	12,937,926	32.7	3,462,600	52.3	IA	2,776,755	-4.7	112,915	24.8
PA	11,881,643	0.1	1,459,585	13.3	MS.	2,573,216	2.1	949,018	3.5
IL.	11,430,602	0.0	2,880,394	14.5	KS	2,477,574	4.8	287,050	27.5
OH.	10,847,115	0.5	1,402,493	10.4	AR	2,350,725	2.8	417,643	2.7
MI	9,295,297	0.4	1,645,346	11.4	WV.	1,793,477	-8.0	74,581	-13.3
NJ	7,730,188	5.0	2,011,222	30.7	UT	1,722,850	17.9	151,596	37.1
NC.	6,628,637	12.7	1,657,510	14.1	NE	1,578,385	0.5	118,290	25.2
GA.	6,478,216	18.6	1,934,791	24.9	NM.	1,515,069	16.3	750,905	21.7
VA	6,187,358	15.7	1,485,708	27.3	ME.	1,227,928	9.2	24,571	30.7
MA	6,016,425	4.9	736,133	66.2	NV	1,201,833	50.1	255,476	90.5
IN	5,544,159	1.0	578,917	7.9	NH.	1,109,252	20.5	29,768	97.1
MO	5,117,073	4.1	668,608	10.5	HI	1,108,229	14.9	760,585	14.4
WI	4,891,769	4.0	427,092	42.3	ID	1,006,749	6.7	78,088	35.2
TN	4,877,185	6.2	849,554	9.2	RI	1,003,464	5.9	107,355	71.8
WA.	4,866,692	17.8	645,070	58.8	MT.	799,065	1.6	65,187	24.7
MD.	4,781,468	13.4	1,455,359	32.2	SD.	696,004	0.8	61,216	14.9
MN.	4,375,099	7.3	273,833	71.7	DE.	666,168	12.1	138,076	24.2
LA	4,219,973	0.3	1,443,951	5.8	ND.	638,800	-2.1	37,208	26.1
AL	4,040,587	3.8	1,080,420	4.1	DC.	606,900	-4.9	440,769	-7.0
KY	3,685,296	0.7	307,274	1.7	VT	562,758	10.0	10,574	39.4
AZ	3,665,228	34.8	1,039,043	50.2	AK.	550,043	36.9	143,321	47.4
SC.	3,486,703	11.7	1,096,647	10.8	WY.	453,588	-3.4	40,877	8.7

*Note: "Minority" includes blacks, Asians, other races, and Hispanics.

Density of Population by State

Source: Bureau of the Census

(Per square mile, land area only)

State	1920	1960	1980	1990	State	1920	1960	1980	1990	State	1920	1960	1980	1990
AL . .	45.8	64.2	76.6	79.6	LA . .	39.6	72.2	94.5	96.9	OH . .	141.4	236.6	263.3	264.9
AK*. .	0.1	0.4	0.7	1.0	ME . .	25.7	31.3	36.3	39.8	OK . .	29.2	33.8	44.1	45.8
AZ . .	2.9	11.5	23.9	32.3	MD . .	145.8	313.5	428.7	489.2	OR . .	8.2	18.4	27.4	29.6
AR . .	33.4	34.2	43.9	45.1	MA . .	479.2	657.3	733.3	767.6	PA . .	194.5	251.4	264.3	265.1
CA . .	22.0	100.4	151.4	190.8	MI. . .	63.8	137.7	162.6	163.6	RI. . .	566.4	819.3	897.8	960.3
CO . .	9.1	16.9	27.9	31.8	MN . .	29.5	43.1	51.2	55.0	SC . .	55.2	78.7	103.4	115.8
CT . .	286.4	520.6	637.8	678.4	MS . .	38.6	46.0	53.4	54.9	SD . .	8.3	9.0	9.1	9.2
DE . .	113.5	225.2	307.6	340.8	MO . .	49.5	62.6	71.3	74.3	TN . .	56.1	86.2	111.6	118.3
DC . .	7,292.9	12,523.9	10,132.3	9,882.8	MT . .	3.8	4.6	5.4	5.5	TX . .	17.8	36.4	54.3	64.9
FL . .	17.7	91.5	180.0	239.6	NE . .	16.9	18.4	20.5	20.5	UT . .	5.5	10.8	17.8	21.0
GA . .	49.3	67.8	94.1	111.9	NV . .	.7	2.6	7.3	10.9	VT . .	38.6	42.0	55.2	60.8
HI* . .	39.9	98.5	150.1	172.5	NH . .	49.1	67.2	102.4	123.7	VA . .	57.4	99.6	134.7	156.3
ID. . .	5.2	8.1	11.5	12.2	NJ . .	420.0	805.5	986.2	1,042.0	WA . .	20.3	42.8	62.1	73.1
IL. . .	115.7	180.4	205.3	205.6	NM . .	2.9	7.8	10.7	12.5	WV . .	60.9	77.2	80.8	74.5
IN. . .	81.3	128.8	152.8	154.6	NY . .	217.9	350.6	370.6	381.0	WI . .	47.6	72.6	86.5	90.1
IA. . .	43.2	49.2	52.1	49.7	NC . .	52.5	93.2	120.4	136.1	WY . .	2.0	3.4	4.9	4.7
KS . .	21.6	26.6	28.9	30.3	ND . .	9.2	9.1	9.4	9.3	U.S. .	*29.9	50.6	64.0	70.3
KY . .	60.1	76.2	92.3	92.8										

* For purposes of comparison, Alaska and Hawaii included in above tabulation for 1920, even though not states then.

Counties with 1990 Population over 1 Million

Source: Bureau of the Census

County	April 1, 1990 census	April 1, 1980 census	Percent change, 1980-90	County	April 1, 1990 census	April 1, 1980 census	Percent change, 1980-90
Los Angeles, CA	8,863,052	7,477,238	18.5	San Bernardino, CA . . .	1,418,380	895,016	58.5
Cook, IL	5,105,067	5,253,628	−2.8	Cuyahoga, OH	1,412,140	1,498,400	−5.8
Harris, TX	2,818,199	2,409,547	17.0	Middlesex, MA	1,398,468	1,367,034	2.3
San Diego, CA	2,498,016	1,861,846	34.2	Allegheny, PA	1,336,449	1,450,195	−7.8
Orange, CA	2,410,668	1,932,921	24.7	Suffolk, NY	1,321,768	1,284,231	2.9
Kings, NY	2,300,664	2,231,028	3.1	Nassau, NY	1,287,444	1,321,582	−2.6
Maricopa, AZ	2,122,101	1,509,175	40.6	Alameda, CA	1,279,702	1,105,379	15.8
Wayne, MI	2,111,687	2,337,843	-9.7	Broward, FL	1,255,518	1,018,257	23.3
Queens, NY	1,951,598	1,891,325	3.2	Bronx, NY	1,203,789	1,168,972	3.0
Dade, FL.	1,937,194	1,625,509	19.2	Bexar, TX	1,185,394	988,971	19.9
Dallas, TX	1,852,810	1,556,419	19.0	Riverside, CA	1,170,413	663,199	76.5
Philadelphia, PA.	1,585,577	1,688,210	−6.1	Tarrant, TX	1,170,103	860,880	35.9
King, WA.	1,507,305	1,269,898	18.7	Oakland, MI	1,083,592	1,011,793	7.1
Santa Clara, CA	1,497,577	1,295,071	15.6	Sacramento, CA	1,041,219	783,381	32.9
New York, NY.	1,487,536	1,428,285	4.1	Hennepin, MN.	1,032,431	941,411	9.7

Los Angeles County, the nation's largest, also had the largest numeric increase, 1.4 million, followed by San Diego and Maricopa (Phoenix) each with over 600,000, and San Bernardino and Riverside each with more than 500,000. New York City encompasses 5 counties, 4 of which exceed a million population. The largest is Kings (Brooklyn), with 2.3 million, followed by Queens, New York (Manhattan), and Bronx. For the first time since 1950, the population of all five counties increased.

1990 Population of U.S. Counties, Under Age 18

Source: Bureau of the Census

Counties with the highest share of residents under age 18, among counties of 10,000 or more; 1990 Census

The national average for counties' population under age 18 is 26 percent. Thirty-one percent of the nation's 64 million children are members of minorities, who, on average, have more children than do non-Hispanic whites. However, Utah, with only 8.8 percent minority population, has 11 of the 25 counties with the highest share of children. Sixty-nine percent of Utah residents belong to the Church of Jesus Christ of Latter Day Saints, and the birthrate for Mormon women was 2.5 births per woman in 1987, compared with 1.9 nationwide.

Rank/County, State	Percent under 18	Rank/County, State	Percent under 18	Rank/County, State	Percent under 18
1. San Juan, UT	43.3	18. Rolette, ND	38.2	35. Washington, UT	36.2
2. Emery, UT	43.0	19. Lincoln, WY	38.1	36. Tooele, UT	36.2
3. Duchesne, UT	43.0	20. Sanpete, UT	38.0	37. Holmes, OH	35.8
4. Millard, UT	42.9	21. Maverick, TX	38.0	38. Humphreys, MS	35.8
5. Apache, AZ	41.7	22. Fremont, ID	37.9	39. Zavala, TX	35.7
6. Uintah, UT	41.4	23. Utah, UT	37.7	40. Campbell, WY	35.7
7. Box Elder, UT	40.6	24. Glacier, MT	37.1	41. Iron, UT	35.5
8. Jefferson, ID	40.4	25. Webb, TX	36.7	42. Deaf Smith, TX	35.3
9. Davis, UT	40.2	26. Big Horn, MT	36.7	43. Matanuska-Susitna Borough, AK	35.3
10. Uinta, WY	39.8	27. Hidalgo, TX	36.6	44. Cameron, TX	35.3
11. Wasatch, UT	39.5	28. Cassia, ID	36.6	45. Roosevelt, MT	35.2
12. Starr, TX	39.4	29. Willacy, TX	36.6	46. Bonneville, ID	35.2
13. Sevier, UT	39.3	30. Cache, UT	36.5	47. Lagrange, IN	35.1
14. Bethel Census Area, AK	39.0	31. Rosebud, MT	36.5	48. Minidoka, ID	35.1
15. McKinley, NM	38.8	32. Gaines, TX	36.4	49. Holmes, MS	35.0
16. Bingham, ID	38.6	33. San Juan, NM	36.4	50. Frio, TX	34.8
17. Navajo, AZ	38.4	34. Dimmit, TX	36.3		

Counties with the lowest share of residents under age 18, among counties of 10,000 or more; 1990 Census

Of the 25 counties with the lowest share of children, 3 are adult resort/vacation areas: Williamsburg, Llano, and Pitkin (Aspen); 8 of the counties are popular Florida retirement places, as is Watauga; 4 (New York, San Francisco, Alexandria, and Arlington) are urban areas that contain high concentrations of affluent single residents; and the other 9 are predominantly rural counties dominated by large colleges or universities.

Rank/County, State	Percent under 18	Rank/County, State	Percent under 18	Rank/County, State	Percent under 18
1. Williamsburg (city), VA	9.2	18. Pasco, FL	17.9	35. Hampshire, MA	19.3
2. Radford (city), VA	12.7	19. Montgomery, VA	17.9	36. Washington, DC	19.3
3. Arlington, VA	15.1	20. Charlottesville (city), VA	18.0	37. Suffolk, MA	19.3
4. Alexandria (city), VA	15.4	21. Centre, PA	18.3	38. Polk, NC	19.4
5. Charlotte, FL	15.6	22. McDonough, IL	18.4	39. Tompkins, NY	19.4
6. Harrisonburg (city), VA	15.6	23. Monroe, IN	18.4	40. Indian River, FL	19.4
7. Sarasota, FL	15.7	24. Hernando, FL	18.4	41. Baxter, AR	19.4
8. San Francisco, CA	16.1	25. Fredericksburg (city), VA	18.6	42. Calloway, KY	19.5
9. Llano, TX	16.4	26. Highlands, FL	18.7	43. Lee, FL	19.6
10. New York, NY	16.6	27. Amador, CA	18.8	44. Palm Beach, FL	19.6
11. Pitkin, CO	16.8	28. Orange, NC	18.9	45. Salem (city), VA	19.7
12. Watauga, NC	17.1	29. Jackson, IL	19.0	46. Volusia, FL	19.7
13. Monroe, FL	17.4	30. Walker, TX	19.0	47. West Feliciana Parish, LA	19.7
14. Martin, FL	17.6	31. Flagler, FL	19.1	48. Story, IA	19.8
15. Citrus, FL	17.6	32. Marin, CA	19.1	49. Johnson, IL	19.8
16. Whitman, WA	17.8	33. Fairfax (city), VA	19.2	50. Macon, NC	19.8
17. Pinellas, FL	17.8	34. Manatee, FL	19.2		

The 50 Most Racially Diverse Counties in the U.S.

Source: Bureau of the Census

Using 1990 census results, counties were ranked according to the proportions of non-Hispanic whites, non-Hispanic blacks, Hispanics, and non-Hispanic other races. Those areas with proportions nearest to being equal were considered to be among the most diverse.

Fourteen of the 50 most diverse counties have populations of 1 million or more, and 33 are in metropolitan areas. Four of New York City's five boroughs, as well as the counties that contain San Francisco, Los Angeles, Chicago, Houston, San Diego, Miami, Dallas, Philadelphia, San Jose, San Bernardino, and Oakland are on the list.

Of the 60 counties with populations more than 99.5 percent non-Hispanic white in 1990, 12 are in Nebraska, 12 are in North Dakota, 7 are in Kentucky, and 6 are in South Dakota.

Rank/County	State	Rank/County	State	Rank/County	State
1. Queens	New York	18. Fresno	California	35. Socorro	New Mexico
2. San Francisco	California	19. San Joaquin	California	36. Aleutians West Census Area	Alaska
3. Los Angeles	California	20. Santa Clara	California	37. Passaic	New Jersey
4. Kings	New York	21. San Mateo	California	38. Pinal	Arizona
5. Alameda	California	22. Cook	Illinois	39. Alexandria (city)	Virginia
6. New York	New York	23. Merced	California	40. Waller	Texas
7. Bronx	New York	24. Hoke	North Carolina	41. Caldwell	Texas
8. Hudson	New Jersey	25. Chattahoochee	Georgia	42. San Diego	California
9. Fort Bend	Texas	26. Kings	California	43. Liberty	Georgia
10. Cibola	New Mexico	27. Dallas	Texas	44. Prince George's	Maryland
11. Harris	Texas	28. Suffolk	Massachusetts	45. Wharton	Texas
12. Robeson	North Carolina	29. Hendry	Florida	46. Philadelphia	Pennsylvania
13. Solano	California	30. Matagorda	Texas	47. Bell	Texas
14. Essex	New Jersey	31. Graham	Arizona	48. Otero	New Mexico
15. Dade	Florida	32. Denver	Colorado	49. Union	New Jersey
16. Sandoval	New Mexico	33. San Juan	New Mexico	50. Coconino	Arizona
17. Monterey	California	34. San Bernardino	California		

Coastal Counties of the U.S.

Source: Bureau of the Census

According to the Census Bureau, 135 million people, or 54 percent of all Americans, lived in the 672 counties adjacent to the Atlantic and Pacific Oceans, the Gulf of Mexico, and the Great Lakes in 1991. Since 1960, the U.S. coastal population has increased by almost 41 million. This 43 percent increase is slightly faster than the U.S. growth rate of 40.6 percent. It also is much higher than the 38 percent growth rate of the interior U.S.

The most rapid coastal growth since 1960 has occurred along the Pacific and Gulf coasts. In 1991 more than 33.9 million people lived in Pacific coastal counties, while nearly 15.6 million people lived in counties along the Gulf of Mexico. The Pacific and Gulf coast areas showed an increase in population of 89.3 percent and 85.8 percent, respectively. The population of the Atlantic coast increased by a third since 1960. In 1991 an estimated 59.5 million people resided along the Atlantic coast. The fourth major coastal region rims the five Great Lakes. With 26.1 million people in 1991, its population has remained relatively stable since 1960, showing only a 10.3 percent increase.

Geographical Mobility Rates, By Type of Movement: 1950-1991

(In thousands)

Source: Bureau of the Census

About 17 percent of Americans changed residence between March 1990 and March 1991. Rates of moving are down from the 1950s and 1960s when 20 percent or more of the population moved every year.

Metropolitan areas have shown modest net in-migration from nonmetropolitan areas since the 1980s. Suburbs gained 6.0 million persons from central cities and nonmetropolitan areas between 1990 and 1991 while losing 3.4 million out-migrants. Central cities gained 3.2 million from in-migration but lost 5.7 million movers.

Mobility period	Total, 1 year old and over	Total movers	Residing in the U.S. at beginning of the period: Total	Different house, same county	Different county: Total	Same State	Different State	Different region	Residing outside the U.S. at beginning of the period
Number									
1990-91	244,884	41,539	40,154	25,151	15,003	7,881	7,122	3,384	1,385
1985-86	232,998	43,237	42,037	26,401	15,636	8,665	6,971	3,778	1,200
1980-81	221,641	38,200	36,887	23,097	13,789	7,614	6,175	3,363	1,313
1975-76	208,069	36,793	35,645	22,399	13,246	7,106	6,140	3,279	1,148
1970-71	201,506	37,705	36,161	23,018	13,143	6,197	6,946	3,936	1,544
1965-66	190,242	37,586	36,703	24,165	12,538	6,275	6,263	3,348	883
1960-61	177,354	36,533	35,535	24,289	11,246	5,493	5,753	3,097	998
1955-56	161,497	34,040	33,098	22,186	10,912	5,859	5,053	(NA)	942
1950-51	148,400	31,464	31,158	20,694	10,464	5,276	5,188	(NA)	306
Percent									
1990-91	100.0	17.0	16.4	10.3	6.1	3.2	2.9	1.4	0.6
1985-86	100.0	18.6	18.0	11.3	6.7	3.7	3.0	1.6	0.5
1980-81	100.0	17.2	16.6	10.4	6.2	3.4	2.8	1.5	0.6
1975-76	100.0	17.7	17.1	10.8	6.4	3.4	3.0	1.6	0.6
1970-71	100.0	18.7	17.9	11.4	6.5	3.1	3.4	2.0	0.8
1965-66	100.0	19.8	19.3	12.7	6.6	3.3	3.3	1.8	0.5
1960-61	100.0	20.6	20.0	13.7	6.3	3.1	3.2	1.7	0.6
1955-56	100.0	21.1	20.5	13.7	6.8	3.6	3.1	(NA)	0.6
1950-51	100.0	21.2	21.0	13.9	7.1	3.6	3.5	(NA)	0.2

(NA) = Not available.

The 50 Fastest-Growing Metropolitan Areas

Source: Bureau of the Census

	1990 population	Percent change 1980-1990
1. Punta Gorda, FL	110,975	89.8
2. Naples, FL	152,099	76.9
3. Fort Pierce-Port Saint Lucie, FL	251,071	66.1
4. Fort Myers-Cape Coral, FL	335,113	63.3
5. Las Vegas, NV-AZ	852,737	61.5
6. Ocala, FL	194,833	59.1
7. Orlando, FL	1,224,852	52.2
8. West Palm Beach-Boca Raton, FL	863,518	49.7
9. Daytona Beach, FL	399,413	48.1
10. Melbourne-Titusville-Palm Bay, FL	398,978	46.2
11. Austin-San Marcos, TX	846,227	44.6
12. Myrtle Beach, SC	144,053	42.0
13. Las Cruces, NM	135,510	40.7
14. Yuma, AZ	106,895	40.3
15. Phoenix-Mesa, AZ	2,238,480	39.9
16. San Luis Obispo-Atascadero-Paso Robles, CA	217,162	39.7
17. Sarasota-Bradenton, FL	489,483	39.6
18. Modesto, CA	370,522	39.3
19. Stockton-Lodi, CA	480,628	38.4
20. McAllen-Edinburg-Mission, TX	383,545	35.4
21. Bakersfield, CA	543,477	34.8
22. Sacramento-Yolo, CA	1,481,102	34.7
23. San Diego, CA	2,498,016	34.2
24. Laredo, TX	133,239	34.2
25. Jacksonville, NC	149,838	32.9
26. Merced, CA	178,403	32.6
27. Dallas-Fort Worth, TX CMSA[1]	4,037,282	32.5
28. Atlanta, GA	2,233,229	32.5
29. Reno, NV	254,667	31.5
30. Fresno, CA	755,580	30.8
31. Fort Walton Beach, FL	143,776	30.8
32. Barnstable-Yarmouth, MA	134,954	30.8
33. Bryan-College Station, TX	121,862	30.2
34. Panama City, FL	126,994	29.9
35. Anchorage, AK	226,338	29.8
36. Raleigh-Durham-Chapel Hill, NC	855,545	28.7
37. Colorado Springs, CO	397,014	28.3
38. Tampa-St. Petersburg-Clearwater, FL	2,067,959	28.2
39. Redding, CA	147,036	27.2
40. Visalia-Tulare-Porterville, CA	311,921	26.9
41. Chico-Paradise, CA	182,120	26.6
42. Los Angeles-Riverside-Orange County, CA CMSA[1]	14,531,529	26.4
43. Lakeland-Winter Haven, FL	405,382	26.0
44. Santa Fe, NM	117,043	25.7
45. Jacksonville, FL	906,727	25.5
46. Tucson, AZ	666,880	25.5
47. Fort Collins-Loveland, CO	186,136	24.8
48. Brownsville-Harlingen-San Benito, TX	260,120	24.0
49. Santa Barbara-Santa Maria-Lompoc, CA	369,608	23.7
50. El Paso, TX	591,610	23.3

[1] CMSA = Consolidated Metropolitan Statistical Area.

Metropolitan Statistical Areas

Source: Bureau of the Census
(MSAs over 400,000 listed by 1990 population)

Metropolitan areas are defined for federal statistical use by the Office of Management and Budget (OMB), with technical assistance from the Bureau of the Census. Most individual metropolitan areas are designated as Metropolitan Statistical Areas (MSAs). Metropolitan areas over 1 million may under specified circumstances be subdivided into component Primary Metropolitan Statistical Areas (PMSAs), in which case the area as a whole is designated a Consolidated Metropolitan Statistical Area (CMSA). Effective December 31, 1992, the OMB designated 253 MSAs, 62 PMSAs, and 19 CMSAs for the U.S. and Puerto Rico based on standards published in the *Federal Register* on March 30, 1990, and used in the 1990 Census. The revised definition and the results of the 1990 Census established 9 new MSAs, 16 new PMSAs, and 2 additional CMSAs. A new definition, which went into effect June 30, 1993, made some minor additional adjustments.

MSA	Population 1990 census	Population 1980 census	Percent change 1980 to 1990
New York-Northern New Jersey-Long Island, NY-NJ-CT-PA CMSA	19,342,013	18,713,425	3.4
Los Angeles-Riverside-Orange County, CA CMSA	14,531,529	11,497,548	26.4
Chicago-Gary-Kenosha, IL-IN-WI CMSA	8,239,820	8,114,844	1.5
Washington-Baltimore, DC-MD-VA-WV CMSA	6,727,050	5,790,555	16.2
San Francisco-Oakland-San Jose, CA CMSA	6,253,311	5,367,900	16.5
Philadelphia-Wilmington-Atlantic City, PA-NJ-DE-MD CMSA	5,892,937	5,649,031	4.3
Boston-Brockton-Nashua, MA-NH-ME-CT CMSA	5,455,403	5,121,673	6.5
Detroit-Ann Arbor-Flint, MI CMSA	5,187,171	5,293,161	−2.0
Dallas-Fort Worth, TX CMSA	4,037,282	3,046,136	32.5
Houston-Galveston-Brazoria, TX CMSA	3,731,131	3,118,480	19.6
Miami-Fort Lauderdale, FL CMSA	3,192,582	2,643,766	20.8
Seattle-Tacoma-Bremerton, WA CMSA	2,970,328	2,408,749	23.3
Atlanta, GA	2,959,950	2,233,229	32.5
Cleveland-Akron, OH CMSA	2,859,644	2,938,277	−2.7
Minneapolis-St. Paul, MN-WI	2,538,834	2,198,190	15.5
San Diego, CA	2,498,016	1,861,846	34.2
St. Louis, MO-IL	2,492,525	2,414,061	3.3
Pittsburgh, PA	2,394,811	2,571,223	−6.9
Phoenix-Mesa, AZ	2,238,480	1,600,093	39.9
Tampa-St. Petersburg-Clearwater, FL	2,067,959	1,613,600	28.2
Denver-Boulder-Greeley, CO CMSA	1,980,140	1,741,899	13.7
Cincinnati-Hamilton, OH-KY-IN CMSA	1,817,571	1,726,430	5.3
Portland-Salem, OR-WA CMSA	1,793,476	1,583,518	13.3
Milwaukee-Racine, WI CMSA	1,607,183	1,570,152	2.4
Kansas City, MO-KS	1,582,875	1,449,380	9.2
Sacramento-Yolo, CA CMSA	1,481,102	1,099,814	34.7
Norfolk-Virginia Beach-Newport News, VA-NC	1,443,244	1,200,998	20.2
Indianapolis, IN	1,380,491	1,305,911	5.7
Columbus, OH	1,345,450	1,214,291	10.8
San Antonio, TX	1,324,749	1,088,881	21.7
New Orleans, LA	1,285,270	1,304,212	−1.5
Orlando, FL	1,224,852	804,774	52.2
Buffalo-Niagara Falls, NY	1,189,288	1,242,826	−4.3
Charlotte-Gastonia-Rock Hill, NC-SC	1,162,093	971,447	19.6
Hartford, CT	1,157,585	1,080,710	7.1
Providence-Fall River-Warwick, RI-MA	1,134,350	1,076,557	5.4
Salt Lake City-Ogden, UT	1,072,227	910,222	17.8
Rochester, NY	1,062,470	1,030,630	3.1
Greensboro–Winston-Salem–High Point, NC	1,050,304	950,763	10.5
Memphis, TN-AR-MS	1,007,306	938,777	7.3
Nashville, TN	985,026	850,505	15.8
Oklahoma City, OK	958,839	860,969	11.4
Dayton-Springfield, OH	951,270	942,083	1.0
Louisville, KY-IN	948,829	953,520	−0.5
Grand Rapids-Muskegon-Holland, MI	937,891	840,824	11.5
Jacksonville, FL	906,727	722,252	25.5
Richmond-Petersburg, VA	865,640	761,311	13.7
West Palm Beach-Boca Raton, FL	863,518	576,758	49.7
Albany-Schenectady-Troy, NY	861,424	824,729	4.4
Raleigh-Durham-Chapel Hill, NC	855,545	664,788	28.7
Las Vegas, NV-AZ	852,737	528,000	61.5
Austin-San Marcos, TX	846,227	585,051	44.6
Birmingham, AL	840,140	815,333	3.0
Honolulu, HI	836,231	762,565	9.7
Greenville-Spartanburg-Anderson, SC	830,563	744,428	11.6
Fresno, CA	755,580	577,737	30.8
Syracuse, NY	742,177	722,865	2.7
Tulsa, OK	708,954	657,173	7.9
Tucson, AZ	666,880	531,443	25.5
Omaha, NE-IA	639,580	605,419	5.6
Scranton–Wilkes-Barre–Hazleton, PA	638,466	659,387	−3.2
Toledo, OH	614,128	616,864	−0.4
Youngstown-Warren, OH	600,895	644,922	−6.8
Allentown-Bethlehem-Easton, PA	595,081	551,052	8.0
El Paso, TX	591,610	479,899	23.3
Albuquerque, NM	589,131	485,429	21.4
Harrisburg-Lebanon-Carlisle, PA	587,986	556,242	5.7
Springfield, MA	587,884	569,777	3.2
Knoxville, TN	585,960	546,488	7.2
Bakersfield, CA	543,477	403,089	34.8
Little Rock-North Little Rock, AK	513,117	474,463	8.1
Charleston-North Charleston, SC	506,875	430,346	17.8
Sarasota-Bradenton, FL	489,483	350,696	39.6
Wichita, KS	485,270	442,401	9.7
Stockton-Lodi, CA	480,628	347,342	38.4
Mobile, AL	476,923	443,536	7.5
Baton Rouge, LA	470,050	444,083	5.8
Fort Wayne, IN	456,281	444,772	2.6
Columbia, SC	453,331	409,953	10.6
Johnson City-Kingsport-Bristol, TN-VA	436,047	433,638	0.6
Lansing-East Lansing, MI	432,674	419,750	3.1
Kalamazoo-Battle Creek, MI	429,453	420,771	2.1
Lancaster, PA	422,822	362,346	16.7
Lexington, KY	405,936	370,900	9.4
Lakeland-Winter Haven, FL	405,382	321,652	26.0

Final 1990 census figures showed that the nation had 40 metropolitan areas of at least 1 million population, including 5 that reached that size since 1980. **The 40 areas had 128.2 million people, or 51.5 percent of the U.S. population.** The 1950 census showed only 14 metropolitan areas of 1 million people, and their combined population of about 45 million amounted to less than 30 percent of the national total.

The census showed that the U.S. population living in all metropolitan areas totaled 197,466,567, an increase of just over 20.8 million (11.8 percent) since 1980. The same areas grew by 10.6 percent in the 1970s. The population living outside metropolitan areas totaled 51,243,306, an increase of 2.1 million (3.9 percent). **The metropolitan population in 1990 constituted 79.4 percent of the U.S. total** compared with 76.2 percent in 1980. More than 90 percent of the nation's growth in the 1980s took place in metropolitan areas.

Population of U.S. Cities

Source: Bureau of the Census (100 most populous cities ranked by April 1990 census; revised April 1993)

Rank	City	1990	1980	1970	1960	1950	1900	1850
1	New York, NY	7,322,564	7,071,639	7,895,563	7,781,984	7,891,957	3,437,202	696,115
2	Los Angeles, CA	3,485,398	2,966,850	2,811,801	2,479,015	1,970,358	102,479	1,610
3	Chicago, IL	2,783,726	3,005,072	3,369,357	3,550,404	3,620,962	1,698,575	29,963
4	Houston, TX	1,630,553	1,595,138	1,233,535	938,219	596,163	44,633	2,396
5	Philadelphia, PA	1,585,577	1,688,210	1,949,996	2,002,512	2,071,605	1,293,697	121,376
6	San Diego, CA	1,110,549	875,538	697,471	573,224	334,387	17,700	...
7	Detroit, MI	1,027,974	1,203,368	1,514,063	1,670,144	1,849,568	285,704	21,019
8	Dallas, TX	1,007,618	904,078	844,401	679,684	434,462	42,638	...
9	Phoenix, AZ	983,395	789,704	584,303	439,170	106,818	5,544	...
10	San Antonio, TX	935,933	785,880	654,153	587,718	408,442	53,321	3,488
11	San Jose, CA	782,248	629,442	459,913	204,196	95,280	21,500	...
12	Indianapolis, IN	741,952	700,807	736,856	476,258	427,173	169,164	8,091
13	Baltimore, MD	736,014	786,741	905,787	939,024	949,708	508,957	169,054
14	San Francisco, CA	723,959	678,974	715,674	740,316	775,357	342,782	34,776
15	Jacksonville, FL	672,971	540,920	504,265	201,030	204,517	28,429	1,045
16	Columbus, OH	632,945	564,871	540,025	471,316	375,901	125,560	17,882
17	Milwaukee, WI	628,088	636,212	717,372	741,324	637,392	285,315	20,061
18	Memphis, TN	610,337	646,170	623,988	497,524	396,000	102,320	8,841
19	Washington, DC	606,900	638,432	756,668	763,956	802,178	278,718	40,001
20	Boston, MA	574,283	562,994	641,071	697,197	801,444	560,892	136,881
21	Seattle, WA	516,259	493,846	530,831	557,087	467,591	80,671	...
22	El Paso, TX	515,342	425,259	322,261	276,687	130,485	15,906	...
23	Nashville-Davidson, TN	510,784	455,651	426,029	170,874	174,307	80,865	10,165
24	Cleveland, OH	505,616	573,822	750,879	876,050	914,808	381,768	17,034
25	New Orleans, LA	496,938	557,927	593,471	627,525	570,445	287,104	116,375
26	Denver, CO	467,610	492,694	514,678	493,887	415,786	133,859	...
27	Austin, TX	465,622	345,496	253,539	186,545	132,459	22,258	629
28	Fort Worth, TX	447,619	385,164	393,455	356,268	278,778	26,688	...
29	Oklahoma City, OK	444,719	403,213	368,164	324,253	243,504	10,037	...
30	Portland, OR	438,802	366,383	379,967	372,676	373,628	90,426	...
31	Kansas City, MO	434,829	448,159	507,330	475,539	456,622	163,752	...
32	Long Beach, CA	429,321	361,334	358,879	344,168	250,767	2,252	...
33	Tucson, AZ	405,371	330,537	262,933	212,892	45,454	7,531	...
34	St. Louis, MO	396,685	452,801	622,236	750,026	856,796	575,238	77,860
35	Charlotte, NC	395,934	314,447	241,420	201,564	134,042	18,091	1,065
36	Atlanta, GA	394,017	425,022	495,039	487,455	331,314	89,872	2,572
37	Virginia Beach, VA	393,089	262,199	172,106	8,091	5,390	...	...
38	Albuquerque, NM	384,619	331,767	244,501	201,189	96,815	6,238	...
39	Oakland, CA	372,242	339,337	361,561	367,548	384,575	66,960	...
40	Pittsburgh, PA	369,879	423,960	520,089	604,332	676,806	321,616	46,601
41	Sacramento, CA	369,365	275,741	257,105	191,667	137,572	29,282	6,820
42	Minneapolis, MN	368,383	370,951	434,400	482,872	521,718	202,718	...
43	Tulsa, OK	367,302	360,919	330,350	261,685	182,740	1,390	...
44	Honolulu, HI	365,272	365,048	324,871	294,194	248,034	39,306	...
45	Cincinnati, OH	364,114	385,410	453,514	502,550	503,998	325,902	115,435
46	Miami, FL	358,648	346,865	334,859	291,688	249,276	1,681	...
47	Fresno, CA	354,091	218,202	165,655	133,929	91,669	12,470	...
48	Omaha, NE	335,719	314,255	346,929	301,598	251,117	102,555	...
49	Toledo, OH	332,943	354,635	383,062	318,003	303,616	131,822	3,829
50	Buffalo, NY	328,175	357,870	462,768	532,759	580,132	352,387	42,261
51	Wichita, KS	304,017	279,272	276,554	254,698	168,279	24,671	...
52	Santa Ana, CA	293,827	203,713	155,710	100,350	45,533	4,933	...
53	Mesa, AZ	288,104	152,453	63,049	33,772	16,790	722	...
54	Colorado Springs, CO	281,140	215,150	135,517	70,194	45,472	21,085	...
55	Tampa, FL	280,015	271,523	277,714	274,970	124,681	15,839	...
56	Newark, NJ	275,221	329,248	381,930	405,220	438,776	246,070	38,894
57	St. Paul, MN	272,235	270,230	309,866	313,411	311,349	163,065	1,112
58	Louisville, KY	269,555	298,694	361,706	390,639	369,129	204,731	43,194
59	Anaheim, CA	266,406	219,311	166,408	104,184	14,556	1,456	...
60	Birmingham, AL	265,965	288,297	300,910	340,887	326,037	38,415	...
61	Arlington, TX	261,721	160,113	90,229	44,775	7,692	1,079	...
62	Norfolk, VA	261,250	266,979	307,951	304,869	213,513	46,624	14,326
63	Las Vegas, NV	258,204	164,674	125,787	64,405	24,624	...	...
64	Corpus Christi, TX	257,453	231,999	204,525	167,690	108,287	4,703	...
65	St. Petersburg, FL	240,318	238,647	216,159	181,298	96,738	1,575	...
66	Rochester, NY	230,356	241,741	295,011	318,611	332,488	162,608	36,403
67	Jersey City, NJ	228,537	223,532	260,350	276,101	299,017	206,433	6,856
68	Riverside, CA	226,546	170,876	140,089	84,332	46,764	7,973	...
69	Anchorage, AK	226,338	174,431	48,081	44,237	11,254	...	...
70	Lexington-Fayette, KY	225,366	204,165	108,137	62,810	55,534	26,369	8,159
71	Akron, OH	223,019	237,590	275,425	290,351	274,605	42,728	3,266
72	Aurora, CO	222,103	158,588	74,974	48,548	11,421	202	...
73	Baton Rouge, LA	219,531	220,394	165,921	152,419	125,629	11,269	3,905
74	Raleigh, NC	212,050	150,255	122,830	93,931	65,679	13,643	4,518
75	Stockton, CA	210,943	149,779	109,963	86,321	70,853	17,506	...
76	Richmond, VA	202,798	219,214	249,332	219,958	230,310	85,050	27,570
77	Shreveport, LA	198,525	205,820	182,064	164,372	127,206	16,013	1,728
78	Jackson, MS	196,637	202,895	153,968	144,422	98,271	7,816	1,881
79	Mobile, AL	196,278	200,452	190,026	194,856	129,009	38,469	20,515
80	Des Moines, IA	193,189	191,003	201,404	208,982	177,965	62,139	...
81	Lincoln, NE	191,972	171,932	149,518	128,521	98,884	40,169	...
82	Madison, WI	191,262	170,616	171,809	126,706	96,056	19,164	1,525
83	Grand Rapids, MI	189,126	181,843	197,649	177,313	176,515	87,565	2,686
84	Yonkers, NY	188,082	195,351	204,297	190,634	152,798	47,931	...

Rank	City	1990	1980	1970	1960	1950	1900	1850
85	Hialeah, FL	188,008	145.254	102,452	66,972	19,676	...	...
86	Montgomery, AL	187,543	177,857	133,386	134,393	106,525	30,346	8,728
87	Lubbock, TX	186,206	173,979	149,101	126,691	71,747	...	...
88	Greensboro, NC	183,894	170,279	144,076	119,574	74,389	10,035	...
89	Dayton, OH	182,005	193,549	243,023	262,332	243,872	85,333	10,977
90	Huntington Beach, CA	181,519	170,505	115,960	11,492	5,237	...	...
91	Garland, TX	180,650	138,857	81,437	38,501	10,571	819	...
92	Glendale, CA	180,038	139,060	133,000	119,000	96,000	...	...
93	Columbus, GA	179,278	169,441	155,028	116,779	79,611	17,614	9,621
94	Spokane, WA	177,165	171,300	170,516	181,608	161,721	36,848	...
95	Tacoma, WA	176,664	158,501	154,407	147,979	143,673	37,714	...
96	Little Rock, AR	175,727	*158,461	132,483	107,813	102,213	38,307	2,167
97	Bakersfield, CA	174,820	105,611	...	56,848	...	...	...
98	Fremont, CA	173,339	131,945	100,869	43,790	...	...	...
99	Fort Wayne, IN	173,072	172,196	178,269	161,776	133,607	45,115	4,282
100	Newport News, VA	171,439	144,903	138,000	114,000	42,000	...	...

Cities with Largest Percentage Loss in Population, 1980-1990

Source: Bureau of the Census; 1990 Census

City	1990	1980	Change
1. Gary, IN	116,646	151,968	−23.2%
2. Newark	275,221	329,248	−16.4
3. Detroit	1,027,974	1,203,368	−14.6
4. Pittsburgh	369,879	423,960	−12.8
5. St. Louis	396,685	452,801	−12.4
6. Cleveland	505,616	573,822	−11.9
7. Flint, MI	140,761	159,611	−11.8
8. New Orleans	496,938	557,927	−10.9
9. Warren, MI	144,864	161,134	−10.1
10. Chattanooga, TN	152,494	169,514	−10.0
11. Louisville, KY	269,555	298,694	−9.8
12. Peoria, IL	113,504	124,160	−8.9
13. Erie, PA	108,718	119,123	−8.7
14. Buffalo	328,175	357,870	−8.3
15. Macon, GA	107,365	116,896	−8.2
16. Birmingham, AL	265,965	288,297	−7.7
17. Richmond	202,798	219,214	−7.5
18. Chicago	2,783,726	3,005,072	−7.4
19. Atlanta	394,017	425,022	−7.3
20. Kansas City, KS	149,800	161,148	−7.0
21. Baltimore	736,014	786,741	−6.4
22. Akron, OH	223,019	237,590	−6.1
23. Toledo, OH	332,943	354,635	−6.1
24. Philadelphia	1,585,577	1,688,210	−6.1
25. Dayton, OH	182,055	193,549	−5.9
26. Knoxville, TN	165,039	175,045	−5.7
27. Memphis	610,337	646,170	−5.5
28. Cincinnati	364,114	385,410	−5.5
29. Denver	467,610	492,694	−5.1
30. Washington, DC	606,900	638,432	−4.9

Fastest Growing Cities, 1980-1990

Source: Bureau of the Census; cities of more than 100.000 with the largest percentage increases in population from 1980 to 1990 Census

City	Suburb of...	1990	1980	% Change
1. Moreno Valley, CA	Riverside	118,779	28,309	319.6
2. Mesa, AZ	Phoenix	288,104	152,404	89.0
3. Rancho Cucamonga, CA	Los Angeles	101,409	55,250	83.5
4. Plano, TX	Dallas	128,885	72,331	78.2
5. Irvine, CA	Los Angeles	110,330	62,134	77.6
6. Escondido, CA	San Diego	108,635	64,355	68.8
7. Oceanside, CA	—	128,154	76,698	67.1
8. Santa Clarita, CA	Los Angeles	110,690	66,730	65.9
9. Bakersfield, CA	—	174,820	105,611	65.5
10. Arlington, TX	Fort Worth	261,721	160,113	63.5
11. Fresno, CA	—	354,091	217,491	62.8
12. Chula Vista, CA	San Diego	135,163	83,927	61.0
13. Las Vegas, NV	—	258,204	164,674	56.8
14. Modesto, CA	—	164,746	106,963	54.0
15. Tallahassee, FL	—	124,773	81,548	53.0
16. Glendale, AZ	Phoenix	147,864	97,172	52.2
17. Mesquite, TX	Dallas	101,484	67,053	51.3
18. Ontario, CA	Los Angeles	133,179	88,820	49.9
19. Virginia Beach, VA	Norfolk	393,089	262,199	49.9
20. Scottsdale, AZ	Phoenix	130,075	88,622	46.5
21. Santa Ana, CA	Los Angeles	293,827	204,023	44.0
22. Stockton, CA	—	210,943	148,283	42.3
23. Pomona, CA	Los Angeles	131,723	92,742	42.0
24. Raleigh, NC	—	212,050	150,255	41.1
25. Irving, TX	Dallas	155,037	109,943	41.0
26. Aurora, CO	Denver	222,103	158,588	40.1
27. San Bernardino, CA	—	164,164	118,794	38.2
28. Santa Rosa, CA	San Francisco	113,313	82,658	37.1
29. Overland Park, KS	Kansas City	111,790	81,784	36.7
30. Vallejo, CA	San Francisco	109,199	80,303	36.0
31. Thousand Oaks, CA	Los Angeles	104,381	77,072	35.4
32. Salinas, CA	—	108,777	80,479	35.2
33. Durham, NC	—	136,612	101,149	35.1
34. Austin, TX	—	465,622	345,890	34.6
35. Laredo, TX	—	122,899	91,449	34.4
36. Sacramento, CA	—	369,365	275,741	34.0
37. El Monte, CA	Los Angeles	106,162	79,494	33.6
38. Reno, NV	—	133,850	100,756	32.8
39. Riverside, CA	—	226,546	170,591	32.8
40. Chesapeake, VA	Norfolk	151,982	114,486	32.8
41. Tempe, AZ	Phoenix	141,993	106,919	32.8
42. Oxnard, CA	Los Angeles	142,560	108,195	31.8
43. Fremont, CA	San Jose/Oakland	173,339	131,945	31.4
44. Colorado Springs, CO	—	281,140	215,105	30.7
45. Garland, TX	Dallas	180,650	138,857	30.1

Immigration by Country of Last Residence: 1820-1992

Source: U.S. Immigration and Naturalization Service
(In thousands; for fiscal years ending in year shown)

Country	Total								Percent			
	1820-1992	1961-1970	1971-1980	1981-1990	1988[10]	1989[11]	1991[14]	1992[14]	1820-1992	1961-1970	1971-1980	1981-1990
All countries*	**59,795**	**3,321.7**	**4,493.3**	**7,338.0**	**643.0**	**1,090.9**	**1,827.2**	**974.0**	**100.0**	**100.0**	**100.0**	**100.0**
Europe	**37,401**	**1,123.5**	**800.4**	**761.5**	**71.8**	**94.3**	**146.7**	**153.3**	**62.5**	**33.8**	**17.8**	**10.4**
Austria[1]	1,836	20.6	9.5	18.9	2.5	2.8	3.5	2.9	3.1	0.6	0.2	0.3
Belgium	212	9.2	5.3	6.6	0.7	0.7	0.9	1.0	0.4	0.3	0.1	0.1
Czechoslovakia	147	3.3	6.0	5.4	0.7	0.5	0.6	0.9	0.2	0.1	0.1	0.1
Denmark	372	9.2	4.4	2.8	0.6	0.6	0.6	0.8	0.6	0.3	0.1	0.1
France	797	45.2	25.1	92.1	3.6	4.1	4.0	4.5	1.3	1.4	0.6	1.3
Germany[1]	7,107	190.8	74.4	159.0	9.7	10.4	10.9	12.9	11.9	5.7	1.7	2.2
Greece	709	86.0	92.4	31.9	4.7	4.6	2.9	2.2	1.2	2.6	2.1	0.4
Hungary[1]	1,670	5.4	6.6	5.9	0.7	0.7	0.9	1.0	2.8	0.2	0.1	0.1
Ireland	4,742	33.0	11.5	67.2	5.1	7.0	4.6	12.0	7.9	1.0	0.3	0.9
Italy	5,416	214.1	129.4	12.3	5.3	11.1	30.3	12.0	9.1	6.4	2.9	0.2
Netherlands	378	30.6	10.5	4.2	1.2	1.2	1.3	1.7	0.6	0.9	0.2	0.1
Norway[9]	803	15.5	3.9	83.2	0.4	0.6	0.6	0.8	1.3	0.5	0.1	1.1
Poland[1]	648	53.5	37.2	40.3	7.3	13.3	17.1	24.5	1.1	1.6	0.8	0.5
Portugal	509	76.1	101.7	20.5	3.3	3.9	4.6	2.8	0.9	2.3	2.3	0.3
Spain	290	44.7	39.1	11.1	2.0	2.2	2.7	2.0	0.5	1.3	0.9	0.2
Sweden[9]	1,288	17.1	6.5	8.0	1.2	1.2	1.2	1.5	2.2	0.5	0.1	0.1
Switzerland	361	18.5	8.2	57.6	0.9	1.1	1.0	1.3	0.6	0.6	0.2	0.8
USSR[1,3,15]	3,512	2.5	39.0	18.7	1.4	4.6	31.6	37.4	5.9	0.1	0.9	0.3
United Kingdom[2]	5,158	213.8	137.4	159.2	14.7	17.0	16.8	21.9	8.6	6.4	3.1	2.2
Yugoslavia[16]	142	20.4	30.5	37.3	2.0	2.5	2.8	2.7	0.2	0.6	0.7	0.5
Other Europe	190	9.1	18.9	7.7	0.8	0.7	1.2	6.5	0.3	0.2	0.2	0.0
Asia	**6,706**	**427.6**	**1,588.2**	**2,738.1**	**254.7**	**296.4**	**342.2**	**344.8**	**11.2**	**12.9**	**35.2**	**37.3**
China[4]	968	34.8	124.3	298.9	34.3	39.3	24.0	29.6	1.6	1.0	2.8	4.1
Hong Kong[4]	335	75.0	113.5	98.2	11.8	15.2	15.9	16.8	0.6	2.3	2.5	1.3
India	533	27.2	164.1	250.7	25.3	28.6	42.7	34.8	0.9	0.8	3.7	3.4
Iran[4]	194	10.3	45.1	116.0	9.8	13.0	9.9	7.0	0.3	0.3	1.0	1.6
Israel[4]	149	29.6	37.7	44.2	4.4	5.5	5.1	5.9	0.2	0.9	0.8	0.6
Japan[4]	480	40.0	49.8	47.0	5.1	5.4	5.6	11.7	0.8	1.2	1.1	0.6
Korea[4]	687	34.5	267.6	333.8	34.2	33.0	25.4	18.7	1.1	1.0	6.0	4.5
Philippines[5]	1,159	98.4	355.0	548.7	61.0	66.1	68.8	63.5	1.9	3.0	7.9	7.5
Turkey	419	10.1	13.4	23.4	2.2	2.5	3.5	3.2	0.7	0.3	0.3	0.3
Vietnam[6]	504	4.3	172.8	281.0	12.8	13.3	14.8	31.2	0.8	1.1	3.8	3.8
Other Asia	1,279	36.5	176.1	631.4	53.7	74.5	126.4	122.4	2.1	1.1	3.8	8.6
America	**14,810**	**1,716.4**	**1,982.5**	**3,615.6**	**294.9**	**672.6**	**1,297.6**	**445.2**	**24.8**	**51.7**	**44.3**	**49.3**
Argentina[7]	139	49.7	29.9	27.3	2.6	3.8	4.2	4.1	0.2	1.5	0.7	0.4
Canada[7]	4,338	413.3	169.9	158.0	15.8	18.3	19.9	21.5	7.3	12.4	3.8	2.2
Colombia	328	72.0	77.3	122.9	10.2	14.9	19.3	12.9	0.5	2.2	1.7	1.7
Cuba[8]	769	208.5	264.9	144.6	16.6	9.5	9.5	10.9	1.3	6.3	5.9	2.0
Dominican Rep.[7]	594	93.3	148.1	252.0	27.2	26.7	42.4	41.9	1.0	2.8	3.3	3.4
Ecuador[7]	173	36.8	50.1	56.2	4.7	7.6	10.0	7.3	0.3	1.1	1.1	0.8
El Salvador[7]	348	15.0	34.4	213.5	12.0	57.6	46.9	26.1	0.6	0.5	0.8	2.9
Haiti[8]	293	34.5	56.3	138.4	34.8	13.3	47.0	10.8	0.5	1.0	1.3	1.9
Jamaica[12]	470	74.9	137.6	208.1	20.4	23.6	23.0	18.3	0.8	2.3	3.1	2.8
Mexico[7]	5,051	453.9	640.3	1,655.7	95.2	405.6	947.9	214.1	8.4	13.7	14.3	22.6
Other America	2,308	264.4	373.8	639.3	55.3	91.6	128.4	77.3	3.9	7.9	8.3	8.7
Africa	**393**	**29.0**	**80.8**	**176.8**	**17.1**	**22.5**	**33.5**	**24.7**	**0.7**	**0.9**	**1.8**	**2.4**
Oceania[13]	**218**	**25.1**	**41.2**	**45.2**	**4.3**	**5.0**	**7.1**	**6.0**	**0.4**	**0.8**	**0.9**	**0.6**
Unknown or Not Reported	**269**	**0.1**	**—**	**1.0**	**0.1**	**0.1**	**0.2**	**0.2**	**4.5**	**—**	**—**	**—**

* Figures may not add to total due to rounding. Figures include immigrants as well as nonimmigrants and refugees already in the U.S. who subsequently changed their status to immigrants. Nonimmigrants are nonresident aliens admitted to the U.S. for a temporary period. (1) 1938-1945, Austria included with Germany; 1899-1919, Poland included with Austria-Hungary, Germany, and USSR. 1820-1917 includes area occupied by the former Soviet Union. (2) Beginning 1952, includes data for United Kingdom not specified, formerly included with "Other Europe". (3) Europe and Asia. (4) Prior to 1951, included with "Other Asia". (5) Prior to 1951, Philippines included with "Other Asia." (6) Prior to 1953, data for Vietnam not available. (7) Prior to 1951, included with "Other America". (8) Prior to 1951, included with "West Indies". (9) Norway and Sweden were combined from 1820-1868. (10) First full year with Immigration Reform and Control Act of 1986 in effect. (11) Data include 478,814 previously illegal aliens who were granted permanent resident status under section 245A of the Immigration Reform and Control Act of 1986 (IRCA). These aliens are not new residents of the United States. (12) Data for Jamaica not collected until 1953. (13) Includes Australia and New Zealand. (14) Includes IRCA aliens. (15) Figures for 1991 and 1992 include Lithuania, Latvia, Estonia, and other former Soviet republics. (16) 1992 figures include Bosnia and Herzegovina, Croatia, Macedonia, Slovenia, and the Republic of Yugoslavia.

Immigrants Admitted for Top 10 Metropolitan Areas of Intended Residence: 1992

Source: Immigration and Naturalization Service

Metropolitan statistical area of intended residence	Total Number	Total Percent
Total	**973,977**	**100.0**
1. Los Angeles-Long Beach, CA	129,266	13.3
2. New York, NY	127,875	13.1
3. Chicago, IL	37,236	3.8
4. Anaheim-Santa Ana, CA	34,417	3.5
5. Miami-Hialeah, FL	31,627	3.2
6. Washington, DC-MD-VA	27,387	2.8
7. Houston, TX	27,067	2.8
8. San Jose, CA	23,537	2.4
9. San Francisco, CA	21,276	2.2
10. San Diego, CA	20,936	2.1

Poverty Rate

Source: Bureau of the Census

The poverty rate is the proportion of the population whose income falls below the government's official poverty level, which is adjusted each year to take account of inflation. The national poverty rate of 14.2 percent in 1991 was lower than the recent peak of 15.2 percent reached in 1983, but remained well above the levels reached in any year from 1969 through 1980. Nationwide, children living in poverty increased 22 percent in the 1980s. Children remain overrepresented among the poor, with a poverty rate of 21.8 percent. As a group the elderly are slightly underrepresented. Poverty rates for children under 18 years and persons 18 to 44 years increased between 1990 and 1991.

Poverty by Family Status, Sex, and Race, 1978 to 1991

Source: Bureau of the Census; in thousands

	1991		1990		1986		1978	
	No.[1]	%[2]	No.[1]	%[2]	No.[1]	%[2]	No.[1]	%[2]
Total poor	**35,708**	**14.2**	**33,585**	**13.5**	**32,370**	**13.6**	**24,497**	**11.4**
In families	27,143	12.8	25,232	12.0	24,754	12.0	19,062	10.0
Head of household	7,712	11.5	7,098	10.7	7,023	10.9	5,280	9.1
Related children	13,658	21.1	12,715	19.9	12,257	19.8	9,722	15.7
Unrelated individuals	**7,773**	**21.1**	**7,446**	**20.7**	**6,846**	**21.6**	**5,435**	**22.1**
In families with a female householder, no husband present	13,824	39.7	12,578	37.2	11,944	38.3	9,269	35.6
Head of household	4,161	35.6	3,768	33.4	3,613	34.6	2,654	31.4
Related children	8,065	55.5	7,363	53.4	6,943	54.4	5,687	50.6
Unrelated female individuals	**4,762**	**24.5**	**4,589**	**24.0**	**4,311**	**25.1**	**3,611**	**26.0**
All other	**13,319**	**7.5**	**12,654**	**7.1**	**12,811**	**7.3**	**9,793**	**5.9**
Head of household	3,551	5.6	3,330	6.0	3,410	6.3	2,626	5.3
Related children	5,593	9.9	5,352	10.7	5,313	10.8	4,035	7.9
Unrelated male individuals	**3,012**	**17.3**	**2,857**	**16.9**	**2,536**	**17.5**	**1,824**	**17.1**
Total white poor	**23,747**	**11.3**	**22,326**	**10.7**	**22,183**	**11.0**	**16,259**	**8.7**
In families	17,268	9.7	15,916	9.0	16,393	9.4	12,050	7.3
Head of household	5,022	8.8	4,622	8.1	4,811	8.6	3,523	6.9
Female	2,192	28.4	2,010	26.8	2,041	28.2	1,391	23.5
Related children	8,321	16.1	7,696	15.1	7,714	15.3	5,674	11.0
Unrelated individuals	**5,872**	**18.8**	**5,739**	**18.6**	**5,198**	**19.2**	**4,209**	**19.8**
Total black poor	**10,242**	**32.7**	**9,837**	**31.9**	**8,983**	**31.1**	**7,625**	**30.6**
In families	8,504	32.0	8,160	31.0	7,401	29.7	6,493	29.5
Head of household	2,343	30.4	2,193	24.3	1,987	28.0	1,622	27.5
Female	1,834	51.2	1,648	48.1	1,488	50.1	1,208	50.6
Related children	4,637	45.6	4,412	44.2	4,039	42.7	3,781	41.2
Unrelated individuals	**1,590**	**35.3**	**1,491**	**35.1**	**1,431**	**38.5**	**1,132**	**38.6**

[1] Beginning in 1980, total includes members of unrelated subfamilies not shown separately. For earlier years, unrelated subfamily members are included in the "in family" category. [2] Percent of total population in that general category who fell below poverty level. For example, of all black female heads of households in 1978, 50.6% were poor.

Poverty Level by Family Size, 1990 and 1991

Source: Bureau of the Census

	1990	1991
1 person	$ 6,652	$ 6,932
Under 65 years	6,800	7,086
65 years and over	6,268	6,532
2 persons	8,509	8,865
Householder under 65 years	8,794	9,165
Householder 65 years and over	7,905	8,241

	1990	1991
3 persons	$ 10,419	$10,860
4 persons	13,359	13,924
5 persons	15,792	10,456
6 persons	17,839	18,587
7 persons	20,241	21,058
8 persons	22,582	23,605
9 persons or more	26,848	27,942

Persons Below Poverty Level, 1960-1991

Source: Bureau of the Census

Year	Number Below Poverty Level (mil.)				Percent Below Poverty Level				Avg. income cutoffs for nonfarm family of 4 at poverty level[3]
	All races[1]	White	Black	Hispanic origin[2]	All races[1]	White	Black	Hispanic origin[2]	
1960	39.9	28.3	NA	NA	22.2	17.8	NA	NA	$3,022
1965	33.2	22.5	NA	NA	17.3	13.3	NA	NA	3,223
1970	25.4	17.5	7.5	NA	12.6	9.9	33.5	NA	3,968
1975	25.9	17.8	7.5	3.0	12.3	9.7	31.3	26.9	5,500
1980[4]	29.3	19.7	8.6	3.5	13.0	10.2	32.5	25.7	8,414
1986[4]	32.4	22.2	9.0	5.1	13.6	11.0	31.1	27.3	11,203
1989	31.5	20.8	9.3	5.4	12.8	10.0	30.7	26.2	12,674
1990	33.6	22.3	9.8	6.0	13.5	10.7	31.9	28.1	13,359
1991	35.7	23.7	10.2	6.3	14.2	11.3	32.7	28.7	13,924

NA = Not Available. [1]Includes other races not shown separately. [2]Persons of Hispanic origin may be of any race. [3]Beginning in 1981, income cutoffs for nonfarm families are applied to both farm and nonfarm families. [4]Data based on revised poverty definition.

Income Distribution by Population Fifths

Source: Bureau of the Census

Families, 1991	Upper limit of each fifth[1]					Percent distribution of total income					
Race	Lowest	Second	Third	Fourth	Top 5%[2]	Lowest fifth	Second fifth	Third fifth	Fourth fifth	Highest fifth	Top 5%
Total	$17,000	$29,111	$43,000	$62,991	$102,824	4.5	10.7	16.6	24.1	44.2	17.1
White	18,922	31,000	44,874	64,950	106,119	5.0	11.0	16.7	23.8	43.4	16.8
Black	7,780	16,000	27,530	43,900	72,800	3.2	8.4	15.7	25.4	47.4	17.3

[1]The highest fifth does not have an upper limit. [2]Lower limit for top 5%.

Aid to Families with Dependent Children

Source: Admin. for Children and Families, Office of Family Assistance, U.S. Dept. of Health and Human Services

FY 1992 State	Total Assistance Payments[1]	Average Monthly Caseload	Average Monthly Recipients	Average Monthly Children	Average Payment per Family	Average Payment per Person
Alabama	$85,459	50,631	141,941	100,722	$140.66	$50.17
Alaska	96,389	10,808	31,919	20,243	743.22	251.65
Arizona	243,261	63,598	180,501	125,908	318.75	112.31
Arkansas	60,540	26,769	73,112	53,422	188.49	67.18
California	5,865,131	806,086	2,306,509	1,601,785	606.34	211.91
Colorado	162,497	42,081	122,379	81,504	321.79	110.65
Connecticut	376,890	55,500	156,989	105,087	565.91	200.06
Delaware	37,341	10,661	26,450	17,925	291.88	117.65
Dist. of Columbia	102,849	22,566	59,997	42,171	379.80	142.85
Florida	738,540	221,205	601,172	416,910	278.23	102.38
Georgia	421,812	135,972	388,022	268,271	258.52	90.59
Guam	7,834	1,283	4,574	3,249	508.94	142.74
Hawaii	125,495	16,350	50,424	33,686	632.67	207.40
Idaho	24,013	7,335	19,708	13,258	272.81	101.54
Illinois	898,275	228,625	687,572	471,798	327.42	108.87
Indiana	218,662	69,134	199,264	133,042	263.57	91.45
Iowa	164,283	37,081	102,540	66,981	369.20	133.51
Kansas	119,209	28,741	84,639	56,677	345.64	117.37
Kentucky	213,634	83,133	229,444	147,082	214.17	77.60
Louisiana	186,427	92,900	273,747	195,487	168.30	56.75
Maine	118,316	23,920	68,108	42,344	412.20	144.77
Maryland	333,195	79,807	220,837	148,841	347.92	125.73
Massachusetts	751,170	111,448	309,786	208,026	561.68	202.07
Michigan	1,160,829	225,609	674,235	440,943	428.78	143.47
Minnesota	388,592	63,656	191,797	123,073	508.71	168.84
Mississippi	88,721	60,810	177,325	127,717	121.58	41.69
Missouri	281,769	85,176	230,690	164,336	275.67	93.66
Montana	45,658	10,909	32,154	20,659	348.77	118.33
Nebraska	65,389	16,551	48,187	32,623	329.24	113.08
Nevada	41,020	11,867	32,198	22,347	288.06	106.17
New Hampshire	54,474	10,500	28,273	17,915	432.33	160.56
New Jersey	511,873	125,847	352,710	240,970	338.95	120.94
New Mexico	105,473	28,764	87,806	56,926	305.57	100.10
New York	2,587,058	397,172	1,116,986	742,555	542.81	193.01
North Carolina	336,577	121,427	313,479	209,535	230.99	89.47
North Dakota	27,513	6,394	18,258	11,853	358.60	125.58
Ohio	983,959	264,271	749,076	489,028	310.27	109.46
Oklahoma	169,652	46,837	134,865	91,998	301.85	104.83
Oregon	200,252	41,460	116,072	76,249	402.50	143.77
Pennsylvania	924,821	200,699	593,928	396,569	384.00	129.76
Puerto Rico	77,338	61,375	194,389	132,321	105.01	33.15
Rhode Island	128,776	21,289	59,396	38,919	504.09	180.67
South Carolina	119,225	49,710	139,553	99,573	199.87	71.19
South Dakota	25,255	7,223	20,368	14,351	291.38	103.33
Tennessee	206,251	95,179	266,125	179,520	180.58	64.58
Texas	517,857	265,819	757,948	528,338	162.35	56.94
Utah	75,567	17,882	51,829	34,482	352.07	121.47
Vermont	67,207	10,047	28,987	17,697	557.44	193.21
Virgin Islands	3,503	1,053	3,767	2,801	277.21	77.49
Virginia	224,816	70,677	188,442	129,000	265.07	99.42
Washington	569,517	96,407	273,466	175,910	492.28	173.55
West Virginia	120,655	40,469	118,609	73,353	248.45	84.77
Wisconsin	453,707	81,680	243,857	139,896	426.89	155.05
Wyoming	27,159	6,625	18,935	12,604	341.63	119.53
U.S. Total	**$21,941,692**	**4,768,495**	**13,625,342**	**9,200,516**	**$383.45**	**$134.20**

(1) Numbers are in thousands. Total assistance payments include AFDC-Basic, AFDC-Unemployed Parent, Title IV-A Payments under JOBS, Home Repair, and payments to Indian tribes.

Some Notable Cities, Population Under 5,000

Unless otherwise noted all population figures are from the Bureau of the Census. The number of annual visitors is from local sources, such as chambers of commerce or convention and visitors bureaus.

ZIP Code	Place	1990 Pop.	Attraction	Estimated Visitors Annually
52203	Amana, IA	1,700[1]	historic communal village	1,500,000
04609	Bar Harbor, ME	4,443	summer resort; borders Acadia National Park and other recreational areas	4,000,000
65616	Branson, MO	3,706	country music center; 32 indoor theaters, 3 theme parks, and 3 outdoor amphitheaters	5,000,000
93921*	Carmel-by-the-Sea, CA	4,239	artist community and resort	1,500,000
98611	Castle Rock, WA	2,067	Mount St. Helens National Volcanic Monument	1,500,000
37738	Gatlinburg, TN	3,417	Tourist office for the Great Smoky Mountains	9,000,000[2]
57751	Keystone, SD	232	gateway to Mount Rushmore National Memorial	2,500,000
87571	Taos, NM	4,065	Indian pueblo; skiing and outdoor recreation; artists' and writers' colony	2,500,000
89440	Virginia City, NV	788	former mining town	1,500,000
54758	West Yellowstone, MT	913	West entrance to Yellowstone National Park	2,000,000

* More than one ZIP code for this area. [1] Estimated population. [2] Figure for entire national park.

U.S. Places of 5,000 or More Population—With ZIP and Area Codes

Source: Bureau of the Census, 1990 Census; updated as of April 1993

This listing presents the official 1990 Census counts. They show the official urban population of the United States. "Urban population" is defined as all persons living in (a) places of 5,000 inhabitants or more incorporated as cities, villages, boroughs (except Alaska), and towns (except in New England, New York, New Jersey, Pennsylvania, and Wisconsin), but excluding those persons living in the rural portions of extended cities; (b) unincorporated places of 5,000 inhabitants or more; and (c) other territory, incorporated or unincorporated, included in urbanized areas.

The non-urban portion of an extended city contains one or more areas at least 5 square miles in extent and with a population density of less than 100 persons per square mile. The area or areas constitute at least 25 percent of the legal city's land area of a total of 25 square miles or more.

In New England, New York, New Jersey, Pennsylvania, and Wisconsin, minor civil divisions called "towns" often include rural areas and one or more urban areas. Only the urban areas of these "towns" are included here, except in the case of New England where entire town populations, which may include some rural population, are shown; these towns are indicated by italics. Boroughs in Alaska may contain one or more urban areas which are included here. Population in Hawaii is counted by county subdivisions.

(u) means place is unincorporated.

The ZIP Code of each place appears before the name of that place, if it is obtainable. Telephone Area Code appears in parentheses after the name of the state or, if a state has more than one number, after the name of the place. Please be aware some cities have more than one area code.

CAUTION—Where an asterisk (*) appears before the ZIP Code, ask your local postmaster for the correct ZIP Code for a specific address within the place listed.

Alabama (205)

ZIP code	Place	1990	1980
35007	Alabaster	14,738	7,079
35950	Albertville	14,507	12,039
35010	Alexander City	14,917	13,807
36420	Andalusia	9,269	10,415
36201	Anniston	26,634	29,135
35016	Arab	6,321	6,053
35611	Athens	16,901	14,558
36502	Atmore	8,046	8,789
35954	Attalla	6,859	7,737
36830	Auburn	33,830	28,471
36507	Bay Minette	7,168	7,455
35020	Bessemer	33,497	31,729
*35203	Birmingham	265,965	288,297
35957	Boaz	6,928	7,151
36426	Brewton	5,885	6,680
35215	Center Point(u)	22,658	23,317
36611	Chickasaw	6,649	7,402
35045	Clanton	7,669	5,832
35055	Cullman	13,367	13,084
36362	Daleville	5,117	4,250
36526	Daphne	11,291	3,406
35601	Decatur	48,778	42,002
36732	Demopolis	7,512	7,678
36301	Dothan	53,721	48,750
36330	Enterprise	20,119	18,033
36027	Eufaula	13,220	12,097
35064	Fairfield	12,200	13,242
36532	Fairhope	8,490	7,286
35630	Florence	36,426	37,029
35214	Forestdale(u)	10,395	10,814
35967	Fort Payne	11,838	11,485
36360	Fort Rucker(u)	7,593	8,932
35068	Fultondale	6,400	6,217
*35901	Gadsden	42,523	47,565
35071	Gardendale	9,251	8,005
36037	Greenville	7,492	7,807
35976	Guntersville	7,038	7,041
35570	Hamilton	5,787	5,093
35640	Hartselle	10,867	8,858
35209	Homewood	23,644	21,412
35226	Hoover	39,785	18,996
35020	Hueytown	15,280	13,452
*35804	Huntsville	159,880	142,513
35210	Irondale	9,454	6,510
36545	Jackson	5,819	6,073
36265	Jacksonville	10,283	9,735
35501	Jasper	13,553	11,894
36863	Lanett	8,985	8,922
35094	Leeds	10,009	8,638
35758	Madison	14,792	4,057
35228	Midfield	5,559	6,182
36054	Millbrook	6,046	3,101
*36601	Mobile	196,278	200,452
36460	Monroeville	6,993	5,674
*36104	Montgomery	187,543	177,857
35223	Mountain Brook	19,810	19,718
35660	Muscle Shoals	9,611	8,911
35476	Northport	17,297	14,291
36801	Opelika	22,122	21,896
36467	Opp	6,985	7,204
36203	Oxford	9,603	8,939
36360	Ozark	13,030	13,188
35124	Pelham	9,421	6,759
35125	Pell City	7,945	6,616
36867	Phenix City	25,311	26,928
36272	Piedmont	5,347	5,544
35126	Pinson-Clay-Chalkville(u)	10,987	....
35127	Pleasant Grove	8,458	7,102
36067	Prattville	19,816	18,647
36610	Prichard	34,320	39,541
35901	Rainbow City	7,667	6,299
36274	Roanoke	6,362	5,809
35653	Russellville	7,812	8,195
36201	Saks(u)	11,138	11,118
36571	Saraland	11,760	9,833
36572	Satsuma	5,194	3,822
35768	Scottsboro	13,786	14,758
36701	Selma	23,755	26,684
35660	Sheffield	10,380	11,903
35901	Southside	5,580	5,141
35150	Sylacauga	12,520	12,708
35160	Talladega	18,175	19,128
36045	Tallassee	5,112	4,763
35217	Tarrant City	8,046	8,148
36582	Theodore(u)	6,509	6,392
36619	Tillman's Corner(u)	17,988	15,941
36081	Troy	13,051	13,124
35173	Trussville	8,283	3,507
35401	Tuscaloosa	77,759	75,211
35674	Tuscumbia	8,413	9,137
36083	Tuskegee	12,257	13,327
36858	Valley	8,215	8,946
35216	Vestavia Hills	19,554	15,722

Alaska (907)

ZIP code	Place	1990	1980
*99502	Anchorage	226,338	174,431
99708	College	11,249	4,043
99702	Eielson AFB(u)	5,251	5,232
*99701	Fairbanks	30,843	22,645
99801	Juneau	26,751	19,528
99611	Kenai	6,327	4,324
99901	Ketchikan	8,263	7,198
99615	Kodiak	6,365	4,756
99639	Ninilchik(u)	10,523	341
99835	Sitka	8,588	7,803

Arizona (602)

ZIP code	Place	1990	1980
85220	Apache Junction	18,092	9,935
85323	Avondale	16,169	8,168
85603	Bisbee	6,288	7,154
85326	Buckeye	5,038	3,434
86430	Bullhead City	21,951	10,719
86322	Camp Verde	6,243	3,824
85222	Casa Grande	19,076	14,971
*85224	Chandler	89,862	29,673
86503	Chinle(u)	5,059	2,815
85228	Coolidge	6,934	6,851
86326	Cottonwood	5,918	4,550
.....	Cottonwood-Verde Village(u)	7,037	....
85607	Douglas	13,137	13,058

ZIP code	Place	1990	1980
85335	El Mirage	5,001	4,307
85231	Eloy	7,211	6,240
*86001	Flagstaff	45,857	34,743
85232	Florence	7,510	3,391
85726	Flowing Wells	14,013	....
.....	Fortuna Foothills(u)	7,737	....
85268	Fountain Hills	10,030	2,771
85234	Gilbert	29,122	5,717
*85301	Glendale	147,864	97,172
85501	Globe	6,062	6,886
85323	Goodyear	6,258	2,747
85614	Green Valley(u)	13,231	7,999
85283	Guadalupe	5,458	4,506
86401	Kingman	12,722	9,257
86403	Lake Havasu City	24,363	15,909
*85201	Mesa	288,104	152,404
86440	Mohave Valley(u)	6,962	....
.....	New Kingman-Butler(u)	11,627	....
85621	Nogales	19,489	15,683
85737	Oro Valley	6,670	1,489
86040	Page	6,598	4,907
85253	Paradise Valley	11,773	11,085
85541	Payson	8,377	5,068
85345	Peoria	50,675	12,171
*85026	Phoenix	983,392	789,704
86301	Prescott	26,592	19,865
86314	Prescott Valley	8,904	2,284
85546	Safford	7,359	7,010
*85251	Scottsdale	130,075	88,622
86336	Sedona	7,720	5,319
85901	Show Low	5,020	4,298
*85635	Sierra Vista	32,983	24,937
85635	Sierra Vista Southeast(u)	9,237	....
85350	Somerton	5,282	3,969
85713	South Tucson	5,171	6,554
*85351	Sun City(u)	38,126	40,505
85375	Sun City West(u)	15,997	3,772
85248	Sun Lakes(u)	6,578	....
85374	Surprise	7,122	3,723
*85282	Tempe	141,993	106,919
86045	Tuba City(u)	7,323	5,045
*85726	Tucson	405,371	330,537
86047	Winslow	9,279	7,921
*85364	Yuma	54,923	42,481

Arkansas (501)

ZIP code	Place	1990	1980
71923	Arkadelphia	10,014	10,005
71822	Ashdown	5,150	4,218
72501	Batesville	9,187	8,447
72714	Bella Vista(u)	9,083	2,589
72015	Benton	18,177	17,717
72712	Bentonville	11,257	8,756
72315	Blytheville	22,523	23,844
72022	Bryant	5,269	2,682
72023	Cabot	8,319	4,806
71701	Camden	14,701	15,356
72830	Clarksville	5,833	5,237
72032	Conway	26,481	20,375
71635	Crossett	6,282	6,706
71639	Dumas	5,520	6,091
71730	El Dorado	23,146	25,270
72701	Fayetteville	42,247	36,608
72335	Forrest City	13,364	13,803
72901	Fort Smith	72,798	71,626
72601	Harrison	9,936	9,567
72543	Heber Springs	5,628	4,589
72342	Helena	7,491	9,598
71801	Hope	9,768	10,290
71901	Hot Springs	32,462	35,781
71909	Hot Springs Village(u)	6,361	2,083
72076	Jacksonville	29,101	27,589
72401	Jonesboro	46,535	31,530
*72201	Little Rock	175,727	159,151
71753	Magnolia	11,151	11,909
72104	Malvern	9,236	10,163
72360	Marianna	6,033	6,220
72113	Maumelle	6,714	1,368
71953	Mena	5,475	5,154
71655	Monticello	8,119	8,259
72110	Morrilton	6,551	7,355
72653	Mountain Home	9,027	8,066
72112	Newport	7,459	8,339
*72114	North Little Rock	61,829	64,388
72370	Osceola	8,930	8,881
72450	Paragould	18,540	15,248
71601	Pine Bluff	57,140	56,636
72455	Pocahontas	6,151	5,995
72756	Rogers	24,692	17,429
72801	Russellville	21,260	14,518
72143	Searcy	15,180	13,612
72116	Sherwood	18,878	10,423
72761	Siloam Springs	8,151	7,940
72764	Springdale	29,945	23,458
72160	Stuttgart	10,420	10,941
75502	Texarkana	22,631	21,459
72472	Trumann	6,346	6,395
72956	Van Buren	14,979	12,020
71671	Warren	6,455	7,646
72390	West Helena	10,137	11,367
72301	West Memphis	28,259	28,138
72396	Wynne	8,817	7,927

California

ZIP code	Place	Area code	1990	1980
94501	Adelanto		8,521	2,164
91301	Agoura Hills	(818)	20,390	11,399
94501	Alameda	(510)	73,979	63,852
94507	Alamo(u)	(510)	12,277	8,505
94706	Albany	(510)	16,327	15,130
*91802	Alhambra	(818)	82,106	64,767
92656	Aliso Viejo(u)		7,612	....
90249	Alondra Park(u)	(310)	12,215	12,096
91901	Alpine(u)	(619)	9,695	5,368
91001	Altadena(u)	(818)	42,658	40,510
95945	Alta Sierra(u)		5,709	2,168
94590	American Canyon(u)	(707)	7,706	5,712
*92803	Anaheim	(714)	266,406	219,494
96007	Anderson	(916)	8,299	7,381
94509	Antioch	(510)	62,195	42,683
92307	Apple Valley	(619)	46,079	16,748
95003	Aptos(u)	(408)	9,061	7,039
91006	Arcadia	(818)	48,284	45,993
95521	Arcata	(707)	15,197	12,849
95825	Arden-Arcade(u)	(916)	92,040	87,570
93420	Arroyo Grande	(805)	14,432	11,290
90701	Artesia	(310)	15,464	14,301
93203	Arvin	(805)	9,286	6,863
94577	Ashland(u)	(510)	16,590	13,893
93422	Atascadero	(805)	23,138	16,232
94025	Atherton	(415)	7,163	7,797
95301	Atwater	(209)	22,282	17,530
95603	Auburn	(916)	10,592	7,540
92505	August(u)	(714)	6,376	5,445
93204	Avenal		9,770	4,137
91746	Avocado Heights(u)	(818)	14,232	11,721
91702	Azusa	(818)	41,333	29,380
*93302	Bakersfield	(805)	174,820	105,611
91706	Baldwin Park	(818)	69,330	50,554
92220	Banning	(714)	20,572	14,020
92311	Barstow	(619)	21,472	17,690
93402	Baywood-Los Osos(u)	(805)	14,377	10,933
95903	Beale AFB East(u)	(916)	6,912	6,329
92223	Beaumont	(714)	9,685	6,818
90201	Bell	(213)	34,365	25,450
90706	Bellflower	(310)	61,815	53,441
90201	Bell Gardens	(213)	42,355	34,117
94002	Belmont	(415)	24,127	24,505
94510	Benicia	(707)	24,437	15,376
95005	Ben Lomond(u)	(408)	7,884	7,238
*94704	Berkeley	(510)	102,724	103,328
*90213	Beverly Hills	(310)	31,971	32,646
92314	Big Bear Lake	(714)	5,351	4,896
94506	Black Hawk(u)		6,199	....
92316	Bloomington(u)	(714)	15,116	12,781
92225	Blythe	(619)	8,448	6,805
.....	Bonadella Ranchos-Madera Ranchos(u)		5,705	3,272
91902	Bonita(u)	(619)	12,542	6,257
92021	Bostonia(u)		13,670	....
95006	Boulder Creek(u)	(408)	6,725	5,662
95416	Boyes Hot Springs(u)		5,973	4,177
92227	Brawley	(619)	18,923	14,946
92621	Brea	(714)	32,873	27,913
94513	Brentwood	(510)	7,563	4,434
*90620	Buena Park	(714)	68,784	64,165
*91505	Burbank	(818)	93,643	84,625
94010	Burlingame	(415)	26,666	26,173
92231	Calexico	(619)	18,633	14,412
93505	California City		5,955	2,743
93010	Camarillo	(805)	52,297	37,797
93428	Cambria		5,382	3,061
95682	Cameron Park(u)	(916)	11,897	5,607
95008	Campbell	(408)	36,048	26,843
92055	Camp Pendleton North(u)	(714)	10,373	2,065
92055	Camp Pendleton South(u)	(714)	11,299	7,952
92380	Canyon Lake(u)		7,938	2,039
95010	Capitola	(408)	10,171	9,095
*92008	Carlsbad	(619)	63,126	35,490
95608	Carmichael(u)	(916)	48,702	43,108
93013	Carpinteria	(805)	13,747	10,835
90744	Carson	(310)	83,995	81,221
92077	Casa de Oro-Mt. Helix(u)	(619)	30,727	19,651
94546	Castro Valley(u)	(510)	48,619	44,011
95012	Castroville	(408)	5,272	4,396
92235	Cathedral City	(619)	30,085	11,096
95307	Ceres	(209)	26,413	13,281
90701	Cerritos	(310)	53,244	53,020
91724	Charter Oak(u)	(818)	8,858	6,840
94541	Cherryland(u)	(415)	11,088	9,425
92223	Cherry Valley(u)	(714)	5,945	5,012
95926	Chico	(916)	40,079	26,716
91710	Chino	(714)	59,682	40,165
91709	Chino Hills		27,608	....

ZIP code	Place		1990	1980
93610	Chowchilla	(209)	5,930	5,122
*91910	Chula Vista	(619)	135,163	83,927
95610	Citrus(u)	(916)	9,481	12,450
*95610	Citrus Heights(u)	(916)	107,439	85,911
91711	Claremont	(714)	32,539	31,028
94517	Clayton		7,317	4,325
95422	Clearlake		11,804	8,343
93612	Clovis	(209)	50,323	33,021
92236	Coachella	(619)	16,896	9,129
93210	Coalinga	(209)	8,212	6,593
92324	Colton	(714)	40,273	21,310
90022	Commerce	(310)	12,135	10,509
*90220	Compton	(310)	90,454	81,350
*94520	Concord	(510)	111,308	103,763
93212	Corcoran	(209)	13,360	6,454
96021	Corning	(916)	5,870	4,745
91720	Corona	(714)	76,095	37,791
92118	Coronado	(619)	26,540	18,790
94925	Corte Madera	(415)	8,272	8,074
*92626	Costa Mesa	(714)	96,357	82,562
94927	Cotati	(707)	5,714	3,346
94556	Country Club(u)	(209)	9,325	9,585
*91722	Covina	(818)	43,207	32,746
92325	Crestline(u)	(714)	8,594	6,715
90201	Cudahy	(213)	22,817	18,275
*90230	Culver City	(310)	38,793	38,139
95014	Cupertino	(408)	39,967	34,297
90630	Cypress	(714)	42,655	40,738
*94017	Daly City	(415)	92,311	78,519
92629	Dana Point	(714)	31,896	21,271
*94526	Danville	(510)	31,306	26,143
95616	Davis	(916)	46,322	36,640
90250	Del Aire(u)	(310)	8,040	8,487
93215	Delano	(805)	22,762	16,491
.....	Del Monte Forest(u)		5,069	....
92240	Desert Hot Springs	(619)	11,668	5,941
91765	Diamond Bar	(714)	53,672	30,736
93618	Dinuba	(209)	12,743	9,907
94514	Discovery Bay(u)		5,351	1,326
95620	Dixon	(916)	10,417	7,541
*90241	Downey	(310)	91,4444	82,602
91010	Duarte	(818)	20,688	16,766
94568	Dublin	(510)	23,229	13,496
93219	Earlimart(u)	(805)	5,881	4,578
90220	East Compton(u)	(310)	7,967	6,435
.....	East Foothills(u)		14,898	....
92343	East Hemet(u)	(714)	17,611	14,712
90638	East La Mirada(u)	(310)	9,367	9,688
90022	East Los Angeles(u)	(310)	126,379	110,017
94303	East Palo Alto	(415)	23,451	18,106
91117	East Pasadena(u)		5,910	....
93257	East Porterville(u)	(209)	5,790	5,218
.....	East San Gabriel(u)		12,736	....
93523	Edwards AFB(u)	(805)	7,423	8,554
*92020	El Cajon	(619)	88,693	73,892
92243	El Centro	(619)	31,405	23,996
94530	El Cerrito	(510)	22,869	22,731
95630	El Dorado Hills(u)		6,395	....
95624	Elk Grove(u)	(916)	17,483	10,959
*91734	El Monte	(818)	106,162	79,494
93446	El Paso de Robles	(310)	18,583	9,163
93030	El Rio(u)	(805)	6,419	5,674
90245	El Segundo	(310)	15,223	13,752
94803	El Sobrante(u)	(510)	9,852	10,535
92630	El Toro(u)	(714)	62,685	38,153
92709	El Toro Station(u)	(714)	6,869	7,632
94608	Emeryville	(510)	5,740	3,714
92024	Encinitas	(619)	55,386	36,550
*92025	Escondido	(619)	108,635	64,355
95501	Eureka	(707)	27,025	24,153
93221	Exeter	(209)	7,276	5,606
94930	Fairfax	(415)	6,931	7,391
94533	Fairfield	(707)	78,650	58,099
95628	Fair Oaks(u)	(916)	26,867	22,602
93238	Fairview(u)		9,045	....
92028	Fallbrook(u)	(619)	22,095	14,041
93223	Farmersville	(209)	6,235	5,544
95018	Felton	(408)	5,350	4,564
93015	Fillmore	(805)	11,992	9,602
90001	Florence-Graham(u)	(213)	57,147	48,662
95828	Florin(u)	(916)	24,330	16,523
95630	Folsom	(916)	29,802	11,003
*92335	Fontana	(714)	87,535	36,804
95841	Foothill Farms(u)	(916)	17,135	13,700
95437	Fort Bragg	(707)	6,078	5,019
95540	Fortuna	(707)	8,788	7,591
94404	Foster City	(415)	28,176	23,287
92708	Fountain Valley	(714)	53,691	55,080
95019	Freedom(u)	(408)	8,361	6,416
*94536	Fremont	(510)	173,339	131,945
*93706	Fresno	(209)	354,091	217,491
*92631	Fullerton	(714)	114,144	102,246
95632	Galt	(209)	8,889	5,514
*90247	Gardena	(310)	49,841	45,165
95205	Garden Acres(u)	(213)	8,547	7,361
*92640	Garden Grove	(714)	143,965	123,307
92392	George AFB(u)	(619)	5,085	7,061
95020	Gilroy	(408)	31,487	21,641
92509	Glen Avon(u)	(714)	12,663	8,444
*91209	Glendale	(818)	180,038	139,060
91740	Glendora	(818)	47,832	38,500
93561	Golden Hills(u)		5,423	....
92324	Grand Terrace	(714)	10,946	8,498
95945	Grass Valley	(916)	9,048	6,697
93308	Greenacres(u)	(805)	7,379	5,381
93927	Greenfield	(805)	7,464	4,181
93433	Grover City	(805)	11,602	8,827
93434	Guadalupe		5,479	3,629
91745	Hacienda Heights(u)	(818)	52,354	49,422
94019	Half Moon Bay	(415)	8,886	7,282
93230	Hanford	(209)	30,897	20,958
90716	Hawaiian Gardens	(213)	13,639	10,548
90250	Hawthorne	(310)	71,349	56,437
*94544	Hayward	(510)	111,343	93,585
95448	Healdsburg	(707)	9,469	7,217
92343	Hemet	(714)	36,094	22,531
94547	Hercules	(415)	16,829	5,963
90254	Hermosa Beach	(310)	18,219	18,070
92345	Hesperia	(619)	50,418	20,612
92346	Highland	(714)	34,439	21,720
94010	Hillsborough	(415)	10,667	10,372
95023	Hollister	(408)	19,212	11,488
91720	Home Gardens(u)	(714)	7,780	5,783
*92647	Huntington Beach	(714)	181,519	170,505
90255	Huntington Park	(213)	56,065	45,932
91932	Imperial Beach	(619)	26,512	22,689
92201	Indio	(619)	36,850	21,611
*90306	Inglewood	(310)	109,602	94,162
.....	Interlaken(u)		6,404	....
95640	Ione		6,516	2,207
*92711	Irvine	(714)	110,330	62,134
93117	Isla Vista(u)	(805)	20,395	....
94904	Kentfield(u)	(415)	6,030	....
93630	Kerman	(209)	5,448	4,002
93930	King City	(408)	7,634	5,495
93631	Kingsburg	(209)	7,245	5,115
91011	La Canada-Flintridge	(818)	19,378	20,153
91214	La Crescenta-Montrose(u)	(818)	16,968	16,531
90045	Ladera Heights(u)	(310)	6,316	6,647
94549	Lafayette	(510)	23,366	20,837
.....	Laguna(u)		9,828	....
*92651	Laguna Beach	(714)	23,170	17,858
92653	Laguna Hills(u)	(714)	46,731	33,600
92677	Laguna Niguel	(714)	44,400	12,237
90631	La Habra	(310)	51,266	45,232
.....	La Habra Heights	(310)	6,226	4,786
92352	Lake Arrowhead(u)	(714)	6,539	6,272
92330	Lake Elsinore	(714)	18,316	5,982
92530	Lakeland Village(u)		5,159	2,796
93535	Lake Los Angeles(u)		7,977	....
92040	Lakeside(u)	(619)	39,412	23,921
*90714	Lakewood	(310)	73,553	74,511
91941	La Mesa	(619)	52,931	50,308
90638	La Mirada	(714)	40,452	40,986
93241	Lamont(u)	(805)	11,517	9,616
93534	Lancaster	(805)	97,291	48,027
90624	La Palma	(714)	15,392	15,399
91747	La Puente	(818)	36,955	30,882
92253	La Quinta		11,215	4,027
.....	La Riviera(u)	(916)	10,986	10,906
95403	Larkfield-Wikiup(u)		6,779	....
94939	Larkspur	(415)	11,068	11,064
95330	Lathrop		6,841	4,112
91750	La Verne	(714)	30,861	23,508
90260	Lawndale	(310)	27,331	23,460
91945	Lemon Grove	(619)	23,984	20,780
93245	Lemoore	(209)	13,622	8,832
90304	Lennox(u)	(310)	22,757	18,445
95207	Lincoln Village(u)	(916)	7,248	4,132
95901	Linda(u)	(916)	13,033	10,225
93247	Lindsay	(209)	8,338	6,936
95062	Live Oak(u)	(916)	15,212	11,482
94550	Livermore	(510)	56,741	48,349
95334	Livingston	(209)	7,317	5,326
*95240	Lodi	(209)	51,874	35,221
92354	Loma Linda	(714)	18,470	10,694
90717	Lomita	(213)	19,382	18,807
93436	Lompoc	(805)	37,649	26,267
*90801	Long Beach	(310)	429,321	361,498
95650	Loomis		5,705	3,663
90720	Los Alamitos	(310)	11,788	11,529
94022	Los Altos	(415)	26,599	25,769
94022	Los Altos Hills	(415)	7,514	7,421
*90052	Los Angeles	(213)	3,485,398	2,968,528
93635	Los Banos	(209)	14,519	10,341
95030	Los Gatos	(408)	27,357	26,906
91709	Los Serranos(u)		7,099	....
94903	Lucas Valley-Marinwood(u)	(415)	5,982	6,409
90262	Lynwood	(310)	61,945	48,289
93250	Mc Farland	(805)	7,005	5,151
95521	McKinleyville(u)	(707)	10,749	7,772
93637	Madera	(209)	29,282	21,732
.....	Madera Acres(u)		5,245	2,173
95954	Magalia(u)		8,987	....
90266	Manhattan Beach	(310)	32,063	31,542
95336	Manteca	(209)	40,773	24,925
92518	March AFB(u)	(714)	5,523	3,607
93933	Marina	(408)	26,512	20,647

ZIP code	Place		1990	1980
90292	Marina Del Rey(u)	(310)	7,431	8,065
94553	Martinez	(510)	31,808	22,582
95901	Marysville	(916)	12,324	9,898
90270	Maywood	(213)	27,850	21,810
93640	Mendota	(209)	6,821	5,038
94025	Menlo Park	(415)	28,403	26,438
92359	Mentone(u)	(714)	5,675	....
*95340	Merced	(209)	56,216	36,423
94030	Millbrae	(415)	20,414	20,058
94941	Mill Valley	(415)	13,038	12,967
95035	Milpitas	(408)	50,686	37,820
91752	Mira Loma(u)	(714)	15,786	8,707
93641	Mira Monte(u)		7,744	....
92675	Mission Viejo	(714)	72,820	48,503
*95350	Modesto	(209)	164,746	106,963
91016	Monrovia	(818)	35,761	30,531
91763	Montclair	(714)	28,434	22,628
90640	Montebello	(213)	59,564	52,929
93940	Monterey	(408)	31,954	27,558
91754	Monterey Park	(818)	60,738	54,338
93020	Moorpark	(805)	25,494	7,798
94556	Moraga Town	(510)	15,987	15,014
*92303	Moreno Valley	(714)	118,779	28,139
95037	Morgan Hill	(408)	23,928	17,060
93442	Morro Bay	(805)	9,664	9,064
*94042	Mountain View	(415)	67,365	58,655
92405	Muscoy(u)	(714)	7,541	6,188
94558	Napa	(707)	61,842	50,879
91950	National City	(619)	54,249	48,772
92363	Needles	(619)	5,191	4,120
94560	Newark	(510)	37,861	32,126
*92660	Newport Beach	(714)	66,643	62,556
93444	Nipomo(u)	(805)	7,109	5,247
91760	Norco	(714)	23,302	19,732
95603	North Auburn(u)	(916)	10,301	7,619
94025	North Fair Oaks(u)	(415)	13,912	10,308
95660	North Highlands(u)	(916)	42,105	37,825
90650	Norwalk	(310)	94,279	84,901
94947	Novato	(415)	47,585	43,916
95361	Oakdale	(209)	11,978	8,474
*94615	Oakland	(510)	372,242	339,337
94561	Oakley(u)		18,374	2,816
93445	Oceano(u)		6,169	4,478
*92054	Oceanside	(619)	128,154	76,698
93308	Oildale(u)	(805)	26,553	23,382
93023	Ojai	(805)	7,613	6,816
95961	Olivehurst(u)	(916)	9,738	8,929
*91761	Ontario	(714)	133,179	88,820
95060	Opal Cliffs(u)	(408)	5,940	5,041
*92667	Orange	(714)	110,658	91,450
93646	Orange Cove	(209)	5,604	4,026
95662	Orangevale(u)	(916)	26,266	20,585
94563	Orinda	(510)	16,642	17,030
95963	Orland	(916)	5,052	4,031
93647	Orosi(u)		5,486	4,076
95965	Oroville	(916)	11,960	8,683
.....	Oroville East(u)		8,462	....
*93030	Oxnard	(805)	142,560	108,195
94044	Pacifica	(415)	37,670	36,866
93950	Pacific Grove	(408)	16,117	15,755
95968	Palermo(u)		5,260	2,572
93550	Palmdale	(805)	68,842	12,277
92260	Palm Desert	(619)	23,252	11,801
.....	Palm Desert Country(u)		5,626	....
92262	Palm Springs	(619)	40,144	32,359
*94302	Palo Alto	(415)	55,900	55,225
90274	Palos Verdes Estates	(310)	13,512	14,376
95969	Paradise	(916)	25,401	22,571
90723	Paramount	(310)	47,669	36,407
95823	Parkway-So. Sacramento(u)	(916)	31,903	26,815
93648	Parlier	(209)	7,938	2,902
*91109	Pasadena	(818)	131,591	118,072
95363	Patterson	(209)	8,626	3,908
92509	Pedley(u)		8,869	....
92370	Perris	(714)	21,460	6,827
94952	Petaluma	(707)	43,184	33,834
90660	Pico Rivera	(310)	59,177	53,387
94611	Piedmont	(510)	10,602	10,498
94564	Pinole	(510)	17,460	14,253
93449	Pismo Beach	(805)	7,669	5,364
94565	Pittsburg	(510)	47,607	33,465
92670	Placentia	(714)	41,259	35,041
95667	Placerville	(916)	8,355	6,739
94523	Pleasant Hill	(510)	31,583	25,547
*94566	Pleasanton	(510)	50,570	35,160
*91766	Pomona	(714)	131,723	92,742
93257	Porterville	(209)	29,521	19707
93041	Port Hueneme	(805)	20,322	17,803
92064	Poway	(619)	43,516	33,439
93907	Prunedale(u)		7,393	....
93534	Quartz Hill(u)	(805)	9,626	7,421
92065	Ramona(u)	(619)	13,040	8,173
95670	Rancho Cordova(u)	(916)	48,731	42,881
91730	Rancho Cucamonga	(714)	101,409	55,250
92270	Rancho Mirage	(619)	9,778	6,281
90274	Rancho Palos Verdes	(310)	41,659	36,577
.....	Rancho San Diego(u)		6,977	....
92688	Rancho Santa Margarita(u)		11,390	....
96080	Red Bluff	(916)	12,363	9,490

ZIP code	Place		1990	1980
*96049	Redding	(916)	66,462	42,103
92373	Redlands	(714)	60,394	43,619
*90277	Redondo Beach	(310)	60,167	57,102
*94064	Redwood City	(415)	66,072	54,951
93654	Reedley	(209)	15,791	11,071
92376	Rialto	(714)	72,395	37,862
*94802	Richmond	(510)	87,619	74,676
93555	Ridgecrest	(619)	28,295	15,929
95003	Rio Del Mar(u)	(408)	8,919	7,067
95673	Rio Linda(u)	(916)	9,481	7,359
95366	Ripon	(209)	7,455	3,509
95307	Riverbank	(209)	8,591	5,695
*92502	Riverside	(714)	226,546	170,591
95677	Rocklin	(916)	18,806	7,344
94572	Rodeo(u)	(415)	7,589	8,286
94928	Rohnert Park	(707)	36,326	22,965
90274	Rolling Hills Estates	(310)	7,789	7,701
93560	Rosamond(u)	(805)	7,430	2,869
95401	Roseland(u)	(707)	8,779	7,915
91770	Rosemead	(818)	51,638	42,604
95826	Rosemont(u)	(916)	22,851	18,888
95678	Roseville	(916)	44,685	24,347
90720	Rossmoor(u)	(310)	9,893	10,457
91745	Rowland Heights(u)	(818)	42,647	28,252
92509	Rubidoux(u)	(714)	24,367	16,763
*95813	Sacramento	(916)	369,365	275,741
93901	Salinas	(408)	108,777	80,479
94960	San Anselmo	(415)	11,735	12,067
*92403	San Bernardino	(714)	164,164	118,794
94066	San Bruno	(415)	38,961	35,417
*93001	San Buenaventura (Ventura)	(805)	92,557	73,774
94070	San Carlos	(415)	26,167	24,710
92672	San Clemente	(714)	41,100	27,325
*92109	San Diego	(619)	1,110,554	875,538
.....	San Diego Country Estates(u)		6,874	....
91773	San Dimas	(714)	32,402	24,014
*91340	San Fernando	(818)	22,580	17,731
*94101	San Francisco	(415)	723,959	678,974
91776	San Gabriel	(818)	37,120	30,072
93657	Sanger	(209)	16,839	12,542
92383	San Jacinto	(714)	16,210	7,098
*95101	San Jose	(408)	782,248	629,400
92375	San Juan Capistrano	(714)	26,183	18,959
*94577	San Leandro	(510)	68,223	63,952
94580	San Lorenzo(u)	(510)	19,987	20,545
93401	San Luis Obispo	(805)	41,958	34,252
92069	San Marcos	(619)	38,974	17,479
91108	San Marino	(818)	12,959	13,307
*94402	San Mateo	(415)	85,619	77,640
94806	San Pablo	(510)	25,158	19,750
*94901	San Rafael	(415)	48,410	44,700
94583	San Ramon	(510)	35,303	20,511
*92711	Santa Ana	(714)	293,827	204,023
*93102	Santa Barbara	(805)	85,571	74,414
*95050	Santa Clara	(408)	93,613	87,700
*91380	Santa Clarita	(805)	110,690	66,730
95060	Santa Cruz	(408)	49,711	41,483
90670	Santa Fe Springs	(310)	15,520	14,520
93454	Santa Maria	(805)	61,552	39,685
*90406	Santa Monica	(310)	86,905	88,314
93060	Santa Paula	(805)	25,062	20,658
*95402	Santa Rosa	(707)	113,313	82,658
92071	Santee	(619)	52,902	40,298
95070	Saratoga	(408)	28,061	29,261
94965	Sausalito	(415)	7,152	7,338
95066	Scotts Valley	(408)	8,667	6,891
90740	Seal Beach	(310)	25,098	25,975
93955	Seaside	(408)	38,826	36,567
95472	Sebastopol	(707)	7,004	5,595
93662	Selma	(209)	14,757	10,942
93263	Shafter	(805)	8,409	7,010
91024	Sierra Madre	(818)	10,762	10,837
90806	Signal Hill	(310)	8,371	5,734
*93065	Simi Valley	(805)	100,218	77,500
92075	Solana Beach	(619)	12,968	12,250
93960	Soledad	(408)	7,161	5,928
95476	Sonoma	(707)	8,168	6,054
95073	Soquel(u)	(408)	9,188	6,212
91733	South El Monte	(213)	20,850	16,623
90280	South Gate	(213)	86,284	66,784
95705	South Lake Tahoe	(916)	21,586	20,681
95965	South Oroville(u)	(916)	7,463	7,246
91030	South Pasadena	(818)	23,936	22,681
94080	South San Francisco	(415)	54,312	49,393
91770	South San Gabriel(u)	(213)	7,700	5,421
91744	South San Jose Hills(u)	(408)	17,814	16,049
90605	South Whittier(u)	(310)	49,514	43,815
95991	South Yuba(u)	(916)	8,816	7,530
*91979	Spring Valley(u)	(619)	55,331	40,191
94305	Stanford(u)	(415)	18,097	11,045
90680	Stanton	(714)	30,491	23,723
*95204	Stockton	(209)	210,943	148,283
94585	Suisun City	(707)	22,704	11,087
92381	Sun City(u)	(714)	14,930	8,460
*94086	Sunnyvale	(408)	117,324	106,618
96130	Susanville	(916)	7,279	6,520
93268	Taft	(805)	5,902	5,316
94941	Tamalpais-Homestead Valley(u)	(415)	9,601	8,511

ZIP code	Place		1990	1980
93561	Tehachapi	(805)	6,182	4,126
*92391	Temecula	(909)	27,099	4,289
91780	Temple City	(818)	31,153	28,972
95965	Thermalito(u)		5,646	4,961
*91360	Thousand Oaks	(805)	104,381	77,072
94920	Tiburon	(415)	7,532	6,685
*90510	Torrance	(310)	133,107	129,881
95396	Tracy	(209)	33,558	18,428
93274	Tulare	(209)	33,249	22,530
95380	Turlock	(209)	42,224	26,287
92680	Tustin	(714)	50,689	32,248
92705	Tustin Foothills(u)	(714)	24,358	26,174
92277	Twentynine Palms	(619)	11,821	8,802
92278	Twentynine Palms Base(u)	(619)	10,606	7,079
.....	Twin Lakes(u)		5,379	4,502
95482	Ukiah	(707)	14,632	12,035
94587	Union City	(510)	53,762	39,406
91786	Upland	(714)	63,374	47,647
*95688	Vacaville	(707)	71,476	43,367
91744	Valinda(u)	(818)	18,735	18,700
*94590	Vallejo	(707)	109,199	80,303
92343	Valle Vista(u)	(714)	8,751	5,474
93437	Vandenberg AFB(u)	(805)	9,846	5,839
93436	Vandenberg Village(u)	(805)	5,971	5,839
92392	Victorville	(619)	40,674	14,220
90043	View Park-Windsor Hills(u)	(310)	11,769	12,101
92667	Villa Park	(714)	6,299	7,137
.....	Vincent(u)		13,713	....
93277	Visalia	(209)	75,659	49,729
92083	Vista	(619)	71,865	35,834
*91789	Walnut	(714)	29,105	12,478
*94596	Walnut Creek	(510)	60,569	54,033
90255	Walnut Park(u)	(310)	14,722	11,811
93280	Wasco	(805)	12,412	9,613
95076	Watsonville	(408)	31,099	23,662
90044	West Athens(u)	(310)	8,859	8,531
90502	West Carson(u)	(213)	20,143	17,997
90247	West Compton(u)	(310)	5,451	5,907
*91793	West Covina	(818)	96,086	80,292
90069	West Hollywood	(310)	36,118	35,754
91359	Westlake Village		7,455	6,130
92683	Westminster	(714)	78,293	71,133
90047	Westmont(u)	(213)	31,044	27,916
94565	West Pittsburg(u)	(510)	17,453	8,773
91746	West Puente Valley(u)	(818)	20,254	20,445
95691	West Sacramento	(916)	28,898	24,482
*90606	West Whittier-Los Nietos(u)	(310)	24,164	21,001
*90605	Whittier	(310)	77,671	68,558
92395	Wildomar(u)		10,411	....
95429	Willits	(707)	5,027	4,008
90222	Willowbrook(u)	(213)	32,772	30,845
95988	Willows	(916)	5,988	4,777
95492	Windsor(u)		13,371	....
95388	Winton(u)		7,559	4,995
92502	Woodcrest(u)		7,796	....
93286	Woodlake	(209)	5,678	4,343
95695	Woodland	(916)	40,230	30,235
94062	Woodside	(415)	5,034	5,291
92686	Yorba Linda	(714)	52,422	28,254
96097	Yreka City	(916)	6,948	5,916
95991	Yuba City	(916)	27,437	18,736
92399	Yucaipa(u)	(714)	32,824	27,654
92284	Yucca Valley(u)	(619)	13,701	8,294

Colorado

ZIP code	Place		1990	1980
80840	Air Force Academy	(719)	9,062	8,655
81101	Alamosa	(719)	7,579	6,830
80401	Applewood(u)	(303)	11,069	12,040
*80001	Arvada	(303)	89,218	84,576
81611	Aspen	(303)	5,049	3,678
*80010	Aurora	(303)	222,103	158,588
.....	Black Forest(u)	(719)	8,143	3,372
*80302	Boulder	(303)	83,295	76,685
80601	Brighton	(303)	14,203	12,773
80020	Broomfield	(303)	24,638	20,730
81212	Canon City	(719)	12,687	13,037
80104	Castle Rock	(303)	8,710	3,921
.....	Castlewood(u)	(303)	24,392	16,413
80110	Cherry Hills Village	(303)	5,245	5,127
81220	Cimarron Hills	(719)	11,160	6,597
81520	Clifton	(303)	12,671	5,223
*80901	Colorado Springs	(719)	281,140	215,105
80120	Columbine	(303)	23,969	23,523
80022	Commerce City	(303)	16,466	16,234
81321	Cortez	(303)	7,284	7,095
81625	Craig	(303)	8,091	8,133
*80817	Denver	(303)	467,610	492,686
80022	Derby(u)	(303)	6,043	8,578
81301	Durango	(303)	12,439	11,649
*80110	Englewood	(303)	29,396	30,021
80620	Evans	(303)	5,877	5,063
80439	Evergreen	(303)	7,582	6,376
80221	Federal Heights	(303)	9,342	7,838
80913	Fort Carson(u)	(719)	11,309	13,219
*80521	Fort Collins	(303)	87,491	65,092
80621	Fort Lupton	(303)	5,159	4,251
80701	Fort Morgan	(303)	9,068	8,768
80817	Fountain	(719)	10,175	8,324
81504	Fruitvale(u)		5,222	....
81522	Gateway(u)	(303)	7,510	....
81601	Glenwood Springs	(303)	6,561	4,637
80401	Golden	(303)	13,127	12,237
81501	Grand Junction	(303)	29,255	27,956
*80631	Greeley	(303)	60,454	53,006
80110	Greenwood Village	(303)	7,589	5,729
80501	Gunbarrel(u)	(303)	9,388	5,172
80126	Highlands Ranch(u)		10,181	....
.....	Ken Caryl	(303)	24,391	10,661
80026	Lafayette	(303)	14,708	8,985
81050	La Junta	(719)	7,678	8,338
80215	Lakewood	(303)	126,475	113,808
81052	Lamar	(719)	8,343	7,713
*80120	Littleton	(303)	33,711	28,631
80501	Longmont	(303)	51,529	42,942
80027	Louisville	(303)	12,363	5,593
*80537	Loveland	(303)	37,357	30,215
81401	Montrose	(303)	8,854	8,722
80233	Northglenn	(303)	27,195	29,847
80649	Orchard Mesa(u)		5,977	4,876
80134	Parker	(303)	5,450	290
*81003	Pueblo	(719)	98,640	101,686
.....	Redlands(u)		9,355	....
80911	Security-Widefield(u)	(719)	23,822	18,768
80221	Sherrelwood(u)	(303)	16,636	17,629
80122	Southglenn(u)	(303)	43,087	37,787
80477	Steamboat Springs	(303)	6,695	5,098
80751	Sterling	(303)	10,362	11,385
80906	Stratmoor(u)	(719)	5,854	5,519
80229	Thornton	(303)	55,031	42,054
81082	Trinidad	(719)	8,580	9,663
80229	Welby(u)	(303)	10,218	9,668
*80030	Westminster	(303)	74,619	50,211
80221	Westminster East(u)	(303)	5,197	6,002
80033	Wheat Ridge	(303)	29,419	30,293
80550	Windsor	(303)	5,062	4,277

Connecticut (203)

See Note on Page 373

ZIP code	Place	1990	1980
06401	Ansonia	18,403	19,039
06001	*Avon*	13,937	11,201
06403	*Beacon Falls*	5,083	.....
06037	*Berlin*	16,787	15,121
06801	*Bethel*	17,541	16,004
06002	*Bloomfield*	19,483	18,608
06405	*Branford*	27,603	23,363
*06602	Bridgeport	141,686	142,546
06010	Bristol	60,640	57,370
06804	*Brookfield*	14,113	12,872
06234	*Brooklyn*	6,681	5,691
06013	*Burlington*	7,026	5,660
06019	*Canton*	8,268	7,635
06040	Central Manchester(u)	30,934	21,103
06410	*Cheshire*	25,684	21,788
06413	*Clinton*	12,767	11,195
06415	*Colchester*	10,980	7,761
06340	Conning Towers-Nautilus Park(u)	10,013	9,665
06238	*Coventry*	10,063	8,895
06416	*Cromwell*	12,286	10,265
06810	Danbury	65,585	60,470
06820	Darien	18,130	18,892
06418	Derby	12,199	12,346
06422	*Durham*	5,732	5,143
06423	*East Haddam*	6,676	5,621
06424	*East Hampton*	10,428	8,572
06108	*East Hartford*	50,452	52,563
06512	*East Haven*	26,144	25,028
06333	*East Lyme*	13,870	11,399
06016	*East Windsor*	10,081	8,925
06425	*Easton*	6,303	5,962
06029	*Ellington*	11,197	9,711
06082	*Enfield*	45,532	42,695
06426	*Essex*	5,904	5,078
06430	*Fairfield*	53,418	54,849
06032	*Farmington*	20,608	16,407
06033	*Glastonbury Center*	27,901	24,327
06035	*Granby*	9,369	7,956
06830	*Greenwich*	58,441	59,578
06351	*Griswold*	10,384	8,967
06340	*Groton*	45,144	41,062
06340	Groton Borough	9,837	10,086
06437	*Guilford*	19,848	17,375
06438	*Haddam*	6,769	6,383
06514	*Hamden*	52,434	51,071
*06101	Hartford	139,739	136,392
06791	*Harwinton*	5,228	.....
06082	Hazardville(u)	5,179	5,436
06248	Hebron	7,079	5,453
06037	Kensington(u)	8,306	7,502
06239	*Killingly*	15,889	14,519
06249	Lebanon	6,041	.....
06339	*Ledyard*	14,913	13,735
06759	*Litchfield*	8,365	7,365

ZIP code	Place	1990	1980
06443	Madison	14,031	9,768
06040	Manchester	49,761	51,618
06250	Mansfield	20,634	19,994
06447	Marlborough	5,535	.....
06450	Meriden	59,479	57,118
06762	Middlebury	6,145	5,995
06457	Middletown	42,762	39,040
06460	Milford	49,938	48,168
06468	Monroe	16,896	14,010
06353	Montville	16,673	16,455
06770	Naugatuck	30,625	26,456
*06050	New Britain	75,491	73,840
06840	New Canaan	17,864	17,931
06810	New Fairfield	12,911	11,260
06057	New Hartford	5,769	....
*06510	New Haven	130,474	126,089
06111	Newington	29,208	28,841
06320	New London	28,540	28,842
06776	New Milford	23,629	19,420
06470	Newtown	20,779	19,107
06471	North Branford	12,996	11,554
06473	North Haven	22,249	22,080
06856	Norwalk	78,331	77,767
06360	Norwich	37,391	38,074
06779	Oakville(u)	8,741	8,737
06371	Old Lyme	6,535	6,159
06475	Old Saybrook	9,552	9,287
06477	Orange	12,830	13,237
06483	Oxford	8,685	.....
02891	Pawcatuck(u)	5,289	5,216
06374	Plainfield	14,363	17,392
06062	Plainville	16,401	16,733
06782	Plymouth	11,832	10,732
06480	Portland	8,418	8,383
06360	Preston	5,006	.....
06712	Prospect	7,775	6,807
06260	Putnam	6,835	6,855
.....	Putnam	9,031	8,580
06875	Redding	7,927	7,272
06877	Ridgefield Center(u)	6,363	6,066
06877	Ridgefield	20,919	20,120
06067	Rocky Hill	16,554	14,559
06483	Seymour	14,288	13,434
06484	Shelton	35,418	31,314
06082	Sherwood Manor(u)	6,357	6,303
06070	Simsbury	22,023	21,161
06071	Somers	9,108	.....
06488	Southbury	15,818	14,156
06489	Southington	38,518	36,879
06074	South Windsor	22,090	17,198
06082	Southwood Acres(u)	8,963	9,779
06075	Stafford	11,091	9,268
*06904	Stamford	108,056	102,466
06378	Stonington	16,919	6,220
06268	Storrs(u)	12,198	11,394
06497	Stratford	49,389	50,541
06078	Suffield	11,427	9,294
06786	Terryville(u)	5,426	5,234
06787	Thomaston	6,947	6,272
06277	Thompson	8,668	8,141
06082	Thompsonville(u)	8,458	....
06084	Tolland	11,001	9,694
06790	Torrington	33,687	30,987
06611	Trumbull	32,016	32,989
06066	Vernon	29,841	27,974
06492	Wallingford	40,822	37,274
*06701	Waterbury	108,961	103,266
06385	Waterford	17,930	17,843
06795	Watertown	20,456	19,489
06107	West Hartford	60,110	61,301
06516	West Haven	54,021	53,184
06498	Westbrook	5,414	5,216
06883	Weston	8,648	8,284
06880	Westport	24,410	24,407
06109	Wethersfield	25,651	25,651
06226	Willimantic	14,746	14,652
06279	Willington	5,979	.....
06897	Wilton	15,989	15,351
06094	Winchester	11,524	10,841
06280	Windham	22,039	21,062
06095	Windsor	27,817	25,204
06096	Windsor Locks	12,358	12,190
06098	Winsted	8,254	8,092
06716	Wolcott	13,700	13,008
06525	Woodbridge	7,924	7,761
06798	Woodbury	8,131	6,942
06281	Woodstock	6,008	5,117

Delaware (302)

ZIP code	Place	1990	1980
19713	Brookside(u)	15,307	15,255
19703	Claymont(u)	9,800	10,022
19901	Dover	27,630	23,507
19802	Edgemoor(u)	5,853	7,397
19805	Elsmere	5,935	6,493
19963	Milford	6,032	5,366
*19711	Newark	26,463	25,247
19800	Pike Creek(u)	10,163	....
19973	Seaford	5,689	5,256
19977	Smyrna	5,231	4,750
19804	Stanton(u)	5,028	5,495
19803	Talleyville(u)	6,346	6,880
*19899	Wilmington	71,529	70,195
19720	Wilmington Manor	8,568	9,233

District of Columbia (202)

ZIP code	Place	1990	1980
*20013	Washington	606,900	638,432

Florida

ZIP code	Place	Area code	1990	1980
*32701	Altamonte Springs	(407)	35,167	21,105
.....	Andover(u)		6,251	....
33572	Apollo Beach(u)		6,025	4,014
32703	Apopka	(407)	13,611	6,019
33821	Arcadia	(813)	6,488	6,002
32233	Atlantic Beach	(904)	11,636	7,847
33823	Auburndale	(813)	8,858	6,501
.....	Aventura(u)	(305)	14,914	9,698
33825	Avon Park	(813)	8,078	8,026
32807	Azalea Park(u)	(407)	8,926	8,301
33830	Bartow	(813)	14,716	14,780
.....	Bay Hill(u)		5,346	....
34667	Bayonet Point(u)	(813)	21,860	16,455
33505	Bayshore Gardens(u)	(813)	17,062	14,945
33589	Beacon Square(u)	(813)	6,265	6,513
.....	Bee Ridge		6,406	3,313
32073	Bellair-Meadowbrook Terrace(u)	(813)	15,606	12,144
33430	Belle Glade	(407)	16,177	16,535
.....	Belle Isle		5,272	2,848
32506	Belleview	(904)	19,386	15,439
32665	Beverly Hills(u)	(904)	6,163	5,024
.....	Bloomingdale(u)		13,912	....
.....	Boca Del Mar(u)		17,754	....
*33487	Boca Raton	(407)	61,486	49,447
33959	Bonita Springs(u)	(813)	13,600	5,435
*33435	Boynton Beach	(407)	46,284	35,624
*34206	Bradenton	(813)	43,769	30,228
33511	Brandon(u)	(813)	57,985	41,826
32525	Brent(u)	(904)	21,624	21,872
33317	Broadview Park(u)	(305)	6,109	6,022
33313	Broadview-Pompano Park(u)	(305)	5,230	5,256
*34601	Brooksville	(904)	7,589	5,582
33311	Browardale(u)	(305)	6,257	7,571
33142	Brownsville(u)	(813)	15,607	18,058
34743	Buena Ventura Lakes(u)		14,148	....
32401	Callaway	(904)	12,253	7,154
32920	Cape Canaveral	(407)	8,014	5,733
33904	Cape Coral	(813)	74,991	32,103
33055	Carol City(u)	(305)	53,331	47,349
33688	Carrollwood(u)	(813)	7,195	....
.....	Carrollwood Village(u)		15,051	....
32707	Casselberry	(407)	18,911	15,037
33401	Century Village(u)	(305)	8,363	10,619
*34615	Clearwater City	(813)	98,784	85,170
32711	Clermont	(904)	6,910	5,461
33440	Clewiston	(813)	6,085	5,219
32922	Cocoa	(407)	17,722	16,096
32931	Cocoa Beach	(407)	12,123	10,926
32922	Cocoa West(u)	(407)	6,160	6,432
33066	Coconut Creek	(305)	27,484	6,288
33064	Collier Manor-Cresthaven(u)	(305)	7,322	7,045
33801	Combee Settlement(u)	(813)	5,463	5,400
32809	Conway(u)	(407)	13,159	24,027
33314	Cooper City	(305)	21,335	10,140
33134	Coral Gables	(305)	40,091	43,241
33065	Coral Springs	(305)	79,443	37,349
.....	Coral Terrace(u)	(305)	23,255	22,702
32536	Crestview	(904)	9,886	7,617
33803	Crystal Lake(u)	(813)	5,300	6,827
33157	Cutler(u)	(305)	16,201	15,593
33157	Cutler Ridge(u)	(305)	21,268	20,886
33880	Cypress Gardens(u)	(813)	9,188	8,043
.....	Cypress Lake(u)	(813)	10,491	8,721
33525	Dade City	(904)	5,633	4,923
33004	Dania	(305)	13,183	11,796
33314	Davie	(305)	47,835	20,515
*32015	Daytona Beach	(904)	61,991	54,176
32713	De Bary	(407)	7,176	4,980
33441	Deerfield Beach	(305)	46,997	39,193
32433	DeFuniak Springs	(904)	5,200	5,563
32720	De Land	(904)	16,622	15,354
*33444	Delray Beach	(407)	47,181	34,329
33617	Del Rio(u)	(813)	8,248	7,409
32725	Deltona(u)	(407)	50,828	15,710
32541	Destin	(904)	8,090	3,913
.....	Doctor Phillips(u)		7,963	....
*34698	Dunedin	(813)	33,997	30,203
33610	East Lake-Orient Park(u)	(813)	6,171	5,612
33940	East Naples(u)	(813)	22,951	12,127
32032	Edgewater	(904)	15,351	6,726
32542	Eglin AFB(u)	(904)	8,347	7,574

ZIP code	Place		1990	1980
33614	Egypt Lake(u)	(813)	14,580	11,932
34680	Elfers(u)	(813)	12,356	11,396
*34223	Englewood(u)	(813)	15,025	10,229
32504	Ensley(u)	(904)	16,362	14,422
32726	Eustis	(904)	12,867	9,453
32804	Fairview Shores(u)	(305)	13,192	10,174
32034	Fernandina Beach	(904)	8,765	7,224
32730	Fern Park(u)	(407)	8,294	8,890
32504	Ferry Pass(u)	(904)	26,301	16,910
33030	Florida City	(305)	5,978	6,174
.....	Florida Ridge		12,218	4,988
32751	Forest City(u)	(407)	10,638	6,819
.....	Forest Island Park(u)		5,988	....
*33319	Fort Lauderdale	(305)	149,238	153,279
*33901	Fort Myers	(813)	45,206	36,638
33931	Fort Myers Beach(u)	(813)	9,284	5,753
.....	Fort Myers Shores(u)		5,460	4,426
*34950	Fort Pierce	(407)	36,830	33,802
33452	Fort Pierce North(u)	(407)	5,833	5,929
.....	Fort Pierce South(u)	(407)	5,320	3,324
32548	Fort Walton Beach	(904)	21,407	20,829
.....	Fruit Cove(u)		5,904	3,906
.....	Fruitville(u)	(813)	9,808	3,070
*32601	Gainesville	(904)	85,075	81,371
33801	Gibsonia(u)	(813)	5,168	5,011
33534	Gibsonton(u)	(813)	7,706	....
32960	Gifford(u)	(407)	6,278	6,240
.....	Gladeview(u)	(305)	15,637	18,919
33143	Glenvar Heights(u)	(305)	14,823	13,216
33999	Golden Gate(u)		14,148	4,327
33055	Golden Glades(u)	(305)	25,474	23,154
32733	Goldenrod(u)	(407)	12,362	13,681
32560	Gonzalez(u)	(904)	7,669	6,084
33170	Goulds(u)	(305)	7,284	7,078
.....	Greater Northdale(u)		16,318	....
33463	Greenacres City	(407)	18,683	8,870
32561	Gulf Breeze	(904)	5,530	5,478
33581	Gulf Gate Estates(u)	(813)	11,622	9,248
33707	Gulfport	(813)	11,709	11,180
33844	Haines City	(813)	11,683	10,799
33009	Hallandale	(305)	30,997	36,460
.....	Hammocks(u)		10,897	....
.....	Hamptons at Boca Raton(u)		11,686	....
*33010	Hialeah	(305)	188,008	145,254
33016	Hialeah Gardens		7,727	2,700
.....	Highpoint		13,818	....
33455	Hobe Sound(u)	(407)	11,507	6,822
34690	Holiday(u)	(813)	19,360	18,392
32017	Holly Hill	(904)	11,141	9,953
*33022	Hollywood	(305)	121,720	121,323
33030	Homestead	(305)	26,694	20,668
33030	Homestead AFB	(305)	5,153	7,594
32646	Homosassa Springs(u)		6,271	1,426
34667	Hudson(u)	(813)	7,344	5,799
33934	Immokalee(u)	(813)	14,120	11,038
32937	Indian Harbour Beach	(407)	6,933	5,967
32650	Inverness	(904)	5,797	4,095
33880	Inwood(u)	(813)	6,824	6,668
.....	Iona(u)		9,565	....
33162	Ives Estates(u)	(305)	13,531	12,623
32250	Jacksonville Beach	(904)	17,839	15,462
*32201	Jacksonville	(904)	635,230	540,920
.....	Jan Phyl Village(u)		5,308	2,785
33568	Jasmine Estates(u)	(813)	17,136	11,995
*34957	Jensen Beach(u)	(407)	9,884	6,639
33458	Jupiter	(407)	24,907	9,868
33183	Kendale Lakes(u)	(305)	48,524	32,769
33156	Kendall(u)	(305)	87,271	73,758
.....	Kendall Lakes West	(305)	6,038	....
33149	Key Biscayne(u)	(305)	8,854	6,313
33037	Key Largo(u)	(305)	11,336	7,447
33040	Key West	(305)	24,832	24,382
.....	Kings Point(u)	(305)	12,422	8,724
32741	Kissimmee	(407)	30,050	15,487
32159	Lady Lake		8,071	1,193
32055	Lake City	(904)	9,626	9,257
*33802	Lakeland	(813)	70,576	47,406
33801	Lakeland Highlands(u)	(813)	9,972	10,426
.....	Lake Lorraine(u)	(904)	6,779	5,427
33054	Lake Lucerne(u)	(305)	9,478	9,762
33612	Lake Magdalene(u)	(813)	15,973	13,331
32746	Lake Mary	(407)	5,929	2,853
33403	Lake Park	(407)	6,704	6,909
.....	Lakes by the Bay(u)		5,615	....
.....	Lakeside(u)	(904)	29,137	10,534
33853	Lake Wales	(813)	9,670	8,466
.....	Lakewood Park(u)		7,211	3,411
33460	Lake Worth	(407)	28,564	27,048
34639	Land O' Lakes(u)		7,892	4,515
33460	Lantana	(407)	8,392	8,048
*34640	Largo	(813)	65,910	57,958
33313	Lauderdale Lakes	(305)	27,341	25,426
33313	Lauderhill	(305)	49,708	37,271
34272	Laurel(u)	(813)	8,245	6,368
33717	Lealman(u)	(813)	21,748	19,873
32748	Leesburg	(904)	14,903	13,191
*33936	Lehigh Acres(u)	(813)	13,611	9,604
33033	Leisure City(u)	(305)	19,379	17,905
33064	Lighthouse Point	(305)	10,378	11,488
.....	Lindgren Acres(u)	(305)	22,290	11,986
32060	Live Oak	(904)	6,332	6,732
32810	Lockhart(u)	(407)	11,636	10,569
34228	Longboat Key	(813)	5,937	4,843
*32750	Longwood	(407)	13,316	10,029
33549	Lutz(u)	(813)	10,552	5,555
32444	Lynn Haven	(904)	9,298	6,239
.....	McGregor(u)		6,504	....
32751	Maitland	(407)	8,932	8,763
33550	Mango(u)	(813)	8,700	6,493
33050	Marathon(u)	(305)	8,857	7,568
33937	Marco(u)		9,493	4,679
33063	Margate	(305)	42,985	35,900
32446	Marianna	(904)	6,292	7,006
*32901	Melbourne	(407)	60,034	46,536
33314	Melrose Park(u)	(904)	6,477	5,662
33561	Memphis(u)	(813)	6,760	5,501
32952	Merritt Island(u)	(407)	32,886	30,708
*33152	Miami	(305)	358,648	346,681
33139	Miami Beach	(305)	92,639	96,298
33023	Miami Gardens —Utopia-Carver(u)	(305)	7,448	9025
33014	Miami Lakes(u)	(305)	12,750	9,809
33153	Miami Shores	(305)	10,084	9,244
33166	Miami Springs	(305)	13,268	12,350
.....	Micco(u)		8,757	....
32068	Middleburg(u)		6,223	3,585
32570	Milton	(904)	7,216	7,206
32754	Mims(u)	(407)	9,412	7,583
33023	Miramar	(305)	40,663	32,813
32757	Mount Dora	(904)	7,316	5,883
32506	Myrtle Grove(u)	(904)	17,402	14,238
*33962	Naples	(813)	19,505	17,581
33940	Naples Park(u)	(813)	8,002	5,438
33032	Naranja(u)	(305)	5,790	10,381
32233	Neptune Beach	(904)	6,816	5,248
*34652	New Port Richey	(813)	14,044	11,196
33552	New Port Richey East(u)	(813)	9,683	6,147
32169	New Smyrna Beach	(904)	16,549	13,557
32578	Niceville	(904)	10,509	8,543
33169	Norland(u)	(305)	22,109	19,471
33308	North Andrews Gardens(u)	(305)	9,002	8,967
33141	North Bay Village		5,383	4,920
33903	North Fort Myers(u)	(813)	30,027	22,808
33068	North Lauderdale	(305)	26,473	18,479
33161	North Miami	(305)	50,001	42,566
33160	North Miami Beach	(305)	35,361	36,553
33940	North Naples(u)	(813)	13,422	7,950
33408	North Palm Beach	(407)	11,284	11,344
33596	North Port	(813)	11,973	6,205
.....	North Sarasota(u)		6,702	4,997
33860	Oak Ridge(u)	(813)	15,388	15,477
33307	Oakland Park	(305)	26,326	22,944
32670	Ocala	(904)	42,045	37,170
32548	Ocean City(u)	(904)	5,422	5,582
32761	Ocoee	(407)	12,778	7,803
33163	Ojus(u)	(305)	15,519	17,344
34677	Oldsmar		8,361	2,608
33165	Olympia Heights(u)	(305)	37,792	33,112
33054	Opa-Locka	(305)	15,283	14,460
33054	Opa-Locka North(u)	(305)	6,568	5,721
32774	Orange City		5,347	2,795
32073	Orange Park	(904)	9,488	8,766
*32820	Orlando	(407)	164,674	128,291
32811	Orlovista(u)	(407)	5,990	6,474
32176	Ormond Beach	(904)	29,721	21,438
32074	Ormond By-The-Sea(u)	(904)	8,157	7,665
32765	Oviedo	(407)	11,114	3,074
32570	Pace(u)	(904)	6,277	5,006
.....	Page Park-Pine Manor(u)		5,116	5,006
33476	Pahokee	(407)	6,822	6,346
32077	Palatka	(904)	10,444	10,175
32905	Palm Bay	(407)	62,543	18,560
33480	Palm Beach	(407)	9,814	9,729
33403	Palm Beach Gardens	(407)	22,990	14,407
32135	Palm Coast(u)		14,287	2,837
34221	Palmetto	(813)	9,268	8,637
33157	Palmetto Estates(u)	(305)	12,293	11,116
*34683	Palm Harbor(u)	(813)	50,256	5,215
33619	Palm River-Clair Mel(u)	(813)	13,691	14,447
33460	Palm Springs	(407)	9,763	8,166
33012	Palm Springs North(u)	(407)	5,300	5,838
.....	Palm Valley		9,960	....
32401	Panama City	(904)	34,396	33,346
33023	Pembroke Pines	(305)	65,566	35,776
*32502	Pensacola	(904)	58,198	57,619
33157	Perrine(u)	(305)	15,576	16,129
32347	Perry	(904)	7,151	8,254
32809	Pine Castle(u)	(407)	8,276	9,992
32808	Pine Hills(u)	(407)	35,322	35,771
.....	Pine Island Ridge		5,244	....
*34665	Pinellas Park	(813)	43,571	32,811
33168	Pinewood(u)	(305)	15,518	16,252
*33317	Plantation	(305)	66,692	48,653
33566	Plant City	(813)	22,754	17,064
*33067	Pompano Beach	(305)	72,411	52,618
33064	Pompano Beach Highlands(u)	(305)	17,915	16,154
33950	Port Charlotte(u)	(813)	41,535	25,770
32019	Port Orange	(904)	35,307	18,756

ZIP code	Place		1990	1980
32927	Port St. John(u)		8,933	1,837
34952	Port St. Lucie	(407)	55,866	14,690
34992	Port Salerno(u)		7,786	4,511
33032	Princeton(u)	(305)	7,073	....
*33950	Punta Gorda	(813)	10,637	6,797
32351	Quincy	(904)	7,452	8,591
33156	Richmond Heights(u)	(305)	8,583	8,577
33312	Riverland (u)	(305)	5,376	5,919
33569	Riverview(u)		6,478	....
33404	Riviera Beach	(407)	27,644	26,489
32955	Rockledge	(407)	16,023	11,877
.....	Royal Palm Beach	(407)	15,532	3,423
33570	Ruskin(u)	(813)	6,046	5,117
34695	Safety Harbor	(813)	15,120	6,461
32084	Saint Augustine	(904)	11,692	11,985
34769	Saint Cloud	(407)	12,652	7,840
*33702	Saint Petersburg	(813)	240,318	238,647
33706	Saint Petersburg Beach	(813)	9,200	9,354
.....	San Carlos Park(u)		11,785	3,590
33432	Sandalfoot Cove(u)	(305)	14,214	5,299
32771	Sanford	(407)	32,387	23,176
33957	Sanibel		5,468	3,363
*34236	Sarasota	(813)	50,897	48,868
33577	Sarasota Springs(u)	(813)	16,088	13,860
32937	Satellite Beach	(407)	9,889	9,163
.....	Scott Lake(u)	(305)	14,588	14,154
32958	Sebastian	(407)	10,248	2,831
*33870	Sebring	(813)	8,841	8,736
33584	Seffner(u)		5,371	....
34642	Seminole	(813)	9,251	4,856
33578	Siesta Key(u)	(813)	7,772	7,010
32688	Silver Springs Shores(u)		6,421	3,983
32809	Sky Lake(u)	(407)	6,202	6,692
32703	South Apopka(u)	(407)	6,360	5,687
33505	South Bradenton(u)	(813)	20,398	14,297
32021	South Daytona	(904)	12,488	11,252
33579	Southgate(u)	(813)	7,324	7,322
.....	South Gate Ridge(u)		5,924	4,259
33143	South Miami	(305)	10,404	10,895
33157	South Miami Heights(u)	(305)	30,030	23,559
.....	South Pasadena		5,644	4,188
32937	South Patrick Shores(u)	(407)	10,249	9,816
.....	South Sarasota(u)		5,298	4,267
33595	South Venice(u)	(813)	11,951	8,075
32401	Springfield	(904)	8,715	7,220
34606	Spring Hill(u)	(904)	31,117	6,468
32091	Starke	(904)	5,226	5,306
*34994	Stuart	(407)	11,936	9,467
33573	Sun City Center(u)	(813)	8,326	5,605
33160	Sunny Isles(u)	(305)	11,772	12,564
33304	Sunrise	(305)	64,407	39,681
33139	Sunset(u)	(305)	15,810	13,531
33144	Sweetwater	(305)	13,909	8,067
*32303	Tallahassee	(904)	124,773	81,548
33313	Tamarac	(305)	44,822	29,376
33144	Tamiami(u)	(305)	33,845	17,607
*33625	Tampa	(813)	280,015	271,577
*34689	Tarpon Springs	(813)	17,874	13,251
32778	Tavares	(904)	7,383	4,398
33617	Temple Terrace	(813)	16,444	11,097
32780	Titusville	(407)	39,394	31,910
32505	Town 'n' Country(u)	(813)	60,946	37,834
33706	Treasure Island	(813)	7,266	6,316
32807	Union Park(u)	(407)	6,890	19,175
33620	University West(u)	(904)	23,760	24,514
.....	Upper Grand Lagoon(u)		7,855	3,314
32580	Valparaiso	(904)	6,316	6,142
*34285	Venice	(813)	17,052	12,153
33595	Venice Gardens(u)	(813)	7,701	6,568
32960	Vero Beach	(407)	17,350	16,176
32960	Vero Beach South(u)	(407)	16,973	12,636
.....	Villages of Oriole(u)		5,698	8,724
33901	Villas(u)	(813)	9,898	8,724
32507	Warrington(u)	(904)	16,040	15,792
33314	Washington Park(u)	(305)	6,930	7,240
32703	Wekiva Springs(u)	(407)	23,026	13,386
.....	Wellington(u)		20,670	4,622
33155	Westchester(u)	(305)	29,883	29,272
.....	Westgate-Belvedere Homes(u)		6,880	....
33138	West Little River(u)	(305)	33,575	32,492
32901	West Melbourne	(407)	8,399	5,078
33144	West Miami	(305)	5,727	6,076
*33404	West Palm Beach	(407)	67,764	63,305
.....	West Park(u)		10,347	....
32505	West Pensacola(u)	(904)	22,107	24,371
33168	Westview(u)	(305)	9,668	9,102
33165	Westwood Lakes(u)	(305)	11,522	11,478
.....	Whiskey Creek(u)		5,061	....
33305	Wilton Manors	(305)	11,804	12,742
33803	Winston(u)	(813)	9,118	9,315
*32787	Winter Garden	(407)	9,863	6,789
33880	Winter Haven	(813)	24,725	21,119
*32789	Winter Park	(407)	22,623	22,339
32708	Winter Springs	(407)	22,151	10,475
32548	Wright(u)	(904)	18,945	13,011
32097	Yulee(u)		6,915	....
33599	Zephyrhills	(813)	8,220	5,742

Georgia

ZIP code	Place		1990	1980
31620	Adel	(912)	5,093	5,592
*31701	Albany	(912)	78,804	74,425
30201	Alpharetta		13,002	3,128
31709	Americus	(912)	16,512	16,120
*30601	Athens	(706)	45,734	42,549
*30304	Atlanta	(404)	393,929	425,022
*30901	Augusta	(706)	44,639	47,532
31717	Bainbridge	(912)	10,803	10,553
30032	Belvedere Park(u)	(404)	18,089	17,766
31723	Blakely	(912)	5,595	5,880
31520	Brunswick	(912)	16,433	17,605
30518	Buford	(404)	8,771	6,578
31728	Cairo	(912)	9,035	8,777
30701	Calhoun	(706)	7,135	5,563
31730	Camilla	(912)	5,124	5,414
30032	Candler-McAfee(u)	(404)	29,491	27,306
30117	Carrollton	(404)	16,029	14,078
30120	Cartersville	(404)	12,037	9,247
30125	Cedartown	(404)	7,978	8,619
30341	Chamblee	(404)	7,668	7,137
30021	Clarkston		5,385	4,539
30337	College Park	(404)	20,645	24,632
*31902	Columbus	(706)	178,681	169,441
30027	Conley(u)	(404)	5,528	6,033
30207	Conyers	(404)	7,380	6,567
31015	Cordele	(912)	10,836	11,184
.....	Country Club Estates(u)		7,500	....
30209	Covington	(404)	10,056	10,586
30720	Dalton	(706)	22,213	20,581
31742	Dawson	(912)	5,295	5,699
*30030	Decatur	(404)	17,304	18,404
31520	Dock Junction(u)	(912)	7,094	6,189
30340	Doraville	(404)	7,626	7,414
31533	Douglas	(912)	10,464	10,980
30134	Douglasville	(404)	11,635	7,641
30333	Druid Hills(u)	(404)	12,174	12,700
31021	Dublin	(912)	16,312	16,083
30136	Duluth		9,029	2,956
30338	Dunwoody(u)	(404)	26,302	17,768
31023	Eastman	(912)	5,241	5,330
30344	East Point	(404)	34,595	37,486
30635	Elberton	(706)	5,682	5,686
30809	Evans(u)	(404)	13,713	....
30060	Fair Oaks(u)	(404)	6,996	8,486
30535	Fairview(u)	(404)	6,444	6,558
30214	Fayetteville		5,827	2,715
31750	Fitzgerald	(912)	8,810	10,187
30050	Forest Park	(404)	16,958	18,782
31905	Fort Benning South(u)	(404)	14,617	15,074
30905	Fort Gordon(u)	(404)	9,140	14,069
30741	Fort Oglethorpe	(404)	5,880	5,443
31313	Fort Stewart(u)	(912)	13,774	15,031
31030	Fort Valley	(912)	8,198	9,000
.....	Gaines School(u)		11,354	....
30501	Gainesville	(404)	17,885	15,280
31408	Garden City	(912)	7,410	6,895
31754	Georgetown	(912)	5,554	2,785
30316	Gresham Park(u)	(404)	9,000	6,232
30223	Griffin	(404)	21,347	20,728
30354	Hapeville	(404)	5,483	6,166
31313	Hinesville	(912)	21,596	11,309
31545	Jesup	(912)	8,958	9,418
30144	Kennesaw	(404)	8,936	5,095
31547	Kingsland	(912)	5,474	....
30728	La Fayette	(706)	6,313	6,517
30240	La Grange	(706)	25,574	24,204
.....	Lakeview(u)		5,237	5,403
30245	Lawrenceville	(404)	17,251	8,928
30247	Lilburn		9,301	3,765
30057	Lithia Springs(u)	(404)	11,403	9,145
30059	Mableton(u)	(404)	25,725	25,111
*31201	Macon	(912)	107,365	116,896
30060	Marietta	(404)	44,129	30,821
30907	Martinez(u)	(404)	33,731	16,472
31061	Milledgeville	(912)	17,727	12,176
30655	Monroe	(404)	9,759	8,854
30260	Morrow		5,168	3,791
31768	Moultrie	(912)	14,865	15,105
30075	Mountain Park(u)	(404)	11,025	9,425
30263	Newnan	(404)	12,497	11,449
30091	Norcross	(404)	5,947	3,363
30319	North Atlanta(u)	(404)	27,812	30,521
30033	North Decatur(u)	(404)	13,936	11,830
30033	North Druid Hills(u)	(404)	14,170	12,438
30032	Panthersville(u)	(404)	9,874	11,366
30269	Peachtree City	(404)	19,027	6,429
31069	Perry	(912)	9,452	9,453
30073	Powder Springs		6,862	3,381
31643	Quitman	(912)	5,292	5,188
30074	Redan(u)		24,376	....
*30274	Riverdale	(404)	9,455	7,121
30161	Rome	(706)	30,326	28,915
30075	Roswell	(404)	47,923	23,337
31558	Saint Marys		8,204	3,596
31522	Saint Simons Island(u)	(912)	12,026	6,566
31082	Sandersville	(912)	6,290	6,137

ZIP code	Place		1990	1980
30328	Sandy Springs(u)	(404)	67,842	46,877
*31401	Savannah	(912)	137,812	141,654
30079	Scottdale(u)	(404)	8,636	8,770
30080	Smyrna	(404)	30,981	20,312
30278	Snellville	(404)	12,084	8,514
30901	South Augusta(u)	(404)	55,998	51,072
30458	Statesboro	(912)	15,854	14,866
30086	Stone Mountain		6,494	4,867
30747	Summerville	(706)	5,025	4,878
30401	Swainsboro	(912)	7,361	7,602
31791	Sylvester	(912)	6,023	5,860
30286	Thomaston	(706)	9,127	9,682
31792	Thomasville	(912)	17,554	18,463
30824	Thomson	(706)	6,862	7,001
31794	Tifton	(912)	14,215	13,749
30577	Toccoa	(706)	8,530	8,869
30084	Tucker(u)	(404)	25,781	25,399
30291	Union City	(404)	8,887	4,780
31601	Valdosta	(912)	40,038	37,596
30474	Vidalia	(912)	11,118	10,393
30180	Villa Rica		6,542	3,420
.....	Vinings(u)		7,417	....
31093	Warner Robins	(912)	43,861	39,893
31501	Waycross	(912)	16,410	19,371
30830	Waynesboro	(706)	5,669	5,760
30901	West Augusta(u)	(404)	27,637	24,242
31410	Wilmington Island(u)	(912)	11,230	7,546
30680	Winder	(404)	7,373	6,705

Hawaii (808)

See Note on Page 373

ZIP code	Place	1990	1980
96706	Aiea	8,906	32,879
.....	Aliamanu	8,835	....
96706	Ewa	14,315	14,369
.....	Halawa	13,408	....
.....	Heeia	5,010	5,432
.....	Hickman	6,553	4,425
96720	Hilo	37,808	35,269
*96815	Honolulu	365,272	365,048
96732	Kahului	16,889	12,978
96734	Kailua	9,126	4,751
96863	Kailua	36,818	35,812
96744	Kaneohe	35,448	29,919
.....	Kaneohe Station	11,662	....
96746	Kapaa	8,149	4,467
96753	Kihei	11,107	5,644
96761	Lahaina	9,073	6,095
96762	Laie	5,577	4,643
96766	Lihue	5,536	4,000
.....	Maili	6,059	5,026
.....	Makaha	7,990	6,582
.....	Makailo	9,828	7,691
96768	Makawao-Paia	5,405	2,900
96789	Mililani Town	29,359	21,365
96792	Nanakuli	9,575	8,185
96782	Pearl City	30,993	42,575
96788	Pukalani	5,879	3,950
.....	Schofield Barracks	19,597	....
.....	Village Park	7,407	18,851
96786	Wahiawa	17,386	16,911
96792	Waianae	8,758	7,941
96793	Wailuku	10,688	10,260
.....	Waimalu	29,967	....
96796	Waimea	5,972	1,179
96797	Waipahu	31,435	29,139
.....	Waipio	11,812	....
.....	Waipio Acre	5,304	4,091

Idaho (208)

ZIP code	Place	1990	1980
83401	Ammon	5,002	4,669
83221	Blackfoot	9,646	10,065
*83708	Boise City	125,551	102,249
83318	Burley	8,702	8,761
83605	Caldwell	18,400	17,699
83201	Chubbuck	7,794	7,052
83814	Coeur D'Alene	24,563	19,913
83714	Garden City	6,369	4,571
*83401	Idaho Falls	43,929	39,739
83338	Jerome	6,529	6,891
83501	Lewiston	28,082	27,986
83642	Meridian	9,596	6,658
83843	Moscow	18,519	16,513
83647	Mountain Home	7,913	7,540
83648	Mountain Home AFB(u)	5,936	6,403
*83651	Nampa	28,365	25,112
83661	Payette	5,667	5,448
*83201	Pocatello	46,117	46,340
83854	Post Falls	7,349	5,736
83440	Rexburg	14,302	11,559
83350	Rupert	5,455	5,476
83809	Sandpoint	5,203	4,460
83301	Twin Falls	27,591	26,209

Illinois

ZIP code	Place		1990	1980
60101	Addison	(708)	32,053	29,826
60102	Algonquin	(708)	11,693	5,834
60658	Alsip	(708)	18,227	17,134
62002	Alton	(618)	33,064	34,171
60002	Antioch	(708)	6,105	4,419
*60004	Arlington Heights	(708)	75,462	66,116
*60507	Aurora	(708)	99,556	81,293
60010	Barrington	(708)	9,538	9,029
60103	Bartlett	(708)	19,373	13,254
61607	Bartonville	(309)	5,643	6,137
60510	Batavia	(708)	17,076	12,574
.....	Beach Park	(708)	9,513	8,468
62618	Beardstown	(217)	5,270	6,338
*62220	Belleville	(618)	42,806	41,580
60104	Bellwood	(708)	20,241	19,811
61008	Belvidere	(815)	15,962	15,176
60106	Bensenville	(708)	17,767	16,106
62812	Benton	(618)	7,216	7,778
60162	Berkeley	(708)	5,137	5,467
60402	Berwyn	(708)	45,426	46,849
62010	Bethalto	(618)	9,507	8,630
60108	Bloomingdale	(708)	16,614	12,656
61701	Bloomington	(309)	51,889	44,189
60406	Blue Island	(708)	21,203	21,855
60439	Bolingbrook	(708)	40,843	37,261
60538	Boulder Hill(u)	(708)	8,894	9,333
60914	Bourbonnais	(815)	13,927	13,280
60915	Bradley	(815)	10,910	11,015
60455	Bridgeview	(708)	14,402	14,155
60153	Broadview	(708)	8,538	8,618
60513	Brookfield	(708)	18,876	19,395
60089	Buffalo Grove	(708)	36,398	22,230
60459	Burbank	(708)	27,600	28,462
60521	Burr Ridge	(708)	7,669	3,838
62206	Cahokia	(618)	17,550	18,904
60409	Calumet City	(708)	37,840	39,697
60643	Calumet Park	(708)	8,418	8,788
61520	Canton	(309)	13,959	14,626
62901	Carbondale	(618)	27,033	26,414
62626	Carlinville	(217)	5,416	5,439
62821	Carmi	(618)	5,626	6,107
60187	Carol Stream	(708)	31,759	15,472
60110	Carpentersville	(708)	23,049	23,272
60013	Cary	(708)	10,043	6,640
62801	Centralia	(618)	14,274	15,126
62206	Centreville	(618)	7,489	9,747
61820	Champaign	(217)	63,502	58,267
61920	Charleston	(217)	20,398	19,355
62629	Chatham	(217)	6,074	5,597
62233	Chester	(618)	8,204	8,401
*60607	Chicago	(312)	2,783,726	3,005,072
60411	Chicago Heights	(708)	32,966	37,026
60415	Chicago Ridge	(708)	13,643	13,473
61523	Chillicothe	(309)	5,959	6,176
60650	Cicero	(708)	67,436	61,232
60514	Clarendon Hills	(708)	6,994	6,870
61727	Clinton	(217)	7,437	8,014
62234	Collinsville	(618)	22,424	19,475
62236	Columbia	(618)	5,524	4,269
60477	Country Club Hills	(708)	15,431	14,676
60525	Countryside	(708)	5,961	6,242
60435	Crest Hill	(815)	10,996	9,252
60445	Crestwood	(708)	10,823	10,852
60417	Crete	(708)	6,773	5,417
61611	Creve Coeur	(309)	5,938	6,851
60014	Crystal Lake	(815)	24,696	18,590
61832	Danville	(217)	33,828	38,985
60559	Darien	(708)	18,193	14,956
*62521	Decatur	(217)	83,900	93,939
60015	Deerfield	(708)	17,327	17,432
60115	De Kalb	(815)	35,076	33,157
*60016	Des Plaines	(708)	53,414	53,568
61021	Dixon	(815)	15,134	15,710
60419	Dolton	(708)	23,956	24,766
60515	Downers Grove	(708)	46,845	42,259
62832	Du Quoin	(618)	6,697	6,594
62024	East Alton	(618)	7,063	7,096
61244	East Moline	(309)	20,147	20,907
61611	East Peoria	(309)	21,378	22,385
*62201	East St. Louis	(618)	40,944	55,200
62025	Edwardsville	(618)	14,579	12,480
62401	Effingham	(217)	11,851	11,270
60120	Elgin	(708)	77,010	63,668
60007	Elk Grove Village	(708)	33,429	28,679
60126	Elmhurst	(708)	42,029	44,276
60635	Elmwood Park	(708)	23,206	24,016
*60204	Evanston	(708)	73,233	73,706
60642	Evergreen Park	(708)	20,874	22,260
62837	Fairfield	(618)	5,439	5,944
62208	Fairview Heights	(618)	14,351	12,111
62839	Flora	(618)	5,093	5,379
60422	Flossmoor	(708)	8,651	8,423
60130	Forest Park	(708)	14,918	15,177
60020	Fox Lake	(708)	7,478	6,831
60423	Frankfort		7,180	4,357
.....	Frankfort Square(u)		6,227	....

ZIP code	Place		1990	1980
60131	Franklin Park	(708)	18,485	17,507
61032	Freeport	(815)	25,840	26,266
60030	Gages Lake(u)	(708)	8,349	3,814
61401	Galesburg	(309)	33,530	35,305
61254	Geneseo	(309)	5,990	6,373
60134	Geneva	(708)	12,617	9,881
62034	Glen Carbon	(618)	7,731	5,197
60022	Glencoe	(708)	8,499	9,200
60137	Glendale Heights	(708)	27,973	23,251
60137	Glen Ellyn	(708)	24,944	23,691
60025	Glenview	(708)	37,093	32,060
60425	Glenwood	(708)	9,289	10,538
62002	Godfrey(u)	(618)	5,436	....
.....	Goodings Grove(u)		14,054	....
62040	Granite City	(618)	32,769	36,815
60030	Grays Lake	(708)	7,388	5,260
62246	Greenville	(618)	5,108	....
60031	Gurnee	(708)	13,701	7,179
60103	Hanover Park	(708)	32,895	28,719
62946	Harrisburg	(618)	9,318	10,410
60033	Harvard	(815)	5,975	5,126
60426	Harvey	(708)	29,771	35,810
60656	Harwood Heights	(312)	7,680	8,228
60429	Hazel Crest	(708)	13,334	13,973
62948	Herrin	(618)	10,857	10,708
60457	Hickory Hills	(708)	13,021	13,778
62249	Highland	(618)	7,525	7,122
60035	Highland Park	(708)	30,575	30,599
60040	Highwood	(708)	5,331	5,455
60162	Hillside	(708)	7,672	8,279
60521	Hinsdale	(708)	16,029	16,726
60172	Hoffman Estates	(708)	46,363	37,272
60430	Homewood	(708)	19,278	19,724
60942	Hoopeston	(217)	5,871	6,411
60067	Inverness	(708)	6,503	4,046
60143	Itasca	(708)	6,947	7,129
62650	Jacksonville	(217)	19,327	20,284
62052	Jerseyville	(618)	7,382	7,506
*60431	Joliet	(815)	76,628	77,956
60458	Justice	(708)	11,137	10,552
60901	Kankakee	(815)	27,531	29,633
61443	Kewanee	(309)	12,969	14,508
60525	La Grange	(708)	15,362	15,693
60525	La Grange Park	(708)	12,861	13,359
60044	Lake Bluff	(708)	5,486	4,434
60045	Lake Forest	(708)	17,836	15,245
60102	Lake in the Hills	(708)	5,866	5,651
60047	Lake Zurich	(708)	14,927	8,225
60438	Lansing	(708)	28,089	29,039
61301	La Salle	(815)	9,717	10,347
60439	Lemont	(708)	7,348	5,640
60048	Libertyville	(708)	19,174	16,520
62656	Lincoln	(217)	15,418	16,327
60645	Lincolnwood	(708)	11,365	11,921
60046	Lindenhurst	(708)	8,038	6,220
60532	Lisle	(708)	19,512	13,638
62056	Litchfield	(217)	6,883	7,204
60441	Lockport	(815)	9,401	9,192
60148	Lombard	(708)	39,408	36,879
61111	Loves Park	(815)	15,462	13,192
60411	Lynwood	(708)	6,535	4,195
60534	Lyons	(708)	9,828	9,925
60050	McHenry	(815)	16,177	10,737
61111	Machesney Park	(815)	19,033	19,514
61455	Macomb	(309)	19,952	19,863
62959	Marion	(618)	14,545	14,031
60426	Markham	(708)	13,136	15,172
62258	Mascoutah	(618)	5,511	4,962
60443	Matteson	(708)	11,378	10,223
61938	Mattoon	(217)	18,441	19,293
60153	Maywood	(708)	27,139	27,998
*60160	Melrose Park	(708)	20,859	20,735
61342	Mendota	(815)	7,018	7,134
62960	Metropolis	(618)	6,734	7,171
60445	Midlothian	(708)	14,372	14,274
61264	Milan	(309)	5,753	6,371
60448	Mokena		6,128	4,578
61265	Moline	(309)	43,127	46,407
61462	Monmouth	(309)	9,489	10,706
60450	Morris	(815)	10,270	8,833
61550	Morton	(309)	13,799	14,178
60053	Morton Grove	(708)	22,373	23,747
62863	Mount Carmel	(618)	8,287	8,908
60056	Mount Prospect	(708)	53,168	52,634
62864	Mount Vernon	(618)	17,080	17,193
60060	Mundelein	(708)	21,215	17,053
62966	Murphysboro	(618)	9,176	9,866
60540	Naperville	(708)	85,351	42,601
60451	New Lenox	(815)	9,618	5,792
60648	Niles	(708)	28,375	30,363
61761	Normal	(309)	40,023	35,672
60656	Norridge	(708)	14,459	16,483
60542	North Aurora	(708)	5,940	5,205
60062	Northbrook	(708)	32,308	30,778
60064	North Chicago	(708)	34,978	38,774
60164	Northlake	(708)	12,505	12,166
60546	North Riverside	(708)	6,180	6,764
60521	Oak Brook	(708)	9,087	6,676
60452	Oak Forest	(708)	26,203	25,040
*60454	Oak Lawn	(708)	56,182	60,590
*60301	Oak Park	(708)	53,648	54,887
62269	O'Fallon	(618)	16,073	12,173
62450	Olney	(618)	8,664	9,026
60477	Orland Hills		5,510	2,784
60462	Orland Park	(708)	35,720	23,045
61350	Ottawa	(815)	17,541	18,166
60067	Palatine	(708)	39,655	32,176
60463	Palos Heights	(708)	11,478	11,096
60465	Palos Hills	(708)	17,803	16,654
62557	Pana	(217)	5,796	6,040
61944	Paris	(217)	9,016	9,885
60466	Park Forest	(708)	24,656	26,222
60068	Park Ridge	(708)	36,175	38,704
61554	Pekin	(309)	32,254	33,967
*61601	Peoria	(309)	113,504	124,160
61614	Peoria Heights	(309)	6,930	7,453
61354	Peru	(815)	9,302	10,886
60545	Plano	(708)	5,104	4,875
61764	Pontiac	(815)	11,428	11,227
61356	Princeton	(815)	7,197	7,342
60070	Prospect Heights	(708)	15,239	11,823
62301	Quincy	(217)	39,681	42,554
61866	Rantoul	(217)	17,212	20,161
60471	Richton Park	(708)	10,523	9,403
60627	Riverdale	(708)	13,671	13,233
60305	River Forest	(708)	11,669	12,392
60171	River Grove	(708)	9,961	10,368
60546	Riverside	(708)	8,774	9,236
60472	Robbins	(708)	7,498	8,853
62454	Robinson	(618)	6,740	7,285
61068	Rochelle	(815)	8,769	8,982
61071	Rock Falls	(815)	9,654	10,633
*61125	Rockford	(815)	139,943	139,712
61201	Rock Island	(309)	40,630	46,821
60008	Rolling Meadows	(708)	22,591	20,167
60441	Romeoville	(815)	14,101	15,519
60172	Roselle	(708)	20,819	17,034
60073	Round Lake Beach	(708)	16,434	12,921
60174	Saint Charles	(708)	22,502	17,492
62881	Salem	(618)	7,470	7,813
60548	Sandwich	(815)	5,607	5,356
60411	Sauk Village	(708)	9,926	10,906
60172	Schaumburg	(708)	68,586	53,355
60176	Schiller Park	(708)	11,189	11,458
62225	Scott AFB(u)	(618)	7,245	8,648
60436	Shorewood	(815)	6,264	4,714
61282	Silvis	(309)	6,926	7,130
60076	Skokie	(708)	59,432	60,278
60177	South Elgin	(708)	7,474	5,970
60473	South Holland	(708)	22,105	24,977
*62703	Springfield	(217)	105,227	100,054
61362	Spring Valley	(815)	5,246	5,822
60475	Steger	(708)	8,584	9,269
61081	Sterling	(815)	15,142	16,281
60402	Stickney	(708)	5,678	5,893
60103	Streamwood	(708)	31,197	23,456
61364	Streator	(815)	14,121	14,795
60501	Summit	(708)	9,971	10,110
62221	Swansea	(618)	8,201	5,529
60178	Sycamore	(815)	9,708	9,219
62568	Taylorville	(217)	11,133	11,386
60477	Tinley Park	(708)	37,121	26,178
62294	Troy	(618)	6,046	3,772
60466	University Park	(708)	6,204	6,245
61801	Urbana	(217)	36,344	35,978
62471	Vandalia	(618)	6,114	5,338
60061	Vernon Hills	(708)	15,319	9,827
60181	Villa Park	(708)	22,253	23,155
60555	Warrenville	(708)	11,390	7,519
61571	Washington	(309)	10,099	10,364
62204	Washington Park	(618)	7,431	8,223
62298	Waterloo	(618)	5,072	4,646
60970	Watseka	(815)	5,424	5,543
60084	Wauconda	(708)	6,294	5,688
60085	Waukegan	(708)	69,392	67,653
60153	Westchester	(708)	17,301	17,730
60185	West Chicago	(708)	14,796	12,550
60558	Western Springs	(708)	11,956	12,876
62896	West Frankfort	(618)	8,526	9,437
60559	Westmont	(708)	21,228	17,353
61604	West Peoria(u)	(309)	5,314	5,219
60187	Wheaton	(708)	51,464	43,043
60090	Wheeling	(708)	29,911	23,266
60514	Willowbrook	(708)	8,701	4,953
60091	Wilmette	(708)	26,694	28,221
60190	Winfield	(708)	7,096	4,422
60093	Winnetka	(708)	12,210	12,772
60096	Winthrop Harbor	(708)	6,240	5,427
60097	Wonder Lake(u)	(815)	6,664	5,917
60191	Wood Dale	(708)	12,425	11,251
60515	Woodridge	(708)	26,256	21,763
62095	Wood River	(618)	11,490	12,446
60098	Woodstock	(815)	14,353	11,725
60482	Worth	(708)	11,208	11,592
60099	Zion	(708)	19,775	17,865

Indiana

ZIP code	Place		1990	1980
46001	Alexandria	(317)	5,709	6,028
46011	Anderson	(317)	59,459	64,695
46703	Angola	(219)	5,851	5,486
46706	Auburn	(219)	9,386	8,122
47421	Bedford	(812)	13,817	14,410
46107	Beech Grove	(317)	13,383	13,196
47401	Bloomington	(812)	60,633	52,663
46714	Bluffton	(219)	9,104	8,705
47601	Boonville	(812)	6,686	6,300
47834	Brazil	(812)	7,640	7,852
46112	Brownsburg	(317)	7,628	6,242
46032	Carmel	(317)	25,380	18,272
46303	Cedar Lake	(219)	8,885	8,754
47111	Charlestown	(812)	5,889	5,596
46304	Chesterton	(219)	9,118	8,531
47130	Clarksville	(812)	19,838	15,164
47842	Clinton	(317)	5,040	5,267
46725	Columbia City	(219)	5,700	5,091
47201	Columbus	(812)	31,802	30,614
47331	Connersville	(317)	15,550	17,023
47933	Crawfordsville	(317)	13,584	13,325
46307	Crown Point	(219)	17,728	16,455
46733	Decatur	(219)	8,642	8,649
46514	Dunlap(u)	(219)	5,705	5,397
46311	Dyer	(219)	10,923	9,555
46312	East Chicago	(219)	33,892	39,786
46514	Elkhart	(219)	43,627	41,305
46036	Elwood	(317)	9,494	10,867
*47708	Evansville	(812)	126,272	130,496
46038	Fishers		7,508	2,008
*46802	Fort Wayne	(219)	172,971	172,391
46041	Frankfort	(317)	14,754	15,168
46131	Franklin	(317)	12,932	11,563
46738	Garrett	(219)	5,349	4,751
*46401	Gary	(219)	116,646	151,968
46933	Gas City	(317)	6,296	6,370
46526	Goshen	(219)	23,794	19,665
46530	Granger(u)		20,241	....
46135	Greencastle	(317)	8,984	8,403
46140	Greenfield	(317)	11,657	11,288
47240	Greensburg	(812)	9,286	9,254
46142	Greenwood	(317)	26,507	19,327
46319	Griffith	(219)	17,914	17,026
*46320	Hammond	(219)	84,236	93,714
47348	Hartford City	(317)	6,960	7,622
46322	Highland	(219)	23,696	25,935
46342	Hobart	(219)	21,822	22,987
47542	Huntingburg	(812)	5,236	5,376
46750	Huntington	(219)	16,389	16,202
*46206	Indianapolis	(317)	731,327	700,807
47546	Jasper	(812)	10,030	9,097
47130	Jeffersonville	(812)	21,968	21,220
46755	Kendallville	(219)	7,773	7,299
46901	Kokomo	(317)	44,996	47,808
*47901	Lafayette	(317)	43,758	43,011
.....	Lakes of the Four Seasons(u)		6,556	....
46405	Lake Station	(219)	13,899	15,087
46350	La Porte	(219)	21,507	21,796
46226	Lawrence	(317)	26,779	25,591
46052	Lebanon	(317)	12,059	11,456
47441	Linton	(812)	5,814	6,315
46947	Logansport	(219)	16,865	17,731
46356	Lowell	(219)	6,430	5,827
47250	Madison	(812)	12,006	12,472
46952	Marion	(317)	32,607	35,874
46151	Martinsville	(317)	11,677	11,311
46410	Merrillville	(219)	27,257	27,677
46360	Michigan City	(219)	33,822	36,850
46544	Mishawaka	(219)	42,635	40,201
47960	Monticello	(219)	5,237	5,162
46158	Mooresville	(317)	5,541	5,349
47620	Mount Vernon	(812)	7,217	7,656
*47302	Muncie	(317)	71,170	77,216
46321	Munster	(219)	19,949	20,671
46550	Nappanee		5,474	4,694
47150	New Albany	(812)	36,322	37,103
47362	New Castle	(317)	17,753	20,056
46774	New Haven	(219)	9,320	6,714
46060	Noblesville	(317)	17,655	12,253
46962	North Manchester	(219)	6,383	5,998
47265	North Vernon	(812)	5,129	5,768
47130	Oak Park(u)	(812)	5,630	5,871
46970	Peru	(317)	12,843	13,764
46168	Plainfield	(317)	10,433	9,191
46563	Plymouth	(219)	8,291	7,693
46368	Portage	(219)	29,062	27,409
47371	Portland	(219)	6,483	7,074
47670	Princeton	(812)	8,127	8,976
47978	Rensselaer	(219)	5,045	4,944
47374	Richmond	(317)	38,705	41,349
46975	Rochester	(219)	5,969	5,050
46173	Rushville	(317)	5,533	6,113
47167	Salem	(812)	5,619	5,290
46375	Schererville	(219)	20,155	13,209
47170	Scottsburg	(812)	5,334	5,068
47172	Sellersburg	(812)	5,914	3,211
47274	Seymour	(812)	15,579	15,050
46176	Shelbyville	(317)	15,347	14,989
*46624	South Bend	(219)	105,511	109,727
46383	South Haven(u)	(219)	6,112	6,679
46224	Speedway	(317)	13,092	12,641
47586	Tell City	(812)	8,088	8,704
*47808	Terre Haute	(812)	57,483	61,125
46383	Valparaiso	(219)	24,414	22,247
47591	Vincennes	(812)	19,867	20,857
46992	Wabash	(219)	12,127	12,985
46580	Warsaw	(219)	10,968	10,647
47501	Washington	(812)	10,864	11,325
47906	West Lafayette	(317)	26,144	21,247
46391	Westville		5,255	2,887
46394	Whiting	(219)	5,155	5,630
47394	Winchester	(317)	5,095	5,659
46077	Zionsville		5,281	3,948

Iowa

ZIP code	Place		1990	1980
50511	Algona	(515)	6,015	6,289
50009	Altoona	(515)	7,242	5,764
50010	Ames	(515)	47,198	45,775
52205	Anamosa	(319)	5,100	4,958
50021	Ankeny	(515)	18,482	15,429
50022	Atlantic	(712)	7,432	7,789
52722	Bettendorf	(319)	28,139	27,381
50036	Boone	(515)	12,392	12,602
52601	Burlington	(319)	27,208	29,529
51401	Carroll	(712)	9,579	9,705
50613	Cedar Falls	(319)	34,298	36,322
*52401	Cedar Rapids	(319)	108,780	110,243
52544	Centerville	(515)	5,936	6,558
50616	Charles City	(515)	7,878	8,778
51012	Cherokee	(712)	6,026	7,004
51632	Clarinda	(712)	5,104	5,458
50428	Clear Lake City	(515)	8,183	7,458
52732	Clinton	(319)	29,201	32,828
50053	Clive	(515)	7,462	6,064
52240	Coralville	(319)	10,347	7,687
51501	Council Bluffs	(712)	54,315	56,449
50801	Creston	(515)	7,911	8,429
*52802	Davenport	(319)	95,333	103,264
52101	Decorah	(319)	8,063	7,991
51442	Denison	(712)	6,604	6,675
*50318	Des Moines	(515)	193,189	191,003
52001	Dubuque	(319)	57,546	62,374
51334	Estherville	(712)	6,720	7,518
52556	Fairfield	(515)	9,768	9,428
50501	Fort Dodge	(515)	25,894	29,423
52627	Fort Madison	(319)	11,618	13,520
50112	Grinnell	(515)	8,902	8,868
51537	Harlan	(712)	5,148	5,357
50644	Independence	(319)	5,972	6,392
50125	Indianola	(515)	11,340	10,843
52240	Iowa City	(319)	59,735	50,508
50126	Iowa Falls	(515)	5,435	6,174
52632	Keokuk	(319)	12,451	13,536
50138	Knoxville	(515)	8,232	8,143
51031	Le Mars	(712)	8,454	8,276
52057	Manchester	(319)	5,137	4,942
52060	Maquoketa	(319)	6,129	6,313
52302	Marion	(319)	20,374	19,474
50158	Marshalltown	(515)	25,178	26,938
50401	Mason City	(515)	29,040	30,144
52641	Mount Pleasant	(319)	8,027	7,322
52761	Muscatine	(319)	22,881	23,467
50201	Nevada	(515)	6,009	5,912
50208	Newton	(515)	14,799	15,292
50211	Norwalk		5,726	2,676
50662	Oelwein	(319)	6,493	7,564
52577	Oskaloosa	(515)	10,600	10,989
52501	Ottumwa	(515)	24,488	27,381
50219	Pella	(515)	9,270	8,349
50220	Perry	(515)	6,652	7,053
51566	Red Oak	(712)	6,264	6,810
51601	Shenandoah	(712)	5,572	6,274
51250	Sioux Center	(712)	5,074	4,588
*51101	Sioux City	(712)	80,505	82,003
51301	Spencer	(712)	11,066	11,726
50588	Storm Lake	(712)	8,769	8,814
50322	Urbandale	(515)	23,500	17,869
52349	Vinton	(319)	5,103	5,040
52353	Washington	(319)	7,074	6,584
*50701	Waterloo	(319)	66,467	75,985
50677	Waverly	(319)	8,539	8,444
50595	Webster City	(515)	7,894	8,572
50265	West Des Moines	(515)	31,702	21,894
50311	Windsor Heights	(515)	5,190	5,474

Kansas

ZIP code	Place		1990	1980
67410	Abilene	(913)	6,242	6,572
67005	Arkansas City	(316)	12,762	13,201
66002	Atchison	(913)	10,656	11,407
67010	Augusta	(316)	7,848	6,968

ZIP code	Place		1990	1980
66012	Bonner Springs	(913)	6,413	6,266
66720	Chanute	(316)	9,488	10,506
67337	Coffeyville	(316)	12,917	15,185
67701	Colby	(913)	5,510	5,544
66901	Concordia	(913)	6,152	6,847
67037	Derby	(316)	14,699	9,786
67801	Dodge City	(316)	21,129	18,001
67042	El Dorado	(316)	11,495	11,551
66801	Emporia	(316)	25,512	25,287
66442	Fort Riley North(u)	(913)	12,848	16,086
66701	Fort Scott	(316)	8,362	8,893
67846	Garden City	(316)	24,097	18,256
67530	Great Bend	(316)	15,427	16,608
67601	Hays	(913)	17,807	16,301
67060	Haysville	(316)	8,364	8,006
67501	Hutchinson	(316)	39,308	40,284
67301	Independence	(316)	10,030	10,598
66749	Iola	(316)	6,351	6,938
66441	Junction City	(913)	20,642	19,305
*66110	Kansas City	(913)	149,800	161,148
66043	Lansing	(913)	7,120	5,307
66044	Lawrence	(913)	65,608	52,738
66048	Leavenworth	(913)	38,495	33,656
66206	Leawood	(913)	19,693	13,360
66215	Lenexa	(913)	34,110	18,639
67901	Liberal	(316)	16,573	14,911
67460	McPherson	(316)	12,422	11,753
66502	Manhattan	(913)	37,737	32,644
66203	Merriam	(913)	11,819	10,794
66222	Mission	(913)	9,504	8,643
67114	Newton	(316)	16,700	16,332
66061	Olathe	(913)	63,402	37,258
66067	Ottawa	(913)	10,667	11,016
66204	Overland Park	(913)	111,790	81,784
.....	Park City		5,054	4,056
67357	Parsons	(316)	11,919	12,898
66762	Pittsburg	(316)	17,789	18,770
66208	Prairie Village	(913)	23,186	24,657
67124	Pratt	(316)	6,687	6,885
66203	Roeland Park	(913)	7,706	7,962
67401	Salina	(913)	42,299	41,843
*66203	Shawnee	(913)	37,962	29,653
*66603	Topeka	(913)	119,883	118,690
67880	Ulysses	(316)	5,474	4,653
67152	Wellington	(316)	8,517	8,212
*67202	Wichita	(316)	304,017	279,838
67156	Winfield	(316)	11,931	10,736

Kentucky

ZIP code	Place		1990	1980
41001	Alexandria		5,592	4,735
41101	Ashland	(606)	23,622	27,064
40004	Bardstown	(502)	6,712	6,155
41073	Bellevue	(606)	6,997	7,678
40403	Berea	(606)	9,129	8,226
42101	Bowling Green	(502)	40,688	40,450
40218	Buechel(u)	(502)	7,081	6,912
41005	Burlington(u)		6,070	....
42718	Campbellsville	(502)	9,592	8,715
40701	Corbin	(606)	7,644	8,075
*41011	Covington	(606)	43,264	49,585
41031	Cynthiana	(606)	6,497	5,881
40422	Danville	(606)	12,449	12,942
41074	Dayton	(606)	6,576	6,979
.....	Douglass Hills	(502)	5,431	4,384
41017	Edgewood	(606)	8,143	7,243
42701	Elizabethtown	(502)	18,167	15,380
41018	Elsmere	(606)	6,847	7,203
41018	Erlanger	(606)	15,979	14,466
40118	Fairdale(u)	(502)	6,563	7,315
40291	Fern Creek(u)	(502)	16,406	16,866
41139	Flatwoods	(606)	7,799	8,354
41042	Florence	(606)	18,586	15,586
42223	Fort Campbell North(u)	(502)	18,861	17,211
40121	Fort Knox(u)	(502)	21,495	31,055
41017	Fort Mitchell	(606)	7,438	7,294
41075	Fort Thomas	(606)	16,032	16,012
41011	Fort Wright		6,570	4,481
40601	Frankfort	(502)	26,535	25,973
42134	Franklin	(502)	7,607	7,738
40324	Georgetown	(502)	11,414	10,972
42141	Glasgow	(502)	12,351	12,958
40330	Harrodsburg	(606)	7,335	7,265
41701	Hazard	(606)	5,416	5,371
42420	Henderson	(502)	25,945	24,834
40228	Highview(u)	(502)	14,814	13,286
40229	Hillview	(502)	6,119	5,196
42240	Hopkinsville	(502)	29,818	27,318
41051	Independence	(606)	10,444	7,998
40299	Jeffersontown	(502)	23,223	15,795
40342	Lawrenceburg	(502)	5,911	5,167
40033	Lebanon	(502)	5,695	6,590
*40511	Lexington-Fayette	(606)	225,366	204,165
40741	London	(606)	5,757	4,002
*40201	Louisville	(502)	269,555	298,694
.....	Lyndon		8,037	1,553
42431	Madisonville	(502)	16,203	16,979
42066	Mayfield	(502)	9,935	10,705
41056	Maysville	(606)	7,169	7,983
40965	Middlesboro	(606)	11,328	12,251
40243	Middletown		5,016	4,262
42633	Monticello	(606)	5,357	5,677
40351	Morehead	(606)	8,357	7,789
40353	Mount Sterling	(606)	5,362	5,820
40047	Mount Washington	(502)	5,256	3,997
42071	Murray	(502)	14,442	14,248
40218	Newburg(u)	(502)	21,647	24,612
*41071	Newport	(606)	18,871	21,587
40356	Nicholasville	(606)	13,603	10,400
40219	Okolona(u)	(502)	18,902	20,039
42301	Owensboro	(502)	53,579	54,450
42001	Paducah	(502)	27,256	29,315
40361	Paris	(606)	8,730	7,935
41501	Pikeville	(606)	6,324	4,756
40258	Pleasure Ridge Park(u)	(502)	25,131	27,332
42445	Princeton	(502)	6,940	7,073
40160	Radcliff	(502)	19,778	14,656
40475	Richmond	(606)	21,183	21,705
42276	Russellville	(502)	7,454	7,520
.....	Saint Dennis(u)		10,326	....
40207	Saint Matthews	(502)	15,691	13,519
40065	Shelbyville	(502)	6,155	5,329
40216	Shively	(502)	15,535	16,645
42501	Somerset	(606)	10,735	10,649
.....	Taylor Mill		5,530	4,509
40272	Valley Station(u)	(502)	22,840	24,474
40383	Versailles	(606)	7,269	6,427
.....	Villa Hills	(606)	7,370	4,384
41101	Westwoods(u)	(606)	5,300	5,973
40769	Williamsburg	(606)	5,493	5,560
40391	Winchester	(606)	15,799	15,216

Louisiana

ZIP code	Place		1990	1980
70510	Abbeville	(318)	11,187	12,391
71301	Alexandria	(318)	49,087	51,648
70032	Arabi(u)	(504)	8,787	10,248
70094	Avondale(u)	(504)	5,813	6,699
70714	Baker	(504)	13,087	12,865
71220	Bastrop	(318)	13,916	15,527
*70821	Baton Rouge	(504)	219,531	220,394
70360	Bayou Cane(u)	(504)	15,876	15,723
70037	Belle Chasse(u)	(504)	8,512	5,412
70427	Bogalusa	(504)	14,280	16,976
71010	Bossier City	(318)	52,721	50,817
70517	Breaux Bridge	(318)	6,694	5,922
70094	Bridge(u)		8,327	....
70811	Brownfields(u)		5,229	....
71291	Brownsville-Bawcomville(u)	(318)	7,397	7,252
71322	Bunkie	(318)	5,044	5,364
70520	Carencro		5,429	3,712
70043	Chalmette(u)	(504)	31,860	33,847
71291	Claiborne(u)	(318)	8,300	6,278
70433	Covington	(504)	7,691	7,892
70526	Crowley	(318)	13,983	16,036
70345	Cut Off(u)	(504)	5,325	5,049
70726	Denham Springs	(504)	8,381	8,563
70634	De Ridder	(318)	9,868	10,337
70047	Destrehan	(504)	8,031	2,382
70346	Donaldsonville	(504)	7,949	7,901
70072	Estelle(u)	(504)	14,091	12,724
70535	Eunice	(318)	11,162	12,479
71459	Fort Polk South	(318)	10,911	12,498
70538	Franklin	(318)	9,004	9,584
70820	Gardere		7,209	....
70737	Gonzales	(504)	7,208	7,287
71245	Grambling		5,512	4,226
70053	Gretna	(504)	17,208	20,615
70401	Hammond	(504)	15,871	15,226
70123	Harahan	(504)	9,927	11,384
70058	Harvey(u)	(504)	21,222	22,709
70360	Houma	(504)	30,495	32,602
70544	Jeanerette	(318)	6,205	6,511
70121	Jefferson(u)	(504)	14,521	15,550
70546	Jennings	(318)	11,305	12,401
70062	Kenner	(504)	72,033	66,382
70445	Lacombe(u)	(504)	6,523	5,146
70501	Lafayette	(318)	94,440	80,584
70601	Lake Charles	(318)	70,580	75,226
71254	Lake Providence	(318)	5,380	6,361
70068	La Place(u)	(504)	24,194	16,112
70373	Larose(u)	(504)	5,772	5,234
71446	Leesville	(318)	7,638	9,054
70448	Mandeville	(504)	7,474	6,076
71052	Mansfield	(318)	5,389	6,485
71351	Marksville	(318)	5,526	5,113
70072	Marrero(u)	(504)	36,671	36,548
70075	Meraux(u)	(504)	8,849	....
70812	Merrydale(u)		10,395	....
*70004	Metairie(u)	(504)	149,428	164,160
71055	Minden	(318)	13,661	15,084
71201	Monroe	(318)	54,909	57,597
70380	Morgan City	(504)	14,531	16,114
70601	Moss Bluff(u)	(318)	8,039	7,004

ZIP code	Place		1990	1980
71457	Natchitoches	(318)	16,609	16,664
70560	New Iberia	(318)	31,828	32,766
*70113	New Orleans	(504)	496,938	557,927
70760	New Roads		5,303	3,924
71463	Oakdale	(318)	6,837	7,155
70810	Oak Hills Place		5,479	....
70570	Opelousas	(318)	19,091	18,903
70392	Patterson	(504)	5,166	4,693
71360	Pineville	(318)	12,251	12,034
70764	Plaquemine	(504)	7,101	7,521
70454	Ponchatoula	(504)	5,425	5,469
70767	Port Allen	(504)	6,277	6,114
70601	Prien(u)	(318)	6,448	6,224
70394	Raceland(u)	(504)	5,564	6,302
70578	Rayne	(318)	8,502	9,066
.....	Red Chute(u)		5,431	....
70084	Reserve(u)	(504)	8,847	7,288
70123	River Ridge(u)	(504)	14,800	17,146
71270	Ruston	(318)	20,071	20,585
70582	Saint Martinville	(318)	7,226	7,965
70087	Saint Rose(u)	(504)	6,259	....
70817	Shenandoah(u)		13,429	....
*71102	Shreveport	(318)	198,525	206,989
70458	Slidell	(504)	24,124	26,718
71075	Springhill	(318)	5,668	6,516
70663	Sulphur	(318)	20,125	19,709
71282	Tallulah	(318)	8,526	11,341
70056	Terrytown(u)	(504)	23,787	23,548
70301	Thibodaux	(504)	14,125	15,810
70053	Timberlane(u)	(504)	12,614	11,579
70809	Village Saint George(u)		6,242	....
70586	Ville Platte	(318)	9,037	9,201
70092	Violet(u)	(504)	8,574	11,678
70094	Waggaman(u)	(504)	9,405	9,004
70669	Westlake	(318)	5,007	5,246
71291	West Monroe	(318)	14,096	14,993
70094	Westwego	(504)	11,218	12,663
71483	Winnfield	(318)	6,138	7,311
71295	Winnsboro	(318)	5,755	5,921
70791	Zachary	(504)	9,036	7,297

Maine (207)

See Note on Page 373

ZIP code	Place	1990	1980
04210	Auburn	24,309	23,128
04330	Augusta	21,325	21,819
04401	Bangor	33,181	31,643
04530	Bath	9,799	10,246
04915	Belfast	6,355	6,243
03901	*Berwick*	5,995	....
04005	Biddeford	20,710	19,638
04412	Brewer	9,021	9,017
04011	Brunswick Center(u)	14,683	10,990
04011	*Brunswick*	20,906	17,366
04093	*Buxton*	6,494	5,775
04843	*Camden*	5,060	....
04107	*Cape Elizabeth*	8,854	7,838
04736	Caribou	9,415	9,916
04021	*Cumberland*	5,836	5,284
03903	Eliot	5,329	....
04605	Ellsworth	5,975	5,179
04937	*Fairfield*	6,718	6,113
04105	*Falmouth*	7,610	6,853
04938	*Farmington*	7,436	6,730
04032	*Freeport*	6,905	5,863
04345	Gardiner	6,746	6,485
04038	*Gorham*	11,856	10,101
04039	Gray	5,904	....
04444	*Hampden*	5,974	5,250
.....	*Harpswell*	5,012	....
04730	Houlton Center(u)	5,627	5,730
04730	*Houlton*	6,613	6,766
04239	*Jay*	5,080	5,080
04043	*Kennebunk*	8,004	6,621
03904	Kittery Center(u)	5,151	5,465
03904	*Kittery*	9,372	9,314
04240	Lewiston	39,757	40,481
04750	*Limestone*	9,922	8,719
04457	*Lincoln*	5,587	5,066
04250	*Lisbon*	9,457	8,769
04750	Loring(u)	5,494	6,572
04462	Millinocket Center(u)	6,922	7,567
04462	*Millinocket*	7,567	7,742
04963	*Oakland*	5,595	5,162
04064	Old Orchard Beach Ctr.(u)	7,789	6,023
04064	*Old Orchard Beach*	7,789	6,291
04468	Old Town	8,317	8,422
04473	Orono Center(u)	9,789	9,891
04473	*Orono*	10,573	10,578
*04101	Portland	64,358	61,572
04769	Presque Isle	10,550	11,172
04841	Rockland	7,972	7,919
04276	Rumford Compact(u)	5,419	6,256
04276	*Rumford*	7,078	8,240
04072	Saco	15,181	12,921
04073	Sanford Center(u)	10,296	10,268
04073	*Sanford*	20,463	18,020
04074	*Scarborough*	12,518	11,347
04976	Skowhegan Center(u)	6,990	6,517
04976	*Skowhegan*	8,725	8,098
03908	*South Berwick*	5,877	....
04106	South Portland	23,163	22,712
04084	*Standish*	7,678	5,946
04086	*Topsham*	8,746	6,147
04901	Waterville	17,173	17,779
04090	*Wells*	7,778	8,211
04092	Westbrook	16,121	14,976
04082	*Windham*	13,020	11,282
04901	Winslow Center(u)	5,436	5,903
04901	*Winslow*	7,997	8,057
04364	*Winthrop*	5,986	5,889
04096	*Yarmouth*	7,862	6,585
03909	*York*	9,818	8,465

Maryland

ZIP code	Place		1990	1980
21001	Aberdeen	(410)	13,087	11,533
21005	Aberdeen Proving Ground(u)		5,267	5,722
20783	Adelphi(u)	(301)	13,524	12,530
20331	Andrews AFB(u)	(410)	10,228	10,064
*21401	Annapolis	(410)	33,195	31,740
21227	Arbutus(u)	(410)	19,750	20,163
21012	Arnold(u)	(410)	20,261	12,285
20906	Aspen Hill(u)	(301)	45,494	47,455
.....	Ballenger Creek		5,546	2,659
*21233	Baltimore	(410)	736,014	786,741
21014	Bel Air	(410)	8,942	7,814
21050	Bel Air North(u)	(410)	14,880	5,043
21014	Bel Air South(u)	(410)	26,421	8,461
20705	Beltsville(u)	(301)	14,476	12,760
*20815	Bethesda(u)	(301)	62,936	62,736
20710	Bladensburg	(301)	8,064	7,691
*20715	Bowie	(301)	37,642	33,695
.....	Bowleys Quarters(u)		5,595	....
21225	Brooklyn Park(u)	(410)	10,987	11,508
20866	Burtonsville(u)		5,853	2,046
20818	Cabin John-Brookmont(u)		5,341	5,135
20619	California(u)	(410)	7,626	5,770
.....	Calverton(u)	(301)	12,046	....
21613	Cambridge	(410)	11,514	11,703
20748	Camp Springs(u)	(301)	16,392	16,118
21401	Cape St. Clair(u)	(410)	7,878	6,022
21234	Carney(u)	(410)	25,578	21,488
21228	Catonsville(u)	(410)	35,233	33,208
.....	Chesapeake Ranch Estates(u)		5,423	....
20785	Cheverly	(301)	6,023	5,751
20815	Chevy Chase(u)	(301)	8,559	12,232
20783	Chillum(u)	(301)	31,309	32,775
20735	Clinton(u)	(301)	19,987	16,438
20904	Cloverly(u)	(301)	7,904	5,153
21030	Cockeysville(u)	(410)	18,668	17,013
20904	Colesville(u)	(301)	18,819	14,359
20740	College Park	(301)	23,714	23,614
*21044	Columbia(u)	(301)	75,883	52,518
20743	Coral Hills(u)	(410)	11,032	11,602
21114	Crofton(u)	(410)	12,781	12,009
21502	Cumberland	(301)	23,712	25,933
20872	Damascus	(301)	9,817	4,129
20747	District Heights	(301)	6,711	6,799
21222	Dundalk(u)	(410)	65,800	71,293
21601	Easton	(410)	9,372	7,536
20737	East Riverdale(u)	(301)	14,187	14,117
21219	Edgemere(u)	(410)	9,226	9,078
21040	Edgewood(u)	(410)	23,903	19,455
21784	Eldersburg(u)		9,720	4,959
.....	Elkridge(u)		12,953	....
21921	Elkton	(410)	9,073	6,468
21043	Ellicott City(u)	(410)	41,396	21,784
21221	Essex(u)	(410)	40,872	39,614
20904	Fairland(u)	(301)	19,828	5,154
21047	Fallston(u)	(410)	5,730	5,572
21061	Ferndale(u)	(410)	16,355	14,314
20747	Forestville(u)	(301)	16,731	16,401
20755	Fort Meade(u)	(301)	12,509	14,083
20744	Fort Washington(u)		24,032	....
21701	Frederick	(301)	40,186	28,086
.....	Friendly(u)	(301)	9,028	8,848
21532	Frostburg	(301)	8,069	7,715
*20877	Gaithersburg	(301)	39,676	26,424
21055	Garrison(u)		5,045	....
20874	Germantown(u)	(301)	41,145	9,721
20706	Glenarden		5,025	4,993
21061	Glen Burnie(u)	(410)	37,305	37,263
20769	Glenn Dale(u)	(301)	9,689	5,106
20772	Greater Upper Marlboro		11,528	....
20770	Greenbelt	(301)	20,561	17,332
21122	Green Haven(u)	(410)	14,416	6,577
.....	Green Valley(u)		9,424	4,504
21740	Hagerstown	(301)	35,445	34,132
21740	Halfway(u)	(301)	8,873	8,659
21078	Havre De Grace	(410)	8,952	8,763
20903	Hillandale(u)		10,318	9,686
20748	Hillcrest Heights(u)	(301)	17,136	17,021
*20780	Hyattsville	(301)	13,864	12,709

ZIP code	Place	Area code	1990	1980
20794	Jessup(u)		6,537	4,288
21085	Joppatowne(u)	(410)	11,084	11,348
20785	Kentland(u)	(301)	7,967	8,596
20772	Kettering(u)		9,901	6,972
21122	Lake Shore(u)	(410)	13,269	10,181
20785	Landover(u)	(301)	5,052	5,374
20787	Langley Park(u)	(301)	17,474	14,038
20706	Lanham-Seabrook(u)	(301)	16,792	15,814
21227	Lansdowne-Baltimore Highlands(u)		15,509	16,759
20646	La Plata	(301)	5,841	2,484
20772	Largo(u)	(301)	9,475	5,557
*20707	Laurel	(301)	19,550	12,103
20653	Lexington Pk.(u)	(410)	9,943	10,361
21090	Linthicum(u)	(410)	7,547	7,457
21207	Lochearn(u)	(410)	25,240	26,908
21037	Londontowne(u)	(410)	6,992	6,052
.....	Long Meadow(u)		5,594	1,203
21093	Lutherville-Timonium(u)		16,442	17,854
20748	Marlow Heights(u)	(301)	5,885	5,824
.....	Marlton		5,523	....
20707	Maryland City(u)		6,813	6,949
.....	Mays Chapel(u)		10,132	5,213
21220	Middle River(u)	(410)	24,616	26,756
.....	Milford Mill(u)		22,547	20,354
20717	Mitchellville		12,593	....
20879	Montgomery Village(u)	(301)	32,315	18,725
20822	Mount Rainier	(301)	7,954	7,361
21402	Naval Academy(u)	(410)	5,420	5,367
20784	New Carrollton	(301)	12,002	12,632
20815	North Bethesda(u)	(301)	29,656	22,671
20895	North Kensington(u)	(301)	8,607	9,039
20707	North Laurel(u)	(301)	15,008	6,093
.....	North Potomac(u)	(301)	18,456	....
21842	Ocean City	(410)	5,146	4,946
21113	Odenton(u)	(410)	12,833	13,270
20832	Olney(u)	(301)	23,019	13,026
21206	Overlea(u)	(410)	12,137	12,965
21117	Owings Mills(u)	(410)	9,474	9,526
20745	Oxon Hill-Glassmanor(u)	(301)	35,794	36,267
20785	Palmer Park(u)	(301)	7,019	7,986
21234	Parkville	(410)	31,617	35,159
21401	Parole		10,054	3,377
21122	Pasadena(u)	(410)	10,012	7,439
21128	Perry Hall(u)	(410)	22,723	13,455
21208	Pikesville(u)	(410)	24,815	22,555
20854	Potomac(u)	(301)	45,634	40,402
21227	Pumphrey(u)		5,483	5,666
21133	Randallstown(u)	(301)	26,277	25,927
.....	Redland(u)	(301)	16,145	10,759
21136	Reisterstown(u)	(410)	19,314	19,385
20737	Riverdale		5,191	4,761
21122	Riviera Beach(u)	(410)	11,376	8,812
*20850	Rockville	(301)	44,830	43,811
.....	Rosaryville(u)		8,976	....
21237	Rosedale(u)	(410)	18,703	19,956
.....	Rossmoor(u)		6,182	8,646
21221	Rossville(u)		9,492	8,646
20601	Saint Charles(u)	(301)	28,717	13,921
21801	Salisbury	(410)	20,592	16,429
20763	Savage-Guilford(u)		9,669	2,928
20743	Seat Pleasant	(301)	5,359	5,217
21144	Severn(u)	(410)	24,499	20,147
21146	Severna Park(u)	(410)	25,879	21,253
*20907	Silver Spring(u)	(301)	76,046	72,893
21061	South Gate(u)	(410)	27,564	24,185
20895	South Kensington(u)	(301)	8,777	9,344
20707	South Laurel(u)		18,591	18,034
20746	Suitland-Silver Hills(u)	(301)	35,111	32,164
20912	Takoma Park	(301)	16,724	16,231
20748	Temple Hills(u)	(301)	6,865	6,630
21204	Towson(u)	(410)	49,445	51,083
20601	Waldorf(u)	(301)	15,058	9,782
20743	Walker Mill(u)	(301)	10,920	10,651
21157	Westminster	(410)	13,060	8,808
20902	Wheaton Glenmont(u)	(301)	53,720	48,598
21162	White Marsh(u)		8,183	....
20903	White Oak(u)	(301)	18,671	13,700
21207	Woodlawn(u)	(410)	32,907	....
21207	Woodlawn(u)		5,329	5,306

Massachusetts

See Note on Page 373

ZIP code	Place	Area code	1990	1980
02351	*Abington*	(617)	13,817	13,887
01720	*Acton*	(508)	17,872	17,544
02743	*Acushnet*	(508)	9,554	8,704
01220	Adams Center(u)	(413)	6,356	6,857
01220	*Adams*	(413)	9,445	10,381
01001	*Agawam*	(413)	27,323	26,271
01913	Amesbury Center(u)	(508)	12,109	12,236
01913	*Amesbury*	(508)	14,997	13,971
01002	Amherst Center	(413)	17,824	17,773
01002	*Amherst*	(413)	35,228	33,229
01810	Andover	(508)	8,242	8,445
01810	*Andover*	(508)	29,151	26,370
02174	*Arlington*	(617)	44,630	44,630
01430	Ashburnham	(508)	5,433	....
01721	*Ashland*	(508)	12,066	9,165
01331	Athol Center(u)	(508)	8,732	8,708
01331	*Athol*	(508)	11,451	10,634
02703	Attleboro	(508)	38,383	34,196
01501	*Auburn*	(508)	15,005	14,845
*01432	*Ayer*	(508)	6,871	6,993
02630	*Barnstable*	(508)	40,949	30,898
01730	*Bedford*	(617)	12,996	13,067
01007	*Belchertown*	(413)	10,579	8,339
02019	*Bellingham*	(508)	14,877	14,300
02178	*Belmont*	(617)	24,720	24,720
01915	Beverly	(508)	38,195	37,655
01821	*Billerica*	(508)	37,609	36,727
01504	*Blackstone*	(508)	8,023	6,570
*02109	Boston	(617)	574,283	562,994
02532	*Bourne*	(508)	16,064	13,874
01921	*Boxford*	(508)	6,266	5,374
02184	*Braintree*	(617)	33,836	36,337
02631	*Brewster*	(508)	8,440	5,226
02324	*Bridgewater*	(508)	21,249	7,242
*02403	Brockton	(508)	92,788	95,172
02146	*Brookline*	(617)	54,718	55,062
01803	*Burlington*	(617)	23,302	23,486
*02138	Cambridge	(617)	95,802	95,322
02021	*Canton*	(617)	18,530	18,182
02330	*Carver*	(508)	10,590	6,988
02632	Centerville	(508)	9,190	3,640
01507	*Charlton*	(508)	9,576	6,719
02633	*Chatham*	(508)	6,579	6,071
01824	*Chelmsford*	(508)	32,383	32,388
02150	Chelsea	(617)	28,710	25,431
*01021	Chicopee	(413)	56,632	55,112
01510	*Clinton*	(508)	13,222	7,943
01778	Cochituate(u)	(508)	6,046	6,126
02025	*Cohasset*	(617)	7,075	7,174
01742	*Concord*	(508)	17,076	16,293
01226	*Dalton*	(413)	7,155	6,797
01923	*Danvers*	(508)	24,174	24,174
02714	*Dartmouth*	(508)	27,244	23,966
02026	*Dedham*	(617)	23,782	25,298
01342	*Deerfield*	(413)	5,018	....
02638	*Dennis*	(508)	13,864	12,360
02715	*Dighton*	(508)	5,631	5,352
.....	*Douglas*	(508)	5,438	....
01826	*Dracut*	(508)	25,594	21,249
01570	*Dudley*	(508)	9,540	8,717
02332	*Duxbury*	(617)	13,895	11,807
02333	*East Bridgewater*	(508)	11,104	9,945
02536	East Falmouth(u)	(508)	5,577	5,181
01027	*Easthampton*	(413)	15,537	15,580
01028	*East Longmeadow*	(413)	13,367	12,905
02334	*Easton*	(508)	19,807	16,623
02149	Everett	(617)	35,701	37,195
02719	*Fairhaven*	(508)	16,132	15,759
*02722	Fall River	(508)	92,703	92,574
02540	*Falmouth*	(508)	27,960	41,194
01420	Fitchburg	(508)	41,194	39,580
01433	Fort Devens(u)	(508)	8,973	9,546
02035	*Foxborough*	(508)	14,637	5,706
01701	*Framingham*	(508)	64,994	65,113
02038	Franklin Center(u)	(508)	9,965	9,296
02038	*Franklin*	(508)	22,095	18,217
02702	*Freetown*	(508)	8,522	7,058
01440	Gardner	(508)	20,125	17,900
01833	*Georgetown*	(508)	6,384	5,687
01930	Gloucester	(508)	28,716	27,768
01519	*Grafton*	(508)	13,035	11,238
01033	*Granby*	(413)	5,565	5,380
01230	*Great Barrington*	(413)	7,725	7,405
01301	Greenfield Center(u)	(413)	14,016	14,198
01302	*Greenfield*	(413)	18,666	18,436
01450	*Groton*	(508)	7,511	6,154
01834	*Groveland*	(508)	5,214	5,040
02338	*Halifax*	(617)	6,526	5,513
01936	*Hamilton*	(508)	7,280	6,960
02339	*Hanover*	(617)	11,912	11,358
02341	*Hanson*	(617)	9,028	8,508
01451	*Harvard*	(508)	12,329	12,170
02645	*Harwich*	(508)	10,275	8,971
01830	Haverhill	(508)	51,418	46,865
02043	*Hingham*	(617)	19,821	18,845
02343	*Holbrook*	(617)	11,041	11,041
01520	*Holden*	(508)	14,628	13,336
01746	*Holliston*	(508)	12,926	12,622
01040	Holyoke	(413)	43,704	44,678
01747	*Hopedale*	(508)	5,666	....
01748	*Hopkinton*	(508)	9,191	7,114
01749	Hudson Center(u)	(508)	14,267	14,156
01749	*Hudson*	(508)	17,233	14,267
02045	*Hull*	(617)	10,466	10,466
02601	Hyannis(u)	(508)	14,120	9,118
01938	*Ipswich*	(508)	11,873	11,158
02364	*Kingston*	(617)	9,045	7,362
02346	*Lakeville*	(617)	7,785	5,931
01523	*Lancaster*	(508)	6,661	6,334
*01842	Lawrence	(508)	70,207	63,175
01238	*Lee*	(413)	5,849	6,247
01524	*Leicester*	(508)	10,191	9,446
01240	*Lenox*	(413)	5,069	6,523

ZIP code	Place		1990	1980
01453	Leominster	(508)	38,145	34,508
02173	*Lexington*	(617)	28,974	29,479
01773	*Lincoln*	(617)	7,666	7,098
01460	*Littleton*	(508)	7,051	6,970
01106	*Longmeadow*	(413)	15,467	15,467
*01853	Lowell	(508)	103,439	92,418
01056	*Ludlow*	(413)	18,820	18,150
01462	*Lunenburg*	(508)	9,117	8,405
*01901	Lynn	(617)	81,245	78,471
01940	*Lynnfield*	(617)	11,274	11,267
02148	Malden	(617)	53,884	53,386
01944	*Manchester*	(508)	5,286	5,424
02048	*Mansfield*	(508)	16,568	7,170
01945	*Marblehead*	(617)	19,971	19,971
01752	Marlborough	(508)	31,813	30,617
02050	*Marshfield*	(617)	21,531	20,916
02648	Marstons Mills(u)	....	8,017	....
02649	*Mashpee*	(508)	7,884	....
02739	*Mattapoisett*	(508)	5,850	5,597
01754	*Maynard*	(508)	10,325	10,325
02052	*Medfield*	(508)	10,531	5,985
02155	Medford	(617)	57,407	58,076
02053	*Medway*	(508)	9,931	8,447
02176	Melrose	(617)	28,150	30,055
01860	Merrimac	(508)	5,166	....
01844	*Methuen*	(508)	39,990	36,701
02346	Middleborough Center(u)	(617)	6,837	7,012
02346	*Middleborough*	(617)	17,867	16,404
01757	Milford Center(u)	(508)	23,339	21,730
01757	*Milford*	(508)	25,355	23,390
01527	*Millbury*	(508)	12,228	11,808
02054	*Millis*	(508)	7,613	6,908
02186	*Milton*	(617)	25,725	25,860
01057	*Monson*	(413)	7,776	7,315
01351	*Montague*	(413)	8,316	8,011
02554	*Nantucket*	(508)	6,012	5,087
01760	*Natick*	(508)	30,510	29,461
02192	*Needham*	(617)	27,557	27,901
*02741	New Bedford	(508)	99,922	98,478
01951	*Newbury*	(508)	5,623	....
01950	Newburyport	(508)	16,317	15,900
02158	Newton	(617)	82,585	83,622
02056	*Norfolk*	(508)	9,270	6,363
01247	North Adams	(413)	16,797	18,063
01002	North Amherst(u)	(413)	6,239	5,616
01060	Northampton	(413)	29,289	29,286
01845	*North Andover*	(508)	22,792	20,129
*02760	*North Attleborough*	(508)	25,038	16,178
01532	*Northborough*	(508)	11,929	5,761
01534	*Northbridge*	(508)	13,371	12,246
01864	*North Reading*	(508)	12,002	11,455
02766	*Norton*	(508)	14,265	12,690
02061	*Norwell*	(617)	9,279	9,182
02062	*Norwood*	(617)	28,700	29,711
01364	*Orange*	(508)	7,312	6,844
02653	*Orleans*	(508)	5,838	5,306
01540	Oxford Center(u)	(508)	5,969	6,369
01540	*Oxford*	(508)	12,588	11,680
01069	*Palmer*	(413)	12,054	11,389
01960	Peabody	(508)	47,264	45,976
02359	*Pembroke*	(617)	14,544	13,487
01463	*Pepperell*	(508)	10,098	8,061
01866	Pinehurst(u)	(508)	6,614	6,588
01201	Pittsfield	(413)	48,622	51,974
02762	*Plainville*	(508)	6,871	5,857
*02360	Plymouth Center(u)	(508)	7,258	7,232
02360	*Plymouth*	(508)	45,608	35,913
02169	Quincy	(617)	84,985	84,743
02368	*Randolph*	(617)	30,093	28,218
02767	*Raynham*	(508)	9,867	9,085
01867	*Reading*	(617)	22,539	22,678
02769	*Rehoboth*	(508)	8,656	7,570
02151	Revere	(617)	42,786	42,423
02370	*Rockland*	(617)	16,123	15,695
01966	*Rockport*	(508)	7,482	5,448
01970	Salem	(508)	38,091	38,276
01950	*Salisbury*	(508)	6,882	5,973
02563	*Sandwich*	(508)	15,489	8,727
01906	*Saugus*	(617)	25,549	25,549
02066	*Scituate*	(617)	16,786	5,180
02771	*Seekonk*	(508)	13,046	12,269
02067	*Sharon*	(617)	15,517	5,893
01464	*Shirley*	(508)	6,118	5,124
01545	*Shrewsbury*	(508)	24,146	22,674
02725	*Somerset*	(508)	17,655	18,813
02143	Somerville(u)	(617)	76,210	77,372
01002	South Amherst	(413)	5,053	4,861
01772	*Southborough*	(508)	6,628	6,193
01550	Southbridge Center(u)	(508)	12,882	14,261
01550	*Southbridge*	(508)	17,816	13,631
01075	*South Hadley*	(413)	16,685	16,399
01077	*Southwick*	(413)	7,667	7,382
02664	South Yarmouth(u)	(508)	10,358	7,525
01562	Spencer Center(u)	(508)	6,306	6,350
01562	*Spencer*	(508)	11,645	10,774
*01101	Springfield	(413)	156,983	152,319
01564	*Sterling*	(508)	6,481	5,440
02180	*Stoneham*	(617)	22,203	21,424
02072	*Stoughton*	(617)	26,777	26,710
01775	*Stow*	(508)	5,328	5,144
01566	*Sturbridge*	(508)	7,775	5,976
01776	*Sudbury*	(508)	14,358	14,027
01527	*Sutton*	(508)	6,824	5,855
01907	*Swampscott*	(617)	13,650	13,837
02777	*Swansea*	(508)	15,411	15,461
02780	Taunton	(508)	49,832	45,001
01468	*Templeton*	(508)	6,438	6,070
01876	*Tewksbury*	(508)	27,266	24,635
01983	*Topsfield*	(508)	5,754	5,709
01469	*Townsend*	(508)	8,496	7,201
01879	*Tyngsborough*	(508)	8,642	5,683
01569	*Uxbridge*	(508)	10,415	8,374
01880	*Wakefield*	(617)	24,825	24,895
02081	*Walpole*	(508)	20,212	5,495
02154	Waltham	(617)	57,878	58,200
01082	Ware Center(u)	(413)	6,533	6,806
01082	*Ware*	(413)	9,808	8,953
02571	*Wareham*	(508)	19,232	18,457
02172	*Watertown*	(617)	33,284	34,384
01778	*Wayland*	(508)	11,874	12,170
01570	Webster Center(u)	(508)	11,849	11,175
01570	*Webster*	(508)	16,196	14,480
02181	*Wellesley*	(617)	26,615	27,209
01581	*Westborough*	(508)	14,133	13,619
01583	*West Boylston*	(508)	6,611	6,204
02379	*West Bridgewater*	(508)	6,389	6,359
01742	West Concord(u)	(508)	5,761	5,331
01085	Westfield	(413)	38,372	36,465
01886	*Westford*	(508)	16,392	13,434
01473	*Westminster*	(508)	6,191	5,139
02193	*Weston*	(617)	10,200	11,169
02790	*Westport*	(508)	13,852	13,763
01089	*West Springfield*	(413)	27,537	27,042
02090	*Westwood*	(617)	12,557	13,212
02673	West Yarmouth	(508)	5,409	3,852
02188	*Weymouth*	(617)	54,063	55,601
01588	Whitinsville(u)	(508)	5,639	5,379
02382	*Whitman*	(617)	13,240	13,534
01095	*Wilbraham*	(413)	12,635	12,053
01267	*Williamstown*	(413)	8,220	8,741
01887	*Wilmington*	(508)	17,654	17,471
01475	*Winchendon*	(508)	8,805	7,019
01890	*Winchester*	(617)	20,267	20,701
02152	*Winthrop*	(617)	18,127	19,294
01801	Woburn	(617)	35,943	36,626
*01613	Worcester	(508)	169,759	161,799
02093	*Wrentham*	(508)	9,006	7,580
02675	*Yarmouth*	(508)	21,174	18,449

Michigan

ZIP code	Place		1990	1980
49221	Adrian	(517)	22,097	21,276
49224	Albion	(517)	10,066	11,059
49401	Allendale(u)	....	6,950	....
48101	Allen Park	(313)	31,092	34,196
48801	Alma	(517)	9,034	9,652
49707	Alpena	(517)	11,354	12,214
*48106	Ann Arbor	(313)	109,608	107,969
48057	Auburn Hills	(313)	17,076	15,388
49016	Battle Creek	(616)	53,516	35,724
48706	Bay City	(517)	38,936	41,593
48505	Beecher(u)	(313)	14,465	17,178
48809	Belding	(616)	5,969	5,634
49022	Benton Harbor	(616)	12,818	14,707
49022	Benton Heights(u)	(616)	5,465	6,787
48072	Berkley	(313)	16,960	18,637
48009	Beverly Hills	(313)	10,610	11,598
49307	Big Rapids	(616)	12,603	14,361
*48012	Birmingham	(313)	19,997	21,689
48013	Bloomfield(u)	(313)	42,137	42,876
48722	Bridgeport(u)	(517)	8,569	....
48116	Brighton	(313)	5,686	4,268
48601	Buena Vista	....	8,196	....
*48502	Burton	(313)	27,437	29,976
49601	Cadillac	(616)	10,104	10,199
48187	Canton(u)	(313)	57,047	....
48724	Carrollton(u)	(517)	6,521	7,482
48015	Center Line	(313)	9,026	9,293
48813	Charlotte	(517)	8,083	8,251
48017	Clawson	(313)	13,874	15,103
48043	Clinton(u)	(517)	85,866	72,400
49036	Coldwater	(517)	9,607	9,461
49321	Comstock Park(u)	(616)	6,530	5,506
49508	Cutlerville(u)	(616)	11,228	8,256
48423	Davison	(313)	5,693	6,087
*48120	Dearborn	(313)	89,286	90,660
48127	Dearborn Heights	(313)	60,838	67,706
*48233	Detroit	(313)	1,027,974	1,203,368
49047	Dowagiac	(616)	6,418	6,307
49506	East Grand Rapids	(616)	10,807	10,914
48823	East Lansing	(517)	50,677	51,392
48021	Eastpointe	(313)	35,283	38,280
49001	Eastwood(u)	(616)	6,340	7,186
48229	Ecorse	(313)	12,180	14,447
49829	Escanaba	(906)	13,659	14,355
49022	Fair Plain(u)	(616)	8,051	8,289

ZIP code	Place		1990	1980
48024	Farmington	(313)	10,170	11,022
48024	Farmington Hills	(313)	74,614	58,056
48430	Fenton	(313)	8,434	8,098
48220	Ferndale	(313)	25,084	26,227
48134	Flat Rock	(313)	7,290	6,853
*48502	Flint	(313)	140,761	159,611
48433	Flushing	(313)	8,542	8,624
49506	Forest Hills		16,690	....
48026	Fraser	(313)	13,899	14,560
48135	Garden City	(313)	31,846	35,640
48439	Grand Blanc	(313)	7,760	6,848
49417	Grand Haven	(616)	11,951	11,763
48837	Grand Ledge	(517)	7,562	6,920
*49501	Grand Rapids	(616)	189,126	181,843
49418	Grandville	(616)	15,624	12,412
48838	Greenville	(616)	8,101	8,019
48138	Grosse Ile(u)	(313)	9,781	9,320
48236	Grosse Pointe	(313)	5,681	5,901
48236	Grosse Pointe Farms	(313)	10,092	10,551
48236	Grosse Pointe Park	(313)	12,857	13,562
48236	Grosse Pointe Woods	(313)	17,715	18,886
48212	Hamtramck	(313)	18,372	21,300
48225	Harper Woods	(313)	14,903	16,361
48625	Harrison(u)	(517)	24,685	23,649
48840	Haslett(u)	(517)	10,230	7,025
49058	Hastings	(616)	6,549	6,418
48030	Hazel Park	(313)	20,051	20,914
48203	Highland Park	(313)	20,121	27,909
49242	Hillsdale	(517)	8,175	7,432
49423	Holland	(616)	30,745	26,281
48442	Holly	(313)	5,595	4,874
48842	Holt(u)	(517)	11,744	10,097
49931	Houghton	(906)	7,498	7,512
48843	Howell	(517)	8,147	6,976
49426	Hudsonville		6,170	4,844
48070	Huntington Woods	(313)	6,419	6,937
48141	Inkster	(313)	30,772	35,190
48846	Ionia	(616)	5,990	5,920
49801	Iron Mountain	(906)	8,525	8,341
49938	Ironwood	(906)	6,849	7,741
49849	Ishpeming	(906)	7,200	7,538
*49201	Jackson	(517)	37,425	39,739
49428	Jenison(u)	(616)	17,882	16,330
*49001	Kalamazoo	(616)	80,277	79,722
49508	Kentwood	(616)	37,826	30,438
49801	Kingsford	(906)	5,480	5,290
49843	K.I. Sawyer(u)	(906)	6,577	7,345
48144	Lambertville(u)	(313)	7,860	6,341
*48924	Lansing	(517)	127,321	130,414
48446	Lapeer	(313)	7,759	6,198
48146	Lincoln Park	(313)	41,832	45,105
*48150	Livonia	(313)	100,850	104,814
49431	Ludington	(616)	8,507	8,937
48071	Madison Heights	(313)	32,196	35,375
49660	Manistee	(616)	6,734	7,665
49855	Marquette	(906)	21,977	23,288
49068	Marshall	(616)	6,941	7,201
48040	Marysville	(313)	8,515	7,345
48854	Mason	(517)	6,768	6,019
48122	Melvindale	(313)	11,216	12,322
49858	Menominee	(906)	9,398	10,099
48640	Midland	(517)	38,053	37,269
48042	Milford	(313)	5,500	5,041
48161	Monroe	(313)	22,902	23,531
48043	Mount Clemens	(313)	18,405	18,991
48858	Mount Pleasant	(517)	23,299	23,746
*49440	Muskegon	(616)	39,809	40,823
49444	Muskegon Heights	(616)	13,176	14,611
48047	New Baltimore	(313)	5,798	5,439
49120	Niles	(616)	12,458	13,115
.....	Northview(u)		13,712	11,662
48167	Northville	(313)	6,226	5,698
49441	Norton Shores	(616)	21,755	22,025
48050	Novi	(313)	32,998	22,525
48237	Oak Park	(313)	30,468	31,537
48864	Okemos(u)	(517)	20,216	8,882
48867	Owosso	(517)	16,322	16,455
49770	Petoskey	(616)	6,056	6,097
48170	Plymouth	(313)	9,560	9,986
48170	Plymouth Township(u)	(313)	23,646	....
*48053	Pontiac	(313)	71,136	76,715
49081	Portage	(616)	41,042	38,157
48060	Port Huron	(313)	33,694	33,981
48239	Redford(u)	(313)	54,387	58,441
48218	River Rouge	(313)	11,314	12,912
48192	Riverview	(313)	13,894	14,569
48063	Rochester	(313)	7,130	7,203
48307	Rochester Hills		61,766	40,704
48174	Romulus	(313)	22,897	24,857
48066	Roseville	(313)	51,412	54,311
*48068	Royal Oak	(313)	65,410	70,893
*48605	Saginaw	(517)	69,512	77,508
48604	Saginaw Township North	(517)	23,018	....
48603	Saginaw Township South	(517)	13,987	....
48079	Saint Clair	(313)	5,116	4,780
*48083	Saint Clair Shores	(313)	68,107	76,210
48879	Saint Johns	(517)	7,392	7,376
49085	Saint Joseph	(616)	9,214	9,622
48176	Saline	(313)	6,660	6,483
49783	Sault Sainte Marie	(906)	14,689	14,448
49455	Shelby		48,655	....
48609	Shields		6,634	....
*48075	Southfield	(313)	75,727	75,568
48198	Southgate	(313)	30,771	32,058
49090	South Haven	(616)	5,563	5,943
48178	South Lyon	(313)	6,479	5,214
48161	South Monroe(u)		5,266	4,232
49015	Springfield	(616)	5,582	5,917
*48078	Sterling Heights	(313)	117,810	108,999
49091	Sturgis	(616)	10,130	9,468
48180	Taylor	(313)	70,811	77,568
49286	Tecumseh	(517)	7,462	7,320
48182	Temperance	(313)	6,542	....
49093	Three Rivers	(616)	7,464	7,015
49684	Traverse City	(616)	15,155	15,516
48183	Trenton	(313)	20,586	22,762
48084	Troy	(313)	72,884	67,102
48087	Utica	(313)	5,081	5,282
49504	Walker	(616)	17,279	15,088
48088	Walled Lake		6,278	4,748
*48089	Warren	(313)	144,864	161,134
48095	Waterford(u)	(313)	66,692	64,250
48917	Waverly		15,614	....
48184	Wayne	(313)	19,899	21,159
48033	West Bloomfield(u)	(313)	54,843	41,962
48185	Westland	(313)	84,724	84,603
49007	Westwood(u)	(616)	8,957	8,519
48096	Wixom	(313)	8,550	6,705
48183	Woodhaven	(313)	11,631	10,902
48753	Wurtsmith AFB(u)	(517)	5,080	5,166
*48192	Wyandotte	(313)	30,938	34,006
49509	Wyoming	(616)	63,891	59,616
48197	Ypsilanti	(313)	24,846	24,031
49464	Zeeland	(616)	5,417	4,764

Minnesota

ZIP code	Place		1990	1980
56007	Albert Lea	(507)	18,310	19,200
56308	Alexandria	(612)	8,029	7,608
55303	Andover	(612)	15,216	9,387
55303	Anoka	(612)	17,192	15,634
55124	Apple Valley	(612)	34,598	21,818
55112	Arden Hills	(612)	9,199	8,012
55912	Austin	(507)	21,926	23,020
56601	Bemidji	(218)	11,165	10,949
55433	Blaine	(612)	38,975	28,558
55420	Bloomington	(612)	86,335	81,831
56401	Brainerd	(218)	12,353	11,489
55429	Brooklyn Center	(612)	28,887	31,230
55429	Brooklyn Park	(612)	56,381	43,332
55313	Buffalo	(612)	6,856	4,560
55337	Burnsville	(612)	51,288	35,674
55008	Cambridge		5,094	3,287
55316	Champlin	(612)	16,849	9,006
55317	Chanhassen	(612)	11,732	6,359
55318	Chaska	(612)	11,339	8,346
55719	Chisholm	(218)	5,290	5,930
55720	Cloquet	(218)	10,885	11,142
55421	Columbia Heights	(612)	18,910	20,029
55433	Coon Rapids	(612)	52,978	35,826
.....	Corcoran	(612)	5,199	4,252
55016	Cottage Grove	(612)	22,935	18,994
56716	Crookston	(218)	8,119	8,628
55428	Crystal	(612)	23,788	25,543
56501	Detroit Lakes	(218)	6,635	7,106
*55806	Duluth	(218)	85,493	92,811
55121	Eagan	(612)	47,409	20,700
55005	East Bethel	(612)	8,050	6,626
56721	East Grand Forks	(218)	8,658	8,537
*55343	Eden Prairie	(612)	39,311	16,263
55435	Edina	(612)	46,075	46,073
55330	Elk River	(612)	11,143	6,785
56031	Fairmont	(507)	11,265	11,506
55113	Falcon Heights	(612)	5,380	5,291
55021	Faribault	(507)	17,085	16,241
55024	Farmington	(612)	5,940	4,370
56537	Fergus Falls	(218)	12,362	12,519
55025	Forest Lake	(612)	5,833	4,596
55432	Fridley	(612)	28,335	30,228
55416	Golden Valley	(612)	20,971	22,775
55744	Grand Rapids	(218)	7,976	7,934
*55303	Ham Lake	(612)	8,924	7,832
55033	Hastings	(612)	15,478	12,827
55811	Hermantown	(218)	6,761	6,759
55746	Hibbing	(218)	18,046	21,193
55343	Hopkins	(612)	16,529	15,336
55350	Hutchinson	(612)	11,459	9,244
56649	International Falls	(218)	8,301	5,611
55075	Inver Grove Heights	(612)	22,477	17,171
55042	Lake Elmo	(612)	5,900	5,296
55044	Lakeville	(612)	24,854	14,790
.....	Lino Lakes	(612)	8,807	4,966
55355	Litchfield	(612)	6,041	5,904
55110	Little Canada	(612)	8,971	7,102
56345	Little Falls	(612)	7,371	7,250
55115	Mahtomedi		5,633	3,851

ZIP code	Place		1990	1980
56001	Mankato	(507)	31,405	28,646
55369	Maple Grove	(612)	38,736	20,525
55109	Maplewood	(612)	30,954	26,990
56258	Marshall	(507)	12,023	11,161
55118	Mendota Heights	(612)	9,388	7,288
*55401	Minneapolis	(612)	368,383	370,951
55343	Minnetonka	(612)	48,370	38,683
56265	Montevideo	(612)	5,499	5,845
55362	Monticello	(612)	5,045	....
56560	Moorhead	(218)	32,295	29,998
56267	Morris	(612)	5,613	5,367
55364	Mound	(612)	9,634	9,280
55112	Mounds View	(612)	12,541	12,593
55112	New Brighton	(612)	22,207	23,269
54428	New Hope	(612)	21,853	23,087
56073	New Ulm	(507)	13,132	13,755
55057	Northfield	(507)	14,684	12,562
56001	North Mankato	(507)	10,662	9,145
55109	North Saint Paul	(612)	12,376	11,921
55119	Oakdale	(612)	18,377	12,123
55323	Orono	(612)	7,285	6,845
55060	Owatonna	(507)	19,386	18,632
55427	Plymouth	(612)	50,889	31,615
55372	Prior Lake	(612)	11,482	7,284
55303	Ramsey	(612)	12,408	10,093
55066	Red Wing	(612)	15,134	13,736
55423	Richfield	(612)	35,710	37,851
55422	Robbinsdale	(612)	14,396	14,422
55901	Rochester	(507)	70,729	57,906
55068	Rosemount	(612)	8,622	5,083
55113	Roseville	(612)	33,485	35,820
55418	Saint Anthony	(612)	7,727	7,981
56301	Saint Cloud	(612)	48,812	42,566
55426	Saint Louis Park	(612)	43,787	42,931
*55101	Saint Paul	(612)	272,235	270,230
56082	Saint Peter	(507)	9,481	9,056
56377	Sartell	(612)	5,409	3,427
56379	Sauk Rapids	(612)	7,825	5,793
56337	Savage	(612)	9,906	3,954
55379	Shakopee	(612)	11,739	9,941
55126	Shoreview	(612)	24,587	17,300
55331	Shorewood		5,917	4,646
55075	South Saint Paul	(612)	20,197	21,235
55432	Spring Lake Park	(612)	6,532	6,477
55082	Stillwater	(612)	13,882	12,290
56701	Thief River Falls	(218)	8,010	9,105
55110	Vadnais Heights	(612)	11,041	5,111
55792	Virginia	(218)	9,410	11,056
56387	Waite Park		5,020	3,496
56093	Waseca	(507)	8,385	8,219
55118	West Saint Paul	(612)	19,248	18,527
55110	White Bear Lake	(612)	24,622	22,538
56201	Willmar	(612)	17,531	15,895
55987	Winona	(507)	25,435	25,075
55119	Woodbury	(612)	20,075	10,297
56187	Worthington	(507)	9,977	10,243

Mississippi (601)

ZIP code	Place	1990	1980
39730	Aberdeen	6,837	7,184
38821	Amory	7,093	7,307
38606	Batesville	6,403	5,162
39520	Bay Saint Louis	8,063	7,850
*39530	Biloxi	46,319	49,311
38829	Booneville	7,955	6,199
39042	Brandon	11,077	9,626
39601	Brookhaven	10,243	10,800
39046	Canton	10,062	11,116
38614	Clarksdale	19,717	21,137
38732	Cleveland	15,384	14,524
39056	Clinton	21,847	14,660
39429	Columbia	6,815	7,733
39701	Columbus	23,799	27,503
38834	Corinth	11,820	13,178
39059	Crystal Springs	5,643	4,902
39532	D'Iberville	6,566	6,236
39074	Forest	5,060	5,229
39553	Gautier	10,088	10,392
38701	Greenville	45,226	40,613
38930	Greenwood	18,906	20,115
38901	Grenada	10,864	11,508
.....	Gulf Hills(u)	5,004	4,512
39501	Gulfport	40,775	39,676
39401	Hattiesburg	41,882	40,829
38635	Holly Springs	7,261	7,285
38637	Horn Lake	9,069	4,326
38751	Indianola	11,809	8,050
*39205	Jackson	196,637	202,895
39090	Kosciusko	6,986	7,415
39440	Laurel	18,827	21,897
38756	Leland	6,366	6,667
39560	Long Beach	15,804	14,199
39339	Louisville	7,165	7,323
39648	McComb	11,797	12,331
39110	Madison	7,471	2,241
39301	Meridian	41,036	46,577
39563	Moss Point	17,837	18,998
39120	Natchez	19,460	22,209
38652	New Albany	6,775	7,072
39564	Ocean Springs	14,658	14,504
39567	Orange Grove(u)	15,676	13,476
38655	Oxford	10,026	9,882
39567	Pascagoula	25,899	29,318
39571	Pass Christian	5,557	5,014
39208	Pearl	19,588	18,602
39465	Petal	7,883	8,476
39350	Philadelphia	6,758	6,434
39466	Picayune	10,633	10,361
39157	Ridgeland	11,714	5,461
38663	Ripley	5,371	4,271
.....	Saint Martin(u)	6,349	....
38671	Southaven	17,949	16,441
39759	Starkville	18,458	16,139
38801	Tupelo	30,685	23,905
39180	Vicksburg	20,908	25,434
39576	Waveland	5,369	4,186
39367	Waynesboro	5,143	5,349
.....	West Hattiesburg(u)	5,450	....
39773	West Point	8,489	8,811
38967	Winona	5,705	6,177
39194	Yazoo City	12,427	12,092

Missouri

ZIP code	Place		1990	1980
63123	Affton(u)	(314)	21,106	23,181
63010	Arnold	(314)	18,828	19,141
65605	Aurora	(417)	6,459	6,437
63011	Ballwin	(314)	21,406	12,656
63137	Bellefontaine Neighbors	(314)	10,918	12,082
64012	Belton	(816)	18,145	12,708
63134	Berkeley	(314)	12,250	15,922
63031	Black Jack	(314)	6,131	5,293
64015	Blue Springs	(816)	40,103	25,936
65613	Bolivar	(417)	6,845	5,919
65233	Boonville	(816)	7,095	6,959
63114	Breckenridge Hills	(314)	5,181	5,666
63144	Brentwood	(314)	8,150	8,209
63044	Bridgeton	(314)	17,732	18,445
63701	Cape Girardeau	(314)	34,475	34,361
64836	Carthage	(417)	10,747	11,104
63830	Caruthersville	(314)	7,389	7,958
63834	Charleston	(314)	5,085	5,230
63005	Chesterfield	(314)	38,630	28,384
64601	Chillicothe	(816)	8,799	9,089
63105	Clayton	(314)	13,926	14,306
64735	Clinton	(816)	8,703	8,366
65201	Columbia	(314)	69,133	62,061
63128	Concord(u)	(314)	19,859	20,896
63126	Crestwood	(314)	11,229	12,815
63141	Creve Coeur	(314)	12,289	11,743
63136	Dellwood	(314)	5,245	6,200
63020	De Soto	(314)	5,993	5,993
63131	Des Peres	(314)	8,388	7,953
63841	Dexter	(314)	7,506	7,043
63011	Ellisville	(314)	7,183	6,233
64024	Excelsior Springs	(816)	10,373	10,424
63640	Farmington	(314)	11,596	8,270
63135	Ferguson	(314)	22,290	24,549
63028	Festus	(314)	8,105	7,574
*63033	Florissant	(314)	51,038	55,721
65473	Fort Leonard Wood(u)	(314)	15,863	21,262
65251	Fulton	(314)	10,033	11,046
64118	Gladstone	(816)	26,243	24,990
65254	Glasgow Village(u)	(314)	5,199	....
63122	Glendale	(314)	5,945	6,035
64030	Grandview	(816)	24,973	24,561
63401	Hannibal	(314)	18,004	18,811
64701	Harrisonville	(816)	7,683	6,372
*63042	Hazelwood	(314)	15,512	13,098
*64051	Independence	(816)	112,301	111,797
63755	Jackson	(314)	9,256	7,827
65101	Jefferson City	(314)	35,517	33,619
63136	Jennings	(314)	15,841	16,934
64801	Joplin	(417)	40,866	39,126
*64108	Kansas City	(816)	434,829	448,028
63857	Kennett	(314)	10,941	10,145
63501	Kirksville	(816)	17,152	17,167
63122	Kirkwood	(314)	27,291	27,739
63124	Ladue	(314)	8,795	9,369
63367	Lake Saint Louis		7,536	3,843
65536	Lebanon	(417)	9,983	9,507
64063	Lee's Summit	(816)	46,418	28,741
63125	Lemay(u)	(314)	18,005	35,424
64068	Liberty	(816)	20,459	16,251
63552	Macon	(816)	5,571	5,680
63863	Malden	(314)	5,123	6,096
63011	Manchester	(314)	6,537	6,351
63143	Maplewood	(314)	9,962	10,960
65340	Marshall	(816)	12,711	12,781
63043	Maryland Heights(u)	(314)	25,440	26,413
64468	Maryville	(816)	10,663	9,558
.....	Mehlville(u)		27,557	....
65265	Mexico	(314)	11,290	12,276
65270	Moberly	(816)	12,839	13,418

ZIP code	Place		1990	1980
65708	Monett	(417)	6,529	6,148
63026	Murphy(u)	(314)	9,342	8,121
64850	Neosho	(417)	9,254	9,493
64772	Nevada	(417)	8,597	9,044
63121	Normandy	(314)	5,063	5,174
63121	Northwoods	(314)	5,106	5,831
.....	Oakville(u)		31,750	....
63366	O'Fallon	(314)	17,427	8,677
63132	Olivette	(314)	7,573	7,952
63114	Overland	(314)	17,987	19,620
63775	Perryville	(314)	6,933	7,343
63120	Pine Lawn	(314)	5,083	6,570
63901	Poplar Bluff	(314)	16,841	17,139
64083	Raymore	(816)	5,592	3,154
64133	Raytown	(816)	30,601	31,831
65738	Republic		6,290	4,485
64085	Richmond	(816)	5,738	5,499
63117	Richmond Heights	(314)	10,448	11,516
63124	Rock Hill	(314)	5,217	5,702
65401	Rolla	(314)	14,090	13,303
63074	Saint Ann	(314)	14,449	15,523
63301	Saint Charles	(314)	50,634	37,379
63114	Saint John	(314)	7,475	7,854
*64501	Saint Joseph	(816)	71,852	76,691
*63155	Saint Louis	(314)	396,685	452,801
63376	Saint Peters	(314)	40,660	15,700
63126	Sappington(u)	(314)	10,917	11,388
65301	Sedalia	(816)	19,800	20,927
63119	Shrewsbury	(314)	6,416	5,077
63801	Sikeston	(314)	17,641	17,431
63138	Spanish Lake(u)	(314)	20,322	20,632
*65801	Springfield	(417)	140,494	133,116
63080	Sullivan	(314)	5,661	5,461
.....	Town and Country		9,503	3,187
64683	Trenton	(816)	6,129	6,811
63084	Union	(314)	5,776	5,506
63130	University City	(314)	40,087	42,690
64093	Warrensburg	(816)	15,244	13,807
63090	Washington	(314)	10,704	9,251
64870	Webb City	(417)	7,449	7,309
63119	Webster Groves	(314)	22,992	23,097
63385	Wentzville	(314)	5,088	3,193
65775	West Plains	(417)	8,913	7,741

Montana (406)

ZIP code	Place	1990	1980
59711	Anaconda-Deer Lodge County	10,356	12,518
*59101	Billings	81,125	66,818
59715	Bozeman	22,660	21,645
59701	Butte-Silver Bow	33,336	37,205
*59401	Great Falls	55,125	56,884
59501	Havre	10,201	10,891
59601	Helena	24,609	23,938
.....	Helena Valley West Central(u)	6,327	....
59901	Kalispell	11,917	10,689
59044	Laurel	5,686	5,481
59457	Lewistown	6,097	7,104
59047	Livingston	6,701	6,994
59402	Malmstrom AFB(u)	5,938	6,675
59301	Miles City	8,461	9,602
*59801	Missoula	42,918	33,351
59801	Orchard Homes(u)	10,317	10,837
59270	Sidney	5,217	5,726

Nebraska

ZIP code	Place		1990	1980
69301	Alliance	(308)	9,765	9,920
68310	Beatrice	(402)	12,352	12,891
68005	Bellevue	(402)	30,982	21,813
68008	Blair	(402)	6,860	6,418
69337	Chadron	(308)	5,588	5,933
.....	Chalco(u)		7,337	....
68601	Columbus	(402)	19,480	17,328
68025	Fremont	(402)	23,680	23,979
69341	Gering	(308)	7,946	7,760
68801	Grand Island	(308)	39,487	33,180
68901	Hastings	(402)	22,837	23,045
68949	Holdrege	(308)	5,671	5,624
68847	Kearney	(308)	24,396	21,158
68128	La Vista	(402)	9,840	9,588
68850	Lexington	(308)	6,600	7,040
*68501	Lincoln	(402)	191,972	171,932
69001	McCook	(308)	8,112	8,404
68410	Nebraska City	(402)	6,547	7,127
68701	Norfolk	(402)	21,476	19,449
69101	North Platte	(308)	22,605	24,509
68113	Offutt AFB West(u)	(402)	10,883	8,787
69153	Ogallala	(308)	5,095	5,638
*68108	Omaha	(402)	335,719	313,939
68046	Papillion	(402)	10,378	6,399
68048	Plattsmouth	(402)	6,415	6,295
68127	Ralston	(402)	6,236	5,143
69361	Scottsbluff	(308)	13,711	14,156
68434	Seward	(402)	5,641	5,713
69162	Sidney	(308)	5,959	6,010
68776	South Sioux City	(402)	9,677	9,339
68787	Wayne	(402)	5,142	5,240
68467	York	(402)	7,940	7,723

Nevada (702)

ZIP code	Place	1990	1980
89005	Boulder City	12,567	9,590
*89701	Carson City	40,443	32,022
89112	East Las Vegas(u)	11,087	6,449
89801	Elko	14,836	8,758
.....	Enterprise(u)	6,412	....
89406	Fallon	6,430	4,262
89408	Fernley(u)	5,164	....
89410	Gardnerville Ranchos(u)	7,455	3,542
89015	Henderson	64,948	24,363
89450	Incline Village-Crystal Bay(u)	7,119	6,225
*89114	Las Vegas	258,204	164,674
89110	Nellis AFB(u)	8,377	7,476
*89030	North Las Vegas	47,849	42,739
89041	Pahrump(u)	7,424	84,818
89109	Paradise(u)	124,682	84,818
*89501	Reno	133,850	100,756
*89431	Sparks	53,367	40,780
.....	Spring Creek(u)	5,866	4,155
.....	Spring Valley(u)	51,726	....
89110	Sunrise Manor(u)	95,362	44,155
89431	Sun Valley(u)	11,391	8,822
89101	Winchester(u)	23,365	19,728
89445	Winnemucca	6,102	4,140

New Hampshire (603)

See Note on Page 373

ZIP code	Place	1990	1980
03031	*Amherst*	9,068	....
03811	*Atkinson*	5,188	....
03825	*Barrington*	6,164	....
03102	*Bedford*	12,563	9,481
03220	*Belmont*	5,796	....
03570	Berlin	11,824	13,084
03304	*Bow*	5,500	....
03743	Claremont	13,902	14,557
03301	Concord	36,006	30,400
03818	*Conway*	7,940	7,158
03038	Derry Compact(u)	20,446	12,248
03038	*Derry*	29,603	18,875
03820	Dover	25,042	22,377
03824	Durham Compact(u)	9,236	8,448
03824	*Durham*	11,818	10,652
03042	*Epping*	5,162	....
03833	Exeter Compact(u)	9,556	8,947
03833	*Exeter*	12,481	11,024
03835	*Farmington*	5,739	....
03235	Franklin	8,304	7,901
03246	*Gilford*	5,867	....
03045	*Goffstown*	14,621	11,315
03841	*Hampstead*	6,732	....
03842	Hampton Compact(u)	7,989	6,779
03842	*Hampton*	12,278	10,493
03755	Hanover Compact(u)	6,538	6,861
03756	*Hanover*	9,212	9,119
03049	*Hollis*	5,705	....
03106	*Hooksett*	8,767	7,303
03051	*Hudson*	19,530	7,626
03452	*Jaffrey*	5,361	....
03431	Keene	22,430	21,449
03848	*Kingston*	5,591	....
03246	Laconia	15,743	15,575
03766	Lebanon	12,183	11,134
.....	*Litchfield*	5,516	....
03561	*Littleton*	5,827	5,558
03053	*Londonderry Compact(u)*	10,114	....
03053	*Londonderry*	19,781	10,114
*03101	Manchester	99,332	90,936
03054	*Merrimack*	22,156	15,406
03055	*Milford Compact(u)*	8,015	....
03055	*Milford*	11,795	8,015
*03060	Nashua	79,662	67,865
03857	*Newmarket*	7,157	....
03773	*Newport*	6,110	6,229
03076	*Pelham*	9,408	8,090
03275	*Pembroke*	6,561	....
03458	*Peterborough*	5,239	....
03865	*Plaistow*	7,316	5,609
03264	*Plymouth*	5,811	....
03801	Portsmouth	25,925	26,254
03077	*Raymond*	8,713	5,453
03867	Rochester	26,630	21,560
03079	*Salem*	25,746	24,124
03874	*Seabrook*	6,503	5,917
03878	Somersworth	11,249	10,350
03275	Suncook(u)	5,214	4,698
.....	*Swanzey*	6,236	....
03281	*Weare*	6,193	....
03087	*Windham*	9,000	5,664

New Jersey

ZIP code	Place		1990	1980
08201	Absecon	(609)	7,298	6,859
07401	Allendale	(201)	5,900	5,901
07712	Asbury Park	(908)	16,799	17,015
*08401	Atlantic City	(609)	37,986	40,199
08106	Audubon	(609)	9,205	9,533
07001	Avenel(u)	(908)	15,504	....
08007	Barrington	(609)	6,792	7,418
07002	Bayonne	(201)	61,464	65,047
08722	Beachwood	(908)	9,324	7,687
07109	Belleville(u)	(201)	34,213	35,367
08031	Bellmawr	(609)	12,603	13,721
07719	Belmar	(908)	5,877	6,771
07621	Bergenfield	(201)	24,458	25,568
07922	Berkeley Heights Twp.(u)	(908)	11,980	12,549
08009	Berlin	(609)	5,672	5,786
07924	Bernardsville	(908)	6,597	6,715
08012	Blackwood(u)	(609)	5,120	5,219
07003	Bloomfield(u)	(201)	45,061	47,792
07403	Bloomingdale	(201)	7,530	7,867
07603	Bogota	(201)	7,824	8,344
07005	Boonton	(201)	8,343	8,620
08805	Bound Brook	(908)	9,487	9,710
08723	Brick Twp.(u)	(201)	66,473	53,629
08302	Bridgeton	(609)	18,942	18,795
08807	Bridgewater Twp.	(908)	32,509	....
08203	Brigantine	(609)	11,354	8,318
08015	Browns Mills(u)	(609)	11,429	10,568
07828	Budd Lake(u)	(201)	7,272	6,523
08016	Burlington	(609)	9,835	10,246
07405	Butler	(201)	7,392	7,616
07006	Caldwell(u)	(201)	7,549	7,624
*08101	Camden	(609)	87,492	84,910
07072	Carlstadt	(201)	5,510	6,166
08069	Carney's Point(u)	(609)	7,686	7,574
07008	Carteret	(908)	19,025	20,598
07009	Cedar Grove Twp.(u)	(201)	12,053	12,600
07928	Chatham	(201)	8,007	8,537
*08002	Cherry Hill Twp.(u)	(609)	69,319	68,785
08077	Cinnaminson Twp.(u)	(609)	14,583	16,072
07066	Clark Twp.(u)	(908)	14,629	16,699
08312	Clayton	(609)	6,155	6,013
08021	Clementon	(609)	5,601	5,764
07010	Cliffside Park	(201)	20,393	21,464
*07015	Clifton	(201)	71,984	74,388
07624	Closter	(201)	8,094	8,164
08108	Collingswood	(609)	15,289	15,838
07067	Colonia(u)	(908)	18,238	....
07016	Cranford Twp.	(908)	22,624	24,573
07626	Cresskill	(201)	7,558	7,609
.....	Crestwood Village(u)	(201)	8,030	7,965
07801	Dover	(201)	15,115	14,681
07628	Dumont	(201)	17,187	18,334
08812	Dunellen	(908)	6,528	6,593
08816	East Brunswick Twp.	(908)	43,548	37,711
07936	East Hanover	(201)	9,926	9,319
*07019	East Orange	(201)	73,552	77,878
07073	East Rutherford	(201)	7,902	7,849
07724	Eatontown	(908)	13,800	12,703
07020	Edgewater Borough	(201)	5,001	4,628
08010	Edgewater Park	(609)	8,388	9,273
08817	Edison Twp.(u)	(908)	88,680	70,193
*07201	Elizabeth	(908)	110,002	106,201
07407	Elmwood Park	(201)	17,623	18,377
07630	Emerson	(201)	6,930	7,793
*07631	Englewood	(201)	24,850	23,701
07632	Englewood Cliffs	(201)	5,634	5,698
08618	Ewing Twp.	(609)	34,185	34,842
07006	Fairfield	(201)	7,615	7,987
07701	Fair Haven	(908)	5,270	5,679
07410	Fair Lawn	(201)	30,548	32,229
07022	Fairview	(201)	10,733	10,519
07023	Fanwood	(908)	7,115	7,767
08518	Florence-Roebling(u)	(609)	8,564	7,677
07932	Florham Park	(201)	8,521	9,359
08863	Fords(u)	(908)	14,392	....
08640	Fort Dix(u)	(609)	10,205	14,297
07024	Fort Lee	(201)	31,997	32,449
07417	Franklin Lakes	(201)	9,873	8,769
.....	Franklin Twp.	(201)	42,780	....
07728	Freehold	(908)	10,742	10,020
07026	Garfield	(201)	26,727	26,803
08753	Gilford Park(u)	(908)	8,668	6,528
08028	Glassboro	(609)	15,614	14,574
08029	Glendora(u)	(609)	5,201	5,632
07028	Glen Ridge(u)	(201)	7,076	7,855
07452	Glen Rock	(201)	10,883	11,497
08030	Gloucester City	(609)	12,649	13,121
07093	Guttenberg	(201)	8,268	7,340
*07602	Hackensack	(201)	37,049	36,039
07840	Hackettstown	(908)	8,120	8,850
08033	Haddonfield	(609)	11,633	12,337
08035	Haddon Heights	(609)	7,860	8,361
07508	Haledon	(201)	6,951	6,607
*08609	Hamilton Twp.(u)	(609)	86,553	82,811
08037	Hammonton	(609)	12,208	12,298
07981	Hanover Twp.(u)	(201)	11,538	11,846

ZIP code	Place		1990	1980
07029	Harrison	(201)	13,425	12,242
07604	Hasbrouck Heights	(201)	11,488	12,166
07506	Hawthorne	(201)	17,084	18,200
07730	Hazlet Twp.(u)	(908)	21,976	23,013
08904	Highland Park	(201)	13,279	13,396
08520	Hightstown	(609)	5,126	4,581
07642	Hillsdale	(201)	9,750	10,495
07205	Hillside Twp.(u)	(908)	21,044	21,440
07030	Hoboken	(201)	33,397	42,460
08753	Holiday City-Berkeley(u)	(908)	14,293	9,019
.....	Holiday City South(u)	(908)	5,452	....
07843	Hopatcong	(201)	15,586	15,531
*08560	Hopewell Twp. (Mercer)(u)	(609)	10,893	11,590
07111	Irvington(u)	(201)	59,774	61,473
08830	Iselin(u)	(908)	16,141	....
*08527	Jackson Twp.(u)	(908)	33,283	25,644
08831	Jamesburg		5,294	4,114
*07303	Jersey City	(201)	228,517	223,532
07734	Keansburg	(908)	11,069	10,613
07032	Kearny	(201)	34,874	35,735
08824	Kendall Park(u)	(908)	7,127	7,419
07033	Kenilworth	(908)	7,574	8,221
07735	Keyport	(908)	7,586	7,413
07405	Kinnelon	(201)	8,470	7,770
07871	Lake Mohawk(u)	(201)	8,930	8,498
08701	Lakewood(u)	(908)	26,095	22,863
08879	Laurence Harbor(u)	(908)	6,361	6,737
08648	Lawrenceville(u)		6,446	....
.....	Leisure Village West-Pine Lake Park(u)		10,139	....
07605	Leonia	(201)	8,365	8,027
07035	Lincoln Park	(201)	10,978	8,806
07738	Lincroft(u)		6,193	....
07036	Linden	(908)	36,701	37,836
08021	Lindenwold	(609)	18,734	18,196
08221	Linwood	(609)	6,866	6,144
07424	Little Falls Twp.(u)	(201)	11,294	11,496
07643	Little Ferry	(201)	9,989	9,399
07739	Little Silver	(908)	5,721	5,548
07039	Livingston Twp.(u)	(201)	26,609	28,040
07644	Lodi	(201)	22,355	23,956
07740	Long Branch	(908)	28,658	29,819
*07946	Long Hill Twp.(u)	(908)	7,826	7,275
07071	Lyndhurst Twp.(u)	(201)	18,262	20,326
08641	McGuire AFB(u)	(609)	7,580	7,853
07940	Madison	(201)	15,850	15,357
08859	Madison Park(u)	(201)	7,490	7,447
*07430	Mahwah Twp.(u)	(201)	17,905	12,137
08736	Manasquan	(908)	5,369	5,354
08835	Manville	(908)	10,567	11,278
08052	Maple Shade Twp.(u)	(609)	19,211	20,525
07040	Maplewood Twp.(u)	(201)	21,756	22,950
08402	Margate City	(609)	8,431	9,179
07746	Marlboro Twp.(u)	(908)	27,974	17,560
08053	Marlton(u)	(609)	10,228	9,411
07747	Matawan	(908)	9,239	8,837
07607	Maywood	(201)	9,536	9,895
08619	Mercerville-Hamilton Sq.(u)	(609)	26,873	25,446
08840	Metuchen	(908)	12,804	13,762
08846	Middlesex	(908)	13,055	13,480
07748	Middletown	(908)	68,183	61,615
07432	Midland Park	(201)	7,047	7,381
07041	Millburn Twp.(u)	(201)	18,630	19,543
08850	Milltown	(908)	6,968	7,136
08332	Millville	(609)	25,992	24,815
08094	Monroe Twp. (Gloucester)(u)	(609)	26,703	21,639
*07042	Montclair(u)	(201)	37,729	38,321
07645	Montvale	(201)	6,946	7,318
07045	Montville Twp.(u)	(201)	15,600	14,290
08057	Moorestown-Lenola(u)	(609)	13,242	13,695
07950	Morris Plains	(201)	5,219	5,305
07960	Morristown	(201)	16,189	16,614
07092	Mountainside	(908)	6,657	7,118
08060	Mount Holly Twp.(u)	(609)	10,639	10,818
08087	Mystic Island		7,400	4,929
*07753	Neptune Twp.(u)	(908)	28,148	28,366
*07102	Newark	(201)	275,221	329,248
*08901	New Brunswick	(908)	41,711	41,442
07646	New Milford	(201)	15,990	16,876
07974	New Providence	(908)	11,439	12,426
07860	Newton	(201)	7,521	7,748
07032	North Arlington	(201)	13,790	16,587
07047	North Bergen Twp.(u)	(201)	48,414	47,019
08902	North Brunswick Twp.(u)	(908)	31,287	22,220
07006	North Caldwell(u)	(201)	6,706	5,832
08225	Northfield	(609)	7,305	7,795
07508	North Haledon	(201)	7,987	8,177
07060	North Plainfield	(908)	18,820	19,108
08260	North Wildwood		5,017	4,714
07110	Nutley	(201)	27,099	28,998
07436	Oakland	(201)	11,997	13,443
*08758	Ocean Twp.(u)	(908)	5,416	23,570
.....	Ocean Acres(u)		5,587	4,850
08226	Ocean City	(609)	15,512	13,949
07757	Oceanport	(908)	6,146	5,888
08857	Old Bridge(u)	(908)	22,151	21,815
08857	Old Bridge Twp.(u)	(908)	56,475	51,515
07649	Oradell	(201)	8,024	8,658
*07050	Orange(u)	(201)	29,925	31,136

ZIP code	Place		1990	1980
07650	Palisades Park	(201)	14,536	13,732
08065	Palmyra	(609)	7,056	7,085
07652	Paramus	(201)	25,004	26,474
07656	Park Ridge	(201)	8,102	8,515
07054	Parsippany-Troy Hills(u)	(201)	48,478	49,868
*07055	Passaic	(201)	58,041	52,463
*07510	Paterson	(201)	140,891	137,970
08066	Paulsboro	(609)	6,577	6,944
08110	Pennsauken Twp.(u)	(609)	34,733	33,775
08069	Penns Grove	(609)	5,228	5,760
08070	Pennsville Center(u)	(609)	12,218	12,467
07440	Pequannock Twp.	(201)	12,844	13,776
*08861	Perth Amboy	(908)	41,967	38,951
08865	Phillipsburg	(908)	15,757	16,647
08021	Pine Hill	(609)	9,854	8,684
*08854	Piscataway Twp.(u)	(908)	47,089	42,223
08071	Pitman	(609)	9,365	9,7447
*07061	Plainfield	(908)	46,577	45,555
08232	Pleasantville	(609)	16,027	13,435
08742	Point Pleasant	(908)	18,177	17,747
08742	Point Pleasant Beach	(908)	5,112	5,415
07442	Pompton Lakes	(201)	10,539	10,660
08540	Princeton	(609)	12,016	12,035
07508	Prospect Park	(201)	5,053	5,142
*07065	Rahway	(908)	25,325	26,723
08057	Ramblewood(u)	(609)	6,181	6,475
07446	Ramsey	(201)	13,228	12,899
07869	Randolph Twp.(u)	(201)	19,974	17,828
08869	Raritan	(908)	5,798	6,128
07701	Red Bank	(908)	10,636	12,031
07657	Ridgefield	(201)	9,996	10,294
07660	Ridgefield Park	(201)	12,454	12,738
*07451	Ridgewood	(201)	24,152	25,208
07456	Ringwood	(201)	12,623	12,625
07661	River Edge	(201)	10,603	11,111
08075	Riverside Twp.(u)	(609)	7,974	7,941
07675	River Vale(u)	(201)	9,410	9,489
07726	Robertsville(u)	(908)	9,841	8,461
07662	Rochelle Park Twp.	(201)	5,587	5,603
07866	Rockaway	(201)	6,243	6,852
07203	Roselle	(908)	20,314	20,641
07204	Roselle Park	(201)	12,805	13,377
07760	Rumson	(908)	6,701	7,623
08078	Runnemede	(609)	9,042	9,461
*07070	Rutherford	(201)	17,790	19,068
07662	Saddle Brook Twp.(u)	(201)	13,296	14,084
08079	Salem	(609)	6,883	6,959
08872	Sayreville	(908)	34,998	29,969
07076	Scotch Plains Twp.(u)	(908)	21,160	20,774
07094	Secaucus	(201)	14,061	13,719
08753	Silverton	(908)	9,175	7,236
08083	Somerdale	(609)	5,440	5,900
08873	Somerset(u)	(908)	22,070	21,731
08244	Somers Point	(609)	11,216	10,330
08876	Somerville	(908)	11,632	11,973
08879	South Amboy	(908)	7,851	8,322
07079	South Orange Twp.(u)	(201)	16,390	15,864
07080	South Plainfield	(908)	20,489	20,521
08882	South River	(908)	13,692	14,361
07871	Sparta Twp.(u)	(201)	15,157	7,333
08884	Spotswood	(908)	7,983	7,840
07081	Springfield Twp.(u)	(201)	13,420	13,955
07762	Spring Lake Heights	(908)	5,341	5,424
08084	Stratford	(609)	7,614	8,005
07747	Strathmore(u)	(201)	7,060	....
07876	Succasunna-Kenvil(u)	(201)	11,781	10,931
07901	Summit	(908)	19,757	21,071
07666	Teaneck Twp.(u)	(201)	37,825	39,007
07670	Tenafly	(201)	13,326	13,552
07724	Tinton Falls	(908)	12,361	7,740
*08753	Toms River(u)	(908)	7,524	7,465
07512	Totowa	(201)	10,177	11,448
*08608	Trenton	(609)	88,675	92,124
08520	Twin Rivers(u)	(609)	7,715	7,742
07083	Union Twp.(u)	(908)	50,024	50,184
07735	Union Beach	(908)	6,156	6,354
07087	Union City	(201)	58,012	55,593
07458	Upper Saddle River	(201)	7,198	7,958
08406	Ventnor City	(609)	11,005	11,704
07044	Verona(u)	(201)	13,597	14,166
08251	Villas(u)	(609)	8,136	5,909
08360	Vineland	(609)	54,780	53,753
07463	Waldwick	(201)	9,757	10,802
07057	Wallington	(201)	10,828	10,741
07465	Wanaque	(201)	9,711	10,025
07882	Washington	(908)	6,474	6,429
07675	Washington Twp. (Bergen)(u)	(201)	9,245	9,550
07060	Watchung	(908)	5,110	5,290
07470	Wayne Twp.(u)	(201)	47,025	46,474
07087	Weehawken Twp.(u)	(201)	12,385	13,168
07006	West Caldwell(u)	(201)	10,422	11,407
*07091	Westfield	(908)	28,870	30,447
07728	West Freehold(u)	(908)	11,166	9,929
07764	West Long Branch	(908)	7,690	7,380
07480	West Milford Twp.(u)	(201)	25,430	22,750
07093	West New York	(201)	38,125	39,194
07052	West Orange	(201)	39,103	39,510
07424	West Paterson	(201)	10,982	11,293
07675	Westwood	(201)	10,446	10,714
07885	Wharton	(201)	5,405	5,485
08610	White Horse(u)	(609)	9,397	10,098
07886	White Meadow Lake(u)	(201)	8,002	8,429
08094	Williamstown	(609)	10,891	5,768
08046	Willingboro Twp.(u)	(609)	36,291	39,912
08095	Winslow Twp.(u)	(609)	30,087	20,034
07095	Woodbridge Twp.(u)	(908)	93,086	90,074
08096	Woodbury	(609)	10,904	10,353
07675	Woodcliff Lake	(201)	5,303	5,644
07075	Wood-Ridge	(201)	7,506	7,929
07481	Wyckoff Twp.(u)	(201)	15,372	15,500
08620	Yardville-Groveville(u)	(609)	9,248	9,414
.....	Yorketown(u)	(609)	6,313	5,330

New Mexico (505)

ZIP code	Place		1990	1980
88310	Alamogordo		27,596	24,024
*87101	Albuquerque		384,619	332,920
88021	Anthony(u)		5,160	....
88210	Artesia		10,610	10,385
87410	Aztec		5,400	5,512
87002	Belen		6,547	5,617
87001	Bernalillo		5,960	2,988
87413	Bloomfield		5,214	4,881
88220	Carlsbad		24,952	25,496
88101	Clovis		30,954	31,194
87048	Corrales		5,453	2,791
88030	Deming		10,970	9,964
87532	Espanola		8,389	6,803
87401	Farmington		33,997	31,222
87301	Gallup		19,157	18,167
87020	Grants		8,626	11,439
88240	Hobbs		29,121	29,153
88330	Holloman AFB(u)		5,891	7,245
*88001	Las Cruces		62,360	45,086
87701	Las Vegas		14,753	14,322
87544	Los Alamos(u)		11,455	11,039
87031	Los Lunas		6,013	3,525
88260	Lovington		9,322	9,727
87107	North Valley(u)		12,507	5,096
87114	Paradise Hills(u)		5,513	5,096
88130	Portales		10,690	9,940
87740	Raton		7,372	8,225
87124	Rio Rancho		32,512	9,985
88201	Roswell		44,260	39,676
87115	Sandia(u)		6,742	5,288
*87501	Santa Fe		56,537	49,160
87420	Shiprock		7,687	7,237
88061	Silver City		10,683	9,887
87801	Socorro		8,159	7,173
87105	South Valley(u)		35,701	38,916
88063	Sunland Park		8,179	4,313
87901	Truth or Consequences		6,221	5,219
88401	Tucumcari		6,827	6,765
87544	White Rock(u)		6,192	6,560
87327	Zuni Pueblo(u)		5,857	5,551

New York

ZIP code	Place		1990	1980
10901	Airmont(u)		7,835	....
*12207	Albany	(518)	100,031	101,727
11507	Albertson(u)	(516)	5,166	5,561
14411	Albion	(716)	5,863	4,897
11701	Amityville	(516)	9,286	9,076
12010	Amsterdam	(518)	20,714	21,872
12603	Arlington(u)	(914)	11,948	11,305
13021	Auburn	(315)	31,258	32,548
*11702	Babylon	(516)	12,249	12,388
11510	Baldwin(u)	(516)	22,719	31,630
11510	Baldwin Harbor(u)		7,899	....
13027	Baldwinsville	(315)	6,591	6,446
12020	Ballston Spa	(518)	5,194	....
14020	Batavia	(716)	16,310	16,703
14810	Bath	(607)	5,801	6,042
11705	Bayport(u)	(516)	7,702	9,282
11706	Bay Shore(u)	(516)	21,279	10,784
11709	Bayville	(516)	7,193	7,034
.....	Baywood(u)		7,351	....
12508	Beacon	(914)	13,243	12,937
11710	Bellmore(u)	(516)	16,438	18,106
11714	Bethpage(u)	(516)	15,761	16,840
*13902	Binghamton	(607)	53,008	55,860
11716	Bohemia(u)	(516)	9,556	9,308
11717	Brentwood(u)	(516)	45,218	44,321
10510	Briarcliff Manor	(914)	7,070	7,115
14610	Brighton (u)	(716)	34,455	35,776
14420	Brockport	(716)	8,749	9,776
10708	Bronxville	(914)	6,028	6,267
*14240	Buffalo	(716)	328,175	357,870
14424	Canandaigua	(716)	10,725	10,419
13617	Canton	(315)	6,379	7,055
11514	Carle Place(u)	(516)	5,107	5,470
11516	Cedarhurst	(516)	5,716	6,162
11720	Centereach(u)	(516)	26,720	30,136
11934	Center Moriches(u)	(516)	5,987	5,703
11721	Centerport(u)	(516)	5,333	6,576

ZIP code	Place		1990	1980
11722	Central Islip(u)	(516)	26,028	19,734
14225	Cheektowaga(u)	(716)	84,387	92,145
10977	Chestnut Ridge		7,517	8,217
12043	Cobleskill	(518)	5,268	5,272
12047	Cohoes	(518)	16,825	18,144
12205	Colonie	(518)	8,019	8,869
11725	Commack(u)	(516)	36,124	34,719
10920	Congers(u)	(914)	8,003	7,123
11726	Copiague(u)	(516)	20,769	20,132
11727	Coram(u)	(516)	30,111	24,752
14830	Corning	(607)	11,938	12,953
13045	Cortland	(607)	19,801	20,138
10520	Croton-on-Hudson	(914)	7,018	6,889
14437	Dansville	(716)	5,002	4,979
11729	Deer Park(u)	(516)	28,840	30,394
12054	Delmar(u)	(518)	8,360	8,423
14043	Depew	(716)	17,673	19,819
13214	DeWitt(u)	(315)	8,244	9,024
11746	Dix Hills(u)	(516)	25,849	26,693
10522	Dobbs Ferry	(914)	9,940	10,053
14048	Dunkirk	(716)	13,989	15,310
14052	East Aurora	(716)	6,647	6,803
10709	Eastchester(u)	(914)	18,537	20,305
12302	East Glenville(u)	(518)	6,518	6,537
11576	East Hills	(516)	6,746	7,160
11730	East Islip(u)	(516)	14,325	13,852
11758	East Massapequa(u)	(516)	19,550	13,987
11554	East Meadow(u)	(516)	36,909	39,317
11731	East Northport(u)	(516)	20,411	20,187
11772	East Patchogue(u)	(516)	20,195	18,139
14445	East Rochester	(716)	6,932	7,596
11518	East Rockaway	(516)	10,152	10,917
11786	East Shoreham		5,461	....
*14901	Elmira	(607)	33,724	35,327
11003	Elmont(u)	(516)	28,612	27,592
11731	Elmwood(u)	(516)	10,916	11,847
13760	Endicott	(607)	13,531	14,457
13760	Endwell(u)	(607)	12,602	13,745
13219	Fairmount(u)	(315)	12,266	13,415
14450	Fairport	(716)	5,943	5,970
11735	Farmingdale	(516)	8,022	7,946
11738	Farmingville(u)	(516)	14,842	13,398
*11001	Floral Park	(516)	15,947	16,805
13603	Fort Drum(u)		11,578	....
11768	Fort Salonga(u)	(516)	9,176	9,550
11010	Franklin Square(u)	(516)	28,205	29,051
14063	Fredonia	(716)	10,436	11,126
11520	Freeport	(516)	39,894	38,272
13069	Fulton	(315)	12,929	13,312
11530	Garden City	(516)	21,675	22,927
11040	Garden City Park(u)	(516)	7,437	7,712
14624	Gates-North Gates(u)	(716)	14,995	15,244
14454	Geneseo	(716)	7,187	6,746
14456	Geneva	(315)	14,143	15,133
11542	Glen Cove	(516)	24,149	24,618
12801	Glens Falls	(518)	15,023	15,897
12801	Glens Falls North(u)	(518)	7,978	6,956
12078	Gloversville	(518)	16,656	17,836
10924	Goshen	(914)	5,255	4,874
*11022	Great Neck	(516)	8,745	9,168
11020	Great Neck Plaza	(516)	5,897	5,604
14616	Greece(u)	(716)	15,632	16,177
11740	Greenlawn(u)	(516)	13,208	13,869
12083	Greenville(u)	(518)	9,528	8,706
14075	Hamburg	(716)	10,442	10,582
11946	Hampton Bays(u)	(516)	7,893	7,256
10528	Harrison	(914)	23,308	23,046
10530	Hartsdale(u)	(914)	9,587	10,216
10706	Hastings-on-Hudson	(914)	8,000	8,573
11787	Hauppauge(u)	(516)	19,750	20,960
10927	Haverstraw	(914)	9,438	8,800
*11551	Hempstead	(516)	47,051	40,404
13350	Herkimer	(315)	7,945	8,383
11557	Hewlett(u)	(516)	6,620	6,986
*11802	Hicksville(u)	(516)	40,174	43,245
10977	Hillcrest(u)	(914)	6,447	5,733
14468	Hilton		5,216	4,151
11741	Holbrook(u)	(516)	25,273	24,382
11742	Holtsville(u)	(516)	14,972	13,515
14843	Hornell	(607)	9,877	10,234
14845	Horseheads	(607)	6,802	7,348
12534	Hudson	(518)	8,034	7,986
12839	Hudson Falls	(518)	7,651	7,419
11743	Huntington(u)	(516)	18,243	21,727
11746	Huntington Station(u)	(516)	28,247	28,769
13357	Ilion	(315)	8,888	9,450
11696	Inwood(u)	(516)	7,767	8,228
14617	Irondequoit(u)	(716)	52,322	57,648
10533	Irvington	(914)	6,348	5,774
11751	Islip(u)	(516)	18,924	13,438
11752	Islip Terrace(u)	(516)	5,530	5,588
14850	Ithaca	(607)	29,541	28,732
14701	Jamestown	(716)	34,681	35,775
10535	Jefferson Valley-Yorktown(u)	(914)	14,118	13,380
11753	Jericho(u)	(516)	13,141	12,739
13790	Johnson City	(607)	16,578	17,126
12095	Johnstown	(518)	9,058	9,360
14217	Kenmore	(716)	17,180	18,474
11754	Kings Park(u)	(516)	17,773	16,131
12401	Kingston	(914)	23,095	24,481
.....	Kiryas Joel		7,437	2,088
14218	Lackawanna	(716)	20,585	22,701
10512	Lake Carmel(u)	(914)	8,489	7,295
11755	Lake Grove	(516)	9,612	9,692
11779	Lake Ronkonkoma(u)	(516)	18,997	38,336
11552	Lakeview(u)	(516)	5,476	5,276
14086	Lancaster	(716)	11,940	13,056
10538	Larchmont	(914)	6,181	6,308
12110	Latham(u)	(518)	10,131	11,182
11559	Lawrence	(516)	6,513	6,175
11756	Levittown(u)	(516)	53,286	57,045
11757	Lindenhurst	(516)	26,879	26,919
13365	Little Falls	(315)	5,829	6,156
14094	Lockport	(716)	24,426	24,844
11561	Long Beach	(516)	33,510	34,073
12211	Loudonville(u)	(518)	10,822	11,480
11563	Lynbrook	(516)	19,208	20,424
10541	Mahopac(u)	(914)	7,755	7,681
12953	Malone	(518)	6,777	7,668
11565	Malverne	(516)	9,054	9,262
10543	Mamaroneck	(914)	17,325	17,616
11030	Manhasset(u)	(516)	7,718	8,485
11050	Manorhaven	(516)	5,672	5,384
11949	Manorville(u)	(516)	6,198	....
11758	Massapequa(u)	(516)	22,018	24,454
11762	Massapequa Park	(516)	18,044	19,779
13662	Massena	(315)	11,716	12,851
11950	Mastic(u)	(516)	13,778	10,413
11951	Mastic Beach(u)	(516)	10,293	8,318
13211	Mattydale(u)	(315)	6,418	7,511
12118	Mechanicville	(518)	5,249	5,500
11763	Medford(u)	(516)	21,274	20,418
14103	Medina	(716)	6,686	6,392
11746	Melville(u)	(516)	12,586	8,139
11566	Merrick(u)	(516)	23,042	24,478
11953	Middle Island(u)	(516)	7,848	5,703
10940	Middletown	(914)	24,160	21,454
11764	Miller Place(u)	(516)	9,315	7,877
11501	Mineola	(516)	19,005	20,757
10950	Monroe	(914)	6,672	5,996
10952	Monsey(u)	(914)	13,986	12,380
12701	Monticello	(914)	6,597	6,306
10970	Mount Ivy(u)		6,013	....
10549	Mount Kisco	(914)	9,108	8,025
11766	Mount Sinai(u)	(516)	8,023	6,591
*10551	Mount Vernon	(914)	67,153	66,713
12590	Myers Corner(u)	(914)	5,599	5,180
10954	Nanuet(u)	(914)	14,065	12,578
11767	Nesconset(u)	(516)	10,712	10,706
14513	Newark	(315)	9,849	10,017
12550	Newburgh	(914)	26,454	23,438
11590	New Cassel(u)	(516)	10,257	9,635
10956	New City(u)	(914)	33,673	35,859
11040	New Hyde Park	(516)	9,728	9,801
12561	New Paltz	(914)	5,470	4,938
*10802	New Rochelle	(914)	67,265	70,794
*12550	New Windsor Center(u)	(914)	8,898	7,812
*10001	New York	(212)	7,322,564	7,071,639
*14302	Niagara Falls	(716)	61,840	71,384
11701	North Amityville(u)	(516)	13,849	13,140
11703	North Babylon(u)	(516)	18,081	19,019
11706	North Bay Shore(u)	(516)	12,799	35,020
11710	North Bellmore(u)	(516)	19,707	20,630
11713	North Bellport(u)	(516)	8,182	7,432
11757	North Lindenhurst(u)	(516)	10,563	11,511
11758	North Massapequa(u)	(516)	19,365	21,385
11566	North Merrick(u)	(516)	12,113	12,848
11040	North New Hyde Park(u)	(516)	14,359	15,114
11772	North Patchogue(u)	(516)	7,374	7,126
11768	Northport	(516)	7,572	7,651
13212	North Syracuse	(315)	7,363	7,970
10591	North Tarrytown	(914)	8,152	7,994
14120	North Tonawanda	(716)	34,989	35,760
11580	North Valley Stream(u)	(516)	14,574	14,530
11793	North Wantagh(u)	(516)	12,276	12,677
13815	Norwich	(607)	7,613	8,082
10960	Nyack	(914)	6,558	6,428
11769	Oakdale(u)	(516)	7,875	8,090
11572	Oceanside(u)	(516)	32,423	33,639
13669	Ogdensburg	(315)	13,521	12,375
11804	Old Bethpage(u)	(516)	5,610	6,215
14760	Olean	(716)	16,946	18,207
13421	Oneida	(315)	10,850	10,810
13820	Oneonta	(607)	13,954	14,933
12550	Orange Lake(u)	(914)	5,196	5,120
10562	Ossining	(914)	22,582	20,196
13126	Oswego	(315)	19,195	19,793
11771	Oyster Bay(u)	(516)	6,687	6,497
11772	Patchogue	(516)	11,060	11,291
10965	Pearl River(u)	(914)	15,314	15,893
10566	Peekskill	(914)	19,536	18,236
10803	Pelham	(914)	6,413	6,848
10803	Pelham Manor	(914)	5,443	6,130
14527	Penn Yan	(315)	5,257	5,242
11714	Plainedge(u)	(516)	8,739	9,629
11803	Plainview(u)	(516)	26,207	28,037
12901	Plattsburgh	(518)	21,255	21,057
12903	Plattsburgh AFB(u)	(518)	5,483	5,905

ZIP code	Place		1990	1980
10570	Pleasantville	(914)	6,592	6,749
10573	Port Chester	(914)	24,728	23,565
11777	Port Jefferson	(516)	7,455	6,731
11776	Port Jefferson Station(u)	(516)	7,232	17,009
12771	Port Jervis	(914)	9,060	8,699
11050	Port Washington(u)	(516)	15,387	14,521
13676	Potsdam	(315)	10,251	10,635
*12601	Poughkeepsie	(914)	28,844	29,757
12144	Rensselaer	(518)	8,255	9,047
11961	Ridge(u)	(516)	11,734	8,977
11901	Riverhead(u)	(516)	8,814	6,339
*14603	Rochester	(716)	230,356	241,741
*11570	Rockville Centre	(516)	24,727	25,412
11778	Rocky Point(u)	(516)	8,596	7,012
12205	Roessleville(u)	(518)	10,753	11,685
13440	Rome	(315)	44,350	43,826
11779	Ronkonkoma	(516)	20,391	....
11575	Roosevelt(u)	(516)	15,030	14,109
11577	Roslyn Heights(u)	(516)	6,405	6,546
12303	Rotterdam(u)	(518)	21,228	22,933
10580	Rye	(914)	14,936	15,083
10573	Rye Brook		7,765	7,996
11780	Saint James(u)	(516)	12,703	12,122
14779	Salamanca	(716)	6,566	6,890
13454	Salisbury(u)		12,226	....
12983	Saranac Lake	(518)	5,377	5,578
12866	Saratoga Springs	(518)	25,001	23,906
11782	Sayville(u)	(516)	16,550	12,013
10583	Scarsdale	(914)	16,987	17,650
*12301	Schenectady	(518)	65,566	67,972
10940	Scotchtown(u)	(914)	8,765	7,352
12302	Scotia	(518)	7,359	7,280
11579	Sea Cliff	(516)	5,054	5,364
11783	Seaford(u)	(516)	15,597	16,117
11507	Searingtown(u)		5,020	....
11784	Selden(u)	(516)	20,608	17,259
13148	Seneca Falls	(315)	7,370	7,466
11733	Setauket-East Setauket(u)	(516)	13,634	10,176
11967	Shirley(u)	(516)	22,936	18,072
11787	Smithtown(u)	(516)	25,638	30,906
13209	Solvay	(315)	6,717	7,140
11789	Sound Beach(u)	(516)	9,102	8,071
11735	South Farmingdale(u)	(516)	15,377	16,439
14850	South Hill(u)	(607)	5,423	....
11746	South Huntington(u)	(516)	9,624	14,854
14094	South Lockport(u)		7,112	3,366
11971	Southold(u)		5,192	4,770
14904	Southport(u)	(607)	7,753	8,329
11581	South Valley Stream(u)	(516)	5,328	5,462
10977	Spring Valley	(914)	21,802	20,537
11790	Stony Brook(u)	(516)	13,726	16,155
10980	Stony Point(u)	(315)	10,587	8,686
10901	Suffern	(914)	11,055	10,794
11791	Syosset(u)	(516)	18,967	9,818
*13201	Syracuse	(315)	163,860	170,105
10983	Tappan(u)	(914)	6,867	8,267
10591	Tarrytown	(914)	10,739	10,648
11776	Terryville		10,275	....
10984	Thiells		5,204	....
10594	Thornwood(u)	(914)	7,025	7,197
14150	Tonawanda	(716)	17,284	18,693
14151	Tonawanda(u)	(716)	65,284	72,795
*12180	Troy	(518)	54,269	56,638
10707	Tuckahoe	(914)	6,302	6,076
11553	Uniondale(u)	(516)	20,328	20,016
*13503	Utica	(315)	68,637	75,632
10989	Valley Cottage(u)	(914)	9,007	8,214
*11580	Valley Stream	(516)	33,946	35,769
11792	Wading River		5,317	....
12586	Walden	(914)	5,836	5,659
11793	Wantagh(u)	(516)	18,567	19,817
10990	Warwick		5,984	4,320
13165	Waterloo	(315)	5,116	5,303
13601	Watertown	(315)	29,429	27,861
12189	Watervliet	(518)	11,061	11,354
14580	Webster	(716)	5,464	5,499
14895	Wellsville	(716)	5,241	5,769
11704	West Babylon(u)	(516)	42,410	41,699
11590	Westbury	(516)	13,060	13,871
14905	West Elmira(u)	(607)	5,218	5,485
12801	West Glens Falls(u)	(518)	5,964	5,331
10993	West Haverstraw	(914)	9,183	9,181
11552	West Hempstead(u)	(516)	17,689	18,536
11743	West Hills(u)	(516)	5,849	6,071
11795	West Islip(u)	(516)	28,419	29,533
12203	Westmere(u)	(518)	6,750	6,881
10996	West Point(u)	(914)	8,024	8,105
14224	West Seneca(u)	(716)	47,866	51,210
13219	Westvale(u)	(315)	5,952	6,169
11798	Wheatley Heights(u)		5,027	....
10602	White Plains	(914)	48,718	46,999
14221	Williamsville	(716)	5,583	6,017
11596	Williston Park	(516)	7,516	8,216
11797	Woodbury(u)	(516)	8,008	7,043
11598	Woodmere(u)	(516)	15,578	17,205
11798	Wyandach(u)	(516)	8,950	13,215
*10701	Yonkers	(914)	188,082	195,351
10598	Yorktown Heights(u)	(914)	7,690	7,696

North Carolina

ZIP code	Place		1990	1980
28001	Albemarle	(704)	14,940	15,110
27263	Archdale	(919)	6,975	5,326
27203	Asheboro	(919)	16,362	15,252
*28801	Asheville	(704)	61,855	54,022
28012	Belmont	(704)	8,434	4,607
28711	Black Mountain		5,533	4,083
28607	Boone	(704)	12,949	10,191
28712	Brevard	(704)	5,388	5,323
27215	Burlington	(919)	39,498	37,266
28542	Camp Le Jeune(u)	(919)	36,716	30,764
27510	Carrboro	(919)	12,134	7,336
27511	Cary	(919)	43,457	21,763
27514	Chapel Hill	(919)	38,711	32,421
*28202	Charlotte	(704)	395,934	315,474
27012	Clemmons(u)	(919)	6,020	4,842
28328	Clinton	(919)	8,385	7,552
28025	Concord	(704)	27,347	16,942
28613	Conover	(704)	5,465	4,245
28334	Dunn	(919)	8,556	8,962
*27701	Durham	(919)	136,612	101,149
27288	Eden	(919)	15,238	15,672
27932	Edenton	(919)	5,268	5,357
27909	Elizabeth City	(919)	14,292	14,004
*28302	Fayetteville	(919)	75,850	59,507
28043	Forest City	(704)	7,475	7,688
28307	Fort Bragg(u)	(919)	34,744	37,834
27529	Garner	(919)	14,716	10,073
28052	Gastonia	(704)	54,725	47,218
27530	Goldsboro	(919)	40,709	31,871
27253	Graham	(919)	10,368	8,674
*27420	Greensboro	(919)	183,894	155,642
27834	Greenville	(919)	46,305	35,740
.....	Half Moon(u)		6,306	3,592
28345	Hamlet	(919)	6,324	4,720
28532	Havelock	(919)	20,300	17,718
27536	Henderson	(919)	15,655	13,522
28739	Hendersonville	(704)	7,284	6,862
28601	Hickory	(704)	28,301	20,757
*27260	High Point	(919)	69,424	63,479
28348	Hope Mills	(919)	8,272	5,412
28540	Jacksonville	(919)	30,001	18,237
28081	Kannapolis	(704)	29,696	30,303
27284	Kernersville	(919)	10,836	5,875
28086	Kings Mountain	(704)	8,763	9,080
28501	Kinston	(919)	25,295	25,234
28352	Laurinburg	(919)	11,643	11,480
28645	Lenoir	(704)	14,192	13,748
27292	Lexington	(704)	16,581	15,711
28092	Lincolnton	(704)	6,955	4,879
28358	Lumberton	(919)	18,733	18,241
.....	Masonboro(u)		7,010	3,881
28105	Matthews	(704)	13,651	1,648
28212	Mint Hill	(704)	11,615	7,915
28110	Monroe	(704)	16,385	12,639
28115	Mooresville	(704)	9,317	8,575
28557	Morehead	(919)	6,046	4,359
28655	Morganton	(704)	15,085	13,763
27030	Mount Airy	(919)	7,156	6,862
28120	Mount Holly	(704)	7,710	4,530
28560	New Bern	(919)	17,363	14,557
27604	New Hope (Wake)(u)	(704)	5,694	6,745
28540	New River Station(u)	(919)	9,732	5,401
28658	Newton	(704)	9,304	7,624
27565	Oxford	(919)	7,965	7,709
28374	Pinehurst	(919)	5,091	1,746
28399	Piney Green-White Oak(u)	(919)	8,999	6,058
*27611	Raleigh	(919)	212,050	150,255
27320	Reidsville	(919)	12,183	12,492
27870	Roanoke Rapids	(919)	15,722	14,702
28379	Rockingham	(919)	9,399	8,300
27801	Rocky Mount	(919)	49,438	41,526
27573	Roxboro	(919)	7,332	7,532
28601	Saint Stephens(u)	(704)	8,734	10,797
28144	Salisbury	(704)	23,621	22,677
27330	Sanford	(919)	14,755	14,773
.....	Seagate(u)		5,444	3,422
28150	Shelby	(704)	14,669	15,310
.....	Smith Creek(u)		7,461	....
27577	Smithfield	(919)	7,540	7,288
28387	Southern Pines	(919)	9,213	8,620
.....	South Gastonia		5,487	4,767
28390	Spring Lake	(919)	7,524	6,273
28677	Statesville	(704)	17,567	18,622
27886	Tarboro	(919)	11,037	8,741
27360	Thomasville	(919)	15,915	14,144
27370	Trinity(u)	(919)	5,469	6,887
27587	Wake Forest	(919)	5,832	3,780
27889	Washington	(919)	9,160	8,418
28786	Waynesville	(704)	6,758	6,765
28472	Whiteville	(919)	5,078	5,565
27892	Williamston	(919)	5,503	6,159
28401	Wilmington	(919)	55,530	44,000
27893	Wilson	(919)	36,930	34,424
*27102	Winston-Salem	(919)	143,485	131,885

North Dakota (701)

ZIP code	Place	1990	1980
58501	Bismarck	49,272	44,485
58301	Devils Lake	7,782	7,442
58601	Dickinson	16,097	15,924
58102	Fargo	74,084	61,383
58201	Grand Forks	49,417	43,765
58201	Grand Forks AFB(u)	9,343	9,390
58401	Jamestown	15,571	16,280
58554	Mandan	15,177	15,513
58701	Minot	34,544	32,843
58701	Minot AFB(u)	9,095	9,880
58072	Valley City	7,163	7,774
58075	Wahpeton	8,751	9,064
58078	West Fargo	12,287	10,099
58801	Williston	13,136	13,336

Ohio

ZIP code	Place		1990	1980
45810	Ada	(419)	5,428	5,669
*44309	Akron	(216)	223,019	237,177
44601	Alliance	(216)	23,376	24,315
44001	Amherst	(216)	10,332	10,638
44805	Ashland	(419)	20,079	20,326
44004	Ashtabula	(216)	21,633	23,449
45701	Athens	(614)	21,265	19,743
44202	Aurora	(216)	9,192	8,177
44515	Austintown(u)	(216)	32,371	33,636
44011	Avon	(216)	7,337	7,241
44012	Avon Lake	(216)	15,066	13,222
44203	Barberton	(216)	27,623	29,751
44140	Bay Village	(216)	17,000	17,846
44122	Beachwood	(216)	10,644	9,983
45385	Beavercreek	(513)	33,626	31,589
44146	Bedford	(216)	14,822	15,056
44146	Bedford Heights	(216)	12,131	13,214
43906	Bellaire	(614)	6,028	8,241
45305	Bellbrook	(513)	6,511	5,174
43311	Bellefontaine	(513)	12,126	11,888
44811	Bellevue	(419)	8,157	8,187
45714	Belpre	(614)	6,796	7,193
44017	Berea	(216)	19,051	19,567
43209	Bexley	(614)	13,088	13,405
43004	Blacklick Estates(u)	(614)	10,080	11,223
45242	Blue Ash	(513)	11,923	9,510
44512	Boardman(u)	(216)	38,596	39,161
43402	Bowling Green	(419)	28,176	25,728
44141	Brecksville	(216)	11,818	10,132
45211	Bridgetown North	(513)	11,748	11,460
44141	Broadview Heights	(216)	12,219	10,920
44144	Brooklyn	(216)	11,706	12,342
44142	Brook Park	(216)	22,865	26,195
44212	Brunswick	(216)	28,218	28,104
43506	Bryan	(419)	8,348	7,879
44820	Bucyrus	(419)	13,496	13,433
43725	Cambridge	(614)	11,748	13,573
44405	Campbell	(216)	10,038	11,619
44406	Canfield	(216)	5,409	5,535
*44711	Canton	(216)	84,161	93,077
45822	Celina	(419)	9,923	9,137
45459	Centerville	(513)	21,082	18,886
45211	Cheviot	(513)	9,616	9,888
45601	Chillicothe	(614)	21,923	23,420
*45234	Cincinnati	(513)	364,114	385,409
43113	Circleville	(614)	11,666	11,700
*44101	Cleveland	(216)	505,616	573,822
44118	Cleveland Heights	(216)	54,052	56,438
43410	Clyde	(419)	5,776	5,489
*43235	Columbus	(614)	632,945	565,021
44030	Conneaut	(216)	13,241	13,835
44410	Cortland	(216)	5,652	5,011
43812	Coshocton	(614)	12,193	13,405
45238	Covedale(u)	(513)	6,669	5,830
*44222	Cuyahoga Falls	(216)	48,950	50,526
*45401	Dayton	(513)	182,005	193,536
45236	Deer Park	(513)	6,181	6,745
43512	Defiance	(419)	16,787	16,810
43015	Delaware	(614)	19,966	18,780
45833	Delphos	(419)	7,093	7,314
45247	Dent(u)		6,416	....
44622	Dover	(216)	11,329	11,782
45427	Drexel(u)		5,143	....
.....	Dry Run(u)		5,389	....
43017	Dublin	(614)	16,366	3,855
44112	East Cleveland	(216)	33,096	36,957
44094	Eastlake	(216)	21,161	22,104
43920	East Liverpool	(216)	13,654	16,687
44413	East Palestine	(216)	5,168	5,306
45320	Eaton	(513)	7,396	6,839
44004	Edgewood(u)		5,189	3,099
*44035	Elyria	(216)	56,746	57,538
45322	Englewood	(513)	11,402	11,329
44117	Euclid	(216)	54,875	59,999
45324	Fairborn	(513)	31,300	29,702
45014	Fairfield	(513)	39,709	30,777
44313	Fairlawn	(216)	5,779	6,100
44126	Fairview Park	(216)	18,028	19,311
45840	Findlay	(419)	35,703	35,594
45224	Finneytown(u)		13,096	....
45405	Forest Park	(513)	18,621	18,566
45230	Forestville(u)		9,185	....
45426	Fort McKinley(u)	(513)	9,740	10,161
44830	Fostoria	(419)	14,971	15,743
45005	Franklin	(513)	11,026	10,711
43420	Fremont	(419)	17,619	17,834
43230	Gahanna	(614)	23,898	18,001
44833	Galion	(419)	11,859	12,391
44125	Garfield Heights	(216)	31,739	34,938
44041	Geneva	(216)	6,597	6,655
44420	Girard	(216)	11,304	12,517
43212	Grandview Heights	(614)	7,010	7,420
45123	Greenfield	(513)	5,172	5,150
45331	Greenville	(513)	12,863	12,999
45239	Groesbeck(u)	(513)	6,684	9,594
43123	Grove City	(614)	19,661	16,816
*45012	Hamilton	(513)	61,436	63,189
45030	Harrison	(513)	7,520	5,855
43055	Heath	(614)	7,231	6,969
44124	Highland Heights	(216)	6,249	5,739
43026	Hilliard	(614)	11,794	8,131
45133	Hillsboro	(513)	6,235	6,356
44484	Howland(u)	(216)	6,732	7,441
44425	Hubbard	(216)	8,248	9,245
45424	Huber Heights	(513)	38,696	35,480
43081	Huber Ridge(u)	(614)	5,255	5,835
44236	Hudson	(216)	5,159	4,615
44839	Huron	(419)	7,067	7,123
44131	Independence	(216)	6,500	6,607
45638	Ironton	(614)	12,751	14,290
45640	Jackson	(614)	6,167	6,675
44240	Kent	(216)	28,835	26,164
43326	Kenton	(419)	8,356	8,605
45236	Kenwood(u)	(513)	7,469	9,928
45429	Kettering	(513)	60,569	61,186
44094	Kirtland	(216)	5,881	5,969
44107	Lakewood	(216)	59,718	61,963
43130	Lancaster	(614)	34,507	34,953
45039	Landen(u)		9,263	2,870
45036	Lebanon	(513)	10,461	9,636
*45802	Lima	(419)	45,553	47,827
43228	Lincoln Village(u)	(614)	9,958	10,548
43138	Logan	(614)	6,725	6,557
43140	London	(614)	7,807	6,958
*44052	Lorain	(216)	71,245	75,416
44641	Louisville	(216)	8,087	7,996
45140	Loveland	(513)	10,122	9,106
44124	Lyndhurst	(216)	15,982	18,092
44056	Macedonia	(216)	7,509	6,571
.....	Mack South(u)		5,767	....
45243	Madeira	(513)	9,141	9,341
*44901	Mansfield	(419)	50,627	53,927
44137	Maple Heights	(216)	27,089	29,735
45750	Marietta	(614)	15,026	16,467
43302	Marion	(614)	34,075	37,040
43935	Martins Ferry	(614)	8,003	9,331
43040	Marysville	(513)	9,656	7,414
45040	Mason	(513)	11,450	8,692
44646	Massillon	(216)	30,969	30,557
43537	Maumee	(419)	15,561	15,747
44124	Mayfield Heights	(216)	19,847	21,550
44256	Medina	(216)	19,231	15,268
44060	Mentor	(216)	47,491	42,065
44060	Mentor-on-the-Lake	(216)	8,271	7,919
45342	Miamisburg	(513)	17,834	15,304
44130	Middleburg Heights	(216)	14,702	16,218
45042	Middletown	(513)	46,022	43,719
45150	Milford	(513)	5,660	5,679
45242	Montgomery	(513)	9,733	10,084
45439	Moraine	(513)	5,989	5,325
45231	Mount Healthy	(513)	7,580	7,562
43050	Mount Vernon	(614)	14,550	14,323
44262	Munroe Falls	(216)	5,359	4,731
43545	Napoleon	(419)	8,884	8,614
43055	Newark	(614)	44,396	41,200
45344	New Carlisle	(513)	6,049	6,498
43764	New Lexington	(614)	5,117	5,179
44663	New Philadelphia	(216)	15,698	16,883
44446	Niles	(216)	21,128	23,088
45239	Northbrook(u)	(513)	11,471	8,357
44720	North Canton	(216)	14,748	14,228
45239	North College Hill	(513)	11,002	11,114
.....	Northgate		7,864	....
44057	North Madison(u)	(216)	8,699	8,741
44070	North Olmsted	(216)	34,204	36,486
45502	Northridge(u)	(513)	5,939	5,559
45414	Northridge(u) (Montgomery)	(513)	9,448	9,720
44039	North Ridgeville	(216)	21,564	21,522
44133	North Royalton	(216)	23,197	17,671
.....	Northview(u)	(513)	10,337	9,973
43619	Northwood	(419)	5,506	5,495
44203	Norton	(216)	11,477	12,242
44857	Norwalk	(419)	14,731	14,358
45212	Norwood	(513)	23,674	26,342
45873	Oakwood	(419)	8,957	9,372
44074	Oberlin	(216)	8,191	8,660

ZIP code	Place		1990	1980
44138	Olmsted Falls	(216)	6,741	5,868
43616	Oregon	(419)	18,334	18,675
44667	Orrville	(216)	7,712	7,511
45431	Overlook-Page Manor(u)	(513)	13,242	14,825
45056	Oxford	(513)	18,937	17,655
44077	Painesville	(216)	15,769	16,391
44129	Parma	(216)	87,876	92,548
44130	Parma Heights	(216)	21,448	23,112
44124	Pepper Pike	(216)	6,185	6,177
44646	Perry Heights(u)	(216)	9,055	9,206
43551	Perrysburg	(419)	12,551	10,215
43147	Pickerington	...	5,668	3,917
45356	Piqua	(513)	20,612	20,480
44319	Portage Lakes(u)	(216)	13,373	11,310
43452	Port Clinton	(419)	7,106	7,223
45662	Portsmouth	(614)	22,676	25,943
44266	Ravenna	(216)	12,069	11,987
45215	Reading	(513)	12,038	12,843
43068	Reynoldsburg	(614)	25,748	20,661
44143	Richmond Heights	(216)	9,611	10,095
44270	Rittman	(216)	6,147	6,063
44116	Rocky River	(216)	20,410	21,084
43460	Rossford	(419)	5,861	5,978
45217	Saint Bernard	(513)	5,344	5,396
43950	Saint Clairsville	(614)	5,136	5,452
45885	Saint Marys	(419)	8,441	8,414
44460	Salem	(216)	12,233	12,869
44870	Sandusky	(419)	29,764	31,360
44870	Sandusky South(u)	(419)	6,336	6,548
44131	Seven Hills	(216)	12,339	13,650
44120	Shaker Heights	(216)	30,867	32,487
45241	Sharonville	(513)	13,121	10,108
44054	Sheffield Lake	(216)	9,825	10,484
44875	Shelby	(419)	9,610	9,703
44878	Shiloh	(419)	11,607	11,735
45365	Sidney	(513)	18,710	17,657
45236	Silverton	(513)	5,859	6,172
44139	Solon	(216)	18,548	14,341
44121	South Euclid	(216)	23,866	25,713
45066	Springboro	(513)	6,574	4,962
45246	Springdale	(216)	10,621	10,111
*45501	Springfield	(513)	70,487	72,563
43952	Steubenville	(614)	22,125	26,400
44224	Stow	(216)	27,998	25,303
44240	Streetsboro	(216)	9,932	9,055
44136	Strongsville	(216)	35,308	28,577
44471	Struthers	(216)	12,284	13,624
43560	Sylvania	(419)	17,489	15,527
44278	Tallmadge	(216)	14,870	15,269
45243	The Village of Indian Hill	(513)	5,383	5,521
44883	Tiffin	(419)	18,604	19,549
45371	Tipp City	(513)	6,027	5,595
*43601	Toledo	(419)	332,943	354,635
43964	Toronto	(614)	6,127	6,934
45067	Trenton	(513)	6,189	6,401
45426	Trotwood	(513)	8,816	7,802
45373	Troy	(513)	19,478	19,086
44087	Twinsburg	(216)	9,606	7,632
44683	Uhrichsville	(614)	5,604	6,130
45322	Union	(513)	5,531	5,219
44118	University Heights	(216)	14,787	15,401
43221	Upper Arlington	(614)	34,128	35,648
43351	Upper Sandusky	(419)	5,906	5,967
43078	Urbana	(513)	11,353	10,762
45377	Vandalia	(513)	13,872	13,161
45891	Van Wert	(419)	10,922	11,035
44089	Vermilion	(216)	11,127	11,012
44281	Wadsworth	(216)	15,718	15,166
45895	Wapakoneta	(419)	9,214	8,402
*44481	Warren	(216)	50,793	56,629
44122	Warrensville Heights	(216)	15,745	16,565
43160	Washington C.H.	(614)	13,080	12,682
43567	Wauseon	(419)	6,322	6,173
45692	Wellston	(614)	6,049	6,016
45449	West Carrollton	(513)	14,403	13,148
43081	Westerville	(614)	30,269	23,414
44145	Westlake	(216)	27,018	19,483
45694	Wheelersburg(u)	...	5,113	4,796
43213	Whitehall	(614)	20,572	21,299
45239	White Oak(u)	(513)	12,430	9,563
44092	Wickliffe	(216)	14,558	16,790
44890	Willard	(419)	6,210	5,720
44094	Willoughby	(216)	20,510	19,329
44094	Willoughby Hills	(216)	8,427	8,612
44094	Willowick	(216)	15,269	17,834
45177	Wilmington	(513)	11,199	10,431
45459	Woodbourne-Hyde Park(u)	(513)	7,837	8,826
44691	Wooster	(216)	22,427	19,289
43085	Worthington	(614)	14,869	14,666
45433	Wright-Patterson AFB(u)	(513)	8,579	....
45215	Wyoming	(513)	8,128	8,282
45385	Xenia	(513)	24,836	24,653
*44501	Youngstown	(216)	95,732	115,511
43701	Zanesville	(614)	26,778	28,655

Oklahoma

ZIP code	Place		1990	1980
74820	Ada	(405)	15,820	15,902
73521	Altus	(405)	21,910	23,101
73717	Alva	(405)	5,495	6,416
73005	Anadarko	(405)	6,586	6,378
73401	Ardmore	(405)	23,079	23,689
74003	Bartlesville	(918)	34,256	34,568
73008	Bethany	(405)	20,075	22,038
74008	Bixby	(918)	9,502	6,969
74631	Blackwell	(405)	7,538	8,400
74012	Broken Arrow	(918)	58,043	35,761
73018	Chickasha	(405)	14,988	15,828
73020	Choctaw	(405)	8,545	7,520
74017	Claremore	(918)	13,280	12,085
73601	Clinton	(405)	9,298	8,796
74429	Coweta	...	6,159	4,554
74023	Cushing	(918)	7,218	7,720
73115	Del City	(405)	23,928	28,523
73533	Duncan	(405)	21,732	22,517
74701	Durant	(405)	12,831	11,972
73034	Edmond	(405)	52,315	34,637
73644	Elk City	(405)	10,428	9,579
73036	El Reno	(405)	15,414	15,486
73701	Enid	(405)	45,309	50,363
73503	Fort Sill(u)	(405)	12,107	15,924
73542	Frederick	(405)	5,221	6,153
74033	Glenpool	(918)	6,688	2,706
73044	Guthrie	(405)	10,518	10,312
73942	Guymon	(405)	7,803	8,492
74437	Henryetta	(918)	5,872	6,432
74743	Hugo	(405)	5,978	7,172
74745	Idabel	(405)	6,957	7,622
74037	Jenks	(918)	7,493	5,876
73501	Lawton	(405)	80,561	80,054
74501	McAlester	(918)	16,370	17,255
74354	Miami	(918)	13,142	14,237
73110	Midwest City	(405)	52,267	49,559
73060	Moore	(405)	40,318	35,063
74401	Muskogee	(918)	37,708	40,011
73064	Mustang	(405)	10,434	7,496
73069	Norman	(405)	80,071	68,020
*73125	Oklahoma City	(405)	444,719	404,014
74447	Okmulgee	(918)	13,441	16,263
74055	Owasso	(918)	11,151	6,149
73075	Pauls Valley	(405)	6,150	5,664
74601	Ponca City	(405)	26,359	26,238
74953	Poteau	(918)	7,210	7,089
74361	Pryor Creek	(918)	8,327	8,483
74955	Sallisaw	(918)	7,122	6,403
74063	Sand Springs	(918)	15,346	13,121
74066	Sapulpa	(918)	18,074	15,853
74868	Seminole	(405)	7,071	8,590
74801	Shawnee	(405)	26,017	26,506
74074	Stillwater	(405)	36,676	38,268
74464	Tahlequah	(918)	10,398	9,708
74873	Tecumseh	(405)	5,570	5,123
73120	The Village	(405)	10,353	11,114
*74101	Tulsa	(918)	367,302	360,919
74301	Vinita	(918)	5,804	6,740
74467	Wagoner	(918)	6,894	6,191
73132	Warr Acres	(405)	9,288	9,940
73096	Weatherford	(405)	10,124	9,640
73801	Woodward	(405)	12,340	13,781
73099	Yukon	(405)	20,935	17,112

Oregon (503)

ZIP code	Place	1990	1980
97321	Albany	29,540	26,511
97005	Aloha(u)	34,284	28,353
97601	Altamont(u)	18,591	19,805
97520	Ashland	16,252	14,943
97103	Astoria	10,069	9,998
97814	Baker	9,140	9,471
97005	Beaverton	53,307	31,962
97701	Bend	20,447	17,263
97013	Canby	8,990	7,659
97225	Cedar Hills(u)	9,294	9,619
97291	Cedar Mill(u)	9,697	22,118
97502	Central Point	7,512	6,357
97058	City of the Dalles	11,021	10,820
97420	Coos Bay	15,076	14,424
97113	Cornelius	6,148	4,462
97330	Corvallis	44,757	40,960
97424	Cottage Grove	7,403	7,148
97338	Dallas	9,422	8,530
*97401	Eugene	112,773	105,664
97439	Florence	5,171	4,411
97116	Forest Grove	13,559	11,499
97301	Four Corners(u)	12,156	11,331
97223	Garden Home-Whitford(u)	6,652	6,926
97027	Gladstone	10,152	9,500
97526	Grants Pass	17,503	15,032
97030	Gresham	68,249	33,005
97303	Hayesville(u)	14,318	9,213
97230	Hazelwood(u)	11,480	25,541
97838	Hermiston	10,047	9,408
97123	Hillsboro	37,598	27,664

ZIP code	Place	1990	1980
.....	Jennings Lodge(u)	6,530	....
97303	Keizer	21,884	19,785
97601	Klamath Falls	17,737	16,661
97850	La Grande	11,766	11,354
97034	Lake Oswego	30,576	22,527
97355	Lebanon	10,950	10,413
97367	Lincoln City	5,908	5,469
97128	McMinnville	17,894	14,080
97501	Medford	47,021	39,746
97862	Milton-Freewater	5,533	5,086
97222	Milwaukie	18,670	17,931
97361	Monmouth	6,288	5,594
97132	Newberg	13,086	10,394
97365	Newport	8,437	7,519
97459	North Bend	9,614	9,779
.....	North Springfield(u)	5,451	6,140
97268	Oak Grove(u)	12,576	11,640
.....	Oak Hills	6,450	....
.....	Oatfield	15,348	....
97914	Ontario	9,394	8,814
97045	Oregon City	14,698	14,673
97801	Pendleton	15,142	14,521
*97208	Portland	438,802	368,148
97236	Powellhurst(u)	28,756	20,132
97754	Prineville	5,355	5,276
97225	Raleigh Hills(u)	6,066	6,517
97756	Redmond	7,165	6,452
97404	River Road(u)	9,443	10,370
.....	Rockcreek	8,282	....
97470	Roseburg	17,069	16,644
97470	Roseburg North(u)	6,831	....
97051	Saint Helens	7,535	7,064
*97301	Salem	107,793	89,091
97401	Santa Clara(u)	12,834	14,288
97138	Seaside	5,359	5,193
97381	Silverton	5,635	5,168
97477	Springfield	44,664	41,621
97383	Stayton	5,011	4,396
97479	Sutherlin	5,020	4,560
97386	Sweet Home	6,850	6,921
97223	Tigard	29,435	14,799
97060	Troutdale	7,852	5,908
97062	Tualatin	14,664	7,483
.....	West Haven-Sylvan	6,009	....
97068	West Linn	16,389	11,358
97225	West Slope(u)	7,959	5,364
97501	White City(u)	5,891	5,445
97070	Wilsonville	7,106	2,920
97071	Woodburn	13,404	11,196

Pennsylvania

The 610 area code takes effect January 8, 1994. Until then, the area code for places that will use 610 is 215. Communities with area codes marked with a dagger (†) will be split between area codes 215 and 610; consult local operators.

ZIP code	Place	Area code	1990	1980
15001	Aliquippa	(412)	13,374	17,094
*18101	Allentown	(610)	105,301	103,758
*16603	Altoona	(814)	51,881	57,078
19002	Ambler	(215)†	6,609	6,628
15003	Ambridge	(412)	8,133	9,575
18403	Archbald	(717)	6,291	6,295
19003	Ardmore(u)	(610)	12,646	....
15068	Arnold	(412)	6,113	6,853
19407	Audubon(u)		6,113	6,853
15202	Avalon	(412)	5,784	6,240
15005	Baden	(412)	5,074	5,318
15234	Baldwin	(412)	21,923	24,714
18013	Bangor	(610)	5,383	5,006
15009	Beaver	(412)	5,028	5,441
15010	Beaver Falls	(412)	10,687	12,525
16823	Bellefonte	(814)	6,358	6,300
15202	Bellevue	(412)	9,126	10,128
18603	Berwick	(717)	10,976	11,850
15102	Bethel Park	(412)	33,823	34,755
*18016	Bethlehem	(610)	71,427	70,419
18447	Blakely	(717)	7,222	7,438
17815	Bloomsburg	(717)	12,439	11,717
19422	Blue Bell(u)		6,091	....
19061	Boothwyn(u)		5,069	....
16701	Bradford	(814)	9,625	11,211
15227	Brentwood	(412)	10,823	11,859
15017	Bridgeville	(412)	5,445	6,154
19007	Bristol	(215)	10,405	10,867
19015	Brookhaven	(610)	8,567	7,912
19008	Broomall(u)	(610)	10,930	....
16001	Butler	(412)	15,714	17,026
15419	California	(412)	5,748	5,703
17011	Camp Hill	(717)	7,831	8,422
15317	Canonsburg	(412)	9,200	10,459
18407	Carbondale	(717)	10,664	11,255
17013	Carlisle	(717)	18,419	18,314
15106	Carnegie	(412)	9,278	10,099
15106	Carnot-Moon(u)	(412)	10,187	11,102
15234	Castle Shannon	(412)	9,135	10,164
18032	Catasauqua	(610)	6,662	6,711
17201	Chambersburg	(717)	16,647	16,174
15022	Charleroi	(412)	5,014	5,717
*19013	Chester	(610)	41,856	45,794
19013	Chester Twp(u)	(610)	5,399	5,687
15025	Clairton	(412)	9,656	12,188
16214	Clarion	(814)	6,457	6,198
18411	Clarks Summit	(717)	5,433	5,272
16830	Clearfield	(814)	6,633	7,580
19018	Clifton Heights	(610)	7,111	7,320
19320	Coatesville	(610)	11,038	10,698
19023	Collingdale	(610)	9,175	9,539
.....	Colonial Park(u)		13,777	....
17512	Columbia	(717)	10,701	10,466
15425	Connellsville	(412)	9,229	10,319
19428	Conshohocken	(215)†	8,064	8,591
15108	Coraopolis	(412)	6,747	7,308
16407	Corry	(814)	7,216	7,149
15205	Crafton	(412)	7,188	7,623
19020	Croydon(u)	(215)	9,967	....
17821	Danville	(717)	5,165	5,239
19023	Darby	(610)	11,140	11,513
19036	Darby Twp(u)	(610)	10,955	12,264
19333	Devon-Berwyn(u)	(610)	5,019	5,246
18519	Dickson City	(717)	6,276	6,699
15033	Donora	(412)	5,928	7,524
15216	Dormont	(412)	9,772	11,275
19335	Downingtown	(610)	7,749	7,650
18901	Doylestown	(215)	8,575	8,717
19026	Drexel Hill(u)	(610)	29,744	....
15801	Du Bois	(814)	8,286	9,290
18512	Dunmore	(717)	15,403	16,781
15110	Duquesne	(412)	8,525	10,094
19401	East Norriton(u)	(215)†	13,324	12,711
18042	Easton	(610)	26,276	26,027
18301	East Stroudsburg	(717)	8,781	8,039
17405	East York(u)	(717)	8,487	....
15005	Economy	(412)	9,305	9,538
16412	Edinboro	(814)	7,736	6,324
18704	Edwardsville	(717)	5,399	5,729
17022	Elizabethtown	(717)	9,952	8,233
16117	Ellwood City	(412)	8,894	9,998
18049	Emmaus	(610)	11,157	11,001
17025	Enola(u)		5,961	....
17522	Ephrata	(717)	12,133	11,095
*16501	Erie	(814)	108,718	119,123
18643	Exeter	(717)	5,691	5,493
19030	Fairless Hills(u)	(215)	9,026	....
16121	Farrell	(412)	6,835	8,645
19047	Feasterville-Trevose(u)	(215)	6,696	....
.....	Fernway(u)		9,072	3,843
19032	Folcroft	(610)	7,506	8,231
15221	Forest Hills	(412)	8,173	8,198
18704	Forty Fort	(717)	5,049	5,590
15238	Fox Chapel	(412)	5,319	5,049
16323	Franklin	(814)	7,329	8,146
15143	Franklin Park	(412)	10,109	6,135
18052	Fullerton(u)	(610)	13,127	8,055
17325	Gettysburg	(717)	7,025	7,194
15045	Glassport	(412)	5,582	6,242
19036	Glenolden	(610)	7,260	7,633
19038	Glenside(u)	(215)	8,704	....
15601	Greensburg	(412)	16,318	17,558
16125	Greenville	(412)	6,734	7,730
16127	Grove City	(412)	8,240	8,162
.....	Hampton Township(u)		15,568	....
17331	Hanover	(717)	14,399	14,890
19438	Harleysville(u)	(215)†	7,405	3,673
*17105	Harrisburg	(717)	52,376	53,264
15636	Harrison Township(u)		11,763	....
19040	Hatboro	(215)	7,382	7,579
18201	Hazleton	(717)	24,730	27,318
18055	Hellertown	(610)	5,662	6,025
16148	Hermitage	(412)	15,260	16,365
17033	Hershey(u)	(717)	11,860	13,249
16648	Hollidaysburg	(814)	5,624	5,892
16001	Homeacre-Lyndora(u)	(412)	7,511	8,333
19044	Horsham(u)	(215)	15,051	9,900
16652	Huntingdon	(814)	6,843	7,042
15701	Indiana	(412)	15,174	16,051
15644	Jeannette	(412)	11,221	13,106
15344	Jefferson	(412)	9,533	8,643
18229	Jim Thorpe	(717)	5,048	5,263
*15901	Johnstown	(814)	28,134	35,496
15108	Kennedy Twp(u)	(412)	7,152	7,159
19348	Kennett Square	(610)	5,218	4,715
19406	King of Prussia(u)	(215)†	18,406	....
18704	Kingston	(717)	14,507	15,681
16201	Kittanning	(412)	5,120	5,432
19443	Kulpsville(u)		5,183	....
*17604	Lancaster	(717)	55,551	54,725
19446	Lansdale	(215)	16,362	16,526
19050	Lansdowne	(610)	11,712	11,891
15650	Latrobe	(412)	9,265	10,799
17540	Leacock-Leola-Bareville(u)		5,685	....
17042	Lebanon	(717)	24,800	25,711
18235	Lehighton	(610)	5,914	5,826
19053	Levittown(u)	(215)	55,362	....
17837	Lewisburg	(717)	5,785	5,407
17044	Lewistown	(717)	9,341	9,830

ZIP code	Place	Area code	1990	1980
17112	Linglestown(u)		5,862	....
19353	Lionville-Marchwood(u)	(610)	6,468	....
17543	Lititz	(717)	8,280	7,590
17745	Lock Haven	(717)	9,230	9,617
.....	Lower Allen(u)		6,329	....
15068	Lower Burrell	(412)	12,251	13,200
15237	McCandless Twp(u)	(412)	28,781	26,250
*15134	McKeesport	(412)	26,016	31,012
15136	McKees Rocks	(412)	7,691	8,742
17948	Mahanoy City	(717)	5,209	6,167
17545	Manheim	(717)	5,011	5,015
19002	Maple Glen(u)		5,881	....
16335	Meadville	(814)	14,318	15,544
17055	Mechanicsburg	(717)	9,452	9,487
*19063	Media	(610)	5,957	6,119
17057	Middletown (Dauphin)	(717)	9,254	10,122
18017	Middletown (Northampton)(u)	(610)	6,866	5,801
17551	Millersville	(717)	8,099	7,668
17847	Milton	(717)	6,746	6,730
15061	Monaca	(412)	6,739	7,661
15062	Monessen	(412)	9,901	11,928
18936	Montgomeryville(u)	(215)	9,114	....
18507	Moosic	(717)	5,397	6,068
19067	Morrisville	(215)	9,765	9,845
17851	Mount Carmel	(717)	7,196	8,190
17552	Mount Joy	(717)	6,398	5,680
15228	Mount Lebanon(u)	(412)	33,362	34,414
15120	Munhall	(412)	13,158	14,535
15146	Municipality of Monroeville	(412)	29,169	30,977
15668	Municipality of Murrysville	(412)	17,240	16,036
18634	Nanticoke	(717)	12,267	13,044
18064	Nazareth	(610)	5,713	5,443
.....	Nether Providence Twp(u)	(610)	13,229	12,730
15066	New Brighton	(412)	6,854	7,364
*16101	New Castle	(412)	28,334	33,621
17070	New Cumberland	(717)	7,665	8,051
15068	New Kensington	(412)	15,894	17,660
*19401	Norristown	(610)	30,754	34,684
18067	Northampton	(610)	8,717	8,240
15104	North Braddock	(412)	7,036	8,711
15137	North Versailles(u)	(412)	12,302	13,294
16421	Northwest Harborcreek(u)	(814)	6,662	7,485
19074	Norwood	(610)	6,162	6,647
15139	Oakmont	(412)	6,961	7,039
.....	O'Hara(u)		9,096	....
16301	Oil City	(814)	11,949	13,881
18518	Old Forge	(717)	8,834	9,304
18447	Olyphant	(717)	5,222	5,204
19075	Oreland(u)		5,695	....
18071	Palmerton	(610)	5,394	5,455
17078	Palmyra	(717)	6,910	7,228
19301	Paoli(u)	(610)	5,603	5,277
.....	Park Forest Village(u)		6,703	....
17331	Parkville(u)	(717)	6,014	5,009
15235	Penn Hills(u)	(717)	51,430	57,632
.....	Penn Wynne(u)		5,807	....
18944	Perkasie	(215)	7,787	5,241
*19104	Philadelphia	(215)	1,585,577	1,688,210
19460	Phoenixville	(610)	15,066	14,165
*15219	Pittsburgh	(412)	369,879	423,959
*18640	Pittston	(717)	9,389	9,9303
15236	Pleasant Hills	(412)	8,884	9,604
15239	Plum	(412)	25,609	25,309
18651	Plymouth	(717)	7,134	7,605
19462	Plymouth Meeting(u)	(215)†	6,241	....
19464	Pottstown	(610)	21,831	22,729
17901	Pottsville	(717)	16,603	18,195
.....	Progress(u)		9,654	....
19076	Prospect Park	(610)	6,764,	6,593
15767	Punxsutawney	(814)	6,782	7,479
18951	Quakertown	(215)	8,982	8,867
19087	Radnor Twp(u)	(610)	28,705	27,676
*19603	Reading	(610)	78,380	78,686
17356	Red Lion	(717)	6,130	5,824
18954	Richboro(u)	(215)	5,332	5,141
19078	Ridley Park	(610)	7,592	7,889
15949	Robinson(u)		10,830	....
15237	Ross Twp(u)	(412)	33,482	35,102
15857	Saint Marys	(814)	5,511	6,417
19464	Sanatoga(u)		5,534	3,723
18840	Sayre	(717)	5,791	6,951
17972	Schuylkill Haven	(717)	5,610	5,977
15683	Scottdale	(412)	5,184	5,833
15106	Scott Twp(u)	(412)	17,118	20,413
*18503	Scranton	(717)	81,805	88,117
17870	Selinsgrove	(717)	5,384	5,227
15116	Shaler Twp(u)	(412)	30,533	33,694
17872	Shamokin	(717)	9,184	10,357
16146	Sharon	(412)	17,533	19,057
19079	Sharon Hill	(610)	5,771	6,221
17976	Shenandoah	(717)	6,221	7,589
19607	Shillington	(610)	5,062	5,601
17404	Shiloh(u)	(717)	8,245	5,315
17257	Shippensburg	(717)	5,331	5,261
15501	Somerset	(814)	6,454	6,474
18964	Souderton	(215)	5,957	6,657
.....	South Park(u)		14,292	....
17701	South Williamsport	(717)	6,496	6,581
19064	Springfield(u)	(717)	24,160	25,326
16801	State College	(814)	38,981	36,130
17113	Steelton	(717)	5,152	6,484
15136	Stowe Twp(u)	(412)	7,681	9,202
18360	Stroudsburg	(717)	5,312	5,148
16323	Sugar Creek	(717)	5,532	5,954
17801	Sunbury	(717)	11,591	12,292
19081	Swarthmore	(610)	6,157	5,950
15218	Swissvale	(412)	10,637	11,345
18704	Swoyersville	(717)	5,630	5,795
18252	Tamaqua	(717)	7,943	8,843
15084	Tarentum	(412)	5,674	6,419
18517	Taylor	(717)	6,941	7,246
16354	Titusville	(814)	6,434	6,884
19401	Trooper(u)	(610)	5,137	7,370
15145	Turtle Creek	(412)	6,556	6,959
16686	Tyrone	(814)	5,743	6,346
15401	Uniontown	(412)	12,034	14,510
19063	Upper Providence Twp(u)	(610)	9,727	9,477
15241	Upper Saint Clair(u)	(412)	19,692	19,023
15690	Vandergrift	(412)	5,904	6,823
.....	Village Green-Green Ridge(u)		9,026	....
16365	Warren	(814)	11,122	12,146
15301	Washington	(412)	15,864	18,363
17268	Waynesboro	(717)	9,578	9,726
.....	Weigelstown(u)	(717)	8,665	5,213
*19380	West Chester	(610)	18,041	17,435
19380	West Goshen(u)	(610)	8,948	7,998
15122	West Mifflin	(412)	23,644	26,322
15905	Westmont	(814)	5,789	6,113
19401	West Norriton(u)	(610)	15,209	14,034
18643	West Pittston	(717)	5,590	5,980
15229	West View	(412)	7,734	7,648
18052	Whitehall	(610)	14,451	15,143
15131	White Oak	(717)	8,761	9,480
*18701	Wilkes-Barre	(717)	47,523	51,551
15221	Wilkinsburg	(412)	21,080	23,669
15145	Wilkins Twp(u)	(412)	7,487	8,472
17701	Williamsport	(717)	31,933	33,401
19090	Willow Grove(u)	(610)	16,325	....
17584	Willow Street(u)		5,817	....
15025	Wilson	(412)	7,830	7,564
19094	Woodlyn(u)	(610)	10,151	....
19118	Wyndmoor(u)	(215)	5,682	....
19610	Wyomissing	(610)	7,332	6,551
19050	Yeadon	(610)	11,980	11,727
*17405	York	(717)	42,192	44,619

Rhode Island (401)

See Note on Page 373

ZIP code	Place	1990	1980
02806	*Barrington(u)*	15,849	16,174
02809	*Bristol(u)*	21,625	20,128
02830	*Burrillville*	16,230	13,164
02863	Central Falls	17,637	16,995
02813	Charlestown	6,478	....
02816	*Coventry*	31,083	27,065
02910	Cranston	76,060	71,992
02864	*Cumberland*	29,038	27,069
02864	Cumberland Hill(u)	6,379	5,421
02818	*East Greenwich*	11,865	10,211
02914	East Providence	50,380	50,980
02822	Exeter	5,461	....
02814	*Glocester*	9,227	7,550
02828	Greenville(u)	8,303	7,576
02833	*Hopkinton*	6,873	6,406
02919	*Johnston*	26,542	24,907
02881	Kingston(u)	6,504	5,479
02865	*Lincoln*	18,045	16,949
02840	*Middletown*	19,460	17,216
02882	*Narragansett*	14,985	12,088
02840	Newport	28,227	29,259
02843	Newport East(u)	11,080	11,030
02852	*North Kingstown*	23,786	21,938
02908	*North Providence(u)*	32,090	29,188
02876	*North Smithfield*	10,497	9,972
02859	Pascoag(u)	5,011	3,807
*02860	Pawtucket	72,644	71,204
02871	*Portsmouth*	16,857	14,257
*02904	Providence	160,728	156,804
.....	Richmond	5,351	....
02857	*Scituate*	9,796	8,405
02917	*Smithfield*	19,163	16,886
02879	*South Kingstown*	24,631	20,414
02878	*Tiverton(u)*	14,312	13,526
02864	Valley Falls(u)	11,175	10,892
*02880	Wakefield-Peacedale(u)	7,134	6,474
02885	*Warren*	11,385	10,640
*02887	Warwick	85,427	87,123
02891	*Westerly*	21,605	18,580
02891	Westerly Center(u)	16,477	14,093
02893	*West Warwick(u)*	29,268	27,026
02895	Woonsocket	43,877	45,914

South Carolina (803)

ZIP code	Place	1990	1980
29620	Abbeville	5,778	5,833
29801	Aiken	20,386	14,978
29621	Anderson	26,385	27,546
29812	Barnwell	5,255	5,572
29902	Beaufort	9,576	8,634
29841	Belvedere(u)	6,133	6,859
29512	Bennettsville	10,095	8,774
29611	Berea(u)	13,535	13,164
.....	Brookdale(u)	5,339	6,123
29902	Burton(u)	6,917	3,619
29020	Camden	6,696	7,462
29033	Cayce	10,807	11,701
*29401	Charleston	80,467	69,779
29520	Cheraw	5,553	5,654
29706	Chester	7,158	6,820
29631	Clemson	11,145	8,118
29325	Clinton	9,603	8,596
*29201	Columbia	103,477	101,229
29526	Conway	9,819	10,240
29532	Darlington	7,310	7,989
29204	Dentsville(u)	11,839	13,579
29536	Dillon	6,829	7,060
29640	Easley	15,179	14,264
29501	Florence	29,913	29,842
29206	Forest Acres	7,181	6,062
29340	Gaffney	13,149	13,453
29605	Gantt(u)	13,891	13,719
.....	Garden City(u)	6,305	....
29440	Georgetown	9,517	10,144
29445	Goose Creek	24,692	17,811
*29602	Greenville	58,256	58,242
29646	Greenwood	20,807	21,613
29651	Greer	10,322	10,525
29410	Hanahan	13,176	13,224
29550	Hartsville	8,372	7,631
29928	Hilton Head Island	23,694	11,239
29621	Homeland Park(u)	6,569	6,720
29063	Irmo	11,277	3,957
29456	Ladson(u)	13,540	13,246
29560	Lake City	7,153	6,731
29720	Lancaster	8,914	9,703
29360	Laurens	9,694	10,587
29571	Marion	7,658	7,700
29662	Mauldin	11,662	8,143
29430	Moncks Corner	5,599	4,179
29464	Mount Pleasant	30,108	14,464
29574	Mullins	5,910	6,068
29577	Myrtle Beach	24,848	18,446
29108	Newberry	10,543	9,866
29841	North Augusta	15,684	13,593
29406	North Charleston	70,218	62,479
29582	North Myrtle Beach	8,731	3,960
29565	Oak Grove(u)	7,173	7,092
29115	Orangeburg	13,772	14,933
.....	Parker(u)	11,072	....
29905	Parris Island(u)	7,172	7,752
.....	Red Bank(u)	5,950	....
.....	Red Hill(u)	6,112	....
29730	Rock Hill	41,610	35,327
29210	Saint Andrews(u)	25,692	20,245
29609	Sans Souci(u)	7,612	8,393
29678	Seneca	7,726	7,436
.....	Seven Oaks(u)	15,722	16,604
29681	Simpsonville	11,744	9,037
29577	Socastee(u)	10,426	1,082
*29301	Spartanburg	43,479	43,826
29483	Summerville	22,519	6,492
29150	Sumter	42,299	24,921
29687	Taylors(u)	19,619	15,801
29379	Union	9,840	10,523
29607	Wade Hampton(u)	20,014	20,180
29488	Walterboro	5,595	6,209
29611	Welcome(u)	6,560	6,922
29169	West Columbia	10,944	10,409
29206	Woodfield(u)	8,862	9,588
29745	York	6,709	6,412

South Dakota (605)

ZIP code	Place	1990	1980
57401	Aberdeen	24,995	25,851
57006	Brookings	16,270	14,951
57706	Ellsworth AFB(u)	7,017	4,766
57350	Huron	12,448	13,000
57042	Madison	6,257	6,210
57301	Mitchell	13,798	13,916
57501	Pierre	12,906	11,973
57701	Rapid City	54,523	46,492
.....	Rapid Valley(u)	5,968	3,265
*57101	Sioux Falls	100,836	81,343
57783	Spearfish	6,966	5,251
57785	Sturgis	5,330	5,184
57069	Vermillion	10,034	10,136
57201	Watertown	17,632	15,649
57078	Yankton	12,703	12,011

Tennessee

ZIP code	Place		1990	1980
37701	Alcoa	(615)	6,400	6,870
37303	Athens	(615)	12,054	12,080
38134	Bartlett	(901)	26,989	17,170
37660	Bloomingdale(u)	(615)	10,953	12,088
38008	Bolivar	(901)	5,969	6,597
37027	Brentwood	(615)	16,392	9,431
37620	Bristol	(615)	23,421	23,986
38012	Brownsville	(901)	10,017	9,307
*37401	Chattanooga	(615)	152,494	169,514
37040	Clarksville	(615)	75,542	54,777
37311	Cleveland	(615)	30,354	26,415
37716	Clinton	(615)	8,972	5,245
37315	Collegedale	(615)	5,048	4,607
38017	Collierville	(901)	14,427	7,839
37663	Colonial Heights(u)	(615)	6,716	6,744
38401	Columbia	(615)	28,583	26,571
38501	Cookeville	(615)	21,744	20,535
38019	Covington	(901)	7,487	6,065
38555	Crossville	(615)	6,930	6,394
37321	Dayton	(615)	5,671	5,233
37055	Dickson	(615)	8,783	7,040
38024	Dyersburg	(901)	16,317	15,856
37801	Eagleton Village(u)	(615)	5,169	5,331
37411	East Brainerd(u)	...	11,594	....
37412	East Ridge	(615)	21,101	21,236
37643	Elizabethton	(615)	11,931	12,431
37650	Erwin	(615)	5,015	4,739
37922	Farragut	(615)	12,802	5,992
37334	Fayetteville	(615)	7,158	7,559
37064	Franklin	(615)	20,098	12,407
37066	Gallatin	(615)	18,794	17,191
38138	Germantown	(901)	32,893	21,467
37072	Goodlettsville	(615)	11,219	8,327
37743	Greeneville	(615)	13,532	14,097
37215	Green Hills(u)	...	6,763	....
37918	Halls(u)	(901)	6,450	10,363
37748	Harriman	(615)	7,119	8,303
37341	Harrison(u)	(615)	7,191	6,206
37075	Hendersonville	(615)	32,188	26,561
38343	Humboldt	(901)	9,651	10,209
38301	Jackson	(901)	49,115	49,258
37760	Jefferson City	(615)	5,522	5,612
37601	Johnson City	(615)	49,479	39,753
*37662	Kingsport	(615)	36,365	32,027
*37901	Knoxville	(615)	165,039	175,045
37766	La Follette	(615)	7,192	8,198
37086	LaVergne	(615)	7,499	5,495
38464	Lawrenceburg	(615)	10,397	10,184
37087	Lebanon	(615)	15,208	11,872
37771	Lenoir City	(615)	6,147	5,180
37091	Lewisburg	(615)	9,879	8,760
38351	Lexington	(901)	5,810	5,934
38201	McKenzie	(901)	5,168	5,405
37110	McMinnville	(615)	11,194	10,683
37355	Manchester	(615)	7,709	7,250
38237	Martin	(901)	8,588	8,898
37701	Maryville	(615)	19,208	17,480
*38101	Memphis	(901)	610,337	646,174
37343	Middle Valley(u)	(615)	12,255	11,420
38358	Milan	(901)	7,512	8,083
38053	Millington	(901)	17,866	20,236
37814	Morristown	(615)	21,385	19,570
37122	Mount Juliet	...	5,389	2,879
37130	Murfreesboro	(615)	44,922	32,845
*37202	Nashville-Davidson	(615)	488,374	455,651
37821	Newport	(615)	7,123	7,580
37830	Oak Ridge	(615)	27,310	27,662
38242	Paris	(901)	9,332	10,728
37148	Portland	(615)	5,165	4,030
37849	Powell(u)	(615)	7,534	7,220
38478	Pulaski	(615)	7,916	7,184
37415	Red Bank	(615)	12,320	13,129
38063	Ripley	(901)	6,188	6,366
37854	Rockwood	(615)	5,348	5,687
38372	Savannah	(901)	6,547	6,992
37862	Sevierville	(615)	7,178	4,556
37865	Seymour(u)		7,026	....
37160	Shelbyville	(615)	14,049	13,530
37377	Signal Mountain	(615)	7,034	5,818
37167	Smyrna	(615)	13,647	8,839
37379	Soddy-Daisy	(615)	8,240	8,388
.....	South Cleveland(u)	...	5,372	4,360
37172	Springfield	(615)	11,227	10,814
37874	Sweetwater	(615)	5,066	4,725
37388	Tullahoma	(615)	16,761	15,800
38261	Union City	(901)	10,513	10,436
37398	Winchester	(615)	6,305	5,821

Texas

ZIP code	Place		1990	1980
*79604	Abilene	(915)	106,707	98,315
75001	Addison	(214)	8,783	5,553
78516	Alamo	(210)	8,210	5,831
78209	Alamo Heights	(210)	6,502	6,252

ZIP code	Place		1990	1980
77039	Aldine(u)	(713)	11,133	12,623
78332	Alice	(512)	19,788	20,961
75002	Allen	(214)	9,198	8,314
79830	Alpine	(915)	5,637	5,465
77511	Alvin	(713)	19,220	16,515
*79105	Amarillo	(806)	157,571	149,230
78750	Anderson Mill(u)		9,468	....
79714	Andrews	(915)	10,678	11,061
77515	Angleton	(409)	17,140	13,929
78336	Aransas Pass	(512)	7,180	7,173
*76010	Arlington	(817)	261,721	160,113
75751	Athens	(903)	10,982	10,197
75551	Atlanta	(214)	6,118	6,272
*78710	Austin	(512)	465,622	345,890
76020	Azle	(817)	8,868	5,822
75149	Balch Springs	(214)	17,406	13,746
77414	Bay City	(409)	18,170	17,837
77520	Baytown	(713)	63,850	56,923
*77704	Beaumont	(409)	114,323	118,102
76021	Bedford	(817)	43,762	20,821
78102	Beeville	(512)	13,547	14,574
77401	Bellaire	(713)	13,842	14,950
76704	Bellmead	(817)	8,336	7,569
76513	Belton	(817)	12,476	10,660
76126	Benbrook	(817)	19,564	13,579
79720	Big Spring	(915)	23,093	24,804
75418	Bonham	(903)	6,686	7,338
79007	Borger	(806)	15,675	15,837
76825	Brady	(915)	5,946	5,969
76024	Breckenridge	(817)	5,665	6,921
77833	Brenham	(409)	11,952	10,966
77611	Bridge City	(409)	8,034	7,667
79316	Brownfield	(806)	9,560	10,387
78520	Brownsville	(210)	98,962	84,997
76801	Brownwood	(915)	18,387	19,396
78717	Brushy Creek(u)		5,833	....
77801	Bryan	(409)	55,002	44,337
76354	Burkburnett	(817)	10,145	10,668
76028	Burleson	(817)	16,113	11,734
76520	Cameron	(817)	5,635	5,721
79015	Canyon	(806)	11,365	10,724
78133	Canyon Lake(u)		9,975	....
78834	Carrizo Springs	(210)	5,745	6,886
75006	Carrolton	(214)	82,169	40,595
75633	Carthage	(903)	6,496	6,447
75104	Cedar Hill	(214)	19,976	6,849
78613	Cedar Park		5,161	3,474
77530	Channelview(u)	(713)	25,564	17,471
79201	Childress	(817)	5,055	5,817
76031	Cleburne	(817)	22,205	19,218
77327	Cleveland	(713)	7,124	5,977
77015	Clover Leaf(u)	(713)	18,230	17,317
77531	Clute	(409)	9,467	9,577
76834	Coleman	(915)	5,410	5,960
77840	College Station	(409)	52,456	37,272
76034	Colleyville	(817)	12,724	6,700
75428	Commerce	(903)	6,825	8,136
77301	Conroe	(409)	27,610	18,034
78109	Converse	(512)	8,887	5,150
75019	Coppell		16,881	3,826
76522	Copperas Cove	(817)	24,079	19,469
*78408	Corpus Christi	(512)	257,453	232,134
75110	Corsicana	(903)	22,911	21,712
75835	Crockett	(409)	7,024	7,405
76036	Crowley	(817)	6,974	5,852
78839	Crystal City	(512)	8,263	8,334
77954	Cuero	(512)	6,700	7,124
79022	Dalhart	(806)	6,246	6,854
*75260	Dallas	(214)	1,007,618	904,599
77535	Dayton	(409)	5,151	4,908
77536	Deer Park	(713)	27,658	22,648
78840	Del Rio	(210)	30,705	30,034
75020	Denison	(903)	21,505	23,884
76201	Denton	(817)	66,270	48,063
79323	Denver City		5,145	4,704
75115	De Soto	(214)	30,544	15,538
77539	Dickinson	(713)	9,497	7,505
78537	Donna	(210)	12,652	9,952
79029	Dumas	(806)	12,871	12,194
75116	Duncanville	(214)	35,008	27,781
76135	Eagle Mountain(u)		5,847	....
78852	Eagle Pass	(210)	20,651	21,407
78539	Edinburg	(210)	29,885	24,075
77957	Edna	(512)	5,343	5,650
77437	El Campo	(409)	10,511	10,462
*79910	El Paso	(915)	515,342	425,259
78543	Elsa	(210)	5,242	5,061
75119	Ennis	(214)	13,883	12,110
76039	Euless	(817)	38,149	24,002
76140	Everman	(817)	5,672	5,387
79838	Fabens(u)		5,599	4,285
78355	Falfurrias	(512)	5,788	6,103
75234	Farmers Branch	(214)	24,250	24,863
.....	First Colony(u)		18,327	....
78114	Floresville		5,247	4,381
75028	Flower Mound		15,527	4,402
76119	Forest Hill	(817)	11,482	11,684
79906	Fort Bliss(u)	(915)	13,915	12,687
76544	Fort Hood(u)	(817)	35,580	31,250

ZIP code	Place		1990	1980
79735	Fort Stockton	(915)	8,524	8,688
*76101	Fort Worth	(817)	447,619	385,164
78624	Fredericksburg	(210)	6,934	6,412
77541	Freeport	(409)	11,389	13,444
77546	Friendswood	(713)	22,814	10,719
75034	Frisco		6,141	3,499
76240	Gainesville	(817)	14,256	14,081
77547	Galena Park	(713)	10,033	9,879
77550	Galveston	(409)	59,067	61,902
*75040	Garland	(214)	180,650	138,857
76528	Gatesville	(817)	11,492	6,078
78626	Georgetown	(512)	14,842	9,468
75647	Gladewater	(903)	6,027	6,548
78629	Gonzales	(210)	6,527	7,152
76046	Graham	(817)	8,986	9,170
*75050	Grand Prairie	(214)	99,616	71,462
76051	Grapevine	(817)	29,202	11,801
75401	Greenville	(903)	23,071	22,161
77619	Groves	(409)	16,744	17,090
76117	Haltom City	(817)	32,856	29,014
76541	Harker Heights	(817)	12,841	7,345
78550	Harlingen	(210)	48,735	43,543
77859	Hearne	(409)	5,132	5,418
75652	Henderson	(903)	11,139	11,473
79045	Hereford	(806)	14,745	15,853
76643	Hewitt	(817)	8,983	5,247
75205	Highland Park	(214)	8,739	8,909
77562	Highlands(u)	(713)	6,632	6,467
75067	Highland Village		7,027	3,246
76645	Hillsboro	(817)	7,072	7,397
77563	Hitchcock	(409)	5,868	6,103
78861	Hondo	(210)	6,018	6,057
*77013	Houston	(713)	1,630,864	1,595,138
77338	Humble	(713)	12,060	6,729
77340	Huntsville	(409)	27,925	23,936
76053	Hurst	(817)	33,574	31,420
78362	Ingleside	(512)	5,696	5,436
76367	Iowa Park	(817)	6,072	6,184
*75061	Irving	(214)	155,037	109,943
77029	Jacinto City	(713)	9,343	8,953
75766	Jacksonville	(214)	12,765	12,264
75951	Jasper	(409)	7,160	6,959
78729	Jollyville		15,206	....
77450	Katy	(713)	8,005	5,660
75142	Kaufman	(214)	5,238	4,658
76248	Keller	(817)	13,683	4,156
79745	Kermit	(915)	6,875	8,015
78028	Kerrville	(210)	17,384	15,276
75662	Kilgore	(903)	11,066	11,331
76541	Killeen	(817)	63,535	46,296
78363	Kingsville	(512)	25,276	28,808
77325	Kingwood	(713)	37,397	16,261
78219	Kirby	(210)	8,326	6,435
78236	Lackland AFB(u)	(210)	9,352	14,459
77566	Lake Jackson	(409)	22,776	19,102
77568	La Marque	(409)	14,120	15,372
79631	Lamesa	(806)	10,809	11,790
76550	Lampasas	(512)	6,382	6,165
75146	Lancaster	(214)	22,117	14,807
77571	La Porte	(713)	27,910	14,062
78040	Laredo	(210)	122,899	91,449
77573	League City	(713)	30,159	16,578
78238	Leon Valley	(210)	9,581	9,088
79336	Levelland	(806)	13,986	13,809
75067	Lewisville	(214)	46,521	24,273
77575	Liberty	(713)	7,690	7,945
79339	Littlefield	(806)	6,489	7,409
78233	Live Oak	(210)	10,023	8,183
77351	Livingston	(409)	5,019	4,928
78644	Lockhart	(512)	9,205	7,953
75601	Longview	(903)	70,311	62,762
*79408	Lubbock	(806)	186,206	174,361
75901	Lufkin	(409)	30,206	28,562
77656	Lumberton		6,640	2,480
78501	McAllen	(210)	84,021	66,281
75069	McKinney	(214)	21,283	16,256
76063	Mansfield	(817)	15,607	8,102
76661	Marlin	(817)	6,386	7,099
75670	Marshall	(903)	23,682	24,921
78368	Mathis	(512)	5,423	5,667
78570	Mercedes	(210)	12,694	11,851
75149	Mesquite	(214)	101,484	67,053
76667	Mexia	(817)	6,933	7,094
79701	Midland	(915)	89,443	70,525
76065	Midlothian	(214)	5,141	3,219
76067	Mineral Wells	(817)	14,870	14,468
78572	Mission	(210)	28,653	22,653
.....	Mission Bend(u)		24,945	....
77459	Missouri City	(713)	36,176	24,423
79756	Monahans	(915)	8,101	8,397
75455	Mount Pleasant	(903)	12,291	11,003
75961	Nacogdoches	(409)	30,872	27,149
77868	Navasota	(409)	6,296	5,971
77627	Nederland	(409)	16,192	16,855
75570	New Boston		5,057	4,628
78130	New Braunfels	(210)	27,334	22,402
76118	North Richland Hills	(817)	45,895	30,592
*79760	Odessa	(915)	89,699	90,027
77630	Orange	(409)	19,381	23,628

ZIP code	Place		1990	1980
75801	Palestine	(903)	18,042	15,948
79065	Pampa	(806)	19,959	21,396
75460	Paris	(903)	24,799	25,498
*77501	Pasadena	(713)	119,608	112,560
77581	Pearland	(713)	18,697	13,248
78061	Pearsall	(210)	6,924	7,383
78721	Pecan Grove(u)		9,502	....
79772	Pecos	(915)	12,069	12,855
79070	Perryton	(806)	7,619	7,991
78577	Pharr	(210)	32,921	21,381
79072	Plainview	(806)	21,700	22,187
*75075	Plano	(214)	127,885	72,331
78064	Pleasanton	(210)	7,678	6,346
77640	Port Arthur	(409)	58,551	61,251
78374	Portland	(512)	12,224	12,023
77979	Port Lavaca	(512)	10,886	10,911
77651	Port Neches	(409)	12,908	13,944
78580	Raymondville	(210)	8,880	9,493
76028	Rendon(u)		7,658	....
*75080	Richardson	(214)	74,840	72,496
76118	Richland Hills	(817)	7,978	7,977
77469	Richmond	(713)	9,801	9,692
78582	Rio Grande City(u)	(210)	9,891	8,930
77019	River Oaks	(817)	6,580	6,890
76701	Robinson	(817)	7,111	6,074
78380	Robstown	(512)	12,849	12,100
76567	Rockdale	(512)	5,235	5,611
75087	Rockwall	(214)	10,486	5,939
78584	Roma		8,059	3,384
77471	Rosenberg	(713)	20,183	17,840
78664	Round Rock	(512)	30,923	12,740
75088	Rowlett	(214)	23,260	7,522
75048	Sachse		5,346	1,640
76179	Saginaw	(817)	8,551	5,736
76901	San Angelo	(915)	84,474	73,240
*78284	San Antonio	(210)	935,933	785,940
78586	San Benito	(210)	20,125	17,988
78589	San Juan	(210)	10,815	7,608
78666	San Marcos	(512)	28,743	23,420
77550	Santa Fe	(713)	8,429	6,172
78154	Schertz	(210)	10,597	7,262
77586	Seabrook	(713)	6,685	4,670
75159	Seagoville	(214)	8,969	7,304
78155	Seguin	(210)	18,853	17,854
79360	Seminole	(915)	6,342	6,080
75090	Sherman	(903)	31,601	30,413
77656	Silsbee	(409)	6,368	7,684
78387	Sinton	(512)	5,549	6,044
79364	Slaton	(806)	6,078	6,804
79549	Snyder	(915)	12,195	12,705
79910	Socorro		22,995	12,341
77587	South Houston	(713)	14,207	13,293
76051	Southlake		7,065	2,808
77373	Spring(u)	(713)	33,111	....
77477	Stafford	(713)	8,397	4,755
76401	Stephenville	(817)	13,502	11,881
77478	Sugar Land	(713)	24,528	8,826
75482	Sulphur Springs	(903)	14,062	12,804
79556	Sweetwater	(915)	11,967	12,242
76574	Taylor	(512)	11,472	10,619
76501	Temple	(817)	46,109	42,354
75160	Terrell	(214)	12,490	13,269
75501	Texarkana	(903)	31,656	31,271
77590	Texas City	(409)	40,822	41,201
75056	The Colony	(214)	22,113	11,586
77380	The Woodlands(u)	(713)	29,205	8,443
77337	Tomball	(713)	6,370	3,996
.....	Town West(u)		6,166	
75701	Tyler	(903)	75,450	70,508
78148	Universal City	(512)	13,057	10,720
76308	University Park	(214)	22,259	22,254
78801	Uvalde	(210)	14,729	14,178
76384	Vernon	(817)	12,001	12,695
77901	Victoria	(512)	55,076	50,695
77662	Vidor	(409)	10,935	11,834
*76701	Waco	(817)	103,590	101,261
76148	Watauga	(817)	20,009	10,284
75165	Waxahachie	(214)	18,168	14,624
76086	Weatherford	(817)	14,804	12,049
78728	Wells Branch(u)		7,094	....
78596	Weslaco	(210)	21,877	19,331
79764	West Odessa(u)		16,568	....
77005	West University Place	(713)	12,920	12,010
77488	Wharton	(409)	9,011	9,033
75693	White Oak		5,136	4,415
76108	White Settlement	(817)	15,472	13,508
*76307	Wichita Falls	(817)	96,259	94,201
78239	Windcrest	(210)	5,331	5,332
76710	Woodway	(817)	8,695	7,091
75098	Wylie		8,716	3,152
77995	Yoakum	(512)	5,611	6,148
78076	Zapata(u)	(512)	7,119	3,831

Utah (801)

ZIP code	Place	1990	1980
84003	American Fork	15,722	12,564
*84010	Bountiful	36,659	32,877
84302	Brigham City	15,644	15,596
84109	Canyon Rim(u)	10,527	....
84720	Cedar City	13,443	10,972
84014	Centerville	11,500	8,069
84015	Clearfield	21,435	17,982
84015	Clinton	7,945	5,777
84121	Cottonwood Heights(u)	28,766	22,665
.....	Cottonwood West(u)	17,476	....
84020	Draper	7,143	5,521
84109	East Millcreek(u)	21,184	24,150
84025	Farmington	9,049	4,691
84004	Highland	5,007	2,435
84117	Holladay-Cottonwood(u)	14,095	22,189
84037	Kaysville	13,961	9,811
84118	Kearns(u)	28,374	21,353
*84041	Layton	41,784	22,862
84043	Lehi	8,475	6,848
.....	Little Cottonwood Creek Valley(u)	5,042	....
84321	Logan	32,771	26,844
84044	Magna(u)	17,829	13,138
84047	Midvale	11,886	10,146
84109	Millcreek(u)	32,230	....
84117	Mount Olympus(u)	7,413	6,068
84107	Murray	31,274	25,750
84404	North Ogden	11,593	9,309
84054	North Salt Lake	6,464	5,548
*84401	Ogden	63,943	64,407
.....	Oquirrh(u)	7,593	....
*84057	Orem	67,561	52,399
84651	Payson	9,510	8,246
84062	Pleasant Grove	13,476	10,833
84501	Price	8,712	9,086
*84601	Provo	86,835	74,111
84701	Richfield	5,593	5,482
84403	Riverdale	6,419	6,031
84065	Riverton	11,261	7,032
84067	Roy	24,595	19,694
84770	Saint George	28,572	11,350
*84101	Salt Lake City	159,928	163,034
*84070	Sandy	75,240	52,210
84335	Smithfield	5,566	4,993
84065	South Jordan	12,215	7,492
84403	South Ogden	12,105	11,366
84115	South Salt Lake	10,129	10,413
84660	Spanish Fork	11,272	9,825
84663	Springville	13,950	12,101
84015	Sunset	5,128	5,733
84107	Taylorsville-Bennion(u)	52,351	17,448
84074	Tooele	13,887	14,335
84047	Union(u)	13,684	9,665
84078	Vernal	6,640	6,600
84403	Washington Terrace	8,189	8,212
*84084	West Jordan	42,915	27,325
*84119	West Valley City	86,969	72,509
84070	White City(u)	6,506	7,180
84087	Woods Cross	5,384	4,263

Vermont (802)

See Note on Page 373

ZIP code	Place	1990	1980
05641	Barre	9,482	9,824
05641	*Barre*	7,411	6,509
05201	*Bennington*	16,451	15,815
05201	Bennington(u)	9,532	9,349
05301	Brattleboro Center(u)	8,612	8,596
05301	*Brattleboro*	12,241	11,886
05401	Burlington	39,127	37,712
05446	*Colchester*	14,731	12,629
05451	*Essex*	16,498	14,392
05452	Essex Junction	8,396	7,033
05047	Hartford	9,404	....
05849	Lyndon	5,371	....
05753	*Middlebury(u)*	8,034	6,007
05468	Milton	8,404	....
05602	Montpelier	8,247	8,241
05663	Northfield	5,610	....
.....	Rockingham	5,484	....
05701	Rutland	18,230	18,436
05478	Saint Albans	7,339	7,308
05819	*Saint Johnsbury(u)*	7,608	6,424
05482	Shelburne	5,871	....
05401	*South Burlington*	12,809	10,679
05156	*Springfield*	9,579	10,190
05488	Swanton	5,636	....
05404	Winooski	6,649	6,318

Virginia

ZIP code	Place		1990	1980
24210	Abingdon	(703)	7,003	4,318
*22313	Alexandria	(703)	111,182	103,217
22003	Annandale(u)	(703)	50,975	49,524
.....	Aquia Harbour(u)		6,308	2,870
*22210	Arlington(u)	(703)	170,936	152,599
23005	Ashland	(804)	5,864	4,640
22041	Bailey's Crossroads(u)	(703)	19,507	12,564

ZIP code	Place		1990	1980
24523	Bedford	(703)	6,073	5,991
22307	Belle Haven(u)	(804)	6,427	6,520
23234	Bellwood(u)	(804)	6,178	6,439
23234	Bensley(u)	(804)	5,093	5,299
24060	Blacksburg	(703)	34,590	30,638
24605	Bluefield	(703)	5,363	5,946
23235	Bon Air(u)	(804)	16,413	16,224
24201	Bristol	(703)	18,426	19,042
24416	Buena Vista	(703)	6,406	6,717
.....	Bull Run(u)		5,525	....
22015	Burke(u)	(703)	57,734	33,835
24018	Cave Spring(u)	(703)	24,053	21,682
22020	Centreville(u)	(703)	26,585	7,473
22021	Chantilly(u)	(703)	29,337	12,259
*22906	Charlottesville	(804)	40,475	39,916
*23320	Chesapeake	(804)	151,982	114,486
23831	Chester(u)	(804)	14,986	11,728
24073	Christiansburg	(703)	15,004	10,345
24078	Collinsville(u)	(703)	7,280	7,517
23834	Colonial Heights	(804)	16,064	16,509
.....	Commonwealth(u)		5,538	3,505
.....	Countryside(u)		8,349	....
24426	Covington	(703)	6,991	9,063
22701	Culpeper	(703)	8,581	6,621
22191	Dale City(u)	(703)	47,170	33,127
24541	Danville	(804)	53,056	45,642
23228	Dumbarton(u)	(804)	8,526	8,149
22027	Dunn Loring(u)	(703)	6,509	6,077
23222	East Highland Park(u)	(804)	11,850	11,797
23847	Emporia	(804)	5,479	4,840
23803	Ettrick(u)		5,290	4,890
22030	Fairfax	(703)	19,622	19,390
*22046	Falls Church	(703)	9,578	9,515
23901	Farmville	(804)	6,046	6,067
24551	Forest(u)	(804)	5,624	....
22060	Fort Belvoir(u)	(703)	8,590	7,726
22308	Fort Hunt(u)	(703)	12,989	14,294
23801	Fort Lee(u)	(804)	6,895	9,784
22310	Franconia(u)	(703)	19,882	8,476
23851	Franklin	(804)	7,864	7,308
22401	Fredericksburg	(703)	19,027	15,322
22630	Front Royal	(703)	11,880	11,126
24333	Galax	(703)	6,670	6,524
23060	Glen Allen(u)	(804)	9,010	6,202
23062	Gloucester Point(u)	(804)	8,509	5,841
22066	Great Falls(u)		6,945	2,419
22306	Groveton(u)	(703)	19,997	18,860
*23660	Hampton	(804)	133,811	122,617
22801	Harrisonburg	(703)	30,707	19,671
*22070	Herndon	(703)	16,139	11,449
23075	Highland Springs(u)	(804)	13,823	12,146
24019	Hollins(u)	(703)	13,305	12,295
23860	Hopewell	(804)	23,101	23,397
22303	Huntington(u)	(703)	7,489	5,813
22306	Hybla Valley(u)	(703)	15,491	15,533
22043	Idylwood(u)	(703)	14,710	11,982
22042	Jefferson(u)	(804)	25,782	24,342
22041	Lake Barcroft(u)	(703)	8,686	8,725
22191	Lake Ridge(u)	(703)	23,862	11,072
23228	Lakeside(u)	(804)	12,081	12,289
23060	Laurel(u)	(804)	13,011	10,569
22075	Leesburg	(703)	16,202	8,357
24450	Lexington	(703)	6,959	7,292
22312	Lincolnia(u)	(703)	13,041	10,350
22079	Lorton(u)	(703)	15,385	5,813
*24505	Lynchburg	(804)	66,049	66,743
22101	McLean(u)	(703)	38,168	35,664
24572	Madison Heights(u)	(804)	11,700	14,146
22110	Manassas	(703)	27,957	15,438
22110	Manassas Park	(703)	6,734	6,524
22030	Mantua(u)	(703)	6,804	6,523
24354	Marion	(703)	6,630	7,287
24112	Martinsville	(703)	16,162	18,149
23111	Mechanicsville(u)	(804)	22,027	9,269
22116	Merrifield(u)	(703)	8,399	7,525
.....	Montclair(u)		11,399	....
23231	Montrose(u)	(804)	6,405	5,349
22121	Mount Vernon(u)	(703)	27,485	24,058
22122	Newington(u)	(703)	17,965	8,313
*23607	Newport News	(804)	171,439	144,903
*23501	Norfolk	(804)	261,250	266,979
22151	North Springfield(u)	(703)	8,996	9,538
22124	Oakton(u)	(703)	24,610	19,150
23803	Petersburg	(804)	37,027	41,055
22043	Pimmit Hills(u)	(703)	6,019	6,658
23662	Poquoson	(804)	11,005	8,726
*23705	Portsmouth	(804)	103,910	104,577
24301	Pulaski	(703)	9,985	10,1069
22134	Quantico Station(u)	(703)	7,425	7,121
24141	Radford	(703)	15,940	13,225
22090	Reston(u)	(703)	48,556	36,407
*23232	Richmond	(804)	202,798	219,214
*24001	Roanoke	(703)	96,509	100,220
22310	Rose Hill(u)	(703)	12,675	11,926
24153	Salem	(703)	23,756	23,958
22044	Seven Corners(u)	(703)	72,80	6,058
24592	South Boston	(804)	6,997	7,093
*22150	Springfield	(703)	23,706	21,435
24401	Staunton	(703)	24,461	21,857
221.	Sterling(u)	(703)	20,512	16,080
24477	Stuarts Draft(u)		5,087	1,776
23162	Studley(u)		7,321	4,674
23434	Suffolk	(804)	52,143	47,621
22170	Sugarland Run(u)	(703)	9,357	6,258
24502	Timberlake(u)	(804)	10,314	9,697
23229	Tuckahoe(u)	(804)	42,629	39,868
22101	Tysons Corner(u)	(703)	13,124	10,065
.....	University Heights(u)		6,900	6,736
22180	Vienna	(703)	14,852	15,469
24179	Vinton	(703)	7,643	8,027
*23458	Virginia Beach	(804)	393,089	262,199
22980	Waynesboro	(703)	18,549	15,329
22110	West Gate(u)	(703)	6,565	7,119
22152	West Springfield(u)	(703)	28,126	25,012
23185	Williamsburg	(804)	11,530	9,870
22601	Winchester	(703)	21,947	20,217
24592	Wolf Trap(u)	(804)	13,133	9,875
22191	Woodbridge(u)	(703)	26,401	24,004
24382	Wytheville	(703)	8,036	7,135
.....	Yorkshire(u)		5,699	4,940

Washington

ZIP code	Place		1990	1980
98520	Aberdeen	(206)	16,565	18,739
98036	Alderwood Manor(u)	(206)	22,945	16,524
98221	Anacortes	(206)	11,451	9,013
98335	Artondale(u)		7,141	....
98002	Auburn	(206)	33,650	26,417
*98009	Bellevue	(206)	86,872	73,903
98225	Bellingham	(206)	52,179	45,794
98390	Bonney Lake	(206)	7,494	5,328
98011	Bothell	(206)	12,345	7,943
98310	Bremerton	(206)	38,142	36,208
98036	Brier		5,633	2,915
98178	Bryn Mawr-Skyway(u)	(206)	12,514	11,754
98166	Burien(u)	(206)	25,089	23,189
98607	Camas	(206)	6,442	5,681
98055	Cascade-Fairwood(u)	(206)	30,107	16,939
98684	Cascade Park East(u)		6,996	....
98684	Cascade Park West(u)		6,656	....
98531	Centralia	(206)	12,101	11,555
98532	Chehalis	(206)	6,527	6,100
99004	Cheney	(509)	7,723	7,630
99403	Clarkston	(509)	6,753	6,903
99324	College Place	(509)	6,308	5,771
.....	Country Homes(u)		5,126	....
98042	Covington-Sawyer-Wilderness(u)		24,321	....
98198	Des Moines	(206)	17,283	7,378
99213	Dishman(u)	(509)	9,671	10,169
.....	East Hill-Meridian(u)		42,696	....
98366	East Port Orchard(u)		5,409	4,631
98056	East Renton Highlands(u)	(206)	13,218	12,033
98801	East Wenatchee Bench(u)	(509)	12,539	11,410
.....	Edgewood-North Hill(u)		9,120	....
98020	Edmonds	(206)	30,743	27,679
98387	Elk Plain(u)		12,197	....
98926	Ellensburg	(509)	12,360	11,752
.....	Ellsworth North(u)		5,796	....
98022	Enumclaw	(206)	7,227	5,427
98823	Ephrata	(509)	5,349	5,359
99210	Esperance(u)	(509)	11,236	11,120
*98201	Everett	(206)	69,961	54,413
98411	Evergreen(u)		11,249	....
98055	Fairwood(u)	(206)	5,807	5,337
*98003	Federal Way	(206)	67,554	....
98248	Ferndale	(206)	5,398	3,855
98466	Fircrest	(206)	5,258	5,477
98597	Five Corners(u)		6,776	....
98433	Fort Lewis(u)	(206)	22,224	23,761
98930	Grandview	(509)	7,169	5,615
.....	Harbour Pointe(u)		9,107	....
98660	Hazel Dell North(u)	(206)	6,924	15,386
98665	Hazel Dell South(u)	(206)	5,796	....
98550	Hoquiam	(206)	8,972	9,719
98011	Inglewood-Finn Hill(u)	(206)	29,132	12,467
98027	Issaquah	(206)	7,786	5,536
98626	Kelso	(206)	11,767	11,129
98028	Kenmore(u)	(206)	8,917	7,281
99336	Kennewick	(509)	42,148	34,397
98031	Kent	(206)	37,960	22,961
98033	Kingsgate(u)	(206)	14,259	12,652
98033	Kirkland	(206)	40,059	18,785
98503	Lacey	(206)	19,279	13,940
98155	Lake Forest North(u)	(206)	8,002	7,995
.....	Lakeland North(u)	(206)	14,402	11,451
.....	Lakeland South(u)	(206)	9,027	5,225
98036	Lake Serene-North Lynnwood(u)		14,290	54,533
.....	Lake Shore(u)		6,268	....
98259	Lakewood(u)	(206)	58,412	....
98632	Longview	(206)	31,499	31,052
98264	Lynden		5,709	4,022
98036	Lynnwood	(206)	28,637	22,641
.....	Martha Lake(u)	(206)	10,155	7,022
98270	Marysville	(206)	10,328	5,080
98040	Mercer Island	(206)	20,816	21,522
.....	Midland(u)		5,587	....

ZIP code	Place		1990	1980
98012	Mill Creek		7,180	1,803
.....	Minnehaha(u)		9,661	....
98837	Moses Lake	(509)	11,235	10,629
98043	Mountlake Terrace	(206)	19,320	16,534
98273	Mount Vernon	(206)	17,647	13,009
98275	Mukilteo	(206)	7,007	1,426
98006	Newport Hills(u)	(206)	14,736	12,245
98166	Normandy Park	(206)	6,709	4,268
98155	North City-Ridgecrest(u)	(206)	13,832	13,551
.....	North Creek-Canyon Park(u)		23,236	13,551
.....	North Hill(u)	(206)	5,706	10,170
98270	North Marysville(u)	(206)	18,711	15,159
98277	Oak Harbor	(206)	17,176	12,271
*98501	Olympia	(206)	33,729	27,447
99214	Opportunity(u)	(509)	22,326	21,241
98662	Orchards North(u)	(206)	6,479	8,828
98662	Orchards South(u)	(206)	12,956	....
99027	Otis Orchards-East Farms(u)		5,811	4,597
.....	Paine Field-Lake Stickney(u)		18,670	....
98444	Parkland(u)	(206)	20,882	23,355
98366	Parkwood(u)		6,853	4,599
99301	Pasco	(509)	20,337	18,428
98027	Pine Lake(u)		13,940	....
98362	Port Angeles	(206)	17,710	17,311
98368	Port Townsend	(206)	7,001	6,067
98390	Prairie Ridge(u)		8,278	....
99163	Pullman	(509)	23,478	23,579
98371	Puyallup	(206)	23,878	18,251
98052	Redmond	(206)	35,800	23,318
98055	Renton	(206)	41,688	31,031
99352	Richland	(509)	32,315	33,578
98160	Richmond Beach-Innis Arden	(206)	7,242	6,700
98113	Richmond Highlands(u)	(206)	26,037	24,463
98188	Riverton-Boulevard Park(u)	(206)	15,337	14,182
.....	Sahalee(u)		13,951	....
98686	Salmon Creek(u)		11,989	....
*98188	SeaTac	(206)	22,694	....
*98109	Seattle	(206)	516,259	493,846
98284	Sedro Woolley	(206)	6,333	6,110
98942	Selah	(509)	5,113	4,500
98584	Shelton	(206)	7,241	7,629
98155	Sheridan Beach(u)	(206)	6,518	6,873
98315	Silverdale(u)	(206)	7,660	....
98201	Silver Lake-Fircrest(u)	(206)	24,474	10,299
98290	Snohomish	(206)	6,499	5,294
98373	South Hill(u)		12,963	....
98387	Spanaway(u)	(206)	15,001	8,868
*99210	Spokane	(509)	177,165	171,300
98388	Steilacoom	(206)	5,728	4,886
98371	Summit(u)		6,312	....
98390	Sumner	(206)	6,459	4,936
98944	Sunnyside	(509)	11,238	9,225
*98402	Tacoma	(206)	176,664	158,501
98501	Tanglewilde-Thompson Place(u)		6,061	5,910
98948	Toppenish	(509)	7,419	6,517
98188	Tukwila	(206)	11,874	3,578
98502	Tumwater	(206)	9,976	6,705
98406	University Place(u)	(206)	27,701	20,381
*98660	Vancouver	(206)	46,380	42,834
98662	Vancouver Mall(u)	(206)	6,938	....
99037	Veradale(u)	(509)	7,836	7,256
99362	Walla Walla	(509)	26,482	25,618
.....	Waller(u)		6,415	....
98801	Wenatchee	(509)	21,756	17,257
.....	West Lake Sammamish(u)		6,087	....
98258	West Lake Stevens(u)	(206)	12,453	....
99301	West Pasco(u)	(509)	7,312	6,210
99181	West Valley(u)		6,594	....
98166	White Center-Shorewood(u)	(206)	20,531	19,362
98072	Woodinville(u)		23,654	....
98032	Woodmont Beach(u)		7,493	....
*98901	Yakima	(509)	54,843	49,826

West Virginia (304)

ZIP code	Place	1990	1980
25801	Beckley	18,296	20,492
24701	Bluefield	12,756	16,060
26330	Bridgeport	6,739	6,604
26201	Buckhannon	5,909	6,820
*25301	Charleston	57,287	63,968
26301	Clarksburg	18,059	22,371
25301	Cross Lanes(u)	10,878	....
25064	Dunbar	8,697	9,285
26241	Elkins	7,420	8,536
26554	Fairmont	20,210	23,863
26354	Grafton	5,524	6,845
*25701	Huntington	54,844	63,684
26726	Keyser	5,870	6,569
25401	Martinsburg	14,073	13,063
26505	Morgantown	25,879	27,605
26041	Moundsville	10,753	12,419
26155	New Martinsville	6,705	7,109
25143	Nitro	6,851	8,074
25901	Oak Hill	6,812	7,120
26101	Parkersburg	33,862	39,946
.....	Pea Ridge(u)	6,535	....
24740	Princeton	7,043	7,538
25177	Saint Albans	11,194	12,402
25303	South Charleston	13,645	15,968
25569	Teays Valley(u)	8,436	....
26105	Vienna	10,862	11,618
26062	Weirton	22,124	25,371
26003	Wheeling	34,882	43,070

Wisconsin

ZIP code	Place		1990	1980
54301	Allouez	(414)	14,431	14,882
54720	Altoona		5,889	4,393
54409	Antigo	(715)	8,275	8,653
59411	Appleton	(414)	65,695	58,913
54806	Ashland	(715)	8,695	9,115
54304	Ashwaubenon	(414)	16,376	14,486
53913	Baraboo	(608)	9,203	8,081
53916	Beaver Dam	(414)	14,196	14,149
.....	Bellevue Town(u)		7,541	....
53511	Beloit	(608)	35,571	35,207
54923	Berlin	(414)	5,371	5,478
53005	Brookfield	(414)	35,184	34,035
53209	Brown Deer	(414)	12,236	12,921
53105	Burlington	(414)	8,855	8,385
53012	Cedarburg	(414)	10,086	9,005
54729	Chippewa Falls	(715)	12,727	12,270
53110	Cudahy	(414)	18,659	19,547
53018	Delafield		5,347	4,083
53115	Delavan	(414)	6,073	5,684
54115	De Pere	(414)	16,569	14,892
54701	Eau Claire	(715)	56,806	51,509
53121	Elkhorn	(414)	5,337	4,605
53122	Elm Grove	(414)	6,261	6,735
53714	Fitchburg	(608)	15,648	11,965
54935	Fond Du Lac	(414)	37,757	35,863
53538	Fort Atkinson	(414)	10,213	9,785
53217	Fox Point	(414)	7,238	7,649
53132	Franklin	(414)	21,855	16,871
53022	Germantown	(414)	13,658	10,729
53209	Glendale	(414)	14,088	13,882
53024	Grafton	(414)	9,340	8,381
*54305	Green Bay	(414)	96,466	87,899
53129	Greendale	(414)	15,128	16,928
53220	Greenfield	(414)	33,403	31,353
53130	Hales Corners	(414)	7,623	7,110
53027	Hartford	(414)	8,188	7,159
53029	Hartland	(414)	6,906	5,559
54303	Howard	(414)	9,874	8,240
54016	Hudson	(715)	6,378	5,434
53545	Janesville	(608)	52,210	51,071
53549	Jefferson	(414)	6,078	5,647
54130	Kaukauna	(414)	11,982	11,310
53140	Kenosha	(414)	80,426	77,685
54136	Kimberly	(414)	5,406	5,881
54601	La Crosse	(608)	51,120	48,347
53147	Lake Geneva	(414)	5,979	5,612
54140	Little Chute	(414)	9,207	7,907
53558	McFarland	(608)	5,232	3,783
*53701	Madison	(608)	190,766	170,616
54220	Manitowoc	(414)	32,520	32,547
54143	Marinette	(715)	11,843	11,965
54449	Marshfield	(715)	19,291	18,290
54952	Menasha	(414)	14,711	14,728
53051	Menomonee Falls	(414)	26,840	27,845
54751	Menomonie	(715)	13,547	12,769
53092	Mequon	(414)	18,885	16,193
54452	Merrill	(715)	9,860	9,578
53562	Middleton	(608)	13,785	11,851
*53203	Milwaukee	(414)	628,088	636,297
53716	Monona	(608)	8,637	8,809
53566	Monroe	(608)	10,241	10,027
53150	Muskego	(414)	16,813	15,277
54956	Neenah	(414)	23,219	22,432
53151	New Berlin	(414)	33,592	30,529
54961	New London	(414)	6,658	6,210
54017	New Richmond	(715)	5,106	4,306
53154	Oak Creek	(414)	19,513	16,932
53066	Oconomowoc	(414)	10,993	9,909
54650	Onalaska	(608)	11,414	9,249
54901	Oshkosh	(414)	55,006	49,620
53072	Pewaukee		5,287	....
53818	Platteville	(608)	9,862	9,580
53158	Pleasant Prairie	(414)	12,037	12,176
54467	Plover	(715)	8,176	5,310
53073	Plymouth	(414)	6,769	6,027
53901	Portage	(608)	8,640	7,896
53074	Port Washington	(414)	9,338	8,612
53821	Prairie du Chien	(608)	5,657	5,859
*53401	Racine	(414)	84,298	85,725
53959	Reedsburg	(608)	5,834	5,038
54501	Rhinelander	(715)	7,427	7,873
54868	Rice Lake	(715)	7,998	7,691
53581	Richland Center	(608)	5,018	4,997
54971	Ripon	(414)	7,241	7,111
54022	River Falls	(715)	10,610	9,019
53207	Saint Francis	(414)	9,245	10,095
54166	Shawano	(715)	7,598	7,013
53081	Sheboygan	(414)	49,587	48,085

ZIP code	Place		1990	1980
53085	Sheboygan Falls	(414)	5,823	5,253
53211	Shorewood	(414)	14,116	14,327
53172	South Milwaukee	(414)	20,958	21,069
54656	Sparta	(608)	7,788	6,934
54481	Stevens Point	(715)	23,006	22,970
53589	Stoughton	(608)	8,786	7,589
54235	Sturgeon Bay	(414)	9,176	8,847
53590	Sun Prairie	(608)	15,333	12,931
54880	Superior	(715)	27,134	29,571
53089	Sussex		5,039	3,482
54660	Tomah	(608)	7,570	7,204
54241	Two Rivers	(414)	13,030	13,354
53593	Verona		5,374	3,336
53094	Watertown	(414)	19,142	18,113
53186	Waukesha	(414)	56,958	50,365
53597	Waunakee		5,897	3,866
53963	Waupun	(414)	8,844	8,132
54401	Wausau	(715)	37,060	32,426
53213	Wauwatosa	(414)	49,366	51,308
53214	West Allis	(414)	63,221	63,982
53095	West Bend	(414)	23,470	21,484
54476	Weston(u)	(715)	9,714	8,775
53217	Whitefish Bay	(414)	14,272	14,930
53190	Whitewater	(414)	12,636	11,520
54494	Wisconsin Rapids	(715)	18,245	17,995

Wyoming (307)

ZIP code	Place	1990	1980
*82601	Casper	46,765	51,016
*82001	Cheyenne	50,008	47,283
82414	Cody	7,897	6,599
82633	Douglas	5,076	6,030
82930	Evanston	10,904	6,265
82716	Gillette	17,545	12,134
82935	Green River	12,711	12,807
82520	Lander	7,023	7,867
82070	Laramie	26,687	24,410
82435	Powell	5,292	5,310
82301	Rawlins	9,380	11,547
82501	Riverton	9,202	9,562
82901	Rock Springs	19,050	19,458
82801	Sheridan	13,904	15,146
82240	Torrington	5,651	5,441
82401	Worland	5,742	6,391

Census and Areas of Counties and States

Source: Bureau of the Census
With names of county seats or court houses

Population figures listed below are final counts in the 1990 census, conducted on Apr. 1, 1990; updated as of Apr. 1993.

Alabama

(67 counties, 50,767 sq. mi. land; pop., 4,040,587)

County	Pop.	County Seat or court house	Land area sq. mi.
Autauga	34,222	Prattville	596
Baldwin	98,280	Bay Minette	1,596
Barbour	25,417	Clayton	885
Bibb	16,576	Centreville	622
Blount	39,248	Oneonta	645
Bullock	11,042	Union Springs	625
Butler	21,892	Greenville	776
Calhoun	116,032	Anniston	608
Chambers	36,876	Lafayette	597
Cherokee	19,543	Centre	553
Chilton	32,458	Clanton	694
Choctaw	16,018	Butler	913
Clarke	27,240	Grove Hill	1,238
Clay	13,252	Ashland	605
Cleburne	12,730	Heflin	560
Coffee	40,240	Elba	679
Colbert	51,666	Tuscumbia	594
Conecuh	14,054	Evergreen	850
Coosa	11,063	Rockford	652
Covington	36,478	Andalusia	1,034
Crenshaw	13,635	Luverne	609
Cullman	67,613	Cullman	738
Dale	49,633	Ozark	561
Dallas	48,130	Selma	980
De Kalb	54,651	Fort Payne	777
Elmore	49,210	Wetumpka	621
Escambia	35,518	Brewton	947
Etowah	99,840	Gadsden	534
Fayette	17,962	Fayette	627
Franklin	27,814	Russellville	635
Geneva	23,647	Geneva	576
Greene	10,153	Eutaw	645
Hale	15,498	Greensboro	643
Henry	15,374	Abbeville	561
Houston	81,331	Dothan	580
Jackson	47,796	Scottsboro	1,078
Jefferson	651,520	Birmingham	1,112
Lamar	15,715	Vernon	604
Lauderdale	79,661	Florence	669
Lawrence	31,513	Moulton	693
Lee	87,146	Opelika	608
Limestone	46,005	Athens	568
Lowndes	12,658	Hayneville	718
Macon	24,928	Tuskegee	610
Madison	238,912	Huntsville	804
Marengo	23,084	Linden	977
Marion	29,830	Hamilton	741
Marshall	70,832	Guntersville	567
Mobile	378,643	Mobile	1,233
Monroe	23,968	Monroeville	1,025
Montgomery	209,085	Montgomery	789
Morgan	100,043	Decatur	599
Perry	12,759	Marion	719
Pickens	20,699	Carrollton	881
Pike	27,595	Troy	671
Randolph	19,881	Wedowee	581
Russell	46,860	Phenix City	641
Saint Clair	49,811	Ashville & Pell City	633
Shelby	99,363	Columbiana	794
Sumter	16,174	Livingston	904
Talladega	74,109	Talladega	739
Tallapoosa	38,826	Dadeville	718
Tuscaloosa	150,522	Tuscaloosa	1,325
Walker	67,670	Jasper	794
Washington	16,694	Chatom	1,080
Wilcox	13,568	Camden	888
Winston	22,053	Double Springs	614

Alaska

(25 divisions, 570,833 sq. mi. land; pop., 550,043)

Census Division	Pop.	Land area sq. mi.
Aleutian East Borough	2,464	6,985
Aleutians West Census Area	9,478	4,402
Anchorage Borough	226,338	1,732
Bethel Census Area	13,656	36,104
Bristol Bay Borough	1,410	531
Dillingham Census Area	4,012	46,042
Fairbanks North Star Borough	77,720	7,404
Haines Borough	2,117	2,374
Juneau Borough	26,751	2,626
Kenai Peninsula Borough	40,802	16,056
Ketchikan Gateway Borough	13,828	1,242
Kodiak Island Borough	13,309	4,796
Lake and Peninsula Borough	1,668	....
Matanuska-Susitna Borough	39,683	24,502
Nome Census Area	8,288	23,871
North Slope Borough	5,979	90,955
Northwest Arctic Borough	6,113	....
Prince of Wales-Outer Ketchikan Census Area	6,278	7,660
Sitka Borough	8,588	2,938
Skagway-Yakutat-Angoon Census Area	4,385	13,239
Southeast Fairbanks Census Area	5,913	24,169
Valdez-Cordova Census Area	9,952	39,229
Wade Hampton Census Area	5,791	17,816
Wrangell-Petersburg Census Area	7,042	6,167
Yukon-Koyukuk Census Area	8,478	159,099

Arizona

(15 counties, 113,508 sq. mi. land; pop. 3,665,228)

County	Pop.	County Seat or court house	Land area sq. mi.
Apache	61,591	Saint Johns	11,211
Cochise	97,624	Bisbee	6,218

County	Pop.	County Seat or court house	Land area sq. mi.
Coconino	96,591	Flagstaff	18,608
Gila	40,216	Globe	4,752
Graham	26,554	Safford	4,630
Greenlee	8,008	Clifton	1,837
La Paz	13,844	Parker	4,430
Maricopa	2,122,101	Phoenix	9,127
Mohave	93,497	Kingman	13,285
Navajo	77,674	Holbrook	9,955
Pima	666,957	Tucson	9,187
Pinal	116,379	Florence	5,343
Santa Cruz	29,676	Nogales	1,238
Yavapai	107,714	Prescott	8,123
Yuma	106,895	Yuma	5,564

Arkansas

(75 counties, 52,078 sq. mi. land; pop. 2,350,725)

County	Pop.	County Seat or court house	Land area sq. mi.
Arkansas	21,653	DeWitt & Stuttgart	1,033
Ashley	24,319	Hamburg	939
Baxter	31,186	Mountain Home	586
Benton	97,499	Bentonville	876
Boone	28,297	Harrison	601
Bradley	11,793	Warren	654
Calhoun	5,826	Hampton	632
Carroll	18,654	Berryville & Eureka Sp.	642
Chicot	15,713	Lake Village	690
Clark	21,437	Arkadelphia	882
Clay	18,107	Corning & Piggott	641
Cleburne	19,411	Heber Springs	591
Cleveland	7,781	Rison	598
Columbia	25,691	Magnolia	766
Conway	19,151	Morrilton	566
Craighead	68,956	Jonesboro & Lake City	713
Crawford	42,493	Van Buren	604
Crittenden	49,939	Marion	636
Cross	19,225	Wynne	622
Dallas	9,614	Fordyce	668
Desha	16,798	Arkansas City	819
Drew	17,369	Monticello	835
Faulkner	60,006	Conway	664
Franklin	14,897	Charleston & Ozark	919
Fulton	10,037	Salem	620
Garland	73,397	Hot Springs	734
Grant	13,948	Sheridan	633
Greene	31,804	Paragould	579
Hempstead	21,621	Hope	741
Hot Spring	26,115	Malvern	622
Howard	13,569	Nashville	595
Independence	31,192	Batesville	771
Izard	11,364	Melbourne	584
Jackson	18,944	Newport	641
Jefferson	85,487	Pine Bluff	913
Johnson	18,221	Clarksville	682
Lafayette	9,643	Lewisville	545
Lawrence	17,455	Walnut Ridge	592
Lee	13,053	Marianna	619
Lincoln	13,690	Star City	572
Little River	13,966	Ashdown	564
Logan	20,557	Booneville & Paris	731
Lonoke	39,268	Lonoke	802
Madison	11,618	Huntsville	837
Marion	12,001	Yellville	640
Miller	38,467	Texarkana	637
Mississippi	57,525	Blytheville & Osceola	919
Monroe	11,333	Clarendon	621
Montgomery	7,841	Mount Ida	800
Nevada	10,101	Prescott	620
Newton	7,666	Jasper	823
Ouachita	30,574	Camden	739
Perry	7,969	Perryville	560
Phillips	28,836	Helena	727
Pike	10,086	Murfreesboro	613
Poinsett	24,664	Harrisburg	763
Polk	17,347	Mena	862
Pope	45,883	Russellville	830
Prairie	9,518	Des Arc & De Valls Bluff	675
Pulaski	349,569	Little Rock	807
Randolph	16,558	Pocahontas	656
Saint Francis	28,497	Forrest City	642
Saline	64,183	Benton	730
Scott	10,205	Waldron	898
Searcy	7,841	Marshall	668
Sebastian	99,590	Fort Smith & Greenwood	546
Sevier	13,637	De Queen	581
Sharp	14,109	Ash Flat	606
Stone	9,775	Mountain View	609
Union	46,719	El Dorado	1,055
Van Buren	14,008	Clinton	724
Washington	113,409	Fayetteville	956
White	54,676	Searcy	1,042
Woodruff	9,520	Augusta	594
Yell	17,759	Danville & Dardanelle	948

California

(58 counties, 156,299 sq. mi. land; pop. 29,760,021)

County	Pop.	County Seat or court house	Land area sq. mi.
Alameda	1,276,702	Oakland	736
Alpine	1,113	Markleeville	738
Amador	30,039	Jackson	589
Butte	182,120	Oroville	1,646
Calaveras	31,998	San Andreas	1,021
Colusa	16,275	Colusa	1 152
Contra Costa	803,732	Martinez	730
Del Norte	23,460	Crescent City	1,007
El Dorado	125,995	Placerville	1,715
Fresno	667,490	Fresno	5,978
Glenn	24,798	Willows	1,319
Humboldt	119,118	Eureka	3,579
Imperial	109,303	El Centro	4,173
Inyo	18,281	Independence	10,223
Kern	543,981	Bakersfield	8,130
Kings	101,469	Hanford	1,392
Lake	50,631	Lakeport	1,262
Lassen	27,598	Susanville	4,553
Los Angeles	8,863,052	Los Angeles	4,070
Madera	88,090	Madera	2,145
Marin	230,096	San Rafael	523
Mariposa	14,302	Mariposa	1,456
Mendocino	80,345	Ukiah	3,512
Merced	178,403	Merced	1,944
Modoc	9,678	Alturas	4,064
Mono	9,956	Bridgeport	3,018
Monterey	355,660	Salinas	3,303
Napa	110,765	Napa	744
Nevada	78,510	Nevada City	960
Orange	2,410,668	Santa Ana	798
Placer	172,796	Auburn	1,416
Plumas	19,739	Quincy	2,573
Riverside	1,170,413	Riverside	7,214
Sacramento	1,041,219	Sacramento	971
San Benito	36,697	Hollister	1,388
San Bernardino	1,418,380	San Bernardino	20,064
San Diego	2,498,016	San Diego	4,212
San Francisco	723,959	San Francisco	46
San Joaquin	480,628	Stockton	1,415
San Luis Obispo	217,162	San Luis Obispo	3,308
San Mateo	649,623	Redwood City	447
Santa Barbara	369,608	Santa Barbara	2,748
Santa Clara	1,497,577	San Jose	1,293
Santa Cruz	229,734	Santa Cruz	446
Shasta	147,036	Redding	3,786
Sierra	3,318	Downieville	959
Siskiyou	43,531	Yreka	6,281
Solano	339,471	Fairfield	834
Sonoma	388,222	Santa Rosa	1,604
Stanislaus	370,522	Modesto	1,506
Sutter	64,415	Yuba City	602
Tehama	49,625	Red Bluff	2,953
Trinity	13,063	Weaverville	3,190
Tulare	311,921	Visalia	4,808
Tuolumne	48,456	Sonora	2,234
Ventura	669,016	Ventura	1,862
Yolo	141,210	Woodland	1,014
Yuba	58,228	Marysville	640

Colorado

(63 counties, 103,595 sq. mi. land; pop. 3,294,394)

County	Pop.	County Seat or court house	Land area sq. mi.
Adams	265,038	Brighton	1,235
Alamosa	13,617	Alamosa	719
Arapahoe	391,511	Littleton	800
Archuleta	5,345	Pagosa Springs	1,353
Baca	4,556	Springfield	2,554
Bent	5,048	Las Animas	1,517
Boulder	225,339	Boulder	742
Chaffee	12,684	Salida	1,008
Cheyenne	2,397	Cheyenne Wells	1,783
Clear Creek	7,619	Georgetown	396
Conejos	7,453	Conejos	1,284
Costilla	3,190	San Luis	1,227
Crowley	3,946	Ordway	790
Custer	1,926	Westcliffe	740
Delta	20,980	Delta	1,141
Denver	467,610	Denver	111
Dolores	1,504	Dove Creek	1,064
Douglas	60,391	Castle Rock	841
Eagle	21,928	Eagle	1,690
Elbert	9,646	Kiowa	1,851
El Paso	397,014	Colorado Springs	2,129
Fremont	32,273	Canon City	1,538
Garfield	29,974	Glenwood Springs	2,952
Gilpin	3,070	Central City	149
Grand	7,966	Hot Sulphur Springs	1,854
Gunnison	10,273	Gunnison	3,238
Hinsdale	467	Lake City	1,115

County	Pop.	County Seat or court house	Land area sq. mi.
Huerfano	6,009	Walsenburg	1,584
Jackson	1,605	Walden	1,614
Jefferson	438,430	Golden	768
Kiowa	1,688	Eads	1,758
Kit Carson	7,140	Burlington	2,160
Lake	6,007	Leadville	379
La Plata	32,284	Durango	1,692
Larimer	186,136	Fort Collins	2,604
Las Animas	13,765	Trinidad	4,771
Lincoln	4,529	Hugo	2,586
Logan	17,567	Sterling	1,818
Mesa	93,145	Grand Junction	3,309
Mineral	558	Creede	877
Moffat	11,357	Craig	4,732
Montezuma	18,672	Cortez	2,038
Montrose	24,423	Montrose	2,240
Morgan	21,939	Fort Morgan	1,276
Otero	20,185	La Junta	1,247
Ouray	2,295	Ouray	542
Park	7,174	Fairplay	2,192
Phillips	4,189	Holyoke	688
Pitkin	12,661	Aspen	968
Prowers	13,347	Lamar	1,629
Pueblo	123,051	Pueblo	2,377
Rio Blanco	5,972	Meeker	3,222
Rio Grande	10,770	Del Norte	913
Routt	14,088	Steamboat Springs	2,367
Saguache	4,619	Saguache	3,167
San Juan	745	Silverton	388
San Miguel	3,653	Telluride	1,287
Sedgwick	2,690	Julesburg	540
Summit	12,881	Breckenridge	607
Teller	12,468	Cripple Creek	559
Washington	4,812	Akron	2,520
Weld	131,821	Greeley	3,990
Yuma	8,954	Wray	2,365

Connecticut

(8 counties, 4,872 sq. mi. land; pop. 3,287,116)

Fairfield	827,645	Bridgeport	632
Hartford	852,783	Hartford	739
Litchfield	174,092	Litchfield	921
Middlesex	143,196	Middletown	373
New Haven	804,219	New Haven	610
New London	254,957	Norwich	669
Tolland	128,699	Rockville	412
Windham	102,525	Putnam	515

Delaware

(3 counties, 1,932 sq. mi. land; pop. 666,168)

Kent	110,993	Dover	595
New Castle	441,946	Wilmington	396
Sussex	113,229	Georgetown	942

District of Columbia

(63 sq. mi. land; pop. 606,900)

Florida

(67 counties, 54,153 sq. mi. land; pop. 12,937,926)

Alachua	181,596	Gainesville	901
Baker	18,486	Macclenny	585
Bay	126,994	Panama City	758
Bradford	22,515	Starke	293
Brevard	398,978	Titusville	995
Broward	1,255,518	Fort Lauderdale	1,211
Calhoun	11,011	Blountstown	568
Charlotte	110,975	Punta Gorda	690
Citrus	93,513	Inverness	629
Clay	105,986	Green Cove Springs	592
Collier	152,099	Naples	1,994
Columbia	42,613	Lake City	796
Dade	1,937,194	Miami	1,955
De Soto	23,865	Arcadia	636
Dixie	10,585	Cross City	701
Duval	672,971	Jacksonville	776
Escambia	262,798	Pensacola	660
Flagler	28,701	Bunnell	491
Franklin	8,967	Apalachicola	545
Gadsden	41,116	Quincy	518
Gilchrist	9,667	Trenton	354
Glades	7,591	Moore Haven	763
Gulf	11,504	Port Saint Joe	559
Hamilton	10,930	Jasper	517
Hardee	19,499	Wauchula	637
Hendry	25,773	La Belle	1,163
Hernando	101,115	Brooksville	477
Highlands	68,432	Sebring	1,029
Hillsborough	834,054	Tampa	1,053
Holmes	15,778	Bonifay	488
Indian River	90,208	Vero Beach	497
Jackson	41,375	Marianna	942
Jefferson	11,296	Monticello	609
Lafayette	5,578	Mayo	545
Lake	152,104	Tavares	954
Lee	335,113	Fort Myers	803
Leon	192,493	Tallahassee	676
Levy	25,912	Bronson	1,100
Liberty	5,569	Bristol	837
Madison	16,569	Madison	710
Manatee	211,707	Bradenton	747
Marion	194,835	Ocala	1,610
Martin	100,900	Stuart	555
Monroe	78,024	Key West	1,034
Nassau	43,941	Fernandina Beach	649
Okaloosa	143,777	Crestview	936
Okeechobee	29,627	Okeechobee	770
Orange	677,491	Orlando	910
Osceola	107,728	Kissimmee	1,350
Palm Beach	863,503	West Palm Beach	1,993
Pasco	281,131	New Port Richey	738
Pinellas	851,659	Clearwater	280
Polk	405,382	Bartow	1,823
Putnam	65,070	Palatka	733
Saint Johns	83,829	Saint Augustine	617
Saint Lucie	150,171	Fort Pierce	581
Santa Rosa	81,608	Milton	1,024
Sarasota	277,776	Sarasota	573
Seminole	287,521	Sanford	298
Sumter	31,577	Bushnell	561
Suwannee	26,780	Live Oak	690
Taylor	17,111	Perry	1,058
Union	10,252	Lake Butler	246
Volusia	370,737	De Land	1,113
Wakulla	14,759	Crawfordville	601
Walton	27,759	De Funiak Springs	1,066
Washington	16,919	Chipley	590

Georgia

(159 counties, 58,056 sq. mi. land; pop. 6,478,216)

Appling	15,744	Baxley	510
Atkinson	6,213	Pearson	344
Bacon	9,566	Alma	286
Baker	3,615	Newton	347
Baldwin	39,530	Milledgeville	257
Banks	10,308	Homer	234
Barrow	29,721	Winder	163
Bartow	55,915	Cartersville	456
Ben Hill	16,245	Fitzgerald	254
Berrien	14,153	Nashville	456
Bibb	150,137	Macon	253
Bleckley	10,430	Cochran	219
Brantley	11,077	Nahunta	445
Brooks	15,398	Quitman	491
Bryan	15,438	Pembroke	441
Bulloch	43,125	Statesboro	678
Burke	20,579	Waynesboro	833
Butts	15,326	Jackson	187
Calhoun	5,013	Morgan	284
Camden	30,167	Woodbine	649
Candler	7,744	Metter	248
Carroll	71,422	Carrollton	501
Catoosa	42,464	Ringgold	162
Charlton	8,496	Folkston	780
Chatham	216,774	Savannah	443
Chattahoochee	16,934	Cusseta	250
Chattooga	22,242	Summerville	313
Cherokee	90,204	Canton	424
Clarke	87,594	Athens	122
Clay	3,364	Fort Gaines	196
Clayton	182,052	Jonesboro	148
Clinch	6,160	Homerville	821
Cobb	447,745	Marietta	343
Coffee	29,592	Douglas	602
Colquitt	36,645	Moultrie	557
Columbia	66,031	Appling	290
Cook	13,456	Adel	233
Coweta	53,853	Newnan	444
Crawford	8,991	Knoxville	328
Crisp	20,011	Cordele	275
Dade	13,147	Trenton	176
Dawson	9,429	Dawsonville	210
Decatur	25,517	Bainbridge	586
De Kalb	546,171	Decatur	270
Dodge	17,607	Eastman	504
Dooly	9,901	Vienna	397

County	Pop.	County Seat or court house	Land area sq. mi.
Dougherty	96,321	Albany	330
Douglas	71,120	Douglasville	203
Early	11,854	Blakely	516
Echols	2,334	Statenville	421
Effingham	25,687	Springfield	482
Elbert	18,949	Elberton	367
Emanuel	20,546	Swainsboro	688
Evans	8,724	Claxton	186
Fannin	15,992	Blue Ridge	384
Fayette	62,415	Fayetteville	199
Floyd	81,251	Rome	519
Forsyth	44,083	Cumming	226
Franklin	16,650	Carnesville	264
Fulton	648,779	Atlanta	534
Gilmer	13,368	Ellijay	427
Glascock	2,357	Gibson	144
Glynn	62,496	Brunswick	412
Gordon	35,067	Calhoun	355
Grady	20,279	Cairo	459
Greene	11,793	Greensboro	389
Gwinnett	352,910	Lawrenceville	435
Habersham	27,622	Clarkesville	278
Hall	95,434	Gainesville	379
Hancock	8,908	Sparta	470
Haralson	21,966	Buchanan	283
Harris	17,788	Hamilton	464
Hart	19,712	Hartwell	230
Heard	8,628	Franklin	292
Henry	58,741	McDonough	321
Houston	89,208	Perry	380
Irwin	8,649	Ocilla	362
Jackson	30,005	Jefferson	342
Jasper	8,453	Monticello	371
Jeff Davis	12,032	Hazlehurst	335
Jefferson	17,408	Louisville	529
Jenkins	8,247	Millen	353
Johnson	8,329	Wrightsville	306
Jones	20,739	Gray	394
Lamar	13,038	Barnesville	186
Lanier	5,531	Lakeland	194
Laurens	39,988	Dublin	816
Lee	16,250	Leesburg	358
Liberty	52,745	Hinesville	517
Lincoln	7,442	Lincolnton	196
Long	6,202	Ludowici	402
Lowndes	75,981	Valdosta	507
Lumpkin	14,573	Dahlonega	287
McDuffie	20,119	Thomson	256
McIntosh	8,634	Darien	425
Macon	13,114	Oglethorpe	404
Madison	21,050	Danielsville	285
Marion	5,590	Buena Vista	366
Meriwether	22,411	Greenville	506
Miller	6,280	Colquitt	284
Mitchell	20,275	Camilla	512
Monroe	17,113	Forsyth	397
Montgomery	7,379	Mount Vernon	244
Morgan	12,883	Madison	349
Murray	26,147	Chatsworth	345
Muscogee	179,278	Columbus	218
Newton	41,808	Covington	277
Oconee	17,618	Watkinsville	186
Oglethorpe	9,763	Lexington	442
Paulding	41,611	Dallas	312
Peach	21,189	Fort Valley	152
Pickens	14,432	Jasper	232
Pierce	13,328	Blackshear	344
Pike	10,224	Zebulon	219
Polk	33,815	Cedartown	311
Pulaski	8,108	Hawkinsville	249
Putnam	14,137	Eatonton	344
Quitman	2,209	Georgetown	146
Rabun	11,648	Clayton	370
Randolph	8,023	Cuthbert	431
Richmond	189,719	Augusta	326
Rockdale	54,091	Conyers	132
Schley	3,588	Ellaville	169
Screven	13,842	Sylvania	655
Seminole	9,010	Donalsonville	225
Spalding	54,457	Griffin	199
Stephens	23,251	Toccoa	177
Stewart	5,654	Lumpkin	452
Sumter	30,228	Americus	489
Talbot	6,524	Talbotton	395
Taliaferro	1,915	Crawfordville	196
Tattnall	17,722	Reidsville	484
Taylor	7,642	Butler	382
Telfair	11,000	MacRae	444
Terrell	10,653	Dawson	337
Thomas	38,943	Thomasville	551
Tift	34,998	Tifton	268
Toombs	24,072	Lyons	371
Towns	6,754	Hiawassee	165
Treutlen	5,994	Soperton	202
Troup	55,532	La Grange	414
Turner	8,703	Ashburn	289
Twiggs	9,806	Jeffersonville	362
Union	11,993	Blairsville	320
Upson	26,300	Thomaston	326
Walker	58,340	La Fayette	446
Walton	38,586	Monroe	330
Ware	35,471	Waycross	907
Warren	6,078	Warrenton	286
Washington	19,112	Sandersville	684
Wayne	22,356	Jesup	647
Webster	2,263	Preston	210
Wheeler	4,903	Alamo	299
White	13,006	Cleveland	242
Whitfield	72,462	Dalton	291
Wilcox	7,008	Abbeville	382
Wilkes	10,597	Washington	470
Wilkinson	10,228	Irwinton	451
Worth	19,744	Sylvester	575

Hawaii

(4 counties, 6,645 sq. mi. land; pop. 1,108,229)

County	Pop.	County Seat or court house	Land area sq. mi.
Hawaii	120,317	Hilo	4,034
Honolulu	836,231	Honolulu	596
Kauai	51,177	Lihue	620
Maui	100,374	Wailuku	1,175

Idaho

(44 counties, 82,412 sq. mi. land; pop. 1,006,749)

County	Pop.	County Seat or court house	Land area sq. mi.
Ada	205,775	Boise	1,052
Adams	3,254	Council	1,362
Bannock	66,026	Pocatello	1,112
Bear Lake	6,084	Paris	990
Benewah	7,937	Saint Maries	784
Bingham	37,583	Blackfoot	2,090
Blaine	13,552	Hailey	2,634
Boise	3,509	Idaho City	1,901
Bonner	26,622	Sandpoint	1,726
Bonneville	72,207	Idaho Falls	1,840
Boundary	8,332	Bonners Ferry	1,268
Butte	2,918	Arco	2,236
Camas	727	Fairfield	1,071
Canyon	90,076	Caldwell	584
Caribou	6,963	Soda Springs	1,763
Cassia	19,532	Burley	2,560
Clark	762	Dubois	1,763
Clearwater	8,505	Orofino	2,460
Custer	4,133	Challis	4,927
Elmore	21,205	Mountain Home	3,071
Franklin	9,232	Preston	664
Fremont	10,937	Saint Anthony	1,852
Gem	11,844	Emmett	558
Gooding	11,633	Gooding	728
Idaho	13,768	Grangeville	8,497
Jefferson	16,543	Rigby	1,093
Jerome	15,138	Jerome	601
Kootenai	69,795	Coeur d'Alene	1,240
Latah	30,617	Moscow	1,077
Lemhi	6,899	Salmon	4,564
Lewis	3,516	Nezperce	478
Lincoln	3,308	Shoshone	1,205
Madison	23,674	Rexberg	468
Minidoka	19,361	Rupert	757
Nez Perce	33,754	Lewiston	845
Oneida	3,492	Malad City	1,200
Owyhee	8,392	Murphy	7,643
Payette	16,434	Payette	405
Power	7,086	American Falls	1,403
Shoshone	13,931	Wallace	2,641
Teton	3,439	Driggs	448
Twin Falls	53,580	Twin Falls	1,944
Valley	6,109	Cascade	3,670
Washington	8,550	Weiser	1,454

Illinois

(102 counties, 55,646 sq. mi. land; pop. 11,430,602)

County	Pop.	County Seat or court house	Land area sq. mi.
Adams	66,090	Quincy	862
Alexander	10,626	Cairo	229
Bond	14,991	Greenville	378
Boone	30,806	Belvidere	283
Brown	5,836	Mount Sterling	306
Bureau	35,688	Princeton	866
Calhoun	5,322	Hardin	247
Carroll	16,805	Mount Carroll	456
Cass	13,437	Virginia	371
Champaign	173,025	Urbana	1,000
Christian	34,418	Taylorville	709
Clark	15,921	Marshall	505
Clay	14,460	Louisville	464

County	Pop.	County Seat or court house	Land area sq. mi.
Clinton	33,944	Carlyle	434
Coles	51,644	Charleston	506
Cook	5,105,067	Chicago	954
Crawford	19,464	Robinson	443
Cumberland	10,670	Toledo	347
DeKalb	77,932	Sycamore	636
De Witt	16,516	Clinton	399
Douglas	19,464	Tuscola	420
Du Page	781,666	Wheaton	337
Edgar	19,595	Paris	628
Edwards	7,440	Albion	225
Effingham	31,704	Effingham	481
Fayette	20,893	Vandalia	703
Ford	14,275	Paxton	488
Franklin	40,319	Benton	434
Fulton	38,080	Lewiston	877
Gallatin	6,909	Shawneetown	328
Greene	15,317	Carrollton	543
Grundy	32,337	Morris	432
Hamilton	8,499	McLeansboro	435
Hancock	21,373	Carthage	797
Hardin	5,189	Elizabethtown	183
Henderson	8,096	Oquawka	376
Henry	51,159	Cambridge	826
Iroquois	30,787	Watseka	1,122
Jackson	61,067	Murphysboro	605
Jasper	10,609	Newton	495
Jefferson	37,020	Mount Vernon	573
Jersey	20,539	Jerseyville	376
Jo Daviess	21,821	Galena	606
Johnson	11,347	Vienna	345
Kane	317,471	Geneva	520
Kankakee	96,255	Kankakee	678
Kendall	39,413	Yorkville	320
Knox	56,393	Galesburg	728
Lake	516,418	Waukegan	457
La Salle	106,913	Ottawa	1,150
Lawrence	15,972	Lawrenceville	374
Lee	34,392	Dixon	728
Livingston	39,301	Pontiac	1,043
Logan	30,798	Lincoln	622
McDonough	35,244	Macomb	582
McHenry	183,241	Woodstock	610
McLean	129,180	Bloomington	1,173
Macon	117,206	Decatur	578
Macoupin	47,679	Carlinville	872
Madison	249,238	Edwardsville	733
Marion	41,561	Salem	579
Marshall	12,846	Lacon	391
Mason	16,269	Havana	541
Massac	14,752	Metropolis	245
Menard	11,164	Petersburg	312
Mercer	17,290	Aledo	556
Monroe	22,422	Waterloo	382
Montgomery	30,728	Hillsboro	705
Morgan	36,397	Jacksonville	561
Moultrie	13,930	Sullivan	326
Ogle	45,957	Oregon	758
Peoria	182,827	Peoria	623
Perry	21,412	Pinckneyville	439
Piatt	15,548	Monticello	437
Pike	17,577	Pittsfield	828
Pope	4,373	Golconda	381
Pulaski	7,523	Mound City	204
Putnam	5,730	Hennepin	160
Randolph	34,583	Chester	594
Richland	16,545	Olney	364
Rock Island	148,723	Rock Island	424
Saint Clair	262,852	Belleville	673
Saline	26,551	Harrisburg	383
Sangamon	178,386	Springfield	879
Schuyler	7,498	Rushville	434
Scott	5,644	Winchester	251
Shelby	22,261	Shelbyville	752
Stark	6,534	Toulon	291
Stephenson	48,052	Freeport	568
Tazewell	123,692	Pekin	652
Union	17,619	Jonesboro	416
Vermilion	88,257	Danville	899
Wabash	13,111	Mount Carmel	222
Warren	19,181	Monmouth	541
Washington	14,965	Nashville	564
Wayne	17,241	Fairfield	715
White	16,522	Carmi	502
Whiteside	60,186	Morrison	687
Will	357,313	Joliet	847
Williamson	57,733	Marion	429
Winnebago	252,913	Rockford	519
Woodford	32,653	Eureka	528

Indiana

(92 counties, 35,870 sq. mi. land; pop. 5,544,159)

County	Pop.	County Seat or court house	Land area sq. mi.
Adams	31,095	Decatur	339
Allen	300,836	Fort Wayne	657
Bartholomew	63,657	Columbus	407
Benton	9,441	Fowler	406
Blackford	14,067	Hartford City	165
Boone	38,147	Lebanon	423
Brown	14,080	Nashville	312
Carroll	18,809	Delphi	372
Cass	38,413	Logansport	413
Clark	87,774	Jeffersonville	375
Clay	24,705	Brazil	358
Clinton	30,974	Frankfort	405
Crawford	9,914	English	306
Daviess	27,533	Washington	431
Dearborn	38,835	Lawrenceburg	305
Decatur	23,645	Greensburg	373
DeKalb	35,324	Auburn	363
Delaware	119,659	Muncie	393
Dubois	36,616	Jasper	430
Elkhart	156,198	Goshen	464
Fayette	26,015	Connersville	215
Floyd	64,404	New Albany	148
Fountain	17,808	Covington	396
Franklin	19,580	Brookville	386
Fulton	18,840	Rochester	369
Gibson	31,913	Princeton	489
Grant	74,169	Marion	414
Greene	30,410	Bloomfield	542
Hamilton	108,936	Noblesville	398
Hancock	45,527	Greenfield	306
Harrison	29,890	Corydon	485
Hendricks	75,717	Danville	408
Henry	48,139	New Castle	393
Howard	80,827	Kokomo	293
Huntington	35,427	Huntington	383
Jackson	37,730	Brownstown	509
Jasper	24,960	Rensselaer	560
Jay	21,512	Portland	384
Jefferson	29,797	Madison	361
Jennings	23,661	Vernon	377
Johnson	88,109	Franklin	320
Knox	39,884	Vincennes	516
Kosciusko	65,294	Warsaw	538
Lagrange	29,477	Lagrange	380
Lake	475,594	Crown Point	497
La Porte	107,066	La Porte	598
Lawrence	42,836	Bedford	449
Madison	130,669	Anderson	452
Marion	797,159	Indianapolis	396
Marshall	42,182	Plymouth	444
Martin	10,369	Shoals	336
Miami	36,897	Peru	376
Monroe	108,978	Bloomington	394
Montgomery	34,436	Crawfordsville	505
Morgan	55,920	Martinsville	407
Newton	13,551	Kentland	402
Noble	37,877	Albion	411
Ohio	5,315	Rising Sun	87
Orange	18,409	Paoli	400
Owen	17,281	Spencer	385
Parke	15,410	Rockville	445
Perry	19,107	Cannelton	381
Pike	12,509	Petersburg	336
Porter	128,932	Valparaiso	418
Posey	25,968	Mount Vernon	409
Pulaski	12,643	Winamac	434
Putnam	30,315	Greencastle	480
Randolph	27,148	Winchester	453
Ripley	24,616	Versailles	446
Rush	18,129	Rushville	408
Saint Joseph	247,052	South Bend	457
Scott	20,991	Scottsburg	190
Shelby	40,307	Shelbyville	413
Spencer	19,490	Rockport	399
Starke	22,747	Knox	309
Steuben	27,446	Angola	309
Sullivan	18,993	Sullivan	447
Switzerland	7,738	Vevay	221
Tippecanoe	130,598	Lafayette	500
Tipton	16,119	Tipton	260
Union	6,976	Liberty	162
Vanderburgh	165,058	Evansville	235
Vermillion	16,773	Newport	257
Vigo	106,107	Terre Haute	403
Wabash	35,069	Wabash	413
Warren	8,176	Williamsport	365
Warrick	44,920	Boonville	384
Washington	23,717	Salem	515
Wayne	71,951	Richmond	404
Wells	25,948	Bluffton	370
White	23,265	Monticello	505
Whitley	27,651	Columbia City	336

Iowa

(99 counties; 55,965 sq. mi. land; pop. 2,776,755)

County	Pop.	County Seat or court house	Land area sq. mi.
Adair	8,409	Greenfield	570
Adams	4,866	Corning	426
Allamakee	13,855	Waukon	660
Appanoose	13,743	Centerville	515
Audubon	7,334	Audubon	444
Benton	22,429	Vinton	718
Black Hawk	123,798	Waterloo	573
Boone	25,186	Boone	574
Bremer	22,813	Waverly	439
Buchanan	20,844	Independence	573
Buena Vista	19,965	Storm Lake	580
Butler	15,731	Allison	582
Calhoun	11,508	Rockwell City	573
Carroll	21,423	Carroll	570
Cass	15,128	Atlantic	565
Cedar	17,444	Tipton	582
Cerro Gordo	46,733	Mason City	575
Cherokee	14,098	Cherokee	577
Chickasaw	13,295	New Hampton	505
Clarke	8,287	Osceola	431
Clay	17,585	Spencer	573
Clayton	19,054	Elkader	795
Clinton	51,040	Clinton	710
Crawford	16,775	Denison	714
Dallas	29,755	Adel	591
Davis	8,312	Bloomfield	505
Decatur	8,338	Leon	535
Delaware	18,035	Manchester	579
Des Moines	42,614	Burlington	429
Dickinson	14,909	Spirit Lake	404
Dubuque	86,403	Dubuque	616
Emmet	11,569	Estherville	402
Fayette	21,843	West Union	731
Floyd	17,058	Charles City	501
Franklin	11,364	Hampton	583
Fremont	8,226	Sidney	517
Greene	10,045	Jefferson	572
Grundy	12,029	Grundy Center	501
Guthrie	10,935	Guthrie Center	594
Hamilton	16,071	Webster City	577
Hancock	12,638	Garner	573
Hardin	19,094	Eldora	569
Harrison	14,730	Logan	701
Henry	19,226	Mount Pleasant	436
Howard	9,809	Cresco	473
Humboldt	10,756	Dakota City	436
Ida	8,365	Ida Grove	432
Iowa	14,630	Marengo	588
Jackson	19,950	Maquoketa	650
Jasper	34,795	Newton	732
Jefferson	16,310	Fairfield	440
Johnson	96,119	Iowa City	623
Jones	19,444	Anamosa	576
Keokuk	11,624	Sigourney	580
Kossuth	18,591	Algona	976
Lee	38,687	Fort Madison and Keokuk	540
Linn	168,767	Cedar Rapids	724
Louisa	11,592	Wapello	417
Lucas	9,070	Chariton	435
Lyon	11,952	Rock Rapids	588
Madison	12,483	Winterset	563
Mahaska	21,532	Oskaloosa	572
Marion	30,001	Knoxville	575
Marshall	38,276	Marshalltown	573
Mills	13,202	Glenwood	441
Mitchell	10,928	Osage	470
Monona	10,034	Onawa	699
Monroe	8,114	Albia	434
Montgomery	12,076	Red Oak	424
Muscatine	39,907	Muscatine	440
O'Brien	15,444	Primghar	574
Osceola	7,267	Sibley	399
Page	16,870	Clarinda	535
Palo Alto	10,669	Emmetsburg	568
Plymouth	23,388	Le Mars	864
Pocahontas	9,525	Pocahontas	578
Polk	327,140	Des Moines	592
Pottawattamie	82,628	Council Bluffs	959
Poweshiek	19,033	Montezuma	586
Ringgold	5,420	Mount Ayr	536
Sac	12,324	Sac City	578
Scott	150,973	Davenport	469
Shelby	13,230	Harlan	591
Sioux	29,903	Orange City	769
Story	74,252	Nevada	574
Tama	17,419	Toledo	722
Taylor	7,114	Bedford	537
Union	12,750	Creston	427
Van Buren	7,676	Keosauqua	489
Wapello	35,696	Ottumwa	436
Warren	36,033	Indianola	573
Washington	19,612	Washington	571
Wayne	7,067	Corydon	527
Webster	40,342	Fort Dodge	718
Winnebago	12,122	Forest City	402
Winneshiek	20,847	Decorah	690
Woodbury	98,276	Sioux City	877
Worth	7,991	Northwood	402
Wright	14,269	Clarion	582

Kansas

(105 counties, 81,782 sq. mi. land; pop. 2,477,574)

County	Pop.	County Seat or court house	Land area sq. mi.
Allen	14,638	Iola	505
Anderson	7,803	Garnett	584
Atchison	16,932	Atchison	431
Barber	5,874	Medicine Lodge	1,136
Barton	29,382	Great Bend	895
Bourbon	14,966	Fort Scott	638
Brown	11,128	Hiawatha	572
Butler	50,580	El Dorado	1,443
Chase	3,021	Cottonwood Falls	777
Chautauqua	4,407	Sedan	644
Cherokee	21,374	Columbus	590
Cheyenne	3,243	Saint Francis	1,021
Clark	2,418	Ashland	975
Clay	9,158	Clay Center	632
Cloud	11,023	Concordia	718
Coffey	8,404	Burlington	615
Comanche	2,313	Coldwater	789
Cowley	36,915	Winfield	1,128
Crawford	35,582	Girard	595
Decatur	4,021	Oberlin	894
Dickinson	18,958	Abilene	852
Doniphan	8,134	Troy	388
Douglas	81,798	Lawrence	461
Edwards	3,787	Kinsley	620
Elk	3,327	Howard	650
Ellis	26,004	Hays	900
Ellsworth	6,586	Ellsworth	717
Finney	33,070	Garden City	1,302
Ford	27,463	Dodge City	1,099
Franklin	21,994	Ottawa	577
Geary	30,453	Junction City	377
Gove	3,231	Gove	1,072
Graham	3,543	Hill City	898
Grant	7,159	Ulysses	575
Gray	5,396	Cimarron	868
Greeley	1,774	Tribune	778
Greenwood	7,847	Eureka	1,135
Hamilton	2,388	Syracuse	998
Harper	7,124	Anthony	802
Harvey	31,028	Newton	540
Haskell	3,886	Sublette	578
Hodgeman	2,177	Jetmore	860
Jackson	11,525	Holton	658
Jefferson	15,905	Oskaloosa	535
Jewell	4,251	Mankato	910
Johnson	355,021	Olathe	478
Kearny	4,027	Lakin	868
Kingman	8,292	Kingman	865
Kiowa	3,660	Greensburg	723
Labette	23,693	Oswego	653
Lane	2,375	Dighton	717
Leavenworth	64,371	Leavenworth	463
Lincoln	3,653	Lincoln	720
Linn	8,254	Mound City	601
Logan	3,081	Oakley	1,073
Lyon	34,732	Emporia	844
McPherson	27,268	McPherson	900
Marion	12,888	Marion	944
Marshall	11,705	Marysville	878
Meade	4,247	Meade	979
Miami	23,466	Paola	590
Mitchell	7,203	Beloit	717
Montgomery	38,816	Independence	646
Morris	6,198	Council Grove	693
Morton	3,480	Elkhart	731
Nemaha	10,446	Seneca	719
Neosho	17,035	Erie	576
Ness	4,033	Ness City	1,074
Norton	5,947	Norton	873
Osage	15,248	Lyndon	695
Osborne	4,867	Osborne	882
Ottawa	5,634	Minneapolis	721
Pawnee	7,555	Larned	755
Phillips	6,590	Phillipsburg	887
Pottawatomie	16,128	Westmoreland	828
Pratt	9,702	Pratt	735
Rawlins	3,404	Atwood	1,069
Reno	62,389	Hutchinson	1,259
Republic	6,482	Belleville	719
Rice	10,610	Lyons	728
Riley	67,139	Manhattan	593
Rooks	6,039	Stockton	888
Rush	3,842	LaCrosse	718
Russell	7,835	Russell	869

County	Pop.	County Seat or court house	Land area sq. mi.
Saline	49,301	Salina	721
Scott	5,289	Scott City	718
Sedgwick	403,662	Wichita	1,007
Seward	18,743	Liberal	640
Shawnee	160,976	Topeka	549
Sheridan	3,043	Hoxie	896
Sherman	6,926	Goodland	1,057
Smith	5,078	Smith Center	897
Stafford	5,365	Saint John	788
Stanton	2,333	Johnson	681
Stevens	5,048	Hugoton	727
Sumner	25,041	Wellington	1,183
Thomas	8,258	Colby	1,075
Trego	3,694	WaKeeney	890
Wabaunsee	6,603	Alma	797
Wallace	1,821	Sharon Springs	914
Washington	7,073	Washington	898
Wichita	2,758	Leoti	719
Wilson	10,289	Fredonia	575
Woodson	4,116	Yates Center	498
Wyandotte	162,026	Kansas City	149

Kentucky

(120 counties, 39,732 sq. mi. land; pop. 3,685,296)

County	Pop.	County Seat or court house	Land area sq. mi.
Adair	15,360	Columbia	407
Allen	14,628	Scottsville	346
Anderson	14,571	Lawrenceburg	203
Ballard	7,902	Wickliffe	251
Barren	34,001	Glasgow	491
Bath	9,692	Owingsville	279
Bell	31,506	Pineville	361
Boone	57,589	Burlington	246
Bourbon	19,236	Paris	291
Boyd	51,150	Catlettsburg	160
Boyle	25,641	Danville	182
Bracken	7,766	Brooksville	203
Breathitt	15,703	Jackson	495
Breckinridge	16,312	Hardinsburg	572
Bullitt	47,567	Shepherdsville	299
Butler	11,245	Morgantown	428
Caldwell	13,232	Princeton	347
Calloway	30,735	Murray	386
Campbell	83,866	Newport	152
Carlisle	5,238	Bardwell	193
Carroll	9,292	Carrollton	130
Carter	24,340	Grayson	411
Casey	14,211	Liberty	446
Christian	68,941	Hopkinsville	721
Clark	29,496	Winchester	254
Clay	21,746	Manchester	471
Clinton	9,135	Albany	198
Crittenden	9,196	Marion	362
Cumberland	6,784	Burkesville	306
Daviess	87,189	Owensboro	462
Edmonson	10,357	Brownsville	303
Elliott	6,455	Sandy Hook	234
Estill	14,614	Irvine	254
Fayette	225,366	Lexington	286
Fleming	12,292	Flemingsburg	351
Floyd	43,586	Prestonsburg	394
Franklin	44,143	Frankfort	211
Fulton	8,271	Hickman	209
Gallatin	5,393	Warsaw	99
Garrard	11,579	Lancaster	231
Grant	15,737	Williamstown	260
Graves	33,550	Mayfield	556
Grayson	21,050	Leitchfield	504
Green	10,371	Greensburg	289
Greenup	36,742	Greenup	346
Hancock	7,864	Hawesville	189
Hardin	89,240	Elizabethtown	628
Harlan	36,574	Harlan	467
Harrison	16,248	Cynthiana	310
Hart	14,890	Munfordville	416
Henderson	43,044	Henderson	440
Henry	12,823	New Castle	289
Hickman	5,566	Clinton	245
Hopkins	46,126	Madisonville	551
Jackson	11,955	McKee	346
Jefferson	665,123	Louisville	385
Jessamine	30,508	Nicholasville	173
Johnson	23,248	Paintsville	262
Kenton	142,031	Covington	163
Knott	17,906	Hindman	352
Knox	29,676	Barbourville	388
Larue	11,679	Hodgenville	263
Laurel	43,438	London	436
Lawrence	13,998	Louisa	419
Lee	7,422	Beattyville	210
Leslie	13,642	Hyden	404
Letcher	27,000	Whitesburg	339
Lewis	13,029	Vanceburg	485
Lincoln	20,045	Stanford	337
Livingston	9,062	Smithland	316
Logan	24,416	Russellville	556
Lyon	6,624	Eddyville	216
McCracken	62,879	Paducah	251
McCreary	15,603	Whitley City	428
McLean	9,628	Calhoun	254
Madison	57,508	Richmond	441
Magoffin	13,077	Salyersville	310
Marion	16,499	Lebanon	347
Marshall	27,205	Benton	305
Martin	12,526	Inez	231
Mason	16,666	Maysville	241
Meade	24,170	Brandenburg	309
Menifee	5,092	Frenchburg	204
Mercer	19,148	Harrodsburg	251
Metcalfe	8,963	Edmonton	291
Monroe	11,401	Tompkinsville	331
Montgomery	19,561	Mount Sterling	199
Morgan	11,648	West Liberty	381
Muhlenberg	31,318	Greenville	475
Nelson	29,710	Bardstown	423
Nicholas	6,725	Carlisle	197
Ohio	21,105	Hartford	594
Oldham	33,263	La Grange	189
Owen	9,035	Owenton	352
Owsley	5,036	Booneville	198
Pendleton	12,036	Falmouth	280
Perry	30,283	Hazard	342
Pike	72,583	Pikeville	788
Powell	11,686	Stanton	180
Pulaski	49,489	Somerset	662
Robertson	2,124	Mount Olivet	100
Rockcastle	14,803	Mount Vernon	318
Rowan	20,353	Morehead	281
Russell	14,716	Jamestown	254
Scott	23,867	Georgetown	285
Shelby	24,824	Shelbyville	384
Simpson	15,145	Franklin	236
Spencer	6,801	Taylorsville	186
Taylor	21,146	Campbellsville	270
Todd	10,940	Elkton	376
Trigg	10,361	Cadiz	443
Trimble	6,090	Bedford	149
Union	16,557	Morganfield	345
Warren	77,720	Bowling Green	545
Washington	10,441	Springfield	301
Wayne	17,468	Monticello	459
Webster	13,955	Dixon	335
Whitley	33,326	Williamsburg	440
Wolfe	6,503	Campton	223
Woodford	19,955	Versailles	191

Louisiana

(64 parishes, 44,521 sq. mi. land; pop. 4,219,973)

County	Pop.	County Seat or court house	Land area sq. mi.
Acadia	55,882	Crowley	657
Allen	21,226	Oberlin	765
Ascension	58,214	Donaldsonville	296
Assumption	22,753	Napoleonville	342
Avoyelles	39,159	Marksville	846
Beauregard	30,083	De Ridder	1,163
Bienville	15,979	Arcadia	816
Bossier	86,088	Benton	845
Caddo	248,253	Shreveport	894
Calcasieu	168,134	Lake Charles	1,082
Caldwell	9,806	Columbia	541
Cameron	9,260	Cameron	1,417
Catahoula	11,065	Harrisonburg	732
Claiborne	17,405	Homer	765
Concordia	20,828	Vidalia	717
De Soto	25,346	Mansfield	880
East Baton Rouge	380,105	Baton Rouge	458
East Carroll	9,709	Lake Providence	426
East Feliciana	19,211	Clinton	455
Evangeline	33,274	Ville Platte	667
Franklin	22,387	Winnsboro	635
Grant	17,526	Colfax	653
Iberia	68,297	New Iberia	589
Iberville	31,049	Plaquemine	638
Jackson	15,705	Jonesboro	579
Jefferson	448,306	Gretna	348
Jefferson Davis	30,722	Jennings	655
Lafayette	164,762	Lafayette	270
Lafourche	85,860	Thibodaux	1,141
La Salle	13,662	Jena	638
Lincoln	41,745	Ruston	472
Livingston	70,523	Livingston	661
Madison	12,463	Tallulah	631
Morehouse	31,938	Bastrop	807
Natchitoches	36,689	Natchitoches	1,264
Orleans	496,938	New Orleans	199
Ouachita	142,191	Monroe	627
Plaquemines	25,575	Pointe a la Hache	1,035
Pointe Coupee	22,540	New Roads	566

County	Pop.	County Seat or court house	Land area sq. mi.
Rapides	131,556	Alexandria	1,341
Red River	9,387	Coushatta	394
Richland	20,629	Rayville	563
Sabine	22,646	Many	855
Saint Bernard	66,631	Chalmette	486
Saint Charles	42,437	Hahnville	286
Saint Helena	9,874	Greensburg	409
Saint James	20,879	Convent	248
Saint John The Baptist	39,996	Edgard	213
Saint Landry	80,312	Opelousas	936
Saint Martin	44,097	Saint Martinville	749
Saint Mary	58,086	Franklin	613
Saint Tammany	144,500	Covington	873
Tangipahoa	85,709	Amite	783
Tensas	7,103	Saint Joseph	623
Terrebonne	96,982	Houma	1,367
Union	20,796	Farmerville	884
Vermilion	50,055	Abbeville	1,205
Vernon	61,961	Leesville	1,332
Washington	43,185	Franklinton	676
Webster	41,989	Minden	602
West Baton Rouge	19,419	Port Allen	194
West Carroll	12,093	Oak Grove	360
West Feliciana	12,915	Saint Francisville	406
Winn	16,269	Winnfield	953

Maine

(16 counties, 30,995 sq. mi. land; pop. 1,227,928)

County	Pop.	County Seat or court house	Land area sq. mi.
Androscoggin	105,259	Auburn	477
Aroostook	86,936	Houlton	6,721
Cumberland	243,135	Portland	876
Franklin	29,008	Farmington	1,699
Hancock	46,948	Ellsworth	1,537
Kennebec	115,904	Augusta	876
Knox	36,310	Rockland	370
Lincoln	30,357	Wiscasset	458
Oxford	52,602	South Paris	2,053
Penobscot	146,601	Bangor	3,430
Piscataquis	18,653	Dover-Foxcroft	3,986
Sagadahoc	33,535	Bath	257
Somerset	49,767	Skowhegan	3,930
Waldo	33,018	Belfast	730
Washington	35,308	Machias	2,586
York	164,587	Alfred	1,008

Maryland

(23 cos., 1 ind. city, 9,837 sq. mi. land; pop. 4,781,468)

County	Pop.	County Seat or court house	Land area sq. mi.
Allegany	74,946	Cumberland	421
Anne Arundel	427,239	Annapolis	418
Baltimore	692,134	Towson	598
Calvert	51,372	Prince Frederick	213
Caroline	27,035	Denton	321
Carroll	123,372	Westminster	452
Cecil	71,347	Elkton	360
Charles	101,154	La Plata	452
Dorchester	30,236	Cambridge	593
Frederick	150,208	Frederick	663
Garrett	28,138	Oakland	657
Harford	182,132	Bel Air	448
Howard	187,328	Ellicott City	251
Kent	17,842	Chestertown	278
Montgomery	757,027	Rockville	495
Prince Georges	729,268	Upper Marlboro	487
Queen Annes	33,953	Centreville	372
Saint Mary's	75,974	Leonardtown	373
Somerset	23,440	Princess Anne	338
Talbot	30,549	Easton	259
Washington	121,393	Hagerstown	455
Wicomico	74,339	Salisbury	379
Worcester	35,028	Snow Hill	475
Independent City			
Baltimore	736,014		80

Massachusetts

(14 counties; 7,824 sq. mi. land; pop. 6,016,425)

County	Pop.	County Seat or court house	Land area sq. mi.
Barnstable	186,605	Barnstable	400
Berkshire	139,352	Pittsfield	929
Bristol	506,325	Taunton	557
Dukes	11,639	Edgartown	102
Essex	670,080	Salem	495
Franklin	70,092	Greenfield	702
Hampden	456,310	Springfield	618
Hampshire	146,568	Northampton	528
Middlesex	1,398,468	East Cambridge	822
Nantucket	6,012	Nantucket	47
Norfolk	616,087	Dedham	400
Plymouth	435,276	Plymouth	655
Suffolk	663,906	Boston	57
Worcester	709,705	Worcester	1,513

Michigan

(83 counties; 56,954 sq. mi. land; pop. 9,295,297)

County	Pop.	County Seat or court house	Land area sq. mi.
Alcona	10,145	Harrisville	679
Alger	8,972	Munising	912
Allegan	90,509	Allegan	832
Alpena	30,605	Alpena	567
Antrim	18,185	Bellaire	480
Arenac	14,906	Standish	367
Baraga	7,954	L'Anse	901
Barry	50,057	Hastings	560
Bay	111,723	Bay City	447
Benzie	12,200	Beulah	322
Berrien	161,378	Saint Joseph	576
Branch	41,502	Coldwater	508
Calhoun	135,982	Marshall	712
Cass	49,477	Cassopolis	496
Charlevoix	21,468	Charlevoix	421
Cheboygan	21,398	Cheboygan	720
Chippewa	34,604	Sault Sainte Marie	1,590
Clare	24,952	Harrison	570
Clinton	57,883	Saint Johns	573
Crawford	12,260	Grayling	559
Delta	37,780	Escanaba	1,173
Dickinson	26,831	Iron Mountain	770
Eaton	92,879	Charlotte	579
Emmet	25,040	Petoskey	468
Genesee	430,459	Flint	642
Gladwin	21,896	Gladwin	505
Gogebic	18,052	Bessemer	1,105
Grand Traverse	64,273	Traverse City	466
Gratiot	38,982	Ithaca	570
Hillsdale	43,431	Hillsdale	603
Houghton	35,446	Houghton	1,014
Huron	34,951	Bad Axe	830
Ingham	281,912	Mason	560
Ionia	57,024	Ionia	577
Iosco	30,209	Tawas City	546
Iron	13,175	Crystal Falls	1,163
Isabella	54,624	Mount Pleasant	577
Jackson	149,756	Jackson	705
Kalamazoo	223,411	Kalamazoo	562
Kalkaska	13,497	Kalkaska	563
Kent	500,631	Grand Rapids	862
Keweenaw	1,701	Eagle River	543
Lake	8,583	Baldwin	568
Lapeer	74,768	Lapeer	658
Leelanau	16,527	Leland	341
Lenawee	91,476	Adrian	753
Livingston	115,645	Howell	574
Luce	5,763	Newberry	904
Mackinac	10,674	Saint Ignace	1,025
Macomb	717,400	Mount Clemens	482
Manistee	21,265	Manistee	543
Marquette	70,887	Marquette	1,821
Mason	25,537	Ludington	494
Mecosta	37,308	Big Rapids	560
Menominee	24,920	Menominee	1,045
Midland	75,651	Midland	525
Missaukee	12,147	Lake City	565
Monroe	133,600	Monroe	557
Montcalm	53,059	Stanton	713
Montmorency	8,936	Atlanta	550
Muskegon	158,983	Muskegon	507
Newaygo	38,206	White Cloud	847
Oakland	1,083,592	Pontiac	875
Oceana	22,455	Hart	541
Ogemaw	18,681	West Branch	570
Ontonagon	8,854	Ontonagon	1,311
Osceola	20,146	Reed City	569
Oscoda	7,842	Mio	568
Otsego	17,957	Gaylord	516
Ottawa	187,768	Grand Haven	567
Presque Isle	13,743	Rogers City	656
Roscommon	19,776	Roscommon	528
Saginaw	211,946	Saginaw	815
Saint Clair	145,607	Port Huron	734
Saint Joseph	58,913	Centreville	503
Sanilac	39,928	Sandusky	964
Schoolcraft	8,302	Manistique	1,173
Shiawassee	69,770	Corunna	540
Tuscola	55,498	Caro	812
Van Buren	70,060	Paw Paw	611
Washtenaw	282,937	Ann Arbor	710
Wayne	2,111,687	Detroit	615
Wexford	26,360	Cadillac	566

Minnesota

(87 counties; 79,548 sq. mi. land; pop., 4,375,099)

County	Pop.	County Seat or court house	Land area sq. mi.
Aitkin	12,425	Aitkin	1,834
Anoka	243,641	Anoka	430
Becker	27,881	Detroit Lakes	1,312
Beltrami	34,384	Bemidji	2,507
Benton	30,185	Foley	408
Big Stone	6,285	Ortonville	407
Blue Earth	54,044	Mankato	749
Brown	26,984	New Ulm	610
Carlton	29,259	Carlton	864
Carver	47,915	Chaska	351
Cass	21,791	Walker	2,033
Chippewa	13,228	Montevideo	584
Chisago	30,521	Center City	417
Clay	50,422	Moorhead	1,049
Clearwater	8,309	Bagley	999
Cook	3,868	Grand Marais	1,412
Cottonwood	12,694	Windom	640
Crow Wing	44,249	Brainerd	1,008
Dakota	275,189	Hastings	574
Dodge	15,731	Mantorville	439
Douglas	28,674	Alexandria	643
Faribault	16,937	Blue Earth	714
Fillmore	20,777	Preston	862
Freeborn	33,060	Albert Lea	705
Goodhue	40,690	Red Wing	763
Grant	6,246	Elbow Lake	547
Hennepin	1,032,431	Minneapolis	541
Houston	18,497	Caledonia	564
Hubbard	14,939	Park Rapids	936
Isanti	25,921	Cambridge	440
Itasca	40,863	Grand Rapids	2,661
Jackson	11,677	Jackson	699
Kanabec	12,802	Mora	527
Kandiyohi	38,761	Willmar	784
Kittson	5,767	Hallock	1,104
Koochiching	16,299	International Falls	3,108
Lac qui Parle	8,924	Madison	772
Lake	10,415	Two Harbors	2,053
Lake of the Woods	4,076	Baudette	1,296
Le Sueur	23,239	Le Center	446
Lincoln	6,890	Ivanhoe	538
Lyon	24,789	Marshall	714
McLeod	32,030	Glencoe	489
Mahnomen	5,044	Mahnomen	559
Marshall	10,993	Warren	1,760
Martin	22,914	Fairmont	706
Meeker	20,846	Litchfield	624
Mille Lacs	18,670	Milaca	578
Morrison	29,604	Little Falls	1,124
Mower	37,385	Austin	711
Murray	9,660	Slayton	702
Nicollet	28,076	Saint Peter	440
Nobles	20,098	Worthington	714
Norman	7,975	Ada	877
Olmsted	106,470	Rochester	655
Otter Tail	50,714	Fergus Falls	1,973
Pennington	13,306	Thief River Falls	618
Pine	21,264	Pine City	1,421
Pipestone	10,491	Pipestone	466
Polk	32,589	Crookston	1,982
Pope	10,745	Glenwood	668
Ramsey	485,765	Saint Paul	154
Red Lake	4,525	Red Lake Falls	433
Redwood	17,254	Redwood Falls	882
Renville	17,673	Olivia	984
Rice	49,183	Faribault	501
Rock	9,806	Luverne	483
Roseau	15,026	Roseau	1,677
Saint Louis	198,213	Duluth	6,125
Scott	57,846	Shakopee	357
Sherburne	41,945	Elk River	435
Sibley	14,366	Gaylord	593
Stearns	119,324	Saint Cloud	1,338
Steele	30,729	Owatonna	431
Stevens	10,634	Morris	560
Swift	10,724	Benson	743
Todd	23,363	Long Prairie	941
Traverse	4,463	Wheaton	575
Wabasha	19,744	Wabasha	537
Wadena	13,154	Wadena	538
Waseca	18,079	Waseca	422
Washington	145,858	Stillwater	390
Watonwan	11,682	Saint James	435
Wilkin	7,516	Breckenridge	751
Winona	47,828	Winona	630
Wright	68,710	Buffalo	672
Yellow Medicine	11,684	Granite Falls	758

Mississippi

(82 counties, 47,233 sq. mi. land; pop. 2,573,216)

County	Pop.	County Seat or court house	Land area sq. mi.
Adams	35,356	Natchez	456
Alcorn	31,722	Corinth	401
Amite	13,328	Liberty	732
Attala	18,481	Kosciusko	737
Benton	8,046	Ashland	407
Bolivar	41,875	Cleveland & Rosedale	892
Calhoun	14,908	Pittsboro	573
Carroll	9,237	Carrollton & Vaiden	634
Chickasaw	18,085	Houston & Okolona	503
Choctaw	9,071	Ackerman	420
Claiborne	11,370	Port Gibson	494
Clarke	17,313	Quitman	692
Clay	21,120	West Point	415
Coahoma	31,665	Clarksdale	559
Copiah	27,592	Hazlehurst	779
Covington	16,527	Collins	416
De Soto	67,910	Hernando	483
Forrest	68,314	Hattiesburg	469
Franklin	8,377	Meadville	566
George	16,673	Lucedale	483
Greene	10,220	Leakesville	718
Grenada	21,555	Grenada	421
Hancock	31,760	Bay Saint Louis	478
Harrison	165,365	Gulfport	581
Hinds	254,441	Jackson & Raymond	875
Holmes	21,604	Lexington	759
Humphreys	12,134	Belzoni	430
Issaquena	1,909	Mayersville	406
Itawamba	20,017	Fulton	541
Jackson	115,243	Pascagoula	731
Jasper	17,114	Bay Springs & Paulding	678
Jefferson	8,653	Fayette	523
Jefferson Davis	14,051	Prentiss	409
Jones	62,031	Ellisville & Laurel	695
Kemper	10,356	De Kalb	766
Lafayette	31,826	Oxford	669
Lamar	30,424	Purvis	499
Lauderdale	75,555	Meridian	705
Lawrence	12,458	Monticello	435
Leake	18,436	Carthage	584
Lee	65,579	Tupelo	451
Leflore	37,341	Greenwood	605
Lincoln	30,278	Brookhaven	586
Lowndes	59,308	Columbus	517
Madison	53,794	Canton	717
Marion	25,544	Columbia	548
Marshall	30,361	Holly Springs	709
Monroe	36,582	Aberdeen	772
Montgomery	12,388	Winona	408
Neshoba	24,800	Philadelphia	571
Newton	20,291	Decatur	580
Noxubee	12,604	Macon	698
Oktibbeha	38,375	Starkville	459
Panola	29,996	Batesville & Sardis	695
Pearl River	38,714	Poplarville	819
Perry	10,865	New Augusta	651
Pike	36,882	Magnolia	410
Pontotoc	22,237	Pontotoc	499
Prentiss	23,278	Booneville	417
Quitman	10,490	Marks	406
Rankin	87,161	Brandon	782
Scott	24,137	Forest	610
Sharkey	7,066	Rolling Fork	435
Simpson	23,953	Mendenhall	591
Smith	14,798	Raleigh	635
Stone	10,750	Wiggins	446
Sunflower	35,129	Indianola	707
Tallahatchie	15,210	Charleston & Sumner	651
Tate	21,432	Senatobia	406
Tippah	19,523	Ripley	458
Tishomingo	17,683	Iuka	434
Tunica	8,164	Tunica	460
Union	22,085	New Albany	417
Walthall	14,352	Tylertown	404
Warren	47,880	Vicksburg	597
Washington	67,935	Greenville	733
Wayne	19,517	Waynesboro	813
Webster	10,222	Walthall	424
Wilkinson	9,678	Woodville	678
Winston	19,433	Louisville	610
Yalobusha	12,033	Coffeeville & Water Valley	478
Yazoo	25,506	Yazoo City	933

Missouri

(114 cos., 1 ind. city, 68,945 sq. mi. land; pop. 5,117,073)

Adair	24,577	Kirksville	567
Andrew	14,632	Savannah	435
Atchison	7,457	Rockport	542
Audrain	23,599	Mexico	697
Barry	27,547	Cassville	773

County	Pop.	County Seat or court house	Land area sq. mi.
Barton	11,312	Lamar	596
Bates	15,025	Butler	849
Benton	13,859	Warsaw	729
Bollinger	10,619	Marble Hill	621
Boone	112,379	Columbia	687
Buchanan	83,083	Saint Joseph	409
Butler	38,765	Poplar Buff	698
Caldwell	8,380	Kingston	430
Callaway	32,809	Fulton	842
Camden	27,495	Camdenton	641
Cape Girardeau	61,633	Jackson	577
Carroll	10,748	Carrollton	695
Carter	5,515	Van Buren	509
Cass	63,808	Harrisonville	701
Cedar	12,093	Stockton	470
Chariton	9,202	Keytesville	758
Christian	32,644	Ozark	564
Clark	7,547	Kahoka	507
Clay	153,411	Liberty	403
Clinton	16,595	Plattsburg	423
Cole	63,579	Jefferson City	392
Cooper	14,835	Boonville	567
Crawford	19,173	Steelville	744
Dade	7,449	Greenfield	491
Dallas	12,646	Buffalo	543
Daviess	7,865	Gallatin	568
De Kalb	9,967	Maysville	425
Dent	13,702	Salem	755
Douglas	11,876	Ava	814
Dunklin	33,112	Kennett	547
Franklin	80,603	Union	922
Gasconade	14,006	Hermann	521
Gentry	6,854	Albany	493
Greene	207,949	Springfield	677
Grundy	10,536	Trenton	437
Harrison	8,469	Bethany	725
Henry	20,044	Clinton	729
Hickory	7,335	Hermitage	379
Holt	6,034	Oregon	457
Howard	9,631	Fayette	465
Howell	31,447	West Plains	928
Iron	10,726	Ironton	552
Jackson	633,234	Kansas City	611
Jasper	90,465	Carthage	641
Jefferson	171,380	Hillsboro	661
Johnson	42,514	Warrensburg	834
Knox	4,482	Edina	507
Laclede	27,158	Lebanon	768
Lafayette	31,107	Lexington	632
Lawrence	30,236	Mount Vernon	613
Lewis	10,233	Monticello	509
Lincoln	28,892	Troy	627
Linn	13,885	Linneus	620
Livingston	14,592	Chillicothe	537
McDonald	16,938	Pineville	540
Macon	15,345	Macon	797
Madison	11,127	Fredericktown	497
Maries	7,976	Vienna	528
Marion	27,682	Palmyra	438
Mercer	3,723	Princeton	454
Miller	20,700	Tuscumbia	593
Mississippi	14,442	Charleston	410
Moniteau	12,298	California	417
Monroe	9,104	Paris	670
Montgomery	11,355	Montgomery City	540
Morgan	15,574	Versailles	594
New Madrid	20,928	New Madrid	658
Newton	44,445	Neosho	627
Nodaway	21,709	Maryville	875
Oregon	9,470	Alton	792
Osage	12,018	Linn	606
Ozark	8,598	Gainesville	731
Pemiscot	21,921	Caruthersville	517
Perry	16,648	Perryville	473
Pettis	35,437	Sedalia	686
Phelps	35,248	Rolla	674
Pike	15,969	Bowling Green	673
Platte	57,867	Platte City	421
Polk	21,826	Bolivar	636
Pulaski	41,307	Waynesville	550
Putnam	5,079	Unionville	520
Ralls	8,476	New London	482
Randolph	24,370	Huntsville	477
Ray	21,968	Richmond	568
Reynolds	6,661	Centerville	809
Ripley	12,303	Doniphan	631
Saint Charles	212,751	Saint Charles	558
Saint Clair	8,457	Osceola	699
Saint Francis	48,904	Farmington	451
Saint Louis	993,528	Clayton	506
Sainte Genevieve	16,037	Sainte Genevieve	504
Saline	23,523	Marshall	755
Schuyler	4,236	Lancaster	309
Scotland	4,822	Memphis	438
Scott	39,376	Benton	423
Shannon	7,613	Eminence	1,004
Shelby	6,942	Shelbyville	501
Stoddard	28,895	Bloomfield	815
Stone	19,078	Galena	451
Sullivan	6,326	Milan	651
Taney	25,561	Forsyth	608
Texas	21,476	Houston	1,180
Vernon	19,041	Nevada	837
Warren	19,534	Warrenton	429
Washington	20,380	Potosi	762
Wayne	11,543	Greenville	762
Webster	23,753	Marshfield	594
Worth	2,440	Grant City	266
Wright	16,758	Hartville	682
Independent City			
Saint Louis	396,685		61

Montana

(56 counties, 145,556 sq. mi. land; pop., 799,065)

County	Pop.	County Seat or court house	Land area sq. mi.
Beaverhead	8,424	Dillon	5,542
Big Horn	11,337	Hardin	4,995
Blaine	6,728	Chinook	4,226
Broadwater	3,318	Townsend	1,191
Carbon	8,080	Red Lodge	2,048
Carter	1,503	Ekalaka	3,340
Cascade	77,691	Great Falls	2,698
Chouteau	5,452	Fort Benton	3,973
Custer	11,697	Miles City	3,783
Daniels	2,266	Scobey	1,426
Dawson	9,505	Glendive	2,373
Deer Lodge	10,356	Anacónda	737
Fallon	3,103	Baker	1,620
Fergus	12,083	Lewistown	4,339
Flathead	59,218	Kalispell	5,099
Gallatin	50,463	Bozeman	2,507
Garfield	1,589	Jordan	4,668
Glacier	12,121	Cut Bank	2,995
Golden Valley	912	Ryegete	1,175
Granite	2,548	Philipsburg	1,728
Hill	17,654	Havre	2,896
Jefferson	7,939	Boulder	1,657
Judith Basin	2,282	Stanford	1,870
Lake	21,041	Polson	1,494
Lewis & Clark	47,495	Helena	3,461
Liberty	2,295	Chester	1,430
Lincoln	17,481	Libby	3,613
McCone	2,276	Circle	2,643
Madison	5,989	Virginia City	3,587
Meagher	1,819	White Sulphur Springs	2,392
Mineral	3,315	Superior	1,220
Missoula	78,687	Missoula	2,598
Musselshell	4,106	Roundup	1,867
Park	14,484	Livingston	2,656
Petroleum	519	Winnett	1,654
Phillips	5,163	Malta	5,140
Pondera	6,433	Conrad	1,625
Powder River	2,090	Broadus	3,297
Powell	6,620	Deer Lodge	2,326
Prairie	1,383	Terry	1,737
Ravalli	25,010	Hamilton	2,394
Richland	10,716	Sidney	2,084
Roosevelt	10,999	Wolf Point	2,356
Rosebud	10,505	Forsyth	5,012
Sanders	8,669	Thompson Falls	2,762
Sheridan	4,732	Plentywood	1,677
Silver Bow	33,941	Butte	718
Stillwater	6,536	Columbus	1,795
Sweet Grass	3,154	Big Timber	1,855
Teton	6,271	Choteau	2,273
Toole	5,046	Shelby	1,911
Treasure	874	Hysham	979
Valley	8,239	Glasgow	4,921
Wheatland	2,246	Harlowton	1,423
Wibaux	1,191	Wibaux	889
Yellowstone	113,419	Billings	2,635

Nebraska

(93 counties, 76,644 sq. mi. land; pop., 1,578,385)

County	Pop.	County Seat or court house	Land area sq. mi.
Adams	29,625	Hastings	564
Antelope	7,965	Neligh	859
Arthur	462	Arthur	711
Banner	852	Harrisburg	747
Blaine	675	Brewster	714
Boone	6,667	Albion	687
Box Butte	13,130	Alliance	1,077
Boyd	2,835	Butte	532
Brown	3,657	Ainsworth	1,214
Buffalo	37,447	Kearney	945
Burt	7,868	Tekamah	486
Butler	8,601	David City	584
Cass	21,318	Plattsmouth	557
Cedar	10,131	Hartington	740

County	Pop.	County Seat or court house	Land area sq. mi.
Chase	4,381	Imperial	894
Cherry	6,307	Valentine	5,961
Cheyenne	9,494	Sidney	1,196
Clay	7,123	Clay Center	574
Colfax	9,139	Schuyler	410
Cuming	10,117	West Point	575
Custer	12,270	Broken Bow	2,571
Dakota	16,742	Dakota City	258
Dawes	9,021	Chadron	1,397
Dawson	19,940	Lexington	982
Deuel	2,237	Chappell	437
Dixon	6,143	Ponca	474
Dodge	34,500	Fremont	534
Douglas	416,444	Omaha	333
Dundy	2,582	Benkelman	920
Fillmore	7,103	Geneva	576
Franklin	3,938	Franklin	576
Frontier	3,101	Stockville	976
Furnas	5,553	Beaver City	721
Gage	22,794	Beatrice	858
Garden	2,460	Oshkosh	1,680
Garfield	2,141	Burwell	570
Gosper	1,928	Elwood	461
Grant	769	Hyannis	775
Greeley	3,006	Greeley	570
Hall	48,925	Grand Island	537
Hamilton	8,862	Aurora	543
Harlan	3,810	Alma	555
Hayes	1,222	Hayes Center	713
Hitchcock	3,750	Trenton	709
Holt	12,599	O'Neill	2,406
Hooker	793	Mullen	721
Howard	6,057	Saint Paul	564
Jefferson	8,759	Fairbury	575
Johnson	4,673	Tecumseh	377
Kearney	6,629	Minden	519
Keith	8,584	Ogallala	1,039
Keya Paha	1,029	Springview	769
Kimball	4,108	Kimball	952
Knox	9,564	Center	1,105
Lancaster	213,641	Lincoln	839
Lincoln	32,508	North Platte	2,525
Logan	878	Stapleton	571
Loup	683	Taylor	574
McPherson	546	Tryon	859
Madison	32,655	Madison	575
Merrick	8,049	Central City	478
Morrill	5,423	Bridgeport	1,405
Nance	4,275	Fullerton	439
Nemaha	7,980	Auburn	409
Nuckolls	5,786	Nelson	576
Otoe	14,252	Nebraska City	615
Pawnee	3,317	Pawnee City	433
Perkins	3,367	Grant	885
Phelps	9,715	Holdrege	540
Pierce	7,827	Pierce	575
Platte	29,820	Columbus	669
Polk	5,668	Osceola	437
Red Willow	11,705	McCook	718
Richardson	9,937	Falls City	553
Rock	2,019	Bassett	1,003
Saline	12,715	Wilber	575
Sarpy	102,583	Papillion	238
Saunders	18,285	Wahoo	753
Scotts Bluff	36,025	Gering	725
Seward	15,450	Seward	575
Sheridan	6,750	Rushville	2,453
Sherman	3,718	Loup City	564
Sioux	1,549	Harrison	2,070
Stanton	6,244	Stanton	431
Thayer	6,635	Hebron	575
Thomas	851	Thedford	713
Thurston	6,936	Pender	391
Valley	5,169	Ord	567
Washington	16,607	Blair	386
Wayne	9,364	Wayne	443
Webster	4,279	Red Cloud	575
Wheeler	948	Bartlett	575
York	14,428	York	576

Nevada

(16 cos., 1 ind. city, 109,894 sq. mi. land; pop., 1,201,833)

County	Pop.	County Seat or court house	Land area sq. mi.
Churchill	17,938	Fallon	4,913
Clark	741,368	Las Vegas	8,084
Douglas	27,637	Minden	751
Elko	33,463	Elko	17,181
Esmeralda	1,344	Goldfield	3,570
Eureka	1,547	Eureka	4,182
Humboldt	12,844	Winnemucca	9,704
Lander	6,266	Battle Mountain	5,621
Lincoln	3,775	Pioche	10,650
Lyon	20,001	Yerington	2,024
Mineral	6,475	Hawthorne	3,837
Nye	17,781	Tonopah	18,064
Pershing	4,336	Lovelock	6,031
Storey	2,526	Virginia City	262
Washoe	254,667	Reno	6,608
White Pine	9,264	Ely	8,905
Independent City			
Carson City	40,443	Carson City	153

New Hampshire

(10 counties, 8,993 sq. mi. land; pop., 1,109,252)

County	Pop.	County Seat or court house	Land area sq. mi.
Belknap	49,216	Laconia	404
Carroll	35,410	Ossipee	933
Cheshire	70,121	Keene	711
Coos	34,693	Lancaster	1,804
Grafton	74,929	Woodsville	1,719
Hillsborough	335,838	Nashua	876
Merrimack	120,240	Concord	936
Rockingham	245,845	Exeter	699
Strafford	104,233	Dover	370
Sullivan	38,592	Newport	540

New Jersey

(21 counties, 7,468 sq. mi. land; pop., 7,730,188)

County	Pop.	County Seat or court house	Land area sq. mi.
Atlantic	224,327	Mays Landing	568
Bergen	825,380	Hackensack	237
Burlington	395,066	Mount Holly	808
Camden	502,824	Camden	223
Cape May	95,089	Cape May Court House	263
Cumberland	138,053	Bridgeton	498
Essex	778,964	Newark	127
Gloucester	230,082	Woodbury	327
Hudson	553,099	Jersey City	46
Hunterdon	107,802	Flemington	426
Mercer	325,824	Trenton	227
Middlesex	671,811	New Brunswick	316
Monmouth	553,093	Freehold	472
Morris	421,361	Morristown	470
Ocean	433,203	Toms River	641
Passaic	453,060	Paterson	187
Salem	65,294	Salem	338
Somerset	240,245	Somerville	305
Sussex	130,943	Newton	526
Union	493,819	Elizabeth	103
Warren	91,607	Belvidere	359

New Mexico

(33 counties, 121,336 sq. mi. land; pop., 1,515,069)

County	Pop.	County Seat or court house	Land area sq. mi.
Bernalillo	480,577	Albuquerque	1,169
Catron	2,563	Reserve	6,929
Chaves	57,849	Roswell	6,066
Cibola	23,794	Grants	4,468
Colfax	12,925	Raton	3,762
Curry	42,207	Clovis	1,408
De Baca	2,252	Fort Sumner	2,323
Dona Ana	135,510	Las Cruces	3,819
Eddy	48,605	Carlsbad	4,184
Grant	27,676	Silver City	3,969
Guadalupe	4,156	Santa Rosa	3,032
Harding	987	Mosquero	2,122
Hidalgo	5,958	Lordsburg	3,445
Lea	55,765	Lovington	4,390
Lincoln	12,219	Carrizozo	4,832
Los Alamos	18,115	Los Alamos	109
Luna	18,110	Deming	2,965
McKinley	60,686	Gallup	5,442
Mora	4,264	Mora	1,930
Otero	51,928	Alamogordo	6,626
Quay	10,823	Tucumcari	2,874
Rio Arriba	34,365	Tierra Amarilla	5,856
Roosevelt	16,702	Portales	2,453
Sandoval	63,319	Bernalillo	3,707
San Juan	91,605	Aztec	5,522
San Miguel	25,743	Las Vegas	4,709
Santa Fe	98,928	Santa Fe	1,905
Sierra	9,912	Truth or Consequences	4,178
Socorro	14,764	Socorro	6,625
Taos	23,118	Taos	2,204
Torrance	10,285	Estancia	3,335
Union	4,124	Clayton	3,830
Valencia	45,235	Los Lunas	1,068

New York

(62 counties, 47,377 sq. mi. land; pop., 17,990,455)

County	Pop.	County Seat or court house	Land area sq. mi.
Albany	292,793	Albany	524
Allegany	50,470	Belmont	1,031
Bronx	1,203,789	Bronx	42
Broome	212,160	Binghamton	707
Cattaraugus	84,234	Little Valley	1,310
Cayuga	82,313	Auburn	693
Chautauqua	141,895	Mayville	1,062
Chemung	95,195	Elmira	408
Chenango	51,768	Norwich	894
Clinton	85,969	Plattsburgh	1,039
Columbia	62,982	Hudson	636
Cortland	48,963	Cortland	500
Delaware	47,225	Delhi	1,446
Dutchess	259,462	Poughkeepsie	802
Erie	968,584	Buffalo	1,045
Essex	37,152	Elizabethtown	1,797
Franklin	46,540	Malone	1,632
Fulton	54,191	Johnstown	496
Genesee	60,060	Batavia	494
Greene	44,739	Catskill	648
Hamilton	5,279	Lake Pleasant	1,721
Herkimer	65,809	Herkimer	1,412
Jefferson	110,943	Watertown	1,272
Kings	2,300,664	Brooklyn	71
Lewis	26,796	Lowville	1,276
Livingston	62,372	Geneseo	632
Madison	69,166	Wampsville	656
Monroe	713,968	Rochester	659
Montgomery	51,981	Fonda	405
Nassau	1,287,444	Mineola	287
New York	1,487,536	New York	28
Niagara	220,756	Lockport	523
Oneida	250,836	Utica	1,213
Onondaga	468,973	Syracuse	780
Ontario	95,101	Canandaigua	644
Orange	307,647	Goshen	816
Orleans	41,846	Albion	391
Oswego	121,785	Oswego	953
Otsego	60,517	Cooperstown	1,003
Putnam	83,941	Carmel	232
Queens	1,951,598	Jamaica	109
Rensselaer	154,429	Troy	654
Richmond	378,977	Saint George	59
Rockland	265,475	New City	174
Saint Lawrence	111,974	Canton	2,686
Saratoga	181,276	Ballston Spa	812
Schenectady	149,285	Schenectady	206
Schoharie	31,859	Schoharie	622
Schuyler	18,662	Watkins Glen	329
Seneca	33,683	Ovid & Waterloo	325
Steuben	99,088	Bath	1,393
Suffolk	1,321,768	Riverhead	911
Sullivan	69,277	Monticello	970
Tioga	52,337	Owego	519
Tompkins	94,097	Ithaca	476
Ulster	165,304	Kingston	1,127
Warren	59,209	Queensbury	870
Washington	59,330	Hudson Falls	836
Wayne	89,123	Lyons	604
Westchester	874,866	White Plains	433
Wyoming	42,507	Warsaw	593
Yates	22,810	Penn Yan	338

North Carolina

(100 counties, 48,843 sq. mi. land; pop., 6,628,637)

County	Pop.	County Seat or court house	Land area sq. mi.
Alamance	108,213	Graham	433
Alexander	27,544	Taylorsville	259
Alleghany	9,590	Sparta	235
Anson	23,474	Wadesboro	533
Ashe	22,209	Jefferson	426
Avery	14,867	Newland	247
Beaufort	42,283	Washington	826
Bertie	20,388	Windsor	701
Bladen	28,663	Elizabethtown	879
Brunswick	50,985	Bolivia	860
Buncombe	174,819	Asheville	659
Burke	75,744	Morganton	504
Cabarrus	98,935	Concord	364
Caldwell	70,709	Lenoir	471
Camden	5,904	Camden	240
Carteret	52,556	Beaufort	526
Caswell	20,693	Yanceyville	428
Catawba	118,412	Newton	396
Chatham	38,759	Pittsboro	708
Cherokee	20,170	Murphy	452
Chowan	13,506	Edenton	182
Clay	7,155	Hayesville	214
Cleveland	84,714	Shelby	468
Columbus	49,587	Whiteville	938
Craven	81,613	New Bern	701
Cumberland	274,566	Fayetteville	657
Currituck	13,736	Currituck	256
Dare	22,746	Manteo	391
Davidson	126,677	Lexington	548
Davie	27,859	Mocksville	267
Duplin	39,995	Kenansville	819
Durham	181,854	Durham	298
Edgecombe	56,692	Tarboro	506
Forsyth	265,878	Winston-Salem	412
Franklin	36,414	Louisburg	494
Gaston	175,093	Gastonia	357
Gates	9,305	Gatesville	338
Graham	7,196	Robbinsville	289
Granville	38,341	Oxford	534
Greene	15,384	Snow Hill	266
Guilford	347,420	Greensboro	651
Halifax	55,516	Halifax	724
Harnett	67,833	Lillington	601
Haywood	46,942	Waynesville	555
Henderson	69,285	Hendersonville	374
Hertford	22,523	Winton	356
Hoke	22,856	Raeford	391
Hyde	5,411	Swan Quarter	624
Iredell	92,935	Statesville	574
Jackson	26,846	Sylva	491
Johnston	81,306	Smithfield	795
Jones	9,414	Trenton	470
Lee	41,370	Sanford	259
Lenoir	57,274	Kinston	402
Lincoln	50,319	Lincolnton	298
McDowell	35,681	Marion	437
Macon	23,499	Franklin	517
Madison	16,953	Marshall	451
Martin	25,078	Williamston	461
Mecklenburg	511,481	Charlotte	528
Mitchell	14,433	Bakersville	222
Montgomery	23,352	Troy	490
Moore	59,000	Carthage	701
Nash	76,677	Nashville	540
New Hanover	120,284	Wilmington	185
Northampton	20,798	Jackson	538
Onslow	149,838	Jacksonville	763
Orange	93,851	Hillsborough	400
Pamlico	11,368	Bayboro	341
Pasquotank	31,298	Elizabeth City	228
Pender	28,885	Burgaw	875
Perquimans	10,447	Hertford	246
Person	30,180	Roxboro	398
Pitt	108,480	Greenville	657
Polk	14,416	Columbus	238
Randolph	106,546	Asheboro	789
Richmond	44,518	Rockingham	477
Robeson	105,170	Lumberton	949
Rockingham	86,064	Wentworth	569
Rowan	110,605	Salisbury	519
Rutherford	56,918	Rutherfordton	568
Sampson	47,297	Clinton	947
Scotland	33,763	Laurinburg	319
Stanly	51,765	Albemarle	396
Stokes	37,223	Danbury	452
Surry	61,704	Dobson	539
Swain	11,268	Bryson City	526
Transylvania	25,520	Brevard	378
Tyrrell	3,856	Columbia	407
Union	84,210	Monroe	639
Vance	38,892	Henderson	249
Wake	426,301	Raleigh	854
Warren	17,265	Warrenton	427
Washington	13,997	Plymouth	332
Watauga	36,952	Boone	314
Wayne	104,666	Goldsboro	554
Wilkes	59,393	Wilkesboro	752
Wilson	66,061	Wilson	374
Yadkin	30,488	Yadkinville	336
Yancey	15,419	Burnsville	314

North Dakota

(53 counties, 69,300 sq. mi. land; pop., 638,800)

County	Pop.	County Seat or court house	Land area sq. mi.
Adams	3,174	Hettinger	988
Barnes	12,545	Valley City	1,498
Benson	7,198	Minnewaukan	1,412
Billings	1,108	Medora	1,152
Bottineau	8,011	Bottineau	1,668
Bowman	3,596	Bowman	1,162
Burke	3,002	Bowbells	1,118
Burleigh	60,131	Bismarck	1,618
Cass	102,874	Fargo	1,767
Cavalier	6,064	Langdon	1,507
Dickey	6,107	Ellendale	1,139
Divide	2,899	Crosby	1,288
Dunn	4,005	Manning	1,993

County	Pop.	County Seat or court house	Land area sq. mi.
Eddy	2,951	New Rockford	634
Emmons	4,830	Linton	1,499
Foster	3,983	Carrington	640
Golden Valley	2,108	Beach	1,003
Grand Forks	70,683	Grand Forks	1,440
Grant	3,549	Carson	1,660
Griggs	3,303	Cooperstown	708
Hettinger	3,445	Mott	1,133
Kidder	3,332	Steele	1,362
La Moure	5,383	La Moure	1,150
Logan	2,847	Napoleon	1,000
McHenry	6,528	Towner	1,887
McIntosh	4,021	Ashley	984
McKenzie	6,383	Watford City	2,754
McLean	10,457	Washburn	2,065
Mercer	9,808	Stanton	1,044
Morton	23,700	Mandan	1,921
Mountrail	7,021	Stanley	1,837
Nelson	4,410	Lakota	991
Oliver	2,381	Center	723
Pembina	9,238	Cavalier	1,120
Pierce	5,052	Rugby	1,037
Ramsey	12,681	Devils Lake	1,241
Ransom	5,921	Lisbon	862
Renville	3,160	Mohall	874
Richland	18,148	Wahpeton	1,436
Rolette	12,772	Rolla	914
Sargent	4,549	Forman	857
Sheridan	2,148	McClusky	989
Sioux	3,761	Fort Yates	1,099
Slope	907	Amidon	1,219
Stark	22,832	Dickinson	1,338
Steele	2,420	Finley	713
Stutsman	22,241	Jamestown	2,263
Towner	3,627	Cando	1,035
Traill	8,752	Hillsboro	861
Walsh	13,840	Grafton	1,290
Ward	57,921	Minot	2,041
Wells	5,864	Fessenden	1,288
Williams	21,129	Williston	2,074

Ohio

(88 counties, 41,004 sq. mi. land; pop., 10,847,115)

County	Pop.	County Seat or court house	Land area sq. mi.
Adams	25,371	West Union	586
Allen	109,755	Lima	405
Ashland	47,507	Ashland	424
Ashtabula	99,821	Jefferson	703
Athens	59,549	Athens	508
Auglaize	44,585	Wapakoneta	398
Belmont	71,074	Saint Clairsville	537
Brown	34,966	Georgetown	493
Butler	291,479	Hamilton	470
Carroll	26,521	Carrollton	393
Champaign	36,019	Urbana	429
Clark	147,548	Springfield	398
Clermont	150,167	Batavia	456
Clinton	35,417	Wilmington	410
Columbiana	108,276	Lisbon	534
Coshocton	35,427	Coshocton	566
Crawford	47,870	Bucyrus	403
Cuyahoga	1,412,140	Cleveland	459
Darke	53,619	Greenville	600
Defiance	39,350	Defiance	414
Delaware	66,929	Delaware	443
Erie	76,779	Sandusky	264
Fairfield	103,461	Lancaster	506
Fayette	27,466	Washington Court House	405
Franklin	961,437	Columbus	543
Fulton	38,498	Wauseon	407
Gallia	30,954	Gallipolis	471
Geauga	81,129	Chardon	408
Greene	136,731	Xenia	416
Guernsey	39,024	Cambridge	522
Hamilton	866,228	Cincinnati	412
Hancock	65,536	Findlay	532
Hardin	31,111	Kenton	471
Harrison	16,085	Cadiz	400
Henry	29,108	Napoleon	415
Highland	35,728	Hillsboro	553
Hocking	25,533	Logan	423
Holmes	32,849	Millersburg	424
Huron	56,240	Norwalk	494
Jackson	30,230	Jackson	420
Jefferson	80,298	Steubenville	410
Knox	47,473	Mount Vernon	529
Lake	215,499	Painesville	231
Lawrence	61,834	Ironton	457
Licking	128,300	Newark	686
Logan	42,310	Bellefontaine	458
Lorain	271,126	Elyria	495
Lucas	462,361	Toledo	341
Madison	37,068	London	467
Mahoning	264,806	Youngstown	417
Marion	64,274	Marion	403
Medina	122,354	Medina	422
Meigs	22,987	Pomeroy	432
Mercer	39,443	Celina	457
Miami	93,182	Troy	410
Monroe	15,497	Woodsfield	457
Montgomery	573,809	Dayton	458
Morgan	14,194	McConnelsville	420
Morrow	27,749	Mount Gilead	406
Muskingum	82,068	Zanesville	654
Noble	11,336	Caldwell	399
Ottawa	40,029	Port Clinton	253
Paulding	20,488	Paulding	419
Perry	31,557	New Lexington	412
Pickaway	48,244	Circleville	503
Pike	24,249	Waverly	443
Portage	142,585	Ravenna	493
Preble	40,113	Eaton	426
Putnam	33,819	Ottawa	484
Richland	126,137	Mansfield	497
Ross	69,330	Chillicothe	692
Sandusky	61,963	Fremont	409
Scioto	80,327	Portsmouth	613
Seneca	59,733	Tiffin	553
Shelby	44,915	Sidney	409
Stark	367,585	Canton	574
Summit	514,990	Akron	412
Trumbull	227,813	Warren	612
Tuscarawas	84,090	New Philadelphia	570
Union	31,969	Marysville	437
Van Wert	30,464	Van Wert	410
Vinton	11,098	McArthur	414
Warren	113,927	Lebanon	403
Washington	62,254	Marietta	640
Wayne	101,461	Wooster	557
Williams	36,956	Bryan	422
Wood	113,269	Bowling Green	619
Wyandot	22,254	Upper Sandusky	406

Oklahoma

(77 counties, 68,655 sq. mi. land; pop., 3,145,585)

County	Pop.	County Seat or court house	Land area sq. mi.
Adair	18,421	Stillwell	577
Alfalfa	6,416	Cherokee	864
Atoka	12,778	Atoka	980
Beaver	6,023	Beaver	1,808
Beckham	18,812	Sayre	904
Blaine	11,470	Watonga	920
Bryan	32,089	Durant	902
Caddo	29,550	Anadarko	1,286
Canadian	74,409	El Reno	901
Carter	42,919	Ardmore	828
Cherokee	34,049	Tahlequah	748
Choctaw	15,302	Hugo	762
Cimarron	3,301	Boise City	1,842
Cleveland	174,253	Norman	529
Coal	5,780	Coalgate	520
Comanche	111,486	Lawton	1,076
Cotton	6,651	Walters	656
Craig	14,104	Vinita	763
Creek	60,915	Sapulpa	930
Custer	26,897	Arapaho	981
Delaware	28,070	Jay	720
Dewey	5,551	Taloga	1,007
Ellis	4,497	Arnett	1,232
Garfield	56,735	Enid	1,060
Garvin	26,605	Pauls Valley	813
Grady	41,747	Chickasha	1,106
Grant	5,689	Medford	1,004
Greer	6,559	Mangum	638
Harmon	3,793	Hollis	537
Harper	4,063	Buffalo	1,039
Haskell	10,940	Stigler	570
Hughes	13,014	Holdenville	806
Jackson	28,764	Altus	817
Jefferson	7,010	Waurika	769
Johnston	10,032	Tishomingo	639
Kay	48,056	Newkirk	921
Kingfisher	13,212	Kingfisher	906
Kiowa	11,347	Hobart	1,019
Latimer	10,333	Wilburton	728
Le Flore	43,270	Poteau	1,585
Lincoln	29,216	Chandler	964
Logan	29,011	Guthrie	748
Love	8,157	Marietta	519
McClain	22,795	Purcell	582
McCurtain	33,433	Idabel	1,826
McIntosh	16,779	Eufaula	599
Major	8,055	Fairview	958
Marshall	10,829	Madill	372
Mayes	33,366	Pryor	644
Murray	12,042	Sulphur	420
Muskogee	68,078	Muskogee	815
Noble	11,045	Perry	736

County	Pop.	County Seat or court house	Land area sq. mi.
Nowata	9,992	Nowata	540
Okfuskee	11,551	Okemah	628
Oklahoma	599,611	Oklahoma City	708
Okmulgee	36,490	Okmulgee	698
Osage	41,645	Pawhuska	2,265
Ottawa	30,561	Miami	465
Pawnee	15,575	Pawnee	551
Payne	61,507	Stillwater	691
Pittsburg	40,581	McAlester	1,251
Pontotoc	34,119	Ada	717
Pottawatomie	58,760	Shawnee	783
Pushmataha	10,997	Antlers	1,417
Roger Mills	4,147	Cheyenne	1,146
Rogers	55,170	Claremore	683
Seminole	25,412	Wewoka	639
Sequoyah	33,828	Sallisaw	678
Stephens	42,299	Duncan	884
Texas	16,419	Guymon	2,040
Tillman	10,384	Frederick	904
Tulsa	503,341	Tulsa	572
Wagoner	47,883	Wagoner	559
Washington	48,066	Bartlesville	423
Washita	11,441	Cordell	1,006
Woods	9,103	Alva	1,291
Woodward	18,976	Woodward	1,242

Oregon

(36 counties, 96,184 sq. mi. land; pop., 2,842,321)

Baker	15,317	Baker City	3,089
Benton	70,811	Corvallis	679
Clackamas	278,850	Oregon City	1,870
Clatsop	33,301	Astoria	873
Columbia	37,557	Saint Helens	687
Coos	60,273	Coquille	1,629
Crook	14,111	Prineville	2,991
Curry	19,327	Gold Beach	1,648
Deschutes	74,976	Bend	3,055
Douglas	94,649	Roseburg	5,071
Gilliam	1,717	Condon	1,223
Grant	7,853	Canyon City	4,525
Harney	7,060	Burns	10,228
Hood River	16,903	Hood River	533
Jackson	146,387	Medford	2,801
Jefferson	13,676	Madras	1,791
Josephine	62,649	Grants Pass	1,640
Klamath	57,702	Klamath Falls	6,135
Lake	7,186	Lakeview	8,359
Lane	282,912	Eugene	4,620
Lincoln	38,889	Newport	992
Linn	91,227	Albany	2,296
Malheur	26,038	Vale	9,926
Marion	228,483	Salem	1,194
Morrow	7,625	Heppner	2,094
Multnomah	583,887	Portland	465
Polk	49,541	Dallas	741
Sherman	1,918	Moro	831
Tillamook	21,570	Tillamook	1,125
Umatilla	59,249	Pendleton	3,218
Union	23,598	La Grande	2,038
Wallowa	6,911	Enterprise	3,150
Wasco	21,683	The Dalles	2,396
Washington	311,554	Hillsboro	727
Wheeler	1,396	Fossil	1,713
Yamhill	65,551	McMinnville	718

Pennsylvania

(67 counties, 44,888 sq. mi. land; pop., 11,881,643)

Adams	78,274	Gettysburg	521
Allegheny	1,336,449	Pittsburgh	727
Armstrong	73,478	Kittanning	646
Beaver	186,093	Beaver	436
Bedford	47,919	Bedford	1,017
Berks	336,523	Reading	861
Blair	130,542	Hollidaysburg	527
Bradford	60,967	Towanda	1,152
Bucks	541,174	Doylestown	610
Butler	152,013	Butler	789
Cambria	163,029	Ebensburg	691
Cameron	5,913	Emporium	398
Carbon	56,973	Jim Thorpe	384
Centre	124,812	Bellefonte	1,106
Chester	376,396	West Chester	758
Clarion	41,699	Clarion	607
Clearfield	78,097	Clearfield	1,149
Clinton	37,182	Lock Haven	891
Columbia	63,202	Bloomsburg	486
Crawford	86,169	Meadville	1,011
Cumberland	195,257	Carlisle	547
Dauphin	237,813	Harrisburg	528
Delaware	547,651	Media	184
Elk	34,878	Ridgway	830
Erie	275,572	Erie	804
Fayette	145,351	Uniontown	794
Forest	4,802	Tionesta	428
Franklin	121,082	Chambersburg	774
Fulton	13,837	McConnellsburg	438
Greene	39,550	Waynesburg	577
Huntingdon	44,164	Huntingdon	877
Indiana	89,994	Indiana	829
Jefferson	46,083	Brookville	657
Juniata	20,625	Mifflintown	392
Lackawanna	219,097	Scranton	461
Lancaster	422,822	Lancaster	952
Lawrence	96,246	New Castle	363
Lebanon	113,744	Lebanon	363
Lehigh	291,130	Allentown	348
Luzerne	328,149	Wilkes-Barre	891
Lycoming	118,710	Williamsport	1,237
McKean	47,131	Smethport	979
Mercer	121,003	Mercer	672
Mifflin	46,197	Lewistown	413
Monroe	95,582	Stroudsburg	609
Montgomery	678,111	Norristown	486
Montour	17,735	Danville	131
Northampton	247,105	Easton	376
Northumberland	96,771	Sunbury	461
Perry	41,172	New Bloomfield	557
Philadelphia	1,585,577	Philadelphia	136
Pike	27,966	Milford	550
Potter	16,717	Coudersport	1,081
Schuylkill	152,585	Pottsville	782
Snyder	36,680	Middleburg	329
Somerset	78,218	Somerset	1,073
Sullivan	6,104	Laporte	451
Susquehanna	40,380	Montrose	826
Tioga	41,126	Wellsboro	1,131
Union	36,176	Lewisburg	317
Venango	59,381	Franklin	679
Warren	45,049	Warren	885
Washington	204,584	Washington	858
Wayne	39,944	Honesdale	731
Westmoreland	370,321	Greensburg	1,033
Wyoming	28,076	Tunkhannock	399
York	339,574	York	906

Rhode Island

(5 counties, 1,055 sq. mi. land; pop., 1,003,464)

Bristol	48,859	Bristol	26
Kent	161,135	East Greenwich	172
Newport	87,194	Newport	107
Providence	596,270	Providence	416
Washington	110,006	West Kingston	333

South Carolina

(46 counties, 30,203 sq. mi. land; pop., 3,486,703)

Abbeville	23,862	Abbeville	508
Aiken	120,991	Aiken	1,092
Allendale	11,722	Allendale	413
Anderson	145,177	Anderson	718
Bamberg	16,902	Bamberg	395
Barnwell	20,293	Barnwell	558
Beaufort	86,425	Beaufort	579
Berkeley	128,776	Moncks Corner	1,108
Calhoun	12,753	Saint Matthews	380
Charleston	295,041	Charleston	938
Cherokee	44,506	Gaffney	396
Chester	32,170	Chester	580
Chesterfield	38,575	Chesterfield	802
Clarendon	28,450	Manning	602
Colleton	34,377	Walterboro	1,052
Darlington	61,851	Darlington	563
Dillon	29,114	Dillon	406
Dorchester	83,060	Saint George	575
Edgefield	18,360	Edgefield	490
Fairfield	22,295	Winnsboro	685
Florence	114,344	Florence	804
Georgetown	46,302	Georgetown	822
Greenville	320,167	Greenville	795
Greenwood	59,567	Greenwood	451
Hampton	18,191	Hampton	561
Horry	144,053	Conway	1,143
Jasper	15,487	Ridgeland	655
Kershaw	43,599	Camden	723
Lancaster	54,516	Lancaster	552
Laurens	58,092	Laurens	712
Lee	18,437	Bishopville	411
Lexington	167,611	Lexington	707
McCormick	8,868	McCormick	350

County	Pop.	County Seat or court house	Land area sq. mi.
Marion	33,899	Marion	493
Marlboro	29,716	Bennettsville	483
Newberry	33,172	Newberry	634
Oconee	57,494	Walhalla	629
Orangeburg	84,803	Orangeburg	1,111
Pickens	93,896	Pickens	499
Richland	286,321	Columbia	762
Saluda	16,357	Saluda	456
Spartanburg	226,793	Spartanburg	814
Sumter	102,637	Sumter	665
Union	30,337	Union	515
Williamsburg	36,815	Kingstree	934
York	131,497	York	685

South Dakota

(67 counties, 75,952 sq. mi. land; pop., 696,004)

County	Pop.	County Seat or court house	Land area sq. mi.
Aurora	3,135	Plankinton	707
Beadle	18,253	Huron	1,259
Bennett	3,206	Martin	1,182
Bon Homme	7,089	Tyndall	552
Brookings	25,207	Brookings	795
Brown	35,580	Aberdeen	1,722
Brule	5,485	Chamberlain	815
Buffalo	1,759	Gannvalley	475
Butte	7,914	Belle Fourche	2,251
Campbell	1,965	Mound City	732
Charles Mix	9,131	Lake Andes	1,090
Clark	4,403	Clark	953
Clay	13,186	Vermillion	409
Codington	22,698	Watertown	694
Corson	4,195	McIntosh	2,467
Custer	6,179	Custer	1,559
Davison	17,503	Mitchell	436
Day	6,978	Webster	1,022
Deuel	4,522	Clear Lake	631
Dewey	5,523	Timber Lake	2,310
Douglas	3,746	Armour	434
Edmunds	4,356	Ipswich	1,149
Fall River	7,353	Hot Springs	4,742
Faulk	2,744	Faulkton	1,004
Grant	8,372	Milbank	681
Gregory	5,359	Burke	1,013
Haakon	2,624	Philip	1,822
Hamlin	4,974	Hayti	512
Hand	4,272	Miller	1,437
Hanson	2,994	Alexandria	433
Harding	1,669	Buffalo	2,678
Hughes	14,817	Pierre	757
Hutchinson	8,262	Olivet	816
Hyde	1,696	Highmore	860
Jackson	2,811	Kadoka	1,872
Jerauld	2,425	Wessington Springs	530
Jones	1,324	Murdo	971
Kingsbury	5,925	De Smet	824
Lake	10,550	Madison	560
Lawrence	20,655	Deadwood	800
Lincoln	15,427	Canton	578
Lyman	3,638	Kennebec	1,679
McCook	5,688	Salem	576
McPherson	3,228	Leola	1,148
Marshall	4,844	Britton	848
Meade	21,878	Sturgis	3,481
Mellette	2,137	White River	1,311
Miner	3,272	Howard	570
Minnehaha	123,809	Sioux Falls	810
Moody	6,507	Flandreau	520
Pennington	81,343	Rapid City	2,783
Perkins	3,932	Bison	2,884
Potter	3,190	Gettysburg	869
Roberts	9,914	Sisseton	1,102
Sanborn	2,833	Woonsocket	569
Shannon	9,902	(Attached to Fall River)	2,094
Spink	7,981	Redfield	1,505
Stanley	2,453	Fort Pierre	1,431
Sully	1,589	Onida	972
Todd	8,352	(Attached to Tripp)	1,388
Tripp	6,924	Winner	1,618
Turner	8,576	Parker	617
Union	10,189	Elk Point	453
Walworth	6,087	Selby	707
Yankton	19,252	Yankton	518
Ziebach	2,220	Dupree	1,969

Tennessee

(95 counties, 41,155 sq. mi. land; pop., 4,877,185)

County	Pop.	County Seat or court house	Land area sq. mi.
Anderson	68,250	Clinton	339
Bedford	30,411	Shelbyville	475
Benton	14,524	Camden	392
Bledsoe	9,669	Pikeville	407
Blount	85,969	Maryville	558
Bradley	73,712	Cleveland	327
Campbell	35,079	Jacksboro	479
Cannon	10,467	Woodbury	266
Carroll	27,514	Huntingdon	600
Carter	51,505	Elizabethton	341
Cheatham	27,140	Ashland City	304
Chester	12,819	Henderson	289
Claiborne	26,137	Tazewell	432
Clay	7,238	Celina	227
Cocke	29,141	Newport	432
Coffee	40,339	Manchester	428
Crockett	13,378	Alamo	266
Cumberland	34,736	Crossville	682
Davidson	510,784	Nashville	501
Decatur	10,472	Decaturville	330
De Kalb	14,360	Smithville	291
Dickson	35,061	Charlotte	491
Dyer	34,854	Dyersburg	520
Fayette	25,559	Somerville	705
Fentress	14,669	Jamestown	498
Franklin	34,725	Winchester	543
Gibson	46,315	Trenton	602
Giles	25,741	Pulaski	610
Grainger	17,095	Rutledge	273
Greene	55,853	Greeneville	619
Grundy	13,362	Altamont	361
Hamblen	50,480	Morristown	156
Hamilton	285,536	Chattanooga	539
Hancock	6,739	Sneedville	223
Hardeman	23,377	Bolivar	670
Hardin	22,633	Savannah	578
Hawkins	44,565	Rogersville	486
Haywood	19,437	Brownsville	534
Henderson	21,844	Lexington	520
Henry	27,888	Paris	560
Hickman	16,754	Centerville	610
Houston	7,018	Erin	200
Humphreys	15,813	Waverly	528
Jackson	9,297	Gainesboro	308
Jefferson	33,016	Dandridge	265
Johnson	13,766	Mountain City	297
Knox	335,749	Knoxville	506
Lake	7,129	Tiptonville	169
Lauderdale	23,491	Ripley	474
Lawrence	35,303	Lawrenceburg	617
Lewis	9,247	Hohenwald	282
Lincoln	28,157	Fayetteville	571
Loudon	31,255	Loudon	235
McMinn	42,383	Athens	429
McNairy	22,422	Selmer	562
Macon	15,906	Lafayette	307
Madison	77,982	Jackson	558
Marion	24,860	Jasper	512
Marshall	21,539	Lewisburg	376
Maury	54,812	Columbia	616
Meigs	8,033	Decatur	189
Monroe	30,541	Madisonville	648
Montgomery	100,498	Clarksville	539
Moore	4,721	Lynchburg	129
Morgan	17,300	Wartburg	523
Obion	31,717	Union City	550
Overton	17,636	Livingston	433
Perry	6,612	Linden	412
Pickett	4,548	Byrdstown	159
Polk	13,643	Benton	438
Putnam	51,373	Cookeville	399
Rhea	24,344	Dayton	309
Roane	47,227	Kingston	357
Robertson	41,492	Springfield	476
Rutherford	118,570	Murfreesboro	606
Scott	18,358	Huntsville	528
Sequatchie	8,863	Dunlap	266
Sevier	51,043	Sevierville	590
Shelby	826,330	Memphis	772
Smith	14,143	Carthage	313
Stewart	9,479	Dover	454
Sullivan	143,596	Blountville	415
Sumner	103,281	Gallatin	529
Tipton	37,568	Covington	454
Trousdale	5,920	Hartsville	114
Unicoi	16,549	Erwin	186
Union	13,694	Maynardville	218
Van Buren	4,846	Spencer	273
Warren	32,992	McMinnville	431
Washington	92,315	Jonesboro	326
Wayne	13,935	Waynesboro	734
Weakley	31,972	Dresden	581
White	20,090	Sparta	373
Williamson	81,021	Franklin	584
Wilson	67,675	Lebanon	570

Texas

(254 counties, 262,017 sq. mi. land; pop., 16,986,510)

County	Pop.	County Seat or court house	Land area sq. mi.
Anderson	48,024	Palestine	1,077
Andrews	14,338	Andrews	1,501
Angelina	69,884	Lufkin	807
Aransas	17,892	Rockport	280
Archer	7,973	Archer City	907
Armstrong	2,021	Claude	909
Atascosa	30,533	Jourdanton	1,218
Austin	19,832	Bellville	656
Bailey	7,064	Muleshoe	826
Bandera	10,562	Bandera	793
Bastrop	38,263	Bastrop	895
Baylor	4,385	Seymour	862
Bee	25,135	Beeville	880
Bell	191,088	Belton	1,055
Bexar	1,185,394	San Antonio	1,248
Blanco	5,972	Johnson City	714
Borden	799	Gail	900
Bosque	15,125	Meridian	989
Bowie	81,665	Boston	891
Brazoria	191,707	Angleton	1,407
Brazos	121,862	Bryan	589
Brewster	8,681	Alpine	6,169
Briscoe	1,971	Silverton	887
Brooks	8,204	Falfurrias	942
Brown	34,371	Brownwood	936
Burleson	13,625	Caldwell	669
Burnet	22,677	Burnet	994
Caldwell	26,392	Lockhart	546
Calhoun	19,053	Port Lavaca	540
Callahan	11,859	Baird	899
Cameron	260,120	Brownsville	906
Camp	9,904	Pittsburg	203
Carson	6,576	Panhandle	924
Cass	29,982	Linden	937
Castro	9,070	Dimmitt	899
Chambers	20,088	Anahuac	616
Cherokee	41,049	Rusk	1,052
Childress	5,953	Childress	707
Clay	10,024	Henrietta	1,086
Cochran	4,377	Morton	775
Coke	3,424	Robert Lee	908
Coleman	9,710	Coleman	1,277
Collin	264,036	McKinney	851
Collingsworth	3,573	Wellington	909
Colorado	18,383	Columbus	965
Comal	51,832	New Braunfels	555
Comanche	13,381	Comanche	930
Concho	3,044	Paint Rock	992
Cooke	30,777	Gainesville	893
Coryell	64,213	Gatesville	1,057
Cottle	2,247	Paducah	895
Crane	4,652	Crane	782
Crockett	4,078	Ozona	2,806
Crosby	7,304	Crosbyton	899
Culberson	3,407	Van Horn	3,815
Dallam	5,461	Dalhart	1,505
Dallas	1,852,810	Dallas	880
Dawson	14,349	Lamesa	903
Deaf Smith	19,153	Hereford	1,497
Delta	4,857	Cooper	278
Denton	273,525	Denton	911
Dewitt	18,840	Cuero	910
Dickens	2,571	Dickens	907
Dimmit	10,433	Carrizo Springs	1,307
Donley	3,696	Clarendon	929
Duval	12,918	San Diego	1,795
Eastland	18,488	Eastland	924
Ector	118,934	Odessa	903
Edwards	2,266	Rocksprings	2,121
Ellis	85,167	Waxahachie	939
El Paso	591,610	El Paso	1,014
Erath	27,991	Stephenville	1,080
Falls	17,712	Marlin	770
Fannin	24,804	Bonham	895
Fayette	20,095	La Grange	950
Fisher	4,842	Roby	897
Floyd	8,497	Floydada	992
Foard	1,794	Crowell	703
Fort Bend	225,421	Richmond	876
Franklin	7,802	Mount Vernon	294
Freestone	15,818	Fairfield	888
Frio	13,472	Pearsall	1,133
Gaines	14,123	Seminole	1,504
Galveston	217,396	Galveston	399
Garza	5,143	Post	895
Gillespie	17,204	Fredericksburg	1,061
Glasscock	1,447	Garden City	900
Goliad	5,980	Goliad	859
Gonzales	17,205	Gonzales	1,068
Gray	23,967	Pampa	921
Grayson	95,021	Sherman	934
Gregg	104,948	Longview	273
Grimes	18,828	Anderson	799
Guadalupe	64,873	Seguin	713
Hale	34,671	Plainview	1,005
Hall	3,905	Memphis	877
Hamilton	7,733	Hamilton	836
Hansford	5,848	Spearman	921
Hardeman	5,283	Quanah	688
Hardin	41,320	Kountze	898
Harris	2,818,199	Houston	1,734
Harrison	57,483	Marshall	908
Hartley	3,634	Channing	1,462
Haskell	6,820	Haskell	901
Hays	65,614	San Marcos	678
Hemphill	3,720	Canadian	903
Henderson	58,543	Athens	888
Hidalgo	383,545	Edinburg	1,569
Hill	27,146	Hillsboro	968
Hockley	24,199	Levelland	908
Hood	28,981	Granbury	425
Hopkins	28,833	Sulphur Springs	789
Houston	21,375	Crockett	1,234
Howard	32,343	Big Spring	901
Hudspeth	2,915	Sierra Blanca	4,567
Hunt	64,343	Greenville	840
Hutchinson	25,689	Stinnett	872
Irion	1,629	Mertzon	1,052
Jack	6,981	Jacksboro	920
Jackson	13,039	Edna	844
Jasper	31,102	Jasper	921
Jeff Davis	1,946	Fort Davis	2,257
Jefferson	239,389	Beaumont	937
Jim Hogg	5,109	Hebbronville	1,136
Jim Wells	37,679	Alice	867
Johnson	97,165	Cleburne	730
Jones	16,490	Anson	931
Karnes	12,455	Karnes City	753
Kaufman	52,220	Kaufman	788
Kendall	14,589	Boerne	663
Kenedy	460	Sarita	1,389
Kent	1,010	Jayton	878
Kerr	36,304	Kerrville	1,107
Kimble	4,122	Junction	1,250
King	354	Guthrie	914
Kinney	3,119	Brackettville	1,359
Kleberg	30,274	Kingsville	853
Knox	4,837	Benjamin	845
Lamar	43,949	Paris	919
Lamb	15,072	Littlefield	1,013
Lampasas	13,521	Lampasas	714
La Salle	5,254	Cotulla	1,517
Lavaca	18,690	Hallettsville	971
Lee	12,854	Giddings	631
Leon	12,665	Centerville	1,079
Liberty	52,726	Liberty	1,174
Limestone	20,946	Groesbeck	930
Lipscomb	3,143	Lipscomb	933
Live Oak	9,556	George West	1,057
Llano	11,631	Llano	939
Loving	107	Mentone	670
Lubbock	222,636	Lubbock	900
Lynn	6,758	Tahoka	888
McCulloch	8,778	Brady	1,071
McLennan	189,123	Waco	1,031
McMullen	817	Tilden	1,163
Madison	10,931	Madisonville	472
Marion	9,984	Jefferson	385
Martin	4,956	Stanton	914
Mason	3,423	Mason	934
Matagorda	36,928	Bay City	1,127
Maverick	36,378	Eagle Pass	1,287
Medina	27,312	Hondo	1,331
Menard	2,252	Menard	902
Midland	106,611	Midland	902
Milam	22,946	Cameron	1,019
Mills	4,531	Goldthwaite	748
Mitchell	8,016	Colorado City	912
Montague	17,274	Montague	928
Montgomery	182,201	Conroe	1,047
Moore	17,865	Dumas	905
Morris	13,200	Daingerfield	256
Motley	1,532	Matador	959
Nacogdoches	54,753	Nacogdoches	939
Navarro	39,926	Corsicana	1,068
Newton	13,569	Newton	935
Nolan	16,594	Sweetwater	915
Nueces	291,145	Corpus Christi	847
Ochiltree	9,128	Perryton	919
Oldham	2,278	Vega	1,485
Orange	80,509	Orange	362
Palo Pinto	25,055	Palo Pinto	949
Panola	22,035	Carthage	812
Parker	64,785	Weatherford	902
Parmer	9,863	Farwell	885
Pecos	14,675	Fort Stockton	4,777
Polk	30,687	Livingston	1,061
Potter	97,841	Amarillo	902
Presidio	6,637	Marfa	3,857
Rains	6,715	Emory	243
Randall	89,673	Canyon	917

County	Pop.	County Seat or court house	Land area sq. mi.
Reagan	4,514	Big Lake	1,173
Real	2,412	Leakey	697
Red River	14,317	Clarksville	1,054
Reeves	15,852	Pecos	2,626
Refugio	7,976	Refugio	771
Roberts	1,025	Miami	915
Robertson	15,511	Franklin	864
Rockwall	25,604	Rockwall	128
Runnels	11,294	Ballinger	1,056
Rusk	43,735	Henderson	932
Sabine	9,586	Hemphill	486
San Augustine	7,999	San Augustine	524
San Jacinto	16,372	Coldspring	572
San Patricio	58,749	Sinton	693
San Saba	5,401	San Saba	1,136
Schleicher	2,990	Eldorado	1,309
Scurry	18,634	Snyder	900
Shackelford	3,316	Albany	915
Shelby	22,034	Center	791
Sherman	2,858	Stratford	923
Smith	151,309	Tyler	932
Somervell	5,360	Glen Rose	188
Starr	40,518	Rio Grande City	1,226
Stephens	9,010	Breckenridge	894
Sterling	1,438	Sterling City	923
Stonewall	2,013	Aspermont	925
Sutton	4,135	Sonora	1,455
Swisher	8,133	Tulia	902
Tarrant	1,170,103	Fort Worth	868
Taylor	119,655	Abilene	917
Terrell	1,410	Sanderson	2,357
Terry	13,218	Brownfield	887
Throckmorton	1,880	Throckmorton	912
Titus	24,009	Mount Pleasant	412
Tom Green	98,458	San Angelo	1,515
Travis	576,407	Austin	989
Trinity	11,445	Groveton	692
Tyler	16,646	Woodville	922
Upshur	31,370	Gilmer	587
Upton	4,447	Rankin	1,243
Uvalde	23,340	Uvalde	1,564
Val Verde	38,721	Del Rio	3,150
Van Zandt	37,944	Canton	855
Victoria	74,361	Victoria	887
Walker	50,917	Huntsville	786
Waller	23,389	Hempstead	514
Ward	13,115	Monahans	836
Washington	26,154	Brenham	610
Webb	133,239	Laredo	3,362
Wharton	39,955	Wharton	1,086
Wheeler	5,879	Wheeler	904
Wichita	122,378	Wichita Falls	606
Wilbarger	15,121	Vernon	947
Willacy	17,705	Raymondville	589
Williamson	139,551	Georgetown	1,137
Wilson	22,650	Floresville	807
Winkler	8,626	Kermit	840
Wise	34,679	Decatur	902
Wood	29,380	Quitman	689
Yoakum	8,786	Plains	800
Young	18,126	Graham	919
Zapata	9,279	Zapata	999
Zavala	12,162	Crystal City	1,298

Utah

(29 counties, 82,168 sq. mi. land; pop. 1,722,850)

County	Pop.	County Seat or court house	Land area sq. mi.
Beaver	4,765	Beaver	2,590
Box Elder	36,485	Brigham City	5,724
Cache	70,183	Logan	1,165
Carbon	20,228	Price	1,479
Daggett	690	Manila	698
Davis	187,941	Farmington	305
Duchesne	12,645	Duchesne	3,238
Emery	10,332	Castle Dale	4,452
Garfield	3,980	Panguitch	5,175
Grand	6,620	Moab	3,682
Iron	20,789	Parowan	3,299
Juab	5,817	Nephi	3,392
Kane	5,169	Kanab	3,992
Millard	11,333	Fillmore	6,590
Morgan	5,528	Morgan	609
Piute	1,277	Junction	758
Rich	1,725	Randolph	1,029
Salt Lake	725,956	Salt Lake City	737
San Juan	12,621	Monticello	7,821
Sanpete	16,259	Manti	1,588
Sevier	15,431	Richfield	1,910
Summit	15,518	Coalville	1,871
Tooele	26,601	Tooele	6,946
Uintah	22,211	Vernal	4,477
Utah	263,590	Provo	1,998
Wasatch	10,089	Heber City	1,181
Washington	48,560	Saint George	2,427
Wayne	2,177	Loa	2,461
Weber	158,330	Ogden	576

Vermont

(14 counties, 9,273 sq. mi. land; pop. 562,758)

County	Pop.	County Seat or court house	Land area sq. mi.
Addison	32,953	Middlebury	773
Bennington	35,845	Bennington	676
Caledonia	27,846	Saint Johnsbury	651
Chittenden	131,761	Burlington	540
Essex	6,405	Guildhall	666
Franklin	39,980	Saint Albans	649
Grand Isle	5,318	North Hero	89
Lamoille	19,735	Hyde Park	461
Orange	26,149	Chelsea	690
Orleans	24,053	Newport	697
Rutland	62,142	Rutland	932
Washington	54,928	Montpelier	690
Windham	41,588	Newfane	786
Windsor	54,055	Woodstock	972

Virginia

(95 cos., 41 ind. cities, 39,704 sq. mi. land; pop. 6,216,568)

County	Pop.	County Seat or court house	Land area sq. mi.
Accomack	31,703	Accomac	476
Albemarle	68,172	Charlottesville	740
Alleghany	13,176	Covington	444
Amelia	8,787	Amelia Court House	366
Amherst	28,578	Amherst	470
Appomattox	12,298	Appomattox	345
Arlington	170,886	Arlington	26
Augusta	54,677	Staunton	968
Bath	4,799	Warm Springs	540
Bedford	45,656	Bedford	771
Bland	6,514	Bland	369
Botetourt	24,992	Fincastle	549
Brunswick	15,987	Lawrenceville	579
Buchanan	31,333	Grundy	508
Buckingham	12,873	Buckingham	582
Campbell	47,572	Rustburg	511
Caroline	19,217	Bowling Green	549
Carroll	26,594	Hillsville	494
Charles City	6,282	Charles City	208
Charlotte	11,688	Charlotte Court House	471
Chesterfield	209,564	Chesterfield	446
Clarke	12,101	Berryville	174
Craig	4,372	New Castle	336
Culpeper	27,791	Culpeper	389
Cumberland	7,825	Cumberland	292
Dickenson	17,620	Clintwood	335
Dinwiddie	22,319	Dinwiddie	502
Essex	8,689	Tappahannock	264
Fairfax	818,584	Fairfax	399
Fauquier	48,860	Warrenton	660
Floyd	11,965	Floyd	383
Fluvanna	12,429	Palmyra	282
Franklin	39,549	Rocky Mount	721
Frederick	45,723	Winchester	432
Giles	16,366	Pearisburg	369
Gloucester	30,131	Gloucester	257
Goochland	14,163	Goochland	289
Grayson	16,278	Independence	494
Greene	10,297	Stanardsville	153
Greensville	8,630	Emporia	301
Halifax	29,033	Halifax	806
Hanover	63,306	Hanover	436
Henrico	217,849	Henrico	244
Henry	56,942	Martinsville	385
Highland	2,635	Monterey	416
Isle of Wight	25,053	Isle of Wight	319
James City	34,970	Williamsburg	144
King and Queen	6,289	King and Queen Court House	327
King George	13,527	King George	183
King William	10,913	King William	286
Lancaster	10,896	Lancaster	153
Lee	24,496	Jonesville	438
Loudoun	86,129	Leesburg	517
Louisa	20,325	Louisa	514
Lunenburg	11,419	Lunenburg	443
Madison	11,949	Madison	327
Mathews	8,348	Mathews	87
Mecklenburg	29,241	Boydton	675
Middlesex	8,653	Saluda	138
Montgomery	73,913	Christiansburg	395
Nelson	12,778	Lovingston	471
New Kent	10,445	New Kent	221
Northampton	13,061	Eastville	209
Northumberland	10,524	Heathsville	223
Nottoway	14,993	Nottoway	308
Orange	21,421	Orange	355

County	Pop.	County Seat or court house	Land area sq. mi.
Page	21,690	Luray	310
Patrick	17,473	Stuart	467
Pittsylvania	55,672	Chatham	985
Powhatan	15,328	Powhatan	272
Prince Edward	17,320	Farmville	357
Prince George	27,394	Prince George	276
Prince William	215,677	Manassas	345
Pulaski	34,496	Pulaski	335
Rappahannock	6,622	Washington	267
Richmond	7,273	Warsaw	203
Roanoke	79,332	Salem	248
Rockbridge	18,350	Lexington	604
Rockingham	57,482	Harrisonburg	865
Russell	28,667	Lebanon	483
Scott	23,204	Gate City	539
Shenandoah	31,636	Woodstock	507
Smyth	32,370	Marion	435
Southampton	17,550	Courtland	599
Spotsylvania	57,403	Spotsylvania	409
Stafford	61,236	Stafford	277
Surry	6,145	Surry	306
Sussex	10,248	Sussex	496
Tazewell	45,960	Tazewell	522
Warren	26,142	Front Royal	219
Washington	45,887	Abingdon	578
Westmoreland	15,480	Montross	250
Wise	39,573	Wise	405
Wythe	25,471	Wytheville	460
York	42,434	Yorktown	122
Independent cities			
Alexandria	111,183		16
Bedford	6,073		7
Bristol	18,426		12
Buena Vista	6,406		7
Charlottesville	40,341		10
Chesapeake	151,976		353
Clifton Forge	4,679		3
Colonial Heights	16,064		8
Covington	6,991		5
Danville	53,056		44
Emporia	5,306		7
Fairfax	19,622		6
Falls Church	9,578		2
Franklin	7,864		8
Fredericksburg	19,027		10
Galax	6,670		8
Hampton	133,793		57
Harrisonburg	30,707		17
Hopewell	23,101		11
Lexington	6,959		2
Lynchburg	66,049		50
Manassas	27,957		11
Manassas Park	6,734		3
Martinsville	16,162		11
Newport News	170,045		69
Norfolk	261,229		66
Norton	4,247		7
Petersburg	38,386		23
Poquoson	11,005		10
Portsmouth	103,907		30
Radford	15,940		9
Richmond	203,056		63
Roanoke	96,397		43
Salem	23,756		14
South Boston	6,997		5
Staunton	24,461		20
Suffolk	52,141		430
Virginia Beach	393,069		310
Waynesboro	18,549		14
Williamsburg	11,530		9
Winchester	21,947		9

Washington

(39 counties, 66,511 sq. mi. land; pop., 4,866,692)

County	Pop.	County Seat or court house	Land area sq. mi.
Adams	13,603	Ritzville	1,921
Asotin	17,605	Asotin	635
Benton	112,560	Prosser	1,715
Chelan	52,250	Wenatchee	2,916
Clallam	56,210	Port Angeles	1,753
Clark	238,053	Vancouver	627
Columbia	4,024	Dayton	865
Cowlitz	82,119	Kelso	1,140
Douglas	26,205	Waterville	1,817
Ferry	6,295	Republic	2,200
Franklin	37,473	Pasco	1,243
Garfield	2,248	Pomeroy	706
Grant	54,798	Ephrata	2,660
Grays Harbor	64,175	Montesano	1,918
Island	60,195	Coupeville	212
Jefferson	20,406	Port Townsend	1,805
King	1,507,305	Seattle	2,128
Kitsap	189,731	Port Orchard	393
Kittitas	26,725	Ellensburg	2,308
Klickitat	16,616	Goldendale	1,880
Lewis	59,358	Chehalis	2,409
Lincoln	8,864	Davenport	2,310
Mason	38,341	Shelton	961
Okanogan	33,350	Okanogan	5,281
Pacific	18,882	South Bend	908
Pend Oreille	8,915	Newport	1,400
Pierce	586,203	Tacoma	1,675
San Juan	10,035	Friday Harbor	179
Skagit	79,545	Mount Vernon	1,735
Skamania	8,289	Stevenson	1,672
Snohomish	465,642	Everett	2,098
Spokane	361,333	Spokane	1,762
Stevens	30,948	Colville	2,470
Thurston	161,238	Olympia	727
Wahkiakum	3,327	Cathlamet	261
Walla Walla	48,439	Walla Walla	1,261
Whatcom	127,780	Bellingham	2,125
Whitman	38,775	Colfax	2,151
Yakima	188,823	Yakima	4,287

West Virginia

(55 counties, 24,119 sq. mi. land; pop., 1,793,477)

County	Pop.	County Seat or court house	Land area sq. mi.
Barbour	15,699	Philippi	343
Berkeley	59,253	Martinsburg	321
Boone	25,870	Madison	503
Braxton	12,998	Sutton	513
Brooke	26,992	Wellsburg	90
Cabell	96,827	Huntington	282
Calhoun	7,885	Grantsville	280
Clay	9,983	Clay	346
Doddridge	6,994	West Union	321
Fayette	47,952	Fayetteville	667
Gilmer	7,669	Glenville	340
Grant	10,428	Petersburg	480
Greenbrier	34,693	Lewisburg	1,025
Hampshire	16,498	Romney	644
Hancock	35,233	New Cumberland	84
Hardy	10,977	Moorefield	585
Harrison	69,371	Clarksburg	417
Jackson	25,938	Ripley	464
Jefferson	35,926	Charles Town	209
Kanawha	207,619	Charleston	901
Lewis	17,223	Weston	389
Lincoln	21,382	Hamlin	439
Logan	43,032	Logan	456
McDowell	35,233	Welch	535
Marion	57,249	Fairmont	312
Marshall	37,356	Moundsville	305
Mason	25,178	Point Pleasant	433
Mercer	64,980	Princeton	420
Mineral	26,697	Keyser	329
Mingo	33,739	Williamson	424
Monongalia	75,509	Morgantown	363
Monroe	12,406	Union	473
Morgan	12,128	Berkeley Springs	230
Nicholas	26,775	Summersville	650
Ohio	50,871	Wheeling	106
Pendleton	8,054	Franklin	698
Pleasants	7,546	St. Marys	131
Pocahontas	9,008	Marlinton	942
Preston	29,037	Kingwood	651
Putnam	42,835	Winfield	346
Raleigh	76,819	Beckley	608
Randolph	27,803	Elkins	1,040
Ritchie	10,233	Harrisville	454
Roane	15,120	Spencer	484
Summers	14,204	Hinton	353
Taylor	15,144	Grafton	174
Tucker	7,728	Parsons	421
Tyler	9,796	Middlebourne	258
Upshur	22,867	Buckhannon	355
Wayne	41,636	Wayne	508
Webster	10,729	Webster Springs	556
Wetzel	19,258	New Martinsville	359
Wirt	5,192	Elizabeth	235
Wood	86,915	Parkersburg	367
Wyoming	28,990	Pineville	502

Wisconsin

(72 counties, 54,426 sq. mi. land; pop., 4,891,769)

County	Pop.	County Seat or court house	Land area sq. mi.
Adams	15,682	Friendship	648
Ashland	16,307	Ashland	1,048
Barron	40,750	Barron	865
Bayfield	14,008	Washburn	1,462
Brown	194,594	Green Bay	524
Buffalo	13,584	Alma	699
Burnett	13,084	Meenon	818
Calumet	34,291	Chilton	326

County	Pop.	County Seat or court house	Land area sq. mi.
Chippewa	52,360	Chippewa Falls	1,017
Clark	31,647	Neillsville	1,218
Columbia	45,088	Portage	771
Crawford	15,940	Prairie du Chien	566
Dane	367,085	Madison	1,205
Dodge	76,559	Juneau	887
Door	25,600	Sturgeon Bay	492
Douglas	41,758	Superior	1,305
Dunn	35,909	Menomonie	853
Eau Claire	85,183	Eau Claire	638
Florence	4,590	Florence	486
Fond du Lac	90,083	Fond du Lac	725
Forest	8,776	Crandon	1,011
Grant	49,266	Lancaster	1,144
Green	30,339	Monroe	583
Green Lake	18,651	Green Lake	357
Iowa	20,150	Dodgeville	760
Iron	6,153	Hurley	751
Jackson	16,588	Black River Falls	998
Jefferson	67,783	Jefferson	562
Juneau	21,650	Mauston	774
Kenosha	128,181	Kenosha	273
Kewaunee	18,878	Kewaunee	343
La Crosse	97,904	La Crosse	457
Lafayette	16,074	Darlington	634
Langlade	19,505	Antigo	873
Lincoln	26,993	Merrill	886
Manitowoc	80,421	Manitowoc	594
Marathon	115,400	Wausau	1,559
Marinette	40,548	Marinette	1,395
Marquette	12,321	Montello	455
Menominee	3,890	Keshena	359
Milwaukee	959,275	Milwaukee	241
Monroe	36,633	Sparta	904
Oconto	30,226	Oconto	1,002
Oneida	31,679	Rhinelander	1,130
Outagamie	140,510	Appleton	642
Ozaukee	72,831	Port Washington	235
Pepin	7,107	Durand	231
Pierce	32,765	Ellsworth	576
Polk	34,773	Balsam Lake	919
Portage	61,405	Stevens Point	810
Price	15,600	Phillips	1,256
Racine	175,034	Racine	334
Richland	17,521	Richland Center	585
Rock	139,510	Janesville	724
Rusk	15,079	Ladysmith	913
Saint Croix	50,251	Hudson	723
Sauk	46,975	Baraboo	838
Sawyer	14,181	Hayward	1,255
Shawano	37,157	Shawano	897
Sheboygan	103,877	Sheboygan	515
Taylor	18,901	Medford	975
Trempealeau	25,263	Whitehall	736
Vernon	25,617	Viroqua	808
Vilas	17,707	Eagle River	867
Walworth	75,000	Elkhorn	556
Washburn	13,772	Shell Lake	815
Washington	95,328	West Bend	431
Waukesha	304,715	Waukesha	554
Waupaca	46,104	Waupaca	754
Waushara	19,385	Wautoma	628
Winnebago	140,320	Oshkosh	449
Wood	73,605	Wisconsin Rapids	801

Wyoming

(23 counties, 96,989 sq. mi. land; pop., 453,588)

County	Pop.	County Seat or court house	Land area sq. mi.
Albany	30,797	Laramie	4,268
Big Horn	10,525	Basin	3,139
Campbell	29,370	Gillette	4,796
Carbon	16,659	Rawlins	7,877
Converse	11,128	Douglas	4,271
Crook	5,294	Sundance	2,855
Fremont	33,662	Lander	9,181
Goshen	12,373	Torrington	2,186
Hot Springs	4,809	Thermopolis	2,005
Johnson	6,145	Buffalo	4,166
Laramie	73,142	Cheyenne	2,684
Lincoln	12,625	Kemmerer	4,070
Natrona	61,226	Casper	5,347
Niobrara	2,499	Lusk	2,684
Park	23,178	Cody	6,936
Platte	8,145	Wheatland	2,023
Sheridan	23,562	Sheridan	2,532
Sublette	4,843	Pinedale	4,872
Sweetwater	38,823	Green River	10,352
Teton	11,173	Jackson	4,011
Uinta	18,705	Evanston	2,085
Washakie	8,388	Worland	2,243
Weston	6,518	Newcastle	2,402

Population of Outlying Areas

Source: Bureau of the Census

(Final counts from the census conducted on Apr. 1, 1990.)

Commonwealth of Puerto Rico

Zip code	Municipios	Pop.	Land area sq. mi.
00601	Adjuntas	19,451	67
00602	Aguada	35,911	31
*00603	Aguadilla	59,335	37
00703	Aguas Buenas	25,424	31
00705	Aibonito	24,971	31
00610	Anasco	25,234	39
*00612	Arecibo	93,385	126
00714	Arroyo	18,910	15
00617	Barceloneta	20,947	23
00794	Barranquitas	25,605	34
*00979	Bayamon	220,262	44
00623	Cabo Rojo	38,521	70
00725	Caguas	133,447	59
00627	Camuy	28,917	46
00729	Canovanas	36,816	33
*00979	Carolina	177,806	45
00962	Catano	34,587	5
00736	Cayey	46,553	52
00735	Ceiba	17,145	29
00638	Ciales	18,084	67
00739	Cidra	35,601	36
00769	Coamo	33,837	78
00782	Comerio	20,265	28
00783	Corozal	33,095	43
00775	Culebra	1,542	12
00646	Dorado	30,759	23
00738	Fajardo	36,882	30
00650	Florida	8,689	10
00653	Guanica	19,984	37
00784	Guayama	41,588	65
00656	Guayanilla	21,581	42
*00965	Guaynabo	92,886	27
00778	Gurabo	28,737	28
00659	Hatillo	32,703	42
00660	Hormigueros	15,212	11
00791	Humacao	55,203	45
00662	Isabela	39,147	55
00664	Jayuya	15,527	45
00795	Juana Diaz	45,198	60
00777	Juncos	30,612	27
00667	Lajas	23,271	60
00669	Lares	29,015	62
00670	Las Marias	9,306	46
00771	Las Piedras	27,896	34
00772	Loiza	29,307	19
00773	Luquillo	18,100	26
00674	Manati	38,692	45
00606	Maricao	6,206	37
00707	Maunabo	12,347	21
00680	Mayaguez	100,371	78
00676	Moca	32,926	50
00687	Morovis	25,288	39
00718	Naguabo	22,620	52
00719	Naranjito	27,914	27
00720	Orocovis	21,158	64
00723	Patillas	19,633	47
00624	Penuelas	22,515	45
*00731	Ponce	187,749	116
00678	Quebradillas	21,425	23
00677	Rincon	12,213	14
00745	Rio Grande	45,648	61
00637	Sabana Grande	22,843	36
00751	Salinas	28,335	69
00683	San German	34,962	55
*00936	San Juan	437,745	48
00754	San Lorenzo	35,163	53
00685	San Sebastian	38,799	70
00757	Santa Isabel	19,318	34
*00953	Toa Alta	44,101	27
*00949	Toa Baja	89,454	23
*00976	Trujillo Alto	61,120	21
00641	Utuado	34,980	114
00692	Vega Alta	34,559	28
00693	Vega Baja	55,997	46
00765	Vieques	8,602	51
00766	Villalba	23,559	36
00767	Yabucoa	36,483	55
00698	Yauco	42,058	68
Total		**3,522,037**	**3,427**

Commonwealth of the Northern Mariannas

Zip code	Municipality	Pop.	Land area sq. mi.
96950	Northern Islands	36	60
96951	Rota	2,295	33
96950	Saipan	38,896	45
96952	Tinian	2,118	42
Total		**43,345**	**180**[1]

U.S. External Territories

Zip code	Area	Pop.	Land area sq. mi.
	American Samoa		
96799	American Samoa	46,773	77
	Guam		
96910	Agana	1,139	1
.....	Agana Hts.	3,646	1
96915	Agat	4,960	10
.....	Asan	2,070	6
96913	Barrigada	8,846	9
.....	Chalan-Pago-Ordot	4,451	6
96912	Dededo	31,728	30
96916	Inarajan	2,469	19
.....	Mangilao	10,483	10
96916	Merizo	1,742	6
.....	Mongmong-Toto-Maite	5,845	2
	Piti	1,827	7
96915	Santa Rita	11,857	17
.....	Sinajana	2,658	1
.....	Talofofo	2,310	17
96911	Tamuning	16,673	6
96918	Umatac	897	6
96921	Yigo	14,213	35
96914	Yona	5,338	20
	Total	133,152	210[1]
	Virgin Islands		
.....	Saint Croix	50,139	83
.....	Saint John	3,504	20
.....	Saint Thomas	48,166	31
00801	Charlotte Amalie	12,331	
00820	Christiansted	2,555	
00840	Frederiksted	1,064	
	Total	101,809	134
	Trust Territory		
96940	Palau (Belau)	15,122	192

[1]Figures may not add due to independent rounding.

U.S. Area and Population: 1790 to 1990

Source: Bureau of the Census

Census date	Area (square miles) Gross	Land	Water	Population Number	Per sq. mile of land	Increase over preceding census Number	%
1990 (Apr. 1)	3,787,425	3,536,342	251,083[1]	248,709,873	70.3	22,164,068	9.8
1980 (Apr. 1)	3,618,770	3,539,289	79,481	226,542,203	64.0	23,240,172	11.4
1970 (Apr. 1)	3,618,770	3,536,855	81,915	203,302,031	57.5	23,978,856	13.4
1960 (Apr. 1)	3,618,770	3,540,911	77,859	179,323,175	50.6	27,997,377	18.5
1950 (Apr. 1)	3,618,770	3,552,206	66,564	151,325,798	42.6	19,161,229	14.5
1940 (Apr. 1)	3,618,770	3,554,608	64,162	132,164,569	37.2	8,961,945	7.3
1930 (Apr. 1)	3,618,770	3,551,608	67,162	123,202,624	34.7	17,181,087	16.2
1920 (Jan. 1)	3,618,770	3,546,931	71,839	106,021,537	29.9	13,793,041	15.0
1910 (Apr. 15)	3,618,770	3,547,045	71,725	92,228,496	26.0	16,016,328	21.0
1900 (June 1)	3,618,770	3,547,314	71,456	76,212,168	21.5	13,232,402	21.0
1890 (June 1)	3,612,299	3,540,705	71,594	62,979,766	17.8	12,790,557	25.5
1880 (June 1)	3,612,299	3,540,705	71,594	50,189,209	14.2	11,630,838	30.2
1870 (June 1)	3,612,299	3,540,705	71,594	38,558,371	10.9	7,115,050	22.6
1860 (June 1)	3,021,295	2,969,640	51,655	31,443,321	10.6	8,251,445	35.6
1850 (June 1)	2,991,655	2,940,042	51,613	23,191,876	7.9	6,122,423	35.9
1840 (June 1)	1,792,552	1,749,462	43,090	17,069,453	9.8	4,203,433	32.7
1830 (June 1)	1,792,552	1,749,462	43,090	12,866,020	7.4	3,227,567	33.5
1820 (June 1)	1,792,552	1,749,462	43,090	9,638,453	5.5	2,398,572	33.1
1810 (Aug. 6)	1,722,685	1,681,828	40,857	7,239,881	4.3	1,931,398	36.4
1800 (Aug. 4)	891,364	864,746	26,618	5,308,483	6.1	1,379,269	35.1
1790 (Aug. 2)	891,364	864,746	26,618	3,929,214	4.5	—	—

(1) Comprises inland, coastal, Great Lakes, and territorial water. Data for prior years cover inland water only.

NOTE: Percent changes are computed on basis of change in population since preceding census date, and period covered therefore is not always exactly 10 years.

Population density figures given for various years represent the area within the boundaries of the United States which was under the jurisdiction on date in question, including in some cases considerable areas not organized or settled and not covered by the census. In 1870, for example, Alaska was not covered by the census.

Revised figure of 39,818,449 for the 1870 population includes adjustments for undernumeration in the Southern states. On the basis of the revised figure, the population increased by 8,375,128, or 26.6 percent between 1860 and 1870, and by 10,370,760, or 26.1 percent between 1870 and 1880.

Resident Population by Sex, Race, Residence, and Median Age: 1790 to 1990

Source: Bureau of the Census (in thousands, except as indicated)

Date	Sex Male	Female	Race White	Black Number	Black Percent	Other	Residence Urban	Rural	Median Age (years) All races	White	Black
Conterminous U.S.[1]											
1790 (Aug. 2)	NA	NA	3,172	757	19.3	NA	202	3,728	NA	NA	NA
1810 (Aug. 6)	NA	NA	5,862	1,378	19.0	NA	525	6,714	NA	16.0	NA
1820 (Aug. 7)	4,897	4,742	7,867	1,772	18.4	NA	693	8,945	16.7	16.5	17.2
1840 (June 1)	8,689	8,381	14,196	2,874	16.8	NA	1,845	15,224	17.8	17.9	17.3
1860 (June 1)	16,085	15,358	26,923	4,442	14.1	79	6,217	25,227	19.4	19.7	17.7
1870 (June 1)	19,494	19,065	33,589	4,880	12.7	89	9,902	28,656	20.2	20.4	18.5
1880 (June 1)	25,519	24,637	43,403	6,581	13.1	172	14,130	36,026	20.9	21.4	18.0
1890 (June 1)	32,237	30,711	55,101	7,489	11.9	358	22,106	40,841	22.0	22.5	17.8
1900 (June 1)	38,816	37,178	66,809	8,834	11.6	351	30,160	45,835	22.9	23.4	19.4
1920 (Jan. 1)	53,900	51,810	94,821	10,463	9.9	427	54,158	51,553	25.3	25.6	22.3
1930 (Apr. 1)	62,137	60,638	110,287	11,891	9.7	597	68,955	53,820	26.4	26.9	23.5
1940 (Apr. 1)	66,062	65,608	118,215	12,866	9.8	589	74,424	57,246	29.0	29.5	25.3
United States											
1950 (Apr. 1)	75,187	76,139	135,150	15,045	9.9	1,131	96,847	54,479	30.2	30.7	26.2
1960 (Apr. 1)	88,331	90,992	158,832	18,872	10.5	1,620	125,269	54,054	29.5	30.3	23.5
1970 (Apr. 1)[2]	98,926	104,309	178,098	22,581	11.1	2,557	149,325	53,887	28.0	28.9	22.4
1980 (Apr. 1)[3]	110,053	116,493	194,713	26,683	11.8	5,150	167,051	59,495	30.0	30.9	24.9
1983 (July 1)	113,119	120,365	199,849	28,056	12.0	6,379	NA	NA	30.8	31.7	25.9
1984 (July 1)	115,022	121,455	201,290	28,457	12.0	6,730	NA	NA	31.1	32.0	26.3
1985 (July 1, est)	116,160	122,576	202,769	28,870	12.1	7,097	NA	NA	31.4	32.3	26.6
1990 (Apr. 1)	121,239	127,470	199,686	29,986	12.1	9,805	187,053	61,656	32.9	34.4	28.1

(NA) Not available. (1) Excludes Alaska and Hawaii. (2) The revised 1970 resident population count is 203,302,031, which incorporates changes due to errors found after tabulations were completed. The race and sex data shown here reflect the official 1970 census count while the residence data come from the tabulated count. (3) The race data shown for April 1, 1980 have been modified.

UNITED STATES FACTS

Superlative U.S. Statistics

Source: U.S. Geological Survey; U.S. Bureau of the Census; World Almanac Research

Area for 50 states and D. of C.	Total Land 3,539,289 sq. mi.—Water 79,481 sq. mi.	3,618,770 sq. mi.
Largest state	Alaska	591,004 sq. mi.
Smallest state	Rhode Island	1,212 sq. mi.
Largest county (excludes Alaska)	San Bernardino County, California	20,064 sq. mi.
Smallest county	Kalawo, Hawaii	14 sq. mi.
Northernmost city	Barrow, Alaska	71°17'N.
Northernmost point	Point Barrow, Alaska	71°23'N.
Southernmost city	Hilo, Hawaii	19°43'N.
Southernmost settlement	Naalehu, Hawaii	19°03'N.
Southernmost point	Ka Lae (South Cape), Island of Hawaii	18°55'N. (155°41'W.)
Easternmost city	Eastport, Maine	66°59'02"W.
*Easternmost settlement	Amchitka I., Alaska	179°15'E.
*Easternmost point	Semisopochnoi I., Alaska	179°52'E.
Westernmost city	Atka, Alaska	174°20'W.
Westernmost settlement	Adak Station, Alaska	176°39'W.
Westernmost point	Amatignak I., Alaska	179°06'W.
Highest settlement	Climax, Colorado	11,560 ft.
Lowest settlement	Calipatria, California	−185 ft.
Highest point on Atlantic coast	Cadillac Mountain, Mount Desert I., Maine	1,530 ft.
Oldest national park	Yellowstone National Park (1872), Wyoming, Montana, Idaho	3,468 sq. mi.
Largest national park	Wrangell-St. Elias, Alaska	13,018 sq. mi.
Largest national monument	Death Valley, California, Nevada	3,231 sq. mi.
Highest waterfall	Yosemite Falls—Total in three sections	2,425 ft.
	Upper Yosemite Fall	1,430 ft.
	Cascades in middle section	675 ft.
	Lower Yosemite Fall	320 ft.
Longest river	Mississippi-Missouri	3,710 mi.
Highest mountain	Mount McKinley, Alaska	20,320 ft.
Lowest point	Death Valley, California	−282 ft.
Deepest lake	Crater Lake, Oregon	1,932 ft.
Rainiest spot	Mt. Waialeale, Hawaii	Annual aver. rainfall 460 inches
Largest gorge	Grand Canyon, Colorado River, Arizona	277 miles long, 600 ft. to 18 miles wide, 1 mile deep
Deepest gorge	Hell's Canyon, Snake River, Idaho-Oregon	7,900 ft.
Strongest surface wind	Mount Washington, New Hampshire recorded 1934	231 mph
Biggest dam	New Cornelia Tailings, Ten Mile Wash, Arizona	274,026,000 cu. yds. material used
Tallest building	Sears Tower, Chicago, Illinois	1,454 ft.
Largest building	Boeing 747 Manufacturing Plant, Everett, Washington	205,600,000 cu. ft.; covers 47 acres.
Tallest structure	TV tower, Blanchard, North Dakota	2,063 ft.
Longest bridge span	Verrazano-Narrows, New York	4,260 ft.
Highest bridge	Royal Gorge, Colorado	1,053 ft. above water
Deepest well	Gas well, Washita County, Oklahoma	31,441 ft.

The 48 Contiguous States

Area for 48 states	Total Land 2,962,031 sq. mi.—Water 59,264 sq. mi.	3,021,295 sq. mi.
Largest state	Texas	266,807 sq. mi
Northernmost city	Bellingham, Washington	48°46'N.
Northernmost settlement	Angle Inlet, Minnesota	49°21'N.
Northernmost point	Northwest Angle, Minnesota	49°23'N.
Southernmost city	Key West, Florida	24°33'N.
Southernmost mainland city	Florida City, Florida	25°27'N.
Southernmost point	Key West, Florida	24°33'N.
Easternmost settlement	Lubec, Maine	66°58'49"W.
Easternmost point	West Quoddy Head, Maine	66°57'W.
Westernmost town	La Push, Washington	124°38'W.
Westernmost point	Cape Alava, Washington	124°44'W.
Highest mountain	Mount Whitney, California	14,494 ft.

*Alaska's Aleutian Islands extend into the eastern hemisphere and therefore technically contain the easternmost point and settlement in the United States.

Geodetic Datum of North America

In July 1986, the National Oceanic and Atmospheric Administration's National Geodetic Survey (NGS) completed the readjustment and redefinition of the North American Datum. This new datum is known as the North American Datum of 1983. Rapid advances in economic growth and scientific exploration in the United States after World War II resulted in an increasing need for accurate coordinate information. To facilitate the use of satellite surveying and navigation systems, the new datum was redefined using the Geodetic Reference System 1980 as the reference ellipsoid because this model more closely approximates the true size and shape of the Earth. The readjustment of the datum resulted in position changes of as much as 330 feet in the Continental United States and as much as 1/4 mile in Hawaii, the Aleutian Islands, Puerto Rico, and the Virgin Islands.

Statistical Information about the U.S.

In the *Statistical Abstract of the United States* the Bureau of the Census, U.S. Dept. of Commerce, annually publishes a summary of social, political, and economic information. A book of almost 1,000 pages, it presents comprehensive data on population, housing, health, education, employment, income, prices, business, banking, energy, science, defense, trade, government finance, foreign country comparison, and other subjects. Special features include data from the 1990 Census, sections on State Rankings and Metropolitan Statistical Areas and a new section on computer technology in the office. The book is prepared under the direction of Glenn W. King, Chief, Statistical Compendia Staff, Bureau of the Census. Information concerning these and other publications may be obtained from the Supt. of Documents, Government Printing Office, Wash., D.C. 20402, or from the U.S. Bureau of the Census, Data User Services Division, Wash., D.C. 20233.

Highest and Lowest Altitudes in the U.S. and Territories

Source: U.S. Geological Survey (Minus sign means below sea level; elevations are in feet.)

State	Highest Point Name	County	Elev.	Lowest Point Name	County	Elev.
Alabama	Cheaha Mountain	Cleburne	2,405	Gulf of Mexico		Sea level
Alaska	Mount McKinley		20,320	Pacific Ocean		Sea level
Arizona	Humphreys Peak	Coconino	12,633	Colorado R.	Yuma	70
Arkansas	Magazine Mountain	Logan	2,753	Ouachita R.	Ashley-Union	55
California	Mount Whitney	Inyo-Tulare	14,494	Death Valley	Inyo	−282
Colorado	Mount Elbert	Lake	14,433	Arkansas R.	Prowers	3,350
Connecticut	Mount Frissell	Litchfield	2,380	L.I. Sound		Sea level
Delaware	On Ebright Road	New Castle	442	Atlantic Ocean		Sea level
Dist. of Col.	Tenleytown	N. W. part	410	Potomac R.		1
Florida	Sec. 30, T 6N, R 20W.	Walton	345	Atlantic Ocean		Sea level
Georgia	Brasstown Bald	Towns-Union	4,784	Atlantic Ocean		Sea level
Guam	Mount Lamlam	Agat District	1,332	Pacific Ocean		Sea level
Hawaii	Mauna Kea	Hawaii	13,796	Pacific Ocean		Sea level
Idaho	Borah Peak	Custer	12,662	Snake R.	Nez Perce	710
Illinois	Charles Mound	Jo Daviess	1,235	Mississippi R.	Alexander	279
Indiana	Franklin Township	Wayne	1,257	Ohio R.	Posey	320
Iowa	Sec. 29, T 100N, R 41W.	Osceola	1,670	Mississippi R.	Lee	480
Kansas	Mount Sunflower	Wallace	4,039	Verdigris R.	Montgomery	679
Kentucky	Black Mountain	Harlan	4,139	Mississippi R.	Fulton	257
Louisiana	Driskill Mountain	Bienville	535	New Orleans	Orleans	−8
Maine	Mount Katahdin	Piscataquis	5,267	Atlantic Ocean		Sea level
Maryland	Backbone Mountain	Garrett	3,360	Atlantic Ocean		Sea level
Massachusetts	Mount Greylock	Berkshire	3,487	Atlantic Ocean		Sea level
Michigan	Mount Arvon	Baraga	1,979	Lake Erie	Monroe	571
Minnesota	Eagle Mountain	Cook	2,301	Lake Superior		600
Mississippi	Woodall Mountain	Tishomingo	806	Gulf of Mexico		Sea level
Missouri	Taum Sauk Mt.	Iron	1,772	St. Francis R.	Dunklin	230
Montana	Granite Peak	Park	12,799	Kootenai R.	Lincoln	1,800
Nebraska	Johnson Township	Kimball	5,426	Missouri R.	Richardson	840
Nevada	Boundary Peak	Esmeralda	13,140	Mount Manchester	Clark	479
New Hamp.	Mt. Washington	Coos	6,288	Atlantic Ocean	Rockingham	Sea level
New Jersey	High Point	Sussex	1,803	Atlantic Ocean		Sea level
New Mexico	Wheeler Peak	Taos	13,161	Red Bluff Res.	Eddy	2,842
New York	Mount Marcy	Essex	5,344	Atlantic Ocean		Sea level
North Carolina	Mount Mitchell	Yancey	6,684	Atlantic Ocean		Sea level
North Dakota	White Butte	Slope	3,506	Red R.	Pembina	750
Ohio	Campbell Hill	Logan	1,549	Ohio R.	Hamilton	455
Oklahoma	Black Mesa	Cimarron	4,973	Little R.	McCurtain	289
Oregon	Mount Hood	Clackamas-Hood R.	11,239	Pacific Ocean		Sea level
Pennsylvania	Mt. Davis	Somerset	3,213	Delaware R.	Delaware	Sea level
Puerto Rico	Cerro de Punta	Ponce District	4,390	Atlantic Ocean		Sea level
Rhode Island	Jerimoth Hill	Providence	812	Atlantic Ocean		Sea level
Samoa	Lata Mountain	Tau Island	3,160	Pacific Ocean		Sea level
South Carolina	Sassafras Mountain	Pickens	3,560	Atlantic Ocean		Sea level
South Dakota	Harney Peak	Pennington	7,242	Big Stone Lake	Roberts	966
Tennessee	Clingmans Dome	Sevier	6,643	Mississippi R.	Shelby	178
Texas	Guadalupe Peak	Culberson	8,749	Gulf of Mexico		Sea level
Utah	Kings Peak	Duchesne	13,528	Beaverdam Wash.	Washington	2,000
Vermont	Mount Mansfield	Lamoille	4,393	Lake Champlain		95
Virginia	Mount Rogers	Grayson-Smyth	5,729	Atlantic Ocean		Sea level
Virgin Islands	Crown Mountain	St. Thomas Island	1,556	Atlantic Ocean		Sea level
Washington	Mount Rainier	Pierce	14,410	Pacific Ocean		Sea level
West Virginia	Spruce Knob	Pendleton	4,861	Potomac R.	Jefferson	240
Wisconsin	Timms Hill	Price	1,951	Lake Michigan		579
Wyoming	Gannett Peak	Fremont	13,804	B. Fourche R.	Crook	3,099

U.S. Coastline by States

Source: NOAA, U.S. Dept. of Commerce
(statute miles)

State	Coastline[1]	Shoreline[2]	State	Coastline[1]	Shoreline[2]
Atlantic coast	**2,069**	**28,673**	**Gulf coast**	**1,631**	**17,141**
Connecticut	0	618	Alabama	53	607
Delaware	28	381	Florida	770	5,095
Florida	580	3,331	Louisiana	397	7,721
Georgia	100	2,344	Mississippi	44	359
Maine	228	3,478	Texas	367	3,359
Maryland	31	3,190			
Massachusetts	192	1,519	**Pacific coast**	**7,623**	**40,298**
New Hampshire	13	131	Alaska	5,580	31,383
New Jersey	130	1,792	California	840	3,427
New York	127	1,850	Hawaii	750	1,052
North Carolina	301	3,375	Oregon	296	1,410
Pennsylvania	0	89	Washington	157	3,026
Rhode Island	40	384			
South Carolina	187	2,876	**Arctic coast, Alaska**	**1,060**	**2,521**
Virginia	112	3,315	**United States**	**12,383**	**88,633**

(1) Figures are lengths of general outline of seacoast. Measurements were made with a unit measure of 30 minutes of latitude on charts as near the scale of 1:1,200,000 as possible. Coastline of sounds and bays is included to a point where they narrow to width of unit measure, and includes the distance across at such point. (2) Figures obtained in 1939-40 with a recording instrument on the largest-scale charts and maps then available. Shoreline of outer coast, offshore islands, sounds, bays, rivers, and creeks is included to the head of tidewater or to a point where tidal waters narrow to a width of 100 feet.

States: Settled, Capitals, Entry into Union, Area, Rank

The original 13 states—The 13 colonies that seceded from Great Britain and fought the War of Independence (American Revolution) became the 13 original states. They were: Delaware, Pennsylvania, New Jersey, Georgia, Connecticut, Massachusetts, Maryland, South Carolina, New Hampshire, Virginia, New York, North Carolina, and Rhode Island. The order for the original 13 states is the order in which they ratified the Constitution.

State	Settled*	Capital	Entered Union Date	Order	Extent in miles Long (approx.)	Wide (mean)	Area in square miles Land	Inland Water	Total	Rank in area
Ala.	1702	Montgomery	Dec. 14, 1819	22	330	190	50,767	938	51,705	29
Alas.	1784	Juneau	Jan. 3, 1959	49	(a)1,480	810	570,833	20,171	591,004	1
Ariz.	1776	Phoenix	Feb. 14, 1912	48	400	310	113,508	492	114,000	6
Ark.	1686	Little Rock	June 15, 1836	25	260	240	52,078	1,109	53,187	27
Cal.	1769	Sacramento	Sept. 9, 1850	31	770	250	156,299	2,407	158,706	3
Col.	1858	Denver	Aug. 1, 1876	38	380	280	103,595	496	104,091	8
Conn.	1634	Hartford	Jan. 9, 1788	5	110	70	4,872	147	5,018	48
Del.	1638	Dover	Dec. 7, 1787	1	100	30	1,932	112	2,045	49
D.C.		Washington			...	...	63	6	69	51
Fla.	1565	Tallahassee	Mar. 3, 1845	27	500	160	54,153	4,511	58,664	22
Ga.	1733	Atlanta	Jan. 2, 1788	4	300	230	58,056	854	58,910	21
Ha.	1820	Honolulu	Aug. 21, 1959	50	...	...	6,425	46	6,471	47
Ida.	1842	Boise	July 3, 1890	43	570	300	82,412	1,153	83,564	13
Ill.	1720	Springfield	Dec. 3, 1818	21	390	210	55,645	700	56,345	24
Ind.	1733	Indianapolis	Dec. 11, 1816	19	270	140	35,932	253	36,185	38
Ia.	1788	Des Moines	Dec. 28, 1846	29	310	200	55,965	310	56,275	25
Kan.	1727	Topeka	Jan. 29, 1861	34	400	210	81,778	499	82,277	14
Ky.	1774	Frankfort	June 1, 1792	15	380	140	39,669	740	40,410	37
La.	1699	Baton Rouge	Apr. 30, 1812	18	380	130	44,521	3,230	47,752	31
Me.	1624	Augusta	Mar. 15, 1820	23	320	190	30,995	2,270	33,265	39
Md.	1634	Annapolis	Apr. 28, 1788	7	250	90	9,837	623	10,460	42
Mass.	1620	Boston	Feb. 6, 1788	6	190	50	7,824	460	8,284	45
Mich.	1668	Lansing	Jan. 26, 1837	26	490	240	56,954	1,573	58,527	23
Minn.	1805	St. Paul	May 11, 1858	32	400	250	79,548	4,854	84,402	12
Miss.	1699	Jackson	Dec. 10, 1817	20	340	170	47,233	457	47,689	32
Mo.	1735	Jefferson City	Aug. 10, 1821	24	300	240	68,945	752	69,697	19
Mon.	1809	Helena	Nov. 8, 1889	41	630	280	145,388	1,658	147,046	4
Neb.	1823	Lincoln	Mar. 1, 1867	37	430	210	76,644	711	77,355	15
Nev.	1849	Carson City	Oct. 31, 1864	36	490	320	109,894	667	110,561	7
N.H.	1623	Concord	June 21, 1788	9	190	70	8,993	286	9,279	44
N.J.	1660	Trenton	Dec. 18, 1787	3	150	70	7,468	319	7,787	46
N.M.	1610	Santa Fe	Jan. 6, 1912	47	370	343	121,335	258	121,593	5
N.Y.	1614	Albany	July 26, 1788	11	330	283	47,377	1,731	49,108	30
N.C.	1660	Raleigh	Nov. 21, 1789	12	500	150	48,843	3,826	52,669	28
N.D.	1812	Bismarck	Nov. 2, 1889	39	340	211	69,300	1,403	70,702	17
Oh.	1788	Columbus	Mar. 1, 1803	17	220	220	41,004	325	41,330	35
Okla.	1889	Oklahoma City	Nov. 16, 1907	46	400	220	68,655	1,301	69,956	18
Ore.	1811	Salem	Feb. 14, 1859	33	360	261	96,184	889	97,073	10
Pa.	1682	Harrisburg	Dec. 12, 1787	2	283	160	44,888	420	45,308	33
R.I.	1636	Providence	May 29, 1790	13	40	30	1,055	158	1,212	50
S.C.	1670	Columbia	May 23, 1788	8	260	200	30,203	909	31,113	40
S.D.	1859	Pierre	Nov. 2, 1889	40	380	210	75,952	1,164	77,116	16
Tenn.	1769	Nashville	June 1, 1796	16	440	120	41,155	989	42,144	34
Tex.	1682	Austin	Dec. 29, 1845	28	790	660	262,017	4,790	266,807	2
Ut.	1847	Salt Lake City	Jan. 4, 1896	45	350	270	82,073	2,826	84,899	11
Vt.	1724	Montpelier	Mar. 4, 1791	14	160	80	9,273	341	9,614	43
Va.	1607	Richmond	June 25, 1788	10	430	200	39,704	1,063	40,767	36
Wash.	1811	Olympia	Nov. 11, 1889	42	360	240	66,511	1,627	68,139	20
W.Va.	1727	Charleston	June 20, 1863	35	240	130	24,119	112	24,232	41
Wis.	1766	Madison	May 29, 1848	30	310	260	54,426	1,727	56,153	26
Wy.	1834	Cheyenne	July 10, 1890	44	360	280	96,989	820	97,809	9

* First European permanent settlement. (a) Aleutian Islands and Alexander Archipelago are not considered in these lengths.

The Continental Divide

The Continental Divide: watershed, created by mountain ranges or table-lands of the Rocky Mountains, from which the drainage is easterly or westerly; the easterly flowing waters reaching the Atlantic Ocean chiefly through the Gulf of Mexico, and the westerly flowing waters reaching the Pacific Ocean through the Columbia River, or through the Colorado River, which flows into the Gulf of California.

The location and route of the Continental Divide across the United States may briefly be described as follows:

Beginning at point of crossing the United States-Mexican boundary, near long. 108°45′W., the Divide, in a northerly direction, crosses New Mexico along the western edge of the Rio Grande drainage basin, entering Colorado near long. 106°41′W.

Thence by a very irregular route northerly across Colorado along the western summits of the Rio Grande and of the Arkansas, the South Platte, and the North Platte River basins, and across Rocky Mountain National Park, entering Wyoming near long. 106°52′W.

Thence in a northwesterly direction, forming the western rims of the North Platte, Big Horn, and Yellowstone River basins, crossing the southwestern portion of Yellowstone National Park.

Thence in a westerly and then a northerly direction forming the common boundary of Idaho and Montana, to a point on said boundary near long. 114°00′W.

Thence northeasterly and northwesterly through Montana and the Glacier National Park, entering Canada near long. 114°04′W.

Chronological List of Territories

Source: National Archives and Records Service

Name of territory	Date of Organic Act			Organic Act effective	Admission as state			Yrs. terr.
Northwest Territory(a)	July	13,	1787	No fixed date	Mar.	1,	1803(b)	16
Territory southwest of River Ohio	May	26,	1790	No fixed date	June	1,	1796(c)	6
Mississippi	Apr.	7,	1798	When president acted	Dec.	10,	1817	19
Indiana	May	7,	1800	July 4, 1800	Dec.	11,	1816	16
Orleans	Mar.	26,	1804	Oct. 1, 1804	Apr.	30,	1812(d)	7
Michigan	Jan.	11,	1805	June 30, 1805	Jan.	26,	1837	31
Louisiana-Missouri(e)	Mar.	3,	1805	July 4, 1805	Aug.	10,	1821	16
Illinois	Feb.	3,	1809	Mar. 1, 1809	Dec.	3,	1818	9
Alabama	Mar.	3,	1817	When Miss. became a state	Dec.	14,	1819	2
Arkansas	Mar.	2,	1819	July 4, 1819	June	15,	1836	17
Florida	Mar.	30,	1822	No fixed date	Mar.	3,	1845	23
Wisconsin	Apr.	20,	1836	July 3, 1836	May	29,	1848	12
Iowa	June	12,	1838	July 3, 1838	Dec.	28,	1846	7
Oregon	Aug.	14,	1848	Date of act	Feb.	14,	1859	10
Minnesota	Mar.	3,	1849	Date of act	May	11,	1858	9
New Mexico	Sept.	9,	1850	On president's proclamation	Jan.	6,	1912	61
Utah	Sept.	9,	1850	Date of act	Jan.	4,	1896	44
Washington	Mar.	2,	1853	Date of act	Nov.	11,	1889	36
Nebraska	May	30,	1854	Date of act	Mar.	1,	1867	12
Kansas	May	30,	1854	Date of act	Jan.	29,	1861	6
Colorado	Feb.	28,	1861	Date of act	Aug.	1,	1876	15
Nevada	Mar.	2,	1861	Date of act	Oct.	31,	1864	3
Dakota	Mar.	2,	1861	Date of act	Nov.	2,	1889	28
Arizona	Feb.	24,	1863	Date of act	Feb.	14,	1912	49
Idaho	Mar.	3,	1863	Date of act	July	3,	1890	27
Montana	May	26,	1864	Date of act	Nov.	8,	1889	25
Wyoming	July	25,	1868	When officers were qualified	July	10,	1890	22
Alaska(f)	May	17,	1884	No fixed date	Jan.	3,	1959	75
Oklahoma	May	2,	1890	Date of act	Nov.	16,	1907	17
Hawaii	Apr.	30,	1900	June 14, 1900	Aug.	21,	1959	59

(a) Included Ohio, Indiana, Illinois, Michigan, Wisconsin, eastern Minnesota; (b) as the state of Ohio; (c) as the state of Tennessee; (d) as the state of Louisiana; (e) organic act for Missouri Territory of June 4, 1812, became effective Dec. 7, 1812; (f) Although the May 17, 1884 act actually constituted Alaska as a district, it was often referred to as a territory, and unofficially administered as such. The Territory of Alaska was legally and formally organized by an act of Aug. 24, 1912.

Geographic Centers, U.S. and Each State

Source: U.S. Geological Survey

United States, including Alaska and Hawaii — South Dakota; Butte County, W of Castle Rock, Approx. lat. 44°58'N. long. 103°46'W.
Contiguous U. S. (48 states) — Near Lebanon, Smith Co., Kansas, lat. 39°50'N. long. 98°35'W.
North American continent — The geographic center is in Pierce County, North Dakota, 6 miles W of Balta, latitude 48°10', longitude 100°10'W.

State—county, locality

Alabama—Chilton, 12 miles SW of Clanton.
Alaska—lat. 63°50'N. long. 152°W. Approx. 60 mi. NW of Mt. McKinley.
Arizona—Yavapai, 55 miles ESE of Prescott.
Arkansas—Pulaski, 12 miles NW of Little Rock.
California—Madera, 38 miles E of Madera.
Colorado—Park, 30 miles NW of Pikes Peak.
Connecticut—Hartford, at East Berlin.
Delaware—Kent, 11 miles S of Dover.
District of Columbia—Near 4th and L Sts., NW.
Florida—Hernando, 12 miles NNW of Brooksville.
Georgia—Twiggs, 18 miles SE of Macon.
Hawaii—Hawaii, 20°15'N, 156°20'W, off Maui Island.
Idaho—Custer, at Custer, SW of Challis.
Illinois—Logan, 28 miles NE of Springfield.
Indiana—Boone, 14 miles NNW of Indianapolis.
Iowa—Story, 5 miles NE of Ames.
Kansas—Barton, 15 miles NE of Great Bend.
Kentucky—Marion, 3 miles NNW of Lebanon.
Louisiana—Avoyelles, 3 miles SE of Marksville.
Maine—Piscataquis, 18 miles north of Dover.
Maryland—Prince Georges, 4.5 miles NW of Davidsonville.
Massachusetts—Worcester, north part of city.
Michigan—Wexford, 5 miles NNW of Cadillac.
Minnesota—Crow Wing, 10 miles SW of Brainerd.
Mississippi—Leake, 9 miles WNW of Carthage.
Missouri—Miller, 20 miles SW of Jefferson City.
Montana—Fergus, 11 miles west of Lewistown.
Nebraska—Custer, 10 miles NW of Broken Bow.
Nevada—Lander, 26 miles SE of Austin.
New Hampshire—Belknap, 3 miles E of Ashland.
New Jersey—Mercer, 5 miles SE of Trenton.
New Mexico—Torrance, 12 miles SSW of Willard.
New York—Madison, 12 miles S of Oneida and 26 miles SW of Utica.
North Carolina—Chatham, 10 miles NW of Sanford.
North Dakota—Sheridan, 5 miles SW of McClusky.
Ohio—Delaware, 25 miles NNE of Columbus.
Oklahoma—Oklahoma, 8 miles N of Oklahoma City.
Oregon—Crook, 25 miles SSE of Prineville.
Pennsylvania—Centre, 2.5 miles SW of Bellefonte.
Rhode Island—Kent, 1 mile SSW of Crompton.
South Carolina—Richland, 13 miles SE of Columbia.
South Dakota—Hughes, 8 miles NE of Pierre.
Tennessee—Rutherford, 5 mi. NE of Murfreesboro.
Texas—McCulloch, 15 miles NE of Brady.
Utah—Sanpete, 3 miles N of Manti.
Vermont—Washington, 3 miles E of Roxbury.
Virginia—Buckingham, 5 miles SW of Buckingham.
Washington—Chelan, 10 mi. WSW of Wenatchee.
West Virginia—Braxton, 4 miles E of Sutton.
Wisconsin—Wood, 9 miles SE of Marshfield.
Wyoming—Fremont, 58 miles ENE of Lander.

There is no generally accepted definition of geographic center, and no satisfactory method for determining it. The geographic center of an area may be defined as the center of gravity of the surface, or that point on which the surface of the area would balance if it were a plane of uniform thickness.

No marked or monumented point has been established by any government agency as the geographic center of either the 50 states, the contiguous United States, or the North American continent. A monument was erected in Lebanon, Kan., contiguous U.S. center, by a group of citizens. A cairn in Rugby, N.D. marks the center of the North American continent.

International Boundary Lines of the U.S.

The length of the northern boundary of the contiguous U.S. — the U.S.-Canadian border, excluding Alaska — is 3,987 miles according to the U.S. Geological Survey, Dept. of the Interior. The length of the Alaskan-Canadian border is 1,538 miles. The length of the U.S.-Mexican border, from the Gulf of Mexico to the Pacific Ocean, is approximately 1,933 miles (1963 boundary agreement).

Origin of the Names of U.S. States

Source: State officials, the Smithsonian Institution, and the Topographic Division, U.S. Geological Survey.

Alabama—Indian for tribal town, later a tribe (Alabamas or Alibamons) of the Creek confederacy.

Alaska—Russian version of Aleutian (Eskimo) word, alakshak, for "peninsula," "great lands," or "land that is not an island."

Arizona—Spanish version of Pima Indian word for "little spring place," or Aztec arizuma, meaning "silver-bearing."

Arkansas—French variant of Quapaw, a Siouan people meaning "downstream people."

California—Bestowed by the Spanish conquistadors (possibly by Cortez). It was the name of an imaginary island, an earthly paradise, in "Las Serges de Esplandian," a Spanish romance written by Montalvo in 1510. Baja California (Lower California, in Mexico) was first visited by Spanish in 1533. The present U.S. state was called Alta (Upper) California.

Colorado—Spanish, red, first applied to Colorado River.

Connecticut—From Mohican and other Algonquin words meaning "long river place."

Delaware—Named for Lord De La Warr, early governor of Virginia; first applied to river, then to Indian tribe (Lenni-Lenape), and the state.

District of Columbia—For Columbus, 1791.

Florida—Named by Ponce de Leon on Pascua Florida, "Flowery Easter," on Easter Sunday, 1513.

Georgia—For King George II of England by James Oglethorpe, colonial administrator, 1732.

Hawaii—Possibly derived from native word for homeland, Hawaiki or Owhyhee.

Idaho—A coined name with an invented Indian meaning: "gem of the mountains;" originally suggested for the Pike's Peak mining territory (Colorado), then applied to the new mining territory of the Pacific Northwest. Another theory suggests Idaho may be a Kiowa Apache term for the Comanche.

Illinois—French for Illini or land of Illini, Algonquin word meaning men or warriors.

Indiana—Means "land of the Indians."

Iowa—Indian word variously translated as "one who puts to sleep" or "beautiful land."

Kansas—Sioux word for "south wind people."

Kentucky—Indian word variously translated as "dark and bloody ground," "meadow land" and "land of tomorrow."

Louisiana—Part of territory called Louisiana by Sieur de La Salle for French King Louis XIV.

Maine—From Maine, ancient French province. Also: descriptive, referring to the mainland as distinct from the many coastal islands.

Maryland—For Queen Henrietta Maria, wife of Charles I of England.

Massachusetts—From Indian tribe named after "large hill place" identified by Capt. John Smith as being near Milton, Mass.

Michigan—From Chippewa words mici gama meaning "great water," after the lake of the same name.

Minnesota—From Dakota Sioux word meaning "cloudy water" or "sky-tinted water" of the Minnesota River.

Mississippi—Probably Chippewa; mici zibi, "great river" or "gathering-in of all the waters." Also: Algonquin word, "Messipi."

Missouri—An Algonquin Indian term meaning "river of the big canoes."

Montana—Latin or Spanish for "mountainous."

Nebraska—From Omaha or Otos Indian word meaning "broad water" or "flat river," describing the Platte River.

Nevada—Spanish, meaning snow-clad.

New Hampshire—Named 1629 by Capt. John Mason of Plymouth Council for his home county in England.

New Jersey—The Duke of York, 1664, gave a patent to John Berkeley and Sir George Carteret to be called Nova Caesaria, or New Jersey, after England's Isle of Jersey.

New Mexico—Spaniards in Mexico applied term to land north and west of Rio Grande in the 16th century.

New York—For Duke of York and Albany who received patent to New Netherland from his brother Charles II and sent an expedition to capture it, 1664.

North Carolina—In 1619 Charles I gave a large patent to Sir Robert Heath to be called Province of Carolana, from Carolus, Latin name for Charles. A new patent was granted by Charles II to Earl of Clarendon and others. Divided into North and South Carolina, 1710.

North Dakota—Dakota is Sioux for friend or ally.

Ohio—Iroquois word for "fine or good river."

Oklahoma—Choctaw coined word meaning red man, proposed by Rev. Allen Wright, Choctaw-speaking Indian.

Oregon—Origin unknown. One theory holds that the name may have been derived from that of the Wisconsin River shown on a 1715 French map as "Ouaricon-sint."

Pennsylvania—William Penn, the Quaker, who was made full proprietor by King Charles II in 1681, suggested Sylvania, or woodland, for his tract. The king's government owed Penn's father, Admiral William Penn, £16,000, and the land was granted as partial settlement. Charles II added the Penn to Sylvania, against the desires of the modest proprietor, in honor of the admiral.

Puerto Rico—Spanish for Rich Port.

Rhode Island—Exact origin is unknown. One theory notes that Giovanni de Verrazano recorded an island about the size of Rhodes in the Mediterranean in 1524, but others believe the state was named Roode Eylandt by Adriaen Block, Dutch explorer, because of its red clay.

South Carolina—See North Carolina.

South Dakota—See North Dakota.

Tennessee—Tanasi was the name of Cherokee villages on the Little Tennessee River. From 1784 to 1788 this was the State of Franklin, or Frankland.

Texas—Variant of word used by Caddo and other Indians meaning friends or allies, and applied to them by the Spanish in eastern Texas. Also written texias, tejas, teysas.

Utah—From a Navajo word meaning upper, or higher up, as applied to a Shoshone tribe called Ute. Spanish form is Yutta, English Uta or Utah. Proposed name Deseret, "land of honeybees," from Book of Mormon, was rejected by Congress.

Vermont—From French words vert (green) and mont (mountain). The Green Mountains were said to have been named by Samuel de Champlain. When the state was formed, 1777, Dr. Thomas Young suggested combining vert and mont into Vermont.

Virginia—Named by Sir Walter Raleigh, who fitted out the expedition of 1584, in honor of Queen Elizabeth, the Virgin Queen of England.

Washington—Named after George Washington. When the bill creating the Territory of Columbia was introduced in the 32d Congress, the name was changed to Washington because of the existence of the District of Columbia.

West Virginia—So named when western counties of Virginia refused to secede from the United States, 1863.

Wisconsin—An Indian name, spelled Ouisconsin and Mesconsing by early chroniclers. Believed to mean "grassy place" in Chippewa. Congress made it Wisconsin.

Wyoming—The word was taken from Wyoming Valley, Pa., which was the site of an Indian massacre and became widely known by Campbell's poem, "Gertrude of Wyoming." In Algonquin it means "large prairie place."

Territorial Sea of the U.S.

According to a December 27, 1988 proclamation by Pres. Ronald Reagan: "The territorial sea of the United States henceforth extends to 12 nautical miles from the baselines of the United States determined in accordance with international law. In accordance with international law, as reflected in the applicable provisions of the 1982 United Nations Convention on the Law of the Sea, within the territorial sea of the United States, the ships of all countries enjoy the right of innocent passage and the ships and aircraft of all countries enjoy the right of transit passage through international straits."

Accession of Territory by the U.S.

Source: Bureau of the Census, U.S. Dept. of Commerce

	Acquisition date	Total Area Sq. mi.		Acquisition date	Total Area Sq. mi.		Acquisition date	Total Area Sq. mi.
Total U.S.	(x)	**3,623,434**	Gadsden Purchase	1853	29,640	Virgin Islands of the U.S.	1917	151
United States	(x)	3,618,770	Alaska	1867	591,004	Pacific Islands, Trust Territory of the (Palau)[5]	1947	217
Territory in 1790[1]	(x)	891,364	Hawaii	1898	6,471	No. Mariana Islands[5]	1947	181
Louisiana Purchase	1803	831,321	Other areas:			All other[6]	(x)	14
Purchase of Florida	1819	69,866	Puerto Rico	[2]1898	3,492			
Texas	1845	384,958	Guam	[3]1898	217			
Oregon	1846	283,439	American Samoa	[4]1899	84			
Mexican Cession	1848	530,706						

(x) Not applicable. (1) Includes that part of drainage basin of Red River of the North, south of 49th parallel, sometimes considered part of Louisiana Purchase. (2) Ceded by Spain in 1898, ratified in 1899, and became Commonwealth of Puerto Rico by Act of Congress on July 25, 1952. (3) Acquired 1898; ratified 1899. (4) Acquired 1899; ratified 1900. (5) The Trust Territory formerly included the Marshall Islands and Micronesia, both officially recognized as independent nations in 1991, and the Northern Mariana Islands, which became a U.S. commonwealth in 1986. (6) Comprises the following islands with gross areas as indicated, in sq. mi.: Midway (2), Wake (3), Palmyra (4), Navassa (2), Baker, Howland, and Jarvis (combined area, 3), Johnston Atoll (combined area, less than .5), and Kingman Reef (less than .5). Excludes Canton and Enderbury Islands (combined area 27 sq. mi.), which are considered to be under the jurisdiction of Kiribati since 1979, and Swan Islands (1 sq. mi.), which were returned to Honduras in 1972.

Public Lands of the U. S.

Source: Bureau of Land Management, U.S. Dept. of the Interior

Disposition of Public Lands 1781 to 1992

Disposition by methods not elsewhere classified[1]	Acres
Disposition by methods not elsewhere classified[1]	303,500,000
Granted or sold to homesteaders	287,500,000
Granted to railroad corporations	94,400,000
Granted to veterans as military bounties	61,000,000
Confirmed as private land claims[2]	34,000,000
Sold under timber and stone law[3]	13,900,000
Granted or sold under timber culture law[4]	10,900,000
Sold under desert land law[5]	10,700,000

Granted to states for:	Acres
Support of common schools	77,630,000
Reclamation of swampland	64,920,000
Construction of railroads	37,130,000
Support of misc. institutions[6]	21,700,000
Purposes not elsewhere classified[7]	117,600,000
Canals and rivers	6,100,000
Construction of wagon roads	3,400,000
Total granted to states	**328,480,000**

(1) Chiefly public, private, and preemption sales, but includes mineral entries, scrip locations, sales of townsites and townlots. (2) The Government has confirmed title to lands claimed under valid grants made by foreign governments prior to the acquisition of the public domain by the United States. (3) The law provided for the sale of lands valuable for timber or stone and unfit for cultivation. (4) The law provided for the granting of public lands to settlers on condition that they plant and cultivate trees on the lands granted. (5) The law provided for the sale of arid agricultural public lands to settlers who irrigate them and bring them under cultivation. (6) Universities, hospitals, asylums, etc. (7) For construction of various public improvements (individual items not specified in the granting act) reclamation of desert lands, construction of water reservoirs, etc.

Public Lands Administered by Federal Agencies

Agency (Acres, Sept. 30, 1992)	Public domain	Acquired	Total
Forest Service	161,038,854.3	28,341,223.5	189,380,077.8
Bureau of Land Management	269,710,529	2,318,889	272,029,418
Bureau of Reclamation	3,533,817.5	1,969,275.9	5,503,093.4
Fish and Wildlife Service	81,321,344	10,097,347	91,318,691
National Park Service	64,325,741.0	8,517,114.8	72,842,855.8
Bureau of Indian Affairs	2,554,358.7	193,079.6	2,747,438.3
Tennessee Valley Authority	0	1,040,231.3	1,040,231.3
Corps of Engineers	604,971.2	4,869,200.0	5,474,171.2
U.S. Army	3,187,901.0	6,495,173.0	9,683,074.0
U.S. Navy	618,005.6	1,743,750.2	2,361,755.8
U.S. Air Force	6,858,510.0	1,255,022.0	8,113,532.0
Department of Energy	1,465,862.4	700,478.8	2,166,341.2
Total, all agencies (incl. those not shown)	**660,976,655.8**	**63,089,515.1**	**724,066,170.9**

National Recreation Areas Administered by Forest Service

			Acreage
Allegheny	Pa.	1984	23,063
Arapaho	Col.	1978	34,928
Flaming Gorge	Ut.-Wyo.	1968	201,114
Grand Island	Mich.	1990	12,957
Hells Canyon	Ida.-Ore.	1975	541,336
Mount Baker	Wash.	1984	8,473
Mount Rogers	Va.	1966	154,816
Oregon Dunes	Ore.	1972	31,566
Pine Ridge	Neb.	1986	6,600
Rattlesnake	Mon.	1980	61,000
Sawtooth	Ida.	1972	756,019
Smith River	Cal.	1990	331,229
Spruce Knob-Seneca Rocks	W. Va.	1965	100,000
Whiskeytown Shasta-Trinity	Cal.	1965	203,587
White Rocks	Vt.	1984	36,400
Winding Stair Mtn.	Okl.	1988	26,445

National Parks, Other Areas Administered by National Park Service

Figures given are date area initially protected by Congress or presidential proclamation, date given current designation, and gross area in acres 12/31/92.

National Parks

Acadia, Me. (1916/1929) 41,888. Includes Mount Desert Island, half of Isle au Haut, Schoodic Point on mainland. Highest elevation on Eastern seaboard.

Arches, Ut. (1929/1971) 73,379. Contains giant red sandstone arches and other products of erosion.

Badlands, S.D. (1929/1978) 242,756; eroded prairie, bison, bighorn and antelope. Contains animal fossils of 40 million years ago.

Big Bend, Tex. (1935/1944) 801,163. Rio Grande, Chisos Mts.

Biscayne, Fla. (1968/1980) 173,467. Aquatic park encompasses chain of islands south of Miami.

Bryce Canyon, Ut. (1923/1928) 35,835. Spectacularly colorful and unusual display of erosion effects.

Canyonlands, Ut. (1964) 337,570. At junction of Colorado and Green rivers, extensive evidence of prehistoric Indians.

Capitol Reef, Ut. (1937/1971) 241,904. A 60-mile uplift of sandstone cliffs dissected by high-walled gorges.

Carlsbad Caverns, N.M. (1923/1930) 46,775. Largest known caverns; not yet fully explored.

Channel Islands, Cal. (1938/1980) 249,354. Sea lion breeding place, nesting sea birds, unique plants.

Crater Lake, Ore. (1902) 183,224. Extraordinary blue lake in crater of extinct volcano encircled by lava walls 500 to 2,000 feet high.

Denali, Alas. (1917/1980) 4,716,726. Name changed from Mt. McKinley NP. Contains highest mountain in U.S.; wildlife.

Dry Tortugas, Fla. (1935/1992) 64,700. Formerly Ft. Jefferson National Monument.

Everglades, Fla. (1934) 1,506,499. Largest remaining subtropical wilderness in continental U.S.

Gates of the Arctic, Alas. (1978/1980) 7,523,888. Vast wilderness in north central region.

Glacier, Mon. (1910) 1,013,572. Superb Rocky Mt. scenery, numerous glaciers and glacial lakes. Part of Waterton-Glacier Intl. Peace Park established by U.S. and Canada in 1932.

Glacier Bay, Alas. (1925/1980) 3,225,284. Great tidewater glaciers that move down mountain sides and break up into the sea; much wildlife.

Grand Canyon, Ariz. (1908/1919) 1,218,375. Most spectacular part of Colorado River's greatest canyon.

Grand Teton, Wy. (1929) 309,994. Most impressive part of the Teton Mountains, winter feeding ground of largest American elk herd.

Great Basin, Nev. (1922/1986) 77,100. Wide basins and high mountain ranges.

Great Smoky Mountains, N.C.-Tenn. (1926/1934) 520,269. Largest eastern mountain range, magnificent forests.

Guadalupe Mountains, Tex. (1966/1972) 86,416. Extensive Permian limestone fossil reef; tremendous earth fault.

Haleakala, Ha. (1916/1960) 28,655. Dormant volcano on Maui with large colorful craters.

Hawaii Volcanoes, Ha. (1916/1961) 229,177. Contains Kilauea and Mauna Loa, active volcanoes.

Hopewell Culture, Oh. (1923/1992) 270. Formerly Mound City Group National Monument.

Hot Springs, Ark. (1832/1921) 5,839. Government supervised bath houses use waters of 45 of the 47 natural hot springs.

Isle Royale, Mich. (1931) 571,790. Largest island in Lake Superior, noted for its wilderness area and wildlife.

Katmai, Alas. (1918/1980) 3,716,000. Valley of Ten Thousand Smokes, scene of 1912 volcanic eruption.

Kenai Fjords, Alas. (1978/1980) 669,541. Abundant mountain goats, marine mammals, birdlife; the Harding Icefield, one of the major icecaps in U.S.

Kings Canyon, Cal. (1890/1940) 461,901. Mountain wilderness, dominated by Kings River Canyons and High Sierra; contains giant sequoias.

Kobuk Valley, Alas. (1978/1980) 1,750,421. Broad river is core of native culture.

Lake Clark, Alas. (1978/1980) 2,636,839. Across Cook Inlet from Anchorage. A scenic wilderness rich in fish and wildlife.

Lassen Volcanic, Cal. (1907/1916) 106,372. Contains Lassen Peak, recently active volcano, and other volcanic phenomena.

Mammoth Cave, Ky. (1926/1941) 52,419. 144 miles of surveyed underground passages, beautiful natural formations, river 300 feet below surface.

Mesa Verde, Col. (1906) 52,122. Most notable and best preserved prehistoric cliff dwellings in the United States.

Mount Rainier, Wash. (1899) 235,612. Greatest single-peak glacial system in the lower 48 states.

North Cascades, Wash. (1968) 504,781. Spectacular mountainous region with many glaciers, lakes.

Olympic, Wash. (1909/1938) 922,654. Mountain wilderness containing finest remnant of Pacific Northwest rain forest, active glaciers, Pacific shoreline, rare elk.

Petrified Forest, Ariz. (1906/1962) 93,533. Extensive petrified wood and Indian artifacts. Contains part of Painted Desert.

Redwood, Cal. (1968) 110,132. Forty miles of Pacific coastline, groves of ancient redwoods and world's tallest trees.

Rocky Mountain, Col. (1915) 265,198. On the continental divide, includes 107 named peaks over 11,000 feet.

Samoa, American Samoa (1988) 9,000. Features the only paleotropical rain forest.

Sequoia, Cal. (1890) 402,482. Groves of giant sequoias, highest mountain in contiguous United States — Mount Whitney (14,494 feet). World's largest tree.

Shenandoah, Va. (1926/1935) 195,039. Portion of the Blue Ridge Mountains; overlooks Shenandoah Valley; Skyline Drive.

Theodore Roosevelt, N.D. (1947/1978) 70,447. Contains part of T.R.'s ranch and scenic badlands.

Virgin Islands, V.I. (1956) 14,689. Covers 75% of St. John Island, lush growth, lovely beaches, Indian relics, evidence of colonial Danes.

Voyageurs, Minn. (1971/1975) 218,035. Abundant lakes, forests, wildlife, canoeing, boating.

Wind Cave, S.D. (1903) 28,295. Limestone caverns in Black Hills. Extensive wildlife includes a herd of bison.

Wrangell-St. Elias, Alas. (1978/1980) 8,331,604. Largest area in park system, most peaks over 16,000 feet, abundant wildlife; day's drive east of Anchorage.

Yellowstone, Ida., Mon., Wy., (1872) 2,219,791. Oldest national park. World's greatest geyser area has about 3,000 geysers and hot springs; spectacular falls and impressive canyons of the Yellowstone River; grizzly bear, moose, and bison.

Yosemite, Cal. (1890) 761,170. Yosemite Valley, the nation's highest waterfall, 3 groves of sequoias, and mountainous.

Zion, Ut. (1909/1919) 146,598. Unusual shapes and landscapes have resulted from erosion and faulting; Zion Canyon, with sheer walls ranging up to 2,500 feet, is readily accessible.

National Historical Parks

Appomattox Court House, Va. (1930/1954) 1,325. Where Lee surrendered to Grant.

Boston, Mass. (1974) 41. Includes Faneuil Hall, Old North Church, Bunker Hill, Paul Revere House.

Chaco Culture, N.M. (1907/1980) 33,974. Ruins of pueblos built by prehistoric Indians.

Chesapeake and Ohio Canal, Md.-W.Va.-D.C. (1961/1971) 20,781. 184 mile historic canal; D.C. to Cumberland, Md.

Colonial, Va. (1930/1936) 9,327. Includes most of Jamestown Island, site of first successful English colony; Yorktown, site of Cornwallis' surrender to George Washington; and the Colonial Parkway.

Cumberland Gap, Ky.-Tenn.-Va. (1940) 20,274. Mountain pass of the Wilderness Road which carried the first great migration of pioneers into America's interior.

George Rogers Clark, Vincennes, Ind. (1966) 26. Commemorates American defeat of British in west during Revolution.

Dayton Aviation, Oh. (1992). Commemorates the area's aviation heritage.

Harpers Ferry, Md., W. Va. (1944/1963) 2,239. At the confluence of the Shenandoah and Potomac rivers, the site of John Brown's 1859 raid on the Army arsenal.

Independence, Pa. (1948/1956) 45. Contains several properties in Philadelphia associated with the Revolutionary War and the founding of the U.S. Includes Independence Hall.

Jean Laffite (and preserve), La. (1939/1978) 20,020. Includes Chalmette, site of 1815 Battle of New Orleans; French Quarter.

Kalaupapa, Ha. (1980) 10,779. Molokai's former leper colony site and other historic areas.

Kaloko-Honokohau, Ha. (1978) 1,161. Culture center has 234 historic features and grave of first king, Kamehameha.

Keweenaw, Mich. (1992). Site of first significant Copper Mine in U.S.

Klondike Gold Rush, Alas.-Wash. (1976) 13,191. Alaskan Trails in 1898 Gold Rush. Museum in Seattle.

Lowell, Mass. (1978) 137. Seven mills, canal, 19th C. structures, park to show planned city of Industrial Revolution.

Lyndon B. Johnson, Tex. (1969/1980) 1,571. President's birthplace, boyhood home, ranch.

Marsh-Billings, Vt. (1992) 550. Boyhood home of George Perkins March.

Minute Man, Mass. (1959) 750. Where the colonial Minute Men battled the British, April 19, 1775. Also contains Nathaniel Hawthorne's home.

Morristown, N.J. (1933) 1,671. Sites of important military encampments during the Revolutionary War; Washington's headquarters 1777, 1779-80.

Natchez, Miss. (1988) 80. Mansions, townhouses, and villas concerning history of Natchez, Miss.

Nez Perce, Ida. (1965) 2,109. Illustrates the history and culture of the Nez Perce Indian country. 20 separate sites.

Pecos, N.M. (1965/1990) 6,547. Ruins of ancient 15th century Pueblo of Pecos, archeological sites, and 2 associated Spanish colonial missions from the 17th and 18th centuries.

Pu'uhonua o Honaunau, Ha. (1955/1978) 182. Until 1819, a sanctuary for Hawaiians vanquished in battle, and those guilty of crimes or breaking taboos.

Salt River Bay, St. Croix, V.I. (1922). The only site known where, 500 years ago, members of a Columbus party landed on what is now territory of the U.S.

San Antonio Missions, Tex. (1978/1983) 493. Four of finest Spanish missions in U.S., 18th C. irrigation system.

San Francisco Maritime (1988) 50. Artifacts, photographs, and historic vessels related to the development of the Pacific Coast.

San Juan Island, Wash. (1966) 1,752. Commemorates peaceful relations of the U.S., Canada and Great Britain since the 1872 boundary disputes.

Saratoga, N.Y. (1938) 3,393. Scene of a major battle which became a turning point in the War of Independence.

Sitka, Alas. (1910/1972) 107. Scene of last major resistance of the Tlingit Indians to the Russians, 1804.

Tumacacori, Ariz. (1908/1990) 17. Historic Spanish Catholic mission building stands near the site first visited by Jesuit Father Kino in 1691.

Valley Forge, Pa. (1976) 3,468. Continental Army campsite in 1777-78 winter.

War in the Pacific, Guam (1978) 1,960. Scenic park memorial for WWII combatants in Pacific.

Women's Rights, N.Y. (1980) 6. Seneca Falls site where Susan B. Anthony, Elizabeth Cady Stanton began rights movement in 1848.

Zuni-Cibola, N. Mex. (1988) 800. Historical, archeological, and cultural site associated with the Zuni Tribe over its 1700-year cultural continuum.

National Battlefields

Antietam, Md. (1890/1978) 3,244. Battle ended first Confederate invasion of North, Sept. 17, 1862.

Big Hole, Mon. (1910/1963) 656. Site of major battle with Nez Perce Indians.

Cowpens, S.C. (1929/1972) 842. Revolutionary War battlefield.

Fort Donelson, Tenn. (1928/1985) 536. Site of first major Union victory.

Fort Necessity, Pa. (1931/1961) 903. First battle of French and Indian War.

Monocacy, Md. (1934/1976) 1,647. Civil War battle in defense of Wash., D.C., July 9, 1864.

Moores Creek, N.C. (1926/1980) 87. 1776 battle between Patriots and Loyalists commemorated here.

Petersburg, Va. (1926/1962) 2,735. Scene of 10-month Union campaign 1864-65.

Stones River, Tenn. (1927/1960) 403. Civil War battle leading to Sherman's "March to the Sea."

Tupelo, Miss. (1929/1961) 1. Crucial battle over Sherman's supply line.

Wilson's Creek, Mo. (1960/1970) 1,750. Civil War battle for control of Missouri.

National Battlefield Parks

Kennesaw Mountain, Ga. (1917/1935) 2,885. Two major battles of Atlanta campaign in Civil War.

Manassas, Va. (1940) 5,072. Two battles of Bull Run in Civil War, 1861 and 1862.

Richmond, Va. (1936) 769. Site of battles defending Confederate capital.

National Battlefield Site

Brices Cross Roads, Miss. (1929) 1. Civil War battlefield.

National Military Parks

Chickamauga and Chattanooga, Ga.-Tenn. (1890) 8,106. Four Civil War battlefields.

Fredericksburg and Spotsylvania County, Va. (1927) 7,688. Sites of several major Civil War battles and campaigns.

Gettysburg, Pa. (1895) 3,942. Site of decisive Confederate defeat in North. Gettysburg Address.

Guilford Courthouse, N.C. (1917) 220. Revolutionary War battle site.

Horseshoe Bend, Ala. (1956) 2,040. On Tallapoosa River, where Gen. Andrew Jackson broke the power of the Creek Indian Confederacy.

Kings Mountain, S.C. (1931) 3,945. Revolutionary War battle.

Pea Ridge, Ark. (1956) 4,300. Civil War battle.

Shiloh, Tenn. (1894) 3,838. Major Civil War battle; site includes some well-preserved Indian burial mounds.

Vicksburg, Miss. (1899) 1,620. Union victory gave North control of the Mississippi and split the Confederacy in two.

National Memorials

Arkansas Post, Ark. (1960) 389. First permanent French settlement in the lower Mississippi River valley.

Arlington House, the Robert E. Lee Memorial, Va. (1925/1972) 28. Lee's home overlooking the Potomac.

Chamizal, El Paso, Tex. (1966/1974) 55. Commemorates 1963 settlement of 99-year border dispute with Mexico.

Coronado, Ariz. (1941/1952) 4,750. Commemorates first European exploration of the Southwest.

DeSoto, Fla. (1948) 27. Commemorates 16th-century Spanish explorations.

Federal Hall, N.Y. (1939/1955) 0.45. First seat of U.S. government under the Constitution.

Fort Caroline, Fla. (1950) 138. On St. Johns River, overlooks site of second attempt by French Huguenots to colonize North America.

Fort Clatsop, Ore. (1958) 125. Lewis and Clark encampment 1805-06.

General Grant, N.Y. (1958) 0.76. Tombs of Pres. and wife.

Hamilton Grange, N.Y. (1962) 0.11. Home of Alexander Hamilton.

John F. Kennedy Center for the Performing Arts, D.C. (1958/1964) 18.

Johnstown Flood, Pa. (1964) 164. Commemorates tragic flood of 1889.

Lincoln Boyhood, Ind. (1962) 200. Lincoln grew up here.

Lincoln Memorial, D.C. (1911) 110.

Lyndon B. Johnson Grove on the Potomac, D.C. (1973) 17.

Mount Rushmore, S.D. (1925) 1,278. World famous sculpture of 4 presidents.

Perry's Victory and International Peace Memorial, Put-in-Bay, Oh. (1936/1978) 25. The world's most massive Doric column, constructed 1912-15, to inculcate the lessons of international peace by arbitration and disarmament.

Roger Williams, R.I. (1965) 5. Memorial to founder of Rhode Island.

Thaddeus Kosciuszko, Pa. (1972) 0.02. Memorial to Polish hero of American Revolution.

Theodore Roosevelt Island, D.C. (1932) 89.

Thomas Jefferson Memorial, D.C. (1934) 18.

USS Arizona, Ha. (1980). 00. Memorializes American losses at Pearl Harbor.

Vietnam Veterans, D.C. (1980) 2. Black granite wall inscribed with names of killed in action and missing in the Vietnam War.

Washington Monument, D.C. (1848) 106.

Wright Brothers, N.C. (1927/1953) 431. Site of first powered flight.

National Historic Sites

Abraham Lincoln Birthplace, Hodgenville, Ky. (1916/1959) 117.

Adams, Quincy, Mass. (1946/1952) 10. Home of Presidents John Adams, John Quincy Adams, and celebrated descendants.

Allegheny Portage Railroad, Pa. (1964) 1,247. Part of the Pennsylvania Canal system.

Andersonville, Andersonville, Ga. (1970) 495. Noted Civil War prison.

Andrew Johnson, Greeneville, Tenn. (1935/1963) 17. Home of the President.

Bent's Old Fort, Col. (1960) 800. Old West fur-trading post.

Boston African American (1980) Pre-Civil War black history structures.

Brown v. Board of Education, Kan. (1992). Commemorates the landmark 1954 U.S. Supreme Court Decision.

Carl Sandburg Home, N.C. (1968/1972) 264. Poet's home.

Charles Pinckney, S.C. (1988) 25.

Christiansted, St. Croix; V.I. (1952/1961) 27. Commemorates Danish colony.

Clara Barton, Md. (1974) 9. Home of founder of American Red Cross.

Edgar Allan Poe, Pa. (1978/1980) 1. Poet's home.

Edison, West Orange, N.J. (1955/1962) 21. Home and laboratory.

Eisenhower, Gettysburg, Pa. (1967/1969) 690. Home of 34th president.

Eleanor Roosevelt, Hyde Park, N.Y. (1977) 181. Personal retreat.

Eugene O'Neill, Danville, Cal. (1976) 13. Playwright's home.

Ford's Theatre, Washington, D.C. (1866/1970) 0.29. Includes theater, now restored, where Lincoln was assassinated, house where he died, and Lincoln Museum.

Fort Bowie, Ariz. (1964/1972) 1,000. Focal point of operations against Geronimo and the Apaches.

Fort Davis, Tex. (1961/1963) 460. Frontier outpost battled Comanches and Apaches.

Fort Laramie, Wy. (1938/1960) 833. Military post on Oregon Trail.

Fort Larned, Kan. (1964/1966) 718. Military post on Santa Fe Trail.

Fort Point, San Francisco, Cal. (1970) 29. Largest West Coast fortification.

Fort Raleigh, N.C. (1941) 157. First English settlement.

Fort Scott, Kan. (1965/1978) 17. Commemorates U.S. frontier of 1840-50.

Fort Smith, Ark. (1961) 75. Active post from 1817 to 1890.

Fort Union Trading Post, Mon., N.D. (1966) 442. Principal fur-trading post on upper Missouri, 1829-1867.

Fort Vancouver, Wash. (1948/1961) 209. Hdqts. for Hudson's Bay Company in 1825. Early military and political seat.

Frederick Douglass Home, D.C. (1962/1988) 9. Home of nation's leading black spokesman.

Frederick Law Olmsted, Mass. (1979) 2. Home of famous park planner (1822-1903).

Friendship Hill, Pa. (1978) 675. Home of Albert Gallatin, Jefferson's Sec'y of Treasury. Not open to public.

Golden Spike, Utah (1957) 2,735. Commemorates completion of first transcontinental railroad in 1869.

Grant-Kohrs Ranch, Mon. (1972) 1,498. Ranch house and part of 19th-century ranch.

Hampton, Md. (1948) 62. 18th-century Georgian mansion.

Harry S. Truman, Mo. (1983). 0.78. Home of Pres. Truman after 1919.

Herbert Hoover, West Branch, Ia. (1965) 187. Birthplace and boyhood home of 31st president.

Home of Franklin D. Roosevelt, Hyde Park, N.Y. (1944) 290. Birthplace, home and "Summer White House".

Hopewell Furnace, Pa. (1938/1985) 848. 19th-century iron making village.

Hubbell Trading Post, Ariz. (1965) 160. Indian trading post.

James A. Garfield, Mentor, Oh. (1980) 8. President's home.

Jefferson National Expansion Memorial, St. Louis, Mo. (1935/1969) 191. Commemorates westward expansion.

Jimmy Carter, Ga. (1987) 70. Birthplace and home of 39th president.

John Fitzgerald Kennedy, Brookline, Mass. (1967) 0.09. Birthplace and childhood home of the President.

John Muir, Martinez, Cal. (1964) 340. Home of early conservationist and writer.

Knife River Indian Villages, N.D. (1974) 1,293. Remnants of 5 Hidatsa villages.

Lincoln Home, Springfield, Ill. (1971) 12. Lincoln's residence when he was elected President, 1860.

Longfellow, Cambridge, Mass. (1972) 2. Longfellow's home, 1837-82, and Washington's hq. during Boston Siege, 1775-76.

Maggie L. Walker, Va. (1978) 1. Richmond home of black leader and 1903 founder of bank.

Manzanar, Lone Pine, Cal. (1992) 640. Commemorates Manzanar War Relocation Ctr., a Japanese-American internment camp during WWII.

Martin Luther King, Jr., Atlanta, Ga. (1980) 23. Birthplace, grave.

Martin Van Buren, N.Y. (1974) 40. Lindenwald, home of 8th president, near Kinderhook.

Mary McLeod Bethune Council House, D.C. (1991). Museum dedicated to the lives and achievements of black American women.

Ninety Six, S.C. (1976) 989. Colonial trading village.

Palo Alto Battlefield, Tex. (1978) 50. One of 2 Mexican War battles fought in U.S.

Pennsylvania Avenue, D.C. (1965) NA. Includes area between Capitol and White House, Ford's Theatre.

Puukohola Heiau, Ha. (1972) 80. Ruins of temple built by King Kamehameha.

Sagamore Hill, Oyster Bay, N.Y. (1962) 83. Home of President Theodore Roosevelt from 1885 until his death in 1919.

Saint-Gaudens, Cornish, N.H. (1964/1977) 148. Home, studio and gardens of American sculptor Augustus Saint-Gaudens.

Saint Paul's Church, N.Y. (1943/1978) 6. 18th-century site of John Peter Zenger's "freedom of press" trial.

Salem Maritime, Mass. (1938) 9. Only port never seized from the patriots by the British. Major fishing and whaling port.

San Juan, P.R. (1949) 75. 16th-century Spanish fortifications.

Saugus Iron Works, Mass. (1968) 9. Reconstructed 17th-century colonial ironworks.

Springfield Armory, Mass. (1974) 55. Small arms manufacturing center for nearly 200 years.

Steamtown, Pa. (1986) 44. Railyard, roadhouse and repair shops of former Delaware, Lackawanna and Western Railroad.

Theodore Roosevelt Birthplace, N.Y., N.Y. (1962) 0.11.

Theodore Roosevelt Inaugural, Buffalo, N.Y. (1966) 1. Wilcox House where he took oath of office, 1901.

Thomas Stone, Md. (1978) 328. Home of signer of Declaration, built in 1771. Not open to public.

Tuskegee Institute, Ala. (1974) 68. College founded by Booker T. Washington in 1881 for blacks.

Ulysses S. Grant, St. Louis Co., Mo. (1989) 10. Home of Grant during pre-Civil War years.

Vanderbilt Mansion, Hyde Park, N.Y. (1940) 212. Mansion of 19th-century financier.

Weir Farm, Wilton, Conn. (1990) 62. Home and studios of American Impressionist painter J. Alden Weir.

Whitman Mission, Wash. (1936/1963) 98. Site where Dr. and Mrs. Marcus Whitman ministered to the Indians until slain by them in 1847.

William Howard Taft, Cincinnati, Oh. (1969) 3. Birthplace and early home of the 27th president.

National Monuments

Name	State	Year	Acreage
Agate Fossil Beds	Neb.	1965	3,055
Alibates Flint Quarries	N.M.-Tex.	1965	1,371
Aniakchak	Alas.	1978	17
Aztec Ruins	N.M.	1923	319
Bandelier	N.M.	1916	32,737
Black Canyon of the Gunnison	Col.	1933	20,766
Booker T. Washington	Va.	1956	224
Buck Island Reef	V.I.	1961	880
Cabrillo	Cal.	1913	137
Canyon de Chelly	Ariz.	1931	83,840
Cape Krusenstern	Alas.	1978	659,807
Capulin Volcano	N.M.	1916	793
Casa Grande Ruins	Ariz.	1892	473
Castillo de San Marcos	Fla.	1924	20
Castle Clinton	N.Y.	1946	1
Cedar Breaks	Ut.	1933	6,155
Chiricahua	Ariz.	1924	11,985
Colorado	Col.	1911	20,454
Congaree Swamp	S.C.	1976	22,200
Craters of the Moon	Ida.	1924	53,545
Death Valley	Cal.-Nev.	1933	2,067,628
Devils Postpile	Cal.	1911	798
Devils Tower	Wy.	1906	1,347
Dinosaur	Col.-Ut.	1915	210,844
Effigy Mounds	Ia.	1949	1,481
El Malpais	N.M.	1987	114,335
El Morro	N.M.	1906	1,279
Florissant Fossil Beds**	Col.	1969	5,998
Fort Frederica	Ga.	1936	216
Fort Matanzas	Fla.	1924	228
Fort McHenry National Monument and Historic Shrine	Md.	1925	43
Fort Pulaski	Ga.	1924	5,623
Fort Stanwix	N.Y.	1935	16
Fort Sumter	S.C.	1948	194
Fort Union	N.M.	1954	721
Fossil Butte	Wy.	1972	8,198
G. Washington Birthplace	Va.	1930	533
George Washington Carver	Mo.	1943	210
Gila Cliff Dwellings	N.M.	1907	533
Grand Portage	Minn.	1951	710
Great Sand Dunes	Col.	1932	38,662
Hagerman Fossil Beds	Ida.	1988	4,280
Hohokam Pima*	Ariz.	1972	1,690
Homestead Nat'l. Monument of America	Neb.	1936	195
Hovenweep	Col.-Ut.	1923	785
Jewel Cave	S.D.	1908	1,274
John Day Fossil Beds	Ore.	1974	14,014
Joshua Tree	Cal.	1936	559,955
Lava Beds	Cal.	1925	46,560
Little Big Horn Battlefield	Mon.	1879	765
Montezuma Castle	Ariz.	1906	858
Muir Woods	Cal.	1908	554
Natural Bridges	Ut.	1908	7,636
Navajo	Ariz.	1909	360
Ocmulgee	Ga.	1934	683
Oregon Caves	Ore.	1909	488
Organ Pipe Cactus	Ariz.	1937	330,689
Petroglyph	N.M.	1990	5,207
Pinnacles	Cal.	1908	16,265
Pipe Spring	Ariz.	1923	40

Name	State	Year	Acreage
Pipestone	Minn.	1937	282
Poverty Point	La.	1988	911
Rainbow Bridge	Ut.	1910	160
Russell Cave	Ala.	1961	310
Saguaro	Ariz.	1933	83,574
Salinas	N.M.	1909	1,077
Scotts Bluff	Neb.	1919	2,997
Statue of Liberty	N.J.-N.Y.	1924	58
Sunset Crater	Ariz.	1930	3,040
Timpanogos Cave	Ut.	1922	250
Tonto	Ariz.	1907	1,120
Tuzigoot	Ariz.	1939	801
Walnut Canyon	Ariz.	1915	2,249
White Sands	N.M.	1933	143,733
Wupatki	Ariz.	1924	35,253
Yucca House*	Col.	1919	10

National Preserves

Name	State	Year	Acreage
Aniakchak	Alas.	1978	465,603
Bering Land Bridge	Alas.	1978	2,784,960
Big Cypress	Fla.	1974	716,000
Big Thicket	Tex.	1974	85,736
Denali	Alas.	1917	1,311,365
Gates of the Arctic	Alas.	1978	948,629
Glacier Bay	Alas.	1925	57,884
Katmai	Alas.	1918	374,000
Lake Clark	Alas.	1978	1,407,293
Little River Canyon	Ala.	1992	NA
Noatak	Alas.	1978	6,574,481
Timucuan Ecological & Historic Preserve	Fla.	1988	46,000
Wrangell-St. Elias	Alas.	1978	4,856,721
Yukon-Charley Rivers	Alas.	1978	2,523,509

National Seashores

Name	State	Year	Acreage
Assateague Island	Md.-Va.	1965	39,631
Canaveral	Fla.	1975	57,662
Cape Cod	Mass.	1961	43,558
Cape Hatteras	N.C.	1937	30,319
Cape Lookout**	N.C.	1966	28,243
Cumberland Island	Ga.	1972	36,415
Fire Island	N.Y.	1964	19,570
Gulf Islands	Fla.-Miss.	1971	135,618
Padre Island	Tex.	1962	130,434
Point Reyes	Cal.	1962	71,050

National Parkways

Name	State	Year	Acreage
Blue Ridge	Va.-N.C.	1936	86,941
George Washington Memorial	Va.-Md.	1930	7,159
John D. Rockefeller Jr. Mem.	Wy.	1972	23,777
Natchez Trace	Ala.-Miss.-Tenn.	1938	51,742

National Lakeshores

Name	State	Year	Acreage
Apostle Islands	Wis.	1970	69,372
Indiana Dunes	Ind.	1966	13,845
Pictured Rocks	Mich.	1966	72,903
Sleeping Bear Dunes	Mich.	1970	71,188

National Reserve

Name	State	Year	Acreage
City of Rocks	Ida.	1988	14,407

Name	State	Year	Acreage
Ebeys Landing	Wash.	1992	8,000

National Rivers

Name	State	Year	Acreage
Big South Fork Natl. R. and Recreation	Tenn.-Ky.	1976	122,960
Buffalo	Ark.	1972	94,219
New River Gorge	W.Va.	1978	62,144
Ozark	Mo.	1964	80,791
Mississippi Natl. R. and Recreation	Minn.	1988	50,000
Niobrara/Missouri	Neb.-S.D.	1991	76

National Wild and Scenic Rivers

Name	State	Year	Acreage
Alagnak Wild	Alas.	1980	24,038
Bluestone	W.Va.	1988	N.A.
Delaware	N.Y.-N.J.-Pa.	1978	1,973
Great Egg Harbor	N.J.	1992	NA
Obed Wild	Tenn.	1976	5,075
Rio Grande	Tex.	1978	9,600
Saint Croix	Minn.-Wis.	1968	67,379
Upper Delaware	N.Y.-N.J.	1978	75,000

Parks (no other classification)

Name	State	Year	Acreage
Catoctin Mountain	Md.	1954	5,770
Constitution Gardens	D.C.	1978	52
Fort Washington	Md.	1930	341
Greenbelt	Md.	1950	1,176
National Capital	D.C.	1992	6,524
Piscataway	Md.	1961	4,263
Prince William Forest	Va.	1948	18,572
Rock Creek	D.C.	1890	1,754
White House	D.C.	1992	18
Wolf Trap Farm Park for the Performing Arts	Va.	1966	130

National Recreation Areas

Name	State	Year	Acreage
Amistad	Tex.	1965	57,292
Bighorn Canyon	Mon.-Wy.	1966	120,296
Chattahoochee R.	Ga.	1978	9,257
Chickasaw	Okla.	1902	9,522
Coulee Dam	Wash.	1946	100,390
Curecanti	Col.	1965	42,114
Cuyahoga Valley	Oh.	1974	32,525
Delaware Water Gap	N.J.-Pa.	1965	66,652
Gateway	N.Y.-N.J.	1972	26,311
Gauley R.	W.Va.	1988	10,300
Glen Canyon	Ariz.-Ut.	1958	1,236,880
Golden Gate	Cal.	1972	73,122
Lake Chelan	Wash.	1968	61,883
Lake Mead	Ariz.-Nev.	1936	1,495,666
Lake Meredith	Tex.	1965	44,978
Ross Lake	Wash.	1968	117,575
Santa Monica Mts.	Cal.	1978	150,050
Whiskeytown	Cal.	1965	42,503

National Mall

Name	State	Year	Acreage
National Mall	D.C.	1933	146

National Scenic Trails

Name	State	Year	Acreage
Appalachian	Me. to Ga.	1968	161,382
Natchez Trace	Ala.-Miss.-Tenn.	1983	10,995
Potomac Heritage	Md.-D.C.-Va.-Pa.	1983	***

International Historic Sites

Name	State	Year	Acreage
Saint Croix Island	Me.	1949	35

* Not open to the public. ** No federal facilities. *** Undetermined.

National Park Service Recreation Visits in 1991

Source: National Park Service

Park	Recreation Visits
Blue Ridge Parkway	16,414,294
Golden Gate Natl. Recreation Area	14,650,213
Lake Mead Natl. Recreation Area	8,445,016
Great Smoky Mountains Natl. Park	8,654,459
Gateway Natl. Recreation Area	6,643,921
Natchez Trace Parkway	5,832,697
Cape Cod Natl. Seashore	5,442,379
George Washington Memorial Parkway	5,004,736

Attendance at all areas administered by the National Park Service in 1991 was 267,419,196 recreation visits.

Federal Indian Reservations and Trust Lands[1]

Source: Bureau of Indian Affairs, U.S. Dept. of the Interior (data as of 1990)

The total American Indian population according to the 1990 Census is 1,878,285.

State	No of Reser.	Tribally-owned acreage[2]	Individually-owned acreage[2]	No. of persons[3]	Major tribes and/or nations
Alabama	1	230	0	16,504	Poarch Creek
Alaska	1[4]	86,773	1,265,432	85,698	Aleut, Eskimo, Athapascan,[5] Haida, Tlingit, Tsimpshian
Arkansas	1	0	2.78	—	unknown
Arizona	23	19,775,959	311,579	203,527	Navajo, Apache, Papago, Hopi, Yavapai, Pima
California	96	520,049	66,769	242,164	Hoopa, Paiute, Yurok, Karok, Cherokee
Colorado	2	764,120	2,805	27,776	Ute
Connecticut	1	1,638	0	6,654	Mashantucket Pequot
Florida	4	153,874	0	36,335	Seminole, Miccosukee, Cherokee
Idaho	4	609,622	327,301	13,780	Shoshone, Bannock, Nez Perce
Iowa	1	3,550	0	7,349	Sac and Fox
Kansas	4	7,219	23,763	21,965	Potawatomi, Kickapoo, Iowa
Louisiana	3	415	0	18,541	Chitimacha, Coushatta, Tunica-Biloxi
Maine	3	191,511	0	5,998	Passamaquoddy, Penobscot, Maliseet
Massachusetts	1	157	0	—	Wampanoag
Michigan	8	14,411	9,276	55,638	Chippewa, Potawatomi, Ottawa, Cherokee
Minnesota	14	779,138	50,338	49,909	Chippewa, Sioux
Mississippi	1	20,486	0	8,825	Choctaw
Missouri	1	0	374.37	—	Cherokee
Montana	7	2,663,385	2,911,450	47,679	Blackfeet, Crow, Sioux, Assiniboine, Cheyenne
Nebraska	3	23,792	43,208	12,410	Omaha, Winnebago, Santee Sioux
Nevada	19	1,147,088	78,529	19,637	Paiute, Shoshone, Washoe
New Mexico	25	7,252,326	630,293	134,355	Zuni, Apache, Navajo
New York	8	118,199	0	62,651	Seneca, Mohawk, Onondaga, Oneida
North Carolina	1	56,509	0	80,155	Cherokee, Lumbee
North Dakota	3	214,006	627,289	25,917	Sioux, Chippewa, Mandan, Arikara, Hidatsa
Oklahoma	1[6]	96,839	1,000,165	252,420	Cherokee, Creek, Choctaw, Chickasaw, Osage, Cheyenne, Arapahoe, Kiowa, Comanche
Oregon	7	660,367	135,053	38,496	Warm Springs, Wasco, Paiute, Umatilla, Siletz
Rhode Island	1	1,800	0	4,071	Narragansett
South Dakota	9	2,399,531	2,121,188	50,573	Sioux
Texas	3	4,726	0	65,877	Alabama-Coushatta, Tiwa, Kickapoo
Utah	4	2,286,448	32,838	24,283	Ute, Goshute, Southern Paiute, Navajo
Washington	27	2,250,731	467,785	81,483	Yakima, Lummi, Quinault, Sioux
Wisconsin	11	338,097	80,345	39,387	Chippewa, Oneida, Winnebago
Wyoming	1	1,958,095	101,537	9,479	Shoshone, Arapahoe

(1) As of 1988 the federal government recognized and acknowledged that it had a special relationship with, and a trust responsibility for, 307 federally recognized Indian entities in the continental U.S., plus some 200 tribal entities in Alaska. The term "Indian entities" encompasses Indian tribes, bands, villages, groups, pueblos, Eskimos, and Aleuts, eligible for federal services and classified in the following 3 categories: (a) Officially approved Indian organizations pursuant to federal statutory authority (Indian Reorganization Act; Oklahoma Indian Welfare Act and Alaska Native Act.) (b) Officially approved Indian organizations outside of specified federal statutory authority. (c) Traditional Indian organizations recognized without formal federal approval of organizational structure. Some reservation boundaries transcend state boundaries (e.g., Navajo which is in Arizona, New Mexico, and Utah). For statistical convenience under "Number of Reservations," such reservations are counted in the state where population is predominant and/or tribal headquarters is located. (2) The acreages refer only to Indian lands which are either owned by the tribes or individual Indians, and held in trust by the U.S. government. Many of these parcels are located off reservations. Not all lands within reservation boundaries are necessarily trust lands. Many parcels are privately-owned by tribes, individual Indians, and non-Indians. Also, some internal lands are the property of various governmental agencies. (3) Total Indian population in each state with reservation/trust lands, including those persons living outside of the BIA Service area. (4) Alaskan Indian Affairs are carried out under the Alaska Native Claims Settlement Act (Dec. 18, 1971). The Act provided for the establishment of regional and village corporations to conduct business for profit and non-profit purposes. There are 13 such regional corporations, each one with organized village corporations. The Annette Island Reservation remains the only federally recognized reservation in Alaska in the sense of specific reservation boundaries, trust lands, etc. (5) Aleuts and Eskimos are racially and linguistically related. Athapascans are related to the Navajo and Apache Indians. (6) Indian land status in Oklahoma is unique and there are no reservations except for Osage in the sense that the term is used elsewhere in the U.S. Likewise, many of the Oklahoma tribes are unique in their high degree of assimilation to the white culture.

American Indian Population: States Without Federal Reservations and Trust Lands

Source: Bureau of the Census, U.S. Dept. of Commerce, 1990 Census

State	No. of Persons	State	No. of Persons	State	No. of Persons
Arkansas	12,773	Kentucky	5,769	Pennsylvania	14,733
Delaware	2,019	Maryland	12,972	South Carolina	8,246
District of Columbia	1,466	Massachusetts	12,241	Tennessee	10,039
Georgia	13,348	Missouri	19,835	Vermont	1,696
Hawaii	5,099	New Hampshire	2,134	Virginia	15,282
Illinois	21,836	New Jersey	14,970	West Virginia	2,458
Indiana	12,972	Ohio	20,358		

UNITED STATES HISTORY

1492

Christopher Columbus and crew sighted land **Oct. 12** in the present-day Bahamas.

1497

John Cabot explored northeast coast to Delaware.

1513

Juan Ponce de León explored Florida coast.

1524

Giovanni da Verrazano led French expedition along coast from Carolina north to Nova Scotia; entered New York harbor.

1539

Hernando de Soto landed in Florida **May 28**; crossed Mississippi River, **1541.**

1540

Francisco Vásquez de Coronado explored Southwest north of Rio Grande. Hernando de Alarcón reached Colorado River, Don Garcia Lopez de Cardenas reached Grand Canyon. Others explored California coast.

1565

St. Augustine, Fla. founded by Pedro Menéndez. Razed by Francis Drake **1586.**

1579

Francis Drake entered San Francisco Bay and claimed region for Britain.

1607

Capt. John Smith and 105 cavaliers in 3 ships landed on Virginia coast, started first permanent English settlement in New World at **Jamestown** in May.

1609

Henry Hudson, English explorer of Northwest Passage, employed by Dutch, sailed into New York harbor in **Sept.,** and up Hudson to Albany. The same year, **Samuel de Champlain** explored Lake Champlain just to the north.

Spaniards settled **Santa Fe, N.M.**

1619

House of Burgesses, first representative assembly in New World, elected **July 30** at Jamestown, Va.

First black laborers — indentured servants — in English N. American colonies, landed by Dutch at Jamestown in **Aug.** Chattel slavery legally recognized, **1650.**

1620

Plymouth Pilgrims, Puritan separatists from Church of England, some living in Holland, left Plymouth, England **Sept. 16** on Mayflower. Original destination Virginia, they reached Cape Cod **Nov. 19,** explored coast; 103 passengers landed **Dec. 26** at Plymouth. Mayflower Compact was agreement to form a government and abide by its laws. Half of colony died during harsh winter.

1624

Dutch colonies started in Albany and in New York area, where New Netherland was established in May.

1626

Peter Minuit bought Manhattan for Dutch from Man-a-hat-a Indians during summer for goods valued at $24; named island New Amsterdam.

1630

Settlement of **Boston** established by Mass. colonists led by John Winthrop.

1634

Maryland founded as Catholic colony with religious tolerance.

1636

Roger Williams founded Providence, R.I., **June,** as a democratically ruled colony with separation of church and state. Charter was granted, **1644.**

Harvard College founded **Oct. 28,** now oldest in U.S.; Grammar school, compulsory education established at Boston.

1654

First Jews arrived in New Amsterdam.

1660

British Parliament passed **Navigation Act,** regulating colonial commerce to suit English needs.

1664

Three hundred **British troops Sept. 8 seized New Netherland** from Dutch, who yield peacefully. Charles II granted province of New Netherland and city of New Amsterdam to brother, Duke of York; both renamed New York. The Dutch recaptured the colony **Aug. 9, 1673,** but ceded it to Britain **Nov. 10, 1674.**

1676

Nathaniel Bacon led planters against autocratic British Gov. Berkeley, burned Jamestown, Va. Bacon died, 23 followers executed.

Bloody **Indian war** in New England ended **Aug. 12.** King Philip, Wampanoag chief, and many Narragansett Indians killed.

1682

Robert Cavelier, Sieur de La Salle, claimed lower Mississippi River country for France, called it Louisiana **Apr. 9.** Had French outposts built in Illinois and Texas, **1684.** Killed during mutiny **Mar. 19, 1687.**

1683

William Penn signed treaty with Delaware Indians and made payment for Pennsylvania lands.

1692

Witchcraft delusion at Salem, Mass.; 20 executed by special court.

1696

Capt. William Kidd, who was born in Scotland and settled in America, was hired by British to fight pirates and take booty, but himself became a pirate. Arrested and sent to England, he was hanged **1701.**

1699

French settlements made in Mississippi, Louisiana.

1704

Indians attacked Deerfield, Mass. **Feb. 28-29,** killed 40, carried off 100.

Boston News Letter, first regular newspaper, started by John Campbell, postmaster. (*Publick Occurences* was suppressed after one issue **1690.**)

1709

British-Colonial troops captured French fort, Port Royal, Nova Scotia, in **Queen Anne's War 1701-13.** France yielded Nova Scotia by treaty **1713.**

1712

Slaves revolted in New York **Apr. 6.** Six committed suicide, 21 were executed. Second rising, **1741;** 13 slaves hanged, 13 burned, 71 deported.

1716

First theater in colonies opened in Williamsburg, Va.

1732

Benjamin Franklin published first *Poor Richard's Almanac;* published annually to 1757.

1735

Freedom of the press recognized in New York by acquittal of John Peter Zenger, editor of *Weekly Journal,* on charge of libeling British Gov. Cosby by criticizing his conduct in office.

1740-41

Capt. Vitus Bering, Dane employed by Russians, reached Alaska.

1744

King George's War pitted British and colonials vs. French. Colonials captured Louisburg, Cape Breton Is. **June 17, 1745.** Returned to France **1748** by Treaty of Aix-la-Chapelle.

1752

Benjamin Franklin, flying kite in thunderstorm, proved lightning is electricity **June 15;** invented lightning rod.

1754

French and Indian War (in Europe called 7 Years War, started 1756) began when French occupied Ft. Duquesne (Pittsburgh). British moved Acadian French from Nova Scotia to Louisiana **Oct. 8, 1755.** British captured Québec **Sept. 18, 1759** in battles in which French Gen. Montcalm and British Gen. Wolfe were killed. Peace signed **Feb. 10, 1763.**

French lost Canada and American Midwest. British tightened colonial administration in North America.

1764

Sugar Act placed duties on lumber, foodstuffs, molasses and rum in colonies, to pay French and Indian War debts.

1765

Stamp Act required revenue stamps to help defray cost of royal troops. Nine colonies, led by New York and Massachusetts at Stamp Act Congress in New York **Oct. 7-25, 1765,** adopted Declaration of Rights opposing taxation without representation in Parliament and trial without jury by admiralty courts. Stamp Act **repealed Mar. 17, 1766.**

1767

Townshend Acts levied taxes on glass, painter's lead, paper, and tea. In **1770** all duties except on tea were repealed.

1770

British troops fired **Mar. 5** into Boston mob, killed 5 including **Crispus Attucks,** a black man, reportedly leader of group; later called **Boston Massacre.**

1773

East India Co. tea ships turned back at Boston, New York, Philadelphia in **May.** Cargo ship burned at Annapolis **Oct. 14,** cargo thrown overboard at **Boston Tea Party Dec. 16,** to protest the Tea Act.

1774

"Intolerable Acts" of Parliament curtailed Massachusetts self-rule; barred use of Boston harbor till tea was paid for.

First Continental Congress held in Philadelphia **Sept. 5-Oct. 26;** protested British measures, called for civil disobedience.

Rhode Island abolished slavery.

1775

Patrick Henry addressed Virginia convention, **Mar. 23** said "Give me liberty or give me death."

Paul Revere and William Dawes on night of **Apr. 18** rode to alert patriots that British were on way to Concord to destroy arms. At Lexington, Mass. **Apr. 19** Minutemen lost 8. On return from Concord British took 273 casualties.

Col. Ethan Allen (joined by Col. Benedict Arnold) captured Ft. **Ticonderoga, N.Y. May 10;** also Crown Point. Colonials headed for **Bunker Hill,** fortified Breed's Hill, Charlestown, Mass., repulsed British under Gen. William Howe twice before retreating **June 17;** British casualties 1,000; called Battle of Bunker Hill. Continental Congress **June 15** named **George Washington** commander-in-chief.

1776

France and Spain each agreed **May 2** to provide one million livres in arms to Americans.

In Continental Congress **June 7,** Richard Henry Lee (Va.) moved "that these united colonies are and of right ought to be free and independent states." Resolution adopted July 2. **Declaration of Independence** approved **July 4.**

Col. Moultrie's batteries at **Charleston, S.C.** repulsed British sea attack **June 28.**

Washington, with 10,000 men, lost **Battle of Long Island Aug. 27,** evacuated New York.

Nathan Hale executed as spy by British **Sept. 22.**

Brig. Gen. Arnold's **Lake Champlain** fleet was defeated at Valcour **Oct. 11,** but British returned to Canada. Howe failed to destroy Washington's army at **White Plains Oct. 28.** Hessians captured Ft. Washington, Manhattan, and 3,000 men **Nov. 16;** Ft. Lee, N.J. **Nov. 18.**

Washington in Pennsylvania, recrossed **Delaware River Dec. 25-26,** defeated 1,400 Hessians at Trenton, N.J. **Dec. 26.**

1777

Washington defeated Lord Cornwallis at **Princeton Jan. 3.** Continental Congress adopted Stars and Stripes. *See Flag article.*

Maj. Gen. John Burgoyne with 8,000 from Canada captured **Ft. Ticonderoga July 6.** Americans beat back Burgoyne at Bemis Heights **Oct. 7** and cut off British escape route. Burgoyne surrendered 5,000 men at **Saratoga N.Y. Oct. 17.**

Marquis de Lafayette, aged 20, made major general.

Articles of Confederation and Perpetual Union adopted by Continental Congress **Nov. 15**

France recognized independence of 13 colonies **Dec. 17.**

1778

France signed treaty of aid with U.S. **Feb. 6.** Sent fleet; British evacuated Philadelphia in consequence **June 18.**

1779

John Paul Jones on the *Bonhomme Richard* defeated *Serapis* in British North Sea waters **Sept. 23.**

1780

Charleston, S.C. fell to the British **May 12,** but a British force was defeated near **Kings Mountain, N.C. Oct. 7** by militiamen.

Benedict Arnold found to be a traitor **Sept. 23.** Arnold escaped, made brigadier general in British army.

1781

Bank of North America incorporated in Philadelphia **May 26.**

Cornwallis, sapped by patriot victories, retired to **Yorktown, Va.** Adm. De Grasse landed 3,000 French and stopped British fleet in Hampton Roads. Washington and Rochambeau joined forces, arrived near Williamsburg **Sept. 26.** When siege of Cornwallis began **Oct. 6,** British had 6,000, Americans 8,846, French 7,800. **Cornwallis surrendered Oct. 19.**

1782

New **British** cabinet agreed **in March** to **recognize U.S.** independence. Preliminary agreement signed in Paris **Nov. 30.**

1783

Massachusetts Supreme Court **outlawed slavery** in that state, noting the words in the state Bill of Rights "all men are born free and equal."

Britain, U.S. signed **peace treaty Sept. 3** (Congress ratified it **Jan. 14, 1784).**

Washington ordered army disbanded Nov. 3, bade farewell to his officers at Fraunces Tavern, N.Y. City **Dec. 4.**

Noah Webster published *American Spelling Book,* great bestseller.

1784

Jefferson's proposal to **ban slavery** in new territory after 1802 is narrowly defeated **Mar. 1.**

First successful daily newspaper, **Pennsylvania Packet & General Advertiser,** published **Sept. 21.**

1786

Delegates from 5 states at **Annapolis, Md. Sept. 11-14** asked Congress to call convention in Philadelphia to write practical constitution for the 13 states.

1787

Shays's Rebellion, of debt-ridden farmers in Massachusetts, failed **Jan. 25.**

Northwest Ordinance adopted **July 13** by Continental Congress. Determined government of Northwest Territory north of Ohio River, west of New York; 60,000 inhabitants could get statehood. Guaranteed freedom of religion, support for schools, no slavery.

Constitutional convention opened at Philadelphia **May 25** with George Washington presiding. Constitution adopted by delegates **Sept. 17;** ratification by 9th state, New Hampshire, **June 21, 1788,** meant adoption; declared in effect **Mar. 4, 1789.**

1789

George Washington chosen president by all electors voting (73 eligible, 69 voting, 4 absent); John Adams, vice president, 34 votes. **Feb. 4.** First Congress met at Federal Hall, N.Y. City; regular sessions began **Apr. 6.** Washington inaugurated there **Apr. 30.** Supreme Court created by Federal Judiciary Act **Sept. 24.** Congress submitted Bill of Rights to states **Sept. 25.**

1790

Congress passed **Census Act Mar. 1; Naturalization Act** (2-year residency) **Mar. 26.**

Congress met in Phila. Dec. 6, new temporary Capital.

1791

Bill of Rights went into effect **Dec. 15.**

1792

Coinage Act established **U.S. Mint** in Philadelphia **Apr. 2.**

Gen. **"Mad" Anthony Wayne** made commander in Ohio-Indiana area, trained "American Legion"; established string of forts. Routed Indians at Fallen Timbers on Maumee River **Aug. 20, 1794,** checked British at Fort Miami, Ohio.

White House cornerstone laid **Oct. 13.**

1793

Eli Whitney invented **cotton gin,** reviving southern slavery.

1794

Whiskey Rebellion, west Pennsylvania farmers protesting liquor tax of **1791,** was suppressed by 15,000 militiamen **Sept. 1794.** Alexander Hamilton used incident to establish authority of the new federal government in enforcing its laws.

1795

U.S. bought peace from **Algerian pirates** by paying $1 mln. ransom for 115 seamen **Sept. 5,** followed by annual tributes.

Gen. Wayne signed peace with Indians at Fort Greenville.

Univ. of North Carolina became first operating state university.

1796

Washington's Farewell Address as president delivered **Sept. 19.** Gave strong warnings against permanent alliances with foreign powers, big public debt, large military establishment and devices of "small, artful, enterprising minority" to control or change government.

1797

U.S. **frigate United States** launched at Philadelphia **July 10;** Constellation at Baltimore **Sept. 7;** Constitution (Old Ironsides) at Boston **Sept. 20.**

1798

Alien & Sedition Acts passed by Federalists; intended to silence political opposition **June-July.**

War with France threatened over French raids on U.S. shipping and rejection of U.S. diplomats. Congress voided all treaties with France, ordered Navy to capture French armed ships. Navy (45 ships) and 365 privateers captured 84 French ships. USS Constellation took French warship Insurgente **1799.** Napoleon stopped French raids after becoming First Consul.

1800

Federal gvt. moves from Philadelphia to **Washington, D.C.**

1801

Tripoli declared war June 10 against U.S., which refused added tribute to commerce-raiding Arab corsairs. Land and naval campaigns forced Tripoli to negotiate **peace June 4, 1805.**

1803

Supreme Court, in **Marbury v. Madison** case, for the first time overturned a U.S. law **Feb. 24.**

Napoleon, who had recovered Louisiana from Spain by secret treaty, sold all of **Louisiana,** stretching to Canadian border, to U.S., for $11,250,000 in bonds, plus $3,750,000 indemnities to American citizens with claims against France. U.S. took title **Dec. 20.** Purchases doubled U.S. area.

1804

Lewis and Clark expedition ordered by Pres. Jefferson to explore what is now northwest U.S. Started from St. Louis **May 14;** ended **Sept. 23, 1806.** Sacagawea, an Indian woman, served as guide.

Vice Pres. **Aaron Burr,** after long political rivalry, **shot Alexander Hamilton** in a duel **July 11** in Weehawken, N.J.; Hamilton died the next day.

1807

Robert Fulton made first practical steamboat trip; left N.Y. City **Aug. 17,** reached Albany, 150 mi., in 32 hrs.

Embargo Act bans all trade with foreign countries, forbids ships to set sail for foreign ports **Dec. 22.**

1808

Slave importation outlawed. Some 250,000 slaves were illegally imported **1808-1860.**

1811

William Henry Harrison, governor of Indiana, defeated Indians under the Prophet, in battle of Tippecanoe **Nov. 7.**

Cumberland Road begun at Cumberland, Md.; became important route to West.

1812

War of 1812 had 3 main causes: Britain seized U.S. ships trading with France; Britain seized 4,000 naturalized U.S. sailors by **1810;** Britain armed Indians who raided western border. U.S. stopped trade with Europe **1807** and **1809.** Trade with Britain only was stopped, **1810.**

Unaware that Britain had raised the blockade against France 2 days before, **Congress declared war June 18** by a small majority. The West favored war, New England opposed it. The British were handicapped by war with France.

U.S. naval victories in **1812** included: USS Essex captured Alert **Aug. 13;** USS Constitution destroyed Guerriere **Aug. 19;** USS Wasp took Frolic **Oct. 18;** USS United States defeated Macedonian off Azores **Oct. 25;** Constitution beat Java **Dec. 29.** British captured Detroit **Aug. 16.**

1813

Oliver H. Perry defeated British fleet at Battle of Lake Erie, **Sept. 10.** U.S. victory at Battle of the Thames, Ont., **Oct. 5,** broke Indian allies of Britain, and made Detroit frontier safe for U.S. But Americans failed in Canadian invasion attempts. York (Toronto) and Buffalo were burned.

1814

British landed in Maryland in August, defeated U.S. force **Aug. 24, burned Capitol** and White House. Maryland militia stopped British advance **Sept. 12.** Bombardment of Ft. McHenry, Baltimore, for 25 hours, **Sept. 13-14,** by British fleet failed; Francis Scott Key wrote words to **Star Spangled Banner.**

U.S. won naval Battle of **Lake Champlain Sept. 11.** Peace treaty signed at Ghent **Dec. 24.**

1815

Some 5,300 British, unaware of peace treaty, attacked U.S. entrenchments near **New Orleans, Jan. 8.** British had over 2,000 casualties, Americans lost 71.

U.S. flotilla finally ended piracy by **Algiers, Tunis, Tripoli** by **Aug. 6.**

1816

Second **Bank of the U.S.** chartered.

1817

Rush-Bagot treaty signed **Apr. 28-29;** limited U.S., British armaments on the Great Lakes.

1819

Spain cedes **Florida** to U.S. **Feb. 22.**

American steamship Savannah made first part steam-powered, part sail-powered crossing of Atlantic, Savannah, Ga. to Liverpool, Eng., 29 days.

1820

First organized **immigration of blacks to Africa** from U.S. began with 86 free blacks sailing **Feb.** to Sierra Leone, Brit. Colony.

Henry Clay's **Missouri Compromise** bill passed by Congress **March 3.** Slavery was allowed in Missouri, but not elsewhere west of the Mississippi River north of 36° 30′ latitude (the southern line of Missouri). Repealed **1854.**

1821

Emma Willard founded Troy Female Seminary, first U.S. women's college.

1823

Monroe Doctrine enunciated **Dec. 2,** opposing European intervention in the Americas.

1824

Pawtucket, R.I. **weavers strike** in first such action by women.

1825

Erie Canal opened; first boat left Buffalo **Oct. 26,** reached N.Y. City **Nov. 4.** Canal cost $7 million but cut travel time one-third, shipping costs nine-tenths; opened Great Lakes area, made N.Y. City chief Atlantic port.

John Stevens, of Hoboken, N.J., built and operated first experimental **steam locomotive** in U.S.

1828

South Carolina **Dec. 19** declared the right of state **nullification of federal laws**, opposing the "Tariff of Abominations."

Noah Webster published his *American Dictionary of the English Language.*

Baltimore & Ohio, 1st U.S. passenger RR, was begun **July 4.**

1830

Mormon church organized by Joseph Smith in Fayette, N.Y. **Apr. 6.**

1831

William Lloyd Garrison began abolitionist newspaper *The Liberator* **Jan. 1.**

Nat Turner, black slave in Virginia, led local slave rebellion, killed 57 whites in **Aug.** Troops called in, 100 slaves killed, Turner captured, tried, and hanged.

1832

Black Hawk War (Ill.-Wis.) **Apr.-Sept.** pushed Sauk and Fox Indians west across Mississippi.

South Carolina convention passed **Ordinance of Nullification in Nov.** against permanent tariff, threatening to withdraw from the Union. Congress **Feb. 1833** passed a compromise tariff act, whereupon South Carolina repealed its act.

1833

Oberlin College, first in U.S. to adopt coeducation; refused to bar students on account of race, **1835.**

1835

Seminole Indians in Florida under Osceola began attacks **Nov. 1,** protesting forced removal. The unpopular 8-year war ended **Aug. 14, 1842;** Indians were sent to Oklahoma. War cost the U.S. 1,500 soldiers.

Texas proclaimed right to secede from Mexico; Sam Houston put in command of Texas army, **Nov. 2-4.**

Gold discovered on **Cherokee land** in Georgia. Indians forced to cede lands **Dec. 20** and to cross Mississippi.

1836

Texans besieged in Alamo in San Antonio by Mexicans under Santa Anna **Feb. 23-Mar. 6;** entire garrison killed. Texas independence declared, **Mar. 2.** At San Jacinto **Apr. 21** Sam Houston and Texans defeated Mexicans.

Marcus Whitman, H.H. Spaulding and wives reached Fort Walla Walla on Columbia River, Oregon. **First white women to cross plains.**

1838

Cherokee Indians made **"Trail of Tears,"** removed from Georgia to Oklahoma starting **Oct.**

1841

First emigrant **wagon train for California,** 47 persons, left Independence, Mo. **May 1,** reached Cal. **Nov. 4.**

Brook Farm commune set up by New England Transcendentalist intellectuals. Lasts to **1846.**

1842

Webster-Ashburton Treaty signed **Aug. 9,** fixing the U.S.-Canada border in Maine and Minnesota.

First use of **anesthetic** (sulphuric ether gas).

Settlement of Oregon begins via **Oregon Trail.**

1843

More than 1,000 settlers left Independence, Mo. for Oregon **May 22,** arrived **Oct.**

1844

First message over first **telegraph line** sent **May 24** by inventor Samuel F.B. Morse from Washington to Baltimore: "What hath God wrought!"

1845

Texas Congress voted for annexation to U.S. **July 4.** U.S. Congress admits Texas to Union **Dec. 29.**

1846

Mexican War. Pres. James K. Polk ordered Gen. Zachary Taylor to seize disputed Texan land settled by Mexicans. After border clash, U.S. declared war **May 13; Mexico May 23.** Northern Whigs opposed war, southerners backed it.

Bear flag of Republic of California raised by American settlers at Sonoma **June 14.**

About 12,000 U.S. troops took Vera Cruz Mar. 27, 1847, Mexico City Sept. 14, 1847. By **treaty, Feb. 1848,** Mexico ceded claims to Texas, California, Arizona, New Mexico, Nevada, Utah, part of Colorado. U.S. assumed $3 million American claims and paid Mexico $15 million.

Treaty with Great Britain **June 15** set **boundary in Oregon** territory at 49th parallel (extension of existing line). Expansionists had used slogan "54° 40′ or fight."

Mormons, after violent clashes with settlers over polygamy, left Nauvoo, Ill. for West under Brigham Young, settled **July 1847 at Salt Lake City, Utah.**

Elias Howe invented **sewing machine.**

1847

First **adhesive U.S. postage stamps** on sale **July 1;** Benjamin Franklin 5¢, Washington 10¢.

Ralph Waldo Emerson published first book of poems; **Henry Wadsworth Longfellow** published *Evangeline.*

1848

Gold discovered Jan. 24 in California; 80,000 prospectors emigrate in **1849.**

Lucretia Mott and Elizabeth Cady Stanton lead **Seneca Falls, N.Y. Women's Rights Convention July 19-20.**

1850

Sen. Henry Clay's **Compromise of 1850** admitted California as 31st state **Sept. 9,** slavery forbidden; made Utah and New Mexico territories without decision on slavery; made Fugitive Slave Law more harsh; ended District of Columbia slave trade.

1851

Herman Melville's *Moby Dick,* **Nathaniel Hawthorne's** *House of the Seven Gables* published.

1852

Uncle Tom's Cabin, by **Harriet Beecher Stowe,** published.

1853

Commodore Matthew C. Perry, U.S.N., received by Lord of Toda, Japan **July 14; negotiated treaty to open Japan** to U.S. ships.

1854

Republican party formed at Ripon, Wis. **Feb. 28.** Opposed Kansas-Nebraska Act (became law **May 30**), which left issue of slavery to vote of settlers.

Henry David Thoreau published *Walden.*

1855

Walt Whitman published *Leaves of Grass.*

First railroad train crossed Mississippi on the river's first bridge, Rock Island, Ill.-Davenport, Ia. **Apr. 21.**

1856

Republican party's first nominee for president, **John C. Fremont,** defeated. Abraham Lincoln made 50 speeches for him.

Lawrence, Kan. sacked **May 21** by pro-slavery group; abolitionist **John Brown** led anti-slavery men against Missourians at **Osawatomie, Kan. Aug. 30**

1857

Dred Scott decision by U.S. Supreme Court **Mar. 6** held, 6-3, that a slave did not become free when taken into a free state, Congress could not bar slavery from a territory, and blacks could not be citizens.

1858

First **Atlantic cable** completed by Cyrus W. Field **Aug. 5;** cable failed **Sept. 1.**

Lincoln-Douglas debates in Illinois **Aug. 21-Oct. 15.**

1859

First commercially productive **oil well,** drilled near Titusville, Pa., by Edwin L. Drake **Aug. 27.**

Abolitionist **John Brown** with 21 men seized U.S. Armory at **Harpers Ferry (then Va.) Oct. 16.** U.S. Marines captured raiders, killing several. Brown was hanged for treason by Virginia **Dec. 2.**

1860

Approximately 20,000 **New England shoe workers** strike **Feb. 22** and win higher wages.

Abraham Lincoln, Republican, elected president in 4-way race.

First **Pony Express** between Sacramento, Cal. and St. Joseph, Mo. started **Apr. 3**; service ended **Oct. 24, 1861** when first transcontinental telegraph line was completed.

1861

Seven southern states set up **Confederate States of America Feb. 8**, with Jefferson Davis as president, captured Federal arsenals and forts. **Civil War** began as Confederates fired on **Ft. Sumter** in Charleston, S.C. **Apr. 12**; they captured it **Apr. 14**.

President **Lincoln called for 75,000 volunteers Apr. 15**. By May, 11 states had seceded. Lincoln blockaded southern ports **Apr. 19**, cutting off vital exports, aid.

Confederates repelled Union forces at first **Battle of Bull Run July 21**.

First **transcontinental telegraph** was put in operation.

1862

Homestead Act was approved **May 20**; it granted free family farms to settlers.

Land Grant Act approved **July 7**, providing for public land sale to benefit agricultural education; eventually led to establishment of state university systems.

Union forces were victorious in western campaigns, took **New Orleans**. Battles in East were inconclusive.

1863

Lincoln issued **Emancipation Proclamation Jan. 1**, freeing "all slaves in areas still in rebellion."

The entire **Mississippi River** was in Union hands by **July 4**. Union forces won a major victory at **Gettysburg, Pa. July 1-July 4**. Lincoln read his **Gettysburg Address Nov. 19**.

In **draft riots** in N.Y. City about 1,000 were killed or wounded; some blacks were hanged by mobs **July 13-16**. Rioters protested provision allowing money payment in place of service. Such payments were ended 1864.

1864

Gen. Sherman marched through Georgia, taking Atlanta **Sept. 1**, Savannah **Dec. 22**.

Sand Creek massacre of Cheyenne and Arapaho Indians **Nov. 29**. Cavalry attacked Indians who were awaiting surrender terms.

1865

Robert E. Lee surrendered 27,800 Confederate troops to Grant at Appomattox Court House, Va. **Apr. 9**. J.E. Johnston surrendered 31,200 to Sherman at Durham Station, N.C. **Apr. 18**. Last rebel troops surrendered **May 26**.

President **Lincoln was shot Apr. 14** by John Wilkes Booth in Ford's Theater, Washington; died the following morning. Booth was reported dead **Apr. 26**. Four co-conspirators were hanged **July 7**.

Thirteenth Amendment, abolishing slavery, took effect **Dec. 18**.

1866

Ku Klux Klan formed secretly in South to terrorize blacks who voted. Disbanded **1869-71**. A second Klan was organized **1915**.

Congress took control of southern Reconstruction, backed freedmen's rights.

1867

Alaska sold to U.S. by Russia for $7.2 million **Mar. 30** through efforts of Sec. of State William H. Seward.

Horatio Alger published first book, *Ragged Dick*.

The **Grange** was organized **Dec. 4**, to protect farmer interests.

1868

The World Almanac, a publication of the *New York World*, appeared for the first time.

Pres. **Andrew Johnson** tried to remove Edwin M. Stanton, secretary of war; was impeached by House **Feb. 24** for violation of Tenure of Office Act; acquitted by Senate **March-May**. Stanton resigned.

1869

Financial "**Black Friday**" in New York **Sept. 24**; caused by attempt to "corner" gold.

Transcontinental railroad completed; golden spike driven at Promontory, Utah **May 10** marking the junction of Central Pacific and Union Pacific.

Knights of Labor formed in Philadelphia. By **1886**, it had 700,000 members nationally.

Woman suffrage law passed in Territory of Wyoming **Dec. 10**.

1871

Great fire destroyed Chicago Oct. 8-11; loss est. at $196 million.

1872

Amnesty Act restored civil rights to citizens of the South **May 22** except for 500 Confederate leaders.

Congress founded first national park — **Yellowstone** in Wyoming.

1873

First U.S. **postal card** issued **May 1**.

Banks failed, panic began in **Sept**. Depression lasted 5 years.

"Boss" William Tweed of N.Y. City convicted of stealing public funds. He died in jail in **1878**.

Bellevue Hospital in N.Y. City started the first **school of nursing**.

1875

Congress passed **Civil Rights Act Mar. 1** giving equal rights to blacks in public accommodations and jury duty. Act invalidated in **1883** by Supreme Court.

First **Kentucky Derby** held **May 17** at Churchill Downs, Louisville, Ky.

1876

Samuel J. Tilden, Democrat, received majority of popular votes for president over **Rutherford B. Hayes**, Republican, but 22 electoral votes were in dispute; issue left to Congress. Hayes given presidency in **Feb., 1877** after Republicans agree to end Reconstruction of South.

Col. **George A. Custer** and 264 soldiers of the 7th Cavalry killed **June 25** in "last stand," Battle of the Little Big Horn, Mont., in Sioux Indian War.

Mark Twain published *Tom Sawyer*.

1877

Molly Maguires, Irish terrorist society in Scranton, Pa. mining areas, broken up by hanging of 11 leaders for murders of mine officials and police.

Pres. Hayes sent troops in violent national **railroad strike**.

1878

First commercial **telephone** exchange opened, New Haven, Conn. **Jan. 28**.

Thomas A. Edison founded **Edison Electric Light Co. Oct. 15**.

1879

F.W. Woolworth opened his first five-and-ten store in Utica, N.Y. **Feb. 22**.

Henry George published *Progress & Poverty*, advocating single tax on land.

1881

Pres. **James A. Garfield shot** in Washington, D.C. **July 2**; died **Sept. 19**.

Booker T. Washington founded Tuskegee Institute for blacks.

Helen Hunt Jackson published *A Century of Dishonor* about mistreatment of Indians.

1883

Pendleton Act, passed **Jan. 16**, reformed federal civil service.

Brooklyn Bridge opened **May 24**.

1886

Haymarket riot and bombing, evening of **May 4**, followed bitter labor battles for 8-hour day in Chicago; 7 police and 4 workers died, 66 wounded. Eight anarchists found guilty. Gov. John P. Altgeld denounced trial as unfair.

Geronimo, Apache Indian, finally surrendered **Sept. 4**.

The **Statue of Liberty** was dedicated **Oct. 28**.

American Federation of Labor (AFL) formed **Dec. 8** by 25 craft unions.

1888

Great blizzard in eastern U.S. **Mar. 11-14;** 400 deaths.

1889

U.S. declared Oklahoma open to white settlement **Apr. 22**; within 24 hours **claims for 2 mln. acres** were staked by 50,000 settlers.

Johnstown, Pa. flood May 31; 2,200 lives lost.

1890

First execution by **electrocution:** William Kemmler **Aug. 6** at Auburn Prison, Auburn, N.Y., for murder.

Battle of **Wounded Knee, S.D. Dec. 29,** the last major conflict between Indians and U.S. troops. About 200 Indian men, women, and children, and 29 soldiers were killed.

Sherman Antitrust Act begins federal effort to curb monopolies.

Jacob Riis published *How the Other Half Lives,* about city slums.

1891

Forest Reserve Act Mar. 3 let Pres. close public forest land to settlement for establishment of national parks.

1892

Homestead, Pa., strike at Carnegie steel mills; 7 guards and 11 strikers and spectators shot to death **July 6;** setback for unions. **Ellis Island** opened as N.Y. immigration depot.

1893

Financial panic began, led to 4-year depression.

1894

Thomas A. **Edison's kinetoscope** (motion pictures) (invented **1887**) given first public showing **Apr. 14.**

Jacob S. Coxey led 500 unemployed from the Midwest into Washington, D.C. **Apr. 30.** Coxey was arrested for trespassing on Capitol grounds.

1896

William Jennings Bryan delivered "Cross of Gold" speech **July 7**; wins Democratic Party nomination.

Supreme Court, in **Plessy v. Ferguson,** approved racial segregation under the "separate but equal" doctrine.

1898

U.S. **battleship Maine** blown up **Feb. 15** at Havana, 260 killed.

U.S. blockaded Cuba Apr. 22 in aid of independence forces. U.S. declared war on Spain, **Apr. 24,** destroyed Spanish fleet in Philippines **May 1,** took Guam **June 20.**

Puerto Rico taken by U.S. **July 25-Aug. 12.** Spain agreed **Dec. 10** to cede Philippines, Puerto Rico, and Guam, and approved independence for Cuba.

U.S. annexed independent republic of **Hawaii.**

1899

Filipino insurgents, unable to get recognition of independence from U.S., started guerrilla war **Feb. 4.** Crushed with capture **May 23, 1901** of leader, Emilio Aguinaldo.

U.S. declared **Open Door Policy** to make China an open international market and to preserve its integrity as a nation.

John Dewey published *School and Society,* backing progressive education.

1900

Carry Nation, Kansas anti-saloon agitator, began raiding with hatchet.

U.S. helped suppress **"Boxers"** in Peking.

International Ladies' Garment Workers Union was founded in NYC in **Nov.**

1901

Texas had its first significant **oil strike,** near Beaumont **Jan. 10.**

Pres. William **McKinley was shot Sept. 6** by an anarchist, Leon Czolgosz; died **Sept. 14.**

1903

Treaty between U.S. and Colombia to have U.S. dig **Panama Canal** signed **Jan. 22,** rejected by Colombia. Panama declared independence with U.S. support **Nov. 3;** recognized by Pres. Theodore Roosevelt **Nov. 6.** U.S., Panama signed canal treaty **Nov. 18.**

Wisconsin set first **direct primary** voting system **May 23.**

First **automobile trip** across U.S. from San Francisco to New York **May 23-Aug. 1.**

First successful flight in heavier-than-air mechanically propelled airplane by **Orville Wright Dec. 17** near Kitty Hawk, N.C., 120 ft. in 12 seconds. Fourth flight same day by **Wilbur Wright,** 852 ft. in 59 seconds. Improved plane patented **May 22, 1906.**

Jack London published *Call of the Wild.*

Great Train Robbery, pioneering film, produced.

1904

Ida Tarbell published muckraking *History of Standard Oil.*

1905

First **Rotary Club** founded in Chicago **Dec.**

1906

San Francisco earthquake and fire **Apr. 18-19** left 503 dead, $350 million damages.

Pure Food and Drug Act and Meat Inspection Act both passed **June 30.**

1907

Financial panic and depression started **Mar. 13.**

First round-world cruise of U.S. **"Great White Fleet";** 16 battleships, 12,000 men.

1908

Henry Ford introduced **Model T** car, priced at $850 **Oct. 1.**

1909

Adm. Robert E. Peary reached **North Pole Apr. 6** on 6th attempt, accompanied by Matthew Henson, a black man, and 4 Eskimos.

National Conference on the Negro convened **May 30,** leading to founding of the National Association for the Advancement of Colored People.

1910

Boy Scouts of America founded **Feb. 8.**

1911

Supreme Court dissolved **Standard Oil Co. May 15.**

Building holding NYC's **Triangle Shirtwaist Co.** sweatshop caught fire **Mar. 25;** 146 died, mostly young women; some trapped and killed, others jumped to their deaths.

First **transcontinental airplane flight** (with numerous stops) by C.P. Rodgers, New York to Pasadena, **Sept. 17-Nov. 5;** time in air 82 hrs., 4 min.

1912

Amer. Girl Guides founded **Mar. 12;** name changed in 1913 to **Girl Scouts.**

U.S. sent marines **Aug. 14** to **Nicaragua,** which was in default of loans to U.S. and Europe.

1913

N.Y. Armory Show brought modern art to U.S. **Feb. 17.**

U.S. blockaded Mexico in support of revolutionaries.

Charles Beard published his *Economic Interpretation of the Constitution.*

Federal Reserve System was authorized **Dec. 23,** in a major reform of U.S. banking and finance.

1914

Ford Motor Co. raised basic wage rates from $2.40 for 9-hr. day to $5 for 8-hr. day **Jan. 5.**

When U.S. sailors were arrested at Tampico **Apr. 9,** Atlantic fleet was sent to **Veracruz,** occupied city.

Pres. Wilson proclaimed **U.S. neutrality** in the European war **Aug. 4.**

Panama Canal was officially opened **Aug. 15.**

The **Clayton Antitrust Act** was passed **Oct. 15,** strengthening federal anti-monopoly powers.

1915

First **telephone talk,** New York to San Francisco, **Jan. 25** by Alexander Graham Bell and Thomas A. Watson.

British ship **Lusitania** sunk **May 7** by German submarine; 128 American passengers lost (Germany had warned passengers in advance). As a result of U.S. campaign, Germany issued apology and promise of payments **Oct. 5.** Pres. Wilson asked for a military fund increase **Dec. 7.**

U.S. troops landed in **Haiti July 28.** Haiti became a virtual U.S. protectorate under **Sept. 16** treaty.

1916

Gen. John J. **Pershing entered Mexico** to pursue Francisco (Pancho) Villa, who had raided U.S. border areas. Forces withdrawn **Feb. 5, 1917.**

Rural Credits Act passed **July 17,** followed by Warehouse Act **Aug. 11;** both provided financial aid to farmers.

Bomb exploded during **San Francisco** Preparedness Day parade **July 22,** killed 10. Thomas J. Mooney, labor organizer, and Warren K. Billings, shoe worker, were convicted; both pardoned in **1939.**

U.S. bought **Virgin Islands** from Denmark **Aug. 4.**

Jeannette Rankin, 1st U.S. Congresswoman (R-Montana) elected.

U.S. established military government in the **Dominican Republic Nov. 29.**

Trade and loans to **European Allies** soared during the year.

John Dewey published *Democracy and Education.*

Carl Sandburg published *Chicago Poems.*

1917

Germany, suffering from British blockade, declared almost unrestricted **submarine warfare Jan. 31.** U.S. cut diplomatic ties with Germany **Feb. 3,** and formally declared war **Apr. 6.**

Conscription law was passed **May 18.** First U.S. troops arrived in Europe **June 26.**

The 18th **(Prohibition)** Amendment to the Constitution was submitted to the states by Congress **Dec. 18.** On **Jan. 16, 1919,** the 36th state (Nevada) ratified it. Franklin D. Roosevelt, as 1932 presidential candidate, endorsed repeal; 21st Amendment repealed 18th; ratification completed **Dec. 5, 1933.**

1918

Pres. Wilson set out his **14 Points** as basis for peace **Jan. 8.**

Over one million **American troops** were in Europe by **July.** War ended **Nov. 11.**

Influenza epidemic killed an estimated 20 million worldwide, 548,000 in U.S.

1919

First **transatlantic flight,** by U.S. Navy seaplane, left Rockaway, N.Y. **May 8,** stopped at Newfoundland, Azores, Lisbon May 27.

Boston police strike Sept. 9; National Guard breaks strike.

Sherwood Anderson published *Winesburg, Ohio.*

About 250 **alien radicals** were deported **Dec. 22.**

1920

In national **Red Scare,** some 2,700 Communists, anarchists, and other radicals were arrested **Jan.-May.**

Senate refused **Mar. 19** to ratify the **League of Nations Covenant.**

Nicola Sacco, 29, shoe factory employee and radical agitator, and **Bartolomeo Vanzetti,** 32, fish peddler and anarchist, accused of killing 2 men in Mass. payroll holdup **Apr. 15.** Found guilty **1921.** A 6-year worldwide campaign for release on grounds of want of conclusive evidence and prejudice failed. Both were executed **Aug. 23, 1927.** Vindicated July 19, 1977 by proclamation of Mass. Gov. Dukakis.

First regular licensed **radio broadcasting** begun **Aug. 20.**

19th Amendment ratified **Aug. 26,** giving women right to vote.

League of Women Voters founded.

Wall St., N.Y. City, **bomb** explosion killed 30, injured 100, did $2 million damage **Sept. 16.**

Sinclair Lewis's *Main Street,* **F. Scott Fitzgerald's** *This Side of Paradise* published.

1921

Congress sharply curbed **immigration,** set national quota system **May 19.**

Joint Congressional resolution declaring **peace with Germany, Austria, and Hungary** signed **July 2** by Pres. Harding; treaties were signed in **Aug.**

Limitation of Armaments Conference met in Washington **Nov. 12 to Feb. 6, 1922.** Major powers agreed to curtail naval construction, outlaw poison gas, restrict submarine attacks on merchant vessels, respect integrity of China.

Ku Klux Klan began revival with violence against blacks in North, South, and Midwest.

1922

Violence during **coal-mine strike** at Herrin, Ill., **June 22-23** cost 36 lives, 21 of them non-union miners.

Reader's Digest founded.

1923

First **sound-on-film motion picture,** "Phonofilm" was shown by Lee de Forest at Rivoli Theater, N.Y. City, beginning in **April.**

1924

Law approved by Congress **June 15** making all **Indians citizens.**

Nellie Tayloe Ross elected governor of Wyoming **Nov. 9** after death of her husband **Oct. 2;** installed **Jan. 5, 1925,** first woman governor. **Miriam (Ma) Ferguson** was elected governor of Texas **Nov. 9;** installed **Jan. 20, 1925.**

George Gershwin wrote *Rhapsody in Blue.*

1925

John T. Scopes found guilty of having taught evolution in Dayton, Tenn. high school, fined $100 and costs **July 24.**

1926

Dr. Robert H. Goddard demonstrated practicality of **rockets Mar. 16** at Auburn, Mass. with first liquid fuel rocket; rocket traveled 184 ft. in 2.5 secs.

Congress established **Army Air Corps July 2.**

Air Commerce Act passed **Nov. 2,** providing federal aid for airlines and airports.

1927

About **1,000 marines landed in China Mar. 5** to protect property in civil war.

Capt. **Charles A. Lindbergh** left Roosevelt Field, N.Y. **May 20** alone in plane Spirit of St. Louis on first New York-Paris nonstop flight. Reached Le Bourget airfield **May 21,** 3,610 miles in 33 1/2 hours.

The Jazz Singer, with **Al Jolson,** demonstrated part-talking pictures in N.Y. City **Oct. 6.**

Show Boat opened in New York **Dec. 27.**

O. E. Rolvaag published *Giants in the Earth.*

1928

Herbert Hoover elected president against **Alfred E. Smith,** the Catholic governor of New York.

Amelia Earhart became first woman to fly the Atlantic **June 17.**

1929

"St. Valentine's Day massacre" in Chicago **Feb. 14;** gangsters killed 7 rivals.

Farm price stability aided by **Agricultural Marketing Act,** passed **June 15.**

Albert B. Fall, former sec. of the interior, was convicted of accepting a bribe of $100,000 in the leasing of the **Elk Hills (Teapot Dome)** naval oil reserve; sentenced **Nov. 1** to $100,000 fine and year in prison.

Stock Market crash Oct. 29 marked end of postwar prosperity as stock prices plummeted. Stock losses for 1929-31 estimated at $50 billion; worst American depression began.

Thomas Wolfe published *Look Homeward, Angel.* **William Faulkner** published *The Sound and the Fury.*

1930

London **Naval Reduction Treaty** signed by U.S., Britain, Italy, France, and Japan **Apr. 22;** in effect **Jan. 1, 1931;** expired **Dec. 31, 1936.**

Hawley-Smoot Tariff signed; rate hikes slash world trade.

1931

Empire State Building opened in N.Y. City **May 1.**

Al Capone was convicted of tax evasion **Oct. 17.**

Pearl Buck published *The Good Earth.*

1932

Reconstruction Finance Corp. established **Jan. 22** to stimulate banking and business. Unemployment at 12 million.

Charles Lindbergh Jr. kidnaped Mar. 1, found dead **May 12.**

Bonus March on Washington **May 29** by World War I veterans demanding Congress pay their bonus in full.

1933

FDR named **Frances Perkins** U.S. Secy of Labor; 1st woman in U.S. Cabinet.

All banks in the U.S. were ordered closed by Pres. Roosevelt **Mar. 6.**

In the "100 days" special session, **Mar. 9—June 16,** Congress passed **New Deal** social and economic measures.

Gold standard dropped by U.S.; announced by Pres. Roosevelt **Apr. 19,** ratified by Congress **June 5.**

Prohibition ended in the U.S. as 36th state ratified 21st Amendment **Dec. 5.**

U.S. foreswore armed intervention in **Western Hemisphere** nations **Dec. 26.**

1934

U.S. troops pull out of **Haiti Aug. 6.**

1935

Comedian **Will Rogers** and aviator Wiley Post **killed Aug. 15** in Alaska plane crash.

Social Security Act passed by Congress **Aug. 14.**

Huey Long, Senator from Louisiana and national political leader, was **assassinated Sept. 8.**

Porgy and Bess, **George Gershwin** opera on American theme, opened **Oct. 10** in N.Y. City.

Committee for Industrial Organization (CIO) formed to expand industrial unionism **Nov. 9.**

1936

Boulder Dam completed.

Margaret Mitchell published *Gone With the Wind.*

1937

Joe Louis knocked out James J. Braddock, became world heavyweight champ **June 22.**

Amelia Earhart, aviator, and co-pilot Fred Noonan lost **July 2** near Howland Is. in the Pacific.

Pres. Roosevelt asked for 6 additional Supreme Court justices; **"packing" plan** defeated.

Auto, steel labor unions won first big contracts.

1938

Naval Expansion Act passed **May 17.**

National minimum wage enacted **June 25.**

Orson Welles radio dramatization of *War of the Worlds* caused nationwide scare **Oct. 30.**

1939

Pres. Roosevelt asked **defense budget hike Jan. 5, 12.**

N.Y. World's Fair opened **Apr. 30,** closed **Oct. 31;** reopened **May 11, 1940,** and finally closed **Oct. 21.**

Einstein alerts FDR to **A-bomb** opportunity in **Aug. 2** letter.

U.S. declares its neutrality in European war **Sept. 5.**

Roosevelt proclaimed a limited **national emergency Sept. 8,** an unlimited emergency **May 27, 1941.** Both ended by Pres. Truman **Apr. 28, 1952.**

John Steinbeck published *Grapes of Wrath.*

1940

U.S. okayed sale of **surplus war material** to Britain **June 3;** announced transfer of 50 overaged destroyers **Sept. 3.**

First **peacetime draft** approved **Sept. 14.**

Richard Wright published *Native Son.*

1941

The **Four Freedoms** termed essential by Pres. Roosevelt in speech to Congress **Jan. 6:** freedom of speech and religion, freedom from want and fear.

Lend-Lease Act signed **Mar. 11,** providing $7 billion in military credits for Britain. Lend-Lease for USSR approved in **Nov.**

U.S. occupied **Iceland July 7.**

The **Atlantic Charter,** 8-point declaration of principles, issued by Roosevelt and Winston Churchill **Aug. 14.**

Japan attacked **Pearl Harbor,** Hawaii, 7:55 a.m. Hawaiian time, **Dec. 7,** 19 ships sunk or damaged, 2,300 dead. U.S. declared war on Japan **Dec. 8,** on Germany and Italy **Dec. 11** after those countries declared war.

1942

Federal government forcibly moved 110,000 **Japanese-Americans** (including 75,000 U.S. citizens) from West Coast to detention camps. Exclusion lasted 3 years.

Battle of **Midway June 4-7** was Japan's first major defeat.

Marines landed on **Guadalcanal Aug. 7;** last Japanese not expelled until **Feb. 9, 1943.**

U.S., Britain invaded North Africa **Nov. 8.**

First **nuclear chain reaction** (fission of uranium isotope U-235) produced at Univ. of Chicago, under physicists Arthur Compton, Enrico Fermi, others **Dec. 2.**

1943

All war contractors barred from **racial discrimination May 27.**

Pres. Roosevelt signed **June 10** the pay-as-you-go income tax bill. Starting **July 1** wage and salary earners were subject to a **paycheck withholding** tax.

Race riot in Detroit June 21; 34 dead, 700 injured. Riot in Harlem section of N.Y. City; 6 killed.

U.S. troops invaded Italy **Sept. 9.**

Marines advanced in **Gilbert Is. in Nov.**

1944

U.S., Allied forces invaded Europe at **Normandy June 6.**

G.I. Bill of Rights signed **June 22,** providing veterans benefits.

U.S. forces landed on **Leyte,** Philippines **Oct. 20.**

1945

Yalta Conference met in the Crimea, USSR, **Feb. 3-11.** Roosevelt, Churchill, and Stalin agreed Russia would enter war against Japan.

Marines landed on **Iwo Jima Feb. 19;** U.S. forces invaded **Okinawa Apr. 1.**

Pres. Roosevelt, 63, died of cerebral hemorrhage in Warm Springs, Ga. **Apr. 12;** V.P. **Harry S. Truman** became pres.

Germany surrendered May 7.

First **atomic bomb,** produced at Los Alamos, N.M., exploded at Alamogordo, N.M. **July 16.** Bomb dropped on **Hiroshima Aug. 6,** on **Nagasaki Aug. 9.** Japan surrendered **Aug. 15.**

U.S. forces entered **Korea** south of 38th parallel to displace Japanese **Sept. 8.**

Gen. Douglas MacArthur took over supervision of Japan **Sept. 9.**

1946

Strike by 400,000 **mine workers** began **Apr. 1;** other industries followed.

Philippines given independence by U.S. **July 4.**

1947

Truman Doctrine: Pres. Truman asked Congress to aid Greece and Turkey to combat Communist terrorism **Mar. 12.** Approved **May 15.**

United Nations Security Council voted unanimously **Apr. 2** to place under **U.S. trusteeship** the Pacific islands formerly mandated to Japan.

Jackie Robinson on Brooklyn Dodgers **Apr. 11,** broke the color barrier in major league baseball.

Taft-Hartley Labor Act curbing strikes was vetoed by Truman **June 20;** Congress overrode the veto.

Proposals later known as the **Marshall Plan,** under which the U.S. would extend aid to European countries, were made by Sec. of State George C. Marshall **June 5.** Congress authorized some $12 billion in next 4 years.

1948

USSR began a land **blockade of Berlin's** Allied sectors **Apr. 1.** This blockade and Western counter-blockade were lifted **Sept. 30, 1949,** after British and U.S. planes had lifted 2,343,315 tons of food and coal into the city.

Organization of American States founded **Apr. 30.**

Alger Hiss, former State Dept. official, indicted Dec. 15 for perjury, after denying he had passed secret documents to Whittaker Chambers for transmission to a communist spy ring. His second trial ended in conviction **Jan. 21, 1950,** and a sentence of 5 years in prison.

Kinsey Report on Sexuality in the Human Male published.

1949

U.S. troops withdrawn from **Korea June 29.**

North Atlantic Treaty Organization (**NATO**) established **Aug. 24** by U.S., Canada, and 10 West European nations, agreeing that an armed attack against one or more of them would be considered an attack against all.

Mrs. I. Toguri D'Aquino (**Tokyo Rose** of Japanese wartime broadcasts) was sentenced **Oct. 7** to 10 years in prison for treason. Paroled **1956,** pardoned **1977.**

Eleven leaders of **U.S. Communist party** convicted **Oct. 14,** after 9-month trial in N.Y. City, of advocating violent overthrow of U.S. government. Ten defendants sentenced to 5 years in prison each and the 11th to 3 years. Supreme Court upheld the convictions **June 4, 1951.**

1950

U.S. **Jan. 14** recalled all consular officials from **China** after the latter seized the American consulate general in Peking.

Masked bandits robbed **Brink's Inc.,** Boston express office, **Jan. 17** of $2.8 million, of which $1.2 million was in cash. Case solved **1956,** 8 sentenced to life.

Pres. Truman authorized production of **H-bomb Jan. 31.**

United Nations asked for troops to restore Korea peace **June 25.**

Truman ordered Air Force and Navy to Korea **June 27** after North Korea invaded South. Truman approved ground forces, air strikes against North **June 30.**

U.S. sent 35 military advisers to **South Vietnam June 27,** and agreed to provide military and economic aid to anti-Communist government.

Army seized all railroads Aug. 27 on Truman's order to prevent a general strike; roads returned to owners in **1952.**

U.S. forces landed at Inchon Sept. 15; UN force took Pyongyang **Oct. 20,** reached China border **Nov. 20,** China sent troops across border **Nov. 26.**

Two members of a **Puerto Rican nationalist** movement tried to kill Pres. Truman **Nov. 1.** (see Assassinations)

U.S. **Dec. 8** banned shipments to **Communist China** and to Asiatic ports trading with it.

1951

Sen. **Estes Kefauver** led Senate investigation into organized crime. Preliminary report **Feb. 28** said gambling take was over $20 billion a year.

Julius Rosenberg, his wife, Ethel, and Morton Sobell, all U.S. citizens, were found guilty **Mar. 29** of conspiracy to commit wartime espionage. Rosenbergs sentenced to death, Sobell to 30 years. Rosenbergs **executed June 19, 1953.** Sobell released **Jan. 14, 1969.**

Gen. Douglas MacArthur was removed from his Korea command **Apr. 11** for unauthorized policy statements.

Korea cease-fire talks began in July; lasted 2 years. **Fighting ended July 27, 1953.**

Tariff concessions by the U.S. to the Soviet Union, Communist China, and all communist-dominated lands were suspended **Aug. 1.**

The U.S., **Australia,** and **New Zealand** signed a mutual security pact **Sept. 1.**

Transcontinental television inaugurated **Sept. 4** with Pres. Truman's address at the Japanese Peace Treaty Conference in San Francisco.

Japanese Peace Treaty signed in San Francisco **Sept. 8** by U.S., Japan, and 47 other nations.

J.D. Salinger published *Catcher in the Rye.*

1952

U.S. **seizure of nation's steel mills** was ordered by Pres. Truman **Apr. 8** to avert a strike. Ruled illegal by Supreme Court **June 2.**

Peace contract between West Germany, U.S., Great Britain, and France was signed **May 26.**

The last racial and ethnic barriers to naturalization were removed, **June 26-27,** with the passage of the **Immigration and Naturalization Act of 1952.**

First **hydrogen device** explosion **Nov. 1** at Eniwetok Atoll in Pacific.

1953

Pres. Eisenhower announced **May 8** that U.S. had given France $60 million for **Indochina War.** More aid was announced in **Sept.** In **1954** it was reported that three fourths of the war's costs were met by U.S.

1954

Nautilus, first atomic-powered submarine, was launched at Groton, Conn. **Jan. 21.**

Five members of Congress were wounded in the House **Mar. 1** by 4 **Puerto Rican independence supporters** who fired at random from a spectators' gallery.

Sen. Joseph McCarthy led televised hearings **Apr. 22-June 17** into alleged Communist influence in the Army.

Racial segregation in public schools was unanimously ruled unconstitutional by the Supreme Court **May 17,** as a violation of the 14th Amendment clause guaranteeing equal protection of the laws.

Southeast Asia Treaty Organization (**SEATO**) formed by collective defense pact signed in Manila **Sept. 8** by the U.S., Britain, France, Australia, New Zealand, Philippines, Pakistan, and Thailand.

Condemnation of **Sen. Joseph R. McCarthy** (R., Wis.) voted by Senate, 67-22 **Dec. 2** for contempt of a Senate elections subcommittee, for abuse of its members, and for insults to the Senate during his Army investigation hearings.

1955

U.S. agreed **Feb. 12** to help train **South Vietnamese** army.

Supreme Court ordered **"all deliberate speed"** in integration of public schools **May 31.**

A **summit meeting** of leaders of U.S., Britain, France, and USSR took place **July 18-23** in Geneva, Switzerland.

Rosa Parks refused **Dec. 1** to give her seat to a white man on a bus in Montgomery, Ala. Bus segregation ordinance declared unconstitutional by a federal court following boycott and NAACP protest.

Merger of America's 2 largest labor organizations was effected **Dec. 5** under the name American Federation of Labor and Congress of Industrial Organizations. The merged **AFL-CIO** had a membership estimated at 15 million.

1956

Massive resistance to Supreme Court desegregation rulings was called for **Mar. 12** by 101 Southern congressmen.

Federal-Aid **Highway Act** signed **June 29,** inaugurating interstate highway system.

First transatlantic **telephone cable** went into operation **Sept. 25.**

1957

Congress approved first **civil rights bill** for blacks since Reconstruction **Apr. 29,** to protect voting rights.

National Guardsmen, called out by Arkansas Gov. Orval Faubus **Sept. 4,** barred 9 black students from entering previously all-white Central High School in **Little Rock.** Faubus complied **Sept. 21** with a federal court order to remove the National Guardsmen. The blacks entered school **Sept. 23** but were ordered to withdraw by local authorities because of fear of mob violence. Pres. Eisenhower sent federal troops **Sept. 24** to enforce the court's order.

Jack Kerouac published *On the Road.*

1958

First U.S. earth satellite to go into orbit, **Explorer I,** launched by Army **Jan. 31** at Cape Canaveral, Fla.; discovered Van Allen radiation belt.

Five thousand U.S. Marines sent to **Lebanon** to protect elected government from threatened overthrow **July-Oct.**

First domestic **jet airline** passenger service in U.S. opened by National Airlines **Dec. 10** between N.Y. and Miami.

1959

Alaska admitted as 49th state **Jan. 3; Hawaii** admitted **Aug. 21.**

St. Lawrence Seaway opened **Apr. 25.**

The George Washington, first U.S. ballistic-missile submarine, launched at Groton, Conn. **June 9.**

N.S. **Savannah,** world's first atomic-powered merchant ship, launched **July 21** at Camden, N.J.

Soviet Premier **Khrushchev** paid unprecedented visit to U.S. **Sept. 15-27,** made transcontinental tour.

1960

Sit-ins began **Feb. 1** when 4 black college students in Greensboro, N.C. refused to move from a Woolworth lunch counter when denied service. By **Sept. 1961** more than 70,000 students, whites and blacks, had participated in sit-ins.

U.S. launched first **weather satellite,** Tiros I, **Apr. 1.**

Congress approved a strong **voting rights act Apr. 21.**

A **U-2 reconnaisance plane** of the U.S. was shot down in the Soviet Union **May 1.** The incident led to cancellation of an imminent Paris summit conference.

Mobs attacked U.S. embassy in **Panama Sept. 17** in dispute over flying of U.S. and Panamanian flags.

U.S. announced **Dec. 15** it backed rightist group in **Laos,** which took power the next day.

1961

The U.S. severed diplomatic and consular relations with **Cuba Jan. 3,** after disputes over nationalizations of U.S. firms, U.S. military presence at Guantanamo base, etc.

Invasion of Cuba's **"Bay of Pigs" Apr. 17** by Cuban exiles trained, armed, and directed by the U.S., attempting to overthrow the regime of Premier Fidel Castro, failed.

Commander Alan B. Shepard Jr. was rocketed from Cape Canaveral, Fla., 116.5 mi. above the earth in a Mercury capsule **May 5** in the first U.S. manned sub-orbital space flight.

1962

Lt. Col. John H. Glenn Jr. became the first American in orbit **Feb. 20** when he circled the earth 3 times in the Mercury capsule **Friendship 7.**

Pres. Kennedy said **Feb. 14** U.S. military advisers in Vietnam would fire if fired upon.

Supreme Court **Mar. 26** backed **one-man one-vote** apportionment of seats in state legislatures.

First U.S. **communications satellite** launched in **July.**

James Meredith became first black student at Univ. of Mississippi **Oct. 1** after 3,000 troops put down riots.

A Soviet **offensive missile buildup in Cuba** was revealed **Oct. 22** by Pres. Kennedy, who ordered a naval and air quarantine on shipment of offensive military equipment to the island. Kennedy and Soviet Premier Khrushchev reached agreement **Oct. 28** on a formula to end the crisis. Kennedy announced **Nov. 2** that Soviet missile bases in Cuba were being dismantled.

Rachel Carson's *Silent Spring* launched environmentalist movement.

1963

Supreme Court ruled **Mar. 18** that all **criminal defendants** must have counsel and that illegally acquired evidence was not admissible in state as well as federal courts.

Supreme Court ruled, 8-1, **June 17** that laws requiring **recitation of the Lord's Prayer** or Bible verses in public schools were unconstitutional.

A limited **nuclear test-ban treaty** was agreed upon **July 25** by the U.S., Soviet Union and Britain, barring all nuclear tests except underground.

Washington demonstration by 200,000 persons **Aug. 28** in support of **black demands** for equal rights. Highlight was speech in which Dr. Martin Luther King said: "I have a dream that this nation will rise up and live out the true meaning of its creed, 'We hold these truths to be self-evident: that all men are created equal.' "

South Vietnam Pres. **Ngo Dinh Diem assassinated Nov. 2;** U.S. had earlier withdrawn support.

Pres. John F. Kennedy was shot and fatally wounded by an assassin **Nov. 22** as he rode in a motorcade through downtown Dallas, Tex. Vice Pres. Lyndon B. Johnson was inaugurated president shortly after in Dallas. Lee Harvey Oswald was arrested and charged with the murder. Oswald was shot and fatally wounded **Nov. 24** by Jack Ruby, 52, a Dallas nightclub owner, who was convicted of murder **Mar. 14, 1964** and sentenced to death. Ruby died of natural causes **Jan. 3, 1967** while awaiting retrial.

U.S. troops in **Vietnam** totalled over 15,000 by year-end; aid to South Vietnam was over $500 million in **1963.**

1964

Panama suspended relations with U.S. **Jan. 9** after riots. U.S. offered **Dec. 18** to negotiate a new canal treaty.

Supreme Court ordered **Feb. 17** that **congressional districts** have equal populations.

U.S. reported **May 27** it was sending military planes to **Laos.**

Omnibus **civil rights bill** passed **June 29** banning discrimination in voting, jobs, public accommodations, etc.

Three **civil rights workers** were reported missing in Mississippi **June 22;** found buried **Aug. 4.** Twenty-one white men were arrested. On **Oct. 20, 1967,** an all-white federal jury convicted 7 of conspiracy in the slayings.

U.S. Congress **Aug. 7** passed **Tonkin Resolution,** authorizing presidential action in Vietnam, after North Vietnam boats reportedly attacked 2 U.S. destroyers **Aug. 2.**

Congress approved War on Poverty bill **Aug. 11.**

The **Warren Commission** released **Sept. 27** a report concluding that Lee Harvey Oswald was solely responsible for the Kennedy assassination.

1965

Pres. Johnson in **Feb.** ordered continuous **bombing of North Vietnam** below 20th parallel.

Some 14,000 U.S. troops sent to **Dominican Republic** during civil war **Apr. 28.** All troops withdrawn by next year.

New **Voting Rights Act** signed **Aug. 6.**

Los Angeles riot by blacks living in **Watts** area resulted in death of 34 persons and property damage est. at $200 million **Aug. 11-16.**

Water Quality Act passed **Sept. 21** to meet pollution, shortage problems.

National origins quota system of **immigration** abolished **Oct. 3.**

Electric power failure blacked out most of northeastern U.S., parts of 2 Canadian provinces the night of **Nov. 9-10.**

U.S. forces in **S. Vietnam** reached 184,300 by year-end.

1966

U.S. forces began firing into **Cambodia May 1.**

Bombing of Hanoi area of North Vietnam by U.S. planes began **June 29.** By **Dec. 31,** 385,300 U.S. troops were stationed in South Vietnam, plus 60,000 offshore and 33,000 in Thailand.

Medicare, government program to pay part of the medical expenses of citizens over 65, began **July 1.**

Edward Brooke (R, Mass.) elected **Nov. 8** as first black U.S. senator in 85 years.

1967

Black representative **Adam Clayton Powell** (D, N.Y.) was denied **Mar. 1** his seat in Congress because of charges he misused gvt. funds. Reelected in 1968, he was seated, but fined $25,000 and stripped of his 22 years' seniority.

Pres. Johnson and Soviet Premier Aleksei Kosygin met **June 23 and 25** at **Glassboro State College** in N.J.; agreed not to let any crisis push them into war.

Riots by blacks in **Newark, N.J. July 12-17** killed 26, injured 1,500; over 1,000 arrested. In Detroit, Mich., **July 23-30** at least 40 died; 2,000 injured, 5,000 left homeless by rioting, looting, burning in city's black ghetto. Quelled by 4,700 federal paratroopers and 8,000 National Guardsmen.

Thurgood Marshall sworn in **Oct. 2** as first black U.S. Supreme Court Justice. Carl B. Stokes (D, Cleveland) and Richard G. Hatcher (D, Gary, Ind.) were elected first black mayors of major U.S. cities **Nov. 7.**

By **December** 475,000 U.S. troops were in **South Vietnam,** all North Vietnam was subject to bombing. Protests against the war mounted in U.S. during year.

1968

USS Pueblo and 83-man crew seized in Sea of Japan **Jan. 23** by North Koreans; 82 men released **Dec. 22.**

"Tet offensive": Communist troops attacked Saigon, 30 province capitals **Jan. 30,** suffer heavy casualties.

Pres. Johnson **curbed bombing** of North Vietnam **Mar. 31.** Peace talks began in Paris **May 10.** All bombing of North halted **Oct. 31.**

Martin Luther King Jr., 39, assassinated Apr. 4 in Memphis, Tenn. James Earl Ray, an escaped convict, pleaded guilty to the slaying, was sentenced to 99 years.

Sen. Robert F. Kennedy (D, N.Y.), 42, **shot June 5** in Hotel Ambassador, Los Angeles, after celebrating presidential primary victories. Died **June 6.** Sirhan Bishara Sirhan, Jordanian, convicted of murder.

Rep. Shirley Chisholm (D., N.Y.) became the first black woman elected to Congress.

1969

Expanded four-party **Vietnam peace talks** began **Jan. 18.** U.S. force peaked at 543,400 in April. Withdrawal started **July 8.** Pres. Nixon set Vietnamization policy **Nov. 3.**

U.S. astronaut **Neil A. Armstrong,** 38, commander of the Apollo 11 mission, became the first man to **set foot on the moon July 20.** Air Force Col. Edwin E. Aldrin Jr. accompanied Armstrong.

Anti-Vietnam War **demonstrations reached peak** in U.S.; some 250,000 marched in Washington, D.C. **Nov. 15.**

Massacre of hundreds of civilians at **Mylai, South Vietnam** in 1968 incident was reported **Nov. 16.**

1970

United Mine Workers official **Joseph A. Yablonski,** his wife, and their daughter were found shot **Jan. 5** in their Clarksville, Pa. home. UMW chief W. A. (Tony) Boyle was later convicted of the killing.

A federal jury **Feb. 18** found the **"Chicago 7"** innocent of conspiring to incite riots during the 1968 Democratic National Convention. However, 5 were convicted of crossing state lines with intent to incite riots.

Millions of Americans participated in anti-pollution demonstrations **Apr. 22** to mark the first **Earth Day.**

U.S. and South Vietnamese forces crossed **Cambodian** borders **Apr. 30** to get at enemy bases. Four students were killed **May 4** at **Kent St.** Univ. in Ohio by National Guardsmen during a protest against the war.

Two **women generals,** the first in U.S. history, were named by Pres. Nixon **May 15.**

A **postal reform** measure was signed **Aug. 12,** creating an independent U.S. Postal Service, thus relinquishing governmental control of the U.S. mails after almost 2 centuries.

1971

Charles Manson, 36, and 3 of his followers were found guilty **Jan. 26** of first-degree murder in the 1969 slaying of actress Sharon Tate and 6 others.

U.S. air and artillery forces aided a 44-day incursion by South Vietnam forces into **Laos** starting **Feb. 8.**

A Constitutional Amendment lowering the **voting age to 18** in all elections was approved in the Senate by a vote of 94-0 **Mar. 10.** The proposed 26th Amendment got House approval by a 400-19 vote **Mar. 23.** Thirty-eighth state ratified **June 30.**

A court-martial jury Mar. 29, convicted **Lt. William L. Calley Jr.** of premeditated murder of 22 South Vietnamese at Mylai on **Mar. 16, 1968.** He was sentenced to life imprisonment **Mar. 31.** Sentence was reduced to 20 years **Aug. 20.**

Publication of classified **Pentagon papers** on the U.S. involvement in Vietnam was begun **June 13** by the New York Times. In a 6-3 vote, the U.S. Supreme Court **June 30** upheld the right of the Times and the Washington Post to publish the documents under the protection of the First Amendment.

U.S. bombers struck massively in North Vietnam for 5 days starting **Dec. 26,** in retaliation for alleged violations of agreements reached prior to the 1968 bombing halt. U.S. forces at year-end were down to 140,000.

1972

Pres. Nixon arrived in **Peking Feb. 21** for an 8-day visit to China, which he called a "journey for peace." The unprecedented visit ended with a joint communique pledging that both powers would work for "a normalization of relations."

By a vote of 84 to 8, the Senate approved **Mar. 22** a Constitutional Amendment banning **discrimination against women** because of their sex and sent the measure to the states for ratification.

North Vietnamese forces launched the biggest attacks in 4 years across the demilitarized zone **Mar. 30.** The U.S. responded **Apr. 15** by resumption of bombing of Hanoi and Haiphong after a 4-year lull.

Nixon announced **May 8** the mining of **North Vietnam ports.** Last U.S. combat troops left **Aug. 11.**

Alabama Gov. George C. Wallace, campaigning for the presidency at a Laurel, Md. shopping center **May 15, was shot** and seriously wounded. Arthur H. Bremer, 21, was sentenced to 63 years for shooting Wallace and 3 bystanders.

In the first visit of a U.S. president to Moscow, Nixon arrived **May 22** for a week of summit talks with Kremlin leaders that culminated in a landmark **strategic arms pact.**

Five men were arrested **June 17** for breaking into the offices of the Democratic National Committee in the **Watergate** office complex in Washington, D.C.

The White House announced **July 8** that the U.S. would sell to the USSR at least $750 million of **American wheat,** corn, and other grains over a period of 3 years.

Full-scale bombing of North Vietnam resumed after Paris peace negotiations reached an impasse **Dec. 18.**

1973

Five of seven defendants in the **Watergate** break-in trial pleaded guilty **Jan. 11 and 15,** and the other 2 were convicted **Jan. 30.**

In **Roe v. Wade,** the Supreme Court ruled 7-2, **Jan. 22,** that a state may not prevent a woman from having an **abortion** during the **first 3 months of pregnancy,** and could regulate but not prohibit abortion during the second trimester; decision in effect overturned anti-abortion laws in 46 states.

Four-party **Vietnam peace pacts** were signed in Paris **Jan. 27,** and North Vietnam released some 590 U.S. prisoners by **Apr. 1.** Last U.S. troops left **Mar. 29.**

The **end of the military draft** was announced **Jan. 27.**

China and the U.S. agreed **Feb. 22** to set up permanent liaison offices in each other's country.

Top **Nixon aides** H.R. Haldeman, John D. Ehrlichman, and John W. Dean, and Attorney General Richard Kleindienst **resigned Apr. 30** amid charges of White House efforts to obstruct justice in the Watergate case.

The Senate Armed Services Committee **July 16** began a probe into allegations that the U.S. Air Force had made 3,500 secret **B-52 raids into Cambodia** in **1969 and 1970.**

John Dean, former Nixon counsel, told Senate hearings **June 25** that Nixon, his staff and campaign aides, and the Justice Department all had conspired to cover up Watergate facts. Nixon refused July 23 to release **tapes** of relevant White House conversations. Some tapes were turned over to the court **Nov. 26.**

The U.S. officially ceased bombing in **Cambodia** at midnight **Aug. 14** in accord with a June Congressional action.

Vice Pres. Spiro T. Agnew Oct. 10 resigned and pleaded "nolo contendere" (no contest) to charges of tax evasion on payments made to him by Maryland contractors when he was governor of that state. Gerald Rudolph Ford **Oct. 12** became first appointed vice president under the 25th Amendment; sworn in **Dec. 6.**

A total ban on **oil exports** to the U.S. was imposed by Arab oil-producing nations **Oct. 19-21** after the outbreak of an Arab-Israeli war. The ban was lifted **Mar. 18, 1974.**

Atty. Gen. Elliot Richardson resigned, and his deputy William D. Ruckelshaus and Watergate Special Prosecutor Archibald Cox were fired by Pres. Nixon **Oct. 20** when Cox threatened to secure a judicial ruling that Nixon was violating a court order to turn tapes over to Watergate case Judge John Sirica.

Leon Jaworski, conservative Texas Democrat, was named **Nov. 1** by the Nixon administration to be special prosecutor to succeed Archibald Cox.

Congress overrode **Nov. 7** Nixon's veto of the **war powers** bill, which curbed the president's power to commit armed forces to hostilities abroad without Congressional approval.

1974

Impeachment hearings were opened **May 9** against Nixon by the House Judiciary Committee.

John D. Ehrlichman and 3 **White House "plumbers"** were found guilty **July 12** of conspiring to violate the civil rights of Dr. Lewis Fielding, formerly psychiatrist to Pentagon Papers leaker Daniel Ellsberg, by breaking into his Beverly Hills, Cal. office.

The U.S. Supreme Court ruled, 8-0, **July 24** that Nixon had to turn over **64 tapes** of White House conversations sought by Watergate Special Prosecutor Leon Jaworski.

The House Judiciary Committee, in televised hearings **July 24-30**, recommended 3 **articles of impeachment** against Nixon. The first, voted 27-11 **July 27**, charged Nixon with taking part in a criminal conspiracy to obstruct justice in the Watergate cover-up. The second, voted 28-10 **July 29**, charged he "repeatedly" failed to carry out his constitutional oath in a series of alleged abuses of power. The third, voted 21-17 **July 30**, accused him of unconstitutional defiance of committee subpoenas. The House of Representatives voted without debate **Aug. 20**, by 412-3, to accept the committee report, which included the recommended impeachment articles.

Nixon resigned Aug. 9. His support began eroding **Aug. 5** when he released 3 tapes, admitting he originated plans to have the FBI stop its probe of the Watergate break-in for political as well as national security reasons. **Vice President Gerald R. Ford** was sworn in as the 38th U.S. president on **Aug. 9.**

An **unconditional pardon** to ex-Pres. Nixon for all federal crimes that he "committed or may have committed" while president was issued by Pres. Gerald Ford **Sept. 8.**

1975

Found guilty of **Watergate** cover-up charges **Jan. 1** were ex-Atty. Gen. John N. Mitchell, ex-presidential advisers H.R. Haldeman and John D. Ehrlichman.

U.S. civilians were evacuated from **Saigon Apr. 29** as communist forces completed takeover of South Vietnam.

U.S. merchant ship **Mayaguez** and crew of 39 seized by Cambodian forces in Gulf of Siam **May 12.** In rescue operation, U.S. Marines attacked Tang Is., planes bombed air base; Cambodia surrendered ship and crew.

Congress voted $405 million for South **Vietnam refugees May 16**; 140,000 were flown to the U.S.

Illegal **CIA operations**, including records on 300,000 persons and groups, and infiltration of agents into black, anti-war and political movements, were described by a "blue-ribbon" panel headed by Vice Pres. Rockefeller **June 10.**

FBI agents captured **Patricia (Patty) Hearst**, kidnapped **Feb. 4, 1974**, in San Francisco **Sept. 18** with others. She was indicted for bank robbery; a San Francisco jury convicted her **Mar. 20, 1976.**

1976

Payments abroad of $22 million in bribes by Lockheed Aircraft Corp. to sell its planes were revealed **Feb. 4** by a Senate subcommittee. Lockheed admitted payments in Japan, Turkey, Italy, and Holland.

The U.S. celebrated its **Bicentennial July 4**, marking the 200th anniversary of its independence with festivals, parades, and N.Y. City's Operation Sail, a gathering of tall ships from around the world viewed by 6 million persons.

A mystery ailment **"legionnaire's disease"** killed 29 persons who attended an American Legion convention **July 21-24** in Philadelphia. The cause was found to be a bacterium, it was reported **June 18, 1977.**

The Viking II set down on **Mars'** Utopia Plains **Sept. 3**, following the successful landing by Viking I **July 20.**

1977

Pres. Jimmy Carter **Jan. 21** pardoned most Vietnam War **draft evaders**, who numbered some 10,000.

Convicted murderer **Gary Gilmore** was executed by a Utah firing squad **Jan. 17**, in the first exercise of capital punishment anywhere in the U.S. since **1967.** Gilmore had opposed all attempts to delay the execution.

Carter signed an act **Aug. 4** creating a new Cabinet-level **Energy Department.**

1978

U.S. Senate voted **Apr. 18** to turn over the **Panama Canal** to Panama on Dec. 31, 1999; **Mar. 16** vote had given approval to a treaty guaranteeing the area's neutrality after the year 2000.

The U.S. Supreme Court **June 28** voted 5-4 not to allow a firm quota system in affirmative action plans; the Court did uphold programs that were more "flexible" in nature.

The **House Select Committee on Assassinations** opened hearings **Sept. 6** into assassinations of Pres. Kennedy and Martin Luther King Jr.; the committee recessed **Dec. 30** after concluding conspiracies likely in both cases, but with no further hard evidence for further prosecutions.

Congress passed the **Humphrey-Hawkins "full employment" Bill Oct. 15**, which set national goal of reducing unemployment to 4% by 1983, while reducing inflation to 3% in same period; Pres. Carter signed bill, **Oct. 27.**

1979

A major accident occurred, **Mar. 28**, at a nuclear reactor on **Three Mile Island** near Middletown, Pa.

The federal government announced, **Nov. 1**, a $1.5 billion loan-guarantee plan to aid the nation's 3d largest automaker, **Chrysler Corp.**, which had reported a loss of $460.6 million for the 3d quarter of 1979.

Some 90 people, including 63 Americans, were taken hostage, **Nov. 4**, at the **American embassy in Teheran**, Iran, by militant student followers of Ayatollah Khomeini who demanded the return of former Shah Mohammad Reza Pahlavi, who was undergoing medical treatment in New York City.

1980

Pres. Carter announced, **Jan. 4, punitive measures against the USSR**, including an embargo on the sale of grain and high technology, in retaliation for the Soviet invasion of Afghanistan. At Carter's request, the **U.S. Olympic Committee** voted, **Apr. 12**, not to attend the Moscow Summer Olympics.

Eight Americans were killed and 5 wounded, **Apr. 24**, in an ill-fated attempt to **rescue the hostages** held by Iranian **militants** at the U.S. Embassy in Teheran.

In Washington, **Mt. St. Helens erupted, May 18**, in a violent blast estimated to be 500 times as powerful as the Hiroshima atomic bomb. The blast, followed by others on **May 25** and **June 12**, left about 60 dead, and economic losses estimated at nearly $3 billion.

In a sweeping victory, **Nov. 4, Ronald Wilson Reagan** was elected 40th President of the United States, defeating incumbent Jimmy Carter. The stunning GOP victory extended to the U.S. Congress where Republicans gained control of the Senate and wrested 33 House seats from the Democrats.

Former Beatle **John Lennon** was shot and killed, **Dec. 8**, outside his apartment building in New York City.

1981

Minutes after the **inauguration of Pres. Ronald Reagan, Jan. 20**, the **52 Americans** who had been held **hostage in Iran** for 444 days were flown to freedom following an agreement in which the U.S. agreed to return to Iran $8 billion in frozen assets.

President Reagan was **shot in the chest** by a would-be assassin, **Mar. 30**, in Washington, D.C., as he walked to his limousine following an address.

The world's first reusable spacecraft, the **Space Shuttle Columbia**, was sent into space, **Apr. 12**, and completed its successful mission 2 days later.

Both houses of Congress passed, **July 29**, President Reagan's **tax-cut legislation.** The largest tax cut in the nation's history was expected to reduce taxes by $37.6 bln. in fiscal 1982, and to save taxpayers $750 bln. over the next 5 years.

Federal air traffic controllers, Aug. 3, began an **illegal nationwide strike** after their union rejected the government's final offer for a new contract. Most of the 13,000 striking controllers defied the back-to-work order, and were dismissed by President Reagan **Aug. 5.**

In a 99-0 vote, the Senate confirmed, **Sept. 21,** the appointment of **Sandra Day O'Connor** as an **associate justice of the U.S. Supreme Court.** She was the first woman appointed to that body.

President Reagan ordered **sanctions against the new Polish military government, Dec. 23,** in response to the imposition of martial law in that country.

1982

The 13-year-old lawsuit against **AT&T** by the **Justice Dept.** was settled **Jan. 8.** AT&T agreed to give up the 22 Bell System companies but in return was allowed to expand into previously prohibited areas inc. data processing, telephone and computer equipment sales, and computer communication devices.

On **Mar. 2,** the Senate voted 57-37 for a bill that virtually eliminated busing for the purposes of racial integration.

On **June 12,** in **N.Y.'s Central Park,** hundreds of thousands demonstrated against **nuclear arms.**

The Equal Rights Amendment was defeated after a 10-year struggle for ratification.

The **elections** on **Nov. 2** resulted in gains for the Democrats—the margin in the new House was 269-166. In the Senate elections, Democrats won 20 out of 33 seats, but were still the minority, 54-46.

The **highest unemployment rate since 1940,** 10.4%, was reported on **Nov. 5.** The rate for Nov. reached 10.8%, with over 11 million unemployed.

Lech Walesa, former leader of **Solidarity,** the Polish labor union, was freed **Nov. 13,** after 11 months of internment following the imposition of martial law and the outlawing of Solidarity. Pres. Reagan lifted the **U.S. embargo on sales of oil and gas equipment to the Soviet Union.**

The **Space Shuttle Columbia** completed its first operational flight **Nov. 16.**

A retired dentist, **Dr. Barney B. Clark,** 61, became the first recipient of a **permanent artificial heart** during a 7½ hour operation in Salt Lake City **Dec. 2.** The heart was designed by **Dr. Robert Jarvik,** also on the surgical team.

1983

On **Apr. 20, Pres. Reagan** signed a compromise, bipartisan bill designed to rescue the **Social Security System** from bankruptcy.

In an 8-1 decision, **the U.S. Supreme Court** held, **May 24,** that the **Internal Revenue Service** could deny **tax exemptions** to **private schools** that practiced **racial discrimination.**

Sally Ride became the first American **woman** to travel in **space, June 18,** when the **space shuttle Challenger** was launched from Cape Canaveral, Fla.

On **Oct. 23,** 241 **U.S. Marines and sailors,** members of the multinational **peacekeeping force in Lebanon,** were killed when a TNT-laden suicide **terrorist** blew up Marine headquarters at **Beirut** Intl. Airport. Almost simultaneously, a second truck bomb blew up a **French paratroop** barracks two miles away, killing more than 40.

U.S. Marines and Rangers and a small force from 6 **Caribbean** nations invaded the island of **Grenada** on **Oct. 25,** in response to a request from the **Organization of Eastern Caribbean States.** After a few days, Grenadian militia and Cuban "construction workers" were overcome, hundreds of U.S. citizens evacuated safely, and the Marxist regime deposed. The U.S. Congress applied the War Powers Resolution, requiring U.S. troops to leave Grenada by **Dec. 24.**

1984

In his **State of the Union address, Jan. 25,** Pres. Reagan called for budget cuts of $100 billion over 3 years, but opposed increased taxes.

On **Feb. 26,** as the position of Pres. Amin Gemayel of Lebanon deteriorated and his army crumbled, Pres. Reagan **removed U.S. Marines from Beirut** and placed them on U.S. ships offshore.

The space shuttle *Challenger* was launched on its 4th trip into space, **Feb. 3.** On **Feb. 7,** Navy Capt. Bruce McCandless, followed by Army Lt. Colonel Robert Stewart, **became the first humans to fly free of a spacecraft.**

During **March,** the U.S. Senate rejected 2 Constitutional amendments that would have permitted **prayer in the public schools.**

The Central Intelligence Agency **(CIA) acknowledged** in April that it had participated in the **mining of Nicaraguan harbors.** This touched off a controversy in Congress, and the Senate, **Apr. 10,** adopted a nonbinding resolution condemning U.S. participation in the mining.

From **Apr. 26 to May 1, Pres. Reagan visited China** for the first time, holding discussions with Chinese leaders.

On **May 7,** American **Vietnam war** veterans reached an **out-of-court settlement with 7 chemical companies** in their class-action suit regarding the herbicide **Agent Orange.**

A federal judge in Salt Lake City held, **May 10,** that the **U.S. government had been negligent** in its above-ground testing of **nuclear weapons** in Nevada from 1951 to 1962.

On **June 6,** former vice president **Walter Mondale** won the **Democratic presidental nomination.** In a historic move, **July 12, Mondale chose a woman, Rep. Geraldine Ferraro (N.Y.)** as candidate for **vice president.**

Pres. Reagan, **Aug. 11,** signed a law prohibiting public high schools from barring students who wished to **assemble for religious or political activities outside of school hours.**

Ronald Reagan was reelected U.S. President **Nov. 6** in the greatest Republican **landslide** in history, carrying 49 states against Walter F. Mondale.

1985

The controversial MX missile survived critical votes in the Senate and House. The **Senate, Mar. 19** and **21,** voted to **authorize the missiles** and to **appropriate $1.5 million** for the construction of 21 missiles. The **House** gave its endorsement **Mar. 26** and **28.**

E.F. Hutton, one of the nation's largest brokerage companies, **pleaded guilty, May 2,** to 2,000 **federal charges** related to the manipulation of its checking accounts. The company agreed to pay $2 million in fines and to pay back up to $8 million to banks it had defrauded.

"Live Aid," a 17-hour rock concert broadcast **July 13** on radio and TV from London and Phila. to 152 countries, raised $70 million for the starving peoples of Africa.

On **Oct. 7, 5 hijackers seized an Italian cruise ship, the** *Achille Lauro,* in the open sea as it approached Port Said, Egypt. Some 400 persons were aboard, including about 340 crew. The hijackers, members of the Palestine Liberation Front, a faction broken from the PLO, demanded the release of 50 Palestinians held by Israel.

In November, for the first time in 6 years, the leaders of the U.S. and the Soviet Union met at a **summit conference.** In Geneva, Switzerland, **Pres. Reagan** and **Mikhail Gorbachev,** the general secretary of the Soviet Communist Party, talked privately for 5 hours, **Nov. 19 and 20.**

1986

On **Jan. 20,** for the 1st time, the U.S. officially observed **Martin Luther King Day.**

Moments after liftoff, **Jan. 28,** the **space shuttle** ***Challenger*** **exploded, killing 6 astronauts and Christa McAuliffe, a New Hampshire teacher.** Subsequent investigations found that NASA had abandoned "good judgment and common sense" regarding safety problems that caused the explosion.

U.S. warplanes struck targets in Tripoli and Benghazi, Libya, Apr. 14—retaliation against the Libyan bombing of a W. Berlin disco that killed 2, injured 200, Apr. 5. On **Jan. 7,** Pres. Reagan had said that the U.S. had aborted 26 "terrorist missions" in 1985. In an executive order, he banned trade with and travel to Libya, ordering Americans out. A 2nd executive order, **Jan. 8,** had frozen all Libyan government assets in the U.S. and U.S. bank branches abroad.

U.S. officials said, **June 12, that AIDS cases and deaths would increase tenfold in the next 5 years.** At that time, the government had recorded 21,517 cases, 11,713 deaths. An anti-viral drug, azidothymidine (AZT) was found to improve the health of some AIDS patient, but was not a cure.

With mounting **abuse of illegal drugs** in the U.S., specifically **cocaine as "crack,"** Congress passed anti-drug laws and the U.S. joined Bolivia in raids against cocaine processing hideouts.

The U.S., **via Congress's Sept. override of Pres. Reagan's veto,** joined other nations in imposing **economic sanctions on So. Africa,** pressuring the Botha gvt. to end apartheid.

The U.S. Senate confirmed, **Sept. 17,** Pres. Reagan's nomination of **William Rehnquist as chief justice, Antonin Scalia as associate justice of the Supreme Court.**

Congress passed, in late **Sept.,** the comprehensive **Tax Reform Law.** In effect in 1987, it simplified the system, drastically changing tax brackets, deductions, and more.

The U.S. and USSR reached tentative agreement on a **world-wide ban of medium-range missiles, Sept. 18.**

One day before the 1986 Congressional elections, it was reported that the U.S. had sent spare parts and ammunition to Iran. Over the next months it was revealed that **additional arms sales had been made to Iran,** and **profits diverted to a fund for Nicaraguan contras.**

In the **Congressional races, Nov. 4, Democrats won a 55-45 Senate majority,** after 6 yrs. of a Republican majority, and **enlarged their House majority by 5, to 258-177.**

The most scandalous year in Wall Street history ended with **Ivan Boesky's agreeing, Nov. 14,** to **plead guilty to an unspecified criminal count, pay a $100 million fine, and return profits;** he was barred for life from trading securities.

1987

Pres. Reagan produced the nation's first **trillion-dollar budget, Jan. 5.**

The stock market continued its phenomenal rise. The **Dow closed at 2002.25, Jan. 8,** its first finish above 2000. The Dow advanced for 13 consecutive trading days, another record, **Jan. 20;** the average soared 51.60 points, **Jan. 22,** a one-day record. At month's end, the cumulative advance was more than 250 points, yet another record.

The Tower Commission Report, Feb. 27, found **Pres. Reagan confused and uninformed** in Iran-contra dealings, and further faulted White House Chief of Staff Donald Regan; former Natl. Security Adviser Robert McFarlane; his successor Adm. John Poindexter; and CIA Director William Casey.

An Iraqi warplane missile killed 37 sailors on the frigate U.S.S. Stark in the Persian Gulf, **May 17.** Iraq called it an accident. The Stark's officers were found negligent, June 14. The U.S. escorted Kuwaiti oil tankers to the Gulf, reflagging them for the U.S.

Public hearings by the Senate and House committees investigating the **Iran-contra affair** went on from **May-Aug.** Former CIA Director Casey died, May 6, 5 months after brain surgery; Lt. Col. Oliver North, a media sensation, said he had believed all his activities authorized by his superiors; Poindexter said his own purpose had been "to provide some future deniability for the president . . ."; Shultz said Casey, McFarlane, and Poindexter had lied to him and deceived Pres. Reagan. Pres. Reagan, Aug. 12, said he had been "stubborn in pursuit of a policy that went astray," but again denied knowing of the funds' diversion to the contras.

Wall Street crashed, Oct. 19, the Dow plummeting a record 508 points—22.6 percent—after a record high of 2722.42, Aug. 25; a 200-point drop by Oct., called a correction by most; and drops of 91.55, Oct. 6; 95.46, Oct. 14; and 108.36, Oct. 16.

Pres. Reagan and **Soviet leader Gorbachev** met in Wash., **Dec. 8,** and signed **an unprecedented agreement** calling for the **dismantling of all 1,752 U.S. and 859 Soviet missiles with a 300-3,400-mile range.** The leaders agreed to meet in Moscow in 1988.

1988

Federal grand juries in Miami and Tampa returned **indictments, Feb. 4,** against **Gen. Manuel Noriega,** the effective ruler of Panama, charging that he had protected and otherwise assisted the Medellin drug cartel. Attempts by the U.S. to oust Noriega plunged Panama into political and economic turmoil.

Nearly **1.4 million illegal aliens** met the **May 4** deadline for applying for **amnesty** under a U.S. Immigration and Naturalization Service policy. An estimated 50+ percent of applications were in Calif.; nationwide, about 71 percent of the aliens had entered the U.S. from Mexico.

Much of the U.S. suffered the worst **drought** in more than 50 years. By June 23, half of the nation's agricultural counties had been designated disaster areas.

A missile, fired from the **U.S. Navy warship *Vincennes*,** in the Persian Gulf, **struck and destroyed a commercial Iranian airliner, July 3, killing all 290 persons** on the plane. Navy personnel had mistaken the airliner for an Iranian F-14 jet fighter.

Fire destroyed about 4 million acres of forest land throughout the west, including Alaska, during the late summer. Property damage was also considerable.

Failures at nuclear-power plants posed problems across the U.S., according to congressional testimony, starting **Sept. 30.** Problems cited including aging equipment, poor management and training, and lax safety standards.

George Bush, vice president under Ronald Reagan, **was elected 41st U.S. president, Nov. 8.** Bush defeated the Democratic nominee, Gov. Michael Dukakis (Mass.), by 54 to 46 percent of the popular vote, and 426 electoral votes to Dukakis's 112. **Sen. Dan Quayle** (Ind.) was the successful vice presidential nominee; Sen. Lloyd Bentsen (Tex.) was the Democratic nominee for v.p. Democrats continued to control both houses of Congress.

Drexel Burnham Lambert agreed, **Dec. 21, to plead guilty to 6 violations of federal law,** including insider trading, stock manipulation, and falsified records; and **to pay penalties of $650 million,** by far the largest such settlement.

1989

The Labor Dept. reported, **Jan. 6,** that **unemployment was 5.3%, a 14-year low,** at the end of **1988.** For the whole year, the economy grew 3.8%, the most in 4 years.

The **largest oil spill in U.S. history** occurred after the ***Exxon Valdez*** struck Bligh Reef in **Alaska's Prince William Sound, Mar. 24.** Exxon Corp. announced, Mar. 25, that it accepted full financial responsibility for the spill, initially estimated at 240,000 barrels, then announced that the spill could not be contained; as of Mar. 29, it extended 45 miles.

Former Natl. Security Council staff member **Oliver North** became the first person, **May 4, convicted in a jury trial** in connection with the **Iran-contra** scandal. The jury acquitted North on 9 charges, found him guilty of 3: aiding and abetting the obstruction of Congress; altering, destroying, removing, or concealing NSC documents; receiving as an illegal gratuity a $13,800 security system for his home. North received, July 6, a 3-year suspended prison sentence, 2 years' probation, a $150,000 fine, and an order to perform 1,200 hours of community service.

House speaker Jim Wright (D. Tex.), who faced 69 ethical charges, announced his **resignation as speaker and from the House, May 31. Rep. Tony Coelho (D. Calif.),** also under scrutiny, announced his **resignation as majority whip and from the House.**

The **U.S. Supreme Court** announced, **July 3,** its 5-4 decision to put new **restraints** on a **woman's right to have an abortion,** although it did not overturn Roe v. Wade.

Jack Kemp, secy. of **Housing and Urban Development,** acknowledged, **July 11,** that an estimated **$2 billion** had been lost due to **fraud and mismanagement** during the tenure of his predecessor **Samuel Pierce.**

Legislation passed by Congress to **rescue the savings and loan industry** was signed into law, **Aug. 9,** by Pres. George Bush. The bill provided $166 billion over 10 years to close or merge insolvent S&Ls. The total cost was put at $400 billion over 30 years, most to be paid by taxpayers.

Army Gen. Colin Powell was nominated by Pres. Bush, **Aug. 10,** to serve as **chairman of the Joint Chiefs of Staff;** he became the first black to hold the post.

Minutes before the start of the 3d game of the 1989 World Series between the San Francisco Giants and the Oakland Athletics, **Oct. 17,** an **earthquake struck the San Francisco Bay area,** causing at least 59 deaths and massive property damage.

Democrats won most of the **top offices** at stake and **black candidates scored major breakthroughs,** in off-year elections, **Nov. 7.** Lt. Gov. L. Douglas Wilder, a Democrat, was elected governor of Virginia, the nation's first black governor since Reconstruction; Manhattan Borough Pres. David Dinkins, also a Democrat, became the first black elected mayor of New York City.

Pennsylvania became the first state, **Nov. 18,** to **restrict abortions,** after the U.S. Supreme Court gave states the right to do so in July.

Pres. Bush signed into law, **Nov. 19,** an **increase in the minimum wage.** Currently $3.35, the wage would rise to **$4.25** an hour by 1991, with a training wage of $3.35 for 16- to 19-year-olds in their first 3 months on a job.

U.S. troops invaded Panama, Dec. 20, overthrowing the government of Manuel Noriega, who eluded capture, took refuge in the Vatican mission, then surrendered to the U.S. Jan. 3, 1990.

1990

The **Dow Jones Industrial average** pushed to an **all-time high** on Wall Street, **July 16 and 17,** finishing at 2,999.75 and averaging above 3,000.

Pres. Bush signed a bill that would bar **discrimination** against people with **physical or mental disabilities, July 26.**

Justice William Brennan announced, **July 20,** his immediate resignation from the U.S. Supreme Court, due to illness; Pres. Bush nominated **Judge David Souter** of the U.S. Court of Appeals for the First Circuit in Boston, **July 23,** and the Senate voted to endorse him, **Sept. 27.**

Operation Desert Shield forces left for **Saudi Arabia, Aug. 7,** to defend that country following the **invasion** of its neighbor **Kuwait by Iraq.**

Pres. Bush **vetoed, Oct. 22,** a **civil rights bill** that sought in effect to reverse 6 recent Supreme Court decisions that civil rights organizations contended had weakened anti-discrimination laws on hiring and promoting.

The Democratic Party made small gains in the Senate and House in **elections, Nov. 6.** Democrats gained one seat in the Senate, for a 56-44 margin over Republicans, and gained 8 seats in the House for a 267-167 margin. One independent was elected in Vermont. About 96 percent of incumbents seeking re-election were successful; only 15 lost. In gubernatorial elections, 14 statehouses changed parties, Democrats emerging with a 28-19 margin, compared with 29-21 before the election. Independents won in Alaska and Connecticut, and a runoff would be required in Arizona.

Pres. Bush signed, **Nov. 15,** a bill designed to **reduce budget deficits** by nearly $500 billion over 5 years. The top tax rate would rise from 28 to 31 percent and exemptions for upper-income Americans would be phased out; gas, cigarette, liquor taxes would increase; a luxury tax would be imposed on some planes, cars, boats, furs, and jewelry.

Pres. Bush signed, **Nov. 15,** the **1990 Clean Air Act,** a comprehensive updating of the original Clean Air Act of 1970.

In **Dec.** unemployment reached a 3-year high of 6.1 percent. In the 2nd half of the year, more than 1 million payroll jobs were lost. Consumer prices rose 6.1 percent during the year, the highest annual rate since 1981.

1991

The **U.S. and its allies defeated Iraq in Jan.** and **Feb. 1991** and liberated Kuwait, which Iraq had overrun in Aug. 1990. After Iraq's invasion, for nearly 6 months, diplomats of many nations had sought to persuade Pres. Saddam Hussein to pull his occupying forces out of the oil-rich sheikhdom. Finally, in **Jan.,** the allies launched an **attack on Iraq from the air** that sharply reduced his offensive and defensive military capacity. In a **ground war in Feb.** that lasted just 100 hours, the U.S.-led attackers killed or captured many thousands of Iraqi soldiers and sent the rest into retreat before Pres. George Bush ordered a cease-fire.

The **unemployment rate** in **March** stood at **6.7 percent,** the highest since late 1986. However, the **Dow Jones Industrial Average** finished above 3000 for the first time, **Apr. 17,** closing at 3004.46.

Justice Thurgood Marshall, the first black ever to serve on the U.S. Supreme Court, announced, **June 27,** that he would retire when a successor was approved.

Unemployment edged up to **7.0 percent** in **June,** but the **Gross National Product,** the broadest measure of the economy, had **risen 0.4 percent** at an annual rate during the **2nd quarter of 1991,** and the chief economic advisor to the U.S. Pres. said, "The recession appears to have ended."

Pres. Bush approved, **July 10,** the recommendations of the **Defense Base Closure and Realignment Commission,** which had proposed that 34 domestic military installations be closed and 48 other realigned, due to the federal budget crunch and the end of the cold war.

Chemical Banking Corp. and **Manufacturers Hanover Corp.** announced, **July 15,** a **merger** agreement. The merger partners, both based in New York, would have combined assets of $135.46 billion.

BankAmerica and Security Pacific Corp. announced, **Aug. 12,** that they would **merge.** The agreement, if approved, would involve a $4.47 billion stock swap.

The **case against Oliver North was "terminated,"** with all charges dropped, **Sept. 16.** In 1989, North, a leading figure in the Iran-contra affair, had been convicted of obstructing a congressional investigation, destroying documents, and accepting an illegal gratuity. In 1990, a federal appeals court had overturned one conviction and sent the others back to the federal district court.

The General Accounting Office revealed that in a recent 12-month period, **8,331 checks** had been written against **insufficient funds** in a bank that operated at the Capitol with only House members for depositors. On **Oct. 3,** House Speaker Tom Foley said the bank would be closed at the end of 1991 and that the House Ethics Committee would investigate.

The **U.S. Senate approved the nomination of Clarence Thomas** to serve as an **associate justice of the Supreme Court,** after investigating an allegation of sexual harassment that had been leveled against him. Thomas and his accusor, Anita Hill, a law professor at the Univ. of Oklahoma, testified before the Senate Judiciary Committee, **Oct. 11,** while a huge TV audience watched. The Senate confirmed Thomas, 52-48.

Both major parties could claim **significant victories** in the **Nov. 5 elections.** The victory of Democrat Harris Wofford over former governor and U.S. attorney general Richard Thornburgh for the U.S. Senate Seat in Pennsylvania was seen as a signal of public concern about the state of the economy. Mississippi's incumbent governor, Democrat Ray Mabus, lost to Kirk Fordice, who would become the first Republican governor of the state since Reconstruction.

A compromise bill providing for **additional benefits for unemployed workers** was signed by Pres. George Bush, **Nov. 15.** The bill would give all unemployed workers from 6 to 20 additional weeks of benefits.

Pres. George Bush signed, **Nov. 21,** a **job-discrimination bill** requiring that hiring and promotion be related to job performance. Those claiming discrimination could sue for damages, not just back pay and lost benefits.

Charles Keating was convicted of 17 counts of securities fraud, Dec. 4. The prosecution asserted that as chairman of the Lincoln Savings & Loan Assn. in Cal., Keating had induced some 17,000 investors to buy $250 million in bonds that were not insured.

1992

In the annual **State of the Union address, Jan. 28,** Pres. George Bush announced proposals to **reduce nuclear arsenals** and to deal with the U.S. **economic recession.** Calling for a $50 billion reduction in the defense budget over the next 5 years, he endorsed cancellation of the Midgetman ICBM program and proposed to cap the number of MX intercontinental ballistic missiles and B-2 stealth bombers. To speed economic growth, Bush said he had instructed federal departments and agencies to impose a 3-month moratorium on new government regulations and had told the IRS to reduce the amount withheld from employees' paychecks.

Pres. Bush submitted to Congress, **Jan. 29,** a **budget for the 1993 fiscal year,** with a projected deficit of $351.9 billion. The estimated budget deficit for 1992 was a record $399.4 billion.

R.H. Macy & Co., owner of 251 retail stores in the U.S., including in New York City "the world's largest department store," **filed for bankruptcy, Jan. 27. Trans World Airlines, Jan. 31,** became the latest major U.S. carrier to **file for bankruptcy.**

The **"Big 3" U.S. auto makers** announced **huge losses in Feb.** Chrysler reported, **Feb. 6,** a loss of $795 million in 1991, and Ford Motor Co. said, **Feb. 13,** that it had lost $2.26 billion in 1991, its greatest loss ever in one year. On **Feb. 24,** General Motors announced a loss of $4.45 billion in 1991, at the time the **greatest in history for any U.S. company.** General Motors named 12 plants that it planned to close over 3 years. However, the **Dow Jones Industrial Average** closed, **Feb. 24,** at **3283.32,** an **all-time high,** which analysts attributed to investors' belief in an imminent economic recovery.

Rioting, looting, and arson swept **South-Central Los Angeles in late April and early May** after a jury that included no blacks acquitted 4 policemen on all but one count in the beating of a black man, Rodney King. Protests in Atlanta, Las Vegas, San Francisco, Miami, and Seattle also turned violent. The attack on King had been videotaped and shown on TV newcasts across the country. The **death toll** in the L.A. violence after the acquittals was put at **52,** mostly homicides; some 600 buildings were set aflame; and damage was said to run as high as **$1 billion.** Army, Marine, and Natl. Guard units helped restore order. The White House announced, May 4, that $700 million in federal funds would be made available to help riot victims and to rebuild damaged areas and businesses.

More than **300 members and former members** of the **U.S. House of Representatives** were identified as having **written overdraft checks** at the **House bank.** On **Apr. 1,** the House Ethics Committee released the names of the 22 "worst abusers." On **Apr. 3,** Senate and House leaders ended free medical care and medicine for members of Congress. The House voted, **Apr. 9,** to give control of nonlegislative House matters to a professional manager, and the position of inspector general, or auditor, was created.

A **27th Amendment** became part of the **U.S. Constitution in May.** Proposed by James Madison, it had been approved by Congress in 1798 and submitted to the states for ratification. It read: "No law, varying the compensation for the services of the senators and representatives shall take effect, until an election of representatives shall have intervened." Approval of three-fourths of the states, 38 at the present time, was required for an amendment to become part of the Constitution. On **May 7,** the Michigan legislature became the 38th to approve it.

Gov. Bill Clinton (Ark.) won primaries, **June 2,** in Calif., Ohio, N.J., and 3 other states, capturing enough delegates to **guarantee the Democratic presidential nomination.** Pres. George Bush, June 2, swept 6 primaries. Texas billionaire H. Ross Perot, mounting an independent campaign for president, was not on any ballot June 2, but according to exit polls he would run well against Bush and Clinton.

A **proposed amendment** to the **U.S. Constitution** that would have **required a balanced budget** in the **federal government** was **defeated** in the House, **June 11.** Under the amendment, expenditures could not exceed receipts in any year unless the U.S. was at war or three-fifths of the membership of both houses of Congress voted to override the balanced requirement in any year.

More than **1.1 million votes** were cast in an election to choose a **portrait of Elvis Presley** for a **U.S. postage stamp.** On **June 4,** the U.S. Postal Service announced that voters preferred, 3-1, a portrait of the younger Elvis.

The **Democratic Party** nominated **Gov. Bill Clinton (Ark.)** as its **candidate for president, July 15,** and **Sen. Al Gore Jr. (Tenn.)** as its **candidate for vice president, July 16,** in New York City. **Texas independent H. Ross Perot** announced, **July 16,** that he would **not seek the presidency** both because the Democratic Party had "revitalized itself" and because his candidacy would cause the election to be thrown into the House for resolution, which would disrupt the country.

The Labor Dept. reported, July 1, that the **nation's unemployment** rate stood at **7.8 in June, the highest level since March 1984.** The Senate and House, July 2, approved a bill that would **extend benefits to long-term unemployed** persons during recessions, and Pres. Bush signed it, **July 3.**

The **Republican Party** renominated **Pres. George Bush** and **Vice Pres. Dan Quayle** at the convention in Houston, Tex. in **early August,** while a Gallup Poll reported, Aug. 4, that Bush's public-approval rating had fallen to 29 percent, a new low.

Pres. Bush and **Gov. Bill Clinton,** the Republican and Democratic candidates for president, participated in **3 TV debates in Oct.** They were joined by independent candidate **H. Ross Perot** who, on **Oct. 1,** 33 days before the election, had **re-declared his candidacy,** after having removed himself from consideration in July.

Congress for the first time **overrode a veto** by **Pres. Bush,** after nearly 4 years and 35 attempts. On **Oct. 3,** Bush vetoed a bill that reversed portions of a law that prohibited local governments from regulating cable-TV fees. The legislation required that the Federal Communications Commission establish a "reasonable" price for basic cable services. On **Oct. 5,** the Senate, 74-25, and the House, 308-114, voted to override by more than the two-thirds majority required.

Gov. Bill Clinton of Arkansas was **elected 42nd president of the U.S.** on **Nov. 3,** and his running mate on the **Democratic** ticket, **Sen. Al Gore Jr. of Tennessee,** was **elected vice president.** They carried **32 states** and the **District of Columbia,** winning **370 electoral votes.** Republican presidential candidate, Pres. George Bush, and his running mate, Vice Pres. Dan Quayle, won 18 states and 188 electoral votes. In the nationwide popular vote, the official tally gave Clinton 44,908,254 (43 percent), Bush 39,102,343 (38 percent), and independent candidate H. Ross Perot 19,741,065 (19 percent). The **Democrats** retained control of both houses of Congress, emerging with a **57-42** margin in the Senate, and after a Nov. 24 runoff, **57-43.** In the House, the Republicans gained 10 seats, but the **Democrats** still held a **258-176** majority, with 1 independent. There would be **110 new House members,** the biggest turnover since 1948, and the new House would include **record numbers of women** (47), **blacks** (38), and **Hispanics** (17). The new **Senate** also would have a **record number of women** (6); two women Democrats won Senate elections in Calif., and **Carol Moseley Braun of Illinois** became the **first black woman** to serve in the **Senate.** The **Democrats** also picked up 2 **governorships,** for a **30-18** margin over the Republicans.

IBM said, **Dec. 15,** it would **cut 25,000 jobs in 1993,** after cutting 40,000 in 1992 through voluntary retirements. Once the industry's leader, the company projected a $5.25 billion net loss for the 4th quarter.

A **U.N.-sanctioned military force,** led by **American troops,** arrived in **Somalia** beginning **Dec. 9** to ensure the delivery of food to starving people in the war-torn nation by "all necessary means."

Declaration of Independence

The Declaration of Independence was adopted by the Continental Congress in Philadelphia, on July 4, 1776. John Hancock was president of the Congress and Charles Thomson was secretary. A copy of the Declaration, engrossed on parchment, was signed by members of Congress on and after Aug. 2, 1776. On Jan. 18, 1777, Congress ordered that "an authenticated copy, with the names of the members of Congress subscribing the same, be sent to each of the United States, and that they be desired to have the same put upon record." Authenticated copies were printed in broadside form in Baltimore, where the Continental Congress was then in session. The following text is that of the original printed by John Dunlap at Philadelphia for the Continental Congress.

IN CONGRESS, July 4, 1776.

A DECLARATION

By the REPRESENTATIVES of the

UNITED STATES OF AMERICA,

In GENERAL CONGRESS assembled

When in the Course of human Events, it becomes necessary for one People to dissolve the Political Bands which have connected them with another, and to assume among the Powers of the Earth, the separate and equal Station to which the Laws of Nature and of Nature's God entitle them, a decent Respect to the Opinions of Mankind requires that they should declare the causes which impel them to the Separation.

We hold these Truths to be self-evident, that all Men are created equal, that they are endowed by their Creator with certain unalienable Rights, that among these are Life, Liberty, and the Pursuit of Happiness—That to secure these Rights, Governments are instituted among Men, deriving their just Powers from the Consent of the Governed, that whenever any Form of Government becomes destructive of these Ends, it is the Right of the People to alter or to abolish it, and to institute new Government, laying its Foundation on such Principles, and organizing its Powers in such Form, as to them shall seem most likely to effect their Safety and Happiness. Prudence, indeed, will dictate that Governments long established should not be changed for light and transient Causes; and accordingly all Experience hath shewn, that Mankind are more disposed to suffer, while Evils are sufferable, than to right themselves by abolishing the Forms to which they are accustomed. But when a long Train of Abuses and Usurpations, pursuing invariably the same Object, evinces a Design to reduce them under absolute Despotism, it is their Right, it is their Duty, to throw off such Government, and to provide new Guards for their future Security. Such has been the patient Sufferance of these Colonies; and such is now the Necessity which constrains them to alter their former Systems of Government. The History of the present King of Great-Britain is a History of repeated Injuries and Usurpations, all having in direct Object the Establishment of an absolute Tyranny over these States. To prove this, let Facts be submitted to a candid World.

He has refused his Assent to Laws, the most wholesome and necessary for the public Good.

He has forbidden his Governors to pass Laws of immediate and pressing Importance, unless suspended in their Operation till his Assent should be obtained; and when so suspended, he has utterly neglected to attend to them.

He has refused to pass other Laws for the Accommodation of large Districts of People, unless those People would relinquish the Right of Representation in the Legislature, a Right inestimable to them, and formidable to Tyrants only.

He has called together Legislative Bodies at Places unusual, uncomfortable, and distant from the Depository of their Public Records, for the sole Purpose of fatiguing them into Compliance with his Measures.

He has dissolved Representative Houses repeatedly, for opposing with manly Firmness his Invasions on the Rights of the People.

He has refused for a long Time, after such Dissolutions, to cause others to be elected; whereby the Legislative Powers, incapable of Annihilation, have returned to the People at large for their exercise; the State remaining in the mean time exposed to all the Dangers of Invasion from without, and Convulsions within.

He has endeavoured to prevent the Population of these States; for that Purpose obstructing the Laws for Naturalization of Foreigners; refusing to pass others to encourage their Migrations hither, and raising the Conditions of new Appropriations of Lands.

He has obstructed the Administration of Justice, by refusing his Assent to Laws for establishing Judiciary Powers.

He has made Judges dependent on his Will alone, for the Tenure of their Offices, and the Amount and payment of their Salaries.

He has erected a Multitude of new Offices, and sent hither Swarms of Officers to harrass our People, and eat out their Substance.

He has kept among us, in Times of Peace, Standing Armies, without the consent of our Legislatures.

He has affected to render the Military independent of, and superior to the Civil Power.

He has combined with others to subject us to a Jurisdiction foreign to our Constitution, and unacknowledged by our Laws; giving his Assent to their Acts of pretended Legislation:

For quartering large Bodies of Armed Troops among us:

For protecting them, by a mock Trial, from Punishment for any Murders which they should commit on the Inhabitants of these States:

For cutting off our Trade with all Parts of the World:

For imposing Taxes on us without our Consent:

For depriving us, in many Cases, of the Benefits of Trial by Jury:

For transporting us beyond Seas to be tried for pretended Offences:

For abolishing the free System of English Laws in a neighbouring Province, establishing therein an arbitrary Government, and enlarging its Boundaries, so as to render it at once an Example and fit Instrument for introducing the same absolute Rule into these Colonies:

For taking away our Charters, abolishing our most valuable Laws, and altering fundamentally the Forms of our Governments:

For suspending our own Legislatures, and declaring themselves invested with Power to legislate for us in all Cases whatsoever.

He has abdicated Government here, by declaring us out of his Protection and waging War against us.

He has plundered our Seas, ravaged our Coasts, burnt our towns, and destroyed the Lives of our People.

He is, at this Time, transporting large Armies of foreign Mercenaries to complete the works of Death, Desolation, and Tyranny, already begun with circumstances of Cruelty and Perfidy, scarcely paralleled in the most barbarous Ages, and totally unworthy the Head of a civilized Nation.

He has constrained our fellow Citizens taken Captive on the high Seas to bear Arms against their Country, to become the Executioners of their Friends and Brethren, or to fall themselves by their Hands.

He has excited domestic Insurrections amongst us, and has endeavoured to bring on the Inhabitants of our Frontiers, the merciless Indian Savages, whose known Rule of Warfare, is an undistinguished Destruction, of all Ages, Sexes and Conditions.

In every stage of these Oppressions we have Petitioned for Redress in the most humble Terms: Our repeated Petitions have been answered only by repeated Injury. A Prince, whose Character is thus marked by every act which may define a Tyrant, is unfit to be the Ruler of a free People.

Nor have we been wanting in Attentions to our British Brethren. We have warned them from Time to Time of Attempts by their Legislature to extend an unwarrantable Jurisdiction over us. We have reminded them of the Circumstances of our Emigration and Settlement here. We have appealed to their native Justice and Magnanimity, and we have conjured them by the Ties of our common Kindred to disavow these Usurpations, which, would inevitably interrupt our Connections and Correspondence. They too have been deaf to the Voice of Justice and of Consanguinity. We must, therefore, acquiesce in the Necessity, which denounces our Separation, and hold them, as we hold the rest of Mankind, Enemies in War, in Peace, Friends.

We, therefore, the Representatives of the UNITED STATES OF AMERICA, in General Congress, Assembled, appealing to the Supreme Judge of the World for the Rectitude of our Intentions, do, in the Name, and by Authority of the good People of these Colonies, solemnly Publish and Declare, That these United Colonies are, and of Right ought to be, Free and Independent States; that they are absolved from all Allegiance to the British Crown, and that all political Connection between them and the State of Great-Britain, is and ought to be totally dissolved; and that as Free and Independent States, they have full Power to levy War, conclude Peace, contract Alliances, establish Commerce, and to do all other Acts and Things which Independent States may of right do. And for the support of this declaration, with a firm Reliance on the Protection of divine Providence, we mutually pledge to each other our lives, our Fortunes, and our sacred Honor.

JOHN HANCOCK, President

Attest.
CHARLES THOMSON, Secretary.

Signers of the Declaration of Independence

Delegate (state)	Vocation	Birthplace	Born	Died
Adams, John (Mass.)	Lawyer	Braintree (Quincy), Mass.	Oct. 30, 1735	July 4, 1826
Adams, Samuel (Mass.)	Political leader	Boston, Mass.	Sept. 27, 1722	Oct. 2, 1803
Bartlett, Josiah (N.H.)	Physician, judge	Amesbury, Mass.	Nov. 21, 1729	May 19, 1795
Braxton, Carter (Va.)	Farmer	Newington Plantation, Va.	Sept. 10, 1736	Oct. 10, 1797
Carroll, Chas. of Carrollton (Md.)	Lawyer	Annapolis, Md.	Sept. 19, 1737	Nov. 14, 1832
Chase, Samuel (Md.)	Judge	Princess Anne, Md.	Apr. 17, 1741	June 19, 1811
Clark, Abraham (N.J.)	Surveyor	Roselle, N.J.	Feb. 15, 1726	Sept. 15, 1794
Clymer, George (Pa.)	Merchant	Philadelphia, Pa.	Mar. 16, 1739	Jan. 23, 1813
Ellery, William (R.I.)	Lawyer	Newport, R.I.	Dec. 22, 1727	Feb. 15, 1820
Floyd, William (N.Y.)	Soldier	Brookhaven, N.Y.	Dec. 17, 1734	Aug. 4, 1821
Franklin, Benjamin (Pa.)	Printer, publisher	Boston, Mass.	Jan. 17, 1706	Apr. 17, 1790
Gerry, Elbridge (Mass.)	Merchant	Marblehead, Mass.	July 17, 1744	Nov. 23, 1814
Gwinnett, Button (Ga.)	Merchant	Down Hatherly, England	c. 1735	May 19, 1777
Hall, Lyman (Ga.)	Physician	Wallingford, Conn.	Apr. 12, 1724	Oct. 19, 1790
Hancock, John (Mass.)	Merchant	Braintree (Quincy), Mass.	Jan. 12, 1737	Oct. 8, 1793
Harrison, Benjamin (Va.)	Farmer	Berkeley, Va.	Apr. 5, 1726	Apr. 24, 1791
Hart, John (N.J.)	Farmer	Stonington, Conn.	c. 1711	May 11, 1779
Hewes, Joseph (N.C.)	Merchant	Princeton, N.J.	Jan. 23, 1730	Nov. 10, 1779
Heyward, Thos. Jr. (S.C.)	Lawyer, farmer	St. Luke's Parish, S.C.	July 28, 1746	Mar. 6, 1809
Hooper, William (N.C.)	Lawyer	Boston, Mass.	June 28, 1742	Oct. 14, 1790
Hopkins, Stephen (R.I.)	Judge, educator	Providence, R.I.	Mar. 7, 1707	July 13, 1785
Hopkinson, Francis (N.J.)	Judge, author	Philadelphia, Pa.	Sept. 21, 1737	May 9, 1791
Huntington, Samuel (Conn.)	Judge	Windham County, Conn.	July 3, 1731	Jan. 5, 1796
Jefferson, Thomas (Va.)	Lawyer	Shadwell, Va.	Apr. 13, 1743	July 4, 1826
Lee, Francis Lightfoot (Va.)	Farmer	Westmoreland County, Va.	Oct. 14, 1734	Jan. 11, 1797
Lee, Richard Henry (Va.)	Farmer	Westmoreland County, Va.	Jan. 20, 1732	June 19, 1794
Lewis, Francis (N.Y.)	Merchant	Llandaff, Wales	Mar., 1713	Dec. 31, 1802
Livingston, Philip (N.Y.)	Merchant	Albany, N.Y.	Jan. 15, 1716	June 12, 1778
Lynch, Thomas Jr. (S.C.)	Farmer	Winyah, S.C.	Aug. 5, 1749	(at sea) 1779
McKean, Thomas (Del.)	Lawyer	New London, Pa.	Mar. 19, 1734	June 24, 1817
Middleton, Arthur (S.C.)	Farmer	Charleston, S.C.	June 26, 1742	Jan. 1, 1787
Morris, Lewis (N.Y.)	Farmer	Morrisania (Bronx County), N.Y.	Apr. 8, 1726	Jan. 22, 1798
Morris, Robert (Pa.)	Merchant	Liverpool, England	Jan. 20, 1734	May 9, 1806
Morton, John (Pa.)	Judge	Ridley, Pa.	1724	Apr., 1777
Nelson, Thos. Jr. (Va.)	Farmer	Yorktown, Va.	Dec. 26, 1738	Jan. 4, 1789
Paca, William (Md.)	Judge	Abingdon, Md.	Oct. 31, 1740	Oct. 23, 1799
Paine, Robert Treat (Mass.)	Judge	Boston, Mass.	Mar. 11, 1731	May 12, 1814
Penn, John (N.C.)	Lawyer	Near Port Royal, Va.	May 17, 1741	Sept. 14, 1788
Read, George (Del.)	Judge	Near North East, Md.	Sept. 18, 1733	Sept. 21, 1798
Rodney, Caesar (Del.)	Judge	Dover, Del.	Oct. 7, 1728	June 29, 1784
Ross, George (Pa.)	Judge	New Castle, Del.	May 10, 1730	July 14, 1779
Rush, Benjamin (Pa.)	Physician	Byberry, Pa. (Philadelphia)	Dec. 24, 1745	Apr. 19, 1813
Rutledge, Edward (S.C.)	Lawyer	Charleston, S.C.	Nov. 23, 1749	Jan. 23, 1800
Sherman, Roger (Conn.)	Lawyer	Newton, Mass.	Apr. 19, 1721	July 23, 1793
Smith, James (Pa.)	Lawyer	Dublin, Ireland	c. 1719	July 11, 1806
Stockton, Richard (N.J.)	Lawyer	Near Princeton, N.J.	Oct. 1, 1730	Feb. 28, 1781
Stone, Thomas (Md.)	Lawyer	Charles County, Md.	1743	Oct. 5, 1787
Taylor, George (Pa.)	Ironmaster	Ireland	1716	Feb. 23, 1781
Thornton, Matthew (N.H.)	Physician	Ireland	1714	June 24, 1803
Walton, George (Ga.)	Judge	Prince Edward County, Va.	1741	Feb. 2, 1804
Whipple, William (N.H.)	Merchant, judge	Kittery, Me.	Jan. 14, 1730	Nov. 28, 1785
Williams, William (Conn.)	Merchant	Lebanon, Conn.	Apr. 23, 1731	Aug. 2, 1811
Wilson, James (Pa.)	Judge	Carskerdo, Scotland	Sept. 14, 1742	Aug. 28, 1798
Witherspoon, John (N.J.)	Clergyman, educator	Gifford, Scotland	Feb. 5, 1723	Nov. 15, 1794
Wolcott, Oliver (Conn.)	Judge	Windsor, Conn.	Dec. 1, 1726	Dec. 1, 1797
Wythe, George (Va.)	Lawyer	Elizabeth City Co. (Hampton), Va.	1726	June 8, 1806

Constitution of the United States

The Original 7 Articles

PREAMBLE

We, the people of the United States, in order to form a more perfect Union, establish justice, insure domestic tranquility, provide for the common defense, promote the general welfare, and secure the blessings of liberty to ourselves and our posterity do ordain and establish this Constitution for the United States of America.

ARTICLE I.

Section 1—Legislative powers; in whom vested:

All legislative powers herein granted shall be vested in a Congress of the United States, which shall consist of a Senate and House of Representatives.

Section 2—House of Representatives, how and by whom chosen. Qualifications of a Representative. Representatives and direct taxes, how apportioned. Enumeration. Vacancies to be filled. Power of choosing officers, and of impeachment.

1. The House of Representatives shall be composed of members chosen every second year by the people of the several States, and the electors in each State shall have the qualifications requisite for electors of the most numerous branch of the State Legislature.

2. No person shall be a Representative who shall not have attained to the age of twenty-five years, and been seven years a citizen of the United States, and who shall not, when elected, be an inhabitant of that State in which he shall be chosen.

3. *(Representatives and direct taxes shall be apportioned among the several States which may be included within this Union, according to their respective numbers, which shall be determined by adding to the whole number of free persons, including those bound to service for a term of years, and excluding Indians not taxed, three-fifths of all other persons.) (The previous sentence was superseded by Amendment XIV, section 2.)* The actual enumeration shall be made within three years after the first meeting of the Congress of the United States, and within every subsequent term of ten years, in such manner as they shall by law direct. The number of Representatives shall not exceed one for every thirty thousand, but each State shall have at least one Representative; and until such enumeration shall be made, the State of New Hampshire shall be entitled to choose three, Massachusetts eight, Rhode Island and Providence Plantations one, Connecticut five, New York six, New Jersey four, Pennsylvania eight, Delaware one, Maryland six, Virginia ten, North Carolina five, South Carolina five, and Georgia three.

4. When vacancies happen in the representation from any State, the Executive Authority thereof shall issue writs of election to fill such vacancies.

5. The House of Representatives shall choose their Speaker and other officers; and shall have the sole power of impeachment.

Section 3—Senators, how and by whom chosen. How classified. Qualifications of a Senator. President of the Senate, his right to vote. President pro tem., and other officers of the Senate, how chosen. Power to try impeachments. When President is tried, Chief Justice to preside. Sentence.

1. The Senate of the United States shall be composed of two Senators from each State, *(chosen by the Legislature thereof), (The preceding five words were superseded by Amendment XVII, section 1.)* for six years; and each Senator shall have one vote.

2. Immediately after they shall be assembled in consequence of the first election, they shall be divided as equally as may be into three classes. The seats of the Senators of the first class shall be vacated at the expiration of the second year, of the second class at the expiration of the fourth year, and of the third class at the expiration of the sixth year, so that one-third may be chosen every second year; *(and if vacancies happen by resignation, or otherwise, during the recess of the Legislature of any State, the Executive thereof may make temporary appointments until the next meeting of the Legislature, which shall then fill such vacancies.) (The words in parentheses were superseded by Amendment XVII, section 2.)*

3. No person shall be a Senator who shall not have attained to the age of thirty years, and been nine years a citizen of the United States, and who shall not, when elected, be an inhabitant of that State for which he shall be chosen.

4. The Vice President of the United States shall be President of the Senate, but shall have no vote, unless they be equally divided.

5. The Senate shall choose their other officers, and also a President pro tempore, in the absence of the Vice President, or when he shall exercise the office of President of the United States.

6. The Senate shall have the sole power to try all impeachments. When sitting for that purpose, they shall be on oath or affirmation. When the President of the United States is tried, the Chief Justice shall preside: and no person shall be convicted without the concurrence of two-thirds of the members present.

7. Judgment in cases of impeachment shall not extend further than to removal from office, and disqualification to hold and enjoy any office of honor, trust or profit under the United States: but the party convicted shall nevertheless be liable and subject to indictment, trial, judgment and punishment, according to law.

Section 4—Times, etc., of holding elections, how prescribed. One session each year.

1. The times, places and manner of holding elections for Senators and Representatives, shall be prescribed in each State by the Legislature thereof; but the Congress may at any time by law make or alter such regulations, except as to the places of choosing Senators.

2. The Congress shall assemble at least once in every year, and such meeting shall *(be on the first Monday in December,) (The words in parentheses were superseded by Amendment XX, section 2).* unless they shall by law appoint a different day.

Section 5—Membership, quorum, adjournments, rules. Power to punish or expel. Journal. Time of adjournments, how limited, etc.

1. Each House shall be the judge of the elections, returns and qualifications of its own members, and a majority of each shall constitute a quorum to do business; but a smaller number may adjourn from day to day, and may be authorized to compel the attendance of absent members, in such manner, and under such penalties as each House may provide.

2. Each House may determine the rules of its proceedings, punish its members for disorderly behavior, and, with the concurrence of two-thirds, expel a member.

3. Each House shall keep a journal of its proceedings, and from time to time publish the same, excepting such parts as may in their judgment require secrecy; and the yeas and nays of the members of either House on any question shall, at the desire of one-fifth of those present, be entered on the journal.

4. Neither House, during the session of Congress, shall, without the consent of the other, adjourn for more than three days, nor to any other place than that in which the two Houses shall be sitting.

Section 6—Compensation, privileges, disqualifications in certain cases.

1. The Senators and Representatives shall receive a compensation for their services, to be ascertained by law, and paid out of the Treasury of the United States. They shall in all cases, except treason, felony and breach of the peace, be privileged from arrest during their attendance at the session of their respective Houses, and in going to and returning from the same; and for any speech or debate in either House, they shall not be questioned in any other place.

2. No Senator or Representative shall, during the time for which he was elected, be appointed to any civil office under the authority of the United States, which shall have been created, or the emoluments whereof shall have been increased during such time; and no person holding any office under the United States, shall be a member of either House

during his continuance in office.

Section 7—House to originate all revenue bills. Veto. Bill may be passed by two-thirds of each House, notwithstanding, etc. Bill, not returned in ten days, to become a law. Provisions as to orders, concurrent resolutions, etc.

1. All bills for raising revenue shall originate in the House of Representatives; but the Senate may propose or concur with amendments as on other bills.

2. Every bill which shall have passed the House of Representatives and the Senate, shall, before it becomes a law, be presented to the President of the United States; if he approves he shall sign it, but if not he shall return it, with his objections to that House in which it shall have originated, who shall enter the objections at large on their journal, and proceed to reconsider it. If after such reconsideration two-thirds of that House shall agree to pass the bill, it shall be sent, together with the objections, to the other House, by which it shall likewise be reconsidered, and if approved by two-thirds of that House, it shall become a law. But in all such cases the votes of both Houses shall be determined by yeas and nays, and the names of the persons voting for and against the bill shall be entered on the journal of each House respectively. If any bill shall not be returned by the President within ten days (Sundays excepted) after it shall have been presented to him, the same shall be a law, in like manner as if he had signed it, unless the Congress by their adjournment prevent its return, in which case it shall not be a law.

3. Every order, resolution, or vote to which the concurrence of the Senate and House of Representatives may be necessary (except on a question of adjournment) shall be presented to the President of the United States; and before the same shall take effect, shall be approved by him, or being disapproved by him, shall be repassed by two-thirds of the Senate and House of Representatives, according to the rules and limitations prescribed in the case of a bill.

Section 8—Powers of Congress.

The Congress shall have power

1. To lay and collect taxes, duties, imposts and excises, to pay the debts and provide for the common defense and general welfare of the United States; but all duties, imposts and excises shall be uniform throughout the United States;

2. To borrow money on the credit of the United States;

3. To regulate commerce with foreign nations, and among the several States, and with the Indian tribes;

4. To establish a uniform rule of naturalization, and uniform laws on the subject of bankruptcies throughout the United States;

5. To coin money, regulate the value thereof, and of foreign coin, and fix the standard of weights and measures;

6. To provide for the punishment of counterfeiting the securities and current coin of the United States;

7. To establish post-offices and post-roads;

8. To promote the progress of science and useful arts, by securing for limited times to authors and inventors the exclusive right to their respective writings and discoveries;

9. To constitute tribunals inferior to the Supreme Court;

10. To define and punish piracies and felonies committed on the high seas, and offenses against the law of nations;

11. To declare war, grant letters of marque and reprisal, and make rules concerning captures on land and water;

12. To raise and support armies, but no appropriation of money to that use shall be for a longer term than two years;

13. To provide and maintain a navy;

14. To make rules for the government and regulation of the land and naval forces;

15. To provide for calling forth the militia to execute the laws of the Union, suppress insurrections and repel invasions;

16. To provide for organizing, arming, and disciplining the militia, and for governing such part of them as may be employed in the service of the United States, reserving to the States respectively, the appointment of the officers, and the authority of training the militia according to the discipline prescribed by Congress;

17. To exercise exclusive legislation in all cases whatsoever, over such district (not exceeding ten miles square) as may, by cession of particular States, and the acceptance of Congress, become the seat of the Government of the United States, and to exercise like authority over all places purchased by the consent of the Legislature of the State in which the same shall be, for the erection of forts, magazines, arsenals, dockyards, and other needful buildings;—And

18. To make all laws which shall be necessary and proper for carrying into execution the foregoing powers, and all other powers vested by this Constitution in the Government of the United States, or in any department or officer thereof.

Section 9—Provision as to migration or importation of certain persons. Habeas corpus, bills of attainder, etc. Taxes, how apportioned. No export duty. No commercial preference. Money, how drawn from Treasury, etc. No titular nobility. Officers not to receive presents, etc.

1. The migration or importation of such persons as any of the States now existing shall think proper to admit, shall not be prohibited by the Congress prior to the year one thousand eight hundred and eight, but a tax or duty may be imposed on such importation, not exceeding ten dollars for each person.

2. The privilege of the writ of habeas corpus shall not be suspended, unless when in cases of rebellion or invasion the public safety may require it.

3. No bill of attainder or ex post facto law shall be passed.

4. No capitation, or other direct, tax shall be laid, unless in proportion to the census or enumeration herein before directed to be taken. *(Modified by Amendment XVI.)*

5. No tax or duty shall be laid on articles exported from any State.

6. No preference shall be given by any regulation of commerce or revenue to the ports of one State over those of another: nor shall vessels bound to, or from, one State, be obliged to enter, clear, or pay duties in another.

7. No money shall be drawn from the Treasury, but in consequence of appropriations made by law; and a regular statement and account of the receipts and expenditures of all public money shall be published from time to time.

8. No title of nobility shall be granted by the United States: and no person holding any office of profit or trust under them, shall, without the consent of the Congress, accept of any present, emolument, office, or title, of any kind whatever, from any king, prince, or foreign state.

Section 10—States prohibited from the exercise of certain powers.

1. No State shall enter into any treaty, alliance, or confederation; grant letters of marque and reprisal; coin money; emit bills of credit; make anything but gold and silver coin a tender in payment of debts; pass any bill of attainder, ex post facto law, or law impairing the obligation of contracts, or grant any title of nobility.

2. No State shall, without the consent of the Congress, lay any imposts or duties on imports or exports, except what may be absolutely necessary for executing its inspection laws: and the net produce of all duties and imposts, laid by any State on imports or exports, shall be for the use of the Treasury of the United States; and all such laws shall be subject to the revision and control of the Congress.

3. No State shall, without the consent of Congress, lay any duty of tonnage, keep troops, or ships of war in time of peace, enter into any agreement or compact with another State, or with a foreign power, or engage in war, unless actually invaded, or in such imminent danger as will not admit of delay.

ARTICLE II.

Section 1—President: his term of office. Electors of President; number and how appointed. Electors to vote on same day. Qualification of President. On whom his duties devolve in case of his removal, death, etc. President's compensation. His oath of office.

1. The Executive power shall be vested in a President of the United States of America. He shall hold his office during the term of four years, and together with the Vice President, chosen for the same term, be elected as follows

2. Each State shall appoint, in such manner as the Legis-

lature thereof may direct, a number of electors, equal to the whole number of Senators and Representatives to which the State may be entitled in the Congress: but no Senator or Representative, or person holding an office of trust or profit under the United States, shall be appointed an elector.

(The electors shall meet in their respective States, and vote by ballot for two persons, of whom one at least shall not be an inhabitant of the same State with themselves. And they shall make a list of all the persons voted for, and of the number of votes for each; which list they shall sign and certify, and transmit sealed to the seat of the Government of the United States, directed to the President of the Senate. The President of the Senate shall, in the presence of the Senate and House of Representatives, open all the certificates, and the votes shall then be counted. The person having the greatest number of votes shall be the President, if such number be a majority of the whole number of electors appointed; and if there be more than one who have such majority, and have an equal number of votes, then the House of Representatives shall immediately choose by ballot one of them for President; and if no person have a majority, then from the five highest on the list the said House shall in like manner choose the President. But in choosing the President, the votes shall be taken by States, the representation from each State having one vote; a quorum for this purpose shall consist of a member or members from two-thirds of the States, and a majority of all the States shall be necessary to a choice. In every case, after the choice of the President, the person having the greatest number of votes of the electors shall be the Vice President. But if there should remain two or more who have equal votes, the Senate shall choose from them by ballot the Vice President.)

(This clause was superseded by Amendment XII.)

3. The Congress may determine the time of choosing the electors, and the day on which they shall give their votes; which day shall be the same throughout the United States.

4. No person except a natural born citizen, or a citizen of the United States, at the time of the adoption of this Constitution, shall be eligible to the office of President; neither shall any person be eligible to that office who shall not have attained to the age of thirty-five years, and been fourteen years a resident within the United States.

(For qualification of the Vice President, see Amendment XII.)

5. In case of the removal of the President from office, or of his death, resignation, or inability to discharge the powers and duties of the said office, the same shall devolve on the Vice President, and the Congress may by law provide for the case of removal, death, resignation or inability, both of the President and Vice President, declaring what officer shall then act as President, and such officer shall act accordingly, until the disability be removed, or a President shall be elected.

(This clause has been modified by Amendments XX and XXV.)

6. The President shall, at stated times, receive for his services, a compensation, which shall neither be increased nor diminished during the period for which he shall have been elected, and he shall not receive within that period any other emolument from the United States, or any of them.

7. Before he enter on the execution of his office, he shall take the following oath or affirmation:

"I do solemnly swear (or affirm) that I will faithfully execute the office of President of the United States, and will to the best of my ability, preserve, protect and defend the Constitution of the United States."

Section 2—President to be Commander-in-Chief. He may require opinions of cabinet officers, etc., may pardon. Treaty-making power. Nomination of certain officers. When President may fill vacancies.

1. The President shall be Commander-in-Chief of the Army and Navy of the United States, and of the militia of the several States, when called into the actual service of the United States; he may require the opinion, in writing, of the principal officer in each of the executive departments, upon any subject relating to the duties of their respective offices, and he shall have power to grant reprieves and pardons for offenses against the United States, except in cases of impeachment.

2. He shall have power, by and with the advice and consent of the Senate, to make treaties, provided two-thirds of the Senators present concur; and he shall nominate, and by and with the advice and consent of the Senate, shall appoint ambassadors, other public ministers and consuls, judges of the Supreme Court, and all other officers of the United States, whose appointments are not herein otherwise provided for, and which shall be established by law: but the Congress may by law vest the appointment of such inferior officers, as they think proper, in the President alone, in the courts of law, or in the heads of departments.

3. The President shall have power to fill up all vacancies that may happen during the recess of the Senate, by granting commissions, which shall expire at the end of their next session.

Section 3—President shall communicate to Congress. He may convene and adjourn Congress, in case of disagreement, etc. Shall receive ambassadors, execute laws, and commission officers.

He shall from time to time give to the Congress information of the state of the Union, and recommend to their consideration such measures as he shall judge necessary and expedient; he may, on extraordinary occasions, convene both Houses, or either of them, and in case of disagreement between them, with respect to the time of adjournment, he may adjourn them to such time as he shall think proper; he shall receive ambassadors and other public ministers; he shall take care that the laws be faithfully executed, and shall commission all the officers of the United States.

Section 4—All civil offices forfeited for certain crimes.

The President, Vice President, and all civil officers of the United States, shall be removed from office on impeachment for, and conviction of, treason, bribery, or other high crimes and misdemeanors.

ARTICLE III.

Section 1—Judicial powers, Tenure. Compensation.

The judicial power of the United States, shall be vested in one Supreme Court, and in such inferior courts as the Congress may from time to time ordain and establish. The judges, both of the Supreme and inferior courts, shall hold their offices during good behavior, and shall at stated times, receive for their services, a compensation, which shall not be diminished during their continuance in office.

Section 2—Judicial power; to what cases it extends. Original jurisdiction of Supreme Court; appellate jurisdiction. Trial by jury, etc. Trial, where.

1. The judicial power shall extend to all cases, in law and equity, arising under this Constitution, the laws of the United States, and treaties made, or which shall be made, under their authority; to all cases affecting ambassadors, other public ministers and consuls; to all cases of admiralty and maritime jurisdiction; to controversies to which the United States shall be a party; to controversies between two or more States; between a State and citizens of another State; between citizens of different States, between citizens of the same State claiming lands under grants of different States, and between a State, or the citizens thereof, and foreign states, citizens or subjects.

(This section is modified by Amendment XI.)

2. In all cases affecting ambassadors, other public ministers and consuls, and those in which a State shall be party, the Supreme Court shall have original jurisdiction. In all the other cases before mentioned, the Supreme Court shall have appellate jurisdiction, both as to law and fact, with such exceptions, and under such regulations as the Congress shall make.

3. The trial of all crimes, except in cases of impeachment, shall be by jury; and such trial shall be held in the State where the said crimes shall have been committed; but when not committed within any State, the trial shall be at such place or places as the Congress may by law have directed.

Section 3—Treason Defined, Proof of, Punishment of.

1. Treason against the United States, shall consist only in levying war against them, or in adhering to their enemies,

giving them aid and comfort. No person shall be convicted of treason unless on the testimony of two witnesses to the same overt act, or on confession in open court.

2. The Congress shall have power to declare the punishment of treason, but no attainder of treason shall work corruption of blood, or forfeiture except during the life of the person attainted.

ARTICLE IV.

Section 1—Each State to give credit to the public acts, etc., of every other State.

Full faith and credit shall be given in each State to the public acts, records, and judicial proceedings of every other State. And the Congress may by general laws prescribe the manner in which such acts, records and proceedings shall be proved, and the effect thereof.

Section 2—Privileges of citizens of each State. Fugitives from justice to be delivered up. Persons held to service having escaped, to be delivered up.

1. The citizens of each State shall be entitled to all privileges and immunities of citizens in the several States.

2. A person charged in any State with treason, felony, or other crime, who shall flee from justice, and be found in another State, shall on demand of the Executive authority of the State from which he fled, be delivered up, to be removed to the State having jurisdiction of the crime.

(3. No person held to service or labor in one State, under the laws thereof, escaping into another, shall in consequence of any law or regulation therein, be discharged from such service or labor, but shall be delivered up on claim of the party to whom such service or labor may be due.) (This clause was superseded by Amendment XIII.)

Section 3—Admission of new States. Power of Congress over territory and other property.

1. New States may be admitted by the Congress into this Union; but no new State shall be formed or erected within the jurisdiction of any other State; nor any State be formed by the junction of two or more States, or parts of States, without the consent of the Legislatures of the States concerned as well as of the Congress.

2. The Congress shall have power to dispose of and make all needful rules and regulations respecting the territory or other property belonging to the United States; and nothing in this Constitution shall be so construed as to prejudice any claims of the United States, or of any particular State.

Section 4—Republican form of government guaranteed. Each state to be protected.

The United States shall guarantee to every State in this Union a Republican form of government, and shall protect each of them against invasion; and on application of the Legislature, or of the Executive (when the Legislature cannot be convened) against domestic violence.

ARTICLE V.

Constitution: how amended; proviso.

The Congress, whenever two-thirds of both Houses shall deem it necessary, shall propose amendments to this Constitution, or, on the application of the Legislatures of two-thirds of the several States, shall call a convention for proposing amendments, which, in either case, shall be valid to all intents and purposes, as part of this Constitution, when ratified by the Legislatures of three-fourths of the several States, or by conventions in three-fourths thereof, as the one or the other mode of ratification may be proposed by the Congress; provided that no amendment which may be made prior to the year one thousand eight hundred and eight shall in any manner affect the first and fourth clauses in the Ninth Section of the First Article; and that no State, without its consent, shall be deprived of its equal suffrage in the Senate.

ARTICLE VI.

Certain debts, etc., declared valid. Supremacy of Constitution, treaties, and laws of the United States. Oath to support Constitution, by whom taken. No religious test.

1. All debts contracted and engagements entered into, before the adoption of this Constitution, shall be as valid against the United States under this Constitution, as under the Confederation.

2. This Constitution, and the laws of the United States which shall be made in pursuance thereof; and all treaties made, or which shall be made, under the authority of the United States, shall be the supreme law of the land; and the judges in every State shall be bound thereby, any thing in the Constitution or laws of any State to the contrary notwithstanding.

3. The Senators and Representatives before mentioned, and the members of the several State Legislatures, and all executive and judicial officers, both of the United States and of the several States, shall be bound by oath or affirmation, to support this Constitution; but no religious test shall ever be required as a qualification to any office or public trust under the United States.

ARTICLE VII.

What ratification shall establish Constitution.

The ratification of the Conventions of nine States, shall be sufficient for the establishment of this Constitution between the States so ratifying the same.

Done in convention by the unanimous consent of the States present the Seventeenth day of September in the year of our Lord one thousand seven hundred and eighty seven, and of the independence of the United States of America the Twelfth. In witness whereof we have hereunto subscribed our names.

George Washington, President and deputy from Virginia.

New Hampshire—John Langdon, Nicholas Gilman.

Massachusetts—Nathaniel Gorham, Rufus King.

Connecticut—Wm. Saml. Johnson, Roger Sherman.

New York—Alexander Hamilton.

New Jersey—Wil: Livingston, David Brearley, Wm. Paterson, Jona: Dayton.

Pennsylvania—B. Franklin, Thomas Mifflin, Robt. Morris, Geo. Clymer, Thos. FitzSimons, Jared Ingersoll, James Wilson, Gouv. Morris.

Delaware—Geo: Read, Gunning Bedford Jun., John Dickinson, Richard Bassett, Jaco: Broom.

Maryland—James McHenry, Daniel of Saint Thomas Jenifer, Danl. Carroll.

Virginia—John Blair, James Madison Jr.

North Carolina—Wm. Blount, Rich'd. Dobbs Spaight, Hugh Williamson.

South Carolina—J. Rutledge, Charles Cotesworth Pinckney, Charles Pinckney, Pierce Butler.

Georgia—William Few, Abr. Baldwin.

Attest: William Jackson, Secretary.

Ten Original Amendments: The Bill of Rights

In force Dec. 15, 1791

(The First Congress, at its first session in the City of New York, Sept. 25, 1789, submitted to the states 12 amendments to clarify certain individual and state rights not named in the Constitution. They are generally called the Bill of Rights.

(Influential in framing these amendments was the Declaration of Rights of Virginia, written by George Mason (1725-1792) in 1776. Mason, a Virginia delegate to the Constitutional Convention, did not sign the Constitution and opposed its ratification on the ground that it did not sufficiently oppose slavery or safeguard individual rights.

(In the preamble to the resolution offering the proposed amendments, Congress said: "The conventions of a number of the States having at the time of their adopting the Constitution, expressed a desire, in order to prevent misconstruction or abuse of its powers, that further declaratory and restrictive clauses should be added, and as extending the ground of public confidence in the government will best insure the beneficent ends of its institution, be it resolved," etc.

(Ten of these amendments now commonly known as one to 10 inclusive, but originally 3 to 12 inclusive, were ratified by the states as follows: New Jersey, Nov. 20, 1789; Maryland, Dec. 19, 1789; North Carolina, Dec. 22, 1789; South Carolina, Jan. 19, 1790; New Hampshire, Jan. 25, 1790; Delaware, Jan. 28, 1790; New York, Feb. 27, 1790; Pennsylvania, Mar. 10, 1790; Rhode

Island, June 7, 1790; Vermont, Nov. 3, 1791; Virginia, Dec. 15, 1791; Massachusetts, Mar. 2, 1939; Georgia, Mar. 18, 1939; Connecticut, Apr. 19, 1939. These original 10 ratified amendments follow as Amendments I to X inclusive.

(Of the two original proposed amendments that were not ratified promptly by the necessary number of states, the first related to apportionment of Representatives; the second, relating to compensation of members of Congress, was ratified in 1992 and became Amendment 27.)

AMENDMENT I.

Religious establishment prohibited. Freedom of speech, of the press, and right to petition.

Congress shall make no law respecting an establishment of religion, or prohibiting the free exercise thereof; or abridging the freedom of speech, or of the press; or the right of the people peaceably to assemble, and to petition the Government for a redress of grievances.

AMENDMENT II.

Right to keep and bear arms.

A well-regulated militia, being necessary to the security of a free State, the right of the people to keep and bear arms, shall not be infringed.

AMENDMENT III.

Conditions for quarters for soldiers.

No soldier shall, in time of peace be quartered in any house, without the consent of the owner, nor in time of war, but in a manner to be prescribed by law.

AMENDMENT IV.

Right of search and seizure regulated.

The right of the people to be secure in their persons, houses, papers, and effects, against unreasonable searches and seizures, shall not be violated, and no warrants shall issue, but upon probable cause, supported by oath or affirmation, and particularly describing the place to be searched, and the persons or things to be seized.

AMENDMENT V.

Provisions concerning prosecution. Trial and punishment—private property not to be taken for public use without compensation.

No person shall be held to answer for a capital, or otherwise infamous crime, unless on a presentment or indictment of a Grand Jury, except in cases arising in the land or naval forces, or in the militia, when in actual service in time of war or public danger; nor shall any person be subject for the same offense to be twice put in jeopardy of life or limb; nor shall be compelled in any criminal case to be a witness against himself, nor be deprived of life, liberty, or property, without due process of law; nor shall private property be taken for public use without just compensation.

AMENDMENT VI.

Right to speedy trial, witnesses, etc.

In all criminal prosecutions, the accused shall enjoy the right to a speedy and public trial, by an impartial jury of the State and district wherein the crime shall have been committed, which district shall have been previously ascertained by law, and to be informed of the nature and cause of the accusation; to be confronted with the witnesses against him; to have compulsory process for obtaining witnesses in his favor, and to have the assistance of counsel for his defense.

AMENDMENT VII.

Right of trial by jury.

In suits at common law, where the value in controversy shall exceed twenty dollars, the right of trial by jury shall be preserved, and no fact tried by a jury shall be otherwise reexamined in any court of the United States, than according to the rules of the common law.

AMENDMENT VIII.

Excessive bail or fines and cruel punishment prohibited.

Excessive bail shall not be required, nor excessive fines imposed, nor cruel and unusual punishments inflicted.

AMENDMENT IX.

Rule of construction of Constitution.

The enumeration in the Constitution, of certain rights, shall not be construed to deny or disparage others retained by the people.

AMENDMENT X.

Rights of States under Constitution.

The powers not delegated to the United States by the Constitution, nor prohibited by it to the States, are reserved to the States respectively, or to the people.

Amendments Since the Bill of Rights

AMENDMENT XI.

Judicial powers construed.

The judicial power of the United States shall not be construed to extend to any suit in law or equity, commenced or prosecuted against one of the United States by citizens of another State, or by citizens or subjects of any foreign state.

(This amendment was proposed to the Legislatures of the several States by the Third Congress on March 4, 1794, and was declared to have been ratified in a message from the President to Congress, dated Jan. 8, 1798.

(It was on Jan. 5, 1798, that Secretary of State Pickering received from 12 of the States authenticated ratifications, and informed President John Adams of that fact.

(As a result of later research in the Department of State, it is now established that Amendment XI became part of the Constitution on Feb. 7, 1795, for on that date it had been ratified by 12 States as follows:

(1. New York, Mar. 27, 1794. 2. Rhode Island, Mar. 31, 1794. 3. Connecticut, May 8, 1794. 4. New Hampshire, June 16, 1794. 5. Massachusetts, June 26, 1794. 6. Vermont, between Oct. 9, 1794, and Nov. 9, 1794. 7. Virginia, Nov. 18, 1794. 8. Georgia, Nov. 29, 1794. 9. Kentucky, Dec. 7, 1794. 10. Maryland, Dec. 26, 1794. 11. Delaware, Jan. 23, 1795. 12. North Carolina, Feb. 7, 1795.

(On June 1, 1796, more than a year after Amendment XI had become a part of the Constitution—but before anyone was officially aware of this—Tennessee had been admitted as a State; but not until Oct. 16, 1797, was a certified copy of the resolution of Congress proposing the amendment sent to the Governor of Tennessee, John Sevier, by Secretary of State Pickering, whose office was then at Trenton, New Jersey, because of the epidemic of yellow fever at Philadelphia; it seems, however, that the Legislature of Tennessee took no action on Amendment XI, owing doubtless to the fact that public announcement of its adoption was made soon thereafter.

(Besides the necessary 12 States, one other, South Carolina, ratified Amendment XI, but this action was not taken until Dec. 4, 1797; the two remaining States, New Jersey and Pennsylvania, failed to ratify.)

AMENDMENT XII.

Manner of choosing President and Vice-President.

(Proposed by Congress Dec. 9, 1803; ratification completed June 15, 1804.)

The Electors shall meet in their respective States and vote by ballot for President and Vice-President, one of whom, at least, shall not be an inhabitant of the same State with themselves; they shall name in their ballots the person voted for as President, and in distinct ballots the person voted for as Vice-President, and they shall make distinct lists of all persons voted for as President, and of all persons voted for as Vice-President, and of the number of votes for each, which lists they shall sign and certify, and transmit sealed to the seat of the Government of the United States, directed to the President of the Senate; the President of the Senate shall, in the presence of the Senate and House of Representatives, open all the certificates and the votes shall then be counted;—The person having the greatest number of votes for President, shall be the President, if such number be a majority of the whole number of Electors appointed; and if no person have such majority, then from the persons having the highest numbers not exceeding three on the list of those voted for as President, the House of Representatives shall choose immediately, by ballot, the President. But in choosing the President, the votes shall be taken by States, the representation from each State having one vote; a quorum for this purpose shall consist of a member or members from two-thirds of the States, and a majority of all the States shall be necessary to a choice. *(And if the House of Representatives shall not choose a President whenever the right of choice shall devolve upon them, before the fourth day of March next following, then the Vice-President shall act as President, as in the case of the death or other constitutional disability of the President.) (The words in parentheses were superseded by Amendment XX, section 3.)* The person having the greatest number of votes as Vice-President, shall be the Vice-President, if such number be a majority of the whole number of Electors appointed, and if no person have a majority, then from the two highest numbers on the list, the Senate shall choose the Vice-President; a quorum for the purpose shall consist of two-thirds of the whole number of Senators, and a majority of the whole number shall be necessary to a choice. But no person constitutionally ineligible to the office of President shall be eligible to that of Vice-President of the United States.

THE RECONSTRUCTION AMENDMENTS

(Amendments XIII, XIV, and XV are commonly known as the Reconstruction Amendments, inasmuch as they followed the Civil War, and were drafted by Republicans who were bent on imposing their own policy of reconstruction on the South. Post-bellum legislatures there—Mississippi, South Carolina, Georgia, for example—had set up laws which, it was charged, were contrived to perpetuate Negro slavery under other names.)

AMENDMENT XIII.

Slavery abolished.

(Proposed by Congress Jan. 31, 1865; ratification completed Dec. 18, 1865. The amendment, when first proposed by a resolution in Congress, was passed by the Senate, 38 to 6, on Apr. 8, 1864, but was defeated in the House, 95 to 66 on June 15, 1864. On reconsideration by the House, on Jan. 31, 1865, the resolution passed, 119 to 56. It was approved by President Lincoln on Feb. 1, 1865, although the Supreme Court had decided in 1798 that the President has nothing to do with the proposing of amendments to the Constitution, or their adoption.)

1. Neither slavery nor involuntary servitude, except as a punishment for crime whereof the party shall have been duly convicted, shall exist within the United States or any place subject to their jurisdiction.

2. Congress shall have power to enforce this article by appropriate legislation.

AMENDMENT XIV.

Citizenship rights not to be abridged.

(The following amendment was proposed to the Legislatures of the several states by the 39th Congress, June 13, 1866, and was declared to have been ratified in a proclamation by the Secretary of State, July 28, 1868.

(The 14th amendment was adopted only by virtue of ratification subsequent to earlier rejections. Newly constituted legislatures in both North Carolina and South Carolina (respectively July 4 and 9, 1868), ratified the proposed amendment, although earlier legislatures had rejected the proposal. The Secretary of State issued a proclamation, which, though doubtful as to the effect of attempted withdrawals by Ohio and New Jersey, entertained no doubt as to the validity of the ratification by North and South Carolina. The following day (July 21, 1868), Congress passed a resolution which declared the 14th Amendment to be a part of the Constitution and directed the Secretary of State so to promulgate it. The Secretary waited, however, until the newly constituted Legislature of Georgia had ratified the amendment, subsequent to an earlier rejection, before the promulgation of the ratification of the new amendment.)

1. All persons born or naturalized in the United States, and subject to the jurisdiction thereof, are citizens of the United States and of the State wherein they reside. No State shall make or enforce any law which shall abridge the privileges or immunities of citizens of the United States; nor shall any State deprive any person of life, liberty, or property, without due process of law; nor deny to any person within its jurisdiction the equal protection of the laws.

2. Representatives shall be apportioned among the several States according to their respective numbers, counting the whole number of persons in each State, excluding Indians not taxed. But when the right to vote at any election for the choice of Electors for President and Vice-President of the United States, Representatives in Congress, the executive and judicial officers of a State, or the members of the Legislature thereof, is denied to any of the male inhabitants of such State, being twenty-one years of age, and, citizens of the United States, or in any way abridged, except for participation in rebellion, or other crime, the basis of representation therein shall be reduced in the proportion which the number of such male citizens shall bear to the whole number of male citizens twenty-one years of age in such State.

3. No person shall be a Senator or Representative in Congress, or Elector of President and Vice-President, or hold any office, civil or military, under the United States, or under any State, who, having previously taken an oath, as a member of Congress, or as an officer of the United States, or as a member of any State Legislature, or as an executive or judicial officer of any State, to support the Constitution of the United States, shall have engaged in insurrection or rebellion against the same, or given aid or comfort to the enemies thereof. But Congress may by a vote of two-thirds of each House, remove such disability.

4. The validity of the public debt of the United States, authorized by law, including debts incurred for payment of pensions and bounties for services in suppressing insurrection or rebellion, shall not be questioned. But neither the United States nor any State shall assume or pay any debt or obligation incurred in aid of insurrection or rebellion against the United States, or any claim for the loss or emancipation of any slave; but all such debts, obligations and claims, shall be held illegal and void.

5. The Congress shall have power to enforce, by appropriate legislation, the provisions of this article.

AMENDMENT XV.

Race no bar to voting rights.

(The following amendment was proposed to the legislatures of the several States by the 40th Congress, Feb. 26, 1869, and was declared to have been ratified in a proclamation by the Secretary of State, Mar. 30, 1870.)

1. The right of citizens of the United States to vote shall not be denied or abridged by the United States or by any State on account of race, color, or previous condition of servitude.

2. The Congress shall have power to enforce this article by appropriate legislation.

AMENDMENT XVI.

Income taxes authorized.

(Proposed by Congress July 12, 1909; ratification declared by the Secretary of State Feb. 25, 1913.)

The Congress shall have power to lay and collect taxes on incomes, from whatever source derived, without apportionment among the several States, and without regard to any census or enumeration.

AMENDMENT XVII.

United States Senators to be elected by direct popular vote.

(Proposed by Congress May 13, 1912; ratification declared by the Secretary of State May 31, 1913.)

1. The Senate of the United States shall be composed of two Senators from each State, elected by the people thereof, for six years; and each Senator shall have one vote. The electors in each State shall have the qualifications requisite for electors of the most numerous branch of the State Legislatures.

2. When vacancies happen in the representation of any State in the Senate, the executive authority of such State shall issue writs of election to fill such vacancies: Provided, That the Legislature of any State may empower the Executive thereof to make temporary appointments until the peo-

ple fill the vacancies by election as the Legislature may direct.

3. This amendment shall not be so construed as to affect the election or term of any Senator chosen before it becomes valid as part of the Constitution.

AMENDMENT XVIII.

Liquor prohibition amendment.

(Proposed by Congress Dec. 18, 1917; ratification completed Jan. 16, 1919. Repealed by Amendment XXI, effective Dec. 5, 1933.)

(1. After one year from the ratification of this article the manufacture, sale, or transportation of intoxicating liquors within, the importation thereof into, or the exportation thereof from the United States and all territory subject to the jurisdiction thereof for beverage purposes is hereby prohibited.

(2. The Congress and the several States shall have concurrent power to enforce this article by appropriate legislation.

(3. This article shall be inoperative unless it shall have been ratified as an amendment to the Constitution by the Legislatures of the several States, as provided in the Constitution, within seven years from the date of the submission hereof to the States by the Congress.)

(The total vote in the Senates of the various States was 1,310 for, 237 against—84.6% dry. In the lower houses of the States the vote was 3,782 for, 1,035 against—78.5% dry.

(The amendment ultimately was adopted by all the States except Connecticut and Rhode Island.)

AMENDMENT XIX.

Giving nationwide suffrage to women.

(Proposed by Congress June 4, 1919; ratification certified by Secretary of State Aug. 26, 1920.)

1. The right of citizens of the United States to vote shall not be denied or abridged by the United States or by any State on account of sex.

2. Congress shall have power to enforce this Article by appropriate legislation.

AMENDMENT XX.

Terms of President and Vice President to begin on Jan. 20; those of Senators, Representatives, Jan. 3.

(Proposed by Congress Mar. 2, 1932; ratification completed Jan. 23, 1933.)

1. The terms of the President and Vice President shall end at noon on the 20th day of January, and the terms of Senators and Representatives at noon on the 3rd day of January, of the years in which such terms would have ended if this article had not been ratified; and the terms of their successors shall then begin.

2. The Congress shall assemble at least once in every year, and such meeting shall begin at noon on the 3rd day of January, unless they shall by law appoint a different day.

3. If, at the time fixed for the beginning of the term of the President, the President elect shall have died, the Vice President elect shall become President. If a President shall not have been chosen before the time fixed for the beginning of his term, or if the President elect shall have failed to qualify, then the Vice President elect shall act as President until a President shall have qualified; and the Congress may by law provide for the case wherein neither a President elect nor a Vice President elect shall have qualified, declaring who shall then act as President, or the manner in which one who is to act shall be selected, and such person shall act accordingly until a President or Vice President shall have qualified.

4. The Congress may by law provide for the case of the death of any of the persons from whom the House of Representatives may choose a President whenever the right of choice shall have devolved upon them, and for the case of the death of any of the persons from whom the Senate may choose a Vice President whenever the right of choice shall have devolved upon them.

5. Sections 1 and 2 shall take effect on the 15th day of October following the ratification of this article (Oct., 1933).

6. This article shall be inoperative unless it shall have been ratified as an amendment to the Constitution by the Legislatures of three-fourths of the several States within seven years from the date of its submission.

AMENDMENT XXI.

Repeal of Amendment XVIII.

(Proposed by Congress Feb. 20, 1933; ratification completed Dec. 5, 1933.)

1. The eighteenth article of amendment to the Constitution of the United States is hereby repealed.

2. The transportation or importation into any State, Territory, or Possession of the United States for delivery or use therein of intoxicating liquors, in violation of the laws thereof, is hereby prohibited.

3. This article shall be inoperative unless it shall have been ratified as an amendment to the Constitution by conventions in the several States, as provided in the Constitution, within seven years from the date of the submission hereof to the States by the Congress.

AMENDMENT XXII.

Limiting Presidential terms of office.

(Proposed by Congress Mar. 24, 1947; ratification completed Feb. 27, 1951.)

1. No person shall be elected to the office of the President more than twice, and no person who has held the office of President, or acted as President, for more than two years of a term to which some other person was elected President shall be elected to the office of the President more than once. But this Article shall not apply to any person holding the office of President when this Article was proposed by the Congress, and shall not prevent any person who may be holding the office of President, or acting as President, during the term within which this Article becomes operative from holding the office of President or acting as President during the remainder of such term.

2. This article shall be inoperative unless it shall have been ratified as an amendment to the Constitution by the Legislatures of three-fourths of the several States within seven years from the date of its submission to the States by the Congress.

AMENDMENT XXIII.

Presidential vote for District of Columbia.

(Proposed by Congress June 16, 1960; ratification completed Mar. 29, 1961.)

1. The District constituting the seat of Government of the United States shall appoint in such manner as the Congress may direct:

A number of electors of President and Vice President equal to the whole number of Senators and Representatives in Congress to which the District would be entitled if it were a State, but in no event more than the least populous State; they shall be in addition to those appointed by the States, but they shall be considered, for the purposes of the election of President and Vice President, to be electors appointed by a State; and they shall meet in the District and perform such duties as provided by the twelfth article of amendment.

2. The Congress shall have power to enforce this article by appropriate legislation.

AMENDMENT XXIV.

Barring poll tax in federal elections.

(Proposed by Congress Aug. 27, 1962; ratification completed Jan. 23, 1964.)

1. The right of citizens of the United States to vote in any primary or other election for President or Vice President, for electors for President or Vice President, or for Senator or Representative in Congress, shall not be denied or abridged by the United States or any State by reason of failure to pay any poll tax or other tax.

2. The Congress shall have power to enforce this article by appropriate legislation.

AMENDMENT XXV.

Presidential disability and succession.

(Proposed by Congress July 6, 1965; ratification completed Feb. 10, 1967.)

1. In case of the removal of the President from office or of his death or resignation, the Vice President shall become President.

2. Whenever there is a vacancy in the office of the Vice President, the President shall nominate a Vice President who shall take office upon confirmation by a majority vote of both houses of Congress.

3. Whenever the President transmits to the President pro tempore of the Senate and the Speaker of the House of Representatives his written declaration that he is unable to discharge the powers and duties of his office, and until he transmits to them a written declaration to the contrary, such powers and duties shall be discharged by the Vice President as Acting President.

4. Whenever the Vice President and a majority of either the principal officers of the executive departments or of such other body as Congress may by law provide, transmit to the President pro tempore of the Senate and the Speaker of the House of Representatives their written declaration that the President is unable to discharge the powers and duties of his office, the Vice President shall immediately assume the powers and duties of the office as Acting President.

Thereafter, when the President transmits to the President pro tempore of the Senate and the Speaker of the House of Representatives his written declaration that no inability exists, he shall resume the powers and duties of his office unless the Vice President and a majority of either the principal officers of the executive department or of such other body as Congress may by law provide, transmit within four days to the President pro tempore of the Senate and the Speaker of the House of Representatives their written declaration that the President is unable to discharge the powers and duties of his office. Thereupon Congress shall decide the issue, assembling within forty-eight hours for that purpose if not in session. If the Congress, within twenty-one days after receipt of the latter written declaration, or, if Congress is not in session, within twenty-one days after Congress is required to assemble, determines by two-thirds vote of both houses that the President is unable to discharge the powers and duties of his office, the Vice President shall continue to discharge the same as Acting President; otherwise, the President shall resume the powers and duties of his office.

AMENDMENT XXVI.

Lowering voting age to 18 years.

(Proposed by Congress Mar. 23, 1971; ratification completed July 1, 1971.)

1. The right of citizens of the United States, who are 18 years of age or older, to vote shall not be denied or abridged by the United States or any state on account of age.

2. The Congress shall have the power to enforce this article by appropriate legislation.

AMENDMENT XXVII.

Congressional pay.

(Proposed by Congress Sept. 25, 1789; ratification completed May 7, 1992.)

No law, varying the compensation for the services of the Senators and Representatives, shall take effect, until an election of Representatives shall have intervened.

Origin of the Constitution

The War of Independence was conducted by delegates from the original 13 states, called the Congress of the United States of America and generally known as the Continental Congress. In 1777 the Congress submitted to the legislatures of the states the Articles of Confederation and Perpetual Union, which were ratified by New Hampshire, Massachusetts, Rhode Island, Connecticut, New York, New Jersey, Pennsylvania, Delaware, Virginia, North Carolina, South Carolina, and Georgia, and finally, in 1781, by Maryland.

The first article of the instrument read: "The stile of this confederacy shall be the United States of America." This did not signify a sovereign nation, because the states delegated only those powers they could not handle individually, such as power to wage war, establish a uniform currency, make treaties with foreign nations and contract debts for general expenses (such as paying the army). Taxes for the payment of such debts were levied by the individual states. The president under the Articles signed himself "President of the United States in Congress assembled," but here the United States were considered in the plural, a cooperating group. Canada was invited to join the union on equal terms but did not act.

When the war was won it became evident that a stronger federal union was needed to protect the mutual interests of the states. The Congress left the initiative to the legislatures. Virginia in Jan. 1786 appointed commissioners to meet with representatives of other states, with the result that delegates from Virginia, Delaware, New York, New Jersey, and Pennsylvania met at Annapolis. Alexander Hamilton prepared for their call by asking delegates from all states to meet in Philadelphia in May 1787 "to render the Constitution of the Federal government adequate to the exigencies of the union." Congress endorsed the plan Feb. 21, 1787. Delegates were appointed by all states except Rhode Island.

The convention met May 14, 1787. George Washington was chosen president (presiding officer). The states certified 65 delegates, but 10 did not attend. The work was done by 55, not all of whom were present at all sessions. Of the 55 attending delegates, 16 failed to sign, and 39 actually signed Sept. 17, 1787, some with reservations. Some historians have said 74 delegates (9 more than the 65 actually certified) were named and 19 failed to attend. These 9 additional persons refused the appointment, were never delegates and never counted as absentees. Washington sent the Constitution to Congress with a covering letter and that body, Sept. 28, 1787, ordered it sent to the legislatures, "in order to be submitted to a convention of delegates chosen in each state by the people thereof."

The Constitution was ratified by votes of state conventions as follows: Delaware, Dec. 7, 1787, unanimous; Pennsylvania, Dec. 12, 1787, 43 to 23; New Jersey, Dec. 18, 1787, unanimous; Georgia, Jan 2, 1788, unanimous; Connecticut, Jan. 9, 1788, 128 to 40; Massachusetts, Feb. 6, 1788, 187 to 168; Maryland, Apr. 28, 1788, 63 to 11; South Carolina, May 23, 1788, 149 to 73; New Hampshire, June 21, 1788, 57 to 46; Virginia, June 25, 1788, 89 to 79; New York, July 26, 1788, 30 to 27. Nine states were needed to establish the operation of the Constitution "between the states so ratifying the same" and New Hampshire was the 9th state. The government did not declare the Constitution in effect until the first Wednesday in Mar. 1789, which was Mar. 4. After that North Carolina ratified it Nov. 21, 1789, 194 to 77; and Rhode Island, May 29, 1790, 34 to 32. Vermont in convention ratified it Jan. 10, 1791, and by act of Congress approved Feb. 18, 1791, was admitted into the Union as the 14th state, Mar. 4, 1791.

There have been calls to hold a second constitutional convention. The Constitution stipulates that a convention must be held when 34 states pass bills to hold a convention.

Selected Landmark Decisions of the U.S. Supreme Court

1803: Marbury v. Madison. The Court ruled that Congress exceeded its power in the Judiciary Act of 1789; thus, the Court established its power to review acts of Congress and declare invalid those it found in conflict with the Constitution.

1819: McCulloch v. Maryland. The Court ruled that Congress had the authority to charter a national bank, under the Constitution's granting of the power to enact all laws "necessary and proper" to exact the responsibilities of government. The Court also held that the national bank was immune to state taxation.

1819: Trustees of Dartmouth College v. Woodward. The Court ruled that a state could not arbitrarily alter the terms of a college's contract. (In later years the Court widened the implications by using the same principle to limit the states' ability to interfere with business contracts.)

1857: Dred Scott v. Sanford. The Court declared unconstitutional the already-repealed Missouri Compromise of 1820 because it deprived a person of his property—a slave—without due process of law. The Court also ruled that slaves were not citizens of any state nor of the U.S. (The latter part of the decision was overturned by ratification of the 14th Amendment in 1868.)

1896: Plessy v. Ferguson. The Court ruled that a state law requiring federal railroad trains to provide separate but equal facilities for black and white passengers neither infringed upon federal authority to regulate interstate commerce nor violated the 13th and 14th Amendments. (The "separate but equal" doctrine remained effective until the 1954 Brown v. Board of Education decision.)

1904: Northern Securities Co. v. U.S. The Court ruled that a holding company formed solely to eliminate competition between two railroad lines was a combination in restraint of trade, thus a violation of the federal antitrust act.

1908: Muller v. Oregon. The Court ruled to uphold a state law limiting the maximum working hours of women. (Instead of presenting legal arguments, Louis D. Brandeis, counsel for the state, brought forth evidence from social workers, physicians, and factory inspectors that the number of hours women worked affected their health and morals.)

1911: Standard Oil Co. of New Jersey et al. v. U.S. The Court ruled that the Standard Oil Trust must be dissolved because of its unreasonable restraint of trade, not because of its size.

1919: Schenck v. U.S. In its first decision regarding the extent of protection afforded by the First Amendment, the Court sustained the Espionage Act of 1917, maintaining that freedom of speech and press could be constrained if "the words used are in such circumstances and are of such a nature as to create a clear and present danger. . ."

1925: Gitlow v. New York. The Court ruled that the First Amendment prohibition against government abridgement of the freedom of speech applied to the states as well as to the federal government. The decision was the first of a number of rulings holding that the 14th Amendment extended the guarantees of the Bill of Rights to state action.

1935: Schechter Poultry Corp. v. U.S. The Court ruled that Congress exceeded its authority to delegate legislative powers and to regulate interstate commerce when it enacted the National Industrial Recovery Act, which afforded the U.S. president too much discretionary power.

1951: Dennis et al. v. U.S. The Court upheld convictions under the Smith Act of 1940 for speaking about communist theory that advocated the forcible overthrow of the government. (In the 1957 Yates v. U.S. decision, the Court moderated this ruling by allowing such advocacy in the abstract, if not connected to action to achieve the goal.)

1954: Brown v. Board of Education of Topeka. The Court ruled that separate public schools for black and white students were inherently unequal, thus state-sanctioned segregation in public schools violated the equal protection guarantee of the 14th Amendment. And in **Bolling v. Sharpe** the Court ruled that the congressionally-mandated segregated public school system in the District of Columbia violated the Fifth Amendment's due process guarantee of personal liberty. (The Brown ruling also led to the abolition of state-sponsored segregation in other public facilities.)

1957: Roth v. U.S., Alberts v. California. The Court ruled that obscene material was not protected by the First Amendment guarantees of freedom of speech and press, defining obscene as "utterly without redeeming social value" and appealing to "prurient interests" in the view of the average person. (This definition, the first offered by the Court, was modified in several subsequent decisions, and the "average person" standard was replaced by the "local community" standard in the **1973 Miller v. California** case.)

1961: Mapp v. Ohio. The Court ruled that evidence obtained in violation of the 4th Amendment guarantee against unreasonable search and seizure must be excluded from use at state as well as federal trials.

1962: Engel v. Vitale. The Court ruled that public school officials could not require pupils to recite a state-composed prayer at the start of each school day, even if the prayer was non-denominational and pupils who so desired could be excused from reciting it, because such official state sanction of religious utterances was an unconstitutional attempt to establish religion.

1962: Baker v. Carr. The Court held that the constitutional challenges to the unequal distribution of voters among legislative districts could be resolved by federal courts, rejecting the doctrine set out in **Colegrove v. Green** in 1946 that such apportionment challenges were "political questions."

1963: Gideon v. Wainwright. The Court ruled that the due process clause of the 14th Amendment extended to state as well as federal defendants, thus all persons charged with serious crimes must be provided with an attorney, and states were required to appoint counsel for defendants unable to pay their own attorneys' fees.

1964: New York Times Co. v. Sullivan. The Court ruled that the First Amendment guarantee of freedom of the press protected the press from libel suits for defamatory reports on public officials unless the officials proved that the reports were made from actual malice. The Court defined malice as "with knowledge that (the defamatory statement) was false or with reckless disregard of whether it was false or not."

1965: Griswold v. Conn. The Court ruled that a state unconstitutionally interfered with personal privacy in the marriage relationship when it prohibited anyone, including married couples, from using contraceptives.

1966: Miranda v. Arizona. The Court ruled that the guarantee of due process required that before any questioning of suspects in police custody, the suspects must be informed of their right to remain silent, that anything they say may be used against them, and that they have the right to counsel.

1973: Roe v. Wade, Doe v. Bolton. The Court ruled that the right to privacy inherent in the 14th Amendment's due process guarantee of personal liberty protected a woman's decision whether or not to bear a child, and was impermissibly abridged by state laws that made abortion a crime. During the first trimester of pregnancy, the Court maintained, the decision to have an abortion should be left entirely to a woman and her physician.

1974: U.S. v. Nixon. The Court ruled that neither the separation of powers nor the need to preserve the confidentiality of presidential communications could alone justify an absolute executive privilege of immunity from judicial demands for evidence to be used in a criminal trial.

1976: Gregg v. Georgia, Profitt v. Fla., Jurek v. Texas. The Court held that death, as a punishment for persons convicted of first degree murder, was not in and of itself cruel and unusual punishment in violation of the 8th Amendment.

The Court also ruled that the Amendment required the sentencing judge and jury to consider the individual character of the offender and the circumstances of the particular crime before deciding whether or not to impose the death sentence. In the associated **Woodson v. N.C., Roberts v. LA.**, the Court ruled that states could not make death the mandatory penalty for first-degree murder, since that would fail to meet the constitutional requirement for the consideration of the individual offender and offense.

1978: Regents of Univ. of Calif. v. Bakke. The Court ruled that a special admissions program for a state medical school under which a set number of places were set aside for minority group members, with white applicants denied the opportunity to compete for those seats, violated Title XIV of the 1964 Civil Rights Act, which forbids the exclusion of anyone, because of race, from participation in a federally-funded program. The Court also ruled that admissions programs that considered race as one of a complex of factors involved in the decision to admit or reject an applicant were not unconstitutional.

1979: United Steelworkers of America v. Weber, Kaiser Aluminum v. Weber, U.S. v. Weber. The Court ruled that Title VII of the 1964 Civil Rights Act, which forbids racial discrimination in employment, did not forbid employers to adopt voluntarily race-conscious affirmative action programs to encourage minority participation in areas in which they traditionally were underrepresented.

1986: Bowers v. Hardwick. The Court refused to extend the right of privacy inherent in the Constitution to homosexual activity, upholding a Georgia law that made sodomy a crime. (Although the Georgia law covered heterosexual sodomy as well as homosexual sodomy, enforcement in Georgia and most other states had been confined to homosexual activity.)

1990: Cruzan v. Missouri. The Court ruled that a person had the right to refuse life-sustaining medical treatment. However, the Court also ruled that such treatment could not be withheld from comatose patients unless there was "clear and convincing evidence" that the person would not have wanted to live under those conditions.

Patrick Henry's Speech to the Virginia Convention

The following is an excerpt from Patrick Henry's speech to the Virginia Convention on Mar. 23, 1775:

Gentlemen may cry, peace, peace—but there is no peace. The war is actually begun! The next gale that sweeps from the north will bring to our ears the clash of resounding arms! Our brethren are already in the field! Why stand we here idle? What is it that gentlemen wish? What would they have? Is life so dear, or peace so sweet, as to be purchased at the price of chains and slavery? Forbid it, Almighty God! I know not what course others may take; but as for me, give me liberty, or give me death!

Common Sense

The following is an excerpt from Thomas Paine's *Common Sense.* Paine adopted the doctrine of separation from Britain after the battles of Lexington and Concord, and published his pamphlet in Jan. 1776.

The cause of America is in great measure the cause of all mankind. Many circumstances hath, and will arise, which are not local, but universal, and through which principles of all Lovers of Mankind are affected, and in the Event of which, their Affections are interested. The laying a Country desolate with Fire and Sword, declaring war against natural rights of all Mankind, and extirpating the Defenders thereof from the Face of the Earth, is the Concern of every Man to whom Nature hath given the Power of feeling; . . . It is repugnant to reason, to the universal order of things, to all examples from former ages, to suppose, that this continent can longer remain subject to any external power . . .

The last cord is now broken, the people of England are presenting addresses against us. There are injuries which nature cannot forgive; she would cease to be nature if she did . . .

O ye that love mankind! Ye that dare oppose, not only the tyranny, but the tyrant, stand forth! Every spot of the old world is overrun with oppression. Freedom hath been hunted round the globe. Asia, and Africa, have long expelled her—Europe regards her like a stranger, and England hath given her warning to depart. O! Receive the fugitive, and prepare in time an asylum for mankind.

Law on Succession to the Presidency

If by reason of death, resignation, removal from office, inability, or failure to qualify there is neither a president nor vice president to discharge the powers and duties of the office of president, then the speaker of the House of Representatives shall upon his resignation as speaker and as representative, act as president. The same rule shall apply in the case of the death, resignation, removal from office, or inability of an individual acting as president.

If at the time when a speaker is to begin the discharge of the powers and duties of the office of president there is no speaker, or the speaker fails to qualify as acting president, then the president pro tempore of the Senate, upon his resignation as president pro tempore and as senator, shall act as president.

An individual acting as president shall continue to act until the expiration of the then current presidential term, except that (1) if his discharge of the powers and duties of the office is founded in whole or in part in the failure of both the president-elect and the vice president-elect to qualify, then he shall act only until a president or vice president qualifies, and (2) if his discharge of the powers and duties of the office is founded in whole or in part on the inability of the president or vice president, then he shall act only until the removal of the disability of one of such individuals.

If, by reason of death, resignation, removal from office, or failure to qualify, there is no president pro tempore to act as president, then the officer of the United States who is highest on the following list, and who is not under any disability to discharge the powers and duties of president shall act as president; the secretaries of state, treasury, defense, attorney general; secretaries of interior, agriculture, commerce, labor, health and human services, housing and urban development, transportation, energy, education.

(Legislation approved July 18, 1947; amended Sept. 9, 1965, Oct. 15, 1966, Aug. 4, 1977, and Sept. 27, 1979. (See also Constitutional Amendment XXV.)

Presidential Oath of Office

The Constitution (Article II) directs that the President shall take the following oath or affirmation: "I do solemnly swear (affirm) that I will faithfully execute the office of President of the United States, and will, to the best of my ability, preserve, protect, and defend the Constitution of the United States." (Custom decrees the use of the words "So help me God" at the end of the oath when taken by the President-elect, his/her left hand on the Bible for the duration of the oath, with his/her right hand slightly raised.)

How the Declaration of Independence Was Adopted

On June 7, 1776, Richard Henry Lee, who had issued the first call for a congress of the colonies, introduced in the Continental Congress at Philadelphia a resolution declaring "that these United Colonies are, and of right ought to be, free and independent states, that they are absolved from all allegiance to the British Crown, and that all political connection between them and the state of Great Britain is, and ought to be, totally dissolved."

The resolution, seconded by John Adams on behalf of the Massachusetts delegation, came up again June 10 when a committee of 5, headed by Thomas Jefferson, was appointed to express the purpose of the resolution in a declaration of independence. The others on the committee were John Adams, Benjamin Franklin, Robert R. Livingston, and Roger Sherman.

Drafting the Declaration was assigned to Jefferson, who worked on a portable desk of his own construction in a room at Market and 7th Sts. The committee reported the result June 28, 1776. The members of the Congress suggested a number of changes, which Jefferson called "deplorable." They didn't approve Jefferson's arraignment of the British people and King George III for encouraging and fostering the slave trade, which Jefferson called "an execrable commerce." They made 86 changes, eliminating 480 words and leaving 1,337. In the final form capitalization was erratic. Jefferson had written that men were endowed with "inalienable" rights; in the final copy it came out as "unalienable" and has been thus ever since.

The Lee-Adams resolution of independence was adopted by 12 yeas July 2 — the actual date of the act of independence. The Declaration, which explains the act, was adopted July 4, in the evening.

After the Declaration was adopted, July 4, 1776, it was turned over to John Dunlap, printer, to be printed on broadsides. The original copy was lost and one of his broadsides was attached to a page in the journal of the Congress. It was read aloud July 8 in Philadelphia, Easton, Pa., and Trenton, N.J. On July 9 at 6 p.m. it was read by order of Gen. George Washington to the troops assembled on the Common in New York City (City Hall Park).

The Continental Congress of July 19, 1776, adopted the following resolution:

"Resolved, That the Declaration passed on the 4th, be fairly engrossed on parchment with the title and stile of 'The Unanimous Declaration of the thirteen United States of America' and that the same, when engrossed, be signed by every member of Congress."

Not all delegates who signed the engrossed Declaration were present on July 4. Robert Morris (Pa.), William Williams (Conn.) and Samuel Chase (Md.) signed on Aug. 2, Oliver Wolcott (Conn.), George Wythe (Va.), Richard Henry Lee (Va.) and Elbridge Gerry (Mass.) signed in August and September, Matthew Thornton (N. H.) joined the Congress Nov. 4 and signed later. Thomas McKean (Del.) rejoined Washington's army before signing and said later that he signed in 1781.

Charles Carroll of Carrollton was appointed a delegate by Maryland on July 4, 1776, presented his credentials July 18, and signed the engrossed Declaration Aug. 2. Born Sept. 19, 1737, he was 95 years old and the last surviving signer when he died Nov. 14, 1832.

Two Pennsylvania delegates who did not support the Declaration on July 4 were replaced.

The 4 New York delegates did not have authority from their state to vote on July 4. On July 9 the New York state convention authorized its delegates to approve the Declaration and the Congress was so notified on July 15, 1776. The 4 signed the Declaration on Aug. 2.

The original engrossed Declaration is preserved in the National Archives Building in Washington.

The Continental Congress: Meetings, Presidents

Meeting places	Dates of meetings	Congress presidents	Date elected
Philadelphia	Sept. 5 to Oct. 26, 1774	Peyton Randolph, Va. (1)	Sept. 5, 1774
"	"	Henry Middleton, S.C.	Oct. 22, 1774
Philadelphia	May 10, 1775 to Dec. 12, 1776	Peyton Randolph, Va.	May 10, 1775
"	"	John Hancock, Mass.	May 24, 1775
Baltimore	Dec. 20, 1776 to Mar. 4, 1777	"	
Philadelphia	Mar. 5 to Sept. 18, 1777	"	
Lancaster, Pa.	Sept. 27, 1777 (one day)	"	
York, Pa.	Sept. 30, 1777 to June 27, 1778	Henry Laurens, S.C.	Nov. 1, 1777(4)
Philadelphia	July 2, 1778 to June 21, 1783	John Jay, N.Y.	Dec. 10, 1778
"	"	Samuel Huntington, Conn.	Sept. 28, 1779
"	"	Thomas McKean, Del.	July 10, 1781
"	"	John Hanson, Md. (2)	Nov. 5, 1781
"	"	Elias Boudinot, N.J..	Nov. 4, 1782
Princeton, N.J.	June 30 to Nov. 4, 1783	Thomas Mifflin, Pa..	Nov. 3, 1783
Annapolis, Md.	Nov. 26, 1783 to June 3, 1784	"	
Trenton, N.J.	Nov. 1 to Dec. 24, 1784	Richard Henry Lee, Va.	Nov. 30, 1784
New York City	Jan. 11 to Nov. 4, 1785	"	
"	Nov. 7, 1785 to Nov. 3, 1786	John Hancock, Mass. (3)	Nov. 23, 1785
"	"	Nathaniel Gorham, Mass.	June 6, 1786
"	Nov. 6, 1786 to Oct. 30, 1787	Arthur St. Clair, Pa.	Feb. 2, 1787
"	Nov. 5, 1787 to Oct. 21, 1788	Cyrus Griffin, Va.	Jan. 22, 1788
"	Nov. 3, 1788 to Mar. 2, 1789	"	

(1) Resigned Oct. 22, 1774. (2) Titled "President of the United States in Congress Assembled," John Hanson is considered by some to be the first U.S. President as he was the first to serve under the Articles of Confederation. He was, however, little more than presiding officer of the Congress, which retained full executive power. He could be considered the head of government, but not head of state. (3) Resigned May 29, 1786, without serving, because of illness. (4) Articles of Confederation agreed upon, Nov. 15, 1777; last ratification from Maryland, Mar. 1, 1781.

Origin of the United States National Motto

In God We Trust, designated as the U. S. National Motto by Congress in 1956, originated during the Civil War as an inscription for U. S. coins, although it was used by Francis Scott Key in a slightly different form when he wrote The Star Spangled Banner in 1814. On Nov. 13, 1861, when Union morale had been shaken by battlefield defeats, the Rev. M. R. Watkinson, of Ridleyville, Pa., wrote to Secy. of the Treasury Salmon P. Chase. "From my heart I have felt our national shame in disowning God as not the least of our present national disasters," the minister wrote, suggesting "recognition of the Almighty God in some form on our coins." Secy. Chase ordered designs prepared with the inscription *In God We Trust* and backed coinage legislation that authorized use of this slogan. It first appeared on some U. S. coins in 1864, disappeared and reappeared on various coins until 1955, when Congress ordered it placed on all paper money and all coins.

The Great Seal of the U.S.

On July 4, 1776, the Continental Congress appointed a committee consisting of Benjamin Franklin, John Adams and Thomas Jefferson "to bring in a device for a seal of the United States of America." After many delays, a verbal description of a design by William Barton was finally approved by Congress on June 20, 1782. The seal shows an American bald eagle with a ribbon in its mouth bearing the device *E pluribus unum* (One out of many). In its talons are the arrows of war and an olive branch of peace. On the reverse side it shows an unfinished pyramid with an eye (the eye of Providence) above it.

The American's Creed

William Tyler Page, Clerk of the U.S. House of Representatives, wrote "The American's Creed" in 1917. It was accepted by the House on behalf of the American people on April 3, 1918.

"I believe in the United States of America as a government of the people, by the people, for the people; whose just powers are derived from the consent of the governed; a democracy in a republic; a sovereign Nation of many sovereign States; a perfect union, one and inseparable; established upon those principles of freedom, equality, justice, and humanity for which American patriots sacrificed their lives and fortunes.

"I therefore believe it is my duty to my country to love it, to support its Constitution, to obey its laws, to respect its flag, and to defend it against all enemies."

The Flag of the U.S.—The Stars and Stripes

The 50-star flag of the United States was raised for the first time officially at 12:01 a.m. on July 4, 1960, at Fort McHenry National Monument in Baltimore, Md. The 50th star had been added for Hawaii; a year earlier the 49th, for Alaska. Before that, no star had been added since 1912, when N.M. and Ariz. were admitted to the Union.

The true history of the Stars and Stripes has become so cluttered by a volume of myth and tradition that the facts are difficult, and in some cases impossible, to establish. For example, it is not certain who designed the Stars and Stripes, who made the first such flag, or even whether it ever flew in any sea fight or land battle of the American Revolution.

One thing all agree on is that the Stars and Stripes originated as the result of a resolution offered by the Marine Committee of the Second Continental Congress at Philadelphia and adopted June 14, 1777. It read:

Resolved: that the flag of the United States be thirteen stripes, alternate red and white; that the union be thirteen stars, white in a blue field, representing a new constellation.

Congress gave no hint as to the designer of the flag, no instructions as to the arrangement of the stars, and no information on its appropriate uses. Historians have been unable to find the original flag law.

The resolution establishing the flag was not even published until Sept. 2, 1777. Despite repeated requests, Washington did not get the flags until 1783, after the Revolutionary War was over. And there is no certainty that they were the Stars and Stripes.

Early Flags

Although it was never officially adopted by the Continental Congress, many historians consider the first flag of the U.S. to have been the Grand Union (sometimes called Great Union) flag. This was a modification of the British Meteor flag, which had the red cross of St. George and the white cross of St. Andrew combined in the blue canton. For the Grand Union flag, 6 horizontal stripes were imposed on the red field, dividing it into 13 alternate red and white stripes. On Jan. 1, 1776, when the Continental Army came into formal existence, this flag was unfurled on Prospect Hill, Somerville, Mass. Washington wrote that "we hoisted the Union Flag in compliment to the United Colonies."

One of several flags about which controversy has raged for years is at Easton, Pa. Containing the devices of the national flag in reversed order, this has been in the public library at Easton for over 150 years. Some contend that this flag was actually the first Stars and Stripes, first displayed on July 8, 1776. This flag has 13 red and white stripes in the canton, 13 white stars centered in a blue field.

A flag was hastily improvised from garments by the defenders of Fort Schuyler at Rome, N.Y., Aug. 3-22, 1777. Historians believe it was the Grand Union Flag.

The Sons of Liberty had a flag of 9 red and white stripes, to signify 9 colonies, when they met in New York in 1765 to oppose the Stamp Tax. By 1775, the flag had grown to 13 red and white stripes, with a rattlesnake on it.

At Concord, Apr. 19, 1775, the minute men from Bedford, Mass., are said to have carried a flag having a silver arm with sword on a red field.

At Cambridge, Mass., the Sons of Liberty used a plain red flag with a green pine tree on it.

In June 1775, Washington went from Philadelphia to Boston to take command of the army, escorted to New York by the Philadelphia Light Horse Troop. It carried a yellow flag which had an elaborate coat of arms — the shield charged with 13 knots, the motto "For These We Strive" — and a canton of 13 blue and silver stripes.

In Feb., 1776, Col. Christopher Gadsden, member of the Continental Congress, gave the S. Carolina Provincial Congress a flag "such as is to be used by the commander-in-chief of the American Navy." It had a yellow field, with a rattlesnake about to strike and the words "Don't Tread on Me."

At the battle of Bennington, Aug. 16, 1777, patriots used a flag of 7 white and 6 red stripes with a blue canton extending down 9 stripes and showing an arch of 11 white stars over the figure 76 and a star in each of the upper corners. The stars are seven-pointed. This flag is preserved in the Historical Museum at Bennington, Vt.

At the Battle of Cowpens, Jan. 17, 1781, the 3d Maryland Regt. is said to have carried a flag of 13 red and white stripes, with a blue canton containing 12 stars in a circle around one star.

Who Designed the Flag? No one knows for certain. Francis Hopkinson, designer of a naval flag, declared he also had designed the flag and in 1781 asked Congress to reimburse him for his services. Congress did not do so. Dumas Malone of Columbia Univ. wrote: "This talented man . . . designed the American flag."

Who Called the Flag Old Glory? — The flag is said to have been named Old Glory by William Driver, a sea captain of Salem, Mass. One legend has it that when he raised the flag on his brig, the Charles Doggett, in 1824, he said: "I name thee Old Glory." But his daughter, who presented the flag to the Smithsonian Institution, said he named it at his 21st birthday celebration Mar. 17, 1824, when his mother presented the homemade flag to him.

The Betsy Ross Legend — The widely publicized legend that Mrs. Betsy Ross made the first Stars and Stripes in June 1776, at the request of a committee composed of George Washington, Robert Morris, and George Ross, an uncle, was first made public in 1870, by a grandson of Mrs. Ross. Historians have been unable to find a historical record of such a meeting or committee.

Adding New Stars

The flag of 1777 was used until 1795. Then, on the admission of Vermont and Kentucky to the Union, Congress passed and Pres. Washington signed an act that after May 1, 1795, the flag should have 15 stripes, alternate red and white, and 15 white stars on a blue field in the union.

When new states were admitted it became evident that the flag would become burdened with stripes. Congress thereupon ordered that after July 4, 1818, the flag should have 13 stripes, symbolizing the 13 original states; that the union have 20 stars, and that whenever a new state was admitted a new star should be added on the July 4 following admission. No law designates the permanent arrangement of the stars. However, since 1912 when a new state has been admitted, the new design has been announced by executive order. No star is specifically identified with any state.

Code of Etiquette for Display and Use of the U.S. Flag

Although the Stars and Stripes originated in 1777, it was not until 146 years later that there was a serious attempt to establish a uniform code of etiquette for the U.S. flag. The War Department issued Feb. 15, 1923, a circular on the rules of flag usage. These were adopted almost in their entirety June 14, 1923, by a conference of 68 patriotic organizations in Washington. Finally, on June 22, 1942, a joint resolution of Congress, amended by Public Law 94-344 July 7, 1976, codified "existing rules and customs pertaining to the display and use of the flag . . ."

When to Display the Flag—The flag should be displayed on all days, especially on legal holidays and other special occasions, on official buildings when in use, in or near polling places on election days, and in or near schools when in session. Citizens may fly the flag at any time they wish. It is customary to display the flag only from sunrise to sunset on buildings and on stationary flagstaffs in the open. However, it may be displayed at night on special occasions, preferably lighted. In Washington, the flag now flies over the White House both day and night. It flies over the Senate wing of the Capitol when the Senate is in session and over the House wing when that body is in session. It flies day and night over the east and west fronts of the Capitol, without floodlights at night but receiving light from the illuminated Capitol Dome. It flies 24 hours a day at several other places, including the Fort McHenry Nat'l Monument in Baltimore, where it inspired Francis Scott Key to write The Star Spangled Banner. The flag also flies 24 hours a day, properly illuminated, at U.S. Customs ports of entry.

How to Fly the Flag—The flag should be hoisted briskly and lowered ceremoniously, and should never be allowed to touch the ground or the floor. When hung over a sidewalk from a rope extending from a building to a pole, the union should be away from the building. When hung over the center of a street it should have the union to the north in an east-west street and to the east in a north-south street. No other flag may be flown above or, if on the same level, to the right of the U.S. flag, except that at the United Nations Headquarters the UN flag may be placed above flags of all member nations and other national flags may be flown with equal prominence or honor with the flag of the U.S. At services by Navy chaplains at sea, the church pennant may be flown above the flag.

When two flags are placed against a wall with crossed staffs, the U.S. flag should be at right—its own right, and its staff should be in front of the staff of the other flag; when a number of flags are grouped and displayed from staffs, it should be at the center and highest point of the group.

Church and Platform Use—In an auditorium, the flag may be displayed flat, above and behind the speaker. When displayed from a staff in a church or public auditorium, the flag should hold the position of superior prominence, in advance of the audience, and in the position of honor at the clergyman's or speaker's right as he faces the audience. Any other flag so displayed should be placed on the left of the clergyman or speaker or to the right of the audience.

When the flag is displayed horizontally or vertically against a wall, the stars should be uppermost and at the observer's left.

How to Dispose of Worn Flags—The flag, when it is in such condition that it is no longer a fitting emblem for display, should be destroyed in a dignified way, preferably by burning.

When to Salute the Flag—All persons present should face the flag, stand at attention and salute on the following occasions: (1) When the flag is passing in a parade or in a review, (2) During the ceremony of hoisting or lowering, (3) When the National Anthem is played, and (4) During the Pledge of Allegiance. Those present in uniform should render the military salute. Those not in uniform should place the right hand over the heart. A man wearing a hat should remove it with his right hand and hold it to his left shoulder during the salute.

On Memorial Day, the flag should fly at half-staff until noon, then be raised to the peak.

As provided by Presidential proclamation the flag should fly at half-staff for 30 days from the day of death of a president or former president; for 10 days from the day of death of a vice president, chief justice or retired chief justice of the U.S., or speaker of the House of Representatives; from day of death until burial of an associate justice of the Supreme Court, cabinet member, former vice president, or Senate president pro tempore, majority or minority Senate leader, or majority or minority House leader; for a U.S. senator, representative, territorial delegate, or the resident commissioner of Puerto Rico, on day of death and the following day within the metropolitan area of the District of Columbia and from day of death until burial within the decedent's state, congressional district, territory or commonwealth; and for the death of the governor of a state, territory, or possession of the U.S., from day of death until burial within that state, territory, or possession.

When used to cover a casket, the flag should be placed so that the union is at the head and over the left shoulder. It should not be lowered into the grave nor touch the ground.

Prohibited Uses of the Flag—The flag should not be dipped to any person or thing. (An exception—customarily, ships salute by dipping their colors.) It should never be displayed with the union down save as a distress signal. It should never be carried flat or horizontally, but always aloft and free.

It should not be displayed on a float, motor car or boat except from a staff.

It should never be used as a covering for a ceiling, nor have placed upon it any word, design, or drawing. It should never be used as a receptacle for carrying anything. It should not be used to cover a statue or a monument.

The flag should never be used for advertising purposes, nor be embroidered on such articles as cushions or handkerchiefs, printed or otherwise impressed on boxes or anything that is designed for temporary use and discard; or used as a costume or athletic uniform. Advertising signs should not be fastened to its staff or halyard.

The flag should never be used as drapery of any sort, never festooned, drawn back, nor up, in folds, but always allowed to fall free. Bunting of blue, white and red always arranged with the blue above and the white in the middle, should be used for covering a speaker's desk, draping the front of a platform, and for decoration in general.

An Act of Congress approved Feb. 8, 1917, provided certain penalties for the desecration, mutilation or improper use of the flag within the District of Columbia. A 1968 federal law provided penalties of up to a year's imprisonment or a $1,000 fine or both, for publicly burning or otherwise desecrating any flag of the United States. In addition, many states have laws against flag desecration. In 1989, the Supreme Court ruled that no laws could prohibit political protesters from burning the flag. The decision had the effect of declaring unconstitutional the flag desecration laws of 48 states, as well as a similar Federal statute, in cases of peaceful political expression.

The Supreme Court, June 1990, declared that a new Federal law making it a crime to burn or deface the American flag violates the free-speech guarantee of the First Amendment. The 5-4 decision led to renewed calls in Congress for a constitutional amendment to make it possible to prosecute flag burning.

Pledge of Allegiance to the Flag

I pledge allegiance to the flag of the United States of America and to the republic for which it stands, one nation under God, indivisible, with liberty and justice for all.

This, the current official version of the Pledge of Allegiance, has developed from the original pledge, which was first published in the Sept. 8, 1892, issue of the Youth's Companion, a weekly magazine then published in Boston. The original pledge contained the phrase "my flag," which was changed more than 30 years later to "flag of the United States of America." An act of Congress in 1954 added the words "under God."

The authorship of the pledge had been in dispute for many years. The Youth's Companion stated in 1917 that the original draft was written by James B. Upham, an executive of the magazine who died in 1910. A leaflet circulated by the magazine later named Upham as the originator of the draft "afterwards condensed and perfected by him and his associates of the Companion force."

Francis Bellamy, a former member of the Youth's Companion editorial staff, publicly claimed authorship of the pledge in 1923. The United States Flag Assn., acting on the advice of a committee named to study the controversy, upheld in 1939 the claim of Bellamy, who had died 8 years earlier. The Library of Congress issued in 1957 a report attributing the authorship to Bellamy.

The National Anthem — The Star-Spangled Banner

The Star-Spangled Banner was ordered played by the military and naval services by President Woodrow Wilson in 1916. It was designated the National Anthem by Act of Congress, Mar. 3, 1931. It was written by Francis Scott Key, of Georgetown, D. C., during the bombardment of Fort McHenry, Baltimore, Md., Sept. 13-14, 1814. Key was a lawyer, a graduate of St. John's College, Annapolis, and a volunteer in a light artillery company. When a friend, Dr. Beanes, a physician of Upper Marlborough, Md., was taken aboard Admiral Cockburn's British squadron for interfering with ground troops, Key and J. S. Skinner, carrying a note from President Madison, went to the fleet under a flag of truce on a cartel ship to ask Beanes' release. Admiral Cockburn consented, but as the fleet was about to sail up the Patapsco to bombard Fort McHenry he detained them, first on H. M. S. Surprise, and then on a supply ship.

Key witnessed the bombardment from his own vessel. It began at 7 a.m., Sept. 13, 1814, and lasted, with intermissions, for 25 hours. The British fired over 1,500 shells, each weighing as much as 220 lbs. They were unable to approach closely because the Americans had sunk 22 vessels in the channel. Only four Americans were killed and 24 wounded. A British bomb-ship was disabled.

During the bombardment Key wrote a stanza on the back of an envelope. Next day at Indian Queen Inn, Baltimore, he wrote out the poem and gave it to his brother-in-law, Judge J. H. Nicholson. Nicholson suggested the tune, Anacreon in Heaven, and had the poem printed on broadsides, of which two survive. On Sept. 20 it appeared in the "Baltimore American." Later Key made 3 copies; one is in the Library of Congress and one in the Pennsylvania Historical Society.

The copy that Key wrote in his hotel Sept. 14, 1814, remained in the Nicholson family for 93 years. In 1907 it was sold to Henry Walters of Baltimore. In 1934 it was bought at auction in New York from the Walters estate by the Walters Art Gallery, Baltimore, for $26,400. The Walters Gallery in 1953 sold the manuscript to the Maryland Historical Society for the same price.

The flag that Key saw during the bombardment is preserved in the Smithsonian Institution, Washington. It is 30 by 42 ft., and has 15 alternate red and white stripes and 15 stars, for the original 13 states plus Kentucky and Vermont. It was made by Mary Young Pickersgill. The Baltimore Flag House, a museum, occupies her premises, which were restored in 1953.

The Star-Spangled Banner

I

Oh, say can you see by the dawn's early light
What so proudly we hailed at the twilight's last gleaming?
Whose broad stripes and bright stars thru the perilous fight,
O'er the ramparts we watched were so gallantly streaming?
And the rocket's red glare, the bombs bursting in air,
Gave proof through the night that our flag was still there.
Oh, say does that star-spangled banner yet wave
O'er the land of the free and the home of the brave?

II

On the shore, dimly seen through the mists of the deep,
Where the foe's haughty host in dread silence reposes,
What is that which the breeze, o'er the towering steep,
As it fitfully blows, half conceals, half discloses?
Now it catches the gleam of the morning's first beam,
In full glory reflected now shines in the stream:
'Tis the star-spangled banner! Oh long may it wave
O'er the land of the free and the home of the brave!

III

And where is that band who so vauntingly swore
That the havoc of war and the battle's confusion,
A home and a country should leave us no more!
Their blood has washed out their foul footsteps' pollution.
No refuge could save the hireling and slave
From the terror of flight, or the gloom of the grave:
And the star-spangled banner in triumph doth wave
O'er the land of the free and the home of the brave!

IV

Oh! thus be it ever, when freemen shall stand
Between their loved home and the war's desolation!
Blest with victory and peace, may the heav'n rescued land
Praise the Power that hath made and preserved us a nation.
Then conquer we must, when our cause it is just,
And this be our motto: "In God is our trust."
And the star-spangled banner in triumph shall wave
O'er the land of the free and the home of the brave!

America
(My Country 'Tis of Thee)

First sung in public on July 4, 1831, at a service in the Park Street Church, Boston, the words were written by Rev. Samuel Francis Smith, a Baptist clergyman, who set them to a melody he found in a German songbook, unaware that it was the tune for the British anthem, "God Save the King/Queen."

My country, 'tis of thee,
Sweet land of liberty, Of thee I sing.
Land where my fathers died!
Land of the Pilgrims' pride!
From ev'ry mountainside,
Let freedom ring!

My native country, thee,
Land of the noble free,
Thy name I love.
I love thy rocks and rills,
Thy woods and templed hills;
My heart with rapture thrills
Like that above.

Let music swell the breeze,
And ring from all the trees
Sweet freedom's song.
Let mortal tongues awake;
Let all that breathe partake;
Let rocks their silence break,
The sound prolong.

Our fathers' God, to Thee,
Author of liberty,
To Thee we sing.
Long may our land be bright
With freedom's holy light;
Protect us by Thy might,
Great God, our King!

America, the Beautiful

Composed by Katherine Lee Bates, a Massachusetts educator and author, in 1893. It was inspired by the view Bates experienced atop Pike's Peak. Its final form was established in 1911 and is set to the music of Samuel A. Ward's "Materna."

O beautiful for spacious skies,
For amber waves of grain,
For purple mountain majesties
Above the fruited plain.
America! America!
God shed His grace on thee,
And crown thy good with brotherhood
From sea to shining sea.

O beautiful for pilgrim feet
Whose stern impassion'd stress
A thorough-fare for freedom beat
Across the wilderness.
America! America!
God mend thine ev'ry flaw,
Confirm thy soul in self control,
Thy liberty in law.

O beautiful for heroes prov'd
In liberating strife,
Who more than self their country lov'd
And mercy more than life.
America! America!
May God thy gold refine
Till all success be nobleness,
And ev'ry gain divine.

O beautiful for patriot dream
That sees beyond the years,
Thine alabaster cities gleam,
Undimmed by human tears.
America! America!
God shed His grace on thee,
And crown thy good with brotherhood
From sea to shining sea.

The Liberty Bell: Its History and Significance

The Liberty Bell, in Independence Hall, Philadelphia, is an object of great reverence to Americans because of its association with the historic events of the War of Independence.

The original Province bell, ordered to commemorate the 50th anniversary of the Commonwealth of Pennsylvania, was cast by Thomas Lister, Whitechapel, London, and reached Philadelphia in Aug. 1752. It bore an inscription from Leviticus XXV, 10: "Proclaim liberty throughout all the land unto all the inhabitants thereof."

The bell was cracked by a stroke of its clapper in Sept. 1752 while it hung on a truss in the State House yard for testing. Pass & Stow, Philadelphia founders, recast the bell, adding 1 1/2 ounces of copper to a pound of the original metal to reduce brittleness. It was found that the bell contained too much copper, injuring its tone, so Pass & Stow recast it again, this time successfully.

In June 1753 the bell was hung in the wooden steeple of the State House, erected on top of the brick tower. In use while the Continental Congress was in session in the State House, it rang out in defiance of British tax and trade restrictions, and proclaimed the Boston Tea Party and the first public reading of the Declaration of Independence.

On Sept. 18, 1777, when the British Army was about to occupy Philadelphia, the bell was moved in a baggage train of the American Army to Allentown, Pa. where it was hidden in the Zion Reformed Church until June 27, 1778. It was moved back to Philadelphia after the British left.

In July 1781 the wooden steeple became insecure and had to be taken down. The bell was lowered into the brick section of the tower. Because of its association with the War of Independence it was not recast but remained mute in this location until 1846, the year of the Mexican War, when it was placed on exhibition in the Declaration Chamber of Independence Hall.

In 1876, when many thousands of Americans visited Philadelphia for the Centennial Exposition, it was placed in its old walnut frame in the tower hallway. In 1877 it was hung from the ceiling of the tower by a chain of 13 links. It was returned again to the Declaration Chamber and in 1896 taken back to the tower hall, where it occupied a glass case. In 1915 the case was removed so that the public might touch it. On Jan. 1, 1976, just after midnight to mark the opening of the Bicentennial Year, the bell was moved to a new glass and steel pavilion behind Independence Hall for easier viewing by the larger number of visitors expected during the year.

The measurements of the bell follow: circumference around the lip, 12 ft.; circumference around the crown, 7 ft. 6 in.; lip to the crown, 3 ft.; height over the crown, 2 ft. 3 in.; thickness at lip, 3 in.; thickness at crown, 1 1/4 in.; weight, 2080 lbs.; length of clapper, 3 ft. 2 in.; cost, £60 14s 5d.

The specific source of the crack in the bell is unknown.

Statue of Liberty National Monument

Since 1886, the Statue of Liberty Enlightening the World has stood as a symbol of freedom in New York harbor. It also commemorates French-American friendship for it was given by the people of France, designed by Frederic Auguste Bartholdi (1834-1904). A $2.5 million building housing the American Museum of Immigration was opened by Pres. Nixon Sept. 26, 1972, at the base of the statue. It houses a permanent exhibition of photos, posters, and artifacts tracing the history of American immigration. The Monument is administered by the National Park Service.

Nearby Ellis Island, gateway to America for more than 12 million immigrants between 1892 and 1954, was proclaimed part of the National Monument in 1965 by Pres. Johnson.

Edouard de Laboulaye, French historian and admirer of American political institutions, suggested that the French present a monument to the United States, the latter to provide pedestal and site. Bartholdi visualized a colossal statue at the entrance of New York harbor, welcoming the peoples of the world with the torch of liberty.

On Washington's birthday, Feb. 22, 1877, Congress approved the use of a site on Bedloe's Island suggested by Bartholdi. This island of 12 acres had been owned in the 17th century by a Walloon named Isaac Bedloe. It was called Bedloe's until Aug. 3, 1956, when Pres. Eisenhower approved a resolution of Congress changing the name to Liberty Island.

The statue was finished May 21, 1884, and formally presented to U.S. Minister Morton July 4, 1884, by Ferdinand de Lesseps, head of the Franco-American Union, promoter of the Panama Canal, and builder of the Suez Canal.

On Aug. 5, 1884, the Americans laid the cornerstone for the pedestal. This was to be built on the foundations of Fort Wood, which had been erected by the Government in 1811. The American committee had raised $125,000, but this was found to be inadequate. Joseph Pulitzer, owner of the New York World, appealed on Mar. 16, 1885, for general donations. By Aug. 11, 1885, he had raised $100,000.

The statue arrived dismantled, in 214 packing cases, from Rouen, France, in June, 1885. The last rivet of the statue was driven Oct. 28, 1886, when Pres. Grover Cleveland dedicated the monument.

The statue weighs 450,000 lbs. or 225 tons. The copper sheeting weighs 200,000 lbs. There are 167 steps from the land level to the top of the pedestal, 168 steps inside the statue to the head, and 54 rungs on the ladder leading to the arm that holds the torch.

Two years of restoration work was completed before the statue's centennial celebration on July 4, 1986. Among other repairs, the multi-million dollar project included replacing the 1,600 wrought iron bands that hold its copper skin to its frame, replacing its torch, and installing an elevator.

A four-day extravaganza of concerts, tall ships, ethnic festivals, and fireworks celebrated the 100th anniversary. The festivities included Chief Justice Warren E. Burger's swearing-in of 5,000 new citizens on Ellis Island, while 20,000 others across the country were simultaneously sworn in through a satellite telecast.

The ceremonies were followed by others on Oct. 28, 1986, the statue's 100th birthday.

Emma Lazarus' Famous Poem

A poem by Emma Lazarus is graven on a tablet within the pedestal on which the statue stands.

The New Colossus

Not like the brazen giant of Greek fame,
With conquering limbs astride from land to land;
Here at our sea-washed, sunset gates shall stand
A mighty woman with a torch, whose flame
Is the imprisoned lightning, and her name
Mother of Exiles. From her beacon-hand
Glows world-wide welcome; her mild eyes command
The air-bridged harbor that twin cities frame.
"Keep ancient lands, your storied pomp!" cries she
With silent lips. "Give me your tired, your poor,
Your huddled masses yearning to breathe free,
The wretched refuse of your teeming shore.
Send these, the homeless, tempest-tost to me,
I lift my lamp beside the golden door!"

Dimensions of the Statue	Ft.	In.
Height from base to torch (45.3 meters)	151	1
Foundation of pedestal to torch (91.5 meters)	305	1
Heel to top of head	111	1
Length of hand	16	5
Index finger	8	0
Circumference at second joint	3	6
Size of finger nail	13x10 in.	
Head from chin to cranium	17	3
Head thickness from ear to ear	10	0
Distance across the eye	2	6
Length of nose	4	6
Right arm, length	42	0
Right arm, greatest thickness	12	0
Thickness of waist	35	0
Width of mouth	3	0
Tablet, length	23	7
Tablet, width	13	7
Tablet, thickness	2	0

Lincoln's Address at Gettysburg, 1863

Fourscore and seven years ago our fathers brought forth on this continent a new nation, conceived in liberty and dedicated to the proposition that all men are created equal.

Now we are engaged in a great civil war, testing whether that nation or any nation so conceived and so dedicated can long endure. We are met on a great battle field of that war. We have come to dedicate a portion of that field, as a final resting-place for those who here gave their lives that that nation might live. It is altogether fitting and proper that we should do this.

But, in a larger sense, we can not dedicate — we can not consecrate — we can not hallow — this ground. The brave men, living and dead, who struggled here, have consecrated it, far above our poor power to add or detract. The world will little note, nor long remember, what we say here, but it can never forget what they did here. It is for us the living, rather, to be dedicated here to the unfinished work which they who fought here have thus far so nobly advanced. It is rather for us to be here dedicated to the great task remaining before us — that from these honored dead we take increased devotion to that cause for which they gave the last full measure of devotion — that we here highly resolve that these dead shall not have died in vain — that this nation, under God, shall have a new birth of freedom — and that government of the people, by the people, for the people, shall not perish from the earth.

Confederate States and Secession

The American Civil War, 1861-65, grew out of sectional disputes over the continued existence of slavery in the South and the contention of Southern legislators that the states retained many sovereign rights, including the right to secede from the Union.

The war was not fought by state against state but by one federal regime against another, the Confederate government in Richmond assuming control over the economic, political, and military life of the South, under protest from Georgia and South Carolina.

South Carolina voted an ordinance of secession from the Union, repealing its 1788 ratification of the U.S. Constitution on Dec. 20, 1860, to take effect Dec. 24. Other states seceded in 1861. Their votes in conventions were:

Mississippi, Jan. 9, 84-15; Florida, Jan. 10, 62-7; Alabama, Jan. 11, 61-39; Georgia, Jan. 19, 208-89; Louisiana, Jan. 26, 113-17; Texas, Feb. 1, 166-7, ratified by popular vote Feb. 23 (for 34,794, against 11,325); Virginia, Apr. 17, 88-55, ratified by popular vote May 23 (for 128,884; against 32,134); Arkansas, May 6, 69-1; Tennessee, May 7, ratified by popular vote June 8 (for 104,019, against 47,238); North Carolina, May 21.

Missouri Unionists stopped secession in conventions Feb. 28 and Mar. 9. The legislature condemned secession Mar. 7. Under the protection of Confederate troops, secessionist members of the legislature adopted a resolution of secession at Neosho, Oct. 31. The Confederate Congress seated the secessionists' representatives.

Kentucky did not secede and its government remained Unionist. In a part occupied by Confederate troops, Kentuckians approved secession and the Confederate Congress admitted their representatives.

The Maryland legislature voted against secession Apr. 27, 53-13. Delaware did not secede. Western Virginia held conventions at Wheeling, named a pro-Union governor June 11, 1861; admitted to Union as West Virginia June 20, 1863; its constitution provided for gradual abolition of slavery.

Confederate Government

Forty-two delegates from South Carolina, Georgia, Alabama, Mississippi, Louisiana, and Florida met in convention at Montgomery, Ala., Feb. 4, 1861. They adopted a provisional constitution of the Confederate States of America, and elected Jefferson Davis (Miss.) provisional president, and Alexander H. Stephens (Ga.) provisional vice president.

A permanent constitution was adopted Mar. 11; it abolished the African slave trade. The Congress moved to Richmond, Va. July 20. Davis was elected president in October, and was inaugurated Feb. 22, 1862.

The Congress adopted a flag, consisting of a red field with a white stripe, and a blue jack with a circle of white stars. Later the more popular flag was the red field with blue diagonal cross bars that held 13 white stars. The stars represented the 11 states actually in the Confederacy plus Kentucky and Missouri.

(See also Civil War, U.S., in Index)

The Mayflower Compact

The threat of James I to "harry them out of the land" sent a little band of religious dissenters from England to Holland in 1608. They were known as "Separatists" because they wished to cut all ties with the Established Church. In 1620, some of them, known now as the Pilgrims, joined with a larger group in England to set sail on the *Mayflower* for the New World. A joint stock company financed their venture.

In November, they sighted Cape Cod and decided to land an exploring party at Plymouth Harbor. However, a rebellious group picked up at Southampton and London troubled the Pilgrim leaders, and to control their actions forty-one of the Pilgrims drew up the "Mayflower Compact," which was signed before going ashore. The voluntary agreement to govern themselves was America's first written constitution.

In the name of God, Amen. We, whose names are underwritten, the Loyal Subjects of our dread Sovereign Lord, King *James*, by the Grace of God, of *Great Britain, France and Ireland*, King, *Defender of the Faith*, etc.

Having undertaken for the Glory of God, and Advancement of the Christian Faith, and the Honour of our King and Country, a voyage to plant the first colony in the northern Parts of Virginia; do by these Presents, solemnly and mutually in the Presence of God and one of another, covenant and combine ouselves together into a civil Body Politick, for our better Ordering and Preservation, and Furtherance of the Ends aforesaid; And by Virtue hereof to enact, constitute, and frame, such just and equal Laws, Ordinances, Acts, Constitutions and Offices, from time to time, as shall be thought most meet and convenient for the General good of the Colony; unto which we promise all due Submission and Obedience.

In Witness whereof we have hereunto subscribed our names at *Cape Cod* the eleventh of *November*, in the Reign of our Sovereign Lord, King *James* of *England, France* and *Ireland*, the eighteenth, and of *Scotland* the fifty-fourth. *Anno Domini, 1620.*

Forms of Address for Persons of Rank and Public Office

In these examples John Smith is used as a representative American name. The salutation Dear Sir or Dear Madam is always permissible when addressing a person not known to the writer. Female equivalents should be substituted where appropriate.

President of the United States

Address: The President, The White House, Washington, DC 20500. Also, The President and Mrs. ____.

Salutation: Dear Sir or Mr. President or Dear Mr. President. More intimately: My dear Mr. President. Also: Dear Mr. President and Mrs. ____

The vice president takes the same forms.

Cabinet Officers

Address: Mr. John Smith, Secretary of State, Washington, D.C. or The Hon. John Smith. Similar addresses for other members of the cabinet. Also: Secretary and Mrs. John Smith.

Salutation: Dear Sir, or Dear Mr. Secretary. Also: Dear Mr. and Mrs. Smith.

The Bench

Address: The Hon. John Smith, Chief Justice of the United States. The Hon. John Smith, Associate Justice of the Supreme Court of the United States. The Hon. John Smith, Associate Judge, U.S. District Court.

Salutation: Dear Sir, or Dear Mr. Chief Justice. Dear Mr. Justice. Dear Judge Smith.

Members of Congress

Address: The Hon. John Smith, United States Senate, Washington, DC 20510, or Sen. John Smith, etc. Also The Hon. John Smith, House of Representatives, Washington, DC 20515, or Rep. John Smith, etc.

Salutation: Dear Mr. Senator or Dear Mr. Smith; for Representative, Dear Mr. Smith.

Officers of Armed Forces

Address: Careful attention should be given to the precise rank, thus: General of the Army John Smith, Fleet Admiral John Smith. The rules for Air Force are same as Army.

Salutation: Dear Sir, or Dear General. All general officers, whatever rank, are entitled to be addressed as generals. Likewise a lieutenant colonel is addressed as colonel and first and second lieutenants are addressed as lieutenant.

Warrant officers and flight officers are addressed as Mister. Chaplains are addressed as Chaplain. A Catholic chaplain may be addressed as Father. Students of the U.S. Military Academy and Air Force Academy are addressed as Cadet, students of the U.S. Naval Academy are addressed as Midshipman/woman. Noncommissioned officers are addressed by their titles.

Ambassador, Governor, Mayor

Address: The Hon. John Smith, followed by his or her title. They can be addressed either at their embassy, or at the Department of State, Washington, D.C. An ambassador from a foreign nation may be addressed as His or Her Excellency. An American is not to be so addressed.

Salutation: Dear Mr. or Madam Ambassador. An ambassador from a foreign nation may be called Your Excellency.

Governors and mayors are often addressed as The Hon. Jane Smith, Governor of ______, or The Hon. John Smith, Mayor of ______; also Governor John Smith, State House, Albany, N.Y., or Mayor Jane Smith, City Hall, Erie, Pa.

The Clergy

Address: His Holiness, the Pope, or His Holiness Pope (name), State of Vatican City, Italy.

Salutation: Your Holiness or Most Holy Father.

Also: His Eminence, John, Cardinal Smith; salutation: Your Eminence. An archbishop or a bishop is addressed The Most Reverend, and the salutation is Your Excellency. A monsignor who is a papal chamberlain is The Very Reverend Monsignor and the salutation is Dear Sir or Very Reverend Monsignor; a monsignor who is a domestic prelate is The Right Reverend Monsignor and salutation is Right Reverend Monsignor. A priest is addressed Reverend John Smith. A brother of an order is addressed Brother —. A sister takes the same form.

A bishop of the Episcopal Church is The Right Reverend John Smith; salutation is Right Reverend Sir, or Dear Bishop Smith. If a clergyman is a doctor of divinity, he is addressed: The Reverend John Smith, D.D., and the salutation is Reverend Sir, or Dear Dr. Smith. When a clergyman does not have the degree the salutation is Dear Mr. Smith, or Dear Father Smith.

A bishop of the Methodist Church is addressed Bishop John Smith with titles following.

Royalty and Nobility

An emperor is to be addressed in a letter as Sir, or Your Imperial Majesty.

A king or queen is addressed as His Majesty (Name), King of (Name), or Her Majesty (Name), Queen of (Name), Salutation: Sir, or Madam, or May it please Your Majesty.

Princes and princesses and other persons of royal blood are addressed as His (or Her) Royal Highness, and saluted with Mav it please Your Royal Highness.

A duke or marquis is My Lord Duke (or Marquis), a duke is His (or Your) Grace.

BIOGRAPHIES OF U.S. PRESIDENTS

George Washington (1789-1797)

George Washington, first president, was born Feb. 22, 1732 (Feb. 11, 1731, old style), the son of Augustine Washington and Mary Ball, at Wakefield on Pope's Creek, Westmoreland Co., Va. His early childhood was spent on a farm, near Fredericksburg. His father died when George was 11. He studied mathematics and surveying and when 16 went to live with his half brother Lawrence, who built and named Mount Vernon. George surveyed the lands of William Fairfax in the Shenandoah Valley, keeping a diary. He accompanied Lawrence to Barbados, West Indies, contracted small pox, and was deeply scarred. Lawrence died in 1752 and George acquired his property by inheritance. He valued land and when he died owned 70,000 acres in Virginia and 40,000 acres in what is now West Virginia.

Washington's military service began in 1753 when Gov. Dinwiddie of Virginia sent him on missions deep into Ohio country. He clashed with the French and had to surrender Fort Necessity July 3, 1754. He was an aide to Braddock and at his side when the army was ambushed and defeated on a march to Ft. Duquesne, July 9, 1755. He helped take Fort Duquesne from the French in 1758.

After his marriage to Martha Dandridge Custis, a widow, in 1759, Washington managed his family estate at Mount Vernon. Although not at first for independence, he opposed British exactions and took charge of the Virginia troops before war broke out. He was made commander-in-chief by the Continental Congress June 15, 1775.

The successful issue of a war filled with hardships was due to his leadership. He was resourceful, a stern disciplinarian, and the one strong, dependable force for unity. He favored a federal government and became chairman of the Constitutional Convention of 1787. He helped get the Constitution ratified and was unanimously elected president by the electoral college and inaugurated, Apr. 30, 1789, on the balcony of New York's Federal Hall.

He was reelected 1792, but refused to consider a 3d term and retired to Mount Vernon. He suffered acute laryngitis after a ride in snow and rain around his estate, was bled profusely, and died Dec. 14, 1799.

John Adams (1797-1801)

John Adams, 2d president, Federalist, was born in Braintree (Quincy), Mass., Oct. 30, 1735 (Oct. 19, o. s.), the son of John Adams, a farmer, and Susanna Boylston. He was a great-grandson of Henry Adams who came from England in 1636. He graduated from Harvard, 1755, taught school, studied law. In 1765 he argued against taxation without representation before the royal governor. In 1770 he defended in court the British soldiers who fired on civilians in the "Boston Massacre." He was a delegate to the first Continental Congress, and signed the Declaration of Independence. He was a commissioner to France, 1778, with Benjamin Franklin and Arthur Lee; won recognition of the U.S. by The Hague, 1782; was first American minister to England, 1785-1788, and was elected vice president, 1788 and 1792.

In 1796 Adams was chosen president by the electors. Intense antagonism to America by France caused agitation for war, led by Alexander Hamilton. Adams, breaking with Hamilton, opposed war.

To fight alien influence and muzzle criticism Adams supported the Alien and Sedition laws of 1798, which led to his defeat for reelection. He died July 4, 1826, on the same day as Jefferson (the 50th anniversary of the Declaration of Independence).

Thomas Jefferson (1801-1809)

Thomas Jefferson, 3d president, was born Apr. 13, 1743 (Apr. 2, o. s.), at Shadwell, Va., the son of Peter Jefferson, a civil engineer of Welsh descent who raised tobacco, and Jane Randolph. His father died when he was 14, leaving him 2,750 acres and his slaves. Jefferson attended the College of William and Mary, 1760-1762, read classics in Greek and Latin and played the violin. In 1769 he was elected to the House of Burgesses. In 1770 he began building Monticello, near Charlottesville. He was a member of the Virginia Committee of Correspondence and the Continental Congress. Named a member of the committee to draw up a Declaration of Independence, he wrote the basic draft. He was a member of the Virginia House of Delegates, 1776-79, elected governor to succeed Patrick Henry, 1779, reelected 1780, resigned June 1781, amid charges of ineffectual military preparation. During his term he wrote the statute on religious freedom. In the Continental Congress, 1783, he drew up an ordinance for the Northwest Territory forbidding slavery after 1800; its terms were put into the Ordinance of 1787. He was sent to Paris with Benjamin Franklin and John Adams to negotiate commercial treaties, 1784; made minister to France, 1785.

Washington appointed him secretary of state, 1789. Jefferson's strong faith in the consent of the governed, as opposed to executive control favored by Hamilton, secretary of the treasury, often led to conflict: Dec. 31, 1793, he resigned. He was the Democrat Republican candidate for president in 1796; beaten by John Adams, he became vice president. In 1800, Jefferson and Aaron Burr received equal electoral college votes for president. The House of Representatives elected Jefferson. Major events of his administration were the Louisiana Purchase, 1803, and the Lewis and Clark Expedition. He established the Univ. of Virginia and designed its buildings. He died July 4, 1826, on the same day as John Adams.

James Madison (1809-1817)

James Madison, 4th president, Democrat Republican, was born Mar. 16, 1751 (Mar. 5, 1750, o. s.) at Port Conway, King George Co., Va., eldest son of James Madison and Eleanor Rose Conway. Madison was graduated from Princeton, 1771; studied theology, 1772; sat in the Virginia Constitutional Convention, 1776. He was a member of the Continental Congress. He was chief recorder at the Constitutional Convention in 1787, and supported ratification in the Federalist Papers, written with Alexander Hamilton and John Jay. He was elected to the House of Representatives in 1789, helped frame the Bill of Rights and fought the Alien and Sedition Acts. He became Jefferson's secretary of state, 1801.

Elected president in 1808, Madison was a "strict constructionist," opposed to the free interpretation of the Constitution by the Federalists. He was reelected in 1812 by the votes of the agrarian South and recently admitted western states. Caught between British and French maritime restrictions, the U.S. drifted into war, declared June 18, 1812. The war ended in a stalemate. He retired in 1817 to his estate at Montpelier. There he edited his famous papers on the Constitutional Convention. He became rector of the Univ. of Virginia, 1826. He died June 28, 1836.

James Monroe (1817-1825)

James Monroe, 5th president, Democrat Republican, was born Apr. 28, 1758, in Westmoreland Co., Va., the son of Spence Monroe and Eliza Jones, who were of Scottish and Welsh descent, respectively. He attended the College of William and Mary, fought in the 3d Virginia Regiment at White Plains, Brandywine, Monmouth, and was wounded at Trenton. He studied law with Thomas Jefferson, 1780, was a member of the Virginia House of Delegates and of Congress, 1783-86. He opposed ratification of the Constitution because it lacked a bill of rights; was U.S. senator, 1790; minister to France, 1794-96; governor of Virginia, 1799-1802, and 1811. Jefferson sent him to France as minister, 1803. He helped Robert Livingston negotiate the Louisiana Purchase, 1803. He ran against Madison for president in 1808. He was elected to the Virginia Assembly, 1810-1811; was secretary of state under Madison, 1811-1817.

In 1816 Monroe was elected president; in 1820 reelected with all but one electoral college vote. Monroe's administration became the "Era of Good Feeling." He obtained Florida from Spain; settled boundaries with Canada, and eliminated border forts. He supported the anti-slavery position that led to the Missouri Compromise. His most significant contribution was the "Monroe Doctrine," which became a cornerstone of U.S. foreign policy. Monroe retired to Oak Hill, Va. Financial problems forced him to sell his property. He moved to New York City to live with a daughter. He died there July 4, 1831.

John Quincy Adams (1825-1829)

John Quincy Adams, 6th president, independent Federalist, later Democratic Republican, was born July 11, 1767, at Braintree (Quincy), Mass., the son of John and Abigail Adams. His father was the 2d president. He was educated in Paris, Leyden, and Harvard, graduating in 1787. He served as American minister in various European capitals, and helped draft the War of 1812 peace treaty. He was U.S. Senator, 1803-08. President Monroe made him secretary of state, 1817, and he negotiated the cession of the Floridas from Spain, supported exclusion of slavery in the Missouri Compromise, and helped formulate the Monroe Doctrine. In 1824 he was elected president by the House after he failed to win an electoral college majority. His expansion of executive powers was strongly opposed and he was beaten in 1828 by Jackson. In 1831 he entered Congress and served 17 years with distinction. He opposed slavery, the annexation of Texas, and the Mexican War. He helped establish the Smithsonian Institution. He had a stroke in the House and died in the Speaker's Room, Feb. 23, 1848.

Andrew Jackson (1829-1837)

Andrew Jackson, 7th president, was a Jeffersonian-Republican, later a Democrat. He was born in the Waxhaws district, New Lancaster Co., S.C., Mar. 15, 1767, the posthumous son of Andrew Jackson and Elizabeth Hutchinson, who were Irish immigrants. At 13, he joined the militia in the Revolution and was captured.

He read law in Salisbury, N.C., moved to Nashville, Tenn., speculated in land, married, and practiced law. In 1796 he helped draft the constitution of Tennessee and for a year occupied its one seat in Congress. He was in the Senate in 1797, and again in 1823. He defeated the Creek Indians at Horseshoe Bend, Ala., 1814. With 6,000 backwoods fighters he defeated Pakenham's 12,000 British troops at the Chalmette, outside New Orleans, Jan. 8, 1815. In 1818 he briefly invaded Spanish Florida to quell Seminoles and outlaws who harassed frontier settlements. In 1824 he ran for president against John Quincy Adams and had the most popular and electoral votes but not a majority; the election was decided by the House, which chose Adams. In 1828 he defeated Adams, carrying the West and South. He was a noisy debater and a duelist and introduced rotation in office called the "spoils system." Suspicious of privilege, he ruined the Bank of the United States by depositing federal funds with state banks. Though "Let the people rule" was his slogan, he at times supported strict constructionist policies against the expansionist West. He killed the congressional caucus for nominating presidential candidates and substituted the national convention, 1832. When South Carolina refused to collect imports under his protective tariff he ordered army and naval forces to Charleston. Jackson recognized the Republic of Texas, 1836. He died at the Hermitage, June 8, 1845.

Martin Van Buren (1837-1841)

Martin Van Buren, 8th president, Democrat, was born Dec. 5, 1782, at Kinderhook, N.Y., the son of Abraham Van Buren, a Dutch farmer, and Mary Hoes. He was surrogate of Columbia County, N.Y., state senator and attorney general. He was U.S. senator 1821, reelected, 1827, elected governor of New York, 1828. He helped swing eastern support to Jackson in 1828 and was his secretary of state 1829-31. In 1832 he was elected vice president. He was a consummate politician, known as "the little magician," and influenced Jackson's policies. In 1836 he defeated William Henry Harrison for president and took office as the Panic of 1837 initiated a 5-year nationwide depression. He inaugurated the independent treasury system. His refusal to spend land revenues led to his defeat by Harrison in 1840. He lost the Democratic nomination in 1844 to Polk. In 1848 he ran for president on the Free Soil ticket and lost. He died July 24, 1862, at Kinderhook.

William Henry Harrison (1841)

William Henry Harrison, 9th president, Whig, who served only 31 days, was born in Berkeley, Charles City Co., Va., Feb. 9, 1773, the 3d son of Benjamin Harrison, signer of the Declaration of Independence. He attended Hampden Sydney College. He was secretary of the Northwest Territory, 1798; its delegate in Congress, 1799; first governor of Indiana Territory, 1800; and superintendent of Indian affairs. With 900 men he routed Tecumseh's Indians at Tippecanoe, Nov. 7, 1811. A major general, he defeated British and Indians at Battle of the Thames, Oct. 5, 1813. He served in Congress, 1816-19; Senate, 1825-28. In 1840, he was elected president with a "log cabin and hard cider" slogan. He caught pneumonia during the inauguration and died Apr. 4, 1841.

John Tyler (1841-1845)

John Tyler, 10th president, independent Whig, was born Mar. 29, 1790, in Greenway, Charles City Co., Va., son of John Tyler and Mary Armistead. His father was governor of Virginia, 1808-11. Tyler was graduated from William and Mary, 1807; member of the House of Delegates, 1811; in congress, 1816-21; in Virginia legislature, 1823-25; governor of Virginia, 1825-26; U.S. senator, 1827-36. In 1840 he was elected vice president and, on Harrison's death, succeeded him. He favored pre-emption, allowing settlers to get government land; rejected a national bank bill and thus alienated most Whig supporters; refused to honor the spoils system. He signed the resolution annexing Texas, Mar. 1, 1845. He accepted renomination, 1844, but withdrew before election. In 1861, he chaired an unsuccessful Washington conference called to avert civil war. After its failure he supported secession, sat in the provisional Confederate Congress, became a member of the Confederate House, but died in Richmond, Jan. 18, 1862, before it met.

James Knox Polk (1845-1849)

James Knox Polk, 11th president, Democrat, was born in Mecklenburg Co., N.C., Nov. 2, 1795, the son of Samuel Polk, farmer and surveyor of Scotch-Irish descent, and Jane Knox. He graduated from the Univ. of North Carolina, 1818; member of the Tennessee state legislature, 1823-25. He served in Congress 1825-39 and as speaker 1835-39. He was governor of Tennessee 1839-41, but was defeated 1841 and 1843. In 1844, when both Clay and Van Buren announced opposition to annexing Texas, the Democrats made Polk the first dark horse nominee because he demanded control of all Oregon and annexation of Texas. Polk re-established the independent treasury system originated by Van Buren. His expansionist policy was opposed by Clay, Webster, Calhoun; he sent troops under Zachary Taylor to the Mexican border and, when Mexicans attacked, declared war existed. The Mexican war ended with the annexation of California and much of the Southwest as part of America's "manifest destiny." He compromised on the Oregon boundary ("54-40 or fight!") by accepting the 49th parallel and giving Vancouver to the British. Polk died in Nashville, June 15, 1849.

Zachary Taylor (1849-1850)

Zachary Taylor, 12th president, Whig, who served only 16 months, was born Nov. 24, 1784, in Orange Co., Va., the son of Richard Taylor, later collector of the port of Louisville, Ky., and Sarah Strother. Taylor was commissioned first lieutenant, 1808; fought in the War of 1812; the Black Hawk War, 1832; and the second Seminole War, 1837. He was called Old Rough and Ready. He settled on a plantation near Baton Rouge, La. In 1845 Polk sent him with an army to the Rio Grande. When the Mexicans attacked him, Polk declared war. Taylor was successful at Palo Alto and Resaca de la Palma, 1846; occupied Monterrey. Polk made him major general but sent many of his troops to Gen. Winfield Scott. Outnumbered 4-1, he defeated Santa Anna at Buena Vista, 1847. A national hero, he received the Whig nomination in 1848, and was elected president. He resumed the spoils system and though once a slave-holder worked to have California admitted as a free state. He died in office July 9, 1850.

Millard Fillmore (1850-1853)

Millard Fillmore, 13th president, Whig, was born Jan. 7, 1800, in Cayuga Co., N.Y., the son of Nathaniel Fillmore and Phoebe Millard. He taught school and studied law; admitted to the bar, 1823. He was a member of the state assembly, 1829-32; in Congress, 1833-35 and again 1837-43. He opposed the entrance of Texas as slave territory and voted for a protective tariff. In 1844 he was defeated for governor of New York. In 1848 he was elected vice president and succeeded as president July 10, 1850, after Taylor's death. Fillmore favored the Compromise of 1850 and signed the Fugitive Slave Law. His policies pleased neither expansionists nor slave-holders and he was not renominated in 1852. In 1856 he was nominated by the American (Know-Nothing) party and accepted by the Whigs, but defeated by Buchanan. He died in Buffalo, Mar. 8, 1874.

Franklin Pierce (1853-1857)

Franklin Pierce, 14th president, Democrat, was born in Hillsboro, N. H., Nov. 23, 1804, the son of Benjamin Pierce, veteran of the Revolution and governor of New Hampshire, 1827. He graduated from Bowdoin, 1824. A lawyer, he served in the state legislature 1829-33; in Congress, supporting Jackson, 1833-37; U.S. senator, 1837-42. He enlisted in the Mexican War, became brigadier general under Gen. Winfield Scott. In 1852 Pierce was nominated on the 49th ballot over Lewis Cass, Stephen A. Douglas, and James Buchanan, and defeated Gen. Scott, Whig. Though against slavery, Pierce was influenced by pro-slavery Southerners. He approved the Kansas-Nebraska Act, leaving slavery to popular vote ("squatter sovereignty"), 1854. He signed a reciprocity treaty with Canada and approved the Gadsden Purchase from Mexico, 1853. Denied renomination by the Democrats, he spent most of his remaining years in Concord, N.H., where he died Oct. 8, 1869.

James Buchanan (1857-1861)

James Buchanan, 15th president, Federalist, later Democrat, was born of Scottish descent near Mercersburg, Pa., Apr. 23, 1791, the son of James Buchanan, merchant, and Elizabeth Speer. He graduated from Dickinson, 1809; was a volunteer in the War of 1812; member, Pennsylvania legislature, 1814-16, Congress, 1820-31; Jackson's minister to Russia, 1831-33; U.S. senator 1834-45. As Polk's secretary of state, 1845-49, he ended the Oregon dispute with Britain, supported the Mexican War and annexation of Texas. As minister to Britain, 1853, he signed the Ostend Manifesto. Nominated by Democrats, he was elected, 1856, over John C. Fremont (Republican) and Millard Fillmore (American Know-Nothing and Whig tickets). On slavery he favored popular sovereignty and choice by state constitutions; he accepted the pro-slavery Dred Scott decision as binding. He denied the right of states to secede. A strict constructionist, he desired to keep peace and found no authority for using force. He died at Wheatland, near Lancaster, Pa., June 1, 1868.

Abraham Lincoln (1861-1865)

Abraham Lincoln, 16th president, Republican, was born Feb. 12, 1809, in a log cabin on a farm then in Hardin Co., Ky., now in Larue. He was the son of Thomas Lincoln, a carpenter, and Nancy Hanks.

The Lincolns moved to Spencer Co., Ind., near Gentryville, when Abe was 7. When his mother died his father married Mrs. Sarah Bush Johnston, 1819; she had a favorable influence on Abe. In 1830 the family moved to Macon Co., Ill. Lincoln lost election to the Illinois General Assembly, 1832, but later won 4 times, beginning in 1834. He enlisted in the militia for the Black Hawk War, 1832. In New Salem he ran a store, surveyed land, and was postmaster.

In 1837 Lincoln was admitted to the bar and became partner in a Springfield, Ill., law office. He was elected to Congress, 1847-49. He opposed the Mexican War. He supported Zachary Taylor, 1848. He opposed the Kansas-Nebraska Act and extension of slavery, 1854. He failed in his bid for the Senate, 1855. He supported John C. Fremont, 1856.

In 1858 Lincoln had Republican support in the Illinois legislature for the Senate but was defeated by Stephen A. Douglas, Dem., who had sponsored the Kansas-Nebraska Act.

Lincoln was nominated for president by the Republican party on an anti-slavery platform, 1860. He ran against Douglas, a northern Democrat; John C. Breckinridge, southern pro-slavery Democrat; John Bell,

Constitutional Union party. When he won the election, South Carolina seceded from the Union Dec. 20, 1860, followed in 1861 by 10 Southern states.

The Civil War erupted when Fort Sumter was attacked Apr. 12, 1861. On Sept. 22, 1862, 5 days after the battle of Antietam, he announced that slaves in territory then in rebellion would be free Jan. 1, 1863, date of the Emancipation Proclamation. His speeches, including his Gettysburg and Inaugural addresses, are remembered for their eloquence.

Lincoln was reelected, 1864, over Gen. George B. McClellan, Democrat. Lee surrendered Apr. 9, 1865. On Apr. 14, Lincoln was shot by actor John Wilkes Booth in Ford's Theatre, Washington. He died the next day.

Andrew Johnson (1865-1869)

Andrew Johnson, 17th president, Democrat, was born in Raleigh, N.C., Dec. 29, 1808, the son of Jacob Johnson, porter at an inn and church sexton, and Mary McDonough. He was apprenticed to a tailor but ran away and eventually settled in Greeneville, Tenn. He became an alderman, 1828; mayor, 1830; state representative and senator, 1835-43; member of Congress, 1843-53; governor of Tennessee, 1853-57; U.S. senator, 1857-62. He supported John C. Breckinridge against Lincoln in 1860. He had held slaves, but opposed secession and tried to prevent his home state, Tennessee, from seceding. In Mar. 1862, Lincoln appointed him military governor of occupied Tennessee. In 1864 he was nominated for vice president with Lincoln on the National Union ticket to win Democratic support. He succeeded Lincoln as president Apr. 15, 1865. In a controversy with Congress over the president's power over the South, he proclaimed, May 26, 1865, an amnesty to all Confederates except certain leaders if they would ratify the 13th Amendment abolishing slavery. States doing so added anti-Negro provisions that enraged Congress, which restored military control over the South. When Johnson removed Edwin M. Stanton, secretary of war, without notifying the Senate, thus repudiating the Tenure of Office Act, the House impeached him for this and other reasons. He was tried by the Senate, and acquitted by only one vote, May 26, 1868. He returned to the Senate in 1875. Johnson died July 31, 1875.

Ulysses Simpson Grant (1869-1877)

Ulysses S. Grant, 18th president, Republican, was born at Point Pleasant, Oh., Apr. 27, 1822, son of Jesse R. Grant, a tanner, and Hannah Simpson. The next year the family moved to Georgetown, Oh. Grant was named Hiram Ulysses, but on entering West Point, 1839, his name was entered as Ulysses Simpson and he adopted it. He was graduated in 1843; served under Gens. Taylor and Scott in the Mexican War; resigned, 1854; worked in St. Louis until 1860, then went to Galena, Ill. With the start of the Civil War, he was named colonel of the 21st Illinois Vols., 1861, then brigadier general; took Forts Henry and Donelson; fought at Shiloh, took Vicksburg. After his victory at Chattanooga, Lincoln placed him in command of the Union Armies. He accepted Lee's surrender at Appomattox, Apr., 1865. President Johnson appointed Grant secretary of war when he suspended Stanton, but Grant was not confirmed. He was nominated for president by the Republicans in 1868 and elected over Horatio Seymour, Democrat. The 15th Amendment, amnesty bill, and civil service reform were events of his administration. The Liberal Republicans and Democrats opposed him with Horace Greeley, 1872, but he was reelected. An attempt by the Stalwarts (Old Guard) to nominate him in 1880 failed. In 1884 the collapse of Grant & Ward, investment house, left him penniless. He wrote his personal memoirs while ill with cancer and completed them 4 days before his death at Mt. McGregor, N.Y., July 23, 1885. The book realized over $450,000.

Rutherford Birchard Hayes (1877-1881)

Rutherford B. Hayes, 19th president, Republican, was born in Delaware, Oh., Oct. 4, 1822, the posthumous son of Rutherford Hayes, a farmer, and Sophia Birchard. He was raised by his uncle Sardis Birchard. He graduated from Kenyon College, 1842, and Harvard Law School, 1845. He practiced law in Lower Sandusky, Oh., now Fremont; was city solicitor of Cincinnati, 1858-61. In the Civil War, he was major of the 23d Ohio Vols., was wounded several times, and rose to the rank of brevet major general, 1864. He served in Congress 1864-67, supporting Reconstruction and Johnson's impeachment. He was elected governor of Ohio, 1867 and 1869; beaten in the race for Congress, 1872; reelected governor, 1875. In 1876 he was nominated for president and believed he had lost the election to Samuel J. Tilden, Democrat. But a few Southern states submitted 2 different sets of electoral votes and the result was in dispute. An electoral commission, appointed by Congress, 8 Republicans and 7 Democrats, awarded all disputed votes to Hayes allowing him to become president by one electoral vote. Hayes, keeping a promise to southerners, withdrew troops from areas still occupied in the South, ending the era of Reconstruction. He proceeded to reform the civil service, alienating political spoilsmen. He advocated repeal of the Tenure of Office Act. He supported sound money and specie payments. Hayes died in Fremont, Oh., Jan. 17, 1893.

James Abram Garfield (1881)

James A. Garfield, 20th president, Republican, was born Nov. 19, 1831, in Orange, Cuyahoga Co., Oh., the son of Abram Garfield and Eliza Ballou. His father died in 1833. He worked as a canal bargeman, farmer, and carpenter; attended Western Reserve Eclectic, later Hiram College, and was graduated from Williams in 1856. He taught at Hiram, and later became principal. He was in the Ohio senate in 1859. Anti-slavery and anti-secession, he volunteered for the war, became colonel of the 42d Ohio Infantry and brigadier in 1862. He fought at Shiloh, was chief of staff for Rosecrans and was made major general for gallantry at Chickamauga. He entered Congress as a radical Republican in 1863; supported specie payment as against paper money (greenbacks). On the electoral commission in 1877 he voted for Hayes against Tilden on strict party lines. He was senator-elect in 1880 when he became the Republican nominee for president. He was chosen as a compromise over Gen. Grant, James G. Blaine, and John Sherman. This alienated the Grant following but Garfield was elected. On July 2, 1881, Garfield was shot by mentally disturbed office-seeker, Charles J. Guiteau, while entering a railroad station in Washington. He died Sept. 19, 1881, at Elberon, N.J.

Chester Alan Arthur (1881-1885)

Chester A. Arthur, 21st president, Republican, was born at Fairfield, Vt., Oct. 5, 1830, the son of the Rev. William Arthur, from County Antrim, Ireland, and Malvina Stone. He graduated from Union College, 1848, taught school at Pownall, Vt., studied law in New York. In 1853 he argued in a fugitive slave case that slaves transported through N.Y. State were thereby freed. He was made collector of the Port of New York, 1871. President Hayes, reforming the civil service, forced Arthur to resign, 1879. This made the

New York machine stalwarts enemies of Hayes. Arthur and the stalwarts tried to nominate Grant for a 3d term in 1880. When Garfield was nominated, Arthur received 2d place in the interests of harmony. When Garfield died, Arthur became president. He supported civil service reform and the tariff of 1883. He was defeated for renomination by James G. Blaine. He died in New York City Nov. 18, 1886.

Grover Cleveland (1885-1889) (1893-1897)

(According to a ruling of the State Dept., Grover Cleveland is both the 22d and the 24th president, because his 2 terms were not consecutive. By individuals, he is only the 22d.)

Grover Cleveland, 22d and 24th president, Democrat, was born in Caldwell, N.J. Mar. 18, 1837, the son of Richard F. Cleveland, a Presbyterian minister, and Ann Neale. He was named Stephen Grover, but dropped the Stephen. He clerked in Clinton and Buffalo, N.Y.; taught at the N.Y. City Institution for the Blind; was admitted to the bar in Buffalo, 1859; became assistant district attorney, 1863; sheriff, 1871; mayor, 1881; governor of New York, 1882. He was an independent, honest administrator who hated corruption. He was nominated for president over Tammany Hall opposition, 1884, and defeated Republican James G. Blaine. He enlarged the civil service, vetoed many pension raids on the Treasury. In 1888 he was defeated by Benjamin Harrison, although his popular vote was larger. Reelected over Harrison in 1892, he faced a money crisis brought about by lowering of the gold reserve, circulation of paper and exorbitant silver purchases under the Sherman Act; obtained a repeal of the latter and a reduced tariff. A severe depression and labor troubles racked his administration but he refused to interfere in business matters and rejected Jacob Coxey's demand for unemployment relief. He broke the Pullman strike, 1894. In 1896, the Democrats repudiated his administration and chose silverite William Jennings Bryan as their candidate. Cleveland died in Princeton, N.J., June 24, 1908.

Benjamin Harrison (1889-1893)

Benjamin Harrison, 23d president, Republican, was born at North Bend, Oh., Aug. 20, 1833. His great-grandfather, Benjamin Harrison, was a signer of the Declaration of Independence; his grandfather, William Henry Harrison, was 9th President; his father, John Scott Harrison, was a member of Congress. His mother was Elizabeth F. Irwin. He attended school on his father's farm; graduated from Miami Univ. at Oxford, Oh., 1852; admitted to the bar, 1853, and practiced in Indianapolis. In the Civil War, he rose to the rank of brevet brigadier general, fought at Kennesaw Mountain, Peachtree Creek, Nashville, and in the Atlanta campaign. He failed to be elected governor of Indiana, 1876; but became senator, 1881. In 1888 he defeated Cleveland for president despite having fewer popular votes. He expanded the pension list, signed the McKinley high tariff bill, the Sherman Antitrust Act, and the Sherman Silver Purchase Act. During his administration, 6 states were admitted to the union. He was defeated for reelection, 1892. He represented Venezuela in a boundary arbitration with Great Britain in Paris, 1899. He died in Indianapolis, Mar. 13, 1901.

William McKinley (1897-1901)

William McKinley, 25th president, Republican, was born in Niles, Oh., Jan. 29, 1843, the son of William McKinley, an ironmaker, and Nancy Allison. McKinley attended school in Poland, Oh., and Allegheny College, Meadville, Pa., and enlisted for the Civil War at 18 in the 23d Ohio, in which Rutherford B. Hayes was a major. He rose to captain and in 1865 was made brevet major. He studied law in the Albany, N.Y., law school; opened an office in Canton, Oh., in 1867, and campaigned for Grant and Hayes. He served in the House of Representatives, 1877-83, 1885-91, and led the fight for passage of the McKinley Tariff, 1890. Defeated for reelection on the tariff issue in 1890, he was governor of Ohio, 1892-96. He had support for president in the convention that nominated Benjamin Harrison in 1892. In 1896 he was elected president on a protective tariff, sound money (gold standard) platform over William Jennings Bryan, Democratic proponent of free silver. McKinley was reluctant to intervene in Cuba but the loss of the battleship Maine at Havana crystallized opinion. He demanded Spain's withdrawal from Cuba; Spain made some concessions but Congress announced state of war as of Apr. 21. He was reelected in the 1900 campaign, defeating Bryan's anti-imperialist arguments with the promise of a "full dinner pail." McKinley was respected for his conciliatory nature, but conservative on business issues. On Sept. 6, 1901, while welcoming citizens at the Pan-American Exposition, Buffalo, N.Y., he was shot by Leon Czolgosz, an anarchist. He died Sept. 14.

Theodore Roosevelt (1901-1909)

Theodore Roosevelt, 26th president, Republican, was born in N.Y. City, Oct. 27, 1858, the son of Theodore Roosevelt, a glass importer, and Martha Bulloch. He was a 5th cousin of Franklin D. Roosevelt and an uncle of Eleanor Roosevelt. Roosevelt graduated from Harvard, 1880; attended Columbia Law School briefly; sat in the N.Y. State Assembly, 1882-84; ranched in North Dakota, 1884-86; failed election as mayor of N.Y. City, 1886; member of U.S. Civil Service Commission, 1889; president, N.Y. Police Board, 1895, supporting the merit system; assistant secretary of the Navy under McKinley, 1897-98. In the war with Spain, he organized the 1st U.S. Volunteer Cavalry (Rough Riders) as lieutenant colonel; led the charge up Kettle Hill at San Juan. Elected New York governor, 1898-1900, he fought the spoils system and achieved taxation of corporation franchises. Nominated for vice president, 1900, he became nation's youngest president when McKinley died. He was reelected in 1904. As president he fought corruption of politics by big business; dissolved Northern Securities Co. and others for violating anti-trust laws; intervened in coal strike on behalf of the public, 1902; obtained Elkins Law forbidding rebates to favored corporations, 1903; Hepburn Law regulating railroad rates, 1906; Pure Food and Drugs Act, 1906, Reclamation Act and employers' liability laws. He organized conservation, mediated the peace between Japan and Russia, 1905; won the Nobel Peace Prize. He was the first to use the Hague Court of International Arbitration. By recognizing the new Republic of Panama he made Panama Canal possible.

In 1908 he obtained the nomination of William H. Taft, who was elected. Feeling that Taft had abandoned his policies, Roosevelt unsuccessfully sought the nomination in 1912. He bolted the party and ran on the Progressive "Bull Moose" ticket against Taft and Woodrow Wilson, splitting the Republicans and insuring Wilson's election. He was shot during the campaign but recovered. In 1916 he supported Charles E. Hughes, Republican. A strong friend of Britain, he fought American isolation in World War I. He wrote some 40 books on many topics; his *Winning of the West* is best known. He died Jan. 6, 1919, at Sagamore Hill, Oyster Bay, N.Y.

William Howard Taft (1909-1913)

William Howard Taft, 27th president, Republican, was born in Cincinnati, Oh., Sept. 15, 1857, the son of Alphonso Taft and Louisa Maria Torrey. His father was secretary of war and attorney general in Grant's cabinet; minister to Austria and Russia under Arthur. Taft was graduated from Yale, 1878; Cincinnati Law School, 1880; became law reporter for Cincinnati newspapers; was assistant prosecuting attorney, 1881-83; assistant county solicitor, 1885; judge, superior court, 1887; U.S. solicitor-general, 1890; federal circuit judge, 1892. In 1900 he became head of the U.S. Philippines Commission and was first civil governor of the Philippines, 1901-04; secretary of war, 1904; provisional governor of Cuba, 1906. He was groomed for president by Roosevelt and elected over Bryan, 1908. His administration dissolved Standard Oil and tobacco trusts; instituted Dept. of Labor; drafted direct election of senators and income tax amendments. His tariff and conservation policies angered progressives; though renominated he was opposed by Roosevelt; the result was Democrat Woodrow Wilson's election. Taft, with some reservations, supported the League of Nations. He was professor of constitutional law, Yale, 1913-21; chief justice of the U.S. Supreme Court, 1921-30; illness forced him to resign. He died in Washington, Mar. 8, 1930.

Woodrow Wilson (1913-1921)

Woodrow Wilson, 28th president, Democrat, was born at Staunton, Va., Dec. 28, 1856, as Thomas Woodrow Wilson, son of a Presbyterian minister, the Rev. Joseph Ruggles Wilson and Janet (Jessie) Woodrow. In his youth Wilson lived in Augusta, Ga., Columbia, S.C., and Wilmington, N.C. He attended Davidson College, 1873-74; was graduated from Princeton, A.B., 1879; A.M., 1882; read law at the Univ. of Virginia, 1881; practiced law, Atlanta, 1882-83; Ph.D., Johns Hopkins, 1886. He taught at Bryn Mawr, 1885-88; at Wesleyan, 1888-90; was professor of jurisprudence and political economy at Princeton, 1890-1910; president of Princeton, 1902-1910; governor of New Jersey, 1911-13. In 1912 he was nominated for president with the aid of William Jennings Bryan, who sought to block James "Champ" Clark and Tammany Hall. Wilson won the election because the Republican vote for Taft was split by the Progressives under Roosevelt.

Wilson protected American interests in revolutionary Mexico and fought for American rights on the high seas. His sharp warnings to Germany led to the resignation of his secretary of state, Bryan, a pacifist. In 1916 he was reelected by a slim margin with the slogan, "He kept us out of war." Wilson's attempts to mediate in the war failed. After 4 American ships had been sunk by the Germans, he secured a declaration of war against Germany on Apr. 6, 1917.

Wilson proposed peace Jan. 8, 1918, on the basis of his "Fourteen Points," a state paper with worldwide influence. His doctrine of self-determination continues to play a major role in territorial disputes. The Germans accepted his terms and an armistice, Nov. 11.

Wilson went to Paris to help negotiate the peace treaty, the crux of which he considered the League of Nations. The Senate demanded reservations that would not make the U.S. subordinate to the votes of other nations in case of war. Wilson refused to consider any reservations and toured the country to get support. He suffered a stroke, Oct., 1919. An invalid for months, he clung to his executive powers while his wife and doctor sought to shield him from affairs which would tire him.

He was awarded the 1919 Nobel Peace Prize, but the treaty embodying the League of Nations was rejected by the Senate, 1920. He died in Washington, Feb. 3, 1924.

Warren Gamaliel Harding (1921-1923)

Warren Gamaliel Harding, 29th president, Republican, was born near Corsica, now Blooming Grove, Oh., Nov. 2, 1865, the son of Dr. George Tyron Harding, a physician, and Phoebe Elizabeth Dickerson. He attended Ohio Central College. He was state senator, 1900-04; lieutenant governor, 1904-06; defeated for governor, 1910; chosen U.S. senator, 1915. He supported Taft, opposed federal control of food and fuel; voted for anti-strike legislation, woman's suffrage, and the Volstead prohibition enforcement act over President Wilson's veto; and opposed the League of Nations. In 1920 he was nominated for president and defeated James M. Cox in the election. The Republicans capitalized on war weariness and fear that Wilson's League of Nations would curtail U.S. sovereignty. Harding stressed a return to "normalcy"; worked for tariff revision and repeal of excess profits law and high income taxes. Two Harding appointees, Albert B. Fall (interior) and Harry Daugherty (attorney general), became involved in the Teapot Dome scandal that embittered Harding's last days. He called the International Conference on Limitation of Armaments, 1921-22. Returning from a trip to Alaska he became ill and died in San Francisco, Aug. 2, 1923.

Calvin Coolidge (1923-1929)

Calvin Coolidge, 30th president, Republican, was born in Plymouth, Vt., July 4, 1872, the son of John Calvin Coolidge, a storekeeper, and Victoria J. Moor, and named John Calvin Coolidge. Coolidge graduated from Amherst in 1895. He entered Republican state politics and served as mayor of Northampton, Mass., state senator, lieutenant governor, and, in 1919, governor. In Sept., 1919, Coolidge attained national prominence by calling out the state guard in the Boston police strike. He declared: "There is no right to strike against the public safety by anybody, anywhere, anytime." This brought his name before the Republican convention of 1920, where he was nominated for vice president. He succeeded to the presidency on Harding's death. He opposed the League of Nations; approved the World Court; vetoed the soldiers' bonus bill, which was passed over his veto. In 1924 he was elected by a huge majority. He reduced the national debt by $2 billion in 3 years. He twice vetoed the McNary-Haugen farm bill, which would have provided relief to financially hard-pressed farmers. With Republicans eager to renominate him he announced, Aug. 2, 1927: "I do not choose to run for president in 1928." He died in Northampton, Jan. 5, 1933.

Herbert Clark Hoover (1929-1933)

Herbert C. Hoover, 31st president, Republican, was born at West Branch, Ia., Aug. 10, 1874, son of Jesse Clark Hoover, a blacksmith, and Hulda Randall Minthorn. Hoover grew up in Indian Territory (now Oklahoma) and Oregon; won his A.B. in engineering at Stanford, 1891. He worked briefly with U.S. Geological Survey and western mines; then was a mining engineer in Australia, Asia, Europe, Africa, U.S. While chief engineer, imperial mines, China, he directed food relief for victims of Boxer Rebellion, 1900. He directed American Relief Committee, London, 1914-15; U.S. Comm. for Relief in Belgium, 1915-1919; was U.S. Food Administrator, 1917-1919; American Relief Administrator, 1918-1923, feeding children in defeated nations; Russian Relief, 1918-1923. He was secy. of commerce, 1921-28. He was elected president over Alfred E. Smith, 1928. In 1929 the stock market crashed and the economy collapsed. During the depression, Hoover inaugurated government assistance programs but opposed direct federal aid to the unemployed. He was defeated in the 1932 election by Franklin D. Roosevelt. President Truman made him coordinator of European Food Program, 1947, chairman of the Commission for Reorganization of the Executive Branch, 1947-49. He died in N.Y. City, Oct. 20, 1964.

Franklin Delano Roosevelt (1933-1945)

Franklin D. Roosevelt, 32d president, Democrat, was born near Hyde Park, N.Y., Jan. 30, 1882, the son of James Roosevelt and Sara Delano. He graduated from Harvard, 1904; attended Columbia Law School; was admitted to the bar. He went to the N.Y. Senate, 1910 and 1913. In 1913 President Wilson made him assistant secretary of the navy.

Roosevelt ran for vice president, 1920, with James Cox and was defeated. From 1920 to 1928 he was a N.Y. lawyer and vice president of Fidelity & Deposit Co. In Aug., 1921, polio paralyzed his legs. He learned to walk with leg braces and a cane.

Roosevelt was elected governor of New York, 1928 and 1930. In 1932, W. G. McAdoo, pledged to John N. Garner, threw his votes to Roosevelt, who was nominated for president. The depression and the promise to repeal prohibition ensured his election. He asked emergency powers, proclaimed the New Deal, and put into effect a vast number of administrative changes. Foremost was the use of public funds for relief and public works, resulting in deficit financing. He greatly expanded the federal government's regulation of business and by an excess profits tax and progressive income taxes produced a redistribution of earnings on an unprecedented scale. The Wagner Act gave labor many advantages in organizing and collective bargaining. He was the last president inaugurated on Mar. 4 (1933) and the first inaugurated on Jan. 20 (1937).

Roosevelt was the first president to use radio for "fireside chats." When the Supreme Court nullified some New Deal laws, he sought power to "pack" the court with additional justices, but Congress refused to give him the authority. He was the first president to break the "no 3d term" tradition (1940) and was elected to a 4th term, 1944, despite failing health. He was openly hostile to fascist governments before World War II and launched a lend-lease program on behalf of the Allies. He wrote the principles of fair dealing into the Atlantic Charter, Aug. 14, 1941 (with Winston Churchill), and urged the Four Freedoms (freedom of speech, of worship, from want, from fear) Jan. 6, 1941. When Japan attacked Pearl Harbor, Dec. 7, 1941, the U.S. entered the war. He conferred with allied heads of state at Casablanca, Jan., 1943; Quebec, Aug., 1943; Teheran, Nov.-Dec., 1943; Cairo, Dec., 1943; Yalta, Feb., 1945. He died at Warm Springs, Ga., Apr. 12, 1945.

Harry S. Truman (1945-1953)

Harry S. Truman, 33d president, Democrat, was born at Lamar, Mo., May 8, 1884, the son of John Anderson Truman and Martha Ellen Young. A family disagreement on whether his middle name was Shippe or Solomon, after names of 2 grandfathers, resulted in his using only the middle initial S. He attended public schools in Independence, Mo., worked for the Kansas City Star, 1901, and as railroad timekeeper, and helper in Kansas City banks up to 1905. He ran his family's farm, 1906-17. He was commissioned a first lieutenant and took part in the Vosges, Meuse-Argonne, and St. Mihiel actions in World War I. After the war he ran a haberdashery, became judge of Jackson Co. Court, 1922-24; attended Kansas City School of Law, 1923-25.

Truman was elected U.S. senator in 1934; reelected 1940. In 1944 with Roosevelt's backing he was nominated for vice president and elected. On Roosevelt's death Truman became president. In 1948 he was elected president.

Truman authorized the first uses of the atomic bomb (Hiroshima and Nagasaki, Aug. 6 and 9, 1945), bringing World War II to a rapid end. He was responsible for creating NATO, the Marshall Plan, and what came to be called the Truman Doctrine (to aid nations such as Greece and Turkey, threatened by communist takeover). He broke a Soviet blockade of West Berlin with a massive airlift, 1948-49. When communist North Korea invaded South Korea, June, 1950, he won UN approval for a "police action" and sent in forces under Gen. Douglas MacArthur. When MacArthur opposed his policy of limited objectives, Truman removed him from command.

Truman was responsible for higher minimum-wage, increased social-security, and aid-for-housing laws. Truman died Dec. 26, 1972, in Kansas City, Mo.

Dwight David Eisenhower (1953-1961)

Dwight D. Eisenhower, 34th president, Republican, was born Oct. 14, 1890, at Denison, Tex., the son of David Jacob Eisenhower and Ida Elizabeth Stover. The next year, the family moved to Abilene, Kan. He graduated from West Point, 1915. He was on the American military mission to the Philippines, 1935-39 and during 4 of those years on the staff of Gen. Douglas MacArthur. He was made commander of Allied forces landing in North Africa, 1942, full general, 1943. He became supreme Allied commander in Europe, 1943, and as such led the Normandy invasion June 6, 1944. He was given the rank of general of the army Dec. 20, 1944, made permanent in 1946. On May 7, 1945, he received the surrender of the Germans at Rheims. He returned to the U.S. to serve as chief of staff, 1945-1948. In 1948, Eisenhower published *Crusade in Europe*, his war memoirs, which quickly became a best seller. From 1948 to 1953, he was president of Columbia Univ., but took leave of absence in 1950, to command NATO forces.

Eisenhower resigned from the army and was nominated for president by the Republicans, 1952. He defeated Adlai E. Stevenson in the election. He again defeated Stevenson, 1956. He called himself a moderate, favored "free market system" vs. government price and wage controls; kept goverment out of labor disputes; reorganized defense establishment; promoted missile programs. He continued foreign aid; sped end of Korean fighting; endorsed Taiwan and SE Asia defense treaties; backed UN in condemning Anglo-French raid on Egypt; advocated "open skies" policy of mutual inspection to USSR. He sent U.S. troops into Little Rock, Ark., Sept., 1957, during the segregation crisis and ordered Marines into Lebanon July-Aug., 1958.

During his retirement at his farm near Gettysburg, Pa., Eisenhower took up the role of elder statesman, counseling his 3 successors in the White House. He died Mar. 28, 1969, in Washington.

John Fitzgerald Kennedy (1961-1963)

John F. Kennedy, 35th president, Democrat, was born May 29, 1917, in Brookline, Mass., the son of Joseph P. Kennedy, financier, who later became ambassador to Great Britain, and Rose Fitzgerald. He entered Harvard, attended the London School of

Economics briefly in 1935, received a B.S., from Harvard, 1940. He served in the Navy, 1941-1945, commanded a PT boat in the Solomons and won the Navy and Marine Corps Medal. He wrote *Profiles in Courage*, which won a Pulitzer prize. He served as representative in Congress, 1947-1953; was elected to the Senate in 1952, reelected 1958. He nearly won the vice presidential nomination in 1956.

In 1960, Kennedy won the Democratic nomination for president and defeated Richard M. Nixon, Republican. He was the first Roman Catholic president.

In Apr. 1961, Kennedy's new administration suffered a severe setback when an invasion force of anti-Castro Cubans, trained and directed by the U.S. Central Intelligence Agency, failed to establish a beachhead at the Bay of Pigs in Cuba.

Kennedy's most important act was his successful demand Oct. 22, 1962, that the Soviet Union dismantle its missile bases in Cuba. He established a quarantine of arms shipments to Cuba and continued surveillance by air. He defied Soviet attempts to force the Allies out of Berlin. He made the steel industry rescind a price rise. He backed civil rights, a mental health program, arbitration of railroad disputes, and expanded medical care for the aged. Astronaut flights and satellite orbiting were greatly developed during his administration.

On Nov. 22, 1963, Kennedy was assassinated in Dallas, Tex.

Lyndon Baines Johnson (1963-1969)

Lyndon B. Johnson, 36th president, Democrat, was born near Stonewall, Tex., Aug. 27, 1908, son of Sam Ealy Johnson and Rebekah Baines. He graduated from Southwest Texas State Teachers College, 1930, attended Georgetown Univ. Law School, Washington, 1935. He taught public speaking in Houston, 1930-32; served as secretary to Rep. R. M. Kleberg, 1932-35. In 1937 Johnson won a contest to fill the vacancy caused by the death of a representative and in 1938 was elected to the full term, after which he returned for 4 terms. He was elected U.S. senator in 1948 and reelected in 1954. He became Democratic leader, 1953. Johnson had strong support for the Democratic presidential nomination at the 1960 convention, where the nominee, John F. Kennedy, asked him to run for vice president. His campaigning helped overcome religious bias against Kennedy in the South.

Johnson became president when Kennedy was assassinated. Johnson worked hard for welfare legislation, signed civil rights, anti-proverty, and tax reduction laws. He was elected to a full term, 1964. The war in Vietnam overshadowed other developments during his administration, such as the "Great Society" social programs.

In face of increasing division in the nation and his own party over his handling of the war, Johnson announced that he would not seek another term, Mar. 31, 1968.

Retiring to his ranch near Johnson City, Tex., Johnson wrote his memoirs and oversaw the construction of the Lyndon Baines Johnson Library. He died Jan. 22, 1973.

Richard Milhous Nixon (1969-1974)

Richard M. Nixon, 37th president, Republican, was the only president to resign without completing an elected term. He was born in Yorba Linda, Cal., Jan. 9, 1913, the son of Francis Anthony Nixon and Hannah Milhous. Nixon graduated from Whittier College, 1934; Duke Univ. Law School, 1937. After practicing law in Whittier and serving briefly in the Office of Price Administration in 1942, he entered the navy, and served in the South Pacific.

Nixon was elected to the House of Representatives in 1946 and 1948. He achieved prominence as the House Un-American Activities Committee member who forced the showdown that resulted in the Alger Hiss perjury conviction. In 1950 Nixon was elected to the Senate.

He was elected vice president in the Eisenhower landslides of 1952 and 1956. With Eisenhower's endorsement, Nixon won the Republican nomination in 1960. He was defeated by Democrat John F. Kennedy, returned to Cal. and was defeated in his race for governor, 1962.

In 1968, he won the presidential nomination and went on to defeat Democrat Hubert H. Humphrey.

Nixon was the first U.S. president to visit China and Russia (1972). He and his foreign affairs advisor, Henry A. Kissinger, achieved a detente with China. Nixon appointed 4 Supreme Court justices, including the chief justice, thus altering the court's balance in favor of a more conservative view.

Reelected 1972, Nixon secured a cease-fire agreement in Vietnam and completed the withdrawal of U.S. troops.

Nixon's 2d term was cut short by a series of scandals beginning with the burglary of Democratic party national headquarters in the Watergate office complex on June 17, 1972. On July 16, 1973, a White House aide, under questioning by a Senate committee, revealed that most of Nixon's office conversations and phone calls had been recorded. Nixon claimed executive privilege to keep the tapes secret and the courts and Congress sought the tapes for criminal proceedings against former White House aides and for a House inquiry into possible impeachment.

On July 24, 1974, the Supreme Court ruled that Nixon's claim of executive privilege must fall before the special prosecutor's subpoenas of tapes relevant to criminal trial proceedings. That same day, the House Judiciary Committee opened debate on impeachment. On July 30, the committee recommended House adoption of 3 articles of impeachment charging Nixon with obstruction of justice, abuse of power, and contempt of Congress.

On Aug. 5, Nixon released transcripts of conversations held 6 days after the Watergate break-in showing that Nixon had known of, approved, and directed Watergate cover-up activities. Nixon resigned from office Aug. 9.

Gerald Rudolph Ford (1974-1977)

Gerald R. Ford, 38th president, Republican, was born July 14, 1913, in Omaha, Neb., son of Leslie King and Dorothy Gardner, and was named Leslie Jr. When he was 2, his parents were divorced and his mother moved with the boy to Grand Rapids, Mich. There she met and married Gerald R. Ford, who formally adopted the boy and gave him his own name.

He graduated from the Univ. of Michigan, 1935, and Yale Law School, 1941.

He began practicing law in Grand Rapids, but in 1942 joined the navy and served in the Pacific, leaving the service in 1946 as a lieutenant commander.

He entered congress in 1949 and spent 25 years in the House, 8 of them as Republican leader.

On Oct. 12, 1973, after Vice President Spiro T. Agnew resigned, Ford was nominated by President Nixon to replace him. It was the first use of the procedures set out in the 25th Amendment.

When Nixon resigned Aug. 9, 1974, Ford became president, the first to serve without being chosen in a national election. On Sept. 8 he pardoned Nixon for any federal crimes he might have committed as president. Ford vetoed 48 bills in his first 21 months in office, saying most would prove too costly. He visited China. In 1976, he was defeated in the election by Democrat Jimmy Carter.

Jimmy (James Earl) Carter (1977-1981)

Jimmy (James Earl) Carter, 39th president, Democrat, was the first president from the Deep South since before the Civil War. He was born Oct. 1, 1924, at Plains, Ga., where his parents, James and Lillian Gordy Carter, had a farm and several businesses.

He attended Georgia Tech, and graduated from the U.S. Naval Academy. He entered the Navy's nuclear submarine program as an aide to Adm. Hyman Rickover, and studied nuclear physics at Union College.

His father died in 1953 and Carter left the Navy to take over the family businesses — peanut-raising, warehousing, and cotton-ginning. He was elected to the Georgia state senate, was defeated for governor, 1966, but elected in 1970.

Carter won the Democratic nomination and defeated President Gerald R. Ford in the election of 1976. He played a major role in the peace negotiations between Israel and Egypt. In Nov. 1979, Iranian student militants attacked the U.S. embassy in Teheran and held members of the embassy staff hostage.

Carter was widely criticized for the poor state of the economy and high inflation. He was also viewed as weak in his handling of foreign policy. He reacted to the Soviet invasion of Afghanistan by imposing a grain embargo and boycotting the Moscow Olympic games. His failure to obtain the release of the remaining 52 hostages held in Iran plagued Carter to the end of his term. He was defeated by Ronald Reagan in the 1980 election. Carter finally succeeded in obtaining the release of the hostages on Inauguration Day, as the new president was taking the oath of office.

Ronald Wilson Reagan (1981-1989)

Ronald Wilson Reagan, 40th president, Republican, was born Feb. 6, 1911, in Tampico, Ill., the son of John Edward Reagan and Nellie Wilson. Reagan graduated from Eureka (Ill.) College in 1932. Following his graduation, he worked as a sports announcer in Des Moines, Ia.

Reagan began a successful career as a film actor in 1937, and starred in numerous movies, and later television, until the 1960s. He was a captain in the Army Air Force during World War II.

He served as president of the Screen Actors Guild from 1947 to 1952, and in 1959.

Once a liberal Democrat, Reagan became active in Republican politics during the 1964 presidential campaign of Barry Goldwater. He was elected governor of California in 1966, and reelected in 1970.

In 1980, he gained the Republican nomination and won a landslide victory over Jimmy Carter. He was easily reelected in 1984. Reagan, at 73, was the oldest man ever elected president.

Reagan successfully forged a bipartisan coalition in Congress which led to enactment of an economic program which included the largest budget and tax cuts in U.S. history, and a Social Security reform bill designed to insure the long-term solvency of the system. In 1986, he signed into law a revolutionary tax-reform bill. He was shot in an assassination attempt in 1981, and had major surgery in 1985 and 1987.

In 1983, Reagan sent a task force to lead the invasion of Grenada, and joined 3 European nations in maintaining a peacekeeping force in Beirut, Lebanon. His opposition to international terrorism led to the U.S. bombing of Libyan military installations in 1986. He strongly supported El Salvador, the Nicaraguan contras, and other anti-communist governments and forces throughout the world. Aid was sent to the rebels fighting Soviet troops in Afghanistan. When the Iran/Iraq war threatened freedom of the seas, U.S. Navy ships were sent to the Persian Gulf.

Reagan held summit meetings with Soviet leader Mikhail Gorbachev in 1985 in Geneva, 1986 in Iceland, 1987 in Washington, D.C., where an historic treaty eliminating short and medium-range missiles from Europe was signed, and 1988 in Moscow where Reagan criticized the Soviet record on human rights, and met with Soviet dissidents.

Reagan faced a major crisis in 1986-1987, when it was revealed that the U.S. had sold weapons to Iran in exchange for the release of U.S. hostages being held in Lebanon and that subsequently some of the money was diverted to the Nicaraguan contras (Congress had barred aid to the contras). The scandal led to the resignation of leading White House aides.

As Reagan left office, the nation was experiencing its 6th consecutive year of economic prosperity. Along with the strong economy, the nation enjoyed low unemployment, energy costs, and inflation. Reagan, however, was unable to control the high budget deficits which plagued him throughout his administration.

George Herbert Walker Bush (1989-1993)

George Herbert Walker Bush, 41st president, Republican, was born June 12, 1924, in Milton, Mass., the son of Prescott Bush, U.S. senator from Connecticut, and Dorothy Walker. He served as a U.S. Navy pilot in World War II, earning the Distinguished Flying Cross and three Air Medals for service in the Pacific. After graduating from Yale Univ. (1948), he settled in Texas where, in 1953, he helped found an oil company.

After losing a bid for a U.S. Senate seat in Texas, 1964, he was elected to the House of Representatives in 1966 and 1968. He lost a 2d U.S. Senate race in 1970. He served as U.S. ambassador to the United Nations, 1971-73, headed the U.S. Liaison Office in Beijing, 1974-75, and was director of the Central Intelligence Agency, 1976-77.

Following an unsuccessful bid for the 1980 Republican presidential nomination, Bush was chosen by Ronald Reagan as his vice presidential running mate. He served as U.S. vice president, 1981-89.

In 1988, he gained the Republican presidential nomination and defeated Democrat Michael Dukakis in the election. Calling on Americans "to make kinder the face of the nation and gentler the face of the world," Bush took office faced with the ongoing U.S. budget and trade deficits as well as the rescue of insolvent U.S. savings and loan institutions.

Bush made no major changes from Reagan's policies during his presidency. He annually faced a severe budget deficit, struggled with military cutbacks in light of reduced "cold war" tensions, and vetoed congressional actions favorable to freedom of choice on abortion, a minimum-wage law, and an anti-discrimination bill that didn't reflect his own views.

Bush supported Soviet reforms and Eastern Europe democratization. He was criticized, however, for not supporting strongly enough the independence effort of the Baltic republics, for keeping U.S. policy tied for too long to Mikhail Gorbachev as the Soviet leader lost power and his nation broke apart, and for his soft reaction to the Chinese government's violent repression of a pro-democracy movement.

In Dec. 1989, Bush sent military forces to Panama which overthrew the government and captured military strongman Gen. Manuel Noriega.

Bush reacted to Iraq's Aug. 1990 invasion of Kuwait by sending U.S. forces to the Persian Gulf area and assembling a U.N.-backed coalition including NATO and Arab League members. A U.S.-led international force launched air and missile attacks on Iraq, Jan. 1991, after a U.N. deadline for withdrawal from Kuwait had passed. In Feb., Allied forces retook Kuwait after a 4-day ground assault. The quick victory gave Bush one of the highest presidential approval ratings in history. His popularity plummeted by the end of 1991 as the economy struggled through a prolonged recession, and he was perceived as being indifferent to the nation's domestic problems. He was defeated by Bill Clinton in the 1992 election.

Bill (William Jefferson) Clinton (1993-)

Bill Clinton was born William Jefferson Blythe 3rd on Aug. 19, 1946 in Hope, Ark., the son of William and Virginia Blythe. Blythe, a traveling salesman, died in an auto accident before his son was born. His mother married Roger Clinton and several years later, at age 16, Bill Blythe changed his name to Bill Clinton. Clinton attended Georgetown Univ., Oxford Univ. in England as a Rhodes scholar, and Yale Law School.

Clinton worked on George McGovern's 1972 presidential campaign and for the House Judiciary Committee in 1973. He taught at the Univ. of Arkansas, 1974-76. He was elected Arkansas State Attorney General in 1976.

In 1978, he was elected the nation's youngest governor, but was defeated for reelection in 1980. He successfully ran for governor again in 1982, 1984, 1986, and 1990. He married Hillary Rodham in 1975. She became a successful lawyer and a social activist. They had a daughter, Chelsea, in 1980.

Despite personal attacks on his character, he won the majority of the 1992 presidential primaries while moving the Democratic Party toward the center, trying to appeal to middle-class suburbanites who had deserted the party during the Reagan era. He defeated Pres. George Bush in the presidential election.

In August 1993, Clinton narrowly won congressional passage of some $500 billion in taxes and spending cuts to reduce the federal budget deficits. He also made a strong commitment to health-care reform. At an April 1993 summit meeting with Boris Yeltsin, he unveiled a $1.62-billion package of aid to Russia.

Wives and Children of the Presidents

Listed in order of presidential administrations.

Name (Born–died, married)	State	Sons/ daughters
Martha Dandridge Custis Washington (1732-1802, 1759)	Va.	None
Abigail Smith Adams (1744-1818, 1764)	Mass.	3/2
Martha Wayles Skelton Jefferson (1748-1782, 1772)	Va.	1/5
Dorothea "Dolley" Payne Todd Madison (1768-1849, 1794)	N.C.	None
Elizabeth Kortright Monroe (1768-1830, 1786)	N.Y.	.../2 (A)
Louisa Catherine Johnson Adams (1775-1852, 1797)	Md.(B)	3/1
Rachel Donelson Robards Jackson (1767-1828, 1791)	Va.	None
Hannah Hoes Van Buren (1783-1819, 1807)	N.Y.	4/...
Anna Symmes Harrison (1775-1864, 1795)	N.J.	6/4
Letitia Christian Tyler (1790-1842, 1813)	Va.	3/5
Julia Gardiner Tyler (1820-1889, 1844)	N.Y.	5/2
Sarah Childress Polk (1803-1891, 1824)	Tenn.	None
Margaret Smith Taylor (1788-1852, 1810)	Md.	1/5
Abigail Powers Fillmore (1798-1853, 1826)	N.Y.	1/1
Caroline Carmichael McIntosh Fillmore (1813-1881, 1858)	N.J.	None
Jane Means Appleton Pierce (1806-1863, 1834)	N.H.	3/...
Mary Todd Lincoln (1818-1882, 1842)	Ky.	4/...
Eliza McCardle Johnson (1810-1876, 1827)	Tenn.	3/2
Julia Dent Grant (1826-1902, 1848)	Mo.	3/1
Lucy Ware Webb Hayes (1831-1889, 1852)	Oh.	7/1
Lucretia Rudolph Garfield (1832-1918, 1858)	Oh.	4/1
Ellen Lewis Herndon Arthur (1837-1880, 1859)	Va.	2/1
Frances Folsom Cleveland (1864-1947, 1886)	N.Y.	2/3
Caroline Lavinia Scott Harrison (1832-1892, 1853)	Oh.	1/1
Mary Scott Lord Dimmick Harrison (1858-1948, 1896)	Pa.	.../1
Ida Saxton McKinley (1847-1907, 1871)	Oh.	.../2
Alice Hathaway Lee Roosevelt (1861-1884, 1880)	Mass.	.../1
Edith Kermit Carow Roosevelt (1861-1948, 1886)	Conn.	4/1
Helen Herron Taft (1861-1943, 1886)	Oh.	2/1
Ellen Louise Axson Wilson (1860-1914, 1885)	Ga.	.../3
Edith Bolling Galt Wilson (1872-1961, 1915)	Va.	None
Florence Kling De Wolfe Harding (1860-1924, 1891)	Oh.	None
Grace Anna Goodhue Coolidge (1879-1957, 1905)	Vt.	2/...
Lou Henry Hoover (1875-1944, 1899)	Ia.	2/...
Anna Eleanor Roosevelt Roosevelt (1884-1962, 1905)	N.Y.	4/1 (A)
Bess Wallace Truman (1885-1982, 1919)	Mo.	.../1
Mamie Geneva Doud Eisenhower (1896-1979, 1916)	Ia.	1/...(A)
Jacqueline Lee Bouvier Kennedy (b. 1929, 1953)	N.Y.	1/1 (A)
Claudia "Lady Bird" Alta Taylor Johnson (b. 1912, 1934)	Tex.	.../2
Thelma Catherine Patricia Ryan Nixon (1912-1993, 1940)	Nev.	.../2
Elizabeth Bloomer Warren Ford (b. 1918, 1948)	Ill.	3/1
Rosalynn Smith Carter (b. 1927, 1946)	Ga.	3/1
Anne Frances "Nancy" Robbins Davis Reagan (b. 1921, 1952)	N.Y.	1/1 (C)
Barbara Pierce Bush (b. 1925, 1945)	N.Y.	4/2
Hillary Rodham Clinton (b. 1947, 1975)	Ill.	.../1

James Buchanan, 15th president, was unmarried. (A) plus one infant, deceased. (B) Born London, father a Md. citizen. (C) President Reagan married and divorced Jane Wyman. They had a son and a daughter.

First Lady: Hillary Rodham Clinton

The first lady was born in Chicago, Ill. in 1947, the daughter of Hugh and Dorothy Rodham. She graduated from Wellesley College and Yale Law School. She married Bill Clinton in 1975. Their daughter, Chelsea, was born in 1980.

She has been active in the areas of children's rights and education reform. From 1979 to 1992, she was a partner in a Little Rock law firm and, in 1988 and 1991, was voted one of the "100 Most Influential Lawyers in America" by the National Law Journal.

President Clinton named her as head of a commission, Jan.-May 1993, to devise a plan for reforming the U.S. health-care system.

Burial Places of the Presidents

Washington	Mt. Vernon, Va.
J. Adams	Quincy, Mass.
Jefferson	Charlottesville, Va.
Madison	Montpelier Station, Va.
Monroe	Richmond, Va.
J.Q. Adams	Quincy, Mass.
Jackson	Nashville, Tenn.
Van Buren	Kinderhook, N.Y.
W.H. Harrison	North Bend, Oh.
Tyler	Richmond, Va.
Polk	Nashville, Tenn.
Taylor	Louisville, Ky.
Fillmore	Buffalo, N.Y.
Pierce	Concord, N.H.
Buchanan	Lancaster, Pa.
Lincoln	Springfield, Ill.
A. Johnson	Greeneville, Tenn.
Grant	New York City
Hayes	Fremont, Oh.
Garfield	Cleveland, Oh.
Arthur	Albany, N.Y.
Cleveland	Princeton, N.J.
B. Harrison	Indianapolis, Ind.
McKinley	Canton, Oh.
T. Roosevelt	Oyster Bay, N.Y.
Taft	Arlington Nat'l. Cem'y.
Wilson	Washington Cathedral
Harding	Marion, Oh.
Coolidge	Plymouth, Vt.
Hoover	West Branch, Ia.
F.D. Roosevelt	Hyde Park, N.Y.
Truman	Independence, Mo.
Eisenhower	Abilene, Kan.
Kennedy	Arlington Nat'l. Cem'y.
L.B. Johnson	Stonewall, Tex.

National Political Convention Sites: 1856-1992[1]

Year	Democrats	Republicans
1856	Cincinnati	Philadelphia
1860	Charleston, S.C.	Chicago
1864	Chicago	Baltimore
1868	New York City	Chicago
1872	Baltimore	Philadelphia
1876	St. Louis	Cincinnati
1880	Cincinnati	Chicago
1884	Chicago	Chicago
1888	St. Louis	Chicago
1892	Chicago	Minneapolis
1896	Chicago	St. Louis
1900	Kansas City, Mo.	Philadelphia
1904	St. Louis	Chicago
1908	Denver	Chicago
1912	Baltimore	Chicago
1916	St. Louis	Chicago
1920	San Francisco	Chicago
1924	New York City	Cleveland
1928	Houston	Kansas City
1932	Chicago	Chicago
1936	Philadelphia	Cleveland
1940	Chicago	Philadelphia
1944	Chicago	Chicago
1948	Philadelphia	Philadelphia
1952	Chicago	Chicago
1956	Chicago	San Francisco
1960	Los Angeles	Chicago
1964	Atlantic City	San Francisco
1968	Chicago	Miami Beach
1972	Miami Beach	Miami Beach
1976	New York City	Kansas City, Mo.
1980	New York City	Detroit
1984	San Francisco	Dallas
1988	Atlanta	New Orleans
1992	New York City	Houston

(1) The first Democratic National Convention was held in 1832. All conventions prior to 1856 were held in Baltimore. The first Republican National Convention was held in 1856. Chicago has hosted more conventions than any other city (24).

Librarians of Congress

Librarian	Served	Appointed by President
John J. Beckley	1802-1807	Jefferson
Patrick Magruder	1807-1815	Jefferson
George Watterston	1815-1829	Madison
John Silva Meehan	1829-1861	Jackson
John G. Stephenson	1861-1864	Lincoln
Ainsworth Rand Spofford	1864-1897	Lincoln
John Russell Young	1897-1899	McKinley
Herbert Putnam	1899-1939	McKinley
Archibald MacLeish	1939-1944	F. Roosevelt
Luther H. Evans	1945-1953	Truman
L. Quincy Mumford	1954-1974	Eisenhower
Daniel J. Boorstin	1975-1987	Ford
James H. Billington	1987-	Reagan

Federal Bureau of Investigation

The Federal Bureau of Investigation (FBI) is the principal investigative arm of the U.S. Department of Justice, and is located at 10th Street and Pennsylvania Avenue, Northwest, Washington, D.C. 20535. It investigates all violations of Federal law except those specifically assigned to some other agency by legislative action. The FBI's jurisdiction includes a wide range of responsibilities in the criminal, civil, and security fields. Priority has been assigned to five areas—counterterrorism, foreign counterintelligence, organized crime/drugs, white-collar crime, and violent crime. On Jan. 28, 1982, the Attorney General assigned concurrent jursidiction for the enforcement of the Controlled Substances Act to the FBI and the Drug Enforcement Administration (DEA).

The FBI also offers cooperative services to duly authorized law enforcement agencies; these services include fingerprint identification, laboratory examination, police training, and the National Crime Information Center.

The FBI has 56 field offices in the principal cities of the country. (Consult telephone directories for locations and phone numbers.)

An applicant for the position of Special Agent of the FBI must be a citizen of the U.S., at least 23 and under 37 years old, and a graduate of an accredited law school or of an accredited college or university. Special agents may be appointed under five entry programs: law, accounting, engineering/science, language, and diversified. Other degree titles may also qualify for the Special Agent position. Please consult your local FBI field office applicant coordinator. Those appointed to the Special Agent position must complete an initial training period of 16 weeks at the FBI Academy, Quantico, Va.

AFGHANISTAN | ALBANIA | ALGERIA | ANDORRA | ANGOLA

ANTIGUA AND BARBUDA | ARGENTINA | ARMENIA | AUSTRALIA | AUSTRIA

AZERBAIJAN | THE BAHAMAS | BAHRAIN | BANGLADESH | BARBADOS

BELARUS | BELGIUM | BELIZE | BENIN | BHUTAN

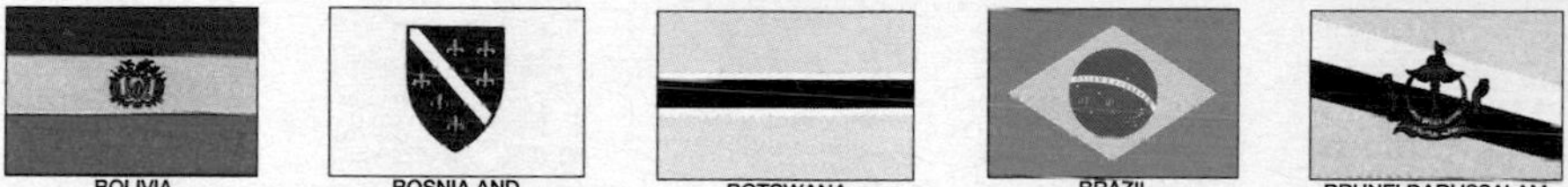

BOLIVIA | BOSNIA AND HERZEGOVINA | BOTSWANA | BRAZIL | BRUNEI DARUSSALAM

BULGARIA | BURKINA FASO | BURUNDI | CAMBODIA | CAMEROON

CANADA | CAPE VERDE | CENTRAL AFRICAN REPUBLIC | CHAD | CHILE

CHINA | COLOMBIA | COMOROS | CONGO | COSTA RICA

COTE D'IVOIRE | CROATIA | CUBA | CYPRUS | CZECH REPUBLIC

DENMARK | DJIBOUTI | DOMINICA | DOMINICAN REPUBLIC | ECUADOR

EGYPT | EL SALVADOR | EQUATORIAL GUINEA | ERITREA | ESTONIA

ETHIOPIA | FIJI | FINLAND | FRANCE | GABON

THE GAMBIA | GEORGIA | GERMANY | GHANA | GREECE

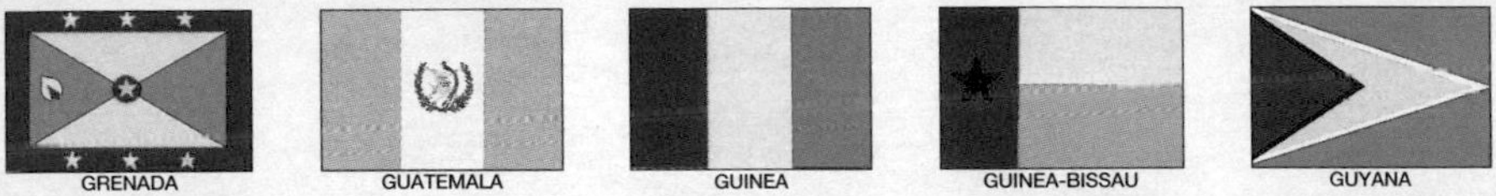

GRENADA | GUATEMALA | GUINEA | GUINEA-BISSAU | GUYANA

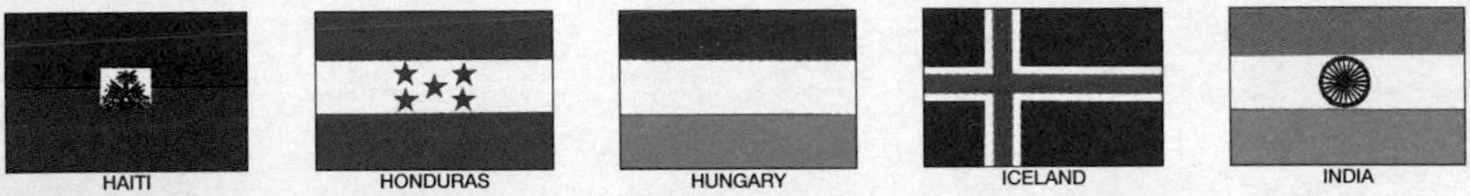

HAITI | HONDURAS | HUNGARY | ICELAND | INDIA

INDONESIA | IRAN | IRAQ | IRELAND | ISRAEL

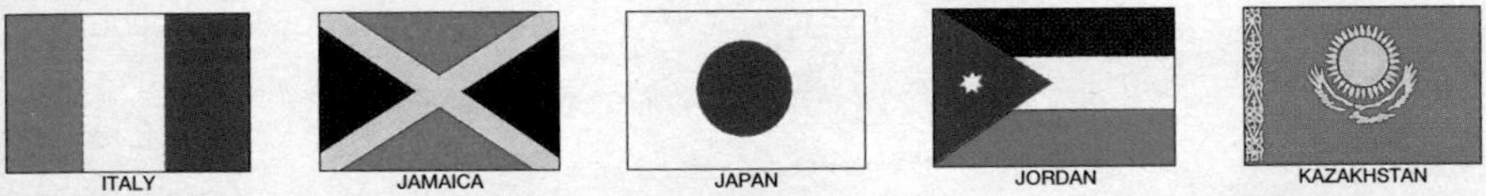

ITALY | JAMAICA | JAPAN | JORDAN | KAZAKHSTAN

KENYA | KIRIBATI | NORTH KOREA | SOUTH KOREA | KUWAIT

KYRGYZSTAN | LAOS | LATVIA | LEBANON | LESOTHO

LIBERIA | LIBYA | LIECHTENSTEIN | LITHUANIA | LUXEMBOURG

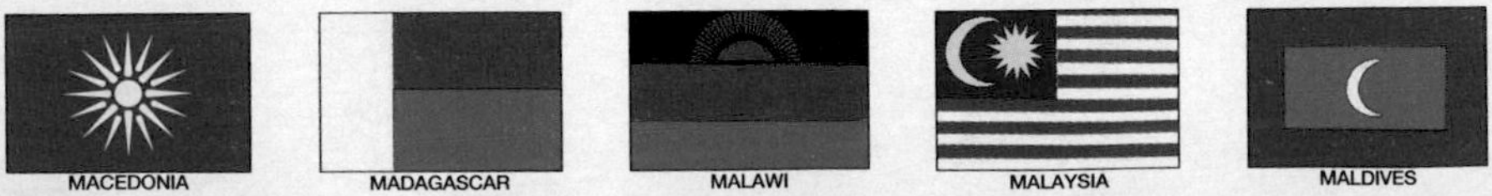

MACEDONIA | MADAGASCAR | MALAWI | MALAYSIA | MALDIVES

MALI | MALTA | MARSHALL ISLANDS | MAURITANIA | MAURITIUS

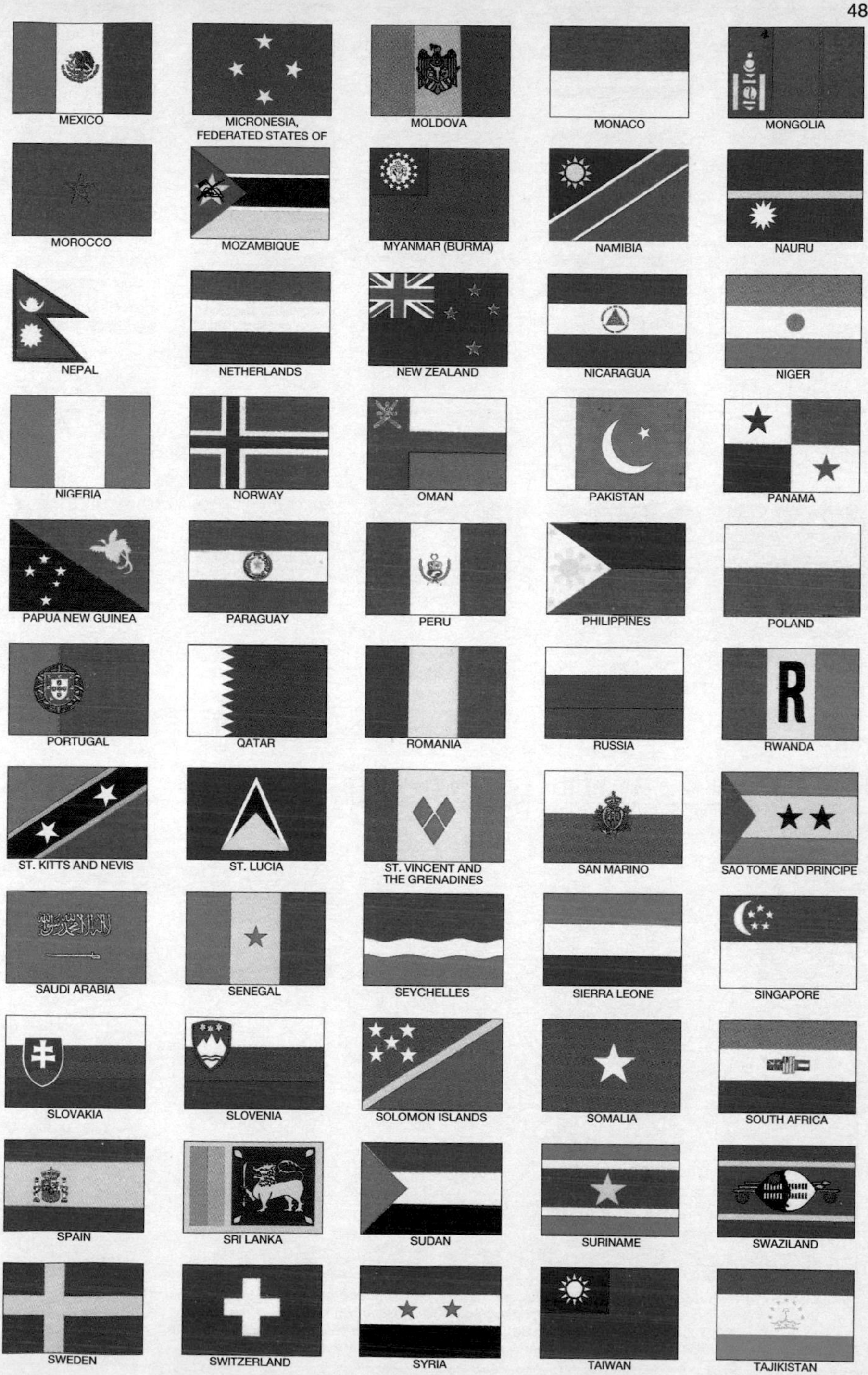

MEXICO
MICRONESIA, FEDERATED STATES OF
MOLDOVA
MONACO
MONGOLIA
MOROCCO
MOZAMBIQUE
MYANMAR (BURMA)
NAMIBIA
NAURU
NEPAL
NETHERLANDS
NEW ZEALAND
NICARAGUA
NIGER
NIGERIA
NORWAY
OMAN
PAKISTAN
PANAMA
PAPUA NEW GUINEA
PARAGUAY
PERU
PHILIPPINES
POLAND
PORTUGAL
QATAR
ROMANIA
RUSSIA
RWANDA
ST. KITTS AND NEVIS
ST. LUCIA
ST. VINCENT AND THE GRENADINES
SAN MARINO
SAO TOME AND PRINCIPE
SAUDI ARABIA
SENEGAL
SEYCHELLES
SIERRA LEONE
SINGAPORE
SLOVAKIA
SLOVENIA
SOLOMON ISLANDS
SOMALIA
SOUTH AFRICA
SPAIN
SRI LANKA
SUDAN
SURINAME
SWAZILAND
SWEDEN
SWITZERLAND
SYRIA
TAIWAN
TAJIKISTAN

TANZANIA

THAILAND

TOGO

TONGA

TRINIDAD AND TOBAGO

TUNISIA

TURKEY

TURKMENISTAN

TUVALU

UGANDA

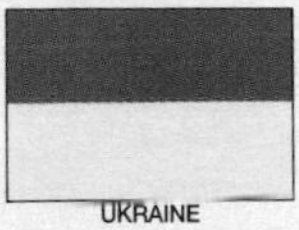
UKRAINE

UNITED ARAB EMIRATES

UNITED KINGDOM

UNITED STATES

URUGUAY

UZBEKISTAN

VANUATU

VATICAN CITY

VENEZUELA

VIETNAM

WESTERN SAMOA

YEMEN

YUGOSLAVIA

ZAIRE

ZAMBIA

ZIMBABWE

INTERNATIONAL TIME ZONES

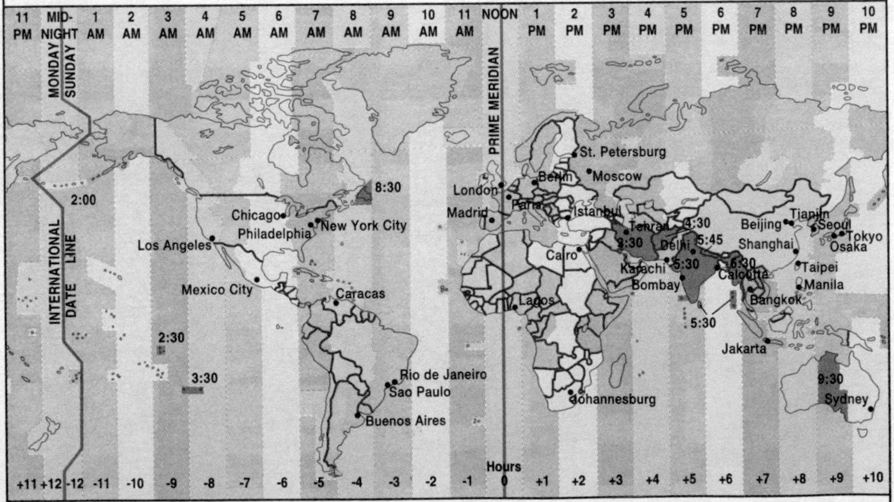

The world is divided into 24 time zones, each 15° longitude wide. The longitudinal meridian passing through Greenwich, England, is the starting point, and is called the *prime meridian*. The 12th zone is divided by the 180th meridian (International Date Line). When the line is crossed going west, the date is advanced one day; when crossed going east, the date becomes a day earlier.

NORTH AMERICA
RUSSIA
ARCTIC OCEAN
Cape Morris Jesup
Nord
Cape Columbia
Alert
Ellesmere Island
Bering Sea
Chukchi Sea
St. Lawrence I.
Bering Strait
SEWARD PENINSULA
Nome
Point Barrow
Barrow
BROOKS RANGE
Queen Elizabeth Islands
Qaanaaq (Thule)
Greenland (Kalaallit Nunaat) (Denmark)
ICELAND
Denmark Strait
Nunivak I.
Yukon
Alaska
Bethel
Beaufort Sea
Melville I.
Sachs Harbour
Banks I.
Resolute
Devon I.
Baffin Bay
Tasiilaq
Mt. McKinley 20,320
Highest point in North America
Fairbanks
ALASKA RANGE
Pond Inlet
Fort McPherson
Inuvik
Anchorage
Seward
Valdez
Mt. Katmai 6,716
Kodiak I.
Dawson
Victoria I.
Cambridge Bay
Baffin Island
Davis Strait
Nuuk (Godthab)
YUKON PLATEAU
Carmacks
Mt. Logan 19,850
Whitehorse
Gulf of Alaska
Mackenzie
Great Bear Lake
Arctic Circle
Pangnirtung
Iqaluit
Cape Farewell
Southampton I.
Hudson Strait
Labrador Sea
Juneau
Sitka
Alexander Archipelago
Ketchikan
COAST MOUNTAINS
Watson Lake
Fort Simpson
Yellowknife
Great Slave Lake
Rankin Inlet
UNGAVA PENINSULA
Povungnituk
Hebron
Fort Nelson
Hay River
Fort Smith
Uranium City
Arviat
CANADA
LABRADOR
Prince Rupert
Queen Charlotte Islands
Kitimat
Dawson Creek
Peace River
Peace
Fort McMurray
Athabasca
Lake Athabasca
Churchill
Hudson Bay
Happy Valley-Goose Bay
Schefferville
St. Anthony
Prince George
Grande Prairie
La Loche
York Factory
Mt. Waddington 13,175
Mt. Robson 12,972
Jasper
La Ronge
Flin Flon
Thompson
CANADIAN SHIELD
Labrador City
Gander
Newfoundland
St. John's
Port Hardy
Vancouver I.
Williams Lake
Kamloops
Fraser
Edmonton
Saskatchewan
Prince Albert
Lake Winnipeg
James Bay
Sept-Iles
Corner Brook
Calgary
Saskatoon
Moosonee
Chibougamau
Vancouver
Victoria
Seattle
Lethbridge
Regina
Sydney
Cape Breton I.
Chicoutimi
Mt. Rainier 14,410
Spokane
ROCKY MOUNTAINS
GREAT PLAINS
Brandon
Winnipeg
Thunder Bay
Val-d'Or
Timmins
Quebec
Fredericton
NOVA SCOTIA
St. Lawrence
Portland
Eugene
Columbia
CASCADE RANGE
Missoula
Great Falls
Williston
Lake Superior
Halifax
Montreal
Ottawa
Sudbury
Butte
Billings
Bismarck
Fargo
Duluth
Lake Huron
Bangor
Portland
Cape Sable
Eureka
Boise
Snake
Rapid City
Minneapolis
Green Bay
Lake Michigan
Toronto
Lake Ontario
Boston
GREAT BASIN
SIERRA NEVADA
Pocatello
Great Salt Lake
Salt Lake City
Casper
Sioux Falls
Missouri
Milwaukee
Rochester
Buffalo
Lake Erie
Reno
Cheyenne
Des Moines
Chicago
Detroit
Cleveland
New York City
San Francisco
Philadelphia
San Jose
Mt. Whitney 14,494
Denver
Platte
Omaha
UNITED STATES
Pittsburgh
Columbus
APPALACHIAN MTS.
Washington, D.C.
Fresno
COLORADO PLATEAU
Mt. Elbert 14,433
Kansas City
Indianapolis
Ohio
Richmond
Santa Barbara
Point Conception
Las Vegas
Death Valley
Lowest point in North America
Colorado
St. Louis
Louisville
Mt. Mitchell 6,684
Cape Hatteras
Los Angeles
San Diego
Wichita
Oklahoma City
Arkansas
Nashville
Raleigh
Albuquerque
Amarillo
Charlotte
Tijuana
Phoenix
Lubbock
Red
Little Rock
Mississippi
Memphis
Atlanta
ATLANTIC OCEAN
Mexicali
Birmingham
Charleston
Tucson
El Paso
Dallas
COASTAL PLAIN
Savannah
PACIFIC OCEAN
Nogales
Ciudad Juarez
Jackson
Jacksonville
Hermosillo
Chihuahua
Austin
Mobile
BAJA CALIFORNIA
SIERRA MADRE OCCIDENTAL
Houston
New Orleans
Rio Grande
San Antonio
Tampa
St. Petersburg
Freeport
Tropic of Cancer
Ciudad Obregon
Nuevo Laredo
Brownsville
Matamoros
Miami
Nassau
THE BAHAMAS
Cerro Mohinora 13,097
La Paz
Durango
Monterrey
SIERRA MADRE ORIENTAL
Gulf of Mexico
Cape Sable
False Cape
Mazatlan
Havana
Pico Duarte 10,416
DOMINICAN REPUBLIC
CUBA
Tampico
Aguascalientes
Cape Corrientes
Leon
Bay of Campeche
Merida
Cancun
HAITI
Port-au-Prince
Santo Domingo
Guadalajara
MEXICO
YUCATAN PENINSULA
Greater Antilles
JAMAICA
Kingston
Colima
Mexico City
Veracruz
Campeche
Puebla
Citlaltepec 18,700
Villahermosa
Oaxaca
Tuxtla Gutierrez
Belmopan
BELIZE
Caribbean Sea
Acapulco
GUATEMALA
HONDURAS
Tegucigalpa
Tajumulco 13,845
Guatemala
NICARAGUA
EL SALVADOR
San Salvador
Managua
Lake Nicaragua
ISTHMUS OF PANAMA
San José
Panama Canal
Panama
COSTA RICA
PANAMA
SOUTH AMERICA
Elevation
Meters
Feet
4,000
13,120
2,000
6,560
500
1,640
200
656
0
0
Below Sea Level
Below Sea Level
0 250 500 750 1000 Miles
0 250 500 750 1000 1200 Kilometers
180°
170°
160°
150°
140°
130°
120°
110°
100°
90°
80°
70°
60°
50°
40°
30°
20°
10°
0°

Vancouver Island
Campbell River
Kamloops
Revelstoke
Mt. Assiniboine 11,870
Banff
Edmonton
Red Deer
Calgary
Nanaimo
Vancouver
Kelowna
Cape Flattery
Victoria
Bellingham
Mt. Olympus 7,966
Seattle
Tacoma
Olympia
Mt. Rainier 14,410
Washington
Spokane
Yakima
Kennewick
Portland
Salem
Mt. Hood 11,239
Pendleton
Eugene
Bend
Coos Bay
Oregon
Burns
Medford
Klamath Falls
Eureka
Mt. Shasta 14,162
Redding
Trail
Cranbrook
Lethbridge
Sandpoint
Mt. Cleveland 10,465
Kalispell
Coeur d'Alene
Lewiston
Missoula
Helena
Butte
Bozeman
Dillon
Salmon
Idaho
Borah Pk. 12,662
Boise
Idaho Falls
Twin Falls
Pocatello
North Battleford
Prince Albert
Hanna
Rosetown
Saskatoon
Brooks
Medicine Hat
Swift Current
Moose Jaw
Regina
Yorkton
Dauphin
The Pas
Cedar Lake
Tisdale
Swan River
Grand Rapids
Lake Winnipeg
Lake Winnipegosis
Lake Manitoba
Portage la Prairie
Brandon
Winnipeg
Kenora
Estevan
Lake of the Woods
Morden
Shelby
Havre
Glasgow
Missouri
Great Falls
Montana
Miles City
Billings
Granite Pk. 12,799
Williston
Minot
Rugby
International Falls
Grand Forks
North Dakota
Bismarck
Dickinson
Fargo
Jamestown
Bemidji
Minnesota
St. Cloud
Minneapolis
Mankato
Mobridge
Aberdeen
South Dakota
Rapid City
Pierre
Watertown
Harney Pk. 7,242
BLACK HILLS
Hot Springs
Sioux Falls
Cody
Sheridan
Jackson
Gannett Pk. 13,804
Lander
Casper
Wyoming
Rock Springs
Laramie
Cheyenne
Chadron
Scottsbluff
O'Neill
Nebraska
North Platte
Broken Bow
Grand Island
Omaha
Lincoln
Platte
Sioux City
Mason City
Des Moines
ROCKY MOUNTAINS
GREAT PLAINS
COLUMBIA PLATEAU
CASCADE RANGE
COAST RANGES
SIERRA NEVADA
Winnemucca
Elko
Reno
Carson City
Sacramento
San Francisco
Oakland
San Jose
Monterey
Fresno
California
Nevada
GREAT BASIN
Hawthorne
Ely
Boundary Pk. 13,140
Highest point in the United States outside Alaska
Mt. Whitney 14,494
Death Valley
Lowest point in the United States
Bakersfield
Las Vegas
Point Conception
Santa Barbara
MOJAVE DESERT
Barstow
Channel Islands
Los Angeles
Long Beach
San Bernardino
Riverside
San Diego
Tijuana
Ensenada
Mexicali
Yuma
Logan
Great Salt Lake
Ogden
Salt Lake City
Provo
Kings Pk. 13,528
Vernal
Utah
Richfield
Caliente
Cedar City
Saint George
Grand Junction
Moab
Montrose
Colorado
COLORADO PLATEAU
Craig
Fort Collins
Sterling
Boulder
Denver
Mt. Elbert 14,433
Colorado Springs
Pikes Pk. 14,110
Pueblo
Alamosa
La Junta
Durango
Goodland
UNITED STATES
Hays
Salina
Topeka
Lawrence
Kansas
Garden City
Hutchinson
Dodge City
Arkansas
Wichita
Parsons
Kansas City
St. Joseph
Grand Canyon
Kayenta
Kingman
Humphreys Pk. 12,633
Farmington
Raton
Wheeler Pk. 13,161
Flagstaff
Winslow
Gallup
Santa Fe
Las Vegas
Prescott
Holbrook
Arizona
Albuquerque
Phoenix
Globe
Casa Grande
Socorro
Clovis
Roswell
New Mexico
Tucson
Sierra Vista
Silver City
Las Cruces
Carlsbad
Nogales
Enid
Oklahoma
Bartlesville
Fayetteville
Tulsa
Oklahoma City
Clinton
Lawton
McAlester
Amarillo
Red
Durant
Lubbock
Wichita Falls
Paris
Texarkana
Fort Worth
Dallas
Abilene
Tyler
Shreveport
Ciudad Juarez
El Paso
Odessa
Midland
Nueva Casas Grandes
San Angelo
Waco
Fort Stockton
Texas
Lufkin
EDWARDS PLATEAU
Bryan
Austin
Rio Grande
Del Rio
San Antonio
Houston
Galveston
GULF OF MEXICO
Victoria
Piedras Negras
Laredo
Nuevo Laredo
Corpus Christi
McAllen
Brownsville
Matamoros
Reynosa
Sabinas Hidalgo
Monclova
Monterrey
Saltillo
Torreon
MEXICO
Hidalgo del Parral
CHIHUAHUAN DESERT
SIERRA MADRE OCCIDENTAL
SIERRA MADRE ORIENTAL
Nacozari
Villa Ahumada
Chihuahua
Delicias
Hermosillo
Guaymas
Ciudad Obregon
Navojoa
Los Mochis
Cerro Mohinora 13,097
Culiacan
SONORAN DESERT
BAJA CALIFORNIA
Gulf of California
Eugenia Point
Loreto
La Paz
False Cape
San Lucas
Tropic of Cancer
Durango
Concepcion del Oro
Mazatlan
Fresnillo
Zacatecas
Ciudad Victoria
San Luis Potosi
Ciudad Mante
Tampico
Aguascalientes
Leon
Guadalajara
Lake Chapala
Irapuato
Queretaro
Cape Corrientes
Pachuca
Colima 14,003
Colima
Uruapan
Mexico City
Toluca
Puebla
Jalapa
Iztaccihuatl 17,343
Citlaltepetl 18,700
Veracruz
Cuernavaca
Popocatepetl 17,887
Orizaba
Bay of Campeche
PACIFIC OCEAN
ALASKA....See page 485
Niihau
Kauai
Lihue
Haleiwa
Oahu
Molokai
Kahului
Honolulu
Lanai
Maui
Hawaii
Honokaa
Mauna Kea 13,796
Hilo
Mauna Loa 13,680
Hawaii
Naalehu
PACIFIC OCEAN

UNITED STATES, CANADA, MEXICO
Elevation
Meters
Feet
2,000
6,560
1,000
3,280
500
1,640
200
656
0
0
Below Sea Level
Below Sea Level
0
250
500 Miles
0
250
500
750 Kilometers
85°
80°
75°
70°
65°
50°
60°
45°
40°
35°
25°
20°
90°
James Bay
Waskaganish
Moosonee
CANADIAN SHIELD
CANADA
Sept-Iles
Port-Cartier
Anticosti I.
Gulf of St. Lawrence
Channel-Port aux Basques
Gaspe
Baie-Comeau
Matane
Causapscal
Cape Breton I.
Sydney
Chibougamau
Mistassini
Alma
Dalhousie
Bathurst
Prince Edward I.
Charlottetown
Matagami
Chicoutimi
Rimouski
Newcastle
Edmundston
Lake Nipigon
Geraldton
Hearst
Kapuskasing
Riviere-du-Loup
Grand Falls
New Glasgow
Canso
Iroquois Falls
Caribou
Moncton
Amherst
Nipigon
Marathon
Timmins
Rouyn-Noranda
Val-d'Or
Quebec
Houlton
Fredericton
Truro
NOVA SCOTIA
Thunder Bay
Kirkland Lake
Shawinigan
Trois-Rivieres
St. Lawrence
Mt. Katahdin 5,267
Saint John
Dartmouth
Halifax
Wawa
Chapleau
New Liskeard
St.-Georges
Calais
Bay of Fundy
Lake Superior
Mont-Laurier
Maine
Sault Ste. Marie
Sudbury
North Bay
Deep River
Sherbrooke
Bangor
Digby
Houghton
Montreal
Bar Harbor
Yarmouth
Shelburne
Cape Sable
Elliot Lake
Pembroke
Hull
Ottawa
Cornwall
Mt. Washington 6,288
Augusta
Marquette
Sault Ste. Marie
Parry Sound
Georgian Bay
Burlington
Montpelier
Vt.
N.H.
Iron Mountain
Cheboygan
Bracebridge
Kingston
Portland
Wisconsin
Lake Huron
Owen Sound
Peterborough
New York
ADIRONDACK MTS.
Rutland
Portsmouth
Alpena
Barrie
Wausau
Traverse City
Oshawa
Lake Ontario
Concord
Manchester
Green Bay
Lake Michigan
Toronto
Syracuse
Mass.
Boston
Appleton
Michigan
Kitchener
Rochester
Albany
Springfield
Cape Cod
La Crosse
Saginaw
Hamilton
Niagara Falls
New Bedford
Madison
Grand Rapids
Flint
London
Buffalo
Hartford
R.I.
Providence
Sarnia
Binghamton
Long Island Sound
Lansing
New Haven
Conn.
Milwaukee
Detroit
Windsor
Lake Erie
Erie
Scranton
Newark
Long I.
Rockford
Kalamazoo
Cleveland
Pa.
MOUNTAINS
Allentown
New York City
Chicago
South Bend
Toledo
Youngstown
Trenton
N.J.
Gary
Akron
Davenport
Fort Wayne
Altoona
Harrisburg
Philadelphia
Rock Island
Mansfield
Wheeling
Wilmington
Peoria
Indiana
Ohio
Pittsburgh
Del.
Dover
ATLANTIC OCEAN
Muncie
Dayton
Columbus
Hagerstown
Md.
Baltimore
Champaign
Parkersburg
Annapolis
Spruce Knob 4,861
Washington, D.C.
Indianapolis
Cincinnati
Salisbury
Springfield
Illinois
Ohio
Charleston
W.Va.
Chesapeake Bay
Bloomington
Charlottesville
St. Louis
Louisville
Frankfort
Huntington
Richmond
Newport News
Carbondale
Evansville
Lexington
Virginia
Norfolk
Cape Girardeau
Owensboro
Kentucky
Roanoke
Poplar Bluff
Bowling Green
Greensboro
Raleigh
North Carolina
Paducah
APPALACHIAN
Cape Hatteras
Johnson City
Winston-Salem
Nashville
Knoxville
Fayetteville
Jackson
Tennessee
Asheville
Mt. Mitchell 6,684
Charlotte
New Bern
Memphis
Chattanooga
Greenville
Wilmington
Huntsville
Columbia
Florence
Tupelo
Tennessee
Gadsden
Athens
Atlanta
South Carolina
Birmingham
Augusta
Columbus
Mississippi
Greenville
Tuscaloosa
Macon
Charleston
Mississippi
Montgomery
Columbus
Georgia
ATLANTIC COASTAL PLAIN
Meridian
Savannah
Jackson
Alabama
Albany
Brunswick
Natchez
Dothan
Valdosta
PLAIN
Hattiesburg
Jacksonville
Mobile
Biloxi
Pensacola
Tallahassee
Baton Rouge
Panama City
St. Augustine
Lafayette
New Orleans
Gainesville
Daytona Beach
Morgan City
Orlando
Cape Canaveral
Tampa
Melbourne
St. Petersburg
Florida
Lake Okeechobee
Sarasota
West Palm Beach
Fort Myers
Fort Lauderdale
Miami
Cape Sable
THE BAHAMAS
Gulf of Mexico
Key West
Florida Keys
Straits of Florida
CUBA
DOMINICAN REPUBLIC
HAITI
Cancun
Merida
Cozumel I.
Campeche
YUCATAN PENINSULA
JAMAICA

ATLANTIC
OCEAN
Caribbean
Sea
PACIFIC
Tropic of Cancer
Equator
THE BAHAMAS
Turks & Caicos Is. (U.K.)
CUBA
Havana
Santa Clara
Camaguey
Holguin
Guantanamo
Santiago de Cuba
Isle of Youth
Cayman Is. (U.K.)
JAMAICA
Montego Bay
Kingston
HAITI
Cap-Haitien
Port-au-Prince
DOMINICAN REPUBLIC
Santiago
Pico Duarte 10,417
Santo Domingo
San Juan
Ponce
Puerto Rico (U.S.)
Virgin Islands (U.S., U.K.)
Anguilla (U.K.)
ST. KITTS & NEVIS
Montserrat (U.K.)
ANTIGUA & BARBUDA
Guadeloupe (Fr.)
DOMINICA
Martinique (Fr.)
SAINT LUCIA
BARBADOS
ST. VINCENT & THE GRENADINES
GRENADA
TRINIDAD & TOBAGO
Port-of-Spain
Aruba (Neth.)
Curacao (Neth.)
Bonaire (Neth.)
Margarita Island
MEXICO
BELIZE
Belize City
Belmopan
Gulf of Honduras
GUATEMALA
Guatemala
Volcan Tajumulco 13,845
Escuintla
Santa Ana
EL SALVADOR
San Salvador
HONDURAS
San Pedro Sula
La Ceiba
Tegucigalpa
Cerro Las Minas 9,347
MOSQUITO COAST
NICARAGUA
Managua
Leon
Granada
Lake Nicaragua
COSTA RICA
San Jose
Puntarenas
Limon
Volcan Irazu 11,260
Volcan Baru 11,401
PANAMA
David
Colon
Panama
ISTHMUS OF PANAMA
Gulf of Panama
COLOMBIA
Barranquilla
Santa Marta
Cartagena
Pico Cristobal Colon 18,947
Valledupar
Sincelejo
Monteria
Barrancabermeja
Medellin
Cucuta
Bucaramanga
Tunja
Bogota
Villavicencio
Manizales
Pereira
Armenia
Ibague
Neiva
Cali
Palmira
Buenaventura
Popayan
Nevada del Huila 18,865
Pasto
Magdalena
LLANOS
VENEZUELA
Maracaibo
Lake Maracaibo
Cabimas
Coro
Valera
Merida
Pico Bolivar 16,427
San Cristobal
Maracay
Valencia
Barquisimeto
Caracas
Barcelona
Cumana
Maturin
El Tigre
San Fernando de Apure
Ciudad Bolivar
Ciudad Guayana
Puerto Ayacucho
Angel Falls
Orinoco
GUIANA HIGHLANDS
Mt. Roraima 9,094
GUYANA
Georgetown
New Amsterdam
SURINAME
Paramaribo
French Guiana (Fr.)
Kourou
Cayenne
ECUADOR
Esmeraldas
Quito
Cotopaxi 19,347
Ambato
Portoviejo
Chimborazo 20,561
Guayaquil
Cuenca
Machala
Galapagos Islands (Ecuador)
PERU
Tumbes
Talara
Sullana
Piura
Aguja Point
Chiclayo
Cajamarca
Trujillo
Chimbote
Nev. Huascaran 22,205
Nev. Yerupaja 21,709
Huanuco
Cerro de Pasco
Pucallpa
Huancayo
Ayacucho
Cuzco
Callao
Lima
Ica
Iquitos
Yurimaguas
Maranon
Ucayali
LA MONTANA
Puerto Maldonado
ANDES
Putumayo
BRAZIL
Manaus
Amazon
Negro
Boa Vista
Benjamin Constant
Jurua
Purus
Cruzeiro do Sul
Rio Branco
Cobija
Riberalta
Guajara-Mirim
Porto Velho
Madeira
Mamore
Beni
Guapore
Trinidad
SELVAS
Santarem
Tapajos
Xingu
Macapa
Marajo Island
Belem
Tocantins
Imperatriz
Gurupi
Sao Luis
Parnaiba
Teresina
Fortaleza
Natal
Joao Pessoa
Recife
Maceio
Aracaju
Salvador
Campina Grande
Juazeiro do Norte
Feira de Santana
Sao Francisco
BRAZILIAN
MATO GROSSO
Araguaia

SOUTH AMERICA
CENTRAL AMERICA
& THE CARIBBEAN
Elevation
Meters
Feet
4,000
13,120
2,000
6,560
500
1,640
200
656
0
0
Below Sea Level
Below Sea Level
0
250
500
750 Miles
0
250
500
750
1,000 Kilometers
Tropic of Capricorn
20°
30°
40°
50°
100°
90°
80°
70°
60°
50°
40°
30°
20°
CHILE
ARGENTINA
PARAGUAY
URUGUAY
ANDES
ATACAMA DESERT
GRAN CHACO
PAMPAS
CAMPOS
PATAGONIA
Iquique
Potosi
Tarija
Calama
Antofagasta
San Salvador de Jujuy
Salta
San Miguel de Tucuman
Cerro Ojos del Salado 22,572
San Felix Island (Chile)
San Ambrosio Island (Chile)
Copiapo
Cerro Bonete 22,546
Catamarca
Santiago del Estero
La Rioja
La Serena
Highest point in South America
Cerro Aconcagua 22,834
Cordoba
San Juan
Mendoza
Rio Cuarto
Vina del Mar
Valparaiso
Santiago
Cerro Tupungato 22,310
San Bernardo
Rancagua
San Rafael
Juan Fernandez Islands (Chile)
Talca
Chillan
Talcahuano
Concepcion
Temuco
Valdivia
Osorno
Puerto Montt
San Carlos de Bariloche
Chiloe Island
Esquel
Chonos Archipelago
Comodoro Rivadavia
Taitao Peninsula
Neuquen
Bahia Blanca
Punta Alta
Viedma
San Matias Gulf
Valdes Peninsula
Lowest point in South America
Trelew
Rawson
Gulf of San Jorge
Cape Tres Puntas
Bahia Grande
Rio Gallegos
Str. of Magellan
Punta Arenas
Tierra del Fuego
Ushuaia
Cape Horn
Stanley
Falkland Islands (U.K.)
(Islas Malvinas)
South Georgia (U.K.)
Pilcomayo
Paraguay
Concepcion
Asuncion
Formosa
Coronel Oviedo
Iguazu Falls
Encarnacion
Resistencia
Corrientes
Posadas
Santo Tome
Uruguay
Curuzu Cuatia
Santa Fe
Concordia
Parana
Salto
Paysandu
Rosario
Parana
Junin
Buenos Aires
Avellaneda
La Plata
Santa Rosa
Mar del Plata
Minas
Montevideo
Rio de la Plata
Melo
Rivera
Pelotas
Santa Maria
Passo Fundo
Caxias do Sul
Porto Alegre
Florianopolis
Joinvile
Curitiba
Ponta Grossa
Campo Grande
Presidente Prudente
Parana
Londrina
Bauru
Sao Jose do Rio Preto
Grande
Ribeirao Preto
Campinas
Jundiai
Sorocaba
Sao Paulo
Santos
Uberlandia
Belo Horizonte
Pico da Bandeira 9,482
Juiz de Fora
Volta Redonda
Niteroi
Rio de Janeiro
Vitoria
Valadares

EUROPE
Elevation
Meters
Feet
4,000
13,120
2,000
6,560
500
1,640
200
656
0
0
Below Sea Level
Below Sea Level
Greenland (Den.)
Arctic Circle
ICELAND
Keflavik
Reykjavik
Akureyri
Hekla 4,892
Norwegian Sea
North Cape
Hammerfest
Tromso
Ivalo
LAPLAND
Murmansk
Arctic Circle
Kiruna
Bodo
Rovaniemi
Arkhangelsk
Lulea
Oulu
Belomorsk
NORWAY
FINLAND
Gulf of Bothnia
Umea
Trondheim
Ostersund
Kuopio
Vaasa
Lake Onega
Petrozavodsk
Alesund
SWEDEN
Faeroe Is. (Den.)
Shetland Is. (U.K.)
Glittertind 8,113
Tampere
Lake Ladoga
Bergen
Gavle
Aland Is. (Fin.)
Turku
Helsinki
Orkney Is.
Gulf of Finland
St. Petersburg
Oslo
Uppsala
Tallinn
Novgorod
Stavanger
Skien
Stockholm
ESTONIA
ATLANTIC OCEAN
Hebrides
Inverness
Aberdeen
Linkoping
Tartu
RUSSIA
Kristiansand
Jonkoping
Glasgow
Dundee
Edinburgh
Goteborg
Baltic Sea
Gotland (Swe.)
Riga
LATVIA
North Sea
Alborg
Jutland
Arhus
Belfast
UNITED KINGDOM
IRELAND
Newcastle
Helsingborg
Daugavpils
Dublin
Liverpool
Leeds
Copenhagen
Malmo
Klaipeda
LITHUANIA
Smolensk
DENMARK
Odense
Kaunas
Vitsyebsk
Vilnius
Limerick
Cork
Manchester
Sheffield
Bornholm (Den.)
(RUSSIA)
Kaliningrad
Minsk
Mahilyow
Bryansk
Birmingham
Hamburg
Rostock
Gdansk
Szczecin
Bialystok
BELARUS
NETHERLANDS
Cardiff
London
Amsterdam
Bremen
POLAND
Homyel
Bristol
Thames
Hague
Hannover
Berlin
Land's End
Plymouth
Portsmouth
Rotterdam
Elbe
Poznan
Warsaw
Brest
Rhine
Essen
Magdeburg
Oder
Wisla
English Channel
Antwerp
Brussels
Cologne
Leipzig
Lodz
Dnieper
Channel Is. (U.K.)
BELGIUM
Bonn
GERMANY
Dresden
Wroclaw
Lublin
Kiev
Le Havre
Rouen
Katowice
Brest
Luxembourg
Frankfurt
Prague
Ostrava
Kracow
UKRAINE
Seine
Paris
LUX.
Nurnberg
CZECH REP.
Lviv
Vynnytsya
Nantes
Orleans
Mannheim
Brno
CARPATHIAN MOUNTAINS
Dniester
Stuttgart
Strasbourg
Danube
SLOVAKIA
Kosice
Loire
Tours
Dijon
Munich
Linz
Vienna
Bratislava
Miskolc
MOLDOVA
Basel
Zurich
Salzburg
Debrecen
Chisinau
Iasi
FRANCE
Bern
LIECH.
AUSTRIA
Budapest
Bay of Biscay
Limoges
SWITZ.
Graz
HUNGARY
Cluj-Napoca
Odesa
Geneva
La Coruna
Bordeaux
Lyon
Mt. Blanc 15,771
Klausrhorn 14,690
Milan
SLOVE.
Ljubljana
Pecs
ROMANIA
Gijon
Brasov
Vigo
Grenoble
Trieste
CROATIA
Timisoara
Bilbao
Garonne
Po
Verona
Venice
Zagreb
Belgrade
Bucharest
Constanta
Oporto
San Sebastian
Toulouse
Turin
Genoa
BOS. & HERZ.
Valladolid
PYRENEES
Rhone
Nice
Bologna
DINARIC ALPS
SERBIA
Danube
Black Sea
Coimbra
Pico de Aneto 11,168
Marseille
MONACO
SAN MARINO
Sarajevo
Ruse
Varna
PORTUGAL
Ebro
IBERIAN
ANDORRA
Florence
Split
YUGO.
BALKAN
Burgas
Tagus
Madrid
Zaragoza
Corsica (Fr.)
Elba
APENNINES
Adriatic Sea
Dubrovnik
MONT.
Sofia
BULGARIA
Lisbon
SPAIN
Barcelona
Tiber
Skopje
Plovdiv
Ajaccio
Rome
Tirana
PENINSULA
MACE.
Cape St. Vincent
PENINSULA
Cordoba
Valencia
ITALY
ALBANIA
Thessaloniki
Palma
Naples
Bari
Vlore
Olympus 9,570
TURKEY
Seville
Balearic Is. (Sp.)
Sardinia (It.)
Vesuvius 4,202
Granada
Alicante
Cagliari
Tyrrhenian Sea
Corfu
Larisa
Volos
Aegean Sea
Cadiz
Malaga
Euboea
Strait of Gibraltar
Gibraltar (U.K.)
Mediterranean Sea
GREECE
Palermo
Messina
Ionian Sea
Athens
Patras
Etna 11,053
Catania
Peloponnesus
Sicily
Rhodes
MALTA
Iraklion
Crete
AFRICA
0
250
500 Miles
0
250
500
750 Kilometers

RUSSIA, UKRAINE & CENTRAL ASIA
Elevation
Meters
Feet
4,000
13,120
2,000
6,560
500
1,640
200
656
0
0
Below Sea Level
Below Sea Level
ARCTIC OCEAN
PACIFIC OCEAN
Chukchi Sea
Bering Strait
Bering Sea
Providenia
Wrangel I.
Anadyr
East Siberian Sea
Cherskiy
KOLYMA MOUNTAINS
KAMCHATKA PENINSULA
Palana
Shiveluch 10,771
Klyuchevskaya 15,584
Karymsky 4,869
Petropavlovsk-Kamchatskiy
Shelikhov Gulf
Magadan
Susuman
Zyryanka
Kolyma
Indigirka
Okhotsk
Sea of Okhotsk
Alaid 7,662
Sarycheva 4,960
Kuril Islands
Okha
Sakhalin
Yuzhno-Sakhalinsk
Tiatia 6,013
Tatar Strait
Komsomolsk
Khabarovsk
Amur
Svobodnyy
Blagoveshchensk
Ussuriysk
Vladivostok
Sea of Japan
STANOVOY RANGE
Aldan
Berkakit
Tynda
Yakutsk
Vilyuysk
Verkhoyansk
VERKHOYANSK RA.
Tiksi
Lena
New Siberian Islands
Laptev Sea
Nordvik
Severnaya Zemlya
Franz Josef Land
Barents Sea
Novaya Zemlya
Kara Sea
Dikson
Norilsk
CENTRAL SIBERIAN PLATEAU
Tura
Lower Tunguska
Lensk
Bodaybo
Ust-Kut
Lake Baykal
Bratsk
Angara
YABLONOVYY RANGE
Chita
Ulan-Ude
Irkutsk
SAYAN MTS.
Tulun
Kansk
Krasnoyarsk
Lesosibirsk
Yenisey
RUSSIA
WEST SIBERIAN PLAIN
Novyy Urengoy
Surgut
Nizhnevartovsk
Ob
Kolpashevo
Tomsk
Achinsk
Kemerovo
Novokuznetsk
Novosibirsk
Barnaul
Tashtagol
Semey
Oskemen
Irtysh
Tara
Omsk
Pavlodar
Qaraghandy
KAZAKH UPLAND
Ayaguz
Aqmola
KAZAKHSTAN
Zhezqazghan
Balqash
Lake Balkhash
Taldy-Kurgan
Alma-Ata
Issyk-Kol
Pobedy Pk. 24,406
Zhambyl
Bishkek
KYRGYZSTAN
Namangan
Andijon
Lenina Pk. 23,405
TAJIKISTAN
PAMIRS
Communism Pk. 24,590
Dushanbe
Farghona
Samarqand
Tashkent
Shymkent
Bukhoro
Qyzylorda
Syr Darya
KYZYL KUM DESERT
Amu Darya
Aral Sea
UZBEKISTAN
Nukus
Urgench
TURKMENISTAN
KARA KUM DESERT
Ashgabat
Krasnovodsk
Caspian Sea
Aqtau
Atyrau
Makhachkala
Groznyy
Baku
AZERBAIJAN
Ganja
ARMENIA
Yerevan
Tbilisi
GEORGIA
Batumi
Mt. Elbrus 18,510
Highest point in Europe
CAUCASUS MTS.
Stavropol
Krasnodar
Sochi
Black Sea
CRIMEA PENINSULA
Sevastopol
Berdyansk
Mariupol
Zaporizhzhya
Kryvyy Rih
Odesa
UKRAINE
Vynnytsya
Lviv
Kiev
Dnieper
Kharkiv
Dnipropetrovsk
Donetsk
Luhansk
Rostov
Volgograd
Astrakhan
Saratov
Volga
Tolyatti
Samara
Penza
Voronezh
Lipetsk
Kursk
Bryansk
Tula
Ryazan
Moscow
Smolensk
Tver
Yaroslavl
Ivanovo
Vologda
Cherepovets
Novgorod
St. Petersburg
Petrozavodsk
Lake Ladoga
Lake Onega
Belomorsk
Arkhangelsk
Murmansk
KOLA PENINSULA
Baltic Sea
Arctic Circle
EUROPE
NORTH EUROPEAN PLAIN
N. Dvina
Kotlas
Syktyvkar
Ukhta
Inta
Vorkuta
Salekhard
Mt. Narodnaya 6,217
URAL MOUNTAINS
Kirov
Nizhniy Novgorod
Kazan
Kama
Berezniki
Perm
Izhevsk
Serov
Nizhniy Tagil
Yekaterinburg
Tyumen
Tobolsk
Kurgan
Chelyabinsk
Magnitogorsk
Petropavl
Ufa
Ural
Oral
Orenburg
Orsk
SOUTH ASIA
0 250 500 750 Miles
0 250 500 750 1,000 Kilometers

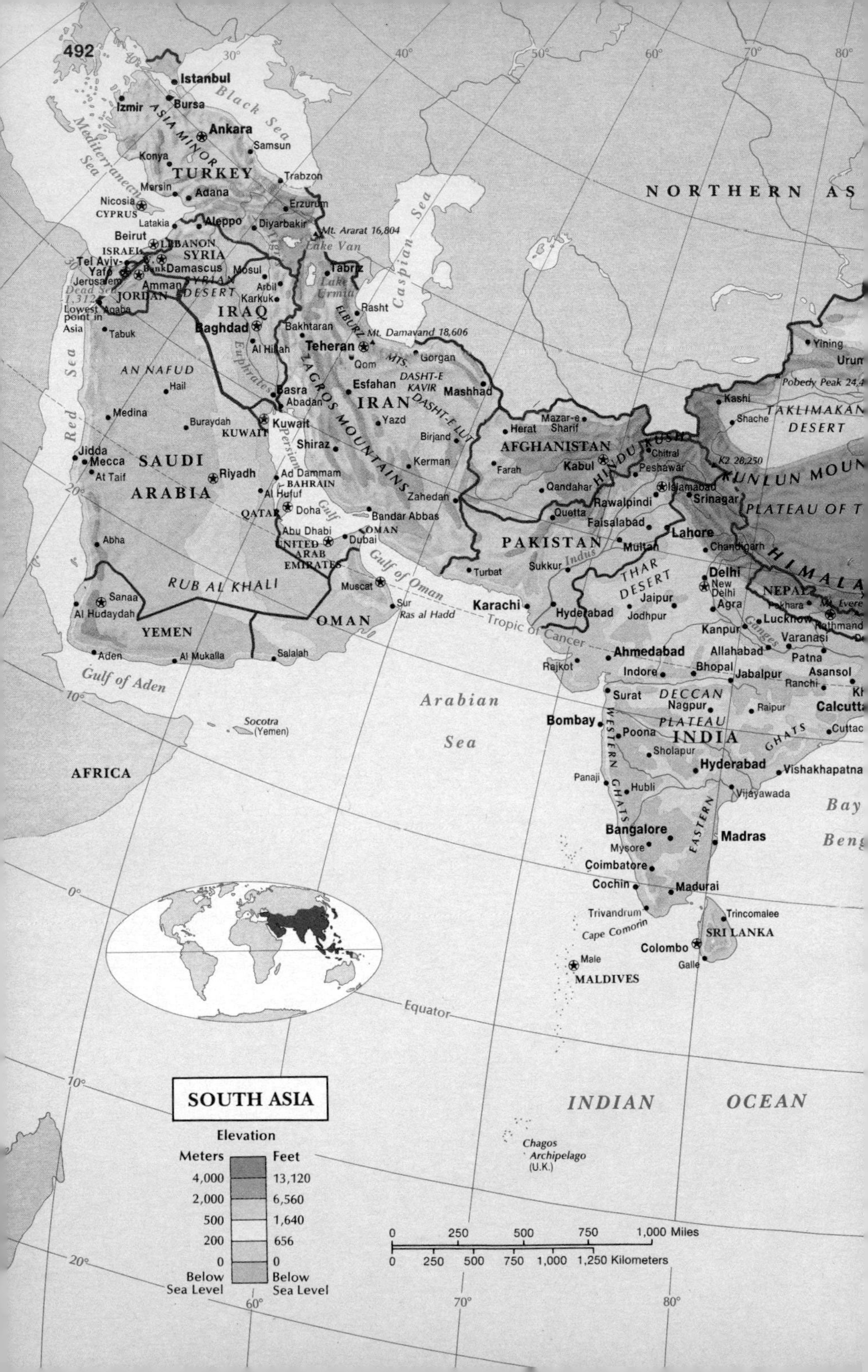
SOUTH ASIA
Elevation
Meters
Feet
4,000
13,120
2,000
6,560
500
1,640
200
656
0
0
Below Sea Level
Below Sea Level
0 250 500 750 1,000 Miles
0 250 500 750 1,000 1,250 Kilometers
NORTHERN ASIA
Black Sea
Mediterranean Sea
Caspian Sea
Red Sea
Persian Gulf
Gulf of Oman
Gulf of Aden
Arabian Sea
Bay of Bengal
INDIAN OCEAN
Tropic of Cancer
Equator
AFRICA
TURKEY
ASIA MINOR
CYPRUS
SYRIA
LEBANON
ISRAEL
JORDAN
IRAQ
IRAN
KUWAIT
SAUDI ARABIA
BAHRAIN
QATAR
UNITED ARAB EMIRATES
OMAN
YEMEN
AFGHANISTAN
PAKISTAN
INDIA
NEPAL
SRI LANKA
MALDIVES
Istanbul
Izmir
Bursa
Ankara
Samsun
Konya
Trabzon
Mersin
Adana
Nicosia
Erzurum
Latakia
Aleppo
Diyarbakir
Mt. Ararat 16,804
Lake Van
Beirut
Damascus
Tel Aviv-Yafo
Jerusalem
Amman
Dead Sea -1,312 Lowest point in Asia
Aqaba
Tabuk
SYRIAN DESERT
Mosul
Arbil
Karkuk
Tabriz
Lake Urmia
Rasht
ELBURZ MTS.
Mt. Damavand 18,606
Baghdad
Bakhtaran
Teheran
Al Hillah
Euphrates
Gorgan
Qom
AN NAFUD
Hail
Esfahan
DASHT-E KAVIR
Mashhad
Basra
Abadan
ZAGROS MOUNTAINS
DASHT-E LUT
Medina
Buraydah
Kuwait
Yazd
Birjand
Jidda
Mecca
At Taif
Shiraz
Kerman
Riyadh
Ad Dammam
Al Hufuf
Doha
Zahedan
Bandar Abbas
Abu Dhabi
Dubai
Abha
RUB AL KHALI
Muscat
Sanaa
Al Hudaydah
Sur
Ras al Hadd
Aden
Al Mukalla
Salalah
Socotra (Yemen)
Herat
Mazar-e Sharif
HINDU KUSH
Kabul
Farah
Chitral
Peshawar
Qandahar
Islamabad
Rawalpindi
Quetta
Faisalabad
Lahore
Multan
Indus
Sukkur
Turbat
Karachi
Hyderabad
THAR DESERT
Jaipur
Jodhpur
Yining
Urum
Pobedy Peak 24,4
Kashi
TAKLIMAKAN DESERT
Shache
K2 28,250
KUNLUN MOUN
Srinagar
PLATEAU OF T
Chandigarh
HIMALA
Delhi
New Delhi
Agra
Pokhara
Mt. Evere
Kathmand
Lucknow
Ganges
Kanpur
Varanasi
Allahabad
Patna
Asansol
Ranchi
Ahmedabad
Rajkot
Indore
Bhopal
Jabalpur
Surat
DECCAN PLATEAU
Nagpur
Raipur
Calcutta
Cuttac
Bombay
Poona
Sholapur
WESTERN GHATS
EASTERN GHATS
Hyderabad
Vishakhapatna
Panaji
Hubli
Vijayawada
Bangalore
Madras
Mysore
Coimbatore
Cochin
Madurai
Trivandrum
Cape Comorin
Trincomalee
Colombo
Galle
Male
Chagos Archipelago (U.K.)
30°
40°
50°
60°
70°
80°
20°
10°
0°

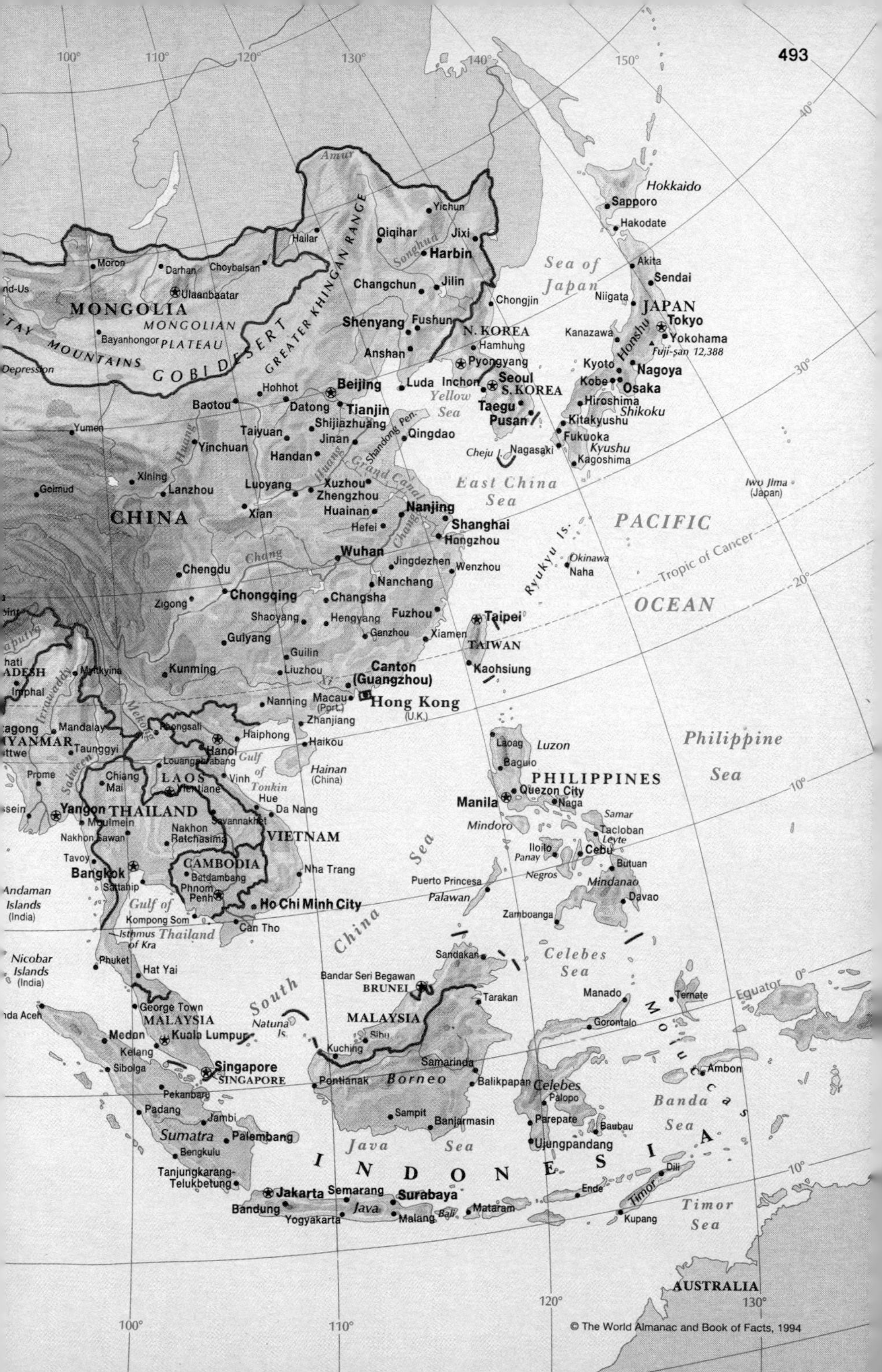
100°
110°
120°
130°
140°
150°
40°
30°
20°
10°
0°
Amur
Hokkaido
Sapporo
Hakodate
Yichun
Hailar
Qiqihar
Jixi
Songhua
Harbin
GREATER KHINGAN RANGE
Moron
Darhan
Choybalsan
Ulaanbaatar
MONGOLIA
MONGOLIAN
PLATEAU
Bayanhongor
MOUNTAINS
GOBI DESERT
Depression
Sea of
Japan
Akita
Sendai
Niigata
JAPAN
Tokyo
Yokohama
Fuji-san 12,388
Kanazawa
Honshu
Changchun
Jilin
Chongjin
Shenyang
Fushun
N. KOREA
Hamhung
Anshan
Pyongyang
Kyoto
Nagoya
Kobe
Osaka
Hohhot
Beijing
Luda
Inchon
Seoul
S. KOREA
Baotou
Datong
Tianjin
Yellow
Sea
Taegu
Pusan
Hiroshima
Shikoku
Kitakyushu
Fukuoka
Kyushu
Kagoshima
Yumen
Taiyuan
Shijiazhuang
Jinan
Shandong Pen.
Qingdao
Yinchuan
Handan
Huang
Cheju I.
Nagasaki
Xining
Grand Canal
Golmud
Lanzhou
Luoyang
Xuzhou
Zhengzhou
East China
Sea
Iwo Jima
(Japan)
Xian
Huainan
Nanjing
CHINA
Hefei
Shanghai
PACIFIC
Hangzhou
Chang
Wuhan
Ryukyu Is.
Okinawa
Naha
Tropic of Cancer
Chengdu
Jingdezhen
Wenzhou
Nanchang
Zigong
Chongqing
Changsha
OCEAN
Fuzhou
Taipei
Shaoyang
Hengyang
Ganzhou
Xiamen
TAIWAN
Guiyang
Guilin
Kaohsiung
Liuzhou
Kunming
Canton
(Guangzhou)
Myitkyina
Xi
Imphal
Irrawaddy
Nanning
Macau
(Port.)
Hong Kong
(U.K.)
Mekong
Mandalay
Phongsali
Zhanjiang
Taunggyi
Haiphong
Hanoi
Haikou
Luzon
Laoag
Philippine
Sea
Louangphrabang
Gulf
of
Tonkin
Baguio
Salween
Prome
Chiang
Mai
LAOS
Vinh
Hainan
(China)
PHILIPPINES
Vientiane
Quezon City
Manila
Hue
Naga
Yangon
THAILAND
Da Nang
Samar
Moulmein
Savannakhet
Mindoro
Tacloban
Nakhon Sawan
Nakhon
Ratchasima
VIETNAM
Leyte
Sea
Iloilo
Cebu
Tavoy
CAMBODIA
Panay
Bangkok
Batdambang
Nha Trang
Negros
Butuan
Andaman
Islands
(India)
Sattahip
Phnom
Penh
Puerto Princesa
Mindanao
Palawan
Davao
Gulf of
Ho Chi Minh City
Kompong Som
Zamboanga
Isthmus
of Kra
Thailand
Can Tho
China
Nicobar
Islands
(India)
Phuket
Hat Yai
Sandakan
Celebes
Sea
South
Bandar Seri Begawan
BRUNEI
Manado
Ternate
Equator
George Town
MALAYSIA
Tarakan
Natuna
Is.
MALAYSIA
Gorontalo
Moluccas
Medan
Kuala Lumpur
Sibu
Kelang
Kuching
Ambon
Sibolga
Singapore
SINGAPORE
Samarinda
Pontianak
Borneo
Balikpapan
Celebes
Palopo
Banda
Pekanbaru
Padang
Jambi
Sampit
Parepare
Sumatra
Palembang
Banjarmasin
Baubau
Sea
Java
Sea
Ujungpandang
Bengkulu
I N D O N E S I A
Tanjungkarang-
Telukbetung
Dili
Timor
Ende
Jakarta
Semarang
Surabaya
Timor
Bandung
Java
Mataram
Bali
Kupang
Sea
Yogyakarta
Malang
AUSTRALIA

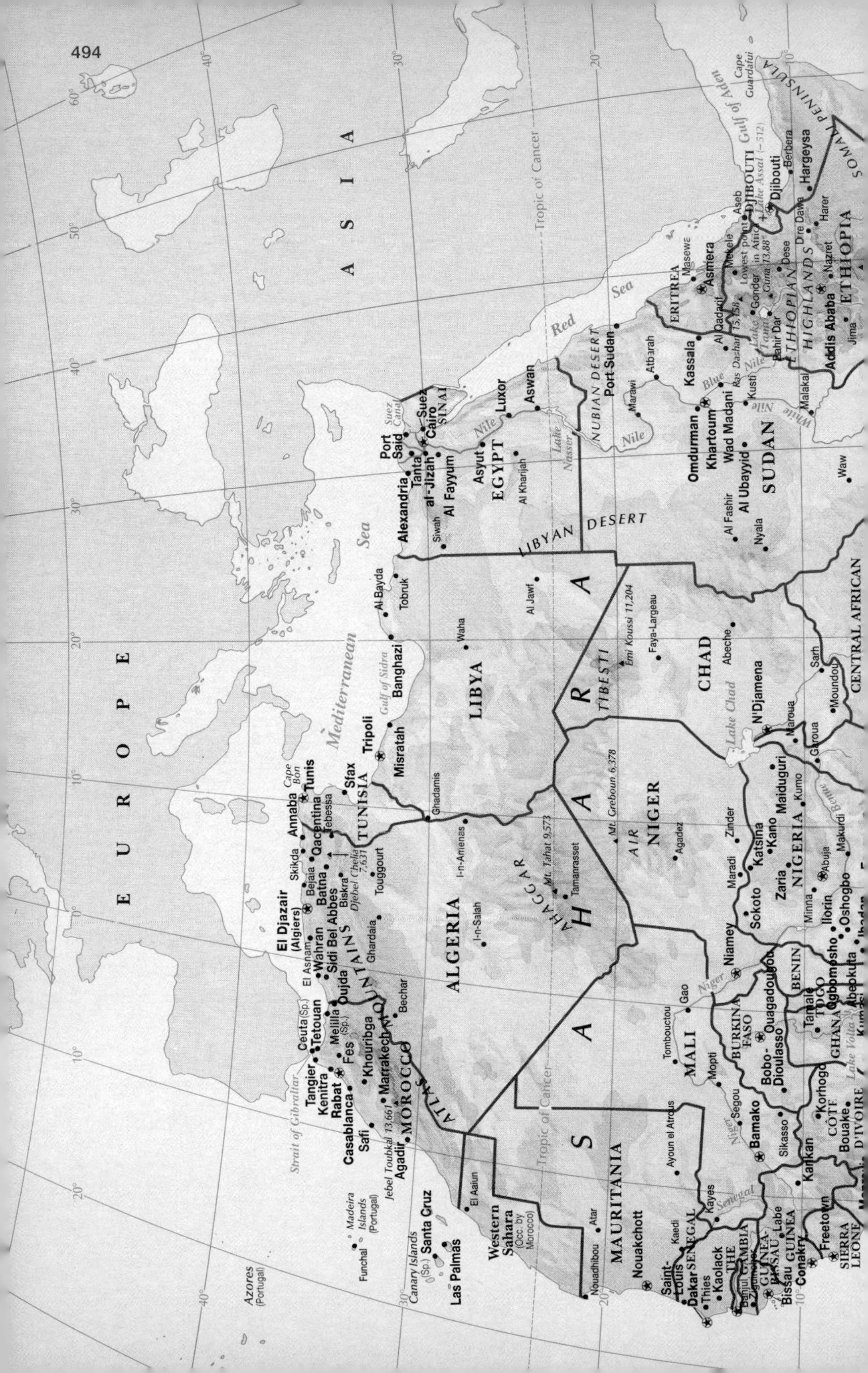
EUROPE
ASIA
Mediterranean Sea
Red Sea
Gulf of Aden
Strait of Gibraltar
Azores (Portugal)
Madeira Islands (Portugal)
Funchal
Canary Islands (Sp.)
Santa Cruz
Las Palmas
Tropic of Cancer
MOROCCO
Tangier
Kenitra
Rabat
Casablanca
Safi
Khouribga
Fes
Marrakech
Agadir
Jebel Toubkal 13,661
Ceuta (Sp.)
Tetouan
Melilla (Sp.)
Oujda
ATLAS MOUNTAINS
ALGERIA
El Djazair (Algiers)
El Asnam
Wahran
Sidi Bel Abbes
Ghardaia
Bechar
Batna
Biskra
Djebel Chelia 7,631
Touggourt
Bejaia
Skikda
Qacentina
Annaba
Tebessa
I-n-Salah
I-n-Amenas
AHAGGAR
Mt. Tahat 9,573
Tamanrasset
TUNISIA
Tunis
Cape Bon
Sfax
Ghadamis
LIBYA
Tripoli
Misratah
Gulf of Sidra
Banghazi
Al Bayda
Tobruk
Waha
Al Jawf
SAHARA
TIBESTI
Emi Koussi 11,204
LIBYAN DESERT
EGYPT
Alexandria
Port Said
Suez Canal
Suez
SINAI
Tanta
Cairo
al-Jizah
Al Fayyum
Siwah
Asyut
Al Kharijah
Luxor
Aswan
Lake Nasser
Nile
NUBIAN DESERT
SUDAN
Port Sudan
Marawi
Atbarah
Kassala
Omdurman
Khartoum
Wad Madani
Al Ubayyid
Al Fashir
Nyala
Kusti
Malakal
Waw
Blue Nile
White Nile
ERITREA
Asmera
Masewe
ETHIOPIA
ETHIOPIAN HIGHLANDS
Mekele
Gonder
Lake Tana
Bahir Dar
Ras Dashan 15,158
Dese
Addis Ababa
Nazret
Dire Dawa
Harer
Jima
Lowest point in Africa
Lake Assal (-512)
DJIBOUTI
Djibouti
Aseb
Berbera
Hargeysa
SOMALI PENINSULA
Cape Guardafui
Western Sahara (Occ. by Morocco)
El Aaiun
MAURITANIA
Nouadhibou
Atar
Nouakchott
Ayoun el Atrous
MALI
Tombouctou
Gao
Mopti
Segou
Bamako
Sikasso
Niger
NIGER
AIR
Mt. Greboun 6,378
Agadez
Zinder
Maradi
Niamey
CHAD
Faya-Largeau
Abeche
Lake Chad
N'Djamena
Sarh
Moundou
CENTRAL AFRICAN
NIGERIA
Sokoto
Katsina
Kano
Zaria
Maiduguri
Abuja
Minna
Ilorin
Oshogbo
Makurdi
Kumo
Maroua
Garoua
Benue
BURKINA FASO
Ouagadougou
Bobo-Dioulasso
BENIN
TOGO
GHANA
Tamale
Lake Volta
Ogbomosho
Abeokuta
CÔTE D'IVOIRE
Korhogo
Bouake
SENEGAL
Saint-Louis
Dakar
Thies
Kaolack
Kaedi
Kayes
Senegal
THE GAMBIA
Banjul
GUINEA-BISSAU
Bissau
GUINEA
Conakry
Labe
Kankan
SIERRA LEONE
Freetown

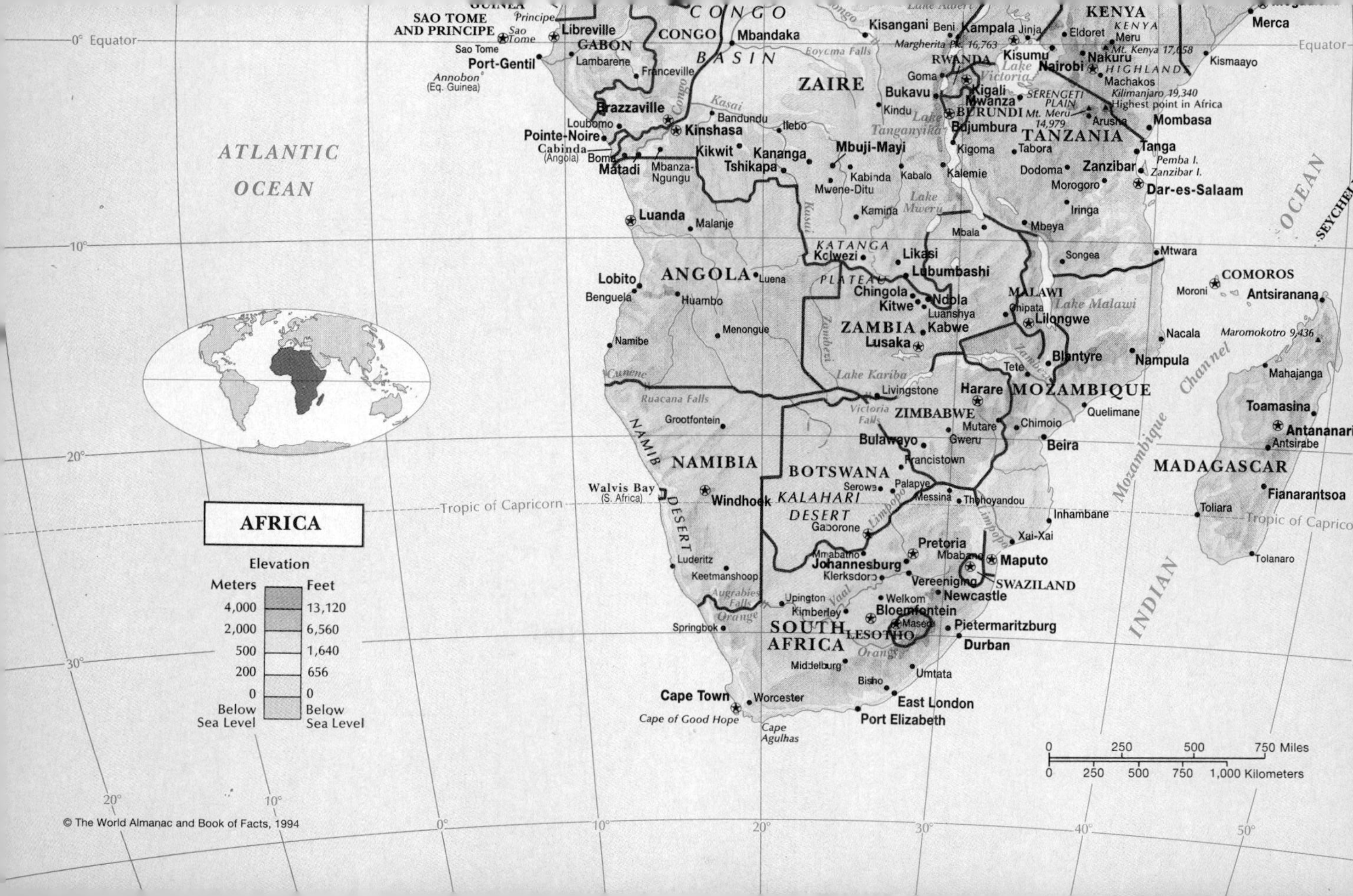
AFRICA
Elevation
Meters
4,000
2,000
500
200
0
Below Sea Level
Feet
13,120
6,560
1,640
656
0
Below Sea Level
0 250 500 750 Miles
0 250 500 750 1,000 Kilometers
ATLANTIC OCEAN
INDIAN OCEAN
0° Equator
Tropic of Capricorn
SAO TOME AND PRINCIPE
Principe
Sao Tome
Annobon (Eq. Guinea)
Port-Gentil
Libreville
GABON
Lambarene
Franceville
CONGO
Brazzaville
Pointe-Noire
Loubomo
Cabinda (Angola)
Boma
Matadi
Kinshasa
BASIN
Mbandaka
ZAIRE
Kisangani
Boyoma Falls
Kasai
Bandundu
Ilebo
Kikwit
Kananga
Tshikapa
Mbanza-Ngungu
Mbuji-Mayi
Kabinda
Mwene-Ditu
Kamina
Kabalo
Kalemie
Bukavu
Kindu
Goma
Beni
Margherita Pk. 16,763
RWANDA
Kigali
BURUNDI
Bujumbura
Lake Tanganyika
Lake Mweru
Lake Victoria
Kampala
Jinja
Kisumu
KENYA
Eldoret
Meru
Nakuru
Nairobi
Mt. Kenya 17,058
KENYA HIGHLANDS
Machakos
Kilimanjaro 19,340
Highest point in Africa
Mombasa
Kismaayo
Merca
SERENGETI PLAIN
Mwanza
Mt. Meru 14,979
Arusha
TANZANIA
Tanga
Pemba I.
Zanzibar I.
Zanzibar
Dar-es-Salaam
Kigoma
Tabora
Dodoma
Morogoro
Iringa
Mbeya
Mbala
Songea
Mtwara
SEYCHELLES
COMOROS
Moroni
Antsiranana
Maromokotro 9,436
Mahajanga
Toamasina
Antananarivo
Antsirabe
MADAGASCAR
Fianarantsoa
Toliara
Tolanaro
Mozambique Channel
Luanda
Malanje
ANGOLA
Luena
Lobito
Benguela
Huambo
Menongue
Namibe
Cunene
Ruacana Falls
KATANGA PLATEAU
Kolwezi
Likasi
Lubumbashi
Chingola
Ndola
Kitwe
Luanshya
ZAMBIA
Kabwe
Lusaka
Zambezi
Lake Kariba
Livingstone
Victoria Falls
MALAWI
Chipata
Lilongwe
Lake Malawi
Blantyre
Nampula
Nacala
Tete
MOZAMBIQUE
Quelimane
Chimoio
Beira
Harare
ZIMBABWE
Mutare
Gweru
Bulawayo
Francistown
Grootfontein
NAMIBIA
NAMIB DESERT
Walvis Bay (S. Africa)
Windhoek
BOTSWANA
KALAHARI DESERT
Serowe
Palapye
Messina
Thohoyandou
Limpopo
Gaborone
Inhambane
Xai-Xai
Pretoria
Mmabatho
Johannesburg
Mbabane
Maputo
SWAZILAND
Klerksdorp
Vereeniging
Newcastle
Luderitz
Keetmanshoop
Augrabies Falls
Orange
Vaal
Upington
Welkom
Kimberley
Bloemfontein
Springbok
SOUTH AFRICA
LESOTHO
Maseru
Pietermaritzburg
Durban
Middelburg
Umtata
Bisho
East London
Cape Town
Worcester
Cape of Good Hope
Cape Agulhas
Port Elizabeth

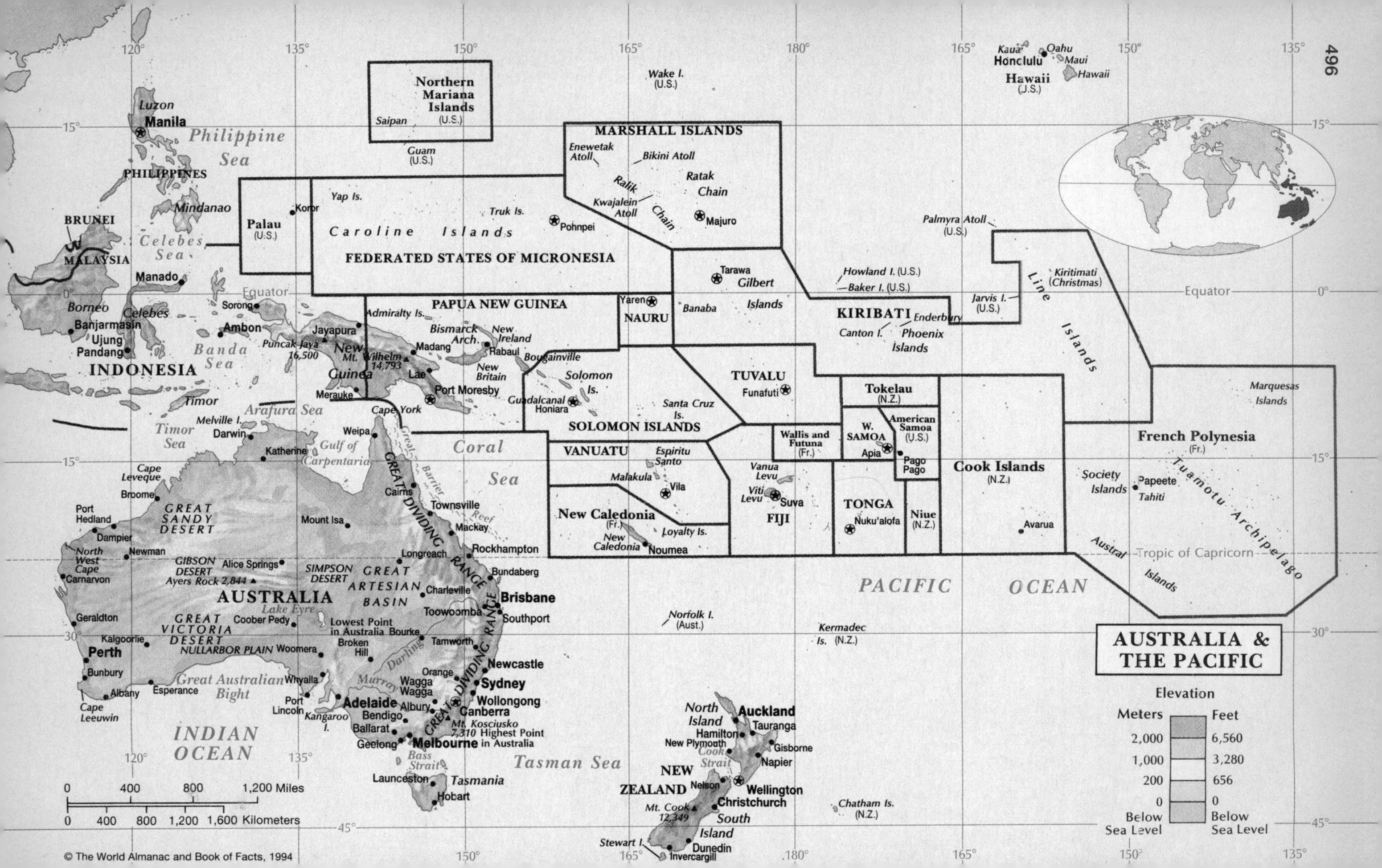
AUSTRALIA & THE PACIFIC
Elevation
Meters
2,000
1,000
200
0
Below Sea Level
Feet
6,560
3,280
656
0
Below Sea Level
0 400 800 1,200 Miles
0 400 800 1,200 1,600 Kilometers
© The World Almanac and Book of Facts, 1994
Northern Mariana Islands (U.S.)
Saipan
Guam (U.S.)
Wake I. (U.S.)
MARSHALL ISLANDS
Enewetak Atoll
Bikini Atoll
Ralik Chain
Ratak Chain
Kwajalein Atoll
Majuro
Palau (U.S.)
Koror
Yap Is.
Truk Is.
Pohnpei
Caroline Islands
FEDERATED STATES OF MICRONESIA
PAPUA NEW GUINEA
Admiralty Is.
Bismarck Arch.
New Ireland
Rabaul
New Britain
Madang
Lae
Port Moresby
Mt. Wilhelm 14,793
New Guinea
Jayapura
Puncak Jaya 16,500
Merauke
Bougainville
Solomon Is.
Guadalcanal
Honiara
SOLOMON ISLANDS
Santa Cruz Is.
NAURU
Yaren
Banaba
Tarawa
Gilbert Islands
KIRIBATI
Howland I. (U.S.)
Baker I. (U.S.)
Canton I.
Enderbury
Phoenix Islands
Jarvis I. (U.S.)
Palmyra Atoll (U.S.)
Line Islands
Kiritimati (Christmas)
Kauai
Honolulu
Oahu
Maui
Hawaii
Hawaii (U.S.)
TUVALU
Funafuti
Tokelau (N.Z.)
W. SAMOA
Apia
American Samoa (U.S.)
Pago Pago
Wallis and Futuna (Fr.)
VANUATU
Espiritu Santo
Malakula
Vila
Vanua Levu
Viti Levu
Suva
FIJI
TONGA
Nuku'alofa
Niue (N.Z.)
Cook Islands (N.Z.)
Avarua
French Polynesia (Fr.)
Marquesas Islands
Society Islands
Papeete
Tahiti
Tuamotu Archipelago
Austral Islands
Tropic of Capricorn
Equator
New Caledonia (Fr.)
New Caledonia
Loyalty Is.
Noumea
PACIFIC OCEAN
Norfolk I. (Aust.)
Kermadec Is. (N.Z.)
Chatham Is. (N.Z.)
Philippine Sea
Luzon
Manila
PHILIPPINES
Mindanao
Celebes Sea
BRUNEI
MALAYSIA
Borneo
Celebes
Manado
Banjarmasin
Ujung Pandang
INDONESIA
Sorong
Ambon
Banda Sea
Timor
Timor Sea
Arafura Sea
Melville I.
Darwin
Katherine
Gulf of Carpentaria
Weipa
Cape York
Coral Sea
Great Barrier Reef
Cairns
Townsville
Mackay
Rockhampton
Bundaberg
Brisbane
Southport
Toowoomba
Charleville
Longreach
Mount Isa
GREAT DIVIDING RANGE
GREAT ARTESIAN BASIN
SIMPSON DESERT
GIBSON DESERT
GREAT SANDY DESERT
GREAT VICTORIA DESERT
NULLARBOR PLAIN
AUSTRALIA
Alice Springs
Ayers Rock 2,844
Lake Eyre
Coober Pedy
Lowest Point in Australia
Bourke
Broken Hill
Woomera
Darling
Murray
Tamworth
Newcastle
Sydney
Wollongong
Canberra
Orange
Wagga Wagga
Albury
Mt. Kosciusko 7,310 Highest Point in Australia
Adelaide
Bendigo
Ballarat
Geelong
Melbourne
Bass Strait
Launceston
Tasmania
Hobart
Tasman Sea
Whyalla
Port Lincoln
Kangaroo I.
Great Australian Bight
Esperance
Albany
Cape Leeuwin
Bunbury
Perth
Kalgoorlie
Geraldton
Carnarvon
North West Cape
Dampier
Newman
Port Hedland
Broome
Cape Leveque
INDIAN OCEAN
NEW ZEALAND
North Island
Auckland
Tauranga
Hamilton
New Plymouth
Gisborne
Napier
Cook Strait
Wellington
Nelson
Christchurch
Mt. Cook 12,349
South Island
Dunedin
Invercargill
Stewart I.

WORLD HISTORY

Prehistory: Our Ancestors Take Over

Homo sapiens. The precise origins of *Homo sapiens,* the species to which all humans belong, are subject to broad speculation based on a small number of fossils, genetic and anatomical studies, and the geological record. But most scientists agree that we evolved from ape-like primate ancestors in a process that began millions of years ago.

Current theories trace the first hominid (human-like primate) to Africa, where 2 lines of hominids appeared 5 to 7 million years ago. One was *Australopithecus,* a social animal, who lived from perhaps 4 to 3 million years ago, and then apparently became extinct.

The 2nd was a human line, *Homo habilis,* a large-brained specimen that walked upright and had a dextrous hand. *Homo habilis* appeared some 2.5 million years ago, lived in semi-permanent camps and had a food-gathering and sharing economy.

Homo erectus, our nearest ancestor, appeared in Africa perhaps 1.75 million years ago, and began spreading into Asia and Europe soon after. It had a fairly large brain and a skeletal structure similar to ours. *Homo erectus* learned to control fire, and probably had primitive language skills. The final brain development to *Homo sapiens* and then to our sub-species *Homo sapiens sapiens* occurred between 500,000 and 50,000 years ago, either in one place — probably Africa — or virtually simultaneously and independently in different places in Africa, Europe, and Asia. There is no question that all modern races are members of the same sub-species, *Homo sapiens sapiens.*

The spread of mankind into the remaining habitable continents probably took place near the end of the last ice age: to the Americas across a land bridge from Asia, and to Australia across the Timor Straits.

Earliest cultures. A variety of cultural modes — in toolmaking, diet, shelter, and possibly social arrangements and spiritual expression, arose as early mankind adapted to different geographic and climatic zones.

Three basic tool-making traditions are recognized by archeologists as arising and often coexisting from one million years ago to the near past: the *chopper tradition,* found largely in E. Asia, with crude chopping tools and simple flake tools; the *flake tradition,* found in Africa and W. Europe, with a variety of small cutting and flaking tools; and the *biface tradition,* found in all of Africa, W. and S. Europe, and S. Asia, producing pointed hand axes chipped on both faces. Later biface sites yield more refined axes and a variety of other tools, weapons, and ornaments using bone, antler, and wood as well as stone.

Only sketchy evidence remains for the different stages in man's increasing control over the environment. Traces of 400,000-year-old covered wood shelters have been found at Nice, France. Scraping tools at Neanderthal sites (200,000-30,000 BC in Europe, N. Africa, the Middle East and Central Asia) suggest the treatment of skins for clothing. Sites from all parts of the world show seasonal migration patterns and exploitation of a wide range of plant and animal food sources.

Painting and decoration, for which there is evidence at the Nice site, flourished along with stone and ivory sculpture after 30,000 years ago; 60 caves in France and 30 in Spain show remarkable examples of wall painting. Other examples have been found in Africa. Proto-religious rites are suggested by these works, and by evidence of ritual cannibalism by Peking Man, 500,000 BC, and of ritual burial with medicinal plants and flowers by Neanderthals at Shanidar in Iraq.

The Neolithic Revolution. Sometime after 10,000 BC, among widely separated human communities, a series of dramatic technological and social changes occurred that are summed up as the Neolithic Revolution. The cultivation of previously wild plants encouraged the growth of permanent settlements. Animals were domesticated as a work force and food source. The manufacture of pottery and cloth began. These techniques permitted a huge increase in world population and in human control over the earth.

No region can safely claim priority as the "inventor" of these techniques. Dispersed sites in Cen. and S. America, S.E. Europe, and the Middle East show roughly contemporaneous (10-8,000 BC) evidence of one or another "neolithic" trait. Dates near 6-3,000 BC have been given for E. and S. Asian, W. European, and sub-Saharan African neolithic remains. The variety of crops — field grains, rice, maize, and roots, and the varying mix of other traits suggest that the revolution occurred independently in all these regions.

History Begins: 4000 - 1000 BC

Near Eastern cradle. If history began with writing, the first chapter opened in Mesopotamia, the Tigris-Euphrates river valley. Clay tablets with pictographs were used by the Sumerians to keep records after 4000 BC. A **cuneiform** (wedge shaped) script evolved by 3000 BC as a full syllabic alphabet. Neighboring peoples adapted the script to their own language.

Sumerian life centered, from 4000 BC, on large cities (Eridu, Ur, Uruk, Nippur, Kish, Lagash) organized around temples and priestly bureaucracies, with the surrounding plains watered by vast irrigation works and worked with traction plows. Sailboats, wheeled vehicles, potters wheels, and kilns were used. Copper was smelted and tempered in Sumeria from c4000 BC and bronze was produced not long after. Ores, as well as precious stones and metals were obtained through long-distance ship and caravan trade. Iron was used from c2000 BC. Improved ironworking, developed partly by the **Hittites,** became widespread by 1200 BC.

Sumerian political primacy passed among cities and their kingly dynasties. Semitic-speaking peoples, with cultures derived from the Sumerian, founded a succession of dynasties that ruled in Mesopotamia and neighboring areas for most of 1800 years; among them the **Akkadians** (first under Sargon c2350 BC), the Amorites (whose laws, codified by **Hammurabi,** c1792-1750 BC, have Biblical parallels), and the Assyrians, with interludes of rule by the Hittites, Kassites, and Mitanni, all possibly Indo-Europeans. The political and cultural center of gravity shifted northwest with each successive empire.

Mesopotamian learning, maintained by scribes and preserved by successive rulers in vast libraries, was not abstract or theoretical. Algebraic and geometric problems could be solved on a practical basis in construction, commerce, or administration. Systematic lists of astronomical phenomena, plants, animals and stones were kept; medical texts listed ailments and their herbal cures.

The Sumerians worshipped anthropomorphic gods representing natural forces — Anu, god of heaven; Enlil (Ea), god of water. Epic poetry related these and other gods in a hierarchy. Sacrifices were made at **ziggurats** — huge stepped temples. Gods were thought to control all events, which could be foretold using oracular materials. This religious pattern persisted into the first millenium BC.

The Syria-Palestine area, site of some of the earliest urban remains (Jericho, 7000 BC), and of the recently uncovered **Ebla** civilization (fl. 2500 BC), experienced Egyptian cultural and political influence along with Mesopotamian. The **Phoenician** coast was an active commercial center. A phonetic alphabet was invented here before 1600 BC. It became the ancestor of all European, Middle Eastern, Indian, S.E.

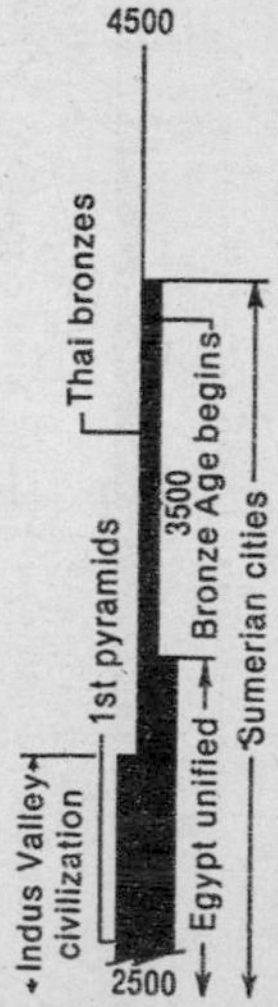

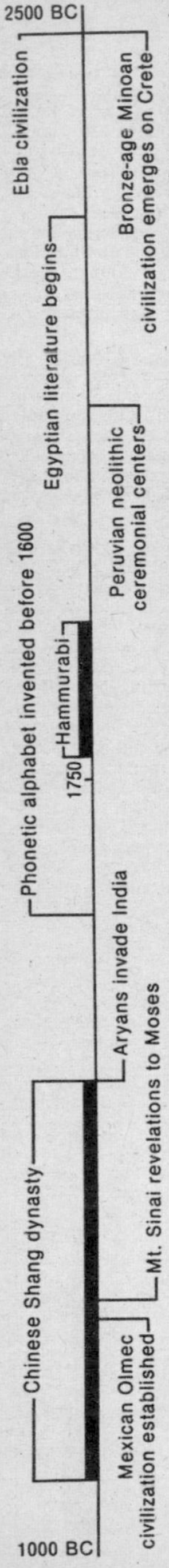

Asian, Ethiopian, and Korean alphabets.

Regional commerce and diplomacy were aided by the use of Akkadian as a *lingua franca,* later replaced by Aramaic.

Egypt. Agricultural villages along the Nile were united by 3300 BC into two kingdoms, Upper and Lower Egypt, unified under the Pharaoh Menes c3100 BC; control over Nubia to the south was asserted beginning 2600 BC. A national bureaucracy supervised construction of canals and monuments (**pyramids** starting 2700 BC). Brilliant First Dynasty achievements in architecture, sculpture, and painting set the standards and forms for all subsequent Egyptian civilization and are still admired. **Hieroglyphic writing** appeared by 3400 BC, recording a sophisticated literature including romantic and philosophical modes after 2300 BC.

An ordered hierarchy of gods, including totemistic animal elements, was served by a powerful priesthood in Memphis. The pharaoh was identified with the falcon god Horus. Later trends were the belief in an afterlife, and the quasi-monotheistic reforms of **Akhenaton** (c1379-1362 BC).

After a period of dominance by Semitic Hyksos from Asia (c1700-1550 BC), the New Kingdom established an empire in Syria. Egypt became increasingly embroiled in Asiatic wars and diplomacy. Eventually it was conquered by Persia in 525 BC, and it faded away as an independent culture.

India. An urban civilization with a so-far-undeciphered writing system stretched across the Indus Valley and along the Arabian Sea c3000-1500 BC. Major sites are Harappa and **Mohenjo-Daro** in Pakistan, well-planned geometric cities with underground sewers and vast granaries. The entire region (600,000 sq. mi.) may have been ruled as a single state. Bronze was used, and arts and crafts were highly developed. Religious life apparently took the form of fertility cults.

Indus civilization was probably in decline when it was destroyed by **Aryan invaders** from the northwest, speaking an Indo-European language from which all the languages of Pakistan, north India and Bangladesh descend. Led by a warrior aristocracy whose legendary deeds are recorded in the **Rig Veda,** the Aryans spread east and south, bringing their pantheon of sky gods, elaborate priestly (Brahmin) ritual, and the beginnings of the caste system; local customs and beliefs were assimilated by the conquerors.

Europe. On Crete, the bronze-age **Minoan civilization** emerged c2500 BC. A prosperous economy and richly decorative art (e.g. at Knossos palace) was supported by seaborne commerce. Mycenae and other cities in Greece and Asia Minor (e.g. **Troy**) preserved elements of the culture to c1100 BC. Cretan Linear A script, c2000-1700 BC, is undeciphered; Linear B, c1300-1200 BC, records a Greek dialect.

Possible connection between Minoan-Mycenaean monumental stonework and the great megalithic monuments and tombs of W. Europe, Iberia, and Malta (c4000-1500 BC) is unclear.

China. Proto-Chinese neolithic cultures had long covered northern and southeastern China when the first large political state was organized in the north by the **Shang dynasty** c1500 BC. Shang kings called themselves Sons of Heaven, and presided over a cult of human and animal sacrifice to ancestors and nature gods. The Chou dynasty, starting c1100 BC, expanded the area of the Son of Heaven's dominion, but feudal states exercised most temporal power.

A writing system with 2,000 different characters was already in use under the Shang, with **pictographs** later supplemented by phonetic characters. The system, with modifications, is still in use, despite changes in spoken Chinese.

Technical advances allowed urban specialists to create fine ceramic and jade products, and bronze casting after 1500 BC was the most advanced in the world.

Bronze artifacts have recently been discovered in northern Thailand dating to 3600 BC, hundreds of years before similar Middle Eastern finds.

Americas. Olmecs settled on the Gulf coast of Mexico, 1500 BC, and soon developed the first civilization in the Western Hemisphere. Temple cities and huge stone sculpture date to 1200 BC. A rudimentary calendar and writing system existed. Olmec religion, centering on a jaguar god, and art forms influenced all later Meso-American cultures.

Neolithic ceremonial centers were built on the Peruvian desert coast, c2000 BC.

Classical Era of Old World Civilizations

Greece. After a period of decline during the Dorian Greek invasions (1200-1000 BC), Greece and the Aegean area developed a unique civilization. Drawing upon Mycenaean traditions, Mesopotamian learning (weights and measures, lunisolar calendar, astronomy, musical scales), the Phoenician alphabet (modified for Greek), and Egyptian art, the revived **Greek city-states** saw a rich elaboration of intellectual life. Long-range commerce was aided by metal coinage (introduced by the Lydians in Asia Minor before 700 BC); colonies were founded around the Mediterranean and Black Sea shores (Cumae in Italy 760 BC, Massalia in France c600 BC).

Philosophy, starting with Ionian speculation on the nature of matter and the universe (Thales c634-546), and including mathematical speculation (Pythagoras c580-c500), culminated in Athens in the rationalist idealism of **Plato** (c428-347) and **Socrates** (c470-399); the latter was executed for alleged impiety. **Aristotle** (384-322) united all fields of study in his system. The arts were highly valued. Architecture culminated in the **Parthenon** in Athens (438, sculpture by Phidias); poetry and drama (Aeschylus 525-456) thrived. Male beauty and strength, a chief artistic theme, were enhanced at the gymnasium and celebrated at the national games at Olympia.

Ruled by local tyrants or oligarchies, the Greeks were never politically united, but managed to resist inclusion in the Persian Empire (Darius defeated at Marathon 490 BC, Xerxes at Salamis, Plataea 479 BC). Local warfare was common; the **Peloponnesian Wars,** 431-404 BC, ended in Sparta's victory over Athens. Greek political power waned, but classical Greek cultural forms spread thoughout the ancient world from the Atlantic to India.

Hebrews. Nomadic Hebrew tribes entered Canaan before 1200 BC, settling among other Semitic peoples speaking the same language. They brought from the desert a **monotheistic faith** said to have been revealed to Abraham in Canaan c1800 BC and to Moses at Mt. Sinai c1250 BC, after the Hebrews' escape from bondage in Egypt. David (ruled 1000-961 BC) and Solomon (ruled 961-922 BC) united the Hebrews in a kingdom that briefly dominated the area. Phoenicians to the north established colonies

(continued on p. 500)

Paleontology: The History of Life

All dates are approximate, and are subject to change based on new fossil finds or new dating techniques; but the sequence of events is generally accepted. Dates are in years before the present.

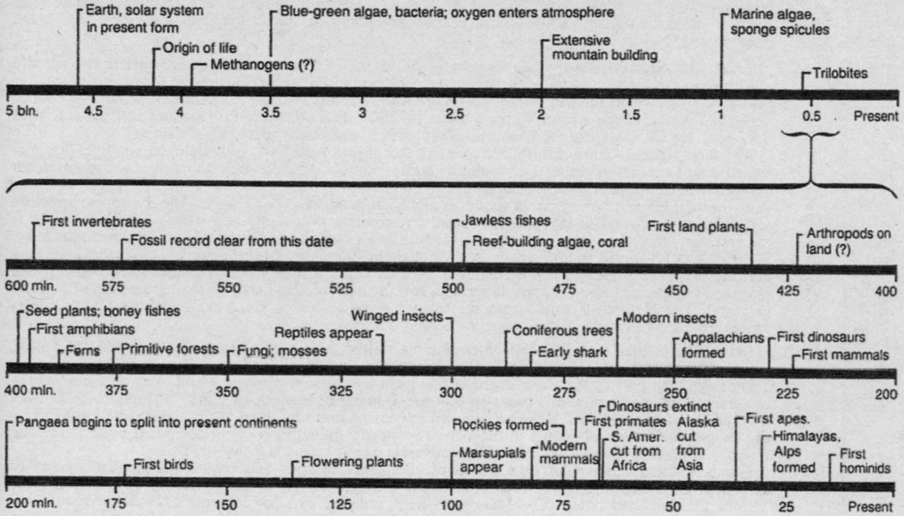

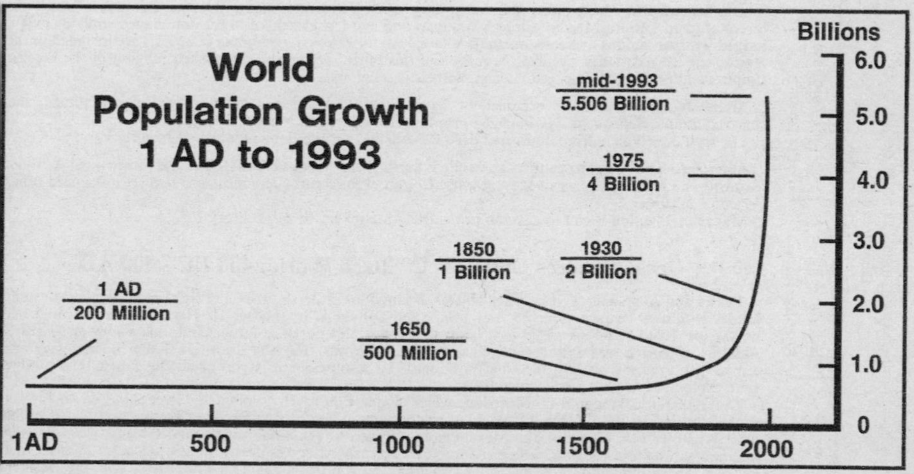

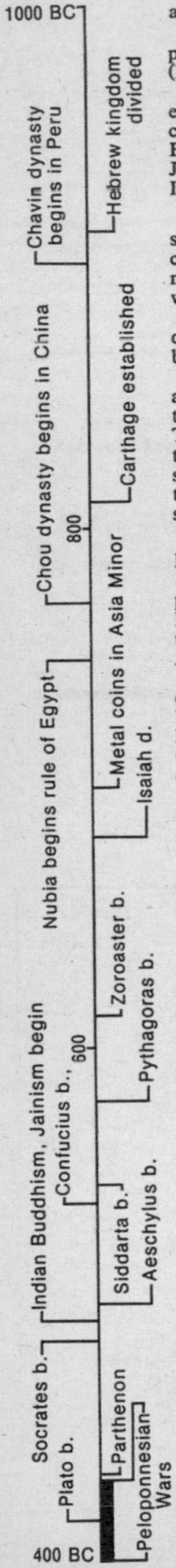

around the E. and W. Mediterranean (**Carthage** c814 BC) and sailed into the Atlantic.

A temple in Jerusalem became the national religious center, with sacrifices performed by a hereditary priesthood. Polytheistic influences, especially of the fertility cult of Baal, were opposed by **prophets** (Elijah, Amos, Isaiah).

Divided into **two kingdoms** after Solomon, the Hebrews were unable to resist the revived Assyrian empire, which conquered Israel, the northern kingdom in 722 BC. Judah, the southern kingdom, was conquered in 586 BC by the Babylonians under Nebuchadnezzar II. But with the fixing of most of the Biblical canon by the mid-fourth century BC, and the emergence of rabbis, arbiters of law and custom, Judaism successfully survived the loss of Hebrew autonomy. A Jewish kingdom was revived under the Hasmoneans (168-42 BC).

China. During the **Eastern Chou** dynasty (770-256 BC), Chinese culture spread east to the sea and south to the Yangtze. Large feudal states on the periphery of the empire contended for pre-eminence, but continued to recognize the Son of Heaven (king), who retained a purely ritual role enriched with courtly music and dance. In the Age of Warring States (403-221 BC), when the first sections of the **Great Wall** were built, the Ch'in state in the West gained supremacy, and finally united all of China.

Iron tools entered China c500 BC, and casting techniques were advanced, aiding agriculture. Peasants owned their land, and owed civil and military service to nobles. Cities grew in number and size, though barter remained the chief trade medium.

Intellectual ferment among noble scribes and officials produced the Classical Age of Chinese literature and philosophy. **Confucius** (551-479 BC) urged a restoration of a supposedly harmonious social order of the past through proper conduct in accordance with one's station and through filial and ceremonial piety. The *Analects*, attributed to him, are revered throughout East Asia. **Mencius** (d. 289 BC) added the view that the Mandate of Heaven can be removed from an unjust dynasty. The Legalists sought to curb the supposed natural wickedness of people through new institutions and harsh laws; they aided the Ch'in rise to power. The Naturalists emphasized the balance of opposites — yin, yang — in the world. **Taoists** sought mystical knowledge through meditation and disengagement.

India. The political and cultural center of India shifted from the Indus to the Ganges River Valley. Buddhism, Jainism, and mystical revisions of orthodox Vedism all developed around 500-300 BC. The *Upanishads*, last part of the *Veda*, urged escape from the illusory physical world. Vedism remained the preserve of the priestly Brahmin caste. In contrast, **Buddhism**, founded by Siddarta Gautama (c563-c483 BC), appealed to merchants in the growing urban centers, and took hold at first (and most lastingly) on the geographic fringes of Indian civilization. The classic Indian epics were composed in this era: The *Ramayana* perhaps around 300 BC, the *Mahabharata* over a period starting 400 BC.

Northern India was divided into a large number of monarchies and aristocratic republics, probably derived from tribal groupings, when the Magadha kingdom was formed in Bihar c542 BC. It soon became the dominant power. The **Maurya dynasty**, founded by Chandragupta c321 BC, expanded the kingdom, uniting most of N. India in a centralized bureaucratic empire. The third Mauryan king, **Asoka** (ruled c274-236) conquered most of the subcontinent: he converted to Buddhism, and inscribed its tenets on pillars throughout India. He downplayed the caste system and tried to end expensive sacrificial rites.

Before its final decline in India, Buddhism developed the popular worship of heavenly Bodhisatvas (enlightened beings), and produced a refined architecture (stupa—shrine—at Sanchi 100 AD) and sculpture (Gandhara reliefs 1-400 AD).

Persia. Aryan peoples (Persians, Medes) dominated the area of present Iran by the beginning of the first millenium BC. The prophet **Zoroaster** (born c628 BC) introduced a dualistic religion in which the forces of good (Ahura Mazda, Lord of Wisdom) and evil (Ahiram) battle for dominance; individuals are judged by their actions and earn damnation or salvation. Zoroaster's hymns (*Gathas*) are included in the *Avesta*, the Zoroastrian scriptures. A version of this faith became the established religion of the Persian Empire, and probably influenced later monotheistic religions.

Africa. Nubia, periodically occupied by Egypt since the third millenium, ruled Egypt c750-661, and survived as an independent Egyptianized kingdom (**Kush**; capital Meroe) for 1,000 years.

The Iron Age Nok culture flourished c500 BC-200 AD on the Benue Plateau of **Nigeria.**

Americas. The Chavin culture controlled north Peru from 900-200 BC. Its ceremonial centers, featuring the jaguar god, survived long after. Chavin architecture, ceramics, and textiles influenced other Peruvian cultures.

Mayan civilization began to develop in Central America in the 5th century BC.

Great Empires Unite the Civilized World: 400 BC - 400 AD

Persia and Alexander. Cyrus, ruler of a small kingdom in Persia from 559 BC, united the Persians and Medes within 10 years, conquered Asia Minor and Babylonia in another 10. His son Cambyses followed by **Darius** (ruled 522-486) added vast lands to the east and north as far as the Indus Valley and Central Asia, as well as Egypt and Thrace. The whole empire was ruled by an international bureaucracy and army, with Persians holding the chief positions. The resources and styles of all the subject civilizations were exploited to create a rich syncretic art.

The Hellenized kingdom of Macedon, which under Phillip II dominated Greece, passed to his son **Alexander** in 336 BC. Within 13 years, Alexander conquered all the Persian dominions. Imbued by his tutor Aristotle with Greek ideals, Alexander encouraged Greek colonization, and Greek-style cities were founded throughout the empire (e.g. Alexandria, Egypt). After his death in 323 BC, wars of succession divided the empire into three parts — **Macedon,** Egypt (ruled by the **Ptolemies**), and the **Seleucid** Empire.

In the ensuing 300 years (the **Hellenistic Era**), a cosmopolitan Greek-oriented culture permeated the ancient world from W. Europe to the borders of India, absorbing native elites everywhere.

Hellenistic philosophy stressed the private individual's search for happiness. The Cynics followed Diogenes (c372-287), who stressed satisfaction of animal needs and contempt for social convention. Zeno (c335-c263) and the Stoics exalted reason, identified it with virtue, and counseled an ascetic disregard for misfortune. The Epicureans tried to build lives of moderate pleasure without political or emotional

(continued on p. 502)

The Seven Wonders of the World

These ancient works of art and architecture were considered awe-inspiring in splendor and/or size by the Greek and Roman world of the Alexandrian epoch and later. Classical writers disagreed as to which works made up the list of Wonders, but the following were usually included:

The Pyramids of Egypt: The only surviving Wonder, these monumental structures of masonry located on the west bank of the Nile River above Cairo were built from 3000 to 1800 B.C. as royal tombs. Three—Khufu, Khafra, and Menkaura—were often grouped as the first Wonder of the World. The largest, **The Great Pyramid of Khufu,** or Cheops, is a solid mass of limestone blocks covering 13 acres. It is estimated to contain 2.3 million blocks of stone, the stones themselves averaging 2½ tons and some weighing 30 tons. Its construction reputedly took 100,000 laborers 20 years.

The Hanging Gardens of Babylon: These gardens were laid out on a brick terrace about 400 feet square and 75 feet above the ground. To irrigate the trees, shrubs, and flowers, screws were turned to lift water from the Euphrates River. The gardens were probably built by King Nebuchadnezzar II around 600 B.C. **The Walls of Babylon,** long, thick, and made of colorfully glazed brick, were considered by some to be among the Seven Wonders.

The Statue of Zeus (Jupiter) at Olympia: This statue of the king of the gods showed him seated on a throne. His flesh was made of ivory, his robe and ornaments of gold. Reputedly 40 feet high, the statue was made by Phidias and was placed in the great temple of Zeus in the sacred grove of Olympia around 457 B.C.

The Colossus of Rhodes: A bronze statue of the sun god Helios, the Colossus was worked on for 12 years in the early 200's B.C. by the sculptor Chares. It was probably 120 feet high. A symbol of the city of Rhodes at its height, the statue stood on a promontory overlooking the harbor.

The Temple of Artemis (Diana) at Ephesus: This largest and most complex temple of ancient times was built around 550 B.C. and was made of marble except for its tile-covered wooden roof. It was begun in honor of a non-Hellenic goddess who later became identified with the Greek goddess of the same name. Ephesus was one of the greatest of the Ionian cities.

The Mausoleum at Halicarnassus: The source of our word "mausoleum," this marble tomb was built in what is now southeastern Turkey by Artemisia for her husband Mausolus, an official of the Persian Empire who died in 353 B.C. About 135 feet high, it was adorned with the works of 4 sculptors.

The Pharos (Lighthouse) of Alexandria: This sculpture was designed around 270 B.C., during the reign of King Ptolemy II, by the Greek architect Sostratos. Estimates of its height range from 200 to 600 feet.

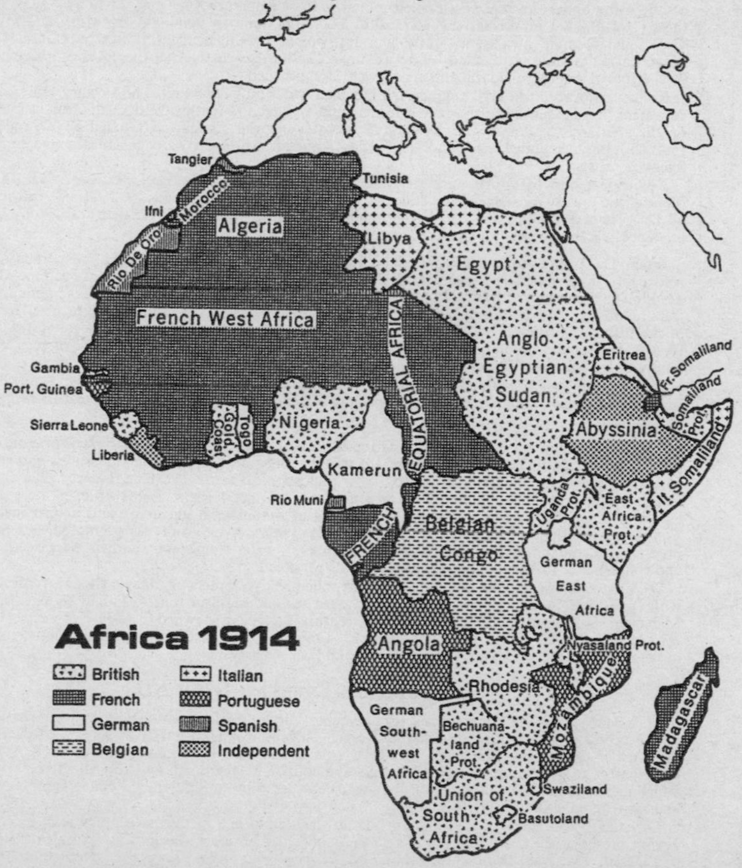

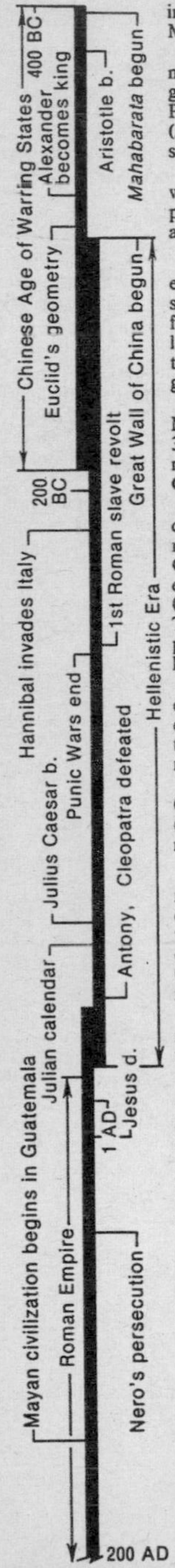

involvement. Hellenistic arts imitated life realistically, especially in sculpture and literature (comedies of Menander, 342-292).

The sciences thrived, especially at Alexandria, where the Ptolemies financed a great library and museum. Fields of study included mathematics (**Euclid's** geometry, c300 BC; Menelaus' non-Euclidean geometry, c100 AD); astronomy (heliocentric theory of Aristarchus, 310-230 BC; Julian calendar 45 BC; Ptolemy's *Almagest,* c150 AD); geography (world map of Eratosthenes, 276-194 BC); hydraulics (**Archimedes,** 287-212 BC); medicine (Galen, 130-200 AD); and chemistry. Inventors refined uses for siphons, valves, gears, springs, screws, levers, cams, and pulleys.

A restored Persian empire under the **Parthians** (N. Iranian tribesmen) controlled the eastern Hellenistic world 250 BC-229 AD. The Parthians and the succeeding Sassanian dynasty (229-651) fought with Rome periodically. The **Sassanians** revived Zoroastrianism as a state religion, and patronized a nationalistic artistic and scholarly renaissance.

Rome. The city of Rome was founded, according to legend, by Romulus in 753 BC. Through military expansion and colonization, and by granting citizenship to conquered tribes, the city annexed all of Italy south of the Po in the 100-year period before 268 BC. The Latin and other Italic tribes were annexed first, followed by the Etruscans (a civilized people north of Rome) and the Greek colonies in the south. With a large standing army and reserve forces of several hundred thousand, Rome was able to defeat Carthage in the 3 **Punic Wars,** 264-241, 218-201, 149-146 (despite the invasion of Italy by Hannibal, 218), thus gaining Sicily and territory in Spain and North Africa.

New provinces were added in the East, as Rome exploited local disputes to conquer Greece and Asia Minor in the 2d century BC, and Egypt in the first (after the defeat and suicide of **Antony and Cleopatra,** 30 BC). All the Mediterranean civilized world up to the disputed Parthian border was now Roman, and remained so for 500 years. Less civilized regions were added to the Empire: Gaul (conquered by Julius Caesar, 56-49 BC), Britain (43 AD) and Dacia NE of the Danube (117 AD).

The original aristocratic republican government, with democratic features added in the fifth and fourth centuries BC, deteriorated under the pressures of empire and class conflict (**Gracchus** brothers, social reformers, murdered 133, 121; slave revolts 135, 73). After a series of civil wars (Marius vs. Sulla 88-82, Caesar vs. Pompey 49-45, triumvirate vs. Caesar's assassins 44-43, Antony vs. Octavian 32-30), the empire came under the rule of a deified monarch (first emperor, **Augustus,** 27 BC-14 AD). Provincials (nearly all granted citizenship by Caracalla, 212 AD) came to dominate the army and civil service. Traditional Roman law, systematized and interpreted by independent jurists, and local self-rule in provincial cities were supplanted by a vast tax-collecting bureaucracy in the 3d and 4th centuries. The legal rights of women, children, and slaves were strengthened.

Roman innovations in **civil engineering** included water mills, windmills, and rotary mills, and the use of cement that hardened under water. Monumental architecture (baths, theaters, apartment houses) relied on the arch and the dome. The network of roads (some still standing) stretched 53,000 miles, passing through mountain tunnels as long as 3.5 miles. Aqueducts brought water to cities, underground sewers removed waste.

Roman art and literature were derivative of Greek models. Innovations were made in sculpture (naturalistic busts and equestrian statues), decorative wall painting (as at Pompeii), satire (Juvenal, 60-127), history (Tacitus, 56-120), prose romance (Petronius, d. 66 AD). Violence and torture dominated, mass public amusements, which were supported by the state.

India. The **Gupta** monarchs reunited N. India c320 AD. Their peaceful and prosperous reign saw a revival of Hindu religious thought and Brahmin power. The old Vedic traditions were combined with devotion to a plethora of indigenous deities (who were seen as manifestations of Vedic gods). **Caste lines** were reinforced, and Buddhism gradually disappeared. The art (often erotic), architecture, and literature of the period, patronized by the Gupta court, are considered to be among India's finest achievements (Kalidasa, poet and dramatist, fl. c400). Mathematical innovations included the use of zero and decimal numbers. Invasions by White Huns from the NW destroyed the empire c550.

Rich cultures also developed in S. India in this era. Emotional Tamil religious poetry aided the Hindu revival. The Pallava kingdom controlled much of S. India c350-880, and helped spread Indian civilization to S.E. Asia.

China. The Ch'in ruler Shih Huang Ti (ruled 221-210 BC), known as the First Emperor, centralized political authority in China, standardized the written language, laws, weights, measures, and coinage, and conducted a census, but tried to destroy most philosophical texts. The **Han dynasty** (206 BC-220 AD) instituted the Mandarin bureaucracy, which lasted for 2,000 years. Local officials were selected by examination in the Confucian classics and trained at the imperial university and at provincial schools. The invention of **paper** facilitated this bureaucratic system. Agriculture was promoted, but the peasants bore most of the tax burden. Irrigation was improved; water clocks and sundials were used; astronomy and mathematics thrived; landscape painting was perfected.

With the expansion south and west (to nearly the present borders of today's China), trade was opened with India, S.E. Asia, and the Middle East, over sea and caravan routes. Indian missionaries brought Mahayana Buddhism to China by the first century AD, and spawned a variety of sects. Taoism was revived, and merged with popular superstitions. Taoist and Buddhist monasteries and convents multiplied in the turbulent centuries after the collapse of the Han dynasty.

Monotheism Emerges: 1-750 AD

Christianity. Religions indigenous to particular Middle Eastern nations became international in the first 3 centuries of the Roman Empire. Roman citizens worshipped **Isis** of Egypt, **Mithras** of Persia, **Demeter** of Greece, and the great mother **Cybele** of Phrygia. Their cults centered on mysteries (secret ceremonies) and the promise of an afterlife, symbolized by the death and rebirth of the god. Judaism, which had begun as the national cult of Judea, also spread by emigration and conversion. It was the only ancient religion west of India to survive.

Christians, who emerged as a distinct sect in the second half of the 1st century AD, revered **Jesus,** a Jewish preacher killed by the Romans at the request of Jewish authorities in Jerusalem c30 AD. They considered him the Savior (Messiah, or Christ) who rose from the dead and could grant eternal life to the faithful, despite their sinfulness. They believed he was an incarnation of the one god worshipped by the Jews, and that he would return soon to pass final judgment on the world. The missionary activities of such early leaders as **Paul of Tarsus** spread the faith, at first mostly among Jews or among quasi-Jews attracted by the Pauline rejection of such difficult Jewish laws as circumcision. Intermittent persecution, as in Rome under Nero in 64 AD, on grounds of suspected disloyalty, failed to disrupt the Christian communities. Each congregation, generally urban and of plebeian character, was tightly organized under a leader (bishop), elders (presbyters or priests), and assistants (deacons). Stories about Jesus (the Gospels) and the early church (Acts) were written down in the late first and early 2d centuries, and circulated along with letters of Paul. An authoritative canon of these writings was not fixed until the 4th century.

A school for priests was established at Alexandria in the second century. Its teachers (**Origen** c182-251) helped define Christian doctrine and promote the faith in Greek-style philosophical works. Pagan Neoplatonism was given Christian coloration in the works of Church Fathers such as Augustine (354-430). Christian hermits, often drawn from the lower classes, began to associate in monasteries, first in Egypt (St. Pachomius c290-345), then in other eastern lands, then in the West (**St. Benedict's rule,** 529). Popular devotion to saints, especially Mary, mother of Jesus, spread.

Under **Constantine** (ruled 306-337), Christianity became in effect the established religion of the Empire. Pagan temples were expropriated, state funds were used to build huge churches and support the hierarchy, and laws were adjusted in accordance with Christian notions. Pagan worship was banned by the end of the fourth century, and severe restrictions were placed on Judaism.

The newly established church was rocked by doctrinal disputes, often exacerbated by regional rivalries both within and outside the Empire. Chief heresies (as defined by church councils backed by imperial authority) were **Arianism,** which denied the divinity of Jesus; **Donatism,** which rejected the convergence of church and state and denied the validity of sacraments performed by sinful clergy; and the **Monophysite** position denying the dual nature of Christ.

Judaism. First century Judaism embraced several sects, including: the **Sadducees,** mostly drawn from the Temple priesthood, who were culturally Hellenized; the **Pharisees,** who upheld the full range of traditional customs and practices as of equal weight to literal scriptural law, and elaborated synagogue worship; and the **Essenes,** an ascetic, millenarian sect. Messianic fervor led to repeated, unsuccessful rebellions against Rome (66-70, 135). As a result, the Temple was destroyed, and the population decimated.

To avoid the dissolution of the faith, a program of codification of law was begun at the academy of Yavneh. The work continued for some 500 years in Palestine and Babylonia, ending in the final redaction of the **Talmud** (c600), a huge collection of legal and moral debates, rulings, liturgy, Biblical exegesis, and legendary materials.

Islam. The earliest Arab civilization emerged by the end of the 2d millenium BC in the watered highlands of Yemen. Seaborne and caravan trade in frankincense and myrrh connected the area with the Nile and Fertile Crescent. The Minaean, Sabean (Sheba), and Himyarite states successively held sway. By Mohammed's time (7th century AD), the region was a province of Sassanian Persia. In the North, the **Nabataean kingdom** at Petra and the kingdom of Palmyra were first Aramaicized and then Romanized, and finally absorbed like neighboring Judea into the Roman Empire. Nomads shared the central region with a few trading towns and oases. Wars between tribes and raids on settled communities were common, and were celebrated in a poetic tradition that by the 6th century helped establish a classic literary Arabic.

In 611 **Mohammed,** a 40-year-old Arab of Mecca, announced a revelation from the one true God, calling on him to repudiate pagan idolatry. Drawing on elements of Judaism and Christianity, and eventually incorporating some Arab pagan traditions (such as reverence for the black stone at the kaaba shrine in Mecca), Mohammed's teachings, recorded in the **Koran,** forged a new religion, Islam (submission to Allah). Opposed by the leaders of Mecca, Mohammed made a *hejira* (migration) to Medina to the north in 622, the beginning of the Moslem lunar calendar. He and his followers defeated the Meccans in 624 in the first *jihad* (holy war), and by his death (632), nearly all the Arabian peninsula accepted his religious and secular leadership.

Under the first two **caliphs** (successors), Abu Bakr (632-34) and Omar (634-44), Moslem rule was confirmed over Arabia. Raiding parties into Byzantine and Persian border areas developed into campaigns of conquest against the two empires, which had been weakened by wars and by disaffection among subject peoples (including Coptic and Syriac Christians opposed to the Byzantine orthodox church). Syria, Palestine, Egypt, Iraq, and Persia all fell to the inspired Arab armies. The Arabs at first remained a distinct minority, using non-Moslems in the new administrative system, and tolerating Christians, Jews, and Zoroastrians as self-governing "Peoples of the Book," whose taxes supported the empire.

Disputes over the succession, and puritan reaction to the wealth and refinement that empire brought to the ruling strata, led to the growth of schismatic movements. The followers of Mohammed's son-in-law Ali (assassinated 661) and his descendants became the founders of the more mystical **Shi'ite** sect, still the largest non-orthodox Moslem sect. The Karijites, puritanical, militant, and egalitarian, persist as a minor sect to the present.

Under the **Omayyad** caliphs (661-750), the boundaries of Islam were extended across N. Africa and into Spain. Arab armies in the West were stopped at Tours in 732 by the Frank **Charles Martel.** Asia Minor, the Indus Valley, and Transoxiana were conquered in the East. The vast majority of the subject population gradually converted to Islam, encouraged by tax and career privileges. The Arab language supplanted the local tongues in the central and western areas, but Arab soldiers and rulers in the East eventually became assimilated to the indigenous languages.

New Peoples Enter History: 400-900

Barbarian invasions. Germanic tribes infiltrated S and E from their Baltic homeland during the 1st millenium BC, reaching S. Germany by 100 BC and the Black Sea by 214 AD. Organized into large federated tribes under elected kings, most resisted Roman domination and raided the empire in time of civil war (Goths took Dacia 214, raided Thrace 251-269). German troops and commanders came to dominate the Roman armies by the end of the 4th century. **Huns,** invaders from Asia, entered Europe 372, driving more Germans into the western empire. Emperor Valens allowed Visigoths to cross

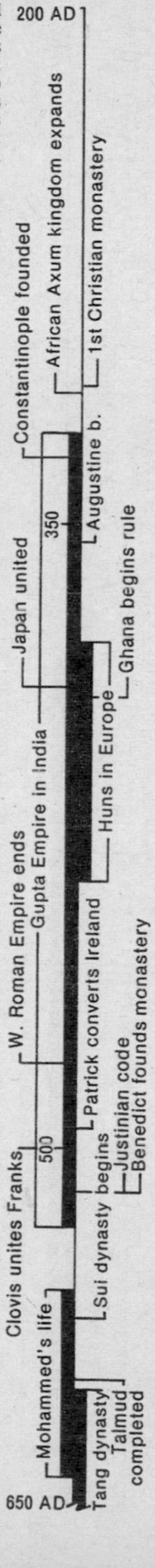

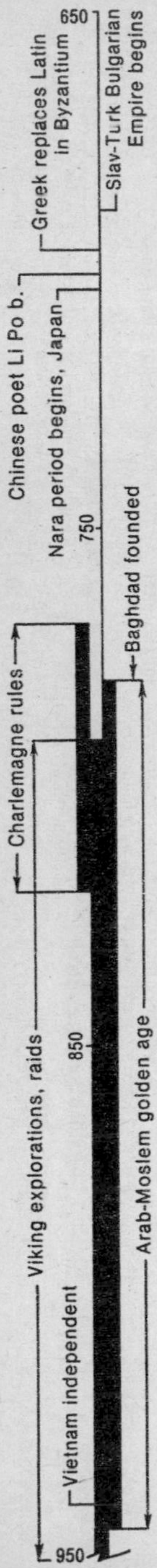

the Danube 376. Huns under Attila (d. 453) raided Gaul, Italy, Balkans. The western empire, weakened by overtaxation and social stagnation, was overrun in the 5th century. Gaul was effectively lost 406-7, Spain 409, Britain 410, Africa 429-39. Rome was sacked 410 by Visigoths under Alaric, 455 by Vandals. The last western emperor, Romulus Augustulus, was deposed 476 by the Germanic chief Odoacer.

Celts. Celtic cultures, which in pre-Roman times covered most of W. Europe, were confined almost entirely to the British Isles after the Germanic invasions. **St. Patrick** completed the conversion of Ireland (c457-92). A strong monastic tradition took hold. Irish monastic missionaries in Scotland, England, and the continent (Columba c521-597; Columban c543-615) helped restore Christianity after the Germanic invasions. The monasteries became renowned centers of classic and Christian learning, and presided over the recording of a Christianized Celtic mythology, elaborated by secular writers and bards. An intricate decorative art style developed, especially in book illumination (Lindisfarne Gospels, c700, Book of Kells, 8th century).

Successor states. The Visigoth kingdom in Spain (from 419) and much of France (to 507) saw a continuation of much Roman administration, language, and law (Breviary of Alaric 506), until its destruction by the Moslems, 711. The Vandal kingdom in Africa, from 429, was conquered by the Byzantines, 533. Italy was ruled in succession by an Ostrogothic kingdom under Byzantine suzerainty 489-554, direct Byzantine government, and the German Lombards (568-774). The latter divided the peninsula with the Byzantines and the papacy under the dynamic reformer Pope Gregory the Great (590-604) and his successors.

King Clovis (ruled 481-511) united the Franks on both sides of the Rhine, and after his conversion to orthodox Christianity, defeated the Arian Burgundians (after 500) and Visigoths (507) with the support of the native clergy and the papacy. Under the **Merovingian** kings a feudal system emerged: power was fragmented among hierarchies of military landowners. Social stratification, which in late Roman times had acquired legal, hereditary sanction, was reinforced. The Carolingians (747-987) expanded the kingdom and restored central power. **Charlemagne** (ruled 768-814) conquered nearly all the Germanic lands, including Lombard Italy, and was crowned Emperor by Pope Leo III in Rome in 800. A centuries-long decline in commerce and the arts was reversed under Charlemagne's patronage. He welcomed Jews to his kingdom, which became a center of Jewish learning (Rashi 1040-1105). He sponsored the "Carolingian Renaissance" of learning under the Anglo-Latin scholar Alcuin (c732-804), who reformed church liturgy.

Byzantine Empire. Under Diocletian (ruled 284-305) the empire had been divided into 2 parts to facilitate administration and defense. Constantine founded **Constantinople,** 330, (at old Byzantium) as a fully Christian city. Commerce and taxation financed a sumptuous, orientalized court, a class of hereditary bureaucratic families, and magnificent urban construction (Hagia Sophia, 532-37). The city's fortifications and naval innovations (Greek fire) repelled assaults by Goths, Huns, Slavs, Bulgars, Avars, Arabs, and Scandinavians. Greek replaced Latin as the official language by c700. Byzantine art, a solemn, sacral, and stylized variation of late classical styles (mosaics at S. Vitale, Ravenna, 526-48) was a starting point for medieval art in E. and W. Europe.

Justinian (ruled 527-65) reconquered parts of Spain, N. Africa, and Italy, codified Roman law (*codex Justinianus,* 529, was medieval Europe's chief legal text), closed the Platonic Academy at Athens and ordered all pagans to convert. Lombards in Italy, Arabs in Africa retook most of his conquests. The Isaurian dynasty from Anatolia (from 717) and the Macedonian dynasty (867-1054) restored military and commercial power. The Iconoclast controversy (726-843) over the permissibility of images, helped alienate the Eastern Church from the papacy.

Arab Empire. Baghdad, founded 762, became the seat of the **Abbasid** Caliphate (founded 750), while Ummayads continued to rule in Spain. A brilliant cosmopolitan civilization emerged, inaugurating an Arab-Moslem golden age. Arab lyric poetry revived; Greek, Syriac, Persian, and Sanskrit books were translated into Arabic, often by Syriac Christians and Jews, whose theology and Talmudic law, respectively, influenced Islam. The arts and music flourished at the court of **Harun al-Rashid** (786-809), celebrated in *The Arabian Nights.* The sciences, medicine, and mathematics were pursued at Baghdad, Cordova, and Cairo (founded 969). Science and Aristotelian philosophy culminated in the systems of Avicenna (980-1037), Averroes (1126-98), and Maimonides (1135-1204), a Jew; all influenced later Christian scholarship and theology. The Islamic ban on images encouraged a sinuous, geometric decorative tradition, applied to architecture and illumination. A gradual loss of Arab control in Persia (from 874) led to the capture of Baghdad by Persians, 945. By the next century, Spain and N. Africa were ruled by Berbers, while Turks prevailed in Asia Minor and the Levant. The loss of political power by the caliphs allowed for the growth of non-orthodox trends, especially the mystical **Sufi** tradition (theologian Ghazali, 1058-1111).

Africa. Immigrants from Saba in S. Arabia helped set up the **Axum** kingdom in Ethiopia in the 2d century (their language, Ge'ez, is preserved by the Ethiopian Church). In the 4th century, when the kingdom became Christianized, it defeated Kushite Meroe and expanded into Yemen. Axum was the center of a vast ivory trade; it controlled the Red Sea coast until c1100. Arab conquest in Egypt cut Axum's political and economic ties with Byzantium.

The Iron Age entered W. Africa by the end of the 1st millenium BC. **Ghana,** the first known sub-Saharan state, ruled in the upper Senegal-Niger region c400-1240, controlling the trade of gold from mines in the S to trans-Sahara caravan routes to the N. The **Bantu** peoples, probably of W. African origin, began to spread E and S perhaps 2000 years ago, displacing the Pygmies and Bushmen of central and southern Africa over a 1,500-year period.

Japan. The advanced Neolithic Yayoi period, when irrigation, rice farming, and iron and bronze casting techniques were introduced from China or Korea, persisted to c400 AD. The myriad Japanese states were then united by the **Yamato** clan, under an emperor who acted as the chief priest of the animistic **Shinto** cult. Japanese political and military intervention in Korea by the 6th century quickened a Chinese cultural invasion, bringing Buddhism, the Chinese language (which long remained a literary and governmental medium), Chinese ideographs and Buddhist styles in painting, sculpture, literature, and architecture (7th c. Horyu-ji temple at Nara). The Taika Reforms, 646, tried to centralize Japan according to Chinese bureaucratic and Buddhist philosophical values, but failed to curb traditional Japanese decentralization. A nativist reaction against the Buddhist **Nara period** (710-94) ushered in the

Heian period (794-1185) centered at the new capital, Kyoto. Japanese elegance and simplicity modified Chinese styles in architecture, scroll painting, and literature; the writing system was also simplified. The courtly novel *Tale of Genji* (1010-20) testifies to the enhanced role of women.

Southeast Asia. The historic peoples of southeast Asia began arriving some 2500 years ago from China and Tibet, displacing scattered aborigines. Their agriculture relied on rice and tubers (yams), which they may have introduced to Africa. Indian cultural influences were strongest; literacy and Hindu and Buddhist ideas followed the southern India-China trade route. From the southern tip of Indochina, the kingdom of **Funan** (1st-7th centuries) traded as far west as Persia. It was absorbed by Chenla, itself conquered by the **Khmer Empire** (600-1300). The Khmers, under Hindu god-kings (Suryavarman II, 1113-c1150), built the monumental Angkor Wat temple center for the royal phallic cult. The **Nam-Viet** kingdom in Annam, dominated by China and Chinese culture for 1,000 years, emerged in the 10th century, growing at the expense of the Khmers, who also lost ground in the NW to the new, highly-organized **Thai** kingdom. On Sumatra, the **Srivijaya** Empire at Palembang controlled vital sea lanes (7th to 10th centuries). A Buddhist dynasty, the Sailendras, ruled central **Java** (8th-9th centuries), building at Borobudur one of the largest stupas in the world.

China. The short-lived Sui dynasty (581-618) ushered in a period of commercial, artistic, and scientific achievement in China, continuing under the **T'ang** dynasty (618-906). Such inventions as the magnetic compass, gunpowder, the abacus, and printing were introduced or perfected. Medical innovations included cataract surgery. The state, from the cosmopolitan capital, Ch'ang-an, supervised foreign trade, which exchanged Chinese silks, porcelains, and art works for spices, ivory, etc., over Central Asian caravan routes and sea routes reaching Africa. A golden age of poetry bequeathed tens of thousands of works to later generations (Tu Fu 712-70, Li Po 701-62). Landscape painting flourished. Commercial and industrial expansion continued under the **Northern Sung** dynasty (960-1126), facilitated by paper money and credit notes. But commerce never achieved respectability; government monopolies expropriated successful merchants. The population, long stable at 50 million, doubled in 200 years with the introduction of early-ripening rice and the double harvest. In art, native Chinese styles were revived.

Americas. A Native American empire stretched from the Valley of Mexico to Guatemala, 300-600, centering on the huge city **Teotihuacan** (founded 100 BC). To the S, in Guatemala, a high **Mayan** civilization developed, 150-900, around hundreds of rural ceremonial centers. The Mayans improved on Olmec writing and the calendar, and pursued astronomy and mathematics (using the idea of zero). In S. America, a widespread pre-Inca culture grew from **Tiahuanaco** near Lake Titicaca (Gateway of the Sun, c700).

Christian Europe Regroups and Expands: 900-1300

Scandinavians. Pagan Danish and Norse (**Viking**) adventurers, traders, and pirates raided the coasts of the British Isles (Dublin founded c831), France, and even the Mediterranean for over 200 years beginning in the late 8th century. Inland settlement in the W was limited to Great Britain (King Canute, 994-1035) and Normandy, settled under Rollo, 911, as a fief of France. Other Vikings reached Iceland (874), Greenland (c986), and N. America (Leif Eriksson c1000). Norse traders (**Varangians**) developed Russian river commerce from the 8th-11th centuries, and helped set up a state at Kiev in the late 9th century. Conversion to Christianity occurred during the 10th century, reaching Sweden 100 years later. Eleventh century Norman bands conquered S. Italy and Sicily. Duke **William of Normandy** conquered England, 1066, bringing continental feudalism and the French language, essential elements in later English civilization.

East Europe. Slavs inhabited areas of E. Central Europe in prehistoric times, and reached most of their present limits by c850. The first Slavic states were in the Balkans (Slav-Turk **Bulgarian Empire**, 680-1018) and Moravia (628). Missions of St. Cyril (whose Greek-based Cyrillic alphabet is still used by S. and E. Slavs) converted Moravia, 863. The Eastern Slavs, part-civilized under the overlordship of the Turkish-Jewish **Khazar** trading empire (7th-10th centuries), gravitated toward Constantinople by the 9th century. The **Kievan state** adopted Eastern Christianity under Prince Vladimir, 989. King Boleslav I (992-1025) began **Poland's** long history of eastern conquest. The Magyars (**Hungarians**), in present-day Hungary since 896, accepted Latin Christianity, 1001.

Germany. The German kingdom that emerged after the breakup of Charlemagne's Empire remained a confederation of largely autonomous states. The Saxon Otto I, king from 936, established the **Holy Roman Empire** of Germany and Italy in alliance with Pope John XII, who crowned him emperor, 962; he defeated the Magyars, 955. Imperial power was greatest under the **Hohenstaufens** (1138-1254), despite the growing opposition of the papacy, which ruled central Italy, and the Lombard League cities. Frederick II (1194-1250) improved administration, patronized the arts; after his death German influence was removed from Italy.

Christian Spain. From its northern mountain redoubts, Christian rule slowly migrated south through the 11th century, when Moslem unity collapsed. After the capture of **Toledo** (1085), the kingdoms of Portugal, Castile, and Aragon undertook repeated crusades of reconquest, finally completed in 1492. Elements of Islamic civilization persisted in recaptured areas, influencing all W. Europe.

Crusades. Pope Urban II called, 1095, for a crusade to restore Asia Minor to Byzantium and conquer the Holy Land from the Turks. Some 10 crusades (to 1291) succeeded only in founding 4 temporary Frankish states in the Levant. The 4th crusade sacked Constantinople, 1204. In Rhineland (1096), England (1290), France (1306), Jews were massacred or expelled, and wars were launched against Christian heretics (**Albigensian** crusade in France, 1229). Trade in eastern luxuries expanded, led by the Venetian naval empire.

Economy. The agricultural base of European life benefitted from improvements in **plow design** c1000, and by draining of lowlands and clearing of forests, leading to a rural population increase. Towns grew in N. Italy, Flanders, and N. Germany (Hanseatic League). Improvements in **loom design** permitted factory textile production. **Guilds** dominated urban trades from the 12th century. Banking (centered in Italy, 12th-15th century) facilitated long-distance trade.

The Church. The split between the Eastern and Western churches was formalized in 1054. W. and

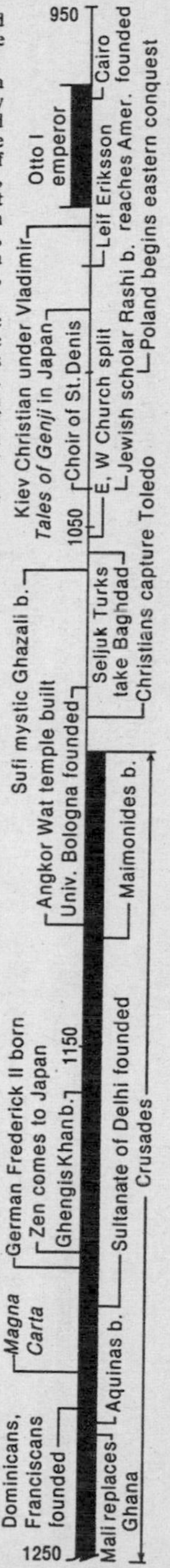

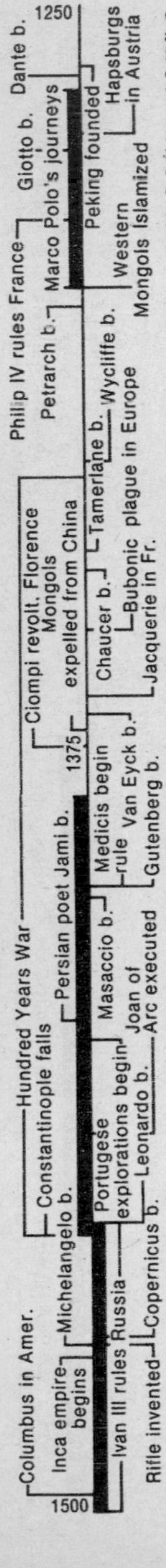

Central Europe was divided into 500 bishoprics under one united hierarchy, but conflicts between secular and church authorities were frequent (German **Investiture Controversy,** 1075-1122). Clerical power was first strengthened through the international monastic reform begun at Cluny, 910. Popular religious enthusiasm often expressed itself in heretical movements (Waldensians from 1173), but was channelled by the **Dominican** (1215) and **Franciscan** (1223) friars into the religious mainstream.

Arts. Romanesque architecture (11th-12th centuries) expanded on late Roman models, using the rounded arch and massed stone to support enlarged basilicas. Painting and sculpture followed Byzantine models. The literature of **chivalry** was exemplified by the epic (Chanson de Roland, c1100) and by courtly love poems of the troubadours of Provence and minnesingers of Germany. **Gothic architecture** emerged in France (choir of St. Denis, c1040) and spread as French cultural influence predominated in Europe. Rib vaulting and pointed arches were used to combine soaring heights with delicacy, and freed walls for display of stained glass. Exteriors were covered with painted relief sculpture and elaborate architectural detail.

Learning. Law, medicine, and philosophy were advanced at independent **universities** (Bologna, late 11th century), originally corporations of students and masters. Twelfth century translations of Greek classics, especially Aristotle, encouraged an analytic approach. Scholastic philosophy, from Anselm (1033-1109) to Aquinas (1225-74) attempted to reconcile reason and revelation.

Apogee of Central Asian Power; Islam Grows: 1250-1500

Turks. Turkic peoples, of Central Asian ancestry, were a military threat to the Byzantine and Persian Empires from the 6th century. After several waves of invasions, during which most of the Turks adopted Islam, the **Seljuk Turks** took Baghdad, 1055. They ruled Persia, Iraq, and, after 1071, Asia Minor, where massive numbers of Turks settled. The empire was divided in the 12th century into smaller states ruled by Seljuks, Kurds (**Saladin** c1137-93), and Mamelukes (a military caste of former Turk, Kurd, and Circassian slaves), which governed Egypt and the Middle East until the Ottoman era (c1290-1922).

Osman I (ruled c1290-1326) and succeeding sultans united Anatolian Turkish warriors in a militaristic state that waged holy war against Byzantium and Balkan Christians. Most of the Balkans had been subdued, and Anatolia united, when **Constantinople fell,** 1453. By the mid-16th century, Hungary, the Middle East, and North Africa had been conquered. The Turkish advance was stopped at Vienna, 1529, and at the naval battle of Lepanto, 1571, by Spain, Venice, and the papacy.

The Ottoman state was governed in accordance with orthodox Moslem law. Greek, Armenian, and Jewish communities were segregated, and ruled by religious leaders responsible for taxation; they dominated trade. State offices and most army ranks were filled by slaves through a system of child conscription among Christians.

India. Mahmud of Ghazni (971-1030) led repeated Turkish raids into N. India. Turkish power was consolidated in 1206 with the start of the **Sultanate at Delhi.** Centralization of state power under the early Delhi sultans went far beyond traditional Indian practice. Moslem rule of most of the subcontinent lasted until the British conquest some 600 years later.

Mongols. Genghis Khan (c1162-1227) first united the feuding Mongol tribes, and built their armies into an effective offensive force around a core of highly mobile cavalry. He and his immediate successors created the largest land empire in history; by 1279 it stretched from the east coast of Asia to the Danube, from the Siberian steppes to the Arabian Sea. East-West trade and contacts were facilitated (Marco Polo c1254-1324). The western Mongols were Islamized by 1295; successor states soon lost their Mongol character by assimilation. They were briefly reunited under the Turk Tamerlane (1336-1405).

Kublai Khan ruled China from his new capital Peking (founded 1264). Naval campaigns against Japan (1274, 1281) and Java (1293) were defeated, the latter by the Hindu-Buddhist maritime kingdom of Majapahit. The **Yuan** dynasty made use of Mongols and other foreigners (including Europeans) in official posts, and tolerated the return of Nestorian Christianity (suppressed 841-45) and the spread of Islam in the South and West. A native reaction expelled the Mongols, 1367-68.

Russia. The Kievan state in Russia, weakened by the decline of Byzantium and the rise of the Catholic Polish-Lithuanian state, was overrun by the Mongols, 1238-40. Only the northern trading republic of Novgorod remained independent. The grand dukes of Moscow emerged as leaders of a coalition of princes that eventually defeated the Mongols, by 1481. With the fall of Constantinople, the **Tsars** (Caesars) at Moscow (from Ivan III, ruled 1462-1505) set up an independent Russian Orthodox Church. Commerce failed to revive. The isolated Russian state remained agrarian, with the peasant class falling into serfdom.

Persia. A revival of Persian literature, using the Arab alphabet and literary forms, began in the 10th century (epic of Firdausi, 935-1020). An art revival, influenced by Chinese styles, began in the 12th. Persian cultural and political forms, and often the Persian language, were used for centuries by Turkish and Mongol elites from the Balkans to India. Persian mystics from Rumi (1207-73) to Jami (1414-92) promoted **Sufism** in their poetry.

Africa. Two militant Islamic Berber dynasties emerged from the Sahara to carve out empires from the Sahel to central Spain — the **Almoravids,** c1050-1140, and the fanatical **Almohads,** c1125-1269. The Ghanaian empire was replaced in the upper Niger by Mali, c1230-c1340, whose Moslem rulers imported Egyptians to help make **Timbuktu** a center of commerce (in gold, leather, slaves) and learning. The Songhay empire (to 1590) replaced Mali. To the S, forest kingdoms produced refined art works (Ife terra cotta, **Benin** bronzes). Other Moslem states in Nigeria (Hausas) and Chad originated in the 11th century, and continued in some form until the 19th century European conquest. Less developed Bantu kingdoms existed across central Africa.

Some 40 Moslem Arab-Persian trading colonies and city-states were established all along the E. African coast from the 10th century (Kilwa, Mogadishu). The interchange with Bantu peoples produced the **Swahili** language and culture. Gold, palm oil, and slaves were brought from the interior, stimulating the growth of the Monamatapa kingdom of the Zambezi (15th century). The Christian Ethiopian empire (from 13th century) continued the traditions of Axum.

Southeast Asia. Islam was introduced into Malaya and the Indonesian islands by Arab, Persian, and

Indian traders. Coastal Moslem cities and states (starting before 1300), enriched by trade, soon dominated the interior. Chief among these was the **Malacca** state, on the Malay peninsula, c1400-1511.

Arts and Statecraft Thrive in Europe: 1350-1600

Italian Renaissance & humanism. Distinctive Italian achievements in the arts in the late Middle Ages (Dante, 1265-1321, Giotto, 1276-1337) led to the vigorous new styles of the Renaissance (14th-16th centuries). Patronized by the rulers of the quarreling petty states of Italy (Medicis in Florence and the papacy, c1400-1737), the plastic arts perfected realistic techniques, including **perspective** (Masaccio, 1401-28, Leonardo 1452-1519). Classical motifs were used in architecture and increased talent and expense were put into secular buildings. The Florentine dialect was refined as a national literary language (Petrarch, 1304-74). Greek refugees from the E strengthened the respect of humanist scholars for the classic sources (Bruni 1370-1444). Soon an international movement aided by the spread of **printing** (Gutenberg c1400-1468), **humanism** was optimistic about the power of human reason (Erasmus of Rotterdam, 1466-1536, Thomas More's *Utopia*, 1516) and valued individual effort in the arts and in politics (Machiavelli, 1469-1527).

France. The French monarchy, strengthened in its repeated struggles with powerful nobles (Burgundy, Flanders, Aquitaine) by alliances with the growing commercial towns, consolidated bureaucratic control under Philip IV (ruled 1285-1314) and extended French influence into Germany and Italy (popes at Avignon, France, 1309-1417). The **Hundred Years War**, 1337-1453, ended English dynastic claims in France (battles of Crécy, 1346, Poitiers, 1356; Joan of Arc executed, 1431). A French Renaissance, dating from royal invasions of Italy, 1494, 1499, was encouraged at the court of Francis I (ruled 1515-47), who centralized taxation and law. French vernacular literature consciously asserted its independence (La Pleiade, 1549).

England. The evolution of England's unique political institutions began with the Magna Carta, 1215, by which King John guaranteed the privileges of nobles and church against the monarchy and assured jury trial. After the Wars of the Roses (1455-85), the **Tudor dynasty** reasserted royal prerogatives (Henry VIII, ruled 1509-47), but the trend toward independent departments and ministerial government also continued. English trade (wool exports from c1340) was protected by the nation's growing maritime power (**Spanish Armada** destroyed, 1588).

English replaced French and Latin in the late 14th century in law and literature (Chaucer, 1340-1400) and English translation of the Bible began (Wycliffe, 1380s). Elizabeth I (ruled 1558-1603) presided over a confident flowering of poetry (Spenser, 1552-99), drama (**Shakespeare**, 1564-1616), and music.

German Empire. From among a welter of minor feudal states, church lands, and independent cities, the **Hapsburgs** assembled a far-flung territorial domain, based in Austria from 1276. The family held the title Holy Roman Emperor from 1452 to the Empire's dissolution in 1806, but failed to centralize its domains, leaving Germany disunited for centuries. Resistance to Turkish expansion brought Hungary under Austrian control from the 16th century. The Netherlands, Luxembourg, and Burgundy were added in 1477, curbing French expansion.

The Flemish painting tradition of naturalism, technical proficiency, and bourgeois subject matter began in the 15th century (Jan Van Eyck, 1366-1440), the earliest northern manifestation of the Renaissance. **Dürer** (1471-1528) typified the merging of late Gothic and Italian trends in 16th century German art. Imposing civic architecture flourished in the prosperous commercial cities.

Spain. Despite the unification of Castile and Aragon in 1479, the 2 countries retained separate governments, and the nobility, especially in Aragon and Catalonia, retained many privileges. Spanish lands in Italy (Naples, Sicily) and the Netherlands entangled the country in European wars through the mid-17th century, while explorers, traders, and conquerors built up a Spanish empire in the Americas and the Philippines.

From the late 15th century, a **golden age** of literature and art produced works of social satire (plays of Lope de Vega, 1562-1635; Cervantes, 1547-1616), as well as spiritual intensity (El Greco, 1541-1614; Velazquez, 1599-1660).

Black Death. The bubonic plague reached Europe from the E in 1348, killing as much as half the population by 1350. Labor scarcity forced a rise in wages and brought greater freedom to the peasantry, making possible **peasant uprisings** (Jacquerie in France, 1358, Wat Tyler's rebellion in England, 1381). In the *ciompi* revolt, 1378, Florentine wage earners demanded a say in economic and political power.

Explorations. Organized European maritime exploration began, seeking to evade the Venice-Ottoman monopoly of eastern trade and to promote Christianity. Expeditions from Portugal beginning 1418 explored the west coast of Africa, until **Vasco da Gama** rounded the Cape of Good Hope in 1497 and reached India. A Portuguese trading empire was consolidated by the seizure of Goa, 1510, and Malacca, 1551. Japan was reached in 1542. Spanish voyages (**Columbus**, 1492-1504) uncovered a new world, which Spain hastened to subdue. Navigation schools in Spain and Portugal, the development of large sailing ships (carracks), and the invention of the rifle, c1475, aided European penetration.

Mughals and Safavids. East of the Ottoman empire, two Moslem dynasties ruled unchallenged in the 16th and 17th centuries. The Mughal empire in India, founded by Persianized Turkish invaders from the NW under Babur, dates from their 1526 conquest of Delhi. The dynasty ruled most of India for over 200 years, surviving nominally until 1857. **Akbar** (ruled 1556-1605) consolidated administration at his glorious court, where Urdu (Persian-influenced Hindi) developed. Trade relations with Europe increased. Under Shah Jahan (1629-58), a secularized art fusing Hindu and Moslem elements flourished in miniature painting and in architecture (**Taj Mahal**). Sikhism, founded c1519, combined elements of both faiths. Suppression of Hindus and Shi'ite Moslems in S India in the late 17th century weakened the empire.

Fanatical devotion to the Shi'ite sect characterized the Safavids of Persia, 1502-1736, and led to hostilities with the Sunni Ottomans for over a century. The prosperity and strength of the empire are evidenced by the mosques at its capital, **Isfahan**. The dynasty enhanced Iranian national consciousness.

China. The Ming emperors, 1368-1644, the last native dynasty in China, wielded unprecedented personal power, while the Confucian bureaucracy began to suffer from inertia. European trade (Portuguese

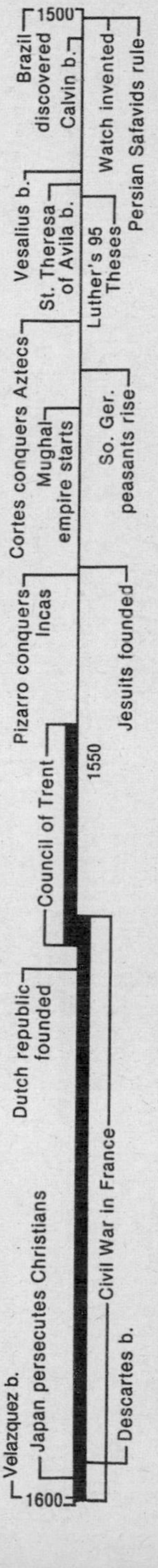

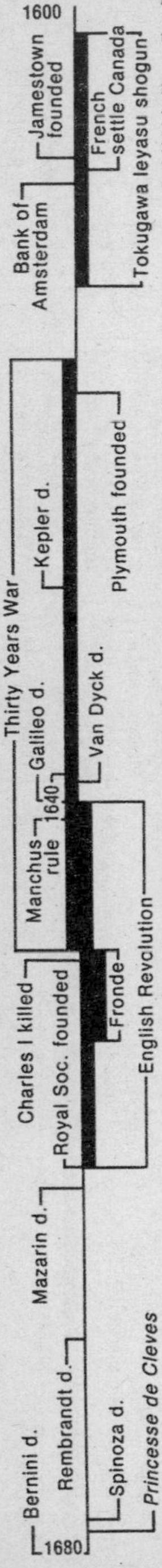

monopoly through **Macao** from 1557) was strictly controlled. Jesuit scholars and scientists (Matteo Ricci 1552-1610) introduced some Western science; their writings familiarized the West with China. Chinese technological inventiveness declined from this era, but the arts thrived, especially painting and ceramics.

Japan. After the decline of the first hereditary shogunate (chief generalship) at **Kamakura** (1185-1333), fragmentation of power accelerated, as did the consequent social mobility. Under Kamakura and the Ashikaga shogunate, 1338-1573, the daimyos (lords) and samurai (warriors) grew more powerful and promoted a martial ideology. Japanese pirates and traders plied the China coast. Popular Buddhist movements included the nationalist Nichiren sect (from c1250) and **Zen** (brought from China, 1191), which stressed meditation and a disciplined esthetic (tea ceremony, landscape gardening, judo, Noh drama).

Reformed Europe Expands Overseas: 1500-1700

Reformation begun. Theological debate and protests against real and perceived clerical corruption existed in the medieval Christian world, expressed by such dissenters as Wycliffe (c1320-84) and his followers, the Lollards, in England, and **Huss** (burned as a heretic, 1415) in Bohemia.

Luther (1483-1546) preached that only faith could lead to salvation, without the mediation of clergy or good works. He attacked the authority of the Pope, rejected priestly celibacy, and recommended individual study of the Bible (which he translated, c1525). His 95 Theses (1517) led to his excommunication (1521). **Calvin** (1509-64) said God's elect were predestined for salvation; good conduct and success were signs of election. Calvin in Geneva and Knox (1505-72) in Scotland erected theocratic states.

Henry VIII asserted English national authority and secular power by breaking away from the Catholic church, 1534. Monastic property was confiscated, and some Protestant doctrines given official sanction.

Religious wars. A century and a half of religious wars began with a South German peasant uprising, 1524, repressed with Luther's support. Radical sects—democratic, pacifist, millenarian—arose (Anabaptists ruled Muenster, 1534-35), and were suppressed violently. Civil war in France from 1562 between **Huguenots** (Protestant nobles and merchants) and Catholics ended with the 1598 Edict of Nantes tolerating Protestants (revoked 1685). Hapsburg attempts to restore Catholicism in Germany were resisted in 25 years of fighting; the 1555 Peace of Augsburg guarantee of religious independence to local princes and cities was confirmed only after the **Thirty Years War,** 1618-48, when much of Germany was devastated by local and foreign armies (Sweden, France).

A Catholic Reformation, or **counter-reformation,** met the Protestant challenge, clearly defining an official theology at the Council of Trent, 1545-63. The **Jesuit** order, founded 1534 by Loyola (1491-1556), helped reconvert large areas of Poland, Hungary, and S. Germany and sent missionaries to the New World, India, and China, while the Inquisition helped suppress heresy in Catholic countries. A revival of piety appeared in the devotional literature (Theresa of Avila, 1515-82) and the grandiose Baroque art (Bernini, 1598-1680) of Roman Catholic countries.

Scientific Revolution. The late nominalist thinkers (Ockham, c1300-49) of Paris and Oxford challenged Aristotelian orthodoxy, allowing for a freer scientific approach. But metaphysical values, such as the Neoplatonic faith in an orderly, mathematical cosmos, still motivated and directed subsequent inquiry. **Copernicus** (1473-1543) promoted the heliocentric theory, which was confirmed when Kepler (1571-1630) discovered the mathematical laws describing the orbits of the planets. The Christian-Aristotelian belief that heavens and earth were fundamentally different collapsed when **Galileo** (1564-1642) discovered moving sunspots, irregular moon topography, and moons around Jupiter. He and **Newton** (1642-1727) developed a mechanics that unified cosmic and earthly phenomena. To meet the needs of the new physics, Newton and Leibnitz (1646-1716) invented **calculus,** Descartes (1596-1650) invented analytic geometry.

An explosion of observational science included the discovery of blood circulation (Harvey, 1578-1657) and microscopic life (Leeuwenhoek, 1632-1723), and advances in anatomy (Vesalius, 1514-64, dissected corpses) and chemistry (Boyle, 1627-91). Scientific research institutes were founded: Florence, 1657, London (**Royal Society**), 1660, Paris, 1666. Inventions proliferated (Savery's steam engine, 1696).

Arts. Mannerist trends of the high Renaissance (**Michelangelo**, 1475-1564) exploited virtuosity, grace, novelty, and exotic subjects and poses. The notion of artistic genius was promoted, in contrast to the anonymous medieval artisan. Private connoisseurs entered the art market. These trends were elaborated in the 17th century **Baroque** era, on a grander scale. Dynamic movement in painting and sculpture was emphasized by sharp lighting effects, use of rich materials (colored marble, gilt), realistic details. Curved facades, broken lines, rich, deep-cut detail, and ceiling decoration characterized Baroque architecture, especially in Germany. Monarchs, princes, and prelates, usually Catholic, used Baroque art to enhance and embellish their authority, as in royal portraits by Velazquez (1599-1660) and Van Dyck (1599-1641).

National styles emerged. In France, a taste for rectilinear order and serenity (Poussin, 1594-1665), linked to the new rational philosophy, was expressed in classical forms. The influence of **classical values** in French literature (tragedies of Racine, 1639-99) gave rise to the "battle of the Ancients and Moderns." New forms included the essay (Montaigne, 1533-92) and novel (*Princesse de Cleves,* La Fayette, 1678).

Dutch painting of the 17th century was unique in its wide social distribution. The Flemish tradition of undemonstrative realism reached its peak in **Rembrandt** (1606-69) and Vermeer (1632-75).

Economy. European economic expansion was stimulated by the new trade with the East, New World gold and silver, and a doubling of population (50 mln. in 1450, 100 mln. in 1600). New business and financial techniques were developed and refined, such as joint-stock companies, insurance, and letters of credit and exchange. The Bank of Amsterdam, 1609, and the Bank of England, 1694, broke the old monopoly of private banking families. The rise of a business mentality was typified by the spread of clock towers in cities in the 14th century. By the mid-15th century, portable clocks were available; the first watch was invented in 1502.

By 1650, most governments had adopted the **mercantile system,** in which they sought to amass metallic wealth by protecting their merchants' foreign and colonial trade monopolies. The rise in prices and the new coin-based economy undermined the craft guild and feudal manorial systems. Expanding industries, such as clothweaving and mining, benefitted from technical advances. Coal replaced disappearing wood as the chief fuel; it was used to fuel new 16th century blast furnaces making cast iron.

New World. The **Aztecs** united much of the Meso-American culture area in a militarist empire by 1519, from their capital, Tenochtitlán (pop. 300,000), which was the center of a cult requiring enormous levels of ritual human sacrifice. Most of the civilized areas of S. America were ruled by the centralized **Inca Empire** (1476-1534), stretching 2,000 miles from Ecuador to N.W. Argentina. Lavish and sophisticated traditions in pottery, weaving, sculpture, and architecture were maintained in both regions.

These empires, beset by revolts, fell in 2 short campaigns to gold-seeking Spanish forces based in the Antilles and Panama. **Cortes** took Mexico, 1519-21; **Pizarro** Peru, 1531-35. From these centers, land and sea expeditions claimed most of N. and S. America for Spain. The Indian high cultures did not survive the impact of Christian missionaries and the new upper class of whites and mestizos. In turn, New World silver, and such Indian products as potatoes, tobacco, corn, peanuts, chocolate, and rubber exercised a major economic influence on Europe. While the Spanish administration intermittently concerned itself with the welfare of Indians, the population remained impoverished at most levels, despite the growth of a distinct South American civilization. European diseases reduced the native population.

Brazil, which the Portuguese reached in 1500 and settled after 1530, and the Caribbean colonies of several European nations developed a plantation economy where sugarcane, tobacco, cotton, coffee, rice, indigo, and lumber were grown commercially by slaves. From the early 16th to the late 19th centuries, some 10 million Africans were transported to **slavery** in the New World.

Netherlands. The urban, Calvinist northern provinces of the Netherlands rebelled against Hapsburg Spain, 1568, and founded an oligarchic mercantile republic. Their strategic control of the Baltic grain market enabled them to exploit Mediterranean food shortages. Religious refugees — French and Belgian Protestants, Iberian Jews — added to the cosmopolitan commercial talent pool. After Spain absorbed Portugal in 1580, the Dutch seized Portuguese possessions and created a vast, though generally short-lived commercial empire in Brazil, the Antilles, Africa, India, Ceylon, Malacca, Indonesia, and Taiwan, and challenged or supplanted Portuguese traders in China and Japan. Revolution in 1640 restored Portuguese independence.

England. Anglicanism became firmly established under Elizabeth I after a brief Catholic interlude under "Bloody Mary," 1553-58. But religious and political conflicts led to a rebellion by Parliament, 1642. Roundheads (Puritans) defeated Cavaliers (Royalists); Charles I was beheaded, 1649. The new **Commonwealth** was ruled as a military dictatorship by Cromwell, who also brutally crushed an Irish rebellion, 1649-51. Conflicts within the Puritan camp (democratic Levelers defeated 1649) aided the Stuart restoration, 1660, but Parliament was permanently strengthened and the peaceful **"Glorious Revolution"**, 1688, advanced political and religious liberties (writings of Locke, 1632-1704). British privateers (Drake, 1540-96) challenged Spanish control of the New World, and penetrated Asian trade routes (Madras taken, 1639). N. American colonies (Jamestown, 1607, Plymouth, 1620) provided an outlet for religious dissenters.

France. Emerging from the religious civil wars in 1628, France regained military and commercial great power status under the ministries of **Richelieu** (1624-42), Mazarin (1643-61), and Colbert (1662-83). Under Louis XIV (ruled 1643-1715) royal absolutism triumphed over nobles and local *parlements* (defeat of Fronde, 1648-53). Permanent colonies were founded in Canada (1608), the Caribbean (1626), and India (1674).

Sweden. Sweden seceded from the Scandinavian Union in 1523. The thinly-populated agrarian state (with copper, iron, and timber exports) was united by the Vasa kings, whose conquests by the mid-17th century made Sweden the dominant Baltic power. The empire collapsed in the Great Northern War (1700-21).

Poland. After the union with Lithuania in 1447, Poland ruled vast territories from the Baltic to the Black Sea, resisting German and Turkish incursions. Catholic nobles failed to gain the loyalty of the Orthodox Christian peasantry in the East; commerce and trades were practiced by German and Jewish immigrants. The bloody 1648-49 cossack uprising began the kingdom's dismemberment.

China. A new dynasty, the **Manchus**, invaded from the NE, seized power in 1644, and expanded Chinese control to its greatest extent in Central and Southeast Asia. Trade and diplomatic contact with Europe grew, carefully controlled by China. New crops (sweet potato, maize, peanut) allowed an economic and population growth (300 million pop. in 1800). Traditional arts and literature were pursued with increased sophistication (*Dream of the Red Chamber*, novel, mid-18th century).

Japan. Tokugawa Ieyasu, shogun from 1603, finally unified and pacified feudal Japan. Hereditary daimyos and samurai monopolized government office and the professions. An urban merchant class grew, literacy spread, and a cultural renaissance occurred (haiku of Basho, 1644-94). Fear of European domination led to persecution of Christian converts from 1597, and stringent isolation from outside contact from 1640.

Philosophy, Industry, and Revolution: 1700-1800

Science and Reason. Faith in human reason and science as the source of truth and a means to improve the physical and social environment, espoused since the Renaissance (Francis Bacon, 1561-1626), was bolstered by scientific discoveries in spite of theological opposition (**Galileo's forced retraction**, 1633). Descartes applied the logical method of mathematics to discover "self-evident" scientific and philosophical truths, while Newton emphasized induction from experimental observation.

The challenge of reason to traditional religious and political values and institutions began with **Spinoza** (1632-77), who interpreted the Bible historically and called for political and intellectual freedom.

French philosophes assumed leadership of the **"Enlightenment"** in the 18th century. Montesquieu (1689-1755) used British history to support his notions of limited government. Voltaire's (1694-1778) diaries and novels of exotic travel illustrated the intellectual trends toward secular ethics and relativism. Rousseau's (1712-1778) radical concepts of the **social contract** and of the inherent goodness of the common man gave impetus to anti-monarchical republicanism. The *Encyclopedia*, 1751-72, edited by Diderot and d'Alembert, designed as a monument to reason, was largely devoted to practical technology.

In England, ideals of political and religious liberty were connected with empiricist philosophy and science in the followers of Locke. But the extreme **empiricism of Hume** (1711-76) and Berkeley

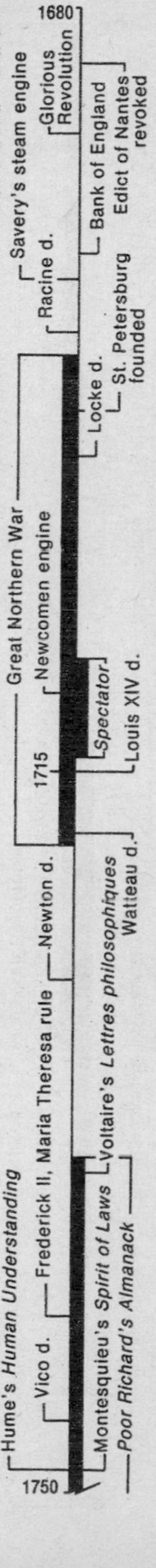

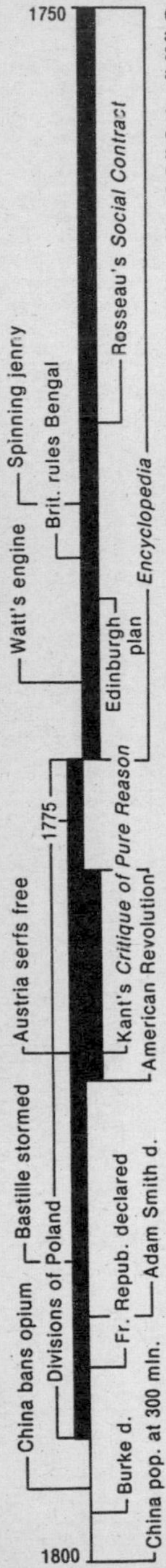

(1685-1753) posed limits to the identification of reason with absolute truth, as did the evolutionary approach to law and politics of Burke (1729-97) and the utilitarianism of Bentham (1748-1832). Adam Smith (1723-90) and other **physiocrats** called for a rationalization of economic activity by removing artificial barriers to a supposedly natural free exchange of goods.

Despite the political disunity and backwardness of most of Germany, German writers participated in the new philosophical trends popularized by Wolff (1679-1754). **Kant's** (1724-1804) **idealism**, unifying an empirical epistemology with *a priori* moral and logical concepts, directed German thought away from skepticism. Italian contributions included work on electricity by Galvani (1737-98) and Volta (1745-1827), the pioneer **historiography of Vico** (1668-1744), and writings on penal reform by Beccaria (1738-94). The American Franklin (1706-90) was celebrated in Europe for his varied achievements.

The growth of the **press** (*Spectator*, 1711-14) and the wide distribution of realistic but sentimental **novels** attested to the increase of a large bourgeois public.

Arts. Rococo art, characterized by extravagant decorative effects, asymmetries copied from organic models, and artificial pastoral subjects, was favored by the continental aristocracy for most of the century (Watteau, 1684-1721), and had musical analogies in the ornamentalized polyphony of late Baroque. The **Neoclassical** art after 1750, associated with the new scientific archeology, was more streamlined, and infused with the supposed moral and geometric rectitude of the Roman Republic (David, 1748-1825). In England, **town planning** on a grand scale began.

Industrial Revolution in England. Agricultural improvements, such as the sowing drill (1701) and livestock breeding, were implemented on the large fields provided by enclosure of common lands by private owners. Profits from agriculture and from colonial and foreign trade (1800 volume, £ 54 million) were channelled through hundreds of banks and the **Stock Exchange** (founded 1773) into new industrial processes.

The Newcomen steam pump (1712) aided coal mining. Coal fueled the new efficient steam engines patented by Watt in 1769, and coke-smelting produced cheap, sturdy iron for machinery by the 1730s. The **flying shuttle** (1733) and **spinning jenny** (1764) were used in the large new cotton textile factories, where women and children were much of the work force. Goods were transported cheaply over **canals** (2,000 miles built 1760-1800).

American Revolution. The British colonies in N. America attracted a mass immigration of religious dissenters and poor people throughout the 17th and 18th centuries, coming from all parts of the British Isles, Germany, the Netherlands, and other countries. The population reached 3 million whites and blacks by the 1770s. The small native population was decimated by European diseases and wars with and between the various colonies. British attempts to control colonial trade, and to tax the colonists to pay for the costs of colonial administration and defense clashed with traditions of local self government, and eventually provoked the colonies to rebellion. (*See American Revolution in Index.*)

Central and East Europe. The monarchs of the three states that dominated eastern Europe — Austria, Prussia, and Russia — accepted the advice and legitimation of philosophes in creating more modern, centralized institutions in their kingdoms, enlarged by the division of Poland (1772-95).

Under **Frederick II** (ruled 1740-86) Prussia, with its efficient modern army, doubled in size. State monopolies and tariff protection fostered industry, and some legal reforms were introduced. Austria's heterogeneous realms were legally unified under **Maria Theresa** (ruled 1740-80) and **Joseph II** (1780-90). Reforms in education, law, and religion were enacted, and the Austrian serfs were freed (1781). With its defeat in the Seven Years' War in 1763, Austria lost Silesia and ceased its active role in Germany, but was compensated by expansion to the E and S (Hungary, Slavonia, 1699, Galicia, 1772).

Russia, whose borders continued to expand in all directions, adopted some Western bureaucratic and economic policies under **Peter I** (ruled 1682-1725) and Catherine II (ruled 1762-96). Trade and cultural contacts with the West multiplied from the new Baltic Sea capital, **St. Petersburg** (founded 1703).

French Revolution. The growing French middle class lacked political power, and resented aristocratic tax privileges, especially in light of liberal political ideals popularized by the American Revolution. Peasants lacked adequate land and were burdened with feudal obligations to nobles. Wars with Britain drained the treasury, finally forcing the king to call the **Estates-General** in 1789 (first time since 1614), in an atmosphere of food riots (poor crop in 1788).

Aristocratic resistance to absolutism was soon overshadowed by the reformist Third Estate (middle class), which proclaimed itself the **National Constituent Assembly** June 17 and took the "Tennis Court oath" on June 20 to secure a constitution. The storming of the **Bastille** July 14 by Parisian artisans was followed by looting and seizure of aristocratic property throughout France. Assembly reforms included abolition of class and regional privileges, a Declaration of Rights, suffrage by taxpayers (75% of males), and the **Civil Constitution of the Clergy** providing for election and loyalty oaths for priests. A republic was declared Sept. 22, 1792, in spite of royalist pressure from Austria and Prussia, which had declared war in April (joined by Britain the next year). Louis XVI was beheaded Jan. 21, 1793, Queen Marie Antoinette was beheaded Oct. 16, 1793.

Royalist uprisings in La Vendee and military reverses led to a **reign of terror** in which tens of thousands of opponents of the Revolution and criminals were executed. Radical reforms in the **Convention** period (Sept. 1793-Oct. 1795) included the abolition of colonial slavery, economic measures to aid the poor, support of public education, and a short-lived de-Christianization.

Division among radicals (execution of Hebert, March 1794, Danton, April, and Robespierre, July) aided the ascendance of a moderate **Directory**, which consolidated military victories. **Napoleon Bonaparte** (1769-1821), a popular young general, exploited political divisions and participated in a coup Nov. 9, 1799, making himself first consul (dictator).

India. Sikh and Hindu rebels (Rajputs, Marathas) and Afghans destroyed the power of the Mughals during the 18th century. After France's defeat in the Seven Years War, 1763, Britain was the chief European trade power in India. Its control of inland **Bengal and Bihar** was recognized by the Mughal shah in 1765, who granted the **British East India Co.** (under Clive, 1727-74) the right to collect land revenue there. Despite objections from Parliament (1784 India Act) the company's involvement in local wars and politics led to repeated acquisitions of new territory. The company exported Indian textiles, sugar, and indigo.

Change Gathers Steam: 1800-1840

French ideals and empire spread. Inspired by the ideals of the French Revolution, and supported by the expanding French armies, new republican regimes arose near France: the **Batavian** Republic in the Netherlands (1795-1806), the **Helvetic** Republic in Switzerland (1798-1803), the **Cisalpine** Republic in N. Italy (1797-1805), the **Ligurian** Republic in Genoa (1797-1805), and the **Parthenopean** Republic in S. Italy (1799). A Roman Republic existed briefly in 1798 after Pope Pius VI was arrested by French troops. In Italy and Germany, new nationalist sentiments were stimulated both in imitation of and reaction to France (anti-French and anti-Jacobin peasant uprisings in Italy, 1796-9).

From 1804, when Napoleon declared himself emperor, to 1812, a succession of military victories (Austerlitz, 1805, Jena, 1806) extended his control over most of Europe, through puppet states (**Confederation of the Rhine** united W. German states for the first time and **Grand Duchy of Warsaw** revived Polish national hopes), expansion of the empire, and alliances.

Among the lasting reforms initiated under Napoleon's absolutist reign were: establishment of the Bank of France, centralization of tax collection, codification of law along Roman models (*Code Napoleon*), and reform and extension of secondary and university education. In an 1801 concordat, the papacy recognized the effective autonomy of the French Catholic Church. Some 400,000 French soldiers were killed in the Napoleonic Wars, along with 600,000 foreign troops.

Last gasp of old regime. France's coastal blockade of Europe (**Continental System**) failed to neutralize Britain. The disastrous 1812 invasion of Russia exposed Napoleon's overextension. After an 1814 exile at Elba, Napoleon's armies were defeated at **Waterloo,** 1815, by British and Prussian troops.

At the **Congress of Vienna,** the monarchs and princes of Europe redrew their boundaries, to the advantage of Prussia (in Saxony and the Ruhr), Austria (in Illyria and Venetia), and Russia (in Poland and Finland). British conquest of Dutch and French colonies (S. Africa, Ceylon, Mauritius) was recognized, and France, under the restored Bourbons, retained its expanded 1792 borders. The settlement brought 50 years of international peace to Europe.

But the Congress was unable to check the advance of liberal ideals and of nationalism among the smaller European nations. The 1825 **Decembrist uprising** by liberal officers in Russia was easily suppressed. But an independence movement in **Greece,** stirred by commercial prosperity and a cultural revival, succeeded in expelling Ottoman rule by 1831, with the aid of Britain, France, and Russia.

A constitutional monarchy was secured in France by an **1830 revolution;** Louis Philippe became king. The revolutionary contagion spread to **Belgium,** which gained its independence from the Dutch monarchy, 1830; to **Poland,** whose rebellion was defeated by Russia, 1830-31; and to Germany.

Romanticism. A new style in intellectual and artistic life began to replace Neo-classicism and Rococo after the mid-18th century. By the early 19th, this style, Romanticism, had prevailed in the European world.

Rousseau had begun the reaction against excessive rationalism and skepticism; in education (*Emile,* 1762) he stressed subjective spontaneity over regularized instruction. In Germany, Lessing (1729-81) and Herder (1744-1803) favorably compared the German folk song to classical forms, and began a cult of Shakespeare, whose passion and "natural" wisdom was a model for the Romantic *Sturm und Drang* (storm and stress) movement. **Goethe's** *Sorrows of Young Werther* (1774) set the model for the tragic, passionate genius.

A new interest in **Gothic architecture** in England after 1760 (Walpole, 1717-97) spread through Europe, associated with an aesthetic Christian and mystic revival (Blake, 1757-1827). Celtic, Norse, and German mythology and folk tales were revived or imitated (Macpherson's Ossian translation, 1762, Grimm's *Fairy Tales,* 1812-22). The medieval revival (Scott's *Ivanhoe,* 1819) led to a new interest in history, stressing national differences and organic growth (Carlyle, 1795-1881; Michelet, 1798-1874), corresponding to theories of natural evolution (Lamarck's *Philosophie zoologique,* 1809, Lyell's *Geology,* 1830-33).

Revolution and war fed an obsession with freedom and conflict, expressed by poets (**Byron,** 1788-1824, **Hugo,** 1802-85) and philosophers (**Hegel,** 1770-1831).

Wild gardens replaced the formal French variety, and painters favored rural, stormy, and mountainous landscapes (**Turner,** 1775-1851; **Constable,** 1776-1837). Clothing became freer, with wigs, hoops, and ruffles discarded. Originality and genius were expected in the life as well as the work of inspired artists (Murger's *Scenes from Bohemian Life,* 1847-49). Exotic locales and themes (as in "Gothic" horror stories) were used in art and literature (Delacroix, 1798-1863, **Poe,** 1809-49).

Music exhibited the new dramatic style and a breakdown of classical forms (Beethoven, 1770-1827). The use of folk melodies and modes aided the growth of distinct national traditions (Glinka in Russia, 1804-57).

Latin America. Haiti, under the former slave **Toussaint L'Ouverture,** was the first Latin American independent state, 1800. All the mainland Spanish colonies won their independence 1810-24, under such leaders as **Bolivar** (1783-1830). Brazil became an independent empire under the Portuguese prince regent, 1822. A new class of military officers divided power with large landholders and the church.

United States. Heavy immigration and exploitation of ample natural resources fueled rapid economic growth. The spread of the franchise, public education, and antislavery sentiment were signs of a widespread democratic ethic.

China. Failure to keep pace with Western arms technology exposed China to greater European influence, and hampered efforts to bar imports of opium, which had damaged Chinese society and drained wealth overseas. In the **Opium War,** 1839-42, Britain forced China to expand trade opportunities and to cede Hong Kong

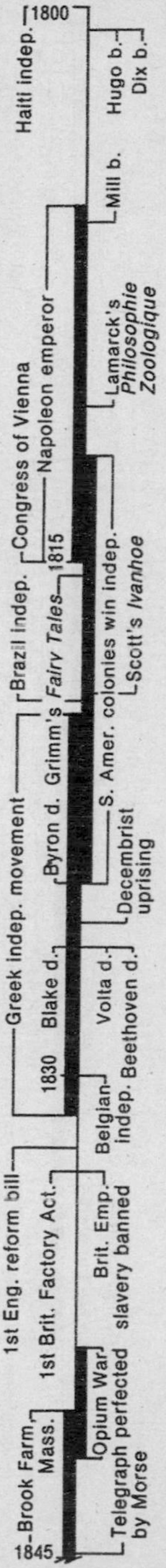

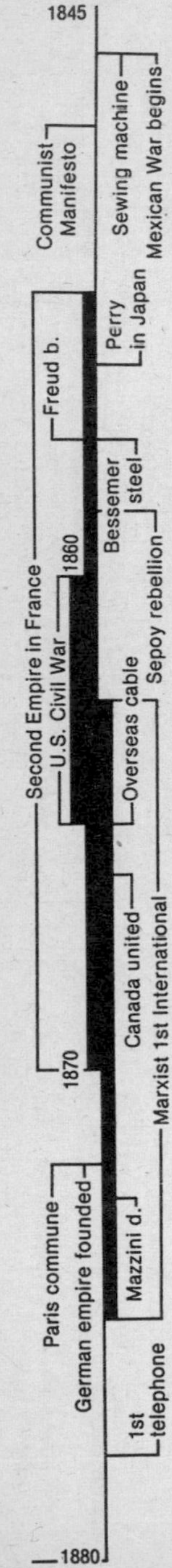

Triumph of Progress: 1840-80

Idea of Progress. As a result of the cumulative scientific, economic, and political changes of the preceding eras, the idea took hold among literate people in the West that continuing growth and improvement was the usual state of human and natural life.

Darwin's statement of the **theory of evolution** and survival of the fittest (*Origin of Species,* 1859), defended by intellectuals and scientists against theological objections, was taken as confirmation that progress was the natural direction of life. The controversy helped define popular ideas of the dedicated scientist and ever-expanding human knowledge of and control over the world (Foucault's demonstration of earth's rotation, 1851, Pasteur's germ theory, 1861).

Liberals following Ricardo (1772-1823) in their faith that unrestrained competition would bring continuous economic expansion sought to adjust political life to the new social realities, and believed that unregulated competition of ideas would yield truth (Mill, 1806-73). In England, successive reform bills (1832, 1867, 1884) gave representation to the new industrial towns, and extended the franchise to the middle and lower classes and to Catholics, Dissenters, and Jews. On both sides of the Atlantic, reformists tried to improve conditions for the mentally ill (Dix, 1802-87), women (Anthony, 1820-1906), and prisoners. Slavery was barred in the British Empire, 1833; the United States, 1865; and Brazil, 1888.

Socialist theories based on ideas of human perfectibility or historical progress were widely disseminated. Utopian socialists like Saint-Simon (1760-1825) envisaged an orderly, just society directed by a technocratic elite. A model factory town, New Lanark, Scotland, was set up by utopian Robert Owen (1771-1858), and utopian communal experiments were tried in the U.S. (Brook Farm, Mass., 1841-7). Bakunin's (1814-76) anarchism represented the opposite utopian extreme of total freedom. Marx (1818-83) posited the inevitable triumph of socialism in the industrial countries through a historical process of class conflict.

Spread of industry. The technical processes and managerial innovations of the English industrial revolution spread to Europe (especially Germany) and the U.S., causing an explosion of industrial production, demand for raw materials, and competition for markets. Inventors, both trained and self-educated, provided the means for larger-scale production (Bessemer steel, 1856, sewing machine, 1846). Many inventions were shown at the 1851 London Great Exhibition at the Crystal Palace, the theme of which was universal prosperity.

Local specialization and long-distance trade were aided by a revolution in transportation and communication. Railroads were first introduced in the 1820s in England and the U.S. Over 150,000 miles of track had been laid worldwide by 1880, with another 100,000 miles laid in the next decade. Steamships were improved (*Savannah* crossed Atlantic, 1819). The telegraph, perfected by 1844 (Morse), connected the Old and New Worlds by cable in 1866, and quickened the pace of international commerce and politics. The first commercial telephone exchange went into operation in the U.S. in 1878.

The new class of industrial workers, uprooted from their rural homes, lacked job security, and suffered from dangerous overcrowded conditions at work and at home. Many responded by organizing trade unions (legalized in England, 1824; France, 1884). The U.S. Knights of Labor had 700,000 members by 1886. The First International, 1864-76, tried to unite workers internationally around a Marxist program. The quasi-Socialist Paris Commune uprising, 1871, was violently suppressed. Factory Acts to reduce child labor and regulate conditions were passed (1833-50 in England). Social security measures were introduced by the Bismarck regime in Germany, 1883-89.

Revolutions of 1848. Among the causes of the continent-wide revolutions were an international collapse of credit and resulting unemployment, bad harvests in 1845-7, and a cholera epidemic. The new urban proletariat and expanding bourgeoisie demanded a greater political role. Republics were proclaimed in France, Rome, and Venice. Nationalist feelings reached fever pitch in the Hapsburg empire, as Hungary declared independence under Kossuth, a Slav Congress demanded equality, and Piedmont tried to drive Austria from Lombardy. A national liberal assembly at Frankfurt called for German unification.

But riots fueled bourgeois fears of socialism (Marx and Engels' 1848 *Communist Manifesto*) and peasants remained conservative. The old establishment — The Papacy, the Hapsburgs (using Croats and Romanians against Hungary), the Russian army — was able to rout the revolutionaries by 1849. The French Republic succumbed to a renewed monarchy by 1852 (Emperor Napoleon III).

Great nations unified. Using the "blood and iron" tactics of Bismarck from 1862, Prussia controlled N. Germany by 1867 (war with Denmark, 1864, Austria, 1866). After defeating France in 1870 (annexation of Alsace-Lorraine), it won the allegiance of S. German states. A new **German Empire** was proclaimed, 1871. **Italy,** inspired by Mazzini (1805-72) and Garibaldi (1807-82), was unified by the reformed Piedmont kingdom through uprisings, plebiscites, and war.

The **U.S.,** its area expanded after the 1846-47 Mexican War, defeated a secession attempt by slave states, 1861-65. The Canadian provinces were united in an autonomous **Dominion of Canada,** 1867. Control in **India** was removed from the East India Co. and centralized under British administration after the 1857-58 Sepoy rebellion, laying the groundwork for the modern Indian State. Queen Victoria was named Empress of India, 1876.

Europe dominates Asia. The Ottoman Empire began to collapse in the face of Balkan nationalisms and European imperial incursions in N. Africa (Suez Canal, 1869). The Turks had lost control of most of both regions by 1882. Russia completed its expansion south by 1884 (despite the temporary setback of the Crimean War with Turkey, Britain, and France, 1853-56) taking Turkestan, all the Caucasus, and Chinese areas in the East and sponsoring Balkan Slavs against the Turks. A succession of reformist and reactionary regimes presided over a slow modernization (serfs freed, 1861). Persian independence suffered as Russia and British India competed for influence.

China was forced to sign a series of unequal treaties with European powers and Japan. Overpopulation and an inefficient dynasty brought misery and caused rebellions (Taiping, Moslems) leaving tens of millions dead. Japan was forced by the U.S. (Commodore Perry's visits, 1853-54) and Europe to end its isolation. The Meiji restoration, 1868, gave power to a Westernizing oligarchy. Intensified empire-building gave Burma to Britain, 1824-86, and Indochina to France, 1862-95. Christian missionary activity followed imperial and trade expansion in Asia.

Respectability. The fine arts were expected to reflect and encourage the progress of morals and manners among the different classes. "Victorian" prudery, exaggerated delicacy, and familial piety were heralded by **Bowdler's** expurgated edition of Shakespeare (1818). Government-supported mass education inculcated a work ethic as a means to escape poverty (Horatio Alger, 1832-99).

The official **Beaux Arts** school in Paris set an international style of imposing public buildings (Paris Opera, 1861-74, Vienna Opera, 1861-69) and uplifting statues (Bartholdi's *Statue of Liberty*, 1885). Realist painting, influenced by photography (Daguerre, 1837), appealed to a new mass audience with social or historical narrative (Wilkie, 1785-1841, Poynter, 1836-1919) or with serious religious, moral, or social messages (pre-Raphaelites, Millet's Angelus, 1858) often drawn from ordinary life. The **Impressionists** (Pissarro, 1830-1903, Renoir, 1841-1919) rejected the central role of serious subject matter in favor of a colorful and sensual depiction of a moment, but their sunny, placid depictions of bourgeois scenes kept them within the respectable consensus.

Realistic **novelists** presented the full panorama of social classes and personalities, but retained sentimentality and moral judgment (Dickens, 1812-70, Eliot, 1819-80, Tolstoy, 1828-1910, Balzac, 1799-1850).

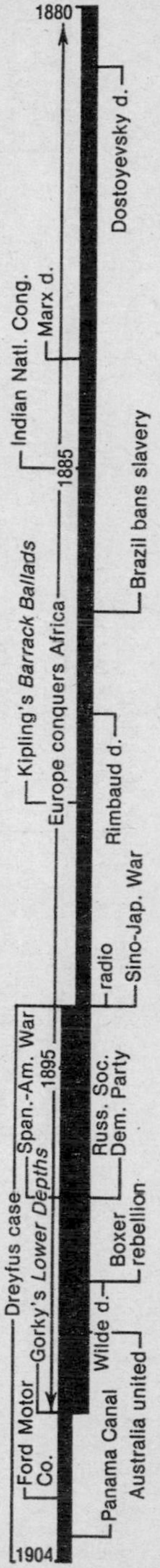

Veneer of Stability: 1880-1900

Imperialism triumphant. The vast **African** interior, visited by European explorers (Barth, 1821-65, Livingstone, 1813-73), was conquered by the European powers in rapid, competitive thrusts from their coastal bases after 1880, mostly for domestic political and international strategic reasons. W. African Moslem kingdoms (Fulani), Arab slave traders (Zanzibar), and Bantu military confederations (Zulu) were alike subdued. Only Christian Ethiopia (defeat of Italy, 1896) and Liberia resisted successfully. France (W. Africa) and Britain ("Cape to Cairo," Boer War, 1899-1902) were the major beneficiaries. The ideology of "the white man's burden" (Kipling, *Barrack Room Ballads*, 1892) or of a "civilizing mission" (France) justified the conquests. (See map on page 501.)

West European foreign capital investment soared to nearly $40 billion by 1914, but most was in E. Europe (France, Germany), the Americas (Britain) and the Europeans' colonies. The foundation of the modern interdependent world economy was laid, with cartels dominating raw material trade.

An industrious world. Industrial and technological proficiency characterized the 2 new great powers — **Germany** and the **U.S.** Coal and iron deposits enabled Germany to reach second or third place status in iron, steel, and shipbuilding by the 1900s. German electrical and chemical industries were world leaders. The U.S. post-civil war boom (interrupted by "panics," 1884, 1893, 1896) was shaped by massive immigration from S. and E. Europe from 1880, government subsidy of railroads, and huge private monopolies (Standard Oil, 1870, U.S. Steel, 1901). The **Spanish-American War**, 1898 (Philippine rebellion, 1899-1901), and the Open Door policy in China (1899) made the U.S. a world power.

England led in **urbanization** (72% by 1890), with **London** the world capital of finance, insurance, and shipping. Sewer systems (Paris, 1850s), electric subways (London, 1890), parks, and bargain department stores helped improve living standards for most of the urban population of the industrial world.

Asians assimilate. Asian reaction to European economic, military, and religious incursions took the form of imitation of Western techniques and adoption of Western ideas of progress and freedom. The Chinese "self-strengthening" movement of the 1860s and 70s included rail, port, and arsenal improvements and metal and textile mills. Reformers like **K'ang Yu-wei** (1858-1927) won liberalizing reforms in 1898, right after the European and Japanese "scramble for concessions."

A universal education system in Japan and importation of foreign industrial, scientific, and military experts aided Japan's unprecedented rapid modernization after 1868, under the authoritarian Meiji regime. Japan's victory in the **Sino-Japanese War**, 1894-95, put Formosa and Korea in its power.

In India, the British alliance with the remaining princely states masked reform sentiment among the Westernized urban elite; higher education had been conducted largely in English for 50 years. The **Indian National Congress**, founded in 1885, demanded a larger government role for Indians.

"Fin-de-siecle" sophistication. Naturalist writers pushed realism to its extreme limits, adopting a quasi-scientific attitude and writing about formerly taboo subjects like sex, crime, extreme poverty, and corruption (Flaubert, 1821-80, Zola, 1840-1902, Hardy, 1840-1928). Unseen or repressed psychological motivations were explored in the clinical and theoretical works of **Freud** (1856-1939) and in the fiction of Dostoevsky (1821-81), James (1843-1916), Schnitzler (1862-1931) and others.

A contempt for bourgeois life or a desire to shock a complacent audience was shared by the French **symbolist** poets (Verlaine, 1844-96, Rimbaud, 1854-91), neo-pagan English writers (Swinburne, 1837-1909), continental dramatists (Ibsen, 1828-1906) and satirists (Wilde, 1854-1900). **Nietzsche** (1844-1900) was influential in his elitism and pessimism.

Post-impressionist art neglected long-cherished conventions of representation (Cezanne, 1839-1906) and showed a willingness to learn from primitive and non-European art (Gauguin, 1848-1903, Japanese prints).

Racism. Gobineau (1816-82) gave a pseudo-biological foundation to modern racist theories, which spread in the latter 19th century along with **Social Darwinism**, the belief that societies are and should be organized as a struggle for survival of the fittest. The Medieval period was interpreted as an era of natural Germanic rule (Chamberlain, 1855-1927) and notions of superiority were associated with German national aspirations (Treitschke, 1834-96). **Anti-Semitism**, with a new racist rationale, became a significant political force in Germany (Anti-Semitic Petition, 1880), Austria (Lueger, 1844-1910), and France (Dreyfus case, 1894-1906).

Last Respite: 1900-1909

Alliances. While the peace of Europe (and its dependencies) continued to hold (1907 **Hague Conference** extended the rules of war and international arbitration procedures), imperial rivalries, protectionist trade practices (in Germany and France), and the escalating arms race (British *Dreadnought* battleship launched, Germany widens Kiel canal, 1906) exacerbated minor disputes (German-French Moroccan "crises", 1905, 1911).

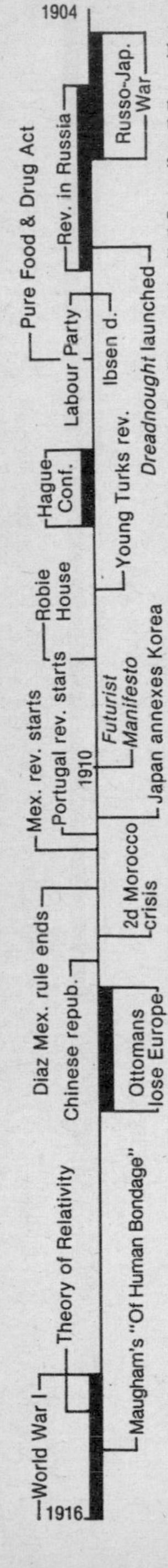

Security was sought through alliances: **Triple Alliance** (Germany, Austria-Hungary, Italy) renewed 1902, 1907; Anglo-Japanese Alliance, 1902; Franco-Russian Alliance, 1899; **Entente Cordiale** (Britain, France), 1904; Anglo-Russian Treaty, 1907; German-Ottoman friendship.

Ottomans decline. The inefficient, corrupt Ottoman government was unable to resist further loss of territory. Nearly all European lands were lost in 1912 to Serbia, Greece, Montenegro, and Bulgaria. Italy took Libya and the Dodecanese islands the same year, and Britain took Kuwait, 1899, and the Sinai, 1906. The **Young Turk** revolution in 1908 forced the sultan to restore a constitution, and introduced some social reform, industrialization, and secularization.

British Empire. British trade and cultural influence remained dominant in the empire, but constitutional reforms presaged its eventual dissolution: the colonies of **Australia** were united in 1901 under a self-governing commonwealth. **New Zealand** acquired dominion status in 1907. The old Boer republics joined Cape Colony and Natal in the self-governing **Union of South Africa** in 1910.

The 1909 Indian Councils Act enhanced the role of elected province legislatures in **India.** The Moslem League, founded 1906, sought separate communal representation.

East Asia. Japan exploited its growing industrial power to expand its empire. Victory in the 1904-05 war against Russia (naval battle of Tsushima, 1905) assured Japan's domination of **Korea** (annexed 1910) and Manchuria (took Port Arthur 1905).

In China, central authority began to crumble (empress died, 1908). Reforms (Confucian exam system ended 1905, modernization of the army, building of railroads) were inadequate and secret societies of reformers and nationalists, inspired by the Westernized **Sun Yat-sen** (1866-1925) fomented periodic uprisings in the south.

Siam, whose independence had been guaranteed by Britain and France in 1896, was split into spheres of influence by those countries in 1907.

Russia. The population of the Russian Empire approached 150 million in 1900. Reforms in education, law, and local institutions (*zemstvos*), and an industrial boom starting in the 1880s (oil, railroads) created the beginnings of a modern state, despite the autocratic tsarist regime. Liberals (1903 Union of Liberation), Socialists (Social Democrats founded 1898, Bolsheviks split off 1903), and populists (Social Revolutionaries founded 1901) were periodically repressed, and national minorities persecuted (anti-Jewish pogroms, 1903, 1905-6).

An industrial crisis after 1900 and harvest failures aggravated poverty among urban workers, and the 1904-05 defeat by Japan (which checked Russia's Asian expansion) sparked the revolution of 1905-06. A **Duma** (parliament) was created, and an agricultural reform (under Stolypin, prime minister 1906-11) created a large class of landowning peasants (kulaks).

The world shrinks. Developments in transportation and communication and mass population movements helped create an awareness of an interdependent world. Early **automobiles** (Daimler, Benz, 1885) were experimental, or designed as luxuries. Assembly-line mass production (Ford Motor Co., 1903) made the invention practicable, and by 1910 nearly 500,000 motor vehicles were registered in the U.S. alone. **Heavier-than-air flights** began in 1903 in the U.S. (Wright brothers), preceded by glider, balloon, and model plane advances in several countries. Trade was advanced by improvements in **ship design** (gyrocompass, 1907), speed (Lusitania crossed Atlantic in 5 days, 1907), and reach (Panama Canal begun, 1904).

The first transatlantic **radio** telegraphic transmission occurred in 1901, 6 years after Marconi discovered radio. Radio transmission of human speech had been made in 1900. Telegraphic transmission of photos was achieved in 1904, lending immediacy to news reports. **Phonographs,** popularized by Caruso's recordings (starting 1902), made for quick international spread of musical styles (ragtime). **Motion pictures,** perfected in the 1890s (Dickson, Lumière brothers), became a popular and artistic medium after 1900; newsreels appeared in 1909.

Emigration from crowded European centers soared in the decade: 9 million migrated to the U.S., and millions more went to Siberia, Canada, Argentina, Australia, South Africa, and Algeria. Some 70 million Europeans emigrated in the century before 1914. Several million Chinese, Indians, and Japanese migrated to Southeast Asia, where their urban skills often enabled them to take a predominant economic role.

Social reform. The social and economic problems of the poor were kept in the public eye by realist fiction writers (Dreiser's *Sister Carrie,* 1900; Gorky's *Lower Depths,* 1902; Sinclair's *Jungle,* 1906), journalists (U.S. **muckrakers** — Steffens, Tarbell) and artists (Ashcan school). Frequent labor strikes and occasional assassinations by anarchists or radicals (Austrian Empress, 1898; King Umberto I of Italy, 1900; U.S. Pres. McKinley, 1901; Russian Interior Minister Plehve, 1904; Portugal's King Carlos, 1908) added to social tension and fear of revolution.

But democratic reformism prevailed. In Germany, Bernstein's (1850-1932) **revisionist Marxism,** downgrading revolution, was accepted by the powerful Social Democrats and trade unions. The British Fabian Society (the Webbs, Shaw) and the Labour Party (founded 1906) worked for reforms such as social security and union rights (1906), while women's suffragists grew more militant. U.S. **progressives** fought big business (Pure Food and Drug Act, 1906). In France, the 10-hour work day (1904) and separation of church and state (1905) were reform victories, as was universal suffrage in Austria (1907).

Arts. An unprecedented period of experimentation, centered in France, produced several new **painting** styles: fauvism exploited bold color areas (Matisse, *Woman with Hat,* 1905); expressionism reflected powerful inner emotions (the Brücke group, 1905); cubism combined several views of an object on one flat surface (Picasso's *Demoiselles,* 1906-07); futurism tried to depict speed and motion (Italian Futurist Manifesto, 1910). **Architects** explored new uses of steel structures, with facades either neo-classical (Adler and Sullivan in U.S.); curvilinear Art Nouveau (Gaudi's Casa Mila, 1905-10); or functionally streamlined (Wright's Robie House, 1909).

Music and **Dance** shared the experimental spirit. Ruth St. Denis (1877-1968) and Isadora Duncan (1878-1927) pioneered modern dance, while Diaghilev in Paris revitalized classic ballet from 1909. Composers explored atonal music (Debussy, 1862-1918) and dissonance (Schönberg, 1874-1951), or revolutionized classical forms (Stravinsky, 1882-1971), often showing jazz or folk music influences.

War and Revolution: 1910-1919

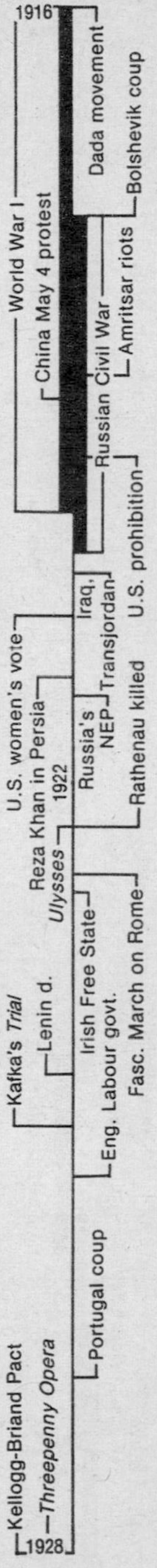

War threatens. Germany under Wilhelm II sought a political and imperial role consonant with its industrial strength, challenging Britain's world supremacy and threatening France, still resenting the loss of Alsace-Lorraine. Austria wanted to curb an expanded Serbia (after 1912) and the threat it posed to its own Slav lands. Russia feared Austrian and German political and economic aims in the Balkans and Turkey. An accelerated arms race resulted: the German standing army rose to over 2 million men by 1914. Russia and France had over a million each, Austria and the British Empire nearly a million each. Dozens of enormous battleships were built by the powers after 1906.

The **assassination of Austrian Archduke Franz Ferdinand** by a Serbian, June 28, 1914, was the pretext for war. The system of alliances made the conflict Europe-wide; Germany's invasion of Belgium to outflank France forced Britain to enter the war. Patriotic fervor was nearly unanimous among all classes in most countries.

World War I. German forces were stopped in France in one month. The rival armies dug **trench networks.** Artillery and improved machine guns prevented either side from any lasting advance despite repeated assaults (600,000 dead at **Verdun,** Feb.-July 1916). Poison gas, used by Germany in 1915, proved ineffective. Over one million U.S. troops tipped the balance after mid-1917, forcing Germany to sue for peace.

In the East, the Russian armies were thrown back (battle of **Tannenberg,** Aug. 20, 1914) and the war grew unpopular. An allied attempt to relieve Russia through Turkey failed (**Gallipoli** 1915). The new Bolshevik regime signed the capitulatory Brest-Litovsk peace in March, 1918. Italy entered the war on the allied side, May 1915, but was pushed back by Oct. 1917. A renewed offensive with Allied aid in Oct.-Nov. 1918 forced Austria to surrender.

The British Navy successfully blockaded Germany, which responded with submarine U-boat attacks; **unrestricted submarine warfare** against neutrals after Jan. 1917 helped bring the U.S. into the war. Other battlefields included Palestine and Mesopotamia, both of which Britain wrested from the Turks in 1917, and the African and Pacific colonies of Germany, most of which fell to Britain, France, Australia, Japan, and South Africa.

From 1916, the civilian populations and economies of both sides were mobilized to an unprecedented degree. Hardships intensified among fighting nations in 1917 (French mutiny crushed in May). More than 10 million soldiers died in the war.

Settlement. At the **Versailles conference** (Jan.-June 1919) and in subsequent negotiations and local wars (Russian-Polish War 1920), the map of Europe was redrawn with a nod to U.S. Pres. Wilson's principle of self-determination. Austria and Hungary were separated and much of their land was given to Yugoslavia (formerly Serbia), Romania, Italy, and the newly independent Poland and Czechoslovakia. Germany lost territory in the West, North, and East, while Finland and the Baltic states were detached from Russia. Turkey lost nearly all its Arab lands to British-sponsored Arab states or to direct French and British rule.

A huge **reparations** burden and partial demilitarization were imposed on Germany. Wilson obtained approval for a League of Nations, but the U.S. Senate refused to allow the U.S. to join.

Russian revolution. Military defeats and high casualties caused a contagious lack of confidence in Tsar Nicholas, who was forced to abdicate, Mar. 1917. A liberal provisional government failed to end the war, and massive desertions, riots, and fighting between factions followed. A moderate socialist government under Kerensky was overthrown in a violent **coup by the Bolsheviks** in Petrograd under Lenin, who disbanded the elected Constituent Assembly, Nov. 1917.

The Bolsheviks brutally suppressed all opposition and ended the war with Germany, Mar. 1918. **Civil war** broke out in the summer between the Red Army, including the Bolsheviks and their supporters, and monarchists, anarchists, nationalities (Ukrainians, Georgians, Poles) and others. Small U.S., British, French and Japanese units also opposed the Bolsheviks, 1918-19 (Japan in Vladivostok to 1922). The civil war, anarchy, and pogroms devastated the country until the 1920 Red Army victory. The wartime total monopoly of political, economic, and police power by the Communist Party leadership was retained.

Other European revolutions. An unpopular monarchy in **Portugal** was overthrown in 1910. The new republic took severe anti-clerical measures, 1911.

After a century of Home Rule agitation, during which **Ireland** was devastated by famine (one million dead, 1846-47) and emigration, republican militants staged an unsuccessful uprising in Dublin, Easter 1916. The execution of the leaders and mass arrests by the British won popular support for the rebels. The Irish Free State, comprising all but the 6 northern counties, achieved dominion status in 1922.

In the aftermath of the world war, radical revolutions were attempted in Germany (**Spartacist** uprising Jan. 1919), **Hungary** (Kun regime 1919), and elsewhere. All were suppressed or failed for lack of support.

Chinese revolution. The Manchu Dynasty was overthrown and a republic proclaimed, Oct. 1911. First president Sun Yat-sen resigned in favor of strongman Yuan Shih-k'ai. Sun organized the parliamentarian **Kuomintang** party.

Students launched protests May 4, 1919 against League of Nations concessions in China to Japan. Nationalist, liberal, and socialist ideas and political groups spread. The **Communist Party** was founded 1921. A communist regime took power in Mongolia with Soviet support in 1921.

India restive. Indian objections to British rule erupted in nationalist riots as well as in the non-violent tactics of Gandhi (1869-1948). Nearly 400 unarmed demonstrators were shot at **Amritsar,** Apr. 1919. Britain approved limited self-rule that year.

Mexican revolution. Under the long Diaz dictatorship (1876-1911) the economy advanced, but Indian and mestizo lands were confiscated, and concessions to foreigners (mostly U.S.) damaged the middle class. A **revolution in 1910** led to civil wars and U.S. intervention (1914, 1916-17). Land reform and a more democratic constitution (1917) were achieved.

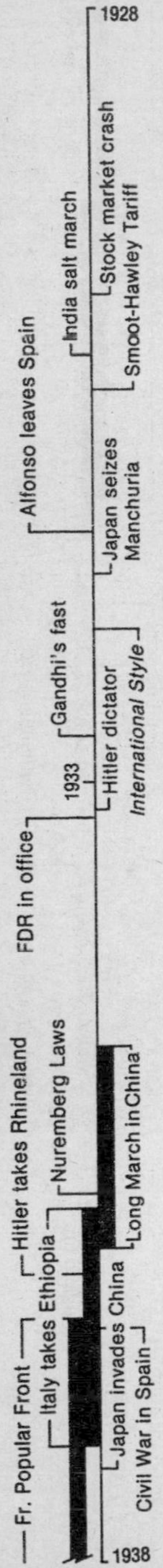

The Aftermath of War: 1920-29

U.S. Easy credit, technological ingenuity, and war-related industrial decline in Europe caused a long economic boom, in which ownership of the new products — autos, phones, radios — became democratized. Prosperity, an increase in women workers, women's suffrage (1920) and drastic change in fashion (flappers, mannish bob for women, clean-shaven men), created a wide perception of social change, despite prohibition of alcoholic beverages (1919-33). Union membership and strikes increased. Fear of radicals led to Palmer raids (1919-20) and Sacco/Vanzetti case (1921-27).

Europe sorts itself out. Germany's liberal **Weimar constitution** (1919) could not guarantee a stable government in the face of rightist violence (Rathenau assassinated 1922) and Communist refusal to cooperate with Socialists. Reparations and allied occupation of the Rhineland caused staggering inflation which destroyed middle class savings, but economic expansion resumed after mid-decade, aided by U.S. loans. A sophisticated, innovative culture developed in architecture and design (Bauhaus, 1919-28), film (Lang, *M*, 1931), painting (Grosz), music (Weill, *Threepenny Opera*, 1928), theater (Brecht, *A Man's a Man*, 1926), criticism (Benjamin), philosophy (Jung), and fashion. This culture was considered decadent and socially disruptive by rightists.

England elected its first labor governments (Jan. 1924, June 1929). A 10-day general strike in support of coal miners failed, May 1926. In **Italy**, strikes, political chaos and violence by small Fascist bands culminated in the Oct. 1922 Fascist March on Rome, which established Mussolini's dictatorship. Strikes were outlawed (1926), and Italian influence was pressed in the Balkans (Albania a protectorate 1926). A conservative dictatorship was also established in **Portugal** in a 1926 military coup.

Czechoslovakia, the only stable democracy to emerge from the war in Central or East Europe, faced opposition from Germans (in the Sudetenland), Ruthenians, and some Slovaks. As the industrial heartland of the old Hapsburg empire, it remained fairly prosperous. With French backing, it formed the Little Entente with Yugoslavia (1920) and **Romania** (1921) to block Austrian or Hungarian irredentism. **Hungary** remained dominated by the landholding classes and expansionist feeling. Croats and Slovenes in **Yugoslavia** demanded a federal state until King Alexander proclaimed a dictatorship (1929). Poland faced nationality problems as well (Germans, Ukrainians, Jews); Pilsudski ruled as dictator from 1926. The Baltic states were threatened by traditionally dominant ethnic Germans and by Soviet-supported communists.

An economic collapse and famine in **Russia**, 1921-22, claimed 5 million lives. The New Economic Policy (1921) allowed land ownership by peasants and some private commerce and industry. Stalin was absolute ruler within 4 years of Lenin's 1924 death. He inaugurated a brutal collectivization program 1929-32, and used foreign communist parties for Soviet state advantage.

Internationalism. Revulsion against World War I led to pacifist agitation, the Kellogg-Briand Pact renouncing aggressive war (1928), and **naval disarmament** pacts (Washington, 1922, London, 1930). But the League of Nations was able to arbitrate only minor disputes (Greece-Bulgaria, 1925).

Middle East. Mustafa Kemal (Ataturk) led **Turkish** nationalists in resisting Italian, French, and Greek military advances, 1919-23. The sultanate was abolished 1922, and elaborate reforms passed, including secularization of law and adoption of the Latin alphabet. Ethnic conflict led to persecution of **Armenians** (over 1 million dead in 1915, 1 million expelled), Greeks (forced Greek-Turk population exchange, 1923), and Kurds (1925 uprising).

With evacuation of the Turks from **Arab** lands, the puritanical Wahabi dynasty of eastern Arabia conquered present Saudi Arabia, 1919-25. British, French, and Arab dynastic and nationalist maneuvering resulted in the creation of two more Arab monarchies in 1921: Iraq and Transjordan (both under British control), and two French mandates: Syria and Lebanon. Jewish immigration into British-mandated **Palestine**, inspired by the Zionist movement, was resisted by Arabs, at times violently (1921, 1929 massacres).

Reza Khan ruled **Persia** after his 1921 coup (shah from 1925), centralized control, and created the trappings of a modern state.

China. The Kuomintang under **Chiang Kai-shek** (1887-1975) subdued the warlords by 1928. The Communists were brutally suppressed after their alliance with the Kuomintang was broken in 1927. Relative peace thereafter allowed for industrial and financial improvements, with some Russian, British, and U.S. cooperation.

Arts. Nearly all bounds of subject matter, style, and attitude were broken in the arts of the period. **Abstract** art first took inspiration from natural forms or narrative themes (Kandinsky from 1911), then worked free of any representational aims (Malevich's suprematism, 1915-19, Mondrian's geometric style from 1917). The **Dada** movement from 1916 mocked artistic pretension with absurd collages and constructions (Arp, Tzara, from 1916). Paradox, illusion, and psychological taboos were exploited by **surrealists** by the latter 1920s (Dali, Magritte). Architectural schools celebrated industrial values, whether vigorous abstract constructivism (Tatlin, *Monument to 3rd International*, 1919) or the machined, streamlined **Bauhaus** style, which was extended to many design fields (Helvetica type face).

Prose writers explored revolutionary narrative modes related to dreams (Kafka's *Trial*, 1925), internal monologue (Joyce's *Ulysses*, 1922), and word play (Stein's *Making of Americans*, 1925). Poets and novelists wrote of modern alienation (Eliot's *Waste Land*, 1922) and aimlessness (Lost Generation).

Sciences. Scientific specialization prevailed by the 20th century. Advances in knowledge and technological aptitude increased with the geometric increase in the number of practitioners. Physicists challenged common-sense views of causality, observation, and a mechanistic universe, putting science further beyond popular grasp (Einstein's general theory of relativity, 1915; Bohr's quantum mechanics, 1913; Heisenberg's uncertainty principle, 1927).

Rise of the Totalitarians: 1930-39

Depression. A worldwide financial panic and economic depression began with the Oct. 1929 U.S. stock market crash and the May 1931 failure of the Austrian Credit-Anstalt. A credit crunch caused international bankruptcies and **unemployment:** 12 million jobless by 1932 in the U.S., 5.6 million in Germany, 2.7 million in England. Governments responded with **tariff restrictions** (Smoot-Hawley Act, 1930; Ottawa Imperial Conference, 1932), which dried up world trade. Government public works programs were vitiated by deflationary budget balancing.

Germany. Years of agitation by violent extremists were brought to a head by the Depression. Nazi leader **Hitler** was named chancellor by Pres. Hindenburg Jan. 1933, and given dictatorial power by the Reichstag in Mar. Opposition parties were disbanded, strikes banned, and all aspects of economic, cultural, and religious life brought under central government and Nazi party control and manipulated by sophisticated propaganda. Severe persecution of Jews began (**Nuremberg Laws** Sept. 1935). Many Jews, political opponents and others were sent to concentration camps (Dachau, 1933) where thousands died or were killed. Public works, renewed conscription (1935), arms production, and a 4-year plan (1936) all but ended unemployment.

Hitler's expansionism started with reincorporation of the Saar (1935), occupation of the **Rhineland** (Mar. 1936), and annexation of Austria (Mar. 1938). At **Munich**, Sept. 1938, an indecisive Britain and France sanctioned German dismemberment of Czechoslovakia.

Russia. Urbanization and education advanced. Rapid industrialization was achieved through successive **5-year-plans** starting 1928, using severe labor discipline and mass forced labor. Industry was financed by a decline in living standards and exploitation of agriculture, which was almost totally collectivized by the early 1930s (*kolkhoz,* collective farm; *sovkhoz,* state farm, often in newly-worked lands). Successive **purges** increased the role of professionals and management at the expense of workers. Millions perished in a series of man-made disasters: elimination of kulaks (peasant land-owners), 1929-34; severe famine, 1932-33; party purges (Great Purge, 1936-38); suppression of nationalities; and poor conditions in labor camps.

Spain. An industrial revolution during World War I created an urban proletariat, which was attracted to socialism and anarchism; Catalan nationalists challenged central authority. The 5 years after King Alfonso left Spain, Apr. 1931, were dominated by tension between intermittent leftist and anti-clerical governments and clericals, monarchists and other rightists. Anarchist and communist rebellions were crushed, but a July, 1936, extreme right rebellion led by Gen. Francisco Franco and aided by Nazi Germany and Fascist Italy succeeded, after a 3-year **civil war** (over 1 million dead in battles and atrocities). The war polarized international public opinion.

Italy. Despite propaganda for the ideal of the Corporate State, few domestic reforms were attempted. An entente with Hungary and Austria, Mar. 1934, a pact with Germany and Japan, Nov. 1937, and intervention by 50-75,000 troops in Spain, 1936-39, sealed Italy's identification with the fascist bloc (anti-Semitic laws after Mar. 1938). Ethiopia was conquered, 1935-37, and **Albania** annexed, Jan. 1939, in conscious imitation of ancient Rome.

East Europe. Repressive regimes fought for power against an active opposition (liberals, socialists, communists, peasants, Nazis). Minority groups and Jews were restricted within national boundaries that did not coincide with ethnic population patterns. In the destruction of **Czechoslovakia, Hungary** occupied southern Slovakia (Nov. 1938) and Ruthenia (Mar. 1939), and a pro-Nazi regime took power in the rest of Slovakia. Other boundary disputes (e.g. Poland-Lithuania, Yugoslavia-Bulgaria, Romania-Hungary) doomed attempts to build joint fronts against Germany or Russia. Economic depression was severe.

East Asia. After a period of liberalism in **Japan,** nativist militarists dominated the government with peasant support. Manchuria was seized, Sept. 1931-Feb. 1932, and a puppet state set up (Manchukuo). Adjacent Jehol (Inner Mongolia) was occupied in 1933. China proper was invaded July 1937; large areas were conquered by Oct. 1938.

In **China** Communist forces left Kuomintang-besieged strongholds in the South in a Long March (1934-35) to the North. The Kuomintang-Communist civil war was suspended Jan. 1937 in the face of threatening Japan.

The democracies. The Roosevelt Administration, in office Mar. 1933, embarked on an extensive program of social reform and economic stimulation, including protection for labor unions (heavy industries organized), social security, public works, wages and hours laws, assistance to farmers. Isolationist sentiment (1937 Neutrality Act) prevented U.S. intervention in Europe, but military expenditures were increased in 1939.

French political instability and polarization prevented resolution of economic and international security questions. The **Popular Front** government under Blum (June 1936-Apr. 1938) passed social reforms (40-hour week) and raised arms spending. National coalition governments ruled Britain from Aug. 1931, brought some economic recovery, but failed to define a consistent foreign policy until Chamberlain's government (from May 1937), which practiced deliberate **appeasement** of Germany and Italy.

India. Twenty years of agitation for autonomy and then for independence (Gandhi's **salt march,** 1930) achieved some constitutional reform (extended provincial powers, 1935) despite Moslem-Hindu strife. Social issues assumed prominence with peasant uprisings (1921), strikes (1928), Gandhi's efforts for untouchables (1932 "fast unto death"), and social and agrarian reform by the provinces after 1937.

Arts. The streamlined, geometric design motifs of Art Deco (from 1925) prevailed through the 1930s. Abstract art flourished (Moore sculptures from 1931) alongside a new realism related to social and political concerns (**Socialist Realism** the official Soviet style from 1934; Mexican muralists Rivera, 1886-1957, and Orozco, 1883-1949), which was also expressed in fiction and poetry (Steinbeck's *Grapes of Wrath,* 1939; Sandburg's *The People, Yes,* 1936). Modern architecture (*International Style,* 1932) was unchallenged in its use of man-made materials (concrete, glass), lack of decoration, and monumentality (Rockefeller Center, 1929-40). U.S.-made films captured a world-wide audience with their larger-than-life fantasies (*Gone with the Wind,* 1939).

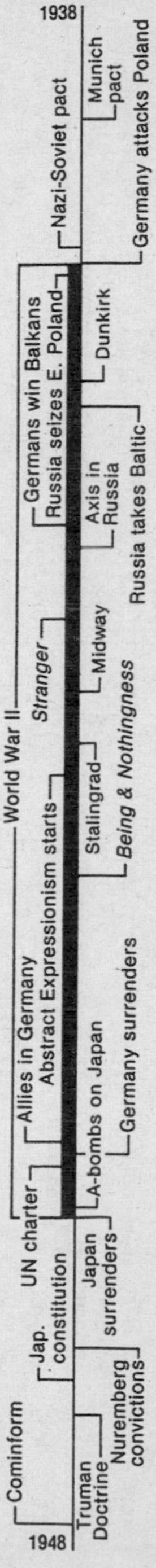

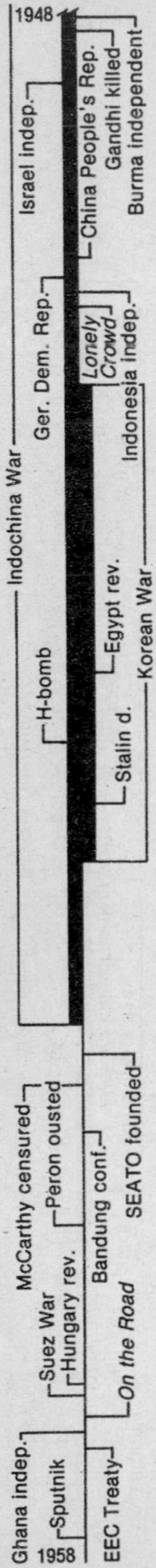

War, Hot and Cold: 1940-49

War in Europe. The Nazi-Soviet non-aggression pact (Aug. '39) freed Germany to attack Poland (Sept.). Britain and France, who had guaranteed Polish independence, declared war on Germany. Russia seized East Poland (Sept.), attacked Finland (Nov.), and took the Baltic states (July '40). Mobile German forces staged **"blitzkrieg"** attacks Apr.-June '40, conquering neutral Denmark, Norway, and the Low Countries and defeating France; 350,000 British and French troops were evacuated at **Dunkirk** (May). The Battle of Britain, June-Dec. '40, denied Germany air superiority. German-Italian campaigns won the Balkans by Apr. '41. Three million Axis troops **invaded Russia** June '41, marching through Ukraine to the Caucasus, and through White Russia and the Baltic republics to Moscow and Leningrad.

Russian winter counterthrusts, '41-'42 and '42-'43, stopped the German advance (Stalingrad Sept. '42-Feb. '43). With British and U.S. Lend-Lease aid and sustaining great casualties, the Russians drove the Axis from all E. Europe and the Balkans in the next 2 years. Invasions of N. Africa (Nov. '42), Italy (Sept. '43), and Normandy (June '44) brought U.S., British, Free French and allied troops to Germany by spring '45. Germany surrendered May 7, 1945.

War in Asia-Pacific. Japan occupied Indochina Sept. '40, dominated Thailand Dec. '41, attacked Hawaii, the Philippines, Hong Kong, Malaya Dec. 7, 1941. Indonesia was attacked Jan. '42, Burma conquered Mar. '42. Battle of **Midway** (June '42) turned back the Japanese advance. "Island-hopping" battles (Guadalcanal Aug. '42-Jan. '43, **Leyte Gulf** Oct. '44, Iwo Jima Feb.-Mar. '45, Okinawa Apr. '45) and massive bombing raids on Japan from June '44 wore out Japanese defenses. Two U.S. atom bombs, dropped Aug. 6 and 9, forced Japan to surrender Aug. 14, 1945.

Atrocities. The war brought 20th-century cruelty to its peak. Nazi murder camps (Auschwitz) systematically killed 6 million Jews. Gypsies, political opponents, sick and retarded people, and others deemed undesirable were murdered by the Nazis, as were vast numbers of Slavs, especially leaders.

Civilian deaths. German bombs killed 70,000 English civilians. Some 100,000 Chinese civilians were killed by Japanese forces in the capture of Nanking. Severe retaliation by the Soviet army, E. European partisans, Free French and others took a heavy toll. U.S. and British bombing of Germany killed hundreds of thousands, as did U.S. bombing of Japan (80-200,000 at Hiroshima alone). Some 45 million people lost their lives in the war.

Settlement. The United Nations charter was signed in San Francisco June 26, 1945 by 50 nations. The International Tribunal at Nuremberg convicted 22 German leaders for war crimes Sept. '46, 23 Japanese leaders were convicted Nov. '48. Postwar border changes included large gains in territory for the USSR, losses for Germany, a shift westward in Polish borders, and minor losses for Italy. Communist regimes, supported by Soviet troops, took power in most of E. Europe, including Soviet-occupied Germany (GDR proclaimed Oct. '49). Japan lost all overseas lands.

Recovery. Basic political and social changes were imposed on Japan and W. Germany by the western allies (Japan constitution Nov. '46, W. German basic law May '49). U.S. Marshall Plan aid ($12 billion '47-'51) spurred W. European economic recovery after a period of severe inflation and strikes in Europe and the U.S. The British Labour Party introduced a national health service and nationalized basic industries in 1946.

Cold War. Western fears of further Soviet advances (Cominform formed Oct. '47, Czechoslovakia coup, Feb. '48, Berlin blockade Apr.'48-Sept. '49) led to formation of NATO. Civil War in Greece and Soviet pressure on Turkey led to U.S. aid under the Truman Doctrine (Mar. '47). Other anti-communist security pacts were the Org. of American States (Apr. '48) and Southeast Asia Treaty Org. (Sept. '54). A new wave of Soviet purges and repression intensified in the last years of Stalin's rule, extending to E. Europe (Slansky trial in Czechoslovakia, 1951). Only Yugoslavia resisted Soviet control (expelled by Cominform, June '48; U.S. aid, June '49).

China, Korea. Communist forces emerged from World War II strengthened by the Soviet takeover of industrial Manchuria. In 4 years of fighting, the Kuomintang was driven from the mainland; the People's Republic was proclaimed Oct. 1, 1949. Korea was divided by Russian and U.S. occupation forces. Separate republics were proclaimed in the 2 zones Aug.-Sept. '48.

India. India and Pakistan became independent dominions Aug. 15, 1947. Millions of Hindu and Moslem refugees were created by the partition; riots, 1946-47, took hundreds of thousands of lives; Gandhi himself was assassinated Jan. '48. Burma became completely independent Jan. '48; Ceylon took dominion status in Feb.

Middle East. The UN approved partition of Palestine into Jewish and Arab states. Israel was proclaimed May 14, 1948. Arabs rejected partition, but failed to defeat Israel in war, May '48-July '49. Immigration from Europe and the Middle East swelled Israel's Jewish population. British and French forces left Lebanon and Syria, 1946. Transjordan occupied most of Arab Palestine.

Southeast Asia. Communists and others fought against restoration of French rule in Indochina from 1946; a non-communist government was recognized by France Mar. '49, but fighting continued. Both Indonesia and the Philippines became independent, the former in 1949 after 4 years of war with Netherlands, the latter in 1946. Philippine economic and military ties with the U.S. remained strong; a communist-led peasant rising was checked in '48.

Arts. New York became the center of the world art market; abstract expressionism was the chief mode (Pollock from '43, de Kooning from '47). Literature and philosophy explored existentialism (Camus's *Stranger,* 1942, Sartre's *Being and Nothingness,* 1943). Non-western attempts to revive or create regional styles (Senghor's Negritude, Mishima's novels) only confirmed the emergence of a universal culture. Radio and phonograph records spread American popular music (swing, bebop) around the world.

The American Decade: 1950-59

Polite decolonization. The peaceful decline of European political and military power in Asia and Africa accelerated in the 1950s. Nearly all of N. Africa was freed by 1956, but France fought a bitter war to retain Algeria, with its large European minority, until 1962. **Ghana,** independent 1957, led a parade of new black African nations (over 2 dozen by 1962), which altered the political character of the UN. Ethnic disputes often exploded in the new nations after decolonization (UN troops in Cyprus 1964; **Nigeria** civil war 1967-70). Leaders of the new states, mostly sharing socialist ideologies, tried to create an Afro-Asian bloc (Bandung Conf. 1955), but Western economic influence and U.S. political ties remained strong (Baghdad Pact, 1955).

Trade. World trade volume soared, in an atmosphere of monetary stability assured by international accords (**Bretton Woods** 1944). In Europe, economic integration advanced (**European Economic Community** 1957, European Free Trade Association 1960). Comecon (1949) coordinated the economies of Soviet-bloc countries.

U.S. Economic growth produced an abundance of consumer goods (9.3 million motor vehicles sold, 1955). Suburban housing tracts changed life patterns for middle and working classes (Levittown 1946-51). **Eisenhower's** landslide election victories (1952, 1956) reflected consensus politics. Censure of McCarthy (Dec. '54) curbed the political abuse of anti-communism. A system of alliances and military bases bolstered U.S. influence on all continents. Trade and payments surpluses were balanced by overseas investments and foreign aid ($50 billion, 1950-59).

USSR. In the "thaw" after Stalin's death in 1953, relations with the West improved (evacuation of Vienna, Geneva summit conf., both 1955). Repression of scientific and cultural life eased, and many prisoners were freed or rehabilitated culminating in **de-Stalinization** (1956). Khrushchev's leadership aimed at consumer sector growth, but farm production lagged, despite the virgin lands program (from 1954). The 1956 Hungarian revolution, the 1960 U-2 spy plane episode, and other incidents renewed East-West tension and domestic curbs.

East Europe. Resentment of Russian domination and Stalinist repression combined with nationalist, economic and religious factors to produce periodic violence. East Berlin workers rioted in 1953, Polish workers rioted in Poznan, June 1956, and a broad-based revolution broke out in Hungary, Oct. 1956. All were suppressed by Soviet force or threats (at least 7,000 dead in Hungary). But Poland was allowed to restore private ownership of farms, and a degree of personal and economic freedom returned to Hungary. Yugoslavia experimented with worker self-management and a market economy.

Korea. The 1945 division of Korea left industry in the North, which was organized into a militant regime and armed by Russia. The South was politically disunited. Over 60,000 North Korean troops invaded the South June 25, 1950. The U.S., backed by the UN Security Council, sent troops. UN troops reached the Chinese border in Nov. Some 200,000 Chinese troops crossed the Yalu River and drove back UN forces. Cease-fire in July 1951 found the opposing forces near the original 38th parallel border. After 2 years of sporadic fighting, an armistice was signed July 27, 1953. U.S. troops remained in the South, and U.S. economic and military aid continued. The war stimulated rapid economic recovery in Japan.

China. Starting in 1952, industry, agriculture, and social institutions were forcibly collectivized. As many as several million people were executed as Kuomintang supporters or as class and political enemies. The Great Leap Forward, 1958-60, unsuccessfully tried to force the pace of development by substituting labor for investment.

Indochina. Ho's forces, aided by Russia and the new Chinese Communist government, fought French and pro-French Vietnamese forces to a standstill, and captured the strategic Dienbienphu camp in May, 1954. The Geneva Agreements divided Vietnam in half pending elections (never held), and recognized Laos and Cambodia as independent. The U.S. aided the anti-Communist Republic of Vietnam in the South.

Middle East. Arab revolutions placed leftist, militantly nationalist regimes in power in Egypt (1952) and Iraq (1958). But Arab unity attempts failed (United Arab Republic joined Egypt, Syria, Yemen 1958-61). Arab refusal to recognize Israel (Arab League economic blockade began Sept. 1951) led to a permanent state of war, with repeated incidents (Gaza, 1955). Israel occupied Sinai, Britain and France took the Suez Canal, Oct. 1956, but were replaced by the UN Emergency Force. The Mossadegh government in Iran nationalized the British-owned oil industry May 1951, but was overthrown in a U.S.-aided coup Aug. 1953.

Latin America. Argentinian Dictator Juan Peron, in office 1946, enforced land reform, some nationalization, welfare state measures, and curbs on the Roman Catholic Church, but crushed opposition. A Sept. 1955 coup deposed Peron. The 1952 revolution in Bolivia brought land reform, nationalization of tin mines, and improvement in the status of Indians, who nevertheless remained poor. The Batista regime in Cuba was overthrown, Jan. 1959, by Fidel Castro, who imposed a communist dictatorship, aligned Cuba with Russia, improved education and health care. A U.S.-backed anti-Castro invasion (Bay of Pigs, Apr. 1961) was crushed. Self-government advanced in the British Caribbean.

Technology. Large outlays on research and development in the U.S. and USSR focused on military applications (H-bomb in U.S. 1952, USSR 1953, Britain 1957, intercontinental missiles late 1950s). Soviet launching of the Sputnik satellite, Oct. 1957, spurred increases in U.S. science education funds (National Defense Education Act).

Literature and letters. Alienation from social and literary conventions reached an extreme in the theater of the absurd (Beckett's *Waiting for Godot* 1952), the "new novel" (Robbe-Grillet's *Voyeur* 1955), and avant-garde film (Antonioni's *L'Avventura* 1960). U.S. Beatniks (Kerouac's *On the Road* 1957) and others rejected the supposed conformism of Americans (Riesman's *Lonely Crowd* 1950).

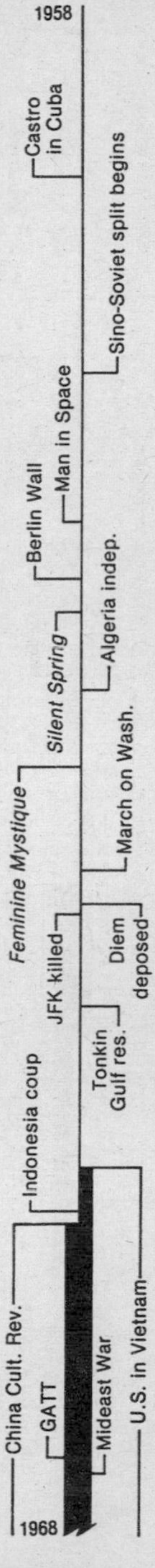

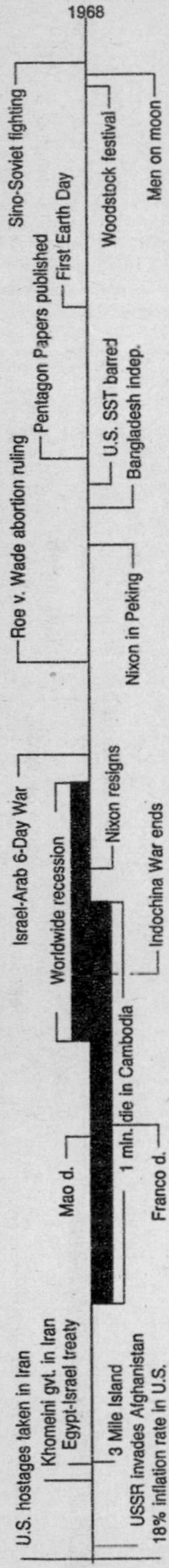

Rising Expectations: 1960-69

Economic boom. The longest sustained economic boom on record spanned almost the entire decade in the capitalist world; the closely-watched GNP figure doubled in the U.S. 1960-70, fueled by Vietnam War-related budget deficits. The **General Agreement on Tariffs and Trade,** 1967, stimulated West European prosperity, which spread to peripheral areas (Spain, Italy, E. Germany). Japan became a top economic power ($20 billion exports 1970). Foreign investment aided the industrialization of Brazil. Soviet 1965 economic reform attempts (decentralization, material incentives) were limited, but growth continued.

Reform and radicalization. Pres. John F. Kennedy, inaugurated 1961, emphasized youthful idealism, vigor; he was assassinated Nov. 22, 1963. A series of political and social reform movements took root in the U.S., later spreading to other countries with the help of ubiquitous U.S. film and television programs and heavy overseas travel (2.2 million U.S. passports issued 1970). Blacks agitated peaceably and with partial success against segregation and poverty (1963 March on Washington, 1964 **Civil Rights Act**); but some urban ghettos erupted in extensive riots (Watts, 1965; Detroit, 1967; King assassination, Apr. 4, 1968). New concern for the poor (Harrington's *Other America*, 1963) led to Pres. Johnson's **"Great Society"** programs (Medicare, Water Quality Act, Higher Education Act, all 1965). Concern with the **environment** surged (Carson's *Silent Spring*, 1962). **Feminism** revived as a cultural and political movement (Friedan's *Feminine Mystique*, 1963, National Organization for Women founded 1966) and a movement for homosexual rights emerged (Stonewall riot, in NYC, 1969). Pope John XXIII called Vatican II, 1962-65, which liberalized Roman Catholic liturgy.

Opposition to U.S. involvement in Vietnam, especially among university students (**Moratorium** protest Nov. '69), turned violent (Weatherman Chicago riots Oct. '69). New Left and Marxist theories became popular, and membership in radical groups swelled (Students for a Democratic Society, Black Panthers). Maoist groups, especially in Europe, called for total transformation of society. In France, students sparked a nationwide strike affecting 10 million workers May-June '68, but an electoral reaction barred revolutionary change.

Arts and styles. The boundary between fine and popular arts was blurred by Pop Art (Warhol) and rock musicals (Hair, 1968). Informality and exaggeration prevailed in fashion (beards, miniskirts). A non-political "counterculture" developed, rejecting traditional bourgeois life goals and personal habits, and use of marijuana and hallucinogens spread (Woodstock festival Aug. '69). Indian influence was felt in music (Beatles), religion (Ram Dass), and fashion.

Science. Achievements in space (men on moon July '69) and electronics (lasers, integrated circuits) encouraged a faith in scientific solutions to problems in agriculture ("green revolution"), medicine (heart transplants 1967) and other areas. The harmful effects of science, it was believed, could be controlled (1963 nuclear weapon test ban treaty, 1968 non-proliferation treaty).

China. Mao's revolutionary militance caused disputes with Russia under "revisionist" Khrushchev, starting 1960. The two powers exchanged fire in 1969 border disputes. China used force to capture areas disputed with India 1962. The "Great Proletarian Cultural Revolution" tried to impose a utopian egalitarian program in China and spread revolution abroad; political struggle, often violent, convulsed China 1965-68.

Indochina. Communist-led guerrillas aided by N. Vietnam fought from 1960 against the S. Vietnam government of Ngo Dinh Diem (killed 1963). The U.S. military role increased after the 1964 Tonkin Gulf incident. U.S. forces peaked at 543,400, Apr. '69. Massive numbers of N. Viet troops also fought. Laotian and Cambodian neutrality were threatened by communist insurgencies, with N. Vietnamese aid, and U.S. intrigues.

Third World. A bloc of authoritarian leftist regimes among the newly independent nations emerged in political opposition to the U.S.-led Western alliance, and came to dominate the conference of nonaligned nations (Belgrade 1961, Cairo 1964, Lusaka 1970). Soviet political ties and military bases were established in Cuba, Egypt, Algeria, Guinea, and other countries, whose leaders were regarded as revolutionary heros by opposition groups in pro-Western or colonial countries. Some leaders were ousted in coups by pro-Western groups—Zaire's Lumumba (killed 1961), Ghana's Nkrumah (exiled 1966), and Indonesia's Sukarno (effectively ousted 1965 after a Communist coup failed).

Middle East. Arab-Israeli tension erupted into a brief war June 1967. Israel emerged as a major regional power. Military shipments before and after the war brought much of the Arab world into the Soviet political sphere. Most Arab states broke U.S. diplomatic ties, while Communist countries cut their ties to Israel. Intra-Arab disputes continued: Egypt and Saudi Arabia supported rival factions in a bloody Yemen civil war 1962-70; Lebanese troops fought Palestinian commandos 1969.

East Europe. To stop the large-scale exodus of citizens, E. German authorities built a fortified wall across Berlin Aug. '61. Soviet sway in the Balkans was weakened by Albania's support of China (USSR broke ties Dec. '61) and Romania's assertion of industrial and foreign policy autonomy 1964. Liberalization in Czechoslovakia, spring 1968, was crushed by troops of 5 Warsaw Pact countries. West German treaties with Russia and Poland, 1970, facilitated the transfer of German technology and confirmed post-war boundaries.

Disillusionment: 1970-79

U.S.: Caution and neoconservatism. A relatively sluggish economy, energy and resource shortages (natural gas crunch 1975, gasoline shortage 1979) and environmental problems contributed to a **"limits of growth"** philosophy. Suspicion of science and technology killed or delayed major projects (supersonic transport dropped 1971, DNA recombination curbed 1976, Seabrook A-plant protests 1977-78) and was fed by the Three Mile Island nuclear reactor accident Mar. '79.

Mistrust of big government weakened support for government reform plans among liberals. School busing and racial quotas were opposed (**Bakke decision** June '78); the Equal Rights Amendment for women languished; civil rights for homosexuals were opposed (Dade County referendum June '77).

Completion of communist forces' takeover of **S. Vietnam** (evacuation of U.S. civilians Apr. '75), revelations of Central Intelligence Agency misdeeds (Rockefeller Commission report June '75), and **Watergate** scandals (Nixon quit Aug. '74) reduced faith in U.S. moral and material capacity to influence world affairs. Revelations of Soviet crimes (Solzhenitsyn's *Gulag Archipelago* from 1974) and Russian intervention in Africa aided a revival of anti-Communist sentiment.

Economy sluggish. The 1960s boom faltered in the 1970s; a severe recession in the U.S. and Europe 1974-75 followed a huge oil price hike Dec. '73. Monetary instability (U.S. cut ties to gold Aug. '71), the decline of the dollar, and **protectionist** moves by industrial countries (1977-78) threatened trade. Business investment and spending for research declined. Severe inflation plagued many countries (25% in Britain 1975; 18% in U.S. 1979).

China picks up pieces. After the 1976 deaths of Mao and Zhou, a power struggle for the leadership succession was won by pragmatists. A nationwide purge of orthodox Maoists was carried out and the **"Gang of Four"** led by Mao's widow Chiang Ching was arrested.

The new leaders freed over 100,000 political prisoners, and reduced public adulation of Mao. Political and trade ties were expanded with Japan, Europe, and U.S. in the late 1970's, as relations worsened with Russia, Cuba, and Vietnam (4-week invasion by China 1979). Ideological guidelines in industry, science, education, and the armed forces, which the ruling faction said had caused chaos and decline, were reversed (bonuses to workers Dec. '77; exams for college entrance Oct. '77). Severe restrictions on cultural expression were eased (Beethoven ban lifted Mar. '77).

Europe. European unity moves (EEC-EFTA trade accord 1972) faltered as economic problems appeared (Britain floated pound 1972; France floated franc 1974). Germany and Switzerland curbed guest workers from S. Europe. Greece and Turkey quarreled over Cyprus (Turks intervened 1974), Aegean oil rights.

All non-Communist Europe was under democratic rule after free elections were held in **Spain** June '76, 7 months after the death of Franco. The conservative, colonialist regime in **Portugal** was overthrown Apr. '74. In **Greece,** the 7-year-old military dictatorship yielded power in 1974. Northern Europe, though ruled mostly by Socialists (**Swedish** Socialists unseated 1976, after 44 years in power), turned conservative. The **British** Labour government imposed wage curbs 1975, and suspended nationalization schemes. Terrorism in **Germany** (1972 Munich Olympics killings) led to laws curbing some civil liberties. **French** "new philosophers" rejected leftist ideologies and the shaky Socialist-Communist coalition lost a 1978 election bid.

Religion back in politics. The improvement in Moslem countries' political fortunes by the 1950s (with the exception of Central Asia under Soviet and Chinese rule) and the growth of Arab oil wealth, was followed by a resurgence of traditional piety. **Libyan** dictator Qaddafy mixed strict Islamic laws with socialism in his militant ideology, called for an eventual Moslem return to Spain and Sicily. The illegal Moslem Brotherhood in **Egypt** was accused of violence, while extreme Moslem groups bombed theaters, 1977, to protest secular values.

In **Turkey,** the National Salvation Party was the first Islamic group to share power (1974) since secularization in the 1920s. Religious authorities, such as Ayatollah Ruhollah Khomeini, led the **Iranian** revolution and religiously motivated Moslems took part in the insurrection in Saudi Arabia that briefly seized the Grand Mosque in Mecca 1979. Moslem puritan opposition to **Pakistan** Pres. Bhutto helped lead to his overthrow July '77. However, Moslem solidarity could not prevent Pakistan's eastern province (**Bangladesh**) from declaring independence, Dec. '71, after a bloody civil war.

Moslem and Hindu resentment against coerced sterilization in **India** helped defeat the Gandhi government, which was replaced Mar. '77 by a coalition including religious Hindu parties and led by devout Hindu Desai. Moslems in the southern **Philippines,** aided by Libya, conducted a long rebellion against central rule from 1973.

Evangelical Protestant groups grew in numbers and prosperity in the U.S. A revival of interest in Orthodox Christianity occurred among **Russian** intellectuals (Solzhenitsyn). The secularist **Israeli** Labor party, after decades of rule, was ousted in 1977 by conservatives led by Begin, an observant Jew; religious militants founded settlements on the disputed West Bank, part of Biblically-promised Israel. U.S. Reform Judaism revived many previously discarded traditional practices.

The Buddhist Soka Gakkai movement launched the Komeito party in Japan 1964, which became a major opposition party in 1972 and 1976 elections.

Old-fashioned religious wars raged intermittently in **N. Ireland** (Catholic vs. Protestant 1969-) and **Lebanon** (Christian vs. Moslem 1975-) while religious militancy complicated the Israel-Arab dispute (1973 Israel-Arab war). In spite of a **1979 peace treaty between Egypt and Israel** which looked forward to a resolution of the Palestinian issue, increased religious militancy on the West Bank made a resolution unlikely.

Latin America. Repressive conservative regimes strengthened their hold on most of the continent, with the violent coup against the elected Allende government in **Chile,** Sept. '73, the 1976 military coup in **Argentina,** and coups against reformist regimes in **Bolivia,** 1971 and 1979, and **Peru,** 1976. In Central America, increasing liberal and leftist militancy led to the ouster of the Somoza regime of Nicaragua in 1979 and civil conflict in El Salvador.

Indochina. Communist victory in Vietnam, Cambodia, and Laos by May '75 did not bring peace. Attempts at radical social reorganization left over one million dead in Cambodia 1975-78 and caused hundreds of thousands of ethnic Chinese and others to flee Vietnam ("boat people" 1979). The Vietnamese invasion of Cambodia swelled the refugee population and contributed to widespread starvation in that devastated country.

Russian expansion. Soviet influence, checked in some countries (troops ousted by Egypt 1972) was projected further afield, often with the use of Cuban troops (Angola 1975-89, Ethiopia 1977-88) and aided by a growing navy, merchant fleet, and international banking ability. Detente with the West — 1972 Berlin pact, 1972 strategic arms pact (**SALT**) — gave way to a more antagonistic relationship in the late 1970s, exacerbated by the Soviet invasion of Afghanistan 1979.

Africa. The last remaining European colonies were granted independence (**Spanish Sahara** 1976, **Djibouti** 1977) and, after 10 years of civil war and many negotiation sessions, a black government took over Zimbabwe (Rhodesia) 1979; white domination remained in **S. Africa.** Great power involvement in local wars (Russia in **Angola, Ethiopia;** France in **Chad, Zaire, Mauritania**) and the use of tens of thousands of Cuban troops was denounced by some African leaders as neocolonialism. Ethnic or tribal clashes made Africa the chief world locus of sustained warfare in the late 1970s.

Arts. Traditional modes in painting, architecture, and music, pursued in relative obscurity for much of the 20th century, returned to popular and critical attention in the 1970s. The pictorial emphasis in neorealist and photorealist painting, the return of many architects to detail, decoration, and traditional natural materials, and the concern with ordered structure in musical composition were, ironically, novel experiences for artistic consumers after the exhaustion of experimental possibilities. However, these more conservative styles coexisted with modernist works in an atmosphere of variety and tolerance.

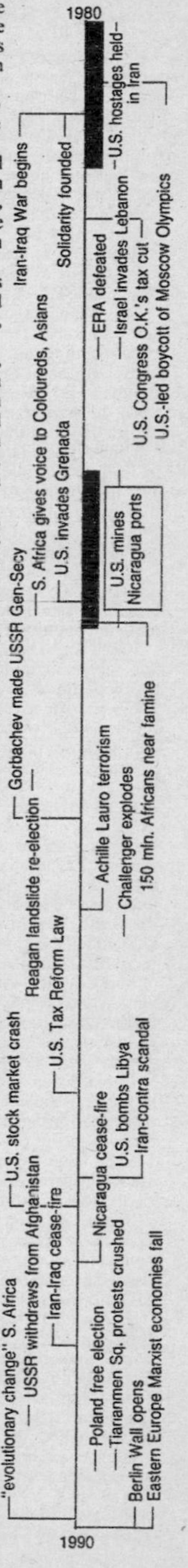

Revitalization of Capitalism, Demand for Democracy: 1980-89

USSR, Eastern Europe. A troublesome 1980-85 for the USSR was followed by 5 years of astonishing change: the **surrender of the Communist monopoly, remaking of the Soviet state, and disintegration of the Soviet empire.** After deaths of Brezhnev 1982, Andropov 1984, Chernenko 1985; harsh treatment of dissent; restriction of emigration; invasion of Afghanistan Dec.'79; Gen. Secy. **Mikhail Gorbachev** (1985-1991) promoted **glasnost, perestroika,** economic and social reform (Jan.'87), supported by Communist Party (July '88); signed **INF treaty** (Dec.'87). Gorbachev pledged to cut the military budget (1988); military withdrawal from Afghanistan was completed Feb.'89; democratization was not hindered in Poland, Hungary; the Soviet people chose part of the new Congress from competing candidates Mar.'89. At decade's end, Gorbachev was widely considered responsible for the **1989 ending of the Cold War.**

Poland. Solidarity, the labor union founded 1980 by **Lech Walesa,** outlawed 1982, was legalized 1988, after years of unrest. Poland's first free election since the Communist takeover brought Solidarity victory (June '89); Tadeusz Mazowiecki, a Walesa advisor, became Prime Minister in a government with the Communists (Aug.'89).

In the fall of 1989 the failure of Marxist economies in **Hungary, E. Germany, Czechoslovakia, Bulgaria, and Romania** brought the fall of the Communist monopoly, the demand for democracy. The **Berlin Wall** was opened Nov.'89.

U.S. "The Reagan Years" (1981-88) brought the **longest economic boom** in U.S. history via budget and tax cuts, deregulation, "junk bond" financing, leveraged buyouts, mergers and takeovers; a **strong anti-Communist stance,** via increased defense spending, aid to anti-communists in Central America, invasion of Cuba-threatened Grenada, championing of MX missile system and "Star Wars." Four Reagan-Gorbachev summits, 1985-88, climaxed in INF treaty 1987. Financial scandals mounted (E.F. Hutton 1985, Ivan Boesky 1986), the stock market crashed Oct.'87, the trade imbalance grew (esp. with Japan), the budget deficit soared ($3.2 trillion 1988); homelessness, drug abuse (esp. "crack") grew. The Iran-contra affair (North TV testimony July'87) was the low point, but V.P. **Bush** was elected pres. 1988.

Middle East. This area remained militarily unstable, with sharp divisions on economic, political, racial, and religious lines. In **Iran,** the revolution (1979-80) and violent political upheavals after, brought strong anti-U.S. stance. A dispute with **Iraq** over the Shatt al-Arab waterway became warfare Sept.'80-July'88, with millions killed.

Libya's support for international terrorism caused the U.S. to close the diplomatic mission (May'81), embargo oil (Mar.'82); U.S. accused Muammar al-Qaddafy of aiding terrorists in Dec.'85 Rome, Vienna airport attacks, retaliated by bombing Libya Apr.'86.

Israel affirmed all Jerusalem as its capital (July'80); destroyed an Iraqi atomic reactor 1981; invaded Lebanon 1982, bringing the PLO to agree to withdraw. A **Palestinian uprising,** inc. women, children hurling rocks, bottles at troops, began Dec.'87 in Israeli-occupied Gaza, spread to the West Bank; troops responded with force, killing 300 by 1988's end, with 6,000 more in detention camps.

Israeli withdrawal from **Lebanon** began Feb.'85, ended June'85, as Lebanon continued torn with military and political conflict between rival factions. Premier Karami was assassinated June'87. Artillery duels between Christian East Beirut and Moslem West Beirut, Mar.-Apr.'89, left 200 dead, 700 wounded. At decade's end, violence still dominated.

Central America. In **Nicaragua,** the leftist Sandinista National Liberation Front, in power after the 1979 civil war, faced problems due to Nicaragua's military aid to leftist guerrillas in El Salvador, U.S. backing of anti-government contras. The U.S. CIA admitted directing the mining of Nicaraguan ports 1984; U.S. sent aid, humanitarian 1985, military 1986. Profits from secret arms sales to Iran were found diverted to contras 1987. Cease-fire talks between Sandinista government and contras came in 1988, elections in Feb.'90.

In **El Salvador,** a military coup (Oct.'79) failed to halt extreme right-wing violence and left-wing activity. Archbishop Oscar Romero was assassinated Mar.'80; Jan.-June some 4,000 civilians reportedly were killed. In 1984, newly-elected Pres. Duarte decreased rights abuses. Leftist guerrillas continued their offensive 1989.

Africa. 1980-85 marked the rapid decline of the economies of virtually all Africa's 61 countries, due to accelerating desertification, the world economic recession, heavy indebtedness to overseas creditors, rapid population growth, political instability. Some 60 million Africans, almost one-fifth of the population, faced prolonged hunger 1981; much of Africa had one of the worst droughts ever 1983, and by year's end **150 million faced near-famine.** "Live Aid" marathon rock concert (July'85), U.S. and Western nations sent aid Sept.'85. Economic hardship fueled political unrest, coups. Wars in Ethiopia, Sudan, military strife in 6 other nations continued through 1989. AIDS took a heavy toll.

South Africa. Anti-apartheid sentiment gathered force, demonstrations and violent police response grew. South African white voters approved (Nov.'83) the first constitution to give "Coloureds," Asians a voice, while still excluding blacks—70% of the population. The U.S. imposed economic sanctions Aug.'85, 11 Western nations followed in Sept. **P.W. Botha,** '80s president, was succeeded by **F.W. de Klerk,** Sept.'89, on a platform of "evolutionary" change via negotiation with the black population.

China. From 1980 through mid-1989 the Communist Party, under **Chairman Deng Xiaoping,** pursued **far-reaching changes** in political and economic institutions, expanding commercial and technical ties to the industrialized world, increasing the role of market forces in stimulating urban economic development. But Apr.'89 brought the demand for more changes: students camped out in Tiananmen Sq., Beijing; some 100,000 students and workers marched, at least 20 other cities saw protests. Martial law was imposed; army troops crushed protests in Tiananmen Sq., June 3-4 with death toll estimates 500-7,000, up to 10,000 injured, up to 10,000 dissidents arrested, 31 tried and executed. The conciliatory Communist Party chief was ousted; the Politburo adopted reforms against official corruption (July).

Japan. Relations with other nations, esp. U.S., 1980-89, were dominated by **trade imbalances favoring Japan.** In 1985 the U.S. trade deficit with Japan was $49.7 billion, one-third of the total U.S. trade deficit. After Japan was found to sell semiconductors, computer memory chips below cost (Apr.'86), the U.S. was assured a "fair share" of the market, but charged Japan with failing to live up to the agreement Mar.'87. The **Omnibus Trade Bill,** Aug.'88, provided for retaliation; Pres. Bush called Japan's practices "unjustifiable," the law gave Japan 18 months to stop or face trade restrictions.

European Community. With the addition of Greece, Portugal, and Spain, the EC became a **common market of over 300 million people,** the West's largest trading entity. **Margaret Thatcher** became the first British prime minister in this century to win 3 consecutive terms 1987. France elected its first socialist president, **Francois Mitterand** 1981, re-elected 1988. Italy elected its first socialist premier, **Bettino Craxi** 1983.

International Terrorism. With the 1979 overthrow of the Shah of Iran, terrorism became a prominent political tactic that increased through the '80s, but with fewer high profile attacks after 1985. Iranian militants held 52 Americans hostage in Iran for 444 days, 1979-81; a TNT-laden suicide terrorist blew up U.S. Marine headquarters in Beirut, killing 241 Americans, while a truck bomb blew up a French paratroop barracks, killing 58. 1984; the *Achille Lauro* was hijacked, an American passenger killed, and the U.S. subsequently intercepted the Egyptian plane flying the terrorists to safety 1985. Incidents rose to 700 in 1985, 1,000+ in 1988. The Pentagon reported 52 terrorist groups Jan.'89.

Assassinations included Egypt's Pres. **Anwar al-Sadat** 1981; India's Prime Minister **Indira Gandhi** 1984; Lebanese Premier **Rashid Karami** 1987; Pakistan's Pres. **Mohammed Zia ul-Haq** 1988.

HISTORICAL FIGURES

Ancient Greeks and Latins

Greeks

Aeschines, orator, 389-314BC.
Aeschylus, dramatist, 525-456BC.
Aesop, fableist, c620-c560BC.
Alcibiades, politician, 450-404BC.
Anacreon, poet, c582-c485BC.
Anaxagoras, philosopher, c500-428BC.
Anaximander, philosopher, 611-546BC.
Antiphon, speechwriter, c480-411BC.
Apollonius, mathematician, c265-170BC.
Archimedes, math. c287-212BC.
Aristophanes, dramatist, c448-380BC.
Aristotle, philosopher, 384-322BC.
Athenaeus, scholar, fl.c200.
Callicrates, architect, fl.5th cent.BC.
Callimachus, poet, c305-240BC.
Cratinus, comic dramatist, 520-421BC.
Democritus, philosopher, c460-370BC.
Demosthenes, orator, 384-322BC.
Diodorus, historian, fl.20BC.
Diogenes, philosopher, c372-c287BC.
Dionysius, historian, d.c7BC.
Empedocles, philosopher, c490-430BC.
Epicharmus, dramatist, c530-440BC.
Epictetus, philosopher, c55-c135.
Epicurus, philosopher, 341-270BC.
Eratosthenes, scientist, c276-194BC.
Euclid, mathematician, fl.c300BC.
Euripides, dramatist, c484-406BC.
Galen, physician, c129-199.
Heraclitus, philosopher, c535-c475BC.
Herodotus, historian, c484-420BC.
Hesiod, poet, 8th cent. BC.
Hippocrates, physician, c460-377BC.
Homer, poet, believed lived c850BC.
Isocrates, orator, 436-338BC.
Menander, dramatist, 342-292BC.
Phidias, sculptor, c500-435BC.
Pindar, poet, c518-c438BC.
Plato, philosopher, c428-c347BC.
Plutarch, biographer, c46-120.
Polybius, historian, c200-c118BC.
Praxiteles, sculptor, 400-330BC.
Pythagoras, phil., math., c580-c500BC.
Sappho, poet, c610-c580BC.
Simonides, poet, 556-c468BC.
Socrates, philosopher, c470-399BC.
Solon, statesman, 640-560BC.
Sophocles, dramatist, C496-406BC.
Strabo, geographer, c63BC-AD24.
Thales, philosopher, c634-c546BC.
Themistocles, politician, c524-c460BC.
Theocritus, poet, c310-250BC.
Theophrastus, phil. c372-c287BC.
Thucydides, historian, fl.5th cent.BC.
Timon, philosopher, c320-c230BC.
Xenophon, historian, c434-c355BC.
Zeno, philosopher, c495-c430BC.

Latins

Ammianus, historian, c330-395.
Apuleius, satirist, c124-c170.
Boethius, scholar, c480-524
Caesar, Julius, general, 100-44BC.
Catilina, politician, c108-62BC.
Cato(Elder), statesman, 234-149BC.
Catullus, poet, c84-54BC.
Cicero, orator, 106-43BC.
Claudian, poet, c370-c404.
Ennius, poet, 239-170BC.
Gellius, author, c130-c165.
Horace, poet, 65-8BC.
Juvenal, satirist, c60-c127.
Livy, historian, 59BC-AD17.
Lucan, poet, 39-65.
Lucilius, poet, c180-c102BC.
Lucretius, poet, c99-c55BC.
Martial, epigrammatist, c38-c103.
Nepos, historian, c100-c25BC.
Ovid,poet, 43BC-AD17.
Persius, satirist, 34-62.
Plautus, dramatist, c254-c184BC.
Pliny, scholar, 23-79.
Pliny(Younger), author, 62-113.
Quintilian, rhetorician, c35-c97.
Sallust, historian, 86-34BC.
Seneca, philosopher, 4BC-AD65.
Silius, poet, c25-101.
Statius, poet, c45-c96.
Suetonius, biographer, c69-c122.
Tacitus, historian, c56-c120.
Terence, dramatist, 185-c159BC.
Tibullus, poet, c55-c19BC.
Virgil, poet, 70-19BC.
Vitruvius, architect, fl.1st cent.BC.

Rulers of England and Great Britain

England

Name		Began	Died	Age	Rgd
Saxons and Danes					
Egbert	King of Wessex, won allegiance of all English	829	839	—	10
Ethelwulf	Son, King of Wessex, Sussex, Kent, Essex	839	858	—	19
Ethelbald	Son of Ethelwulf, displaced father in Wessex	858	860	—	2
Ethelbert	2d son of Ethelwulf, united Kent and Wessex	860	866	—	6
Ethelred I	3d son, King of Wessex, fought Danes	866	871	—	5
Alfred	The Great, 4th son, defeated Danes, fortified London	871	899	52	28
Edward	The Elder, Alfred's son, united English, claimed Scotland	899	924	55	25
Athelstan	The Glorious, Edward's son, King of Mercia, Wessex	924	940	45	16
Edmund I	3d son of Edward, King of Wessex, Mercia	940	946	25	6
Edred	4th son of Edward	946	955	32	9
Edwy	The Fair, eldest son of Edmund, King of Wessex	955	959	18	3
Edgar	The Peaceful, 2d son of Edmund, ruled all English	959	975	32	17
Edward	The Martyr, eldest son of Edgar, murdered by stepmother	975	978	17	4
Ethelred II	The Unready, 2d son of Edgar, married Emma of Normandy	978	1016	48	37
Edmund II	Ironside, son of Ethelred II, King of London	1016	1016	27	0
Canute	The Dane, gave Wessex to Edmund, married Emma	1016	1035	40	19
Harold I	Harefoot, natural son of Canute	1035	1040	—	5
Hardecanute	Son of Canute by Emma, Danish King	1040	1042	24	2
Edward	The Confessor, son of Ethelred II (Canonized 1161)	1042	1066	62	24
Harold II	Edward's brother-in-law, last Saxon King	1066	1066	44	0
House of Normandy					
William I	The Conqueror, defeated Harold at Hastings	1066	1087	60	21
William II	Rufus, 3d son of William I, killed by arrow	1087	1100	43	13
Henry I	Beauclerc, youngest son of William I	1100	1135	67	35
House of Blois					
Stephen	Son of Adela, daughter of William I, and Count of Blois	1135	1154	50	19
House of Plantagenet					
Henry II	Son of Geoffrey Plantagenet (Angevin) by Matilda, dau. of Henry I	1154	1189	56	35
Richard I	Coeur de Lion, son of Henry II, crusader	1189	1199	42	10
John	Lackland, son of Henry II, signed Magna Carta, 1215	1199	1216	50	17
Henry III	Son of John, acceded at 9, under regency until 1227	1216	1272	65	56
Edward I	Longshanks, son of Henry III	1272	1307	68	35
Edward II	Son of Edward I, deposed by Parliament, 1327	1307	1327	43	20
Edward III	Of Windsor, son of Edward II	1327	1377	65	50
Richard II	Grandson of Edw. III, minor until 1389, deposed 1399	1377	1400	33	22
House of Lancaster					
Henry IV	Son of John of Gaunt, Duke of Lancaster, son of Edw. III	1399	1413	47	13
Henry V	Son of Henry IV, victor of Agincourt	1413	1422	34	9
Henry VI	Son of Henry V, deposed 1461, died in Tower	1422	1471	49	39

House of York

Name		Began	Died	Age	Rgd
Edward IV	Great-great-grandson of Edward III, son of Duke of York	1461	1483	41	22
Edward V	Son of Edward IV, murdered in Tower of London	1483	1483	13	0
Richard III	Crookback, bro. of Edward IV, fell at Bosworth Field	1483	1485	35	2

House of Tudor

Name		Began	Died	Age	Rgd
Henry VII	Son of Edmund Tudor, Earl of Richmond, whose father had married the widow of Henry V; descended from Edward III through his mother, Margaret Beaufort via John of Gaunt. By marriage with dau. of Edward IV he united Lancaster and York	1485	1509	53	24
Henry VIII	Son of Henry VII by Elizabeth, dau. of Edward IV.	1509	1547	56	38
Edward VI	Son of Henry VIII, by Jane Seymour, his 3d queen. Ruled under regents. Was forced to name Lady Jane Grey his successor. Council of State proclaimed her queen July 10, 1553. Mary Tudor won Council, was proclaimed queen July 19, 1553. Mary had Lady Jane Grey beheaded for treason, Feb., 1554	1547	1553	16	6
Mary I	Daughter of Henry VIII, by Catherine of Aragon	1553	1558	43	5
Elizabeth I	Daughter of Henry VIII, by Anne Boleyn	1558	1603	69	44

Great Britain

House of Stuart

Name		Began	Died	Age	Rgd
James I	James VI of Scotland, son of Mary, Queen of Scots. *First to call himself King of Great Britain. This became official with the Act of Union, 1707*	1603	1625	59	22
Charles I	Only surviving son of James I; beheaded Jan. 30, 1649	1625	1649	48	24

Commonwealth, 1649-1660

Council of State, 1649; Protectorate, 1653

Name		Began	Died	Age	Rgd
The Cromwells	Oliver Cromwell, Lord Protector	1653	1658	59	—
	Richard Cromwell, son, Lord Protector, resigned May 25, 1659	1658	1712	86	—

House of Stuart (Restored)

Name		Began	Died	Age	Rgd
Charles II	Eldest son of Charles I, died without issue	1660	1685	55	25
James II	2d son of Charles I. Deposed 1688. Interregnum Dec. 11, 1688, to Feb. 13, 1689	1685	1701	68	3
William III	Son of William, Prince of Orange, by Mary, dau. of Charles I	1689	1702	51	13
and Mary II	Eldest daughter of James II and wife of William III		1694	33	6
Anne	2d daughter of James II	1702	1714	49	12

House of Hanover

Name		Began	Died	Age	Rgd
George I	Son of Elector of Hanover, by Sophia, grand-dau. of James I	1714	1727	67	13
George II	Only son of George I, married Caroline of Brandenburg	1727	1760	77	33
George III	Grandson of George II, married Charlotte of Mecklenburg	1760	1820	81	59
George IV	Eldest son of George III, Prince Regent, from Feb., 1811	1820	1830	67	10
William IV	3d son of George III, married Adelaide of Saxe-Meiningen	1830	1837	71	7
Victoria	Dau. of Edward, 4th son of George III; married (1840) Prince Albert of Saxe-Coburg and Gotha, who became Prince Consort	1837	1901	81	63

House of Saxe-Coburg and Gotha

Name		Began	Died	Age	Rgd
Edward VII	Eldest son of Victoria, married Alexandra, Princess of Denmark	1901	1910	68	9

House of Windsor

Name Adopted July 17, 1917

Name		Began	Died	Age	Rgd
George V	2d son of Edward VII, married Princess Mary of Teck	1910	1936	70	25
Edward VIII	Eldest son of George V; acceded Jan. 20, 1936, abdicated Dec. 11	1936	1972	77	1
George VI	2d son of George V; married Lady Elizabeth Bowes-Lyon	1936	1952	56	15
Elizabeth II	Elder daughter of George VI, acceded Feb. 6, 1952	1952	—	—	—

Rulers of Scotland

Kenneth I MacAlpin was the first Scot to rule both Scots and Picts, 846 AD.

Duncan I was the first general ruler, 1034. Macbeth seized the kingdom 1040, was slain by Duncan's son, Malcolm III MacDuncan (Canmore), 1057.

Malcolm married Margaret, Saxon princess who had fled from the Normans. Queen Margaret introduced English language and English monastic customs. She was canonized, 1250. Her son Edgar, 1097, moved the court to Edinburgh. His brothers Alexander I and David I succeeded. Malcolm IV, the Maiden, 1153, grandson of David I, was followed by his brother, William the Lion, 1165, whose son was Alexander II, 1214. The latter's son, Alexander III, 1249, defeated the Norse and regained the Hebrides. When he died, 1286, his granddaughter, Margaret, child of Eric of Norway and grandniece of Edward I of England, known as the Maid of Norway, was chosen ruler, but died 1290, aged 8.

John Baliol, 1292-1296. (Interregnum, 10 years).

Robert Bruce (The Bruce), 1306-1329, victor at Bannockburn, 1314.

David II, only son of Robert Bruce, ruled 1329-1371.

Robert II, 1371-1390, grandson of Robert Bruce, son of Walter, the Steward of Scotland, was called The Steward, first of the so-called Stuart line.

Robert III, son of Robert II, 1390-1406.

James I, son of Robert III, 1406-1437.

James II, son of James I, 1437-1460.

James III, eldest son of James II, 1460-1488.

James IV, eldest son of James III, 1488-1513.

James V, eldest son of James IV, 1513-1542.

Mary, daughter of James V, born 1542, became queen when one week old; was crowned 1543. Married, 1558, Francis, son of Henry II of France, who became king 1559, died 1560. Mary ruled Scots 1561 until abdication, 1567. She also married (2) Henry Stewart, Lord Darnley, and (3) James, Earl of Bothwell. Imprisoned by Elizabeth I, Mary was beheaded 1587.

James VI, 1566-1625, son of Mary and Lord Darnley, became King of England on death of Elizabeth in 1603. Although the thrones were thus united, the legislative union of Scotland and England was not effected until the Act of Union, May 1, 1707.

Prime Ministers of Great Britain

(W=Whig; T=Tory; Cl=Coalition; P=Peelite; L=Liberal; C=Conservative; La=Labour)

Sir Robert Walpole (W)	1721-1742
Earl of Wilmington (W)	1742-1743
Henry Pelham (W)	1743-1754
Duke of Newcastle (W)	1754-1756
Duke of Devonshire (W)	1756-1757
Duke of Newcastle (W)	1757-1762
Earl of Bute (T)	1762-1763
George Grenville (W)	1763-1765
Marquess of Rockingham (W)	1765-1766
William Pitt the Elder (Earl of Chatham) (W)	1766-1768
Duke of Grafton (W)	1768-1770
Frederick North (Lord North) (T)	1770-1782
Marquess of Rockingham (W)	1782
Earl of Shelburne (W)	1782-1783
Duke of Portland (Cl)	1783
William Pitt the Younger (T)	1783-1801
Henry Addington (T)	1801-1804
William Pitt the Younger (T)	1804-1806
William Wyndham Grenville, Baron Grenville (W)	1806-1807
Duke of Portland (T)	1807-1809
Spencer Perceval (T)	1809-1812
Earl of Liverpool (T)	1812-1827
George Canning (T)	1827
Viscount Goderich (T)	1827-1828
Duke of Wellington (T)	1828-1830
Earl Grey (W)	1830-1834
Viscount Melbourne (W)	1834
Sir Robert Peel (T)	1834-1835
Viscount Melbourne (W)	1835-1841
Sir Robert Peel (T)	1841-1846
Lord John Russell (later Earl) (W)	1846-1852
Earl of Derby (T)	1852
Earl of Aberdeen (P)	1852-1855
Viscount Palmerston (L)	1855-1858
Earl of Derby (C)	1858-1859
Viscount Palmerston (L)	1859-1865
Earl Russell (L)	1865-1866
Earl of Derby (C)	1866-1868
Benjamin Disraeli (C)	1868
William E. Gladstone (L)	1868-1874
Benjamin Disraeli (C)	1874-1880
William E. Gladstone (L)	1880-1885
Marquess of Salisbury (C)	1885-1886
William E. Gladstone (L)	1886
Marquess of Salisbury (C)	1886-1892
William E. Gladstone (L)	1892-1894
Earl of Rosebery (L)	1894-1895
Marquess of Salisbury (C)	1895-1902
Arthur J. Balfour (C)	1902-1905
Sir Henry Campbell-Bannerman (L)	1905-1908
Herbert H. Asquith (L)	1908-1915
Herbert H. Asquith	1915-1916
David Lloyd George (Cl)	1916-1922
Andrew Bonar Law (C)	1922-1923
Stanley Baldwin (C)	1923-1924
James Ramsay MacDonald (La)	1924
Stanley Baldwin (C)	1924-1929
James Ramsay MacDonald (La)	1929-1931
James Ramsay MacDonald (Cl)	1931-1935
Stanley Baldwin (Cl)	1935-1937
Neville Chamberlain (Cl)	1937-1940
Winston Churchill (Cl)	1940-1945
Winston Churchill (C)	1945
Clement Attlee (La)	1945-1951
Sir Winston Churchill (C)	1951-1955
Sir Anthony Eden (C)	1955-1957
Harold Macmillan (C)	1957-1963
Sir Alec Douglas-Home (C)	1963-1964
Harold Wilson (La)	1964-1970
Edward Heath (C)	1970-1974
Harold Wilson (La)	1974-1976
James Callaghan (La)	1976-1979
Margaret Thatcher (C)	1979-1990
John Major (C)	1990-

Historical Periods of Japan

Yamato	c.300-592	Conquest of Yamato plain c. 300 A.D.
Asuka	592-710	Accession of Empress Suiko, 592.
Nara	710-794	Completion of Heijo (Nara), 710; capital moves to Nagaoka, 784.
Heian	794-1192	Completion of Heian (Kyoto), 794.
Fujiwara	858-1160	Fujiwara-no-Yoshifusa becomes regent, 858.
Taira	1160-1185	Taira-no-Kiyomori assumes control, 1160; Minamoto-no-Yoritomo victor over Taira, 1185.
Kamakura	1192-1333	Yoritomo becomes shogun, 1192.
Namboku	1334-1392	Restoration of Emperor Godaigo, 1334; Southern Court established by Godaigo at Yoshino, 1336.
Ashikaga	1338-1573	Ashikaga Takauji becomes shogun, 1338.
Muromachi	1392-1573	Unification of Southern and Northern Courts, 1392.
Sengoku	1467-1600	Beginning of the Onin war, 1467.
Momoyama	1573-1603	Oda Nobunaga enters Kyoto, 1568; Nobunaga deposes last Ashikaga shogun, 1573; Tokugawa Ieyasu victor at Sekigahara, 1600.
Edo	1603-1867	Ieyasu becomes shogun, 1603.
Meiji	1868-1912	Enthronement of Emperor Mutsuhito (Meiji), 1867; Meiji Restoration and Charter Oath, 1868.
Taisho	1912-1926	Accession of Emperor Yoshihito, 1912.
Showa	1926-1989	Accession of Emperor Hirohito, 1926.
Heisei	1989-	Accession of Emperor Akihito, 1989.

Rulers of France: Kings, Queens, Presidents

Caesar to Charlemagne

Julius Caesar subdued the Gauls, native tribes of Gaul (France) 57 to 52 BC. The Romans ruled 500 years. The Franks, a Teutonic tribe, reached the Somme from the East ca. 250 AD. By the 5th century the Merovingian Franks ousted the Romans. In 451 AD, with the help of Visigoths, Burgundians and others, they defeated Attila and the Huns at Chalons-sur-Marne.

Childeric I became leader of the Merovingians 458 AD. His son Clovis I (Chlodwig, Ludwig, Louis), crowned 481, founded the dynasty. After defeating the Alemanni (Germans) 496, he was baptized a Christian and made Paris his capital. His line ruled until Childeric III was deposed, 751.

The West Merovingians were called Neustrians, the eastern Austrasians. Pepin of Herstal (687-714) major domus, or head of the palace, of Austrasia, took over Neustria as dux (leader) of the Franks. Pepin's son, Charles, called Martel (the Hammer) defeated the Saracens at Tours-Poitiers, 732; was succeeded by his son, Pepin the Short, 741, who deposed Childeric III and ruled as king until 768.

His son, Charlemagne, or Charles the Great (742-814) became king of the Franks, 768, with his brother Carloman, who died 771. He ruled France, Germany, parts of Italy, Spain, Austria, and enforced Christianity. Crowned Emperor of the Romans by Pope Leo III in St. Peter's, Rome, Dec. 25, 800 AD. Succeeded by son, Louis I the Pious, 814. At death, 840, Louis left empire to sons, Lothair (Roman emperor); Pepin I (king of Aquitaine); Louis II (of Germany); Charles the Bald (France). They quarreled and by the peace of Verdun, 843, divided the empire.

(continued)

AD Name, year of accession

The Carolingians

843 Charles I (the Bald), Roman Emperor, 875
877 Louis II (the Stammerer), son
879 Louis III (died 882) and Carloman, brothers
885 Charles II (the Fat), Roman Emperor, 881
888 Eudes (Odo) elected by nobles
898 Charles III (the Simple), son of Louis II, defeated by
922 Robert, brother of Eudes, killed in war
923 Rudolph (Raoul) Duke of Burgundy
936 Louis IV, son of Charles III
954 Lothair, son, aged 13, defeated by Capet
986 Louis V (the Sluggard), left no heirs

The Capets

987 Hugh Capet, son of Hugh the Great
996 Robert II (the Wise), his son
1031 Henry I, his son
1060 Philip I (the Fair), son
1108 Louis VI (the Fat), son
1137 Louis VII (the Younger), son
1180 Philip II (Augustus), son, crowned at Reims
1223 Louis VIII (the Lion), son
1226 Louis IX, son, crusader; Louis IX (1214-1270) reigned 44 years, arbitrated disputes with English King Henry III; led crusades, 1248 (captured in Egypt 1250) and 1270, when he died of plague in Tunis. Canonized 1297 as St. Louis.
1270 Philip III (the Hardy), son
1285 Philip IV (the Fair), son, king at 17
1314 Louis X (the Headstrong), son. His posthumous son, John I, lived only 7 days
1316 Philip V (the Tall), brother of Louis X
1322 Charles IV (the Fair), brother of Louis X

House of Valois

1328 Philip VI (of Valois), grandson of Philip III
1350 John II (the Good), his son, retired to England
1364 Charles V (the Wise), son
1380 Charles VI (the Beloved), son
1422 Charles VII (the Victorious), son. In 1429 Joan of Arc (Jeanne d'Arc) promised Charles to oust the English, who occupied northern France. Joan won at Orleans and Patay and had Charles crowned at Reims July 17, 1429. Joan was captured May 24, 1430, and executed May 30, 1431, at Rouen for heresy. Charles ordered her rehabilitation, effected 1455.
1461 Louis XI (the Cruel), son, civil reformer
1483 Charles VIII (the Affable), son
1498 Louis XII, great-grandson of Charles V
1515 Francis I, of Angouleme, nephew, son-in-law. Francis I (1494-1547) reigned 32 years, fought 4 big wars, was patron of the arts, aided Cellini, del Sarto, Leonardo da Vinci, Rabelais, embellished Fontainebleau.
1547 Henry II, son, killed at a joust in a tournament. He was the husband of Catherine de Medicis (1519-1589) and the lover of Diane de Poitiers (1499-1566). Catherine was born in Florence, daughter of Lorenzo de Medicis. By her marriage to Henry II she became the mother of Francis II, Charles IX, Henry III and Queen Margaret (Reine Margot) wife of Henry IV. She persuaded Charles IX to order the massacre of Huguenots on the Feast of St. Bartholomew, Aug. 24, 1572, the day her daughter was married to Henry of Navarre.
1559 Francis II, son. In 1548, Mary, Queen of Scots since infancy, was betrothed when 6 to Francis, aged 4. They were married 1558. Francis died 1560, aged 16; Mary ruled Scotland, abdicated 1567.
1560 Charles IX, brother
1574 Henry III, brother, assassinated

House of Bourbon

1589 Henry IV, of Navarre, assassinated. Henry IV made enemies when he gave tolerance to Protestants by Edict of Nantes, 1598. He was grandson of Queen Margaret of Navarre, literary patron. He married Margaret of Valois, daughter of Henry II and Catherine de Medicis; was divorced; in 1600 married Marie de Medicis, who became Regent of France, 1610-17 for her son, Louis XIII, but was exiled by Richelieu, 1631.
1610 Louis XIII (the Just), son. Louis XIII (1601-1643) married Anne of Austria. His ministers were Cardinals Richelieu and Mazarin.
1643 Louis XIV (The Grand Monarch), son. Louis XIV was king 72 years. He exhausted a prosperous country in wars for thrones and territory. By revoking the Edict of Nantes (1685) he caused the emigration of the Huguenots. He said: "I am the state."
1715 Louis XV, great-grandson. Louis XV married a Polish princess; lost Canada to the English. His favorites, Mme. Pompadour and Mme. Du Barry, influenced policies. Noted for saying "After me, the deluge".
1774 Louis XVI, grandson; married Marie Antoinette, daughter of Empress Maria Therese of Austria. King and queen beheaded by Revolution, 1793. Their son, called Louis XVII, died in prison, never ruled.

First Republic

1792 National Convention of the French Revolution
1795 Directory, under Barras and others
1799 Consulate, Napoleon Bonaparte, first consul. Elected consul for life, 1802.

First Empire

1804 Napoleon I, emperor. Josephine (de Beauharnais) empress, 1804-09; Marie Louise, empress, 1810-1814. Her son, Francois (1811-1832), titular King of Rome, later Duke de Reichstadt and "Napoleon II," never ruled. Napoleon abdicated 1814, died 1821.

Bourbons Restored

1814 Louis XVIII king; brother of Louis XVI.
1824 Charles X, brother; reactionary; deposed by the July Revolution, 1830.

House of Orleans

1830 Louis-Philippe, the "citizen king."

Second Republic

1848 Louis Napoleon Bonaparte, president, nephew of Napoleon I. He became:

Second Empire

1852 Napoleon III, emperor; Eugenie (de Montijo) empress. Lost Franco-Prussian war, deposed 1870. Son, Prince Imperial (1856-79), died in Zulu War. Eugenie died 1920.

Third Republic—Presidents

1871 Thiers, Louis Adolphe (1797-1877)
1873 MacMahon, Marshal Patrice M. de (1808-1893)
1879 Grevy, Paul J. (1807-1891)
1887 Sadi-Carnot, M. (1837-1894), assassinated
1894 Casimir-Perier, Jean P. P. (1847-1907)
1895 Faure, Francois Felix (1841-1899)
1899 Loubet, Emile (1838-1929)
1906 Fallieres, C. Armand (1841-1931)
1913 Poincare, Raymond (1860-1934)
1920 Deschanel, Paul (1856-1922)
1920 Millerand, Alexandre (1859-1943)
1924 Doumergue, Gaston (1863-1937)
1931 Doumer, Paul (1857-1932), assassinated
1932 Lebrun, Albert (1871-1950), resigned 1940
1940 **Vichy govt.** under German armistice: Henri Philippe Petain (1856-1951) Chief of State, 1940-1944.
Provisional govt. after liberation: Charles de Gaulle (1890-1970) Oct. 1944-Jan. 21, 1946; Felix Gouin (1884-1977) Jan. 23, 1946; Georges Bidault (1899-1983) June 24, 1946.

Fourth Republic—Presidents

1947 Auriol, Vincent (1884-1966)
1954 Coty, Rene (1882-1962)

Fifth Republic—Presidents

1959 de Gaulle, Charles Andre J. M. (1890-1970)
1969 Pompidou, Georges (1911-1974)
1974 Giscard d'Estaing, Valery (1926-)
1981 Mitterrand, Francois (1916-)

Rulers of Middle Europe; Rise and Fall of Dynasties

Carolingian Dynasty

Charles the Great, or Charlemagne, ruled France, Italy, and Middle Europe; established Ostmark (later Austria); crowned Roman emperor by pope in Rome, 800 AD; died 814.

Louis I (Ludwig) the Pious, son; crowned by Charlemagne 814, d. 840.

Louis II, the German, son; succeeded to East Francia (Germany) 843-876.

Charles the Fat, son; inherited East Francia and West Francia (France) 876, reunited empire, crowned emperor by pope, 881, deposed 887.

Arnulf, nephew, 887-899. Partition of empire.

Louis the Child, 899-911, last direct descendant of Charlemagne.
Conrad I, duke of Franconia, first elected German king, 911-918, founded House of Franconia.

Saxon Dynasty; First Reich

Henry I, the Fowler, duke of Saxony, 919-936.
Otto I, the Great, 936-973, son; crowned Holy Roman Emperor by pope, 962.
Otto II, 973-983, son; failed to oust Greeks and Arabs from Sicily.
Otto III, 983-1002, son; crowned emperor at 16.
Henry II, the Saint, duke of Bavaria, 1002-1024, great-grandson of Otto the Great.

House of Franconia

Conrad II, 1024-1039, elected king of Germany.
Henry III, the Black, 1039-1056, son; deposed 3 popes; annexed Burgundy.
Henry IV, 1056-1106, son; regency by his mother, Agnes of Poitou. Banned by Pope Gregory VII, he did penance at Canossa.
Henry V, 1106-1125, son; last of Salic House.
Lothair, duke of Saxony, 1125-1137. Crowned emperor in Rome, 1134.

House of Hohenstaufen

Conrad III, duke of Swabia, 1138-1152. In 2d Crusade.
Frederick I, Barbarossa, 1152-1190; Conrad's nephew.
Henry VI, 1190-1196, took lower Italy from Normans. Son became king of Sicily.
Philip of Swabia, 1197-1208, brother.
Otto IV, of House of Welf, 1198-1215; deposed.
Frederick II, 1215-1250, son of Henry VI; king of Sicily; crowned king of Jerusalem; in 5th Crusade.
Conrad IV, 1250-1254, son; lost lower Italy to Charles of Anjou.
Conradin (1252-1268) son, king of Jerusalem and Sicily, beheaded. Last Hohenstaufen.
Interregnum, 1254-1273, Rise of the Electors.

Transition

Rudolph I of Hapsburg, 1273-1291, defeated King Ottocar II of Bohemia. Bequeathed duchy of Austria to eldest son, Albert.
Adolph of Nassau, 1292-1298, killed in war with Albert of Austria.
Albert I, king of Germany, 1298-1308, son of Rudolph.
Henry VII, of Luxemburg, 1308-1313, crowned emperor in Rome. Seized Bohemia, 1310.
Louis IV of Bavaria (Wittelsbach), 1314-1347. Also elected was Frederick of Austria, 1314-1330 (Hapsburg). Abolition of papal sanction for election of Holy Roman Emperor.
Charles IV, of Luxemburg, 1347-1378, grandson of Henry VII, German emperor and king of Bohemia, Lombardy, Burgundy; took Mark of Brandenburg.
Wenceslaus, 1378-1400, deposed.
Rupert, Duke of Palatine, 1400-1410.
Sigismund, 1411-1437.

Hungary

Stephen I, house of Arpad, 997-1038. Crowned king 1000; converted Magyars; canonized 1083. After several centuries of feuds Charles Robert of Anjou became Charles I, 1308-1342.
Louis I, the Great, son, 1342-1382; joint ruler of Poland with Casimir III, 1370. Defeated Turks.
Mary, daughter, 1382-1395, ruled with husband. Sigismund of Luxemburg, 1387-1437, also king of Bohemia. As bro. of Wenceslaus he succeeded Rupert as Holy Roman Emperor, 1410.
Albert, 1438-1439, son-in-law of Sigismund; also Roman emperor as Albert II. *(see under Hapsburg.)*
Ulaszlo I of Poland, 1440-1444.
Ladislaus V, posthumous son of Albert II, 1444-1457. John Hunyadi (Hunyadi Janos), governor (1446-1452), fought Turks, Czechs; died 1456.
Matthias I (Corvinus), son of Hunyadi, 1458-1490. Shared rule of Bohemia, captured Vienna, 1485, annexed Austria, Styria, Carinthia.
Ulaszlo II (king of Bohemia), 1490-1516.
Louis II, son, aged 10, 1516-1526. Wars with Suleiman, Turk. In 1527 Hungary was split between Ferdinand I, Archduke of Austria, bro.-in-law of Louis II, and John Zapolya of Transylvania. After Turkish invasion, 1547, Hungary was split between Ferdinand, Prince John Sigismund (Transylvania) and the Turks.

House of Hapsburg

Albert V of Austria, Hapsburg, crowned king of Hungary, Jan. 1438, Roman emperor, March, 1438, as Albert II; died 1439.
Frederick III, cousin, 1440-1493. Fought Turks.
Maximilian I, son, 1493-1519. Assumed title of Holy Roman Emperor (German), 1493.
Charles V, grandson, 1519-1556. King of Spain with mother co-regent; crowned Roman emperor at Aix, 1520. Confronted Luther at Worms; attempted church reform and religious conciliation; abdicated 1556.
Ferdinand I, king of Bohemia, 1526, of Hungary, 1527; disputed. German king, 1531. Crowned Roman emperor on abdication of brother Charles V, 1556.
Maximilian II, son, 1564-1576.
Rudolph II, son, 1576-1612.
Matthias, brother, 1612-1619, king of Bohemia and Hungary.
Ferdinand II of Styria, king of Bohemia, 1617, of Hungary, 1618, Roman emperor, 1619. Bohemian Protestants deposed him, elected Frederick V of Palatine, starting Thirty Years War.
Ferdinand III, son, king of Hungary, 1625, Bohemia, 1627, Roman emperor, 1637. Peace of Westphalia, 1648, ended war. Leopold I, 1658-1705; Joseph I, 1705-1711; Charles VI, 1711-1740.
Maria Theresa, daughter, 1740-1780, Archduchess of Austria, queen of Hungary; ousted pretender, Charles VII, crowned 1742; in 1745 obtained election of her husband Francis I as Roman emperor and co-regent (d. 1765). Fought Seven Years' War with Frederick II (the Great) of Prussia. Mother of Marie Antoinette, Queen of France.
Joseph II, son, 1765-1790, Roman emperor, reformer; powers restricted by Empress Maria Theresa until her death, 1780. First partition of Poland. Leopold II, 1790-1792.
Francis II, son, 1792-1835. Fought Napoleon. Proclaimed first hereditary emperor of Austria, 1804. Forced to abdicate as Roman emperor, 1806; last use of title. Ferdinand I, son, 1835-1848, abdicated during revolution.

Austro-Hungarian Monarchy

Francis Joseph I, nephew, 1848-1916, emperor of Austria, king of Hungary. Dual monarchy of Austria-Hungary formed, 1867. After assassination of heir, Archduke Francis Ferdinand, June 28, 1914, Austrian diplomacy precipitated World War I.
Charles I, grand-nephew, 1916-1918, last emperor of Austria and king of Hungary. Abdicated Nov. 11-13, 1918, died 1922.

Rulers of Prussia

Nucleus of Prussia was the Mark of Brandenburg. First margrave was Albert the Bear (Albrecht), 1134-1170. First Hohenzollern margrave was Frederick, burgrave of Nuremberg, 1417-1440.
Frederick William, 1640-1688, the Great Elector. Son, Frederick III, 1688-1713, was crowned King Frederick of Prussia, 1701.
Frederick William I, son, 1713-1740.
Frederick II, the Great, son, 1740-1786, annexed Silesia, part of Austria.
Frederick William II, nephew, 1786-1797.
Frederick William III, son, 1797-1840. Napoleonic wars.
Frederick William IV, son, 1840-1861. Uprising of 1848 and first parliament and constitution.

Second and Third Reich

William I, 1861-1888, brother. Annexation of Schleswig and Hanover; Franco-Prussian war, 1870-71, proclamation of German Reich, Jan. 18, 1871, at Versailles; William, German emperor (Deutscher Kaiser), Bismarck, chancellor.
Frederick III, son, 1888.
William II, son, 1888-1918. Led Germany in World War I, abdicated as German emperor and king of Prussia, Nov. 9, 1918. Died in exile in Netherlands June 4, 1941. Minor rulers of Bavaria, Saxony, Wurttemberg also abdicated.
Germany proclaimed republic at Weimar, July 1, 1919. Presidents: Frederick Ebert, 1919-1925, Paul von Hindenburg-Beneckendorff, 1925, reelected 1932, d. Aug. 2, 1934. Adolf Hitler, chancellor, chosen successor as Leader-Chancellor (Fuehrer-Reichskanzler) of Third Reich. Annexed Austria, March, 1938. Precipitated World War II, 1939-1945. Suicide April 30, 1945.

Rulers of Poland

House of Piasts

Miesko I, 962?-992; Poland Christianized 966. Expansion under 3 Boleslavs: I, 992-1025, son, crowned king 1024; II, 1058-1079, great-grandson, exiled after killing bishop Stanislav who became chief patron saint of Poland; III, 1106-1138, nephew, divided Poland among 4 sons, eldest suzerain.

(*continued*)

1138-1306, feudal division. 1226 founding in Prussia of military order Teutonic Knights. 1226 invasion by Tartars/Mongols.

Vladislav I, 1306-1333, reunited most Polish territories, crowned king 1320. Casimir III the Great, 1333-1370, son, developed economic, cultural life, foreign policy.

House of Anjou

Louis I, 1370-1382, nephew/identical with Louis I of Hungary.

Jadwiga, 1384-1399, daughter, married 1386 Jagiello, Grand Duke of Lituania.

House of Jagelloneans

Vladislav II, 1386-1434, Christianized Lituania, founded personal union between Poland & Lituania. Defeated 1410 Teutonic Knights at Grunwald.

Vladislav III, 1434-1444, son, simultaneously king of Hungary. Fought Turks, killed 1444 in battle of Varna.

Casimir IV, 1446-1492, brother, competed with Hapsburgs, put son Vladislav on throne of Bohemia, later also of Hungary.

Sigismund I, 1506-1548, brother, patronized science & arts, his & son's reign "Golden Age."

Sigismund II, 1548-1572, son, established 1569 real union of Poland and Lituania (lasted until 1795).

Elective kings

Polish nobles proclaimed 1572 Poland a Republic headed by king to be elected by whole nobility.

Stephen Batory, 1576-1586, duke of Transylvania, married Ann, sister of Sigismund II August. Fought Russians.

Sigismund III Vasa, 1587-1632, nephew of Sigismund II. 1592-1598 also king of Sweden. His generals fought Russians, Turks.

Vladislav II Vasa, 1632-1648, son. Fought Russians.

John II Casimir Vasa, 1648-1668, brother. Fought Cossacks, Swedes, Russians, Turks, Tartars (the "Deluge"). Abdicated 1668.

John III Sobieski, 1674-1696. Won Vienna from besieging Turks, 1683.

Stanislav II, 1764-1795, last king. Encouraged reforms; 1791 1st modern Constitution in Europe. 1772, 1793, 1795 Poland partitioned among Russia, Prussia, Austria. Unsuccessful insurrection against foreign invasion 1794 under Kosciuszko, Amer-Polish gen.

1795-1918 Poland under foreign rule

1807-1815 Grand Duchy of Warsaw created by Napoleon I, Frederick August of Saxony grand duke.

1815 Congress of Vienna proclaimed part of Poland "Kingdom" in personal union with Russia.

Polish uprisings: 1830 against Russia, 1846, 1848 against Austria, 1863 against Russia—all repressed.

1918-1939 Second Republic

1918-1922 Head of State Jozef Pilsudski. Presidents: Gabriel Narutowicz 1922, assassinated. Stanislav Wojciechowski 1922-1926, had to abdicate after Pilsudski's coup d'état. Ignacy Moscicki, 1926-1939, ruled with Pilsudski as (until 1935) virtual dictator.

1939-1945 Poland under foreign occupation

Nazi aggression Sept. 1939. Polish govt.-in-exile, first in France, then in England. Vladislav Raczkiewicz pres., Gen. Vladislav Sikorski, then Stanislav Mikolajczyk, prime ministers. Polish Committee of Natl. Liberation proclaimed at Lublin July 1944, transformed into govt. Jan. 1, 1945.

Rulers of Denmark, Sweden, Norway

Denmark

Earliest rulers invaded Britain; King Canute, who ruled in London 1016-1035, was most famous. The Valdemars furnished kings until the 15th century. In 1282 the Danes won the first national assembly, Danehof, from King Erik V.

Most redoubtable medieval character was Margaret, daughter of Valdemar IV, born 1353, married at 10 to King Haakon VI of Norway. In 1376 she had her first infant son Olaf made king of Denmark. After his death, 1387, she was regent of Denmark and Norway. In 1388 Sweden accepted her as sovereign. In 1389 she made her grand-nephew, Duke Erik of Pomerania, titular king of Denmark, Sweden, and Norway, with herself as regent. In 1397 she effected the Union of Kalmar of the three kingdoms and had Erik VII crowned. In 1439 the three kingdoms deposed him and elected, 1440, Christopher of Bavaria king (Christopher III). On his death, 1448, the union broke up.

Succeeding rulers were unable to enforce their claims as rulers of Sweden until 1520, when Christian II conquered Sweden. He was thrown out 1522, and in 1523 Gustavus Vasa united Sweden. Denmark continued to dominate Norway until the Napoleonic wars, when Frederick VI, 1808-1839, joined the Napoleonic cause after Britain had destroyed the Danish fleet, 1807. In 1814 he was forced to cede Norway to Sweden and Helgoland to Britain, receiving Lauenburg. Successors Christian VIII, 1839; Frederick VII, 1848; Christian IX, 1863; Frederick VIII, 1906; Christian X, 1912; Frederick IX, 1947; Margrethe II, 1972.

Sweden

Early kings ruled at Uppsala, but did not dominate the country. Sverker, c1130-c1156, united the Swedes and Goths. In 1435 Sweden obtained the Riksdag, or parliament. After the Union of Kalmar, 1397, the Danes either ruled or harried the country until Christian II of Denmark conquered it anew, 1520. This led to a rising under Gustavus Vasa, who ruled Sweden 1523-1560, and established an independent kingdom. Charles IX, 1599-1611, crowned 1604, conquered Moscow. Gustavus II Adolphus, 1611-1632, was called the Lion of the North. Later rulers: Christina, 1632; Charles X, Gustavus 1654; Charles XI, 1660; Charles XII (invader of Russia and Poland, defeated at Poltava, June 28, 1709), 1697; Ulrika Eleanora, sister, elected queen 1718; Frederick I (of Hesse), her husband, 1720; Adolphus Frederick, 1751; Gustavus III, 1771; Gustavus IV Adolphus, 1792; Charles XIII, 1809. (Union with Norway began 1814.) Charles XIV John, 1818. He was Jean Bernadotte, Napoleon's Prince of Ponte Corvo, elected 1810 to succeed Charles XIII. He founded the present dynasty: Oscar I, 1844, Charles XV, 1859; Oscar II, 1872; Gustavus V, 1907; Gustav VI Adolf, 1950; Carl XVI Gustaf, 1973.

Norway

Overcoming many rivals, Harald Haarfager, 872-930, conquered Norway, Orkneys, and Shetlands; Olaf I, great-grandson, 995-1000, brought Christianity into Norway, Iceland, and Greenland. In 1035 Magnus the Good also became king of Denmark. Haakon V, 1299-1319, had married his daughter to Erik of Sweden. Their son, Magnus, became ruler of Norway and Sweden at 6. His son, Haakon VI, married Margaret of Denmark; their son Olaf IV became king of Norway and Denmark, followed by Margaret's regency and the Union of Kalmar, 1397.

In 1450 Norway became subservient to Denmark. Christian IV, 1588-1648, founded Christiania, now Oslo. After Napoleonic wars, when Denmark ceded Norway to Sweden, a strong nationalist movement forced recognition of Norway as an independent kingdom united with Sweden under the Swedish kings, 1814-1905. In 1905 the union was dissolved and Prince Carl of Denmark became Haakon VII. He died Sept. 21, 1957; succeeded by son, Olav V. Olav V died January 17, 1991; succeeded by son, Harald V.

Rulers of the Netherlands and Belgium

The Netherlands (Holland)

William Frederick, Prince of Orange, led a revolt against French rule, 1813, and was crowned King of the Netherlands, 1815. Belgium seceded Oct. 4, 1830, after a revolt. The secession was ratified by the two kingdoms by treaty Apr. 19, 1839.

Succession: William II, son, 1840; William III, son, 1849; Wilhelmina, daughter of William III and his 2d wife Princess Emma of Waldeck, 1890; Wilhelmina abdicated, Sept. 4, 1948, in favor of daughter, Juliana. Juliana abdicated Apr. 30, 1980, in favor of daughter, Beatrix.

Belgium

A national congress elected Prince Leopold of Saxe-Coburg King; he took the throne July 21, 1831, as Leopold I. Succession: Leopold II, son 1865; Albert I, nephew of Leopold II, 1909; Leopold III, son of Albert, 1934; Prince Charles, Regent 1944; Leopold returned 1950, yielded powers to son Baudouin, Prince Royal, Aug. 6, 1950, abdicated July 16, 1951. Baudouin I took throne July 17, 1951; died July 31, 1993; succeeded by brother, Albert II.

For political history prior to 1830 see articles on the Netherlands and Belgium.

Roman Rulers

From Romulus to the end of the Empire in the West. Rulers of the Roman Empire in the East sat in Constantinople and for a brief period in Nicaea, until the capture of Constantinople by the Turks in 1453, when Byzantium was succeeded by the Ottoman Empire.

BC	Name
	The Kingdom
753	Romulus (Quirinus)
716	Numa Pompilius
673	Tullus Hostilius
640	Ancus Marcius
616	L. Tarquinius Priscus
578	Servius Tullius
534	L. Tarquinius Superbus
	The Republic
509	Consulate established
509	Quaestorship instituted
498	Dictatorship introduced
494	Plebeian Tribunate created
494	Plebeian Aedileship created
444	Consular Tribunate organized
435	Censorship instituted
366	Praetorship established
366	Curule Aedileship created
362	Military Tribunate elected
326	Proconsulate introduced
311	Naval Duumvirate elected
217	Dictatorship of Fabius Maximus
133	Tribunate of Tiberius Gracchus
123	Tribunate of Gaius Gracchus
82	Dictatorship of Sulla
60	First Triumvirate formed (Caesar, Pompeius, Crassus)
46	Dictatorship of Caesar
43	Second Triumvirate formed (Octavianus, Antonius, Lepidus)
	The Empire
27	Augustus (Gaius Julius Caesar Octavianus)
AD	
14	Tiberius I
37	Gaius Caesar (Caligula)
41	Claudius I
54	Nero
68	Galba
69	Galba; Otho, Vitellius
69	Vespasianus
79	Titus
81	Domitianus
96	Nerva

AD	Name
98	Trajanus
117	Hadrianus
138	Antoninus Pius
161	Marcus Aurelius and Lucius Verus
169	Marcus Aurelius (alone)
180	Commodus
193	Pertinax; Julianus I
193	Septimius Severus
211	Caracalla and Geta
212	Caracalla (alone)
217	Macrinus
218	Elagabalus (Heliogabalus)
222	Alexander Severus
235	Maximinus I (the Thracian)
238	Gordianus I and Gordianus II; Pupienus and Balbinus
238	Gordianus III
244	Philippus (the Arabian)
249	Decius
251	Gallus and Volusianus
253	Aemilianus
253	Valerianus and Gallienus
258	Gallienus (alone)
268	Claudius Gothicus
270	Quintillus
270	Aurelianus
275	Tacitus
276	Florianus
276	Probus
282	Carus
283	Carinus and Numerianus
284	Diocletianus
286	Diocletianus and Maximianus
305	Galerius and Constantius I
306	Galerius, Maximinus II, Severus I
307	Galerius, Maximinus II, Constantinus I, Licinius, Maxentius
311	Maximinus II, Constantinus I, Licinius, Maxentius
314	Maximinus II, Constantinus I, Licinius
314	Constantinus I and Licinius

AD	Name
324	Constantinus I (the Great)
337	Constantinus II, Constans I, Constantius II
340	Constantius II and Constans I
350	Constantius II
361	Julianus II (the Apostate)
363	Jovianus
	West (Rome) and East (Constantinople)
364	Valentinianus I (West) and Valens (East)
367	Valentinianus I with Gratianus (West) and Valens (East)
375	Gratianus with Valentinianus II (West) and Valens (East)
378	Gratianus with Valentinianus II (West) Theodosius I (East)
383	Valentinianus II (West) and Theodosius I (East)
394	Theodosius I (the Great)
395	Honorius (West) and Arcadius (East)
408	Honorius (West) and Theodosius II (East)
423	Valentinianus III (West) and Theodosius II (East)
450	Valentinianus III (West) and Marcianus (East)
455	Maximus (West), Avitus (West); Marcianus (East)
456	Avitus (West), Marcianus (East)
457	Majorianus (West), Leo I (East)
461	Severus II (West), Leo I (East)
467	Anthemius (West), Leo I (East)
472	Olybrius (West), Leo I (East)
473	Glycerius (West), Leo I (East)
474	Julius Nepos (West), Leo II (East)
475	Romulus Augustulus (West) and Zeno (East)
476	End of Empire in West; Odovacar, King, drops title of Emperor; murdered by King Theodoric of Ostrogoths 493 AD

Rulers of Modern Italy

After the fall of Napoleon in 1814, the Congress of Vienna, 1815, restored Italy as a political patchwork, comprising the Kingdom of Naples and Sicily, the Papal States, and smaller units. Piedmont and Genoa were awarded to Sardinia, ruled by King Victor Emmanuel I of Savoy.

United Italy emerged under the leadership of Camillo, Count di Cavour (1810-1861), Sardinian prime minister. Agitation was led by Giuseppe Mazzini (1805-1872) and Giuseppe Garibaldi (1807-1882), soldier, Victor Emmanuel I abdicated 1821. After a brief regency for a brother, Charles Albert was King 1831-1849, abdicating when defeated by the Austrians at Novara. Succeeded by Victor Emmanuel II, 1849-1861.

In 1859 France forced Austria to cede Lombardy to Sardinia, which gave rights to Savoy and Nice to France. In 1860 Garibaldi led 1,000 volunteers in a spectacular campaign, took Sicily and expelled the King of Naples. In 1860 the House of Savoy annexed Tuscany, Parma, Modena, Romagna, the Two Sicilies, the Marches, and Umbria. Victor Emmanuel assumed the title of King of Italy at Turin Mar. 17, 1861. In 1866 he allied with Prussia in the Austro-Prussian War, with Prussia's victory received Venetia. On Sept. 20, 1870, his troops under Gen. Raffaele Cadorna entered Rome and took over the Papal States, ending the temporal power of the Roman Catholic Church.

Succession: Umberto I, 1878, assassinated 1900; Victor Emmanuel III, 1900, abdicated 1946, died 1947; Umberto II, 1946, ruled a month. In 1921 Benito Mussolini (1883-1945) formed the Fascist party and became prime minister Oct. 31, 1922. He entered World War II as an ally of Hitler. He was deposed July 25, 1943.

At a plebiscite June 2, 1946, Italy voted for a republic; Premier Alcide de Gasperi became chief of state June 13, 1946. On June 28, 1946, the Constituent Assembly elected Enrico de Nicola, Liberal, provisional president. Successive presidents: Luigi Einaudi, elected May 11, 1948; Giovanni Gronchi, Apr. 29, 1955; Antonio Segni, May 6, 1962; Giuseppe Saragat, Dec. 28, 1964; Giovanni Leone, Dec. 29, 1971; Alessandro Pertini, July 9, 1978; Francesco Cossiga, July 9, 1985; Oscar Luigi Scalfaro, May 25, 1992.

Rulers of Spain

From 8th to 11th centuries Spain was dominated by the Moors (Arabs and Berbers). The Christian reconquest established small kingdoms (Asturias, Aragon, Castile, Catalonia, Leon, Navarre, and Valencia). In 1474 Isabella, b. 1451, became Queen of Castile & Leon. Her husband, Ferdinand, b. 1452, inherited Aragon 1479, with Catalonia, Valencia, and the Balearic Islands, became Ferdinand V of Castile. By Isabella's request Pope Sixtus IV established the Inquisition, 1478. Last Moorish kingdom, Granada, fell 1492. Columbus opened New World of colonies, 1492. Isabella died 1504, succeeded by her daughter, Juana "the Mad," but Ferdinand ruled until his death 1516.

Charles I, b. 1500, son of Juana and grandson of Ferdinand and Isabella, and of Maximilian I of Hapsburg; succeeded later as Holy Roman Emperor, Charles V, 1520; abdicated 1556. Philip II, son, 1556-1598, inherited only Spanish throne; conquered Portugal, fought Turks, persecuted non-Catholics, sent Armada against England. Was married to Mary I of England, 1554-1558. Succession: Philip III, 1598-1621; Philip IV, 1621-1665; Charles II, 1665-1700, left Spain to Philip of Anjou, grandson of Louis XIV, who as Philip V, 1700-1746, founded Bourbon dynasty; Ferdinand VI, 1746-1759; Charles III, 1759-1788; Charles IV, 1788-1808, abdicated.

Napoleon now dominated politics and made his brother Joseph King of Spain 1808, but the Spanish ousted him in 1813. Ferdinand VII, 1808, 1814-1833, lost American colonies; succeeded by daughter Isabella II, aged 3, with wife Maria Christina of Naples regent until 1843. Isabella deposed by revolution 1868. Elected king by the Cortes, Amadeo of Savoy, 1870; abdicated 1873. First republic, 1873-74. Alphonso XII, son of Isabella, 1875-85. His posthumous son was Alphonso XIII, with his mother, Queen Maria Christina regent; Spanish-American war, Spain lost Cuba, gave up Puerto Rico, Philippines, Sulu Is., Marianas. Alphonso took throne 1902, aged 16, married British Princess Victoria Eugenia of Battenberg. The dictatorship of Primo de Rivera, 1923-30, precipitated the revolution of 1931. Alphonso agreed to leave without formal abdication. The monarchy was abolished and the second republic established, with socialist backing. Presidents were Niceto Alcala Zamora, to 1936, when Manuel Azaña was chosen.

In July, 1936, the army in Morocco revolted against the government and General Francisco Franco led the troops into Spain. The revolution succeeded by Feb., 1939, when Azaña resigned. Franco became chief of state, with provisions that if he was incapacitated the Regency Council by two-thirds vote may propose a king to the Cortes, which must have a two-thirds majority to elect him.

Alphonso XIII died in Rome Feb. 28, 1941, aged 54. His property and citizenship had been restored.

A succession law restoring the monarchy was approved in a 1947 referendum. Prince Juan Carlos, son of the pretender to the throne, was designated by Franco and the Cortes in 1969 as the future king and chief of state. Upon Franco's death, Nov. 20, 1975, Juan Carlos was proclaimed king, Nov. 22, 1975.

Leaders in the South American Wars of Liberation

Simon Bolivar (1783-1830), Jose Francisco de San Martin (1778-1850), and Francisco Antonio Gabriel Miranda (1750-1816), are among the heroes of the early 19th century struggles of South American nations to free themselves from Spain. All three, and their contemporaries, operated in periods of factional strife, during which soldiers and civilians suffered.

Miranda, a Venezuelan, who had served with the French in the American Revolution and commanded parts of the French Revolutionary armies in the Netherlands, attempted to start a revolt in Venezuela in 1806 and failed. In 1810, with British and American backing, he returned and was briefly a dictator, until the British withdrew their support. In 1812 he was overcome by the royalists in Venezuela and taken prisoner, dying in a Spanish prison in 1816.

San Martin was born in Argentina and during 1789-1811 served in campaigns of the Spanish armies in Europe and Africa. He first joined the independence movement in Argentina in 1812 and in 1817 invaded Chile with 4,000 men over the mountain passes. Here he and Gen. Bernardo O'Higgins (1778-1842) defeated the Spaniards at Chacabuco, 1817, and O'Higgins was named Liberator and became first director of Chile, 1817-23. In 1821 San Martin occupied Lima and Callao, Peru, and became protector of Peru.

Bolivar, the greatest leader of South American liberation from Spain, was born in Venezuela, the son of an aristocratic family. He first served under Miranda in 1812 and in 1813 captured Caracas, where he was named Liberator. Forced out next year by civil strife, he led a campaign that captured Bogota in 1814. In 1817 he was again in control of Venezuela and was named dictator. He organized Nueva Granada with the help of General Francisco de Paula Santander (1792-1840). By joining Nueva Granada, Venezuela, and the present terrain of Panama and Ecuador, the republic of Colombia was formed with Bolivar president. After numerous setbacks he decisively defeated the Spaniards in the second battle of Carabobo, Venezuela, June 24, 1821.

In May, 1822, Gen. Antonio Jose de Sucre, Bolivar's lieutenant, took Quito. Bolivar went to Guayaquil to confer with San Martin, who resigned as protector of Peru and withdrew from politics. With a new army of Colombians and Peruvians Bolivar defeated the Spaniards in a battle at Junín in 1824 and cleared Peru.

De Sucre organized Charcas (Upper Peru) as Republica Bolivar (now Bolivia) and acted as president in place of Bolivar, who wrote its constitution. De Sucre defeated the Spanish faction of Peru at Ayacucho, Dec. 19, 1824.

Continued civil strife finally caused the Colombian federation to break apart. Santander turned against Bolivar, but the latter defeated him and banished him. In 1828 Bolivar gave up the presidency he had held precariously for 14 years. He became ill from tuberculosis and died Dec. 17, 1830. He is buried in the national pantheon in Caracas.

Rulers of Prerevolutionary Russia; Leaders of the USSR

First ruler to consolidate Slavic tribes was Rurik, leader of the Russians who established himself at Novgorod, 862 AD. He and his immediate successors had Scandinavian affiliations. They moved to Kiev after 972 AD and ruled as Dukes of Kiev. In 988 Vladimir was converted and adopted the Byzantine Greek Orthodox service, later modified by Slav influences. Important as organizer and lawgiver was Yaroslav, 1019-1054, whose daughters married kings of Norway, Hungary, and France. His grandson, Vladimir II (Monomakh), 1113-1125, was progenitor of several rulers, but in 1169 Andrew Bogolubski overthrew Kiev and began the line known as Grand Dukes of Vladimir.

Of the Grand Dukes of Vladimir, Alexander Nevsky, 1246-1263, had a son, Daniel, first to be called Duke of Muscovy (Moscow) who ruled 1294-1303. His successors became Grand Dukes of Muscovy. After Dmitri III Donskoi defeated the Tartars in 1380, they also became Grand Dukes of all Russia. Independence of the Tartars and considerable territorial expansion were achieved under Ivan III, 1462-1505.

Tsars of Muscovy—Ivan III was referred to in church ritual as Tsar. He married Sofia, niece of the last Byzantine emperor. His successor, Basil III, died in 1533 when Basil's son Ivan was only 3. He became Ivan IV, "the Terrible"; crowned 1547 as Tsar of all the Russias, ruled till 1584. Under the weak rule of his son, Feodor I, 1584-1598, Boris Godunov had control. The dynasty died, and after years of tribal strife and intervention by Polish and Swedish armies, the Russians united under 17-year-old Michael Romanov, distantly related to the first wife of Ivan IV. He ruled 1613-1645 and established the Romanov line. Fourth ruler after Michael was Peter I.

Tsars, or Emperors of Russia (Romanovs)—Peter I, 1682-1725, known as Peter the Great, took title of Emperor in 1721. His successors and dates of accession were: Catherine, his widow, 1725; Peter II, his grandson, 1727; Anne, Duchess of Courland, 1730, daughter of Peter the Great's brother, Tsar Ivan V; Ivan VI, 1740, great-grandson of Ivan V, child, kept in prison and murdered 1764; Elizabeth, daughter of Peter I, 1741; Peter III, grandson of Peter I, 1761, deposed 1762 for his consort, Catherine II, former princess of Anhalt Zerbst (Germany) who is known as Catherine the Great; Paul I, her son, 1796, killed 1801; Alexander I, son of Paul, 1801, defeated Napoleon; Nicholas I, his brother, 1825; Alexander II, son of Nicholas, 1855, assassinated 1881 by terrorists; Alexander III, son, 1881.

Nicholas II, son, 1894-1917, last Tsar of Russia, was forced to abdicate by the Revolution that followed losses to Germany in WWI. The Tsar, the Empress, the Tsesarevich (Crown Prince) and the Tsar's 4 daughters were murdered by the Bolsheviks in Ekaterinburg, July 16, 1918.

Provisional Government—Prince Georgi Lvov and Alexander Kerensky, premiers, 1917.

Union of Soviet Socialist Republics

Bolshevik Revolution, Nov. 7, 1917, displaced Kerensky; council of People's Commissars formed, Lenin (Vladimir Ilyich Ulyanov), premier. Lenin died Jan. 21, 1924. Aleksei Rykov (executed 1938) and V. M. Molotov held the office, but actual ruler was Joseph Stalin (Joseph Vissarionovich Djugashvili), general secretary of the Central Committee of the Communist Party. Stalin became president of the Council of Ministers (premier) May 7, 1941, died Mar. 5, 1953. Succeeded by Georgi M. Malenkov, as head of the Council and premier and Nikita S. Khrushchev, first secretary of the Central Committee. Malenkov resigned Feb. 8, 1955, became deputy premier, was dropped July 3, 1957. Marshal Nikolai A. Bulganin became premier Feb. 8, 1955; was demoted and Khrushchev became premier Mar. 27, 1958. Khrushchev was ousted Oct. 14-15, 1964, replaced by Leonid I. Brezhnev as first secretary of the party and by Aleksei N. Kosygin as premier. On June 16, 1977, Brezhnev took office as president. Brezhnev died Nov. 10, 1982; 2 days later the Central Committee unanimously elected former KGB head Yuri V. Andropov president. Andropov died Feb. 9, 1984; on Feb. 13, Konstantin U. Chernenko was chosen by Central Committee as its general secretary. Chernenko died Mar. 10, 1985. On Mar. 11, he was succeeded as general secretary by Mikhail Gorbachev, who replaced Andrei Gromyko as president on Oct. 1, 1988. Gorbachev resigned Dec. 25, 1991, and the Soviet Union officially disbanded the next day. A loose Commonwealth of Independent States, made up of 11 of the 15 former Soviet constituent republics, was created.

Governments of China

(Until 221 BC and frequently thereafter, China was not a unified state. Where dynastic dates overlap, the rulers or events referred to appeared in different areas of China.)

Hsia	c1994BC	c1523BC
Shang	c1523	c1028
Western Chou	c1027	770
Eastern Chou	770	256
Warring States	403	222
Ch'in (first unified empire)	221	206
Han	202BC	220AD
Western Han (expanded Chinese state beyond the Yellow and Yangtze River valleys)	202BC	9AD
Hsin (Wang Mang, usurper)	9AD	23AD
Eastern Han (expanded Chinese state into Indo-China and Turkestan)	25	220
Three Kingdoms (Wei, Shu, Wu)	220	265
Chin (western)	265	317
(eastern)	317	420
Northern Dynasties (followed several short-lived governments by Turks, Mongols, etc.)	386	581
Southern Dynasties (capital: Nanking)	420	589
Sui (reunified China)	581	618
Tang (a golden age of Chinese culture; capital: Sian)	618	906
Five Dynasties (Yellow River basin)	902	960
Ten Kingdoms (southern China)	907	979
Liao (Khitan Mongols; capital: Peking)	947	1125
Sung	960	1279
Northern Sung (reunified central and southern China)	960	1126
Western Hsai (non-Chinese rulers in northwest)	990	1227
Chin (Tartars; drove Sung out of central China)	1115	1234
Yuan (Mongols; Kublai Khan made Peking his capital in 1267)	1271	1368
Ming (China reunified under Chinese rule; capital: Nanking, then Peking in 1420)	1368	1644
Ch'ing (Manchus, descendents of Tartars)	1644	1911
Republic (disunity; provincial rulers, warlords)	1912	1949
People's Republic of China	1949	—

Leaders Since 1949

Mao Zedong	Chairman, Central People's Administrative Council, Communist Party (CPC), 1949-1976
Zhou Enlai	Premier, foreign minister, 1949-1976
Deng Xiaoping	Vice Premier, 1949-1976; 1977-1987
Liu Shaoqi	President, 1959-1969
Hua Guofeng	Premier, 1976-1980; CPC Chairman, 1976-1981
Zhao Ziyang	Premier, 1980-88; CPC Chairman, 1987-89
Hu Yaobang	CPC Chairman, 1981-1987
Li Xiannian	President, 1983-1988
Yong Shang-Kun	President, 1988-1993
Li Peng	Premier, 1988-
Jiang Zemin	CPC Chairman, 1989- ; President, 1993-

Chronological List of Popes

Source: Annuario Pontificio. Table lists year of accession of each Pope.

The Roman Catholic Church names the Apostle Peter as founder of the Church in Rome. He arrived there c. 42, was martyred there c. 67, and raised to sainthood.

The Pope's temporal title is: Sovereign of the State of Vatican City.

The Pope's spiritual titles are: Bishop of Rome, Vicar of Jesus Christ, Successor of St. Peter, Prince of the Apostles, Supreme Pontiff of the Universal Church, Patriarch of the West, Primate of Italy, Archbishop and Metropolitan of the Roman Province.

Anti-Popes are in *Italics.* Anti-Popes were illegitimate claimants of or pretenders to the papal throne.

Year	Pope
See above.	St. Peter
67	St. Linus
76	St. Anacletus or Cletus
88	St. Clement I
97	St. Evaristus
105	St. Alexander I
115	St. Sixtus I
125	St. Telesphorus
136	St. Hyginus
140	St. Pius I
155	St. Anicetus
166	St. Soter
175	St. Eleutherius
189	St. Victor I
199	St. Zephyrinus
217	St. Callistus I
217	*St. Hippolytus*
222	St. Urban I
230	St. Pontian
235	St. Anterus
236	St. Fabian
251	St. Cornelius
251	*Novatian*
253	St. Lucius I
254	St. Stephen I
257	St. Sixtus II
259	St. Dionysius
269	St. Felix I
275	St. Eutychian
283	St. Caius
296	St. Marcellinus
308	St. Marcellus I
309	St. Eusebius
311	St. Melchiades
314	St. Sylvester I
336	St. Marcus
337	St. Julius I
352	Liberius
355	*Felix II*
366	St. Damasus I
366	*Ursinus*
384	St. Siricius
399	St. Anastasius I
401	St. Innocent I
417	St. Zosimus
418	St. Boniface I
418	*Eulalius*
422	St. Celestine I
432	St. Sixtus III
440	St. Leo I
461	St. Hilary
468	St. Simplicius
483	St. Felix III (II)
492	St. Gelasius I
496	Anastasius II
498	St. Symmachus
498	*Lawrence (501-505)*
514	St. Hormisdas
523	St. John I, Martyr
526	St. Felix IV (III)
530	Boniface II
530	*Dioscorus*
533	John II
535	St. Agapitus I
536	St. Silverius, Martyr
537	Vigilius
556	Pelagius I
561	John III
575	Benedict I
579	Pelagius II
590	St. Gregory I
604	Sabinian
607	Boniface III
608	St. Boniface IV
615	St. Deusdedit or Adeodatus

Year	Pope
619	Boniface V
625	Honorius I
640	Severinus
642	Theodore I
649	St. Martin I, Martyr
654	St. Eugene I
657	St. Vitalian
672	Adeodatus II
676	Donus
678	St. Agatho
682	St. Leo II
684	St. Benedict II
685	John V
686	Conon
687	*Theodore*
687	*Paschal*
687	St. Sergius I
701	John VI
705	John VII
708	Sisinnius
708	Constantine
715	St. Gregory II
731	St. Gregory III
741	St. Zachary
752	Stephen II (III)
757	St. Paul I
767	*Constantine*
768	*Philip*
768	Stephen III (IV)
772	Adrian I
795	St. Leo III
816	Stephen IV (V)
817	St. Paschal I
824	Eugene II
827	Valentine
827	Gregory IV
844	*John*
844	Sergius II
847	St. Leo IV
855	Benedict III
855	*Anastasius*
858	St. Nicholas I
867	Adrian II
872	John VIII
882	Marinus I
884	St. Adrian III
885	Stephen V (VI)
891	Formosus
896	Boniface VI
896	Stephen VI (VII)
897	Romanus
897	Theodore II
898	John IX
900	Benedict IV
903	Leo V
903	*Christopher*
904	Sergius III
911	Anastasius III
913	Landus
914	John X
928	Leo VI
928	Stephen VII (VIII)
931	John XI
936	Leo VII
939	Stephen VIII (IX)
942	Marinus II
946	Agapitus II
955	John XII
963	Leo VIII
964	Benedict V
965	John XIII
973	Benedict VI
974	*Boniface VII*
974	Benedict VII

Year	Pope
983	John XIV
985	John XV
996	Gregory V
997	*John XVI*
999	Sylvester II
1003	John XVII
1004	John XVIII
1009	Sergius IV
1012	Benedict VIII
1012	*Gregory*
1024	John XIX
1032	Benedict IX
1045	Sylvester III
1045	Benedict IX
1045	Gregory VI
1046	Clement II
1047	Benedict IX
1048	Damasus II
1049	St. Leo IX
1055	Victor II
1057	Stephen IX (X)
1058	*Benedict X*
1059	Nicholas II
1061	Alexander II
1061	*Honorius II*
1073	St. Gregory VII
1080	*Clement III*
1086	Bl. Victor III
1088	Bl. Urban II
1099	Paschal II
1100	*Theodoric*
1102	*Albert*
1105	*Sylvester IV*
1118	Gelasius II
1118	*Gregory VIII*
1119	Callistus II
1124	Honorius II
1124	*Celestine II*
1130	Innocent II
1130	*Anacletus II*
1138	*Victor IV*
1143	Celestine II
1144	Lucius II
1145	Bl. Eugene III
1153	Anastasius IV
1154	Adrian IV
1159	Alexander III
1159	*Victor IV*
1164	*Paschal III*
1168	*Callistus III*
1179	*Innocent III*
1181	Lucius III
1185	Urban III
1187	Clement III
1187	Gregory VIII
1191	Celestine III
1198	Innocent III
1216	Honorius III
1227	Gregory IX
1241	Celestine IV
1243	Innocent IV
1254	Alexander IV
1261	Urban IV
1265	Clement IV
1271	Bl. Gregory X
1276	Bl. Innocent V
1276	Adrian V
1276	John XXI
1277	Nicholas III
1281	Martin IV
1285	Honorius IV
1288	Nicholas IV
1294	St. Celestine V
1294	Boniface VIII
1303	Bl. Benedict XI
1305	Clement V

Year	Pope
1316	John XXII
1328	*Nicholas V*
1334	Benedict XII
1342	Clement VI
1352	Innocent VI
1362	Bl. Urban V
1370	Gregory XI
1378	Urban VI
1378	*Clement VII*
1389	Boniface IX
1394	*Benedict XIII*
1404	Innocent VII
1406	Gregory XII
1409	*Alexander V*
1410	*John XXIII*
1417	Martin V
1431	Eugene IV
1439	*Felix V*
1447	Nicholas V
1455	Callistus III
1458	Pius II
1464	Paul II
1471	Sixtus IV
1484	Innocent VIII
1492	Alexander VI
1503	Pius III
1503	Julius II
1513	Leo X
1522	Adrian VI
1523	Clement VII
1534	Paul III
1550	Julius III
1555	Marcellus II
1555	Paul IV
1559	Pius IV
1566	St. Pius V
1572	Gregory XIII
1585	Sixtus V
1590	Urban VII
1590	Gregory XIV
1591	Innocent IX
1592	Clement VIII
1605	Leo XI
1605	Paul V
1621	Gregory XV
1623	Urban VIII
1644	Innocent X
1655	Alexander VII
1667	Clement IX
1670	Clement X
1676	Bl. Innocent XI
1689	Alexander VIII
1691	Innocent XII
1700	Clement XI
1721	Innocent XIII
1724	Benedict XIII
1730	Clement XII
1740	Benedict XIV
1758	Clement XIII
1769	Clement XIV
1775	Pius VI
1800	Pius VII
1823	Leo XII
1829	Pius VIII
1831	Gregory XVI
1846	Pius IX
1878	Leo XIII
1903	St. Pius X
1914	Benedict XV
1922	Pius XI
1939	Pius XII
1958	John XXIII
1963	Paul VI
1978	John Paul I
1978	John Paul II

WORLD EXPLORATION AND GEOGRAPHY

Early Explorers of the Western Hemisphere

The first people to discover the New World or Western Hemisphere are believed to have walked across a "land bridge" from Siberia to Alaska, an isthmus since broken by the Bering Strait. From Alaska, these ancestors of the Indians spread through North, Central, and South America. Anthropologists have placed these crossings at between 18,000 and 14,000 B.C., but evidence found in 1967 near Puebla, Mex., indicates people may have reached there as early as 35,000-40,000 years ago.

At first, these people were hunters using flint weapons and tools. In Mexico, about 7000-6000 B.C., they founded farming cultures, developing corn, squash, etc. Eventually, they created complex civilizations — Olmec, Toltec, Aztec, and Maya and, in South America, Inca. Carbon-14 tests show humans lived about 8000 B.C. near what are now Front Royal, Va., Kanawha, W.Va., and Dutchess Quarry, N.Y. The Hopewell Culture, based on farming, flourished about 1000 B.C.; remains of it are seen today in large mounds in Ohio and other states.

Norsemen (Norwegian Vikings sailing out of Iceland and Greenland) are credited by most scholars with being the first Europeans to discover America, with at least 5 voyages around 1000 A.D. to areas they called Helluland, Markland, Vinland—possibly Labrador, Nova Scotia or Newfoundland, and New England.

Christopher Columbus, the most famous explorer, was born Cristoforo Colombo in or near Genoa, Italy, probably in 1451, but made his voyages of exploration for the Spanish rulers Ferdinand and Isabella. Dates of his voyages, places he reached, and other information follow:

1492—First voyage. Left Palos, Spain, Aug. 3 with 88 men (est.). His fleet consisted of 3 vessels—the *Nina*, the *Pinta*, and the *Santa Maria*. Landed San Salvador, (Guanahani or Watling Is., Bahamas) Oct. 12. Also Cuba, Hispaniola (Haiti-Dominican Republic); built Fort La Navidad on latter.

1493—Second voyage, first part, Sept. 25, with 17 ships, 1,500 men. Dominica (Lesser Antilles) Nov. 3; Guadeloupe, Montserrat, Antigua, San Martin, Santa Cruz, Puerto Rico, Virgin Islands. Settled Isabela on Hispaniola. **Second part** (Columbus having remained in Western Hemisphere), Jamaica, Isle of Pines, La Mona Is.

1498—Third voyage. Left Spain, May 30, 1498, 6 ships. Landed Trinidad. Saw South American continent, Aug. 1, 1498, but called it Isla Sancta (Holy Island). Entered Gulf of Paria and landed, first time on continental soil. At mouth of Orinoco, Aug. 14, he decided this was the mainland.

1502—Fourth voyage, 4 caravels, 150 men. St. Lucia, Guanaja off Honduras; Cape Gracias a Dios, Honduras; San Juan River, Costa Rica; Almirante, Portobelo, and Laguna de Chiriqui, Panama.

Year	Explorer	Nationality and employer	Area reached or explored
1497	John Cabot	Italian-English	Newfoundland or Nova Scotia
1498	John and Sebastian Cabot	Italian-English	Labrador to Hatteras
1499	Alonso de Ojeda	Spanish	South American coast, Venezuela
1500, Feb.	Vicente y Pinzon	Spanish	South American coast, Amazon River
1500, Apr.	Pedro Alvarez Cabral	Portuguese	Brazil (for Portugal)
1500-02	Gaspar Corte-Real	Portuguese	Labrador
1501	Rodrigo de Bastidas	Spanish	Central America
1513	Vasco Nunez de Balboa	Spanish	Pacific Ocean
1513	Juan Ponce de Leon	Spanish	Florida
1515	Juan de Solis	Spanish	Rio de la Plata
1519	Alonso de Pineda	Spanish	Mouth of Mississippi River
1519	Hernando Cortes	Spanish	Mexico
1520	Ferdinand Magellan	Portuguese-Spanish	Straits of Magellan, Tierra del Fuego
1524	Giovanni da Verrazano	Italian-French	Atlantic coast-New York harbor
1532	Francisco Pizarro	Spanish	Peru
1534	Jacques Cartier	French	Canada, Gulf of St. Lawrence
1536	Pedro de Mendoza	Spanish	Buenos Aires
1536	A.N. Cabeza de Vaca	Spanish	Texas coast and interior
1539	Francisco de Ulloa	Spanish	California coast
1539-41	Hernando de Soto	Spanish	Mississippi River near Memphis
1539	Marcos de Niza	Italian-Spanish	Southwest (now U.S.)
1540	Francisco V. de Coronado	Spanish	Southwest (now U.S.)
1540	Hernando Alarcon	Spanish	Colorado River
1540	Garcia de L. Cardenas	Spanish	Grand Canyon of the Colorado
1541	Francisco de Orellana	Spanish	Amazon River
1542	Juan Rodriguez Cabrillo	Portuguese-Spanish	San Diego harbor
1565	Pedro Menendez de Aviles	Spanish	St. Augustine
1576	Martin Frobisher	English	Frobisher's Bay, Canada
1577-80	Francis Drake	English	California coast
1582	Antonio de Espejo	Spanish	Southwest (named New Mexico)
1584	Amadas & Barlow (for Raleigh)	English	Virginia
1585-87	Sir Walter Raleigh's men	English	Roanoke Is., N.C.
1595	Sir Walter Raleigh	English	Orinoco River
1603-09	Samuel de Champlain	French	Canadian interior, Lake Champlain
1607	Capt. John Smith	English	Atlantic coast
1609-10	Henry Hudson	English-Dutch	Hudson River, Hudson Bay
1634	Jean Nicolet	French	Lake Michigan; Wisconsin
1673	Jacques Marquette, Louis Jolliet	French	Mississippi S to Arkansas
1682	Sieur de La Salle	French	Mississippi S to Gulf of Mexico
1789	Alexander Mackenzie	Canadian	Canadian Northwest

Arctic Exploration

Early Explorers

1587 — John Davis (England). Davis Strait to Sanderson's Hope, 72° 12′ N.

1596 — Willem Barents and Jacob van Heemskerck (Holland). Discovered Bear Island, touched northwest tip of Spitsbergen, 79° 49′ N, rounded Novaya Zemlya, wintered at Ice Haven.

1607 — Henry Hudson (England). North along Greenland's east coast to Cape Hold-with-Hope, 73° 30', then north of Spitsbergen to 80° 23'. Returning he discovered Hudson's Touches (Jan Mayen).

1616 — William Baffin and Robert Bylot (England). Baffin Bay to Smith Sound.

1728 — Vitus Bering (Russia). Proved Asia and America were separated by sailing through strait.

1733-40 — Great Northern Expedition (Russia). Surveyed Siberian Arctic coast.

1741 — Vitus Bering (Russia). Sighted Alaska from sea, named Mount St. Elias. His lieutenant, Chirikof, discovered coast.

1771 — Samuel Hearne (Hudson's Bay Co.). Overland from Prince of Wales Fort (Churchill) on Hudson Bay to mouth of Coppermine River.

1778 — James Cook (Britain). Through Bering Strait to Icy Cape, Alaska, and North Cape, Siberia.

1789 — Alexander Mackenzie (North West Co., Britain). Montreal to mouth of Mackenzie River.

1806 — William Scoresby (Britain). N. of Spitsbergen to 81° 30'.

1820-3 — Ferdinand von Wrangel (Russia). Completed a survey of Siberian Arctic coast. His exploration joined that of James Cook at North Cape, confirming separation of the continents.

1845 — Sir John Franklin (Britain) was one of many to seek the Northwest Passage—an ocean route connecting the Atlantic and Pacific via the Arctic. His 2 ships (the *Erebus* and *Terror*) were last seen entering Lancaster Sound July, 26.

1881 — The steamer *Jeanette* on an expedition led by Lt. Cmdr. George W. DeLong was trapped in ice and crushed, June 1881. DeLong and 11 crewmen died; 12 others survived.

1888 — Fridtjof Nansen (Norway) crossed Greenland's icecap, 1893-96 — Nansen in Fram drifted from New Siberian Is. to Spitsbergen; tried polar dash in 1895, reached Franz Josef Land.

1897 — Salomon A. Andree (Sweden) and 2 others started in balloon from Danes, Is., Spitsbergen, July 11, to drift across pole to America, and disappeared. Over 33 years later, Aug. 6, 1930, their frozen bodies were found on White Is., 82° 57' N 29° 52' E.

1903-06 — Roald Amundsen (Norway) first sailed Northwest Passage.

Discovery of North Pole

Robert E. Peary explored Greenland's coast, 1891-92, tried for North Pole, 1893. In 1900 he reached northern limit of Greenland and 83° 50' N; in 1902 he reached 84° 06' N; in 1906 he went from Ellesmere Is. to 87° 06' N. He sailed in the *Roosevelt*, July, 1908, to winter off Cape Sheridan, Grant Land. The dash for the North Pole began Mar. 1 from Cape Columbia, Ellesmere Land. Peary reached the pole, 90° N, Apr. 6, 1909.

Peary had several supporting groups carrying supplies until the last group turned back at 87° 47' N. Peary, Matthew Henson, and 4 Eskimos proceeded with dog teams and sleds. They crossed the pole several times, finally built an igloo at 90°, remained 36 hours. Started south, Apr. 7 at 4 p.m., for Cape Columbia. The Eskimos were Coqueeh, Ootah, Eginwah, and Seegloo.

1914 — Donald MacMillan (U.S.). Northwest, 200 miles, from Axel Heiberg Island to seek Peary's Crocker Land.

1915-17 — Vihjalmur Stefansson (Canada) discovered Borden, Brock, Meighen, and Lougheed Islands.

1918-20 — Roald Amundsen sailed Northeast Passage.

1925 — Amundsen and Lincoln Ellsworth (U.S.) reached 87° 44' N in attempt to fly to North Pole from Spitsbergen.

1926 — Richard E. Byrd and Floyd Bennett (U.S.) first over North Pole by air, May 9.

1926 — Amundsen, Ellsworth, and Umberto Nobile (Italy) flew from Spitsbergen over North Pole May 12, to Teller, Alaska, in dirigible *Norge*.

1928 — Nobile crossed North Pole in airship, May 24, crashed, May 25. Amundsen lost while trying to effect rescue by plane.

North Pole Exploration Records

On Aug. 3, 1958, the *Nautilus*, under Comdr. William R. Anderson, became the first ship to cross the North Pole beneath the Arctic ice.

The nuclear-powered U.S. submarine *Seadragon*, Comdr. George P. Steele 2d, made the first east-west underwater transit through the Northwest Passage during August, 1960. It sailed from Portsmouth N.H., headed between Greenland and Labrador through Baffin Bay, then west through Lancaster Sound and McClure Strait to the Beaufort Sea. Traveling submerged for the most part, the submarine made 850 miles from Baffin Bay to the Beaufort Sea in 6 days.

On Aug. 16, 1977, the Soviet nuclear icebreaker *Arktika* reached the North Pole and became the first surface ship to break through the Arctic ice pack to the top of the world.

On April 30, 1978, Naomi Uemura, a Japanese explorer, became the first man to reach the North Pole alone by dog sled. During the 54-day, 600-mile trek over the frozen Arctic, Uemura survived attacks by a marauding polar bear.

In April, 1982, Sir Ranulph Fiennes and Charles Burton, British explorers, reached the North Pole and became the first to circle the earth from pole to pole. They had reached the South Pole 16 months earlier. The 52,000-mile trek took 3 years, involved 23 people, and cost an estimated $18 million. The expedition was also the first to travel down the Scott Glacier and the first to journey up the Yukon and through the Northwest Passage in a single season.

On May 2, 1986, 6 American and Canadian explorers reached the North Pole assisted only by dogs. They became the first to reach the Pole without mechanical assistance since Robert E. Peary planted a flag there in 1909. The explorers, Americans Will Steger, Paul Schurke, Anne Bancroft, and Geoff Carroll, and Canadians Brent Boddy and Richard Weber completed the 500-mile journey in 56 days.

Antarctic Exploration

Early History

Antarctica has been approached since 1773-75, when Capt. James Cook (Britain) reached 71° 10' S. Many sea and landmarks bear names of early explorers. Bellingshausen (Russia) discovered Peter I and Alexander I Islands, 1819-21. Nathaniel Palmer (U.S.) discovered Palmer Peninsula, 60° W, 1820, without realizing that this was a continent. James Weddell (Britain) found Weddell Sea, 74° 15' S, 1823.

First to announce existence of the continent of Antarctica was Charles Wilkes (U.S.), who followed the coast for 1,500 mi., 1840. Adelie Coast, 140° E, was found by Dumont d'Urville (France), 1840. Ross Ice Shelf was found by James Clark Ross (Britain), 1841-42.

1895 — Leonard Kristensen (Norway) landed a party on the coast of Victoria Land. They were the first ashore on the main continental mass. C.E. Borchgrevink, a member of that party, returned in 1899 with a British expedition, first to winter on Antarctica.

1902-04 — Robert F. Scott (Britain) discovered Edward VII Peninsula. He reached 82° 17' S, 146° 33' E from McMurdo Sound.

1908-09 — Ernest Shackleton (Britain) introduced the use of Manchurian ponies in Antarctic sledging. He reached 88° 23' S, discovering a route on to the plateau by way of the Beardmore Glacier and pioneering the way to the pole.

Discovery of South Pole

1911 — Roald Amundsen (Norway) with 4 men and dog teams reached the pole, Dec. 14.

1912 — Capt. Scott reached the pole from Ross Island, Jan. 18, with 4 companions. They found Amundsen's tent. None of Scott's party survived. They were found, Nov. 12.

1928 — First man to use an airplane over Antarctica was Hubert Wilkins (Britain).

1929 — Richard E. Byrd (U.S.) established Little America on Bay of Whales. On 1,600-mi. airplane flight begun, Nov. 28, he crossed South Pole, Nov. 29 with 3 others.

1934-35 — Byrd led 2d expedition to Little America, explored 450,000 sq. mi., wintered alone at weather station, 80° 08′ S.

1934-37 — John Rymill led British Graham Land expedition; discovered that Palmer Peninsula is part of Antarctic mainland.

1935 — Lincoln Ellsworth (U.S.) flew south along Palmer Peninsula's east coast, then crossed continent to Little America, making 4 landings on unprepared terrain in bad weather.

1939-41 — U.S. Antarctic Service built West Base on Ross Ice Shelf under Paul Siple, and East Base on Palmer Peninsula under Richard Black. U.S. Navy plane flights discovered about 150,000 sq. miles of new land.

1940 — Byrd charted most of coast between Ross Sea and Palmer Peninsula.

1946-47 — U.S. Navy undertook Operation High-jump under Byrd. Expedition included 13 ships and 4,000 men. Airplanes photomapped coastline and penetrated beyond pole.

1946-48 — Ronne Antarctic Research Expedition, Comdr. Finn Ronne, USNR, determined the Antarctic to be only one continent with no strait between Weddell Sea and Ross Sea; discovered 250,000 sq. miles of land by flights to 79° S Lat., and made 14,000 aerial photographs over 450,000 sq. miles of land. Mrs. Ronne and Mrs. H. Darlington were the first women to winter on Antarctica.

1955-57 — U.S. Navy's Operation Deep Freeze led by Adm. Byrd. Supporting U.S. scientific efforts for the International Geophysical Year, the operation was commanded by Rear Adm. George Dufek. It established 5 coastal stations fronting the Indian, Pacific, and Atlantic oceans and also 3 interior stations; explored more than 1,000,000 sq. miles in Wilkes Land.

1957-58 — During the International Geophysical year, July 1957, through Dec. 1958, scientists from 12 countries conducted ambitious programs of Antarctic research. A network of some 60 stations on the continent and sub-Arctic islands studied oceanography, glaciology, meteorology, seismology, geomagnetism, the ionosphere, cosmic rays, aurora, and airglow.

Dr. V.E. Fuchs led a 12-man Trans-Antarctic Expedition on the first land crossing of Antarctica. Starting from the Weddell Sea, they reached Scott Station, Mar. 2, 1958, after traveling 2,158 miles in 98 days.

1958 — A group of 5 U.S. scientists led by Edward C. Thiel, seismologist, moving by tractor from Ellsworth Station on Weddell Sea, identified a huge mountain range, 5,000 ft. above the ice sheet and 9,000 ft. above sea level. The range, originally seen by a Navy plane, was named the Dufek Massif, for Rear Adm. George Dufek.

1959 — Twelve nations — Argentina, Australia, Belgium, Chile, France, Japan, New Zealand, Norway, South Africa, the Soviet Union, the United Kingdom, and the U.S. — signed a treaty suspending any territorial claims for 30 years and reserving the continent for research.

1961-62 — Scientists discovered a trough, the Bentley Trench, running from Ross Ice Shelf, Pacific, into Marie Byrd Land, around the end of the Ellsworth Mtns., toward the Weddell Sea.

1962 — First nuclear power plant began operation at McMurdo Sound.

1963 — On Feb. 22 a U.S. plane made the longest nonstop flight ever made in the S. Pole area, covering 3,600 miles in 10 hours. The flight was from McMurdo Station south past the geographical S. Pole to Shackleton Mtns., southeast to the "Area of Inaccessibility" and back to McMurdo Station.

1964 — A British survey team was landed by helicopter on Cook Island, the first recorded visit since its discovery in 1775.

1964 — New Zealanders completed one of the last and most important surveys when they mapped the mountain area from Cape Adare west some 400 miles to Pennell Glacier.

1989 — Two Americans, Victoria Murden and Shirley Metz, became the first women to reach the South Pole overland when they arrived with 9 others on Jan. 17, 1989. The 51-day trek on skis covered 740 miles.

Volcanoes

Source: Global Volcanism Network, Smithsonian Institution

More than 75 percent of the world's 850 active volcanoes lie within the "Ring of Fire," a zone running along the west coast of the Americas from Chile to Alaska and down the east coast of Asia from Siberia to New Zealand. Twenty per cent of these volcanoes are located in Indonesia. Other prominent groupings are located in Japan, the Aleutian Islands, and Central America. Almost all active regions are found at the boundaries of the large moving plates which comprise the earth's surface. The "Ring of Fire" marks the boundary between the plates underlying the Pacific Ocean and those underlying the surrounding continents. Other active regions, such as the Mediterranean Sea and Iceland, are located on plate boundaries.

Major Historical Eruptions

Approximately 7,000 years ago, Mazama, a 9,900-feet-high volcano in southern Oregon, erupted violently, ejecting ash and lava. The ash spread over the entire northwestern United States and as far away as Saskatchewan, Canada. During the eruption, the top of the mountain collapsed, leaving a caldera 6 miles across and about a half mile deep, which filled with rain water to form what is now called Crater Lake.

In 79 A.D., Vesuvio, or Vesuvius, a 4,190 feet volcano overlooking Naples Bay became active after several centuries of quiescence. On Aug. 24 of that year, a heated mud and ash flow swept down the mountain engulfing the cities of Pompeii, Herculaneum, and Stabiae with debris over 60 feet deep. About 10 percent of the population of the 3 towns was killed.

The largest eruptions in recent centuries have been in Indonesia. In 1883, an eruption similar to the Mazama eruption occurred on the island of Krakatau. On August 27, the 2,640-feet-high peak of the volcano collapsed to 1,000 feet below sea level, leaving only a small portion of the island standing above the sea. Ash from the eruption colored sunsets around the world for 2 years. A tsunami ("tidal wave") generated by the collapse killed 36,000 people in nearby Java and Sumatra and eventually reached England. A similar, but even more powerful, eruption had taken place 68 years earlier at Tambora volcano on the Indonesian island of Sumbawa.

Notable Active Volcanoes

Name, latest activity	Location	Height (feet)
Africa		
Cameroon (1982)	Cameroon	13,354
Nyirangongo (1977)	Zaire	11,400
Nyamuragira (1991)	Zaire	10,028
Karthala (1977)	Comoro Is.	8,000
Piton de la Fournaise (1991)	Reunion Is.	5,981
Erta-Ale (1992)	Ethiopia	1,650
Antarctica		
Erebus (1991)	Ross Island	12,450
Deception Island (1970)	South Shetland Islands	1,890

(continued)

Name, latest activity	Location	Height (feet)
Asia-Oceania		
Kliuchevskol (1991)	Russia	15,584
Kerinci (1987)	Sumatra	12,467
Semeru (1991)	Java	12,060
Slamet (1988)	Java	11,247
Raung (1991)	Java	10,932
On-Take (1991)	Japan	10,049
Mayon (1993)	Philippines	9,991
Merapi (1993)	Java	9,551
Marapi (1988)	Sumatra	9,485
Ruapehu (1992)	New Zealand	9,175
Asama (1991)	Japan	8,300
Niigata Yakeyama (1989)	Japan	8,111
Canlaon (1991)	Philippines	8,070
Alaid (1972)	Kuril Is.	7,662
Ulawun (1992)	New Britain	7,532
Ngauruhoe (1975)	New Zealand	7,515
Chokai (1974)	Japan	7,300
Galunggung (1982)	Java	7,113
Azuma (1978)	Japan	6,700
Pinatubo (1992)	Philippines	5,770
Sangeang Api (1988)	Indonesia	6,351
Nasu (1977)	Japan	6,210
Tiatia (1973)	Kuril Islands	6,013
Manam (1992)	Papua New Guinea	6,000
Soputan (1989)	Indonesia	5,994
Siau (1976)	Indonesia	5,853
Kelud (1990)	Java	5,679
Kirisima (1982)	Japan	5,577
Bagana (1992)	Papua New Guinea	6,558
Akita Komaga take (1970)	Japan	5,449
Gamkonora (1981)	Indonesia	5,364
Aso (1993)	Japan	5,223
Lokon-Empung (1991)	Indonesia	5,187
Bulusan (1988)	Philippines	5,115
Sarycheva (1976)	Kuril Islands	4,960
Karkar (1981)	Papua New Guinea	4,920
Lopevi (1982)	Vanuatu	4,755
Unzen (1993)	Japan	4,462
Ambrym (1991)	Vanuatu	4,376
Awu (1992)	Indonesia	4,350
Sakurajima (1993)	Japan	3,668
Langila (1992)	New Britain	3,586
Suwanosezima (1991)	Japan	2,640
Oshima (1990)	Japan	2,550
Usu (1978)	Japan	2,400
Pagan (1990)	Mariana Is.	1,870
White Island (1993)	New Zealand	1,075
Taal (1988)	Philippines	984
Central America—Caribbean		
Acatenango (1972)	Guatemala	12,992
Fuego (1991)	Guatemala	12,582
Tacana (1988)	Guatemala	12,400
Santiaguito (Santa Maria) (1991)	Guatemala	12,362
Irazu (1992)	Costa Rica	11,260
Turrialba (1992)	Costa Rica	10,650
Poas (1992)	Costa Rica	8,930
Pacaya (1991)	Guatemala	8,346
San Miguel (1986)	El Salvador	6,994
Rincon de la Vieja (1993)	Costa Rica	6,234
El Viejo (San Cristobal) (1991)	Nicaragua	5,840
Ometepe (Concepcion) (1986)	Nicaragua	5,106
Arenal (1993)	Costa Rica	5,092
Momotombo (1982)	Nicaragua	4,199
Soufriere (1979)	St. Vincent	4,048
Telica (1987)	Nicaragua	3,409
South America		
Guallatiri (1987)	Chile	19,882
Lascar (1991)	Chile	19,652
Cotopaxi (1975)	Ecuador	19,347
Tupungatito (1986)	Chile	18,504
Ruiz (1992)	Colombia	17,716
Sangay (1988)	Ecuador	17,159
Guagua Pichincha (1988)	Ecuador	15,696
Purace (1977)	Colombia	15,601
Galeras (1993)	Colombia	13,996
Llaima (1990)	Chile	10,239
Villarrica (1992)	Chile	9,318
Hudson (1991)	Chile	8,580
Alcedo (1970)	Galapagos Is.	3,599
Mid-Pacific		
Mauna Loa (1987)	Hawaii	13,680
Kilauea (1993)	Hawaii	4,077
Mid-Atlantic Ridge		
Beerenberg (1985)	Jan Mayen Is.	7,470
Hekla (1991)	Iceland	4,892
Leirhnukur (1975)	Iceland	2,145
Krafla (1984)	Iceland	2,145
Europe		
Etna (1993)	Italy	11,053
Stromboli (1993)	Italy	3,038
North America		
Colima (1991)	Mexico	14,003
Redoubt (1991)	Alaska	10,197
Iliamna (1978)	Alaska	10,016
Shishaldin (1987)	Aleutian Is.	9,387
Mt. St. Helens (1991)	Washington	8,300+
Pavlof (1988)	Aleutian Is.	8,261
Veniaminof (1987)	Alaska	8,225
El Chichon (1983)	Mexico	7,300
Katmai (1974)	Alaska	6,715
Makushin (1987)	Aleutian Is.	6,680
Great Sitkin (1974)	Aleutian Is.	5,710
Cleveland (1987)	Aleutian Is.	5,675
Gareloi (1982)	Aleutian Is.	5,334
Korovin (1987)	Aleutian Is.	4,852
Akutan (1992)	Aleutian Is.	4,275
Kiska (1990)	Aleutian Is.	4,275
Augustine (1988)	Alaska	3,999
Okmok (1988)	Aleutian Is.	3,519
Seguam (1977)	Alaska	3,458

Notable Volcanic Eruptions

Date	Volcano	Deaths
79 A.D.	Mt. Vesuvius, Italy	16,000
1169	Mt. Etna, Sicily	15,000
1631	Mt. Vesuvius, Italy	4,000
1669	Mt. Etna, Sicily	20,000
1772	Mt. Papandayan, Java	3,000
1792	Mt. Unzen-Dake, Japan	10,400
1815	Tamboro, Java	12,000
Aug. 26-28, 1883	Krakatau, Indonesia	35,000
Apr. 8, 1902	Santa Maria, Guatemala	1,000
May 8, 1902	Mt. Pelée, Martinique	30,000
1911	Mt. Taal, Philippines	1,400
1919	Mt. Kelud, Java	5,000
Jan. 18-21, 1951	Mt. Lamington, New Guinea	3,000
Apr. 26, 1966	Mt. Kelud, Java	1,000
May 18, 1980	Mt. St. Helens, U.S.	60
Nov. 13, 1985	Nevado del Ruiz, Colombia	22,940
Aug. 24, 1986	NW Cameroon	1,700+

Mountains

Height of Mount Everest

Mt. Everest was considered to be 29,002 ft. tall when Edmund Hillary and Tenzing Norgay scaled it in 1953. This triangulation figure had been accepted since 1850. In 1954 the Surveyor General of the Republic of India set the height at 29,028 ft., plus or minus 10 ft. because of snow. The National Geographic Society accepts the new figure, but many mountaineering groups still use 29,002 ft.

In 1987, new calculations based on satellite measurements indicate that the Himalayan peak K-2 rose 29,064 feet above sea level and that Mt. Everest is 800 feet higher. The National Geographic Society has not accepted the revised figure.

United States, Canada, Mexico

Name	Place	Height (feet)
McKinley	Alaska	20,320
Logan	Yukon	19,850
Citlaltepec (Orizaba)	Mexico	18,700
St. Elias	Alas-Yukon	18,008
Popocatepetl	Mexico	17,887
Foraker	Alaska	17,400
Iztaccihuatl	Mexico	17,343
Lucania	Yukon	17,147
King	Yukon	16,971
Steele	Yukon	16,644
Bona	Alaska	16,550
Blackburn	Alaska	16,390
Kennedy	Alaska	16,286
Sanford	Alaska	16,237
South Buttress	Alaska	15,885
Wood	Yukon	15,885
Vancouver	Alas-Yukon	15,700
Churchill	Alaska	15,638
Fairweather	Alas-Yukon	15,300
Zinantecatl (Toluca)	Mexico	15,016
Hubbard	Alas-Yukon	15,015
Bear	Alaska	14,831
Walsh	Yukon	14,780
East Buttress	Alaska	14,730
Matlalcueyetl	Mexico	14,636
Hunter	Alaska	14,573
Alverstone	Alas-Yukon	14,565
Browne Tower	Alaska	14,530
Whitney	Cal	14,494
Elbert	Col	14,433
Massive	Col	14,421
Harvard	Col	14,420
Rainier	Wash	14,410
Williamson	Cal	14,375
Blanca Peak	Col	14,345
La Plata	Col	14,336
Uncompahgre	Col	14,309
Crestone	Col	14,294
Lincoln	Col	14,286
Grays Peak	Col	14,270
Antero	Col	14,269
Torreys	Col	14,267
Castle	Col	14,265
Quandary	Col	14,265
Evans	Col	14,264
Longs Peak	Col	14,256
McArthur	Yukon	14,253
Wilson	Col	14,246
White	Cal	14,246
North Palisade	Cal	14,242
Shavano	Col	14,229
Belford	Col	14,197
Princeton	Col	14,197
Crestone Needle	Col	14,197
Yale	Col	14,196
Bross	Col	14,172
Kit Carson	Col	14,165
Wrangell	Alaska	14,163
Shasta	Cal	14,162
Sill	Cal	14,162
El Diente	Col	14,159
Maroon	Col	14,156
Tabeguache	Col	14,155
Oxford	Col	14,153
Sneffels	Col	14,150
Point Success	Wash	14,150
Democrat	Col	14,148
Capitol	Col	14,130
Liberty Cap	Wash	14,112
Pikes Peak	Col	14,110
Snowmass	Col	14,092
Windom	Col	14,087
Russell	Cal	14,086
Eolus	Col	14,084
Columbia	Col	14,073
Augusta	Alas-Yukon	14,070
Missouri	Col	14,067
Humboldt	Col	14,064

South America

Peak, country	Height (feet)
Aconcagua, Argentina	22,834
Ojos del Salado, Arg.-Chile	22,572
Bonete, Argentina	22,546
Tupungato, Argentina-Chile	22,310
Pissis, Argentina	22,241
Mercedario, Argentina	22,211
Huascaran, Peru	22,205
Llullaillaco, Argentina-Chile	22,057
El Libertador, Argentina	22,047
Cachi, Argentina	22,047
Yerupaja, Peru	21,709
Galan, Argentina	21,654
El Muerto, Argentina-Chile	21,457
Sajama, Bolivia	21,391
Nacimiento, Argentina	21,302
Illimani, Bolivia	21,201
Coropuna, Peru	21,083
Laudo, Argentina	20,997
Ancohuma, Bolivia	20,958
Ausangate, Peru	20,945
Toro, Argentina-Chile	20,932
Illampu, Bolivia	20,873
Tres Cruces, Argentina-Chile	20,853
Huandoy, Peru	20,852
Parinacota, Bolivia-Chile	20,768
Tortolas, Argentina-Chile	20,745
Ampato, Peru	20,702
Condor, Argentina	20,669
Salcantay, Peru	20,574
Chimborazo, Ecuador	20,561
Huancarhuas, Peru	20,531
Famatina, Argentina	20,505
Pumasillo, Peru	20,492
Solo, Argentina	20,492
Polleras, Argentina	20,456
Pular, Chile	20,423
Chani, Argentina	20,341
Aucanquilcha, Chile	20,295
Juncal, Argentina-Chile	20,276
Negro, Argentina	20,184
Quela, Argentina	20,128
Condoriri, Bolivia	20,095
Palermo, Argentina	20,079
Solimana, Peru	20,068
San Juan, Argentina-Chile	20,049
Sierra Nevada, Arg.-Chile	20,023
Antofalla, Argentina	20,013
Marmolejo, Argentina-Chile	20,013
Chachani, Peru	19,931
Licancabur, Argentina-Chile	19,425

The highest point in the West Indies is in the Dominican Republic, Pico Duarte (10,417 ft.)

Africa, Southeast Asia, Australia, New Zealand

Peak, country/island	Height (feet)
Kilimanjaro, Tanzania	19,340
Kenya, Kenya	17,058
Margherita Pk., Uganda-Zaire	16,763
Jaja, New Guinea	16,500
Trikora, New Guinea	15,585
Mandala, New Guinea	15,420
Ras Dashan, Ethiopia	15,158
Meru, Tanzania	14,979
Wilhelm, New Guinea	14,793
Karisimbi, Zaire-Rwanda	14,787
Elgon, Kenya-Uganda	14,178
Batu, Ethiopia	14,131
Guna, Ethiopia	13,881
Gughe, Ethiopia	13,780
Toubkal, Morocco	13,661
Kinabalu, Malaysia	13,455
Cameroon, Cameroon	13,353
Kerinci, Sumatra	12,467
Cook, New Zealand	12,349
Teide, Canary Islands	12,198
Semeru, Java	12,060
Kosciusko, Australia	7,310

Europe

Peak, country	Height (feet)
Alps	
Mont Blanc, Fr.-It.	15,771
Monte Rosa (highest peak of group), Switz.	15,203
Dom, Switz.	14,911
Liskamm, It., Switz.	14,852
Weisshom, Switz.	14,780
Taschhorn, Switz.	14,733
Matterhorn, It., Switz.	14,690
Dent Blanche, Switz.	14,293
Nadelhorn, Switz.	14,196
Grand Combin, Switz.	14,154
Lenzpitze, Switz.	14,088
Finsteraarhorn, Switz.	14,022
Castor, Switz.	13,865
Zinalrothorn, Switz.	13,849
Hohberghom, Switz.	13,842
Alphubel, Switz.	13,799
Rimpfischhom, Switz.	13,776
Aletschorn, Switz.	13,763
Strahlhorn, Switz.	13,747
Dent D'Herens, Switz.	13,686
Breithorn, It., Switz.	13,665
Bishorn, Switz.	13,645
Jungfrau, Switz.	13,642
Ecrins, Fr.	13,461
Monch, Switz.	13,448
Pollux, Switz.	13,422
Schreckhorn, Switz.	13,379
Ober Gabelhorn, Switz.	13,330
Gran Paradiso, It.	13,323

(*continued*)

Peak, country	Height (feet)
Bernina, It., Switz.	13,284
Fiescherhorn, Switz.	13,283
Grunhorn, Switz.	13,266
Lauteraarhorn, Switz.	13,261
Durrenhorn, Switz.	13,238
Allalinhorn, Switz.	13,213
Weissmies, Switz.	13,199
Lagginhorn, Switz.	13,156
Zupo, Switz.	13,120
Fletschhorn, Switz.	13,110
Adlerhorn, Switz.	13,081
Gletscherhorn, Switz.	13,068
Schalihorn, Switz.	13,040
Scerscen, Switz.	13,028
Eiger, Switz.	13,025
Jagerhorn, Switz.	13,024
Rottalhorn, Switz.	13,022

Pyrenees

Peak, country	Height (feet)
Aneto, Sp.	11,168
Posets, Sp.	11,073
Perdido, Sp.	11,007
Vignemale, Fr.-Sp.	10,820
Long, Sp.	10,479
Estats, Sp.	10,304
Montcalm, Sp.	10,105

Caucasus (Europe-Asia)

Peak, country	Height (feet)
El'brus, Russia	18,510
Shkara, Russia	17,064
Dykh Tau, Russia	17,054
Kashtan Tau, Russia	16,877
Dzhangi Tau, Russia	16,565
Kazbek, Russia	16,558

Asia

Peak	Country	Height (feet)
Everest	Nepal-Tibet	29,028
K2 (Godwin Austen)	Kashmir	28,250
Kanchenjunga	India-Nepal	28,208
Lhotse I (Everest)	Nepal-Tibet	27,923
Makalu I	Nepal-Tibet	27,824
Lhotse II (Everest)	Nepal-Tibet	27,560
Dhaulagiri	Nepal	26,810
Manaslu I	Nepal	26,760
Cho Oyu	Nepal-Tibet	26,750
Nanga Parbat	Kashmir	26,660
Annapurna I	Nepal	26,504
Gasherbrum	Kashmir	26,470
Broad	Kashmir	26,400
Gosainthan	Tibet	26,287
Annapurna II	Nepal	26,041
Gyachung Kang	Nepal-Tibet	25,910
Disteghil Sar	Kashmir	25,868
Himalchuli	Nepal	25,801
Nuptse (Everest)	Nepal-Tibet	25,726
Masherbrum	Kashmir	25,660
Nanda Devi	India	25,645
Rakaposhi	Kashmir	25,550
Kamet	India-Tibet	25,447
Namcha Barwa	Tibet	25,445
Gurla Mandhata	Tibet	25,355
Ulugh Muz Tagh	Sinkiang-Tibet	25,340
Kungur	Sinkiang	25,325
Tirich Mir	Pakistan	25,230
Makalu II	Nepal-Tibet	25,120
Minya Konka	China	24,900
Kula Gangri	Bhutan-Tibet	24,784
Changtzu (Everest)	Nepal-Tibet	24,780
Muz Tagh Ata	Sinkiang	24,757
Skyang Kangri	Kashmir	24,750
Communism Peak	Tajikistan	24,590
Jongsang Peak	India-Nepal	24,472
Pobedy Peak	Sinkiang-Kyrgyzstan	24,406
Sia Kangri	Kashmir	24,350
Haramosh Peak	Pakistan	24,270
Istoro Nal	Pakistan	24,240
Tent Peak	India-Nepal	24,165
Chomo Lhari	Bhutan-Tibet	24,040
Chamlang	Nepal	24,012
Kabru	India-Nepal	24,002
Alung Gangri	Tibet	24,000
Baltoro Kangri	Kashmir	23,990
Mussu Shan	Sinkiang	23,890
Mana	India	23,860
Baruntse	Nepal	23,688
Nepal Peak	India-Nepal	23,500
Amne Machin	China	23,490
Gauri Sankar	Nepal-Tibet	23,440
Badrinath	India	23,420
Nunkun	Kashmir	23,410
Lenin Peak	Tajikistan	23,405
Pyramid	India-Nepal	23,400
Api	Nepal	23,399
Pauhunri	India-Tibet	23,385
Trisul	India	23,360
Kangto	India-Tibet	23,260
Nyenchhen Thanglha	Tibet	23,255
Trisuli	India	23,210
Pumori	Nepal-Tibet	23,190
Dunagiri	India	23,184
Lombo Kangra	Tibet	23,165
Saipal	Nepal	23,100
Macha Pucchare	Nepal	22,958
Numbar	Nepal	22,817
Kanjiroba	Nepal	22,580
Ama Dablam	Nepal	22,350
Cho Polu	Nepal	22,093
Lingtren	Nepal-Tibet	21,972
Khumbutse	Nepal-Tibet	21,785
Hlako Gangri	Tibet	21,266
Mt. Grosvenor	China	21,190
Thagchhab Gangri	Tibet	20,970
Damavand	Iran	18,606
Ararat	Turkey	16,804

Antarctica

Peak	Height (feet)
Vinson Massif	16,864
Tyree	16,290
Shinn	15,750
Gardner	15,375
Epperly	15,100
Kirkpatrick	14,855
Elizabeth	14,698
Markham	14,290
Bell	14,117
Mackellar	14,098
Anderson	13,957
Bentley	13,934
Kaplan	13,878
Andrew Jackson	13,750
Sidley	13,720
Ostenso	13,710
Minto	13,668
Miller	13,650
Long Gables	13,620
Dickerson	13,517
Giovinetto	13,412
Wade	13,400
Fisher	13,386
Fridtjof Nansen	13,350
Wexler	13,202
Lister	13,200
Shear	13,100
Odishaw	13,008
Donaldson	12,894
Ray	12,808
Sellery	12,779
Waterman	12,730
Anne	12,703
Press	12,566
Falla	12,549
Rucker	12,520
Goldthwait	12,510
Morris	12,500
Erebus	12,450
Campbell	12,434
Don Pedro Christophersen	12,355
Lysaght	12,326
Huggins	12,247
Sabine	12,200
Astor	12,175
Mohl	12,172
Frankes	12,064
Jones	12,040
Gjelsvik	12,008
Coman	12,000

Some Notable U.S. Mountains

Name	Place	Height (feet)
Gannett Peak	Wyo.	13,804
Grand Teton	Wyo.	13,766
Kings	Utah	13,528
Cloud	Wyo.	13,175
Boundary	Nevada	13,140
Wheeler	N.M.	13,065
Granite	Montana	12,799
Borah	Idaho	12,662
Humphreys	Ariz.	12,633
Adams	Wash.	12,307
San Gorgonio	Cal.	11,502
Hood	Ore.	11,235
Lassen	Cal.	10,457
Granite	Cal.	10,321
Guadalupe	Texas	8,751
Olympus	Wash.	7,965
Harney	S.D.	7,242
Mitchell	N.C.	6,684
Clingmans Dome	N.C.-Tenn.	6,643
Washington	N.H.	6,288
Rogers	Va.	5,927
Marcy	N.Y.	5,344
Katahdin	Maine	5,268
Spruce Knob	W. Va.	4,862
Mansfield	Vt.	4,393
Black Mountain	Ky.	4,145

Ocean Areas and Average Depths

Four major bodies of water are recognized by geographers and mapmakers: the Pacific, Atlantic, Indian, and Arctic oceans. The Atlantic and Pacific oceans are considered divided at the equator into the No. and So. Atlantic; the No. and So. Pacific. The Arctic Ocean is the name for waters north of the continental land masses in the region of the Arctic Circle.

	Sq. miles	Avg. depth (feet)
Pacific Ocean	64,186,300	12,925
Atlantic Ocean	33,420,000	11,730
Indian Ocean	28,350,500	12,598
Arctic Ocean	5,105,700	3,407
South China Sea	1,148,500	4,802
Caribbean Sea	971,400	8,448
Mediterranean Sea	969,100	4,926
Bering Sea	873,000	4,893
Gulf of Mexico	582,100	5,297
Sea of Okhotsk	537,500	3,192
Sea of Japan	391,100	5,468
Hudson Bay	281,900	305
East China Sea	256,600	620
Andaman Sea	218,100	3,667
Black Sea	196,100	3,906
Red Sea	174,900	1,764
North Sea	164,900	308
Baltic Sea	147,500	180
Yellow Sea	113,500	121
Persian Gulf	88,800	328
Gulf of California	59,100	2,375

Principal Ocean Depths

Source: Defense Mapping Agency Hydrographic/Topographic Center, U.S. Dept. of Defense

Name of area	Location		Depth Meters	Depth Fathoms	Feet
Pacific Ocean					
Mariana Trench	11°22'N	142°36'E	10,924	5,973	35,840
Tonga Trench	23°16'S	174°44'W	10,800	5,906	35,433
Philippine Trench	10°38'N	126°36'E	10,057	5,499	32,995
Kermadec Trench	31°53'S	177°21'W	10,047	5,494	32,963
Bonin Trench	24°30'N	143°24'E	9,994	5,464	32,788
Kuril Trench	44°15'N	150°34'E	9,750	5,331	31,988
Izu Trench	31°05'N	142°10'E	9,695	5,301	31,808
New Britain Trench	06°19'S	153°45'E	8,940	4,888	29,331
Yap Trench	08°33'N	138°02'E	8,527	4,663	27,976
Japan Trench	36°08'N	142°43'E	8,412	4,600	27,599
Peru-Chile Trench	23°18'S	71°14'W	8,064	4,409	26,457
Palau Trench	07°52'N	134°56'E	8,054	4,404	26,424
Aleutian Trench	50°51'N	177°11'E	7,679	4,199	25,194
New Hebrides Trench	20°36'S	168°37'E	7,570	4,139	24,836
North Ryukyu Trench	24°00'N	126°48'E	7,181	3,927	23,560
Mid. America Trench	14°02'N	93°39'W	6,662	3,643	21,857
Atlantic Ocean					
Puerto Rico Trench	19°55'N	65°27'W	8,605	4,705	28,232
So. Sandwich Trench	55°42'S	25°56'E	8,325	4,552	27,313
Romanche Gap	0°13'S	18°26'W	7,728	4,226	25,354
Cayman Trench	19°12'N	80°00'W	7,535	4,120	24,721
Brazil Basin	09°10'S	23°02'W	6,119	3,346	20,076
Indian Ocean					
Java Trench	10°19'S	109°58'E	7,125	3,896	23,376
Ob' Trench	09°45'S	67°18'E	6,874	3,759	22,553
Diamantina Trench	35°50'S	105°14'E	6,602	3,610	21,660
Vema Trench	09°08'S	67°15'E	6,402	3,501	21,004
Agulhas Basin	45°20'S	26°50'E	6,195	3,387	20,325
Arctic Ocean					
Eurasia Basin	82°23'N	19°31'E	5,450	2,980	17,881
Mediterranean Sea					
Ionian Basin	36°32'N	21°06'E	5,150	2,816	16,896

Note: Deeper depths have been reported in some of the above areas. However, they are not official unless confirmed by research vessels.

Principal World Rivers

Source: Geological Survey, U.S. Dept. of the Interior

River	Outflow	Length (Miles)
Albany	James Bay	610
Amazon	Atlantic Ocean	4,000
Amu	Aral Sea	1,578
Amur	Tatar Strait	2,744
Angara	Yenisey River	1,151
Arkansas	Mississippi	1,459
Back	Arctic Ocean	605
Brahmaputra	Bay of Bengal	1,800
Bug, Southern	Dnieper River	532
Bug, Western	Wisla River	481
Canadian	Arkansas River	906
Chang Jiang	E. China Sea	3,964
Churchill, Man.	Hudson Bay	1,000
Churchill, Que.	Atlantic Ocean	532
Colorado	Gulf of Calif.	1,450
Columbia	Pacific Ocean	1,243
Congo	Atlantic Ocean	2,718
Danube	Black Sea	1,776
Dnieper	Black Sea	1,420
Dniester	Black Sea	877
Don	Sea of Azov	1,224
Drava	Danube River	447
Dvina, North	White Sea	824
Dvina, West	Gulf of Riga	634
Ebro	Mediterranean	565
Elbe	North Sea	724
Euphrates	Shatt al-Arab	1,700
Fraser	Str. of Georgia	850
Gambia	Atlantic Ocean	700
Ganges	Bay of Bengal	1,560
Garonne	Bay of Biscay	357
Huang	Yellow Sea	3,395
Indus	Arabian Sea	1,800

River	Outflow	Length (Miles)
Irrawaddy	Bay of Bengal	1,337
Japura	Amazon River	1,750
Jordan	Dead Sea	200
Kootenay	Columbia River	485
Lena	Laptev Sea	2,734
Loire	Bay of Biscay	634
Mackenzie	Arctic Ocean	2,635
Madeira	Amazon River	2,013
Magdalena	Caribbean Sea	956
Marne	Seine River	326
Mekong	S. China Sea	2,600
Meuse	North Sea	580
Mississippi	Gulf of Mexico	2,340
Missouri	Mississippi	2,315
Murray-Darling	Indian Ocean	2,310
Negro	Amazon	1,400
Nelson	Hudson Bay	410
Niger	Gulf of Guinea	2,590
Nile	Mediterranean	4,160
Ob-Irtysh	Gulf of Ob	3,362
Oder	Baltic Sea	567
Ohio	Mississippi	981
Orange	Atlantic Ocean	1,300
Orinoco	Atantic Ocean	1,600
Ottawa	St. Lawrence R.	790
Paraguay	Parana River	1,584
Parana	Rio de la Plata	2,485
Peace	Slave River	1,210
Pilcomayo	Paraguay River	1,000
Po	Adriatic Sea	405
Purus	Amazon River	2,100
Red	Mississippi	1,290
Red River of N.	Lake Winnipeg	545
Rhine	North Sea	820
Rhone	Gulf of Lions	505
Rio de la Plata	Atlantic Ocean	150
Rio Grande	Gulf of Mexico	1,900
Rio Roosevelt	Aripuana	400
Saguenay	St. Lawrence R.	434
St. John	Bay of Fundy	418
St. Lawrence	Gulf of St. Law.	800
Salween	Andaman Sea	1,500
Sao Francisco	Atlantic Ocean	1,988
Saskatchewan	Lake Winnipeg	1,205
Seine	English Chan.	496
Shannon	Atlantic Ocean	230
Snake	Columbia River	1,038
Songhua	Amur River	1,150
Syr	Aral Sea	1,370
Tajo, Tagus	Atlantic Ocean	626
Tennessee	Ohio River	652
Thames	North Sea	236
Tiber	Tyrrhenian Sea	252
Tigris	Shatt al-Arab	1,180
Tisza	Danube River	600
Tocantins	Para River	1,677
Ural	Caspian Sea	1,575
Uruguay	Rio de la Plata	1,000
Volga	Caspian Sea	2,290
Weser	North Sea	454
Wisla	Bay of Danzig	675
Xi	S. China Sea	1,200
Yellow (See Huang)		
Yenisey	Kara Sea	2,543
Yukon	Bering Sea	1,979
Zambezi	Indian Ocean	1,700

Major Rivers in North America

Source: Geological Survey, U.S. Dept. of the Interior

River	Source or Upper Limit of Length	Outflow	Miles
Alabama	Gilmer County, Ga.	Mobile River	729
Albany	Lake St. Joseph, Ontario	James Bay	610
Allegheny	Potter County, Pa.	Ohio River	325
Altamaha-Ocmulgee	Junction of Yellow and South Rivers, Newton County, Ga.	Atlantic Ocean	392
Apalachicola-Chattahoochee	Towns County, Ga.	Gulf of Mexico	524
Arkansas	Lake County, Col.	Mississippi River	1,459
Assiniboine	Eastern Saskatchewan	Red River	450
Attawapiskat	Attawapiskat, Ontario	James Bay	465
Back (N.W.T.)	Contwoyto Lake	Chantrey Inlet	605
Big Black (Miss.)	Webster County, Miss.	Mississippi River	330
Brazos	Junction of Salt and Double Mountain Forks, Stonewall County, Tex.	Gulf of Mexico	923
Canadian	Las Animas County, Col.	Arkansas River	906
Cedar (Iowa)	Dodge County, Minn.	Iowa River	329
Cheyenne	Junction of Antelope Creek and Dry Fork, Converse County, Wyo.	Missouri River	290
Churchill	Methy Lake, Saskatchewan	Hudson Bay	1,000
Cimarron	Colfax County, N.M.	Arkansas River	600
Colorado (Ariz.)	Rocky Mountain National Park, Col. (90 miles in Mexico)	Gulf of Cal.	1,450
Colorado (Texas)	West Texas	Matagorda Bay	862
Columbia	Columbia Lake, British Columbia	Pacific Ocean, bet. Ore. and Wash.	1,243
Columbia, Upper	Columbia Lake, British Columbia	To mouth of Snake River	890
Connecticut	Third Connecticut Lake, N.H.	L.I. Sound, Conn.	407
Coppermine (N.W.T.)	Lac de Gras	Coronation Gulf (Arctic Ocean)	525
Cumberland	Letcher County, Ky.	Ohio River	720
Delaware	Schoharie County, N.Y.	Liston Point, Delaware Bay	390
Fraser	Near Mount Robson (on Continental Divide)	Strait of Georgia	850
Gila	Catron County, N.M.	Colorado River	649
Green (Ut.-Wyo.)	Junction of Wells and Trail Creeks, Sublette County, Wyo.	Colorado River	730
Hamilton (Lab.)	Lake Ashuanipi	Atlantic Ocean	532
Hudson	Henderson Lake, Essex County, N.Y.	Upper N.Y. Bay	306
Illinois	St. Joseph County, Ind.	Mississippi River	420
James (N.D.-S.D.)	Wells County, N.D.	Missouri River	710
James (Va.)	Junction of Jackson and Cowpasture Rivers, Botetourt County, Va.	Hampton Roads	340
Kanawha-New	Junction of North and South Forks of New River, N.C.	Ohio River	352
Kentucky	Junction of North and Middle Forks, Lee County, Ky.	Ohio River	259
Klamath	Lake Ewauna, Klamath Falls, Ore.	Pacific Ocean	250
Koyukuk	Endicott Mountains, Alaska	Yukon River	470
Kuskokwim	Alaska Range	Kuskokwim Bay	724
Liard	Southern Yukon, Alaska	Mackenzie River	693
Little Missouri	Crook County, Wyo.	Missouri River	560
Mackenzie	Great Slave Lake, N.W.T.	Arctic Ocean	2,635
Milk	Junction of North and South Forks, Alberta	Missouri River	625
Minnesota	Big Stone Lake, Minn.	Mississippi River	332
Mississippi	Lake Itasca, Minn.	Mouth of Southwest Pass	2,340
Mississippi, Upper	Lake Itasca, Minn.	To mouth of Missouri River	1,171
Mississippi-Missouri-Red Rock	Source of Red Rock, Beaverhead Co., Mon.	Mouth of Southwest Pass	3,710
Missouri	Junction of Jefferson, Madison, and Gallatin rivers, Madison County, Mon.	Mississippi River	2,315
Missouri-Red Rock	Source of Red Rock, Beaverhead Co., Mon.	Mississippi River	2,540
Mobile-Alabama-Coosa	Gilmer County, Ga.	Mobile Bay	774
Nelson (Manitoba)	Lake Winnipeg	Hudson Bay	410

River	Source or Upper Limit of Length	Outflow	Miles
Neosho	Morris County, Kan.	Arkansas River, Okla.	460
Niobrara	Niobrara County, Wyo.	Missouri River, Neb.	431
North Canadian	Union County, N.M.	Canadian River, Okla.	800
North Platte	Junction of Grizzly and Little Grizzly creeks, Jackson County, Col.	Platte River, Neb.	618
Ohio	Junction of Allegheny and Monongahela rivers, Pittsburgh, Pa.	Mississippi River	981
Ohio-Allegheny	Potter County, Pa.	Mississippi River	1,310
Osage	East-central Kansas	Missouri River	500
Ottawa	Lake Capimitchigama	St. Lawrence River	790
Ouachita	Polk County, Ark.	Red River	605
Peace	Stikine Mountains, B.C.	Slave River	1,210
Pearl	Neshoba County, Miss.	Gulf of Mexico	411
Pecos	Mora County, N.M.	Rio Grande	926
Pee Dee-Yadkin	Watauga County, N.C.	Winyah Bay	435
Pend Oreille-Clark Fork	Near Butte, Mon.	Columbia River	531
Platte	Junction of North and South Platte Rivers, Neb.	Missouri River	310
Porcupine	Ogilvie Mountains, Alaska	Yukon River, Alaska	569
Potomac	Garrett County, Md.	Chesapeake Bay	383
Powder	Junction of South and Middle Forks, Wyo.	Yellowstone River	375
Red (Okla.-Tex.-La.)	Curry County, N.M.	Mississippi River	1,290
Red River of the North	Junction of Otter Tail and Bois de Sioux Rivers, Wilkin County, Minn.	Lake Winnipeg	545
Republican	Junction of North Fork and Arikaree River, Neb.	Kansas River	445
Rio Grande	San Juan County, Col.	Gulf of Mexico	1,900
Roanoke	Junction of North and South Forks, Montgomery County, Va.	Albemarle Sound	380
Rock (Ill.-Wis.)	Dodge County, Wis.	Mississippi River	300
Sabine	Junction of South and Caddo Forks, Hunt County, Tex.	Sabine Lake	380
Sacramento	Siskiyou County, Cal.	Suisun Bay	377
St. Francis	Iron County, Mo.	Mississippi River	425
St. Lawrence	Lake Ontario	Gulf of St. Lawrence (Atlantic Ocean)	800
Salmon (Idaho)	Custer County, Ida.	Snake River	420
San Joaquin	Junction of South and Middle Forks, Madera County, Cal.	Suisun Bay	350
San Juan	Silver Lake, Archuleta County, Col.	Colorado River	360
Santee-Wateree-Catawba	McDowell County, N.C.	Atlantic Ocean	538
Saskatchewan, North	Rocky Mountains	Saskatchewan R.	800
Saskatchewan, South	Rocky Mountains	Saskatchewan R.	865
Savannah	Junction of Seneca and Tugaloo rivers, Anderson County, S.C.	Atlantic Ocean, Ga.-S.C.	314
Severn (Ontario)	Sandy Lake	Hudson Bay	610
Smoky Hill	Cheyenne County, Col.	Kansas River, Kan.	540
Snake	Teton County, Wyo.	Columbia River, Wash.	1,038
South Platte	Junction of South and Middle Forks, Park County, Col.	Platte River	424
Susitna	Alaska Range	Cook Inlet	313
Susquehanna	Otsego Lake, Otsego County, N.Y.	Chesapeake Bay	444
Tallahatchie	Tippah County, Miss.	Yazoo River	301
Tanana	Wrangell Mountains, Alaska	Yukon River	659
Tennessee	Junction of French Broad and Holston Rivers	Ohio River	652
Tennessee-French Broad	Transylvania County, N.C.	Ohio River	883
Tombigbee	Prentiss County, Miss.	Mobile River	525
Trinity	North of Dallas, Tex.	Galveston Bay	360
Wabash	Darke County, Oh.	Ohio River	512
Washita	Hemphill County, Tex.	Red River, Okla.	500
White (Ark.-Mo.)	Madison County, Ark.	Mississippi River	722
Willamette	Douglas County, Ore.	Columbia River	309
Wind-Bighorn	Junction of Wind and Little Wind Rivers, Fremont Co., Wyo. (Source of Wind R. is Togwotee Pass, Teton Co., Wyo.)	Yellowstone River	336
Wisconsin	Lac Vieux Desert, Vilas County, Wis.	Mississippi River	430
Yellowstone	Park County, Wyo.	Missouri River	692
Yukon	Coast Mountains of British Columbia	Bering Sea	1,979

Lakes of the World

Source: Geological Survey, U.S. Dept. of the Interior

A lake is a body of water surrounded by land. Although some lakes are called seas (such as the Caspian Sea and the Aral Sea), they are lakes by definition.

Name	Continent	Area (sq. mi.)	Length (miles)	Depth (feet)	Elevation (feet)
Caspian Sea	Asia-Europe	143,244	760	3,363	−92
Superior	North America	31,700	350	1,330	600
Victoria	Africa	26,828	250	270	3,720
Aral Sea	Asia	24,904(A)	280	220	174
Huron	North America	23,000	206	750	579
Michigan	North America	22,300	307	923	579
Tanganyika	Africa	12,700	420	4,823	2,534
Baykal	Asia	12,162	395	5,315	1,493
Great Bear	North America	12,096	192	1,463	512
Nyasa	Africa	11,150	360	2,280	1,550

(continued)

Name	Continent	Area (sq. mi.)	Length (miles)	Depth (feet)	Elevation (feet)
Great Slave	North America	11,031	298	2,015	513
Erie	North America	9,910	241	210	570
Winnipeg	North America	9,417	266	60	713
Ontario	North America	7,550	193	802	245
Balkhash	Asia	7,115	376	85	1,115
Ladoga	Europe	6,835	124	738	13
Chad	Africa	6,300	175	24	787
Maracaibo	South America	5,217	133	115	Sea level
Onega	Europe	3,710	145	328	108
Eyre	Australia	3,600	90	4	−52
Volta	Africa	3,276	250	....	....
Titicaca	South America	3,200	122	922	12,500
Nicaragua	North America	3,100	102	230	102
Athabasca	North America	3,064	208	407	700
Reindeer	North America	2,568	143	720	1,106
Rudolf	Africa	2,473	154	240	1,230
Issyk Kul	Asia	2,355	115	2,303	5,279
Torrens	Australia	2,230	130	....	92
Vanern	Europe	2,156	91	328	144
Nettilling	North America	2,140	67	....	95
Winnipegosis	North America	2,075	141	38	830
Albert	Africa	2,075	100	168	2,030
Kariba	Africa	2,050	175	390	1,590
Nipigon	North America	1,872	72	540	1,050
Gairdner	Australia	1,840	90	....	112
Urmia	Asia	1,815	90	49	4,180
Manitoba	North America	1,799	140	12	813

(A) Probably less because of the diversion of feeder rivers.

The Great Lakes

Source: National Ocean Service, U.S. Dept. of Commerce

The Great Lakes form the largest body of fresh water in the world and with their connecting waterways are the largest inland water transportation unit. Draining the great North Central basin of the U.S., they enable shipping to reach the Atlantic via their outlet, the St. Lawrence R., and also the Gulf of Mexico via the Illinois Waterway, from Lake Michigan to the Mississippi R. A third outlet connects with the Hudson R. and thence the Atlantic via the N. Y. State Barge Canal System. Traffic on the Illinois Waterway and the N.Y. State Barge Canal System is limited to recreational boating and small shipping vessels.

Only one of the lakes, Lake Michigan, is wholly in the United States; the others are shared with Canada. Ships move from the shores of Lake Superior to Whitefish Bay at the east end of the lake, thence through the Soo (Sault Ste. Marie) locks, through the St. Mary's River and into Lake Huron. To reach Gary, and Port of Indiana and South Chicago, Ill., ships move west from Lake Huron to Lake Michigan through the Straits of Mackinac.

Lake Superior is 600 feet above mean water level at Point-au-Pere, Quebec, on the International Great Lakes Datum (1955). From Duluth, Minn., to the eastern end of Lake Ontario is 1,156 mi.

	Superior	Michigan	Huron	Erie	Ontario
Length in miles	350	307	206	241	193
Breadth in miles	160	118	183	57	53
Deepest soundings in feet	1,330	923	750	210	802
Volume of water in cubic miles	2,900	1,180	850	116	393
Area (sq. miles) water surface—U.S.	20,600	22,300	9,100	4,980	3,560
Canada	11,100	.....	13,900	4,930	3,990
Area (sq. miles) entire drainage basin—U.S.	16,900	45,600	16,200	18,000	15,200
Canada	32,400	.....	35,500	4,720	12,100
Total Area (sq. miles) U.S. and Canada	**81,000**	**67,900**	**74,700**	**32,630**	**34,850**
Mean surface above mean water level at Point-au-Pere, Quebec, aver. level in feet (1900-1988)	600.61	578.34	578.34	570.53	244.74
Latitude, North	46° 25′	41° 37′	43° 00′	41° 23′	43° 11′
	49° 00′	46° 06′	46° 17′	42° 52′	44° 15′
Longitude, West	84° 22′	84° 45′	79° 43′	78° 51′	76° 03′
	92° 06′	88° 02′	84° 45′	83° 29′	79° 53′
National boundary line in miles	282.8	None	260.8	251.5	174.6
United States shore line (mainland only) miles	863	1,400	580	431	300

Highest and Lowest Continental Altitudes

Source: National Geographic Society

Continent	Highest point	Elevation (feet)	Lowest point	Elevation (feet) below sea level
Asia	Mount Everest, Nepal-Tibet	29,028	Dead Sea, Israel-Jordan	1,312
South America	Mount Aconcagua, Argentina	22,834	Valdes Peninsula, Argentina	131
North America	Mount McKinley, Alaska	20,320	Death Valley, California	282
Africa	Kilimanjaro, Tanzania	19,340	Lake Assal, Djibouti	512
Europe	Mount El'brus, Russia	18,510	Caspian Sea, Russia, Azerbaijan	92
Antarctica	Vinson Massif	16,864	Unknown	...
Australia	Mount Kosciusko, New South Wales	7,310	Lake Eyre, South Australia	52

Famous Waterfalls

Source: National Geographic Society

The earth has thousands of waterfalls, some of considerable magnitude. Their importance is determined not only by height but volume of flow, steadiness of flow, crest width, whether the water drops sheerly or over a sloping surface, and in one leap or a succession of leaps. A series of low falls flowing over a considerable distance is known as a cascade.

Estimated mean annual flow, in cubic feet per second, of major waterfalls are: Niagara, 212,200; Paulo Afonso, 100,000; Urubupunga, 97,000; Iguazu, 61,000; Patos-Maribondo, 53,000; Victoria, 35,400; and Kaieteur, 23,400.

Height = total drop in feet in one or more leaps. † = falls of more than one leap; * = falls that diminish greatly seasonally; ** = falls that reduce to a trickle or are dry for part of each year. If river names not shown, they are same as the falls. R. = river; L. = lake; (C) = cascade type.

Name and location	Elevation (Feet)
Africa	
Angola	
Ruacana, Cuene R.	406
Ethiopia	
Fincha	508
Lesotho	
*Maletsunyane	630
Zimbabwe-Zambia	
*Victoria, Zambezi R.	343
South Africa	
*Augrabies, Orange R.	480
† Tugela	2,014
Tanzania-Zambia	
*Kalambo	726
Asia	
India—*Cauvery	330
*Jog (Gersoppa), Sharavathi R.	830
Japan	
*Kegon, Daiya R.	330
Australasia	
Australia	
New South Wales	
Wentworth	614
Wollomombi	1,100
Queensland	
Tully	885
† Wallaman, Stony Cr.	1,137
New Zealand	
Helena	890
† Sutherland, Arthur R.	1,904
Europe	
Austria—† Gastein	492
† Krimml	1,312
France—*Gavarnie	1,385
Great Britain—Scotland	
Glomach	370
Wales	
Rhaiadr	240
Italy—Frua, Toce R. (C)	470
Norway	
Mardalsfossen (Northern)	1,535
† Mardalsfossen (Southern)	2,149
† **Skjeggedal, Nybuai R.	1,378
**Skykje	984
Vetti, Morka-Koldedola R.	900
Sweden	
† Handol	427
Switzerland	
Giessbach (C)	984
† Reichenbach	656
† Simmen	459
Staubbach	984
† Trummelbach	1,312
North America	
Canada	
Alberta	
Panther, Nigel Cr.	600
British Columbia	
† Della	1,443
† Takakkaw, Daly Glacier	1,200
Quebec	
Montmorency	274
Canada—United States	
Niagara: American	182
Horseshoe	173
United States	
California	
*Feather, Fall R.	640
Yosemite National Park	
*Bridalveil	620
*Illilouette	370
*Nevada, Merced R.	594
**Ribbon	1,612
**Silver Strand, Meadow Br.	1,170
*Vernal, Merced R.	317
† **Yosemite	2,425
Colorado	
† Seven, South Cheyenne Cr.	300
Hawaii	
Akaka, Kolekole Str.	442
Idaho	
**Shoshone, Snake R.	212
Kentucky	
Cumberland	68
Maryland	
*Great, Potomac R. (C)	71
Minnesota	
**Minnehaha	53
New Jersey	
Passaic	70
New York	
*Taughannock	215
Oregon	
† Multnomah	620
Tennessee	
Fall Creek	256
Washington	
Mt. Rainier Natl. Park	
Sluiskin, Paradise R.	300
**Snoqualmie	268
Wisconsin	
*Big Manitou, Black R. (C)	165
Wyoming	
Yellowstone Natl. Pk. Tower	132
*Yellowstone (upper)	109
*Yellowstone (lower)	308
Mexico	
El Salto	218
South America	
Argentina-Brazil	
Iguazu	230
Brazil	
Glass	1,325
Patos-Maribondo, Grande R.	115
Paulo Afonso, Sao Francisco R.	275
Colombia	
Catarata de Candelas, Cusiana R.	984
*Tequendama, Bogota R.	427
Ecuador	
*Agoyan, Pastaza R.	200
Guyana	
Kaieteur, Potaro R.	741
Great, Kamarang R.	1,600
† Marina, Ipobe R.	500
Venezuela—	
† *Angel	3,212
Cuquenan	2,000

Notable Deserts of the World

Arabian (Eastern), 70,000 sq. mi. in Egypt between the Nile river and Red Sea, extending southward into Sudan.

Atacama, 600 mi. long area rich in nitrate and copper deposits in N. Chile.

Chihuahuan, 140,000 sq. mi. in Tex., N.M., Ariz., and Mexico.

Death Valley, 3,300 sq. mi. in E. Cal. and SW Nev. Contains lowest point below sea level (282 ft.) in Western Hemisphere.

Gibson, 120,000 sq. mi. in the interior of W. Australia.

Gobi, 500,000 sq. mi. in Mongolia and China.

Great Sandy, 150,000 sq. mi. in W. Australia.

Great Victoria, 150,000 sq. mi. in W. and S. Australia.

Kalahari, 225,000 sq. mi. in southern Africa.

Kara-Kum, 120,000 sq. mi. in Turkmenistan.

Kyzyl Kum, 100,000 sq. mi. in Kazakhstan & Uzbekistan.

Libyan, 450,000 sq. mi. in the Sahara extending from Lybia through SW Egypt into Sudan.

Lut (Dasht-e Lut), 20,000 sq. mi. in E. Iran.

Mojave, 15,000 sq. mi. in S. Cal.

Namib, long narrow area extending 800 miles along SW coast of Africa.

Nubian, 100,000 sq. mi. in the Sahara in NE Sudan.

Painted Desert, section of high plateau in N. Ariz. extending 150 mi.

Rub al Khali (Empty Quarter), 250,000 sq. mi. in the south Arabian Peninsula.

Sahara, 3,500,000 sq. mi. in N. Africa extending westward to the Atlantic. Largest desert in the world.

Sonoran, 70,000 sq. mi. in SW Ariz. and SE Cal. extending into Mexico.

Syrian, 100,000 sq. mi. arid wasteland extending over much of N. Saudi Arabia, E. Jordan, S. Syria, and W. Iraq.

Taklimakan, 140,000 sq. mi. in Sinkiang Province, China.

Thar (Great Indian), 100,000 sq. mi. arid area extending 400 mi. along India-Pakistan border.

Important Islands and Their Areas

Figure in parentheses shows rank among the world's 10 largest islands; some islands have not been surveyed accurately; in such cases estimated areas are shown.

Location-Ownership

Area in square miles

Arctic Ocean

Canadian

Axel Heiberg	15,779
Baffin (5)	183,810
Banks	27,038
Bathurst	7,609
Devon	20,861
Ellesmere (9)	82,119
Melville	16,369
Prince of Wales	12,830
Somerset	9,370
Southampton	15,700
Victoria (10)	81,930

Norwegian

Svalbard	23,940
Nordaustlandet	5,410
Spitsbergen	15,060

Russian

Franz Josef Land	8,000
Novaya Zemlya (two is.)	31,730
Wrangel	2,800

Atlantic Ocean

Anticosti, Canada	3,043
Ascension, UK	34
Azores, Portugal	888
Faial	67
Sao Miguel	291
Bahamas	5,386
Bermuda Is., UK	20
Bioko Is. Equatorial Guinea	785
Block, Rhode Island	10
Canary Is., Spain	2,808
Fuerteventura	668
Gran Canaria	592
Tenerife	795
Cape Breton, Canada	3,970
Cape Verde Is.	1,557
Faeroe Is., Denmark	540
Falkland Is., UK	4,700
Fernando de Noronha Archipelago, Brazil	7
Greenland, Denmark (1)	840,000
Iceland	39,769
Long Island, N. Y.	1,396
Madeira Is., Portugal	307
Marajo, Brazil	15,444
Martha's Vineyard, Mass.	108
Mount Desert, Me.	108
Nantucket, Mass.	57
Newfoundland, Canada	42,030
Prince Edward, Canada	2,184
St. Helena, UK	47
South Georgia, UK	1,450
Tierra del Fuego, Chile and Argentina	18,800
Tristan da Cunha, UK	40

British Isles

Great Britain, mainland (8)	84,200
Channel Islands	75
Guernsey	24
Jersey	45
Sark	2
Hebrides	2,744
Ireland	32,599
Irish Republic	27,136
Northern Ireland	5,463
Man	227
Orkney Is.	390
Scilly Is.	6
Shetland Is.	567
Skye	670
Wight	147

Baltic Sea

Aland Is., Finland	581
Bornholm, Denmark	227
Gotland, Sweden	1,159

Caribbean Sea

Antigua	108
Aruba, Netherlands	75
Barbados	166
Cuba	44,218
Isle of Youth	1,182
Curacao, Netherlands	171
Dominica	290
Guadeloupe, France	687
Hispaniola, Haiti and Dominican Republic	29,371
Jamaica	4,244
Martinique, France	425
Puerto Rico, U.S.	3,435
Tobago	116
Trinidad	1,864
Virgin Is., UK	59
Virgin Is., U.S.	132

Indian Ocean

Andaman Is., India	2,500
Madagascar (4)	226,658
Mauritius	720
Pemba, Tanzania	380
Reunion, France	969
Seychelles	171
Sri Lanka	25,332
Zanzibar, Tanzania	640

Persian Gulf

Bahrain	255

Mediterranean Sea

Balearic Is., Spain	1,936
Corfu, Greece	229
Corsica, France	3,369
Crete, Greece	3,189
Cyprus	3,572
Elba, Italy	86
Euboea, Greece	1,411
Malta	95
Rhodes, Greece	540
Sardinia, Italy	9,262
Sicily, Italy	9,822

Pacific Ocean

Aleutian Is., U.S.	6,821
Adak	289
Amchitka	121
Attu	388
Kanaga	135
Kiska	110
Tanaga	209
Umnak	675
Unalaska	1,064
Unimak	1,600
Canton, Kiribati*	4
Caroline Is.	472
Christmas, Kiribati*	94
Clipperton, France	2
Diomede, Big, Russia	11
Diomede, Little, U.S.	2
Easter, Chile	69
Fiji	7,056
Vanua Levu	2,242
Viti Levu	4,109
Funafuti, Tuvalu*	2
Galapagos Is., Ecuador	3,043
Guadalcanal	2,180
Guam	209
Hainan, China	13,000
Hawaiian Is., U.S.	6,450
Hawaii	4,037
Oahu	593
Hong Kong	29
Japan	145,809
Hokkaido	30,144
Honshu (7)	87,805
Iwo Jima	8
Kyushu	14,114
Okinawa	459
Shikoku	7,049
Kodiak, U.S.	3,670
Marquesas Is., France	492
Marshall Is.	70
Bikini*	2
Nauru	8
New Caledonia, France	6,530
New Guinea (2)	306,000
New Zealand	103,883
Chatham	372
North	44,035
South	58,305
Stewart	674
Northern Mariana Is.	184
Philippines	115,831
Leyte	2,787
Luzon	40,880
Mindanao	36,775
Mindoro	3,790
Negros	4,907
Palawan	4,554
Panay	4,446
Samar	5,050
Quemoy	56
Sakhalin, Russia	29,500
Samoa Is.	1,177
American Samoa	77
Tutuila	52
Samoa (Western)	1,133
Savaii	670
Upolu	429
Santa Catalina, U.S.	72
Tahiti, France	402
Taiwan	13,823
Tasmania, Australia	26,178
Tonga Is.	270
Vancouver, Canada	12,079
Vanuatu	5,700

East Indies

Bali, Indonesia	2,171
Borneo, Indonesia-Malaysia, Brunei (3)	280,100
Celebes, Indonesia	69,000
Java, Indonesia	48,900
Madura, Indonesia	2,113
Moluccas, Indonesia	32,307
New Britain, Papua New Guinea	14,093
New Ireland, Papua New Guinea	3,707
Sumatra, Indonesia (6)	165,000
Timor	13,094

* **Atolls:** Bikini (lagoon area, 230 sq. mi., land area 2 sq. mi.); Canton (lagoon 20 sq. mi., land 4 sq. mi.), Kiribati; Christmas (lagoon 140 sq. mi., land 94 sq. mi.), Kiribati; Funafuti (lagoon 84 sq. mi., land 2 sq. mi.), Tuvalu. **Australia,** often called an island, is a continent.

Islands in minor waters: Manhattan (22 sq mi.), Staten (59 sq. mi.), and Governors (173 acres), all in New York Harbor, U.S.; Isle Royale (209 sq. mi.), Lake Superior, U.S.; Manitoulin (1,068 sq. mi.), Lake Huron, Canada; Pinang (110 sq. mi.), Strait of Malacca, Malaysia; Singapore (239 sq. mi.), Singapore Strait, Singapore.

DISASTERS

Some Notable Shipwrecks Since 1850

(Figures indicate estimated lives lost; as of mid-1993)

1854, Mar.—City of Glasgow; British steamer missing in North Atlantic; 480.

1854, Sept. 27—Arctic; U.S. (Collins Line) steamer sunk in collision with French steamer Vesta near Cape Race; 285-351.

1856, Jan. 23—Pacific; U.S. (Collins Line) steamer missing in North Atlantic; 186-286.

1858, Sept. 23—Austria; German steamer destroyed by fire in North Atlantic; 471.

1863, Apr. 27—Anglo-Saxon; British steamer wrecked at Cape Race; 238.

1865, Apr. 27—Sultana; a Mississippi River steamer blew up near Memphis, Tenn; 1,450.

1869, Oct. 27—Stonewall; steamer burned on Mississippi River below Cairo, Ill.; 200.

1870, Jan. 25—City of Boston; British (Inman Line) steamer vanished between New York and Liverpool; 177.

1870, Oct. 19—Cambria; British steamer wrecked off northern Ireland; 196.

1872, Nov. 7—Mary Celeste; U.S. half-brig sailed from New York for Genoa; found abandoned in Atlantic 4 weeks later in mystery of sea; crew never heard from; loss of life unknown.

1873, Jan. 22—Northfleet; British steamer foundered off Dungeness, England; 300.

1873, Apr. 1—Atlantic; British (White Star) steamer wrecked off Nova Scotia; 585.

1873, Nov. 23—Ville du Havre; French steamer, sunk after collision with British sailing ship Loch Earn; 226.

1875, May 7—Schiller; German steamer wrecked off Scilly Isles; 312.

1875, Nov. 4—Pacific; U.S. steamer sunk after collision off Cape Flattery; 236.

1878, Sept. 3—Princess Alice; British steamer sank after collision in Thames River; 700.

1878, Dec. 18—Byzantin; French steamer sank after Dardanelles collision; 210.

1881, May 24—Victoria; steamer capsized in Thames River, Canada; 200.

1883, Jan. 19—Cimbria; German steamer sunk in collision with British steamer Sultan in North Sea; 389.

1887, Nov. 15—Wah Yeung; British steamer burned at sea; 400.

1890, Feb. 17—Duburg; British steamer wrecked, China Sea; 400.

1890, Sept. 19—Ertogrul; Turkish frigate foundered off Japan; 540.

1891, Mar. 17—Utopia; British steamer sank in collision with British ironclad Anson off Gibraltar; 562.

1895, Jan. 30—Elbe; German steamer sank in collision with British steamer Craithie in North Sea; 332.

1895, Mar. 11—Reina Regenta; Spanish cruiser foundered near Gibraltar; 400.

1898, Feb. 15—Maine; U.S. battleship blown up in Havana Harbor; 260.

1898, July 4—La Bourgogne; French steamer sunk in collision with British sailing ship Cromartyshire off Nova Scotia; 549.

1898, Nov. 26—Portland; U.S. steamer wrecked off Cape Cod; 157.

1904, June 15—General Slocum; excursion steamer burned in East River, New York City; 1,030.

1904, June 28—Norge; Danish steamer wrecked on Rockall Island, Scotland; 620.

1906, Aug. 4—Sirio; Italian steamer wrecked off Cape Palos, Spain; 350.

1908, Mar. 23—Matsu Maru; Japanese steamer sank in collision near Hakodate, Japan; 300.

1909, Aug. 1—Waratah; British steamer, Sydney to London, vanished; 300.

1910, Feb. 9—General Chanzy; French steamer wrecked off Minorca, Spain; 200.

1911, Sept. 25—Liberté; French battleship exploded at Toulon; 285.

1912, Mar. 5—Principe de Asturias; Spanish steamer wrecked off Spain; 500.

1912, Apr. 14-15—Titanic; British (White Star) steamer hit iceberg in North Atlantic; 1,503.

1912, Sept. 28—Kichemaru; Japanese steamer sank off Japanese coast; 1,000.

1914, May 29—Empress of Ireland; British (Canadian Pacific) steamer sunk in collision with Norwegian collier in St. Lawrence River; 1,014.

1915, May 7—Lusitania; British (Cunard Line) steamer torpedoed and sunk by German submarine off Ireland; 1,198.

1915, July 24—Eastland; excursion steamer capsized in Chicago River; 812.

1916, Feb. 26—Provence; French cruiser sank in Mediterranean; 3,100.

1916, Mar. 3—Principe de Asturias; Spanish steamer wrecked near Santos, Brazil; 558.

1916, Aug. 29—Hsin Yu; Chinese steamer sank off Chinese coast; 1,000.

1917, Dec. 6—Mont Blanc, Imo; French ammunition ship and Belgian steamer collided in Halifax Harbor; 1,600.

1918, Apr. 25—Kiang-Kwan Chinese steamer sank in collision off Hankow; 500.

1918, July 12—Kawachi; Japanese battleship blew up in Tokayama Bay; 500.

1918, Oct. 25—Princess Sophia; Canadian steamer sank off Alaskan coast; 398.

1919, Jan. 17—Chaonia; French steamer lost in Straits of Messina, Italy; 460.

1919, Sept. 9—Valbanera; Spanish steamer lost off Florida coast; 500.

1921, Mar. 18—Hong Kong; steamer wrecked in South China Sea; 1,000.

1922, Aug. 26—Niitaka; Japanese cruiser sank in storm off Kamchatka, USSR; 300.

1927, Oct. 25—Principessa Mafalda; Italian steamer blew up, sank off Porto Seguro, Brazil; 314.

1928, Nov. 12—Vestris; British steamer sank in gale off Virginia; 113.

1934, Sept. 8—Morro Castle; U.S. steamer, Havana to New York, burned off Asbury Park, N.J.; 134.

1939, May 23—Squalus; U.S. submarine sank off Portsmouth, N.H.; 26.

1939, June 1—Thetis; British submarine, sank in Liverpool Bay; 99.

1942, Feb. 18—Truxtun and Pollux; U.S. destroyer and cargo ship ran aground, sank off Newfoundland; 204.

1942, Oct. 2—Curacao; British cruiser sank after collision with liner Queen Mary; 338.

1944, Dec. 17-18—3 U.S. Third Fleet destroyers sank during typhoon in Philippine Sea; 790.

1947, Jan. 19—Himera; Greek steamer hit a mine off Athens; 392.

1947, Apr. 16—Grandcamp; French freighter exploded in Texas City, Tex., Harbor, starting fires; 510.

1948, Nov.—Chinese army evacuation ship exploded and sunk off S. Manchuria; 6,000.

1948, Dec. 3—Kiangya; Chinese refugee ship wrecked in explosion S. of Shanghai; 1,100+.

1949, Sept. 17—Noronic; Canadian Great Lakes Cruiser burned at Toronto dock; 130.

1952, Apr. 26—Hobson and Wasp; U.S. destroyer and aircraft carrier collided in Atlantic; 176.

1953, Jan. 31—Princess Victoria; British ferry sank in storm off northern Irish coast; 134.

1954, Sept. 26—Toya Maru; Japanese ferry sank in Tsugaru Strait, Japan; 1,172.

1956, July 26—Andrea Doria and Stockholm; Italian liner and Swedish liner collided off Nantucket; 51.

1957, July 14—Eshghabad; Soviet ship ran aground in Caspian Sea; 270.

1961, July 8—Save; Portuguese ship ran aground off Mozambique; 259.

1962, Apr. 8—Dara; British liner exploded and sunk in Persian Gulf; 236.

1963, Apr. 10—Thresher; U.S. Navy atomic submarine sank in North Atlantic; 129.

1964, Feb. 10—Voyager, Melbourne; Australian destroyer sank after collision with Australian aircraft carrier Melbourne off New South Wales; 82.

1965, Nov. 13—Yarmouth Castle; Panamanian registered cruise ship burned and sank off Nassau; 90.

1967, July 29—Forrestal; U.S. aircraft carrier caught fire off N. Vietnam; 134.

1968, Jan. 25—Dakar; Israeli submarine vanished in Mediterranean Sea; 69.

1968, Jan. 27—Minerve; French submarine vanished in Mediterranean; 52.

1968, late May—Scorpion; U.S. nuclear submarine sank in Atlantic near Azores; 99 (located Oct. 31).

1969, June 2—Evans; U.S. destroyer cut in half by Australian carrier Melbourne, S. China Sea; 74.

1970, Mar. 4—Eurydice; French submarine sank in Mediterranean near Toulon; 57.

1970, Dec. 15—Namyong-Ho; South Korean ferry sank in Korea Strait; 308.

1974, May 1— Motor launch capsized off Bangladesh; 250.

1974, Sept. 26— Soviet destroyer burned and sank in Black Sea; 200+.
1976, Oct. 20—George Prince and Frosta; ferryboat and Norwegian tanker collided on Mississippi R. at Luling, La.; 77.
1976, Dec. 25—Patria; Egyptian liner caught fire and sank in the Red Sea; c. 100.
1977, Jan. 11—Grand Zenith; Panamanian-registered tanker sank off Cape Cod, Mass.; 38.
1979, Aug. 14—23 yachts competing in Fastnet yacht race sunk or abandoned during storm in S. Irish Sea; 18.
1981, Jan. 27—Tamponas II; Indonesian passenger ship caught fire and sank in Java Sea; 580.
1981, May 26—Nimitz; U.S. Marine combat jet crashed on deck of U.S. aircraft carrier; 14.
1983, Feb. 12—Marine Electric; coal freighter sank during storm off Chincoteague, Va.; 33.
1983, May 25—10th of Ramadan; Nile steamer caught fire and sank in L. Nassar; 357.
1986, Aug. 31—Soviet passenger ship **Admiral Nakhimov** and Soviet freighter **Pyotr Vasev** collided in Black Sea; 398.
1987, Mar. 6—British ferry capsized off Zeebrugge, Belgium; 188.
1987, Dec. 20—Philippine ferry **Dona Paz** and oil tanker **Victor** collided in Tablas Strait; 3,000+.
1988, Aug. 6—Indian ferry capsized on Ganges R.; 400+.
1989, Apr. 7—Soviet submarine sank off Norway; 42.
1989, Apr. 19—USS Iowa; U.S. battleship; explosion in gun turret; 47.
1989, Aug. 20—British barge **Bowbelle** struck British pleasure cruiser **Marchioness** on Thames R. in central London; 56.
1989, Sept. 10—Romanian pleasure boat and Bulgarian barge collided on Danube R.; 161.
1991, Apr. 10—Auto ferry and oil tanker collided outside Livorno Harbor, Italy; 140.
1991, Dec. 14—Salem Express; ferry rammed coral reef nr. Safaga, Egypt; 462.
1993, Feb. 17—Neptune; ferry capsized off Port-au-Prince, Haiti; 500+.

Some Notable Aircraft Disasters Since 1937

Date			Aircraft	Site of accident	Deaths
1937	May	6	German zeppelin Hindenburg	Burned at mooring, Lakehurst, N.J.	36
1944	Aug.	23	U.S. Air Force B-24	Hit school, Freckelton, England	76[1]
1945	July	28	U.S. Army B-25	Hit Empire State bldg., N.Y.C.	14[1]
1947	May	30	Eastern Air Lines DC-4	Crashed near Port Deposit, Md.	53
1952	Dec.	20	U.S. Air Force C-124	Fell, burned, Moses Lake, Wash.	87
1953	Mar.	3	Canadian Pacific Comet Jet	Karachi, Pakistan	11[2]
1953	June	18	U.S. Air Force C-124	Crashed, burned near Tokyo	129
1955	Nov.	1	United Air Lines DC-6B	Exploded, crashed near Longmont, Col.	44[3]
1956	June	20	Venezuelan Super-Constellation	Crashed in Atlantic off Asbury Park, N.J.	74
1956	June	30	TWA Super-Const., United DC-7	Collided over Grand Canyon, Arizona	128
1960	Dec.	16	United DC-8 jet, TWA Super-Const.	Collided over N.Y. City	134[4]
1962	Mar.	16	Flying Tiger Super-Const.	Vanished in Western Pacific	107
1962	June	3	Air France Boeing 707 jet	Crashed on takeoff from Paris	130
1962	June	22	Air France Boeing 707 jet	Crashed in storm, Guadeloupe, W.I.	113
1963	June	3	Chartered Northw. Airlines DC-7	Crashed in Pacific off British Columbia	101
1963	Nov.	29	Trans-Canada Airlines DC-8F	Crashed after takeoff from Montreal	118
1965	May	20	Pakistani Boeing 720-B	Crashed at Cairo, Egypt, airport	121
1966	Jan.	24	Air India Boeing 707 jetliner	Crashed on Mont Blanc, France-Italy	117
1966	Feb.	4	All-Nippon Boeing 727	Plunged into Tokyo Bay	133
1966	Mar.	5	BOAC Boeing 707 jetliner	Crashed on Mount Fuji, Japan	124
1966	Dec.	24	U.S. military-chartered CL-44	Crashed into village in So. Vietnam	129[1]
1967	Apr.	20	Swiss Britannia turboprop	Crashed at Nicosia, Cyprus	126
1967	July	19	Piedmont Boeing 727, Cessna 310	Collided in air, Hendersonville, N.C.	82
1968	Apr.	20	S. African Airways Boeing 707	Crashed on takeoff, Windhoek, SW Africa	122
1968	May	3	Braniff International Electra	Crashed in storm near Dawson, Tex.	85
1969	Mar.	16	Venezuelan DC-9	Crashed after takeoff from Maracaibo, Venezuela	155[5]
1969	Dec.	8	Olympia Airways DC-6B	Crashed near Athens in storm	93
1970	Feb.	15	Dominican DC-9	Crashed into sea on takeoff from Santo Domingo	102
1970	July	3	British chartered jetliner	Crashed near Barcelona, Spain	112
1970	July	5	Air Canada DC-8	Crashed near Toronto International Airport	108
1970	Aug.	9	Peruvian turbojet	Crashed after takeoff from Cuzco, Peru	101[1]
1970	Nov.	14	Southern Airways DC-9	Crashed in mountains near Huntington, W. Va.	75[6]
1971	July	30	All-Nippon Boeing 727 and Japanese Air Force F-86	Collided over Morioka, Japan	162[7]
1971	Sept.	4	Alaska Airlines Boeing 727	Crashed into mountain near Juneau, Alaska	111
1972	Aug.	14	E. German Ilyushin-62	Crashed on take-off East Berlin	156
1972	Oct.	13	Aeroflot Ilyushin-62	E. German airline crashed near Moscow	176
1972	Dec.	3	Chartered Spanish airliner	Crashed on take-off, Canary Islands	155
1972	Dec.	29	Eastern Airlines Lockheed Tristar	Crashed on approach to Miami Int'l. Airport	101
1973	Jan.	22	Chartered Boeing 707	Burst into flames during landing, Kano Airport, Nigeria	176
1973	Feb.	21	Libyan jetliner	Shot down by Israeli fighter planes over Sinai	108
1973	Apr.	10	British Vanguard turboprop	Crashed during snowstorm at Basel, Switzerland	104
1973	June	3	Soviet Supersonic TU-144	Crashed near Goussainville, France	14[8]
1973	July	11	Brazilian Boeing 707	Crashed on approach to Orly Airport, Paris	122
1973	July	31	Delta Airlines jetliner	Crashed, landing in fog at Logan Airport, Boston	89
1973	Dec.	23	French Caravelle jet	Crashed in Morocco	106
1974	Mar.	3	Turkish DC-10 jet	Crashed at Ermenonville near Paris	346
1974	Apr.	23	Pan American 707 jet	Crashed in Bali, Indonesia	107
1974	Dec.	1	TWA-727	Crashed in storm, Upperville, Va.	92
1974	Dec.	4	Dutch-chartered DC-8	Crashed in storm near Colombo, Sri Lanka	191
1975	Apr.	4	Air Force Galaxy C-5B	Crashed near Saigon, So. Vietnam, after takeoff with load of orphans	172
1975	June	24	Eastern Airlines 727 jet	Crashed in storm, JFK Airport, N.Y. City	113
1975	Aug.	3	Chartered 707	Hit mountainside, Agadir, Morocco	188
1976	Sept.	10	British Airways Trident, Yugoslav DC-9	Collided near Zagreb, Yugoslavia	176
1976	Sept.	19	Turkish 727	Hit mountain, southern Turkey	155
1976	Oct.	13	Bolivian 707 cargo jet	Crashed in Santa Cruz, Bolivia	100[9]
1977	Jan.	13	Aeroflot TU-104	Exploded and crashed at Alma-Ata, Central Asia	90
1977	Mar.	27	KLM 747, Pan American 747	Collided on runway, Tenerife, Canary Islands	582
1977	Nov.	19	TAP Boeing 727	Crashed on Madeira	130
1977	Dec.	4	Malaysian Boeing 737	Hijacked, then exploded in mid-air over Straits of Johore	100
1977	Dec.	13	U.S. DC-3	Crashed after takeoff at Evansville, Ind.	29[10]
1978	Jan.	1	Air India 747	Exploded, crashed into sea off Bombay	213
1978	Sept.	25	Boeing 727, Cessna 172	Collided in air, San Diego, Cal.	150

Date			Aircraft	Site of accident	Deaths
1978	Nov.	15	Chartered DC-8	Crashed near Colombo, Sri Lanka	183
1979	May	25	American Airlines DC-10	Crashed after takeoff at O'Hare Intl. Airport, Chicago	275[11]
1979	Aug.	17	Two Soviet Aeroflot jetliners	Collided over Ukraine	173
1979	Oct.	31	Western Airlines DC-10	Mexico City Airport	74
1979	Nov.	26	Pakistani Boeing 707	Crashed near Jidda, Saudi Arabia	156
1979	Nov.	28	New Zealand DC-10	Crashed into mountain in Antarctica	257
1980	Mar.	14	Polish Ilyushin 62	Crashed making emergency landing, Warsaw	87[12]
1980	Aug.	19	Saudi Arabian Tristar	Burned after emergency landing, Riyadh	301
1981	Dec.	1	Yugoslavian DC-9	Crashed into mountain in Corsica	174
1982	Jan.	13	Air Florida Boeing 737	Crashed into Potomac River after takeoff	78
1982	July	9	Pan-Am Boeing 727	Crashed after takeoff in Kenner, La.	153[13]
1982	Sept.	11	U.S. Army CH-47 Chinook helicopter	Crashed during air show in Mannheim, W. Germany	46
1983	Sept.	1	S. Korean Boeing 747	Shot down after violating Soviet airspace	269
1983	Nov.	27	Colombian Boeing 747	Crashed near Barajas Airport, Madrid	183
1985	Feb.	19	Spanish Boeing 727	Crashed into Mt. Oiz, Spain	148
1985	June	23	Air-India Boeing 747	Crashed into Atlantic Ocean S. of Ireland	329
1985	Aug.	2	Delta Air Lines jumbo jet	Crashed at Dallas-Ft. Worth Intl. Airport	133
1985	Aug.	12	Japan Air Lines Boeing 747	Crashed into Mt. Ogura, Japan	520[14]
1985	Dec.	12	Arrow Air DC 8	Crashed after takeoff in Gander, Newfoundland	256[15]
1986	Mar.	31	Mexican Boeing 727	Crashed NW of Mexico City	166
1986	Aug.	31	Aeromexico DC-9	Collided with Piper PA-28 over Cerritos, Cal.	82[16]
1987	May	9	Ilyushin 62M	Crashed after takeoff in Warsaw, Poland	183
1987	Aug.	16	Northwest Airlines MD-82	Crashed after takeoff in Romulus, Mich.	156
1988	July	3	Iranian A300 Airbus	Shot down by U.S. Navy warship *Vincennes* over Persian Gulf	290
1988	Dec.	21	Pan Am Boeing 747	Exploded and crashed in Lockerbie, Scotland	270[17]
1989	Feb.	8	Boeing 707	Crashed into mountain in Azores Islands off Portugal	144
1989	June	7	Suriname DC-8	Crashed near Paramaribo Airport, Suriname	168
1989	July	19	United Airlines DC-10	Crashed while landing with a disabled hydraulic system, Sioux City, Ia.	111
1989	Sept.	19	French DC-10	Exploded in air over Niger	171
1991	May	26	Austrian Boeing 767-300	Exploded over rural Thailand	223
1991	July	11	Nigerian DC-8	Crashed while landing at Jidda, Saudi Arabia	261

(1) Including those on the ground and in buildings. (2) First fatal crash of commercial jet plane. (3) Caused by bomb planted by John G. Graham in insurance plot to kill his mother, a passenger. (4) Including all 128 aboard the planes and 6 on ground. (5) Killed 84 on plane and 71 on ground. (6) Including 43 Marshall U. football players and coaches. (7) Airliner-fighter crash, pilot of fighter parachuted to safety, was arrested for negligence. (8) First supersonic plane crash killed 6 crewmen and 8 on the ground; there were no passengers. (9) Crew of 3 killed; 97, mostly children, killed on ground. (10) Including U. of Evansville basketball team. (11) Highest death toll in U.S. aviation history. (12) Including 22 members of U.S. boxing team. (13) Including 8 on ground. (14) Worst single-plane disaster. (15) Incl. 248 members of U.S. 101st Airborne Division. (16) Incl. 15 on the ground. (17) Incl. 11 on the ground.

Notable Railroad Disasters

Date			Location	Deaths
1876	Dec.	29	Ashtabula, Oh.	92
1880	Aug.	11	Mays Landing, N. J.	40
1887	Aug.	10	Chatsworth, Ill.	81
1888	Oct.	10	Mud Run, Pa.	55
1891	June	14	Nr. Basel, Switzerland	100
1896	July	30	Atlantic City, N. J.	60
1903	Dec.	23	Laurel Run, Pa.	53
1904	Aug.	7	Eden, Col.	96
1904	Sept.	24	New Market Tenn.	56
1906	Mar.	16	Florence, Col.	35
1906	Oct.	28	Atlantic City, N. J.	40
1906	Dec.	30	Washington, D. C.	53
1907	Jan.	2	Volland, Kan.	33
1907	Jan.	19	Fowler, Ind.	29
1907	Feb.	16	New York, N.Y.	22
1907	Feb.	23	Colton, Cal.	26
1907	May	11	Lompoc, Cal.	36
1907	July	20	Salem, Mich.	33
1910	Mar.	1	Wellington, Wash.	96
1910	Mar.	21	Green Mountain, Ia.	55
1911	Aug.	25	Manchester, N. Y.	29
1912	July	4	East Corning, N. Y.	39
1912	July	5	Ligonier, Pa.	23
1914	Aug.	5	Tipton Ford, Mo.	43
1914	Sept.	15	Lebanon, Mo.	28
1915	May	22	Nr. Gretna, Scotland	227
1916	Mar.	29	Amherst, Oh.	27
1917	Sept.	28	Kellyville, Okla.	23
1917	Dec.	12	Modane, France	543(1)
1917	Dec.	20	Shepherdsville, Ky.	46
1918	June	22	Ivanhoe, Ind.	68
1918	July	9	Nashville, Tenn.	101
1918	Nov.	1	Brooklyn, N. Y.	97
1919	Jan.	12	South Byron, N. Y.	22
1919	July	1	Dunkirk, N. Y.	12
1919	Dec.	20	Onawa, Maine	23
1921	Feb.	27	Porter, Ind.	37
1921	Dec.	5	Woodmont, Pa.	27
1922	Aug.	5	Sulphur Spring, Mo.	34
1922	Dec.	13	Humble, Tex.	22
1923	Sept.	27	Lockett, Wy.	31
1925	June	16	Hackettstown, N. J.	50
1925	Oct.	27	Victoria, Miss.	21
1926	Sept.	5	Waco, Col.	30
1928	Aug.	24	I.R.T. subway, Times Sq., N. Y.	18
1937	July	16	Nr. Patna, India	107
1938	June	19	Saugus, Mont.	47
1939	Aug.	12	Harney, Nev.	24
1939	Dec.	22	Nr. Magdeburg, Germany	132
1939	Dec.	22	Nr. Friedrichshafen, Germany	99
1940	Apr.	19	Little Falls, N. Y.	31
1940	July	31	Cuyahoga Falls, Oh.	43
1943	Aug.	29	Wayland, N. Y.	27
1943	Sept.	6	Frankford Junction, Philadelphia, Pa.	79
1943	Dec.	16	Between Rennert and Buie, N. C.	72
1944	Jan.	16	Leon Province, Spain	500
1944	Mar.	2	Salerno, Italy	521
1944	July	6	High Bluff, Tenn.	35
1944	Aug.	4	Near Stockton, Ga.	47
1944	Sept.	14	Dewey, Ind.	29
1944	Dec.	31	Bagley, Utah	50
1945	Aug.	9	Michigan, N. D.	34
1946	Mar.	20	Aracaju, Mexico	185
1946	Apr.	25	Naperville, Ill.	45
1947	Feb.	18	Gallitzin, Pa.	24
1949	Oct.	22	Nr. Dwor, Poland	200+
1950	Feb.	17	Rockville Centre, N. Y.	31
1950	Sept.	11	Coshocton, Oh.	33
1950	Nov.	22	Richmond Hill, N. Y.	79
1951	Feb.	6	Woodbridge, N. J.	84
1951	Nov.	12	Wyuta, Wyo.	17
1951	Nov.	25	Woodstock, Ala.	17
1952	Mar.	4	Nr. Rio de Janeiro, Brazil	119
1952	July	9	Rzepin, Poland	160
1952	Oct.	8	Harrow, England	112
1953	Mar.	27	Conneaut, Oh.	21
1955	Apr.	3	Guadalajara, Mexico	300
1956	Jan.	22	Los Angeles, Cal.	30
1956	Feb.	28	Swampscott, Mass.	13
1956	Sept.	5	Springer, N. M.	20
1957	June	11	Vroman, Col.	12
1957	Sept.	1	Kendal, Jamaica	178
1957	Sept.	29	Montgomery, W. Pakistan	250
1957	Dec.	4	London, England	90
1958	May	8	Rio de Janeiro, Brazil	128
1958	Sept.	15	Elizabethport, N. J.	48

Date			Location	Deaths
1960	Mar.	14	Bakersfield, Cal.	14
1960	Nov.	14	Pardubice, Czech.	110
1962	Jan.	8	Woerden, Netherlands	91
1962	May	3	Tokyo, Japan	163
1962	July	28	Steelton, Pa.	19
1964	July	26	Oporto, Portugal	94
1966	Dec.	28	Everett, Mass.	13
1970	Feb.	1	Buenos Aires, Argentina	236
1971	June	10	Salem, Ill.	11
1972	June	16	Vierzy, France	107
1972	July	21	Seville, Spain	76
1972	Oct.	6	Saltillo, Mexico	208
1972	Oct.	30	Chicago, Ill.	45
1974	Aug.	30	Zagreb, Yugoslavia	153

Date			Location	Deaths
1977	Jan.	18	Granville, Australia	82
1977	Feb.	4	Chicago, Ill., elevated train	11
1981	June	6	Bihar, India	500+
1982	Jan.	27	El Asnam, Algeria	130
1982	July	11	Tepic, Mexico	120
1983	Feb.	19	Empalme, Mexico	100
1987	Jan.	4	Essex, Md.	16
1988	Dec.	12	London, England	115
1989	Jan.	15	Maizdi Khan, Bangladesh	110+
1990	Jan.	4	Sindh Province, Pakistan	210+
1991	May	14	Shigaraki, Japan	42
1991	July	31	Camden, S.C.	7
1991	Aug.	28	N.Y. City subway	5
1993	Jan.	18	Gary, Ind.	7

(1) World's worst train wreck; passenger train derailed.

Principal U.S. Mine Disasters Since 1900

Source: Bureau of Mines, U.S. Interior Department

Note: Prior to 1968, only disasters with losses of 60 or more lives are listed; since 1968, all disasters in which 5 or more people were killed are listed. Only fatalities to mining company employees are included. All bituminous-coal mines unless otherwise noted.

Date		Location	Deaths
1900	May 1	Scofield, Ut.	200
1902	May 19	Coal Creek, Tenn.	184
1902	July 10	Johnstown, Pa.	112
1903	June 30	Hanna, Wy.	169
1904	Jan. 25	Cheswick, Pa.	179
1905	Feb. 20	Virginia City, Ala.	112
1907	Jan. 29	Stuart W. Va.	84
1907	Dec. 6	Monongah, W. Va.	361
1907	Dec. 19	Jacobs Creek, Pa.	239
1908	Nov. 28	Marianna, Pa.	154
1909	Jan. 12	Switchback, W. Va.	67
1909	Nov. 13	Cherry, Ill.	259
1910	Jan. 31	Primero, Col.	75
1910	May 5	Palos, Ala.	90
1910	Nov. 8	Delagua, Col.	79
1911[1]	Apr. 7	Throop, Pa.	72
1911	Apr. 8	Littleton, Ala.	128
1911	Dec. 9	Briceville, Tenn.	84
1912	Mar. 20	McCurtain, Okla.	73
1912	Mar. 26	Jed, W. Va.	83
1913	Apr. 23	Finleyville, Pa.	96
1913	Oct. 22	Dawson, N.M.	263
1914	Apr. 28	Eccles, W. Va.	181
1915	Mar. 2	Layland, W. Va.	112
1917	Apr. 27	Hastings, Col.	121
1917[2]	June 8	Butte, Mon.	163
1917	Aug. 4	Clay, Ky.	62
1919[1]	June 5	Wilkes-Barre, Pa.	92
1922	Nov. 6	Spangler, Pa.	77
1922	Nov. 22	Dolomite, Ala.	90
1923	Feb. 8	Dawson, N.M.	120

Date		Location	Deaths
1923	Aug. 14	Kemmerer, Wy.	99
1924	Mar. 8	Castle Gate, Ut.	171
1924	Apr. 28	Benwood, W. Va.	119
1926	Jan. 13	Wilburton, Okla.	91
1926[2]	Nov. 3	Ishpeming, Mich.	51
1927	Apr. 30	Everettville, W. Va.	97
1928	May 19	Mather, Pa.	195
1929	Dec. 17	McAlester, Okla.	61
1930	Nov. 5	Millfield, Oh.	79
1940	Jan. 10	Bartley, W. Va.	91
1940	Mar. 16	St. Clairsville, Oh.	72
1940	July 15	Portage, Pa.	63
1943	Feb. 27	Washoe, Mon.	74
1944	July 5	Belmont, Oh.	66
1947	Mar. 25	Centralia, Ill.	111
1951	Dec. 21	West Frankfort, Ill.	119
1968[3]	Mar. 6	Calumet, La.	21
1968	Nov. 20	Farmington, W. Va.	78
1970	Dec. 30	Hyden, Ky.	38
1972[2]	May 2	Kellogg, Ida.	91
1976	Mar. 9, 11	Oven Fork, Ky.	26
1977	Mar. 1	Tower City, Pa.	9
1981	Apr. 15	Redstone, Col.	15
1981	Dec. 7	Topmost, Ky.	8
1981	Dec. 8	nr. Chattanooga, Tenn.	13
1982	Jan. 20	Floyd County, Ky.	7
1983	June 21	McClure, Va	7
1984	Dec. 19	Huntington, Ut.	27
1989	Sept. 13	Wheatcroft, Ky.	10
1992	Dec. 7	Norton, Va.	8

(1) Anthracite mine. (2) Metal mine. (3) Nonmetal mine.
World's worst mine disaster killed 1,549 workers in Honkeiko Colliery in Manchuria Apr. 25, 1942.

Some Notable Tornadoes In U.S. Since 1925

Date			Location	Deaths
1925	Mar.	18	Mo., Ill. Ind.	689
1927	Apr.	12	Rock Springs, Tex.	74
1927	May	9	Arkansas, Poplar Bluff, Mo.	92
1927	Sept.	29	St. Louis, Mo.	90
1930	May	6	Hill, Navarro, Ellis Co., Tex.	41
1932	Mar.	21	Ala. (series of tornadoes)	268
1936	Apr.	5	Miss., Ga.	455
1936	Apr.	6	Gainesville, Ga.	203
1938	Sept.	29	Charleston, S.C.	32
1942	Mar.	16	Central to NE Miss.	75
1942	Apr.	27	Rogers & Mayes Co., Okla.	52
1944	June	23	Oh., Pa., W. Va., Md.	150
1945	Apr.	12	Okla.-Ark.	102
1947	Apr.	9	Tex., Okla. & Kan.	169
1948	Mar.	19	Bunker Hill & Gillespie, Ill.	33
1949	Jan.	3	La. & Ark.	58
1952	Mar.	21	Ark., Mo., Tenn. (series)	208
1953	May	11	Waco, Tex.	114
1953	June	8	Mich., Oh.	142
1953	June	9	Worcester and vicinity, Mass.	90
1953	Dec.	5	Vicksburg, Miss.	38
1955	May	25	Kan., Mo., Okla., Tex.	115
1957	May	20	Kan., Mo.	48
1958	June	4	Northwestern Wisconsin	30
1959	Feb.	10	St. Louis, Mo.	21
1960	May	5, 6	SE Oklahoma, Arkansas	30
1965	Apr.	11	Ind., Ill., Oh., Mich., Wis.	271

Date			Location	Deaths
1966	Mar.	3	Jackson, Miss.	57
1966	Mar.	3	Mississippi, Alabama	61
1967	Apr.	21	Ill., Mich.	33
1968	May	15	Midwest	71
1969	Jan.	23	Mississippi	32
1971	Feb.	21	Mississippi delta	110
1973	May	26-27	South, Midwest (series)	47
1974	Apr.	3-4	Ala., Ga., Tenn., Ky., Oh.	350
1977	Apr.	4	Ala., Miss., Ga.	22
1979	Apr.	10	Tex., Okla.	60
1980	June	3	Grand Island, Neb. (series)	4
1982	Mar.	2-4	South, Midwest (series)	17
1982	May	29	So. Ill.	10
1983	May	18-22	Tex.	12
1984	Mar.	28	N. Carolina; S. Carolina	67
1984	Apr.	21-22	Mississippi	15
1984	Apr.	26	Series Okla to Minn.	17
1985	May	31	N.Y., Pa., Oh., Ont. (series)	90
1987	May	22	Saragosa, Tex.	29
1989	Nov.	15	Huntsville, Ala.	18
1989	Nov.	16	Newburgh, N.Y.	9
1990	June	2-3	Midwest, Great Lakes	13
1990	Aug.	28	N. Ill.	25
1991	Apr.	26	Kan., Okla.	23
1992	Nov.	21-23	South, Midwest	25
1993	Aug.	6	Petersburg, Va.	4

Hurricanes, Typhoons, Blizzards, Other Storms

Names of hurricanes and typhoons in italics—H.—hurricane; T.—typhoon

Date	Location	Deaths
1888 Mar. 11-14	Blizzard, Eastern U.S.	400
1900 Aug.-Sept.	H., Galveston, Tex.	6,000
1906 Sept. 21	H., La., Miss.	350
1906 Sept. 18	Typhoon, Hong Kong	10,000
1926 Sept. 11-22	H., Fla., Ala.	243
1926 Oct. 20	H., Cuba	600
1928 Sept. 6-20	H., So. Fla.	1,836
1930 Sept. 3	H., Dominican Rep.	2,000
1938 Sept. 21	H., Long, Island N.Y., New England	600
1940 Nov. 11-12	Blizzard, U.S. NE, Midwest	144
1942 Oct. 15-16	H., Bengal, India	40,000
1944 Sept. 9-16	H., N.C. to New Eng.	46
1952 Oct. 22	Typhoon, Philippines	440
1954 Aug. 30	H. *Carol*, Northeast U.S.	68
1954 Oct. 5-18	H. *Hazel*, Eastern, U.S., Haiti	347
1955 Aug. 12-13	H. *Connie*, Carolinas, Va., Md.	43
1955 Aug. 7-21	H. *Diane*, Eastern U.S.	400
1955 Sept. 19	H. *Hilda*, Mexico	200
1955 Sept. 22-28	H. *Janet*, Caribbean	500
1956 Feb. 1-29	Blizzard, Western Europe	1,000
1957 June 25-30	H. *Audrey*, Tex. to Ala.	390
1958 Feb. 15-16	Blizzard, NE U.S.	171
1959 Sept. 17-19	T. *Sarah*, Japan, S. Korea	2,000
1959 Sept. 26-27	T. *Vera*, Honshu, Japan	4,466
1960 Sept. 4-12	H. *Donna*, Caribbean, E. U.S.	148
1961 Sept. 11-14	H. *Carla*, Tex.	46
1961 Oct. 31	H. *Hattie*, Br. Honduras	400
1963 May 28-29	Windstorm, Bangladesh	22,000
1963 Oct. 4-8	H. *Flora*, Caribbean	6,000
1964 Oct. 4-7	H. *Hilda*, La., Miss., Ga.	38
1964 June 30	T. *Winnie*, N. Philippines	107
1964 Sept. 5	T. *Ruby*, Hong Kong and China	735
1965 May 11-12	Windstorm, Bangladesh	17,000
1965 June 1-2	Windstorm, Bangladesh	30,000
1965 Sept. 7-12	H. *Betsy*, Fla., Miss., La.	74
1965 Dec. 15	Windstorm, Bangladesh	10,000
1966 June 4-10	H. *Alma*, Honduras, SE U.S.	51
1966 Sept. 24-30	H. *Inez*, Carib., Fla., Mex.	293
1967 July 9	T. *Billie*, SW Japan	347
1967 Sept. 5-23	H. *Beulah*, Carib., Mex., Tex.	54
1967 Dec. 12-20	Blizzard, Southwest, U.S.	51
1968 Nov. 18-28	T. *Nina*, Philippines	63
1969 Aug. 17-18	H. *Camille*, Miss., La.	256
1970 July 30-Aug. 5	H. *Celia*, Cuba, Fla., Tex.	31
1970 Aug. 20-21	H. *Dorothy*, Martinique	42
1970 Sept. 15	T. *Georgia*, Philippines	300
1970 Oct. 14	T. *Sening*, Philippines	583
1970 Oct. 15	T. *Titang*, Philippines	526
1970 Nov. 13	Cyclone, Bangladesh	300,000
1971 Aug. 1	T. *Rose*, Hong Kong	130
1972 June 19-29	H. *Agnes*, Fla. to N.Y.	118
1972 Dec. 3	T. *Theresa*, Philippines	169
1973 June-Aug.	Monsoon rains in India	1,217
1974 June 11	Storm Dinah, Luzon Is., Philip.	71
1974 July 11	T. *Gilda*, Japan, S. Korea	108
1974 Sept. 19-20	H. *Fifi*, Honduras	2,000
1974 Dec. 25	Cyclone leveled Darwin, Aus.	50
1975 Sept. 13-27	H. *Eloise*, Caribbean, NE U.S.	71
1976 May 20	T. *Olga*, floods, Philippines	215
1977 July 25, 31	T. *Thelma*, T. *Vera*, Taiwan	39
1978 Oct. 27	T. *Rita*, Philippines	c. 400
1979 Aug. 30-Sept. 7	H. *David*, Caribbean, East. U.S.	1,100
1980 Aug. 4-11	H. *Allen*, Caribbean, Texas	272
1981 Nov. 25	T. *Irma*, Luzon Is., Philippines	176
1983 June	Monsoon rains in India	900
1983 Aug. 18	H. *Alicia*, southern Texas	17
1984 Sept. 2	T. *Ike*, southern Philippines	1,363
1985 May 25	Cyclone, Bangladesh	10,000
1985 Oct. 26-Nov. 6	H. *Juan*, SE U.S.	97
1987 Nov. 25	T. *Nina*, Philippines	650
1988 Sept. 10-17	H. *Gilbert*, Caribbean, G. of Mexico	260
1989 Sept. 16-22	H. *Hugo*, Caribbean, SE U.S.	504
1990 May 6-11	Cyclones, SE India	450
1991 Apr. 30	Cyclone, Bangladesh	70,000
1992 Aug. 24-26	H. *Andrew*, S. Fla., La.	14
1993 Mar. 13-14	Blizzard, Eastern U.S.	200

Floods, Tidal Waves

Date		Location	Deaths
1228	....	Holland	100,000
1642	....	China	300,000
1887	....	Huang He River, China	900,000
1889	May 31	Johnstown, Pa.	2,200
1900	Sept. 8	Galveston, Tex.	5,000
1903	June 15	Heppner, Ore.	325
1911	....	Chang Jiang River, China	100,000
1913	Mar. 25-27	Ohio, Indiana	732
1915	Aug. 17	Galveston, Tex.	275
1928	Mar. 13	Collapse of St. Francis Dam, Saugus, Cal.	450
1928	Sept. 13	Lake Okeechobee, Fla.	2,000
1931	Aug.	Huang He River, China	3,700,000
1937	Jan. 22	Ohio, Miss. Valleys	250
1939	....	Northern China	200,000
1946	Apr. 1	Hawaii, Alaska	159
1947	....	Honshu Island, Japan	1,900
1951	Aug.	Manchuria	1,800
1953	Jan. 31	Western Europe	2,000
1954	Aug. 17	Farahzad, Iran	2,000
1955	Oct. 7-12	India, Pakistan	1,700
1959	Nov. 1	Western Mexico	2,000
1959	Dec. 2	Frejus, France	412
1960	Oct. 10	Bangladesh	6,000
1960	Oct. 31	Bangladesh	4,000
1962	Feb. 17	German North Sea coast	343
1962	Sept. 27	Barcelona, Spain	445
1963	Oct. 9	Dam collapse, Vaiont, Italy	1,800
1966	Nov. 3-4	Florence, Venice, Italy	113
1967	Jan. 18-24	Eastern Brazil	894
1967	Mar. 19	Rio de Janeiro, Brazil	436
1967	Nov. 26	Lisbon, Portugal	464
1968	Aug. 7-14	Gujarat State, India	1,000
1968	Oct. 7	Northeastern India	780
1969	Jan. 18-26	So. Cal.	100
1969	Mar. 17	Mundau Valley, Alagoas, Brazil	218
1969	Aug. 20-22	Western Virginia	189
1969	Sept. 15	South Korea	250
1969	Oct. 1-8	Tunisia	500
1970	May 20	Central Romania	160
1970	July 22	Himalayas, India	500
1971	Feb. 26	Rio de Janeiro, Brazil	130
1972	Feb. 26	Buffalo Creek, W. Va.	118
1972	June 9	Rapid City, S.D.	236
1972	Aug. 7	Luzon Is., Philippines	454
1973	Aug. 19-31	Pakistan	1,500
1974	Mar. 29	Tubaro, Brazil	1,000
1974	Aug. 12	Monty-Long, Bangladesh	2,500
1976	June 5	Teton Dam collapse, Ida.	11
1976	July 31	Big Thompson Canyon, Col.	139
1976	Nov. 17	East Java, Indonesia	136
1977	July 19-20	Johnstown, Pa.	68
1978	June-Sept.	Northern India	1,200
1979	Jan.-Feb.	Brazil	204
1979	July 17	Lomblem Is., Indonesia	539
1979	Aug. 11	Morvi, India	5,000-15,000
1980	Feb. 13-22	So. Cal., Ariz.	26
1981	Apr.	Northern China	550
1981	July	Sichuan, Hubei Prov., China	1,300
1982	Jan. 23	Nr. Lima, Peru	600
1982	May 12	Guangdong, China	430
1982	June 6	So. Conn.	12
1982	Sept. 17-21	El Salvador, Guatemala	1,300+
1982	Dec. 2-9	Ill., Mo., Ark.	22
1983	Feb.-Mar.	Cal. coast	13
1983	Apr. 6-12	Ala., La., Miss., Tenn.	15
1984	May 27	Tulsa, Okla.	13
1984	Aug-Sept.	S. Korea	200+
1985	July 19	Northern Italy, dam burst	361
1987	Aug.-Sept.	Northern Bangladesh	1,000+
1988	Sept.	Northern India	1,000+
1990	June 14	Shadyside, Oh.	23
1991	Dec. 18-26	Texas	18
1992	Feb. 9-15	So. Cal.	13
1992	Apr. 13	Downtown Chicago	0
1993	July-Aug.	Midwest	50+

Fires

Date	Location	Deaths
1835 Dec. 16	New York City, 500 bldgs. destroyed	—
1845 May	Canton, China, theater	1,670
1871 Oct. 8	Chicago, $196 million loss	250
1871 Oct. 8	Peshtigo, Wis., forest fire	1,182
1872 Nov. 9	Boston, 800 bldgs. destroyed	—
1876 Dec. 5	Brooklyn (N.Y.), theater	295
1877 June 20	St. John, N. B., Canada	100
1881 Dec. 8	Ring Theater, Vienna	850
1887 May 25	Opera Comique, Paris	200
1887 Sept. 4	Exeter, England, theater	200
1894 Sept. 1	Minn., forest fire	413
1897 May 4	Paris, charity bazaar	150
1900 June 30	Hoboken, N. J., docks	326
1902 Sept. 20	Birmingham, Ala., church	115
1903 Dec. 30	Iroquois Theater, Chicago	602
1908 Jan. 13	Rhoads Theater, Boyertown, Pa.	170
1908 Mar. 4	Collinwood, Oh., school	176
1911 Mar. 25	Triangle factory, N. Y. City	145
1913 Oct. 14	Mid Glamorgan, Wales, colliery	439
1918 Apr. 13	Norman Okla., state hospital	38
1918 Oct. 12	Cloquet, Minn., forest fire	400
1919 June 20	Mayaguez Theater, San Juan	150
1923 May 17	Camden, S. C., school	76
1924 Dec. 24	Hobart, Okla., school	35
1929 May 15	Cleveland, Oh., clinic	125
1930 Apr. 21	Columbus, Oh., penitentiary	320
1931 July 24	Pittsburgh, Pa., home for aged	48
1934 Dec. 11	Hotel Kerns, Lansing, Mich.	34
1938 May 16	Atlanta, Ga., Terminal Hotel	35
1940 Apr. 23	Natchez, Miss., dance hall	198
1942 Nov. 28	Cocoanut Grove, Boston	491
1942	St. John's, Newfoundland, hostel	100
1943 Sept. 7	Gulf Hotel, Houston	55
1944 July 6	Ringling Circus, Hartford	168
1946 June 5	LaSalle Hotel, Chicago	61
1946 Dec. 7	Winecoff Hotel, Atlanta	119
1946 Dec. 12	New York, ice plant, tenement	37
1949 Apr. 5	Effingham, Ill., hospital	77
1950 Jan. 7	Davenport, Ia., Mercy Hospital	41
1953 Mar. 29	Largo, Fla., nursing home	35
1953 Apr. 16	Chicago, metalworking plant	35
1957 Feb. 17	Warrenton, Mo., home for aged	72
1958 Mar. 19	New York City, loft building	24
1958 Dec. 1	Chicago, parochial school	95
1958 Dec. 16	Bogota, Colombia, store	83
1959 June 23	Stalheim, Norway, resort hotel	34
1960 Mar. 12	Pusan, Korea, chemical plant	68
1960 July 14	Guatemala City, mental hospital	225
1960 Nov. 13	Amude, Syria, movie theater	152
1961 Jan. 6	Thomas Hotel, San Francisco	20
1961 Dec. 8	Hartford, Conn., hospital	16
1961 Dec. 17	Niteroi, Brazil, circus	323
1963 May 4	Diourbel, Senegal, theater	64
1963 Nov. 18	Surfside Hotel, Atlantic City, N.J.	25
1963 Nov. 23	Fitchville, Oh., rest home	63
1963 Dec. 29	Roosevelt Hotel, Jacksonville, Fla.	22
1964 May 8	Manila, apartment bldg.	30
1964 Dec. 18	Fountaintown, Ind., nursing home	20
1965 Mar. 1	LaSalle, Canada, apartment	28
1966 Mar. 11	Numata, Japan, 2 ski resorts	31
1966 Aug. 13	Melbourne, Australia, hotel	29
1966 Sept. 12	Anchorage, Alaska, hotel	14
1966 Oct. 17	N. Y. City bldg. (firemen)	12
1966 Dec. 7	Erzurum, Turkey, barracks	68
1967 Feb. 7	Montgomery, Ala., restaurant	25
1967 May 22	Brussels, Belgium, store	322
1967 July 16	Jay, Fla., state prison	37
1968 Feb. 26	Shrewsbury, England, hospital	22
1968 May 11	Vijayawada, India, wedding hall	58
1968 Nov. 18	Glasgow, Scotland, factory	24
1969 Jan. 26	Victoria Hotel, Dunnville, Ont.	13
1969 Dec. 2	Notre Dame, Can., nursing home	54
1970 Jan. 9	Marietta, Oh., nursing home	27
1970 Mar. 20	Seattle, Wash., hotel	19
1970 Nov. 1	Grenoble, France, dance hall	145
1970 Dec. 20	Tucson, Arizona, hotel	28
1971 Mar. 6	Burghoezli, Switzerland, psychiatric clinic	28
1971 Apr. 20	Hotel, Bangkok, Thailand	24
1971 Oct. 19	Honesdale, Pa., nursing home	15
1971 Dec. 25	Hotel, Seoul, So. Korea	162
1972 May 13	Osaka, Japan, nightclub	116
1972 July 5	Sherborne, England, hospital	30
1973 Feb. 6	Paris, France, school	21
1973 Nov. 6	Fukui, Japan, train	28
1973 Nov. 29	Kumamoto, Japan, department store	107
1973 Dec. 2	Seoul, Korea, theater	50
1974 Feb. 1	Sao Paulo, Brazil, bank building	189
1974 June 30	Port Chester, N. Y., discotheque	24
1974 Nov. 3	Seoul, So. Korea, hotel discotheque	88
1975 Dec. 12	Mina, Saudi Arabia, tent city	138
1976 Oct. 24	Bronx, N.Y., social club	25
1977 Feb. 25	Moscow, Rossiya hotel	45
1977 May 28	Southgate, Ky., nightclub	164
1977 June 9	Abidjan, Ivory Coast, nightclub	41
1977 June 26	Columbia, Tenn., jail	42
1977 Nov. 14	Manila, Philippines, hotel	47
1978 Jan. 28	Kansas City, Coates House Hotel	16
1979 July 14	Saragossa, Spain, hotel	80
1979 Dec. 31	Chapais, Quebec, social club	42
1980 May 20	Kingston, Jamaica, nursing home	157
1980 Nov. 21	MGM Grand Hotel, Las Vegas	84
1980 Dec. 4	Stouffer Inn, Harrison, N.Y.	26
1981 Jan. 9	Keansburg, N.J., boarding home	30
1981 Feb. 10	Las Vegas Hilton	8
1981 Feb. 14	Dublin, Ireland, discotheque	44
1982 Sept. 4	Los Angeles, apartment house	24
1982 Nov. 8	Biloxi, Miss., county jail	29
1983 Feb. 13	Turin, Italy, movie theater	64
1983 Dec. 17	Madrid, Spain, discotheque	83
1984 May 11	Great Adventure Amusement Park, N.J.	8
1985 Apr. 21	Tabaco, Philippines, movie theater	44
1985 Apr. 26	Buenos Aires, Argentina hospital	79
1985 May 11	Bradford, England, soccer stadium	53
1986 Dec. 31	Puerto Rico, Dupont Plaza Hotel	96
1987 May 6-June 2	Northern China forest fire	193
1987 Nov. 17	London, England subway	30
1990 Mar. 25	N.Y. City social club	87
1991 Sept. 3	Hamlet, N.C. chicken-processing plant	25
1991 Oct. 20-21	Oakland, Berkeley, Cal. wildfire	24
1992 Nov. 20	Windsor Castle, England	0
1993 Apr. 19	Waco, Tex., cult compound	72

Explosions

Date	Location	Deaths
1910 Oct. 1	Los Angeles Times Bldg.	21
1913 Mar. 7	Dynamite, Baltimore harbor	55
1915 Sept. 27	Gasoline tank car, Ardmore, Okla.	47
1917 Apr. 10	Munitions plant, Eddystone, Pa.	133
1917 Dec. 6	Halifax Harbor, Canada	1,654
1918 May 18	Chemical plant, Oakdale, Pa.	193
1918 July 2	Explosives, Split Rock, N.Y.	50
1918 Oct. 4	Shell plant, Morgan Station, N.J.	64
1919 May 22	Food plant, Cedar Rapids, Ia.	44
1920 Sept. 16	Wall Street, New York, bomb	30
1924 Jan. 3	Food plant, Pekin, Ill.	42
1928 April 13	Dance hall, West Plains, Mo.	40
1937 Mar. 18	New London, Tex., school	413
1940 Sept. 12	Hercules Powder, Kenvil, N.J.	55
1942 June 5	Ordnance plant, Elwood, Ill.	49
1944 Apr. 14	Bombay, India, harbor	700
1944 July 17	Port Chicago, Cal., pier	322
1944 Oct. 21	Liquid gas tank, Cleveland	135
1947 Apr. 16	Texas City, Tex., pier	561
1948 July 28	Farben works, Ludwigshafen, Ger.	184
1950 May 19	Munitions barges, S. Amboy, N. J.	30
1956 Aug. 7	Dynamite trucks, Cali, Colombia	1,100
1958 Apr. 18	Sunken munitions ship, Okinawa	40
1958 May 22	Nike missiles, Leonardo, N.J.	10
1959 Apr. 10	World War II bomb, Philippines	38
1959 June 28	Rail tank cars, Meldrin, Ga.	25
1959 Aug. 7	Dynamite truck, Roseburg, Ore.	13
1959 Nov. 2	Jamuri Bazar, India, explosives	46
1959 Dec. 13	Dortmund, Ger., 2 apt. bldgs.	26
1960 Mar. 4	Belgian munitions ship, Havana	100
1960 Oct. 25	Gas, Windsor, Ont., store	11
1962 Jan. 16	Gas pipeline, Edson, Alberta, Canada	8

Date			Location	Deaths
1962	Oct.	3	Telephone Co. office, N. Y. City	23
1963	Jan.	2	Packing plant, Terre Haute, Ind.	16
1963	Mar.	9	Dynamite plant, S. Africa	45
1963	Aug.	13	Explosives dump, Gauhiti, India	32
1963	Oct.	31	State Fair Coliseum, Indianapolis	73
1964	July	23	Bone, Algeria, harbor munitions	100
1965	Mar.	4	Gas pipeline, Natchitoches, La.	17
1965	Aug.	9	Missile silo, Searcy, Ark.	53
1965	Oct.	21	Bridge, Tila Bund, Pakistan	80
1965	Oct.	30	Cartagena, Colombia	48
1965	Nov.	24	Armory, Keokuk, Ia.	20
1966	Oct.	13	Chemical plant, La Salle, Que.	11
1967	Feb.	17	Chemical plant, Hawthorne, N.J.	11
1967	Dec.	25	Apartment bldg., Moscow	20
1968	Apr.	6	Sports store, Richmond, Ind.	43
1970	Apr.	8	Subway construction, Osaka, Japan	73
1971	June	24	Tunnel, Sylmar, Cal.	17
1971	June	28	School, fireworks, Pueblo, Mex.	13
1971	Oct.	21	Shopping center, Glasgow, Scot.	20
1973	Feb.	10	Liquified gas tank, Staten Is., N.Y.	40
1975	Dec.	27	Chasnala, India, mine	431
1976	Apr.	13	Lapua, Finland, munitions works	40
1977	Nov.	11	Freight train, Iri, S. Korea	57
1977	Dec.	22	Grain elevator, Westwego, La.	35
1978	Feb.	24	Derailed tank car, Waverly, Tenn.	12
1978	July	11	Propylene tank truck, Spanish coastal campsite	150
1980	Oct.	23	School, Ortuella, Spain	64
1981	Feb.	13	Sewer system, Louisville, Ky.	0
1982	Apr.	7	Tanker truck, tunnel, Oakland, Cal.	7
1982	Apr.	25	Antiques exhibition, Todi, Italy	33
1982	Nov.	2	Salang Tunnel, Afghanistan	1,000-3,000
1984	Feb.	25	Oil pipeline, Cubatao, Brazil	508
1984	June	21	Naval supply depot, Severomorsk, USSR	200+
1984	Nov.	19	Gas storage area, NE Mexico City	334
1984	Dec.	5	Coal mine, Taipei, Taiwan	94
1985	June	25	Fireworks factory, Hallett, Okla.	21
1988	July	6	Oil rig, North Sea	167
1989	June	3	Gas pipeline, between Ufa, Asha, USSR	650+
1992	Mar.	3	Coal mine, Kozlu, Turkey	270+
1992	Apr.	22	Guadalajara, Mexico sewer	190
1992	May	9	Coal mine, Plymouth, Nova Scotia	26
1993	Feb.	26	World Trade Center, N.Y. City	6

Notable Nuclear Accidents

Oct. 7, 1957 — A fire in the Windscale plutonium production reactor north of Liverpool, England spread radioactive material throughout the countryside. In 1983, the British government said that 39 people probably died of cancer as a result.

1957 — A chemical explosion in Kasli, USSR, in tanks containing nuclear waste, spread radioactive material and forced a major evacuation.

Jan. 3, 1961 — An experimental reactor at a federal installation near Idaho Falls, Id. killed three workers—the only deaths in U.S. reactor operations. The plant had high radiation levels but damage was contained.

Oct. 5, 1966 — A sodium cooling system malfunction caused a partial core meltdown at the Enrico Fermi demonstration breeder reactor near Detroit, Mich. Radiation was contained.

Jan. 21, 1969 — A coolant malfunction from an experimental underground reactor at Lucens Vad, Switzerland resulted in the release of a large amount of radiation into a cavern, which was then sealed.

Mar. 22, 1975 — A technician checking for air leaks with a lighted candle caused a $100 million fire at the Brown's Ferry reactor in Decatur, Ala. The fire burned out electrical controls, lowering the cooling water to dangerous levels.

Mar. 28, 1979 — The worst commercial nuclear accident in the U.S. occurred as equipment failures and human mistakes led to a loss of coolant and partial core meltdown at the Three Mile Island reactor in Middletown, Pa.

Feb. 11, 1981 — Eight workers were contaminated when over 100,000 gallons of radioactive coolant leaked into the containment building of the TVA's Sequoyah 1 plant in Tennessee.

Apr. 25, 1981 — Some 100 workers were exposed to radioactive material during repairs of a nuclear plant at Tsuruga, Japan.

Jan. 6, 1986 — A cylinder of nuclear material burst after being improperly heated at a Kerr-McGee plant at Gore, Okla. One worker died and 100 were hospitalized.

Apr. 26, 1986 — In the worst accident in the history of the nuclear power industry, fires and explosions resulting from an unauthorized experiment at the Chernobyl nuclear power plant near Kiev in the Soviet Union left at least 31 people dead in the immediate aftermath of the disaster and spread significant quantities of radioactive material over much of Europe. An estimated 135,000 people were evacuated from areas around Chernobyl, some of which were rendered uninhabitable for years. As a result of the radiation released into the atmosphere, tens of thousands of excess cancer deaths (as well as increased rates of birth defects) were expected in succeeding decades.

Record Oil Spills

As a rule, the number of tons can be multiplied by 7 to estimate the number of barrels spilled; the exact number of barrels in a ton varies with the type of oil. Each barrel contains 42 gallons.

Name, place	Date	Cause	Tons
Ixtoc I oil well, southern Gulf of Mexico	June 3, 1979	Blowout	600,000
Nowruz oil field, Persian Gulf	Feb., 1983	Blowout	600,000 (est.)
Atlantic Empress & Aegean Captain, off Trinidad & Tobago	July 19, 1979	Collision	300,000
Castillo de Bellver, off Cape Town, South Africa	Aug. 6, 1983	Fire	250,000
Amoco Cadiz, near Portsall, France	March 16, 1978	Grounding	223,000
Torrey Canyon, off Land's End, England	March 18, 1967	Grounding	119,000
Sea Star, Gulf of Oman	Dec. 19, 1972	Collision	115,000
Urquiola, La Coruna, Spain	May 12, 1976	Grounding	100,000
Hawaiian Patriot, northern Pacific	Feb. 25, 1977	Fire	99,000
Othello, Tralhavet Bay, Sweden	March 20, 1970	Collision	60,000-100,000

Other Notable Oil Spills

Name, place	Date	Cause	Gallons
Persian Gulf	Jan. 23, 1991 (began)	Spillage by Iraq	130,000,000*
Braer, off Shetland Islands	Jan. 5, 1993	Grounding	26,000,000
Aegean Sea, off northern Spain	Dec. 3, 1992	Unknown	21,500,000
World Glory, off South Africa	June 13, 1968	Hull failure	13,524,000
Burmah Agate, Galveston Bay, Tex.	Nov. 1, 1979	Collision	10,700,000
Exxon Valdez, Prince William Sound, Alas.	Mar. 24, 1989	Grounding	10,080,000
Keo, off Massachusetts	Nov. 5, 1969	Hull failure	8,820,000
Storage tank, Sewaren, N.J.	Nov. 4, 1969	Tank rupture	8,400,000

(continued)

Other Notable Oil Spills *(continued)*

Name, place	Date	Cause	Gallons
Ekofisk oil field, North Sea	Apr. 22, 1977	Well blowout	8,200,000
Argo Merchant, Nantucket, Mass.	Dec. 15, 1976	Grounding	7,700,000
Pipeline, West Delta, La.	Oct. 15, 1967	Dragging anchor	6,720,000
Tanker off Japan	Nov. 30, 1971	Ship broke in half	6,258,000
Storage tank, Monongahela River	Jan. 2, 1988	Tank rupture	3,800,000

* Estimated by Saudi Arabia. Some estimates are as low as 25,000,000 gallons.

Major Earthquakes

Magnitude of earthquakes (Mag.), distinct from deaths or damage caused, is measured on the Richter scale, on which each higher number represents a tenfold increase in energy measured in ground motion. Adopted in 1935, the scale has been applied in the following table to earthquakes as far back as reliable seismograms are available.

	Date	Location	Deaths	Mag.
526	May 20	Syria, Antioch	250,000	N.A.
856	....	Greece, Corinth	45,000	"
1057	....	China, Chihli	25,000	"
1268	....	Asia Minor, Cilicia	60,000	"
1290	Sept. 27	China, Chihli	100,000	"
1293	May 20	Japan, Kamakura	30,000	"
1531	Jan. 26	Portugal, Lisbon	30,000	"
1556	Jan. 24	China, Shaanxi	830,000	"
1667	Nov.	Caucasia, Shemaka	80,000	"
1693	Jan. 11	Italy, Catania	60,000	"
1730	Dec. 30	Japan, Hokkaido	137,000	"
1737	Oct. 11	India, Calcutta	300,000	"
1755	June 7	Northern Persia	40,000	"
1755	Nov. 1	Portugal, Lisbon	60,000	8.75*
1783	Feb. 4	Italy, Calabria	30,000	N.A.
1797	Feb. 4	Ecuador, Quito	41,000	"
1811-12		New Madrid, Mo. (series)	—	8.7*
1822	Sept. 5	Asia Minor, Aleppo	22,000	N.A.
1828	Dec. 28	Japan, Echigo	30,000	"
1868	Aug. 13-15	Peru and Ecuador	40,000	"
1875	May 16	Venezuela, Colombia	16,000	"
1886	Aug. 31	Charleston, S.C.	60	6.6
1896	June 15	Japan, sea wave	27,120	N.A.
1906	Apr. 18-19	San Francisco, Cal.	503	8.3
1906	Aug. 16	Chile, Valparaiso	20,000	8.6
1908	Dec. 28	Italy, Messina	83,000	7.5
1915	Jan. 13	Italy, Avezzano	29,980	7.5
1920	Dec. 16	China, Gansu	100,000	8.6
1923	Sept. 1	Japan, Yokohama	200,000	8.3
1927	May 22	China, Nan-Shan	200,000	8.3
1932	Dec. 26	China, Gansu	70,000	7.6
1933	Mar. 2	Japan	2,990	8.9
1933	Mar. 10	Long Beach, Cal.	115	6.2
1934	Jan. 15	India, Bihar-Nepal	10,700	8.4
1935	May 31	India, Quetta	50,000	7.5
1939	Jan. 24	Chile, Chillan	28,000	8.3
1939	Dec. 26	Turkey, Erzincan	30,000	7.9
1946	Dec. 21	Japan, Honshu	2,000	8.4
1948	June 28	Japan, Fukui	5,131	7.3
1949	Aug. 5	Ecuador, Pelileo	6,000	6.8
1950	Aug. 15	India, Assam	1,530	8.7
1953	Mar. 18	NW Turkey	1,200	7.2
1956	June 10-17	N. Afghanistan	2,000	7.7
1957	July 2	Northern Iran	2,500	7.4
1957	Dec. 13	Western Iran	2,000	7.1
1960	Feb. 29	Morocco, Agadir	12,000	5.8
1960	May 21-30	Southern Chile	5,000	8.3
1962	Sept. 1	Northwestern Iran	12,230	7.1
1963	July 26	Yugoslavia, Skopje	1,100	6.0
1964	Mar. 27	Alaska	131	8.4
1966	Aug. 19	Eastern Turkey	2,520	6.9
1968	Aug. 31	Northeastern Iran	12,000	7.4
1970	Jan. 5	Yunnan Province, China	10,000	7.7
1970	Mar. 28	Western Turkey	1,086	7.4
1970	May 31	Northern Peru	66,794	7.7
1971	Feb. 9	San Fernando Valley, Cal.	65	6.6
1972	Apr. 10	Southern Iran	5,057	6.9
1972	Dec. 23	Nicaragua	5,000	6.2
1974	Dec. 28	Pakistan (9 towns)	5,200	6.3
1975	Sept. 6	Turkey (Lice, etc.)	2,312	6.8
1976	Feb. 4	Guatemala	22,778	7.5
1976	May 6	Northeast Italy	946	6.5
1976	June 26	New Guinea, Irian Jaya	443	7.1
1976	July 28	China, Tangshan	242,000	8.2
1976	Aug. 17	Philippines, Mindanao	8,000	7.8
1976	Nov. 24	E. Turkey	4,000	7.9
1977	Mar. 4	Romania	1,541	7.5
1977	Aug. 19	Indonesia	200	8.0
1977	Nov. 23	Northwestern Argentina	100	8.2
1978	June 12	Japan, Sendai	21	7.5
1978	Sept. 16	Northeast Iran	25,000	7.7
1979	Sept. 12	Indonesia	100	8.1
1979	Dec. 12	Colombia, Ecuador	800	7.9
1980	Oct. 10	Northwestern Algeria	4,500	7.3
1980	Nov. 23	Southern Italy	4,800	7.2
1982	Dec. 13	North Yemen	2,800	6.0
1983	Mar. 31	Southern Colombia	250	5.5
1983	May 26	N. Honshu, Japan	81	7.7
1983	Oct. 30	Eastern Turkey	1,300	7.1
1985	Mar. 3	Chile	146	7.8
1985	Sept. 19, 21	Mexico City	4,200+	8.1
1987	Mar. 5-6	NE Ecuador	4,000+	7.3
1988	Aug. 20	India/Nepal border	1,000+	6.5
1988	Nov. 6	China/Burma border	1,000	7.3
1988	Dec. 7	NW Armenia	55,000+	6.8
1989	Oct. 17	San Francisco Bay area	62	6.9
1990	May 30	N. Peru	115	6.3
1990	May 30	Romania	8	6.5
1990	June 21	NW Iran	40,000+	7.7
1990	July 16	Luzon, Philippines	1,621	7.7
1991	Feb. 1	Pakistan, Afghanistan border	1,200	6.8
1992	Mar. 13, 15	E. Turkey	4,000	6.2/6.0
1992	June 28	S. Cal.	1	7.5/6.6
1992	Oct. 12	Cairo, Egypt	450	5.9
1992	Dec. 12	Flores, Indonesia	2,500	7.5
1993	July 12	off Hokkaido, Japan	200+	7.8

(*) estimated from earthquake intensity. (N.A.) not available.

Some Recent Earthquakes

Source: Global Volcanism Network, Smithsonian Institution

Date	Location	Magnitude
Aug. 8, 1993	Agana, Guam	8.0
July 12	off Hokkaido, Japan	7.8
Mar. 26	S. Greece	5.1
Mar. 12	Fiji	6.5
Mar. 6	Solomon Islands	6.5
Mar. 6	Fiji	6.7
Mar. 6	Santa Cruz Islands	7.1
Jan. 15	Kushiro, Japan	7.0
Dec. 20, 1992	Banda Sea, Indonesia	7.0
Dec. 12	Flores, Indonesia	7.5
Nov. 8	Fiji	6.5
Oct. 23	Papua New Guinea	6.7
Oct. 17	Murindo, Colombia	7.2
Oct. 12	Cairo, Egypt	5.9
Sept. 11	SE Zaire	6.8
Sept. 2	off Nicaragua	7.2
Aug. 19	Kyrgyzstan	7.5
Aug. 7	Gulf of Alaska	6.5
June 28	S. California	7.5/6.6
May 25	Cabo Cruz, Cuba	7.0
May 15	Kyrgyzstan	6.2
Apr. 25	N. California	7.0
Apr. 13	SE Netherlands	5.0
Mar. 13	Turkey	6.2
Feb. 27	E. New Guinea	6.7
Feb. 13	Vanuatu	6.8

Historic Assassinations Since 1865

1865—Apr. 14. U. S. Pres. Abraham Lincoln, shot by John Wilkes Booth in Washington, D. C.; died Apr. 15.

1881—Mar. 13. Alexander II, of Russia—July 2. U. S. Pres. James A. Garfield, shot by Charles J. Guiteau, Washington D.C.; died Sept. 19.

1900—July 29. Umberto I, king of Italy.

1901—Sept. 6. U. S. Pres. William McKinley in Buffalo, N. Y., died Sept. 14. Leon Czolgosz executed for the crime Oct. 29.

1913—Feb. 23. Mexican Pres. Francisco I. Madero and Vice Pres. Jose Pino Suarez.—Mar. 18. George, king of Greece.

1914—June 28. Archduke Francis Ferdinand of Austria-Hungary and his wife in Sarajevo, Bosnia (later part of Yugoslavia), by Gavrilo Princip.

1916—Dec. 30. Grigori Rasputin, politically powerful Russian monk.

1918—July 12. Grand Duke Michael of Russia, at Perm.—July 16. Nicholas II, abdicated as czar of Russia; his wife, the Czarina Alexandra; their son, Czarevitch Alexis; their daughters, Grand Duchesses Olga, Tatiana, Marie, Anastasia; and 4 members of their household were executed by Bolsheviks at Ekaterinburg.

1920—May 20. Mexican Pres. Gen. Venustiano Carranza in Tlaxcalantongo.

1922—Aug. 22. Michael Collins, Irish revolutionary.—Dec. 16. Polish President Gabriel Narutowicz in Warsaw by an anarchist.

1923—July 20. Gen. Francisco "Pancho" Villa, ex-rebel leader, in Parral, Mexico.

1928—July 17. Gen. Alvaro Obregon, president-elect of Mexico, in San Angel, Mexico.

1933—Feb. 15. In Miami, Fla., Joseph Zangara, anarchist, shot at Pres.-elect Franklin D. Roosevelt, but a woman seized his arm, and the bullet fatally wounded Mayor Anton J. Cermak, of Chicago, who died Mar. 6. Zangara was electrocuted on Mar. 20, 1933.

1934—July 25. In Vienna, Austrian Chancellor Engelbert Dollfuss by Nazis.

1935—Sept. 8. U. S. Sen. Huey P. Long, shot in Baton Rouge, La., by Dr. Carl Austin Weiss, who was slain by Long's bodyguards; Long died Sept. 10.

1940—Aug. 20. Leon Trotsky (Lev Bronstein), 63, exiled Russian war minister, near Mexico City. Killer identified as Ramon Mercador del Rio, a Spaniard, served 20 years in Mexican prison.

1948—Jan. 30. Mohandas K. Gandhi, 78, shot in New Delhi, India, by Nathuram Vinayak Godse.—Sept. 17. Count Folke Bernadotte, UN mediator for Palestine, ambushed in Jerusalem.

1951—July 20. King Abdullah ibn Hussein of Jordan. —Oct. 16. Prime Min. Liaquat Ali Khan of Pakistan shot in Rawalpindi.

1956—Sept. 21. Pres. Anastasio Somoza of Nicaragua, in Leon; died Sept. 29.

1957—July 26. Pres. Carlos Castillo Armas of Guatemala, in Guatemala City by one of his own guards.

1958—July 14. King Faisal of Iraq; his uncle, Crown Prince Abdullah; and July 15, Premier Nuri as-Said, by rebels in Baghdad.

1959—Sept. 25. Prime Minister Solomon Bandaranaike of Ceylon, by Buddhist monk in Colombo.

1961—Jan. 17. Ex-Premier Patrice Lumumba of the Congo, in Katanga Province—May 30. Dominican dictator Rafael Leonidas Trujillo Molina shot to death by assassins near Ciudad Trujillo.

1963—June 12. Medgar W. Evers, NAACP's Mississippi field secretary, in Jackson, Miss.—Nov. 2. Pres. Ngo Dinh Diem of the Republic of Vietnam and his brother, Ngo Dinh Nhu, in a military coup.—Nov. 22. U. S. Pres. John F. Kennedy fatally shot in Dallas, Tex.; accused Lee Harvey Oswald murdered by Jack Ruby while awaiting trial.

1965—Jan. 21. Iranian premier Hassan Ali Mansour fatally wounded by assassin in Teheran; 4 executed.—Feb. 21. Malcolm X, black nationalist, fatally shot in N. Y. City.

1966—Sept. 6. Prime Minister Hendrik F. Verwoerd of South Africa stabbed to death in parliament at Capetown.

1968—Apr. 4. Rev. Dr. Martin Luther King Jr. fatally shot in Memphis, Tenn. by James Earl Ray.—June 5. Sen. Robert F. Kennedy (D-N. Y.) fatally shot in Los Angeles; Sirhan Sirhan, resident alien, convicted of murder.

1971—Nov. 28. Prime Minister Wasfi Tal of Jordan, in Cairo, by Palestinian guerrillas.

1973—Mar. 2. U. S. Ambassador Cleo A. Noel Jr., U. S. Charge d'Affaires George C. Moore and Belgian Charge d'Affaires Guy Eid killed by Palestinian guerrillas in Khartoum, Sudan.

1974—Aug. 19. U. S. Ambassador to Cyprus, Rodger P. Davies, killed by sniper's bullet in Nicosia.

1975—Feb. 11. Pres. Richard Ratsimandrava, of Madagascar, shot in Tananarive.—Mar. 25. King Faisal of Saudi Arabia shot by nephew Prince Musad Abdel Aziz, in royal palace, Riyadh.—Aug. 15. Bangladesh Pres. Sheik Mujibur Rahman killed in coup.

1976—Feb. 13. Nigerian head of state, Gen. Murtala Ramat Mohammed, slain by self-styled "young revolutionaries."

1977—Mar. 16. Kamal Jumblat, Lebanese Druse chieftain, was shot near Beirut.—Mar. 18. Congo Pres. Marien Ngouabi shot in Brazzaville.

1978—July 9. Former Iraqi Premier Abdul Razak Al-Naif shot in London.

1979—Feb. 14. U.S. Ambassador Adolph Dubs shot and killed by Afghan Moslem extremists in Kabul.—Aug. 27. Lord Mountbatten, WW2 hero, and 2 others were killed when a bomb exploded on his fishing boat off the coast of Co. Sligo, Ire. The IRA claimed responsibility. —Oct. 26. So. Korean President Park Chung Hee and 6 bodyguards fatally shot by Kim Jae Kyu, head of Korean CIA, and 5 aides in Seoul.

1980—Apr. 12. Liberian President William R. Tolbert slain in military coup.—Sept. 17. Former Nicaraguan President Anastasio Somoza Debayle shot in Paraguay.

1981—Oct. 6. Egyptian President Anwar al-Sadat fatally shot by a band of commandos while reviewing a military parade in Cairo.

1982—Sept. 14. Lebanese President-elect Bashir Gemayel killed by bomb in east Beirut.

1983—Aug. 21. Philippine opposition political leader Benigno Aquino Jr. fatally shot by a gunman at Manila International Airport.

1984—Oct. 31. Indian Prime Minister Indira Gandhi shot and killed by 2 of her bodyguards, who were members of the minority Sikh sect, in New Delhi.

1986—Feb. 28. Swedish Premier Olaf Palme shot and killed by a gunman in Stockholm.

1988—June 1. Lebanese Premier Rashid Karami killed when a bomb exploded aboard a helicopter in which he was traveling. —Apr. 16. PLO military chief Khalil Wazir (Abu Jihad) was gunned down by Israeli commandos in Tunisia.

1989—Aug. 18. Colombian Liberal Party presidential candidate Luis Carlos Galan was killed by Medellín cartel drug traffickers at a campaign rally in Bogotá.—Nov. 22. Lebanese President Rene Moawad was killed when a bomb exploded next to his motorcade.

1990—Mar. 22. Colombian Patriotic Union presidential candidate Bernando Jamamillo Ossa was shot by a gunman at an airport in Bogotá.

1991—May 21. Rajiv Gandhi, former prime minister of India, was killed when a bomb exploded during an election rally in Madras.

1992—June 29. Mohammed Boudiaf, president of Algeria, was shot by a gunman in Annaba.

1993—May 1. Ranasinghe Premadasa, president of Sri Lanka, killed by bomb in Colombo.—Apr. 10. Chris Hani, S. African communist leader, shot by gunman in Boksburg.

Assassination Attempts

1910—Aug. 6. N. Y. City Mayor William J. Gaynor shot and seriously wounded by discharged city employee.

1912—Oct. 14. Former U. S. President Theodore Roosevelt shot and seriously wounded by demented man in Milwaukee, Wis.

1950—Nov. 1. In an attempt to assassinate President Truman, 2 members of a Puerto Rican nationalist movement—Griselio Torresola and Oscar Collazo—tried to shoot their way into Blair House. Torresola was killed, and a guard, Pvt. Leslie Coffelt was fatally shot. Collazo was convicted Mar. 7, 1951, for the murder of Coffelt.

1970—Nov. 27. Pope Paul VI unharmed by knife-wielding assailant who attempted to attack him in Manila airport.

1972—May 15. Alabama Gov. George Wallace shot in Laurel, Md. by Arthur Bremer; seriously crippled.

1972—Dec. 7. Mrs. Ferdinand E. Marcos, wife of the Philippine president, was stabbed and seriously injured in Pasay City, Philippines.

1975—Sept. 5. Pres. Gerald R. Ford was unharmed when a Secret Service agent grabbed a pistol aimed at him by Lynette (Squeaky) Fromme, a Charles Manson follower, in Sacramento.

1975—Sept. 22. Pres. Ford escaped unharmed when Sara Jane Moore, a political activist, fired a revolver at him.

1980—May 29. Civil rights leader Vernon E. Jordan Jr. shot and wounded in Ft. Wayne, Ind.

1981—Jan. 16. Irish political activist Bernadette Devlin McAliskey and her husband were shot and seriously wounded by 3 members of a Protestant paramilitary group in Co. Tyrone, Ire.

1981—Mar. 30. Pres. Ronald Reagan, Press Secy. James Brady, Secret Service agent Timothy J. McCarthy, and Washington, D.C. policeman Thomas Delahanty were shot and seriously wounded by John W. Hinckley Jr. in Washington, D.C.

1981—May 13. Pope John Paul II and 2 bystanders were shot and wounded by Mehmet Ali Agca, an escaped Turkish murderer, in St. Peter's Square, Rome.

1982—May 12. Pope John Paul II was unharmed when a man with a knife was overpowered by guards, in Fatima, Portugal.

1982—June 3. Israel's ambassador to Britain Shlomo Argov was shot and seriously wounded by Arab terrorists in London.

1986—Sept. 7. Chilean President Gen. Augusto Pinochet Ugarte escaped unharmed when his motorcade was attacked by rebels using rockets, bazookas, grenades, and rifles.

Notable Kidnappings in the U.S.

Edward A. Cudahy Jr., 16, in Omaha, Neb., **Dec. 18, 1900.** Returned Dec. 20 after $25,000 paid. Pat Crowe confessed.

Robert Franks, 13, in Chicago, **May 22, 1924**, by 2 youths, Richard Loeb and Nathan Leopold, who killed boy. Demand for $10,000 ignored. Loeb died in prison, Leopold paroled 1958.

Charles A. Lindbergh Jr., 20 mos. old, in Hopewell, N.J., **Mar. 1, 1932;** found dead May 12. Ransom of $50,000 was paid to man identified as Bruno Richard Hauptmann, 35, paroled German convict who entered U.S. illegally. Hauptmann was convicted after spectacular trial at Flemington, and electrocuted in Trenton, N.J. prison, Apr. 3. 1936.

William A. Hamm Jr., 39, in St. Paul, **June 15, 1933.** $100,000 paid. Alvin Karpis given life, paroled in 1969.

Charles F. Urschel, in Oklahoma City, **July 22, 1933.** Released July 31 after $200,000 paid. George (Machine Gun) Kelly and 5 others given life.

Brooke L. Hart, 22, in San Jose, Cal. Thomas Thurmond and John Holmes arrested after demanding $40,000 ransom. When Hart's body was found in San Francisco Bay, **Nov. 26, 1933**, a mob attacked the jail at San Jose and lynched the 2 kidnappers.

George Weyerhaeuser, 9, in Tacoma, Wash., **May 24, 1935.** Returned home June 1 after $200,000 paid. Kidnappers given 20 to 60 years.

Charles Mattson, 10, in Tacoma, Wash., **Dec. 27, 1936.** Found dead Jan. 11, 1937. Kidnapper asked $28,000, failed to contact.

Arthur Fried, in White Plains, N.Y., **Dec. 4, 1937.** Body not found. Two kidnappers executed.

Robert C. Greenlease, 6, taken from Kansas City, Mo. school **Sept. 28, 1953**, and held for $600,000. Body found Oct. 7. Bonnie Brown Heady and Carl A. Hall pleaded guilty and were executed.

Peter Weinberger, 32 days old, Westbury, N.Y., **July 4, 1956**, for $2,000 ransom, not paid. Child found dead. Angelo John LaMarca, 31, convicted, executed.

Lee Crary, 8, in Everett, Wash., **Sept. 22, 1957;** $10,000 ransom, not paid. He escaped after 3 days, led police to George E. Collins, who was convicted.

Frank Sinatra Jr., 19, from hotel room in Lake Tahoe, Cal., **Dec. 8, 1963.** Released **Dec. 11** after his father paid $240,000 ransom. Three men sentenced to prison.

Barbara Jane Mackle, 20, abducted **Dec. 17, 1968**, from Atlanta, Ga., motel, was found unharmed 3 days later, buried in a coffin-like wooden box 18 inches underground, after her father had paid $500,000 ransom; Gary Steven Krist sentenced to life, Ruth Eisenmann-Schier to 7 years.

Mrs. Roy Fuchs, 35, and 3 children held hostage 2 hours, **May 14, 1969**, in Long Island, N. Y., released after her husband, a bank manager, paid kidnappers $129,000 in bank funds; 4 men arrested, ransom recovered.

Virginia Piper, 49, abducted **July 27, 1972**, from her home in suburban Minneapolis; found unharmed near Duluth 2 days later after her husband paid $1 million ransom.

Patricia (Patty) Hearst, 19, taken from her Berkeley, Cal., apartment **Feb. 4, 1974.** Symbionese Liberation Army demanded her father, Randolph A. Hearst, publisher, give millions to poor. She was identified by FBI as taking part in a San Francisco bank holdup, **Apr. 15.** FBI, **Sept. 18, 1975**, captured her and others in San Francisco; they were indicted on various charges. Patricia Hearst convicted of bank robbery, **Mar. 20, 1976.** She was released from prison under executive clemency, **Feb. 1, 1979.** In 1978, William and Emily Harris were sentenced to 10 years to life for the Hearst kidnapping. Both were paroled in 1983.

J. Reginald Murphy, 40, an editor of *Atlanta* (Ga.) *Constitution*, kidnapped **Feb. 20, 1974;** freed **Feb. 22** after payment of $700,000 ransom by the newspaper. Police arrested William A. H. Williams, a contractor; most of the money was recovered.

E. B. Reville, Hepzibah, Ga., banker, and wife, Jean, kidnapped **Sept. 30, 1974.** Ransom of $30,000 paid. He was found alive; Jean Reville was found dead **Oct. 2.**

Jack Teich, Kings Point, N,Y., steel executive, seized **Nov. 12, 1974;** released **Nov. 19** after payment of $750,000.

Sidney J. Reso, oil co. executive, seized **Apr. 29, 1992;** died May 3; Arthur D. Seale and wife, Irene, arrested **June 19.** Arthur Seale pleaded guilty and was sentenced to life in prison; Irene Seale was sentenced to a 20-year prison term.

Katie Beers, 9, Long Island, N.Y., disappeared **Dec. 28, 1992**, found unharmed **Jan. 13, 1993**, in an underground bunker in the home of a family friend. John Esposito indicted **Jan. 19, 1993.**

ASSOCIATIONS AND SOCIETIES

Source: World Almanac questionnaire

Arranged according to key words in titles. Founding year of organization in parentheses; last figure after ZIP code indicates membership.

AFS Intercultural Programs (1917), 313 E. 43rd Street, N.Y., NY 10017; 22,000.

ASM International (1913), 9639 Kinsman Rd., Materials Park, OH 44073-0002; 48,625.

ASTM (1898), 1916 Race St., Philadelphia, PA 19103.

Aaron Burr Assn. (1946), 4520 King Edward Ct., Annandle, VA 22003; 600.

Abortion Federation, Natl. (1977), 1436 U St. NW, Suite 103, Washington, DC 20009; 300 organizations.

Accountants, Amer. Institute of Certified Public (1887), 1211 Ave. of the Americas, N.Y., NY 10036; 305,465.

Accountants, Natl. Assn. of (1919), 10 Paragon Dr., Box 433, Montvale, NJ 07645-1760; 85,000.

Accountants for Cooperatives, Natl. Soc. of (1936), 6320 Augusta Dr., Ste. 800, Springfield, VA 22150; 2,000.

Acoustical Society of America (1929), 500 Sunnyside Blvd., Woodbury, NY 11797; 7,000.

Actors' Equity Assn. (1913), 165 W. 46 St., N.Y., NY 10036.

Actuaries, Society of (1949), 475 N. Martingale Rd., Suite 800, Schaumburg, IL 60173-2226; 13,830.

Advertisers, Assn. of Natl. (1910), 155 E. 44th St., N.Y., NY 10017; 245 cos.

Advertising Agencies, Amer. Assn. of (1917), 666 Third Ave., N.Y., NY 10017; 700 agencies.

Aeronautic Assn., Natl. (1905), 1815 N. Fort Myer Dr., Ste. 700, Arlington, VA 22209.

Aerospace Industries Assn. of America (1919), 1250 Eye St. NW, Wash., DC 20005; 55 cos.

Aerospace Medical Assn. (1929), 320 S. Henry St., Alexandria, VA 22314-3579; 4,500.

Afro-American Life and History, Assn. for the Study of (1915), 1401 14th St. NW, Wash., DC 20005; 1,800.

Aging Assn., Amer. (1970), 600 South 42nd St., Omaha, NE 68198-4635; 400.

Agricultural Chemicals Assn., Natl. (1933), 1155 15th St. NW, Wash., DC 20005; 80 cos.

Agricultural Economics Assn., Amer. (1910), 80 Heady Hall, Iowa State Univ., Ames, IA 50011; 4,500.

Agricultural History Society (1919), Room 928, 1301 New York Ave. NW, Wash., DC 20250; 1,400.

Agronomy, Amer. Society of (1907), 677 S. Segoe Rd., Madison, WI 53711; 12,747.

Aircraft Assn., Experimental (1953), EAA Aviation Center, Oshkosh, WI 54903-3086; 130,000.

Aircraft Owners and Pilots Assn. (1939), 421 Aviation Way, Frederick, MD 21701; 300,000.

Air Force Assn. (1946), 1501 Lee Hwy., Arlington, VA 22209.

Air Force Gunners Assn. (1986), 3644 Elk Grove Ct., Land O'Lakes, FL 34639; 1,407.

Air Line Pilots Assn. (1931), 1625 Massachusetts Ave. NW, Wash., DC 20036; 41,000.

Airmen, Assn. of Independent (1989), 1625 Massachusetts Ave. NW, Washington, DC 20036; 3,000.

Air Transport Assn. of America (1936), 1709 New York Ave. NW, Wash., DC 20006; 19 airlines.

Air & Waste Management Assn. (1907), P.O. Box 2861, Pittsburgh, PA 15230; 14,057.

Al-Anon Family Groups (1950), P.O. Box 862, Midtown Sta., N.Y., NY 10018; 24,918.

Alcohol Problems, Amer. Council on (1895), 3426 Bridgeland Dr., Bridgeton, MO 63044; 37 state affiliates.

Alcoholics Anonymous (1935), P.O. Box 459, Grand Central Station, N.Y., NY 10163.

Alcoholism and Drug Dependence, Natl. Council on (1944), 12 W. 21st St., N.Y., NY 10010; 200 affiliates.

Allergy and Immunology, Amer. Academy of (1943), 611 E. Wells St., Milwaukee, WI 53202; 4,800.

Alpine Club, Amer. (1902), 113 E. 90th St., N.Y., NY 10028.

Alzheimer's Assn. (1980), 919 Michigan Ave., Chicago, IL 60611.

Amer. Indian Affairs, Assn. on (1922), 245 Fifth Ave., Ste. 1801, N.Y., NY, 10016-8728; 50,000.

American Legion, The (1919), 700 N. Pennsylvania St., Indianapolis, IN 46204; 3.1 mln. **American Legion Auxiliary** (1919), 777 N. Meridian St., Indianapolis, IN 46204; 1 mln.

Amer. Veterans (AMVETS) (1947); **AMVETS Auxiliary** (1946), 4647 Forbes Blvd., Lanham, MD 20706-9961; 200,000.

Americares Foundation (1982), 161 Cherry St., New Canaan, CT 06840.

Amideast (Amer. Mideast Educational & Training Services) (1951), 1100 17th St. NW, Ste. 300, Wash., DC 20036-4601.

Amnesty Intl. USA (1961), 322 Eighth Ave., N.Y., NY 10001.

Amputation Foundation, Natl. (1919), 12-45 150th St., Whitestone, NY 11357; 2,500.

Anachronism, Society for Creative (1966), P.O. Box 360743, Milpitas, CA 95036-0743; 23,000.

Animal Protection Institute of America (1968), 2831 Fruitridge Rd., Sacramento, CA 95822; 150,000.

Animal Welfare Institute (1951), P.O. Box 3650, Wash., DC 20007; 8,500.

Animals, Amer. Society for Prevention of Cruelty to (ASPCA) (1866), 424 E. 92d St., N.Y., NY 10128; 350,000.

Animals, People for the Ethical Treatment of (1980), P.O. Box 42516, Wash., DC 20015; 350,000.

Anthropological Assn., Amer. (1902), 1703 New Hampshire Ave. NW, Wash., DC 20009; 11,000.

Antiquarian Society, Amer. (1812), 185 Salisbury St., Worcester, MA 01609-1634; 552.

Anti-Vivisection Society, New England (1895), 333 Washington St., Boston, MA 02108-5100; 10,000.

Appalachian Mountain Club (1876), 5 Joy St., Boston, MA 02108; 54,952.

Appalachian Trail Conference (1925), Washington & Jackson Sts., Harpers Ferry, WV 25425; 23,000.

Appraisers, Amer. Society of (1936), 535 Herndon Pwky., #150, Herndon, VA 22070; 6,500.

Arab Americans, Natl. Assn. of (1972), 2033 M St. NW, Wash., DC 20036.

Arbitration Assn., Amer. (1926), 140 W. 51st St., N.Y., NY 10020-1203; 6,523.

Arc, The (1950), 500 E. Border St., Ste. 300, Arlington, TX 76010; 140,000.

Archaeological Institute of America (1879), 675 Commonwealth Ave., Boston, MA 02215; 11,500.

Archaeology, Institute of Nautical (1976), P.O. Drawer HG, College Station, TX 77841-5137; 1,100.

Archery Assn., Natl. (1879), One Olympic Plaza, Colorado Springs, CO 80909; 3,800.

Architects, Amer. Institute of (1857), 1735 New York Ave. NW, Wash., DC 20006; 51,000.

Architectural Historians, Society of (1940), 1232 Pine Street, Phila., PA 19107-5944; 3,500.

Armed Forces Communications and Electronics Assn. (1946), 4400 Fair Lakes Ct., Fairfax, VA 22033; 40,000.

Army, Assn. of the United States (1950), 2425 Wilson Blvd., Arlington, VA 22201-3385; 113,500.

Arthritis Foundation (1948), 1314 Spring St. NW, Atlanta, GA 30309; 500,000.

Arts, Amer. Council for the (1960), 1285 Avenue of the Americas, N.Y., NY 10019; 1,725.

Arts, Amer. Federation of (1909), 41 E. 65th St., N.Y., NY 10021.

Arts and Letters, Natl. Society of (1944), 655 15th St. NW, Washington, DC 20005; 1,600.

Arts & Sciences, Amer. Academy of (1780), Norton's Woods, 136 Irving St., Cambridge, MA 02138; 4,000.

Association Executives, American Society of (1920), 1575 Eye St. NW, Wash., DC 20005; 18,000.

Association Publications, Society of Natl. (1963), 3299 K St. NW, Suite 700, Wash., DC 20007; 210 publications.

Astrologers, Amer. Federation of (1938), 6535 S. Rural Rd., Tempe, AZ 85283; 4,500.

Astronautical Society, Amer. (1954), 6352 Rolling Mill Pl., Suite 102, Springfield, VA 22152; 1,550.

Astronomical Society, Amer. (1899), 2000 Florida Ave., NW, Suite 300, Wash., DC 20009; 5,700.

Ataxia Foundation, Natl. (1957), 600 Twelve Oaks Cntr., 15500 Wayzata Blvd., Wayzata MN 55391; 1,400.

Atheists, Amer. (1963), P.O. Box 140195, Austin, TX 78714.

Athletic Assn., Natl. Jr. College (1939), P.O. Box 7305, Colorado Springs, CO 80933-7305; 530.

Athletic Associations, Natl. Federation of State H. S. (1920), 11724 Plaza Circle, Box 20626, Kansas City, MO 64195.

Athletic Union of the U.S., Amateur (1888), 3400 W. 86th St., Indianapolis, IN 46268; 230,000+.

Auctioneers Assn., Natl. (1949), 8880 Ballentine, Overland Park, KS 66214; 5,487.

Audubon Society, Natl. (1905), 950 Third Ave., N.Y., NY 10022; 1 mln.

Authors Guild, Inc., The (1921), 330 W. 42nd St., New York, NY 10036; 14,000.

Authors League of America (1912), 234 W. 44th St., N.Y., NY 10036; 15,000.

Autism Society of America, (1965), 7910 Woodmont Ave., Ste. 650, Bethesda, MD 20814; 11,500.

Autograph Collectors Club, Universal (1965), P.O. Box 6181, Wash., DC 20044-6181; 2,447.

Automobile Assn., Amer. (1902), 1000 AAA Dr., Heathrow, FL 32746: 34 mln.
Automobile Club, Natl. (1924), One Market Plaza, San Francisco, CA 94105; 316,000.
Automobile Club of America, Antique (1935), 501 W. Governor Rd., Hershey, PA 17033; 53,000.
Automobile Dealers Assn., Natl. (1917), 8400 Westpark Dr., McLean, VA 22102; 19,000.
Automobile License Plate Collectors' Assn. (1954), P.O. Box 77, Horner, W. VA 26372; 2,750.
Automotive Hall of Fame (1939), 3225 Cook Rd., P. O. Box 1727, Midland, MI 48641-1727; 2,500

Badminton Assn., U.S. (1936), 920 O Street, Lincoln, NE 68508-3624.
Baker Street Irregulars (1934), 34 Pierson Ave., Norwood, NJ 07648; 275.
Bald-Headed Men of America (1973), 102 Bald Drive, Morehead City, N.C. 28557; 20,000.
Ball Players of Amer., Assn. of Professional (1924), 12062 Valley View St., #211, Garden Grove, CA 92645; 58,000.
Band & Choral Directors Hall of Fame, Natl. (1985), 519 N. Halifax Ave., Daytona Beach, FL 32118.
Bankers Assn., Amer. (1875), 1120 Connecticut Ave. NW, Wash., DC 20036.
Bankers Assn. of America, Independent (1930), One Thomas Circle NW, Suite 950, Wash. DC 20005; 6,400 banks.
Bar Assn., Federal (1920), 1815 H St. NW, Wash., DC 20006; 14,300.
Barbershop Quartet Singing in Amer., Soc. for Preservation & Encouragement of (1938), 6315 Third Ave., Kenosha, WI 53140-5199; 35,000.
Baseball Congress, Amer. Amateur (1935), 118-19 Redfield Plaza, Marshall, MI 49068; 10,625 teams.
Baseball Congress, Natl. (1931), P.O. Box 1420, Wichita, KS 67201.
Baseball Research, Society for Amer. (1971), P.O. Box 93183, Cleveland, OH 44101; 6,226.
Basketball Assn., Natl. (1946), 645 Fifth Ave., N.Y., NY 10022.
Battleship Assn., Amer. (1964), P.O. Box 711247, San Diego, CA 92171; 1,300.
Beer Can Collectors of America (1970), 747 Merus Ct., Fenton, MO 63026-2092; 4,100.
Beta Gamma Sigma (1913), 11701 Borman Dr., Ste. 320, St. Louis, MO 63146-4194; 295,000.
Beta Sigma Phi (1931), 1800 W. 91st Place, Kansas City, MO 64114; 250,000.
Bible Society, Amer. (1816), 1865 Broadway, N.Y., NY 10023; 188,500.
Biblical Literature, Society of (1880), 1549 Clairmont Rd., Ste. 204, Decatur, GA 30033-4635; 5,500.
Bibliographical Society of America (1904), P.O. Box 397, Grand Central Sta., N.Y., NY 10163; 1,257.
Big Brothers/Big Sisters of America (1902), 230 No. 13th St., Philadelphia, PA 19107; 494 agencies.
Biochemistry and Molecular Biology, Amer. Society for (1906), 9650 Rockville Pike, Bethesda, MD 20814-3996; 9,000.
Biological Sciences, American Institute of (1947), 730 11th St. NW, Washington, DC 20001-4521; 14,000.
Bison Assn., Amer. (1976), P.O. Box 16660, Denver, CO 80216.
Black History Honors & Awards, Contemporary & (1990), 6514 Georgia Road, Birmingham, AL 35212; 250.
Blind, Amer. Council of the (1961), 1155 15th St. NW, Washington, DC 20005; 40,000.
Blind, Natl. Federation of the (1940), 1800 Johnson St., Baltimore, MD 21230; 30,000+.
Blindness, Natl. Society to Prevent (1908), 500 E. Remington Rd., Schaumburg, IL 60173; 26 affiliates.
Blue Angels Assn. (1982), 4600 Twin Oaks Dr., Apt. 702, Pensacola, FL 32506; 250.
Blue Cross and Blue Shield Assn. (1946), 676 St. Clair, Chicago, IL 60611; 74 plans.
Blueberry Council, No. Amer. (1965), P.O. Box 166, Marmora, NJ 08223.
B'nai B'rith Intl. (1853), 1640 Rhode Island Ave. NW, Wash., DC 20036; 500,000.
Boat Club, Chris Craft Antique (1973), 217 S. Adams St., Tallahassee, FL 32301; 2,000.
Boat Owners Assn. of the U.S. (1966), 880 S. Pickett St., Alexandria, VA 22304; 350,000.
Bodybuilders Assn., Amer. (1981), 6991 Simson St., Oakland, CA 94605-2226; 854.
Bookplate Collectors and Designers, Amer. Soc. of (1922), 605 N. Stoneman Ave. #F, Alhambra, CA 91801; 200.
Booksellers Assn., Amer. (1900), 122 E. 42d St., N.Y., NY 10168; 8,500+.
Bottle Collectors, Federation of Historical (1969), 4098 Faxon Ave., Memphis, TN 38122; 600.
Bowling Congress, Amer. (1895), 5301 S. 76th St., Greendale, WI 53129; 2.7 mln.
Boys' Clubs of America (1906), 771 First Ave., N.Y., NY 10017; 1.2 mln.
Boy Scouts of America (1910), 1325 Walnut Hill Lane, Irving, TX 75015-2079; 3.8 mln.
Bridge, Tunnel and Turnpike Assn., Intl. (1932), 2120 L St. NW, Suite 305, Wash., DC 20037; 250 organizations.
Brith Sholom, Natl. (1905), 3939 Conshohocken Ave., Philadelphia, PA 19131; 4,500.
Broadcasters, Natl. Assn. of (1922), 1771 N St. NW, Wash., DC 20036.
Burroughs Bibliophiles, The (1960), 454 Elaine Dr., Pittsburgh, PA 15236-2417; 462.
Business Bureaus, Council of Better (1970), 4200 Wilson Blvd., Arlington, VA 22203; 180 bureaus.
Business Clubs, Natl. Assn. of Amer. (1922), 3315 No. Main St., High Point, NC 27262; 6,727.
Business Communicators, Intl. Assn. of (1970), One Hallidie Pl., Suite 600, San Francisco, CA 94102.
Business Education Assn., Natl. (1946), 1906 Association Dr., Reston, VA 22091; 18,000.
Button Society, Natl. (1938), 2733 Juno Pl., Akron, OH 44313-4137; 3,560.
Byron Society, The (1971 England, 1973 in U.S.), 259 New Jersey Ave., Collingswood, NJ 08108; 300.

CLU & CHFC, Amer. Soc. of (1928), 270 S. Bryn Mawr Ave., Bryn Mawr, PA 19010; 32,000.
CPCU, The Society of (1944), 720 Providence Rd., Malvern, PA 19355-0709; 24,000.
Camp Fire Boys & Girls (1910), 4601 Madison Ave., Kansas City, MO 64112; 600,000.
Campers & Hikers Assn., Inc. (1954), 4804 Transit Rd., Bldg. 2, Depew, NY 14043; 21,000 families.
Camping Assn., Amer. (1910), 5000 State Rd. 67 N., Martinsville, IN 46131; 5,231.
Cancer Society, Amer. (1913), 90 Park Ave., N.Y., NY 10017.
Carillonneurs in North America, Guild of (1936), 3718 Settle Rd., Cincinnati, OH 45227; 507.
Carnegie Hero Fund Commission (1904), 2307 Oliver Bldg., Pittsburgh, PA 15222; 21 members.
Cartoonists Society, Natl. (1946), 157 W. 57th St., Suite 904, N.Y., NY 10019; 500.
Cat Fanciers' Assn. (1906), 1805 Atlantic Ave., Manasquan, NJ 08736-1005.
Catholic Bishops, Natl. Conference of/U.S. Cath. Conference (1966), 1312 Massachusetts Ave. NW, Wash., DC 20005.
Catholic Church Extension Society of the U.S.A. (1905), 35 E. Wacker Dr., #400, Chicago, IL 60601; 220,000.
Catholic Daughters of the Americas (1903), 10 W. 71st St., N.Y., NY 10023; 140,000.
Catholic Educational Assn., Natl. (1904), 1077-30th St. NW, Suite 100, Wash, DC 20007; 18,353.
Catholic Historical Soc., Amer. (1884), 263 S. Fourth St., P.O. Box 84, Philadelphia, PA 19106-3819; 900.
Catholic Library Assn. (1921), 461 W. Lancaster Ave., Haverford, PA 19041; 1,518.
Catholic Rural Life Conference, Natl. (1923), 4625 Beaver Ave., Des Moines, IA 50310-2199; 1,900.
Catholic War Veterans of the U.S.A. (1935), 419 North Lee Street, Alexandria, VA 22314; 30,000.
Cemetery Assn., Amer. (1889), 5201 Leesburg Pike, Falls Church, VA 22041; 1,600.
Ceramic Society, Amer. (1898), 735 Ceramic Pl., Westerville, OH 43081; 13,000.
Cerebral Palsy Assns., United (1949), 7 Penn Plaza, N.Y., NY 10001; 180 affiliates.
Chamber Music Players, Amateur (1948), 545 Eighth Ave., N.Y., NY 10018.
Chamber of Commerce of the U.S.A. (1912), 1615 H St. NW, Wash., DC 20062; 185,000.
Chaplain's Intl. Assn. (1960), Adjutant General Office, 5045 N. Robberson, Springfield, MO 65803; 963.
Checker Federation, Amer. (1948), 3475 Belmont Ave., Baton Rouge, LA 70808; 1,000.
Chemical Manufacturers Assn. (1872), 2501 M St. NW, Wash., DC 20037; 171 companies.
Chemical Society, Amer. (1876), 1155 16th St. NW, Wash., DC 20036; 135,000.
Chemists, Amer. Assn. of Cereal (1915), 3340 Pilot Knob Rd., St. Paul, MN 55121; 3,891.
Chemists, Amer. Society of Brewing (1934), 3340 Pilot Knob Rd., St. Paul MN 55121; 730.
Chess Federation, U.S. (1939), 186 Rt. 9W, New Windsor, NY 12553; 69,000.

Chess League of Amer., Correspondence (1897), P.O. Box 3481, Barrington, IL 60011-3481; 900.

Child Welfare League of America (1920), 440 First St. NW, Wash., DC 20001-2085; 670 agencies.

Childhood Education, Intl. Assn. for (1892), 11501 Georgia Ave., Suite 315, Wheaton, MD 20902; 11,000.

Children, Natl. Center for Missing and Exploited (1984), 2101 Wilson Blvd., Arlington, VA 22201.

Children of the Amer. Revolution, Natl. Society of the (1895), 1776 D St. NW, Wash., DC 20006.

Children's Aid Society (1853), 105 E. 22d St., N.Y., NY 10010; 1,207.

Children's Book Council (1945), 568 Broadway, Suite 404, N.Y., NY 10012; 65 publishing houses.

Chiropractic Assn., Amer. (1930), 1916 Wilson Blvd., Arlington, VA 22201; 20,000.

Christian Endeavor, Intl. (1881), 1221 E. Broad St., P.O. Box 1110, Columbus, OH 43216.

Christian Laity Counseling Board (1970), 5901 Plainfield Dr., Charlotte, NC 28215; 38 mln.

Christians and Jews, Natl. Conference of (1927), 71 Fifth Ave., Suite 1100 N.Y., NY 10003.

Church Federation, Ecumenical (1982), 13014-270 N. Dalemabry, Tampa, FL 33618-2808.

Churches, U.S. Conference for the World Council of (1948), 475 Riverside Dr., N.Y., NY 10115; 317 denominations.

Church Women United (1941), 475 Riverside Dr., Rm. 812, N.Y., NY 10115.

Cincinnati, Society of the (1783), 2118 Massachusetts Ave. NW, Wash., DC 20008; 3,300.

Circulation Managers Assn., Intl. (1889), 11600 Sunrise Valley Dr., Reston, VA 22091; 1,705.

Cities, Natl. League of (1924), 1301 Pennsylvania Ave. NW, Wash., DC 20004; 1,450 cities.

City/County Management Assn., Intl. (1914), 777 North Capitol St. NE, Ste. 500, Wash., DC 20002; 8,000.

Civil Air Patrol (1941), HQ CAP-USAF, Maxwell AFB, AL 36112-5572; 63,000.

Civil Engineers, Amer. Society of (1852), 345 E. 47th St., N.Y., NY 10017; 104,000.

Civil Liberties Union, Amer. (1920), 132 W. 43rd St., N.Y. NY 10036; 250,000.

Civic League, Natl. (1894), 55 West 44th St., N.Y., NY 10036; 3,000.

Civitan Internatl. (1920), One Civitan Pl., Birmingham, AL 35213-1983; 50,000.

Classical League, Amer. (1919), Hall, Miami Univ., Oxford, OH 45056; 3,604.

Clinical Pathologists, Amer. Society of (1922), 2100 W. Harrison St., Chicago, IL 60612; 58,757.

Coal Association, Natl. (1917), 1130 17th St. NW, Wash., DC 20036; 150 corporate members.

Coast Guard Combat Veterans Assn. (1985), 6858 Lafayette Rd., Medina, OH 44256; 1,366.

Co-Dependents Anonymous (1986), P.O. Box 33577, Phoenix, AZ 85067-3577.

College Board, The (1900), 45 Columbus Ave., N.Y., NY 10023; 2,900 institutions.

College Music Society (1958), 202 W. Spruce St., Missoula, MT 59802; 4,000.

College Placement Council (1956), 62 Highland Ave., Bethlehem, PA 18017; 2,966.

Colleges, Amer. Assn. of Community and Jr. (1921), One Dupont Circle NW, Suite 410, Wash., DC 20036.

Colleges, Assn. of Amer. (1915), 1818 R St. NW, Wash., DC 20009; 635 institutions.

Colleges and Universities, Assn. of Intl. (1973), l301 S. Noland Rd., Independence, MO 64055; 10,572.

Collegiate Athletic Assn., Natl. (1906), 6201 College Blvd., Overland Park, KS 66211-2422; 828 inst.

Collegiate Schools of Business, Amer. Assembly of (1916), 605 Old Ballas Rd., St. Louis, MO 63141-7077.

Colonial Dames XVII Century, Natl. Society (1915), 1300 New Hampshire Ave. NW, Wash., DC 20036-1595; 13,750.

Colonial Wars, General Society of (1892), 840 Woodbine Ave., Glendale, OH 45246; 4,300.

Commerce, U.S. Junior Chamber of (1920), 4 W. 21st St., Tulsa, OK 74114-1116; 225,000.

Commercial Collectors Assn., Amer. (1970), 4040 W. 70th St., Minneapolis, MN 55435; 3,225.

Commercial Law League of America (1895), 175 W. Jackson, #1541, Chicago, IL 60604; 5,100.

Commercial Travelers of America, Order of United (1888), 632 N. Park St., Columbus, OH 43215; 186,000.

Common Cause (1970), 2030 M St. NW, Wash., DC 20036.

Communication, Intl. Training In (1938), 2519 Woodland Dr., Anaheim, CA 92801; 18,000.

Communities, Federation of Egalitarian (1976), E. Wind, Rt. 3, Box 6B2, Tecumseh, MO 65760; 250+.

Community Cultural Center Assoc., Amer. (1978), 19 Foothills Dr., Pompton Plains, NJ 07444.

Composers/USA, Natl. Assn. of (1932), P.O. Box 49652, Barrington Sta., Los Angeles, CA 90049; 600.

Composers, Authors & Publishers, Amer. Society of (ASCAP) (1914), One Lincoln Plaza, N.Y., NY 10023; 24,000.

Computer Professionals, Inst. for Certification of (1973), 2200 E. Devon Ave., Ste. 268, Des Plaines, IL 60018-4503; 47,000.

Computing Machinery, Assn. for (1947), 1515 Broadway, N.Y., NY 10036; 55,000.

Concrete Institute, Amer. (1904), 22400 W. Seven Mile Rd., Detroit, MI 48219-1849.

Conscientious Objectors, Central Committee for (1948), 2208 South St., Phila., PA 19146.

Conservation Engineers, Assn. of (1961), Alabama Dept. of Conservation, 64 N. Union St., Montgomery, AL 36130; 225.

Constantian Society, The (1970), 123 Orr Rd., Pittsburgh, PA 15241; 550.

Construction Industry Manufacturers Assn. (1911), 111 E. Wisconsin Ave., Milwaukee, WI 53202; 150 companies.

Construction Specifications Institute (1948), 601 Madison St., Alexandria, VA 22314-1791; 19,200.

Consulting Organizations, Council of (1989), 521 5th Ave., N.Y., NY 10175.

Consumer Credit Assn., Intl. (1912), 243 N. Lindbergh, St. Louis, MO 63141; 20,000.

Consumer Federation of America (1968), 1424 16th St. NW, #604, Wash., DC 20036; 240 organizations.

Consumer Interests, Amer. Council on (1953), 240 Stanley Hall, Univ. of Missouri, Columbia, MO 65211; 1,500.

Consumer Protection Institute (1970), 5901 Plainfield Dr., Charlotte, NC 28215.

Consumers Union of the U.S. (1936), 101 Truman Ave., Yonkers, NY 10703; 405,990.

Contract Bridge League, Amer. (1937), 2990 Airways Blvd., Memphis, TN 38116-3847; 200,000+.

Contract Management Assn., Natl. (1959), 6728 Old McLean Village Dr., McLean, VA 22101; 20,176.

Contractors of Amer., General (1919), 1957 E St. NW, Wash., DC 20006; 32,000.

Cooperative Business Assn., Natl. (1916), 1401 New York Ave. NW, #1100, Wash., DC 20005; 450.

Cooperative League of the U.S.A. (1916), 1401 New York Ave. NW, Suite 1100, Wash., DC 20005; 285 co-ops.

Correctional Assn., Amer. (1870), 8025 Laurel Lakes Court, Laurel, MD 20707; 20,000+.

Correctional Officers, Intl. Assn. of (1977), 8600 Glenarden Pky,Glenarden, MD 20706-1599.

Cosmetology Assn., Natl. (1921), 3510 Olive St., St. Louis, MO 63103; 47,000.

Cotton Council of America, Natl. (1938), 1918 North Parkway, Memphis, TN 38112; 297 delegates.

Counseling and Development, Amer. Assn. for (1952), 5999 Stevenson Ave., Alexandria, VA 22304; 58,065.

Country Music Assn. (1958), One Music Circle S., Nashville, TN 37203; 6,588.

Creative Children and Adults, Natl. Assn. for (1974), 8080 Springvalley Dr., Cincinnati, OH 45236-1395; 1,500.

Credit Assn., International (1912), 243 N. Lindberg, St. Louis, MO 63141; 10,000.

Credit Union Natl. Assn. (1934), 5710 Mineral Point Rd., Madison, WI 53705; 52 state credit union leagues.

Crime and Delinquency, Natl. Council on (1907), 685 Market St., Suite 620, San Francisco, CA 94105; 500.

Criminology, Amer. Society of (1941), 1314 Kinnear Rd., Ste. 212, Columbus, OH 43212.

Crop Science Society of America (1955), 677 S. Segoe Rd., Madison, WI 53711; 5,345.

Cryogenic Soc. of Amer. (1964), 1033 South Blvd., #13, Oak Park, IL 60302.

Customs Brokers & Forwarders Assn. of Am., Natl. (1897), One World Trade Center, Ste. 1153, N.Y., NY 10048.

Cystic Fibrosis Foundation (1955), 6931 Arlington Rd., Bethesda, MD 20814; 60,000.

Dairy Council, Natl. (1915), 6300 N. River Rd., Rosemont, IL 60018.

Dairy and Food Industries Supply Assn. (1917), 6245 Executive Blvd., Rockville, MD 20852; 800 companies.

Dairy Goat Assn., American (1904), 209 W. Main St., Spindale, NC 28160; 13,000.

Danish Brotherhood in America (1882), 3717 Harney St., Omaha, NE 68131; 8,600.

Daughters of the American Revolution, Natl. Society, (1890), 1776 D St. NW, Wash., DC 20006-5392; 200,000.

Daughters of the British Empire in the U.S.A. (1909), 14611 NE 50th Pl., F-4, Bellevue, WA 98007; 5,206.

Daughters of the Confederacy, United (1894), 328 N. Blvd., Richmond, VA 23220-4057; 24,000.

Daughters of the Republic of Texas (1891), 510 E. Anderson Ln., Austin, TX 78752; 6,400.

Daughters of Union Veterans of the Civil War (1885), 503 S. Walnut St., Springfield, IL 62704; 4,100+.

Deaf, Alexander Graham Bell Assn. for the (1890), 3417 Volta Pl. NW, Washington, DC 20007.

Deaf, Natl. Assn. of the (1880), 814 Thayer Ave., Silver Spring, MD 20910.

Death and Dying, Natl. Council on (1990), 250 W. 50th St., N.Y., NY 10019; 120,000.

Defense Preparedness Assn., Amer. (1919), 2101 Wilson Blvd., Ste. 400, Arlington, VA 22201-3061; 29,000.

Delta Kappa Gamma Society Intl. (1929), 416 W. 12th St., Austin, TX 78701; 165,000.

Deltiologists of America (1960), P.O. Box 8, Norwood, PA 19074; 800+.

Democratic Natl. Committee, (1792), 430 S. Capitol St. SE, Wash., DC 20003.

DeMolay, Intl. Supreme Council, Order of (1919), 10200 N. Executive Hills Blvd., Kansas City, MO 64153-1367; 30,000.

Dental Assn., Amer. (1859), 211 E. Chicago Ave., Chicago, IL 60611; 148,542.

Descendants of the Colonial Clergy, Society of the (1933), 30 Leewood Rd., Wellesley, MA 02181; 1,400.

Descendants of the Signers of the Declaration of Independence (1907), 9th & Chestnut Sts., Phila., PA 19105; 873.

Descendants of Washington's Army at Valley Forge, Society of (1976), P.O. Box 915, Valley Forge, PA 19482-0915.

Desert Protective Council (1954), P.O. Box 2312, Valley Center, CA 92082; 305.

Diabetes Assn., Amer. (1940), 1660 Duke St., Alexandria, VA 22314; 259,000.

Dialect Society, Amer. (1889), c/o Allan Metcalf, English Dept., MacMurray College, Jacksonville, IL 62650; 600.

Direct Marketing Assn. (1917), 6 E. 43d St., N.Y., NY 10017.

Directors Guild of America (1936), 7920 Sunset Blvd., Los Angeles, CA 90046; 9,700.

Disabled Amer. Veterans (1923), 3725 Alexandria Pike, Cold Spring, KY 41076; 1.2 mln.

Disabled Collectors' Correspondence Club (1991), 457 Washington Blvd., Fremont, CA 94539.

Dogs Intl., Therapy (1980), 260 Fox Chase Rd., Chester, NJ 07930; 2,500+.

Dogs on Stamp Study Unit (1979), 3208 Hana Rd., Edison, NJ 08817-2552; 400.

Dozenal Society of America (1944), Math Dept., Nassau Community College, Garden City, NY 11530; 144.

Dracula Society, Count (1962), 334 W. 54th St., Los Angeles, CA 90037; 500.

Drug, Chemical and Allied Trades Assn. (1890), 2 Roosevelt Ave., Syosset, NY 11791; 2,018.

Ducks Unlimited (1937), One Waterfowl Way, Memphis, TN 38120; 500,000+.

Dutch Settlers Soc. of Albany (1924), RD#2 Box 313, Altamont, NY 12009-9531; 250.

Eagles, Fraternal Order of (1898), 12660 West Capitol Dr., Brookfield, WI 53055; 1.1 mln.

Easter Seal Society, Natl. (1919), 70 E. Lake St., Chicago, IL 60601.

Eastern Star, General Grand Chapter, Order of the (1876), 1618 New Hampshire Ave. NW, Wash., DC 20009; 1.7 mln.

Economic Assn., Amer. (1885), 2014 Broadway, Ste. 305, Nashville, TN 37203; 27,316.

Edsel Club, Intl. (1969), P.O. Box 371, Sully, IA 50251; 1,011.

Education, Amer. Council on (1918), One Dupont Circle NW, #800, Wash., DC 20036; 1,600 institutions.

Education, Amer. Soc. for Engineering (1893), 11 Dupont Circle NW, Suite 200, Washington, DC 20036; 10,000+.

Education, Council for Advancement & Support of (1974), 11 Dupont Circle NW, Wash., DC 20036; 2,950 schools.

Education, Council for Basic (1956), 725 15th St. NW, Wash., DC 20005; 10,000.

Education, Institute of Intl. (1919), 809 United Nations Plaza, N.Y., NY 10017; 700 U.S. colleges, univ.

Education, Natl. Assn. for Family and Community (1936), 5963 Jefferson St., Burlington, KY 41005-9596; 341,651.

Education Assn., Natl. (1857), 1201 16th St. NW, Wash., DC 20036; 2 mln.

Education of Young Children, Natl. Assn. for the (1926), 1509 16th St. NW, Washington, DC 20036; 82,000.

Educational Exchange, Council on Intl. (1947), 205 E. 42d St., N.Y., NY 10017; 240 organizations.

Educational Research Assn., Amer. (1916), 1230 17th St. NW, Wash., DC 20036; 17,000.

8th Air Force Historical Society (1975), P.O. Box 7215, St. Paul, MN 55107; 17,000.

82nd Airborne Division Assn., Inc. (1944), NFCS, P.O. Box 9308, Fayetteville, NC 28311-7694; 22,000.

88th Infantry Division Assn., Inc. (1948), P.O. Box 925, Havertown, PA 19083; 5,152.

Electrical and Electronics Engineers, Institute of (1884), 345 E. 47th St., N.Y., NY 10017; 300,000.

Electrical Manufacturers Assn., Natl. (1926), 2101 L St. NW, Wash., DC 20037; 560 companies.

Electrochemical Society (1902), 10 S. Main St., Pennington, NJ 08534-2896; 6,300.

Electronic Circuits, The Institute for Interconnecting & Packaging (1957), 7380 N. Lincoln, Lincolnwood, IL 60646-1705; 1900 cos.

Electronic Industries Assn. (1924), 2001 Pennsylvania Ave., Wash., DC 20006-1813; 1,058 companies.

Electronics Technicians, Intl. Society of Certified (1970), 2708 W. Berry, Ft. Worth, TX 76109; 2,000.

Electroplaters' and Surface Finishers' Society, Amer. (1909), 12644 Research Pkwy, Orlando, FL 32826; 8,500.

Elks of the U.S.A., Benevolent and Protective Order of (1868), 2750 N. Lakeview Ave., Chicago, IL 60614; 1.5 mln.

Elvis Burning Love Fan Club (1983), 1904 Williamsburg Dr., Streamwood, IL 60107.

Elvis Presley Fan Club of Ceylon (1964), 113/1, Pirivena Rd., Mt. Lavania, Sri Lanka; 2,000.

Energy Research Institute, Clean (1974), 1251 Memorial Dr., 219 MacArthur Engineering Bldg., Coral Gables, FL, 33146.

Engineering, Natl. Academy of (1964), 2101 Constitution Ave. NW, Wash., DC 20418; 1,700.

Engineering, Soc. for the Advancement of Material & Process (1944), P.O. Box 2459, Covina, CA 91722; 10,000.

Engineering Society of N. America, Illuminating (1906), 345 E. 47th St., N.Y., NY 10017; 10,000.

Engineers, Amer. Inst. of Chemical (1908), 345 E. 47th St., N.Y., N.Y. 10017; 53,622.

Engineers, Amer. Institute of Mining, Metallurgical and Petroleum (1871), 345 E. 47th St., N.Y., NY 10017.

Engineers, Amer. Soc. of Agricultural (1907), 2950 Niles Rd., St. Joseph, MI 49085-9659; 8,000.

Engineers, Amer. Soc. of Civil (1852), 345 E. 47th St., N.Y., NY 10017; 111,112.

Engineers, American Soc. of Mechanical (1881), 345 E. 47th St., N.Y., NY 10017; 120,000.

Engineers, Amer. Soc. of Naval (1888), 1452 Duke St., Alexandria, VA 22314; 7,500.

Engineers, Amer. Soc. of Safety (1911), 1800 E. Oakton St., Des Plains, IL 60018-2187; 28,000.

Engineers, Assn. of Energy (1977), 4025 Pleasantdale Rd., Suite 420, Atlanta, GA 30340; 8,500.

Engineers, Inst. of Industrial (1948), 25 Technology Park, Atlanta, GA 30092; 43,000.

Engineers, Inst. of Transportation (1930), Suite 410, 525 School St. NW, Wash., DC 20024, 7,700.

Engineers, Natl. Society of Professional (1934), 1420 King St., Alexandria, VA 22314; 75,000.

Engineers, Soc. of Fire Protection (1950), One Liberty Sq., Boston, MA 02109; 4,026.

Engineers, Soc. of Logistics (1966), 8100 Professional Pl., Ste. 211, New Carrollton, MD 20785; 8,500.

Engineers, Soc. of Manufacturing (1932), One SME Drive, P.O. Box 930, Dearborn, MI 48121; 80,000.

Engineers, Society of Mining (1871), 8307 Shaffer Pkwy., Littleton, CO 80127; 23,058.

Engineers, Society of Plastics (1942), 14 Fairfield Dr., Brookfield Ctr., CT 06805; 25,000.

English, U.S. (1983), 818 Connecticut Ave. NW, Ste. 200, Washington, DC 20006; 250,000.

English Assn., College (1939), English Dept., Nazareth College of Rochester, Rochester, NY 14618; 1,250.

Entomological Society of America (1897), 9301 Annapolis Rd., Lanham, MD 20706-3115; 8,665.

Environmental Health Assn., Natl. (1937), 720 S. Colorado Blvd., Suite 970, Denver, CO 80222; 5,000.

Environmental Information Assn. (1983), 1777 NE Expressway, Ste. 150, Atlanta, GA 30329; 3,000.

Epigraphic Society, Inc., The (1974), 6625 Bamburgh Dr., San Diego, CA 92117; 800.

Esperanto League for North America (1952), P.O. Box 1129, El Cerrito, CA 94530; 1,000.

Evangelism Crusades, Intl. (1959), 14617 Victory Blvd., Van Nuys, CA 91411; 1,500.

Exchange Club, Natl. (1911), 3050 Central Ave., Toledo, OH 43606-1700.

Fairs & Expositions, Intl. Assn. of (1919), P.O. Box 985, Springfield, MO 65801; 2,400.

Family Relations, Natl. Council on (1938), 3989 Central Ave. NE, Suite 550, Minneapolis, MN 55421; 3,800.

Family Service America (1911), 11700 W. Lake Park Dr., Park Pl, Milwaukee, WI 53224; 300 agencies.
Farm Bureau Federation, Amer. (1919), 225 Touhy Ave., Park Ridge, IL 60068; 4 mln.
Farmers Union, Natl. (1902), Denver, CO 80251; 250,000.
Farmers' Educational and Co-Operative Union of America (1902), 10065 E. Harvard Ave., Denver, CO 80231; 250,000.
Fat Acceptance, Natl. Assn. to Advance (NAAFA) (1969), P.O. Box 188620, Sacramento, CA 95818; 3,500.
Federal Employees, Natl. Assn. of Retired (1921), 1533 New Hampshire Ave. NW, Washington, DC 20036-1279.
Federal Employees, Natl. Fed. of (1917), 1016 16th St. NW, Wash., DC 20036.
Feminists for Life of America (1972), 811 E. 47th St., Kansas City, MO 64110; 5,000.
Financial Analysts Federation (1945), #5 Boar's Head Lane, Charlottesville, VA 22903; 22,700.
Financial Executives Institute (1931), 10 Madison Ave., P.O. Box 1938, Morristown, NJ 07962-1938; 14,000.
Financiers, Intl. Soc. of (1979), P.O. Box 18508, Asheville, NC 28814; 275.
Fire Chiefs, Intl. Assn. of (1873), 4025 Fair Ridge Dr., Fairfax, VA 22033-2868.
Fire Protection Assn., Natl. (1896), Batterymarch Park, Quincy MA 02269; 38,000.
First Amendment Studies, Institute for (1984), P.O. Box 589, Great Barrington, MA 01230; 27,000.
Fish Assn., Intl. Game (1939), 1301 E. Atlantic Blvd., Pompano Beach, FL 33060; 20,000.
Fisheries Soc., American (1870), 5410 Grosvenor Lane, Ste. 110, Bethesda, MD 20814; 8,500.
Fishes, Soc. for the Protection of Old (1967), School of Fisheries, WH-10 Univ. of Washington, Seattle, WA 98195; 275.
Fishing Tackle Manufacturers Assn., Amer. (1933), 1250 Grove Ave., Barrington, IL 60010; 500 cos.
Flag Research Center, The (1962), Box 580, Winchester, MA 01890; 1,300.
Flight Attendants, Assn. of (1973), 1625 Massachusetts Ave. NW, Wash., DC 20036; 28,000.
Fly Fishers, Fed. of (1965), Box 1088, 200 Yellowstone Ave., W. Yellowstone, MT 59758; 10,000.
Flying Disc Fed., World (1985), Gnejsvägen 24, 85240; Sundsvall, Sweden; 15,000.
Food Brokers Assn., Natl. (1904), 1010 Massachusetts Ave. NW, Wash., DC 20001; 1,800 companies.
Food Institute, Amer. Frozen (1942), 1764 Old Meadow Ln., Suite 350, McLean, VA 22102; 550 firms.
Footwear Industries Assn., Amer. (1871), 3700 Market St., Philadelphia, PA 19104; 180.
Foreign Student Affairs, Natl. Assn. for (1948), 1860 19th St. NW, Wash., DC 20009; 5,500.
Foreign Study, Amer. Institute for (1964), 102 Greenwich Ave., Greenwich, CT 06830; 300,000.
Foreign Trade Council, Inc., Natl. (1914), 1625 K St. NW, Washington, DC 20006; 500 companies.
Forensic Sciences, Amer. Academy of (1948), 410 N. 21st St., Ste. 203, Colorado Springs, CO 80904; 3,435.
Forest & Paper Assn., Amer. (1993), 1250 Connecticut Ave. NW, 2nd Floor, Washington, DC 20036.
Forest Council (1932), 1250 Connecticut Ave. NW, Suite 320, Washington, DC 20036.
Forest History Society (1946), 701 Vickers Ave., Durham, NC 27701; 2,000.
Forest Products Research Society (1947), 2801 Marshall Ct., Madison, WI 53705; 3,000.
Foresters, Society of Amer. (1900), 5400 Grosvenor La., Bethesda, MD 20814; 18,324.
Forestry Assn., Amer. (1875), 1516 P St. NW, Wash., DC 20005; 112,000.
Forests, Amer. (1875), 1516 P St. NW, Wash., DC 20005; 115,000.
Fortean Organization, Intl. (1966), P.O. Box 367, Arlington, VA 22210-0367; 850.
Founders and Patriots of Amer., The Order of the (1896), 3813 Acapulco Ct., Irving, TX 75062; 1,250.
Foundrymen's Society, Amer. (1896), 505 State St., Des Plaines, IL 60016-8399; 13,389.
4-H Clubs (1901-1905), Extension Service, U.S. Dept of Agriculture, Wash., DC 20250; 5.8 mln.
Frederick A. Cook Soc., The (1957), Sullivan County Historical Museum, P.O. Box 247, Hurleyville, NY 12747-0247; 200.
Freedom of Information Center (1958), 20 Walter Williams Hall, Univ. of Missouri, Columbia, MO 65211.
Freedoms Foundation at Valley Forge (1949), Valley Forge, PA 19481; 4,800.
French Institute/Alliance Francaise (1971), 22 E. 60th St., N.Y., NY 10022-1077; 8,500.
Friendship and Good Will, Intl. Soc. of (1978), 211 W. 4th Ave., P.O. Box 2637, Gastonia, NC 28053-2637; 4,239.
Funeral and Memorial Societies, Continental Assn. of (1963), 2001 S. St. NW, Suite 530, Washington, DC 20009.
Future Farmers of Amer. Org., Natl. (1928), 5632 Mt. Vernon Memorial Hwy., Alexandria, VA 22309-0160; 401,574.

Gamblers Anonymous (1957), P.O. Box 17173, Los Angeles, CA 90017.
Garden Club of Amer. (1913), 598 Madison Ave., N.Y., NY 10022; 15,000.
Garden Clubs, Natl. Council of State (1929), 4401 Magnolia Ave., St. Louis, MO 63110; 308,623.
Garden Clubs of America, Men's (1932), 5560 Merle Hay Rd., Johnston, IA 50131; 9,500.
Gas Appliance Manufacturers Assn. (1935), 1901 N. Moore St., Arlington, VA 22209; 210 companies.
Gas Assn., Amer. (1918), 1515 Wilson Blvd., Arlington, VA 22209; 229 companies; 3,000 individuals.
Gay and Lesbian Task Force, Natl. (1973), 1734 14th St. NW, Washington, DC 20009; 20,000.
Genealogical Society, Natl. (1903), 4527 17th St. N., Arlington, VA 22207; 12,000.
Genetic Assn., Amer. (1903), P.O. Box 39, Buckeystown, MD 21717; 800.
Geographers, Assn. of Amer. (1904), 1710 16th St. NW, Wash., DC 20009-3198; 6,600.
Geographic Education, Natl. Council for (1915), 16A Leonard Hall, IUPA, Indiana, PA 15705; 3,700.
Geographic Society, Natl. (1888), 1145 17th St. NW, Wash., DC 20036; 9.7 mln.
Geographical Society, Amer. (1851), 156 Fifth Ave., Suite 600, N.Y., NY 10010-7002; 1,900.
Geological Society of America (1888), 3300 Penrose Pl., P.O. Box 9140, Boulder, CO 80301; 17,000.
Geologists, Amer. Assn. of Petroleum (1917), 1444 So. Boulder, Tulsa, OK 74119; 33,050.
Geophysicists, Society of Exploration (1930), P.O. Box 702740, Tulsa, OK 74170; 14,500.
Geriatrics Society, Amer. (1942), 770 Lexington Ave., Suite 300, N.Y., NY 10021; 6,686.
Gideons Intl. (1899), 2900 Lebanon Rd., Nashville, TN 37214; 104,000.
Gifted Children, Natl. Assn. for (1957), 1155 15th St. NW, Ste. 1002, Wash., DC 20005; 6,500.
Girls Clubs of America (1945), 30 E. 33d St., N.Y., NY 10016; 250,000+.
Girl Scouts of the U.S.A. (1912), 830 Third Ave., N.Y., NY 10022; 3.2 mln.
Glenn Miller Birthplace Soc. (1976), P.O. Box 61, Clarinda, IA 51632; 1,200.
Gold Star Mothers, Amer. (1928), 2128 Leroy Pl. NW, Wash., DC 20008; 3,000.
Golf Association, U.S. (1894), Box 708, Far Hills, NJ 07931.
Gospel Music Assn. (1964), 7 Music Circle N., Nashville, TN 37203; 2,900.
Government Finance Officers Assn. (1906), 180 N. Michigan Ave., Suite 800, Chicago, IL 60601; 12,500.
Graduate Schools in the U.S., Council of (1961), One Dupont Circle NW, Wash., DC 20036; 402 institutions.
Grandmothers Clubs of America, Natl. Federation of (1934), 203 N. Wabash Ave., Chicago, IL 60601; 10,000.
Grange, Natl. (1867), 1616 H St. NW, Wash., DC 20006.
Graphic Arts, Amer. Institute of (1914), 1059 Third Ave., N.Y., NY 10021; 6,000.
Gray Panthers (1970), 1424 16th St. NW, Suite 602, Wash., DC 20036; 45,000.
Green Mountain Club, The (1910), RR1, Box 650, Waterbury Ctr., VT 05677; 5,200.
Grocers, Natl. Assn. of (1893), 1825 Samuel Morse Dr., Reston, VA 22090.
Grocery Manufacturers of America (1908), 1010 Wisconsin Ave., Suite 800, Wash., DC 20007; 140 companies.
Guide Dog Foundation for the Blind (1946), 371 E. Jericho Tpke., Smithtown, NY 11787-2976.
Gyro Intl. (1912), 1096 Mentor Ave., Painesville, OH 44077.

HIAS (Hebrew Immigrant Aid Society) (1880), 333 7th Ave., 17th Floor, N.Y., NY 10001-5004.
Hadassah, the Women's Zionist Organization of America (1912), 50 W. 58th St., N.Y., NY 10019; 385,000.
Hairdressers and Cosmetologists Assn., Natl. (1921), 3510 Olive St., St. Louis, MO 63103; 50,406.
Handball Assn., U.S. (1951), 930 N. Benton Ave., Tucson, AZ 85711; 8,300.
Handicapped, Federation of the (1935), 211 W. 14th St., N.Y., NY 10011; 650.
Handicapped, Natl. Assn. of the Physically (1958), Bethesda Scarlet Oaks, #117, 440 Lafayette Ave., Cincinnati, OH 45220-1000; 700.

Handicapped Sports, Natl. (1967), 451 Hungerford Dr., Ste. 100, Rockville, MD 20850; 20,000.
Health Council, Natl. (1920), 1730 M St. NW, Ste. 500, Washington, DC 20036.
Health Info. Management Assoc., American (1928), 919 N. Michigan Ave., #1400, Chicago, IL 60611-1683; 34,000.
Health, Physical Education, Recreation and Dance, Amer. Alliance for (1885), 1900 Association Dr., Reston, VA 22091.
Health Professions, Assn. of Schools of Allied (1967), 1101 Connecticut Ave. NW, Ste. 700, Wash., DC 20036-4387.
Hearing Society, Intl. (1951), 20361 Middlebelt Rd., Livonia, MI 48152; 2,800.
Hearing and Speech Action, Natl. Assn. for (1910), 10801 Rockville Pike, Rockville, MD 20852.
Heart Assn., Amer. (1924), 7320 Greenville Ave., Dallas TX 75231; 200,000.
Hearts, Mended (1951), 7320 Greenville Ave., Dallas TX 75231; 20,000.
Heating, Refrigerating & Air Conditioning Engineers, Amer. Soc. of (1894), 1791 Tullie Circle NE, Atlanta, GA 30329.
Helicopter Assn. Intl. (1948), 1619 Duke St., Alexandria, VA 22314; 1,800.
Helicopter Society, Amer. (1943), 217 N. Washington St., Alexandria VA 22314; 6,500.
Hemispheric Affairs, Council on (1975), 724 9th St. NW, Wash., DC 20001; 2,800.
Highpointers Club (1987), Box 327, Mtn. Home, AR 72653; 691.
High School Assns., Natl. Federation of State (1920), P.O. Box 20626, Kansas City, MO 64195.
High Twelve Internatl. (1921), 11155-B2 South Towne Square, St. Louis, MO 63123-7823; 24,000.
Hiking Society, Amer. (1977), P.O. Box 20160, Wash., DC 20041-2160; 4,500.
Historians, Organization of Amer. (1907), 112 N. Bryan St., Bloomington, IN 47408; 12,000.
Historical Assn., Amer. (1884), 400 A St. SE, Wash., DC 20003; 15,200.
Historic Preservation, Natl. Trust for (1949), 1785 Massachusetts Ave. NW, Wash., DC 20036; 250,000.
Hockey, U.S.A. (1937), 2997 Broadmoor Valley Rd., Colorado Springs, CO 80906; 250,000.
Home Builders, Natl. Assn. of (1942), 1201 15th St. NW, Wash., DC 20005; 157,000.
Home Economics Assn., Amer. (1909), 1555 King St., Alexandria, VA 22314; 20,000.
Homemakers of America, Future (1945), 1910 Association Dr., Reston, VA 22091; 281,000+.
Honor Society, Natl. (1921), 1904 Association Dr., Reston, VA 22091; 22,000.
Horatio Alger Soc. (1961), 4907 Allison Dr., Lansing, MI 48910; 300.
Horse Council, American (1969), 1700 K St. NW, #300, Washington, DC 20006; 2,500.
Horse Protection Assn., Amer. (1966), 1000 29th St. NW, Suite T-100, Wash., DC 20007; 5,000.
Horse Shows Assn., Amer. (1917), 220 E. 42 St., N.Y., NY 10017-5806; 56,500+.
Hospital Association, Amer. (1899), 840 N. Lake Shore Dr., Chicago, IL 60611; 40,000.
Hospital Marketing and Public Relations, Amer. Society for (1964), 840 N. Lake Shore Dr., Chicago, IL 60611; 3,167.
Hot Rod Assn., Natl. (1951), 2035 Financial Way, Glendora, CA 91740; 74,524.
Hotel & Motel Assn., Amer. (1910), 1201 New York Ave., NW, Washington, DC 20005-3917.
Humanism, Council for Democratic and Secular (1980), Box 664, Buffalo, NY 14228; 20,000.
Human Resource Management, Society for (1948), 606 N. Washington St., Alexandria, VA 22314; 45,000.
Humane Society of the U.S. (1954), 2100 L St. NW, Wash., DC 20037; 650,000.
Hydrogen Energy, Intl. Assn. for (1975), P.O. Box 248266, Coral Gables, FL 33124; 2,500.
Hygiene Assn., Amer. Industrial (1939), P.O. Box 8390, 345 White Pond Dr., Akron, OH 44320.

Idaho, U.S.S. (BB-42) Assn. (1957), P.O. Box 711247, San Diego, CA 92171; 925.
Identification, Intl. Assn. for (1916), P.O. Box 2423, Alameda, CA 94501; 3,300.
Illustrators, Society of (1901), 128 E. 63 St., N.Y., NY 10021; 901.
Impotence Inst. of Amer. (1983), 2020 Pennsylvania Ave. NW, Ste. 292, Washington, DC 20006.
Industrial Designers Society of America (1965), 1142-E Walker Rd., Great Falls, VA 22066; 2,200.
Industrial Engineers, Amer. Institute of (1948), 25 Technology Park, Norcross, GA 30092; 40,000.
Industrial Health Foundation (1935), 34 Penn Circle West, Pittsburgh, PA 15206; 170 companies.
Industrial Security, Amer. Soc. for (1955), 1655 N. Ft. Myer Dr., Suite 1200, Arlington, VA 22209; 25,000.
Information and Image Management, Assn. for (1943), 1100 Wayne Ave., Ste. 1100, Silver Springs, MD 20910; 10,000.
Information Industry Assn. (1968), 555 New Jersey Ave. NW, Suite 800, Wash., DC 20001; 500 companies.
Inner Network, The (1991), 300 Darby Hill Rd., RD #1, Delanson, NY 12053; 450.
Insurance Assn., Amer. (1964), 1130 Connecticut Ave. NW, Suite 1000, Wash., DC 20036; 250+ companies.
Insurance Society, Inc., Intl. (1957), Box 870223, Tuscaloosa, AL 35487-0223; 1,200.
Intellectual Property Owners (1972), 1255 23rd St. NW, Washington, DC 20037; 300.
Intelligence Officers, Assn. of Former (1975), 6723 Whittier Ave., Suite 303A, McLean, VA 22101; 3,300.
Intercollegiate Athletics, Natl. Assn. of (1940), 1221 Baltimore Ave., Kansas City, MO 64105; 412 schools.
Interior Designers, Amer. Society of (1931), 608 Mass. Ave. NE, Washington, DC 20002; 33,000.
International Interculture Programs, AFS (1947), 313 E. 43rd St., N.Y., NY 10017; 100,000.
Inventors, Amer. Assn. of (1891), 2020 Pennsylvania Ave. NW, Wash., DC 20006; 5,727.
Investment Clubs, Natl. Assn. of (1951), 1515 E. Eleven Mile Rd., Royal Oak, MI 44067; 140,000.
Investors Corp., Natl. Assn. of (1951), 1515 E. Eleven Mile Rd., Royal Oak, MI 48067; 181,161.
Irish-American Cultural Inst. (1962), 2115 Summit Ave., #5026, Univ. of St. Thomas, St. Paul, MN 55105; 5,000.
Iron Castings Society (1897), 455 State St., Des Plaines, IL 60016; 200 firms.
Iron and Steel Engineers, Assn. of (1907), Three Gateway Center, Suite 2350, Pittsburgh, PA 15222; 10,000.
Iron and Steel Institute, Amer. (1855), 1101 17th St. NW, Ste. 1300, Wash., DC 20036; 1,100.
Italian Historical Society of America (1949), 111 Columbia Heights, Bklyn., NY 11201.
Izaak Walton League of America, The (1922), 1401 Wilson Blvd., Level B, Arlington, VA 22209; 54,000.

Jamestowne Society (1936), P.O. Box 14523, Richmond, VA 23221; 3,000.
Jane Austen Society of N. Amer. (1979), 207 Pinecroft Dr., Raleigh, NC 27609; 2,800.
Japanese Amer. Citizens League (1929), 1765 Sutter St., San Francisco, CA 94115; 24,000.
Jewish Book Council (1943), 15 E. 26th St., N.Y., NY 10010.
Jewish Committee, Amer. (1906), 165 E. 56th St., N.Y., NY 10022; 50,000.
Jewish Community Centers Assn. (1917), 15 E. 26th St., N.Y., NY 10010.
Jewish Congress, Amer. (1918), 15 E. 84th St., N.Y., NY 10028; 50,000.
Jewish Federations, Council of (1932), 730 Broadway, N.Y., NY 10003; 200 agencies.
Jewish Historical Society, Amer. (1892), 2 Thornton Rd., Waltham, MA 02154; 1,500.
Jewish War Veterans of the U.S.A. (1896), 1811 R St. NW, Wash., DC 20009; 150,000.
Jewish Women, Natl. Council of (1893), 53 W. 23rd St., N.Y., NY 10010; 100,000.
Job's Daughters, Internatl. Order of (1920), 233 W. 6th St., Papillion, NE 68046; 24,000.
Jockey Club (1894), 380 Madison Ave., N.Y., NY 10017; 90.
John Birch Society (1958), P.O. Box 8040, Appleton, WI 54913.
Joseph Diseases Foundation, Intl. (1977), P.O. Box 2550, Livermore, CA 94550; 800.
Journalists, Society of Professional (1909), P.O. Box 77, Greencastle, IN 46135; 16,000.
Journalists and Authors, Amer. Society of (1948), 1501 Broadway, Suite 1907, N.Y., NY 10036; 850.
Judaism, Amer. Council for (1943), P.O. Box 9009, Alexandria, VA 22304.
Judicature Society, Amer. (1913), 25 E. Washington, Chicago, IL 60602; 20,000.
Juggler's Assn., Intl. (1947), P.O. Box 218, Montague, MA 01351; 3,300.
Junior Achievement (1919), 550 Summer St., Stamford, CT 06901; 300,000.
Junior Auxiliaries, Natl. Assn. of (1941), 845 S. Main, Greenville, MS 38701; 10,500.
Junior Leagues, Assn. of (1921), 660 First Ave., N.Y., NY 10016; 190,000.

Kennel Club, Amer. (1884), 51 Madison Ave., N.Y., NY 10010; 500+ clubs.
Kidney Fund, Amer. (1971), 6110 Executive Blvd., #1010, Rockville, MD 20852.
Kiwanis Intl. (1915), 3636 Woodview Trace, Indianapolis, IN 46268-3196; 329,000.
Knights of Columbus (1882), One Columbus Plaza, New Haven, CT 06507; 1.4 mln.
Knights of Pythias (1864), 2785 E. Desert Inn Rd., #150, Las Vegas, NV 89121; 96,000.
Knights Templar U.S.A., Grand Encampment (1816), 5097 N. Elston, Ste. 101, Chicago, IL 60630.
Krishna Consciousness, Intl. Soc. for (ISKON) (1966) 3764 Watseka Ave., Los Angeles, CA 92109; 1 mln.

LCI National Assn., U.S.S. (1991), 134 Lancaster Ave., Columbia, PA 17512; 1,500.
La Leche League Intl. (1956), 9616 Minneapolis Ave., P.O. Box 1209, Franklin Park, IL 60131; 48,000.
Lambs, The (1874), 3 W. 51st St., N.Y., NY 10019; 202.
Landscape Architects, Amer. Society of (1899), 4401 Connecticut Ave., NW, Wash., DC 20008-2302; 10,000.
Law, Amer. Society of International (1906), 2223 Massachusetts Ave. NW, Washington, DC 20008; 4,300.
Law Enforcement Officers Assn., Amer. (1966), 1000 Connecticut Ave. NW, Suite 9, Wash., DC 20036; 50,000.
Law Libraries, Amer. Assn. of (1906), 53 W. Jackson Blvd., Chicago, IL 60604; 4,630.
Learned Societies, Amer. Council of (1919), 228 E. 45th St., N.Y., NY 10017; 45 societies.
Lefthanders Intl. (1975), P.O. Box 8249, Topeka, KS 66608.
Legal Administrators, Assn. of (1971), 175 E. Hawthorn Pkwy. #325, Vernon Hills, IL 60061-1428; 8,000.
Legion of Valor of the U.S.A. (1890), 92 Oak Leaf Lane, Chapel Hill, NC 27516; 780.
Leif Ericson Society (1962), Box 301, Chicago, IL 60690-0301; 1,250.
Leprosy Missions, Amer. (1906), One Alm Way, Greenville, SC 29601.
Leukemia Society of America (1949), 733 Third Ave., N.Y., NY 10017; 57 chapters.
Lewis and Clark Trail Heritage Foundation, Inc. (1969), P.O. Box 3434, Great Falls, MT 59403; 1,493.
Lewis Carroll Society of N. America (1974), 617 Rockford Rd., Silver Spring, MD 20902; 400.
Libertarian Natl. Committee (1971), 1528 Pennsylvania Ave. SE, Washington, DC 20003-3116.
Liberty Lobby (1955), 300 Independence Ave. SE, Wash., DC 20003; 16,000.
Libraries Assn., Special (1909), 1700 18th St., NW, Wash., DC 20009; 13,800.
Library Assn., Amer. (1876), 50 E. Huron St., Chicago, IL 60611; 50,000.
Library Assn., Am. Theological (1947), 820 Church St., Ste. 300, Evanston, IL 60201; 188 libraries.
Library Assn., Medical (1861), 6 N. Michigan Ave., Suite 300, Chicago, IL 60602; 5,000+.
Life, Americans United for (1971), 343 S. Dearborn St., Ste. 1804, Chicago, IL 60604.
Life Insurance, Amer. Council of (1976), 1001 Pennsylvania Ave., NW, Wash., DC 20004; 616 firms.
Life Underwriters, Amer. Soc. of Certified (1929), 270 Bryn Mawr Ave., Byrn Mawr, PA 19010; 28,000.
Life Underwriters, Natl. Assn. of (1890), 1922 F St. NW, Wash., DC 20006; 135,000.
Lions Clubs, Intl. Assn. of (1917), 300 22d St., Oak Brook, IL 60521-8842; 1,363,000.
Liquid Crystal Soc., Intl. (1990), Liquid Crystal Institute, Kent State Univ., Kent, OH 44242-0001; 700.
Litchfield Institute, The (1984), 2121 W. Oakland Park Blvd., #333,Ft. Lauderdale, FL 33311-1507; 51.
Literacy Volunteers of America (1962), 5795 Widewaters Parkway, Syracuse, NY 13214.
Little League Baseball (1939), Route #15, S. Williamsport, PA 17701; 17,816 charters.
Little People of America (1957), P.O. Box 9897, Washington, DC 20016; 2,000.
London Club (1975), 214 N. 2100 Road, Lecompton, KS 66050; 100+.
Lung Assn., Amer. (1904), 1740 Broadway, N.Y., NY 10019.
Lutheran Education Assn. (1942), 7400 Augusta St., River Forest, IL 60305; 3,800.

Magazine Photographers, Am. Soc. of (1944), 419 Park Ave. South, N.Y., NY 10016; 5,000+.
Magazine Publishers of America (1919), 575 Lexington Ave., N.Y., NY 10022; 200 publishers.
Magicians, Intl. Brotherhood of (1926), P.O. Box 192090, Saint Louis, MO 63119-9998; 13,500.
Magicians, Society of Amer. (1902), 1333 Cory St., Yellow Springs, OH 45387; 5,500.
Management Assn., Amer. (1923), 135 W. 50th St., N.Y., NY 10020; 70,000.
Management Consultants, Institute of (1968), 521 5th Ave., 35th Floor, N.Y., NY 10175-3598; 2,201.
Manufacturers, Natl. Assn. of (1897), 1331 Penna. Ave. NW, Ste. 1500N, Wash., DC 20004-1703; 12,500 companies.
Manufacturers' Agents Natl. Assn. (1947), 23016 Mill Creek Rd., P.O. Box 3467, Laguna Hills, CA 92654; 10,000.
March of Dimes Birth Defects Foundation (1938), 1275 Mamaroneck Ave., White Plains, NY 10605; 2 mln.+.
Marine Corps League (1923), P.O. Box 3070, Merrifield, VA 22116-3070; 38,000.
Marine Manufacturers Assn., Natl. (1904), 401 N. Michigan Ave., Chicago, IL 60611; 1,650 companies.
Marketing Assn., Amer. (1934), 250 S. Wacker Dr., Chicago, IL 60606; 49,122.
Masonic Relief Assn. of U.S. and Canada (1880), 3827 Canal St., New Orleans, LA 70119.
Masons, Ancient and Accepted Scottish Rite, Southern Jurisdiction, Supreme Council 33° (1801), 1733 16th St. NW, Wash., DC 20009; 528,837.
Masons, Supreme Council 33°, Ancient and Accepted Scottish Rite, Northern Masonic Jurisdiction (1813), 33 Marrett Rd., Lexington, MA 02173; 385,870.
Masons, Royal Arch, General Grand Chapter (1797), P.O. Box 489, 111 S. 4th St., Danville, KY 40423-0489; 245,000.
Mathematical Society, Amer. (1888), 201 Charles St., Providence, RI 02904; 30,000.
Mathematical Statistics, Institute of (1935), 3401 Investment Blvd., Ste. 7, Hayward, CA 94545; 4,000.
Mathematics, Society for Industrial and Applied (1952), 3600 University City Science Ctr., Phila., PA 19104-2688; 8,100.
Mayflower Descendants, General Society of (1897), 4 Winslow St., P.O. Box 3297, Plymouth, MA 02361; 23,500.
Mayors, U.S. Conference of (1932), 1620 Eye St. NW, Wash., DC 20006.
Mechanics, Amer. Academy of (1969), Dept. of Civil Engineering, Northwestern Univ., Evanston, IL 60201; 1,200.
Medical Assn., Amer. (1847), 535 N. Dearborn St., Chicago, IL 60610; 290,000.
Medical Assn., Natl. (1895), 1012 Tenth St. NW, Wash., DC 20001; 14,000.
Medical Record Assn., Amer. (1928), 919 N. Michigan Ave., Chicago, IL 60611; 31,000.
Medieval Academy of America (1926), 1430 Massachusetts Ave., Cambridge, MA 02138; 3,936.
Men, Natl. Coalition of Free (1977), P.O. Box 129, Manhasset, NY 11030; 2,000.
Mensa, Amer. (1960), 2626 E. 14th St., Brooklyn, NY 11235.
Mental Health Assn., Natl. (1909), 1021 Prince St., Alexandria, VA 22314; 1 mln.
Mental Health Program Directors, Natl. Assn. of State (1959), 66 Canal Ctr. Plaza, Ste. 302, Alexandria, VA 22314; 55.
Mentally Ill, Natl. Alliance for the (1979), 2101 Wilson Blvd., Suite 302, Arlington, VA 22201; 80,000.
Merchant Marine Library Assn., Amer. (1921), One World Trade Center, Suite 2161, N.Y., NY 10048.
Merchant Marine Veterans of WWII, U.S. (1945), P.O. Box 629, San Pedro, CA 90733; 7,090.
Merchants Assn., Natl. Retail (1911), 100 W. 31st St., N.Y., NY 10001; 45,000.
Merrill's Marauders Assn. (1946), 11244 N. 33rd St., Phoenix, AZ 85028-2723; 1,695.
Metallurgy Institute, Amer. Powder (1959), 105 College Rd. East, Princeton, NJ 08540; 2,800.
Metal Powder Industries Federation (1943), 105 College Rd. East, Princeton, NJ 08540; 230 cos.
Metals, Amer. Society for (ASM Internatl.) (1913), Metals Park, OH 44073; 53,000.
Meteorological Society, Amer. (1919), 45 Beacon St., Boston, MA 02108; 10,200.
Metric Assn., U.S. (1966), 10245 Andasol Ave., Northridge, CA 91325; 1,400.
Microbiology, Amer. Society for (1899), 1325 Massachusetts Ave. NW, Wash. DC 20005; 37,000.
Military Order of the Loyal Legion of the U.S.A. (1865), 1805 Pine St., Phila., PA 19103; 900.
Military Order of the Purple Heart of the USA (1932), 5413-B Backlick Rd., Springfield, VA 22151; 30,000.
Military Order of the World Wars (1919), 435 N. Lee St., Alexandria, VA 22314; 14,000.
Military Service, Veterans of Underage (1991), 3444 Walker Dr., Ellicott City, MD 21042; 532.
Miniatures, Friends of (1988), Dollhouse Museum of the Southwest, 2208 Routh St., Dallas, TX 75201; 274.

Mining, Metallurgy and Exploration, Inc., Society for (1871), 8307 Shaffer Pkwy., Littleton, CO 80127; 20,279.
Ministerial Assn., Amer. (1929), 2210 Wilshire Blvd., Suite 582, Santa Monica, CA 90403; 3,000.
Model Railroad Assn., Natl. (1935), 4121 Cromwell Rd., Chattanooga, TN 37421; 25,000.
Modern Language Assn. of America (1883), 10 Astor Pl., N.Y., NY 10003; 32,000.
Modern Language Teachers Assns., Natl. Federation of (1916), Gannon Univ., Erie, PA 16541; 7,200.
Moose Intl., Inc. (1988), Mooseheart, IL 60539; 1.8 mln.
Mothers, American (1935), 301 Park Ave., N.Y., NY 10022; 3,000.
Mothers of Twins Clubs, Natl. Organization of (1960), P.O. Box 23188, Albuquerque, NM 87192-1188; 14,000.
Motion Picture Arts & Sciences, Academy of (1927), 8949 Wilshire Blvd., Beverly Hills, CA 90211; 5,300.
Motion Pictures, Natl. Board of Review of (1909), P.O. Box 589, Lenox Hill Sta., N.Y., NY 10021.
Motion Picture & Television Engineers, Society of (1916), 595 West Hartsdale Ave., White Plains, NY 10607; 9,500.
Motor Fire Apparatus in Amer., Soc. for the Preservation & Appreciation of Antique (1958), P.O. Box 2005, Syracuse, NY 13220-2005; 3,000.
Motor Vehicle Manufacturers Assn. (1903), 7430 2nd Ave., Suite 300, Detroit, MI 48202; 7 companies.
Motorcyclist Assn., American (1924), 33 Collegeview Rd., Westerville, OH 43081-6114.
Multiple Sclerosis Society, Natl. (1946), 733 Third Ave., N.Y., NY 10017; 400,000.
Muscular Dystrophy Assn. (1950), 3300 E. Sunrise Dr., Tucson, AZ 85718.
Museums, Amer. Assn. of (1906), 1225 Eye St. NW, Ste. 200, Wash., DC 20005; 12,000.
Music Center, Amer. (1939), 30 W. 26th St., N.Y., NY 10010.
Music Council, Natl. (1940), 40 W. 37th St., N.Y., NY 10018; 50 organizations.
Music Educators Natl. Conference (1907), 1902 Association Dr., Reston, VA 22090; 60,000.
Music Scholarship Assn., Amer. (1956), 1826 Carew Tower, Cincinnati, OH 45202; 15,000.
Music Teachers Natl. Assn. (1876), 617 Vine St., Suite 1432, Cincinnati, OH 45202-2439; 25,000.
Musicological Society, Amer. (1934), 201 S. 34th St., Phila., PA 19104; 3,500.
Muzzle Loading Rifle Assn., Natl. (1933), P.O. Box 67, Friendship, IN 47021; 26,000.
Myasthenia Gravis Foundation, The (1952), 53 W. Jackson Blvd., Ste. 660, Chicago, IL 60604; 30,000.

NAACP (Natl. Assn. for the Advancement of Colored People) (1909), 4805 Mt. Hope Drive, Baltimore, MD 21215.
Na'amat USA (1925), 200 Madison Ave., N.Y., NY 10016.
Narcolepsy and Cataplexy Foundation of Amer. (1975), 1410 York Ave., Suite 2D, N.Y. NY 10021; 3,991.
Narcotics Anonymous (1953), P.O. Box 9999, Van Nuys, CA 91409; 1 million.
National Guard Assn. of the U.S. (1878), One Massachusetts Ave. NW, Wash., DC 20001; 54,000.
Nature Conservancy (1951), 1815 N. Lynn St., Arlington, VA 22209; 692,000.
Naturist Society, The (1980), P.O. Box 132, Oshkosh, WI 54902; 20,000.
Naval Architects & Marine Engineers, The Society of (1893), 601 Pavonia Ave., Ste. 400, Jersey City, NJ 07306.
Naval Institute, U.S. (1873), 118 Maryland Ave., Annapolis, MD 21402; 100,000.
Naval Reserve Assn. (1954), 1619 King St., Alexandria, VA 22314; 24,500.
Navigation, Institute of (1945), 1026 16th St. NW, Suite 104, Wash., DC 20036; 3,200.
Navy League of the U.S. (1902); 2300 Wilson Blvd., Arlington, VA 22201; 73,000.
Needlework Guild of America (1885), 1007-B Street Rd., Southampton, PA 18966; 100,000.
Negro College Fund, United (1944), 500 E. 62d St., N.Y., NY 10021; 42 institutions.
Neurofibromatosis Foundation, Natl. (1978), 141 Fifth Ave., Suite 7-S, N.Y., NY 10010; 7,000.
New Age Walkers (1982), 3301 Bellaire Dr., Altadena, CA 91001; 4,700.
Newspaper Assn. of Amer. (1992), NAA, The Newspaper Center, 11600 Sunrise Valley Dr., Reston, VA 22091.
Newspaper Editors, Amer. Society of (1922), P.O. Box 17004, Washington, DC 20041.
Newspaper Marketing Assn., Intl. (1930), 11600 Sunrise Valley Dr., Reston, VA 22091; 1,300+.
Newswomen's Club of N.Y. (1922), 15 Gramercy Park S., N.Y., NY 10003; 200.
Nikola Tesla Walkers (1982), 10799 Sherman Grove Ave., #18, Sunland, CA 91040; 4,800.
Ninety-Nines (Intl. Organization of Women Pilots) (1929), P.O. Box 59965, Will Rogers Airport, Oklahoma City, OK 73159.
Nobel Committee, Amer. (1942), 1 Morningside Dr. N., Westport, CT 06880.
Non-Commissioned Officers Assn. (1960), 10635 IH 35 North, San Antonio, TX 78233; 160,000.
Northern Cross Society (1986), Route One, Big Springs, KS 66050; 50.
Notaries, Amer. Society of (1965), 918 16th St. NW, Wash., DC 20006; 21,499.
Nuclear Society, Amer. (1954), 555 N. Kensington Ave., La Grange Park, IL 60525; 16,777.
Numismatic Assn., Amer. (1891), 818 N. Cascade Ave., Colorado Springs, CO 80903-3279; 29,000.
Numismatic Society, Amer. (1858), Broadway at 155th St., N.Y., NY 10032; 2,369.
Nurses' Assn., Amer. (1896), 2420 Pershing Rd., Kansas City, MO 64108.
Nursing, Natl. League for (1952), 350 Hudson St., N.Y., NY 10014; 18,000.
Nutrition, Amer. Institute of (1928), 9650 Rockville Pike, Bethesda, MD 20814; 3,000.

ORT Federation, Amer. (Org. for Rehabilitation through Training) (1924), 817 Broadway, N.Y., NY 10019; 20,000.
Odd Fellows, Independent Order of (1819), 422 N. Trade St., Winston-Salem, NC 27101-2830; 453,612.
Old Crows, Assn. of (1964), 1000 N. Payne St., Alexandria, VA 22314-1696; 25,000.
Olympic Committee, U.S. (1921), 1750 E. Boulder St., Colorado Springs, CO 80909; 70 organizations.
Opthalmology, Amer. Academy of (1979), 655 Beach St., San Francisco, CA 94109; 16,250.
Optical Society of America (1916), 2010 Massachusetts Ave. NW, Wash., DC 20036; 12,200.
Optimist Intl. (1919), 4494 Lindell Blvd., St. Louis, MO 63108.
Optometric Assn., Amer. (1898), 243 N. Lindbergh Blvd., St. Louis, MO 63141; 28,000.
Organists, Amer. Guild of (1896), 475 Riverside Dr., Suite 1260, N.Y., NY 10115; 20,200.
Oriental Society, Amer. (1842), 329 Sterling Memorial Library, Yale Sta., New Haven, CT 06520; 1,440.
Ornithologists' Union, Amer. (1883), c/o National Museum of Natural History, Smithsonian, Wash., DC 20560; 5,000.
Osteopathic Assn., Amer. (1887), 212 E. Ohio St., Chicago, IL 60611; 23,292.
Ostomy Assn., United (1963), 36 Executive Park, Suite 120, Irving, CA 92714, 41,009.
Outlaw and Lawman History, Natl. Organization for (1974), 615-C N. 8th St., Killeen, TX 76541; 559.
Overeaters Anonymous (1960), World Service Office, 383 Van Ness Ave., #1601, Torrance, CA 90501; 152,000.

PTA (Natl. Congress of Parents and Teachers), Natl. (1897), 700 N. Rush St., Chicago, IL 60611; 6.8 mln.
Paper Industry, Technical Assn. of the Pulp and (1915), 15 Technology Pkwy. S., Norcross, GA 30092; 33,000.
Parametric Analysts, Intl. Soc. of (1979), P.O. Box 1056, Germantown, MD 20878; 600.
Parents Without Partners (1957), 8807 Colesville Rd., Silver Spring, MD 20910; 100,000.
Parkinson's Disease Foundation (1957), 650-170 W. 168th St., N.Y., NY 10032.
Parliamentarians, Natl. Assn. of (1930), 6601 Winchester, Kansas City, MO 64133-4600; 4,400.
Parliamentary Law, Intl. Organization of Professionals in (1975), 3611 Victoria Ave., Los Angeles, CA 90016; 250.
Pasta Assn., Natl. (1904), 2101 Wilson Blvd., Suite 920, Arlington, VA 22201.
Pathologists, Amer. Assn. of (1976), 9650 Rockville Pike, Bethesda, MD 20814; 2,000.
Pathology, Amer. Soc. for Investigative (1900), 9650 Rockville Pike, Bethesda, MD 20814-3993; 2,200.
Patton Historical Soc., George S. Jr. (1970), 3116 Thorn St., San Diego, CA 92104-4618.
Pearl Harbor History Associates (1983), P.O. Box 205, Sperryville, VA 22740-0205; 500.
PEN Amer. Center (1922), 568 Broadway, N.Y., NY 10012.
PEN Women, Natl. League of Amer. (1897), 1300 17th St. NW, Wash., DC 20036-1973; 5,000.
Pen Friends, Intl. (1967), Box 65, Brooklyn, NY 11229; 300,000.
Pension Actuaries, Amer. Society of (1966), 4350 N. Fairfax Dr., Ste. 820, Arlington, VA 22203; 3,000.
P.E.O. (Philanthropic Educational Organization) Sisterhood (1869), 3700 Grand Ave., Des Moines, IA 50312; 242,000.

Personnel Administration, Amer. Society for (1948), 606 N. Washington St., Alexandria, VA 22314; 40,000.
Petroleum Equipment Inst. (1951), 3739 E. 31st St., Tulsa, OK 74135; 1,200 member companies.
Petroleum Institute, Amer. (1919), 1220 L St. NW, Wash., DC 20005; 250 corporations.
Pharmaceutical Assn., Amer. (1852), 2215 Constitution Ave. NW, Wash., DC 20037; 40,000.
Phi Delta Kappa (1906), 8th & Union, Box 789, Bloomington, IN 47401-0789; 132,000.
Philatelic Pages & Panels, Amer. Soc. for (1984), 4116 Kilmer Ave., Allentown, PA 18104; 950.
Philatelic Society, Amer. (1886), 100 Oakwood Ave., P.O. Box 8000, State College, PA 16803; 57,000.
Philological Assn., Amer. (1869), Dept. of Classics, Fordham Univ., Bronx, NY 10458; 2,500.
Philosophical Assn., Amer. (1900), Univ. of Delaware, Newark, DE 19716; 8,500.
Philosophical Enquiry, Intl. Soc. For (1974), 277 Washington Blvd., Hudson, NY 12534-1322; 530.
Philosophical Society, Amer. (1743), 104 S. 5th St., Phila., PA 19106; 690.
Photogrammetry and Remote Sensing, Amer. Society of (1934), 5410 Grosvenor Ln., Ste. 210, Bethesda, MD 20814.
Photographers of America, Professional (1880), 1090 Executive Way, Des Plaines, IL 60018; 15,000.
Photographic Society of Amer. (1934), 3000 United Founders Blvd. #103, Oklahoma City, OK 73112.
Physical Therapy Assn., Amer. (1921), 1111 N. Fairfax St., Alexandria, VA 22314; 56,000.
Physicians, Amer. Academy of Family (1947), 8880 Ward Pkwy., Kansas City, MO 64114; 72,000.
Physics, Amer. Inst. of (1931), 335 E. 45th St., N.Y., NY 10017-3483.
Physiological Society, Amer. (1887), 9650 Rockville Pike, Bethesda, MD 20814; 7,000.
Pilgrim Society (1820), 75 Court St., Plymouth, MA 02360-3891; 600.
Pilot Intl. (1921), P.O. Box 4844, 244 College St., Macon, GA 31213-0599; 19,000.
Planetary Society (1980), 65 N. Catalina Ave., Pasadena, CA 91106; 100,000.
Planned Parenthood Federation of America (1916), 810 Seventh Ave., N.Y., NY 10019; 187 affiliates.
Plastic Modelers Society, Intl. (1963), P.O. Box 6138, Warner Robins, GA 31095-6138; 3,750.
Plastics Industry, Society of (1937), 1275 K St. NW, Suite 400, Washington, DC 20005; 2,200 cos.
Platform Assn., Intl. (1831), Box 250, Winnetka, IL 60093.
Poetry Day Committee, Natl. (1947), 1110 N. Venetian Dr., Miami, FL 33139-1019; 17,500.
Poetry Society of America (1910), 15 Gramercy Park, N.Y., NY 10003; 1,700.
Poets, Academy of Amer. (1934), 584 Broadway, N.Y., NY 10024; 2,220.
Police, Internatl. Assn. of Chiefs of (1893), 1110 N. Glebe Rd., Suite 200, Arlington, VA 22201; 13,500.
Polish Army Veterans Assn. of America (1921), 155 Noble St., Brooklyn, NY 11222; 3,500.
Polish Cultural Society of America (1940), P.O. Box 31, Wall Street, N.Y., NY 10005; 104,001.
Political Items Collectors, Amer. (1945), P.O. Box 340339, San Antonio, TX 78234; 3,100.
Political Science, Academy of (1880), 475 Riverside Dr., Suite 1274, N.Y., NY 10115-0012; 8,500.
Political Science Assn., Amer. (1903), 1527 New Hampshire Ave. NW, Wash., DC 20036; 12,152.
Political & Social Science, Amer. Academy of (1889), 3937 Chestnut St., Phila., PA 19104; 4,000.
Pollution Control, Internatl. Assn. for (1970), 444 N. Capital St. NW, Wash. DC 20001.
Polo Assn., U.S. (1890), 4059 Iron Works Pike, Lexington, KY, 40511; 3,000.
Population Assn. of America (1931), 1722 N. St. NW, Washington, DC 20036; 2,600.
Portuguese-American Federation, Inc. (1965), Linden Pl., 500 Hope St., Bristol, RI 02809; 250.
Portuguese Continental Union of the U.S.A. (1925), 899 Boylston St., Boston, MA 02115.
Postmasters of the U.S., Natl. Assn. of (1898), 8 Herbert St., Arlington, VA 22305; 43,000.
Postmasters of the U.S., Natl. League of (1904), 1023 N. Royal St., Alexandria, VA 22314; 21,874.
Poultry Science Assn. (1921), 309 W. Clark St., Champaign, IL 61820.
Power Boat Assn., Amer. (1903), 17640 E. Nine Mile Rd., P.O. Box 377, E. Detroit, MI 48021.
Precancel Collectors, Natl. Assn. of (1950), 5121 Park Blvd., Wildwood, NJ 08260-0121; 7,600.
Press, Associated (1848), 50 Rockefeller Plaza, N.Y., NY 10020; 1,558 newspapers & 6,000 broadcast stations.
Press Club, Natl. (1908), 529 14th St. NW, Wash., DC 20045.
Press Intl., United (1907), 1400 I St. NW, Wash. DC 20005.
Press and Radio Club (1948), P.O. Box 70023, Montgomery, AL 36107; 741.
Printing Industries of America (1887), 100 Dangerfield Rd., Alexandria, VA 22314; 14,000.
Prisoners of War, Amer. Ex- (1942), 3201 E. Pioneer Pkwy., #40, Arlington, TX 76010-5396; 32,000.
Procrastinators Club of America (1956), Box 712, Bryn Athyn, PA 19009; 10,000.
Production and Inventory Control Soc., American, 500 W. Annandale Rd., Falls Church, VA 22046-4274; 65,000.
Psychiatric Assn., Amer. (1844), 1400 K St. NW, Wash., DC 20005; 37,380.
Psychical Research, Amer. Society for (1907), 5 W. 73d St., N.Y., NY 10023; 2,000.
Psychoanalytic Assn., Amer. (1911), 309 E. 49th St., N.Y., NY 10017; 3,000.
Psychological Assn., Amer. (1892), 750 1st St. NE, Washington, DC 20002-4242; 119,000.
Psychological Assn. for Psychoanalysis, Natl. (1948), 150 W. 13th St., N.Y., NY 10011-7891; 353.
Psychological Minorities, Society for the Aid of (1953), 42-25 Hampton St., Elmhurst, NY 11373; 530.
Psoriasis Foundation, Natl (1968), 6443 SW Beaverton Hwy., #210, Portland, OR 97221; 14,000.
Public Administration, Amer. Soc. for (1939), 1120 G St. NW, Wash, DC 20005; 14,800.
Public Health Assn., World Fed. of (1967), 1015 15th St. NW, Wash., DC 20005; 48 natl. assn.
Public Relations Soc. of Amer. (1947), 33 Irving Pl., N.Y., NY 10003-2376; 15,462.
Publishers, Assn. of Amer. (1970), 220 E. 23rd St., N.Y., NY 10010; 230 cos.
Puppeteers of Amer. (1937), 5 Cricklewood Path, Pasadena, CA 91107; 2,200.
Puzzle Buffs Intl. (1978), 1772 State Road, Cuyahoga Falls, OH 44223; 39,000.

Quality Control, Amer. Society for (1946), 611 E. Wisconsin Ave., Milwaukee, WI 53201-3005, 90,000.

Rabbis, Central Conference of Amer. (1889), 192 Lexington Ave., N.Y., NY 10016; 1,540.
Racial Equality, Congress of (CORE) (1942), 1457 Flatbush Ave., Brooklyn, NY 11210; 100,000.
Radio, Natl. Assn. of Business and Educational (1965), 1501 Duke St., Alexandria, VA 22314; 3,000.
Radio Union, Intl. Amateur (1925), P.O. Box AAA, Newington, CT 06111; 126 societies.
Radio and TV Society, Intl. (1939), 420 Lexington Ave., Ste. 1714, N.Y., NY 10170; 1,600.
Radio Relay League, Amer. (1914), 225 Main St., Newington, CT 06111; 160,000.
Railway Historical Society, Natl. (1935), P.O. Box 58153, Phila., PA 19102-8153; 19,000+.
Railway Progress Institute (1908), 700 N. Fairfax St., Suite 601, Alexandria, VA 22314-2098; 104 companies.
Range Management, Society for (1948), 1839 York Street, Denver, CO 80206; 5,400.
Reading Assn., Intl. (1956), P.O. Box 8139, 800 Barksdale Rd., Newark, DE 19714-8139; 93,000.
Real Estate Institute, Intl. (1975), 8383 E. Evans Rd., Scottsdale, AZ 85260-3614; 4,500.
Rebekah Assemblies, Intl. Assn. of (1916), 422 N. Trade, Winston-Salem, NC 27101; 182,158.
Reconciliation, Fellowship of (1915), 523 N. Broadway, Nyack, NY 10960; 10,000.
Records Managers & Administrators, Assn. of (1975), 4200 Somerset Dr., Suite 215, Prairie Village, KS 66208; 11,000.
Recreation and Park Assn., Natl. (1965), 2775 S. Quincy St., Ste. 300, Arlington, VA 22206-2204; 22,000+.
Recycling Coalition, Natl., 1101 30th St. NW, Ste. 305, Wash., DC 20007.
Red Cross, American (1881), 17th & D Sts. NW, Wash., DC 20006; 1.5 mln. volunteers.
Red Men, Improved Order of (1765), 4521 Speight Ave., Waco, TX, 76711-1708; 29,000.
Redwoods League, Save-the- (1918), 114 Sansome St., Rm. 605, San Francisco, CA 94104; 45,000.
Rehabilitation Assn., Natl. (1925), 1910 Association Dr., Ste. 205, Reston, VA 22091.
Religion, Amer. Academy of (1909), 501 Hall of Languages, Syracuse Univ., Syracuse, NY 13244-1170; 5,600.
Religion Foundation, Freedom from (1978), P.O. Box 750, Madison, WI 53701; 3,100.

Renaissance Society of America (1954), 24 W. 12th St., N.Y., NY 10011; 2,411.

Republican National Committee (1856), 310 1st Street SE, Washington, DC 20003-1801.

Reserve Officers Assn. of the U.S. (1922), One Constitution Ave., NE, Wash., DC 20002; 123,000.

Restaurant Assn., Natl. (1919), 1200 17th St. NW, Wash., DC 20036; 20,000.

Retail Federation, Natl. (1918), 100 West 31st St., N.Y., NY 10001; 50,000.

Retired Credit Union People, Natl. Assn. for (1978), P.O. Box 391, 5910 Mineral Pt. Rd., Madison, WI 53705; 81,180.

Retired Federal Employees, Natl. Assn. of (1921), 1533 New Hampshire Ave. NW, Wash., DC 20036; 500,000.

Retired Officers Assn. (1929), 201 N. Washington St., Alexandria, VA 22314-2529; 380,000.

Retired Persons, Amer. Assn. of (1958), 1909 K St. NW, Wash., DC 20049; 32 mln.

Retired Teachers Assn., Natl. (1947), 1909 K St. NW, Wash., DC 20049, 540,000.

Revolver Assn., U.S. (1900), 96 W. Union St., Ashland, MA 01721; 1,400.

Reye's Syndrome Foundation, Natl. (1974), 426 N. Lewis, Bryan, OH 43506; 5,000+.

Richard III Society (1969), P.O. Box 13787, New Orleans, LA 70185; 700.

Rifle Assn., Natl. (1871), 1600 Rhode Island Ave. NW, Wash., DC 20036; 3.17 mln.

Road & Transportation Builders' Assn., Amer. (1902), 501 School St. SW, Wash., DC 20024-2713; 3,600.

Rocky Horror Picture Show Preservation Soc. of Terra (1993), One Caddo Ct., Kenner, LA 70065-3920.

Rodeo Cowboys Assn., Professional (1936), 101 Pro Rodeo Dr., Colorado Springs, CO 80919; 8,983.

Roller Skating, U.S. Amateur Confederation of (1937), 4730 South St., P.O. Box 6579, Lincoln, NE 68506; 21,000.

Rose Society, Amer. (1892), 8877 Jefferson Paige Rd., Shreveport, LA 71119; 38,000.

Rotary Intl. (1905), 1560 Sherman Ave., Evanston, IL 60201.

Running and Fitness Assn., Amer. (1968), 9310 Old Georgetown Rd., Bethesda, MD 20814; 18,000.

Ruritan Natl. (1928), Ruritan Natl. Rd., Dublin, VA 24084.

Safety and Fairness Everywhere, Natl. Assn. Taunting (1980), P.O. Box 5743WA, Montecito, CA 93150; 12,000.

Safety Council, Natl. (1913), 444 N. Michigan Ave., Chicago, IL 60611; 12,500.

Sailors, Tin Can (1976), P.O. Box 100, Somerset, MA 02726; 17,000.

Sailors Assn., Destroyer-Escort (1975), 352 W. Story Rd., Ocoee, FL 34761, 12,000.

St. Andrew, The Brotherhood of (1883), 1109 Merchant St., P.O. Box 632, Ambridge, PA 15003; 5,000.

St. Paul, Natl. Guild of (1937), 601 Hill 'n Dale, Lexington, KY 40503; 13,652.

Salespersons, Natl. Assn. of Professional (1970), P.O. Box 76461, Atlanta, GA 30358; 35,000.

Salt Institute (1914), 700 N. Fairfax St., Ste. 600, Alexandria, VA, 22314-2040; 23 companies.

Sane Nuclear Policy, Committee for a (1957), 711 G St. SE, Wash., DC 20003; 130,000.

Savings Institutions, Natl. Council of (1983), 1101 15th St. NW, Wash., DC 20005; 550 members.

School Administrators, Amer. Assn. of (1865), 1801 N. Moore St., Arlington, VA 22209; 18,000.

School Boards Assn., Natl. (1940), 1680 Duke St., Alexandria, VA 22314.

School Counselor Assn., Amer. (1953), 5999 Stevenson Ave., Alexandria, VA 22304; 13,000.

Schools of Art, Natl. Assn. of (also: School of Art and Design, School of Dance, Music, and Theater) (1944), 11250 Roger Bacon Dr., Reston, VA 22090; 161.

Schools & Colleges, Amer. Council on (1927), 13014 Dale Mabry Hwy., Ste. 270-B, Tampa, FL 33180-2808; 400+.

Science, Amer. Assn. for the Advancement of (1848), 1333 H St. NW, Wash., DC 20005; 135,000.

Science Fiction Society, World (1939), P.O. Box 1270, Kendall Sq. Sta., Cambridge, MA 02142; 5,000.

Science Service (1921), 1719 N St. NW, Wash., DC 20036.

Science Teachers Assn., Natl. (1985), 1742 Connecticut Ave. NW, Wash., DC 20009; 49,000.

Science Writers, Natl. Assn. of (1934), P.O. Box 294, Greenlawn, NY 11740; 1,650.

Sciences, Natl. Academy of (1863), 2101 Constitution Ave. NW, Wash., DC 20418; 1,936.

Scrabble Assn., Natl. (1978), Box 700, Greenport, NY 11944; 10,000.

Screen Actors Guild (1933), 7065 Hollywood Blvd., Hollywood, CA 90028; 78,000.

Screen Printing Assn. Intl. (1948), 10015 Main St., Fairfax, VA 22031.

Sculpture Soc., Natl. (1893), 1177 Ave. of the Americas, N.Y., NY 10036; 3,600.

2d Air Division Assn. (1947), 1 Jeffrey's Neck Rd., Ipswich, MA 01938; 7,852.

Secondary School Principals, Natl. Assn. of (1916), 1904 Association Dr., Reston, VA 22091; 42,000.

Secretaries Intl., Professional (1942), P.O. Box 20404, Kansas City, MO 64195-0404; 40,000.

Secretaries, Natl. Assn. of Legal (1920), 2250 E 73, Ste. 550, Tulsa, OK 74136-6864; 16,000.

Securities Industry Assn. (1972), 120 Broadway, N.Y., NY 10271; 600 firms.

Separation of Church & State, Americans United for (1947), 8120 Fenton St., Silver Spring, MD 20910; 50,000.

Sertoma Internatl. (1912), 1912 E. Meyer Blvd., Kansas City, MO 64132; 29,000.

Sex Information & Education Council of the U.S. (SIECUS) (1964), 130 W. 42 St., Ste. 2500, N.Y., NY 10036; 2,000+.

Sharkhunters Intl. (1983), P.O. Box 1539, Hernanado, FL 32642; 2,700.

Shipbuilders Council of America (1921), 1110 Vermont Ave. NW, Wash., DC 20005; 50 organizations.

Ships-in-Bottles Assn. of Amer. (1983), P.O. Box 180550, Coronado, CA 92178; 400.

Shore & Beach Preservation Assn., Amer. (1926), P.O. Box 279, Middletown, CA 95461; 900.

Shrine, Ancient Arabic Order of the Nobles of the Mystic (1872), 2900 Rocky Pt. Dr., Tampa, FL 33607; 799,000.

Sierra Club (1892), 730 Polk St., San Francisco, CA 94109.

Skeet Shooting Assn., Natl. (1946), P.O. Box 680007, San Antonio, TX 78268; 15,800.

Ski Assn., U.S. (1904), P.O. Box 100, Park City, UT 84060.

Small Business, Amer. Federation of (1938), 18200 Sherman St., Lansing, IL 60438-3104.

Small Business United, Natl. (1986), 1155 15th St. NW, Suite 710, Wash., DC 20005; 65,000.

Smoking & Health, Natl. Clearinghouse for (1965), Center for Disease Control, 1600 Clifton Road NE, Atlanta, GA 30333.

Soccer Federation, U.S. (1913), 1801-1811 S. Prairie Ave., Chicago, IL 60616; 2 mln.

Social Sciences, Natl. Institute of (1865), 444 Madison Ave., Ste. 2901, N.Y., NY 10022; 300.

Social Work Education, Council on (1952), 1600 Duke Street, Alexandria, VA 22314; 2,500.

Social Workers, Natl. Assn. of (1955), 750 First St. NE, Ste. 700, Washington, DC 20002-4241; 138,000.

Sociological Assn., Amer. (1905), 1722 N St. NW, Wash., DC 20036; 13,000.

Softball Association, Amateur (1933), 2801 N.E. 50th St., Oklahoma City, OK 73111; 4.5 mln.

Soft Drink Assn., Natl. (1921), 1101 16th St. NW, Wash., DC 20036; 1,000.

Soil & Water Conservation Society of America (1945), 7515 N.E. Ankeny Rd., Ankeny, IA 50021-9764; 11,000.

Soil Science Society of America (1936), 677 S. Segoe Rd., Madison, WI 53711; 6,018.

Soldier's, Sailor's and Airmen's Club (1919), 283 Lexington Ave., N.Y., NY 10016.

Songwriters Guild of America, The (1931), 276 Fifth Ave., Ste. 306, N.Y., NY 10001; 3,500.

Sons of the Amer. Legion (1932), Box 1055, Indianapolis, IN 46206; 147,893.

Sons of the American Revolution, Natl. Society of (1889), 1000 S. 4th, Louisville, KY 40203; 27,000.

Sons of Confederate Veterans (1896), Southern Station, Box 5164, Hattiesburg, MS 39406-5164; 13,000.

Sons of the Desert (1965), P.O. Box 8341, Universal City, CA 91608; 10,000.

Sons of Italy in America, Order (1905), 219 E. St., NE, Wash. DC 20002; 500,000.

Sons of Norway (1895), 1455 W. Lake St., Minneapolis, MN 55408; 76,030.

Sons of Poland, Assn. of the (1903), 591 Summit Ave., Rm. 702, Jersey City, NJ 07306; 10,000.

Sons of the Republic of Texas, The (1922), 5942 Abrams Rd., #222, Dallas, TX 75231; 2,400.

Sons of St. Patrick, Society of the Friendly (1784), 80 Wall St., N.Y., NY 10005; 1,500.

Sons of Sherman's March to the Sea (1966), 1725 Farmers Ave., Tempe, AZ 85281-6533; 705.

Sons of Union Veterans of the Civil War (1881), 411 Bartlett St., Lansing, MI 48915; 2,700.

Soroptimist Intl. of the Americas (1921), 1616 Walnut St., Phila., PA 19103; 50,000.

Southern Christian Leadership Conference (1957), 334 Auburn Ave. NE, Atlanta, GA 30303; 1 mln.

Space Education Assoc., U.S. (1973), P.O. Box 249, Rheems, PA 17570-0249; 1,500.
Special Olympics Intl. (1968), 1350 New York Ave. NW, Ste. 500, Washington, DC 20005.
Speech Communication Assn. (1914), 5105 Backlick Rd., Annandale, VA 22003; 6,800.
Speech-Language-Hearing Assn., Amer. (1925), 10801 Rockville Pike, Rockville, MD 20852.
Speedskating Union of the U.S., Amateur (1927), 1033 Shady Lane, Glen Ellyn, IL 60137; 3,000.
Speleological Society, Natl. (1941), 2813 Cave Ave., Huntsville, AL 35810; 11,000.
Spiritual Awareness, Assn. for (1984), P.O. Box 41, Clifton Hill, MO 65244; 1,500.
Sports Car Club of America (1944), 9033 E. Eastern Pl., Englewood, CO 80112; 50,000+.
Sports Club, Indoor (1930), 1145 Highland St., Napoleon, OH 43545; 950.
Sportscasters Assn., Amer. (1980), 5 Beekman St., N.Y., NY 10038; 500+.
State Governments, Council of (1933), P.O. Box 11910, Lexington, KY 40517; 50 states, 4 territories.
State & Local History, Amer. Assn. for (1940), 530 Church St., Ste. 600, Nashville, TN 37219; 5,600.
Statistical Assn., Amer. (1839), 1429 Duke St., Alexandria, VA 22314-3402; 15,000.
Steamship Historical Society of America (1935), 300 Ray Dr., Ste. 4, Providence, RI 02906; 3,500.
Steel Construction, Amer. Institute of (1921), 1 E. Wacker Dr., Ste. 3100, Chicago, IL 60601-2001; 2,770.
Stock Car Auto Racing, Natl. Assn. for (NASCAR) (1947), P.O. Box 2875, Daytona Beach, FL 32120-2875; 45,000.
Stock Exchange, Amer. (1911), 86 Trinity Pl., N.Y., NY 10006; 871.
Stock Exchange, N.Y. (1792), 11 Wall St., N.Y., NY 10005.
Stock Exchange, Phila. (1790), 1900 Market St., Phila., PA 19103; 505.
Student Councils, Natl. Assn. of (1931), 1904 Association Dr., Reston, VA 22091; 9,000 schools.
Stuttering Project, Natl. (1977), 2151 Irving St., Ste. 208, San Francisco, CA 94122-1609; 4,000.
Sudden Infant Death Syndrome Alliance, Natl. (1987), 10500 Little Patuxent Pkwy., Ste. 420, Columbia, MD 21044.
Sugar Brokers Assn., Natl. (1903), 1 World Trade Center, N.Y., NY 10047; 100.
Sunbathing Assn., Amer. (1931), 1703 N. Main St., Kissimmee, FL 34744; 40,000.
Surfing Committee, U.S. (1960), Box 545921, Surfhouse, Surfside, FL 33154-5492; 5,876,182.
Surgeons, Amer. College of (1913), 55 E. Erie St., Chicago IL 60611-2797; 52,127.
Surgeons of the U.S., Assn. of Military (1891), 9320 Old Georgetown Rd., Bethesda, MD 20814; 14,500.
Surveying & Mapping, Amer. Congress on (1941), 5410 Grosvenor Ln., Bethesda, MD 20814-2122; 9,500.
Symphony Orchestra League, Amer. (1942), 777 14th St. NW, Ste. 500, Wash., DC 20005; 860 orchestras.
Systems Management, Assn. for (1947), 1433 West Bagley Rd., Berea, OH 44017; 8,000.

Table Tennis Assn., U.S. (1933), One Olympic Plaza, Colorado Springs, CO 80909; 7,000.
Tailhook Assn., The (1957), P.O. Box 40, Bonita, CA 91908.
Tax Accountants, Natl. Assn. of Enrolled Federal (1960), P.O. Box 59-009, Chicago, IL 60659-0009; 450.
Tax Administrators, Federation of (1937), 444 N. Capitol St. NW, Wash., DC 20001.
Tax Assn., Natl.–Tax Institute of America (1907), 5310 E. Main St., Suite 104, Columbus, OH 43213; 3,570.
Tax Foundation, Inc. (1937), 1250 H St. NW, Ste. 750, Washington, DC 20005.
Taxpayers Union, Natl. (1969), 325 Pennsylvania Ave. SE, Wash., DC 20003; 200,000.
Tea Assn. of the U.S.A. (1899), 230 Park Ave., N.Y., NY 10169; 140.
Teachers of English, Natl. Council of (1911), 1111 Kenyon Rd., Urbana, IL 61801; 125,000.
Teachers of English to Speakers of Other Languages (1969), 1600 Cameron St., Suite 300, Alexandria, VA 22314.
Teachers of French, Amer. Assn. of (1927), 57 E. Armory Ave., Champaign, IL 61820; 11,000.
Teachers of Mathematics, Natl. Council of (1920), 1906 Association Dr., Reston, VA 22091; 91,740.
Teachers of Singing, Natl. Assn. of (1944), 2800 Univ. Blvd. N, J.U. Sta., Jacksonville, FL 32211; 5,000.
Teachers of Spanish & Portuguese, Amer. Assn. of (1917), P.O. Box 6349, 218 Lee Hall, MSU., MS 39762-6349.
Technicians Assn., Market (1973), 71 Broadway, 2nd Fl., N.Y., NY 10006; 600.
Telephone Pioneers of Amer. (1911), 930 15th St., 12th Fl., Denver, CO 80202; 820,000.
Television Arts & Sciences, Natl. Academy of (1947), 111 W. 57th St., Suite 1020, N.Y., NY 10019; 12,000.
Television Bureau of Advertising (1954), 477 Madison Ave., N.Y., NY 10022.
Television & Radio Artists, Amer. Federation of (1937), 1350 Ave. of the Americas, N.Y., NY 10019; 66,000.
Telluride Assn. (1911), 217 West Ave., Ithaca, NY 14850.
Tennis Assn., U.S. (1881), 1212 Ave. of Americas, N.Y., NY 10036.
Terraplane Club, Hudson-Essex (1959), 100 E. Cross St., Ypsilanti, MI 48198; 3,200.
Tesla Memorial Soc., Inc. (1979), 453 Martin Rd., Buffalo, NY 14218; 1,900.
Testing & Materials, Amer. Society for (1898), 1916 Race St., Phila., PA 19103; 32,000.
Textile Manufacturers Institute, Amer. (1949), 1801 K St. NW, Suite 900, Wash., DC 20006.
Theodore Roosevelt Assn. (1919), P.O. Box 719, Oyster Bay, NY 11771; 2,200.
Theological Schools in the U.S. and Canada, Assn. of (1918), 10 Summit Park Dr., Pittsburgh, PA 15275-1103.
Theosophical Society in America, The (1886), 1926 N. Main St., Wheaton, IL 60189-0270; 5,000.
Thoreau Society (1941), 156 Belknap St., Concord, MA 01742; 1,500.
Thoroughbred Racing Assns. (1942), 420 Fair Hill Dr., Ste. 1, Elkton, MD 21921; 53 racing associations.
Titanic Historical Society (1963), P.O. Box 51053, Indian Orchard, MA 01151-0053; 5,100.
Toastmasters Intl. (1924), 23182 Arroyo Vista, Rancho Santa Margarita, CA 92688.
Topical Assn., Amer. (1949), P.O. Box 630, Johnstown, PA 15907; 7,000.
Toy Manufacturers of America (1916), 200 Fifth Ave., N.Y., NY 10010; 240.
Track & Field, USA (1979), P.O. Box 120, Indianapolis, IN 46206; 100,000+.
Transit Assn., Amer. Public (1974), 1201 New York Ave. NW, Wash., DC 20005; 11,000 organizations.
Translators Assn., Amer. (1960), 1735 Jefferson Davis Hwy., #903, Arlington, VA 22202-3413; 4,850.
Trapshooting Assn., Amateur (1923), 601 W. National Rd., Vandalia, OH 45377; 100,000+.
Travel Agents, Amer. Society of (1936), 1101 King St., Alexandria, VA 22314; 20,000.
Travelers Protective Assn. of America (1890), 3755 Lindell Blvd., St. Louis, MO 63108; 161,866.
Trilateral Commission, The (1973), 345 E. 46th St., N.Y., NY 10017; 311.
Truck Historical Soc., Amer. (1971), 300 Office Park Dr., Ste. 120, Birmingham, AL 35223; 15,000+.
Trucking Assn., Amer. (1933), 2200 Mill Rd., Alexandria, VA 22314-4677; 4,000 cos.
True Sisters, United Order (1846), 212 Fifth Ave., N.Y., NY 10010; 10,000.
T.S. Eliot Soc. (1980), 5007 Waterman Blvd., St. Louis. MO 63108; 200.
Tuberous Sclerosis Assn. of Amer. (1970), P.O. Box 44, Rockland, MA 02370; 2,500.

UFOs, Natl. Investigation Committee on (1967), 14617 Victory Blvd., Suite 4, Van Nuys, CA 91411.
UNICEF, U.S. Committee for (1947), 333 E. 38th St., N.Y., NY 10016.
USO (United Service Organizations) (1941), 601 Indiana Ave., NW, Wash., DC 20004.
Underwriters, Amer. Soc. of Chartered Life (1927), 270 Bryn Mawr Ave., Bryn Mawr, PA 19010; 30,000.
Underwriters, Soc. of Chartered Property and Casualty (1944), Kahler Hall, 720 Providence Rd., Malvern, PA 19355.
United Nations Assn. of the U.S.A. (1923, as League of Nations Assn.), 485 Fifth Ave., N.Y., NY 10017; 29,000.
United Way of America (1918), 801 N. Fairfax St., Alexandria, VA 22309; 1,200.
Universities, Assn. of Amer. (1914), One Dupont Circle, Suite 730, Wash., DC 20036; 59 institutions.
Universities & Colleges, Assn. of Governing Bds. of (1921), One Dupont Circle NW, Suite 400, Wash., DC 20036.
University Continuing Education Assn., Natl. (1915), One Dupont Circle, Ste. 615, Wash., DC 20036; 2,000.
University Extension Assn., Natl. (1915), One Dupont Circle NW, Suite 400, Wash., DC 20036; 1,100.
University Foundation, Intl. (1973), 1301 S. Noland Rd., Independence, MO 64055; 67,780.

University Professors, Amer. Assn. of (1915), 1012 14th St. NW, Suite 500, Wash., DC 20005; 41,000.
University Women, Amer. Assn. of (1881), 1111 16th St. NW, Wash., DC 20036.
Urban Coalition, Natl. (1967), 1120 G St. NW, Suite 900, Wash., DC 20005; 42 affiliates.
Urban League, Natl. (1910), 500 E. 62d St., N.Y., NY 10020.
Useless Skills, Institute of Totally (1987), Box 181, Temple, NH 03084; 424.
Utility Commissioners, Natl. Assn. of Regulatory (1889), 1102 Interstate Commerce Commission Bldg., 12th & Constitution Ave. NW, Wash., DC 20044-0684.

Vampire Research Center (1972), P.O. Box 252, Elmhurst, NY 11373; 650.
Variety Clubs Intl. (1928), 1560 Bdway., N.Y., NY 10036.
VASA Order of America (1896), 65 Bryant Rd., Cranston, R.I. 02910; 30,000.
Ventriloquists, No. American Assn. of (1944), Box 420, Littleton, CO 80160; 1,475.
Veterans Assn., Blinded (1958), 477 H St. NW, Wash., DC 20001; 7,500.
Veterans of Foreign Wars of the U.S. (1899) & Ladies Auxiliary (1914), 406 W. 34th St., Kansas City, MO 64111.
Veterans of the Vietnam War (1980), 760 Jumper Rd., Wilkes-Barre, PA 18702-8033; 30,000.
Veterans of World War I (1958), 941 N. Capitol St. NE, Room 1201-C, Wash., DC 20002-4234; 52,000.
Veterans of WWII, U.S. Submarine (1955), 6523 San Joaquin St., Sacramento, CA 95820; 8,000.
Veterinary Medical Assn., Amer. (1863), 1931 N. Meacham Rd., Schaumburg, IL 60173; 53,512.
Victorian Society in America (1965), 219 S. Sixth St., Phila., PA 19106; 2,300.
Violet Soc. of Amer., African (1946), P.O. Box 3609, Beaumont, TX 77704; 15,000.
Virgil Fox Society, The (1977), 88 Chestnut St., Brooklyn, NY 11208; 450+.
Volleyball Assn., U.S. (1928), 3595 E. Fountain Blvd., Ste. I-2, Colorado Springs, CO 80910-1740; 78,911.

Walking Society, American (1980), Viana House, Box 1315, Beverly Hills, CA 90213.
War Mothers, Amer. (1917), 2615 Woodley Pl. NW, Wash., DC 20008; 2,000.
Warrant and Warrant Officers' Assn., Chief, U.S. Coast Guard (1929), c/o Fort McNair Yacht Basin, 200 V Street, SW, Wash., DC 20024; 3,346.
Watch & Clock Collectors, Natl. Assn. of (1943), 514 Poplar St., Columbia, PA 17512; 35,000.
Watercolor Soc., American (1867), 47 Fifth Ave., N.Y., NY 10003; 506.
Water Environment Federation (1928), 601 Wythe St., Alexandria, VA 22314; 40,000.
Water Pollution Control Admin., Assn. of State and Interstate (1961), 750 First St. NE, Ste. 910, Wash., DC 20001.
Water Pollution Control Federation (1928), 601 Wythe St., Alexandria, VA 22314-1994; 32,000.
Water Resources Assn., Amer. (1964), 5410 Grosvenor Ln., Suite 220, Bethesda, MD 20814-2192; 4,000.
Water Ski Assn., Amer. (1939), 799 Overlook Dr. SE, Winter Haven, FL 33884.
Water Assn., Natl. Ground (1948), 6375 Riverside Drive, Dublin, OH 43017; 24,000.
Water Works Assn., Amer. (1881), 6666 W. Quincy Ave., Denver, CO 80235; 52,000.
Welding Society, Amer. (1919), 550 NW LeJeune Rd., Miami, FL 33126; 41,000.
Wheelchair Athletic Assn., Natl. (1956), 3595 E. Fountain Blvd., Suite L-1, Colorado Springs, CO 80918; 1,500.
Widows, Society of Military (1968), 5535 Hemstead Way, Springfield, VA 22151; 2,000.
Wilderness Society (1935), 900 17th St. NW, Wash., DC 20006; 350,000.
Wildflower Research Center, Natl. (1982), 2600 FM 973 N., Austin, TX 78725-4201; 16,000.
Wildlife, Defenders of (1947), 1244 19th St. NW, Wash., DC 20036; 80,000.
Wildlife Federation, Natl. (1936), 1400 16th St. NW, Wash., DC 20036-2266; 5.8 mln.
Wildlife Fund, World (1961), 1250 24th St. NW, Wash., DC 20037; 1.2 mln.
Wildlife Management Institute (1911), 1101 14th St., Suite 725, NW, Wash., DC 20005.
William Penn Assn. (1886), 709 Brighton Rd., Pittsburgh, PA 15233; 90,000.
Wireless Pioneers, Society of (1968), P.O. Box 86, Geyserville, CA 85441; 5,200.
Wizard of Oz Club, Intl. (1957), Box 95, Kinderhook, IL 62345; 3,000.
Women, Natl. Assn. of Bank (1920), 500 No. Michigan Ave., Suite 1400, Chicago, IL 60611; 30,000.
Women, Natl. Organization for (NOW) (1966), 1000 16th St. NW, Ste. 700, Wash., DC 20036; 250,000.
Women Artists, Natl. Assn. of (1889), 41 Union Sq., N.Y., NY 10003; 725.
Women Engineers, Society of (1950), 345 E. 47th St., N.Y., NY 10017; 16,000.
Women for America, Concerned (1979), 370 L'Enfant Promenade SW, #800, Washington, DC 20024; 600,000.
Women in Communications (1908), 2101 Wilson Blvd., Ste. 417, Arlington, VA 22201; 11,000.
Women in Radio and TV, Inc. (1951), 1101 Connecticut Ave. NW, #700, Washington, DC 20036; 2,500.
Women Intl., Financial (1921), 500 N. Michigan Ave., Ste. 1400, Chicago, IL 60611; 35,000.
Women Strike for Peace (1961), 110 Maryland Ave. NE, Ste. 302, Washington, DC 20002; 10,000.
Women of the U.S., Natl. Council of (1888), 777 U.N. Plaza, N.Y., NY 10017; 500.
Women Voters of the U.S., League of (1920), 1730 M St. NW, Wash., DC 20036; 120,000.
Women World War Veterans (1919), 237 Madison Ave., N.Y., NY 10016; 35,000.
Women's Army Corps Veterans Assn. (1947), Hwy. 21, Anniston, AL 36206; 3,500.
Women's Association, American Business (1949), 9100 Ward Parkway, P.O. Box 8728, Kansas City, MO 64114.
Women's Christian Temperance Union, Natl. (1874), 1730 Chicago Ave., Evanston, IL 60201; 40,000.
Women's Clubs, General Federation of (1890), 1734 N St. NW, Wash. DC, 20036-2990; 350,000 U.S.
Women's Clubs, Natl. Federation of Business & Professional (1919), 2012 Massachusetts Ave. NW, Wash., DC 20036.
Women's Intl. League for Peace & Freedom (1915), 1213 Race St., Phila., PA 19107; 50,000.
Women's Legal Defense Fund (1971), 1875 Connecticut Ave. NW, Suite 710, Washington, DC 20009; 2,500.
Women's Overseas Service League (1921), P.O. Box 39058, Friendship Station, Washington, DC 20016; 1,164.
Woodmen of America, Modern (1883), 1701 1st Ave., Rock Island, IL 61201; 704,833.
Woodmen of the World Life Insurance Soc. (1890), 1700 Farnam St., Omaha, NE 68102; 980,000.
Workmen's Circle (1900), 45 E. 33d St., N.Y., NY 10016.
World Federalist Assn. (1975), 418 7th St. SE, Washington, DC 20003; 10,000.
World Future Society (1966), 7910 Woodmont Ave., Ste. 450, Bethesda, MD 20814; 30,000.
World Learning Inc. (1932), Kipling Rd., P.O. Box 676, Brattleboro, VT 05302-0676; 60,000.
World Peace, Intl Assn. of Educators for (1969), P.O. Box 3282, Mastin Lake Sta., Huntsville, AL 35810-0282; 21,500.
World's Fair Collectors Soc. (1968), P.O. Box 20806, Sarasota, FL 34276-3806; 540.
Writers Guild of America, West (1933), 8955 Beverly Blvd., W. Hollywood, CA 90048; 7,500+.

Yachting Assn., Southern California (1921), 1086 Peninsula St., Ventura, CA 93001; 20,000 families.
Young America's Foundation (1971), 110 Elden St., Herndon, VA 22070.
Young Men's Christian Assns. of the U.S.A. (1851), 101 N. Wacker Dr., Chicago, IL 60606; 13 mln.
YM-YMHAs of Greater New York, Associated (1957), 130 E. 59th St., N.Y., NY 10020; 55,100.
Young Women's Christian Assn. of the U.S.A. (1906), 726 Broadway, N.Y., NY 10003; 1.6 mln.
Youth Hostels, American (1934), P.O. Box 37613, Wash., DC 20013-7613; 200,000.

Zero Population Growth (1968), 1400 16th St. NW, Suite 320, Wash., DC 20036; 50,000.
Zionist Organization of America (1897), 4 E. 34th St., N.Y., NY 10016; 110,000.
Zoological Parks & Aquariums, Amer. Assn. of (1924), 7970-D Old Georgetown Rd., Bethesda, MD 20814-2493; 6,300.
Zoologists, Amer. Society of (1902), 401 N. Michigan Ave., Chicago, IL 60611; 3,500.

POSTAL INFORMATION

U.S. Postal Service

The Postal Reorganization Act, creating a government-owned postal service under the executive branch and replacing the old Post Office Department, was signed into law by President Richard Nixon on Aug. 12, 1970. The service officially came into being on July 1, 1971.

The U.S. Postal Service is governed by an 11-person Board of Governors. Nine members are appointed to 9-year terms by the president with Senate approval. These 9, in turn, choose a postmaster general. The board and the postmaster general choose the 11th member, who serves as deputy postmaster general. An independent Postal Rate Commission of 5 members, appointed by the president, recommends postal rates to the Board of Governors for their approval.

As of Sept. 30, 1992, there were 39,595 post offices, stations, and branches throughout the U.S. and possessions.

U.S. Domestic Rates

Postal rates and fees shown below were implemented on Feb. 3, 1991. Domestic rates apply to the U.S., its territories and possessions, and APOs and FPOs.

First Class

Letters written, and matter sealed against inspection, 29¢ for 1st oz. or fraction, 23¢ for each additional oz. or fraction.

U.S. Postal Service cards, single 19¢, double 38¢; private postcards, same.

First class includes written matter, namely letters, postal cards, postcards (private mailing cards) and all other matter wholly or partly in writing, whether sealed or unsealed, except manuscripts for books, periodical articles and music, manuscript copy accompanying proofsheets or corrected proofsheets of the same and the writing authorized by law on matter of other classes. Also matter sealed or closed against inspection, bills and statements of accounts.

Express Mail

Express Mail Service is available for any mailable article up to 70 pounds, and guarantees delivery between major U.S. cities or your money back. Articles received by the acceptance time authorized by the postmaster at a postal facility offering Express Mail will be delivered by 3 p.m. the next day to some locations or will be delivered by noon the next day to other destinations. Or, if you prefer, your shipment can be picked up as early as 10 a.m. the next business day. Second day service is available to locations not on the Next Day Delivery Network. Rates include insurance, Shipment Receipt, and Record of Delivery at the destination post office.

Consult Postmaster for other Express Mail Services and rates. (The Postal Service will refund, upon application to originating office, the postage for any Express Mail shipments not meeting the service standard except for those delayed by strike or work stoppage, delay or cancellation of flights, or governmental action beyond the control of the Postal Service.)

Third Class

Third class (limit up to but not including 16 ounces): Mailable matter not in 1st and 2d classes.

Single mailing: Publications, small parcels, printed matter, booklets and catalogs, 29¢ the first ounce, 52¢ for over 1 to 2 ozs., 75¢ for over 2 to 3 ozs., 98¢ for over 3 to 4 ozs., $1.21 for over 4 to 6 ozs., $1.33 for over 6 to 8 ozs., $1.44 for over 8 to 10 ozs., $1.56 for over 10 to 12 ozs., $1.67 for over 12 to 14 ozs., $1.79 for over 14 but less than 16 ozs.

Bulk mailing: At least 200 pieces or 50 pounds of such items as solicitations, newsletters, advertising materials, books and cassettes, each item of which individually weighs less than one pound. Minimum rate per piece: Basic presort, $0.198 for pieces weighing 3.3067 ounces or less; for pieces weighing more than 3.3067 ounces, the rate is $0.109 per piece + $0.600 per pound. Contact your post office for the discounts offered for presorted, destination entry and automation compatible mail.

Separate rates for some nonprofit organizations. Bulk mailing fee, $75 per calendar year. Apply to postmaster for permit. One-time fee for permit imprint, $75.

Parcel Post—Fourth Class

Fourth class or parcel post (16 ounces and over): merchandise, printed matter, etc., may be sealed, subject to inspection.

Priority Mail Flat Rate

First class mail of more than 11 ounces can be sent "Priority Mail" service. The most expeditious handling and transportation available will be used for fastest delivery.

The pickup service for Priority Mail costs $4.50 for each stop by the Postal Service. There is also a $2.90 flat Priority Mail rate for matter sent in the Special Postal Service-provided envelope.

Forwarding Addresses

The mailer, in order to obtain a forwarding address, must endorse the envelope or cover "Address Correction Requested." The destination post office then will determine whether a forwarding address has been left on file and provide it for a fee of 35¢ per manual correction and 20¢ per automated correction.

Priority Mail

Packages weighing up to 70 pounds and not exceeding 108 inches in length and girth combined, including written and other material of the first class, whether sealed or unsealed, fractions of a pound being charged as a full pound.

Rates according to zone apply between the U.S. and Puerto Rico and Virgin Islands. The mileage between the specific geographic locations of 3-digit ZIP codes determines the zone number to be used. The mileage range represented by the zone number is: Zone 1—up to 50 miles; 2—51 to 150 miles; 3—151 to 300 miles; 4—301 to 600 miles; 5—601 to 1,000 miles; 6—1,001 to 1,400 miles; 7—1,401 to 1,800 miles; 8—over 1,800 miles.

Parcels weighing less than 15 pounds, measuring over 84 inches but not exceeding 108 inches in length and girth combined are chargeable with a minimum rate equal to that for a 15 pound parcel for the zone to which addressed.

Zones	To 2 lbs	3 lbs	4 lbs	5 lbs*
1, 2, 3, 4, 5, 6, 7, 8	$2.90	$4.10	$4.65	$5.45

*Consult postmaster for rates for parcels over 5 lbs.

Special Handling

Third and fourth class parcels will be handled and delivered as expeditiously as practicable (but not special delivery) upon payment, in addition to the regular postage: up to 10 lbs., $1.80; over 10 lbs., $2.50. Such parcels must be endorsed, Special Handling.

Special Delivery

First class mail up to 2 lbs., $7.65; over 2 lbs. and up to 10 lbs., $7.95; over 10 lbs., $8.55. All other classes up to 2 lbs., $8.05; over 2 and up to 10 lbs., $8.65; over 10 lbs., $9.30.

Bound Printed Matter Rates

(Single Piece Zone Rate)

Fourth-Class Mail: Single-Piece Bound Printed Matter Rate

Weight lbs.	Local	Zones 1&2	3	4	5	6	7	8
1.5	$0.93	$1.27	$1.30	$1.36	$1.45	$1.54	$1.65	$1.75
2	0.94	1.30	1.34	1.42	1.53	1.66	1.81	1.93
2.5	0.96	1.33	1.38	1.48	1.62	1.78	1.97	2.12
3	0.98	1.35	1.42	1.54	1.71	1.90	2.12	2.31
3.5	0.99	1.38	1.46	1.60	1.80	2.02	2.28	2.50
4	1.01	1.41	1.50	1.66	1.89	2.14	2.44	2.69
4.5	1.02	1.44	1.54	1.72	1.98	2.26	2.59	2.88
5	1.04	1.47	1.58	1.78	2.07	2.38	2.75	3.07
6	1.07	1.53	1.66	1.89	2.24	2.61	3.06	3.44
7	1.10	1.59	1.74	2.01	2.42	2.85	3.38	3.82
8	1.14	1.64	1.82	2.13	2.60	3.09	3.69	4.20
9	1.17	1.70	1.90	2.25	2.77	3.33	4.01	4.57
10	1.20	1.76	1.98	2.37	2.95	3.57	4.32	4.95

(Includes both catalogs and similar bound printed matter.)

(Bound printed matter must weigh at least 1 pound and not more than 10 pounds. Bound printed matter includes catalogs, directories and books not eligible for special fourth-class rates.)

Domestic Mail Special Services

Registry — Only matter prepaid with postage at First-class postage rates may be registered. Stamps or meter stamps must be attached. The face of the article must be at least 5" long, 3½" high. The mailer is required to declare the value of mail presented for registration.

Registered Mail

Value	Insured	Uninsured
$0.00 to $100	$4.50	$4.40
$100.01 to $500	4.85	4.70
$500.01 to $1,000	5.25	5.05
$1,000.01 to $2,000	5.70	5.40
$2,000.01 to $3,000	6.15	5.75
$3,000.01 to $4,000	6.60	6.10
$4,000.01 to $5,000	7.05	6.45
$5,000.01 to $6,000	7.50	6.80
$6,000.01 to $7,000	7.95	7.15
$7,000.01 to $8,000	8.40	7.50
$8,000.01 to $9,000	8.85	7.85
$9,000.01 to $10,000	9.30	8.20

Consult postmaster for registry rates above $10,000.

C.O.D.: Unregistered — is applicable to first-, third-, fourth-class, and express mail matter. Such mail must be based on bona fide orders or be in conformity with agreements between senders and addressees. **Registered** — for details consult postmaster.

Insurance — is applicable to third and fourth class matter. Matter for sale addressed to prospective purchasers who have not ordered it or authorized its sending will not be insured.

Insured Mail

$0.01 to $50	$0.75
50.01 to $100	1.60
100.01 to $150	2.40
150.01 to $200	2.40
200.01 to $300	3.50
300.01 to $400	4.60
400.01 to $500	5.40
500.01 to $600	6.20

Liability for insured mail is limited to $600.

Certified mail — service is available for any matter having no intrinsic value on which 1st class or air mail postage is paid. Receipt is furnished at time of mailing and evidence of delivery obtained. The fee is $1.00 in addition to postage. Return receipt, restricted delivery, and special delivery are available upon payment of additional fees. No indemnity.

Special Fourth Class Rate

(limit 70 lbs.)

First pound or fraction, $1.05 (59¢ if 500 pieces or more of special rate matter are presorted to 5 digit ZIP code or 88¢ if 500 pieces or more are presorted to Bulk Mail Cntrs.); each additional pound or fraction through 7 pounds, 43¢; each additional pound, 25¢. Only the following specific articles: Books of at least 8 printed pages consisting wholly of reading matter or scholarly bibliography, or reading matter with incidental blank spaces for notations and containing no advertising matter other than incidental announcements of books; 16-millimeter or narrower width films in final form and catalogs of such films of 24 pages or more (at least 22 of which are printed) except films and film catalogs sent to or from commercial theaters; printed music in bound or sheet form; printed objective test materials; sound recordings, playscripts and manuscripts for books, periodicals, and music; printed educational reference charts; loose-leaf pages and binders thereof consisting of medical information for distribution to doctors, hospitals, medical schools, and medical students; computer-readable media containing prerecorded information and guides for use with such media. Package must be marked "Special 4th Class Rate" stating item contained.

Library Rate (limit 70 lbs.)

First pound 65¢, each additional pound through 7 pounds, 24¢; each additional pound, 12¢. Books when loaned or exchanged between and sent to or from schools, colleges, public libraries, and certain non-profit organizations; books, printed music, bound academic theses, periodicals, sound recordings, other library materials, museum materials (specimens, collections), scientific or mathematical kits, instruments or other devices; also catalogs, guides or scripts for some of these materials. Must be marked "Library Rate".

Also qualifying for library rate are: Books mailed from publishers or distributors to schools, libraries, colleges or universities or to bookstores owned, operated and controlled by schools, colleges or universities.

Parcel Post Rate Schedule

(Inter BMC/ASF Zip Codes Only, Machinable Parcels, No Discount, No Surcharge)

Weight up to but not exceeding—(pounds)	Zones 1 and 2	3	4	5	6	7	8
2	$2.19	$2.32	$2.46	$2.74	$2.85	$2.85	$2.85
3	2.29	2.49	2.70	3.12	3.54	4.00	4.05
4	2.39	2.65	2.94	3.50	4.06	4.35	4.60
5	2.49	2.81	3.17	3.88	4.58	5.20	5.40
6	2.59	2.98	3.41	4.26	5.10	6.33	8.55
7	2.68	3.14	3.65	4.64	5.62	7.06	9.60
8	2.78	3.31	3.89	5.02	6.14	7.78	10.65
9	2.88	3.47	4.12	5.40	6.67	8.51	11.70
10	2.98	3.63	4.36	5.78	7.19	9.24	12.75
11	3.08	3.80	4.60	6.16	7.71	9.97	13.75

Weight up to but not exceeding—(pounds)	Zones 1 and 2	3	4	5	6	7	8
12	3.18	3.96	4.83	6.54	8.23	10.69	14.80
13	3.25	4.08	4.99	6.79	8.57	11.17	15.85
14	3.32	4.19	5.16	7.04	8.92	11.65	16.90
15	3.38	4.28	5.27	7.23	9.17	11.99	17.95
16	3.43	4.36	5.39	7.40	9.40	12.31	19.00
17	3.48	4.44	5.49	7.56	9.62	12.61	19.91
18	3.53	4.51	5.60	7.72	9.83	12.90	20.38
19	3.58	4.59	5.69	7.87	10.03	13.17	20.83
20	3.63	4.65	5.79	8.01	10.22	13.43	21.26
21	3.68	4.72	5.88	8.15	10.40	13.68	21.66
22	3.72	4.79	5.97	8.28	10.57	13.91	22.05
23	3.77	4.85	6.05	8.40	10.74	14.14	22.43
24	3.81	4.91	6.13	8.52	10.90	14.36	22.78
25	3.85	4.97	6.21	8.64	11.05	14.57	23.13

Postal Union Mail Special Services

Registration — available to practically all countries. Fee $4.40. The maximum indemnity payable — generally only in case of complete loss (of both contents and wrapper) — is $32.35. To Canada only the fee is $4.50 providing indemnity for loss up to $100, $4.85 for loss up to $500, and $5.25 for loss up to $1,000.

Return receipt — showing to whom and date delivered, $1.00.

Special delivery — Available to most countries. Consult post office. Fees for International Special Delivery same for air or surface: for letters, letter packages and postcards not over 2 pounds, $7.65. If over 2 pounds, $7.95, for printed matter, matter for the blind, or small packets, $8.05 if not over 2 pounds; if over 2 pounds, $8.65.

Marking — an article intended for special delivery service must have affixed to the cover near the name of the country of destination "EXPRES" (special delivery) label, obtainable at the post office, or it may be marked on the cover boldly in red "EXPRES" (special delivery).

Special handling — entitles AO surface packages to priority handling between mailing point and U.S. point of dispatch. Fees: $1.80 for packages to 10 pounds, and $2.50 for packages over 10 pounds.

Airmail — there is daily air service to practically all countries.

Prepayment of replies from other countries — a mailer who wishes to prepay a reply by letter from another country may do so by sending his correspondent one or more international reply coupons, which may be purchased at United States post offices. One coupon should be accepted in any country in exchange for stamps to prepay a surface letter of the first unit of weight to the U.S.

Additional international special services: Insurance: Available to many countries for loss of or damage to items paid at parcel post rate. Consult postmaster for indemnity limits for individual countries.

Limit of Indemnity Not Over	Fees Canada	All Other Countries
$50	$0.75	$1.60
100	1.60	2.40
200	2.40	3.50
300	3.50	4.60
400	4.60	5.40
500	5.40	6.20
600	6.20	6.60
700		6.90
800		7.20
900		7.50
1,000		7.80
1,100		8.10
1,200		8.40

Restricted Delivery: Available to many countries for registered mail, limits who may receive an item. Fee: $2.50.

Post Office-Authorized 2-Letter State Abbreviations

The abbreviations below are approved by the U.S. Postal Service for use in addresses only. They do not replace the traditional abbreviations in other contexts. The official list follows, including the District of Columbia, Guam, Puerto Rico, the Canal Zone, and the Virgin Islands (all capital letters are used):

Alabama	AL	Hawaii	HI	Mississippi	MS	Pennsylvania	PA
Alaska	AK	Idaho	ID	Missouri	MO	Puerto Rico	PR
American Samoa	AS	Illinois	IL	Montana	MT	Rhode Island	RI
Arizona	AZ	Indiana	IN	Nebraska	NE	South Carolina	SC
Arkansas	AR	Iowa	IA	Nevada	NV	South Dakota	SD
California	CA	Kansas	KS	New Hampshire	NH	Tennessee	TN
Colorado	CO	Kentucky	KY	New Jersey	NJ	Texas	TX
Connecticut	CT	Louisiana	LA	New Mexico	NM	Utah	UT
Delaware	DE	Maine	ME	New York	NY	Vermont	VT
Dist. of Col.	DC	Marshall Islands	MH	North Carolina	NC	Virginia	VA
Federated States of Micronesia	FM	Maryland	MD	North Dakota	ND	Virgin Islands	VI
Florida	FL	Massachusetts	MA	Northern Mariana Is.	MP	Washington	WA
Georgia	GA	Michigan	MI	Ohio	OH	West Virginia	WV
Guam	GU	Minnesota	MN	Oklahoma	OK	Wisconsin	WI
				Oregon	OR	Wyoming	WY

Also approved for use in addressing mail are the following abbreviations:

Alley	Aly	Court	Ct	Gardens	Gdns	Road	Rd
Arcade	Arc	Courts	Cts	Grove	Grv	Rural	R
Avenue	Ave	Crescent	Cres	Heights	Hts	Square	Sq
Boulevard	Blvd	Drive	Dr	Highway	Hwy	Street	St
Branch	Br	Expressway	Expy	Lane	Ln	Terrace	Ter
Bypass	Byp	Extended	Ext	Manor	Mnr	Trail	Trl
Causeway	Cswy	Extension	Ext	Place	Pl	Turnpike	Tpke
Center	Ctr	Freeway	Fwy	Plaza	Plz	Viaduct	Via
Circle	Cir			Point	Pt	Vista	Vis

International Air Mail

Aerogrammes — 45¢ each to all countries.
Air mail postcards (single) - 40¢ to all countries except Canada and Mexico (30¢ each)
International letters and letter packages: airmail to Canada and Mexico (there are no surface rates to these countries)—weight not over 0.5 ozs., 40¢ to Canada, 35¢ to Mexico; not over 1.0 ozs., 40¢ to Canada, 45¢ to Mexico; not over 2 ozs., 63¢ to Canada, 65¢ to Mexico; not over 3 ozs., 86¢ to Canada, 90¢ to Mexico.

Air Mail, Letter and Letter Package Rates, Countries Other Than Canada and Mexico

Weight not over	Rate	Weight not over	Rate	Weight not over	Rate	Weight not over	Rate
0.5 ozs.	$ 0.50	12.5 ozs.	$ 9.92	24.5 ozs.	$19.28	41 ozs.	$28.64
1.0	0.95	13.0	10.31	25.0	19.67	42	29.03
1.5	1.34	13.5	10.70	25.5	20.06	43	29.42
2.0	1.73	14.0	11.09	26.0	20.45	44	29.81
2.5	2.12	14.5	11.48	26.5	20.84	45	30.20
3.0	2.51	15.0	11.87	27.0	21.23	46	30.59
3.5	2.90	15.5	12.26	27.5	21.62	47	30.98
4.0	3.29	16.0	12.65	28.0	22.01	48	31.37
4.5	3.68	16.5	13.04	28.5	22.40	49	31.76
5.0	4.07	17.0	13.43	29.0	22.79	50	32.15
5.5	4.46	17.5	13.82	29.5	23.18	51	32.54
6.0	4.85	18.0	14.21	30.0	23.57	52	32.93
6.5	5.24	18.5	14.60	30.5	23.96	53	33.32
7.0	5.63	19.0	14.99	31.0	24.35	54	33.71
7.5	6.02	19.5	15.38	31.5	24.74	55	34.10
8.0	6.41	20.0	15.77	32.0	25.13	56	34.49
8.5	6.80	20.5	16.16	33	25.52	57	34.88
9.0	7.19	21.0	16.55	34	25.91	58	35.27
9.5	7.58	21.5	16.94	35	26.30	59	35.66
10.0	7.97	22.0	17.33	36	26.69	60	36.05
10.5	8.36	22.5	17.72	37	27.08	61	36.44
11.0	8.75	23.0	18.11	38	27.47	62	36.83
11.5	9.14	23.5	18.50	39	27.86	63	37.22
12.0	9.53	24.0	18.89	40	28.25	64	37.61

Weight limit: 64 oz. (4 lbs.)

Air Mail, Parcel Post Rates

Weight steps	Air Parcel post rate groups A	B	C	D	E
First pound	$6.00	$7.75	$9.25	$10.70	$12.30
Each additional pound or fraction up to 5 pounds	3.00	4.25	5.00	6.00	7.00
Each additional pound or fraction over 5 pounds	2.00	3.00	4.00	5.00	6.00

Air Parcel Post Rate Groups (For further information, consult your local post office.)

Country	Rate group	Maximum weight limit
Afghanistan	D	44
Albania	C	44
Algeria	D	44
Andorra	B	44
Angola	E	22
Anguilla	A	22
Antigua & Barbuda	A	22
Argentina	D	44
Armenia	E	22
Aruba	A	44
Ascension	No Air Service	
Australia	D	44
Austria	B	44
Azerbaijan	E	22
Azores	C	44
Bahamas	A	22
Bahrain	D	22
Bangladesh	E	22
Barbados	B	44
Belarus	E	22
Belgium	D	44
Belize	A	44
Benin	C	44
Bermuda	A	44
Bhutan	E	44
Bolivia	B	44
Bosnia and Herzegovina	C	33
Botswana	E	22
Brazil	E	44
British Virgin Islands	A	44
Brunei	D	22
Bulgaria	D	44

Country	Rate group	Maximum weight limit
Burkina Faso	D	44
Burma	D	22
Burundi	E	44
Cambodia	No Parcel Post Service.	
Cameroon	D	44
Canada	Separate Rate Group.	66
Cape Verde	D	22
Cayman Islands	A	44
Central African Rep.	E	44
Chad	D	44
Chile	D	44
China (Peoples Republic of)	D	44
Colombia	B	44
Comoros	E	44
Congo	D	44
Corsica	E	44
Costa Rica	A	44
Cote d'Ivoire (Ivory Coast)	D	44
Croatia	C	44
Cuba	No Parcel Post Service.	
Cyprus	C	44
Czech Republic	C	33
Denmark	C	66
Djibouti	D	44
Dominica	A	22
Dominican Rep.	A	44
East Timor	No Parcel Post Service.	
Ecuador	C	44
Egypt	D	44
El Salvador	B	44

Country	Rate group	Maximum weight limit
Equatorial Guinea	D.	44
Estonia	E.	22
Ethiopia	D.	44
Falkland Islands	D.	44
Faeroe Islands	C.	44
Fiji	B.	44
Finland	D.	44
France	E.	44
French Guiana	C.	44
French Polynesia	D.	44
Gabon	D.	44
Gambia	B.	22
Georgia, Republic of	E.	22
Germany	C.	44
Ghana	D.	22
Gibraltar	C.	44
Great Britain and Northern Ireland	C.	50
Greece	C.	44
Greenland	D.	44
Grenada	A.	44
Guadeloupe	A.	44
Guatemala	A.	44
Guinea	B.	44
Guinea-Bissau	B.	22
Guyana	B.	44
Haiti	A.	44
Honduras	B.	44
Hong Kong	C.	44
Hungary	C.	44
Iceland	C.	44
India	D.	44
Indonesia	E.	44
Iran	D.	44
Iraq	D.	44
Ireland (Eire)	C.	50
Israel	C.	33
Italy (incl. San Marino)	C.	44
Jamaica	A.	22
Japan	E.	44
Jordan	C.	44
Kazakhstan	E.	22
Kenya	D.	44
Kirabati	B.	44
Korea, Democratic People's Rep. of (North)	No Parcel Post Service.	
Korea, Republic of (South)	C.	44
Kuwait	C.	44
Kyrgyzstan	E.	22
Laos	E.	44
Latvia	E.	44
Lebanon	C.	11
Lesotho	E.	44
Liberia	C.	22
Libya	D.	44
Liechtenstein	B.	44
Lithuania	E.	22
Luxembourg	B.	44
Macao	C.	44
Macedonia	C.	33
Madagascar	E.	44
Madeira Islands	B.	44
Malawi	D.	22
Malaysia	D.	22
Maldives	D.	22
Mali	C.	44
Malta	C.	22
Martinique	A.	44
Mauritania	D.	44
Mauritius	E.	22
Mexico	A.	44
Moldova	E.	22
Monaco	E.	44
Mongolia	No Parcel Post Service.	
Montserrat	A.	44
Morocco	C.	44
Mozambique	E.	22
Namibia	D.	44
Nauru	C.	44
Nepal	D.	44
Netherlands	C.	44
Netherlands Antilles	A.	44
New Caledonia	D.	44
New Zealand	D.	44
Nicaragua	B.	44
Niger	D.	44
Nigeria	C.	22
Norway	D.	44
Oman	D.	22
Pakistan	D.	22
Panama	A.	44
Papua New Guinea	D.	44
Paraguay	D.	44
Peru	B.	44
Philippines	D.	44
Pitcairn Islands	B.	22
Poland	B.	33
Portugal	C.	22
Qatar	C.	44
Reunion	E.	44
Romania	C.	44
Russia	E.	22
Rwanda	D.	44
Saint Christopher & Nevis	A.	44
Saint Helena	C.	44
Saint Lucia	A.	44
Saint Pierre & Miguelon	A.	44
Saint Vincent & the Grenadines	A.	22
San Marino	C.	44
Sao Tome & Principe	D.	44
Saudi Arabia	D.	22
Senegal	D.	44
Seychelles	D.	22
Sierre Leone	D.	44
Singapore	D.	44
Slovakia	E.	22
Slovenia	C.	44
Solomon Islands	C.	44
Somalia	D.	44
South Africa	D.	44
Spain	C.	44
Sri Lanka	D.	44
Sudan	D.	44
Suriname	B.	44
Swaziland	D.	44
Sweden	D.	44
Switzerland	B.	44
Syria	C.	44
Taiwan	C.	44
Tajikistan	E.	22
Tanzania	E.	22
Thailand	D.	44
Togo	D.	44
Tonga	B.	22
Trinidad & Tobago	B.	22
Tristan da Cunha	E.	22
Tunisia	C.	44
Turkey	C.	44
Turkmenistan	E.	22
Turks and Caicos Islands	A.	22
Tuvalu	B.	44
Uganda	D.	22
Ukraine	E.	22
United Arab Emirates	D.	44
Uruguay	B.	44
Uzbekistan	E.	22
Vanuatu	B.	44
Vatican City State	C.	44
Venezuela	B.	44
Vietnam	No Parcel Post Service.	
Wallis & Futuna Islands	D.	44
Western Samoa	B.	22
Yemen	E.	44
Yugoslavia	C.	33
Zaire	E.	33
Zambia	E.	44
Zimbabwe	E.	44

International Post Cards, Surface Rates

Canada and Mexico: 30¢. All other countries: 35¢. Maximum size permitted, 6 × 4¼ inches; minimum size, 5½ × 3½ inches.

LANGUAGE

Sources for this section: *The World Almanac Guide to Good Word Usage; The Columbia Encyclopedia; Webster's Third New International Dictionary; The Oxford English Dictionary, 2nd ed.; The Associated Press Stylebook and Libel Manual; The Encyclopedia Americana.*

Neologisms

("New" words; from the Second Edition of the *Oxford English Dictionary*, Oxford Univ. Press, 1989.)

arcade game: a (mechanical or electronic) game of a type orig. popularized in amusement arcades.

assertiveness training: a technique by which diffident persons are trained to behave (more) assuredly.

astroturfed: carpeted with artificial turf.

birth parent: a natural (as opposed to an adoptive) parent.

build-down: a systematic reduction of nuclear armaments, by destroying two or more for each new one deployed.

bulimarexic: suffering from or characteristic of bulimia nervosa; one who suffers from bulimia nervosa.

camp-on: a facility of some telephone systems by which the caller of an engaged number can arrange for the system to ring it automatically as soon as it becomes free (in some cases ringing the caller also if he or she has replaced the receiver).

car-phone: a radio-telephone designed for use in a motor vehicle.

CD-ROM (compact disk-read only memory)**:** a compact disk with data that can be viewed but not altered.

crack: a potent, crystalline form of cocaine usually smoked for its stimulating effect.

debit card: a card issued by an organization, giving the holder access to an account, via an appropriate computer terminal, esp. in order to authorize the transfer of funds to the account of another party when making a purchase, etc., without incurring revolving finance charges for credit.

designer drug: a drug synthesized to mimic a legally restricted or prohibited drug without itself being subject to restriction.

E-mail: colloq. shortening of electronic mail.

fast tracker: a high-flyer; an ambitious or thrusting person.

foodie: also foody. One who is particular about food, a gourmet.

gender gap: the difference in (esp. political) attitudes between men and women.

hate mail: letters (often anonymous) in which the senders express their hostility toward the recipient.

HIV (human immunodeficiency virus)**:** either of 2 retroviruses (HIV-1, HIV-2) that cause AIDS.

microwavable: of food and food containers: suitable for cooking or heating in a microwave oven.

NIMBY, nimby (not in my backyard)**:** a slogan expressing objection to the siting of something considered unpleasant, such as nuclear waste, in one's own locality.

passive smoking: the inhalation of smoke involuntarily from the tobacco being smoked by others, considered as a health risk.

right to die: the alleged right of a brain-damaged or otherwise incurably ill person to the termination of life-sustaining treatment.

street credibility: popularity with, or accessibility to, ordinary people, esp. those involved in urban street culture; the appearance or fact of being "street-wise," hence (apparent) familiarity with contemporary trends, fashions, social issues.

yuppiedom: the condition or fact of being a yuppie; the domain of yuppies; yuppies as a class.

Eponyms (words named for people)

Bloody Mary—a vodka and tomato juice drink; after the nickname of Mary I, Queen of England, 1553-58, notorious for her persecution of Protestants.

Bloomers—full, loose trousers gathered at the knee; after Mrs. Amelia Bloomer, an American social reformer who advocated such clothing, 1851.

Bobbies—in Great Britain, police officers; after Sir Robert Peel, the statesman who organized the London police force, 1850.

Bowdlerize—to delete written matter considered indelicate; after Thomas Bowdler, British editor of an expurgated Shakespeare, 1825.

Boycott—to combine against in a policy of nonintercourse for economic or political reasons; after Charles C. Boycott, an English land agent in County Mayo, Ireland, ostracized in 1880 for refusing to reduce rents.

Braille—a system of writing for the blind; after Louis Braille, the French teacher of the blind who invented it, 1852.

Cesarean—surgical removal of a child from the uterus through an abdominal incision; after Julius Caesar, born c. 102 B.C. in this manner, according to legend.

Casanova—a man who is a promiscuous and unscrupulous lover; after Giovanni Casanova, an Italian adventurer, 1725-98.

Chauvinist—excessively patriotic; after Nicolas Chauvin, a legendary French soldier devoted to Napoleon.

Derby—a stiff felt hat with a dome-shaped crown and rather narrow rolled brim; after Edward Stanley, 12th Earl of Derby, who in 1780 founded the Derby horse race at Epsom Downs, England, to which these hats are worn.

Gerrymander—to divide an election district in an unnatural way, to favor one political party; after Elbridge Gerry, and the salamander, for the salamander-like shape of a Mass. election district created, 1812, during Gerry's governorship.

Guillotine—a machine for beheading; after Joseph Guillotine, a French physician who proposed its use in 1789 as more humane than hanging.

Leotard—a close-fitting garment for the torso, worn by dancers, acrobats, and the like; after Julius Leotard, a 19th-century French aerial gymnast.

Silhouette—an outline image; from Etienne de Silhouette, the French finance minister, 1757, who advocated economies that included buying such paper portraits instead of painted miniatures.

Foreign Words and Phrases

(L=Latin; F=French; Y=Yiddish; R=Russian; G=Greek; I=Italian; S=Spanish)

ad hoc (L; ad HOK): for the particular end or purpose at hand

ad infinitum (L; ad in-fi-NITE-um): endless

ad nauseam (L; ad NAWZ-ee-um): to a sickening degree

apropos (L; ap-ruh-POH): to the point; appropriate

bête noire (F; BET NWAHR): a thing or person viewed with particular dislike

bon appetit (F; BOH nap-uh-teet): good appetite

bona fide (L; BOH nuh-feyed): genuine

carte blanche (F; kahrt BLANNSH): full discretionary power

cause célèbre (F; kawz suh-LEB-ruh): a notorious incident

c'est la vie (F; se lah VEE): that's life

chutzpah (Y; KHOOT-spuh): amazing nerve bordering on arrogance

coup de grâce (F; kooh duh GRAHS): the final blow

coup d'état (F; kooh duh tah): forceful overthrow of a government

crème de la crème (F; KREM duh luh KREM): the best of the best

cum laude/magna cum laude/summa cum laude (L; KUHM loud-ay; MAHN-ya . . .; SOO-ma . . .): with praise or honor; with great praise or honor; with the highest praise or honor

de facto (L; di FAK-toh): in fact; generally agreed to without a formal decision

déjà vu (F; DAY-zhah VOOH): the sensation that something happening has happened before

de jure (L; dee JOOR-ee, day YOOR-ay): determined by law, as opposed to de facto

de rigueur (F; duh ree-GUR): necessary according to convention

détente (F; day-TAHNT): an easing or relaxation of strained relations

éminence grise (F; ay-meh-NAHNN-suh GREEZ): one who wields power behind the scenes

enfant terrible (F; ahnn-FAHNN te-REE-bluh): one whose unconventional behavior causes embarrassment

en masse (F; ahn MAHS): in a large body

ergo (L; ER-goh): therefore

esprit de corps (F; es-PREE duh KAWR): group spirit; feeling of camaraderie

eureka (G; YOOR-EE-kuh): I have found it

ex post facto (L; eks pohst FAK-toh): an explanation or regulation concocted after the event

fait accompli (F; fayt uh-kom-PLEE): an accomplished fact

faux pas (F; fowe PAH): a social blunder

hoi polloi (G; hoy puh-LOY): the masses

in loco parentis (L; in LOH-koh puh-REN-tis): in place of a parent

in memoriam (L; in muh-MAWR-ee-uhm): in memory of

in situ (L; in SEYE-tyooh): in the original arrangement

in toto (L; in TOH-toh): totally

je ne sais quoi (F; zhuh nuh say KWAH): I don't know what; the little something that eludes description

joie de vivre (F; zhwah duh VEEV-ruh): joy of living, love of life

mea culpa (L; MAY-uh CUL-puh): my fault

modus operandi (L; MOH-duhs op-uh-RAN-dee): method of operation

noblesse oblige (F; noh-BLES uh-BLEEZH): the obligation of nobility to help the less fortunate

non compos mentis (L; non KOM-puhs MEN-tis): out of control of the mind; insane

nouveau riche (F; nooh-voh REESH); pejorative for recent rich who spend money conspicuously

perestroika (R; PAIR-es TROY-kuh): restructuring

persona non grata (L; per-SOH-nah non GRAH-tah): unacceptable person

post-mortem (L; pohst-MORE-tuhm): after death; autopsy; analysis after event

prima donna (I; pree-muh DAH-nuh): temperamental person

pro tempore (L; proh TEM-puh-ree): for the time being

que sera sera (S; keh sair-ah sair-AH): what will be, will be

quid pro quo (L; kwid proh KWOH): something given or received for something else

raison d'être (F; RAY-zohnn DET-ruh): reason for being

shlemiel (Y; shleh-MEEL): an unlucky bungling person

savoir-faire (F; sav-wahr-FAIR): dexterity in social and practical affairs

semper fidelis (L; SEM-puhr fee-DAY-lis): always faithful

status quo (L; STAY-tus QWOH): existing order of things

tour de force (L; TOOR duh FAWRS): feat accomplished through great skill

terra firma (L; TER-uh FUR-muh): solid ground

verbatim (L; ver-BAY-tuhm): word for word

vis-à-vis (F; vee-ZUH-VEE): compared with

Figures of Speech

hyperbaton—any intentional deviation from normal word order
"Whom God wishes to destroy, he first makes mad." **Euripides**
"Arms and the man I sing." **Virgil**

enallage—an effective grammatical error
"We was robbed!" Joe Jacobs, professional prize fight manager
"Curioser and curioser" **Lewis Carroll**'s *Alice's Adventures in Wonderland*

antihimeria—a type of enallage that substitutes one part of speech for another
"Lord Angelo dukes it well." **Shakespeare**'s *Measure for Measure*
"I am going in search of the great perhaps." **Rabelais**

catechresis—the substitution of one word with a seemingly inappropriate one
"The Cold War" **Bernard Baruch**
"And that White Sustenance—Despair" **Emily Dickinson**

periphrasis—a roundabout means of expression
"To meet the demands of nature" **Sallust**
"From pro's and con's they fell to a warmer way of disputing." **Cervantes**

antithesis—saying something two different ways, specifically by denying its contrary and asserting it
"A man should be mourned at his birth, not at his death." **Montesquieu**
"The greatest crimes are caused by surfeit, not by want." **Aristotle**

epanorthosis—a statement followed by a correction
"Religion is a disease, but it is a noble disease." **Heraclitus**
"God, make me pure, but not yet." **Saint Augustine**

polyptoton—repetition of the same word or root with different grammatical forms or functions
"Who shall stand guard to the guards themselves?" **Juvenal**
"Love is an irresistible desire to be irresistibly desired." **Robert Frost**

isolcolon—repetition of the same grammatical forms in different words
"I speak Spanish to God, Italian to women, French to men, and German to my horse." **Charles V**
"The louder he talked of his honor, the faster we counted our spoons." **Ralph Waldo Emerson**

epizeuxis—the immediate repetition of a word or phrase
"O dark, dark, dark, amid the blaze of noon." **John Milton**
"Then kill, kill, kill, kill, kill, kill." **Shakespeare's** *King Lear*

diacope—repetition of a word with another word interposing
"Tomorrow, and tomorrow, and tomorrow . . ." **Shakespeare's** *Macbeth*
"A horse! a horse! my kingdom for a horse!" **Shakespeare's** *Richard III*

anaphora—repetition of the first word or words from one sentence to another
"Blessed are the poor in spirit: for theirs is the kingdom of heaven. Blessed are they that mourn: for they shall be comforted. Blessed are the meek: for they shall inherit the earth." **Matthew 5:3**
"We shall fight in France, we shall fight on the seas and oceans, we shall fight with growing confidence and growing strength in the air, we shall defend our island, whatever the cost may be, we shall fight on the beaches, we shall fight on the landing grounds, we shall fight in the fields and in the streets, we shall fight in the hills; we shall never surrender." **Winston Churchill**

epistrophe—repetition of the last word or words from one sentence to another
"When I was a child, I spake as a child, I understood as a child, I thought as a child: but when I became a man, I put away childish things." **1 Cor. 13:11**
"Selfishness is not living as one wishes to live. It is asking others to live as one wishes to live." **Thomas Macaulay**

epanepsis—ending a sentence or clause with the same word or phrase with which it began
"Nothing can be created out of nothing." **Lucretius**
"Common sense is not so common." **Voltaire**

palindrome—repetition in which the sentence reads the same forward or backward
"Able was I ere I saw Elba." attributed to **Napoleon**
"Madam, I'm Adam." attributed to the first man addressing the first woman

Common Abbreviations

Usage of periods after abbreviations varies, but recently the tendency has been toward omission. Definitions preceding those in parentheses are in Latin.

A.A. = Alcoholics Anonymous
A.A.A. = American Automobile Association
AC = alternating current
A.D. = anno Domini (in the year of the Lord)
A.M. = ante meridiem (before noon)
A.F.L. = American Federation of Labor
AIDS = acquired immunodeficiency syndrome
A.M.A. = American Medical Association
anon. = anonymous
ASAP = as soon as possible
ASCAP = American Society of Composers, Authors, and Publishers
B.A. = Bachelor of Arts
bbl. = barrel(s)
B.C. = before Christ
B.C.E. = before the Christian era
B.S. = Bachelor of Science
B.T.U. = British thermal unit
bu. = bushel
C = centigrade, Celsius
c = copyright
c. (or ca.) = circa (about)
C.I.A. = Central Intelligence Agency
C.E.O. = chief executive officer
C.I.O. = Congress of Industrial Organizations
cm = centimeter
C.O.D. = cash (or collect) on delivery
C.P.A. = Certified Public Accountant
CPR = cardio-pulmonary resuscitation
D.A. = District Attorney
D.A.R. = Daughters of the American Revolution
DC = direct current
D.D. = Doctor of Divinity
D.D.S. = Doctor of Dental Surgery
DNA = deoxyribonucleic acid
DOA = dead on arrival
ed. = edited, edition, editor
e.g. = exempli gratia (for example)
esp. = especially
et al. = et alii (and others)
etc. = et cetera (and so forth)
F = Fahrenheit
F.B.I. = Federal Bureau of Investigation
f.o.b. = freight on board
ft. = foot
FYI = for your information
gal. = gallon
g.n.p. = gross national product
G.O.P. = Grand Old Party (Republican)
h. = hour
Hon. = the Honorable
H.R.H. = His (Her) Royal Highness
ht. = height
i.e. = id est (that is)
in. = inch
I.Q. = Intelligence Quotient
I.R.A. = Irish Republican Army
I.R.S. = Internal Revenue Service
J.D. = Juris Doctor (Doctor of Laws)
J.P. = Justice of the Peace
J.S.D. = Doctor of the Science of Law
K = 1,000
k. = karat
kg = kilogram
km = kilometer
kW = kilowatt
kWh = kilowatt-hour
l = liter
lb. = libra (pound)
LL.B. = Bachelor of Laws
m = meter
M.A. = Master of Arts
M.D. = Medicinae Doctor (Doctor of Medicine)
mfg. = manufacturing
mi. = mile
MIA = missing in action
min. = minute
ml = milliliter
mm = millimeter
mph = miles per hour
M.S. = Master of Science
MS = manuscript
MSG = monosodium glutamate
Msgr. = Monsignor
NCO = Noncommissioned Officer
No. = numero (number)
op. = opus (work)
oz. = ounce
p. = page
Ph.D. = Doctor of philosophy
P.M. = post meridiem (afternoon)
POW = prisoner of war
P.S. = post scriptum (postscript)
pt. = pint(s), part, point
qt. = quart(s)
REM = rapid eye movement
Rev. = Reverend
R.F.D. = rural free delivery
R.I.P. = Requiescat in pace (May he rest in peace)
R.N. = Registered Nurse
ROTC = Reserve Officers' Training Corps
rpm = revolutions per minute
RR = railroad
R.S.V.P. = Répondez, s'il vous plait (Please answer)
S.A.S.E. = self-addressed stamped envelope
sec. = second
S.P.C.A. = Society for the Prevention of Cruelty to Animals
St. = saint, street
T. = ton
T.N.T. = trinitrotoluene
UFO = unidentified flying object
UHF = ultra high frequency
U.S.S. = United States Ship
v. (or vs.) = versus (against)
VHF = very high frequency
W = watt
yd. = yard

Latin and Greek Prefixes and Suffixes

Latin prefix/English meaning
a, abs/from
alti, alto/high
ambi/both
ante/before
aqui/water
arbori/tree
audio/hearing
avi/bird
brevi/short
centi/hundred
cerebro/brain
circum/around
ferri, ferro/iron
fissi/split
igni/fire
inter/between
juxta/close
lacto/milk
luni/moon
magni/great
mal/bad
multi/many
naso/nose
nati/birth
oculo/eye
oleo/oil
omni/all
ovi, ovo/egg
plano/flat
post/after
pre/before
pro/for
pulmo/lung
re/again
recti/straight
retro/backward
somni/sleep
stelli/star
sub/under
super/above
terri/land
trans/through
ultra/beyond
uni/one

Latin suffix/ English meaning
cide, cidal/kill
fid/split
fuge, fugal/flee from
grade/walking
pennale/wing
vorous/eating

Greek prefix/ English meaning
a/not
anti/against
astro/star
auto/self
biblio/book
bio/life
cardio/heart
chloro/green
chrono/time
cosmo/universe
ex/outside
geo/earth
geronto/old age
gluc/sweet
grapho/writing
helio/sun
hemi/half
hetero/different
homeo/similar
homo/same
hydro/water
hyper/above
kinesi/movement
litho/stone
logo/word
macro/large
mega/great
meso/middle
meta/beyond
micro/small
mono/one
necro/dead body
neo/new
ornitho/bird
osteo/bone
pan/all
para/close
phono/sound
photo/light
poly/many
proto/first
pseudo/false
psycho/mind, spirit
pyro/fire
rhino/nose
theo/god
thermo/heat
toxico/poison
zoo/living

Greek suffix/ English meaning
algia/pain
archy/government
gamy/marriage
gnomy/knowledge
iasis/disease
itis/inflammation
lepsy/seizure
logy/science of
machy/battle
meter/measure
oid/like
oma/tumor
phobe/fear
scope/observation
sect/cutting
soma/body
sophy/wisdom

Commonly Confused English Words

adverse: unfavorable
averse: opposed

affect: to influence
effect: to cause

aggravate: to make worse
annoy: to irritate

allusion: an indirect reference
illusion: an unreal impression

anxious: apprehensive
eager: avid

complement: to make complete; something that completes
compliment: to praise; praise

capital: the seat of government
capitol: the building in which a legislative body meets

discreet: prudent
discrete: separate

disinterested: impartial
uninterested: without interest

emigrate: to leave for another place of residence
immigrate: to come to another place of residence

elicit: to draw or bring out
illicit: illegal

denote: to mean
connote: to suggest beyond the explicit meaning

farther: more distant in space
further: an extension of time or degree

historic: an important occurrence
historical: any occurrence in the past

imply: to relay information but not explicitly
infer: to understand information that is not relayed explicitly

imminent: ready to take place
eminent: standing out

incredible: unbelievable
incredulous: skeptical

include: used when the items following are part of a whole
comprise: used when the items following are all of a whole

ingenious: clever
ingenuous: innocent

insidious: intended to trick
invidious: detrimental to reputation

literally: actually
figuratively: metaphorically

oral: spoken, as opposed to written
verbal: referring to skill with language, as opposed to other skills

prevaricate: to lie
procrastinate: to put off

pestilence: a contagious or infectious epidemic disease
petulance: rudeness

prostrate: stretched out flat, face down
prostate: of or relating to the prostate gland

qualitative: relating to quality
quantitative: relating to number

National Spelling Bee Champions

The Scripps Howard National Spelling Bee, conducted by Scripps Howard Newspapers and other leading newspapers since 1939, was instituted by the Louisville (Ky.) Courier-Journal in 1925. Children under 16 years of age and not beyond the eighth grade are eligible to compete for cash prizes at the finals, which are held annually in Washington, D.C. The 1993 winners are: first prize, **Geoff Hooper,** Arlington, Tenn.; second prize, **David Urban,** Amarillo, Tex.; third prize, **Yuni Kim,** Pottsville, Pa.

Winning Words

These were the last words given in each of the years 1965-1993 at the Scripps Howard National Spelling Bee. They were all correctly spelled, thereby determining the national champion.

1965 — eczema
1966 — ratoon
1967 — chihuahua
1968 — abalone
1969 — interlocutory
1970 — croissant
1971 — shalloon
1972 — macerate
1973 — vouchsafe
1974 — hydrophyte
1975 — incisor
1976 — narcolepsy
1977 — cambist
1978 — deification
1979 — maculature
1980 — elucubrate
1981 — sarcophagus
1982 — psoriasis
1983 — purim
1984 — luge
1985 — milieu
1986 — odontalgia
1987 — staphylococci
1988 — elegiacal
1989 — spoliator
1990 — fibranne
1991 — antipyretic
1992 — lyceum
1993 — kamikaze

Commonly Misspelled English Words

accidentally
accommodate
acquainted
all right
already
amateur
appearance
appropriate
bureau
character
commitment
conscious
conscientious
convenience
deceive
describe
description
desirable
despair
desperate
eliminate
embarrass
fascinating
finally
foreign
forty
government
grammar
humorous
hurrying
incidentally
independent
inoculate
irresistible
laboratory
lightning
maintenance
marriage
miniature
mysterious
necessary
opportunity
optimistic
performance
permanent
rhythm
ridiculous
similar
sincerely
transferred

Foreign Idioms

English	Italian
Naked as a jaybird	Naked as a worm (Nudo come un verme)
A bird in the hand is worth two in the bush.	Better a finch in hand than a thrush on a branch. (Meglio fringuello in man che tordo in frasca.)
To kill two birds with one stone	To catch two pigeons with one bean (Pigliare due piccioni con una fava)
To eat crow	To swallow the toad (Inghiottire il rospo)
To eat like a pig	To eat like a buffalo (Mangiare come un bufalo)
Don't bite off more than you can chew.	Don't take a step longer than your leg. (Non fare il passo piu lungo della gamba.)
Pride goes before a fall.	Pride rode out on horseback and came back on foot. (La superbia andò a cavallo e tornò a piedi.)
To go by fits and starts	To go by hiccups (Andare a singhiozzo)
There is honor among thieves.	A dog doesn't eat a dog. (Cane non mangia cane.)
Once in a blue moon	Every death of a pope (Ad oogni morte di papa)

English	French
Don't waste your breath!	Save your saliva! (Epargne ta salive!)
To turn up like a bad penny	To arrive like a hair in the soup. (Arriver comme un cheveu sur la soupe.)
To talk to yourself	To talk to angels (Parler aux anges)
Let's get back to the subject.	Let's get back to our sheep. (Revenons à nos moutons.)
To pull a long face	To make a funny nose (Faire un drôle de nez)
He laughs in your face.	He laughs in your nose. (Il vous rit au nez.)
By rule of thumb	From the view of the nose (A vue de nez)
To be knock-kneed	To have your legs in an X (Avoir les jambes en X)
Put that in your pipe and smoke it!	Put this in your pocket with your handkerchief on top! (Mets-le dans ta poche avec ton mouchoir dessus!)
It's Greek to me!	It's Chinese! (C'est du chinois!)

English	Spanish
To hit the ceiling	To scream at the sky (Poner el grito en el cielo)
Go fly a kite!	Go fry asparagus! (Véte a freír esparragos!)
There's always room for one more.	Where six can eat, seven can eat. (Donde comen seis, comen siete.)
To have the tables turned	To go out for wool and come home shorn (Ir por lana y volver esquilado)

To cut off your nose to spite your face	To throw stones at your own roof (Tirar piedras contra su propio tejado)
To slam the door in your face	To slam the door on your nostrils (Cerrarle la puerta en las narices)
Give him an inch, he'll take a mile.	Give him a hand and he takes a foot. (Le da la mano y se toma el pie.)
To be alive and kicking	To be alive and wagging your tail (Estar vivo y coleando)
You can't make a silk purse out of a sow's ear.	A monkey dressed in silk is still a monkey. (Aunque la mona se vista de seda, mona se queda.)
To swear a blue streak	To toss out toads and snakes (Echar sapos y culebras)
English	**Yiddish**
Go jump in the lake!	Go whistle in the ocean! (Gai feifen ahfenyam!)
You can only do one thing at a time.	You can't dance at two weddings at the same time. (Me ken nit tantzen auf tsvai chassenes mit ain mol.)
He's as slow as molasses.	He creeps like a bedbug. (Er kricht vi a vantz.)
He repeats himself.	He grinds ground flour. (Er molt gemolen mel.)
Where there's smoke, there's fire.	When bells ring, it's usually a holiday. (Az es klingt, iz misstomeh chogeh.)
Are you in a hurry?	Are you standing on one leg? (Bist ahf ain fus?)
Drop dead!	You should lie in the earth! (Zolst ligen in drerd!)
He makes a lot of trouble for me.	He makes my wedding black. (Er macht mir a shvartzeh chasseneh.)
Go fight City Hall.	Go fight with God. (Shlog zich mit Got arum.)
Thanks for nothing.	Many thanks in your belly button. (A shainem dank dir im pupik.)

Names of the Days

English	French	Italian	Spanish	German
Sunday	Dimanche	domenica	domingo	Sonntag
Monday	Lundi	lunedì	lunes	Montag
Tuesday	Mardi	martedì	martes	Dienstag
Wednesday	Mercredi	mercoledì	miércoles	Mittwoch
Thursday	Jeudi	giovedì	jueves	Donnerstag
Friday	Vendredi	venerdì	viernes	Freitag
Saturday	Samedi	sabato	sábado	Samstag

Idioms: Their Meaning and Derivation

dyed in the wool: to have traits deeply ingrained; from the fact that if wool is dyed before being made into yarn, or while still raw wool, the color is more firmly fixed.

feet of clay: a blemish in the character of one previously held above reproach; from Daniel's interpretation of Nebuchadnezzar's dream in the Old Testament. The king dreamed of an image made of precious metals, except for feet made of clay and iron. Daniel said that the feet symbolized human vulnerability to weakness and destruction.

hands down: effortlessly; incontestably; from the way a jockey, sure of victory, drops his hands, loosening his grip on the reins.

in seventh heaven: in a state of bliss; especially in Islamic beliefs, the heaven of heavens, the home of God and the highest angels.

kiss of death: something that seems good but is in reality the instrument of one's downfall; from the earlier phrase "Judas kiss," betraying Jesus to the authorities.

mad as a hatter: crazy; from mercury's use in the making of felt hats, thus hatters often were afflicted with a violent twitching of the muscles as a result of its effects.

red herring: a false lead; a herring cured by smoke; from the persistent odor, hence the use, trailed over the ground, for training a dog to follow this scent over any other.

red-letter day: a memorable day; from the custom of using red or purple colors to mark holy days on the calendar.

to bark up the wrong tree: to pursue a false lead; an Americanism that comes from hunting, some say specifically nocturnal racoon hunting, in which dogs often lost track of their quarry.

to buckle down: to adopt an attitude of effort and determination; probably from the act of buckling on armor to prepare for battle.

to go at it with hammer and tongs: no holds barred; from the blacksmith who, with his tongs (long-handled pincers) took a piece of red-hot metal from the forge, laid it on the anvil, and beat it into shape with his hammer.

to hold water: to pass a test for soundness; from testing a pitcher by filling it with water.

to knuckle under: to submit to another; from the time when one knelt before a conquerer, putting the "knuckles" of one's knees (the rounded part of the bone where the joint is bent) on the ground.

to make hay while the sun shines: to seize the opportunity; from hay's composition of mown grass dried for fodder, with the sun as the cheapest and most available drying agent.

to strike while the iron is hot: to seize the opportunity; from the blacksmith's need to swing the hammer while the metal on the anvil is glowing, or he must start up the forge again and reheat the iron.

Pen Names

Currer, Ellis, and Acton Bell (Charlotte, Emily, and Anne Bronte)
Isak Dinesen (Karen Blixen)
George Eliot (Mary Ann or Marian Evans)
O. Henry (W.S. Porter)
John le Carré (David Cornwell)
George Sand (Amandine Aurore Dupine)
Dr. Seuss (Theodor Geisel)
Stendahl (Marie Henri Beyle)
Mark Twain (Samuel Clemens)

Designations of Some King Louis of France

Louis I (778-840): the Debonair or the Pious
Louis II (846-879): the Stammerer
Louis V (966-987): the Lazy
Louis VI (1081-1137): the Fat
Louis VII (1121-1180): the Young
Louis VIII (1187-1226): the Lion
Louis X (1289-1316): the Quarrelsome
Louis XII (1462-1515): Father of the People
Louis XIV (1638-1715): the Great or the Sun King
Louis XV (1710-1774): the Well-Beloved
Louis XVII (1785-1795?): the Lost Dauphin

Young of Animals Have Special Names

The young of many animals, birds and fish have come to be called by special names. A young eel, for example, is an elver. Many young animals, of course, are often referred to simply as infants, babies, younglets, or younglings.

bunny: rabbit.
calf: cattle, elephant, antelope, rhino, hippo, whale, etc.
cheeper: grouse, partridge, quail.
chick, chicken: fowl.
cockerel: rooster.
codling, sprag: codfish.
colt: horse (male).
cub: lion, bear, shark, fox, etc.
cygnet: swan.
duckling: duck.
eaglet: eagle.
elver: eel.
eyas: hawk, others.
fawn: deer.
filly: horse (female).
fingerling: fish generally.
flapper: wild fowl.
fledgling: birds generally.
foal: horse, zebra, others.
fry: fish generally.
gosling: goose.
heifer: cow.
joey: kangaroo, others.
kid: goat.
kit: fox, beaver, rabbit, cat.
kitten, kitty, catling: cats, other fur-bearers.
lamb, lambkin, cosset, hog: sheep.
leveret: hare.
nestling: birds generally.
owlet: owl.
parr, smolt, grilse: salmon.
piglet, shoat, farrow, suckling: pig.
polliwog, tadpole: frog.
poult: turkey.
pullet: hen.
pup: dog, seal, sea lion, fox.
puss, pussy: cat.
spike, blinker, tinker: mackerel.
squab: pigeon.
squeaker: pigeon, others.
whelp: dog, tiger, beasts of prey.
yearling: cattle, sheep, horse, etc.

A Collection of Animal Collectives

The English language boasts an abundance of names to describe groups of things, particularly pairs or aggregations of animals. Some of these words have fallen into comparative disuse, but many of them are still in service, helping to enrich the vocabularies of those who like their language to be precise, who tire of hearing a group referred to as "a bunch of," or who enjoy the sound of words that aren't overworked.

bale of turtles
band of gorillas
bed of clams, oysters
bevy of quail, swans
brace of ducks
brood of chicks
cast of hawks
cete of badgers
charm of goldfinches
cloud of gnats
clowder of cats
clutch of chicks
clutter of cats
colony of ants
congregation of plovers
covey of quail, partridge
crash of rhinoceri
cry of hounds
down of hares
drift of swine
drove of cattle, sheep
exaltation of larks
flight of birds
flock of sheep, geese
gaggle of geese
gam of whales
gang of elks
grist of bees
herd of elephants
horde of gnats
husk of hares
kindle or **kendle** of kittens
knot of toads
leap of leopards
leash of greyhounds, foxes
litter of pigs
mob of kangaroos
murder of crows
muster of peacocks
mute of hounds
nest of vipers
nest, nide of pheasants
pack of hounds, wolves
pair of horses
pod of whales, seals
pride of lions
school of fish
sedge or **siege** of cranes
shoal of fish, pilchards
skein of geese
skulk of foxes
sleuth of bears
sounder of boars, swine
span of mules
spring of teals
swarm of bees
team of ducks, horses
tribe or **trip** of goats
troop of kangaroos, monkeys
volery of birds
watch of nightingales
wing of plovers
yoke of oxen

The Principal Languages of the World

Source: S. Culbert, NI-25, University of Washington, Seattle, WA 98195; data as of mid-1993

Languages with over 100,000,000 speakers

	Speakers (millions) Native	Total		Speakers (millions) Native	Total		Speakers (millions) Native	Total
Mandarin	827	930	Bengali	184	192	Japanese	125	126
Hindi	327	400	Arabic	182	214	German	98	120
Spanish	326	371	Russian	172	291	French	72	124
English	319	463	Portuguese	167	179	Malay-Indonesian	49	152

Total number of speakers (native plus non-native) of languages spoken by at least one million speakers

Achinese (N Sumatra, Indonesia)	3
Afrikaans (So. Africa)	10
Akan (or Twi-Fanti) (Ghana)	7
Albanian (Albania; Kosovo)	5
Amharic (Ethiopia)	19
Arabic (see above)	214
Armenian (Armenia)	5
Assamese[1] (India, Bangladesh)	23
Aymara (Bolivia; Peru)	2
Azerbaijani (Azerbaijan)	15
Balinese (Bali, Indonesia)	3
Baluchi (Baluchistan, Pakistan)	5
Bashkir (Bashkortostan, in Russia)	1
Batak Toba (Indonesia)	4
Baule (Côte d'Ivoire)	2
Beja (Kassala, Sudan; Ethiopia)	1
Bemba (Zambia)	2
Bengali[1] (see above)	192
Berber[2]	
Beti (Cameroon; Gabon; Eq. Guinea)	2
Bhili (India)	3
Bikol (SE Luzon, Philippines)	4
Brahui (Pakistan; Afghan.; Iran)	2
Bugis (Indonesia; Malaysia)	4
Bulgarian (Bulgaria)	9
Burmese (Myanmar)	31
Buyi (S Guizhou, S China)	2
Byelorussian (Belarus)	10
Cantonese (China; Hong Kong)	65
Catalan (NE Spain; S France; Andorra)	9
Cebuano (Bohol Sea, Philippines)	13

(continued)

Chagga (Kilimanjaro area, Tanzania)	1
Chiga (Ankole, Uganda)	1
Chinese[3]	
Chuvash (Chuvash, in Russia)	2
Czech (Czech Republic)	12
Danish (Denmark)	5
Dimli (EC Turkey)	1
Dogri (Jammu-Kashmir, CE India)	1
Dong (SC China)	2
Dutch-Flemish (Netherlands; Belg.)	21
Dyerma (SW Niger)	2
Edo (Bendel, S Nigeria)	1
Efik (incl. Ibibio) (SE Nigeria)	6
English (see above)	463
Esperanto	2
Estonian (Estonia)	1
Ewe (SE Ghana; S Togo)	3
Fang-Bulu (Dialects of Beti, q. v.)	
Farsi (Iranian form of Persian, q. v.)	
Finnish (Finland; Sweden)	6
Fon (SC Benin; S Togo)	1
French (see above)	124
Fula (or Peulh) (Cameroon; Nigeria)	13
Fulakunda (Senegambia; Guinea B.)	2
Futa Jalon (Guinea; Sierra Leone)	3
Galician (Galicia, NW Spain)	4
Galla (see Oromo)	
Ganda (or Luganda) (S Uganda)	3
Georgian (Georgia)	4
German (see above)	120
Gilaki (Gilan, NW Iran)	2
Gogo (Riff Valley, Tanzania)	1
Gondi (Central India)	2
Greek (Greece)	12
Guarani (Paraguay)	4
Gujarati[1] (WC India; S Pakistan)	40
Gusii (Kisii District, Nyanza, Kenya)	2
Hadiyya (Arusi, Ethiopia)	2
Hakka (or Kejia) (SE China)	34
Hani (S China)	1
Hausa (N Nigeria; Niger; Cameroon)	37
Haya (Kagera, NW Tanzania)	1
Hebrew (Israel)	4
Hindi[1,4] (see above)	400
Ho (Bihar and Orissa States, India)	1
Hungarian (or Magyar) (Hungary)	14
Iban (Indonesia; Malaysia)	1
Ibibio (see Efik)	
Igbo (or Ibo) (lower Niger, Nigeria)	17
Ijaw (Niger River delta, Nigeria)	2
Ilocano (NW Luzon, Philippines)	7
Indonesian (see Malay-Indonesian)	
Italian (Italy)	63
Japanese (see above)	126
Javanese (Java, Indonesia)	63
Kabyle (W Kabylia, N Algeria)	3
Kamba (E Kenya)	3
Kannada[1] (S India)	43
Kanuri (Nigeria; Niger; Chad; Cam.)	4
Karen (see Pho and Sgaw)	
Karo-Dairi (N Sumatra, Indonesia)	2
Kashmiri[1] (N India; NE Pakistan)	4
Kazakh (Kazakhstan)	8
Kenuzi-Dongola (S Egypt; Sudan)	1
Khalka (see Mongolian)	
Khmer (Kampuchea; Vietnam; Thai.)	8
Khmer, Northern (Thailand)	1
Kikuyu (or Gekoyo) (WC Kenya)	5
Kituba (Bas-Zaire, Bandundu, Zaire)	4
Kongo (W Zaire; S Congo; NW Ang.)	3
Konkani (Maharashtra and SW India)	4
Korean (Korea; China; Japan)	74
Kurdish (south-west of Caspian Sea)	11
Kyrgyz (Kyrgyzstan)	2
Lao[5] (Laos)	4
Lampung (Sumatra, Indonesia)	2
Latvian (Latvia)	2
Lingala (incl. Bangala) (Zaire)	7
Lithuanian (Lithuania)	3
Luba-Lulua (or Chiluba) (Zaire)	7
Luba-Shaba (Shaba, Zaire)	1
Lubu (E Sumatra, Indonesia)	1
Luhya (W Kenya)	1
Luo (Kenya; Nyanza, Tanzania)	4
Luri (SW Iran; Iraq)	4
Lwena (E Angola; W Zambia)	2
Macedonian (Macedonia)	2
Madurese (Madura, Indonesia)	10
Magindanaon (S Philippines)	1
Makassar (S Sulawesi, Indonesia)	2
Makua (S Tanzania; N Mozambique)	4
Malagasy (Madagascar)	12
Malay-Indonesian (see above)	152
Malay, Pattani (SE Thailand)	1
Malayalam[1] (Kerala, S India)	35
Malinke-Bambara-Dyula (W Africa)	9
Mandarin (see above)	930
Marathi[1] (Maharashtra, India)	68
Mazandarani (S Mazandaran, N Iran)	2
Mbundu (Benguela, Angola)	4
Mbundu (Luanda, Angola)	3
Meithei (NE India; Bangladesh)	1
Mende (Sierra Leone)	2
Meru (Eastern Province, C Tanzania)	1
Miao (or Hmong) (S China; SE Asia)	6
Mien (China; Viet.; Laos; Thailand)	2
Min (SE China; Taiwan; Malaysia)	50
Minangkabau (W Sumatra, Indon.)	6
Moldavian (included with Romanian)	
Mongolian (Mongolia; NE China)	6
Mordvin (Mordova, in Russia)	1
Moré (central part of Burkina Faso)	4
Nepali (Nepal; NE india; Bhutan)	16
Ngulu (Mozambique; Malawi)	2
Nkole (Western Prov., Uganda)	1
Norwegian (Norway)	5
Nung (NE of Hanoi, Vietnam; China)	2
Nupe (Kwara, Niger States, Nigeria)	1
Nyamwezi-Sukuma (NW Tanzania)	5
Nyanja (Malawi; Zambia; Zimbabwe)	5
Oriya[1] (Central and E India)	31
Oromo (West Ethiopia; N Kenya)	10
Pampangan (NW of Manila, Philip.)	2
Panay-Hiligaynon (Philippines)	7
Pangasinan (Lingayen G., Philip.)	2
Pashtu (Pakistan; Afghanistan; Iran)	21
Pedi (see Sotho, Northern)	
Persian (Iran; Afghanistan)	34
Polish (Poland)	44
Portuguese (see above)	179
Provençal (S France)	4
Punjabi[1] (Punjab, Pakistan; India)	92
Pushto (see Pashtu) (many spellings)	
Quechua A (Peru; Boliv.; Ec.; Arg.)	8
Rejang (SW Sumatra, Indonesia)	1
Riff (N Morocco; Algerian coast)	1
Romanian (Romania; Moldova)	26
Romany (Vlach only) (Eur.; Amer.)	2
Ruanda (Rwanda; Uganda; Zaire)	8
Rundi (Burundi)	6
Russian (see above)	291
Samar-Leyte (Central E Philippines)	3
Sango (Central African Republic)	4
Santali (E India; Nepal)	5
Sasak (Lombok, Alas Strait, Indon.)	2
Serbo-Croatian (NW Balkan area)	20
Sgaw (SW Myanmar)	2
Shan (Shan, E Myanmar)	3
Shilha (W Algeria; S Morocco)	3
Shona (Zimbabwe)	8
Sidamo (Sidamo, S Ethiopia)	2
Sindhi[1] (SE Pakistan; W India)	18
Sinhalese (Sri Lanka)	13
Slovak (Slovakia)	5
Slovene (Slovenia)	2
Soga (Busoga, Uganda)	1
Somali (Som.; Eth.; Ken.; Djibouti)	6
Songye (Kasai Or., NW Shala, Zaire)	1
Soninke (Mali; countries to W S E)	1
Sotho, Northern (So. Africa)	3
Sotho, Southern (So. Afr.; Lesotho)	4
Spanish (see above)	371
Sundanese (Sunda Strait, Indonesia)	26
Swahili (Kenya; Tanz.; Zaire; Ug.)	47
Swedish (Sweden; Finland)	9
Sylhetti (Bangladesh)	5
Tagalog (Philippines)	43
Tajiki (Tajikistan; Uzbek.; Kyrgyz.)	5
Tamazight (N Morocco; W Algeria)	3
Tamil[1] (Tamil Nadu, India; Sri Lanka)	68
Tatar (Tatarstan, in Russia)	8
Tausug (Philippines; Malaysia)	1
Telugu[1] (Andhra Pradesh, SE India)	72
Temne (central Sierra Leone)	2
Thai[5] (Thailand)	49
Tho (N Vietnam; S China)	2
Thonga (Mozambique; So. Africa)	3
Tibetan (SW China; N India; Nepal)	5
Tigrinya (S Eritrea; Tigre, Ethiopia)	4
Tiv (SE Nigeria; Cameroon)	2
Tong (see Dong)	
Tonga (SW Zambia; NW Zimbabwe)	2
Tswana (Botswana; So. Africa)	4
Tudza (N Vietnam; S China)	1
Tulu (S India)	2
Tumbuka (N Malawi; NE Zambia)	2
Turkish (Turkey)	58
Turkmen (Turkmenistan; Afghanistan)	3
Twi-Fante (see Akan)	
Uighur (Xinjiang, NW China)	8
Ukrainian (Ukraine; Russia; Poland)	46
Urdu[1,4] (Pakistan; India)	98
Uzbek (Uzbekistan)	14
Vietnamese (Vietnam)	63
Wolaytta (SE Ethiopia)	2
Wolof (Senegal)	7
Wu (Shanghai region, China)	65
Xhosa (SW Cape Prov., So. Africa)	8
Yao (see Mien)	
Yao (Malawi; Tanzania; Mozambique)	1
Yi (S and SW China)	7
Yiddish[6]	
Yoruba (SW Nigeria; Zou, Benin)	19
Zande (NE Zaire; SW Sudan)	1
Zhuang (S China)	15
Zulu (N. Natal, So. Africa; Lesotho)	8

(1) One of the fifteen languages of the Constitution of India. (2) See Kabyle, Riff, Shilha, and Tamazight. (3) See Mandarin, Cantonese, Wu, Min, and Hakka. The "common speech" (Putonghua) or the "national language" (Guoyu) is a standardized form of Mandarin as spoken in the area of Beijing. (4) Hindi and Urdu are essentially the same language, Hindustani. As the official language of Pakistan it is written in a modified Arabic script and called Urdu. As the official language of India it is written in the Devanagari script and called Hindi. (5) The distinctions between some Thai dialects and Lao are political rather than linguistic. (6) Yiddish is usually considered a variant of German, though it has its own standard grammar and dictionaries, has a highly developed literature, and is written in Hebrew characters.

Non-English-Speaking Americans

Source: Bureau of the Census, U.S. Dept. of Commerce

According to data from the 1990 census, more than 31.8 million people (almost 14 percent of the U.S. population age 5 and over) spoke a language other than English in 1990, compared with 23.1 million (11 percent) in 1980, an increase of almost 38 percent over the decade. After English, Spanish was the most common language, spoken by more than half of the non-English-speaking Americans. Spanish was ten times more commonly used than the next choice, French, which was followed by German, Italian, and Chinese.

Top 25 Languages, Other Than English, Spoken at Home by Americans

Source: Bureau of the Census, U.S. Dept. of Commerce

Language used at home	Total speakers over 5 years old 1990	1980	Percentage change*
1. Spanish	17,339,000	11,549,000	50.1%
2. French	1,703,000	1,572,000	8.3%
3. German	1,547,000	1,607,000	−3.7%
4. Italian	1,309,000	1,633,000	−19.9%
5. Chinese	1,249,000	632,000	97.7%
6. Tagalog	843,000	452,000	86.6%
7. Polish	723,000	826,000	−12.4%
8. Korean	626,000	276,000	127.2%
9. Vietnamese	507,000	203,000	149.5%
10. Portugese	430,000	361,000	19.0%
11. Japanese	428,000	342,000	25.0%
12. Greek	388,000	410,000	−5.4%
13. Arabic	355,000	227,000	57.4%
14. Hindi, Urdu & related	331,000	130,000	155.1%
15. Russian	242,000	175,000	38.5%
16. Yiddish	213,000	320,000	−33.5%
17. Thai	206,000	89,000	131.6%
18. Persian	202,000	109,000	84.7%
19. French Creole	188,000	25,000	654.1%
20. Armenian	150,000	102,000	46.3%
21. Navajo	149,000	123,000	20.6%
22. Hungarian	148,000	180,000	−17.9%
23. Hebrew	144,000	99,000	45.5%
24. Dutch	143,000	146,000	−2.6%
25. Mon-Khmer	127,000	16,000	676.3%

*Calculations are from numbers before rounding.

Language Spoken at Home by Persons 5 Years and Over, by State, 1990

State	Population 5 years and over	Speaks only English	Total non-English	Percent non-English
United States	**230,445,777**	**196,600,798**	**31,844,979**	**13.8**
Alabama	3,759,802	3,651,936	107,866	2.9
Alaska	495,425	435,260	60,165	12.1
Arizona	3,374,806	2,674,519	700,287	20.8
Arkansas	2,186,665	2,125,884	60,781	2.8
California	27,383,547	18,764,213	8,619,334	31.5
Colorado	3,042,986	2,722,355	320,631	10.5
Connecticut	3,060,000	2,593,825	466,175	15.2
Delaware	617,720	575,393	42,327	6.9
Distr. of Columbia	570,284	498,936	71,348	12.5
Florida	12,095,284	9,996,969	2,098,315	17.3
Georgia	5,984,188	5,699,642	284,546	4.8
Hawaii	1,026,209	771,485	254,724	24.8
Idaho	926,703	867,708	58,995	6.4
Illinois	10,585,838	9,086,726	1,499,112	14.2
Indiana	5,146,160	4,900,334	245,826	4.8
Iowa	2,583,526	2,483,135	100,391	3.9
Kansas	2,289,615	2,158,011	131,604	5.7
Kentucky	3,434,955	3,348,473	86,482	2.5
Louisiana	3,886,353	3,494,359	391,994	10.1
Maine	1,142,122	1,036,681	105,441	9.2
Maryland	4,425,285	4,030,234	395,051	8.9
Massachusetts	5,605,751	4,753,523	852,228	15.2
Michigan	8,594,737	8,024,930	569,807	6.6
Minnesota	4,038,861	3,811,700	227,161	5.6
Mississippi	2,378,805	2,312,289	66,516	2.8
Missouri	4,748,704	4,570,494	178,210	3.8
Montana	740,218	703,198	37,020	5.0
Nebraska	1,458,904	1,389,032	69,872	4.8
Nevada	1,110,450	964,298	146,152	13.2
New Hampshire	1,024,621	935,825	88,796	8.7
New Jersey	7,200,696	5,794,548	1,406,148	19.5
New Mexico	1,390,048	896,049	493,999	35.5
New York	16,743,048	12,834,328	3,908,720	23.3
North Carolina	6,172,301	5,931,435	240,866	3.9
North Dakota	590,839	543,942	46,897	7.9
Ohio	10,063,212	9,517,064	546,148	5.4
Oklahoma	2,921,755	2,775,957	145,798	5.0
Oregon	2,640,482	2,448,772	191,710	7.3
Pennsylvania	11,085,170	10,278,294	806,876	7.3
Rhode Island	936,423	776,931	159,492	17.0
South Carolina	3,231,539	3,118,376	113,163	3.5
South Dakota	641,226	599,232	41,994	6.5
Tennessee	4,544,743	4,413,193	131,550	2.9
Texas	15,605,822	11,635,518	3,970,304	25.4
Utah	1,553,351	1,432,947	120,404	7.8
Vermont	521,521	491,112	30,409	5.8
Virginia	5,746,419	5,327,898	418,521	7.3
Washington	4,501,879	4,098,706	403,173	9.0
West Virginia	1,686,932	1,642,729	44,203	2.6
Wisconsin	4,531,134	4,267,496	263,638	5.8
Wyoming	418,713	394,904	23,809	5.7

Economic and Financial Glossary

Acquisition: The purchase of one company by another.

Balanced Budget: The federal government budget is balanced when receipts are equal to current expenditure.

Balance of payments: The difference between all payments made to and from foreign countries over a set period of time. A *favorable* balance exists when more payments are coming in than going out; an *unfavorable* balance, when the reverse is true. Payments include gold, the cost of merchandise and services, interest and dividend payments, money spent by travelers, and repayment of principal on loans.

Balance of trade (trade gap): The difference between exports and imports, both in actual funds and credit. A nation's balance of trade is *favorable* when exports exceed imports and *unfavorable* when the reverse is true.

Bear Market: A market in which prices are falling.

Bearer Bond: A bond issued in bearer form rather than being registered in the owner's name. Ownership is determined by possession.

Bond: A written promise or IOU by the issuer to repay a fixed amount of borrowed money on a specified date and to pay a set annual rate of interest in the meantime, usually at semi-annual intervals. Bonds are generally considered safe because the borrower (whether a company or the government) usually must make interest payments before the money is spent on anything else.

Bull Market: A market in which prices are on the rise.

Capital Gain (Loss): An increase (decrease) in the market value of an asset above (below) the price originally paid, at the time the asset is sold.

Commercial Paper: An extremely short-term corporate IOU, generally due in 270 days or less. Available in face amounts of $100,000, $250,000, $500,000, $1,000,000 and combinations thereof.

Convertible Bond: A corporate bond (see below) which may be converted into a stated number of shares of common stock. Its price tends to fluctuate along with fluctuations in the price of the stock and with changes in interest rates.

Corporate Bond: Evidence of debt by a corporation. The bond normally has a stated life and pays a fixed rate of interest. Considered safer than the common or preferred stock of the same company.

Cost of living: The cost of maintaining a standard of living measured in terms of purchased goods and services. A rise in the cost of living mirrors the rate of inflation.

Cost-of-living benefits: Benefits that go to those persons whose money receipts increase automatically as prices rise.

Credit crunch (liquidity crisis): The period when cash for lending to business and consumers is in short supply.

Debenture: An unsecured long-term debt obligation backed only by the general credit of the issuing corporation.

Deficit spending: The practice whereby a government goes into debt to finance some of its expenditures.

Depression: A long period of economic decline when prices are low, unemployment is high, and there are many business failures.

Devaluation: The official lowering of a nation's currency, decreasing its value in relation to foreign currencies.

Discount Rate: The rate of interest set by the Federal Reserve that member banks are charged when borrowing money through the Federal Reserve System.

Disposable income: Income after taxes which is available to persons for spending and saving.

Dividend: Payment by a corporation to its shareholders, usually in the form of cash, stock shares, or other property.

Dow-Jones Industrial Average: A measure of stock market prices, based on 30 leading companies on the New York Stock Exchange.

Econometrics: The application of mathematical and statistical methods to the study of economic and financial data.

Economic Growth: The steady process of increasing productive capacity of the economy, and hence of increasing national income.

Federal Deposit Insurance Corporation (FDIC): A government-sponsored corporation that insures accounts in national banks and other qualified institutions.

Federal Reserve System: The entire banking system of the U.S., incorporating 12 Federal Reserve banks (one in each of 12 Federal Reserve districts), and 24 Federal Reserve branch banks, all national banks and state-chartered commercial banks and trust companies that have been admitted to its membership. The system greatly influences the nation's monetary and credit policies.

Full employment: The economy is said to be at full employment when only fractional unemployment exists. That is, everyone who wishes to work at the going wage-rate for his type of labor is employed. Since it takes time to switch from one job to another, there will be at any given time a small amount of unemployment.

Golden Parachute: Provisions in the employment contracts of executives guaranteeing substantial severance benefits if they lose their position in a corporate takeover.

Government Bond: An IOU of the U.S. Treasury, considered the safest security in the investment world. They are divided into two categories, those that are not marketable and those that are. *Savings Bonds* cannot be bought and sold once the original purchase is made. These include the familiar Series EE bonds. You buy them at 50 percent of their face value and when they mature, 12 years later, they will pay you back 100 percent of face value if you cash them in. Another type, Series H, are not discounted, but issued in amounts of $500, $1,000, $5,000, and $10,000 and pay their interest in semiannual checks. Marketable bonds fall into 12 categories. *Treasury Bills* are short-term U.S. obligations, maturing in 3, 6, or 12 months. They are sold at a discount of the face value, and the minimum denomination is $10,000. *Treasury Notes* mature in up to 10 years. Denominations range from $500, $1,000 to $5,000, $10,000 and up. *Treasury Bonds* mature in 10 to 30 years. The minimum investment is $1,000.

Greenmail: A company buys back its own shares from a suitor for more than the going market price to avoid a hostile takeover.

Gross Domestic Product (GDP): The market value of all goods and services that have been bought for final use during a year. It became the official measure of the U.S. economy in 1991, and replaced the *Gross National Product (GNP)* which had been in use since 1941. The GDP covers workers and capital employed within the nation's borders. The GNP covers production by American residents, regardless of location. The switch aligned the U.S. with most other industrialized countries, making comparisons easier.

Individual Retirement Account (IRA): A self-funded retirement plan that allows employed individuals to contribute a maximum yearly sum toward their retirement. Interest earned in the account is tax deferred.

Inflation: An increase in the average level of prices.

Insider Information: Important facts about the condition or plans of a corporation that have not been released to the general public.

Interest: Money paid for the use of money. There are two kinds of interest. Simple interest is interest that is earned and paid. Compound interest is the accumulated interest that is added to the principal amount.

Junk Bonds: Debt securities that sell at relatively low prices, because of the low credit rating of their issuers. They pay significantly higher yields than top-grade bonds to reflect their added risk. In the 1980s, they were used to finance hostile takeovers.

Key leading indicators: A series of eleven indicators from different segments of the economy used by the Commerce Department to foretell what will happen in the economy in the near future.

Leveraged Buy-Out: An acquisition of a public company by a small group, often including the company's management, which takes the company private. Much of the purchase price is borrowed with the debt repaid from company profits or by selling company assets.

Liquid Assets: Assets that include cash or those items that are easily converted into cash.

Margin Account: A brokerage account that allows a person to trade securities on credit.

Money supply: The currency held by the public plus checking accounts in commercial banks and savings institutions.

Mortgage-Backed Securities: Created when a bank, builder or government agency gathers together a group of mortgages and then sells bonds to other institutions and the public. The investors receive their proportionate share of the interest payments on the loans as well as the principal payments. Usually, these mortgages are guaranteed by the government.

Municipal Bond: Issued by governmental units such as states, cities, local taxing authorities and other agencies. Interest is exempt from U.S. — and sometimes state and local — income tax. *Municipal Bond Unit Investment Trusts* allow you to invest in a portfolio of many different municipal bonds chosen by professionals. The income is exempt from federal income taxes.

Mutual Fund: A portfolio, or selection, of professionally bought and managed stocks in which you pool your money along with thousands of other people. A share price is based on net asset value, or the value of all the investments owned by the funds, less any debt, and divided by the total number of shares. The major advantage is less risk — it is spread out over many stocks and, if one or two do badly, the remainder may shield you from the losses. *Bond Funds* are mutual funds that deal in the bond market exclusively. *Money Market Mutual Funds* buy in the so-called "Money Market" — institutions that need to borrow large sums of money for short terms. Usually the individual investor cannot afford the denominations required in the "Money Market" (i.e. treasury bills, commercial paper, certificates of deposit), but through a money market mutual fund he can take advantage of these instruments when interest rates are high. These funds offer special checking account advantages.

National debt: The debt of the national government as distinguished from the debts of the political subdivisions of the nation and private business and individuals.

National debt ceiling: Limit set by Congress beyond which the national debt cannot rise. This limit is periodically raised by congressional vote.

Option: A contractual agreement between a buyer and a seller to buy or sell shares of a security. A **Call** option contract gives the right to purchase shares of a specific stock at a stated price within a given period of time. A **Put** option contract gives the buyer the right to sell shares of a specific stock at a stated price within a given period of time.

Per capita income: The nation's total income divided by the number of people in the nation.

Prime interest rate: The rate charged by banks on short-term loans to large commercial customers with the highest credit rating.

Producer price index: A statistical measure of the change in the price of wholesale goods. It is reported for 3 different stages of the production chain: crude, intermediate, and finished goods.

Program Trading: A term used for trading techniques involving large numbers and large blocks of stocks, usually used in conjunction with computer programs. Techniques include *Index Arbitrage* in which traders profit from price differences between stocks and futures contracts on stock indexes, and *Portfolio Insurance* which is the use of stock-index futures to protect stock investors from large losses when the market drops.

Public debt: The total of the nation's debts owed by state, local, and national government. This is considered a good measure of how much of the nation's spending is financed by borrowing rather than taxation.

Recession: A mild decrease in economic activity marked by a decline in real GNP, employment, and trade, usually lasting 6 months to a year, and marked by widespread decline in many sectors of the economy.

Savings Association Insurance Fund (SAIF): Created in 1989 to insure accounts in savings and loan associations up to $100,000.

Seasonal adjustment: Statistical changes made to compensate for regular fluctuations in data that are so great they tend to distort the statistics and make comparisons meaningless. For instance, seasonal adjustments are made in midwinter for a slowdown in housing construction and for the rise in farm income in the fall after the summer crops are harvested.

Stagnation: A period of economic slowdown in which there is little growth in GDP, capital investment, and real income.

Stock: *Common Stocks* are shares of ownership in a corporation; they are the most direct way to participate in the fortunes of a company. There can be wide swings in the prices of this kind of stock. *Preferred Stock* is a type of stock on which a fixed dividend must be paid before holders of common stock are issued their share of the issuing corporation's earnings. Prices are higher and yields lower than comparable bonds. However, they are attractive to corporate investors because 85 percent of preferred dividends are tax exempt to corporations. *Convertible Preferred Stock* can be converted into the common stock of the company that issued the preferred. This stock has the advantage of producing a higher yield than common stock and it also has appreciation potential. *Over-the-Counter Stock* is not traded on the major or regional exchanges, but rather through dealers from whom you buy directly. *Blue Chip* stocks are so called because they have been leading stocks for a long time. *Growth* stocks are stocks whose earnings have grown over several years.

Stock-index Futures: A futures contract is an agreement to buy or sell a specific amount of a commodity or financial instrument at a particular price at a set date. Futures on a stock index (such as the Standard & Poor's 500) are bets on the future price of that group of stocks.

Supply-side economics: The school of economic thinking which stresses the importance of the costs of production as a means of revitalizing the economy. Advocates policies that raise capital and labor output by increasing the incentives to produce.

Takeover: The passing of control of one company by another company or group by sale or merger. A friendly takeover occurs when the acquired company's management is agreeable to the merger; when management is opposed to the merger it is an unfriendly takeover. Takeover **arbitrage** is the purchase and/or selling of the securities of companies involved in takeover situations in order to realize a profit.

Tender Offer: A public offer to buy a company's stock; usually priced at a premium above the market.

Unit Investment Trust: A portfolio of many different corporate bonds, preferred stocks, government-backed securities or utility common stocks in which you can invest with as little as $1,000. Professional managers choose the securities, arrange for safe-keeping and collect the income. You receive your pro rata share of income every month.

Zero Coupon Bond: A corporate or government bond that is issued at a deep discount from the maturity value and pays no interest during the life of the bond. It is redeemable at face value.

Esperanto

Esperanto is the most commonly spoken of the international languages, artificial languages intended to provide a universal means of communication to bridge the gap between speakers of the world's many different natural languages. International languages are based on natural languages, with simplifications of grammar and spelling. Esperanto, invented in 1887 by the Polish physician and linguist Dr. Ludwik L. Zamenhof, is derived from a combination of Latin, the Romance languages, and the Germanic languages. Its name comes from the pseudonym ("Doktoro Esperanto") used by Zamenhof in his textbook describing the language. Because of its logical structure, phonemic spelling, and regular grammar, Esperanto can generally be learned more quickly than a typical natural language. An example of Esperanto:

Inteligenta persono lernas la lingvon Esperanto rapide kaj facile. Esperanto estas la moderna, kultura lingvo por la tuta mondo.

PRESIDENTIAL ELECTIONS

Popular and Electoral Vote, 1988 and 1992

Source: News Election Service; Federal Election Commission

	1992						1988			
	Electoral Vote			Democrat	Republican	Ind.	Electoral Vote		Democrat	Republican
States	Clinton	Bush	Perot	Clinton	Bush	Perot	Dukakis	Bush	Dukakis	Bush
Ala.. .	0	9	0	690,080	804,283	183,109	0	9	549,506	815,576
Alas. .	0	3	0	78,294	102,000	73,481	0	3	72,584	119,251
Ariz. .	0	8	0	543,050	572,086	353,741	0	7	454,029	702,541
Ark. .	6	0	0	505,823	337,324	99,132	0	6	349,237	466,578
Cal. .	54	0	0	5,121,325	3,630,574	2,296,006	0	47	4,702,233	5,054,917
Col. .	8	0	0	629,681	562,850	366,010	0	8	621,453	728,177
Conn.	8	0	0	682,318	578,313	348,771	0	8	676,584	750,241
Del. .	3	0	0	126,054	102,313	59,213	0	3	108,647	139,639
D.C. .	3	0	0	192,619	20,698	9,681	3	0	159,407	27,590
Fla.. .	0	25	0	2,071,651	2,171,781	1,052,481	0	21	1,655,851	2,616,597
Ga.. .	13	0	0	1,008,966	995,252	309,657	0	12	714,792	1,081,331
Ha.. .	4	0	0	179,310	136,822	53,003	4	0	192,364	158,625
Ida.. .	0	4	0	137,013	202,645	130,395	0	4	147,272	253,881
Ill.. . .	22	0	0	2,453,350	1,734,096	840,515	0	24	2,215,940	2,310,939
Ind.. .	0	12	0	848,420	989,375	455,934	0	12	860,643	1,297,763
Ia. . .	7	0	0	586,353	504,891	253,468	8	0	670,557	545,355
Kan. .	0	6	0	390,434	449,951	312,358	0	7	422,636	554,049
Ky.. .	8	0	0	665,104	617,178	203,944	0	9	580,368	734,281
La.. .	9	0	0	815,971	733,386	211,478	0	10	717,460	883,702
Me.. .	4	0	0	263,420	206,504	206,820	0	4	243,569	307,131
Md.. .	10	0	0	988,571	707,094	281,414	0	10	826,304	876,167
Mass.	12	0	0	1,318,639	805,039	630,731	13	0	1,401,415	1,194,635
Mich..	18	0	0	1,871,182	1,554,940	824,813	0	20	1,675,783	1,965,486
Minn..	10	0	0	1,020,997	747,841	562,506	10	0	1,109,471	962,337
Miss..	0	7	0	400,258	487,793	85,626	0	7	363,921	557,890
Mo.. .	11	0	0	1,053,873	811,159	518,741	0	11	1,001,619	1,084,953
Mon. .	3	0	0	154,507	144,207	107,225	0	4	168,936	190,412
Neb. .	0	5	0	216,864	343,678	174,104	0	5	259,235	397,956
Nev. .	4	0	0	189,148	175,828	132,580	0	4	132,738	206,040
N.H. .	4	0	0	209,040	202,484	121,337	0	4	163,696	281,537
N.J. .	15	0	0	1,436,206	1,356,865	521,829	0	16	1,317,541	1,740,604
N.M. .	5	0	0	261,617	212,824	91,895	0	5	244,497	270,341
N.Y. .	33	0	0	3,444,450	2,346,649	1,090,721	36	0	3,347,882	3,081,871
N.C. .	0	14	0	1,114,042	1,134,661	357,864	0	13	890,167	1,237,258
N.D. .	0	3	0	99,168	136,244	71,084	0	3	127,739	166,559
Oh.. .	21	0	0	1,984,942	1,894,310	1,036,426	0	23	1,939,629	2,416,549
Okla..	0	8	0	473,066	592,929	319,878	0	8	483,423	678,367
Ore. .	7	0	0	621,314	475,757	354,091	7	0	616,206	560,126
Pa.. .	23	0	0	2,239,164	1,791,841	902,667	0	25	2,194,944	2,300,087
R.I.. .	4	0	0	213,299	131,601	105,045	4	0	225,123	177,761
S.C. .	0	8	0	479,514	577,507	138,872	0	8	370,554	606,443
S.D. .	0	3	0	124,888	136,718	73,295	0	3	145,560	165,415
Tenn..	11	0	0	933,521	841,300	199,968	0	11	679,794	947,233
Tex. .	0	32	0	2,281,815	2,496,071	1,354,781	0	29	2,352,748	3,036,829
Ut. . .	0	5	0	183,429	322,632	203,400	0	5	207,352	428,442
Vt. . .	3	0	0	133,590	88,122	65,985	0	3	115,775	124,331
Va.. .	0	13	0	1,038,650	1,150,517	348,639	0	12	859,799	1,309,162
Wash.	11	0	0	993,037	731,234	541,780	10	0	933,516	903,835
W.Va.	5	0	0	331,001	241,974	108,829	5[1]	0	341,016	310,065
Wis. .	11	0	0	1,041,066	930,855	544,479	11	0	1,126,794	1,047,499
Wyo..	0	3	0	68,160	79,347	51,263	0	3	67,113	106,867
Total.	**370**	**168**	**0**	**44,908,254**	**39,102,343**	**19,741,065**	**111[1]**	**426**	**41,805,422**	**48,881,221**

(1) Lloyd Bentsen (D.-Tex.) received 1 electoral vote from W.Va.

Presidential Election Returns by Counties

All 1992 results are official. Results for New England states are for selected cities or towns due to unavailability of county results. Totals are always statewide.

Source: News Election Service; Federal Election Commission

Alabama

County	1992 Clinton (D)	1992 Bush (R)	1992 Perot (I)	1988 Dukakis (D)	1988 Bush (R)
Autauga	4,819	8,715	1,916	3,667	7,828
Baldwin	12,195	26,270	7,656	9,271	25,933
Barbour	4,836	4,475	1,020	3,836	4,958
Bibb	2,900	3,124	686	2,244	2,885
Blount	5,433	8,882	1,949	4,485	8,754
Bullock	3,259	1,253	266	3,122	1,421
Butler	4,021	3,494	867	3,465	3,923
Calhoun	16,453	20,623	4,717	12,451	19,806
Chambers	5,938	5,682	1,427	5,103	7,694
Cherokee	4,222	2,745	846	3,176	2,868
Chilton	4,946	8,126	1,363	3,820	8,761
Choctaw	3,941	3,069	489	3,491	3,629
Clarke	5,023	5,495	872	4,217	5,708
Clay	2,073	2,859	652	1,602	3,496
Cleburne	2,144	2,425	630	1,383	3,071
Coffee	5,776	7,591	2,021	4,319	8,890
Colbert	12,206	8,073	2,098	10,397	7,775
Conecuh	3,155	2,463	552	3,022	3,256
Coosa	2,330	1,973	476	1,860	2,405
Covington	5,004	6,840	1,880	3,845	8,130
Crenshaw	2,404	2,339	485	1,836	2,617
Cullman	10,451	14,411	4,113	8,517	14,351
Dale	5,098	8,123	2,423	3,476	9,266
Dallas	11,053	7,394	1,110	9,660	7,630
DeKalb	8,245	10,519	2,741	7,333	11,478
Elmore	6,223	11,356	2,765	4,501	10,852
Escambia	4,809	5,955	1,616	4,020	6,807
Etowah	20,558	17,467	4,277	17,762	17,828
Fayette	3,830	3,604	1,012	3,186	4,338
Franklin	5,953	4,794	1,075	4,961	5,146
Geneva	3,622	4,843	1,323	2,685	5,703
Greene	3,865	805	194	3,295	1,048
Hale	3,481	2,001	486	3,187	2,414
Henry	2,804	2,970	667	2,206	3,613
Houston	8,857	17,360	3,492	7,001	19,989
Jackson	10,628	5,711	2,462	7,418	6,090
Jefferson	125,889	149,832	22,191	107,766	148,879
Lamar	2,849	3,262	763	2,274	3,214
Lauderdale	15,936	13,728	4,009	12,862	12,942
Lawrence	6,364	3,576	1,624	4,646	3,616
Lee	13,770	16,885	4,572	9,078	17,180
Limestone	8,087	9,862	3,584	5,455	9,086
Lowndes	3,500	1,328	284	3,328	1,405
Macon	7,253	1,134	283	6,351	1,304
Madison	38,974	51,444	16,989	25,800	53,575
Marengo	5,632	4,470	919	4,402	4,241
Marion	6,167	5,692	1,389	4,505	5,955
Marshall	10,421	12,249	3,795	7,357	12,148
Mobile	54,962	72,935	15,105	45,524	72,203
Monroe	3,872	4,919	759	3,509	5,379
Montgomery	37,342	40,742	7,647	28,709	41,131
Morgan	15,091	21,073	7,683	10,594	18,679
Perry	3,712	1,829	213	3,574	2,107
Pickens	3,783	3,634	690	3,107	3,851
Pike	4,688	5,423	1,024	3,813	5,897
Randolph	3,318	3,813	919	2,462	4,625
Russell	8,647	5,587	1,360	6,589	6,333
St. Clair	6,517	12,447	2,614	4,335	10,604
Shelby	10,317	32,736	5,022	7,138	27,052
Sumter	4,810	1,807	388	4,390	2,212
Talladega	10,695	12,661	2,629	8,291	12,973
Tallapoosa	5,703	8,140	1,562	4,598	8,502
Tuscaloosa	23,495	27,454	7,011	18,166	27,396
Walker	14,831	11,301	3,344	11,338	11,011
Washington	4,046	3,270	829	3,402	3,741
Wilcox	3,439	1,671	174	3,369	1,739
Winston	3,415	5,550	1,110	2,954	6,235
Totals	**690,080**	**804,283**	**183,109**	**549,506**	**815,576**

Alabama Vote Since 1944

1944, Roosevelt, Dem., 198,918; Dewey, Rep., 44,540; Watson, Proh., 1,095; Thomas, Soc., 190.

1948, Thurmond, States' Rights, 171,443; Dewey, Rep., 40,930; Wallace, Prog., 1,522; Watson, Proh., 1,085.

1952, Eisenhower, Rep., 149,231; Stevenson, Dem., 275,075; Hamblen, Proh., 1,814.

1956, Stevenson, Dem., 290,844; Eisenhower, Rep. 195,694; Independent electors, 20,323.

1960, Kennedy, Dem., 324,050; Nixon, Rep., 237,981; Faubus, States' Rights, 4,367; Decker, Proh., 2,106; King, Afro-Americans, 1,485; scattering, 236.

1964, Dem. 209,848 (electors unpledged); Goldwater, Rep., 479,085; scattering, 105.

1968, Nixon, Rep., 146,923; Humphrey, Dem., 196,579; Wallace, 3d party, 691,425; Munn, Proh., 4,022.

1972, Nixon, Rep., 728,701; McGovern, Dem., 219,108 plus 37,815 Natl. Demo. Party of Alabama; Schmitz, Conservative, 11,918; Munn., Proh., 8,551.

1976, Carter, Dem., 659,170; Ford, Rep., 504,070; Maddox, Am. Ind., 9,198; Bubar, Proh., 6,669; Hall, Com., 1,954; MacBride, Libertarian, 1,481.

1980, Reagan, Rep., 654,192; Carter, Dem., 636,730; Anderson, Independent, 16,481; Rarick, Amer. Ind., 15,010; Clark, Libertarian, 13,318; Bubar, Statesman, 1,743; Hall, Com., 1,629; DeBerry, Soc. Work., 1,303; McReynolds, Socialist, 1,006; Commoner, Citizens, 517.

1984, Reagan, Rep., 872,849; Mondale, Dem., 551,899; Bergland, Libertarian, 9,504.

1988, Bush, Rep., 815,576; Dukakis, Dem., 549,506; Paul, Lib., 8,460; Fulani, Ind., 3,311.

1992, Bush, Rep., 804,283; Clinton, Dem., 690,080; Perot, Ind., 183,109; Marrou, Libertarian, 5,737; Fulani, New Alliance, 2,161.

Alaska

Election District	1992 Clinton (D)	1992 Bush (R)	1992 Perot (I)	1988 Dukakis (D)	1988 Bush (R)
No. 1	2,055	2,495	2,120		
No. 2	2,565	2,916	2,137		
No. 3	4,064	2,447	1,424		
No. 4	2,688	2,894	1,561		
No. 5	2,095	1,844	1,684		
No. 6	1,546	2,345	1,748		
No. 7	2,088	2,173	2,244		
No. 8	1,509	2,499	2,325		
No. 9	1,540	2,349	2,368		
No. 10	1,947	3,548	1,899		
No. 11	2,009	2,730	2,081		
No. 12	1,831	2,999	2,039		
No. 13	3,001	2,963	1,907		
No. 14	1,423	3,013	1,599		
No. 15	2,389	1,842	1,591		
No. 16	1,814	1,375	1,320		
No. 17	1,749	2,623	1,958		
No. 18	2,483	3,629	2,134		
No. 19	1,931	2,539	1,840		
No. 20	2,383	2,914	1,823		
No. 21	2,386	2,437	1,693		
No. 22	2,253	3,164	1,713		
No. 23	1,139	2,127	1,217		
No. 24	1,876	3,441	1,930		
No. 25	1,513	3,197	2,122		
No. 26	1,439	2,675	2,419		
No. 27	1,625	2,757	2,401		
No. 28	1,522	2,459	2,825		
No. 29	3,216	2,205	2,026		
No. 30	1,860	2,434	1,912		
No. 31	1,969	2,223	1,992		
No. 32	1,150	2,339	1,724		
No. 33	1,712	3,100	2,278		
No. 34	1,455	3,408	2,201		
No. 35	1,572	2,525	2,139		
No. 36	1,748	2,081	1,322		
No. 37	1,822	1,689	925		
No. 38	1,897	2,011	850		
No. 39	1,797	1,777	860		
No. 40	1,211	1,786	1,122		
Totals	**78,294**	**102,000**	**73,481**	**72,584**	**119,251**

Alaska Vote Since 1968

1968, Nixon, Rep., 37,600; Humphrey, Dem., 35,411; Wallace, 3d party, 10,024.

1972, Nixon, Rep., 55,349; McGovern, Dem., 32,967; Schmitz, American, 6,903.

1976, Carter, Dem., 44,058; Ford, Rep., 71,555; MacBride, Libertarian, 6,785.

1980, Reagan, Rep., 86,112; Carter, Dem., 41,842; Clark, Libertarian, 18,479; Anderson, Ind., 11,155; Write-in, 857.

1984, Reagan, Rep., 138,377; Mondale, Dem., 62,007; Bergland, Libertarian, 6,378.

1988, Bush, Rep., 119,251; Dukakis, Dem., 72,584; Paul, Lib., 5,484; Fulani, New Alliance, 1,024.

1992, Bush, Rep., 102,000; Clinton, Dem., 78,294; Perot, Ind., 73,481; Gritz, Populist/America First, 1,379; Marrou, Libertarian, 1,378.

Arizona

County	1992 Clinton (D)	1992 Bush (R)	1992 Perot (I)	1988 Dukakis (D)	1988 Bush (R)
Apache	11,218	4,588	1,979	8,944	5,347
Cochise	12,701	12,202	7,857	11,812	15,815
Coconino	18,888	13,769	9,363	14,660	16,649
Gila	7,571	5,781	4,694	7,147	7,861
Graham	3,391	4,169	1,860	3,407	5,120
Greenlee	1,695	1,451	794	1,733	1,526
La Paz	1,808	1,599	1,488	1,746	2,562
Maricopa	285,457	360,049	221,475	230,952	442,337
Mohave	13,255	13,684	12,706	10,197	17,651
Navajo	10,882	7,994	4,787	9,023	10,393
Pima	128,569	97,036	53,925	113,824	117,899
Pinal	15,468	11,669	9,231	13,850	14,966
Santa Cruz	3,512	3,024	1,447	3,268	3,320
Yavapai	18,268	23,419	16,409	14,514	27,842
Yuma	10,367	11,652	5,726	8,952	13,253
Totals	543,050	572,086	353,741	454,029	702,541

Arizona Vote Since 1944

1944, Roosevelt, Dem., 80,926; Dewey, Rep., 56,287; Watson, Proh., 421.

1948, Truman, Dem., 95,251; Dewey, Rep., 77,597; Wallace, Prog., 3,310; Watson, Proh., 786; Teichert, Soc. Labor, 121.

1952, Eisenhower, Rep., 152,042; Stevenson, Dem., 108,528.

1956, Eisenhower, Rep., 176,990; Stevenson, Dem., 112,880; Andrews, Ind. 303.

1960, Kennedy, Dem., 176,781; Nixon, Rep., 221,241; Hass, Soc. Labor, 469.

1964, Johnson, Dem., 237,753; Goldwater, Rep., 242,535; Hass, Soc. Labor, 482.

1968, Nixon, Rep., 266,721; Humphrey, Dem., 170,514; Wallace, 3d party, 46,573; McCarthy, New Party, 2,751; Halstead, Soc. Worker, 85; Cleaver, Peace and Freedom, 217; Blomen, Soc. Labor, 75.

1972, Nixon, Rep., 402,812; McGovern, Dem., 198,540; Schmitz, Amer., 21,208; Soc. Workers, 30,945. Due to ballot peculiarities in 3 counties (particularly Pima), thousands of voters cast ballots for the Socialist Workers Party *and* one of the major candidates. Court ordered both votes counted as official.

1976, Carter, Dem., 295,602; Ford, Rep., 418,642; McCarthy, Ind., 19,229; MacBride, Libertarian, 7,647; Camejo, Soc. Workers, 928; Anderson, Amer., 564; Maddox, Am. Ind., 85.

1980, Reagan, Rep., 529,688; Carter, Dem., 246,843; Anderson, Ind., 76,952; Clark, Libertarian, 18,784; De Berry, Soc. Workers, 1,100; Commoner, Citizens, 551; Hall, Com., 25; Griswold, Workers World, 2.

1984, Reagan, Rep., 681,416; Mondale, Dem., 333,854; Bergland, Libertarian, 10,585.

1988, Bush, Rep., 702,541; Dukakis, Dem., 454,029; Paul, Lib., 13,351; Fulani, New Alliance, 1,662.

1992, Bush, Rep., 572,086; Clinton, Dem., 543,050; Perot, Ind., 353,741; Gritz, Populist/America First, 8,141; Marrou, Libertarian, 6,759; Hagelin, Natural Law, 2,267.

Arkansas

County	1992 Clinton (D)	1992 Bush (R)	1992 Perot (I)	1988 Dukakis (D)	1988 Bush (R)
Arkansas	4,709	2,594	639	3,075	4,007
Ashley	5,876	2,686	931	4,466	4,111
Baxter	6,991	5,640	2,938	4,808	8,614
Benton	15,774	21,126	6,128	9,399	24,295
Boone	6,128	6,094	2,079	3,998	7,567
Bradley	2,954	1,482	391	2,167	2,089
Calhoun	1,389	1,047	257	1,024	1,316
Carroll	3,769	3,535	1,500	2,632	4,553
Chicot	3,504	1,242	347	2,426	1,901
Clark	5,767	2,403	714	4,675	3,389
Clay	4,848	1,647	568	3,442	2,766
Cleburne	5,090	3,580	1,263	3,404	4,932
Cleveland	1,893	1,127	337	1,404	1,462
Columbia	4,747	3,702	1,090	3,706	5,810
Conway	4,898	2,719	803	4,134	4,066
Craighead	13,931	9,104	2,274	9,083	11,887
Crawford	6,656	6,882	2,442	3,582	9,092
Crittenden	9,683	5,910	848	6,702	7,441
Cross	4,058	2,303	602	2,989	3,186
Dallas	2,107	1,458	345	1,990	1,947
Desha	3,815	1,279	392	2,859	2,334
Drew	3,748	1,938	596	2,578	2,995
Faulkner	13,000	9,491	2,437	7,302	10,678
Franklin	3,217	2,495	987	2,458	3,588
Fulton	2,827	1,258	631	2,018	1,918
Garland	18,811	12,886	3,475	11,406	19,281
Grant	3,190	2,272	702	2,142	2,717
Greene	7,541	3,510	1,213	5,065	5,161
Hempstead	5,476	2,387	1,022	3,841	3,938
Hot Spring	6,308	3,036	1,209	5,090	4,181
Howard	2,764	1,728	466	1,818	2,510
Independence	7,083	4,232	1,444	4,523	6,637
Izard	3,419	1,532	606	2,652	2,824
Jackson	4,944	1,864	673	4,199	3,049
Jefferson	21,819	7,525	2,067	16,664	12,520
Johnson	3,951	2,563	1,013	2,818	4,046
Lafayette	2,273	1,188	504	1,915	1,860
Lawrence	4,146	2,124	636	3,179	3,205
Lee	3,436	1,293	308	2,878	1,863
Lincoln	2,805	1,142	390	2,204	1,557
Little River	3,327	1,483	890	2,740	2,347
Logan	3,995	3,408	1,220	1,254	2,203
Lonoke	7,963	6,253	1,554	4,786	7,215
Madison	2,415	2,238	598	2,106	3,067
Marion	2,757	2,023	1,327	2,033	2,993
Miller	7,050	5,273	2,249	5,437	7,110
Mississippi	10,046	4,697	981	6,759	7,841
Monroe	2,578	1,324	355	2,052	1,862
Montgomery	1,904	1,205	576	1,362	1,752
Nevada	2,242	1,217	455	1,732	1,714
Newton	1,765	1,730	608	1,489	2,504
Ouachita	7,411	3,711	1,238	5,229	6,297
Perry	1,906	1,162	412	1,470	1,627
Phillips	6,456	2,695	634	5,580	3,892
Pike	2,168	1,577	472	1,681	2,105
Poinsett	5,341	2,425	761	3,873	3,644
Polk	3,162	2,757	1,225	2,390	4,099
Pope	7,704	8,056	1,989	4,941	10,084
Prairie	2,366	1,154	434	1,688	1,947
Pulaski	79,482	47,789	8,751	55,657	70,562
Randolph	3,921	1,766	578	2,781	2,560
St. Francis	6,548	3,289	766	4,656	4,298
Saline	12,671	10,105	2,751	8,436	12,353
Scott	2,228	1,695	610	1,707	2,507
Searcy	1,679	1,772	503	1,340	2,743
Sebastian	16,570	16,817	6,023	9,684	24,426
Sevier	2,558	1,592	643	2,037	2,254
Sharp	3,761	2,486	921	2,955	3,623
Stone	2,622	1,672	697	1,728	2,186
Union	8,786	7,305	1,919	5,931	10,581
Van Buren	3,819	2,612	888	2,607	3,562
Washington	22,029	20,292	5,304	12,557	23,601
White	10,494	8,538	2,366	6,957	11,094
Woodruff	2,589	676	227	1,924	1,097
Yell	4,165	2,506	940	2,763	3,535
Totals	505,823	337,324	99,132	349,237	466,578

Arkansas Vote Since 1944

1944, Roosevelt, Dem., 148,965; Dewey, Rep., 63,551; Thomas, Soc. 438.

1948, Truman, Dem., 149,659; Dewey, Rep., 50,959; Thurmond, States' Rights, 40,068; Thomas, Soc., 1,037; Wallace, Prog., 751; Watson, Proh., 1.

1952, Eisenhower, Rep., 177,155; Stevenson, Dem., 226,300; Hamblen, Proh., 886; MacArthur, Christian Nationalist, 458; Hass, Soc. Labor, 1.

1956, Stevenson, Dem., 213,277; Eisenhower, Rep., 186,287; Andrews, Ind., 7,008.

1960, Kennedy, Dem., 215,049; Nixon, Rep., 184,508; Nat'l. States' Rights, 28,952.

1964, Johnson, Dem., 314,197; Goldwater, Rep., 243,264; Kasper, Nat'l. States Rights, 2,965.

1968, Nixon, Rep., 189,062; Humphrey, Dem., 184,901; Wallace, 3d party, 235,627.

1972, Nixon, Rep., 445,751; McGovern, Dem., 198,899; Schmitz, Amer., 3,016.

1976, Carter, Dem., 498,604; Ford, Rep., 267,903; McCarthy, Ind., 639; Anderson, Amer., 389.

1980, Reagan, Rep., 403,164; Carter, Dem., 398,041; Anderson, Ind., 22,468; Clark, Libertarian, 8,970; Commoner, Citizens, 2,345; Bubar, Statesman, 1,350; Hall, Comm., 1,244.

1984, Reagan, Rep., 534,774; Mondale, Dem., 338,646; Bergland, Libertarian, 2,220.

1988, Bush, Rep., 466,578; Dukakis, Dem., 349,237; Duke, Chr. Pop., 5,146; Paul, Lib., 3,297.

1992, Clinton, Dem., 505,823; Bush, Rep., 337,324; Perot, Ind., 99,132; Phillips, U.S. Taxpayers, 1,437; Marrou, Libertarian, 1,261; Fulani, New Alliance, 1,022.

California

County	1992 Clinton (D)	1992 Bush (R)	1992 Perot (I)	1988 Dukakis (D)	1988 Bush (R)
Alameda	334,224	109,292	81,643	310,283	162,815
Alpine	215	222	186	230	306
Amador	5,286	6,477	4,550	5,197	6,893
Butte	32,489	31,608	20,231	30,406	40,143
Calaveras	5,989	6,006	4,848	5,674	7,640
Colusa	1,798	2,589	1,206	2,022	3,077
Contra Costa	194,960	112,965	72,518	169,411	158,652
Del Norte	3,639	3,083	2,575	3,587	3,714
El Dorado	21,012	25,906	17,503	19,801	30,021
Fresno	92,418	89,137	36,299	92,635	94,835
Glenn	2,666	3,812	2,278	2,894	4,944
Humboldt	28,854	18,299	12,340	29,781	21,460
Imperial	11,109	9,759	4,247	10,243	12,889
Inyo	2,695	3,689	1,999	2,653	5,042
Kern	60,510	80,762	36,891	55,083	90,550
Kings	9,982	10,673	4,899	9,142	12,110
Lake	10,548	6,678	5,797	9,828	9,366
Lassen	3,388	3,836	3,004	3,446	5,157
Los Angeles	1,446,529	799,607	488,624	1,372,352	1,239,716
Madera	10,863	13,066	6,156	10,642	13,255
Marin	76,158	30,479	22,986	69,394	46,855
Mariposa	3,023	2,982	2,211	2,998	3,768
Mendocino	18,344	7,958	9,753	17,152	12,979
Merced	20,133	17,981	10,914	20,105	21,717
Modoc	1,489	1,803	1,269	1,416	2,518
Mono	1,489	1,570	1,248	1,284	2,177
Monterey	54,861	36,461	24,472	48,998	50,022
Napa	24,215	15,662	13,150	22,283	23,235
Nevada	15,433	17,343	11,072	14,980	21,383
Orange	306,930	426,613	232,394	269,013	586,230
Placer	30,783	38,298	21,741	27,516	42,096
Plumas	3,742	3,599	2,551	4,251	4,603
Riverside	166,241	159,457	102,233	133,122	199,979
Sacramento	197,540	160,366	91,412	188,557	201,832
San Benito	5,354	4,112	3,182	4,559	5,578
San Bernardino	183,634	176,563	109,183	151,118	235,167
San Diego	367,397	352,125	259,249	333,264	523,143
San Francisco	233,263	57,352	29,018	201,887	72,503
San Joaquin	63,655	58,355	31,205	61,699	75,309
San Luis Obispo	40,136	36,384	27,314	35,667	46,613
San Mateo	149,232	75,080	50,465	141,859	109,261
Santa Barbara	69,215	57,375	35,105	63,586	77,524
Santa Clara	296,265	170,870	128,895	277,810	254,442
Santa Cruz	66,183	24,916	21,615	63,133	37,728
Shasta	21,605	28,190	17,990	21,171	32,402
Sierra	653	691	519	791	860
Siskiyou	8,254	6,660	5,567	8,365	9,056
Solano	64,320	38,883	27,851	54,344	50,314
Sonoma	104,334	47,619	43,859	91,262	67,725
Stanislaus	52,415	47,275	27,651	44,685	51,648
Sutter	7,883	12,956	4,881	6,557	14,100
Tehama	7,508	7,419	5,884	7,213	9,854
Trinity	1,967	1,886	2,092	2,518	3,267
Tulare	31,188	40,482	16,430	30,711	46,891
Tuolumne	9,216	8,525	6,294	8,717	10,646
Ventura	99,011	94,911	71,844	89,065	147,604
Yolo	33,297	17,574	11,073	30,429	22,358
Yuba	5,785	7,333	3,637	5,444	8,937
Totals	**5,121,325**	**3,630,574**	**2,296,006**	**4,702,233**	**5,054,917**

California Vote Since 1944

1944, Roosevelt, Dem., 1,988,564; Dewey, Rep., 1,512,965; Watson, Proh., 14,770; Thomas, Soc., 3,923; Teichert, Soc. Labor, 327.

1948, Truman, Dem., 1,913,134; Dewey, Rep., 1,895,269; Wallace, Prog., 190,381; Watson, Proh., 16,926; Thomas, Soc., 3,459; Thurmond, States' Rights, 1,228; Teichert, Soc. Labor, 195; Dobbs, Soc. Workers, 133.

1952, Eisenhower, Rep., 2,897,310; Stevenson, Dem., 2,197,548; Hallinan, Prog., 24,106; Hamblen, Proh., 15,653; MacArthur, (Tenny Ticket), 3,326; (Kellems Ticket) 178; Hass, Soc. Labor, 273; Hoopes, Soc., 206; scattered, 3,249.

1956, Eisenhower, Rep., 3,027,668; Stevenson, Dem., 2,420,136; Holtwick, Proh., 11,119; Andrews, Constitution, 6,087; Hass, Soc. Labor, 300; Hoopes, Soc., 123; Dobbs, Soc. Workers, 96; Smith, Christian Nat'l., 8.

1960, Kennedy, Dem., 3,224,099; Nixon, Rep., 3,259,722; Decker, Proh., 21,706; Hass, Soc. Labor, 1,051.

1964, Johnson, Dem., 4,171,877; Goldwater, Rep., 2,879,108; Hass, Soc. Labor, 489; DeBerry, Soc. Worker, 378; Munn, Proh., 305; Hensley, Universal, 19.

1968, Nixon, Rep., 3,467,664; Humphrey, Dem., 3,244,318; Wallace, 3d party, 487,270; Peace and Freedom party, 27,707; McCarthy, Alternative, 20,721; Gregory, write-in, 3,230; Mitchell, Com., 260; Munn, Proh., 59; Blomen, Soc. Labor, 341; Soeters, Defense, 17.

1972, Nixon, Rep., 4,602,096; McGovern, Dem., 3,475,847; Schmitz, Amer., 232,554; Spock, Peace and Freedom, 55,167; Hall, Com., 373; Hospers, Libertarian, 980; Munn, Proh., 53; Fisher, Soc. Labor, 197; Jenness, Soc. Workers, 574; Green, Universal, 21.

1976, Carter, Dem., 3,742,284; Ford, Rep., 3,882,244; MacBride, Libertarian, 56,388; Maddox, Am. Ind., 51,098; Wright, People's, 41,731; Camejo, Soc. Workers, 17,259; Hall, Com., 12,766; write-in, McCarthy, 58,412; other write-in, 4,935.

1980, Reagan, Rep. 4,524,858; Carter, Dem., 3,083,661; Anderson, Ind., 739,833; Clark, Libertarian, 148,434; Commoner, Ind. 61,063; Smith, Peace & Freedom, 18,116; Rarick, Amer. Ind., 9,856.

1984, Reagan, Rep. 5,305,410; Mondale, Dem., 3,815,947; Bergland, Libertarian, 48,400.

1988, Bush, Rep., 5,054,917; Dukakis, Dem., 4,702,233; Paul, Lib., 70,105; Fulani, Ind., 31,181.

1992, Clinton, Dem., 5,121,325; Bush, Rep., 3,630,575; Perot, Ind., 2,296,006; Marrou, Libertarian, 48,139; Daniels, Ind., 18,597; Phillips, U.S. Taxpayers, 12,711.

Colorado

County	1992 Clinton (D)	1992 Bush (R)	1992 Perot (I)	1988 Dukakis (D)	1988 Bush (R)
Adams	45,357	30,856	26,379	49,464	43,163
Alamosa	1,928	1,572	1,089	2,146	2,567
Arapahoe	66,607	72,221	44,363	61,113	95,926
Archuleta	819	1,242	741	795	1,440
Baca	726	1,240	647	851	1,670
Bent	985	759	506	1,088	1,032
Boulder	64,567	33,553	27,762	57,265	48,174
Chaffee	2,284	2,419	1,549	2,548	3,080
Cheyenne	301	615	292	399	760
Clear Creek	1,744	1,356	1,308	1,698	1,820
Conejos	1,705	1,160	578	1,976	1,445
Costilla	1,180	366	199	1,120	454
Crowley	570	602	276	630	862
Custer	343	651	368	310	753
Delta	3,424	4,359	2,627	3,521	5,449
Denver	121,961	55,418	37,298	127,173	77,753
Dolores	242	315	285	230	488
Douglas	9,991	18,592	11,329	6,931	17,035
Eagle	3,870	3,100	3,821	3,314	4,366
Elbert	1,237	2,205	1,567	1,566	2,805
El Paso	45,827	86,044	34,346	39,995	96,965
Fremont	5,356	5,961	3,709	5,278	7,623
Garfield	5,082	4,404	4,408	4,620	6,358
Gilpin	726	462	545	804	728
Grand	1,678	1,763	1,454	1,451	2,306
Gunnison	2,389	1,662	1,671	1,897	2,520
Hinsdale	151	188	136	111	295
Huerfano	1,224	685	385	1,876	1,079
Jackson	216	422	326	294	534
Jefferson	80,834	82,705	58,404	81,824	110,820
Kiowa	290	472	267	398	645
Kit Carson	925	1,801	919	1,196	2,262
Lake	1,426	605	863	1,516	969
La Plata	5,913	5,522	4,083	5,443	7,714
Larimer	38,232	35,995	24,879	35,703	45,967
Las Animas	3,847	1,739	953	4,075	2,162
Lincoln	640	1,079	581	874	1,356
Logan	2,718	3,420	2,184	3,382	4,485
Mesa	15,162	18,169	10,474	14,372	22,150
Mineral	171	159	117	174	217
Moffat	1,386	1,809	1,875	1,634	2,757
Montezuma	2,270	3,124	2,205	2,233	4,208
Montrose	3,713	4,847	3,093	3,748	6,012
Morgan	2,985	3,724	2,175	3,728	4,795
Otero	3,485	3,120	1,590	3,910	4,265
Ouray	461	653	466	439	814
Park	1,307	1,530	1,396	1,343	1,909
Philips	692	1,075	525	923	1,317
Pitkin	3,820	1,686	1,907	3,420	2,801
Prowers	1,770	2,371	1,184	2,207	2,978
Pueblo	30,261	16,120	9,841	32,788	20,119
Rio Blanco	778	1,231	794	803	1,821
Rio Grande	1,541	1,927	1,043	1,545	2,626
Routt	3,188	2,358	2,564	2,922	3,264
Saguache	1,011	675	471	1,033	945
San Juan	147	118	183	192	210
San Miguel	1,380	628	634	961	798
Sedgwick	397	447	295	611	921
Summit	3,344	2,256	2,715	2,595	2,893
Teller	1,873	3,050	1,927	1,656	3,760
Washington	660	1,266	671	958	1,707
Weld	19,295	20,958	13,571	20,548	26,497
Yuma	1,269	2,019	1,197	1,835	2,513
Totals	**629,681**	**562,850**	**366,010**	**621,453**	**728,177**

Colorado Vote Since 1944

1944, Roosevelt, Dem., 234,331; Dewey, Rep., 268,731; Thomas, Soc., 1,977.

1948, Truman, Dem., 267,288; Dewey, Rep., 239,714; Wallace, Prog., 6,115; Thomas, Soc., 1,678; Dobbs, Soc. Workers, 228; Teichert, Soc. Labor, 214.

1952, Eisenhower, Rep., 379,782; Stevenson, Dem., 245,504; MacArthur, Constitution, 2,181; Hallinan, Prog., 1,919; Hoopes, Soc., 365; Hass, Soc. Labor, 352.

1956, Eisenhower, Rep., 394,479; Stevenson, Dem., 263,997; Hass, Soc. Lab., 3,308; Andrews, Ind., 759; Hoopes, Soc., 531.

1960, Kennedy, Dem., 330,629; Nixon, Rep., 402,242; Hass, Soc. Labor, 2,803; Dobbs, Soc. Workers, 572.

1964, Johnson, Dem., 476,024; Goldwater, Rep., 296,767; Hass, Soc. Labor, 302; DeBerry, Soc. Worker, 2,537; Munn, Proh., 1,356.

1968, Nixon, Rep., 409,345; Humphrey, Dem., 335,174; Wallace, 3d party, 60,813; Blomen, Soc. Labor, 3,016; Gregory, New-party, 1,393; Munn, Proh., 275; Halstead, Soc. Worker, 235.

1972, Nixon, Rep., 597,189; McGovern, Dem., 329,980; Fisher, Soc. Labor, 4,361; Hospers, Libertarian, 1,111; Hall, Com., 432; Jenness, Soc. Workers, 555; Munn, Proh., 467; Schmitz, Amer., 17,269; Spock, Peoples, 2,403.

1976, Carter, Dem., 460,353; Ford, Rep., 584,367; McCarthy, Ind., 26,107; MacBride, Libertarian, 5,330; Bubar, Proh., 2,882.

1980, Reagan, Rep., 652,264; Carter, Dem., 367,973; Anderson, Ind., 130,633; Clark, Libertarian, 25,744; Commoner, Citizens, 5,614; Bubar, Statesman, 1,180; Pulley, Socialist, 520; Hall, Com., 487.

1984, Reagan, Rep., 821,817; Mondale, Dem., 454,975; Bergland, Libertarian, 11,257.

1988, Bush, Rep., 728,177; Dukakis, Dem., 621,453; Paul, Lib., 15,482; Dodge, Proh., 4,604.

1992, Clinton, Dem., 629,681; Bush, Rep., 562,850; Perot, Ind., 366,010; Marrou, Libertarian, 8,669; Fulani, New Alliance, 1,608.

Connecticut

	1992			1988	
County	Clinton (D)	Bush (R)	Perot (I)	Dukakis (D)	Bush (R)
Bridgeport.	22,321	13,149	6,263	23,831	17,084
Hartford.	26,971	6,180	3,390	27,295	8,100
New Britain	14,159	7,040	4,983	15,843	9,569
New Haven	29,774	8,931	4,130	31,951	11,616
Norwalk	16,488	14,743	6,046	14,518	18,618
Stamford	23,185	19,809	6,763	20,773	24,877
Waterbury.	16,366	16,155	9,188	18,202	20,018
West Hartford . . .	19,623	12,266	5,017	19,311	16,482
Totals.	**682,318**	**578,313**	**348,771**	**676,584**	**750,241**

Connecticut Vote Since 1944

1944, Roosevelt, Dem., 435,146; Dewey, Rep., 390,527; Thomas, Soc., 5,097; Teichert, Soc. Labor, 1,220.

1948, Truman, Dem., 423,297; Dewey, Rep., 437,754; Wallace, Prog., 13,713; Thomas, Soc., 6,964; Teichert, Soc. Labor, 1,184; Dobbs, Soc. Workers, 606.

1952, Eisenhower, Rep., 611,012; Stevenson, Dem., 481,649; Hoopes, Soc., 2,244; Hallinan, Peoples, 1,466; Hass, Soc. Labor, 535; write-in, 5.

1956, Eisenhower, Rep., 711,837; Stevenson, Dem., 405,079; scattered, 205.

1960, Kennedy, Dem., 657,055; Nixon, Rep., 565,813.

1964, Johnson, Dem., 826,269; Goldwater, Rep., 390,996; scattered, 1,313.

1968, Nixon, Rep., 556,721; Humphrey, Dem., 621,561; Wallace, 3d party, 76,650; scattered, 1,300.

1972, Nixon, Rep., 810,763; McGovern, Dem., 555,498; Schmitz, Amer., 17,239; scattered, 777.

1976, Carter, Dem., 647,895; Ford, Rep., 719,261; Maddox, George Wallace Party, 7,101; LaRouche, U.S. Labor, 1,789.

1980, Reagan, Rep., 677,210; Carter, Dem., 541,732; Anderson, Ind., 171,807; Clark, Libertarian, 8,570; Commoner, Citizens, 6,130; scattered, 836.

1984, Reagan, Rep., 890,877; Mondale, Dem., 569,597.

1988, Bush, Rep., 750,241; Dukakis, Dem., 676,584; Paul, Lib., 14,071; Fulani; New Alliance, 2,491.

1992, Clinton, Dem., 682,318; Bush, Rep., 578,313; Perot, Ind., 348,771; Marrou, Libertarian, 5,391; Fulani, New Alliance, 1,363.

Delaware

	1992			1988	
County	Clinton (D)	Bush (R)	Perot (I)	Dukakis (D)	Bush (R)
Kent	15,364	15,562	8,916	12,996	19,923
New Castle	91,516	66,311	37,581	79,147	92,587
Sussex	19,174	20,440	12,716	16,504	27,129
Totals.	**126,054**	**102,313**	**59,213**	**108,647**	**139,639**

Delaware Vote Since 1944

1944, Roosevelt, Dem., 68,166; Dewey, Rep., 56,747; Watson, Proh., 294; Thomas, Soc., 154.

1948, Truman, Dem., 67,813; Dewey, Rep., 69,688; Wallace, Prog., 1,050; Watson, Proh., 343; Thomas, Soc., 250; Teichert, Soc. Labor, 29.

1952, Eisenhower, Rep., 90,059; Stevenson, Dem., 83,315; Hass, Soc. Labor, 242; Hamblen, Proh., 234; Hallinan, Prog., 155; Hoopes, Soc., 20.

1956, Eisenhower, Rep., 98,057; Stevenson, Dem., 79,421; Oltwick, Proh., 400; Hass, Soc. Labor, 110.

1960, Kennedy, Dem., 99,590; Nixon, Rep., 96,373; Faubus, States' Rights, 354; Decker, Proh., 284; Hass, Soc. Labor, 82.

1964, Johnson, Dem., 122,704; Goldwater, Rep., 78,078; Hass, Soc. Labor, 113; Munn, Proh., 425.

1968, Nixon, Rep., 96,714; Humphrey, Dem., 89,194; Wallace, 3d party, 28,459.

1972, Nixon, Rep., 140,357; McGovern, Dem., 92,283; Schmitz, Amer., 2,638; Munn, Proh., 238.

1976, Carter, Dem., 122,596; Ford, Rep., 109,831; McCarthy, non-partisan, 2,437; Anderson, Amer., 645; LaRouche, U.S. Labor, 136; Bubar, Proh., 103; Levin, Soc. Labor, 86.

1980, Reagan, Rep., 111,252; Carter, Dem., 105,754; Anderson, Ind., 16,288; Clark, Libertarian, 1,974; Greaves, American, 400.

1984, Reagan, Rep., 152,190; Mondale, Dem., 101,656; Bergland, Libertarian, 268.

1988, Bush, Rep., 139,639; Dukakis, Dem., 108,647; Paul, Lib., 1,162; Fulani, New Alliance, 443.

1992, Clinton, Dem., 126,054; Bush, Rep., 102,313; Perot, Ind., 59,213; Fulani, New Alliance, 1,105.

District of Columbia

	1992			1988	
County	Clinton (D)	Bush (R)	Perot (I)	Dukakis (D)	Bush (R)
Totals.	**192,619**	**20,698**	**9,681**	**159,407**	**27,590**

District of Columbia Vote Since 1972

1972, Nixon, Rep., 35,226; McGovern, Dem., 127,627; Reed, Soc. Workers, 316; Hall, Com., 252.

1976, Carter, Dem., 137,818; Ford, Rep., 27,873; Camejo, Soc. Workers, 545; MacBride, Libertarian, 274; Hall, Com., 219; LaRouche, U.S. Labor, 157.

1980, Reagan, Rep., 23,313; Carter, Dem., 130,231; Anderson, Ind., 16,131; Commoner, Citizens, 1,826; Clark, Libertarian, 1,104; Hall, Com., 369; De Berry, Soc. Work., 173; Griswold, Workers World, 52; write-ins, 690.

1984, Mondale, Dem., 180,408; Reagan, Rep., 29,009; Bergland, Libertarian, 279.

1988, Bush, Rep., 27,590; Dukakis, Dem., 159,407; Fulani, New Alliance, 2,901; Paul, Lib., 554.

1992, Clinton, Dem., 192,619; Bush, Rep., 20,698; Perot, Ind., 9,681; Fulani, New Alliance, 1,459; Daniels, Ind., 1,186.

Florida

	1992			1988	
County	Clinton (D)	Bush (R)	Perot (I)	Dukakis (D)	Bush (R)
Alachua	37,876	22,606	15,293	29,375	30,124
Baker	1,974	3,417	1,315	1,353	3,414
Bay	12,830	22,820	9,702	11,582	31,712
Bradford.	3,040	3,671	1,572	2,386	4,218
Brevard	61,070	84,545	49,491	42,967	104,721
Broward.	276,309	164,782	90,923	218,211	220,196

Calhoun	1,665	1,721	1,176	1,329	2,420
Charlotte	22,904	24,302	14,711	15,967	28,879
Citrus	15,935	16,402	12,310	12,177	21,052
Clay	10,597	26,313	8,414	7,766	25,882
Collier	18,794	38,447	14,514	12,768	38,910
Columbia	5,526	6,489	2,906	4,072	7,759
Dade	254,444	235,149	53,957	216,847	270,672
De Soto	2,646	3,070	1,687	2,181	4,237
Dixie	1,855	1,401	1,094	1,366	2,027
Duval	92,010	123,480	33,335	74,832	127,875
Escambia	32,018	52,775	19,868	29,934	64,774
Flagler	6,692	6,241	3,387	4,241	6,494
Franklin	1,534	1,660	1,143	1,283	1,911
Gadsden	8,478	3,975	1,871	6,368	5,987
Gilchrist	1,511	1,395	1,090	1,137	1,854
Glades	1,305	1,185	878	1,034	1,546
Gulf	1,938	2,650	1,245	1,687	3,040
Hamilton	1,622	1,402	695	1,314	2,062
Hardee	2,017	2,898	1,498	1,688	3,636
Hendry	2,690	3,279	2,032	2,036	3,962
Hernando	19,171	17,896	11,845	15,432	21,179
Highlands	11,234	14,497	6,592	8,087	16,713
Hillsborough	115,261	130,611	63,037	98,969	150,065
Holmes	1,877	3,196	1,426	1,639	4,221
Indian River	12,359	19,137	12,375	10,447	24,619
Jackson	5,481	6,720	2,447	5,002	8,392
Jefferson	2,270	1,506	894	2,055	2,326
Lafayette	866	1,037	612	722	1,450
Lake	23,199	30,818	15,606	16,762	37,314
Lee	53,656	73,423	38,446	40,709	87,247
Leon	47,770	31,964	17,207	33,446	36,032
Levy	4,330	3,796	2,784	3,433	5,250
Liberty	820	1,126	617	709	1,419
Madison	2,644	2,006	1,174	1,950	2,556
Manatee	33,826	42,708	23,282	26,618	51,160
Marion	30,823	35,438	20,524	20,679	41,488
Martin	14,778	24,768	13,433	11,486	31,270
Monroe	10,435	9,891	8,306	10,151	15,919
Nassau	5,497	9,364	3,251	4,138	8,366
Okaloosa	12,003	32,755	16,649	9,726	40,295
Okeechobee	3,418	3,298	2,645	3,007	4,733
Orange	82,656	108,738	44,827	53,991	117,141
Osceola	15,009	19,139	11,021	9,811	21,350
Palm Beach	187,840	140,317	76,223	144,143	181,408
Pasco	53,125	47,721	34,650	50,369	63,788
Pinellas	160,217	158,733	101,150	152,374	210,971
Polk	51,442	65,952	28,198	38,236	77,065
Putnam	10,707	8,909	5,975	8,569	11,621
St. Johns	12,284	20,173	7,397	7,999	19,164
St. Lucie	23,873	24,397	19,813	17,427	32,241
Santa Rosa	6,526	17,229	8,735	5,251	18,948
Sarasota	54,536	66,831	34,281	42,095	84,585
Seminole	35,649	57,085	24,477	22,627	60,328
Sumter	5,027	4,366	2,901	3,900	5,933
Suwannee	3,985	4,571	2,790	3,126	5,859
Taylor	2,568	2,693	1,929	1,762	4,054
Union	1,247	1,543	770	691	1,643
Volusia	65,213	59,155	30,813	55,437	74,116
Wakulla	2,319	2,586	1,790	1,605	3,157
Walton	3,886	5,719	3,886	3,231	7,481
Washington	2,544	3,694	1,596	2,139	4,366
Totals	**2,071,651**	**2,171,781**	**1,052,481**	**1,655,851**	**2,616,597**

Florida Vote Since 1944

1944, Roosevelt, Dem., 339,377; Dewey, Rep., 143,215.

1948, Truman, Dem., 281,988; Dewey, Rep., 194,280; Thurmond, States' Rights, 89,755; Wallace, Prog., 11,620.

1952, Eisenhower, Rep., 544,036; Stevenson, Dem., 444,950; scattered, 351.

1956, Eisenhower, Rep., 643,849; Stevenson, Dem., 480,371.

1960, Kennedy, Dem., 748,700; Nixon, Rep., 795,476.

1964, Johnson, Dem., 948,540; Goldwater, Rep., 905,941.

1968, Nixon, Rep., 886,804; Humphrey, Dem., 676,794; Wallace, 3d party, 624,207.

1972, Nixon, Rep., 1,857,759; McGovern, Dem., 718,117; scattered, 7,407.

1976, Carter, Dem., 1,636,000; Ford, Rep., 1,469,531; McCarthy, Ind., 23,643; Anderson, Amer., 21,325.

1980, Reagan, Rep., 2,046,951; Carter, Dem., 1,419,475; Anderson, Ind., 189,692; Clark, Libertarian, 30,524; write-ins, 285.

1984, Reagan, Rep., 2,728,775; Mondale, Dem., 1,448,344.

1988, Bush, Rep., 2,616,597; Dukakis, Dem., 1,655,851; Paul, Lib., 19,796, Fulani, New Alliance, 6,655.

1992, Bush, Rep., 2,171,781; Clinton, Dem., 2,071,651; Perot, Ind., 1,052,481; Marrou, Libertarian, 15,068.

Georgia

	1992			1988	
County	Clinton (D)	Bush (R)	Perot (I)	Dukakis (D)	Bush (R)
Appling	2,455	2,514	1,047	1,837	3,000
Atkinson	1,056	779	342	887	1,126
Bacon	1,423	1,301	604	780	1,407
Baker	864	391	210	707	629
Baldwin	5,813	4,262	1,679	4,008	5,852
Banks	1,530	1,551	583	984	1,590
Barrow	3,991	4,328	1,633	2,442	4,738
Bartow	6,675	7,742	2,500	4,884	8,039
Ben Hill	2,348	1,476	619	1,867	2,005
Berrien	2,103	1,637	796	1,381	2,030
Bibb	28,070	19,847	6,021	22,084	22,179
Bleckley	1,710	1,570	662	1,175	1,950
Brantley	1,883	1,541	840	1,450	1,539
Brooks	1,895	1,779	630	1,500	2,136
Bryan	2,031	2,789	1,095	1,423	2,802
Bulloch	4,903	5,690	2,020	3,417	6,354
Burke	3,647	2,390	807	2,861	2,986
Butts	2,448	1,768	619	1,730	2,184
Calhoun	1,301	464	248	901	644
Camden	2,952	3,517	1,077	2,090	2,913
Candler	1,192	1,014	541	877	1,261
Carroll	8,404	10,750	3,358	4,706	10,754
Catoosa	4,817	7,599	2,290	3,588	9,319
Charlton	1,127	1,333	427	943	1,327
Chatham	31,533	31,925	8,269	25,063	35,623
Chattahoochee	604	413	177	362	454
Chattooga	2,976	2,439	965	2,206	3,665
Cherokee	8,113	16,054	4,950	4,378	14,593
Clarke	15,403	10,459	2,987	11,154	11,150
Clay	778	264	155	595	398
Clayton	25,890	23,965	7,942	14,689	28,225
Clinch	759	790	286	594	863
Cobb	63,960	103,734	28,747	39,297	106,621
Coffee	3,275	3,776	1,256	2,777	4,019
Colquitt	3,891	4,680	1,682	2,998	5,653
Columbia	7,115	16,657	4,379	4,617	16,401
Cook	1,731	1,318	537	1,226	1,555
Coweta	7,093	9,814	3,587	4,212	9,668
Crawford	1,648	974	549	1,340	1,235
Crisp	2,610	2,253	823	1,690	2,916
Dade	1,782	2,191	823	1,120	2,539
Dawson	1,399	1,696	790	761	1,908
Decatur	3,198	3,142	1,068	2,348	3,866
DeKalb	124,559	70,282	19,741	92,521	90,179
Dodge	3,002	2,287	978	2,164	2,677
Dooly	1,993	1,034	350	1,613	1,386
Dougherty	15,236	12,455	3,178	12,579	15,520
Douglas	8,869	13,349	4,362	5,086	13,493
Early	1,970	1,457	652	1,359	1,918
Echols	312	361	238	245	422
Effingham	2,690	3,814	1,443	1,905	3,933
Elbert	3,025	2,372	757	2,118	2,796
Emanuel	2,951	2,662	755	2,387	3,530
Evans	1,230	1,244	480	1,023	1,707
Fannin	2,902	3,255	1,028	2,123	4,271
Fayette	8,430	17,576	5,598	4,593	16,443
Floyd	11,614	12,378	3,779	8,548	14,697
Forsyth	4,936	8,652	3,453	2,347	7,947
Franklin	2,505	2,391	1,014	1,842	2,615
Fulton	147,459	85,451	23,578	120,752	91,785
Gilmer	2,311	2,661	879	1,363	3,353
Glascock	316	516	180	210	580
Glynn	8,581	11,242	3,053	6,339	11,126
Gordon	4,103	5,265	1,818	2,369	6,051
Grady	2,520	2,370	1,126	1,883	2,989
Greene	2,259	1,307	483	1,818	1,432
Gwinnett	44,253	81,822	23,926	20,948	66,372
Habersham	3,098	4,569	1,444	2,114	4,871
Hall	11,214	16,108	5,043	7,782	17,415
Hancock	2,461	506	189	1,947	621
Haralson	3,281	3,142	1,167	2,404	4,529
Harris	2,679	3,316	954	1,905	3,414
Hart	3,614	2,607	1,376	2,476	3,044
Heard	1,456	1,190	617	874	1,551
Henry	7,817	12,634	3,769	4,348	10,882
Houston	12,270	14,119	6,263	8,664	15,748
Irwin	1,366	973	465	918	1,226
Jackson	3,792	3,976	1,381	2,607	4,407
Jasper	1,485	1,153	373	1,183	1,474
Jeff Davis	2,031	1,947	958	1,242	2,050
Jefferson	3,220	2,077	685	2,346	2,788
Jenkins	1,401	929	394	953	1,288
Johnson	1,473	1,314	502	927	1,567
Jones	3,338	2,770	1,159	2,662	3,618
Lamar	2,065	1,707	600	1,416	2,035
Lanier	811	600	298	698	725
Laurens	6,184	6,146	1,602	4,879	6,929
Lee	1,811	3,061	1,024	995	2,875
Liberty	3,853	2,832	1,176	2,906	3,100
Lincoln	1,327	1,149	479	893	1,417
Long	874	719	355	681	858
Lowndes	9,019	10,276	2,864	6,427	10,855
Lumpkin	2,010	1,972	1,035	1,286	2,888
McDuffie	2,640	2,955	860	1,704	3,231
McIntosh	1,925	1,027	550	1,527	1,273
Macon	2,491	944	363	2,268	1,412
Madison	2,393	3,351	1,129	1,639	3,724
Marion	1,145	711	198	844	804
Meriwether	4,002	2,364	942	2,934	3,101
Miller	934	826	455	515	1,105
Mitchell	3,052	1,917	818	2,260	2,590
Monroe	2,774	2,423	949	1,970	2,570
Montgomery	1,185	1,009	416	903	1,228

Morgan	2,057	1,797	596	1,508	2,108
Murray	2,764	3,256	1,186	1,679	3,996
Muscogee	25,476	21,386	4,327	18,772	23,058
Newton	5,811	5,804	1,998	3,111	5,809
Oconee	2,745	4,125	1,182	1,990	4,265
Oglethorpe	1,491	1,590	620	1,154	1,951
Paulding	5,212	7,180	2,654	2,717	7,329
Peach	3,677	2,327	947	2,972	2,782
Pickens	2,359	2,332	1,037	1,430	3,021
Pierce	1,852	1,899	708	1,558	1,947
Pike	1,651	1,822	623	1,176	2,074
Polk	4,872	4,158	1,598	2,977	5,454
Pulaski	1,756	1,075	614	1,476	1,400
Putnam	2,149	1,756	775	1,532	2,111
Quitman	523	284	113	436	296
Rabun	1,878	1,902	825	1,301	2,278
Randolph	1,756	887	315	1,369	1,319
Richmond	28,910	24,227	6,290	20,489	27,566
Rockdale	7,003	11,945	3,664	4,330	12,413
Schley	601	511	180	439	635
Screven	1,940	1,705	709	1,461	2,178
Seminole	1,193	850	468	1,171	1,469
Spalding	6,392	7,262	2,044	4,318	7,730
Stephens	2,976	4,047	1,448	2,185	4,329
Stewart	1,540	1,186	175	1,136	832
Sumter	4,489	3,616	1,046	3,332	4,289
Talbot	1,768	671	238	1,248	802
Taliaferro	755	269	80	469	306
Tattnall	2,360	2,566	996	1,694	3,172
Taylor	1,508	1,078	281	1,134	1,145
Telfair	2,238	1,324	613	1,765	1,805
Terrell	1,942	1,143	384	1,383	1,517
Thomas	4,841	5,500	1,591	3,530	6,572
Tift	3,930	4,485	1,139	2,446	4,760
Toombs	2,648	3,609	1,210	1,152	4,433
Towns	1,487	1,674	537	942	1,783
Treutlen	1,116	898	318	726	970
Troup	6,412	8,118	2,488	4,562	9,484
Turner	1,669	936	370	1,122	1,312
Twiggs	2,097	853	432	1,730	1,261
Union	2,304	2,533	804	1,258	2,396
Upson	3,740	4,053	1,186	2,666	4,614
Walker	6,217	8,489	2,748	4,753	10,487
Walton	4,821	5,619	1,923	3,091	5,974
Ware	4,573	4,573	1,263	4,292	4,819
Warren	1,239	751	180	1,091	897
Washington	3,508	2,384	820	2,615	2,752
Wayne	3,052	3,381	1,107	2,417	3,340
Webster	600	208	103	427	361
Wheeler	880	601	214	658	709
White	1,756	2,477	981	1,028	2,648
Whitfield	7,335	12,003	2,866	4,618	12,761
Wilcox	1,365	916	433	1,079	1,235
Wilkes	1,955	1,535	464	1,549	1,810
Wilkinson	2,286	1,232	520	1,831	1,546
Worth	2,578	2,344	905	1,311	2,668
Totals	**1,008,966**	**995,252**	**309,657**	**714,792**	**1,081,331**

Georgia Vote Since 1944

1944, Roosevelt, Dem., 268,187; Dewey, Rep., 56,506; Watson, Proh., 36.

1948, Truman, Dem., 254,646; Dewey, Rep., 76,691; Thurmond, States' Rights, 85,055; Wallace, Prog., 1,636; Watson, Proh., 732.

1952, Eisenhower, Rep., 198,979; Stevenson, Dem., 456,823; Liberty Party, 1.

1956, Stevenson, Dem., 444,388; Eisenhower, Rep., 222,778; Andrews, Ind., write-in, 1,754.

1960, Kennedy, Dem., 458,638; Nixon, Rep., 274,472; write-in, 239.

1964, Johnson, Dem., 522,557; Goldwater, Rep., 616,600.

1968, Nixon, Rep., 380,111; Humphrey, Dem., 334,440; Wallace, 3d party, 535,550; write-in, 162.

1972, Nixon, Rep., 881,496; McGovern, Dem., 289,529; Schmitz, Amer., 2,288; scattered.

1976, Carter, Dem., 979,409; Ford, Rep., 483,743; write-in, 4,306.

1980, Reagan, Rep., 654,168; Carter, Dem., 890,955; Anderson, Ind., 36,055; Clark, Libertarian, 15,627.

1984, Reagan, Rep., 1,068,722; Mondale, Dem., 706,628.

1988, Bush, Rep., 1,081,331; Dukakis, Dem., 714,792; Paul, Lib., 8,435; Fulani, New Alliance, 5,099.

1992, Clinton, Dem., 1,008,966; Bush, Rep., 995,252; Perot, Ind., 309,657; Marrou, Libertarian, 7,110.

Hawaii

	1992			1988	
County	Clinton (D)	Bush (R)	Perot (I)	Dukakis (D)	Bush (R)
Hawaii	25,725	15,460	8,889	24,091	17,125
Honolulu	123,908	103,937	35,728	138,971	120,258
Kauai	10,715	6,274	1,756	11,770	8,298
Maui	18,962	11,151	6,630	17,532	12,944
Totals	**179,310**	**136,822**	**53,003**	**192,364**	**158,625**

Hawaii Vote Since 1968

1968, Nixon, Rep., 91,425; Humphrey, Dem., 141,324; Wallace, 3d party, 3,469.

1972, Nixon, Rep., 168,865; McGovern, Dem., 101,409.

1976, Carter, Dem., 147,375; Ford, Rep., 140,003; MacBride, Libertarian, 3,923.

1980, Reagan, Rep., 130,112; Carter, Dem., 135,879; Anderson, Ind., 32,021; Clark, Libertarian, 3,269; Commoner, Citizens, 1,548; Hall, Com., 458.

1984, Reagan, Rep., 184,934; Mondale, Dem., 147,098; Bergland, Libertarian, 2,167.

1988, Bush, Rep., 158,625; Dukakis, Dem., 192,364; Paul, Lib., 1,999; Fulani, New Alliance, 1,003.

1992, Clinton, Dem., 179,310; Bush, Rep., 136,822; Perot, Ind., 53,003; Gritz, Populist/America First, 1,452; Marrou, Libertarian, 1,119.

Idaho

	1992			1988	
County	Clinton (D)	Bush (R)	Perot (I)	Dukakis (D)	Bush (R)
Ada	31,941	49,000	28,192	30,525	54,951
Adams	457	754	695	643	1,107
Bannock	11,091	12,016	8,116	13,074	14,986
Bear Lake	562	1,419	684	867	2,084
Benewah	1,270	1,223	1,165	1,518	1,650
Bingham	3,565	7,333	4,144	4,346	10,131
Blaine	2,865	2,243	2,831	2,498	3,130
Boise	623	912	754	620	1,044
Bonner	4,995	3,937	4,645	5,555	5,721
Bonneville	7,014	16,557	10,241	7,032	22,613
Boundary	1,095	1,479	1,136	1,336	1,800
Butte	433	602	392	521	899
Camas	134	202	145	136	288
Canyon	9,095	19,220	8,974	10,207	21,426
Caribou	562	1,350	1,088	867	2,239
Cassias	1,351	4,052	1,785	1,833	5,345
Clark	95	195	119	133	281
Clearwater	1,433	1,152	1,098	1,861	1,659
Custer	564	829	729	616	1,253
Elmore	1,858	3,087	1,867	2,078	3,756
Franklin	524	2,115	890	806	2,992
Fremont	903	2,333	1,349	1,178	3,401
Gem	1,609	2,455	1,555	2,064	2,926
Gooding	1,530	2,178	1,591	1,872	2,908
Idaho	1,974	2,709	1,900	2,198	3,541
Jefferson	978	3,471	2,164	1,198	5,295
Jerome	1,739	2,972	1,768	1,985	3,830
Kootenai	11,553	13,065	11,261	11,621	15,093
Latah	7,233	5,353	3,602	6,544	6,367
Lemhi	996	1,540	1,175	1,157	2,378
Lewis	674	593	491	807	786
Lincoln	514	656	441	574	918
Madison	741	4,591	1,920	1,009	6,197
Minidoka	1,815	3,304	1,875	2,290	4,623
Nez Perce	7,069	5,431	4,363	7,754	7,027
Oneida	351	713	590	508	1,269
Owyhee	686	1,469	862	848	1,707
Payette	1,656	2,895	2,055	1,900	3,786
Power	837	1,352	697	1,095	1,838
Shoshone	3,182	1,441	1,878	3,379	2,134
Teton	472	762	608	531	982
Twin Falls	6,593	10,335	6,043	7,078	13,243
Valley	1,259	1,548	1,313	1,251	1,897
Washington	1,122	1,802	1,204	1,359	2,380
Totals	**137,013**	**202,645**	**130,395**	**147,272**	**253,881**

Idaho Vote Since 1944

1944, Roosevelt, Dem., 107,399; Dewey, Rep., 100,137; Watson, Proh., 503; Thomas, Soc., 282.

1948, Truman, Dem., 107,370; Dewey, Rep., 101,514; Wallace, Prog., 4,972; Watson, Proh., 628; Thomas, Soc., 332.

1952, Eisenhower, Rep., 180,707; Stevenson Dem., 95,081; Hallinan, Prog., 443; write-in, 23.

1956, Eisenhower, Rep., 166,979; Stevenson, Dem., 105,868; Andrews, Ind., 126; write-in, 16.

1960, Kennedy, Dem., 138,853; Nixon, Rep., 161,597.

1964, Johnson, Dem., 148,920; Goldwater, Rep., 143,557.

1968, Nixon, Rep., 165,369; Humphrey, Dem., 89,273; Wallace, 3d party, 36,541.

1972, Nixon, Rep., 199,384; McGovern, Dem., 80,826; Schmitz, Amer., 28,869; Spock, Peoples, 903.

1976, Carter, Dem., 126,549; Ford, Rep., 204,151; Maddox, Amer., 5,935; MacBride, Libertarian, 3,558; LaRouche, U.S. Labor, 739.

1980, Reagan, Rep., 290,699; Carter, Dem., 110,192; Anderson, Ind., 27,058; Clark, Libertarian, 8,425; Rarick, Amer., 1,057.

1984, Reagan, Rep., 297,523; Mondale, Dem., 108,510; Bergland, Libertarian, 2,823.

1988, Bush, Rep., 253,881; Dukakis, Dem., 147,272; Paul, Lib., 5,313; Fulani, Ind., 2,502.

1992, Bush, Rep., 202,645; Clinton, Dem., 137,013; Perot, Ind., 130,395; Gritz, Populist/America First, 10,281; Marrou, Libertarian, 1,167.

Illinois

	1992			1988	
County	Clinton (D)	Bush (R)	Perot (I)	Dukakis (D)	Bush (R)
Adams	11,748	13,529	6,157	13,768	15,831
Alexander	2,566	1,301	474	2,693	1,954
Bond	3,428	2,715	1,373	3,459	3,608
Boone	5,114	5,589	2,880	4,234	6,923
Brown	1,146	1,029	504	1,267	1,373
Bureau	7,551	6,836	3,465	7,354	8,896
Calhoun	1,519	745	532	1,544	1,238
Carroll	2,854	3,297	1,502	2,990	4,464
Cass	3,200	2,162	1,072	3,316	2,916
Champaign	35,003	27,096	13,571	29,733	33,247
Christian	9,042	5,087	3,401	8,295	7,040
Clark	3,338	3,175	1,450	3,275	4,508
Clay	2,962	2,471	1,193	2,761	3,494
Clinton	6,686	5,771	3,315	5,935	7,681
Coles	9,402	8,098	4,707	8,327	11,043
Cook	1,249,533	605,300	281,999	1,129,973	878,582
Crawford	3,964	3,606	2,062	3,555	4,951
Cumberland	2,111	1,860	1,209	1,904	2,667
DeKalb	13,744	12,655	7,680	11,811	17,182
DeWitt	3,009	3,164	1,543	2,660	3,942
Douglas	3,341	3,309	1,600	3,184	4,378
DuPage	114,564	178,271	76,839	94,285	217,907
Edgar	4,014	3,790	1,930	3,880	5,538
Edwards	1,299	1,601	634	1,218	2,212
Effingham	5,221	6,329	3,354	4,553	8,431
Fayette	4,833	3,508	1,730	4,632	5,452
Ford	2,175	3,046	1,222	2,026	4,059
Franklin	12,744	5,504	3,180	11,023	7,677
Fulton	9,725	5,062	2,874	9,046	6,999
Gallatin	2,371	990	568	2,455	1,580
Greene	3,164	2,391	1,461	3,020	3,136
Grundy	6,122	6,346	3,724	5,525	8,743
Hamilton	2,582	1,521	862	2,618	2,622
Hancock	4,213	3,714	2,091	4,740	4,568
Hardin	1,665	985	515	1,308	1,504
Henderson	2,013	1,310	715	2,085	1,726
Henry	11,077	8,989	4,231	11,594	11,358
Iroquois	4,440	6,948	3,073	4,221	9,596
Jackson	13,373	6,899	3,995	11,334	9,687
Jasper	2,284	1,996	1,160	2,135	3,024
Jefferson	8,665	5,497	3,403	7,729	7,624
Jersey	4,749	2,933	2,363	4,376	4,343
JoDaviess	4,044	4,249	2,102	4,141	4,923
Johnson	2,299	2,124	944	1,872	2,797
Kane	44,568	55,684	27,179	36,366	66,283
Kankakee	17,229	15,411	7,264	15,147	20,316
Kendall	5,423	8,521	4,394	4,347	10,653
Knox	12,524	8,331	4,357	12,752	10,842
Lake	81,693	99,000	42,384	64,327	114,115
LaSalle	23,276	16,078	10,434	22,271	22,166
Lawrence	3,270	2,681	1,498	3,140	3,655
Lee	5,530	6,652	3,191	4,608	8,903
Livingston	6,007	8,004	3,029	5,009	10,324
Logan	5,169	6,567	2,420	4,727	8,490
McDonough	5,814	5,297	2,770	5,247	7,173
McHenry	24,783	41,356	21,817	18,919	46,135
McLean	23,090	25,726	10,282	18,659	30,572
Macon	27,449	18,684	9,236	25,364	23,862
Macoupin	12,050	6,518	5,018	12,195	9,362
Madison	58,484	32,167	23,110	54,175	44,907
Marion	9,669	5,764	3,407	8,592	8,695
Marshall	2,819	2,491	1,169	2,742	3,588
Mason	3,969	2,473	1,245	3,406	3,424
Massac	3,347	2,754	892	3,227	3,507
Menard	2,264	2,834	1,179	2,103	3,560
Mercer	3,990	2,983	1,535	4,204	3,683
Monroe	4,894	4,807	2,813	4,529	6,275
Montgomery	7,424	4,407	2,956	7,293	6,388
Morgan	6,351	6,566	3,317	6,032	8,808
Moultrie	3,056	2,065	1,322	3,013	3,167
Ogle	6,512	9,008	4,455	5,641	11,644
Peoria	38,099	30,718	12,195	35,253	37,605
Perry	6,009	3,105	1,955	5,167	4,576
Piatt	3,520	3,076	1,822	3,099	4,137
Pike	4,016	3,342	1,643	4,614	3,965
Pope	1,063	951	391	996	1,202
Pulaski	1,987	1,169	379	1,793	1,666
Putnam	1,574	969	752	1,601	1,516
Randolph	8,529	4,899	3,092	7,844	7,396
Richland	3,286	3,053	1,689	2,863	4,264
Rock Island	37,412	23,212	10,416	40,174	27,412
St. Clair	57,625	31,951	17,592	55,465	41,439
Saline	7,258	3,667	2,302	6,676	5,798
Sangamon	40,052	39,641	16,861	37,729	50,175
Schuyler	1,650	1,512	815	1,866	2,178
Scott	1,057	1,132	588	1,243	1,535
Shelby	5,101	3,601	2,401	4,650	5,370
Stark	1,336	1,384	625	1,274	1,841
Stephenson	7,899	9,005	4,677	7,460	11,342
Tazewell	26,428	23,469	9,927	24,603	28,861
Union	4,681	3,003	1,370	4,197	4,244
Vermilion	10,383	11,703	8,162	17,918	16,943
Wabash	2,436	2,485	1,302	2,241	3,453
Warren	3,661	3,325	1,436	3,617	4,584
Washington	2,986	3,003	1,542	2,689	4,127
Wayne	3,332	3,809	1,702	3,135	5,481
White	4,308	3,057	1,428	4,144	4,354
Whiteside	12,329	10,146	4,589	11,328	12,978
Will	59,633	58,337	32,788	49,816	73,129
Williamson	14,361	9,462	4,779	12,712	12,274
Winnebago	48,298	42,221	21,227	45,280	55,699
Woodford	5,490	8,032	2,733	4,604	9,474
Totals	**2,453,350**	**1,734,096**	**840,515**	**2,215,940**	**2,310,939**

Illinois Vote Since 1944

1944, Roosevelt, Dem., 2,079,479; Dewey, Rep., 1,939,314; Teichert, Soc. Labor, 9,677; Watson, Proh., 7,411; Thomas, Soc., 180.

1948, Truman, Dem., 1,994,715; Dewey, Rep., 1,961,103; Watson, Proh., 11,959; Thomas, Soc., 11,522; Teichert, Soc. Labor, 3,118.

1952, Eisenhower, Rep., 2,457,327; Stevenson, Dem., 2,013,920; Hass, Soc. Labor, 9,363; write-in, 448.

1956, Eisenhower, Rep., 2,623,327; Stevenson, Dem., 1,775,682; Hass, Soc. Labor, 8,342; write-in, 56.

1960, Kennedy, Dem., 2,377,846; Nixon, Rep., 2,368,988; Hass, Soc. Labor, 10,560; write-in, 15.

1964, Johnson, Dem., 2,796,833; Goldwater, Rep., 1,905,946; write-in, 62.

1968, Nixon, Rep., 2,174,774; Humphrey, Dem., 2,039,814; Wallace, 3d party, 390,958; Blomen, Soc. Labor, 13,878; write-in, 325.

1972, Nixon, Rep. 2,788,179; McGovern, Dem., 1,913,472; Fisher, Soc. Labor, 12,344; Schmitz, Amer., 2,471; Hall, Com., 4,541; others, 2,229.

1976, Carter, Dem., 2,271,295; Ford, Rep., 2,364,269; McCarthy, Ind., 55,939; Hall, Com., 9,250; MacBride, Libertarian, 8,057; Camejo, Soc. Workers, 3,615; Levin, Soc. Labor, 2,422; LaRouche, U.S. Labor, 2,018; write-in, 1,968.

1980, Reagan, Rep., 2,358,049; Carter, Dem., 1,981,413; Anderson, Ind., 346,754; Clark, Libertarian, 38,939; Commoner, Citizens, 10,692; Hall, Com., 9,711; Griswold, Workers World, 2,257; DeBerry, Socialist Workers, 1,302; write-ins, 604.

1984, Reagan, Rep., 2,707,103; Mondale, Dem., 2,086,499; Bergland, Libertarian, 10,086.

1988, Bush, Rep., 2,310,939; Dukakis, Dem., 2,215,940; Paul, Lib., 14,944; Fulani, Solid., 10,276.

1992, Clinton, Dem., 2,453,350; Bush, Rep., 1,734,096; Perot, Ind., 840,515; Marrou, Libertarian, 9,218; Fulani, New Alliance, 5,267; Gritz, Populist/America First, 3,577; Hagelin, Natural Law, 2,751; Warren, Socialist Workers, 1,361.

Indiana

	1992			1988	
County	Clinton (D)	Bush (R)	Perot (I)	Dukakis (D)	Bush (R)
Adams	3,708	6,078	2,865	3,811	8,137
Allen	39,629	55,003	25,809	39,238	74,638
Bartholomew	8,284	13,146	5,882	8,804	17,364
Benton	1,221	2,030	1,056	1,349	2,698
Blackford	2,088	2,347	1,319	2,253	3,336
Boone	3,982	9,485	3,826	4,168	11,608
Brown	2,029	2,633	1,635	2,115	3,348
Carroll	2,561	3,800	2,173	2,952	4,981
Cass	4,757	7,421	3,944	5,784	10,970
Clark	17,460	13,333	5,653	14,528	16,544
Clay	3,306	4,696	2,134	3,724	5,852
Clinton	3,490	6,141	2,535	4,412	8,570
Crawford	2,260	1,903	819	2,036	2,532
Daviess	3,201	5,591	1,695	3,483	6,768
Dearborn	5,116	6,974	3,384	5,066	8,195
Decatur	2,774	5,195	2,299	2,979	6,245
Dekalb	4,652	6,682	3,554	4,657	9,018
Delaware	19,556	20,473	10,453	20,548	27,348
Dubois	5,878	6,785	3,195	5,954	9,995
Elkhart	14,660	27,920	9,450	14,236	33,793
Fayette	3,969	4,376	2,299	4,118	5,949
Floyd	13,166	11,932	4,421	11,024	14,291

Fountain	2,829	3,391	2,162	3,279	5,113
Franklin	2,456	3,831	1,858	2,472	4,777
Fulton	2,552	3,982	1,963	2,788	5,234
Gibson	6,909	5,172	2,680	7,031	7,610
Grant	9,211	13,806	5,597	10,799	18,441
Greene	5,431	5,410	2,610	5,979	7,689
Hamilton	10,215	34,622	10,365	8,853	36,654
Hancock	4,752	11,072	4,752	5,355	13,374
Harrison	5,768	5,403	2,469	4,933	6,702
Hendricks	7,071	18,373	7,519	7,643	22,090
Henry	6,794	8,720	4,416	7,779	11,280
Howard	10,288	15,306	8,575	11,518	19,971
Huntington	3,855	9,093	2,967	3,873	11,675
Jackson	5,663	7,246	3,148	5,550	9,470
Jasper	3,033	4,809	2,019	3,237	6,009
Jay	3,208	3,609	1,994	3,212	5,363
Jefferson	5,510	4,937	2,565	5,221	6,949
Jennings	3,471	4,392	2,370	3,667	5,636
Johnson	8,712	20,353	8,246	9,001	24,654
Knox	6,718	6,683	3,719	7,006	9,813
Kosciusko	5,307	14,179	5,115	5,321	17,761
LaGrange	2,093	3,584	1,736	2,029	4,495
Lake	102,778	53,867	28,635	105,026	79,929
LaPorte	17,717	14,962	9,641	17,585	20,537
Lawrence	5,557	7,712	3,452	5,787	10,742
Madison	22,276	23,479	13,100	24,443	32,596
Marion	122,234	141,369	57,878	128,627	184,519
Marshall	4,912	8,048	3,522	5,488	10,490
Martin	2,018	2,523	883	2,132	3,066
Miami	3,967	6,416	3,428	4,613	8,533
Monroe	19,712	16,661	6,943	15,855	20,756
Montgomery	3,371	7,602	3,511	3,623	10,793
Morgan	4,690	10,939	5,375	5,375	14,284
Newton	1,757	2,295	1,274	1,744	3,274
Noble	4,411	5,883	3,328	4,143	7,889
Ohio	970	1,009	527	1,113	1,412
Orange	2,948	3,738	1,296	2,739	5,245
Owen	2,207	2,753	1,563	2,484	3,837
Parke	2,429	2,953	1,696	2,563	4,458
Perry	4,829	2,973	1,560	4,804	4,720
Pike	2,960	2,156	1,238	3,037	3,294
Porter	21,022	22,644	13,096	19,390	29,790
Posey	4,632	4,435	2,357	4,468	5,987
Pulaski	1,950	2,712	1,214	2,213	3,677
Putnam	3,487	5,341	3,174	3,850	7,119
Randolph	3,870	4,937	2,939	3,990	6,856
Ripley	3,480	5,033	2,406	3,605	6,414
Rush	2,168	3,873	1,948	2,451	5,112
St. Joseph	46,203	38,934	18,828	48,056	49,481
Scott	4,085	2,649	1,092	3,378	3,455
Shelby	4,560	8,075	3,521	5,382	10,176
Spencer	4,301	3,789	1,464	4,061	4,964
Starke	3,695	3,100	1,885	4,104	4,458
Steuben	3,630	4,868	2,896	3,114	6,855
Sullivan	4,211	3,052	1,857	4,320	4,246
Switzerland	1,535	1,211	636	1,479	1,572
Tippecanoe	17,343	23,050	9,684	16,256	27,897
Tipton	2,125	3,906	1,816	2,485	5,148
Union	898	1,394	664	946	1,814
Vanderburgh	33,799	30,271	12,513	31,270	38,928
Vermillion	3,652	2,360	1,794	4,044	3,674
Vigo	18,050	15,834	8,141	19,192	21,929
Wabash	4,518	7,062	3,424	4,168	9,153
Warren	1,367	1,601	1,020	1,542	2,243
Warrick	8,612	8,087	3,862	7,999	10,504
Washington	4,092	4,043	1,846	3,370	4,998
Wayne	9,960	12,221	5,095	10,209	16,388
Wells	3,282	5,799	2,890	3,437	7,712
White	2,988	4,622	2,582	3,256	6,220
Whitley	3,569	5,217	3,195	3,642	7,679
Totals	**848,420**	**989,375**	**455,934**	**860,643**	**1,297,763**

Indiana Vote Since 1944

1944, Roosevelt, Dem., 781,403; Dewey, Rep., 875,891; Watson, Proh., 12,574; Thomas, Soc., 2,223.

1948, Truman, Dem., 807,833; Dewey, Rep., 821,079; Watson, Proh., 14,711; Wallace, Prog., 9,649; Thomas, Soc., 2,179; Teichert, Soc. Labor, 763.

1952, Eisenhower, Rep., 1,136,259; Stevenson, Dem., 801,530; Hamblen, Proh., 15,335; Hallinan, Prog., 1,222; Hass, Soc. Labor, 979.

1956, Eisenhower, Rep., 1,182,811; Stevenson, Dem., 783,908; Holtwick, Proh., 6,554; Hass, Soc. Labor, 1,334.

1960, Kennedy, Dem., 952,358; Nixon, Rep., 1,175,120; Decker, Proh., 6,746; Hass, Soc. Labor, 1,136.

1964, Johnson, Dem. 1,170,848; Goldwater, Rep., 911,118; Munn, Proh., 8,266; Hass, Soc. Labor, 1,374.

1968, Nixon, Rep., 1,067,885; Humphrey, Dem., 806,659; Wallace, 3d party, 243,108; Munn, Proh., 4,616; Halstead, Soc. Worker, 1,293; Gregory, write-in, 36.

1972, Nixon, Rep., 1,405,154; McGovern, Dem., 708,568; Reed, Soc. Workers, 5,575; Fisher, Soc. Labor, 1,688; Spock, Peace & Freedom, 4,544.

1976, Carter, Dem., 1,014,714; Ford, Rep., 1,185,958; Anderson, Amer., 14,048; Camejo, Soc. Workers, 5,695; LaRouche, U.S. Labor, 1,947.

1980 Reagan, Rep., 1,255,656; Carter, Dem., 844,197; Anderson, Ind., 111,639; Clark, Libertarian, 19,627; Commoner, Citizens, 4,852; Greaves, American, 4,750; Hall, Com., 702; DeBerry, Soc., 610.

1984 Reagan, Rep., 1,377,230; Mondale, Dem., 841,481; Bergland, Libertarian, 6,741.

1988, Bush, Rep., 1,297,763; Dukakis, Dem., 860,643; Fulani, New Alliance, 10,215.

1992, Bush, Rep., 989,375; Clinton, Dem., 848,420; Perot, Ind., 455,934; Marrou, Libertarian, 7,936; Fulani, New Alliance, 2,583.

Iowa

	1992			1988	
County	Clinton (D)	Bush (R)	Perot (I)	Dukakis (D)	Bush (R)
Adair	1,655	1,713	814	2,261	1,833
Adams	1,034	863	679	1,283	1,080
Allamakee	2,362	2,627	1,543	2,768	3,186
Appanoose	2,810	2,346	1,161	3,209	2,779
Audubon	1,589	1,373	887	1,863	1,478
Benton	4,467	3,469	2,454	5,873	4,011
Black Hawk	29,584	21,398	10,182	31,657	24,112
Boone	5,913	4,148	2,070	7,232	4,381
Bremer	4,774	4,482	2,338	4,961	5,079
Buchanan	4,166	3,313	2,126	4,778	3,495
Buena Vista	3,374	3,863	1,955	4,580	4,170
Butler	2,548	3,209	1,333	2,593	3,523
Calhoun	2,140	2,169	946	2,990	2,474
Carroll	3,800	3,439	2,192	5,437	3,701
Cass	2,231	3,176	1,608	2,934	3,962
Cedar	3,296	2,965	1,945	4,032	3,373
Cerro Gordo	11,415	8,250	4,498	12,857	9,358
Cherokee	2,590	2,768	1,503	3,574	3,218
Chickasaw	2,913	2,129	1,566	3,530	2,549
Clarke	1,921	1,417	899	2,262	1,631
Clay	3,346	3,011	1,964	4,173	3,641
Clayton	3,742	3,044	2,309	4,320	3,839
Clinton	11,683	8,746	4,414	12,549	10,243
Crawford	3,004	2,693	1,905	3,868	3,375
Dallas	6,554	5,587	2,665	7,501	4,858
Davis	1,962	1,344	718	2,246	1,563
Decatur	1,866	1,316	786	2,192	1,406
Delaware	3,093	3,195	2,144	3,947	3,425
Des Moines	11,309	6,378	3,386	11,593	7,652
Dickinson	3,106	3,196	1,974	3,342	3,678
Dubuque	20,539	14,007	8,208	23,797	14,530
Emmet	2,239	1,749	1,010	2,778	2,173
Fayette	4,412	3,879	2,493	5,304	4,921
Floyd	3,688	2,404	1,611	4,377	3,266
Franklin	2,049	2,137	1,045	2,594	2,320
Fremont	1,422	1,459	1,003	1,547	1,946
Greene	2,422	1,952	956	3,011	2,091
Grundy	1,895	3,160	1,069	2,211	3,433
Guthrie	2,234	1,962	1,216	2,910	2,005
Hamilton	3,262	3,031	1,348	4,156	3,277
Hancock	2,175	2,428	1,170	2,831	2,731
Hardin	3,792	3,590	1,547	5,088	3,856
Harrison	2,349	2,763	1,691	2,883	3,108
Henry	3,544	3,435	1,522	3,754	3,951
Howard	2,099	1,516	1,193	2,330	1,970
Humboldt	1,765	2,299	1,093	2,713	2,594
Ida	1,449	1,714	1,061	1,787	1,951
Iowa	2,560	2,656	1,709	3,338	3,247
Jackson	4,421	2,673	2,096	4,864	3,237
Jasper	8,120	6,866	2,972	8,940	6,703
Jefferson	2,562	2,541	1,241	3,594	3,614
Johnson	28,656	14,041	8,625	28,759	15,453
Jones	3,508	3,071	2,306	4,641	3,496
Keokuk	2,329	1,981	1,238	2,899	2,278
Kossuth	3,660	3,464	1,906	5,088	3,938
Lee	9,366	4,777	2,920	10,911	6,228
Linn	38,567	30,215	19,643	42,993	33,129
Louisa	2,091	1,691	1,044	2,268	2,060
Lucas	2,072	1,734	848	2,454	1,776
Lyon	1,331	3,272	1,068	1,706	3,517
Madison	2,525	2,421	1,168	3,421	2,410
Mahaska	3,714	4,953	1,508	4,451	4,798
Marion	5,531	6,062	1,896	6,922	5,914
Marshall	8,303	6,784	3,100	9,760	7,657
Mills	1,798	2,699	1,638	2,092	3,212
Mitchell	2,177	1,933	1,199	2,870	2,338
Monona	1,939	1,660	1,231	2,408	2,068
Monroe	1,829	1,323	612	2,338	1,313
Montgomery	1,599	2,404	1,341	1,898	3,166
Muscatine	7,089	6,087	3,583	7,059	6,904
O'Brien	2,122	3,869	1,557	2,768	4,241
Osceola	990	1,756	813	1,277	1,951
Page	1,951	3,670	1,669	2,185	4,583
Palo Alto	2,374	1,789	1,186	3,377	2,041
Plymouth	3,171	5,196	2,039	4,220	5,316
Pocahontas	1,919	1,743	942	2,722	1,871
Polk	78,585	63,708	24,155	84,476	57,854

Pottawattamie	13,228	15,671	8,035	14,958	17,193
Poweshiek	4,056	3,245	1,680	4,876	3,683
Ringgold	1,341	967	551	1,609	1,110
Sac	1,896	2,138	1,157	2,613	2,411
Scott	33,765	28,844	11,423	34,415	31,025
Shelby	2,094	2,809	1,614	2,806	3,019
Sioux	2,226	10,637	1,771	2,923	10,270
Story	17,118	12,702	6,275	19,051	13,782
Tama	3,573	2,948	1,748	4,584	3,362
Taylor	1,430	1,200	910	1,671	1,647
Union	2,565	2,224	1,280	3,236	2,751
Van Buren	1,464	1,418	811	1,612	1,692
Wapello	8,070	4,852	2,513	10,177	5,350
Warren	8,612	7,242	3,217	9,627	6,424
Washington	3,384	3,576	1,994	3,776	3,741
Wayne	1,632	1,299	642	1,988	1,467
Webster	8,562	6,992	3,272	10,267	6,926
Winnebago	2,322	2,407	1,329	2,804	2,863
Winneshiek	3,791	3,331	2,416	4,443	4,194
Woodbury	17,398	18,148	7,182	20,153	18,790
Worth	2,009	1,382	1,044	2,440	1,488
Wright	2,776	2,708	1,151	3,353	2,658
Totals	**586,353**	**504,891**	**253,468**	**670,557**	**545,355**

Iowa Vote Since 1944

1944, Roosevelt, Dem., 499,876; Dewey, Rep., 547,267; Watson, Proh., 3,752; Thomas, Soc., 1,511; Teichert, Soc. Labor, 193.

1948, Truman, Dem., 522,380; Dewey, Rep., 494,018; Wallace, Prog., 12,125; Teichert, Soc. Labor, 4,274; Watson, Proh., 3,382; Thomas, Soc., 1,829; Dobbs, Soc. Workers, 26.

1952, Eisenhower, Rep., 808,906; Stevenson, Dem., 451,513; Hallinan, Prog., 5,085; Hamblen, Proh., 2,882; Hoopes, Soc., 219; Hass, Soc. Labor, 139; scattering 29.

1956, Eisenhower, Rep., 729,187; Stevenson, Dem., 501,858; Andrews (A.C.P. of Iowa), 3,202; Hoopes, Soc., 192; Hass, Soc. Labor, 125.

1960, Kennedy, Dem., 550,565; Nixon, Rep., 722,381; Hass, Soc. Labor, 230; write-in, 634.

1964, Johnson, Dem., 733,030; Goldwater, Rep., 449,148; Hass, Soc. Labor, 182; DeBerry, Soc. Worker, 159; Munn, Proh., 1,902.

1968, Nixon, Rep., 619,106; Humphrey, Dem., 476,699; Wallace, 3d party, 66,422; Munn, Proh., 362; Halstead, Soc. Worker, 3,377; Cleaver, Peace and Freedom, 1,332; Blomen, Soc. Labor, 241.

1972, Nixon, Rep., 706,207; McGovern, Dem., 496,206; Schmitz, Amer., 22,056; Jenness, Soc. Workers, 488; Fisher, Soc. Labor, 195; Hall, Com. 272; Green, Universal, 199; scattered, 321.

1976, Carter, Dem., 619,931; Ford, Rep., 632,863; McCarthy, Ind., 20,051; Anderson, Amer., 3,040; MacBride, Libertarian, 1,452.

1980, Reagan, Rep., 676,026; Carter, Dem., 508,672; Anderson, Ind., 115,633; Clark, Libertarian, 13,123; Commoner, Citizens, 2,273; McReynolds, Socialist, 534; Hall Com., 298; DeBerry, Soc. Work., 244; Greaves, American, 189; Bubar, Statesman, 150; scattering, 519.

1984, Reagan, Rep., 703,088; Mondale, Dem., 605,620; Bergland, Libertarian, 1,844.

1988, Bush, Rep., 545,355; Dukakis, Dem., 670,557; LaRouche, Ind., 3,526; Paul, Lib., 2,494.

1992, Clinton, Dem., 586,353; Bush, Rep., 504,891; Perot, Ind., 253,468; Hagelin, Natural Law, 3,079; Gritz, Populist/America First, 1,177; Marrou, Libertarian, 1,076.

Kansas

	1992			1988	
County	Clinton (D)	Bush (R)	Perot (I)	Dukakis (D)	Bush (R)
Allen	2,312	2,351	1,746	2,392	3,429
Anderson	1,178	1,218	1,282	1,466	1,781
Atchison	2,959	2,521	2,020	3,177	3,243
Barber	759	1,225	893	1,118	1,539
Barton	3,846	5,113	4,574	5,024	7,741
Bourbon	2,509	2,876	1,763	2,623	3,660
Brown	1,476	2,203	1,603	1,719	3,059
Butler	7,029	9,166	7,355	7,690	10,976
Chase	470	610	600	538	884
Chautauqua	598	853	607	661	1,247
Cherokee	4,003	3,589	2,067	4,069	4,281
Cheyenne	407	863	477	594	1,105
Clark	293	676	341	409	876
Clay	947	2,198	1,434	1,112	2,997
Cloud	1,720	2,131	1,578	2,022	3,043
Coffey	1,021	1,824	1,443	1,246	2,581
Comanche	325	636	324	375	738
Cowley	5,405	5,422	4,911	6,186	7,778
Crawford	7,366	5,468	3,706	7,783	6,940
Decatur	576	940	565	793	1,291
Dickinson	2,518	3,851	2,833	2,870	5,121
Doniphan	1,177	1,579	1,200	1,312	2,162
Douglas	19,439	12,949	9,630	15,752	16,149
Edwards	567	769	584	792	993
Elk	485	748	503	608	1,075
Ellis	4,544	3,985	3,887	5,289	5,194
Ellsworth	1,010	1,197	1,020	1,219	1,711
Finney	2,612	5,278	3,011	3,408	5,381
Ford	2,635	4,342	3,341	3,817	5,685
Franklin	2,968	3,699	3,184	3,592	4,777
Geary	2,559	2,928	2,057	2,721	3,782
Gove	379	792	532	663	966
Graham	554	752	603	702	1,139
Grant	619	1,561	835	907	1,654
Gray	443	1,039	686	696	1,180
Greeley	191	504	175	317	506
Greenwood	1,262	1,411	1,167	1,421	2,217
Hamilton	386	716	271	517	801
Harper	845	1,371	1,151	1,235	1,941
Harvey	5,047	6,259	3,653	5,503	6,893
Haskell	336	1,023	462	427	964
Hodgeman	258	625	343	439	732
Jackson	1,639	1,970	1,927	2,261	2,759
Jefferson	2,538	2,569	2,642	2,810	3,605
Jewell	546	1,050	698	684	1,546
Johnson	59,573	85,418	49,136	55,183	95,591
Kearny	384	943	376	524	1,073
Kingman	1,100	1,680	1,370	1,420	2,205
Kiowa	355	1,057	475	485	1,276
Labette	4,196	3,368	2,577	4,433	5,125
Lane	265	674	356	450	768
Leavenworth	8,077	7,738	7,306	8,797	9,913
Lincoln	612	893	657	796	1,229
Linn	1,353	1,413	1,358	1,497	2,163
Logan	355	905	446	503	988
Lyon	4,811	5,090	4,717	5,314	6,820
McPherson	3,645	5,745	3,561	4,354	6,563
Marion	1,627	3,142	1,557	2,024	3,685
Marshall	2,022	2,030	1,786	2,560	3,140
Meade	430	1,135	592	664	1,322
Miami	3,835	3,528	3,701	4,427	4,807
Mitchell	938	1,601	1,098	1,145	2,257
Montgomery	5,453	6,848	3,570	5,429	9,067
Morris	957	1,071	1,071	1,165	1,682
Morton	398	915	350	569	1,074
Nemaha	1,580	2,220	1,804	2,261	2,849
Neosho	2,799	2,926	2,136	3,402	3,739
Ness	565	967	678	887	1,230
Norton	779	1,469	815	855	1,923
Osage	2,297	2,561	2,532	2,840	3,496
Osborne	779	1,003	819	943	1,541
Ottawa	764	1,284	762	953	1,836
Pawnee	1,118	1,357	1,097	1,474	1,825
Phillips	843	1,579	955	960	2,316
Pottawatomie	2,099	3,106	2,759	2,544	3,897
Pratt	1,466	1,779	1,528	1,651	2,505
Rawlins	393	1,023	517	612	1,318
Reno	9,257	11,377	7,636	11,545	12,753
Republic	939	1,767	1,084	1,069	2,346
Rice	1,555	2,158	1,543	2,033	2,503
Riley	7,933	8,394	5,387	7,283	9,507
Rooks	771	1,249	1,063	1,012	1,938
Rush	689	756	665	1,020	1,045
Russell	1,178	1,434	1,395	1,448	2,403
Saline	7,890	8,565	7,108	7,998	11,371
Scott	480	1,426	621	717	1,590
Sedgwick	62,670	75,577	47,238	65,618	86,124
Seward	1,488	3,477	1,818	1,655	4,089
Shawnee	31,972	29,344	20,653	33,940	35,489
Sheridan	347	739	546	600	901
Sherman	810	1,630	828	1,082	1,929
Smith	789	1,236	816	1,004	1,951
Stafford	777	1,064	910	1,121	1,532
Stanton	224	556	214	310	592
Stevens	390	1,408	674	612	1,642
Summer	3,564	4,087	3,887	4,417	5,394
Thomas	932	1,849	1,129	1,408	2,342
Trego	608	727	574	795	979
Wabaunsee	851	1,254	1,258	1,166	1,737
Wallace	164	679	219	257	655
Washington	893	1,740	1,054	1,063	2,269
Wichita	241	681	303	399	721
Wilson	1,331	1,925	1,365	1,545	2,743
Woodson	590	662	604	761	1,062
Wyandotte	34,397	12,872	13,620	38,678	19,097
Totals	**390,434**	**449,951**	**312,358**	**422,636**	**554,049**

Kansas Vote Since 1944

1944, Roosevelt, Dem., 287,458; Dewey, Rep., 442,096; Watson, Proh., 2,609; Thomas, Soc., 1,613.

1948, Truman, Dem., 351,902; Dewey, Rep., 423,039; Watson, Proh., 6,468; Wallace, Prog., 4,603; Thomas, Soc., 2,807.

1952, Eisenhower, Rep., 616,302; Stevenson, Dem., 273,296; Hamblen, Proh., 6,038; Hoopes, Soc., 530.

1956, Eisenhower, Rep., 566,878; Stevenson. Dem., 296,317; Holtwick, Proh., 3,048.

1960, Kennedy, Dem., 363,213; Nixon, Rep., 561,474; Decker, Proh., 4,138.

1964, Johnson, Dem., 464,028; Goldwater, Rep., 386,579; Munn, Proh., 5,393; Hass, Soc. Labor, 1,901.

1968, Nixon, Rep., 478,674; Humphrey, Dem., 302,996; Wallace, 3d, 88,921; Munn, Proh., 2,192.

1972, Nixon, Rep., 619,812; McGovern, Dem., 270,287; Schmitz, Cons., 21,808; Munn, Proh., 4,188.

1976, Carter, Dem., 430,421; Ford, Rep., 502,752; McCarthy, Ind., 13,185; Anderson, Amer., 4,724; MacBride, Libertarian, 3,242; Maddox, Cons., 2,118; Bubar, Proh., 1,403.

1980, Reagan, Rep., 566,812; Carter, Dem., 326,150; Anderson, Ind., 68,231; Clark, Libertarian, 14,470; Shelton, American, 1,555; Hall, Com., 967; Bubar, Statesman, 821; Rarick, Conservative, 789.

1984, Reagan, Rep., 674,646; Mondale, Dem., 332,471; Bergland, Libertarian, 3,585.

1988, Bush, Rep., 554,049; Dukakis, Dem., 422,636; Paul, Ind., 12,553; Fulani, Ind., 3,806.

1992, Bush, Rep., 449,951; Clinton, Dem., 390,434; Perot, Ind., 312,358; Marrou, Libertarian, 4,314.

Kentucky

		1992		1988	
County	Clinton (D)	Bush (R)	Perot (I)	Dukakis (D)	Bush (R)
Adair	2,044	3,740	617	1,723	4,346
Allen	2,040	2,747	606	1,573	3,342
Anderson	2,491	2,731	1,219	2,176	3,225
Ballard	2,268	1,108	500	2,162	1,460
Barren	5,688	5,467	1,778	4,799	6,653
Bath	2,229	1,259	694	2,099	1,614
Bell	5,745	4,501	1,193	5,182	5,759
Boone	6,514	12,306	4,676	5,382	12,667
Bourbon	2,895	2,707	1,290	2,793	3,308
Boyd	10,496	7,387	3,195	9,552	9,379
Boyle	3,894	4,019	1,335	3,575	4,746
Bracken	1,259	1,162	500	1,176	1,630
Breathitt	3,496	1,303	515	3,387	2,149
Breckinridge	3,113	2,941	945	2,765	3,841
Bullitt	7,830	7,745	3,333	6,005	8,859
Butler	1,468	2,729	596	1,245	3,278
Caldwell	3,000	1,966	670	2,564	2,952
Calloway	6,181	4,654	1,853	5,287	6,225
Campbell	10,673	16,382	5,659	9,553	19,387
Carlisle	1,383	844	309	1,428	1,104
Carroll	2,119	1,046	566	1,913	1,702
Carter	4,224	3,305	989	4,570	4,325
Casey	1,409	3,317	542	1,216	3,857
Christian	6,709	7,737	1,789	5,704	9,250
Clark	4,892	4,625	1,955	4,252	5,329
Clay	2,012	4,747	648	1,709	4,156
Clinton	1,241	2,830	346	899	3,248
Crittenden	1,740	1,576	495	1,443	2,211
Cumberland	917	1,866	268	753	2,231
Daviess	16,592	14,936	5,112	14,815	17,356
Edmonson	1,653	2,486	438	1,243	2,555
Elliott	1,796	444	273	1,797	550
Estill	1,837	2,453	736	1,692	3,077
Fayette	38,306	41,908	14,215	32,554	48,065
Fleming	2,257	2,045	815	2,086	2,409
Floyd	13,351	3,540	1,723	12,327	5,296
Franklin	9,896	7,591	3,340	9,271	9,805
Fulton	1,813	1,073	306	1,531	1,474
Gallatin	1,171	699	445	1,060	881
Garrard	1,730	2,359	697	1,710	2,681
Grant	2,097	2,128	1,149	1,896	2,835
Graves	8,001	5,311	1,943	7,153	6,274
Grayson	2,909	4,533	993	2,575	5,186
Green	1,760	2,709	500	1,595	3,139
Greenup	7,214	4,975	2,188	6,956	6,559
Hancock	1,714	1,261	551	1,478	1,733
Hardin	9,417	12,299	4,026	7,262	13,240
Harlan	6,796	3,970	1,391	7,341	5,166
Harrison	2,795	2,148	1,225	2,748	2,983
Hart	2,852	2,401	579	2,519	2,927
Henderson	8,270	5,125	2,678	7,648	6,911
Henry	2,838	1,640	720	2,544	2,286
Hickman	1,296	861	294	1,158	1,142
Hopkins	8,881	6,032	2,565	7,453	7,979
Jackson	776	3,398	341	678	3,926
Jefferson	152,728	116,566	39,822	127,936	139,711
Jessamine	3,764	6,474	2,059	2,955	7,057
Johnson	3,669	3,614	1,118	3,538	4,619
Kenton	16,344	27,261	9,336	14,838	30,738
Knott	5,500	1,243	560	5,185	1,691
Knox	3,787	5,011	972	2,919	4,903
Larue	2,190	2,154	582	1,822	2,590
Laurel	4,560	8,583	1,859	3,620	9,296
Lawrence	2,400	2,084	557	2,198	2,294
Lee	1,170	1,617	356	984	1,588
Leslie	1,591	2,879	450	1,105	3,280
Letcher	5,817	3,011	1,206	4,697	3,601
Lewis	1,713	2,493	673	1,568	3,108
Lincoln	2,532	2,624	762	2,677	3,530
Livingston	2,386	1,339	578	2,052	1,834
Logan	4,064	3,710	1,043	3,379	4,295
Lyon	1,583	820	293	1,337	1,077
McCracken	13,341	10,657	3,077	12,208	12,160
McCreary	1,934	3,588	624	1,644	3,477
McLean	2,223	1,355	529	2,269	1,829
Madison	8,005	8,719	3,038	6,672	9,958
Magoffin	3,261	1,992	440	2,895	2,158
Marion	3,403	2,091	805	3,152	2,500
Marshall	6,576	4,368	1,773	5,888	5,256
Martin	1,715	1,961	393	1,581	2,587
Mason	2,657	2,432	916	2,721	3,158
Meade	3,387	2,641	1,298	3,079	3,441
Menifee	1,311	557	254	1,096	670
Mercer	3,010	3,211	1,298	2,832	3,904
Metcalfe	1,703	1,683	409	1,705	2,179
Monroe	1,515	3,776	480	1,025	4,214
Montgomery	3,686	2,590	1,308	3,082	3,435
Morgan	2,655	1,239	498	2,329	1,452
Muhlenberg	7,901	3,551	1,624	6,912	5,369
Nelson	5,437	4,495	1,638	4,788	5,283
Nicholas	1,341	894	513	1,242	1,271
Ohio	4,022	3,385	1,423	3,612	4,910
Oldham	5,457	8,263	2,855	4,025	8,716
Owen	1,830	1,108	613	1,823	1,468
Owsley	678	1,437	209	345	1,266
Pendleton	1,740	1,810	1,086	1,576	2,487
Perry	6,619	4,128	1,308	5,557	5,154
Pike	17,358	8,212	2,444	16,339	9,976
Powell	2,323	1,809	874	2,113	2,128
Pulaski	5,465	11,423	2,449	4,786	13,482
Robertson	439	329	170	515	511
Rockcastle	1,144	3,267	446	1,041	3,880
Rowan	3,558	2,469	1,212	2,968	3,093
Russell	1,950	4,041	673	1,455	4,292
Scott	3,639	3,810	1,800	3,380	4,482
Shelby	4,398	4,550	1,451	3,834	4,998
Simpson	2,834	2,280	708	2,138	2,699
Spencer	1,383	1,305	466	1,121	1,368
Taylor	3,518	4,319	1,044	2,879	5,362
Todd	1,858	1,691	612	1,632	2,282
Trigg	2,438	1,820	573	1,991	2,427
Trimble	1,413	789	413	1,342	1,083
Union	3,325	1,605	794	3,316	2,292
Warren	11,529	14,748	3,533	9,684	16,703
Washington	2,008	2,098	542	1,950	2,445
Wayne	2,516	3,412	560	2,057	3,672
Webster	3,380	1,408	854	3,019	2,159
Whitley	4,600	5,998	1,533	3,794	7,337
Wolfe	1,674	697	297	1,516	916
Woodford	3,161	3,992	1,535	2,653	4,512
Totals	**665,104**	**617,178**	**203,944**	**580,368**	**734,281**

Kentucky Vote Since 1944

1944, Roosevelt, Dem., 472,589; Dewey, Rep., 392,448; Watson, Proh., 2,023; Thomas, Soc., 535; Teichert, Soc. Labor, 326.

1948, Truman, Dem., 466,756; Dewey, Rep., 341,210; Thurmond, States' Rights, 10,411; Wallace, Prog., 1,567; Thomas, Soc., 1,284; Watson, Proh., 1,245; Teichert, Soc. Labor, 185.

1952, Eisenhower, Rep., 495,029; Stevenson, Dem., 495,729; Hamblen, Proh., 1,161; Hass, Soc. Labor, 893; Hallinan, Proh., 336.

1956, Eisenhower, Rep., 572,192; Stevenson, Dem., 476,453; Byrd, States' Rights, 2,657; Holtwick, Proh., 2,145; Hass, Soc. Labor, 358.

1960, Kennedy, Dem., 521,855; Nixon, Rep., 602,607.

1964, Johnson, Dem., 669,659; Goldwater, Rep., 372,977; John Kasper, Nat'l. States Rights, 3,469.

1968, Nixon, Rep., 462,411; Humphrey, Dem., 397,547; Wallace, 3d p., 193,098; Halstead, Soc. Worker, 2,843.

1972, Nixon, Rep., 676,446; McGovern, Dem., 371,159; Schmitz, Amer., 17,627; Jenness, Soc. Workers, 685; Hall, Com., 464; Spock, Peoples, 1,118.

1976, Carter, Dem., 615,717; Ford, Rep., 531,852; Anderson, Amer., 8,308; McCarthy, Ind., 6,837; Maddox, Amer. Ind., 2,328; MacBride, Libertarian, 814.

1980, Reagan, Rep., 635,274; Carter, Dem., 616,417; Anderson, Ind., 31,127; Clark, Libertarian, 5,531; McCormack, Respect For Life, 4,233; Commoner, Citizens, 1,304; Pulley, Socialist, 393; Hall, Com., 348.

1984, Reagan, Rep., 815,345; Mondale, Dem., 536,756.

1988, Bush, Rep., 734,281; Dukakis, Dem., 580,368; Duke, Pop., 4,494; Paul, Lib., 2,118.

1992, Clinton, Dem., 665,104; Bush, Rep., 617,178; Perot, Ind., 203,944; Marrou, Libertarian, 4,513.

Louisiana

Parish	1992 Clinton (D)	1992 Bush (R)	1992 Perot (I)	1988 Dukakis (D)	1988 Bush (R)
Acadia	12,276	9,017	3,145	11,510	11,319
Allen	5,626	3,069	1,245	5,204	3,674
Ascension	13,036	10,275	4,295	12,147	10,726
Assumption	5,639	2,928	1,358	5,610	4,017
Avoyelles	8,696	4,851	2,139	7,353	7,659
Beauregard	5,037	5,119	2,103	4,704	6,466
Bienville	3,899	2,412	832	3,705	3,680
Bossier	11,313	15,628	4,863	9,035	20,807
Caddo	47,733	42,665	11,830	39,204	54,498
Calcasieu	33,570	24,847	10,980	33,932	29,649
Caldwell	2,061	1,752	653	1,423	2,997
Cameron	1,985	1,329	995	2,257	1,775
Catahoula	2,570	1,976	770	1,916	2,862
Claiborne	3,263	2,599	926	3,158	3,756
Concordia	4,283	3,223	1,317	3,461	5,037
DeSoto	5,671	3,643	1,358	5,366	5,022
E. Baton Rouge	68,622	81,072	16,102	59,270	86,791
East Carroll	1,835	1,142	283	1,809	1,536
East Feliciana	4,093	2,813	932	3,659	3,527
Evangeline	8,564	5,147	2,124	7,693	7,437
Franklin	4,127	3,889	1,311	3,043	5,520
Grant	3,122	3,214	1,174	2,628	4,402
Iberia	13,040	11,905	4,337	12,166	15,438
Iberville	8,218	5,211	1,543	8,678	5,855
Jackson	3,370	3,072	882	2,842	4,251
Jefferson	64,302	100,493	21,278	53,035	110,942
Jefferson Davis	7,022	4,513	2,221	6,799	5,851
Lafayette	28,583	32,406	9,124	24,133	36,648
Lafourche	16,182	12,744	5,077	15,013	16,152
LaSalle	2,389	3,068	993	1,622	4,559
Lincoln	7,205	7,220	1,751	5,427	8,853
Livingston	11,499	14,808	4,971	9,659	15,779
Madison	2,773	1,702	469	2,416	2,334
Morehouse	6,013	5,364	1,727	4,496	7,335
Natchitoches	6,974	5,694	1,606	6,151	7,224
Orleans	133,261	52,019	10,889	116,851	64,763
Ouachita	20,835	27,600	6,612	15,429	33,858
Plaquemines	4,467	5,018	1,729	3,997	6,084
Pointe Coupee	6,512	3,563	1,157	6,308	4,333
Rapides	20,873	22,783	6,599	17,928	29,977
Red River	2,360	1,649	566	2,254	2,266
Richland	3,706	3,808	1,054	2,833	5,226
Sabine	4,173	3,586	1,219	3,532	4,767
St. Bernard	12,305	16,131	4,308	11,406	19,609
St. Charles	8,810	9,158	2,593	7,973	9,685
St. Helena	3,416	1,515	589	3,013	2,006
St. James	6,609	3,339	993	6,707	3,799
St. John The Baptist	8,977	6,730	1,922	8,366	7,464
St. Landry	20,383	11,882	4,266	19,091	15,790
St. Martin	11,252	5,909	2,573	10,148	7,541
St. Mary	10,648	8,792	3,257	10,364	11,540
St. Tammany	19,735	37,839	9,005	15,638	38,334
Tangipahoa	15,194	14,128	4,612	13,527	16,669
Tensas	1,666	1,153	353	1,556	1,645
Terrebonne	13,325	14,662	5,505	12,686	18,745
Union	4,005	4,434	1,209	3,210	5,900
Vermilion	12,324	7,062	3,127	12,180	9,224
Vernon	6,005	5,912	2,313	4,998	7,453
Washington	9,095	7,227	2,303	8,369	9,374
Webster	8,380	6,640	2,629	7,434	10,204
W. Baton Rouge	5,131	3,522	1,249	4,686	3,972
West Carroll	2,068	2,082	771	1,607	3,077
West Feliciana	2,328	1,501	516	2,146	1,854
Winn	3,537	2,932	843	2,699	4,165
Totals	**815,971**	**733,386**	**211,478**	**717,460**	**883,702**

Louisiana Vote Since 1944

1944, Roosevelt, Dem., 281,564; Dewey, Rep., 67,750.

1948, Thurmond, States' Rights, 204,290; Truman, Dem., 136,344; Dewey, Rep., 72,657; Wallace, Prog., 3,035.

1952, Eisenhower, Rep., 306,925, Stevenson, Dem., 345,027.

1956, Eisenhower, Rep., 329,047; Stevenson, Dem., 243,977; Andrews, States' Rights, 44,520.

1960, Kennedy, Dem., 407,339; Nixon, Rep., 230,890; States' Rights (unpledged) 169,572.

1964, Johnson, Dem., 387,068; Goldwater, Rep., 509,225.

1968, Nixon, Rep., 257,535; Humphrey, Dem., 309,615; Wallace, 3d party, 530,300.

1972, Nixon, Rep., 686,852; McGovern, Dem., 298,142; Schmitz, Amer., 52,099; Jenness, Soc. Workers, 14,398.

1976, Carter, Dem., 661,365; Ford, Rep., 587,446; Maddox, Amer., 10,058; Hall, Com., 7,417; McCarthy, Ind., 6,588; MacBride, Libertarian, 3,325.

1980, Reagan, Rep., 792,853; Carter, Dem., 708,453; Anderson, Ind., 26,345; Rarick, Amer. Ind., 10,333; Clark, Libertarian, 8,240; Commoner, Citizens, 1,584; DeBerry, Soc. Work., 783.

1984, Reagan, Rep., 1,037,299; Mondale, Dem., 651,586; Bergland, Libertarian, 1,876.

1988, Bush, Rep., 883,702; Dukakis, Dem., 717,460; Duke, Pop., 18,612; Paul, Lib., 4,115.

1992, Clinton, Dem., 815,971; Bush, Rep., 733,386; Perot, Ind., 211,478; Gritz, Populist/America First, 18,545; Marrou, Libertarian, 3,155; Daniels, Ind., 1,663; Phillips, U.S. Taxpayers, 1,552; Fulani, New Alliance, 1,434; LaRouche, Ind., 1,136.

Maine

City	1992 Clinton (D)	1992 Bush (R)	1992 Perot (I)	1988 Dukakis (D)	1988 Bush (R)
Auburn	5,025	3,653	3,964	4,629	5,947
Augusta	4,657	3,003	3,002	4,576	5,182
Bangor	6,826	5,185	4,689	6,534	7,194
Bath	1,988	1,630	1,458	1,838	2,543
Biddeford	4,945	2,533	2,717	5,017	4,375
Brewer	1,788	1,907	1,625	1,784	2,908
Gardiner	1,391	1,054	1,115	1,395	1,609
Lewiston	9,265	4,372	6,180	9,225	7,265
Old Town	2,272	1,173	1,302	2,220	1,640
Portland	19,510	8,660	6,910	18,234	11,676
Rockland	1,192	1,081	1,059	1,198	1,850
Saco	4,000	2,769	2,303	3,169	3,852
Sanford	3,854	3,030	3,215	3,456	4,541
South Portland	5,933	3,999	2,734	5,820	5,744
Waterville	3,868	1,832	2,257	4,031	3,158
Westbrook	3,665	2,904	2,512	3,648	4,086
Totals	**263,420**	**206,504**	**206,820**	**243,569**	**307,131**

Maine Vote Since 1944

1944, Roosevelt, Dem., 140,631; Dewey, Rep., 155,434; Teichert, Soc. Labor, 335.

1948, Truman, Dem., 111,916; Dewey, Rep., 150,234; Wallace, Prog., 1,884; Thomas, Soc., 547; Teichert, Soc. Labor, 206.

1952, Eisenhower, Rep., 232,353; Stevenson, Dem., 118,806; Hallinan, Prog., 332; Hass, Soc. Labor, 156; Hoopes, Soc., 138; scattered, 1.

1956, Eisenhower, Rep., 249,238; Stevenson, Dem., 102,468.

1960, Kennedy, Dem., 181,159; Nixon, Rep., 240,608.

1964, Johnson, Dem., 262,264; Goldwater, Rep., 118,701.

1968, Nixon, Rep., 169,254; Humphrey, Dem., 217,312; Wallace, 3d party, 6,370.

1972, Nixon, Rep., 256,458; McGovern, Dem., 160,584; scattered, 229.

1976, Carter, Dem., 232,279; Ford, Rep., 236,320; McCarthy, Ind., 10,874; Bubar, Proh., 3,495.

1980, Reagan, Rep., 238,522; Carter, Dem., 220,974; Anderson, Ind., 53,327; Clark, Libertarian, 5,119; Commoner, Citizens, 4,394; Hall, Com., 591; write-ins, 84.

1984, Reagan, Rep., 336,500; Mondale, Dem., 214,515.

1988, Bush, Rep., 307,131; Dukakis, Dem., 243,569; Paul, Lib., 2,700; Fulani, New Alliance, 1,405.

1992, Clinton, Dem., 263,420; Perot, Ind., 206,820; Bush, Rep., 206,504; Marrou, Libertarian, 1,681.

Maryland

County	1992 Clinton (D)	1992 Bush (R)	1992 Perot (I)	1988 Dukakis (D)	1988 Bush (R)
Allegany	11,501	13,862	5,081	11,844	17,462
Anne Arundel	68,629	81,467	35,191	55,440	98,540
Baltimore	143,498	126,728	51,757	121,570	163,881
Calvert	8,619	10,026	4,499	6,376	10,956
Caroline	2,822	3,856	1,729	2,440	4,661
Carroll	15,447	28,405	10,965	12,368	31,224
Cecil	10,232	10,784	6,115	7,807	13,224
Charles	14,498	17,293	6,501	11,823	20,828
Dorchester	3,933	4,934	2,010	3,709	6,343
Frederick	21,848	31,290	11,373	17,061	32,575
Garrett	2,856	5,714	1,987	2,557	6,665
Harford	27,164	36,350	17,002	19,803	38,493
Howard	44,763	38,594	16,182	34,007	44,153
Kent	3,093	3,094	1,411	2,925	3,761
Montgomery	199,757	119,705	41,971	165,187	154,191
Prince George's	168,691	62,955	23,355	133,816	86,545
Queen Anne's	4,668	6,829	2,958	3,857	7,803
St. Mary's	8,931	11,485	4,550	7,434	12,767
Somerset	3,210	3,450	1,230	2,911	4,222
Talbot	4,642	6,774	2,233	3,948	8,170
Washington	16,495	21,977	7,537	14,408	25,912
Wicomico	11,481	13,560	5,140	9,413	16,272
Worcester	6,040	7,237	3,256	4,787	8,430

City					
Baltimore	185,753	40,725	17,381	170,813	59,089
Totals	988,571	707,094	281,414	826,304	876,167

Maryland Vote Since 1944

1944, Roosevelt, Dem., 315,490; Dewey, Rep., 292,949.

1948, Truman, Dem., 286,521; Dewey, Rep., 294,814; Wallace, Prog., 9,983; Thomas, Soc., 2,941; Thurmond, States' Rights, 2,476; Wright, write-in, 2,294.

1952, Eisenhower, Rep., 499,424; Stevenson, Dem., 395,337; Hallinan, Prog., 7,313.

1956, Eisenhower, Rep., 559,738; Stevenson, Dem., 372,613.

1960, Kennedy, Dem., 565,800; Nixon, Rep., 489,538.

1964, Johnson, Dem., 730,912; Goldwater, Rep., 385,495; write-in, 50.

1968, Nixon, Rep., 517,995; Humphrey, Dem., 538,310; Wallace, 3d party, 178,734.

1972, Nixon, Rep., 829,305; McGovern, Dem., 505,781; Schmitz, Amer., 18,726.

1976, Carter, Dem., 759,612; Ford, Rep., 672,661.

1980, Reagan, Rep., 680,606; Carter, Dem., 726,161; Anderson, Ind., 119,537; Clark, Libertarian, 14,192.

1984, Reagan, Rep., 879,918; Mondale, Dem., 787,935; Bergland, Libertarian, 5,721.

1988, Bush, Rep., 876,167; Dukakis, Dem., 826,304; Paul, Lib., 6,748; Fulani, New Alliance, 5,115.

1992, Clinton, Dem., 988,571; Bush, Rep., 707,094; Perot, Ind., 281,414; Marrou, Libertarian, 4,715; Fulani, New Alliance, 2,786.

Massachusetts

City	1992 Clinton (D)	1992 Bush (R)	1992 Perot (I)	1988 Dukakis (D)	1988 Bush (R)
Boston	114,260	41,868	25,189	122,349	62,202
Brockton	13,209	8,863	7,579	14,776	16,056
Cambridge	30,737	5,847	4,106	32,027	8,770
Fall River	18,652	5,456	6,922	20,184	8,394
Framingham	15,165	8,114	6,089	15,826	12,745
Lawrence	7,698	5,079	3,245	9,255	8,265
Lowell	14,492	8,467	8,893	16,391	13,998
Lynn	15,275	7,350	7,665	18,540	12,182
New Bedford	20,880	5,255	6,965	22,609	9,901
Newton	29,136	9,623	5,685	29,039	13,892
Quincy	18,891	12,306	9,068	20,911	18,403
Somerville	19,792	5,883	4,416	21,612	8,931
Springfield	27,302	12,200	10,361	30,113	16,244
Worcester	32,326	17,228	10,488	34,369	24,355
Totals	1,318,639	805,039	630,731	1,401,415	1,194,635

Massachusetts Vote Since 1944

1944, Roosevelt, Dem., 1,035,296; Dewey, Rep., 921,350; Teichert, Soc. Labor, 2,780; Watson, Proh., 973.

1948, Truman, Dem., 1,151,788; Dewey, Rep., 909,370; Wallace, Prog., 38,157; Teichert, Soc. Labor, 5,535; Watson, Proh., 1,663.

1952, Eisenhower, Rep., 1,292,325; Stevenson, Dem., 1,083,525; Hallinan, Prog., 4,636; Hass, Soc. Labor, 1,957; Hamblen, Proh., 886; scattered, 69; blanks, 41,150.

1956, Eisenhower, Rep., 1,393,197; Stevenson, Dem., 948,190; Hass, Soc. Labor, 5,573; Holtwick, Proh., 1,205; others, 341.

1960, Kennedy, Dem., 1,487,174; Nixon, Rep., 976,750; Hass, Soc. Labor, 3,892; Decker, Proh., 1,633; others, 31; blank and void, 26,024.

1964, Johnson, Dem., 1,786,422; Goldwater, Rep., 549,727; Hass, Soc. Labor, 4,755; Munn, Proh., 3,735; scattered, 159; blank, 48,104.

1968, Nixon, Rep., 766,844; Humphrey, Dem., 1,469,218; Wallace, 3d party, 87,088; Blomen, Soc. Labor, 6,180; Munn, Proh., 2,369; scattered, 53; blanks, 25,394.

1972, Nixon, Rep., 1,112,078; McGovern, Dem., 1,332,540; Jenness, Soc. Workers, 10,600; Fisher, Soc. Labor, 129; Schmitz, Amer., 2,877; Spock, Peoples, 101; Hall, Com., 46; Hospers, Libertarian, 43; scattered, 342.

1976, Carter, Dem., 1,429,475; Ford, Rep., 1,030,276; McCarthy, Ind., 65,637; Camejo, Soc. Workers, 8,138; Anderson, Amer., 7,555; La Rouche, U.S. Labor, 4,922; MacBride, Libertarian, 135.

1980, Reagan, Rep., 1,057,631; Carter, Dem., 1,053,802; Anderson, Ind., 382,539; Clark, Libertarian, 22,038; DeBerry, Soc. Workers, 3,735; Commoner, Citizens, 2,056; McReynolds, Socialist, 62; Bubar, Statesman, 34; Griswold, Workers World, 19; scattered, 2,382.

1984, Reagan, Rep., 1,310,936; Mondale, Dem., 1,239,606.

1988, Bush, Rep., 1,194,635; Dukakis, Dem., 1,401,415; Paul, Lib., 24,251; Fulani, New Alliance, 9,561.

1992, Clinton, Dem., 1,318,639; Bush, Rep., 805,039; Perot, Ind., 630,731; Marrou, Libertarian, 9,021; Fulani, New Alliance, 3,172; Phillips, U.S. Taxpayers, 2,218; Hagelin, Natural Law, 1,812; LaRouche, Ind., 1,027.

Michigan

County	1992 Clinton (D)	1992 Bush (R)	1992 Perot (I)	1988 Dukakis (D)	1988 Bush (R)
Alcona	2,383	2,247	1,117	1,918	2,966
Alger	2,144	1,471	941	2,210	1,830
Allegan	12,823	19,077	8,742	10,785	22,163
Alpena	6,894	4,878	3,236	6,341	6,664
Antrim	3,431	3,984	2,528	3,159	5,231
Arenac	3,244	2,330	1,608	3,211	3,064
Baraga	1,695	1,160	754	1,753	1,630
Barry	8,652	9,489	6,303	7,983	12,546
Bay	26,492	16,383	11,258	28,225	20,710
Benzie	2,715	2,438	1,657	2,437	3,240
Berrien	25,840	29,252	14,056	21,948	37,799
Branch	5,850	5,976	4,683	5,231	9,225
Calhoun	25,542	19,791	13,058	22,717	26,771
Cass	8,047	7,391	4,756	7,444	10,229
Charlevoix	4,063	4,017	3,360	3,875	5,802
Cheboygan	4,459	3,864	2,495	3,943	5,395
Chippewa	5,434	5,462	2,706	5,222	6,786
Clare	5,346	3,916	2,812	4,710	5,661
Clinton	10,116	12,216	7,877	9,225	15,497
Crawford	2,252	2,193	1,442	1,825	3,097
Delta	8,387	6,027	3,485	8,891	7,114
Dickinson	5,689	4,273	3,022	6,129	6,158
Eaton	16,752	18,669	12,208	15,322	24,193
Emmet	4,245	5,312	3,578	4,170	7,105
Geneseo	105,156	47,834	46,259	104,880	70,922
Gladwin	4,457	3,616	2,649	4,164	4,746
Gogebic	4,792	2,838	1,543	5,151	3,509
Grand Traverse	11,148	13,629	9,495	10,098	17,191
Gratiot	5,678	6,280	3,866	5,719	8,447
Hillsdale	5,244	7,579	4,968	4,763	10,571
Houghton	6,558	5,575	2,945	6,510	7,098
Huron	6,023	6,491	4,064	5,714	9,419
Ingham	61,596	43,926	27,683	55,984	58,363
Ionia	8,370	9,135	6,211	8,160	12,028
Iosco	5,369	4,912	3,131	4,929	7,234
Iron	3,648	1,971	1,344	3,774	2,866
Isabella	8,784	7,706	5,434	7,960	10,362
Jackson	23,686	25,424	15,194	21,865	33,885
Kalamazoo	43,568	38,035	21,666	39,457	50,205
Kalkaska	2,297	2,173	1,915	2,092	3,369
Kent	82,305	115,285	43,707	73,467	131,910
Keweenaw	582	378	212	631	536
Lake	2,351	1,194	981	1,958	1,713
Lapeer	11,982	12,326	10,541	10,736	16,670
Leelanau	3,445	3,993	2,685	3,331	5,215
Lenawee	15,399	14,297	9,517	13,690	19,115
Livingston	17,851	27,539	15,971	13,749	31,331
Luce	972	958	660	864	1,528
Mackinac	2,293	2,278	1,379	2,093	3,127
Macomb	130,732	147,795	67,954	112,856	175,632
Manistee	5,193	3,491	2,923	4,765	5,368
Marquette	16,038	9,665	5,768	15,418	11,704
Mason	4,829	5,102	3,096	4,531	6,800
Mecosta	6,097	6,047	3,612	4,736	8,181
Menominee	4,559	3,995	2,487	4,918	5,440
Midland	13,382	16,149	8,945	13,452	19,994
Missaukee	1,893	2,829	1,306	1,621	3,566
Monroe	24,957	20,250	13,551	21,847	26,189
Montcalm	8,730	8,420	5,504	7,664	10,963
Montmorency	1,903	1,794	1,077	1,563	2,514
Muskegon	32,515	23,769	15,268	28,977	33,567
Newaygo	6,455	7,333	4,056	5,389	9,896
Oakland	214,733	242,160	94,911	174,745	283,359
Oceana	3,846	3,944	2,713	3,356	5,693
Ogemaw	4,016	2,936	2,122	4,012	4,091
Ontonagon	2,451	1,463	805	2,517	2,023
Osceola	3,529	3,606	2,199	2,860	5,218
Oscoda	1,471	1,583	755	1,170	1,972
Otsego	3,129	3,393	2,635	2,635	4,620
Ottawa	22,180	56,862	16,855	18,769	61,515
Presque Isle	3,308	2,398	1,612	3,025	3,614
Roscommon	5,243	4,170	2,551	4,394	5,866
Saginaw	43,819	32,103	20,523	45,616	42,401
St. Clair	23,385	24,508	18,523	20,909	32,336
St. Joseph	7,817	9,836	6,209	7,017	13,084
Sanilac	5,868	7,891	4,894	5,445	10,653
Schoolcraft	2,139	1,253	721	2,071	1,802
Shiawassee	12,629	10,930	8,632	13,056	15,506
Tuscola	9,138	8,636	6,765	9,060	12,093
Van Buren	12,466	10,357	7,255	10,668	14,522
Washtenaw	73,325	41,386	21,889	61,799	55,029
Wayne	508,464	227,002	102,074	450,222	291,996

Wexford	4,894	4,696	2,923	4,287	6,043
Totals	**1,871,182**	**1,554,940**	**824,813**	**1,675,783**	**1,965,486**

Michigan Vote Since 1944

1944, Roosevelt, Dem., 1,106,899; Dewey, Rep., 1,084,423; Watson, Proh., 6,503; Thomas, Soc., 4,598; Smith, America First, 1,530; Teichert, Soc. Labor, 1,264.

1948, Truman, Dem., 1,003,448; Dewey, Rep., 1,038,595; Wallace, Prog., 46,515; Watson, Proh., 13,052; Thomas, Soc. 6,063; Teichert, Soc. Labor, 1,263; Dobbs, Soc. Workers, 672.

1952, Eisenhower, Rep., 1,551,529; Stevenson, Dem., 1,230,657; Hamblen, Proh., 10,331; Hallinan, Prog., 3,922; Hass, Soc. Labor, 1,495; Dobbs, Soc. Workers, 655; scattered, 3.

1956, Eisenhower, Rep., 1,713,647; Stevenson, Dem., 1,359,898; Holtwick, Proh., 6,923.

1960, Kennedy, Dem., 1,687,269; Nixon, Rep., 1,620,428; Dobbs, Soc. Workers, 4,347; Decker, Proh., 2,029; Daly, Tax Cut, 1,767; Hass, Soc. Labor, 1,718; Ind. American, 539.

1964, Johnson, Dem., 2,136,615; Goldwater, Rep., 1,060,152; DeBerry, Soc. Workers, 3,817; Hass, Soc. Labor, 1,704; Proh. (no candidate listed), 699, scattering, 145.

1968, Nixon, Rep., 1,370,665; Humphrey, Dem., 1,593,082; Wallace, 3d party, 331,968; Halstead, Soc. Worker, 4,099; Blomen, Soc. Labor, 1,762; Cleaver, New Politics, 4,585; Munn, Proh., 60; scattering, 29.

1972, Nixon, Rep., 1,961,721; McGovern, Dem., 1,459,435; Schmitz, Amer., 63,321; Fisher, Soc. Labor, 2,437; Jenness, Soc. Workers, 1,603; Hall, Com., 1,210.

1976, Carter, Dem., 1,696,714; Ford, Rep., 1,893,742; McCarthy, Ind., 47,905; MacBride, Libertarian, 5,406; Wright, People's, 3,504, Camejo, Soc. Workers, 1,804; LaRouche, U.S. Labor, 1,366; Levin, Soc. Labor, 1,148; scattering, 2,160.

1980, Reagan, Rep., 1,915,225; Carter, Dem., 1,661,532; Anderson, Ind., 275,223; Clark, Libertarian, 41,597; Commoner, Citizens, 11,930; Hall, Com., 3,262; Griswold, Workers World, 30; Greaves, American, 21; Bubar, Statesman, 9.

1984, Reagan, Rep., 2,251,571; Mondale, Dem., 1,529,638; Bergland, Libertarian, 10,055.

1988, Bush, Rep., 1,965,486; Dukakis, Dem., 1,675,783; Paul, Lib., 18,336; Fulani, Ind., 2,513.

1992, Clinton, Dem., 1,871,182; Bush, Rep., 1,554,940; Perot, Ind., 824,813; Marrou, Libertarian, 10,175; Phillips, U.S. Taxpayers, 8,263; Hagelin, Natural Law, 2,954.

Minnesota

	1992			1988	
County	Clinton (D)	Bush (R)	Perot (I)	Dukakis (D)	Bush (R)
Aitkin	3,400	2,151	1,951	3,863	3,011
Anoka	54,621	39,458	35,140	57,953	46,853
Becker	4,958	5,430	3,238	5,787	6,738
Beltrami	7,210	5,204	3,473	7,566	6,652
Benton	5,156	5,053	4,048	5,861	6,060
Big Stone	1,610	1,052	740	2,026	1,469
Blue Earth	11,531	8,813	7,299	12,375	11,959
Brown	4,278	5,390	3,845	5,109	6,898
Carlton	7,736	3,922	3,005	8,790	4,626
Carver	8,349	10,201	7,942	8,439	12,560
Cass	4,901	4,276	2,939	5,127	5,895
Chippewa	2,929	2,143	1,505	3,238	3,190
Chisago	7,077	4,813	5,098	7,875	6,163
Clay	9,845	9,666	3,835	11,186	10,380
Clearwater	1,587	1,315	841	1,769	1,763
Cook	1,005	878	704	1,080	1,078
Cottonwood	2,382	2,481	1,749	3,095	3,390
Crow Wing	8,896	9,112	6,367	9,674	11,017
Dakota	63,660	52,312	40,244	61,942	61,606
Dodge	2,620	3,049	2,231	2,925	3,848
Douglas	5,252	6,356	4,138	5,803	7,898
Faribault	3,339	3,439	2,322	3,879	4,846
Fillmore	3,977	3,583	3,011	4,114	5,004
Freebom	7,759	5,089	4,878	8,836	7,226
Goodhue	7,916	7,321	5,790	9,438	9,455
Grant	1,561	1,201	885	1,950	1,693
Hennepin	278,648	179,581	123,659	292,909	240,209
Houston	3,744	3,853	2,697	3,936	4,777
Hubbard	3,362	3,227	1,949	3,306	4,365
Isanti	5,386	3,988	3,898	6,075	5,246
Itasca	9,621	5,952	5,147	10,517	8,358
Jackson	2,481	1,824	1,918	3,275	2,629
Kanabec	2,532	1,876	1,836	2,970	2,571
Kandiyohi	7,914	6,784	4,869	8,962	8,634
Kittson	1,307	1,098	558	1,650	1,381
Koochiching	3,474	1,954	1,993	3,867	2,842
LacQuiParle	2,342	1,435	1,163	2,805	2,116
Lake	3,415	1,465	1,437	3,887	1,838
Lake O'Woods	794	762	629	798	984
Le Sueur	4,662	3,858	3,363	5,410	5,415
Lincoln	1,555	1,084	967	1,891	1,479
Lyon	4,481	4,591	3,180	5,657	5,969
McLeod	4,919	5,422	4,933	5,736	7,967
Mahnomen	1,035	854	483	1,277	1,051
Marshall	2,309	2,136	1,306	3,001	2,752
Martin	4,019	4,438	3,089	4,922	5,724
Meeker	3,861	3,497	3,120	4,544	4,999
Mille Lacs	3,648	2,814	2,615	4,327	3,862
Morrison	5,588	5,038	3,710	6,469	6,598
Mower	9,935	5,147	5,001	11,893	6,969
Murray	1,993	1,609	1,588	2,840	2,316
Nicollet	6,055	5,091	3,799	6,786	6,878
Nobles	3,756	3,548	2,586	4,953	4,348
Norman	1,784	1,541	776	2,149	1,789
Olmsted	19,039	23,404	13,806	19,423	27,683
Otter Tail	9,176	11,074	6,274	10,373	14,015
Pennington	2,578	2,155	1,598	3,105	2,920
Pine	4,929	2,841	2,952	5,540	3,857
Pipestone	1,773	1,953	1,429	2,382	2,760
Polk	5,850	5,817	3,176	7,523	7,032
Pope	2,619	1,886	1,390	3,074	2,627
Ramsey	130,932	68,206	50,757	143,767	88,736
Red Lake	1,020	691	472	1,229	918
Redwood	2,740	3,408	2,710	3,178	5,076
Renville	3,414	2,852	2,598	4,454	4,356
Rice	10,908	7,015	6,057	11,570	9,460
Rock	2,006	2,065	1,244	2,435	2,737
Roseau	2,346	2,785	2,099	2,630	3,500
St. Louis	61,813	24,579	21,714	70,344	31,799
Scott	11,225	10,936	9,881	11,405	13,050
Sherburne	7,843	7,339	6,534	7,959	8,360
Sibley	2,421	2,315	2,407	3,154	3,655
Stearns	21,451	22,502	14,834	23,798	27,529
Steele	5,152	5,964	4,542	5,496	7,981
Stevens	2,466	2,229	1,086	2,721	2,679
Swift	2,980	1,603	1,359	3,579	2,156
Todd	4,059	3,990	2,976	5,023	5,633
Traverse	1,053	841	582	1,399	1,061
Wabasha	3,736	3,397	3,012	4,442	4,681
Wadena	2,340	2,492	1,535	2,484	3,733
Waseca	3,146	3,118	2,621	3,721	4,471
Washington	35,820	26,568	22,585	34,952	30,850
Watonwan	2,100	1,871	1,574	2,544	2,821
Wilkin	1,122	1,626	748	1,486	1,933
Winona	9,707	8,585	5,993	10,310	11,012
Wright	12,465	11,650	10,829	14,177	14,987
Yellow Med	2,593	1,909	1,645	3,282	2,925
Totals	**1,020,997**	**747,841**	**562,506**	**1,109,471**	**962,337**

Minnesota Vote Since 1944

1944, Roosevelt, Dem., 589,864; Dewey, Rep., 527,416; Thomas, Soc., 5,073; Teichert, Ind. Gov't., 3,176.

1948, Truman, Dem., 692,966; Dewey, Rep., 483,617; Wallace, Prog., 27,866; Thomas, Soc., 4,646; Teichert, Soc. Labor, 2,525; Dobbs, Soc. Workers, 606.

1952, Eisenhower, Rep., 763,211; Stevenson, Dem., 608,458; Hallinan, Prog., 2,666; Hass, Soc. Labor, 2,383; Hamblen, Proh., 2,147; Dobbs, Soc. Workers, 618.

1956, Eisenhower, Rep., 719,302; Stevenson, Dem., 617,525; Hass, Soc. Labor (Ind. Gov.), 2,080; Dobbs, Soc. Workers, 1,098.

1960, Kennedy, Dem., 779,933; Nixon, Rep., 757,915; Dobbs, Soc. Workers, 3,077; Industrial Gov., 962.

1964, Johnson, Dem., 991,117; Goldwater, Rep., 559,624; DeBerry, Soc. Workers, 1,177; Hass, Industrial Gov., 2,544.

1968, Nixon, Rep., 658,643; Humphrey, Dem., 857,738; Wallace, 3d party, 68,931; scattered, 2,443; Halstead, Soc. Worker, 808; Blomen, Ind. Gov't., 285; Mitchell, Com., 415; Cleaver, Peace, 935; McCarthy, write-in, 585; scattered, 170.

1972, Nixon, Rep., 898,269; McGovern, Dem., 802,346; Schmitz, Amer., 31,407; Spock, Peoples, 2,805; Fisher, Soc. Labor, 4,261; Jenness, Soc. Workers, 940; Hall, Com., 662; scattered, 962.

1976, Carter, Dem., 1,070,440; Ford, Rep., 819,395; McCarthy, Ind., 35,490; Anderson, Amer., 13,592; Camejo, Soc. Workers, 4,149; MacBride, Libertarian, 3,529; Hall, Com., 1,092.

1980, Reagan, Rep., 873,268; Carter, Dem., 954,173; Anderson, Ind., 174,997; Clark, Libertarian, 31,593; Commoner, Citizens, 8,406; Hall, Com., 1,117; DeBerry, Soc. Workers, 711; Griswold, Workers World, 698; McReynolds, Socialist, 536; write-ins, 281.

1984, Mondale, Dem., 1,036,364; Reagan, Rep., 1,032,603; Bergland, Libertarian, 2,996.

1988, Bush., 962,337; Dukakis, Dem., 1,109,471; McCarthy, Minn. Prog., 5,403; Paul, Lib., 5,109.

1992, Clinton, Dem., 1,020,997; Bush, Rep., 747,841; Perot, Ind., 526,506; Marrou, Libertarian, 3,373; Gritz, Populist/America First, 3,363; Hagelin, Natural Law, 1,406.

Mississippi

	1992			1988	
County	Clinton (D)	Bush (R)	Perot (I)	Dukakis (D)	Bush (R)
Adams	8,255	5,831	1,753	7,732	8,116
Alcorn	6,373	6,249	1,349	5,335	6,641
Amite	2,608	2,561	498	2,834	3,333
Attala	3,015	3,520	529	2,997	4,524
Benton	2,402	1,253	293	1,718	1,565
Bolivar	8,801	4,752	593	7,606	6,105
Calhoun	2,462	3,191	607	2,086	3,375
Carroll	1,182	1,695	200	1,560	2,628
Chickasaw	3,220	3,150	629	2,713	3,390
Choctaw	1,435	2,026	298	1,335	2,297
Claiborne	3,302	935	161	3,083	1,233
Clarke	2,259	4,207	450	2,576	4,522
Clay	4,620	3,297	626	3,849	3,645
Coahoma	6,409	4,120	518	6,139	4,939
Copiah	4,397	4,600	409	4,175	5,100
Covington	2,775	3,525	654	2,591	4,005
DeSoto	8,833	16,104	2,569	5,449	14,681
Forrest	8,333	12,432	1,909	6,953	14,249
Franklin	1,587	1,942	393	1,563	2,376
George	2,650	4,141	1,335	2,435	4,545
Greene	1,664	2,406	559	1,637	2,837
Grenada	4,203	4,721	609	3,683	5,352
Hancock	4,651	6,422	2,302	3,760	7,763
Harrison	15,268	25,049	6,855	14,439	32,092
Hinds	43,434	45,031	5,341	41,058	52,749
Holmes	4,092	1,694	203	5,350	2,737
Humphreys	2,696	1,721	258	2,644	2,018
Issaquena	550	298	79	511	424
Itawamba	3,635	4,142	918	3,143	4,535
Jackson	13,017	25,321	6,484	10,328	29,830
Jasper	3,059	2,789	568	3,184	3,368
Jefferson	2,796	562	156	2,693	702
Jefferson Davis	2,991	2,228	382	2,948	2,745
Jones	8,035	13,824	2,523	7,383	16,764
Kemper	2,243	1,830	278	2,069	2,128
Lafayette	5,224	5,251	861	3,967	5,841
Lamar	3,208	8,259	1,543	2,535	9,145
Lauderdale	8,489	17,098	1,659	7,967	18,302
Lawrence	2,582	2,689	765	2,517	3,682
Leake	3,333	3,943	497	2,787	4,168
Lee	7,710	12,231	2,041	6,604	13,767
Leflore	6,374	5,298	611	5,830	6,409
Lincoln	4,744	7,040	1,281	4,534	8,710
Lowndes	6,552	10,509	1,716	5,993	11,258
Madison	9,386	12,810	1,478	8,242	11,399
Marion	4,654	5,776	1,162	4,240	7,019
Marshall	7,913	3,847	689	6,982	4,668
Monroe	4,933	5,994	1,255	4,669	6,447
Montgomery	2,076	2,324	370	1,893	2,504
Neshoba	3,090	6,135	794	2,942	6,363
Newton	2,146	5,128	494	2,332	5,658
Noxubee	3,188	1,623	203	2,722	1,870
Oktibbeha	5,726	6,381	984	5,100	7,126
Panola	6,066	4,644	729	5,222	5,382
Pearl River	4,683	7,726	2,352	3,939	10,220
Perry	1,490	2,538	462	1,326	2,983
Pike	6,279	6,005	1,380	6,531	7,637
Pontotoc	2,965	4,595	777	2,772	4,939
Prentiss	3,385	4,317	781	3,429	4,348
Quitman	2,422	1,451	210	2,497	1,832
Rankin	8,155	24,537	3,454	6,201	22,937
Scott	3,349	5,268	691	2,939	5,522
Sharkey	1,526	1,008	145	1,609	1,277
Simpson	3,213	5,358	726	3,016	6,151
Smith	1,968	4,106	680	1,660	4,573
Stone	1,447	2,295	447	1,452	3,007
Sunflower	5,050	3,726	600	4,898	4,362
Tallahatchie	2,902	2,213	380	2,881	2,633
Tate	3,519	4,196	634	2,872	4,553
Tippah	3,475	4,444	802	2,958	4,593
Tishomingo	3,910	3,393	751	3,378	3,646
Tunica	1,451	693	96	1,510	896
Union	3,714	5,173	816	3,044	5,511
Walthall	2,476	2,728	711	2,354	3,103
Warren	8,175	10,209	2,146	7,437	12,507
Washington	10,588	7,598	795	10,222	10,229
Wayne	3,064	3,874	824	2,889	4,496
Webster	1,746	2,791	444	1,550	3,061
Wilkinson	3,210	1,399	307	2,678	1,528
Winston	3,953	4,311	688	3,851	5,317
Yalobusha	2,617	2,179	438	2,402	2,660
Yazoo	4,880	5,113	669	4,989	5,538
Totals	400,258	487,793	85,626	363,921	557,890

Mississippi Vote Since 1944

1944, Roosevelt, Dem., 158,515; Dewey, Rep., 3,742; Reg. Dem., 9,964; Ind. Rep., 7,859.

1948, Thurmond, States' Rights, 167,538; Truman, Dem., 19,384; Dewey, Rep., 5,043; Wallace, Prog., 225.

1952, Eisenhower, Ind. vote pledged to Rep. candidate, 112,966; Stevenson, Dem., 172,566.

1956, Stevenson, Dem., 144,498; Eisenhower, Rep., 56,372; Black and Tan Grand Old Party, 4,313; total, 60,685; Byrd, Ind., 42,966.

1960, Democratic unpledged electors, 116,248; Kennedy, Dem., 108,362; Nixon, Rep., 73,561. Mississippi's victorious slate of 8 unpledged Democratic electors cast their votes for Sen. Harry F. Byrd (D-Va.).

1964, Johnson, Dem., 52,618; Goldwater, Rep., 356,528.

1968, Nixon, Rep., 88,516; Humphrey, Dem., 150,644; Wallace, 3d party, 415,349.

1972, Nixon, Rep., 505,125; McGovern, Dem., 126,782; Schmitz, Amer., 11,598; Jenness, Soc. Workers, 2,458.

1976, Carter, Dem., 381,309; Ford, Rep., 366,846; Anderson, Amer., 6,678; McCarthy, Ind., 4,074; Maddox, Ind., 4,049; Camejo, Soc. Workers, 2,805; MacBride, Libertarian, 2,609.

1980, Reagan, Rep., 441,089; Carter, Dem., 429,281; Anderson, Ind., 12,036; Clark, Libertarian, 5,465; Griswold, Workers World, 2,402; Pulley, Soc. Worker, 2,347.

1984, Reagan, Rep., 582,377; Mondale, Dem., 352,192; Bergland, Libertarian, 2,336.

1988, Bush, Rep., 557,890; Dukakis, Dem., 363,921; Duke, Ind., 4,232; Paul, Lib., 3,329.

1992, Bush, Rep., 487,793; Clinton, Dem., 400,258; Perot, Ind., 85,626; Fulani, New Alliance, 2,625; Marrou, Libertarian, 2,154; Phillips, U.S. Taxpayers, 1,652; Hagelin, Natural Law, 1,140.

Missouri

	1992			1988	
County	Clinton (D)	Bush (R)	Perot (I)	Dukakis (D)	Bush (R)
Adair	4,232	4,141	2,224	3,571	5,721
Andrew	2,675	2,652	2,151	3,108	3,407
Atchison	1,208	1,140	840	1,468	1,761
Audrain	4,731	3,798	2,099	5,226	5,072
Barry	4,791	5,565	2,381	4,210	7,231
Barton	1,433	2,775	971	1,603	3,339
Bates	2,993	2,499	2,225	3,332	3,574
Benton	3,195	2,511	1,551	2,654	3,467
Bollinger	2,150	2,289	909	1,883	2,710
Boone	26,176	19,405	12,040	24,370	22,948
Buchanan	16,570	11,275	9,404	18,601	15,336
Butler	6,602	6,450	2,189	5,751	7,968
Caldwell	1,456	1,295	1,283	1,726	2,074
Callaway	5,799	4,880	3,266	5,209	6,687
Camden	5,140	5,554	3,891	3,930	7,773
Cape Girardeau	9,605	13,464	5,199	7,904	16,583
Carroll	2,100	1,774	1,495	2,330	2,811
Carter	1,169	1,101	405	1,087	1,429
Cass	10,246	10,349	9,216	10,092	12,799
Cedar	2,064	2,085	1,173	1,774	2,966
Chariton	2,141	1,378	1,067	2,347	2,193
Christian	6,242	7,422	3,422	4,724	7,670
Clark	1,815	1,039	725	1,925	1,493
Clay	30,565	23,798	20,951	29,620	30,293
Clinton	3,400	2,391	2,423	3,653	3,282
Cole	10,201	15,270	5,770	8,359	18,023
Cooper	2,709	2,867	1,735	2,510	3,737
Crawford	3,515	2,831	2,002	3,107	3,856
Dade	1,332	1,577	834	1,315	2,154
Dallas	2,533	2,116	1,392	2,293	2,898
Daviess	1,477	1,107	1,143	1,743	1,765
DeKalb	1,630	1,318	1,207	1,970	1,863
Dent	2,689	2,125	1,049	2,421	2,975
Douglas	2,126	2,569	1,081	1,735	3,225
Dunklin	6,277	4,024	1,166	5,281	5,026
Franklin	13,431	11,477	11,043	11,891	16,611
Gasconade	1,952	2,690	1,672	1,621	4,216
Gentry	1,519	1,272	921	1,872	1,554
Greene	41,137	46,457	17,770	35,475	52,211
Grundy	1,968	1,749	1,372	2,052	2,668
Harrison	1,590	1,563	1,059	1,776	2,271
Henry	4,232	2,681	2,807	4,135	4,167
Hickory	1,929	1,259	864	1,677	2,043
Holt	1,050	1,202	781	1,258	1,583
Howard	2,085	1,253	1,090	2,446	1,865
Howell	5,492	5,360	2,650	4,324	7,277
Iron	2,507	1,276	841	2,283	1,877
Jackson	145,999	78,611	66,142	147,964	107,810
Jasper	11,727	17,592	6,440	11,159	19,934
Jefferson	32,569	20,637	20,057	27,738	29,279

Johnson	5,546	5,032	4,578	5,373	7,512
Knox	1,010	724	523	1,255	1,212
Laclede	4,179	5,176	2,852	3,442	6,070
Lafayette	5,213	4,651	3,561	5,654	6,825
Lawrence	4,666	5,608	2,570	4,432	6,911
Lewis	2,196	1,461	892	2,460	1,803
Lincoln	5,453	3,718	3,572	4,605	5,305
Linn	2,916	1,967	1,524	3,150	3,061
Livingston	2,505	2,370	1,976	3,077	3,462
McDonald	2,281	3,010	1,551	2,299	3,812
Macon	3,194	2,256	1,697	3,215	3,406
Madison	2,501	1,673	899	2,167	2,528
Maries	1,732	1,356	915	1,552	1,919
Marion	5,156	4,762	1,841	5,617	5,034
Mercer	843	626	378	877	875
Miller	2,905	4,175	2,391	2,555	5,662
Missouri	3,226	1,675	776	2,814	2,218
Moniteau	2,018	2,566	1,499	1,936	3,502
Monroe	2,060	1,153	969	2,461	1,542
Montgomery	2,063	1,974	1,266	2,064	2,714
Morgan	2,906	2,819	2,028	2,604	3,958
New Madrid	4,883	2,431	902	3,812	3,387
Newton	5,987	8,804	3,567	5,798	10,617
Nodaway	3,723	3,147	2,484	4,240	4,103
Oregon	2,258	1,402	564	2,042	1,717
Osage	1,860	2,784	1,423	1,771	3,885
Ozark	1,581	1,772	906	1,329	2,404
Pemiscot	3,924	2,161	670	3,288	3,066
Perry	2,525	3,205	1,498	2,136	3,836
Pettis	5,314	6,823	4,278	5,486	9,648
Phelps	6,852	6,040	3,774	5,867	8,329
Pike	3,609	2,255	1,464	3,816	3,271
Platte	10,920	9,380	9,062	11,225	11,838
Polk	3,316	3,465	1,879	3,419	5,030
Pulaski	4,113	3,793	2,057	3,446	4,642
Putnam	838	1,143	522	803	1,365
Ralls	2,158	1,349	880	2,489	1,494
Randolph	4,951	3,025	2,212	5,291	4,384
Ray	4,457	2,563	2,567	4,879	3,763
Reynolds	2,014	776	532	1,864	1,162
Ripley	2,300	1,814	739	1,961	2,647
St. Charles	37,263	38,673	30,351	29,286	50,005
St. Clair	1,965	1,555	1,083	1,864	2,312
St. Francois	9,367	5,889	3,635	8,158	7,923
St. Louis	235,760	188,285	109,099	216,534	262,784
Ste. Genevieve	3,795	1,780	1,547	3,612	2,532
Saline	4,643	2,688	2,815	5,039	4,625
Schuyler	936	742	487	1,013	1,063
Scotland	1,070	798	617	1,117	1,248
Scott	7,452	6,265	2,763	5,914	8,013
Shannon	2,135	1,224	579	1,796	1,696
Shelby	1,435	1,169	786	1,818	1,586
Stoddard	5,720	4,608	1,977	4,701	5,822
Stone	3,256	4,035	1,884	2,889	5,080
Sullivan	1,510	1,326	596	1,562	1,897
Taney	4,682	6,081	2,395	3,888	7,043
Texas	4,597	3,470	1,900	3,887	4,584
Vernon	3,546	2,851	1,890	3,402	4,149
Warren	3,213	2,953	2,471	2,935	4,452
Washington	4,211	2,157	1,618	3,744	3,240
Wayne	3,073	2,101	837	2,456	2,648
Webster	4,149	4,361	2,108	3,890	5,123
Worth	599	483	328	732	677
Wright	2,814	3,427	1,425	2,232	4,151
City					
St. Louis	102,356	25,441	18,864	110,076	40,906
Totals	**1,053,873**	**811,159**	**518,741**	**1,001,619**	**1,084,953**

Missouri Vote Since 1944

1944, Roosevelt, Dem., 807,357; Dewey, Rep., 761,175; Thomas, Soc., 1,750; Watson, Proh., 1,175; Teichert, Soc. Labor, 221.

1948, Truman, Dem., 917,315; Dewey, Rep., 655,039; Wallace, Prog., 3,998; Thomas, Soc., 2,222.

1952, Eisenhower, Rep., 959,429; Stevenson, Dem., 929,830; Hallinan, Prog., 987; Hamblen, Proh., 885; MacArthur, Christian Nationalist, 302; America First, 233; Hoopes, Soc., 227; Hass, Soc. Labor, 169.

1956, Stevenson, Dem., 918,273; Eisenhower, Rep., 914,299.

1960, Kennedy, Dem., 972,201; Nixon, Rep., 962,221.

1964, Johnson, Dem., 1,164,344; Goldwater, Rep., 653,535.

1968, Nixon, Rep., 811,932; Humphrey, Dem., 791,444; Wallace, 3d party, 206,126.

1972, Nixon, Rep., 1,154,058; McGovern, Dem., 698,531.

1976, Carter, Dem., 999,163; Ford, Rep., 928,808; McCarthy, Ind., 24,329.

1980, Reagan, Rep., 1,074,181; Carter, Dem., 931,182; Anderson, Ind., 77,920; Clark, Libertarian, 14,422; DeBerry, Soc. Workers, 1,515; Commoner, Citizens, 573; write-ins, 31.

1984, Reagan, Rep., 1,274,188; Mondale, Dem., 848,583.

1988, Bush, Rep., 1,084,953; Dukakis, Dem., 1,001,619; Fulani, New Alliance, 6,656; Paul, write-in, 434.

1992, Clinton, Dem., 1,053,873; Bush, Rep., 811,159; Perot, Ind., 518,741; Marrou, Libertarian, 7,497.

Montana

	1992			1988	
County	Clinton (D)	Bush (R)	Perot (I)	Dukakis (D)	Bush (R)
Beaverhead	1,098	1,746	1,202	1,274	2,668
Big Horn	2,154	1,377	840	2,233	1,711
Blaine	1,355	971	699	1,460	1,402
Broadwater	491	830	505	592	1,054
Carbon	1,549	1,562	1,482	2,039	2,360
Carter	154	497	220	242	686
Cascade	14,719	12,494	9,151	15,718	15,946
Chouteau	959	1,380	870	1,166	1,980
Custer	1,968	2,105	1,505	2,343	3,007
Daniels	457	496	402	571	802
Dawson	1,785	1,679	1,370	2,120	2,658
Deer Lodge	3,174	832	1,207	3,185	1,168
Fallon	446	731	427	612	1,002
Fergus	1,615	2,736	1,934	2,052	3,948
Flathead	9,746	11,699	9,109	10,202	14,461
Gallatin	9,535	11,109	7,711	9,527	13,214
Garfield	125	403	281	196	631
Glacier	2,076	1,222	997	2,151	1,728
Golden Valley	142	192	157	203	335
Granite	358	556	386	511	789
Hill	3,618	2,408	2,017	4,219	3,467
Jefferson	1,415	1,541	1,172	1,746	2,007
Judith Basin	409	610	415	590	902
Lake	3,938	3,596	2,878	4,109	4,883
Lewis & Clark	11,117	9,351	5,560	11,932	10,946
Liberty	321	512	363	418	771
Lincoln	2,765	2,799	2,637	3,601	3,500
Madison	779	1,415	1,043	878	2,045
McCone	424	528	395	567	814
Meagher	260	422	310	337	656
Mineral	664	403	543	789	616
Missoula	20,347	12,898	9,735	19,178	15,965
Musselshell	648	876	691	898	1,280
Park	2,258	2,846	2,182	2,526	3,823
Petroleum	61	135	95	91	204
Phillips	634	1,026	949	905	1,462
Pondera	1,046	1,252	855	1,245	1,795
Powder River	258	547	340	395	815
Powell	989	1,058	872	1,174	1,574
Prairie	260	412	179	343	541
Ravalli	4,644	5,392	4,573	4,763	7,418
Richland	1,440	1,760	1,525	1,824	2,628
Roosevelt	1,827	1,212	1,089	2,083	1,957
Rosebud	1,669	1,130	1,099	1,869	1,822
Sanders	1,689	1,361	1,378	1,959	2,152
Sheridan	1,077	795	782	1,354	1,381
Silver Bow	9,960	3,491	4,570	11,422	5,043
Stillwater	1,178	1,390	1,056	1,407	1,920
Sweet Grass	395	880	507	462	1,242
Teton	1,043	1,364	969	1,303	1,876
Toole	854	943	903	1,070	1,505
Treasure	157	206	178	231	291
Valley	1,715	1,497	1,320	2,163	2,467
Wheatland	384	478	284	443	667
Wibaux	195	234	173	258	358
Yellowstone	20,163	22,822	13,133	21,987	28,069
Totals	**154,507**	**144,207**	**107,225**	**168,936**	**190,412**

Montana Vote Since 1944

1944, Roosevelt, Dem., 112,556; Dewey, Rep., 93,163; Thomas, Soc., 1,296; Watson, Proh., 340.

1948, Truman, Dem., 119,071; Dewey, Rep., 96,770; Wallace, Prog., 7,313; Thomas, Soc., 695; Watson, Proh., 429.

1952, Eisenhower, Rep., 157,394; Stevenson, Dem., 106,213; Hallinan, Prog., 723; Hamblen, Proh., 548; Hoopes, Soc., 159.

1956, Eisenhower, Rep., 154,933; Stevenson, Dem., 116,238.

1960, Kennedy, Dem., 134,891; Nixon, Rep., 141,841; Decker, Proh., 456; Dobbs, Soc. Workers, 391.

1964, Johnson, Dem., 164,246; Goldwater, Rep., 113,032; Kasper, Nat'l States Rights, 519; Munn, Proh., 499; DeBerry, Soc. Worker, 332.

1968, Nixon, Rep., 138,835; Humphrey, Dem., 114,117; Wallace, 3d party, 20,015; Halstead, Soc. Worker, 457; Munn, Proh., 510; Caton, New Reform, 470.

1972, Nixon, Rep., 183,976; McGovern, Dem., 120,197; Schmitz, Amer., 13,430.

1976, Carter, Dem., 149,259; Ford, Rep., 173,703; Anderson, Amer., 5,772.

1980, Reagan, Rep., 206,814; Carter, Dem., 118,032; Anderson, Ind., 29,281; Clark, Libertarian, 9,825.

1984, Reagan, Rep., 232,450; Mondale, Dem., 146,742; Bergland, Libertarian, 5,185.

1988, Bush, Rep., 190,412; Dukakis, Dem., 168,936; Paul, Lib., 5,047; Fulani, New Alliance, 1,279.

1992, Clinton, Dem., 154,507; Bush, Rep., 144,207; Perot, Ind., 107,225; Gritz, Populist/America First, 3,658.

Nebraska

County	1992 Clinton (D)	Bush (R)	Perot (I)	1988 Dukakis (D)	Bush (R)
Adams	3,445	6,346	3,273	4,145	8,063
Antelope	650	1,979	1,134	933	2,626
Arthur	18	148	97	58	210
Banner	68	284	128	112	361
Blaine	64	256	130	72	338
Boone	604	1,588	956	976	2,160
Box Butte	1,935	2,198	1,508	2,466	3,253
Boyd	353	744	468	480	967
Brown	311	999	525	435	1,335
Buffalo	3,742.	9,708	4,083	4,700	9,980
Burt	1,224	1,667	1,009	1,458	2,050
Butler	1,087	1,881	1,157	1,715	2,083
Cass	2,949	4,314	2,657	3,674	4,658
Cedar	1,007	1,981	1,507	1,759	2,462
Chase	398	1,000	674	597	1,446
Cherry	563	1,707	730	642	2,240
Cheyenne	967	2,197	1,061	1,333	2,862
Clay	802	1,818	952	1,097	2,352
Colfax	1,011	1,915	1,197	1,542	2,329
Cuming	835	2,711	1,192	1,238	3,201
Custer	1,126	3,180	1,492	1,496	4,202
Dakota	2,322	2,771	1,307	2,941	2,744
Dawes	987	1,961	1,103	1,122	2,618
Dawson	1,739	4,710	2,305	2,184	5,529
Deuel	232	558	327	302	769
Dixon	830	1,484	726	1,166	1,802
Dodge	4,665	7,269	4,432	6,116	8,412
Douglas	67,003	93,421	38,641	76,444	99,806
Dundy	244	664	332	333	828
Fillmore	988	1,495	993	1,433	1,952
Franklin	477	967	527	768	1,294
Frontier	302	785	479	384	1,057
Furnas	624	1,365	804	791	1,830
Gage	3,309	3,995	2,726	4,008	5,114
Garden	212	697	385	366	986
Garfield	221	595	270	234	803
Gosper	254	492	297	331	694
Grant	75	247	124	89	301
Greeley	435	587	395	670	763
Hall	5,519	9,264	5,822	6,822	12,020
Hamilton	992	2,379	1,213	1,289	3,019
Harlan	488	991	623	725	1,403
Hayes	85	362	207	160	512
Hitchcock	359	824	540	480	1,132
Holt	835	3,131	1,714	1,327	4,081
Hooker	70	283	102	91	378
Howard	778	1,138	940	1,186	1,526
Jefferson	1,506	1,783	1,177	1,819	2,470
Johnson	822	885	642	1,162	1,182
Kearney	644	1,751	844	1,056	2,120
Keith	731	2,019	1,130	1,067	2,879
Keya Paha	105	368	158	145	446
Kimball	408	931	440	540	1,321
Knox	968	2,112	1,166	1,477	2,644
Lancaster	41,207	41,400	21,783	44,260	44,605
Lincoln	5,142	7,025	3,384	6,070	8,395
Logan	80	271	98	93	373
Loup	58	233	96	97	295
McPherson	49	217	62	60	229
Madison	2,352	7,851	3,486	2,779	9,135
Merrick	864	1,854	1,072	1,192	2,376
Morrill	577	1,184	752	753	1,554
Nance	559	851	569	794	1,185
Nemaha	1,110	1,696	1,020	1,457	2,293
Nuckolls	834	1,277	825	1,114	1,750
Otoe	2,038	2,960	1,800	2,616	3,724
Pawnee	566	670	565	767	975
Perkins	300	842	522	467	1,117
Phelps	829	2,748	1,298	1,047	3,316
Pierce	611	1,853	1,084	914	2,474
Platte	2,409	7,712	3,656	3,285	9,029
Polk	661	1,435	812	944	1,768
Red Willow	1,164	2,488	1,660	1,505	3,325
Richardson	1,513	2,050	1,356	1,926	2,702
Rock	162	588	233	198	756
Saline	2,425	1,740	1,576	3,119	2,352
Sarpy	10,720	20,482	9,270	10,936	20,179
Saunders	2,509	4,037	2,567	3,524	4,454
Scotts Bluff	4,173	7,213	3,514	4,454	8,594
Seward	2,118	3,044	1,722	2,682	3,467
Sheridan	535	1,698	751	612	2,251
Sherman	568	736	582	839	914
Sioux	148	445	206	194	568
Stanton	496	1,274	786	637	1,709
Thayer	923	1,387	1,077	1,322	1,981
Thomas	69	283	115	81	383
Thurston	865	898	487	1,225	1,105
Valley	716	1,173	693	873	1,603
Washington	2,108	4,035	2,148	2,552	4,567
Wayne	921	2,122	1,047	1,111	2,473
Webster	624	972	657	891	1,314
Wheeler	88	246	127	141	309
York	1,385	3,783	1,825	1,748	4,744
Totals	**216,864**	**343,678**	**174,104**	**259,235**	**397,956**

Nebraska Vote Since 1944

1944, Roosevelt, Dem., 233,246; Dewey, Rep., 329,880.

1948, Truman, Dem., 224,165; Dewey, Rep., 264,774.

1952, Eisenhower, Rep., 421,603; Stevenson Dem., 188,057.

1956, Eisenhower, Rep., 378,108; Stevenson, Dem., 199,029.

1960, Kennedy, Dem., 232,542; Nixon, Rep., 380,553.

1964, Johnson, Dem., 307,307; Goldwater, Rep., 276,847.

1968, Nixon, Rep., 321,163; Humphrey, Dem., 170,784; Wallace, 3d party, 44,904.

1972, Nixon, Rep., 406,298; McGovern, Dem., 169,991; scattered 817.

1976, Carter, Dem., 233,287; Ford, Rep., 359,219; McCarthy, Ind., 9,383; Maddox, Amer. Ind., 3,378; MacBride, Libertarian, 1,476.

1980, Reagan, Rep., 419,214; Carter, Dem., 166,424; Anderson, Ind., 44,854; Clark, Libertarian, 9,041.

1984, Reagan, Rep., 459,135; Mondale, Dem., 187,475; Bergland, Libertarian, 2,075.

1988, Bush, Rep., 397,956; Dukakis, Dem., 259,235; Paul, Lib., 2,534; Fulani, New Alliance, 1,740.

1992, Bush, Rep., 343,678; Clinton, Dem., 216,864; Perot, Ind., 174,104; Marrou, Libertarian, 1,340.

Nevada

County	1992 Clinton (D)	Bush (R)	Perot (I)	1988 Dukakis (D)	Bush (R)
Churchill	1,770	3,789	1,964	1,481	4,578
Clark	124,586	97,403	75,364	78,359	108,110
Douglas	3,928	6,182	4,814	3,107	7,074
Elko	2,782	5,208	3,628	2,310	5,722
Esmeralda	118	221	220	143	380
Eureka	129	330	214	151	413
Humboldt	810	1,505	1,149	1,024	2,378
Lander	423	885	652	439	1,214
Lincoln	511	890	394	466	1,035
Lyon	2,777	3,509	2,716	2,301	4,390
Mineral	909	918	746	978	1,480
Nye	2,561	2,743	2,501	1,748	3,619
Pershing	467	643	429	458	867
Storey	488	458	550	432	651
Washoe	39,500	42,636	30,974	32,902	52,654
White Pine	1,354	1,206	1,070	1,351	1,774
City					
Carson City	6,035	7,302	5,195	5,088	9,701
Totals	**189,148**	**175,828**	**132,580**	**132,738**	**206,040**

Nevada Vote Since 1944

1944, Roosevelt, Dem., 29,623; Dewey, Rep., 24,611.

1948, Truman, Dem., 31,291; Dewey, Rep., 29,357; Wallace, Prog., 1,469.

1952, Eisenhower, Rep., 50,502; Stevenson, Dem., 31,688.

1956, Eisenhower, Rep., 56,049; Stevenson, Dem., 40,640.

1960, Kennedy, Dem., 54,880; Nixon, Rep., 52,387.

1964, Johnson, Dem., 79,339; Goldwater, Rep., 56,094.

1968, Nixon, Rep., 73,188; Humphrey, Dem., 60,598; Wallace, 3d party, 20,432.

1972, Nixon, Rep., 115,750; McGovern, Dem. 66,016.

1976, Carter Dem., 92,479; Ford, Rep., 101,273; MacBride, Libertarian, 1,519; Maddox, Amer. Ind., 1,497; scattered 5,108.

1980, Reagan, Rep., 155,017; Carter, Dem., 66,666; Anderson, Ind., 17,651; Clark, Libertarian, 4,358.

1984, Reagan, Rep., 188,770; Mondale, Dem., 91,655; Bergland, Libertarian, 2,292.

1988, Bush, Rep., 206,040; Dukakis, Dem., 132,738; Paul, Lib., 3,520; Fulani, New Alliance, 835.

1992, Clinton, Dem., 189,148; Bush, Rep., 175,828; Perot, Ind., 132,580; Gritz, Populist/America First, 2,892; Marrou, Libertarian, 1,835.

New Hampshire

City	1992 Clinton (D)	Bush (R)	Perot (I)	1988 Dukakis (D)	Bush (R)
Berlin City	2,680	1,272	1,162	2,271	2,529
Claremont	2,650	1,822	904	2,254	2,513

Concord	8,325	5,651	2,843	6,698	7,439
Dover	5,449	4,197	2,246	4,803	5,357
Keene	5,210	3,257	1,736	4,466	4,535
Laconia	2,390	3,033	1,496	2,111	3,835
Manchester	16,627	16,298	7,441	12,567	23,893
Nashua	14,777	12,514	8,306	12,833	19,369
Portsmith	6,132	3,563	2,088	5,377	4,827
Rochester	4,588	4,272	2,541	3,591	5,368
Totals	**209,040**	**202,484**	**121,337**	**163,696**	**281,537**

New Hampshire Vote Since 1944

1944, Roosevelt, Dem., 119,663; Dewey, Rep., 109,916; Thomas, Soc., 46.

1948, Truman, Dem., 107,995; Dewey, Rep., 121,299; Wallace, Prog., 1,970; Thomas, Soc., 86; Teichert, Soc. Labor, 83; Thurmond, States' Rights, 7.

1952, Eisenhower, Rep., 166,287; Stevenson, Dem., 106,663.

1956, Eisenhower, Rep., 176,519; Stevenson, Dem., 90,364; Andrews, Const., 111.

1960, Kennedy, Dem., 137,772; Nixon, Rep., 157,989.

1964, Johnson, Dem., 182,065; Goldwater, Rep., 104,029.

1968, Nixon, Rep., 154,903; Humphrey, Dem., 130,589; Wallace, 3d party, 11,173; New Party, 421; Halstead, Soc. Worker, 104.

1972, Nixon, Rep., 213,724; McGovern, Dem., 116,435; Schmitz, Amer., 3,386; Jenness, Soc. Workers, 368; scattered, 142.

1976, Carter, Dem., 147,645; Ford, Rep., 185,935; McCarthy, Ind., 4,095; MacBride, Libertarian, 936; Reagan, write-in, 388; La Rouche, U.S. Labor, 186; Camejo, Soc. Workers, 161, Levin, Soc. Labor, 66; scattered, 215.

1980, Reagan, Rep., 221,705; Carter, Dem., 108,864; Anderson, Ind., 49,693; Clark, Libertarian, 2,067; Commoner, Citizens, 1,325; Hall, Com., 129; Griswold, Workers World, 76; DeBerry, Soc. Workers, 72; scattered, 68.

1984, Reagan, Rep., 267,051; Mondale, Dem., 120,377; Bergland, Libertarian, 735.

1988, Bush, Rep., 281,537; Dukakis, Dem., 163,696; Paul, Lib., 4,502; Fulani, New Alliance, 790.

1992, Clinton, Dem., 209,040; Bush, Rep., 202,484; Perot, Ind., 121,337; Marrou, Libertarian, 3,548.

New Jersey

County	1992 Clinton (D)	1992 Bush (R)	1992 Perot (I)	1988 Dukakis (D)	1988 Bush (R)
Atlantic	39,633	34,279	15,890	34,047	44,748
Bergen	171,104	178,223	52,082	160,655	226,885
Burlington	72,845	63,709	35,322	61,140	87,416
Camden	104,915	67,205	37,144	90,704	100,072
Cape May	17,324	21,502	9,798	15,105	28,738
Cumberland	22,220	19,253	9,901	21,869	26,024
Essex	158,130	89,146	26,961	156,098	111,491
Gloucester	42,425	37,335	24,132	35,479	51,708
Hudson	99,799	66,505	14,569	95,696	81,807
Hunterdon	15,423	25,130	12,736	13,758	31,907
Mercer	71,383	50,473	22,503	68,712	65,384
Middlesex	128,824	108,701	45,055	117,149	143,361
Monmouth	101,750	117,715	45,445	91,844	147,320
Morris	67,593	108,431	32,447	58,721	127,420
Ocean	75,431	95,984	41,668	64,474	124,587
Passaic	70,030	71,147	21,494	66,254	88,070
Salem	10,062	10,363	7,274	9,956	15,240
Somerset	42,867	56,044	21,014	37,406	67,658
Sussex	14,775	29,510	12,537	13,676	36,086
Union	96,671	87,742	23,991	93,158	112,967
Warren	13,002	18,468	9,866	11,640	21,715
Totals	**1,436,206**	**1,356,865**	**521,829**	**1,317,541**	**1,740,604**

New Jersey Vote Since 1944

1944, Roosevelt, Dem., 987,874; Dewey, Rep., 961,335; Teichert, Soc. Labor, 6,939; Watson, Nat'l. Proh., 4,255; Thomas, Soc., 3,385.

1948, Truman, Dem., 895,455; Dewey, Rep., 981,124; Wallace, Prog., 42,683; Watson, Proh., 10,593; Thomas, Soc., 10,521; Dobbs, Soc. Workers, 5,825; Teichert, Soc. Labor, 3,354.

1952, Eisenhower, Rep., 1,373,613; Stevenson, Dem., 1,015,902; Hoopes, Soc., 8,593; Hass, Soc. Labor, 5,815; Hallinan, Prog., 5,589; Krajewski, Poor Man's, 4,203; Dobbs, Soc. Workers, 3,850; Hamblen, Proh., 989.

1956, Eisenhower, Rep., 1,606,942; Stevenson Dem., 850,337; Holtwick, Proh., 9,147; Hass, Soc. Labor, 6,736; Andrews, Conservative, 5,317; Dobbs, Soc. Workers, 4,004; Krajewski, American Third Party, 1,829.

1960, Kennedy, Dem., 1,385,415; Nixon, Rep., 1,363,324; Dobbs, Soc. Workers, 11,402; Lee, Conservative, 8,708; Hass, Soc. Labor, 4,262.

1964, Johnson, Dem., 1,867,671; Goldwater, Rep., 963,843; DeBerry, Soc. Workers, 8,181; Hass, Soc. Labor, 7,075.

1968, Nixon, Rep., 1,325,467; Humphrey, Dem., 1,264,206; Wallace, 3d party, 262,187; Halstead, Soc. Worker, 8,667; Gregory, Peace Freedom, 8,084; Blomen, Soc. Labor, 6,784.

1972, Nixon, Rep., 1,845,502; McGovern, Dem., 1,102,211; Schmitz, Amer., 34,378; Spock, Peoples, 5,355; Fisher, Soc. Labor, 4,544; Jenness, Soc. Workers, 2,233; Mahalchik, Amer. First, 1,743; Hall, Com., 1,263.

1976, Carter, Dem., 1,444,653; Ford, Rep., 1,509,688; McCarthy, Ind., 32,717; MacBride, Libertarian, 9,449; Maddox, Amer., 7,716; Levin, Soc. Labor, 3,686; Hall, Com., 1,662; LaRouche, U.S. Labor, 1,650; Camejo, Soc. Workers, 1,184; Wright, People's, 1,044; Bubar, Proh., 554; Zeidler, Soc., 469.

1980, Reagan, Rep., 1,546,557; Carter, Dem., 1,147,364; Anderson, Ind., 234,632; Clark, Libertarian, 20,652; Commoner, Citizens, 8,203; McCormack, Right to Life, 3,927; Lynen, Middle Class, 3,694; Hall, Com., 2,555; Pulley, Soc. Workers, 2,198; McReynolds, Soc., 1,973; Gahres, Down With Lawyers, 1,718; Griswold, Workers World, 1,288; Wendelken, Ind., 923.

1984, Reagan, Rep., 1,933,630; Mondale, Dem., 1,261,323; Bergland, Libertarian, 6,416.

1988, Bush, Rep., 1,740,604; Dukakis, Dem., 1,317,541; Lewin, Peace & Freedom, 9,953; Paul, Lib., 8,421.

1992, Clinton, Dem., 1,436,206; Bush, Rep., 1,356,865; Perot, Ind., 521,829; Marrou, Libertarian, 6,822; Fulani, New Alliance, 3,513; Phillips, U.S. Taxpayers, 2,670; LaRouche, Ind., 2,095; Warren, Socialist Workers, 2,011; Daniels, Ind., 1,996; Gritz, Populist/America First, 1,867; Hagelin, Natural Law, 1,353.

New Mexico

County	1992 Clinton (D)	1992 Bush (R)	1992 Perot (I)	1988 Dukakis (D)	1988 Bush (R)
Bernalillo	90,863	77,304	31,241	78,346	92,830
Catron	465	771	289	490	925
Chaves	6,360	8,872	3,590	6,730	13,367
Cibola	3,334	2,051	847	3,458	2,640
Colfax	2,607	1,730	871	2,785	2,256
Curry	3,699	6,831	2,056	3,995	8,032
De Baca	451	526	204	480	643
Dona Ana	19,894	16,308	7,682	19,608	21,582
Eddy	7,409	7,313	3,430	8,544	9,805
Grant	5,603	2,917	1,685	5,443	4,196
Guadalupe	1,225	691	173	1,243	861
Harding	268	312	98	291	377
Hidalgo	995	871	442	901	1,100
Lea	5,047	7,921	3,233	5,879	11,309
Lincoln	1,730	2,669	1,431	1,690	3,511
Los Alamos	3,897	4,320	2,339	3,275	6,622
Luna	2,637	2,166	1,445	3,066	3,415
McKinley	9,405	4,720	1,304	9,595	5,694
Mora	1,555	668	188	1,601	923
Otero	5,377	7,481	3,257	5,284	9,984
Quay	1,758	1,759	755	1,901	2,454
Rio Arriba	7,832	2,680	984	7,503	3,024
Roosevelt	2,172	3,215	1,085	2,033	3,589
Sandoval	10,951	8,491	3,954	9,332	9,411
San Juan	11,302	13,415	5,351	11,094	16,202
San Miguel	6,186	2,183	965	6,131	2,763
Santa Fe	27,189	9,684	5,656	23,581	12,891
Sierra	1,771	1,562	1,055	1,595	2,507
Socorro	2,908	2,186	918	2,960	3,114
Taos	7,051	2,260	1,300	6,271	2,897
Torrance	1,662	1,667	810	1,618	2,252
Union	519	975	355	638	1,291
Valencia	7,495	6,305	2,902	7,136	7,874
Totals	**261,617**	**212,824**	**91,895**	**244,497**	**270,341**

New Mexico Vote Since 1944

1944, Roosevelt, Dem., 81,389; Dewey, Rep., 70,688; Watson, Proh., 148.

1948, Truman, Dem., 105,464; Dewey, Rep., 80,303; Wallace, Prog., 1,037; Watson, Proh., 127; Thomas, Soc., 83; Teichert, Soc. Labor, 49.

1952, Eisenhower, Rep., 132,170; Stevenson, Dem., 105,661; Hamblen, Proh., 297; Hallinan, Ind. Prog., 225; MacArthur, Christian National, 220; Hass, Soc. Labor, 35.

1956, Eisenhower, Rep., 146,788; Stevenson, Dem., 106,098; Holtwick, Proh., 607; Andrews, Ind., 364; Hass, Soc. Labor, 69.

1960, Kennedy, Dem., 156,027; Nixon, Rep., 153,733; Decker, Proh., 777; Hass, Soc. Labor, 570.

1964, Johnson, Dem., 194,017; Goldwater, Rep., 131,838; Hass, Soc. Labor, 1,217; Munn, Proh., 543.

1968, Nixon, Rep., 169,692; Humphrey, Dem., 130,081; Wallace, 3d party, 25,737; Chavez, 1,519; Halstead, Soc. Worker, 252.

1972, Nixon, Rep., 235,606; McGovern, Dem., 141,084; Schmitz, Amer., 8,767; Jenness, Soc. Workers, 474.

1976, Carter, Dem., 201,148; Ford, Rep., 211,419; Camejo, Soc. Workers, 2,462; MacBride, Libertarian, 1,110; Zeidler, Soc., 240; Bubar, Proh., 211.

1980, Reagan, Rep., 250,779; Carter, Dem., 167,826; Anderson, Ind., 29,459; Clark, Libertarian, 4,365; Commoner, Citizens, 2,202; Bubar, Statesman, 1,281; Pulley, Soc. Worker, 325.

1984, Reagan, Rep., 307,101; Mondale, Dem., 201,769; Bergland, Libertarian, 4,459.

1988, Bush, Rep., 270,341; Dukakis, Dem., 244,497; Paul, Lib., 3,268; Fulani, New Alliance, 2,237.

1992, Clinton, Dem., 261,617; Bush, Rep., 212,824; Perot, Ind., 91,895; Marrou, Libertarian, 1,615.

New York

County	1992 Clinton (D)	1992 Bush (R)	1992 Perot (I)	1988 Dukakis (D)	1988 Bush (R)
Albany	80,641	49,452	24,064	86,564	59,534
Allegany	4,848	8,976	4,703	5,614	11,880
Bronx	225,038	63,310	15,115	218,245	76,043
Broome	43,444	34,653	21,280	48,130	47,610
Cattaraugus	10,150	13,944	10,662	12,447	19,691
Cayuga	13,088	12,065	10,279	15,044	16,934
Chautauqua	22,645	21,222	18,455	25,814	31,642
Chemung	15,099	16,088	7,493	15,966	20,951
Chenango	8,017	8,114	5,356	8,021	11,727
Clinton	12,881	13,455	5,389	12,670	15,702
Columbia	11,368	11,568	5,829	11,585	15,111
Cortland	7,815	7,782	5,098	7,673	10,934
Delaware	7,152	8,829	4,404	7,463	11,391
Dutchess	41,655	46,709	26,320	38,968	62,165
Erie	196,233	129,444	123,358	238,779	188,796
Essex	6,717	8,278	3,784	6,623	10,350
Franklin	7,654	6,635	3,857	7,928	9,135
Fulton	8,400	9,137	5,120	9,012	11,757
Genesee	8,071	11,663	6,192	9,945	14,182
Greene	6,924	9,390	4,689	7,265	11,874
Hamilton	963	2,038	793	976	2,320
Herkimer	10,880	12,052	6,866	12,694	15,104
Jefferson	13,380	14,227	9,461	14,137	19,304
Kings	411,183	133,344	33,014	363,916	178,961
Lewis	3,676	4,101	3,164	4,252	5,787
Livingston	8,648	12,122	5,775	9,506	14,004
Madison	10,099	11,293	7,391	10,665	14,902
Monroe	141,502	134,021	63,229	153,650	155,271
Montgomery	9,509	8,802	5,020	11,371	11,128
Nassau	282,593	246,881	77,097	250,130	337,430
New York	416,142	84,501	27,689	385,675	115,927
Niagara	35,649	30,401	30,126	43,801	42,537
Oneida	40,966	43,806	22,717	47,665	55,039
Onondaga	90,645	77,642	45,175	94,751	104,080
Ontario	16,064	18,995	9,571	17,341	21,780
Orange	45,946	53,493	22,499	38,465	65,446
Orleans	4,927	7,468	4,275	5,913	9,028
Oswego	16,990	18,530	14,053	18,430	25,362
Otsego	10,471	10,141	5,841	11,069	13,021
Putnam	14,048	18,934	8,011	12,158	24,086
Queens	349,520	157,561	46,014	325,147	217,049
Rensselaer	29,793	28,937	15,198	33,066	35,412
Richmond	56,901	70,707	19,678	47,812	77,427
Rockland	56,759	49,608	15,026	47,634	63,825
St. Lawrence	18,197	13,901	9,758	18,921	20,290
Saratoga	33,011	36,917	19,091	31,684	43,498
Schenectady	32,335	26,258	14,838	36,483	33,364
Schoharie	4,997	5,678	3,327	5,389	7,008
Schuyler	2,859	3,226	2,051	2,900	4,291
Seneca	5,810	5,432	3,660	6,215	7,221
Steuben	12,043	19,761	9,378	12,824	25,359
Suffolk	220,811	229,467	112,973	199,215	311,242
Sullivan	13,717	11,396	6,336	11,635	15,713
Tioga	7,791	9,287	5,867	8,102	12,670
Tompkins	23,197	11,520	6,704	21,455	14,932
Ulster	32,886	29,223	17,952	30,744	41,173
Warren	9,820	12,260	6,401	8,580	15,860
Washington	8,429	10,305	6,143	8,201	14,103
Wayne	11,866	18,019	9,188	12,959	20,613
Westchester	184,300	151,990	39,933	169,860	197,956
Wyoming	4,045	7,324	4,837	5,228	9,451
Yates	3,242	4,366	2,354	3,507	5,488
Totals	**3,444,450**	**2,346,649**	**1,090,721**	**3,347,882**	**3,081,871**

New York Vote Since 1944

1944, Roosevelt, Dem., 2,478,598; American Lab., 496,405; Liberal, 329,325; total, 3,304,238; Dewey, Rep., 2,987,647; Teichert, Ind. Gov't., 14,352; Thomas, Soc., 10,553.

1948, Truman, Dem., 2,557,642; Liberal, 222,562; total, 2,780,204; Dewey, Rep., 2,841,163; Wallace, Amer. Lab., 509,559; Thomas, Soc., 40,879; Teichert, Ind. Gov't., 2,729; Dobbs, Soc. Workers, 2,675.

1952, Eisenhower, Rep., 3,952,815; Stevenson, Dem., 2,687,890, Liberal, 416,711; total, 3,104,601; Hallinan, American Lab., 64,211; Hoopes, Soc., 2,664; Dobbs, Soc. Workers, 2,212; Hass, Ind. Gov't., 1,560; scattering, 178; blank and void, 87,813.

1956, Eisenhower, Rep., 4,340,340; Stevenson, Dem., 2,458,212; Liberal, 292,557; total, 2,750,769; write-in votes for Andrews, 1,027; Werdel, 492; Hass, 150; Hoopes, 82; others, 476.

1960, Kennedy, Dem., 3,423,909; Liberal, 406,176; total, 3,830,085; Nixon, Rep., 3,446,419; Dobbs, Soc. Workers, 14,319; scattering, 256; blank and void, 88,896.

1964, Johnson, Dem., 4,913,156; Goldwater, Rep., 2,243,559; Hass, Soc. Labor, 6,085; DeBerry, Soc. Workers, 3,215; scattering, 188; blank and void, 151,383.

1968, Nixon, Rep., 3,007,932; Humphrey, Dem., 3,378,470; Wallace, 3d party, 358,864; Blomen, Soc. Labor, 8,432; Halstead, Soc. Worker, 11,851; Gregory, Freedom and Peace, 24,517; blank, void, and scattering, 171,624.

1972, Nixon, Rep., 3,824,642; Conservative, 368,136; McGovern, Dem., 2,767,956; Liberal, 183,128; Reed, Soc. Workers, 7,797; Fisher, Soc. Labor, 4,530; Hall, Com., 5,641; blank, void, or scattered, 161,641.

1976, Carter, Dem., 3,389,558; Ford, Rep., 3,100,791; MacBride, Libertarian, 12,197; Hall, Com., 10,270; Camejo, Soc. Workers, 6,996; LaRouche, U.S. Labor, 5,413; blank, void, or scattered, 143,037.

1980, Reagan, Rep., 2,893,831; Carter, Dem., 2,728,372; Anderson, Lib., 467,801; Clark, Libertarian, 52,648; McCormack, Right To Life, 24,159; Commoner, Citizens, 23,186; Hall, Com., 7,414; DeBerry, Soc. Workers, 2,068; Griswold, Workers World, 1,416; scattering, 1,064.

1984, Reagan, Rep., 3,664,763; Mondale, Dem., 3,119,609; Bergland, Libertarian, 11,949.

1988, Bush, Rep., 3,081,871; Dukakis, Dem., 3,347,882; Marra, Right to Life, 20,497; Fulani, New Alliance, 15,845.

1992, Clinton, Dem., 3,444,450; Bush, Rep., 2,346,649; Perot, Ind., 1,090,721; Warren, Socialist Workers, 15,472; Marrou, Libertarian, 13,451; Fulani, New Alliance, 11,318; Hagelin, Natural Law, 4,420.

North Carolina

County	1992 Clinton (D)	1992 Bush (R)	1992 Perot (I)	1988 Dukakis (D)	1988 Bush (R)
Alamance	15,521	20,637	6,444	12,642	24,131
Alexander	4,849	6,764	2,002	4,148	7,968
Alleghany	2,271	1,853	600	2,087	2,174
Anson	5,269	2,334	921	4,831	2,782
Ashe	4,624	5,200	1,220	4,034	6,019
Avery	1,755	3,895	1,123	1,367	4,277
Beaufort	6,445	7,337	2,174	5,352	8,190
Bertie	4,382	1,756	600	3,762	2,145
Bladen	5,700	3,214	1,248	5,031	3,770
Brunswick	10,177	8,833	3,349	7,881	10,007
Buncombe	32,955	30,892	11,481	26,964	36,828
Burke	12,565	13,397	4,124	10,848	15,933
Cabarrus	13,513	21,281	6,251	10,686	22,524
Caldwell	9,033	12,543	3,965	7,862	15,176
Camden	1,153	1,039	479	1,081	1,144
Carteret	8,028	10,334	3,401	6,859	11,076
Caswell	4,725	2,793	827	4,189	3,299
Catawba	16,334	25,466	7,523	12,922	28,872
Chatham	9,520	6,568	2,425	7,600	6,999
Cherokee	3,686	4,021	1,040	2,567	4,557
Chowan	2,136	1,661	700	1,756	1,884
Clay	1,600	1,890	465	1,289	2,174
Cleveland	13,037	13,650	3,784	10,321	14,039
Columbus	11,469	5,462	1,963	9,172	6,659
Craven	9,998	11,575	3,679	7,313	12,057
Cumberland	30,291	27,139	6,792	23,789	27,057
Currituck	1,935	2,188	1,163	1,555	2,443
Dare	3,925	4,357	2,388	2,806	5,234

Davidson	16,462	24,869	8,324	13,215	28,374
Davie	3,675	6,796	1,903	3,166	7,988
Duplin	6,816	5,286	1,636	5,945	5,774
Durham	47,331	27,581	7,504	35,441	29,928
Edgecombe	11,174	6,275	2,175	9,044	6,831
Forsyth	49,006	52,787	14,262	39,726	57,688
Franklin	6,517	4,669	2,062	5,438	5,499
Gaston	19,121	34,714	7,490	14,582	34,775
Gates	2,206	1,158	466	2,024	1,451
Graham	1,551	1,919	403	1,313	2,091
Granville	6,178	4,538	1,321	5,260	4,880
Greene	2,768	2,180	780	2,729	2,498
Guilford	66,319	60,140	19,601	50,351	66,060
Halifax	9,960	5,769	2,047	8,726	7,462
Harnett	8,473	9,751	2,684	7,259	9,749
Haywood	10,385	7,292	3,303	9,010	8,957
Henderson	10,747	17,010	5,260	9,338	19,711
Hertford	4,609	2,208	846	4,943	2,977
Hoke	3,730	1,711	887	3,281	2,020
Hyde	1,206	740	340	1,316	940
Iredell	13,263	19,411	6,204	10,530	21,536
Jackson	5,753	4,275	1,516	4,933	5,166
Johnston	11,284	15,418	4,939	8,717	15,563
Jones	1,962	1,438	444	1,946	1,649
Lee	5,852	6,658	2,125	4,231	7,104
Lenoir	8,793	8,932	2,107	7,649	10,669
Lincoln	8,150	11,018	3,142	6,444	11,651
McDowell	5,309	6,090	1,881	4,449	6,526
Macon	4,624	4,797	1,829	3,773	6,026
Madison	3,980	3,121	857	3,033	3,453
Martin	4,069	2,958	981	3,598	3,149
Mecklenburg	97,065	99,496	31,283	71,907	106,236
Mitchell	1,727	4,405	877	1,377	4,620
Montgomery	4,422	3,543	1,185	3,995	4,504
Moore	9,649	12,448	4,448	7,642	14,543
Nash	10,809	14,446	4,544	8,740	15,906
New Hanover	20,291	24,338	7,401	15,401	23,807
Northampton	5,195	1,845	916	4,599	2,415
Onslow	8,045	11,842	4,387	7,162	12,253
Orange	28,595	13,009	5,535	22,326	14,503
Pamlico	2,229	1,929	809	2,188	2,297
Pasquotank	4,709	3,419	1,434	3,860	4,006
Pender	5,825	4,857	1,725	4,377	4,926
Perquimans	1,818	1,429	624	1,543	1,781
Person	4,323	4,460	1,431	3,777	4,832
Pitt	17,959	16,609	5,262	14,777	18,245
Polk	2,939	3,448	1,134	2,534	3,874
Randolph	11,274	20,697	6,870	8,641	23,881
Richmond	9,163	4,356	2,015	7,151	5,073
Robeson	19,378	7,777	3,277	16,988	9,908
Rockingham	13,880	12,678	4,671	11,551	14,591
Rowan	14,308	21,297	7,053	12,127	23,192
Rutherford	7,855	9,748	2,695	6,926	10,337
Sampson	8,698	8,007	1,852	8,009	8,524
Scotland	5,175	2,980	1,196	3,865	3,199
Stanly	7,735	11,030	2,855	6,627	11,885
Stokes	6,463	7,979	2,183	5,319	8,661
Surry	9,392	10,866	3,164	7,245	11,393
Swain	2,117	1,640	568	1,821	1,795
Transylvania	5,120	5,984	2,006	4,280	7,009
Tyrrell	928	553	189	785	637
Union	10,789	16,542	4,601	8,820	17,015
Vance	6,598	4,747	1,444	5,631	5,625
Wake	88,979	86,798	31,140	61,352	81,613
Warren	4,656	1,767	693	4,249	2,163
Washington	2,902	1,780	563	2,806	2,186
Watauga	8,262	7,899	3,007	6,048	8,662
Wayne	10,307	14,397	2,798	9,135	15,292
Wilkes	7,991	12,547	3,307	7,230	15,231
Wilson	10,105	10,176	2,630	8,214	10,997
Yadkin	3,913	7,311	1,725	3,195	7,918
Yancey	4,285	3,994	917	3,803	4,160
Totals	**1,114,042**	**1,134,661**	**357,864**	**890,167**	**1,237,258**

North Carolina Vote Since 1944

1944, Roosevelt, Dem., 527,399; Dewey, Rep., 263,155.

1948, Truman, Dem., 459,070; Dewey, Rep., 258,572; Thurmond, States' Rights, 69,652; Wallace, Prog., 3,915.

1952, Eisenhower, Rep., 558,107; Stevenson, Dem., 652,803.

1956, Eisenhower, Rep., 575,062; Stevenson, Dem., 590,530.

1960, Kennedy, Dem., 713,136; Nixon, Rep., 655,420.

1964, Johnson, Dem., 800,139; Goldwater Rep., 624,844.

1968, Nixon, Rep., 627,192; Humphrey, Dem., 464,113; Wallace, 3d party, 496,188.

1972, Nixon, Rep., 1,054,889; McGovern, Dem., 438,705; Schmitz, Amer., 25,018.

1976, Carter, Dem., 927,365; Ford, Rep., 741,960; Anderson, Amer., 5,607; MacBride, Libertarian, 2,219; LaRouche, U.S. Labor, 755.

1980, Reagan, Rep., 915,018; Carter, Dem., 875,635; Anderson, Ind., 52,800; Clark, Libertarian, 9,677; Commoner, Citizens, 2,287; DeBerry, Soc. Workers, 416.

1984, Reagan, Rep., 1,346,481; Mondale, Dem., 824,287; Bergland, Libertarian, 3,794.

1988, Bush, Rep., 1,237,258; Dukakis, Dem., 890,167; Fulani, New Alliance, 5,682; Paul, write-in, 1,263.

1992, Bush, Rep., 1,134,661; Clinton, Dem., 1,114,042; Perot, Ind., 357,864; Marrou, Libertarian, 5,171.

North Dakota

	1992			1988	
County	Clinton (D)	Bush (R)	Perot (I)	Dukakis (D)	Bush (R)
Adams	469	647	499	708	1,018
Barnes	2,124	2,728	1,568	2,858	3,631
Benson	1,126	874	610	1,691	1,316
Billings	123	279	270	211	437
Bottineau	1,266	1,787	1,036	1,684	2,530
Bowman	506	712	678	737	1,111
Burke	458	551	506	693	971
Burleigh	8,940	16,484	6,780	10,760	18,000
Cass	18,077	25,312	9,513	22,107	26,699
Cavalier	866	1,527	723	1,333	2,096
Dickey	918	1,514	616	1,249	2,064
Divide	634	616	466	875	869
Dunn	667	784	637	892	1,263
Eddy	575	591	432	748	891
Emmons	595	1,047	774	925	1,634
Foster	565	803	556	837	1,218
Golden Valley	255	503	352	388	781
Grand Forks	10,930	13,705	6,349	12,494	14,801
Grant	415	900	629	654	1,351
Griggs	647	773	330	846	1,020
Hettinger	465	854	500	698	1,395
Kidder	468	739	489	678	1,039
La Moure	797	1,270	679	1,223	1,642
Logan	383	703	390	540	1,111
McHenry	1,173	1,321	886	1,665	1,888
McIntosh	450	1,134	454	598	1,726
McKenzie	787	1,324	969	1,273	1,949
McLean	1,808	2,124	1,330	2,428	2,906
Mercer	1,323	2,274	1,378	1,843	3,013
Morton	3,594	5,042	2,787	4,708	5,588
Mountrail	1,393	1,017	861	1,977	1,443
Nelson	841	864	486	1,151	1,078
Oliver	306	503	407	526	696
Pembina	1,186	1,917	991	1,616	2,471
Pierce	761	1,099	554	1,008	1,422
Ramsey	2,008	2,516	1,507	2,665	3,103
Ransom	1,166	1,102	625	1,459	1,362
Renville	580	655	429	837	893
Richland	2,688	3,873	1,698	3,523	4,670
Rolette	2,002	895	660	2,426	1,126
Sargent	961	816	463	1,306	1,119
Sheridan	276	589	304	428	885
Sioux	463	264	244	701	325
Slope	145	226	162	202	315
Stark	3,003	4,491	3,123	3,678	6,137
Steele	598	503	267	895	690
Stutsman	3,313	4,039	2,580	4,214	5,375
Towner	748	600	402	970	946
Traill	1,638	2,019	875	1,940	2,562
Walsh	1,936	2,544	1,384	2,646	3,250
Ward	7,856	12,056	5,856	9,906	13,179
Wells	888	1,171	850	1,317	1,901
Williams	3,008	3,664	3,180	4,004	5,653
Totals	**99,168**	**136,244**	**71,084**	**127,739**	**166,559**

North Dakota Vote Since 1944

1944, Roosevelt, Dem., 100,144; Dewey, Rep., 118,535; Thomas, Soc., 943, Watson, Proh., 549.

1948, Truman, Dem., 95,812; Dewey, Rep., 115,139; Wallace, Prog., 8,391; Thomas, Soc., 1,000, Thurmond, States' Rights, 374.

1952, Eisenhower, Rep., 191,712; Stevenson, Dem., 76,694; MacArthur, Christian Nationalist, 1,075; Hallinan, Prog., 344; Hamblen, Proh., 302.

1956, Eisenhower, Rep., 156,766; Stevenson, Dem., 96,742; Andrews, Amer., 483.

1960, Kennedy, Dem., 123,963; Nixon, Rep., 154,310; Dobbs, Soc. Workers, 158.

1964, Johnson, Dem., 149,784; Goldwater, Rep., 108,207; DeBerry, Soc. Worker, 224; Munn, Proh., 174.

1968, Nixon, Rep., 138,669; Humphrey, Dem., 94,769; Wallace, 3d party, 14,244; Halstead, Soc. Worker, 128; Munn, Prohibition, 38; Troxell, Ind., 34.

1972, Nixon, Rep., 174,109; McGovern, Dem., 100,384; Jenness, Soc. Workers, 288; Hall, Com., 87; Schmitz, Amer., 5,646.

1976, Carter, Dem., 136,078; Ford, Rep., 153,470; Anderson, Amer., 3,698; McCarthy, Ind., 2,952; Maddox, Amer. Ind., 269; MacBride, Libertarian, 256; scattering, 371.

1980, Reagan, Rep., 193,695; Carter, Dem., 79,189; Anderson, Ind., 23,640; Clark, Libertarian, 3,743; Commoner,

Libertarian, 429; McLain, Nat'l People's League, 296; Greaves, American, 235; Hall, Com., 93; DeBerry, Soc. Workers, 89; McReynolds, Soc., 82; Bubar, Statesman, 54.

1984, Reagan, Rep., 200,336; Mondale, Dem., 104,429; Bergland, Libertarian, 703.

1988, Bush, Rep., 166,559; Dukakis, Dem., 127,739; Paul, Lib., 1,315; LaRouche, Natl. Econ. Recovery, 905.

1992, Bush, Rep., 136,244; Clinton, Dem., 99,168; Perot, Ind., 71,084.

Ohio

	1992			1988	
County	Clinton (D)	Bush (R)	Perot (I)	Dukakis (D)	Bush (R)
Adams	3,998	4,722	1,993	3,740	5,916
Allen	13,777	25,322	8,131	13,727	31,021
Ashland	5,985	9,864	4,950	6,072	12,726
Ashtabula	18,843	13,254	10,765	20,536	17,654
Athens	13,423	7,184	5,074	10,795	9,314
Auglaize	4,960	10,455	4,840	4,756	13,562
Belmont	18,527	8,614	6,142	19,515	12,214
Brown	5,540	5,912	3,676	5,047	7,539
Butler	39,682	63,375	27,527	33,770	75,725
Carroll	4,731	4,224	3,434	4,667	6,179
Champaign	5,201	7,004	3,992	4,272	8,995
Clark	26,692	24,011	12,571	23,247	32,729
Clermont	17,558	32,065	14,279	15,352	37,417
Clinton	4,638	7,290	3,402	3,746	8,856
Columbiana	19,765	15,016	12,611	21,581	21,175
Coshocton	6,212	5,705	4,081	6,020	8,282
Crawford	6,351	8,618	5,764	6,018	12,472
Cuyahoga	337,548	187,186	112,352	353,401	242,439
Darke	7,016	11,098	6,217	6,851	14,914
Defiance	5,735	7,195	4,187	5,448	9,566
Delaware	9,263	18,225	9,244	7,590	20,693
Erie	14,531	12,459	8,720	15,097	16,670
Fairfield	14,249	24,125	12,246	12,504	29,208
Fayette	2,976	4,916	2,162	2,623	6,186
Franklin	176,656	186,324	79,049	147,585	226,265
Fulton	5,576	8,358	4,798	5,076	10,230
Gallia	5,350	5,776	2,549	4,834	7,399
Geauga	11,466	18,200	10,577	11,874	22,339
Greene	20,139	27,651	11,459	18,025	34,432
Guernsey	6,428	5,749	4,103	5,926	8,507
Hamilton	148,409	192,447	60,145	140,354	227,004
Hancock	7,944	16,821	7,002	7,435	19,896
Hardin	4,364	5,851	2,867	4,145	7,291
Harrison	3,830	2,289	1,679	3,881	3,298
Henry	3,933	6,196	3,178	3,764	8,618
Highland	4,866	7,020	3,315	4,278	8,776
Hocking	3,935	3,761	2,831	3,706	5,426
Holmes	1,969	5,079	1,945	2,179	5,064
Huron	7,930	9,480	6,751	7,794	12,633
Jackson	5,016	5,422	2,389	4,505	6,671
Jefferson	20,978	10,764	6,910	22,095	14,141
Knox	7,259	9,044	5,282	6,882	12,180
Lake	37,682	40,766	26,878	39,667	52,963
Lawrence	12,325	10,044	4,536	11,628	12,937
Licking	18,898	26,918	13,806	16,793	34,540
Logan	4,889	9,364	4,472	4,484	11,099
Lorain	50,962	36,803	30,425	55,600	50,410
Lucas	99,989	63,297	38,108	99,755	83,788
Madison	3,998	6,865	3,170	3,421	8,303
Mahoning	64,731	31,191	29,417	75,524	43,722
Marion	9,444	11,675	6,471	9,596	14,864
Medina	18,995	24,090	17,290	19,505	29,962
Meigs	4,226	3,916	2,098	3,699	5,486
Mercer	4,883	8,683	4,913	4,978	11,162
Miami	12,547	19,741	10,544	11,138	24,915
Monroe	4,235	1,823	1,505	4,269	2,557
Montgomery	108,017	104,751	47,854	95,737	131,596
Morgan	2,402	2,719	1,551	2,085	3,713
Morrow	3,907	5,208	3,623	3,515	7,130
Muskingum	11,670	14,168	8,731	11,691	19,736
Noble	2,201	2,223	1,429	2,079	3,155
Ottawa	8,128	6,782	4,832	8,038	9,352
Paulding	3,293	3,652	2,510	3,114	5,381
Perry	4,972	4,712	3,810	5,011	6,602
Pickaway	5,765	8,690	4,319	4,905	10,796
Pike	5,057	4,094	2,192	5,191	5,611
Portage	26,325	18,447	17,065	25,607	26,334
Preble	5,557	8,023	4,460	4,937	10,297
Putnam	3,962	9,338	3,648	4,004	11,183
Richland	19,606	23,532	13,370	19,617	30,047
Ross	10,452	10,825	5,616	9,271	14,563
Sandusky	9,878	10,772	6,682	9,709	14,203
Scioto	14,715	11,931	6,860	14,442	16,029
Seneca	9,280	9,763	6,967	9,504	13,704
Shelby	5,262	8,854	5,835	5,065	12,198
Stark	70,064	61,863	42,413	69,639	87,087
Summit	107,881	77,530	55,151	112,612	101,155
Trumbull	54,591	25,831	26,791	58,674	38,815
Tuscarawas	14,787	13,179	8,785	14,185	17,145
Union	3,465	7,818	3,433	3,130	8,846
Van Wert	3,822	7,227	3,102	3,848	9,410
Vinton	2,308	1,975	1,050	2,385	2,652
Warren	13,542	27,998	11,115	11,145	31,419
Washington	10,380	12,204	5,415	9,967	14,767
Wayne	13,953	18,350	9,482	13,571	22,320
Williams	4,862	7,614	4,902	4,666	10,782
Wood	20,754	20,579	11,682	18,579	26,013
Wyandot	3,031	4,411	2,929	2,936	6,178
Totals	1,984,942	1,894,310	1,036,426	1,939,629	2,416,549

Ohio Vote Since 1944

1944, Roosevelt, Dem., 1,570,763; Dewey, Rep., 1,582,293.

1948, Truman, Dem., 1,452,791; Dewey, Rep., 1,445,684; Wallace, Prog., 37,596.

1952, Eisenhower, Rep., 2,100,391; Stevenson, Dem., 1,600,367.

1956, Eisenhower, Rep., 2,262,610; Stevenson, Dem., 1,439,655.

1960, Kennedy, Dem., 1,944,248; Nixon, Rep., 2,217,611.

1964, Johnson, Dem., 2,498,331; Goldwater, Rep., 1,470,865.

1968, Nixon, Rep., 1,791,014; Humphrey, Dem., 1,700,586; Wallace, 3d party, 467,495; Gregory, 372; Munn, Proh., 19; Blomen, Soc. Labor, 120; Halstead, Soc. Worker, 69; Mitchell, Com., 23.

1972, Nixon, Rep., 2,441,827; McGovern, Dem., 1,558,889; Fisher, Soc. Labor, 7,107; Hall, Com., 6,437; Schmitz, Amer., 80,067; Wallace, Ind., 460.

1976, Carter, Dem., 2,011,621; Ford, Rep., 2,000,505; McCarthy, Ind., 58,258; Maddox, Amer. Ind., 15,529; MacBride, Libertarian, 8,961; Hall, Com., 7,817; Camejo, Soc. Workers, 4,717; LaRouche, U.S. Labor, 4,335; scattered, 130.

1980, Reagan, Rep., 2,206,545; Carter, Dem., 1,752,414; Anderson, Ind., 254,472; Clark, Libertarian, 49,033; Commoner, Citizens, 8,564; Hall, Com., 4,729; Congress, Ind. 4,029; Griswold, Workers World, 3,790; Bubar, Statesman, 27.

1984, Reagan, Rep., 2,678,559; Mondale, Dem., 1,825,440; Bergland, Libertarian, 5,886.

1988, Bush, Rep., 2,416,549; Dukakis, Dem., 1,939,629; Fulani, Ind., 12,017; Paul, Ind., 11,926.

1992, Clinton, Dem., 1,984,942; Bush, Rep., 1,894,310; Perot, Ind., 1,036,426; Marrou, Libertarian, 7,252; Fulani, New Alliance, 6,413; Gritz, Populist/America First, 4,699; Hagelin, Natural Law, 3,437; LaRouche, Ind., 2,446.

Oklahoma

	1992			1988	
County	Clinton (D)	Bush (R)	Perot (I)	Dukakis (D)	Bush (R)
Adair	2,645	2,994	914	2,624	3,558
Alfalfa	741	1,567	722	1,117	1,960
Atoka	2,336	1,561	1,255	2,565	1,971
Beaver	580	1,699	565	777	2,013
Beckham	2,947	2,913	1,929	3,388	3,463
Blaine	1,564	2,209	1,258	1,775	2,889
Bryan	6,259	3,452	3,713	6,849	4,615
Caddo	4,861	3,664	2,911	5,387	4,689
Canadian	7,215	16,756	8,985	7,453	17,872
Carter	7,171	5,947	5,188	7,988	8,430
Cherokee	6,794	4,977	3,297	6,483	5,838
Choctaw	3,413	1,641	1,298	3,362	2,217
Cimarron	395	965	254	470	1,153
Cleveland	24,404	35,561	20,352	22,067	36,313
Coal	1,448	714	618	1,365	891
Comanche	12,237	15,704	7,463	11,441	17,464
Cotton	1,314	910	853	1,482	1,266
Craig	2,780	2,106	1,316	2,940	2,463
Creek	9,118	10,055	5,984	9,512	11,308
Custer	3,540	5,362	2,741	3,697	6,735
Delaware	4,842	4,840	2,689	4,889	5,248
Dewey	845	1,244	684	963	1,543
Ellis	594	1,072	632	786	1,422
Garfield	6,720	13,095	5,559	8,067	15,248
Garvin	4,811	3,983	3,014	5,438	5,109
Grady	6,177	6,997	4,528	6,689	7,994
Grant	864	1,311	871	1,249	1,690
Greer	1,162	964	640	1,256	1,225
Harmon	783	496	326	890	611
Harper	486	1,038	501	593	1,281
Haskell	3,069	1,461	995	2,963	1,822
Hughes	2,850	1,522	1,158	3,259	2,037
Jackson	3,273	3,893	2,227	3,542	4,423
Jefferson	1,580	671	758	1,767	1,063
Johnston	2,096	1,191	1,040	2,042	1,518
Kay	6,643	9,115	6,984	7,751	12,646
Kingfisher	1,379	3,479	1,534	1,777	4,011
Kiowa	2,143	1,635	1,114	2,296	2,030
Latimer	2,606	1,212	1,049	2,365	1,830

Le Flore	7,843	5,850	3,021	6,594	6,964
Lincoln	3,904	5,315	3,160	4,225	6,409
Logan	4,453	6,071	3,239	4,603	6,947
Love	1,708	922	1,033	1,889	1,361
McClain	3,378	4,377	2,996	3,594	4,771
McCurtain	5,082	3,519	2,852	4,928	4,920
McIntosh	4,184	2,225	1,469	4,041	2,665
Major	731	2,154	857	982	2,638
Marshall	2,519	1,478	1,486	2,730	1,911
Mayes	6,432	5,445	3,235	6,691	6,115
Murray	2,594	1,536	1,447	2,697	2,056
Muskogee	13,619	8,782	5,454	13,760	11,147
Noble	1,333	2,474	1,449	1,661	3,015
Nowata	1,912	1,531	1,063	2,203	2,000
Okfuskee	2,141	1,580	889	2,209	1,851
Oklahoma	76,271	126,788	56,139	75,812	135,376
Okmulgee	7,767	4,586	3,013	8,262	5,674
Osage	6,894	5,891	4,477	7,778	7,162
Ottawa	6,304	4,141	2,721	6,658	5,026
Pawnee	2,612	2,675	1,656	2,781	3,324
Payne	9,886	13,032	7,852	10,568	16,027
Pittsburg	8,523	5,659	4,594	8,623	7,594
Pontotoc	6,350	6,206	3,016	6,484	6,600
Pottawatomie	8,616	10,350	6,520	8,873	12,099
Pushmataha	2,553	1,319	1,000	2,430	1,841
Roger Mills	767	890	505	866	1,132
Rogers	8,257	12,455	7,101	8,771	12,940
Seminole	4,624	3,253	2,330	4,911	4,078
Sequoyah	6,092	4,925	2,486	4,951	5,710
Stephens	7,644	7,085	5,692	7,833	9,844
Texas	1,487	4,059	1,417	1,717	4,971
Tillman	1,749	1,377	1,039	2,148	1,754
Tulsa	71,165	117,465	49,760	69,044	127,512
Wagoner	7,041	9,053	5,381	7,378	10,219
Washington	6,593	11,342	5,664	6,971	14,613
Washita	1,929	1,912	1,468	2,290	2,402
Woods	1,361	2,225	1,167	1,735	2,835
Woodward	2,063	4,006	2,411	2,408	4,996
Totals	**473,066**	**592,929**	**319,878**	**483,423**	**678,367**

Oklahoma Vote Since 1944

1944, Roosevelt, Dem., 401,549; Dewey, Rep., 319,424; Watson, Proh., 1,663.

1948, Truman, Dem., 452,782; Dewey, Rep., 268,817.

1952, Eisenhower, Rep., 518,045; Stevenson, Dem., 430,939.

1956, Eisenhower, Rep., 473,769; Stevenson, Dem., 385,581.

1960, Kennedy, Dem., 370,111; Nixon, Rep., 533,039.

1964, Johnson, Dem., 519,834; Goldwater, Rep. 412,665.

1968, Nixon, Rep., 449,697; Humphrey, Dem., 301,658; Wallace, 3d party, 191,731.

1972, Nixon, Rep. 759,025; McGovern, Dem., 247,147; Schmitz, Amer., 23,728.

1976, Carter, Dem., 532,442; Ford, Rep., 545,708; McCarthy, Ind., 14,101.

1980, Reagan, Rep., 695,570; Carter, Dem., 402,026; Anderson, Ind., 38,284; Clark, Libertarian, 13,828.

1984, Reagan, Rep., 861,530; Mondale, Dem., 385,080; Bergland, Libertarian, 9,066.

1988, Bush, Rep., 678,367; Dukakis, Dem., 483,423; Paul., Lib., 6,261; Fulani, New Alliance, 2,985.

1992, Bush, Rep., 592,929; Clinton, Dem., 473,066; Perot, Ind., 319,878; Marrou, Libertarian, 4,486.

Oregon

	1992			1988	
County	Clinton (D)	Bush (R)	Perot (I)	Dukakis (D)	Bush (R)
Baker	2,395	2,862	2,191	2,896	3,696
Benton	17,966	11,550	8,103	16,930	14,004
Clackamas	60,310	53,724	39,776	59,799	61,381
Clatsop	7,700	4,683	4,316	8,074	5,956
Columbia	8,298	5,227	5,670	8,983	6,424
Coos	12,072	9,284	7,989	13,996	10,153
Crook	2,508	2,703	2,024	2,719	3,049
Curry	3,841	3,809	3,310	4,015	4,761
Deschutes	15,693	15,655	12,293	14,264	16,425
Douglas	14,137	19,011	12,377	17,255	20,120
Gilliam	374	377	283	417	470
Grant	1,135	1,496	1,302	1,437	2,264
Harney	973	1,350	1,024	1,379	1,833
Hood River	3,106	2,453	2,235	3,275	3,257
Jackson	29,146	28,704	18,633	28,028	32,516
Jefferson	2,161	1,962	1,741	2,346	2,509
Josephine	11,007	13,003	8,426	10,646	15,876
Klamath	7,918	11,864	6,636	8,429	13,484
Lake	1,019	1,791	980	1,237	2,161
Lane	74,083	41,789	34,906	69,883	47,563
Lincoln	9,603	5,716	6,127	9,598	7,364
Linn	15,399	16,461	13,256	17,007	18,312
Malheur	2,539	5,374	2,654	2,965	6,285
Marion	41,137	42,145	26,156	41,193	45,292
Morrow	1,174	1,187	1,089	1,375	1,529
Multnomah	165,081	72,326	58,236	161,361	95,561
Polk	9,551	10,082	5,818	9,626	10,553
Sherman	362	424	326	435	555
Tillamook	5,040	3,359	2,997	5,529	4,297
Umatilla	6,787	7,095	5,581	8,327	10,254
Union	3,990	4,223	3,305	4,682	5,061
Wallowa	1,203	1,630	1,209	1,425	1,993
Wasco	4,663	3,242	3,008	5,141	4,462
Washington	67,528	57,146	41,575	59,837	67,018
Wheeler	267	357	227	274	367
Yamhill	11,148	11,693	8,312	11,423	13,321
Totals	**621,314**	**475,757**	**354,091**	**616,206**	**560,126**

Oregon Vote Since 1944

1944, Roosevelt, Dem., 248,635; Dewey, Rep., 225,365; Thomas, Soc., 3,785; Watson, Proh., 2,362.

1948, Truman, Dem., 243,147; Dewey, Rep., 260,904; Wallace, Prog., 14,978; Thomas, Soc., 5,051.

1952, Eisenhower, Rep., 420,815; Stevenson, Dem., 270,579; Hallinan, Ind., 3,665.

1956, Eisenhower, Rep., 406,393; Stevenson, Dem., 329,204.

1960, Kennedy, Dem., 367,402; Nixon, Rep., 408,060.

1964, Johnson, Dem., 501,017; Goldwater, Rep., 282,779; write-in, 2,509.

1968, Nixon, Rep., 408,433; Humphrey, Dem., 358,866; Wallace, 3d party, 49,683; write-in, McCarthy, 1,496; N. Rockefeller, 69; others, 1,075.

1972, Nixon, Rep., 486,686; McGovern, Dem., 392,760; Schmitz, Amer., 46,211; write-in, 2,289.

1976, Carter, Dem., 490,407; Ford, Rep., 492,120; McCarthy, Ind., 40,207; write-in, 7,142.

1980, Reagan, Rep., 571,044; Carter, Dem., 456,890; Anderson, Ind., 112,389; Clark, Libertarian, 25,838; Commoner, Citizens, 13,642; scattered, 1,713.

1984, Reagan, Rep., 658,700; Mondale, Dem., 536,479.

1988, Bush, Rep., 560,126; Dukakis, Dem., 616,206; Paul, Lib., 14,811; Fulani, Ind., 6,487.

1992, Clinton, Dem., 621,314; Bush, Rep., 475,757; Perot, Ind., 354,091; Marrou, Libertarian, 4,277; Fulani, New Alliance, 3,030.

Pennsylvania

	1992			1988	
County	Clinton (D)	Bush (R)	Perot (I)	Dukakis (D)	Bush (R)
Adams	9,576	13,552	6,313	8,299	15,650
Allegheny	324,004	183,035	103,470	348,814	231,137
Armstrong	12,995	9,122	6,166	13,892	11,509
Beaver	44,877	21,361	15,954	50,327	25,764
Bedford	5,840	9,216	3,731	5,754	11,123
Berks	46,031	52,939	31,663	41,040	70,153
Blair	14,857	21,447	8,284	15,588	25,623
Bradford	6,903	10,221	5,452	6,635	13,568
Bucks	97,902	94,584	53,931	82,472	127,563
Butler	22,303	23,656	15,013	22,341	27,777
Cambria	34,334	20,770	11,070	38,517	25,626
Cameron	824	1,173	676	901	1,731
Carbon	9,072	7,243	5,222	9,104	10,232
Centre	21,177	20,478	9,356	18,357	23,875
Chester	59,643	74,002	34,536	44,853	93,522
Clarion	5,584	6,477	3,619	5,616	8,026
Clearfield	12,247	11,553	6,989	12,235	14,296
Clinton	5,397	4,471	2,654	5,759	5,735
Columbia	8,261	9,742	5,683	7,767	12,114
Crawford	12,813	14,112	7,392	13,021	17,249
Cumberland	26,635	43,447	14,344	24,613	47,292
Dauphin	36,990	45,479	16,063	35,079	48,917
Delaware	111,210	108,587	43,728	96,144	147,656
Elk	5,016	4,908	3,885	5,879	6,737
Erie	56,381	39,283	21,510	53,913	48,306
Fayette	30,577	12,820	10,162	33,098	16,915
Forest	890	801	448	895	1,159
Franklin	13,440	23,387	6,941	12,368	27,086
Fulton	1,588	2,558	869	1,532	3,086
Greene	8,438	3,482	3,186	9,126	4,879
Huntingdon	5,153	7,249	3,273	4,752	8,800
Indiana	15,194	10,966	7,089	16,514	14,983
Jefferson	5,998	7,271	4,403	6,235	9,743
Juniata	2,601	3,980	1,819	2,834	4,881
Lackawanna	45,054	33,443	15,667	45,591	42,083
Lancaster	44,255	88,447	26,807	38,982	96,979
Lawrence	20,830	12,359	7,950	21,884	15,829
Lebanon	12,350	21,512	9,005	11,912	24,415
Lehigh	46,711	42,631	24,853	42,801	56,363
Luzerne	56,623	49,285	21,007	58,553	59,059
Lycoming	13,315	20,536	9,170	13,528	24,792
McKean	5,331	6,965	4,019	5,300	9,323
Mercer	23,264	16,081	10,277	24,278	21,301
Mifflin	4,946	6,300	3,382	4,790	8,170
Monroe	13,468	14,557	9,257	9,859	17,185
Montgomery	136,572	125,704	53,738	109,834	170,294
Montour	2,150	3,096	1,373	2,031	3,617
Northampton	42,203	34,429	20,234	39,264	42,748

Northumberland	12,814	15,057	7,782	14,255	20,207
Perry	4,086	7,871	3,334	3,910	8,545
Philadelphia	434,904	133,328	65,455	449,566	219,053
Pike	4,382	6,084	3,019	3,097	6,659
Potter	1,892	3,452	1,687	2,119	4,432
Schuylkill	23,679	25,780	13,398	24,797	32,666
Snyder	2,952	6,934	2,686	2,658	9,054
Somerset	12,493	13,858	6,333	13,815	16,809
Sullivan	1,030	1,340	731	1,091	1,808
Susquehanna	5,368	7,356	3,946	4,871	9,077
Tioga	4,868	7,823	3,804	4,807	9,471
Union	3,623	6,362	2,255	3,163	7,912
Venango	8,230	8,545	4,695	8,624	11,468
Warren	6,972	6,585	4,795	6,790	8,991
Washington	46,143	21,977	16,083	47,527	28,651
Wayne	4,817	8,184	3,727	3,775	9,926
Westmoreland	69,817	47,315	37,036	76,710	61,472
Wyoming	3,158	5,143	2,525	2,797	6,607
York	46,113	60,130	27,743	37,691	72,408
Totals	**2,239,164**	**1,791,841**	**902,667**	**2,194,944**	**2,300,087**

Pennsylvania Vote Since 1944

1944, Roosevelt, Dem., 1,940,479; Dewey, Rep., 1,835,054; Thomas, Soc., 11,721; Watson, Proh., 5,750; Teichert, Ind. Gov., 1,789.

1948, Truman, Dem., 1,752,426; Dewey, Rep., 1,902,197; Wallace, Prog., 55,161; Thomas, Soc., 11,325; Watson, Proh., 10,338; Dobbs, Militant Workers, 2,133; Teichert, Ind. Gov., 1,461.

1952, Eisenhower, Rep., 2,415,789; Stevenson, Dem., 2,146,269; Hamblen, Proh., 8,771; Hallinan, Prog., 4,200; Hoopes, Soc., 2,684; Dobbs, Militant Workers, 1,502; Hass, Ind. Gov., 1,347; scattered, 155.

1956, Eisenhower, Rep., 2,585,252; Stevenson, Dem., 1,981,769; Hass, Soc. Labor, 7,447; Dobbs, Militant Workers, 2,035.

1960, Kennedy, Dem., 2,556,282; Nixon, Rep., 2,439,956; Hass, Soc. Labor, 7,185; Dobbs, Soc. Workers, 2,678; scattering, 440.

1964, Johnson, Dem., 3,130,954; Goldwater, Rep., 1,673,657; DeBerry, Soc. Workers, 10,456; Hass, Soc. Labor, 5,092; scattering, 2,531.

1968, Nixon, Rep., 2,090,017; Humphrey, Dem., 2,259,405; Wallace, 3d party, 378,582; Blomen, Soc. Labor, 4,977; Halstead, Soc. Workers, 4,862; Gregory, 7,821; others, 2,264.

1972, Nixon, Rep., 2,714,521; McGovern, Dem., 1,796,951; Schmitz, Amer., 70,593; Jenness, Soc. Workers, 4,639; Hall, Com., 2,686; others, 2,715.

1976, Carter, Dem., 2,328,677; Ford, Rep., 2,205,604; McCarthy, Ind., 50,584; Maddox, Constitution, 25,344; Camejo, Soc. Workers, 3,009; LaRouche, U.S. Labor, 2,744; Hall, Com., 1,891; others, 2,934.

1980, Reagan, Rep., 2,261,872; Carter, Dem., 1,937,540; Anderson, Ind., 292,921; Clark, Libertarian, 33,263; DeBerry, Soc. Workers, 20,291; Commoner, Consumer, 10,430; Hall, Com., 5,184.

1984, Reagan, Rep., 2,584,323; Mondale, Dem., 2,228,131; Bergland, Libertarian, 6,982.

1988, Bush, Rep., 2,300,087; Dukakis, Dem., 2,194,944; McCarthy, Consumer, 19,158; Paul, Lib., 12,051.

1992, Clinton, Dem., 2,239,164; Bush, Rep., 1,791,841; Perot, Ind., 902,667; Marrou, Libertarian, 21,477; Fulani, New Alliance, 4,661.

Rhode Island

	1992			1988	
City	Clinton (D)	Bush (R)	Perot (I)	Dukakis (D)	Bush (R)
Cranston	18,589	12,450	8,331	19,711	17,129
East Providence	11,701	5,843	4,661	11,948	8,181
Pawtucket	14,177	6,322	6,244	15,985	9,359
Providence	32,536	11,519	7,816	34,806	15,310
Warwick	20,504	13,348	10,526	21,662	18,052
Totals	**213,299**	**131,601**	**105,045**	**225,123**	**177,761**

Rhode Island Vote Since 1944

1944, Roosevelt, Dem., 175,356; Dewey, Rep., 123,487; Watson, Proh., 433.

1948, Truman, Dem., 188,736; Dewey, Rep., 135,787; Wallace, Prog., 2,619; Thomas, Soc., 429; Teichert, Soc. Labor, 131.

1952, Eisenhower, Rep., 210,935; Stevenson, Dem., 203,293; Hallinan, Prog., 187; Hass, Soc. Labor, 83.

1956, Eisenhower, Rep., 225,819; Stevenson, Dem., 161,790.

1960, Kennedy, Dem., 258,032; Nixon, Rep., 147,502.

1964, Johnson, Dem., 315,463; Goldwater, Rep., 74,615.

1968, Nixon, Rep., 122,359; Humphrey, Dem., 246,518; Wallace, 3d party, 15,678; Halstead, Soc. Worker, 383.

1972, Nixon, Rep., 220,383; McGovern, Dem., 194,645; Jenness, Soc. Workers, 729.

1976, Carter, Dem., 227,636; Ford, Rep., 181,249; MacBride, Libertarian, 715; Camejo, Soc. Workers, 462; Hall, Com., 334; Levin, Soc. Labor, 188.

1980, Reagan, Rep., 154,793; Carter, Dem., 198,342; Anderson, Ind., 59,819; Clark, Libertarian, 2,458; Hall, Com., 218; McReynolds, Socialist, 170; DeBerry, Soc. Worker, 90; Griswold, Workers World, 77.

1984, Reagan, Rep., 212,080; Mondale, Dem., 197,106; Bergland, Libertarian, 277.

1988, Bush, Rep., 177,761; Dukakis, Dem., 225,123; Paul, Lib., 825; Fulani, New Alliance, 280.

1992, Clinton, Dem., 213,299; Bush, Rep., 131,601; Perot, Ind., 105,045; Fulani, New Alliance, 1,878.

South Carolina

	1992			1988	
County	Clinton (D)	Bush (R)	Perot (I)	Dukakis (D)	Bush (R)
Abbeville	3,968	3,317	1,036	3,629	3,738
Aiken	14,802	25,731	6,056	10,598	27,665
Allendale	2,159	1,049	212	1,796	1,295
Anderson	16,072	24,793	6,966	12,281	25,939
Bamberg	3,426	1,906	360	2,830	2,403
Barnwell	3,344	4,026	752	2,564	4,467
Beaufort	11,466	14,735	4,966	8,691	16,184
Berkeley	12,533	18,048	4,632	9,312	16,779
Calhoun	2,770	2,418	564	2,175	2,585
Charleston	40,095	47,403	10,354	32,977	49,149
Cherokee	5,453	6,887	2,186	4,322	7,763
Chester	5,458	3,451	1,350	3,737	3,968
Chesterfield	5,691	4,183	1,315	4,699	4,999
Clarendon	6,033	4,147	744	5,030	4,337
Colleton	5,455	4,545	1,245	4,508	4,962
Darlington	9,090	8,912	1,863	7,625	9,854
Dillon	4,953	3,575	831	3,251	3,793
Dorchester	9,160	15,004	3,648	7,371	14,756
Edgefield	3,433	3,339	596	3,020	3,814
Fairfield	4,867	2,518	652	3,827	2,714
Florence	15,569	19,802	3,499	12,531	19,490
Georgetown	7,494	6,870	1,840	5,402	7,032
Greenville	34,651	65,066	13,699	27,188	67,371
Greenwood	7,621	9,079	2,101	6,511	9,096
Hampton	4,332	2,402	564	3,435	2,826
Horry	18,896	23,489	8,472	13,316	24,843
Jasper	3,453	1,725	549	2,894	2,004
Kershaw	6,585	8,499	2,150	4,494	8,877
Lancaster	8,307	7,757	2,563	6,181	9,152
Laurens	6,638	8,347	2,157	5,930	9,731
Lee	4,454	2,730	611	3,423	2,936
Lexington	18,312	41,759	8,652	11,366	41,467
McCormick	1,846	899	295	1,722	1,172
Marion	5,843	3,647	822	5,008	4,403
Marlboro	5,111	2,526	895	3,937	2,921
Newberry	4,896	5,980	1,393	3,825	6,427
Oconee	6,617	10,379	3,405	4,299	10,184
Orangeburg	18,440	11,328	2,383	14,655	13,281
Pickens	8,275	17,008	4,128	6,103	17,448
Richland	53,648	43,744	7,918	36,420	43,841
Saluda	2,393	2,968	833	1,984	3,225
Spartanburg	25,488	37,707	8,900	22,964	40,801
Sumter	11,852	12,576	2,062	9,502	13,161
Union	4,644	4,647	1,371	4,420	6,019
Williamsburg	8,077	5,289	864	7,343	5,914
York	15,844	21,297	6,418	11,458	21,657
Totals	**479,514**	**577,507**	**138,872**	**370,554**	**606,443**

South Carolina Vote Since 1944

1944, Roosevelt, Dem., 90,601; Dewey, Rep., 4,547; Southern Democrats, 7,799; Watson, Proh., 365; Rep. Tolbert faction, 63.

1948, Thurmond, States' Rights, 102,607; Truman, Dem., 34,423; Dewey, Rep., 5,386; Wallace, Prog., 154; Thomas, Soc., 1.

1952, Eisenhower ran on two tickets. Under state law vote cast for two Eisenhower slates of electors could not be combined. Eisenhower, Ind., 158,289; Rep., 9,793; total, 168,082; Stevenson, Dem., 173,004; Hamblen, Proh., 1.

1956, Stevenson, Dem., 136,372; Byrd, Ind., 88,509; Eisenhower, Rep., 75,700; Andrews, Ind., 2.

1960, Kennedy, Dem., 198,129; Nixon, Rep., 188,558; write-in, 1.

1964, Johnson, Dem., 215,700; Goldwater, Rep., 309,048; write-ins: Nixon, 1, Wallace, 5; Powell, 1; Thurmond, 1.

1968, Nixon, Rep., 254,062; Humphrey, Dem., 197,486; Wallace, 3d party, 215,430.
1972, Nixon, Rep., 477,044; McGovern, Dem., 184,559, United Citizens, 2,265; Schmitz, Amer., 10,075; write-in, 17.
1976, Carter, Dem., 450,807; Ford, Rep., 346,149; Anderson, Amer., 2,996; Maddox, Amer. Ind., 1,950; write-in, 681.
1980, Reagan, Rep., 439,277; Carter, Dem., 428,220; Anderson, Ind., 13,868; Clark, Libertarian, 4,807; Rarick, Amer. Ind., 2,086.
1984, Reagan, Rep., 615,539; Mondale, Dem., 344,459; Bergland, Libertarian, 4,359.
1988, Bush, Rep., 606,443; Dukakis, Dem., 370,554; Paul, Lib., 4,935; Fulani, United Citizens, 4,077.
1992, Bush, Rep., 577,507; Clinton, Dem., 479,514; Perot, Ind., 138,872; Marrou, Libertarian, 2,719; Phillips, U.S. Taxpayers, 2,680; Fulani, New Alliance, 1,235.

South Dakota

County	1992 Clinton (D)	1992 Bush (R)	1992 Perot (I)	1988 Dukakis (D)	1988 Bush (R)
Aurora	680	594	435	987	856
Beadle	3,925	3,363	1,819	4,523	4,611
Bennett	413	556	221	579	663
Bon Homme	1,294	1,212	836	1,574	1,826
Brookings	4,645	4,698	2,614	4,860	5,394
Brown	7,521	6,665	3,812	8,673	8,537
Brule	1,060	908	687	991	971
Buffalo	282	137	72	334	151
Butte	973	1,674	1,039	1,256	2,291
Campbell	222	574	252	334	909
Chas. Mix	1,639	1,570	886	2,205	1,966
Clark	799	803	761	1,164	1,247
Clay	2,826	1,869	1,303	2,859	2,307
Codington	3,701	3,943	3,262	4,570	5,050
Corson	444	483	321	722	710
Custer	1,078	1,422	845	1,180	1,806
Davison	3,285	3,111	1,706	3,705	4,024
Day	1,578	1,161	973	2,137	1,616
Deuel	880	778	761	1,246	1,251
Dewey	766	642	340	1,007	765
Douglas	481	1,175	403	695	1,438
Edmunds	894	944	415	1,259	1,327
Fall River	1,416	1,533	792	1,380	2,002
Faulk	488	658	281	714	842
Grant	1,484	1,595	1,018	1,988	2,148
Gregory	879	1,027	688	1,138	1,566
Haakon	209	860	245	379	958
Hamlin	826	1,133	774	1,258	1,380
Hand	785	1,130	624	1,101	1,461
Hanson	566	522	341	776	786
Harding	139	515	225	259	633
Hughes	2,578	4,325	1,160	2,853	4,545
Hutchinson	1,211	2,002	920	1,594	2,700
Hyde	301	440	211	436	546
Jackson	351	627	184	450	671
Jerauld	600	518	346	751	777
Jones	166	454	154	261	521
Kingsbury	1,267	1,113	744	1,472	1,592
Lake	2,388	1,890	1,299	2,663	2,439
Lawrence	3,157	3,770	2,673	3,705	5,570
Lincoln	2,943	3,365	1,593	3,190	3,537
Lyman	486	669	311	631	843
McCook	1,167	1,177	617	1,492	1,501
McPherson	478	945	322	571	1,358
Marshall	1,056	810	427	1,372	1,142
Meade	2,694	4,724	2,611	3,212	5,189
Mellette	277	417	140	385	460
Miner	698	543	332	955	795
Minnehaha	27,016	25,081	11,496	29,135	26,765
Moody	1,473	898	715	1,715	1,161
Pennington	11,106	18,052	8,358	12,068	19,510
Perkins	566	872	541	851	1,326
Potter	493	901	375	701	1,175
Roberts	1,716	1,437	954	2,267	2,012
Sanborn	632	595	376	770	815
Shannon	1,267	225	137	1,206	256
Spink	1,732	1,527	839	2,071	1,969
Stanley	427	719	240	511	698
Sully	273	565	167	393	571
Todd	915	456	246	1,117	535
Tripp	1,046	1,459	848	1,219	2,113
Turner	1,507	1,906	867	1,780	2,436
Union	2,210	1,784	1,085	2,612	1,907
Walworth	829	1,439	628	1,094	1,940
Yankton	3,404	3,430	2,511	3,777	4,186
Ziebach	280	328	117	427	362
Totals	**124,888**	**136,718**	**73,295**	**145,560**	**165,415**

South Dakota Vote Since 1944

1944, Roosevelt, Dem., 96,711; Dewey, Rep., 135,365.
1948, Truman, Dem., 117,653; Dewey, Rep., 129,651; Wallace, Prog., 2,801.
1952, Eisenhower, Rep., 203,857; Stevenson, Dem., 90,426.
1956, Eisenhower, Rep., 171,569; Stevenson, Dem., 122,288.
1960, Kennedy, Dem., 128,070; Nixon, Rep., 178,417.
1964, Johnson, Dem., 163,010; Goldwater, Rep., 130,108.
1968, Nixon, Rep., 149,841; Humphrey, Dem., 118,023; Wallace, 3d party, 13,400.
1972, Nixon, Rep., 166,476; McGovern, Dem., 139,945; Jenness, Soc. Workers, 994.
1976, Carter, Dem., 147,068; Ford, Rep., 151,505; MacBride, Libertarian, 1,619; Hall, Com., 318; Camejo, Soc. Workers, 168.
1980, Reagan, Rep., 198,343; Carter, Dem., 103,855; Anderson, Ind., 21,431; Clark, Libertarian, 3,824; Pulley, Soc. Workers, 250.
1984, Reagan, Rep., 200,267; Mondale, Dem., 116,113.
1988, Bush, Rep., 165,415; Dukakis, Dem., 145,560; Paul, Lib., 1,060; Fulani, New Alliance, 730.
1992, Bush, Rep., 136,718; Clinton, Dem., 124,888; Perot, Ind., 73,295.

Tennessee

County	1992 Clinton (D)	1992 Bush (R)	1992 Perot (I)	1988 Dukakis (D)	1988 Bush (R)
Anderson	13,482	11,838	3,149	9,589	15,056
Bedford	5,978	3,836	1,541	4,046	4,856
Benton	3,896	1,625	559	2,826	2,167
Bledsoe	1,884	1,776	352	1,274	1,858
Blount	14,655	18,415	4,468	9,602	20,027
Bradley	9,889	16,528	3,212	6,122	15,829
Campbell	6,756	4,897	1,240	4,188	5,197
Cannon	2,593	1,229	495	1,726	1,604
Carroll	5,741	4,842	1,139	4,151	5,635
Carter	6,502	10,712	1,898	4,634	12,036
Cheatham	4,817	3,496	1,433	3,067	4,132
Chester	2,317	2,834	439	1,757	2,781
Claiborne	4,509	4,065	860	2,977	4,071
Clay	1,922	1,072	223	1,183	1,291
Cocke	3,495	5,298	1,124	2,115	5,430
Coffee	8,534	6,047	2,420	5,686	7,837
Crockett	2,657	2,180	507	1,742	2,214
Cumberland	6,393	7,116	2,200	3,964	7,557
Davidson	106,355	76,567	20,184	89,270	98,599
Decatur	2,633	1,667	351	1,880	2,286
De Kalb	4,382	1,714	608	2,452	2,098
Dickson	7,863	4,450	1,730	5,129	5,343
Dyer	5,845	5,668	1,241	3,690	6,508
Fayette	4,211	3,713	657	3,292	3,573
Fentress	2,730	2,391	606	1,856	3,103
Franklin	7,773	4,507	1,837	5,442	5,381
Gibson	9,555	7,161	1,536	7,542	8,415
Giles	5,601	2,827	1,309	3,918	3,518
Grainger	2,242	2,772	513	1,423	2,734
Greene	7,857	9,912	2,930	5,077	11,947
Grundy	2,997	1,004	366	2,415	1,429
Hamblen	7,114	8,898	1,760	5,061	10,418
Hamilton	46,770	53,476	14,400	40,990	68,111
Hancock	1,000	1,274	151	737	1,303
Hardeman	4,832	3,122	594	3,526	3,547
Hardin	3,922	3,875	734	2,808	4,252
Hawkins	6,623	7,758	1,847	5,212	9,356
Haywood	3,511	2,518	331	2,923	2,687
Henderson	3,502	4,719	785	2,296	5,418
Henry	6,797	3,661	1,588	5,138	4,784
Hickman	4,093	1,820	795	2,643	2,246
Houston	2,012	648	280	1,467	882
Humphreys	3,875	1,641	609	3,037	2,132
Jackson	3,208	708	332	1,962	1,168
Jefferson	4,740	6,184	1,385	3,168	6,832
Johnson	1,781	3,170	574	1,329	3,715
Knox	59,702	66,607	15,669	41,829	73,092
Lake	1,449	680	151	935	806
Lauderdale	4,452	2,928	561	3,296	3,308
Lawrence	6,816	5,608	1,403	4,903	6,273
Lewis	2,491	1,218	434	1,419	1,324
Lincoln	5,063	3,814	1,371	3,672	4,288
Loudon	5,414	6,444	1,602	3,480	7,122
McMinn	6,682	7,453	1,812	4,568	8,462
McNairy	4,691	4,093	774	3,510	4,625
Macon	2,961	2,299	443	1,538	2,962
Madison	13,629	14,869	2,634	11,001	16,952
Marion	5,589	3,262	1,186	4,175	4,407
Marshall	4,491	2,516	1,050	2,795	2,975
Maury	9,997	7,440	2,821	6,280	8,397
Meigs	1,673	1,355	453	1,048	1,507
Monroe	5,384	6,025	936	4,000	6,355
Montgomery	14,507	13,011	3,753	9,145	12,599
Moore	1,151	661	327	731	786
Morgan	3,190	2,306	658	1,941	2,576
Obion	6,497	4,812	1,494	4,785	6,037
Overton	4,489	1,657	468	2,511	1,873

Perry	1,889	708	317	1,208	854
Pickett	1,144	1,094	121	634	1,118
Polk	2,583	1,584	419	2,073	2,297
Putnam	10,858	7,998	2,473	6,606	9,547
Rhea	4,289	4,860	1,163	2,595	5,144
Roane	9,812	8,719	2,396	6,535	10,881
Robertson	8,498	5,271	1,978	5,884	5,714
Rutherford	21,084	18,877	7,005	12,245	20,397
Scott	2,730	3,011	643	1,611	2,562
Sequatchie	1,754	1,381	405	1,196	1,659
Sevier	6,719	11,714	2,760	3,643	11,920
Shelby	191,322	153,310	20,223	149,759	157,457
Smith	5,061	1,482	486	2,522	2,138
Stewart	2,779	1,046	487	1,979	1,302
Sullivan	20,935	28,801	6,730	17,396	32,996
Sumner	19,387	17,401	5,177	11,702	19,523
Tipton	5,652	6,757	1,279	3,824	6,052
Trousdale	1,846	565	243	1,193	969
Unicoi	2,375	3,344	709	1,794	3,664
Union	2,478	2,274	580	1,431	2,110
Van Buren	1,329	555	191	796	780
Warren	7,189	3,704	1,415	4,646	4,529
Washington	13,071	18,206	4,002	10,087	19,615
Wayne	1,868	2,955	424	1,516	3,405
Weakley	5,691	4,800	1,355	4,239	5,701
White	4,102	2,118	821	2,562	2,646
Williamson	13,053	22,015	5,026	7,864	20,847
Wilson	13,861	12,061	3,848	8,360	13,317
Totals	**933,521**	**841,300**	**199,968**	**679,794**	**947,233**

Tennessee Vote Since 1944

1944, Roosevelt, Dem., 308,707; Dewey, Rep., 200,311; Watson, Proh., 882; Thomas, Soc., 892.

1948, Truman, Dem., 270,402; Dewey, Rep., 202,914; Thurmond, States' Rights, 73,815; Wallace, Prog., 1,864; Thomas, Soc., 1,288.

1952, Eisenhower, Rep., 446,147; Stevenson, Dem., 443,710; Hamblen, Proh., 1,432; Hallinan, Prog., 885; MacArthur, Christian Nationalist, 379.

1956, Eisenhower, Rep., 462,288; Stevenson, Dem., 456,507; Andrews, Ind., 19,820; Holtwick, Proh., 789.

1960, Kennedy, Dem., 481,453; Nixon, Rep., 556,577; Faubus, States' Rights, 11,304; Decker, Proh., 2,458.

1964, Johnson, Dem. 635,047; Goldwater, Rep., 508,965; write-in, 34.

1968, Nixon, Rep., 472,592; Humphrey, Dem., 351,233; Wallace, 3d party, 424,792.

1972, Nixon, Rep., 813,147; McGovern, Dem., 357,293; Schmitz, Amer., 30,373; write-in, 369.

1976, Carter, Dem., 825,879; Ford, Rep., 633,969; Anderson, Amer., 5,769; McCarthy, Ind., 5,004; Maddox, Am. Ind., 2,303; MacBride, Libertarian, 1,375; Hall, Com., 547; LaRouche, U.S. Labor, 512; Bubar, Proh., 442; Miller, Ind., 316; write-in, 230.

1980, Reagan, Rep., 787,761; Carter, Dem., 783,051; Anderson, Ind., 35,991; Clark, Libertarian, 7,116; Commoner, Citizens, 1,112; Bubar, Statesman, 521; McReynolds, Socialist, 519; Hall, Com., 503; DeBerry, Soc. Worker, 490; Griswold, Workers World, 400; write-ins, 152.

1984, Reagan, Rep., 990,212; Mondale, Dem., 711,714; Bergland, Libertarian, 3,072.

1988, Bush, Rep., 947,233; Dukakis, Dem., 679,794; Paul, Ind., 2,041; Duke, Ind., 1,807.

1992, Clinton, Dem., 933,521; Bush, Rep., 841,300; Perot, Ind., 199,968; Marrou, Libertarian, 1,847.

Texas

	1992			1988	
County	Clinton (D)	Bush (R)	Perot (I)	Dukakis (D)	Bush (R)
Anderson	5,322	5,598	3,519	6,128	7,858
Andrews	1,081	2,266	875	1,122	3,052
Angelina	10,318	9,722	6,204	10,849	12,738
Aransas	2,246	2,826	1,676	2,305	3,858
Archer	1,284	1,560	1,106	1,627	2,010
Armstrong	278	561	187	314	720
Atascosa	3,766	3,806	2,035	4,657	4,777
Austin	2,278	4,015	1,585	2,593	4,524
Bailey	677	1,308	376	876	1,459
Bandera	1,059	2,674	1,537	1,251	3,435
Bastrop	6,252	4,980	3,240	8,004	5,991
Baylor	990	611	529	1,153	914
Bee	4,083	3,633	1,367	4,616	4,620
Bell	18,684	24,936	11,026	17,751	29,382
Bexar	172,513	168,816	72,110	174,036	193,192
Blanco	891	1,370	830	1,012	1,680
Borden	106	184	87	169	283
Bosque	2,173	2,300	1,999	2,670	3,458
Bowie	11,825	11,776	6,659	12,331	15,454
Brazoria	21,861	30,384	18,954	23,436	34,028
Brazos	14,819	23,943	10,372	14,885	29,369
Brewster	1,383	1,127	712	1,569	1,708
Briscoe	430	360	164	574	464
Brooks	2,856	585	318	2,859	608
Brown	4,264	5,313	3,034	4,763	6,810
Burleson	2,511	2,013	1,179	3,085	2,242
Burnet	3,638	4,272	2,865	4,343	5,120
Caldwell	3,794	2,749	1,776	4,649	3,553
Calhoun	2,550	2,640	1,579	3,314	3,183
Callahan	1,694	2,134	1,452	2,017	2,887
Cameron	29,435	20,123	9,286	30,972	24,263
Camp	1,938	1,219	821	2,121	1,908
Carson	825	1,647	578	1,034	2,100
Cass	5,476	3,999	2,168	5,941	5,305
Castro	1,113	1,307	485	1,436	1,604
Chambers	2,832	3,398	2,122	3,035	3,694
Cherokee	5,003	5,847	3,273	5,604	7,520
Childress	881	1,033	421	1,060	1,201
Clay	1,919	1,586	1,397	2,288	2,043
Cochran	454	750	255	681	771
Coke	580	640	393	674	863
Coleman	1,579	1,462	1,095	1,978	2,340
Collin	24,508	60,514	43,287	22,934	67,776
Collingsworth	635	697	265	809	872
Colorado	2,442	3,286	1,421	2,847	3,723
Comal	6,312	12,651	5,841	5,716	13,994
Comanche	2,296	1,666	1,281	2,622	2,120
Concho	489	414	329	643	617
Cooke	3,105	5,299	4,658	4,217	7,196
Coryell	4,157	6,144	3,974	4,026	7,461
Cottle	542	245	235	690	379
Crane	514	918	412	596	1,219
Crockett	653	623	368	881	932
Crosby	1,010	1,006	313	1,435	1,121
Culberson	424	251	171	557	417
Dallam	434	922	325	645	1,205
Dallas	231,412	256,007	170,571	243,198	347,094
Dawson	1,639	2,691	518	2,155	3,154
Deaf Smith	1,642	3,137	772	1,930	3,744
Delta	864	599	551	1,244	849
Denton	27,891	48,492	39,653	26,204	57,444
DeWitt	2,127	3,238	1,346	2,579	3,628
Dickens	536	373	250	696	435
Dimmit	3,172	844	361	2,735	900
Donley	578	893	260	661	1,043
Duval	4,006	698	326	4,177	907
Eastland	2,738	2,830	1,698	3,215	3,929
Ector	11,130	18,161	6,668	10,825	23,155
Edwards	254	460	171	368	556
Ellis	9,537	13,564	10,303	11,169	16,422
El Paso	67,715	47,224	19,738	62,622	55,573
Erath	3,531	3,835	3,046	4,113	5,427
Falls	2,761	1,826	1,185	2,877	2,344
Fannin	4,164	2,510	2,919	5,163	4,024
Fayette	2,923	3,789	2,088	3,390	4,551
Fisher	1,242	539	442	1,516	721
Floyd	947	1,676	385	1,391	1,741
Foard	435	207	152	513	306
Fort Bend	29,992	41,039	16,853	23,351	39,818
Franklin	1,338	1,058	942	1,453	1,439
Freestone	2,445	2,316	1,596	2,916	3,159
Frio	2,377	1,275	654	3,016	1,505
Gaines	1,095	2,138	696	1,310	2,265
Galveston	38,623	31,303	20,103	38,633	34,913
Garza	558	982	345	989	1,183
Gillespie	1,600	4,712	2,018	1,588	5,662
Glasscock	100	379	93	143	384
Goliad	1,069	1,236	521	1,358	1,427
Gonzales	2,006	2,502	1,018	2,897	2,983
Gray	2,426	6,105	1,810	2,460	7,259
Grayson	12,547	12,322	13,327	14,347	18,825
Gregg	12,797	20,542	8,437	12,486	26,465
Grimes	2,594	2,402	1,213	2,735	2,820
Guadalupe	6,567	10,818	5,618	7,111	13,265
Hale	2,761	6,098	1,357	3,502	6,284
Hall	819	631	263	1,029	714
Hamilton	1,100	1,232	921	1,355	1,718
Hansford	345	1,660	398	443	1,967
Hardeman	954	614	362	1,143	855
Hardin	6,753	5,885	4,129	8,245	6,897
Harris	360,171	406,778	172,922	342,919	464,217
Harrison	9,538	8,733	4,371	8,974	11,957
Hartley	406	1,081	308	505	1,229
Haskell	1,438	852	562	1,715	1,193
Hays	10,842	10,008	6,252	11,187	11,716
Hemphill	479	989	232	527	1,170
Henderson	9,105	8,368	6,746	9,819	11,005
Hidalgo	51,205	26,976	9,757	54,330	29,246
Hill	3,929	3,669	2,752	4,381	4,796
Hockley	2,301	4,261	1,291	2,850	4,368
Hood	4,359	5,313	4,457	4,255	7,400
Hopkins	4,085	3,398	3,147	4,984	5,133
Houston	3,250	3,067	1,690	3,846	3,882
Howard	3,735	5,129	1,984	4,445	6,024
Hudspeth	364	325	178	406	405
Hunt	7,452	9,739	7,387	8,820	12,331
Hutchinson	2,833	6,034	1,993	2,950	7,526
Irion	256	283	290	326	539
Jack	1,254	1,041	1,045	1,521	1,542
Jackson	1,722	2,451	976	2,141	2,954
Jasper	5,658	3,870	2,539	6,613	4,985

Jeff Davis	321	360	187	325	524
Jefferson	48,405	29,622	17,242	55,649	35,754
Jim Hogg	1,520	478	107	1,630	510
Jim Wells	7,812	3,311	1,413	8,495	4,335
Johnson	12,030	13,473	11,573	12,507	17,509
Jones	2,400	2,088	1,436	2,898	3,000
Karnes	1,897	1,990	802	2,529	2,383
Kaufman	6,498	6,578	5,913	7,358	8,466
Kendall	1,374	4,162	1,773	1,446	4,875
Kenedy	87	69	18	119	76
Kent	271	175	163	398	274
Kerr	3,707	8,787	3,790	3,587	11,207
Kimble	467	790	354	551	1,061
King	54	79	56	64	111
Kinney	598	634	299	669	771
Kleberg	5,109	3,897	1,470	5,367	4,443
Knox	854	521	438	1,013	765
Lamar	6,328	5,778	4,093	7,553	8,021
Lamb	1,737	2,998	709	2,230	3,064
Lampasas	1,508	2,233	1,432	1,954	3,000
LaSalle	1,522	586	211	1,651	693
Lavaca	2,700	3,362	1,696	3,531	4,377
Lee	1,847	2,108	1,088	2,527	2,513
Leon	2,042	2,212	1,251	2,316	2,778
Liberty	7,036	6,959	4,311	8,343	8,524
Limestone	3,188	2,358	1,505	3,476	3,257
Lipscomb	338	839	270	377	1,111
Live Oak	1,345	1,805	806	1,573	2,277
Llano	2,409	3,056	1,799	2,629	3,550
Loving	20	31	45	23	54
Lubbock	22,240	48,847	11,618	22,202	50,760
Lynn	902	1,233	291	1,086	1,279
McCulloch	1,393	1,108	986	1,665	1,618
McLennan	25,903	26,473	15,505	27,545	38,606
McMullen	78	274	89	94	302
Madison	1,553	1,544	778	1,835	1,896
Marion	2,156	1,245	882	2,255	1,857
Martin	641	986	356	632	1,017
Mason	570	776	364	671	975
Matagorda	4,759	5,328	3,045	5,675	6,787
Maverick	4,540	2,002	771	4,395	1,592
Medina	3,650	4,912	2,167	4,227	5,722
Menard	553	354	367	614	552
Midland	9,160	24,143	7,880	8,487	30,618
Milam	3,542	2,414	1,495	4,865	3,512
Mills	753	702	530	842	1,043
Mitchell	1,353	1,128	604	1,773	1,596
Montague	2,885	2,304	2,330	3,689	3,475
Montgomery	18,551	39,976	19,203	18,394	40,360
Moore	1,361	3,147	976	1,537	3,710
Morris	3,028	1,400	1,138	3,522	2,104
Motley	256	446	117	262	429
Nacogdoches	6,937	9,864	4,803	6,886	11,767
Navarro	6,006	4,897	3,800	6,749	6,445
Newton	3,249	1,212	1,032	3,640	1,659
Nolan	2,490	1,993	1,455	2,853	2,734
Nueces	46,317	36,781	17,374	49,209	46,337
Ochiltree	557	2,419	576	579	2,928
Oldham	225	583	177	303	691
Orange	15,305	9,793	7,321	17,834	11,959
Palo Pinto	3,392	2,852	3,010	3,930	4,649
Panola	3,950	3,473	1,906	4,123	4,642
Parker	7,934	10,321	9,148	8,517	14,090
Parmer	637	1,829	564	764	2,061
Pecos	1,778	1,836	895	1,960	2,483
Polk	5,942	5,390	2,884	5,943	5,831
Potter	9,527	13,510	4,655	9,563	16,400
Presidio	1,189	400	290	1,176	586
Rains	1,108	975	890	1,448	1,281
Randall	9,119	24,971	6,340	8,492	27,986
Reagan	337	651	259	418	935
Real	463	787	386	483	795
Red River	2,686	1,735	1,228	3,165	2,475
Reeves	2,569	1,244	734	2,812	1,724
Refugio	1,531	1,469	716	1,831	1,883
Roberts	126	391	99	135	441
Robertson	2,927	1,707	963	3,630	2,184
Rockwall	2,397	6,427	4,393	2,659	7,214
Runnels	1,401	1,653	1,279	1,720	2,417
Rusk	5,391	7,560	3,575	5,140	9,117
Sabine	2,288	1,490	894	2,053	1,925
San Augustine	1,737	1,243	667	2,118	1,946
San Jacinto	2,846	2,494	1,653	2,972	2,691
San Patricio	8,202	7,456	3,178	9,920	9,159
San Saba	716	723	660	1,165	1,099
Schleicher	420	452	355	494	653
Scurry	1,609	2,670	1,826	2,119	3,749
Shackelford	484	623	422	681	865
Shelby	3,986	3,217	1,487	4,261	3,999
Sherman	261	851	256	340	1,145
Smith	17,514	27,753	13,569	18,719	34,658
Somervell	782	872	903	983	1,304
Starr	7,668	1,209	345	6,958	1,218
Stephens	1,115	1,573	1,062	1,519	2,342
Sterling	127	322	182	188	464
Stonewall	561	242	322	724	421
Sutton	524	687	387	571	996
Swisher	1,413	989	541	1,893	1,271
Tarrant	156,230	183,387	129,998	151,310	242,660
Taylor	12,382	22,614	10,331	13,073	28,563
Terrell	325	176	128	390	296
Terry	1,461	2,309	619	1,941	2,645
Throckmorton	401	389	228	534	455
Titus	3,625	3,024	2,146	4,357	4,247
Tom Green	11,437	14,989	10,244	12,283	21,463
Travis	130,546	88,105	56,158	127,783	105,915
Trinity	2,784	1,988	1,133	2,657	2,448
Tyler	3,465	2,357	1,529	4,198	3,070
Upshur	4,776	4,511	2,896	5,242	5,991
Upton	489	908	313	544	1,189
Uvalde	3,482	3,635	1,387	3,684	4,266
Val Verde	4,748	4,102	2,093	5,044	5,109
Van Zandt	5,310	5,810	5,239	6,153	7,371
Victoria	7,604	13,086	5,136	8,923	15,056
Walker	5,619	6,662	3,619	5,826	8,473
Waller	4,270	3,065	1,692	3,957	3,607
Ward	1,695	1,769	948	1,858	2,709
Washington	3,283	5,817	1,738	2,960	6,041
Webb	14,509	7,789	2,517	16,227	7,528
Wharton	4,643	5,503	2,624	5,935	6,978
Wheeler	938	1,458	367	1,067	1,703
Wichita	17,021	17,956	11,478	17,956	23,324
Wilbarger	1,924	1,959	1,453	2,248	2,669
Willacy	3,359	1,490	652	3,165	1,750
Williamson	19,437	26,208	15,415	19,589	27,322
Wilson	3,711	3,766	2,105	3,953	4,436
Winkler	942	1,173	582	947	1,656
Wise	4,478	4,555	4,485	5,288	6,064
Wood	4,084	4,708	3,494	4,553	6,216
Yoakum	595	1,486	484	727	1,762
Young	2,464	2,894	2,302	3,007	4,156
Zapata	2,052	866	326	2,171	958
Zavala	3,058	571	237	3,338	628
Totals	**2,281,815**	**2,496,071**	**1,354,781**	**2,352,748**	**3,036,829**

Texas Vote Since 1944

1944, Roosevelt, Dem., 821,605; Dewey, Rep., 191,425; Texas Regulars, 135,439; Watson, Proh., 1,017; Thomas, Soc., 594; America First, 250.

1948, Truman, Dem., 750,700; Dewey, Rep., 282,240; Thurmond, States' Rights, 106,909; Wallace, Prog., 3,764; Watson, Proh., 2,758; Thomas, Soc., 874.

1952, Eisenhower, Rep., 1,102,878; Stevenson, Dem., 969,228; Hamblen, Proh., 1,983; MacArthur, Christian Nationalist, 833; MacArthur, Constitution, 730; Hallinan, Prog., 294.

1956, Eisenhower, Rep., 1,080,619; Stevenson, Dem., 859,958; Andrews, Ind., 14,591.

1960, Kennedy, Dem., 1,167,932; Nixon, Rep., 1,121,699; Sullivan, Constitution, 18,169; Decker, Proh., 3,870; write-in, 15.

1964, Johnson, Dem., 1,663,185; Goldwater, Rep., 958,566; Lightburn, Constitution, 5,060.

1968, Nixon, Rep., 1,227,844; Humphrey, Dem., 1,266,804; Wallace, 3d party, 584,269; write-in, 489.

1972, Nixon, Rep., 2,298,896; McGovern, Dem., 1,154,289; Schmitz, Amer., 6,039; Jenness, Soc. Workers, 8,664; others, 3,393.

1976, Carter, Dem., 2,082,319; Ford, Rep., 1,953,300; McCarthy, Ind., 20,118; Anderson, Amer., 11,442; Camejo, Soc. Workers, 1,723; write-in, 2,982.

1980, Reagan, Rep., 2,510,705; Carter, Dem., 1,881,147; Anderson, Ind., 111,613; Clark, Libertarian, 37,643; write-in, 528.

1984, Reagan, Rep., 3,433,428; Mondale, Dem., 1,949,276.

1988, Bush, Rep., 3,036,829; Dukakis, Dem., 2,352,748; Paul, Lib., 30,355; Fulani, New Alliance, 7,208.

1992, Bush, Rep., 2,496,071; Clinton, Dem., 2,281,815; Perot, Ind., 1,354,781; Marrou, Libertarian, 19,699.

Utah

	1992			1988	
County	Clinton (D)	Bush (R)	Perot (I)	Dukakis (D)	Bush (R)
Beaver	668	1,040	330	816	1,286
Box Elder	2,186	7,712	4,507	2,736	12,585
Cache	4,973	15,971	8,032	5,871	21,766
Carbon	4,480	2,038	2,002	5,521	3,019
Daggett	122	172	117	132	272
Davis	14,924	39,087	24,105	16,868	50,469
Duchesne	772	1,983	1,229	1,227	3,118
Emery	1,349	1,643	1,138	1,788	2,322
Garfield	309	1,235	355	370	1,470
Grand	1,160	1,100	991	1,287	1,895
Iron	1,537	5,616	1,693	1,736	6,038
Juab	823	1,237	616	974	1,505
Kane	295	1,241	534	398	1,788
Millard	742	2,496	1,064	1,124	3,515
Morgan	520	1,339	851	647	1,889
Piute	169	429	146	206	476
Rich	154	525	187	234	621

Salt Lake	100,082	117,247	91,968	107,453	163,557
San Juan	1,639	2,004	576	1,407	2,377
Sanpete	1,302	2,995	1,742	1,822	4,579
Sevier	1,039	3,160	1,671	1,403	4,747
Summit	3,013	3,133	3,060	2,545	3,881
Tooele	3,270	3,676	3,011	4,166	5,539
Uintah	1,374	3,505	2,250	1,799	5,341
Utah	14,090	61,398	24,558	18,533	68,134
Wasatch	1,042	1,822	1,234	1,451	2,487
Washington	3,364	11,310	4,623	3,054	13,306
Wayne	236	706	251	353	784
Weber	17,795	26,812	20,559	21,431	39,676
Totals	**183,429**	**322,632**	**203,400**	**207,352**	**428,442**

Utah Vote Since 1944

1944, Roosevelt, Dem., 150,088; Dewey, Rep., 97,891; Thomas, Soc., 340.

1948, Truman, Dem., 149,151; Dewey, Rep., 124,402; Wallace, Prog., 2,679; Dobbs, Soc. Workers, 73.

1952, Eisenhower, Rep., 194,190; Stevenson, Dem., 135,364.

1956, Eisenhower, Rep., 215,631; Stevenson, Dem., 118,364.

1960, Kennedy, Dem., 169,248; Nixon, Rep., 205,361; Dobbs, Soc. Workers, 100.

1964, Johnson, Dem., 219,628; Goldwater, Rep., 181,785.

1968, Nixon, Rep., 238,728; Humphrey, Dem., 156,665; Wallace, 3d party, 26,906; Halstead, Soc. Worker, 89; Peace and Freedom, 180.

1972, Nixon, Rep., 323,643; McGovern, Dem., 126,284; Schmitz, Amer., 28,549.

1976, Carter, Dem., 182,110; Ford, Rep., 337,908; Anderson, Amer., 13,304; McCarthy, Ind., 3,907; MacBridc, Libertarian, 2,438; Maddox, Am. Ind., 1,162; Camejo, Soc. Workers, 268; Hall, Com., 121.

1980, Reagan, Rep., 439,687; Carter, Dem., 124,266; Anderson, Ind., 30,284; Clark, Libertarian, 7,226; Commoner, Citizens, 1,009; Greaves, American, 965; Rarick, Amer. Ind., 522; Hall, Com., 139; DeBerry, Soc. Worker, 124.

1984, Reagan, Rep., 469,105; Mondale, Dem., 155,369; Bergland, Libertarian, 2,447.

1988, Bush, Rep., 428,442; Dukakis, Dem., 207,352; Paul, Lib., 7,473; Dennis, American, 2,158.

1992, Bush, Rep., 322,632; Perot, Ind., 203,400; Clinton, Dem., 183,429; Gritz, Populist/America First, 28,602; Marrou, Libertarian, 1,900; Hagelin, Natural Law, 1,319; LaRouche, Ind., 1,089.

Vermont

City	1992 Clinton (D)	1992 Bush (R)	1992 Perot (I)	1988 Dukakis (D)	1988 Bush (R)
Barre City	1,807	1,508	1,035	2,132	2,100
Bennington	3,646	2,151	1,536	3,180	2,748
Brattleboro	3,519	1,447	847	3,136	2,044
Burlington	12,508	4,462	3,241	9,748	6,382
Montpelier	2,490	1,407	657	2,351	2,013
Rutland City	3,888	2,915	1,722	3,590	3,631
St. Albans City	1,455	887	744	1,441	1,295
St. Johnsbury	1,249	1,243	836	1,188	1,974
South Burlington	3,730	2,131	1,359	3,373	3,136
Winooski	1,462	733	646	1,426	1,014
Totals	**133,590**	**88,122**	**65,985**	**115,775**	**124,331**

Vermont Vote Since 1944

1944, Roosevelt, Dem., 53,820; Dewey, Rep., 71,527.

1948, Truman, Dem., 45,557; Dewey, Rep., 75,926; Wallacc, Prog., 1,279; Thomas, Soc., 585.

1952, Eisenhower, Rep., 109,717; Stevenson, Dem., 43,355; Hallinan, Prog., 282; Hoopes, Soc., 185.

1956, Eisenhower, Rep., 110,390; Stevenson, Dem., 42,549; scattered, 39.

1960, Kennedy, Dem., 69,186; Nixon, Rep., 98,131.

1964, Johnson, Dem., 107,674; Goldwater, Rep., 54,868.

1968, Nixon, Rep., 85,142; Humphrey, Dem., 70,255; Wallace, 3d party, 5,104; Halstead, Soc. Worker, 295; Gregory, New Party, 579.

1972, Nixon, Rep., 117,149; McGovern, Dem., 68,174; Spock, Liberty Union, 1,010; Jenness, Soc. Workers, 296; scattered, 318.

1976, Carter, Dem., 77,798; Carter, Ind. Vermonter, 991; Ford, Rep., 100,387; McCarthy, Ind., 4,001; Camejo, Soc. Workers, 430; LaRouche, U.S. Labor, 196; scattered, 99.

1980, Reagan, Rep., 94,598; Carter, Dem., 81,891; Anderson, Ind., 31,760; Commoner, Citizens, 2,316; Clark, Libertarian, 1,900; McReynolds, Liberty Union, 136; Hall, Com. 118; DeBerry, Soc. Worker, 75; scattering, 413.

1984, Reagan, Rep., 135,865; Mondale, Dem., 95,730; Bergland, Libertarian, 1,002.

1988, Bush, Rep., 124,331; Dukakis, Dem., 115,775; Paul, Lib., 1,000; LaRouche, Ind., 275.

1992, Clinton, Dem., 133,590; Bush, Rep., 88,122; Perot, Ind., 65,985.

Virginia

County	1992 Clinton (D)	1992 Bush (R)	1992 Perot (I)	1988 Dukakis (D)	1988 Bush (R)
Accomack	4,950	5,666	2,304	4,443	6,926
Albemarle	13,886	13,894	3,855	10,363	15,117
Alleghany	2,396	2,294	926	2,316	2,555
Amelia	1,534	2,062	574	1,359	2,187
Amherst	4,101	5,482	1,268	3,567	6,507
Appomattox	1,919	2,830	801	1,740	3,205
Arlington	47,756	26,376	7,992	40,314	34,191
Augusta	5,190	12,896	3,397	4,170	13,251
Bath	855	1,075	354	881	1,273
Bedford	6,792	10,496	3,251	5,406	10,702
Bland	1,001	1,368	408	937	1,556
Botetourt	4,349	5,904	1,819	3,763	5,687
Brunswick	3,687	2,480	479	3,070	2,742
Buchanan	7,405	3,297	815	6,935	3,912
Buckingham	2,193	2,368	459	1,941	2,481
Campbell	5,999	10,931	2,553	4,574	12,713
Caroline	3,770	2,947	965	3,186	3,065
Carroll	3,790	5,664	1,388	3,190	6,377
Charles City	2,010	729	251	1,839	826
Charlotte	2,098	2,293	640	1,923	2,699
Chesterfield	28,028	56,626	16,898	18,723	58,828
Clarke	1,811	1,994	802	1,478	2,502
Craig	965	1,008	304	864	1,112
Culpeper	3,444	5,226	1,640	2,555	5,896
Cumberland	1,284	1,643	372	1,132	1,978
Dickenson	4,839	2,574	660	4,461	3,091
Dinwiddie	3,624	3,648	1,198	3,405	4,165
Essex	1,583	1,897	382	1,294	2,038
Fairfax	160,186	170,488	53,012	125,711	200,631
Fauquier	6,600	10,497	3,464	4,837	11,733
Floyd	2,026	2,575	672	1,727	2,921
Fluvanna	2,134	2,811	871	1,562	2,447
Franklin	6,590	6,724	2,232	5,734	7,391
Frederick	4,942	9,425	2,981	3,707	9,921
Giles	3,346	3,023	1,142	3,042	3,490
Gloucester	4,058	6,461	2,640	3,372	7,646
Goochland	2,589	3,834	994	2,209	3,765
Grayson	2,615	3,378	860	2,441	3,968
Greene	1,353	2,265	627	899	2,234
Greensville	2,237	1,335	360	2,083	1,610
Halifax	4,752	5,199	1,140	4,282	5,671
Hanover	8,021	20,336	5,674	5,985	20,570
Henrico	36,807	56,910	14,720	26,980	62,284
Henry	9,296	9,005	3,212	7,536	10,871
Highland	494	686	212	456	807
Isle of Wight	4,380	5,370	1,536	3,747	5,779
James City	6,536	8,781	2,675	4,642	8,945
King George	1,363	1,206	323	1,519	2,587
King and Queen	1,811	2,570	918	1,309	1,376
King William	1,822	2,591	758	1,561	2,735
Lancaster	1,812	2,841	739	1,551	3,380
Lee	5,215	3,504	1,002	4,906	4,080
Loudoun	14,462	19,290	7,391	10,101	20,448
Louisa	3,399	3,461	1,381	2,789	3,831
Lunenburg	2,082	2,227	505	1,870	2,530
Madison	1,700	2,341	653	1,427	2,501
Mathews	1,402	2,179	884	1,235	2,752
Mecklenburg	4,273	5,401	1,128	3,275	5,887
Middlesex	1,597	2,224	768	1,361	2,571
Montgomery	10,658	10,606	3,449	8,909	12,326
Nelson	2,586	2,159	748	2,272	2,502
New Kent	1,738	2,708	1,017	1,427	2,917
Northampton	2,568	2,088	844	2,242	2,562
Northumberland	1,862	2,667	729	1,506	2,984
Nottoway	2,411	2,610	606	2,217	3,161
Orange	3,348	4,092	1,425	2,592	4,319
Page	3,010	4,203	1,163	2,499	5,013
Patrick	2,465	3,521	1,026	2,093	3,990
Pittsylvania	7,675	11,467	2,296	6,612	12,229
Powhatan	1,950	3,832	1,232	1,467	4,040
Prince Edward	2,775	2,858	635	2,434	3,147
Prince George	3,087	4,799	1,459	2,469	4,982
Prince William	26,486	35,432	13,190	19,198	39,654
Pulaski	5,633	6,148	2,066	4,686	6,844
Rappahannock	1,273	1,410	487	1,003	1,657
Richmond	1,034	1,609	366	924	1,862
Roanoke	14,704	20,667	5,477	12,938	22,011
Rockbridge	2,908	3,228	1,254	2,412	3,541
Rockingham	5,407	13,016	2,839	4,716	13,241
Russell	6,480	3,891	958	6,222	4,374
Scott	3,979	4,515	957	3,616	4,986
Shenandoah	3,956	7,746	2,063	3,276	8,612
Smyth	4,924	6,128	1,618	3,989	7,446
Southampton	3,199	2,844	754	3,000	3,439

Spotsylvania	8,133	11,829	3,918	5,486	10,978
Stafford	7,718	12,528	4,481	5,380	12,234
Surry	1,823	1,046	364	1,602	1,246
Sussex	2,193	1,527	446	1,958	1,822
Tazewell	8,586	6,375	1,872	8,098	7,165
Warren	3,554	4,319	1,650	2,769	4,700
Washington	7,269	9,150	2,288	5,819	10,722
Westmoreland	2,758	2,554	818	2,311	2,974
Wise	7,681	5,144	1,835	7,017	6,189
Wythe	3,616	5,121	1,557	3,201	5,827
York	6,218	10,197	3,426	4,639	11,103
City					
Alexandria	30,784	16,700	4,934	24,358	20,913
Bedford	963	1,091	313	960	1,322
Bristol	2,948	3,616	851	2,446	4,407
Buena Vista	1,023	849	291	828	1,121
Charlottesville	8,685	4,705	1,397	7,671	5,817
Chesapeake	23,495	28,909	9,237	18,828	29,738
Clifton Forge	958	632	251	961	759
Colonial Heights	1,721	5,298	1,312	1,581	6,001
Covington	1,442	995	402	1,567	1,274
Danville	8,134	9,584	1,679	7,353	12,221
Emporia	1,048	1,094	157	977	1,289
Fairfax	3,884	4,333	1,439	3,430	5,576
Falls Church	2,864	1,912	599	2,484	2,470
Franklin	1,696	1,347	272	1,630	1,557
Fredericksburg	3,266	2,819	738	2,683	3,401
Galax	957	1,087	276	907	1,278
Hampton	23,395	19,219	6,581	19,106	24,034
Harrisonburg	3,414	4,935	1,162	2,799	5,376
Hopewell	2,863	3,818	1,227	2,566	4,672
Lexington	1,128	894	228	997	994
Lynchburg	9,587	12,518	2,545	8,279	15,323
Manassas	3,647	5,453	1,971	2,658	5,980
Manassas Park	567	792	356	434	993
Martinsville	3,073	2,690	748	2,794	3,360
Newport News	25,743	26,779	8,217	21,413	32,570
Norfolk	37,602	22,362	8,732	37,778	30,538
Norton	871	472	182	795	608
Petersburg	8,671	3,125	834	8,177	4,231
Poquoson	1,086	3,354	960	877	3,840
Portsmouth	20,416	12,575	4,360	19,698	16,087
Radford	2,183	1,996	582	1,855	2,481
Richmond	47,642	24,341	6,992	42,155	31,586
Roanoke	17,724	13,443	3,753	17,185	15,389
Salem	4,028	5,143	1,430	3,760	5,694
South Boston	1,051	1,435	252	936	1,694
Staunton	2,851	4,989	1,146	2,457	5,775
Suffolk	9,196	8,697	2,150	8,080	9,742
Virginia Beach	44,294	68,936	24,087	33,780	76,481
Waynesboro	2,302	3,758	961	2,038	4,672
Williamsburg	1,856	1,349	445	1,534	1,648
Winchester	2,768	3,833	1,048	2,300	4,497
Totals	**1,038,650**	**1,150,517**	**348,639**	**859,799**	**1,309,162**

Virginia Vote Since 1944

1944, Roosevelt, Dem., 242,276; Dewey, Rep., 145,243; Watson, Proh., 459; Thomas, Soc., 417; Teichert, Soc. Labor, 90.

1948, Truman, Dem., 200,786; Dewey, Rep., 172,070; Thurmond, States' Rights, 43,393; Wallace, Prog., 2,047; Thomas, Soc., 726; Teichert, Soc. Labor, 234.

1952, Eisenhower, Rep., 349,037; Stevenson, Dem., 268,677; Hass, Soc. Labor, 1,160; Hoopes, Social Dem., 504; Hallinan, Prog., 311.

1956, Eisenhower, Rep., 386,459; Stevenson, Dem., 267,760; Andrews, States' Rights, 42,964; Hoopes, Soc. Dem., 444; Hass, Soc. Labor, 351.

1960, Kennedy, Dem., 362,327; Nixon, Rep., 404,521; Coiner, Conservative, 4,204; Hass, Soc. Labor, 397.

1964, Johnson, Dem., 558,038; Goldwater, Rep., 481,334; Hass, Soc. Labor, 2,895.

1968, Nixon, Rep., 590,319; Humphrey, Dem., 442,387; Wallace, 3d party, *320,272; Blomen, Soc. Labor, 4,671; Munn, Proh., 601; Gregory, Peace and Freedom, 1,680.

*10,561 votes for Wallace were omitted in the count.

1972, Nixon, Rep., 988,493; McGovern, Dem., 438,887; Schmitz, Amer., 19,721; Fisher, Soc. Labor, 9,918.

1976, Carter, Dem., 813,896; Ford, Rep., 836,554; Camejo, Soc. Workers, 17,802; Anderson, Amer., 16,686; LaRouche, U.S. Labor, 7,508; MacBride, Libertarian, 4,648.

1980, Reagan, Rep., 989,609; Carter, Dem., 752,174; Anderson, Ind., 95,418; Commoner, Citizens, 14,024; Clark, Libertarian, 12,821; DeBerry, Soc. Worker, 1,986.

1984, Reagan, Rep., 1,337,078; Mondale, Dem., 796,250.

1988, Bush, Rep., 1,309,162; Dukakis, Dem., 859,799; Fulani, Ind., 14,312; Paul, Lib., 8,336.

1992, Bush, Rep., 1,150,517; Clinton, Dem., 1,038,650; Perot, Ind., 348,639; LaRouche, Ind., 11,937; Marrou, Libertarian, 5,730; Fulani, New Alliance, 3,192.

Washington

		1992		1988	
County	Clinton (D)	Bush (R)	Perot (I)	Dukakis (D)	Bush (R)
Adams	1,449	2,087	1,010	1,612	2,612
Asotin	3,239	2,425	1,849	3,422	2,874
Benton	16,459	22,883	12,878	14,817	28,688
Chelan	7,860	10,716	4,606	8,183	11,601
Clallam	10,820	9,765	7,775	11,123	11,200
Clark	42,648	36,906	26,163	40,021	37,285
Columbia	668	761	466	730	1,172
Cowlitz	15,052	10,000	9,246	16,090	12,009
Douglas	3,731	4,920	2,315	3,760	5,378
Ferry	963	773	762	972	972
Franklin	3,743	4,486	2,597	4,772	6,488
Garfield	473	620	222	593	714
Grant	7,278	9,503	4,898	7,564	10,859
Grays Harbor	12,599	6,904	7,460	14,097	8,860
Island	9,555	9,526	7,889	8,510	12,552
Jefferson	6,148	3,467	3,168	5,270	4,184
King	391,050	212,986	167,216	349,663	290,574
Kitsap	34,442	29,340	23,873	33,748	34,743
Kittitas	5,432	4,078	2,778	5,318	5,048
Klickitat	2,758	2,085	1,938	2,991	2,920
Lewis	7,810	12,316	6,684	8,629	14,184
Lincoln	1,653	2,152	1,098	1,884	2,689
Mason	8,076	5,776	5,577	7,826	7,426
Okanogan	5,015	4,265	3,541	5,630	5,856
Pacific	4,587	2,243	2,351	5,017	3,073
Pend Oreille	1,798	1,528	1,340	1,925	1,802
Pierce	102,243	77,410	59,523	96,688	94,167
San Juan	3,353	1,901	1,776	3,008	2,660
Skagit	15,936	13,388	10,973	15,159	16,550
Skamania	1,474	1,102	1,050	1,748	1,356
Snohomish	88,643	69,137	65,838	80,694	84,158
Spokane	69,526	59,984	38,251	68,520	68,787
Stevens	4,960	5,706	3,769	5,068	6,576
Thurston	38,293	25,643	19,551	33,860	31,980
Wahkiakum	696	488	584	961	629
Walla Walla	7,325	7,894	4,507	7,448	9,683
Whatcom	26,619	23,801	12,455	25,571	23,820
Whitman	7,637	6,428	3,220	7,403	7,680
Yakima	21,026	25,841	10,583	23,221	30,026
Totals	**993,037**	**731,234**	**541,780**	**933,516**	**903,835**

Washington Vote Since 1944

1944, Roosevelt, Dem., 486,774; Dewey, Rep., 361,689; Thomas, Soc., 3,824; Watson, Proh., 2,396; Teichert, Soc. Labor, 1,645.

1948, Truman, Dem., 476,165; Dewey, Rep., 386,315; Wallace, Prog., 31,692; Watson, Proh., 6,117; Thomas, Soc., 3,534; Teichert, Soc. Labor, 1,133; Dobbs, Soc. Workers, 103.

1952, Eisenhower, Rep., 599,107; Stevenson, Dem., 492,845; MacArthur, Christian Nationalist, 7,290; Hallinan, Prog., 2,460; Hass, Soc. Labor, 633; Hoopes, Soc., 254; Dobbs, Soc. Workers, 119.

1956, Eisenhower, Rep., 620,430; Stevenson, Dem., 523,002; Hass, Soc. Labor, 7,457.

1960, Kennedy, Dem., 599,298; Nixon, Rep., 629,273; Hass, Soc. Labor, 10,895; Curtis, Constitution, 1,401; Dobbs, Soc. Workers, 705.

1964, Johnson, Dem., 779,699; Goldwater, Rep., 470,366; Hass, Soc. Labor, 7,772; DeBerry, Freedom Soc., 537.

1968, Nixon, Rep., 588,510; Humphrey, Dem., 616,037; Wallace, 3d party, 96,990; Blomen, Soc. Labor, 488; Cleaver, Peace and Freedom, 1,609; Halstead, Soc. Worker, 270; Mitchell, Free Ballot, 377.

1972, Nixon, Rep., 837,135; McGovern, Dem., 568,334; Schmitz, Amer., 58,906; Spock, Ind., 2,644; Fisher, Soc. Labor, 1,102; Jenness, Soc. Worker, 623; Hall, Com., 566; Hospers, Libertarian, 1,537.

1976, Carter, Dem., 717,323; Ford, Rep., 777,732; McCarthy, Ind., 36,986; Maddox, Amer. Ind., 8,585; Anderson, Amer., 5,046; MacBride, Libertarian, 5,042; Wright, People's, 1,124; Camejo, Soc. Workers, 905; LaRouche, U.S. Labor, 903; Hall, Com., 817; Levin, Soc. Labor, 713; Zeidler, Soc., 358.

1980, Reagan, Rep., 865,244; Carter, Dem., 650,193; Anderson, Ind., 185,073; Clark, Libertarian, 29,213; Commoner, Citizens, 9,403; DeBerry, Soc. Worker, 1,137; McReynolds, Socialist, 956; Hall, Com., 834; Griswold, Workers World, 341.

1984, Reagan, Rep., 1,051,670; Mondale, Dem., 798,352; Bergland, Libertarian, 8,844.

1988, Bush, Rep., 903,835; Dukakis, Dem., 933,516; Paul, Lib., 17,240; LaRouche, Ind., 4,412.

1992, Clinton, Dem., 993,037; Bush, Rep., 731,234; Perot, Ind., 541,780; Marrou, Libertarian, 7,533; Gritz, Populist/America First, 4,854; Hagelin, Natural Law, 2,456; Phillips, U.S. Taxpayers, 2,354; Fulani, New Alliance, 1,776; Daniels, Ind., 1,171.

West Virginia

	1992			1988	
County	Clinton (D)	Bush (R)	Perot (I)	Dukakis (D)	Bush (R)
Barbour	3,467	2,322	1,153	3,221	3,023
Berkeley	7,159	9,134	3,645	6,313	10,761
Boone	6,576	2,021	1,037	6,539	2,786
Braxton	3,396	1,535	823	3,377	2,024
Brooke	5,693	2,582	2,103	6,258	4,006
Cabell	15,111	13,203	5,311	15,368	17,197
Calhoun	1,627	1,095	537	1,644	1,395
Clay	1,928	1,255	462	2,263	1,536
Doddridge	968	1,500	515	955	1,880
Fayette	9,574	3,991	2,002	11,009	5,143
Gilmer	1,576	1,085	484	1,661	1,387
Grant	1,011	2,762	519	893	3,215
Greenbrier	5,784	4,442	1,898	6,091	5,395
Hampshire	2,365	2,767	1,022	2,085	3,253
Hancock	7,830	3,897	3,267	8,338	5,882
Hardy	1,917	2,144	602	1,689	2,581
Harrison	15,480	9,687	5,131	17,005	13,364
Jackson	5,102	4,192	1,908	4,573	5,696
Jefferson	5,363	4,656	2,114	4,334	5,349
Kanawha	38,315	31,358	11,778	41,144	38,140
Lewis	2,931	2,413	1,197	3,272	3,602
Lincoln	4,502	2,637	787	5,049	3,457
Logan	11,095	3,336	1,835	11,317	4,244
McDowell	7,019	1,941	803	7,204	2,463
Marion	14,042	6,380	4,736	14,441	9,229
Marshall	7,298	4,463	3,402	7,903	6,793
Mason	5,331	3,808	2,045	5,468	5,332
Mercer	9,511	7,888	2,817	10,152	10,221
Mineral	3,992	4,837	1,884	4,059	6,015
Mingo	7,342	2,584	915	7,429	2,896
Monongalia	14,142	9,831	4,576	14,178	12,091
Monroe	2,418	2,311	685	2,427	2,719
Morgan	1,854	2,585	886	1,545	3,002
Nicholas	5,042	2,959	1,495	5,173	3,731
Ohio	9,522	7,421	3,632	10,121	10,341
Pendleton	1,626	1,589	362	1,595	1,901
Pleasants	1,387	1,248	731	1,421	1,761
Pocahontas	1,741	1,401	627	1,958	1,876
Preston	3,933	4,429	2,109	4,357	5,804
Putnam	6,817	7,653	2,910	6,640	8,163
Raleigh	13,171	8,700	3,247	14,302	10,395
Randolph	5,097	3,496	1,582	5,233	4,746
Ritchie	1,474	2,184	745	1,446	2,874
Roane	2,607	2,207	1,009	2,447	2,861
Summers	2,650	1,652	565	3,072	2,231
Taylor	2,843	2,022	1,242	2,852	2,816
Tucker	1,805	1,261	550	1,869	1,699
Tyler	1,587	1,593	1,013	1,501	2,365
Upshur	3,161	3,505	1,558	3,065	4,813
Wayne	8,392	5,729	2,199	8,621	7,123
Webster	2,320	811	436	2,185	1,016
Wetzel	3,753	2,271	1,550	3,928	3,381
Wirt	1,043	939	394	929	1,125
Wood	13,529	15,441	6,998	12,959	19,450
Wyoming	5,782	2,821	996	6,138	3,516
Totals	**331,001**	**241,974**	**108,829**	**341,016**	**310,065**

West Virginia Vote Since 1944

1944, Roosevelt, Dem., 392,777; Dewey, Rep., 322,819.

1948, Truman, Dem., 429,188; Dewey, Rep., 316,251; Wallace, Prog., 3,311.

1952, Eisenhower, Rep., 419,970; Stevenson, Dem., 453,578.

1956, Eisenhower, Rep., 449,297; Stevenson, Dem., 381,534.

1960, Kennedy, Dem., 441,786; Nixon, Rep., 395,995.

1964, Johnson, Dem., 538,087; Goldwater, Rep., 253,953.

1968, Nixon, Rep., 307,555; Humphrey, Dem., 374,091; Wallace, 3d party, 72,560.

1972, Nixon, Rep., 484,964; McGovern, Dem., 277,435.

1976, Carter, Dem., 435,864; Ford, Rep., 314,726.

1980, Reagan, Rep., 334,206; Carter, Dem., 367,462; Anderson, Ind., 31,691; Clark, Libertarian, 4,356.

1984, Reagan, Rep., 405,483; Mondale, Dem., 328,125.

1988, Bush, Rep., 310,065; Dukakis, Dem., 341,016; Fulani, New Alliance, 2,230.

1992, Clinton, Dem., 331,001; Bush, Rep., 241,974; Perot, Ind., 108,829; Marrou, Libertarian, 1,873.

Wisconsin

	1992			1988	
County	Clinton (D)	Bush (R)	Perot (I)	Dukakis (D)	Bush (R)
Adams	3,539	2,465	2,003	3,598	3,258
Ashland	4,213	2,372	1,746	4,526	2,926
Barron	8,063	6,572	5,479	8,951	8,527
Bayfield	3,873	2,393	1,786	4,323	3,095
Brown	37,513	42,352	22,395	41,788	43,625
Buffalo	2,996	2,029	1,889	3,481	2,783
Burnet	3,172	2,340	1,855	3,537	2,884
Calumet	5,701	7,541	5,055	6,481	8,107
Chippewa	10,487	8,215	6,408	11,447	9,757
Clark	5,540	4,977	4,284	6,642	6,296
Columbia	9,348	9,099	5,439	9,132	10,475
Crawford	3,540	2,390	1,797	3,608	3,238
Dane	114,724	61,957	31,874	105,414	69,143
Dodge	11,438	14,971	9,136	12,663	17,003
Door	4,735	5,468	3,506	5,425	6,907
Douglas	12,319	5,679	4,150	13,907	6,440
Dunn	7,965	5,283	4,809	9,205	7,273
Eau Claire	21,221	15,915	9,783	21,150	17,664
Florence	978	942	719	1,018	1,106
Fond duLac	13,757	19,785	10,660	15,887	21,985
Forest	1,904	1,393	1,062	2,142	1,845
Grant	8,914	7,678	6,405	9,421	10,049
Green	5,467	4,887	3,735	5,153	6,636
Green Lake	2,772	3,897	2,827	3,033	5,205
Iowa	4,467	3,288	2,341	4,268	4,240
Iron	1,762	1,273	835	2,090	1,599
Jackson	3,681	2,644	2,040	3,924	3,555
Jefferson	11,593	13,072	7,960	11,816	14,309
Juneau	4,177	4,051	2,670	3,734	4,869
Kenosha	27,341	19,854	14,232	30,089	21,661
Kewaunee	4,050	3,570	2,700	4,786	4,330
La Crosse	22,838	18,891	10,224	22,204	21,548
La Fayette	3,143	2,582	2,079	3,521	3,665
Langlade	3,630	3,890	2,444	4,254	4,884
Lincoln	5,297	4,321	3,605	5,819	5,257
Manitowoc	15,903	14,008	11,179	19,680	16,020
Marathon	21,482	20,948	14,600	24,658	24,482
Marinette	7,626	7,984	5,412	8,030	9,637
Marquette	2,533	2,322	1,818	2,463	3,059
Menominee	691	244	221	1,028	381
Milwaukee	235,521	151,314	76,039	268,287	168,363
Monroe	6,427	6,118	4,183	6,437	7,073
Oconto	5,898	5,720	4,405	6,549	7,084
Oneida	7,160	6,725	4,782	7,414	8,130
Outagamie	23,735	30,370	18,479	27,771	33,113
Ozaukee	11,879	22,805	8,002	12,661	22,899
Pepin	1,673	1,098	781	1,906	1,311
Pierce	7,824	4,844	4,492	8,659	6,045
Polk	7,746	5,446	4,753	8,981	6,866
Portage	15,553	10,914	7,083	16,317	12,057
Price	3,575	2,654	2,286	3,987	3,450
Racine	34,875	32,310	20,227	39,631	36,342
Richland	3,458	3,144	1,899	3,643	4,026
Rock	31,154	21,942	15,700	29,576	28,178
Rusk	3,376	2,430	2,085	3,888	3,063
St. Croix	10,281	8,114	7,125	11,392	9,960
Sauk	9,128	8,886	5,280	8,324	10,225
Sawyer	2,796	2,658	1,861	3,231	3,260
Shawano	6,062	7,253	4,540	6,587	8,362
Sheboygan	20,568	22,526	11,295	23,429	23,471
Taylor	3,305	3,415	2,590	3,785	4,254
Trempealeau	6,218	3,577	3,160	6,212	4,902
Vernon	5,673	4,072	2,890	5,754	5,226
Vilas	3,764	4,616	2,827	3,781	5,842
Walworth	11,825	15,727	9,029	12,203	18,259
Washburn	3,080	2,586	1,978	3,393	3,074
Washington	13,339	22,739	13,045	15,907	24,328
Waukesha	50,270	91,461	36,622	57,598	90,467
Waupaca	6,666	10,252	6,088	7,078	11,559
Waushara	3,402	4,045	2,829	3,535	4,953
Winnebago	27,234	33,709	16,140	28,508	35,085
Wood	13,208	13,843	8,822	16,074	16,549
Totals	**1,041,066**	**930,855**	**544,479**	**1,126,794**	**1,047,499**

Wisconsin Vote Since 1944

1944, Roosevelt, Dem., 650,413; Dewey, Rep., 674,532; Thomas, Soc., 13,205; Teichert, Soc. Labor, 1,002.

1948, Truman, Dem., 647,310; Dewey, Rep., 590,959; Wallace, Prog., 25,282; Thomas, Soc., 12,547; Teichert, Soc. Labor, 399; Dobbs, Soc. Workers, 303.

1952, Eisenhower, Rep., 979,744; Stevenson, Dem., 622,175; Hallinan, Ind., 2,174; Dobbs, Ind., 1,350; Hoopes, Ind., 1,157; Hass, Ind., 770.

1956, Eisenhower, Rep., 954,844; Stevenson, Dem., 586,768; Andrews, Ind., 6,918; Hoopes, Soc., 754; Hass, Soc. Labor, 710; Dobbs, Soc. Workers, 564.

1960, Kennedy, Dem., 830,805; Nixon, Rep., 895,175; Dobbs, Soc. Workers, 1,792; Hass, Soc. Labor, 1,310.

1964, Johnson, Dem., 1,050,424; Goldwater, Rep., 638,495; DeBerry, Soc. Worker, 1,692; Hass, Soc. Labor, 1,204.

1968, Nixon, Rep., 809,997; Humphrey, Dem., 748,804; Wallace, 3d party, 127,835; Blomen, Soc. Labor, 1,338; Halstead, Soc. Worker, 1,222; scattered, 2,342.

1972 Nixon, Rep., 989,430; McGovern, Dem., 810,174; Schmitz, Amer., 47,525; Spock, Ind., 2,701; Fisher, Soc. Labor, 998; Hall, Com., 663; Reed, Ind., 506; scattered, 893.

1976, Carter, Dem., 1,040,232; Ford, Rep., 1,004,987; McCarthy, Ind., 34,943; Maddox, Amer. Ind., 8,552; Zeidler, Soc., 4,298; MacBride, Libertarian, 3,814; Camejo, Soc. Workers, 1,691; Wright, People's, 943; Hall, Com., 749; LaRouche, U.S. Lab., 738; Levin, Soc. Labor, 389; scattered, 2,839.

1980, Reagan, Rep., 1,088,845; Carter, Dem., 981,584; Anderson, Ind., 160,657; Clark, Libertarian, 29,135; Commoner, Citizens, 7,767; Rarick, Constitution, 1,519; McReynolds, Socialist, 808; Hall, Com., 772; Griswold, Workers World, 414; DeBerry, Soc. Workers, 383; scattering, 1,337.

1984, Reagan, Rep., 1,198,584; Mondale, Dem., 995,740; Bergland, Libertarian, 4,883.

1988, Bush, Rep., 1,047,499; Dukakis, Dem., 1,126,794; Paul, Lib., 5,157; Duke, Pop., 3,056.

1992, Clinton, Dem., 1,041,066; Bush, Rep., 930,855; Perot, Ind., 544,479; Marrou, Libertarian, 2,877; Gritz, Populist/America First, 2,311; Daniels, Ind., 1,883; Phillips, U.S. Taxpayers, 1,772; Hagelin, Natural Law, 1,070.

Wyoming

	1992			1988	
County	Clinton (D)	Bush (R)	Perot (I)	Dukakis (D)	Bush (R)
Albany	5,713	4,176	2,862	5,486	5,653
Big Horn	1,216	2,216	1,236	1,469	3,258
Campbell	2,709	5,315	3,133	2,288	6,702
Carbon	2,737	2,320	1,579	2,555	3,336
Converse	1,307	2,159	1,260	1,301	2,885
Crook	568	1,377	718	553	1,939
Fremont	4,765	5,387	3,594	5,020	7,681
Goshen	1,754	2,395	1,144	1,875	3,075
Hot Springs	740	978	652	800	1,490
Johnson	656	1,614	844	707	2,081
Laramie	12,177	12,890	6,607	11,851	15,561
Lincoln	1,430	2,595	1,495	1,592	3,237
Natrona	9,817	9,717	7,647	9,148	14,005
Niobrara	298	635	355	354	825
Park	2,771	5,218	3,145	2,646	6,884
Platte	1,398	1,668	956	1,482	2,253
Sheridan	4,139	4,303	3,035	4,655	5,980
Sublette	536	1,168	828	576	1,636
Sweetwater	6,417	4,476	3,879	6,720	6,780
Teton	3,120	2,854	2,340	2,217	3,616
Uinta	2,047	2,701	2,041	1,922	3,464
Washakie	1,118	1,720	1,084	1,197	2,538
Weston	727	1,465	829	699	1,988
Totals	**68,160**	**79,347**	**51,263**	**67,113**	**106,867**

Wyoming Vote Since 1944

1944, Roosevelt, Dem., 49,419; Dewey, Rep., 51,921.

1948, Truman, Dem., 52,354; Dewey, Rep., 47,947; Wallace, Prog., 931; Thomas, Soc., 137; Teichert, Soc. Labor, 56.

1952, Eisenhower, Rep., 81,047; Stevenson, Dem., 47,934; Hamblen, Proh., 194; Hoopes, Soc., 40; Haas, Soc. Labor, 36.

1956, Eisenhower, Rep., 74,573; Stevenson, Dem., 49,554.

1960, Kennedy, Dem., 63,331; Nixon, Rep., 77,451.

1964, Johnson, Dem., 80,718; Goldwater, Rep., 61,998.

1968, Nixon, Rep., 70,927; Humphrey, Dem., 45,173; Wallace, 3d party, 11,105.

1972, Nixon, Rep., 100,464; McGovern, Dem., 44,358; Schmitz, Amer., 748.

1976, Carter, Dem., 62,239; Ford, Rep., 92,717; McCarthy, Ind., 624; Reagan, Ind., 307; Anderson, Amer., 290; MacBride, Libertarian, 89; Brown, Ind., 47; Maddox, Amer. Ind., 30.

1980, Reagan, Rep., 110,700; Carter, Dem., 49,427; Anderson, Ind., 12,072; Clark, Libertarian, 4,514.

1984, Reagan, Rep., 133,241; Mondale, Dem., 53,370; Bergland, Libertarian, 2,357.

1988, Bush, Rep., 106,867; Dukakis, Dem., 67,113; Paul, Lib., 2,026; Fulani, New Alliance, 545.

1992, Bush, Rep., 79,347; Clinton, Dem., 68,160; Perot, Ind., 51,263.

Electoral Votes for President

(based on 1990 Census)

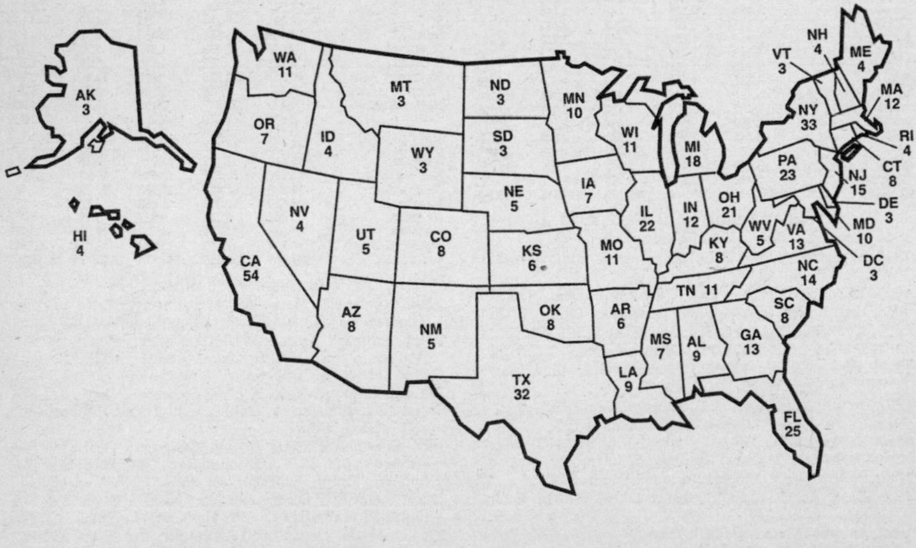

1992 Official Presidential General Election Results

Source: State Elections Offices; News Election Service

Candidate (Party)	Popular Vote	Percent of Popular Vote
Bill Clinton (Democrat)	44,908,254	42.95
George Bush (Republican)	39,102,343	37.40
Ross Perot (Independent)	19,741,065	18.86
Andre Marrou (Libertarian)	291,612	.28
James "Bo" Gritz (Populist/ America First)	98,918	.09
Lenora Fulani (New Alliance)	73,248	.07
Howard Phillips (U.S. Taxpayers)	42,960	.04
John Hagelin (Natural Law)	37,137	.04
Ron Daniels (Independent)	27,396	.03
Lyndon LaRouche (Independent)	25,863	.02
James Mac Warren (Socialist Workers)	22,883	.02
Drew Bradford (Independent)	4,749	.00
Jack Herer (Grassroots)	3,875	.00
Helen Halyard (Workers League)	3,050	.00
John Quinn Brisben (Socialist)	2,909	.00
John Yiamouyiannis (Independent)	2,199	.00
Delbert Ehlers (Independent)	1,149	.00
Jim Boren (Apathy)	956	.00
Earl Dodge (Prohibition)	935	.00
Eugene Hem (Third Party)	405	.00
Isabelle Masters (Looking Back Group)	327	.00
Robert J. Smith (American)	292	.00
Gloria Estella La Riva (Workers World)	181	.00
Write-In	177,207	.17
None of the Above (Nevada)	2,537	.00
Total	**104,552,736**	**100**

Note: Party designations may vary from one state to another.

America's Third Parties

Since 1860, there have been only 5 presidential elections in which all "third parties" together polled more than 10% of the vote. The major vote-getters in those elections were the Populists (James Baird Weaver) in 1892, the National Progressives (Theodore Roosevelt) in 1912, the La Follette Progressives in 1924, George Wallace's American Party in 1968, and independent H. Ross Perot in 1992. In 1948, the combined third parties (Henry Wallace's Progessives, Strom Thurmond's States' Rights Party or Dixiecrats, Prohibition, Socialists, and others) received only 5.75% of the vote. In most elections since 1860, fewer than one vote in 20 has been cast for a third party. The only successful third party in American history was the Republican Party in the election of Abraham Lincoln in 1860.

Notable Third Parties

Party	Presidential nominee	Year	Issues	Strength in
Anti-Masonic	William Wirt	1832	Against secret societies and oaths	Pa., Vt.
Liberty	James G. Birney	1844	Anti-slavery	North
Free Soil	Martin Van Buren	1848	Anti-slavery	New York, Oh.
American (Know Nothing)	Millard Fillmore	1856	Anti-immigrant	Northeast, South
Greenback	Peter Cooper	1876	For "cheap money,"	
Greenback	James B. Weaver	1880	labor rights	National
Prohibition	John P. St. John	1884	Anti-liquor	National
Populist	James B. Weaver	1892	For "cheap money," end of national banks	South, West
Socialist	Eugene V. Debs	1900-20	For public ownership	National
Progressive (Bull Moose)	Theodore Roosevelt	1912	Against high tariffs	Midwest, West
Progressive	Robert M. La Follette	1924	Farmer & labor rights	Midwest, West
Socialist	Norman Thomas	1928-48	Liberal reforms	National
Union	William Lemke	1936	Anti "New Deal"	National
States' Rights	Strom Thurmond	1948	For states' rights	South
Progressive	Henry Wallace	1948	Anti-cold war	N.Y., Calif.
American Independent	George Wallace	1968	For states' rights	South
American	John G. Schmitz	1972	For "law and order"	Far West, Oh., La.
None (Independent)	John B. Anderson	1980	A 3d choice	National
None (Independent)	H. Ross Perot	1992	Federal budget deficit	National

Political Action Committee Contributions to Federal Candidates: 1992 Election

Largest Contributions from Political Action Committees

Source: Federal Election Commission

1. National Association of Realtors	$2,950,138
2. American Medical Association	2,936,086
3. International Brotherhood of Teamsters	2,442,552
4. Association of Trial Lawyers	2,336,135
5. National Education Association	2,323,122
6. United Auto Workers	2,231,917

Political Action Committees, Health Care Industry

Source: Center for Responsive Politics

Second in growth only to lawyers and lobbyists, the health care industry increased its contributions in the 1992 election by 36 percent. Listed below are PACs that contributed more than $200,000.

Political Action Committee	Type of organization	Contribution
American Medical Assoc.[1]	Professional	$2,936,086
American Dental Assoc.[1]	Professional	1,420,958
American Academy of Opthalmology	Professional	801,527
American Chiropractic Assoc.[1]	Professional	641,746
American Hospital Assoc.[1]	Hospitals and nursing homes	505,888
American Podiatry Assoc.	Professional	401,000
American Optometric Assoc.	Professional	398,366
American Health Care Assoc.	Hospitals and nursing homes	382,019
American College of Emergency Physicians	Professional	330,725
American Nurses Assoc.	Professional	306,519
Assoc. for the Advancement of Psychology	Professional	273,743

[1]Does not include affiliated PACs.

Major Parties' Popular and Electoral Vote for President

(F) Federalist; (D) Democrat; (R) Republican; (DR) Democratic Republican; (NR) National Republican; (W) Whig; (P) People's; (PR) Progressive; (SR) States' Rights; (LR) Liberal Republican; Asterisk (*)—See notes.

Year	President elected	Popular	Elec.	Losing candidate	Popular	Elec.
1789	George Washington (F)	Unknown	69	No opposition	—	—
1792	George Washington (F)	Unknown	132	No opposition	—	—
1796	John Adams (F)	Unknown	71	Thomas Jefferson (DR)	Unknown	68
1800*	Thomas Jefferson (DR)	Unknown	73	Aaron Burr (DR)	Unknown	73
1804	Thomas Jefferson (DR)	Unknown	162	Charles Pinckney (F)	Unknown	14
1808	James Madison (DR)	Unknown	122	Charles Pinckney (F)	Unknown	47
1812	James Madison (DR)	Unknown	128	DeWitt Clinton (F)	Unknown	89
1816	James Monroe (DR)	Unknown	183	Rufus King (F)	Unknown	34
1820	James Monroe (DR)	Unknown	231	John Quincy Adams (DR)	Unknown	1
1824*	John Quincy Adams (DR)	105,321	84	Andrew Jackson (DR)	155,872	99
				Henry Clay (DR)	46,587	37
				William H. Crawford (DR)	44,282	41
1828	Andrew Jackson (D)	647,231	178	John Quincy Adams (NR)	509,097	83
1832	Andrew Jackson (D)	687,502	219	Henry Clay (NR)	530,189	49
1836	Martin Van Buren (D)	762,678	170	William H. Harrison (W)	548,007	73
1840	William H. Harrison (W)	1,275,017	234	Martin Van Buren (D)	1,128,702	60
1844	James K. Polk (D)	1,337,243	170	Henry Clay (W)	1,299,068	105
1848	Zachary Taylor (W)	1,360,101	163	Lewis Cass (D)	1,220,544	127
1852	Franklin Pierce (D)	1,601,474	254	Winfield Scott (W)	1,386,578	42
1856	James Buchanan (D)	1,927,995	174	John C. Fremont (R)	1,391,555	114
1860	Abraham Lincoln (R)	1,866,352	180	Stephen A. Douglas (D)	1,375,157	12
				John C. Breckinridge (D)	845,763	72
				John Bell (Const. Union)	589,581	39
1864	Abraham Lincoln (R)	2,216,067	212	George McClellan (D)	1,808,725	21
1868	Ulysses S. Grant (R)	3,015,071	214	Horatio Seymour (D)	2,709,615	80
1872*	Ulysses S. Grant (R)	3,597,070	286	Horace Greeley (D-LR)	2,834,079	—
1876*	Rutherford B. Hayes (R)	4,033,950	185	Samuel J. Tilden (D)	4,284,757	184
1880	James A. Garfield (R)	4,449,053	214	Winfield S. Hancock (D)	4,442,030	155
1884	Grover Cleveland (D)	4,911,017	219	James G. Blaine (R)	4,848,334	182
1888*	Benjamin Harrison (R)	5,444,337	233	Grover Cleveland (D)	5,540,050	168
1892	Grover Cleveland (D)	5,554,414	277	Benjamin Harrison (R)	5,190,802	145
				James Weaver (P)	1,027,329	22
1896	William McKinley (R)	7,035,638	271	William J. Bryan (D-P)	6,467,946	176
1900	William McKinley (R)	7,219,530	292	William J. Bryan (D)	6,358,071	155
1904	Theodore Roosevelt (R)	7,628,834	336	Alton B. Parker (D)	5,084,491	140
1908	William H. Taft (R)	7,679,006	321	William J. Bryan (D)	6,409,106	162
1912	Woodrow Wilson (D)	6,286,214	435	Theodore Roosevelt (PR)	4,216,020	88
				William H. Taft (R)	3,483,922	8
1916	Woodrow Wilson (D)	9,129,606	277	Charles E. Hughes (R)	8,538,221	254
1920	Warren G. Harding (R)	16,152,200	404	James M. Cox (D)	9,147,353	127
1924	Calvin Coolidge (R)	15,725,016	382	John W. Davis (D)	8,385,586	136
				Robert M. LaFollette (PR)	4,822,856	13
1928	Herbert Hoover (R)	21,392,190	444	Alfred E. Smith (D)	15,016,443	87
1932	Franklin D. Roosevelt (D)	22,821,857	472	Herbert Hoover (R)	15,761,841	59
				Norman Thomas (Socialist)	884,781	—
1936	Franklin D. Roosevelt (D)	27,751,597	523	Alfred Landon (R)	16,679,583	8
1940	Franklin D. Roosevelt (D)	27,243,466	449	Wendell Willkie (R)	22,304,755	82
1944	Franklin D. Roosevelt (D)	25,602,505	432	Thomas E. Dewey (R)	22,006,278	99
1948	Harry S. Truman (D)	24,105,812	303	Thomas E. Dewey (R)	21,970,065	189
				J. Strom Thurmond (SR)	1,169,021	39
				Henry A. Wallace (PR)	1,157,172	—
1952	Dwight D. Eisenhower (R)	33,936,252	442	Adlai E. Stevenson (D)	27,314,992	89
1956*	Dwight D. Eisenhower (R)	35,585,316	457	Adlai E. Stevenson (D)	26,031,322	73
1960*	John F. Kennedy (D)	34,227,096	303	Richard M. Nixon (R)	34,108,546	219
1964	Lyndon B. Johnson (D)	43,126,506	486	Barry M. Goldwater (R)	27,176,799	52
1968	Richard M. Nixon (R)	31,785,480	301	Hubert H. Humphrey (D)	31,275,166	191
				George C. Wallace (3d party)	9,906,473	46
1972*	Richard M. Nixon (R)	47,165,234	520	George S. McGovern (D)	29,170,774	17
1976*	Jimmy Carter (D)	40,828,929	297	Gerald R. Ford (R)	39,148,940	240
1980	Ronald Reagan (R)	43,899,248	489	Jimmy Carter (D)	35,481,435	49
				John B. Anderson (independent)	5,719,437	—
1984	Ronald Reagan (R)	54,281,858	525	Walter F. Mondale (D)	37,457,215	13
1988*	George Bush (R)	48,881,221	426	Michael S. Dukakis (D)	41,805,422	111
1992	Bill Clinton (D)	44,908,254	370	George Bush (R)	39,102,343	168
				H. Ross Perot (independent)	19,741,065	—

1800—Elected by House of Representatives because of tied electoral vote. **1824**—Elected by House of Representatives. No candidate polled a majority. In 1824, the Democratic Republicans had become a loose coalition of competing political groups. By 1828, the supporters of Jackson were known as Democrats, and the J.Q. Adams and Henry Clay supporters as National Republicans. **1872**—Greeley died Nov. 29, 1872. His electoral votes were split among 4 individuals. **1876**—Fla., La., Ore., and S.C. election returns were disputed. Congress in joint session (Mar. 2, 1877) declared Hayes and Wheeler elected President and Vice-President. **1888**—Cleveland had more votes than Harrison but the 233 electoral votes cast for Harrison against the 168 for Cleveland elected Harrison president. **1956**—Democrats elected 74 electors but one from Alabama refused to vote for Stevenson. **1960**—Sen. Harry F. Byrd (D-Va.) received 15 electoral votes. **1972**—John Hospers of Cal. and Theodora Nathan of Ore. received one vote from an elector of Virginia. **1976**—Ronald Reagan of Cal. received one vote from an elector of Washington. **1988**—Sen. Lloyd Bentsen (D.-Tex.) received 1 electoral vote.

The Electoral College

The president and the vice president of the United States are the only elective federal officials not elected by direct vote of the people. They are elected by the members of the Electoral College, an institution that has survived since the founding of the nation despite repeated attempts in Congress to alter or abolish it. In the elections of 1824, 1876, and 1888 the presidential candidate receiving the largest popular vote failed to win a majority of the electoral votes.

On presidential election day, the first Tuesday after the first Monday in November of every 4th year, each state chooses as many electors as it has senators and representatives in Congress. In 1964, for the first time, as provided by the 23d Amendment to the Constitution, the District of Columbia voted for 3 electors. Thus, with 100 senators and 435 representatives, there are 538 members of the Electoral College, with a majority of 270 electoral votes needed to elect the president and vice president.

Political parties customarily nominate their lists of electors at their respective state conventions. An elector cannot be a member of Congress or anyone holding federal office.

Some states print the names of the candidates for president and vice president at the top of the November ballot while others list only the names of the electors. In either case, the electors of the party receiving the highest vote are elected. The electors meet on the first Monday after the 2d Wednesday in December in their respective state capitals or in some other place prescribed by state legislatures. By long-established custom they vote for their party nominees, although the Constitution does not require them to do so. The only Constitutional requirement is that at least one of the persons each elector votes for shall not be an inhabitant of that elector's home state.

Certified and sealed lists of the votes of the electors in each state are mailed to the president of the U.S. Senate. He opens them in the presence of the members of the Senate and House of Representatives in a joint session held on Jan. 6 (the next day if that falls on a Sunday), and the electoral votes of all the states are then counted. If no candidate for president has a majority, the House of Representatives chooses a president from among the 3 highest candidates, with all representatives from each state combining to cast one vote for that state. If no candidate for vice president has a majority, the Senate chooses from the top 2, with the senators voting as individuals.

Voting for President

Source: Federal Election Commission; Commission for Study of American Electorate

	Candidates	Voter Participation (% of voting-age population)		Candidates	Voter Participation (% of voting-age population)
1932	Roosevelt-Hoover	52.4	1964	Johnson-Goldwater	61.9
1936	Roosevelt-Landon	56.0	1968	Humphrey-Nixon	60.9
1940	Roosevelt-Willkie	58.9	1972	McGovern-Nixon	55.2(a)
1944	Roosevelt-Dewey	56.0	1976	Carter-Ford	53.5
1948	Truman-Dewey	51.1	1980	Carter-Reagan	54.0
1952	Stevenson-Eisenhower	61.6	1984	Mondale-Reagan	53.1
1956	Stevenson-Eisenhower	59.3	1988	Dukakis-Bush	50.2
1960	Kennedy-Nixon	62.8	1992	Clinton-Bush-Perot	55.9

(a) The sharp drop in 1972 reflects the expansion of eligibility with the enfranchisement of 18 to 21 year olds.

Party Nominees for President and Vice President

Asterisk (*) denotes winning ticket

	Democratic		Republican	
Year	President	Vice President	President	Vice President
1844	James K. Polk*	George M. Dallas	Henry Clay (Whig)	Theo. Frelinghuysen
1848	Lewis Cass	William Butler	Zachary Taylor* (Whig)	Millard Fillmore
1852	Franklin Pierce*	William King	Winfield Scott (Whig)	William Graham
1856	James Buchanan*	John Breckinridge	John Fremont	William Dayton
1860	John Breckinridge	Joseph Lane	Abraham Lincoln*	Hannibal Hamlin
1864	George McClellan	G.H. Pendleton	Abraham Lincoln*	Andrew Johnson
1868	Horatio Seymour	Francis Blair	Ulysses S. Grant*	Schuyler Colfax
1872	Horace Greeley	B. Gratz Brown	Ulysses S. Grant*	Henry Wilson
1876	Samuel J. Tilden	Thomas Hendricks	Rutherford B. Hayes*	William Wheeler
1880	Winfield Hancock	William English	James A. Garfield*	Chester A. Arthur
1884	Grover Cleveland*	Thomas Hendricks	James Blaine	John Logan
1888	Grover Cleveland	A.G. Thurman	Benjamin Harrison*	Levi Morton
1892	Grover Cleveland*	Adlai Stevenson	Benjamin Harrison	Whitelaw Reid
1896	William J. Bryan	Arthur Sewall	William McKinley*	Garret Hobart
1900	William J. Bryan	Adlai Stevenson	William McKinley*	Theodore Roosevelt
1904	Alton Parker	Henry Davis	Theodore Roosevelt*	Charles Fairbanks
1908	William J. Bryan	John Kern	William H. Taft*	James Sherman
1912	Woodrow Wilson*	Thomas Marshall	William H. Taft	James Sherman[1]
1916	Woodrow Wilson*	Thomas Marshall	Charles Hughes	Charles Fairbanks
1920	James M. Cox	Franklin D. Roosevelt	Warren G. Harding*	Calvin Coolidge
1924	John W. Davis	Charles W. Bryan	Calvin Coolidge*	Charles G. Dawes
1928	Alfred E. Smith	Joseph T. Robinson	Herbert Hoover*	Charles Curtis
1932	Franklin D. Roosevelt*	John N. Garner	Herbert Hoover	Charles Curtis
1936	Franklin D. Roosevelt*	John N. Garner	Alfred M. Landon	Frank Knox
1940	Franklin D. Roosevelt*	Henry A. Wallace	Wendell L. Willkie	Charles McNary
1944	Franklin D. Roosevelt*	Harry S. Truman	Thomas E. Dewey	John W. Bricker
1948	Harry S. Truman*	Alben W. Barkley	Thomas E. Dewey	Earl Warren
1952	Adlai E. Stevenson	John J. Sparkman	Dwight D. Eisenhower*	Richard M. Nixon
1956	Adlai E. Stevenson	Estes Kefauver	Dwight D. Eisenhower*	Richard M. Nixon
1960	John F. Kennedy*	Lyndon B. Johnson	Richard M. Nixon	Henry Cabot Lodge
1964	Lyndon B. Johnson*	Hubert H. Humphrey	Barry M. Goldwater	William E. Miller
1968	Hubert H. Humphrey	Edmund S. Muskie	Richard M. Nixon*	Spiro T. Agnew
1972	George S. McGovern	R. Sargent Shriver Jr.	Richard M. Nixon*	Spiro T. Agnew
1976	Jimmy Carter*	Walter F. Mondale	Gerald R. Ford	Robert J. Dole
1980	Jimmy Carter	Walter F. Mondale	Ronald Reagan*	George Bush
1984	Walter F. Mondale	Geraldine Ferraro	Ronald Reagan*	George Bush
1988	Michael S. Dukakis	Lloyd Bentsen	George Bush*	Dan Quayle
1992	Bill Clinton*	Al Gore	George Bush	Dan Quayle

(1) Died Oct. 30; replaced on ballot by Nicholas Butler.

Presidents of the U.S.

No.	Name	Politics	Born	in	Inaug.	at age	Died	at age
1	George Washington	Fed.	1732, Feb. 22	Va.	1789	57	1799, Dec. 14	67
2	John Adams	Fed.	1735, Oct. 30	Mass.	1797	61	1826, July 4	90
3	Thomas Jefferson	Dem.-Rep.	1743, Apr. 13	Va.	1801	57	1826, July 4	83
4	James Madison	Dem.-Rep.	1751, Mar. 16	Va.	1809	57	1836, June 28	85
5	James Monroe	Dem.-Rep.	1758, Apr. 28	Va.	1817	58	1831, July 4	73
6	John Quincy Adams	Dem.-Rep.	1767, July 11	Mass.	1825	57	1848, Feb. 23	80
7	Andrew Jackson	Dem.	1767, Mar. 15	S.C.	1829	61	1845, June 8	78
8	Martin Van Buren	Dem.	1782, Dec. 5	N.Y.	1837	54	1862, July 24	79
9	William Henry Harrison	Whig	1773, Feb. 9	Va.	1841	68	1841, Apr. 4	68
10	John Tyler	Whig	1790, Mar. 29	Va.	1841	51	1862, Jan. 18	71
11	James Knox Polk	Dem.	1795, Nov. 2	N.C.	1845	49	1849, June 15	53
12	Zachary Taylor	Whig	1784, Nov. 24	Va.	1849	64	1850, July 9	65
13	Millard Fillmore	Whig	1800, Jan. 7	N.Y.	1850	50	1874, Mar. 8	74
14	Franklin Pierce	Dem.	1804, Nov. 23	N.H.	1853	48	1869, Oct. 8	64
15	James Buchanan	Dem.	1791, Apr. 23	Pa.	1857	65	1868, June 1	77
16	Abraham Lincoln	Rep.	1809, Feb. 12	Ky.	1861	52	1865, Apr. 15	56
17	Andrew Johnson	(1)	1808, Dec. 29	N.C.	1865	56	1875, July 31	66
18	Ulysses Simpson Grant	Rep.	1822, Apr. 27	Oh.	1869	46	1885, July 23	63
19	Rutherford Birchard Hayes	Rep.	1822, Oct. 4	Oh.	1877	54	1893, Jan. 17	70
20	James Abram Garfield	Rep.	1831, Nov. 19	Oh.	1881	49	1881, Sept. 19	49
21	Chester Alan Arthur	Rep.	1830, Oct. 5	Vt.	1881	50	1886, Nov. 18	56
22	Grover Cleveland	Dem.	1837, Mar. 18	N.J.	1885	47	1908, June 24	71
23	Benjamin Harrison	Rep.	1833, Aug. 20	Oh.	1889	55	1901, Mar. 13	67
24	Grover Cleveland	Dem.	1837, Mar. 18	N.J.	1893	55	1908, June 24	71
25	William McKinley	Rep.	1843, Jan. 29	Oh.	1897	54	1901, Sept. 14	58
26	Theodore Roosevelt	Rep.	1858, Oct. 27	N.Y.	1901	42	1919, Jan. 6	60
27	William Howard Taft	Rep.	1857, Sept. 15	Oh.	1909	51	1930, Mar. 8	72
28	Woodrow Wilson	Dem.	1856, Dec. 28	Va.	1913	56	1924, Feb. 3	67
29	Warren Gamaliel Harding	Rep.	1865, Nov. 2	Oh.	1921	55	1923, Aug. 2	57
30	Calvin Coolidge	Rep.	1872, July 4	Vt.	1923	51	1933, Jan. 5	60
31	Herbert Clark Hoover	Rep.	1874, Aug. 10	Ia.	1929	54	1964, Oct. 20	90
32	Franklin Delano Roosevelt	Dem.	1882, Jan. 30	N.Y.	1933	51	1945, Apr. 12	63
33	Harry S. Truman	Dem.	1884, May 8	Mo.	1945	60	1972, Dec. 26	88
34	Dwight David Eisenhower	Rep.	1890, Oct. 14	Tex.	1953	62	1969, Mar. 28	78
35	John Fitzgerald Kennedy	Dem.	1917, May 29	Mass.	1961	43	1963, Nov. 22	46
36	Lyndon Baines Johnson	Dem.	1908, Aug. 27	Tex.	1963	55	1973, Jan. 22	64
37	Richard Milhous Nixon (2)	Rep.	1913, Jan. 9	Cal.	1969	56		
38	Gerald Rudolph Ford	Rep.	1913, July 14	Nebr.	1974	61		
39	Jimmy (James Earl) Carter	Dem.	1924, Oct. 1	Ga.	1977	52		
40	Ronald Reagan	Rep.	1911, Feb. 6	Ill.	1981	69		
41	George Bush	Rep.	1924, June 12	Mass.	1989	64		
42	Bill Clinton	Dem.	1946, Aug. 19	Ark.	1993	46		

(1) Andrew Johnson — a Democrat, nominated vice president by Republicans and elected with Lincoln on National Union ticket. (2) Resigned Aug. 9, 1974.

Presidents, Vice Presidents, Congresses

No.	President	Service	No.	Vice President	Congress
1	George Washington	Apr. 30, 1789—Mar. 3, 1797	1	John Adams	1, 2, 3, 4
2	John Adams	Mar. 4, 1797—Mar. 3, 1801	2	Thomas Jefferson	5, 6
3	Thomas Jefferson	Mar. 4, 1801—Mar. 3, 1805	3	Aaron Burr	7, 8
	"	Mar. 4, 1805—Mar. 3, 1809	4	George Clinton	9, 10
4	James Madison	Mar. 4, 1809—Mar. 3, 1813		"(1)	11, 12
	"	Mar. 4, 1813—Mar. 3, 1817	5	Elbridge Gerry (2)	13, 14
5	James Monroe	Mar. 4, 1817—Mar. 3, 1825	6	Daniel D. Tompkins	15, 16, 17, 18
6	John Quincy Adams	Mar. 4, 1825—Mar. 3, 1829	7	John C. Calhoun	19, 20
7	Andrew Jackson	Mar. 4, 1829—Mar. 3, 1833		"(3)	21, 22
	"	Mar. 4, 1833—Mar. 3, 1837	8	Martin Van Buren	23, 24
8	Martin Van Buren	Mar. 4, 1837—Mar. 3, 1841	9	Richard M. Johnson	25, 26
9	William Henry Harrison (4)	Mar. 4, 1841—Apr. 4, 1841	10	John Tyler	27
10	John Tyler	Apr. 6, 1841—Mar. 3, 1845			27, 28
11	James K. Polk	Mar. 4, 1845—Mar. 3, 1849	11	George M. Dallas	29, 30
12	Zachary Taylor (4)	Mar. 5, 1849—July 9, 1850	12	Millard Fillmore	31
13	Millard Fillmore	July 10, 1850—Mar. 3, 1853			31, 32
14	Franklin Pierce	Mar. 4, 1853—Mar. 3, 1857	13	William R. King (5)	33, 34
15	James Buchanan	Mar. 4, 1857—Mar. 3, 1861	14	John C. Breckinridge	35, 36
16	Abraham Lincoln	Mar. 4, 1861—Mar. 3, 1865	15	Hannibal Hamlin	37, 38
	"(4)	Mar. 4, 1865—Apr. 15, 1865	16	Andrew Johnson	39
17	Andrew Johnson	Apr. 15, 1865—Mar. 3, 1869			39, 40
18	Ulysses S. Grant	Mar. 4, 1869—Mar. 3, 1873	17	Schuyler Colfax	41, 42
	"	Mar. 4, 1873—Mar. 3, 1877	18	Henry Wilson (6)	43, 44
19	Rutherford B. Hayes	Mar. 4, 1877—Mar. 3, 1881	19	William A. Wheeler	45, 46
20	James A. Garfield (4)	Mar. 4, 1881—Sept. 19, 1881	20	Chester A. Arthur	47
21	Chester A. Arthur	Sept. 20, 1881—Mar. 3, 1885			47, 48
22	Grover Cleveland (7)	Mar. 4, 1885—Mar. 3, 1889	21	Thomas A. Hendricks (8)	49, 50
23	Benjamin Harrison	Mar. 4, 1889—Mar. 3, 1893	22	Levi P. Morton	51, 52
24	Grover Cleveland (7)	Mar. 4, 1893—Mar. 3, 1897	23	Adlai E. Stevenson	53, 54
25	William McKinley	Mar. 4, 1897—Mar. 3, 1901	24	Garret A. Hobart (9)	55, 56
	"(4)	Mar. 4, 1901—Sept. 14, 1901	25	Theodore Roosevelt	57
26	Theodore Roosevelt	Sept. 14, 1901—Mar. 3, 1905			57, 58
	"	Mar. 4, 1905—Mar. 3, 1909	26	Charles W. Fairbanks	59, 60
27	William H. Taft	Mar. 4, 1909—Mar. 3, 1913	27	James S. Sherman (10)	61, 62
28	Woodrow Wilson	Mar. 4, 1913—Mar. 3, 1921	28	Thomas R. Marshall	63, 64, 65, 66

(continued)

Presidents, Vice Presidents, Congresses (continued)

	President	Service		Vice President	Congress
29	Warren G. Harding (4)	Mar. 4, 1921—Aug. 2, 1923	29	Calvin Coolidge	67
30	Calvin Coolidge	Aug. 3, 1923—Mar. 3, 1925			68
	"	Mar. 4, 1925—Mar. 3, 1929	30	Charles G. Dawes	69, 70
31	Herbert C. Hoover	Mar. 4, 1929—Mar. 3, 1933	31	Charles Curtis	71, 72
32	Franklin D. Roosevelt (16)	Mar. 4, 1933—Jan. 20, 1941	32	John N. Garner	73, 74, 75, 76
	"	Jan. 20, 1941—Jan. 20, 1945	33	Henry A. Wallace	77, 78
	"(4)	Jan. 20, 1945—Apr. 12, 1945	34	Harry S. Truman	79
33	Harry S. Truman	Apr. 12, 1945—Jan. 20, 1949			79, 80
	"	Jan. 20, 1949—Jan. 20, 1953	35	Alben W. Barkley	81, 82
34	Dwight D. Eisenhower	Jan. 20, 1953—Jan. 20, 1961	36	Richard M. Nixon	83, 84, 85, 86
35	John F. Kennedy (4)	Jan. 20, 1961—Nov. 22, 1963	37	Lyndon B. Johnson	87, 88
36	Lyndon B. Johnson	Nov. 22, 1963—Jan. 20, 1965			88
	"	Jan. 20, 1965—Jan. 20, 1969	38	Hubert H. Humphrey	89, 90
37	Richard M. Nixon	Jan. 20, 1969—Jan. 20, 1973	39	Spiro T. Agnew (11)	91, 92, 93
	"(12)	Jan. 20, 1973—Aug. 9, 1974	40	Gerald R. Ford (13)	93
38	Gerald R. Ford (14)	Aug. 9, 1974—Jan. 20, 1977	41	Nelson A. Rockefeller (15)	93, 94
39	Jimmy (James Earl)Carter	Jan. 20, 1977—Jan. 20, 1981	42	Walter F. Mondale	95, 96
40	Ronald Reagan	Jan. 20, 1981—Jan. 20, 1989	43	George Bush	97, 98, 99, 100
41	George Bush	Jan. 20, 1989—Jan. 20, 1993	44	Dan Quayle	101, 102
42	Bill Clinton	Jan. 20, 1993—	45	Al Gore	103

(1) Died Apr. 20, 1812. (2) Died Nov. 23, 1814. (3) Resigned Dec. 28, 1832, to become U.S. Senator. (4) Died in office. (5) Died Apr. 18, 1853. (6) Died Nov. 22, 1875. (7) Terms not consecutive. (8) Died Nov. 25, 1885. (9) Died Nov. 21, 1899. (10) Died Oct. 30, 1912. (11) Resigned Oct. 10, 1973. (12) Resigned Aug. 9, 1974. (13) First non-elected vice president, chosen under 25th Amendment procedure. (14) First non-elected president. (15) 2d non-elected vice president. (16) First president to be inaugurated under 20th Amendment, Jan. 20, 1937.

Vice Presidents of the U.S.

The numerals given vice presidents do not coincide with those given presidents, because some presidents had none and some had more than one.

	Name	Birthplace	Year	Home	Inaug.	Politics	Place of death	Year	Age
1	John Adams	Quincy, Mass.	1735	Mass.	1789	Fed.	Quincy, Mass.	1826	90
2	Thomas Jefferson	Shadwell, Va.	1743	Va.	1797	Dem.-Rep.	Monticello, Va.	1826	83
3	Aaron Burr	Newark, N.J.	1756	N.Y.	1801	Dem.-Rep.	Staten Island, N.Y.	1836	80
4	George Clinton	Ulster Co., N.Y.	1739	N.Y.	1805	Dem.-Rep.	Washington, D.C.	1812	73
5	Elbridge Gerry	Marblehead, Mass.	1744	Mass.	1813	Dem.-Rep.	Washington, D.C.	1814	70
6	Daniel D. Tompkins	Scarsdale, N.Y.	1774	N.Y.	1817	Dem.-Rep.	Staten Island, N.Y.	1825	51
7	John C. Calhoun (1)	Abbeville, S.C.	1782	S.C.	1825	Dem.-Rep.	Washington, D.C.	1850	68
8	Martin Van Buren	Kinderhook, N.Y.	1782	N.Y.	1833	Dem.	Kinderhook, N.Y.	1862	79
9	Richard M. Johnson	Louisville, Ky.	1780	Ky.	1837	Dem.	Frankfort, Ky.	1850	70
10	John Tyler	Greenway, Va.	1790	Va.	1841	Whig	Richmond, Va.	1862	71
11	George M. Dallas	Philadelphia, Pa.	1792	Pa.	1845	Dem.	Philadelphia, Pa.	1864	72
12	Millard Fillmore	Summerhill, N.Y.	1800	N.Y.	1849	Whig	Buffalo, N.Y.	1874	74
13	William R. King	Sampson Co., N.C.	1786	Ala.	1853	Dem.	Dallas Co., Ala.	1853	67
14	John C. Breckinridge	Lexington, Ky.	1821	Ky.	1857	Dem.	Lexington, Ky.	1875	54
15	Hannibal Hamlin	Paris, Me.	1809	Me.	1861	Rep.	Bangor, Me.	1891	81
16	Andrew Johnson	Raleigh, N.C.	1808	Tenn.	1865	(2)	Carter Co., Tenn.	1875	66
17	Schuyler Colfax	New York, N.Y.	1823	Ind.	1869	Rep.	Mankato, Minn.	1885	62
18	Henry Wilson	Farmington, N.H.	1812	Mass.	1873	Rep.	Washington, D.C.	1875	63
19	William A. Wheeler	Malone, N.Y.	1819	N.Y.	1877	Rep.	Malone, N.Y.	1887	68
20	Chester A. Arthur	Fairfield, Vt.	1829	N.Y.	1881	Rep.	New York, N.Y.	1886	57
21	Thomas A. Hendricks	Muskingum Co., Oh.	1819	Ind.	1885	Dem.	Indianapolis, Ind.	1885	66
22	Levi P. Morton	Shoreham, Vt.	1824	N.Y.	1889	Rep.	Rhinebeck, N.Y.	1920	96
23	Adlai E. Stevenson (3)	Christian Co., Ky.	1835	Ill.	1893	Dem.	Chicago, Ill.	1914	78
24	Garret A. Hobart	Long Branch, N.J.	1844	N.J.	1897	Rep.	Paterson, N.J.	1899	55
25	Theodore Roosevelt	New York, N.Y.	1858	N.Y.	1901	Rep.	Oyster Bay, N.Y.	1919	60
26	Charles W. Fairbanks	Unionville Centre, Oh.	1852	Ind.	1905	Rep.	Indianapolis, Ind.	1918	66
27	James S. Sherman	Utica, N.Y.	1855	N.Y.	1909	Rep.	Utica, N.Y.	1912	57
28	Thomas R. Marshall	N. Manchester, Ind.	1854	Ind.	1913	Dem.	Washington, D.C.	1925	71
29	Calvin Coolidge	Plymouth, Vt.	1872	Mass.	1921	Rep.	Northampton, Mass.	1933	60
30	Charles G. Dawes	Marietta, Oh.	1865	Ill.	1925	Rep.	Evanston, Ill.	1951	85
31	Charles Curtis	Topeka, Kan.	1860	Kan.	1929	Rep.	Washington, D.C.	1936	76
32	John Nance Garner	Red River Co., Tex.	1868	Tex.	1933	Dem.	Uvalde, Tex.	1967	98
33	Henry Agard Wallace	Adair County, Ia.	1888	Iowa	1941	Dem.	Danbury, Conn.	1965	77
34	Harry S. Truman	Lamar, Mo.	1884	Mo.	1945	Dem.	Kansas City, Mo.	1972	88
35	Alben W. Barkley	Graves County, Ky.	1877	Ky.	1949	Dem.	Lexington, Va.	1956	78
36	Richard M. Nixon	Yorba Linda, Cal.	1913	Cal.	1953	Rep.			
37	Lyndon B. Johnson	Johnson City, Tex.	1908	Tex.	1961	Dem.	San Antonio, Tex.	1973	64
38	Hubert H. Humphrey	Wallace, S.D.	1911	Minn.	1965	Dem.	Waverly, Minn.	1978	66
39	Spiro T. Agnew (4)	Baltimore, Md.	1918	Md.	1969	Rep.			
40	Gerald R. Ford	Omaha, Neb.	1913	Mich.	1973	Rep.			
41	Nelson A. Rockefeller	Bar Harbor, Me.	1908	N.Y.	1974	Rep.	New York, N.Y.	1979	70
42	Walter F. Mondale	Ceylon, Minn.	1928	Minn.	1977	Dem.			
43	George Bush	Milton, Mass.	1924	Tex.	1981	Rep.			
44	Dan Quayle	Indianapolis, Ind.	1947	Ind.	1989	Rep.			
45	Al Gore	Washington, D.C.	1948	Tenn.	1993	Dem.			

(1) John C. Calhoun resigned Dec. 28, 1832, having been elected to the Senate to fill a vacancy. (2) Andrew Johnson — a Democrat nominated by Republicans and elected with Lincoln on the National Union Ticket. (3) Adlai E. Stevenson, 23d vice president, was grandfather of Democratic candidate for president, 1952 and 1956. (4) Resigned Oct. 10, 1973.

CONGRESS

The One Hundred and Third Congress, First Session

Membership as of Mid-1993, With 1992 Election Results

The Senate

Terms are for 6 years and end Jan. 3 of the year preceding name. Annual salary, $133,600; President Pro Tempore, Majority Leader, and Minority Leader, $148,400. To be eligible for the U.S. Senate a person must be at least 30 years of age, a citizen of the United States for at least 9 years, and a resident of the state from which he or she is chosen. The Congress must meet annually on Jan. 3, unless it has, by law, appointed a different day.

The ZIP code of the Senate is 20510, the telephone number is 202-224-3121.

Senate officials: President Pro Tempore, Robert C. Byrd; Majority Leader, George J. Mitchell; Majority Whip, Wendell H. Ford; Minority Leader, Bob Dole; Minority Whip, Alan K. Simpson.

Dem., 56; Rep., 44; Total, 100. *Incumbent. Bold face denotes winner.

(Source: News Election Service; World Almanac research)

Term ends	Senator (Party)/Service from[1]	1992 Election
	Alabama	
1999	**Richard C. Shelby*** (D)/1987	**1,022,698**
	Richard Sellers (R)	522,015
1997	Howell Heflin (D)/1979	
	Alaska	
1999	**Frank H. Murkowski*** (R)/1981	**127,163**
	Tony Smith (D)	92,065
1997	Ted Stevens (R)/12/24/68	
	Arizona	
1999	**John McCain*** (R)/1987	**771,395**
	Claire Sargent (D)	436,321
1995	Dennis DeConcini (D)/1977	
	Arkansas	
1999	**Dale Bumpers*** (D)/1975	**553,635**
	Mike Huckabee (R)	366,373
1997	David H. Pryor (D)/1979	
	California	
1999	**Barbara Boxer** (D)	**5,173,467**
	Bruce Herschensohn (R)	4,644,182
1995	**Dianne Feinstein** (D)	**5,493,418**
	John Seymour* (R) /1/10/91	3,777,635
	Colorado	
1999	**Ben Nighthorse Campbell** (D)	**803,725**
	Terry Considine (R)	662,893
1997	Hank Brown (R)	
	Connecticut	
1999	**Christopher J. Dodd*** (D)/1981	**882,558**
	Brook Johnson (R)	572,036
1995	Joe Lieberman (D)/1989	
	Delaware	
1995	William V. Roth, Jr. (R)/1/1/71	
1997	Joseph R. Biden, Jr. (D)/1973	
	Florida	
1999	**Bob Graham*** (D)/1987	**3,244,299**
	Bill Grant (R)	1,715,156
1995	Connie Mack (R)/1989	
	Georgia	
1999	**Paul Coverdell** (R)[2]	**634,208**
	Wyche Fowler, Jr.* (D)	617,283
1997	Sam Nunn (D)/1972	
	Hawaii	
1999	**Daniel K. Inouye*** (D)/1963	**208,266**
	Rick Reed (R)	97,928
1995	Daniel K. Akaka (D)/5/16/90	
	Idaho	
1999	**Dirk Kempthorne** (R)	**270,468**
	Richard H. Stallings (D)	208,036
1997	Larry E. Craig (R)	

Term ends	Senator (Party)/Service from[1]	1992 Election
	Illinois	
1999	**Carol Moseley Braun** (D)	**2,631,229**
	Richard S. Williamson (R)	2,126,833
1997	Paul Simon (D)/1985	
	Indiana	
1999	**Daniel R. Coats*** (R)/1989	**1,267,972**
	Joseph H. Hogsett (D)	900,148
1995	Richard G. Lugar (R)/1977	
	Iowa	
1999	**Charles E. Grassley*** (R)/1981	**899,761**
	Jean Lloyd-Jones (D)	351,561
1997	Tom Harkin (D)/1985	
	Kansas	
1999	**Bob Dole*** (R)/1969	**706,246**
	Gloria O'Dell (D)	349,525
1997	Nancy Landon Kassebaum (R)/12/23/78	
	Kentucky	
1999	**Wendell H. Ford*** (D)/12/28/74	**836,888**
	David L. Williams (R)	476,604
1997	Mitch McConnell (R)/1985	
	Louisiana	
1999	John B. Breaux* (D)/1987	
1997	J. Bennett Johnston (D)/11/14/72	
	Maine	
1995	George J. Mitchell (D)/5/17/80	
1997	William S. Cohen (R)/1979	
	Maryland	
1999	**Barbara A. Mikulski*** (D)/1987	**1,307,610**
	Alan L. Keyes (R)	533,688
1995	Paul S. Sarbanes (D)/1977	
	Massachusetts	
1995	Edward M. Kennedy (D)/11/7/62	
1997	John F. Kerry (D)/1/2/85	
	Michigan	
1995	Donald W. Riegle, Jr.* (D)/12/30/76	
1997	Carl Levin (D)/1979	
	Minnesota	
1995	David Durenberger (R)/11/8/78	
1997	Paul David Wellstone (D)	
	Mississippi	
1995	Trent Lott (R)/3/3/89	
1997	Thad Cochran (R)/12/27/78	
	Missouri	
1999	**Christopher "Kit" Bond*** (R)/1987	**1,221,901**
	Geri Rothman-Serot (D)	1,057,967
1995	John C. Danforth (R)/12/27/76	
	Montana	
1995	Conrad Burns (R)/1989	
1997	Max Baucus (D)/12/15/78	

Term ends	Senator (Party)/Service from[1]	1992 Election
	Nebraska	
1995	J. Robert Kerrey (D)/1989	
1997	J. James Exon (D)/1979	
	Nevada	
1999	**Harry M. Reid*** (D)/1987	**253,150**
	Demar Dahl (R)	199,413
1995	Richard H. Bryan (D)/1989	
	New Hampshire	
1999	**Judd Gregg** (R)	**249,591**
	John Rauh (D)	234,982
1997	Robert Smith (R)	
	New Jersey	
1995	Frank R. Lautenberg (D)/12/27/82	
1997	Bill Bradley (D)/1979	
	New Mexico	
1995	Jeff Bingaman (D)/1983	
1997	Pete V. Domenici (R)/1973	
	New York	
1999	**Alfonse M. D'Amato*** (R)/1981	**3,167,061**
	Robert Abrams (D)	3,086,213
1995	Daniel Patrick Moynihan (D)/1977	
	North Carolina	
1999	**Lauch Faircloth** (R)	**1,297,892**
	Terry Sanford* (D) 11/5/86	1,194,015
1997	Jesse Helms (R)/1973	
	North Dakota	
1999	**Byron L. Dorgan** (D)/1987	**179,347**
	Steve Sydness (R)	118,162
1995	**Kent Conrad** (D)[3]	**103,246**
	Jack Dalrymple (R)	55,194
	Ohio	
1999	**John Glenn*** (D)/12/24/74	**2,444,419**
	Michael DeWine (R)	2,028,300
1995	Howard M. Metzenbaum (D)/12/29/76	
	Oklahoma	
1999	**Don Nickles*** (R)/1981	**757,876**
	Steve Lewis (D)	494,350
1997	David L. Boren (D)/1979	
	Oregon	
1999	**Bob Packwood*** (R)/1969	**717,455**
	Les AuCoin (D)	639,851
1997	Mark O. Hatfield (R)/1/10/67	
	Pennsylvania	
1999	**Arlen Specter*** (R)/1981	**2,358,125**
	Lynn Yeakel (D)	2,224,966
1995	Harris Wofford (D)	
	Rhode Island	
1995	John H. Chafee (R)/12/29/76	
1997	Claiborne Pell (D)/1961	
	South Carolina	
1999	**Ernest F. "Fritz" Hollings*** (D)/11/9/66	**591,030**
	Thomas Hartnett (R)	554,175
1997	Strom Thurmond (R)/11/7/56	
	South Dakota	
1999	**Thomas A. Daschle*** (D)/1987	**217,095**
	Charlene Haar (R)	108.733
1997	Larry Pressler (R)/1979	
	Tennessee	
1995	Jim Sasser (D)/1977	
1997	Harlan Matthews (D)[4]	
	Texas	
1995	**Kay Bailey Hutchison**[5] (R)	**1,186,716**
	Bob Krueger* (D)	576,538
1997	Phil Gramm (R)/1985	
	Utah	
1999	**Robert F. Bennett** (R)	**420,069**
	Wayne Owens (D)	301,228
1995	Orrin G. Hatch (R)/1977	
	Vermont	
1999	**Patrick J. Leahy*** (D)/1975	**154,762**
	James H. Douglas (R)	123,854
1995	James M. Jeffords (R)/1989	
	Virginia	
1995	Charles S. Robb (D)/1989	
1997	John W. Warner (R)/1/2/79	
	Washington	
1999	**Patty Murray** (D)	**1,197,973**
	Rod Chandler (R)	1,020,829
1995	Slade Gorton (R)/1981	
	West Virginia	
1995	Robert C. Byrd (D)/1959	
1997	John D. Rockefeller IV (D)/1/15/85	
	Wisconsin	
1999	**Russell D. Feingold** (D)	**1,290,662**
	Robert W. Kasten, Jr.* (R)/1981	1,129,599
1995	Herbert H. Kohl (D)/1989	
	Wyoming	
1995	Malcolm Wallop (R)/1977	
1997	Alan K. Simpson (R)/1979	

(1) Jan. 3, unless otherwise noted. (2) In the Georgia Senate race, Nov. 3, 1992, incumbent Sen. Wyche Fowler, Jr. (D), received 1,108,416 votes and Paul Coverdell (R) received 1,073,282. Since neither candidate received an absolute majority, a runoff election was held Nov. 24. In the runoff, Coverdell emerged with 50.68 percent of the vote; Fowler received 49.32 percent. (3) A special election was held Dec. 4, 1992, to fill the seat left vacant by the death of Sen. Quentin Burdick (D). The winner will serve the remainder of Burdick's term. (4) Sen. Harlan Matthews (D) was appointed by Gov. Ned Ray McWherter to fill the seat vacated by Al Gore, Jr., who became vice president; in Nov. 1994, a special election will be held to fill the remaining two years of the term. (5) Incumbent Sen. Bob Krueger was appointed by Gov. Ann Richards on Jan. 20, 1993, to fill the seat vacated when Sen. Lloyd Bentsen (D) resigned to become secretary of the Treasury. On June 7, 1993, in a special election, Krueger lost to Kay Bailey Hutchison. She will serve the remainder of the term.

The House of Representatives

Members' terms to Jan. 3, 1995. Annual salary, $133,600; Speaker of the House, $171,500; Majority Leader and Minority Leader, $148,400. To be eligible for membership, a person must be at least 25 years of age, a U.S. citizen for at least 7 years, and a resident of the state from which he or she is chosen. The ZIP code of the House is 20515, the telephone number is 202-225-3121.

House Officials: Speaker, Thomas S. Foley; Majority Leader, Richard A. Gephardt; Majority Whip, David E. Bonior; Minority Leader, Robert H. Michel; Minority Whip, Newt Gingrich.

D-Democrat; R-Republican; B-Libertarian; C-Conservative; I-Independent; L-Liberal; PF-Peace & Freedom.

Dem., 258; Rep., 176; Ind., 1; Total, 435. *Incumbent. Bold face denotes winner.

(Source: News Election Service; World Almanac research)

Dist.	Representative (Party)	1992 Election
	Alabama	
1.	**H.L. "Sonny" Callahan*** (R)	**128,874**
	William A. Brewer (D)	78,742
2.	**Terry Everett** (R)	**112,906**
	George C. Wallace, Jr. (D)	109,335
3.	**Glen Browder*** (D)	**119,175**
	Don Sledge (R)	73,800
4.	**Tom Bevill*** (D)	**157,907**
	Martha "Mickey" Strickland (R)	66,934
5.	**Bud Cramer*** (D)	**160,060**
	Terry Smith (R)	77,951
6.	**Spencer Bachus** (R)	**146,599**
	Ben Erdreich* (D)	126,062
7.	**Earl F. Hilliard** (D)	**144,320**
	Kervin Jones (R)	36,086
	Alaska At Large	
	Don Young* (R)	**111,849**
	John C. Devens (D)	102,378
	Arizona	
1.	**Sam Coppersmith** (D)	**130,715**
	John J. Rhodes III* (R)	113,613
2.	**Ed Pastor*** (D)	**90,693**
	Don Shooter (R)	41,257
3.	**Bob Stump*** (R)	**158,906**
	Roger Hartstone (D)	88,830
4.	**John Kyl*** (R)	**156,330**
	Walter R. Mybeck II (D)	70,572
5.	**Jim Kolbe*** (R)	**172,867**
	Jim Toevs (D)	77,256
6.	**Karen English** (D)	**124,251**
	Doug Wead (R)	97,074
	Arkansas	
1.	**Blanche Lambert** (D)	**149,558**
	Terry Hayes (R)	64,618
2.	**Ray Thornton*** (D)	**154,946**
	Dennis Scott (R)	53,978
3.	**Tim Hutchinson** (R)	**125,295**
	John VanWinkle (D)	117,775
4.	**Jay Dickey** (R)	**113,009**
	W. J. "Bill" McCuen (D)	102,918
	California	
1.	**Dan Hamburg** (D)	**119,676**
	Frank Riggs* (R)	113,266
2.	**Wally Herger*** (R)	**167,247**
	Elliot Roy Freedman (D)	71,780
3.	**Vic Fazio*** (D)	**122,149**
	H.L. "Bill" Richardson (R)	96,092
4.	**John T. Doolittle*** (R)	**141,155**
	Patricia Malberg (D)	129,489
5.	**Robert T. Matsui*** (D)	**158,250**
	Robert S. Dinsmore (R)	58,698
6.	**Lynn Woolsey** (D)	**190,322**
	Bill Filante (R)	98,171
7.	**George Miller*** (D)	**153,320**
	David Scholl (R)	54,822
8.	**Nancy Pelosi*** (D)	**191,906**
	Marc Wolin (R)	25,693
9.	**Ronald V. Dellums*** (D)	**164,265**
	G. William "Billy" Hunter (R)	53,707
10.	**Bill Baker** (R)	**145,702**
	Wendell H. Williams (D)	134,635
11.	**Richard W. Pombo** (R)	**94,453**
	Patricia Garamendi (D)	90,539
12.	**Tom Lantos*** (D)	**157,205**
	Jim Tomlin (R)	53,278
13.	**Fortney "Pete" Stark*** (D)	**123,795**
	Verne Teyler (R)	64,953
14.	**Anna G. Eshoo** (D)	**146,873**
	Tom Huening (R)	101,202

Dist.	Representative (Party)	1992 Election
15.	**Norman Y. Mineta*** (D)	**168,617**
	Robert Wick (R)	82,875
16.	**Don Edwards*** (D)	**96,661**
	Ted Bundesen (R)	49,843
17.	**Sam Farr*** (D)	**53,675**
	Bill McCampbell (R)	43,774
18.	**Gary A. Condit*** (D)	**139,704**
	Kim R. Almstrom (B)	25,307
19.	**Rick Lehman*** (D)	**101,619**
	Tal L. Cloud (R)	100,590
20.	**Calvin Dooley*** (D)	**72,679**
	Ed Hunt (R)	39,388
21.	**William M. "Bill" Thomas*** (R)	**127,758**
	Deborah A. Vollmer (D)	68,058
22.	**Michael Huffington** (R)	**131,242**
	Gloria Ochoa (D)	87,328
23.	**Elton Gallegly*** (R)	**115,504**
	Anita Perez Ferguson (D)	88,225
24.	**Anthony C. Beilenson*** (D)	**141,742**
	Tom McClintock (R)	99,835
25.	**Howard P. "Buck" McKeon** (R)	**113,611**
	James H. "Gil" Gilmartin (D)	72,233
26.	**Howard L. Berman*** (D)	**73,807**
	Gary Forsch (R)	36,453
27.	**Carlos J. Moorhead*** (R)	**105,521**
	Doug Kahn (D)	83,805
28.	**David Dreier*** (R)	**122,353**
	Al Wachtel (D)	76,525
29.	**Henry A. Waxman*** (D)	**160,312**
	Mark A. Robbins (R)	67,141
30.	**Xavier Becerra** (D)	**48,800**
	Morry Waksberg (R)	20,034
31.	**Matthew G. Martinez*** (D)	**68,324**
	Reuben D. Franco (R)	40,873
32.	**Julian C. Dixon*** (D)	**150,644**
	Bob Weber (B)	12,384
33.	**Lucille Roybal-Allard** (D)	**32,010**
	Robert Guzman (R)	15,428
34.	**Esteban E. Torres*** (D)	**91,738**
	J. "Jay" Hernandez (R)	50,907
35.	**Maxine Waters*** (D)	**102,941**
	Nate Truman (R)	17,417
36.	**Jane Harman** (D)	**125,751**
	Joan Milke Flores (R)	109,684
37.	**Walter R. Tucker** (D)	**97,159**
	B. Kwaku Duren (PF)	16,178
38.	**Steve Horn** (R)	**92,038**
	Evan Anderson Braude (D)	82,108
39.	**Ed Royce** (R)	**122,472**
	Molly McClanahan (D)	81,728
40.	**Jerry Lewis*** (R)	**129,563**
	Donald M. "Don" Rusk (D)	63,881
41.	**Jay C. Kim** (R)	**101,753**
	Bob Baker (D)	58,777
42.	**George E. Brown, Jr.*** (D)	**79,780**
	Dick Rutan (R)	69,251
43.	**Ken Calvert** (R)	**88,987**
	Mark A. Takano (D)	88,468
44.	**Al McCandless*** (R)	**110,333**
	Georgia Smith (D)	81,693
45.	**Dana Rohrabacher*** (R)	**123,731**
	Patricia McCabe (D)	88,508
46.	**Robert K.O. "Bob" Dornan*** (R)	**55,659**
	Robert John Banuelos (D)	45,435
47.	**Christopher Cox*** (R)	**165,004**
	John F. Anwiler (D)	76,924
48.	**Ron Packard*** (R)	**140,935**
	Michael Farber (D)	67,415
49.	**Lynn Schenk** (D)	**127,280**
	Judy Jarvis (R)	106,170
50.	**Bob Filner** (D)	**77,293**
	Tony Valencia (R)	39,531

Dist.	Representative (Party)	1992 Election
51.	**Randy "Duke" Cunningham*** (R)	**141,890**
	Bea Herbert (D)	85,148
52.	**Duncan Hunter*** (R)	**112,995**
	Janet M. Gastil (D)	88,076

Colorado

Dist.	Representative (Party)	1992 Election
1.	**Patricia Schroeder*** (D)	**156,629**
	Raymond Diaz Aragon (R)	70,902
2.	**David E. Skaggs*** (D)	**164,790**
	Bryan Day (R)	88,470
3.	**Scott McInnis** (R)	**143,293**
	Mike Callihan (D)	114,480
4.	**Wayne Allard*** (R)	**139,884**
	Tom Redder (D)	101,957
5.	**Joel Hefley*** (R)	**173,096**
	Charles A. Oriez (D)	62,550
6.	**Daniel Schaefer*** (R)	**142,021**
	Tom Kolbe (D)	91,073

Connecticut

Dist.	Representative (Party)	1992 Election
1.	**Barbara Bailey Kennelly*** (D)	**164,735**
	Philip F. Steele (R)	75,113
2.	**Samuel Gejdenson*** (D)	**123,291**
	Edward W. Munster (R)	119,416
3.	**Rosa L. De Lauro*** (D)	**162,568**
	Thomas Scott (R)	84,952
4.	**Christopher Shays*** (R)	**147,816**
	Dave Schropfer (D)	58,666
5.	**Gary A. Franks*** (R)	**104,891**
	James J. Lawlor (D)	74,791
6.	**Nancy L. Johnson*** (R)	**166,967**
	Eugene F. Slason (D)	60,373

Delaware At Large

Dist.	Representative (Party)	1992 Election
	Michael N. Castle (R)	**153,037**
	S. B. Woo (D)	117,426

Florida

Dist.	Representative (Party)	1992 Election
1.	**Earl Hutto*** (D)	**118,753**
	Terry Ketchel (R)	100,136
2.	**Pete Peterson*** (D)	**167,151**
	Ray Wagner (R)	60,378
3.	**Corrine Brown** (D)	**91,877**
	Don Weidner (R)	63,070
4.	**Tillie Fowler** (R)	**135,772**
	Mattox Hair (D)	103,484
5.	**Karen L. Thurman** (D)	**129,678**
	Tom Hogan (R)	114,331
6.	**Cliff Stearns*** (R)	**144,120**
	Phil Denton (D)	76,396
7.	**John L. Mica** (R)	**125,790**
	Dan Webster (D)	96,926
8.	**Bill McCollum*** (R)	**141,925**
	Chuck Kovaleski (D)	65,132
9.	**Michael Bilirakis*** (R)	**157,822**
	Cheryl Davis Knapp (D)	110,023
10.	**C.W. Bill Young*** (R)	**149,347**
	Karen Moffitt (D)	114,637
11.	**Sam M. Gibbons*** (D)	**100,962**
	Mark Sharpe (R)	77,625
12.	**Charles T. Canady** (R)	**100,468**
	Tom Mims (D)	92,333
13.	**Dan Miller** (R)	**158,836**
	Rand Snell (D)	115,741
14.	**Porter J. Goss*** (R)	**220,324**
	James H. King (I)	48,156
15.	**Jim Bacchus*** (D)	**132,385**
	Bill Tolley (R)	128,830
16.	**Tom Lewis*** (R)	**157,253**
	John P. Comerford (D)	101,217
17.	**Carrie Meek** (D)	**Unopposed**
18.	**Ileana Ros-Lehtinen*** (R)	**104,715**
	Magda Montiel Davis (D)	52,095
19.	**Harry Johnston*** (D)	**177,411**
	Larry Metz (R)	103,848
20.	**Peter Deutsch** (D)	**130,946**
	Beverly Kennedy (R)	91,573
21.	**Lincoln Diaz-Balart** (R)	**Unopposed**
22.	**E. Clay Shaw*** (R)	**128,376**
	Gwen Margolis (D)	91,605
23.	**Alcee L. Hastings** (D)	**84,232**
	Ed Fielding (R)	44,800

Georgia

Dist.	Representative (Party)	1992 Election
1.	**Jack Kingston** (R)	**103,932**
	Barbara Christmas (D)	75,808
2.	**Sanford Bishop** (D)	**95,789**
	Jim Dudley (R)	54,593
3.	**Mac Collins** (R)	**114,107**
	Richard Ray* (D)	94,271
4.	**John Linder** (R)	**126,495**
	Cathey Steinberg (D)	123,819
5.	**John Lewis*** (D)	**147,445**
	Paul Stabler (R)	56,960
6.	**Newt Gingrich*** (R)	**158,761**
	Tony Center (D)	116,196
7.	**George "Buddy" Darden*** (D)	**111,374**
	Al Beverly (R)	82,915
8.	**J. Roy Rowland*** (D)	**108,472**
	Robert F. "Bob" Cunningham (R)	86,220
9.	**Nathan Deal** (D)	**113,024**
	Daniel Becker (R)	77,919
10.	**Don Johnson** (D)	**108,426**
	Ralph Hudgens (R)	93,059
11.	**Cynthia McKinney** (D)	**120,168**
	Woodrow Lovett (R)	44,221

Hawaii

Dist.	Representative (Party)	1992 Election
1.	**Neil Abercrombie*** (D)	**129,332**
	Warner C. Kimo Sutton (R)	41,575
2.	**Patsy Takemoto Mink*** (D)	**131,454**
	Kamuela Price (R)	40,070

Idaho

Dist.	Representative (Party)	1992 Election
1.	**Larry LaRocco*** (D)	**140,985**
	Rachel S. Gilbert (R)	90,983
2.	**Michael D. Crapo** (R)	**139,783**
	J.D. Williams (D)	81,450

Illinois

Dist.	Representative (Party)	1992 Election
1.	**Bobby L. Rush** (D)	**209,258**
	Jay Walker (R)	43,453
2.	**Mel Reynolds** (D)	**182,614**
	Ron Blackstone (R)	31,957
3.	**William O. Lipinski*** (D)	**162,165**
	Harry C. Lepinske (R)	93,128
4.	**Luis V. Gutierrez** (D)	**90,452**
	Hildegarde Rodriguez-Schieman (R)	26,154
5.	**Dan Rostenkowski*** (D)	**132,889**
	Elias R. "Non-Incumbent" Zenkich (R)	90,738
6.	**Henry J. Hyde*** (R)	**165,009**
	Barry W. Watkins (D)	86,891
7.	**Cardiss Collins*** (D)	**182,811**
	Norman G. Boccio (R)	35,346
8.	**Philip M. Crane*** (R)	**132,887**
	Sheila A. Smith (D)	96,419
9.	**Sidney R. Yates*** (D)	**162,942**
	Herbert Sohn (R)	64,760
10.	**John E. Porter*** (R)	**155,230**
	Michael J. Kennedy (D)	85,400
11.	**George E. Sangmeister*** (D)	**135,387**
	Robert T. Herbolsheimer (R)	107,860
12.	**Jerry F. Costello*** (D)	**168,762**
	Mike Starr (R)	68,115
13.	**Harris W. Fawell*** (R)	**179,257**
	Dennis Michael Temple (D)	82,985
14.	**J. Dennis Hastert*** (R)	**155,271**
	Jonathan Abram Reich (D)	75,294
15.	**Thomas W. Ewing*** (R)	**142,167**
	Charles D. Mattis (D)	97,190
16.	**Donald Manzullo** (R)	**142,388**
	John W. Cox, Jr.* (D)	113,555
17.	**Lane Evans*** (D)	**156,233**
	Ken Schloemer (R)	103,719
18.	**Robert H. Michel*** (R)	**156,533**
	Ronald C. Hawkins (D)	114,413

Dist.	Representative (Party)	1992 Election
19.	**Glenn Poshard** (D)	**187,156**
	Douglas E. Lee (R)	83,526
20.	**Richard J. Durbin*** (D)	**154,869**
	John M. Shimkus (R)	119,219
	Indiana	
1.	**Peter J. Visclosky*** (D)	**147,054**
	David J. Vucich (R)	64,770
2.	**Philip R. Sharp*** (D)	**130,881**
	William G. Frazier (R)	90,593
3.	**Timothy J. Roemer*** (D)	**121,269**
	Carl H. Baxmeyer (R)	89,834
4.	**Jill L. Long*** (D)	**134,907**
	Charles W. "Chuck" Pierson (R)	82,468
5.	**Steve Buyer** (R)	**112,492**
	James Jontz* (D)	107,973
6.	**Dan Burton*** (R)	**186,499**
	Natalie M. Bruner (D)	71,952
7.	**John T. Myers*** (R)	**129,189**
	Ellen E. Wedum (D)	88,005
8.	**Frank McCloskey*** (D)	**125,244**
	Richard E. Mourdock (R)	108,054
9.	**Lee H. Hamilton*** (D)	**160,980**
	Michael E. Bailey (R)	70,057
10.	**Andrew Jacobs, Jr.*** (D)	**117,604**
	Janos Horvath (R)	64,378
	Iowa	
1.	**James A. "Jim" Leach*** (R)	**178,042**
	Jan J. Zonneveld (D)	81,600
2.	**Jim Nussle*** (R)	**134,536**
	David R. Nagle (D)	131,570
3.	**Jim Ross Lightfoot*** (R)	**125,931**
	Elaine Baxter (D)	121,063
4.	**Neal Smith*** (D)	**158,610**
	Paul Lunde (R)	94,045
5.	**Fred Grandy*** (R)	**Unopposed**
	Kansas	
1.	**Pat Roberts*** (R)	**194,912**
	Duane E. West (D)	83,620
2.	**Jim Slattery*** (D)	**151,019**
	Jim Van Slyke (R)	109,801
3.	**Jan Meyers*** (R)	**169,929**
	Tom Love (D)	110,076
4.	**Dan Glickman*** (D)	**143,671**
	Eric R. Yost (R)	117,070
	Kentucky	
1.	**Tom Barlow** (D)	**128,524**
	Steve Hamrick (R)	83,088
2.	**William H. Natcher*** (D)	**126,894**
	Bruce R. Bartley (R)	79,684
3.	**Romano L. Mazzoli*** (D)	**148,066**
	Susan B. Stokes (R)	132,689
4.	**Jim Bunning*** (R)	**139,634**
	Dr. Floyd G. Poore (D)	86,890
5.	**Harold Rogers*** (R)	**115,255**
	John Doug Hays (D)	95,760
6.	**Scotty Baesler** (D)	**135,613**
	Charles W. Ellinger (R)	87,816
	Louisiana	
1.	**Bob Livingston*** (R)	**Declared Elected**
2.	**William J. Jefferson*** (D)	**Declared Elected**
3.	**Billy Tauzin*** (D)	**Declared Elected**
4.	**Cleo Fields** (D)	**143,980**
	Charles Jones (D)	50,851
5.	**Jim McCrery** (R)	**153,501**
	Jerry Huckaby* (D)	90,079
6.	**Richard Baker*** (R)	**123,953**
	Clyde C. Holloway (R)	121,225
7.	**James A. "Jimmy" Hayes*** (D)	**Declared Elected**

In Louisiana, all candidates of all parties run against each other in an open primary, unless they are unopposed incumbents in which case they are declared elected. All candidates who receive more than 50 percent of the primary vote are also declared elected and do not appear on the general election ballot.

Dist.	Representative (Party)	1992 Election
	Maine	
1.	**Thomas H. Andrews*** (D)	**232,696**
	Linda Bean (R)	125,236
2.	**Olympia J. Snowe*** (R)	**153,022**
	Patrick K. McGowan (D)	130,824
	Maryland	
1.	**Wayne T. Gilchrest*** (R)	**120,084**
	Thomas McMillen (D)	112,771
2.	**Helen Delich Bentley*** (R)	**165,443**
	Michael C. Hickey, Jr. (D)	88,658
3.	**Benjamin L. Cardin*** (D)	**163,354**
	William T.S. Bricker (R)	58,869
4.	**Albert R. Wynn*** (D)	**136,902**
	Michele Dyson (R)	45,166
5.	**Steny H. Hoyer*** (D)	**118,312**
	Lawrence J. Hogan, Jr. (R)	97,982
6.	**Roscoe G. Bartlett** (R)	**125,564**
	Thomas H. Hattery* (D)	106,224
7.	**Kweisi Mfume*** (D)	**152,689**
	Kenneth Kondner (R)	26,304
8.	**Constance A. Morella*** (R)	**203,377**
	Edward J. Heffernan (D)	77,042
	Massachusetts	
1.	**John W. Olver*** (D)	**135,049**
	Patrick Larkin (R)	113,828
2.	**Richard E. Neal*** (D)	**131,215**
	Anthony W. Ravosa, Jr. (R)	76,795
3.	**Peter I. Blute** (R)	**131,473**
	Joseph D. Early* (D)	115,587
4.	**Barney Frank*** (D)	**182,633**
	Edward J. McCormick III (R)	70,665
5.	**Martin T. Meehan** (D)	**133,844**
	Paul W. Cronin (R)	96,206
6.	**Peter G. Torkildsen** (R)	**159,165**
	Nicholas Mavroules* (D)	130,248
7.	**Edward J. Markey*** (D)	**174,837**
	Stephen A. Sohn (R)	78,262
8.	**Joseph P. Kennedy II***(D)	**149,903**
	Alice Harriet Nakash (I)	30,402
9.	**John Joseph Moakley*** (D)	**175,550**
	Martin D. Conboy (R)	54,291
10.	**Gerry E. Studds*** (D)	**189,342**
	Daniel W. Daly (R)	75,887
	Michigan	
1.	**Bart Stupak** (D)	**144,857**
	Philip E. Ruppe (R)	117,056
2.	**Peter Hoekstra** (R)	**155,577**
	John H. Miltner (D)	86,265
3.	**Paul B. Henry**[2](R)	**162,451**
	Carol S. Kooistra (D)	95,927
4.	**Dave Camp** (R)	**157,337**
	Lisa A. Donaldson (D)	87,573
5.	**James A. Barcia** (D)	**147,618**
	Keith Muxlow (R)	93,098
6.	**Fred Upton** (R)	**144,083**
	Andy Davis (D)	89,020
7.	**Nick Smith** (R)	**133,972**
	Kenneth L. Proctor (B)	18,751
8.	**Bob Carr** (D)	**135,517**
	Dick Chrysler (R)	131,906
9.	**Dale E. Kildee** (D)	**133,956**
	Megan O'Neill (R)	111,798
10.	**David E. Bonior** (D)	**138,193**
	Douglas Carl (R)	114,918
11.	**Joseph K. Knollenberg** (R)	**168,940**
	Walter Briggs (D)	117,725
12.	**Sander Levin** (D)	**137,514**
	John Pappageorge (R)	119,357
13.	**William D. Ford** (D)	**127,642**
	R. Robert Geake (R)	105,169

Dist.	Representative (Party)	1992 Election
14.	**John Conyers, Jr.** (D)	**165,496**
	John W. Gordon (R)	32,036
15.	**Barbara-Rose Collins*** (D)	**148,908**
	Charles C. Vincent (R)	31,849
16.	**John D. Dingell*** (D)	**156,964**
	Frank Beaumont (R)	75,694

Minnesota

Dist.	Representative (Party)	1992 Election
1.	**Timothy J. "Tim" Penny*** (D)	**206,369**
	Timothy R. Droogsma (R)	72,367
2.	**David Minge** (D)	**132,156**
	Cal R. Ludeman (R)	131,587
3.	**Jim Ramstad*** (R)	**200,240**
	Paul Mandell (D)	104,606
4.	**Bruce F. Vento*** (D)	**159,796**
	Ian Maitland (R)	101,744
5.	**Martin Olav Sabo*** (D)	**174,139**
	Stephen A. Moriarty (R)	77,093
6.	**Rod Grams** (R)	**133,564**
	Gerry Sikorski* (D)	100,016
7.	**Collin C. Peterson*** (D)	**133,886**
	Bernie Omann (R)	130,396
8.	**James L. Oberstar*** (D)	**167,104**
	Phil Herwig (R)	83,823

Mississippi

Dist.	Representative (Party)	1992 Election
1.	**Jamie L. Whitten*** (D)	**121,664**
	Clyde E. Whitaker (R)	82,952
2.	**Bennie Thompson**[3] (D)	**72,561**
	Hayes Dent (R)	58,995
3.	**G. V. "Sonny" Montgomery*** (D)	**162,864**
	Michael E. Williams (R)	37,710
4.	**Mike Parker*** (D)	**130,927**
	Jack L. McMillan (R)	43,705
5.	**Gene Taylor*** (D)	**120,766**
	Paul Harvey (R)	67,619

Missouri

Dist.	Representative (Party)	1992 Election
1.	**William "Bill" Clay*** (D)	**158,693**
	Arthur S. Montgomery (R)	74,482
2.	**James M. Talent** (R)	**157,594**
	Joan Kelly Horn* (D)	148,729
3.	**Richard A. Gephardt*** (D)	**174,000**
	Malcolm L. "Mack" Holekamp (R)	90,006
4.	**Ike Skelton*** (D)	**176,977**
	John Carley (R)	74,475
5.	**Alan Wheat*** (D)	**151,014**
	Edward "Gomer" Moody (R)	93,562
6.	**Patsy Ann "Pat" Danner** (D)	**148,887**
	E. Thomas "Tom" Coleman* (R)	119,637
7.	**Melton D. "Mel" Hancock*** (R)	**160,303**
	Thomas Patrick "Pat" Deaton (D)	99,762
8.	**Bill Emerson*** (R)	**147,398**
	Thad Bullock (D)	86,730
9.	**Harold L. Volkmer*** (D)	**124,694**
	Rick Hardy (R)	118,811

Montana At Large

Dist.	Representative (Party)	1992 Election
1.	**Pat Williams*** (D)	**203,711**
	Ron Marlenee (R)	189,570

Nebraska

Dist.	Representative (Party)	1992 Election
1.	**Douglas K. Bereuter*** (R)	**142,713**
	Gerry Finnegan (D)	96,309
2.	**Peter Hoagland*** (D)	**119,512**
	Ronald L. Staskiewicz (R)	113,828
3.	**Bill Barrett*** (R)	**170,857**
	Lowell Fisher (D)	67,457

Nevada

Dist.	Representative (Party)	1992 Election
1.	**James H. Bilbray*** (D)	**128,278**
	J. Coy Pettyjohn (R)	84,217
2.	**Barbara F. Vucanovich*** (R)	**129,575**
	Pete Sferrazza (D)	117,199

New Hampshire

Dist.	Representative (Party)	1992 Election
1.	**"Bill" Zeliff*** (R)	**135,936**
	"Bob" Preston (D)	108,578
2.	**"Dick" Swett*** (D)	**157,328**
	"Bill" Hatch (R)	91,127

New Jersey

Dist.	Representative (Party)	1992 Election
1.	**Robert E. Andrews*** (D)	**153,525**
	Lee A. Solomon (R)	65,123
2.	**William J. Hughes*** (D)	**132,465**
	Frank A. LoBiondo (R)	98,315
3.	**Jim Saxton*** (R)	**151,368**
	Timothy E. Ryan (D)	94,012
4.	**Christopher H. Smith*** (R)	**149,095**
	Brian M. Hughes (D)	84,514
5.	**Marge Roukema*** (R)	**196,198**
	Frank R. Lucas (D)	67,579
6.	**Frank Pallone, Jr.*** (D)	**118,266**
	Joseph M. Kyrillos (R)	100,949
7.	**Bob Franks** (R)	**132,174**
	Leonard R. Sendelsky (D)	105,761
8.	**Herbert C. Klein** (D)	**96,742**
	Joseph L. Bubba (R)	84,674
9.	**Robert G. Torricelli*** (D)	**139,188**
	Patrick J. Roma (R)	88,179
10.	**Donald M. Payne*** (D)	**117,287**
	Alfred D. Palermo (R)	30,160
11.	**Dean A. Gallo*** (R)	**188,165**
	Ona Spiridellis (D)	68,871
12.	**Dick Zimmer*** (R)	**174,216**
	Frank C. Abate (D)	83,035
13.	**Robert Mendenez** (D)	**93,670**
	Fred J. Theomling, Jr. (R)	44,529

New Mexico

Dist.	Representative (Party)	1992 Election
1.	**Steven H. Schiff*** (R)	**128,426**
	Robert J. Aragon (D)	76,600
2.	**Joe Skeen*** (R)	**94,838**
	Dan Sosa, Jr. (D)	73,157
3.	**Bill Richardson*** (D)	**122,850**
	F. Gregg Bemis, Jr. (R)	54,569

New York

Dist.	Representative (Party)	1992 Election
1.	**George J. Hochbrueckner*** (D)	**117,940**
	Edward P. Romaine (R)	110,043
2.	**Rick A. Lazio** (R)	**109,386**
	Thomas J. Downey* (D)	96,328
3.	**Peter T. King** (R)	**124,727**
	Steve A. Orlins (D)	116,915
4.	**David A. Levy** (R)	**110,710**
	Philip Schiliro (D)	100,386
5.	**Gary L. Ackerman*** (D)	**110,476**
	Allan E. Binder (R)	94,907
6.	**Floyd H. Flake*** (D)	**96,972**
	Dianand D. Bnaowandin (R)	22,687
7.	**Thomas J. Manton*** (D)	**72,280**
	Dennis C. Shea (R)	54,639
8.	**Jerrold L. Nadler** (D)	**138,423**
	David L. Askren (R)	25,592
9.	**Charles E. Schumer*** (D,L)	**116,545**
	Alice E. Gaffney (C)	14,985
10.	**Edolphus Towns*** (D,L)	**97,509**
	Owen Augustin (C)	4,315
11.	**Major R. Owens*** (D,L)	**80,028**
	Michael Gaffney (C)	4,287
12.	**Nydia M. Velazquez** (D)	**55,926**
	Angel Diaz (R)	14,976
13.	**Susan Molinari*** (R)	**107,903**
	Sal F. Albanese (D)	73,520
14.	**Carolyn B. Maloney** (D)	**101,687**
	Bill Green* (R)	97,232
15.	**Charles B. Rangel*** (D,L)	**105,011**
	Jose Suero (C)	4,345
16.	**José E. Serrano*** (D)	**85,222**
	Michael Walters (R)	7,975
17.	**Eliot L. Engel*** (D)	**98,068**
	Martin Richman (R)	16,511
18.	**Nita M. Lowey*** (D)	**115,841**
	Joseph J. DioGuardi (R)	92,687
19.	**Hamilton Fish, Jr.*** (R)	**139,610**
	Neil McCarthy (D)	92,854

Dist.	Representative (Party)	1992 Election
20.	**Benjamin A. Gilman*** (R)	**150,301**
	Jonathan L. Levine (D)	66,826
21.	**Michael R. McNulty*** (D)	**166,371**
	Nancy Norman (R)	91,184
22.	**Gerald B. H. Solomon*** (R)	**164,436**
	David Roberts (D)	86,896
23.	**Sherwood L. Boehlert*** (R)	**139,774**
	Paula DiPerna (D)	61,835
24.	**John M. McHugh** (R)	**122,257**
	Margaret M. Ravenscroft (D)	47,675
25.	**James T. Walsh*** (R)	**135,076**
	Rhea Jezer (D)	107,310
26.	**Maurice D. Hinchey** (D)	**119,557**
	Bob Moppert (R)	110,738
27.	**Bill Paxon*** (R)	**156,596**
	W. Douglas Call (D)	89,906
28.	**Louise M. Slaughter*** (D)	**140,908**
	William P. Polito (R)	112,273
29.	**John J. LaFalce*** (D)	**128,230**
	William E. Miller, Jr. (R)	98,031
30.	**Jack Quinn** (R)	**125,734**
	Dennis T. Gorski (D)	111,445
31.	**Amo Houghton*** (R)	**150,696**
	Joseph P. Leahey (D)	52,010

North Carolina

Dist.	Representative (Party)	1992 Election
1.	**Eva Clayton** (D)	**116,078**
	Ted Tyler (R)	54,457
2.	**I.T. "Tim" Valentine, Jr.*** (D)	**113,693**
	Don Davis (R)	93,893
3.	**Martin Lancaster*** (D)	**101,739**
	Tommy Pollard (R)	80,759
4.	**David E. Price*** (D)	**171,299**
	LaVinia "Vicky" Rothrock Goudie (R)	89,345
5.	**Stephen Neal*** (D)	**117,835**
	Richard M. Burr (R)	102,086
6.	**J. Howard Coble*** (R)	**162,822**
	Robin Hood (D)	67,200
7.	**Charles C. "Charlie" Rose III*** (D)	**92,414**
	Robert C. Anderson (R)	66,536
8.	**W. G. "Bill" Hefner*** (D)	**113,162**
	Coy C. Privette (R)	71,842
9.	**J. Alex McMillan*** (R)	**153,650**
	Rory Blake (D)	74,583
10.	**T. Cass Ballenger*** (R)	**148,999**
	Ben Neill (D)	79,206
11.	**Charles H. Taylor*** (R)	**130,158**
	John S. Stevens (D)	108,003
12.	**Melvin Watt** (D)	**127,262**
	Barbara Gore Washington (R)	49,402

North Dakota At Large

Dist.	Representative (Party)	1992 Election
	Earl Pomeroy(D)	**169,273**
	John T. Korsmo (R)	117,442

Ohio

Dist.	Representative (Party)	1992 Election
1.	**David Mann** (D)	**120,190**
	Steve Grote (I)	101,498
	Jim Berns (I)	12,734
2.	**Rob Portman**[4](R)	**53,020**
	Lee Hornberger (D)	22,652
3.	**Tony P. Hall*** (D)	**146,072**
	Peter W. Davis (R)	98,733
4.	**Michael G. Oxley*** (R)	**147,346**
	Raymond M. Ball (D)	92,608
5.	**Paul E. Gillmor*** (R)	**Unopposed**
6.	**Ted Strickland** (D)	**122,720**
	Bob McEwen* (R)	119,252
7.	**David L. Hobson*** (R)	**164,195**
	Clifford S. Heskett (D)	66,237
8.	**John A. Boehner*** (R)	**176,362**
	Fred Sennet (D)	62,033
9.	**Marcy Kaptur*** (D)	**178,879**
	Ken D. Brown (R)	53,011
10.	**Martin R. Hoke** (R)	**136,433**
	Mary Rose Oakar* (D)	103,788
11.	**Louis Stokes*** (D)	**154,718**
	Beryl E. Rothschild (R)	43,866
12.	**John R. Kasich*** (R)	**170,297**
	Bob Fitrakis (D)	68,761
13.	**Sherrod Brown** (D)	**134,486**
	Margaret R. Mueller (R)	88,889
14.	**Thomas C. Sawyer*** (D)	**165,335**
	Robert Morgan (R)	78,659
15.	**Deborah Pryce** (R)	**110,390**
	Richard Cordray (D)	94,907
16.	**Ralph Regula*** (R)	**158,489**
	Warner D. Mendenhall (D)	90,224
17.	**James A. Traficant, Jr.*** (D)	**216,503**
	Salvatore Pansino (R)	40,743
18.	**Douglas Applegate*** (D)	**166,189**
	Bill Ress (R)	77,229
19.	**Eric D. Fingerhut** (D)	**138,465**
	Robert A. Gardner (R)	124,606

Oklahoma

Dist.	Representative (Party)	1992 Election
1.	**James M. Inhofe*** (R)	**119,211**
	John Selph (D)	106,619
2.	**Mike Synar*** (D)	**118,542**
	Jerry Hill (R)	87,657
3.	**Bill K. Brewster*** (D)	**155,934**
	Robert W. Stokes (R)	51,725
4.	**Dave McCurdy*** (D)	**140,841**
	Howard Bell (R)	58,235
5.	**Ernest Jim Istook** (R)	**123,237**
	Laurie Williams (D)	107,579
6.	**Glenn English*** (D)	**134,734**
	Bob Anthony (R)	64,068

Oregon

Dist.	Representative (Party)	1992 Election
1.	**Elizabeth Furse** (D)	**152,917**
	Tony Meeker (R)	140,986
2.	**Bob Smith*** (R)	**184,163**
	Denzel Ferguson (D)	90,036
3.	**Ron Wyden*** (D)	**208,028**
	Al Ritter (R)	50,235
4.	**Peter A. DeFazio*** (D)	**199,372**
	Richard L. Schulz (R)	79,733
5.	**Mike Kopetski*** (D)	**174,443**
	Jim Seagraves (R)	97,984

Pennsylvania

Dist.	Representative (Party)	1992 Election
1.	**Thomas M. Foglietta*** (D)	**150,172**
	Craig Snyder (R)	35,419
2.	**Lucien E. Blackwell*** (D)	**164,355**
	Larry Hollin (R)	47,906
3.	**Robert A. Borski*** (D)	**130,828**
	Charles F. Dougherty (R)	86,787
4.	**Ron Klink** (D)	**186,684**
	Gordon R. Johnston (R)	48,484
5.	**William F. "Bill" Clinger, Jr.*** (D)	**Unopposed**
6.	**Tim Holden** (D)	**108,312**
	John E. Jones (R)	99,694
7.	**Curt Weldon*** (R)	**180,648**
	Frank Daly (D)	91,623
8.	**Jim Greenwood** (R)	**129,593**
	Peter H. Kostmayer* (D)	114,095
9.	**Bud Shuster*** (R, D)	**Unopposed**
10.	**Joseph M. McDade*** (R,D)	**189,414**
	Albert A. Smith (B)	20,134
11.	**Paul E. Kanjorski*** (D)	**138,675**
	Michael A. Fescina (R)	68,112
12.	**John P. Murtha*** (D)	**Unopposed**
13.	**Marjorie Margolies Mezvinsky** (D)	**127,685**
	John D. Fox (R)	126,312
14.	**William J. Coyne*** (D)	**165,633**
	Byron W. King (R)	61,311
15.	**Paul McHale** (D)	**111,419**
	Don Ritter* (R)	99,520
16.	**Robert S. Walker*** (R)	**137,823**
	Robert Peters (D)	74,741
17.	**George W. Gekas*** (R)	**150,158**
	Bill Sturges (D)	65,881
18.	**Rick Santorum*** (R)	**154,024**
	Frank A. Pecora (D)	96,655
19.	**William F. Goodling*** (R)	**98,599**
	Paul V. Kilker (D)	74,798
	Thomas M. Humbert (I)	44,290

Dist.	Representative (Party)	1992 Election
20.	**Austin J. Murphy*** (D)	**124,898**
	Bill Townsend (R)	111,591
21.	**Thomas J. Ridge*** (R)	**150,729**
	John C. Harkins (D)	78,802

Rhode Island

Dist.	Representative (Party)	1992 Election
1.	**Ronald K. Machtley*** (R)	**135,982**
	David R. Carlin, Jr. (D)	48,092
2.	**John F. Reed*** (D)	**144,450**
	James W. Bell (R)	49,998

South Carolina

Dist.	Representative (Party)	1992 Election
1.	**Arthur Ravenel, Jr.*** (R)	**121,938**
	Bill Oberst, Jr. (D)	59,908
2.	**Floyd D. Spence*** (R)	**148,667**
	Geb Sommer (B)	20,816
3.	**Butler Derrick*** (D)	**119,119**
	Jim Bland (R)	75,660
4.	**Bob Inglis*** (R)	**99,879**
	Liz J. Patterson (D)	94,182
5.	**John Spratt*** (D)	**112,031**
	Bill Horne (R)	70,866
6.	**James R. Clyburn** (D)	**120,647**
	John Chase (R)	64,149

South Dakota At Large

Dist.	Representative (Party)	1992 Election
	Tim Johnson* (D)	**230,070**
	John Timmer (R)	89,375

Tennessee

Dist.	Representative (Party)	1992 Election
1.	**James H. "Jimmy" Quillen*** (R)	**114,797**
	J. Carr "Jack" Christian (D)	47,809
2.	**John J. Duncan, Jr.*** (R)	**148,377**
	Troy Goodale (D)	52,887
3.	**Marilyn Lloyd*** (D)	**105,693**
	Zack Wamp (R)	102,763
4.	**Jim Cooper*** (D)	**98,984**
	Dale Johnson (R)	50,340
5.	**Bob Clement*** (D)	**125,233**
	Tom Stone (R)	49,417
6.	**Bart Gordon*** (D)	**120,177**
	Marsha Blackburn (R)	86,289
7.	**Don Sundquist*** (R)	**125,101**
	David R. Davis (D)	72,062
8.	**John Tanner*** (D)	**Unopposed**
9.	**Harold E. Ford*** (D)	**123,276**
	Charles L. Black (R)	60,606

Texas

Dist.	Representative (Party)	1992 Election
1.	**Jim Chapman*** (D)	**Unopposed**
2.	**Charles Wilson*** (D)	**118,625**
	Donna Peterson (R)	92,176
3.	**Sam Johnson*** (R)	**201,569**
	Noel Kopala (B)	32,570
4.	**Ralph M. Hall*** (D)	**128,008**
	David L. Bridges (R)	83,875
5.	**John Bryant*** (D)	**98,567**
	Richard Stokley (R)	62,419
6.	**Joe Barton*** (R)	**189,140**
	John Dietrich (D)	73,933
7.	**Bill Archer*** (R)	**Unopposed**
8.	**Jack Fields*** (R)	**179,349**
	Charles Robinson (D)	53,473
9.	**Jack Brooks*** (D)	**118,690**
	Steve Stockman (R)	96,270
10.	**J. J. "Jake" Pickle*** (D)	**177,233**
	Herbert Spiro (R)	68,646
11.	**Chet Edwards*** (D)	**119,999**
	James W. Broyles (R)	58,033
12.	**Pete Geren*** (D)	**125,492**
	David Hobbs (R)	74,432
13.	**Bill Sarpalius*** (D)	**117,892**
	Beau Bolter (R)	77,514
14.	**Greg Laughlin*** (D)	**135,930**
	Humberto J. "Bert" Garza (R)	54,412
15.	**E. "Kika" de la Garza*** (D)	**86,351**
	Tom Haughey (R)	56,549
16.	**Ronald Coleman*** (D)	**66,731**
	Chip Taberski (R)	61,870
17.	**Charles W. Stenholm*** (D)	**136,213**
	Jeannie Sadowski (R)	69,958
18.	**Craig A. Washington*** (D)	**111,422**
	Edward Blum (R)	56,080
19.	**Larry Combest*** (R)	**162,057**
	Terry Lee Moser (D)	47,325
20.	**Henry B. Gonzalez*** (D)	**Unopposed**
21.	**Lamar Smith*** (R)	**190,979**
	James M. Gaddy (D)	62,827
22.	**Tom DeLay*** (R)	**150,221**
	Richard Konrad (D)	67,812
23.	**Henry Bonilla** (R)	**98,259**
	Albert G. Bustamente* (D)	63,797
24.	**Martin Frost*** (D)	**104,174**
	Steve Masterson (R)	70,042
25.	**Mike Andrews*** (D)	**98,975**
	Dolly Madison McKenna (R)	73,192
26.	**Dick Armey*** (R)	**150,209**
	John Wayne Caton (D)	55,237
27.	**Solomon P. Ortiz*** (D)	**87,022**
	Jay Kimbrough (R)	66,853
28.	**Frank Tejeda** (D)	**122,457**
	David C. Slatter (B)	18,128
29.	**Gene Green** (D)	**64,064**
	Clark Kent Ervin (R)	34,609
30.	**Eddie Bernice Johnson** (D)	**107,831**
	Lucy Cain (R)	37,853

Utah

Dist.	Representative (Party)	1992 Election
1.	**James V. Hansen*** (R)	**160,037**
	Ron Holt (D)	68,712
2.	**Karen Shepherd** (D)	**127,738**
	Enid Greene (R)	118,307
3.	**Bill Orton*** (D)	**135,029**
	Richard Harrington (R)	84,019

Vermont At Large

Dist.	Representative (Party)	1992 Election
	Bernie Sanders* (I)	**162,724**
	Tim Philbin (R)	86,901
	Lewis E. Young (D)	22,279

Virginia

Dist.	Representative (Party)	1992 Election
1.	**Herbert H. "Herb" Bateman*** (R)	**133,537**
	Andrew H. "Andy" Fox (D)	89,814
2.	**Owen B. Pickett*** (D)	**99,253**
	J. L. "Jim" Chapman (R)	77,797
3.	**Robert C. "Bobby" Scott** (D)	**132,432**
	Daniel "Dan" Jenkins (R)	35,780
4.	**Norman Sisisky*** (D)	**147,649**
	A.J. "Tony" Zevgolis (R)	68,286
5.	**L. F. Payne, Jr.*** (D)	**133,031**
	W.A. "Bill" Hurlburt (R)	60,030
6.	**Robert W. "Bob" Goodlatte** (R)	**127,309**
	Stephen Alan Musselwhite (D)	84,618
7.	**Thomas J. "Tom" Bliley, Jr.*** (R)	**211,618**
	Gerald E. "Jerry" Berg (I)	43,267
8.	**James P. Moran, Jr.*** (D)	**138,542**
	Kyle E. McSlarrow (R)	102,717
9.	**Frederick C. "Rick" Boucher*** (D)	**133,284**
	L. Garrett "Gary" Weddle (R)	77,985
10.	**Frank R. Wolf*** (R)	**144,471**
	Raymond E. "Ray" Vickery, Jr. (D)	75,775
11.	**Leslie L. Byrne** (D)	**114,172**
	Henry N. Butler (R)	103,119

Washington

Dist.	Representative (Party)	1992 Election
1.	**Maria Cantwell** (D)	**148,844**
	Gary Nelson (R)	113,897
2.	**Al Swift*** (D)	**133,207**
	Jack Metcalf (R)	107,365
3.	**Jolene Unsoeld*** (D)	**138,043**
	Pat Fiske (R)	108,583
4.	**Jay Inslee** (D)	**106,556**
	Richard "Doc" Hastings (R)	103,028
5.	**Thomas S. Foley*** (D)	**135,965**
	John Sonneland (R)	110,443
6.	**Norman D. Dicks*** (D)	**152,933**
	Lauri J. Phillips (R)	66,664
7.	**Jim McDermott*** (D)	**222,604**
	Glenn C. Hampson (R)	54,149

Dist.	Representative (Party)	1992 Election
8.	**Jennifer Dunn** (R)	**155,874**
	George O. Tamblyn (D)	87,611
9.	**Mike Kreidler** (D)	**110,902**
	Pete von Reichbauer (R)	91,910
	Brian Wilson (I)	6,585
	Timothy J. Brill (I)	3,522
	West Virginia	
1.	**Alan B. Mollohan*** (D)	**Unopposed**
2.	**Bob Wise*** (D)	**143,988**
	Samuel A. Cravotta (R)	59,102
3.	**Nick Joe Rahall II*** (D)	**122,279**
	Ben Waldman (R)	64,012
	Wisconsin	
1.	**Peter Barca**[5] (D)	**55,605**
	Mark W. Neumann (R)	54,930
2.	**Scott L. Klug*** (R)	**183,366**
	Ada E. Deer (D)	108,291
3.	**Steven C. Gunderson*** (R)	**146,903**
	Paul Sacia (D)	108,664
4.	**Gerald D. Kleczka*** (D)	**173,482**
	Joseph L. Cook (R)	84,872
5.	**Thomas M. Barrett** (D)	**162,344**
	Donalda Ann Hammersmith (R)	71,085
6.	**Thomas E. Petri*** (R)	**143,875**
	Peggy A. Lautenschlager (D)	128,232
7.	**David R. Obey*** (D)	**166,200**
	Dale R. Vannes (R)	91,772
8.	**Toby Roth*** (R)	**191,704**
	Catherine L. Helms (D)	81,792
9.	**F. James Senstenbrenner, Jr.*** (R)	**192,898**
	Ingrid K. Buxton (D)	77,362
	Wyoming At Large	
	Craig Thomas* (R)	**113,882**
	John Herschler (D)	77,418

Resident Commissioner (Non-Voting)

Puerto Rico

Carlos Romero Barceló (D)

Non-Voting Delegates

District of Columbia
Eleanor Holmes Norton* (D)

Guam[6]
Robert Underwood (D)

American Samoa
Eni F. H. Faleomavaega (D)

Virgin Islands
Ron de Lugo* (D)

(1) A special election was held June 9, 1993, to fill the seat left vacant when Rep. Leon E. Panetta (D) resigned to become budget director. The winner will serve the remainder of Panetta's term. (2) A special election will be held Dec. 7, 1993, to fill the seat left vacant by the death of Rep. Paul B. Henry on July 31. (3) A special election was held Apr. 13, 1993, to fill the seat left vacant when Rep. Mike Espy (D) resigned to become secretary of agriculture. The winner will serve the remainder of Espy's term. (4) A special election was held May 4, 1993, to fill the seat left vacant when Rep. Willis D. Gradison, Jr. (R) resigned after 18 years in office to become a lobbyist. The winner will serve the remainder of Gradison's term. (5) A special election was held May 4, 1993, to fill the seat left vacant when Rep. Les Aspin (D) resigned to become secretary of defense. The winner will serve the remainder of Aspin's term. (6) A typhoon postponed elections on Guam until Nov. 7, 1992.

Congressional Reapportionment for the 103rd Congress

Source: Bureau of the Census, U.S. Dept. of Commerce

As a result of population changes from 1980 to 1990, as reported in the 1990 Census, 8 states have more representatives in the 103rd Congress, which convened in January 1993. The states with the largest gains were California (+7), Florida (+4), and Texas (+3), while Washington, Arizona, Georgia, North Carolina, and Virginia each gained a seat. Thirteen states have fewer representatives. New York lost 3 seats, while Illinois, Michigan, Ohio, and Pennsylvania lost 2 seats each. West Virginia, Kentucky, Louisiana, Kansas, Massachusetts, New Jersey, Iowa, and Montana lost one seat.

The population shifts gave the West 8, and the South 7 additional seats. The Midwest lost 8, and the Northeast 7 seats.

Political Divisions of the U.S. Senate and House of Representatives From 1955 (84th Cong.) to 1993 (103rd Cong.)

Source: Clerk of the House of Representatives; Secretary of the Senate

		Senate					House of Representatives				
Congress	Years	Number of Senators	Democrats	Republicans	Other parties	Vacant	Number of Representatives	Democrats	Republicans	Other parties	Vacant
84th	1955-57	96	48	47	1		435	232	203		
85th	1957-59	96	49	47			435	234	201		
86th	1959-61	98	64	34			[1]436	283	153		
87th	1961-63	100	64	36			[2]437	262	175		
88th	1963-65	100	67	33			435	258	176		1
89th	1965-67	100	68	32			435	295	140		
90th	1967-69	100	64	36			435	248	187		
91st	1969-71	100	58	42			435	243	192		
92d	1971-73	100	54	44	2		435	255	180		
93d	1973-75	100	56	42	2		435	242	192	1	
94th	1975-77	100	61	37	2		435	291	144		
95th	1977-79	100	61	38	1		435	292	143		
96th	1979-81	100	58	41	1		435	277	158		
97th	1981-83	100	46	53	1		435	242	190		3
98th	1983-85	100	46	54			435	269	166		
99th	1985-87	100	47	53			435	253	182		
100th	1987-89	100	54	46			435	258	177		
101st	1989-91	100	57	43			435	262	173		
102nd	1991-93	100	57	43			435	266	164	1	4
103rd	1993-95	100	[3]56	[3]44			435	[3]258	[3]176	[3]1	

(1) Proclamation declaring Alaska a state issued Jan. 3, 1959. (2) Proclamation declaring Hawaii a state issued Aug. 21, 1959. (3) As of mid-1993.

Congressional Bills Vetoed, 1789-1993

Source: Senate Library; June 16, 1993

	Regular vetoes	Pocket vetoes	Total vetoes	Vetoes over-ridden
Washington	2	—	2	—
John Adams	—	—	—	—
Jefferson	—	—	—	—
Madison	5	2	7	—
Monroe	1	—	1	—
John Q. Adams	—	—	—	—
Jackson	5	7	12	—
Van Buren	—	1	1	—
William Harrison	—	—	—	—
Tyler	6	4	10	1
Polk	2	1	3	—
Taylor	—	—	—	—
Fillmore	—	—	—	—
Pierce	9	—	9	5
Buchanan	4	3	7	—
Lincoln	2	5	7	—
Andrew Johnson	21	8	29	15
Grant	45	48	93	4
Hayes	12	1	13	1
Garfield	—	—	—	—
Arthur	4	8	12	1
Cleveland	304	110	414	2
Benjamin Harrison	19	25	44	1
Cleveland	42	128	170	5
McKinley	6	36	42	—
Theodore Roosevelt	42	40	82	1
Taft	30	9	39	1
Wilson	33	11	44	6
Harding	5	1	6	—
Coolidge	20	30	50	4
Hoover	21	16	37	3
Franklin Roosevelt	372	263	635	9
Truman	180	70	250	12
Eisenhower	73	108	181	2
Kennedy	12	9	21	—
Lyndon Johnson	16	14	30	—
Nixon	26	17	43	7
Ford	48	18	66	12
Carter	13	18	31	2
Reagan	39	39	78	9
Bush[1]	29	15	44	1
Total[1]	**1,467**	**1,066**	**2,514**	**104**

(1) Excluded from the figures are 2 additional bills, which Pres. Bush claimed to be vetoed but Congress considered enacted into law because the President failed to return them to Congress; the courts will decide the status of these bills.

How a Bill Becomes a Law

1. A Senator or Representative introduces a bill by sending it to the clerk of the House or Senate, who assigns it a number and title. This procedure is termed the *first reading.* The clerk then refers the bill to the appropriate Senate or House committee.

2. If the committee opposes the bill, It will *table,* or kill, it. Otherwise, the committee holds hearings to listen to opinions and facts offered by members and other interested people. The committee then debates the bill and possibly offers amendments. A vote is taken, and if favorable, the bill is sent back to the clerk of the House or Senate.

3. The clerk reads the bill to the house. This is termed the *second reading.* Members may then debate the bill and suggest amendments.

4. After debate and possibly amendment, the bill is given a *third reading,* simply of the title, and put to a voice or roll-call vote.

5. If passed, the bill goes to the other house, where it may be defeated, or passed with or without amendments. If defeated, the bill dies. If passed with amendments, a conference committee made up of members of both houses works out the differences and arrives at a compromise.

6. After passage of the final version by both houses, the bill is sent to the President. If he signs it, the bill becomes a law. However, he may *veto* the bill by refusing to sign it and sending it back to the house where it originated, with his reasons for the veto.

7. The President's objections are then read and debated and a roll-call vote taken. If the bill receives less than a two-thirds vote, it is defeated. If it receives at least two-thirds, it is sent to the other house. If that house also passes it by at least a two-thirds majority, the veto is *overridden,* and the bill becomes a law.

8. If the President neither signs nor vetoes the bill within 10 days—not including Sundays—it automatically becomes a law even without his signature. However, if Congress has adjourned within those 10 days, the bill is automatically killed; this indirect rejection is termed a *pocket veto.*

Congressional Committees

Senate Standing Committees

(As of March 24, 1993)

Agriculture, Nutrition, and Forestry
Chairman: Patrick J. Leahy, Vt.
Ranking Rep.: Richard G. Lugar, Ind.

Appropriations
Chairman: Robert C. Byrd, W.V.
Ranking Rep.: Mark O. Hatfield, Ore.

Armed Services
Chairman: Sam Nunn, Ga.
Ranking Rep.: Strom Thurmond, S.C.

Banking, Housing, and Urban Affairs
Chairman: Donald W. Riegle, Jr., Mich.
Ranking Rep.: Alfonse M. D'Amato, N.Y.

Budget
Chairman: Jim Sasser, Tenn.
Ranking Rep.: Pete V. Domenici, N.M.

Commerce, Science, and Transportation
Chairman: Ernest F. "Fritz" Hollings, S.C.
Ranking Rep.: John C. Danforth, Mo.

Energy and Natural Resources
Chairman: J. Bennett Johnston, La.
Ranking Rep.: Malcolm Wallop, Wyo.

Environment and Public Works
Chairman: Max Baucus, Mon.
Ranking Rep.: John H. Chafee, R.I.

Finance
Chairman: Daniel Patrick Moynihan, N.Y.
Ranking Rep.: Bob Packwood, Ore.

Foreign Relations
Chairman: Claiborne Pell, R.I.
Ranking Rep.: Jesse Helms, N.C.

Governmental Affairs
Chairman: John Glenn, Ohio
Ranking Rep.: William V. Roth, Jr., Del.

Judiciary
Chairman: Joseph R. Biden, Jr., Del.
Ranking Rep.: Orrin G. Hatch, Ut.

Labor and Human Resources
Chairman: Edward M. Kennedy, Mass.
Ranking Rep.: Nancy Landon Kassebaum, Kan.

Rules and Administration
Chairman: Wendell H. Ford, Ky.
Ranking Rep.: Ted Stevens, Alas.

Small Business
Chairman: Dale Bumpers, Ark.
Ranking Rep.: Larry Pressler, S.D.

Veterans' Affairs
Chairman: John D. Rockefeller IV, W.V.
Ranking Rep.: Frank H. Murkowski, Alas.

Senate, Other, Select, and Special Committees

(As of March 24, 1993)

Aging
Chairman: David H. Pryor, Ark.
Ranking Rep.: William S. Cohen, Me.
Ethics
Chairman: Richard H. Bryan, Nev.
V. Chairman: Mitch McConnell, Ky.
Indian Affairs
Chairman: Daniel K. Inouye, Ha.
Ranking Rep.: John McCain, Ariz.
Intelligence
Chairman: Dennis DeConcini, Ariz.
V. Chairman: John W. Warner, Va.

Joint Committees of Congress

Economic
Chairman: Rep. David R. Obey, Wis.
V. Chairman: Sen. Paul S. Sarbanes, Md.
Library
Chairman: Rep. Charles C. "Charlie" Rose, N.C.
V. Chairman: Sen. Claiborne Pell, R.I.
Organization of Congress
Co-Chairman: Sen. David L. Boren, Okla.
Co-Chairman: Rep. Lee H. Hamilton, Ind.
V. Chairman: Sen. Pete V. Domenici, N.M.
V. Chairman: Rep. David Dreier, Cal.
Printing
Chairman: Sen. Wendell H. Ford, Ky.
V. Chairman: Rep. Charles C. "Charlie" Rose, N.C.
Taxation
Chairman: Rep. Dan Rostenkowski (D), Ill.
V. Chairman: Sen. Daniel Patrick Moynihan, N.Y.

House Standing Committees

(As of April 5, 1993)

Agriculture
Chairman: E. "Kika" de la Garza, Tex.
Ranking Rep.: Pat Roberts, Kan.
Appropriations
Chairman: William H. Natcher, Ky.
Ranking Rep.: Joseph M. McDade, Pa.
Armed Services
Chairman: Ronald V. Dellums, Cal.
Ranking Rep.: Floyd D. Spence, S.C.
Banking, Finance, and Urban Affairs
Chairman: Henry B. Gonzalez, Tex.
Ranking Rep.: James A. "Jim" Leach, Ia.
Budget
Chairman: Martin Olav Sabo, Minn.
Ranking Rep.: John R. Kasich, Oh.
District of Columbia
Chairman: Fortney "Pete" Stark, Cal.
Ranking Rep.: Thomas J. "Tom" Bliley, Jr., Va.
Education and Labor
Chairman: William D. Ford, Mich.
Ranking Rep.: William F. Goodling, Pa.
Energy and Commerce
Chairman: John D. Dingell, Mich.
Ranking Rep.: Carlos J. Moorhead, Cal.
Foreign Affairs
Chairman: Lee H. Hamilton, Ind.
Ranking Rep.: Benjamin A. Gitman, N.Y.
Government Operations
Chairman: John Conyers, Jr., Mich.
Ranking Rep.: William F. "Bill" Clinger, Jr., Pa.
House Administration
Chairman: Charles C. "Charlie" Rose, N.C.
Ranking Rep.: William M. "Bill" Thomas, Cal.
Judiciary
Chairman: Jack Brooks, Tex.
Ranking Rep.: Hamilton Fish, Jr., N.Y.
Merchant Marine and Fisheries
Chairman: Gerry E. Studds, Mass.
Ranking Rep.: Jack Fields, Tex.
Natural Resources
Chairman: George Miller, Cal.
Ranking Rep.: Don Young, Alas.
Post Office and Civil Service
Chairman: William "Bill" Clay, Mo.
Ranking Rep.: John T. Meyers, Ind.
Public Works and Transportation
Chairman: Norman Y. Mineta, Cal.
Ranking Rep.: Bud Shuster, Pa.
Rules
Chairman: John Joseph Moakley, Mass.
Ranking Rep.: Gerald B. H. Solomon, N.Y.
Science, Space, and Technology
Chairman: George E. Brown, Jr., Cal.
Ranking Rep.: Robert S. Walker, Pa.
Small Business
Chairman: John J. LaFalce, N.Y.
Ranking Rep.: Jan Meyers, Kan.
Standards of Official Conduct
Chairman: Jim McDermott, Wash.
Ranking Rep.: Fred Grandy, Ia.
Veterans' Affairs
Chairman: G. V. (Sonny) Montgomery, Miss.
Ranking Rep.: Bob Stump, Ariz.
Ways and Means
Chairman: Dan Rostenkowski, Ill.
Ranking Rep.: Bill Archer, Tex.

House Select Committees

Intelligence
Chairman: Dan Glickman, Kan.
Ranking Rep.: Larry Combest, Tex.

Mayors and City Managers of Selected U.S. Cities

Reflects elections as of August 1993.

* Asterisk before name denotes city manager. All others are mayors. For mayors, dates are those of next election; for city managers, they are dates of appointment.

D, Democrat; R, Republican; N-P, Non-Partisan; I, Independent

City	Name	Term
Abilene, Tex.	Gary McCaleb, N-P	**1993, May**
Abington, Pa.	*Albert Herrmann	**1978, May**
Akron, Oh.	D.L. Plusquellic, D	**1995, Nov.**
Alameda, Cal.	E. William Withrow, N-P	**1994, Nov.**
Albany, Ga.	*Roy Lane	**1991, Mar.**
Albany, N.Y.	Thomas M. Whalen,3d,D	**1993, Nov.**
Albuquerque, N.M.	Louis Saavedra, D.	**1993, Oct.**
Alexandria, La.	Edward Randolph Jr., D	**1994, Nov.**
Alexandria, Va.	*Vola Lawson	**1985, Sept.**
Alhambra, Cal.	*Julio Fuentes	**1992, Aug.**
Allentown, Pa.	Joseph S. Daddona, D	**1993, Nov.**
Amarillo, Tex.	*John Ward	**1983, June**
Ames, Ia.	*Steven L. Schainker	**1982, Oct.**
Anaheim, Cal.	*James D. Ruth	**1990, May**
Anchorage, Alas.	Tom Fink, R	**1994, Apr.**
Anderson, Ind.	J. Mark Lawler, D	**1995, Nov.**
Anderson, S.C.	*Richard Burnette	**1976, Sept.**
Ann Arbor, Mich.	Ingrid B. Sheldon, R	**1994, Nov.**
Appleton, Wis.	Richard De Broux, N-P	**1996, Apr.**
Arcadia, Cal.	*Donald R. Duckworth	**1992, Sept.**
Arlington, Mass.	*Donald R. Marquis	**1966, Sept.**
Arlington, Tex.	*George Campbell	**1991, Feb.**
Arlington Hts., Ill.	William Maki, N-P	**1993, Apr.**
Arvada, Col.	*Neal G. Berlin	**1986, Feb.**
Asheville, N.C.	*Douglas Bean	**1986, Apr.**
Athens, Ga.	Gwen O'Looney, D	**1994, Nov.**
Atlanta, Ga.	Maynard Jackson, D	**1993, Nov.**
Atlantic City, N.J.	Jim Whelan, N-P.	**1994, May**
Augusta, Ga.	Charles Devaney, N-P	**1993, Nov.**
Aurora, Col.	*John Pazour	**1990, May**
Aurora, Ill.	David L. Pierce, N-P.	**1997, Feb.**
Austin, Tex.	Bruce Todd, N-P.	**1994, May**
Bakersfield, Cal.	*Alan Tandy	**1992, Aug.**
Baldwin Park, Cal.	*Donald Penman	**1990, Jan.**
Baltimore, Md.	Kurt Schmoke, D	**1995, Nov.**
Baton Rouge, La.	Tom E. McHugh, D	**1996, Oct.**
Battle Creek, Mich.	*Rance L. Leaders	**1988, June**
Bayonne, N.J.	Richard Rutkowski, N-P	**1994, May**
Baytown, Tex.	*Bobby Rountree	**1989, Oct.**
Beaumont, Tex.	*Ray A. Riley	**1989, Feb.**

City	Name	Term
Belleville, Ill.	Roger C. Cook, I.	1997, Apr.
Belleville, N.J.	Marina Perna, N-P.	1994, May
Bellevue, Wash.	*Phillip Kushlan	1985, Mar.
Bellingham, Wash.	Tim Douglas, N-P	1995, Nov.
Bellflower, Cal.	*Linda C. Lowry	1993, Apr.
Berkeley, Cal.	*Weldon Rucker	1993, July
Bethlehem, Pa.	Kenneth Smith, R	1993, Nov.
Beverly Hills, Cal.	*Mark Scott	1990, Mar.
Billings, Mont.	*Mark S. Watson	1993, Jan.
Biloxi, Miss.	A.J. Holloway, R.	1997, June
Binghamton, N.Y.	Juanita M. Crabb, D.	1993, Nov.
Birmingham, Ala.	Richard Arrington Jr., D.	1995, Nov.
Bismarck, N.D.	Bill Sorensen, R	1994, June
Bloomfield, N.J.	James P. Norton, R	1995, Nov.
Bloomington, Ill.	Jesse Smart, R	1997, Apr.
Bloomington, Ind.	Tomilea Allison, D	1995, Sept.
Bloomington, Minn.	*Mark Bernhardson	1991, July
Boca Raton, Fla.	Emil Danciu, N-P	1995, Mar.
Boise, Ida.	H. Brent Coles, N-P	1993, Nov.
Bossier City, La	*Lorenz Walker	1989, July
Boston, Mass.	Thomas M. Menino, D.	1993, Nov.
Boulder, Col.	*Stephen Honey	1991, Apr.
Bridgeport, Conn.	Joseph Ganim, D.	1993, Nov.
Bristol, Conn.	William Stortz, D.	1993, Nov.
Brockton, Mass.	Winthrop Farwell Jr., D	1995, Nov.
Broken Arrow, Okla.	*John Vinson	1991, Aug.
Brooklyn Park, Minn.	*Craig R. Rapp	1989, Nov.
Brownsville, Tex.	*Steve Fitzgibbons	1987, Jan.
Bryan, Tex.	*Michael Conduff	1992, June
Buena Park, Cal.	*Kevin O'Rourke	1985, Nov.
Buffalo, N.Y.	James D. Griffin, D	1993, Nov.
Burbank, Cal.	*Bud Ovrom	1985, June
Burlington, Vt.	Peter C. Brownell, R	1995, Mar.
Calumet City, Ill.	Gerry P. Genova, I	1997, Apr.
Camarillo, Cal.	*J. William Little	1988, Nov.
Cambridge, Mass.	*Robert Healy	1981, July
Camden, N.J.	Aaron Thompson, D.	1993, Nov.
Canton, Oh.	Richard Watkins, R	1995, Nov.
Cape Coral, Fla.	Joseph Mazurkiewicz, R	1993, Nov.
Carlsbad, Cal.	*Ray Patchett	1987, Sept.
Carson, Cal.	*Jack Smith	1988, Dec.
Casper, Wyo.	*Thomas Forslund	1988, Aug.
Cedar Rapids, Ia.	Larry Serbousek, N-P.	1993, Nov.
Champaign, Ill.	*Steven C. Carter	1985, Feb.
Chandler, Ariz.	*John Pinch	1989, Jan.
Charleston, S.C.	Joseph P. Riley Jr., D.	1995, Nov.
Charleston, W. Va.	Kent S. Hall, R.	1995, Apr.
Charlotte, N.C.	Richard Vinroot, R.	1993, Nov.
Charlottesville, Va.	*Cole Hendrix	1970, Jan.
Chattanooga, Tenn.	Gene Roberts, R	1997, Apr.
Chesapeake, Va.	*James W. Rein	1987, Mar.
Chester, Pa.	Barbara Bohannan-Shepperd, D	1995, Nov.
Cheyenne, Wyo.	Leo Pando, N-P	1996, Nov.
Chicago, Ill.	Richard M. Daley, D.	1995, Apr.
Chicopee, Mass.	Joseph Chessey, D	1993, Nov.
Chino, Cal.	Eunice M. Ulloa, R.	1994, Nov.
Chula Vista, Cal.	Tim Nader, D.	1994, Nov.
Cicero, Ill.	Betty L. Maltese, R	1997, Apr.
Cincinnati, Oh.	*Gerald Newfarmer	1990, Sept.
Clarksville, Tenn.	Don Trotter, N-P.	1994, Nov.
Clearwater, Fla.	*Michael Wright	1991, Mar.
Cleveland, Oh.	Michael White, D	1993, Nov.
Cleveland Hgts., Oh.	*Robert Downey	1985, Jan.
Clifton, N.J.	James Anzaldi, R	1994, May
Col. Spgs., Col.	*Richard Zickefoose	1990, May
Columbia, Mo.	*Raymond A. Beck	1985, Aug.
Columbia, S.C.	*Miles Hadley	1989, Dec.
Columbus, Ga.	Frank Martin, D	1994, Nov.
Columbus, Oh.	Gregory Lashutka, R	1995, Nov.
Compton, Cal.	*Howard Caldwell	1989, Nov.
Concord, Cal.	*F.A. Stewart	1992, Nov.
Coon Rapids., Minn.	*Robert Svehla	1991, June
Coral Gables, Fla.	*H.C. Eads Jr.	1988, May
Corona, Cal.	*William Garrett	1989, Dec.
Corpus Christi, Tex.	*Juan Garza	1988, Apr.
Costa Mesa, Cal.	*Allan L. Roeder	1985, Oct.
Council Bluffs, Ia.	Tom Hanafan, N-P	1993, Nov.
Covington, Ky.	Denny Bowman, D	1995, Nov.
Cranston, R.I.	Michael Traficante, R	1994, Nov.
Crystal, Minn.	*John Irving	1963, Jan.
Cuyahoga Falls, Oh.	Don L. Robart, R	1993, Nov.
Dallas, Tex.	*Jan Hart	1990, Apr.
Daly City, Cal.	*David R. Rowe	1969, Sept.
Danbury, Conn.	Gene Eriquez, D	1993, Nov.
Danville, Va.	*A. Ray Griffin Jr.	1992, Mar.
Davenport, Ia.	Patrick J. Gibbs, R	1993, Nov.
Davis, Cal.	*John Meyer	1990, Oct.
Dayton, Oh.	*Richard B. Helwig	1984, June
Daytona Bch., Fla.	*Howard D. Tipton	1978, Oct.
Dearborn , Mich.	Michael Guido, N-P	1993, Nov.
Dearborn Hts., Mich.	Lyle Van Houton, R	1993, Nov.
Decatur, Ill.	*James Bacon Jr.	1988, Oct.
Delray Beach, Fla.	Thomas E. Lynch, N-P	1994, Mar.
Denton, Tex.	*Larry Harrell	1986, Feb.
Denver, Col.	Wellington Webb, N-P	1995, May
Des Moines, Ia.	John Dorrian, D	1993, Nov.
Des Plaines, Ill.	Ted Sherwood, N-P	1997, Apr.
Detroit, Mich.	Coleman A. Young, N-P	1993, Nov.
Dothan, Ala.	Alfred Saliba, N-P	1997, July
Downey, Cal.	*Gerald Caton	1989, Oct.
Dubuque, Ia.	*M. Van Milligen	1993, Jan.
Duluth, Minn.	Gary L. Doty, N-P	1995, Nov.
Durham, N.C.	*Orville Powell Jr.	1983, Mar.
E. Hartford, Conn.	Susan Kniep, R	1993, Nov.
E. Lansing, Mich.	Liz Schweitzer, I	1993, Nov.
E. Orange, N.J.	Cardell Cooper, D.	1993, Nov.
Eau Claire, Wis.	*Eric Anderson	1984, Jan.
Edison, N.J.	Thomas Paterniti, D	1993, Nov.
Edmond, Okla.	*C. Max Speegle	1986, Sept.
El Cajon, Cal.	Robert T. Acker	1982, July
El Monte, Cal.	Patricia Wallach, D	1994, Apr.
El Paso, Tex.	*Kenneth Beasley	1980, May
Elgin, Ill.	*Larry L. Rice	1989, Oct.
Elizabeth, N.J.	J.C. Bollwage, D.	1996, Nov.
Elkhart, Ind.	James Perron, D	1995, Nov.
Elyria, Oh.	Michael Keys, D	1995, Nov.
Enfield, Conn.	*A. Louis Hayward	1990, July
Enid, Okla.	*Jim Ferree	1990, July
Erie, Pa.	Joyce Savocchio, D	1993, Nov.
Escondido, Cal.	*Douglas Clark	1989, June
Euclid, Oh.	David Lynch, R	1995, Nov.
Eugene, Ore.	*Michael Gleason	1981, Jan.
Evanston, Ill.	*Eric Anderson	1991, June
Evansville, Ind.	Frank McDonald, D	1995, Nov.
Everett, Wash.	Pete Kinch, N-P	1993, Nov.
Fairfield, Cal.	*Charles Long	1988, Sept.
Fairfield, Conn.	Jacquelyn Durrell, R	1993, Nov.
Fall River, Mass.	John Mitchell, D	1993, Nov.
Fargo, N.D.	Jon Lindgren, D	1994, Apr.
Farmington Hills, Mich.	*William M. Costick	1981, Jan.
Fayetteville, N.C.	*John P. Smith	1981, Jan.
Fitchburg, Mass.	Jeffrey Bean, D	1993, Nov.
Flagstaff, Ariz.	*David Wilcox	1992, July
Flint, Mich.	Woodrow Stanley, D	1995, Nov.
Florissant, Mo.	James J. Eagan, N-P	1995, Apr.
Fontana, Cal.	Gary Boyles, R	1994, Nov.
Ft. Collins, Col.	*Steven Burkett	1986, Apr.
Ft. Lauderdale, Fla.	*George Hanbury 2d	1990, June
Ft. Smith, Ark.	Ray Baker, N-P	1994, Oct.
Ft. Wayne, Ind.	Paul Helmke, R	1995, Nov.
Ft. Worth, Tex.	Kay Granger, N-P	1995, May
Fountain Valley, Cal.	*Raymond H. Kromer	1991, Mar.
Fremont, Cal.	*Charles Kent McClain	1981, May
Fresno, Cal.	*Michael Bierman	1990, Nov.
Fullerton, Cal.	*William C. Winter	1979, Oct.
Gadsden, Ala.	Steve Means, N-P	1994, Aug.
Gainesville, Fla.	James F. Painter, R	1994, Mar.
Galveston, Tex.	*Douglas W. Matthews	1985, Mar.
Gardena, Cal.	*Kenneth Landau	1985, Mar.
Garden Grove, Cal.	*George Tindall	1988, May
Garland, Tex.	*Ron Holifield	1992, Feb.
Gary, Ind.	Thomas Barnes, D	1995, Nov.
Gastonia, N.C.	*Gary Hicks	1973, Dec.
Glendale, Ariz.	*Martin Vanacour	1985, Mar.
Glendale, Cal.	*David Ramsay	1988, May
Grand Forks, N.D.	Michael Polovitz, D	1996, Apr.
Grand Prairie, Tex.	*Gary Gwyn	1991, July
Grand Rapids, Mich.	*Kurt Kimball	1987, Apr.
Greeley, Col.	William Morton, N-P	1993, Nov.
Green Bay, Wis.	Samuel Halloin, N-P	1995, Apr.
Greenville, S.C.	*Aubrey Watts Jr.	1991, Dec.
Greenwich, Conn.	John Margenot, R, first selectman	1993, Nov.
Groton, Conn.	*Ronald P. LeBlanc	1993, Nov.
Gulfport, Miss.	Ken Combs, R	1997, June
Hamden, Conn.	Lillian Clayman, D	1993, Nov.
Hamilton, Oh.	*Hal Shepherd	1989, Apr.
Hammond, Ind.	Duane W. Dadeiow, R	1995, Nov.
Hampton, Va.	*Robert O'Neill Jr.	1984, Oct.
Harrisburg, Pa.	Stephen Reed, D	1993, Nov.
Hartford, Conn.	*Howard Stanback	1992, May
Haverhill, Mass.	Theodore Pelosi, R	1993, Nov.
Hawthorne, Cal.	*James Mitsch	1990, Dec.
Hayward, Cal.	*Jesús Armas	1993, Feb.

City	Name	Term
Henderson, Nev.	Robert A. Groesbeck, N-P	1997, June
Hesperia, Cal.	*D.J. Collins	1992, July
Hialeah, Fla.	Julio Martinez, R	1993, Nov.
High Point, N.C.	Rebecca R. Smothers, N-P	1995, Nov.
Hollywood, Fla.	*Robert S. Noe Jr.	1991, Nov.
Holyoke, Mass.	William Hamilton, R	1993, Nov.
Honolulu, Ha.	Frank Fasi, R	1996, Nov.
Houston, Tex.	Bob Lanier, N-P	1993, Nov.
Huntington, W. Va.	Jean Dean, R	1997, June
Huntington Beach, Cal.	*Michael Ubervaga	1990, Feb.
Huntington Park, Cal.	Raul Perez, R	1994, Apr.
Huntsville, Ala.	Steve Hettinger, N-P	1996, Aug.
Idaho Falls, Ida.	Thomas Campbell, N-P	1993, Nov.
Independence, Mo.	*L.C. Kaufman	1990, Aug.
Indianapolis, Ind.	Steve Goldsmith, R	1995, Nov.
Inglewood, Cal.	*Paul Eckles	1975, Nov.
Iowa City, Ia.	*Stephen Atkins	1986, July
Irving, Tex.	*Jack Huffman	1974, Jan.
Irvington, N.J.	Michael Steele, D	1994, May
Jackson, Miss.	Kane Ditto, D.	1997, June
Jacksonville, Fla.	Ed Austin, D	1995, Apr.
Janesville, Wis.	*Steven Sheiffer	1987, May
Jersey City, N.J.	Bret Schundler, R	1997, May
Johnson City, Tenn.	*John G. Campbell	1984, June
Joliet, Ill.	*John M. Mezera	1987, Jan.
Kalamazoo, Mich.	*Marc A. Ott	1993, Mar.
Kansas City, Kan.	*David Isabell	1985, Sept.
Kansas City, Mo.	Emanuel Cleaver, D.	1995, Mar.
Kenner, La.	*Charlotte Burnell	1988, Jan.
Kenosha, Wis.	John Antaramian, D.	1996, Apr.
Kettering, Oh.	Richard Hartmann, R	1993, Nov.
Killeen, Tex.	*Daniel Hobbs	1990, Jan.
Knoxville, Tenn.	Victor Ashe, R	1995, Nov.
Kokomo, Ind.	Robert Sargent, D.	1995, May
LaCrosse, Wis.	Patrick Zielke, N-P	1997, Apr.
La Habra, Cal.	*Lee Risner	1970, Dec.
La Mesa, Cal.	*David Wear	1990, Apr.
La Mirada, Cal.	*Gary K. Sloan	1981, Apr.
Lafayette, Ind.	James Riehle, D.	1995, Nov.
Lafayette, La.	Kenneth Bowen, D	1996, Mar.
Lake Charles, La.	Willie L. Mount, D	1997, Apr.
Lakeland, Fla.	*E.S. Strickland	1986, Feb.
Lakewood, Cal.	*Howard L. Chambers	1976, June
Lakewood, Col.	*Michael J. Rock	1992, Dec.
Lakewood, Oh.	David Harbarger, R	1995, Nov.
Lancaster, Pa.	Janice Stork, D	1993, Nov.
Lansing, Mich.	James A. Crawford, N-P	1993, Nov.
Laredo, Tex.	*Marvin Townsend	1982, June
Largo, Fla.	*Stephen Bonczek	1988, July
Las Cruces, N.M.	Ruben A. Smith, D.	1995, Nov.
Las Vegas, Nev.	Jan Laverty Jones, D	1994, May
Lauderhill, Fla.	Ilene Lieberman, D	1996, Mar.
Lawrence, Kan.	*Mike Wildgen	1990, Apr.
Lawrence, Mass.	Kevin Sullivan, N-P	1993, Nov.
Lawton, Okla.	John T. Marley, D	1995, Mar.
Lexington, Ky.	Scotty Baesler, N-P	1993, Nov.
Lima, Oh.	David Berger, N-P	1993, Nov.
Lincoln, Neb.	Mike Johanns, R.	1995, May
Little Rock, Ark.	*Thomas Dalton	1986, June
Livermore, Cal.	*Leland Horner	1979, Aug.
Livonia, Mich.	Robert Bennett, N-P	1995, Nov.
Lodi, Cal.	*Thomas A. Peterson	1985, Apr.
Long Beach, Cal.	*James Hankla	1987, Mar.
Longmont,Col.	*Geoff Dolan	1987, Jan.
Longview, Tex.	*James Baugh	1989, Oct.
Lorain, Oh.	Alex Olejko, D	1995, Nov.
Los Angeles, Cal.	Richard Riordan, N-P	1997, June
Louisville, Ky.	Jerry Abramson, D	1993, Nov.
Lowell, Mass.	*James Campbell	1987, Jan.
Lubbock, Tex.	*Bob Cass	1992, Sept.
Lynchburg, Va.	*Charles Church	1991, Oct.
Lynn, Mass.	Patrick McManus, D.	1993, Nov.
Lynwood, Cal.	*Faustin Gonzales	1993, June
Macon, Ga.	Tommy Olmstead, D	1995, Nov.
Madison, Wis.	Paul Soglin, R	1995, Apr.
Malden, Mass.	Edwin C. Lucey, D.	1993, Nov.
Manchester, Conn.	*Richard Sartor	1989, June
Manchester, N.H.	Ray Wieczorek, R	1993, Nov.
Mansfield, Oh.	Lydia J. Reid, D	1995, Nov.
Marietta, Ga.	Joe Mack Wilson, D.	1993, Nov.
McAllen, Tex.	Othal Brand, R.	1997, Apr.
Medford, Mass.	Michael McGlynn, D.	1993, Nov.
Medford, Ore.	*Harold Anderson	1987, Sept.
Melbourne, Fla.	*Samuel Halter	1978, July
Memphis, Tenn.	W.W. Herenton, D.	1996, Aug.
Mentor, Oh.	*Julian Suso	1990, Apr.
Merced, Cal.	*James Marshall	1992, Apr.
Meriden, Conn.	*Michael Aldi	1988, Mar.
Meridian, Miss.	John Robert Smith, R	1997, June
Mesa, Ariz.	*C.K. Luster	1979, June
Mesquite, Tex.	*James Prugel	1987, Dec.
Miami, Fla.	Xavier Suarez, N-P	1993, Nov.
Miami Beach, Fla.	*Roger Carlton	1992, Apr.
Middletown, Oh.	*Ronald Olson	1992, Nov.
Midland, Tex.	J.D. Faircloth, R.	1994, May
Midwest City, Okla.	*Charles Johnson	1984, Nov.
Milford, Conn.	Frederick Lisman, R.	1993, Nov.
Milpitas, Cal.	*Lawrence M. Moore	1993, Feb.
Milwaukee, Wis.	John Norquist, D.	1996, Apr.
Minneapolis, Minn.	Donald Fraser, D	1993, Nov.
Minnetonka, Minn.	*James F. Miller	1980, Jan.
Mobile, Ala.	Michael Dow, R, I	1997, Aug.
Modesto, Cal.	*J. Edward Tewes	1991, Mar.
Monroe, La.	Robert Powell, D	1996, Mar.
Montclair, N.J.	*Bertrand Kendall	1980, Sept.
Montebello, Cal.	William M. Molinari, R	1993, Nov.
Monterey Park, Cal.	*Mark Lewis	1988, July
Montgomery, Ala.	Emory Folmar, R	1995, Nov.
Mt. Prospect, Ill.	*Michael Janonis	1992, July
Mt. Vernon, N.Y.	Roland Blackwood, D.	1995, Nov.
Mountain View, Cal.	*Bruce Liedstrand	1976, June
Muncie, Ind.	David M. Dominick, R	1995, Nov.
Muskogee, Okla.	*Walter Beckham	1984, Feb.
Napa, Cal.	Ed Solomon, R.	1996, June
Naperville, Ill.	Samuel MacCrane, N-P	1995, Apr.
Nashua, N.H.	Rob Wagner, D	1995, Nov.
Nashville, Tenn.	Philip Bredesen, D.	1995, Aug.
National City, Cal.	George H. Waters, R	1994, Nov.
New Bedford, Mass.	Rosemary Tierney, D	1993, Nov.
New Britain, Conn.	Donald DeFronzo, D	1993, Nov.
New Haven, Conn.	John Daniels, D	1993, Nov.
New London, Conn.	*C.F. Driscoll	1969, May
New Orleans, La.	Sidney Barthelemy, D.	1994, Mar.
New Rochelle, N.Y.	*C. Samuel Kissinger	1975, Apr.
New York, N.Y.	David Dinkins, D.	1993, Nov.
Newark, N.J.	Sharpe James, D	1994, May
Newport, R.I.	*Francis Edwards	1987, Jan.
Newport Beach, Cal.	*Kevin Murphy	1992, Mar.
Newport News, Va.	*Ed Maroney	1987, Jan.
Newton, Mass.	Theodore Mann, R	1993, Nov.
Niagara Falls, N.Y.	Jacob A. Palillo, R.	1995, Nov.
Norfolk, Va.	*James B. Oliver Jr.	1987, Jan.
Norman, Okla.	Bill Nations, N-P	1995, Mar.
North Charleston, S.C.	Bobby Kinard, R	1995, May
No. Little Rock, Ark.	Patrick Hayes, D	1996, Nov.
Norwalk, Cal.	*Richard Powers	1988, July
Norwalk, Conn.	Frank Esposito, R	1993, Nov.
Novato, Cal.	*Rod Wood	1992, July
Oak Park, Ill.	*J.N. Nielsen	1986, July
Oak Ridge, Tenn.	*Jeffrey J. Broughton	1986, Sept.
Oakland, Cal.	Elihu M. Harris, N-P	1994, June
Oceanside, Cal.	*James Turner	1990, Aug.
Odessa, Tex.	*Jerry McGuire	1992, Mar.
Ogden, Ut.	Glenn Mecham, N-P	1995, Nov.
Oklahoma City, Okla.	*Donald D. Brown	1991, Feb.
Omaha, Neb.	P.J. Morgan, R.	1997, May
Ontario, Cal.	*Roger Hughbanks, N-P	1975, July
Orange, Cal.	*Ron Thompson,	1989, Apr.
Orlando, Fla.	Glenda E. Hood, N-P	1996, Sept.
Oshkosh, Wis.	*William Frueh	1976, Aug.
Overland Park, Kan.	*Donald Pipes	1977, June
Owensboro, Ky.	*Max Rhoads	1959, Sept.
Oxnard, Cal.	*Vernon Hazen	1990, Aug.
Palm Springs, Cal.	*Dallas Flicek	1990, Aug.
Palo Alto, Cal.	*William Zaner	1979, Sept.
Parma, Oh.	Michael Ries, D	1995, Nov.
Pasadena, Cal.	*Philip Hawkey	1990, June
Pasadena, Tex.	Johnny Isbell, N-P	1997, May
Passaic, N.J.	Margie Semler, N-P	1997, June
Paterson, N.J.	William Pascrell, D	1994, May
Pawtucket, R.I.	Robert Metivier, D.	1993, Nov.
Peabody, Mass.	Peter Torigian, D	1993, Nov.
Pembroke Pines, Fla.	*Charles Dodge	1989, Aug.
Pensacola, Fla.	*Rodney Kendig	1986, June
Peoria, Ill.	*Thomas Mikulecky	1987, July
Philadelphia, Pa.	Edward Rendell, D	1995, Nov.
Phoenix, Ariz.	*Frank Fairbanks	1990, Apr.
Pico Rivera, Cal.	*Dennis Courtemarche	1984, Nov.
Pine Bluff, Ark	Jerry Taylor, I	1996, Nov.
Pittsburgh, Pa.	Sophie Masloff, D	1993, Nov.
Pittsfield, Mass.	Edward Reilly, N-P	1993, Nov.
Plainfield, N.J.	*Jewel Thompson-Chin	1990, Sept.
Plano, Tex.	*Thomas Muehlenbeck	1987, Dec.

City	Name	Term
Plantation, Fla.	Frank Veletri, D	1995, Mar.
Plymouth, Mass.	*Dwight Johnson	1993, Feb.
Pocatello, Ida.	Peter Angstadt, N-P	1993, Nov.
Pomona, Cal.	*Lloyd Wood	1992, Aug.
Pompano Beach, Fla.	*Roy Stype	1989, Oct.
Pontiac, Mich.	Wallace Holland, N-P	1993, Nov.
Port Arthur, Tex.	*Mary Ellen Summerlin, D	1995, May
Portland, Me.	*Robert Ganley	1987, Sept.
Portland, Ore.	Vera Katz, D	1996, Nov.
Portsmouth, Va.	*V. Wayne Orton	1990, June
Poughkeepsie, N.Y.	*William J. Theysohn	1982, Mar.
Providence, R.I.	Vincent Cianci Jr., R, I	1993, Nov.
Provo, Ut.	Joseph Jenkins, R	1993, Nov.
Pueblo, Col.	*Lewis A. Quigley	1987, Jan.
Quincy, Ill.	Charles Wischolz, D	1997, Apr.
Quincy, Mass.	James Sheets, D	1993, Nov.
Racine, Wis.	N. Owen Davies, N-P	1995, Apr.
Raleigh, N.C.	*Dempsey Benton	1983, Dec.
Rapid City, S.D.	Edward McLaughlin, N-P	1995, Apr.
Reading, Pa.	Warren Haggerty Jr., D	1995, Nov.
Redding, Cal.	*Robert Christofferson	1987, Jan.
Redlands, Cal.	*James Wheaton	1991, Mar.
Redondo Beach, Cal.	*William Kirchhoff	1991, Feb.
Redwood City, Cal.	*James M. Smith	1982, Feb.
Reno, Nev.	*Clay Holstine	1991, Feb.
Rialto, Cal.	*Gerald Johnson	1988, July
Richardson, Tex.	*Bob Hughey	1974, Jan.
Richmond, Cal.	George Livingstone, D	1993, Nov.
Richmond, Va.	*Robert C. Bobb	1986, July
Riverside, Cal.	Terry Frizzel, R	1993, Nov.
Roanoke, Va.	David Bowers, D	1996, May
Rochester, Minn.	*Steven Kvenvold	1979, June
Rochester, N.Y.	Thomas Ryan Jr., D	1993, Nov.
Rochester Hills, Mich.	Billie Ireland, R	1995, Nov.
Rock Hill, S.C.	*J. Russell Allen	1993, July
Rock Island, Ill.	*John Phillips	1986, Nov.
Rockford, Ill.	Charles Box, D	1997, Apr.
Rockville, Md.	Douglas M. Duncan, D	1993, Nov.
Rome, N.Y.	Joseph Griffo, R	1995, Nov.
Rosemead, Cal.	*Frank G. Tripepi	1974, Oct.
Roseville, Mich.	Jeanne Riesterer, N-P	1993, Nov.
Roswell, N.M.	*John Capps	1992, July
Royal Oak, Mich.	*William Baldridge	1975, Sept.
Sacramento, Cal.	*Walter Slipe	1976, Mar.
Saginaw, Mich.	*J. Marvin Baldwin	1991, Apr.
St. Charles, Mo.	Grace M. Nichols, N-P	1995, Apr.
St. Clair Shores, Mich.	*Mark Wollenweber	1990, Jan.
St. Cloud, Minn.	Charles Winkleman, N-P	1993, Nov.
St. Joseph, Mo.	Glenda Kelly, N-P	1994, Mar.
St. Louis, Mo.	Freeman R. Bosley Jr., D	1997, Mar.
St. Louis Park, Minn.	*Charles Meyer	1993, Apr.
St. Paul, Minn.	James Scheibel, N-P	1993, Nov.
St. Petersburg, Fla.	*Norman Hickey	1992, May
Salem, Ore.	*Gary Eide	1988, Jan.
Salinas, Cal.	*David R. Mora	1990, Sept.
Salt Lake City, Ut.	Deedee Corradini, D	1995, Nov.
San Angelo, Tex.	*Alex Briseno	1990, Apr.
San Antonio, Tex.	Nelson Wolff, N-P	1995, Apr.
San Bernardino, Cal.	Tom Minor, R	1997, Mar.
San Diego, Cal.	Susan Golding, R	1996, Nov.
San Francisco, Cal.	Frank Jordan, D	1995, Nov.
San Jose, Cal.	*Leslie White	1989, May
San Leandro, Cal.	*Richard H. Randall	1986, July
San Mateo, Cal.	*Arne Croce	1990, Mar.
San Rafael, Cal.	*Pamela Nicolai	1985, Dec.
Sandy, Ut.	*Byron D. Jorgenson	1986, May
Santa Ana, Cal.	*David Ream	1986, July
Santa Barbara, Cal.	*Sandra Lizarraga	1993, Aug.
Santa Clara, Cal.	*Jennifer Sparacino	1987, Mar.
Santa Cruz, Cal.	*Richard Wilson	1981, June
Santa Fe, N.M.	*David A. Sena	1993, Aug.
Santa Maria, Cal.	George S. Hobbs, N-P	1994, Nov.
Santa Monica, Cal.	*John Jalili	1984, Dec.
Santa Rosa, Cal.	*Kenneth Blackman	1970, July
Sarasota, Fla.	*David Sollenberger	1987, Mar.
Savannah, Ga.	*Arthur A. Mendonsa	1966, Jan.
Schaumburg, Ill.	*George Longmeyer	1986, Oct.
Schenectady, N.Y.	Frank Duci, R	1995, Nov.
Scottsdale, Ariz.	Herbert Drinkwater, R	1996, Apr.
Scranton, Pa.	James Connors, R	1993, Nov.
Seattle, Wash.	Norman Rice, D	1993, Nov.
Sheboygan, Wis.	Richard Schneider, N-P	1997, Apr.
Shreveport, La.	Hazel Beard, R	1994, Nov.
Simi Valley, Cal.	*M.L. Koester	1979, Sept.
Sioux City, Ia.	James R. Wharton, R	1993, Nov.
Sioux Falls, S.D.	Jack White, R	1996, June
Skokie, Ill.	*Albert Rigoni	1987, Jan.
Somerville, Mass.	Michael Capuano, D	1993, Nov.
South Bend, Ind.	Joseph Kernan, D	1995, Nov.
South Gate, Cal.	Mary Ann Buckles, R	1994, Apr.
Southfield, Mich.	Donald F. Fracassi, R	1993, Nov.
Sparks, Nev.	*Patricia Thompson	1983, Sept.
Spartanburg, S.C.	*Wayne Bowers	1984, Sept.
Spokane, Wash.	*Roger Crum	1992, Aug.
Springfield, Ill.	Ossie Langfelder, D	1995, Apr.
Springfield, Mass	Robert Markel, D	1993, Nov.
Springfield, Mo.	*Thomas Finnie	1990, Apr.
Springfield, Oh.	*Matthew Kridler	1988, Oct.
Stamford, Conn.	Stanley Esposito, R	1993, Nov.
Sterling Hts., Mich.	*Steve Duchane	1987, Dec.
Stockton, Cal.	*Dwane Milnes	1991, Oct.
Stratford, Conn.	*Mark S. Barnhart	1992, July
Sunnyvale, Cal.	*Thomas Lewcock	1980, Apr.
Suffolk, Va.	*Richard Hedrick	1991, July
Sunrise, Fla.	*Patrick Salerno	1990, Dec.
Syracuse, N.Y.	Thomas G. Young, D	1993, Nov.
Tacoma, Wash.	*Ray Corpuz Jr.	1990, Jan.
Tallahassee, Fla.	*Daniel A. Kleman	1974, Aug.
Tampa, Fla.	Sandra Freedman, N-P	1995, Mar.
Taunton, Mass.	Robert Nunes, D	1993, Nov.
Taylor, Mich.	Cameron Priebe, D	1993, Nov.
Tempe, Ariz.	Harry E. Mitchell, D	1994, Mar.
Temple, Tex.	*David Taylor	1991, Dec.
Terre Haute, Ind.	P. Pete Chalos, D	1995, Nov.
Thornton, Col.	*Jack Ethredge	1985, Jan.
Thousand Oaks, Cal.	*Grant Brimhall	1978, Jan.
Titusville, Fla.	*Norman Hickey	1974, June
Toledo, Oh.	*Thomas Hoover	1990, Sept.
Topeka, Kan.	Butch Felker, R	1997, Apr.
Torrance, Cal.	*Leroy J. Jackson	1983, Jan.
Trenton, N.J.	Douglas Palmer, N-P	1994, May
Troy, Mich.	*Frank Gerstenecker	1970, Feb
Troy, N.Y.	*Steven Dworsky	1986, July
Tucson, Ariz.	George Miller, D	1995, Nov.
Tulsa, Okla.	M. Susan Savage, D	1994, Mar.
Tuscaloosa, Ala.	Alvin DuPont, D	1993, Oct.
Tyler, Tex.	*Ernest R. Clark	1991, Oct.
Union City, N.J.	Robert Menendez, D	1994, May
Upland, Cal.	*Ray Silver	1988, Dec.
Utica, N.Y.	Louis La Polla, R	1995, Nov.
Vacaville, Cal.	*John P. Thompson	1984, Oct.
Vallejo, Cal.	*Edward Wohlenberg	1989, Apr.
Vancouver, Wash.	*John Fischbach	1990, Aug.
Ventura, Cal.	*John Baker	1986, Nov.
Vineland, N.J.	Joseph Romano, I	1996, May
Virginia Beach, Va.	*James Spore	1991, Nov.
Visalia, Cal.	*Raymond W. Forsyth	1992, Feb.
Vista, Cal.	Gloria McClellan, R	1994, Nov.
Waco, Tex.	*John Harrison	1977, Sept.
Walnut Creek, Cal.	*Donald Blubaugh	1988, Apr.
Waltham, Mass.	William Stanley, D	1995, Nov.
Warren, Mich.	Ronald Bonkowski, N-P	1995, Nov.
Warren, Oh.	Daniel Sferra, D	1995, Nov.
Warwick, R.I.	Lincoln D. Chafee, R	1994, Nov.
Washington, D.C.	Sharon Dixon, D	1994, Nov.
Waterbury, Conn.	Edward D. Bergin, D	1993, Nov.
Waterloo, Ia.	Albert Manning Jr., R	1993, Nov.
Waukegan, Ill.	William F. Durkin, D	1997, Apr.
Waukesha, Wis.	Paul Vrakas, N-P	1994, Apr.
Wauwatosa, Wis.	Maricolette Walsh, N-P	1994, Apr.
W. Allis, Wis.	Joyce Ann Radtke, N-P	1996, Apr.
W. Covina, Cal.	*Herman Fast	1976, Aug.
W. Hartford, Conn.	Sandy Klebanoff, D	1993, Nov.
W. Haven, Conn.	H. Richard Borer, D	1993, Nov.
W. Palm Beach, Fla.	Nancy M. Graham, N-P	1995, Mar.
Westland, Mich.	Robert Thomas, D	1993, Nov.
Westminster, Cal.	*Jerry Kenny	1989, Jan.
Westminster, Col.	Nancy Heil, N-P	1993, Nov.
Wheaton, Ill.	C. James Carr, N-P	1995, Apr.
White Plains, N.Y.	Alfred Del Vecchio, R	1993, Nov.
Whittier, Cal.	*Thomas Mauk	1980, Oct.
Wichita, Kan.	*Chris Cherches	1985, Oct.
Wichita Falls, Tex.	*James Berzina	1983, June
Wilkes-Barre, Pa.	Lee Namey, D	1995, May
Wilmington, Del.	Jim Sills, D	1996, Nov.
Wilmington, N.C.	Mary M. Gornto	1993, July
Winston-Salem, N.C.	*Bryce A. Stuart	1980, Nov.
Woodbridge, N.J.	James McGreevey, D	1995, Nov.
Woonsocket, R.I.	Francis Lanctot, N-P	1993, Nov.
Worcester, Mass.	*William Mulford	1985, Nov.
Wyandotte, Mich.	James R. DeSana, D	1995, Apr.
Wyoming, Mich.	*Donald Mason	1991, Aug.
Yakima, Wash.	Pat Berndt, N-P	1993, Nov.
Yonkers, N.Y.	Terence Zaleski, D	1995, Nov.
York, Pa.	William Althaus, R	1993, Nov.
Youngstown, Oh.	Patrick Ungaro, D	1993, Nov.
Yuma, Ariz.	Robert Tippert, R	1993, Dec.

STATES AND OTHER AREAS OF THE U.S.

Sources: Population: Commerce Dept., Bureau of the Census (July, 1992 est., inc. armed forces personnel in each state but excluding such personnel stationed overseas); area: Bureau of the Census, Geography Division; forested land: Agriculture Dept., Forest Service; lumber production: Bureau of the Census, Industry Division; mineral production: Interior Dept., Bureau of Mines; commercial fishing: Commerce Dept., Natl. Marine Fisheries Service; value of construction: McGraw-Hill Information Systems Co., F.W. Dodge Division; per capita income: Commerce Dept., Bureau of Economic Analysis; unemployment: Labor Dept., Bureau of Labor Statistics; finance: Federal Deposit Insurance Corp.; federal employees: Labor Dept., Office of Personnel Management; energy: Energy Dept., Energy Information Administration; education: Education Dept., National Education Assn. Other information from sources in individual states, usually Commerce Dept.

Alabama

Heart of Dixie, Camellia State

People. Population (1992): 4,135,543; **rank:** 22. **Pop. density:** 81.5 per sq. mi. **Racial distrib.** (1990): 73.6% White; 25.3% Black; 0.6% Hispanic. **Net change** (1990-92): 2.4%.

Geography. Total area: 51,705 sq. mi.; **rank:** 29. **Land area:** 50,750 sq. mi. **Acres forested land:** 21,725,000. **Location:** East South Central state extending N-S from Tenn. to the Gulf of Mexico; east of the Mississippi River. **Climate:** long, hot summers; mild winters; generally abundant rainfall. **Topography:** coastal plains inc. Prairie Black Belt give way to hills, broken terrain; highest elevation, 2,407 ft. **Capital:** Montgomery.

Economy. Principal industries: pulp and paper, chemicals, electronics, apparel, textiles, primary metals, lumber and wood prods., food processing, fabricated metals, automotive tires, oil and gas exploration. **Principal manufactured goods** (1991-1992): electronics, cast iron and plastic pipe, fabricated steel prods., ships, paper products, chemicals, steel, mobile homes, fabrics, poultry processing, soft drinks, furniture, tires. **Agriculture: Chief crops** (1991-92): peanuts, cotton, soybeans, cottonseed, catfish, hay, corn, wheat, potatoes, pecans, peaches, sweet potatoes. **Livestock** (1990): 1.8 mln. cattle; 400,000 hogs/pigs; 14.8 mln. poultry, 2.7 mln. foodsize catfish. **Timber/lumber** (1991): pine, hardwoods; 1.94 bln. bd. ft. **Nonfuel Minerals** (1992): $603.7 mln., mostly stone, cement, clays, lime, sand & gravel. **Commercial fishing** (1992): $35.6 mln. **Chief ports:** Mobile. **Value of construction** (1992): $3.2 bln. **Employment distribution** (1991): 20% mfg.; 35% trade; 16% serv. **Per capita income** (1992): $16,220. **Unemployment** (1992): 7.3%. **Tourism** (1991): tourists spent $3.4 bln. **Sales Tax** (1991): 4%.

Finance. FDIC-insured commercial banks & trust companies (1992): 219. **Deposits:** $33.6 bln. **Savings institutions** (1992): 25. **Assets:** $4.9 bln.

Federal government. No. federal civilian employees (Mar. 1992): 46,134. **Avg. salary:** $34,556. **Notable federal facilities:** George C. Marshall NASA Space Center, Huntsville; Gunter & Maxwell AFB, Montgomery; Ft. Rucker, Ozark; Ft. McClellan, Anniston; Natl. Fertilizer Development Center, Muscle Shoals; Navy Station & U.S. Corps of Engineers, Mobile; Redstone Arsenal, Huntsville.

Energy. Electricity production (1992, MWh, by source): Hydroelectric: 12.2 mln. Mineral: 44.7 mln. Nuclear: 19.7 mln.

Education. Student-teacher ratio (1991): 17.8. **Avg. salary, public school teachers** (1992-93): $27,490.

State data. Motto: We dare defend our rights. **Flower:** Camellia. **Bird:** Yellowhammer. **Tree:** Southern pine. **Song:** Alabama. **Entered union** Dec. 14, 1819; rank, 22d. **State fair** at: Birmingham; early Oct.

History. First Europeans were Spanish explorers in the early 1500s. The French made the first permanent settlement, on Mobile Bay, 1701-02; later, English settled in the northern areas. France ceded the entire region to England at the end of the French and Indian War, 1763, but Spanish Florida claimed the Mobile Bay area until U. S. troops took it, 1813. Gen. Andrew Jackson broke the power of the Creek Indians, 1814, and they were removed to Oklahoma. The Confederate States were organized Feb. 4, 1861, at Montgomery, the first capital.

Tourist attractions. Jefferson Davis' "first White House" of the Confederacy; Montgomery's Civil Rights Memorial; Ivy Green, Helen Keller's birthplace, Tuscumbia; statue of Vulcan, Birmingham; George Washington Carver Museum, Tuskegee Univ.; W.C. Handy Home & Museum, Florence; Alabama Space and Rocket Center, Huntsville; Alabama Shakespeare Festival, Montgomery; Moundville State Monument, Moundville; Pike Pioneer Museum, Troy; USS Alabama Memorial Park, Mobile; 28 hunting areas, 24 public lakes, 82 campgrounds, 21 state parks.

At Russell Cave National Monument, near Bridgeport: a detailed record of occupancy by humans from about 10,000 BC to 1650 AD.

Famous Alabamians include Hank Aaron, Tallulah Bankhead, Hugo L. Black, Paul "Bear" Bryant, George Washington Carver, Nat King Cole, William C. Handy, Bo Jackson, Helen Keller, Harper Lee, Joe Louis, Willie Mays, John Hunt Morgan, Jesse Owens, George Wallace, Booker T. Washington, Hank Williams.

Alabama Business Council (State Chamber of Commerce). 468 S. Perry St., P.O. Box 76, Montgomery, AL 36195.

Toll-free travel information. 1-800-392-8096; 1-800-ALABAMA out of state.

Alaska

The Last Frontier (unofficial)

People. Population (1992): 586,872; **rank:** 48. **Racial distrib.** (1990): 75.5% White; 4.1% Black; 3.2% Hispanic; 15.6% Amer. Ind., Eskimo or Aleut; 3.6% Asian or Pacific Is. **Pop. density:** 1.03 per sq. mi. **Net change** (1990-92): 6.7%.

Geography. Total area: 591,000 sq. mi.; **rank:** 1. **Land area:** 570,373 sq. mi. **Acres forested land:** 129,045,000. **Location:** NW corner of North America, bordered on east by Canada. **Climate:** SE, SW, and central regions, moist and mild; far north extremely dry. Extended summer days, winter nights, throughout. **Topography:** includes Pacific and Arctic mountain systems, central plateau, and Arctic slope. Mt. McKinley, 20,320 ft., is the highest point in North America. **Capital:** Juneau.

Economy. Principal industries: oil, gas, tourism, commercial fishing, mining, forestry. **Principal manufactured goods:** fish products, lumber and pulp, furs. **Agriculture** (1991): Chief crops: barley, hay, greenhouse nursery prods., potatoes, lettuce, milk. **Livestock** (1990): 7,500 cattle; 2,500 sheep; 5,000 poultry; 37,000 reindeer. **Timber/lumber:** spruce, yellow cedar, hemlock. **Nonfuel minerals** (1992): $530.9 mln.; crushed and broken stone, gold, sand & gravel. **Commercial fishing** (1992): $1.6 bln. **Chief ports:** Anchorage, Dutch Harbor, Kodiak, Seward, Skagway, Juneau, Sitka, Valdez, Wrangell. **International airports at:** Anchorage, Fairbanks, Ketchikan, Juneau. **Value of construction** (1992): $905.3 mln. **Employment distribution** (1991): 29.7% gvt.; 21.3% serv.; 19.6% trade. **Per capita income** (1992): $21,603. **Unemployment** (1992): 9.1%. **Tourism** (1987-88): $500 mln.

Finance. FDIC-insured commercial banks & trust companies (1992): 8. Deposits: $3.5 bln. **Commercial bank deposits, per capita** (1990): $7,475. **Savings institutions** (1992): 1. **Assets:** $100 mln.

Federal government. No. federal civilian employees (Mar. 1992): 12,252. **Avg. salary:** $37,776.

Energy. Electricity production (1992, MWh, by source): Hydroelectric: 0.9 mln. Mineral: 91 mln.

Education. Student-teacher ratio (1991): 16.7. **Avg. salary, public school teachers** (1992-93): $46,373.

State data. Motto: North to the future. **Flower:** Forget-Me-Not. **Bird:** Willow ptarmigan. **Tree:** Sitka spruce. **Song:** Alaska's Flag. **Entered union** Jan. 3, 1959; rank, 49th. **State fair** at: Palmer; late Aug.—early Sept.

History. Vitus Bering, a Danish explorer working for Russia, was the first European to land in Alaska, 1741. Alexander Baranov, first governor of Russian America, set up headquarters at Archangel, near present Sitka, in 1799. Secretary of State William H. Seward in 1867 bought Alaska from Russia for $7.2 million, a bargain some called "Seward's Folly." In 1896 gold was discovered and the famed Gold Rush was on.

Tourist attractions: Portage Glacier, Mendenhall Glacier, Glacier Bay National Park, Katmai National Park & Preserve, Denali National Park, one of North America's great wildlife sanctuaries, surrounding Mt. McKinley, No. America's highest peak. Pribilof Islands fur seal rookeries, restored St. Michael's Russian Orthodox Cathedral, Sitka.

Famous Alaskans include Tom Bodett, Susan Butcher, Ernest Gruening, Sydney Laurence, Libby Riddles, Jefferson "Soapy" Smith.

Tourist information. Alaska Division of Tourism, P.O. Box 110801, Juneau, AK 99811-0801.

Arizona

Grand Canyon State

People. Population (1992): 3,832,294; **rank:** 23. **Pop. density:** 33.7 per sq. mi. **Racial distrib.** (1990): 80.8% White; 3.0% Black; 5.6% American Indian; 18.8% Hispanic. **Net change** (1990-92): 4.6%.

Geography. Total area: 114,000 sq. mi.; **rank:** 6. **Land area:** 113,642 sq. mi. **Acres forested land:** 19,384,000. **Location:** in the southwestern U.S. **Climate:** clear and dry in the southern regions and northern plateau; high central areas have heavy winter snows. **Topography:** Colorado plateau in the N, containing the Grand Canyon; Mexican Highlands running diagonally NW to SE; Sonoran Desert in the SW. **Capital:** Phoenix.

Economy: Principal industries: manufacturing, tourism, mining, agriculture. **Principal manufactured goods:** electronics, printing and publishing, foods, primary and fabricated metals, aircraft and missiles, apparel. **Agriculture: Chief crops:** cotton, lettuce, cauliflower, broccoli, sorghum, barley, corn, wheat, sugar beets, citrus fruits. **Livestock** (1992): 900,000 cattle; 100,000 hogs/pigs; 225,000 sheep; 325,000 poultry. **Timber/lumber** (1991): pine, fir, spruce; 325 mln. bd. ft. **Nonfuel Minerals** (1992): $3.1 bln.; copper, gold, molybdenum, silver. **International airports at:** Phoenix, Tucson, Yuma. **Value of construction** (1992): $5.4 bln. **Employment distribution** (1992): 27.9% services; 24.7% trade; 18.3% gvt.; 11.3% mfg. **Per capita income** (1992): $17,119. **Unemployment** (1992): 7.4%. **Tourism** (1992): tourists spent $7.2 bln. **Sales tax:** 5.0% (Maricopa, Pinal Countries, 5.5%).

Finance. FDIC-insured commercial banks & trust companies (1992): 41. **Deposits:** $30.4 bln. **Savings institutions** (1992): 2. **Assets:** $200 mln.

Federal government: No. federal civilian employees (Mar. 1992): 29,607. **Avg. salary:** $32,167. **Notable federal facilities:** Williams, Luke, Davis-Monthan AF bases; Ft. Huachuca Army Base; Yuma Proving Grounds.

Energy. Electricity production (1992, MWh, by source): Hydroelectric: 5.3 mln.; Mineral: 29.8; Nuclear: 18.1.

Education. Student-teacher ratio (1991): 19.3. **Avg. salary, public school teachers** (1992-93): $32,403.

State data. Motto: Ditat Deus (God enriches). **Flower:** Blossom of the Saguaro cactus. **Bird:** Cactus wren. **Tree:** Paloverde. **Song:** Arizona. **Entered union** Feb. 14, 1912; rank, 48th. **State fair** at: Phoenix; late Oct.–early Nov.

History. Marcos de Niza, a Franciscan, and Estevan, a black slave, explored the area, 1539. Eusebio Francisco Kino, Jesuit missionary, taught Indians Christianity and farming, 1690-1711, left a chain of missions. Spain ceded Arizona to Mexico, 1821. The U. S. took over at the end of the Mexican War, 1848. The area below the Gila River was obtained from Mexico in the Gadsden Purchase, 1854. Long Apache wars did not end until 1886, with Geronimo's surrender.

Tourist attractions. The Grand Canyon of the Colorado, an immense, vari-colored fissure 217 mi. long, 4 to 13 mi. wide at the brim, 4,000 to 5,500 ft. deep; the Painted Desert, extending for 30 mi. along U.S. 66; the Petrified Forest; Canyon Diablo, 225 ft. deep and 500 ft. wide; Meteor Crater, 4,150 ft. across, 570 ft. deep, made by a prehistoric meteor. Also, London Bridge at Lake Havasu City.

Famous Arizonans include Bruce Babbitt, Cochise, Geronimo, Barry Goldwater, Zane Grey, Carl Hayden, George W. P. Hunt, Helen Jacobs, Percival Lowell, Sandra Day O'Connor, William H. Pickering, John J. Rhodes, Morris Udall, Stewart Udall, Frank Lloyd Wright.

Tourist information. Phoenix & Valley of the Sun Visitor and Convention Bureau, 1-602-254-6500.

Arkansas

Land of Opportunity

People. Population (1992): 2,398,767; **rank:** 33. **Pop. density:** 46.1 per sq. mi. **Racial distrib.** (1990): 82.7% White; 15.9% Black; 0.8% Hispanic. **Net change** (1990-92): 2.0%.

Geography. Total area: 53,187 sq. mi.; **rank:** 27. **Land area:** 52,075 sq. mi. **Acres forested land:** 16,987,000. **Location:** in the west south-central U.S. **Climate:** long, hot summers, mild winters; generally abundant rainfall. **Topography:** eastern delta and prairie, southern lowland forests, and the northwestern highlands, which include the Ozark Plateaus. **Capital:** Little Rock.

Economy. Principal industries: manufacturing, agriculture, tourism, forestry. **Principal manufactured goods:** food prods., chemicals, lumber, paper, electric motors, furniture, home appliances, auto components, airplane parts, apparel, machinery, petroleum prods., steel. **Agriculture: Chief crops:** soybeans, rice, cotton, tomatoes, grapes, apples, commercial vegetables, peaches, wheat. **Livestock** (1991): 1.71 mln. cattle; 760,000 hogs/pigs; 980 mln. poultry. **Timber/lumber** (1991): oak, hickory, gum, cypress, pine; 1.7 bln. bd. ft. **Nonfuel Minerals** (1992): 287.0 mln.; bromine, abrasives, bauxite, sand & gravel. **Chief ports:** Little Rock, Pine Bluff, Osceola, Helena, Fort Smith, Van Buren, Camden, Dardanelle, North Little Rock, West Memphis, Crossett, McGehee. **Value of construction** (1992): $2.0 bln. **Employment distribution** (1992): 21.2% mfg.; 19.1% trade; 18.8% serv.; 15.0% gvt. **Per capita income** (1992): $15,439. **Unemployment** (1992): 7.2%. **Tourism** (1992): travelers spent $2.7 bln.

Finance. FDIC-insured commercial banks & trust companies (1992): 262. **Deposits:** $20.9 bln. **Savings institutions** (1992): 18. **Assets:** $2.8 bln.

Federal government. No. federal civilian employees (Mar. 1992): 12,669. **Avg. salary:** $30,448. **Notable federal facilities:** Nat'l. Center for Toxicological Research, Jefferson; Pine Bluff Arsenal, Little Rock AFB.

Energy. Electricity production (1992, MWh, by source): Hydroelectric: 3.5 mln.; Mineral: 16.9 mln.; Nuclear: 12.9 mln.

Education. Student-teacher ratio (1991): 17.0. **Avg. salary, public school teachers** (1992-93): $27,598.

State data. Motto: Regnat Populus (The people rule). **Flower:** Apple blossom. **Bird:** Mockingbird. **Tree:** Pine. **Song:** Arkansas. **Entered union** June 15, 1836; rank, 25th. **State fair** at: Little Rock; late Sept. –early Oct.

History. First European explorers were de Soto, 1541, Jolliet, 1673; La Salle, 1682. First settlement was by the French under Henri de Tonty, 1686, at Arkansas Post. In 1762 the area was ceded by France to Spain, then back again in 1800, and was part of the Louisiana Purchase by the U.S. in 1803. Arkansas seceded from the Union in 1861, only after the Civil War began, and more than 10,000 Arkansans fought on the Union side.

Tourist attractions. 5 natl. parks & 47 state parks, inc. Hot Springs National Park, water ranging from 95° to 147°F. Eureka Springs, resort since 1879; Blanchard Caverns, near Mountain View, are among the nation's largest;

Crater of Diamonds, near Murfreesboro, only U.S. diamond mine; Buffalo Natl. River; Mid-America Museum, Ozark Folk Center.

Famous Arkansans include Daisy Bates, Dee Brown, Glen Campbell, Johnny Cash, Hattie Caraway, President Bill Clinton, "Dizzy" Dean, Orval Faubus, James W. Fulbright, Douglas MacArthur, John L. McClellan, James S. McDonnel, Dick Powell, Winthrop Rockefeller, Mary Steenburgen, Edward Durell Stone, Archibald Yell.

Chamber of Commerce. One Spring Bldg., Little Rock, AR 72201-2486.

Toll-free travel information. 1-800-NATURAL.

California

Golden State

People. Population (1992): 30,866,851; **rank:** 1. **Pop. density:** 197.9 per sq. mi. **Racial distrib.** (1990): 69.0% White; 7.4% Black; 9.6% Asian; 25.8% Hispanic. **Net change** (1990-92): 3.7%.

Geography. Total area 158,706 sq. mi.; **rank:** 3. **Land area:** 155,973 sq. mi. **Acres forested land:** 39,381,000. **Location:** on western coast of the U.S. **Climate:** moderate temperatures and rainfall along the coast; extremes in the interior. **Topography:** long mountainous coastline; central valley; Sierra Nevada on the east; desert basins of the southern interior; rugged mountains of the north. **Capital:** Sacramento.

Economy. Principal industries: agriculture, manufacturing, services, trade. **Principal manufactured goods:** foods, printed material, primary and fabricated metals, machinery, electric and electronic equipment, transportation equipment, instruments. **Agriculture: Chief crops:** grapes, cotton, flowers, oranges, nursery products, hay, tomatoes, lettuce, strawberries, almonds, broccoli, walnuts, sugar beets, peaches, potatoes. **Livestock** (1992): 8.17 mln. cattle & calves; 250,000 hogs/pigs; 945,000 sheep and lambs; 27.6 mln. chickens exc. broilers. **Timber/lumber** (1991): fir, pine, redwood, oak; 4.1 bln. bd. ft. **Nonfuel Minerals:** (1992): $2.5 bln.; mostly asbestos, boron minerals, cement, diatomite, calcined gypsum, construction sand & gravel. **Commercial fishing** (1992): $136.3 mln. **Chief ports:** Long Beach, Los Angeles, San Diego, Oakland, San Francisco, Sacramento, Stockton. **International airports at:** Los Angeles, San Francisco, San Jose, San Diego. **Value of construction** (1992): $27.2 bln. **Employment distribution** (1992): 28.2% serv.; 23.3% trade; 15.6% mfg.; 17.2% gvt. **Per capita income** (1992): $21,278. **Unemployment** (1992): 7.1%. **Tourism** (1991): $48.5 bln. **Sales tax:** 7¼-8¾%.

Finance. FDIC-insured commercial banks & trust companies (1992): 480. **Deposits**: $287.1 bln. **Savings institutions** (1992): 104. **Assets:** $272.5 bln.

Federal government. No. federal civilian employees (Mar. 1992): 205,672. **Avg. salary:** $35,826. **Notable federal facilities:** Vandenberg, Beale, Travis, McClellan AF bases, San Francisco Mint.

Energy. Electricity production (1992, MWh, by source): Hydroelectric: 11.0 mln.; Mineral: 13.0 mln.; Nuclear: 32.8 mln.

Education. Student-teacher ratio (1991): 22.8. **Avg. salary, public school teachers** (1992-93): $41,400.

State Data. Motto: Eureka (I have found it). **Flower:** Golden poppy. **Bird:** California valley quail. **Tree:** California redwood. **Song:** I Love You, California. **Entered Union** Sept. 9, 1850; rank, 31st. **State fair** at: Sacramento; late Aug.—early Sept.

History. First European explorers were Cabrillo, 1542, and Drake, 1579. First settlement was the Spanish Alta California mission at San Diego, 1769, first in a string founded by Franciscan Father Junipero Serra. U. S. traders and settlers arrived in the 19th century and staged the abortive Bear Flag Revolt, 1846; the Mexican War began later in 1846 and U.S. forces occupied California; Mexico ceded the province to the U.S., 1848, the same year the Gold Rush began.

Tourist attractions. Scenic regions are Yosemite Valley; Lassen and Sequoia-Kings Canyon national parks; Lake Tahoe; the Mojave and Colorado deserts; San Francisco Bay; Napa Valley; and Monterey Peninsula. Oldest living things on earth are believed to be a stand of Bristlecone pines in the Inyo National Forest, est. to be 4,600 years old. The world's tallest tree, the Howard Libbey redwood, 362 ft. with a girth of 44 ft., stands on Redwood Creek, Humboldt County.

Also, RMS Queen Mary, Spruce Goose, both Long Beach; Palomar Observatory; Disneyland; J. Paul Getty Museum, Malibu; Tournament of Roses and Rose Bowl; Universal Studios, Hollywood; Los Angeles County Art Museum; San Diego Zoo.

Famous Californians include Luther Burbank, John C. Fremont, Bret Harte, Wm. R. Hearst, Jack London, Aimee Semple McPherson, John Muir, Richard M. Nixon, William Saroyan, Junipero Serra, Leland Stanford, John Steinbeck, Earl Warren.

Chamber of Commerce: 1201 K St., Sacramento, CA 95814.

Toll-free travel information. 1-800-862-2543, x T100.

Colorado

Centennial State

People. Population (1992): 3,470,216; **rank:** 26. **Pop. density:** 33.5 per sq. mi. **Racial distrib.** (1990): 88.2% White; 4.0% Black; 12.9% Hispanic. **Net change** (1990-92): 5.3%.

Geography. Total area: 104,091 sq. mi.; **rank:** 8. **Land area:** 103,730 sq. mi. **Acres forested land:** 21,338,000. **Location:** in west central U.S. **Climate:** low relative humidity, abundant sunshine, wide daily, seasonal temperatures ranges; alpine conditions in the high mountains. **Topography:** eastern dry high plains; hilly to mountainous central plateau; western Rocky Mountains of high ranges alternating with broad valleys and deep, narrow canyons. **Capital:** Denver.

Economy. Principal industries: manufacturing, government, tourism, agriculture, aerospace, electronics equipment. **Principal manufactured goods:** computer equipment, instruments, foods, machinery, aerospace products. **Agriculture: Chief crops:** corn, wheat, hay, sugar beets, barley, potatoes, apples, peaches, pears, dry edible beans, sorghum, onions, oats. **Livestock** (1989): 2.8 mln. cattle; 220,000 hogs/pigs; 825,000 sheep; 4.0 mln. poultry. **Timber/lumber** (1991): oak, ponderosa pine, Douglas fir; 114 mln. bd. ft. **Nonfuel Minerals** (1992): $388.5 mln.; gold, construction sand & gravel, crushed stone. **International airports at:** Denver. **Value of construction** (1992): $5.8 bln. **Employment distribution** (1987 est.): 26.7% serv.; 20.8% trade; 17.0% gvt.; 10.0% mfg. **Per capita income** (1992): $20,124. **Unemployment** (1992): 5.9%. **Tourism** (1989): $5.6 bln. **Sales Tax:** 3%.

Finance. FDIC-insured commercial banks & trust companies (1992): 387. **Deposits:** $24.4 bln. **Savings Institutions** (1992): 19. **Assets:** $4.6 bln.

Federal government. No. federal civilian employees (Mar. 1992): 39,588. **Avg. salary:** $35,306. **Notable federal facilities:** U.S. Air Force Academy; U.S. Mint; Ft. Carson, Lowry AFB; Solar Energy Research Institute; U.S. Rail Transport. Test Center; N. Amer. Aerospace Defense Command; Consolidated Space Operations Center; U.S. Documents Center, Fitzsimons Army Medical Center, Federal Center.

Energy. Electricity production (1992, MWh, by source): Hydroelectric: 1.37 mln.; Mineral: 28.2 mln.

Education. Student-teacher ratio (1991): 17.9. **Avg. salary, public school teachers** (1992-93): $33,541.

State data. Motto: Nil Sine Numine (Nothing without Providence). **Flower:** Rocky Mountain columbine. **Bird:** Lark bunting. **Tree:** Colorado blue spruce. **Song:** Where the Columbines Grow. **Entered union** Aug. 1, 1876; rank 38th. **State fair** at: Pueblo; last week in Aug.

History. Early civilization centered around Mesa Verde 2,000 years ago. The U.S. acquired eastern Colorado in the Louisiana Purchase, 1803; Lt. Zebulon M. Pike explored the area, 1806, discovering the peak that bears his name. After the Mexican War, 1846-48, U.S. immigrants settled in the east, former Mexicans in the south.

Tourist attractions. 310 or more sunshine days per year; more than 1,000 peaks of 2 or more miles; Rocky Mountain National Park; Garden of the Gods; Great Sand Dunes, Dinosaur, Black Canyon of the Gunnison, and Colorado national monuments; Pikes Peak and Mt. Evans highways; Mesa Verde National Park (Ancient Anasazi Indian cliff dwellings); 35 major ski areas; the Grand Mesa tableland comprises Grand Mesa Forest, 659,584 acres, with 200 lakes stocked with trout. Mining towns of Central City, Silverton, Cripple Creek; Burlington's Old Town; Bent's Fort, outside La Junta; Georgetown Loop Historic Mining Railroad Park, Cumbres & Toltec Scenic Railroad.

Famous Coloradans include Frederick Bonfils, Molly Brown, William N. Byers, M. Scott Carpenter, Jack Dempsey, Mamie Eisenhower, Douglas Fairbanks, Scott Hamilton, "Baby Doe" Tabor, Lowell Thomas, Byron R. White, Paul Whiteman.

Toll-free travel information. 1-800-433-2656.

Connecticut

Constitution State, Nutmeg State

People. Population (1992): 3,280,959; **rank:** 27. **Pop. density:** 677.2 per sq. mi. **Racial distrib.** (1990): 87.0% White; 8.3% Black; 6.5% Hispanic. **Net change** (1990-92): 0.2%.

Geography. Total area: 5,018 sq. mi.; **rank:** 48. **Land area:** 4,845 sq. mi. **Acres forested land:** 1,815,800. **Location:** New England state in the northeastern corner of the U.S. **Climate:** moderate; winters avg. slightly below freezing, warm, humid summers. **Topography:** western upland, the Berkshires, in the NW, highest elevations; narrow central lowland N-S; hilly eastern upland drained by rivers. **Capital:** Hartford.

Economy. Principal industries: manufacturing, retail trade, government, services, finances, insurance, real estate. **Principal manufactured goods:** aircraft engines and parts, submarines, helicopters, instruments, machinery & computer equipment, electronics & electrical equipment, medical instruments, pharmaceuticals. **Agriculture: Chief crops:** nursery stock, Christmas trees, mushrooms, vegetables, sweet corn, tobacco, apples. **Livestock** (1989): 73,000 cattle; 50,000 horses; 6,800 hogs/pigs; 8,400 sheep; 5.6 mln. poultry. **Timber/lumber** (1991): oak, birch, beech, maple; 46 mln. bd. ft. **Nonfuel Minerals** (1992): $94.9 mln.; crushed stone; construction sand & gravel. **Commercial fishing** (1992): $62.7 mln. **Chief ports:** New Haven, Bridgeport, New London. **International airports at:** Windsor Locks. **Value of construction** (1992): $2.9 bln. **Employment distribution** (1992): 19.3% mfg.; 28.3% serv. **Per capita income** (1992): $26,979. **Unemployment** (1992): 7.5%. **Tourism** (1991): out-of-state visitors spent $3.7 bln. **Sales tax:** 6.0%.

Finance. FDIC-insured commercial banks & trust companies (1992): 56. **Deposits:** $28.2 bln. **Savings institutions** (1992): 17. **Assets:** $8.6 bln.

Federal Government. No. federal civilian employees (Mar. 1992): 10,049. **Avg. salary:** $36,735. **Notable federal facilities:** U.S. Coast Guard Academy; U.S. Navy Submarine Base.

Energy. Electricity production (1992, MWh, by source): Hydroelectric: 0.3 mln.; Mineral: 1.2 mln.; Nuclear: 0.5 mln.

Education. Student-teacher ratio (1991): 14.0. **Avg. salary, public school teachers** (1992-93): $48,850.

State data. Motto: Qui Transtulit Sustinet (He who transplanted still sustains). **Flower:** Mountain laurel. **Bird:** American robin. **Tree:** White oak. **Song:** Yankee Doodle. **Fifth** of the 13 original states to ratify the Constitution, Jan. 9, 1788.

History. Adriaen Block, Dutch explorer, was the first European visitor, 1614. By 1634, settlers from Plymouth Bay started colonies along the Connecticut River and in 1637 defeated the Pequot Indians. In the Revolution, Connecticut men fought in most major campaigns and turned back British raids on Danbury and other towns, while Connecticut privateers captured British merchant ships.

Tourist attractions. Mark Twain House, Hartford; Yale University's Art Gallery, Peabody Museum, both in New Haven; Mystic Seaport; Mystic Marine Life Aquarium; P.T. Barnum Museum, Bridgeport; Gillette Castle, Hadlyme; U.S.S. Nautilus Memorial, Groton (1st nuclear-powered submarine).

Famous "Nutmeggers" include Ethan Allen, Phineas T. Barnum, Samuel Colt, Jonathan Edwards, Nathan Hale, Katharine Hepburn, Isaac Hull, J. Pierpont Morgan, Israel Putnam, Harriet Beecher Stowe, Mark Twain, Noah Webster, Eli Whitney.

Tourist information. State Dept. of Economic Development, 865 Brook St., Rocky Hill, CT 06067.

Toll-free travel information. 1-800-CT-BOUND (282-6863).

Delaware

First State, Diamond State

People. Population (1992): 689,214; **rank:** 46. **Pop. density:** 352.5 per sq. mi. **Racial distrib.** (1990): 80.3% White; 16.9% Black; 2.4% Hispanic. **Net change** (1990-92): 3.5%.

Geography. Total area: 2,045 sq. mi.; **rank:** 49. **Land area:** 1,955 sq. mi. **Acres forested land:** 398,000. **Location:** occupies the Delmarva Peninsula on the Atlantic coastal plain. **Climate:** moderate. **Topography:** Piedmont plateau to the N, sloping to a near sea-level plain. **Capital:** Dover.

Economy. Principal industries: chemistry, agriculture, finance, poultry, shellfish, tourism, auto assembly, food processing, transportation equipment. **Principal manufactured goods:** nylon, apparel, luggage, foods, autos, processed meats and vegetables, railroad and aircraft equipment. **Agriculture: Chief crops:** soybeans, potatoes, corn, mushrooms, lima beans, green peas, barley, cucumbers, snap beans, watermelons, apples, wheat, sweet corn. **Livestock** (1992): 31,000 cattle, 39,000 hogs, 236.5 mln. broilers. **Nonfuel Minerals** (1992): $16.3 mln; construction sand & gravel, magnesium compounds. **Commercial fishing** (1992): $4.2 mln. **Chief ports:** Wilmington. **International airports at:** Philadelphia/Wilmington. **Value of construction** (1992): $782.5 mln. **Employment distribution** (1992): 80.3% non-manufacturing; 19.7% mfg. **Per capita income** (1992): $21,451. **Unemployment** (1992): 5.3%. **Tourism** (1989): travelers spent $785 mln.

Finance. FDIC-insured commercial banks & trust companies (1992): 42. **Deposits:** $36.0 bln. **Savings institutions** (1992): 3. **Assets:** $200 mln.

Federal government. No. federal civilian employees (Mar. 1992): 2,891. **Avg. salary:** $31,689. **Notable federal facilities:** Dover Air Force Base, Federal Wildlife Refuge, Bombay Hook.

Energy. Electricity production (1992, MWh, by source): Mineral: 6.0 mln.

Education. Student-teacher ratio (1991): 16.8. **Avg. salary, public school teachers** (1992-93): $36,217.

State data. Motto: Liberty and independence. **Flower:** Peach blossom. **Bird:** Blue hen chicken. **Tree:** American holly. **Song:** Our Delaware. **First** of original 13 states to ratify the Constitution, Dec. 7, 1787. **State fair** at: Harrington; end of July.

History. The Dutch first settled in Delaware near present Lewes, 1631, but were wiped out by Indians. Swedes settled at present Wilmington, 1638; Dutch settled anew, 1651, near New Castle and seized the Swedish settlement, 1655, only to lose all Delaware and New Netherland to the British, 1664.

Tourist attractions. Ft. Christina Monument, the site of founding of New Sweden; John Dickinson "Penman of the Revolution" home, Dover; Henry Francis du Pont Winterthur Museum; Hagley Museum, Wilmington; Rehoboth Beach, "nation's summer capitol," Rehoboth; Dover Downs Intl. Speedway, Dover; Old Swedes (Trinity Parish)

Church, erected 1698, is the oldest Protestant church in the U.S. still in use.

Famous Delawareans include Thomas F. Bayard, Henry Seidel Canby, E. I. du Pont, John P. Marquand, Howard Pyle, Caesar Rodney.

Chamber of Commerce. One Commerce Center, Wilmington, DE 19801.

Toll-free travel information. 1-800-441-8846.

Florida

Sunshine State

People. Population (1992): 13,487,621; **rank:** 4. **Pop. density:** 249.8 per sq. mi. **Racial distrib.** (1990): 83.1% White; 13.6% Black; 12.2% Hispanic. **Net change** (1990-92): 4.3%.

Geography: Total area: 58,664 sq. mi.; **rank:** 22. **Land area:** 53,997 sq. mi. **Acres forested land:** 16,721,000. **Location:** peninsula jutting southward 500 mi. bet. the Atlantic and the Gulf of Mexico. **Climate:** subtropical N of Bradenton-Lake Okeechobee-Vero Beach line; tropical S of line. **Topography:** land is flat or rolling; highest point is 345 ft. in the NW. **Capital:** Tallahassee.

Economy. Principal industries: services, trade, gvt., manufacturing, tourism. **Principal manufactured goods:** electric & electronic equip., transp. equipment; food; printing & publishing; machinery. **Agriculture: Chief crops:** citrus fruits, vegetables, potatoes, melons, strawberries, sugarcane. **Livestock** (1987): 1.97 mln. cattle; 150,000 hogs/pigs; 7,360 sheep; 13.5 mln. poultry. **Timber/lumber** (1991): pine, cypress, cedar; 570 mln. bd. ft. **Nonfuel Minerals** (1992): $1.4 bln.; mostly cement, phosphate rock, crushed stone. **Commercial fishing** (1992): $154.9 mln. **Chief ports:** Pensacola, Tampa, Miami, Port Everglades, Jacksonville, St. Petersburg, Canaveral. **International airports at:** Miami, Tampa, Jacksonville, Orlando, Ft. Lauderdale, W. Palm Beach. **Value of construction** (1992): $16.7 bln. **Per capita income** (1992): $19,397. **Unemployment** (1992): 8.2% **Tourism** (1990): out-of-state visitors spent $26.6 bln. **Sales tax:** 6%.

Finance. FDIC-insured commercial banks & trust companies (1992): 421. **Deposits:** $119.9 bln. **Savings institutions** (1992): 87. **Assets:** $38.2 bln.

Federal government. No. federal civilian employees (Mar. 1992): 64,887. **Avg. salary:** $34,250. **Notable federal facilities:** John F. Kennedy Space Center, NASA-Kennedy Space Center's Spaceport USA; Eglin Air Force Base.

Energy. Electricity production (1992, MWh, by source): Hydroelectric: 0.2 mln.; Mineral: 70.6 mln.; Nuclear: 27.7 mln.

Education. Student-teacher ratio (1991): 17.6. **Avg. salary, public school teachers** (1992-93): $31,153.

State data. Motto: In God we trust. **Flower:** Orange blossom. **Bird:** Mockingbird. **Tree:** Sabal palmetto palm. **Song:** Old Folks at Home. **Entered union** Mar. 3, 1845; rank, 27th. **State fair** at: Tampa; early to mid-Feb.

History. First European to see Florida was Ponce de León, 1513. France established a colony, Fort Caroline, on the St. Johns River, 1564; Spain settled St. Augustine, 1565, and Spanish troops massacred most of the French. Britain's Francis Drake burned St. Augustine, 1586. Britain held the area briefly, 1763-83, returning it to Spain. After Andrew Jackson led a U.S. invasion, 1818, Spain ceded Florida to the U.S., 1819. The Seminole War, 1835-42, resulted in removal of most Indians to Oklahoma. Florida seceded from the Union, 1861, was readmitted, 1868.

Tourist attractions. Miami, with a variety of luxury hotels at Miami Beach; St. Augustine, oldest city in U.S.; Walt Disney World's Magic Kingdom, EPCOT Center, and Disney-MGM Studios, near Orlando; Spaceport U.S.A.

Everglades National Park preserves the beauty of the vast Everglades swamp. Castillo de San Marcos, St. Augustine, is a national monument. Also, the Ringling Museum of Art and the Ringling Museum of the Circus, both in Sarasota; Sea World, Orlando; Cypress Gardens, Winter Haven; Busch Gardens, Tampa; Universal Studios, near Orlando.

Famous Floridians include Henry M. Flagler, James Weldon Johnson, MacKinlay Kantor, Henry B. Plant, Marjorie Kinnan Rawlings, Joseph W. Stilwell, Charles P. Summerall.

Tourist information. Florida Division of Tourism, 126 Van Buren St., Tallahassee, FL 32399-2000, 1-904-487-1462.

Georgia

Empire State of the South, Peach State

People. Population (1992): 6,751,404; **rank:** 11. **Pop. density:** 116.6 per sq. mi. **Racial distrib.** (1990): 71.0% White; 27.0% Black; 1.7% Hispanic. **Net change** (1990-92): 4.2%.

Geography. Total area: 58,910 sq. mi.; **rank:** 21. **Land area:** 57,919 sq. mi. **Acres forested land:** 23,907,000. **Location:** South Atlantic state. **Climate:** maritime tropical air masses dominate in summer; continental polar air masses in winter; east central area drier. **Topography:** most southerly of the Blue Ridge Mtns. cover NE and N central; central Piedmont extends to the fall line of rivers; coastal plain levels to the coast flatlands. **Capital:** Atlanta.

Economy. Principal industries: services, manufacturing, gvt., retail trade. **Principal manufactured goods** (1991): textiles, food, and kindred prods. **Agriculture: Chief crops** (1991): peanuts, cotton, corn, tobacco, hay soybeans. **Livestock** (1991): 8.8 mln. poultry; 1.4 mln. cattle; 1.1 hogs/pigs. **Timber/lumber** (1991): pine, hardwood; 2.5 bln. bd. ft. **Nonfuel Minerals** (1992): $1.5 bln.; mostly crushed stone. **Commercial fishing** (1992): $23.0 mln. **Chief ports:** Savannah, Brunswick. **International airports at:** Atlanta. **Value of construction** (1992): $8.1 bln. **Employment distribution** (1991): 20% services; 19% mfg.; 18% retail trade; 18% gvt. **Per capita income** (1992): $18,130. **Unemployment** (1992): 6.9%. **Tourism** (1991): tourists spent $10.4 bln. **Sales tax:** 4%.

Finance. FDIC-insured commercial banks & trust companies (1992): 405. **Deposits:** $54.9 bln. **Savings institutions** (1992): 43. **Assets:** $13.6 bln.

Federal government. No. federal civilian employees (Mar. 1992): 71,257. **Avg. salary:** $32,637. **Notable federal facilities:** Dobbins AFB; Fts. Benning, Gordon, McPherson; Fed. Law Enforcement Training Ctr., Glynco, Warner Robins AFB; Centers for Disease Control, Atlanta.

Energy. Electricity production (1992, MWh, by source): Hydroelectric: 3.6 mln.; Mineral: 39.7 mln.; Nuclear: 26.6 mln.

Education. Student-teacher ratio (1991): 18.5. **Avg. salary, public school teachers** (1992-93): $30,626.

State data. Motto: Wisdom, justice and moderation. **Flower:** Cherokee rose. **Bird:** Brown thrasher. **Tree:** Live oak. **Song:** Georgia On My Mind. **Fourth** of the 13 original states to ratify the Constitution, Jan. 2, 1788.

History. Gen. James Oglethorpe established the first settlements, 1733, for poor and religiously-persecuted Englishmen. Oglethorpe defeated a Spanish army from Florida at Bloody Marsh, 1742. In the Revolution, Georgians seized the Savannah armory, 1775, and sent the munitions to the Continental Army; they fought seesaw campaigns with Cornwallis' British troops, twice liberating Augusta and forcing final evacuation by the British from Savannah, 1782.

Tourist attractions. Atlanta area: State Capitol, Stone Mt. Park, Six Flags over Georgia, Kennesaw Mt. Natl. Battlefield Park, Martin Luther King Center, Underground Atlanta, Jimmy Carter Lib. & Museum. NW: Chickamauga Battlefield Park, Chattahoochee Natl. Forest. NE: alpine village of Helen; Dahlonega, site of America's first gold rush; Brasstown Bald Mt., Lake Lanier. SW: Roosevelt's Little White House, Callaway Gardens, Andersonville Natl. Historic Site. SE: Okefenokee Swamp. Coastal: Jekyll Island, St. Simons Island, Cumberland Island Natl. Seashore, historic riverfront district in Savannah, Ft. Pulaski.

Famous Georgians include Hank Aaron, Griffin Bell, James Bowie, Erskine Caldwell, Jimmy Carter, Ray Charles, Lucius D. Clay, Ty Cobb, John C. Fremont, Joel Chandler Harris, Martin Luther King Jr., Gladys Knight,

Sidney Lanier, Juliette Gordon Low, Margaret Mitchell, Flannery O'Connor, Jackie Robinson, Joseph Wheeler.

Chamber of Commerce. 235 International Blvd., Atlanta, GA 30303.

Toll-free travel information. 1-800-VISIT GA.

Hawai'i

The Aloha State

People. Population (1992): 1,159,614; **rank:** 40. **Pop. density:** 180.5 per sq. mi. **Racial distrib.** (1990): 33.4% White; 2.5% Black; 61.8% Asian or Pacific Is.; 7.3% Hispanic. **Net change** (1990-92): 4.6%.

Geography. Total area: 6,471 sq. mi.; **rank:** 47. **Land area:** 6,423 sq. mi. **Acres forested land:** 1,748,000. **Location:** Hawaiian Islands lie in the North Pacific, 2,397 mi. SW from San Francisco. **Climate:** subtropical, with wide variations in rainfall; Waialeale, on Kaua'i, wettest spot in U.S. (annual rainfall 444 in.) **Topography:** islands are tops of a chain of submerged volcanic mountains; active volcanoes: Mauna Loa, Kilauea. **Capital:** Honolulu.

Economy. Principal industries: tourism, defense and other government, sugar refining, pineapple and diversified agriculture, aquaculture, fishing, motion pictures. **Principal manufactured goods:** sugar, canned pineapple, clothing, foods, printing and publishing. **Agriculture: Chief crops:** sugar, pineapples, macadamia nuts, fruits, coffee, vegetables, melons, floriculture. **Livestock** (1990): 214,000 cattle and calves; 36,000 hogs/pigs; 1.18 mln. chickens. **Nonfuel Minerals** (1992): $148.6 mln.; mostly crushed stone, sand, gravel & cement. **Commercial fishing** (1992): $70.2 mln. **Chief ports:** Honolulu, Nawiliwili, Barbers Point, Kahului, Hilo. **International airports at:** Honolulu. **Value of construction** (1992): $2.9 bln. **Employment distribution** (1991): 25.3% trade; 29.4% serv.; 20.2% gvt. **Per capita income** (1992): $21,218. **Unemployment** (1992): 4.5%. **Tourism** (1992): visitors spent $9.6 bln. **General excise tax:** 4%. **Sales tax:** 4%.

Finance. FDIC-insured commercial banks & trust companies: (1992): 20. **Deposits:** $16.2 bln. **Savings institutions** (1992): 5. **Assets:** $4.7 bln.

Federal government. No. federal civilian employees (Mar. 1992): 21,560. **Avg. salary:** $34,445. **Notable federal facilities:** Pearl Harbor Naval Shipyard; Hickam AFB; Schofield Barracks.

Energy. Electricity production (1992, MWh, by source): Hydroelectric: 0.01 mln.; Mineral: 5.6 mln.

Education. Student-teacher ratio (1991): 18.5. **Avg. Salary, public school teachers** (1992-93): $36,470.

State data. Motto: The life of the land is perpetuated in righteousness. **Flower:** Yellow hibiscus. **Bird:** Hawaiian goose. **Tree:** Kukui (Candlenut). **Song:** Hawai'i Pono'i. **Entered union** Aug. 21, 1959; rank, 50th. **State fair** at: Honolulu; late May–mid-June.

History. Polynesians from islands 2,000 mi. to the south settled the Hawaiian Islands, probably between 300 A.D. and 600 A.D. First European visitor was British Capt. James Cook, 1778. Missionaries arrived, 1820, taught religion, reading and writing. King Kamehameha III and his chiefs created the first Constitution and a Legislature that set up a public school system. Sugar production began in 1835 and it became the dominant industry. In 1893, Queen Liliuokalani was deposed, followed, 1894, by a republic headed by Sanford B. Dole. Annexation by the U.S. came in 1898.

Tourist attractions. Hawaii Volcanoes, Haleakala National Parks; Polynesian Cultural Center, Waikiki Beach, Nu'uanu Pali, Bishop Museum, Waimea Canyon, Wailua River State Park, Honolulu Academy of Arts.

Famous Islanders include Bernice Pauahi Bishop, John A. Burns, Father Damien de Veuster, Daniel K. Inouye, Duke Kahanamoku, King Kamehameha the Great, Queen Ka'ahumanu, Queen Liliuokalani, Ellison Onizuka.

Chamber of Commerce. Dillingham Bldg., 735 Bishop St., Honolulu, HI 96813.

Idaho

Gem State

People. Population (1992): 1,067,250; **rank:** 42. **Pop. density:** 12.9 per sq. mi. **Racial distrib.** (1990): 94.4% White; 0.3% Black; 5.3% Hispanic. **Net change** (1990-92): 6.0%.

Geography. Total area: 83,564 sq. mi.; **rank:** 13. **Land area:** 82,751 sq. mi. **Acres forested land:** 21,818,000. **Location:** northwestern Mountain state bordering on British Columbia. **Climate:** tempered by Pacific westerly winds; drier, colder, continental clime in SE; altitude an important factor. **Topography:** Snake R. plains in the S; central region of mountains, canyons, gorges (Hells Canyon, 7,900 ft., deepest in N.A.); subalpine northern region. **Capital:** Boise.

Economy. Principal industries: agriculture, manufacturing, tourism, lumber, mining, electronics. **Principal manufactured goods:** processed foods, lumber and wood products, chemical products, primary metals, fabricated metal products, machinery, electronic components. **Agriculture: Chief crops:** potatoes, peas, sugar beets, alfalfa seed, wheat, hops, barley, plums and prunes, mint, onions, corn, cherries, apples, hay. **Livestock** (1989): 1.66 mln. cattle; 296,000 sheep; 72,000 hogs; 1.1 mln. poultry. **Timber/lumber** (1991): yellow, white pine; Douglas fir; white spruce; 1.9 bln. bd. ft. **Nonfuel Minerals** (1992): $338.6 mln.; phosphate rock, silver, gold, sand & gravel. **Chief ports:** Lewiston. **Value of construction** (1992) $1.3 bln. **Employment distribution** (1990): 21% trade; 17% serv., 13% mfg.; 7% agric. **Per capita income** (1992): $16,067. **Unemployment** (1992): 6.5%. **Tourism** (1989): travelers spent $1.4 bln. **Sales tax:** 5%.

Finance. FDIC-insured commercial banks & trust companies (1992): 22. **Deposits:** $7.6 bln. **Savings institutions** (1992): 3. **Assets:** $500 mln.

Federal government. No. federal civilian employees (Mar. 1992): 7,856. **Avg. salary:** $33,265. **Notable federal facilities:** Ida. Nat'l. Engineering Lab, Idaho Falls; Mt. Home Air Force Base, Mt. Home.

Energy. Electricity production (1992, MWh, by source): Hydroelectric: 5.2 mln.

Education: Student-teacher ratio (1991): 19.4. **Avg. salary, public school teachers** (1992-93): $27,156.

State data. Motto: Esto Perpetua (It is perpetual). **Flower:** Syringa. **Bird:** Mountain bluebird. **Tree:** White pine. **Song:** Here We Have Idaho. **Entered union** July 3, 1890; rank, 43d. **State fair** at: Boise, late Aug.; and Blackfoot, early Sept.

History. Exploration of the Idaho area began with Lewis and Clark, 1805-06. Next came fur traders, setting up posts, 1809-34, and missionaries, establishing missions, 1830s-1850s. Mormons made their first permanent settlement at Franklin, 1860. Idaho's Gold Rush began that same year, and brought thousands of permanent settlers. Strangest of the Indian Wars was the 1,300-mi. trek in 1877 of Chief Joseph and the Nez Perce tribe, pursued by troops that caught them a few miles short of the Canadian border. In 1890, Idaho adopted a progressive Constitution and became a state.

Tourist attractions. Hells Canyon, deepest gorge in N.A.; World Center for Birds of Prey; Craters of the Moon; Sun Valley, year-round resort in the Sawtooth Mtns.; Crystal Falls Cave; Shoshone Falls; Lava Hot Springs; Lake Pend Oreille; Lake Coeur d'Alene; Sawtooth Natl. Recreation Area; River of No Return Wilderness Area.

Famous Idahoans include William E. Borah, Frank Church, Fred T. Dubois, Chief Joseph, Sacagawea.

Tourist information. Department of Commerce, 700 W. State St., Boise, ID 83720.

Toll-free travel information. 1-800-635-7820.

Illinois

The Prairie State

People. Population (1992): 11,631,131; **rank:** 6. **Pop. density:** 209.2 per sq. mi. **Racial distrib.** (1990): 78.3% White; 14.8% Black; 7.9% Hispanic. **Net change** (1990-92): 1.8%.

Geography. Total area: 56,345 sq. mi.; **rank:** 24. **Land area:** 55,593 sq. mi. **Acres forested land:** 4,265,000. **Location:** East North Central state; western, southern, and eastern boundaries formed by Mississippi, Ohio, and Wabash rivers, respectively. **Climate:** temperate; typically cold, snowy winters, hot summers. **Topography:** prairie and fertile plains throughout; open hills in the southern region. **Capital:** Springfield.

Economy. Principal industries: services, manufacturing, travel, wholesale and retail trade, finance, insurance, real estate, construction, gvt., health care, agriculture. **Principal manufactured goods:** machinery, electric and electronic equipment, primary and fabricated metals, chemical products, printing and publishing, food and kindred prods. **Agriculture: Chief crops:** corn, soybeans, wheat, oats, hay. **Livestock** (1991): 1.98 mln. cattle; 5.9 mln. hogs/pigs; 129,000 sheep; 3.31 mln. poultry. **Timber/lumber** (1991): oak, hickory, maple, cottonwood; 94 mln. bd. ft. **Nonfuel Minerals** (1992): $677.4 mln.; mostly crushed stone, cement, construction & industrial sand & gravel, lime. **Commercial fishing** (1992): $367,000. **Chief ports:** Chicago. **International airports at:** Chicago. **Value of construction** (1992): $10.6 bln. **Employment distribution** (1991): 26.0% serv.; 24.0% trade; 18.1% mfg. **Per capita income** (1992): $21,608. **Unemployment** (1992): 7.5%. **Tourism** (1991): out-of-state visitors spent $15 bln. **Sales tax:** 6.25%.

Finance. FDIC-insured commercial banks & trust companies (1992): 1,061. **Deposits:** $157.0 bln. **Savings institutions** (1992): 151. **Assets:** $43.2 bln.

Federal government. No. federal civilian employees (Mar. 1992): 54,139. **Avg. salary:** $35,198. **Notable federal facilities:** Fermi Nat'l. Accelerator Lab; Argonne Nat'l. Lab; Ft. Sheridan; Rock Island; Great Lakes, Naval Training Station, Scott AFB.

Energy. Electricity production (1992, MWh, by source): Hydroelectric: 0.1 mln.; Mineral: 47.5 mln.; Nuclear: 62.9 mln.

Education. Student-teacher ratio (1991): 16.8. **Avg. salary, public school teachers** (1992-93): $38,576.

State data. Motto: State sovereignty—national union. **Flower:** Native violet. **Bird:** Cardinal. **Tree:** White oak. **Song:** Illinois. **Entered union** Dec. 3, 1818; rank, 21st. **State fair** at: Springfield, mid-Aug.; DuQuoin, late Aug.

History. Fur traders were the first Europeans in Illinois, followed shortly, 1673, by Jolliet and Marquette, and, 1680, La Salle, who built a fort near present Peoria. First settlements were French, at Fort St. Louis on the Illinois River, 1692, and Kaskaskia, 1700. France ceded the area to Britain, 1763; Amer. Gen. George Rogers Clark, 1778, took Kaskaskia from the British without a shot. Defeat of Indian tribes in Black Hawk War, 1832, and railroads in 1850s, inspired change.

Tourist attractions: Chicago museums, parks; Lincoln shrines at Springfield, New Salem, Sangamon; Cahokia Mounds, E. St. Louis; Starved Rock State Park; Crab Orchard Wildlife Refuge; Mormon settlement at Nauvoo; Fts. Kaskaskia, Chartres, Massac (parks); Shawnee Nat'l. Forest, Southern Illinois; Illinois State Museum, Springfield; Dickson Mounds Museum, btwn. Havana & Lewistown.

Famous Illinoisans include Jane Addams, Saul Bellow, Jack Benny, Ray Bradbury, Gwendolyn Brooks, William Jennings Bryan, St. Francis Xavier Cabrini, Clarence Darrow, John Deere, Stephen A. Douglas, James T. Farrell, George W. Ferris, Marshall Field, Betty Friedan, Benny Goodman, Ulysses S. Grant, Ernest Hemingway, Wild Bill Hickok, Abraham Lincoln, Vachel Lindsay, Edgar Lee Masters, Oscar Mayer, Cyrus McCormick, Ronald Reagan, Carl Sandburg, Adlai Stevenson, Frank Lloyd Wright, Philip Wrigley.

Tourist information. Illinois Dept. of Commerce and Community Affairs, 620 E. Adams St., Springfield, IL 62701. **Toll-free literature:** 1-800-223-0121.

Indiana

Hoosier State

People. Population (1992): 5,661,800; **rank:** 14. **Pop. density:** 157.8 per sq. mi. **Racial distrib.** (1990): 90.6% White; 7.8% Black; 1.8% Hispanic. **Net change** (1990-92): 2.1%.

Geography. Total area: 36,185 sq. mi.; **rank:** 38. **Land area:** 35,870 sq. mi. **Acres forested land:** 4,439,900. **Location:** East North Central state; Lake Michigan on northern border. **Climate:** 4 distinct seasons with a temperate climate. **Topography:** hilly southern region; fertile rolling plains of central region; flat, heavily glaciated north; dunes along Lake Michigan shore. **Capital:** Indianapolis.

Economy: Principal industries: manufacturing, services, agriculture, government, wholsesale and retail trade, transportation and public utilities. **Principal manufactured goods:** primary metals, transportation equipment, motor vehicles and equipment, machinery except electrical, fabricated metal, chemical and allied products. **Agriculture: Chief crops** (1987): corn, sorghum, oats, wheat, rye, soybeans, hay. **Livestock** (1987): 1.2 mln. cattle; 4.4 mln. hogs/pigs; 82,757 sheep; 28 mln. chickens. **Timber/lumber** (1991): oak, tulip, beech, sycamore; 208 mln. bd. ft. **Nonfuel Minerals** (1992): $465.2 mln.; mostly crushed stone, abrasives, cement, construction sand & gravel. **Commercial fishing** (1992): $2.55 mln. **Chief ports:** Burns Harbor, Portage; Southwind Maritime, Mt. Vernon; Clark Maritime, Jeffersonville. **International airports at:** Indianapolis. **Value of construction** (1992): $6.4 bln. **Employment distribution** (1989): 27.9% mfg.; 24.8% trade; 19.8% serv; 12.3% gvt. **Per capita income** (1992): $18,043. **Unemployment** (1992): 6.5%. **Tourism** (1992): tourists spent $4.4 bln. **Sales tax:** 5%, with exemptions.

Finance. FDIC-insured commercial banks & trust companies (1992): 284. **Deposits:** $48.5 bln. **Savings institutions** (1992): 86. **Assets:** $13.9 bln.

Federal government. No. federal civilian employees (Mar. 1992): 26,040. **Avg. salary:** $32,697. **Notable federal facilities:** Naval Avionics Ctr.; Ft. Benjamin Harrison; Grissom AFB; Naval Surface Warfare Ctr., Crane.

Energy. Electricity production (1992 MWh, by source): Hydroelectric: 0.5 mln.; Mineral: 86.5 mln.

Education. Student-teacher ratio (1991): 17.5. **Avg. salary, public school teachers** (1992-93): $37,446.

State data. Motto: Crossroads of America. **Flower:** Peony. **Bird:** Cardinal. **Tree:** Tulip poplar. **Song:** On the Banks of the Wabash, Far Away. **Entered union** Dec. 11, 1816; rank, 19th. **State fair** at: Indianapolis; mid-Aug.

History: Pre-historic Indian Mound Builders of 1,000 years ago were the earliest known inhabitants. A French trading post was built, 1731-32, at Vincennes and La Salle visited the present South Bend area, 1679 and 1681. France ceded the area to Britain, 1763. During the Revolution, American Gen. George Rogers Clark captured Vincennes, 1778, and defeated British forces 1779; at war's end Britain ceded the area to the U.S. Miami Indians defeated U.S. troops twice, 1790, but were beaten, 1794, at Fallen Timbers by Gen. Anthony Wayne. At Tippecanoe, 1811, Gen. William H. Harrison defeated Tecumseh's Indian confederation.

Tourist attractions. Lincoln Boyhood, George Rogers Clark memorials; Wyandotte Cave; Vincennes, Tippecanoe sites; Indiana Dunes; Hoosier Nat'l. Forest; Benjamin Harrison Home; Basketball Hall of Fame, New Harmony; Indianapolis 500 race and museum.

Famous "Hoosiers" include Larry Bird, Ambrose Burnside, Hoagy Carmichael, Jim Davis, James Dean, Eugene V. Debs, Theodore Dreiser, Paul Dresser, Gil Hodges, David Letterman, Jane Pauley, Cole Porter, Gene Stratton Porter, Ernie Pyle, James Whitcomb Riley, Oscar Robertson, Red Skelton, Booth Tarkington, Lew Wallace, Wendell L. Willkie, Wilbur Wright.

Chamber of Commerce. One North Capital, Suite 200, Indianapolis, IN 46204.

Toll-free travel information. 1-800-289-6646.

Iowa

Hawkeye State

People. Population (1992): 2,812,448; **rank:** 30. **Pop. density:** 50.3 per sq. mi. **Racial distrib.** (1990): 96.6% White; 1.7% Black; 1.2% Hispanic. **Net change** (1990-92): 1.3%.

Geography. Total area: 56,275 sq. mi.; **rank:** 25. **Land area:** 55,875 sq. mi. **Acres forested land:** 1,562,000. **Location:** West North Central state bordered by Mississippi R. on the E and Missouri R. on the W. **Climate:** humid, continental. **Topography:** Watershed from NW to SE; soil especially rich and land level in the N central counties. **Capital:** Des Moines.

Economy. Principal industries: agriculture, communications, construction, finance, insurance, trade, service, mfg. **Principal manufactured goods:** tires, farm machinery, electronic products, appliances, office furniture, chemicals, fertilizers, auto accessories. **Agriculture: Chief crops:** silage and grain corn, soybeans, oats, hay. **Livestock** (1992): 4.45 mln. cattle; 15.0 mln. swine; 345,000 sheep & lambs; 8.6 mln. turkeys. **Timber/lumber** (1991): red cedar; 31 mln. bd. ft. **Nonfuel Minerals** (1992): $387.7 mln.; mostly crushed stone, portland cement, construction sand & gravel. **Value of construction** (1992): 2.2 bln. **Employment distribution** (1992): 25.2% trade; 24.4% serv; 18.3% mfg.; 18.2% gvt. **Per capita income** (1992): $18,287. **Unemployment** (1992): 4.6%. **Tourism** (1992): tourists spent $2.5 bln. **Sales tax:** 5%.

Finance. FDIC-insured commercial banks & trust companies (1992): 553. **Deposits:** $30.8 bln. **Savings institutions** (1992): 31. **Assets:** $4.6 bln.

Federal government. No. federal civilian employees (Mar. 1992): 7,957. **Avg. salary:** $32,456.

Energy. Electricity production (1992, MWh, by source): Hydroelectric: 0.8 mln.; Mineral: 24.8 mln.; Nuclear: 3.3 mln.

Education. Student-teacher ratio (1991): 15.7. **Avg. salary, public school teachers** (1992-93): $30,124.

State data. Motto: Our liberties we prize and our rights we will maintain. **Flower:** Wild rose. **Bird:** Eastern goldfinch. **Tree:** Oak. **Rock:** Geode. **Entered union** Dec. 28, 1846; rank, 29th. **State fair** at: Des Moines; mid-Aug.

History. A thousand years ago several groups of prehistoric Indian Mound Builders dwelt on Iowa's fertile plains. Marquette and Jolliet gave France its claim to the area, 1673. It became U.S. territory through the 1803 Louisiana Purchase. Indian tribes were moved into the area from states further east, but by mid-19th century were forced to move on to Kansas. Before and during the Civil War, Iowans strongly supported Abraham Lincoln and became traditional Republicans.

Tourist attractions. Herbert Hoover birthplace and library, West Branch; Effigy Mounds Nat'l. Monument, Marquette, a pre-historic Indian burial site; Amana Colonies; Davenport Municipal Art Gallery's collection of Grant Wood's paintings and memorabilia; Living History Farms, Des Moines; Adventureland, Altoona; Boone & Scenic Valley Railroad, Boone; Greyhound Parks in Dubuque, Council Bluffs & Waterloo; Prairie Meadows horse racing, Altoona; riverboat cruises and casino gambling, Mississippi River; Iowa Great Lakes, Okoboji.

Famous Iowans include James A. Van Allen, Marquis Childs, Buffalo Bill Cody, Mamie Dowd Eisenhower, George Gallup, Susan Glaspell, James Norman Hall, Harry Hansen, Herbert Hoover, Glenn Miller, Billy Sunday, Carl Van Vechten, Henry Wallace, John Wayne, Meredith Willson, Grant Wood.

Tourist information. Division of Tourism, Iowa Dept. of Economic Development, 200 E. Grand Ave., Des Moines, IA 50309.

Toll-free travel information. 1-800-345-IOWA.

Kansas

Sunflower State

People. Population (1992): 2,522,574; **rank:** 32. **Pop. density:** 30.8 per sq. mi. **Racial distrib.** (1990): 90.1% White; 5.8% Black; 3.8% Hispanic. **Net change** (1990-92): 1.8%.

Geography. Total area: 82,277 sq. mi.; **rank:** 14. **Land area:** 81,823 sq. mi. **Acres forested land:** 1,358,000. **Location:** West North Central state, with Missouri R. on E. **Climate:** temperate but continental, with great extremes bet. summer and winter. **Topography:** hilly Osage Plains in the E; central region level prairie and hills; high plains in the W. **Capital:** Topeka.

Economy. Principal industries: manufacturing, finance, insurance, real estate, services. **Principal manufactured goods:** transportation equip., machinery and computer equipment, food and kindred products, printing and publishing. **Agriculture: Chief crops:** wheat, sorghum, corn, hay, soybeans. **Livestock** (1992): 5.65 mln. cattle; 1.44 mln. hogs/pigs; 179,000 sheep & lambs; 1.8 mln. poultry. **Timber/lumber:** oak, walnut. **Nonfuel Minerals** (1992): $368.9 mln.; cement, salt, crushed stone. **Chief ports:** Kansas City. **International airports at:** Wichita. **Value of construction** (1992): $2.5 bln. **Employment distribution** (1992): 21.9% trade; 20.6% serv.; 18.5% gvt.; 14.2% mfg. **Per capita income** (1992): $19,376. **Unemployment** (1992): 4.2%. **Tourism** (1991): out-of-state visitors spent $2.1 bln. **Sales tax:** 6.9% maximum.

Finance. FDIC-insured commercial banks & trust companies (1992): 528. **Deposits**: $25.9 bln. **Savings institutions** (1992): 31. **Assets** : $8.5 bln.

Federal government. No. federal civilian employees (Mar. 1992): 17,029. **Avg. salary:** $32,065. **Notable federal facilities:** McConnell AFB; Fts. Riley, Leavenworth.

Energy. Electricity production (1992, MWh, by source): Mineral: 20.5 mln; Nuclear: 4.0 mln.

Education. Student-teacher ratio (1991): 15.2. **Avg. salary, public school teachers** (1992-93): $33,133.

State data. Motto: Ad Astra per Aspera (To the stars through difficulties). **Flower:** Native sunflower. **Bird:** Western meadowlark. **Tree:** Cottonwood. **Song:** Home on the Range. **Entered union** Jan. 29, 1861; rank, 34th. **State fair** at: Hutchinson; begins Friday after Labor Day.

History. Coronado marched through the Kansas area, 1541; French explorers came next. The U.S. took over in the Louisiana Purchase, 1803. In the pre-war North-South struggle over slavery, so much violence swept the area it was called Bleeding Kansas. Railroad construction after the war made Abilene and Dodge City terminals of large cattle drives from Texas.

Tourist attractions. Eisenhower Center and "Place of Meditation," Abilene; Agricultural Hall of Fame and National Ctr., Bonner Springs, displays farm equipment; Dodge City-Boot Hill & Frontier Town; Cowtown-historic frontier town, Wichita; Ft. Scott & Ft. Larned-restored 1800s cavalry forts. Kansas Cosmosphere and Space Discovery Center, Hutchinson.

Famous Kansans include Thomas Hart Benton, John Brown, Walter P. Chrysler, John Steuart Curry, Amelia Earhart, Dwight D. Eisenhower, Ron Evans, Wild Bill Hickok, Cyrus Holliday, William Inge, Walter Johnson, Alf Landon, Carry Nation, Gordon Parks, Jim Ryun, William Allen White.

Tourist information. Kansas Dept. of Commerce & Housing, Travel and Tourism Div., 700 SW 8th St., Suite 1300, Topeka, KS 66603; 1-913-296-2009.

Toll-free travel information. 1-800-2KANSAS.

Kentucky

Bluegrass State

People. Population (1992): 3,754,715; **rank:** 24. **Pop. density:** 94.5 per sq. mi. **Racial Distrib.** (1990): 92.0% White; 7.1% Black; Hispanic 0.6%. **Net change** (1990-92): 1.9%.

Geography. Total area: 40,410 sq. mi.; **rank:** 37. **Land area:** 39,732 sq. mi. **Acres forested land:** 12,256,000. **Location:** East South Central state, bordered on N by Illinois, Indiana, Ohio; on E by West Virginia and Virginia; in S by Tennessee; on W by Missouri. **Climate:** moderate, with plentiful rainfall. **Topography:** mountainous in E; rounded hills of the Knobs in the N; Bluegrass, heart of state; wooded rocky hillsides of the Pennyroyal; Western Coal Field; the fertile Purchase the SW. **Capital:** Frankfort.

Economy. Principal industries: manufacturing, finance, insurance and real estate, services, retail trade. **Principal manufactured goods:** non-electrical machinery, electrical & electronic prods., apparel, transportation equip., printing and publishing. **Agriculture: Chief crops** (1991): tobacco, soybeans, corn. **Livestock** (1991): 2.5 mln. cattle; 920,000 hogs/pigs; 35,000 sheep; 2.2 mln. chickens; 1990 receipts for horse & mule sales, $490 mln. **Timber/lumber** (1991): hardwoods, pines; 553 mln. bd. ft. **Nonfuel Minerals** (1992): $412.5 mln.; mostly crushed stone. **Chief ports:** Paducah, Louisville, Covington, Owensboro, Ashland, Henderson County, Lyon County, Hickman-Fulton County. **International airports at:** Covington. **Value of construction** (1992): $3.9 bln. **Employment distribution** (1991): 25.6% trade; 21% mfg.; 21.2% serv.; 14.1% gvt. **Per capita income** (1992): $16,534. **Unemployment** (1992): 6.9%. **Tourism** (1992): tourists spent $5.7 bln. **Sales tax:** 6%.

Finance. FDIC-insured commercial banks & trust companies (1992): 320. **Deposits:** $34.1 bln. **Savings institutions** (1992): 56. **Assets:** $7.3 bln.

Federal government. No. federal civilian employees (Mar. 1992): 27,815. **Avg. salary:** $28,968. **Notable federal facilities:** U.S. Gold Bullion Depository, Fort Knox; Federal Correctional Institution, Lexington.

Energy. Electricity production (1992, MWh, by source): Hydroelectric: 3.9 mln.; Mineral: 61.3 mln.

Education. Student-teacher ratio (1991): 17.2. **Avg. salary, public school teachers** (1992-93): $31,487.

State data. Motto: United we stand, divided we fall. **Flower:** Goldenrod. **Bird:** Cardinal. **Tree:** Kentucky coffee tree. **Song:** My Old Kentucky Home. **Entered union** June 1, 1792; rank, 15th. **State fair** at: Louisville.

History. Kentucky was the first area west of the Alleghenies settled by American pioneers; first permanent settlement, Harrodsburg, 1774. Daniel Boone blazed the Wilderness Trail through the Cumberland Gap and founded Fort Boonesborough, 1775. Indian attacks, spurred by the British, were unceasing until, during the Revolution, Gen. George Rogers Clark captured British forts in Indiana and Illinois, 1778. In 1792, after Virginia dropped its claims to the region, Kentucky became the 15th state.

Tourist attractions. Kentucky Derby and accompanying festivities, Louisville; Land Between the Lakes Nat'l. Recreation Area encompassing Kentucky Lake and Lake Barkley; Mammoth Cave National Park with 330 mi. of explored passageways, 200-ft. high rooms, blind fish, and Echo River, 360 ft. below ground; Lake Cumberland in south central Kentucky; Lincoln birthplace, Hodgenville; My Old Kentucky Home, Bardstown; Cumberland Gap Natl. Historical Park, Middlesboro; Kentucky Horse Park, Lexington.

Famous Kentuckians include Muhammad Ali, John James Audubon, Alben Barkley, Daniel Boone, Louis D. Brandeis, John C. Breckinridge, Kit Carson, Albert B. "Happy" Chandler, Cassius Marcellus Clay, Henry Clay, Jefferson Davis, "Casey" Jones, Abraham Lincoln, Mary Todd Lincoln, Thomas Hunt Morgan, Carry Nation, Col. Harland Sanders, Diane Sawyer, Jesse Stuart, Adlai Stevenson, Zachary Taylor, Robert Penn Warren, Whitney Young, Jr.

Chamber of Commerce. 452 Versailles Rd., P.O. Box 817, Frankfort, KY 40602.

Toll-free travel information. 1-800-225-TRIP, extension 67 in U.S., Ontario & Quebec, Canada.

Louisiana

Pelican State

People. Population (1992): 4,287,195; **rank:** 21. **Pop. density:** 98.4 per sq. mi. **Racial distrib.** (1990): 67.3% White; 30.8% Black; 2.2% Hispanic. **Net change** (1990-92): 1.6%.

Geography. Total area: 47,752 sq. mi.; **rank:** 31. **Land area:** 43,566 sq. mi. **Acres forested land:** 13,883,000. **Location:** West South Central state on the Gulf Coast. **Climate:** subtropical, affected by continental weather patterns. **Topography:** lowlands of marshes and Mississippi R. flood plain; Red R. Valley lowlands; upland hills in the Florida Parishes; average elevation, 100 ft. **Capital:** Baton Rouge.

Economy. Principal industries: wholesale and retail trade, government, manufacturing, construction, transportation, mining. **Principal manufactured goods** (1991): chemical products, foods, transportation equipment, electronic equipment, petroleum products, lumber, wood, and paper. **Agriculture: Chief crops** (1991): soybean, sugarcane, rice, corn, cotton, sweet potatoes, pecans, sorghum. **Livestock** (1991): 1.02 mln. cattle; 60,000 hogs/pigs; 16,000 sheep; 1.85 mln. poultry. **Timber/lumber** (1991): pines, hardwoods, oak; 870 mln. bd. ft. **Nonfuel Minerals** (1992): $272.2 mln., mostly salt, sand & gravel, sulfur. **Commercial fishing** (1992): $295.0 mln. **Chief ports:** New Orleans, Baton Rouge, Lake Charles, S. Louisiana Port Commission at La Place, Shreveport. **International airports at:** New Orleans. **Value of construction** (1992): $3.1 bln. **Employment distribution** (1991): 22.8% trade; 23.8% serv.; 21.2% gvt.; 11.4% mfg. **Per capita income** (1992): $15,712. **Unemployment** (1992): 8.1%. **Tourism** (1990): out-of-state visitors spent $8.1 bln. **Sales tax:** 4%.

Finance. FDIC-insured commercial banks & trust companies (1992): 226 **Deposits:** $33.0 bln. **Savings institutions** (1992): 40. **Assets:** $4.0 bln.

Federal government. No. federal civilian employees (Mar. 1992): 22,644. **Avg. salary:** $32,027. **Notable federal facilities:** Barksdale, England, Ft. Polk military bases; Strategic Petroleum Reserve, New Orleans; Michoud Assembly Plant, New Orleans; U.S. Public Service Hospital, Carville.

Energy. Electricity production (1992, MWh, by source): Mineral: 17.6 mln; Nuclear: 10.2 mln.

Education. Student-teacher ratio (1991): 16.6. **Avg. salary, public school teachers** (1992-93): $26,074.

State data. Motto: Union, justice and confidence. **Flower:** Magnolia. **Bird:** Eastern brown pelican. **Tree:** Cypress. **Song:** Give Me Louisiana. **Entered union** Apr. 30, 1812; rank, 18th. **State fair** at: Shreveport; Oct.

History. The area was first visited, 1530, by Cabeza de Vaca and Panfilo de Narvaez. The region was claimed for France by La Salle, 1682. First permanent settlement was by French at Biloxi, now in Mississippi, 1699. France ceded the region to Spain, 1762, took it back, 1800, and sold it to the U.S., 1803, in the Louisiana Purchase. During the Revolution, Spanish Louisiana aided the Americans. Admitted to statehood, 1812, Louisiana was the scene of the Battle of New Orleans, 1815.

Louisiana Creoles are descendants of early French and/or Spanish settlers. About 4,000 Acadians, French settlers in Nova Scotia, Canada, were forcibly transported by the British to Louisiana in 1755 (an event commemorated in Longfellow's *Evangeline*) and settled near Bayou Teche; their descendants became known as Cajuns. Another group, the Islenos, were descendants of Canary Islanders brought to Louisiana by a Spanish governor in 1770. Traces of Spanish and French survive in local dialects.

Tourist attractions. Mardi Gras, French Quarter, Superdome, Dixieland jazz, Aquarium of the Americas, all New Orleans; Battle of New Orleans site; Longfellow-Evangeline Memorial Park; Kent House Museum, Alexandria; Hodges Gardens, Natchilotches.

Famous Louisianans include Louis Armstrong, Pierre Beauregard, Judah P. Benjamin, Braxton Bragg, Grace King, Huey Long, Leonidas K. Polk, Henry Miller Shreve, Edward D. White Jr.

Tourist Information. State Dept. of Culture, Recreation & Tourism, P.O. Box 94291, Baton Rouge, LA 70804-9291.

Toll-free travel information. 1-800-33-GUMBO.

Maine

Pine Tree State

People. Population (1992): 1,235,396; **rank:** 39. **Pop. density:** 40.0 per sq. mi. **Racial distrib.** (1990): 98.4% White; 0.4% Black; 0.6% Hispanic. **Net change** (1990-92): 0.6%.

Geography. Total area: 33,265 sq. mi.; **rank:** 39. **Land area:** 30,865 sq. mi. **Acres forested land:** 17,713,000. **Location:** New England state at northeastern tip of U.S. **Climate:** Southern interior and coastal, influenced by air masses from the S and W; northern clime harsher, avg. +100 in. snow in winter. **Topography:** Appalachian Mtns. extend through state; western borders have rugged terrain; long sand beaches on southern coast; northern coast mainly rocky promontories, peninsulas, fjords. **Capital:** Augusta.

Economy. Principal industries: manufacturing, services, trade, government, finance, insurance, real estate, construction. **Principal manufactured goods:** paper and wood products, transportation equipment. **Agriculture: Chief crops:** potatoes, apples, hay, blueberries. **Livestock** (1986): 135,000 cattle; 79,000 hogs/pigs; 17,000 sheep; 4.9 mln. poultry. **Timber/lumber** (1991): pine, spruce, fir; 847 mln. bd. ft. **Nonfuel Minerals** (1992): $52.9 mln.; construction sand & gravel, cement, crushed stone, dimension stone. **Commercial fishing** (1992): $163.3 mln. **Chief ports:** Searsport, Portland, Eastport. **International airports at:** Portland, Bangor. **Value of construction** (1992): $1.2 bln. **Employment distribution** (1991): 24.7% trade; 24.5% serv.; 18.7% mfg.; 18.7% gvt. **Per capita income** (1992): $18,226. **Unemployment** (1992): 7.1%. **Tourism** (1991): $2.75 bln. **Sales tax:** 6%.

Finance. FDIC-insured commercial banks & trust companies (1992): 21. **Deposits**: $7.4 bln. **Savings institutions** (1992): 12. **Assets**: $600 mln.

Federal government. No. federal civilian employees (Mar. 1992): 11,886. **Avg. salary:** $32,247. **Notable federal facilities:** Kittery Naval Shipyard; Brunswick Naval Air Station; Loring Air Force Base.

Energy. Electricity production (1992, MWh, by source): Hydroelectric: 1.9 mln.; Mineral: 1.9 mln.; Nuclear: 5.4 mln.

Education. Student-teacher ratio (1991): 14.0. **Avg. salary, public school teachers** (1992-93): $30,258.

State data. Motto: Dirigo (I direct). **Flower:** White pine cone and tassel. **Bird:** Chickadee. **Tree:** Eastern white pine. **Song:** State of Maine Song. **Entered union** Mar. 15, 1820; rank, 23d.

History. Maine's rocky coast was explored by the Cabots, 1498-99. French settlers arrived, 1604, at the St. Croix River; English, 1607, on the Kennebec. In 1691, Maine was made part of Massachusetts. In the Revolution, a Maine regiment fought at Bunker Hill; a British fleet destroyed Falmouth (now Portland), 1775, but the British ship Margaretta was captured near Machiasport. In 1820, Maine broke off from Massachusetts, became a separate state.

Tourist attractions. Acadia Nat'l. Park, Bar Harbor, on Mt. Desert Is.; Funtown, Saco; Bath Iron Works and Maine Maritime Museum; Boothbay (Harbor) Railway Museum; Portland Art Museum; Sugarloaf/USA Ski Area; Ogunquit, Portland, York.

Famous "Down Easters" include James G. Blaine, Cyrus H.K. Curtis, Hannibal Hamlin, Longfellow, Sir Hiram and Hudson Maxim, Edna St. Vincent Millay, Kate Douglas Wiggin, Ben Ames Williams.

Chamber of Commerce and Industry. 126 Sewall St., Augusta, ME 04330.

Toll-free travel information. 1-800-533-9595, winter only, out of state only; 1-207-623-0363 year round.

Maryland

Old Line State, Free State

People. Population (1992): 4,908,453; **rank:** 19. **Pop. density:** 502.1 per sq. mi. **Racial distrib.** (1990): 71.0% White; 24.9% Black; 2.9% Asian; 2.6% Hispanic. **Net change** (1990-92): 2.7%.

Geography. Total area: 10,460 sq. mi.; **rank:** 42. **Land area:** 9,775 sq. mi. **Acres forested land:** 2,632,000. **Location:** South Atlantic state stretching from the Ocean to the Allegheny Mtns. **Climate:** continental in the west; humid subtropical in the east. **Topography:** Eastern Shore of coastal plain and Maryland Main of coastal plain, piedmont plateau, and the Blue Ridge, separated by the Chesapeake Bay. **Capital:** Annapolis.

Economy. Principal industries: manufacturing, services, tourism. **Principal manufactured goods:** electric and electronic equipment; food and kindred products; chemicals and allied products. **Agriculture: Chief crops** (1992): greenhouse & nursery prods, soybeans, corn. **Livestock** (1992): 315,000 cattle; 180,000 hogs/pigs; 33,000 sheep; 257.8 mln. poultry, 280.5 mln. broilers. **Timber/lumber:** hardwoods. **Nonfuel Minerals** (1992): $323.3 mln.; crushed stone, sand & gravel, portland cement. **Commercial fishing** (1992): $36.4 mln. **Chief ports:** Baltimore. **International airports at:** Baltimore-Washington Intl. **Value of construction** (1992): $5.3 bln. **Employment distribution** (1992): 30.3% serv.; 24.2% trade; 19.9% gvt. **Per capita income** (1992): $22,974. **Unemployment** (1992): 6.6%. **Tourism** (1992): tourists spent $4.6 bln. **Sales tax:** 5.0%.

Finance. FDIC-insured commercial banks & trust companies (1992): 102. **Deposits:** $44.0 bln. **Savings institutions** (1992): 83. **Assets:** $15.8 bln.

Federal government. No. federal civilian employees (Mar. 1992): 109,981. **Avg. salary:** $39,640. **Notable federal facilities:** U.S. Naval Academy, Annapolis; Natl. Agric. Research Cen.; Ft. George G. Meade, Aberdeen Proving Ground; Goddard Space Flight Center; Natl. Institutes of Health; Natl. Institute of Standards & Technology; Food & Drug Administration; Bureau of the Census.

Energy. Electricity production (1992, MWh, by source): Hydroelectric: 2.2 mln.; Mineral: 22.5 mln.; Nuclear: 1.2 mln.

Education. Student-teacher ratio (1991): 16.9 **Avg. salary, public school teachers** (1992-93): $39,141.

State data. Motto: Fatti Maschii, Parole Femine (Manly deeds, womanly words). **Flower:** Black-eyed susan. **Bird:** Baltimore oriole. **Tree:** White oak. **Song:** Maryland, My Maryland. **Seventh** of the original 13 states to ratify Constitution, Apr. 28, 1788. **State fair** at: Timonium; late Aug.-early Sept.

History. Capt. John Smith first explored Maryland, 1608. William Claiborne set up a trading post on Kent Is. in Chesapeake Bay, 1631. Britain granted land to Cecilius Calvert, Lord Baltimore, 1632; his brother led 200 settlers to St. Marys River, 1634. The bravery of Maryland troops in the Revolution, as at the Battle of Long Island, won the state its nickname, The Old Line State. In the War of 1812, when a British fleet tried to take Fort McHenry, Marylander Francis Scott Key, 1814, wrote *The Star-Spangled Banner.*

Tourist Attractions. Racing events include the Preakness and Maryland Million, both at Pimlico track, Baltimore, and the International at Laurel Race Course; Baltimore Orioles pro baseball at Oriole Park, Camden Yards. Also Annapolis yacht races; Ocean City beach resort; restored Ft. McHenry, Baltimore, near which Francis Scott Key wrote *The Star-Spangled Banner;* Antietam Battlefield, 1862, near Hagerstown; South Mountain Battlefield, 1862; Edgar Allan Poe house, Baltimore; National Aquarium, Baltimore Harborplace; The State House, Annapolis, 1772, the oldest still in use in the U.S.; Montgomery & Prince George's County, gateway to Washington, D.C.

Famous Marylanders include Benjamin Banneker, Francis Scott Key, H.L. Mencken, William Pinkney, Upton Sinclair, Roger B. Taney, Charles Willson Peale.

Maryland Dept. of Economic & Employment Development. 217 E. Redwood St., Baltimore, MD 21202; (410) 333-6970.

Toll-free travel information. 1-800-543-1036.

Massachusetts

Bay State, Old Colony

People. Population (1992): 5,998,375; **rank:** 13. **Pop. density:** 765.3 per sq. mi. **Racial distrib.** (1990): 89.8% White; 5.0% Black; 2.4% Asian; 4.8% Hispanic. **Net change** (1990-92): −0.3%.

Geography. Total area: 8,284 sq. mi.; **rank:** 45. **Land area:** 7,838 sq. mi. **Acres forested land:** 3,097,000. **Location:** New England state along Atlantic seaboard. **Climate:** temperate, with colder and drier clime in western region. **Topography:** jagged indented coast from Rhode Island around Cape Cod; flat land yields to stony upland pastures near central region and gentle hilly country in west; except in west, land is rocky, sandy, and not fertile. **Capital:** Boston.

Economy. Principal industries (1990): services, trade, manufacturing. **Principal manufactured goods** (1990): electric and electronic equipment, machinery, industrial machinery and equipment, printing and publishing, fabricated metal products. **Agriculture: Chief crops:** cranberries, greenhouse, nursery, vegetables. **Livestock** (1983): 120,000 cattle; 50,000 hogs/pigs; 8,000 sheep; 125,000 horses, ponies; 3.6 mln. poultry. **Timber/lumber** (1991): white pine, oak, other hard woods; 45 mln. bd. ft. **Nonfuel Minerals** (1992): $156.9 mln.; mostly construction sand & gravel, crushed stone. **Commercial fishing** (1992): $280.6 mln. **Chief ports:** Boston, Fall River, New Bedford, Salem, Gloucester, Plymouth. **International airports at:** Boston. **Value of construction** (1992): $5.7 bln. **Employment distribution** (1990): 30.8% trade; 23.5% serv.; 17.5% mfg. **Per capita income** (1992): $24,059. **Unemployment** (1992): 8.5%. **Tourism** (1987): out-of-state visitors spent $12.9 bln. **Sales tax:** 5%.

Finance. FDIC-insured commercial banks & trust companies (1992): 73. **Deposits:** $67.8 bln. **Savings institutions** (1992): 22. **Assets:** $3.2 bln.

Federal government. No. federal civilian employees (Mar. 1992): 32,034. **Avg. salary:** $35,222. **Notable federal facilities:** Ft. Devens; Thomas P. O'Neill Jr. Federal Bldg., J.W. McCormack Bldg., John Fitzgerald Kennedy Federal Bldg., Boston; Q.M. Laboratory, Natick.

Energy. Electricity production (1992, MWh, by source): Hydroelectric: 0.5 mln.; Mineral: 29.3 mln.; Nuclear: 4.8 mln.

Education. Student-teacher ratio (1991): 15.1. **Avg. salary, public school teachers** (1992-93): $39,245.

State data. Motto: Ense Petit Placidam Sub Libertate Quietem (By the sword we seek peace, but peace only under liberty). **Flower:** Mayflower. **Bird:** Chickadee. **Tree:** American elm. **Song:** All Hail to Massachusetts. **Sixth** of the original 13 states to ratify Constitution, Feb. 6, 1788.

History. Pilgrims settled in Plymouth, 1620; the following year they gave thanks for their survival with the first Thanksgiving Day. Indian opposition reached a high point in King Philip's War, 1675-76, won by the colonists. Demonstrations against British restrictions set off the "Boston Massacre," 1770, and Boston "tea party," 1773. First bloodshed of the Revolution was at Lexington, 1775.

Tourist attractions. Cape Cod—Plymouth Rock, Plymouth Plantation, Mayflower II, Provincetown artists colony; Boston—Freedom Trail, Museum of Fine Arts, Children's Museum, Museum of Science, New England Aquarium, JFK Library, Boston Ballet, Boston Pops, Boston Symphony Orchestra; Berkshires—Tanglewood, Jacob's Pillow Dance Festival, Hancock Shaker Village, Berkshire Scenic Railroad; Old Sturbridge Village; Walden Pond; Naismith Memorial Basketball Hall of Fame, Springfield.

Famous "Bay Staters" include John Adams, John Quincy Adams, Samuel Adams, Louisa May Alcott, Horatio Alger, Susan B. Anthony, Crispus Attucks, Clara Barton, Alexander Graham Bell, Emily Dickinson, Ralph Waldo Emerson, John Hancock, Nathaniel Hawthorne, Oliver W. Holmes, Winslow Homer, Elias Howe, John Fitzgerald Kennedy, Samuel F.B. Morse, Edgar Allan Poe, Paul Revere, Henry David Thoreau, James McNeil Whistler, John Greenleaf Whittier.

Tourist information. Massachusetts Office of Travel & Tourism, 100 Cambridge St., 13th Floor, Boston, MA 02202.

Toll-free travel information. 1-800-624-MASS.

Michigan

Great Lakes State, Wolverine State

People. Population (1992): 9,436,628; **rank:** 8. **Pop. density:** 166.1 per sq. mi. **Racial distrib.** (1990): 83.4% White; 13.9% Black; 2.2% Hispanic. **Net change** (1990-92): 1.5%.

Geography. Total area: 58,527 sq. mi.; **rank:** 23. **Land area:** 56,809 sq. mi. **Acres forested land:** 18,220,000. **Location:** East North Central state bordering on 4 of the 5 Great Lakes, divided into an Upper and Lower Peninsula by the Straits of Mackinac, which link lakes Michigan and Huron. **Climate:** well-defined seasons tempered by the Great Lakes. **Topography:** low rolling hills give way to northern tableland of hilly belts in Lower Peninsula; Upper Peninsula is level in the east, with swampy areas; western region is higher and more rugged. **Capital:** Lansing.

Economy. Principal industries: manufacturing, services, tourism, agriculture, mining. **Principal manufactured goods:** transportation equipment, machinery, fabricated metals, primary metals, food prods., rubber & plastics. **Agriculture: Chief crops:** corn, winter wheat, soybeans, dry beans, oats, hay, sugar beets, honey, asparagus, sweet corn, apples, cherries, grapes, peaches, blueberries, flowers. **Livestock** (1992): 1.2 mln. cattle; 1.3 mln. hogs/pigs; 103,000 sheep; 11.5 mln. poultry. **Timber/lumber** (1991): maple, oak, aspen; 313 mln. bd. ft. **Nonfuel Minerals** (1992): $1.4 bln.; iron ore, portland cement, crushed stone, sand & gravel. **Commercial fishing** (1992): $10.4 mln. **Chief ports:** Detroit, Saginaw River, Escanaba, Muskegon, Sault Ste. Marie, Port Huron, Marine City. **International airports at:** Detroit, Sault Ste. Marie. **Value of construction** (1992): $7.5 bln. **Employment distribution** (1992): 23% mfg.; 24% serv.; **Per capita income** (1992): $19,508. **Unemployment** (1992): 8.8%. **Tourism** (1990): travelers spent $16.5 bln. **Sales tax:** 4%.

Finance. FDIC-insured commercial banks & trust companies (1992): 230. **Deposits:** $78.7 bln. **Savings institutions** (1992): 34. **Assets:** $29.3 bln.

Federal government. No. federal civilian employees (Mar. 1992): 27,218. **Avg. salary:** $34,270. **Notable federal facilities:** Isle Royal, Sleeping Bear Dunes national parks.

Energy. Electricity production (1992, MWh, by source): Hydroelectric: 0.8 mln.; Mineral: 52.9 mln.; Nuclear: 29.0 mln.

Education. Student-teacher ratio (1991): 19.2. **Avg. salary, public school teachers** (1992-93): $43,331.

State data. Motto: Si Quaeris Peninsulam Amoenam Circumspice (If you seek a pleasant peninsula, look about you). **Flower:** Apple blossom. **Bird:** Robin. **Tree:** White pine. **Song:** Michigan, My Michigan. **Entered union** Jan. 26, 1837; rank, 26th. **State fair** at: Detroit, late Aug.-early Sept.; Upper Peninsula (Escanaba), mid-Aug; Michigan Festival, mid.-Aug.

History. French fur traders and missionaries visited the region, 1616, set up a mission at Sault Ste. Marie, 1641, and a settlement there, 1668. The whole region went to Britain, 1763. Anthony Wayne defeated their Indian allies at Fallen Timbers, Ohio, 1794. The British returned, 1812, seized Ft. Mackinac and Detroit. Oliver H. Perry's Lake Erie victory and William H. Harrison's troops, who carried the war to the Thames River in Canada, 1813, freed Michigan once more.

Tourist attractions. Henry Ford Museum, Greenfield Village, reconstruction of a typical 19th cent. American village, both in Dearborn; Michigan Space Ctr., Jackson; Tahquamenon *(Hiawatha)* Falls; DeZwaan windmill and

Tulip Festival, Holland; "Soo Locks," St. Marys Falls Ship Canal, Sault Ste. Marie.

Famous Michiganians include Ralph Bunche, Thomas A. Edison, Gerald R. Ford, Paul de Kruif, Edna Ferber, Henry Ford, Aretha Franklin, Edgar Guest, Lee Iacocca, Robert Ingersoll, Magic Johnson, Will Kellogg, Ring Lardner, Elmore Leonard, Charles Lindbergh, Joe Louis, Madonna, Pontiac, Diana Ross, Tom Selleck, Lily Tomlin, Stewart Edward White, Malcolm X.

Chamber of Commerce: 200 N. Washington Sq., Suite 400, Lansing, MI 48933.

Toll-free travel information. 1-800-543-2937.

Minnesota

North Star State, Gopher State

People. Population (1992): 4,480,034; **rank:** 20. **Pop. density:** 56.3 per sq. mi. **Racial distrib.** (1990): 94.4% White; 2.2% Black; 1.8% Asian; 1.2% Hispanic. **Net change** (1990-92): 2.4%.

Geography. Total area: 84,402 sq. mi.; **rank:** 12. **Land area:** 79,617 sq. mi. **Acres forested land:** 16,583,000. **Location:** West North Central state bounded on the E by Wisconsin and Lake Superior, on the N by Canada, on the W by the Dakotas, and on the S by Iowa. **Climate:** northern part of state lies in the moist Great Lakes storm belt; the western border lies at the edge of the semi-arid Great Plains. **Topography:** central hill and lake region covering approx. half the state; to the NE, rocky ridges and deep lakes; to the NW, flat plain; to the S, rolling plains and deep river valleys. **Capital:** St. Paul.

Economy. Principal industries: agri business, forest products, mining, manufacturing, tourism. **Principal manufactured goods:** food processing, non-electrical machinery, chemicals, paper, electric and electronic equipment, printing and publishing, instruments, fabricated metal products. **Agriculture: Chief crops:** corn, soybeans, wheat, sugar beets, sunflowers, barley. **Livestock** (1990): 2.95 mln. cattle; 4.25 mln. hogs/pigs; 285,000 sheep; 12.7 mln. poultry. **Timber/lumber** (1991): needleleaves and hardwoods; 95 mln. bd. ft. **Nonfuel Minerals** (1992): 1.4 bln.; mostly iron ore, construction sand & gravel, industrial sand and gravel, crushed stone. **Commercial fishing** (1992): $101,000. **Chief ports:** Duluth, St. Paul, Minneapolis. **International airports at:** Minneapolis-St. Paul. **Value of construction** (1992): $5.2 bln. **Employment distribution** (1990): 24.4% trade; 26.0% serv.; 18.3% mfg.; 15.8% gvt. **Per capita income** (1992): $20,049. **Unemployment** (1992): 5.1%. **Tourism** (1987): out-of-state visitors spent $3.6 bln. **Sales tax:** 6½%.

Finance. FDIC-insured commercial banks & trust companies (1992): 608. **Deposits:** $45.0 bln. **Savings institutions** (1992): 24. **Assets:** $6.7 bln.

Federal government. No. federal civilian employees (Mar. 1992): 15,193. **Avg. salary:** $38,854.

Energy. Electricity production (1992, MWh, by source): Hydroelectric: 0.7 mln.; Mineral: 21.9 mln.; Nuclear: 11.1 mln.

Education. Student-teacher ratio (1991): 17.2. **Avg. salary, public school teachers** (1992-93): $35,656.

State data. Motto: L'Etoile du Nord (The star of the north). **Flower:** Pink and white lady's-slipper. **Bird:** Common loon. **Tree:** Red pine. **Song:** Hail! Minnesota. **Entered union** May 11, 1858; rank, 32d. **State fair** at: Saint Paul; late Aug. to early Sept.

History. Fur traders and missionaries from French Canada opened the region in the 17th century. Britain took the area east of the Mississippi, 1763. The U.S. took over that portion after the Revolution and in 1803 bought the western area as part of the Louisiana Purchase. The U.S. built present Ft. Snelling, 1820, bought lands from the Indians, 1837. Sioux Indians staged a bloody uprising, 1862, and were driven from the state.

Tourist attractions. Minnehaha Falls, Minneapolis, inspiration for Longfellow's *Hiawatha;* over 15,000 lakes; 66 state parks; 25 historical sites; Minneapolis Aquatennial; Ordway Theater, St. Paul; Guthrie Theater, Minneapolis; professional baseball, football, hockey. Voyageurs Nat'l. Park, a water wilderness along the Canadian border; Mayo Clinic, Rochester; St. Paul Winter Carnival; North Shore (of Lake Superior).

Famous Minnesotans include F. Scott Fitzgerald, Cass Gilbert, Hubert Humphrey, Sister Elizabeth Kenny, Sinclair Lewis, Paul Manship, E. G. Marshall, William and Charles Mayo, Walter F. Mondale, Charles Schulz, Harold Stassen, Thorstein Veblen.

Tourist Information. Minnesota Office of Tourism, 375 Jackson St., 250 Skyway Level, St. Paul, MN 55101.

Toll-free travel information. 1-800-328-1461.

Mississippi

Magnolia State

People. Population (1992): 2,614,294; **rank:** 31. **Pop. density:** 55.7 per sq. mi. **Racial distrib.** (1990): 63.5% White; 35.6% Black; 0.6% Hispanic. **Net change** (1990-92): 1.6%.

Geography. Total area: 47,689 sq. mi.; **rank:** 32. **Land area:** 46,914 sq. mi. **Acres forested land:** 16,693,000. **Location:** East South Central state bordered on the W by the Mississippi R. and on the S by the Gulf of Mexico. **Climate:** semi-tropical, with abundant rainfall, long growing season, and extreme temperatures unusual. **Topography:** low, fertile delta bet. the Yazoo and Mississippi rivers; loess bluffs stretching around delta border; sandy Gulf coastal terraces followed by piney woods and prairie; rugged, high sandy hills in extreme NE followed by black prairie belt. Pontotoc Ridge, and flatwoods into the north central highlands. **Capital:** Jackson.

Economy. Principal industries: manufacturing, government, wholesale and retail trade. **Principal manufactured goods:** apparel, food & kindred prods., furniture, lumber and wood products, electrical machinery, transportation equip. **Agriculture: Chief crops** (1990): cotton, catfish, rice, soybeans. **Livestock** (1991): 1.3 mln. cattle; 149,000 hogs/pigs; 456.5 mln. broilers. **Timber/lumber** (1991): pine, oak, hardwoods; 2.25 bln. bd. ft. **Nonfuel Minerals** (1992): $109.5 mln., mostly construction sand & gravel. **Commercial fishing** (1992): $31.3 mln. **Chief ports:** Pascagoula, Vicksburg, Gulfport, Natchez, Greenville. **Value of construction** (1992): $1.7 bln. **Employment distribution** (1992): 26.1% mfg.; 21.7% gvt.; 20.8% trade; 18.4% serv. **Per capita income** (1992): $14,088. **Unemployment** (1992): 8.1%. **Tourism** (1990): out-of-state visitors spent $1.68 bln. **Sales tax:** 7%.

Finance. FDIC-insured commercial banks & trust companies (1992): 123. **Deposits:** $19.1 bln. **Savings institutions** (1992): 21. **Assets:** $2.6 bln.

Federal government. No. federal civilian employees (Mar. 1992): 18,396. **Avg. salary:** $32,586. **Notable federal facilities:** Columbus, Keesler AF bases; Meridian Naval Air Station, John C. Stennis Space Center; U.S. Army Corps of Engineers Waterway Experiment Station.

Energy. Electricity production (1992, MWh, by source): Mineral: 9.1 mln.; Nuclear: 5.8 mln.

Education. Student-teacher ratio (1991): 17.9. **Avg. salary, public school teachers** (1992-93): $24,369.

State data. Motto: Virtute et Armis (By valor and arms). **Flower:** Magnolia. **Bird:** Mockingbird. **Tree:** Magnolia. **Song:** Go, Mississippi! **Entered union** Dec. 10, 1817; rank, 20th. **State fair** at: Jackson; Fall.

History. De Soto explored the area, 1540, sighted the Mississippi River, 1541. La Salle traced the river from Illinois to its mouth and claimed the entire valley for France, 1682. First settlement was the French Ft. Maurepas, near Ocean Springs, 1699. The area was ceded to Britain, 1763; American settlers followed. During the Revolution, Spain seized part of the area and refused to leave even after the U.S. acquired title at the end of the Revolution, finally moving out, 1798. Mississippi seceded 1861. Union forces captured Corinth and Vicksburg and destroyed Jackson and much of Meridian.

Tourist attractions. Vicksburg National Military Park and Cemetery, other Civil War sites; Natchez Trace; Indian mounds; Antebellum Home; pilgrimages in Natchez and some 25 other cities; Jubilee Jam, May, Jackson;

Mardi Gras and blessing of the shrimp fleet, June, both in Biloxi.

Famous Mississippians include Dana Andrews, Jimmy Buffet, Hodding Carter III, William Faulkner, Shelby Foote, John Grisham, Fannie Lou Hamer, Jim Henson, Robert Johnson, James Earl Jones, B.B. King, L.Q.C. Lamar, Willie Morris, Elvis Presley, Leontyne Price, Charlie Pride, Margaret Walker, Eudora Welty, Tennessee Williams, Oprah Winfrey, Richard Wright, Tammy Wynette.

Dept. of Economic & Community Development. P.O. Box 849, Jackson, MS 39205-0849.

Toll-free travel information. 1-800-359-3297; 1-800-647-2290 out of state.

Missouri

Show Me State

People. Population (1992): 5,192,632; **rank:** 15. **Pop. density:** 75.4 per sq. mi. **Racial distrib.** (1990): 87.7% White; 10.7% Black; 1.2% Hispanic. **Net change** (1990-92): 1.5%.

Geography. Total area: 69,697 sq. mi.; **rank:** 19. **Land area:** 68,898 sq. mi. **Acres forested land:** 12,523,000. **Location:** West North Central state near the geographic center of the conterminous U.S.; bordered on the E by the Mississippi R., on the NW by the Missouri R. **Climate:** continental, susceptible to cold Canadian air, moist, warm Gulf air, and drier SW air. **Topography:** Rolling hills, open, fertile plains, and well-watered prairie N of the Missouri R.; south of the river land is rough and hilly with deep, narrow valleys; alluvial plain in the SE; low elevation in the west. **Capital:** Jefferson City.

Economy. Principal industries: agriculture, manufacturing, aerospace, tourism. **Principal manufactured goods:** transportation equipment, food and related products, electrical and electronic equipment, chemicals. **Agriculture: Chief crops:** soybeans, corn, wheat, hay. **Livestock** (1991): 4.55 mln. cattle; 2.7 mln. hogs/pigs; 111,000 sheep; 7.6 mln. chickens and eggs, 21.5 mln. turkeys. **Timber/lumber** (1991): oak, hickory; 249 mln. bd. ft. **Nonfuel minerals** (1992): $924.6 mln., mostly lead, crushed stone, portland cement. **Chief ports:** St. Louis, Kansas City. **International airports at:** St. Louis, Kansas City. **Value of construction** (1992): $4.4 bln. **Employment distribution** (1991): 25.2% services; 24.0% trade; 18.1% mfg.; 16.2% gvt. **Per capita income** (1992): $18,835. **Unemployment** (1992): 5.7%. **Tourism** (1990): total travelers spent $5 bln. **Sales tax:** 4.225%.

Finance. FDIC-insured commercial banks & trust companies (1992): 532. **Deposits:** $54.4 bln. **Savings institutions** (1992): 61. **Assets:** $14.8 bln.

Federal government: No. federal civilian employees (Mar. 1992): 44,700. **Avg. salary:** $32,797. **Notable federal facilities:** Federal Reserve banks, St. Louis, Kansas City; Ft. Leonard Wood, Rolla; Jefferson Barracks, St. Louis; Whiteman AFB, Knob Noster.

Energy. Electricity production (1992 MWh, by source): Hydroelectric: 0.8 mln.; Mineral: 38.1 mln.; Nuclear: 7.7 mln.

Education. Student-teacher ratio (1991): 15.8. **Avg. salary, public school teachers** (1992-93): $29,410.

State data. Motto: Salus Populi Suprema Lex Esto (The welfare of the people shall be the supreme law). **Flower:** Hawthorn. **Bird:** Bluebird. **Tree:** Dogwood. **Song:** Missouri Waltz. **Entered union** Aug. 10, 1821; rank, 24th. **State fair** at: Sedalia; 3d week in Aug.

History. DeSoto visited the area, 1541. French hunters and lead miners made the first settlement, c. 1735, at Ste. Genevieve. The U.S. acquired Missouri as part of the Louisiana Purchase, 1803. The fur trade and the Santa Fe Trail provided prosperity; St. Louis became the "jump-off" point for pioneers on their way West. Pro- and anti-slavery forces battled each other there during the Civil War.

Tourist attractions. Mark Twain Area, Hannibal; Pony Express Museum, St. Joseph; Harry S. Truman Library, Independence; Gateway Arch, St. Louis; Silver Dollar City, Branson Worlds of Fun, Kansas City; Lake of the Ozarks, Churchill Memorial, Fulton; State Capitol, Jefferson City.

Famous Missourians include Josephine Baker, Thomas Hart Benton, George Caleb Bingham, Gen. Omar Bradley, Dale Carnegie, George Washington Carver, Walter Cronkite, Walt Disney, T.S. Eliot, Betty Grable, Jesse James, J. C. Penney, John J. Pershing, Joseph Pulitzer, Ginger Rogers, Bess Truman, Harry S. Truman, Mark Twain, Tennessee Williams.

Chamber of Commerce: 400 E. High St., P.O. Box 149, Jefferson City, MO 65101.

Toll-free travel information. 1-800-877-1234.

Montana

Treasure State

People. Population (1992): 823,697; **rank:** 44. **Pop. density:** 5.66 per sq. mi. **Racial distrib.** (1990): 92.7% White; 0.3% Black; 6.0% Amer. Indian; 1.5% Hispanic. **Net change** (1990-92): 3.1%.

Geography. Total area: 147,046 sq. mi.; **rank:** 4. **Land area:** 145,556 sq. mi. **Acres forested land:** 21,910,000. **Location:** Mountain state bounded on the E by the Dakotas, on the S by Wyoming, on the S/SW by Idaho, and on the N by Canada. **Climate:** colder, continental climate with low humidity. **Topography:** Rocky Mtns. in western third of the state; eastern two-thirds gently rolling northern Great Plains. **Capital:** Helena.

Economy. Principal industries: agriculture, timber, mining, tourism, oil & gas. **Principal manufactured goods:** food prods., wood & paper prods., primary metals, printing & publishing, petroleum & coal prods. **Agriculture: Chief crops:** wheat, barley, sugar beets, hay, oats. **Livestock** (1992): 2.6 mln. cattle; 225,000 hogs/pigs; 688,000 sheep; 780,000 poultry. **Timber/lumber** (1991): Douglas fir, pines, larch; 1.36 bln. bd. ft. **Nonfuel Minerals** (1992): $603.3 mln. mostly metallics. **International airports at:** Great Falls, Billings, Kalispell, Missoula. **Value of construction** (1992): $603.8 mln. **Employment distribution** (1991): 26.8% serv.; 22.6% trade; 18.4% govt.; 7.0% agric.; 5.6% mfg. **Per capita income** (1992): $16,062. **Unemployment** (1992): 6.7%. **Tourism** (1990): non-resident visitors spent $751 mln.

Finance. FDIC-insured commercial banks & trust companies (1992): 145. **Deposits:** $6.5 bln. **Savings institutions** (1992): 9. **Assets:** $1.3 bln.

Federal government. No. federal civilian employees (Mar. 1992): 8,782. **Avg. salary:** $32,759. **Notable federal facilities:** Malmstrom AFB; Ft. Peck, Hungry Horse, Libby, Yellowtail dams; numerous missile silos.

Energy. Electricity production (1992, MWh, by source): Hydroelectric: 6.9 mln; Mineral: 15.8 mln.

Education. Student-teacher ratio (1991): 15.8. **Avg. salary, public school teachers** (1992-93): $28,514.

State data. Motto: Oro y Plata (Gold and silver). **Flower:** Bitterroot. **Bird:** Western meadowlark. **Tree:** Ponderosa pine. **Song:** Montana. **Entered union** Nov. 8, 1889; rank, 41st. **State fair** at: Great Falls; late July to early Aug.

History. French explorers visited the region, 1742. The U.S. acquired the area partly through the Louisiana Purchase, 1803, and partly through the explorations of Lewis and Clark, 1805-06. Fur traders and missionaries established posts in the early 19th century. Indian uprisings reached their peak with the Battle of the Little Bighorn, 1876. Mining activity and the coming of the Northern Pacific Railway, 1883, brought population growth.

Tourist attractions. Glacier Natl. Park, on the Continental Divide, is a scenic and recreational wonderland, with 60 glaciers, 200 lakes, and many trout streams. Yellowstone Natl. Park has 3 of the 5 entrances in Montana, with 2,221,000 acres of scenic beauty, inc. geysers, mountains, canyons, streams, lakes, forests, waterfalls.

Also, Museum of the Plains Indian, Blackfeet Reservation near Browning; Little Bighorn Battlefield Natl. Monument & Custer Natl. Cemetery; Flathead Lake, in the NW; Lewis and Clark Caverns State Park, near Whitehall; 7 Indian reservations, covering over 5 million acres; state capitol and historical society, Helena.

Famous Montanans include Gary Cooper, Marcus Daly, Chet Huntley, Will James, Myrna Loy, Mike Mansfield, Brent Musberger, Jeannette Rankin, Charles M. Russell, Lester Thurow.

Chamber of Commerce. 2030 11th Ave., P.O. Box 1730, Helena, MT 59624.

Toll-free travel information. 1-800-541-1447.

Nebraska

Cornhusker State

People. Population (1992): 1,605,603; **rank:** 36. **Pop. density:** 20.9 per sq. mi. **Racial distrib.** (1990): 93.8% White; 3.6% Black; 2.3% Hispanic. **Net change** (1990-92): 1.7%.

Geography. Total area: 77,355 sq. mi.; **rank:** 15. **Land area:** 76,878 sq. mi. **Acres forested land:** 722,000. **Location:** West North Central state with the Missouri R. for a NE/E border. **Climate:** continental semi-arid. **Topography:** till plains of the central lowland in the eastern third rising to the Great Plains and hill country of the north central and NW. **Capital:** Lincoln.

Economy. Principal industries: agriculture, food processing, manufacturing. **Principal manufactured goods:** foods, machinery, electric and electronic equipment, primary and fabricated metal products, transportation equipment, instruments & related prod. **Agriculture: Chief crops:** corn, sorghum, soybeans, hay, wheat, beans, oats, potatoes, sugar beets. **Livestock** (1990): 6 mln. cattle; 4.2 mln. hogs/pigs; 160,000 sheep; 6.2 mln. chickens, 2.1 mln. turkeys. **Nonfuel Minerals** (1992): $111.2 mln.; mostly portland cement, crushed stone, construction sand & gravel. **Chief ports:** Omaha, Sioux City, Brownville, Blair, Plattsmouth, Nebraska City. **Value of construction** (1992): $1.5 bln. **Employment distribution** (1990): 25.5% trade; 24.4% serv.; 19.7% gvt.; 13.8% mfg.; 8.8% agric. **Per capita income** (1992): $19,084. **Unemployment** (1992): 3.0%. **Tourism** (1991): traveler expenditures $1.7 bln. **Sales tax:** 5%, + some local sales taxes of .5-1.5%.

Finance. FDIC-insured commercial banks & trust companies (1992): 389. **Deposits:** $18.6 bln. **Savings institutions** (1992): 16. **Assets:** $7.1 bln.

Federal government. No. federal civilian employees (Mar. 1992): 9,135. **Avg. salary:** $33,058. **Notable federal facilities:** Strategic Air Command Base, Omaha.

Energy. Electricity production (1992, MWh, by source): Hydroelectric: 0.7 mln.; Mineral: 12.2 mln.; Nuclear: 8.8 mln.

Education. Student-teacher ratio (1991): 14.7. **Avg. salary, public school teachers** (1992-93): $28,718.

State data. Motto: Equality before the law. **Flower:** Goldenrod. **Bird:** Western meadowlark. **Tree:** Cottonwood. **Song:** Beautiful Nebraska. **Entered union** Mar. 1, 1867; rank, 37th. **State fair** at: Lincoln; late Aug. to mid-Sept.

History. Spanish and French explorers and fur traders visited the area prior to the Louisiana Purchase, 1803. Lewis and Clark passed through, 1804-06. First permanent settlement was Bellevue, near Omaha, 1823. Many Civil War veterans settled under free land terms of the 1862 Homestead Act; struggles followed between homesteaders and ranchers.

Tourist attractions. Architecturally unique, 400'-tall state capitol, Lincoln; Stuhr Museum of the Prairie Pioneer, Grand Island; Museum of the Fur Trade, Chadron; State Museum (Elephant Hall), Lincoln; Joslyn Art Museum, Omaha; Strategic Air Command Museum, Bellevue; Boys Town, founded by Fr. Flanagan, west of Omaha; Arbor Lodge State Park, Nebraska City; Buffalo Bill Ranch State Historical Park, North Platte; Pioneer Village, Minden; Oregon Trail landmarks, Scotts Bluff National Monument, Chimney Rock Historic Site, Ft. Robinson; Hastings Museum, McDonald Planetarium, Hastings.

Famous Nebraskans include Fred Astaire, Charles W. and William Jennings Bryan, Johnny Carson, Willa Cather, William F. "Buffalo Bill" Cody, Loren Eiseley, Rev. Edward J. Flanagan, Henry Fonda, Gerald R. Ford, Rollin Kirby, Harold Lloyd, Wright Morris, J. Sterling Morton, John Neidhardt, George Norris, Gen. John J. Pershing, Chief Red Cloud, Mari Sandoz, Roscoe Pound, Malcolm X.

Chamber of Commerce. 1320 Lincoln Mall, Box 95128, Lincoln, NE 68501.

Toll-free travel information. 1-800-742-7595; 1-800-228-4307 out of state.

Nevada

Sagebrush State, Battle Born State, Silver State

People. Population (1992): 1,327,387; **rank:** 38. **Pop. density:** 12.1 per sq. mi. **Racial distrib.** (1990): 84.3% White; 6.6% Black; 3.2% Asian; 10.4% Hispanic. **Net change** (1990-92): 10.5%.

Geography. Total area: 110,561 sq. mi.; **rank:** 7. **Land area:** 109,806 sq. mi. **Acres forested land:** 8,928,000. **Location:** Mountain state bordered on N by Oregon and Idaho, on E by Utah and Arizona, on SE by Arizona, and on SW/W by California. **Climate:** semi-arid and arid. **Topography:** rugged N-S mountain ranges; highest elevation, Boundary Peak, 13,140 ft.; southern area is within the Mojave Desert; lowest elevation, Colorado River at southern tip of state, 479 ft. **Capital:** Carson City.

Economy. Principal industries: gaming, tourism, mining, manufacturing, government, agriculture, warehousing, trucking. **Principal manufactured goods:** gaming devices, chemicals, aerospace prods.; lawn & garden irrigation equip.; seismic & machinery-monitoring devices. **Agriculture: Chief crops:** hay, alfalfa seed, potatoes, onions, garlic, barley, wheat. **Livestock** (1992): 480,000 cattle; 10,000 hogs/pigs; 91,000 sheep; 12,000 poultry. **Timber/lumber:** piñon, juniper, other pines. **Nonfuel Minerals** (1992): $2.4 bln.; mostly gold, construction sand & gravel. **International airports at:** Las Vegas, Reno. **Value of construction** (1992): $4.0 bln. **Employment distribution** (1992): 44.4% serv.; 20.3% trade; 13.4% gvt. **Per capita income** (1992): $20,266. **Unemployment** (1992): 6.6%. **Tourism** (1991): out-of-state travelers spent over $10 bln. **Sales tax:** 6.5-7%.

Finance. FDIC-insured commercial banks & trust companies (1992): 19. **Deposits:** $9.1 bln. **Savings institutions** (1992): 5. **Assets:** $3.8 bln.

Federal government. No. federal civilian employees (Mar. 1992): 7,272. **Avg. salary:** $34,817. **Notable federal facilities:** Nevada Test Site; Hawthorne Army Ammunition Plant, Nellis Air Force Base & Gunnery Range; Fallon Naval Air Station; Palomino Valley Wild Horse & Burro Placement Center.

Energy. Electricity production (1992, MWh, by source): Hydroelectric: 4.6 mln.; Mineral: 16.5 mln.

Education. Student-teacher ratio (1991): 18.6. **Avg. salary, public school teachers** (1992-93): $34,119.

State data. Motto: All for our country. **Flower:** Sagebrush. **Bird:** Mountain bluebird. **Trees:** Single-leaf piñon and bristlecone pine. **Song:** Home Means Nevada. **Entered union** Oct. 31, 1864; rank, 36th. **State fair** at: Reno; early Sept.

History. Nevada was first explored by Spaniards in 1776. Hudson's Bay Co. trappers explored the north and central region, 1825; trader Jedediah Smith crossed the state, 1826 and 1827. The area was acquired by the U.S., in 1848, at the end of the Mexican War. First settlement, Mormon Station, now Genoa, was est. 1849. In the early 20th century, Nevada adopted progressive measures such as the initiative, referendum, recall, and woman suffrage.

Tourist attractions. Legalized casino gambling provided the impetus for the development of resort facilities at Lake Tahoe, Reno, Las Vegas, Laughlin, and elsewhere. Ghost towns, rodeos, mountain climbing, skiing, golfing, trout fishing, water sports and hunting important. Notable are Hoover Dam, Lake Mead Natl. Recreation Area, Lake Tahoe, Great Basin Natl. Park, Valley of Fire State Park & Virginia City. Annual events inc. Helldorado Days & Rodeo, Las Vegas; Reno Rodeo; Basque Festival, Elko; Nevada Day, Carson City; Cowboy Poetry Gathering, Elko.

Famous Nevadans include Walter Van Tilburg Clark, Sarah Winnemucca Hopkins, Paul Laxalt, Dat So La Lee, John William Mackay, Pat McCarran, Key Pittman, William Morris Stewart.

Tourist Information. Commission on Tourism, Capitol Complex, Carson City, NV 89710.

Toll-free travel information. 1-800-638-2328.

New Hampshire

Granite State

People. Population (1992): 1,110,801; **rank:** 41. **Pop. density:** 123.8 per sq. mi. **Racial distrib.** (1990): 98.0% White; 0.6% Black; 1.0% Hispanic. **Net change** (1990-92): −0.1%.

Geography. Total area: 9,279 sq. mi.; **rank:** 44. **Land area:** 8,969 sq. mi. **Acres forested land:** 5,021,000. **Location:** New England state bounded on S by Massachusetts, on W by Vermont, on N/NW by Canada, on E by Maine and the Atlantic O. **Climate:** highly varied, due to its nearness to high mountains and ocean. **Topography:** low, rolling coast followed by countless hills and mountains rising out of a central plateau. **Capital:** Concord.

Economy. Principal industries: tourism, manufacturing, agriculture, trade, mining. **Principal manufactured goods:** machinery, electrical & electronic products, plastics, fabricated metal products. **Agriculture: Chief crops:** dairy products, nursery and greenhouse products, hay, vegetables, fruit, maple syrup & sugar prods. **Livestock** (1992): 55,000 cattle; 9,500 hogs/pigs; 9,000 sheep; 15,000 horses; 310,000 poultry. **Timber/lumber** (1991): white pine, hemlock, oak, birch; 203 mln. bd. ft. **Nonfuel Minerals** (1992): $42.4 mln.; mostly construction sand & gravel, crushed & dimension stone. **Commercial fishing** (1992): $11.5 mln. **Chief ports:** Portsmouth, Hampton, Rye. **Value of construction** (1992): $1.0 bln. **Employment distribution** (1992): 20.0% mfg.; 25.4% trade; 26.6% serv.; 14.9% gvt. **Per capita income** (1992): $22,934. **Unemployment** (1992): 7.5%. **Tourism** (1992): out-of-state visitors spent $3.3 bln.

Finance. FDIC-insured commercial banks & trust companies (1992): 32. **Deposits:** $6.9 bln. **Savings institutions** (1992): 9. **Assets:** $1.6 bln.

Federal government. No. federal civilian employees (Mar. 1992): 3,747. **Avg. salary:** $37,070.

Energy. Electricity production (1992, MWh, by source): Hydroelectric: 0.9 mln.; Mineral: 5.8 mln.; Nuclear: 8.5 mln.

Education: Student-teacher ratio (1991): 15.5. **Avg. salary, public school teachers** (1992-93): $33,931.

State data. Motto: Live free or die. **Flower:** Purple lilac. **Bird:** Purple finch. **Tree:** White birch. **Song:** Old New Hampshire. **Ninth** of the original 13 states to ratify the Constitution, June 21, 1788.

History. First explorers to visit the New Hampshire area were England's Martin Pring, 1603, and Champlain, 1605. First settlement was Odiorne's Point (now port of Rye), 1623. Indian raids were halted, 1759, by Robert Rogers' Rangers. Before the Revolution, New Hampshire men seized a British fort at Portsmouth, 1774, and drove the royal governor out, 1775. Three regiments served in the Continental Army and scores of privateers raided British shipping.

Tourist attractions. Mt. Washington, highest peak in Northeast, hub of network of trails; Lake Winnipesaukee; White Mt. Natl. Forest; Crawford, Franconia, Pinkham notches in White Mt. region—Franconia famous for the Old Man of the Mountain, described by Hawthorne as the Great Stone Face; the Flume, a spectacular gorge; the aerial tramway on Cannon Mt; Strawbery Banke, Portsmouth; Shaker Village, Canterbury; Saint-Gaudens, natl. historic site, Cornish; Mt. Monadnock.

Famous New Hampshirites include Salmon P. Chase, Ralph Adams Cram, Mary Baker Eddy, Daniel Chester French, Robert Frost, Horace Greeley, Sarah Buell Hale, Franklin Pierce, Augustus Saint-Gaudens, Daniel Webster.

Tourist Information. Department of Resources and Economic Development, Division of Travel & Tourism Development, P.O. Box 856, Concord, NH 03302-0856; 603-271-2666.

New Jersey

Garden State

People. Population (1992): 7,789,060; **rank:** 9. **Pop. density:** 1,049.9 per sq. mi. **Racial distrib.** (1990): 79.3% White; 13.4% Black; 3.5% Asian; 9.6% Hispanic. **Net change** (1990-92): 0.8%.

Geography. Total area: 7,787 sq. mi.; **rank:** 46. **Land area:** 7,419 sq. mi. **Acres forested land:** 1,985,000. **Location:** Middle Atlantic state bounded on the N and E by New York and the Atlantic O., on the S and W by Delaware and Pennsylvania. **Climate:** moderate, with marked difference bet. NW and SE extremities. **Topography:** Appalachian Valley in the NW also has highest elevation, High Pt., 1,801 ft.; Appalachian Highlands, flat-topped NE-SW mountain ranges; Piedmont Plateau, low plains broken by high ridges (Palisades) rising 400-500 ft.; Coastal Plain, covering three-fifths of state in SE, gradually rises from sea level to gentle slopes. **Capital:** Trenton.

Economy. Principal industries: services, trade, manufacturing. **Principal manufactured goods:** chemicals, electronic and electrical equipment, non-electrical machinery, fabricated metals. **Agriculture: Chief crops:** hay, corn, soybeans, tomatoes, blueberries, peaches, cranberries. **Livestock** (1992): 77,000 cattle; 24,000 hogs/pigs; 13,000 sheep; 2.1 mln. poultry. **Timber/lumber** (1991): pine, cedar, mixed hardwoods. **Nonfuel Minerals** (1992): $213.7 mln.; mostly crushed stone, construction sand & gravel. **Commercial fishing** (1992): $97.5 mln. **Chief ports:** Newark, Elizabeth, Hoboken, Camden. **International airports at:** Newark. **Value of construction** (1992): $5.5 bln. **Employment distribution** (1992): 28.2% serv.; 23.5% trade; 15.3% mfg.; 16.5% gvt. **Per capita income** (1992): $26,457. **Unemployment** (1992): 8.4%. **Tourism** (1992): tourists spent $17.9 bln. **Sales tax:** 6%.

Finance. FDIC-insured commercial banks & trust companies (1992): 117. **Deposits:** $81.2 bln. **Savings institutions** (1992): 81. **Assets:** $24.0 bln.

Federal government. No. federal civilian employees (Mar. 1992): 39,395. **Avg. salary:** $37,745. **Notable federal facilities:** McGuire AFB; Fort Dix; Fort Monmouth; Picatinny Arsenal; Lakewood Naval Air Station, Lakehurst Naval Air Engineering Center; Naval Air Warfare Center, Ewing.

Energy. Electricity production (1992, MWh, by source): Mineral: 8.4 mln.; Nuclear: 18.8 mln.

Education. Student-teacher ratio (1991): 13.8. **Avg. salary, public school teachers** (1992-93): $43,997.

State Data. Motto: Liberty and prosperity. **Flower:** Purple violet. **Bird:** Eastern goldfinch. **Tree:** Red oak. **Third** of the original 13 states to ratify the Constitution, Dec. 18, 1787. **State fair:** usually Aug.

History. The Lenni-Lenape (Delaware) Indians had mostly peaceful relations with European colonists who arrived after the explorers Verrazano, 1524, and Hudson, 1609. The Dutch were first; when the British took New Netherland, 1664, the area between the Delaware and Hudson Rivers was given to Lord John Berkeley and Sir George Carteret. New Jersey was the scene of nearly 100 battles, large and small, during the Revolution, including Trenton, 1776, Princeton, 1777, Monmouth, 1778.

Tourist attractions. 127 miles of beaches; Miss America Pageant and hotel-casinos, Atlantic City; Grover Cleveland birthplace, Caldwell; Cape May Historic District; Edison Labs, W. Orange; Great Adventure amusement park; Liberty State Park; Meadowlands Sports Complex; Pine Barrens wilderness area; Princeton University; numerous Revolutionary War historical sites; State Aquarium, Camden.

Famous New Jerseyans include Count Basie, Judy Blume, Aaron Burr, Grover Cleveland, James Fenimore Cooper, Stephen Crane, Thomas Edison, Albert Einstein,

Alexander Hamilton, Joyce Kilmer, Gen. George McClellan, Thomas Paine, Molly Pitcher, Paul Robeson, Philip Roth, Walter Schirra, Frank Sinatra, Bruce Springsteen, Walt Whitman, William Carlos Williams, Woodrow Wilson.

Chamber of Commerce. 50 W. State St., Trenton, NJ 08608.

Toll-free travel information. 1-800-JERSEY-7.

New Mexico

Land of Enchantment

People. Population (1992): 1,581,227; **rank:** 37. **Pop. density:** 13.0 per sq. mi. **Racial distrib.** (1990): 75.6% White; 2.0% Black; 8.9% Amer. Indian; 38.2% Hispanic. **Net change** (1990-92): 4.4%.

Geography. Total area: 121,593 sq. mi.; **rank:** 5. **Land area:** 121,364 sq. mi. **Acres forested land:** 18,526,000. **Location:** southwestern state bounded by Colorado on the N, Oklahoma, Texas, and Mexico on the E and S, and Arizona on the W. **Climate:** dry, with temperatures rising or falling 5° F with every 1,000 ft. elevation. **Topography:** eastern third, Great Plains; central third, Rocky Mtns. (85% of the state is over 4,000 ft. elevation); western third, high plateau. **Capital:** Santa Fe.

Economy. Principal industries: government, services, trade. **Principal manufactured goods:** foods, machinery, apparel, lumber, printing, transportation equipment. **Agriculture: Chief crops:** hay, onions, wheat, pecans, corn, cotton, sorghum. **Livestock** (1990): 1.34 mln. cattle; 27,000 hogs; 462,000 sheep; 1.43 mln. poultry. **Timber/lumber** (1991): Ponderosa pine, Douglas fir; 139 mln. bd. ft. **Nonfuel Minerals** (1992): $866.1 mln.; copper, potash, construction sand & gravel. **International airports at:** Albuquerque. **Value of construction** (1992): $1.4 bln. **Employment distribution** (1990): 26% serv.; 2% agric.; 10% mfg.; 26.2% gvt. **Per capita income** (1992): $15,353. **Unemployment** (1992): 6.8%. **Tourism** (1990): out-of-state visitors spent $2.2 bln. **Sales tax:** 5-6.75%.

Finance. FDIC-insured commercial banks & trust companies (1992): 83. **Deposits:** $10.7 bln. **Savings institutions** (1992): 13. **Assets:** $1.2 bln.

Federal government. No. federal civilian employees (Mar. 1992): 23,716. **Avg. salary:** $33,157. **Notable federal facilities:** Kirtland, Cannon, Holloman AF bases; Los Alamos Scientific Laboratory; White Sands Missile Range; National Solar Observatory; National Radio Astronomy Observatory.

Energy. Electricity production (1992, MWh, by source): Hydroelectric: 0.1 mln.; Mineral: 18.7 mln.

Education. Student-teacher ratio (1991): 17.6. **Avg. salary, public school teachers** (1992-93): $26,355.

State data. Motto: Crescit Eundo (It grows as it goes). **Flower:** Yucca. **Bird:** Roadrunner. **Tree:** Piñon. **Song:** O, Fair New Mexico; Asi Es Nuevo Mexico. **Entered union** Jan. 6, 1912; rank, 47th. **State fair** at: Albuquerque; mid-Sept.

History. Franciscan Marcos de Niza and a black slave Estevan explored the area, 1539, seeking gold. First settlements were at San Juan Pueblo, 1598, and Santa Fe, 1610. Settlers alternately traded and fought with the Apaches, Comanches, and Navajos. Trade on the Santa Fe Trail to Missouri started 1821. The Mexican War was declared May, 1846, Gen. Stephen Kearny took Santa Fe, August. In the 1870s, cattlemen staged the famed Lincoln County War in which Billy (the Kid) Bonney played a leading role. Pancho Villa raided Columbus, 1916.

Tourist Attractions. Carlsbad Caverns, a national park, has caverns on 3 levels and the largest natural cave "room" in the world, 1,500 by 300 ft., 300 ft. high; White Sands Natl. Monument, the largest gypsum deposit in the world.

Pueblo ruins from 100 AD, Chaco Canyon; Acoma, the "sky city," built atop a 357-ft. mesa; 19 Pueblo, 4 Navajo, and 2 Apache reservations. Also, ghost towns, dude ranches, skiing, hunting, and fishing.

Famous New Mexicans include Billy (the Kid) Bonney, Kit Carson, Peter Hurd, Archbishop Jean Baptiste Lamy, Nancy Lopez, Bill Mauldin, Georgia O'Keeffe, Kim Stanley, Al Unser, Bobby Unser, Lew Wallace.

Tourist information. New Mexico Dept. of Tourism, P.O. Box 20003, Santa Fe, N.M. 87503.

Toll-free travel information. 1-800-545-2040.

New York

Empire State

People. Population (1992): 18,119,416; **rank:** 2. **Pop. density:** 383.7 per sq. mi. **Racial distrib.** (1990): 74.4% White; 15.9% Black; 3.9% Asian; 12.3% Hispanic. **Net change** (1990-92): 0.7%.

Geography. Total area: 49,108 sq. mi.; **rank:** 30. **Land area:** 47,224 sq. mi. **Acres forested land:** 18,775,000. **Location:** Middle Atlantic state, bordered by the New England states, Atlantic Ocean, New Jersey and Pennsylvania, Lakes Ontario and Erie, and Canada. **Climate:** variable; the SE region moderated by the ocean. **Topography:** highest and most rugged mountains in the NE Adirondack upland; St. Lawrence-Champlain lowlands extend from Lake Ontario NE along the Canadian border; Hudson-Mohawk lowland follows the flows of the rivers N and W, 10-30 mi. wide; Atlantic coastal plain in the SE; Appalachian Highlands, covering half the state westward from the Hudson Valley, include the Catskill Mtns., Finger Lakes; plateau of Erie-Ontario lowlands. **Capital:** Albany.

Economy. Principal industries: manufacturing, finance, communications, tourism, transportation, services. **Principal manufactured goods:** books and periodicals, clothing and apparel, pharmaceuticals, machinery, instruments, toys and sporting goods, electronic equipment, automotive and aircraft components. **Agriculture: Chief crops:** apples, cabbage, cauliflower, celery, cherries, grapes, corn, peas, snap beans, sweet corn. **Products:** milk, cheese, maple syrup, wine. **Livestock** (1990): 1.6 mln. cattle; 103,000 hogs/pigs; 92,000 sheep; 9.8 mln. poultry. **Timber/lumber** (1991): saw log production; 380 mln. bd. ft. **Nonfuel Minerals** (1992): $715.0 mln.; mostly crushed stone, salt, cement, construction sand & gravel, zinc. **Commercial fishing** (1992): $54.0 mln. **Chief ports:** New York, Buffalo, Albany. **International airports at:** New York, Buffalo, Syracuse, Massena, Ogdensburg, Watertown, Niagara Falls, Newburgh, Sullivan county. **Value of construction** (1992): $14.2 bln. **Employment distribution** (1992): 30% serv.; 20% trade; 18% gvt.; 13% mfg. **Per capita income** (1992): $23,534. **Unemployment** (1992): 8.5%. **Tourism** (1991): tourists spent $19.0 bln. **Sales tax:** 4-8¼%.

Finance. FDIC-insured commercial banks & trust companies (1992): 189. **Deposits:** $480.7 bln. **Savings institutions** (1992): 68. **Assets:** $41.5 bln.

Federal government. No. federal civilian employees (Mar. 1992): 70,019. **Avg. salary:** $35,369. **Notable federal facilities:** West Point Military Academy; Merchant Marine Academy; Ft. Drum; Griffiss, Plattsburgh AF bases; Watervliet Arsenal.

Energy. Electricity production (1992, MWh, by source): Hydroelectric: 20.0 mln.; Mineral: 49.3 mln.; Nuclear: 27.2 mln.

Education. Student-teacher ratio (1991): 15.4. **Avg. salary, public school teachers** (1992-93): $44,600.

State data. Motto: Excelsior (Ever upward). **Flower:** Rose. **Bird:** Bluebird. **Tree:** Sugar maple. **Song:** I Love New York. **Eleventh** of the original 13 states to ratify the Constitution, July 26, 1788. **State fair** at: Syracuse; late Aug.-early Sept.

History. In 1609 Henry Hudson visited the river that bears his name and Champlain explored the lake, far upstate, that was named for him. Dutch built posts near present-day Albany and New York City in 1624; in 1626 they settled Manhattan. A British fleet seized New Netherland, 1664. Ninety-two of the 300 or more engagements of the Revolution were fought in New York, including the Battle of Bemis Heights-Saratoga, a turning point of the war.

Tourist attractions. New York City; Adirondack and Catskill mtns.; Finger Lakes, Great Lakes; Long Island beaches; Thousand Islands; Niagara Falls; Saratoga Springs racing and spas; Philipsburg Manor, Sunnyside, the restored home of Washington Irving, The Dutch Church of Sleepy Hollow, all in North Tarrytown; Corning Glass Center and Steuben factory, Corning; Fenimore House, National Baseball Hall of Fame and Museum, both in Cooperstown; Ft. Ticonderoga overlooking Lakes George and Champlain; Albany's Empire State Plaza; Lake Placid Olympic Village.

The Franklin D. Roosevelt National Historic Site, Hyde Park, includes the graves of Pres. and Mrs. Roosevelt, the family home since 1867, the Roosevelt Library. Sagamore Hill, Oyster Bay, the Theodore Roosevelt estate, includes his home.

Famous New Yorkers include Susan B. Anthony, Peter Cooper, George Eastman, Millard Fillmore, George and Ira Gershwin, Julia Ward Howe, Charles Evans Hughes, Henry and William James, Herman Melville, Franklin Delano Roosevelt, Theodore Roosevelt, Alfred E. Smith, Elizabeth Cady Stanton, Martin Van Buren, Walt Whitman.

Tourist information: N.Y. State Dept. of Economic Development, 1 Commerce Plaza, Albany, NY 12245.

Toll-free travel information. 1-800-CALLNYS from 50 states & U.S. territories; 1-518-474-4116 from other areas and Canada.

North Carolina

Tar Heel State, Old North State

People. Population (1992): 6,842,691; **rank:** 10. **Pop. density:** 140.5 per sq. mi. **Racial distrib.** (1990): 75.6% White; 22.0% Black; 1.2% Amer. Indian; 1.2% Hispanic. **Net change** (1990-92): 3.2%.

Geography. Total area: 52,669 sq. mi.; **rank:** 28. **Land area:** 48,718 sq. mi. **Acres forested land:** 18,891,000. **Location:** South Atlantic state bounded by Virginia, South Carolina, Georgia, Tennessee, and the Atlantic O. **Climate:** sub-tropical in SE, medium-continental in mountain region; tempered by the Gulf Stream and the mountains in W. **Topography:** coastal plain and tidewater, two-fifths of state, extending to the fall line of the rivers; piedmont plateau, another two-fifths, 200 mi. wide of gentle to rugged hills; southern Appalachian Mtns. contains the Blue Ridge and Great Smoky mtns. **Capital:** Raleigh.

Economy. Principal industries: manufacturing, agriculture, tobacco, tourism. **Principal manufactured goods:** textiles, tobacco products, electrical/electronic equip., chemicals, furniture, food products, non-electrical machinery. **Agriculture: Chief crops:** tobacco, soybeans, corn, peanuts, sweet potatoes, feed grains, vegetables, fruits. **Livestock** (1991): 950,000 cattle; 3.6 mln. hogs/pigs; 19.3 mln. chickens. **Timber/lumber** (1991): yellow pine, oak, hickory, poplar, maple; 1.56 bln. bd. ft. **Nonfuel Minerals** (1992): Total $573.0 mln.; mostly clay, sand & gravel, crushed stone. **Commercial fishing** (1992): $57.5 mln. **Chief ports:** Morehead City, Wilmington. **Value of construction** (1992): $8.0 bln. **Employment distribution** (1992): 26.6% mfg.; 22.8% trade; 20.4% serv.; 16.3% gvt. **Per capita income** (1992): $17,667. **Unemployment** (1992): 5.9%. **Tourism** (1991): out-of-state visitors spent $7.0 bln. **Sales tax:** 6%.

Finance. FDIC-insured commercial banks & trust companies (1992): 81. **Deposits:** $59.7 bln. **Savings institutions** (1992): 60. **Assets:** $10.2 bln.

Federal government. No. federal civilian employees (Mar. 1992): 30,680. **Avg. salary:** $31,155. **Notable federal facilities:** Ft. Bragg; Camp LeJeune Marine Base; U.S. EPA Research and Development Labs, Cherry Point Marine Corps Air Station; Natl. Humanities Center; Natl. Inst. of Environmental Health Science; Natl. Center for Health Statistics Lab, Research Triangle Park.

Energy. Electricity production (1992, MWh, by source): Hydroelectric: 5.7 mln.; Mineral: 46.5 mln.; Nuclear: 21.7 mln.

Education. Student-teacher ratio (1991): 16.8. **Avg. salary, public school teachers** (1992-93): $29,367.

State data. Motto: Esse Quam Videri (To be rather than to seem). **Flower:** Dogwood. **Bird:** Cardinal. **Tree:** Pine. **Song:** The Old North State. **Twelfth** of the original 13 states to ratify the Constitution, Nov. 21, 1789. **State fair** at: Raleigh; mid-Oct.

History. The first English colony in America was the first of 2 established by Sir Walter Raleigh on Roanoke Is., 1585 and 1587. The first group returned to England; the second, the "Lost Colony," disappeared without trace. Permanent settlers came from Virginia, c. 1660. Roused by British repressions, the colonists drove out the royal governor, 1775; the province's congress was the first to vote for independence; ten regiments were furnished to the Continental Army. Cornwallis' forces were defeated at Kings Mountain, 1780, and forced out after Guilford Courthouse, 1781.

Tourist attractions. Cape Hatteras and Cape Lookout national seashores; Great Smoky Mtns. (half in Tennessee); Guilford Courthouse and Moore's Creek parks, 66 Revolutionary battle sites; Bennett Place, NW of Durham, where Gen. Joseph Johnston surrendered the last Confederate army to Gen. Wm. Sherman; Ft. Raleigh, Roanoke Is., where Virginia Dare, first child of English parents in the New World, was born Aug. 18, 1587; Wright Brothers National Memorial, Kitty Hawk; N.C. Zoo, Asheboro; N.C. Symphony, & N.C. Museum, Raleigh.

Famous North Carolinians include Richard J. Gatling, Billy Graham, Andy Griffith, Andrew Jackson, Andrew Johnson, Michael Jordan, Wm. Rufus King, Charles Kuralt, Dolley Madison, Edward R. Murrow, James K. Polk, Enos Slaughter, Thomas Wolfe.

Tourist information. Travel & Tourism Division, 430 No. Salisbury St., Raleigh, NC 27603.

Toll-free travel information. 1-800-VISITNC.

North Dakota

Peace Garden State

People. Population (1992): 635,927; **rank:** 47. **Pop. density:** 9.2 per sq. mi. **Racial distrib.** (1990): 94.6% White; 0.6% Black; 4.1% Amer. Indian; 0.7% Hispanic. **Net change** (1990-1992): −0.5%.

Geography. Total area: 70,702 sq. mi.; **rank:** 17. **Land area:** 68,994 sq. mi. **Acres forested land:** 460,000. **Location:** West North Central state, situated exactly in the middle of North America, bounded on the N by Canada, on the E by Minnesota, on the S by South Dakota, on the W by Montana. **Climate:** continental, with a wide range of temperature and moderate rainfall. **Topography:** Central Lowland in the E comprises the flat Red River Valley and the Rolling Drift Prairie; Missouri Plateau of the Great Plains on the W. **Capital:** Bismarck.

Economy. Principal industries: agriculture, mining, tourism, manufacturing, telecommunications, energy. **Principal manufactured goods:** farm equipment, processed foods, fabricated metal, high-tech. electronics. **Agriculture: Chief crops:** spring wheat, durum, barley, rye, flaxseed, oats, potatoes, dried edible beans, honey, soybeans, sugar beets, sunflowers, hay. **Livestock** (1992): 1.85 mln. cattle; 290,000 hogs/pigs; 214,000 sheep; 1.5 mln. poultry. **Nonfuel Minerals** (1992): $17.7 mln.; mostly construction sand & gravel, lime. **International airports at:** Fargo, Grand Forks, Bismarck, Minot. **Value of construction** (1992): $586.9 mln. **Employment distribution** (1991): 22.8% trade; 35.2% serv.; 18.6% gvt.; 11.7% agric. **Per capita income** (1992): $16,854. **Unemployment** (1992): 4.9%. **Tourism** (1991): $790 mln. **Sales tax:** 5-6%.

Finance. FDIC-insured commercial banks & trust companies (1992): 146. **Deposits:** $6.8 bln. **Savings institutions** (1992): 4. **Assets:** $6.7 bln.

Federal government. No. federal civilian employees (Mar. 1992): 5,505. **Avg. salary:** $30,795. **Notable federal facilities:** Strategic Air Command bases at Minot, Grand Forks; Northern Prairie Wildlife Research Center; Garrison Dam; Theodore Roosevelt Natl. Park; Grand Forks Energy Research Center; Ft. Union Natl. Historic Site.

Energy. Electricity production (1992, MWh, by source): Hydroelectric: 1.9 mln.; Mineral: 24.3 mln.

Education. Student-teacher ratio (1991): 15.3. **Avg. salary, public school teachers** (1992-93): $25,211.

State data. Motto: Liberty and union, now and forever, one and inseparable. **Flower:** Wild prairie rose. **Bird:** Western meadowlark. **Tree:** American elm. **Song:** North Dakota Hymn. **Entered union** Nov. 2, 1889; rank, 39th. **State fair** at: Minot; 3d week in July.

History. Pierre La Verendrye was the first French fur trader in the area, 1738, followed later by the English. The U.S. acquired half the territory in the Louisiana Purchase, 1803. Lewis and Clark built Ft. Mandan, spent the winter of 1804-05 there. In 1818, American ownership of the other half was confirmed by agreement with Britain. First permanent settlement was at Pembina, 1812. Missouri River steamboats reached the area, 1832; the first railroad, 1873, bringing many homesteaders. The state was first to hold a presidential primary, 1912.

Tourist attractions. North Dakota Heritage Center, state capitol grounds; Bonanzaville, Fargo, restored pioneer town; Ft. Union Trading Post Natl. Historic Site, built 1829; Lake Sakakawea, 180 miles of fishing, boating, 1,600 miles of shoreline. Interntl. Peace Garden, 2,200-acre tract extending across the border into Manitoba; 65,000-acre Theodore Roosevelt National Park, Badlands, contains the president's Elkhorn Ranch; Ft. Abraham Lincoln State Park and Museum, S of Mandan.

Famous North Dakotans include Maxwell Anderson, Angie Dickinson, John Bernard Flannagan, Louis L'Amour, Peggy Lee, Eric Sevareid, Vilhjalmur Stefansson, Lawrence Welk.

Chamber of Commerce. P.O. Box 2639, 2000 Schafer St., Bismarck, ND 58501.

Toll-free travel information. 1-800-437-2077.

Ohio

Buckeye State

People. Population (1992): 11,016,385; **rank:** 7. **Pop. density:** 269.0 per sq. mi. **Racial distrib.** (1990): 87.8% White; 10.6% Black; 1.3% Hispanic. **Net change** (1990-92): 1.6%.

Geography. Total area: 41,330 sq. mi.; **rank:** 35. **Land area:** 40,953 sq. mi. **Acres forested land:** 7,309,000. **Location:** East North Central state bounded on the N by Michigan and Lake Erie; on the E and S by Pennsylvania, West Virginia, and Kentucky; on the W by Indiana. **Climate:** temperate but variable; weather subject to much precipitation. **Topography:** generally rolling plain; Allegheny plateau in E; Lake [Erie] plains extend southward; central plains in the W. **Capital:** Columbus.

Economy. Principal industries: manufacturing, trade, services. **Principal manufactured goods:** transportation equipment, machinery, primary and fabricated metal products. **Agriculture: Chief crops:** corn, hay, winter wheat, oats, soybeans. **Livestock** (1992): 1.6 mln. cattle; 1.9 mln. hogs/pigs; 24.9 mln. broilers, 5 mln. turkeys. **Timber/lumber** (1991): oak, ash, maple, walnut, beech; 295 mln. bd. ft. **Nonfuel Minerals** (1992): $679.9 mln.; mostly crushed stone, construction sand & gravel, lime, portland cement. **Commercial fishing** (1992): $2.6 mln. **Chief ports:** Toledo, Conneaut, Cleveland, Ashtabula. **International airports at:** Cleveland, Cincinnati, Columbus, Dayton. **Value of construction** (1992): $10.8 bln. **Employment distribution** (1992): 21.7% mfg.; 24.0% trade; 25.6% serv.; 15.2% gvt. **Per capita income** (1992): $18,624. **Unemployment** (1992): 7.2%. **Tourism** (1992): travelers spent $8.8 bln.

Finance. FDIC-insured commercial banks & trust companies (1992): 280. **Deposits:** $92.2 bln. **Savings institutions** (1992): 181. **Assets:** $36.5 bln.

Federal government. No. federal civilian employees (Mar. 1992): 55,426. **Avg. salary:** $35,745. **Notable federal facilities:** Wright Patterson AF base; Defense Construction Supply Center; Lewis Research Ctr.; Portsmouth Gaseous Diffusion Plant; Mound Laboratory.

Energy. Electricity production (1992, MWh, by source): Hydroelectric: 0.2 mln.; Mineral: 107.6 mln.; Nuclear: 13.9 mln.

Education. Student-teacher ratio (1991): 17.3. **Avg. salary, public school teachers** (1992-93): $34,600.

State data. Motto: With God, all things are possible. **Flower:** Scarlet carnation. **Bird:** Cardinal. **Tree:** Buckeye. **Song:** Beautiful Ohio. **Entered union** Mar. 1, 1803; rank, 17th. **State fair** at: Columbus; August.

History. LaSalle visited the Ohio area, 1669. American fur-traders arrived, beginning 1685; the French and Indians sought to drive them out. During the Revolution, Virginians defeated the Indians, 1774, but hostilities were renewed, 1777. The region became U.S. territory after the Revolution. First organized settlement was at Marietta, 1788. Indian warfare ended with Anthony Wayne's victory at Fallen Timbers, 1794. In the War of 1812, Oliver Hazard Perry's victory on Lake Erie and William Henry Harrison's invasion of Canada, 1813, ended British incursions.

Tourist attractions. Mound City Group National Monuments, a group of 24 prehistoric Indian burial mounds; Neil Armstrong Air and Space Museum, Wapakoneta; Air Force Museum, Dayton; Pro Football Hall of Fame, Canton; King's Island amusement park, King's Island; Cedar Point amusement park, Sandusky; birthplaces, homes, and memorials to Ohio's 8 U.S. presidents: William Henry Harrison, Grant, Garfield, Hayes, McKinley, Harding, Taft, Benjamin Harrison; Lake Erie Islands, Sandusky; Amish Region, Tuscarawas/Holmes counties; German Village, Columbus; Sea World, Aurora; Jack Nicklaus Sports Center, Mason; Bob Evans Farm, Rio Grande.

Famous Ohioans include Sherwood Anderson, Neil Armstrong, George Bellows, Ambrose Bierce, Clarence Darrow, Paul Laurence Dunbar, Thomas Edison, Clark Gable, John Glenn, Bob Hope, Jack Nicklaus, Jesse Owens, Eddie Rickenbacker, John D. Rockefeller Sr. and Jr., Pete Rose, Gen. Wm. Sherman, Harriet Beecher Stowe, Charles Taft, Robert A. Taft, William H. Taft, James Thurber, Orville Wright.

Chamber of Commerce. 35 E. Gay St., Columbus, OH 43215.

Toll-free travel information. 1-800-BUCKEYE.

Oklahoma

Sooner State

People. Population (1992): 3,212,198; **rank:** 28. **Pop. density:** 46.8 per sq. mi. **Racial distrib.** (1990): 82.1% White; 7.4% Black; 8.0% Amer. Indian; 2.7% Hispanic. **Net change** (1990-92): 2.1%.

Geography. Total area: 69,919 sq. mi.; **rank:** 18. **Land area:** 68,679 sq. mi. **Acres forested land:** 7,283,000. **Location:** West South Central state bounded on the N by Colorado and Kansas; on the E by Missouri and Arkansas; on the S and W by Texas and New Mexico. **Climate:** temperate; southern humid belt merging with colder northern continental; humid eastern and dry western zones. **Topography:** high plains predominate the W, hills and small mountains in the E; the east central region is dominated by the Arkansas R. Basin, and the Red R. Plains, in the S. **Capital:** Oklahoma City.

Economy. Principal industries: manufacturing, mineral and energy exploration and production, agriculture, services, printing & publishing. **Principal manufactured goods:** non-electrical machinery, fabricated metal products, petroleum. **Agriculture: Chief crops:** wheat, hay, peanuts, grain sorghum, soybeans, corn, pecans, oats, barley, rye. **Livestock** (1990): 5.2 mln. cattle; 215,000 hogs/pigs; 135,000 sheep; 4.75 mln. poultry. **Timber/lumber** (1991): pine, oaks, hickory; 219 mln. bd. ft. **Nonfuel Minerals** (1992): $284.3 mln.; mostly crushed stone, portland cement, iodine. **Chief ports:** Catoosa, Muskogee. **International airports at:** Oklahoma City, Tulsa. **Value of construction** (1992): $2.5 bln. **Employment distribution** (1990): 23.3% trade; 22.2% gvt.; 23.0% serv.; 14.0% mfg. **Per capita income** (1992): $16,198. **Unemployment** (1992): 5.7%. **Tourism** (1990): tourists spent $2.56 bln.

Finance. FDIC-insured commercial banks & trust companies (1992): 411. **Deposits:** $24.8 bln. **Savings institutions** (1992): 19. **Assets:** $5.5 bln.

Federal government. No. federal civilian employees (Mar. 1992): 35,022. **Avg. salary:** $32,253. **Notable federal facilities:** Federal Aviation Agency and Tinker AFB, both Oklahoma City; Ft. Sill, Lawton; Altus AFB, Altus; Vance AFB, Enid.

Energy. Electricity production (1992, MWh, by source): Hydroelectric: 2.5 mln.; Mineral: 26.1 mln.

Education. Student-teacher ratio (1991): 15.6. **Avg. salary, public school teachers** (1992-93): $26,051.

State data. Motto: Labor Omnia Vincit (Labor conquers all things). **Flower:** Mistletoe. **Bird:** Scissor-tailed flycatcher. **Tree:** Redbud. **Song:** Oklahoma! **Entered union** Nov. 16, 1907; rank, 46th. **State fair** at: Oklahoma City; last week of Sept.

History. Part of the Louisiana Purchase, 1803, Oklahoma was known as Indian Territory (but was not given territorial government) after it became the home of the "Five Civilized Tribes"—Cherokee, Choctaw, Chickasaw, Creek, and Seminole—1828-1846. The land was also used by Comanche, Osage, and other Plains Indians. As white settlers pressed west, land was opened for homesteading by runs and lottery, the first run taking place Apr. 22, 1889. The most famous run was to the Cherokee Outlet, 1893.

Tourist attractions. State park system—camping, hiking, water sports; Cherokee Heritage Center, Tahlequah; White Water Bay and Frontier City theme pks., both Oklahoma City; Will Rogers Memorial, Claremore; National Cowboy Hall of Fame and Remington Park Race Track, both Oklahoma City; restored Ft. Gibson Stockade, near Muskogee, the Army's largest outpost in Indian lands; Indian pow-wows; rodeos; fishing; hunting; Ouachita National Forest; Enterprise Square, museum devoted to American economic system; Tulsa's art deco district; Woolaroc Museum & Wildlife Preserve, Bartlesville.

Famous Oklahomans include Carl Albert, Johnny Bench, L. Gordon Cooper, Woody Guthrie, Gen. Patrick J. Hurley, Karl Jansky, Mickey Mantle, Carry Nation, Wiley Post, Oral Roberts, Will Rogers, Maria Tallchief, Jim Thorpe.

Chamber of Commerce. 4020 N. Lincoln Blvd., Oklahoma City, OK 73105.

Tourism Dept. P.O. Box 60789, Oklahoma City, OK 73146-0789.

Toll-free travel information. 1-800-652-6552.

Oregon

Beaver State

People. Population (1992): 2,977,331; **rank:** 29. **Pop. density:** 31.0 per sq. mi. **Racial distrib.** (1990): 92.8% White; 1.6% Black; 4.0% Hispanic. **Net change** (1990-92): 4.8%.

Geography. Total area: 97,073 sq. mi.; **rank:** 10. **Land area:** 96,003 sq. mi. **Acres forested land:** 28,057,000. **Location:** Pacific state, bounded on N by Washington; on E by Idaho; on S by Nevada and California; on W by the Pacific. **Climate:** coastal mild and humid climate; continental dryness and extreme temperatures in the interior. **Topography:** Coast Range of rugged mountains; fertile Willamette R. Valley to E and S; Cascade Mtn. Range of volcanic peaks E of the valley; plateau E of Cascades, remaining two-thirds of state. **Capital:** Salem.

Economy. Principal industries: forestry, agriculture, tourism, high technology, manufacturing. **Principal manufactured goods:** lumber & wood products, foods, machinery, fabricated metals, paper, printing & publishing, primary metals. **Agriculture: Chief crops:** greenhouse/nursery prods., hay, farm forest prods., wheat, potatoes, grass seed, pears, onions. **Livestock** (1991): 1.5 mln. cattle; 80,000 hogs/pigs; 466,000 sheep; 3.0 mln. poultry. **Timber/lumber** (1991): Douglas fir, hemlock, ponderosa pine; 6.56 bln. bd. ft. **Nonfuel Minerals** (1992): $199.5 mln.; mostly portland cement, crushed stone, construction sand & gravel. **Commercial fishing** (1992): $76.2 mln. **Chief ports:** Portland, Astoria, Newport, Coos Bay. **International airports at:** Portland. **Value of construction** (1992): $2.9 bln. **Employment distribution** (1991): 25.7% trade; 23.2% serv.; 18.0% mfg.; 17.8% gvt. **Per capita income** (1992): $18,202. **Unemployment** (1992): 7.5%. **Tourism** (1991): travel expenditures, $2.97 bln.

Finance: FDIC-insured commercial banks & trust companies (1992): 51. **Deposits:** $20.3 bln. **Savings institutions** (1992): 8. **Assets:** $3.8 bln.

Federal government. No. federal civilian employees (Mar. 1992): 20,939. **Avg. salary:** $33,628. **Notable federal facilities:** Bonneville Power Administration.

Energy: Electricity production (1992, MWh, by source): Hydroelectric: 30.9 mln.; Mineral: 3.8 mln.

Education. Student-teacher ratio (1991): 18.6. **Avg. salary, public school teachers** (1992-93): $35,435.

State data. Motto: She flies with her own wings. **Flower:** Oregon grape. **Bird:** Western meadowlark. **Tree:** Douglas fir. **Song:** Oregon, My Oregon. **Entered union** Feb. 14, 1859; rank, 33d. **State fair** at: Salem; 11 days ending with Labor Day.

History. American Capt. Robert Gray sighted and sailed into the Columbia River, 1792; Lewis and Clark, traveling overland, wintered at its mouth 1805-06; fur traders followed. Settlers arrived in the Willamette Valley, 1834. In 1843 the first large wave of settlers arrived via the Oregon Trail. Early in the 20th century, the "Oregon System"—political reforms that included the initiative, referendum, recall, direct primary, and woman suffrage—was adopted.

Tourist attractions. John Day Fossil Beds National Monument; Columbia River Gorge; Mt. Hood & Timberline Lodge; Crater Lake National Park; Oregon Dunes National Recreation Area; Ft. Clatsop National Memorial; Oregon Caves National Monument; Oregon Museum of Science and Industry; Shakespearean Festival, Ashland; High Desert Museum, Bend. Also, skiing, fishing; Annual Albany Timber Carnival, Pendelton Round-Up, Portland Rose Festival.

Famous Oregonians include Ernest Bloch, Ernest Haycox, Chief Joseph, Edwin Markham, Tom McCall, Dr. John McLoughlin, Joaquin Miller, Linus Pauling, John Reed, Alberto Salazar, Mary Decker Slaney, William Simon U'Ren.

Tourist Information: Economic Development Department, 775 Summer St. NE, Salem, OR 97310.

Toll-free travel information. 1-800-543-8838; 1-800-547-7842 out of state.

Pennsylvania

Keystone State

People. Population (1992): 12,009,361; **rank:** 5. **Pop. density:** 267.9 per sq. mi. **Racial distrib.** (1990): 88.5% White; 9.2% Black; 2.0% Hispanic. **Net change** (1990-92): 1.1%.

Geography. Total area: 45,308 sq. mi.; **rank:** 33. **Land area:** 44,820 sq. mi. **Acres forested land:** 16,997,000. **Location:** Middle Atlantic state, bordered on the E by the Delaware R.; on the S by the Mason-Dixon Line; on the W by West Virginia and Ohio; on the N/NE by Lake Erie and New York. **Climate:** continental with wide fluctuations in seasonal temperatures. **Topography:** Allegheny Mtns. run SW to NE, with Piedmont and Coast Plain in the SE triangle; Allegheny Front a diagonal spine across the state's center; N and W rugged plateau falls to Lake Erie Lowland. **Capital:** Harrisburg.

Economy. Principal industries: steel, travel, health, apparel, machinery, food & agriculture. **Principal manufactured goods:** primary metals, foods, fabricated metal products, non-electrical machinery, electrical machinery. **Agriculture: Chief crops:** corn, hay, mushrooms, apples, potatoes, winter wheat, oats, vegetables, tobacco, grapes. **Livestock** (1985): 1.96 mln. cattle; 800,000 hogs/pigs; 88,000 sheep; 22.5 mln. poultry. **Timber/lumber** (1991): pine, oak, maple; 650 mln. bd. ft. **Nonfuel Minerals** (1992): $862.6 mln.; mostly crushed stone, cement, lime, construction sand & gravel. **Commercial fishing** (1992): $395,000. **Chief ports:** Philadelphia, Pittsburgh, Erie. **International airports at:** Philadelphia, Pittsburgh, Erie, Harrisburg. **Value of construction**

(1992): $10.0 bln. **Employment distribution** (1986): 24.4% serv.; 23.9% trade; 23.3% mfg.; 14.9% gvt. **Per capita income** (1992): $20,253 **Unemployment** (1992): 7.5%. **Tourism** (1985): out-of-state visitors spent $8.9 bln.

Finance. FDIC-insured commercial banks & trust companies (1992): 289. **Deposits:** $138.1 bln. **Savings institutions** (1992): 101. **Assets:** $24.1 bln.

Federal government. No. federal civilian employees (Mar. 1992): 85,792. **Avg. salary:** $31,999. **Notable federal facilities:** Army War College, Carlisle; Ships Control Ctr., Mechanicsburg; New Cumberland Army Depot; Philadelphia Navy Yard, Philadelphia.

Energy. Electricity production (1992, MWh, by source): Hydroelectric: 0.7 mln.; Mineral: 93.7 mln.; Nuclear: 60.5 mln.

Education. Student-teacher ratio (1991): 16.8. **Avg. salary, public school teachers** (1992-93): $41,580.

State data. Motto: Virtue, liberty and independence. **Flower:** Mountain laurel. **Bird:** Ruffed grouse. **Tree:** Hemlock. **Second** of the original 13 states to ratify the Constitution, Dec. 12, 1787. **State fair** at: Harrisburg; 2d week in Jan.

History. First settlers were Swedish, 1643, on Tinicum Is. In 1655 the Dutch seized the settlement but lost it to the British, 1664. The region was given by Charles II to William Penn, 1681, Philadelphia (brotherly love) was the capital of the colonies during most of the Revolution, and of the U.S., 1790-1800. Philadelphia was taken by the British, 1777; Washington's troops encamped at Valley Forge in the bitter winter of 1777-78. The Declaration of Independence, 1776, and the Constitution, 1787, were signed in Philadelphia.

Tourist attractions. Independence Hall & Natl. Historic Park, Franklin Institute Science Museum, Philadelphia Museum of Art, all in Philadelphia; Valley Forge Natl. Historic Park; Gettysburg Natl. Military Park; Pennsylvania Dutch Country; Hershey; Duquesne Incline, Carnegie Institute, Heinz Hall, all in Pittsburgh; year 'round outdoor sports in Pocono Mtns., Pine Creek River Gorge, Alleghenies, Laurel Highlands & Presque Isle State Park.

Famous Pennsylvanians include Marian Anderson, Maxwell Anderson, James Buchanan, Andrew Carnegie, Stephen Foster, Benjamin Franklin, George C. Marshall, Andrew W. Mellon, Robert E. Peary, Mary Roberts Rinehart, Betsy Ross.

Chamber of Commerce. 222 N. 3d St., Harrisburg, PA 17101.

Toll-free travel information. 1-800-VISITPA.

Rhode Island

Little Rhody, Ocean State

People. Population (1992): 1,005,091; **rank:** 43. **Pop. density:** 961.8 per sq. mi. **Racial distrib.** (1990): 91.4% White; 3.9% Black; 4.6% Hispanic. **Net change** (1990-92): 0.2%.

Geography. Total area: 1,212 sq. mi.; **rank:** 50. **Land area:** 1,045 sq. mi. **Acres forested land:** 399,000. **Location:** New England state. **Climate:** invigorating and changeable. **Topography:** eastern lowlands of Narragansett Basin; western uplands of flat and rolling hills. **Capital:** Providence.

Economy. Principal industries: manufacturing, services. **Principal manufactured goods:** costume jewelry, toys, machinery, textiles, electronics. **Agriculture: Chief crops:** nursery prods., turf, potatoes, apples. **Timber/lumber:** oak. **Nonfuel Minerals** (1992): $14.5 mln.; construction sand & gravel, crushed stone. **Commercial fishing** (1992): $85.7 mln. **Chief ports:** Providence, Quonset Point, Newport. **Value of construction** (1992): $650.6 mln. **Employment distribution** (1992): 31% services; 21.0% mfg.; 21.0% trade. **Per capita income** (1992): $20,299. **Unemployment** (1992): 8.9%. **Tourism** (1992): visitors spent $1.1 bln. **Sales tax:** 7%.

Finance. FDIC-insured commercial banks & trust companies (1992): 13. **Deposits:** $10.9 bln. **Savings institutions** (1992): 3. **Assets:** $1.9 bln.

Federal government. No. federal civilian employees (Mar. 1992): 5,891. **Avg. salary:** $35,734. **Notable federal facilities:** Naval War College; Naval Underwater Warfare Center.

Energy. Electricity production (1992, MWh, by source): Mineral: 0.3 mln.

Education. Student-teacher ratio (1991): 14.6. **Avg. salary, public school teachers** (1992-93): $37,510.

State data. Motto: Hope. **Flower:** Violet. **Bird:** Rhode Island red. **Tree:** Red maple. **Song:** Rhode Island. **Thirteenth** of original 13 states to ratify the Constitution, May 29, 1790.

History. Rhode Island is distinguished for its battle for freedom of conscience and action, begun by Roger Williams, founder of Providence, who was exiled from Massachusetts Bay Colony in 1636, and Anne Hutchinson, exiled in 1638. Rhode Island gave protection to Quakers in 1657 and to Jews from Holland in 1658.

The colonists broke the power of the Narragansett Indians in the Great Swamp Fight, 1675, the decisive battle in King Philip's War. British trade restrictions angered the colonists and they burned the British revenue cutter Gaspee, 1772. The colony declared its independence May 4, 1776. Gen. John Sullivan and Lafayette won a partial victory, 1778, but failed to oust the British.

Tourist attractions. Newport mansions; summer resorts and water sports; various yachting races inc. Newport to Bermuda; Touro Synagogue, Newport, 1763; first Baptist Church in America, Providence, 1638; Gilbert Stuart birthplace, Saunderstown; Narragansett Indian Fall Festival.

Famous Rhode Islanders include Ambrose Burnside, George M. Cohan, Nelson Eddy, Jabez Gorham, Nathanael Greene, Christopher and Oliver La Farge, Matthew C. and Oliver Hazard Perry, Gilbert Stuart.

Chamber of Commerce. 30 Exchange Terr., Providence, RI 02908.

Toll-free travel information. 1-800-556-2484.

South Carolina

Palmetto State

People. Population (1992): 3,603,227. **rank:** 25. **Pop. density:** 119.7 per sq. mi. **Racial distrib.** (1990): 69.0% White; 29.8% Black; 0.9% Hispanic. **Net change** (1990-92): 3.3%.

Geography. Total area: 31,113 sq. mi.; **rank:** 40. **Land area:** 30,111 sq. mi. **Acres forested land:** 12,257,000. **Location:** South Atlantic state, bordered by North Carolina on the N; Georgia on the SW and W; the Atlantic O. on the E, SE and S. **Climate:** humid sub-tropical. **Topography:** Blue Ridge province in NW has highest peaks; piedmont lies between the mountains and the fall line; coastal plain covers two-thirds of the state. **Capital:** Columbia.

Economy: Principal industries: tourism, agriculture, manufacturing. **Principal manufactured goods:** textiles, chemicals and allied products, machinery & fabricated metal products, apparel and related products. **Agriculture: Chief crops:** tobacco, soybeans, corn, cotton, peaches, hay. **Livestock** (1991): 575,000 cattle; 410,000 hogs/pigs; 7.13 mln. chickens, excl. broilers. **Timber/lumber** (1991): pine, oak; 1.3 bln. bd. ft. **Nonfuel Minerals** (1992): $347.3 mln.; mostly crushed stone, cement, clay. **Commercial fishing** (1992): $25.6 mln. **Chief ports:** Charleston, Georgetown, Port Royal. **International airports at:** Charleston. **Value of construction** (1992): $3.4 bln. **Employment distribution** (1992): 24.2% mfg.; 20.3% serv.; 22.6% trade; 6.6% gvt. **Per capita income** (1992): $15,989. **Unemployment** (1992): 6.2%. **Tourism** (1991): $6.4 bln. **Sales tax:** 5%.

Finance. FDIC-insured commercial banks & trust companies (1992): 83. **Deposits:** $19.0 bln. **Savings institutions** (1992): 39. **Assets:** $10.1 bln.

Federal government: No. federal civilian employees (Mar. 1992): 23,657. **Avg. Salary:** $31,494. **Notable federal facilities:** Polaris Submarine Base; Barnwell Nuclear

Power Plant; Ft. Jackson; Parris Island; Savannah River Plant.

Energy. Electricity production (1992, MWh, by source): Hydroelectric: 1.9 mln.; Mineral: 19.1 mln.; Nuclear: 40.3 mln.

Education. Student-teacher ratio (1991): 16.9. **Avg. salary, public school teachers** (1992-93): $29,151.

State data. Motto: Dum Spiro Spero (While I breathe, I hope). **Flower:** Yellow jessamine. **Bird:** Carolina wren. **Tree:** Palmetto. **Song:** Carolina. **Eighth** of the original 13 states to ratify the Constitution, May 23, 1788. **State fair** at: Columbia; mid-Oct.

History. The first English colonists settled, 1670, on the Ashley River, moved to the site of Charleston, 1680. The colonists seized the government, 1775, and the royal governor fled. The British took Charleston, 1780, but were defeated at Kings Mountain that year, and at Cowpens and Eutaw Springs, 1781. In the 1830s, South Carolinians, angered by federal protective tariffs, adopted the Nullification Doctrine, holding that a state can void an act of Congress. The state was the first to secede in 1861, and Confederate troops fired on and forced the surrender of U.S. troops at Ft. Sumter, in Charleston harbor, launching the Civil War.

Tourist attractions. Restored historic Charleston harbor area and Charleston gardens: Middleton Place, Magnolia, Cypress; other gardens at Brookgreen, Edisto, Glencairn; state parks; coastal islands; shore resorts such as Myrtle Beach and Hilton Head Island; fishing and quail hunting; Revolutionary War battle sites; Andrew Jackson State Park & Museum; Carl Sandburg Home, Hendersonville; Ft. Sumter National Monument, in Charleston Harbor; Charleston Museum, est. 1773, is the oldest museum in the U.S.; South Carolina State Museum, one of largest museums in South, Columbia; Riverbanks Zoo, Columbia.

Famous South Carolinians include Charles Bolden, James F. Byrnes, John C. Calhoun, DuBose Heyward, Ernest F. Hollings, Andrew Jackson, Jesse Jackson, James Longstreet, Francis Marion, Ronald McNair, Charles Pinckney, John Rutledge, Thomas Sumter, Strom Thurmond, John B. Watson.

Tourist information: Chamber of Commerce, 930 Richland St., P.O. Box 1360, Columbia, SC 29201; and So. Carolina Dept. of Parks, Recreation, & Tourism, (803) 734-0122; Greater Columbia Convention & Visitors' Bureau, 301 Gervais St., Columbia, SC 29201, (803) 254-0479.

Toll-free travel information. 1-800-346-3634.

South Dakota

Coyote State, Mount Rushmore State

People. Population (1992): 711,154; **rank:** 45. **Pop. density:** 9.37 per sq. mi. **Racial distrib.** (1990): 91.6% White; 0.5% Black; 7.3% Amer. Indian; 0.8% Hispanic. **Net change** (1990-92): 2.2%.

Geography. Total area: 77,116 sq. mi.; **rank:** 16. **Land area:** 75,898 sq. mi. **Acres forested land:** 1,690,000. **Location:** West North Central state bounded on the N by North Dakota; on the E by Minnesota and Iowa; on the S by Nebraska; on the W by Wyoming and Montana. **Climate:** characterized by extremes of temperature, persistent winds, low precipitation and humidity. **Topography:** Prairie Plains in the E; rolling hills of the Great Plains in the W; the Black Hills, rising 3,500 ft., in the SW corner. **Capital:** Pierre.

Economy: Principal industries: agriculture, services, manufacturing. **Principal manufactured goods** (1991): food & kindred prods., machinery, electric & electronic equipment. **Agriculture: Chief crops** (1992): corn, oats, wheat, sunflowers, soybeans, sorghum. **Livestock** (1992): 3.75 mln. cattle; 1.8 mln. hogs/pigs; 591,000 sheep. **Timber/lumber** (1991): ponderosa pine; 168 mln. bd. ft. **Nonfuel Minerals** (1992): $298.1 mln.; mostly gold, portland cement. **Value of construction** (1992): $585.6 mln. **Employment distribution** (1992): 22.3% serv.; 10.5% mfg. **Per capita income** (1992): $16,558. **Unemployment** (1992): 3.1%. **Tourism** (1992): travelers' impact $979 mln. **Sales tax:** 4%.

Finance. FDIC-insured commercial banks & trust companies (1992): 126. **Deposits:** $11.3 bln. **Savings institutions** (1992): 9. **Assets:** $1.0 bln.

Federal government. No. federal civilian employees (Mar. 1992): 7,191. **Avg. salary:** $30,215. **Notable federal facilities:** Bureau of Indian Affairs, Ellsworth AFB, Corp of Engineers, Nat'l Park Service.

Energy. Electricity production (1992, MWh, by source): Hydroelectric: 2.8 mln.; Mineral: 2.3 mln.

Education: Student-teacher ratio (1991): 14.8. **Avg. salary, public school teachers** (1992-93): $24,125.

State data. Motto: Under God, the people rule. **Flower:** Pasqueflower. **Bird:** Ring-necked pheasant. **Tree:** Black Hills spruce. **Song:** Hail, South Dakota. **Entered union** Nov. 2, 1889; rank, 40th. **State fair** at: Huron; late Aug.-early Sept.

History. Les Verendryes explored the region, 1742-43. Lewis and Clark passed through the area, 1804 and 1806. First white American settlement was at Fort Pierre, 1817. Gold was discovered, 1874, on the Great Sioux Reservation; miners rushed in. The U.S. first tried to stop them, then relaxed its opposition. The "Great Dakota Boom" began 1879. A new Indian uprising came in 1890, climaxed by the massacre of Indian families at Wounded Knee.

Tourist attractions. Black Hills; Mt. Rushmore, with colossal likeness of the faces of U.S. Presidents Washington, Jefferson, Lincoln & T. Roosevelt carved by sculptor Gutzon Borglum; Needles Highway; Harney Peak, at 7,242 ft. the tallest peak east of the Rockies; Deadwood, an 1876 Gold Rush town; Custer State Park's buffalo and burro herds; Jewel Cave, the 4th longest cave in the world; Badlands Natl. Park's "moonscape"; "Great Lakes of So. Dakota"; Ft. Sisseton, restored 1864 army frontier post; Great Plains Zoo & Museum in Sioux Falls; Corn Palace in Mitchell; Wind Cave; Mammoth Site, ongoing excavation of prehistoric mammoths; Crazy Horse, mountain carving in progress.

Famous South Dakotans include Sparky Anderson, Catherine Bach, Tom Brokaw, "Calamity Jane", Mary Hart, Crazy Horse, Myron Floren, Alvin H. Hansen, Cheryl Ladd, Dr. Ernest O. Lawrence, George McGovern, Billy Mills, Allen Neuharth, Pat O'Brien, Sitting Bull.

Tourist information. South Dakota Tourism, 711 E. Wells Ave., Pierre, SD 57501-3369.

Toll-free travel information. 1-800-SDAKOTA (732-5682).

Tennessee

Volunteer State

People. Population (1992): 5,023,990; **rank:** 17. **Pop. density:** 121.9 per sq. mi. **Racial distrib.** (1990): 83.0% White; 16.0% Black; 0.7% Hispanic. **Net change** (1990-92): 3.0%.

Geography. Total area: 42,144 sq. mi.; **rank:** 34. **Land area:** 41,220 sq. mi. **Acres forested land:** 13,258,000. **Location:** East South Central state bounded on the N by Kentucky and Virginia; on the E by North Carolina; on the S by Georgia, Alabama, and Mississippi; on the W by Arkansas and Missouri. **Climate:** humid continental to the N; humid sub-tropical to the S. **Topography:** rugged country in the E; the Great Smoky Mtns. of the Unakas; low ridges of the Appalachian Valley; the flat Cumberland Plateau; slightly rolling terrain and knobs of the Interior Low Plateau, the largest region; Eastern Gulf Coastal Plain to the W, is laced with meandering streams; Mississippi Alluvial Plain, a narrow strip of swamp and flood plain in the extreme W. **Capital:** Nashville.

Economy. Principal industries: trade, services, construction; transp., commun., public utilities; finance, ins., real estate. **Principal manufactured goods:** chemicals, food, transportation equip., industrial machinery & equip., fabr. metal prods., rubber/plastic prods., paper & allied prods., printing and publishing. **Agriculture: Chief crops** (1991): tobacco, lint cotton, soybeans, corn, greenhouse/nursery. **Livestock** (1992): 2.30 mln. cattle; 0.67 mln.

hogs/pigs; 1.72 mln. poultry. **Timber/lumber** (1991): red oak, white oak, yellow poplar, hickory; 519 mln. bd. ft. **Nonfuel Minerals** (1992): $579.9 mln.; mostly clay, sand and gravel, crushed stone. **Chief ports:** Memphis, Nashville, Chattanooga, Knoxville. **International airports at:** Memphis, Nashville. **Value of construction** (1992): $5.3 bln. **Employment distribution** (1992): 23.0% mfg.; 23.2% trade; 24% serv.; 16% gvt. **Per capita income** (1992): $17,341. **Unemployment** (1992): 6.4%. **Tourism** (1989): out-of-state visitors spent $3.3 bln. **Sales tax:** 6.0% state, up to 2.75% local.

Finance. FDIC-insured commercial banks & trust companies (1992): 250. **Deposit:** $41.3 bln. **Savings institutions** (1992): 38. **Assets:** $8.2 bln.

Federal government. No. federal civilian employees (Mar. 1992): 38,388. **Avg. salary:** $33,695. **Notable federal facilities:** Tennessee Valley Authority; Oak Ridge Nat'l. Laboratories; Arnold Engineering Development Center; Ft. Campbell Army Base; Millington Naval Station.

Energy: Electricity production (1992, MWh, by source): Hydroelectric: 1.1 mln.; Mineral: 47.8 mln.; Nuclear: 16.8 mln.

Education. Student-teacher ratio (1991): 19.4. **Avg. salary, public school teachers** (1992-93): $29,313.

State data. Motto: Agriculture and commerce. **Flower:** Iris. **Bird:** Mockingbird. **Tree:** Tulip poplar. **Song:** The Tennessee Waltz. **Entered union** June 1, 1796; rank, 16th. **State fair** at: Nashville; mid-Sept.

History. Spanish explorers first visited the area, 1541. English traders crossed the Great Smokies from the east while France's Marquette and Jolliet sailed down the Mississippi on the west, 1673. First permanent settlement was by Virginians on the Watauga River, 1769. During the Revolution, the colonists helped win the Battle of Kings Mountain, N.C., 1780, and joined other eastern campaigns. The state seceded from the Union 1861, and saw many engagements of the Civil War, but 30,000 soldiers fought for the Union.

Tourist attractions. Natural wonders include Reelfoot Lake, the reservoir basin of the Mississippi R. formed by the 1811 earthquake; Lookout Mountain, Chattanooga; Fall Creek Falls, 256 ft. high; Great Smoky Mountains National Park; Lost Sea, Sweetwater; Cherokee Natl. Forest.

Also, the Hermitage, 13 mi. E of Nashville, home of Andrew Jackson; the homes of presidents Polk and Andrew Johnson; American Museum of Science, Oak Ridge; the Parthenon, Nashville, a replica of the Parthenon of Athens; the Grand Old Opry, Nashville; Opryland, USA, theme park, Nashville; Graceland, home of Elvis Presley, Memphis; Alex Haley Home & Museum, Henning; Casey Jones Home & Museum, Jackson.

Famous Tennesseans include Roy Acuff, Davy Crockett, David Farragut, William C. Handy, Sam Houston, Cordell Hull, Grace Moore, Minnie Pearl, Dinah Shore, Alvin York.

Tourist information. Dept. of Tourist Development, 5th Floor, Rachel Jackson Bldg., 320 6th Ave. N., Nashville, TN 37202.

Texas

Lone Star State

People. Population (1992): 17,655,650; **rank:** 3. **Pop. density:** 67.4 per sq. mi. **Racial distrib.** (1990): 75.2% White; 11.9% Black; 25.5% Hispanic. **Net change** (1990-92): 3.9%.

Geography: Total area: 266,807 sq. mi.; **rank:** 2. **Land area:** 261,914 sq. mi.; **Acres forested land:** 13,656,000. **Location:** Southwestern state, bounded on the SE by the Gulf of Mexico; on the SW by Mexico, separated by the Rio Grande; surrounding states are Louisiana, Arkansas, Oklahoma, New Mexico. **Climate:** extremely varied; driest region is the Trans-Pecos; wettest is the NE. **Topography:** Gulf Coast Plain in the S and SE; North Central Plains slope upward with some hills; the Great Plains extend over the Panhandle, are broken by low mountains; the Trans-Pecos is the southern extension of the Rockies. **Capital:** Austin.

Economy. Principal industries: trade, services, manufacturing. **Principal manufactured goods:** machinery, transportation equipment, foods, electrical and electronic equip., chemicals and allied prods., apparel. **Agriculture: Chief crops:** cotton, grain sorghum, grains, vegetables, citrus and other fruits, pecans, peanuts. **Livestock** (1991): 13.4 mln. cattle; 500,000 hogs/pigs; 2.0 mln. sheep; 17.2 mln. poultry. **Timber/lumber** (1991): pine, cypress; 1.05 bln. bd. ft. **Nonfuel Minerals** (1992): $1.4 bln.; mostly cement, stone, sand & gravel. **Commercial fishing** (1992): $181.4 mln. **Chief ports:** Houston, Galveston, Brownsville, Beaumont, Port Arthur, Corpus Christi. **Major international airports at:** Houston, Dallas/Ft. Worth, San Antonio. **Value of construction** (1992) $16.5 bln. **Employment distribution** (1992): 24.1% trade; 25.4% serv.; 18.4% gvt.; 13.3% mfg. **Per capita income** (1992): $17,892. **Unemployment** (1992): 7.5%. **Tourism** (1992): out-of-state visitors spent $20.6 bln. **Sales tax:** 6.25%, + optional 1% local, 1% transit.

Finance. FDIC-insured commercial banks & trust companies (1992): 1,122. **Deposits:** $147.5 bln. **Savings institutions** (1992): 64. **Assets:** $47.5 bln.

Federal government. No. federal civilian employees (Mar. 1992): $123,721. **Avg. salary:** $32,236. **Notable federal facilities:** Fort Hood (Killeen); Kelly AFB and Ft. Sam Houston, both San Antonio.

Energy. Electricity production (1992, MWh, by source): Hydroelectric: 3.2 mln.; Mineral: 104 mln.; Nuclear: 23.6 mln.

Education. Student-teacher ratio (1991): 15.8. **Avg. salary, public school teachers** (1992-93): $29,935.

State data. Motto: Friendship. **Flower:** Bluebonnet. **Bird:** Mockingbird. **Tree:** Pecan. **Song:** Texas, Our Texas. **Entered union** Dec. 29, 1845; rank, 28th. **State fair** at: Dallas; mid-Oct.

History. Pineda sailed along the Texas coast, 1519; Cabeza de Vaca and Coronado visited the interior, 1541. Spaniards made the first settlement at Ysleta, near El Paso, 1682. Americans moved into the land early in the 19th century. Mexico, of which Texas was a part, won independence from Spain, 1821; Santa Anna became dictator, 1835. Texans rebelled; Santa Anna wiped out defenders of the Alamo, 1836. Sam Houston's Texans defeated Santa Anna at San Jacinto and independence was proclaimed the same year. In 1845, Texas was admitted to the Union.

Tourist attractions. Padre Island National Seashore; Big Bend, Guadalupe Mtns. national parks; The Alamo; Ft. Davis; Six Flags Amusement Park; Sea World and Fiesta Texas, both in San Antonio. Named for Pres. Lyndon B. Johnson are a state park, a natl. historic site marking his birthplace, boyhood home, and ranch, all near Johnson City, and a library in Austin.

Famous Texans include Stephen F. Austin, James Bowie, Carol Burnett, J. Frank Dobie, Dwight D. Eisenhower, Sam Houston, Howard Hughes, Lyndon B. Johnson, Mary Martin, Chester Nimitz, Katharine Ann Porter, Sam Rayburn.

Chamber of Commerce. 900 Congress, Suite 501, Austin, TX 78701.

Toll-free travel information. 1-800-888-8TEX.

Utah

Beehive State

People. Population (1992): 1,813,116; **rank:** 34. **Pop. density:** 22.1 per sq. mi. **Racial distrib.** (1990): 93.8% White; 0.7% Black; 4.9% Hispanic. **Net change** (1990-92): 5.2%.

Geography. Total area: 84,899 sq. mi.; **rank:** 11. **Land area:** 82,168 sq. mi. **Acres forested land:** 16,234,000. **Location:** Middle Rocky Mountain state; its southeastern corner touches Colorado, New Mexico, and Arizona, and is the only spot in the U.S. where 4 states join. **Climate:** arid; ranging from warm desert in SW to alpine in NE. **Topography:** high Colorado plateau is cut by brilliantly-colored canyons of the SE; broad, flat, desert-like Great Basin of the W; the Great Salt Lake and Bonneville Salt Flats to the NW; Middle Rockies in the NE run E-W; valleys and plateaus of the Wasatch Front. **Capital:** Salt Lake City.

Economy. Principal industries: services, trade, manufacturing, government, construction. **Principal manufactured goods:** guided missiles and parts, electronic components, food products, fabricated metals, steel, electrical equipment, automobile airbags. **Agriculture: Chief crops:** hay, wheat, apples, barley, alfalfa seed, corn, potatoes, cherries, onions. **Livestock:** 855,000 cattle; 34,000 hogs/pigs; 600,000 sheep; 3.8 mln. poultry. **Timber/lumber:** aspen, spruce, pine. **Nonfuel Minerals** (1992): $1.3 bln.; mostly copper, gold, magnesium. **International airports at:** Salt Lake City. **Value of construction** (1992): $2.0 bln. **Employment distribution** (1992): 25.6% serv.; 24.0% trade; 20.4% govt; 13.8% mfg. **Per capita income** (1992): $15,325. **Unemployment** (1992): 4.9%. **Tourism** (1986): travelers spent $2.0 bln. **Sales tax:** 6.25%.

Finance. FDIC-insured commercial banks & trust companies (1992): 55. **Deposits:** $10.5 bln. **Savings institutions** (1992): 5. **Assets:** $1.3 bln.

Federal government. No. federal civilian employees (Mar. 1992): 31,990. **Avg. salary:** $30,717. **Notable federal facilities:** Hill AFB; Tooele Army Depot; IRS Western Service Center.

Energy. Electricity production (1992, MWh, by source): Hydroelectric: 0.6 mln.; Mineral: 30.3 mln.

Education. Student-teacher ratio (1991): 24.9. **Avg. salary, public school teachers** (1992-93): $26,997.

State data. Motto: Industry. **Flower:** Sego lily. **Bird:** Seagull. **Tree:** Blue spruce. **Song:** Utah, We Love Thee. **Entered union** Jan. 4, 1896; rank, 45th. **State fair** at: Salt Lake City; Sept.

History. Spanish Franciscans visited the area, 1776, the first white men to do so. American fur traders followed. Permanent settlement began with the arrival of the Mormons, 1847. They made the arid land bloom and created a prosperous economy, organized the State of Deseret, 1849, and asked admission to the Union. This was not achieved until 1896, after a long period of controversy over the Mormon Church's doctrine of polygamy, which it discontinued in 1890.

Tourist attractions. Temple Square, Mormon Church hdqtrs., Salt Lake City; Great Salt Lake; fishing streams, lakes and reservoirs, numerous winter sports; campgrounds. Natural wonders may be seen at Zion, Canyonlands, Bryce Canyon, Arches, and Capitol Reef national parks; Dinosaur, Rainbow Bridge, Timpanogos Cave, and Natural Bridges national monuments. Also Lake Powell and Flaming Gorge reservoirs.

Famous Utahans include Maude Adams, Ezra Taft Benson, John Moses Browning, Mariner Eccles, Philo Farnsworth, James Fletcher, David M. Kennedy, J. Willard Marriott, Merlin Olsen, Osmond family, Ivy Baker Priest, George Romney, Brigham Young, Loretta Young.

Tourist information. Utah Travel Council, Council Hall, Salt Lake City, UT 84114.

Vermont

Green Mountain State

People. Population (1992): 569,784; **rank:** 49. **Pop. density:** 61.6 per sq. mi. **Racial distrib.** (1990): 98.6% White; 0.3% Black; 0.6% Asian; 0.7% Hispanic. **Net change** (1990-92): 1.3%.

Geography. Total area: 9,614 sq. mi.; **rank:** 43. **Land area:** 9,249 sq. mi. **Acres forested land:** 4,479,000. **Location:** northern New England state. **Climate:** temperate, with considerable temperature extremes; heavy snowfall in mountains. **Topography:** Green Mtns. N-S backbone 20-36 mi. wide; avg. altitude 1,000 ft. **Capital:** Montpelier.

Economy. Principal industries: manufacturing, tourism, agriculture, trade; finance, insurance, real estate, government. **Principal manufactured goods:** machine tools, furniture, scales, books, computer components, fishing rods. **Agriculture: Chief crops:** dairy products, apples, maple syrup, silage corn, hay. **Livestock** (1989): 320,000 cattle; 5,100 hogs/pigs; 20,456 sheep; 406,000 poultry. **Timber/lumber** (1991): pine, spruce, fir, hemlock; 186 mln. bd. ft. **Nonfuel Minerals** (1992): $67.9 mln.; mostly dimension stone, crushed stone, construction sand & gravel. **International airports at:** Burlington. **Value of construction** (1992): $583.6 mln. **Employment distribution** (1990): 27% serv.; 23% trade; 18% mfg. **Per capita income** (1992): $18,834. **Unemployment** (1992): 6.6%. **Tourism** (1990): visitors spent $1.25 bln. **Sales tax.** 5%.

Finance. FDIC-insured commercial banks & trust companies (1992): 24. **Deposits:** $5.3 bln. **Savings institutions** (1992): 4. **Assets:** $600 mln.

Federal government. No. federal civilian employees (Mar. 1992): 2,656. **Avg. salary:** $32,293.

Energy. Electricity production (1992, MWh, by source): Hydroelectric: 1.0 mln.; Mineral: 0.1 mln.; Nuclear: 3.6 mln.

Education. Student-teacher ratio (1991): 13.8. **Avg. salary, public school teachers** (1992-93): $34,824.

State data. Motto: Freedom and unity. **Flower:** Red clover. **Bird:** Hermit thrush. **Tree:** Sugar maple. **Song:** Hail, Vermont. **Entered union** Mar. 4, 1791; rank, 14th. **State fair** at: Rutland; early Sept.

History. Champlain explored the lake that bears his name, 1609. First American settlement was Ft. Dummer, 1724, near Brattleboro. Ethan Allen and the Green Mountain Boys captured Ft. Ticonderoga, 1775; John Stark defeated part of Burgoyne's forces near Bennington, 1777. In the War of 1812, Thomas MacDonough defeated a British fleet on Champlain off Plattsburgh, 1814.

Tourist attractions. Year-round outdoor sports, esp. hiking, camping and skiing; there are 24 alpine ski areas & 47 cross country areas in the state. Popular are the Shelburne Museum; Rock of Ages Tourist Center, Graniteville; Vermont Marble Exhibit, Proctor; Bennington Battle Monument; Pres. Coolidge homestead, Plymouth; Maple Grove Maple Museum, St. Johnsbury.

Famous Vermonters include Ethan Allen, Chester A. Arthur, Calvin Coolidge, Adm. George Dewey, John Dewey, Stephen A. Douglas, Dorothy Canfield Fisher, James Fisk.

Tourist Information. Vermont Dept. of Travel and Tourism, 134 State St., Montpelier, VT 05602.

Virginia

Old Dominion

People. Population (1992): 6,377,141; **rank:** 12. **Pop. density:** 161.0 per sq. mi. **Racial distrib.** (1990): 77.4% White; 18.8% Black; 2.6% Asian; 2.6% Hispanic. **Net change** (1990-92): 3.1%.

Geography. Total area: 40,767 sq. mi.; **rank:** 36. **Land area:** 39,598 sq. mi. **Acres forested land:** 15,968,000. **Location:** South Atlantic state bounded by the Atlantic O. on the E and surrounded by North Carolina, Tennessee, Kentucky, West Virginia, and Maryland. **Climate:** mild and equable. **Topography:** mountain and valley region in the W, including the Blue Ridge Mtns.; rolling piedmont plateau; tidewater, or coastal plain, including the eastern shore. **Capital:** Richmond.

Economy. Principal industries: services, trade, government, manufacturing, tourism, agriculture. **Principal manufactured goods:** textiles, transportation equipment, electric & electronic equipment, food processing, chemicals, printing. **Agriculture: Chief crops** (1991): soybeans, tobacco, peanuts, corn, far grain, tomatoes, apples, summer & sweet potatoes. **Livestock** (1991): 1.73 mln. cattle; 430,000 hogs/pigs; 157,000 sheep; 1.96 mln. broilers, 1.7 mln. turkeys. **Timber/lumber** (1991): pine and hardwoods; 1.09 bln. bd. ft. **Nonfuel Minerals** (1992): $416.0 mln.; mostly crushed stone. **Commercial fishing** (1992): $90.5 mln. **Chief ports:** Hampton Roads, Richmond, Alexandria. **International airports at:** Norfolk, Dulles, Richmond, Newport News. **Value of construction** (1992): $7.4 bln. **Employment distribution** (1991): 23.4% serv.; 20.5% trade; 18.6% gvt.; 13.2% mfg. **Per capita income** (1992): $20,629. **Unemployment** (1992): 6.4%. **Tourism** (1990): domestic travelers spent $8 bln. **Sales tax:** 4.5%.

Finance. FDIC-insured commercial banks & trust companies (1992): 174. **Deposits:** $55.8 bln. **Savings institutions** (1992): 44. **Assets:** $15.0 bln.

Federal government. No. federal civilian employees (Mar. 1992): 140,954. **Avg. salary:** $37,918. **Notable federal facilities:** Pentagon; Naval Sta., Norfolk; Naval Air Sta., Norfolk, Virginia Beach; Naval Shipyard, Portsmouth; Marine Corps Base, Quantico; Langley AFB; NASA at Langley.

Energy. Electricity production (1992, MWh, by source): Hydroelectric: 0.5 mln.; Mineral: 25.5 mln.; Nuclear: 15.9 mln.

Education. Student-teacher ratio (1990): 15.7. **Avg. salary, public school teachers** (1992-93): $32,356.

State data. Motto: Sic Semper Tyrannis (Thus always to tyrants). **Flower:** Dogwood. **Bird:** Cardinal. **Tree:** Dogwood. **Song:** Carry Me Back to Old Virginia. **Tenth** of the original 13 states to ratify the Constitution, June 25, 1788. **State fair** at: Richmond; late Sept.-early Oct.

History. English settlers founded Jamestown, 1607. Virginians took over much of the government from royal Gov. Dunmore in 1775, forcing him to flee. Virginians under George Rogers Clark freed the Ohio-Indiana-Illinois area of British forces. Benedict Arnold burned Richmond and Petersburg for the British, 1781. That same year, Britain's Cornwallis was trapped at Yorktown and surrendered.

Tourist attractions. Colonial Williamsburg; Busch Gardens, Williamsburg; Wolf Trap Farm, near Falls Church; Arlington National Cemetery; Mt. Vernon, home of George Washington; Jamestown Festival Park; Yorktown; Jefferson's Monticello, Charlottesville; Robert E. Lee's birthplace, Stratford Hall, and grave, at Lexington; Appomattox; Shenandoah National Park; Blue Ridge Parkway; Virginia Beach; King's Dominion, near Richmond.

Famous Virginians include Richard E. Byrd, James B. Cabell, William Henry Harrison, Patrick Henry, Thomas Jefferson, Joseph E. Johnston, Robert E. Lee, Meriwether Lewis and William Clark, James Madison, John Marshall, George Mason, James Monroe, Edgar Allan Poe, Walter Reed, Zachary Taylor, John Tyler, Maggie Walker, Booker T. Washington, George Washington, Woodrow Wilson.

Chamber of Commerce: 9 South Fifth St., Richmond, VA 23219.

Toll-free travel information. 1-800-VISITVA.

Washington

Evergreen State

People. Population (1992): 5,135,731; **rank:** 16. **Pop. density:** 77.1 per sq. mi. **Racial distrib.** (1990): 88.5% White; 3.1% Black; 4.3% Asian; 4.4% Hispanic. **Net change** (1990-92): 5.5%.

Geography. Total area: 68,139 sq. mi.; **rank:** 20. **Land area:** 66,582 sq. mi. **Acres forested land:** 21,856,000. **Location:** Pacific state bordered by Canada on the N; Idaho on the E; Oregon on the S; and the Pacific O. on the W. **Climate:** mild, dominated by the Pacific O. and protected by the Rockies. **Topography:** Olympic Mtns. on NW peninsula; open land along coast to Columbia R.; flat terrain of Puget Sound Lowland; Cascade Mtns. region's high peaks to the E; Columbia Basin in central portion; highlands to the NE; mountains to the SE. **Capital:** Olympia.

Economy. Principal industries: aerospace, forest products, food products, tourism, primary metals, agriculture. **Principal manufactured goods:** aircraft, pulp and paper, lumber and plywood, aluminum, processed fruits and vegetables. **Agriculture: Chief crops:** hops, spearmint oil, wine grapes, wheat, raspberries, apples, asparagus, pears, cherries, peppermint oil, potatoes. **Livestock** (1986): 1.3 mln. cattle; 50,000 hogs/pigs; 59,000 sheep; 5.7 mln. poultry. **Timber/lumber** (1991): Douglas fir, hemlock, cedar, pine; 4.05 bln. bd. ft. **Nonfuel Minerals** (1992): $478.3 mln.; mostly construction sand & gravel, crushed stone, portland cement. **Commercial fishing** (1992): $104.5 mln. **Chief ports:** Seattle, Tacoma, Vancouver, Kelso-Longview. **International airports at:** Seattle/Tacoma, Spokane, Boeing Field. **Value of construction** (1992): $7.5 bln. **Employment distribution** (1989): 24.4% trade; 20.7% serv.; 18.3% gvt.; 17.3% mfg. **Per capita income** (1992): $20,398. **Unemployment** (1992): 7.5%. **Tourism** (1990): $5.3 bln. **Sales tax:** 6.5%.

Finance. FDIC-insured commercial banks & trust companies (1992): 93. **Deposits:** $33.4 bln. **Savings institutions** (1992): 15. **Assets:** $15.6 bln.

Federal government. No. federal civilian employees (Mar. 1992): 50,825. **Avg. salary:** $34,620. **Notable federal facilities:** Bonneville Power Admin.; Ft. Lewis; McChord AFB; Hanford Nuclear Reservation; Bremerton Naval Shipyards.

Energy. Electricity production (1992, MWh, by source): Hydroelectric: 65.6 mln.; Mineral: 8.8 mln.; Nuclear: 8.1 mln.

Education. Student-teacher ratio (1991): 20.2. **Avg. salary, public school teachers** (1992-93): $35,870.

State data. Motto: Alki (By and by). **Flower:** Western rhododendron. **Bird:** Willow goldfinch. **Tree:** Western hemlock. **Song:** Washington, My Home. **Entered union** Nov. 11, 1889; rank, 42d. **State fairs** at: many county fairs, mostly in Aug. or Sept.

History. Spain's Bruno Hezeta sailed the coast, 1775. American Capt. Robert Gray sailed up the Columbia River, 1792. Canadian fur traders set up Spokane House, 1810; Americans under John Jacob Astor established a post at Fort Okanogan, 1811. Missionary Marcus Whitman settled near Walla Walla, 1836. Final agreement on the border of Washington and Canada was made with Britain, 1846, and gold was discovered in the state's northeast, 1855, bringing new settlers.

Tourist attractions. Mt. Rainier, Olympic, and North Cascades national parks; Mt. St. Helens; Pacific beaches; Puget Sound; wineries; Indian cultures; year-round outdoor recreation: Seattle Waterfront, Seattle Center, Space Needle, San Juan Islands, Grand Coulee Dam, Spokane's Riverfront Park.

Famous Washingtonians include Bing Crosby, William O. Douglas, Henry M. Jackson, Gary Larson, Mary McCarthy, Edward R. Murrow, Theodore Roethke, Marcus Whitman, Minoru Yamasaki.

Local Chambers of Commerce. P.O. Box 658, Olympia, WA 98507.

Toll-free travel information. 1-800-544-1800.

West Virginia

Mountain State

People. Population (1992): 1,812,194. **rank:** 35. **Pop. density:** 75.2 per sq. mi. **Racial distrib.** (1990): 96.2% White; 3.1% Black; 0.5% Hispanic. **Net change** (1990-92): 1.0%.

Geography. Total area: 24,232 sq. mi.; **rank:** 41. **Land area:** 24,087 sq. mi. **Acres forested land:** 11,942,000. **Location:** South Atlantic state bounded on the N by Ohio, Pennsylvania, Maryland; on the S and W by Virginia, Kentucky, Ohio; on the E by Maryland and Virginia. **Climate:** humid continental climate except for marine modification in the lower panhandle. **Topography:** ranging from hilly to mountainous; Allegheny Plateau in the W, covers two-thirds of the state; mountains here are the highest in the state, over 4,000 ft. **Capital:** Charleston.

Economy. Principal industries: manufacturing, services, mining, tourism. **Principal manufactured goods:** machinery, plastic and hardwood prods., fabricated metals, basic organic and inorganic chemicals, aluminum, steel. **Agriculture: Chief crops:** apples, peaches, hay, tobacco, corn, wheat, oats. **Chief products:** dairy prods., eggs. **Livestock** (1991): 520,000 cattle; 32,000 hogs/pigs; 76,000 sheep; 1.2 mln. chickens. **Timber/lumber** (1991): oak, yellow poplar, hickory, walnut, cherry; 399 mln. bd. ft. **Nonfuel Minerals** (1992): $123.7 mln.; mostly crushed stone. **Chief port:** Huntington. **Value of construction** (1992): $1.1 bln. **Employment distribution** (1993): 22.8% trade; 20.6% gvt.; 25.1% serv.; 4.5% mfg. **Per capita income** (1992): $15,065. **Unemployment**

(1992): 11.3%. **Tourism** (1992): travel-related expenditures were $2.6 bln. **Sales tax:** 6%.

Finance. FDIC-insured commercial banks & trust companies (1992): 169. **Deposits:** $15.7 bln. **Savings institutions** (1992): 11. **Assets:** $1.2 bln.

Federal government. No. federal civilian employees (Mar. 1992): 10,878. **Avg. salary:** $31,965. **Notable federal facilities:** National Radio Astronomy Observatory, Green Bank; Bureau of Public Debt Bldg., Parkersburg; Natl. Park, Harpers Ferry; Correctional Institution for Women, Alderson.

Energy. Electricity production (1992, MWh, by source): Hydroelectric: 0.5 mln.; Mineral: 61.3 mln.

Education. Student-teacher ratio (1991): 15.3. **Avg. salary, public school teachers** (1992-93): $30,301.

State Data. Motto: Montani Semper Liberi (Mountaineers are always free). **Flower:** Big rhododendron. **Bird:** Cardinal. **Tree:** Sugar maple. **Songs:** The West Virginia Hills; This Is My West Virginia; West Virginia, My Home, Sweet Home. **Entered union** June 20, 1863; rank, 35th. **State fair** at: Lewisburg (Fairlea); late Aug.

History. Early explorers included George Washington, 1753, and Daniel Boone. The area became part of Virginia and often objected to rule by the eastern part of the state. When Virginia seceded, 1861, the Wheeling Conventions repudiated the act and created a new state, Kanawha, subsequently changed to West Virginia. It was admitted to the Union as such, 1863.

Tourist attractions. Harpers Ferry National Historic Park has been restored to its condition in 1859, when John Brown seized the U.S. Armory.

Also Science and Cultural Center, Charleston; White Sulphur and Berkeley Springs mineral water spas; Monongahela Natl. Forest; state parks and forests; trout fishing; turkey, deer, and bear hunting; white water rafting, paddleboat tours, skiing; glass tours at Fenton Glass in Williamstown, Viking Glass in New Martinsville, Blenko Glass in Milton; Sternwheel Regatta, Charleston; Mountain State Forest Festival; Mountain State Arts & Crafts Fair, Ripley.

Famous West Virginians include Newton D. Baker, Pearl Buck, John W. Davis, Thomas "Stonewall" Jackson, Don Knotts, Dwight Whitney Morrow, Nick Nolte, Michael Owens, Cyrus Vance, Col. Charles "Chuck" Yeager.

Tourist information. Dept. of Commerce, State Capitol, Charleston WV 25305.

Toll-free travel information. 1-800-CALLW.VA.

Wisconsin

Badger State

People. Population (1992): 5,006,591; **rank:** 18. **Pop. density:** 92.2 per sq. mi. **Racial distrib.** (1990): 92.2% White; 5.0% Black; 1.9% Hispanic. **Net change** (1990-92): 2.4%.

Geography. Total area: 56,153 sq. mi.; **rank:** 26. **Land area:** 54,314 sq. mi. **Acres forested land:** 15,319,000. **Location:** East North Central state, bounded on the N by Lake Superior and Upper Michigan; on the E by Lake Michigan; on the S by Illinois; on the W by the St. Croix and Mississippi rivers. **Climate:** long, cold winters and short, warm summers tempered by the Great Lakes. **Topography:** narrow Lake Superior Lowland plain met by Northern Highland, which slopes gently to the sandy crescent Central Plain; Western Upland in the SW; 3 broad parallel limestone ridges running N-S are separated by wide and shallow lowlands in the SE. **Capital:** Madison.

Economy. Principal industries: services, manufacturing, trade, government, agriculture, tourism. **Principal manufactured goods:** industrial machinery, food products, fabricated metals, paper products, printing and publishing, electronic and electrical machinery. **Agriculture: Chief crops:** corn, beans, cherries, peas, hay, oats, cranberries. **Chief products:** milk, butter, cheese. **Livestock** (1991): 4.0 mln. cattle, 1.2 mln. hogs/pigs; 105,000 sheep; 4.2 mln. poultry. **Timber/lumber** (1991): maple, birch, oak, evergreens; 511 mln. bd. ft. **Nonfuel Minerals** (1992): $218.2 mln.; mostly crushed stone, construction & industrial sand & gravel, lime. **Commercial fishing** (1992): $5.9 mln. **Chief ports:** Superior, Ashland, Milwaukee, Green Bay, Kewaunee, Pt. Washington, Manitowoc, Sheboygan, Marinette, Kenosha. **International airports at:** Milwaukee. **Value of construction** (1992): $4.9 bln. **Employment distribution** (1993): 22.3% trade; 22.7% mfg.; 24.0% serv.; 15.8% gvt. **Per capita income** (1992): $18,727. **Unemployment** (1992): 5.1%. **Tourism** (1992): out-of-state visitors spent $6.0 bln. **Sales tax:** 5%.

Finance. FDIC-insured commercial banks & trust companies (1992): 458. **Deposits:** $41.3 bln. **Savings institutions** (1992): 50. **Assets:** $13.9 bln.

Federal government. No. federal civilian employees (Mar. 1992): 12,643. **Avg. salary:** $31,804. **Notable federal facilities:** Ft. McCoy.

Energy. Electricity production (1992, MWh, by source): Hydroelectric: 1.8 mln.; Mineral: 29.1 mln.; Nuclear: 11.3 mln.

Education. Student-teacher ratio (1991): 15.7. **Avg. salary, public school teachers** (1992-93): $36,477.

State data. Motto: Forward. **Flower:** Wood violet. **Bird:** Robin. **Tree:** Sugar maple. **Song:** On, Wisconsin! **Entered union** May 29, 1848; rank, 30th. **State fair** at: West Allis; mid-Aug.

History. Jean Nicolet was the first European to see the Wisconsin area, arriving in Green Bay, 1634; French missionaries and fur traders followed. The British took over, 1763. The U.S. won the land after the Revolution but the British were not ousted until after the War of 1812. Lead miners came next, then farmers. Railroads were started in 1851, serving growing wheat harvests and iron mines.

Tourist attractions. Old Wade House and Carriage Museum, Greenbush; Villa Louis, Prairie du Chien; Circus World Museum, Baraboo; Wisconsin Dells; Old World Wisconsin, Eagle; Door County peninsula; Chequamegon and Nicolet national forests; Lake Winnebago; numerous lakes for water sports, ice boating and fishing; skiing and hunting.

Famous Wisconsinites include Edna Ferber, King Camp Gillette, Harry Houdini, Robert La Follette, Alfred Lunt, Georgia O'Keeffe, Donald K. "Deke" Slayton, Spencer Tracy, Thorstein Veblen, Orson Welles, Thornton Wilder, Frank Lloyd Wright.

Tourist information. Wisconsin Dept. of Development, Division of Tourism, 123 W. Washington Ave., Madison, WI 53702.

Toll-free travel information. 1-800-372-2737.

Wyoming

Equality State

People. Population (1992): 466,185; **rank:** 50. **Pop. density:** 4.8 per sq. mi. **Racial distrib.** (1990): 94.2% White; 0.8% Black; 2.1% Amer. Indian; 5.7% Hispanic. **Net change** (1990-92): 2.8%.

Geography. Total area: 97,809 sq. mi.; **rank:** 9. **Land area:** 97,105 sq. mi. **Acres forested land:** 9,966,000. **Location:** Mountain state lying in the high western plateaus of the Great Plains. **Climate:** semi-desert conditions throughout; true desert in the Big Horn and Great Divide basins. **Topography:** the eastern Great Plains rise to the foothills of the Rocky Mtns.; the Continental Divide crosses the state from the NW to the SE. **Capital:** Cheyenne.

Economy. Principal industries: mineral extraction, tourism and recreation, agriculture. **Principal manufactured goods:** refined petroleum products, foods, wood products, stone, clay and glass products. **Agriculture: Chief crops:** wheat, beans, barley, oats, sugar beets, hay. **Livestock** (1992): 1.3 mln. cattle; 24,000 hogs/pigs; 850,000 sheep. **Timber/lumber** (1991): Ponderosa & lodgepole pine, Douglas fir, Engelmann spruce; 213 mln. bd. ft. **Nonfuel Minerals** (1992): $935.0 mln.; mostly portland cement, crushed stone. **International airports at:** Casper. **Value of construction** (1992): $467.9 mln. **Employment distribution** (1992): 23% trade; 20% services; 9% mining. **Per capita income** (1992): $17,423.

Unemployment (1992): 5.6%. **Tourism** (1992): out-of-state visitors spent $1.5 bln. **State sales tax:** 4%.

Finance. FDIC-insured commercial banks & trust companies (1992): 62. **Deposits:** $4.3 bln. **Savings institutions** (1992): 6. **Assets:** $800 mln.

Federal government. No. federal civilian employees (Mar. 1992): 4,878. **Avg. salary:** $32,062. **Notable federal facilities:** Warren AFB.

Energy. Electricity production (1992, MWh, by source): Hydroelectric: 0.4 mln.; Mineral: 36.1 mln.

Education. Student-teacher ratio (1991): 15.6. **Avg. salary, public school teachers** (1992-93): $30,850.

State data. Motto: Equal Rights. **Flower:** Indian paintbrush. **Bird:** Meadowlark. **Tree:** Cottonwood. **Song:** Wyoming. **Entered union** July 10, 1890; rank, 44th. **State fair** at: Douglas; late Aug.

History. Francés Francois and Louis La Verendrye were the first Europeans, 1743. John Colter, American, was first to traverse Yellowstone Park, 1807-08. Trappers and fur traders followed in the 1820s. Forts Laramie and Bridger became important stops on the pioneer trail to the West Coast. Indian wars followed massacres of army detachments in 1854 and 1866. Population grew after the Union Pacific crossed the state, 1869. Women won the vote, for the first time in the U.S., from the Territorial Legislature, 1869.

Tourist attractions. Yellowstone National Park, 3,472 sq. mi. in the NW corner of Wyoming and the adjoining edges of Montana and Idaho, the oldest U.S. national park, est. 1872, has some 10,000 geysers, hot springs, mud volcanoes, fossil forests, a volcanic glass (obsidian) mountain, the 1,000-ft.-deep canyon and 308-ft.-high waterfall of the Yellowstone River, and a wide variety of animals living free in their natural habitat.

Also, Grand Teton National Park, with mountains 13,000 ft. high; National Elk Refuge, covering 25,000 acres; Devils Tower, a columnar rock of igneous origin 1,280 ft. high; Fort Laramie and surrounding areas of pioneer trails; Buffalo Bill Museum, Cody; Cheyenne Frontier Days Celebration, last full week in July, the state's largest rodeo, and world's largest purse.

Famous Wyomingites include James Bridger, Buffalo Bill Cody, Nellie Tayloe Ross.

Tourist information. Travel Commission, Etchepare Circle, Cheyenne, WY 82002.

Toll-free travel information. 1-800-CALLWYO.

District of Columbia

Area: 69 sq. mi. **Population** (1992): 588,620. **Motto:** Justitia omnibus (Justice for all). **Flower:** American beauty rose. **Tree:** Scarlet oak. **Bird:** Wood thrush. The city of Washington is coextensive with the District of Columbia.

The District of Columbia is the seat of the federal government of the United States. It lies on the west central edge of Maryland on the Potomac River, opposite Virginia. Its area was originally 100 sq. mi. taken from the sovereignty of Maryland and Virginia. Virginia's portion south of the Potomac was given back to that state in 1846.

The 23d Amendment, ratified in 1961, granted residents the right to vote for president and vice president for the first time and gave them 3 members in the Electoral College. The first such votes were cast in Nov. 1964.

Congress, which has legislative authority over the District under the Constitution, established in 1878 a government of 3 commissioners appointed by the president. The Reorganization Plan of 1967 substituted a single commissioner (also called mayor), assistant, and 9-member City Council. Funds were still appropriated by Congress; residents had no vote in local government, except to elect school board members.

In Sept. 1970, Congress approved legislation giving the District one delegate to the House of Representatives. The delegate could vote in committee but not on the House floor. The first was elected 1971.

In May 1974 voters approved a charter giving them the right to elect their own mayor and a 13-member city council; the first took office Jan. 2, 1975. The district won the right to levy its own taxes but Congress retained power to veto council actions, and approve the city's annual budget.

Proposals for a "federal town" for the deliberations of the Continental Congress were made in 1783, 4 years before the adoption of the Constitution that gave the Confederation a national government. Rivalry between northern and southern delegates over the site appeared in the First Congress, 1789. John Adams, presiding officer of the Senate, cast the deciding vote of that body for Germantown, Pa. In 1790 Congress compromised by making Philadelphia the temporary capital for 10 years. The Virginia members of the House wanted a capital on the eastern bank of the Potomac; they were defeated by the Northerners, while the Southerners defeated the Northern attempt to have the nation assume the war debts of the 13 original states, the Assumption Bill fathered by Alexander Hamilton. Hamilton and Jefferson arranged a compromise: the Virginia men voted for the Assumption Bill, and the Northerners conceded the capital to the Potomac. President Washington chose the site in Oct. 1790 and persuaded landowners to sell their holdings to the government at £25, then about $66, an acre. The capital was named Washington.

Washington appointed Pierre Charles L'Enfant, a French engineer who had come over with Lafayette, to plan the capital on an area not over 10 mi. square. The L'Enfant plan, for streets 100 to 110 feet wide and one avenue 400 feet wide and a mile long, seemed grandiose and foolhardy, but Washington endorsed it. When L'Enfant ordered a wealthy landowner to remove his new manor house because it obstructed a vista, and demolished it when the owner refused, Washington stepped in and dismissed the architect. The official map and design of the city was completed by Benjamin Banneker, a distinguished black architect and astronomer, and Andrew Ellicott.

On Sept. 18, 1793, Pres. Washington laid the cornerstone of the north wing of the Capitol. On June 3, 1800, Pres. John Adams moved to Washington and on June 10, Philadelphia ceased to be the temporary capital. The City of Washington was incorporated in 1802; the District of Columbia was created as a municipal corporation in 1871, embracing Washington, Georgetown, and Washington County.

Outlying U.S. Areas

Commonwealth of Puerto Rico

(Estado Libre Asociado de Puerto Rico)

People. Population (1992): 3,580,332 (and about 2.7 mln. more Puerto Ricans reside in the mainland U.S.). **Pop. density:** 1,035 per sq. mi. **Urban** (1990): 66.8%. **Racial distribution** (1990): 99.9% Hispanic. **Language:** On Jan. 28, 1993, the Gov. of Puerto Rico declared Spanish and English joint official languages.

Geography. Total area: 3,492 sq. mi. **Land area:** 3,427 sq. mi. **Location:** island lying between the Atlantic to the N and the Caribbean to the S; it is easternmost of the West Indies group called the Greater Antilles, of which Cuba, Hispaniola, and Jamaica are the larger islands. **Climate:** mild, with a mean temperature of 77° F. **Topography:** mountainous throughout three-fourths of its rectangular area, surrounded by a broken coastal plain; highest peak is Cerro Puntita, 4,389 ft. **Capital:** San Juan.

Economy. Principal industries: manufacturing. **Principal manufactured goods:** pharmaceuticals, chemicals, machinery and metals, electric machinery and equipment, food products, apparel, petroleum refining. **Agriculture: Chief crops:** coffee, plantains, pineapples, tomatoes, sugarcane, bananas, peppers, pumpkins, lettuce, tobacco, yams. **Livestock** (1990): 600,000 cattle; 206,000 pigs; 7.4 mln. poultry. **Nonfuel Minerals** (1991): $119.2 mln., mostly cement. **Commercial fishing** (1992): $6.2 mln. **Chief ports/river shipping:** San Juan, Ponce, Mayaguez. **Major airports at:** San Juan, Ponce, Mayaguez, Aguadilla. **Value of construction** (1992): $2.7

bln. **Employment distribution** (1992): 22.5% public admin., 19.8% trade, 16.8% mfg., 3.4% agric. **Per capita income** (1992): $6,360. **Unemployment** (1992): 16.7%. **Tourism** (1992): Visitors spent $1.51 bln.

Finance. No. FDIC-insured commercial banks & trust companies (1992): 17. **Deposits:** $18.8 bln. **No. savings institutions** (1992): 8. **Assets:** $4.1 bln.

Federal government. No. federal civilian employees (1992): 10,000. **Notable federal facilities:** U.S. Naval Station at Roosevelt Roads, Ceiba; U.S. Army Training Area and Ft. Allen at Salinas; Sabana SECA Communications Center (U.S. Navy); Ft. Buchanan at Guaynabo.

Energy Production (1992): 16,458 mln. kwh.

Education. Student-teacher ratio (1992): 21.0. **Avg. salary, public school teachers** (1992): $1,000 monthly.

Misc. Data. Motto: Joannes Est Nomen Eius (John is his name). **Flower:** Maga. **Bird:** Reinita. **Tree:** Ceiba. **National anthem:** La Borinqueña.

History: Puerto Rico (or Borinquen, after the original Arawak Indian name Boriquen), was visited by Columbus, on his second voyage, Nov. 19, 1493. In 1508 the Spanish arrived.

Sugarcane was introduced, 1515, and slaves were imported 3 years later. Gold mining petered out, 1570. Spaniards fought off a series of British and Dutch attacks; slavery was abolished, 1873. Under the treaty of Paris, Puerto Rico was ceded to the U.S. after the Spanish-American War, 1898. In 1952 the people voted in favor of Commonwealth status.

The Commonwealth of Puerto Rico is a self-governing part of the U.S. with a primary Hispanic culture. The current commonwealth political status of Puerto Rico gives the island's citizens virtually the same control over their internal affairs as the 50 states of the U.S. However, they do not vote in national elections, although they do vote in national primary elections.

Puerto Rico is represented in the U.S. Congress by a resident commissioner who has a voice but no vote, except in committees.

No federal income tax is collected from residents on income earned from local sources in Puerto Rico. Nevertheless, as part of the U.S. legal system, Puerto Rico is subject to the provisions of the U.S. Constitution; most federal laws apply as they do in the 50 states.

Puerto Rico's famous "Operation Bootstrap," begun in the late 1940s, succeeded in changing the island from "The Poorhouse of the Caribbean" to an area with the highest per capita income in Latin America. This pioneering program encouraged manufacturing and the development of the tourist trade by selective tax exemption, low-interest loans, and other incentives. Despite the marked success of Puerto Rico's development efforts over an extended period of time, per capita income in Puerto Rico is low in comparison to that of the U.S. Economic growth slowed in fiscal 1991 from the 2.2% of fiscal 1990.

General tourist attractions: Ponce Museum of Art; forts El Morro and San Cristobal; Old Walled City of San Juan; Arecibo Observatory; Cordillera Central and state parks; El Yunque Rain Forest; San Juan Cathedral; Porta Coeli Chapel and Museum of Religious Art, Interamerican Univ., San Germán; Condado Convention Center; Casa Blanca, Ponce de León family home, Puerto Rican Family Museum of 16th and 17th centuries and the Fine Arts Center in San Juan.

Cultural facilities, festivals, etc.: Festival Casals classical music concerts, mid-June; Puerto Rico Symphony Orchestra at Music Conservatory; Botanical Garden and Museum of Anthropology, Art, and History at the University of Puerto Rico; Institute of Puerto Rican Culture, at the Dominican Convent; and many popular festivals throughout the island.

Famous Puerto Ricans include: Miguel Hernández Agosto, José Celso Barbosa, Julia de Burgos, Pablo Casals, Orlando Cepeda, Roberto Clemente, Rafael Hernández Colón, José de Diego, José Feliciano, Luis A. Ferré, José Ferrer, Doña Felisa Rincón de Gautier, Commodore Diégo E. Hernández, Rafael Hernández (El Jibarito), Marta Casals Istomin, Raúl Julía, Luis Muñoz Marín, René Marqués, Luis Palés Matos, Concha Meléndez, Rita Moreno, Adm. Horacio Rivero.

Chamber of Commerce: 100 Tetuán P.O. Box. S-3789, San Juan, PR 00904; Ponce & South: El Señorial Bldg., Ponce, PR 00731.

Guam

Where America's Day Begins

People. Population (1990): 133,152, a 26% increase over the 1980 figure of 105,979. **Pop. density:** 631.6 per sq. mi. **Urban** (1980): 39.5%. **Major ethnic groups** (1990): Chamorro 43%, Filipino 28.6%, stateside immigrants 20%, remainder Micronesians. Native Guamanians, ethnically called Chamorros, are basically of Indonesian stock, with a mixture of Spanish and Filipino. In addition to the offical language, they speak the native Chamorro. **Migration** (1990): About 52% of population were born elsewhere; of these, 48% in Asia, 40% in U.S.

Geography. Total area: 217 sq. mi. land, 30 mi. long and 4 to 8.5 mi. wide. **Location:** largest and southernmost of the Mariana Islands in the West Pacific, 3,700 mi. W of Hawaii. **Climate:** tropical, with temperatures from 70° to 90° F; avg. annual rainfall, about 70 in. **Topography:** coralline limestone plateau in the N; southern chain of low volcanic mountains sloping gently to the W, more steeply to coastal cliffs on the E; general elevation, 500 ft.; highest pt., Mt. Lamlam, 1,334 ft. **Capital:** Agana.

Economy. Principal industries: tourism, defense, construction, banking. **Principal manufactured goods:** textiles, foods. **Agriculture: Chief crops:** cabbages, eggplants, cucumber, long beans, tomatoes, bananas, coconuts, watermelon, yams, canteloupe, papayas, maize, sweet potatoes. **Livestock** (1984): 2,000 cattle; 14,000 hogs/pigs. **Chief ports:** Apra Harbor. **International airports at:** Tamuning. **Value of construction** (1980): $80.6 mln. **Employment distribution** (1987): 61.3% private sector; 38.7% gvt. **Per capita income** (1986): $7,116. **Median household income** (1989): $30,755; persons per household 3.97; persons per family 4.26. **Unemployment** (1990): 3.8%. **Tourism** (1990): visitors' receipts $550 mln.

Finance. Notable industries: insurance, real estate, finance. **No. banks:** 13; **No. savings and loan assns.:** 2.

Federal government. No. federal employees (1990): 7,200. **Notable federal facilities:** Anderson AFB; naval, air and port bases.

Misc. Data. Flower: Puti Tai Nobio (Bougainvillea). **Bird:** Toto (Fruit dove). **Tree:** Ifit (Intsiabijuga). **Song:** Stand Ye Guamanians.

History. Guam was probably settled by voyagers from the Indonesian-Philippine archipelago by at least the third century B.C. Pottery, rice cultivation, and megalithic technology show strong East Asian cultural influence. Centralized, village clan-based communities engaged in agriculture and offshore fishing. The est. population by the early 16th century was between 50,000 and 75,000 inhabitants. Magellan arrived in the Marianas Mar. 6, 1521. They were colonized in 1668 by Spanish missionaries who named them the Mariana Islands in honor of Maria Anna, queen of Spain. When Spain ceded Guam to the U.S., it sold the other Marianas to Germany. Japan obtained a League of Nations mandate over the German islands in 1919; in Dec. 1941 it seized Guam; the island was retaken by the U.S. in July 1944.

Guam is a self-governing organized unincorporated U.S. territory. The Organic Act of 1950 provides for a governor and a 21-member unicameral legislature, elected biennially by the residents who are American citizens.

In 1972 a U.S. law gave Guam one delegate to the U.S. House of Representatives; the delegate may vote in committee but not on the House floor.

Guam's quest to change its status to a U.S. Commonwealth began in the late 1970's. A Commission on Self-Determination, created in 1984, developed a Draft Commonwealth Act, which was submitted to Congress.

General tourist attractions. Tropical climate, oceanic marine environment; annual mid-Aug. Merizo Water Festival; Tarzan Falls; beaches; water sports; duty-free port shopping.

Virgin Islands

St. John, St. Croix, St. Thomas

People. Population (1990): 101,809 (50,139, St. Croix; 48,166, St. Thomas; 3,504, St. John). **Pop. density:** 748.6 per sq. mi. **Urban** (1980): 39%. **Racial distribution:** (1980) 15% White; 85% Black. **Major ethnic groups:** West Indian, French, Hispanic.

Geography. Total area: 151 sq. mi.; **Land area:** 134 sq. mi. **Location:** 3 larger and 50 smaller islands and cays in the S and W of the V.I. group (British V.I. colony to the N and E) which is situated 70 mi. E of Puerto Rico, located W of the Anegada Passage, a major channel connecting the Atlantic O. and the Caribbean Sea. **Climate:** subtropical; the sun tempered by gentle trade winds; humidity is low; average temperature, 78° F. **Topography:** St. Thomas is mainly a ridge of hills running E and W, and has little tillable land; St. Croix rises abruptly in the N but slopes to the S to flatlands and lagoons; St. John has steep, lofty hills and valleys with little level tillable land. **Capital:** Charlotte Amalie, St. Thomas.

Economy. Principal industries: tourism, rum, alumina prod., petroleum refining, watch industry, textiles, electronics. **Principal manufactured goods:** rum, textiles, pharmaceuticals, perfumes. **Gross Domestic Product** (1987): $1.246 bln. **Agriculture: Chief crops:** truck garden produce. **Minerals:** sand, gravel. **Chief ports:** Cruz Bay, St. John; Frederiksted and Christiansted, St. Croix; Charlotte Amalie, St. Thomas. **International airports on:** St. Thomas, St. Croix. **Value of construction** (1987): $167.0 mln. **Per capita income** (1989): $11,052. **Unemployment** (1992): 2.8%. **Tourism** (1988): $662.8. **No. banks** (1990): 8.

Misc. data. Flower: Yellow elder or yellow trumpet, local designation Ginger Thomas. **Bird:** Yellow breast. **Song:** Virgin Islands March.

History. The islands were visited by Columbus in 1493. Spanish forces, 1555, defeated the Caribes and claimed the territory; by 1596 the native population was annihilated. First permanent settlement in the U.S. territory, 1672, by the Danes; U.S. purchased the islands, 1917, for defense purposes.

The Virgin Islands has a republican form of government, headed by a governor and lieut. governor elected, since 1970, by popular vote for 4-year terms. There is a 15-member unicameral legislature, elected by popular vote. Residents of the V.I. have been U.S. citizens since 1927. Since 1973 they have elected a delegate to the U.S. House of Representatives, who may vote in committee but not in the House.

General tourist attractions. Magens Bay, St. Thomas; duty-free shopping; Virgin Islands National Park, 14,488 acres on St. John of lush growth, beaches, Indian relics, and evidence of colonial Danes.

Tourist information. Dept. of Economic Development & Agriculture, St. Thomas, P.O. Box 6400, St. Thomas, VI 00801; St. Croix, P.O. Box 4535, Christiansted, St. Croix 00820.

American Samoa

Capital: Pago Pago, Island of Tutuila. **Total Area:** 84 sq. mi. **Population:** (1992) 50,923. **Motto:** Samoa Muamua le Atua (In Samoa, God Is First). **Song:** Amerika Samoa. **Flower:** Paogo (Ula-fala). **Plant:** Ava.

Blessed with spectacular scenery and delightful South Seas climate, American Samoa is the most southerly of all lands under U.S. sovereignty. It is an unincorporated territory consisting of 7 small islands of the Samoan group: **Tutuila, Aunu'u, Manu'a Group (Ta'u, Olosega and Ofu), Rose,** and **Swains Island.** The islands are 2,300 mi. SW of Honolulu.

A tripartite agreement between Great Britain, Germany, and the U.S. in 1899 gave the U.S. sovereignty over the eastern islands of the Samoan group; these islands became American Samoa. Local chiefs officially ceded Tutuila and Aunu'u to the U.S. in April 1900 and the Manu'a group in July 1904; Swains Island was annexed in 1925.

Samoa (Western), comprising the larger islands of the Samoan group, was a New Zealand mandate and UN Trusteeship until it became an independent nation Jan. 1, 1962 *(see Index)*.

Tutuila and Aunu'u have an area of 53 sq. mi. Ta'u has an area of 17 sq. mi., and the islets of Ofu and Olosega, 5 sq. mi. with a population of a few thousand. Swains Island has nearly 2 sq. mi. and a population of about 100.

About 70% of the land is bush and mountains. Chief products and exports are fish products. Taro, breadfruit, yams, coconuts, pineapples, oranges, and bananas are also produced.

From 1900-1951, American Samoa was under the jurisdiction of the U.S. Navy. Since 1951, it has been under the Interior Dept. On Jan. 3, 1978, the first popularly elected Samoan governor and lieutenant governor were inaugurated. Previously, the governor was appointed by the Secretary of the Interior. American Samoa has a bicameral legislature and elects its own member of Congress, who can introduce legislation and vote in committee, but not in the House.

The American Samoans are of Polynesian origin. They are nationals of the U.S.; approximately 20,000 live in Hawaii, 65,000 in California and Washington.

Minor Caribbean Island

Navassa lies between Jamaica and Haiti, 100 miles south of Guantanamo Bay, Cuba; it covers about 3 sq. mi., Is reserved by the U.S. for a lighthouse and is uninhabited. It is administered by the U.S. Coast Guard.

Wake, Midway, Other Islands

Wake Island, and its sister islands, **Wilkes** and **Peale,** lie in the Pacific Ocean on the direct route from Hawaii to Hong Kong, about 2,300 mi. W of Honolulu and 1,290 mi. E of Guam. The group is 4.5 mi. long, 1.5 mi. wide, and totals less than 3 sq. mi.

The U.S. flag was hoisted over Wake Island, July 4, 1898, formal possession taken Jan. 17, 1899; Wake has been administered by the U.S. Air Force since 1972. The population consists of about 200 persons.

The **Midway Islands,** acquired in 1867, consist of 2, **Sand** and **Eastern,** in the North Pacific 1,150 mi. NW of Honolulu, with area of about 3 sq. mi., administered by the U.S. Navy. There is no indigenous population; its population is about 450.

Johnston Atoll, 717 miles WSW of Honolulu, area 1 sq. mi., is operated by The Defense Nuclear Agency, and the Fish and Wildlife Service, U.S. Dept. of the Interior; its population is about 1,200. **Kingman Reef,** 920 miles S of Hawaii, is under Navy control.

Howland, Jarvis, and **Baker Islands,** 1,400-1,650 miles SW of Honolulu, uninhabited since World War II, are under the Interior Dept.

Palmyra is an atoll about 1,000 miles south of Hawaii, 2 sq. mi. Privately owned, it is under the Interior Dept.

Islands Under Trusteeship

The Trust Territory of the Pacific Islands was established in 1947, as the only strategic trusteeship of the 11 trusteeships established by the U.N. For nearly 4 decades, the territory had a heterogeneous population of about 140,000 people scattered among more than 2,100 islands and atolls in 3 major archipelagos: the Carolines, the Marshalls, and the Marianas. The entire geographic area is sometimes referred to as "Micronesia," meaning "little islands." The area of the Trust Territory covered some 3 million sq. miles of the Pacific Ocean, slightly larger than the continental U.S. However, its islands constituted a land area of only 715.8 sq. miles—half the size of Rhode Island. It formerly consisted of 7 districts and now has 4 political jurisdictions: The Commonwealth of the Northern Mariana Islands (CNMI), the Federated

States of Micronesia (FSM), the Republic of the Marshall Islands (RMI), and Palau. As of Oct. 21, 1986, the RMI entered into free association with the U.S., as did the FSM effective Nov. 3, 1986. The CNMI became a commonwealth of the U.S., also effective Nov. 3. Only Palau remains under trusteeship.

Commonwealth of the Northern Mariana Islands

Located in the perpetually warm climes between Guam and the Tropic of Cancer, the 14 islands of the Northern Marianas form a 300-mile-long archipelago, comprising a total land area of 179 sq. miles. The native population, 1990, is 43,345, and is concentrated on the 3 largest of the 6 inhabited islands: **Saipan,** the seat of government and commerce (38,896), **Rota** (2,295), and **Tinian** (2,118).

The people of the Northern Marianas are predominantly of Chamorro cultural extraction, although numbers of Carolinians and immigrants from other areas of E. Asia and Micronesia have also settled in the islands. Pursuant to the Covenant of 1976, which established the Northern Marianas as a commonwealth in political union with the U.S., most natives and many domiciliaries of these islands achieved U.S. citizenship on Nov. 13, 1986, when the U.S. terminated its administration of the U.N. trusteeship as it affected the Northern Marianas. From July 18, 1947, the U.S. had administered the Northern Marianas under a trusteeship agreement with the U.N. Security Council. English is among the several languages commonly spoken.

The Northern Mariana Islands has been self-governing since 1978, when both a constitution drafted and adopted by the people became effective and a bicameral legislature with offices of governor and lieutenant governor was inaugurated. Commercial activity has increased steadily in recent years. In 1990, more than 417,146 tourists visited.

Palau

Palau (or Belau) consists of more than 200 islands in 16 states in the Caroline chain, of which 8 are permanently inhabited. The capital of Palau, Koror, lies 3,997 miles SW of Honolulu and 813 miles S of Guam. Population of Palau is 15,122 (1990), 10,501 (1990) in Koror. Average year-round temperature is 80 degrees, average annual rainfall 150 inches.

Until 1979, a High Commissioner, appointed by the U.S. President, in turn appoints a district administrator for Palau to oversee programs and administration there. In support of the islands' evolving political status, the U.S. recognized the Constitution of Palau and the establishment of the government of Palau, consistent with U.S. responsibilities in Palau as the administering authority of the U.N. Trust Territory of the Pacific Islands (TTPI).

The Assistant Secretary of the Interior for Territorial and International Affairs has been delegated U.S. authority with respect to Palau and may suspend any newly enacted national law in Palau, as well as any newly enacted state law that involves finance or the expenditure of funds, if the law is inconsistent with the trusteeship agreement or U.S. laws or regulations applicable to the TTPI. The Constitution became effective in 1980. The President and Vice President are elected by popular vote. A Council of Chiefs advises the President on matters concerning traditional law and custom. Palau has a bicameral national legislature composed of a House of Delegates and a Senate.

Washington, Capital of the U.S.

Arlington National Cemetery

Arlington National Cemetery, on the former Custis estate in Virginia, is the site of the **Tomb of the Unknowns** and the final resting place of John Fitzgerald Kennedy, president of the United States, who was buried there Nov. 25, 1963. A torch burns day and night over his grave. The remains of his brother Sen. Robert F. Kennedy (N.Y.) were interred on June 8, 1968, in an area adjacent. Many other famous Americans are also buried at Arlington, as well as 175,000 American soldiers from every major war.

U.S. Marine Corps War Memorial (Iwo Jima)

North of the National Cemetery, approximately 350 yards, stands the bronze statue of the raising of the United States flag on Mt. Suribachi during WWII, executed by Felix de Weldon from the photograph by Joe Rosenthal, and presented to the nation by members and friends of the U.S. Marine Corps.

Vietnam Veterans Memorial

Dedicated on November 13, 1982, it is a symbol of the nation's recognition of the men and women who served in the armed forces in the Vietnam War. On a V-shaped wall are inscribed the names of the more than 58,000 Americans who lost their lives or remain missing.

The Capitol

The United States Capitol was originally designed by Dr. William Thornton, an amateur architect, who submitted a plan in the spring of 1793 that won him $500 and a city lot.

The south, or House, wing was completed in 1807 under the direction of Benjamin H. Latrobe.

The present Senate and House wings and the iron dome were designed and constructed by Thomas U. Walter, the 4th architect of the Capitol, between 1851 and 1863.

The present cast iron dome at its greatest exterior measures 135 ft. 5 in., and it is topped by the bronze Statue of Freedom that stands 19½ ft. and weighs 14,985 pounds. On its base are the words "E Pluribus Unum" (Out of Many One).

The Capitol is normally open from 9 a.m. to 4:30 p.m; from June to Aug., to 10 p.m. Tours through the Capitol, including the House and Senate galleries, are conducted from 9 a.m. to 4 p.m. without charge.

Folger Shakespeare Library

The Folger Shakespeare Library, on Capitol Hill, is a research institution devoted to the advancement of learning in the background of Anglo-American civilization in the 16th and 17th centuries and in most aspects of the continental Renaissance. It has the largest collection of Shakespeareana in the world; with 79 copies of the First Folio.

Library of Congress

Established by and for Congress in 1800, the Library of Congress has extended its services over the years to other government agencies and other libraries, to scholars, and to the general public, and it now serves as the national library. It contains over 80 million items in 470 languages.

The library's exhibit halls are open to the public, from 8:30 a.m. to 9:30 p.m. Mon.-Fri.; to 6 p.m. Sat.; from 1 p.m. to 5 p.m. Sun. & holidays. Guided tours are given every hour from 9 a.m. through 4 p.m. Monday through Friday.

Thomas Jefferson Memorial

Dedicated in 1943, **The Thomas Jefferson Memorial** stands on the south shore of the Tidal Basin in West Potomac Park. It is a circular stone structure, with Vermont marble on the exterior and Georgia white marble inside, and combines architectural elements of the dome of the Pantheon in Rome and the rotunda designed by Jefferson for the University of Virginia.

The memorial is open daily from 8 a.m. to midnight. An elevator and curb ramps for the handicapped are in service.

Lincoln Memorial

The Lincoln Memorial in West Potomac Park, on the axis of the Capitol and the Washington Monument, consists of a large marble hall enclosing a heroic statue of Abraham Lincoln in meditation sitting on a large armchair. It was dedicated on Memorial Day, May 30, 1922. The Memorial was designed by Henry Bacon. The statue was made by Daniel Chester French and sculpted by the Piccirilli family. Murals and ornamentation on the bronze ceiling beams are by Jules Guerin.

The memorial is open daily from 8 a.m. to midnight. An elevator for the handicapped is in service.

John F. Kennedy Center

John F. Kennedy Center for the Performing Arts, designated by Congress as the National Cultural Center and the official memorial in Washington to President Kennedy, opened September 8, 1971. Tours are available daily between 10:00 a.m. and 1:00 p.m.

Mount Vernon

Mount Vernon, George Washington's estate, is on the south bank of the Potomac R., 16 miles below Washington, D.C., in northern Virginia.

The present house is an enlargement of one apparently built on the site by Augustine Washington, who lived there 1735-1738. His son Lawrence came there in 1743, when he renamed the plantation Mount Vernon in honor of Admiral Vernon, under whom he had served in the West Indies. Lawrence Washington died in 1752 and was succeeded as proprietor of Mount Vernon by his half-brother, George Washington.

National Archives

The Declaration of Independence, the Constitution of the United States, and the Bill of Rights are on permanent display in the National Archives Exhibition Hall. They are sealed in glass-and-bronze cases. The National Archives also holds the permanently valuable federal records of the United States government.

National Gallery of Art

The National Gallery of Art, situated on the north side of the Mall facing Constitution Avenue, was established by Joint Resolution of Congress Mar. 24, 1937, and opened Mar. 17, 1941.

Normally open daily from 10 a.m. to 5 p.m.; 11 a.m. to 6 p.m. Sunday. Summer, 10 a.m. to 9 p.m., noon to 9 p.m. on Sunday.

The Pentagon

The Pentagon, headquarters of the Department of Defense, is one of the world's largest office buildings. Situated in Arlington, Va., it houses more than 23,000 employees in offices that occupy 3,707,745 square feet.

Tours are available Monday through Friday (excluding federal holidays), from 9:30 a.m. to 3:30 p.m.

Smithsonian Institution

The Smithsonian Institution, established in 1846, the world's largest museum complex, is comprised of 14 museums and the National Zoo. It holds some 100 million artifacts and specimens in its trust "for the increase and diffusion of knowledge among men." Nine museums are located on the National Mall between the Washington Monument and the Capitol; 4 other museums and the zoo are elsewhere in Washington, and the Cooper-Hewitt Museum is in New York City. The National Air and Space Museum, the National Museum of Natural History, and the National Portrait Gallery are some of the more popular museums. They are open daily, except Dec. 25, from 10 a.m. to 5:30 p.m. unless otherwise noted.

Washington Monument

The Washington Monument, dedicated in 1885, is a tapering shaft or obelisk of white marble, 555 ft., 5-1/8 inches in height and 55 ft., 1-1/2 inches square at base. Eight small windows, 2 on each side, are located at the 500-ft. level, where points of interest are indicated.

Open daily except Dec. 25, 9 a.m. to 4:30 p.m., 8 a.m. to midnight Apr.-Labor Day.

The White House

The White House, the president's residence, stands on 18 acres on the south side of Pennsylvania Avenue, between the Treasury and the Executive Office Building.

The walls are of sandstone, quarried at Aquia Creek, Va. The exterior walls were painted, causing the building to be termed the "White House." On Aug. 24, 1814, during Madison's administration, the house was burned by the British. James Hoban rebuilt it by Oct. 1817.

The White House is normally open from 10 a.m. to 12 noon, Tues.-Sat., and from 10 a.m. to 2 p.m. in summer. Only the public rooms on the ground floor and state floor may be visited.

Naturalization: How to Become an American Citizen

Source: Federal Statutes

A person who desires to be naturalized as a citizen of the United States may obtain the necessary application form as well as detailed information from the nearest office of the Immigration and Naturalization Service or from the clerk of a court handling naturalization cases.

An applicant must be at least 18 years old and must have been a lawful resident of the United States continuously for 5 years. For husbands and wives of U.S. citizens the period is 3 years in most instances. Special provisions apply to certain veterans of the Armed Forces.

An applicant must have been physically present in the country for at least half of the required 5 years' residence.

Every applicant for naturalization must:

(1) demonstrate an understanding of the English language, including an ability to read, write, and speak words in ordinary usage in the English language (persons physically unable to do so and persons who, on the date of their examinations, are over 50 years of age and have been lawful permanent residents of the United States for 20 years or more are exempt);

(2) have been a person of good moral character, attached to the principles of the Constitution, and well disposed to the good order and happiness of the United States for five years just before filing the petition or for whatever other period of residence is required in the particular case and continue to be such a person until admitted to citizenship; and

(3) demonstrate a knowledge and understanding of the fundamentals of the history, and the principles and form of government, of the United States.

At the preliminary hearing the applicant may be represented by a lawyer or social service agency. There is a 30-day wait. If action is favorable, there is a final hearing before a judge, who administers the following oath of allegiance:

I hereby declare, on oath, that I absolutely and entirely renounce and abjure all allegiance and fidelity to any foreign prince, potentate, state or sovereignty, to whom or which I have heretofore been a subject or citizen; that I will support and defend the Constitution and laws of the United States of America against all enemies, foreign and domestic; that I will bear true faith and allegiance to the same; that I will bear arms on behalf of the United States when required by the law; that I will perform noncombatant service in the armed forces of the United States when required by the law; that I will perform work of national importance under civilian direction when required by the law; and that I take this obligation freely without any mental reservation or purpose of evasion; so help me God.

CITIES OF THE U.S.

Sources: Bureau of the Census: population (1990 Census, updated as of April 1993); population growth (1980-1990). Geography Division, Bureau of the Census: population density (1990); area (1990). Bureau of Labor Statistics: employment (1992 averages for city proper only). Bureau of Economic Analysis: per capita personal income (Metropolitan Statistical Area, 1991).

Based on 1990 Census, the 100 most populous cities (inc.=incorporated; est.=established).

Akron, Ohio

Population: 223,019; **Pop. density:** 4,055 per sq. mi.; **Pop. growth:** −6.0%. **Area:** 55 sq. mi. **Employment:** 97,224 employed, 9.6% unemployed; **Per capita income:** $18,234; % change 1981-91: 69.1.

History: settled 1825; inc. as city 1865; located on Ohio-Erie Canal and is a port of entry; since 1870 the rubber capital of the U.S.

Transportation: 1 airport; major trucking industry; Conrail; metro transit system. **Communications:** 4 TV, 7 radio stations. **Medical facilities:** 11 hospitals; specialized children's treatment center. **Educational facilities:** 13 universities and colleges; 68 public schools. **Further information:** Akron Regional Development Board or Akron-Summit Convention and Visitors Bureau, Cascade Plaza, Akron, OH 44308.

Albuquerque, New Mexico

Population: 384,619; **Pop. density:** 2,829 per sq. mi.; **Pop. growth:** 15.6%. **Area:** 136 sq. mi. **Employment:** 213,698 employed, 4.6% unemployed; **Per capita income:** $17,040; % change 1981-91: 73.7.

History: founded 1706 by the Spanish; inc. 1890.

Transportation: 1 international airport; 1 railroad; 2 bus lines. **Communications:** 8 TV, 31 radio stations. **Medical facilities:** 10 major hospitals. **Educational facilities:** 2 universities, 2 colleges. **Further information:** Convention & Visitors Bureau, 121 Tijeras Ave. NE, Albuquerque, NM 87125.

Anaheim, California

Population: 266,406; **Pop. density:** 6,498 per sq. mi.; **Pop. growth:** 21.4%. **Area:** 41 sq. mi. **Employment:** 141,649 employed, 7.1% unemployed; **Per capita income:** $24,077; % change 1981-91: 65.4.

History: founded 1858; inc. 1876; now known as home of Disneyland (since 1955).

Transportation: 3 municipal airports; 4 railroads; Greyhound buses. **Communications:** 12 TV, 4 radio stations. **Medical facilities:** 6 general hospitals. **Educational facilities:** 3 colleges, 5 junior colleges; 62 elementary, 8 junior high, 8 high schools. **Further information:** Chamber of Commerce, 100 South Anaheim Blvd., Suite 300, Anaheim, CA 92805.

Anchorage, Alaska

Population: 226,338; **Pop. density:** 131 per sq. mi.; **Pop. growth:** 29.8%. **Area:** 1,732 sq. mi. **Employment:** 109,090 employed, 7.3% unemployed; **Per capita income:** $24,464; % change 1981-91: 45.1.

History: founded 1914 as a construction camp for railroad; HQ of Alaska Defense Command, WWII; severely damaged in earthquake 1964.

Transportation: 1 international airport, 3 other airports. **Communications:** 6 TV, 16 radio stations. **Medical facilities:** 3 hospitals. **Educational facilities:** 2 universities, 1 community college. **Further information:** Chamber of Commerce, 441 W. 5th Ave., Ste. 300, Anchorage, AK 99501.

Arlington, Texas

Population: 261,721; **Pop. density:** 3,313 per sq. mi.; **Pop. growth:** 63.5%. **Area:** 79 sq. mi. **Employment:** 150,988 employed, 6.2% unemployed; **Per capita income:** $18,714; % change 1981-91: 55.4.

History: settled in 1840s between Dallas & Ft. Worth; inc. 1884.

Transportation: Dallas/Ft. Worth airport is 20 minutes away; 11 railway lines; intercity transport system in planning stage. **Communications:** 13 TV, 53 radio stations. **Medical facilities:** 4 hospitals. **Educational facilities:** 1 university; 51 public schools. **Further information:** Chamber of Commerce, 316 W. Main St., Arlington, TX 76010.

Atlanta, Georgia

Population: 393,929; **Pop. density:** 3,008 per sq. mi.; **Pop. growth:** −7.3%. **Area:** 131 sq. mi. **Employment:** 164,506 employed, 10.0% unemployed; **Per capita income:** $20,304; % change 1981-91: 81.6.

History: founded as "Terminus" 1837; renamed Atlanta 1845 after Atlantis; inc. 1847; played major role in Civil War and burned during Gen. Sherman's "March to the Sea."

Transportation: 1 international airport; 7 railroad lines, 2 systems; 2 bus terminals; rapid rail. **Communications:** 9 TV, 41 radio stations; 21 cable TV companies. **Medical facilities:** 60 hospitals; VA hospital; Natl. Centers for Disease Control; Natl. Cancer Center. **Educational facilities:** 37 colleges, universities, seminaries, junior colleges. **Further information:** Chamber of Commerce, 235 International Blvd., Atlanta, GA 30303.

Aurora, Colorado

Population: 222,103; **Pop. density:** 1,645 per sq. mi.; **Pop. growth:** 40.1%. **Area:** 135 sq. mi. **Employment:** 118,569 employed, 5.4% unemployed; **Per capita income:** $21,441; % change 1981-91: 59.4.

History: located 5 miles east of Denver; early growth stimulated by presence of military bases; fast-growing trade center.

Transportation: adjacent to new Denver Intl. Airport; 1 airport; 4 railroads; bus system. **Further information:** Aurora Economic Development Council, 15701 E. 1st Ave., Ste. 206, Aurora, CO 80011.

Austin, Texas

Population: 465,622; **Pop. density:** 4,014 per sq. mi.; **Pop. growth:** 34.6%. **Area:** 116 sq. mi. **Employment:** 269,075 employed, 5.7% unemployed; **Per capita income:** $18,081; % change 1981-91: 71.1.

History: first permanent settlement 1835; capital of Rep. of Texas 1838; named after Stephen Austin; inc. 1840.

Transportation: 1 international airport; 4 railroads. **Communications:** 5 TV, 18 radio stations. **Medical facilities:** 15 hospitals. **Educational facilities:** 7 universities and colleges. **Further information:** Chamber of Commerce, P.O. Box 1967, Austin, TX 78767.

Bakersfield, California

Population: 174,820; **Pop. density:** 2,033 per sq. mi.; **Pop. growth:** 65.5%. **Area:** 86 sq. mi. **Employment:** 80,470 employed, 11.2% unemployed; **Per capita income:** $15,791; % change 1981-91: 42.2.

History: incorporated in 1898.

Transportation: 1 airport; 3 railroads; Greyhound buses; local bus system. **Medical facilities:** 4 major hospitals; 9 convalescent; 2 psychiatric; 3 physical rehab. centers; 3 clinics; 2 urgent care centers. **Educational facilities:** 1 university, 1 community college; 9 vocational schools; 1 adult school; 1 college of law; 58 public schools. **Further information:** Greater Bakersfield Chamber of Commerce, 1033 Truxtun Avenue, Bakersfield, CA 93301.

Baltimore, Maryland

Population: 736,014; **Pop. density:** 9,200 per sq. mi.; **Pop. growth:** −6.4%. **Area:** 80 sq. mi. **Employment:** 297,512 employed, 10.7% unemployed; **Per capita income:** $21,874; % change 1981-91: 84.5.

History: founded by Maryland legislature 1729; inc. 1797; bombing of its Ft. McHenry 1814 inspired Francis Scott Key to write "Star-Spangled Banner;" rebuilt after fire 1904.

Transportation: 1 major airport; 3 railroads; bus system; subway system; 2 underwater tunnels. **Communications:** 6 TV, 33 radio stations. **Medical facilities:** 29 hospitals; 2 major medical centers. **Educational facilities:** over 30 universities and colleges; 189 public schools. **Further information:** Greater Baltimore Committee, 111 S. Calvert St., Baltimore, MD 21202.

Baton Rouge, Louisiana

Population: 219,531; **Pop. density:** 3,599 per sq. mi.; **Pop. growth:** −0.4%. **Area:** 61 sq. mi. **Employment:** 108,838 employed; 6.6% unemployed; **Per capita income:** $17,032; % change 1981-91: 56.5.

History: claimed by Spain at time of La. Purchase 1803; est. independence by rebellion 1810; inc. as town 1817; held by Union during most of Civil War.

Transportation: 1 airport, 7 airlines; 1 bus line; 3 railroad trunk lines. **Communications:** 5 TV, 19 radio stations. **Medical facilities:** 7 hospitals. **Educational facilities:** 2 universities; 96 public, 46 private schools. **Further information:** Chamber of Commerce, P.O. Box 3217, Baton Rouge, LA 70821.

Birmingham, Alabama

Population: 265,965; **Pop. density:** 2,687 per sq. mi.; **Pop. growth:** −6.5%. **Area:** 99 sq. mi. **Employment:** 113,176 employed, 8.6% unemployed; **Per capita income:** $18,210; % change 1981-91: 83.5.

History: settled due to discovery of elements needed for steel production; inc. 1871; named after Great Britain's steel-making center.

Transportation: 1 airport; 4 major rail freight lines, Amtrak; 1 bus line; 75 truck line terminals; 4 interstate highways. **Communications:** 4 TV, 22 radio stations; 1 educational TV, 1 educational radio station. **Medical facilities:** Univ. of Alabama at Birmingham Medical Center; VA hospital with organ transplant program; 15 other hospitals. **Educational facilities:** 1 university, 2 colleges, 2 junior colleges. **Further information:** Chamber of Commerce, 2027 First Ave. N., Birmingham, AL 35202.

Boston, Massachusetts

Population: 574,283; **Pop. density:** 12,484 per sq. mi.; **Pop. growth:** 2.0%. **Area:** 46 sq. mi. **Employment:** 271,288 employed, 7.8% unemployed; **Per capita income:** $23,480; % change 1981-91: 96.6.

History: settled 1630 by John Winthrop; capital of Mass. Bay Colony; figured strongly in Am. Revolution, earning distinction as the "Cradle of Liberty;" inc. 1822.

Transportation: 1 major airport; 2 railroads; city rail and subway system; 2 underwater tunnels; port. **Communications:** 8 TV, 17 radio stations. **Medical facilities:** 16 hospitals; 8 major medical research centers. **Educational facilities:** 11 universities and colleges. **Further information:** Greater Boston Chamber of Commerce, 1 Beacon St., 4th fl., Boston, MA 02108-3114.

Buffalo, New York

Population: 328,175; **Pop. density:** 7,812 per sq. mi.; **Pop. growth:** −8.3%. **Area:** 42 sq. mi. **Employment:** 125,888 employed, 12.0% unemployed; **Per capita income:** $18,466; % change 1981-91: 72.8.

History: founded 1790 by the Dutch; raided twice by British during War of 1812; as western terminus for Erie Canal became a center for trade and manufacturing; inc. 1832.

Transportation: 1 international airport; 6 major railroads; metro rail system; water service to Great Lakes-St. Lawrence seaways system, and Atlantic seaboard. **Communications:** 8 TV, 31 radio stations. **Medical facilities:** 16 hospitals. **Educational facilities:** 2 universities, 11 colleges; 70 public and private schools. **Further information:** Greater Buffalo Partnership, 300 Main Place Tower, Buffalo, NY 14202.

Charlotte, North Carolina

Population: 395,934; **Pop. density:** 2,869 per sq. mi.; **Pop. growth:** 25.5%. **Area:** 138 sq. mi. **Employment:** 218,604 employed, 5.5% unemployed; **Per capita income:** $18,757; % change 1981-91: 87.4.

History: settled by Scotch-Irish immigrants 1740s; inc. 1767 and named after Queen Charlotte, George III's wife; scene of first major U.S. gold discovery 1799.

Transportation: 1 airport; 2 major railway lines; 2 bus lines; 280 trucking firms. **Communications:** 6 TV, 20 radio stations. **Medical facilities:** 12 hospitals, 1 medical center. **Educational facilities:** 2 universities, 5 colleges. **Further information:** Chamber of Commerce, P.O. Box 32785, Charlotte, NC 28232.

Chicago, Illinois

Population: 2,783,726; **Pop. density:** 12,209 per sq. mi.; **Pop. growth:** −7.4%. **Area:** 228 sq. mi. **Employment:** 1,232,521 employed, 9.2% unemployed; **Per capita income:** $22,849; % change 1981-91: 75.6.

History: site acquired from Indians 1795; area began settlement with opening of Erie Canal 1825; chartered as city 1837; boomed with arrival of railroads from east and canal to Mississippi R.; much of city destroyed by fire 1871; major grain & livestock market.

Transportation: 3 airports; major railroad system; major trucking industry. **Communications:** 9 TV, 31 radio stations. **Medical facilities:** over 123 hospitals. **Educational facilities:** 95 institutions of higher learning. **Further information:** Association of Commerce and Industry, 200 N. LaSalle St., Chicago, IL 60601.

Cincinnati, Ohio

Population: 364,114; **Pop. density:** 4,667 per sq. mi.; **Pop. growth:** −5.5%. **Area:** 78 sq. mi. **Employment:** 173,843 employed, 7.6% unemployed; **Per capita income:** $19,273; % change 1981-91: 77.0.

History: founded 1788 and named after the Society of Cincinnati, an organization of Revolutionary War officers; chartered as village 1802; inc. as city 1819.

Transportation: 1 international airport; 3 railroads; 1 bus system. **Communications:** 6 TV, 27 radio stations. **Medical facilities:** 32 hospitals; Children's Hospital Medical Center; VA hospital. **Educational facilities:** 4 universities; 5 colleges, 8 technical & 2-year colleges. **Further information:** Chamber of Commerce, 300 Carew Tower, 441 Vine St., Cincinnati, OH 45202.

Cleveland, Ohio

Population: 505,616; **Pop. density:** 6,400 per sq. mi.; **Pop. growth:** −11.9%. **Area:** 79 sq. mi. **Employment:** 192,253 employed, 12.5% unemployed; **Per capita income:** $19,995; % change 1981-91: 66.4.

History: surveyed in 1796; inc. as village 1814, as city 1836; annexed Ohio City 1854.

Transportation: 1 intl. airport; rail service; major port; rapid transit system. **Communications:** 9 TV, 26 radio stations. **Medical facilities:** 24 hospitals; major medical research center. **Educational facilities:** 9 universities and colleges; 127 public schools. **Further information:** Greater Cleveland Growth Assn., 200 Tower City Center, Cleveland, OH 44113.

Colorado Springs, Colorado

Population: 281,140; **Pop. density:** 2,730 per sq. mi.; **Pop. growth:** 30.7%. **Area:** 103 sq. mi. **Employment:** 132,358 employed, 6.9% unemployed; **Per capita income:** $17,651; % change 1981-91: 66.3.

History: founded 1859 at the foot of Pikes Peak; inc. 1886.

Transportation: 1 municipal airport; 2 railroads; Greyhound-Trailways bus line. **Communications:** 5 TV, 22 radio stations. **Medical facilities:** 9 hospitals. **Educational facilities:** 3 universities, 7 colleges. **Further information:** Chamber of Commerce, P.O. Drawer B, Colorado Springs, CO 80901.

Columbus, Georgia

Population: 178,681; **Pop. density:** 822 per sq. mi.; **Pop. growth:** 5.4%. **Area:** 218 sq. mi. **Employment:** 70,718 employed, 7.1% unemployed; **Per capita income:** $15,401; % change 1981-91: 86.9.

History: settled and inc. 1828; a port city on Chattahouchee R.

Transportation: 1 airport; metro bus system; 2 bus lines; 2 railroads. **Communications:** 5 TV, 11 radio stations. **Medical facilities:** 5 hospitals. **Educational facilities:** 1 college; 53 public schools. **Further information:** Chamber of Commerce, P.O. Box 1200, Columbus, GA 31902.

Columbus, Ohio

Population: 632,945; **Pop. density:** 3,497 per sq. mi.; **Pop. growth:** 12.0%. **Area:** 181 sq. mi. **Employment:** 338,849 employed, 5.8% unemployed; **Per capita income:** $18,630; % change 1981-91: 77.6.

History: first settlement 1797; laid out as new capital 1812 with current name; became city 1834.

Transportation: 2 airports; 3 railroads; 4 intercity bus lines. **Communications:** 5 TV, 19 radio stations. **Medical facilities:** 22 hospitals. **Educational facilities:** 12 universities and colleges. **Further information:** Chamber of Commerce, P.O. Box 1527, Columbus, OH 43216.

Corpus Christi, Texas

Population: 257,453; **Pop. density:** 2,476 per sq. mi.; **Pop. growth:** 10.9%. **Area:** 104 sq. mi. **Employment:** 118,026 employed, 9.2% unemployed; **Per capita income:** $15,273; % change 1981-91: 42.6.

History: settled 1839 and inc. 1852.

Transportation: 1 international airport; 2 bus lines, metro bus system; 3 freight railroads. **Communications:** 6 TV, 17 radio stations. **Medical facilities:** 14 hospitals including a children's center. **Educational facilities:** 1 university, 1 college. **Further information:** Chamber of Commerce, PO Box 640, Corpus Christi, TX 78403.

Dallas, Texas

Population: 1,007,618; **Pop. density:** 3,024 per sq. mi.; **Pop. growth:** 11.3%. **Area:** 333 sq. mi. **Employment:** 520,135 employed, 8.9% unemployed; **Per capita income:** $20,892; % change 1981-91: 60.2.

History: first settled 1841; platted 1846; inc. 1871; developed as the financial and commercial center of Southwest; known for its oil industry and cotton market.

Transportation: 1 international airport; Amtrak; major transit system. **Communications:** 10 TV, 49 radio stations. **Medical facilities:** 70 hospitals; major medical center. **Educational facilities:** 7 universities, 2 colleges. **Further information:** Chamber of Commerce, 1201 Elm, Dallas, TX 75270.

Dayton, Ohio

Population: 182,005; **Pop. density:** 3,793 per sq. mi.; **Pop. growth:** −5.9%. **Area:** 48 sq. mi. **Employment:** 71,854 employed, 10.9% unemployed; **Per capita income:** $18,302; % change 1981-91: 71.8.

History: settled 1796; inc. 1805; disastrous flood 1913; site where Wright Bros. invented first airplane to sustain flight 1903.

Transportation: 1 international airport, 14 airlines; 3 railroads; 3 bus lines; countywide Dayton Regional Transit Authority. **Communications:** 5 TV, 17 radio stations. **Medical facilities:** 14 hospitals including VA facility. **Educational facilities:** 26 institutions of higher learning. **Further information:** Dayton Area Chamber of Commerce, Fifth and Main, Chamber Plaza, Dayton, OH 45402.

Denver, Colorado

Population: 467,610; **Pop. density:** 4,213 per sq. mi.; **Pop. growth:** −5.1%. **Area:** 111 sq. mi. **Employment:** 227,968 employed, 7.1% unemployed; **Per capita income:** $21,441; % change 1981-91: 59.4.

History: settled 1858 by gold prospectors and miners; inc. 1861; growth spurred by gold and silver boom; the financial and industrial center of Rocky Mt. region.

Transportation: 1 international airport; 5 major rail freight lines, Amtrak; 2 bus lines. **Communications:** 7 TV, 35 radio stations. **Medical facilities:** 34 hospitals. **Educational facilities:** 5 universities, 2 colleges. **Further information:** Greater Denver Chamber of Commerce, 1445 Market St., Denver, CO 80202.

Des Moines, Iowa

Population: 193,189; **Pop. density:** 2,927 per sq. mi.; **Pop. growth:** 1.1%. **Area:** 66 sq. mi. **Employment:** 113,241 employed, 5.0% unemployed; **Per capita income:** $20,570; % change 1981-91: 69.6.

History: Fort Des Moines built 1843; settled and inc. 1851; chartered as city 1857.

Transportation: 1 international airport; 3 bus lines; 4 railroads; metro bus system. **Communications:** 5 TV, 18 radio stations. **Medical facilities:** 8 hospitals. **Educational facilities:** 1 university, 2 colleges. **Further information:** Chamber of Commerce, 601 Locust St., Ste. 100, Des Moines, IA 50309.

Detroit, Michigan

Population: 1,027,974; **Pop. density:** 7,559 per sq. mi.; **Pop. growth:** −14.6%. **Area:** 136 sq. mi. **Employment:** 328,371 employed, 16.5% unemployed; **Per capita income:** $20,585; % change 1981-91: 72.6.

History: founded by French 1701; controlled by British 1760; acquired by U.S. 1796; destroyed by fire 1805; capital of state 1837-47; inc. as city 1824; auto manufacturing began 1899.

Transportation: 1 international airport; 10 railroads; major international port; public transit system. **Communications:** 9 TV, 37 radio stations. **Medical facilities:** 28 hospitals, major medical center. **Educational facilities:** 13 universities and colleges. **Further information:** Greater Detroit Chamber of Commerce, 600 W. Lafayette Blvd., Detroit, MI 48226.

El Paso, Texas

Population: 515,342; **Pop. density:** 2,156 per sq. mi. **Pop. growth:** 21.2%. **Area:** 239 sq. mi. **Employment:** 210,618 employed, 10.3% unemployed; **Per capita income:** $11,764; % change 1981-91: 62.2.

History: first settled 1827; inc. 1873; arrival of railroad 1881 boosted city's population and industries.

Transportation: 1 international airport; 5 major rail lines; 8 bus lines; 9 major highways; gateway to Mexico. **Communications:** 6 TV, 23 radio stations. **Medical facilities:** 16 hospitals; cancer treatment center. **Educational facilities:** 2 colleges and universities. **Further information:** Convention and Visitors Bureau, 5 Civic Center Plaza, El Paso, TX 79901.

Fort Wayne, Indiana

Population: 172,971; **Pop. density:** 3,328 per sq. mi.; **Pop. growth:** 0.4%. **Area:** 52 sq. mi. **Employment:** 86,782 employed, 7.5% unemployed; **Per capita income:** $17,962; % change 1981-91: 71.6.

History: French fort 1680; U.S. fort 1794; settled by 1832; inc. 1840 prior to Wabash-Erie canal completion 1843.

Transportation: 1 airport, 7 airlines; 3 railroads; 5 bus lines. **Communications:** 5 TV, 13 radio stations. **Medical facilities:** 3 major hospitals; VA hospital. **Educational facilities:** 5 colleges; 82 public schools. **Further information:** Chamber of Commerce, 826 Ewing Street, Fort Wayne, IN 46802-2182.

Fort Worth, Texas

Population: 447,619; **Pop. density:** 1,549 per sq. mi.; **Pop. growth:** 16.2%. **Area:** 289 sq. mi. **Employment:** 213,559 employed, 9.2% unemployed; **Per capita income:** $18,714; % change 1981-91: 55.4.

History: est. as military post 1849; inc. 1873; oil discovered 1917.

Transportation: 1 international airport; 8 major railroads, Amtrak; local bus service; 2 transcontinental, 2 intrastate bus lines. **Communications:** 9 TV, 37 radio stations. **Medical facilities:** 35 hospitals; 2 children's hospitals; 4 government hospitals. **Educational facilities:** 8 universities and colleges. **Further information:** Chamber of Commerce, 777 Taylor St. #900, Fort Worth, TX 76102.

Fremont, California

Population: 173,339; **Pop. density:** 2,211 per sq. mi.; **Pop. growth:** 31.4%. **Area:** 78.4 sq. mi. **Employment:** 96,255 employed, 4.5% unemployed; **Per capita income:** $23,545; % change 1981-91: 70.0.

History: area first settled by Spanish 1769; during 1800s a collection of towns formed the area; inc. 1956.

Transportation: intracity bus line; Bay Area Rapid Transit System (southern terminal). **Communications:** NA. **Medical facilities:** 1 hospital. **Educational facilities:** 1 junior college; 43 public schools. **Further information:** Chamber of Commerce, 2201 Walnut Ave., Ste. 110, Fremont, CA 94538.

Fresno, California

Population: 354,091; **Pop. density:** 5,449 per sq. mi.; **Pop. growth:** 62.9%. **Area:** 65 sq. mi. **Employment:** 151,788 employed, 13.0% unemployed; **Per capita income:** $15,994; % change 1981-91: 50.7.

History: founded 1872; inc. as city 1885.

Transportation: 2 municipal airports; Amtrak; 1 bus line; intracity bus system. **Communications:** 11 TV, 58 radio stations. **Medical facilities:** 6 general hospitals including a VA facility. **Educational facilities:** 8 universities and colleges; 85 public schools. **Further information:** Chamber of Commerce, P.O. Box 1469, Fresno, CA 93716-1469.

Garland, Texas

Population: 180,650; **Pop. density:** 3,226 per sq. mi.; **Pop. growth:** 30.1%. **Area:** 56 sq. mi. **Employment:** 99,852 employed, 5.9% unemployed; **Per capita income:** $20,892; % change 1981-91: 60.2.

History: city in Dallas co., 14 mi. NE of Dallas.

Transportation: 45 miles from Dallas/Ft. Worth airport; 2 railroads. **Communications:** 3 TV stations (from Dallas). **Medical facilities:** total of 306 hospital beds. **Educational facilities:** 1 university, 2 community colleges; 53 public schools. **Further information:** Chamber of Commerce, 914 S. Garland Ave., Garland, TX 75040.

Glendale, California

Population: 180,038; **Pop. density:** 5,886 per sq. mi.; **Pop. growth:** 29%. **Area:** 30.59 sq. mi. **Employment:** 84,942 employed, 9.1% unemployed; **Per capita income:** $20,967; % change 1981-91: 59.5.

History: Township in 1887, incorporated in 1906. Adjacent to Los Angeles.

Transportation: 1 airport; 1 railroad; in triangle surrounded by 3 freeways; Southern California Rapid Transit system; Glendale Beeline bus. **Communications:** 2 radio stations. **Medical facilities:** 1,100 beds in three hospitals. **Educational facilities:** 1 community college. **Further information:** Chamber of Commerce, 200 S. Louise, Glendale, CA 91205.

Grand Rapids, Michigan

Population: 189,126; **Pop. density:** 4,358 per sq. mi.; **Pop. growth:** 4.0%. **Area:** 43.4 sq. mi. **Employment:** 90,336 employed, 10.2% unemployed; **Per capita income:** $18,008; % change 1981-91: 75.4.

History: originally site of Ottowa Indian village; trading post 1826; became lumbering center and chartered as town 1850.

Transportation: 1 international airport; 4 railroads; 5 bus lines; transit bus system. **Communications:** 6 TV, 25 radio stations. **Medical facilities:** 10 hospitals. **Educational facilities:** 8 colleges; 64 public schools. **Further information:** Chamber of Commerce, 17 Fountain St., NW, Grand Rapids, MI 49503.

Greensboro, North Carolina

Population: 183,894; **Pop. density:** 3,059 per sq. mi.; **Pop. growth:** 17.9%. **Area:** 60 sq. mi. **Employment:** 101,263 employed, 5.6% unemployed; **Per capita income:** $18,943; % change 1981-91: 83.7.

History: settled 1749; site of Revolutionary War conflict 1781 between Nathanael Greene and Cornwallis; inc. 1807.

Transportation: 1 regional airport; 2 railroads; Trailways/Greyhound bus service. **Communications:** all cable TV stations; 11 radio stations. **Medical facilities:** 4 hospitals. **Educational facilities:** 2 universities, 3 colleges; 38 public schools. **Further information:** Chamber of Commerce, P.O. Box 3246, Greensboro, NC 27402.

Hialeah, Florida

Population: 188,008; **Pop. density:** 8,545 per sq. mi.; **Pop. growth:** 29.4%. **Area:** 22 sq. mi. **Employment:** 87,733 employed, 10.4% unemployed; **Per capita income:** $18,252; % change 1981-91: 65.5.

History: inc. 1925; built over drained swamplands NW of Miami.

Transportation: Miami Int'l. airport is 5 miles away; Amtrak; 2 rail freight lines. **Communications:** NA. **Medical facilities:** 4 hospitals. **Educational facilities:** 5 universities and colleges. **Further information:** Hialeah Dept. of Eco. Development, Office of the Mayor, 501 Palm Ave., Hialeah, FL 33010.

Honolulu, Hawaii

Population: 365,272; **Pop. density:** 613 per sq. mi.; **Pop. growth:** 0.1%. **Area:** 596 sq. mi. **Employment (MSA):** 394,028 employed, 3.5% unemployed; **Per capita income:** $22,102; % change 1981-91: 84.0.

History: harbor entered by Europeans 1794; declared capital of kingdom by King Kamehameha III 1850; Pearl Harbor naval base attacked by Japanese Dec. 7, 1941.

Transportation: 1 major airport; large, active port for passengers and cargo. **Communications:** 10 TV, 30 radio stations. **Medical facilities:** 36 hospitals. **Educational facilities:** 4 universities, 1 college; 165 public schools, 98 private schools. **Further information:** Visitors Bureau, 2270 Kalakaua Avenue, Honolulu, HI 96815.

Houston, Texas

Population: 1,630,864; **Pop. density:** 2,933 per sq. mi.; **Pop. growth:** 2.2%. **Area:** 556 sq. mi. **Employment:** 806,617 employed; 8.7% unemployed; **Per capita income:** $20,169; % change 1981-91: 42.2.

History: founded 1836; inc. 1837; capital of Republic of Texas 1837-39; developed rapidly after completion of canal to Gulf of Mexico 1914; important oil and natural gas center.

Transportation: 3 commercial airports; 4 mainline railroads; major bus transit system; major international port. **Communications:** 11 TV, 53 radio stations. **Medical facilities:** 66 hospitals; major medical center. **Educational facilities:** 26 universities and colleges. **Further information:** Greater Houston Partnership, 1100 Milam, Houston, TX 77002-5507.

Huntington Beach, California

Population: 181,519; **Pop. density:** 6,723 per sq. mi.; **Pop. growth:** 6.5%. **Area:** 27 sq. mi. **Employment:** 108,192 employed, 4.7% unemployed; **Per capita income:** $20,967; % change 1981-91: 59.5.

History: settled in early 1880s; inc. 1909; oil discovered 1920, led to city's development.

Transportation: 1 railroad; 2 bus lines. **Communications:** 1 TV station. **Medical facilities:** 2 hospitals. **Educational facilities:** 1 junior college; 45 public schools. **Further information:** Chamber of Commerce, Seacliff Office Park, 2100 Main #200, Huntington Beach, CA 92648.

Indianapolis, Indiana

Population: 731,327; **Pop. density:** 2,108 per sq. mi.; **Pop. growth:** 4.3%. **Area:** 352 sq. mi. **Employment:** 375,706 employed, 6.0% unemployed; **Per capita income:** $19,844; % change 1981-91: 79.0.

History: settled in 1820, made into capital 1825.

Transportation: 1 international airport; 5 railroads; 3 interstate bus lines. **Communications:** 10 TV, 26 radio stations. **Medical facilities:** 17 hospitals; 1 major medical and research center. **Educational facilities:** 8 universities and colleges; major public library system. **Further information:** Chamber of Commerce, 320 N. Meridian Street, Indianapolis, IN 46204.

Jackson, Mississippi

Population: 196,637; **Pop. density:** 1,852 per sq. mi.; **Pop. growth:** −3.1%. **Area:** 106.2 sq. mi. **Employment:** 90,756 employed, 6.2% unemployed; **Per capita income:** $15,991; % change 1981-91: 66.0.

History: originally known as Le Fleur's Bluff, selected as capital 1822 and named for Andrew Jackson; inc. 1823; scene of secession convention 1861; captured by Sherman 1863.

Transportation: 6 airlines; 2 bus lines; 3 railroads. **Communications:** 5 TV, 26 radio stations. **Medical facilities:** 14 hospitals including a VA facility. **Educational facilities:** 2 universities, 4 colleges; 7 public school districts. **Further information:** Metro Jackson Chamber of Commerce, P.O. Box 22548, Jackson, MS 39225-2548.

Jacksonville, Florida

Population: 635,230; **Pop. density:** 885 per sq. mi.; **Pop. growth:** 17.9%. **Area:** 760 sq. mi. **Employment:** 304,160 employed, 7.3% unemployed; **Per capita income:** $17,937; % change 1981-91: 75.8.

History: settled 1816 as Cowford; renamed after Andrew Jackson 1822; inc. 1832; rechartered 1851; scene of conflicts in Seminole and Civil wars.

Transportation: 1 international airport; 3 railroads; 2 interstate bus lines. **Communications:** 6 TV, 21 radio stations. **Medical facilities:** 14 hospitals. **Educational facilities:** 5 universities and colleges. **Further information:** Chamber of Commerce, 3 Independent Drive, P.O. Box 329, Jacksonville, FL 32201.

Jersey City, New Jersey

Population: 228,517; **Pop. density:** 17,313 per sq. mi.; **Pop. growth:** 2.2%. **Area:** 13.2 sq. mi. **Employment:** 91,801 employed, 14.4% unemployed; **Per capita income:** $25,583; % change 1981-91: 92.1.

History: bought from Indians 1630; chartered as town by British 1668; scene of Revolutionary War conflict 1779; chartered under present name 1838; important station on Underground Railroad.

Transportation: bus and subway system. **Medical facilities:** 10 hospitals. **Educational facilities:** 3 colleges. **Further information:** Chamber of Commerce & Industry of Hudson County, 911 Bergen Ave., Jersey City, NJ 07303.

Kansas City, Missouri

Population: 434,829; **Pop. density:** 1,377 per sq. mi.; **Pop. growth:** −2.9%. **Area:** 316 sq. mi. **Employment:** 221,485 employed, 6.5% unemployed; **Per capita income:** $19,963; % change 1981-91: 70.0.

History: settled by 1838 at confluence of the Missouri and Kansas rivers; inc. 1851.

Transportation: 1 international airport; a major rail center; 191 trunk lines; several barge companies. **Communications:** 7 TV, 29 radio stations. **Medical facilities:** 14 hospitals; VA facility. **Educational facilities:** 9 universities and colleges. **Further information:** Greater Kansas City Chamber of Commerce, 911 Main St., Ste. 2600, Kansas City, MO 64105.

Las Vegas, Nevada

Population: 258,204; **Pop. density:** 4,696 per sq. mi.; **Pop. growth:** 56.9%. **Area:** 55 sq. mi. **Employment:** 139,269 employed, 6.7% unemployed; **Per capita income:** $18,474; % change 1981-91: 58.7.

History: occupied by Mormons 1855-57; bought by railroad 1903; city of Las Vegas inc. 1911; gambling legalized 1931.

Transportation: 1 international airport; 2 railroads; bus system. **Communcations:** 7 TV, 33 radio stations. **Medical facilities:** 8 hospitals. **Educational facilities:** 1 university, 1 college; 170 public schools. **Further information:** Chamber of Commerce, 711 E. Desert Inn Rd., Las Vegas, NV 89109.

Lexington–Fayette, Kentucky

Population: 225,366; **Pop. density:** 794 per sq. mi.; **Pop. growth:** 10.4%. **Area:** 284 sq. mi. **Employment:** 123,985 employed, 4.1% unemployed; **Per capita income:** $18,142; % change 1981-91: 77.9.

History: site was founded and named 1775 by hunters who heard of the Revolutionary War battle at Lexington, Mass.; settled 1779; inc. 1832.

Transportation: 8 airlines; 2 railroads; city buses. **Communications:** 5 TV, 9 radio stations. **Medical facilities:** 5 general, 5 specialized hospitals. **Educational facilities:** 2 universities, 2 colleges. **Further information:** Chamber of Commerce, 330 East Main, Lexington, KY 40507.

Lincoln, Nebraska

Population: 191,972; **Pop. density:** 3,200 per sq. mi.; **Pop. growth:** 11.7%. **Area:** 60 sq. mi. **Employment:** 117,678 employed, 2.5% unemployed; **Per capita income:** $18,429; % change 1981-91: 70.5.

History: originally called Lancaster, chosen state capital 1867 and renamed after Abraham Lincoln; inc. 1869.

Transportation: 1 airport; Greyhound; Amtrak, 2 railroads. **Communications:** 1 TV, 13 radio stations. **Medical facilities:** 4 hospitals including a VA facility. **Educational facilities:** 2 universities, 1 college; 46 public, 15 private schools. **Further information:** Chamber of Commerce, 1221 N St., Lincoln, NE 68508.

Little Rock, Arkansas

Population: 175,727; **Pop. density:** 2,225 per sq. mi.; **Pop. growth:** 10.5%. **Area:** 79 sq. mi. **Employment:** 92,612 employed, 5.8% unemployed; **Per capita income:** $17,610; % change 1981-91: 77.0.

History: founded 1821; inc. as city 1835.

Transportation: 1 airport, 9 airlines; 3 railroads; 1 bus line. **Communications:** 7 TV, 34 radio stations. **Medical facilities:** 16 hospitals; veterans' medical center. **Educational facilities:** 8 universities and colleges, Univ. of Arkansas; 49 public schools. **Further information:** Chamber of Commerce, One Spring St., Little Rock, AR 72201.

Long Beach, California

Population: 429,321; **Pop. density:** 8,589 per sq. mi.; **Pop. growth:** 18.8%. **Area:** 50 sq. mi. **Employment:** 192,208 employed, 9.0% unemployed; **Per capita income:** $20,967; % change 1981-91: 59.5.

History: settled as early as 1769 by Spanish; by 1884 present site developed due to its harbor; inc. 1888; oil discovered 1921.

Transportation: 1 airport; 3 railroads; major international port; 6 bus lines, "lite" rail service. **Communications:** 4 radio stations. **Medical facilities:** 10 hospitals. **Educational facilities:** 1 university, 1 college; 78 public schools. **Further information:** Chamber of Commerce, One World Trade Center, Long Beach, CA 90831.

Los Angeles, California

Population: 3,485,398; **Pop. density:** 7,495 per sq. mi.; **Pop. growth:** 17.4%. **Area:** 465 sq. mi. **Employment:** 1,628,879 employed, 10.9% unemployed; **Per capita income:** $20,967; % change 1981-91: 59.5.

History: founded by Spanish 1781; captured by U.S. 1846; inc. 1850; Hollywood a district of L.A.

Transportation: 1 international airport; 4 railroads; major freeway system; intracity transit system. **Communications:** 19 TV, 71 radio stations. **Medical facilities:** 822 hospitals and clinics. **Educational facilities:** 11 universities and colleges; 1,642 public schools; 800 private schools. **Further information:** Chamber of Commerce, 404 S. Bixel St., P.O. Box 3696, Los Angeles, CA 90051.

Louisville, Kentucky

Population: 269,555; **Pop. density:** 4,484 per sq. mi.; **Pop. growth:** −9.9%. **Area:** 60 sq. mi. **Employment:** 122,272 employed, 7.2% unemployed. **Per capita income:** $18,912; % change 1981-91: 78.5.

History: settled 1778; named for Louis XVI of France; inc. 1828; base for Union forces in Civil War.

Transportation: 2 municipal airports; 1 terminal, 6 trunk-line railroads; 2 bus lines; 5 barge lines. **Communications:** 4 TV, 21 radio stations, 2 educational. **Medical facilities:** 21 hospitals. **Educational facilities:** 10 universities and colleges, 9 business colleges and technical schools. **Further information:** Louisville Area Chamber of Commerce, 600 W. Main, Louisville, KY 40202.

Lubbock, Texas

Population: 186,206; **Pop. density:** 2,069 per sq. mi.; **Pop. growth:** 6.8%. **Area:** 90 sq. mi. **Employment:** 92,047 employed, 6.6% unemployed; **Per capita income:** $15,577; % change 1981-91: 55.0.

History: settled 1879; inc. 1909 through merger of two towns.

Transportation: 1 international airport; 2 railroads, bus line. **Communications:** 5 TV, 18 radio stations. **Medical facilities:** 7 hospitals. **Educational facilities:** 2 universities, 1 college; 51 public schools. **Further information:** Chamber of Commerce, P.O. Box 561, Lubbock, TX 79408.

Madison, Wisconsin

Population: 190,766; **Pop. density:** 3,188 per sq. mi.; **Pop. growth:** 12.1%. **Area:** 60 sq. mi. **Employment:** 121,973 employed, 2.9% unemployed; **Per capita income:** $20,629; % change 1981-91: 76.7.

History: first white settlement 1832; named after James Madison who died in 1836; chartered 1856.

Transportation: 1 airport, 10 airlines; 2 railroads; intercity and intracity bus systems. **Communications:** 6 TV, 18 radio stations. **Medical facilities:** 5 hospitals. **Educational facilities:** 3 colleges and universities, Univ. of Wisconsin; 39 public schools. **Further information:** Chamber of Commerce, P.O. Box 71, Madison, WI 53701.

Memphis, Tennessee

Population: 610,337; **Pop. density:** 2,312 per sq. mi.; **Pop. growth:** −5.5%. **Area:** 264 sq. mi. **Employment:** 264,752 employed, 6.7% unemployed; **Per capita income:** $18,331; % change 1981-91: 87.1.

History: French, Spanish, and U.S. forts by 1797; settled by 1819; inc. as town 1826, as city 1840; surrendered charter to state 1879 after yellow fever epidemics; re-chartered as city 1893.

Transportation: 1 international airport; 6 railroads; bus system. **Communications:** 6 TV, 29 radio stations. **Medical facilities:** 21 hospitals. **Educational facilities:** 12 universities and colleges; 205 public, 76 private schools. **Further information:** Memphis Area Chamber of Commerce, 22 N. Front St., Box 224, Memphis TN 38101.

Mesa, Arizona

Population: 288,104; **Pop. density:** 4,237 per sq. mi.; **Pop. growth:** 89.0%. **Area:** 68 sq. mi. **Employment:** 133,357 employed, 5.4% unemployed; **Per capita income:** $22,014; % change 1981-91: 61.6.

History: founded by Mormons 1878; inc. 1883; 15 mi. from Phoenix; population boomed fivefold from 1960-80.

Transportation: 1 international airport; 2 railroads; trolley and bus lines. **Medical facilities:** 4 major hospitals. **Educational facilities:** 1 university, 1 college; 49 public schools. **Further information:** Convention and Visitor's Bureau, 120 N. Center, Mesa, AZ 85201.

Miami, Florida

Population: 358,648; **Pop. density:** 10,546 per sq. mi.; **Pop. growth:** 3.4%. **Area:** 34 sq. mi. **Employment:** 148,041 employed; 14.2% unemployed; **Per capita income:** $18,252; % change 1981-91: 65.5.

History: site of fort 1836; settlement began 1870; inc. 1896 and modern city developed into resort and recreation center; land speculation 1920s added to city's growth, as did Cuban immigration in 1970s and 1980s.

Transportation: 1 international airport; 2 passenger railroads, 1 all-freight; 2 bus lines; 65 truck lines. **Communications:** 6 commercial, 5 educational TV stations; 31 radio stations. **Medical facilities:** 41 hospitals, VA Hospital. **Educational facilities:** 6 universities and colleges. **Further information:** Metro-Dade Department of Tourism, 234 W. Flagler St., Miami, FL 33130.

Milwaukee, Wisconsin

Population: 628,088; **Pop. density:** 6,543 per sq. mi.; **Pop. growth:** −1.3%. **Area:** 96 sq. mi. **Employment:** 258,525 employed, 5.8% unemployed; **Per capita income:** $20,325; % change 1981-91: 67.6.

History: Indian trading post by 1674; settlement began 1835; inc. as city 1848; famous beer industry.

Transportation: 1 international airport; 2 railroads; major port; 4 bus lines. **Communications:** 12 TV, 34 radio stations. **Medical facilities:** 24 hospitals; major medical center. **Educational facilities:** 12 universities and colleges. **Further information:** Association of Commerce, 756 N. Milwaukee Street, Milwaukee, WI 53202.

Minneapolis, Minnesota

Population: 368,383; **Pop. density:** 6,698 per sq. mi.; **Pop. growth:** −0.7%. **Area:** 55 sq. mi. **Employment:** 194,572 employed; 4.8% unemployed; **Per capita income:** $21,665; % change 1981-91: 72.7.

History: site visited by Hennepin 1680; included in area of military reservations 1819; inc. 1867.

Transportation: 1 international airport; 6 railroads; mass transit systems; 5 major barge lines. **Communications:** 6 TV, 30 radio stations. **Medical facilities:** 36 hospitals, including leading heart hospital at Univ. of Minnesota. **Educational facilities:** 13 universities and colleges. 48 public school districts. **Further information:** Greater Minneapolis Chamber of Commerce, 81 S. 9th St., Ste. 200, Minneapolis, MN 55402.

Mobile, Alabama

Population: 196,278; **Pop. density:** 1,596 per sq. mi.; **Pop. growth:** −2.1%. **Area:** 123 sq. mi. **Employment:** 85,454 employed, 8.7% unemployed; **Per capita income:** $15,134; % change 1981-91: 68.8.

History: settled by French 1711; later occupied by U.S. 1813; inc. as town 1814, as city 1819; only seaport of Alabama.

Transportation: 4 rail freight lines, Amtrak; 5 major airlines; 65 truck lines; leading river system. **Communications:** 8 TV, 20 radio stations. **Medical facilities:** 7 hospitals. **Educational facilities:** 1 university, 3 colleges. **Further information:** Chamber of Commerce, P.O. Box 2187, Mobile, AL 36652.

Montgomery, Alabama

Population: 187,543; **Pop. density:** 1,462 per sq. mi.; **Pop. growth:** 5.2%. **Area:** 128 sq. mi. **Employment:** 84,637 employed, 6.5% unemployed; **Per capita income:** $17,158; % change 1981-91: 86.7.

History: inc. as town 1819, as city 1837; first capital of Confederacy 1861.

Transportation: 5 airlines; 2 railroads; 4 bus lines; Alabama River is navigable to Gulf of Mexico. **Communications:** 7 TV, 16 radio stations. **Medical facilities:** 10 hospitals; VA and 32 clinics. **Educational facilities:** 5 universities; 49 public, 31 private schools. **Further information:** Chamber of Commerce, P.O. Box 79, Montgomery, AL 36101.

Nashville-Davidson, Tennessee

Population: 516,880; **Pop. density:** 984 per sq. mi.; **Pop. growth:** 6.9%. **Area:** 525 sq. mi. **Employment:** 254,831 employed, 4.8% unemployed; **Per capita income:** $19,059; % change 1981-91: 87.4.

History: settled 1779; first chartered 1806; home of the Grand Ole Opry.

Transportation: 1 airport; 1 railroad; bus line; transit system of buses and trolleys. **Communications:** 7 TV, 30 radio stations. **Medical facilities:** 14 hospitals; VA Hospital, speech-hearing center. **Educational facilities:** 16 universities and colleges. **Further information:** Chamber of Commerce, 161 4th Ave., Nashville, TN 37219.

Newark, New Jersey

Population: 275,221; **Pop. density:** 11,468 per sq. mi.; **Pop. growth:** −16.4%. **Area:** 24 sq. mi. **Employment:** 96,361 employed, 16.8% unemployed; **Per capita income:** $25,583; % change 1981-91: 92.1.

History: settled by Puritans 1666; used as supply base by Washington 1776; inc. as town 1833, as city 1836.

Transportation: 1 international airport; 2 railroads; bus system; 2 subways. **Communications:** 3 TV, 5 radio stations. **Medical facilities:** 6 hospitals. **Educational facilities:** 5 universities and colleges; 71 public schools. **Further information:** Metro Newark Chamber of Commerce, 40 Clinton St., Newark, NJ 07102.

New Orleans, Louisiana

Population: 496,938; **Pop. density:** 2,497 per sq. mi.; **Pop. growth:** −10.9%. **Area:** 199 sq. mi. **Employment:** 190,555 employed, 7.3% unemployed; **Per capita income:** $16,959; % change 1981-91: 53.3.

History: founded by French 1718, became major seaport on Mississippi R.; acquired by U.S. as part of La. Purchase 1803; inc. as city 1805; 29-day Battle of New Orleans fought during War of 1812.

Transportation: 2 airports; major railroad center; major international port. **Communications:** 7 TV, 18 radio stations. **Medical facilities:** numerous hospitals; major medical research center. **Educational facilities:** 13 universities and colleges. **Further information:** Chamber of Commerce, 301 Camp Street, New Orleans, LA 70130.

Newport News, Virginia

Population: 171,439; **Pop. density:** 2,464 per sq. mi.; **Pop. growth:** 17.4%. **Area:** 69 sq. mi. **Employment:** 76,373 employed, 7.6% unemployed; **Per capita income:** $17,030; % change 1981-91: 68.4.

History: the cities of Warwick and Newport News consolidated in 1958 into the larger city of Newport News; one of the world's major shipbuilding centers.

Transportation: 1 international airport; 2 railroads; Greyhound buses; local bus system. **Communications:** 7 TV, 20 radio stations received in area. **Medical facilities:** 3 hospitals; adolescent psychiatry hospital. **Educational facilities:** 33 public schools. **Further information:** Peninsula Chamber of Commerce, A-12, Coliseum Mall, 1800 West Mercury Blvd., Hampton, VA 23666.

New York City, New York

Population: 7,322,564; **Pop. density:** 24,327 per sq. mi.; **Pop. growth:** 3.5%. **Area:** 301 sq. mi. **Employment:** 2,952,000 employed, 10.8% unemployed; **Per capita income:** $25,583; % change 1981-91: 92.1.

History: trading post established by H. Hudson 1609; British took control from Dutch 1664 and named New York; briefly capital of U.S.; Washington inaugurated as president 1789; comprised of 5 boroughs: The Bronx, Brooklyn, Manhattan, Queens, Staten Island.

Transportation: 2 airports; 2 rail terminals; major subway network; ferry system; 4 underwater tunnels. **Communications:** 13 TV, 117 radio stations. **Medical facilities:** 100 hospitals; 5 medical research centers. **Educational facilities:** 94 universities and colleges; 976 public schools, 914 private schools. **Further information:** Convention and Visitors Bureau, 2 Columbus Circle, New York, NY 10019.

Norfolk, Virginia

Population: 261,250; **Pop. density:** 4,929 per sq. mi.; **Pop. growth:** −2.2%. **Area:** 53 sq. mi. **Employment:** 89,091 employed, 7.8% unemployed; **Per capita income:** $17,030; % change 1981-91: 68.4.

History: founded 1682; burned by patriots to prevent capture by British during Revolutionary War; rebuilt and inc. as town 1805, as city 1845; location of world's largest naval base.

Transportation: 1 international airport; 4 major railroad systems in area. **Communications:** 7 TV, 38 radio stations. **Medical facilities:** 11 hospitals. **Educational facilities:** 2 universities, 1 college; 53 public schools. **Further information:** Hampton Roads Chamber of Commerce, 480 Bank St., Norfolk, VA 23510.

Oakland, California

Population: 372,242; **Pop. density:** 6,893 per sq. mi.; **Pop. growth:** 9.7%. **Area:** 54 sq. mi. **Employment:** 162,476 employed, 10.0% unemployed; **Per capita income:** $23,545; % change 1981-91: 70.0.

History: area settled by Spanish 1820; inc. as city under present name 1854.

Transportation: 1 international airport; western terminus for 3 railroads; underground, underwater 75-mile subway. **Communications:** 1 TV, 3 radio stations. **Medical facilities:** 7 hospitals, including Children's Hospital Medical Center, VA hospital. **Educational facilities:** 8 "eastbay" colleges and universities; 94 public schools. **Further information:** Chamber of Commerce, 475 14th St., Oakland, CA 94612-1903.

Oklahoma City, Oklahoma

Population: 444,719; **Pop. density:** 736 per sq. mi.; **Pop. growth:** 10.1%. **Area.** 604 sq. mi. **Employment:** 217,167 employed, 5.7% unemployed; **Per capita income:** $16,799; % change 1981-91: 39.8.

History: settled during landrush in Midwest 1889; inc. 1890; oil discovered 1928.

Transportation: 1 international airport; 3 railroads; public transit system; 5 major bus lines. **Communications:** 8 TV, 24 radio stations. **Medical facilities:** 12 hospitals, VA hospital. **Educational facilities:** 17 universities and colleges; 87 public schools. **Further information:** Chamber of Commerce, One Santa Fe Plaza, Oklahoma City, OK 73102.

Omaha, Nebraska

Population: 335,719; **Pop. density:** 3,690 per sq. mi.; **Pop. growth:** 7.0%. **Area:** 91 sq. mi. **Employment:** 181,986 employed, 3.7% unemployed; **Per capita income:** $19,037; % change 1981-91: 70.8.

History: founded 1854; inc. 1857; large livestock market; home for U.S. Strategic Command.

Transportation: 8 major airlines; 4 major railroads; intercity bus line. **Communications:** 8 TV, 22 radio stations. **Medical facilities:** 17 hospitals; institute for cancer research. **Educational facilities:** 3 universities, 6 colleges; 216 public, 82 private schools. **Further information:** Chamber of Commerce, 1301 Harney St., Omaha, NE 68102.

Philadelphia, Pennsylvania

Population: 1,585,577; **Pop. density:** 11,659 per sq. mi.; **Pop. growth:** −6.1%. **Area:** 136 sq. mi. **Employment:** 637,988 employed, 8.8% unemployed; **Per capita income:** $22,014; % change 1981-91: 87.2.

History: first settled by Swedes 1636; by English 1681; named Philadelphia 1682; chartered 1701; Continental Congress met 1774, 1775; Dec. of Independence signed 1776; national capital 1790-1800; cap. of Penn. 1683-1799.

Transportation: 1 major airport; 3 railroads; major freshwater port; subway, el, rail commuter, bus, and streetcar system. **Communications:** 6 TV, 53 radio stations. **Medical facilities:** 124 hospitals. **Educational facilities:** 88 degree-granting institutions. **Further information:** Office of City Representative, 1660 Municipal Services Bldg., Philadelphia, PA 19107.

Phoenix, Arizona

Population: 983,392; **Pop. density:** 3,035 per sq. mi.; **Pop. growth:** 24.5%. **Area:** 324 sq. mi. **Employment:** 473,232 employed, 7.0% unemployed; **Per capita income:** $18,156; % change 1981-91: 61.6.

History: settled in 1870; inc. as city 1881.

Transportation: 1 international airport; 2 railroads; 2 transcontinental bus lines; public transit system. **Communications:** 11 TV, 40 radio stations. **Medical facilities:** 42 hospitals, 1 medical research center. **Educational facilities:** 12 institutions of higher learning; 161 public schools. **Further information:** Chamber of Commerce, 201 N. Central Ave. #2700, Phoenix, AZ 85004.

Pittsburgh, Pennsylvania

Population: 369,879; **Pop. density:** 6,725 per sq. mi.; **Pop. growth:** −12.8%. **Area:** 55 sq. mi. **Employment:** 165,141 employed, 6.6% unemployed; **Per capita income:** $19,579; % change 1981-91: 69.6.

History: settled around Ft. Pitt 1758; inc. as city 1816; has one of largest inland ports; by Civil War, already a center for iron production.

Transportation: 1 international airport; 20 railroads; 2 bus lines; trolley/subway system. **Communications:** 6 TV, 25 radio stations. **Medical facilities:** 32 hospitals; VA installation. **Educational facilities:** 3 universities, 6 colleges; 86 public schools. **Further information:** Chamber of Commerce, 3 Gateway Ctr., Pittsburgh, PA 15222.

Portland, Oregon

Population: 438,802; **Pop. density:** 4,246 per sq. mi.; **Pop. growth:** 18.8%. **Area:** 103 sq. mi. **Employment:** 230,352 employed, 7.4% unemployed; **Per capita income:** $19,235; % change 1981-91: 63.8.

History: settled by pioneers 1845, developed as trading center, aided by California Gold Rush 1849; chartered as city 1851.

Transportation: 1 international airport; 3 major rail freight lines, Amtrak; 2 intercity bus lines; 27-mi. frontage freshwater port; mass transit bus and rail system. **Communications:** 6 TV, 27 radio stations. **Medical facilities:** 40 hospitals; VA hospital. **Educational facilities:** 21 universities and colleges, 3 community colleges. **Further information:** Portland Metropolitan Chamber of Commerce, 221 N.W. 2nd Ave., Portland, OR 97209-3999.

Raleigh, North Carolina

Population: 212,050; **Pop. density:** 3,851 per sq. mi.; **Pop. growth:** 38.4%. **Area:** 54 sq. mi. **Employment:** 126,429 employed, 4.4% unemployed; **Per capita income:** $20,170; % change 1981-91: 99.7.

History: named after Sir Walter Raleigh, site chosen for capital 1788; laid out 1792; inc. 1795; occupied by Gen. Sherman 1865.

Transportation: 1 airport, 6 airlines; 3 railroads; 1 bus line. **Communications:** 6 TV, 20 radio stations. **Medical facilities:** 11 hospitals. **Educational facilities:** 4 universities and colleges, 4 junior colleges; 82 public schools. **Further information:** Chamber of Commerce, 800 S. Salisbury St., P.O. Box 2978, Raleigh, NC 27602.

Richmond, Virginia

Population: 202,798; **Pop. density:** 3,384 per sq. mi.; **Pop. growth:** −7.4%. **Area:** 60 sq. mi. **Employment:** 95,866 employed, 8.5% unemployed; **Per capita income:** $21,416; % change 1981-91: 81.9.

History: first settled 1607; attacked by British under Benedict Arnold 1781; inc. as city 1782; capital of Confederate States of America, 1861.

Transportation: 1 international airport; 4 railroads; 3 intracity bus lines; deepwater terminal accessible to oceangoing ships. **Communications:** 6 TV, 26 radio stations. **Medical facilities:** Medical Coll. of Virginia renowned for heart and kidney transplants; 19 other hospitals including VA facility. **Educational facilities:** 9 universities and colleges; 173 public, 45 private schools. **Further information:** Chamber of Commerce, P.O. Box 12324, Richmond, VA 23241.

Riverside, California

Population: 226,546; **Pop. density:** 3,190 per sq. mi.; **Pop. growth:** 32.8%. **Area:** 71 sq. mi. **Employment:** 97,842 employed, 12.2% unemployed; **Per capita income:** $16,707; % change 1981-91: 51.9.

History: founded 1870; inc. 1886; known for its citrus industry.

Communications: 11 TV, 13 radio stations. **Educational facilities:** 3 universities, 1 community college. **Further information:** Chamber of Commerce, 4261 Main St., Riverside, CA 92501.

Rochester, New York

Population: 230,356; **Pop. density:** 6,813 per sq. mi.; **Pop. growth:** −4.2%. **Area:** 34 sq. mi. **Employment:** 100,056 employed, 8.4% unemployed; **Per capita income:** $20,784; % change 1981-91: 77.2.

History: first permanent white settlement 1812; inc. as village 1817, as city 1834; developed as Erie Canal town.

Transportation: 1 airport; Amtrak; 3 bus lines; intracity transit service; Port of Rochester. **Communications:** 5 TV, 18 radio stations. **Medical facilities:** 8 general hospitals. **Educational facilities:** 10 colleges, 3 community colleges. **Further information:** Chamber of Commerce, 55 St. Paul St., Rochester, NY 14604.

Sacramento, California

Population: 369,365; **Pop. density:** 3,848 per sq. mi.; **Pop. growth:** 34.0%. **Area:** 96 sq. mi. **Employment:** 168,401 employed, 9.4% unemployed; **Per capita income:** $19,540; % change 1981-91: 70.1.

History: settled 1839; important trading center during California Gold Rush 1840s.

Transportation: metropolitan airport; 2 mainline transcontinental rail carriers; bus and light rail system. **Communications:** 7 TV, 25 radio stations. **Medical facilities:** 8 hospitals. **Educational facilities:** 2 universities, 4 community colleges. **Further information:** Chamber of Commerce, 917 7th St., P.O. Box 1017, Sacramento, CA 95805.

St. Louis, Missouri

Population: 396,685; **Pop. density:** 6,503 per sq. mi.; **Pop. growth:** −12.4%. **Area:** 61 sq. mi. **Employment:** 164,899 employed, 8.0% unemployed; **Per capita income:** $20,507; % change 1981-91: 75.9.

History: founded 1764 as a fur trading post by French; acquired by U.S. 1803; chartered as city 1822; lies on Mississippi R., near confluence with Missouri R.

Transportation: 1 international airport; major rail center, 17 trunk-line railroads; major inland port; 14 bus lines; 14 barge lines. **Communications:** 7 TV, 35 radio stations. **Medical facilities:** 65 hospitals. **Educational facilities:** 6 universities, 25 colleges and seminaries. **Further information:** Regional Commerce and Growth Assoc., 100 S. 4th St., Ste. 500, St. Louis, MO 63102.

St. Paul, Minnesota

Population: 272,235; **Pop. density:** 5,235 per sq. mi.; **Pop. growth:** 0.7%. **Area:** 52 sq. mi. **Employment:** 134,231 employed, 5.2% unemployed; **Per capita income:** $21,665; % change 1981-91: 72.7.

History: founded in early 1840s as "Pig's Eye Landing;" became capital of the Minnesota territory 1849 and chartered as St. Paul.

Transportation: 1 international airport; 6 major rail lines; 3 interstate bus lines; public transit system. **Communications:** 6 TV, 35 radio stations. **Medical facilities:** 7 hospitals. **Educational facilities:** 2 universities, 5 colleges. **Further information:** Chamber of Commerce, 600 N. Central Tower, 445 Minnesota St., St. Paul, MN 55101.

St. Petersburg, Florida

Population: 240,318; **Pop. density:** 4,056 per sq. mi.; **Pop. growth:** 0.0%. **Area:** 59 sq. mi. **Employment:** 114,287 employed, 7.5% unemployed; **Per capita income:** $18,445; % change 1981-91: 72.4.

History: settled 1888; inc. 1892.

Transportation: 1 international airport; bus system; 1 full-service port. **Communications:** 12 TV, 22 radio stations. **Medical facilities:** 9 hospitals. **Educational facilities:** 6 colleges; 120 public schools. **Further information:**

Chamber of Commerce, P.O. Box 1371, St. Petersburg, FL 33731.

San Antonio, Texas

Population: 935,933; **Pop. density:** 2,681 per sq. mi.; **Pop. growth:** 19.1%. **Area:** 349 sq. mi. **Employment:** 416,566 employed, 7.4% unemployed; **Per capita income:** $15,950; % change 1981-91: 64.2.

History: first Spanish garrison 1718; Battle at the Alamo fought here 1836; city subsequently captured by Texans; inc. 1837.

Transportation: 1 international airport; 4 railroads; 4 bus lines; public transit system. **Communications:** 8 TV, 33 radio stations. **Medical facilities:** 34 hospitals; major medical center. **Educational facilities:** 14 universities and colleges. **Further information:** Chamber of Commerce, 602 E. Commerce, P.O. Box 1628, San Antonio, TX 78296.

San Diego, California

Population: 1,110,554; **Pop. density:** 3,470 per sq. mi.; **Pop. growth:** 26.8%. **Area:** 320 sq. mi. **Employment:** 507,386 employed, 7.5% unemployed; **Per capita income:** $19,799; % change 1981-91: 68.3.

History: claimed by the Spanish 1542, first mission est. 1769; scene of conflict during Mexican-American War 1846; inc. 1850.

Transportation: 1 major airport; 1 railroad; major freeway system; bus system; trolley system. **Communications:** 8 TV, 22 radio stations. **Medical facilities:** 28 hospitals. **Educational facilities:** 5 universities, 7 colleges. **Further information:** Greater SD Chamber of Commerce, 402 W. Broadway, Suite 1000, San Diego, CA 92101-3585.

San Francisco, California

Population: 723,959; **Pop. density:** 15,403 per sq. mi.; **Pop. growth:** 6.6%. **Area:** 47 sq. mi. **Employment:** 368,789 employed, 7.0% unemployed; **Per capita income:** $30,555; % change 1981-91: 77.5.

History: nearby Farallon Islands sighted by Spanish 1542, city settled by 1776; claimed by U.S. 1846; became a major city during California Gold Rush 1849; inc. as city 1850; earthquake devastated city 1906.

Transportation: 1 major airport; intracity railway system; 2 railway transit systems; bus and railroad service; ferry system; 1 underwater tunnel. **Communications:** 14 TV and cable stations; 69 radio stations. **Medical facilities:** 23 hospitals; 1 major medical center. **Educational facilities:** 4 universities and colleges. **Further information:** Chamber of Commerce, 465 California Street, San Francisco, CA 94104.

San Jose, California

Population: 782,248; **Pop. density:** 4,951 per sq. mi.; **Pop. growth:** 24.3%. **Area:** 158 sq. mi. **Employment:** 387,202 employed, 8.0% unemployed; **Per capita income:** $25,955; % change 1981-91: 78.6.

History: founded by the Spanish 1777 between San Francisco and Monterey; briefly capital of Calif. 1849-51; inc. 1850.

Transportation: 1 international airport; 2 railroads; bus system. **Communications:** 4 TV, 14 radio stations. **Medical facilities:** 6 hospitals. **Educational facilities:** 3 universities and colleges. **Further information:** Chamber of Commerce, 180 S. Market St., San Jose, CA 95113.

Santa Ana, California

Population: 293,827; **Pop. density:** 10,879 per sq. mi.; **Pop. growth:** 44.0%. **Area:** 27 sq. mi. **Employment:** 140,515 employed, 10.8% unemployed; **Per capita income:** $24,077; % change 1981-91: 65.4.

History: founded 1869; inc. as city 1886.

Transportation: 1 airport; 5 major freeways including main Los Angeles-San Diego artery; Amtrak. **Communications:** CATV system. **Medical facilities:** 4 hospitals. **Educational facilities:** 1 community college. **Further information:** Chamber of Commerce, 801 Civic Center Dr. W., Ste. 110, Santa Ana, CA 92701.

Seattle, Washington

Population: 516,259; **Pop. density:** 6,146 per sq. mi.; **Pop. growth:** 4.5%. **Area:** 84 sq. mi. **Employment:** 289,247 employed, 7.1% unemployed; **Per capita income:** $23,329; % change 1981-91: 71.3.

History: settled 1851; inc. 1869; suffered severe fire 1889; played prominent role during Alaska Gold Rush 1897; growth followed opening of Panama Canal 1914; center of aircraft industry WWII.

Transportation: 1 international airport; 2 railroads; ferries serve Puget Sound, Alaska, Canada. **Communications:** 7 TV, 39 radio stations. **Medical facilities:** 40 hospitals. **Educational facilities:** 7 universities, 6 colleges, 11 community colleges. **Further information:** Greater Seattle Chamber of Commerce, 600 University St., Ste. 1200, Seattle, WA 98101-3186.

Shreveport, Louisiana

Population: 198,525; **Pop. density:** 2,482 per sq. mi.; **Pop. growth:** −4.1%. **Area:** 80 sq. mi. **Employment:** 86,056 employed, 7.6% unemployed; **Per capita income:** $15,897; % change 1981-91: 54.7.

History: founded 1833 near site of a 160-mile log jam cleared by Capt. Henry Shreve; inc. 1839; oil discovered 1906.

Transportation: 2 airports; 2 bus lines. **Communications:** 5 TV, 16 radio stations. **Medical facilities:** 13 hospitals. **Educational facilities:** 4 universities, 3 colleges. **Further information:** Chamber of Commerce, P.O. Box 20074, Shreveport, LA 71120.

Spokane, Washington

Population: 177,165; **Pop. density:** 3,408 per sq. mi.; **Pop. growth:** 3.4%. **Area:** 52 sq. mi. **Employment:** 80,676 employed, 7.7% unemployed; **Per capita income:** $16,857; % change 1981-91: 63.7.

History: settled 1872; inc. as village of Spokane Falls 1881 but destroyed in fire 1889; reinc. as city of Spokane 1891.

Transportation: 1 international airport; 2 railroads; bus system. **Communications:** 5 TV, 25 radio stations. **Medical facilities:** 5 major hospitals. **Educational facilities:** 8 universities and colleges; 14 public school districts, 11 high schools. **Further information:** Chamber of Commerce, W. 1020 Riverside Ave., P.O. Box 2147, Spokane, WA 99210.

Stockton, California

Population: 210,943; **Pop. density:** 5,274 per sq. mi.; **Pop. growth:** 42.3%. **Area:** 40 sq. mi. **Employment:** 73,854 employed, 16.7% unemployed; **Per capita income:** $15,582; % change 1981-91: 41.9.

History: site purchased 1842; settled 1847; inc. 1850; chief distributing point for agricultural products of San Joaquin Valley.

Transportation: 1 airport, 7 railroads; 2 bus lines, city bus system. **Communications:** 5 TV stations. **Medical**

facilities: 4 hospitals; regional burn and heart centers. **Educational facilities:** 5 universities and colleges; 45 public schools. **Further information:** Chamber of Commerce, 445 W. Weber Ave., Suite 220, Stockton, CA 95203.

Tacoma, Washington

Population: 176,664; **Pop. density:** 3,696 per sq. mi.; **Pop. growth:** 11.5%. **Area:** 47.8 sq. mi. **Employment:** 71,768 employed, 9.1% unemployed; **Per capita income:** $17,184; % change 1981-91: 60.9.

History: area explored 1792 by the British; first permanent settlement 1864; terminus for the Northern Pacific Railroad; inc. 1884.

Transportation: 1 airport; 2 railroads; transit system; Port of Tacoma. **Communications:** NA. **Medical facilities:** 6 hospitals, VA facility. **Educational facilities:** 3 universities, 2 colleges. **Further information:** Chamber of Commerce, P.O. Box 1933, Tacoma, WA 98401-1933.

Tampa, Florida

Population: 280,015; **Pop. density:** 3,334 per sq. mi.; **Pop. growth:** 3.1%. **Area:** 84 sq. mi. **Employment:** 135,431 employed, 8.8% unemployed; **Per capita income:** $18,445; % change 1981-91: 72.4.

History: U.S. army fort on site 1824; inc. 1855.

Transportation: 1 international airport; Port of Tampa; bus system. **Communications:** 7 TV, 27 radio stations. **Medical facilities:** 17 hospitals. **Educational facilities:** 4 universities and colleges; 183 public schools. **Further information:** Chamber of Commerce, 801 E. Kennedy Blvd., P.O. Box 420, Tampa, FL 33601.

Toledo, Ohio

Population: 332,943; **Pop. density:** 3,964 per sq. mi.; **Pop. growth:** −6.1%. **Area:** 84 sq. mi. **Employment:** 145,508 employed, 9.7% unemployed; **Per capita income:** $17,713; % change 1981-91: 62.7.

History: site of Ft. Industry, 1794; settled 1817; figured in "Toledo War" 1835-36 between Ohio and Michigan over their borders; inc. 1837.

Transportation: 3 major airlines; 5 railroads; 100 motor freight lines; 2 interstate bus lines. **Communications:** 4 TV, 17 radio stations. **Medical facilities:** 9 major hospital complexes. **Educational facilities:** 4 universities and colleges. **Further information:** Office of Tourism and Conventions, 401 Jefferson Ave., Toledo, OH 43604.

Tucson, Arizona

Population: 405,371; **Pop. density:** 4,095 per sq. mi.; **Pop. growth:** 22.6%. **Area:** 99 sq. mi. **Employment:** 188,721 employed, 5.8% unemployed; **Per capita income:** $16,087; % change 1981-91: 59.6.

History: settled 1775 by Spanish as a presidio; acquired by U.S. in Gadsden Purchase 1853; inc. 1877.

Transportation: 1 international airport; 3 railroads; bus system. **Communications:** 10 TV, 27 radio stations. **Medical facilities:** 13 hospitals. **Educational facilities:** 2 universities, 1 college; 165 public schools. **Further information:** Chamber of Commerce, P.O. Box 991, Tucson, AZ 85702.

Tulsa, Oklahoma

Population: 367,302; **Pop. density:** 1,979 per sq. mi.; **Pop. growth:** 1.8%. **Area:** 185.6 sq. mi. **Employment:** 173,362 employed, 5.9% unemployed; **Per capita income:** $17,837; % change 1981-91: 41.8.

History: settled in 1830s by Creek Indians; modern town founded 1882 and inc. 1898; oil discovered early 20th century.

Transportation: 1 international airport; 5 rail lines; 2 bus lines; transit bus system. **Communications:** 7 TV, 23 radio stations. **Medical facilities:** 6 hospitals. **Educational facilities:** 6 universities and colleges; 57 public, 23 private schools. **Further information:** Chamber of Commerce, 616 S. Boston Ave., Tulsa, OK 74119.

Virginia Beach, Virginia

Population: 393,089; **Pop. density:** 1,541 per sq. mi.; **Pop. growth:** 49.9%. **Area:** 255 sq. mi. **Employment:** 183,038 employed, 5.9% unemployed; **Per capita income:** $17,030; % change 1981-91: 68.4.

History: area founded by Capt. John Smith 1607; formed by merger with Princess Anne co. 1963.

Transportation: 1 airport; 2 railroads; 2 bus lines; public transit system. **Communications:** 6 TV, 40 radio stations. **Medical facilities:** 2 hospitals. **Educational facilities:** 1 university, 2 colleges; 62 public schools. **Further information:** Chamber of Commerce, 4512 Virginia Beach Blvd., Virginia Beach, VA 23462.

Washington, District of Columbia

Population: 606,900; **Pop. density:** 9,633 per sq. mi.; **Pop. growth:** −4.9%. **Area:** 63 sq. mi. **Employment:** 253,000 employed, 8.4% unemployed; **Per capita income:** $25,338; % change 1981-91: 84.2.

History: capital of the U.S.; 10-mile-square diamond at Potomac R. chosen by George Washington 1790 on land ceded from Va. and Md.; Congress first met 1800; inc. 1802; sacked by British, War of 1812.

Transportation: 3 airports; rail transit system; extensive local bus service; 1 bus, 2 rail lines. **Communications:** 5 TV, 61 radio stations. **Medical facilities:** 43 hospitals; major medical research center. **Educational facilities:** 10 universities and colleges. **Further information:** Convention and Visitors Association, 1301 Pennsylvania Ave. NW, Suite 309, Washington, DC 20004.

Wichita, Kansas

Population: 304,017; **Pop. density:** 3,010 per sq. mi.; **Pop. growth:** 8.6%. **Area:** 101 sq. mi. **Employment:** 160,010 employed, 4.9% unemployed; **Per capita income:** $19,206; % change 1981-91: 54.8.

History: founded 1864; inc. 1871.

Transportation: 2 airports; 3 major rail freight lines; 2 bus lines. **Communications:** 5 TV, 26 radio stations. **Medical facilities:** 7 hospitals, 2 psychiatric rehab. centers. **Educational facilities:** 2 universities, 2 colleges; 96 public schools. **Further information:** Chamber of Commerce, 350 W. Douglas, Wichita, KS 67202.

Yonkers, New York

Population: 188,082; **Pop. density:** 10,449 per sq. mi.; **Pop. growth:** −3.7%. **Area:** 18 sq. mi. **Employment:** 83,898 employed, 8.4% unemployed; **Per capita income:** $25,583; % change 1981-91: 92.1.

History: founded 1641 by the Dutch; inc. as town 1855; chartered as city 1872; borders NYC to the North.

Transportation: intracity bus system; rail service. **Communications:** see New York City. **Medical facilities:** 3 hospitals. **Educational facilities:** 3 colleges; 30 public schools. **Further information:** Chamber of Commerce, 480 N. Broadway, Yonkers, NY 10701.

Notable Tall Buildings in North American Cities

Height from sidewalk to roof, including penthouse and tower if enclosed as integral part of structure; actual number of stories beginning at street level. Asterisks (*) denote buildings still under construction Jan. 1994. Year is date of completion.

Albany, N.Y.

City	Hgt. ft.	Stories
Erastus Corning II Tower	589	44
State Office Building	388	34
Agency (4 bldgs.), So. Mall	310	23

Atlanta, Ga.

City	Hgt. ft.	Stories
Nation's Bank Tower (1992)	1,050	57
One Peachtree Center (1992)	880	63
Atlantic Center/IBM (1988)	828	52
191 Peachtree (1990)	770	54
Westin Peachtree Plaza (1973)	723	71
Georgia Pacific Tower (1981)	697	51
Promenade II/AT&T (1989)	691	40
Southern Bell Telephone (1980)	677	47
GLG Grand/Occidental Hotel (1992)	629	53
Concourse Tower #5 (1988)	570	32
State of Georgia Tower (1968)	556	44
Marriott Marquis (1985)	554	52
Concourse Tower #6 (1991)	553	32
Equitable Building, 100 Peachtree (1967)	453	34
101 Marietta Tower, 101 Marietta (1975)	446	36
Ravinia #3 (1991)	444	34
AT&T Long Line Bldg (1975)	433	...
Bell South Enterprises (1990)	428	28
Atlanta Plaza I (1986)	425	32
Park Place, 2660 Peachtree (1986)	420	40
Club Towers Apts. (1989)	410	38
South Trust Bank (1961)	409	32
Peachtree Summit/Federal Bldg. (1975)	406	31
North Avenue Tower (1979)	403	26
Tower Place, 3361 Piedmont Rd. (1974)	401	29
First Union Bank (1987)	396	30
Richard B. Russell, Federal Bldg. (1978)	383	26
Atlanta Hilton Hotel (1974)	383	32
Peachtree Center, Harris Bldg. (1975)	382	31
Marquis One (1985)	378	30
Marquis Two (1987)	378	30
Trust Company Bank (1968)	377	28
260 Peachtree (1971)	377	27
Peachtree Center Cain Building (1972)	376	30
Peachtree Center Building (1966)	374	31
One Georgia Center (1966)	371	29
Mayfair Apts. Tower (1990)	370	34
The Campanile, 1145 Peachtree (1987)	367	25
Riverwood Tower/Barnett Bank (1989)	362	26

Austin, Tex.

City	Hgt. ft.	Stories
One American Center (1982)	395	32
One Congress Plaza (1987)	391	30
NCNB Tower (1975)	328	26

Baltimore, Md.

City	Hgt. ft.	Stories
U.S. Fidelity & Guaranty Co.	529	40
Maryland National Bank Bldg.	509	34
6 St. Paul Place	493	37
World Trade Center Bldg.	395	32
Tremont Plaza Hotel	395	37
250 W. Pratt St.	360	26
Harbor Court	356	28
Blaustein Bldg.	342	30
Union Trust Tower	335	24
Central Savings Bank Bldg.	330	28
Charles Center South	330	26

Baton Rouge, La.

City	Hgt. ft.	Stories
State Capitol (1932)	460	34
Hancock Bank Bldg. (1974)	315	24

Birmingham, Ala.

City	Hgt. ft.	Stories
Southtrust Tower (1986)	454	34
AmSouth/Harbert Plaza (1989)	390	30
AmSouth/Sonat Tower (1972)	390	30
South Central Bell Hdqts. Bldg.	390	30
City Federal Bldg. (1913)	325	27

Boston, Mass.

City	Hgt. ft.	Stories
John Hancock Tower	790	60
Prudential Center	750	52
Boston Co. Bldg., Court St.	605	41
Federal Reserve Bldg.	604	32
International Place, 100 Oliver St.	600	46
First National Bank of Boston	591	37
One Financial Center	590	46
Shawmut Bank Bldg.	520	38
Exchange Place, 53 State St.	510	39
Sixty State St.	509	38
One Post Office Sq.	507	40
One Beacon St.	507	40
New England Merch. Bank Bldg.	500	40
U.S. Custom House	496	32
John Hancock Bldg.	495	26
State St. Bank Bldg.	477	34
125 High St. (1990)	455	30
One Hundred Summer St.	450	33
McCormack Bldg.	401	22
Keystone Custodian Funds	400	32
Saltonstall Office Bldg.	396	22
Devonshire, 250 Wash. St.	396	40
Harbor Towers (2 bldgs.)	396	40
Westin Hotel, Copley Place	395	36
Federal Center (1988)	393	28
75 State St. (1988)	390	31
John F. Kennedy Bldg.	387	24
Marriott Hotel, Copley Place	383	39
101 Federal St. (1988)	382	31
Longfellow Towers (2 bldgs.)	380	38

Buffalo, N.Y.

City	Hgt. ft.	Stories
Marine Midland Center (1971)	529	40
City Hall (1926)	378	32
Rand Bldg., not incl. 40-ft. beacon (1929)	351	29
Main Place Tower (1969)	350	26

Calgary, Alta.

City	Hgt. ft.	Stories
Petro-Canada Centre, W. Tower (1984)	689	52
Bankers Hall (1989)	645	50
Calgary Tower (1988)	626	...
Canterra Tower (1988)	580	46
First Canadian Centre (1983)	547	44
Scotia Centre (1976)	504	38
Nova Bldg., 801 7th Ave. SW	500	37
Petro-Canada Centre, E. Tower (1984)	469	33
Two Bow Valley Square (1974)	468	39
Fifth & Fifth Bldg.	460	35
Home Oil Tower	463	34
Canada Trust Tower (1991)	462	40
Shell Tower	460	34
Dome Oil Tower	449	33
Four Bow Valley Square (1982)	441	37
Esso Plaza (twin towers)	435	34
Oxford Square	421	33
Family Life Bldg.	410	33
Pan Canadian Bldg., 150 9th Ave. SW	410	28
Norcen Tower	408	33
Alberta Stock Exchange Bldg.	407	33
Amoco Centre (1988)	396	30
Western Centre	385	40
Calgary Place	385	30
Three Bow Valley Square	382	33

Charlotte, N.C.

City	Hgt. ft.	Stories
NationsBank Corp. Center (1992)	871	60
One First Union Center (1988)	580	42
NationsBank Plaza (1974)	503	40
Interstate Tower (1990)	462	32
Two First Union Center (1971)	433	32
Wachovia Center (1974)	420	32
Carillon (1991)	394	24
Charlotte Plaza (1982)	388	27

Chicago, Ill.

City	Hgt. ft.	Stories
Sears Tower (world's tallest) (1974)	1,454	110
Amoco (1974)	1,136	80
John Hancock Center (1969)	1,127	100
311 S. Wacker (1990)	970	65
Two Prudential Plaza (1990)	901	64
AT&T Corporate Center (1989)	891	60
900 N. Michigan (1989)	871	66
Water Tower Place (1976)	859	74
First Natl. Bank (1969)	852	60
Three First National Plaza (1981)	775	57
Olympia Centre (1984)	727	63
Leo Burnett Bldg. (1989)	700	46

City	Hgt. ft.	Stories
IBM Plaza (1991)	695	52
One Magnificent Mile (1983)	673	58
Paine Webber Bldg., 181 W. Madison	644	50
Daley Center (1965)	662	31
1,000 Lake Shore Plaza (1964)	648	55
Lake Point Tower (1968)	645	70
Board of Trade, incl. 81 ft. statue (1930)	605	44
Prudential Bldg., 130 E. Randolph (1955)	601	41
Antenna tower, 311 ft., makes total	912	...
CNA Plaza (1972)	600	44
Huron Apts.	599	56
Marina City Apts., 2 buildings	588	61
Mid Continental Plaza (1972)	580	50
Associates Center (1983)	575	41
Pittsfield, 55 E. Washington St. (1927)	572	38
Onterie Center (1985)	570	58
Civic Opera Bldg. (1929)	555	45
Lincoln Tower, 75 E. Wacker Dr. (1928)	554	42
Newberry Plaza, State & Oak (1974)	553	56
One South Wacker Dr. (1983)	550	40
Harbor Point (1975)	550	54
Madison Plaza (1982)	551	45
190 S. LaSalle (1986)	550	40
LaSalle Natl. Bank (1934)	535	44
One N. LaSalle Street (1930)	530	49
111 E. Chestnut St. (1972)	529	56
Chicago Mercantile Exchange (2 bldgs)	525	40
River Plaza, Rush & Hubbard (1988)	524	56
35 E. Wacker Drive (1926)	523	40
United Ins. Bldg., 1 E. Wacker Dr. (1962)	522	41
Quaker Tower (1987)	518	35
Carbide & Carbon, 230 N. Mich. (1929)	503	37
Walton Colonnade (1972)	500	44
Xerox Center (1980)	500	40
One Financial Place (1985)	498	40
LaSalle-Wacker, 221 N. LaSalle St.	491	41
Amer. Nat'l. Bank, 33 N. LaSalle St.	479	40
Bankers, 105 W. Adams St. (1927)	476	41
Brunswick Bldg. (1965)	475	37
310 Center (1924)	475	37

Cincinnati, Oh.

City	Hgt. ft.	Stories
Carew Tower (1931)	568	49
Central Trust Tower (1979)	504	33
312 Walnut St.	500	35
Dubois Tower, 5th & Walnut (1969)	423	32
Cincinnati Commerce Center (1984)	418	29
Chemed Center	411	31
Chiquita Center	391	29
Star Bank Center (1981)	351	26

Cleveland, Oh.

City	Hgt. ft.	Stories
Society Center (1991)	948	57
Terminal Tower (1930)	708	52
BP America (1985)	658	46
Plaza Tower at Erieview (1964)	529	40
One Cleveland Center (1983)	450	31
Bank One Center (1991)	446	28
Justice Center, 1250 Ontario (1976)	420	26
Federal Bldg. (1967)	419	32
National City Center (1980)	410	35
900 Euclid (1971)	383	29
Cleveland St. J. F. Rhodes Tower (1971)	373	20
Eaton Center (1983)	360	28
Ohio-Bell. (1927)	360	22

Columbus, Oh.

City	Hgt. ft.	Stories
James A. Rhodes (State Office Tower)	629	41
LeVeque Tower, 50 W. Broad	555	47
Ohio Bureau of Worker's Compensation & Ind. Comm. (1990)	530	33
Huntington Center, 41 S. High St.	512	37
Verne-Riffe State Office Tower	503	33
One Nationwide Plaza	482	40
One Riverside Plaza	456	31
Borden Bldg., 180 E. Broad	438	34
Three Nationwide Plaza (1989)	408	27
One Columbus	366	26
Columbus Center, 100 E. Broad	357	24

Dallas, Tex.

City	Hgt. ft.	Stories
National Bank Plaza (1985)	939	72
Bank One Center (1987)	787	60
Texas Commerce Tower (1987)	738	55
First Interstate Bank Tower (1986)	721	60
Renaissance Tower (1987)	710	56
Trammell Crow Center (1984)	686	50
First City Center (1984)	655	50
Thanksgiving Tower (1982)	645	50
First National Bank	625	52
Republic Bank Tower	598	50
SW Bell Admin. Tower	580	37
Lincoln Plaza (1984)	579	45
Olympia York Tower (1982)	562	36
Cityplace Center East (1988)	560	50
Southland Center Tower (1959)	550	42
Maxus Energy (1980)	550	34
2001 Bryan St. (1973)	512	40
San Jacinto Tower (1982)	456	33
NationsBank Center Tower 1 (1954)	452	36
Stouffer Hotel	451	29
Skyway Tower (1981)	448	31
One Main Place (1968)	445	34
1600 Pacific Bldg. (1964)	434	32
Magnolia Bldg. (1923)	430	27
Mart Hotel	400	29
Complex Union Tower	400	33

Dayton, Oh.

City	Hgt. ft.	Stories
Kettering Tower, 2d & Main (1970)	405	30
Mead World Hqtrs, 10 W. 2d St. (1976)	385	28

Denver, Col.

City	Hgt. ft.	Stories
Republic Plaza	714	56
Mountain Bell Center	709	54
United Bank of Denver	698	52
1999 Broadway	544	43
Arco Tower	527	41
Anaconda Tower	507	40
Amoco Bldg., 17th Ave. & Broadway	448	36
17th Street Plaza	438	35
Stellar Plaza	437	31
First Interstate Tower North	434	32
One Denver Place	428	34
Brooks Towers, 1020 15th St.	420	42
Tabor Center, #1	408	32
Manville Plaza	404	29
Colorado Nat'l. Bank, 17th & Curtis	389	26
First Interstate Tower South	385	28
Security Life Bldg.	384	33
Mellon Financial Center	374	31
Dominion Plaza	368	30
Lincoln Center	366	30
Denver Natl. Bank Plaza	363	29
Bank Western	357	27
Colorado State Bank	352	26

Des Moines, Ia.

City	Hgt. ft.	Stories
Principal Financial Group Bldg. (1990)	630	44
Ruan Center (1974)	457	35
Financial Center, 7th & Walnut (1973)	345	25
Marriott Hotel, 700 Grand Ave. (1981)	340	33
Plaza, 3d & Walnut (1984)	340	25

Detroit, Mich.

City	Hgt. ft.	Stories
Westin Hotel	720	71
Penobscot Bldg.	557	47
1 Detroit Center	491	44
Guardian	485	40
Renaissance Center (4 bldgs.)	479	39
Book Tower	472	35
150 W. Jefferson Bldg.	470	29
Prudential 3000 Town Center	448	32
Cadillac Tower	437	40
David Stott	436	38
ANR Bldg.	430	32
Fisher	420	28
J. L. Hudson Bldg.	397	28
McNamara Federal Office Bldg.	393	27
2000 Prudential Town Ctr.	392	28
American Center	374	27
Top of Troy Bldg.	374	27
Comerica Bldg., 211 N. Fort	370	28
Edison Plaza	365	25
David Broderick Tower	358	34
1st National Bldg.	350	25
Buhl, 535 Griswold	350	26

Edmonton, Alta.

City	Hgt. ft.	Stories
Manulife Place (1983)	479	36
AGT Tower (1971)	441	33
Canada Trust Tower (1982)	440	31
City Centre (1990)	409	30
Metropolitan Place (1980)	397	31
Oxford Tower (1978)	390	27
TD Tower (1975)	386	27
Scotia Place (1983)	366	28
CN Tower (1966)	365	27

City	Hgt. ft.	Stories
Phipps McKinnon (1977)	359	20

Fort Wayne, Ind.

City	Hgt. ft.	Stories
One Summit Square (1981)	442	26
Ft. Wayne Natl. Bank (1970)	339	26

Fort Worth, Tex.

City	Hgt. ft.	Stories
City Center Tower II (1984)	546	38
Burnett Plaza (1983)	538	40
Continental Plaza (1982)	520	40
1st City Bank Tower (1982)	475	33
Team Bank-Ft. Worth (1974)	457	37
Texas Bldg. (1955)	420	31

Hartford, Conn.

City	Hgt. ft.	Stories
City Place (1983)	535	38
Travelers Ins. Co. Bldg. (1919)	527	34
Goodwin Square (1990)	522	30
Hartford Plaza (1967)	420	22
Shawmut Bank (1960)	360	26
One Commercial Plaza (1984)	349	28
Bushnell Tower (1969)	349	27

Honolulu, Hi.

City	Hgt. ft.	Stories
Imperial Plaza (1992)	400	40
Waterfront Towers (1990)	400	46
Nauru Tower (1991)	400	45
Ala Moana Hotel	396	38
Pacific Tower	350	30
Franklin Towers	350	41
Honolulu Tower	350	40
Discovery Bay	350	42
Hyatt Regency Waikiki	350	39
Maile Court Hotel	350	43
Regency Tower, 2525 Date St.	350	42
Pearlridge Square	350	43
Yacht Harbor Towers	350	40
Canterbury Place	350	40
Royal Iolani	350	38
Island Colony	350	44
Century Center	350	41
Pacific Beach Hotel	350	43
Hawaiian Monarch Hotel	350	43
Waikiki Hobron	350	43
Honolulu Tower 2	350	40
Tapa Tower, 2005 Kalia Rd.	350	36
Executive Center, 1088 Bishop St.	350	41
1001 Bishop	350	28

Houston, Tex.

City	Hgt. ft.	Stories
Texas Commerce Tower (1981)	1,002	75
First Interstate Plaza (1983)	992	71
Transco Tower (1983)	901	64
NationsBank Center (1983)	780	56
Heritage Plaza, 1111 Bagby	762	53
InterFirst Plaza (1980)	744	55
1600 Smith St. (1984)	729	54
Chevron Tower, 1301 McKinney (1982)	725	52
One Shell Plaza (not incl. 285 ft. TV tower) (1970)	714	50
Enron Bldg. (1983)	692	50
Capital Natl. Bank Plaza	685	50
One Houston Center (1978)	678	47
First City, Tex. Financial Center (1984)	662	47
1100 Milam Bldg. (1973)	651	47
San Felipe Plaza (1984)	620	45
Exxon Bldg. (1962)	606	44
The America Tower	577	42
Marathon Oil Tower (1983)	572	41
Two Houston Center (1974)	570	40
Kellogg Tower (1973)	550	40
1415 Louisiana Tower (1983)	550	44
Pennzoil, 700 Milam (2 bldgs.) (1975)	523	36
Two Allen Center (1978)	521	36
1201 Louisiana Bldg. (1971)	518	35
Huntington	506	34
Tenneco Bldg. (1962)	502	33
Conoco Tower (1973)	465	32
One Allen Center (1974)	452	34
Summit Tower West (1979)	441	31
Coastal Tower (1978)	441	31
Four Leafs Towers (2 bldgs.)	439	40
Phoenix Tower (1984)	434	34
Chevron Bldg.	428	37
The Spires	426	41
Central Tower (4 Oaks Place)	420	30
First City Natl. Bank (1960)	410	32
Houston Lighting & Power (1968)	410	27
Niels Esperson Bldg. (1927)	409	31
Hyatt Regency Houston (1972)	401	34

Indianapolis, Ind.

City	Hgt. ft.	Stories
Bank One Tower (1989)	728	51
AUL Tower (1981)	533	38
Market Tower (1988)	515	32
Indiana Natl. Bank Tower (1969)	504	35
Riley Towers (2 bldgs.) (1963)	427	30
300 N. Meridian Bldg. (1988)	408	28

Jacksonville, Fla.

City	Hgt. ft.	Stories
Barnett Center (1990)	617	42
Independent Life Bldg. (1975)	535	37
Southern Bell (1983)	447	32
Gulf Life Tower (1967)	432	28
American Heritage Life (1989)	357	23

Kansas City, Mo.

City	Hgt. ft.	Stories
One Kansas City Place	626	42
AT&T Town Pavilion	590	38
Hyatt Regency	504	40
Kansas City Power and Light Bldg.	476	32
City Hall	443	29
Federal Office Bldg.	413	35
Commerce Tower	402	32
City Center Sq.	402	30
Southwest Bell Telephone Bldg.	394	27
Pershing Road Associates	352	28

Las Vegas, Nev.

City	Hgt. ft.	Stories
*Vegas World Tower	1,012	...
Fitzgerald Casino-Hotel	400	34
Landmark Hotel	356	31
Las Vegas Hilton	345	30

Lexington, Ky.

City	Hgt. ft.	Stories
Lexington Financial Center (1986)	410	30
Kincaid Tower (1980)	333	22

Little Rock, Ark.

City	Hgt. ft.	Stories
TCBY Towers (1986)	546	40
First Commercial Bank (1975)	454	30
Worthen Bank & Trust (1969)	375	24
Stephens Bldg. (1985)	365	25
Tower Bldg. (1960)	350	18
Union National Bank (1968)	331	21

Los Angeles, Cal.

City	Hgt. ft.	Stories
First Interstate World Center (1989)	1,017	73
First Interstate Bank	858	62
Cal. Plaza 11A	750	57
Wells Fargo Tower	750	54
Security Pacific Plaza	735	55
So. Cal. Gas Center (1990)	733	55
777 Tower	725	52
Mitsui Fudoson (1990)	716	52
Atlantic Richfield Tower	699	52
Bank of America Tower	699	52
444 S. Flower St.	625	48
AT&T Bldg.	620	42
One California Plaza	578	42
Century Plaza Towers (2 bldgs.)	571	44
IBM Tower	560	45
Citicorp Plaza	534	42
1999 Ave. of the Stars (1989)	533	39
Manulife Tower (1990)	517	37
Union Bank Square	516	41
MCA-Getty	506	36
WTC Bldg.	496	36
Fox Plaza	492	34
ARCO Center	462	33
City Hall	454	28
Equitable Life Bldg.	454	34
Transamerica Center	452	32
Mutual Benefit Life Ins. Bldg.	435	31
Warner Center Plaza III	415	25
Broadway Plaza	414	33
1900 Ave. of Stars	398	27
1 Wilshire Bldg.	395	28
The Evian	390	31
400 S. Hope St.	375	26
Westin Bonaventure Hotel	367	35
Beaudry Center	365	29
Cal. Fed. Savings & Loan Bldg.	363	28
Century City North	363	26
Home Savings Tower	356	25

Louisville, Ky.

City	Hgt. ft.	Stories
First Natl. Bank (1972)	512	40
Citizen's Plaza (1971)	420	30
Humana Bldg.	350	27
Meindinger Tower (1982)	338	26
Brown & Williamson Tower (1982)	338	26

Memphis, Tenn.

100 N. Main Bldg.	430	37
Commerce Square	396	31
Sterick Bldg.	365	31
Clark, 5100 Poplar	365	32
Morgan Keegan Tower, 50 Front St.	341	23
First Natl. Bank Bldg.	332	25

Miami, Fla.

Southeast Financial Center (1983)	764	55
Centrust Tower (1987)	562	35
Metro-Dade Administration Bldg.	510	30
Florida National Tower (1986)	484	35
One Biscayne Corp.	456	40
Amerifirst Bldg. (1973)	375	32
Hotel Inter-Continental Miami	366	35
Venitia, 1635 Bayshore Dr.	365	42
Dade County Court House	357	28

Milwaukee, Wis.

Firstar Center	625	42
100 E. Wisconsin (1989)	549	37
Milwaukee Center	425	29
411 E. Wisconsin	385	30
Northwestern Mutual Tower (1989)	350	19
City Hall	350	9

Minneapolis, Minn.

IDS Center (1973)	787	51
Norwest (1988)	777	57
*First Bank Place	774	53
Multifoods Tower (1983)	651	52
Piper Jaffray Tower (1984)	627	42
*Dain Bosworth Plaza	550	40
Pillsbury Center, 200 S. 6th St. (1981)	545	40
Lincoln Centre, 333 S. 7th (1987)	496	31
Foshay Tower, not including 163-ft. antenna tower (1929)	496	32
Plaza VII, 45 S. 7th (1987)	494	36
100 South Fifth (1987)	490	36
Telephone Bldg. (1931)	423	27
Hennepin Co. Govt. Center (1974)	413	24
First Bank Place West (1960)	386	26
Marriott Hotel (1983)	379	31

Montreal, Que.

1100 Rue de la Gauchetiere	669	45
1250 Boulevard Rene Levesque	640	45
Place Victoria (1963)	624	47
Place Ville Marie (1962)	620	45
Canadian Imperial Bank of Commerce (1962)	590	45
Le Complexe Desjardins		
La Tour du Sud	498	40
La Tour du L'Est	428	32
La Tour du Nord	355	27
Les Cooperants (1987)	479	34
Place Montreal Trust (1988)	449	32
Chateau Champlain Hotel (1967)	420	38
Port Royal Apts.	400	33
Royal Bank Tower	397	22
Sun Life Bldg.	390	26
500 Place d'Armes	390	32

Nashville, Tenn.

Third National Financial Center	490	30
American General Center	452	31
Landmark Center	409	30
Nashville City Center (1987)	402	27
James K. Polk State Office Bldg.	392	32
Stouffer Hotel (1987)	385	35
First American Center	354	28
One Nashville Plaza	346	23

Newark, N.J.

Natl. Newark & Essex Bldg.	465	36
Raymond-Commerce	448	37
Park Plaza Bldg.	400	26
Prudential Plaza	370	24
Public Service Elec. & Gas	360	26
Prudential Ins. Co., 753 Broad St.	360	26
AT&T Bldg.	359	31
Gateway 1	355	28

New Orleans, La.

City	Hgt. ft.	Stories
One Shell Square (1972)	697	51
Place St. Charles (1985)	645	53
Plaza Tower (1969)	531	45
Energy Centre (1984)	530	39
LL&E Tower (1987)	481	36
Sheraton Hotel (1985)	478	47
Marriott Hotel (1972)	450	42
Texaco Bldg. (1983)	442	33
Canal Place One (1979)	439	32
1010 Common (1971)	438	31
Int'l. Trade Mart Bldg.	407	33
225 Baronne St. (1965)	362	28
One Poydras Plaza (1983)	360	28
Hyatt-Regency Hotel (1976)	360	25
Hibernia Bank Bldg. (1920)	355	23

New York, N.Y.

World Trade Center (2 towers) (1973)	1,368/ 1,362	110/110
Empire State, 34th St. & 5th Ave.	1,250	102
TV tower, 164 ft., makes total (1931)	1,414	...
Chrysler, Lexington & 43d (1930)	1,046	77
Amer. International, 70 Pine (1932)	950	67
40 Wall Tower (1929)	927	71
Citicorp Center (1977)	914	46
G.E. Bldg., Rockefeller Center (1933)	850	70
Chase Manhattan Plaza (1960)	813	60
MetLife Bldg. (1963)	808	59
Cityspire (1989)	802	72
Woolworth, 233 Broadway (1913)	792	60
1 Worldwide Plaza	778	47
1 Penn Plaza (1972)	764	57
Carnegie Tower	756	59
Exxon, 1251 Ave. of Americas (1971)	750	54
Equitable Center Tower West (1985)	750	58
60 Wall St. (1989)	745	50
1 Liberty Plaza (1972)	743	50
Citibank (1907)	741	57
World Financial Center, Tower C (1988)	739	54
One Astor Plaza (1969)	730	54
Solow Bldg. (1979)	725	50
Marine Midland	724	52
Metropolitan Tower (1988)	716	66
Union Carbide Bldg. (1960)	707	52
General Motors Bldg. (1968)	705	50
Metropolitan Life (1909)	700	50
500 5th Ave. (1928)	697	58
Chem. Bank, N.Y. Trust Bldg. (1963)	687	50
55 Water St.	687	53
1585 Broadway	685	42
Four Seasons Hotel (1993)	682	52
Chanin, Lexington & 42d (1929)	680	56
15 Columbus Circle (1970)	679	44
McGraw Hill, 1221 Ave. of Am. (1972)	674	51
Citicorp (Queens) (1990)	673	50
Lincoln, 60 E. 42d Street (1939)	673	53
1633 Broadway	670	48
Trump Tower, 725 5th Ave. (1983)	664	68
599 Lexington Ave. (1986)	653	47
Museum Tower Apts. (1985)	650	58
712 5th Ave. (1990)	650	56
American Brands, 245 Park Ave.	648	47
A. T. & T. Tower (1983)	648	37
World Financial Center Tower B (1986)	645	50
General Electric, 570 Lexington (1931)	640	50
Irving Trust, 1 Wall St. (1932)	640	50
345 Park Ave.	634	44
Grace Plaza, 1114 Ave. of Am.	630	50
1 New York Plaza (1969)	630	50
Home Insurance Co. Bldg.	630	44
N.Y. Telephone, 1095 Ave. of Am.	630	40
Central Park Place (1988)	628	56
888 7th Ave.	628	42
1 Hammarskjold Plaza	628	50
Waldorf-Astoria, 301 Park Ave. (1931)	625	47
Burlington House (1970)	625	50
Olympic Tower, 645 5th Ave. (1976)	620	51
10 E. 40th St.	620	48
101 Park Ave.	618	50
750 7th Ave.	615	35
New York Life, 51 Madison Ave. (1928)	615	40
Rihga Royal Hotel	610	54
17 State St.	610	41
Penney Bldg., 1301 Ave. of Am.	609	46
IBM, 590 Madison Ave. (1983)	603	41

City	Hgt. ft.	Stories
780 3rd Ave.	600	50
Celanese Bldg. (1973)	592	45
U.S. Court House, 505 Pearl St. (1976).	590	37
Kalikow Hotel	588	58
Federal Bldg., Foley Square	587	41
Time & Life, 1271 Ave. of Am. (1959)	587	47
Cooper Bregstein Bldg., 1250 Bway.	580	40
Stevens Tower, 1185 Ave. of Am.	580	42
Municipal, Bldg. (1919)	580	34
520 Madison Ave. (1983)	577	42
1 Madison Square Plaza (1968)	576	42
World Financial Center Tower A (1986)	575	42
One Financial Sq. (1987)	575	37
Park Ave. Plaza (1981)	575	44
Westvaco Bldg. 299 Park Ave.	574	42
Marriott Marquis Hotel (1985)	574	42
Socony Mobil Bldg., East 42d St.	572	45
Sperry Rand Bldg., 1290 Ave. of Am.	570	43
600 3d Ave.	570	42
Helmsley Bldg., 230 Park (1929)	565	35
1 Bankers Trust Plaza	565	40
Hemsley Palace Hotel (1980)	563	51
30 Broad St.	562	48
Park Ave Tower (1986)	561	36
Sherry-Netherland, 5th Ave. & 59th St.	560	40
Continental Can, 633 3d Ave. (1983)	557	39
Sperry & Hutchinson, 330 Madison	555	39
Continental Corp., 180 Maiden Lane	555	41
Galleria, 117 E. 57th St. (1975)	552	57
Interchem Bldg., 1133 Ave. of Am.	552	45
151 E. 44th St.	550	44
N.Y. Telephone, 323 Bway. (1979)	550	45
919 3d Ave.	550	47
Burroughs Bldg., 605 3d Ave.	550	44
Bankers Trust, 33 E. 48 St. (1963)	547	41
Transportation Bldg., 225 Bway.	546	45
Equitable, 120 Broadway (1915).	545	42
1 Brooklyn Bridge Plaza (1976)	540	42
Paine Webber Bldg. (1961).	540	42
Ritz Tower, Park Ave. & 57th St.	540	41
Bankers Trust, 6 Wall St.	540	39
1166 Ave. of Americas	540	44
1700 Broadway	533	41
Downtown Athletic Club, 19 West St.	530	45
Nelson Towers, 7th Ave. & 34th St.	525	45
767 3d Ave.	525	39
Hotel Pierre, 5th Ave. & 61st St. (1928).	525	44
House of Seagram (1958)	525	38
7 World Trade Center (1985)	525	44
Random House, 825 3d Ave.	522	40
3 Park Ave.	522	42
North American Plywood, 800 3d Ave.	520	41
Du Mont Bldg., 515 Madison Ave.	520	42
26 Broadway	520	31
Newsweek Bldg., 444 Madison Ave.	518	43
Sterling Drug Bldg., 90 Park Ave.	515	41
First National City Bank	515	41
Bank of New York, 48 Wall St.	513	32
Navarre, 512 7th Ave.	513	43
Manhattan Savings Bank, Bklyn.	512	42
ITT—American, 437 Madison Ave.	512	40
International, Rockefeller Ctr.	512	41
1407 Broadway Realty Corp.	512	44
United Nations, 405 E. 42 St. (1953)	505	39
Oakland, Cal.		
Ordway Bldg., 2150 Valdez St.	404	28
Kaiser Bldg.	390	28
Lake Merritt Plaza	371	27
Federal Bldg. (2 Bldgs.).	368	19
American President Lines (1990)	360	29
Raymond Kaiser Engineer Bldg.	336	25
Clorox Bldg.	330	24
Oklahoma City, Okla.		
Liberty Tower (1971)	500	36
First National Center (1974)	493	33
City Place (1985)	440	32
First Oklahoma Tower (1982)	425	31
Kerr-McGee Center (1973).	393	30
Mid America Tower (1981)	362	19
Omaha, Neb.		
Woodmen Tower (1969)	469	30
Northwestern Bell Telephone (1980)	334	16
Masonic Manor (1963)	320	22
First Natl. Center (1971)	320	22

City	Hgt. ft.	Stories
Orlando, Fla.		
Sun Bank Center Tower (1988)	441	31
DuPont Center Bldg. (1986)	409	28
Ottawa, Ont.		
Place de Ville, Tower C.	368	29
R.H. Coats Bldg.	326	27
Philadelphia, Pa.		
One Liberty Place (1987)	960	61
Two Liberty Place (1989)	845	52
Mellon Bank Center (1989)	795	54
Bell Atlantic Tower (1991)	739	53
Blue Cross Tower (1990)	700	50
Commerce Sq., #1 (1990)	572	40
Commerce Sq., #2 (1992)	572	40
City Hall Tower, incl. 37-ft. statue of Wm. Penn. (1901)	548	7
1818 Market St. (1974)	500	40
Provident Mutual Life (1983)	491	40
Meridan Bank (1972)	492	38
Phila. Saving Fund Society (1932)	492	39
Central Penn Natl. Bank (1970)	490	36
Centre Square (2 towers) (1973)	490/416	38/32
Industrial Valley Bank (1968)	482	32
Philadelphia National Bank (1930)	475	25
Two Mellon Plaza (1930)	450	30
2000 Market St. (1973)	435	29
Two Logan Square (1987)	435	34
2 Girard Plaza (1930)	412	30
Fidelity Bank Bldg. (1927)	405	30
Lewis Tower, 15th & Locust (1929)	400	33
One Logan Square (1982)	400	32
1500 Locust St. (1973)	390	44
Philadelphia Electric Co. (1970)	384	29
Academy House, 1420 Locust St.	377	37
Penn Mutual Life (1931)	375	20
The Drake, 15th & Spruce (1928)	375	33
INA Annex	369	27
Medical Tower, 255 So. 17th (1931)	364	33
United Engineers, 17th & Ludlow (1976)	344	22
Inquirer Building (1924)	340	18
Phoenix, Ariz.		
Valley National Bank (1972)	483	40
Arizona Bank Downtown(1976)	407	31
Phoenix Plaza (1990)	397	25
First Interstate Bank Plaza (1971)	372	27
Phoenix Center (1979)	361	28
Citibank Plaza (1980)	356	27
One Renaissance Sq. (1987)	347	26
Two Renaissance Sq. (1989)	347	26
Merabank Tower	341	26
Pittsburgh, Pa.		
USX Towers	841	64
One Mellon Bank Center	725	54
One PPG Place	635	40
Fifth Avenue Place (1987)	616	32
One Oxford Centre	615	46
Gulf, 7th Ave. and Grant St.	582	44
University of Pittsburgh	535	42
Mellon Bank Bldg.	520	41
1 Oliver Plaza	511	39
Grant, Grant St. at 3rd Ave.	485	40
Koppers, 7th Ave. and Grant	475	34
Equibank Bldg.	445	34
CNG Tower (1987)	430	32
Pittsburgh National Bldg.	424	30
Alcoa Bldg., 425 Sixth Ave.	410	30
Liberty Tower	358	29
Westinghouse Bldg.	355	23
Oliver, 535 Smithfield St.	347	25
Gateway Bldg. No. 3	344	24
Centre City Tower	341	26
Federal Bldg., 1000 Liberty Ave.	340	23
Bell Telephone, 416 7th Ave.	339	21
Hilton Hotel.	333	22
Frick, 437 Grant St.	330	20
Portland, Ore.		
First Interstate Tower	546	41
U.S. Bancorp Tower.	536	39
Koin Tower Plaza	509	35
Standard Insurance Center.	367	27
Pacwest Center	356	31
Providence, R.I.		
Fleet National Bank	420	26

City	Hgt. ft.	Stories
Rhode Island Hospital Trust Tower	410	30
40 Westminster Bldg.	301	24

Raleigh, N.C.

City	Hgt. ft.	Stories
BB & T/2 Hanover Sq. (1991)	431	29
First Union Capitol Center (1991)	390	29

Richmond, Va.

James Monroe Bldg.	450	29
City Hall (incl. penthouse)	425	17
Crestar Bank Hdqt. Bldg.	400	24
Federal Reserve Bank	393	26
Sovran Center	333	25

Rochester, N.Y.

Xerox Tower (1967)	443	30
Lincoln First Tower (1973)	392	27
Eastman Kodak Bldg. (1914)	340	19

Sacramento, Cal.

Wells Fargo Center	405	30
Park Plaza Tower	373	26
Renaissance Tower	372	28

St. Louis, Mo.

Gateway Arch	630	...
Metropolitan Square Tower	591	42
S.W. Bell Telephone Bldg.	587	44
Mercantile Center Tower	550	37
Centerre Plaza	433	31
Laclede Gas. Bldg., 8th & Olive	400	31
S.W. Bell Telephone Bldg.	398	31
Civil Courts	387	13

St. Paul, Minn.

First Natl. Bank Bldg., incl. 100-ft. sign	517	32
Minn. World Trade Center	471	36
Galtier Plaza's Jackson Tower	440	46
Osborn Bldg., 320 Wabasha	368	20
Kellogg Square Apts.	366	32
Northwestern Bell Telephone (2 bldgs.)	340	16
Pointe of St. Paul	340	34
American National Bank Bldg.	335	25
North Central Tower, 445 Minn.	328	27
Amhoist/Park Tower	324	26

Salt Lake City, Ut.

L.D.S. Church Office Bldg.	420	30
Beneficial Life Tower	351	21
Utah One Center (1992)	350	24

San Antonio, Tex.

Tower of the Americas (1968)	622	...
Marriott Rivercenter (1988)	546	38
NBC Plaza (1988)	444	32
Tower Life (1929)	404	30
NCNB Plaza (1983)	387	28
Nix Professional Bldg. (1931)	375	23

San Diego, Cal.

One American Plaza (1991)	500	34
Symphony Tower (1989)	499	34
Hyatt Regency San Diego (1992)	495	39
Emerald-Shapery Center (1991)	450	30
One Harber Drive (1992)	424	41
First Interstate Bank (1985)	398	23
Meridian Condominiums (1985)	395	27
Union Bank (1969)	388	27
First National Bank (1982)	379	27
Imperial Bank	355	24
Executive Complex (1963)	350	25
Wells Fargo Bldg. (1982)	348	20
Great American Bldg. (1974)	339	24

San Francisco, Cal.

Transamerica Pyramid (1972)	853	48
Bank of America (1969)	778	52
101 California St. (1986)	600	48
5 Fremont Center (1983)	600	43
Embarcadero Center, No. 4 (1982)	570	45
Security Pacific Bank	569	45
One Market Plaza, Spear St. (1976)	565	43
Wells Fargo Bldg.	561	43
Standard Oil, 575 Market St. (1975)	551	39
One Sansome-Citicorp	550	39
Shaklee Bldg., 444 Market	537	38
Aetna Life	529	38

City	Hgt. ft.	Stories
First & Market Bldg. (1973)	529	38
Metropolitan Life (1973)	524	38
Crocker National Bank	500	38
Hilton Hotel	493	46
Pacific Gas & Electric (1970)	492	34
Union Bank (1972)	487	37
Pacific Insurance (1972)	476	34
Bechtel Bldg., Fremont St. (1977)	475	33
333 Market Bldg. (1979)	474	33
Hartford Bldg. (1965)	465	33
Mutual Benefit Life (1969)	438	32
Russ Bldg. (1928)	435	31
Pacific Telephone Bldg. (1925)	435	26
Pacific Gateway (1983)	416	30
Embarcadero Center, No. 3 (1976)	412	31
Embarcadero Center, No. 2 (1974)	412	31
595 Market Bldg. (1979)	410	31
101 Montgomery St.	405	28
Cal. State Automobile Assn. (1974)	399	29
Alcoa Bldg.	398	27
St. Francis Hotel (1970)	395	32
Shell Bldg. (1928)	386	29
Del Monte	378	28
Meridien Hotel (1984)	374	34

Seattle, Wash.

Columbia Seafirst Center (1985)	954	76
Two Union Square (1989)	740	56
Washington Mutual Tower (1988)	730	55
AT&T Gateway Tower (1990)	722	62
1001 4th Pl. (1969)	609	50
Space Needle (1962)	605	...
Pacific First Center (1989)	580	44
First Interstate Center (1983)	574	48
Seafirst 5th Ave. Plaza (1981)	543	42
Security Pacific Bank Tower (1977)	514	42
Smith Tower (1914)	500	42
520 Pike Tower (1984)	498	29
Key Tower (1986)	493	40
Federal Office Bldg.	487	37
US West Communications	466	33
One Union Square (1981)	456	38
1111 3d Ave. Bldg. (1980)	454	35
Westin Bldg., 2001 6th Ave. (1981)	409	34
Westin Hotel	397	40
Unigard Financial Center (1973)	389	27
Century Square (1986)	379	30
Sheraton Seattle Hotel	371	34

Tampa, Fla.

100 N. Tampa (1992)	579	42
Barnett Plaza (1986)	577	42
Tampa City Center (1981)	537	39
Landmark Centre (1992)	525	36
First Financial Tower (1973)	458	36
NCNB Plaza (1988)	454	33

Toledo, Oh.

Owens-Illinois Corp. Headquarters	411	32
Owens-Corning Fiberglas Tower	400	30
Ohio Citizens Bank Bldg.	368	27
Toledo Govt. Center	327	22

Toronto, Ont.

CN Tower, World's tallest self-supporting structure (1975)	1,821	...
First Canadian Place (1979)	952	72
Bay/Adelaide Project (1991)	951	57
Scotia Plaza (1988)	902	68
Canada Trust Tower (1990)	869	52
Bay-Wellington Tower (1990)	705	47
Commerce Court West (1972)	784	57
Toronto-Dominion Tower (TD Centre) (1967)	758	56
Royal Trust Tower (TD Centre) (1969)	600	46
Royal Bank Plaza—South Tower (1977)	589	41
Manulife Centre (1975)	545	53
IBM Tower (TD Centre) (1986)	520	36
Two Bloor West (1974)	488	34
Exchange Tower (1981)	480	36
Commerce Court North (1930)	476	34
Simpson Tower (1968)	473	33
Eaton Tower (1990)	471	34
Cadillac-Fairview Tower (1982)	466	36
Palace Point (1991)	455	46
Palace Pier (1978)	453	46
Continental Bank Bldg. (1980)	450	35
Sheraton Centre (1972)	443	43
Hudson's Bay Centre (1974)	442	35

City	Hgt. ft.	Stories
Royal York Hotel (1929)	439	26
Ernst & Yonge Tower (1990)	438	31
Old Toronto Exchange Bldg. (1990)	436	31
Leaside Towers (2 bldgs.) (1970)	423	44
Metro Hall (1991)	420	27
Commercial Union Tower (1974)	420	32
Maple Leaf Mills Tower	419	30
Plaza 2 Hotel	415	41
Sun Life Bldg. (1981)	410	28
Tulsa, Okla.		
Bank of Oklahoma Tower	667	52
City of Faith Clinic Tower	640	60
1st National Tower	516	41
Mid-Continent Tower	513	36
4th Natl. Bank of Tulsa	412	33
320 South Boston Bldg.	400	24
Occidential Place	388	28
Univ. Club Tower	377	32
City of Faith Hospital	348	30
Philtower	343	24
Vancouver, B.C.		
Royal Centre Tower (1973)	460	36
Canada Trust Tower, 1055 Melville	454	35
Scotiabank Tower	451	36
Bentall IV (1981)	450	35
Vancouver Center (1977)	450	36
Park Place (1984)	450	35
T-D Bank Tower (1978)	440	30
200 Granville Square (1973)	438	28
Harbour Centre (1977)	428	21
Bentall III (1974)	399	31
Winnipeg, Man.		
Toronto Dominion Center (1989)	407	31
Richardson Bldg. (1969)	390	32
Commodity Exchange Tower (1980)	384	31
Winston-Salem, N.C.		
Wachovia Bldg. (1965)	410	30
One Triad Park (1987)	340	20
Reynolds Bldg. (1929)	315	21

Other Notable Tall Buildings in U.S.

Cape Canaveral, Fla., Vehicle Assembly Bldg., 40 (552); Amarillo, Tex., American Natl. Bank, 33 (374); Atlantic City, N.J., Taj Mahal, 51 (429); Charleston, W. Va., Kanawha Valley Bldg., 20 (384); Galveston, Tex., American National Ins., 20 (358); Hamilton, Ont., Century Twenty One, 43 (418); Harrisburg, PA., State Office Tower #2, 21 (334); Knoxville, Tenn., United American Bank, 30 (400); Lincoln, Neb., State Capitol (432); Mobile, Ala., First Natl. Bank, 33 (420); Niagara Falls, Ont., Skylon, (520); Shreveport La., Commercial National Tower, 24 (365); Springfield, Mass., Valley Bank Tower, 29 (370); Tallahassee, Fla., State Capitol Tower, 22 (345).

Some Notable Foreign Structures

Structure	Hgt. ft.	Stories
Central Plaza, Hong Kong (1992)	1,028	78
Bank of China, Hong Kong (1989)	1,001	70
Eiffel Tower, Paris (1889)	984	-
Landmark Tower, Yokohama (1993)	971	70
Overseas Union Bank, Singapore (1984)	919	63
MesseTurm. Bldg, Frankfurt (1990)	841	70
One Canada Sq, London (1991)	800	59
Tokyo City Hall (1992)	797	59
Metropolitan Tower, Tokyo (1992)	796	50
Rialto Tower, Melbourne (1985)	794	60
Palace of Science & Culture, Warsaw	790	42
Moscow State Univ (incl. spire)	787	39
Treasury Bldg., Singapore (1986)	770	52
Seoul Tower, S. Korea (1988)	764	63
Maine Montparnasse, Paris (1973)	751	64
MLC Center, Sydney (1977)	748	60
Governor Philip Tower, Sydney (1993)	745	54
Raffles City Hotel, Singapore (1986)	742	73
Ikebukuro Office Tower, Tokyo (1978)	742	60
Bourke Place, Melbourne (1991)	735	48
Central Park, Perth (1992)	733	51
Carlton Centre, Johannesburg (1973)	722	50
Shinjuku Center, Tokyo (1979)	709	55
Shinjuku Mitsui, Tokyo	696	55
Shinjuku Nomura, Tokyo	666	53
Overseas-Chinese Banking Corp., Singapore	660	52
Shinjuku Sumitomo, Tokyo	656	52
Parque Central Torre Oficinas, Caracas	656	56
Ukraine Hotel, Moscow	650	60
Natwest Tower, London	600	50
Tour Elf Aquitaine, Paris	578	48
Ulm Cathedral, Germany	530	-
Cologne Cathedral, Germany	515	-
Tour du Cite Administrative, Brussels	492	36

Notable Bridges in North America

Source: Survey of State Highway Engineers (1993)

Asterisk (*) designates railroad bridge. Span of a bridge is distance (in feet) between its supports.

Year	Bridge	Location	Longest span
	Suspension		
1964	Verrazano-Narrows	New York, N.Y.	4,260
1937	Golden Gate	San Fran. Bay, Cal.	4,200
1957	Mackinac	Sts. of Mackinac	3,800
1931	Geo. Washington	Hudson R., N.Y.- N.J.	3,500
1950	Tacoma Narrows	Washington	2,800
1936	[1]Transbay	San Fran. Bay, Cal.	2,310
1939	Bronx-Whitestone	East R., N.Y.C.	2,300
1970	Pierre Laporte	Quebec	2,190
1951	Del. Memorial	Wilmington, Del.	2,150
1968	Del. Mem. (new)	Wilmington, Del.	2,150
1957	Walt Whitman	Phila., Pa.	2,000
1929	Ambassador	Detroit-Canada	1,850
1961	Throgs Neck	Long Is. Sound, N.Y.	1,800
1926	Benjamin Franklin	Philadelphia, Pa.	1,750
1924	Bear Mt., N.Y.	Hudson R.	1,632
1952	[2]Wm. Preston Lane Mem.	Sandy Point, Md.	1,600
1903	Williamsburg	East R., N.Y.C.	1,600
1969	Newport	Narragansett Bay, R.I.	1,600
1883	Brooklyn	East R., N.Y.C.	1,595
1939	Lion's Gate	Burrard Inlet, B.C.	1,550
1930	Mid-Hudson	Poughkeepsie, N.Y.	1,500
1964	Vincent Thomas	Los Angeles Harbor	1,500
1909	Manhattan	East R., N.Y.C.	1,470
1936	Triboro	East R., N.Y.C.	1,380
1931	St. Johns	Portland, Ore.	1,207
1929	Mount Hope	Rhode Island	1,200
1960	Ogdensburg, N.Y.	St. Lawrence R.	1,150
1939	Deer Isle	Maine	1,080
1931	Maysville (Ky.)	Ohio R.	1,060
1867	Cincinnati	Ohio R.	1,057
1971	Dent	Clearwater Co., Ida.	1,050
1900	Miampimi	Mexico	1,030
1849	Wheeling, W. Va.	Ohio R.	1,010
	Cantilever		
1917	Quebec	Quebec	1,800
1981	Ravenswood	W. Va.	1,723
1974	Commodore Barry	Chester, Pa.	1,622
1958	Mississippi R.	New Orleans, La.	1,575
1988	Mississippi R.	New Orleans, La	1,575
1936	Transbay	San Fran. Bay	1,400
1968	W. 17th St.	Huntington, W. Va.	1,312
1968	Mississippi R.	Baton Rouge, La.	1,235
1955	Tappan Zee	Hudson R.	1,212
1930	Lewis and Clark	Longview, Wash.	1,200

Year	Bridge	Location	Longest span
1909	Queensboro	East R., N.Y.C.	1,182
1927	Carquinez Strait	California	1,100
1958	Parallel Span	"	1,100
1930	Jacques Cartier	Montreal, Can.	1,097
1968	Isaiah D. Hart	Jacksonville, Fla.	1,088
1957	[3]Richmond	San Fran. Bay, Cal.	1,070
1929	Grace Memorial	Charleston, S.C.	1,050
1980	Newburgh-Beacon	Hudson R., N.Y.	1,000
1963	Newburgh-Beacon	Hudson R., N.Y.	1,000
1949	Martin Luther King	St. Louis, Mo.	962
1982	Yeager	Charleston, W. Va.	947
1975	Caruthersville, Mo.	Mississippi R.	920
1977	Saint Marys	Saint Marys, W. Va.	900
1969	Silver Memorial	Pt. Pleasant, W. Va.	900
1987	Carl Perkins	Ohio R., Ky.	900
1986	Mississippi R.	Natchez, Miss.	875
1940	Mississippi R.	Natchez, Miss.	875
1938	Blue Water	Pt. Huron, Mich.	871
1972	Mississippi R.	Vicksburg, Miss	870
1972	N. Fork American R.	Auburn, Cal.	862
1940	*Baton Rouge	Mississippi R.	848
1899	*Cornwall	St. Lawrence R.	843
1940	Mississippi R.	Greenville, Miss.	840
1961	Helena, Ark.	Mississippi R.	840
1963	Brent Spence	Covington, Ky.	831
1963	Cincinnati	Ohio R.	830
1963	Mississippi R.	Donaldsonville, La.	825
1940	Mississippi R.	Vicksburg, Miss.	825
1929	Louisville	Ohio R.	820
1961	Campbellton-Cross Point	New Brunswick-Quebec	815
1950	Maurice J. Tobin	Boston, Mass.	800
1935	Rip Van Winkle	Catskill, N.Y.	800
1938	Cairo	Ohio R., Ill.-Ky.	800
1932	Washington Mem.	Seattle, Wash.	800
1936	McCullough	Coos Bay, Ore.	793
1935	[4]Huey P Long	New Orleans	790
1916	*Memphis (Harahan)	Mississippi R.	790
1892	*Memphis	Mississippi R.	790
1949	Memphis-Arkansas	Mississippi R.	790
1904	*Mingo Jct., W. Va.	Ohio R.	769
1910	*Beaver, Pa.	Ohio R.	767
1941	Columbia R.	Kettle Falls, Wash.	600
1954	Columbia R.	Umatilla, Ore.	600
1954	Columbia R.	The Dalles, Ore.	573

Simple Truss

Year	Bridge	Location	Longest span
1976	Chester	Chester, W. Va.	745
1917	*Metropolis	Ohio R.	720
1929	Irvin S. Cobb	Ohio R.-Ill.-Ky.	716
1922	*Tanana R.	Nenana, Alaska	700
1933	*Henderson	Ohio R.-Ind.-Ky.	665
1967	I-77, Ohio R.	Williamstown, W. Va.	650
1917	4 MacArthur, Ill.-Mo.	St. Louis	647
1919	Louisville	Ohio R.	644
1989	St. Charles	Missouri R.	625
1933	Atchafalaya	Morgan City, La.	608
1924	*Castleton	Hudson R.	598
1937	Delaware R.	Easton, Pa.	550
1930	Swindell Bridge	Pittsburgh, Pa.	545
1889	*Cincinnati	Ohio R.	542
1952	Allegheny R., Tpk.	Pittsburgh, Pa.	534
1930	*Martinez	California	528
1951	Rankin	Pittsburgh, Pa.	525
1914	Old Brownsville	Brownsville, Pa.	520
1906	Donora-Webster	Donora-Webster, Pa.	515
1909	Hulton	Pittsburgh, Pa.	505
1967	Tanana R.	Alaska	500

Steel Truss

Year	Bridge	Location	Longest span
1988	Glade Creek	Raleigh Co., W.Va.	784
1973	Atchafalaya R.	Krotz Springs, La.	780
1972	Piscataqua R.	N.H., Me.	756
1972	Atchafalaya R.	Simmesport, La.	720
1957	SR-3, Rappahannock R.	Middlesex Co., Va.	648
1940	Jamestown	Jamestown, R.I.	640
1949	Memphis	Mississippi R., Ark.	621
1978	Atchafalaya R.	Morgan City, La.	607
1938	US-22	Delaware R., N.J.	540
1955	Interstate (I-5)	Columbia R., Ore.-Wash.	531
1910	[4]McKinley, St. Louis	Mississippi R.	517
1972	Mississippi R.	Muscatine, Ia.	512
1896	Newport	Ohio R., Ky.	511
1970	Lake Koocanusa	Lincoln Co., Mon.	500
1931	US-60	Cumberland R., Ky.	500
1958	Lake Oahe	Mobridge, S.D.	500
1958	Lake Oahe	Gettysburg, S.D.	500

Continuous Truss

Year	Bridge	Location	Longest span
1966	Columbia R. (Astoria)	Ore.-Wash.	1,232
1977	Francis Scott Key	Baltimore, Md.	1,200
1943	Dubuque, Ia.	Mississippi R.	845
1956	[7]Earl C. Clements	Ohio R., Ill-Ky.	825
1953	John E. Mathews	Jacksonville, Fla.	810
1940	Gov. Nice Mem.	Potomac River, Md.	800
1957	Kingston-Rhinecliff	Hudson R., N.Y.	800
1986	Rochester-Monaca	Rochester-Monaca, Pa.	780
1918	*Sciotoville	Ohio R.	775
1976	I-275, Lawrenceburg	Ohio R., Ind.-Ky.	750
1981	Sewickley	Sewickley, Pa.	750
1984	13th St. Bridge, Ohio R.	Ashland, Ky.	740
1959	Monaca-E. Rochester	Monaca-East Rochester, Pa.	730
1976	Betsy Ross	Philadelphia, Pa.	729
1929	Madison-Milton	Ohio R., Ind.-Ky.	727
1966	[5]Matthew E. Welsh	Mauckport, Ind.	725
1977	I-275, Brent	Ohio R.	720
1970	Vanport	Vanport, Pa.	715
1962	Champlain	Montreal, P.Q.	707
1973	Girard Point	Philadelphia, Pa.	700
1954	Pa. Tpk., Delaware R.	Philadelphia, Pa.	682
1949	George Platt	Philadelphia, Pa.	680
1938	Port Arthur-Orange	Tex.	680
1929	*Cincinnati	Ohio R.	675
1928	Cape Girardeau, Mo.	Mississippi R.	672
1946	Chester, Ill.	Mississippi R.	670
1970	Gulfgate	Port Arthur, Tex.	664
1953	Jefferson City	Missouri R.	640
1930	Quincy, Ill.	Mississippi R.	628
1961	Shippingport	Shippingport, Pa.	620
1959	US 181, over harbor	Corpus Christi, Tex.	620
1934	Bourne	Cape Cod Canal	616
1935	Sagamore	Cape Cod Canal	616
1965	Clarion R. (I-80)	Clarion, Pa.	612
1975	Donora-Monesson	Donora-Monesson, Pa.	608
1957	Blatnik	Duluth, Minn.	600
1965	Rio Grande Gorge	Taos, N.M.	600
1987	Jefferson City	Missouri R.	596
1962	W. Br. Feather R.	Oroville, Cal.	576
1967	Glenwood	Pittsburgh, Pa.	567
1936	Meredosia	Illinois R.	567
1936	Mark Twain Mem.	Hannibal, Mo.	562
1957	Mackinac	Mackinac Straits, Mich.	560

Continuous Box and Plate Girder

Year	Bridge	Location	Longest span
1988	Piney Creek-US19	Beckley, W. Va.	1,760
1973	Danville-US119	Danville, W. Va.	1,545
1983	Mississippi R.	Luling, La.	1,222
1974	Dunbar-S. Charleston	S. Charleston, W. Va.	842
1988	Beaver Creek-I-64	Beckley, W. Va.	764
1982	Houston Ship Chan.	Houston, Tex.	750
1967	San Mateo-Hayward No. 2	San Fran. Bay, Cal.	750
1977	Intracoastal Canal	Gibbstown, La.	750
1976	Intracoastal Canal	Forked Is., La.	750
1969	[6]San Diego-Coronado	San Diego Bay, Cal.	660
1987	Columbia R.	Umatilla, Ore.	660
1981	Douglas	Juneau, Alaska	620
1976	Wax L. Outlet	Calumet, La.	618
1975	S. Charleston-I-64	S. Charleston, W. Va.	612
1981	Glenn Jackson (I-205)	Columbia R., Ore.-Wash.	600
1967	Poplar St.	St. Louis, Mo.	600
1982	Illinois R.	Pekin, Ill.	550
1982	I-440	Arkansas R.	540
1977	US-64, Tennessee R.	Savannah, Tenn.	525
1988	Mon City	Monongahela, Pa.	520
1965	McDonald-Cartier	Ottawa, Ont.	520
1984	Columbia R.	Richland, Wash.	450
1986	Veterans	Pittsburgh, Pa.	440
1986	SR 76, Cumberland R.	Dover, Tenn.	440
1985	SR 20, Tennessee R.	Perryville, Tenn.	440
1970	Willamette R., I-205	West Linn, Ore.	430
1974	I-430	Arkansas R.	430
1985	FAU 3456, Tenn. R.	Chattanooga, Tenn.	420
1967	I-24, Tennessee R.	Marion Co., Tenn.	420
1978	Snake R.	Clarkston, Wash.	420
1975	36th St.	Charleston, W.Va.	420

Continuous Plate

Year	Bridge	Location	Longest span
1973	Ship Channel (I-610)	Houston, Tex.	630
1971	W. Atchafalaya	Henderson, La.	573

Year	Bridge	Location	Longest span
1981	Illinois 23	Illinois R., Ill.	510
1968	Trinity R.	Dallas, Tex.	480
1978	San Joaquin R.	Antioch, Cal.	460
1977	Thomas Johnson Mem.	Solomons, Md.	451
1975	Lewis	St. Louis, Mo.	450
1975	I-129	Missouri R., Ia.	450
1967	Mississippi R.	LaCrescent, Minn.	450
1972	Whiskey Bay Pilot Channel	Ramah, La.	425
1966	I-480	Missouri R., Ia.-Neb.	425
1970	I-435	Missouri R., Mo.	425
1972	I-80	Missouri R., Ia.-Neb.	425
1985	I-435	Missouri R., Ks.-Mo.	425
1984	US-36	Missouri R., Ks.-Mo.	425
1972	I-635, Kansas City	Missouri R., Ks.-Mo.	425
1978	I-24	Cumberland R., Ky.	420

Cable-Stayed

Year	Bridge	Location	Longest span
1987	Sunshine Skyway	Tampa Bay, Fla.	1,200
1991	Talmadge Mem.	Savannah, Ga.	1,100
1979	Intercity	Pasco-Kennewick, Wash.	970
1985	E. Huntington	Huntington, W. Va.	900
1985	Mississippi R.	Quincy, Ill.	900
1980	Veterans Mem'l.	W. Va.-Oh.	820
1991	Neches R.	Port Arthur - Orange, Tex.	640
1990	James R.	Henrico Co., Va.	630
1972	Sitka Harbor	Sitka, Alaska	450

I-Beam Girder

Year	Bridge	Location	Longest span
1980	Shreveport Int.	Louisiana	438
1948	US-27	Licking R., Ky.	316
1947	US-31E	Green R., Ky.	316
1941	US-62	Rolling Fork, Ky.	240
1942	Licking R.	Owingsville, Ky.	240
1954	Fuller Warren	Jacksonville, Fla.	224

Steel Arch

Year	Bridge	Location	Longest span
1977	New R. Gorge	Fayetteville, W. Va.	1,700
1931	Bayonne, N.J.	Kill Van Kull	1,652
1973	Fremont	Portland, Ore.	1,255
1964	Port Mann	British Columbia	1,200
1916	*Hell Gate	East R., N.Y.C.	1,038
1959	Glen Canyon	Colorado R.	1,028
1967	Trois-Rivieres	St. Lawrence R., P.Q.	1,100
1990	Roosevelt Lake	Arizona	1,080
1962	Lewiston-Queenston	Niagara R., Ont.	1,000
1976	Perrine	Twin Falls, Ida.	993
1941	Rainbow	Niagara Falls	984
1986	Moundsville	Ohio R., W. Va.	912
1984	I-255	Mississippi R., Mo.	909
1972	[9]I-40, Mississippi R.	Memphis, Tenn.	900
1970	Lake Quinsigamond	Worcester, Mass.	849
1966	Charles Braga	Somerset, Mass.	840
1936	Henry Hudson	Harlem R., N.Y.C.	840
1967	Lincoln Trail	Ohio R., Ind.-Ky.	825
1978	I-57, Cairo, Ill.	Mississippi R.	821
1980	I-65 Mobile R.	Mobile, Ala.	800
1961	Sherman Minton	Louisville, Ky.	800
1936	French King	Conn. R. (Rt. 2, Mass.)	782
1978	I-470 Bridge, Ohio R.	Wheeling, W. Va.	780
1930	West End	Pittsburgh, Pa.	780

Concrete Arch

Year	Bridge	Location	Longest span
1971	Selah Creek (twin)	Selah, Wash.	549
1968	Cowlitz R.	Mossyrock, Wash.	520
1931	Westinghouse	Pittsburgh, Pa.	460
1923	Cappelen	Minneapolis, Minn.	435

Twin Concrete Trestle

Year	Bridge	Location	Longest span
1979	I-55/I-10	Manchac, La.	181,157
1969	L. Pontchartrain Cswy.	Mandeville, La.	126,720
1972	Atchafalaya Flwy.	Baton Rouge, La.	93,984
1963	[8]L. Pontchartrain	Slidell, La.	28,547

Concrete Slab Dam

Year	Bridge	Location	Longest span
1927	Conowingo Dam	Maryland	4,611
1952	SR-4, Roanoke R.	Mecklenburg Co., Va.	2,785
1936	Hoover Dam	Boulder City, Nev.	1,324

Drawbridges

Vertical Lift

Year	Bridge	Location	Longest span
1959	*Arthur Kill	N.Y.-N.J.	558
1965	Pennsylvania Railroad	Kirkwood-Mt. Pleasant, Del.	548
1935	*Cape Cod Canal	Massachusetts	544
1960	*Delair, N.J.	Delaware R.	542
1937	Marine Parkway	Jamaica Bay, N.Y.C.	540
1931	Burlington, N.J.	Delaware R.	534
1908	*Willamette R.	Portland, Ore.	521
1968	Second Narrows	Vancouver, B.C.	493
1912	*A-S-B Fratt	Kansas City	428
1945	*Harry S. Truman	Kansas City	427
1955	Roosevelt Island	East R., N.Y.C.	418
1980	US-17, James R.	Isle of Wight, Co., Va.	415
1932	*M-K-T R.R.	Missouri R.	414
1969	Cape Fear Mem.	Wilmington, N.C.	408
1930	Aerial	Duluth, Minn.	386
1941	Main St.	Jacksonville, Fla.	386
1962	Burlington	Ontario	370
1941	Acosta	St. Johns R., Fla.	365
1922	*Cincinnati	Ohio R.	365
1967	SR-156, James R.	Prince George Co., Va.	364
1964	Red R.	Alexandria, La.	360
1957	Industrial Canal	New Orleans, La.	360
1950	Red R.	Moncla, La.	360
1936	Tribo	Harlem R., N.Y.C.	344
1961	[4]Corpus Christi Harbor	Corpus Christi, Tex.	344
1939	U.S. 1&9, Passaic R.	Newark, N.J.	333
1929	Carlton	Bath-Woolwich, Me.	328
1930	*Martinez	California	328
1960	St. Andrews Bay	Panama City, Fla.	327
1929	*Penn-Lehigh	Newark Bay	322
1987	Industrial Canal	New Orleans, La.	320
1920	*Chattanooga	Tennessee R.	310

Bascule

Year	Bridge	Location	Longest span
1969	E. Pearl R.	Slidell, La.	482
1940	Lorain, Oh.	Black R.	330
1917	SR-8, Tennessee R.	Chattanooga, Tenn.	306
1956	Duwamish R.	Seattle, Wash.	300
1955	Chehalis R.	Aberdeen, Wash.	288
1968	Elizabeth R.	Chesapeake, Va.	280
1913	Broadway	Portland, Ore.	278

Swing Bridges

Year	Bridge	Location	Longest span
1926	[4]Fort Madison	Mississippi R.	525
1991	SW Spokane St.	Seattle, Wash.	480
1930	Rigolets Pass	New Orleans, La.	400
1950	Douglass Memorial	Wash. D.C.	386
1945	Lord Delaware	Mattaponi R., Va.	252
1957	Eltham	Pamunkey R., Va.	237

Swing Span

Year	Bridge	Location	Longest span
1903	*East Omaha	Missouri R.	519
1952	US-17	York R., Va.	500
1897	*Duluth, Minn.	St. Louis Bay	486
1899	*C.M.&N.R.R.	Chicago	474
1913	Rt. 82, Conn-R.	E. Haddam, Ct.	465
1914	*Coos Bay	Oregon	458

Floating Pontoon

Year	Bridge	Location	Longest span
1963	Evergreen Pt.	Seattle, Wash.	7,518
1961	Hood Canal	Pt. Gamble, Wash.	6,471
1989	3rd Lake Washington	Seattle, Wash.	6,130

(1) The Transbay Bridge has 2 spans of 2,310 ft. each. (2) A second bridge in parallel was completed in 1973. (3) The Richmond Bridge has twin spans 1,070 ft. each. (4) Railroad and vehicular bridge. (5) Two spans each 707 ft. (6) Two spans each 660 ft. (7) Two spans each 825 ft. (8) Total length of bridge. (9) Two spans each 900 ft.

Notable International Bridges

Angostura, suspension type, span 2,336 feet, 1967 at Ciudad Bolivar, Venezuela. Total length, 5,507.

Bendorf Bridge on the Rhine River, 5 mi. n. of Coblenz, completed 1965, is a 3-span cement girder bridge, 3,378 ft. overall length, 101 ft. wide, with the main span 682 ft.

Bosporus Bridge linking Europe and Asia opened at Istanbul in 1973, at 3,524 ft. is the fifth longest suspension bridge in the world.

(continued)

Gladesville Bridge at Sydney, Australia, has the longest concrete arch in the world (1,000 ft. span).

Humber Bridge, with a suspension span of 4,626 ft., the longest in the world, crosses the Humber estuary 5 miles west of the city of Kingston upon Hull, England. Unique in a large suspension bridge are the towers of reinforced concrete instead of steel.

Second Narrow's Bridge, Canada's longest railway lift span connecting Vancouver and North Vancouver over Burrard Inlet.

Oland Island Bridge in Sweden was completed in 1972. It is 19,882 feet long, Europe's longest.

Oosterscheldebrug, opened Dec. 15, 1965, is a 3.125-mile causeway for automobiles over a sea arm in Zeeland, the Netherlands. It completes a direct connection between Flushing and Rotterdam.

Rio-Niteroi, Guanabara Bay, Brazil, completed in 1972, is world's longest continuous box and plate girder bridge, 8 miles, 3,363 feet long, with a center span of 984 feet and a span on each side of 656 feet.

Tagus River Bridge near Lisbon, Portugal, has a 3,323-ft. main span. Opened Aug. 6, 1966, it was named Salazar Bridge for the former premier.

Zoo Bridge across the Rhine at Cologne, with steel box girders, has a main span of 850 ft.

Oldest U.S. Bridge in Continuous Use

Completed in 1841, the 178 ft. long, wood truss (with orthotropic steel deck) covered bridge spans the Housatonic River on Rt. 128 in West Cornwall, Conn.

Underwater Vehicular Tunnels in North America

(over 5,000 feet in length)

Name	Location	Waterway	Feet
Bart Trans-Bay Tubes (Rapid Transit)	San Francisco, Cal.	S.F. Bay	3.6 miles
Brooklyn-Battery	New York, N.Y.	East River	9,117
Holland Tunnel	New York, N.Y.	Hudson River	8,557
Lincoln Tunnel	New York, N.Y.	Hudson River	8,216
Thimble Shoal Channel	Northampton Co., Va.	Chesapeake Bay	8,187
Chesapeake Channel	Northampton Co., Va.	Chesapeake Bay	7,941
Baltimore Harbor Tunnel	Baltimore, Md.	Patapsco River	7,650
Hampton Roads (twin)	Hampton, Va.	Hampton Roads	7,479
Fort McHenry Tunnel (2)	Baltimore, Md.	Baltimore Harbor	7,200
Queens Midtown	New York, N.Y.	East River	6,414
Sumner Tunnel	Boston, Mass.	Boston Harbor	5,650
Louis-Hippolyte Lafontaine Tunnel	Montreal, Que.	St. Lawrence River	5,280
Detroit-Windsor	Detroit, Mich.	Detroit River	5,160
Callahan Tunnel	Boston, Mass.	Boston Harbor	5,046

Land Vehicular Tunnels in U.S.

(over 3,000 feet in length.)

Name	Location	Feet
E. Johnson Memorial	I-70, Col.	8,959
Eisenhower Memorial	I-70, Col.	8,941
Allegheny (twin)	Penn. Turnpike	6,072
Liberty Tubes	Pittsburgh, Pa.	5,920
Zion Natl. Park	Rte. 9, Utah	5,766
East River Mt. (twin)	Bland Co., Va.	5,412
Tuscarora (twin)	Penn. Turnpike	5,400
Trans-Koolau	H-3, Hawaii	5,165
Kittatinny (twin)	Penn. Turnpike	4,660
Blue Mountain (twin)	Penn. Turnpike	4,435
Lehigh	Penn. Turnpike	4,379
Wawona	Yosemite Natl. Park	4,233
Big Walker Mt.	Bland Co., Va.	4,229
Hanging Lake (twin)	Glenwood Canyon, Col.	4,000
Fort Pitt	Pittsburgh, Pa.	3,560
Dingess Tunnel	Mingo Co., W.Va.	3,400
Mall Tunnel	Dist. of Columbia	3,400
Caldecott	Oakland, Cal.	3,371
Cody No. 1	U.S. 14, 16, 20, Wyo.	3,202

World's Longest Railway Tunnels

Source: Railway Directory & Year Book. Tunnels over 8 miles in length.

Tunnel	Date	Miles	Operating railway	Country
Seikan	1985	33.5	Japanese Railway	Japan
Dai-shimizu	1979	14	Japanese Railway	Japan
Simplon No. 1 and 2	1906, 1922	12	Swiss Fed. & Italian St.	Switz.-Italy
Kanmon	1975	12	Japanese Railway	Japan
Apennine	1934	11	Italian State	Italy
Rokko	1972	10	Japanese Railway	Japan
Mt. MacDonald	1989	9.1	Canadian Pacific	Canada
Gotthard	1882	9	Swiss Federal	Switzerland
Lotschberg	1913	9	Bern-Lotschberg-Simplon	Switzerland
Hokuriku	1962	9	Japanese Railway	Japan
Mont Cenis (Frejus)	1871	8	Italian State	France-Italy
Shin-Shimizu	1961	8	Japanese Railway	Japan
Aki	1975	8	Japanese Railway	Japan
Cascade	1929	8	Burlington Northern	U.S.
Flathead	1970	8	Burlington Northern	U.S.

SOCIAL SECURITY

Social Security Programs

Source: Social Security Administration, U.S. Dept. of Health and Human Services

Old-Age, Survivors, and Disability Insurance; Medicare; Supplemental Security Income

Social Security Benefits

Social Security benefits are based on a worker's primary insurance amount (PIA), which is related by law to the average indexed monthly earnings (AIME) on which social security contributions have been paid. The full PIA is payable to a retired worker who becomes entitled to benefits at age 65 and to an entitled disabled worker at any age. Spouses and children of retired or disabled workers and survivors of deceased workers receive set proportions of the PIA subject to a family maximum amount. The PIA is calculated by applying varying percentages to succeeding parts of the AIME. The formula is adjusted annually to reflect changes in average annual wages.

Automatic increases in Social Security benefits are initiated for December of a year whenever the Consumer Price Index (CPI) of the Bureau of Labor Statistics for the third calendar quarter of a year increases relative to the CPI for the base quarter, which is either the third calendar quarter of the preceding year or the quarter in which an increase legislated by Congress becomes effective. The size of the benefit increase is determined by the actual percentage rise of the CPI between the quarters measured.

The average monthly benefit payable to all retired workers was $653.00 in December 1992. The average amount for disabled workers in that month was $627.00.

Minimum and maximum monthly retired-worker benefits payable to individuals who retired at age 65[1]

	Minimum benefit		Maximum benefit			
Year of attainment of age 65[2]	Payable at time of retirement	Payable effective Dec. 1992	Payable at time of retirement Men[3]	Payable at time of retirement Women	Payable effective Dec. 1992 Men[3]	Payable effective Dec. 1992 Women
1965 . . .	$44.00	$261.00	$131.70	$135.90	$697.70	$720.00
1970 . . .	64.00	261.00	189.80	196.40	773.20	800.70
1980 . . .	133.90	261.00	572.00	...	1,115.40	...
1990 . . .	(4)	(4)	975.00	...	1,097.50	...
1993 . . .	(4)	(4)	1,128.80	...	...	...

(1) Assumes retirement at beginning of year. (2) The final benefit amount payable after Supplementary Medical Insurance (SMI) premium or any other deductions is rounded to next lower $1 (if not already a multiple of $1). (3) Benefit for both men and women are shown in men's columns except where women's benefit appears separately. (4) Minimum eliminated for workers who reach age 62 after 1981.

Amount of Work Required

To qualify for benefits, the worker must have worked in covered employment long enough to become insured. Just how long depends on when the worker reaches age 62 or, if earlier, when he or she dies or becomes disabled.

A person is fully insured if he or she has one quarter of coverage for every year after 1950 (or year age 21 is reached, if later) up to but not including the year in which the worker reaches age 62, dies, or becomes disabled. In 1993, a person earns one quarter of coverage for each $590 of annual earnings in covered employment, up to a maximum of 4 quarters per year.

The law permits special monthly payments under the Social Security program to certain very old persons who are not eligible for regular social security benefits since they had little or no opportunity to earn social security work credits during their working lifetime.

To get disability benefits, in addition to being fully insured, the worker must also have credit for 20 quarters of coverage out of the 40 calendar quarters before he or she becomes disabled. A disabled blind worker need meet only the fully insured requirement. Persons disabled before age 31 can qualify with a briefer period of coverage. Certain survivor benefits are payable if the deceased worker had 6 quarters of coverage in the 13 quarters preceding death.

Work credit for fully insured status for benefits

Born after 1929; die, become disabled, or reach age 62 in	Years needed
1983	8
1984	8¼
1985	8½
1986	8¾
1987	9
1988	9¼
1989	9½
1990	9¾
1991 and after	10

Contribution and benefit base

Calendar year	OASDI[1] Base	HI[2] Base
1984	$37,800	—
1985	39,600	—
1986	42,000	—
1987	43,800	—
1988	45,000	—
1989	48,000	—
1990	51,300	—
1991	53,400	$125,000[3]
1992	55,500	130,200
1993	57,600	135,000

(1) Old-Age, Survivors, and Disability Insurance. (2) Hospital Insurance. (3) Although the OASDI and HI bases were the same prior to 1991, they have differed since that time.

Tax-rate schedule
[Percent of covered earnings]

Year	Total	OASDI	HI
	Employees and employers, each		
1979-80	6.13	5.08	1.05
1981	6.65	5.35	1.30
1982-83	6.70	5.40	1.30
1984	7.00	5.70	1.30
1985	7.05	5.70	1.35
1986-87	7.15	5.70	1.45
1988-89	7.51	6.06	1.45
1990 and after	7.65	6.20	1.45
	Self-employed		
1979-80	8.10	7.05	1.05
1981	9.30	8.00	1.30
1982-83	9.35	8.05	1.30
1984	14.00	11.40	2.60
1985	14.10	11.40	2.70
1986-87	14.30	11.40	2.90
1988-89	15.02	12.12	2.90
1990 and after	15.30	12.40	2.90

What Aged Workers Get

When a person has enough work in covered employment and reaches retirement age (currently 65 for full benefit, 62 for reduced benefit), he or she may retire and get monthly old-age benefits. The age at which unreduced benefits are payable will be increased gradually from 65 to 67 over a 21-year period beginning with workers age 62 in the year 2000; (reduced benefits will still be available as early as age 62 but with a larger reduction at age 62.) If a person aged 65 or older continues to work and has earnings of more than $10,560 in 1993, $1 in benefits will be withheld for every $3 above $10,560. The annual exempt amount for people under age 65 is $7,680 in 1993, and $1 in benefits is withheld for every $2 in earnings above the exempt amount for them. The annual exempt amount is raised automatically as the general earnings level rises. The eligible worker who is 70 receives the full benefit regardless of earnings.

For workers who reach age 65 from 1982 through 1989, the worker's benefit is raised by 3% for each year for which the worker between 65 and 70 (72 before 1984) did not receive benefits because of earnings from work or because the worker had not applied for benefits. The delayed retirement credit is 1 percent a year for workers reaching age 65 before 1982. The delayed retirement credit will gradually rise to 8% per year from 1990 through 2008. The rate for workers reaching age 65 in 1992-93 is 4%.

Effective December 1992, the special benefit for persons aged 72 or over who do not meet the regular coverage requirements is $178.80 a month. Like the monthly benefits, these payments are subject to cost-of-living increases. The special payment is not made to persons on the public assistance or supplemental security income rolls.

Workers retiring before age 65 have their benefits permanently reduced by 5/9 of 1% for each month they receive benefits before age 65. Thus, workers entitled to benefits in the month they reach age 62 receive 80% of the PIA, while a worker retiring at age 65 receives a benefit equal to 100% of the PIA. The nearer to age 65 the worker is when he or she begins collecting a benefit, the larger the benefit will be.

Benefits for Worker's Spouse

The spouse of a worker who is getting Social Security retirement or disability payments may become entitled to a spouse's insurance benefit when he or she reaches 65 of one-half of the worker's PIA. Reduced spouse's benefits are available at age 62 (25/36 of 1% reduction for each month of entitlement before age 65). Benefits are also payable to the aged-divorced spouse of an insured worker if he or she was married to the worker for at least 10 years.

Benefits for Children of Retired or Disabled Workers

If a retired or disabled worker has a child under 18 the child will get a benefit that is half of the worker's unreduced benefit, and so will the worker's spouse, even if he or she is under 62 if he or she is caring for an entitled child of the worker who is under 16 or who became disabled before age 22. Total benefits paid on a worker's earnings record are subject to a maximum and if the total that would be paid to a family exceeds that maximum, the individual dependents' benefits are adjusted downward. (Total benefits paid to the family of a worker who retired in January 1993 at age 65 and who always had the maximum amount of earnings creditable under Social Security can be no higher than $1,974.70.)

When entitled children reach 18, their benefits will generally stop, except that a child disabled before 22 may get a benefit as long as his or her disability meets the definition in the law. Additionally, benefits will be paid to a child until age 19 if the child is in full-time attendance at an elementary or secondary school.

Benefits may also be paid to a grandchild or step-grandchild of a worker or of his or her spouse, in special circumstances.

OASDI	May 1993	May 1992	May 1991
Monthly beneficiaries, total (in thousands)	**41,784**	**40,956**	**40,119**
Aged 65 and over, total	30,484	30,030	29,516
Retired workers	23,303	22,889	22,432
Survivors and dependents	7,178	7,137	7,078
Special age-72 beneficiaries	3	4	6
Under age 65, total	11,300	10,926	10,603
Retired workers	2,529	2,536	2,539
Disabled workers	3,571	3,306	3,076
Survivors and dependents	5,200	5,084	4,988
Total monthly benefits (in millions)	**$24,623**	**$23,307**	**$21,880**

What Disabled Workers Get

If a worker becomes so severely disabled that he or she is unable to work, he or she may be eligible to receive a monthly disability benefit. Benefits continue until it is determined that the individual is no longer disabled. Each beneficiary's eligibility is reviewed periodically. When a disabled-worker beneficiary reaches 65, the disability benefit becomes a retired-worker benefit.

Benefits generally like those provided for dependents of retired-worker beneficiaries may be paid to dependents of disabled beneficiaries. However, the maximum family benefit in disability cases is generally lower than in retirement cases.

Survivor Benefits

If an insured worker should die, one or more types of benefits may be payable to survivors, again subject to a maximum family benefit as described above.

1. If claiming benefits at 65, the surviving spouse will receive a benefit that is 100% of the deceased worker's PIA. The surviving spouse may choose to get the benefit as early as age 60, but the benefit is then reduced by 19/40 of 1% for each month it is paid before age 65. However, for those whose spouses claimed their benefits before 65, the benefit is limited to the reduced amount the worker would be getting if alive but not less than 82 1/2% of the worker's PIA. Marriage after the worker's death ends the surviving spouses benefit rights. However, if he or she marries and the marriage is ended, he or she regains benefit rights (A marriage after age 60, 50 if disabled, is deemed not to have occurred for benefit purposes.). This benefit may also be paid to the divorced spouse, if the marriage lasted for at least 10 years.

Disabled widows and widowers may under certain circumstances qualify for benefits after attaining age 50 at the rate of 71.5% of the deceased worker's PIA. The widow or widower must have become totally disabled before or within 7 years after the spouse's death, the last month in which he or she received mother's or father's insurance benefits, or the last month he or she previously received surviving spouse's benefits.

2. A benefit for each child until the child reaches 18. The monthly benefit of each child of a worker who has died is three-quarters of the amount the worker would have received if he or she had lived and drawn full retirement benefits. A child with a disability that began before age 22 may receive benefits. Also, a child may receive benefits until age 19 if he or she is in full-time attendance at an elementary or secondary school.

3. A mother's or father's benefit for the widow(er), if children of the worker under 16 are in his or her care. The benefit is 75% of the PIA and he or she draws it until the youngest child reaches 16, at which time payments stop even if the child's benefit continues. They may start again when he or she is 60 (50 if disabled) unless he or she is married. If he or she has a disabled child beneficiary aged 16 or over in care, benefits also continue.

4. Dependent parents may be eligible for benefits, if they have been receiving at least half their support from the worker before his or her death, have reached age 62, and (except in certain circumstances) have not remarried since the worker's death. Each parent gets 75% of the worker's PIA; if only one parent survives the benefit is 82 1/2%.

5. A lump sum cash payment of $255. Payment is made only when there is a spouse who was living with the worker or a spouse or child eligible for immediate monthly survivor benefits.

Self-Employed

A self-employed person who has net earnings of $400 or more in a year must report such earnings for social security tax and credit purposes. The person reports net returns from the business. Income from real estate, savings, dividends, loans, pensions, or insurance policies may not be included unless they are part of the business.

A self-employed person gets a quarter of coverage for each $590 (for 1993), up to a maximum of 4 quarters of coverage.

The nonfarm self-employed have the option of reporting their earnings as ⅔ of their gross income from self-employment but not more than $1,600 a year and not less than their actual net earnings. This option can be used only if actual net earnings from self-employment income is less than $1,600 and may be used only 5 times. Also, the self-employed person must have actual net earnings of $400 or more in 2 of the 3 taxable years immediately preceding the year in which he or she uses the option.

When a person has both taxable wages and earnings from self-employment, the wages are credited for Social Security purposes first; only as much of the self-employment income as will bring total earnings up to the current taxable maximum is subject to the self-employment tax.

Farm Owners and Workers

Self-employed farmers whose gross annual earnings from farming are $2,400 or less may report ⅔ of their gross earnings instead of net earnings for social security purposes. Farmers whose gross income is over $2,400 and whose net earnings are less than $1,600 can report $1,600. Cash or crop shares received from a tenant or share farmer count if the owner participated materially in production or management. The self-employed farmer pays contributions at the same rate as other self-employed persons.

Agricultural employees. A worker's earnings from farm work count toward benefits (1) if the employer pays him $150 or more in cash during the year; or (2) if the employer spends $2,500 or more in the year for agricultural labor. Under these rules a person gets credit for one calendar quarter for each $590 in cash pay in 1993 up to four quarters.

Foreign farm workers admitted to the United States on a temporary basis are not covered.

Household Workers

Anyone working as maid, cook, laundress, nursemaid, baby-sitter, chauffeur, gardener and at other household tasks in the house of another is covered by Social Security if he or she is paid $50 or more in cash in a calendar quarter by any one employer. Room and board do not count, but carfare counts if paid in cash. The job does not have to be regular or full time. The employee should get a Social Security card at the social security office and show it to the employer.

The employer deducts the amount of the employee's social security tax from the worker's pay, adds an identical amount as the employer's social security tax and sends the total amount to the federal government, with the employee's social security number.

Medicare

The Medicare health insurance program provides acute-care coverage for Social Security and Railroad Retirement beneficiaries aged 65 and over and, for persons entitled for 24 months to receive a social security disability benefit, and certain persons with end-stage kidney disease. The Medicare program cost $129 billion in 1992 and served more than 35 million people.

Persons eligible for Medicare may choose to have their covered services provided through a Health Maintenance Organization.

Hospital insurance. The hospital insurance program pays the cost of covered services for hospital and posthospital care as follows:

- Medicare pays for all necessary inpatient hospital care for the first 60 days of each benefit period, except for a deductible ($676 in 1993). For days 61-90, Medicare pays for covered services except for a coinsurance amount ($169 per day in 1993). After 90 days, the beneficiary has 60 reserve days for which Medicare helps pay. The coinsurance amount for reserve days was $338 in 1993.
- Up to 100 days' care in a skilled-nursing facility (skilled-nursing home) in each benefit period. Hospital insurance pays for all covered services for the first 20 days; for the 21-100th day, the beneficiary pays coinsurance ($84.50 in 1993).
- Visits by nurses or other health workers (not doctors) from a home health agency.
- Hospice care for terminally ill individuals.

Medical insurance. Aged persons can receive benefits under this supplementary program only if they sign up for them and agree to a monthly premium ($36.60 in 1993). The Federal Government pays the rest of the cost.

The medical insurance program pays 80% of the approval amount (after the first $100 in each calendar year) for the following services:

Medicare helps pay for covered services you receive from your doctor in his or her office, in a hospital, in a skilled nursing facility, in your home, or any other location.

Doctors' services covered by Medicare include:

- Medical and surgical services, including anesthesia.
- Diagnostic tests and procedures that are part of your treatment.
- Radiology and pathology services by doctors while you are a hospital inpatient or outpatient.
- Treatment of mental illness. Medicare payments for nonhospital treatment are limited—you may get the services from doctors, comprehensive outpatient rehabilitation facilities (CORFs), physician assistants, psychologists, and clinical social workers.

These services for nonhospital treatment of a mental illness are subject to a special payment rule. In effect, once the annual deductible is met, Medicare pays only 50% (not 80%) of approved charges for these services. On assigned claims, beneficiaries are responsible for paying the remaining 50%. For unassigned claims, beneficiaries may have to pay more.

Partial hospitalization services for treatment of mental illness are not subject to this special payment rule. Also, brief office visits for the sole purpose of monitoring or changing drug prescriptions used in the treatment of mental illness are not subject to this special payment rule.

- Other services such as:
  - — X-rays.
  - — Services of your doctor's office nurse.
  - — Drugs and biologicals that cannot be self-administered.
  - — Transfusions of blood and blood components.
  - — Medical supplies.
  - — Physical/occupational therapy and speech pathology services.

To get medical insurance protection, persons approaching age 65 may enroll in the 7-month period that includes 3 months before the 65th birthday, the month of the birthday, and 3 months after the birthday, but if they wish coverage to begin in the month they reach 65 they must enroll in the 3 months before their birthday. Persons not enrolling within their first enrollment period may enroll later, during the first 3 months of each year, but their premium is 10% higher for each 12-month period elapsed since they first could have enrolled.

The monthly premium is deducted from the cash benefit for persons receiving Social Security, Railroad Retirement, or Civil Service retirement benefits. Income from the medical premiums and the federal matching payments are put in a Supplementary Medical Insurance Trust Fund, from which benefits and administrative expenses are paid.

Medicare card. Persons qualifying for hospital insurance under Social Security receive a health insurance card similar to cards now used by Blue Cross and other health insurers. The card indicates whether the individual has taken out medical insurance protection. It is to be shown to the hospital, skilled-nursing facility, home health agency, doctor, or whoever provides the covered services.

Payments are made only in the 50 states, Puerto Rico, the Virgin Islands, Guam, and American Samoa, except that hospital services may be provided in border areas immediately outside the U.S. if comparable services are not accessible in the U.S. for a beneficiary who becomes ill or is injured in the U.S.

Social Security Financing

Social Security is paid for by a tax on earnings (for 1993, up to $57,600 for Old Age, Survivors, and Disability Insurance and up to $135,000 for Hospital Insurance with the Medicare Program; the taxable earnings bases have been adjusted annually to reflect increases in average wages). The employed worker and his or her employer share the tax equally. Beginning in 1994, there will be no ceiling on earnings subject to the Medicare tax.

Employers remit amounts withheld from employee wages for Social Security and income taxes to the Internal Revenue Service; employer Social Security taxes are also payable at the same time. (Self-employed workers pay their Social Security taxes along with their regular income tax forms). The Social Security taxes (along with revenues arising from partial taxation of the Social Security benefits of certain high-income people) are transferred to the Social Security Trust Funds—the Federal Old-Age and Survivors Insurance (OASI) Trust Fund, the Federal Disability Insurance (DI) Trust Fund, and the Federal Hospital Insurance (HI) Trust Fund; they can be used only to pay benefits, the cost of rehabilitation services, and administrative expenses. Money not immediately needed for these purposes is by law invested in obligations of the Federal Government, which must pay interest on the money borrowed and must repay the principal when the obligations are redeemed or mature.

Supplemental Security Income

On Jan. 1, 1974, the Supplemental Security Income (SSI) program established by the 1972 Social Security Act amendments replaced the former federal grants to states for aid to the needy aged, blind, and disabled in the 50 states and the District of Columbia. The program provides both for federal payments based on uniform national standards and eligibility requirements and for state supplementary payments varying from state to state. The Social Security Administration administers the federal payments financed from general funds of the Treasury—and the state supplements as well, if the state elects to have its supplementary program federally administered. The states may supplement the federal payment for all recipients and must supplement it for persons otherwise adversely affected by the transition from the former public assistance programs. In May 1993, the number of persons receiving federal payments and federally administered state payments was 5,786,998 and the amount of these payments was $2.14 billion.

The maximum monthly federal SSI payment for individuals with no other countable income, living in their own household, was $434.00 in 1993. For couples it was $652.00.

Examples of monthly cash benefit awards for selected beneficiary families with first entitlement in 1993, effective January 1993

Beneficiary Family	Low Earnings ($10,544 in 1993) (45% of average)	Career Earnings Level Average Earnings ($23,432 in 1993)[1]	Maximum Earnings ($57,600 in 1993)
Primary insurance amount (worker retiring at 65)	$496.70	$819.90	$1,128.80
Maximum family benefit (worker retiring at 65)	744.40	1,492.90	1,973.90
Disability maximum family benefit (worker disabled at 55; in 1992)*	694.40	1,221,00	1,722.31
Disabled worker: (worker disabled at 55)			
Worker alone	494.00	814.00	1,148.50
Worker, spouse, and 1 child	693.00	1,220.00	1,721.00
Retired worker claiming benefits at age 62:			
Worker alone[2]	398.00	656.00	899.00
Worker with spouse claiming benefits at—			
Age 65 or over	645.00	1,063.00	1,457.00
Age 62[2]	587.00	984.00	1,312.00
Widow or widower claiming benefits at—			
Age 65 or over[3]	496.00	819.00	1,128.00
Age 60	355.00	586.00	807.00
Disabled widow or widower claiming benefits at age 50-59[4]	355.00	586.00	807.00
1 surviving child	372.00	614.00	846.00
Widow or widower age 65 or over and 1 child[5]	744.00	1,433.00	1,972.00
Widowed mother or father and 1 child[5]	744.00	1,228.00	1,692.00
Widowed mother or father and 2 children[5]	744.00	1,491.00	1,974.00

* Assumes work beginning at age 22. (1) Estimate. (2) Assumes maximum reduction. (3) A widow(er)'s benefit amount is limited to the amount the spouse would have been receiving if still living but not less than 82.5 percent of the PIA. (4) Effective January 1984, disabled widow(er)s claiming benefit at ages 50-59 will receive benefit equal to 71.5 percent of the PIA (based on 1983 Social Security Amendment provision). (5) Based on worker dying at age 65.

Social Security Trust Funds

Old-Age and Survivors Insurance Trust Fund, 1940-1992

(In millions)

	Income					Disbursements						
Fiscal year[1]	Total	Net contributions[2]	Income from taxation of benefits	Payments from the general fund of the Treasury[3]	Net interest[4]	Total	Benefit payments[5]	Administrative expenses	Transfers to Railroad Retirement program	Interfund borrowing transfers[6]	Net increase in fund	Fund at end of period
1940	$592	$550	—	—	$42	$28	$16	$12	—	—	$564	$1,745
1950	2,367	2,106	—	$4	257	784	727	57	—	—	1,583	12,893
1960	10,360	9,843	—	—	517	11,073	10,270	202	$600	—	−713	20,829
1970	31,746	29,955	—	442	1,350	27,321	26,268	474	579	—	4,425	32,616
1980	100,051	97,608	—	557	1,886	103,228	100,626	1,160	1,442	—	−3,177	24,566
1985	179,881	175,305	$3,151	105	1,321	169,210	165,310	1,589	2,310	$−4,364	6,308	33,877
1990	278,607	261,506	2,924	34	14,143	223,481	218,948	1,564	2,969	—	55,126	203,445
1991	293,288	270,841	5,790	−2,089	18,746	241,316	236,195	1,746	3,375	—	51,972	255,417
1992	307,102	278,506	6,019	19	22,557	256,239	251,268	1,823	3,148	—	50,862	306,280

(1) Under the Congressional Budget Act of 1974 (Public Law 93-344), fiscal years 1977 and later consist of the 12 months ending on September 30 of each year. Fiscal years prior to 1977 consisted of the 12 months ending on June 30 of each year.

(2) Beginning in 1983, includes transfers from general fund of Treasury representing contributions that would have been paid on deemed wage credits for military service in 1957 and later, if such credits were considered to be covered wages.

(3) Includes payments (a) in 1947-52 and in 1967 and later, for costs of noncontributory wage credits for military service performed before 1957; (b) in 1972-83, for costs of deemed wage credits for military service performed after 1956; and (c) in 1969 and later, for costs of benefits to certain uninsured persons who attained age 72 before 1968.

(4) Net interest includes net profits or losses on marketable investments. Beginning in 1967, administrative expenses are charged currently to the trust fund on an estimated basis, with a final adjustment, including interest, made in the following fiscal year. The amounts of these interest adjustments are included in net interest. For years prior to 1967, a description of the method of accounting for administrative expenses is contained in the 1970 Annual Report. Beginning in October 1973, the figures shown include relatively small amounts of gifts to the fund. Figures for 1983-86 reflect payments from a borrowing trust fund to a lending trust fund for interest on amounts owed under the interfund borrowing provisions. During 1983-91, interest paid from the trust fund to the general fund on advance tax transfers is reflected. The amounts shown for 1985 and 1986 include interest adjustments of $76.5 million and $11.5 million, respectively, on unnegotiated checks issued before April 1985.

(5) Beginning in 1967, includes payments for vocational rehabilitation services furnished to disabled persons receiving benefits because of their disabilities. Beginning in 1983, amounts are reduced by amount of reimbursement for unnegotiated benefit checks.

(6) Negative figures represent amounts repaid from the OASI Trust Fund to the DI and HI Trust Funds.

Disability Insurance Trust Fund, 1960-1992

(In millions)

	Income					Disbursements						
Fiscal year[1]	Total	Net contributions[2]	Income from taxation of benefits	Payments from the general fund of the Treasury[3]	Net interest[4]	Total	Benefit payments[5]	Administrative expenses	Transfers to Railroad Retirement program	Interfund borrowing transfers[6]	Net increase in fund	Fund at end of period
1960	$1,034	$987	—	—	$47	$533	$528	$32	−$27	—	$501	$2,167
1970	4,380	4,141	—	$16	223	2,954	2,795	149	10	—	1,426	5,104
1980	17,376	16,805	—	118	453	15,320	14,998	334	−12	—	2,056	7,680
1985	17,984	16,876	$217	—	891	19,294	18,648	603	43	$2,540	1,230	5,873
1990	28,215	27,291	158	—	766	25,124	24,327	717	80	—	3,091	11,455
1991	29,322	28,953	131	−775	1,014	27,780	26,909	789	82	—	1,543	12,997
1992	31,168	29,871	218	—	1,080	31,285	30,382	845	58	—	−116	12,881

(1) Under the Congressional Budget Act of 1974 (Public Law 93-344), fiscal years 1977 and later consist of the 12 months ending on September 30 of each year. The act further provides that the calendar quarter July-September 1976 is a period of transition from fiscal year 1976, which ended on June 30, 1976, to fiscal year 1977, which began on October 1, 1976.

(2) Beginning in 1983, includes government contributions on deemed wage credits for military service in 1957 and later.

(3) Includes payments (a) in 1967 and later, for costs of noncontributory wage credits for military service performed before 1957; and (b) in 1972-83, for costs of deemed wage credits for military service performed after 1956.

(4) Net interest includes net profits or losses on marketable investments. Beginning in 1967, administrative expenses are charged currently to the trust fund on an estimated basis, with a final adjustment, including interest, made in the following fiscal year. The amounts of these interest adjustments are included in net interest. For years prior to 1967, a description of the method of accounting for administrative expenses is contained in the 1970 Annual Report of the Board of Trustees of the Federal Old-Age and Survivors Insurance and Disability Insurance Trust Funds. Beginning in 1983, these figures reflect payments from a borrowing trust fund to a lending trust fund for interest on amounts owed under the interfund borrowing provisions. Also, beginning in 1983, interest paid from the trust fund to the general fund on advance tax transfers is reflected. The amount shown for 1985 includes an interest adjustment of $14.8 million on unnegotiated checks issued before April 1985.

(5) Beginning in 1967, includes payments for vocational rehabilitation services furnished to disabled persons receiving benefits because of their disabilities. Beginning in 1983, amounts are reduced by amount of reimbursement for unnegotiated benefit checks. The amount shown for 1983 is reduced by $48 million for all unnegotiated checks issued before 1983; reductions in subsequent years are relatively small.

(6) Negative figure represents amounts lent by the DI Trust Fund to the OASI Trust Fund. Positive figures represent repayment of these amounts.

Supplementary Medical Insurance Trust Fund, 1970-1992

(In millions)

	Income				Disbursements			
Fiscal year[1]	Premium from participants	Government contributions[2]	Interest and other income[3]	Total income	Benefit payments	Administrative expenses	Total disbursements	Balance in fund at end of year[4]
1970	$936	$928	$12	$1,876	$1,979	$217	$2,196	$57
1975	1,887	2,330	105	4,322	3,765	405	4,170	1,424
1980	2,928	6,932	415	10,275	10,144	593	10,737	4,532
1985	5,524	17,898	1,155	24,577	21,808	922	22,730	10,646
1990	11,494[5]	33,210	1,434[5]	46,138[5]	41,498	1,524[5]	43,022[5]	14,527[5]
1991	11,807	34,730	1,629	48,166	45,514	1,505	47,019	15,675
1992	12,748	38,684	1,717	53,149	48,627	1,661	50,288	18,535

(1) For 1967 through 1976, fiscal years cover the interval from July 1 through June 30; fiscal years 1977 and later cover the interval from October 1 through September 30. (2) The payments shown as being from the general fund of the Treasury include certain interest-adjustment items. (3) Other income includes recoveries of amounts reimbursed from the trust fund that are not obligations of the trust fund and other miscellaneous income. (4) The financial status of the program depends on both the total net assets and the liabilities of the program. (5) Includes the impact of the Medicare Catastrophic Coverage Act of 1988 (Public Law 100-360).

Hospital Insurance Trust Fund, 1970-1992

(In millions)

	Income							Disbursements			Trust Fund	
Fiscal Year[1]	Payroll taxes	Transfers from railroad retirement account	Reimbursement for uninsured persons	Premiums from voluntary enrollees	Payments for military wage credits	Interest on investments and other income[2]	Total income	Benefit payments[3]	Administrative expense[4]	Total disbursements	Net increase fund	Fund at end of year
1970	$4,785	$64	617	—	$11	$137	$5,614	$4,804	$149	$4,953	$661	$2,677
1975	11,291	132	481	6	48	609	12,568	10,353	259	10,612	1,956	9,870
1980	23,244	244	697	17	141	1,072	25,415	23,790	497	24,288	1,127	14,490
1985	46,490	371	766	38	86	3,182	50,933	47,841	813	48,654	4,103[5]	21,277[5]
1990	70,655	367	413	113	107	7,908	79,563	65,912	774	66,687	12,876	95,631
1991	74,655	352	605	367	−1,011[6]	8,969	83,938	68,705	934	69,638	14,299	109,930
1992	80,978	374	621	484	86	10,133	92,677	80,784	1,191	81,974	10,703	120,633

(1) Fiscal years 1976 and earlier consist of the 12 months ending on June 30 of each year; fiscal years 1977 and later consist of the 12 months ending on September 30 of each year. (2) Other income includes recoveries of amounts reimbursed from the trust fund that are not obligations of the trust fund and a small amount of miscellaneous income. (3) Includes costs of Peer Review Organizations (beginning with the implementation of the Prospective Payment System on October 1, 1983). (4) Includes costs of experiments and demonstration projects. (5) In fiscal year 1983, $12,437 million was loaned to the Old-Age and Survivors Insurance Trust Fund under the interfund borrowing provisions of the Social Security Act. Repayments of $1,824 million and $10,613 million were made in fiscal years 1985 and 1986, respectively. (6) Includes the lump sum general revenue adjustment of $-1,100 million, as provided for by section 151 of P.L. 98-21. NOTE: Totals do not necessarily equal the sum of rounded components.

HEALTH

Ethics Regarding Care of the Terminally Ill

Physician-assisted suicide for the terminally ill remained a prominent issue. On Aug. 4, 1993, Dr. Jack Kevorkian, a retired Michigan pathologist, assisted a suicide for the 17th time since beginning such procedures in June 1990; in most cases he employed an apparatus—which must be activated by the patient—consisting of a face mask attached by a tube to a container of carbon monoxide. A new Michigan law that went into effect in Feb. 1993 made it a felony to assist in a suicide. A county judge struck down the law in May on a technicality, but an appellate court stayed that decision, leaving the law in effect while court challenges continued. On Aug. 17, Kevorkian was indicted for his role in the Aug. death. On Sept. 10, the same day he was ordered to stand trial, Kevorkian assisted a suicide for the 18th time. In Nov. 1992, California voters defeated a ballot measure that would have legalized in that state physician-assisted suicide for the terminally ill.

In a 1992 survey conducted by the American Society of Internal Medicine, one in five physicians said they had deliberately taken action to cause a patient's death. Another survey of medical practitioners, published in 1993, found that nearly half the attending physicians and nurses and 70 percent of the resident physicians surveyed said they had acted against their own convictions by ignoring requests from terminally ill patients to withhold life support.

Another prominent ethical issue in recent years has involved the questions of whether and under what circumstances life-support for comatose patients with no apparent hope of recovery could be discontinued. The Supreme Court heard its first ever "right-to-die" case on Dec. 6, 1989. *Cruzan v. Missouri Dept. of Health* concerned Nancy Beth Cruzan, 32, who had been unconscious since Jan. 1983, after a car accident. Her parents and a guardian appointed to represent her sought to stop the medical treatment sustaining her in a "persistent vegetative state." On June 25, 1990, the Supreme Court, in a 5-4 ruling, interpreted the 14th Amendment as conferring on patients a right to refuse life-sustaining treatment, but it held that in the case of comatose patients a state could, as Missouri did, require that "clear and convincing" evidence about the patient's previous wishes regarding life-sustaining treatment be presented before such care could be withdrawn. (Since the state courts had found that there was not "clear and convincing" evidence, the Cruzans' request to withdraw their daughter's feeding tube was denied. However, after the family presented further evidence in a new state court proceeding, removal of the feeding tube was permitted, and Nancy Cruzan died in Dec. 1990.)

As of Jan. 1988, hospitals are required by the Joint Commission on Accreditation of Health Care Organizations to have formal policies specifying when doctors and nurses can refrain from trying to resuscitate terminally ill patients. The policy must be developed in consultation with the medical staff and the nursing staff, adopted by the medical staff, and then approved by the hospital's governing body. The policy must define the roles of physicians, nursing personnel, and members of the patient's family in any decision to withhold resuscitation. It must also include "provisions designed to assure that a patient's rights are respected."

In March 1986, the American Medical Association announced that it would be ethical for doctors to withhold "all means of life prolonging medical treatment," including food and water, from permanently unconscious patients even if death was not imminent. The withholding of such therapy should occur only when a patient's unconscious state "is beyond doubt irreversible and there are adequate safeguards to confirm the accuracy of the diagnosis," the association's judicial council said.

In June 1991, the AMA adopted 2 reports of its Council on Ethical and Judicial Affairs dealing with refusal of life-prolonging treatment when patients are incurably ill. The first, "Decisions Near the End of Life," concluded: "the principle of patient autonomy requires that physicians must respect the decision to forego life-sustaining treatment of a patient who possesses decisionmaking capacity." Life-sustaining treatment was defined as "any treatment that serves to prolong life without reversing the underlying medical condition," including "mechanical ventilation, renal dialysis, chemotherapy, antibiotics and artificial nutrition and hydration." The Council also reaffirmed its position that "physicians must not perform euthanasia or participate in assisted suicide." The second report, "Decisions to Forego Life-Sustaining Treatment for Incompetent Patients," encouraged the use of advance directives (living wills and the designation of durable power of attorney) by persons to ensure that their interests will be promoted in the event that they become incompetent. When there is no advance directive designating a proxy decisionmaker, the Council concluded, the patient's family should become the surrogate decisionmaker. Family was defined as "persons with whom the patient is closely associated." Surrogate decisionmakers should consider the patient's previous values and preferences and base decisions on what the patient would have likely decided had he or she been competent. When this is not possible, decisions should be based on what would objectively be in the best interests of the patient. The Council encouraged the establishment and use of ethics committees designed to facilitate sound decisionmaking.

A number of states have "living will" statutes that set out a procedure for a mentally competent person to declare that he or she does not wish to be subjected to a "death-prolonging" procedure. In Oct. 1990, Congress passed the Patient Self-Determination Act, which took effect in December 1991. The Act requires health care facilities that receive funds from Medicare or Medicaid to provide written information to all patients about advance directives and patients' rights under their state laws and document whether or not a patient has an advance directive. Information on living wills and health-care powers of attorney can be obtained from the American Bar Association's Commission on Legal Problems of the Elderly.

Estimated New Cancer Cases and Deaths by Sex for Leading Sites, 1993*

Source: American Cancer Society

Estimated New Cases

Total		Women		Men	
All Sites	**1,170,000**	**All Sites**	**570,000**	**All Sites**	**600,000**
Breast	183,000	Breast	182,000	Prostate	165,000
Lung	170,000	Colorectal	75,000	Lung	100,000
Prostate	165,000	Lung	70,000	Colorectal	77,000
Colorectal	152,000	Uterus	44,500	Bladder	39,000
Bladder	52,300	Lymphoma	22,400	Lymphoma	28,500

Estimated Deaths

Total		Women		Men	
All Sites	**526,000**	**All Sites**	**249,000**	**All Sites**	**277,000**
Lung	149,000	Lung	56,000	Lung	93,000
Colorectal	57,000	Breast	46,000	Prostate	35,000
Breast	46,300	Colorectal	28,200	Colorectal	28,800
Prostate	35,000	Ovary	13,300	Pancreas	12,000
Pancreas	25,000	Pancreas	13,000	Lymphoma	11,500

***Note:** The estimates of new cancer cases are offered as a rough guide and should not be regarded as definitive. About 700,000 basal and squamous cell skin cancers and 100,000 carcinoma in situ cases are not included in the totals.

Cancer Prevention

Source: American Cancer Society

PRIMARY PREVENTION: steps that can be taken to avoid those factors that might lead to the development of cancer.

Smoking Cigarette smoking is responsible for 90% of lung cancer cases among men, 79% among women—about 87% overall. Smoking accounts for about 30% of all cancer deaths. Those who smoke two or more packs of cigarettes a day have lung cancer mortality rates 15-25 times greater than nonsmokers.

Nutrition Risk for colon, breast, and uterine cancers increases in obese people. High-fat diets may contribute to the development of cancers of the breast, colon, and prostate. High-fiber foods may help reduce risk of colon cancer. A varied diet containing plenty of vegetables and fruits rich in vitamins A and C may reduce risk for many cancers. Salt-cured, smoked, and nitrite-cured foods have been linked to esophageal and stomach cancer.

Sunlight Almost all of the more than 700,000 cases of non-melanoma skin cancer diagnosed each year in the U.S. are sun-related. Epidemiological evidence shows that sun exposure is a major factor in the development of melanoma, and the incidence increases for those living near the equator.

Alcohol Oral cancer and cancers of the larynx, throat, esophagus, and liver occur more frequently among heavy drinkers of alcohol, especially when accompanied by cigarette smoking or use of chewing tobacco.

Smokeless Tobacco Use of chewing tobacco or snuff increases risk of cancers of the mouth, larynx, throat, and esophagus.

Estrogen Estrogen treatment to control menopausal symptoms can increase risk of endometrial cancer. However, including progesterone in estrogen replacement therapy helps to minimize this risk. Use of estrogen by menopausal women needs careful discussion by the woman and her physician, while research continues.

Radiation Excessive exposure to ionizing radiation can increase cancer risk. Most medical and dental X rays are adjusted to deliver the lowest dose possible without sacrificing image quality. Excessive radon exposure in the home may increase lung cancer risk, especially in cigarette smokers. If levels are found to be too high, remedial actions should be taken.

Occupational Hazards Exposure to several different industrial agents (including nickel, chromate, asbestos, and vinyl chloride) increases risk of various cancers. Risk of lung cancer from asbestos is greatly increased when combined with smoking.

SECONDARY PREVENTION: steps to be taken to diagnose a cancer or precursor as early as possible after it has developed.

Colorectal Tests The ACS recommends 3 tests for the early detection of colon and rectum cancer in people without symptoms: The digital rectal examination performed by a physician during an office visit, every year after the age of 40; the stool blood test, every year after 50; and the proctosigmoidoscopy examination, every 3 to 5 years, based on the advice of a physician.

Pap Test For cervical cancer, women who are or have been sexually active, or have reached 18 years, should have an annual Pap test and pelvic examination. After a woman has had 3 or more consecutive satisfactory normal exams, the Pap test may be performed less frequently at the discretion of her physician.

Breast Cancer Detection The ACS recommends monthly breast self-examination by women 20 years and older. Examination of the breast by a health care professional should be done every 3 years from ages 20 to 40 and then every year. The ACS recommends a mammogram every year for asymptomatic women age 50 and over. Women age 40-49 should have mammography every 1-2 years, depending on physical and mammographic findings.

Some Benefits of Quitting Smoking

Source: American Cancer Society; U.S. Centers for Disease Control and Prevention

Within 20 Minutes
- Blood pressure drops to normal
- Pulse rate drops to normal
- Body temperature of hands and feet increases to normal

Within 8 Hours
- Carbon monoxide level in blood drops to normal
- Oxygen level in blood increases to normal

Within 24 Hours
- Chance of heart attack decreases

Within 48 Hours
- Nerve endings start regrowing
- Ability to smell and taste is enhanced

Within 2 Weeks to 3 Months
- Circulation improves
- Walking becomes easier
- Lung function increases up to 30 percent

Within 1 to 9 Months
- Coughing, sinus congestion, fatigue, shortness of breath decrease
- Cilia regrow in lungs, increasing ability to handle mucus, clean the lungs, reduce infection
- Body's overall energy increases

Within 1 Year
- Excess risk of coronary heart disease is half that of a smoker

Within 5 Years
- Lung cancer death rate for average former smoker (one pack a day) decreases by almost half
- Stroke risk is reduced to that of a nonsmoker 5-15 years after quitting
- Risk of cancer of the mouth, throat, and esophagus is half that of a smoker's

Within 10 Years
- Lung cancer death rate similar to that of nonsmokers
- Precancerous cells are replaced
- Risk of cancer of the mouth, throat, esophagus, bladder, kidney, and pancreas decreases

Within 15 Years
- Risk of coronary heart disease is that of a nonsmoker

Cancer Death Rates by Site, U.S., 1930-1989

Source: American Cancer Society; rates adjusted to 1970 population

Females

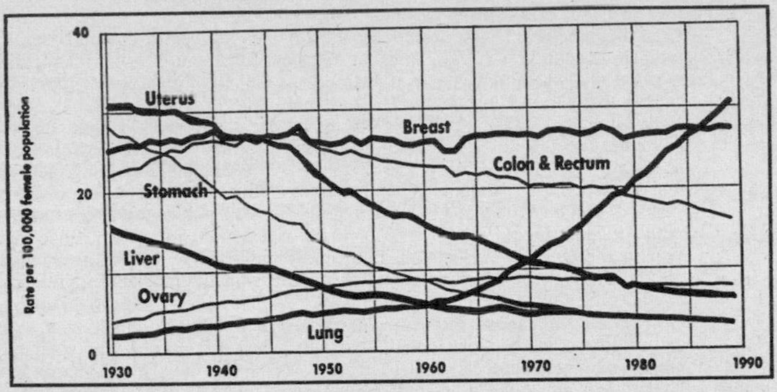

Males

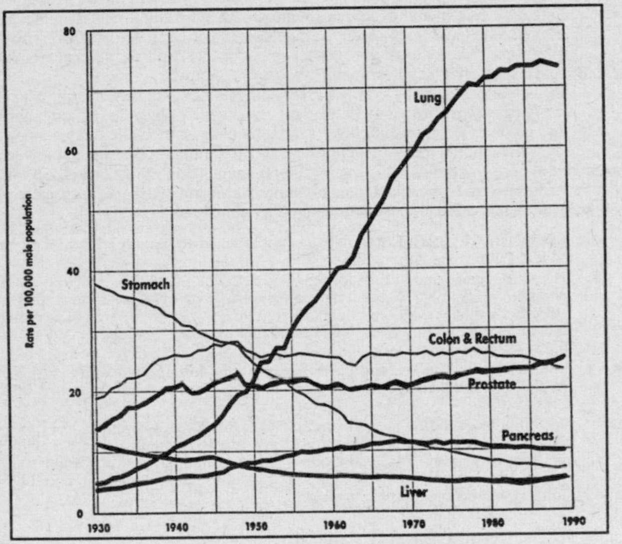

Cancer's 7 Warning Signals*

Source: American Cancer Society

1. A change in bowel or bladder habits.
2. A sore that does not heal.
3. Unusual bleeding or discharge.
4. Thickening or lump in breast or elsewhere.
5. Indigestion or difficulty in swallowing.
6. Obvious change in wart or mole.
7. Nagging cough or hoarseness.

* If you have a warning signal, see your doctor.

Heart and Blood Vessel Disease

Source: American Heart Association, Dallas

Warning Signs

Of Heart Attack

- Uncomfortable pressure, fullness, squeezing, or pain in the center of the chest lasting two minutes or longer
- Pain may radiate to the shoulder, arm, neck, or jaw
- Sweating may accompany pain or discomfort
- Nausea and vomiting may also occur
- Shortness of breath, dizziness, or fainting may accompany other signs

The American Heart Association advises immediate action at the onset of these symptoms. The Association points out that more than half of heart attack victims die before they reach the hospital and that the average victim waits 2 hours before seeking help.

Of Stroke

- Sudden temporary weakness or numbness of face or limbs on one side of the body
- Temporary loss of speech, or trouble speaking or understanding speech
- Temporary dim or lost vision, especially in one eye
- Unexplained dizziness, unsteadiness, or sudden falls

Some Major Risk Factors

Blood pressure—High blood pressure increases the risk of stroke, heart attack, kidney failure, and congestive heart failure.

Cholesterol—A blood cholesterol level over 240 mg/dl (milligrams of cholesterol per deciliter of blood) approximately doubles the risk of coronary heart disease; about 25% of the U.S. adult population falls into this category. Blood cholesterol levels between 200 and 240 mg/dl are in a zone of moderate and increasing risk. An estimated 26.1 mln. (36%) of youths age 19 and under have levels of 170 mg/dl or higher, comparable to a level of 200 mg/dl in adults.

Cigarettes—Cigarette smokers have more than twice the risk of heart attack and 2-4 times the risk of sudden cardiac death as nonsmokers. Young smokers have a higher risk for early death from stroke.

Obesity—47 mln. adults are 20% or more over their desirable weight. (24.4% of white males, 25.7% of black males, 25.1% of white females, 43.8% of black females.)

Cardiovascular Diseases Statistical Summary, 1991

Prevalence — 56,450,000 Americans had one or more forms of heart and blood vessel disease.
- high blood pressure — 50,000,000
- coronary heart disease — 6,300,000
- stroke — 3,020,000
- rheumatic heart disease — 1,340,000

Mortality — 923,422 in 1991 (42.7% of all deaths).
- Someone died from cardiovascular disease every 34 seconds in the U.S. in 1991.

Congenital or inborn heart defects —
- postnatal mortality from heart defects 5,800 in 1991.

Coronary heart disease (heart attack) — caused 478,530 deaths in 1991.
- 6,300,000 alive today have history of heart attack and/or angina pectoris.
- As many as 1,500,000 Americans had a heart attack in 1991, about one-third of them fatal.

Stroke — killed about 144,070 in 1991; afflicted 3,060,000.

Hypertension (high blood pressure) — afflicts 50,000,000 Americans age 6 and above.

Rheumatic heart disease — afflicted 1,340,000 in 1991.
- killed 6,020 in 1991.

Note: 1991 mortality data are estimates based on 1991 provisional data published by the National Center for Health Statistics.

Immunization Schedule for Children

Source: American Academy of Pediatrics, Aug. 3, 1993

By ensuring that your child gets immunized on schedule, you can provide the best defense against dangerous childhood diseases. Childhood immunization means protection from nine major diseases: hepatitis B, polio, measles, mumps, rubella (German measles), pertussis (whooping cough), diphtheria, tetanus (lockjaw), and *Haemophilus influenzae* type b (a bacterium that can cause such serious infections as meningitis and pneumonia).

For the best possible protection against diphtheria, tetanus, and pertussis, your child needs a series of five shots of the combination diphtheria-tetanus-pertussis (DTP) vaccine. The first four doses should be given at 2, 4, 6, and 15 to 18 months of age, with a final booster dose given before school entry (4 to 6 years). For the fourth and fifth dose, the acellular (DTaP) vaccine may be substituted for the DTP vaccine.

For protection against polio, your child needs a series of four oral polio vaccine doses, the first three at 2, 4, and 15 to 18 months and the final dose before school entry (4 to 6 years).

To be completely protected against hepatitis B, your child needs to be vaccinated with a series of three hepatitis B virus (HBV) vaccine shots. The American Academy of Pediatrics recommends that these immunizations be given at birth, at 1 to 2 months, and at 6 to 18 months of age. In some cases your pediatrician may decide to begin the 3-dose schedule after your baby has left the hospital.

Several vaccines are available for protection against *Haemophilus influenzae* type b (Hib). However, only two vaccines—HbOC and PRP-OMP—are approved for children under 15 months of age. The Academy recommends that your child receive either the HbOC vaccine at 2, 4, and 6 months of age, with a final dose at 12 to 15 months or the PRP-OMP vaccine at 2 and 4 months, with a final dose at 12 to 15 months.

At 15 months, your child should have an immunization for measles, mumps, and rubella (MMR). A second MMR vaccination, primarily to boost measles and mumps immunity, should be given to children 11 to 12 years or older who have not had measles. If there is a measles outbreak in your community or if you live in a high-risk area, the MMR booster may be given just before kindergarten or at an earlier age.

If you do not have a pediatrician, call your local public health department. It usually has supplies of vaccine and may give immunizations free.

	DTP[1]	Polio	Hepatitis B[2]	Measles[3]	Mumps[3]	Rubella[3]	Hib[4]	Tetanus-Diphtheria
Birth			X					
1-2 months			X					
2 months	X	X					X	
4 months	X	X					X	
6 months	X						X	
6-18 months			X					
12-15 months							X	
15 months				X	X	X		
15-18 months	X	X						
4-6 years	X	X						
11-12 years				X	X	X		
14-16 years								X

(1) For the fourth and fifth doses, the acellular (DTaP) pertussis vaccine may be substituted for the DTP vaccine. (2) Infants of mothers with positive blood tests for hepatitis B must receive hepatitis B immune globulin (HBIG) at or shortly after the first dose. These infants will also require a second hepatitis B vaccine dose at 1 month and a third hepatitis B vaccine injection at 6 months of age. (3) Combined MMR vaccine. Second dose at 11-12 years except where public health authorities require otherwise. (4) The 6-month dose depends on the type of *Haemophilus influenzae* type b vaccine given previously.

Drug Use: America's Students

Source: National Institute on Drug Abuse/Univ. of Michigan Inst. for Social Research

The long-term decline in the use of a number of drugs among 12th-graders continued in 1992, according to the report of the 18th national survey of American high school seniors. However, some results of the 2nd annual national survey of 8th-graders and 10th-graders were interpreted as warning signals: there were modest but statistically significant increases in 8th-graders' use of marijuana, cocaine, crack, LSD, other hallucinogens, stimulants, and inhalants. Researchers expressed concern that the newest wave of adolescents entering the teen years could be at the vanguard of a reversal of previously improving conditions, with LSD possibly a prime example of "generational forgetting."

Cigarette smoking remained quite high among all 3 grade levels in 1992: 16 percent of 8th-graders, 22 percent of 10th-graders, and 28 percent of 12th-graders reported having smoked during the 30 days before they responded to the survey. Eighth-graders showed some modest, but not statistically significant, increases in alcohol use.

Although the surveys missed the 15 to 20 percent of a class group that drops out of school early, investigators said there was little reason to believe trends would differ among this group, although it would undoubtedly have higher rates of use overall.

In 1992, around 17,000 seniors in 135 public and private high schools participated in the survey, along with 15,000 10th-graders in 125 schools and 18,000 8th-graders in 160 schools.

A separate 1992 survey of 1,500 college students found that the long-term decline in illicit drug use by such students had halted. It was found that 30.6 percent of the college students used some illicit drugs at least once in the prior 12 months—a slight increase over the 29.2 percent figure for 1991. The change was attributed largely to an increase in the percentage of college students using marijuana, for which use rose from 26 percent to 27 percent. One in every eight college students (13 percent) reported using an illicit drug other than marijuana, representing virtually no change from 1991. However, the use of one class of illicit drugs did rise: hallucinogen use rose among college students for the third year in a row. In 1989, 5.1 percent reported using a hallucinogen; by 1992, 6.8 percent reported such use. LSD use accounted for most or all of this increase, rising from 3.4 percent to 5.7 percent between 1989 and 1992. Cocaine's popularity continued to decline, with use dropping from 3.6 percent of college students surveyed in 1991 to 3 percent of the 1992 students. Crack, stimulants, barbiturates, tranquilizers, inhalants, heroin, opiates other than heroine, and other illicitly used drugs showed little or no further decline in active use among college students in 1992, although a number of them had been declining previously.

Drug Use: America's High School Seniors

	Percent ever used										
	Class of 1975	Class of 1980	Class of 1985	Class of 1986	Class of 1987	Class of 1988	Class of 1989	Class of 1990	Class of 1991	Class of 1992	'91-'92 change
Marijuana/Hashish	47.3	60.3	54.2	50.9	50.2	47.2	43.7	40.7	36.7	32.6	−4.1sss
Inhalants	NA	11.9	15.4	15.9	17.0	16.7	17.6	18.0	17.6	16.6	−1.0
Inhalants Adjusted[1]	NA	17.6	18.1	20.1	18.6	17.5	18.6	18.5	18.0	17.0	−1.0
Amyl & Butyl Nitrites	NA	11.1	7.9	8.6	4.7	3.2	3.3	2.1	1.6	1.5	−0.1
Hallucinogens	16.3	13.3	10.3	9.7	10.3	8.9	9.4	9.4	9.6	9.2	−0.4
Hallucinogens Adjusted[2]	NA	15.7	12.1	11.9	10.6	9.2	9.9	9.7	10.0	9.4	−0.6
LSD	11.3	9.3	7.5	7.2	8.4	7.7	8.3	8.7	8.8	8.6	−0.2
PCP	NA	9.6	4.9	4.8	3.0	2.9	3.9	2.8	2.9	2.4	−0.5
Cocaine	9.0	15.7	17.3	16.9[5]	15.2	12.1	10.3	9.4	7.8	6.1	−1.7ss
"Crack"	NA	NA	NA	NA	5.6	4.8	4.7	3.5	3.1	2.6	−0.5
Heroin	2.2	1.1	1.2	1.1	1.2	1.1	1.3	1.3	0.9	1.2	+0.3
Other opiates[3]	9.0	9.8	10.2	9.0	9.2	8.6	8.3	8.3	6.6	6.1	−0.5
Stimulants Adjusted[3,4]	NA	NA	26.2	23.4	21.6	19.8	19.1	17.5	15.4	13.9	−1.5s
Sedatives[3]	18.2	14.9	11.8	10.4	8.7	7.8	7.4	5.3	6.7	6.1	−0.6
Barbiturates[3]	16.9	11.0	9.2	8.4	7.4	6.7	6.5	6.8	6.2	5.5	−0.7
Methaqualone[3]	8.1	9.5	6.7	5.2	4.0	3.3	2.7	2.3	1.3	1.6	+0.3
Tranquilizers[3]	17.0	15.2	11.9	10.9	10.9	9.4	7.6	7.2	7.2	6.0	−1.2s
Alcohol	90.4	93.2	92.2	91.3	92.2	92.0	90.7	89.5	88.0	87.5	−0.5
Cigarettes	73.6	71.0	68.8	67.6	67.2	66.4	65.7	64.4	63.1	61.8	−1.3

NA=Not available. Level of significance between the two most recent classes: s=.05, ss=.01, sss=.001. (1) Adjusted for underreporting of amyl and butyl nitrites. (2) Adjusted for underreporting of PCP. (3) Only drug use that was not under a doctor's orders. (4) Adjusted for overreporting of the nonprescription stimulants. (5) In 1986, three-fourths of those who used cocaine used it in powder form; the remainder used the "crack" form.

Drug Use in the General U.S. Population

According to the National Institute on Drug Abuse (NIDA) 1991 National Household Survey on Drug Abuse, 75.4 million (37% of) Americans age 12 and older reported some use of an illicit drug at least once during their lifetimes, 12.8% reported use during the previous year, and 6.2% reported use in the month before the survey was conducted.

For those age 25 and under, an estimated 2.5 million reported using cocaine (including crack), and 9 million reported using marijuana at least once within the previous year. For those age 26 and over, 3.9 million reported using cocaine (including crack), and 10.5 million reported using marijuana at least once within the previous year.

The NIDA Drug Abuse Warning Network reported an estimated 400,000 admissions to hospital emergency rooms nationwide that involved drug abuse in 1991. A total of 6,601 drug-abuse related deaths were reported in 1991 by 130 medical examiners in 27 metropolitan areas.

Federal Drug Control Budget

Federal spending on drug control programs increased from $1.7 billion in fiscal 1982 to $12 billion in fiscal 1992, according to the Office of Natl. Drug Control Policy.

Basic First Aid

First aid experts stress that knowing what to do for an injured person until a doctor or trained person gets to an accident scene can save a life, especially in cases of stoppage of breath, severe bleeding, and shock.

People with special medical problems, such as diabetes, cardiovascular disease, epilepsy, or allergy, are also urged to wear some sort of emblem identifying it, as a safeguard against use of medication that might be injurious or fatal in an emergency. Emblems may be obtained from Medic Alert Foundation, Turlock, CA 95380.

Most accidents occur in homes. National Safety Council figures show that home accidents exceed those in other locations, such as in cars, at work, or in public places.

In all cases, get medical assistance as soon as possible.

Animal bite — Wound should be washed with soap under running water and animal should be caught alive for rabies test.

Asphyxiation — Start mouth-to-mouth resuscitation immediately after getting patient to fresh air.

Bleeding — Elevate the wound above the heart if possible. Press hard on wound with sterile compress until bleeding stops. Send for doctor if it is severe.

Burn — If mild, with skin unbroken and no blisters, plunge into ice water until pain subsides. Apply a dry dressing if necessary. Send for physician if burn is severe. Apply sterile compresses and keep patient quiet and comfortably warm until doctor's arrival. Do not try to clean burn, or to break blisters.

Chemical in eye — With patient lying down, pour cupsful of water immediately into corner of eye, letting it run to other side to remove chemicals thoroughly. Cover with sterile compress. Get medical attention immediately .

Choking — Do not use back slaps to dislodge obstruction. (See **Abdominal Thrust**)

Convulsions — Place person on back on bed or rug. Loosen clothing. Turn head to side. Do not place a blunt object between the victim's teeth. If convulsions do not stop, get medical attention immediately.

Cut (minor) — Apply mild antiseptic and sterile compress after washing with soap under warm running water.

Drowning — (See **Mouth-to-Mouth Resuscitation**) Artificial breathing must be started at once, before victim is out of the water, if possible. If the victim's stomach is bloated with water, put victim on stomach, place hands under stomach, and lift. If no pulse is felt, begin cardio-pulmonary resuscitation. This should only be done by those professionally trained. If necessary, treat for shock. (See **Shock**)

Electric shock — If possible, turn off power. Don't touch victim until contact is broken; pull him from contact with electrical source using rope, wooden pole, or loop of dry cloth. Start mouth-to-mouth resuscitation if breathing has stopped.

Foreign body in eye — Touch object with moistened corner of handkerchief if it can be seen. If it cannot be seen or does not come out after a few attempts, take patient to doctor. Do not rub eye.

Fainting — If victim feels faint, lower head to knees. Lay him down with head turned to side if he becomes unconscious. Loosen clothing and open windows. Keep patient lying quietly for at least 15 minutes after he regains consciousness. Call doctor if faint lasts for more than a few minutes.

Fall — Send for physician if patient has continued pain. Cover wound with sterile dressing and stop any severe bleeding. Do not move patient unless absolutely necessary — as in case of fire — if broken bone is suspected. Keep patient warm and comfortable.

Loss of Limb — If a limb is severed, it is important to properly protect the limb so that it can possibly be reattached to the victim. After the victim is cared for, the limb should be placed in a clean plastic bag, garbage can, or other suitable container. Pack ice around the limb on the OUTSIDE of the bag to keep the limb cold. Call ahead to the hospital to alert them of the situation.

Poisoning — Call doctor. Use antidote listed on label if container is found. Call local Poison Control Center if possible. Except for lye, other caustics, and petroleum products, induce vomiting unless victim is unconscious. Give milk if poison or antidote is unknown.

Shock (injury-related) — Keep the victim lying down; if uncertain as to his injuries, keep him flat on his back. Maintain the victim's normal body temperature; if the weather is cold or damp, place blankets or extra clothing over and under the victim; if weather is hot, provide shade.

Snakebite — Immediately get victim to a hospital. If there is mild swelling or pain, apply a constricting band 2 to 4 inches above the bite.

Sting from insect — If possible, remove stinger and apply solution of ammonia and water, or paste of baking soda. Call physician immediately if body swells or patient collapses.

Unconsciousness — Send for doctor and place person on his back. Start resuscitation if he stops breathing. Never give food or liquids to an unconscious person.

Abdominal Thrust

The American Red Cross and the American Heart Association both agree that the recommended first aid for choking victims is the abdominal thrust, also known as the Heimlich maneuver, after its creator, Dr. Henry Heimlich. Slaps on the back are no longer advised and may even prove detrimental in an attempt to assist a choking victim.

- Get behind the victim and wrap your arms around him above his waist.
- Make a fist with one hand and place it, with the thumb knuckle pressing inward, just below the point of the "v" of the rib cage.
- Grasp the wrist with the other hand and give one or more upward thrusts or hugs.
- Start mouth-to-mouth resuscitation if breathing stops.

Mouth-to-Mouth Resuscitation

Stressing that your breath can save a life, the American Red Cross gives the following directions for mouth-to-mouth resuscitation if the victim is not breathing:

- Determine consciousness by tapping the victim on the shoulder and asking loudly, "Are you okay?"
- Tilt the victim's head back so that his chin is pointing upward. Do not press on the soft tissue under the chin, as this might obstruct the airway. If you suspect that an accident victim might have neck or back injuries, open the airway by placing the tips of your index and middle fingers on the corners of the victim's jaw to lift it forward without tilting the head.
- Place your cheek and ear close to the victim's mouth and nose. Look at the victim's chest to see if it rises and falls. Listen and feel for air to be exhaled for about 5 seconds.
- If there is no breathing, pinch the victim's nostrils shut with the thumb and index finger of your hand that is pressing on the victim's forehead. Another way to prevent leakage of air when the lungs are inflated is to press your cheek against the victim's nose.
- Blow air into victim's mouth by taking a deep breath and then sealing your mouth tightly around the victim's mouth. Initially, give two, quick (approx. 1.5 seconds each), full breaths without allowing the lungs to deflate completely between each breath.
- Watch the victim's chest to see if it rises.
- Stop blowing when the victim's chest is expanded. Raise your mouth; turn your head to the side and listen for exhalation.
- Watch the chest to see if it falls.
- Repeat the blowing cycle until the victim starts breathing.

Note: Infants (up to one year) and children (1 to 8 years) should be administered mouth-to-mouth resuscitation as described above, except for the following:

- Do not tilt the head as far back as an adult's head.
- Both the mouth and nose of the infant should be sealed by the mouth.
- Give breaths to a child once every four seconds.
- Blow into the infant's mouth and nose once every three seconds with less pressure and volume than for a child.

Nutritive Value of Food (Calories, Proteins, etc.)

Source: Home and Garden Bulletin No. 72; available from Supt. of Documents, U. S. Government Printing Office, Washington, DC 20402

Food	Measure	Grams	Food Energy (calories)	Protein (grams)	Fat (grams)	Saturated fats (grams)	Carbohydrate (grams)	Calcium (milligrams)	Iron (milligrams)	Vitamin A (I.U.)	Thiamin (milligrams)	Riboflavin (milligrams)
Dairy products												
Cheese, cheddar	1 oz.	28	115	7	9	6.1	T	204	.2	300	.01	.11
Cheese, cottage, small curd	1 cup	210	220	26	9	6.0	6	126	.3	340	.04	.34
Cheese, cream	1 oz.	28	100	2	10	6.2	1	23	.3	400	T	.06
Cheese, Swiss	1 oz.	28	105	8	8	5.0	1	272	T	240	.01	.10
Half-and-Half	1 tbsp.	15	20	T	2	1.1	1	16	T	20	.01	.02
Cream, sour	1 tbsp.	15	25	T	3	1.6	1	14	T	90	T	.02
Milk, whole	1 cup	244	150	8	8	5.1	11	291	.1	310	.09	.40
Milk, nonfat (skim)	1 cup	244	85	8	T	.3	12	302	.1	500	.09	.37
Milkshake, chocolate	10.6 oz.	300	355	9	8	5.0	63	396	.9	260	.14	.67
Ice Cream, hardened	1 cup	133	270	5	14	8.9	32	176	.1	540	.05	.33
Sherbet	1 cup	193	270	2	4	2.4	59	103	.3	190	.03	.09
Yogurt, fruit-flavored	8 oz.	227	230	10	3	1.8	42	343	.2	120	.08	.40
Eggs												
Fried in butter	1	46	85	5	6	2.4	1	26	.9	290	.03	.13
Hard-cooked	1	50	80	6	6	1.7	1	28	1.0	260	.04	.14
Scrambled in butter (milk added)	1	64	95	6	7	2.8	1	47	.9	310	.04	.16
Fats & oils												
Butter	1 tbsp.	14	100	T	12	7.2	T	3	T	430	T	T
Margarine	1 tbsp.	14	100	T	12	2.1	T	3	T	470	T	T
Salad dressing, blue cheese	1 tbsp.	15	75	1	8	1.6	1	12	T	30	T	.02
Salad dressing, French	1 tbsp.	16	65	T	6	1.1	3	2	1	—	—	—
Salad dressing, Italian	1 tbsp.	15	85	T	9	1.6	1	2	T	T	T	T
Mayonnaise	1 tbsp.	14	100	T	11	2.0	T	3	.1	40	T	.01
Meat, poultry, fish												
Bluefish, baked with butter or margarine	3 oz.	85	135	22	4	—	0	25	0.6	40	.09	.08
Clams, raw, meat only	3 oz.	85	65	11	1	—	2	59	5.2	90	.08	.15
Crabmeat, white or king, canned	1 cup	135	135	24	3	.6	1	61	1.1	—	.11	.11
Fish sticks, breaded, cooked, frozen	1 oz.	28	50	5	3	—	2	3	.1	0	.01	.02
Salmon, pink, canned	3 oz.	85	120	17	5	.9	0	167	.7	60	.03	.16
Sardines, Atlantic, canned in oil	3 oz.	85	175	20	9	3.0	0	372	2.5	190	.02	.17
Shrimp, French fried	3 oz.	85	190	17	9	2.3	9	61	1.7	—	.03	.07
Tuna, canned in oil	3 oz.	85	170	24	7	1.7	0	7	1.6	70	.04	.10
Bacon, broiled or fried crisp	2 slices	15	85	4	8	2.5	T	2	.5	0	.08	.05
Ground beef, broiled, 10% fat	3 oz.	85	185	23	10	4.0	0	10	3.0	20	.08	.20
Roast beef, relatively lean	3 oz.	85	165	25	7	2.8	0	11	3.2	10	.06	.19
Beef steak, lean and fat	3 oz.	85	330	20	27	11.3	0	9	2.5	50	.05	.15
Beef & vegetable stew	1 cup	245	220	16	11	4.9	15	29	2.9	2,400	.15	.17
Lamb, chop, lean and fat	3.1 oz.	89	360	18	32	14.8	0	8	1.0	—	.11	.19
Liver, beef	3 oz.	85	195	22	9	2.5	5	9	7.5	45,390	.22	3.56
Ham, light cure, lean and fat	3 oz.	85	245	18	19	6.8	0	8	2.2	0	.40	.15
Pork, chop, lean and fat	2.7 oz	78	305	19	25	8.9	0	9	2.7	0	.75	.22
Bologna	1 slice	28	85	3	8	3.0	T	2	.5	—	.05	.06
Frankfurter, cooked	1	56	170	7	15	5.6	1	3	.8	—	.08	.11
Sausage, pork link, cooked	1 link	13	60	2	6	2.1	T	1	.3	0	.10	.04
Veal, cutlet, braised or boiled	3 oz.	85	185	23	9	4.0	0	9	2.7	—	.06	.21
Chicken, drumstick, fried, bones removed	1.3 oz.	38	90	12	4	1.1	T	6	.9	50	.03	.15
Chicken, half broiler, broiled, bones removed	6.2 oz.	176	240	42	7	2.2	0	16	3.0	160	.09	.34
Fruits & products												
Apple, raw, 2-3/4 in. diam.	1	138	80	T	1	—	20	10	.4	120	.04	.03
Applejuice	1 cup	248	120	T	T	—	30	15	1.5	—	.02	.05
Apricots, raw	3	107	55	1	T	—	14	18	.5	2,890	.03	.04
Banana, raw	1	119	100	1	T	—	26	10	.8	230	.06	.07
Cherries, sweet, raw	10	68	45	1	T	—	12	15	.3	70	.03	.04
Fruit cocktail, canned, in heavy syrup	1 cup	255	195	1	T	—	50	23	1.0	360	.05	.03
Grapefruit, raw, medium, white	1/2	241	45	1	T	—	12	19	.5	10	.05	.02
Grapes, Thompson seedless	10	50	35	T	T	—	9	6	.2	50	.03	.02
Lemonade, frozen, diluted	1 cup	248	105	T	T	—	28	2	.1	10	.01	.02
Cantaloupe, 5-in. diam.	1/2	477	80	2	T	—	20	38	1.1	9,240	.11	.08
Orange, 2-5/8 in. diam.	1	131	65	1	T	—	16	54	.5	260	.13	.05
Orange juice, frozen, diluted	1 cup	249	120	2	T	—	29	25	.2	540	.23	.03
Peach, raw, 2-1/2 in. diam.	1	100	40	1	T	—	10	9	.5	1,330	.02	.05
Raisins, seedless	1 cup	145	420	4	T	—	112	90	5.1	30	.16	.12
Strawberries, whole	1 cup	149	55	1	1	—	13	31	1.5	90	.04	.10
Watermelon, 4 by 8 in. wedge	1 wedge	926	110	2	1	—	27	30	2.1	2,510	.13	.13
Grain products												
Bagel, egg	1	55	165	6	2	.5	28	9	1.2	30	.14	.10
Biscuit, 2 in. diam., from home recipe	1	28	105	2	5	1.2	13	34	.4	T	.08	.08
Bread, white, enriched, soft-crumb	1 slice	25	70	2	1	.2	13	21	.6	T	.10	.06
Bread, whole wheat, soft-crumb	1 slice	28	65	3	1	.1	14	24	.8	T	.09	.03
Oatmeal or rolled oats	1 cup	240	130	5	2	.4	23	22	1.4	0	.19	.05
Bran flakes (40% bran), added sugar, salt, iron, vitamins	1 cup	35	105	4	1	—	28	19	12.4	1,650	.41	.49
Corn flakes, added sugar, salt, iron, vitamins	1 cup	25	95	2	T	—	21	*	0.6	1,180	.29	.35
Rice, puffed, added iron, thiamin, niacin	1 cup	15	60	1	T	—	13	3	.3	0	.07	.01
Wheat, shredded, plain, 1 biscuit or 1/2 cup	1 serving	25	90	2	1	—	20	11	.9	0	.06	.03
Cake, angel food, 1/12 of cake	1	53	135	3	T	—	32	50	.2	0	.03	.08
Cupcake, 2-1/2 in. diam., with chocolate icing	1	36	130	2	5	2.0	21	47	.4	60	.05	.06
Boston cream pie with custard filling, 1/12 of cake	1	69	210	3	6	1.9	34	46	.7	140	.09	.11
Fruitcake, dark, 1/30 of loaf	1	15	55	1	2	.5	9	11	.4	20	.02	.02
Cake, pound, 1/17 of loaf	1	33	160	2	10	2.5	16	6	.5	80	.05	.06
Brownies, with nuts, from commercial recipe	1	20	85	1	4	.9	13	9	.4	20	.03	.02
Cookies, chocolate chip, from home recipe	4	40	205	2	12	3.5	24	14	.8	40	.06	.06
Crackers, graham	2	14	55	1	1	.3	10	6	.5	0	.02	.08

Food	Measure	Grams	Food Energy (calories)	Protein (grams)	Fat (grams)	Saturated fats (grams)	Carbohydrate (grams)	Calcium (milligrams)	Iron (milligrams)	Vitamin A (I.U.)	Thiamin (milligrams)	Riboflavin (milligrams)
Crackers, saltines	4	11	50	1	1	.3	8	2	.5	0	.05	.05
Danish pastry, round piece	1	65	275	5	15	4.7	30	33	1.2	200	.18	.19
Doughnut, cake type	1	25	100	1	5	1.2	13	10	.4	20	.05	.05
Macaroni and cheese, from home recipe	1 cup	200	430	17	22	8.9	40	362	1.8	860	.20	.40
Muffin, corn	1	40	125	3	4	1.2	19	42	.7	120	.10	.10
Noodles, enriched, cooked	1 cup	160	200	7	2	—	37	16	1.4	110	.22	.13
Pie, apple, 1/7 of pie	1	135	345	3	15	3.9	51	11	.9	40	.15	.11
Pie, cherry, 1/7 of pie	1	135	350	4	15	4.0	52	19	.9	590	.16	.12
Pie, lemon meringue, 1/7 of pie	1	120	305	4	12	3.7	45	17	1.0	200	.09	.12
Pie, pecan, 1/7 of pie	1	118	495	6	27	4.0	61	55	3.7	190	.26	.14
Pizza, cheese, 1/8 of 12 in. diam. pie	1	60	145	6	4	1.7	22	86	1.1	230	.16	.18
Popcorn, popped, plain	1 cup	6	25	1	T	T	5	1	.2	—	—	.01
Pretzels, stick	10	3	10	T	T	—	2	1	T	0	.01	.01
Rolls, enriched, brown & serve	1	26	85	2	2	.4	14	20	.5	T	.10	.06
Rolls, frankfurter & hamburger	1	40	120	3	2	.5	21	30	.8	T	.16	.10
Spaghetti with meat balls & tomato sauce	1 cup	248	330	19	12	3.3	39	124	3.7	1,590	.25	.30
Legumes, nuts, seeds												
Beans, Great Northern, cooked	1 cup	180	210	14	1	—	38	90	4.9	0	.25	.13
Peanuts, roasted in oil, salted	1 cup	144	840	37	72	13.7	27	107	3.0	—	.46	.19
Peanut butter	1 tbsp.	16	95	4	8	1.5	3	9	.3	—	.02	.02
Sunflower seeds	1 cup	145	810	35	69	8.2	29	174	10.3	70	2.84	.33
Sugars & sweets												
Candy, caramels	1 oz.	28	115	1	3	1.6	22	42	.4	T	.01	.05
Candy, milk chocolate	1 oz.	28	145	2	9	5.5	16	65	.3	80	.02	.10
Fudge, chocolate	1 oz.	28	115	1	3	1.3	21	22	.3	T	.01	.03
Candy, hard	1 oz.	28	110	0	T	—	28	6	.5	0	0	0
Honey	1 tbsp.	21	65	T	0	0	17	1	.1	0	T	.01
ams & Preserves	1 tbsp.	20	55	T	T	—	14	4	.2	T	T	.01
ugar, white, granulated	1 tbsp.	12	45	0	0	0	12	0	T	0	0	0
Vegetables												
sparagus, canned, spears	4 spears	80	15	2	T	—	3	15	1.5	640	.05	.08
eans, green, from frozen, cuts	1 cup	135	35	2	T	—	8	54	.9	780	.09	.12
roccoli, cooked	1 stalk	180	45	6	1	—	8	158	1.4	4,500	.16	.36
abbage, raw, coarsely shredded or sliced	1 cup	70	15	1	T	—	4	34	.3	90	.04	.04
arrots, raw, 7-1/2 by 1-1/8 in.	1	72	30	1	T	—	7	27	.5	7,930	.04	.04
elery, raw	1 stalk	40	5	T	T	—	2	16	.1	110	.01	.01
ollards, cooked	1 cup	190	65	7	1	—	10	357	1.5	14,820	.21	.38
orn, sweet, cooked	1 ear	140	70	2	1	—	16	2	.5	310	.09	.08
ettuce, Iceberg, chopped	1 cup	55	5	T	T	—	2	11	.3	180	.03	.03
ushrooms, raw	1 cup	70	20	2	T	—	3	4	.6	T	.07	.32
nions, raw, chopped	1 cup	170	65	3	T	—	15	46	.9	T	.05	.07
eas, frozen, cooked	1 cup	160	110	8	T	—	19	30	3.0	960	.43	.14
otatoes, baked, peeled	1	156	145	4	T	—	33	14	1.1	T	.15	.07
otatoes, frozen, French fried	10	50	110	2	4	1.1	17	5	.9	T	.07	.01
otatoes, mashed, milk added	1 cup	210	135	4	2	.7	27	50	.8	40	.17	.11
otato chips	10	20	115	1	8	2.1	10	8	.4	T	.04	.01
otato salad	1 cup	250	250	7	7	2.0	41	80	1.5	350	.20	.18
pinach, chopped, from frozen	1 cup	205	45	6	1	—	8	232	4.3	16,200	.14	.31
weet potatoes, baked in skin, peeled	1	114	160	2	1	—	37	46	1.0	9,230	.10	.08
omatoes, raw	1	135	25	1	T	—	6	16	.6	1,110	.07	.05
Miscellaneous												
eer	12 fl. oz.	360	150	1	0	0	14	18	T	—	.01	.11
in, rum, vodka, whisky, 86 proof	1-1/2 fl. oz.	42	105	—	—	0	T	—	—	—	—	—
ine, table	3-1/2 fl. oz.	102	85	T	0	0	4	9	.4	—	T	.01
ola-type beverage	12 fl. oz.	369	145	0	0	0	37	—	—	0	0	0
inger ale	12 fl. oz	366	115	0	0	0	29	—	—	0	0	0
elatin dessert	1 cup	240	140	4	0	0	34	—	—	—	—	—
ives, pickled, green	4 medium	16	15	T	2	.2	T	8	.2	40	—	—
ckles, dill, whole	1	65	5	T	T	—	1	17	.7	70	T	.01
psicle, 3 fl. oz.	1	95	70	0	0	0	18	0	T	0	0	0
oup, tomato, prepared with water	1 cup	245	90	2	3	.5	16	15	.7	1,000	.05	.05

— Indicates trace * — Varies by brand

Recommended Weight Tables

Source: Metropolitan Life Insurance Co., 1983

Weights for people age 25-59 based on lowest mortality. Weight in lbs. according to frame (in indoor clothing weighing 5 lbs. for men, 3 lbs. for women). Heights include shoes with 1-inch heels.

Men: Height Feet	Men: Height Inches	Men: Small Frame	Men: Medium Frame	Men: Large Frame	Women: Height Feet	Women: Height Inches	Women: Small Frame	Women: Medium Frame	Women: Large Frame
5	2	128-134	131-141	138-150	4	10	102-111	109-121	118-131
5	3	130-136	133-143	140-153	4	11	103-113	111-123	120-134
5	4	132-138	135-145	142-156	5	0	104-115	113-126	122-137
5	5	134-140	137-148	144-160	5	1	106-118	115-129	125-140
5	6	136-142	139-151	146-164	5	2	108-121	118-132	128-143
5	7	138-145	142-154	149-168	5	3	111-124	121-135	131-147
5	8	140-148	145-157	152-172	5	4	114-127	124-138	134-151
5	9	142-151	148-160	155-176	5	5	117-130	127-141	137-155
5	10	144-154	151-163	158-180	5	6	120-133	130-144	140-159
5	11	146-157	154-166	161-184	5	7	123-136	133-147	143-163
6	0	149-160	157-170	164-188	5	8	126-139	136-150	146-167
6	1	152-164	160-174	168-192	5	9	129-142	139-153	149-170
6	2	155-168	164-178	172-197	5	10	132-145	142-156	152-173
6	3	158-172	167-182	176-202	5	11	135-148	145-159	155-176
6	4	162-176	171-187	181-207	6	0	138-151	148-162	158-179

Food and Nutrition

Food contains proteins, carbohydrates, fats, water, vitamins and minerals. Nutrition is the way your body takes in and uses these ingredients to maintain proper functioning.

The U.S. Dept. of Health and Human Services and the Dept. of Agriculture issued dietary guidelines Nov. 5, 1990 that were the most specific ever, and covered children from age 2 as well as adults. Recommended were: (1) no more than 30 percent of calories from fat, or about 67 grams of fat in a 2,000-calorie daily diet; and no more than 10 percent or 22 grams of that from saturated fats high in cholesterol; (2) maximum alcohol consumption of about 1 drink a day for women, 2 for men; (3) daily consumption of vegetables of 3-5 servings; fruits, 2-4; pastas, cereals or breads, 6-11; milk, 2-3; meat, poultry, fish and eggs, 2-3. (For vegetables, 1 serving=about 1 cup raw leafy greens or one-half cup other kinds; fruit, 1 medium apple, banana, or orange; grains, 1 slice of bread or 1 oz. cereal; milk, 1 cup or 1.5 oz. of cheese; meat and poultry, 2-3 oz. cooked lean beef or chicken without skin.)

Protein

Proteins, composed of amino acids, are indispensable in the diet. They build, maintain, and repair the body. Best sources: eggs, milk, fish, meat, poultry, soybeans, nuts. High quality proteins such as eggs, meat, or fish supply all 8 amino acids needed in the diet.

Fats

Fats provide energy by furnishing calories to the body, and by carrying vitamins A, D, E, and K. They are the most concentrated source of energy in the diet. Best sources: butter, margarine, salad oils, nuts, cream, egg yolks, most cheeses, lard, meat.

Carbohydrates

Carbohydrates provide energy for body function and activity by supplying immediate calories. The carbohydrate group includes sugars, starches, fiber, and starchy vegetables. Best sources: grains, legumes, nuts, potatoes, fruits.

Water

Water dissolves and transports other nutrients throughout the body, aiding the processes of digestion, absorption, circulation, and excretion. It helps regulate body temperature.

Vitamins

Vitamin A—promotes good eyesight and helps keep the skin and mucous membranes resistant to infection. Best sources: liver, carrots, sweet potatoes, kale, collard greens, turnips, fortified milk.

Vitamin B_1 (thiamine)—prevents beriberi. Essential to carbohydrate metabolism and health of nervous system.

Vitamin B_2 (riboflavin)—protects skin, mouth, eye, eyelids, and mucous membranes. Essential to protein and energy metabolism. Best sources: liver, milk, meat, poultry, broccoli, mushrooms.

Vitamin B_6 (pyridoxine)—important in the regulation of the central nervous system and in protein metabolism. Best sources: whole grains, meats, nuts, brewers' yeast.

Vitamin B_{12} (cobalamin)—needed to form red blood cells. Best sources: liver, meat, fish, eggs, soybeans.

Niacin—maintains the health of skin, tongue, and digestive system. Best sources: poultry, peanuts, fish, organ meats, enriched flour and bread.

Other B vitamins—biotin, choline, folic acid (folacin), inositol, PABA (para-aminobenzoic acid), pantothenic acid.

Vitamin C (ascorbic acid)—maintains collagen, a protein necessary for the formation of skin, ligaments, and bones. It helps heal wounds and mend fractures, and aids in resisting some types of virus and bacterial infections. Best sources: citrus fruits and juices, turnips, broccoli, Brussels sprouts, potatoes and sweet potatoes, tomatoes, cabbage.

Vitamin D—important for bone development. Best sources: sunlight, fortified milk and milk products, fish-liver oils, egg yolks, organ meats.

Vitamin E (tocopherol)—helps protect red blood cells. Best sources: vegetable oils, wheat germ, whole grains, eggs, peanuts, organ meats, margarine, green leafy vegetables.

Vitamin K—necessary for formation of prothrombin, which helps blood to clot. Also made by intestinal bacteria. Best dietary sources: green leafy vegetables, tomatoes.

Minerals

Calcium—the most abundant mineral in the body, works with phosphorus in building and maintaining bones and teeth. Best sources: milk and milk products, cheese, and blackstrap molasses.

Phosphorus—the 2d most abundant mineral, performs more functions than any other mineral, and plays a part in nearly every chemical reaction in the body. Best source: whole grains, cheese, milk.

Iron—Necessary for the formation of myoglobin, which transports oxygen to muscle tissue, and hemoglobin, which transports oxygen in the blood. Best sources: organ meats, beans, green leafy vegetables, and shellfish.

Other minerals—chromium, cobalt, copper, fluorine, iodine, magnesium, manganese, molybdenum, potassium, selenium, sodium, sulfur, and zinc.

Recommended Daily Dietary Allowances

Source: Food and Nutrition Board, Natl. Academy of Sciences—Natl. Research Council; 1989

	Age (years) and sex group	Weight (lbs.)	Protein (grams)	Fat soluble vitamins: Vitamin A[1]	Vitamin D[2]	Vitamin E[3]	Vitamin K	Water soluble vitamins: Vitamin C	Thiamin (mg.)	Riboflavin (mg.)	Niacin (mg.)[4]	Vitamin B_6 (mg.)	Folate (micrograms)	Vitamin B_{12} (micrograms)	Minerals: Calcium (mg.)	Phosphorus (mg.)	Magnesium (mg.)	Iron (mg.)	Zinc (mg.)	Iodine (micrograms)	Selenium (micrograms)
Infants. . .	to 5 mos.	13	13	375	7.5	3	5	30	0.3	0.4	5	0.3	25	0.3	400	300	40	6	5	40	10
	to 1 yr.	20	14	375	10	4	10	35	0.4	0.5	6	0.6	35	0.5	600	500	60	10	5	50	15
Children. .	1-3	29	16	400	10	6	15	40	0.7	0.8	9	1.0	50	0.7	800	800	80	10	10	70	20
	4-6	44	24	500	10	7	20	45	0.9	1.1	12	1.1	75	1.0	800	800	120	10	10	90	20
	7-10	62	28	700	10	7	30	45	1.0	1.2	13	1.4	100	1.4	800	800	170	10	10	120	30
Males . . .	11-14	99	45	1000	10	10	45	50	1.3	1.5	17	1.7	150	2.0	1200	1200	270	12	15	150	40
	15-18	145	59	1000	10	10	65	60	1.5	1.8	20	2.0	200	2.0	1200	1200	400	12	15	150	50
	19-24	160	58	1000	10	10	70	60	1.5	1.7	19	2.0	200	2.0	1200	1200	350	10	15	150	70
	25-50	174	63	1000	5	10	80	60	1.5	1.7	19	2.0	200	2.0	800	800	350	10	15	150	70
	51+	170	63	1000	5	10	80	60	1.2	1.4	15	2.0	200	2.0	800	800	350	10	15	150	70
Females .	11-14	101	46	800	10	8	45	50	1.1	1.3	15	1.4	150	2.0	1200	1200	280	15	12	150	45
	15-18	120	44	800	10	8	55	60	1.1	1.3	15	1.5	180	2.0	1200	1200	300	15	12	150	50
	19-24	128	46	800	10	8	60	60	1.1	1.3	15	1.6	180	2.0	1200	1200	280	15	12	150	55
	25-50	138	50	800	5	8	65	60	1.1	1.3	15	1.6	180	2.0	800	800	280	15	12	150	55
	51+	143	50	800	5	8	65	60	1.0	1.2	13	1.6	180	2.0	800	800	280	10	12	150	55

(1) Retinol equivalents. (2) Micrograms of cholecalciferol. (3) Milligrams alpha-tocopherol equivalents. (4) Niacin equivalents.

The New Food Labels

Source: Food Labeling Education Information Center, Beltville, Md.

The federal Nutrition Labeling and Education Act of 1990 established new requirements regarding what information must appear on the labels of processed foods. The effective date of the new regulations is the middle of 1994, although some products may carry the new labels earlier, and products with old labels may still be sold after the effective date as long as they were labeled earlier. Consumers should be aware that new labels use the words "Nutrition Facts" on the back or side panel, while the old ones use "Nutrition Information Per Serving." The new labels offer four basic improvements, according to the U.S. government's Food Labeling Education Information Center:

(1) **You can believe the claims on the package.** You will be able to believe the descriptive terms that say a food is "low in fat" or the health claims that link a certain nutrient to a specific disease because government regulations now define and regulate use of the terms and claims.

(2) **You can more easily compare products because serving sizes will be more comparable for similar food products.** For the first time, virtually all processed and packaged products will have to contain nutrition information. The information on the label will reflect an average serving in amounts customarily consumed. Since the serving size for each product is defined in the regulations, product comparisons will be easier and more meaningful than previously.

(3) **By using the "% Daily Value," you can quickly determine if a product is high or low in a nutrient.** You can use the % Daily Value column to easily compare one product to another. If you want to lower the fat in your diet, you can compare products and select the ones with the lower percentage. You can also use the % Daily Value to make dietary tradeoffs with other foods throughout the day. This means you don't have to deprive yourself of a favorite food that might be high in fat, if you watch what else they eat the rest of the day.

(4) **By consulting the Daily Values, you can determine how much (or how little) of the major nutrients you should eat on a daily basis.** Daily Values serve as a reference for dietary guidance. They help consumers understand how much of a nutrient they should eat at a minimum (say for fiber or calcium) or maximum (fat and cholesterol). The Daily Values are listed for people who take in approximately 2,000 calories a day (many older adults, children, and sedentary women) or 2,500 calories a day (active men, teenage boys, and very active women).

Note: The new labeling requirements do not cover restaurant menus. Nor do they cover fresh produce, meat and poultry, and fish.

Sample of the New Nutrition Labels

Source: Food Labeling Education Information Center, Beltsville, Md.

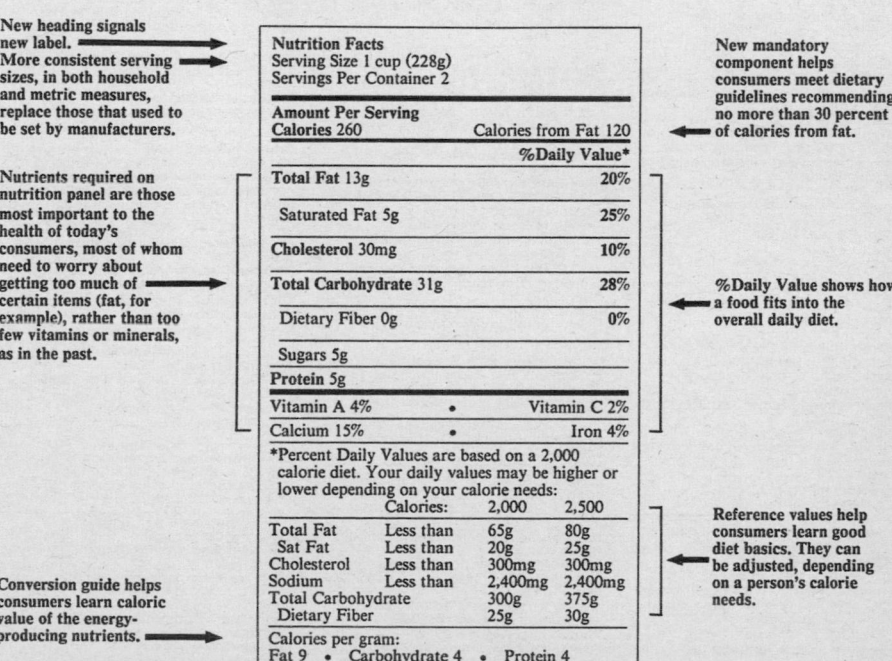

New heading signals new label.

More consistent serving sizes, in both household and metric measures, replace those that used to be set by manufacturers.

New mandatory component helps consumers meet dietary guidelines recommending no more than 30 percent of calories from fat.

Nutrients required on nutrition panel are those most important to the health of today's consumers, most of whom need to worry about getting too much of certain items (fat, for example), rather than too few vitamins or minerals, as in the past.

%Daily Value shows how a food fits into the overall daily diet.

Reference values help consumers learn good diet basics. They can be adjusted, depending on a person's calorie needs.

Conversion guide helps consumers learn caloric value of the energy-producing nutrients.

Nutrition Facts
Serving Size 1 cup (228g)
Servings Per Container 2

Amount Per Serving	
Calories 260	Calories from Fat 120
	%Daily Value*
Total Fat 13g	**20%**
Saturated Fat 5g	**25%**
Cholesterol 30mg	**10%**
Total Carbohydrate 31g	**28%**
Dietary Fiber 0g	**0%**
Sugars 5g	
Protein 5g	
Vitamin A 4% •	Vitamin C 2%
Calcium 15% •	Iron 4%

*Percent Daily Values are based on a 2,000 calorie diet. Your daily values may be higher or lower depending on your calorie needs:

	Calories:	2,000	2,500
Total Fat	Less than	65g	80g
Sat Fat	Less than	20g	25g
Cholesterol	Less than	300mg	300mg
Sodium	Less than	2,400mg	2,400mg
Total Carbohydrate		300g	375g
Dietary Fiber		25g	30g

Calories per gram:
Fat 9 • Carbohydrate 4 • Protein 4

Where to Get Help

Source: Reprinted from Health & Medical Year Book 1993, "Where to Get Help," pp. 278-283.

Listed below are some of the major U.S. organizations providing information about good health practices generally or about specific conditions and how to deal with them. Where a toll-free number is not available, an address is given when possible.

General Sources

Centers for Disease Control Voice Information System
404-332-4555
Tape-recorded information about public health topics, such as AIDS, Lyme disease, and chronic fatigue syndrome. Also, you can request to talk with a CDC expert.

National Health Information Center
800-336-4797; in Maryland, 301-565-4167
Provides phone numbers for more than 1,000 health-related organizations and offers various printed materials.

National Institutes of Health
Bethesda, MD 20892
301-496-4000
Free information, including the latest research findings, on a wide range of diseases.

Tel-Med
Check the phone book for local listings or call Tel-Med headquarters at 714-825-6034
Tape-recorded information on over 600 health topics. Sponsored by local medical societies, health organizations, or hospitals.

Aging

National Council on the Aging
800-424-9046
Provides information and publications on all aspects of aging.

National Institute on Aging
Public Information Office
Federal Building, Room 6C12
Bethesda, MD 20892
410-496-1752
Provides information about disabling conditions, support groups, and community resources.

AIDS

National AIDS Hotline
800-342-AIDS 24 hours; in Spanish, 800-344-SIDA; for the hearing impaired, 800-AIDS-TTY
Provides recorded information on the prevention and spread of AIDS.

Alcoholism and Drug Abuse

Alcohol Abuse Emergency
800-ALCOHOL

Alcoholism and Drug Addiction Treatment Center
800-382-4357
Offers referrals to local facilities for adolescents and adults; operates 24 hours.

National Clearinghouse for Alcohol and Drug Information
800-729-6686
Provides federal publications and literature searches.

National Cocaine Hotline
800-COCAINE
Answers questions about cocaine and other drugs, provides referral to drug treatment centers. Operates 24 hours.

National Council on Alcoholism and Drug Dependence Hopeline
800-475-HOPE

National Institute for Drug Abuse
800-662-HELP; in Spanish, 800-66-AYUDA
Makes referrals to support groups and treatment programs.

National Parents' Resource Institute for Drug Education
800-677-7433
Recording gives telephone numbers to call and an address to write to for drug information. Operates 24 hours.

Recovering Network
800-527-5344
Provides treatment referrals and counseling for recovering alcoholics; operates 24 hours.

Alzheimer's Disease

Alzheimer's Association
800-621-0379; in Illinois, 800-572-6037
Makes referrals to local chapters and support groups; offers information on publications available from the association.

Anemia

National Association for Sickle Cell Disease
800-421-8453; in California, 213-736-5455
Offers genetic counseling and information packet.

Arthritis

Arthritis Foundation
800-283-7800
Provides information, publications, and referrals to local groups.

Asthma and Allergies

Asthma and Allergy Foundation Patient Information Line
800-7-ASTHMA
Provides general information, publications and videos, and referrals to physicians.

Asthma Information Line
800-822-ASMA
Provides written materials on asthma and allergies. Operates 24 hours.

Blindness and Eye Care

American Council of the Blind
800-424-8666; in Washington, D.C., 202-467-5081
Offers information on blindness; provides referrals to clinics and other organizations.

American Foundation for the Blind
800-AF-BLIND; in New York State, 212-620-2147
Gives information on visual impairments and on AFB services, products, and publications.

Blind Children's Center
800-222-3566; in California, 800-222-3567

National Association for Parents of the Visually Impaired
800-562-6265
Offers support and information for parents of individuals who are visually impaired.

National Retinitis Pigmentosa Foundation
800-638-2300; in Maryland, 301-225-9400; for the hearing impaired, 301-225-9409
Answers questions and provides written materials.

NSPB (National Society to Prevent Blindness) Center for Sight
800-221-3004

Cancer

American Cancer Society
800-ACS-2345
Provides publications and information about cancer and coping with cancer; makes referrals to local chapters of the American Cancer Society for support services.

National Cancer Institute's Cancer Information Service
800-4-CANCER; 800-638-6070 in Alaska; 808-524-1234 in Oahu, Ha. (neighboring islands call collect)
Answers questions about cancer; Spanish-speaking staff members available in some areas.

Y-Me Breast Cancer Support Program
800-221-2141; in Illinois, 708-799-8228, 24 hours
Provides information and literature on breast cancer, counseling, and referrals.

Cerebral Palsy

United Cerebral Palsy Associations
800-USA-5UCP; in Washington, D.C., 202-842-1266
Provides literature about cerebral palsy.

Child Abuse

Childhelp's National Child Abuse Hotline
800-4-A-CHILD
Provides crisis intervention, professional counseling, referrals to local groups offering counseling and to shelters for runaways, and literature in English and Spanish. Operates 24 hours.

National Center for Missing and Exploited Children
800-843-5678; for the hearing impaired, 800-826-7653; In Arlington, Va., 703-235-3900
Operates a hotline for reporting missing children and sightings of missing children. Assists law enforcement agencies.

Parents Anonymous Hotline
800-421-0353; in California, 800-352-0386
Provides information on self-help groups for parents. Operates 24 hours.

Crisis

National Adolescent Suicide Hotline
800-621-4000; in California, 800-352-0386
Provides crisis intervention and referrals for runaways. Operates 24 hours.

National Youth Crisis Hotline
800-HIT-HOME
Provides counseling for youths dealing with drug abuse, pregnancy, molestation, suicide, and child abuse; makes referrals to local drug treatment centers, shelters, and counseling services. Operates 24 hours.

Cystic Fibrosis

Cystic Fibrosis Foundation
800-FIGHT-CF; in Maryland, 301-951-4422
Answers questions and offers literature and referrals to local clinics.

Diabetes

American Diabetes Association
800-ADA-DISC; in Virginia and Washington, D.C., 703-549-1500
Provides literature and referrals to local affiliates for information on support groups.

Juvenile Diabetes Foundation Hotline
800-223-1138 or 800-533-2873; in New York City, 212-889-7575
Answers questions, provides literature (some in Spanish), and refers to local chapters, physicians, and clinics.

Digestive Diseases

National Digestive Diseases Information Clearinghouse
Box NDDIC, Bethesda, MD 20892
301-468-6344

National Foundation for Ileitis and Colitis
800-343-3637; in New York, 212-679-1570
Provides educational materials, refers to local support groups and physicians.

Down Syndrome

National Down Syndrome Congress
800-232-6372; in Illinois, 312-823-7550
Answers questions and makes referrals to local organizations.

National Down Syndrome Society Hotline
800-221-4602; in New York City, 212-460-9330
Provides information and gives referrals for local programs for newborn.

Dyslexia

Orton Dyslexia Society
800-ABCD-123; in Maryland, 301-296-0232
Provides information on testing, tutoring, and computers to aid people with dyslexia and related disorders.

Eating Disorders

Bulimia/Anorexia Self-Help Hotline
800-227-4785
Provides information on bulimia and anorexia.

National Anorexic Aid Society
1925 East Dublin-Granville Road
Columbus, Ohio 43229-3517
614-436-1112

Endometriosis

Endometriosis Association
800-992-ENDO; in Wisconsin, 414-962-8972; in Canada, 800-426-2END
Provides a 24-hour recording for callers to request information.

Epilepsy

Epilepsy Foundation of America
800-332-1000; in Maryland, 301-459-3700
Provides information and referrals to local chapters.

Handicaps and Disabilities

Library of Congress
800-424-9100; in Washington, D.C., 202-707-5100
Lends braille and audio-recorded books; refers callers to state and local libraries with these services.

National Information Center for Children and Youth With Handicaps
800-999-5599 or 703-893-6061
Offers information and referrals for disabled and handicapped children.

National Information System for Health Related Services
800-922-9234; in South Carolina, 800-922-1107
Makes referrals to support groups and to sources of financial, medical, and legal assistance for developmentally disabled and chronically ill children.

Headaches

National Headache Foundation
800-843-2256; in Illinois, 800-523-8858
Offers literature on headaches and treatment.

National Institute of Neurological Disorders and Stroke
P.O. Box 5801
Bethesda, MD 20824
800-352-9424

Hearing

American Speech-Language-Hearing Association Helpline
800-638-8255; in Maryland call collect, 301-897-0039
Offers materials on hearing aids and on pathologists and audiologists certified by the association.

Dial A Hearing Screening Test
800-222-EARS; in Pennsylvania, 800-345-EARS
Answers questions on hearing problems, makes referrals to local numbers for a two-minute hearing test, as well as to ear, nose, and throat specialists and to organizations with specialized ear and hearing aid information.

Hearing Helpline
800-EAR-WELL; in Virginia, 703-642-0580
Provides information on better hearing and preventing deafness.

National Hearing Aid Helpline
800-521-5247
Provides information and distributes a directory of hearing aid specialists certified by the National Hearing AID Society.

Heart Disease

American Heart Association
7272 Greenville Avenue
Dallas, TX 75231
800-242-1793; 214-373-6300

National Heart, Lung, and Blood Institute Information Office
9000 Rockville Pike
Building 31-4A21
Bethesda, MD 20892
301-496-4236

Hospices

Children's Hospice International
800-242-4453; in Virginia, 703-684-0330
Provides information on and referrals to children's hospices.

Hospice Education Institute Hospicelink
800-331-1620; in Connecticut, 203-767-1620
Offers general information about hospice care and makes referrals to local programs.

Huntington's Disease

Huntington's Disease Society of America
800-345-4372; in New York, 212-242-1968
Provides information and referrals to physicians and support groups.

Hysterectomy

Hysterectomy Resources and Services Foundation
422 Bryn Mawr Ave.
Bala-Cynwyd, PA 19004
215-667-7757
Offers peer support for women considering hysterectomy, referrals for second opinions, legal referrals.

Impotence

Impotence Information Center
800-843-4315
Provides information on the causes and treatment of impotence.

Impotence Institute of America Hotline
800-669-1603
Offers literature, physician referrals, and phone numbers of local Impotents Anonymous chapters.

Kidney Diseases

National Kidney Foundation
800-622-9010
Provides information and referrals.

National Kidney and Urologic Diseases Information Clearinghouse
P.O. Box NKUDIC
Bethesda, MD 20892
301-468-6345

Lead Exposure

National Lead Information Center Hotline
800-LEAD-FYI
Makes recommendations for reducing a child's exposure to lead, in the home and elsewhere.

Liver Diseases

American Liver Foundation
800-223-0179; in New Jersey, 201-256-2550
Provides information and physician and support group referrals.

Lung Diseases

American Lung Association
Check the phone book for local listings or call the national office at 212-315-8700

National Jewish Center for Immunology and Respiratory Medicine Information Service
800-222-LUNG; in Denver, 303-355-LUNG
Answers questions on asthma, emphysema, allergies, smoking, and other respiratory and immune system disorders.

Lupus

American Lupus Society
800-331-1802
Provides literature on lupus research and referrals to physicians and local chapters.

Lupus Foundation of America
800-558-0121; in Rockville, Md., 301-670-9292; in Washington, D.C., 202-328-4550.
Answers basic questions and provides literature about lupus; refers to local affiliates.

Mental Health

American Mental Health Fund
800-433-5959; in Illinois, 800-826-2336
Provides a 24-hour recorded message for callers to request a pamphlet on mental health.

American Schizophrenic Association
800-847-3802
Provides information about mental illness, physician referrals, and book lists.

National Depressive and Manic Depressive Association
800-826-3632
Offers support for patients and families, provides emergency assistance, and helps patients seek qualified treatment.

National Foundation for Depressive Illness
800-248-4344
Provides a 24-hour recorded message describing the symptoms of depression and offering an address for more information and physician referral.

National Mental Health Association
800-969-6642
Makes referrals to mental health groups.

OCD (Obsessive-Compulsive Disorder) Foundation
P.O. Box 9573
New Haven, CT 06535
203-772-0565

Multiple Sclerosis

National Multiple Sclerosis Society
800-624-8236
A 24-hour recording allows callers to request information and leave name and address; to speak to a staff member, call 800-227-3166.

Nutrition

National Center for Nutrition and Dietetics Hotline
800-366-1655
Offers general information on nutrition, answers questions, and provides literature.

USDA Food, Safety, and Inspection Service Meat and Poultry Hotline
800-535-4555
Provides information on proper handling, preparation, storage, and cooking of meat, poultry, and eggs.

University of Alabama at Birmingham Nutrition Information Service
800-231-DIET
Answers questions on healthful eating and food handling.

Pain

National Chronic Pain Outreach Association
7979 Old Georgetown Road
Suite 100
Bethesda, MD 20814-2429
301-652-4948
Provides information clearinghouse, makes referrals, and publishes newsletters.

Parkinson's Disease

National Parkinson's Foundation
800-327-4545; in Florida, 800-433-7022; in Miami, 305-547-6666
Answers questions, makes physician referrals, and provides written information.

Parkinson's Educational Program
800-344-7872; in California, 714-250-2975
Provides written materials as well as information on support groups and physician referrals. Operates 24 hours.

Prostate Problems

Prostate Information Line
800-543-9632

Sexually Transmitted Diseases

American Social Health Association's National STD Hotline
800-227-8922
Provides information and confidential referrals for treatment.

Skin Problems

National Psoriasis Foundation
6443 W.W. Beaverton Hwy., Suite 210
Portland, OR 97221
503-297-1545
Offers information and referrals.

Sleep Disorders

American Narcolepsy Association
800-222-6085; in California, 415-591-7979
Provides literature on narcolepsy, a condition marked by brief attacks of deep sleep.

Speech Disorders

National Center for Stuttering
800-221-2483; in New York City, 212-532-1460
Provides information on stuttering in young children, as well as older children and adults.

Stuttering Foundation of America
800-992-9392
Provides referrals to speech pathologists, resource lists, and other publications. Operates 24 hours.

Spina Bifida

Spina Bifida Information and Referral
800-621-3141; in Maryland, 301-770-7222
Offers information and referrals to local chapters.

Spinal Injuries

American Paralysis Association's Spinal Cord Injury Hotline
800-526-3456
Provides literature on spinal cord injuries and makes referrals to organizations and support groups.

National Spinal Cord Injury Association
800-962-9629; in Massachusetts, 617-935-2722
Offers peer counseling and makes referrals to local chapters and other organizations.

Stroke

National Stroke Association
800-787-6537
Provides written and referral information.

Sudden Infant Death Syndrome

American Sudden Infant Death Syndrome Institute
800-232-SIDS; in Georgia, 800-847-7437
Answers questions, distributes literature, and makes referrals to other organizations. Operates 24 hours.

National SIDS Foundation
800-221-SIDS; in Maryland, 301-964-8000
Provides literature on medical information, referrals, and support groups.

Tourette Syndrome

Tourette Syndrome Association
800-237-0717; in New York, 718-224-2999
Provides a 24-hour recording for callers to request information, published in English and Spanish.

Urinary Incontinence

Help for Incontinent People
800-BLADDER
Offers information on bladder control, services available for incontinence, and assistive devices.

Simon Foundation
800-23-SIMON
Offers support and literature on incontinence.

Women's Health

National Women's Health Network
1325 G St. NW
Washington, D.C. 20005
202-347-1140

National Women's Health Resource Center
2440 M St. NW
Washington, D.C.
202-293-6045

NATIONAL DEFENSE

Data as of mid-1993

Chairman, Joint Chiefs of Staff
Gen. Colin L. Powell (until Sept. 30, 1993)
Gen. John Shalikashvili (as of Oct. 1, 1993)

Vice Chairman
Adm. David E. Jeremiah

The Joint Chiefs of Staff consists of the Chairman and Vice Chairman of the Joint Chiefs of Staff; the Chief of Staff, U.S. Army; the Chief of Naval Operations; the Chief of Staff, U.S. Air Force; and the Commandant of the Marine Corps.

Army

Chief of Staff—Gordon R. Sullivan

Generals

	Date of Rank
Burba, Edwin H. Jr.	Sept. 27, 1989
Franks, Frederick M. Jr.	Aug. 23, 1991
Galvin, John R.	Feb. 25, 1985
Joulwan, George A.	Nov. 21, 1990
Powell, Colin L.	Apr. 4, 1989
Reimer, Dennis J.	June 21, 1991
RisCassi, Robert W.	Jan. 17, 1989
Ross, Jimmy D.	Feb. 1, 1992
Saint, Crosbie E.	June 24, 1988
Stiner, Carl W.	July 1, 1990

Air Force

Chief of Staff—Merrill A. McPeak

Generals

Boyd, Charles G.	Dec. 1, 1992
Butler, George L.	Jan. 25, 1991
Carns, Michael P.C.	May 16, 1991
Davis, James B.	June 1, 1992
Fogleman, Ronald R.	Sept. 1, 1992
Horner, Charles A.	June 1, 1992
Loh, John M.	June 1, 1990
Oaks, Robert C.	July 1, 1990
Rutherford, Robert L.	Feb. 1, 1993
Viccellio Jr., Henry	Dec. 10, 1992
Yates, Ronald W.	Apr. 1, 1990

Navy

Chief of Naval Operations
Adm. Frank B. Kelso II (submariner)

Admirals

	Date of Rank
Arthur, Stanley R. (aviator)	July 6, 1992
Boorda, Jeremy M. (surface warfare)	Mar. 2, 1992
DeMars, Bruce (submariner)	Nov. 1, 1988
Jeremiah, David E. (surface warfare)	Oct. 1, 1987
Kelly, Robert J. (aviator)	Mar. 1, 1991
Larson, Charles R. (submariner)	Mar. 1, 1990
Mauz, Henry N. Jr. (surface warfare)	Aug. 1, 1992
Miller, Paul D. (surface warfare)	Feb. 1, 1991
Smith, William D. (submariner)	Feb. 22, 1991

Marine Corps

Corps Commandant, with rank of General

Carl E. Mundy Jr.	July 1, 1991

ACMC/Chief of Staff, with rank of Gen.

Walter E. Boomer	Sept. 1, 1992
Joseph P. Hoar	Sept. 1, 1991

Coast Guard

Commandant, with rank of Admiral

J. William Kime	June 1, 1990

Vice Commandant, with rank of Vice Admiral

Robert T. Nelson	June 5, 1992

Unified Defense Commands Commanders in Chief

(as of mid-1993)

U.S. European Command, Brussels, Belgium — Maj. Gen. John Shalikashvili* (USA) (concurrently NATO Supreme Allied Commander, Europe)

U.S. Southern Command, Quarry Heights, Panama Canal Zone — Gen. George A. Joulwan (USA)

U.S. Atlantic Command, Norfolk, Virginia — Adm. Paul D. Miller (USN) (concurrently NATO Supreme Allied Commander, Atlantic)

U.S. Pacific Command, Honolulu, Hawaii — Adm. Charles R. Larson (USN)

U.S. Space Command, Peterson AFB, Colo. — Gen. Charles A. Horner (USAF)

U.S. Strategic Command, Omaha, Neb. — Gen. George L. Butler (USAF)

U.S. Forces Command, Fort McPherson, Ga. — Gen. Dennis J. Reimer (USA)

U.S. Transportation Command, Scott AFB, Ill. — Gen. Ronald R. Fogleman (USAF)

U.S. Special Operations Command, Fort Walton Beach, Fla. — Gen. Wayne A. Dowling (USA)

U.S. Central Command, MacDill AFB, Fla. — Gen. Joseph P. Hoar (USMC)

North Atlantic Treaty Organization International Commands

(as of mid-1993)

Supreme Allied Commander, Europe (SACEUR) — Gen. John Shalikashvili* (USA)

Deputy Supreme Allied Commander, Europe (DSACEUR) — Gen. Sir John Waters (UKA)

Commander in Chief Allied Forces Northern Europe — Gen. Sir Garry Johnson (UKA)

Commander in Chief Allied Forces Central Europe — Gen. Henning von Ondarva (GEA)

Commander in Chief Allied Forces Southern Europe — Adm. Jeremy M. Boorda

Commander in Chief United Kingdom Air Forces — Gen. John Thomson (UKAF)

Chairman, NATO Military Committee — Field Marshall Sir Richard Vincent (UKA)

* Named by Pres. Bill Clinton, Aug. 11, 1993, to become Chairman of the Joint Chiefs of Staff, effective Oct. 1, 1993.

Principal U.S. Military Training Centers

Army

Name, P.O. address	Zip	Nearest city
Aberdeen Proving Ground, MD	21005	Aberdeen
Carlisle Barracks, PA	17013	Carlisle
Fort Benning, GA	31905	Columbus
Fort Bliss, TX	79916	El Paso
Fort Bragg, NC	28307	Fayetteville
Fort Devens, MA	01433	Ayer
Fort Dix, NJ	08640	Trenton
Fort Eustis, VA	23604	Newport News
Fort Gordon, GA	30905	Augusta
Fort Benjamin Harrison, IN	46216	Indianapolis

Name, P.O. address	Zip	Nearest city
Fort Sam Houston, TX	78234	San Antonio
Fort Huachuca, AZ	85613	Sierra Vista
Fort Jackson, SC	29207	Columbia
Fort Knox, KY	40121	Louisville
Fort Leavenworth, KS	66027	Leavenworth
Fort Lee, VA	23801	Petersburg
Fort McClellan, AL	36205	Anniston
Fort Monmouth, NJ	07703	Red Bank
Fort Rucker, AL	36362	Dothan
Fort Sill, OK	73503	Lawton
Fort Leonard Wood, MO	65473	Rolla
Joint Readiness, Ft. Chaffee, AR	72905	Fort Smith
National Training Center	92311	Barstow, CA
The Judge Advocate General School, VA	22901	Charlottes-ville
U.S. Military Acad., NY	10996	West Point

Navy

Name, P.O. address	Zip	Nearest city
Great Lakes, IL	60088	North Chicago
Annapolis, MD	21402	Annapolis

Marine Corps

Name, P.O. address	Zip	Nearest city
MCB Camp Lejeune, NC	28542	Jacksonville
MCB Camp Pendleton, CA	92055	Oceanside
MCAGCC Twentynine Palms, CA.	92278	Palm Springs
MCCDC Quantico, VA	22134	Quantico
MCRD Parris Island, SC	29905	Beaufort
MCAS Cherry Point, NC	28533	Havelock
MCAS Tustin, CA	92780	Santa Ana
MCAS New River, NC	28545	Jacksonville
MCAS Kaneohe Bay, Oahu, HI	San Francisco 96863	Kailua
MCAS Beaufort, SC	29904	Beaufort
MCAS Yuma, AZ	85369	Yuma
MCMWTC Bridgeport, CA	93517	Bridgeport

MCB = Marine Corps Base. MCCDC = Marine Corps Combat Development Command. MCAS = Marine Corps Air Station. MCRD = Marine Corps Recruit Depot. MCAGCC = Marine Corps Air-Ground Combat Center. MCMWTC = Marine Corps Mountain Warfare Training Center.

Air Force

Name, P.O. address	Zip	Nearest city
Chanute AFB, IL	61868	Rantoul
Goodfellow AFB, TX	76908	San Angelo
Gunter AFB, AL*	36114	Montgomery
Keesler AFB, MS	39534	Biloxi
Lackland AFB, TX	78236	San Antonio
Lowry AFB, CO	80230	Denver
Maxwell AFB, AL*	36112	Montgomery
Sheppard AFB, TX	76311	Wichita Falls

* Air University Bases. All others are Air Training Command Bases.

Personal Salutes and Honors

The United States national salute, 21 guns, is also the salute to a national flag. The independence of the United States is commemorated by the salute to the Union — one gun for each state — fired at noon on July 4 at all military posts provided with suitable artillery.

A 21-gun salute on arrival and departure, with 4 ruffles and flourishes, is rendered to the President of the United States, to an ex-President and to a President-elect. The national anthem or *Hail to the Chief,* as appropriate, is played for the President, and the national anthem for the others. A 21-gun salute on arrival and departure, with 4 ruffles and flourishes, also is rendered to the sovereign or chief of state of a foreign country or a member of a reigning royal family; the national anthem of his or her country is played. The music is considered an inseparable part of the salute and will immediately follow the ruffles and flourishes without pause.

Rank	Salute—guns Arrive	Leave	Ruffles, flourishes	Music
Vice President of United States	19		4	Hail Columbia
Speaker of the House	19		4	March
American or foreign ambassador	19		4	Nat. anthem of official
Premier or prime minister	19		4	Nat. anthem of official
Secretary of Defense, Army, Navy or Air Force	19	19	4	Honors March
Other Cabinet members, Senate President pro tempore, Governor, or Chief Justice of U.S.	19		4	Honors March
Chairman, Joint Chiefs of Staff	19	19	4	
Army Chief of Staff, Chief of Naval Operations, Air Force Chief of Staff, Marine Commandant	19	19	4	General's or Admiral's March
General of the Army, General of the Air Force, Fleet Admiral	19	19	4	
Generals, Admirals	17	17	4	
Assistant secretaries of Defense, Army, Navy or Air Force	17	17	4	Honors March
Chairman of a committee of Congress	17		4	Honors March

Other salutes (on arrival only) include 15 guns for U.S. envoys or ministers and foreign envoys or ministers accredited to the U.S.; 15 guns for a lieutenant general or vice admiral; 13 guns for a major general or rear admiral (upper half); 13 guns for U.S. ministers resident and ministers resident accredited to the U.S.; 11 guns for a brigadier general or rear admiral (lower half); 11 guns for U.S. charges d'affaires and like officials accredited to the U.S.; and 11 guns for consuls general accredited to the U.S.

Military Units, U.S. Army and Air Force

Army Units. Squad. In infantry usually ten enlisted personnel under a staff sergeant. **Platoon.** In infantry 4 squads under a lieutenant. **Company.** Headquarters section and 4 platoons under a captain. (Company-size unit in the artillery is a battery; in the cavalry, a troop.) **Battalion.** Hdqts. and 4 or more companies under a lieutenant colonel. (Battalion-size unit in the cavalry is a squadron.) **Brigade.** Hdqts. and 3 or more battalions under a colonel. **Division.** Hdqts. and 3 brigades with artillery, combat support, and combat service support units under a major general. **Army Corps.** Two or more divisions with corps troops under a lieutenant general. **Field Army.** Hdqts. and two or more corps with field Army troops under a general.

Air Force Units. Flight. Numerically designated flights are the lowest level unit in the Air Force. They are used primarily where there is a need for small mission elements to be incorporated into an organized unit. **Squadron.** A squadron is the basic unit in the Air Force. It is used to designate the mission units in operational commands. **Group.** The group is a flexible unit composed of two or more squadrons whose functions may be either tactical, support or administrative in nature. **Wing.** An operational wing normally has two or more assigned mission squadrons in an area such as combat, flying training or airlift. **Air Division.** The organization of the air division may be similar to that of the numbered air force, though on a much smaller scale. Functions are usually limited to operations and logistics. **Numbered Air Forces.** Normally an operationally oriented agency, the numbered air force is designed for the control of two or more air divisions or units of comparable strength. It is a flexible organization and may be of any size. Its wings may be assigned to air divisions or directly under the numbered air force. **Major Command.** A major subdivision of the Air Force that is assigned a major segment of the USAF mission.

The Federal Service Academies

U.S. Military Academy, West Point, N.Y. Founded 1802. Awards B.S. degree and Army commission for a 5-year service obligation. For admissions information, write Admissions Office, USMA, West Point, NY 10996.

U.S. Naval Academy, Annapolis, Md. Founded 1845. Awards B.S. degree and Navy or Marine Corps commission for a 5-year service obligation. For admissions information, write Dean of Admissions, Naval Academy, Annapolis, MD 21402.

U.S. Air Force Academy, Colorado Springs, Col. Founded 1954. Awards B.S. degree and Air Force commission for a 5-year service obligation. For admissions information, write Registrar, U.S. Air Force Academy, CO 80840.

U.S. Coast Guard Academy, New London, Conn. Founded 1876. Awards B.S. degree and Coast Guard commission for a 5-year service obligation. For admissions information, write Director of Admissions, Coast Guard Academy, New London, CT 06320.

U.S. Merchant Marine Academy, Kings Point, N.Y. Founded 1943. Awards B.S. degree, a license as a deck, engineer, or dual officer, and a U.S. Naval Reserve commission. Service obligations vary according to options taken by the graduate. For admissions information, write Admission Office, U.S. Merchant Marine Academy, Kings Point, NY 11024.

U.S. Army Insignia and Chevrons

Source: Department of the Army, U.S. Dept. of Defense

Grade **Insignia**

General of the Armies

General John J. Pershing, the only person to have held this rank, was authorized to prescribe his own insignia, but never wore in excess of four stars. The rank originally was established by Congress for George Washington in 1799, and he was promoted to the rank by joint resolution of Congress, approved by Pres. Ford Oct. 19, 1976.

General of Army . . . Five silver stars fastened together in a circle and the coat of arms of the United States in gold color metal with shield and crest enameled.

Grade	Insignia
General	Four silver stars
Lieutenant General	Three silver stars
Major General	Two silver stars
Brigadier General	One silver star
Colonel	Silver eagle
Lieutenant Colonel	Silver oak leaf
Major	Gold oak leaf
Captain	Two silver bars
First Lieutenant	One silver bar
Second Lieutenant	One gold bar

Warrant Officers

Grade Four—Silver bar with 4 enamel black squares.
Grade Three—Silver bar with 3 enamel black squares.
Grade Two—Silver bar with 2 enamel black squares.
Grade One—Silver bar with 1 enamel black squares.

Noncommissioned Officers

Sergeant Major of the Army (E-9). Same as Command Sergeant Major (below) but with 2 stars. Also wears distinctive red and white shield on lapel.

Command Sergeant Major (E-9). Three chevrons above three arcs with a 5-pointed star with a wreath around the star between the chevrons and arcs.

Sergeant Major (E-9). Three chevrons above three arcs with a five-pointed star between the chevrons and arcs.

First Sergeant (E-8). Three chevrons above three arcs with a lozenge between the chevrons and arcs.

Master Sergeant (E-8). Three chevrons above three arcs.

Sergeant First Class (E-7). Three chevrons above two arcs.

Staff Sergeant (E-6). Three chevrons above one arc.

Sergeant (E-5). Three chevrons.

Corporal (E-4). Two chevrons.

Specialists

Specialist (E-4). Eagle device only.

Other enlisted

Private First Class (E-3). One chevron above one arc.

Private (E-2). One chevron.

Private (E-1). None.

U.S. Navy Insignia

Source: Dept. of the Navy, U.S. Dept. of Defense

Navy

Stripes and corps device are of gold embroidery.

	Stripes
Fleet Admiral	1 two inch with 4 one-half inch.
Admiral	1 two inch with 3 one-half inch.
Vice Admiral	1 two inch with 2 one-half inch.
Rear Admiral (upper half)	1 two inch with 1 one-half inch.
Rear Admiral (lower half)	1 two inch.
Captain	4 one-half inch.
Commander	3 one-half inch.
Lieut. Commander	2 one-half inch, with 1 one-quarter inch between.
Lieutenant	2 one-half inch.
Lieutenant (j.g.)	1 one-half inch with one-quarter inch above.
Ensign	1 one-half inch.

Warrant Officers—One 1/2" broken with 1/2" intervals of blue as follows:

Warrant Officer W-4—1 break
Warrant Officer W-3—2 breaks, 2" apart
Warrant Officer W-2—3 breaks, 2" apart

The breaks are symmetrically centered on outer face of the sleeve.

Enlisted personnel (noncommissioned petty officers) . . . A rating badge worn on the upper left arm, consisting of a spread eagle, appropriate number of chevrons, and centered specialty mark.

Marine Corps

Marine Corps and Army officer insignia are similar. Marine Corps and Army enlisted insignia, although basically similar, differ in color, design, and fewer Marine Corps subdivisions. The Marine Corps' distinctive cap and collar ornament is a combination of the American eagle, globe, and anchor.

Coast Guard

Coast Guard insignia follow Navy custom, with certain minor changes such as the officer cap insignia. The Coast Guard shield is worn on both sleeves of officers and on the right sleeve of all enlisted personnel.

U.S. Army Personnel on Active Duty[1]

Source: Department of the Army, U.S. Dept. of Defense

June 30[2]	Total strength	Commissioned officers			Warrant officers		Enlisted personnel		
		Total	Male	Female[3]	Male[4]	Female	Total	Male	Female
1940	267,767	17,563	16,624	939	763	———	249,441	249,441	———
1942	3,074,184	203,137	190,662	12,475	3,285	———	2,867,762	2,867,762	———
1943	6,993,102	557,657	521,435	36,222	21,919	0	6,413,526	6,358,200	55,325
1944	7,992,868	740,077	692,351	47,726	36,893	10	7,215,888	7,144,601	71,287
1945	8,266,373	835,403	772,511	62,892	56,216	44	7,374,710	7,283,930	90,780
1946	1,889,690	257,300	240,643	16,657	9,826	18	1,622,546	1,605,847	16,699
1950	591,487	67,784	63,375	4,409	4,760	22	518,921	512,370	6,551
1955	1,107,606	111,347	106,173	5,174	10,552	48	985,659	977,943	7,716
1960	871,348	91,056	86,832	4,224	10,141	39	770,112	761,833	8,279
1965	967,049	101,812	98,029	3,783	10,285	23	854,929	846,409	8,520
1970	1,319,735	143,704	138,469	5,235	23,005	13	1,153,013	1,141,537	11,476
1975	781,316	89,756	85,184	4,572	13,214	22	678,324	640,621	37,703
1980 (Sept 30)	772,661	85,339	77,843	7,496	13,265	113	673,944	612,593	61,351
1985 (Sept. 30)	776,244	94,103	83,563	10,540	15,296	288	666,557	598,639	67,918
1990 (Mar. 31)	746,220	91,330	79,520	11,810	15,177	470	639,713	567,015	72,698
1991 (Mar. 31)	740,023	89,448	77,489	11,959	14,771	505	635,299	564,180	71,119
1992 (Mar. 31)	661,391	85,953	74,326	11,627	13,840	494	561,104	496,335	64,769
1993 (Mar. 31)	590,324	76,714	66,336	10,378	12,359	441	500,810	443,942	56,868

(1) Represents strength of the active Army, including Philippine Scouts, retired Regular Army personnel on extended active duty, and National Guard and Reserve personnel on extended active duty; excludes U.S. Military Academy cadets, contract surgeons, and National Guard and Reserve personnel not on extended active duty.

(2) Data for 1940 to 1946 include personnel in the Army Air Forces and its predecessors (Air Service and Air Corps).

(3) Includes: women doctors, dentists, and Medical Service Corps officers for 1946 and subsequent years, women in the Army Nurse Corps for all years, and the Women's Army Corps and Women's Medical Specialists Corps (dietitians, physical therapists, and occupational specialists) for 1943 and subsequent years.

(4) Act of Congress approved April 27, 1926, directed the appointment as warrant officers of field clerks still in active service. Includes flight officers as follows: 1943, 5,700; 1944, 13,615; 1945, 31,117; 1946, 2,580.

U.S. Navy Personnel on Active Duty

June 30	Officers	Nurses	Enlisted	Off. Cand.	Total
1940 (June)	13,162	442	144,824	2,569	160,997
1945 (June)	320,293	11,086	2,988,207	61,231	3,380,817
1950 (June)	42,687	1,964	331,860	5,037	381,538
1960 (June)	67,456	2,103	544,040	4,385	617,984
1970 (June)	78,488	2,273	605,899	6,000	692,660
1980 (June)	63,100[1]	—	464,100[2]	—	527,200
1990 (Sept.)	74,429[1]	—	530,133[2]	—	604,562
1992 (Mar.)	71,826[1]	—	500,459[2]	—	572,285
1993 (Mar.)	66,787[1]	—	445,409[2]	—	512,196

(1) Nurses are included. (2) Officer candidates are included.

U.S. Marine Corps Personnel On Active Duty

(midyear personnel figures)

Year	Officers	Enlisted	Total	Year	Officers	Enlisted	Total	Year	Officers	Enlisted	Total
1955	18,417	186,753	205,170	1980	18,198	170,271	188,469	1991	19,753	174,297	194,050
1960	16,203	154,418	170,621	1985	20,175	177,850	198,025	1992	19,132	165,397	184,529
1965	17,258	172,955	190,213	1990	19,958	176,694	196,652	1993	18,878	161,205	180,083
1970	24,941	234,796	259,737								

U.S. Air Force Personnel on Active Duty

Year[1]	Strength	Year[1]	Strength	Year[1]	Strength	Year[1]	Strength
1907	3	1941	152,125	1950	411,277	1988	575,603
1918	195,023	1942	764,415	1960	814,213	1989	570,965
1920	9,050	1943	2,197,114	1970	791,078	1990	535,200
1930	13,531	1944	2,372,292	1980	557,969	1991	508,500
1940	51,165	1945	2,282,259	1986	608,200	1992	486,800

(1) Prior to 1947, data are for U.S. Army Air Corps and Air Service of the Signal Corps.

U.S. Coast Guard Personnel on Active Duty

Source: U.S. Dept. of Transportation

Year	Total	Officers	Cadets	Enlisted	Year	Total	Officers	Cadets	Enlisted
1970	37,689	5,512	653	31,524	1985	38,595	6,775	733	31,087
1975	36,788	5,630	1,177	29,981	1986	37,284	6,577	754	29,953
1980	39,381	6,463	877	32,041	1987	38,576	6,644	859	31,073
1981	39,760	6,519	981	32,260	1988	37,723	6,530	887	30,306
1982	38,248	6,431	902	30,915	1990	37,308	6,475	820	29,860
1983	39,708	6,535	811	32,362	1991	38,280	7,095	900	30,285
1984	38,705	6,790	759	31,156	1992	39,185	7,348	919	30,918

Defense Contracts

Source: U.S. Dept. of Defense; thousands of dollars

The 50 companies (including their subsidiaries) receiving the largest dollar volume of prime contract awards from the Department of Defense during fiscal 1992.

Company	Amount	Company	Amount	Company	Amount
McDonnell Douglas	$5,311,151	TRW	1,012,521	FMC	447,616
Northrop	4,851,015	IBM	931,776	Dyncorp	446,517
Lockheed	4,659,404	Unisys	834,011	Mitre	434,253
General Dynamics	4,463,771	ITT	797,273	Johns Hopkins University	406,267
General Electric	4,007,764	Foundation Health	751,262	Teledyne	401,602
General Motors	3,694,122	Texas Instruments	730,601	MIT	389,144
Raytheon	2,840,686	GTE	724,489	Johnson Controls	373,738
United Technologies	2,802,878	Science Applications International	685,606	Oshkosh Trucking	372,228
Boeing	2,495,191	Alliant Techsystems	609,676	Hercules	364,165
Martin Marietta	2,356,077	Tenneco	584,822	Motorola	353,384
Litton Industries	2,334,436	Olin	573,331	Royal Dutch Shell Group	344,473
Grumman	2,182,739	E-Systems	500,880	Gencorp	339,079
Loral	1,815,445	Computer Sciences	495,419	Harris	307,604
AT&T	1,337,587	Renco Group	462,143	Coastal	306,543
Rockwell International	1,233,435	Allied Signal	458,869	Exxon	306,116
Textron	1,161,072	Sikorsky	$458,619		
Bath Holding	1,148,372	CFM International	447,648		
Westinghouse Electric	$1,147,210				

Women in the Armed Forces

Source: U.S. Dept. of Defense

Women in the Army, Navy, Air Force, Marines, and Coast Guard are all fully integrated with male personnel. Expansion of military women's programs began in the Department of Defense in fiscal year 1973.

As of 1992, women made up 11.5 percent of the armed forces. Almost 25 percent of medical and dental specialists were women; of active duty women personnel, fewer than 1 percent served in the infantry, gun crews, or aboard ship.

Women Active Duty Troops in 1992

Service	Pct. Women
Army	12.2
Navy	10.4
Marines	4.5
Air Force	14.7
Coast Guard	7.7

Women on Active Duty, All Services: 1973-1992

Year	Pct. Women	Year	Pct. Women
1973	2.5	1983	9.3
1975	4.6	1987	10.2
1981	8.9	1992	11.5

In Apr. 1993, the Defense Dept. ordered the military to drop most of its restrictions on women in aerial and naval combat. The Clinton administration in 1993 announced that it would ask Congress to repeal a law barring women from serving on many warships. In addition, each service was directed to justify all remaining jobs that were off limits to women, including service in ground combat units.

Admission of women to the service academies began in the fall of 1976.

Army — Information: Chief, Office of Public Affairs, Dept. of the Army, Wash., DC 20310.

Army Nurse Corps — Chief, Army Nurse Corps, Office of the Surgeon General, Dept. of the Army, 5109 Leesburg Pike, Falls Church, VA 22041.

Navy — Information: Chief of Information, Dept. of the Navy, Wash., DC 20350-1200.

Navy Nurse Corps — Dir., Navy Nurse Corps, Dept. of the Navy, Wash., DC 20372-2000.

Air Force — Information: Office of Public Affairs, Dept. of the Air Force, Wash., DC 20330.

Air Force Nurse Corps — Chief, Air Force Nurse Corps, Office of the Surgeon General, USAF, Bolling AFB, Wash., DC 20332.

Marine Corps — Information: Commandant of the Marine Corps (Code PA), Headquarters, Marine Corps, Wash., DC 20380-0001.

Coast Guard — Information: Commandant (G-PDP), U.S. Coast Guard, 2100 Second St., SW, Wash., DC 20593-0001.

Veteran Population

Source: U.S. Dept. of Veterans Affairs; as of July 1992; in thousands

Total veterans in civilian life[a,b]	**26,981**
Total wartime veterans	**20,828**
Total Persian Gulf War	730
Persian Gulf War with service in Vietnam era	111
Persian Gulf War with no prior wartime service	618
Total Vietnam era	8,278
Vietnam era with service in Korean conflict	560
Vietnam era with no prior wartime service	7,718
Total Korean conflict	4,782
Korean conflict with service in WWII	823
Korean conflict with no prior wartime service	3,958
World War II	8,500
World War I	34
Total peacetime veterans	**6,153**
Total post-Vietnam era	3,060
Service between Korean conflict and Vietnam era only	2,911
Other peacetime	181

NOTE: Detail may not add to total shown due to rounding. (a) The category "Wartime veterans" equals the sum of Persian Gulf War (no service in Vietnam era), Vietnam era (no service in Korean conflict), Korean conflict (no service in World War II), World War II and World War I. The data refer only to veterans living in the U.S. and Puerto Rico since data on veterans living elsewhere are not available. (b) There are an indeterminate number of Mexican Border period veterans, 42 of whom were receiving benefits in March 1993.

Veterans Compensation and Pension Case Payments

Fiscal year	Living veteran cases (no.)	Deceased veteran cases (no.)	Total cases (no.)	Total disbursement (dollars)
1900	752,510	241,019	993,529	138,462,130
1910	602,622	318,461	921,083	159,974,056
1920	419,627	349,916	769,543	316,418,029
1930	542,610	298,223	840,833	418,432,808
1940	610,122	239,176	849,298	429,138,465
1950	2,368,238	658,123	3,026,361	2,009,462,298
1960	3,008,935	950,802	3,959,737	3,314,761,383
1970	3,127,338	1,487,176	4,614,514	5,113,649,490
1980	3,195,395	1,450,785	4,646,180	11,045,412,000
1990	2,746,329	837,596	3,583,925	15,535,069,000
1991	2,709,500	799,677	3,509,177	15,975,440,000
1992	2,673,833	753,981	3,427,814	16,145,203,000

Active Duty U.S. Military Personnel Strengths, Worldwide

(As of Sept. 30, 1992)

Source: U.S. Dept. of Defense

U.S. Territories & Special Locations	
U.S., 48 contiguous states	1,171,208
Alaska	22,208
Hawaii	44,864
Guam	7,844
Johnston Atoll	238
Puerto Rico	3,518
Transients	42,379
Afloat	170,731
Total[1]	**1,463,112**
Western & Southern Europe	
Belgium	2,151
Germany	134,483
Greece	1,260
Greenland	137
Iceland	3,094
Italy	13,246
Netherlands	2,384
Norway	218
Portugal	1,523
Spain	3,863
Turkey	4,824
United Kingdom	20,048
Afloat	17,464
Total[1]	**205,052**
East Asia & Pacific	
Australia	518
Japan	45,964
Philippines	1,929
Rep. of Korea	35,743
Singapore	145
Thailand	105
Afloat	12,990
Total[1]	**97,609**
Africa, Near East & South Asia	
Bahrain	305
Diego Garcia	1,253
Egypt	1,120
Kuwait	1,980
Saudi Arabia	1,801
Afloat	14,438
Total[1]	**21,243**
Sub-Saharan Africa	**547**
Other Western Hemisphere	
Bermuda	891
Canada	513
Cuba (Guantânamo)	2,392
Honduras	853
Panama	10,447
Afloat	2,407
Total[1]	**18,113**
Total Worldwide	**1,807,177**

(1) Area totals include countries with fewer than 100 assigned U.S. military members.

Estimates of Total Dollar Costs of American Wars

(millions of dollars, except percent)

Source: *The Military Budget and National Economic Priorities*, revised and updated by James L. Clayton.

Item	World War II	Vietnam Conflict	Korean Conflict	World War I	Civil War: Union	Civil War: Confederacy	Spanish American War	American Revolution	War of 1812	Mexican War
Original increment, direct costs:[1]										
Current dollars	360,000	140,600	50,000	32,700	2,300	1,000	270	100-140	89	82
Constant (1967) dollars	816,300	148,800	69,300	100,000	8,500	3,700	1,100	400-680	170	300
Percent 1 year's GNP	188	14	15	43	74	123	2	104	14	4
Service-connected veterans' benefits[2]	96,666	32,288	19,512	19,580	3,290	—	2,111	28	20	26
Interest, pmts. on war loans[3]	(5)	(5)	(5)	11,000	1,200	(5)	60	20	14	10
Current cost to 1990[4]	466,000	179,000	72,000	63,500	6,790	(5)	2,441	170	120	120

(1) Figures are rounded and taken from Claudia D. Goldin, *Encyclopedia of American Economic History*. (2) Total cost to Oct. 1, 1990. For World War I and later wars, benefits are actual service-connected figures from *Annual Report* of Veterans Administration. For earlier wars, service-connected veterans' benefits are estimated at 40 percent of total, the approximate ratio of service-connected to total benefits since World War I. (3) Total cost to 1990. Interest payments are a very rough approximation based on the percentage of the original costs of each war financed by money creation and debt, the difference between the level of public debt at the beginning of the war and at its end, and the approximate time required to pay off the war debts. (4) Figures are rounded estimates. (5) Unknown.

The Medal of Honor

The Medal of Honor is the highest military award for bravery that can be given to any individual in the United States. The first Army Medals were awarded on March 25, 1863, and the first Navy Medals went to sailors and Marines on April 3, 1863.

The Medal of Honor, established by Joint Resolution of Congress, July 12, 1862 (amended by Acts of Congress, July 9, 1918, and July 25, 1963), is awarded in the name of Congress to a person who, while a member of the Armed Forces, distinguishes himself or herself conspicuously by gallantry and intrepidity at the risk of life above and beyond the call of duty while engaged in an action against any enemy of the United States; while engaged in military operations involving conflict with an opposing foreign force; or while serving with friendly foreign forces engaged in an armed conflict against an opposing armed force in which the United States is not a belligerent party. The deed performed must have been one of personal bravery or self-sacrifice so conspicuous as to clearly distinguish the individual above his or her comrades and must have involved risk of life. Incontestable proof of the performance of service is required, and each recommendation for award of this decoration is considered on the standard of extraordinary merit.

Prior to World War I, the 2,625 Army Medal of Honor awards up to that time were reviewed to determine which past awards met new stringent criteria. The Army removed 911 names from the list, most of them former members of a volunteer infantry group during the Civil War who had been induced to extend their enlistments when they were promised the Medal.

Since that review Medals of Honor have been awarded in the following numbers:

World War I	96	Korean War	131
World War II	432	Vietnam War	238

Armed Services Senior Enlisted Advisers

The U.S. Army, Navy, and Air Force in 1966-1967 each created a new position of senior enlisted adviser, whose primary job is to represent the point of view of the services' enlisted men and women on matters of welfare, morale, and any problems concerning enlisted personnel. The senior adviser has direct access to the military chief of the service and policy-making bodies. The senior enlisted adviser for each service as of mid-1993 is:

Army—Sgt. Major of the Army Richard A. Kidd.

Navy—Master Chief Petty Officer of the Navy John Hagan.

Air Force—Chief Master Sgt. of the Air Force Gary R. Pfingston.

Marines—Sgt. Major of the Marine Corps Harold G. Overstreet.

Armed Forces Per 1,000 Persons, 1992[1]

Source: U.S. Arms Control and Disarmament Agency

Argentina	2.0	India	1.4	Pakistan	4.5
Australia	3.9	Indonesia	1.5	Philippines	1.7
Austria	6.6	Iran	8.9	Poland	7.7
Belgium	8.1	Iraq	20.3	Portugal	5.6
Bolivia	4.1	Israel	33.4	Romania	8.6
Brazil	2.0	Italy	6.2	Russia	18.2
Bulgaria	11.9	Japan	2.0	Singapore	19.9
Canada	3.0	Jordan	27.3	South Africa	1.9
Chile	6.8	Korea, North	50.9	Spain	5.6
China	2.6	Korea, South	14.5	Sweden	8.8
Colombia	4.1	Kuwait	9.8	Switzerland	0.2
Cuba	16.1	Lebanon	13.1	Syria	32.4
Denmark	5.7	Libya	19.1	Taiwan	17.4
Egypt	7.3	Mexico	2.1	Thailand	5.0
El Salvador	8.0	Mongolia	7.1	Turkey	9.6
Finland	6.5	Morocco	7.5	United Kingdom	5.1
France	7.5	Netherlands	6.1	United States	7.5
Germany	5.6	Nicaragua	3.6	Venezuela	3.7
Greece	15.5	Norway	7.6	Vietnam	12.4
Hungary	7.8	Oman	21.8		

(1) Includes active-duty personnel performing national security functions. Does not include reserves or paramilitary forces.

Monthly Military Pay Scale

Source: U.S. Dept. of Defense

(effective Jan. 1, 1993)

	Years of Service						
Rank/Grade	**2**	**4**	**8**	**12**	**16**	**20**	**26**
General—0-10	$6,889.20	$6,889.20	$7,153.50	$7,549.80	$8,089.80	$8,631.60	$9,169.50
Lt. General—0-9	6,052.50	6,181.50	6,338.70	6,602.40	7,153.50	7,549.80	8,089.80
Major General—0-8	5,502.30	5,632.80	6,052.50	6,338.70	6,602.40	7,153.50	7,329.90
Brig. General—0-7	4,740.60	4,740.60	4,953.30	5,240.40	6,052.50	6,468.90	6,468.90
Colonel—0-6	3,614.70	3,851.70	3,851.70	3,851.70	4,612.20	4,953.30	5,683.50
Lt. Colonel—0-5	3,089.40	3,303.30	3,303.30	3,586.50	4,113.30	4,480.80	4,637.40
Major—0-4	2,700.90	2,881.20	3,063.90	3,456.90	3,773.40	3,877.50	3,877.50
Captain—0-3	2,304.60	2,725.80	2,958.60	3,273.00	3,353.40	3,353.40	3,353.40
1st Lt.—0-2	1,962.60	2,437.50	2,488.20	2,488.20	2,488.20	2,488.20	2,488.20
2d Lt.—0-1	1,624.20	1,962.60	1,962.60	1,962.60	1,962.60	1,962.60	1,962.60
Chief Warrant—W-4	2,253.00	2,304.60	2,515.50	2,804.40	3,037.50	3,219.60	3,586.50
Warrant Officer—W-1	1,596.90	1,730.10	1,886.10	2,043.90	2,200.50	2,358.30	2,358.30
Sgt. Major—E-9	0.00	0.00	0.00	2,497.80	2,613.00	2,723.40	3,144.90
Master Sgt.—E-8	0.00	0.00	2,048.70	2,162.70	2,277.60	2,387.10	2,808.60
Sgt. 1st class—E-7	1,544.10	1,657.20	1,768.20	1,881.90	2,022.90	2,106.00	2,527.20
Staff Sgt.—E-6	1,341.30	1,456.50	1,565.40	1,706.70	1,817.10	1,844.70	1,844.70
Sergeant—E-5	1,175.40	1,286.10	1,426.50	1,537.50	1,565.40	1,565.40	1,565.40
Corporal—E-4	1,063.80	1,213.20	1,261.20	1,261.20	1,261.20	1,261.20	1,261.20
Pvt. 1st class—E-3	1,001.10	1,082.10	1,082.10	1,082.10	1,082.10	1,082.10	1,082.10
Private—E-2	913.20	913.20	913.20	913.20	913.20	913.20	913.20
Recruit—E-1	814.80	814.80	814.80	814.80	814.80	814.80	814.80

Chairmen of the Joint Chiefs of Staff

Gen. of the Army Omar N. Bradley, USA	Aug. 16, 1949 – Aug. 14, 1953
Adm. Arthur W. Radford, USN	Aug. 15, 1953 – Aug. 14, 1957
Gen. Nathan F. Twining, USAF	Aug. 15, 1957 – Sept. 30, 1960
Gen. Lyman L. Lemnitzer, USA	Oct. 1, 1960 – Sept. 30, 1962
Gen. Maxwell D. Taylor, USA	Oct. 1, 1962 – July 3, 1964
Gen. Earle G. Wheeler, USA	July 3, 1964 – July 2, 1970
Adm. Thomas H. Moorer, USN	July 3, 1970 – June 30, 1974
Gen. George S. Brown, USAF	July 1, 1974 – June 20, 1978
Gen. David C. Jones, USAF	June 21, 1978 – June 18, 1982
Gen. John W. Vessey Jr., USA	June 18, 1982 – Sept. 30, 1985
Adm. William J. Crowe, Jr., USN	Oct. 1, 1985 – Sept. 30, 1989
Gen. Colin L. Powell, USA	Oct. 1, 1989 – Sept. 30, 1993
Gen. John Shalikashvili, USA	Oct. 1, 1993 –

Nuclear Arms Treaties and Negotiations: An Historical Overview

Aug. 4, 1963—Nuclear Test Ban Treaty signed in Moscow by the U.S., USSR, and Great Britain; prohibited testing of nuclear weapons in space, above ground, and under water.

Jan. 1967—Outer Space Treaty banned the introduction of nuclear weapons into space.

1968—Nuclear Nonproliferation Treaty, with U.S., USSR, and Great Britain as major signers, limited the spread of military nuclear technology by agreement not to assist nonnuclear nations in getting or making nuclear weapons.

May 26, 1972—Strategic Arms Limitation Treaty (SALT I) signed in Moscow by U.S. and USSR. In the area of defensive nuclear weapons, the treaty limited antiballistic missiles to 2 sites of 100 antiballistic missile launchers in each country (amended in 1974 to one site in each country). The treaty also imposed a 5-year freeze on testing and deployment of intercontinental ballistic missiles and submarine-launched ballistic missiles. An interim short-term agreement putting a ceiling on numbers of offensive nuclear weapons was also signed. SALT I was in effect until Oct. 3, 1977.

July 3, 1974—Protocol on antiballistic missile systems and a treaty and protocol on limiting underground testing of nuclear weapons was signed by U.S. and USSR in Moscow.

Sept. 1977—U.S. and USSR agreed to continue to abide by SALT I, despite its expiration date.

June 18, 1979—SALT II, signed in Vienna by the U.S. and USSR, constrained offensive nuclear weapons, limiting each side to 2,400 missile launchers and heavy bombers with that ceiling to apply until Jan. 1, 1985. The treaty also set a subceiling of 1,320 ICBMs and SLBMs with multiple warheads on each side. Although approved by the U.S. Senate Foreign Relations Committee, the treaty never reached the Senate floor for ratification because Pres. Jimmy Carter withdrew his support for the treaty following the December 1979 invasion of Afghanistan by Soviet troops.

Dec. 8, 1987—Intermediate-Range Nuclear Forces (INF) Treaty signed in Washington, D.C., by USSR leader Mikhail Gorbachev and U.S. Pres. Ronald Reagan, eliminating all medium- and shorter-range nuclear missiles; ratified with conditions by U.S. Senate on May 27, 1988.

July 31, 1991—Strategic Arms Reduction Treaty (START I) signed in Moscow by Soviet Pres. Mikhail Gorbachev and U.S. Pres. George Bush to reduce strategic offensive arms by approximately 30 percent in three phases over seven years. START I was the first treaty to mandate reductions by the superpowers. The treaty was approved by the U.S. Senate Oct. 1, 1992. With the breakup of the Soviet Union in December 1991, four former Soviet republics became independent nations with strategic nuclear weapons on their territory—Russia, Ukraine, Kazakhstan, and Belarus. The last 3 agreed in principle in 1992 to transfer their nuclear weapons to Russia and ratify START I. The Russian Supreme Soviet voted to ratify Nov. 4, 1992, but Russia decided not to provide the instruments of ratification until Ukraine, Kazakhstan, and Belarus each ratified START I and acceded to the Nuclear Nonproliferation Treaty as nonnuclear nations. By late 1993, Belarus and Kazakhstan had ratified START I and acceded to the nonproliferation treaty. In September 1993, Ukrainian President Leonid Kravchuk agreed to a plan that could restart stalled negotiations on the transfer of nuclear weapons to Russia.

Jan. 3, 1993—START II signed in Moscow by U.S. Pres. George Bush and Russian Pres. Boris Yeltsin. Potentially the broadest disarmament pact in history, it called for both sides to reduce their long-range nuclear arsenals to about one-third of their then-current levels within a decade and would entirely eliminate land-based multiple-warhead missiles. Action will not be taken on START II until START I is fully ratified. START II will require ratification only by the U.S. Senate and the legislature of Russia, which would, under the guidelines for START I finalization, be the only remaining nuclear republic of the former Soviet Union.

Leading Arms Importers, 1989

Source: U.S. Arms Control and Disarmament Agency

	Principal supplier[1]	Imports (millions of dollars)
1. Saudi Arabia	United Kingdom	$4,200
2. Afghanistan	Soviet Union	3,800
3. India	Soviet Union	3,500
4. Greece	United States	2,000
5. Iraq	Soviet Union	1,900
6. United States	—	1,600
7. Japan	United States	1,400
8. Iran	—	1,300
9. Vietnam	Soviet Union	1,300
10. Cuba	Soviet Union	1,200
11. Turkey	United States	$1,100
12. Syria	Soviet Union	1,000
13. Libya	Soviet Union	975
14. Ethiopia	Soviet Union	925
15. Soviet Union	Czechoslovakia	900
16. W. Germany	United States	875
17. United Arab Emirates	France	850
18. E. Germany	Soviet Union	825
19. Angola	Soviet Union	750
20. Spain	United States	750

(1) Supplies more than 50 percent of total value of imports.

Policy Guidelines on Homosexual Conduct in the Armed Forces

Source: U.S. Dept. of Defense

On July 19, 1993, Secretary of Defense Les Aspin directed the implementation of President Bill Clinton's new policy on homosexual conduct in the U.S. armed forces. The move followed months of controversy and marked a compromise between the Clinton administration and those in the Pentagon and Congress opposed to lifting an unqualified ban on homosexuals in the military that had stood for 50 years. The following are excerpts from the Department of Defense's official policy guidelines, effective October 1, 1993.

Accession Policy: Applicants for military service will no longer be asked or required to reveal if they are homosexual or bisexual, but applicants will be informed of the conduct that is proscribed for members of the armed forces, including homosexual conduct.

Discharge Policy: Sexual orientation will not be a bar to service unless manifested by homosexual conduct. The military will discharge members who engage in homosexual conduct, which is defined as a homosexual act, a statement that the member is homosexual or bisexual, or a marriage or attempted marriage to someone of the same gender.

Investigations Policy: No investigations or inquiries will be conducted solely to determine a servicemember's sexual orientation. Commanders will initiate inquiries or investigations when there is credible information that a basis for discharge or disciplinary action exists. Sexual orientation, absent credible information that a crime has been committed, will not be the subject of a criminal investigation. An allegation or statement by another that a servicemember is a homosexual, alone, is not grounds for either a criminal investigation or a commander's inquiry.

Credible Information: Credible information of homosexual conduct exists when the information, considered in light of its source and all attendant circumstances, supports a reasonable belief that a servicemember has engaged in such conduct. It requires a determination based on articulable facts, not just a belief or suspicion.

Off-Base Conduct: No distinction will be made between off-base and on-base conduct.

Casualties in Principal Wars of the U.S.

Source: U.S. Dept. of Defense

Data prior to World War I are based on incomplete records in many cases. Casualty data are confined to dead and wounded personnel and therefore exclude personnel captured or missing in action who were subsequently returned to military control. Dash (—) indicates information is not available.

			Casualties			
Wars	Branch of service	Number serving	Battle deaths	Other deaths	Wounds not mortal[7]	Total
Revolutionary War	**Total**	—	**4,435**	—	**6,188**	—
1775-1783	Army	184,000	4,044	—	6,004	—
	Navy	to	342	—	114	—
	Marines	250,000	49	—	70	—
War of 1812	**Total**	**286,730[8]**	**2,260**	—	**4,505**	**6,765**
1812-1815	Army	—	1,950	—	4,000	5,950
	Navy	—	265	—	439	704
	Marines	—	45	—	66	111
Mexican War	**Total**	**78,718[8]**	**1,733**	**11,550**	**4,152**	**17,435**
1846-1848	Army	—	1,721	11,500	4,102	17,373
	Navy	—	1	—	3	4
	Marines	—	11	—	47	58
Civil War	**Total**	**2,213,363[8]**	**140,414**	**224,097**	**281,881**	**646,392**
(Union forces)	Army	2,128,948	138,154	221,374	280,040	639,568
1861-1865	Navy	—	2,112	2,411	1,710	6,233
	Marines	84,415	148	312	131	591
Confederate forces	**Total**	—	**74,524**	**59,297**	—	**133,821**
(estimate)[1]	Army	600,000	—	—	—	—
1863-1866	Navy	to	—	—	—	—
	Marines	1,500,000	—	—	—	—
Spanish-American War	**Total**	**306,760**	**385**	**2,061**	**1,662**	**4,108**
1898	Army[3]	280,564	369	2,061	1,594	4,024
	Navy	22,875	10	0	47	57
	Marines	3,321	6	0	21	27
World War I	**Total**	**4,743,826**	**53,513**	**63,195**	**204,002**	**320,710**
April 6, 1917-	Army[4]	4,057,101	50,510	55,868	193,663	300,041
Nov. 11, 1918	Navy	599,051	431	6,856	819	8,106
	Marines	78,839	2,461	390	9,520	12,371
	Coast Guard	8,835	111	81	—	192
World War II	**Total**	**16,353,659**	**292,131**	**115,185**	**670,846**	**1,078,162**
Dec. 7, 1941-	Army[5]	11,260,000	234,874	83,400	565,861	884,135
Dec. 31, 1946[2]	Navy[6]	4,183,466	36,950	25,664	37,778	100,392
	Marines	669,100	19,733	4,778	67,207	91,718
	Coast Guard	241,093	574	1,343	—	1,917
Korean War[9]	**Total**	**5,764,143**	**33,651**	—	**103,284**	—
June 25, 1950-	Army	2,834,000	27,709	—	77,596	—
July 27, 1953	Navy	1,177,000	474	176	1,576	2,226
	Marines	424,000	4,270	339	23,744	28,353
	Air Force	1,285,000	1,198	298	368	1,864
	Coast Guard	44,143	—	—	—	—
Vietnam War[10]	**Total**	**8,744,000**	**47,369**	**10,799**	**153,303**	**211,471**
Aug. 4, 1964-	Army	4,368,000	30,911	7,274	96,802	134,987
Jan. 27, 1973	Navy	1,842,000	1,631	927	4,178	6,736
	Marines	794,000	13,083	1,754	51,392	66,229
	Air Force	1,740,000	1,739	842	931	3,512
	Coast Guard	—	5	2	—	7
Persian Gulf War	**Total**	**467,539[11]**	**148**	**145**	**467**	**760**
1991	Army	246,682	98	105	—	—
	Navy	98,852	6	8	—	—
	Marines	71,254	24	26	—	—
	Air Force	50,751	20	6	—	—

(1) Authoritative statistics for the Confederate forces are not available. An estimated 26,000-31,000 Confederate personnel died in Union prisons.
(2) Data are for the period Dec. 1, 1941 through Dec. 31, 1946 when hostilities were officially terminated by Presidential Proclamation, but few battle deaths or wounds not mortal were incurred after the Japanese acceptance of Allied peace terms on Aug. 14, 1945. Numbers serving from Dec. 1, 1941-Aug. 31, 1945 were: Total—14,903,213; Army—10,420,000; Navy—3,883,520; and Marine Corps—599,693.
(3) Number serving covers the period April 21-Aug. 13, 1898, while dead and wounded data are for the period May 1-Aug. 31, 1898. Active hostilities ceased on Aug. 13, 1898, but ratifications of the treaty of peace were not exchanged between the United States and Spain until April 11, 1899.
(4) Includes Army Air Forces battle deaths and wounds not mortal, as well as casualties suffered by American forces in Northern Russia to Aug. 25, 1919, and in Siberia to April 1, 1920. Other deaths covered the period April 1, 1917-Dec. 31, 1918.
(5) Includes Army Air Forces.
(6) Battle deaths and wounds not mortal include casualties incurred in Oct. 1941 due to hostile action.
(7) Marine Corps data for World War II, the Spanish-American War and prior wars represent the number of individuals wounded, whereas all other data in this column represent the total number (incidence) of wounds.
(8) As reported by the Commissioner of Pensions in his Annual Report for Fiscal Year 1903.
(9) Battle deaths and other deaths associated with the conflict differ from previously reported figures due to a reexamination of individual files by the U.S. Dept. of Defense.
(10) Number serving covers the period Aug. 4, 1964-Jan. 27, 1973 (date of ceasefire). Number of casualties incurred in connection with the conflict in Vietnam covers the period Jan. 1, 1961-Sept. 30, 1977. Includes casualties incurred in Mayaguez Incident. Wounds not mortal exclude 150,375 persons not requiring hospital care.
(11) Estimated because of continual changing deployment figures.

CONSUMER INFORMATION

Consumer Information Catalog

Source: Consumer Information Center, U.S. General Services Administration

The *Consumer Information Catalog* is a free listing of about 200 of the best federal consumer publications. They range from booklets on financial planning to planning a diet, from learning about federal benefits to getting an education, from fixing a car to dealing effectively with consumer problems or getting a passport or a birth certificate. Many of these booklets are free.

The *Consumer Information Catalog* is published quarterly by the Consumer Information Center of the U.S. General Services Administration. For a free copy of the most current *Consumer Information Catalog*, send your name and address to: Consumer Information Catalog, Pueblo, CO 81009. Educators, libraries, and other nonprofit groups who are able to distribute 25 or more copies of the *Consumer Information Catalog* on a quarterly basis should write to the same address for an application to be placed on the mailing list. Costs prevent the Consumer Information Center from maintaining a mailing list for individuals.

The booklets listed below are available *free* from the *Consumer Information Catalog* as of fall 1993. Quantities of some may be limited. There is a $1 fee for handling. To order, please send your name and address, the item numbers of the booklets you want, and the $1 fee to: S. James, Consumer Information Center, Pueblo, CO 81009.

Some Free Publications

Children

Feeding Baby: Nature and Nurture. Explains why breast milk is best for babies. Compares milk-based and soy-based formulas and discusses the dangers of confusing soy beverages with soy-based formulas. 4 pp. (1990) **506Z.**

Growing up Drug Free. Shows parents what children should understand about drugs, including alcohol and tobacco; identifies classes and types of drugs and resource contacts. 55 pp. (1989) **507Z.**

Preparing Your Child for College: A Resource Book for Parents. Worksheets and checklists to help you and your child plan for college academically and financially. Gives examples and charts of typical college costs; suggests ways to save and invest; discusses financial assistance. 49 pp. (1992) **596Z.**

Unemployment and Health Insurance

Health Benefits Under COBRA (Consolidated Omnibus Budget Reconciliation Act). Helps you keep or buy coverage for yourself and your family after a job loss, reduced work hours, divorce, or death of employed family member. 18 pp. (1990) **509Z.**

How to File a Claim for Your COBRA Benefits. An outline of what to do if your COBRA claim or appeal is denied. Covers what the law does for you, waiting period, and more. 2 pp. (1991) **510Z.**

Federal Benefits

Guide to Health Insurance for People with Medicare. Provides guidance on filling in gaps in Medicare coverage while avoiding paying for duplicate benefits. 24 pp. (1992) **515Z.**

Medicare and Advance Directives. Explains how to set up a living will or durable power of attorney to help you receive the medical treatment you want if you become physically or mentally unable to communicate. 4 pp. (1992) **516Z.**

Medicare Q & A. Answers 60 frequently asked questions about Medicare, including eligibility, enrollment, deductibles, services, and benefits. 16 pp. (1991) **517Z.**

Request for Earnings and Benefit Estimate Statement. A form to complete and return to the Social Security Administration to get your earnings history and an estimate of future benefits. 3 pp. (1989) **519Z.**

Understanding Social Security. Explains retirement, disability, and survivor's benefits, Medicare coverage, Supplemental Security Income, and more. 41 pp. (1991) **521Z.**

Health

Cancer Tests You Should Know About: A Guide for People 65 and Over. Describes six tests that can help detect cancer early. Checklists included. 16 pp. (1992) **619Z.**

Clearing the Air. Tips on how to quit smoking for keeps. 24 pp. (1991) **529Z.**

Contact Lenses: The Better the Care the Safer the Wear. Discusses infection risks and charts proper care for hard, gas-permeable, and extended-wear soft lenses. 3 pp. (1991) **530Z.**

Cosmetic Safety. Describes which cosmetic products are regulated and explains terms such as "hypoallergenic" and "natural." 8 pp. (1992) **614Z.**

Facing Forward: A Guide for Cancer Survivors. Advice on coping with the many effects of this illness. Practical information on health care, insurance, job concerns, and more. 45 pp. (1990) **513Z.**

Guide to Choosing a Nursing Home. Help for evaluating your need, with information on services. Medicare/Medicaid coverage, insurance, contracts, and more. 199 pp. (1991) **533Z.**

Hocus-Pocus as Applied to Arthritis. Discusses fraudulent cures and medically sound treatments for arthritis, rheumatism, and gout. 7 pp. (1989) **355Z.**

Silicone Breast Implants. Where to get more information or report problems, and what to do if you already have gel-filled or saline implants. 4 pp. (1992) **598Z.**

Surviving Cold and Flu Season. Discusses symptoms of different cold and flu viruses, when to consider vaccines, and treatments. 8 pp. (1993) **599Z.**

Who Donates Better Blood for You Than You Do? Discusses the advantages of donating blood to yourself before undergoing surgery. (1991) **538Z.**

Mental Health

Bipolar Disorder (Manic-Depressive Illness). Discusses signs and symptoms, available treatments, and how to get help. 5 pp. (1989) **621Z.**

A Consumer's Guide to Mental Health Services. Answers common questions, identifies warning signs, discusses treatments, and lists resources for help and information. 28 pp. (1987) **556Z.**

Depression. Describes symptoms and causes, diagnosis and treatment, and how to help someone suffering from depression. 4 pp. (1989) **557Z.**

Eating Disorders. Describes the dangers of these disorders, symptoms, treatments, how to help a victim, and resources for more information. (Anorexia and bulimia afflict at least 3% of girls and young adult women in the U.S.) 17 pp. (1993) **613Z.**

Obsessive-Compulsive Disorder. Covers how to identify and get help for this disorder, as well as treatments. 11 pp. (1991) **559Z.**

You Are Not Alone. Facts about mental health and illness, behavior that may indicate a problem, and how to find help. 12 pp. (1992) **566Z.**

Housing

Fair Housing: It's Your Right. Outlines how you are protected against discrimination when buying, selling, or renting a home or apartment and when applying for a mortgage. Includes a form to use if you think your rights have been violated. 9 pp. (1993) **567Z.**

A Home of Your Own. Advice on choosing and buying a home. Answers questions about FHA-insured homes that have been foreclosed and reverted to government ownership. 30 pp. (1990) **568Z.**

How to Buy a Home with a Low Down Payment. Describes private and federal options for obtaining a low-down-payment mortgage, how to qualify, and how to determine what you can afford. 8 pp. (1993) **631Z.**

Tips for Energy Savers. How to save energy and money through conservation measures relating to transportation, home heating and cooling, lighting, cooking, and running appliances. 29 pp. (1991) **604Z.**

Money Management

Building Your Future with Annuities. An annuity is tax-deferred money set aside for future use, typically at retirement. Discusses various types—their features and costs—and answers questions. 13 pp. (1992) **571Z.**

Buying Treasury Securities. Information about bills, notes, and bonds issued by the U.S. government. 16 pp. (1993) **572Z.**

Investment Swindles: How They Work and How to Avoid Them. How to protect yourself against illegal, yet legitimate-sounding telemarketing and direct mail offers. 20 pp. (1987) **573Z.**

Investors' Bill of Rights. Tips to help make an informed decision when making investments. 7 pp. (1987) **574Z.**

Business Directory

Listed below are major U.S. corporations, and major foreign corporations, **whose operations—products and services—directly concern the American consumer.** At the end of each listing is a **representative sample** of the company's products.

Company...Address...Phone Number...Chief executive officer...Business.

A & W Brands Inc....709 Westchester Ave., White Plains, NY 10604...(914) 397-1700...M.L. Lowenkron...soft drinks.

AMR Corp....PO Box 619616, Dallas/Ft. Worth Airport, TX 75261...(817) 355-1234...Robert Crandall...Air transportation (American Airlines).

Abbott Laboratories... One Abbott Park Rd., Abbott Park, IL 60064...(708) 937-6100...D.L. Burnham...health care prods.

Aetna Life & Casualty Co....151 Farmington Ave., Hartford, CT 06156...(203) 273-0123...Ronald E. Compton...insurance, financial services.

H.F. Ahmanson & Co....4900 Rivergrade Rd., Irwindale, CA 91706...(818) 814-7986...R.H. Deihi...operates largest S&L assn. in U.S. (Home Savings of America).

Alberto-Culver Co....2525 Armitage Ave., Melrose Park, IL 60160...(708) 450-3000...Leonard H. Lavin...hair care preparations, feminine hygiene products, household and grocery items.

Albertson's Inc....250 Parkcenter Blvd., Boise, ID 83726...(208) 385-6200...Gary Michael...supermarkets.

Alcan Aluminium Ltd....1188 Sherbrooke St. W., Montreal, Que., Canada H3A 3G2...(514) 848-8000...David Morton...aluminum producer.

Alexander & Alexander Services Inc....1211 Ave. of the Americas, New York, NY 10036...(212) 840-8500...T.H. Irvin...insurance & financial services.

AlliedSignal Inc.... Box 4000, Morristown, NJ 07962...(201) 455-2000...Lawrence Bossidy...aerospace, engineered materials, automotive prods.

Alltel Corp.... One Allied Dr., Little Rock, AR 72202...(501) 661-8000...J.T. Ford...telephone service in Midwest, South, and Eastern U.S.

Aluminum Co. of America...1501 Alcoa Bldg., Pittsburgh, PA 15219...(412) 553-4545...Paul O'Neill...mining, refining, & processing of aluminum.

Amerada Hess Corp....1185 Ave. of the Americas, N.Y., NY 10036...(212) 997-8500...L. Hess...integrated petroleum co.

American Brands, Inc....1700 E. Putnam Ave., Old Greenwich, CT 06870...(203) 698-5000...W.J. Alley...tobacco (Pall Mall, Carlton, Half and Half, Paleden pipe tobacco), whiskey (Jim Beam), snack foods, life insurance, office prods., food, financial services, toiletries.

American Cyanamid Co.... One Cyanamid Plaza, Wayne, NJ 07470...(201) 831-2000...A.J. Costello...medical, agricultural, chemical, and consumer prods.

American Express Co.... World Financial Center, N.Y., NY 10285...(212) 640-2000...H. Golub...travelers checks, credit card services, insurance, investment services (Shearson Lehman).

American Greetings Corp....10500 American Rd., Cleveland, OH 44144...(216) 252-7300...M. Weiss...greeting cards, stationery, gift items.

American Home Products Corp....685 3d Ave., N.Y., NY 10017...(212) 986-1000...J.R. Stafford...prescription and ethical drugs (Advil, Anacin, Robitussin), household prods. (Woolite, Easy-Off oven cleaner, Black Flag, Wizard air fresheners), food (Chef Boy-ar-dee).

American Stores Co....709 E. South Temple, Salt Lake City, Utah 84102...(801) 539-0112...Victor Lund ...retail food markets, dept. & drug stores.

American Telephone & Telegraph Co....32 Ave. of the Americas, N.Y., NY 10013...(212) 605-5500...Robert Allen...communications, financial services.

Amoco Corp....200 E. Randolph Dr., Chicago, IL 60601...(312) 856-6111...H.L. Fuller...oil and gas exploration, production, and marketing.

Anheuser-Busch, Inc.... One Busch Place, St. Louis, MO 63118...(314) 577-2000...August A. Busch 3d...brewing (Budweiser, Michelob, Bud Light, Natural Light, Busch), theme parks, snack foods (Eagle).

Apple Computer, Inc....10260 Bandley Dr., Cupertino, CA 95014...(408) 996-1010...Michael Spindler...manuf. personal computers.

Armstrong World Industries...P.O. Box 3001, 313 W. Liberty St., Lancaster, PA 17604...(717) 397-0611...W.W. Adams...interior furnishings.

Arvin Industries, Inc.... Box 3000, Columbus, IN 47202...(812) 379-3000...J.K. Baker...auto emission & noise control systems.

Ashland Oil, Inc....P.O. Box 391, Ashland, KY 41114...(606) 329-3333...J.R. Hall...petroleum refiner, chemicals.

Atlantic Richfield Co....515 S. Flower St., Los Angeles, CA 90071...(213) 486-3511 ...L.M. Cook...petroleum, chemicals, other natural resources.

Avery Denison Corp....150 N. Orange Grove Blvd., Pasadena, CA 91103...(818) 304-2000...Charles D. Miller...self-adhesive labels, office prods., specialty chemicals.

Avon Products, Inc....9 West 57th St., N.Y., NY 10019...(212) 546-6015...J. E. Preston...cosmetics, fragrances, toiletries, health care.

Bausch & Lomb... One Lincoln First Square, Rochester, NY 14601...(716) 338-6000...D.E. Gill...manuf. of vision care products, accessories.

Baxter International Inc.... One Baxter Pky., Deerfield, IL 60015...(708) 948-2000...Vernon R. Loucks Jr....health care prods. & services.

Bell Atlantic Corp....1717 Arch St., Philadelphia, PA 19103...(215) 963-6000...R.W. Smith...telephone service in mid-Atlantic region.

BellSouth Corp....1155 Peachtree St. NE, Atlanta, GA 30367...(404) 249-2000...J.L. Clendenin...telephone service in the South.

Bethlehem Steel Corp....8th & Eaton Ave., Bethlehem, PA 18016...(215) 694-2424...C.H. Barnette...steel & steel prods.

Bic Corporation...500 Bic Dr., Milford, CT 06400...(203) 783-2000...Bruno Bich...writing instruments, disposable lighters, shavers, and correction fluid (Wite-Out).

Black & Decker Corp....701 E. Joppa Rd., Towson, MD 21286...(410) 583-3900...N.D. Archibald...manuf. power tools, household prods., small appliances.

H & R Block, Inc....4410 Main St., Kansas City, MO 64111...(816) 753-6900...Henry W. Bloch...tax preparation.

Blockbuster Entertainment Corp.... One Blockbuster Plaza, Ft. Lauderdale, FL 33301...(305) 832-3000...H. Wayne Huizenga...video rental superstores.

Boeing Company...7755 E. Marginal Way So., Seattle, WA 98108...(206) 655-6123...F.A. Shrontz...aircraft manuf.

Boise Cascade Corp.... One Jefferson Square, Boise, ID 83728...(208) 384-6161...J.B. Fery...timber, paper, wood prod.

Borden, Inc....277 Park Ave., N.Y., NY 10172...(212) 573-4000...A.S. D'Amato...food, cheese and cheese products, snacks (Cracker Jack), beverages, adhesives (Elmer's, Krazy Glue), pasta (Prince, Creamette), pasta sauce (Aunt Millie's, Classico).

Bristol-Myers Squibb Co....345 Park Ave., N.Y., NY 10154...(212) 546-4000...Richard L. Gelb...toiletries (Ban antiperspirant), hair items (Clairol), drugs (Bufferin, Comtrex, Excedrin), household prods. (Drano, Windex), infant formula (Enfamil).

Brown-Forman Inc....850 Dixie Highway, Louisville, KY 40210...(502) 585-1100...Owsley Brown 2d...distilled spirits (Jack Daniel's, Early Times), wines (Bolla, Fontana Candita), champagne (Korbel), liquor (Southern Comfort), Lenox china and crystal.

Brown Group, Inc....8400 Maryland Ave., St. Louis, MO 63166...(314) 854-4000...B.A. Brightwater Jr....manuf. and wholesaler of women's and children's shoes (Buster Brown, Naturalizer); specialty retailing.

Brunswick Corp.... One N. Field Ct., Lake Forest, IL 60045...(708) 735-4700...J.F. Reichert...marine, recreation prods., bowling centers & equip., fishing equip.

Burlington Coat Factory Warehouse Corp....1830 Route 130 North, Burlington, NJ 08016...(609) 387-7800...M.G. Milstein...discount apparel stores.

Burlington Northern Inc....777 Main St., Ft. Worth, TX 76102...(817) 878-2000...G. Grinstein...rail transportation.

CBS Inc....51 W. 52d St., N.Y., NY 10019...(212) 975-4321...L.A. Tisch...broadcasting.

CPC International, Inc.... International Plaza, Englewood Cliffs, NJ 07632...(201) 894-4000...Charles Shoemate...branded food items (Hellman's mayonnaise, Best Foods, Mazola corn oil, Skippy peanut butter, Knorr soups, Thomas' English muffins, Mueller pasta prods., Arnold breads).

Caesar's World, Inc....1801 Century Park East, Los Angeles, CA 90067...(310) 552-2711...H. Gluck...hotels & casinos, resort hotels.

Caldor Corp....20 Glover Ave., Norwalk, CT 06856...(203) 849-2000...D.R. Clarke...discount retailer.

Callaway Golf Co....2285 Rutherford Rd., Carlsbad, CA 92008...(619) 931-1771...E. Callaway...manuf. & markets golf clubs.

Campbell Soup Co.... Campbell Pl., Camden, NJ 08103...(609) 342-4800...D.W. Johnson...canned soups, spaghetti (Franco-American), vegetable juice (V-8), pork and beans, pet foods, confections, Swanson frozen dinners, Prego spaghetti sauce, Mrs. Paul's frozen fish, Pepperidge Farm breads.

Capital Cities/ABC, Inc....77 W. 66th Street, New York, NY 10023...(212) 456-7777...D.B. Burke...operates television and radio stations, newspapers, cable TV (ESPN); newspapers, specialized business and consumer periodicals.

Carnival Cruise Lines Inc....3655 NW 87th St., Miami, FL 33138...(305) 599-2600...M. Arison...cruise line.

Carter-Wallace, Inc....1345 Ave. of the Americas, New York, NY 10105...(212) 339-5000...H.H. Hoyt Jr....personal care items, antiperspirant (Arrid), shave lathers (Rise), tooth polish (Pearl Drops), condoms (Trojan), laxative (Carter's Pills), pet prods. (Victory flea collars).

Caterpillar Inc....100 N.E. Adams St., Peoria, IL 61629...(309) 675-1000...Donald Fites...heavy duty earth-moving equip.

Chase Manhattan Corp....1 Chase Manhattan Plaza, New York, NY 10081...(212) 552-2222...Thomas Labrecque ...bank holding co.

Chevron Corp....225 Bush St., San Francisco, CA 94104...(415) 894-7700...K.T. Derr...integrated oil co.

Chrysler Corp....12000 Chrysler Dr., Highland Pk., MI 48288...(313) 956-5741...R.J. Eaton...cars, trucks.

Church & Dwight Co., Inc....469 N. Harrison St., Princeton, NJ 08543...(609) 683-5900...D.C. Minton...consumer prods. (Arm & Hammer).

Circuit City Stores, Inc....9950 Maryland Dr., Richmond, VA 23233...(804) 527-4000...R.L. Sharp...retailer of electronic equip., consumer appliances.

Circus Circus Enterprises, Inc....2880 Las Vegas Blvd. S., Las Vegas, NV 89109...(702) 734-0410...W.G. Bennett... casino operator.

Citicorp...399 Park Ave., N.Y., NY 10043...(212) 559-1000...J.S. Reed...largest U.S. commercial bank.

Clayton Homes...P.O. Box 15169, Knoxville, TN 37901...(615) 970-7200...J.L. Clayton...produces & sells manufactured homes.

Clorox Co....1221 Broadway, Oakland, CA 94612...(510) 271-7000...C.R. Weaver...retail consumer prods. (Formula 409, Pine-Sol, Kingsford charcoal briquets, Deer Park bottled water, Combat insecticides, Hidden Valley Ranch salad dressing, Soft Scrub cleanser).

Coachman Industries Inc....601 E. Beardsley Ave., Elkhart, IN 46515...(219) 262-0123...T.H. Corson...manuf. recreational vehicles.

Coca-Cola Co.... One Coca-Cola Plaza N.W., Atlanta, GA 30313...(404) 676-2121...R.C. Goizueta...soft drinks (Coca-Cola, Sprite, Nestea), syrups, citrus and fruit juices (Minute Maid, Hi-C).

Colgate-Palmolive Co....300 Park Ave., N.Y., NY 10022...(212) 310-2000...R. Mark...soaps (Palmolive, Irish Spring), detergents (Fab, Ajax, Fresh Start), toothpaste (Colgate, Ultra Brite), household prods. (Handy Wipes, Curad bandages).

Commodore International Ltd....1200 Wilson Dr., West Chester, PA 19380...(215) 431-9100...I. Gould...microcomputer systems, semiconductors component, consumer electronics, office equipment.

Compaq Computer Corp....20555 SH 149, Houston, TX 77070...(713) 370-0670...E. Pfeiffer...portable, desktop computers.

Adolph Coors Co.... Golden, CO 80401...(303) 279-6565...W. K. Coors...brewery.

Corning Inc.... Houghton Park, Corning, NY 14831...(607) 974-9000...J.R. Houghton ...glass mfg.

Crane Co....100 First Stamford Place, Stamford, CT 06902...(203) 363-7300...R.S. Evans...manuf. engineered industrial prods.

A.T. Cross Co.... One Albion Rd., Lincoln, RI 02865...(401) 333-1200...B.R. Boss...writing instruments.

Crystal Brands, Inc.... Crystal Brands Rd., Southport, CT 06490...(203) 254-6200...G.E. Allen...apparel, accessories (Evan Picone, Izod).

Culbro Corp....387 Park Avenue South, New York, NY 10016...(212) 561-8700...E. M. Cullman...cigars (Corina, Robert Burns, White Owl, Tiparillo's), snack foods.

Dana Corp....4500 Dorr St., Toledo, OH 43615...(419) 535-4500...S.J. Morcott...truck and auto parts supplies.

Data General Corp....4400 Computer Dr., Westboro, MA 01580...(508) 366-8911...R.L. Skates...computer & communications sytems manuf.

Dayton Hudson Corp....777 Nicollet Mall, Minneapolis, MN 55402...(612) 370-6948...K.A. Macke...department, specialty stores, Mervyn's, Target.

Deere & Co.... John Deere Rd., Moline, IL 61265...(309) 765-8000...H.W. Becherer...farm, industrial, and outdoor power equip.

Delta Air Lines, Inc.... Hartsfield Atlanta Intl. Airport, Atlanta, GA 30320...(404) 765-2600...Ronald W. Allen...air transportation.

Dial Corp.... Dial Tower, Phoenix, AZ 85077-2346...(602) 207-4000...J.W. Teets...consumer prods. (Dial, Purex detergents, Armour Star meats, Breck shampoo), contract and fast food services, manuf. buses.

Diebold, Inc....P.O. Box 8230, Canton, OH 44711...(216) 489-4000...R.W. Mahoney...manuf. equip. for financial insts.

Digital Equipment Corp....146 Main St., Maynard, MA 01754...(508) 493-5111...R.B. Palmer...computer systems manuf.

Walt Disney Co....500 S. Buena Vista St., Burbank, CA 91521...(818) 560-1000...M.D. Eisner...motion pictures, cable television, theme parks (Walt Disney World, Disneyland) and resorts, publishing, recordings, retailing (Disney stores).

Dole Food Co....31355 Oak Crest Drive, Westlake Village, CA 91361...(818) 879-6600...David Murdock...food products, fresh fruits and vegetables, real estate.

R.R. Donnelley & Sons Co....77 W. Wacker Rd., Chicago, IL 60616...(312) 326-8000...J.R. Walter...largest commercial printer.

Dow Chemical Co....2030 Dow Center, Midland, MI 48674...(517) 636-1000...F.P. Popoff...chemicals, plastics, metals, consumer prods. (Ziploc, Saran Wrap, Fantastik).

Dow Jones & Co....200 Liberty St., New York, NY 10281...(212) 416-2000...P. R. Kann...financial news service, publishing (Wall Street Journal, Barron's, Ottaway Newspapers).

Dun & Bradstreet Corp....299 Park Ave., New York, NY 10171...(212) 593-6800...C.W. Moritz...business information and computer services, publishing, broadcasting.

E.I. du Pont de Nemours & Co....1007 Market St., Wilmington, DE 19898...(302) 774-1000...Edgar Woolard Jr....chemicals, petroleum, consumer prods., coal.

Duracell Intl. Co.... Berkshire Corporate Park, Bethel, CT 06801...(203) 796-4000...C.R. Kidder...manuf. batteries.

Eastman Kodak Co....343 State St., Rochester, NY 14650...(716) 724-4000...K.R. Whitmore...photographic prods., chemicals, health care.

Eaton Corp.... Eaton Center, Cleveland, OH 44114...(216) 523-5000...W.E. Butler...manuf. of electronic, electrical prods., vehicle components.

Emerson Electric Co....8000 W. Florissant Ave., St. Louis, MO 63136...(314) 553-2000...C.F. Knight...electrical/ electronics products & systems.

Ethyl Corp....330 S. 4th St., Richmond, VA 23217...(804) 788-5000...B.C. Gottwald...petroleum and industrial chemicals.

Exxon Corp....225 E. John W. Carpenter Freeway, Irving, TX 75062...(214) 444-1000...L.G. Rawl...oil, natural gas, coal, chemicals.

Fabri-Centers of America, Inc...5555 Darrow Rd., Hudson, OH 44236...(216) 656-2600...Alan Rosskamm...specialty fabric stores.

Family Dollar Stores, Inc....P.O. Box 1017, Charlotte, NC 28201...(704) 847-6961...L. Levine...discount variety stores.

Fedders Corp....158 Highway 206, P.O. Box 265, Peapack, NJ 07977...(908) 234-2100...S. Giordano Jr....manuf. of room air conditioners.

Federal Express Corp....2005 Corporate Ave., Memphis, TN 38132...(901) 369-3600...F.W. Smith...express delivery service.

Fieldcrest Cannon, Inc.... One Lake Dr., Kannapolis, NC 28081...(704) 939-2000...J.M. Fitzgibbons...household textile prods., rugs (Karastan).

First Brands Corp....83 Wooster Hts. Rd., Danbury, CT 06813...(203) 731- 2300...A.E. Dudley...consumer prods. (Glad plastic bags, Scoop-Away cat litter, Prestone auto prods.).

Fleetwood Enterprises, Inc....P.O. Box 7638, Riverside, CA 92523...(714) 351-3500...John C. Crean...manufactured homes, recreational vehicles.

Fluor Corp....3333 Michelson Dr., Irvine, CA 92730...(714) 975-2000...L.G. McGraw...engineering and construction, natural resources.

Ford Motor Co.... The American Rd., Dearborn, MI 48121...(313) 322-3000...H.A. Poling...motor vehicles, Ford Tractor, Lincoln-Mercury.

Fruit of The Loom, Inc....6300 Sears Tower, Chicago, IL 60606...(312) 876-1724...W. Farley...manuf. of men's and boy's underwear.

GTE Corp.... One Stamford Forum, Stamford, CT 06904...(203) 965-2000...C.E. Lee...largest U.S. local exchange telephone co., cellular telephone operator.

Gannett Co., Inc....1100 Wilson Blvd., Arlington, VA 22234...(703) 284-6000...J.J. Curley...newspaper publishing (USA Today), TV stations, outdoor advertising.

The GAP, Inc....1 Harrison, San Francisco, CA 94105...(415) 952-4400...D.G. Fisher...casual and activewear retailer.

Gencorp...175 Ghent Rd., Fairlawn, OH 44313...(216) 869-4200...A.W. Reynolds...aerospace, auto prods., polymer prods.

General Dynamics Corp....3190 Fairview Park Dr., Falls Church, VA 22042...(703) 876-3000...William Anders ...military and commercial aircraft, tactical missiles.

General Electric Co....3135 Easton Ave., Fairfield, CT 06431...(203) 373-2211...J. F. Welch Jr....electrical, electronic equip., radio, television (NBC), plastics manuf.

General Host Corp....1 Station Place, Stamford, CT 06902...(203) 357-9900...H.J. Ashton...crafts, lawn and garden retail stores (Frank's Nursery & Crafts).

General Mills, Inc.... One General Mills Blvd., Minneapolis, MN 55426...(612) 540-2311...H.B. Atwater Jr....foods (Total, Bisquick, Wheaties, Cheerios, Hamburger Helper, Gorton's, Betty Crocker), restaurants (Red Lobster, Olive Garden).

General Motors Corp....3044 W. Grand Rapids, Detroit, MI 48202...(313) 556-5000...J.F. Smith Jr....world's largest auto manuf.

Genesco Inc.... Genesco Park, Nashville, TN 37202...(615) 367-7000...W.S. Wire 2d...footwear and men's clothing manuf. and retailer.

Genuine Parts Co....2999 Circle 75 Pkwy., Atlanta, GA 30339...(404) 953-1700...L. L. Prince...distributes auto replacement parts (NAPA).

Georgia-Pacific Corp....133 Peachtree St., NE, Atlanta, GA 30303...(404) 521-4000...T.M. Hahn Jr....building prods., pulp, paper, chemicals.

Gerber Products Co....445 State St., Fremont, MI 49413...(616) 928-2718...A.A. Piergallini...baby foods, clothing, nursery accessories.

Giant Food Inc....P.O. Box 1804, Washington, DC 20013...(301) 341-4100...I. Cohen...supermarkets.

Gillette Co.... Prudential Tower Bldg., Boston, MA 02199...(617) 421-7000...Alfred Zeier...razors, pens (Paper Mate), toiletries (Right Guard deodorants, Foamy shaving cream, Earth Born shampoo), hair products (Toni, Adorn).

Goodyear Tire & Rubber Co....1144 E. Market St., Akron, OH 44316...(216) 796-2121...Stanley Gault...tires, rubber prods.

W.R. Grace & Co.... One Town Center Rd., Boca Raton, FL 33486...(407) 362-2000...J.P. Bolduc...chemicals, natural resources, health care.

Great Atlantic & Pacific Tea Co....2 Paragon Dr., Montvale, NJ 07645...(201) 573-9700...James Wood...supermarket chain.

Grumman Corp....1111 Stewart Ave., Bethpage, NY 11714...(516) 575-0574...Renso Caporali...aerospace, truck bodies, electronics.

Hannaford Bros. Co....145 Pleasant Hill Rd., Scarborough, ME 04074...(207) 883-2911...Hugh G. Farrington...operates supermarkets, drug stores.

Harley-Davidson, Inc....3700 W. Juneau Ave., Milwaukee, WI 53201...(414) 342-4680...R.F. Terrlink...manuf. of motorcycles, parts & accessories.

Hartmarx...101 N. Wacker Dr., Chicago, IL 60606...(312) 372-6300...E.O. Hand...apparel manufacturer and retailer (Hickey-Freeman, Hart Schaffner & Marx).

Hasbro Inc....1027 Newport Ave., Pawtucket, RI 02862...(401) 431-8400...A.G. Hassenfeld...toy manuf. & marketer (Milton Bradley, Playskool, G.I. Joe, Parker Bros. games, Tonka trucks, Play-Doh).

H.J. Heinz Co....P.O. Box 57, Pittsburgh, PA 15230...(412) 456-3700...Anthony J.F. O'Reilly...foods (Star-Kist, Ore-Ida, '57 Varieties), 9-Lives cat food, Weight Watchers.

Helene Curtis...325 N. Wells St., Chicago, IL 60610...(312) 661-0222...R.J. Gidwitz...hair care prods. (Finesse, Suave, Salon Selectives), antiperspirant (Degree).

Hershey Foods Corp....100 Crystal A Dr., Hershey, PA 17033...(717) 534-7552...R.A. Zimmerman...chocolate & confectionery prods. (Reese's peanut butter cups, Kit Kat, Peter Paul Mounds, Almond Joy), pasta (San Giorgio, Ronzoni).

Hewlett-Packard Co....P.O. Box 10301, Palo Alto, CA 94304...(415) 857-1501...L.E. Platt...manuf. electronic prods. and systems.

Hillenbrand Industries, Inc.... Highway 46, Batesville, IN 47006...(812) 934-7000...W.A. Hillenbrand...manuf. burial caskets, electronically operated hospital beds, luggage.

Home Depot, Inc....2727 Paces Ferry Rd., Atlanta, GA 30339...(404) 433-8211...Bernard Marcus...retailer of building materials & home improvement prods.

Honda Motor Co., LTD...1290 Ave. of the Americas, N.Y., NY 10104...(212) 765-3804...N. Kawamoto...manuf. autos, motorcycles.

Honeywell, Inc.... Honeywell Plaza, Minneapolis, MN 55408...(612) 951-1000...J.J. Renier...industrial systems & controls, aerospace guidance systems, information systems.

Geo. A. Hormel & Co....501 16th Ave. N.E., Austin, MN 55912...(507) 437-5611...R.L. Knowlton...meat packaging, pork and beef prods. (Spam, Dinty Moore, Mary Kitchen).

Houghton Mifflin Co.... One Beacon St., Boston, MA 02108...(617) 351-5000...Nader F. Darehshori...book publishing.

Household International Inc....2700 Sanders Rd., Prospect Heights, IL 60070...(708) 564-5000...D.C. Clark...financial and insurance services.

Huffy Corp....7701 Byers Rd., Miamisburg, OH 45342...(513) 866-6251...H.A. Shaw 3d...bicycles, sports and hardware equip. manuf.

Humana, Inc....500 W. Main St., Louisville, KY 40201...(502) 580-1000...D. A. Jones...operates hospitals, provides health care plans.

ITT Corp....1330 Ave. of the Americas, N.Y., NY 10022...(212) 258-1000...R.V. Araskog...manuf., installs communication and electronic equip., auto equip., insurance, financial services, hotels, educational services.

Imperial Oil Ltd....111 St. Clair Ave. W., Toronto, Ont., Canada M5W 1K3...(416) 968-5076...R.B. Peterson... Canada's largest oil co.

International Business Machines Corp.... Old Orchard Rd., Armonk, NY 10504...(914) 765-7777...Louis Gerstner Jr. ...information processing systems, equip., and services.

International Paper Co....2 Manhattanville Rd., Purchase, NY 10577...(914) 397-1500...J.A. Georges...paper, wood prods.

Johnson & Johnson... One Johnson & Johnson Plaza, New Brunswick, NJ 08933...(201) 524-0400...R.S. Larsen... surgical dressings, pharmaceuticals (Tylenol), consumer prods.

Jostens, Inc....5501 Norman Center Dr., Minneapolis, MN 55437...(612) 830-3300...H. W. Lurton...school rings, yearbooks.

Kmart Corp....3100 W. Big Beaver Rd., Troy, MI 48084...(313) 643-1000...J. E. Antonini...largest U.S. chain of discount stores, book stores (Waldenbooks), cafeterias, drug stores (Pay Less Drug Stores), home improvement retail stores.

Kellogg Co.... One Kellogg Sq., Battle Creek, MI 49016...(616) 961-6122...Arnold G. Laugbo...ready to eat cereals & other food prods., Mrs. Smith's Pie Co., Eggo.

Kimberly-Clark Corp....P.O. Box 619100, Dallas, TX 75261...(214) 830-1200...Wayne R. Sanders...paper and lumber prods., consumer prods. (Kleenex, Huggies, Depend).

King World Productions, Inc....1700 Broadway, N.Y., NY 10019...(212) 315-4000...M. King...syndicator of TV programs (Oprah Winfrey Show, Wheel of Fortune, Jeopardy, Inside Edition).

Knight-Ridder, Inc.... One Herold Plaza, Miami, FL 33132...(305) 376-3800...J.K. Batten...newspaper publishing, TV broadcasting, book publishing, information services.

Kroger Co....1014 Vine St., Cincinnati, OH 45202...(513) 762-4000...Joseph Pichler...grocery chain.

L.A. Gear, Inc....2850 Ocean Park Blvd., Santa Monica, CA 90405...(213) 822-1995...Stanley P. Gold...athletic & leisure footwear, casual apparel.

La-Z-Boy Chair Co....1284 N. Telegraph Rd., Monroe, MI 48161...(313) 242-1444...C. T. Knabusch...reclining chair mfg.

Lands' End, Inc.... One Lands' End Lane, Dodgeville, WI 53595...(608) 935-9341...R.C. Anderson...direct-mail catalog co.

Eli Lilly & Company... Lilly Corp. Center, Indianapolis, IN 46285...(317) 276-2000...Vaughn D. Bryson...mfg. human health and agricultural products.

The Limited, Inc.... Two Limited Pkwy., Columbus, OH 43216...(614) 479-7000...L.H. Wexner...women's apparel stores (Lane Bryant, Lerner, Victoria's Secret), Abercrombie & Fitch.

Litton Industries, Inc....360 N. Crescent Dr., Beverly Hills, CA 90210...(310) 859-5000...A.J. Brann...industrial systems & services, advanced electronic systems, electronic & electrical prods., marine engineering.

Lockheed Corp....4500 Park Granada Blvd., Calabasas, CA 91399...(818) 876-2380...D.M. Tellep...commercial and military aircraft, missiles.

Loews Corp....667 Madison Ave., N.Y., NY 10021...(212) 545-2000...Laurence A. Tisch...tobacco prods. (Kent, Newport, True), watches, hotels, real estate, insurance.

Long's Drug Stores Corp....141 North Civic Dr., Walnut Creek, CA 94596...(510) 937-1170...R.M. Long...drug store chain.

Lowe's Cos., Inc.... Hwy. 268 East, N. Wilkesboro, NC 28659...(919) 651-4000...L.G. Herring...retailer of building materials & related prods.

Luby's Cafeterias, Inc....2211 Northeast Loop 410, San Antonio, TX 78265...(512) 654-9000...R. Erben...operates cafeterias in SW U.S.

Manor Care, Inc....10750 Columbia Pike, Silver Spring, MD 20901...(301) 681-9400...S. Bainum Jr....operates nursing homes.

Marriott Corp.... Marriott Dr., Wash., DC 20058...(301) 380-9000...J. Willard Marriott Jr....hotels, food service.

Martin Marietta Corp....6801 Rockledge Dr., Bethesda, MD 20817...(301) 897-6000...N.R. Augustine...electronics, aerospace.

Mattel, Inc....333 Continental Blvd., El Segundo, CA 90245...(213) 524-2000...J.W. Amerman...toy & hobby prods. (Barbie doll, Hot Wheels).

May Department Stores Co....611 Olive Street, St. Louis, MO 63101...(314) 342-6300...D.C. Farrell...department stores (Hecht's, Lord & Taylor, Foley's).

Maytag Corp....403 W. 4th St. North, Newton, IA 50208...(515) 792-8000...L.A. Handley...manuf. home laundry equip., appliances (Magic Chef, Admiral).

McDonald's Corp.... McDonald's Plaza, Oak Brook, IL 60521...(708) 575-3000...M.R. Quinlan...fast food restaurants.

McDonnell Douglas Corp....P.O. Box 516, St. Louis, MO 63166...(314) 232-0232...J. F. McDonnell...commercial & military aircraft, space systems & missiles.

McGraw-Hill, Inc....1221 Ave. of the Americas, New York, NY 10020...(212) 512-2000...J.L. Dionne...book, magazine publishing (Business Week), information & financial services (Standard and Poor's), TV stations.

Mead Corporation... Courthouse Plaza Northeast, Dayton, OH 45463...(513) 495-6323...S.C. Mason...printing and writing paper, paperboard, packaging, shipping containers, pulp and lumber.

Media General, Inc....333 E. Grace St., Richmond, VA 23219...(804) 649-6000...J.S. Bryan 3d...broadcasting, newspaper publishing.

Medtronic, Inc....7000 Central Ave. N.E., Minneapolis, MN 55432...(612) 574-4000...W.W. George...manuf. prosthetic and therapeutic devices.

Melville Corp....1 Theall Rd., Rye, NY 10580...(914) 925-4000...S.P. Goldstein...shoe stores (Thom McAn), apparel (Marshalls, Chess King), drug stores.

Merck & Co., Inc....P.O. Box 2000, Rahway, NJ 07065...(908) 594-4000...P. Roy Vagelos...human & animal health care prods.

Meredith Corp....1716 Locust St., Des Moines, IA 50336...(515) 284-3000...J.D. Rehm...magazine publishing (Better Homes and Gardens, Ladies Home Journal), book publishing, broadcasting.

Merrill Lynch & Co., Inc.... World Financial Center, N. Tower, N.Y., NY 10281...(212) 449-1000...Daniel P. Tully...securities broker, financial services.

Microsoft Corp....16011 Northeast 36th Way, Redmond, WA 98073-9717...(206) 882-8080...William H. Gates...the world's largest computer software company.

Minnesota Mining & Manuf. Co....3M Center, St. Paul, MN 55144...(612) 733-1110...L.D. DeSimone...abrasives, adhesives, building services & chemicals, electrical, health care, photographic, printing, recording materials, consumer prods. (Scotch Tape, Post-It).

Mirage Resorts, Inc....3400 Las Vegas Blvd., S., Las Vegas, NV 89109...(702) 791-7111...S.A. Wynn...hotel-casino operator (Mirage, Treasure Island, Golden Nugget).

Mobil Corp....3225 Gallows Rd., Fairfax, VA 22037...(703) 846-3000...A.E. Murray...international oil co., chemicals.

Monsanto Company...800 N. Lindbergh Blvd., St. Louis, MO 63167...(314) 694-1000...R. J. Mahoney...chemicals, agricultural prods., pharmaceuticals, consumer prods. (Nutra-Sweet).

Motorola, Inc....1303 E. Algonquin Rd., Schaumburg, IL 60196...(708) 576-5000...G. Fisher...electronic equipment and components.

National Medical Enterprises, Inc....P.O. Box 4070, Santa Monica, CA 90404...(310) 315-8000...J.C. Barbakow...operates hospitals.

National Semiconductor Corp....2900 Semiconductor Dr., Santa Clara, CA 95052...(408) 721-5000...P. Sprague ...manuf. of semiconductors.

Navistar Intl. Corp....455 N. Cityfront Plaza Dr., Chicago, IL 60611...(312) 836-2000...J.C. Cotting...manuf. heavy duty trucks, parts.

New York Times Co....229 W. 43rd St., N.Y., NY 10036...(212) 556-4317...A. O. Sulzberger...newspapers, radio, CATV stations, magazines (Family Circle, Golf Digest).

Nike, Inc.... One Bowerman Dr., Beaverton, OR 97005...(503) 671-6453...Philip Knight...athletic & leisure footwear.

Norfolk Southern Corp....3 Commercial Place, Norfolk, VA 23510...(804) 629-2600...D.R. Goode...operates Norfolk & Southern railways, freight carrier (North American Van Lines).

Northrop Corp....1840 Century Park E., Los Angeles, CA 90067...(213) 553-6262...K. Kresa...aircraft, electronics, communications.

Nynex Corp....335 Madison Ave., N.Y., NY 10017...(212) 370-7400...W.C. Ferguson...telephone co. in northeast U.S.

Occidental Petroleum Corp....10889 Wilshire Blvd., Los Angeles, CA 90024...(310) 208-2880...Ray Irani...oil, gas, chemicals, coal, agriculture.

Office Depot, Inc. . . . 2200 Old Germantown Rd., Delray Beach, FL 33445 . . . (407) 278-4800 . . . D.I. Fuente . . . retail office supply stores.
Ogden Corp. . . . 2 Pennsylvania Plaza, New York, NY 10121 . . . (212) 868-6100 . . . R.R. Ablon . . . transportation, foods, metals, financial services.
Olin Corp. . . . 120 Long Ridge Rd., Stamford, CT 06904 . . . (203) 356-2000 . . . J.W. Johnstone Jr. . . . chemicals, water treatment prods., aerospace.
Olsten Corp. . . . One Merrick Ave., Westbury, NY 11590 . . . (516) 832-8200 . . . F. N. Liguori . . . provides temporary workers.
Outboard Marine Corp. . . . 100 Sea Horse Dr., Waukegan, IL 60085 . . . (708) 689-6200 . . . J.C. Chapman . . . outboard motors (Evinrude, Johnson), boats.
'Owens-Corning Fiberglas Corp. . . . Fiberglas Tower, Toledo, OH 43659 . . . (419) 248-8000 . . . G.H. Minor . . . glass fiber and related prods.
Oxford Industries, Inc. . . . 222 Piedmont Ave., N.E., Atlanta, GA 30308 . . . (404) 659-2424 . . . J.H. Lanier . . . manuf. men's and women's apparel.

Pacific Telesis Group . . . 130 Kearny St., San Francisco, CA 94108 . . . (415) 394-3000 . . . S. L. Ginn . . . telephone service.
Paramount Communications Inc. . . . 15 Columbus Circle, N.Y., NY 10023 . . . (212) 373-8000 . . . M.S. Davis . . . entertainment (Paramount Pictures, Madison Square Garden), publishing (Simon & Schuster, Prentice Hall).
J.C. Penney Co. . . . 14841 N. Dallas Pkwy., P.O. Box 659000, Dallas, TX 75240 . . . (214) 591-1000 . . . W. R. Howell . . . dept. stores, catalog sales, drug stores, insurance.
Pennzoil Co. . . . P.O. Box 2967, Houston, TX 77252 . . . (713) 546-4000 . . . J.L. Pate . . . integrated oil and gas co.
Pep Boys—Manny, Moe & Jack . . . 3111 W. Allegheny Ave., Philadelphia, Pa. 19132 . . . (215) 229-9000 . . . M. G. Leibovitz . . . automotive parts and accessories, retail stores.
PepsiCo, Inc. . . . PepsiCo. World HQ, Purchase, NY 10577 . . . (914) 253-2000 . . . W. Calloway . . . soft drinks (Pepsi-Cola, Slice), snack foods (Ruffles, Lays, Sunchips, Doritos), restaurants (Pizza Hut, KFC, Taco Bell).
Perry Drug Stores, Inc. . . . 5400 Perry Dr., P.O. Box 436021, Pontiac, MI 48343 . . . (313) 334-1300 . . . J.A. Robinson . . . drug stores, health care.
Petrie Stores Corp. . . . 70 Enterprise Ave., Secaucus, NJ 07094 . . . (201) 866-3600 . . . M.J. Petrie . . . operates chain of women's specialty stores.
Pfizer Inc. . . . 235 E. 42d St., N.Y., NY 10017 . . . (212) 573-2323 . . . W.C. Steere Jr. . . . pharmaceutical, hospital, agricultural, chemical prods., consumer prods. (Visine eye drops, Ben-Gay pain relief).
Philip Morris Cos., Inc. . . . 120 Park Ave., N.Y., NY 10017 . . . (212) 880-5000 . . . Michael A. Miles . . . cigarettes (Marlboro, Virginia Slims), beer (Miller High Life, Lowenbrau brands), packaged foods (Jell-o, Entenmann baked goods, Maxwell House coffee, Kool Aid, Oscar Mayer meats, Tang, Cheez Whiz & Velveeta cheese prods.).
Phillips-Van Heusen Corp. . . . 1290 Ave. of the Americas, New York, NY 10104 . . . (212) 541-5200 . . . L. S. Phillips . . . manuf. apparel for men & women; operates retail stores.
Pitney Bowes, Inc. . . . One Elmcroft Rd., Stamford, CT 06926 . . . (203) 356-5000 . . . G. B. Harvey . . . postage meters, mail handling equip., office equipment.
Playboy Enterprises, Inc. . . . 680 N. Lake Shore Dr., Chicago, IL 60611 . . . (312) 751-8000 . . . C. Hefner . . . magazine publishing, CATV, merchandising.
Polaroid Corp. . . . 549 Technology Sq., Cambridge, MA 02139 . . . (617) 577-2000 . . . I.M. Booth . . . photographic equip., supplies, and optical goods.
Premark Intl., Inc. . . . 1717 Deerfield Rd., Deerfield, IL 60015 . . . (708) 405-6000 . . . W.L. Batts . . . consumer prods. (Tupperware, Hobart, West Bend).
Primerica, Corp. . . . 65 E. 55th St., N.Y., NY 10022 . . . (212) 891-8900 . . . S. I. Weill . . . insurance, financial services (Smith Barney, Shearson).
Procter & Gamble Co. . . . One Proctor & Gamble Plaza, Cincinnati, OH 45202 . . . (513) 983-1100 . . . E. L. Artzt . . . soap & detergent (Ivory, Cheer, Tide, Mr. Clean, Comet, Spic and Span, Zest), toiletries (Crest toothpaste, Prell, Head and Shoulders shampoos, Noxzema, Oil of Olay, Old Spice), pharmaceuticals (Pepto-Bismol); Pampers disposable diapers, Folgers coffee, Hawaiian Punch, Ultra Charmin toilet tissues, Bounty towels, Vicks cough medicines, Duncan Hines cakes, Crisco shortening.
Promus Cos. Inc. . . . 1023 Cherry Rd., Memphis, TN 38117 . . . (901) 762-8600 . . . M.D. Rose . . . casinos (Harrah), lodging (Hampton Inn, Embassy Suites).

Quaker Oats Co. . . . 321 N. Clark St., Chicago, IL 60604 . . . (312) 222-7111 . . . William D. Smithburg . . . foods, cereal (Quaker Oat Bran, Life, Cap'n Crunch, Puffed Wheat, Puffed Rice), foods (Aunt Jemima, Celeste pizza, Van Camp's pork and beans, Gatorade), pet foods (Ken-L-Ration, Gaines).
Quaker State Corp. . . . 255 Elm St., Oil City, PA 16301 . . . (814) 676-7676 . . . H.M. Baum . . . refining, marketing petroleum prods., filters, mining & marketing coal.

Ralston Purina Co. . . . Checkerboard Sq., St. Louis, MO 63164 . . . (314) 982-2161 . . . W. P. Stiritz . . . pet and livestock food (Purina), consumer prods. (Chex cereal, Beech-Nut baby food, Wonder bread, Hostess baked goods, Eveready and Energizer batteries).
Raytheon Company . . . 141 Spring St., Lexington, MA 02173 . . . (617) 862-6600 . . . Dennis J. Picard . . . electronics, aviation, appliances; Amana Refrigeration, Beech Aircraft.
Reader's Digest Assn. . . . Pleasantville, NY 10570 . . . (914) 238-1000 . . . George V. Grune . . . magazines, books.
Reebok Intl. Ltd. . . . 100 Technology Ctr. Dr., Stoughton, MA 02072 . . . (617) 341-5000 . . . P.B. Fireman . . . athletic & casual footwear, sportswear.
Reynolds Metals Co. . . . 6601 W. Broad St., Richmond, VA 23230 . . . (804) 281-2000 . . . Richard G. Holder . . . aluminum prods.
Rite Aid Corp. . . . 30 Hunter Lane, Camp Hill, PA 17011 . . . (717) 761-2633 . . . A. Grass . . . discount drug stores, beauty aid stores, auto parts stores.
RJR Nabisco Holdings Corp. . . . 1301 Ave. of the Americas, N.Y., NY 10019 . . . (212) 258-5600 . . . C.M. Harper . . . cigarettes (Winston, Salem, Camel), foods (Oreos, Ritz crackers).
Rockwell Intl. Corp. . . . 2201 Seal Beach Blvd., Seal Beach, CA 90740 . . . (213) 647-5000 . . . D. R. Beall . . . aerospace, electronic, automotive prods.
Rubbermaid Inc. . . . 1147 Akron Rd., Wooster, OH 44691 . . . (216) 264-6464 . . . W.R. Schmidt . . . rubber and plastic consumer prods.
Russell Corp. . . . 1 Lee St., Alexander City, AL 35010 . . . (205) 329-4000 . . . J.C. Adams . . . manuf. leisure apparel, athletic uniforms.
Ryder System, Inc. . . . 3600 NW 82d Ave., Miami, FL 33166 . . . (305) 593-3726 . . . M. A. Burns . . . truck leasing service.

Santa Fe Pacific Corp. . . . 1700 E. Golf Rd., Schaumberg, IL 60173 . . . (708) 995-6000 . . . Robert D. Krebs . . . railroad, real estate, construction, natural resources.
Sara Lee Corp. . . . 3 First National Plaza, Chicago, IL 60602 . . . (312) 726-2600 . . . J.H. Bryan . . . baked goods, fresh and processed meats, fresh and frozen fruits and vegetables and other packaged foods, beverages, tobacco products, hosiery, intimate apparel and knitwear, Hanes, Kiwi, Shasta, Hillshire Farm, L'eggs, Isotoner.
Schering-Plough Corp. . . . One Giralda Farms, Madison, NJ 07940 . . . (201) 822-7000 . . . R. P. Luciano . . . pharmaceuticals, consumer prods.
Schlumberger Ltd. . . . 277 Park Ave., New York, NY 10172 . . . (212) 350-9400 . . . D.E. Baird . . . oilfield services, electronics, measurement and control devices.
Scott Paper Co. . . . Scott Plaza, Phila., PA 19113 . . . (215) 522-5000 . . . P. E. Lippincott . . . toilet tissue, paper towels, napkins.
Seagram Co. Ltd. . . . 1430 Peel St., Montreal, Que., Canada H3A 1S9 . . . (514) 849-5271 . . . E.M. Bronfman . . . distilled spirits & wine (Crown Royal, Chivas Regal, Calvert, Wolfschmidt Vodka, Paul Masson, Christian Brothers, Martell, Myer's Jamaica Rum), juice (Tropicana).
Sears, Roebuck & Co. . . . Sears Tower, Chicago, IL 60684 . . . (312) 875-2500 . . . E.A. Brennan . . . merchandising, insurance (Allstate).
Service Merchandise, Inc. . . . 7100 Service Merchandise Dr., Brentwood, TN 37027 . . . (615) 660-6000 . . . R. Zimmerman . . . operates catalog showrooms.
Shaw Industries, Inc. . . . 616 E. Walnut Ave., Dalton, GA 30722 . . . (404) 278-3812 . . . R.E. Shaw . . . manuf. tufted carpeting (Magee, Philadelphia).
Sherwin-Williams Co. . . . 101 Prospect Ave. N.W., Cleveland, OH 44115 . . . (216) 566-2000 . . . John G. Breen . . . paint manuf. (Dutch Boy, Kem-Tone).
Sizzler Intl., Inc. . . . 12655 W. Jefferson Blvd., Los Angeles, CA 90060 . . . (310) 827-2300 . . . B.P. Bermington . . . quick service restaurants.
Skyline Corp. . . . 2520 By-Pass Rd., Elkhart, IN 46515 . . . (219) 294-6521 . . . Arthur J. Decio . . . mfg. housing and recreational vehicles.
Smucker (J.M.) Co. . . . Strawberry Lane, Orrville, OH 44667 . . . (216) 682-3000 . . . R.K. Smucker . . . preserves, jams, jellies, toppings.
Snap-on Tools Corp. . . . 2801 80th St., Kenosha, WI 53141 . . . (414) 656-5200 . . . R. A. Cornog . . . manuf. mechanic's tools, equip.

Sony Corp....9 W. 57th St., New York, NY 10019...(212) 371-5800...N. Ohga...manuf. televisions, radios, tape recorders, audio equip. (Walkman), videotape recorders; entertainment (Sony Pictures).

Southwest Airlines Co....P.O. Box 36611, Dallas, TX 75235...(214) 904-4000...H.D. Kelleher...air transportation.

Southwestern Bell Corp....P.O. Box 2933, San Antonio, TX 78299...(210) 821-4105...E.E. Whitacre Jr....telephone services.

Sprint Corp....2330 Shawnee Mission Pkwy., Westwood, KS 66025...(913) 624-3000...W.T. Esrey...long-distance telecommunications.

Stanley Works...1000 Stanley Drive, P.O. Box 7000, New Britain CT 06050...(203) 225-5111...R.H. Ayers...hand tools, hardware, door opening equip.

Stride Rite Corp....5 Cambridge Center, Cambridge, MA 02142...(617) 491-8800...Erwin Shames...manuf. & retailer children's footwear.

Sun Company, Inc....1801 Market St., Philadelphia, PA 19103...(215) 977-3000...R.H. Campbell...energy resources co.

Syms Corp.... Syms Way, Secaucus, NJ 07094...(201) 902-9600...S. Syms...operates off-price apparel stores.

Tambrands Inc....777 Westchester Ave., White Plains, NY 10604...(914) 696-6000...C. Chapman...feminine hygiene products (Tampax, Maxithins).

Tandem Computers...19333 Vallco Pkwy., Cupertino, CA 95014...(408) 285-6000...T. G. Treybig...supplier of computer systems and networks.

Tandy Corp....1800 One Tandy Center, Fort Worth, TX 76102...(817) 390-3700...J.F. Roach...consumer electronics retailing (Computer City, Radio Shack).

Teledyne, Inc....1901 Ave. of the Stars, Los Angeles, CA 90067...(310) 277-3311...William Rutledge...electronics, aerospace prods., industrial prods., insurance, finance.

Tenneco, Inc....P.O. Box 2511, Houston, TX 77252...(713) 757-2131...M. H. Walsh...oil, natural gas pipelines, shipbuilding, farm equip.

Texaco Inc....2000 Westchester Ave., White Plains, NY 10650...(914) 253-4000...J.W. Kinnear...petroleum and petroleum prods.

Texas Instruments Inc....13500 N. Central Expressway, Dallas, TX 75265...(214) 995-2011...Jerry Junkins...electrical & electronics prods.

Textron Inc....40 Westminster St., Providence, RI 02903...(401) 421-2800...J.F. Handymon...aerospace, consumer, industrial, metal prods., consumer finance, insurance, management services.

Tiffany & Co....727 5th Ave., New York, NY 10022...(212) 755-8000...W.R. Chaney...designs, manuf., and distributes jewelry & gift items.

Time Warner Inc.... Time & Life Bldg., Rockefeller Center, New York, NY 10020...(212) 522-1212...G.M. Levin...magazine publisher (Time, Sports Illustrated, Fortune, Money, People), CATV (HBO, Cinemax), book publishing (Little, Brown, Warner Books), motion pictures (Warner Bros.).

Tootsie Roll Industries, Inc....7401 S. Cicero Ave., Chicago, IL 60629...(312) 838-3400...M.J. Gordon...candy (Tootsie Roll, Mason Dots, Charms).

Toro Co....8111 Lyndale Ave. South, Bloomington, MN 55420...(612) 887-8801...K. B. Melrose...lawn and turf maintenance (Lawn Boy); snow removal equipment.

Toys "R" Us...461 From Rd., Paramus, NJ 07652...(201) 262-7800...Charles Lazarus...toy retailer, clothing stores (Kids "R" Us).

Transamerica Corp....600 Montgomery St., San Francisco, CA 94111...(415) 983-4000...Frank C. Herringer...insurance, financial, business services.

Travelers Corp.... One Tower Sq., Hartford, CT 06183...(203) 277-0111...E. H. Budd...insurance.

Tribune Co....435 N. Michigan Ave., Chicago, IL 60611...(312) 222-9100...C.T. Brumback...newpaper publishing, broadcasting, entertainment (Chicago Cubs baseball team).

Trinity Industries, Inc....2525 Stemmons Freeway, Dallas, TX 75356...(214) 631-4420...W.R. Wallace...manufactures variety of metal products.

TRW Inc....1900 Richmond Rd., Cleveland, OH 44124...(216) 291-7000...J.T. Gorman...car and truck operations, electronics, and space systems.

Turner Broadcasting System, Inc....1 CNN Center, Atlanta, GA 30303...(404) 827-1700...R.E. Turner...operates cable TV networks: CNN, TBS, TNT; owns MGM film library; owns Atlanta Braves, Hawks.

USAIR Group, Inc....1911 Jefferson Davis Hwy., Arlington, VA 22202...(703) 418-7000...Seth E. Schofield...air carrier of passengers, property, and mail.

UST Inc....100 W. Putnam Ave., Greenwich, CT 06830...(203) 661-1100...L.F. Bantle...smokeless tobacco (Copenhagen, Skoal, Happy Days), pipes, pipe tobacco.

USX-U.S. Steel Group...600 Grant St., Pittsburgh, PA 15230...(412) 433-1121...C.A. Corry...steel manuf.

Unilever, PLC...390 Park Ave., New York, NY 10022...(212) 906-3398...Michael Perry, chmn....soap, detergent, margarine, frozen food, toothpaste, tea, dried soups, ice cream, cosmetics, fragrances (Lever Brothers, Lipton, Pond's Vaseline Intensive Care, Obsession, Q-Tips, Cutex).

Union Carbide Corp....39 Old Ridgebury Rd., Danbury, CT 06817...(203) 794-2000...R.D. Kennedy...chemicals, industrial gases.

Union Pacific Corp.... Martin Tower, Bethlehem, PA 18018...(215) 861-3200...D. Lewis...railroad, natural resources.

Unisys Corp....P.O. Box 500, Blue Bell, PA 19424...(215) 986-6999...James Unruh...computer based information systems.

U.S. Shoe Corp.... One Eastwood Dr., Cincinnati, OH 45227...(513) 527-7459...B.B. Hudson...apparel, retailer (Casual Corner), shoes (Red Cross, Joyce), eye-care stores (LensCrafters).

United Technologies Corp.... United Technologies Bldg., Hartford, CT 06101...(203) 728-7000...R.F. Daniell...aerospace, industrial prods. & services, Carrier Corp., Otis Elevator, Pratt & Whitney, Sikorsky Aircraft.

Univar Corp....6100 Carillon Pt., Kirkland, WA 98033...(206) 899-3400...J.W. Bernard...industrial and agricultural chemicals, laboratory and graphic arts products distributor, home furnishing supplies and fabrics distributors.

Universal Foods Corp....433 East Michigan St., Milwaukee, WI 53202...(414) 271-6755...G.A. Osborn...yeast products, cheese products, dehydrated seasonings, food colors and flavors, imported gourmet foods.

Upjohn Co....7000 Portage Rd., Kalamazoo, MI 49001...(616) 323-4000...W.U. Parfet...pharmaceuticals (Motrin, Nuprin, Halcion), chemicals, agricultural and health care prods.

VF Corp....1047 No. Park Rd., Wyomissing, PA 19610...(215) 378-1151...L.R. Pugh...apparel, Vanity Fair, Lee, Wrangler jeans, Jantzen.

Wal-Mart Stores Inc.... Box 116, Bentonville, AR 72716...(501) 273-4000...D.D. Glass...retail dept. stores (Sam's Wholesale Clubs).

Walgreen Co....200 Wilmot Rd., Deerfield, IL 60015...(312) 940-2500...Charles R. Walgreen 3d...retail drug chain.

Warner-Lambert Co....201 Tabor Rd., Morris Plains, NJ 07950...(201) 540-2000...M.R. Goodes, chmn....health care prods. (Benadryl), consumer prods. (Efferdent dental cleanser, Hall cough tablets, Schick razors, Rolaids antacid, Listerine mouthwash).

Washington Post Co....1150 15th St., N.W., Washington, DC 20071...(202) 334-6000...D.E. Graham...newspapers, magazines (Newsweek), TV stations.

Weis Markets, Inc....1000 South Second Street, Sunbury, PA 17801...(717) 286-4571...S. Weis...operates supermarkets, distributes frozen foods and grocery items.

Wells Fargo & Co....420 Montgomery St., San Francisco, CA 94163...(415) 477-1000...C.E. Reichardt...banking.

Wendy's Intl., Inc....4288 W. Dublin-Granville Rd., Dublin, OH 43017...(614) 764-3100...J.W. Near...quick service restaurants.

Westinghouse Electric Corp.... Westinghouse Bldg., Gateway Center, Pittsburgh, PA 15222...(412) 244-2000...Michael H. Jordan...manuf. electrical, mechanical equip.; radio and television stations.

Westvaco Corp....299 Park Avenue, New York, NY 10171...(212) 688-5000...J.A. Luke Jr....manufactures paper for graphic reproduction, communications, and packaging.

Weyerhaeuser Co.... Tacoma, WA 98477...(206) 924-2345...George H. Weyerhaeuser...manuf., distribution of forest prods.

Whirlpool Corp.... Benton Harbor, MI 49022...(616) 926-5000...D.R. Whitwam...major home appliances.

Whitman Corp....111 Crossroads of Commerce, 3501 Algonquin Rd., Rolling Meadows, IL 60008...(708) 818-5000...Bruce S. Chelberg...diversified prods. and services, consumer prods., food, auto prods. (Midas).

Winn-Dixie Stores, Inc....5050 Edgewood Ct., Jacksonville, FL 32205...(904) 783-5000...A.D. Davis, chmn....supermarket chain.

Winnebago Industries, Inc....P.O. Box 152, Forest City, IA 50436...(515) 582-3535...J.K. Hanson, chmn....manuf. of motor homes, recreation vehicles.

Wolverine World Wide Corp....9341 Courtland Dr., Rockford, MI 49351...(616) 866-5500...T.D. Gleason...manuf. footwear (Hush Puppies).

Woolworth Corp....233 Broadway, N.Y., NY 10279...(212) 553-2000...W.K. Lavin...variety stores, shoe stores (Kinney), men's clothing (Richman Brothers), children's apparel (Kid's Mart), athletic footwear (Foot Locker).

Wm. Wrigley Jr. Co....410 N. Michigan Ave., Chicago, IL 60611...(312) 644-2121...William Wrigley...chewing gum.

Xerox Corp....P.O. Box 1600, Stamford, CT 06904...(203) 968-3000...Paul Allaire...equip. for reproduction, reduction, and transmission of business prods. & systems.

Zenith Electronics Corp....1000 Milwaukee Ave., Glenview, IL 60025...(708) 391-7000...Jerry K. Pearlman...consumer electronic prods.

Who Owns What: Familiar Consumer Products

Listed below are familiar consumer products and their parent companies. The parent company address can be found on pages 710-716.

Admiral appliances: Maytag
Advil: American Home Products
Ajax cleanser: Colgate-Palmolive
Almond Joy candy: Hershey
Anacin: American Home Products
Arrid antiperspirant: Carter-Wallace
Arnold breads: CPC International
Aunt Millie's pasta sauce: Borden
Ban antiperspirant: Bristol-Myers
Beech Aircraft: Raytheon
Beech-Nut babyfood: Ralston Purina
Ben-Gay: Pfizer
Betty Crocker products: General Mills
Breck shampoo: Dial
Budweiser beer: Anheuser-Busch
Bufferin: Bristol-Myers Squibb
Business Week magazine: McGraw-Hill
Buster Brown shoes: Brown Group
Cap'n Crunch cereal: Quaker Oats
Carrier air conditioners: United Technologies
Celeste Pizza: Quaker Oats
Charmin toilet tissues: Procter & Gamble
Chef Boy-ar-dee products: American Home Products
Cheer detergent: Procter & Gamble
Cheerios cereal: General Mills
Clairol hair products: Bristol-Myers Squibb
Clorets mints: Warner-Lambert
Combat insecticides: Clorox
Comet cleanser: Procter & Gamble
Copenhagen snuff: UST
Cracker Jacks: Borden
Crest toothpaste: Procter & Gamble
Crisco shortening: Procter & Gamble
Deer Park bottled water: Clorox
Degree antiperspirant: Helene Curtis
Doritos chips: PepsiCo
Drano: Bristol-Myers Squibb
Dristan: American Home Products
Duncan Hines cakes: Procter & Gamble
Easy-Off oven cleaner: American Home Products
Efferdent dental cleanser: Warner-Lambert
ESPN: Capital Cities/ABC
Eveready batteries: Ralston Purina
Excedrin: Bristol-Myers
Fab detergent: Colgate-Palmolive
Family Circle magazine: New York Times
Foamy shaving cream: Gillette
Folgers coffee: Procter & Gamble
Formula 409 spray cleaner: Clorox
Franco-American foods: Campbell Soup
Frito-Lay snacks: PepsiCo
Gatorade: Quaker Oats
Gleem toothpaste: Procter & Gamble
Handy Wipes: Colgate-Palmolive
Hanes hosiery: Sara Lee
Hawaiian Punch: Procter & Gamble
Head and Shoulders shampoo: Procter & Gamble
Hellman's mayonnaise: CPC International
Hi-C fruit drinks: Coca-Cola
Hillshire Farm meats: Sara Lee
Home Box Office: Time Warner
Hostess baked goods: Ralston Purina
Hush Puppies shoes: Wolverine World Wide
Ivory soap products: Procter & Gamble
Jack Daniel bourbon: Brown-Forman
Jell-o: Philip Morris
Jim Beam whiskey: American Brands
Ken-L-Ration pet foods: Quaker Oats
Kent cigarettes: Loews
Kinney shoe stores: Woolworth
Knorr soups: CPC International
Kool Aid: Philip Morris
Ladies Home Journal magazine: Meredith
Lee jeans: VF Corp.
Lenox china: Brown-Forman
Lens Crafters: U.S. Shoe
Lerner stores: The Limited
Lipton tea: Unilever
Listerine mouthwash: Warner-Lambert
Log Cabin syrup: Philip Morris
Lord & Taylor dept. stores: May Dept. Stores
Marlboro cigarettes: Philip Morris
Mazola oil: CPC International
Maxwell House coffee: Philip Morris
Michelob beer: Anheuser-Busch
Midas automotive centers: Whitman
Miller beer: Philip Morris
Milton Bradley games: Hasbro
Minute Rice: Philip Morris
Mrs. Paul's frozen fish: Campbell Soup
NBC Broadcasting: General Electric
Newsweek magazine: Washington Post
9-Lives cat food: H.J. Heinz
North American Van Lines: Norfolk Southern
Obsession fragrance: Unilever
Old Spice: Procter & Gamble
Olive Garden restaurants: General Mills
Ore-Ida frozen foods: H.J. Heinz
Oreo cookies: RJR Nabisco
Pampers: Procter & Gamble
Paper Mate pens: Gillette
People magazine: Time Warner
Pepto-Bismol: Procter & Gamble
Pepperidge Farm products: Campbell Soup
Pizza Hut restaurants: PepsiCo
Playskool toys: Hasbro
Prego spaghetti sauce: Campbell Soup
Prell shampoo: Procter & Gamble
Prentice-Hall publishing: Paramount
Prestone auto products: First Brands
Post-It stickers: Minn. Min. & Manuf.
Purex detergent: Dial
Q-Tips: Unilever
Radio Shack retail outlets: Tandy
Red Lobster Inns: General Mills
Reese's peanut butter cups: Hershey
Right Guard deodorant: Gillette
Rise shave lathers: Carter-Wallace
Ritz crackers: RJR Nabisco
Robitussin: American Home Products
Rolaids antacid: Warner-Lambert
Ruffles chips: PepsiCo
San Giorgio pasta: Hershey
Saran Wrap: Dow Chemical
Scotch tape: Minn. Min. & Manuf.
Skippy peanut butter: CPC International
Simon & Schuster publishing: Paramount
Southern Comfort liquor: Brown-Forman
Sports Illustrated magazine: Time Warner
Sprite soda: Coca-Cola
Sugartwin: Alberto Culver
Swanson frozen dinners: Campbell Soup
Taco Bell restaurants: PepsiCo
Thomas' English muffins: CPC International
Tide detergent: Procter & Gamble
Tonka trucks: Hasbro
Trojan condoms: Carter-Wallace
Tropicana juices: Seagram
Tupperware: Premark
Tylenol: Johnson & Johnson
Ultra Brite toothpaste: Colgate-Palmolive
V-8 vegetable juice: Campbell Soup
Vanity Fair apparel: VF Corp.
Velveeta cheese prods.: Philip Morris
Vicks cough medicines: Procter & Gamble
Victory flea collars: Carter-Wallace
Virginia Slims cigarettes: Philip Morris
Walkman: Sony
Wall Street Journal: Dow Jones
Weight Watchers: H.J. Heinz
Wheaties cereal: General Mills
White Owl cigars: Culbro
Wizard air freshener: American Home Products
Wyler's drink mixes: Borden

Interest Laws and Consumer Finance Loan Rates

Source: Revised by Christian T. Jones, Editor, Consumer Finance Law Bulletin, San Diego, CA

All states have laws regulating interest rates. These laws fix a legal or conventional rate, which applies when there is no contract for interest. They also fix a general maximum contract rate, but there are so many exceptions that the general contract maximum actually applies only to exceptional cases. Also, federal law has preempted state limits on first home mortgages, subject to each state's right to reinstate its own law, and given depository institutions parity with other state lenders.

Legal rate of interest. The legal or conventional rate of interest applies to money obligations when no interest rate is contracted for and also to judgments. The rate is usually somewhat below the general interest rate.

General maximum contract rates. General interest laws in most states set the maximum rate between 8% and 16% per year. The general maximum is fixed by the state constitution at 5% over the Federal Reserve discount rate in Arkansas. Loans to corporations are frequently exempted or subject to a higher maximum. In recent years, it has also been common to provide special rates for home mortgage loans and variable usury rates that are indexed to market rates.

Specific enabling acts. In many states special statutes permit industrial loan companies, second mortgage lenders, and banks to charge 1.5% a month or more. Laws regulating revolving loans, charge accounts, and credit cards generally limit rates to between 1.5% and 2% per month plus annual fees for credit cards. Rates for installment sales contracts in most states are somewhat higher. Credit unions may generally charge 1% to 1.5% a month. Pawnbrokers' rates vary widely. Savings and loan associations, and loans insured by federal agencies, are also specially regulated. A number of states allow regulated lenders to charge any rate agreed to with the customer either for all credit or over a certain dollar amount.

Consumer finance loan statutes. Most consumer finance loan statutes are based on early models drafted by the Russell Sage Foundation (1916-42) to provide small loans to wage earners under license and other protective regulations. Since 1969 the model has frequently been the Uniform Consumer Credit Code, which applies to credit sales and loans for consumer purposes. In general, licensed lenders may charge 3% a month and reduced rates for additional amounts. An add-on of 17% ($17 per $100) per year yields about 2.5% per month if paid in equal monthly installments. Discount rates produce higher yields than add-on rates of the same amount. In the table below, unless otherwise stated, monthly and annual rates are based on reducing principal balances, annual add-on rates are based on the original principal for the full term, and two or more rates apply to different portions of the balance or original principal.

States with consumer finance loan laws and the rates of charge as of Aug. 1, 1993

Maximum monthly rates computed on unpaid balances, unless otherwise stated.

Ala. . . Annual add-on: 15% to $750, 10% to $2,000 (min. 1.5% on unpaid balances). Higher rates for loans up to $749. Over $2,000, any agreed rate. Fee: 4% (max. $25); 5% real estate.
Alas. . . 3% to $850, 2% to $10,000. Over $10,000, any agreed rate.
Ariz. . . To $1,000: 3%. Over $1,000: 3% to $500, 2% to $10,000. Over $10,000, any agreed rate.
Cal. . . 2.5% to $225, 2% to $900, 1.5% to $1,650, 1% to $2,500 (1.6% min.). Over $2,500, any agreed rate. 5% fee (max. $50) to $2,500
Col. . . 36% per year to $630, 21% to $2,100, 15% to $25,000 (21% min.).
Conn. . Annual add-on: 17% to $600, 11% to $5,000; 11% over $1,800 to $5,000 for certain secured loans. Any agreed rate for second mortgages.
Del. . . Any agreed rate.
D.C. . . 24% per year.
Fla. . . 30% per year to $1,000, 24% to $2,000, 18% to $25,000.
Ga. . . 10% per year discount to 18 months, add-on to 36½ months; 8% fee to $600, 4% on excess plus $2 per month. Over $3,000, any agreed rate.
Ha. . . 3.5% to $100, 2.5% to $300; 2% on entire balance over $300 or discount rates.
Ida. . . Any agreed rate.
Ill. . . Any agreed rate.
Ind. . . 36% per year to $840, 21% to $2,800, 15% to $25,000 (21% min.).
Ia. . . 3% to $1,000, 2% to $2,800, 1.5% to $10,000; or equivalent flat rate. Over $10,000, 21% per year.
Kan. . . 36% per year to $780, 21% to $2,600, 14.45% to $25,000 (18% min.). Fee: 2% (max. $100); 3% real estate.
Ky. . . 3% to $1,000, 2% to $3,000. Over $3,000, 2%.
La. . . 36% per year to $1,400, 27% to $4,000, 24% to $7,000, 21% over $7,000, plus $25 fee.
Me. . . 30% per year to $700, 21% to $2,000, 15% to $25,000 (18% min.).
Md. . . 2.75% to $1,000, 2% to $2,000. Over $2,000, 2%.
Mass. . 23% per year plus $20 annual fee to $6,000; any agreed rate over $6,000.
Mich. . . 22% per year to $8,000; 18% for second mortgages, plus 2% fee (max. $200).
Minn. . . 33% per year to $750, 19% over $750 (21.75% min.).
Miss. . . 36% per year to $1,000, 33% to $1,800, 24% to $5,000, 14% over $5,000. Over $25,000, 18%. 2% fee (max. $50).
Mo. . . 2.218% to $1,200, 1.67% over $1,200, plus 5% fee (max. $15); 1.67% plus 2% for second mortgages.
Mon. . . Any agreed rate.
Neb. . . 24% per year to $1,000. 21% over, plus fee of 7% to $2,000 and 5% over (max. $500).
Nev. . . Any agreed rate.
N.H. . . 2% to $600, 1.5% to $1,500; any agreed rate over $1,500 or for real estate mortgages.
N.J. . . 30% per year to $5,000 or for second mortgages.
N.M. . . Any agreed rate.
N.Y. . . 25% per year.
N.C. . . 2.5% to $1,000, 1.5% to $7,500; 1.5% on entire amount to $10,000. 1.5% or variable plus 2% fee for second mortgages.
N.D. . . 2.5% to $250, 2% to $500, 1.75% to $750, 1.5% to $1,000; any agreed rate over $1,000.
Oh. . . 28% per year to $1,000, 22% to $5,000; 25% on entire amount over $5,000; plus fee.
Okla. . . 30% per annum to $900, 21% to $3,000, 15% to $45,000 (21% min.). Special rates to $500.
Ore. . . Any agreed rate.
Pa. . . 9.5% per year discount to 48 months, 6% for remaining time plus 2% fee (max. $100); or 2% on unpaid balances; 1.85% for second mortgages over $5,000, plus 2% fee.
P.R. . . Variable: 25% max., 19% min.
R.I. . . 3% to $300, 2.5% for loans between $300 and $800; 2% for larger loans to $5,000. 1.75% over $5,000.
S.C. . . Any agreed and posted rate.
S.D. . . Any agreed rate.
Tenn. . . Over $100, 24% per year or discount rates plus fees.
Tex. . . Annual add-on: 18% to $1,200, 8% to $10,000 or formula rate (18% to 24% per year on unpaid balances.)
Ut. . . Any agreed rate.
Vt. . . 2% to $1,000, 1% to $3,000 (min. 1.5%); 1.5% for second mortgages.
Va. . . 2.56% to $800, 1.9% to $2,000, 1.4% to $3,500; or annual add-on of 17% to $800, 15% to $2,000, 11% to $3,500; 2% fee. Any agreed rate over $3,500 for second mortgages, plus 2% fee.
Wash. . 25% per year plus fees.
W.Va. . 36% per year to $500, 24% to $1,500, 18% to $2,000. Over $2,000, 27% per year to $2,000, 25% to $10,000, 18% on remainder, plus 2% fee.
Wis. . . Any agreed rate.
Wyo. . . 36% per year to $1,000, 21% to $25,000. No limit over $25,000.

How to Check Your Credit File

Any individual can investigate the contents of his or her credit file by directly contacting one or more of the approximately 2,000 credit bureaus, or consumer credit clearinghouses, in the United States. The nearest ones can be found by calling a local Better Business Bureau or by looking in the telephone Yellow Pages under "Credit Rating or Reporting Agencies."

Although the Fair Credit Reporting Act requires that a bureau give a person no more than an oral or written credit history review, many bureaus will go beyond the technical requirements of the law and furnish the same computer-generated compilation of facts that they give the banks, retailers and other companies that subscribe to their service. An individual who has been denied credit on the basis of negative information from a credit bureau can obtain this review without charge within 30 days of the denial. Sometimes there is a small fee for such a credit check.

After inspecting this record of past credit behavior, a consumer can question any item believed to be inaccurate, misleading or vague. The credit bureau must then investigate and remove any item that cannot be substantiated.

When a bureau affirms, rather than removes, a questionable item, an individual can present a 100-word explanation that must be placed in his or her file. And whenever an adverse item is deleted from the file or an explantory statement is added to one, a consumer may request that the credit bureau inform every credit grantor who received a report within the last six months.

Credit Card Rates

(As of Aug. 1, 1993)

(Prepared by Christian T. Jones, San Diego, CA)

Nearly all states have special laws dealing with rates charged for credit cards issued by state banks and other financial institutions. Although some state laws apply only to banks, under federal parity law, the same charges can be made by other financial institutions. A national bank can charge the highest rates allowed for revolving credit extended by any other creditor in the state where the bank is located for similar types of credit, and such rates may also be charged to residents of any other state. Maximum rates and fees shown below; rates are yearly unless otherwise stated.

Ala.	No limit.
Alas.	17% plus fee.
Ariz.	No limit.
Ark.	5% over FRB discount rate (max. 17%).
Cal.	No limit.
Col.	21%.
Conn.	18%.
D.C.	24%.
Del.	No limit.
Fla.	No limit.
Ga.	No limit on rate or fee.
Ha.	24%.
Ida.	No limit.
Ill.	No limit; plus fee.
Ind.	36-21-15%, @ $840, $2,800; or 21%.
Ia.	No limit.
Kan.	18-14.45% @ $1,000.
Ky.	21%; $20 annual fee.
La.	18%; 4% cash advance and $12 annual fee.
Me.	18%; $12 annual fee.
Md.	24%; 2% fee.
Mass.	18% or formula rate.
Mich.	18%; no limit on annual fee.
Minn.	18%; $50 annual fee.
Miss.	21%; or 18% plus $12 annual fee.
Mo.	22-10% @ $1,000.
Mon.	No limit.
Neb.	18% plus fee.
Nev.	No limit.
N.H.	No limit.
N.J.	30%; $15 annual fee or $50 over $5,000.
N.M.	No limit.
N.Y.	25% plus annual fee.
N.C.	18%; $24 annual fee.
N.D.	No limit.
Oh.	25% to 1/1/96.
Okla.	30-21-15% @ $870, $2,900; or 21%.
Ore.	No limit.
Pa.	12% loans; 15% purchases; $15 annual fee.
P.R.	2.17% per mo.
R.I.	18%.
S.C.	No limit.
S.D.	No limit.
Tenn.	24%.
Tex.	Set by rule (max. 24%, min. 18%.)
Ut.	No limit.
Vt.	18%; no limit on annual fee.
Va.	No limit.
Wash.	12% or 4% over U.S. T-bill rate.
W.Va.	18%.
Wis.	No limit.
Wyo.	36-21% @ $1,000; no limit over $25,000.

The Cost of Raising a Child

Source: Family Economics Research Group, U.S. Dept. of Agriculture

Projected annual expenditures in current dollars on a child born in 1990, by income group for married-couple families.

		Income group[1]		
Year	Age of child	Low	Medium	High
1990	under 1	$4,330	$6,140	$8,770
1991	1	4,590	6,510	9,300
1992	2	4,870	6,900	9,850
1993	3	5,510	7,790	11,030
1994	4	5,850	8,260	11,690
1995	5	6,200	8,750	12,390
1996	6	6,550	9,220	12,950
1997	7	6,950	9,770	13,730
1998	8	7,360	10,360	14,550
1999	9	7,570	10,690	15,120
2000	10	8,020	11,340	16,030
2001	11	8,500	12,020	16,990
2002	12	10,360	14,190	19,680
2003	13	10,980	15,040	20,860
2004	14	11,640	15,940	22,110
2005	15	13,160	17,950	24,610
2006	16	13,950	19,030	26,090
2007	17	14,780	20,170	27,650
Total		$151,170	$210,070	$293,400

(1) Low income is under $29,900 in 1990; middle is $29,900 to $48,299; high is $48,300 or more. Projection assumes 6 percent annual inflation.

Tourism: Foreign Visitors to the U.S., 1990

Source: U.S. Travel & Tourism Admin.; Bureau of Economic Analysis

Country of origin	Visitors (millions)	Expenditures (millions)	Expenditures per visitor
Japan	3.2	$7,694	$2,381
Canada	17.3	5,690	330
Mexico	6.8	4,004	592
United Kingdom	2.2	3,581	1,596
Germany	1.2	2,139	1,778
France	0.7	$1,219	$1,703
Australia	0.5	1,061	2,279
Italy	0.4	781	1,973
Netherlands	0.3	404	1,422
New Zealand	0.2	379	2,181
All countries	39.1	$40,579	$1,038

Note: Excludes international passenger fare payments and cruise travel. Numbers may not add up due to rounding.

U.S. Passport, Visa, and Health Requirements

Source: Bureau of Consular Affairs, U.S. Dept. of State as of mid-1993

Passports are issued by the U.S. Department of State to citizens and nationals of the United States for the purpose of documenting them for foreign travel and identifying them as Americans.

How to Obtain a Passport

Applicants who have never been issued a passport in their own name must execute an application in person before (1) a passport agent; (2) a clerk of any federal court or state court of record or a judge or clerk of any probate court accepting applications; (3) a postal employee designated by the postmaster at a post office that has been selected to accept passport applications; or (4) a U.S. diplomatic or consular officer abroad. A DSP-11 is the correct form to use for applicants who must apply in person. All persons are required to obtain individual passports in their own name. An applicant who is 13 years of age or older is required to appear in person before the clerk or agent executing the application. A parent or legal guardian may execute the application for children under 13.

A full validity passport previously issued to the applicant, or one in which he or she was included, will be accepted as proof of U.S. citizenship. If the applicant has no prior passport and was born in the U.S., a certified copy of his/her birth certificate shall be presented to the agent accepting the passport application. To be acceptable, the certificate must show the given name and surname, the date and place of birth, and that the birth record was filed shortly after birth. A delayed birth certificate (a record filed more than one year after the date of birth) is acceptable provided that it shows acceptable secondary evidence was used for creating this record. Contact the nearest Dept. of State passport office for more information concerning acceptable secondary evidence.

If a birth certificate is not obtainable, a notice from a state registrar shall be submitted stating that no birth record exists. The notice shall be accompanied by the best obtainable secondary evidence, such as a baptismal certificate or a hospital birth record.

A naturalized citizen with no previous passport must present a Certificate of Naturalization. A person born abroad claiming U.S. citizenship through either a native-born or naturalized citizen parent must submit a Certificate of Citizenship issued by the Immigration and Naturalization Service; or a Consular Report of Birth or Certification of Birth Abroad issued by the Dept. of State. If one of the above documents has not been obtained, evidence of citizenship of the parent(s) through whom citizenship is claimed and evidence that would establish the parent/child relationship must be submitted. Additionally, if citizenship is derived through birth to citizen parent(s), the following documents will be required: parents' marriage certificate plus an affidavit from parent(s) showing periods and places of residence or physical presence in the U.S. and abroad, specifying periods spent abroad in the employment of the U.S. government, including the armed forces, or with certain international organizations. If citizenship is derived through naturalization of parents, evidence of admission to the U.S. for permanent residence also will be required.

Persons who possess the most recent passport issued within the last 12 years and after their 16th birthday may be eligible to apply for a new passport by mail. A form DSP-82, Application for Passport by Mail must be filled out and mailed to the address shown on the form, together with the previous passport, 2 recent identical photographs and $55.00. The DSP-82 may not be used if the most recent passport has been altered or mutilated.

Photographs, Fees and Identity

Photographs — Submit 2 identical photographs that are sufficiently recent (normally not more than 6 months old) to be a good likeness of and satisfactorily identify the applicant. Photographs should be 2 × 2 inches in size. The image size measured from the bottom of the chin to the top of the head (including hair) should be not less than one inch nor more than 1 3/8 inches. Photographs should be portrait-type prints. They must be clear, front view, full face, with a plain, white or off-white background. Photographs that depict the applicant as relaxed and smiling are encouraged.

Fees — The passport fee is $30.00 for passports issued to persons under 18 years of age. These passports are valid for 5 years from the date of issue. The passport fee is $55.00 for passports issued to persons 18 and older. These passports are valid for 10 years from the date of issuance. An additional fee of $10.00 is charged for the execution of the application. There is no execution fee when using DSP-82, Application for Passport by Mail. Applicants eligible to use this form pay only the $55.00 passport fee.

Identity—Applicants must also establish their identity to the satisfaction of the person accepting the application and to Passport Services. Generally acceptable documents of identity include a previous U.S. passport, a Certificate of Naturalization, a Certificate of Citizenship, a valid driver's license, or a government identification card. Applicants may not use a Social Security card, learner's or temporary driver's license, credit card, or expired identity card. Extremely old documents cannot be used by themselves. Applicants unable to establish identity must present some documentation in their own name (e.g., Social Security card) and must be accompanied by a person who has known the applicant for at least 2 years and who is a U.S. citizen or legal U.S. permanent resident alien. That person must sign an affidavit before the individual who executes the passport application. The witness will be required to establish his or her own identity.

The loss or theft of a valid passport is a serious matter and should be reported immediately to Passport Services, 1425 K Street, N.W., Dept. of State, Wash., D.C. 20524, tel: (202) 647-0518 or to the nearest passport agency, or the nearest U.S. embassy or consulate when abroad.

Foreign Regulations

A visa, usually rubber stamped in a passport by a representative of the country to be visited, indicates that the bearer of the passport is permitted to enter that country for a certain purpose and length of time. In most instances, you must obtain necessary visas before you leave the U.S. Apply directly to the embassy or nearest consulate of each country you plan to visit, or consult a travel agent.

The State Dept.'s "Foreign Entry Requirements" contains entry requirements and application instructions for most foreign countries and is available for 50¢ from the Consumer Information Center, Dept. 438T, Pueblo, CO 81009.

The process may take several weeks, so it is important to apply well in advance and verify requirements with the embassy or nearest consulate of each country before applying.

How to Obtain Birth, Marriage, Death Records

The pamphlet "Where to Write for Vital Records: Births, Deaths, Marriages, and Divorces" (Pub. #93-1142, Stock # 017-022-01196-4) is available from the Superintendent of Documents, Government Printing Office, Washington, DC 20402; advance payment of $2.25 is required. "How You May Save Time Proving Your Age and Other Birth Facts" is available from the U.S. Dept. of Health and Human Services, National Center for Health Statistics, Rockville, MD 20852. "Geneological Research in the National Archives" is sold by the National Archives Trust Fund Board, P.O. Box 100793, Atlanta, GA 30384.

Copyright Law of The United States

Source: Copyright Office, Library of Congress

What Copyright Is

Copyright is a form of protection provided by the laws of the United States (title 17, U.S. Code) to the authors of "original works of authorship" including literary, dramatic, musical, artistic, and certain other intellectual works. This protection is available to both published and unpublished works. Section 106 of the Copyright Act generally gives the owner of copyright the exclusive right to do and to authorize others to do the following:

- *To reproduce* the copyrighted work in copies or phonorecords;
- *To prepare derivative works* based upon the copyrighted work;
- *To distribute copies or phonorecords* of the copyrighted work to the public by sale or other transfer of ownership, or by rental, lease, or lending;
- *To perform the copyrighted work publicly,* in the case of literary, musical, dramatic, and choreographic works, pantomimes, and motion pictures and other audiovisual works; and
- *To display the copyrighted work publicly,* in the case of literary, musical, dramatic, and choreographic works, pantomimes, and pictorial, graphic, or sculptural works, including the individual images of a motion picture or other audiovisual work.

It is illegal for anyone to violate any of the rights provided by the Act to the owner of copyright. These rights, however, are not unlimited in scope. Sections 107 through 119 of the Copyright Act establish limitations on these rights. In some cases, these limitations are specified exemptions from copyright liability. One major limitation is the doctrine of "fair use," which is given a statutory basis by section 107 of the Act. In other instances, the limitation takes the form of a "compulsory license" under which certain limited uses of copyrighted works are permitted upon payment of specified royalties and compliance with statutory conditions.

Copyright protection subsists from the time the work is created in fixed form; that is, it is an incident of the process of authorship. The copyright in the work of authorship *immediately* becomes the property of the author who created it. Only the author or those deriving their rights from the author can rightfully claim copyright.

In the case of works made for hire, the employer and not the employee is presumptively considered the author. Section 101 of the copyright statute defines a "work made for hire" as:

(1) a work prepared by an employee within the scope of his or her employment; or

(2) a work specially ordered or commissioned for use as a contribution to a collective work, as a part of a motion picture or other audiovisual work, as a translation, as a supplementary work, as a compilation, as an instructional text, as a test, as answer material for a test, or as an atlas, if the parties expressly agree in a written instrument signed by them that the work shall be considered a work made for hire.

The authors of a joint work are co-owners of the copyright in the work, unless there is an agreement to the contrary.

Copyright in each separate contribution to a periodical or other collective work is distinct from copyright in the collective work as a whole and vests initially with the author of the contribution.

Works published on or after January 1, 1978, are subject to protection under the copyright statute if, on the date of first publication, one or more of the authors is a national or domiciliary of the U.S., or is a national, domiciliary, or sovereign authority of a foreign nation that is a party to a copyright treaty to which the U.S. is also a party, or is a stateless person, regardless of domicile, or if the work is first published either in the U.S. or in a foreign nation that on the date of first publication is a party to the Universal Copyright Convention or the Berne Union.

What Works Are Protected

Copyright protects "original works of authorship" that are fixed in a tangible form of expression. The fixation need not be directly perceptible, so long as it may be communicated with the aid of a machine or device. Copyrightable works include the following categories:

(1) literary works;

(2) musical works, including any accompanying words;

(3) dramatic works, including any accompanying music;

(4) pantomimes and choreographic works;

(5) pictorial, graphic, and sculptural works;

(6) motion pictures and other audiovisual works;

(7) sound recordings; and

(8) architectural works.

These categories should be viewed quite broadly: for example, computer programs and most "compilations" are registrable as "literary works"; maps and architectural plans are registrable as "pictorial, graphic, and sculptural works."

What Is Not Protected by Copyright

Several categories of material are generally not eligible for statutory copyright protection. These include among others:

- Works that have *not* been fixed in a tangible form of expression. For example: choreographic works that have not been notated or recorded, or improvisational speeches or performances that have not been written or recorded.
- Titles, names, short phrases, and slogans; familiar symbols or designs; mere variations of typographic ornamentation, lettering, or coloring; mere listings of ingredients or contents.
- Ideas, procedures, methods, systems, processes, concepts, principles, discoveries, or devices, as distinguished from a description, explanation, or illustration.
- Works consisting *entirely* of information that is common property and containing no original authorship. For example: standard calendars, height and weight charts, tape measures and rulers, and lists or tables taken from public documents or other common sources.

Notice of Copyright

For works first published on and after March 1, 1989, use of the copyright notice is optional, though highly recommended. Before March 1, 1989, the use of the notice was mandatory on all published works, and any work first published before that date *must* bear a notice or risk loss of copyright protection.

Use of the notice is recommended because it informs the public that the work is protected by copyright, identifies the copyright owner, and shows the year of first publication. Furthermore, in the event that a work is infringed, if the work carries a proper notice, the court will not allow a defendant to claim "innocent infringement"—that is, that he or she did not realize that the work is protected. (A successful innocent infringement claim may result in a reduction in damages that the copyright owner would otherwise receive.)

The use of the copyright notice is the responsibility of the copyright owner and does not require advance permission from, or registration with, the Copyright Office.

For visually perceptible copies, the form of the notice consists of the following: © (the letter C in a circle), the word "Copyright," or "Copr.," and the year of first publication, and the name of the owner of copyright in the work. Example: © 1993 Judy Smith. The notice must be affixed in such manner and location as to give reasonable notice of the claim of copyright.

The notice of copyright prescribed for all published phonorecords of sound recordings consists of the symbol ℗ (the letter P in a circle), the year of first publication of the sound recording, and the name of the owner of copyright in the sound recording. Example ℗ 1993 XYZ Records, Inc. The notice on phonorecords may appear on the surface of the phonorecord or on the phonorecord label or container, provided the manner of placement and location give reasonable notice of the claim.

How Long Copyright Protection Endures

Works Originally Copyrighted on or After January 1, 1978

A work that is created (fixed in tangible form for the first time) on or after January 1, 1978, is automatically protected from the moment of its creation, and is ordinarily given a term enduring for the author's life, plus an additional 50 years after the author's death. In the case of "a joint work prepared by two or more authors who did not work for hire," the term lasts for 50 years after the last surviving author's death. For works made for hire, and for anonymous and pseudonymous works (unless the author's identity is revealed in Copyright Office records), the duration of copyright will be 75 years from publication or 100 years from creation, whichever is shorter.

Works that were created but not published or registered for copyright before January 1, 1978, have been automatically brought under the statute and are now given Federal copyright protection. The duration of copyright in these works will generally be computed in the same way as for works created on or after January 1, 1978: the life-plus-50 or 75/100-year terms will apply to them as well. The law provides that in no case will the term of copyright for works in this category expire before December 31, 2002, and for works published on or before December 31, 2002, the term of copyright will not expire before December 31, 2027.

Works Copyrighted Before January 1, 1978

Under the law in effect before 1978, copyright was secured either on the date a work was published or on the date of registration if the work was registered in unpublished form. In either case, the copyright endured for a first term of 28 years from the date it was secured. During the last (28th) year of the first term, the copyright was eligible for renewal. The current copyright law has extended the renewal term from 28 to 47 years for copyrights that were subsisting on January 1, 1978, making these works eligible for a total term of protection of 75 years. On June 26, 1992, President Bush signed Public Law 102-307, which amends the Copyright Law to extend automatically the term of copyrights secured between January 1, 1964, and December 31, 1977, to a further term of 47 years and increases the filing fee from $12.00 to $20.00. This fee increase applies to all renewal applications filed on or after June 29, 1992.

P.L. 102-307 makes renewal registration optional. There is no need to make the renewal filing in order to extend the original 28-year copyright term to the full 75 years.

International Copyright Protection

There is no such thing as an "international copyright" that will automatically protect an author's writings throughout the entire world. Protection against unauthorized use in a particular country depends, basically, on the national laws of that country. However, most countries do offer protection to foreign works under certain conditions, and these conditions have been greatly simplified by international copyright treaties and conventions. The U.S. belongs to both global, multilateral copyright treaties—the Universal Copyright Convention (UCC) and the Berne Convention for the Protection of Literary and Artistic Works.

A U.S. author may obtain copyright protection in all countries that are members of the Berne Union and the Universal Copyright Convention. A work first published in the U.S. or another Berne Union country (or first published in a non-Berne Union country, followed by publication within 30 days in a Berne Union country) is eligible for protection in all Berne member countries. There are no special requirements. In UCC member countries, where no formalities are required, the works of U.S. authors are also automatically protected. Member countries whose laws impose formalities protect U.S. works if all published copies bear a Convention notice, which consists of the symbol ©, together with the name of the copyright owner and the year of publication. Example: © JOHN DOE 1993.

For a list of countries that maintain copyright relations with the U.S., write or call the Copyright Office and ask for Circular 38a.

Copyright Registration

Copyright registration is a legal formality intended to make a public record of the basic facts of a particular copyright. Except in specific situations, registration is not a condition for protection, but the copyright law provides several inducements or advantages to encourage copyright owners to register. Among these advantages are the following:

- Registration establishes a public record of the copyright claim;
- Before an infringement suit may be filed in court, registration is necessary for works of U.S. origin and for foreign works not originating in a Berne Union country. (For more information on when a work is of U.S. origin, request Circular 93 from the Copyright Office);
- If made before or within 5 years of publication, registration will establish prima facie evidence in court of the validity of the copyright and of the facts stated in the certificate; and
- If registration is made within 3 months after publication of the work or prior to an infringement of the work, statutory damages and attorney's fees will be available to the copyright owner in court actions. Otherwise, only an award of actual damages and profits is available to the copyright owner.

Copyright registration allows the owner of the copyright to record the registration with the U.S. Customs Service for protection against the importation of infringing copies. For additional information, request Publication No. 563 from:

Commissioner of Customs
ATTN: IPR Branch,
Room 2104
U.S. Customs Service
1301 Constitution Avenue, N.W.
Washington, D.C. 20229

Registration may be made at any time within the life of the copyright. When a work has been registered in unpublished form, it is not necessary to make another registration when the work becomes published (although the copyright owner may register the published edition, if desired).

The process of registration is quite simple. An appropriate form is requested from the Copyright Office and completed. It is returned to the Copyright Office along with a $20 nonrefundable filing fee and the appropriate deposit(s) of the work for which registration is sought. In a common example—a published book—the deposit is two copies of the best edition of the book. A certificate of registration is sent once the paperwork is completed, a process that usually takes 12 to 16 weeks due to the large volume of registrations the Office must handle.

Although a copyright registration is not required, the Copyright Act establishes a mandatory deposit requirement for works published in the U.S. In general, the owner of copyright, or the owner of the exclusive right of publication in the work, has a legal obligation to deposit in the Copyright Office, within three months of publication in the U.S., two copies (or, in the case of sound recordings, two phonorecords) for the use of the Library of Congress. Failure to make the deposit can result in fines and other penalties, but does not affect copyright protection. Certain categories of works are *exempt entirely* from the mandatory deposit requirements, and the obligation is reduced for certain other categories.

Information on registration and application forms may be obtained free of charge by writing the Copyright Office, Information Section, LM-401, Library of Congress, Washington, DC 20559. Registration application forms and circulars may be ordered on a 24-hour basis by calling (202) 707-9100. Request Circular 1 for additional general information on copyright, including a list of which application forms to use when registering specific types of works.

Birthstones

Source: Jewelry Industry Council

Month	Ancient	Modern
January	Garnet	Garnet
February	Amethyst	Amethyst
March	Jasper	Bloodstone or Aquamarine
April	Sapphire	Diamond
May	Agate	Emerald
June	Emerald	Pearl, Moonstone, or Alexandrite
July	Onyx	Ruby
August	Carnelian	Sardonyx or Peridot
September	Chrysolite	Sapphire
October	Aquamarine	Opal or Tourmaline
November	Topaz	Topaz
December	Ruby	Turquoise or Zircon

Mortgage Payment Tables

Source: *The Mortgage Money Guide*, Federal Trade Commission

8% Annual Percentage Rate

Monthly Payments (Principal and Interest)

Amount Financed	10 Years	15 Years	20 Years	25 Years	30 Years
$ 25,000	303.32	238.91	209.11	192.95	183.44
35,000	424.65	334.48	292.75	270.14	256.82
45,000	545.97	430.04	376.40	347.32	330.19
50,000	606.64	477.83	418.22	385.91	366.88
60,000	727.97	573.39	501.86	463.09	440.26
70,000	849.29	668.96	585.51	540.27	513.64
80,000	970.62	764.52	669.15	617.45	587.01
90,000	1091.95	860.09	752.80	694.63	660.39
100,000	1213.28	955.65	836.44	771.82	733.76
120,000	1455.94	1146.78	1003.72	926.18	880.52
140,000	1698.58	1337.92	1171.02	1080.54	1027.28
160,000	1941.24	1529.04	1338.30	1234.90	1174.02
180,000	2183.90	1720.18	1505.60	1389.26	1320.78
200,000	2426.56	1911.30	1672.88	1543.64	1467.52

10% Annual Percentage Rate

Monthly Payments (Principal and Interest)

Amount Financed	10 Years	15 Years	20 Years	25 Years	30 Years
$ 25,000	330.38	268.65	241.26	227.18	219.39
35,000	462.53	376.11	337.76	318.05	307.15
45,000	594.68	483.57	434.26	408.92	394.91
50,000	660.75	537.30	482.51	454.35	438.79
60,000	792.90	644.76	579.01	545.22	526.54
70,000	925.06	752.22	675.52	636.09	614.30
80,000	1057.20	859.68	772.02	726.96	702.06
90,000	1189.36	967.14	868.52	817.83	789.81
100,000	1321.51	1074.61	965.02	908.70	877.57
120,000	1585.80	1289.52	1158.02	1090.44	1053.08
140,000	1850.12	1504.44	1351.04	1272.18	1228.60
160,000	2114.40	1719.36	1544.04	1453.92	1404.12
180,000	2378.72	1934.28	1737.04	1635.66	1579.62
200,000	2643.02	2149.22	1930.04	1817.40	1755.14

12% Annual Percentage Rate

Monthly Payments (Principal and Interest)

Amount Financed	10 Years	15 Years	20 Years	25 Years	30 Years
$ 25,000	358.68	300.05	275.28	263.31	257.16
35,000	502.15	420.06	385.39	368.63	360.02
45,000	645.62	540.08	495.49	473.96	462.88
50,000	717.36	600.09	550.55	526.62	514.31
60,000	860.83	720.11	660.66	631.93	617.17
70,000	1004.30	840.12	770.77	737.26	720.03
80,000	1147.77	960.14	880.87	842.58	822.90
90,000	1291.24	1080.15	990.98	947.90	925.75
100,000	1434.71	1200.17	1101.09	1053.23	1028.62
120,000	1721.66	1440.22	1321.32	1263.86	1234.34
140,000	2008.60	1680.24	1541.54	1474.52	1440.06
160,000	2295.54	1920.28	1761.74	1685.16	1645.80
180,000	2582.48	2160.30	1981.96	1895.80	1851.50
200,000	2869.42	2400.34	2202.18	2106.46	2057.24

14% Annual Percentage Rate

Monthly Payments (Principal and Interest)

Amount Financed	10 Years	15 Years	20 Years	25 Years	30 Years
$ 25,000	388.17	332.94	310.89	300.95	296.22
35,000	543.44	466.11	435.24	421.32	414.71
45,000	698.70	599.29	559.59	541.70	533.20
50,000	776.34	665.88	621.77	601.89	592.44
60,000	931.60	799.05	746.12	722.26	710.93
70,000	1086.87	932.22	870.47	842.64	829.42
80,000	1242.14	1065.40	994.82	963.01	947.90
90,000	1397.40	1198.57	1119.17	1083.38	1066.38
100,000	1552.67	1331.75	1243.53	1203.77	1184.88
120,000	1863.20	1598.10	1492.24	1444.52	1421.86
140,000	2173.74	1864.44	1740.94	1685.28	1658.84
160,000	2484.28	2130.80	1989.64	1926.02	1895.80
180,000	2794.80	2397.14	2238.34	2166.76	2132.76
200,000	3105.34	2663.50	2487.06	2407.54	2369.76

Median Price of Existing Single-Family Homes

Source: National Association of Realtors

City[1]	Apr. 1990	Apr. 1992	Apr. 1993
Akron, Oh.	$67,700	$75,500	$77,400
Albuquerque, N.M.	84,500	86,700	94,400
Anaheim/Santa Ana, Cal.	242,400	235,100	222,200
Atlanta, Ga.	86,400	85,800	NA
Baltimore, Md.	105,900	111,500	113,200
Baton Rouge, La.	64,900	71,800	72,800
Birmingham, Ala.	80,800	89,500	89,000
Boston, Mass.	174,200	168,200	165,200
Bradenton, Fla.	69,600	80,400	84,300
Buffalo, N.Y.	77,200	79,700	84,200
Charleston, S.C.	76,200	82,000	86,200
Chicago, Ill.	116,800	131,100	131,200
Cincinnati, Oh.	79,800	87,500	85,600
Cleveland, Oh.	80,600	88,100	89,200
Columbia, S.C.	77,100	85,100	82,300
Columbus, Oh.	81,600	90,300	89,300
Corpus Christi, Tex.	63,200	62,500	66,600
Dallas, Tex.	89,500	90,500	89,600
Daytona Beach, Fla.	64,100	63,600	67,600
Denver, Col.	86,400	91,300	96,300
Des Moines, Ia.	60,500	71,200	71,600
Detroit, Mich.	76,700	77,500	92,200
El Paso, Tex.	63,600	65,900	67,900
Grand Rapids, Mich.	68,300	73,000	73,900
Hartford, Conn.	157,300	141,500	135,500
Honolulu, Hi.	352,000	342,000	347,000
Houston, Tex.	70,700	78,200	78,000
Indianapolis, Ind.	74,800	80,100	83,800
Jacksonville, Fla.	72,400	75,100	74,100
Kansas City, Mo.	74,100	76,100	79,100
Knoxville, Tenn.	75,400	78,300	82,400
Las Vegas, Nev.	93,000	101,400	105,200
Los Angeles, Cal.	212,800	218,000	199,700
Louisville, Ky.	$60,800	$69,700	$69,900
Madison, Wis.	82,300	89,400	97,700
Memphis, Tenn.	78,100	83,600	84,200
Miami, Fla.	89,300	97,300	98,000
Milwaukee, Wis.	84,400	96,100	98,400
Minneapolis, Minn.	88,700	94,800	96,400
Mobile, Ala.	59,100	63,300	66,200
Nashville, Tenn.	81,800	89,000	87,000
New Haven, Conn.	153,300	142,400	142,600
New Orleans, La.	67,800	68,400	73,000
New York, N.Y.	174,900	169,300	168,000
Oklahoma City, Okla.	53,200	59,800	61,100
Omaha, Neb.	63,000	67,400	64,300
Orlando, Fla.	62,800	86,200	86,900
Philadelphia, Pa.	108,700	119,800	108,900
Phoenix, Ariz.	84,000	84,700	86,300
Pittsburgh, Pa.	70,100	74,800	75,900
Portland, Ore.	79,500	92,300	99,600
Providence, R.I.	127,900	120,300	112,500
Sacramento, Cal.	137,100	135,600	130,400
St. Louis, Mo.	75,700	81,600	80,900
Salt Lake City, Ut.	69,400	73,000	79,000
San Antonio, Tex.	63,600	68,000	72,600
San Diego, Cal.	183,600	182,700	175,500
San Francisco, Cal.	259,300	243,900	249,300
Seattle, Wash.	142,000	141,300	145,000
Spokane, Wash.	55,500	71,300	79,100
Syracuse, N.Y.	80,700	77,400	86,100
Tampa, Fla.	71,400	70,100	69,900
Toledo, Oh.	62,800	74,000	65,700
Tulsa, Okla.	63,900	68,500	68,200
Washington, D.C.	150,200	152,500	153,500

(1) All areas are metropolitan statistical areas as defined by the U.S. Office of Management and Budget. They include the named central city and surrounding suburban areas. NA=not available.

Housing Affordability

Source: National Association of Realtors; data as of midyear

	Median-priced existing home	Average mortgage rate	Monthly principal and interest payment	Payment as percentage of median income
1982	$67,800	15.38%	$702	35.9%
1983	70,300	12.85	616	30.1
1984	72,400	12.49	618	28.2
1985	75,500	11.74	609	26.2
1986	80,300	10.25	563	23.0
1987	85,600	9.28	565	21.9
1988	$90,600	9.31%	$591	22.0%
1989	93,100	10.11	660	23.1
1990	97,500	10.04	673	22.7
1991	99,700	9.51	671	22.3
1992	100,900	8.48	620	20.0
1993	106,100	7.30	582	18.8

Note: The average mortgage rate is based on the effective rate of loans closed on existing homes monitored by the Federal Home Loan Bank Board.

Income Needed to Get a Mortgage

Source: National Association of Realtors

The following shows the minimum annual gross income needed for various size home loans at different rates. The figures are based on a 30-year loan and assume that the borrower's monthly payments can't exceed 28% of gross income, the ceiling most lenders use. The figures do not include property taxes and insurance as part of the monthly payment.

Interest rate (Percent)	$50,000	$75,000	Loan amount $100,000 income needed	$150,000	$200,000
8	$15,724	$23,586	$31,447	$47,171	$62,895
8½	16,477	24,715	32,954	49,430	65,907
9	17,242	25,863	34,484	51,726	68,968
9½	18,018	27,028	36,037	54,055	72,074
10	18,085	28,208	37,611	56,415	75,221
10½	19,602	29,403	39,203	58,805	78,406
11	20,407	30,611	40,814	61,221	81,628
11½	21,221	31,531	42,441	63,662	84,883
12	22,042	33,063	44,084	66,125	88,167
12½	22,870	34,305	45,740	68,610	91,479
13	23,704	35,556	47,409	71,113	94,817

Marriage Laws

Source: Gary N. Skoloff, Skoloff & Wolfe, Livingston, N.J.; as of May 1, 1993.

State	Age with parental consent		Age without consent		Physical exam & blood test for male and female			
	Male	Female	Male	Female	Maximum period between exam and license	Scope of medical exam	Waiting period: Before license	Waiting period: After license
Alabama*	14a	14a	18	18	—	b	—	s
Alaska	16z	16z	18	18	—	b	3 da., w	—
Arizona	16z	16z	18	18	—	—	—	—
Arkansas	17c	16c	18	18	—	—	v	—
California	aa	aa	18	18	30 da., w	zz	—	h
Colorado*	16z	16z	18	18	—	bb	—	s
Connecticut	16z	16z	18	18	—	bb	4 da., w	ttt
Delaware	18c	16c	18	18	—	—	—	e, s
Florida	16a, c	16a, c	18	18	—	b	3 da.	s
Georgia*	aa	aa	18	18	—	b	3 da., g	s*
Hawaii	16d	16d	18	18	—	b	—	—
Idaho*	16z	16z	18	18	—	bb	—	—
Illinois	16	16	18	18	30 da.	b, n	—	ee
Indiana	17c	17c	18	18	—	bb	72 hrs.	t
Iowa*	18z	18z	18	18	—	—	3 da., v	tt
Kansas*[y]	18z	18z	18	18	—	—	3 da., w	—
Kentucky	18c, z	18c, z	18	18	—	—	—	—
Louisiana	18z	18z	18	18	10 da.	b	72 hrs., w	—
Maine	16z	16z	18	18	—	—	3 da., v, w	h
Maryland	16c, f	16c, f	18	18	—	—	48 hrs., w	ff
Massachusetts	14j	12j	18	18	60 da.	bb	3 da., v	—
Michigan	16c, d	16c	18	18	30 da.	b	3 da., w	—
Minnesota	16z	16z	18	18	—	—	5 da., w	—
Mississippi	17	15	21	21	30 da.	b	3 da., w	—
Missouri	15d, 18z	15d, 18z	18	18	—	—	—	—
Montana*[yy]	16	16	18	18	—	b	—	ff
Nebraska[yy]	17	17	19	19	—	bb	—	—
Nevada	16z	16z	18	18	—	—	—	—
New Hampshire	14j	13j	18	18	—	l,zz	3 da., v	h
New Jersey	16z, c	16z, c	18	18	30 da.	b	72 hrs., w	s
New Mexico[y]	16d	16d	18	18	30 da.	b	—	—
New York	14j	14j	18	18	—	nn	—	24 hrs., w, t
North Carolina	16c, g	16c, g	18	18	—	m	—	—
North Dakota	16	16	18	18	—	—	—	t
Ohio*	18c, z	16c, z	18	18	30 da.	b	5 da.,w	t
Oklahoma*	16c	16c	18	18	30 da., w	b	—	s
Oregon	17	17	18	18	—	—	3 da., w	—
Pennsylvania*	16d	16d	18	18	30 da.	b	3 da., w	t
Puerto Rico[y]	18c, d, z	16c, d, z	21	21	—	b	—	—
Rhode Island*	18d	16d	18	18	—	bb	—	—
South Carolina*	16c	14c	18	18	—	—	1 da.	—
South Dakota	16c	16c	18	18	—	—	—	tt
Tennesee	16d	16d	18	18	—	—	3 da., cc	s
Texas*[y]	14j, k	14j, k	18	18	—	—	—	s
Utah*	14	14	18x	18x	30 da.	b	—	s
Vermont	16z	16z	18	18	30 da.	b	1 da., w	—
Virginia	16a, c	16a, c	18	18	—	b	—	t
Washington	17d	17d	18	18	—	bbb	3 da.	t
West Virginia	18c	18c	18	18	—	b	3 da., w	—
Wisconsin	16d	16d	18	18	—	b	5 da., w	s
Wyoming	16d	16d	18	18	—	bb	—	—
Dist. of Columbia*	16a	16a	18	18	30 da.	b	3 da. w	—

* Indicates 1987 common-law marriage recognized; in many states, such marriages are only recognized if entered into many years before. (a) Parental consent not required if minor was previously married. (aa) No age limits. (b) Venereal diseases. (bb) Venereal diseases and Rubella (for female). In Colorado and Wyoming, Rubella for female under 45 and Rh type. (bbb) No medical exam required; however, applicants must file affidavit showing non-affliction of contagious venereal disease. (c) Younger parties may obtain license in case of pregnancy or birth of child. (cc) Unless parties are over 18 years of age. (d) Younger parties may obtain license in special circumstances. (e) Residents before expiration of 24-hour waiting period; non-residents formerly residents, before expiration of 96-hour waiting period; others 96 hours. (ee) License effective 1 day after issuance, unless court orders otherwise, valid for 60 days only. (f) If parties are at least 16 years of age, proof of age and the consent of parents in person is required. If a parent is ill, an affidavit by the incapacitated parent and a physician's affidavit to that effect required. (ff) License valid for 180 days only. (g) Unless parties are 18 years of age or more, or female is pregnant, or applicants are the parents of a living child born out of wedlock. (h) License valid for 90 days only. (j) Parental consent and/or permission of judge required. (k) Below age of consent parties need parental consent and permission of judge. (l) With each certificate issued to couples, a list of family planning agencies and services available to them is provided. (m) Mental incompetence, infectious tuberculosis, venereal diseases and Rubella (certain counties only). (n) Venereal diseases; test for sickle cell anemia given at request of examining physician. (nn) Tests for sickle cell anemia may be required for certain applicants. Marriage prohibited unless it is established that procreation is not possible. (s) License valid for 30 days only. (t) License valid for 60 days only. (tt) License valid for 20 days only. (ttt) License valid for 65 days. (v) Parties must file notice of intention to marry with local clerk. (w) Waiting period may be avoided. (x) Authorizes counties to provide for premarital counseling as a requisite to issuance of license to persons under 19 and persons previously divorced. (y) Marriages by proxy are valid. (yy) Proxy marriages are valid under certain conditions. (z) Younger parties may marry with parental consent and/or permission of judge. In Connecticut, judicial approval. (zz) Required offer of HIV test, and/or must be provided with information on AIDS.

Divorce Laws

Source: Gary N. Skoloff, Skoloff & Wolfe, Livingston, N.J.; as of May 1, 1993. Important: almost all states also have other laws, as well as qualifications of the laws shown below and proposed divorce-reform laws pending. It would be wise to consult a lawyer in conjunction with the use of this chart.

Some grounds for absolute divorce

	Residence	Adultery	Cruelty	Desertion	Alcoholism	Impotency	Non-support	Insanity	Pregnancy at marriage	Bigamy	Separation	Felony conviction or imprisonment	Drug addiction	Fraud force, duress
PR	1 yr.	Yes	Yes	1 yr.	Yes	Yes	No	Yes	No	A	2 yrs.	Yes*	Yes	No
AL	6 mos.*	Yes	Phys. only	1 yr.	Yes	Yes*	2 yrs.	5 yrs.	Yes	A	2 yrs.*	2 yrs*	Yes	A
AK	*	Yes	Yes	1 yr.	1 yr.	Yes	No	18 mos.	No	A	No	Yes	Yes	A
AZ	90 da.	No	No	No	No	No	No	No	No	No	No	No	No	No
AR	60 da.	Yes	Yes	No	1 yr.	Yes	Yes	3 yrs.	No	No	18 mos.	Yes	No	A
CA	6 mos.	No	No	No	No	A	No	Yes, A	No	A	No	No	No	A
CO	90 da.	No	No	No	No	No	No	No	No	A	No	No	No	A
CT	1 yr.*	Yes	Yes	1 yr.	Yes	No	No	5 yrs.	No	A	18 mos.*	life*	No	Yes
DE	6 mos.	Yes	Yes	Yes	Yes	A	No	A	No	Yes	6 mos.	Yes	Yes	A
FL	6 mos.	No	No	No	No	No	No	3 yrs.	No	No	No	No	No	No
GA	6 mos.	Yes	Yes	1 yr.	Yes	Yes	No	2 yrs.	Yes	A	No	Yes*	Yes	Yes
HI	6 mos.*	No	No	No	No	No	No	A	No	A	2 yrs.*	No	No	A
ID	6 wks.	Yes	Yes	Yes	Yes	A	Yes	3 yrs.	Yes	A	5 yrs.	Yes	No	A
IL	90 da.	Yes	Yes	1 yr.	2 yrs.	Yes	No	No	No	Yes	2 yrs.*	Yes	2 yrs.	No
IN	6 mos.*	No	No	No	No	Yes	No	2 yrs.	No	A	No	Yes	No	A
IA	1 yr.*	No	No	No	No	A	No	A	No	A	No	No	No	No
KS	60 da.	No	No	No	No	No	Yes	2 yrs.	A	A	No	No	No	A
KY	180 da.	No	No	No	No	A	No	No	No	A	No	No	No	A
LA	1 yr.*	Yes	No	No	No	No	No	No	No	A	6 mos.	Yes*	No	A
ME	6 mos.*	Yes	Yes	3 yrs.	Yes	Yes	Yes	A	No	A	No	No	Yes	No
MD	1 yr.*	Yes	No	1 yr.*	No	No	No	3 yrs.	No	A	1 yr.*	1 yr.*	No	No
MA	1 yr.*	Yes	Yes	1 yr.	Yes	Yes	Yes	No	No	A	No	5 yrs.	Yes	No
MI	180 da.	No	No	No	No	No	No	No	No	No	No	No	No	A
MN	180 da.	No	No	No	No	No	No	No	No	No	No	No	No	A
MS	6 mos.	Yes	Yes	1 yr.	Yes	Yes	No	3 yrs.	Yes	Yes	No	Yes*	Yes	A
MO	90 da.	No	No	No	No	No	No	No	No	No	No	No	No	A
MT	90 da.	No	No	No	No	A	No	No	No	No	180 da.*	No	No	A
NE	1 yr.*	No	No	No	No	A	No	No	No	A	No	No	No	A
NV	6 wks.	No	No	No	No	No	No	2 yrs.	No	A	1 yr.	No	No	A
NH	1 yr.*	Yes	Yes	2 yrs.	2 yrs.	Yes	2 yrs.	No	No	A	Yes	1 yr.*	No	No
NJ	1 yr.*	Yes	Yes	1 yr.	1 yr.	A	No	2 yrs.	No	A	18 mos.	18 mos.	1 yr.	A
NM	6 mos.	Yes	Yes	Yes*	No	No	No	No	No	No	No	No	No	No
NY	1 yr.*	Yes	Yes	1 yr.	No	No	No	No	No	A	1 yr.	3 yrs.	No	A
NC	6 mos.	No	No	No	No	A	No	3 yrs.	No	A	1 yr.	No	No	No
ND	6 mos.	Yes	Yes	1 yr.	1 yr.	A	1 yr.	5 yrs.*	No	A	No	Yes	1 yr.	A
OH	6 mos.	Yes	Yes	1 yr.	Yes	Yes	Yes	No	No	Yes, A	1 yr.*	Yes	No	Yes, A
OK	6 mos.	Yes	Yes	1 yr.	Yes	Yes	Yes	5 yrs.	Yes	Yes	No	Yes	No	Yes
OR	6 mos.*	No	No	No	No	No	No	No	No	No	No	No	No	A
PA	6 mos.	Yes	Yes	1 yr.	No	No	No	18 mos.*	No	Yes	2 yrs.*	Yes	No	No
RI	1yr.	Yes	Yes	5 yrs.*	Yes	Yes	1 yr.	No	No	Yes	3 yrs.	Yes	Yes	No
SC	1 yr.*	Yes	Phys. only	1 yr.	Yes	No	No	No	No	No	1 yr.	No	Yes	No
SD	none*	Yes	Yes	1 yr.	1 yr.	A	1 yr.	5 yrs.	No	A	No	Yes	No	A*
TN	6 mos.*	Yes	Yes	1 yr.	Yes	Yes	Yes	No	Yes	Yes	2 yrs.	Yes	Yes	A
TX	6 mos.*	Yes	Yes	1 yr.	*	A	No	3 yrs.	No	No	3 yrs.	1 yr.	No	No
UT	3 mos.*	Yes	Yes	1 yr.	Yes	Yes	Yes	Yes	No	A	3 yrs.*	Yes	No	No
VT	6 mos.*	Yes	Yes	7 yrs.*	No	No	Yes	5 yrs.	No	A	6 mos.	3 yrs.	No	A
VA	6 mos.*	Yes	Yes*	1 yr.	No	A	No	No	A	A	1 yr.*	1 yr.*	No	A
WA	bona fide res.	No	No	No	No	No	No	No	No	No	No	No	No	No
WV	1 yr.*	Yes	Yes	6 mos.	Yes	A	No	3 yrs.	A	A	1 yr.	Yes	Yes	No
WI	6 mos.	No	No	No	No	A	No	No	No	A	1 yr.	No	No	A
WY	60 da.*	No	No	No	No	No	No	2 yrs.	No	A	No	No	No	No
DC	6 mos.	No	No	No	No	A	No	A*	No	A	6 mos.-1 yr.	No	No	A

(*) indicates qualification-check local statutes; (A) indicates grounds for annulment.

Wedding Anniversaries

The traditional names for wedding anniversaries go back many years in social usage. As such names as wooden, crystal, silver, and golden were applied it was considered proper to present the married pair with gifts made of these products or of something related. The list of traditional gifts, with a few allowable revisions in parentheses, is presented below, followed by modern gifts in **bold face.**

1st-Paper, **clocks**
2d-Cotton, **china**
3d-Leather, **crystal & glass**
4th-Linen (silk), **electrical appliances**
5th-Wood, **silverware**
6th-Iron, **wood**
7th-Wool (copper), **desk sets**
8th-Bronze, **linens & lace**
9th-Pottery (china), **leather**
10th-Tin (aluminum), **diamond jewelry**
11th-Steel, **fashion jewelry, accessories**
12th-Silk, **pearls or colored gems**
13th-Lace, **textiles & furs**
14th-Ivory, **gold jewelry**
15th-Crystal, **watches**
20th-China, **platinum**
25th-Silver, **sterling silver jubliee**
30th-Pearl, **diamond**
35th-Coral (jade), **jade**
40th-Ruby, **ruby**
45th-Sapphire, **sapphire**
50th-Gold, **gold**
55th-Emerald, **emerald**
60th-Diamond, **diamond**

RELIGIOUS INFORMATION

Census of Religious Groups in the U.S.

Source: *1993 Yearbook of American and Canadian Churches*

Comparisons of membership statistics from group to group are not necessarily meaningful. Membership definitions vary—e.g., Roman Catholics count members from infancy, but some Protestant groups count only "adult" members, usually 13 years or older; some groups compile data carefully, but others estimate; not all groups report annually.

The number of churches appears in parentheses. Asterisk (*) indicates church declines to publish membership figures; denominations that are not listed have not provided data for at least 10 years.

Group	Members
Adventist churches:	
Advent Christian Ch. (335)	28,000
Church of God General Conf. (Oregon, IL) (89)	5,526
Primitive Advent Christian Ch. (10)	343
Seventh-day Adventists (4,229)	733,026
American Rescue Workers (20)	**2,700**
Anglican Orthodox Church (40)	**6,000**
Apostolic Christian Ch. (Nazarene) (48)	**2,799**
Apostolic Christian Churches of America (80)	**11,450**
Baha'i Faith (1,700)	**110,000**
Baptist churches:	
Amer. Baptist Assn. (1,705)	250,000
Amer. Baptist Chs. in U.S.A. (5,862)	1,527,840
Baptist Bible Fellowship Intl. (3,500)	*
Baptist General Conference (821)	134,658
Baptist Missionary Assn. of America (1,312)	230,127
Conservative Baptist Assn. of America (1,126)	210,000
Free Will Baptists, Natl. Assn. of (2,495)	209,223
Gen. Assn. of Regular Baptist Chs. (1,532)	160,123
Gen. Baptists, Gen. Assn. of (876)	74,156
Liberty Baptist Fellowship (100)	*
Natl. Baptist Convention of America (2,500)	3,500,000
Natl. Baptist Convention, U.S.A. (36,000)	8,000,000
Natl. Missionary Baptist Convention of America (*)	2,500,000
No. Amer. Baptist Conference (265)	43,087
Progressive National Baptist Convention (1,400)	2,500,000
Separate Baptists in Christ (101)	10,000
Seventh Day Baptist General Conference (90)	5,250
Southern Baptist Convention (36,168)	15,232,347
Sovereign Grace Baptists (300)	3,000
Brethren (German Baptists):	
Brethren Ch. (Ashland, Ohio) (124)	13,322
Fellowship of Grace Brethren (322)	39,237
Old German Baptist Brethren (55)	5,475
Brethren, River:	
Brethren in Christ Ch. (194)	17,454
United Zion Ch. (13)	850
Buddhist Churches of America (67)	**19,441**
Christian Brethren (1,150)	**98,000**
Christian Catholic Church (6)	**2,500**
Christian Church (Disciples of Christ) (4,031)	**1,022,926**
Christian Churches and Churches of Christ (5,579)	**1,070,616**
Christian Congregation (1,447)	**110,716**
Christian Nation Church U.S.A. (5)	**200**
Christian Union (114)	**6,000**
Churches of Christ:	
Church of the Living God (170)	42,000
Churches of Christ (13,200)	1,690,000
Churches of Christ in Christian Union (240)	10,349
Churches of God:	
Chs. of God, General Conference (354)	33,584
Ch. of God (Anderson, Ind.) (2,330)	214,743
Ch. of God (Seventh Day), Denver, Col. (153)	5,749
Church of God by Faith (145)	8,235
Church of God in Christ Which He Purchased With His Own Blood (7)	800
Church of Christ, Scientist (3,000)	*
Church of the Nazarene (5,172)	**573,834**
Community Churches, Intl. Council of (398)	*
Congregational Christian Chs. (405)	**90,000**
Conservative Congregational Christian Conference (176)	**28,035**
Eastern Orthodox churches:	
Albanian Orth. Diocese of America (2)	1,873
American Carpatho-Russian Orth. Greek Catholic Ch. (72)	17,981
Antiochian Orth. Christian Archdiocese of No. Amer. (170)	350,000
Apostolic Catholic Assyrian Ch. of the East, N.A. Diocese (22)	120,000
Armenian Apostolic Ch. of America (30)	150,000
Armenian Church of Amer., Diocese of the (72)	*
Bulgarian Eastern Orth. Ch. (9)	10,000
Coptic Orthodox Ch. (55)	260,000
Orthodox Ch. in America (1,000)	1,030,000
Patriarchal Parishes of the Russian Orth. Ch. in the U.S.A. (38)	9,780
Romanian Orth. Episcopate of America (37)	65,000
Serbian Orthodox Ch. of U.S.A. & Canada (68)	67,000
Syrian Orth. Ch. of Antioch (Archdiocese of the U.S.A. and Canada) (28)	30,000
True Orthodox Church of Greece (8)	900
Ukrainian Orth. Ch. in America (Ecumenical Patriarchate) (27)	5,000
Episcopal Church (7,367)	**2,471,880**
American Ethical Union (Ethical Culture Movement) (21)	**3,212**
Evangelical Church (185)	**16,398**
Evangelical Congregational Church (155)	**24,437**
The Evangelical Covenant Church (590)	**89,735**
Evangelical Free Church of America (1,113)	**187,775**
Fellowship of Fundamental Bible Churches (26)	**2,087**
Fire Baptized Holiness Church (Wesleyan) (49)	**695**
Friends:	
Evangelical Friends International, No. Amer. (246)	26,322
Friends General Conference (520)	30,902
Friends United Meeting (526)	50,803
Religious Society of Friends (Conservative) (28)	1,744
Grace Gospel Fellowship (50)	**4,500**
Independent Fundamental Churches of America (700)	**78,174**
Jehovah's Witnesses (9,890)	**914,079**
Jewish organizations:	
Union of Amer. Hebrew Congregations (Reform) (848)	1,300,000
Union of Orthodox Jewish Congregations of America (1,200)	1,000,000
United Synagogue of America (Conservative) (800)	2,000,000
Latter-day Saints:	
Ch. of Jesus Christ (Bickertonites) (63)	2,707
Ch. of Jesus Christ of Latter-day Saints (Mormon) (9,468)	4,336,000
Reorganized Ch. of Jesus Christ of Latter Day Saints (1,001)	150,143
Liberal Catholic Ch.-Province of the U.S.A. (34).	**2,800**
Lutheran churches:	
Apostolic Lutheran Ch. of America (53)	7,583
Ch. of the Lutheran Brethren of America (111)	22,478
Ch. of the Lutheran Confession (70)	8,722
Conservative Lutheran Assn. (12)	1,530
Estonian Evangelical Lutheran Ch. (24)	7,298
Evangelical Lutheran Ch. in America (11,074)	5,245,177
Evangelical Lutheran Synod (126)	21,347
Free Lutheran Congregations, Assn. of (210)	27,650
Latvian Evangelical Lutheran Church of America (56)	12,553
Lutheran Ch.-Missouri Synod (5,364)	2,607,309
Lutheran Chs., Amer. Assn. of (78)	15,150
Protestant Conference (Lutheran) (7)	1,150
Wisconsin Evangelical Lutheran Synod (1,211)	420,039
Mennonite churches:	
Beachy Amish Mennonite Chs. (99)	6,872
Church of God in Christ (Mennonite) (78)	9,999
Evangelical Mennonite Ch. (27)	4,059
Fellowship of Evangelical Bible Churches (14)	1,925
Hutterian Brethren (95)	6,700
Mennonite Brethren Chs., The Conf. of (144)	16,843
Mennonite Church (1,053)	99,431
Mennonite Ch., The General Conference (229)	33,937
Old Order Amish Ch. (876)	78,840
Methodist churches:	
African Methodist Episcopal Ch. (*)	3,500,000
African Methodist Episcopal Zion Ch. (3,000)	1,200,000
Allegheny Wesleyan Methodist Connection (117)	2,130
Christian Methodist Episcopal Church (2,340)	718,922
Evangelical Methodist Ch. (126)	8,514

(continued)

Group	Members
Free Methodist Ch. of North America (1,063)	73,572
Fundamental Methodist Ch. (12)	1,075
Primitive Methodist Ch., U.S.A. (85)	8,244
Reformed Methodist Union Episcopal Ch. (18)	3,800
Southern Methodist Ch. (133)	7,745
United Methodist Ch. (37,100)	8,785,135
The Wesleyan Church (U.S.A.) (1,211)	316,813
Metropolitan Community Churches, Univ. Fellowship of (195)	**25,076**
Moravian churches:	
Moravian Ch. Northern Province (98)	29,805
Moravian Ch. in America Southern Province (56)	21,513
Unity of the Brethren (26)	3,615
Moslems	**6,000,000**
Natl. Organization of the New Apostolic Ch. of N.A. (523)	**39,816**
Natl. Spiritualist Assn. of Churches (137)	**3,883**
Old Catholic churches:	
Christ Catholic Ch. (10)	1,435
North American Old Roman Catholic Church-N.Y. Archdiocese (5)	400
Pentecostal churches:	
Apostolic Faith Mission (Portland, Ore.) (50)	4,100
Apostolic Faith Mission Ch. of God (18)	6,200
Apostolic Overcoming Holy Church of God (12)	479
Assemblies of God (11,536)	2,234,708
Bible Church of Christ (6)	6,700
Christian Church of N.A., Gen. Council (104)	13,500
Church of God (Cleveland, Tenn.) (5,841)	620,393
Church of God in Christ (15,300)	5,499,875
Church of God in Christ, Intl. (300)	200,000
Church of God of Prophecy (2,072)	72,465
Congregational Holiness Ch. (176)	7,116
Elim Fellowship (177)	20,000
Gen. Council, Christian Ch. of No. Amer. (104)	13,500
Intl. Ch. of the Foursquare Gospel (1,516)	208,150
National Gay Pentecostal Alliance (2)	*
Open Bible Standard Chs. (368)	40,000
Pentecostal Assemblies of the World (1,005)	500,000
Pentecostal Church of God (1,160)	92,060
Pentecostal Free-Will Baptist Ch. (148)	11,757
United Pentecostal Ch. Intl. (3,500)	550,000
Presbyterian churches:	
Associate Reformed Presbyterian Ch. (Gen. Synod) (189)	38,552
Cumberland Presbyterian Ch. (784)	92,433
Evangelical Presbyterian Ch. (180)	56,000
Korean Prebyterian Church in America (203)	26,988
Orthodox Presbyterian Ch. (170)	18,137
Presbyterian Ch. in America (*)	233,770
Presbyterian Ch. (U.S.A.) (11,468)	3,778,358
Reformed Presbyterian Ch. of No. Amer. (68)	5,174
Reformed churches:	
Christian Reformed Ch. in N. America (739)	224,921
Hungarian Reformed Ch. in America (27)	9,780
Netherlands Reformed Congregations (15)	5,250
Reformed Ch. in America (967)	340,991
Reformed Ch. in the U.S. (34)	3,778
United Church of Christ (6,301)	1,583,830
Reformed Episcopal Church (83)	**6,565**
The Roman Catholic Church (19,971)	**58,267,424**
The Salvation Army (1,151)	**446,403**
The Schwenkfelder Church (5)	**2,489**
The Swedenborgian Church (50)	**2,423**
Unitarian Universalist Assn. (1,020)	**141,315**
United Brethren:	
United Brethren in Christ (260)	25,775
United Christian Ch. (12)	420
Vedanta Societies (13)	**2,500**

Women and Blacks Enrolled in Seminaries, 1972-1992[1]

Source: *1993 Yearbook of American and Canadian Churches*

Year	Women			Blacks		
	Number of Students	Percentage Annual Change	Percentage of Total Enrollment	Number of Students	Percentage Annual Change	Percentage of Total Enrollment
1972	3,358	NA	10.2	1,061	+ 16.9	3.2
1973	4,021	+ 19.7	11.8	1,210	+ 14.0	3.6
1974	5,255	+ 30.7	14.3	1,246	+ 3.0	3.4
1975	6,505	+ 23.8	15.9	1,365	+ 9.6	3.3
1976	7,349	+ 13.0	17.1	1,524	+ 11.6	3.5
1977	8,371	+ 13.9	18.5	1,759	+ 15.4	3.9
1978	8,972	+ 7.2	19.3	1,919	+ 9.1	4.1
1979	10,204	+ 13.7	21.1	2,043	+ 6.5	4.2
1980	10,830	+ 6.1	21.8	2,205	+ 7.9	4.4
1981	11,683	+ 7.9	23.1	2,371	+ 7.5	4.7
1982	12,473	+ 6.8	23.7	2,576	+ 8.6	4.9
1983	13,451	+ 7.8	24.4	2,881	+ 11.8	5.2
1984	14,142	+ 5.1	25.0	2,917	+ 1.2	5.2
1985	14,572	+ 3.0	25.8	3,046	+ 4.4	5.4
1986	14,864	+ 2.0	26.4	3,277	+ 7.6	5.8
1987	15,310	+ 3.0	27.0	3,379	+ 3.1	6.0
1988	16,344	+ 6.8	29.3	3,662	+ 8.4	6.6
1989	16,461	+ 0.7	29.3	3,961	+ 8.2	7.1
1990	17,571	+ 6.7	29.7	4,303	+ 8.6	7.3
1991	18,384	+ 4.6	30.6	4,671	+ 8.6	7.8
1992	19,653	+ 6.9	31.1	5,554	+ 18.9	8.8

(1) Data cover U.S. and Canadian seminaries that are members of the Assn. of Theological Schools. NA=not available.

Adherents of All Religions by Continental Areas, Mid-1992

Source: *1993 Encyclopedia Britannica Book of the Year*

	Africa	Asia	Europe	Latin America	Northern America	Oceania	Former U.S.S.R.	World
Christians	327,204,000	285,365,000	413,756,000	435,811,000	239,004,000	22,628,000	109,254,000	1,833,022,000
Roman Catholics	122,907,000	123,597,000	262,638,000	405,623,000	97,022,000	8,208,000	5,590,000	1,025,585,000
Protestants	87,332,000	81,476,000	73,939,000	17,263,000	96,312,000	7,518,000	9,858,000	373,698,000
Orthodox	28,549,000	3,655,000	36,165,000	1,764,000	6,008,000	576,000	93,705,000	170,422,000
Anglicans	26,863,000	707,000	32,956,000	1,300,000	7,338,000	5,719,000	400	74,883,400
Other Christians	61,553,000	75,930,000	8,058,000	9,861,000	32,324,000	607,000	100,600	188,433,600
Moslems	278,250,800	636,976,000	12,574,500	1,350,500	2,847,000*	100,500	39,229,400	971,328,700
Nonreligious	1,896,000	691,144,000	52,411,000	17,159,000	25,265,000	3,291,000	85,066,000	876,232,000
Hindus	1,475,000	728,118,000	704,000	884,000	1,269,000	360,000	2,000	732,812,000
Buddhists	21,000	313,114,000	272,000	541,000	558,000	26,000	407,000	314,939,000
Atheists	316,000	161,414,000	17,604,000	3,224,000	1,319,000	535,000	55,898,000	240,310,000

	Africa	Asia	Europe	Latin America	Northern America	Oceania	Former U.S.S.R.	World
Chinese folk religionists	13,000	186,817,000	60,000	73,000	122,000	21,000	1,000	187,107,000
New-Religionists	21,000	141,382,000	50,000	530,000	1,421,000	10,000	1,000	143,415,000
Tribal religionists	70,588,000	24,948,000	1,000	936,000	41,000	67,000	0	96,581,000
Sikhs	26,000	18,272,000	231,000	8,000	254,000	9,000	500	18,800,500
Jews	337,000	5,587,000	1,469,000	1,092,000	7,003,000	98,000	2,236,000	17,822,000
Shamanists	1,000	10,233,000	2,000	1,000	1,000	1,000	254,000	10,493,000
Confucians	1,000	5,994,000	2,000	2,000	26,000	1,000	2,000	6,028,000
Baha'is	1,496,000	2,680,000	91,000	801,000	365,000	77,000	7,000	5,517,000
Jains	53,000	3,717,000	15,000	4,000	4,000	1,000	0	3,794,000
Shintoists	200	3,220,000	500	500	1,000	500	100	3,222,800
Other religionists	433,000	12,292,000	1,469,000	3,570,000	485,000	4,000	333,000	18,586,000
Total Population	**682,132,200**	**3,231,273,000**	**500,712,000**	**465,987,000**	**279,985,000**	**27,230,000**	**292,691,000**	**5,480,010,000**

Notes: *This figure is disputed by the U.S. Moslem community, who claim 6 million adherents in the U.S. alone.

Adherents: As defined and enumerated for each of the world's countries in *World Christian Encyclopedia* (1982), projected to mid-1992, adjusted for recent data.

Christians: Followers of Jesus Christ affiliated with churches (church members, including children: 1,692,466,000) plus persons professing in censuses or polls though not so affiliated.

Other Christians: Catholics (non-Roman), marginal Protestants, crypto-Christians, and adherents of African, Asian, black, and Latin-American indigenous churches.

Moslems: 83% Sunnites, 16% Shi'ites, 1% other schools. The definition excludes former ethnic Moslems who have now abandoned Islam, also followers of syncretistic religions combining Islam with other belief systems. In the U.S., a recent detailed survey showed that most Asian immigrants previously thought to be Moslems are now in fact Christians.

Nonreligious: Persons professing no religion, nonbelievers, agnostics, freethinkers, dereligionized secularists indifferent to all religion.

Hindus: 70% Vaishnavites, 25% Shaivites, 2% neo-Hindus and reform Hindus.

Buddhists: 56% Mahayana, 38% Theravada, 6% Tantrism.

Atheists: Persons professing atheism, skepticism, disbelief, or irreligion, including antireligious (opposed to all religion).

Chinese folk religionists: Followers of traditional Chinese religion (local deities, ancestor veneration, Confucian ethics, Taoism, universism, divination, some Buddhist elements).

New-Religionists: Followers of Asian 20th-century New Religions, New Religious movements, radical new crisis religions, and non-Christian syncretistic mass religions, all founded since 1800 and mostly since 1945.

Jews: 84% Ashkenazis, 10% Orientals, 4% Sephardis. The definition includes nonpracticing Jews, underground Jews, and crypto-Jews in Moslem countries.

Confucians: Non-Chinese followers of Confucius and Confucianism, mostly Koreans in Korea.

Other religionists: Including 50 minor world religions and a large number of spiritist religions, New Age religions, quasi religions, pseudoreligions, parareligions, religious or mystic systems, and religious and semireligious brotherhoods.

Total Population: UN medium variant figures for mid-1992, as given in *World Population Prospects 1990* (UN, 1991).

Change in Membership of Some U.S. Denominations, 1980–1990

Source: *1993 Yearbook of American and Canadian Churches*

Denomination	1980–1990 % Change in Adherents
Advent Christian Church	−32.9%
African Methodist Episcopal Zion	4.5%
American Baptist Churches USA	−2.5%
Apostolic Christian Church (Nazarene)	20.6%
Apostolic Lutheran Church of America	0.1%
Armenian Apostolic Ch. Amer., E.Prelacy	619.1%
Assemblies of God	34.0%
Assoc. Reformed Presbyterian Church	18.8%
Baptist General Conference	11.0%
Baptist Missionary Association of Amer.	5.6%
Beachy Amish Mennonite Churches	39.6%
Berean Fundamental Church	46.6%
Bible Church of Christ, Inc.	119.6%
Brethren Church (Ashland, Ohio)	−11.1%
Brethren in Christ Church	7.2%
Catholic Church	12.4%
Christ Catholic Church	−40.2%
Christian & Missionary Alliance	59.3%
Christian Brethren	29.1%
Christian Church (Disciples of Christ)	−14.4%
Christian Churches & Churches of Christ	7.6%
Christian Reformed Church	6.7%
Church of God (Anderson, Indiana)**	−56.5%
Church of God (Cleveland, Tennessee)	46.5%
Church of God (Seventh Day), Denver, Colo.	89.8%
Church of God Gen. Conf. (Abrahamic Faith)	−14.1%
Church of God in Christ (Mennonite)	68.2%
Church of Jesus Christ of Latter-day Saints	31.9%
Church of the Brethren	−10.3%
Church of the Lutheran Brethren of Amer.	62.7%
Church of the Lutheran Confession	−6.4%
Church of the Nazarene	0.3%
Churches of Christ	5.1%
Congr. Christian Churches, Nat'l Assoc. of	−17.3%
Conservative Congregational Christian Conf.	28.0%

Denomination	1980–1990 % Change in Adherents
Cumberland Presbyterian Church	0.4%
Episcopal Church	−13.4%
Estonian Evangelical Lutheran Church	−43.1%
Evangelical Bible Churches, Fellowship of	−24.0%
Evangelical Congregational Church	−2.7%
Evangelical Free Church of America	155.4%
Evangelical Lutheran Church in America*	−2.8%
Evangelical Lutheran Synod	7.4%
Evangelical Mennonite Church, Inc.	11.5%
Evangelical Methodist Church	−5.8%
Fire Baptized Holiness Church (Wesleyan)	−2.0%
Free Lutheran Congregations, The Assoc. of	88.9%
Free Methodist Church of North America**	−59.5%
Friends-USA	−5.0%
General Conf. of Mennonite Brethren Chs.	14.7%
Internat'l Church of the Foursquare Gospel	59.4%
Jewish (estimate)**	645.3%
Latvian Evang. Lutheran Church in Amer.	5.0%
Lutheran Church—Missouri Synod	−0.7%
Mennonite Church	30.4%
Mennonite Church, The General Conference	−12.7%
Missionary Church	26.8%
Moravian Church in America, Alaska Prov.	22.1%
Moravian Church in America, Northern Prov.	−4.1%
Moravian Church in America, Southern Prov.	1.0%
North American Baptist Conference	4.4%
Old Order Amish Church	42.1%
Pentecostal Holiness Church, Inc.	29.2%
Presbyterian Church (USA)*	−11.5%
Presbyterian Church in America*	95.7%
Primitive Advent Christian Church	−21.2%
Primitive Methodist Church, U.S.A.	−34.7%
Protestant Conference (Lutheran), The	−21.8%
Reformed Church in America	−2.2%
Reformed Episcopal Church	−10.9%

Denomination	1980–1990 % Change in Adherents
Salvation Army, The**	−64.7%
Seventh Day Baptist General Conference	4.8%
Seventh-day Adventists	35.1%
Southern Baptist Convention	16.3%
Syrian Orthodox Church of Antioch	25.1%
Unitarian Universalist Association**	21.7%
United Christian Church	−2.3%
United Church of Christ	−4.9%
United Methodist Church, The	−4.0%
Wisconsin Evangelical Lutheran Synod	3.8%
Total	**12.4%**

Notes: Many Protestant denominations do not include children in membership, and a number of groups could not provide data on adherents; therefore, an estimating formula was used to include children, which made this study's adherent figures higher than the *Yearbook's* membership figures. * 1980 figures include denominations that merged during the decade. ** Methodology for reporting adherents differed in 1980 and 1990.

Predominant Religious Groups in U.S. Counties

Source: *1993 Yearbook of American and Canadian Churches*

Religious Group	No. of Counties Where Predominant
Baptist	1,322
Catholic	959
Lutheran	266
Methodist	249
Latter-day Saints	83
Disciples of Christ	54
Reformed	8
Mennonite	7
United Church of Christ	6
Pentecostal	5
Presbyterian	5
Brethren	2
Jewish	2
Moravian	2
Adventist	1
Episcopal	1
Friends	1

Episcopal Church Calendar and Liturgical Colors

Source: The Episcopal Church Center, New York City

White—from Christmas Day through the First Sunday after Epiphany; Maundy Thursday (as an alternative to crimson at the Eucharist); from the Vigil of Easter to the Day of Pentecost (Whitsunday); Trinity Sunday; Feasts of the Lord (except Holy Cross Day); the Confession of St. Peter; the Conversion of St. Paul; St. Joseph; St. Mary Magdalene; St. Mary the Virgin; St. Michael and All Angels; All Saints' Day; St. John the Evangelist; memorials of other saints who were not martyred; Independence Day and Thanksgiving Day; weddings and funerals. **Red**—the Day of Pentecost; Holy Cross Day; feasts of apostles and evangelists (except those listed above); feasts and memorials of martyrs (including Holy Innocents' Day). **Violet**—Advent and Lent. **Crimson** (dark red)—Holy Week. **Green**—the seasons after Epiphany and after Pentecost. **Black**—optional alternative for funerals. Alternative colors used in some churches: **Blue**—Advent; **Lenten White**—Ash Wednesday to Palm Sunday.

In the Episcopal Church the days of fasting are Ash Wednesday and Good Friday. Other days of special devotion (abstinence) are the 40 days of Lent and all Fridays of the year, except those in Christmas and Easter seasons and any Feasts of the Lord that occur on a Friday or during Lent. Ember Days (optional) are days of prayer for the Church's ministry. They fall on the Wednesday, Friday, and Saturday after the first Sunday in Lent, the Day of Pentecost, Holy Cross Day, and the Third Sunday of Advent. Rogation Days (also optional) are the three days before Ascension Day, and are days of prayer for God's blessing on the crops, on commerce and industry, and for the conservation of the earth's resources.

Days, etc.	1993	1994	1995	1996	1997
Golden Number	18	19	1	2	3
Sunday Letter	C	B	A	GF	E
Sundays after Epiphany	7	6	8	7	5
Ash Wednesday	Feb. 24	Feb. 16	Mar. 1	Feb. 21	Feb. 12
First Sunday in Lent	Feb. 28	Feb. 20	Mar. 5	Feb. 25	Feb. 16
Passion/Palm Sunday	Apr. 4	Mar. 27	Apr. 9	Mar. 31	Mar. 23
Good Friday	Apr. 9	Apr. 1	Apr. 14	Apr. 5	Mar. 28
Easter Day	Apr. 11	Apr. 3	Apr. 16	Apr. 7	Mar. 30
Ascension Day	May 20	May 12	May 25	May 16	May 8
The Day of Pentecost	May 30	May 22	June 4	May 26	May 18
Trinity Sunday	June 6	May 29	June 11	June 2	May 25
Numbered Proper of 2 Pentecost	#6	#5	#6	#5	#4
First Sunday of Advent	Nov. 28	Nov. 27	Dec. 3	Dec. 1	Nov. 30

Greek Orthodox Movable Ecclesiastical Dates

	1993	1994	1995	1996	1997
Triódion begins	February 7	February 20	February 12	February 4	February 16
Sat. of Souls	February 20	March 5	February 25	February 17	March 1
Meat Fare	February 21	March 6	February 26	February 18	March 2
2nd Sat. of Souls	February 27	March 12	March 4	February 24	March 8
Lent Begins	March 1	March 14	March 6	February 26	March 10
St. Theodore 3rd Sat. of Souls	March 6	March 19	March 11	March 2	March 15
Sunday of Orthodoxy	March 7	March 20	March 12	March 3	March 16
Sat. of Lazarus	April 10	April 23	April 15	April 6	April 19
Palm Sunday	April 11	April 24	April 16	April 7	April 20
Holy (Good) Friday	April 16	April 29	April 21	April 12	April 25
Western Easter	April 11	April 3	April 16	April 7	March 30
Orthodox Easter	April 18	May 1	April 23	April 14	April 27
Ascension	May 27	June 9	June 1	May 23	June 5
Sat. of Souls	June 5	June 18	June 10	June 1	June 14
Pentecost	June 6	June 19	June 11	June 2	June 15
All Saints	June 13	June 26	June 18	June 9	June 22

Jewish Holy Days, Festivals, and Fasts

	1993 (5753-54)	1994 (5754-54)	1995 (5755-56)	1996 (5756-57)	1997 (5757-58)
Tu B'Shvat	Feb. 6 Sat.	Jan. 27 Thu.	Jan. 16 Mon.	Feb. 5 Mon.	Jan. 23 Thu.
Ta'anis Esther (Fast of Esther)	Mar. 4 Thu.*	Feb. 24 Thu.	Mar. 15 Wed.	Mar. 4 Mon.	Mar. 20 Thu.*
Purim	Mar. 7 Sun.	Feb. 25 Fri.	Mar. 16 Thu.	Mar. 5 Tue.	Mar. 23 Sun.
Passover	Apr. 6 Tue.	Mar. 27 Sun.	Apr. 15 Sat.	Apr. 4 Thu.	Apr. 22 Tue.
	Apr. 13 Tue.	Apr. 3 Sun.	Apr. 22 Sat.	Apr. 11 Thu.	Apr. 29 Tue.
Lag B'Omer	May 9 Sun.	Apr. 29 Fri.	May 18 Thu.	May 7 Tue.	May 25 Sun.
Shavuot	May 26 Wed.	May 16 Mon.	June 4 Sun	May 24 Fri.	June 11 Sun.
	May 27 Thu.	May 17 Tue.	June 5 Mon.	May 25 Sat.	June 12 Mon.
Fast of the 17th Day of Tammuz	July 6 Tue.	June 26 Sun.	July 16 Sun.*	July 4 Thu.	July 22 Tue.
Fast of the 9th Day of Ac	July 27 Tue.	July 17 Sun.	Aug. 6 Sun.	July 25 Thu.	Aug. 12 Tue.
Rosh Hashanah	Sept. 16 Thu.	Sept. 6 Tue.	Sept. 25 Mon.	Sept. 14 Sat.	Oct. 2 Thu.
	Sept. 17 Fri.	Sept. 7 Wed.	Sept. 26 Tue.	Sept. 15 Sun.	Oct. 3 Fri.
Fast of Gedalya	Sept. 19 Sun.*	Sept. 8 Thu.	Sept. 27 Wed.	Sept. 16 Mon.	Oct. 5 Sun.*
Yom Kippur	Sept. 25 Sat.	Sept. 15 Thu.	Oct. 4 Wed.	Sept 23 Mon.	Oct 11 Sat.
Sukkot	Sept. 30 Thu.	Sept. 20 Tue.	Oct. 9 Mon.	Sept. 28 Sat.	Oct. 16 Thu.
	Oct. 6 Wed.	Sept. 26 Mon.	Oct. 15 Sun.	Oct. 4 Fri.	Oct. 22 Wed.
Shmini Atzeret	Oct. 7 Thu.	Sept. 27 Tue.	Oct. 16 Mon.	Oct. 5 Sat.	Oct. 23 Thu.
	Oct. 8 Fri.	Sept. 28 Wed.	Oct. 17 Tue.	Oct. 6 Sun.	Oct. 24 Fri.
Chanukah	Dec. 9 Thu.	Nov. 28 Mon.	Oct. 18 Mon.	Dec. 6 Fri.	Dec. 24 Wed.
	Dec. 16 Thu.	Dec. 5 Mon.	Oct. 25 Mon.	Dec. 13 Fri.	Dec. 31 Wed.
Fast of the 10th of Tevet	Dec. 24 Fri.	Dec. 13 Tue.	Jan. 2 Tue.	Dec. 20 Fri.	Jan. 8 Thu.

The months of the Jewish year are: 1) Tishri; 2) Cheshvan (also Marcheshvan); 3) Kislev; 4) Tebet (also Tebeth); 5) Shebat (also Shebhat); 6) Adar; 6a) Adar Sheni (II) added in leap years; 7) Nisan; 8) Iyar; 9) Sivan; 10) Tammuz; 11) Av (also Abh); 12) Elul. All Jewish holy days, etc., begin at sunset on the day previous. *Date changed to avoid Sabbath.

Islamic (Moslem) Calendar 1993-1998 (1414-1418)

The Islamic calendar is a lunar reckoning from the year of the *hegira*, 622 A.D., when Muhammed moved from Mecca to Medina. It runs in cycles of 30 years, of which the 2nd, 5th, 7th, 10th, 13th, 16th, 18th, 21st, 24th, 26th, and 29th are leap years; 1414 is the 4th year of the cycle. Common years have 354 days, leap years 355, the extra day being added to the last month, Zu'lhijjah. Except for this case, the 12 months beginning with Muharram have alternately 30 and 29 days.

Year	Name of month	Month begins	Year	Name of month	Month begins
1414	Muharram (New Year)	June 21, 1993	1416	Rajab	Nov. 24, 1995
1414	Safar	July 21, 1993	1416	Shaban	Dec. 24, 1995
1414	Rabia I	Aug. 19, 1993	1416	Ramadan	Jan. 22, 1996
1414	Rabia II	Sept. 18, 1993	1416	Shawwai	Feb. 21, 1996
1414	Jamada I	Oct. 17, 1993	1416	Zu'lkadah	Mar. 21, 1996
1414	Jamada II	Nov. 16, 1993	1416	Zu'lhijjah	Apr. 20, 1996
1414	Rajab	Dec. 15, 1993	1417	Muharram (New Year)	May 19, 1996
1414	Shaban	Jan. 14, 1994	1417	Safar	June 18, 1996
1414	Ramadan	Feb. 12, 1994	1417	Rabia I	July 17, 1996
1414	Shawwai	Mar. 14, 1994	1417	Rabia II	Aug. 16, 1996
1414	Zu'lkadah	April 12, 1994	1417	Jamada I	Sept. 14, 1996
1414	Zu'lhijjah	May 12, 1994	1417	Jamada II	Oct. 14, 1996
1415	Muharram (New Year)	June 10, 1994	1417	Rajab	Nov. 12, 1996
1415	Safar	July 10, 1994	1417	Shaban	Dec. 12, 1996
1415	Rabia I	Aug. 8, 1994	1417	Ramadan	Jan. 10, 1997
1415	Rabia II	Sept. 7, 1994	1417	Shawwai	Feb. 9, 1997
1415	Jamada I	Oct. 6, 1994	1417	Zu'lkadah	March 10, 1997
1415	Jamada II	Nov. 5, 1994	1417	Zu'lhijjah	Apr. 9, 1997
1415	Rajab	Dec. 12, 1994	1418	Muharram (New Year)	May 9, 1997
1415	Shaban	Jan. 3, 1995	1418	Safar	June 8, 1997
1415	Ramadan	Feb. 2, 1995	1418	Rabia I	July 7, 1997
1415	Shawwai	Mar. 3, 1995	1418	Rabia II	Aug. 6, 1997
1415	Zu'lkadah	Apr. 4, 1995	1418	Jamada I	Sept. 4, 1997
1415	Zu'lhijjah	May 1, 1995	1418	Jamada II	Oct. 4, 1997
1416	Muharram (New Year)	May 21, 1995	1418	Rajab	Nov. 2, 1997
1416	Safar	June 30, 1995	1418	Shaban	Dec. 2, 1997
1416	Rabia I	July 29, 1995	1418	Ramadan	Dec. 31, 1997
1416	Rabia II	Aug. 28, 1995	1418	Shawwai	Jan. 30, 1998
1416	Jamada I	Sept. 26, 1995	1418	Zu'lkadah	Feb. 27, 1998
1416	Jamada II	Oct. 26, 1995	1418	Zu'lhijjah	March 30, 1998

Ash Wednesday and Easter Sunday

Year	Ash Wed.	Easter Sunday	Year	Ash Wed.	Easter Sunday	Year	Ash Wed.	Easter Sunday	Year	Ash Wed.	Easter Sunday
1901	Feb. 20	Apr. 7	1914	Feb. 25	Apr. 12	1927	Mar. 2	Apr. 17	1940	Feb. 7	Mar. 24
1902	Feb. 12	Mar. 30	1915	Feb. 17	Apr. 4	1928	Feb. 22	Apr. 8	1941	Feb. 26	Apr. 13
1903	Feb. 25	Apr. 12	1916	Mar. 8	Apr. 23	1929	Feb. 13	Mar. 31	1942	Feb. 18	Apr. 5
1904	Feb. 17	Apr. 3	1917	Feb. 21	Apr. 8	1930	Mar. 5	Apr. 20	1943	Mar. 10	Apr. 25
1905	Mar. 8	Apr. 23	1918	Feb. 13	Mar. 31	1931	Feb. 18	Apr. 5	1944	Feb. 23	Apr. 9
1906	Feb. 28	Apr. 15	1919	Mar. 5	Apr. 20	1932	Feb. 10	Mar. 27	1945	Feb. 14	Apr. 1
1907	Feb. 13	Mar. 31	1920	Feb. 18	Apr. 4	1933	Mar. 1	Apr. 16	1946	Mar. 6	Apr. 21
1908	Mar. 4	Apr. 19	1921	Feb. 9	Mar. 27	1934	Feb. 14	Apr. 1	1947	Feb. 19	Apr. 6
1909	Feb. 24	Apr. 11	1922	Mar. 1	Apr. 16	1935	Mar. 6	Apr. 21	1948	Feb. 11	Mar. 28
1910	Feb. 9	Mar. 27	1923	Feb. 14	Apr. 1	1936	Feb. 26	Apr. 12	1949	Mar. 2	Apr. 17
1911	Mar. 1	Apr. 16	1924	Mar. 5	Apr. 20	1937	Feb. 10	Mar. 28	1950	Feb. 22	Apr. 9
1912	Feb. 21	Apr. 7	1925	Feb. 25	Apr. 12	1938	Mar. 2	Apr. 17	1951	Feb. 7	Mar. 25
1913	Feb. 5	Mar. 23	1926	Feb. 17	Apr. 4	1939	Feb. 22	Apr. 9	1952	Feb. 27	Apr. 13

Year	Ash Wed.	Easter Sunday	Year	Ash Wed.	Easter Sunday	Year	Ash Wed.	Easter Sunday	Year	Ash Wed.	Easter Sunday
1953 . .	Feb. 18	Apr. 5	1990 . .	Feb. 28	Apr. 15	2027 . .	Feb. 10	Mar. 28	2064 . .	Feb. 20	Apr. 6
1954 . .	Mar. 3	Apr. 18	1991 . .	Feb. 13	Mar. 31	2028 . .	Mar. 1	Apr. 16	2065 . .	Feb. 11	Mar. 29
1955 . .	Feb. 23	Apr. 10	1992 . .	Mar. 4	Apr. 19	2029 . .	Feb. 14	Apr. 1	2066 . .	Feb. 24	Apr. 11
1956 . .	Feb. 15	Apr. 1	1993 . .	Feb. 24	Apr. 11	2030 . .	Mar. 6	Apr. 21	2067 . .	Feb. 16	Apr. 3
1957 . .	Mar. 6	Apr. 21	1994 . .	Feb. 16	Apr. 3	2031 . .	Feb. 26	Apr. 13	2068 . .	Mar. 7	Apr. 22
1958 . .	Feb. 19	Apr. 6	1995 . .	Mar. 1	Apr. 16	2032 . .	Feb. 11	Mar. 28	2069 . .	Feb. 27	Apr. 14
1959 . .	Feb. 11	Mar. 29	1996 . .	Feb. 21	Apr. 7	2033 . .	Mar. 2	Apr. 17	2070 . .	Feb. 12	Mar. 30
1960 . .	Mar. 2	Apr. 17	1997 . .	Feb. 12	Mar. 30	2034 . .	Feb. 22	Apr. 9	2071 . .	Mar. 4	Apr. 19
1961 . .	Feb. 15	Apr. 2	1998 . .	Feb. 25	Apr. 12	2035 . .	Feb. 7	Mar. 25	2072 . .	Feb. 24	Apr. 10
1962 . .	Mar. 7	Apr. 22	1999 . .	Feb. 17	Apr. 4	2036 . .	Feb. 27	Apr. 13	2073 . .	Feb. 8	Mar. 26
1963 . .	Feb. 27	Apr. 14	2000 . .	Mar. 8	Apr. 23	2037 . .	Feb. 18	Apr. 5	2074 . .	Feb. 28	Apr. 15
1964 . .	Feb. 12	Mar. 29	2001 . .	Feb. 28	Apr. 15	2038 . .	Mar. 10	Apr. 25	2075 . .	Feb. 20	Apr. 7
1965 . .	Mar. 3	Apr. 18	2002 . .	Feb. 13	Mar. 31	2039 . .	Feb. 23	Apr. 10	2076 . .	Mar. 4	Apr. 19
1966 . .	Feb. 23	Apr. 10	2003 . .	Mar. 5	Apr. 20	2040 . .	Feb. 15	Apr. 1	2077 . .	Feb. 24	Apr. 11
1967 . .	Feb. 8	Mar. 26	2004 . .	Feb. 25	Apr. 11	2041 . .	Mar. 6	Apr. 21	2078 . .	Feb. 16	Apr. 3
1968 . .	Feb. 28	Apr. 14	2005 . .	Feb. 9	Mar. 27	2042 . .	Feb. 19	Apr. 6	2079 . .	Mar. 8	Apr. 23
1969 . .	Feb. 19	Apr. 6	2006 . .	Mar. 1	Apr. 16	2043 . .	Feb. 11	Mar. 29	2080 . .	Feb. 21	Apr. 7
1970 . .	Feb. 11	Mar. 29	2007 . .	Feb. 21	Apr. 8	2044 . .	Mar. 2	Apr. 17	2081 . .	Feb. 12	Mar. 30
1971 . .	Feb. 24	Apr. 11	2008 . .	Feb. 6	Mar. 23	2045 . .	Feb. 22	Apr. 9	2082 . .	Mar. 4	Apr. 19
1972 . .	Feb. 16	Apr. 2	2009 . .	Feb. 25	Apr. 12	2046 . .	Feb. 7	Mar. 25	2083 . .	Feb. 17	Apr. 4
1973 . .	Mar. 7	Apr. 22	2010 . .	Feb. 17	Apr. 4	2047 . .	Feb. 27	Apr. 14	2084 . .	Feb. 9	Mar. 26
1974 . .	Feb. 27	Apr. 14	2011 . .	Mar. 9	Apr. 24	2048 . .	Feb. 19	Apr. 5	2085 . .	Feb. 28	Apr. 15
1975 . .	Feb. 12	Mar. 30	2012 . .	Feb. 22	Apr. 8	2049 . .	Mar. 3	Apr. 18	2086 . .	Feb. 13	Mar. 31
1976 . .	Mar. 3	Apr. 18	2013 . .	Feb. 13	Mar. 31	2050 . .	Feb. 23	Apr. 10	2087 . .	Mar. 5	Apr. 20
1977 . .	Feb. 23	Apr. 10	2014 . .	Mar. 5	Apr. 20	2051 . .	Feb. 15	Apr. 2	2088 . .	Feb. 25	Apr. 11
1978 . .	Feb. 8	Mar. 26	2015 . .	Feb. 18	Apr. 5	2052 . .	Mar. 6	Apr. 21	2089 . .	Feb. 16	Apr. 3
1979 . .	Feb. 28	Apr. 15	2016 . .	Feb. 10	Mar. 27	2053 . .	Feb. 19	Apr. 6	2090 . .	Mar. 1	Apr. 16
1980 . .	Feb. 20	Apr. 6	2017 . .	Mar. 1	Apr. 16	2054 . .	Feb. 11	Mar. 29	2091 . .	Feb. 21	Apr. 8
1981 . .	Mar. 4	Apr. 19	2018 . .	Feb. 14	Apr. 1	2055 . .	Mar. 3	Apr. 18	2092 . .	Feb. 13	Mar. 30
1982 . .	Feb. 24	Apr. 11	2019 . .	Mar. 6	Apr. 21	2056 . .	Feb. 16	Apr. 2	2093 . .	Feb. 25	Apr. 12
1983 . .	Feb. 16	Apr. 3	2020 . .	Feb. 26	Apr. 12	2057 . .	Mar. 7	Apr. 22	2094 . .	Feb. 17	Apr. 4
1984 . .	Mar. 7	Apr. 22	2021 . .	Feb. 17	Apr. 4	2058 . .	Feb. 27	Apr. 14	2095 . .	Mar. 9	Apr. 24
1985 . .	Feb. 20	Apr. 7	2022 . .	Mar. 2	Apr. 17	2059 . .	Feb. 12	Mar. 30	2096 . .	Feb. 29	Apr. 15
1986 . .	Feb. 12	Mar. 30	2023 . .	Feb. 22	Apr. 9	2060 . .	Mar. 3	Apr. 18	2097 . .	Feb. 13	Mar. 31
1987 . .	Mar. 4	Apr. 19	2024 . .	Feb. 14	Mar. 31	2061 . .	Feb. 23	Apr. 10	2098 . .	Mar. 5	Apr. 20
1988 . .	Feb. 17	Apr. 3	2025 . .	Mar. 5	Apr. 20	2062 . .	Feb. 8	Mar. 26	2099 . .	Feb. 25	Apr. 12
1989 . .	Feb. 8	Mar. 26	2026 . .	Feb. 18	Apr. 5	2063 . .	Feb. 28	Apr. 15	2100 . .	Feb. 10	Mar. 28

The Ten Commandments

According to Judeo-Christian tradition, as related in the Bible, the Ten Commandments were revealed by God to Moses, and form the basic moral component of God's covenant with Israel. The Ten Commandments appear in two different places in the Old Testament—Exodus 20:1-17 and Deuterotomy 5:6-21—the phrasing similar but not identical. Most Protestant, Anglican, and Orthodox Christians enumerate the commandments differently from Roman Catholics and Lutherans. Jewish tradition considers the introduction, "I am the Lord . . ." to be the first commandment and makes the prohibition against "other gods" and idolatry the second.

Abridged Text of the Ten Commandments in Exodus 20:1-17

I. I am the Lord your God, who brought you out of the land of Egypt, out of the house of bondage. You shall have no other gods before me.
II. You shall not make for yourself a graven image. You shall not bow down to them or serve them.
III. You shall not take the name of the Lord your God in vain.
IV. Remember the sabbath day, to keep it holy.
V. Honor your father and your mother.
VI. You shall not kill.
VII. You shall not commit adultery.
VIII. You shall not steal.
IX. You shall not bear false witness against your neighbor.
X. You shall not covet.

Books of the Bible

Old Testament—Standard Protestant English Versions

Genesis
Exodus
Leviticus
Numbers
Deuteronomy
Joshua
Judges
Ruth
I Samuel
II Samuel
I Kings
II Kings
I Chronicles
II Chronicles
Ezra
Nehemiah
Esther
Job
Psalms
Proverbs
Ecclesiastes
Song of Solomon
Isaiah
Jeremiah
Lamentations
Ezekiel
Daniel
Hosea
Joel
Amos
Obadiah
Jonah
Micah
Nahum
Habakkuk
Zephaniah
Haggai
Zechariah
Malachi

New Testament—Standard Protestant English Versions

Matthew
Mark
Luke
John
Acts
Romans
I Corinthians
II Corinthians
Galatians
Ephesians
Phillippians
Colossians
I Thessalonians
II Thessalonians
I Timothy
II Timothy
Titus
Philemon
Hebrews
James
I Peter
II Peter
I John
II John
III John
Jude
Revelation

Catholic Versions

All the Catholic books of the Bible (Old Testament and New Testament) have the same names as Protestant Versions. A Catholic Version (and Pre-Reformation Bibles) simply has the books **Tobit, Judith, Wisdom, Sirach (Ecclesiasticus), Baruch, I Maccabees,** and **II Maccabees** as part of the Old Testament. The Old Testament books that a Catholic Bible includes and a Protestant Bible does not are called "Deuterocanonical Books."

Roman Catholic Hierarchy

Source: U.S. Catholic Conference; mid-1993

Supreme Pontiff

At the head of the Roman Catholic Church is the Supreme Pontiff, Pope John Paul II, Karol Wojtyla, born at Wadowice (Krakow), Poland, May 18, 1920; ordained priest Nov. 1, 1946; appointed bishop July 4, 1958; promoted to archbishop of Krakow Jan. 13, 1964; proclaimed cardinal June 26, 1967; elected pope as successor of Pope John Paul I Oct. 16, 1978; installed as pope Oct. 22, 1978.

College of Cardinals

Members of the Sacred College of Cardinals are chosen by the Pope to be his chief assistants and advisers in the administration of the church. Among their duties is the election of the Pope when the Holy See becomes vacant.

In its present form, the College of Cardinals dates from the 12th century. The first cardinals, from about the 6th century, were deacons and priests of the leading churches of Rome, and bishops of neighboring diocese. The title of cardinal was limited to members of the college in 1567. The number of cardinals was set at 70 in 1586 by Pope Sixtus V. From 1959 Pope John XXIII began to increase the number. However, the number of cardinals eligible to participate in papal elections was limited to 120. There were lay cardinals until 1918, when the Code of Canon Law specified that all cardinals must be priests. Pope John XXIII in 1962 established that all cardinals must be bishops. The first age limits were set in 1971 by Pope Paul VI, who decreed that at age 80 cardinals must retire from curial departments and offices and from participation in papal elections. They continue as members of the college, with all rights and privileges.

U.S. Cardinals

Name	Office	Born	Named Cardinal
Baum, William W.	Major Penitentiary of Apostolic Penitentiary, the Vatican	1926	1976
Bevilacqua, Anthony J.	Archbishop of Philadelphia	1923	1991
Bernardin, Joseph L.	Archbishop of Chicago	1928	1983
Carberry, John J.*	Archbishop emeritus of St. Louis	1904	1969
Hickey, James A.	Archbishop of Washington	1920	1988
Krol, John J.*	Archbishop emeritus of Philadelphia	1910	1967
Law, Bernard F.	Archbishop of Boston	1931	1985
Mahony, Roger	Archbishop of Los Angeles	1936	1991
O'Connor, John J.	Archbishop of New York	1920	1985
Szoka, Edmund C.	Pres. of Prefecture of Economic Affairs of Holy See, the Vatican	1927	1988

*Asterisk indicates cardinals ineligible to take part in papal elections.

Census of Religious Groups in Canada

Source: *1993 Yearbook of American and Canadian Churches;* number of churches in parenthesis; groups with under 1,000 members not included.

Religious Body	Members
Anglican Church of Canada (1,767)	848,256
Antiochian Orthodox Christian Archdiocese of North America (12)	20,000
Apostolic Church in Canada (14)	1,600
Apostolic Church of Pentecost of Canada Inc. (132)	13,842
Associated Gospel Churches (126)	N.A.
Bahá'i Faith (398)	27,000
Baptist Convention of Ontario and Quebec (372)	44,713
Baptist General Conference of Canada (70)	6,066
Baptist Union of Western Canada (172)	20,719
Brethren in Christ Church, Canadian Conference (36)	3,069
Canadian and American Reformed Churches (44)	13,182
Canadian Baptist Federation (1,165)	129,720
Canadian Convention of Southern Baptists (104)	6,001
Canadian Yearly Meeting of the Religious Society of Friends (52)	1,556
Central Canada Baptist Conference (37)	N.A.
Christian and Missionary Alliance in Canada (336)	76,119
Christian Brethren (also known as Plymouth Brethren) (600)	52,000
Christian Church (Disciples of Christ) in Canada (36)	4,251
Christian Churches and Churches of Christ in Canada (140)	7,500
Christian Reformed Church in North America (240)	86,281
Church of God (Anderson, Ind.) (50)	3,151
Church of God (Cleveland, Tenn.) (98)	5,958
Church of God of Prophecy in Canada (50)	2,915
Church of Jesus Christ of Latter-day Saints in Canada (380)	126,000
Church of the Nazarene (161)	10,915
Churches of Christ in Canada (147)	7,181
Conference of Mennonites in Canada (150)	28,648
Coptic Church in Canada (12)	N.A.
Estonian Evangelical Lutheran Church (13)	6,478
Evangelical Baptist Churches in Canada, Fellowship of (484)	57,780
Evangelical Church in Canada (46)	3,688
Evangelical Covenant Church in Canada (23)	1,278
Evangelical Free Church of Canada (124)	13,299
Evangelical Lutheran Church in Canada (656)	206,187
Evangelical Mennonite Conference (50)	6,000
Evangelical Mennonite Mission Conference (28)	3,559
Foursquare Gospel Church of Canada (46)	2,019
Free Methodist Church in Canada (147)	7,479
Free Will Baptists (17)	1,125
Greek Orthodox Diocese of Toronto (Canada) (58)	230,000
Italian Pentecostal Church of Canada (21)	3,300
Jehovah's Witnesses (1,312)	106,052
Latvian Evangelical Lutheran Church in America (8)	2,380
Lutheran Church–Canada (321)	78,566
Mennonite Brethren Churches, Canadian Conference of (193)	27,597
Metropolitan Community Churches, Universal Fellowship (12)	1,500
Missionary Church of Canada (92)	6,431
Moravian Church in America, Northern Province, Canadian District of (9)	2,126
Netherlands Reformed Congregations of North America (9)	4,660
North American Baptist Conference (120)	18,125
Old Order Amish Church (17)	N.A.
Open Bible Standard Churches of Canada (4)	1,000
Orthodox Church in America (Canada Section) (59)	N.A.
Pentecostal Assemblies of Canada (976)	194,972
Pentecostal Assemblies of Newfoundland (160)	33,700
Presbyterian Church in Canada (1,023)	245,883
Reformed Church in Canada (40)	6,779
Reformed Doukhobors, Christian Community and Brotherhood of (1)	2,108
Reorganized Church of Jesus Christ of Latter Day Saints (83)	12,258
Roman Catholic Church in Canada (11,286)	11,852,350
Romanian Orthodox Episcopate of America (Jackson, MI) (13)	8,600
Russian Orthodox Church in Canada, Patriarchal Parishes (24)	7,000
Salvation Army in Canada (402)	99,658
Serbian Orthodox Church in the U.S.A. and Canada, Diocese of Canada (17)	18,494
Seventh-day Adventist Church in Canada (320)	41,085
Ukranian Orthodox Church of Canada (258)	120,000
Union D'Eglises Baptistes Francaises Au Canada (23)	1,969
Unitarian Universalist Association (40)	6,003
United Baptist Convention of the Atlantic Provinces (558)	64,093
United Church of Canada (4,044)	2,018,808
United Pentecostal Church in Canada (213)	N.A.
Wesleyan Church of Canada (72)	5,232

N.A. = not available

The Major World Religions

Buddhism

Founded: About 525 BC, reportedly near Benares, India.
Founder: Gautama Siddhartha (ca. 563-480), the Buddha, who achieved enlightenment through intense meditation.
Sacred Texts: The *Tripitaka*, a collection of the Buddha's teachings, rules of monastic life, and philosophical commentaries on the teachings; also a vast body of Buddhist teachings and commentaries, many of which are called *sutras*.
Organization: The basic institution is the *sangha* or monastic order through which the traditions are passed to each generation. Monastic life tends to be democratic and anti-authoritarian. Large lay organizations have developed in some sects.
Practice: Varies widely according to the sect and ranges from austere meditation to magical chanting and elaborate temple rites. Many practices, such as exorcism of devils, reflect pre-Buddhist beliefs.
Divisions: A wide variety of sects grouped into 3 primary branches: Theravada (sole survivor of the ancient Hinayana schools), which emphasizes the importance of pure thought and deed; Mahayana, which includes Zen and Soka-gakkai, ranges from philosophical schools to belief in the saving grace of higher beings or ritual practices, and to practical meditative disciplines; and Tantrism, an unusual combination of belief in ritual magic and sophisticated philosophy.
Location: Throughout Asia, from Sri Lanka to Japan. Zen and Soka-gakkai have several thousand adherents in the U.S.
Beliefs: Life is misery and decay, and there is no ultimate reality in it or behind it. The cycle of endless birth and rebirth continues because of desire and attachment to the unreal "self". Right meditation and deeds will end the cycle and achieve Nirvana, the Void, nothingness.

Hinduism

Founded: Ca. 1500 BC by Aryan invaders of India where their Vedic religion intermixed with the practices and beliefs of the natives.
Sacred texts: The *Veda*, including the *Upanishads*, a collection of rituals and mythological and philosophical commentaries; a vast number of epic stories about gods, heroes, and saints, including the *Bhagavadgita*, a part of the *Mahabharata*, and the *Ramayana;* and a great variety of other literature.
Organization: None, strictly speaking. Generally, rituals should be performed or assisted by Brahmins, the priestly caste, but in practice simpler rituals can be performed by anyone. Brahmins are the final judges of ritual purity, the vital element in Hindu life. Temples and religious organizations are usually presided over by Brahmins.
Practice: A variety of private rituals, primarily passage rites (eg. initiation, marriage, death, etc.) and daily devotions, and a similar variety of public rites in temples. Of the latter, the *puja*, a ceremonial dinner for a god, is the most common.
Divisions: There is no concept of orthodoxy in Hinduism, which presents a variety of sects, most of them devoted to the worship of one of the many gods. The 3 major living traditions are those devoted to the gods Vishnu and Shiva and to the goddess Shakti; each of them divided into further subsects. Numerous folk beliefs and practices, often in amalgamation with the above groups, exist side-by-side with sophisticated philosophical schools and exotic cults.
Location: Mainly India, Nepal, Malaysia, Guyana, Suriname, Sri Lanka.
Beliefs: There is only one divine principle; the many gods are only aspects of that unity. Life in all its forms is an aspect of the divine, but it appears as a separation from the divine, a meaningless cycle of birth and rebirth (*samsara*) determined by the purity or impurity of past deeds (*karma*). To improve one's *karma* or escape *samsara* by pure acts, thought, and/or devotion is the aim of every Hindu.

Islam

Founded: 622 AD in Medina, Arabian peninsula.
Founder: Mohammed (ca. 570-632), the Prophet.
Sacred texts: *Koran*, the words of God. *Hadith*, collections of the sayings of the Prophet.
Organization: Theoretically the state and religious community are one, administered by a caliph. In practice, Islam is a loose collection of congregations united by a very conservative tradition. Islam is basically egalitarian and non-authoritarian.
Practice: Every Moslem has 5 duties: to make the profession of faith ("There is no god but Allah . . ."), pray 5 times a day, give a regular portion of his goods to charity, fast during the day in the month of Ramadan, and make at least one pilgrimage to Mecca if possible.
Divisions: The 2 major sects of Islam are the Sunni (orthodox) and the Shi'ah. The Shi'ah believe in 12 *imams*, perfect teachers, who still guide the faithful from Paradise. Shi'ah practice tends toward the ecstatic, while the Sunni is staid and simple. The Shi'ah sect affirms man's free will; the Sunni is deterministic. The mystic tradition in Islam is Sufism. A Sufi adept believes he has acquired a special inner knowledge direct from Allah.
Location: From the west coast of Africa to the Philippines across a broad band that includes Tanzania, Central Asia and western China, India, Malaysia, and Indonesia. Islam has several million adherents in the U.S.
Beliefs: Strictly monotheistic. God is creator of the universe, omnipotent, just, and merciful. Man is God's highest creation, but limited and commits sins. He is misled by Satan, an evil spirit. God revealed the *Koran* to Mohammed to guide men to the truth. Those who repent and sincerely submit to God return to a state of sinlessness. In the end, the sinless go to Paradise, a place of physical and spiritual pleasure, and the wicked burn in Hell.

Judaism

Founded: About 1300 BCE.
Founder: Abraham is regarded as the founding patriarch, but the Torah of Moses is the basic source of the teachings.
Sacred Texts: The five books of Moses constitute the written Torah. Special sanctity is also assigned other writings of the Hebrew Bible—the teachings of oral Torah are recorded in the Talmud, the Midrash, and various commentaries.
Organization: Originally theocratic, Judaism has evolved a congregational polity. The basic institution is the local synagogue, operated by the congregation and led by a rabbi of their choice. Chief Rabbis in France and Great Britain have authority only over those who accept it; in Israel, the 2 Chief Rabbis have civil authority in family law.
Practice: Among traditional practitioners, almost all areas of life are governed by strict religious discipline. Sabbath and holidays are marked by special observances, and attendance at public worship is regarded as especially important then. The chief annual observances are Passover, celebrating the liberation of the Israelites from Egypt and marked by the ritual Seder meal in the home, and the 10 days from Rosh Hashana (New Year) to Yom Kippur (Day of Atonement), a period of fasting and penitence.
Divisions: Judaism is an unbroken spectrum from ultra conservative to ultra liberal, largely reflecting different points of view regarding the binding character of the prohibitions and duties—particularly the dietary and Sabbath observations—prescribed in the daily life of the Jew.
Location: Almost worldwide, with concentrations in Israel and the U.S.
Beliefs: Strictly monotheistic. God is the creator and absolute ruler of the universe. Men are free to choose to rebel against God's rule. God established a particular relationship with the Hebrew people: by obeying a divine law God gave them they would be a special witness to God's mercy and justice. The emphasis in Judaism is on ethical behavior (and, among the traditional, careful ritual obedience) as the true worship of God.

(See following pages for discussion of Christian denominations.)

Major Christian Denominations:

Italics indicate that area which, generally speaking, most

Denomination	Origins	Organization	Authority	Special rites
Baptists	In radical Reformation objections to infant baptism, demands for church-state separation; John Smyth, English Separatist in 1609; Roger Williams, 1638, Providence, R.I.	Congregational, *i.e.*, each local church is autonomous.	Scripture; some Baptists, particularly in the South, interpret the Bible literally.	Baptism, after about age 12, by total immersion; Lord's Supper.
Church of Christ (Disciples)	Among evangelical Presbyterians in Ky. (1804) and Penn. (1809), in distress over Protestant factionalism and decline of fervor. Organized 1832.	Congregational.	*"Where the Scriptures speak, we speak; where the Scriptures are silent, we are silent."*	Adult baptism, Lord's Supper (weekly).
Episcopalians	Henry VIII separated English Catholic Church from Rome, 1534, for political reasons. Protestant Episcopal Church in U.S. founded 1789.	*Bishops, in apostolic succession, are elected by diocesan representatives; part of Anglican Communion, symbolically headed by Archbishop of Canterbury.*	Scripture as interpreted by tradition, esp. *39 Articles* (1563); not dogmatic. Tri-annual convention of bishops, priests, and laymen.	Infant baptism, Holy Communion, others. Sacrament is symbolic, but has real spiritual effect.
Lutherans	Martin Luther in Wittenberg, Germany, 1517, objected to Catholic doctrine of salvation by merit and sale of indulgences; break complete by 1519.	Varies from congregational to episcopal; in U.S. a combination of regional synods and congregational polities is most common.	*Scripture, and tradition as spelled out in Augsburg Confession (1530) and other creeds. These confessions of faith are binding although interpretations vary.*	Infant baptism, Lord's Supper. Christ's true body and blood present "in, with, and under the bread and wine."
Methodists	Rev. John Wesley began movement, 1738, within Church of England. First U.S. denomination Baltimore, 1784.	Conference and superintendent system. *In United Methodist Church, general superintendents are bishops—not a priestly order, only an office—who are elected for life.*	Scripture as interpreted by tradition, reason, and experience.	Baptism of infants or adults, Lord's Supper commanded. Other rites, inc. marriage, ordination, solemnize personal commitments.
Mormons	In visions of the Angel Moroni by Joseph Smith, 1827, in New York, in which he received a new revelation on golden tablets: *The Book of Mormon.*	Theocratic; all male adults are in priesthood which culminates in Council of 12 Apostles and 1st Presidency (1st President, 2 counselors).	*The Bible, Book of Mormon and other revelations to Smith, and certain pronouncements of the 1st Presidency.*	Baptism, at age 8, laying on of hands (which confers the gift of the Holy Spirit), Lord's Supper. Temple rites: baptism for the dead, marriage for eternity, others.
Orthodox	Original Christian proselytizing in 1st century; broke with Rome, 1054, after centuries of doctrinal disputes and diverging traditions.	Synods of bishops in autonomous, usually national, churches elect a patriarch, archbishop or metropolitan. These men, as a group, are the heads of the church.	Scripture, tradition, and the first 7 church councils up to Nicaea II in 787. Bishops in council have authority in doctrine and policy.	Seven sacraments: infant baptism and anointing, Eucharist (both bread and wine), ordination, penance, anointing of the sick, marriage.
Pentecostal	In Topeka, Kansas (1901), and Los Angeles (1906) in reaction to loss of evangelical fervor among Methodists and other denominations.	Originally a movement, not a formal organization, Pentecostalism now has a variety of organized forms and continues also as a movement.	Scripture, individual charismatic leaders, the teachings of the Holy Spirit.	*Spirit baptism, esp. as shown in "speaking in tongues"; healing and sometimes exorcism; adult baptism, Lord's Supper.*
Presbyterians	In Calvinist Reformation in 1500s; differed with Lutherans over sacraments, church government. John Knox founded Scotch Presbyterian church about 1560.	*Highly structured representational system of ministers and laypersons (presbyters) in local, regional and national bodies. (synods).*	Scripture.	Infant baptism, Lord's Supper; bread and wine symbolize Christ's spiritual presence.
Roman Catholics	Traditionally, by Jesus who named St. Peter the 1st Vicar; historically, in early Christian proselytizing and the conversion of imperial Rome in the 4th century.	Hierarchy with supreme power vested in Pope elected by cardinals. Councils of Bishops advise on matters of doctrine and policy.	*The Pope, when speaking for the whole church in matters of faith and morals, and tradition, which is partly recorded in scripture and expressed in church councils.*	Seven sacraments: baptism, contrition and penance, confirmation, Eucharist, marriage, ordination, and anointing of the sick (unction).
United Church of Christ	*By ecumenical union, 1957, of Congregationalists and Evangelical & Reformed, representing both Calvinist and Lutheran traditions.*	Congregational; a General Synod, representative of all congregations, sets general policy.	Scripture.	Infant baptism, Lord's Supper.

How Do They Differ?

distinguishes that denomination from any other.

Practice	Ethics	Doctrine	Other	Denomination
Worship style varies from staid to evangelistic. Extensive missionary activity.	Usually opposed to alcohol and tobacco; sometimes tends toward a perfectionist ethical standard.	*No creed; true church is of believers only, who are all equal.*	Since no authority can stand between the believer and God, the Baptists are strong supporters of church-state separation.	Baptists
Tries to avoid any rite or doctrine not explicitly part of the 1st century church. Some congregations may reject instrumental music.	Some tendency toward perfectionism; increasing interest in social action programs.	Simple New Testament faith; avoids any elaboration not firmly based on Scripture.	Highly tolerant in doctrinal and religious matters; strongly supportive of scholarly education.	Church of Christ (Disciples)
Formal, based on *Book of Common Prayer* (1549); services range from austerely simple to highly elaborate.	Tolerant; sometimes permissive; some social action programs.	*Apostles' Creed* is basic; otherwise, considerable variation ranges from rationalist and liberal to acceptance of most Roman Catholic dogma.	Strongly ecumenical, holding talks with all other branches of Christendom.	Episcopalians
Relatively simple formal liturgy with emphasis on the sermon.	Generally, conservative in personal and social ethics; doctrine of "2 kingdoms" (worldly and holy) supports conservatism in secular affairs.	Salvation by faith alone through grace. Lutheranism has made major contributions to Protestant theology.	Though still somewhat divided along ethnic lines (German, Swede, etc.), main divisions are between fundamentalists and liberals.	Lutherans
Worship style varies widely by denomination, local church, geography.	Originally pietist and perfectionist; always strong social activist elements.	No distinctive theological development; 25 Articles abridged from Church of England's 39 not binding.	In 1968, United Methodist Church joined pioneer English- and German-speaking groups. UMs leaders in ecumenical movement.	Methodists
Staid service with hymns, sermon. Secret temple ceremonies may be more elaborate. Strong missionary activity.	Temperance; strict tithing. Combine a strong work ethic with communal self-reliance.	God is a material being; he created the universe out of pre-existing matter; all persons can be saved and many will become divine. Most other beliefs are traditionally Christian.	Mormons regard mainline churches as apostate, corrupt. Reorganized Church (founded 1860) rejects most Mormon doctrine and practice except Book of Mormon.	Mormons
Elaborate liturgy, usually in the vernacular, though extremely traditional. The liturgy is the essence of Orthodoxy. Veneration of icons.	Tolerant; very little social action; divorce, remarriage permitted in some cases. Priests need not be celibate; bishops are.	Emphasis on Christ's resurrection, rather than crucifixion; the Holy Spirit proceeds from God the Father only.	Orthodox Church in America, originally under Patriarch of Moscow, was granted autonomy in 1970. Greek Orthodox do not recognize this autonomy.	Orthodox
Loosely structured service with rousing hymns and sermons, culminating in spirit baptism.	Usually, emphasis on perfectionism with varying degrees of tolerance.	Simple traditional beliefs, usually Protestant, with emphasis on the immediate presence of God in the Holy Spirit.	Once confined to lower-class "holy rollers," Pentecostalism now appears in mainline churches and has established middle-class congregations.	Pentecostal
A simple, sober service in which the sermon is central.	Traditionally, a tendency toward strictness with firm church- and self-discipline; otherwise tolerant.	Emphasizes the sovereignty and justice of God; no longer doctrinaire.	While traces of belief in predestination (that God has foreordained salvation for the "elect") remain, this idea is no longer a central element in Presbyterianism.	Presbyterians
Relatively elaborate ritual; wide variety of public and private rites, eg., mass, rosary recitation, processions, novenas.	Theoretically very strict; tolerant in practice on most issues. Divorce and remarriage not accepted. Celibate clergy, except in Eastern rite.	Highly elaborated. Salvation by merit gained through faith. Unusual development of doctrines surrounding Mary. Dogmatic.	Roman Catholicism went through a period of relatively rapid change as a result of Vatican Council II.	Roman Catholics
Usually simple services with emphasis on the sermon.	Tolerant; some social action emphasis.	Standard Protestant; *Statement of Faith* (1959) is not binding.	The 2 main churches in the 1957 union represented earlier unions with small groups of almost every Protestant denomination.	United Church of Christ

NATIONS OF THE WORLD

As of mid-1993

The nations of the world are listed in alphabetical order. Initials in the following articles include UN (United Nations), OAS (Org. of American States), NATO (North Atlantic Treaty Org.), EC (European Communities, or Common Market), OAU (Org. of African Unity), ILO (Intl. Labor Org.), FAO (Food & Agriculture Org.), WHO (World Health Org.), IMF (Intl. Monetary Fund), GATT (General Agreement on Tarriffs & Trade), CIS (Commonwealth of Independent States). **Sources:** U.S. Dept. of State; U.S. Census Bureau; The World Factbook; International Monetary Fund; UN Statistical Yearbook; UN Demographic Yearbook; International Iron and Steel Institute; The Statesman's Year-Book; Encyclopaedia Britannica; Funk & Wagnalls New Encyclopedia. All embassy addresses are Wash., DC; area codes (202), unless otherwise noted. Literacy rates are usually based on the ability to read and write on a lower elementary school level. The concept of literacy is changing in the industrialized countries, where literacy is defined as the ability to read instructions necessary for a job or a license. By these standards, illiteracy may be more common than present rates suggest. Per person figures in communications and health sections are post-1988.

See pages 481-496 for full-color maps and flags.

Afghanistan

Republic of Afghanistan

De Afghanistan Jamhuriat

People: Population (1992 est.): 16,095,000. **Pop. density:** 63 per sq. mi. **Urban** (1990): 18%. **Ethnic groups:** Pushtun 38%; Tajik 25%; Uzbek 6%; Hazara 19%. **Languages:** Pushtu, Dari Persian (spoken by Tajiks, Hazaras), Uzbek (Turkic). **Religions:** Sunni Moslem 74%, Shi'a Moslem 5%.

Geography: Area: 251,773 sq. mi., about the size of Texas. **Location:** In SW Asia, NW of the Indian subcontinent. **Neighbors:** Pakistan on E, S, Iran on W, Turkmenistan, Tajikistan, Uzbekistan on N; the NE tip touches China. **Topography:** The country is landlocked and mountainous, much of it over 4,000 ft. above sea level. The Hindu Kush Mts. tower 16,000 ft. above Kabul and reach a height of 25,000 ft. to the E. Trade with Pakistan flows through the 35-mile-long Khyber Pass. The climate is dry, with extreme temperatures, and there are large desert regions, though mountain rivers produce intermittent fertile valleys. **Capital:** Kabul. **Cities** (1988 est.): Kabul 1.4 mln.

Government: Type: In transition. **Head of state:** Pres. Burhanuddin Rabbani; in office: June 28, 1992. **Local divisions:** 30 provinces. **Defense:** 15% of GDP (1990).

Economy: Industries: Textiles, furniture, cement. **Chief crops:** Nuts, wheat, fruits. **Minerals:** Copper, coal, zinc, iron. **Other resources:** Wool, hides, karacul pelts. **Arable land:** 13%. **Livestock** (1990): cattle: 1.6 mln.; sheep: 13 mln. **Electricity prod.** (1991): 1.4 bln. kWh. **Labor force:** agriculture supports about 80% of the population.

Finance: Monetary unit: Afghani (Mar. 1993: 50.60 = $1 US). **Gross domestic product** (1989): $3.1 bln. **Per capita GDP:** $220. **Imports** (1991): $874 mln.; partners: CIS 55%, Jap. 8%. **Exports** (1991): $236 mln.; partners: CIS 72%. **International reserves less gold** (Feb. 1992): $229 mln. **Gold:** 965,000 oz t. **Consumer prices** (change in 1991): 56%.

Transport: Motor vehicles: in use (1990): 31,000 passenger cars, 30,000 comm. vehicles. **Civil aviation** (1989): 194 mln. passenger-km.

Communications: Television sets: 1 per 169 persons; **Radios:** 1 per 11 persons. **Telephones in use:** 1 per 443 persons. **Daily newspaper circ.** (1988): 10 per 1,000 pop.

Health: Life expectancy at birth (1992): 45 male; 43 female. **Births** (per 1,000 pop. 1992): 44. **Deaths** (per 1,000 pop. 1991): 20. **Natural increase:** 2.3%. **Hospital beds:** 1 per 2,054 persons. **Physicians:** 1 per 4,797 persons. **Infant mortality** (per 1,000 live births 1992): 164.

Education (1990): **Literacy:** 29%. Over 88% of adults have no formal schooling.

Major International Organizations: UN (World Bank, IMF)

Embassy: 2341 Wyoming Ave. NW, 20008; 234-3770.

Afghanistan, occupying a favored invasion route since antiquity, has been variously known as Ariana or Bactria (in ancient times) and Khorasan (in the Middle Ages). Foreign empires alternated rule with local emirs and kings until the 18th century, when a unified kingdom was established. In 1973, a military coup ushered in a republic.

Pro-Soviet leftists took power in a bloody 1978 coup, and concluded an economic and military treaty with the USSR.

Late in Dec. 1979, the USSR began a massive military airlift into Kabul. The three-month-old regime of Hafizullah Amin ended with a Soviet-backed coup, Dec. 27. He was replaced by Babrak Karmal, a more pro-Soviet leader. Soviet troops fanned out over Afghanistan, fighting Islamic rebels. Fighting continued for 9 years as the Soviets found themselves engaged in a protracted guerrilla war.

An UN-mediated agreement was signed Apr. 14, 1988 providing for the withdrawal of Soviet troops from Afghanistan, creation of a neutral Afghan state, and repatriation of millions of Afghan refugees. The U.S. and USSR pledged to serve as guarantors of the agreement. Afghan rebels rejected the pact and vowed to continue fighting while the "Soviets and their puppets" remained in Afghanistan.

The Soviets disclosed that during the war some 15,000 soldiers were killed. They completed their troop withdrawal Feb. 15, 1989; fighting between Afghan rebels and government forces ensued.

Communist Pres. Najibullah resigned Apr. 16, 1992 as competing guerrilla forces advanced on Kabul. The rebels achieved power, Apr. 28, ending 14 years of Soviet-backed regimes. Over 2 million Afghans had been killed and 6 million had fled the country since 1979. There were immediate clashes between moderates and Islamac fundamentalist forces. Burhanuddin Rabbani, a guerrilla leader, became president June 28, 1992. Fierce fighting continued around Kabul in 1993.

Albania

Republic of Albania

Republika e Shqipërisë

People: Population (1991 est.): 3,285,000. **Pop. density:** 295 per sq. mi. **Urban** (1991): 35%. **Ethnic groups:** Albanians (Gegs in N, Tosks in S) 90%, Greeks 8%. **Languages:** Albanian, Greek. **Religions:** Moslem 70%, Greek Orthodox 20%, Roman Catholic 10%.

Geography: Area: 11,100 sq. mi., slightly larger than Maryland. **Location:** On SE coast of Adriatic Sea. **Neighbors:** Greece on S, Yugoslavia on N, Macedonia on E. **Topography:** Apart from a narrow coastal plain, Albania consists of hills and mountains covered with scrub forest, cut by small E-W rivers. **Capital:** Tiranë. **Cities** (1990 est.): Tiranë 243,000; Durres 85,000; Elbasin 84,000.

Government: Type: Democracy. **Head of state:** Pres. Sali Berisha; in office: Apr. 9, 1992. **Head of government:** Premier Alexander Meksi; in office: Apr. 13, 1992. **Local divisions:** 26 districts. **Defense:** 4.1% of GNP (1990).

Economy: Industries: Cement, textiles, food processing. **Chief crops:** Corn, wheat, cotton, potatoes, tobacco, fruits. **Minerals:** Chromium, coal, oil. **Other resources:** Forests. **Arable land:** 21%. **Livestock** (1991): 650,000 cattle; 1.6 mln. sheep. **Electricity prod.** (1990): 5.0 bln. kWh. **Labor force:** 60% agric; 40% ind. & comm.

Finance: Monetary unit: Lek (Nov. 1992: 109 = $1 US). **Gross national product** (1991): $4.0 bln. **Per capita GNP** (1987): $1,300. **Imports** (1991): $147 mln.; partners: Czech., Yugoslavia, Rom. **Exports** (1991): $80 mln.; partners: Czech., Yugoslavia, Italy. **National budget** (1991): $1.4 bln. expenditures.

Chief ports: Durres, Vlone, Sarande.

Communications: Television sets: 1 per 13 persons. **Radios:** 1 per 6 persons. **Daily newspaper circ.:** 48 per 1,000 pop.

Health: Life expectancy at birth (1992): 72.0 yrs. male; 79 yrs. female. **Births** (per 1,000 pop. 1992): 23. **Deaths** (per 1,000 pop. 1992): 5. **Natural increase:** 2.0%. **Hospital beds:** 1 per 176 persons. **Physicians:** 1 per 574 persons. **Infant mortality** (per 1,000 live births 1992): 27.

Major International Organizations: UN (FAO, WHO).

Education (1990): **Literacy:** 72%. Free and compulsory ages 7-15.

Ancient Illyria was conquered by Romans, Slavs, and Turks (15th century); the latter Islamized the population. Independent Albania was proclaimed in 1912, republic was formed in 1920. King Zog I ruled 1925-39, until Italy invaded.

Communist partisans took over in 1944, allied Albania with USSR, then broke with USSR in 1960 over de-Stalinization. Strong political alliance with China followed, leading to several billion dollars in aid, which was curtailed after 1974. China cut off aid in 1978 when Albania attacked its policies after the death of Chinese ruler Mao Tse-tung.

Large-scale purges of officials occurred during the 1970s. Enver Hoxha, the nation's ruler for 4 decades, died Apr. 11, 1985.

There was some liberalization in 1990, including measures providing for freedom to travel abroad and restoration of the right to practice religion.

In 1991, a general strike and urban opposition forced the communist cabinet to resign; a non-communist caretaker was installed. By March, over 40,000 Albanians had left their country and sailed to Italy. James Baker became the first U.S. secy. of state to visit Albania, June 22.

Albania's former Communists were routed in parliamentary elections Mar. 1992 amid economic collapse and social unrest. Berisha was elected as the first non-Communist president since World War II. Inflation was about 150%, unemployment was estimated at 70% nationwide, and almost all food came from foreign aid.

Algeria

Democratic and Popular Republic of Algeria

al-Jumhuriya al-Jazāiriya ad-Dimuqratiya ash-Shabiya

People: Population (1992 est.); 26,666,000. **Age distrib.** (%): 0–14: 43.9; 15–59: 50.3; 60+: 5.8. **Pop. density:** 31 per sq. mi. **Urban** (1990): 51%. **Ethnic groups:** Arabs 75%, Berbers 25%. **Languages:** Arabic (official), Berber (indigenous language). **Religions:** Sunni Moslem (state religion).

Geography: Area: 918,497 sq. mi., more than 3 times the size of Texas. **Location:** In NW Africa, from Mediterranean Sea into Sahara Desert. **Neighbors:** Morocco on W, Mauritania, Mali, Niger on S, Libya, Tunisia on E. **Topography:** The Tell, located on the coast, comprises fertile plains 50-100 miles wide, with a moderate climate and adequate rain. Two major chains of the Atlas Mts., running roughly E-W, and reaching 7,000 ft., enclose a dry plateau region. Below lies the Sahara, mostly desert with major mineral resources. **Capital:** Algiers (El Djazair). **Cities** (1987 est.): El Djazair 1,483,000; Wahran 590,000; Qacentina 483,000.

Government: Type: Republic. **Head of state:** Pres. Ali Kafi; in office: July 1, 1992. **Head of government:** Prime Min. Redha Malek; in office: Aug. 21, 1993. **Local divisions:** 48 provinces. **Defense:** 1.8% of GDP (1992).

Economy: Industries: Oil, light industry, food processing. **Chief crops:** Grains, wine-grapes, potatoes, dates, olives, oranges. **Minerals:** Mercury, iron, zinc, lead. **Crude oil reserves** (1987): 4.8 bln. bbls. **Other resources:** Cork trees. **Arable land:** 3%; **Livestock** (1988): cattle: 1.7 mln.; sheep: 14 mln. **Electricity prod.** (1991): 16.7 bln. kWh. **Crude steel prod.** (1991): 767,000 metric tons. **Labor force:** 24% agric.; 40% ind. and commerce; 24% government, & services.

Finance: Monetary Unit: Dinar (Mar. 1993: 23 = $1 US). **Gross domestic product** (1990): $54 bln. **Per capita GDP:** $2,130. **Imports** (1991): $9.2 bln.; partners: EEC 64%. **Exports** (1991): $11.7 bln.; partners: EEC 74%. **National budget** (1990): $17.3 bln. **International reserves less gold** (Mar. 1993): $1.8 bln. **Gold:** 5.5 mln. oz t. **Consumer prices** (change in 1990): 26%

Transport: Railroads (1991): **Length:** 2,668 mi. **Motor vehicles:** in use (1990): 750,000 passenger cars, 500,000 comm. vehicles. **Chief ports:** El Djazair.

Communications: Television sets: 1 per 15 persons. **Radios:** 1 per 4 persons. **Telephones in use:** 1 per 23 persons. **Daily newspaper circ.** (1990): 53 per 1,000 pop.

Health: Life expectancy at birth (1992): 66 male; 68 female. **Births** (per 1,000 pop. 1992): 31 **Deaths** (per 1,000 pop. 1992): 7.0. **Natural increase:** 2.4%. **Hospital beds:** 1 per 393 persons. **Physicians:** 1 per 1,062 persons. **Infant mortality** (per 1,000 live births 1992): 57.

Education (1991): **Literacy:** 52%.

Major International Organizations: UN (FAO, IMF, WHO), OAU, Arab League, OPEC.

Embassy: 2118 Kalorama Rd. NW, 20008; 328-5300.

Earliest known inhabitants were ancestors of Berbers, followed by Phoenicians, Romans, Vandals, and, finally, Arabs. Turkey ruled 1518 to 1830, when France took control.

Large-scale European immigration and French cultural inroads did not prevent an Arab nationalist movement from launching guerrilla war. Peace, and French withdrawal, was negotiated with French Pres. Charles de Gaulle. One million Europeans left. Independence came July 5, 1962.

Ahmed Ben Bella was the victor of infighting and ruled 1962-65, when an army coup installed Col. Houari Boumedienne as leader.

In 1967, Algeria declared war on Israel, broke ties with U.S., and moved toward eventual military and political ties with the USSR. Some 500 died in riots protesting economic hardship in 1988. In 1989, voters approved a new constitution which cleared the way for a multiparty system and guaranteed "fundamental rights and freedoms" of Algerians.

The government canceled Jan. 1992 elections Islamic fundamentalists were expected to win and banned all nonreligious activities at Algeria's 10,000 mosques. Pres. Mohammed Boudiaf was assassinated June 29, 1992. There were several attacks on high-ranking officials by militant Moslem fundamentalists in 1993.

Andorra

Principality of Andorra

Principat d'Andorra

People: Population (1992 est.): 54,000. **Age distrib.** (%): 0–14: 17.4; 14–59: 68.8; 60+: 13.8. **Pop. density:** 291 per sq. mi. **Ethnic groups:** Catalan 61%, Spanish 30%, Andorran 6%, French 3%. **Languages:** Catalan (official), Spanish, French. **Religion:** Roman Catholic.

Geography: Area: 185 sq. mi., half the size of New York City. **Location:** In Pyrenees Mtns. **Neighbors:** Spain on S, France on N. **Topography:** High mountains and narrow valleys over the country. **Capital:** Andorra la Vella.

Government: Type: Parliamentary democracy. **Head of government:** Oscar Ribas Reig; in office: May 4, 1992. **Local divisions:** 7 parishes.

Economy: Industries: Tourism, tobacco products. **Labor force:** 20% agric.; 80% ind. and commerce; services; government.

Finance: Monetary unit: French franc, Spanish peseta.

Communications: Television sets: 1 per 8 persons. **Radios:** 1 per 4 persons. **Telephones in use:** 1 per 2 persons.

Health: Births (per 1,000 pop. 1992): 10. **Deaths** (per 1,000 pop. 1992): 4. **Natural increase:** 0.7%.

Education (1992): **Literacy:** 99%. School compulsory to age 16.

Major International Organizations: UN.

Andorra was a co-principality, with joint sovereignty by France and the bishop of Urgel, from 1278 to 1993.

Tourism, especially skiing, is the economic mainstay. A free port, allowing for an active trading center, draws some 10 million tourists annually. The ensuing economic prosperity, accompanied by Andorra's virtual law-free status, gave rise to calls for reform.

Andorra voters chose to end a feudal system that had been in place for 715 years and adopt a parliamentary system of government Mar. 14, 1993.

Angola

Republic of Angola

República de Angola

People: Population (1991 est.): 8,902,000. **Pop. density:** 18 per sq. mi. **Ethnic groups:** Ovimbundu 38%, Kimbundu 25%; Bakongo 13%. **Urban** (1991): 29%. **Languages:** Portuguese (official), various Bantu languages. **Religions:** Roman Catholic 38%, Protestant 15%, indigenous beliefs 47%.

Geography: Area: 481,353 sq. mi., larger than Texas and California combined. **Location:** In SW Africa on Atlantic coast. **Neighbors:** Namibia on S, Zambia on E, Zaire on N; Cabinda, an enclave separated from rest of country by short Atlantic coast of Zaire, borders Congo Republic. **Topography:** Most of Angola consists of a plateau elevated 3,000 to 5,000 feet above sea level, rising from a narrow coastal strip. There is also a temperate highland area in the west-central region, a desert in the S, and a tropical rain forest covering Cabinda. **Capital:** Luanda (1988 est.): 1.1 mln.

Government: Type: Republic. **Head of state:** Pres. Jose Eduardo dos Santos b. Aug. 28, 1942; in office: Sept. 20, 1979. Prime Min. Marcolino Moco; in office: Dec. 2, 1992. **Local divisions:** 18 provinces. **Defense:** 14.3% of GNP (1984).

Economy: Industries: Food processing, textiles, mining, tires, petroleum. **Chief crops:** Coffee, bananas. **Minerals:** Iron, diamonds (over 2 mln. carats a year), copper, phosphates, oil. **Livestock** (1991): cattle: 3.1 mln.; goats: 1 mln. **Crude oil reserves** (1987): 1.9 bln. bbls. **Arable land:** 3%. **Fish catch** (1990): 178,000 metric tons. **Electricity prod.** (1991): 770 mln. kWh. **Labor force:** 85% agric., 15% industry.

Finance: Monetary unit: new Kwanza (Nov. 1992: 550 = $1 US). **Gross domestic product** (1991): $8.3 bln. **Per capita GDP:** $950. **Imports** (1991): $1.3 bln.; partners: Portugal 29%, Fra. 9%; U.S. 9%. **Exports** (1991): $3.4 bln.; partners: U.S. 56%.

Transport: Motor vehicles: in use (1990): 130,000 passenger cars, 44,000 comm. vehicles. **Chief ports:** Cabinda, Lobito, Luanda.

Communications: Television sets: 1 per 200 persons. Radios: 1 per 22 persons. **Telephones in use:** 1 per 132 persons. **Daily newspaper circ.** (1984): 13 per 1,000 pop.

Health: Life expectancy at birth (1992): 43 male; 47 female. **Births** (per 1,000 pop. 1992): 46. **Deaths** (per 1,000 pop. 1992): 19. **Natural increase:** 2.7%. **Hospital beds:** 1 per 845 persons. **Physicians:** 1 per 15,136 persons. **Infant mortality** (per 1,000 live births 1992): 151.

Education (1992): **Literacy:** 40%.

Major International Organizations: UN (ILO, WHO), OAU.

From the early centuries AD to 1500, Bantu tribes penetrated most of the region. Portuguese came in 1583, allied with the Bakongo kingdom in the north, and developed the slave trade. Large-scale colonization did not begin until the 20th century, when 400,000 Portuguese immigrated.

A guerrilla war begun in 1961 lasted until 1975, when Portugal granted independence. Fighting then erupted between three rival rebel groups —the National Front, based in Zaire, the Soviet-backed Popular Movement for the Liberation of Angola (MPLA), and the National Union for the Total Independence of Angola (UNITA), aided by the U.S. and S. Africa. The civil war killed thousands of blacks, drove most whites to emigrate, and completed economic ruin. Cuban troops and Soviet aid helped the MPLA win control of most of the country by 1976 and gain wide recognition as the government of Angola, but UNITA continued fighting.

An agreement was signed in Dec. 1988 between Angola, Cuba, and S. Africa on a timetable for withdrawal of Cuban troops, completed May 25, 1991. The 16-year war ended May 1, 1991, as the government and UNITA signed a peace agreement which would lead to democracy.

Elections were held in Sept. 1992, but fighting again broke out, as UNITA rejected the presidential election results, and continued into 1993, with UNITA forces holding about 50 percent of the nation's territory. The U.S. formally recognized the government of Angola, May 19, 1993, for the first time since independence.

Antigua and Barbuda

People: Population (1992 est.) 64,000 (incl. Redonda). **Urban:** (1990) 32%. **Ethnic groups:** Mostly African. **Language:** English (official). **Religion:** Predominantly Church of England.

Geography: Area: 171 sq. mi. **Location:** Eastern Caribbean. **Neighbors:** approx. 30 mi. north of Guadeloupe. **Capital:** St. John's, (1988 est.) 27,000.

Government: Type: Constitutional monarchy with British-style parliament. **Head of state:** Queen Elizabeth II; represented by Sir Wilfred E. Jacobs. **Head of government:** Prime Min. Vere Cornwall Bird; b. Dec. 7, 1910; in office Nov. 1, 1981.

Economy: Industries: Manufacturing, tourism. **Arable land:** 18%.

Finance: Monetary unit: East Caribbean dollar (June 1993): 2.70 = $1 U.S. **Gross domestic product** (1990): $350 mln.

Health: Infant mortality (per 1,000 live births 1992): 20.

Education (1990): **Literacy:** 90%.

Major International Organizations: UN, Commonwealth of Nations.

Embassy: 2400 International Dr., NW 20008; 362-5122.

Columbus landed on Antigua in 1493. The British colonized it in 1632.

The British associated state of Antigua achieved independence as Antigua and Barbuda on Nov. 1, 1981. The government maintains close relations with the U.S., United Kingdom, and Venezuela.

Argentina

Argentine Republic

República Argentina

People: Population (1992 est.): 32,901,000. **Age distrib.** (%): 0–14: 30.3; 15–59: 56.8; 60+: 12.9. **Pop. density:** 30 per sq. mi. **Urban** (1991): 87%. **Ethnic groups:** Europeans 95% (Spanish, Italian), Indians, Mestizos, Arabs. **Languages:** Spanish (official), Italian. **Religions:** Roman Catholic 92%.

Geography: Area: 1,065,189 sq. mi., 4 times the size of Texas, second largest in S. America. **Location:** Occupies most of southern S. America. **Neighbors:** Chile on W, Bolivia, Paraguay on N, Brazil, Uruguay on NE. **Topography:** The mountains in W: the Andean, Central, Misiones, and Southern. Aconcagua is the highest peak in the Western hemisphere, alt. 22,834 ft. E of the Andes are heavily wooded plains, called the Gran Chaco in the N, and the fertile, treeless Pampas in the central region. Patagonia, in the S, is bleak and arid. Rio de la Plata, 170 by 140 mi., is mostly fresh water, from 2,485-mi. Parana and 1,000-mi. Uruguay rivers. **Capital:** Buenos Aires. (The Senate has approved the moving of the capital to the Patagonia Region). **Cities** (1991 est.): Buenos Aires 12,582,000 met.; Cordoba 1.1 mln.; Rosario 1.0 mln. (met.).

Government: Type: Republic. **Head of state:** Pres. Carlos Saúl Menem; b. July 2, 1930; in office: July 8, 1989. **Local divisions:** 28 provinces, 1 federal dist. **Defense:** 1.4% of GNP (1991).

Economy: Industries: Food processing, flour milling, chemicals, textiles, machinery, autos. **Chief crops:** Grains, corn, grapes, linseed, sugar, tobacco, rice, soybeans, citrus fruits. **Minerals:** Oil, lead, zinc, iron, copper, tin, uranium. **Crude oil reserves** (1987): 2.1 bln. bbls. **Arable land:** 9%. **Livestock** (1991): cattle: 50 mln.; sheep: 27 mln. **Fish catch** (1990): 555,000 metric tons. **Electricity prod.** (1991): 46.0 bln. kWh. **Crude steel prod.** (1991): 2.9 mln. metric tons. **Labor force:** 19% agric.; 36% ind. and comm.; 20% services.

Finance: Monetary unit: Peso (July 1993: .99 = $1 US). **Gross domestic product** (1991): $101.2 bln. **Per capita GDP:** $3,100. **Imports** (1991): $8.0 bln.; partners: U.S. 21%, W. Ger. 9%, Braz. 16%, Jap. 7%. **Exports** (1991): $12.3 bln.; partners: CIS 13%, Neth. 9%, U.S. 12%. **Tourists** (1990): receipts: $903 mln. **National budget** (1990): $17.3 bln. expenditures. **International reserves less gold** (Jan. 1992): $6.6 bln. **Gold:** 4.12 mln. oz t. **Consumer prices** (change in 1992): 24.9%.

Transport: Railroads (1988): **Length:** 21,198 mi. **Motor vehicles:** in use (1989): 4.0 mln. passenger cars, 1.5 mln. comm. vehicles. **Civil aviation:** (1991) 8.2 mln. passenger-km. 1,473 airports **Chief ports:** Buenos Aires, Bahia Blanca, La Plata.

Communications: Television sets: 1 per 4 persons. **Radios:** 1 per 1 person. **Telephones in use:** 1 per 9 persons. **Daily newspaper circ.** (1986): 88 per 1,000 pop.

Health: Life expectancy at birth (1992): 67 male; 74 female. **Births** (per 1,000 pop. 1992): 20. **Deaths** (per 1,000 pop. 1992): 9. **Natural increase:** 1.2%. **Hospital beds:** 1 per 150 persons. **Physicians:** 1 per 326 persons. **Infant mortality** (per 1,000 live births 1992): 31.

Education (1992): **Literacy:** 95%. **Years compulsory:** 7.

Major International Organizations: UN (WHO, IMF, FAO), OAS.

Embassy: 1600 New Hampshire Ave. NW 20009; 939-6400.

Nomadic Indians roamed the Pampas when Spaniards arrived, 1515-16, led by Juan Diaz de Solis. Nearly all the Indians were killed by the late 19th century. The colonists won independence, 1816, and a long period of disorders ended in a strong centralized government.

Large-scale Italian, German, and Spanish immigration in the decades after 1880 spurred modernization, making Argentina the most prosperous, educated, and industrialized of the major Latin American nations. Social reforms were enacted in the 1920s, but military coups prevailed 1930-46, until the election of Gen. Juan Peron as president.

Peron, with his wife Eva Duarte, effected labor reforms, but also suppressed speech and press freedoms, closed religious schools, and ran the country into debt. A 1955 coup exiled Peron, who was followed by a series of military and civilian regimes. Peron returned in 1973, and was once more elected president. He died 10 months later, succeeded by his wife, Isabel, who had been elected vice president, and who became the first woman head of state in the Western hemisphere.

A military junta ousted Mrs. Peron in 1976 amid charges of corruption. Under a continuing state of siege, the army battled guerrillas and leftists, killed 5,000 people, and jailed and tortured others. On Dec. 9, 1985, after a trial of 5 months and nearly 1,000 witnesses, 5 former junta members, including ex-presidents Jorge Videla and Gen. Roberto Eduardo Viola, were found guilty of murder and human rights abuses.

A severe worsening in economic conditions placed extreme pressure on the military government.

Argentine troops seized control of the British-held Falkland Islands on Apr. 2, 1982. Both countries had claimed sovereignty over the islands, located 250 miles off the Argentine coast, since 1833. The British dispatched a task force and declared a total air and sea blockade around the Falklands. Fighting began May 1; several hundred lost their lives as the result of the destruction of a British destroyer and the sinking of an Argentine cruiser.

British troops landed in force on East Falkland Island May 21. By June 2, the British had surrounded Stanley, the capital city and Argentine stronghold. The Argentine troops surrendered, June 14; Argentine President Leopoldo Galtieri resigned June 17.

Democratic rule returned to Argentina in 1983 as Raul Alfonsin's Radical Civic Union gained an absolute majority in the presidential electoral college and Congress. In 1989 the nation was plagued by severe financial problems as inflation reached crisis levels; over 6,000%. The hyperinflation sparked a week of looting and rioting in several cities; the government declared a 30-day state of siege May 29.

The government unveiled harsh economic measures in an effort to combat spiraling inflation, control government spending, and restructure the foreign debt 1991-92.

Armenia

Republic of Armenia

Haikakan Hanrapetoutioun

People: Population (1992 est.): 3,415,000. **Pop. density:** 302 per sq. mi. **Urban** (1991): 70%. **Language:** Armenian. **Ethnic groups:** Armenian 93%. **Religion:** Mostly Christian.

Geography: Area: 11,306 sq. mi., slightly larger than Maryland. **Neighbors:** Georgia on N., Azerbaijan on E., Iran on S., Turkey on W. **Topography:** Mountainous with many peaks above 10,000 ft. **Capital:** Yerevan.

Government: Type: Republic. **Head of state:** Pres. Levon Ter-Petrosyan; in office: Oct. 16, 1991. **Head of government:** Gagik Arutyunyaw.

Economy: Industries: Mining, chemicals. **Chief crops:** Cotton, figs, grain. **Minerals:** Copper, zinc. **Arable land:** 10%.

Finance: Monetary unit: Ruble.

Transport: Vehicles (1989): 230,000 passenger cars.

Communications: Television sets: 1 per 5 persons. **Radios:** 1 per 5 persons. **Telephones:** 1 per 6 persons. **Newspaper circ.:** 468 per 1,000 pop.

Health: Life expectancy at birth (1992): 68 male; 74 female. Physicians: 1 per 246 persons. **Hospital beds:** 1 per 117 persons. **Infant mortality** (per 1,000 live births 1992): 35.

Major International Organizations: UN (IMF), CIS.

Embassy: 122 C St. NW 20001; 628-5766.

Armenia is an ancient country, parts of which are now in Turkey and Iran. Present-day Armenia was set up as a Soviet Republic Apr. 2, 1921. It joined Georgian and Azerbaijan SSRs Mar. 12, 1922 to form the Transcaucasian SFSR, which became part of the USSR Dec. 30, 1922. Armenia became a constituent republic of the USSR Dec. 5, 1936. An earthquake struck Armenia Dec. 7, 1988; over 55,000 were killed and several cities and towns were left in ruins. Armenia declared independence Sept. 23, 1991, and became an independent state when the USSR disbanded Dec. 26, 1991.

Fighting between mostly Christian Armenia and mostly Moslem Azerbaijan escalated in 1992 and continued in 1993. Each country claimed Nagorno-Karabakh, an enclave in Azerbaijan that has a majority population of ethnic Armenians.

Australia

Commonwealth of Australia

People: Population (1992 est.): 17,576,000 (incl. Macquarie Island). **Age distrib.** (%): 0–14: 21.9; 15–59; 62.6; ; 59 +: 15.5. **Pop. density:** 5.9 per sq. mi. **Urban** (1990): 85%. **Ethnic groups:** European 95%, Asian 4%, aborigines (including mixed) 1.5%. **Languages:** English, aboriginal languages. **Religions:** Anglican 26%, other Protestant 25%, Roman Catholic 25%.

Geography: Area: 2,966,200 sq. mi., almost as large as the continental U.S. **Location:** SE of Asia, Indian O. is W and S, Pacific O. (Coral, Tasman seas) is E; they meet N of Australia in Timor and Arafura seas: Tasmania lies 150 mi. S of Victoria state, across Bass Strait. **Neighbors:** Nearest are Indonesia, Papua New Guinea on N, Solomons, Fiji, and New Zealand on E. **Topography:** An island continent. The Great Dividing Range along the E coast has Mt. Kosciusko, 7,310 ft. The W plateau rises to 2,000 ft., with arid areas in the Great Sandy and Great Victoria deserts. The NW part of Western Australia and Northern Terr. are arid and hot. The NE has heavy rainfall and Cape York Peninsula has jungles. The Murray R. rises in New South Wales and flows 1,600 mi. to the Indian O. **Capital:** Canberra. **Cities** (1991 est.): Sydney 3,600,000; Melbourne 3,000,000; Brisbane 1,200,000; Perth 1,200,000; Adelaide 1,000,000.

Government: Type: Democratic, federal state system. **Head of state:** Queen Elizabeth II, represented by Gov.-Gen. William Hayden; in office: Feb. 16, 1989. **Head of government:** Prime Min. Paul Keating; b. Jan. 18, 1944; in office: Dec. 20, 1991. **Local divisions:** 6 states, 2 territories. **Defense:** 2.3% of GDP (1992).

Economy: Industries: Iron, steel, textiles, electrical equip., chemicals, autos, aircraft, ships, machinery. **Chief crops:** Wheat (a leading export), barley, oats, corn, hay, sugar, wine, fruit, vegetables. **Minerals:** Coal, copper, iron, lead, tin, uranium, zinc. **Crude oil reserves** (1987): 1.6 bln. bbls. **Other resources:** Wool (30% of world output). **Arable land:** 9%. **Livestock** (1991): cattle: 22 mln.; sheep: 162 mln.; pigs: 2.5 mln. **Fish catch** (1990): 175,000 metric tons. **Electricity prod.** (1991): 155 bln. kWh. **Crude steel prod.** (1991): 6.1 mln. metric tons. **Labor force:** 6% agric.; 33% finance & services; 36% trade & manuf.

Finance: Monetary unit: Dollar (July 1993: 1.47 = $1.00 US). **Gross domestic product** (1991): $311 bln. **Per capita income:** $18,054. **Imports** (1992): $43.7 bln; partners: U.S. 21%, Jap. 20%, UK 7%. **Exports** (1992): $42.4 bln.; partners: Jap. 27%, U.S. 11%, NZ 5%. **Tourists** (1990): $3.7 bln. receipts. **National budget** (1991): $93 bln. expenditures. **International reserves less gold** (Mar. 1993): $9.3 bln. **Gold:** 7.93 mln. oz t. **Consumer prices** (change in 1992): 1.0%.

Transport: Railroads (1991): **Length:** 22,051 mi. **Motor vehicles:** in use (1990): 7.6 mln. passenger cars, 2.1 mln. comm.

vehicles. **Civil aviation** (1990): 23.0 mln. passenger-km.; 441 airports with scheduled flights. **Chief ports:** Sydney, Melbourne, Newcastle, Port Kembla, Fremantle, Geelong.

Communications: Television sets: 1 per 2 persons. **Radios:** 1 per 2 persons. **Telephones in use:** 1 per 2 persons. **Daily newspaper circ.** (1988): 405 per 1,000 pop.

Health: Life expectancy at birth (1992): 74 male; 80 female. **Births** (per 1,000 pop. 1992): 15. **Deaths** (per 1,000 pop. 1992): 8. **Natural increase:** .8%. **Hospital beds:** 1 per 199 persons. **Physicians:** 1 per 438 persons. **Infant mortality** (per 1,000 live births 1992): 8.

Education (1992): **Literacy:** 99%. **School:** compulsory to age 15; attendance 94%.

Major International Organizations: UN and all its specialized agencies, OECD, Commonwealth of Nations.

Embassy: 1601 Massachusetts Ave NW 20036; 797-3000.

Capt. James Cook explored the E coast in 1770, when the continent was inhabited by a variety of different tribes. The first settlers, beginning in 1788, were mostly convicts, soldiers, and government officials. By 1830, Britain had claimed the entire continent, and the immigration of free settlers began to accelerate. The commonwealth was proclaimed Jan. 1, 1901. Northern Terr. was granted limited self-rule July 1, 1978.

States	Area (sq. mi.)	Population (1991 cen.)
New South Wales, Sydney	309,500	5,731,926
Victoria, Melbourne	87,900	4,243,719
Queensland, Brisbane	666,990	2,976,617
Western Aust., Perth	975,100	1,586,393
South Aust., Adelaide	379,900	1,400,656
Tasmania, Hobart	26,200	452,847
Aust. Capital Terr., Canberra	900	280,085
Northern Terr., Darwin	519,800	175,253

Australia's racially discriminatory immigration policies were abandoned in 1973, after 3 million Europeans (half British) had entered since 1945. The 50,000 aborigines and 150,000 part-aborigines are mostly detribalized, but there are several preserves in the Northern Territory. They remain economically disadvantaged.

Australia's agricultural success makes the country among the top exporters of beef, lamb, wool, and wheat. Major mineral deposits have been developed as well, largely for exports. Industrialization has been completed.

Australia harbors many plant and animal species not found elsewhere, including the kangaroo, koalas, platypus, dingo (wild dog), Tasmanian devil (racoon-like marsupial), wombat (bear-like marsupial), and barking and frilled lizards.

The nation suffered through a deep recession 1990-93. Unemployment was 11.1 percent in Feb. 1993.

Australian External Territories

Norfolk Is., area 13½ sq. mi., pop. (1990) 1,800, was taken over, 1914. The soil is very fertile, suitable for citrus fruits, bananas, and coffee. Many of the inhabitants are descendants of the Bounty mutineers, moved to Norfolk 1856 from Pitcairn Is. Australia offered the island limited home rule, 1978.

Coral Sea Is. Territory, 1 sq. mi., is administered from Norfolk Is.

Territory of Ashmore and Cartier Is., area 2 sq. mi., in the Indian O. came under Australian authority 1934 and are administered as part of Northern Territory. **Heard** and **McDonald Is.** are administered by the Dept. of Science.

Cocos (Keeling) Is., 27 small coral islands in the Indian O. 1,750 mi. NW of Australia. Pop. (1990) 600, area: 5½ sq. mi. The residents voted to become part of Australia, Apr. 1984.

Christmas Is. 52 sq. mi., pop. 1,700 (1991), 230 mi. S of Java, was transferred by Britain in 1958. It has phosphate deposits.

Australian Antarctic Territory was claimed by Australia in 1933, including 2,362,000 sq. mi. of territory S of 60th parallel S Lat. and between 160th-45th meridians E Long. It does not include Adelie Coast.

Austria

Republic of Austria

Republik Österreich

People: Population (1992 est.): 7,867,000. **Age distrib.** (%): 0–14: 17.4; 15–59: 62.1; 60+: 20.5. **Pop. density:** 243 per sq. mi. **Urban** (1991): 54%. **Ethnic groups:** German 99%, Slovene, Croatian. **Languages:** German. **Religions:** Roman Catholic 89%.

Geography: Area: 32,377 sq. mi., slightly smaller than Maine. **Location:** In S Central Europe. **Neighbors:** Switzerland, Liechtenstein on W, Germany, Czech Rep., Slovakia on N, Hungary on E, Slovena, Italy on S. **Topography:** Austria is primarily mountainous, with the Alps and foothills covering the western and southern provinces. The eastern provinces and Vienna are located in the Danube River Basin. **Capital:** Vienna. **Cities** (1991 est.): Vienna 1,500,000.

Government: Type: Parliamentary democracy. **Head of state:** Pres. Thomas Klestil; in office: July 8, 1992. **Head of government:** Chancellor Franz Vranitzky; b. Oct. 4, 1937; in office: June 16, 1986. **Local divisions:** 9 lander (states), each with a legislature. **Defense:** 1.2% of GDP (1990).

Economy: Industries: Steel, machinery, autos, electrical and optical equip., glassware, sport goods, paper, textiles, chemicals, cement. **Chief crops:** Grains, potatoes, beets. **Minerals:** Iron ore, oil, magnesite. **Other resources:** Forests, hydro power. **Arable land:** 17%. **Livestock** (1991): cattle: 2.5 mln.; pigs: 3.6 mln. **Electricity prod.** (1991): 49.5 bln. kWh. **Crude steel prod.** (1991): 4.1 mln. metric tons. **Labor force:** 8% agric.; 35% ind. & comm.; 56% service.

Finance: Monetary unit: Schilling (June 1993: 11.90 = $1 US). **Gross domestic product** (1991): $164 bln. **Per capita GDP:** $20,895. **Imports** (1991): $54.1 bln.; partners: EC 70%. **Exports** (1992): $44.4 bln.; partners: EC 68%. **Tourists** (1990): receipts: $13.0 bln. **National budget** (1990): $49.6 bln. expenditures. **International reserves less gold** (Mar. 1993): $12.1 bln. **Gold:** 19.9 mln. oz t. **Consumer prices** (change in 1992): 4.0%.

Transport: Railroads (1991): **Length:** 4,041 mi. **Motor vehicles:** in use (1991): 2.9 mln. passenger cars, 256,000 comm. **Civil aviation** (1991): 2.9 bln. passenger-km; 6 airports with scheduled flights.

Communications: Television sets: 1 per 2.8 persons. **Radios:** 1 per 1.6 persons. **Telephones in use:** 1 per 1.8 persons. **Daily newspaper circ.** (1991): 445 per 1,000 pop.

Health: Life expectancy at birth (1991): 74 male; 81 female. **Births** (per 1,000 pop. 1992): 12. **Deaths** (per 1,000 pop. 1992): 11. **Natural increase:** –.1%. **Hospital beds:** 1 per 101 persons. **Physicians:** 1 per 334 persons. **Infant mortality** (per 1,000 live births 1992): 8.

Education (1992): **Literacy:** 99%. **School years compulsory:** 9; attendance 95%.

Major International Organizations: UN and all of its specialized agencies, EFTA, OECD.

Embassy: 3524 International Court NW 20008; 895-6700.

Rome conquered Austrian lands from Celtic tribes around 15 BC. In 788 the territory was incorporated into Charlemagne's empire. By 1300, the House of Hapsburg had gained control; they added vast territories in all parts of Europe to their realm in the next few hundred years.

Austrian dominance of Germany was undermined in the 18th century and ended by Prussia by 1866. But the Congress of Vienna, 1815, confirmed Austrian control of a large empire in southeast Europe consisting of Germans, Hungarians, Slavs, Italians, and others.

The dual Austro-Hungarian monarchy was established in 1867, giving autonomy to Hungary and almost 50 years of peace.

World War I, started after the June 28, 1914 assassination of Archduke Franz Ferdinand, the Hapsburg heir, by a Serbian nationalist, destroyed the empire. By 1918 Austria was reduced to a small republic, with the borders it has today.

Nazi Germany invaded Austria Mar. 13, 1938. The republic was reestablished in 1945, under Allied occupation. Full independence and neutrality were restored in 1955.

Austria produces most of its food, as well as an array of industrial products. A large part of Austria's economy is controlled by state enterprises. Socialists have shared or alternated power with the conservative People's Party.

Azerbaijan

Azerbaijani Republic

Azerbaijchan Respublikasy

People: Population (1992 est.): 7,450,000; **Pop. density:** 223 per sq. mi. **Urban** (1991): 54%. **Ethnic groups:** Azerbaijani 82%, Russian 6%, Armenian 6%. **Language:** Azeri, Turkish, Russian. **Religions:** mostly Moslem.

Geography: Area: 33,400 sq. mi., slightly larger than Maine. **Neighbors:** Russia, Georgia on N., Iran on S., Armenia on W., Caspian Sea on E. **Capital:** Baku.

Government: Type: in transition. **Head of state:** Pres. Geidar A. Aliyev; in office: June 30, 1993. **Head of government:** Prime Min. Surat Huseynov; in office: June 30, 1993.

Economy: Industries: Oil refining. **Chief crops:** Grain, cotton, rice, silk. **Minerals:** Iron, copper, lead, zinc. **Livestock** (1989): cattle: 2.1 mln., goats & sheep: 5.7 mln. **Electricity prod.** (1991): 23.3 bln. kWh.

Finance: Monetary unit: Manat: (Jan. 1993: 31.68 = $1 US).

Transport: Vehicles (1990): 240,000 passenger cars.

Communications: Newspaper circ. (1990): 73 per 1,000 pop.

Health: Life expectancy at birth (1992): 65 male; 73 female. **Births** (per 1,000 pop. 1992): 26. **Deaths** (per 1,000 pop. 1992): 7. **Natural increase:** 1.9%. Physicians: 1 per 255 persons. **Hospital beds:** 1 per 98 persons. **Infant mortality** (per 1,000 live births 1992): 45.

Major International Organizations: UN.

Azerbaijan was the home of Scythian tribes and part of the Roman Empire. It was overrun by Turks in the 11th century and conquered by Russia in 1806 and 1813. It joined the USSR Dec. 30, 1922, and became a constituent republic in 1936. Azerbaijan declared independence Aug. 30, 1991 and became an independent state when the Soviet Union disbanded Dec. 26, 1991.

Fighting between mostly Moslem Azerbaijan and mostly Christian Armenia escalated in 1992 and continued in 1993. Each country claimed Nagorno-Karabakh, an enclave in Azerbaijan with a majority population of ethnic Armenians.

A National Council ousted communist Pres. Mutaibov and took power May 19, 1992. Abulfez Elchibey became the nation's first democratically elected president June 7, but was ousted from office by Surat Huseynov, commander of a private militia, June 30, 1993. Huseynov became prime minister with expanded authority over the ministries of defense, interior, and security.

The Bahamas

The Commonwealth of the Bahamas

People: Population (1992 est.): 255,000. **Age distrib.** (%): 0–14: 38.0; 15–59: 56.3; 60+: 5.7. **Pop. density:** 47 per sq. mi. **Urban** (1990): 60%. **Ethnic groups:** black 85%, white (British, Canadian, U.S.) 15%. **Languages:** English. **Religions:** Baptist 32%, Anglican 20%, Roman Catholic 19%.

Geography: Area: 5,380 sq. mi., about the size of Connecticut. **Location:** In Atlantic O., E of Florida. **Neighbors:** Nearest are U.S. on W, Cuba on S. **Topography:** Nearly 700 islands (30 inhabited) and over 2,000 islets in the western Atlantic extend 760 mi. NW to SE. **Capital:** Nassau. **Cities:** (1990 est.) New Providence 171,000; Freeport 25,000.

Government: Type: Independent commonwealth. **Head of state:** Queen Elizabeth II, represented by Gov.-Gen. Clifford Darling. **Head of government:** Prime Min. Hubert Ingraham; b. 1947; in office: Aug. 21, 1992. **Local divisions:** 21 districts.

Economy: Industries: Tourism (50% of GDP), rum, banking, pharmaceuticals. **Chief crops:** Fruits, vegetables. **Minerals:** Salt. **Other resources:** Lobsters. **Arable land:** 2%. **Electricity prod.** (1991): 857 mln. kWh. **Labor force:** 5% agric.; 25% tourism, 30% government.

Finance: Monetary unit: Dollar (Apr. 1993: 1 = $1 US). **Gross domestic product** (1989): $2.4 bln. **Per capita income** (1988): $7,178. **Imports** (1991): $1.1 bln.; partners: U.S. 35%, Nigeria 21%. **Exports** (1991): $306 mln.; partners: U.S. 41%, Norway 30%. **Tourism** (1990): $1.1 bln. **National budget** (1991): $727 mln. expenditures. **International reserves less gold** (Mar. 1993): $242 mln. **Consumer prices** (change in 1992): 5.7%.

Transport: Motor vehicles: in use (1989): 67,000 passenger cars, 14,000 comm. vehicles. **Chief ports:** Nassau, Freeport.

Communications: Radios: 1 per 2 persons. **Television sets:** 1 per 4.6 persons. **Telephones in use:** 1 per 2 persons. **Daily newspaper circ.** (1991): 135 per 1,000 pop.

Health: Life expectancy at birth (1992): 69 male; 76 female. **Births** (per 1,000 pop. 1992): 19. **Deaths** (per 1,000 pop. 1992): 5. **Natural increase:** 1.4%. **Infant mortality** (per 1,000 live births 1992): 19.

Education (1992): **Literacy:** 95%; School compulsory through age 14.

Major International Organizations: UN (World Bank, IMF, WHO), OAS.

Embassy: 600 New Hampshire Ave. NW 20037; 338-3940.

Christopher Columbus first set foot in the New World on San Salvador (Watling I.) in 1492, when Arawak Indians inhabited the islands. British settlement began in 1647; the islands became a British colony in 1783. Internal self-government was granted in 1964; full independence within the Commonwealth was attained July 10, 1973.

International banking and investment management has become a major industry alongside tourism, despite controversy over financial irregularities.

Bahrain

State of Bahrain

Dawlat al-Bahrayn

People: Population (1992 est.): 551,000. **Age distrib.** (%): 0-14: 32.7; 15-59: 64.2; 60+ 3.1. **Pop. density:** 2,055 per sq. mi. **Urban** (1990): 82%. **Ethnic groups:** Bahraini 63%, Asian 13%, other Arab 10%, Iranian 6%. **Languages:** Arabic (official), Farsi, Urdu. **Religions:** Sunni Moslem 30%, Shi'ah Moslem 70%.

Geography: Area: 268 sq. mi., smaller than New York City. **Location:** In Persian Gulf. **Neighbors:** Nearest are Saudi Arabia on W, Qatar on E. **Topography:** Bahrain Island, and several adjacent, smaller islands, are flat, hot and humid, with little rain. **Capital:** Manama. **Cities** (1988 est.): Manama 151,000.

Government: Type: Traditional monarchy. **Head of state:** Amir Isa bin Sulman al-Khalifa; b. July 3, 1933; in office: Nov. 2, 1961. **Head of government:** Prime Min. Kahlifa ibn Sulman al-Khalifa; b. 1935; in office: Jan. 19, 1970. **Local divisions:** 12 districts. **Defense:** 6.0% of GDP (1990).

Economy: Industries: Oil products, aluminum smelting. **Chief crops:** Fruits, vegetables. **Minerals:** Oil, gas. **Crude oil reserves** (1985): 173 mln. bbls. **Arable land:** 5%. **Electricity prod.** (1991): 10.5 bln. kWh. **Labor force:** 5% agric.; 85% ind. and commerce; 5% services; 3% gov.

Finance: Monetary unit: Dinar (Mar. 1993: 1.00 = $2.66 US). **Gross domestic product** (1989): $3.4 bln. **Per capita income** (1989): $7,300. **Imports** (1991): $4.0 bln.; partners: Sau. Ar. 60%, UK 6%, U.S. 9%. **Exports** (1991): $3.4 bln.; partners: UAE 18%, Jap. 12%, Sing. 10%, U.S. 6%. **National budget** (1989): $1.3 bln. expenditures. **International reserves less gold** (Mar. 1993): $1.3 bln. **Gold:** 150,000 oz t. **Consumer prices** (change in 1992): -0.2%.

Transport: Motor vehicles: in use (1990): 104,000 passenger cars, 23,000 comm. vehicles. **Chief ports:** Sitra.

Communications: Television sets: 1 per 2.3 persons. **Radios:** 1 per 1.7 persons. **Telephones in use:** 1 per 3.4 persons.

Health: Life expectancy at birth (1992): 70 male; 75 female. **Births** (per 1,000 pop. 1992): 27. **Deaths** (per 1,000 pop. 1992): 3. **Natural increase:** 2.4. Medical services are free. **Infant mortality** (per 1,000 live births 1992): 21.

Education (1992): **Literacy:** 77%.

Major International Organizations: UN (GATT, IMF, WHO), Arab League.

Embassy: 3502 International Dr. NW 20008; 342-0741.

Long ruled by the Khalifa family, Bahrain was a British protectorate from 1861 to Aug. 15, 1971, when it regained independence.

Pearls, shrimp, fruits, and vegetables were the mainstays of the economy until oil was discovered in 1932. By the 1970s, oil reserves were depleted; international banking thrived.

Bahrain took part in the 1973-74 Arab oil embargo against the U.S. and other nations. The government bought controlling interest in the oil industry in 1975.

Bangladesh

People's Republic of Bangladesh

Gama Prajātantrī Bangladesh

People: Population (1992 est.): 119,000,000. **Age distrib.** (%): 0-14: 44.3; 15-59: 50.4; 60+: 5.3. **Pop. density:** 2,132 per sq. mi. **Urban** (1990): 24%. **Ethnic groups:** Bengali 98%, Bihari, tribesmen. **Languages:** Bengali (official), Chakma, Magh. **Religions:** Moslem 83%, Hindu 16%.

Geography: Area: 55,813 sq. mi. slightly smaller than Wisconsin. **Location:** In S Asia, on N bend of Bay of Bengal. **Neighbors:** India nearly surrounds country on W, N, E; Myanmar on SE. **Topography:** The country is mostly a low plain cut by the Ganges and Brahmaputra rivers and their delta. The land is alluvial and marshy along the coast, with hills only in the extreme SE and NE. A tropical monsoon climate prevails, among the rainiest in the world. **Capital:** Dhaka. **Cities** (1991 est.): Dhaka (met.) 6.1 mln.; Chittagong (met.) 2.1 mln.; Khulna (met.) 877,000.

Government: Type: Parliamentary democracy. **Head of state:** Pres. Abdur Rahman Biswas in office: Oct. 10, 1991. **Head of Government:** Prime Min. Khaleda Zia; b. Nov. 1944; in office: Mar. 20, 1991. **Local divisions:** 64 districts. **Defense:** 1.5% of GDP (1992).

Economy: Industries: Food processing, jute, textiles, fertilizers, petroleum products. **Chief crops:** Jute (most of world output), rice, tea. **Minerals:** Natural gas, offshore oil, coal. **Arable land:** 67%. **Livestock** (1991): cattle: 23 mln.; goats: 22 mln. **Fish catch** (1990): 847,000 metric tons. **Electricity prod.** (1990): 5.7 bln. kWh. **Labor force:** 74% agric; 11% ind.; 15% services.

Finance: Monetary unit: Taka (Mar. 1993: 39 = $1 US). **Gross domestic product** (1991): $23.1 bln. **Per capita GDP:** $200. **Imports** (1991): $3.6 bln.; partners: Jap. 9%, U.S. 6%. **Exports** (1991): $1.6 bln.; partners: U.S. 31%, It. 9%; Pak 5%. **Tourism** (1990): $11.0 mln. receipts. **National budget** (1991): $3.7 bln. expenditures. **International reserves less gold** (Mar. 1993): $2.1 bln. **Gold:** 87,000 oz t. **Consumer prices** (change in 1992): 4.7%.

Transport: Railroads (1989): **Length:** 1,750 mi. **Motor vehicles:** in use (1990): 41,000 passenger cars, 53,000 comm. vehicles. **Chief ports:** Chittagong, Chalna.

Communications: Radios: 1 per 24 persons. **Television sets:** 1 per 315 persons. **Telephones in use:** 1 per 572 persons. **Daily newspaper circ.** (1988) 8 per 1,000 pop.

Health: Life expectancy at birth (1992): 55 male; 54 female. **Births** (per 1,000 pop. 1992): 36. **Deaths** (per 1,000 pop. 1992): 13. **Natural increase:** 2.3%. **Hospital beds:** 1 per 3,195 persons. **Physicians:** 1 per 5,500 persons. **Infant mortality** (per 1,000 live births 1992): 112.

Education (1992): **Literacy:** 47%. **Attendance:** 73% primary school; 26% secondary school.

Major International Organizations: UN (GATT, IMF, WHO).

Embassy: 2201 Wisconsin Ave. NW 20007; 342-8372.

Moslem invaders conquered the formerly Hindu area in the 12th century. British rule lasted from the 18th century to 1947, when East Bengal became part of Pakistan.

Charging West Pakistani domination, the Awami League, based in the East, won National Assembly control in 1971. Assembly sessions were postponed; riots broke out. Pakistani troops attacked Mar. 25; Bangladesh independence was proclaimed the next day. In the ensuing civil war, one million died and 10 million fled to India.

War between India and Pakistan broke out Dec. 3, 1971. Pakistan surrendered in the East on Dec. 15. Sheik Mujibur Rahman became prime minister. The country moved into the Indian and Soviet orbits in response to U.S. support of Pakistan, and much of the economy was nationalized. Bangladesh adopted a parliamentary system of government in 1991.

Chronic destitution among the densely crowded population has been worsened by the decline of jute as a major world commodity.

On May 30, 1981, Pres. Ziaur Rahman was shot and killed in an unsuccessful coup attempt by army rivals. Vice President Abdus Sattar assumed the presidency but was ousted in a coup led by army chief of staff Gen. H.M. Ershad, Mar. 1982. Ershad declared Bangladesh an Islamic Republic in 1988. Bangladesh remains one of the world's poorest countries.

In 1988 and 1989 natural disasters and monsoon rains brought devastation to Bangladesh: over 4,000 died, 30 million were made homeless. A cyclone struck Apr. 1991, killing over 131,000 people and causing $2.7 billion in damages. Some 7,500 U.S. military personnel aided in the relief effort.

Barbados

People: Population (1992 est.): 254,000 **Age distrib.** (%): 0–14: 24.8%; 15–59: 60.6; 60+: 14.6. **Pop. density:** 1,530 per sq. mi. **Urban** (1992): 42%. **Ethnic groups:** African 80%, mixed 16%, Caucasian 4%. **Languages:** English. **Religions:** Protestant 67%, Roman Catholic 4%.

Geography: Area: 166 sq. mi. **Location:** In Atlantic, farthest E of W. Indies. **Neighbors:** Nearest are Trinidad, Grenada on SW. **Topography:** The island lies alone in the Atlantic almost completely surrounded by coral reefs. Highest point is Mt. Hillaby, 1,115 ft. **Capital:** Bridgetown. **Cities** (1990): Bridgetown 6,700.

Government: Type: Parliamentary democracy. **Head of state:** Queen Elizabeth II, represented by Gov.-Gen. Dame Nita Barrow; in office: June 6, 1990. **Head of government:** Prime Min. Erskine Sandiford; b. Mar. 24, 1937; in office: June 1, 1987. **Local divisions:** 11 parishes and Bridgetown.

Economy: Industries: Sugar, tourism. **Chief crops:** Sugar, cotton. **Minerals:** Lime. **Other resources:** Fish. **Arable land:** 76%. **Electricity prod.** (1991): 539 mln. kWh. **Labor force:** 5% agric.; 17% ind. and comm.; 37% services and government.

Finance: Monetary unit: Dollar (June 1993: 2.01 = $1 US). **Gross domestic product** (1990): $1.7 bln. **Per capita GDP** $6,500. **Imports** (1991): $694 mln.; partners: U.S. 35%, CARACOM 12%. **Exports** (1991): $205 mln.; partners: U.S. 21%, CARACOM 30%. **Tourism** (1990): $502 mln. receipts. **National budget** (1992): $615 mln. expenditures. **International reserves less gold** (Mar. 1993): $172 mln. **Consumer prices** (change in 1992): 6.1%.

Transport: Motor vehicles: in use (1991): 38,000 passenger cars; 9,000 comm. vehicles. **Chief ports:** Bridgetown.

Communications: Television sets: 1 per 3.9 persons. **Radios:** 1 per 1.1 persons. **Telephones in use:** 1 per 2.4 persons. **Daily newspaper circ.** (1990): 161 per 1,000 pop.

Health: Life expectancy at birth (1992): male: 70 female: 76. **Births** (per 1,000 pop. 1992): 16. **Deaths** (per 1,000 pop. 1992): 9. **Natural increase:** 0.7%. **Hospital beds:** 1 per 123 persons. **Physicians:** 1 per 1,042 persons. **Infant mortality** (per 1,000 live births 1992): 23.

Education (1992): **Literacy:** 99%. **Years compulsory:** to age 16.

Major International Organizations: UN (FAO, GATT, ILO, IMF, WHO), OAS.

Embassy: 2144 Wyoming Ave. NW 20008; 939-9200.

Barbados was probably named by Portuguese sailors in reference to bearded fig trees. An English ship visited in 1605, and British settlers arrived on the uninhabited island in 1627. Slaves worked the sugar plantations until slavery was abolished in 1834. Self-rule came gradually, with full independence proclaimed Nov. 30, 1966. British traditions have remained.

Belarus

Republic of Belarus

Respublika Belarus

People: Population (1992 est.): 10,373,000. **Pop. density:** 129 per sq. mi. **Urban** (1991): 67%. **Ethnic groups:** Belarus 80%, Russian 13%. **Languages:** Belorussian, Russian.

Geography: Area: 80,134 sq. mi. **Neighbors:** Poland on W, Latvia, Lithuania on N, Russia on E, Ukraine on S. **Capital:** Minsk. **Cities** (1991): Minsk 1.6 mln., Homel 503,000.

Government: Republic. **Head of state:** Pres. Stanislav Shushkevich; in office: Sept. 1991. **Head of government:** Prime Min. Vyacheslav Kebich. **Local divisions:** 6 regions.

Economy: Industries: Food processing, chemicals, machine-tool & agricultural machinery. **Chief crops:** Grain, flax, potatoes, sugar beets. **Livestock** (1991): cattle: 6.3 mln., pigs: 4.7 mln. **Electricity prod.** (1991): 38.7 mln. kWh.

Finance: Monetary unit: Belarus ruble.

Transport: Railroads (1991): **Length:** 3,472 mi. **Passenger Cars** (1990): 500,000.

Communications: Television sets: 1 per 3.3 persons. **Radios:** 1 per 1.3 persons. **Telephones:** 1 per 6.3 persons. **Newspaper circ.** (1990): 260 per 1,000 pop.

Health: Life expectancy at birth (1992): 66 male; 76 female. **Birth** (per 1,000 pop. 1992): 15. **Deaths** (per 1,000 pop. 1992): 11. Physicians: 1 per 248 persons. **Hospital beds** 1 per 76 persons. **Infant mortality** (per 1,000 live births 1992): 20.

Major International Organizations: UN, CIS.

The region was subject to Lithuanians and Poles in medieval times, and was a prize of war between Russia and Poland beginning in 1503. It became part of the USSR in 1922 although the western part of the region was controlled by Poland. Belarus was overrun by German armies in 1941; recovered by Soviet troops in 1944. Following World War II, Belarus increased in area through Soviet annexation of part of NE Poland. Belarus declared independence Aug. 25, 1991. It became an independent state when the Soviet Union disbanded Dec. 26, 1991.

Belgium

Kingdom of Belgium

Koninkrijk België (Dutch)
Royaume de Belgique (French)

People: Population (1992 est.): 10,016,000. **Age distrib.** (%): 0–14: 18.2; 15–59: 61.7; 60+: 20.1 **Pop. density:** 848 per sq. mi. **Urban** (1992): 96%. **Ethnic groups:** Fleming 55%, Walloon 33%. **Languages:** Flemish (Dutch) 57%, French 33%, Italian, German. **Religions:** Roman Catholic 75%.

Geography: Area: 11,799 sq. mi., slightly larger than Maryland. **Location:** In NW Europe, on N. Sea. **Neighbors:** France on W, S, Luxembourg on SE, Germany on E, Netherlands on N. **Topography:** Mostly flat, the country is trisected by the Scheldt and Meuse, major commercial rivers. The land becomes hilly and forested in the SE (Ardennes) region. **Capital:** Brussels. **Cities** (1991 est.): Brussels (met.) 970,000; Antwerp (met.) 467,000; Ghent 233,000; Charleroi 209,000; Liege 195,000.

Government: Type: Parliamentary democracy under a constitutional monarch. **Head of state:** King Albert; in office: Aug. 1, 1993. **Head of government:** Premier Jean-Luc Dehaene; b. Aug. 7, 1940; in office: Mar. 7, 1992. **Local divisions:** 9 provinces; 3 regions; 3 cultural communities. **Defense:** 2.7% of GDP (1991).

Economy: Industries: Steel, glassware, diamond cutting, textiles, chemicals. **Chief crops:** Wheat, potatoes, sugar beets. **Minerals:** Coal. **Other resources:** Forests. **Arable land** (incl. Lux.): 26.5%. **Livestock:** (1991): cattle: 3.1 mln; pigs: 6.4 mln. **Fish catch** (1988): 23.3 metric tons. **Electricity prod.** (1991): 67 bln. kWh. **Crude steel prod.** (1991): 11.3 mln. metric tons. **Labor force:** 2% agric.; 26% ind. & comm.; 37% services & transportation; 23% public service.

Finance: Monetary unit: Franc (Aug. 1993: 35.50 = $1 US). **Gross domestic product** (1991): $171 bln. **Per capita GDP** $17,300. *Note:* the following trade and tourist data includes Luxembourg. **Imports** (1992): $120 bln.; partners: EC 73%. **Exports** (1992): $118 bln.; partners: EC 74%. **Tourism** (1990): receipts: $3.5 bln. **National budget** (1989): $51 bln. expenditures. **International reserves less gold** (Mar. 1993): $13.2 bln. **Gold:** 23.1 mln. oz t. **Consumer prices** (change in 1992): 2.4%.

Transport: Railroads (1990): **Length:** 2,162 mi. **Motor vehicles:** in use (1991): 3.9 mln. passenger cars, 596,000 comm. vehicles. **Civil aviation** (1990): 7.5 bln. passenger-km; 4 airports with scheduled flights. **Chief ports:** Antwerp, Zeebrugge, Ghent.

Communications: Television sets: 1 per 4.2 persons. **Radios:** 1 per 2.2 persons; **Telephones in use:** 1 per 1.9 persons. **Daily newspaper circ.** (1990): 213 per 1,000 pop.

Health: Life expectancy at birth (1992): 73 male; 80 female. **Births** (per 1,000 pop. 1992): 10. **Deaths** (per 1,000 pop. 1992): 10. **Natural increase** 0.2%. **Hospital beds:** 1 per 108 persons. **Physicians:** 1 per 317 persons. **Infant mortality** (per 1,000 live births 1992): 8.

Education (1992): **Literacy:** 98%. School compulsory to age 18.

Major International Organizations: UN and all of its specialized agencies, NATO, EC, OECD.

Embassy: 3330 Garfield St. NW 20008; 333-6900

Belgium derives its name from the Belgae, the first recorded inhabitants, probably Celts. The land was conquered by Julius Caesar, and was ruled for 1800 years by conquerors, including Rome, the Franks, Burgundy, Spain, Austria, and France. After 1815, Belgium was made a part of the Netherlands, but it became an independent constitutional monarchy in 1830.

Belgian neutrality was violated by Germany in both world wars. King Leopold III surrendered to Germany, May 28, 1940. After the war, he was forced by political pressure to abdicate in favor of his son, King Baudouin.

The Flemings of northern Belgium speak Dutch while French is the language of the Walloons in the south. The language difference has been a perennial source of controversy and led to antagonism between the 2 groups. Parliament has passed measures aimed at transferring power from the central government to 3 regions—Wallonia, Flanders, and Brussels.

Belgium lives by its foreign trade; about 50% of its entire production is sold abroad.

Belize

People: Population (1992 est.): 189,000. **Age distrib.** (%): 0–14: 44.5; 15–59: 47.8; 60+: 7.6. **Pop. density:** 21 per sq. mi. **Ethnic groups:** Mestizo 43%, Creole 29%, Maya 8%. **Languages:** English (official), Spanish, native Creole dialects. **Religions:** Roman Catholic 57%, Protestant 28%.

Geography: Area: 8,867 sq. mi. **Location:** eastern coast of Central America. **Neighbors:** Mexico on N, Guatemala on W and S. **Capital:** Belmopan. **Cities:** (1991 est.): Belize City 44,000.

Government: Type: Parliamentary democracy. **Head of state:** Gov. Gen. Minita Gordon. **Head of government:** Prime Min. George Cadle Price; in office: Sept. 8, 1989. **Local divisions:** 6 districts.

Economy: Sugar is the main export.

Finance: Monetary unit: Belize dollar (Mar. 1993) 2 = $1 U.S. **Gross domestic product** (1990): $290 mln. **Per capita GDP:** $1,637. **Imports** (1992): $273 mln.; partners: U.S. 55%, UK 8%. **Exports:** (1992): $102 mln.; partners: U.S. 46%, UK 31%. **National budget** (1991): $23 mln. expenditures.

Health: Life expectancy at birth (1992): male: 67; female: 72. **Births** (per 1,000 pop. 1992): 31. **Deaths** (per 1,000 pop. 1992): 5. **Hospital beds:** 1 per 309 persons. **Physicians:** 1 per 1,543 persons. **Infant mortality** (per 1,000 live births, 1992): 30.

Education: (1991) **Literacy:** 93%.; **Years compulsory:** 9; attendance 55%.

Major International Organizations: OAS, UN (IMF, World Bank), Commonwealth of Nations.

Embassy: 3400 International Dr., NW 20005; 363-4505.

Belize (formerly called British Honduras) was Great Britain's last colony on the American mainland. The country achieved independence on Sept. 21, 1981. British troops in Belize guarantee security.

Benin

Republic of Benin

République du Benin

People: Population (1992 est.): 4,997,000. **Age distrib.** (%): 0–14: 46.5; 15–59: 49.0; 60+: 4.5. **Pop. density:** 114 per sq. mi. **Urban** (1985): 20%. **Ethnic groups:** Fon, Adja, Bariba, Yoruba. **Languages:** French (official), Fon, Yoruba, Somba. **Religions:** Mainly animist with Christian, Moslem minorities.

Geography: Area: 43,483 sq. mi., slightly smaller than Pennsylvania. **Location:** In W Africa on Gulf of Guinea. **Neighbors:** Togo on W, Burkina Faso, Niger on N, Nigeria on E. **Topography:** most of Benin is flat and covered with dense vegetation. The coast is hot, humid, and rainy. **Capital:** Porto-Novo. **Cities** (1984 est.): Cotonou 330,000.

Government: Type: Democracy. **Head of state:** Nicephore Soglo; in office: Apr. 4, 1991. **Local divisions:** 6 provinces. **Defense:** 2.1% of GDP (1988).

Economy: Chief crops: Palm products, peanuts, cotton, coffee, tobacco. **Minerals:** Oil. **Arable land:** 12%. **Livestock** (1989): sheep: 890,000; goats: 1.1 mln. **Fish catch** (1990): 39,000 metric tons. **Electricity prod.** (1991): 24 mln. kWh. **Labor force:** 60% agric; 38% serv. & comm.

Finance: Monetary unit: CFA franc (Mar. 1993: 273 = $1 US). **Gross domestic product** (1991): $1.7 bln. **Per capita GDP:** $400. **Imports** (1990): $428 mln.; partners: Fr. 34%. **Exports** (1990): $263 mln.; partners: EC. **National budget** (1990): $390 bln. expenditures. **International reserves less gold** (Feb. 1993): $245 mln.

Transport: Railroads (1992): **Length:** 359 mi. **Chief ports:** Cotonou.

Communications: Radios: 1 per 14 persons. **Televisions:** 1 per 281 persons. **Daily newspaper circ.** (1990): 3 per 1,000 pop.

Health: Life expectancy at birth (1992): 49 male; 52 female. **Births** (per 1,000 pop. 1992): 49. **Deaths** (per 1,000 pop. 1992): 16. **Natural increase:** 3.7%. **Hospital beds:** 1 per 749 persons. **Physicians:** 1 per 16,025 persons. **Infant mortality** (per 1,000 live births 1992): 115.

Education (1991): **Literacy:** 28%. Years compulsory 6; attendance 43%.

Major International Organizations: UN (GATT, IMF, WHO), OAU.

Embassy: 2737 Cathedral Ave. NW 20008; 232-6656.

The Kingdom of Abomey, rising to power in wars with neighboring kingdoms in the 17th century, came under French domination in the late 19th century and was incorporated into French West Africa by 1904.

Under the name Dahomey, the country became independent Aug. 1, 1960. The name was changed to Benin in 1975. In the fifth coup since independence Col. Ahmed Kerekou took power in 1972; two years later he declared a socialist state with a "Marxist-Leninist" philosophy. In Dec. 1989, Kerekou announced that Marxism-Leninism would no longer be the state ideology. In 1991, Kerekou was defeated in Benin's first free presidential elections in 30 years by Nicephore Soglo.

The economy relies on the development of agriculturally based industries.

Bhutan

Kingdom of Bhutan

Druk-Yul

People: Population (1992 est.): 1,660,000. **Age distrib.** (%): 0–14: 39.8; 15–59: 53.8; over 60: 6.4 **Pop. density:** 91 per sq. mi. **Ethnic groups:** Bhote 60%, Napalese 25%. **Languages:** Dzongkha (official), Gurung, Assamese. **Religions:** Buddhist (state religion) 75%, Hindu 25%.

Geography: Area: 18,147 sq. mi., the size of Vermont and New Hampshire combined. **Location:** In eastern Himalayan Mts. **Neighbors:** India on W (Sikkim) and S, China on N. **Topography:** Bhutan is comprised of very high mountains in the N, fertile valleys in the center, and thick forests in the Duar Plain in the S. **Capital:** Thimphu (Paro Dzong is administrative capital). **City** (1987 est.): Thimphu 20,000.

Government: Type: Monarchy. **Head of state:** King Jigme Singye Wangchuk; b. Nov. 11, 1955; in office: July 21, 1972. **Local divisions:** 18 districts.

Economy: Industries: Handicrafts, chemicals. **Chief crops:** Rice, corn, wheat. **Other resources:** Timber. **Arable land:** 2%. **Labor force:** 93% agric.

Finance: Monetary unit: Ngultrum (Mar. 1993: 28.29 = $1 US). (Indian Rupee also used). **Gross domestic product** (1989): $273 mln. **Per capita GDP:** $199. **Tourism** (1990): 2.0 mln. **Imports** (1991): $138 mln.; partners: India 67%. **Exports** (1989): $70 mln.; partners: India 93%.

Communications: Radios: 1 per 64 persons. **Telephones in use:** 1 per 675 persons.

Health: Life expectancy at birth (1992): 50 male; 48 female. **Births** (per 1,000 pop. 1992): 40. **Deaths** (per 1,000 pop. 1992): 17. **Natural increase:** 2.3%. **Hospital beds:** 1 per 1,476 persons. **Physicians:** 1 per 9,686 persons. **Infant mortality** (per 1,000 live births 1992): 126.

Education (1989): **Literacy:** 15%. School attendance: 25%.

Major International Organizations: UN (IMF, World Bank).

The region came under Tibetan rule in the 16th century. British influence grew in the 19th century. A monarchy, set up in 1907, became a British protectorate by a 1910 treaty. The country became independent in 1949, with India guiding foreign relations and supplying aid.

Links to India have been strengthened by airline service and a road network. Most of the population engages in subsistence agriculture.

Bolivia

Republic of Bolivia

República de Bolivia

People: Population (1992 est.): 7,323,000. **Age distrib.** (%): 0–14: 41.1; 15–59: 52.4; 60+: 5.5. **Pop. density:** 17 per sq. mi. **Urban** (1990): 51%. **Ethnic groups:** Quechua 30%, Aymara 25%, mixed 30%, European 14%. **Languages:** Spanish, Quechua, Aymara (all official). **Religions:** Roman Catholic 95%.

Geography: Area: 424,165 sq. mi., the size of Texas and California combined. **Location:** In central Andes Mtns. **Neighbors:** Peru, Chile on W, Argentina, Paraguay on S, Brazil on E and N. **Topography:** The great central plateau, at an altitude of 12,000 ft., over 500 mi. long, lies between two great cordilleras having 3 of the highest peaks in S. America. Lake Titicaca, on Peruvian border, is highest lake in world on which steamboats ply (12,506 ft.). The E central region has semitropical forests; the llanos, or Amazon-Chaco lowlands are in E. **Capitals:** Sucre, (legal), La Paz (de facto). **Cities** (1989 est.): La Paz 1,669,000; Santa Cruz 529,000; Cochabamba 403,000.

Government: Type: Republic. **Head of state:** Pres. Gonzalo Sanchez de Lozada; in office: Aug. 6, 1993. **Local divisions:** 9 departments. **Defense:** 1.5% of GDP (1990).

Economy: Industry: Textiles, food processing, mining, clothing. **Chief crops:** Potatoes, sugar, coffee, corn, coca (sold for cocaine processing). **Minerals:** Antimony, tin, tungsten, silver, zinc, oil, gas, iron. **Crude oil reserves** (1985): 157 mln. bbls. **Other resources:** rubber, cinchona bark. **Arable land:** 3%. **Livestock** (1991): cattle: 5.3 mln.; sheep: 12.3 mln.; pigs: 1.6 mln. **Electricity prod.** (1991): 1.7 bln. kWh. **Labor force:** 50% agric., 10% ind. & comm, 26% serv. & govt.

Finance: Monetary unit: Bolivianos (Mar. 1993: 4.17 = $1 US). **Gross domestic product** (1990): $4.8 bln. **Per capita GDP:** $690. **Imports** (1991): $760 mln.; partners: U.S. 20%, Jap. 10%, Arg. 14%, Braz. 20%. **Exports** (1991): $970 mln.; partners: U.S. 19%. **National budget** (1991): $825 mln. expenditures. **International reserves less gold** (Mar. 1993): $134 mln. **Gold:** 894,000 oz t. **Consumer prices** (change in 1991): 21%.

Transport: Railroads (1991): **Length:** 2,269 mi. **Motor vehicles:** in use (1988): 83,000 passenger cars, 150,000 comm. vehicles. **Civil aviation** (1990): 1.2 bln. passenger-km.; 19 airports with scheduled flights.

Communications: Television sets: 1 per 16 persons. **Radios:** 1 per 1.8 persons. **Telephones in use:** 1 per 37 persons. **Daily newspaper circ.** (1986): 35 per 1,000 pop.

Health: Life expectancy at birth (1992): 59 male; 64 female. **Births** (per 1,000 pop. 1992): 34. **Deaths** (per 1,000 pop. 1992): 19. **Natural increase:** 2.5%. **Hospital beds:** 1 per 686 persons. **Physicians:** 1 per 2,124 persons. **Infant mortality** (per 1,000 live births 1992): 83.

Education (1991): **Literacy:** 78%. **Years compulsory:** ages 7-14; attendance 82%.

Major International Organizations: UN (IMF, FAO, WHO), OAS.

Embassy: 3014 Massachusetts Ave. NW 20008; 483-4410.

The Incas conquered the region from earlier Indian inhabitants in the 13th century. Spanish rule began in the 1530s and lasted until Aug. 6, 1825. The country is named after Simon Bolivar, independence fighter.

In a series of wars, Bolivia lost its Pacific coast to Chile, the oil-bearing Chaco to Paraguay, and rubber-growing areas to Brazil, 1879-1935.

Economic unrest, especially among the militant mine workers, has contributed to continuing political instability. A reformist government under Victor Paz Estenssoro, 1951-64, nationalized tin mines and attempted to improve conditions for the Indian majority but was overthrown by a military junta. A series of coups and countercoups continued through 1981, until the military junta elected Gen. Villa as president.

In July 1982, the military junta assumed power amid a growing economic crisis and foreign debt difficulties. The junta resigned in October and allowed the Congress, elected democratically in 1980, to take power.

U.S. pressure on the government to reduce the country's output of coca, the raw material for cocaine, has led to clashes between police and coca growers and increased anti-U.S. feeling among Bolivians.

Bosnia and Herzegovina

People: Population (1992 est.): 4,365,000. **Pop. density:** 221 per sq. mi. **Ethnic groups:** Moslem Slav 43%, Serbian 31%, Croatian 17%. **Languages:** Serbo-Croatian (official). **Religions:** Eastern Orthodox, Catholic, Moslem.

Geography: Area: 19,741 sq. mi. **Location:** in SE Europe. **Neighbors:** Yugoslavia, Croatia, Adriatic Sea. **Topography:** Hilly with some mountains. About 50% of the land is forested. **Capital:** Sarajevo.

Government: Type: In transition. **Head of state:** Pres. Alija Izetbegovic.

Economy: Industries: Textiles, rugs, timber. **Chief crops:** Corn, wheat, oats, barley. **Minerals:** Bauxite, iron ore, coal.

Finance: Monetary unit: New Yugoslav Dinar. (Dec. 1992: 225 = $1 US.) **Gross domestic product** (1991): $14 bln.

Health: Doctors: 1 per 624 persons; **Hospital beds:** 1 per 219 persons.

Education: Literacy (1991): 90%.

International Organizations: UN.

Bosnia was ruled by Croatian kings c. 958 A.D., and by Hungary 1000-1200. It became organized c. 1200 and later took control of Herzegovina. The kingdom disintegrated from 1391, with the southern part becoming the independent duchy Herzegovina. It was conquered by Turks in 1463 and made a Turkish province. The area was placed under control of Austria-Hungary in 1878, and made part of the province of **Bosnia and Herzegovina,** which was formally annexed to Austria-Hungary 1908, and it became a province of Yugoslavia in 1918. It was reunited with Herzegovina as a federated republic in the 1946 constitution.

The Bosnia and Herzegovina parliament adopted a declaration of sovereignty Oct. 15, 1991. A referendum for independence was passed Feb. 29, 1992. Ethnic Serbs' opposition to the referendum spurred violent clashes and bombings. The U.S. and EC recognized the republic as independent Apr. 7. Fierce fighting continued—interrupted by 2 cease-fires in June—as Serbs massacred many thousands of Bosnians, most of them civilians. Serb forces launched major offensives, July 13, marking the 100th day of the siege of Sarajevo, Bosnia's capital. By Sept. 1992, Serb nationalist forces occupied some 70% of Bosnia, with a small area under Croatian control.

The U.S. air dropped relief supplies to Moslem towns under siege in E. Bosnia Feb. 28-Mar. 3, 1993. Bosnian Croats, Serbs, and Moslems agreed in principle to the partitioning of the country into autonomous ethnic regions July 30. Despite the accord, fierce fighting continued around Sarajevo and elsewhere in Bosnia. The mostly Moslem Bosnian Parliament rejected a specific partition plan Aug. 29; negotiations resumed in Sept.

Botswana

Republic of Botswana

People: Population (1992 est.): 1,300,000. **Age distrib. (%):** 0–14: 39.6; 15–64: 48.3; 65+: 3.1. **Pop. density:** 5 per sq. mi. **Urban** (1991): 25%. **Ethnic groups:** Tswana, Kalanga, others. **Languages:** English (official), Setswana. **Religions:** indigenous beliefs 50%, Christian 50%.

Geography: Area: 231,804 sq. mi., slightly smaller than Texas. **Location:** In southern Africa. **Neighbors:** Namibia on N and W, S. Africa on S, Zimbabwe on NE; Botswana claims border with Zambia on N. **Topography:** The Kalahari Desert, supporting nomadic Bushmen and wildlife, spreads over SW; there are swamplands and farming areas in N, and rolling plains in E where livestock are grazed. **Capital:** Gaborone. **Cities** (1991): Gaborone 138,000.

Government: Type: Parliamentary republic. **Head of state:** Pres. Quett Masire; b. 1925; in office: July 13, 1980. **Local divisions:** 10 district councils and 4 town councils. **Defense:** 4.4% of GDP (1991).

Economy: Industries: Livestock processing, mining. **Chief crops:** Corn, sorghum, beans. **Minerals:** Copper, coal, nickel, diamonds. **Other resources:** Big game. **Arable land:** 2%. **Electricity prod.** (1991): 630 mln. kWh. **Labor force:** 70% agric.

Finance: Monetary unit: Pula (Mar. 1993: 1.00 = $.42 US). **Gross domestic product** (1990): $3.1 bln. **Imports** (1991): $2.2 bln.; partners: S. Africa 88%. **Exports** (1991): $2.7 bln.; partners: Europe 67%, U.S. 17%, S. Africa 7%. **National budget** (1992): $1.7 bln. expenditures. **International reserves less gold** (Mar. 1992): $3.7 bln. **Consumer prices** (change in 1993): 16.2%

Transport: Railroads (1991): **Length:** 443 mi. **Motor vehicles:** in use (1991): 26,000 passenger cars, 47,000 comm. vehicles.

Communications: Radios: 1 per 1.2 persons. **Telephones:** 1 per 26 persons. **Daily newspaper circ.** (1989): 22 per 1,000 pop.

Health: Life expectancy at birth (1992): male: 59; female: 65. **Births** (1,000 pop. 1992): 36. **Deaths** (per 1,000 pop. 1992): 9. **Natural increase:** 2.7%. **Hospital beds** (1990): 5,022. **Physicians:** 1 per 7,185 persons. **Infant mortality** (per 1,000 live births 1992): 43.

Education (1990): **Literacy:** 23%.

Major International Organizations: UN (GATT, IMF, WHO), OAU, Commonwealth of Nations.

Embassy: 3400 International Dr. NW 20008; 244-4990.

First inhabited by bushmen, then by Bantus, the region became the British protectorate of Bechuanaland in 1886, halting encroachment by Boers and Germans from the south and southwest. The country became fully independent Sept. 30, 1966, changing its name to Botswana.

Cattle raising and mining (diamonds, copper, nickel) have contributed to the country's economic growth. The economy is closely tied to S. Africa.

Brazil

Federative Republic of Brazil

República Federativa do Brasil

People: Population (1992 est.): 158,000,000. **Age distrib.** (%): 0–14: 35.2; 15–59: 57.7; 60+: 7.1. **Pop. density:** 48 per sq. mi. **Urban** (1989): 76%. **Ethnic groups:** Portuguese, Africans, and mulattoes make up the vast majority; Italians, Germans, Japanese, Indians, Jews, Arabs. **Languages:** Portuguese (official), English, German, Italian. **Religions:** Roman Catholic 89%.

Geography: Area: 3,286,470 sq. mi., larger than contiguous 48 U.S. states; largest country in S. America. **Location:** Occupies eastern half of S. America. **Neighbors:** French Guiana, Suriname, Guyana, Venezuela on N, Colombia, Peru, Bolivia, Paraguay, Argentina on W, Uruguay on S. **Topography:** Brazil's Atlantic coastline stretches 4,603 miles. In N is the heavily-wooded Amazon basin covering half the country. Its network of rivers navigable for 15,814 mi. The Amazon itself flows 2,093 miles in Brazil, all navigable. The NE region is semiarid scrubland, heavily settled and poor. The S central region, favored by climate and resources, has almost half of the population, produces 75% of farm goods and 80% of industrial output. The narrow coastal belt includes most of the major cities. Almost the entire country has a tropical or semitropical climate. **Capital:** Brasilia. **Cities** (1991 est.): Sao Paulo 15.2 mln.; Rio de Janeiro 6.0 mln.; Belo Horizonte 2.4 mln.; Salvador 2.0 mln.

Government: Type: Federal republic. **Head of state:** Pres. Itamar Franco; in office: Dec. 29, 1992. **Local divisions:** 26 states, federal district (Brasilia). **Defense:** 2.6% of GDP (1990).

Economy: Industries: Steel, autos, ships, appliances, petrochemicals, machinery. **Chief crops:** Coffee (largest grower), cotton, soybeans, sugar, cocoa, rice, corn, fruits. **Minerals:** Chromium, iron, manganese, diamonds, gold, nickel, gem stones, tin, bauxite, oil. **Crude oil reserves** (1991): 2.8 bln. bbls. **Arable land:** 8%. **Livestock** (1989): cattle: 136 mln.; pigs: 33 mln.; sheep: 20 mln. **Fish catch** (1989): 850,000 metric tons. **Electricity prod.** (1991): 229 bln. kWh. **Crude steel prod.** (1991): 22.6 mln. metric tons. **Labor force:** 42% services, 31% agric.; 25% ind.

Finance: Monetary unit: Cruzeiro (June 1992: 3,059 = $1 US). **Gross domestic product** (1990): $388 bln. **Per capita GDP** (1990): $2,540. **Imports** (1992): $23 bln.; partners: U.S.

21%, EC 23%. **Exports** (1992): $36 bln.; partners: U.S. 26%, EC 27%. **Tourism** (1991): receipts: $1.4 bln. **National budget** (1991): $170 bln expenditures. **International reserves less gold** (Jan. 1993): $22.5 bln. **Gold:** 2.2 mln. oz t. **Consumer prices** (change in 1992): 1,100%.

Transport: Railroads (1990): **Length:** 18,721 mi. **Motor vehicles:** in use (1988): 14 mln. passenger cars, 1.6 mln. **Civil aviation** (1991): 17.2 bln. passenger-km.; 100 airports with scheduled flights. **Chief ports:** Santos, Rio de Janeiro, Vitoria, Salvador, Rio Grande, Recife.

Communications: Television sets: 1 per 5 persons. **Radios:** 1 per 2.5 persons. **Telephones in use:** 1 per 10 persons. **Daily newspaper circ.** (1990): 55 per 1,000 pop.

Health: Life expectancy at birth (1992): 62 male; 68 female. **Births** (per 1,000 pop. 1992): 26. **Deaths** (per 1,000 pop. 1992): 7. **Natural increase:** 1.9%. **Hospital beds:** 1 per 285 persons. **Physicians:** 1 per 684 persons. **Infant mortality** (per 1,000 live births 1992): 67.

Education (1991): **Literacy:** 81%.

Major International Organizations: UN and most of its specialized agencies, OAS.

Embassy: 3006 Massachusetts Ave. NW 20008; 745-2700.

Pedro Alvares Cabral, a Portuguese navigator, is generally credited as the first European to reach Brazil, in 1500. The country was thinly settled by various Indian tribes. Only a few have survived to the present, mostly in the Amazon basin.

In the next centuries, Portuguese colonists gradually pushed inland, bringing along large numbers of African slaves. Slavery was not abolished until 1888.

The King of Portugal, fleeing before Napoleon's army, moved the seat of government to Brazil in 1808. Brazil thereupon became a kingdom under Dom Joao VI. After his return to Portugal, his son Pedro proclaimed the independence of Brazil, Sept. 7, 1822, and was acclaimed emperor. The second emperor, Dom Pedro II, was deposed in 1889, and a republic proclaimed, called the United States of Brazil. In 1967 the country was renamed the Federative Republic of Brazil.

A military junta took control in 1930; dictatorial power was assumed by Getulio Vargas, until finally forced out by the military in 1945. A democratic regime prevailed 1945-64, during which time the capital was moved from Rio de Janeiro to Brasilia in the interior.

In 1964, Pres. Joao Belchoir Marques Goulart instituted economic policies that aggravated Brazil's inflation; he was overthrown by an army revolt. The next 5 presidents were all military leaders. Censorship was imposed, and much of the opposition was suppressed amid charges of torture. In 1974 elections, the official opposition party made gains in the chamber of deputies; some relaxation of censorship occurred.

Since 1930, successive governments have pursued industrial and agricultural growth and the development of interior areas. Exploiting vast mineral resources, fertile soil in several regions, and a huge labor force, Brazil became the leading industrial power of Latin America by the 1970s, while agricultural output soared. Democratic presidential elections were held in 1985 as the nation returned to civilian rule. Fernando Collor de Mello was elected president in Dec. 1989.

However, income maldistribution and inflation have led to severe economic recession. Foreign debt is among the largest in the world. Brazil and its principal commercial bank lenders agreed to restructure the nation's $44 billion commercial debts, July 1992. The 1991 census revealed that population growth dipped below 2 percent for the first time in half a century.

Brazil unveiled a comprehensive environmental program for the Amazon region in 1989, amid an international outcry by environmentalists and others concerned about the ongoing destruction of the Amazon ecosystem. The Amazon rain forest was considered a global resource because of its impact on world weather patterns. Brazil hosted delegates from 178 countries at the Earth Summit June 3-14, 1992.

In Sept. 1992, Pres. Collor was impeached for corruption. He resigned on Dec. 29 as his trial was beginning, and Franco, who had been acting president, was sworn in as president.

Brunei Darussalam

State of Brunei Darussalam

Negara Brunei Darussalam

People: Population (1992 est.): 369,000. **Pop. density:** 165 per sq. mi. **Ethnic groups:** Malay 65%, Chinese 20%. **Language:** Malay, English, (both official), Chinese. **Religion:** Moslem 60%, Buddhist 14%, Christian 10%.

Geography: Area: 2,226 sq. mi.; larger than Delaware. **Location:** on the north coast of the island of Borneo; it is surrounded on its landward side by the Malaysian state of Sarawak. **Capital:** Bandar Seri Begawan. **Cities** (1982 est.): Bandar Seri Begawan 51,000.

Government: Type: Independent sultanate. **Head of government:** Sultan Sir Muda Hassanal Bolkiah Mu'izzadin Waddaulah; in office: Jan. 1, 1984. **Local divisions:** 4 districts.

Economy: Industries: petroleum (about 90% of revenue is derived from oil exports). **Chief crops:** rice, bananas, cassava.

Finance: Monetary unit: Brunei dollar (Dec. 1992: 1.60 = $1). **Gross domestic product** (1989): $3.1 bln. **Per capita GDP:** $9,600.

Transport: Motor vehicles: In use (1990): 100,000 passenger cars, 12,000 commercial vehicles.

Communications: Television sets: 1 per 2.6 persons. **Radios:** 1 per 3 persons. **Telephones:** 1 per 6 persons.

Education (1987): **Literacy:** 95% among young.

Health: Life expectancy at birth: (1992): 69 male; 73 female. **Infant mortality** (per 1,000 live births 1992): 26.

Major International Organizations: UN and some of its specialized agencies.

The Sultanate of Brunei was a powerful state in the early 16th century, with authority over all of the island of Borneo as well as parts of the Sulu Islands and the Philippines. In 1888, a treaty was signed which placed the state under the protection of Great Britain.

Brunei became a fully sovereign and independent state on Jan. 1, 1984.

The Sultan of Brunei donated $10 million to the Nicaraguan *contras* in 1987; the subsequent misplacement of the funds generated much media attention in the U.S.

Bulgaria

Republic of Bulgaria

Republika Bulgaria

People: Population (1992 est.): 8,868,000. **Age distrib.** (%): 0–14: 20.6; 15–59: 60.5; 60+: 18.9. **Pop. density:** 199 per sq. mi. **Urban** (1992): 67%. **Ethnic groups:** Bulgarian 85%, Turk 8.5%. **Languages:** Bulgarian (official), Turkish. **Religions:** Bulgarian Orthodox, 85%, Moslem 13%.

Geography: Area: 44,365 sq. mi., about the size of Ohio. **Location:** In eastern Balkan Peninsula on Black Sea. **Neighbors:** Romania on N, Yugoslavia, Macedonia on W, Greece, Turkey on S. **Topography:** The Stara Planina (Balkan) Mts. stretch E-W across the center of the country, with the Danubian plain on N, the Rhodope Mts. on SW, and Thracian Plain on SE. **Capital:** Sofia. **Cities** (1991 est.): Sofia 1,200,000; Plovdiv 379,000; Varna 320,000.

Government: Type: Republic. **Head of state:** Pres. Zhelyu Zhelev; b. Mar. 3, 1935; in office: Aug. 1, 1990. **Head of government:** Premier Lyuben Berov; in office: Dec. 30, 1992. **Local divisions:** 9 provinces. **Defense:** 4.4% of GNP (1991).

Economy: Industries: Chemicals, machinery, metals, textiles, processed food. **Chief crops:** Grains, fruit, corn, potatoes, tobacco. **Minerals:** Lead, manganese, lignite, coal. **Arable land:** 34%. **Livestock** (1990): cattle: 1.5 mln.; pigs: 4.3 mln.; sheep: 7.9 mln. **Fish catch** (1989): 121,000 metric tons. **Electricity prod.** (1990): 45 bln. kWh. **Crude steel prod.** (1991): 2.3 mln. metric tons. **Labor force:** 20% agric.; 33% ind.

Finance: Monetary unit: Leva (Dec. 1992: 25 = $1 US). **Gross national product** (1990): $47.3 bln. **Per capita GNP:** $5,300. **Imports** (1990): $9.6 bln.; partners: CIS 56%. **Exports** (1990): $8.4 bln.; partners: CIS 70%. **Tourism** (1989): revenues: $362 mln. **National budget** (1988): $28 bln. expenditures.

Transport: Railroads (1991): **Length:** 4,106 km. **Motor vehicles:** in use (1990): 1.3 mln. passenger cars, 200,000 commercial. **Civil aviation** (1990): 3.7 bln. passenger km.; 3 airports. **Chief ports:** Burgas, Varna.

Communications: Television sets: 1 per 3.9 persons. **Radios:** 1 per 4.8 persons. **Telephones in use:** 1 per 4.8 persons. **Daily newspaper circ.** (1988): 316 per 1,000 pop.

Health: Life expectancy at birth (1992): 69 male; 76 female. **Births** (per 1,000 pop. 1992): 13. **Deaths** (per 1,000 pop. 1992): 12. **Hospital beds:** 1 per 103 persons. **Physicians:** 1 per 337 persons. **Infant mortality** (per 1,000 live births 1992): 13.

Education (1990): **Literacy:** 98%.

Major International Organizations: UN.

Embassy: 1621-22d St. NW 20008; 387-7969.

Bulgaria was settled by Slavs in the 6th century. Turkic Bulgars arrived in the 7th century, merged with the Slavs, became Christians by the 9th century, and set up powerful empires in the 10th and 12th centuries. The Ottomans prevailed in 1396 and remained for 500 years.

A revolt in 1876 led to an independent kingdom in 1908. Bulgaria expanded after the first Balkan War but lost its Aegean coastline in World War I, when it sided with Germany. Bulgaria joined the Axis in World War II but withdrew in 1944. Communists took power with Soviet aid; the monarchy was abolished Sept. 8, 1946.

On Nov. 10, 1989, Communist party leader and head of state Todor Zhivkov, who had held power for 35 years, resigned. Zhivkov was imprisoned, Jan. 1990, and convicted, Sept. 1992, of corruption and abuse of power. In Jan. 1990, parliament voted to revoke the constitutionally guaranteed dominant role of the Communist Party.

Burkina Faso

People: Population (1992 est.): 9,653,000. **Pop. density:** 91 per sq. mi. **Urban** (1988): 8%. **Ethnic groups:** Voltaic groups (Mossi, Bobo), Mande. **Languages:** French (official), Sudanic tribal languages. **Religions:** animist 65%, Moslem 25%, Christian 10%.

Geography: Area: 105,869 sq. mi., the size of Colorado. **Location:** In W. Africa, S of the Sahara. **Neighbors:** Mali on NW, Niger on NE, Benin, Togo, Ghana, Côte d' Ivoire on S. **Topography:** Landlocked Burkina Faso is in the savannah region of W. Africa. The N is arid, hot, and thinly populated. **Capital:** Ouagadougou. **Cities** (1990): Ouagadougou 500,000; Bobo-Dioulasso 250,000.

Government: Type: Military. **Head of state:** Pres. Blaise Compaoré; in office: Oct. 15, 1987. **Head of government:** Prime Min. Youssouf Ouedraogo; in office: June 16, 1992. **Local divisions:** 30 provinces. **Defense:** 2.7% of GDP (1988).

Economy: Chief crops: Millet, sorghum, rice, peanuts, grain. **Minerals:** Manganese, gold, limestone. **Arable land:** 10%. **Electricity prod.** (1991): 320 mln. kWh. **Labor force:** 82% agric.

Finance: Monetary unit: CFA Franc (Mar. 1993: 273 = $1 US). **Gross domestic product** (1990): $2.9 bln. **Per capita GDP** (1989): $205. **Imports** (1989): $322 mln.; partners: EC, Côte d' Ivoire. **Exports** (1989): $95 mln.; partners: Côte d' Ivoire, EC, China. **International reserves less gold** (Jan. 1993): $345 mln. **Gold:** 11,000 oz t. **Consumer prices** (change in 1992): −1.4%.

Transport: Motor vehicles: in use (1990): 12,000 passenger cars, 13,000 comm. vehicles.

Communications: Television sets: 1 per 223 persons. **Radios:** 1 per 44 persons. **Telephones in use:** 1 per 482 persons. **Daily newspaper circ.** (1989): 1 per 1,000 pop.

Health: Life expectancy at birth (1992): 52 male; 53 female. **Births** (per 1,000 pop. 1992): 50. **Deaths** (per 1,000 pop. 1992): 16. **Natural increase:** 3.4%. **Hospital beds:** 1 per 1,359 persons. **Physicians:** 1 per 29,914 persons. **Infant mortality** (per 1,000 live births 1992): 117.

Education (1991): **Literacy:** 18%. Only 8% attend school.

Major International Organizations: UN and many of its specialized agencies, OAU.

Embassy: 2340 Massachusetts Ave. NW 20008; 332-5577.

The Mossi tribe entered the area in the 11th to 13th centuries. Their kingdoms ruled until defeated by the Mali and Songhai empires.

French control came by 1896, but Upper Volta (name changed to Burkina Faso on Aug. 4, 1984) was not finally established as a separate territory until 1947. Full independence came Aug. 5, 1960, and a pro-French government was elected. The military seized power in 1980. A 1987 coup established the current regime, which restored limited democracy in the early 1990s.

Several hundred thousand farm workers migrate each year to Côte D'Ivoire and Ghana. Burkina Faso is heavily dependent on foreign aid.

Burma

(See Myanmar)

Burundi

Republic of Burundi

Republika y'Uburundi

People: Population (1992 est.): 6,022,000. **Age distrib.** (%): 0–14: 45.1; 15–59: 50.1; 60+: 4.8. **Pop. density:** 559 per sq. mi. **Urban** (1986): 8%. **Ethnic groups:** Hutu 85%, Tutsi 14%, Twa (pygmy) 1%. **Languages:** French, Rundi (both official). **Religions:** Roman Catholic 62%, traditional African 32%.

Geography: Area: 10,759 sq. mi., the size of Maryland. **Location:** In central Africa. **Neighbors:** Rwanda on N, Zaire on W, Tanzania on E. **Topography:** Much of the country is grassy highland, with mountains reaching 8,900 ft. The southernmost source of the White Nile is located in Burundi. Lake Tanganyika is the second deepest lake in the world. **Capital:** Bujumbura. **Cities** (1991 est.): Bujumbura 240,000.

Government: Type: Republic. **Head of state:** Pres. Maj. Pierre Buyoya; in office: Sept. 9, 1987. **Head of government:** Pres. Melchior Ndadaye; in office: July 10, 1993. **Local divisions:** 15 provinces. **Defense** (1990): 19% of govt. budget.

Economy: Chief crops: Coffee (87% of exports), cotton, tea. **Minerals:** Nickel. **Arable land:** 43%. **Electricity prod.** (1991): 105 mln. kWh. **Labor force:** 93% agric.

Finance: Monetary unit: Franc (Apr. 1993: 236 = $1 US). **Gross domestic product** (1990): $1.2 bln. **Per capita GDP:** $200. **Imports** (1991): $248 mln.; partners: Belg.-Lux. 17%; Ger. 18%. **Exports** (1991): $90 mln; partners: Ger. 31%, Belg. 20%. **Tourism** (1990): $4 mln. receipts. **National budget** (1990): $203 mln. expenditures. **International reserves less gold** (Mar. 1993): $196 mln. **Gold:** 17,000 oz t. **Consumer prices** (change in 1992): 4.7%.

Transport: Motor vehicles: in use (1990): 12,000 passenger cars, 12,000 comm. vehicles.

Communications: Radios: 1 per 11 persons. **Telephones in use:** 1 per 611 persons.

Health: Life expectancy at birth (1992): 51 male; 55 female. **Births** (per 1,000 pop. 1992): 46. **Deaths** (per 1,000 pop. 1992): 14. **Natural increase:** 3.2%. **Hospital beds:** 1 per 515 persons. **Physicians:** 1 per 31,777 persons. **Infant mortality** (per 1,000 live births 1992): 106.

Education (1991): **Literacy:** 50%. **Years compulsory:** 6; **Attendance:** 45%.

Major International Organizations: UN (GATT, IMF, WHO), OAU.

Embassy: 2233 Wisconsin Ave. NW 20007; 342-2574.

The pygmy Twa were the first inhabitants, followed by Bantu Hutus, who were conquered in the 16th century by the Tutsi (Watusi), probably from Ethiopia. Under German control in 1899, the area fell to Belgium in 1916, which exercised successively a League of Nations mandate and UN trusteeship over Ruanda-Urundi (now the two countries of Rwanda and Burundi).

Independence came in 1962.

An unsuccessful Hutu rebellion in 1972-73 left 10,000 Tutsi and 150,000 Hutu dead. Over 100,000 Hutu fled to Tanzania and Zaire. In the 1980s, Burundi's Tutsi-dominated regime pledged itself to ethnic reconciliation and democratic reform. In the nation's first democratic presidential election, in June 1993, a Hutu was elected. Burundi remains one of the poorest and most densely populated countries in Africa.

Cambodia

State of Cambodia

Roat Kampuchea

People: Population (1992 est.): 7,249,000. **Pop. density:** 103 per sq. mi. **Urban** (1990): 12%. **Ethnic groups:** Cambodian 90%, Vietnamese 4%, Chinese 5%. **Languages:** Khmer (official), French. **Religions:** Theravada Buddhism 95%.

Geography: Area: 70,238 sq. mi., the size of Missouri. **Location:** In Indochina Peninsula. **Neighbors:** Thailand on W, N, Laos on NE, Vietnam on E. **Topography:** The central area, formed by the Mekong R. basin and Tonle Sap lake, is level. Hills and mountains are in SE, a long escarpment separates the country from Thailand on NW. 75% of the area is forested. **Capital:** Phnom Penh. **Cities** (1990 est.): Phnom Penh 800,000.

Government: Type: Constitutional monarchy. **Head of State:** King Norodom Sihanouk; b. Oct. 31, 1922; in office: Sept. 24, 1993. **Head of Government:** First Prime Min. Prince Norodom Ranariddh; in office: Sept. 24, 1993. **Local divisions:** 19 provinces and 2 cities.

Economy: Industries: Rice milling, wood & rubber. **Chief crops:** Rice, corn. **Minerals:** Iron, copper, manganese. **Other resources:** Forests, rubber. **Arable land:** 16%. **Livestock** (1991): cattle: 2.0 mln. pigs: 1.5 mln. **Fish catch** (1991): 105,000 metric tons. **Electricity prod.** (1991): 200 mln. kWh. **Labor force:** 74% agri.

Finance: Monetary unit: Riel (Jan. 1993: 1,508 = $1 US). **Gross domestic product** (1991): $930 mln. **Per capita GDP:** $130. **Imports** (1988): $147 mln. **Exports** (1988): $32 mln.

Transport: Railroads (1989): **Length:** 649 mi. **Motor vehicles:** in use (1988): 4,000 passenger cars, 7,000 trucks. **Chief ports:** Kompong Som.

Communications: Television sets: 1 per 125 persons. **Radios:** 1 per 10 persons. **Telephones in use:** 1 per 3,300 persons.

Health: Life expectancy at birth (1992): 48 male; 51 female. **Births** (per 1,000 pop. 1992): 37. **Deaths** (per 1,000 pop. 1992): 15. **Natural increase:** 2.2. **Hospital beds:** 1 per 632 persons. **Physicians:** 1 per 27,000 persons. **Infant Mortality** (per 1,000 live births 1992): 121.

Education (1990): **Literacy:** 50%.

Major International Organizations: UN.

Early kingdoms dating from that of Funan in the 1st century AD culminated in the great Khmer empire which flourished from the 9th century to the 13th, encompassing present-day Thailand, Cambodia, Laos, and southern Vietnam. The peripheral areas were lost to invading Siamese and Vietnamese, and France established a protectorate in 1863. Independence came in 1953.

Prince Norodom Sihanouk, king 1941-1955 and head of state from 1960, tried to maintain neutrality. Relations with the U.S. were broken in 1965, after South Vietnam planes attacked Vietcong forces within Cambodia. Relations were restored in 1969, after Sihanouk charged Viet communists with arming Cambodian insurgents.

In 1970, pro-U.S. premier Lon Nol seized power, demanding removal of 40,000 North Viet troops; the monarchy was abolished. Sihanouk formed a government-in-exile in Peking, and open war began between the government and Khmer Rouge. The U.S. provided heavy military and economic aid.

Khmer Rouge forces captured Phnom Penh April 17, 1975. The new government evacuated all cities and towns, and shuffled the rural population, sending virtually the entire population to clear jungle, forest, and scrub, which covered half the country. Over one million people were killed in executions and enforced hardships.

Severe border fighting broke out with Vietnam in 1978; developed into a full-fledged Vietnamese invasion. The Vietnamese-backed Kampuchean National United Front for National Salvation, a Cambodian rebel movement, announced, Jan. 8, 1979, the formation of a government one day after the Vietnamese capture of Phnom Pehn. Thousands of refugees flowed into Thailand and widespread starvation was reported.

On Jan. 10, 1983, Vietnam launched an offensive against rebel forces in the west. They overran a refugee camp, Jan. 31, driving 30,000 residents into Thailand. In March, Vietnam launched a major offensive against camps on the Cambodian-Thailand border, engaged Khmer Rouge guerrillas, and crossed the border instigating clashes with Thai troops. Vietnam announced that it would withdraw all its troops by Sept. 1989.

Following UN-sponsored elections that ended May 28, 1993, the 2 leading parties agreed, June 18, to share power in an interim government until a new constitution was adopted. On Sept. 21, a constitution that created a constitutional monarchy was adopted by the National Assembly. It went into effect on Sept. 24.

Cameroon

Republic of Cameroon

People: Population (1992 est.): 12,658,000. **Age distrib.** (%): 0–14: 46.1; 15–59: 48.3; 60+: 5.6. **Pop. density:** 70 per sq. mi. **Urban** (1990): 40%. **Ethnic groups:** Some 200 tribes; largest are Bamileke 30%, Fulani 7%. **Languages:** English, French (both official), numerous African groups. **Religions:** Animist 51%, Moslem 16%, Christian 33%.

Geography: Area: 179,714 sq. mi., somewhat larger than California. **Location:** Between W and central Africa. **Neighbors:** Nigeria on NW, Chad, Central African Republic on E, Congo, Gabon, Equatorial Guinea on S. **Topography:** A low coastal plain with rain forests is in S; plateaus in center lead to forested mountains in W, including Mt. Cameroon, 13,000 ft.; grasslands in N lead to marshes around Lake Chad. **Capital:** Yaounde. **Cities** (1988 est.): Douala 852,000; Yaounde 700,000.

Government: Type: Republic, one party presidential regime. **Head of state:** Pres. Paul Biya; b. Feb. 13, 1933; in office: Nov. 6, 1982. Prime Min. Simon Achidi Achu; in office: Apr. 9, 1992. **Local divisions:** 10 provinces. **Defense:** 1.7% of GDP (1990).

Economy: Industries: Aluminum processing, oil prod., palm products. **Chief crops:** Cocoa, coffee, cotton. **Crude oil reserves** (1985): 531 mln. bbls. **Other resources:** Timber. **Arable land:** 14%. **Livestock** (1989): cattle: 4.5 mln.; sheep: 3.1 mln.; pigs: 1.2 mln. **Fish catch** (1990): 77,000 metric tons. **Electricity prod.** (1991): 2.9 bln. kWh. **Labor force:** 74% agric., 11% ind. and commerce.

Finance: Monetary unit: CFA franc (Mar. 1993: 274 = $1 US). **Gross domestic product** (1991): $11.6 bln. **Per capita GDP** (1991): $1,010. **Imports** (1990): $2.1 bln.; partners: Fr. 42%. **Exports** (1990): $928 mln.; partners: EC 50%. **National budget** (1990): $2.1 bln. **International reserves less gold** (Jan. 1993): $32.5 mln. **Gold:** 30,000 oz t.

Transport: Railroads (1990): **Length:** 686 mi. **Motor vehicles:** in use (1987): 78,000 passenger cars, 43,000 comm. vehicles. **Chief ports:** Douala.

Communications: Radios: 1 per 6 persons. **Telephones in use:** 1 per 185 persons. **Daily newspaper circ.** (1991): 6 per 1,000 pop.

Health: Life expectancy at birth (1992): 55 male; 60 female. **Births** (per 1,000 pop. 1992): 44. **Deaths** (per 1,000 pop. 1992): 11. **Natural increase:** 3.1%. **Hospital beds:** 1 per 377 persons. **Physicians:** 1 per 12,540 persons. **Infant mortality** (per 1,000 live births 1992): 81.

Education (1991): **Literacy:** 65%. About 70% attend school.

Major International Organizations: UN, OAU, EC (Associate).

Embassy: 2349 Massachusetts Ave. NW 20008; 265-8790.

Portuguese sailors were the first Europeans to reach Cameroon, in the 15th century. The European and American slave trade was very active in the area. German control lasted from 1884 to 1916, when France and Britain divided the territory, later receiving League of Nations mandates and UN trusteeships. French Cameroon became independent Jan. 1, 1960; one part of British Cameroon joined Nigeria in 1961, the other part joined Cameroon. Stability has allowed for development of roads, railways, agriculture, and petroleum production. Some 3,000 died in 1986 as a result of clouds of toxic gas of volcanic origin emanating from Lake Nyos.

Canada

People: Population (1992 est.): 27,351,000. **Age distrib.** (%): 0–14: 20.9; 15–59: 63.1; 60+: 16.0. **Pop. density:** 7 per sq. mi. **Urban** (1990): 77%. **Ethnic groups:** British 25%; French 24%; other European 16%; mixed 28%. **Language:** English, French (both official). **Religion:** Roman Catholic 46%, Protestant 41%.

Geography: Area: 3,849,672 sq. mi., the largest country in land size in the western hemisphere. Canada stretches 3,426 miles from east to west and extends southward from the North Pole to the U.S. border. Its seacoast includes 36,356 miles of mainland and 115,133 miles of islands, including the Arctic islands almost from Greenland to near the Alaskan border. Climate, while generally temperate, varies from freezing winter cold to blistering summer heat. **Capital:** Ottawa. **Cities** (met. 1991 est.): Montreal 3,100,000; Toronto 3,800,000; Vancouver 1,600,000; Ottawa-Hull 920,000; Winnipeg 652,000; Edmonton 839,000, Calgary 754,000, Quebec 645,000.

Government: Type: Confederation with parliamentary democracy. **Head of state:** Queen Elizabeth II, represented by Gov.-Gen. Ramon Hnatyshyn; in office: Jan. 29, 1990. **Head of government:** Prime Min. Kim Campbell; b. Mar. 10, 1947; in office: June 25, 1993. **Local divisions:** 10 provinces, 2 territories. **Defense:** 2% of GDP (1991).

Economy: Minerals: Nickel, zinc, copper, gold, lead, molybdenum, potash, silver. **Crude oil reserves** (1991): 6.4 bln. barrels. **Arable land:** 5%. **Livestock** (1990): cattle: 12.0 mln.; pigs: 10.8 mln.; sheep: 722,000. **Fish catch** (1989): 1.6 mln. metric tons. **Electricity prod.** (1991): 479 bln. kWh. **Crude steel prod.** (1991): 12.9 mln. metric tons. **Labor force:** 4% agric.; 52% ind. & comm., 28% services.

Finance: Monetary unit: Dollar (July 1993: 1.27 = $1 US). **Gross domestic product** (1991): $521 bln. **Per capita GDP:** $19,400. **Imports** (1992): $124 bln.; partners: U.S. 69%, EC 8%, Jap. 5%. **Exports** (1992): $134 bln.; partners: U.S. 75%, EC 9%, Jap. 5%. **Tourism** (1990): receipts: $6.3 bln. **National budget** (1990-91): $127 bln. expenditures. **International reserves less gold** (Mar. 1993): $12.7 bln. **Gold:** 9.1 mln. oz t. **Consumer prices** (change in 1992): 1.5%.

Transport: Railroads (1990): **Length:** 56,771 mi. **Motor vehicles:** in use (1989): 12.0 mln. passenger cars, 3.7 mln. comm. **Civil aviation** (1990): 46 bln. passenger-km: 106 airports with scheduled flights.

Communications: Television sets: 1 per 1.7 persons. **Radios:** 1 per 1.2 persons. **Telephones in use:** 1 per 1.3 persons. **Daily newspaper circ.** (1991): 187 per 1,000 pop.

Health: Life expectancy at birth (1992): 74 male; 81 female. **Births** (per 1,000 pop. 1992): 14. **Deaths** (per 1,000 pop. 1992): 7. **Natural increase:** .7%. **Hospital beds:** 1 per 148 persons. **Physicians:** 1 per 449 persons. **Infant mortality** (per 1,000 live births 1992): 7.3.

Education (1991): **Literacy:** 99%.

Major International Organizations: UN and all of its specialized agencies, NATO, OECD, Commonwealth of Nations.

Embassy: 501 Pennsylvania Ave. NW 20001; 682-1740.

French explorer Jacques Cartier, who reached the Gulf of St. Lawrence in 1534, is generally regarded as the founder of Canada. But English seaman John Cabot sighted Newfoundland 37 years earlier, in 1497, and Vikings are believed to have reached the Atlantic coast centuries before either explorer.

Canadian settlement was pioneered by the French who established Quebec City (1608) and Montreal (1642) and declared New France a colony in 1663.

Britain, as part of its American expansion, acquired Acadia (later Nova Scotia) in 1717 and, through military victory over French forces in Canada (an extension of a European conflict between the 2 powers), captured Quebec (1759) and obtained control of the rest of New France in 1763. The French, through the Quebec Act of 1774, retained the rights to their own language, religion, and civil law.

The British presence in Canada increased during the American Revolution when many colonials, proudly calling themselves United Empire Loyalists, moved north to Canada.

Fur traders and explorers led Canadians westward across the continent. Sir Alexander Mackenzie reached the Pacific in 1793 and scrawled on a rock by the ocean, "from Canada by land."

In Upper and Lower Canada (later called Ontario and Quebec) and in the Maritimes, legislative assemblies appeared in the 18th century and reformers called for responsible government. But the War of 1812 intervened. The war, a conflict between Great Britain and the United States fought mainly in Upper Canada, ended in a stalemate in 1814.

In 1837 political agitation for more democratic government culminated in rebellions in Upper and Lower Canada. Britain sent Lord Durham to investigate and, in a famous report (1839), he recommended union of the 2 parts into one colony called Canada. The union lasted until Confederation, July 1, 1867, when proclamation of the British North America (BNA) Act launched the Dominion of Canada, consisting of Ontario, Quebec, and the former colonies of Nova Scotia and New Brunswick.

Since 1840 the Canadian colonies had held the right to internal self-government. The BNA act, which became the country's written constitution, established a federal system of government on the model of a British parliament and cabinet structure under the crown. Canada was proclaimed a self-governing Dominion within the British Empire in 1931.

In 1982 Canada severed its last formal legislative link with Britain by obtaining the right to amend its constitution (the British North America Act of 1867).

The Meech Lake Agreement was signed June 3, 1987. The historic accord would have assured constitutional protection for Quebec's efforts to preserve its French language and culture. Critics of the accord charged that it did not make any provision for other minority groups and that it gave Quebec too much power, which might enable it to pass laws that conflicted with the nation's 1982 Charter of Rights and Freedoms. The accord died June 22, 1990.

Its failure sparked a separatist revival in Quebec which culminated in Aug. 1992 in the Charlottetown agreement. This called for changes to the constitution, such as recognition of Quebec as a "distinct society" within the Canadian confederation and self- government for native peoples. The accord was defeated in a national referendum on Oct. 26, 1992.

In May 1992 voters in the Northwest Territories approved the creation of a self-governing homeland for the 17,500 Inuut living in the territories. The area—to be known as Nunavut, "Our Land"—would cover an area of 136,493 sq. mi. and will take effect by 1999.

Canada became the first nation to ratify the North American Free Trade Agreement between Canada, Mexico, and the U.S., June 23, 1993.

Canadian Provinces

	Sq. mi.	Population, 1991 cen.
Alberta	255,287	2,545,553
British Columbia	365,947	3,282,061
Manitoba	250,947	1,091,942
New Brunswick	28,355	723,900
Newfoundland	156,949	568,474
Nova Scotia	21,425	899,942
Ontario	412,581	10,084,885
Prince Edward Island	2,185	129,765
Quebec	594,860	6,895,963
Saskatchewan	251,866	988,928
Territories		
Northwest Territories	1,322,909	57,649
Yukon	186,661	27,797

Prime Ministers of Canada

Canada is a constitutional monarchy with a parliamentary system of government. It is also a federal state. Canada's official head of state is the King or Queen of England, represented by a resident Governor-General. However, in practice the nation is governed by the Prime Minister, leader of the party that commands the support of a majority of the House of Commons, dominant chamber of Canada's bicameral Parliament.

Name	Party	Term
Sir John A. MacDonald	Conservative	1867-1873
		1878-1891
Alexander Mackenzie	Liberal	1873-1878
Sir John J. C. Abbott	Conservative	1891-1892
Sir John S. D. Thompson	Conservative	1892-1894
Sir Mackenzie Bowell	Conservative	1894-1896

Name	Party	Term
Sir Charles Tupper	Conservative	1896
Sir Wilfrid Laurier	Liberal	1896-1911
Sir Robert L. Borden	Cons. Union.	1911-1920
Arthur Meighen	Cons. Union.	1920-1921
W.L. Mackenzie King	Liberal	1921-1926[1] 1926-1930 1935-1948
R. B. Bennett	Conservative	1930-1935
Louis St. Laurent	Liberal	1948-1957
John G. Diefenbaker	Prog. Cons.	1957-1963
Lester B. Pearson	Liberal	1963-1968
Pierre Elliott Trudeau	Liberal	1968-1979
Joe Clark	Prog. Cons.	1979-1980
Pierre Elliott Trudeau	Liberal	1980-1984
John Turner	Liberal	1984
Brian Mulroney	Prog. Cons.	1984-1993
Kim Campbell	Prog. Cons.	1993

(1) King's term was interrupted from June 26-Sept. 25, 1926, when Arthur Meighen again served as prime minister.

Cape Verde

Republic of Cape Verde

República de Cabo Verde

People: Population (1992 est.): 398,000. **Age distrib.** (%): 0–14: 45.6; 15–59: 47.7; 60+: 6.7. **Pop. density:** 255 per sq. mi. **Urban** (1991): 29%. **Ethnic groups:** Creole (mulatto) 71%, African 28%, European 1%. **Languages:** Portuguese (official), Crioulo. **Religions:** 80% Roman Catholic.

Geography: Area: 1,557 sq. mi., a bit larger than Rhode Island. **Location:** In Atlantic O., off western tip of Africa. **Neighbors:** Nearest are Mauritania, Senegal. **Topography:** Cape Verde Islands are 15 in number, volcanic in origin (active crater on Fogo). The landscape is eroded and stark, with vegetation mostly in interior valleys. **Capital:** Praia. **Cities** (1990 est.): Mindelo 47,000; Praia 61,000.

Government: Type: Republic. **Head of state:** Pres. Antonio Mascarenhas Monteiro; in office: Mar. 17, 1991. **Head of government:** Prime Min. Carlos Veiga; in office: Apr. 4, 1991. **Local divisions:** 14 administrative districts.

Economy: Chief crops: Bananas, coffee, beats, corn, beans. **Minerals:** Salt. **Other resources:** Fish. **Arable land:** 10%. **Electricity prod.** (1991): 15 mln. kWh.

Finance: Monetary unit: Escudo (Mar. 1993: 77 = $1 US). **Gross domestic product** (1990): $310 mln. **Per capita GDP:** $800. **Imports** (1989): $108 mln.; partners: Port. 33%, Neth. 12%. **Exports** (1989): $10.9 mln.; partners: Port. 32%, Ang. 21%.

Transport: Motor vehicles: in use (1988): 13,000 passenger cars, 4,000 comm. vehicles. **Chief ports:** Mindelo, Praia.

Communications: Radios: 1 per 6.8 persons. **Telephones in use:** 1 per 76 persons.

Health: Life expectancy at birth (1992): 60 male; 64 female. **Births** (per 1,000 pop. 1992): 48. **Deaths** (per 1,000 pop. 1992): 11. **Natural increase:** 3.8%. **Hospital beds:** 1 per 550 persons. **Physicians:** 1 per 4,208 persons. **Infant mortality** (per 1,000 live births 1992): 61.

Education (1989): **Literacy:** 37%.

Major International Organizations: UN (GATT, IMF, WHO), OAU.

Embassy: 3415 Massachusetts Ave. NW 20007; 965-6820.

The uninhabited Cape Verdes were discovered by the Portuguese in 1456 or 1460. The first Portuguese colonists landed in 1462; African slaves were brought soon after, and most Cape Verdeans descend from both groups. Cape Verde independence came July 5, 1975. The islands have suffered from repeated extreme droughts and famines. Emphasis is placed on the development of agriculture and on fishing.

Antonio Mascarenhas Monteiro won the nation's first free presidential election in 1991.

Central African Republic

République Centrafricaine

People: Population (1992 est.): 3,029,000. **Pop. density:** 12 per sq. mi. **Urban** (1990): 47%. **Ethnic groups:** Banda 27%, Baya 34%, Mandja 21%, Sara 10%. **Languages:** French (official), local dialects. **Religions:** Protestant 25%, Roman Catholic 25%, traditional 24%.

Geography: Area: 240,534 sq. mi., slightly smaller than Texas. **Location:** In central Africa. **Neighbors:** Chad on N, Cameroon on W, Congo, Zaire on S, Sudan on E. **Topography:** Mostly rolling plateau, average altitude 2,000 ft., with rivers draining S to the Congo and N to Lake Chad. Open, well-watered savanna covers most of the area, with an arid area in NE, and tropical rainforest in SW. **Capital:** Bangui. **Cities** (1988 est.): Bangui (met.) 596,000.

Government: Type: Republic (under military rule). **Head of state:** Gen. Andre Kolingba; in office: Sept. 1, 1981. **Head of government:** Prime Min. Enoch Devant Lakoue; in office: Feb. 1993. **Local divisions:** 16 prefectures. **Defense:** 2% of GDP (1989).

Economy: Industries: Textiles, light manuf, mining. **Chief crops:** Cotton, coffee, peanuts, tobacco. **Minerals:** Diamonds (chief export), uranium. **Other resources:** Timber. **Arable land:** 3%. **Electricity prod.** (1991): 93 mln. kWh. **Labor force:** 72% agric.

Finance: Monetary unit: CFA Franc (Mar. 1993: 273 = $1 US). **Gross domestic product** (1990): $1.3 bln. **Per capita GDP:** $440. **Imports** (1990): $214 mln.; partners: Fr. 44%. **Exports** (1990): $151 mln.; partners: Fr. 53%, Belg.-Lux. 23%. **National budget** (1991): $193 mln. expenditures. **International reserves less gold** (Jan. 1993): $103 mln. **Gold:** 12,000 oz t.

Transport: Motor vehicles: in use (1989): 10,000 passenger cars, 8,000 comm. vehicles.

Communications: Radios: 1 per 5 persons. **Telephones:** 1 per 380 persons.

Health: Life expectancy at birth (1992): 46 male; 49 female. **Births** (per 1,000 pop. 1992): 44. **Deaths** 1 per 1,000 pop. 1992): 19. **Natural increase:** 2.5%. **Hospital beds:** 1 per 689 persons. **Physicians:** 1 per 17,292 persons. **Infant mortality** (per 1,000 live births 1992): 135.

Education (1991): **Literacy:** 27%. **Attendance:** primary school 79%; secondary school 18%.

Major International Organizations: UN (GATT, IMF, WHO), OAU.

Embassy: 1618 22d St. NW 20008; 483-7800.

Various Bantu tribes migrated through the region for centuries before French control was asserted in the late 19th century, when the region was named Ubangi-Shari. Complete independence was attained Aug. 13, 1960.

All political parties were dissolved in 1960, and the country became a center for Chinese political influence in Africa. Relations with China were severed after 1965. Elizabeth Domitien, premier 1975-76, was the first woman to hold that post in an African country. Pres. Jean-Bedel Bokassa, who seized power in a 1965 military coup, proclaimed himself constitutional emperor of the renamed Central African Empire Dec. 1976.

Bokassa's rule was characterized by ruthless and cruel authority and human rights violations. Bokassa was ousted in a bloodless coup aided by the French government, Sept. 20, 1979, and replaced by his cousin David Dacko, former president from 1960 to 1965. In 1981, the political situation deteriorated amid strikes and economic crisis. Gen. Kolingba replaced Dacko as head of state in a bloodless coup. Multiparty legislative and presidential elections were held in Oct. 1992 but were canceled by the government when Kolingba was losing. New elections were scheduled for Oct. 1993.

Chad

Republic of Chad

République du Tchad

People: Population (1992 est.): 5,238,000. **Age distrib.** (%): 0–14: 42.5; 15–59: 51.7; 60+: 5.8. **Pop. density:** 10 per sq. mi. **Urban** (1990): 32%. **Ethnic groups:** 200 distinct groups. **Languages:** French, Arabic, (both official), some 100 other languages. **Religions:** Moslem 44%, animist 23%, Christian 33%.

Geography: Area: 495,755 sq. mi., four-fifths the size of Alaska. **Location:** In central N. Africa. **Neighbors:** Libya on N, Niger, Nigeria, Cameroon on W, Central African Republic on S, Sudan on E. **Topography:** Southern wooded savanna, steppe, and desert, part of the Sahara, in the N. Southern rivers flow N to Lake Chad, surrounded by marshland. **Capital:** N'Djamena. **Cities** (1992 est.): N'Djamena 500,000.

Government: Type: Republic. **Head of state:** Pres. Idriss Deby; in office: Dec. 4, 1990. **Head of government:** Prime Min. Joseph Yodoyman; in office: May 20, 1992. **Local divisions:** 14 prefectures. **Defense:** 5.6% of GDP (1990).

Economy: Chief crops: Cotton. **Minerals:** Uranium, salt. **Arable land:** 2%. **Fish catch** (1990): 115,000 metric tons. **Electricity prod.** (1991): 69 mln. kWh. **Labor force:** 85% agric.

Finance: Monetary unit: CFA franc (Mar. 1993: 273 = $1 US). **Gross domestic product** (1992): $1.0 bln. **Per capita GDP:** $190. **Imports** (1990): $264 mln.; partners: Fr. 47%. **Exports** (1990): $174 mln.; partners Fra. **International reserves less gold** (Jan. 1993): $74 mln. **Gold:** 11,000 oz t.

Transport: Motor vehicles: in use (1989): 8,000 passenger cars, 6,000 comm. vehicles.

Communications: Radios: 1 per 4.3 persons. **Telephones in use:** 1 per 555 persons.

Health: Life expectancy at birth (1992): 39 male; 41 female. **Births** (per 1,000 pop. 1992): 42. **Deaths** (per 1,000 pop. 1992): 22. **Natural increase:** 2.0%. **Hospital beds** (1980): 3.500. **Physicians** (1980): 94. **Infant mortality** (per 1,000 live births 1992): 136.

Education (1991): **Literacy:** 30%.

Major International Organizations: UN, (GATT, IMF, WHO), OAU, EEC.

Embassy: 2002 R St. NW 20009; 462-4009.

Chad was the site of paleolithic and neolithic cultures before the Sahara Desert formed. A succession of kingdoms and Arab slave traders dominated Chad until France took control around 1900. Independence came Aug. 11, 1960.

Northern Moslem rebels have fought animist and Christian southern government and French troops from 1966, despite numerous cease-fires and peace pacts.

Libyan troops entered the country at the request of the Chad government, December 1980. On Jan. 6, 1981, Libya and Chad announced their intention to unite. France together with several African nations condemned the agreement as a menace to African security. The Libyan troops were withdrawn from Chad in November 1981.

Rebel forces, led by Hissene Habre, captured the capital and forced Pres. Goukouni Oueddei to flee the country in June 1982.

In 1983, France sent some 3,000 troops to Chad to assist Habre in opposing Libyan-backed rebels. France and Libya agreed to a simultaneous withdrawal of troops from Chad in September 1984, but Libyan forces remained in the north until Mar. 1987 when Chad forces drove them from their last major stronghold. In Dec. 1990, Pres. Hissene Habre was overthrown by a Libyan-supported insurgent group, the Patriotic Salvation Movement. The group's leader, Idriss Deby, assumed the presidency.

Chile

Republic of Chile

República de Chile

People: Population (1992 est.): 13,528,000. **Age distrib.** (%): 0–14: 30.9 15–59: 60.4; 60+: 7.7. **Pop. density:** 44 per sq. mi. **Urban** (1990): 84%. **Ethnic groups:** Mestizo 66%, Spanish 25%, Indian 5%. **Languages:** Spanish. **Religions:** Roman Catholic 89%, Protestant 11%.

Geography: Area: 302,779 sq. mi., twice the size of California. **Location:** Occupies western coast of southern S. America. **Neighbors:** Peru on N, Bolivia on NE, Argentina on E. **Topography:** Andes Mtns. are on E border including some of the world's highest peaks; on W is 2,650-mile Pacific Coast. Width varies between 100 and 250 miles. In N is Atacama Desert, in center are agricultural regions, in S are forests and grazing lands. **Capital:** Santiago. **Cities** (1992 metro est.) Santiago 5,300,000.

Government: Type: Republic. **Head of state:** Pres. Patricio Aylwin Ozocar; b. Nov. 26, 1918; in office: Mar. 11, 1990. **Local divisions:** 13 regions. **Defense:** 3.4% of GNP (1991).

Economy: Industries: Fish processing, wood products, iron, steel. **Chief crops:** Grain, onions, beans, potatoes, peas, fruits. **Minerals:** Copper (about half of export revenues), molybdenum, nitrates, iodine (half world output), iron, coal, oil, gas, gold, cobalt, zinc, manganese, borate, mica, mercury, salt, sulphur, marble, onyx. **Other resources:** Water, forests. **Arable land:** 7%. **Livestock** (1990): cattle: 3.3 mln.; sheep: 6.5 mln.; pigs: 1.1 mln. **Fish catch** (1991): 6.1 mln. metric tons. **Electricity prod.** (1991): 21.4 bln. kWh. **Labor force:** 19% agric., forestry, fishing; 34% ind & comm., 30% serv.

Finance: Monetary unit: Peso (July 1993: 392 = $1 US). **Gross domestic product** (1991): $29.2 bln. **Per capita GDP** (1990): $2,200. **Imports** (1991): $7.6 bln.; partners: U.S. 19%, EC 23%. **Exports** (1991): $9.0 bln.; partners: EC 34%, U.S. 18%. **Tourism** (1990): $548 mln. receipts. **National budget** (1991): $8.3 bln. expenditures. **International reserves less gold** (Mar. 1993): $9.7 bln. **Gold:** 1.86 mln. oz. t. **Consumer prices** (change in 1992): 15.4%.

Transport: Railroads (1990): **Length:** 4,470 mi. **Motor vehicles:** in use (1989): 690,000 passenger cars, 300,000 comm. vehicles. **Civil aviation** (1990): 2.9 bln. passenger-km.; 17 airports with scheduled flights. **Chief ports:** Valparaiso, Arica, Antofagasta.

Communications: Television sets: 1 per 4.1 persons. **Radios:** 1 per 3.3 persons. **Telephones in use:** 1 per 16 persons.

Health: Life expectancy at birth (1992): 71 male; 77 female. **Births** (per 1,000 pop. 1992): 21. **Deaths** (per 1,000 pop. 1992): 6. **Natural increase:** 1.5%. **Hospital beds:** 1 per 304 persons. **Physicians:** 1 per 919 persons. **Infant mortality** (per 1,000 live births 1992): 18.

Education (1991): **Literacy:** 92%. Compulsory ages 6-14.

Major International Organizations: UN and all of its specialized agencies, OAS.

Embassy: 1732 Massachusetts Ave. NW 20036; 785-1746.

Northern Chile was under Inca rule before the Spanish conquest, 1536-40. The southern Araucanian Indians resisted until the late 19th century. Independence was gained 1810-18, under Jose de San Martin and Bernardo O'Higgins; the latter, as supreme director 1817-23, sought social and economic reforms until deposed. Chile defeated Peru and Bolivia in 1836-39 and 1879-84, gaining mineral-rich northern land.

Eduardo Frei Montalva came into office in 1964, instituting social programs and gradual nationalization of foreign-owned mining companies. In 1970, Salvador Allende Gossens, a Marxist, became president with a third of the national vote.

The Allende government furthered nationalizations and improved conditions for the poor. But illegal and violent actions by extremist supporters of the government, the regime's failure to attain majority support, and poorly planned socialist economic programs led to political and financial chaos.

A military junta seized power Sept. 11, 1973, and said Allende killed himself. The junta named a mostly military cabinet and announced plans to "exterminate Marxism."

Repression continued during the 1980s with little sign of any political liberalization. In a plebiscite held Oct. 5, 1988, voters rejected junta-candidate Gen. Augusto Pinochet Ugarte who, if victorious, would have governed Chile until 1997. Pinochet accepted the rejection and called for presidential elections. In Dec. 1989 voters removed Pinochet from office and elected Patricio Aylwin as president. A 1991 report documented more than 2,200 deaths that were a result of human rights violoations during Pinochet's rule.

Tierra del Fuego is the largest (18,800 sq. mi.) island in the archipelago of the same name at the southern tip of South America, an area of majestic mountains, tortuous channels, and high winds. It was discovered 1520 by Magellan and named the Land of Fire because of its many Indian bonfires. Part of the island is in Chile, part in Argentina. Punta Arenas, on a mainland peninsula, is a center of sheep raising and the world's southernmost city (pop. about 70,000); Puerto Williams is the southernmost settlement.

China

People's Republic of China

Zhonghua Renmin Gonghe Guo

People: Population (1992 est.): 1,169,619,000. **Pop. density:** 315 per sq. mi. **Urban** (1990): 27%. **Ethnic groups:** Han

Chinese 94%, Mongol, Korean, Manchu, others. **Languages:** Mandarin (official), Yue, Wu Hakka, Xiang, Gan, Min, Zhuang, Hui, Yi. **Religions:** officially atheist; Confucianism, Buddhism, Taoism are traditional.

Geography: Area: 3,696,100 sq. mi., slightly larger than the U.S. **Location:** Occupies most of the habitable mainland of E. Asia. **Neighbors:** Mongolia on N, Russia on NE and NW, Afghanistan, Pakistan, Tajikistan, Kazakhstan on W, India, Nepal, Bhutan, Myanmar, Laos, Vietnam on S, N. Korea on NE. **Topography:** Two-thirds of the vast territory is mountainous or desert, and only one-tenth is cultivated. Rolling topography rises to high elevations in the N in the Daxinganlingshanmai separating Manchuria and Mongolia; the Tienshan in Xinjiang; the Himalayan and Kunlunshanmai in the SW and in Tibet. Length is 1,860 mi. from N to S, width E to W is more than 2,000 mi. The eastern half of China is one of the best-watered lands in the world. Three great river systems, the Changjiang, the Huanghe, and the Xijiang provide water for vast farmlands. **Capital:** Beijing. **Cities** (1990 est.): Shanghai 7.7 mln.; Beijing 6.9 mln.; Tianjin 5.7 mln.; Canton 3.5 mln.; Shenyang 4.5 mln.; Wuhan 3.7 mln.

Government: Type: Communist Party led state. **Head of state:** Pres. Jiang Zemin; in office: Mar. 27, 1993. **Head of government:** Premier Li Peng; in office: Apr. 9, 1989. **Local divisions:** 22 provinces, 5 autonomous regions, and 3 cities. **Defense:** 3.0% of GNP (1992).

Economy: Industries: Iron and steel, textiles, agriculture implements, trucks. **Chief crops:** Grain, rice, cotton, tea. **Minerals:** tungsten, antimony, coal, iron, lead, manganese, molybdenum, tin. **Crude oil reserves** (1991): 30.8 bln. barrels. **Other resources:** Silk. **Arable land:** 11%. **Livestock** (1991): cattle: 81 mln.; pigs: 369 mln.; sheep: 112 mln. **Fish catch** (1990): 12.0 mln. metric tons. **Electricity prod.** (1991): 670 bln. kWh. **Crude steel prod.** (1991): 70.4 mln. metric tons. **Labor force:** 60% agric.; 25% ind. & comm.

Finance: Monetary unit: Yuan (July 1993): 5.71 = $1 US). **Gross national product** (1989): $393 bln. **Per capita GNP:** $360. **Imports** (1992): $76.3 bln.; partners: Jap. 20%, U.S. 11%, Hong Kong 20%. **Exports** (1992): $80.5 bln.; partners: Hong Kong 38%, Jap. 16%, U.S. 7%. **Tourism** (1991): $2.8 bln. receipts. **National budget** (1987): $66.1 bln. expenditures. **International reserves less gold** (Feb. 1993): $42.8 bln. **Gold:** 12.7 mln. oz t. **Consumer prices** (change in 1991): 2.1%.

Transport: Railroads (1990): **Length:** 41,973 mi. **Motor vehicles:** in use (1990): 1.6 mln. passenger cars, 4.1 mln. comm. vehicles. **Civil aviation** (1991): 30.1 bln. passenger km, 90 airports with scheduled flights. **Chief ports:** Shanghai, Qinhuangdao, Dalian, Canton.

Communications: Television sets: 1 per 8 persons. **Radios:** 1 per 9.1 persons. **Telephones:** 1 per 89 persons. **Daily newspaper circ.** (1989): 37 per 1,000 pop.

Health: Life expectancy at birth (1992): 69 male; 72 female. **Births** (per 1,000 pop. 1992): 22. **Deaths** (per 1,000 pop. 1992): 7. **Natural increase:** 1.5%. **Infant mortality** (per 1,000 live births 1992): 33. **Hospital beds:** 1 per 428 persons. **Physicians:** 1 per 646 persons.

Education (1987): **Literacy:** 70%. Years compulsory 9; first grade enrollment 93%.

Major International Organizations: UN (IMF, FAO, WHO).

Embassy: 2300 Conn. Ave. NW 20008; 328-2500.

History. Remains of various man-like creatures who lived as early as several hundred thousand years ago have been found in many parts of China. Neolithic agricultural settlements dotted the Huanghe basin from about 5,000 BC. Their language, religion, and art were the sources of later Chinese civilization.

Bronze metallurgy reached a peak and Chinese pictographic writing, similar to today's, was in use in the more developed culture of the Shang Dynasty (c. 1500 BC-c. 1000 BC) which ruled much of North China.

A succession of dynasties and interdynastic warring kingdoms ruled China for the next 3,000 years. They expanded Chinese political and cultural domination to the south and west, and developed a brilliant technologically and culturally advanced society. Rule by foreigners (Mongols in the Yuan Dynasty, 1271-1368, and Manchus in the Ch'ing Dynasty, 1644-1911) did not alter the underlying culture.

A period of relative stagnation left China vulnerable to internal and external pressures in the 19th century. Rebellions left tens of millions dead, and Russia, Japan, Britain, and other powers exercised political and economic control in large parts of the country. China became a republic Jan. 1, 1912, following the Wuchang Uprising inspired by Dr. Sun Yat-sen.

For a period of 50 years, 1894-1945, China was involved in conflicts with Japan. In 1895, China ceded Korea, Taiwan, and other areas. On Sept. 18, 1931, Japan seized the Northeastern Provinces (Manchuria) and set up a puppet state called Manchukuo. The border province of Jehol was cut off as a buffer state in 1933. Japan invaded China proper July 7, 1937. After its defeat in World War II, Japan gave up all seized land.

Following World War II, internal disturbances arose involving the Kuomintang, communists, and other factions. China came under domination of communist armies, 1949-1950. The Kuomintang government moved to Taiwan, 90 mi. off the mainland, Dec. 8, 1949.

The People's Republic of China was proclaimed in Peking Sept. 21, 1949, by the Chinese People's Political Consultative Conference under Mao Zedong.

China and the USSR signed a 30-year treaty of "friendship, alliance and mutual assistance," Feb. 15, 1950.

The U.S. refused recognition of the new regime. On Nov. 26, 1950, the People's Republic sent armies into Korea against U.S. troops and forced a stalemate.

By the 1960s, relations with the USSR deteriorated, with disagreements on borders, ideology and leadership of world communism. The USSR cancelled aid accords, and China, with Albania, launched anti-Soviet propaganda drives.

On Oct. 25, 1971, the UN General Assembly ousted the Taiwan government from the UN and seated the People's Republic in its place. The U.S. had supported the mainland's admission but opposed Taiwan's expulsion.

U.S. Pres. Nixon visited China Feb. 21-28, 1972, on invitation from Premier Zhou Enlai, ending years of antipathy between the 2 nations. China and the U.S. opened liaison offices in each other's capitals, May-June 1973. The U.S., Dec. 15, 1978, formally recognized the People's Republic of China as the sole legal government of China; diplomatic relations between the 2 nations were established, Jan. 1, 1979.

Internal developments. After an initial period of consolidation, 1949-52, industry, agriculture, and social and economic institutions were forcibly molded according to Maoist ideals. However, frequent drastic changes in policy and violent factionalism interfered with economic development.

In 1957, Mao Tse-tung admitted an estimated 800,000 people had been executed 1949-54; opponents claimed much higher figures.

The Great Leap Forward, 1958-60, tried to force the pace of economic development through intensive labor on huge new rural communes, and through emphasis on ideological purity and enthusiasm. The program caused resistance and was largely abandoned. Serious food shortages developed, and the government was forced to buy grain from the West.

The Great Proletarian Cultural Revolution, 1965, was an attempt to oppose pragmatism and bureaucratic power and instruct a new generation in revolutionary principles. Massive purges took place. A program of forcibly relocating millions of urban teenagers into the countryside was launched.

By 1968 the movement had run its course; many purged officials returned to office in subsequent years, and reforms in education and industry that had placed ideology above expertise were gradually weakened.

In a continuing "reassessment" of the policies of Mao Zedong, Mao's widow, Jiang Quing, and other Gang of Four members were convicted of "committing crimes during the 'Cultural Revolution,'" Jan. 25, 1981.

In the mid-1970s, factional and ideological fighting increased, and emerged into the open after the 1976 deaths of Mao and Premier Zhou Enlai. Mao's widow and 3 other leading leftists were purged and placed under arrest, after reportedly trying to seize power. The new ruling group modified Maoist policies in education, culture, and industry, and sought better ties with non-communist countries.

Relations with Vietnam deteriorated in 1978 as China charged persecution of ethnic Chinese. In retaliation for Vietnam's invasion of Cambodia, China attacked 4 Vietnamese border provinces Feb. 17, 1979; heavy border fighting ensued.

By the mid 1980's, China had enacted far-reaching economic reforms highlighted by the departure from rigid central planning and the stressing of market-oriented socialism.

Some 100,000 students and workers staged a march in Beijing to demand democratic reforms, May 4, 1989. The demonstrations continued during a visit to Beijing by Soviet leader Mikhail Gorbachev May 15-18. It was the first Sino-Soviet summit since 1959. A million people gathered in Beijing to demand democratic reforms and the removal of Deng and other leaders. There were protests in at least 20 other Chinese cities. Martial law was imposed, May 20, but was mostly ignored by the protesters.

Chinese army troops entered Beijing, June 3-4, and crushed the pro-democracy protests. Tanks and armored personnel carriers attacked Tiananmen Square, outside the Great Hall of the People, which was the main scene of the demonstrations and hunger strikes. It is estimated that 5,000 died, 10,000 were injured, and hundreds of students and workers arrested.

China's population, the world's largest, is still increasing, but with more couples following the government's one-child policy some experts predict that the nation's population will actually decline after peaking in the early 21st century.

Manchuria. Home of the Manchus, rulers of China 1644-1911, Manchuria has accommodated millions of Chinese settlers in the 20th century. Under Japanese rule 1931-45, the area became industrialized. China no longer uses the name Manchuria for the region, which is divided into the 3 NE provinces of Heilongjiang, Jilin, and Liaoning.

Guangxi is in SE China, bounded on N by Kweichow and Hunan provinces, E and S by Kwangtung, on SW by North Vietnam, and on W by Yunnan. It produces rice in the river valleys and has valuable forest products.

Inner Mongolia was organized by the People's Republic in 1947. Its boundaries have undergone frequent changes, reaching its greatest extent (and restored in 1979) in 1956, with an area of 454,000 sq. mi., allegedly in order to dilute the minority Mongol population. Chinese settlers outnumber the Mongols more than 10 to 1. Pop. (1990 cen.): 21.4 mln. Capital: Hohhot.

Xinjiang, in Central Asia, is 633,802 sq. mi., pop. (1990 cen.): 15.1 mln. (75% Uygurs, a Turkic Moslem group, with a heavy Chinese increase in recent years). Capital: Urumqi. It is China's richest region in strategic minerals.

Tibet, 470,000 sq. mi., is a thinly populated region of high plateaus and massive mountains, the Himalayas on the S, the Kunluns on the N. High passes connect with India and Nepal; roads lead into China proper. Capital: Lhasa. Average altitude is 15,000 ft. Jiachan, 15,870 ft., is believed to be the highest inhabited town on earth. Agriculture is primitive. Pop. (1990 cen.): 2.1 mln. (of whom about 500,000 are Chinese). Another 4 million Tibetans form the majority of the population of vast adjacent areas that have long been incorporated into China.

China ruled all of Tibet from the 18th century, but independence came in 1911. China reasserted control in 1951, and a communist government was installed in 1953, revising the theocratic Lamaist Buddhist rule. Serfdom was abolished, but all land remained collectivized.

A Tibetan uprising within China in 1956 spread to Tibet in 1959. The rebellion was crushed with Chinese troops, and Buddhism was almost totally suppressed. The Dalai Lama and 100,000 Tibetans fled to India.

Colombia

Republic of Colombia

República de Colombia

People: Population (1992 est.): 34,296,000. **Age distrib.** (%): 0–14: 36.1; 15–59: 57.8; 60+: 6.1. **Pop. density:** 77 per sq. mi. **Urban** (1983): 65.4%. **Ethnic groups:** Mestizo 58%, Caucasian 20%, Mulatto 14%. **Languages:** Spanish. **Religions:** Roman Catholic 95%.

Geography: Area: 439,735 sq. mi., about the size of Texas, and New Mexico combined. **Location:** At the NW corner of S. America. **Neighbors:** Panama on NW, Ecuador, Peru on S, Brazil, Venezuela on E. **Topography:** Three ranges of Andes, the Western, Central, and Eastern Cordilleras, run through the country from N to S. The eastern range consists mostly of high table lands, densely populated. The Magdalena R. rises in Andes, flows N to Carribean, through a rich alluvial plain. Sparsely-settled plains in E are drained by Orinoco and Amazon systems. **Capital:** Bogota. **Cities** (1992 est.): Bogota 4,921,000; Medellin 1,581,000; Cali 1,624,000; Barranquilla 1,018,000.

Government: Type: Republic. **Head of state:** Pres. Cesar Gaviria Trujillo; b. Mar. 31, 1947; in office: Aug. 7, 1990. **Local divisions:** 23 departments, 8 national territories, and special district of Bogota. **Defense:** 1.4% of GDP (1991).

Economy: Industries: Textiles, processed goods, hides, steel, cement, chemicals. **Chief crops:** Coffee (50% of exports), rice, corn, cotton, sugar, bananas. **Minerals:** Oil, gas, emeralds (90% world output), gold, copper, lead, coal, iron, nickel, salt. **Crude oil reserves** (1991): 1.8 bln. bbls. **Other resources:** Rubber, balsam, dye-woods, copaiba, hydro power. **Arable land:** 5%. **Livestock** (1990): cattle: 24.6 mln.; pigs: 2.6 mln.; sheep: 2.6 mln. **Fish catch** (1990): 101,000 metric tons. **Electricity prod.** (1991): 38 bln. kWh. **Labor force:** 30% agric.; 24% ind.; 46% services.

Finance: Currency: Peso (July 1993: 678 = $1 US). **Gross domestic product** (1990): $43 bln. **Per capita GDP:** $1,300. **Imports** (1991): $6.1 bln.; partners: U.S. 36%, EC 16%. **Exports** (1991): $7.5 bln.; partners: U.S. 40%, EC 21%. **Tourism** (1990): $362 mln. receipts. **National budget** (1989): $3.9 bln. expenditures. **International reserves less gold** (Mar. 1993): $7.3 bln. **Gold:** 539,000 oz t. **Consumer prices** (change in 1992): 27.0.

Transport: Railway traffic (1991): 179 mln. passenger-km. **Motor vehicles:** in use (1989): 936,000 passenger cars, 364,000. **Civil aviation** (1991): 4.5 bln. passenger-km; airports with scheduled flights: 63. **Chief ports:** Buena Ventura, Santa Marta, Barranquilla, Cartagena.

Communications: Television sets: 1 per 5.6 persons. **Radios:** 1 per 7.3 persons. **Telephones:** 1 per 13 persons. **Daily newspaper circ.** (1992): 23 per 1,000 pop.

Health: Life expectancy at birth (1992): 69 male; 74 female. **Births** (per 1,000 pop. 1992): 24. **Deaths** (per 1,000 pop. 1992): 5. **Natural increase:** 1.9%. **Physicians:** 1 per 1,079 persons. **Infant mortality** (per 1,000 live births 1991): 37%.

Education (1990): **Literacy:** 80%. Only 28% finish primary school.

Major International Organizations: UN (World Bank, GATT), OAS.

Embassy: 2118 Leroy Pl. NW, 20008; 387-8338.

Spain subdued the local Indian kingdoms (Funza, Tunja) by the 1530s and ruled Colombia and neighboring areas as New Granada for 300 years. Independence was won by 1819. Venezuela and Ecuador broke away in 1829-30, and Panama withdrew in 1903.

One of the Latin American democracies, Colombia is plagued by rural and urban violence, though scaled down from "La Violencia" of 1948-58, which claimed 200,000 lives. Attempts at land and social reform and progress in industrialization have not succeeded in reducing massive social problems aggravated by a very high birth rate. In 1989, the government's increased activity against local drug traffickers sparked a series of retaliation killings. On Aug. 18, Luis Carlos Galán, the ruling party's presidential hopeful in the 1990 election, was assassinated. In 1990, 2 other presidential candidates were slain as the drug traffickers carried on a campaign of intimidation to stop the presidential election. Cesar Gaviria Trujillo, a strong advocate of maintaining the government's war against the nation's drug cartels, was elected president in May. His popularity greatly declined in 1992 when a drug boss escaped from prison in July, allegedly with aid from the military and prison officials, and the drug industry continued to grow.

Comoros

Federal Islamic Republic of the Comoros

Jumhurīyat al-Qumur al-Itthādīyah al-Islāmīyah

People: Population (1992 est.): 493,000. **Pop. density:** 588 per sq. mi. **Ethnic groups:** Arabs, Africans, East Indians. **Languages:** Arabic, French (both official). **Religions:** Sunni Moslem 86%, Roman Catholic 14%.

Geography: Area: 838 sq. mi., half the size of Delaware. **Location:** 3 islands (Grande Comore, Anjouan, and Moheli) in the Mozambique Channel between NW Madagascar and SE Africa. **Neighbors:** Nearest are Mozambique on W, Madagascar on E. **Topography:** The islands are of volcanic origin, with an active volcano on Grand Comoro. **Capital:** Moroni. **Cities** (1992 est.): Moroni (met.) 30,000.

Government: Type: Republic. **Head of state:** Pres. Said Mohammed Djohar; in office: Nov. 26, 1989. **Local divisions:** each of the 3 main islands is a prefecture.

Economy: Industries: Perfume. **Chief crops:** Vanilla, copra, perfume plants, fruits. **Arable land:** 35%. **Electricity prod.** (1991): 24 mln. kWh. **Labor force:** 80% agric.

Finance: Monetary unit: CFA franc (Mar. 1993: 273 = $1 US). **Gross domestic product** (1991): $260 mln. **Per capita GDP:** $540. **Imports** (1990): $41 mln.; partners: Fr. 22%. **Exports** (1990): $16 mln.; partners: Fr. 41%, U.S. 53%.

Transport: Chief ports: Dzaoudzi.

Communications: Radios: 1 per 9 persons. **Telephones in use:** 1 per 132 persons.

Health: Life expectancy at birth (1992): 55 male; 59 female. **Births** (per 1,000 pop. 1992): 47. **Deaths** (per 1,000 pop. 1992): 13. **Natural increase:** 3.5%. **Infant mortality** (per 1,000 live births 1992): 84.

Education: (1989): **Literacy:** 15%; less than 20% attend secondary school.

Major International Organizations: UN (IMF, World Bank); OAU.

Embassy: 336 E. 45th St., New York, NY 10017; (212) 972-8010.

The islands were controlled by Moslem sultans until the French acquired them 1841-1909. They became a French overseas territory in 1947. A 1974 referendum favored independence, with only the Christian island of Mayotte preferring association with France. The French National Assembly decided to allow each of the islands to decide its own fate. The Comoro Chamber of Deputies declared independence July 6, 1975, with Ahmed Abdallah as president. In a referendum in 1976, Mayotte voted to remain French. A leftist regime that seized power from Abdallah in 1975 was deposed in a pro-French 1978 coup in which he regained the presidency.

In Nov. 1989, Pres. Abdallah was assassinated.

Congo

Republic of Congo

République du Congo

People: Population (1992 est.): 2,376,000. **Pop. density:** 17 per sq. mi. **Urban** (1990): 41%. **Ethnic groups:** Bakongo 45%, Bateke 20%, others. **Languages:** French (official), Kongo, Teke. **Religions:** Christians 50% (two-thirds Roman Catholic), animists 47%, Moslem 2%.

Geography: Area: 132,046 sq. mi., slightly smaller than Montana. **Location:** In western central Africa. **Neighbors:** Gabon, Cameroon on W, Central African Republic on N, Zaire on E, Angola on SW. **Topography:** Much of the Congo is covered by thick forests. A coastal plain leads to the fertile Niari Valley. The center is a plateau; the Congo R. basin consists of flood plains in the lower and savanna in the upper portion. **Capital:** Brazzaville. **Cities** (1992 est.): Brazzaville (met.) 937,000; Pointe-Noire 576,000; Loubomo 83,000.

Government: Type: Democracy. **Head of state:** Pres. Pascal Lissouba; in office: Aug. 20, 1992. **Head of government:** Prime Min. Claude Antoine Dacosta; in office: Dec. 6, 1992. **Local divisions:** 9 regions and capital district. **Defense:** 4.6% of GNP (1987).

Economy: Chief crops: Palm oil and kernels, cocoa, coffee, tobacco. **Minerals:** Gold, lead, copper, zinc. **Crude oil reserves** (1988): 750 mln. bbls. **Arable land:** 2%. **Fish catch** (1989): 19,000 metric tons. **Electricity prod.** (1991): 315 mln. kWh. **Labor force:** 90% agric.

Finance: Monetary unit: CFA franc (Mar. 1993: 273 = $1 US). **Gross domestic product** (1990): $2.4 bln. **Per capita GDP:** $1,070. **Imports** (1990): $621 mln.; partners: Fr. 52%. **Exports** (1990): $981 mln.; partners: U.S. 45%, Fr. 15%. **Tourism** (1990): $7 mln. receipts. **International reserves less gold** (Jan. 1993): $4.1 mln. **Gold:** 11,000 oz t.

Transport: Railroads (1989): **Length:** 494 mi. **Motor vehicles:** in use (1989): 26,000 passenger cars, 20,000 comm. vehicles. **Chief ports:** Pointe-Noire, Brazzaville.

Communications: Television sets: 1 per 402 persons. **Radios:** 1 per 9.4 persons. **Telephones in use:** 1 per 111 persons.

Health: Life expectancy at birth (1992): 52 male; 56 female. **Births** (per 1,000 pop. 1992): 43. **Deaths** (per 1,000 pop. 1992): 13. **Natural increase:** 3.0%. **Hospital beds:** 1 per 456 persons. **Physicians:** 1 per 3,873 persons. **Infant mortality** (per 1,000 live births 1992): 110.

Education (1991): **Literacy:** 57%. Years compulsory 10; attendance 80%.

Major International Organizations: UN (GATT, IMF, WHO), OAU.

Embassy: 4891 Colorado Ave. NW 20011; 726-5500.

The Loango Kingdom flourished in the 15th century, as did the Anzico Kingdom of the Batekes; by the late 17th century they had become weakened. France established control by 1885. Independence came Aug. 15, 1960.

After a 1963 coup sparked by trade unions, the country adopted a Marxist-Leninist stance, with the USSR and China vying for influence. France remained a dominant trade partner and source of technical assistance, and French-owned private enterprise retained a major economic role. However, the government of Pres. Denis Sassou-Nguesso favored a strengthening of relations with the USSR; a socialist constitution was adopted, 1979.

In 1990, Marxism was renounced and opposition parties legalized. In 1991 the country's name was changed to Republic of Congo, and a new constitution was approved.

Costa Rica

Republic of Costa Rica

República de Costa Rica

People: Population (1992 est.): 3,187,000. **Age distrib.** (%): 0–14: 36.2; 15–49: 57.4; 50+: 6.4. **Pop. density:** 162 per sq. mi. **Urban** (1991): 50%. **Ethnic groups:** Spanish (with Mestizo minority). **Language:** Spanish (official). **Religions:** Roman Catholic 95%.

Geography: Area: 19,652 sq. mi., smaller than W. Virginia. **Location:** In central America. **Neighbors:** Nicaragua on N, Panama on S. **Topography:** Lowlands by the Caribbean are tropical. The interior plateau, with an altitude of about 4,000 ft., is temperate. **Capital:** San Jose. **Cities** (1992 met. est.): San Jose 890,000.

Government: Type: Democratic republic. **Head of state:** Pres. Rafael Angel Calderon; b. 1949; in office May 8, 1990. **Local divisions:** 7 provinces.

Economy: Industries: Furniture, food processing, aluminum, textiles, fertilizers, roofing, cement. **Chief crops:** Coffee (chief export), bananas, sugar, cocoa, cotton, hemp. **Minerals:** Gold, salt, sulphur, iron. **Other resources:** Fish, forests. **Arable land:** 12%. **Livestock** (1991): cattle: 1.7. mln. **Fish catch** (1990): 20,000 metric tons. **Electricity prod.** (1990): 2.9 bln. kWh. **Labor force:** 32% agric.; 25% ind. & comm.; 38% service and government.

Finance: Monetary unit: Colones (Mar. 1993: 138 = $1 US). **Gross domestic product** (1991): $5.6 bln. **Per capita GDP:** $1,810. **Imports** (1992): $2.5 bln.; partners: U.S. 38%, CACM 10%, Jap. 10%. **Exports** (1992): $1.8 bln.; partners: U.S. 45%, CACM 18%. **Tourism** (1989): receipts: $206 mln. **National budget** (1990): $1.0 bln. expenditures. **International reserves less gold** (Mar. 1993): $1.0 bln. **Gold:** 35,000 oz t. **Consumer prices** (change in 1992): 28.7%.

Transport: Motor vehicles: in use (1990): 168,000 passenger cars, 94,000 comm. vehicles. **Civil aviation** (1991): 1.0 bln. passenger-km; 9 airports with scheduled flights. **Chief ports:** Limon, Puntarenas, Golfito.

Communications: Television sets: 1 per 4.9 persons. **Radios:** 1 per 11 persons. **Telephones:** 1 per 6.9 persons. **Daily newspaper circ.** (1990): 110 per 1,000 pop.

Health: Life expectancy at birth (1992): 75 male; 79 female. **Births** (per 1,000 pop. 1992): 27. **Deaths** (per 1,000 pop. 1992): 4. **Natural increase:** 2.3%. **Hospital beds:** 1 per 454 persons. **Physicians:** 1 per 798 persons. **Infant mortality** (per 1,000 live births 1992): 12.

Education (1992): **Literacy:** 93%. Years compulsory 6; attendance 99%.

Major International Organizations: UN (FAO, ILO, IMF, WHO), OAS.

Embassy: 1825 Connecticut Ave. NW, 20009; 234-2945.

Guaymi Indians inhabited the area when Spaniards arrived, 1502. Independence came in 1821. Costa Rica seceded from the Central American Federation in 1838. Since the civil war of 1948-49, there has been little violent social conflict, and free political institutions have been preserved.

An earthquake in Apr. 1991 damaged the banana industry and shut down the port of Limon, adding pressure to a floundering economy.

Costa Rica, though still a largely agricultural country, has achieved a relatively high standard of living and social services, and land ownership is widespread, despite a troubled economy.

Côte d'Ivoire

Ivory Coast

République de la Côte d'Ivoire

People: Population (1992 est.): 13,497,000. **Age distrib.** (%): 0–14: 48.2; 15–59: 45.2; 60+: 6.6. **Pop. density:** 104 per sq. mi. **Urban** (1990): 40%. **Ethnic groups:** Baule 23%, Bete 18%, Senufo 15%, Malinke 11%, over 60 tribes. **Languages:** French (official), Akan, Kru, Voltaic, Malinke. **Religions:** Moslem 25%, Christian 12%, indigenous 63%.

Geography: Area: 124,503 sq. mi., slightly larger than New Mexico. **Location:** On S. coast of W. Africa. **Neighbors:** Liberia, Guinea on W, Mali, Burkina Faso on N, Ghana on E. **Topography:** Forests cover the W half of the country, and range from a coastal strip to halfway to the N on the E. A sparse inland plain leads to low mountains in NW. **Capital:** Yamoussoukro (official); Abidjan (de facto). **Cities** (1990 est.): Abidjan 2.7 mln.

Government: Type: Republic. **Head of state:** Pres. Felix Houphouet-Boigny; b. Oct. 18, 1905; in office: Aug. 7, 1960. **Head of government:** Prime Min. Alassane Ouattara. **Local divisions:** 49 departments.

Economy: Chief crops: Coffee, cocoa. **Minerals:** Diamonds, manganese. **Other resources:** Timber, rubber, petroleum. **Arable land:** 9%. **Livestock** (1990): goats: 1.5 mln.; sheep: 1.5 mln.; cattle: 991,000. **Fish catch** (1990): 108,000 metric tons. **Electricity prod.** (1991): 2.6 bln. kWh. **Labor force:** 85% agric., forestry.

Finance: Monetary unit: CFA franc (Mar. 1993: 273 = $1 US). **Gross domestic product** (1990): $10 bln. **Per capita GDP:** $800. **Imports** (1989): $2.1 bln.; partners: Fr. 31%, Jap. 5%, U.S. 5%. **Exports** (1989): $2.8 bln.; partners: Fr. 14%, Neth. 19%, U.S. 11%, It. 8%. **Tourism** (1990): $48 mln. receipts; **International reserves less gold** (Jan. 1993): $6.9 mln. **Gold:** 45,000 oz t. **Consumer prices** (changed in 1992): 3.5%.

Transport: Railroads (1990): **Length:** 600 km. **Motor vehicles:** in use (1989): 168,000 passenger cars, 90,000 comm. vehicles. **Chief ports:** Abidjan, Sassandra.

Communications: Television sets: 1 per 15 persons. **Radios:** 1 per 8.1 persons. **Telephones:** 1 per 143 persons. **Daily newspaper circ.** (1990): 12 per 1,000 pop.

Health: Life expectancy at birth (1992): 53 male; 57 female. **Births** (per 1,000 pop. 1992): 48. **Deaths** (per 1,000 pop. 1992): 12. **Natural increase:** 3.6%. **Hospital beds** (1982): 10,062. **Physicians** (1982): 502. **Infant mortality** (per 1,000 live births 1992): 94.

Education (1990): **Literacy:** 45%. **Years compulsory:** none; attendance 75%.

Major International Organizations: UN and all of its specialized agencies, OAU.

Embassy: 2424 Massachusetts Ave. NW 20008; 483-2400.

A French protectorate from 1842, Côte D'Ivoire became independent in 1960. It is the most prosperous of the tropical African nations, due to diversification of agriculture for export, close ties to France, and encouragement of foreign investment. About 20% of the population are workers from neighboring countries. Côte D'Ivoire officially changed its name from Ivory Coast in Oct. 1985.

Students and workers protested, Feb. 1990, demanding the ouster of Pres. Houphouet-Boigny and multiparty democracy. Côte D'Ivoire held its first multiparty presidential election in Oct. 1990.

Croatia

Republic of Croatia

Republika Hrvatska

People: Population (1992 est.): 4,784,000. **Pop. density:** 219 per sq. mi. **Ethnic groups:** Croatian 78%, Serbian 12%. **Language:** Croatian. **Religion:** Roman Catholic 77%.

Geography: Area: 21,829 sq. mi., slightly smaller than W. Virginia. **Location:** in SE Europe. **Neighbors:** Slovenia, Bosnia and Herzegovina, Hungary, Yugoslavia, and the Adriatic Sea. Over 33 percent is forested. **Capital:** Zagreb.

Government: Type: Parliamentary democracy. **Head of state:** Pres. Franjo Tudjman; b. 1922; in office: May 1990. **Head of government:** Prime Min. Hryoje Sarinic; in office: Sept. 8, 1992. **Local divisions:** 102 districts.

Economy: Industries: Textiles, chemicals, aluminum prods., paper. **Chief crops:** Olives, wine. **Minerals:** Bauxite, copper, coal. **Arable land:** 32%. **Electricity prod.** (1991): 8.8 mln. kWh.

Finance: Monetary unit: Croatian Dinar (Jan. 1993: 365 = $1 US). **Gross domestic product** (1991): $26.3 bln. **Per capita GDP:** $5,600. **Imports** (1990): $4.4 bln. **Exports** (1990): 2.9 bln.

Transport: Motor vehicles: in use (1990): 865,000 passenger cars, 72,000 commercial vehicles.

Communications: Television sets: 1 per 4 persons. **Radios:** 1 per 4 persons. **Telephones:** 1 per 4 persons. **Newspaper circ.** (1990): 150 per 1,000 pop.

Health: Life expectancy at birth (1990): 67 male; 74 female. **Births** (per 1,000 pop. 1992): 12. **Deaths** (per 1,000 pop. 1992): 11. Physicians: 1 per 466 persons. **Hospital beds:** 1 per 133 persons. **Infant mortality** (per 1,000 live births 1990): 10.

Education (1991): **Literacy:** 96%.

International Organizations: UN.

From the 7th century the area was inhabited by Croats, a south Slavic people. It was formed into a kingdom under Tomislav in 924, and joined with Hungary in 1102. The Croats became westernized and separated from Slavs under Serbian influence. The Croats retained autonomy under the Hungarian crown. Slavonia was taken by Turks in the 16th century, the northern part was restored by the Treaty of Karlowitz in 1699. Croatia helped Austria put down the Hungarian revolution 1848-49 and as a result was set up with Slavonia as the separate Austrian crownland of Croatia and Slavonia, which was reunited to Hungary as part of *Ausgleich* in 1867. It united with other Yugoslav areas to proclaim the kingdom of Serbs, Croats, and Slovenes in 1918. At the reorganization of Yugoslavia in 1929, Croatia and Slavonia became Savska co., which in 1939 was united with Primorje co. to form the county of Croatia. A nominally independent state between 1941-45, it became a constituent republic in the 1946 constitution.

On June 25, 1991, Croatia declared independence from Yugoslavia. Fighting began between ethnic Serbs and Croats. There were clashes between Croats and Yugoslavian army units and their Serb supporters. Croatia was granted EC recognition Jan. 15, 1992. Fighting continued in 1992 and 1993 as some 30% of Croatia's territory remained under Serbian control.

Cuba

Republic of Cuba

República de Cuba

People: Population (1992 est.): 10,846,000. **Age distrib.** (%): 0-under 15: 23.3; 15–59: 64.9; 60+: 11.8. **Pop. density:** 245 per sq. mi. **Urban** (1991): 72%. **Ethnic groups:** Spanish, African. **Languages:** Spanish. **Religions:** Roman Catholic 42%, none 49%.

Geography: Area: 44,218 sq. mi., nearly as large as Pennsylvania. **Location:** Westernmost of West Indies. **Neighbors:** Bahamas, U.S., on N, Mexico on W, Jamaica on S, Haiti on E. **Topography:** The coastline is about 2,500 miles. The N coast is steep and rocky, the S coast low and marshy. Low hills and fertile valleys cover more than half the country. Sierra Maestra, in the E is the highest of 3 mountain ranges. **Capital:** Havana. **Cities** (1989 est.): Havana 2,077,000; Santiago de Cuba 397,000; Camaguey 274,000.

Government: Type: Communist state. **Head of state:** Pres. Fidel Castro Ruz; b. Aug. 13, 1926; in office: Dec. 3, 1976 (formerly Prime Min. since Feb. 16, 1959). **Local divisions:** 14 provinces, Havana. **Defense:** 6.0% of GNP (1989).

Economy: Industries: Cement, food processing, sugar. **Chief crops:** Sugar (75% of exports), tobacco, rice, coffee, tropical fruit. **Minerals:** Cobalt, nickel, iron, copper, manganese, salt. **Other resources:** Forests. **Arable land:** 29%. **Livestock** (1991): cattle: 4.9 mln.; pigs: 1.9 mln. **Fish catch** (1991): 188,000 metric tons. **Electricity prod.** (1991): 16.2 bln. kWh. **Labor force:** 20% agric.; 33% ind. & comm.; 30% services & govt.

Finance: Monetary unit: Peso (Dec. 1992: .76 peso = $1.00 US). **Gross social product:** economic measure not convertible to GNP. **Per capita income** (1990): $2,644. **Imports** (1991): $3.7 bln. **Exports** (1991): $3.6 bln. **Tourism** (1990): $250 mln. revenues. **National budget** (1990): $14.4 bln. expenditures.

Transport: Railroads (1989): **Length:** 3,009 mi. **Motor vehicles:** in use (1988): 241,000 passenger cars, 208,000 comm. vehicles. **Civil aviation** (1991): 3.1 bln. passenger-km.; 11 airports with scheduled flights. **Chief ports:** Havana, Matanzas, Cienfuegos, Santiago de Cuba.

Communications: Television sets: 1 per 5 persons. **Radios:** 1 per 3 persons. **Telephones in use:** 1 per 19 persons. **Daily newspaper circ.** (1988): 155 per 1,000 pop.

Health: Life expectancy at birth: (1992): 74 male; 79 female. **Births** (per 1,000 pop. 1992): 18. **Deaths** (per 1,000 pop. 1992): 7. **Natural increase:** 1.1%. **Hospital beds:** 1 per 141 persons. **Physicians:** 1 per 303 persons. **Infant mortality** (per 1,000 live births 1992): 12.

Education (1992): **Literacy:** 99%. 92% of those between ages 6–14 attend school.

Major International Organizations: UN (UNESCO, WHO).

Some 50,000 Indians lived in Cuba when it was reached by Columbus in 1492. Its name derives from the Indian Cubanacan. Except for British occupation of Havana, 1762-63, Cuba remained Spanish until 1898. A slave-based sugar plantation economy developed from the 18th century, aided by early mechanization of milling. Sugar remains the chief product and chief export despite government attempts to diversify.

A ten-year uprising ended in 1878 with guarantees of rights by Spain, which Spain failed to carry out. A full-scale movement under Jose Marti began Feb. 24, 1895.

The U.S. declared war on Spain in April, 1898, after the sinking of the U.S.S. Maine in Havana harbor, and defeated it in the Spanish-American War. Spain gave up all claims to Cuba. U.S. troops withdrew in 1902, but under 1903 and 1934 agreements, the U.S. leases a site at Guantanamo Bay in the SE as a naval base. U.S. and other foreign investments acquired a dominant role in the economy. In 1952, former president Fulgencio Batista seized control and established a dictatorship, which grew increasingly harsh and corrupt. Fidel Castro assembled a rebel band in 1956; guerrilla fighting intensified in 1958. Batista fled Jan. 1, 1959, and in the resulting political vacuum Castro took power, becoming premier Feb. 16.

The government began a program of sweeping economic and social changes, without restoring promised liberties. Opponents were imprisoned and some were executed. Some 700,000 Cubans emigrated in the years after the Castro takeover, mostly to the U.S.

Cattle and tobacco lands were nationalized, while a system of cooperatives was instituted. By 1960 all banks and industrial companies had been nationalized, including over $1 billion worth of U.S.-owned properties, mostly without compensation.

Poor sugar crops resulted in collectivization of farms, stringent labor controls, and rationing, despite continued aid from the USSR and other communist countries.

The U.S. imposed an export embargo in 1962, severely damaging the economy. In 1961, some 1,400 Cubans, trained and backed by the U.S. Central Intelligence Agency, unsuccessfully tried to invade and overthrow the regime.

In the fall of 1962, the U.S. learned that the USSR had brought nuclear missiles to Cuba. After an Oct. 22 warning from Pres. Kennedy, the missiles were removed.

In 1977, Cuba and the U.S. signed agreements to exchange diplomats, without restoring full ties, and to regulate offshore fishing. In 1978, and again in 1980, the U.S. agreed to accept political prisoners released by Cuba some of whom, it was later discovered, were criminals and mental patients. A 1987 agreement provided for 20,000 Cubans to immigrate to the U.S. each year; Cuba agreed to take back some 2,500 jailed in the U.S. since the 1980 Mariel boat lift.

In 1975-78, Cuba sent troops to aid one faction in the Angola civil war. All Cuban troops were withdrawn by May 1991. Cuba's involvement in Central America, Africa, and the Caribbean contributed to poor relations with the U.S.

In 1983, 24 Cubans died and over 700 were captured, later repatriated, as a result of the U.S.-led invasion of Grenada.

Cuba resisted the social and economic reforms that took place in the late 1980s and 1990s in the Soviet Union and its successor states and in Eastern Europe. The nation, whose economy had been heavily dependent on the Soviet Union, suffered severe economic difficulties in the 1990s. A mystery illness of epidemic proportions struck Cuba in 1993. Over 43,000 people were diagnosed with the illness which caused vision loss and impaired coordination.

Cyprus

Republic of Cyprus

Kypriaki Dimokratia (Greek)
Kibris Cumhuriyeti (Turkish)

People: Population (1992 est.): 716,000. **Age distrib.** (%): 0–14: 25.4; 15–59: 60.4; 60+: 14.2. **Pop. density:** 200 per sq. mi. **Urban** (1991): 69%. **Ethnic groups:** Greeks 78%, Turks 18.7%, Armenians, Maronites. **Languages:** Greek, Turkish (both official), English. **Religions:** Orthodox 77%, Moslems 18%.

Geography: Area: 3,572 sq. mi., smaller than Connecticut. **Location:** In eastern Mediterranean Sea, off Turkish coast. **Neighbors:** Nearest are Turkey on N, Syria, Lebanon on E. **Topography:** Two mountain ranges run E-W, separated by a wide, fertile plain. **Capital:** Nicosia. **Cities** (1992 est.): Nicosia 166,000.

Government: Type: Republic. **Head of state:** Pres. Glafcos Clerides; in office: Mar. 1, 1993. **Local divisions:** 6 districts. **Defense:** 5.0% of GDP (1990).

Economy: Industries: Light manuf. **Chief crops:** Grains, grapes, carobs, citrus fruits, potatoes, olives. **Minerals:** Copper, pyrites, asbetos. **Arable land:** 40%. **Electricity prod.** (1990): 1.6 mln. kWh. **Labor force:** 21% agric.; 20% ind., 18% comm., 19% serv.

Finance: Monetary unit: Pound (Mar. 1993: 1.00 = $2.05 US). **Gross domestic product** (1990): $5.3 bln. **Per capita GDP:** $7,585. **Imports** (1991): $2.2 bln.; partners: UK 13%, Itl. 12%. **Exports** (1991): $838 mln.; partners: UK 21%, Libya 9%. **Tourism** (1991): receipts: $990 mln. **National budget** (1991): $2.0 bln. expenditures. **International reserves less gold** (Mar. 1993): $1.1 bln. **Gold:** 459,000 oz. t. **Consumer prices** (change in 1992): 6.5%.

Transport: Motor vehicles: in use (1989): 159,000 passenger cars, 54,000 comm. vehicles. **Civil aviation** (1991): 2.2 bln. passenger-km; one airport. **Chief ports:** Famagusta, Limassol.

Communications: Television sets: 1 per 3.4 persons. **Radios:** 1 per 2.7 persons. **Telephones:** 1 per 2.0 persons. **Daily newspaper circ.** (1991): 161 per 1,000 pop.

Health: Life expectancy at birth (1992): 74 male; 78 female. **Births** (per 1,000 pop. 1992): 18. **Deaths** (per 1,000 pop. 1992): 8. **Natural increase:** 1.0%. **Hospital beds:** 1 per 165 persons. **Physicians:** 1 per 480 persons. **Infant mortality** (per 1,000 live births 1992): 10.

Education (1991): **Literacy:** 95%. **Years compulsory:** 9; attendance 99%.

Major International Organizations: UN (GATT, IMF, WHO), Commonwealth of Nations, EC (Assoc.).

Embassy: 2211 R St. NW, 20008; 462-5772.

Agitation for enosis (union) with Greece increased after World War II, with the Turkish minority opposed, and broke into violence in 1955-56. In 1959, Britain, Greece, Turkey, and Cypriot leaders approved a plan for an independent republic, with constitutional guarantees for the Turkish minority and permanent division of offices on an ethnic basis. Greek and Turkish Communal Chambers dealt with religion, education, and other matters.

Archbishop Makarios III, formerly the leader of the enosis movement, was elected president, and full independence became final Aug. 16, 1960. Makarios was reelected in 1968 and 1973.

Further communal strife led the United Nations to send a peacekeeping force in 1964; its mandate has been repeatedly renewed.

The Cypriot National Guard, led by officers from the army of Greece, seized the government July 15, 1974. Makarios fled the country. On July 20, Turkey invaded the island; Greece mobilized its forces but did not intervene. A cease-fire was arranged July 22. A peace conference collapsed Aug. 14; fighting resumed. By Aug. 16, Turkish forces had occupied the NE 40% of the island, despite the presence of UN peacekeeping forces. Makarios resumed the presidency in Dec., until his death in 1977.

Turkish Cypriots voted overwhelmingly, June 8, 1975, to form a separate Turkish Cypriot federated state. A president and assembly were elected in 1976. Some 200,000 Greeks have been expelled from the Turkish-controlled area, replaced by thousands of Turks, some from the mainland.

Turkish Republic of Northern Cyprus

A declaration of independence was announced by Turkish-Cypriot leader Rauf Denktash, Nov. 15, 1983. The new state is not internationally recognized although it does have trade relations with some countries. TRNC contains 1,295 sq mi., pop. (1992 est.): 176,000, 99% Turkish.

Czech Republic

(Figures prior to 1992 are for the Czech and Slovak Federal Republic)

People: Population (1992 est.): 10,400,000. **Age distrib.** (1990) (%): 0–14: 22.5; 15–59: 60.8; 60+: 16.7. **Pop. density:** 342 per sq. mi. **Urban** (1990): 73%. **Ethnic groups:** Czechs 94%, Slovaks 4%. **Language:** Czech.

Geography: Area: 30,449 sq. mi. **Location:** In E central Europe. **Neighbors:** Poland on N, Germany on N, W, Austria on S, Slovakia on E, SE. **Topography:** Bohemia, in W, is a plateau surrounded by mountains; Moravia is hilly. **Capital:** Prague. **Cities** (1992 est.): Prague 1.2 mln.; Brno 391,000; Ostrava 331,000.

Government: Type: Republic. **Head of state:** Vaclav Havel; b. Oct. 5, 1936; in office: Feb. 15, 1993. **Head of government:** Prime Min. Jan Strasky; in office: July 3, 1992. **Defense:** 6.8% of GNP (1987).

Economy: Industries: Machinery, oil products, iron and steel, glass, chemicals, motor vehicles, cement. **Chief crops:** Wheat, sugar beets, potatoes, rye, corn, barley. **Minerals:** coke, coal, iron. **Livestock:** (1989): cattle: 5 mln.; pigs: 7 mln.; sheep: 1 mln. **Electricity prod.** (1991): 89.0 bln. kWh. **Crude steel prod.** (1991): 12.0 mln. metric tons. **Labor force:** 12% agric.; 37% ind.; 22% service, govt.

Finance: Monetary unit: Koruna (Aug. 1993: 29.43 = $1 US). **Gross domestic product** (1990): $120 bln. **Per capita GDP:** $7,700. **Imports** (1991): $10.4 bln.; partners: USSR 31%, Ger. 19%, Pol. 6%. **Exports** (1991): $10.8 bln.; partners: USSR 35%, Ger. 7%, Pol. 7%. **Tourism** (1989): $689 mln. receipts. **National budget** (1991): $16.8 bln. expenditures. **International reserves less gold** (Mar. 1993): $1.1 bln. **Gold:** 3.2 mln. oz t. **Consumer prices** (change in 1992): 8.2%.

Transport: Railroads (1990): **Length:** 8,142 mi. **Motor vehicles:** in use (1989): 3.1 mln. passenger cars, 327,000 comm. **Civil aviation** (1989): 2.2 bln. passenger-km.; 8 airports.

Communications: Television sets: 1 per 2.7 persons. **Radios:** 1 per 3.3 persons. **Telephones:** 1 per 3.9 persons. **Daily newspaper circ.** (1990): 327 per 1,000 pop.

Health: Life expectancy at birth (1992): 69 male; 77 female. **Births** (per 1,000 pop. 1991): 14. **Deaths** (per 1,000 pop. 1991): 12. **Natural increase:** .2%. **Hospital beds:** 1 per 99 persons; **Physicians:** 1 per 317 persons. **Infant mortality** (per 1,000 live births 1991): 11.

Education (1992): **Literacy:** 99%.

Major International Organizations: UN (GATT, WHO).

Embassy: 3900 Linnean Ave. NW 20008; 263-6315.

Bohemia and Moravia were part of the Great Moravian Empire in the 9th century and later became part of the Holy Roman Empire. Under the kings of Bohemia, Prague in the 14th century was the cultural center of Central Europe. Bohemia and Hungary became part of Austria-Hungary.

In 1914-18 Thomas G. Masaryk and Eduard Benes formed a provisional government with the support of Slovak leaders including Milan Stefanik. They proclaimed the Republic of Czechoslovakia Oct. 28, 1918.

Czechoslovakia

By 1938 Nazi Germany had worked up disaffection among German-speaking citizens in Sudetenland and demanded its cession. Prime Min. Neville Chamberlain of Britain, with the acquiescence of France, signed with Hitler at Munich, Sept. 30, 1938, an agreement to the cession, with a guarantee of peace by Hitler and Mussolini. Germany occupied Sudetenland Oct. 1-2.

Hitler on Mar. 15, 1939, dissolved Czechoslovakia, made protectorates of Bohemia and Moravia, and supported the autonomy of Slovakia, which was proclaimed independent Mar. 14, 1939.

Soviet troops with some Czechoslovak contingents entered eastern Czechoslovakia in 1944 and reached Prague in May 1945; Benes returned as president. In May 1946 elections, the Communist Party won 38% of the votes, and Benes accepted Klement Gottwald, a communist, as prime minister.

In February 1948, the communists seized power in advance of scheduled elections. In May 1948 a new constitution was approved. Benes refused to sign it. On May 30 the voters were offered a one-slate ballot and the communists won full control. Benes resigned June 7 and Gottwald became president. A harsh Stalinist period followed, with complete and violent suppression of all opposition.

In Jan. 1968 a liberalization movement spread explosively through Czechoslovakia. Antonin Novotny, long the Stalinist ruler of the nation, was deposed as party leader and succeeded by Alexander Dubcek, a Slovak, who declared he intended to make communism democratic. On Mar. 22 Novotny resigned as president and was succeeded by Gen. Ludvik Svoboda. On Apr. 6, Premier Joseph Lenart resigned and was succeeded by Oldrich Cernik, whose new cabinet was pledged to carry out democratization and economic reforms.

In July 1968 the USSR and 4 Warsaw Pact nations demanded an end to liberalization. On Aug. 20, the Soviet, Polish, East German, Hungarian, and Bulgarian armies invaded Czechoslovakia.

Despite demonstrations and riots by students and workers, press censorship was imposed, liberal leaders were ousted from office and promises of loyalty to Soviet policies were made by some old-line Communist Party leaders.

On Apr. 17, 1969, Dubcek resigned as leader of the Communist Party and was succeeded by Gustav Husak. In Jan. 1970, Premier Cernik was ousted. Censorship was tightened, and the Communist Party expelled a third of its members. In 1973, amnesty was offered to some of the 40,000 who fled the country after the 1968 invasion, but repressive policies remained in force.

More than 700 leading Czechoslovak intellectuals and former party leaders signed a human rights manifesto in 1977, called Charter 77, prompting a renewed crackdown by the regime.

The police crushed the largest anti-government protests since 1968, when tens of thousands of demonstrators took to the streets of Prague, Nov. 17, 1989. As protesters demanded free elections, the Communist Party leadership resigned Nov. 24; millions went on strike Nov. 27.

On Dec. 10, 1989 the first Cabinet in 41 years without a communist majority took power; Vaclav Havel, playwright and human rights campaigner, was chosen president, Dec. 29. Havel failed to win reelection July 3, 1992; his bid was blocked by a Slovak-led coalition.

Slovakia declared sovereignty, July 17. Czech and Slovak leaders agreed, July 23, on a basic plan for a peaceful division of Czechoslovakia into 2 independent states.

Czech Republic

Czechoslovakia split into 2 separate states—the Czech Republic and Slovakia—on Jan. 1, 1993.

Denmark

Kingdom of Denmark

Kongeriget Danmark

People: Population (1992 est.): 5,163,000. **Age distrib.** (%): 0–14: 17.1; 15–59: 62.5; 60+: 20.4. **Pop. density:** 310 per sq. mi. **Urban** (1990): 86%. **Ethnic groups:** Almost all Scandinavian. **Languages:** Danish. **Religions:** Evangelical Lutheran 90%.

Geography: Area: 16,633 sq. mi., the size of Massachusetts and New Hampshire combined. **Location:** In northern Europe, separating the North and Baltic seas. **Neighbors:** Germany on S, Norway on NW, Sweden on NE. **Topography:** Denmark consists of the Jutland Peninsula and about 500 islands, 100 inhabited. The land is flat or gently rolling, and is almost all in productive use. **Capital:** Copenhagen. **Cities** (1991, met.): Copenhagen 1.3 mln. (met.).

Government: Type: Constitutional monarchy. **Head of state:** Queen Margrethe II; b. Apr. 16, 1940; in office: Jan. 14, 1972. **Head of government:** Prime Min. Poul Schluter; b. 1929; in office: Sept. 10, 1982. **Local divisions:** 14 counties and one city (Copenhagen). **Defense:** 2.0% of GDP (1991).

Economy: Industries: Machinery, textiles, furniture, electronics. **Chief crops:** Dairy products. **Arable land:** 62%. **Livestock** (1987): cattle: 2.3 mln.; pigs: 9.2 mln. **Fish catch** (1989): 1.9 mln. metric tons. **Electricity prod.** (1991): 31 bln. kWh. **Labor force:** 6% agric.; 50% ind. & comm.; 11% serv.; 27% govt.

Finance: Monetary unit: Krone (July 1993: 6.56 = $1 US). **Gross domestic product** (1991): $91 bln. **Per capita GDP:** $17,700. **Imports** (1992): $32.3 bln.; partners: EC 52%, Swe. 10%. **Exports** (1992): $39.6 bln.; partners: EC 54%, Swe. 11%. **Tourism** (1991): $3.4 bln. receipts. **International reserves less gold** (Mar. 1993): $12.6 bln. **Gold:** 2.0 mln. oz t. **Consumer prices** (change in 1992): 2.1%.

Transport: Railroads (1990): **Length:** 1,763 km. **Motor vehicles:** in use (1990): 1.5 mln. passenger cars, 294,000 comm. vehicles. **Civil aviation** (1990): 4.2 bln. passenger-km; 12 airports with scheduled flights. **Chief ports:** Copenhagen, Alborg, Arhus, Odense.

Communications: Television sets: 1 per 2.7 persons. **Radios:** 1 per 2.4 persons. **Telephones:** 1 per 1.2 persons. **Daily newspaper circ.** (1991): 361 per 1,000 pop.

Health: Life expectancy at birth (1992): 72 male; 78 female. **Births** (per 1,000 pop. 1992): 12. **Deaths** (per 1,000 pop. 1992): 11. **Hospital beds:** 1 per 177 persons. **Physicians:** 1 per 360 persons. **Infant mortality** (per 1,000 live births 1992): 7.

Education (1991): **Literacy:** 99%. Years compulsory 9; attendance 100%.

Major International Organizations: UN and all of its specialized agencies, OECD, EC, NATO.

Embassy: 3200 Whitehaven St. NW 20008; 234-4300.

The origin of Copenhagen dates back to ancient times, when the fishing and trading place named Havn (port) grew up on a cluster of islets, but Bishop Absalon (1128-1201) is regarded as the actual founder of the city.

Danes formed a large component of the Viking raiders in the early Middle Ages. The Danish kingdom was a major north European power until the 17th century, when it lost its land in southern Sweden. Norway was separated in 1815, and Schleswig-Holstein in 1864. Northern Schleswig was returned in 1920.

Voters ratified the Maastricht Treaty on greater European Community unity, May 1993, after having rejected it in 1992.

The **Faeroe Islands** in the N. Atlantic, about 300 mi. NE of the Shetlands, and 850 mi. from Denmark proper, 18 inhabited, have an area of 540 sq. mi. and pop. (1987) of 46,000. They are self-governing in most matters.

Greenland

(Kalaallit Nunaat)

Greenland, a huge island between the N. Atlantic and the Polar Sea, is separated from the North American continent by Davis Strait and Baffin Bay. Its total area is 840,000 sq. mi., 84% of which is ice-capped. Most of the island is a lofty plateau 9,000 to 10,000 ft. in altitude. The average thickness of the cap is 1,000 ft. The population (1992) is 57,000. Under the 1953 Danish constitution the colony became an integral part of the realm with representatives in the Folketing. The Danish parliament, 1978, approved home rule for Greenland, effective May 1, 1979. Accepting home rule the islanders elected a socialist-dominated legislature, Apr. 4th. With home rule, Greenlandic place names came into official use. The technically correct name for Greenland is now Kalaallit Nunaat; its capital is Nuuk, rather than Gothab. Fish is the principal export.

Djibouti

Republic of Djibouti

Jumhouriyya Djibouti

People: Population (1992 est.): 390,000. **Pop. density:** 43. **Urban (1991):** 81%. **Ethnic groups:** Somali 60%; Afar 35%. **Languages:** French, Arabic (both official); Afar, Somali. **Religions:** Sunni Moslem 94%.

Geography: Area: 8,950 sq. mi., about the size of New Hampshire. **Location:** On E coast of Africa, separated from Arabian Peninsula by the strategically vital strait of Bab el-Mandeb. **Neighbors:** Ethiopia on W, NW, Eritrea on NW, Somalia on S. **Topography:** The territory, divided into a low coastal plain, mountains behind, and an interior plateau, is arid, sandy, and desolate. The climate is generally hot and dry. **Capital:** Djibouti. **Cities** (1988): Djibouti (met.) 290,000.

Government: Type: Republic. **Head of state:** Pres. Hassan Gouled Aptidon b. 1916; in office: June 24, 1977; **Head of government:** Prem. Barkat Gourad Hamadou; in office: Sept. 30, 1978. **Local divisions:** 5 districts.

Economy: Minerals: Salt. **Electricity prod.** (1991): 200 mln. kWh.

Finance: Monetary unit: Franc (Mar. 1993: 177=$1 US). **Gross domestic product:** (1989): $344 mln. **Per capita GDP:** $1,030. **Imports** (1990): $311 mln.; partners: EC 36%. **Exports** (1990): $190 mln.; partners: Middle East 50%.

Transport: Motor vehicles: in use (1989): 13,000 passenger cars, 13,000 commercial vehicles. **Chief ports:** Djibouti.

Communications: Television sets: 1 per 38 persons. **Radios:** 1 per 18 persons. **Telephones:** 1 per 55 persons.

Health: Life expectancy at birth (1992): 47 male; 50 female. **Births** (per 1,000 pop. 1992): 43. **Deaths** (per 1,000 pop. 1992): 17. **Natural increase:** 2.6%. **Infant mortality** (per 1,000 live births 1992): 115.

Education (1991): **Literacy:** 48%.

Major International Organizations: UN, OAU, Arab League.

Embassy: 866 United Nations Plaza, New York, NY 10017; (212) 753-3163.

France gained control of the territory in stages between 1862 and 1900.

Ethiopia and Somalia have renounced their claims to the area, but each has accused the other of trying to gain control. There were clashes between Afars (ethnically related to Ethiopians) and Issas (related to Somalis) in 1976. Immigrants from both countries continued to enter the country up to independence, which came June 27, 1977.

Unemployment is high and there are few natural resources. French aid is the mainstay of the economy, as well as assistance from the U.S.

Dominica

Commonwealth of Dominica

People: Population (1992 est.): 86,000. **Pop. density:** 296 per sq. mi. **Ethnic groups:** nearly all African or mulatto, Caribs. **Languages:** English (official), French creole. **Religions:** Roman Catholic 77%.

Geography: Area: 290 sq. mi., about one-fourth the size of Rhode Island. **Location:** In Eastern Caribbean, most northerly Windward Is. **Neighbors:** Guadeloupe to N, Martinique to S. **Topography:** Mountainous, a central ridge running from N to S, terminating in cliffs; volcanic in origin, with numerous thermal springs; rich deep topsoil on leeward side, red tropical clay on windward coast. **Capital** (1987 est.) Roseau 22,000.

Government: Type: Parliamentary democracy. **Head of state:** Pres. Clarence Augustus Seignoret; in office: 1984. **Head of government:** Prime Min. Mary Eugenia Charles; b. 1919; in office: July 21, 1980. **Local divisions:** 10 parishes.

Economy: Industries: Agriculture, tourism. **Chief crops:** Bananas, citrus fruits, coconuts. **Minerals:** Pumice. **Other resources:** Forests. **Arable land:** 23%. **Electricity prod.** (1991): 16 mln. kWh. **Labor force:** 37% agric.; 20% ind & comm.; 30% services.

Finance: Monetary unit: East Caribbean dollar (May 1993: 2.70 = $1 US). **Gross domestic product** (1990): $170 mln. **Imports** (1992): $111 mln.; partners: UK 17%, U.S. 23%. **Exports** (1992): $56 mln.; partners: UK 70%. **Tourism** (1989): $19 mln. receipts. **Consumer prices** (change in 1991): 6.0%.

Transport: Chief ports: Roseau.

Communications: Telephones: 1 per 11 persons.

Health: Life expectancy at birth (1992): 74 male; 79 female. **Births** (per 1,000 pop. 1992): 24. **Deaths** (per 1,000 pop. 1992): 5. **Natural increase:** 1.9%. **Hospital beds:** 1 per 247 persons. **Physicians:** 1 per 1,947 persons. **Infant mortality** (per 1,000 live births 1992): 11.

Education: Literacy: 90%.

Major International Organizations: UN, OAS.

A British colony since 1805, Dominica was granted self government in 1967. Independence was achieved Nov. 3, 1978.

Hurricane David struck, Aug. 30, 1979, devastating the island and destroying the banana plantations, Dominica's economic mainstay. Coups were attempted in 1980 and 1981.

Dominica took a leading role in the instigation of the 1983 U.S.-led invasion of Grenada.

In 1992 the government instituted a controversial program that offered passports to people from the Far East who agreed to invest large sums of money in the country.

Dominican Republic

República Dominicana

People: Population (1992 est.): 7,515,000. **Age distrib.** (%): 0–14: 37.9; 15–59: 56.6; 60+: 5.5. **Pop. density:** 401 per sq. mi. **Urban** (1990): 60%. **Ethnic groups:** Caucasian 16%, mixed 73%, black 11%. **Languages:** Spanish. **Religions:** Roman Catholic 95%.

Geography: Area: 18,704 sq. mi., the size of Vermont and New Hampshire combined. **Location:** In West Indies, sharing I. of Hispaniola with Haiti. **Neighbors:** Haiti on W. **Topography:** The Cordillera Central range crosses the center of the country, rising to over 10,000 ft., highest in the Caribbean. The Cibao valley to the N is major agricultural area. **Capital:** Santo Domingo. **Cities** (1991 est.): Santo Domingo 2,400,000; Santiago de Los Caballeros 490,000.

Government: Type: Representative democracy. **Head of state:** Pres. Joaquin Balaguer; in office: Aug. 16, 1986. **Local divisions:** 29 provinces and Santo Domingo. **Defense:** 1.0% of GDP. (1990).

Economy: Industries: Sugar refining, cement, pharmaceuticals. **Chief crops:** sugar, cocoa, coffee, tobacco, rice. **Minerals:** Nickel, gold, silver. **Other resources:** Timber. **Arable land:** 23%. **Livestock.** (1991): cattle: 2.2 mln.; pigs: 431,000. **Electricity prod.** (1991): 4.4 bln. kWh. **Labor force:** 35% agric.; 13% ind.; 23% serv. & govt.

Finance: Monetary unit: Peso (Mar. 1993: 12.59 = $1 US). **Gross domestic product** (1991): $7.1 bln. **Per capita GDP:** $950. **Imports** (1991): $1.8 bln.; partners: U.S. 50%. **Exports** (1991): $775 mln.; partners: U.S. 59% EC 19%. **Tourists** (1990): $750 mln. receipts. **National budget** (1990): $938 mln. expenditures. **International reserves less gold** (Mar. 1993): $508 mln. **Gold:** 18,000 oz t. **Consumer prices** (change in 1991): 53.9%

Transport: Motor vehicles: in use (1989): 114,000 passenger cars, 72,000 comm. vehicles. **Civil Aviation** (1988): 247 mln. passenger km.; 5 airports. **Chief ports:** Santo Domingo, San Pedro de Macoris, Puerto Plata.

Communications: Television sets: 1 per 10 persons. **Radios:** 1 per 6 persons. **Telephones:** 1 per 24 persons. **Daily newspaper circ.** (1990): 37 per 1,000 pop.

Health: Life expectancy at birth (1992): 66 male; 70 female. **Births** (per 1,000 pop. 1992): 27. **Deaths** (per 1,000 pop. 1992): 7. **Natural increase:** 2.0%. **Hospital beds:** 1 per 1,508 persons. **Physicians:** 1 per 934 persons. **Infant mortality** (per 1,000 live births 1992): 56.

Education (1991): **Literacy:** 83%. Years compulsory 6; attendance 70%.

Major International Organizations: UN (World Bank, IMF, GATT), OAS.

Embassy: 1715 22d St. NW 20008; 332-6280.

Carib and Arawak Indians inhabited the island of Hispaniola when Columbus landed in 1492. The city of Santo Domingo, founded 1496, is the oldest settlement by Europeans in the hemisphere and has the supposed ashes of Columbus in an elaborate tomb in its ancient cathedral.

The western third of the island was ceded to France in 1697. Santo Domingo itself was ceded to France in 1795. Haitian leader Toussaint L'Ouverture seized it, 1801. Spain returned intermittently 1803-21, as several native republics came and went. Haiti ruled again, 1822-44, and Spanish occupation occurred 1861-63.

The country was occupied by U.S. Marines from 1916 to 1924, when a constitutionally elected government was installed.

In 1930, Gen. Rafael Leonidas Trujillo Molina was elected president. Trujillo ruled brutally until his assassination in 1961. Pres. Balaguer, appointed by Trujillo in 1960, resigned under pressure in 1962. Juan Bosch, elected president in the first free elections in 38 years, was overthrown in 1963.

On April 24, 1965, a revolt was launched by followers of Bosch and others, including a few communists. Four days later U.S. Marines intervened against the pro-Bosch forces. Token units were later sent by 5 So. American countries as a peacekeeping force.

A provisional government supervised a June 1966 election, in which Balaguer defeated Bosch by a 3-2 margin. The Inter-American Peace Force completed its departure Sept. 20, 1966.

Continued depressed world prices have affected the main export commodity, sugar.

Ecuador

Republic of Ecuador

República del Ecuador

People: Population (1992 est.): 10,933,000. **Age distrib.** (%): 0–14: 41.3; 15–64: 55.0; 65+: 3.7. **Pop. density:** 99 per sq. mi. **Urban** (1990): 54% **Ethnic groups:** Indians 25%, Mestizo 55%, Spanish 10%, African 10%. **Languages:** Spanish (official), Quechuan, Jivaroan. **Religions:** Roman Catholic 95%.

Geography: Area: 109,483 sq. mi., the size of Colorado. **Location:** In NW S. America, on Pacific coast, astride Equator. **Neighbors:** Colombia to N, Peru to E and S. **Topography:** Two ranges of Andes run N and S, splitting the country into 3 zones: hot, humid lowlands on the coast; temperate highlands between the ranges, and rainy, tropical lowlands to the E. **Capital:** Quito. **Cities** (1991 est.): Guayaquil 2,000,000; Quito 1,500,000.

Government: Type: Republic. **Head of state:** Pres. Sixto Duran Ballen; b. 1922; in office: Aug. 10, 1992. **Local divisions:** 21 provinces. **Defense:** 1.6% of GDP (1990).

Economy: Industries: Food processing, wood prods., textiles. **Chief crops:** Bananas (largest exporter), coffee, rice, sugar, corn. **Minerals:** Oil, copper, iron, lead, silver, sulphur. **Crude oil reserves** (1991): 1.8 bln. bbls. **Other resources:** Rubber, bark. **Arable land:** 6%. **Livestock** (1990): cattle: 3.8 mln.; pigs: 4.1 mln.; sheep: 2.1 mln. **Fish catch** (1989): 767,000 metric tons. **Electricity prod.** (1991): 6.4 bln. kWh. **Labor force:** 39% agric., 12% ind., 42% services.

Finance: Monetary unit: Sucre (July 1993: 1,875 = $1 US). **Gross domestic product** (1991): $11.5 bln. **Per capita GDP:** $1,070. **Imports** (1992): $2.4 bln.; partners: U.S. 34%. **Exports** (1992): $3.0 bln.; partners: U.S. 60%. **Tourism** (1990): $193 mln. receipts. **National budget** (1991): $2.2 bln. expenditures. **International reserves less gold** (Mar. 1993): $831 mln. **Gold:** 443,000 oz t. **Consumer prices** (change in 1992): 54.6%.

Transport: Railroads (1987): **Length:** 965 km. bf Motor vehicles: in use (1987): 272,000 passenger cars, 41,000 comm. vehicles. **Civil aviation** (1990): 1.2 bln. passenger-km. **Chief ports:** Guayaquil, Manta, Esmeraldas, Puerto Bolivar.

Communications: Television sets: 1 per 17 persons. **Radios:** 1 per 3.4 persons. **Telephones:** 1 per 28 persons. **Daily newspaper circ.** (1989): 87 per 1,000 pop.

Health: Life expectancy at birth (1992): 67 male, 72 female. **Births** (per 1,000 pop. 1992): 28. **Deaths** (per 1,000 pop. 1992): 6. **Natural increase:** 2.2%. **Hospital beds:** 1 per 610 persons. **Physicians** (1984): 11,000. **Infant mortality** (per 1,000 live births 1991): 60.

Education (1991): Literacy: 88%. Attendance through 6th grade—76% urban, 33% rural.

Major International Organizations: UN (IMF, WHO), OAS.

Embassy: 2535 15th St. NW 20009; 234-7200.

Spain conquered the region, which was the northern Inca empire, in 1633. Liberation forces defeated the Spanish May 24, 1822, near Quito. Ecuador became part of the Great Colombia Republic but seceded, May 13, 1830.

Ecuador had been ruled by civilian and military dictatorships since 1968. A peaceful transfer of power from the military junta to the democratic civilian government took place, 1979.

Since 1972, the economy has revolved around its petroleum exports, which have declined since 1982 causing severe economic problems. Ecuador suspended interest payments for 1987 on its estimated $8.2 billion foreign debt following a Mar. 5-6 earthquake which left 20,000 homeless, and destroyed a stretch of the country's main oil pipeline.

Ecuadoran Indians staged a number of protests in 1991 to demand greater rights.

Ecuador and Peru have long disputed their Amazon Valley boundary.

The **Galapagos Islands,** 600 mi. to the W, are the home of huge tortoises and other unusual animals.

Egypt

Arab Republic of Egypt

Jumhūrīyah Misr al-Arabiya

People: Population (1992 est.): 56,386,000. **Age distrib** (%) 0-14: 41.8; 15-59: 52.7; 60+: 5.5. **Pop. density:** 146 per sq. mi. **Urban** (1986): 44%. **Ethnic groups:** Eastern Hamitic stock 90%, Bedouin, Nubian. **Languages:** Arabic (official), English. **Religions:** 94% Sunni Moslem.

Geography: Area: 386,650 sq. mi, about the size of Texas, Oklahoma, and Arkansas combined. **Location:** NE corner of Africa. **Neighbors:** Libya on W, Sudan on S, Israel on E. **Topography:** Almost entirely desolate and barren, with hills and mountains in E and along Nile. The Nile Valley, where most of the people live, stretches 550 miles. **Capital:** Cairo. **Cities** (1990 est.): Cairo 6,452,000; Alexandria 3,170,000; al-Jizah 2,156,000.

Government: Type: Republic. **Head of state:** Pres. Hosni Mubarak; b. 1929; in office: Oct. 14, 1981. **Head of Government:** Atef Sedki in office: Nov. 10, 1986. **Local divisions:** 26 governorates. **Defense:** 7.3% of GDP (1991).

Economy: Industries: Textiles, chemicals, petrochemicals, food processing, cement. **Chief crops:** Cotton (one of largest producers), rice, beans, fruits, grains, vegetables, sugar, corn. **Minerals:** Oil, phosphates, gypsum, iron, manganese, limestone. **Crude oil reserves** (1991): 6.2 bln. bbls. **Arable land:** 4%. **Livestock** (1990): cattle: 1.9 mln.; sheep: 1.3 mln. **Fish catch** (1990): 312,000 metric tons. **Electricity prod.** (1991): 45 bln. kWh. **Labor force:** 44% agric.; 22% services; 14% industry.

Finance: Monetary unit: Pound (June 1992: 3.32 = $1 US). **Gross domestic product** (1991): $39.2 bln. **Per capita GDP:** $720. **Imports** (1991): $11.5 bln.; partners: U.S. 19%, Ger. 10%, It. 8%, France 8%. **Exports** (1991): $4.5 bln.; partners: It. 22%, Rom. 12%. **Tourism** (1990): $1.9 bln. receipts. **National budget** (1991): $16.7 bln. expenditures. **International reserves less gold** (Jan. 1993): $10.8 bln. **Gold:** 2.43 mln. oz t. **Consumer prices** (change in 1992): 13.6%.

Transport: Railroads (1991): **Length:** 5,489 mi. **Motor vehicles:** in use (1989): 826,000 passenger cars, 550,000 comm. vehicles. **Civil aviation** (1991): 5.2 bln. passenger-km.; 10 airports. **Chief ports:** Alexandria, Port Said, Suez.

Communications: Television sets: 1 per 15 persons. **Radios:** 1 per 3.9 persons. **Telephones:** 1 per 34 persons. **Daily newspaper circ.** (1991): 62 per 1,000 pop.

Health: Life expectancy at birth (1992): 58 male; 62 female. **Births** (per 1,000 pop. 1992): 33. **Deaths** (per 1,000 pop. 1992): 10. **Natural increase:** 2.3%. **Hospital beds:** 1 per 505 persons. **Physicians:** 1 per 616 persons. **Infant mortality** (per 1,000 live births 1992): 80.

Education (1990): **Literacy:** 44%. Compulsory ages 6-12.

Major International Organizations: UN (IMF, World Bank, GATT), OAU.

Embassy: 2310 Decatur Pl. NW 20008; 232-5400.

Archeological records of ancient Egyptian civilization date back to 4000 BC. A unified kingdom arose around 3200 BC, and extended its way south into Nubia and north as far as Syria. A high culture of rulers and priests was built on an economic base of serfdom, fertile soil, and annual flooding of the Nile banks.

Imperial decline facilitated conquest by Asian invaders (Hyksos, Assyrians). The last native dynasty fell in 341 BC to the Persians, who were in turn replaced by Greeks (Alexander and the Ptolemies), Romans, Byzantines, and Arabs, who introduced Islam and the Arabic language. The ancient Egyptian language is preserved only in the liturgy of the Coptic Christians.

Egypt was ruled as part of larger Islamic empires for several centuries. The Mamluks, a military caste of Caucasian origin, ruled Egypt from 1250 until defeat by the Ottoman Turks in 1517. Under Turkish sultans the khedive as hereditary viceroy had wide authority. Britain intervened in 1882 and took control of administration, though nominal allegiance to the Ottoman Empire continued until 1914.

The country was a British protectorate from 1914 to 1922. A 1936 treaty strengthened Egyptian autonomy, but Britain retained bases in Egypt and a condominium over the Sudan. Britain fought German and Italian armies from Egypt, 1940-42. In 1951 Egypt abrogated the 1936 treaty. The Sudan became independent in 1956.

The uprising of July 23, 1952, led by the Society of Free Officers, named Maj. Gen. Mohammed Naguib commander in chief and forced King Farouk to abdicate. When the republic was proclaimed June 18, 1953, Naguib became its first president and premier. Lt. Col. Gamal Abdel Nasser removed Naguib and became premier in 1954. In 1956, he was voted president. Nasser died in 1970 and was replaced by Vice Pres. Anwar Sadat.

The Aswan High Dam, completed 1971, provides irrigation for more than a million acres of land. Artesian wells, drilled in the Western Desert, reclaimed 43,000 acres, 1960-66.

When the state of Israel was proclaimed in 1948, Egypt joined other Arab nations invading Israel and was defeated.

After terrorist raids across its border, Israel invaded Egypt's Sinai Peninsula, Oct. 29, 1956. Egypt rejected a cease-fire demand by Britain and France; on Oct. 31 the 2 nations dropped bombs and on Nov. 5-6 landed forces. Egypt and Israel accepted a UN cease-fire; fighting ended Nov. 7.

A UN Emergency Force guarded the 117-mile long border between Egypt and Israel until May 19, 1967, when it was withdrawn at Nasser's demand. Egyptian troops entered the Gaza Strip and the heights of Sharm el Sheikh and 3 days later closed the Strait of Tiran to all Israeli shipping. Full-scale war broke out June 5 and before it ended under a UN cease-fire June 10, Israel had captured Gaza and the Sinai Peninsula, controlled the east bank of the Suez Canal and reopened the gulf.

Sporadic fighting with Israel continued almost daily, 1968-70. Israel and Egypt agreed, Aug. 7, 1970, to a cease-fire and peace negotiations proposed by the U.S. Negotiations failed to achieve results, but the cease-fire continued.

In a surprise attack Oct. 6, 1973, Egyptian forces crossed the Suez Canal into the Sinai. (At the same time, Syrian forces attacked Israelis on the Golan Heights.) Egypt was supplied by a USSR military airlift; the U.S. responded with an airlift to Israel. Israel counter-attacked, crossed the canal, surrounded Suez City. A UN cease-fire took effect Oct. 24.

A disengagement agreement was signed Jan. 18, 1974. Under it, Israeli forces withdrew from the canal's W bank; limited numbers of Egyptian forces occupied a strip along the E bank. A second accord was signed in 1975, with Israel yielding Sinai oil fields. Pres. Sadat's surprise visit to Jerusalem, Nov. 1977, opened the prospect of peace with Israel. On Mar. 26, 1979, Egypt and Israel signed a formal peace treaty, ending 30 years of war, and establishing diplomatic relations. Israel returned control of the Sinai to Egypt in April 1982.

Tension between Moslem fundamentalists and Christians in 1981 caused street riots and culminated in a nationwide security crackdown in Sept. Pres Sadat was assassinated on Oct. 6.

Egypt was a political and military supporter of the Allied forces in their defeat of Iraq in the Persian Gulf War, 1991.

Egypt saw a rising tide of Islamic fundamentalist violence in 1992 and 1993. Egyptian security forces conducted raids against Islamic militants Mar. 1993. Seven Islamic militants convicted of participating in 6 separate attacks on tourists were hanged June 8.

The **Suez Canal,** 103 mi. long, links the Mediterranean and Red seas. It was built by a French corporation 1859-69, but Britain obtained controlling interest in 1875. The last British troops were removed June 13, 1956. On July 26, Egypt nationalized the canal.

El Salvador

Republic of El Salvador

República de El Salvador

People: Population (1992 est.): 5,574,000. **Age distrib.** (%): 0–14: 44.4; 15–59: 49.9; 60+: 5.7. **Pop. density:** 686 per sq. mi. **Urban** (1991): 45%. **Ethnic groups:** Mestizo 89%, Indian 10%. **Languages:** Spanish (official). **Religions:** Roman Catholic 75%.

Geography: Area: 8,124 sq. mi., the size of Massachusetts. **Location:** In Central America. **Neighbors:** Guatemala on W, Honduras on N. **Topography:** A hot Pacific coastal plain in the south rises to a cooler plateau and valley region, densely populated. The N is mountainous, including many volcanoes. **Capital:** San Salvador. **Cities** (1993 est.): San Salvador 1.4 mln.

Government: Type: Republic. **Head of state:** Pres., Alfredo Cristiani; b. Nov, 22, 1947; in office: June 1, 1989. **Local divisions:** 14 departments. **Defense:** 3.6% of GDP (1991).

Economy: Industries: Food and beverages, textiles, petroleum products. **Chief crops:** Coffee (21% of GNP), cotton, corn, sugar. **Other resources:** Rubber, forests. **Arable land:** 27%. **Livestock** (1990): cattle: 1.1 mln.; pigs: 440,000. **Electricity prod.** (1991): 1.9 bln. kWh. **Labor force:** 40% agric.; 16% ind.; 27% services.

Finance: Monetary unit: Colon (Mar. 1993: 8.73 = $1 US). **Gross domestic product** (1992): $5.5 bln. **Per capita GDP:** $1,010. **Imports** (1992): $1.5 bln.; partners: U.S. 41%, CACM 22%. **Exports** (1992): $683 mln.; partners: U.S. 41%, EC 30%, CACM 10%. **Tourism** (1990): $70 mln. receipts. National budget (1990): $790 mln. expenditures. **International reserves less gold** (Mar. 1993): $458 mln. **Gold:** 469,000 oz t. **Consumer prices** (change in 1992): 20%.

Transport: Railroads (1991): **Length:** 374 mi. **Motor vehicles:** in use (1990): 80,000 passenger cars, 80,000 comm. vehicles. **Chief ports:** La Union, Acajutla.

Communications: Television sets: 1 per 12 persons. **Radios:** 1 per 2.6 persons. **Telephones:** 1 per 36 persons. **Daily newspaper circ.** (1991): 47 per 1,000 pop.

Health: Life expectancy at birth (1992): 68 male; 75 female. **Births** (per 1,000 pop. 1992): 33. **Deaths** (per 1,000 pop. 1992): 5. **Natural increase:** 2.8%. **Hospital beds:** 1 per 973 persons. **Physicians:** 1 per 1,322 persons. **Infant mortality** (per 1,000 live births 1992): 26.

Education (1991): **Literacy:** 75%. Years compulsory 6; attendance 82%.

Major International Organizations: UN (IMF, WHO, ILO), OAS, CACM.

Embassy: 2308 California St. NW 20008; 265-9671.

El Salvador became independent of Spain in 1821, and of the Central American Federation in 1839.

A fight with Honduras in 1969 over the presence of 300,000 Salvadorean workers left 2,000 dead. Clashes were renewed 1970 and 1974.

A military coup overthrew the government of Pres. Carlos Humberto Romero in 1979, but the ruling military-civilian junta failed to quell a rebellion by leftist insurgents, armed by Cuba and Nicaragua. Extreme right-wing death squads organized to eliminate suspected leftists were blamed for thousands of deaths in the 1980s. The Reagan administration staunchly supported the government with military aid.

Voters turned out in large numbers in the May 1984 presidential election. Christian Democrat Jose Napoleon Duarte, a moderate, was victorious with 54% of the vote.

The 12-year civil war ended Jan. 16, 1992, as the government and leftist rebels signed a formal peace treaty. The civil war had taken the lives of some 75,000 people. The treaty provided for military and political reforms.

Nine soldiers, including 3 officers, were indicted Jan. 1990 in the Nov. 1989 slaying of 6 Jesuit priests at a university in San Salvador. Two of the officers received maximum 30-year jail sentences. They were released after serving 15 months of their sentences, Mar. 20, 1993, when the National Assembly passed a sweeping amnesty for those who had committed atrocities during the civil war.

Equatorial Guinea

Republic of Equatorial Guinea

República de Guinea Ecuatorial

People: Population (1992 est.): 388,000. **Age distrib.** (%): 0–14: 38.1; 15–59: 55.2; 60+: 6.7. **Pop. density:** 35 per sq. mi. **Ethnic groups:** Fangs 80%, Bubi 15%. **Languages:** Spanish (official), Fang, Bubi. **Religions:** Mostly Roman Catholic.

Geography: Area: 10,832 sq. mi., the size of Maryland. **Location:** Bioko Is. off W. Africa coast in Gulf of Guinea, and Rio Muni, mainland enclave. **Neighbors:** Gabon on S, Cameroon on E, N. **Topography:** Bioko Is. consists of 2 volcanic mountains and a connecting valley. Rio Muni, with over 90% of the area, has a coastal plain and low hills beyond. **Capital:** Malabo. **Cities** (1989 est.): Malabo 38,000.

Government: Type: in transition. **Head of state:** Pres., Supreme Military Council Teodoro Obiang Nguema Mbasogo; b. June 5, 1942; in office: Oct. 10, 1979. **Head of government:** Prime Min. Silvestre Siale Bileka; In office: Mar. 4, 1992. **Local divisions:** 7 provinces.

Economy: Chief crops: Cocoa, coffee, bananas, sweet potatoes. **Other resources:** Timber. **Arable land:** 8%. **Electricity prod.** (1991): 60 mln. kWh. **Labor force:** agric. 50%; public sector 40%.

Finance: Monetary unit: CFA franc (Mar. 1993: 278 = $1 US). **Gross domestic product** (1990): $136 mln. **Per capita GDP:** $430. **Imports** (1990): 68 mln.; partners: Fra. 26%, Sp. 21%. **Exports** (1990): $37 mln.; partners: Sp. 38%, Neth. 12%.

Transport: Chief ports: Malabo, Bata.

Communications: Radios: 1 per 3.5 persons.

Health: Life expectancy at birth (1992): 49 male; 53 female. **Births** (per 1,000 pop. 1992): 42. **Deaths** (per 1,000 pop. 1992): 15. **Natural increase:** 2.7% **Hospital beds** (1982): 3,200. **Physicians:** 1 per 3,622 persons. **Infant mortality** (per 1,000 live births 1992): 107.

Education (1991): **Literacy:** 55%. About 65% attend primary school.

Major International Organizations: UN (IMF, World Bank), OAU.

Embassy: 801 2d Ave., New York, NY 10017; (212) 599-1523.

Fernando Po (now Bioko) Island was reached by Portugal in the late 15th century and ceded to Spain in 1778. Independence came Oct. 12, 1968. Riots occurred in 1969 over disputes between the island and the more backward Rio Muni province on the mainland. Masie Nguema Biyogo, himself from the mainland, became president for life in 1972.

Masie's 11-year reign was one of the most brutal in Africa, resulting in a bankrupted nation. Most of the nation's 7,000 Europeans emigrated. In 1976, 45,000 Nigerian workers were evacuated amid charges of a reign of terror. Masie was ousted in a military coup, Aug. 1979. Mbasogo, leader of the coup, became president.

The nation is heavily dependent on external aid.

Eritrea

State of Eritrea

People: Population (1993 est.): 3,200,000. **Pop. density:** 88 per sq. mi. **Ethnic groups:** 9 different ethnic groups. **Languages:** 7 native languages. **Religions:** about evenly split between Moslem and Christian.

Geography: Area: 36,170 sq. mi., slightly larger than Maine. **Location:** in E. Africa. **Neighbors:** Ethiopia on S, Djibouti on E, Sudan on W, Red Sea on N. **Topography:** includes many islands of the Dahlak Archipelago, low coastal plains in S., mountain range with peaks to 9,000 ft. in N. **Capital:** Asmera.

Government: Type: in transition. **Head of state:** Issaias Afwerki; in office: May 24, 1993.

Economy: no industry. **Chief crops:** Cotton, coffee, tobacco.

Transport: Chief ports: Masewa, Aseb.

Communications: no telephones outside the capital.

Major International Organizations: UN.

Eritrea was part of the Ethiopian kingdom of Aksum. It was an Italian colony from 1890 to 1941, when it was captured by the British. Following a period of British and UN supervision, Eritrea was awarded to Ethiopia as part of a federation in 1952. Ethiopia annexed Eritrea as a province in 1962. This led to a 31-year struggle for independence, which ended when Eritrea formally declared itself an independent nation May 24, 1993.

Estonia

Republic of Estonia

Eesti Vabariik

People: Population (1992 est.): 1,607,000. **Pop. density:** 92 per sq. mi. **Urban** (1991): 72%. **Ethnic groups:** Estonian 65%, Russian 30%. **Languages:** Estonian (official), Russian. **Religion:** Mostly Evangelical Lutheran.

Geography: Area: 17,413 sq. mi. **Neighbors:** bounded on N., W. by the Baltic Sea, E. by Russia, S. by Latvia. **Capital:** Tallinn. **Cities** (1991 est.): Tallinn 502,000.

Government: Type: Republic. **Head of state:** Pres. Lennart Meri; in office: Oct. 5, 1992. **Head of government:** Prime Min.

Mart Laar; in Office; Oct. 8, 1992. **Local divisions:** 15 districts, 33 towns, 26 urban settlements.

Economy: Industries: Agricultural machinery, electric motors. **Chief crops:** Grain, vegetables. **Arable Land:** 22%. **Livestock** (1990): cattle: 823,000, sheep: 138,000. **Electricity prod.** (1000): 17.2 kWh. **Labor force:** Ind. & const. 42%, agric. 13%.

Finance: Monetary unit: Kroon (Jan. 1993: 11.26 = $1 US).

Transport: Railroads (1991): **Length:** 640 mi. **Motor vehicles:** in use (1989): 198,000 passenger cars. **Chief port:** Tallinn.

Communications: Television sets: 1 per 2.7 persons. **Radios:** 1 per 1.7 persons. **Telephones:** 1 per 5.1 persons.

Health: Life expectancy at birth (1992): 65 male, 75 female. **Hospital beds:** 1 per 83 persons. **Physicians:** 1

Education: 11 year school curriculum.

Major International Organizations: UN, IMF.

Estonia was a province of imperial Russia before World War I, was independent between World Wars I and II, but was conquered by the USSR in 1940. Estonia declared itself an "occupied territory," and proclaimed itself a free nation Mar. 1990. During an abortive Soviet coup, Estonia declared immediate full independence, Aug. 20, 1991; the Soviet Union recognized its independence in Sept. 1991. The first free elections in over 50 years were held Sept. 20, 1992.

Ethiopia

(Figures prior to 1993 include Eritrea)

People: Population (1993 est.): 51,070,000. **Age distrib.** (%): 0–14: 46.5; 15–59: 47.3; 60+: 6.2. **Pop. density:** 117 per sq. mi. **Urban** (1992): 11%. **Ethnic groups:** Oromo 40%, Amhara 25%, Tigre 12%, Sidama 9%. **Languages:** Amharic (official), Tigre (Semitic languages); Galla (Hamitic). **Religions:** Orthodox Christian 40%, Moslem 40%.

Geography: Area: 435,606 sq. mi., about three-quarters the size of Alaska. **Location:** In E. Africa. **Neighbors:** Sudan on W, Kenya on S, Somalia, Djibouti on E, Eritrea on N. **Topography:** A high central plateau, between 6,000 and 10,000 ft. high, rises to higher mountains near the Great Rift Valley, cutting in from the SW. The Blue Nile and other rivers cross the plateau, which descends to plains on both W and SE. **Capital:** Addis Ababa. **Cities** (1984 est.): Addis Ababa 1,412,000.

Government: Type: In transition. **Head of state:** Pres. Meles Zenawi; in office: May 28, 1991. **Head of Government:** Prime Min. Timirat Laynie; in office: June 6, 1991. **Local divisions:** 13 provinces. **Defense:** 8% of GDP (1989).

Economy: Industries: Food processing, cement, textiles. **Chief crops:** Coffee (over 50% export earnings), grains. **Minerals:** Platinum, gold, copper, potash. **Arable Land:** 13%. **Livestock** (1990): cattle: 30 mln.; sheep: 23 mln. **Electricity prod.** (1991): 650 mln. kWh. **Labor force:** 80% agric.

Finance: Monetary unit: Birr (Mar. 1993: 5.00 = $1 US). **Gross domestic product** (1991): $6.6 bln. **Per capita GDP:** $130. **Imports** (1991): $472 mln.; partners: USSR 22%, U.S. 15%, Italy 10%, Jap. 6%, Ger. 10%. **Exports** (1991): $189 mln.; partners: U.S. 20%, Ger. 18%, Italy 7%. **National budget** (1989): $1.7 bln. expenditures. **International reserves less gold** (Mar. 1993): $252 mln. **Gold:** 113,000 oz t. **Consumer prices** (change in 1992): 10.5%.

Transport: Railroads (1989): **Length:** 486 mi. **Motor vehicles:** in use (1991): 38,000 passenger cars, 15,000 comm. vehicles. **Civil aviation** (1989): 1.6 bln. passenger-km; 29 airports with scheduled flights.

Communications: Television sets: 1 per 503 persons. **Radios:** 1 per 5.5 persons. **Telephones:** 1 per 320 persons. **Daily newspaper circ.** (1990): 1 per 1,000 pop.

Health: Life expectancy at birth (1992): 50 male; 53 female. **Births** (per 1,000 pop. 1992): 45. **Deaths** (per 1,000 pop. 1992): 15. **Natural increase:** 3.1%. **Hospital beds:** 1 per 3,873 persons. **Physicians:** 1 per 36,660 persons. **Infant mortality** (per 1,000 live births 1992): 113.

Education (1985): **Literacy:** 18%.

Major International Organizations: UN (IMF, WHO), OAU.

Embassy: 2134 Kalorama Rd. NW 20008; 234-2281.

Ethiopian culture was influenced by Egypt and Greece. The ancient monarchy was invaded by Italy in 1880 but maintained its independence until another Italian invasion in 1936. British forces freed the country in 1941.

The last emperor, Haile Selassie I, established a parliament and judiciary system in 1931 but barred all political parties.

A series of droughts in the 1970s killed hundreds of thousands. An army mutiny, strikes, and student demonstrations led to the dethronement of Selassie in 1974. The ruling junta pledged to form a one-party socialist state and instituted a successful land reform; opposition was violently suppressed. The influence of the Coptic Church, embraced in 330 AD, was curbed, and the monarchy was abolished in 1975.

The regime, torn by bloody coups, faced uprisings by tribal and political groups in part aided by Sudan and Somalia. Ties with the U.S., once a major arms and aid source, deteriorated, while cooperation accords were signed with the USSR in 1977. In 1978, Soviet advisors and Cuban troops helped defeat Somalia forces. Ethiopia and Somalia signed a peace agreement in 1988.

A worldwide relief effort began in 1984, as an extended drought caused millions to face starvation and death. In 1988, victories by Eritrean guerrillas forced the government to curtail the work of foreign aid workers in drought-stricken regions.

The Ethiopian People's Revolutionary Democractic Front (EPRDF), an umbrella group of 6 rebel armies, launched a major push against government forces, Feb. 1991. In May, Pres. Mengistu Haile Mariam resigned and left the country. The EPRDF took posession of the capital and announced plans for a coalition government.

Eritrea, a province on the Red Sea, declared its independence May 24, 1993.

Fiji

Republic of Fiji

People: Population (1992 est.): 744,000. **Age distrib.** (%): 0–14: 38.2; 15–59: 56.9; 60+: 4.9. **Pop. density:** 105 per sq. mi. **Urban** (1986): 39%. **Ethnic groups:** Indian 48%, Fijian (Melanesian-Polynesian) 46%, Europeans 2%. **Languages:** English (official), Fijian, Hindi. **Religions:** Christian 52%, Hindu 38%, Moslem 8%.

Geography: Area: 7,056 sq. mi., the size of Massachusetts. **Location:** In western S. Pacific O. **Neighbors:** Nearest are Solomons on NW, Tonga on E. **Topography:** 322 islands (106 inhabited), many mountainous, with tropical forests and large fertile areas. Viti Levu, the largest island, has over half the total land area. **Capital:** Suva. **Cities** (1986 est.): Suva 69,000.

Government: Type: Republic. **Head of state:** Pres. Penaia Ganilau; in office: Dec. 5, 1987. **Head of government:** Prime Min. Sitiveni Rabuka; in office: June 2, 1992. **Local divisions:** 4 divisions, 1 dependency.

Economy: Industries: Sugar refining, light industry, tourism. **Chief crops:** Sugar, bananas, ginger. **Minerals:** Gold. **Other resources:** Timber. **Arable land:** 8%. **Electricity prod.** (1990): 325 mln. kWh. **Labor force:** 44% agric.

Finance: Monetary unit: Dollar (Mar. 1993: 1.53 = $1.00 US). **Gross domestic product** (1991): $1.3 bln. **Per capita GDP:** $1,700. **Imports** (1991): $840 mln.; partners: Austral. 29%, Jap. 12%, N.Z. 19%. **Exports** (1991): $646 mln.; partners: EC 32%, Aust. 21%. **Tourism** (1990): $320 mln. receipts. **National budget** (1992): $464 mln. expenditures. **International reserves less gold** (Mar. 1993): $283 mln. **Gold:** 10,000 oz t. **Consumer prices** (change in 1992): 4.9%.

Transport: Motor vehicles: in use (1990): 40,000 passenger cars, 28,000 comm. vehicles. **Civil aviation** (1990): 882 mln. passenger-km; 17 airports with scheduled flights. **Chief ports:** Suva, Lautoka.

Communications: Televisions: 1 per 73 persons. **Radios:** 1 per 1.7 persons. **Telephones:** 1 per 10 persons. **Daily newspaper circ.** (1988): 56 per 1,000 pop.

Health: Life expectancy at birth (1992): 62 male; 67 female. **Births** (per 1,000 pop. 1992): 26. **Deaths** (per 1,000 pop. 1992): 7. **Natural increase:** 1.9%. **Hospital beds:** 1 per 413 persons. **Physicians:** 1 per 2,438 persons. **Infant mortality** (per 1,000 live births 1992): 19.

Education (1990): **Literacy:** 85%. 95% attend school.

Major International Organizations: UN (IMF, WHO).

Embassy: 2233 Wisconsin Ave. NW 20007; 337-8320.

A British colony since 1874, Fiji became an independent parliamentary democracy Oct. 10, 1970.

Cultural differences between the majority Indian community, descendants of contract laborers brought to the islands in the 19th century, and the less modernized native Fijians, who by law own 83% of the land in communal villages, have led to political polarization.

In 1987, a military coup ousted the government; order was restored May 21 when a compromise was reached granting Lt. Col. Rabuka, the coup's leader, increased power. Rabuka staged a second coup Sept. 25 and in Oct. declared Fiji a republic. A civilian government was restored to power in Dec., and a new constitution was drafted which protected the rights of all citizens.

Finland

Republic of Finland

Suomen Tasavalta

People: Population (1992 est.): 5,004,000. **Age distrib. (%):** 0–14: 19.3; 15–59: 62.9; 60+: 17.8. **Pop. density:** 38 per sq. mi. **Urban** (1992): 61%. **Ethnic groups:** Finns 94%, Swedes, Lapps. **Languages:** Finnish, Swedish (both official). **Religions:** Lutheran 97%.

Geography: Area: 130,119 sq. mi., slightly smaller than Montana. **Location:** In northern Europe. **Neighbors:** Norway on N, Sweden on W, Russia on E. **Topography:** South and central Finland are mostly flat areas with low hills and many lakes. The N has mountainous areas, 3,000-4,000 ft. **Capital:** Helsinki. **Cities** (1992 est.): Helsinki 490,000; Tampere 170,000; Turku 160,000.

Government: Type: Constitutional republic. **Head of state:** Pres. Mauno Koivisto; b. Nov. 25, 1923; in office: Jan. 27, 1982. **Head of government:** Prime Min. Esko Aho: b. 1954; in office: Apr. 26, 1991. **Local divisions:** 12 laanit (provinces). **Defense:** 1.4% of GDP (1989).

Economy: Industries: Machinery, metal, shipbuilding, textiles, clothing. **Chief crops:** Grains, potatoes, dairy prods. **Minerals:** Copper, iron, zinc. **Other resources:** Forests (40% of exports). **Arable land:** 8%. **Livestock** (1990): cattle; 1.3 mln. pigs: 1.3 mln. **Fish catch** (1989): 160,000 metric tons. **Electricity prod.** (1991): 49.3 bln. kWh. **Crude steel prod.** (1991): 2.8 mln. metric tons. **Labor force:** 9% agric.; 54% ind., comm. & finance; 25% services.

Finance: Monetary unit: Markka (June 1993: 5.62 = $1 US). **Gross domestic product** (1991): $80 bln. **Per capita GDP:** $16,200. **Imports** (1992): $21.2 bln.; partners: EC 45%. **Exports** (1992): $23.8 bln.; partners: EC 50%. **Tourism** (1991): $1.2 bln. receipts. **National budget** (1991): $41.5 bln. expenditures. **International reserves less gold** (Mar. 1993): $4.3 bln. **Gold** 2.0 mln. oz t. **Consumer prices** (change in 1992): 2.6%.

Transport: Railroads (1991): **Length:** 3,656 mi. **Motor vehicles:** in use (1990): 1.9 mln. passenger cars, 271,000 comm. vehicles; **Civil aviation** (1991): 9.8 bln. passenger-km; 25 airports. **Chief ports:** Helsinki, Turku.

Communications: Television sets: 1 per 2.7 persons. **Radios:** 1 per person. **Telephones:** 1 per 2.1 persons. **Daily newspaper circ.** (1990): 521 per 1,000 pop.

Health: Life expectancy at birth (1992): 72 male; 80 female. **Births** (per 1,000 pop. 1992): 12. **Deaths** (per 1,000 pop. 1992): 10. **Natural increase:** .02%. **Hospital beds:** 1 per 74 persons. **Physicians:** 1 per 503 persons. **Infant mortality** (per 1,000 live births 1992): 6.

Education (1991): **Literacy:** 99%. Years compulsory 9; attendance 99%.

Major International Organizations: UN (IMF, GATT), EFTA, OECD.

Embassy: 3216 New Mexico Ave. NW 20016; 363-2430.

The early Finns probably migrated from the Ural area at about the beginning of the Christian era. Swedish settlers brought the country into Sweden, 1154 to 1809, when Finland became an autonomous grand duchy of the Russian Empire. Russian exactions created a strong national spirit; on Dec. 6, 1917, Finland declared its independence and in 1919 became a republic. On Nov. 30, 1939, the Soviet Union invaded, and the Finns were forced to cede 16,173 sq. mi., including the Karelian Isthmus, Viipuri, and an area on Lake Ladoga. After World War II, in which Finland tried to recover its lost territory, further cessions were exacted. In 1948, Finland signed a treaty of mutual assistance with the USSR; Finland and Russia nullified this treaty with a new pact in Jan. 1992. In 1956, Russia returned Porkkala, which had been ceded as a military base. In 1992 Finland's economy suffered because of changes in the former Soviet Union and Eastern Europe.

Aland, constituting an autonomous department, is a group of small islands, 590 sq. mi., in the Gulf of Bothnia, 25 mi. from Sweden, 15 mi. from Finland. Mariehamn is the principal port.

France

French Republic

République Francaise

People: Population (1992 est.): 57,287,000. **Age distrib.** (%): 0–14: 19.1; 15–60: 61.0; 60+: 19.9. **Pop. density:** 259 per sq. mi. **Urban** (1990): 74%. **Ethnic groups:** A mixture of various European and Mediterranean groups. **Languages:** French (official); minorities speak Breton, Alsatian German, Flemish, Italian, Basque, Catalan. **Religions:** Mostly Roman Catholic.

Geography: Area: 220,668 sq. mi., four-fifths the size of Texas. **Location:** In western Europe, between Atlantic O. and Mediterranean Sea. **Neighbors:** Spain on S, Italy, Switzerland, Germany on E, Luxembourg, Belgium on N. **Topography:** A wide plain covers more than half of the country, in N and W, drained to W by Seine, Loire, Garonne rivers. The Massif Central is a mountainous plateau in center. In E are Alps (Mt. Blanc is tallest in W. Europe, 15,771 ft.), the lower Jura range, and the forested Vosges. The Rhone flows from Lake Geneva to Mediterranean. Pyrenees are in SW, on border with Spain. **Capital:** Paris. **Cities** (1990 est.): Paris 2,152,000; Marseille 801,000; Lyon 415,000; Toulouse 359,000; Nice 342,000; Strasbourg 252,000; Nantes 245,000; Bordeaux 201,000.

Government: Type: Republic. **Head of state:** Pres. François Mitterrand; b. Oct. 26, 1916; in office: May 21, 1981. **Head of government:** Prime Min. Edouard Balladur; in office: Mar. 29, 1993. **Local divisions:** 22 administrative regions containing 95 departments. **Defense:** 3.6% of GDP (1991).

Economy: Industries: Steel, chemicals, textiles, wine, perfume, aircraft, electronic equipment. **Chief crops:** Grains, corn, rice, fruits, vegetables. France is largest food producer, exporter, in W. Eur. **Minerals:** Bauxite, iron, coal. **Crude oil reserves** (1985): 221 mln. bbls. **Other resources:** Forests. **Arable land:** 32%. **Livestock** (1990): cattle: 21.1 mln.; pigs: 12.2 mln.; sheep: 10.3 mln. **Fish catch** (1990): 896,000 metric tons. **Electricity prod.** (1991): 399 bln. kWh. **Crude steel prod.** (1991): 18.4 mln. metric tons. **Labor force:** 9% agric.; 45% ind. & comm.; 46% services.

Finance: Monetary unit: Franc (July 1993: 5.79 = $1 US). **Gross domestic product** (1991): $1 trl. **Per capita GDP:** $18,300. **Imports** (1992): $239 bln.; partners: EC 51%. **Exports** (1992): $235 bln.; partners: EC 50%, U.S. 6%. **Tourism** (1990): $21.6 bln. receipts. **National budget** (1992): $246 bln. expenditures. **International reserves less gold** (Feb. 1993): $33.0 bln. **Gold:** 81.85 mln. oz t. **Consumer prices** (change in 1992): 2.4%.

Transport: Railroads (1991): **Length:** 21,173 mi. **Motor vehicles:** in use (1991): 23.8 mln. passenger cars, 5.1 mln. **Civil aviation** (1991): 32.5 bln. passenger-km; 64 airports with scheduled flights. **Chief ports:** Marseille, LeHavre, Nantes, Bordeaux, Rouen.

Communications: Television sets: 1 per 2.6 persons. **Radios:** 1 per 1.1 persons. **Telephones:** 1 per 1.7 persons. **Daily newspaper circ.** (1990): 176 per 1,000 pop.

Health: Life expectancy at birth (1992): 74 male; 82 female. **Births** (per 1,000 pop. 1992): 13. **Deaths** (per 1,000 pop. 1992): 9. **Natural increase:** .4%. **Hospital beds:** 1 per 80 persons. **Physicians:** 1 per 374 persons. **Infant mortality** (per 1,000 live births 1992): 7.

Education (1991): **Literacy:** 99%. Years compulsory 10.

Major International Organizations: UN and most of its specialized agencies, OECD, EC, NATO.

Embassy: 4101 Reservoir Rd. NW 20007; 944-6000.

Celtic Gaul was conquered by Julius Caesar 58-51 BC; Romans ruled for 500 years. Under Charlemagne, Frankish rule extended over much of Europe. After his death France emerged as one of the successor kingdoms.

The monarchy was overthrown by the French Revolution (1789-93) and succeeded by the First Republic; followed by the First Empire under Napoleon (1804-15), a monarchy (1814-48), the Second Republic (1848-52), the Second Empire (1852-70), the Third Republic (1871-1946), the Fourth Republic (1946-58), and the Fifth Republic (1958 to present).

France suffered severe losses in manpower and wealth in the first World War, 1914-18, when it was invaded by Germany. By the Treaty of Versailles, France exacted return of Alsace and Lorraine, French provinces seized by Germany in 1871. Germany invaded France again in May, 1940, and signed an armistice with a government based in Vichy. After France was liberated by the Allies Sept. 1944, Gen. Charles de Gaulle became head of the provisional government, serving until 1946.

De Gaulle again became premier in 1958, during a crisis over Algeria, and obtained voter approval for a new constitution, ushering in the Fifth Republic. Using strong executive powers, he promoted French economic and technological advances in the context of the European Economic Community and guarded French foreign policy independence.

France had withdrawn from Indochina in 1954, and from Morocco and Tunisia in 1956. Most of its remaining African territories were freed 1958-62.

In 1966, France withdrew all its troops from the integrated military command of NATO, though 60,000 remained stationed in Germany. France continued to attend political meetings of NATO.

In May 1968 rebellious students in Paris and other centers rioted, battled police, and were joined by workers who launched nationwide strikes. The government awarded pay increases to the strikers May 26. In elections to the Assembly in June, de Gaulle's backers won a landslide victory. Nevertheless, he resigned from office in April, 1969, after losing a nationwide referendum on constitutional reform.

On May 10, 1981, France elected François Mitterrand, a Socialist candidate, president. In September, the government nationalized 5 major industries and most private banks. In 1986, France began a privatization program in which many state-owned companies were sold. In 1993 the government completed the privatization program by selling stakes in 21 companies for about $54 billion. Mitterrand was elected to a 2d 7-year term in 1988.

France set tighter rules for entry into the country and made it easier for the government to expel foreigners in 1993.

The island of **Corsica,** in the Mediterranean W of Italy and N of Sardinia, is an official region of France comprising 2 departments. Area: 3,369 sq. mi.; pop. (1990 cen.): 249,700. The capital is Ajaccio, birthplace of Napoleon.

Overseas Departments

French Guiana is on the NE coast of South America with Suriname on the W and Brazil on the E and S. Its area is 43,740 sq. mi.; pop. (1991): 101,000. Guiana sends one senator and one deputy to the French Parliament. Guiana is administered by a prefect and has a Council General of 16 elected members; capital is Cayenne.

The famous penal colony, Devil's Island, was phased out between 1938 and 1951.

Immense forests of rich timber cover 90% of the land. Placer gold mining is the most important industry. Exports are shrimp, timber, and machinery.

Guadeloupe, in the West Indies' Leeward Islands, consists of 2 large islands, Basse-Terre and Grande-Terre, separated by the Salt River, plus Marie Galante and the Saintes group to the S and, to the N, Desirade, St. Barthelemy, and over half of St. Martin (the Netherlands portion is St. Maarten). A French possession since 1635, the department is represented in the French Parliament by 2 senators and 3 deputies; administration consists of a prefect (governor) and an elected general and regional councils.

Area of the islands is 660 sq. mi.; pop. (1991 est.) 395,000, mainly descendants of slaves; capital is Basse-Terre on Basse-Terre Is. The land is fertile; sugar, rum, and bananas are exported; tourism is an important industry.

Martinique, the northernmost of the Windward Islands, in the West Indies, has been a possession since 1635, and a department since March 1946. It is represented in the French Parliament by 2 senators and 3 deputies. The island was the birthplace of Napoleon's Empress Josephine.

It has an area of 425 sq. mi.; pop. (1991 est.) 365,000, mostly descendants of slaves. The capital is Fort-de-France (pop. 1991: 101,000). It is a popular tourist stop. The chief exports are rum, bananas, and petroleum products.

Reunion is a volcanic island in the Indian O. about 420 mi. E of Madagascar, and has belonged to France since 1665. Area, 969 sq. mi.; pop. (1992 est.) 626,000, 30% of French extraction. Capital: Saint-Denis. The chief export is sugar. It elects 3 deputies, 2 senators to the French Parliament.

Territorial Collectivities

Mayotte, claimed by Comoros and administered by France, voted in 1976 to become a territorial collectivity of France. An island NW of Madagascar, area is 144 sq. mi., pop. (1992 est.) 86,000.

St. Pierre and Miquelon, formerly an Overseas Territory (1816-1976) and department (1976-85), made the transition to territorial collectivity in 1985. It consists of 2 groups of rocky islands near the SW coast of Newfoundland, inhabited by fishermen. The exports are chiefly fish products. The St. Pierre group has an area of 10 sq. mi.; Miquelon, 83 sq. mi. Total pop. (1992 est.), 6,513. The capital is St. Pierre. A deputy and a senator are elected to the French Parliament.

Overseas Territories

French Polynesia Overseas Territory, comprises 130 islands widely scattered among 5 archipelagos in the South Pacific; administered by a governor. Territorial Assembly and a Council with headquarters at Papeete, Tahiti, one of the **Society Islands** (which include the **Windward** and **Leeward** islands). A deputy and a senator are elected to the French Parliament.

Other groups are the **Marquesas Islands,** the **Tuamotu Archipelago,** including the **Gambier Islands,** and the **Austral Islands.**

Total area of the islands administered from Tahiti is 1,544 sq. mi.; pop. (1991 est.), 195,000, more than half on Tahiti. Tahiti is picturesque and mountainous with a productive coastline bearing coconut, banana and orange trees, sugar cane and vanilla.

Tahiti was visited by Capt. James Cook in 1769 and by Capt. Bligh in the Bounty, 1788-89. Its beauty impressed Herman Melville, Paul Gauguin, and Charles Darwin.

French Southern and Antarctic Lands Overseas Territory comprises **Adelie Land,** on Antarctica, and 4 island groups in the Indian O. Adelie, reached 1840, has a research station, a coastline of 185 mi. and tapers 1,240 mi. inland to the South Pole. The U.S. does not recognize national claims in Antarctica. There are 2 huge glaciers, Ninnis, 22 mi. wide, 99 mi. long, and Mentz, 11 mi. wide, 140 mi. long. The Indian O. groups are:

Kerguelen Archipelago, visited 1772, consists of one large and 300 small islands. The chief is 87 mi. long, 74 mi. wide, and has Mt. Ross, 6,429 ft. tall. Principal research station is Port-aux-Francais. Seals often weigh 2 tons; there are blue whales, coal, peat, semi-precious stones. **Crozet Archipelago,** reached 1772, covers 195 sq. mi. Eastern Island rises to 6,560 ft. **Saint Paul,** in southern Indian O., has warm springs with earth at places heating to 120° to 390° F. **Amsterdam** is nearby; both produce cod and rock lobster.

New Caledonia and its dependencies, an overseas territory, are a group of islands in the Pacific O. about 1,115 mi. E of Australia and approx. the same distance NW of New Zealand. Dependencies are the **Loyalty Islands,** the **Isle of Pines, Huon Islands** and the **Chesterfield Islands.**

New Caledonia, the largest, has 6,530 sq. mi. Total area of the territory is 8,548 sq. mi.; population (1991 est.) 172,000. The group was acquired by France in 1853.

The territory is administered by a governor and government council. There is a popularly elected Territorial Assembly. A deputy and a senator are elected to the French Parliament. Capital: Noumea.

Mining is the chief industry. New Caledonia is one of the world's largest nickel producers. Other minerals found are chrome, iron, cobalt, manganese, silver, gold, lead, and copper. Agricultural products include coffee, copra, cotton, manioc (cassava), corn, tobacco, bananas and pineapples.

In 1987, New Caledonian voters chose by referendum to remain within the French Republic. There were clashes between French and Melanesians (Kanaks) in 1988.

Wallis and Futuna Islands, 2 archipelagos raised to status of overseas territory July 29, 1961, are in the SW Pacific S of the Equator between Fiji and Samoa. The islands have a total area of 106 sq. mi. and population (1988 est.) of 15,400. **Alofi,** attached to Futuna, is uninhabited. Capital: Mata-Utu. Chief products are copra, yams, taro roots, bananas. A senator and a deputy are elected to the French Parliament.

Gabon

Gabonese Republic

République Gabonaise

People: Population (1992 est.): 1,106,000. **Pop. density:** 10 per sq. mi. **Urban** (1990): 45%. **Ethnic groups:** Fang 25%, Bapounon 10%, others. **Languages:** French (official), Bantu dialects. **Religions:** Mostly Christian, minority follow traditional beliefs.

Geography: Area: 103,346 sq. mi., the size of Colorado. **Location:** On Atlantic coast of central Africa. **Neighbors:** Equatorial Guinea, Cameroon on N, Congo on E, S. **Topography:** Heavily forested, the country consists of coastal lowlands plateaus in N, E, and S, mountains in N, SE, and center. The Ogooue R. system covers most of Gabon. **Capital:** Libreville. **Cities** (1991 est.): Libreville 275,000.

Government: Type: Republic. **Head of state:** Pres. Omar Bongo; b. Dec. 30, 1935; in office: Dec. 2, 1967. **Head of government:** Prime Min. Casimir Oye Mba; in office: May 3, 1990. **Local divisions:** 9 provinces. **Defense:** 3.2% of GDP (1990).

Economy: Industries: Oil products. **Chief crops:** Cocoa, coffee, rice, peanuts, palm products, cassava, bananas. **Minerals:** Manganese, uranium, oil, iron, gas. **Crude oil reserves** (1985): 623 mln. bbls. **Other resources:** Timber. **Arable land:** 2%. **Electricity prod.** (1991): 995 mln. kWh. **Labor force:** 65% agric.; 30% ind. & comm.

Finance: Monetary unit: CFA franc (Mar. 1993: 273 = $1 US). **Gross domestic product** (1991) $5.3 bln. **Per capita income** (1991): $4,400. **Imports** (1990): $780 mln.; partners: Fr. 51%. **Exports** (1990): $1.1 bln.; partners: Fr. 53%, U.S. 22%. **Tourism receipts** (1990): $4 mln. **National budget** (1991): $1.8 bln. **International reserves less gold** (Jan. 1993): $167 mln. **Gold:** 13,000 oz t. **Consumer prices** (change in 1990): 8.0%.

Transport: Motor vehicles: in use (1989): 19,000 passenger cars, 15,000 comm. vehicles. **Civil aviation** (1990): 445 mln. passengers-km. **Chief ports:** Port-Gentil, Owendo, Mayumba.

Communications: Television sets: 1 per 29 persons. **Radios:** 1 per 5 persons. **Telephones:** 1 per 64 persons.

Health: Life expectancy at birth (1992): 51 male; 56 female. **Births** (per 1,000 pop. 1992): 28. **Deaths** (per 1,000 pop. 1992): 15. **Natural increase:** 1.4%. **Hospital beds** (1985): 4,617. **Physicians** (1985): 265. **Infant mortality** (per 1,000 live births 1992): 100.

Education (1991): **Literacy:** 70%. Compulsory to age 16; attendance: 100% primary, 14% secondary.

Major International Organizations: UN (World Bank), OAU, OPEC.

Embassy: 2034 20th St NW 20009; 797-1000.

France established control over the region in the second half of the 19th century. Gabon became independent Aug. 17, 1960. A multiparty political system was introduced in 1990, and a new constitution was enacted in 1991. It is one of the most prosperous black African countries, thanks to abundant natural resources, foreign private investment, and government development programs.

The Gambia

Republic of The Gambia

People: Population (1992 est.): 902,000. **Age distrib.** (%): 0–14: 45.9; 15–59: 54.4; 60+: 3.8. **Pop. density:** 218 per sq. mi. **Urban** (1990): 21%. **Ethnic groups:** Mandinka 42%, Fula 8%, Wolof 16%, others. **Languages:** English (official), Mandinka, Wolof. **Religions:** Moslem 95%.

Geography: Area: 4,127 sq. mi., smaller than Connecticut. **Location:** On Atlantic coast near western tip of Africa. **Neighbors:** Surrounded on 3 sides by Senegal. **Topography:** A narrow strip of land on each side of the lower Gambia. **Capital:** Banjul. **Cities** (1993 est.): Banjul 40,000.

Government: Type: Republic. **Head of state:** Pres. Dawda Kairaba Jawara; b. May 16, 1924; in office: Apr. 24, 1970 (prime min. from June 12, 1962). **Local divisions:** 5 divisions and Banjul.

Economy: Industries: Tourism, peanut processing. **Chief crops:** Peanuts (main export), rice. **Arable land:** 16%. **Fish catch** (1989): 17,000 metric tons. **Electricity prod.** (1991): 65 mln. kWh. **Labor force:** 75% agric.; 18% ind. & comm.

Finance: Monetary unit: Dalasi (Mar. 1993: 9.14 = $1.00 US). **Gross domestic product** (1991): $207 mln. **Per capita GDP:** $235. **Imports** (1991): $167 mln.; partners: EC 53%. **Exports** (1991): $122 mln.; partners: Japan 60%. **Tourism** (1990): $26 mln. receipts. **National budget** (1990): $95 mln. expenditures. **International reserves less gold** (Jan. 1993): $64 mln. **Consumer prices** (change in 1992): 9.5%.

Transport: Motor vehicles: in use (1989): 5,200 passenger cars, 1,000 comm. vehicles. **Chief ports:** Banjul.

Communications: Radios: 1 per 6.1 persons. **Telephones:** 1 per 80 persons.

Health: Life expectancy at birth (1992): 47 male; 51 female. **Births** (per 1,000 pop. 1992): 47. **Deaths** (per 1,000 pop. 1992): 17. **Natural increase:** 3.0%. **Physicians:** 1 per 17,604 persons. **Infant mortality** (per 100,000 live births 1992): 129.

Education (1993): **Literacy:** 30%.

Major International Organizations: UN (GATT, IMF, WHO), OAU.

Embassy: 1155 15th St. 20005; 785-1399.

The tribes of Gambia were at one time associated with the West African empires of Ghana, Mali, and Songhay. The area became Britain's first African possession in 1588.

Independence came Feb. 18, 1965; republic status within the Commonwealth was achieved in 1970. After a coup attempt in 1981, The Gambia formed the confederation of Senegambia with Senegal that lasted until 1989. The country suffered from severe famine in the 1970s.

Georgia

Republic of Georgia

Sakartvelos Respublica

People: Population (1992 est.): 5,570,000. **Pop. density:** 206 per sq. mi. **Urban** (1991): 57%. **Ethnic groups:** Georgian 70%, Armenian 7%, Russian 6%. **Languages:** Georgian (official), Russian. **Religions:** Georgia Orthodox 65%, Russian Orthodox 10%.

Geography: Area: 26,911 sq. mi., slightly larger than S.C. **Neighbors:** Black Sea on W, Russia on N, NE, Turkey, Armenia on S, Azerbaijan on SE. **Topography:** Separated from Russia on NE by main range of the Caucasus mts. **Capital:** Tbilisi. **Cities** (1991): Tbilisi 1.2 mln.

Government: Type: Republic. **Head of state:** Pres. Eduard A. Shevardnadze; b. Jan. 25, 1928; in office: Nov. 6, 1992. **Head of government:** Prime Min. Otar Patsatsia; in office: Aug. 1993.

Economy: Industries: Manganese mining. **Chief crops:** Citrus fruits, wheat, grapes. **Livestock** (1990): cattle: 1.5 mln., sheep: 1.9 mln.

Finance: Monetary unit: Ruble. **Imports** (1990): $1.5 bln. **Exports** (1990): $176 mln.

Transport: Railroads: Length: 976 mi. **Motor vehicles:** in use: 427,000 passenger cars.

Communications: Newspaper circ. (1990): 671 per 1,000 pop.

Health: Life expectancy at birth: 67 male; 73 female. Births (per 1,000 pop. 1992): 17. **Deaths** (per 1,000 pop. 1992): 9. Infant mortality (per 1,000 live births 1992): 34. Physicians: 1 per 170 persons; **Hospital beds:** 1 per 90 persons.

The region contained the ancient kingdoms of Colchis and Iberia. It was Christianized in the 4th century and conquered by Arabs in the 8th century. The region expanded to include area from the Black Sea to Caspian and parts of Armenia and Persia before its disintegration under the impact of Mongol and Turkish invasions. The annexation to Russia in 1801 caused the Russian war with Persia, 1804-1813. Georgia entered the USSR in 1922 and became a constituent republic in 1936.

In 1989, strong nationalist feelings led the USSR to attempts at repression; Soviet troops attacked nationalist demonstrators in April, killing some 20 persons. Georgia declared independence Apr. 9, 1991. It became an independent state when the Soviet Union disbanded Dec. 26, 1991, although it did not join the Commonwealth of Independent States.

There was fighting during 1991 between rebel forces and loyalists of Pres. Zviad Gamsakhurdia, whom the rebels accused of aspiring to establish a dictatorship. Gamsakhurdia fled the capital Jan. 6, 1992. The ruling Military Council picked former Soviet Foreign Minister Eduard A. Shevardnadze to chair a newly created State Council. An attempted coup by forces loyal to ousted Pres. Gamsakhurdia was crushed June 24. Shevardnadze was elected president Nov. 1992.

Georgia accused Russia of aiding rebels in Abkhazia, an autonomous region within Georgia, in 1993. The ethnic Abkhazis were in armed revolt to secure independence. Martial law was declared in parts of the region July 6.

Germany

Federal Republic of Germany

Bundesrepublik Deutschland

(Figures prior to 1990 for original 11 states)

People: Population (1992 est.): 80,387,000. **Age distrib.** (%): 0–14: 14.7; 15–59: 64.7; 60+: 20.6. **Pop. density:** 583 per sq. mi. **Urban** (1990): 86% **Ethnic groups:** German 93%. **Languages:** German. **Religions:** Protestant 44%, Roman Catholic 37%.

Geography: Area: 137,838 sq. mi. **Location:** In central Europe. **Neighbors:** Denmark on N, Netherlands, Belgium, Luxembourg, France on W, Switzerland, Austria on S, Czech Rep., Poland on E. **Topography:** Germany is flat in N, hilly in center and W, and mountainous in Bavaria. Chief rivers are Elbe, Weser, Ems, Rhine, and Main, all flowing toward North Sea, and Danube, flowing toward Black Sea. **Capital:** Berlin. **Cities** (1991 est.): Berlin 3.0 mln.; Hamburg 1.6 mln.; Munich 1.3 mln.; Cologne 946,000; Essen 622,000; Frankfurt 635,000; Dortmund 575,000; Dusseldorf 593,000; Stuttgart 561,000; Leipzig 549,000; Dresden 521,000.

Government: Type: Federal republic. **Head of state:** Pres. Richard von Weizsacker; b. Apr. 15, 1920; in office: May 23, 1984. **Head of government:** Chan. Helmut Kohl; b. Apr. 3, 1930; in office: Oct. 1, 1982. **Local divisions:** 16 laender (states) with substantial powers. **Defense:** 2.5% of GDP (1991).

Economy: Industries: Steel, ships, vehicles, machinery, electronics, coal, chemicals. **Chief crops:** Grains, potatoes, sugar beets. **Minerals:** Coal, potash, lignite, iron, uranium. **Arable land:** 35%. **Livestock** (1990): cattle: 15.3 mln.; pigs: 10.0 mln.; sheep: 1.2 mln. **Fish catch** (1990): 390,000 metric tons. **Electricity prod.** (1991): 580 bln. kWh. **Crude steel prod.** (1991): 42.1 mln. metric tons. **Labor force:** 5% agric.; 40% ind. & comm.; 54% services.

Finance: Monetary unit: Mark (Aug. 1993: 1.71 = $1 US). **Gross domestic product** (1991): $1,331 bln. **Per capita GDP:** $14,600. **Imports** (1992): $402 bln.; partners: EC 52%; other European 16%. **Exports** (1992): $422 bln.; partners: EC 55%; other European 19%. **Tourists** (1989): receipts $8.6 bln. **National budget** (1990): $245 bln. expenditures. **International reserves less gold** (Mar. 1993): $70 bln. **Gold:** 95.18 mln. oz t. **Consumer prices** (change in 1992): 4.0%.

Transport: Railroads (1991): **Length:** 56,397 mi. **Motor vehicles:** in use (1990): 35.5 mln. passenger cars, 2.7 mln. comm. **Civil aviation** (1988): 34.0 bln. passenger-km; 27 airports with scheduled flights. **Chief ports:** Hamburg, Bremen, Bremerhaven, Lubeck.

Communications: Television sets: 1 per 2.6 persons. **Radios:** 1 per 2.3 persons. **Telephones:** 1 per 1.5 persons. **Daily newspaper circ.** (1990): 401 per 1,000 pop.

Health: Life expectancy at birth (1992): 73 male; 79 female. **Births** (per 1,000 pop. 1992): 11. **Deaths** (per 1,000 pop. 1992): 11. **Hospital beds:** 1 per 95 persons. **Physicians:** 1 per 324 persons. **Infant mortality** (per 1,000 live births 1992): 7.

Education (1991): **Literacy:** 99%. **Years compulsory:** 10; attendance 100%.

Major International Organizations: UN and all of its specialized agencies, EC, OECD, NATO.

Embassy: 4645 Reservoir Rd. NW 20007; 298-4000.

Germany, prior to World War II, was a central European nation composed of numerous states which had a common language and traditions and which had been united in one country since 1871; since World War II until 1990, had been split in 2 parts.

History and government. Germanic tribes were defeated by Julius Caesar, 55 and 53 BC, but Roman expansion N of the Rhine was stopped in 9 AD. Charlemagne, ruler of the Franks, consolidated Saxon, Bavarian, Rhenish, Frankish, and other lands; after him the eastern part became the German Empire. The Thirty Years' War, 1618-1648, split Germany into small principalities and kingdoms. After Napoleon, Austria contended with Prussia for dominance, but lost the Seven Weeks' War to Prussia, 1866. Otto von Bismarck, Prussian chancellor, formed the North German Confederation, 1867.

In 1870 Bismarck maneuvered Napoleon III into declaring war. After the quick defeat of France, Bismarck formed the **German Empire** and on Jan. 18, 1871, in Versailles, proclaimed King Wilhelm I of Prussia German emperor (Deutscher kaiser).

The German Empire reached its peak before World War I in 1914, with 208,780 sq. mi., plus a colonial empire. After that war Germany ceded Alsace-Lorraine to France; West Prussia and Posen (Poznan) province to Poland; part of Schleswig to Denmark; lost all of its colonies and the ports of Memel and Danzig.

Republic of Germany, 1919-1933, adopted the Weimar constitution; met reparation payments and elected Friedrich Ebert and Gen. Paul von Hindenburg presidents.

Third Reich, 1933-1945, Adolf Hitler led the National Socialist German Workers' (Nazi) party after World War I. In 1923 he attempted to unseat the Bavarian government and was imprisoned. Pres. von Hindenburg named Hitler chancellor Jan. 30, 1933; on Aug. 3, 1934, the day after Hindenburg's death, the cabinet joined the offices of president and chancellor and made Hitler fuehrer (leader). Hitler abolished freedom of speech and assembly, and began a long series of persecutions climaxed by the murder of millions of Jews and opponents.

Hitler repudiated the Versailles treaty and reparations agreements. He remilitarized the Rhineland 1936 and annexed Austria (Anschluss, 1938). At Munich he made an agreement with Neville Chamberlain, British prime minister, which permitted Hitler to annex part of Czechoslovakia. He signed a non-aggression treaty with the USSR, 1939. He declared war on Poland Sept. 1, 1939, precipitating World War II.

With total defeat near, Hitler committed suicide in Berlin Apr. 1945. The victorious Allies voided all acts and annexations of Hitler's Reich.

Postwar changes. The zones of occupation administered by the Allied Powers and later relinquished gave the USSR Saxony, Saxony-Anhalt, Thuringia, and Mecklenburg, and the former Prussian provinces of Saxony and Brandenburg.

The territory E of the Oder-Neisse line within 1937 boundaries comprising the provinces of Silesia, Pomerania, and the southern part of East Prussia, totaling about 41,220 sq. mi., was taken by Poland. Northern East Prussia was taken by the USSR.

The Western Allies ended the state of war with Germany in 1951. The USSR did so in 1955.

There was also created the area of Greater Berlin, within but not part of the Soviet zone, administered by the 4 occupying powers under the Allied Command. In 1948 the USSR withdrew, established its single command in East Berlin, and cut off supplies. The Allies utilized a gigantic airlift to bring food to West Berlin, 1948-49. In Aug. 1961 the East Germans built a wall dividing Berlin, after over 3 million E. Germans had emigrated.

On Nov. 9, 1989 the E. German government announced the decision to open the border with the West signaling the end of the infamous Berlin Wall.

A New Era: As communism was being rejected in E. Germany, talks began concerning German reunification. At a meeting in Ottawa, Feb. 1990, the foreign ministers of the World War II "Big Four" Allied nations—U.S., USSR, UK, and France—as well as the foreign ministers of E. Germany and W. Germany reached agreement on a format for high-level talks on German reunification.

In May, NATO ministers adopted a package of proposals on reunification, including the inclusion of the united Germany as a full member of NATO and the barring of the new Germany from having its own nuclear, chemical, or biological weapons. In July, the USSR agreed to conditions that would allow Germany to become a member of NATO.

The 2 nations agreed to monetary unification under the W. German mark beginning in July. The merger of the 2 Germanys took place on Oct. 3, 1990, and the first all-German elections since 1932 were held Dec. 2, 1990.

In 1992, neo-Nazi groups intensified their campaign against refugees. The Constitutional Protection Office reported 2,285 violent attacks by right-wingers in 1992. Parliament approved constitutional changes to restrict foreigners' rights to seek asylum in Germany, May 1993.

East Germany

The German Democratic Republic was proclaimed in the Soviet sector of Berlin Oct. 7, 1949. It was proclaimed fully sovereign in 1954, but Soviet troops remained on grounds of security and the 4-power Potsdam agreement.

Coincident with the entrance of W. Germany into the European Defense community in 1952, the East German government decreed a prohibited zone 3 miles deep along its 600-mile border with W. Germany and cut Berlin's telephone system in two. Berlin was further divided by erection of a fortified wall in 1961, but the exodus of refugees to the West continued, though on a smaller scale.

E. Germany suffered severe economic problems until the mid-1960s. A "new economic system" was introduced, easing the former central planning controls and allowing factories to make profits provided they were reinvested in operations or redistributed to workers as bonuses. By the early 1970s, the economy was highly industrialized. In May 1972 the few remaining private firms were ordered sold to the government. The nation was credited with the highest standard of living among Warsaw Pact countries. But growth slowed in the late 1970s, due to shortages of natural resources and labor, and a huge debt to lenders in the West. Comparison with the lifestyle in the West caused many of the young to leave the country.

The government firmly resisted following the USSR's policy of *glasnost*, but by Oct. 1989, was faced with nationwide demonstrations demanding reform. Pres. Erich Honecker, in office since 1976, was forced to resign, Oct. 18. On Nov. 4, the border with Czechoslovakia was opened and permission granted for refugees to travel on to the West, On Nov. 9, the decision was made to open the border with the West, signaling the end of the "Berlin Wall," which separated the 2 Germanys and was the supreme emblem of the cold war.

On Aug. 23, 1990, the E. German Parliament agreed to formal unification with W. Germany; this took place on Oct. 3.

West Germany

The Federal Republic of Germany was proclaimed May 23, 1949, in Bonn, after a constitution had been drawn up by a consultative assembly formed by representatives of the 11 laender (states) in the French, British, and American zones. Later reorganized into 9 units, the laender numbered 10 with the addition of the Saar, 1957. Berlin also was granted land (state) status, but the 1945 occupation agreements placed restrictions on it.

The occupying powers, the U.S., Britain, and France, restored the civil status, Sept. 21, 1949. The U. S. resumed diplomatic relations July 2, 1951. The powers lifted controls and the republic became fully independent May 5, 1955.

Dr. Konrad Adenauer, Christian Democrat, was made chancellor Sept. 15, 1949, re-elected 1953, 1957, 1961. Willy Brandt, heading a coalition of Social Democrats and Free Democrats, became chancellor Oct. 21, 1969.

In 1970 Brandt signed friendship treaties with the USSR and Poland. In 1971, the U.S., Britain, France, and the USSR signed an agreement on Western access to West Berlin. In 1972 the Bundestag approved the USSR and Polish treaties and East and West Germany signed their first formal treaty, implementing the agreement easing access to West Berlin. In 1973 a West Germany-Czechoslovakia pact normalized relations and nullified the 1938 "Munich Agreement."

In May 1974 Brandt resigned, saying he took full responsibility for "negligence" for allowing an East German spy to become a member of his staff.

West Germany experienced economic growth since the 1950s. The country led Europe in provisions for worker participation in the management of industry.

The NATO decision to deploy medium-range nuclear missiles in Western Europe sparked a demonstration by some 400,000 protesters in 1983. In 1989, Chanceller Kohl's call for early negotiations with the Soviets on reducing short-range missiles caused a rift with the NATO allies, especially the U.S. and Great Britain.

In 1989, the changes in the E. German government and the opening of the Berlin Wall sparked talk of reunification of the 2 Germanys. In 1990, under the leadership of Chanceller Kohl, W. Germany moved rapidly to reunite with E. Germany.

Helgoland, an island of 130 acres in the North Sea, was taken from Denmark by a British Naval Force in 1807 and later ceded to Germany to become a part of Schleswig-Holstein province in return for rights in East Africa. The heavily fortified island was surrendered to UK, May 23, 1945, demilitarized in 1947, and returned to W. Germany, Mar 1, 1952. It is a free port.

Ghana

Republic of Ghana

People: Population (1992 est.): 16,185,000. **Age distrib.** (%): 0–14: 46.6; 15-59: 48.9; 60+: 4.5. **Pop. density:** 175 per sq. mi. **Urban** (1990): 33%. **Ethnic groups:** Akan 44%, Moshi-Dagomba 16%, Ewe 13%, Ga 8%, others. **Languages:** English (official), Akan, Mossi, Ewe, Ga-Adangme. **Religions:** Christian 24%, traditional beliefs 38%, Moslem 30%.

Geography: Area: 92,098 sq. mi., slightly smaller than Oregon. **Location:** On southern coast of W. Africa. **Neighbors:** Côte D'Ivoire on W, Burkina Faso on N, Togo on E. **Topography:** Most of Ghana consists of low fertile plains and scrubland, cut by rivers and by the artificial Lake Volta. **Capital:** Accra. **Cities** (1988 est.): Accra 949,000.

Government: Type: Military. **Head of government:** Pres. Jerry Rawlings; b. 1947; in office: Dec. 31, 1981. **Local divisions:** 10 regions.

Economy: Industries: Aluminum, light industry. **Chief crops:** Cocoa, coffee. **Minerals:** Gold, manganese, industrial diamonds, bauxite. **Crude oil reserves:** (1980): 7 mln. bbls. **Other resources:** Timber, rubber. **Arable land:** 5%. **Livestock** (1990): cattle: 1.1 mln.; sheep: 2.2 mln. **Fish catch** (1990): 360,000 metric tons. **Electricity prod.** (1991): 4.1 bln. kWh. **Labor force:** 55% agric.; 19% ind.

Finance: Monetary unit: Cedi (Mar. 1993: 555 = $1.00 US). **Gross domestic product** (1991): $6.2 bln. **Per capita GDP:** $400. **Imports** (1991): $1.2 bln.; partners: UK 10%, Ger. 12%, Nigeria 12%. **Exports** (1991): $843 mln.; partners: U.S. 23%, Neth. 9%, Ger. 9%. **International reserves less gold** (Mar. 1993): 399 mln. **Gold:** 275,000 oz t. **Consumer prices** (change in 1991): 18%.

Transport: Railroads (1991): **Length:** 592 mi. **Motor vehicles:** in use (1986): 26,000 passenger cars, 28,000 comm. vehicles. **Civil aviation** (1990): 407 mln. passenger-km; 3 airports with scheduled flights. **Chief ports:** Tema, Takoradi.

Communications: Television sets: 1 per 83 persons. **Radios:** 1 per 4.7 persons. **Telephones:** 1 per 191 persons.

Health: Life expectancy at birth (1992): 53 male; 56 female. **Births** (per 1,000 pop. 1992): 46. **Deaths** (per 1,000 pop. 1992): 13. **Natural increase:** 3.3%. **Physicians:** 1 per 22,127 persons. **Infant mortality** (per 1,000 live births 1992): 86.

Education (1991): **Literacy:** 60%.

Major International Organizations: UN and all of its specialized agencies, OAU.

Embassy: 3512 International Dr., 20008; 686-4500.

Named for an African empire along the Niger River, 400-1240 AD, Ghana was ruled by Britain for 113 years as the Gold Coast. The UN in 1956 approved merger with the British Togoland trust territory. Independence came March 6, 1957. Republic status within the Commonwealth was attained in 1960.

Pres. Kwame Nkrumah built hospitals and schools, promoted development projects like the Volta R. hydroelectric and aluminum plants but ran the country into debt, jailed opponents, and was accused of corruption. A 1964 referendum gave Nkrumah dictatorial powers and set up a one-party socialist state.

Nkrumah was overthrown in 1966 by a police-army coup, which expelled Chinese and East German teachers and technicians. Elections were held in 1969, but 4 further coups occurred in 1972, 1978, 1979, and 1981. The 1979 and 1981 coups, led by Flight Lieut. Jerry Rawlings, were followed by suspension of the constitution and banning of political parties. A new constitution, which allowed for multiparty politics, was approved in April 1992.

Greece

Hellenic Republic

Elliniki Dimokratia

People: Population (1992 est.): 10,064,000. **Age distrib.** (%): 0–14: 20.5; 15-59: 61.1; 60+: 20.4. **Pop. density:** 196 per sq. mi. **Urban** (1990): 63.0%. **Ethnic groups:** Greeks 98.5%. **Languages:** Greek. **Religions:** Greek Orthodox 97% (official).

Geography: Area: 51,146 sq. mi., the size of Alabama. **Location:** Occupies southern end of Balkan Peninsula in SE Europe. **Neighbors:** Albania, Macedonia, Bulgaria on N, Turkey on E. **Topography:** About 75% of Greece is non-arable, with mountains in all areas. Pindus Mts. run through the country N to S. The heavily indented coastline is 9,385 mi. long. Of over 2,000 islands, only 169 are inhabited, among them Crete, Rhodes, Milos, Kerkira (Corfu), Chios, Lesbos, Samos, Euboea, Delos, Mykonos. **Capital:** Athens. **Cities** (1991 est.): Athens 748,110; Thessaloniki 377,000; Patras 169,000.

Government: Type: Presidential parliamentary republic. **Head of state:** Pres. Konstantinos Karamanlis; in office: May, 1990. **Head of government:** Prime Min. Konstantinos Mitsotakis; b. Oct. 18, 1918, in office: Apr. 11, 1990. **Local divisions:** 51 prefectures. **Defense:** 5.5% of GDP (1991).

Economy: Industries: Textiles, chemicals, metals, wine, food processng, cement. **Chief crops:** Grains, corn, rice, cotton, tobacco, olives, citrus fruits, raisins, figs. **Minerals:** Bauxite, lignite, oil, manganese. **Crude oil reserves** (1985): 35 mln. bbls. **Arable land:** 23%. **Livestock** (1990): sheep: 11.0 mln.; goats: 5.6 mln. **Fish catch** (1990): 128,000 metric tons. **Electricity prod.** (1991): 36.4 bln. kWh. **Labor force:** 28% agric.; 29% ind., 42% service.

Finance: Monetary unit: Drachma (Aug. 1993: 239.00 = $1 US). **Gross domestic product** (1991): $77 bln. **Per capita GDP:** $7,730. **Imports** (1991): $21.5 bln.; partners: Ger. 21%, It. 15%, Fr. 7%. **Exports** (1991): $8.6 bln.; partners: Ger. 20%, It. 17%, Fra. 10%. **Tourism** (1990): $2.5 bln. receipts. **National budget** (1991): $33 bln. expenditures. **International reserves less gold** (Mar. 1993): $4.7 bln. **Gold:** 3.4 mln. oz t. **Consumer prices** (change in 1992): 15.8%.

Transport: Railroads (1991): **Length:** 1,540 mi. **Motor vehicles:** in use (1990): 1.6 mln. passenger cars, 781,000 comm. vehicles. **Civil aviation** (1990): 7.7 bln. passenger-km; 33 airports with scheduled flights. **Chief ports:** Piraeus, Thessaloniki, Patrai.

Communications: Television sets: 1 per 4.5 persons. **Radios:** 1 per 2.4 persons. **Telephones:** 1 per 2.2 persons. **Daily newspaper circ.** (1986): 88 per 1,000 pop.

Health: Life expectancy at birth (1992): 75 male; 80 female. **Births** (per 1,000 pop. 1992): 11. **Deaths** (per 1,000 pop. 1992): 9. **Natural increase:** .2%. **Hospital beds:** 1 per 193 persons. **Physicians:** 1 per 327 persons. **Infant mortality** (per 1,000 live birth 1992): 10.

Education (1991): **Literacy:** men 96%, women 89%. **Years compulsory:** 9.

Major International Organizations: UN (GATT, IMF, WHO, ILO), EC, NATO, OECD.

Embassy: 2221 Massachusetts Ave. NW 20008; 667-3168.

The achievements of ancient Greece in art, architecture, science, mathematics, philosophy, drama, literature, and democracy became legacies for succeeding ages. Greece reached the height of its glory and power, particularly in the Athenian city-state, in the 5th century BC.

Greece fell under Roman rule in the 2d and 1st centuries BC. In the 4th century AD it became part of the Byzantine Empire and, after the fall of Constantinople to the Turks in 1453, part of the Ottoman Empire.

Greece won its war of independence from Turkey 1821-1829, and became a kingdom. A republic was established 1924; the monarchy was restored, 1935, and George II, King of the Hellenes, resumed the throne. In Oct. 1940, Greece rejected an ultimatum from Italy. Nazi support resulted in its defeat and occupation by Germans, Italians, and Bulgarians. By the end of 1944 the invaders withdrew. Communist resistance forces were defeated by Royalist and British troops. A plebiscite recalled King George II. He died Apr. 1, 1947 and was succeeded by his brother, Paul I.

Communists waged guerrilla war 1947-49 against the government but were defeated with the aid of the U.S.

A period of reconstruction and rapid development followed, mainly with conservative governments under Premier Constantine Karamanlis. The Center Union led by George Papandreou won elections in 1963 and 1964. King Constantine, who acceded in 1964, forced Papandreou to resign. A period of political maneuvers ended in the military takeover of April 21, 1967, by Col. George Papadopoulos. King Constantine tried to reverse the consolidation of the harsh dictatorship Dec. 13, 1967, but failed and fled to Italy. Papadopoulos was ousted Nov. 25, 1973.

Greek army officers serving in the National Guard of Cyprus staged a coup on the island July 15, 1974. Turkey invaded Cyprus a week later, precipitating the collapse of the Greek junta, which was implicated in the Cyprus coup.

The 1981 victory of the Panhellenic Socialist Movement (Pasok) of Andreas Papandreou has brought about substantial changes in the internal and external policies that Greece has pursued for the past 5 decades. Greece was victimized in the 1980s by incidents of international terrorism.

A scandal centered on George Kostokas, a banker and publisher, led to the arrest or investigation of about a dozen leading Socialists, implicated Papandreou, and led to the defeat of the Socialists at the polls in 1989.

Grenada

People: Population (1992 est.): 84,000. **Pop. density:** 631 per sq. mi. **Ethnic groups:** Mostly African descent. **Languages:** English (official), French patois. **Religions:** Roman Catholic 64%, Anglican 22%.

Geography: Area: 133 sq. mi., twice the size of Washington, D.C. **Location:** 90 mi. N. of Venezuela. **Topography:** Main island is mountainous; country includes Carriacon and Petit Martinique islands. **Capital:** St. George's. **Cities** (1991 est.): St. George's 30,000.

Government: Type: Parliamentary democracy. **Head of state:** Queen Elizabeth II, represented by Gov.-Gen. Reginald Palmer. **Head of government:** Prime Minister: Nicholas Brathwaite; in office: Mar. 13, 1990. **Local divisions:** 6 parishes and one dependency.

Economy: Industries: Rum. **Chief crops:** Nutmegs, bananas, cocoa, mace. **Arable land:** 15%. **Electricity prod.** (1991): 26 mln. kWh. **Labor force:** 33% agric.; 31% services.

Finance: Monetary unit: East Caribbean dollar (Apr. 1993: 2.70 = $1 US). **Gross domestic product** (1989): $238 mln. **Per capita GDP:** $2,800. **Imports** (1989): $200 mln.; partners: UK 19%, Trin./Tob. 12%, U.S. 24%. **Exports** (1990): $26 mln.; partners: UK 23%, CARICOM countries 38%. **Tourism** (1991): $38 mln. receipts. **National budget** (1990): $77 mln. expenditures. **International reserves less gold** (Jan. 1993): $25 mln.

Transport: Chief ports: Saint George's.

Communications: Radios: 1 per 2.4 persons. **Telephones:** 1 per 9 persons.

Health: Life expectancy at birth (1992): 69 male; 74 female. **Births** (per 1,000 pop. 1992): 35. **Deaths** (per 1,000 pop. 1992): 7. **Natural increase:** 2.8%. **Infant mortality** (per 1,000 live births 1992): 28.

Education (1991): **Literacy:** 95%; **Years compulsory:** 6.

Major International Organizations: UN (IMF, WHO), OAS.

Embassy: 1701 New Hampshire Ave. NW 20009; 265-2561.

Columbus sighted the island 1498. First European settlers were French, 1650. The island was held alternately by France and England until final British occupation, 1784. Grenada became fully independent Feb. 7, 1974 during a general strike. It is the smallest independent nation in the Western Hemisphere.

On Oct. 14, 1983, a military coup ousted Prime Minister Maurice Bishop, who was put under house arrest, later freed by supporters, rearrested, and, finally, on Oct. 19, executed. U.S. forces, with a token force from 6 area nations, invaded Grenada, Oct. 25. Resistance from the Grenadian army and Cuban advisors was quickly overcome as most of the population welcomed the invading forces as liberators. U.S. troops left Grenada in June 1985.

Guatemala

Republic of Guatemala

República de Guatemala

People: Population (1992 est.): 9,784,000. **Age distrib.** (%): 0–14: 45.4; 15–59: 49.5; 60+: 5.1. **Pop. density:** 232 per sq. mi. **Urban** (1992): 39%. **Ethnic groups:** Maya 55%, Mestizos 44%. **Languages:** Spanish (official), Mayan languages. **Religions:** Mostly Roman Catholics.

Geography: Area: 42,042 sq. mi., the size of Tennessee. **Location:** In Central America. **Neighbors:** Mexico N, W, El Salvador on S, Honduras, Belize on E. **Topography:** The central highland and mountain areas are bordered by the narrow Pacific coast and the lowlands and fertile river valleys on the Caribbean. There are numerous volcanoes in S, more than half a dozen over 11,000 ft. **Capital:** Guatemala City. **Cities** (1992 est.): Guatemala City 1,115,000.

Government: Type: Republic. **Head of state:** Pres. Ramiro de Leon Carpio; in office: June 6, 1993. **Local divisions:** Guatemala City and 22 departments. **Defense:** 1.0% of GDP (1990).

Economy: Industries: Prepared foods, tires, textiles. **Chief crops:** Coffee (one third of exports), sugar, bananas, cotton, corn. **Minerals:** Oil, nickel. **Crude oil reserves** (1985): 500 mln. bbls. **Other resources:** Rare woods, fish, chicle. **Arable land:** 12%. **Electricity prod.** (1991): 2.5 bln. kWh. **Labor force:** 36% agric.; 24% ind. & comm., 34% services.

Finance: Monetary unit: Quetzal (Apr. 1993: 5.47 = $1 US). **Gross domestic product** (1991): $11.7 bln. **Per capita GDP:** $1,260. **Imports** (1992): $2.4 bln.; partners: U.S. 37%, CACM 8%. **Exports** (1992): $1.0 bln.; partners: U.S. 28%, CACM 20%. **Tourism** (1990): $185 mln. **National budget** (1990): $1.1 bln. expenditures. **International reserves less gold** (Mar. 1993): $807 mln. **Gold:** 122,000 oz t. **Consumer prices** (change in 1992): 10.0%.

Transport: Motor vehicles: in use (1990): 130,000 passenger cars, 100,000 comm. vehicles. **Civil aviation** (1990): 213 mln. passenger-km; 2 airports with scheduled flights. **Chief ports:** Puerto Barrios, San Jose.

Communications: Television sets: 1 per 18 persons. **Radios:** 1 per 22 persons. **Telephones:** 1 per 36 persons. **Daily newspaper circ.** (1989): 22 per 1,000 pop.

Health: Life expectancy at birth (1992): 61 male; 66 female. **Births** (per 1,000 pop. 1992): 34. **Deaths** (per 1,000 pop. 1992): 8. **Natural increase:** 2.6%. **Physicians:** 1 per 2,356 persons. **Infant mortality** (per 1,000 live births 1992): 56.

Education (1991): **Literacy:** 55%. **Years compulsory:** 6; **Attendance:** 35%.

Major International Organizations: UN (IMF, World Bank), OAS.

Embassy: 2220 R St. NW 20008; 745-4952.

The old Mayan Indian empire flourished in what is today Guatemala for over 1,000 years before the Spanish.

Guatemala was a Spanish colony 1524-1821; briefly a part of Mexico and then of the U.S. of Central America, the republic was established in 1839.

Since 1945 when a liberal government was elected to replace the long-term dictatorship of Jorge Ubico, the country has seen a swing toward socialism, an armed revolt, renewed attempts at social reform, a military coup, and, in 1986, civilian rule. The Guerrilla Army of the Poor, an insurgent group founded 1975, led a military offensive by attacking army posts and succeeded in incorporating segments of the large Indian population in its struggle against the government.

Dissident army officers seized power, Mar. 23, 1982, denouncing the Mar. 7 presidential election as fraudulent and pledging to restore "authentic democracy" to the nation. Political violence has caused some 200,000 Guatemalans to seek refuge in Mexico. A second military coup occurred Oct. 8, 1983. The nation returned to civilian rule in 1986.

Pres. Jorge Serrano Elias was ousted by the military June 1, 1993. Ramiro de Leon Carpio was elected president by Congress June 6. De Leon fired the defense minister and reassigned several military commanders.

Guinea

Republic of Guinea

République de Guinée

People: Population (1992 est.): 7,783,000. **Pop. density:** 81 per sq. mi. **Urban** (1991): 26%. **Ethnic groups:** Foulah 35%, Malinké 30%, Soussous 20%, 15 other tribes. **Languages:** French (official), Peul, Mande. **Religions:** Moslem 85%, Christian 10%.

Geography: Area: 94,964 sq. mi., slightly smaller than Oregon. **Location:** On Atlantic coast of W. Africa. **Neighbors:** Guinea-Bissau, Senegal, Mali on N, Côte d'Ivoire on E, Liberia on S. **Topography:** A narrow coastal belt leads to the mountainous middle region, the source of the Gambia, Senegal, and Niger rivers. Upper Guinea, farther inland, is a cooler upland. The SE is forested. **Capital:** Conakry. **Cities** (1989 est.): Conakry 705,000; Labe 273,000; N'Zerekore 250,000; Kankan 278,000.

Government: Type: Republic. **Head of state:** Pres. Brig. Gen. Lansana Conte; b. 1944; in office: Apr. 5, 1984. **Local divisions:** 33 administrative regions. **Defense:** 1.2% of GDP (1988).

Economy: Chief crops: Bananas, pineapples, rice, corn, palm nuts, coffee, honey. **Minerals:** Bauxite, iron, diamonds. **Arable land:** 6%. **Electricity prod.** (1991) 300 mln. kWh. **Labor force:** 82% agric.; 9% ind. & comm.

Finance: Monetary unit: Franc (Jan. 1993: 811 = $1 US). **Gross domestic product** (1990): $3.0 bln. **Per capita GDP:** $410. **Imports** (1990): $692 mln.; partners: U.S. 16%. **Exports** (1990): $788 mln.; partners: U.S. 33%. **National budget** (1990): 708 mln.

Transport: Motor vehicles: in use (1989): 13,000 passenger cars, 13,000 comm. vehicles. **Chief ports:** Conakry.

Communications: Radios: 1 per 34 persons. **Telephones:** 1 per 355 persons.

Health: Life expectancy at birth (1992): 41 male; 45 female. **Births** (per 1,000 pop. 1992): 46. **Deaths** (per 1,000 pop. 1992): 21. **Natural increase:** 2.5%. **Physicians:** 1 per 9,732 persons. **Infant mortality** (per 1,000 live births 1992): 144.

Education (1989): **Literacy:** 35% (in French). **Years compulsory:** 8; attendance: 36% primary, 15% secondary.

Major International Organizations: UN and most specialized agencies, OAU.

Embassy: 2112 Leroy Pl. NW 20008; 483-9420.

Part of the ancient West African empires, Guinea fell under French control 1849-98. Under Sekou Toure, it opted for full independence in 1958, and France withdrew all aid.

Toure turned to communist nations for support and set up a militant one-party state.

Thousands of opponents were jailed in the 1970s, in the aftermath of an unsuccessful Portuguese invasion. Many were tortured and killed.

The military took control of the government in a bloodless coup after the March 1984 death of Toure. A new constitution was approved in 1991, which promised full democracy by 1996. In 1992, movement toward democracy was slow; although political parties were made legal, political demonstrations were banned.

Guinea-Bissau

Republic of Guinea-Bissau

Republica da Guiné-Bissau

People: Population (1992 est.): 1,074,000. **Pop. density:** 77 per sq. mi. **Ethnic groups:** Balante 27%, Fula 23%, Manjaca 11%, Mandinka 12%. **Languages:** Portuguese (official), Crioulo, tribal languages. **Religions:** Traditional 54%, Moslem 38%, Christian 8%.

Geography: Area: 13,948 sq. mi. about the size of Connecticut and New Hampshire combined. **Location:** On Atlantic coast of W. Africa. **Neighbors:** Senegal on N, Guinea on E, S. **Topography:** A swampy coastal plain covers most of the country; to the east is a low savanna region. **Capital:** Bissau. **Cities** (1988 est.): Bissau 138,000.

Government: Type: Republic. **Head of state:** Brig.-Gen. Joao Bernardo Vieira; b. 1939; in office: Nov. 14, 1980. **Head of government:** Prime Min. Carlos Correia; in office: Dec. 27, 1991. **Local divisions:** 9 regions. **Defense:** 3.3% of GDP (1987).

Economy: Chief crops: Peanuts, cotton, rice. **Minerals:** Bauxite. **Arable land:** 10%. **Electricity prod.** (1991): 30 mln. kWh. **Labor force:** 90% agric.

Finance: Monetary unit: Peso (Jan. 1993: 4,491 = $1 US). **Gross domestic product** (1989): $154 mln. **Per capita GDP** (1991): $160. **Imports** (1989): $69 mln.; partners: Port. 20%, It. 27%. **Exports** (1989): $14 mln.; partners: Port. 35%. **National Budget** (1989): $30 mln. expenditures.

Transport: Motor vehicles: in use (1990): 3,000 passenger cars, 2,500 commercial vehicles.

Communications: Radios: 1 per 27 persons. **Daily newspaper circ.** (1990): 12 per 1,000 pop.

Health: Life expectancy at birth (1992): 45 male; 48 female. **Births** (per 1,000 pop. 1992): 42. **Deaths** (per 1,000 pop. 1992): 18. **Natural increase:** 2.4%. **Infant mortality** (per 1,000 live births 1992): 125.

Education (1991): **Literacy:** 36%. **Years compulsory:** 4.

Major International Organizations: UN, OAU.

Embassy: 211 E 43d St., New York, NY 10017; (212) 611-3977.

Portuguese mariners explored the area in the mid-15th century; the slave trade flourished in the 17th and 18th centuries, and colonization began in the 19th.

Beginning in the 1960s, an independence movement waged a guerrilla war and formed a government in the interior that achieved international support. Full independence came Sept. 10, 1974, after the Portuguese regime was overthrown.

The November 1980 coup gave Vieira absolute power. Vieira initiated political liberalization.

Guyana

Co-operative Republic of Guyana

People: Population (1992 est.): 739,000. **Age distrib.** (%): 0–14: 33.4; 5–59: 60.7; 60+: 5.9. **Pop. density:** 9 per sq. mi. **Urban** (1990): 35%. **Ethnic groups:** East Indians 51%, African 30%; mixed 14%. **Languages:** English (official), Amerindian dialects. **Religions:** Christian 46%, Hindu 37%; Moslem 9%.

Geography: Area: 83,000 sq. mi., the size of Idaho. **Location:** On N coast of S. America. **Neighbors:** Venezuela on W, Brazil on S, Suriname on E. **Topography:** Dense tropical forests cover much of the land, although a flat coastal area up to 40 mi. wide, where 90% of the population lives, provides rich alluvial soil for agriculture. A grassy savanna divides the 2 zones. **Capital:** Georgetown. **Cities** (1985 est.): Georgetown 170,000.

Government: Type: Republic. **Head of state:** President Cheddi Jagan; in office: Oct. 9, 1992. **Head of Government:** Prime Min. Sam Hinds; in office: Oct. 9, 1992. **Local divisions:** 10 regions. **Defense:** 6% of GDP (1989).

Economy: Industries: Mining, textiles. **Chief crops:** Sugar, rice, citrus and other fruits. **Minerals:** Bauxite, diamonds. **Other resources:** Timber, shrimp. **Arable land:** 2%. **Electricity prod.** (1991): 647 bln. kWh. **Labor force:** 33% agric.; 45% ind. & comm.; 22% services.

Finance: Monetary unit: Dollar (Mar. 1993: 126 = $1 US). **Gross domestic product** (1991): $250 mln. **Per capita GDP:** $300. **Imports** (1991): $246 mln.; partners: U.S. 33%, CARICOM 10%. **Exports** (1991): $189 mln.; partners: UK 31%, U.S. 23%. **National budget** (1990): $250 mln. **International reserves less gold** (Feb. 1993): $185 mln. **Consumer prices** (change in 1992): 10.0%.

Transport: Motor vehicles: in use (1990): 24,000 passenger cars, 9,000 comm. vehicles. **Chief ports:** Georgetown.

Communications: Radios: 1 per 2.5 persons. **Telephones:** 1 per 47 persons. **Daily newspaper circ.** (1991): 53 per 1,000 pop.

Health: Life expectancy at birth (1992): 61 male; 68 female. **Births** (per 1,000 pop. 1992): 21. **Deaths** (per 1,000 pop. 1992): 7. **Natural increase:** 1.4% **Hospital beds:** 1 per 341 persons. **Physicians:** 1 per 6,809 persons. **Infant mortality** (per 1,000 live births 1992): 51.

Education (1991): **Literacy:** 95%. **Years compulsory:** ages 5-14.

Major International Organizations: UN (GATT, ILO, IMF, World Bank), Commonwealth of Nations, OAS.

Embassy: 2490 Tracy Pl. NW 20008; 276-6900.

Guyana became a Dutch possession in the 17th century, but sovereignty passed to Britain in 1815. Indentured servants from India soon outnumbered African slaves. Ethnic tension has affected political life.

Guyana became independent May 26, 1966. A Venezuelan claim to the western half of Guyana was suspended in 1970 but renewed in 1982. The Suriname border is also disputed. The government has nationalized most of the economy which has remained severely depressed.

The Port Kaituma ambush of U.S. Rep. Leo J. Ryan and others investigating mistreatment of American followers of the Rev. Jim Jones' People's Temple cult triggered a mass suicide-execution of 911 cultists at Jonestown in the Guyana jungle, Nov. 18, 1978.

The People's National Congress, the party in power since Guyana became independent, was voted out of office with the election of Cheddi Jagan in Oct. 1992.

Haiti

Republic of Haiti

Républiqe d'Haiti

People: Population (1992 est.): 6,431,000. **Age distrib.** (%): 4–14: 40.2; 15–59: 53.6; 60+: 6.2. **Pop. density:** 607 per sq. mi. **Urban** (1990): 29%. **Ethnic groups:** African descent 95%. **Languages:** French, Creole (both official). **Religions:** Roman Catholic 80%, Protestant 10%; Voodoo widely practiced.

Geography: Area: 10,579 sq. mi., the size of Maryland. **Location:** In West Indies, occupies western third of I. of Hispaniola. **Neighbors:** Dominican Republic on E, Cuba on W. **Topography:** About two-thirds of Haiti is mountainous. Much of the rest is semiarid. Coastal areas are warm and moist. **Capital:** Port-au-Prince. **Cities** (1992 est.): Port-au-Prince 752,000.

Government: Type: In transition. **Head of state:** ——. **Head of government:** Prime Min. Robert Malval; in office: Aug. 30, 1993. **Local divisions:** 9 departments. **Defense:** 1.5% of GDP (1990).

Economy: Industries: Sugar refining, textiles. **Chief crops:** Coffee, sugar, bananas, cocoa, tobacco, rice. **Minerals:** Bauxite. **Other resources:** Timber. **Arable land:** 20%. **Livestock** (1989): cattle: 1.5 mln.; goats: 1.2 mln. **Electricity prod.** (1991): 468 mln. kWh. **Labor force:** 66% agric.; 9% ind. & comm.; 25% services.

Finance: Monetary unit: Gourde (Dec. 1992: 5.00 = $1 US). **Gross domestic product** (1990): $2.7 bln. **Per capita GDP** (1991): $440. **Imports** (1991): $347 mln.; partners: U.S. 64%. **Exports** (1991): $103 mln.; partners: U.S. 84%. **Tourism** (1991): receipts $66 mln. **National budget** (1990): $416 mln. expenditures. **International reserves less gold** (Mar. 1993): $17.3 mln. **Gold:** 18,000 oz t. **Consumer prices** (change in 1991): 15.4%.

Transport: Motor vehicles: in use (1989): 32,000 passenger cars, 21,000 comm. vehicles. **Chief ports:** Port-au-Prince, Les Cayes.

Communications: Television sets: 1 per 265 persons. **Radios:** 1 per 2.2 persons. **Telephones in use:** 1 per 79 persons. **Daily newspaper circ.** (1990): 8 per 1,000 pop.

Health: Life expectancy at birth (1992): 53 male; 55 female. **Births** (per 1,000 pop. 1992): 43. **Deaths** (per 1,000 pop. 1992): 15. **Natural increase:** 2.8%. **Hospital beds:** 1 per 1,258 persons. **Physicians:** 1 per 6,039 persons. **Infant mortality rate** (per 1,000 live births, 1992): 104.

Education (1991): **Literacy:** 53%.

Major International Organizations: UN and some of its specialized agencies, OAS.

Embassy: 2311 Massachusetts Ave. NW 20008; 332-4090.

Haiti, visited by Columbus, 1492, and a French colony from 1677, attained its independence, 1804, following the rebellion led by former slave Toussaint L'Ouverture. Following a period of political violence, the U.S. occupied the country 1915-34.

Dr. Francois Duvalier was voted president in 1957; in 1964 he was named president for life. Upon his death in 1971, he was succeeded by his son, Jean-Claude. Drought in 1975-77 brought famine, and Hurricane Allen in 1980 destroyed most of the rice, bean, and coffee crops.

Following several weeks of unrest, President Jean Claude Duvalier fled Haiti aboard a U.S. Air Force jet Feb. 7, 1986, ending the 28-year dictatorship by the Duvalier family. A military-civilian council headed by Gen. Henri Namphy assumed control. In 1987, voters approved a new constitution.

The Jan. 17, 1988 elections led to Leslie Manigat being named president; opposition leaders charged widespread fraud. Gen. Namphy seized control, June 20, and named himself president of a military government. Namphy was ousted by a military coup in Sept. By mid-1990, there had been 5 governments since Duvalier fled. Father Jean-Bertrand Aristide was elected President Dec. 1990.

A coup led by leaders of the Tonton Macoutes, the private militia of the Duvalier family, was crushed by loyalist army forces, Jan. 1991. The attempted coup sparked riots that left some 70 dead. In Sept. 1991, Aristide was arrested by the military and expelled from the country.

Some 35,000 Haitian refugees were intercepted by the U.S. Coast Guard as they tried to enter the U.S., 1991-92. Most were returned to Haiti despite protests by U.S. human rights and legal organizations.

The UN imposed a worldwide oil, arms, and financial embargo on Haiti June 23, 1993. The embargo was later suspended when the military agreed to Aristide's return to power on Oct. 30.

Honduras

Republic of Honduras

República de Honduras

People: Population (1991 est.): 4,949,000. **Age distrib.** (%): 0–14: 44.6; 15–59: 50.5; 60+: 4.9. **Pop. density:** 114 per sq. mi. **Urban** (1990): 40.0%. **Ethnic groups:** Mestizo 90%, Indian 7%. **Languages:** Spanish (official). **Religions:** Roman Catholic 95%.

Geography: Area: 43,277 sq. mi., slightly larger than Tennessee. **Location:** In Central America. **Neighbors:** Guatemala on W, El Salvador, Nicaragua on S. **Topography:** The Caribbean coast is 500 mi. long. Pacific coast, on Gulf of Fonseca, is 40 mi. long. Honduras is mountainous, with wide fertile valleys and rich forests. **Capital:** Tegucigalpa. **Cities** (1989 est.): Tegucigalpa 550,000; San Pedro Sula 399,000.

Government: Type: Democratic constitutional republic. **Head of State:** Pres. Rafael Leonardo Callejas; in office: Jan. 27, 1990. **Local divisions:** 18 departments. **Defense:** 1.9% of GDP (1990).

Economy: Industries: Textiles, wood prods. **Chief crops:** Bananas (chief export), coffee, corn, beans. **Minerals:** Gold, silver, copper, lead, zinc, iron, antimony, coal. **Other resources:** Timber. **Arable land:** 16%. **Livestock** (1989): cattle: 2.8 mln. **Electricity prod.** (1990): 2.0 bln. kWh. **Labor force:** 62% agric.; 20% services; 9% manuf.

Finance: Monetary unit: Lempira (Apr. 1992): 5.40 = $1 US). **Gross domestic product** (1990): $4.9 bln. **Per capita GDP** (1989): $960. **Imports** (1989): $981 mln.; partners: U.S. 39%, Jap. 8%. **Exports** (1989): $940 mln.; partners: U.S. 54%, Europe 34%. **Tourists** (1989): $28 mln. receipts. **International reserves less gold** (Mar. 1992): $180 mln. **Gold:** 21,000 oz t. **Consumer prices** (change in 1991): 35.0%.

Transport: Motor vehicles: in use (1989) 77,000 passenger cars, 24,000 comm. vehicles. **Civil aviation** (1988): 446 mln. passenger-km; 9 airports with scheduled flights. **Chief ports:** Puerto Cortes, La Ceiba.

Communications: Television sets: 1 per 25 persons. **Radios:** 1 per 2.4 persons. **Telephones:** 1 per 58 persons. **Daily newspaper circ.** (1989): 51 per 1,000 pop.

Health: Life expectancy at birth (1991): 64 male; 68 female. **Births** (per 1,000 pop. 1991): 38. **Deaths** (per 1,000 pop. 1991): 7. **Natural increase:** 3.0%. **Hospital beds:** 1 per 821 persons. **Physicians:** 1 per 1,586 persons. **Infant mortality** (per 1,000 live births 1991): 56.

Education (1991): **Literacy:** 73%. **Years compulsory:** 6; attendance 70%.

Major International Organizations: UN, (IMF, WHO, ILO), OAS.

Embassy: 4301 Connecticut Ave. NW 20008; 966-7700.

Mayan civilization flourished in Honduras in the 1st millenium AD. Columbus arrived in 1502. Honduras became independent after freeing itself from Spain, 1821 and from the Fed. of Central America, 1838.

Gen. Oswaldo Lopez Arellano, president for most of the period 1963-75 by virtue of one election and 2 coups, was ousted by the army in 1975 over charges of pervasive bribery by United Brands Co. of the U.S.

The government has resumed land distribution, raised minimum wages, and started a literacy campaign. An elected civilian government took power in 1982.

Some 3,200 U.S. troops were sent to Honduras after the Honduran border was violated by Nicaraguan forces, Mar. 1988.

Honduras is one of the poorest countries in the Western Hemisphere.

Hungary

Republic of Hungary

Magyar Köztársaság

People: Population (1992 est.): 10,333,000. **Age distrib.** (%): 0–14: 20.8; 15–59: 60.5; 60+: 18.7. **Pop. density:** 287 per sq. mi. **Urban** (1990): 62%. **Ethnic groups:** Magyar 92%, Gypsy 3%, German 2.5%. **Languages:** Hungarian (Magyar). **Religions:** Roman Catholic 67%, Protestant 25%.

Geography: Area: 35,919 sq. mi., slightly smaller than Indiana. **Location:** In East Central Europe. **Neighbors:** Slovakia, Ukraine on N, Austria on W, Slovenia, Yugoslavia, Croatia on S, Romania, on E. **Topography:** The Danube R. forms the Slovak border in the NW, then swings S to bisect the country. The eastern half of Hungary is mainly a great fertile plain, the Alfold; the W and N are hilly. **Capital:** Budapest. **Cities** (1991 est.): Budapest 2,016,000; Miskolc 196,000; Debrecen 212,000.

Government: Type: Parliamentary democracy. **Head of state:** Pres. Arpad Goncz; in office: May 2, 1990. **Head of government:** Prime Min. Jozsef Antall; in office: May 3, 1990. **Local divisions:** 19 counties, 1 capital. **Defense:** 1.7% of GDP (1992).

Economy: Industries: Iron and steel, machinery, pharmaceuticals, vehicles, communications equip., milling, distilling. **Chief crops:** Grains, vegetables, fruits, grapes. **Minerals:** Bauxite, coal, natural gas. **Arable land:** 54%. **Livestock** (1990): cattle: 1.6 mln.; pigs: 7.6 mln.; sheep: 2.0 mln. **Electricity prod.** (1990): 30.4 bln. kWh. **Crude steel prod.** (1991): 1.8 mln. metric tons. **Labor force:** 19% agric.; 48% ind. & comm.; 27% services.

Finance: Monetary unit: Forint (Mar. 1993: 88 = $1 US). **Gross domestic product** (1991): $60.1 bln. **Per capita GDP:** $5,700. **Imports** (1991): $11.7 bln.; partners: CIS 34%, EC 21%. **Exports** (1991): $10.2 bln.; partners: CIS 30%, EC 32%. **National budget** (1992): $13.6 bln. **Tourism** (1990): $1 bln. receipts. **Consumer prices** (change in 1991): 34.0%.

Transport: Railroads (1990): **Length:** 8,221 mi. **Motor vehicles:** in use (1990): 1.9 mln. passenger cars, 223,000 comm. vehicles. **Civil aviation** (1990): 1.5 bln. passenger-km; 1 airport with scheduled flights.

Communications: Television sets: 1 per 2.5 persons. **Radios:** 1 per 1.7 persons. **Telephones:** 1 per 5.5 persons. **Daily newspaper circ.** (1990): 237 per 1,000 pop.

Health: Life expectancy at birth (1992): 66 male; 75 female. **Births** (per 1,000 pop. 1992): 12. **Deaths** (per 1,000 pop. 1992): 14. **Natural increase:** –.2%. **Hospital beds:** 1 per 99 persons. **Physicians:** 1 per 306 persons. **Infant mortality** (per 1,000 live births 1992): 14.

Education (1992): **Literacy:** 98%. **Years compulsory:** to age 16; attendance 96%.

Major International Organizations: UN (IMF, World Bank, GATT).

Embassy: 3910 Shoemaker St. NW 20008.

Earliest settlers, chiefly Slav and Germanic, were overrun by Magyars from the east. Stephen I (997-1038) was made king by Pope Sylvester II in 1000 AD. The country suffered repeated Turkish invasions in the 15th-17th centuries. After the defeats of the Turks, 1686-1697, Austria dominated, but Hungary obtained concessions until it regained internal independence in 1867, with the emperor of Austria as king of Hungary in a dual monarchy with a single diplomatic service. Defeated with the Central Powers in 1918, Hungary lost Transylvania to Romania, Croatia and Bacska to Yugoslavia, Slovakia and Carpatho-Ruthenia to Czechoslovakia, all of which had large Hungarian minorities. A republic under Michael Karolyi and a bolshevist revolt under Bela Kun were followed by a vote for a monarchy in 1920 with Admiral Nicholas Horthy as regent.

Hungary joined Germany in World War II, and was allowed to annex most of its lost territories. Russian troops captured the country, 1944-1945. By terms of an armistice with the Allied powers Hungary agreed to give up territory acquired by the 1938 dismemberment of Czechoslovakia and to return to its borders of 1937.

A republic was declared Feb. 1, 1946; Zoltan Tildy was elected president. In 1947 the communists forced Tildy out. Premier Imre Nagy, in office since mid-1953, was ousted for his moderate policy of favoring agriculture and consumer production, April 18, 1955.

In 1956, popular demands for the ousting of Erno Gero, Communist Party secretary, and for formation of a government by Nagy, resulted in the latter's appointment Oct. 23; demonstrations against communist rule developed into open revolt. On Nov. 4 Soviet forces launched a massive attack against Budapest with 200,000 troops, 2,500 tanks and armored cars.

About 200,000 persons fled the country. Nagy was executed, and thousands were arrested. In the spring of 1963 the regime freed many anti-communists and captives from the 1956 revolt in a sweeping amnesty.

Hungarian troops participated in the 1968 Warsaw Pact invasion of Czechoslovakia. Major economic reforms were launched early in 1968, switching from a central planning system to one in which market forces and profit control much of production.

In 1989 parliament passed legislation legalizing freedom of assembly and association as Hungary shifted away from communism toward democracy. In Oct., the Communist Party was formally dissolved. The last Soviet troops left Hungary June 19, 1991.

Iceland

Republic of Iceland

Lýoveldio Island

People: Population (1992 est.): 259,000. **Age distrib.** (%): 0–14: 25.5; 15–59: 60.1; 60+: 14.4. **Pop. density:** 6 per sq. mi. **Urban** (1991): 90% **Ethnic groups:** Homogeneous, descendants of Norwegians, Celts. **Language:** Icelandic (Islenska). **Religion:** Evangelical Lutheran 95%.

Geography: Area: 39,769 sq. mi., the size of Virginia. **Location:** At N end of Atlantic O. **Neighbors:** Nearest is Greenland. **Topography:** Iceland is of recent volcanic origin. Three-quarters of the surface is wasteland: glaciers, lakes, a lava desert. There are geysers and hot springs, and the climate is moderated by the Gulf Stream. **Capital:** Reykjavik. **Cities** (1991 est.): Reykjavik 97,000.

Government: Type: Constitutional republic. **Head of state:** Pres. Vigdis Finnbogadottir; b. Apr. 15, 1930; in office: Aug. 1, 1980. **Head of government:** Prime Min. David Oddsson; in office: Apr. 30, 1991. **Local divisions:** 23 counties, 14 ind. towns.

Economy: Industries: Fish products (some 80% of exports), aluminum. **Chief crops:** Potatoes, turnips, hay. **Arable land:** 0.5%. **Livestock** (1991): sheep: 549,000. **Fish catch** (1991): 991,000. metric tons. **Electricity prod.** (1991): 5.1 bln. kWh. **Labor force:** 11% agric.; 55% comm. & services, 14% fisheries.

Finance: Monetary unit: Kronur (Mar. 1993: 64.12 = $1 US). **Gross domestic product** (1991): $4.2 bln. **Per capita GDP:** $16,300. **Imports** (1992): $1.7 bln.; partners: EC 50%. **Exports** (1992): $1.6 bln.; partners: EC 67%. **Tourism** (1991): receipts: $223 mln. **National budget** (1991): $1.9 bln. expenditures. **International reserves less gold** (Mar. 1993): $443 mln. **Gold:** 49,000 oz t. **Consumer prices** (change in 1992): 4.0%.

Transport: Motor vehicles: in use (1991): 121,000 passenger cars, 16,000 comm. vehicles. **Civil aviation** (1991): 1.8 bln. passenger-km; 21 airports with scheduled flights. **Chief ports:** Reykjavik.

Communications: Television sets: 1 per 3.3 persons. **Radios:** 1 per 1.6 persons. **Telephones:** 1 per 2.2 persons. **Daily newspaper circ.** (1990): 518 per 1,000 pop.

Health: Life expectancy at birth (1992): 76 male; 81 female. **Births** (per 1,000 pop. 1992): 17. **Deaths** (per 1,000 pop. 1992): 7. **Natural increase:** 1.0%. **Hospital beds:** 1 per 73 persons. **Physicians:** 1 per 373 persons. **Infant mortality** per (1,000 live births 1992): 4.

Education (1992): **Literacy:** 99%. **Years compulsory:** 8; **Attendance:** 99%.

Major International Organizations: UN (GATT), NATO, OECD.

Embassy: 2022 Connecticut Ave. NW 20008; 265-6653.

Iceland was an independent republic from 930 to 1262, when it joined with Norway. Its language has maintained its purity for 1,000 years. Danish rule lasted from 1380-1918; the last ties with the Danish crown were severed in 1941. The Althing, or assembly, is the world's oldest surviving parliament.

India

Republic of India

Bharat

People: Population (1992 est.): 886,362,000. **Age distrib.** (%): 0–14: 36.8; 15–59: 56.4; 60+: 5.8. **Pop. density:** 700 per sq. mi. **Urban** (1991): 28%. **Ethnic groups:** Indo-Aryan groups 72%, Dravidians 25%, Mongoloids 3%. **Languages:** 16 languages, including Hindi (official) and English (associate official). **Religions:** Hindu 83%, Moslem 11%, Christian 3%, Sikh 2%.

Geography: Area: 1,266,595 sq. mi., one-third the size of the U.S. **Location:** Occupies most of the Indian subcontinent in S. Asia. **Neighbors:** Pakistan on W, China, Nepal, Bhutan on N, Myanmar, Bangladesh on E. **Topography:** The Himalaya Mts., highest in world, stretch across India's northern borders. Below, the Ganges Plain is wide, fertile, and among the most densely populated regions of the world. The area below includes the Deccan Peninsula. Close to one quarter the area is forested. The climate varies from tropical heat in S to near-Arctic cold in N. Rajasthan Desert is in NW; NE Assam Hills get 400 in. of rain a year. **Capital:** New Delhi. **Cities** (1991 est.): Calcutta 10.8 mln.; Bombay 12.5 mln.; New Delhi 8.3 mln.; Madras 5.3 mln.; Bangalore 4.1 mln.; Hyderabad 4.2 mln.

Government: Type: Federal republic. **Head of state:** Pres. Ramaswamy Venkataraman; b. Dec. 4, 1910; in office: July 25, 1987. **Head of government:** Prime Min. P. V. Narasimha Rao; b. June 28, 1921; in office: June 21, 1991. **Local divisions:** 25 states, 7 union territories. **Defense:** 3.5% of GNP (1991).

Economy: Industries: Textiles, steel, processed foods, cement, machinery, chemicals, fertilizers, consumer appliances, autos. **Chief crops:** Rice, grains, coffee, sugar cane, spices, tea, cashews, cotton, copra, coir, juta, linseed. **Minerals:** Chromium, coal, iron, manganese, mica salt, bauxite, gypsum, oil. **Crude oil reserves** (1991): 4.2 bln. bbls. **Other resources:** Rubber, timber. **Arable land:** 57%. **Livestock** (1989): cattle: 195 mln.; sheep: 55 mln. **Fish catch** (1990): 3.6 mln. metric tons. **Electricity prod.** (1991): 290 bln. kWh. **Crude steel prod.** (1991): 16.3 mln. metric tons. **Labor force:** 70% agric.; 19% ind. & comm.

Finance: Monetary unit: Rupee (Aug. 1993: 31.03 = $1 US). **Gross domestic product** (1992): $328 bln. **Per capita GDP:** $380. **Imports** (1991): $25.2 bln.; partners: Jap. 8%, U.S. 12%, EC 33%. **Exports** (1991): $20.2 bln.; partners: U.S. 16%, EC 25%, CIS 19%. **Tourism** (1991): receipts: $1.4 bln. **National budget** (1992): $53.4 bln. expenditures. **International reserves less gold** (Mar. 1993): $6.7 bln. **Gold:** 11.3 mln. oz. t. **Consumer prices** (change in 1992): 11.8%.

Transport: Railroads (1991): **Length:** 38,752 mi. **Motor vehicles:** in use (1990): 2.3 mln. passenger cars, 1.4 mln. comm. vehicles. **Civil aviation:** (1990): 16.5 bln. passenger-km; 98 airports with scheduled flights. **Chief ports:** Calcutta, Bombay, Madras, Cochin, Vishakhapatnam.

Communications: Television sets: 1 per 44 persons. **Radios:** 1 per 15 persons. **Telephones:** 1 per 200 persons. **Daily newspaper circ.** (1988): 21 per. 1,000 pop.

Health: Life expectancy at birth (1992): 57 male; 58 female. **Births** (per 1,000 pop. 1992): 30. **Deaths** (per 1,000 pop. 1992): 11. **Natural increase:** 1.9%. **Hospital beds:** 1 per 1,314 persons. **Physicians:** 1 per 2,337 persons. **Infant mortality** (per 1,000 live births 1992): 81.

Education (1991): **Literacy:** 48%. **Years Compulsory:** to age 14.

Major International Organizations: UN (IMF, World Bank).

Embassy: 2107 Massachusetts Ave. NW 20008; 939-7000.

India has one of the oldest civilizations in the world. Excavations trace the Indus Valley civilization back for at least 5,000 years. Paintings in the mountain caves of Ajanta, richly carved temples, the Taj Mahal in Agra, and the Kutab Minar in Delhi are among relics of the past.

Aryan tribes, speaking Sanskrit, invaded from the NW around 1500 BC, and merged with the earlier inhabitants to create classical Indian civilization.

Asoka ruled most of the Indian subcontinent in the 3d century BC, and established Buddhism. But Hinduism revived and eventually predominated. During the Gupta kingdom, 4th-6th century AD, science, literature, and the arts enjoyed a "golden age."

Arab invaders established a Moslem foothold in the W in the 8th century, and Turkish Moslems gained control of North India by 1200. The Mogul emperors ruled 1526-1857.

Vasco de Gama established Portuguese trading posts 1498-1503. The Dutch followed. The British East India Co. sent Capt. William Hawkins, 1609, to get concessions from the Mogul emperor for spices and textiles. Operating as the East India Co. the British gained control of most of India. The British parliament assumed political direction; under Lord Bentinck, 1828-35, rule by rajahs was curbed. After the Sepoy troops mutinied, 1857-58, the British supported the native rulers.

Nationalism grew rapidly after World War I. The Indian National Congress and the Moslem League demanded constitutional reform. A leader emerged in Mohandas K. Gandhi (called Mahatma, or Great Soul), born Oct. 2, 1869, assassinated Jan. 30, 1948. He advocated self-rule, non-violence, removal of untouchability. In 1930 he launched "civil disobedience," including boycott of British goods and rejection of taxes without representation.

In 1935 Britain gave India a constitution providing a bicameral federal congress. Mohammed Ali Jinnah, head of the Moslem League, sought creation of a Moslem nation, Pakistan.

The British government partitioned British India into the dominions of India and Pakistan. India became a self-governing member of the Commonwealth and a member of the UN. It became a democratic republic, Jan. 26, 1950.

More than 12 million Hindu & Moslem refugees crossed the India-Pakistan borders in a mass transferral of some of the 2 peoples during 1947; about 200,000 were killed in communal fighting.

After Pakistan troops began attacks on Bengali separatists in East Pakistan, Mar. 25, 1971, some 10 million refugees fled into India. India and Pakistan went to war Dec. 3, 1971, on both the East and West fronts. Pakistan troops in the east surrendered Dec. 16; Pakistan agreed to a cease-fire in the west Dec. 17. In Aug. 1973 India released 93,000 Pakistanis held prisoner since 1971. The 2 countries resumed full relations in 1976.

In 2 days of carnage, the Bengali population of the village of Mandai, Tripura State, 700 people, were massacred in a raid by indigenous tribal residents of the area, June 8-9, 1980. A similar year-long campaign against Bengali immigrants had been going on in Assam State.

Mrs. Indira Gandhi, was named prime minister Jan. 19, 1966. Threatened with adverse court rulings in a voting law case, and opposition protest campaign and strikes, Gandhi invoked emergency provisions of the constitution June, 1975. Thousands of opponents were arrested and press censorship imposed. Measures to control prices, protect small farmers, and improve productivity were adopted.

The emergency, especially enforcement of coercive birth control measures in some areas, and the prominent extra-constitutional role of Indira Gandhi's son Sanjay, was widely resented. Opposition parties, united in the Janata coalition, scored massive victories in federal and state parliamentary elections in 1977, turning Gandhi's New Congress Party from power.

Gandhi became prime minister for the second time, Jan. 14, 1980. She was assassinated by 2 of her Sikh bodyguards Oct. 31, 1984. Widespread rioting followed. Thousands of Sikhs were killed and some 50,000 left homeless. The assassination was in response to the government supression of a Sikh uprising in Punjab in June 1984 which included an assault on the Golden Temple, the holiest Sikh shrine. Rajiv, her son, replaced her as prime minister. He was swept from office in 1989 amid charges of incompetence and corruption. He was assassinated May 21, 1991 during an election campaign to regain the prime ministership.

Sikhs ignited several violent clashes during the 1980s. The government's May 1987 decision to bring the state of Punjab under the rule of the central government led to violence. Many died during a government siege of the Golden Temple at Amritsar, May 1988.

In the biggest wave of criminal violence in Indian history, a series of bombings jolted Bombay and Calcutta, Mar. 12-19, 1993, leaving over 300 dead and some 1,200 injured. The explosions came in the wake of nationwide riots prompted by the destruction of a 16th- century mosque by Hindu militants in Dec. 1992.

Sikkim, bordered by Tibet, Bhutan and Nepal, formerly British protected, became a protectorate of India in 1950. Area, 2,740 sq. mi.; pop. 1991 cen. 405,000; capital, Gangtok. In Sept. 1974 India's parliament voted to make Sikkim an associate Indian state, absorbing it into India.

Kashmir, a predominantly Moslem region in the NW, has been in dispute between India and Pakistan since 1947. A cease-fire was negotiated by the UN Jan. 1, 1949; it gave Pakistan control of one-third of the area, in the west and northwest, and India the remaining two-thirds, the Indian state of Jammu and Kashmir, which enjoys internal autonomy.

In 1990 and 1991, there were repeated clashes between Indian army troops and pro-independence demonstrators triggered by India's decision to impose central government rule. The clashes strained relations between India and Pakistan which India charged was aiding the Moslem separatists.

France, 1952-54, peacefully yielded to India its 5 colonies, former French India, comprising Pondicherry, Karikal, Mahe, Yanaon (which became Pondicherry Union Territory, area 185 sq. mi., pop. 1991, 807,000) and Chandernagor (which was incorporated into the state of West Bengal).

Indonesia

Republic of Indonesia

Republik Indonesia

People: Population (1992 est.): 195,000,000. **Age distrib.** (%): 0–14: 39.2; 15–59: 56.5; 60+: 5.3. **Pop. density:** 262 per sq. mi. **Urban** (1991): 31%. **Ethnic groups:** Malay, Chinese, Irianese. **Languages:** Bahasa Indonesian (Malay) (official), Javanese, other Austronesian languages. **Religions:** Moslem 88%.

Geography: Area: 735,268 sq. mi. **Location:** Archipelago SE of Asia along the Equator. **Neighbors:** Malaysia on N, Papua New Guinea on E. **Topography:** Indonesia comprises some 17,000 islands, including Java (one of the most densely populated areas in the world with 1,500 persons to the sq. mi.), Sumatra, Kalimantan (most of Borneo), Sulawesi (Celebes), and West Irian (Irian Jaya, the W. half of New Guinea). Also: Bangka, Billiton, Madura, Bali, Timor. The mountains and plateaus on the major islands have a cooler climate than the tropical lowlands. **Capital:** Jakarta. **Cities** (1988 est.): Jakarta 8,800,000; Surabaya 2,500,000; Bandung 1,400,000; Medan 1,700,000.

Government: Type: Republic. **Head of state:** Pres. Suharto; b. June 8, 1921; in office: Mar. 6, 1967. **Local divisions:** 24 provinces, 3 special regions. **Defense:** 2.0% of GDP (1992).

Economy: Industries: Food processing, textiles, cement, light industry. **Chief crops:** Rice, coffee, sugar. **Minerals:** Nickel, tin, oil, bauxite, copper, natural gas. **Crude oil reserves** (1991): 10.7 bln. bbls. **Other resources:** Rubber. **Arable land:** 8%. **Livestock** (1989): cattle: 6.5 mln.; sheep: 5.4 mln. **Fish catch** (1990): 3.1 mln. metric tons. **Electricity prod.** (1991): 38 bln. kWh. **Crude steel prod.** (1991): 3 mln. metric tons. **Labor force:** 56% agric.; 23% ind. & comm.; 16% services.

Finance: Monetary unit: Rupiah (Aug. 1993: 2,096 = $1 US). **Gross domestic product** (1991): $122 bln. **Per capita GDP:** $630. **Imports** (1991): $25.8 bln.; partners: Jap. 23%, U.S. 12%, Sing. 6%. **Exports** (1991): $29.5 bln.; partners: Jap. 41%, U.S. 16%, Sing. 10%. **Tourism** (1990): $1.8 bln. receipts. **National budget** (1991): $23.4 bln. **International reserves less gold** (Feb. 1993): $10.8 bln. **Gold:** 3.11 mln. oz t. **Consumer prices** (change in 1992): 7.5%.

Transport: Railway traffic (1989): 7.8 bln. passenger-km. **Motor vehicles:** in use (1991): 1.3 mln. passenger cars, 1.5 mln. comm. vehicles **Civil aviation** (1991): 12.7 bln. passenger-km; 116 airports. **Chief ports:** Jakarta, Surabaya, Medan, Palembang, Semarang.

Communications: Television sets: 1 per 24 persons. **Radios:** 1 per 8 persons. **Telephones:** 1 per 172 persons.

Health: Life expectancy at birth (1992): male: 59; female 64 years. **Births** (per 1,000 pop. 1992): 26. **Deaths** (per 1,000 pop. 1992): 8. **Natural increase:** 1.8%. **Hospital beds:** 1 per 1,485 persons. **Physicians:** 1 per 7,427 persons. **Infant mortality** (per 1,000 live births 1992): 70.

Education (1990): **Literacy:** 85%. 84% attend primary school.

Major International Organizations: UN and all of its specialized agencies, ASEAN, OPEC.

Embassy: 2020 Massachusetts Ave. NW 20036; 775-5200.

Hindu and Buddhist civilization from India reached the peoples of Indonesia nearly 2,000 years ago, taking root especially in Java. Islam spread along the maritime trade routes in the 15th century, and became predominant by the 16th century. The Dutch replaced the Portuguese as the most important European trade power in the area in the 17th century. They secured territorial control over Java by 1750. The outer islands were not finally subdued until the early 20th century, when the full area of present-day Indonesia was united under one rule for the first time.

Following Japanese occupation, 1942-45, nationalists led by Sukarno and Hatta proclaimed a republic. The Netherlands ceded sovereignty Dec. 27, 1949, after 4 years of fighting. West Irian, on New Guinea, remained under Dutch control.

After the Dutch in 1957 rejected proposals for new negotiations over West Irian, Indonesia stepped up the seizure of Dutch property. A U.S. mediator's plan was adopted in 1962. In 1963 the UN turned the area over to Indonesia, which promised a plebiscite. In 1969, voting by tribal chiefs favored staying with Indonesia, despite an uprising and widespread opposition.

Sukarno suspended Parliament in 1960, and was named president for life in 1963. Russian-armed Indonesian troops staged raids in 1964 and 1965 into Malaysia, whose formation Sukarno had opposed.

Indonesia's Communist Party tried to seize control in 1965; the army smashed the coup. In parts of Java, communists seized several districts before being defeated; over 300,000 communists were executed.

Gen. Suharto, head of the army, was named president in 1968 and was reelected for a 6th consecutive 5-year term in 1993. A coalition his supporters won a strong majority in House elections in 1971. Moslem opposition parties made gains in 1977 elections but lost ground in the 1982 elections. The military retains a predominant political role.

In 1966 Indonesia and Malaysia signed an agreement ending hostility.

Oil export earnings, and political stability have made Indonesia's economy stable.

Iran

Islamic Republic of Iran

Jomhori-e-Islami-e-Irân

People: Population (1992 est.): 61,183,000. **Age distrib.** (%): 0–14: 43.8; 15–59: 50.4; 60+: 5.8. **Pop. density:** 96 per sq. mi. **Urban** (1990): 57%. **Ethnic groups:** Persian 51%, Azerbaijani 25%, Kurd 9%. **Languages:** Farsi (official), Turk, Kurdish, Arabic. **Religions:** Shi'a Moslem 95%.

Geography: Area: 636,293 sq. mi. slightly larger than Alaska. **Location:** Between the Middle East and S. Asia. **Neighbors:** Turkey, Iraq on W, Armenia, Azerbaijan, Turkmenistan on N, Afghanistan, Pakistan on E. **Topography:** Interior highlands and plains are surrounded by high mountains, up to 18,000 ft. Large salt deserts cover much of the area, but there are many oases and forest areas. Most of the population inhabits the N and NW. **Capital:** Tehran. **Cities** (1986 cen.): Tehran 6,022,000; Esfahan 1,001,000; Mashhad 1,466,000; Tabriz 994,000; Shiraz 848,000.

Government: Type: Islamic republic. **Religious head:** Ayatollah Sayyed Ali Khamenei; b. 1939; in office: June 4, 1989. **Head of state:** Pres. Hashemi Rafsanjani; in office: Aug 3, 1989. **Local divisions:** 24 provinces. **Defense:** 15% of GNP (1991).

Economy: Industries: Cement, sugar refining, carpets. **Chief crops:** Grains, rice, fruits, sugar beets, cotton, grapes. **Minerals:** Chromium, oil, gas. **Crude oil reserves** (1991): 63 bln. barrels. **Other resources:** Gums, wool, silk, caviar. **Arable land:** 9%. **Livestock** (1990): cattle: 8.3 mln.; sheep: 34.0 mln. **Electricity prod.** (1990): 40.2 bln. kWh. **Labor force:** 33% agric.; 21% ind. & comm; 27% services.

Finance: Monetary unit: Rial (Mar. 1993: 67.07 = $1 US). **Gross national product** (1991): $90 bln. **Per capita GNP:** $1,500. **Imports** (1991): $21.6 bln.; partners: Ger. 20%, Jap. 10%, UK 6%. **Exports** (1991): $15.9 bln.; partners: Jap. 13%, Neth. 12%. **National budget** (1990): $80 bln. expenditures.

Transport: Motor vehicles: in use (1990): 2.0 mln. passenger cars, 472,000 comm. vehicles. **Civil Aviation** (1990): 5.5 bln. passenger km.; 17 airports. **Chief ports:** Bandar Abbas.

Communications: Television sets: 1 per 23 persons. **Radios:** 1 per 4.7 persons. **Telephones:** 1 per 25 persons. **Daily newspaper circ.** (1990): 13 per 1,000 pop.

Health: Life expectancy at birth (1992): 64 male; 66 female. **Births** (per 1,000 pop. 1992): 44. **Deaths** (per 1,000 pop. 1992): 10. **Natural increase:** 3.4%. **Hospital beds:** 1 per 653 persons. **Physicians:** 1 per 2,882 persons. **Infant mortality** (per 1,000 live births 1992): 66.

Education (1990): **Literacy:** 54%.

Major International Organizations: UN (IMF, WHO), OPEC.

Iran was once called Persia. The Iranians, who supplanted an earlier agricultural civilization, came from the E during the 2d millenium BC; they were an Indo-European group related to the Aryans of India.

In 549 BC Cyrus the Great united the Medes and Persians in the Persian Empire, conquered Babylonia in 538 BC, restored Jerusalem to the Jews. Alexander the Great conquered Persia in 333 BC, but Persians regained their independence in the next century under the Parthians, themselves succeeded by Sassanian Persians in 226 AD. Arabs brought Islam to Persia in the 7th century, replacing the indigenous Zoroastrian faith. After Persian political and cultural autonomy was reasserted in the 9th century, the arts and sciences flourished for several centuries.

Turks and Mongols ruled Persia in turn from the 11th century to 1502, when a native dynasty reasserted full independence. The British and Russian empires vied for influence in the 19th century, and Afghanistan was severed from Iran by Britain in 1857.

Reza Khan abdicated as Shah, 1941, and was succeeded by his son, Mohammad Reza Pahlavi. Under his rule, Iran underwent economic and social change but political opposition was not tolerated.

Conservative Moslem protests led to 1978 violence. Martial law in 12 cities was declared Sept. 8. A military government was appointed Nov. 6 to deal with striking oil workers. Prime Min. Shahpur Bakhtiar was designated by the shah to head a regency council in his absence. The shah left Iran Jan. 16, 1979.

Exiled religious leader Ayatollah Ruhollah Khomeini named a provisional government council in preparation for his return to Iran, Jan. 31. Clashes between Khomeini's supporters and government troops culminated in a rout of Iran's elite Imperial Guard Feb. 11, leading to the fall of Bakhtiar's government.

The Iranian revolution was marked by revolts among the ethnic minorities and by a continuing struggle between the clerical forces and westernized intellectuals and liberals. The Islamic Constitution established final authority to be vested in a Faghi, the Ayatollah Khomeini.

Iranian militants seized the U.S. embassy, Nov. 4, 1979, and took hostages including 62 Americans. Despite international condemnations and U.S. efforts, including an abortive Apr., 1980, rescue attempt, the crisis continued. The U.S. broke diplomatic relations with Iran, Apr. 7th. The shah died in Egypt, July 27th. The hostage drama finally ended Jan. 21, 1981 when an accord, involving the release of frozen Iranian assets, was reached.

A dispute over the Shatt al-Arab waterway that divides the two countries brought Iran and Iraq, Sept. 22, 1980, into open warfare. Iraqi planes attacked Iranian air fields including Teheran airport. Iranian planes bombed Iraqi bases. Iraqi troops occupied Iranian territory including the port city of Khorramshahr in October. Iranian troops recaptured the city and drove Iraqi troops back across the border, May 1982. Iraq, and later Iran, attacked several oil tankers in the Persian Gulf during 1984. Saudi Arabian war planes shot down 2 Iranian jets, June 5, which they felt were threatening Saudi shipping. In Aug. 1988, Iran agreed to accept a UN resolution calling for a cease fire.

In Nov. 1986, senior U.S. officials secretly visited Iran and exchanged arms for Iran's help in obtaining the release of U.S. hostages held by terrorists in Lebanon. The exchange sparked a major scandal in the Reagan administration.

A U.S. Navy warship shot down an Iranian commercial airliner, July 3, 1988, after mistaking it for an F-14 fighter jet; all 290 aboard the plane died.

A major earthquake struck northern Iran June 21, 1990, killing over 45,000, injuring 100,000, and leaving 400,000 homeless. A U.S. offer of assistance was accepted by the Iranian government.

Some one million Kurdish refugees crossed Iran's border to escape Iraqi forces following the Persian Gulf War.

Iraq

Republic of Iraq

al Jumhouriya al 'Iraqia

People: Population (1992 est.): 18,445,000. **Age distrib.** (%): 0–14: 44.5; 15–59: 50.3; 60+: 5.2. **Pop. density:** 109 per sq. mi. **Urban** (1991): 70%. **Ethnic groups:** Arabs, 75% Kurds, 15% Turks. **Languages:** Arabic (official), Kurdish. **Religions:** Moslem 95% (Shiites 60%, Sunnis 35%), Christian 5%.

Geography: Area: 167,924 sq. mi., larger than California. **Location:** In the Middle East, occupying most of historic Mesopotamia. **Neighbors:** Jordan, Syria on W, Turkey on N, Iran on E, Kuwait, Saudi Arabia on S. **Topography:** Mostly an alluvial plain, including the Tigris and Euphrates rivers, descending from mountains in N to desert in SW. Persian Gulf region is marshland. **Capital:** Baghdad. **Cities** (1985 est.): Baghdad (met.) 3,400,000, Basra 616,000, Mosul 570,000.

Government: Type: Republic. **Head of state:** Pres. Saddam Hussein At-Takriti, b. Apr. 29, 1937; in office: July 16, 1979. **Local divisions:** 18 provinces. **Defense:** 18% of GNP (1990).

Economy: Industries: Textiles, petrochemicals, oil refining, cement. **Chief crops:** Grains, rice, dates, cotton. **Minerals:** Oil, gas. **Crude oil reserves** (1991): 100 bln. barrels. **Other resources:** Wool, hides. **Arable land:** 13%. **Livestock** (1991): cattle: 1.5 mln.; sheep: 9.6 mln.; goats: 1.4 mln. **Electricity prod.** (1991): 3.8 bln. kWh. **Labor force:** 30% agric.; 48% services; 22% ind.

Finance: Monetary unit: Dinar (Mar. 1993: 1.00 = $3.21 US). **Gross national product** (1989): $35 bln. **Per capita GNP** (1989): $1,950. **Imports** (1990): $6.6 bln.; partners: Tur. 2%, U.S. **Exports** (1990): $10.4 bln.; partners: U.S., Tur., Jap. **National budget** (1990): $35 bln. expenditures.

Transport: Railroads: Length (1991): 1,484 mi. Motor vehicles: in use (1991): 744,000 passenger cars, 295,000 comm. vehicles. **Chief ports:** Basra.

Communications: Television sets: 1 per 18 persons. **Radios:** 1 per 5 persons. **Telephones:** 1 per 25 persons. **Daily newspaper circ.** (1990): 32 per 1,000 pop.

Health: Life expectancy at birth (1992): 62 male; 64 female. **Births** (per 1,000 pop. 1992): 45. **Deaths** (per 1,000 pop. 1992): 8. **Natural increase:** 3.8%. **Hospital beds:** 1 per 586 persons. **Physicians:** 1 per 1,922 persons. **Infant mortality** (per 1,000 live births 1992): 84.

Major International Organizations: UN (IMF, ILO), Arab League, OPEC.

Education (1991): **Literacy:** 60%. Compulsory age 6 to grade 6.

Embassy: 1801 P St. NW 20036; 483-7500.

The Tigris-Euphrates valley, formerly called Mesopotamia, was the site of one of the earliest civilizations in the world. The Sumerian city-states of 3,000 BC originated the culture later developed by the Semitic Akkadians, Babylonians, and Assyrians.

Mesopotamia ceased to be a separate entity after the conquests of the Persians, Greeks, and Arabs. The latter founded Baghdad, from where the caliph ruled a vast empire in the 8th and 9th centuries. Mongol and Turkish conquests led to a decline in population, the economy, cultural life, and the irrigation system.

Britain secured a League of Nations mandate over Iraq after World War I. Independence under a king came in 1932. A leftist, pan-Arab revolution established a republic in 1958, which oriented foreign policy toward the USSR. Most industry has been nationalized, and large land holdings broken up.

A local faction of the international Baath Arab Socialist party has ruled by decree since 1968. Russia and Iraq signed an aid pact in 1972, and arms were sent along with several thousand advisers. The 1978 execution of 21 communists and a shift of trade to the West signalled a more neutral policy, straining relations with the USSR. In the 1973 Arab-Israeli war Iraq sent forces to aid Syria. Within a month of assuming power, Saddam Hussein instituted a bloody purge in the wake of a reported coup attempt against the new regime.

Years of battling with the Kurdish minority resulted in total defeat for the Kurds in 1975, when Iran withdrew support. The fighting led to Iraqi bombing of Kurdish villages in Iran, causing relations with Iran to deteriorate.

After skirmishing intermittently for 10 months over the sovereignty of the disputed Shatt al-Arab waterway that divides the two countries, Iraq and Iran, Sept. 22, 1980, entered into open warfare when Iraqi fighter-bombers attacked 10 Iranian airfields, including Teheran airport, and Iranian planes retaliated with strikes on 2 Iraqi bases. In the following days, there was heavy ground fighting around Abadan and the adjacent port of Khorramshahr as Iraq pressed its attack on Iran's oil-rich province of Khuzistan. In May 1982, Iraqi troops were driven back across the border.

Israeli airplanes destroyed a nuclear reactor near Baghdad on June 7, 1981, claiming that it could be used to produce nuclear weapons.

Iraq and Iran expanded their war to the Persian Gulf in Apr. 1984. There were several attacks on oil tankers. An Iraqi warplane launched a missile attack on the U.S.S. *Stark*, a U.S. Navy frigate on patrol in the Persian Gulf, May 17, 1987; 37 U.S. sailors died. Iraq apologized for the attack, claiming it was inadvertent. The fierce war ended Aug. 1988, when Iraq accepted a UN resolution for a ceasefire.

Iraq attacked and overran Kuwait Aug. 2, 1990, sparking an international crisis. The United Nations, Aug. 6, imposed a ban on all trade with Iraq and called on member countries to protect the assets of the legitimate government of Kuwait. Iraq declared Kuwait its 19th province, Aug. 28. A campaign of looting, murder, and pillage was mounted against Kuwaiti civilians. Westerners caught in Iraq and Kuwait were initially held as hostages, but by the end of 1990, all were released.

A U.S.-led coalition launched air and missile attacks on Iraq, Jan. 16, 1991, after the expiration of a UN Security Council deadline for Iraq to withdraw from Kuwait. Iraq retaliated by firing scud missiles at Saudi Arabia and Israel. The coalition began a ground attack to retake Kuwait Feb. 23. Iraqi forces showed little resistance and were soundly defeated in 4 days. Some 175,000 Iraqis were taken prisoner, and casualties were estimated at over 85,000. As part of the cease-fire agreement, Iraq agreed to scrap all poison gas and germ weapons and allow UN observers to inspect the sites. UN trade sanctions would remain in effect until Iraq complied.

In the aftermath of the war, there were revolts against Pres. Saddam Hussein throughout Iraq. In Feb., Iraqi troops drove Kurdish insurgents and civilians to the Iran and Turkey borders, causing a refugee crisis. The U.S. and allies established havens inside Iraq for the Kurds.

Tensions heightened over the UN's efforts to dismantle Iraq's arms-production program, July 5, 1992, when a UN inspection team was denied entrance to a ministry building in Baghdad. Iraq allowed the inspection team access to the building July 26; the team found no arms-related evidence.

The U.S. launched a missile attack aimed at Iraq's intelligence headquarters in Baghdad June 26, 1993. The. U.S. justified the attack by citing evidence that Iraq had sponsored a plot to assassinate former Pres. George Bush during his visit to Kuwait in April.

Ireland

Eire

People: Population (1992 est.): 3,521,000. **Age distrib. (%):** 0–14: 30.5; 15–59: 54.5; 60+:15.0. **Pop. density:** 129 per sq. mi. **Urban** (1990): 57%. **Ethnic groups:** Celtic, English minority. **Languages:** English predominates, Irish (Gaelic) spoken by minority. **Religions:** Roman Catholic 95%, Anglican 3%.

Geography: Area: 27,137 sq. mi. slightly larger than W. Va. **Location:** In the Atlantic O. just W of Great Britain. **Neighbors:** United Kingdom (Northern Ireland). **Topography:** Ireland consists of a central plateau surrounded by isolated groups of hills and mountains. The coastline is heavily indented by the Atlantic O. **Capital:** Dublin. **Cities** (1991 est.): Dublin 502,000; Cork (met.) 133,000.

Government: Type: Parliamentary republic. **Head of State:** Pres. Mary Robinson; in office: Dec. 3, 1990. **Head of government:** Prime Min. Albert Reynolds; b. 1935; in office: Feb. 11, 1992. **Local divisions:** 26 counties. **Defense:** 1.6% of GDP (1992).

Economy: Industries: Food processing, textiles, chemicals, brewing, machinery, tourism. **Chief crops:** Potatoes, grain, sugar beets, fruits, vegetables. **Minerals:** Zinc, lead, silver, gas. **Arable land:** 14%. **Livestock** (1990): cattle: 5.6 mln.; pigs: 961,000; sheep: 4.9 mln. **Fish catch** (1990): 247,000 metric tons. **Electricity prod.** (1991): 14.4 bln. kWh. **Labor force:** 15% agric.; 29% ind. 51% services.

Finance: Monetary unit: Punt (June 1993: 0.69 = $1 US). **Gross domestic product** (1991): $39.2 bln. **Per capita GDP:** $11,200. **Imports** (1991): $24.5 bln.; partners: UK 41%, U.S. 14%, other EC 25%. **Exports** (1991): $27.8 bln.; partners: UK 34%, other EC 40%, U.S. 8%. **Tourism** (1990): receipts: $1.4 bln. **National budget** (1992): $12.6 bln. expenditures. **International reserves less gold** (Mar. 1993): $5.0 bln. **Gold:** 360,000 oz. t. **Consumer prices** (change in 1992): 3.2%.

Transport: Railroads (1991): **Length:** 2,814 km. **Motor vehicles:** in use (1990): 796,000 passenger cars, 147,000 comm. vehicles. **Civil aviation:** (1990): 3.8 bln. passenger-km; 11 airports. **Chief ports:** Dublin, Cork.

Communications: Television sets: 1 per 3.8 persons. **Radios:** 1 per 1.7 persons. **Telephones:** 1 per 3.8 persons. **Daily newspaper circ.** (1991): 179 per 1,000 pop.

Health: Life expectancy at birth (1992): 72 male; 78 female. **Births** (per 1,000 pop. 1992): 15. **Deaths** (per 1,000 pop. 1992): 9. **Natural increase:** .6%. **Hospital beds:** 1 per 257 persons. **Physicians:** 1 per 681 persons. **Infant mortality** (per 1,000 live births 1992): 8.

Education (1991): **Literacy:** 99%. **Years compulsory:** 9; attendance 91%.

Major International Organizations: UN (GATT, IMF, World Bank), EC, OECD.

Embassy: 2234 Massachusetts Ave. NW 20008; 462-3939.

Celtic tribes invaded the islands about the 4th century BC; their Gaelic culture and literature flourished and spread to Scotland and elsewhere in the 5th century AD, the same century in which St. Patrick converted the Irish to Christianity. Invasions by Norsemen began in the 8th century, ended with defeat of the Danes by the Irish King Brian Boru in 1014. English invasions started in the 12th century; for over 700 years the Anglo-Irish struggle continued with bitter rebellions and savage repressions.

The Easter Monday Rebellion (1916) failed but was followed by guerrilla warfare and harsh reprisals by British troops, the "Black and Tans." The Dail Eireann, or Irish parliament, reaffirmed independence in Jan. 1919. The British offered dominion status to Ulster (6 counties) and southern Ireland (26 counties) Dec. 1921. The constitution of the Irish Free State, a British dominion, was adopted Dec. 11, 1922. Northern Ireland remained part of the United Kingdom.

A new constitution adopted by plebiscite came into operation Dec. 29, 1937. It declared the name of the state Eire in the Irish language (Ireland in the English) and declared it a sovereign democratic state.

On Dec. 21, 1948, an Irish law declared the country a republic rather than a dominion and withdrew it from the Commonwealth. The British Parliament recognized both actions, 1949, but reasserted its claim to incorporate the 6 northeastern counties in the United Kingdom. This claim has not been recognized by Ireland. *(See United Kingdom — Northern Ireland.)*

Irish governments have favored peaceful unification of all Ireland. Ireland cooperated with Britain against terrorist groups.

Ireland suffered economic hardship in the 1980's; unemployment was over 20% in 1992.

Israel

State of Israel

Medinat Israel

People: Population (1992 est.): 4,748,000. **Age distrib. (%):** 0–14: 32.4; 15–59: 55.3; 60+: 13.3. **Pop. density:** 605 per sq. mi. **Urban** (1990): 89%. **Ethnic groups:** Jewish 83%, Arab 16%. **Languages:** Hebrew and Arabic (official). **Religions:** Jewish 83%, Moslem 13%.

Geography: Area: 7,847 sq. mi. about the size of New Jersey. **Location:** On eastern end of Mediterranean Sea. **Neighbors:** Lebanon on N, Syria, Jordan on E, Egypt on W. **Topography:** The Mediterranean coastal plain is fertile and well-watered. In the center is the Judean Plateau. A triangular-shaped semi-desert region, the Negev, extends from south of Beersheba to an apex at the head of the Gulf of Aqaba. The eastern border drops sharply into the Jordan Rift Valley, including Lake Tiberias (Sea of Galilee) and the Dead Sea, which is 1,312 ft. below sea level, lowest point on the earth's surface. **Capital:** Jerusalem. Most countries maintain their embassy in Tel Aviv. **Cities** (1990 est.): Jerusalem 504,000; Tel Aviv-Yafo 321,000; Haifa 222,000.

Government: Type: Republic. **Head of state:** Pres. Chaim Herzog; b. Sept. 17, 1918; in office: May 5, 1983. **Head of government:** Prime Min. Yitzhak Rabin; b. Mar. 1, 1922; in office: July 13, 1992. **Local divisions:** 6 districts. **Defense:** 12.1% of GDP (1992).

Economy: Industries: Diamond cutting, textiles, electronics, machinery, food processing. **Chief crops:** Citrus fruit, vegetables. **Minerals:** Potash, copper, phosphate, manganese, sulphur. **Arable land:** 17%. **Livestock** (1991): cattle: 331,000; sheep: 375,000. **Fish catch** (1991): 26,000 metric tons. **Electricity prod.** (1991): 21.0 bln. kWh. **Labor force:** 6% agric.; 23% ind., 30% public services.

Finance: Monetary unit: New Sheqalim (Aug. 1993: 2.81 = $1 US). **Gross domestic prod.** (1991): $54.6 bln. **Per capita GDP:** $12,500. **Imports** (1991): $18.1 bln.; partners: U.S. 16%, W. Ger. 13%, UK 9%. **Exports** (1991): $12.1 bln.; partners: U.S. 30%, W. Ger. 5%, UK 7%. **Tourists** (1990): receipts $1.4 bln. **National budget** (1992): $47.6 bln. expenditures. **International reserves less gold** (Jan. 1993): $4.6 bln. **Gold:** 9,000 oz t. **Consumer prices** (change in 1992): 11.6%.

Transport: Railroads: (1990): **Length:** 323 mi. **Motor vehicles:** in use (1990): 786,000 passenger cars, 157,000 comm. vehicles. **Civil aviation** (1990): 7.0 mln. passenger-km; 7 airports with scheduled flights. **Chief ports:** Haifa, Ashdod, Eilat.

Communications: Television sets: 1 per 4.1 persons. **Radios:** 1 per 2.2 persons. **Telephones:** 1 per 2.1 persons. **Daily newspaper circ.** (1989): 357 per 1,000 pop.

Health: Life expectancy at birth (1992) Jewish pop. only: 76 male; 79 female. **Births** (per 1,000 pop. 1992): 21. **Deaths** (per 1,000 pop. 1992): 6%. **Natural increase:** 1.5%. **Hospital beds:** 1 per 161 persons. **Physicians:** 1 per 345 persons. **Infant mortality** (per 1,000 live births 1992): 9.

Education (1991): **Literacy:** 92% (Jewish), 70% (Arab).

Major International Organizations: UN (GATT).

Embassy: 3514 International Dr. NW 20008; 364-5500.

Occupying the SW corner of the ancient Fertile Crescent, Israel contains some of the oldest known evidence of agriculture and of primitive town life. A more advanced civilization emerged in the 3d millennium BC. The Hebrews probably arrived early in the 2d millennium BC. Under King David and his successors (c.1000 BC-597 BC), Judaism was developed and secured. After conquest by Babylonians, Persians, and Greeks, an independent Jewish kingdom was revived, 168 BC, but Rome took effective control in the next century, suppressed Jewish revolts in 70 AD and 135 AD, and renamed Judea Palestine, after the earlier coastal inhabitants, the Philistines.

Arab invaders conquered Palestine in 636. The Arabic language and Islam prevailed within a few centuries, but a Jewish minority remained. The land was ruled from the 11th century as a part of non-Arab empires by Seljuks, Mamluks, and Ottomans (with a crusader interval, 1098-1291).

After 4 centuries of Ottoman rule, during which the population declined to a low of 350,000 (1785), the land was taken in 1917 by Britain, which in the Balfour Declaration that year pledged to support a Jewish national homeland there, as foreseen by the Zionists. In 1920 a British Palestine Mandate was recognized; in 1922 the land east of the Jordan was detached.

Jewish immigration, begun in the late 19th century, swelled in the 1930s with refugees from the Nazis; heavy Arab immigration from Syria and Lebanon also occurred. Arab opposition to Jewish immigration turned violent in 1920, 1921, 1929, and 1936. The UN General Assembly voted in 1947 to partition Palestine into an Arab and a Jewish state. Britain withdrew in May 1948.

Israel was declared an independent state May 14, 1948; the Arabs rejected partition. Egypt, Jordan, Syria, Lebanon, Iraq, and Saudi Arabia invaded, but failed to destroy the Jewish state, which gained territory. Separate armistices with the Arab nations were signed in 1949; Jordan occupied the West Bank, Egypt occupied Gaza, but neither granted Palestinian autonomy.

After persistent terrorist raids, Israel invaded Egypt's Sinai, Oct. 29, 1956, aided briefly by British and French forces. A UN cease-fire was arranged Nov. 6.

An uneasy truce between Israel and the Arab countries, supervised by a UN Emergency Force, prevailed until May 19, 1967, when the UN force withdrew at the demand of Egypt's Pres. Gamal Abdel Nasser. Egyptian forces reoccupied the Gaza Strip and closed the Gulf of Aqaba to Israeli shipping. In a 6-day war that started June 5, the Israelis took the Gaza Strip, occupied the Sinai Peninsula to the Suez Canal, and captured East Jerusalem, Syria's Golan Heights, and Jordan's West Bank. The fighting was halted June 10 by UN-arranged cease-fire agreements.

Egypt and Syria attacked Israel, Oct. 6, 1973 (Yom Kippur, most solemn day on the Jewish calendar). Israel counter-attacked, driving the Syrians back, and crossed the Suez Canal.

A cease fire took effect Oct. 24; a UN peace-keeping force went to the area. A disengagement agreement was signed Jan. 18, 1974. Israel withdrew from the canal's W bank. A second withdrawal was completed in 1976; Israel returned the Sinai to Egypt in 1982.

Israeli forces raided Entebbe, Uganda, July 3, 1976, and rescued 103 hostages seized by Arab and German terrorists.

In 1977, the conservative opposition, led by Menachem Begin, was voted into office for the first time. Egypt's Pres. Anwar al-Sadat visited Jerusalem Nov. 1977 and on Mar. 26, 1979, Egypt and Israel signed a formal peace treaty, ending 30 years of war and establishing diplomatic relations.

Israel invaded S. Lebanon, March 1978, following a Lebanon-based terrorist attack in Israel. Israel withdrew in favor of a 6,000-man UN force, but continued to aid Christian militiamen. Violence on the Israeli-occupied West Bank rose in 1982 when Israel announced plans to build new Jewish settlements. Israel affirmed the entire city of Jerusalem as its capital, July 1980, encompassing the annexed East Jerusalem.

On June 7, 1981, Israeli jets destroyed an Iraqi atomic reactor near Baghdad that, Israel claimed, would have enabled Iraq to manufacture nuclear weapons.

Israeli jets bombed Palestine Liberation Organization (PLO) strongholds in Lebanon April, May 1982. In reaction to the wounding of the Israeli ambassador to Great Britain, Israeli forces in a coordinated land, sea, and air attack invaded Lebanon, June 6, to destroy PLO strongholds in that country. Israeli forces encircled Beirut June 14. Following massive Israeli bombing of West Beirut, the PLO agreed to evacuate the city.

Israeli troops entered West Beirut after newly elected Lebanese president Bashir Gemayel was assassinated on Sept. 14. Israel received widespread condemnation when Lebanese Christian forces, Sept. 16, entered 2 West Beirut refugee camps and slaughtered hundreds of Palestinian refugees.

In 1989, violence escalated over the Israeli military occupation of the West Bank and Gaza Strip; Palestinian protesters and Israeli troops clashed frequently. Israeli police and stone-throwing Palestinians clashed, Oct. 8, 1990, around the al-Aqsa mosque on the Temple Mount in Jerusalem. Some 20 Palestinians died and 150 were injured.

The Knesset approved a new right-wing coalition government led by Prime Minister Yitzhak Shamir, June 11, 1990, following a 3-month political crisis that began with the fall of the previous "National Unity" government of Shamir and the Labor Party of Shimon Peres.

During the Persian Gulf War, Iraq fired a series of scud missiles at Israel; most were intercepted by U.S. Patriot missiles. Israel agreed in Aug. 1991 to take part in a U.S.-Soviet sponsored Middle East peace conference.

The Labor Party of Yitzhak Rabin won a clear victory in elections held June 23, 1992. Rabin called for peace and reconciliation with Israel's Arab neighbors.

Israeli forces conducted air raids and artillery strikes against guerrilla bases and villages in S. Lebanon, July 25-29, 1993, in retaliation for attacks by a pro-Iranian group on N. Israel.

Ongoing peace talks produced historic agreements between Israel and the Palestine Liberation Organization in Sept. 1993. The latter recognized Israel's right to exist, and Israel recognized the PLO as the representative of the Palestinians; the two sides then signed, Sept. 13, an agreement for limited Palestinian self-rule in Gaza and in the West Bank, beginning with the city of Jericho. The next day, Israel and Jordan signed a framework accord intended to pave the way for a future peace treaty.

Italy

Italian Republic

Repubblica Italiana

People: Population (1992 est.): 57,904,000. **Age distrib.** (%): 0–14: 17.8; 15–59: 62.8; 60+: 19.4. **Pop. density:** 497 per sq. mi. **Urban** (1991): 67%. **Ethnic groups:** Italians, small minorities of Germans, Slovenes, Albanians. **Languages:** Italian. **Religions:** Predominantly Roman Catholic.

Geography: Area: 116,303 sq. mi., about the size of Florida and Georgia combined. **Location:** In S Europe, jutting into Mediterranean S. **Neighbors:** France on W, Switzerland, Austria on N, Slovenia on E. **Topography:** Occupies a long boot-shaped peninsula, extending SE from the Alps into the Mediterranean, with the islands of Sicily and Sardinia offshore. The alluvial Po Valley drains most of N. The rest of the country is rugged and mountainous, except for intermittent coastal plains, like the Campania, S of Rome. Apennine Mts. run down through center of peninsula. **Capital:** Rome. **Cities** (1991 est.): Rome 2.8 mln.; Milan 1.4 mln.; Naples 1.2 mln.; Turin 1.0 mln.

Government: Type: Republic. **Head of state:** Pres. Oscar Luigi Scalfaro; in office: May 28, 1992. **Head of government:** Prime Min. Carlo Azeglio Ciampi; in office: April 22, 1993. **Local divisions:** 20 regions with some autonomy, 94 provinces. **Defense:** 2.2% of GDP (1991).

Economy: Industries: Steel, machinery, autos, textiles, shoes, machine tools, chemicals. **Chief crops:** Grapes, olives, citrus fruits, vegetables, wheat, rice. **Minerals:** Mercury, potash, sulphur. **Crude oil reserves** (1991): 700 mln. bbls. **Arable land:** 32%. **Livestock** (1991): cattle: 8.7 mln.; pigs: 9.5 mln.; sheep: 11.6 mln. **Fish catch** (1990): 360,000 metric tons. **Electricity prod.** (1991): 235 bln. kWh. **Crude steel prod.** (1991): 25.4 mln. metric tons. **Labor force:** 10% agric.; 32% ind. and comm.; 58% services and govt.

Finance: Monetary unit: Lira (June 1992: 1,202 = $1 US). **Gross domestic product** (1991): $965 bln. **Per capita GDP:** $16,700. **Imports** (1991): $181 bln.; partners: EC 58%, Fr. 15%, U.S. 7%. **Exports** (1991): $170 bln.; partners: EC 58%. **Tourism** (1990): receipts $19.7 bln. **National budget** (1991): $565 bln. expenditures. **International reserves less gold** (Apr. 1993): $26 bln. **Gold:** 66.67 mln. oz t. **Consumer prices** (change in 1992): 5.4%.

Transport: Railroads (1990): **Length:** 12,158 mi. **Motor vehicles:** in use (1989): 24.3 mln. passenger cars, 2.0 mln. comm. vehicles. **Civil aviation** (1990): 22.7 bln. passenger-km; 30 airports. **Chief ports:** Genoa, Venice, Trieste, Taranto, Naples, La Spezia.

Communications: Television sets: 1 per 3.8 persons. **Radios:** 1 per 3.4 persons. **Telephones:** 1 per 1.8 persons. **Daily newspaper circ.** (1989): 142 per 1,000 pop.

Health: Life expectancy at birth (1992): 74 male; 81 female. **Births** (per 1,000 pop. 1992): 11. **Deaths** (per 1,000 pop. 1992): 10. **Natural increase:** .1%. **Hospital beds:** 1 per 135 persons. **Physicians:** 1 per 233 persons. **Infant mortality** (per 1,000 live births 1992): 8.

Education (1991): **Literacy:** 98%. **Years compulsory:** 8.

Major International Organizations: UN and all of its specialized agencies, NATO, OECD, EC.

Embassy: 1601 Fuller St. NW 20009; 328-5500.

Rome emerged as the major power in Italy after 500 BC, dominating the more civilized Etruscans to the N and Greeks to the S. Under the Empire, which lasted until the 5th century AD, Rome ruled most of Western Europe, the Balkans, the Near East, and North Africa. In 1988, archeologists unearthed evidence showing Rome as a dynamic society in the 6th and 7th centuries B.C.

After the Germanic invasions, lasting several centuries, a high civilization arose in the city-states of the N, culminating in the Renaissance. But German, French, Spanish, and Austrian intervention prevented the unification of the country. In 1859 Lombardy came under the crown of King Victor Emmanuel II of Sardinia. By plebiscite in 1860, Parma, Modena, Romagna, and Tuscany joined, followed by Sicily and Naples, and by the Marches and Umbria. The first Italian parliament declared Victor Emmanuel king of Italy Mar. 17, 1861. Mantua and Venetia were added in 1866 as an outcome of the Austro-Prussian war. The Papal States were taken by Italian troops Sept. 20, 1870, on the withdrawal of the French garrison. The states were annexed to the kingdom by plebiscite. Italy recognized the State of Vatican City as independent Feb. 11, 1929.

Fascism appeared in Italy Mar. 23, 1919, led by Benito Mussolini, who took over the government at the invitation of the king Oct. 28, 1922. Mussolini acquired dictatorial powers. He made war on Ethiopia and proclaimed Victor Emmanuel III emperor, defied the sanctions of the League of Nations, sent troops to fight for Franco against the Republic of Spain and joined Germany in World War II.

After Fascism was overthrown in 1943, Italy declared war on Germany and Japan and contributed to the Allied victory. It surrendered conquered lands and lost its colonies. Mussolini was killed by partisans Apr. 28, 1945.

Victor Emmanuel III abdicated May 9, 1946; his son Humbert II was king until June 10, when Italy became a republic after a referendum, June 2-3. Reorganization of the Fascist party is forbidden.

Italy has enjoyed growth in industry and living standards since World War II, in part due to membership in the European Community. A wave of left-wing political violence began in the late 1970s with kidnappings and assassinations and continued into the 1980s. Christian Democratic leader and former Prime Min. Aldo Moro was murdered May 1978 by Red Brigade terrorists.

The Cabinet of Prime Min. Arnaldo Forlani resigned, May 26, 1981, in the wake of revelations that numerous high-ranking officials were members of an illegally secret Masonic lodge. The June 1983 elections saw Bettino Craxi chosen the nation's first Socialist premier. Craxi ended the longest tenure of an Italian leader since World War II by resigning Mar. 1987.

By mid-1991, some 20,000 Albanian refugees had entered Italy as the result of political unrest in their homeland. In Aug. an additional wave of 18,000 Albanians reached Italy. They were rounded up and sent back to Albania.

Italian voters in a referendum and Italy's parliament approved, in 1993, electoral reforms, amid growing political corruption scandals. Under the reforms, most members of parliament would be elected from single districts, rather than in a proportional representation system that fragmented power among several major parties.

Sicily, 9,926 sq. mi., pop. (1990) 5,172,000, is an island 180 by 120 mi., seat of a region that embraces the island of **Pantelleria,** 32 sq. mi., and the **Lipari** group, 44 sq. mi., 63 14,000, including 2 active volcanoes: **Vulcano,** 1,637 ft. and **Stromboli,** 3,038 ft. From prehistoric times Sicily has been settled by various peoples; a Greek state had its capital at Syracuse. Rome took Sicily from Carthage 215 BC. **Mt. Etna,** 11,053 ft. active volcano, is tallest peak.

Sardinia, 9,301 sq. mi., pop. (1990) 1,657,000, lies in the Mediterranean, 115 mi. W of Italy and 7-½ mi. S of Corsica. It is 160 mi. long, 68 mi. wide, and mountainous, with mining of coal, zinc, lead, copper. In 1720 Sardinia was added to the possessions of the Dukes of Savoy in Piedmont and Savoy to form the Kingdom of Sardinia. Giuseppe Garibaldi is buried on the nearby isle of Caprera. **Elba,** 86 sq. mi., lies 6 mi. W of Tuscany. Napoleon I lived in exile on Elba 1814-1815.

Trieste. An agreement, signed Oct. 5, 1954, by Italy and Yugoslavia, confirmed, Nov. 10, 1975, gave Italy provisional administration over the northern section and the seaport of Trieste, and Yugoslavia the part of Istrian peninsula it has occupied.

Jamaica

People: Population (1992 est.): 2,506,000. **Age distrib.** (%): 0–14: 33.7; 15–59: 56.4; 60+: 9.9. **Pop. density:** 592 per sq. mi. **Urban** (1990): 52%. **Ethnic groups:** African 76%, mixed 15%, Chinese, Caucasians, East Indians. **Languages:** English, (official), Jamaican Creole. **Religions:** Protestant 60%.

Geography: Area: 4,232 sq. mi., slightly smaller than Connecticut. **Location:** In West Indies. **Neighbors:** Nearest are Cuba on N, Haiti on E. **Topography:** The country is four-fifths covered by mountains. **Capital:** Kingston. **Cities** (1991 est.): St. Andrew 393,000, Kingston 100,000.

Government: Type: Parliamentary democracy. **Head of state:** Queen Elizabeth II, represented by Gov.-Gen. Howard Cooke; in office: Aug. 1, 1991. **Head of government:** Prime Min. Percival J. Patterson; in office: Mar. 30, 1992. **Local divisions:** 14 parishes; Kingston and St. Andrew corporate area. **Defense:** 1.0% of GDP (1991).

Economy: Industries: Rum, molasses, mining, tourism. **Chief crops:** Sugar cane, coffee, bananas, coconuts, citrus fruits. **Minerals:** Bauxite, limestone, gypsum. **Arable land:** 19%. **Livestock** (1991): cattle: 250,000; goats: 440,000. **Electricity prod.** (1991): 2.5 bln. kWh. **Labor force:** 31% agric.; 27% services; 41% ind.

Finance: Monetary unit: Dollar (Apr. 1993: 22.81 = $1 US). **Gross domestic product** (1991): $3.6 bln. **Per capita GDP:** $1,400.**Imports** (1991): $1.8 bln.; partners: U.S. 48%. **Exports** (1991): $1.2 bln.; partners: U.S. 36%. **Tourism** (1990): receipts: $740 mln. **National budget** (1991): $736 mln. **International reserves less gold** (Feb. 1993): $106 mln. **Consumer prices** (change in 1992): 49.9%.

Transport: Railroads (1989): **Length:** 211 mi. **Motor vehicles:** in use (1989): 93,000 passenger cars, 16,000 comm. vehicles. **Civil aviation** (1991): 1.3 bln. passenger km.; 6 airports with scheduled flights. **Chief ports:** Kingston, Montego Bay.

Communications: Television sets: 1 per 5.9 persons. **Radios:** 1 per 2.6 persons. **Telephones:** 1 per 13 persons. **Daily newspaper circ.** (1991): 51 per 1,000 pop.

Health: Life expectancy at birth (1992): 72 male; 76 female. **Births** (per 1,000 pop. 1992): 24. **Deaths:** (per 1,000 pop. 1992): 6. **Natural increase:** 1.8%. **Hospital beds:** 1 per 468 persons. **Physicians:** 1 per 5,904 persons. **Infant mortality** (per 1,000 live births 1992): 17.

Education (1990): **Literacy:** 98%. Compulsory to age 14.

Major International Organizations: UN (World Bank, GATT), OAS.

Embassy: 1850 K St. NW 20008; 452-0660.

Jamaica was visited by Columbus, 1494, and ruled by Spain (under whom Arawak Indians died out) until seized by Britain, 1655. Jamaica won independence Aug. 6, 1962.

In 1974 Jamaica sought an increase in taxes paid by U.S. and Canadian companies which mine bauxite on the island. The socialist government acquired 50% ownership of the companies' Jamaican interests in 1976, and was reelected that year. Rudimentary welfare state measures were passed. Relations with the U.S. improved greatly in the 1980s following the election of Edward Seaga.

Hurricane Gilbert struck Jamaica Sept. 12, 1988, killing some 45 and causing extensive damage including half the nation's houses.

Japan

Nippon

People: Population (1992 est.): 124,460,000. **Age distrib.** (%): 0–14: 17.3; 15–59: 64.1; 60+: 17.3. **Pop. density:** 830 per sq. mi. **Urban** (1990): 77%. **Language:** Japanese. **Ethnic groups:** Japanese 99.4%, Korean 0.5%. **Religions:** Buddhism, Shintoism shared by large majority.

Geography: Area: 145,856 sq. mi., slightly smaller than California. **Location:** Archipelago off E. coast of Asia. **Neighbors:** USSR on N, S. Korea on W. **Topography:** Japan consists of 4 main islands: Honshu ("mainland"), 87,805 sq. mi.; Hokkaido, 30,144 sq. mi.; Kyushu, 14,114 sq. mi.; and Shikoku, 7,049 sq. mi. The coast, deeply indented, measures 16,654 mi. The northern islands are a continuation of the Sakhalin Mts. The Kunlun range of China continues into southern islands, the ranges meeting in the Japanese Alps. In a vast transverse fissure crossing Honshu E-W rises a group of volcanoes, mostly extinct or inactive, including 12,388 ft. Fuji-San (Fujiyama) near Tokyo. **Capital:** Tokyo. **Cities** (1991 est.): Tokyo 8.1 mln.; Osaka 2.6 mln.; Yokohama 3.2 mln.; Nagoya 2.1 mln.; Kyoto 1.4 mln.; Kobe 1.4 mln.; Sapporo 1.6 mln.; Kitakyushu 1 mln.; Kawasaki 1.1 mln; Fukuoka 1.2 mln.

Government: Type: Parliamentary democracy. **Head of state:** Emp. Akihito; b. Dec. 23, 1933; in office: Jan. 7, 1989. **Head of government:** Prime Min. Morihiro Hosokawa; b. Jan. 14, 1938; in office: Aug. 6, 1993. **Local divisions:** 47 prefectures. **Defense:** Less than 1% of GNP (1992).

Economy: Industries: Electrical & electronic equip., autos, machinery, chemicals. **Chief crops:** Rice, grains, vegetables, fruits. **Minerals:** negligible. **Arable land:** 13%. **Livestock** (1991): cattle: 4.8 mln.; pigs: 11.3 mln. **Fish catch** (1990): 10.3 mln. metric tons. **Electricity prod.** (1991): 823 bln. kWh. **Crude steel prod.** (1991): 109 mln. metric tons. **Labor force:** 8% agric.; 32% manuf. & mining; 43% services & trade.

Finance: Monetary unit: Yen (June 1992: 127 = $1 US). **Gross domestic product** (1991): $2.3 trl. **Per capita GDP:** $19,100. **Imports** (1992): $233 bln.; partners: U.S. 22%, Middle East 26%, SE Asia 22%, EC 6%. **Exports** (1992): $339 bln.; partners: U.S. 33%, EC 20%, SE Asia 23%. **Tourism** (1990): $3.6 bln. receipts. **National budget** (1991): $532 bln. expenditures. **International reserves less gold** (Mar. 1993): $73 bln. **Gold:** 24.23 mln. oz. t. **Consumer prices** (change in 1992): 1.7%.

Transport: Railroads (1991): **Length:** 23,690 mi. **Motor vehicles:** in use (1991): 37.0 mln. passenger cars, 22.6 mln. comm. vehicles. **Civil aviation** (1990): 95.3 bln. passenger-km; 71 airports with scheduled flights. **Chief ports:** Yokohama, Tokyo, Kobe, Osaka, Nagoya, Chiba, Kawasaki, Hakodate.

Communications: Television sets: 1 per 1.8 persons. **Radios:** 1 per 1.3 persons. **Telephones:** 1 per 2.3 persons. **Daily newspaper circ.** (1991): 585 per 1,000 pop.

Health: Life expectancy at birth (1992): 77 male; 82 female. **Births** (per 1,000 pop. 1992): 10. **Deaths** (per 1,000 pop. 1992): 7. **Natural increase:** 0.3%. **Hospital beds:** 1 per 74 persons. **Physicians:** 1 per 588 persons. **Infant mortality** (per 1,000 live births 1992): 4.

Education (1991): **Literacy:** 99%. Most attend school for 12 years.

Major International Organizations: UN (IMF, GATT, ILO), OECD.

Embassy: 2520 Massachusetts Ave. NW 20008; 939-6700.

According to Japanese legend, the empire was founded by Emperor Jimmu, 660 BC, but earliest records of a unified Japan date from 1,000 years later. Chinese influence was strong in the formation of Japanese civilization. Buddhism was introduced before the 6th century.

A feudal system, with locally powerful noble families and their samurai warrior retainers, dominated from 1192. Central power was held by successive families of shoguns (military dictators), 1192-1867, until recovered by the Emperor Meiji, 1868. The Portuguese and Dutch had minor trade with Japan in the 16th and 17th centuries; U.S. Commodore Matthew C. Perry opened it to U.S. trade in a treaty ratified 1854. Japan fought China, 1894-95, gaining Taiwan. After war with Russia, 1904-05, Russia ceded S half of Sakhalin and gave concessions in China. Japan annexed Korea 1910. In World War I Japan ousted Germany from Shantung, took over German Pacific islands. Japan took Manchuria 1931, started war with China 1932. Japan launched war against the U.S. by attack on Pearl Harbor Dec. 7, 1941. Japan surrendered Aug. 14, 1945.

In a new constitution adopted May 3, 1947, Japan renounced the right to wage war; the emperor gave up claims to divinity; the Diet became the sole law-making authority.

The U.S. and 48 other non-communist nations signed a peace treaty and the U.S. a bilateral defense agreement with Japan, in San Francisco Sept. 8, 1951, restoring Japan's sovereignty as of April 28, 1952.

On June 26, 1968, the U.S. returned to Japanese control the Bonin Is., the Volcano Is. (including Iwo Jima) and Marcus Is. On May 15, 1972, Okinawa, the other Ryukyu Is. and the Daito Is. were returned to Japan by the U.S.; it was agreed the U.S. would continue to maintain military bases on Okinawa.

Industrialization was begun in the late 19th century. After World War II, Japan emerged as one of the most powerful economies in the world, and as a leader in technology.

The U.S. and EC member nations have criticized Japan for its restrictive policy on imports which has given Japan a substantial trade surplus.

Pres. Bush visted Japan, Jan. 1992; he won trade concessions in the areas of auto parts and sales, computers, paper, and glass.

The Recruit scandal, the nation's worst political scandal since World War II, which involved illegal political donations and stock trading, led to the resignation of Premier Noboru Takeshita in May 1989. A series of scandals rocked Japan's financial sector in 1991; one involved the largest bank, another the 4 largest securities firms.

Following a series of political scandals, the Liberal Democratic Party was denied a majority in general elections held July 18, 1993. The LDP had held power in Japan since the party was founded in 1955. Morihiro Hosokawa, a reformer, was chosen prime minister Aug. 6.

Jordan

Hashemite Kingdom of Jordan

al Mamlaka al Urduniya al Hashemiyah

Population (1992 est.): 3,557,000. **Age distrib.** (%): 0–14: 48.1; 15–59: 46.9; 60+: 4.0. **Pop. density:** 94 per sq. mi. **Urban** (1990): 68%. **Ethnic groups:** Arab 98%. **Languages:** Arabic (official). **Religions:** Sunni Moslem 92%, Christian 8%.

Geography: Area: 37,737 sq. mi., slightly larger than Indiana. **Location:** In W Asia. **Neighbors:** Israel on W, Saudi Arabia on S, Iraq on E, Syria on N. **Topography:** About 88% of Jordan is arid. Fertile areas are in W. Only port is on short Aqaba Gulf coast. Country shares Dead Sea (1,296 ft. below sea level) with Israel. **Capital:** Amman. **Cities** (1989 est.): Amman 936,000; az-Zarqa 318,000; Irbid 161,000.

Government: Type: Constitutional monarchy. **Head of state:** King Hussein I; b. Nov. 14, 1935; in office: Aug. 11, 1952. **Head of government:** Prime Min. Sharif Zaid ibn Shaker; in office: Nov. 16, 1991. **Local divisions:** 8 governorates. **Defense:** 9.5% of GDP (1990).

Economy: Industries: Textiles, cement, food processing. **Chief crops:** Grains, olives, vegetables, fruits. **Minerals:** Phosphate, potash. **Arable land:** 5%. **Electricity prod.** (1991): 3.9 bln. kWh. **Labor force:** 20% agric. 20% manuf. & mining.

Finance: Monetary unit: Dinar (Mar. 1993: 1.00 = $1.43 US). **Gross domestic product** (1991): $3.6 bln. **Imports** (1991): $2.3 bln.; partners: Saudi Ar. 6%, U.S. 11%, Jap. 8%. **Exports** (1991): $1.0 bln.; partners: Saudi Ar. 12%, Ind. 13%, Iraq. 18%. **Tourism** (1989): receipts: $546 mln. **National budget** (1992): $1.8 bln. expenditures. **International reserves less gold** (Mar. 1993): $680 mln. **Gold:** 789,000 oz t. **Consumer prices** (change in 1992): 4.2%.

Transport: Motor vehicles: in use (1990): 173,000 passenger cars, 68,000 comm. vehicles. **Civil aviation** (1990): 2.7 bln. passenger-km; 2 airports with scheduled flights. **Chief ports:** Aqaba.

Communications: Television sets: 1 per 12 persons. **Radios:** 1 per 4.5 persons. **Telephones:** 1 per 10 persons. **Daily newspaper circ.** (1990): 73 per 1,000 pop.

Health: Life expectancy at birth (1991): 70 male; 73 female. **Births** (per 1,000 pop. 1991): 46.7. **Deaths** (per 1,000 pop. 1991): 5. **Natural increase:** 4.1%. **Hospital beds:** 1 per 502 persons. **Physicians:** 1 per 813 persons. **Infant mortality** (per 1,000 live births 1991): 38.

Education (1989): **Literacy:** 71%.

Major International Organizations: UN (WHO, IMF), Arab League.

Embassy: 3504 International Dr. NW 20008; 966-2664.

From ancient times to 1922 the lands to the E of the Jordan River were culturally and politically united with the lands to the W. Arabs conquered the area in the 7th century; the Ottomans took control in the 16th. Britain's 1920 Palestine Mandate covered both sides of the Jordan. In 1921, Abdullah, son of the ruler of Hejaz in Arabia, was installed by Britain as emir of an autonomous Transjordan, covering two-thirds of Palestine. An independent kingdom was proclaimed, 1946.

During the 1948 Arab-Israeli war the West Bank and East Jerusalem were added to the kingdom, which changed its name to Jordan. All these territories were lost to Israel in the 1967 war, which swelled the number of Arab refugees on the East Bank. A 1974 Arab summit conference designated the Palestine Liberation Organization as the sole representative of Arabs on the West Bank. In 1988 Jordan cut legal and administrative ties with the Israeli-occupied West Bank. Jordan and Israel signed, Sept. 14, 1993, a framework accord, intended to lead to a peace treaty.

Some 700,000 refugees entered Jordan following Iraq's invasion of Kuwait, Aug. 1990. Jordan was viewed as supporting Iraq during the 1990-1991 Persian Gulf crisis.

Kazakhstan

Republic of Kazakhstan

Kazak Respublikasy

People: Population (1992 est.): 17,101,000. **Pop. density:** 16 per sq. mi. **Urban** (1991): 58%. **Ethnic groups:** Kazakh 40%, Russian 37%, German 6%, Ukrainian 5%. **Languages:** Kazakh, Russian, German. **Religion:** Moslem 47%.

Geography: Area: 1,049,200 sq. mi. **Neighbors:** Russia on N, China on E, Kyrgyzstan, Uzbekistan, Turkmenistan on S, Caspian Sea on W. **Topography:** Extends from the lower reaches of Volga in Europe to the Altai Mtns. on the Chinese border. **Capital:** Alma-Ata. **Cities** (1991): Alma-Ata 1.1 mln., Qaraghandy 608,000.

Government: Type: Republic. **Head of state:** Pres. Nursultan A. Nazarbayev. **Head of government:** Prime Min. Sergei Tereshchenko.

Economy: Industries: Steel, cement, footwear, textiles. **Chief crops:** Grain, cotton. **Minerals:** Coal, tungsten, copper, lead, zinc. **Livestock** (1989): cattle: 9.7 mln., sheep: 36.5 mln., pigs: 3.2 mln.

Finance: Monetary unit: Ruble.

Transport: Railroads (1991): **Length** (1991): 9,040 mi. **Motor vehicles** (1989): 734,000 passenger cars. **Civil aviation** (1990): 13.3 bln. passenger km.; airports with sched. flights: 5.

Communications: Telephones: 1 per 8.5 persons.

Health: Life expectancy at birth (1992): 63 male; 72 female. **Birth rate** (per 1,000 pop. 1992): 23. **Death rate** (per 1,000 pop. 1992): 8. **Hospital beds:** 1 per 74 persons. **Physicians:** 1 per 224 persons. **Infant mortality** (per 1,000 live births 1992): 26.

Major International Organizations: UN, CIS.

The region came under the Mongols in the 13th century and gradually came under Russian rule, 1730-1853. It was admitted to the USSR as a constituent republic 1936. Kazakhstan declared independence Dec. 16, 1991. It became an independent state when the Soviet Union dissolved Dec. 26, 1991.

Kenya

Republic of Kenya

Jamhuri ya Kenya

People: Population (1992 est.): 26,164,000. **Age distrib.** (%): 0–14: 49.6; 15–59: 50.0; 60+: 3.4. **Pop. density:** 116 per sq. mi. **Urban** (1991): 26%. **Ethnic groups:** Kikuyu 21%, Luo 13%, Luhya 14%, Kelenjin 11%, Kamba 11%, others, including Asians, Arabs, Europeans. **Languages:** Swahili (official), Kikuyu, Luhya, Luo, Meru. **Religions:** Protestant 38%, Roman Catholic 28%, Moslem 6%, others.

Geography: Area: 224,960 sq. mi., slightly smaller than Texas. **Location:** On Indian O. coast of E. Africa. **Neighbors:** Uganda on W, Tanzania on S, Somalia on E, Ethopia, Sudan on N. **Topography:** The northern three-fifths of Kenya is arid. To the S, a low coastal area and a plateau varying from 3,000 to 10,000 ft. The Great Rift Valley enters the country N-S, flanked by high mountains. **Capital:** Nairobi. **Cities** (1987 est.): Nairobi 959,000; Mombasa 401,000.

Government: Type: Republic. **Head of state:** Pres. Daniel arap Moi, b. Sept., 1924; in office: Aug. 22, 1978. **Local divisions:** Nairobi and 7 provinces. **Defense:** 1.0% of GDP (1989).

Economy: Industries: Tourism, light industry, petroleum prods. **Chief crops:** Coffee, corn, tea, cereals, cotton, sisal. **Minerals:** Gold, limestone, diatomite, salt, barytes, magnesite, felspar, sapphires, fluospar, garnets. **Other resources:** Timber, hides. **Arable land:** 4%. **Livestock** (1991): cattle: 13.7 mln. **Fish catch** (1990): 144,000 metric tons. **Electricity prod.** (1991): 2.8 bln. kWh. **Labor force:** 78% agric.

Finance: Monetary unit: Shilling (Mar. 1993: 45.52 = $1 US). **Gross domestic product** (1991): $9.7 bln. **Per capita GDP:** $385. **Imports** (1991): $1.9 bln.; partners: EC 45%. **Exports** (1991): $1.0 bln.; partners: EC 44%. **Tourism** (1992): receipts: $295 mln. **National budget** (1990): $2.8 bln expenditures. **International reserves less gold** (Mar. 1993): $77 mln. **Gold:** 80,000 oz t. **Consumer prices** (change in 1992): 35.5%.

Transport: Motor vehicles: in use (1989): 133,000 passenger cars, 149,000 comm. vehicles. **Civil Aviation** (1991): 1.4 bln. passenger-km; 16 airports with scheduled flights. **Chief ports:** Mombasa.

Communications: Television sets: 1 per 100 persons. **Radios:** 1 per 6 persons. **Telephones:** 1 per 67 persons. **Daily newspaper circ.** (1991): 13 per 1,000 pop.

Health: Life expectancy at birth (1992): 60 male; 64 female. **Births** (per 1,000 pop. 1992): 44. **Deaths** (per 1,000 pop. 1992): 8. **Natural increase:** 3.6%. **Hospital beds:** 1 per 737 persons. **Physicians:** 1 per 7,313 persons. **Infant mortality** (per 1,000 live births 1992): 68.

Education (1989): **Literacy:** 50%. 86% attend primary school.

Major International Organizations: UN and all of its specialized agencies, OAU, Commonwealth of Nations.

Embassy: 2249 R St. NW 20008; 387-6101.

Arab colonies exported spices and slaves from the Kenya coast as early as the 8th century. Britain obtained control in the 19th century. Kenya won independence Dec. 12, 1963, 4 years after the end of the violent Mau Mau uprising.

Kenya had steady growth in industry and agriculture under a modified private enterprise system, and enjoyed a relatively free political life. But stability was shaken in 1974-5, with opposition charges of corruption and oppression.

Tribal clashes in the western provinces claimed some 2,000 lives and left 50,000 homeless in 1992. The unrest was the worst since independence in 1963. Several western nations issued travel advisories for Kenya.

In the 1990s, Kenya suffered from widespread unemployment and high inflation. Pres. Moi suspended parliament, Jan. 27, 1993, one day after it opened with its first opposition members since the early 1960s.

Kiribati

Republic of Kiribati

People: Population (1992 est.): 74,000. **Pop. density:** 278 per sq. mi. **Ethnic groups:** nearly all Micronesian, some Polynesians. **Languages:** Gilbertese and English (official). **Religions:** evenly divided between Protestant and Roman Catholic.

Geography: Area: 266 sq. mi., slightly smaller than New York City. **Location:** 33 Micronesian islands (the Gilbert, Line, and Phoenix groups) in the mid-Pacific scattered in a 2-mln. sq. mi. chain around the point where the International Date Line cuts the Equator. **Neighbors:** Nearest are Nauru to SW, Tuvalu and Tokelau Is. to S. **Topography:** except Banaba (Ocean) I., all are low-lying, with soil of coral sand and rock fragments, subject to erratic rainfall. **Capital** (1990): Tarawa 25,000.

Government: Type: Republic. **Head of state and of government:** Pres. Teateo Teannaki; in office: July 3, 1991.

Economy: Industries: Copra. **Chief crops:** Coconuts, breadfruit, pandanus, bananas, paw paw. **Other resources:** Fish. **Electricity prod.** (1990): 13 mln. kWh.

Finance: Monetary unit: Australian dollar. **Gross domestic product** (1990): $36 mln.

Transport: Chief port: Tarawa.

Communications: Radios: 1 per 7 persons. **Telephones:** 1 per 53 persons.

Health: Hospital beds: 1 per 231 persons. **Physicians:** 1 per 4,104 persons.

Education: Literacy (1985): 90%.

A British protectorate since 1892, the Gilbert and Ellice Islands colony was completed with the inclusion of the Phoenix Islands, 1937. Self-rule was granted 1971; the Ellice Islands separated from the colony 1975 and became independent Tuvalu, 1978. Kiribati (pronounced *Kiribass)* independence was attained July 12, 1979. Under a Treaty of Friendship the U.S. relinquished its claims to several of the Line and Phoenix islands, including Christmas (Kiritimati), Canton, and Enderbury.

Tarawa Atoll was the scene of some of the bloodiest fighting in the Pacific during WW II.

Korea, North

Democratic People's Republic of Korea

Chosun Minchu-chui Inmin Konghwa-guk

People: Population (1992 est.): 22,227,000. **Pop. density:** 477 per sq. mi. **Urban** (1990): 60%. **Ethnic groups:** Korean. **Languages:** Korean. **Religions:** activities almost nonexistent; traditionally Buddhism, Confucianism, Chondokyo.

Geography: Area: 46,540 sq. mi., slightly smaller than Mississippi. **Location:** In northern E. Asia. **Neighbors:** China, Russia on N, S. Korea on S. **Topography:** Mountains and hills cover nearly all the country, with narrow valleys and small plains in between. The N and the E coast are the most rugged areas. **Capital:** Pyongyang. **Cities** (1987 est.): Pyongyang 2,355,000.

Government: Type: Communist state. **Head of state:** Pres. Kim Il-Sung; b. Apr. 15, 1912; in office: Dec. 28, 1972. **Head of government:** Premier Kang Song San; in office: Dec. 11, 1992. **Head of Communist Party:** Gen. Sec. Kim Il-Sung; in office: 1945. **Local divisions:** 9 provinces, 3 special cities. **Defense** (1991): 24% of GNP.

Economy: Industries: Textiles, petrochemicals, food processing. **Chief crops:** Corn, potatoes, fruits, vegetables, rice. **Minerals:** Coal, lead tungsten, graphite, magnesite, iron, copper, gold, phosphate, salt, fluorspar. **Arable land:** 19%. **Livestock** (1990): cattle: 1.2 mln; pigs: 3.1 mln. **Fish catch** (1990): 1.7 mln. metric tons. **Crude steel prod.** (1991) 7.0 mln. metric tons. **Electricity prod.** (1991): 36 bln. kWh. **Labor force:** 48% agric.

Finance: Monetary unit: Won (Mar. 1993): 2.15 = $1 US). **Gross national product** (1991): $23 bln. **Imports** (1990): $2.6 bln.; partners: China 17%, USSR 36%, Jap. 19%. **Exports** (1990): $2.0 bln.; partners: USSR 43% China 13%, Jap. 15%. **National budget** (1990): $17.7 bln. expenditures.

Communications: Television sets: 1 per 90 persons. **Radios:** 1 per 6 persons.

Transport: Chief ports: Chonglin, Hamhung, Nampo.

Health: Life expectancy at birth (1992): 66 male; 72 female. **Births** (per 1,000 pop. 1992): 24. **Deaths** (per 1,000 pop. 1992): 6. **Natural increase:** 1.8%. **Hospital beds:** 1 per 74 persons. **Physicians:** 1 per 370 persons. **Infant mortality** (per 1,000 live births, 1992): 30.

Education (1991): **Literacy:** 99%. **Years compulsory:** 11.

Major International Organizations: UN.

The Democratic People's Republic of Korea was founded May 1, 1948, in the zone occupied by Russian troops after World War II. Its armies tried to conquer the south, 1950. After 3 years of fighting, with Chinese and U.S. intervention, a cease-fire was proclaimed.

Industry, begun by the Japanese during their 1910-45 occupation, and nationalized in the 1940s, had grown substantially, using N. Korea's abundant mineral and hydroelectric resources.

In Mar. 1993, N. Korea became the first nation to formally withdraw from the Nuclear Nonproliferation Treaty, the international pact designed to limit the spread of nuclear weapons; the nation suspended its withdrawal in June in reaction to threats of UN economic sanctions.

Korea, South

Republic of Korea

Taehan Min'guk

People: Population (1992 est.): 44,149,000. **Age distrib.** (%): 0–14: 27.3; 15–59: 65.5; 60+: 7.2. **Pop. density:** 1,161 per sq. mi. **Urban** (1990): 74%. **Ethnic groups:** Korean. **Languages:** Korean. **Religions:** Christian 43%, Buddhist 18%.

Geography: Area: 38,025 sq. mi., slightly larger than Indiana. **Location:** In Northern E. Asia. **Neighbors:** N. Korea on N. **Topography:** The country is mountainous, with a rugged east coast. The western and southern coasts are deeply indented, with many islands and harbors. **Capital:** Seoul. **Cities** (1990 est.): Seoul 10.7 mln.; Pusan 3,800,000; Taegu 2,200,000; Inchon 1,600,000; Kwangju 1,200,000; Taejon 1,000,000.

Government: Type: Republic, with power centralized in a strong executive. **Head of state:** Pres. Kim Young Sam; in office: Feb. 25, 1993. **Head of government:** Prime Min. Hwang In Sung; in office: Feb. 22, 1993. **Local divisions:** 9 provinces and 6 special cities. **Defense:** 4.5% of GNP (1992).

Economy: Industries: Electronics, ships, textiles, clothing, motor vehicles. **Chief crops:** Rice, barley, vegetables, wheat. **Minerals:** Tungsten, coal, graphite. **Arable land:** 22%. **Livestock** (1990): cattle: 2.0 mln.; pigs: 4.8 mln. **Fish catch:** (1990): 3.2 mln. metric tons. **Electricity prod.** (1991): 106 bln. kWh. **Crude steel prod.** (1991): 26.0 mln. metric tons. **Labor force:** 21% agric.; 27% manuf. & mining; 52% services.

Finance: Monetary unit: Won (Aug. 1993: 805 = $1 US). **Gross national product** (1991): $273 bln. **Per capita GNP:** $6,300. **Imports** (1992): $81 bln.; partners: Jap. 26%, U.S. 21%. **Exports** (1992): $72 bln.; partners: U.S. 26%, Jap. 18%. **Tourism** (1990): receipts: $3.5 bln. **National budget** (1992): $44 bln. expenditures. **International reserves less gold** (Mar. 1993): $18 bln. **Gold:** 323,000 oz t. **Consumer prices** (change in 1992): 6.2%.

Transport: Railroads (1990): **Length:** 4,000 mi. **Motor vehicles:** in use (1990): 2.0 mln. passenger cars, 1.3 mln. comm. vehicles. **Civil aviation** (1990): 18.7 bln. passenger-km; 12 airlines with scheduled flights. **Chief ports:** Pusan, Inchon.

Communications: Television sets: 1 per 4.9 persons. **Radios:** 1 per 1.0 persons. **Telephones:** 1 per 3.3 persons. **Daily newspaper circ.** (1990): 309 per 1,000 pop.

Health: Life expectancy at birth (1992): 67 male; 73 female. **Births** (per 1,000 pop. 1992): 15. **Deaths** (per 1,000 pop. 1992): 6. **Natural increase:** 0.9%. **Hospital beds:** 1 per 429 persons. **Physicians:** 1 per 1,007 persons. **Infant mortality** (per 1,000 live births 1992): 23.

Education (1991): **Literacy:** 96%. **Attendance:** High school 90%, college 14%.

Embassy: 2320 Massachusetts Ave. NW 20008; 939-5600.

Major International Organizations: UN.

Korea, once called the Hermit Kingdom, has a recorded history since the 1st century BC. It was united in a kingdom under the Silla Dynasty, 668 AD. It was at times associated with the Chinese empire; the treaty that concluded the Sino-Japanese war of 1894-95 recognized Korea's complete independence. In 1910 Japan forcibly annexed Korea as Chosun.

At the Potsdam conference, July, 1945, the 38th parallel was designated as the line dividing the Soviet and the American occupation. Russian troops entered Korea Aug. 10, 1945, U.S. troops entered Sept. 8, 1945. The Soviet military organized socialists and communists and blocked efforts to let the Koreans unite their country. *(See Index for Korean War.)*

The South Koreans formed the Republic of Korea in May 1948 with Seoul as the capital. Dr. Syngman Rhee was chosen president but a movement spearheaded by college students forced his resignation Apr. 26, 1960.

In an army coup May 16, 1961, Gen. Park Chung Hee became chairman of the ruling junta. He was elected president, 1963; a 1972 referendum allowed him to be reelected for 6 year terms unlimited times. Park was assassinated by the chief of the Korean CIA, Oct. 26, 1979. The calm of the new government was halted by the rise of Gen. Chun Doo Hwan, head of the military intelligence, who reinstated martial law, and reverted South Korea to the police state it was under Park.

In July 1972 South and North Korea agreed on a common goal of reunifying the 2 nations by peaceful means. But there was no sign of a thaw in relations between the two regimes until 1985 when they agreed to discuss economic issues. In 1988, radical students demanding reunification clashed with police.

On June 10, 1987, middle class office workers, shopkeepers, and business executives joined students in antigovernment protests in Seoul. They were protesting President Chun's decision to choose his successor and not allow the next president to be chosen by direct vote of the people. Following weeks of rioting and violence, Chun, July 1, agreed to permit election of the next president by direct popular vote and other constitutional reforms. In Dec., Roh Tae Woo was elected president. In 1990, the nation's 3 largest political parties merged; some 100,000 students demonstrated, charging that the merger was undemocratic.

Kim Young Sam took office in 1993 as the first civilian president since 1961.

Kuwait

State of Kuwait

Dowlat al-Kuwait

People: Population (1992 est.): 1,318,000. **Age distrib.** (%): 0–14: 35.5; 15–59: 62.1; 60+: 2.4. **Pop. density:** 191 per sq. mi. **Urban** (1990): 95%. **Ethnic groups:** Kuwaiti 50%, other Arab 35%, Iranians, Indians, Pakistanis. **Languages:** Arabic, (official). **Religions:** Moslem 85%.

Geography: Area: 6,880 sq. mi., slightly smaller than New Jersey. **Location:** In Middle East, at N end of Persian Gulf. **Neighbors:** Iraq on N, Saudi Arabia on S. **Topography:** The country is flat, very dry, and extremely hot. **Capital:** Kuwait. **Cities** (1985 est.): Hawalli 145,000; as-Salimiyah 153,000.

Government: Type: Constitutional monarchy. **Head of state:** Emir Shaikh Jabir al-Ahmad al-Jabir as-Sabah; b. 1928; in office: Jan. 1, 1978. **Head of government:** Prime Min. Shaikh Saad Abdulla as-Salim as-Sabah; in office: Feb. 8, 1978. **Local divisions:** 5 governorates. **Defense:** 21% of GDP (1991).

Economy: Industries: Oil products. **Minerals:** Oil, gas. **Crude oil reserves** (1990): 94 bln. barrels. **Cultivated land:** 1%. **Electricity prod.** (1991): 3.1 bln. kWh. **Labor force:** social services 45%; construction 20%.

Finance: Monetary unit: Dinar (Mar. 1993: 1.00 = $3.30 US). **Gross domestic product** (1991): $8.7 bln. **Per capita GDP:** $6,200. **Imports** (1991): $4.7 bln.; partners: Jap. 21%, U.S. 9%. **Exports** (1989): $11.4 bln.; partners: Jap. 16%, It. 10%. **Tourism** (1990): $180 mln. receipts. **National budget** (1992): $21 bln. expenditures. **International reserves less gold** (Mar. 1993): $4.2 bln. **Gold:** 2.53 mln. oz t.

Transport: Motor vehicles: in use (1990): 500,000 passenger cars, 114,000 comm. vehicles. **Civil aviation** (1991): 1.8 mln. passenger-km. 1 airport with scheduled flight. **Chief ports:** Mina al-Ahmadi.

Communications: Television sets: 1 per 2.6 persons. **Radios:** 1 per 1.8 persons. **Telephones:** 1 per 6.9 persons. **Daily newspaper circ.** (1992): 550 per 1,000 pop.

Health: Life expectancy at birth (1992): 72 male; 76 female. **Births** (per 1,000 pop. 1992): 32. **Deaths** (per 1,000 pop. 1992): 2. **Natural increase:** 3.0%. **Hospital beds:** 1 per 336 persons. **Physician:** 1 per 695 persons. **Infant mortality** (per 1,000 live births 1992): 15.

Education (1989): **Literacy:** 71%. **Years compulsory:** 8.

Major International Organizations: UN (World Bank, IMF, GATT), Arab League, OPEC.

Embassy: 2940 Tilden St. NW 20008; 966-0702.

Kuwait is ruled by the Al-Sabah dynasty, founded 1759. Britain ran foreign relations and defense from 1899 until independence in 1961. The majority of the population is non-Kuwaiti, with many Palestinians, and cannot vote.

Oil, first exported in 1946, is the fiscal mainstay, providing most of Kuwait's income. Oil pays for free medical care, education, and social security. There are no taxes, except customs duties.

Kuwaiti oil tankers have come under frequent attack by Iran because of Kuwait's support of Iraq in the Iran-Iraq War. In July 1987, U.S. Navy warships began escorting Kuwaiti tankers in the Persian Gulf.

In 1988, a Kuwaiti Airways jet was hijacked by pro-Iranian Shiite Moslem terrorists who demanded the release of 17 Shiite terrorists. The ordeal lasted 16 days as Kuwait refused to release the terrorists.

Kuwait was attacked and overrun by Iraqian forces Aug. 2, 1990. The Emir and senior members of the ruling family fled to Saudi Arabia to establish a government in exile. On Aug. 28, Iraq announced that Kuwait was its 19th province. Following several weeks of aerial attacks on Iraq and Iraqi forces in Kuwait, a U.S.-led coalition began a ground attack Feb. 23, 1991. By Feb. 27, Iraqi forces were routed and Kuwait liberated.

Following liberation, there were reports of abuse of Palestinians and others suspected of collaborating with Iraqi occupiers.

Former U.S. President George Bush visited Kuwait, Apr. 14-16, 1993, and was honored as the leader of the Persian Gulf War alliance that expelled Iraqi troops in 1991. Prior to the visit, Kuwaiti authorities arrested a group of Iraqis who had planned to assassinate Bush during his visit. An inquiry by the FBI substantiated accusations that Iraq was involved in the plot.

Kyrgyzstan

Republic of Kyrgyzstan

Kyrgyz Respublikasy

People: Population (1992 est.): 4,567,000. **Pop density:** 59 per sq. mi. **Urban** (1991): 38%. **Ethnic groups:** Kyrghiz 52%, Russian 22%, Uzbec 13%.

Geography: Area: 76,642 sq. mi. **Neighbors:** Kazakhstan on N., China on E., Uzbekistan on W., Tajikistan on S. **Capital:** Bishkek. **Cities** (1991): Bishkek 631,000; Osh 218,000.

Government: Type: Republic. **Head of state:** Pres. Askar Akayev. **Head of government:** Prime Min. Tursunbek Chyngyshev. **Local divisions:** 6 oblasts.

Economy: Industries: Tanning, tobacco, textiles, mining. **Chief crops:** Wheat, sugar beets, tobacco. **Livestock** (1989): cattle: 1.2 mln., sheep: 10.4 mln.

Finance: Monetary unit: Som (May 1993): 1.00 = $.24 US.

Transport: Railroads (1991): **Length:** 490 mi. **Motor vehicles:** in use (1990): 173,000 passenger cars. **Civil aviation** (1990): 3.7 bln. passenger-km; 1 airport.

Communications: Telephones: 1 per 14 persons. **Newspaper circ. (1990): 367 per 1,000 pop.**

Health: Life expectancy at birth (1992): 62 male; 71 female. **Birth rate** (per 1,000 pop. 1992): 31. **Death rate** (per 1,000 pop. 1992): 8. **Hospital beds:** 1 per 84 persons. **Physicians:** 1 per 275 persons. **Infant mortality** (per 1,000 live births 1992): 56.

Major International Organizations: UN (IMF), CIS.

The region was inhabited around the 13th century by the Kirghiz. It was annexed to Russia 1864. After 1917, it was nominally a Kara-Kirghiz autonomous area, which was reorganized 1926, and made a constituent republic of the USSR in 1936. Kyrgyzstan declared independence Aug. 31, 1991. It became an independent state when the USSR disbanded Dec. 26, 1991.

Laos

Lao People's Democratic Republic

Sathalanalat Paxathipatai Paxaxōn Lao

People: Population (1992 est.): 4,440,000. **Pop. density:** 48 per sq. mi. **Urban** (1990): 19%. **Ethnic groups:** Lao 50%, Mon-Khmer tribes 25%, Thai 14%, Meo and Yao 13%, others. **Languages:** Lao (official), Palaung-Wa, Tai. **Religions:** Buddhists 80%, tribal 20%.

Geography: Area: 91,428 sq. mi., slightly larger than Utah. **Location:** In Indochina Peninsula in SE Asia. **Neighbors:** Myanmar, China on N, Vietnam on E, Cambodia on S, Thailand on W. **Topography:** Landlocked, dominated by jungle. High mountains along the eastern border are the source of the E-W rivers slicing across the country to the Mekong R., which defines most of the western border. **Capital:** Vientiane. **Cities** (1985 cen.): Vientiane 377,000.

Government: Type: Communist. **Head of state:** Pres. Nouhak Phoumsavan; in office: Nov. 25, 1992. **Head of government:** Prime Min. Khamtai Siphandon; in office: Aug. 15 1991. **Local divisions:** 17 provinces, 1 municipality. **Armed forces: Defense:** 3.8% of GDP (1988).

Economy: Industries: Wood products, mining. **Chief crops:** Rice, corn, tobacco, cotton, opium, citrus fruits, coffee. **Minerals:** Tin. **Other resources:** Forests. **Arable land:** 4%. **Livestock** (1990): pigs: 1.3 mln. **Fish catch** (1990): 20,000 metric tons. **Electricity prod.** (1991): 1.1 bln. kWh. **Labor force:** 85% agric.; 6% ind.

Finance: Monetary unit: New kip (Dec. 1992): 714 = $1 US). **Gross domestic product** (1991): $800 mln. **Per capita GDP:** $200. **Imports** (1990): $240 mln.; partners: Thai. 45%, Jap. 20%. **Exports** (1990): $72 mln.; partners: Thai, Viet, USSR.

Transport: Motor vehicles: in use (1989): 17,000 passenger cars, 3,500 comm. vehicles. **Civil Aviation** (1987): 18 mln. passenger km; 4 airports with scheduled flights.

Communications: Radios: 1 per 9 persons.

Health: Life expectancy at birth (1992): 49 male; 52 female. **Births** (per 1,000 pop. 1992): 44. **Deaths** (per 1,000 pop. 1992): 16. **Natural increase:** 2.8%. **Hospital beds:** 1 per 369 persons. **Physicians:** 1 per 6,495 persons. **Infant mortality** (per 1,000 live births, 1992): 107.

Education: (1991): **Literacy:** 45%.

Major International Organizations: UN (FAO, IMF, WHO).

Embassy: 2222 S St. NW 20008; 332-6416.

Laos became a French protectorate in 1893, but regained independence as a constitutional monarchy July 19, 1949.

Conflicts among neutralist, communist and conservative factions created a chaotic political situation. Armed conflict increased after 1960.

The 3 factions formed a coalition government in June 1962, with neutralist Prince Souvanna Phouma as premier. A 14-nation conference in Geneva signed agreements, 1962, guaranteeing neutrality and independence. By 1964 the Pathet Lao had withdrawn from the coalition, and, with aid from N. Vietnamese troops, renewed sporadic attacks. U.S. planes bombed the Ho Chi Minh trail, supply line from N. Vietnam to communist forces in Laos and S. Vietnam.

In 1970 the U.S. stepped up air support and military aid. After Pathet Lao military gains, Souvanna Phouma in May 1975 ordered government troops to cease fighting; the Pathet Lao took control. A Lao People's Democratic Republic was proclaimed Dec. 3, 1975.

Latvia

Republic of Latvia

Latvijas Republika

People: Population (1992 est.): 2,728,000. **Pop density:** 109 per sq. mi. **Urban** (1991): 71%. **Language:** Latvian. **Religion:** Mostly Evangelical Lutheran. **Ethnic groups:** Latvian 54%, Russian 33%.

Geography: Area: 24,900 sq. mi., slightly larger than W. Va. **Neighbors:** Estonia & Baltic Sea on N., Baltic Sea on W., Lithuania & Belarus on S., Russia on E. **Capital:** Riga. **Cities** (1991): Riga 910,000.

Government: Type: Republic. **Head of state:** Anatolijs Gorbunovs. **Head of government:** Prime Min. Ivars Godmanis. **Local divisions:** 26 districts, 56 towns, 37 urban settlements.

Economy: Industries: Electric railway passenger cars, paper. **Chief crops:** oats, barley, potatoes. **Livestock** (1989): cattle 1.5 mln. **Arable land:** 27%. **Electricity prod.** (1991): 6.5 bln. kWh. **Labor force:** 16% agric. & forestry; 41% ind. & comm.

Finance: Monetary unit: Latvian ruble. **Imports** (1990): $9.0 bln. **Exports** (1990): $239 mln.

Transport: Railroads: Length (1991): 1,489 mi. **Motor vehicles:** in use (1990): 271,000 passenger cars, 14,000 comm. vehicles. **Civil aviation** (1990): 3.7 bln. passenger-km; 1 airport.

Communications: Telephones: 1 per 3.7 persons. **Newspaper circ.** (1990): 1,637 per 1,000 pop.

Health: Life expectancy at birth (1992): 64 male, 75 female. **Births** (per 1,000 pop. 1992): 15. **Deaths** (per 1,000 pop. 1992): 12. **Hospital beds:** 1 per 60 persons. **Physicians:** 1 per 200 persons. **Infant mortality rates** (per 1,000 live births 1992): 19.

Transport: Motor vehicles: in use (1988): 241,000 passenger cars. **Chief port:** Riga.

Communications: Television sets (1990): 1.2 per household, **Radios:** 1.4 per household. **Telephones:** 1 per 4.3 persons.

Prior to 1918, Latvia was occupied by the Russians and Germans. It was an independent republic, 1918-39. The Aug. 1939 Soviet-German agreement assigned it to the Soviet sphere of influence. It was officially accepted as part of the USSR on Aug. 5, 1940. It was overrun by the German army, but retaken in 1945. It attempted to establish independence 1990.

During an abortive Soviet coup, Latvia declared independence, Aug. 21, 1991. The Soviet Union recognized Latvia's independence in Sept. 1991.

Lebanon

Republic of Lebanon

al-Jumhouriya al-Lubnaniya

People: Population (1992 est.): 3,439,000. **Age distrib.** (%): 0–14: 37.0; 15–59: 55.1; 60+: 7.9. **Pop. density:** 856 per sq. mi. **Urban** (1990): 84%. **Ethnic groups:** Arab 95%, Armenian 4%, Palestinian 9%. **Languages:** Arabic (official), French. **Religions:** Moslem 75%; Christian 25%.

Geography: Area: 4,015 sq. mi., smaller than Connecticut. **Location:** On Eastern end of Mediterranean Sea. **Neighbors:** Syria on E Israel on S. **Topography:** There is a narrow coastal strip, and 2 mountain ranges running N-S enclosing the fertile Beqaa Valley. The Litani R. runs S through the valley, turning W to empty into the Mediterranean. **Capital:** Beirut. **Cities** (1991 est.): Beirut 1,100,000; Tripoli 240,000.

Government: Type: Republic. **Head of state:** Pres. Elias Hrawi; in office: Nov. 24, 1989. **Head of government:** Prime Min. Rafiq al-Hariri; in office: Oct. 31, 1992. **Local divisions:** 5 governorates. **Defense:** 8.2% of GDP (1992).

Economy: Industries: Trade, food products, textiles, cement, oil products. **Chief crops:** Fruits, olives, tobacco, grapes, vegetables, grains. **Minerals:** Iron. **Arable land:** 21%. **Livestock** (1991): goats: 400,000; sheep: 205,000. **Electricity prod.** (1991): 3.8 bln. kWh. **Labor force:** 11% agric.; 79% ind., comm., services.

Finance: Monetary unit: Pound (Aug. 1993: 1,728 = $1 US). **Gross domestic product** (1991): $4.8 bln. **Per capita GDP:** $1,400. **Imports** (1990): $1.9 bln.; partners: It. 15%, Fr. 10%, U.S. 6%. **Exports** (1990): $700 mln.; partners: Saudi Ar. 16%, Jor. 6%, Kuw. 8%. **National budget** (1991): $1.3 bln. expenditures. **International reserves less gold** (Mar. 1993): $1.2 bln. **Gold;** 9.22 mln. oz t.

Transport: Motor vehicles: in use (1985): 300,000 passenger cars, 50,000 comm. vehicles. **Civil aviation** (1990): 1.5 bln. passenger-km. **Chief ports:** Beirut, Tripoli, Sidon.

Communications: Television sets: 1 per 3.4 persons. **Radios:** 1 per 1.3 persons. **Telephones:** 1 per 18.4 persons. **Daily newspaper circ.** (1986): 211 per 1,000 pop.

Health: Life expectancy at birth (1992): 66 male; 71 female. **Births** (per 1,000 pop. 1992): 28. **Deaths** (per 1,000 pop. 1992): 7. **Natural increase:** 2.1%. **Hospital beds:** 1 per 263 persons. **Physicians:** 1 per 771 persons. **Infant mortality** (per 1,000 live births 1992): 43.

Education: (1991): **Literacy:** 75%. **Years compulsory:** 5; attendance 93%.

Major International Organizations: UN (IMF, ILO, WHO).

Embassy: 2560 28th St. NW 20008; 939-6300.

Formed from 5 former Turkish Empire districts, Lebanon became an independent state Sept. 1, 1920, administered under French mandate 1920-41. French troops withdrew in 1946.

Under the 1943 National Covenant, all public positions were divided among the various religious communities, with Christians in the majority. By the 1970s, Moslems became the majority and demanded a larger political and economic role.

U.S. Marines intervened, May-Oct. 1958, during a Syrian-aided revolt. Continued raids against Israeli civilians, 1970-75, brought Israeli attacks against guerrilla camps and villages. Israeli troops occupied S. Lebanon, March 1978, and again in Apr. 1980.

An estimated 60,000 were killed and billions of dollars in damage inflicted in a 1975-76 civil war. Palestinian units and leftist Moslems fought against the Maronite militia, the Phalange, and other Christians. Several Arab countries provided political and arms support to the various factions, while Israel aided Christian forces. Up to 15,000 Syrian troops intervened in 1976, and fought Palestinian groups. Arab League troops from several nations tried to impose a cease-fire.

Clashes between Syrian troops and Christian forces erupted, Apr. 1, 1981, bringing to an end the cease-fire. By Apr. 22, fighting had also broken out between two Moslem factions. In July, Israeli air raids on Beirut killed or wounded some 800 persons.

Israeli forces invaded Lebanon June 6, 1982, in a coordinated land, sea, and air attack aimed at crushing strongholds of the Palestine Liberation Organization (PLO). Israeli and Syrian forces engaged in the Bekaa Valley. By June 14, Israeli troops had encircled Beirut. On Aug. 21, the PLO evacuated west Beirut following massive Israeli bombings of the city. Israeli troops entered west Beirut following the Sept. 14 assassination of newly elected Lebanese Pres. Bashir Gemayel. On Sept. 16, Lebanese Christian troops entered 2 refugee camps and massacred hundreds of Palestinian refugees. Israeli troops withdrew from Lebanon in June 1985.

In 1983, terrorist bombings became a way of life in Beirut as some 50 people were killed in an explosion at the U.S. Embassy, Apr. 18; 241 U.S. servicemen and 58 French soldiers died in separate Moslem suicide attacks, Oct. 23.

On Apr. 26, 1984, pro-Syrian Rashid Karami was appointed premier. The appointment failed to end virtual civil war in Beirut between Christian forces and Druse and Shiite Moslem militias. There was heavy fighting between Shiite militiamen and Palestinian guerrillas in May 1985. In June, Beirut Airport was the scene of a hostage crisis where Shiite terrorists held U.S. citizens for 17 days. Fierce artillery duels between Christian east Beirut and Moslem west Beirut, Mar.-Apr. 1989, left some 200 dead and 700 wounded.

Kidnapping of foreign nationals by Islamic militants became common in the 1980s. U.S., British, French, and Soviet citizens were victims. All were released by 1992.

A treaty signed May 22, 1991, between Lebanon and Syria recognized Lebanon as a separate and independent state for the first time since the 2 countries gained independence in 1943.

Israeli forces conducted air raids and artillery strikes against guerrilla bases and villages in S Lebanon, causing over 200,000 to flee their homes July 25-29, 1993.

Lesotho

Kingdom of Lesotho

People: Population (1992 est.): 1,848,000. **Age distrib.** (%): 0–14: 42.3; 15–59: 52.2; 60+: 5.7. **Pop. density:** 157 per sq. mi. **Ethnic groups:** Sotho 99%. **Languages:** English, Sotho (both official). **Religions:** Roman Catholic 38%, Protestant 42%.

Geography: Area: 11,716 sq. mi., slightly larger than Maryland. **Location:** In Southern Africa. **Neighbors:** Completely surrounded by Republic of South Africa. **Topography:** Landlocked and mountainous, with altitudes ranging from 5,000 to 11,000 ft. **Capital:** Maseru. **Cities** (1990 est.): Maseru 109,000.

Government: Type: Parliamentary democracy & constitutional monarchy. **Head of state:** King Letsie 3d; in office: Nov. 12, 1990. **Head of government:** Prime Min. Ntsu Mokhehle; in office: Apr. 1, 1993. **Local divisions:** 10 districts. **Defense:** 8.6% of GDP (1990).

Economy: Industries: Food processing. **Chief crops:** Corn, grains, peas, beans. **Other resources:** Diamonds. **Arable land:** 13%. **Labor force:** 40% agric.

Finance: Monetary unit: Maloti (Mar. 1993: 1.00 = $.31 US). **Gross domestic product** (1990): $420 mln. **Per capita GDP** (1990): $240. **Imports** (1990): $600 mln.; partners: Mostly So. Afr. **Exports** (1990): $60 mln.; partners: Mostly So. Afr. **National budget** (1991): $288 mln.

Transport: Motor vehicles: in use (1987): 6,000 passenger cars, 15,000 comm. vehicles.

Communications: Radios: 1 per 5 persons. **Daily newspaper circ.** (1990): 5 per 1,000 pop.

Health: Life expectancy at birth (1992): 60 male; 63 female. **Births** (per 1,000 pop. 1992): 35. **Deaths** (per 1,000 pop. 1992):

10. **Natural increase:** 2.5%. **Hospital beds:** 1 per 672 persons. **Physicians:** 1 per 15,728 persons. **Infant mortality** (per 1,000 live births 1992): 74.

Education (1990): **Literacy:** 59%.

Major International Organizations: UN (IMF, UNESCO, WHO), OAU.

Embassy: 2511 Massachusetts Ave. NW 20008; 797-5533.

Lesotho (once called Basutoland) became a British protectorate in 1868 when Chief Moshesh sought protection against the Boers. Independence came Oct. 4, 1966. Elections were suspended in 1970. Most of Lesotho's GNP is provided by citizens working in S. Africa. Livestock raising is the chief industry; diamonds are the chief export.

S. Africa imposed a blockade, Jan. 1, 1986, because of Lesotho's giving sanctuary to rebel groups fighting to overthrow the S. African Government. The blockade sparked a Jan. 20 military coup, and was lifted, Jan. 25, when the new leaders agreed to expel the rebels.

In 1990, King Moshoeshoe was sent into exile by the military government. In Mar. 1993, Ntsu Mokhehle, a civilian, was elected prime minister ending 23 years of military rule.

Liberia

Republic of Liberia

People: Population (1992 est.): 2,462,000. **Age distrib.** (%): 0–14: 46.8; 15–59: 48.3; 60+: 4.9. **Pop. density:** 64 per sq. mi. **Urban** (1990): 46%. **Ethnic groups:** Americo-Liberians 5%, indigenous tribes 95% **Languages:** English (official), tribal dialects. **Religions:** Moslem 20%, Christian 10%, traditional beliefs 70%.

Geography: Area: 38,250 sq. mi., slightly smaller than Pennsylvania. **Location:** On SW coast of W. Africa. **Neighbors:** Sierra Leone on W, Guinea on N, Côte d'Ivoire on E. **Topography:** Marshy Atlantic coastline rises to low mountains and plateaus in the forested interior; 6 major rivers flow in parallel courses to the ocean. **Capital:** Monrovia. **Cities** (1987 est.): Monrovia 400,000.

Government: Type: Civilian republic. **Head of state:** Pres. Amos Sawyer, act.; in office: Nov. 22, 1990. **Local divisions:** 13 counties. **Defense:** 3.8% of GDP (1987).

Economy: Industries: Food processing, mining. **Chief crops:** Rice, cassava, coffee, cocoa, sugar. **Minerals:** Iron, diamonds, gold. **Other resources:** Rubber, timber. **Arable land:** 1%. **Fish catch** (1990): 16,000 metric tons. **Electricity prod.** (1991): 750 mln. kWh. **Labor force:** 82% agric.

Finance: Monetary unit: Dollar (May 1993: 1.00 = $1 US). **Gross national product** (1989): $1.0 bln. **Per capita GNP** (1989): $440. **Imports** (1989): $394 mln.; partners: U.S. 32%, W. Ger. 10%, Jap. 6%, Neth. 7%. **Exports** (1989): $505 mln.; partners: W. Ger. 31%, U.S. 20%, It. 14%, Fr. 9%. **National budget** (1989): $435 mln. **International reserves less gold** (Feb. 1991): $7,000. **Consumer prices** (change in 1990): 5.8%.

Transport: Motor vehicles: in use (1990): 8,000 passenger cars, 4,000 comm. vehicles. **Chief ports:** Monrovia, Buchanan, Greenville.

Communications: Television sets: 1 per 60 persons. **Radios:** 1 per 4.4 persons. **Telephones:** 1 per 278 persons. **Daily newspaper circ.** (1990): 11 per 1,000 pop.

Health: Life expectancy at birth (1992): 54 male; 59 female. **Births** (per 1,000 pop. 1992): 45. **Deaths** (per 1,000 pop. 1992): 13. **Natural increase:** 3%. **Hospital beds** (1981): 3,000. **Physicians** (1981): 236. **Infant mortality** (per 1,000 live births 1992): 119.

Education (1990): **Literacy:** 40%; 35% attend primary school.

Major International Organizations: UN and most specialized agencies, OAU.

Embassy: 5201 16th St. NW 20011; 723-0437.

Liberia was founded in 1822 by U.S. black freedmen who settled at Monrovia with the aid of colonization societies. It became a republic July 26, 1847, with a constitution modeled on that of the U.S. Descendants of freedmen dominated politics.

Charging rampant corruption, an Army Redemption Council of enlisted men staged a bloody predawn coup, April 12, 1980, in which Pres. Tolbert was killed and replaced as head of state by Sgt. Samuel Doe. Doe was chosen president in a disputed election, and survived a subsequent coup, in 1985.

A civil war began Dec. 1989. Rebel forces seeking to depose Pres. Doe made major territorial gains and advanced on the capital, June 1990. In Sept., Doe was captured and put to death. A cease-fire was declared Feb. 13, 1991. More than half of the nation's population became refugees as a result of the civil war.

Libya

Socialist People's Libyan Arab Jamahiriya

al-Jamahiriyah al-Arabiya al-Libya al-Shabiya al-Ishtirakiya

People: Population: (1992 est.): 4,485,000. **Age distrib.** (%): 0–14: 45.0; 15–59: 51.2; 60+: 3.8. **Pop. density:** 6 per sq. mi. **Urban** (1990): 70%. **Ethnic groups:** Arab-Berber 97%. **Languages:** Arabic. **Religions:** Sunni Moslem 97%.

Geography: Area: 679,359 sq. mi., larger than Alaska. **Location:** On Mediterranean coast of N. Africa. **Neighbors:** Tunisia, Algeria on W, Niger, Chad on S, Sudan, Egypt on E. **Topography:** Desert and semidesert regions cover 92% of the land, with low mountains in N, higher mountains in S, and a narrow coastal zone. **Capital:** Tripoli. **Cities** (1988 est.): Tripoli 591,000.

Government: Type: Islamic Arabic Socialist "Mass-State." **Head of state:** Col. Muammar al-Qaddafi; b. Sept. 1942; in office: Sept. 1969. **Head of government:** Premier Abu Zaid Umar Dourda; in office: Oct. 7, 1990. **Local divisions:** 25 municipalities. **Defense:** 11.1% of GNP (1987).

Economy: Industries: Carpets, textiles, petroleum. **Chief crops:** Dates, olives, citrus and other fruits, grapes, wheat. **Minerals:** Gypsum, oil, gas. **Crude oil reserves** (1987): 22 bln. bbls. **Arable land:** 2%. **Livestock** (1991): sheep: 5.5 mln.; goats: 1.0 mln. **Electricity prod.** (1991): 13.6 bln. kWh. **Labor force:** 18% agric.; 31% ind.; 27% services; 24% govt.

Finance: Monetary unit: Dinar (Feb. 1993: 1.00 = $3.37 US). **Gross domestic product** (1990): $28.9 bln. **Per capita GDP:** $6,800. **Imports** (1990): $7.6 bln.; partners: It. 21%, W. Ger. 11%, Fr. 6%. **Exports** (1990): $11.0 bln.; partners: It. 57%, W. Ger. 27%, Sp. 13%. **National budget** (1989): $9.8 bln. expenditures. **International reserves less gold** (Mar. 1993): $6.1 bln. **Gold:** 3.6 mln. oz t.

Transport: Motor vehicles: in use (1989): 448,000 passenger cars, 322,000 comm. vehicles. **Chief ports:** Tripoli, Benghazi.

Communications: Television sets: 1 per 8 persons. **Radios:** 1 per 4 persons. **Daily newspaper circ.** (1990): 10 per 1,000 pop.

Health: Life expectancy at birth (1992): 66 male; 71 female. **Births** (per 1,000 pop. 1992): 36. **Deaths** (per 1,000 pop. 1992): 6. **Natural increase:** 3.0%. **Hospital beds** (1982): 16,051. **Physicians** (1982): 5,200. **Infant mortality** (per 1,000 live births 1992): 60.

Education (1991): **Literacy:** 64%. **Years compulsory:** 7; **Attendance:** 90%.

Major International Organizations: UN, Arab League, OAU, OPEC.

First settled by Berbers, Libya was ruled by Carthage, Rome, and Vandals, the Ottomans, Italy from 1912, and Britain and France after WW II. It became an independent constitutional monarchy Jan. 2, 1952. In 1969 a junta lead by Col. Muammar al-Qaddafi seized power.

In the mid-1970s, Libya helped arm violent revolutionary groups in Egypt and Sudan, and had aided terrorists of various nationalities.

Libya and Egypt fought several air and land battles along their border in July, 1977. Chad charged Libya with military occupation of its uranium-rich northern region in 1977. Libyan troops were driven from their last major stronghold by Chad forces in 1987, leaving over $1 billion in military equipment behind.

On Jan. 7, 1986, the U.S. imposed economic sanctions against Libya, ordered all Americans to leave that country and froze all Libyan assets in the U.S. The U.S. commenced flight operations over the Gulf of Sidra, Jan. 27, and a U.S. Navy task force began conducting exercises in the Gulf, Mar. 23. When Libya fired antiaircraft missiles at American warplanes, the U.S. responded by sinking 2 Libyan ships and bombing a missile installation in Libya. The U.S. withdrew from the Gulf, Mar. 27.

The U.S. accused Libyan leader Qaddafi of having ordered the April 5 bombing of a West Berlin discotheque which killed 3, including a U.S. serviceman. After failing to get their European allies to join them in imposing economic sanctions against Libya, the U.S. sent warplanes to attack terrorist-related targets in Tripoli and Benghazi, Libya, Apr. 14.

The UN imposed limited sanctions, Apr. 15, 1992, for Libya's failure to extradite 2 intelligence agents linked to the 1988 bombing of Pan American World Airways Flight 103 over Lockerbie, Scotland, and 4 others linked to an airplane bombing over Niger.

Liechtenstein

Principality of Liechtenstein

Fürstentum Liechtenstein

People: Population (1992 est.): 28,642. **Age distrib.** (%): 0–14: 20.1; 15–59: 66.3; 60+: 11.6. **Pop. density:** 461 per sq. mi. **Ethnic groups:** Alemannic 95%, Italian 5%. **Languages:** German (official), Alemannic dialect. **Religions:** Roman Catholic 87%, Protestant 8%.

Geography: Area: 62 sq. mi., the size of Washington, D.C. **Location:** In the Alps. **Neighbors:** Switzerland on W, Austria on E. **Topography:** The Rhine Valley occupies one-third of the country, the Alps cover the rest. **Capital:** Vaduz. **Cities** (1991 cen.): Vaduz 4,874, Schaan 4,930.

Government: Type: Hereditary constitutional monarchy. **Head of state:** Prince Hans Adam; in office: Nov. 13, 1989. **Head of government:** Hans Brunhart; b. Mar. 28, 1945; in office: Apr. 26, 1978. **Local divisions:** 2 districts, 11 communities.

Economy: Industries: Machines, instruments, chemicals, furniture, ceramics. **Arable land:** 25%. **Labor force:** 54% industry, trade and building; 41% services; 4% agric., fishing, forestry.

Finance: Monetary unit: Swiss Franc. **Gross domestic product** (1990): $630 mln.

Communications: Radios: 1 per 2.9 persons. **Telephones:** 1 per 1.0 persons. **Daily newspaper circ.** (1990): 598 per 1,000 pop.

Health: Births (per 1,000 pop. 1992): 13. **Deaths** (per 1,000 pop. 1992): 7. **Natural increase:** .6%. **Infant mortality** (per 1,000 live births 1992): 5.

Education (1992): **Literacy:** 100%. **Years compulsory** 9; attendance 100%.

Liechtenstein became sovereign in 1866. Austria administered Liechtenstein's ports up to 1920; Switzerland has administered its postal services since 1921. Liechtenstein is united with Switzerland by a customs and monetary union. Taxes are low; many international corporations have headquarters there. Foreign workers comprise a third of the population.

The 1986 general elections were the first in which women were allowed to vote.

Lithuania

Republic of Lithuania

Lietuvos Respublika

People: Population (1992 est.): 3,788,000. **Pop. density:** 150 per sq. mi. **Urban** (1992): 68%. **Ethnic groups:** Lithuanian 80%, Russian 9%, Polish 7%. **Religion:** mostly Roman Catholic.

Geography: Area: 25,170 sq. mi. **Neighbors:** Latvia on N., Belarus on E., S., Poland, Russia, & Baltic Sea on W. **Capital:** Vilnius. **Cities (1992):** Vilnius 597,000; Kaunas 433,000.

Government: Type: Republic. **Head of state:** Pres. Algirdas Brazauskas; in office: Nov. 25, 1992. **Head of government:** Prime Min. Bronislovas Lubys; in office: Dec. 2, 1992.

Economy: Industries: Engineering, shipbuilding. **Chief crops:** grain, potatoes, vegetables. **Arable land:** 49%. **Livestock** (1991): cattle: 2.4 mln., pigs: 2.7 mln. **Electricity prod.** (1991): 25 mln. kWh. **Labor force: 29% agric., 25% ind.**

Finance: Monetary unit: Lit.

Transport: Railroads (1989): **Length:** 1,951 mi. **Civil aviation:** (1991): 2.3 mln. passenger km.; 3 airports. **Chief Port:** Klaipeda.

Communications: Television sets: 1 per 2.9 persons. **Radios:** 1 per 1.2 persons. **Telephones:** 1 per 4.5 persons.

Health: Life expectancy at birth: (1992); 66 male, 76 female. **Births** (per 1,000 pop. 1992): 15. **Deaths** (per 1,000 pop. 1992): 11. **Hospital beds:** 1 per 81 persons. **Physicians:** 1 per 262 persons. **Infant mortality rate** (per 1,000 live births): 18.

Major international organizations: UN

Lithuania, was occupied by the German Army, 1914-18. It was annexed by the USSR, but the Soviets were overthrown, 1919. Lithuania was a democratic republic until 1926 when the regime was ousted by a coup. In 1939, the Soviet-German treaty assigned most of Lithuania to the Soviet sphere of influence. It became part of the USSR Aug. 3, 1940. Lithuania formally declared its independence from the Soviet Union Mar. 11, 1990. Soviet forces began large-scale maneuvers Mar. 18; border controls were tightened Mar. 21. The Soviets cut off oil and gas supplies Apr. 19.

Soviet troops killed 15 protesters in Vilnius, Jan. 13, 1991, in an attempted coup. During an abortive Soviet coup in Aug., the Western nations recognized Lithuania's independence, which was recognized by the Soviet Union in Sept. 1991.

In 1992 elections, former communists won an absolute majority in the legislature.

Luxembourg

Grand Duchy of Luxembourg

Grand-Duché de Luxembourg

People: Population: (1992 est.): 392,000. **Age distrib.** (%): 0–14: 17.3; 15–59: 64.5; 60+: 18.2. **Pop. density:** 400 per sq. mi. **Urban** (1991): 91%. **Ethnic groups:** Mixture of French and Germans predominate. **Languages:** French, German (both official), Luxembourgish. **Religions:** Roman Catholic 97%.

Geography: Area: 998 sq. mi., smaller than Rhode Island. **Location:** In W. Europe. **Neighbors:** Belgium on W, France on S, Germany on E. **Topography:** Heavy forests (Ardennes) cover N, S is a low, open plateau. **Capital:** Luxembourg. **Cities** (1991 est.): Luxembourg 75,000.

Government: Type: Constitutional monarchy. **Head of state:** Grand Duke Jean; b. Jan. 5, 1921; in office: Nov. 12, 1964. **Head of government:** Prime Min. Jacques Santer; in office: July 21, 1984. **Local divisions:** 3 districts. **Defense:** 1.2% of GDP (1991).

Economy: Industries: Steel, chemicals, beer, tires, tobacco, metal products, cement. **Chief crops:** Corn, wine. **Minerals:** Iron. **Arable land:** 25%. **Electricity prod.** (1991): 1.1 bln. kWh. **Labor force:** 1% agric.; 42% ind. & comm.; 45% services.

Finance: Monetary unit: Franc (Mar. 1993: 33.24 = $1 US). **Gross domestic product** (1991): $7.8 bln. **Per capita GDP:** $20,200. **Note:** trade and tourism data included in Belgian statistics. **Tourism** (1989): $286 mln. receipts. **Consumer prices** (change in 1992): 3.2%.

Transport: Railroads (1991): **Length:** 169 mi. **Motor vehicles:** in use (1991): 192,000 passenger cars, 18,000 comm. vehicles.

Communications: Television sets: 1 per 4.0 persons. **Radios:** 1 per 1.6 persons. **Telephones:** 1 per 2.3 persons. **Daily newspaper circ.** (1990): 340 per 1,000 pop.

Health: Life expectancy at birth (1992): 73 male; 80 female. **Births** (per 1,000 pop. 1992): 12. **Deaths** (per 1,000 pop. 1992): 11. **Hospital beds:** 1 per 85 persons. **Physicians:** 1 per 498 persons. **Infant mortality** (per 1,000 live births 1992): 7.

Education (1989): **Literacy:** 100%. **Years compulsory** 9; attendance 100%.

Major International Organizations: UN, OECD, EC, NATO.

Embassy: 2200 Massachusetts Ave. NW 20008; 265-4171.

Luxembourg, founded about 963, was ruled by Burgundy, Spain, Austria, and France from 1448 to 1815. It left the Germanic Confederation in 1866. Overrun by Germany in 2 world wars, Luxembourg ended its neutrality in 1948, when a customs union with Belgium and Netherlands was adopted.

Macedonia

Republic of Macedonia

People: Population (1992 est.): 2,050,000. **Pop. density:** 206 per sq. mi. **Ethnic groups:** Macedonian 68%, Albanian 20%. **Languages:** Macedonian, Albanian, Bulgarian, Greek. **Religions:** mostly Eastern Orthodox; Moslem.

Geography: Area: 9,928 sq. mi., slightly larger than Vermont. **Location:** In SE Europe. **Neighbors:** Bulgaria on E., Greece on S, Albania on W, Yugoslavia on N. **Capital:** Skopje. **Cities** (1991 met. est.): Skopje 563,000, Tetova 180,000.

Government: Type: Republic. **Head of state:** Pres. Kiro Gliforov. **Head of government:** Prime Min. Branko Crenkovski. **Local divisions:** 30 districts.

Economy: Industries: Steel, cement. **Chief crops:** Wheat, cotton, tobacco. **Livestock** (1992): 2.2 mln. sheep. **Electricity prod.** (1990): 5.7 bln. kWh.

Finance: Monetary unit: Denar **Gross domestic product** (1990): $4.8 bln. **Per capita GDP:** $2,399.

Transport: Railroads (1990): **Length:** 431 mi. **Vehicles:** in use (1990): 230,000 passenger cars, 23,000 comm. vehicles. **Civil aviation:** 1 airport.

Communications: Television sets: 1 per 5.2 persons. **Radios:** 1 per 4.5 persons. **Telephones:** 1 per 5.7 persons. **Newspaper circ.** (1990): 26 per 1,000 pop.

Health: Hospital beds: 1 per 171 persons. **Physicians:** 1 per 464 persons. **Infant mortality** (per 1,000 live births 1990): 35.3.

Education (1990): **Literacy:** 90%.

Major International Organizations: UN.

Macedonia, as part of a larger region also called Macedonia, was ruled by Moslem Turks from 1389 to 1912, when native Greeks, Bulgarians, and Slavs won independence. Serbia received the largest part of the territory with the rest going to Greece and Bulgaria. The area was incorporated in Serbia in 1918.

Macedonia declared its independence from Yugoslavia, Sept. 8, 1991. At the request of Greece, the U.S. and most European nations have not recognized Macedonia as an independent nation until it changes its name and flag, which it has refused to do.

Macedonia was admitted to the UN under a provisional name in 1993. A UN force, which included 300 U.S. troops, was deployed in Macedonia in 1993 to deter the warring factions in Bosnia from carrying their dispute into other areas of the Balkans.

Madagascar

Democratic Republic of Madagascar

Repoblika Demokratika Malagasy

People: Population (1992 est.): 12,596,000. **Pop. density:** 55 per sq. mi. **Urban** (1990): 22%. **Ethnic groups:** 18 Malayan-Indonesian tribes (Merina 26%), with Arab and African presence. **Languages:** Malagasy, French (both official). **Religions:** animists 52%, Christian 41%, Moslem 7%.

Geography: Area: 226,657 sq. mi., slightly smaller than Texas. **Location:** In the Indian O., off the SE coast of Africa. **Neighbors:** Comoro Is., Mozambique (across Mozambique Channel). **Topography:** Humid coastal strip in the E, fertile valleys in the mountainous center plateau region, and a wider coastal strip on the W. **Capital:** Antananarivo. **Cities** (1990 est.): Antananarivo 802,000.

Government: Type: Republic. **Head of state:** Pres. Albert Zafy; in office: Feb. 10, 1993. **Head of government:** Prime Min. Guy Razanamasy; in office: Aug. 8, 1991. **Local divisions:** 6 provinces. **Defense:** 2.2% of GDP (1989).

Economy: Industries: Food processing, textiles. **Chief crops:** Coffee (over 50% of exports), cloves, vanilla, rice, sugar, sisal, tobacco, peanuts. **Minerals:** Chromium, graphite, coal, bauxite. **Arable land:** 5%. **Livestock** (1990): cattle: 10.4 mln.; pigs: 1.3 mln. **Fish catch** (1990): 99,000 metric tons. **Electricity prod.** (1991): 450 mln. kWh. **Labor force:** 90% agric.

Finance: Monetary unit: Franc (Mar. 1993: 1,920 = $1 US). **Gross domestic product** (1991): $2.4 bln. **Per capita GDP:** $200. **Imports** (1991): $442 mln.; partners: Fr. 32%, U.S. 15%. **Exports** (1991): $305 mln.; partners: Fr. 34%, U.S. 14%. **Tourism** (1990): $28 mln. receipts. **National budget** (1990): $525 mln. **International reserves less gold** (Jan. 1993): $89 mln. **Consumer prices** (change in 1992): 14.5%.

Transport: Railroads (1990): **Length:** 655 mi. **Motor vehicles:** in use (1990): 46,000 passenger cars, 33,000 comm. vehicles. **Civil aviation:** (1990): 512 mln. passenger-km; 50 airports with scheduled flights. **Chief ports:** Tamatave, Diego-Suarez, Majunga, Tulear.

Communications: Television sets: 1 per 95 persons. **Radios:** 1 per 8 persons. **Telephones in use:** 1 per 239 persons.

Health: Life expectancy at birth (1992): 51 male; 55 female. **Births** (per 1,000 pop. 1991): 47. **Deaths** (per 1,000 pop. 1991): 15. **Natural increase:** 3.2%. **Hospital beds** (1982): 20,800. **Physicians** (1982): 940. **Infant mortality** (per 1,000 live births 1992): 93.

Education (1987): **Literacy:** 53%. **Years compulsory:** 5; attendance 83%.

Major International Organizations: UN (GATT, WHO, IMF), OAU.

Embassy: 2374 Massachusetts Ave. NW 20008; 265-5525.

Madagascar was settled 2,000 years ago by Malayan-Indonesian people, whose descendants still predominate. A unified kingdom ruled the 18th and 19th centuries. The island became a French protectorate, 1885, and a colony 1896. Independence came June 26, 1960.

Discontent with inflation and French domination led to a coup in 1972. The new regime nationalized French-owned financial interests, closed French bases and a U.S. space tracking station, and obtained Chinese aid. The government conducted a program of arrests, expulsion of foreigners, and repression of strikes, 1979.

In 1990, Madagascar ended a ban on multiparty politics that had been in place since 1975. Albert Zafy was elected president of Madagascar in 1993, ending the 17-year rule of Didier Ratsiraka, whose rule was marked by a blend of socialism and authoritarianism.

Malawi

Republic of Malawi

People: Population (1992 est.): 9,605,000. **Age distrib.** (%): 0–14: 47.8; 15–59: 48.0; 60+: 4.2. **Pop. density:** 209 per sq. mi. **Urban** (1990): 15%. **Ethnic groups:** Chewa, 90%, Nyanja, Lomwe, other Bantu tribes. **Languages:** English, Chewa (both official), Lomwe, Yao. **Religions:** Christian 75%, Moslem 20%.

Geography: Area: 45,747 sq. mi., the size of Pennsylvania. **Location:** In SE Africa. **Neighbors:** Zambia on W, Mozambique on SE, Tanzania on N. **Topography:** Malawi stretches 560 mi. N-S along Lake Malawi (Lake Nyasa), most of which belongs to Malawi. High plateaus and mountains line the Rift Valley the length of the nation. **Capital:** Lilongwe. **Cities** (1987 est.): Blantyre 402,000; Lilongwe 220,000.

Government: Type: One-party state. **Head of state:** Pres. Hastings Kamuzu Banda, b. May 14, 1906; in office: July 6, 1966. **Local divisions:** 24 districts. **Defense:** 1.6% of GDP (1989).

Economy: Industries: Textiles, sugar, cement. **Chief crops:** Tea, tobacco, sugar, coffee. **Other resources:** Rubber. **Arable land:** 25%. **Fish catch** (1990): 68 metric tons. **Electricity prod.** (1991): 535 mln. kWh. **Labor force:** 43% agric.; 23% ind. and comm.; 17% services.

Finance: Monetary unit: Kwacha (Mar. 1993: 4.40 = $1 US). **Gross domestic product** (1991): $1.9 bln. **Per capita GDP:** $200. **Imports** (1992): $720 mln.; partners: So. Afr. 29%, UK 24%, Jap. 6%. **Exports** (1992): $392 mln.; partners: UK 27%, S. Afr. 8%., Ger. 10%. **National budget** (1991): $510 mln. **International reserves less gold** (Mar. 1993): $45 mln. **Gold:** 13,000 oz t. **Consumer prices** (change in 1992): 12.4%.

Transport: Railroads (1987): **Length:** 495 mi. **Motor vehicles:** in use (1990): 16,000 passenger cars, 17,000 comm. vehicles. **Civil aviation** (1990) 86 mln. passenger-km; 5 airports with scheduled flights.

Communications: Radios: 1 per 4.3 persons. **Telephones:** 1 per 176 persons. **Daily newspaper circ.** (1991): 3 per 1,000 pop.

Health: Life expectancy at birth (1992): 48 male; 51 female. **Births** (per 1,000 pop. 1992): 52. **Deaths** (per 1,000 pop. 1992): 18. **Natural increase:** 3.4%. **Hospital beds:** 1 per 627 persons. **Physicians:** 1 per 27,094 persons. **Infant mortality** (per 1,000 live births 1992): 136.

Education (1989): **Literacy:** 25%. About 45% attend school.
Major International Organizations: UN (World Bank, IMF), OAU, Commonwealth of Nations.
Embassy: 2408 Massachusetts Ave. NW 20008; 797-1007.

Bantus came in the 16th century, Arab slavers in the 19th. The area became the British protectorate Nyasaland, in 1891. It became independent July 6, 1964, and a republic in 1966.

Malaysia

People: Population (1992 est.): 18,410,000. **Age distrib.** (%): 0–14: 37.8; 15–59: 56.5; 60+: 5.7. **Pop. density:** 144 per sq. mi. **Urban** (1985): 38%. **Ethnic groups:** Malays 59%, Chinese 32%, Indian 9%. **Languages:** Malay (official), English, Chinese, Indian languages. **Religions:** Moslem, Hindu, Buddhist, Confucian, Taoist, local religions.
Geography: Area: 127,316 sq. mi., slightly larger than New Mexico. **Location:** On the SE tip of Asia, plus the N. coast of the island of Borneo. **Neighbors:** Thailand on N, Indonesia on S. **Topography:** Most of W. Malaysia is covered by tropical jungle, including the central mountain range that runs N-S through the peninsula. The western coast is marshy, the eastern, sandy. E. Malaysia has a wide, swampy coastal plain, with interior jungles and mountains. **Capital:** Kuala Lumpur. **Cities** (1991 est.): Kuala Lumpur 1 mln.
Government: Type: Federal parliamentary democracy with a constitutional monarch. **Head of state:** Paramount Ruler Sultan Azlan Shah; in office: Apr. 26, 1989. **Head of government:** Prime Min. Datuk Seri Mahathir bin Mohamad; b. Dec. 20, 1925; in office: July 16, 1981. **Local divisions:** 13 states and 2 federal terr. **Defense:** 5.0% of GDP (1992).
Economy: Industries: Rubber goods, steel, electronics. **Chief crops:** Palm oil, copra, rice, pepper. **Minerals:** Tin (35% world output), iron. **Crude oil reserves** (1987): 3.2 bln. bbls. **Other resources:** Rubber (35% world output). **Arable land:** 13%. **Livestock** (1990): pigs: 2.2 mln. **Fish catch** (1990): 604,000 metric tons. **Electricity prod.** (1991): 16.5 bln. kWh. **Labor force:** 18% agric.; 11% tourism & trade; 10% govt.
Finance: Monetary unit: Ringgit (June 1993: 2.58 = $1 US). **Gross domestic product** (1991): $48 bln. **Per capita GDP:** $2,670. **Imports** (1991): $38.7 bln.; partners: Jap. 21%, U.S. 18%, Sing. 14%. **Exports** (1991): $35.4 bln.; partners: Jap. 20%, U.S. 17% Sing. 19%, Neth. 6%. **Tourism** (1990): $1.6 bln. receipts. **National budget** (1991): $11.8 bln. **International reserves less gold** (Mar. 1993): $19.4 bln. **Gold:** 2.22 mln. oz t. **Consumer prices** (change in 1992): 4.4%.
Transport: Railroads (incl. Singapore) (1991): **Length:** 1,381 mi. **Motor vehicles:** in use (1990): 1.8 mln. passenger cars, 407,000 comm. vehicles. **Civil aviation:** (1990): 11.9 bln. passenger-km; 38 airports with scheduled flights. **Chief ports:** George Town, Kelang, Melaka, Kuching.
Communications: Television sets: 1 per 9 persons. **Radios:** 1 per 2.4 persons. **Telephones:** 1 per 8 persons. **Daily newspaper circ.** (1989): 145 per 1,000 pop.
Health: Life expectancy at birth (1992): 66 male; 71 female. **Births** (per 1,000 pop. 1992): 30. **Deaths** (per 1,000 pop. 1992): 6. **Natural increase:** 2.4%. **Hospital beds:** 1 per 457 persons. **Physicians:** 1 per 2,638 persons. **Infant mortality** (per 1,000 live births 1992): 27.
Education (1991): **Literacy:** 80%; 96% attend primary school, 65% attend secondary.
Major International Organizations: UN (World Bank, IMF, GATT), ASEAN.
Embassy: 2401 Massachusetts Ave. NW 20008; 328-2700.

European traders appeared in the 16th century; Britain established control in 1867. Malaysia was created Sept. 16, 1963. It included Malaya (which had become independent in 1957 after the suppression of Communist rebels), plus the formerly-British Singapore, Sabah (N Borneo), and Sarawak (NW Borneo). Singapore was separated in 1965, in order to end tensions between Chinese, the majority in Singapore, and Malays in control of the Malaysian government.
A monarch is elected by a council of hereditary rulers of the Malayan states every 5 years.
Abundant natural resources have assured prosperity, and foreign investment has aided industrialization.

Maldives

Republic of Maldives

Divehi Jumhuriya

People: Population (1992 est.): 226,000. **Age distrib.** (%): 0–14: 44.4; 15–59: 51.7; 60+: 3.9. **Pop. density:** 1,965 per sq. mi. **Urban** (1990): 26%. **Ethnic groups:** Sinhalese, Dravidian, Arab mixture. **Languages:** Divehi (Sinhalese dialect). **Religions:** Sunni Moslem.
Geography: Area: 115 sq. mi., twice the size of Washington, D.C. **Location:** In the Indian O. SW of India. **Neighbors:** Nearest is India on N. **Topography:** 19 atolls with 1,087 islands, about 200 inhabited. None of the islands are over 5 sq. mi. in area, and all are nearly flat. **Capital:** Male. **Cities** (1991 est.): Male 55,000.
Government: Type: Republic. **Head of state:** Pres. Maumoon Abdul Gayoom; b. Dec. 29, 1939; in office: Nov. 11, 1978. **Local divisions:** 19 districts.
Economy: Industries: Fish processing, tourism. **Chief crops:** Coconuts, fruit, millet. **Other resources:** Shells. **Arable land:** 10%. **Fish catch** (1990): 76,000 metric tons. **Electricity prod.** (1991): 11.0 mln. kWh. **Labor force:** 80% fishing, agriculture, & manufacturing.
Finance: Monetary unit: Rufiyaa (Mar. 1993: 10.48 = $1 US). **Gross domestic product** (1990): $174 mln. **Per capita GDP:** $770. **Imports** (1990): $128 mln.; partners: Sing., Ger., Sri Lan. **Exports** (1990): $52 mln.; partners: U.S., U.K.. **Tourism** (1990): $142 mln. receipts.
Transport: Chief ports: Male Atoll.
Communications: Radios: 1 per 8 persons. **Telephones:** 1 per 60 persons.
Health: Life expectancy at birth (1992): 62 male; 64 female. **Births** (per 1,000 pop. 1992): 45. **Deaths** (per 1,000 pop. 1992): 8. **Natural increase:** 3.7%. **Infant morality** (per 1,000 live births 1992): 61.
Education (1989): **Literacy:** 93%. Only 6% of those aged 11-15 attend school.
Major International Organizations: UN.

The islands had been a British protectorate since 1887. The country became independent July 26, 1965. Long a sultanate, the Maldives became a republic in 1968. Natural resources and tourism are being developed; however, it remains one of the world's poorest countries.

Mali

Republic of Mali

République du Mali

People: Population (1992 est.): 8,641,000. **Age distrib.** (%): 0–14: 46.0; 15–59: 49.4; 60+: 4.6. **Pop. density:** 18 per sq. mi. **Urban** (1992): 25%. **Ethnic groups:** Mande (Bambara, Malinke, Sarakole) 50%, Peul 17%, Voltaic 12%, Songhai 6%, Tuareg and Moor, 5%. **Languages:** French (official), Bambara, Senufo. **Religions:** Moslem 90%.
Geography: Area: 478,764 sq. mi., about the size of Texas and California combined. **Location:** In the interior of W. Africa. **Neighbors:** Mauritania, Senegal on W, Guinea, Côte d'Ivoire, Burkina Faso on S, Niger on E, Algeria on N. **Topography:** A landlocked grassy plain in the upper basins of the Senegal and Niger rivers, extending N into the Sahara. **Capital:** Bamako. **Cities** (1989 est.): Bamako (met.) 800,000.
Government: Type: Republic. **Head of state:** Pres. Alpha Oumar Konare; in office: June 8, 1992. **Local divisions:** 8 regions. **Defense:** 2.4% of GDP (1989).
Economy: Chief crops: Millet, rice, peanuts, cotton. **Other resources:** Bauxite, iron, gold. **Arable land:** 2%. **Livestock** (1989): sheep: 5.7 mln.; cattle: 4.8 mln. **Fish catch** (1990): 71,000 metric tons. **Electricity prod.** (1991): 750 mln. kWh. **Labor force:** 72% agric.; 12% ind. & comm.; 16% services.
Finance: Monetary unit: Franc (Mar. 1993: 273 = $1 US). **Gross domestic product** (1990): $2.2 bln. **Per capita GDP:** $265. **Imports** (1989): $513 mln.; partners: Fr. 22%, Ivory Coast 25%. **Exports** (1989): $285 mln.; partners: Belg.-Lux. 25%, Fr. 15%. **Tourism** (1990): $37 mln. receipts. **National budget** (1989): $519 mln. expenditures. **International reserves less gold** (Feb. 1993): $307 mln. **Gold:** 19,000 oz t.

Transport: Railroads (1991): **Length:** 401 mi. **Motor vehicles:** in use (1987): 29,000 passenger cars, 7,500 comm. vehicles.

Communications: Radios: 1 per 53 persons. **Telephones:** 1 per 730 persons.

Health: Life expectancy at birth (1992): 43 male; 47 female. **Births** (per 1,000 pop. 1992): 51. **Deaths** (per 1,000 pop. 1992): 21. **Natural increase:** 3.0%. **Hospital beds** (1983): 4,215. **Physicians** (1983): 283. **Infant mortality** (per 1,000 live births 1992): 110.

Education (1991): **Literacy:** 25%. **Attendance:** 21% attend primary school.

Major International Organizations: UN and all of its specialized agencies, OAU, EC.

Embassy: 2130 R St. NW 20008; 332-2249.

Until the 15th century the area was part of the great Mali Empire. Timbuktu was a center of Islamic study. French rule was secured, 1898. The Sudanese Rep. and Senegal became independent as the Mali Federation June 20, 1960, but Senegal withdrew, and the Sudanese Rep. was renamed Mali.

Mali signed economic agreements with France and, in 1963, with Senegal. In 1968, a coup ended the socialist regime. Famine struck in 1973-74, killing as many as 100,000 people. Drought conditions returned in the 1980s.

The military, Mar. 26, 1991, overthrew the government of Pres. Amadou Toumani Traore, who had been in power since 1968. A multiparty democracy was promised.

Malta

Repubblika Ta' Malta

People: Population (1992 est.): 354,000. **Age distrib. (%):** 0–14: 23.6; 15–59: 61.8; 60+: 14.6. **Pop. density:** 2,901 per sq. mi. **Ethnic groups:** Italian, Arab, French. **Languages:** Maltese, English (both official). **Religions:** Mainly Roman Catholic.

Geography: Area: 122 sq. mi., twice the size of Washington, D.C. **Location:** In center of Mediterranean Sea. **Neighbors:** Nearest is Italy on N. **Topography:** Island of Malta is 95 sq. mi.; other islands in the group: Gozo, 26 sq. mi., Comino, 1 sq. mi. The coastline is heavily indented. Low hills cover the interior. **Capital:** Valletta. **Cities** (1990 est.): Birkirkara 21,000, Qormi 19,000.

Government: Type: Parliamentary democracy. **Head of state:** Pres. Censu Tabone; in office: Apr. 4, 1989. **Head of government:** Prime Min. Edward Fenech-Adami; b. Feb. 7, 1934; in office: May 12, 1987. **Local Divisions:** 13 electoral districts. **Defense:** 1.3% of GNP (1990).

Economy: Industries: Textiles, machinery, food & beverages, tourism. **Chief crops:** Potatoes, tomatoes. **Arable land:** 38%. **Electricity prod.** (1991): $1.1 bln. kWh. **Labor force:** 2% agric.; 24% manuf.; 43% services; 29% gov.

Finance: Monetary unit: Maltese Lera (Mar. 1993: 1.00 = $2.64 US). **Gross domestic product** (1990): $2.5 bln. **Per capita GDP:** $7,000. **Imports** (1991): $2.1 bln.; partners: UK 16%, It. 30%, Ger. 14%, U.S. 4%. **Exports** (1991): $1.2 bln.; partners: Ger. 23%, UK 11%, It. 30%. **Tourism** (1989): receipts: $475 mln. **National budget** (1992): $1.3 bln. expenditures. **International reserves less gold** (Mar. 1992): 1.1 bln. **Gold:** 126,000 oz t. **Consumer prices** (change in 1992): 2.2%.

Transport: Motor vehicles: in use (1990): 104,000 passenger cars, 19,000 comm. vehicles. **Civil aviation** (1990): 903 mln. passenger-km; 1 airport. **Chief ports:** Valletta.

Communications: Television sets: 1 per 2.6 persons. **Radios:** 1 per 3.3 persons. **Telephones in use:** 1 per 2.1 persons.

Health: Life expectancy at birth (1992): 74 male; 79 female. **Births** (per 1,000 pop. 1992): 14. **Deaths** (per 1,000 pop. 1992): 8. **Natural increase:** .6%. **Hospital beds:** 1 per 108 persons. **Physicians:** 1 per 444 persons. **Infant mortality** (per 1,000 live births 1992): 7.

Education (1988): **Literacy:** 90%. **Compulsory:** until age 16.

Major International Organizations: UN (GATT, WHO, IMF), Commonwealth of Nations.

Embassy: 2017 Connecticut Ave. NW 20008; 462-3611.

Malta was ruled by Phoenicians, Romans, Arabs, Normans, the Knights of Malta, France, and Britain (since 1814). It became independent Sept. 21, 1964. Malta became a republic in 1974. The withdrawal of the last of its sailors, Apr. 1, 1979, ended 179 years of British military presence on the island.

Marshall Islands

Republic of the Marshall Islands

People: Population (1992 est.): 50,000. **Pop. density:** 714 per sq. mi. **Ethnic groups:** Marshallese 97%. **Languages:** English (official), Marshallese, Japanese. **Religions:** Protestant 90%.

Geography: Area: 70 sq. mi. **Location:** In central Pacific Ocean; comprised of 2 800-mi-long parallel chains of coral atolls. **Capital:** Majuro.

Government: Type: Republic. **Head of state:** Pres. Amata Kabua.

Economy: Agriculture and tourism are mainstays of the economy. **Electricity prod.** (1990): 80 mln. kwh.

Finance: Monetary unit: U.S. dollar. **Gross domestic product** (1989): $63 mln. **Per capita GDP** (1989): $1,500. **Imports** (1988): 34 mln. **Exports** (1988): $2 mln.

Transport: 24 airports with scheduled flights. **Port:** Majuro.

Communications: Telephones: 1 per 53 persons.

Health: Life expectancy at birth (1992): 61 male; 64 female. **Births** (per 1,000 pop. 1992): 47. **Deaths** (per 1,000 pop. 1992): 8. **Infant mortality** (per 1,000 live births 1992): 53.

Education (1990): **Literacy:** 86%.

Major International Organizations: UN.

The Marshall Islands were a German possession until World War 1 and were administered by Japan between the World Wars. After WW2, they were administered as part of the UN Trust Territory of the Pacific Islands by the U.S.

The Marshall Islands secured international recognition as an independent nation on Sept. 17, 1991.

Mauritania

Islamic Republic of Mauritania

République Islamique de Mauritanie

People: Population (1992 est.): 2,059,000. **Age distrib. (%):** 0–14: 46.4; 15–59: 49.0; 60+: 4.6. **Pop. density:** 5 per sq. mi. **Urban** (1987): 34%. **Ethnic groups:** Arab-Berber 80%, Negroes 20%. **Languages:** Arabic, French (both official), Hassanya Arabic (national). **Religion:** Nearly 100% Moslem.

Geography: Area: 419,212 sq. mi., the size of Texas and California combined. **Location:** In W. Africa. **Neighbors:** Morocco on N, Algeria, Mali on E, Senegal on S. **Topography:** The fertile Senegal R. valley in the S gives way to a wide central region of sandy plains and scrub trees. The N is arid and extends into the Sahara. **Capital:** Nouakchott. **Cities** (1992 est.): Nouakchott 550,000; Nouadhibou 70,000; Kaedi 74,000.

Government: Type: Islamic republic. **Head of state:** Pres. Maaouya Ould Sidi Ahmed Taya; in office: Apr. 18, 1992. **Head of government:** Prime Min. Sidi Mohamed Ould Boubacar; in office: Apr. 18, 1992 **Local divisions:** 12 regions, one capital district. **Defense:** 4.2% of GDP (1990).

Economy: Chief crops: Dates, grain. **Industries:** iron mining. **Minerals:** Iron, ore, gypsum. **Livestock** (1988): sheep: 4.1 mln.; goats: 3.9 mln.; cattle: 1.2 mln. **Fish catch** (1991): 92,000 metric tons. **Electricity prod.** (1991): 136 mln. kWh. **Labor force:** 47% agric., 14% ind. & comm., 29% services.

Finance: Monetary unit: Ouguiya (Mar. 1993: 116 = $1 US). **Gross domestic product** (1990): $1.0 bln. **Per capita GDP:** $520. **Imports** (1990): $639 mln.; partners: EC 60%. **Exports** (1990): $437 mln.; partners: EC 43%, Jap. 27%. **International reserves less gold** (Feb. 1993): $35 mln.

Transport: Motor vehicles: in use (1990): 10,000 passenger cars, 5,000 comm. vehicles. **Chief ports:** Nouakchott, Nouadhibou.

Communications: Radios: 1 per 7.8 persons. **Television sets: 1 per 1,100 persons.**

Health: Life expectancy at birth (1992): 44 male; 50 female. **Births** (per 1,000 pop. 1992): 49. **Deaths** (per 1,000 pop. 1992): 19. **Natural increase:** 3.0%. **Hospital beds:** 1 per 1,217 persons. **Physicians:** 1 per 10,128 persons. **Infant mortality** (per 1,000 live births 1992): 89.

Education (1991): **Literacy:** 30%. **Attendance:** 79% in primary school, 18% in secondary school.

Major International Organizations: UN (GATT, IMF, WHO), OAU, Arab League.

Embassy: 2129 Leroy Pl. NW 20008; 232-5700.

Mauritania was a French protectorate from 1903. It became independent Nov. 28, 1960. It annexed the south of former Spanish Sahara in 1976. Saharan guerrillas stepped up attacks in 1977; 8,000 Moroccan troops and French bomber raids aided the government. Mauritania signed a peace treaty with the Polisario Front, 1980, resumed diplomatic relations with Algeria while breaking a defense treaty with Morocco, and renounced sovereignty over its share of former Spanish Sahara. Morocco annexed the territory.

Mauritius

People: Population (1992 est.): 1,081,900. **Age distrib.** (%): 0–14: 36.3; 15–59: 57.2; 60+: 6.4. **Pop. density:** 1,313 per sq. mi. **Urban** (1990): 41%. **Ethnic groups:** Indo-Mauritian 68%, Creole 27%, others. **Languages:** English (official), French Creole, Bhojpuri. **Religions:** Hindu 51%, Christian 30%, Moslem 16%.

Geography: Area: 720 sq. mi., about the size of Rhode Island. **Location:** In the Indian O., 500 mi. E of Madagascar. **Neighbors:** Nearest is Madagascar on W. **Topography:** A volcanic island nearly surrounded by coral reefs. A central plateau is encircled by mountain peaks. **Capital:** Port Louis. **Cities** (1991 est.): Port Louis 142,000.

Government: Type: Republic. **Head of state:** Pres. Cassam Uteem; in office: June 30, 1992. **Head of government:** Prime Min. Aneerood Jugnauth; in office: June 12, 1982. **Local divisions:** 9 districts, 3 dependencies.

Economy: Industries: Tourism, food processing. **Chief crops:** Sugar cane, tea. **Arable land:** 54%. **Electricity prod.** (1990): 423 mln. kWh. **Labor force:** 17% agric. & fishing; 32% manuf.; 14% govt. services.

Finance: Monetary unit: Rupee (Mar. 1993: 17.17 = $1 US). **Gross domestic product** (1991): $2.5 bln. **Per capita GDP:** $2,300. **Imports** (1991): $1.5 bln.; partners: UK 9%, Fr. 12%, So. Afr. 9%. **Exports** (1991): $1.1 bln.; partners: UK 50%, Fr. 22%, U.S. 8%. **Tourists** (1990): $264 mln. receipts. **National budget** (1989): $540 mln. **International reserves less gold** (Feb. 1993): $859 mln. **Gold:** 61,000 oz t. **Consumer prices** (change in 1992): 4.6%.

Transport: Motor vehicles: in use (1990): 29,000 passenger cars, 6,000 comm. vehicles. **Chief ports:** Port Louis.

Communications: Television sets: 1 per 8.2 persons. **Radios:** 1 per 4.2 persons. **Telephones:** 1 per 15 persons. **Daily newspaper circ.** (1989): 75 per 1,000 pop.

Health: Life expectancy at birth (1992): 66 male; 74 female. **Births** (per 1,000 pop. 1992): 19. **Deaths** (per 1,000 pop. 1992): 6. **Natural increase:** 1.3%. **Hospital beds:** 1 per 364 persons. **Physicians:** 1 per 1,118 persons. **Infant mortality** (per 1,000 live births 1992): 22.

Education (1989): **Literacy:** 94%. **Attendance:** almost all children attend school.

Major International Organizations: UN and all of its specialized agencies, OAU, Commonwealth of Nations.

Embassy: 4301 Connecticut Ave. NW 20008; 244-1491.

Mauritius was uninhabited when settled in 1638 by the Dutch, who introduced sugar cane. France took over in 1721, bringing African slaves. Britain ruled from 1810 to Mar. 12, 1968, bringing Indian workers for the sugar plantations.

Mauritius formally severed its association with the British crown Mar. 12, 1992.

Mexico

United Mexican States

Estados Unidos Mexicanos

People: Population (1992 est.): 92,380,000. **Age distrib.** (%): 0–14: 36.5; 15–59: 57.8; 60+: 5.7. **Pop. density:** 121 per sq. mi. **Urban** (1990): 72%. **Ethnic groups:** Mestizo 60%, American Indian 29%, Caucasian 9%. **Languages:** Spanish (official), Ameridian languages. **Religions:** Roman Catholic 97%.

Geography: Area: 761,604 sq. mi., three times the size of Texas. **Location:** In southern N. America. **Neighbors:** U.S. on N, Guatemala, Belize on S. **Topography:** The Sierra Madre Occidental Mts. run NW-SE near the west coast; the Sierra Madre Oriental Mts., run near the Gulf of Mexico. They join S of Mexico City. Between the 2 ranges lies the dry central plateau, 5,000 to 8,000 ft. alt., rising toward the S, with temperate vegetation. Coastal lowlands are tropical. About 45% of land is arid. **Capital:** Mexico City. **Cities** (1991 est.): Mexico City (metro) 20 mln.; Guadalajara (metro) 3 mln.; Monterrey (metro) 2.7 mln.

Government: Type: Federal republic. **Head of state:** Pres. Carlos Salinas de Gortari; b. Apr. 3, 1948; in office: Dec. 1, 1988. **Local divisions:** Federal district and 31 states. **Defense:** 1.0% of GDP (1988).

Economy: Industries: Steel, chemicals, electric goods, textiles, rubber, petroleum, tourism. **Chief crops:** Cotton, coffee, wheat, rice, sugar cane, vegetables, corn. **Minerals:** Silver, lead, zinc, gold, oil, natural gas. **Crude oil reserves** (1991): 51 bln. barrels. **Arable land:** 13%. **Livestock** (1991): cattle: 31 mln.; pigs: 15 mln.; sheep: 6 mln. **Fish catch** (1991): 1.1 mln. metric tons. **Electricity prod.** (1991): 114 bln. kWh. **Crude steel prod.** (1991): 7.8 mln. metric tons. **Labor force:** 24% agric.; 19% manuf.; 31% services; 14% comm.

Finance: Monetary unit: New peso (July 1993: 3,122 = $1 US). **Gross domestic product** (1991): $289 bln. **Per capita GDP:** $3,200. **Imports** (1991): $36.7 bln.; partners: U.S. 69%, EC 13%. **Exports** (1991): $27 bln.; partners: U.S. 68%, EC 14%. **Tourism** (1992): receipts: $6.6 bln. **National budget** (1990): $47.9 bln. expenditures. **International reserves less gold** (Jan. 1993): $18.9 bln. **Gold:** 685,000 oz t. **Consumer prices** (change in 1992): 15.5%.

Transport: Railroads (1992): **Length:** 16,363 mi. **Motor vehicles:** in use (1990): 6.8 mln. passenger cars, 3.0 mln. comm. **Civil aviation** (1991): 17.4 bln. passenger-km; 54 airports. **Chief ports:** Veracruz, Tampico, Mazatlan, Coatzacoalcos.

Communications: Television sets: 1 in 6.6 persons. **Radios:** 1 in 5.1 persons. **Telephones:** 1 in 7.6 persons. **Daily newspaper circ.** (1986): 142 per 1,000 pop.

Health: Life expectancy at birth (1992): 69 male; 76 female. **Births** (per 1,000 pop. 1992): 29. **Deaths** (per 1,000 pop. 1992): 5. **Natural increase:** 2.4%. **Hospital beds:** 1 per 1,298 persons. **Physicians:** 1 per 600 persons. **Infant mortality** (per 1,000 live births 1992): 29.

Education (1993): **Literacy:** 90%. **Years compulsory:** 8.

Major International Organizations: UN (IMF, GATT), OAS.

Embassy: 1911 Pennsylvania Ave. NW 20006; 728-1600.

Mexico was the site of advanced Indian civilizations. The Mayas, an agricultural people, moved up from Yucatan, built immense stone pyramids, invented a calendar. The Toltecs were overcome by the Aztecs, who founded Tenochtitlan 1325 AD, now Mexico City. Hernando Cortes, Spanish conquistador, destroyed the Aztec empire, 1519-1521.

After 3 centuries of Spanish rule the people rose, under Fr. Miguel Hidalgo y Costilla, 1810, Fr. Morelos y Payon, 1812, and Gen. Agustin Iturbide, who made himself emperor as Agustin I, 1821. A republic was declared in 1823.

Mexican territory extended into the present American Southwest and California until Texas revolted and established a republic in 1836; the Mexican legislature refused recognition but was unable to enforce its authority there. After numerous clashes, the U.S.-Mexican War, 1846-48, resulted in the loss by Mexico of the lands north of the Rio Grande.

French arms supported an Austrian archduke on the throne of Mexico as Maximilian I, 1864-67, but pressure from the U.S. forced France to withdraw. A dictatorial rule by Porfirio Diaz, president 1877-80, 1884-1911, led to fighting by rival forces until the new constitution of Feb. 5, 1917 provided social reform. Since then Mexico has developed large-scale programs of social security, labor protection, and school improvement. A constitutional provision requires management to share profits with labor.

The Institutional Revolutionary Party has been dominant in politics since 1929. Radical opposition, including some guerrilla activity, has been contained by strong measures.

The presidency of Luis Echeverria, 1970-76, was marked by a more leftist foreign policy and domestic rhetoric. Some land redistribution begun in 1976 was reversed under the succeeding administration.

Some gains in agriculture, industry, and social services have been achieved. The land is rich, but the rugged topography and lack of sufficient rainfall are major obstacles. Crops and farm prices are controlled, as are export and import. Economic prospects brightened with the discovery of vast oil reserves, perhaps the world's greatest. But much of the work force is jobless or underemployed.

Inflation and the drop in world oil prices caused economic problems in the 1980s. The peso was devalued and private banks were nationalized to restore financial stability.

Mexico reached agreement with the U.S. and Canada on the North American Free Trade Agreement Aug. 12, 1992. The agreement required ratification by the 3 governments.

Micronesia

Federated States of Micronesia

People: Population: (1992 est.) 111,000. **Pop. density:** 411 per sq. mi. **Ethnic groups:** Trukese 41%, Pohnpeian 26%. **Languages:** English (official). **Religions:** Mostly Christian.

Geography: Area: 270 sq. mi. The Federation consists of 607 islands in the W. Pacific Ocean. **Capital:** Palikir.

Government: Type: Republic. **Head of state:** Bailey Olter; in office: May 21, 1991. **Local divisions:** 4 states.

Economy: Chief crops: Tropical fruits, vegetables, coconuts.

Finance: Monetary unit: U.S. dollar. **Gross national product (1989):** $150 million. **Imports** (1988): 67 mln. **Exports** (1988): 3 mln.

Transport: 4 airports with scheduled flights.

Communications: Television sets: 1 per 16 persons. **Radios:** 1 per 1.6 persons. **Telephones:** 1 per 61 persons.

Health: Life expectancy at birth (1992): 65 male; 69 female. **Births** (per 1,000 pop. 1992): 34. **Deaths** (per 1,000 pop. 1992): 5. **Hospital beds:** 1 per 280 persons. **Physicians:** 1 per 2,540 persons. **Infant mortality** (per 1,000 live births 1992): 39.

Education (1991): **Literacy:** 90%.

Major International Organizations: UN.

The Federated States of Micronesia, formerly known as the Caroline Islands, was ruled successively by Spain, Germany, Japan, and the U.S. It was internationally recognized as an independent nation Sept. 17, 1991.

Moldova

Republic of Moldova

Republica Moldoveneasca

People: Population (1992 est.): 4,458,000. **Pop. density:** 342 per sq. mi. **Urban (1991): 48%. Ethnic groups:** Moldovan 65%, Ukrainian 14%, Russian 13%. **Languages:** Romanian, Ukrainian. **Religion:** E. Orthodox 98%.

Geography: Area: 13,012 sq. mi. **Neighbors:** Romania on W, Ukraine on N, E, and S. **Capital:** Kishinev. **Cities** (1991): Kishinev 753,000, Tiraspol 186,000.

Government: Type: Republic. **Head of state:** Pres. Mircea Snegur. **Head of government:** Prime Min. Andre Sang Heli; in office: July 1, 1992.

Economy: Industries: Canning, wine making, textiles. **Chief crops:** Grain, grapes. **Minerals:** Lignite, gypsum. **Livestock** (1989): cattle: 1.1 mln., pigs: 1.9 mln., sheep: 1.3 mln. **Electricity prod.** (1991): 13 mln. kWh.

Finance: Monetary unit: Ruble.

Transport: Railroads (1991): **Length:** 715 mi. **Motor vehicles:** in use (1990): 177,000 passenger cars. **Civil aviation** (1990): 2.3 bln. passenger-km. 1 airport.

Communications: Telephones: 1 per 8 persons. **Newspaper circ.** (1990): 71 per 1,000 pop.

Health: Life expectancy at birth (1992): 64 male; 71 female. **Births** (per 1,000 pop. 1992): 19. **Deaths** (per 1,000 pop. 1992): 10. **Hospital beds:** 1 per 77 persons. **Physicians:** 1 per 251 persons. **Infant mortality** (per 1,000 live births 1992): 35.

Major International Organizations: UN, CIS.

In 1918, Romania annexed all of Bessarabia which Russia had acquired from Turkey in 1812 by the Treaty of Bucharest. In 1924, the Soviet Union established the Moldavian Autonomous Soviet Socialist Republic on the eastern bank of the Dniester. It was merged with the Romanian-speaking districts of Bessarabia in 1940 to form the Moldavian SSR.

During World War II, Romania, allied with Germany, occupied the area. It was recaptured by the USSR in 1944. Moldova declared independence Aug. 27, 1991. It became an independent state when the Soviet Union disbanded Dec. 26, 1991. Fighting erupted between Moldovan security forces and Slavic separatists—ethnic Russians and ethnic Ukrainians—Mar. 1992. The Slavs feared that Moldovans, who are Romanian in language and culture, would merge with neighboring Romania.

Monaco

Principality of Monaco

People: Population (1992 est.): 29,712. **Age distrib.** (%): 0–14: 12.7; 15–59: 56.3 60+: 30.7. **Pop. density:** 49,520 per sq. mi. **Ethnic groups:** French 47%, Italian 16%, Monegasque 16%. **Languages:** French (official). **Religions:** Predominantly Roman Catholic.

Geography: Area: 0.6 sq. mi. **Location:** On the NW Mediterranean coast. **Neighbors:** France to W, N, E. **Topography:** Monaco-Ville sits atop a high promontory, the rest of the principality rises from the port up the hillside. **Capital:** Monaco.

Government: Type: Constitutional monarchy. **Head of state:** Prince Rainier III; b. May 31, 1923; in office: May 9, 1949. **Head of government:** Min. of State Jacques Dupont.

Economy: Industries: Tourism, gambling, chemicals, precision instruments, plastics.

Finance: Monetary unit: French franc or Monégasque franc.

Transport: Chief ports: La Condamine.

Communications: Television sets: 17,000 in use (1984). **Telephones in use** (1984): 18,000.

Health: Births (per 1,000 pop. 1992): 7. **Deaths** (per 1,000 pop. 1992): 7. **Infant mortality** (per 1,000 live births 1992): 8.

Education: (1989): **Literacy:** 99%. **Years compulsory:** 10; attendance 99%.

Major International Organizations: UN.

An independent principality for over 300 years, Monaco has belonged to the House of Grimaldi since 1297 except during the French Revolution. It was placed under the protectorate of Sardinia in 1815, and under that of France, 1861. The Prince of Monaco was an absolute ruler until a 1911 constitution.

Monaco's fame as a tourist resort is widespread. It is noted for its mild climate and magnificent scenery. The area has been extended by land reclamation.

Mongolia

People: Population (1992 est.): 2,305,000. **Pop. density:** 3 per sq. mi. **Urban** (1991): 58%. **Ethnic groups:** Mongol 90%. **Languages:** Mongolian (official). **Religion:** traditionally Lama Buddhism.

Geography: Area: 604,247 sq. mi., more than twice the size of Texas. **Location:** In E Central Asia. **Neighbors:** Russia N, China on S. **Topography:** Mostly a high plateau with mountains, salt lakes, and vast grasslands. Arid lands in the S are part of the Gobi Desert. **Capital:** Ulaanbaatar. **Cities** (1991 est.): Ulaanbaatar 575,000, Darhan 90,000.

Government: Type: In transition. **Head of state:** Pres. Punsalmaagiyn Ochirbat; b. 1942; in office: Mar. 21, 1990. **Head of government:** Prime Min. Puntsagiyn Jasray; in office: July 21, 1992. **Local divisions:** 18 provinces, 3 municipalities. **Defense:** 11.5% of GNP (1984).

Economy: Industries: Food processing, textiles, chemicals, cement. **Chief crops:** Grain. **Minerals:** Coal, tungsten, copper, molybdenum, gold, tin. **Arable land:** 1%. **Livestock** (1990): sheep: 14.8 mln.; cattle 2.2 mln. **Electricity prod.** (1991): 3.7 bln. kWh. **Labor force:** 52% agric.; 10% manuf.

Finance: Monetary unit: Tugrik (Jan. 1993: 120 = $1 US). **Gross domestic product** (1991): $2.1 bln. **Per capita GDP:** $900. **Imports** (1991): $360 mln.; partners: CIS 91%. **Exports** (1991): $279 mln.; partners: CIS 80%.

Transport: Railroads (1991): **Length:** 1,445 mi.

Communications: Television sets: 1 per 18 persons. **Radios:** 1 per 7.5 persons. **Telephones:** 1 per 32 persons. **Daily newspaper circ.** (1990): 106 per 1,000 pop.

Health: Life expectancy at birth (1992): 63 male; 68 female. **Births** (per 1,000 pop. 1992): 34. **Deaths** (per 1,000 pop. 1992): 8. **Natural increase:** 2.6%. **Hospital beds:** 1 per 79 persons. **Physicians:** 1 per 345 persons. **Infant mortality** (per 1,000 live births 1992): 47.

Major International Organizations: UN (ILO, WHO).

Education (1990): **Literacy:** 89%.

One of the world's oldest countries, Mongolia reached the zenith of its power in the 13th century when Genghis Khan and his successors conquered all of China and extended their influence as far west as Hungary and Poland. In later centuries, the empire dissolved and Mongolia became a province of China.

With the advent of the 1911 Chinese revolution, Mongolia, with Russian backing, declared its independence. A Mongolian Communist regime was established July 11, 1921.

Mongolia has been changed from a nomadic culture to one of settled agriculture and growing industries with aid from the USSR and East European nations.

In 1990, the Mongolian Communist Party surrendered its monopoly on power. Free elections were held July 1990; the communists were victorious.

Morocco

Kingdom of Morocco

al-Mamlaka al-Maghrebia

People: Population (1992 est.): 26,708,000. **Age distrib.** (%): 0–14: 41.2; 15–59: 53.7; 60+: 5.1. **Pop. density:** 154 per sq. mi. **Urban** (1992): 50%. **Ethnic groups:** Arab-Berber 99%. **Languages:** Arabic (official), Berber. **Religions:** Sunni Moslems 99%.

Geography: Area: 172,413 sq. mi., larger than California. **Location:** on NW coast of Africa. **Neighbors:** W. Sahara on S, Algeria on E. **Topography:** Consists of 5 natural regions: mountain ranges (Riff in the N, Middle Atlas, Upper Atlas, and Anti-Atlas); rich plains in the W; alluvial plains in SW; well-cultivated plateaus in the center; a pre-Sahara arid zone extending from SE. **Capital:** Rabat. **Cities** (1984): Casablanca 2,600,000; Rabat 556,000, Fes 852,000.

Government: Type: Constitutional monarchy. **Head of state:** King Hassan II; b. July 9, 1929; in office: Mar. 3, 1961. **Head of government:** Prime Min. Mohammed Karim Lamrani; in office: Aug. 11, 1992. **Local divisions:** 37 provinces, 5 municipalities. **Defense:** 4.2% of GDP (1992).

Economy: Industries: Carpets, clothing, leather goods, mining, tourism. **Chief crops:** Grain, fruits, dates, grapes. **Minerals:** Copper, cobalt, manganese, phosphates, lead, oil. **Crude oil reserves** (1980): 100 mln. bbls. **Arable land:** 18%. **Livestock** (1990): cattle: 3.5 mln.; sheep; 17 mln.; goats: 5.9 mln. **Fish catch** (1989): 551,000 metric tons. **Electricity prod.** (1991): 8.1 bln. kWh. **Labor force:** 50% agric., 26% services; 15% ind.

Finance: Monetary unit: Dirham (Mar. 1993: 9.09 = $1 US). **Gross domestic product** (1991): $27.3 bln. **Per capita GDP:** $1,060. **Imports** (1991): $6.0 bln.; partners: EC 53%, U.S. 11%. **Exports** (1991): $4.1 bln.; partners: EC 58%. **Tourism** (1990): $1.2 bln. receipts. **National budget** (1992): $7.7 bln. expenditures. **International reserves less gold** (Mar. 1993): $3.2 bln. **Gold:** 704,000 oz t. **Consumer prices** (change in 1992): 4.9%.

Transport: Railroads (1990): **Length:** 1,893 km. **Motor vehicles:** in use (1990): 666,000 passenger cars, 280,000 comm. vehicles. **Civil aviation** (1989): 2.7 bln. passenger-km; 15 airports. **Chief ports:** Tangier, Casablanca, Kenitra.

Communications: Television sets: 1 per 21 persons. **Radios:** 1 per 5.4 persons. **Telephones in use:** 1 per 62 persons. **Daily newspaper circ.** (1990): 15 per 1,000 pop.

Health: Life expectancy at birth (1992): 63 male; 67 female. **Births** (per 1,000 pop. 1992): 30. **Deaths** (per 1,000 pop. 1992): 8. **Natural increase:** 2.2%. **Hospital beds:** 1 per 959 persons. **Physicians:** 1 per 4,415 persons. **Infant mortality** (per 1,000 live births 1992): 56.

Education (1990): **Literacy:** 50%.

Major International Organizations: UN (ILO, IMF, WHO), OAU, Arab League.

Embassy: 1601 21st St. NW 20009; 462-7979.

Berbers were the original inhabitants, followed by Carthaginians and Romans. Arabs conquered in 683. In the 11th and 12th centuries, a Berber empire ruled all NW Africa and most of Spain from Morocco.

Part of Morocco came under Spanish rule in the 19th century; France controlled the rest in the early 20th. Tribal uprisings lasted from 1911 to 1933. The country became independent Mar. 2, 1956. Tangier, an internationalized seaport, was turned over to Morocco, 1956. Ifni, a Spanish enclave, was ceded in 1969.

Morocco annexed over 70,000 sq. mi. of phosphate-rich land Apr. 14, 1976, two-thirds of former Spanish Sahara, with the remainder annexed by Mauritania. Spain had withdrawn in February. Polisario, a guerrilla movement, proclaimed the region independent Feb. 27, and launched attacks with Algerian support. Morocco accepted U.S. military and economic aid. When Mauritania signed a treaty with the Polisario Front and gave up its portion of the former Spanish Sahara, Morocco occupied the area, 1980. Morocco accused Algeria of instigating Polisario attacks.

After years of bitter fighting, Morocco controlled the main urban areas, but the Polisario Front's guerrillas moved freely in the vast, sparsely populated deserts. The 2 sides signed a cease-fire agreement in 1990. The UN will conduct a referendum in Western Sahara on whether the territory should become independent or remain part of Morocco.

Mozambique

Republic of Mozambique

República de Mocambique

People: Population (1992 est.): 15,469,000. **Age distrib.** (%): 0–14: 45.3; 15–59: 50.6; 60+: 4.1. **Pop. density:** 50 per sq. mi. **Ethnic groups:** Bantu tribes. **Languages:** Portuguese (official), Makua, Malawi, Shona, Tsonga. **Religions:** Traditional beliefs 60%, Christian 30%, Moslem 10%.

Geography: Area: 303,769 sq. mi., about the size of Texas. **Location:** On SE coast of Africa. **Neighbors:** Tanzania on N, Malawi, Zambia, Zimbabwe on W, South Africa, Swaziland on S. **Topography:** Coastal lowlands comprise nearly half the country with plateaus rising in steps to the mountains along the western border. **Capital:** Maputo. **Cities:** (1991 est.): Maputo 931,000, Beira 298,000.

Government: Type: Republic. **Head of state:** Pres. Joaquim Chissano; b. Oct. 22, 1939; in office: Oct. 19, 1986. **Head of Government:** Mario de Graca Machungo; in office: July 17, 1986. **Local divisions:** 10 provinces. **Defense:** 8.4% of GNP (1987).

Economy: Industries: Cement, alcohol, textiles. **Chief crops:** Cashews, cotton, sugar, copra, tea. **Minerals:** Coal, titanium. **Arable land:** 4%. **Livestock** (1991): cattle: 1.3 mln. **Fish catch** (1990): 35,000 metric tons. **Electricity prod.** (1991): 1.7 bln. kWh. **Labor force:** 85% agric., 9% ind. & comm., 2% services.

Finance: Monetary unit: Metical (Mar. 1993: 2,982 = $1 US). **Gross domestic product** (1991): $1.7 bln. **Per capita GDP:** $120. **Imports** (1990): $870 mln.; partners: So. Afr. 11%, U.S. 8%, USSR 12%, It. 10%. **Exports** (1990): $117 mln.; partners: Sp. 21%, U.S. 16%, Jap. 15%. **National budget** (1989): $208 mln.

Transport: Railroads (1990): **Length:** 2,033 mi. **Motor vehicles:** in use (1990): 87,000 passenger cars, 24,000 comm. vehicles. **Chief ports:** Maputo, Beira, Nacala, Quelimane.

Communications: Television sets: 1 per 418 persons. **Radios:** 1 per 29 persons. **Telephones:** 1 per 217 persons. **Daily newspaper circ.** (1991): 3 per 1,000 pop.

Health: Life expectancy at birth (1992): 46 male; 49 female. **Births** (per 1,000 pop. 1992): 46. **Deaths** (per 1,000 pop. 1992): 17. **Natural increase:** 2.9%. **Hospital beds:** 1 per 1,227 persons. **Physicians:** 1 per 43,536 persons. **Infant mortality** (per 1,000 live births 1992): 134.

Education (1989): **Literacy:** 14%.

Major International Organization: UN (IMF, World Bank), OAU.

The first Portuguese post on the Mozambique coast was established in 1505, on the trade route to the East. Mozambique became independent June 25, 1975, after a ten-year war against Portuguese colonial domination. The 1974 revolution in Portugal paved the way for the orderly transfer of power to Frelimo (Front for the Liberation of Mozambique). Frelimo took over local administration Sept. 20, 1974, over the opposition, in part violent, of some blacks and whites. The new government, led by Maoist Pres. Samora Machel, promised a gradual transition to a communist system. Private schools were closed, rural collective farms organized, and private homes nationalized. Economic problems included the emigration of most of the country's whites, a politically untenable economic dependence on white-ruled South Africa, and a large external debt.

In the 1980s, severe drought and civil war caused famine and heavy loss of life.

Myanmar (Formerly Burma)

Union of Myanmar

Pyidaungzu Myanma Naingngandaw

People: Population (1992 est.): 42,642,000. **Age distrib.** (%): 0–14: 41.2; 15–59: 52.8; 60+: 6.0. **Pop. density:** 162 per sq. mi. **Urban** (1991): 25%. **Ethnic groups:** Burmans (related to Tibetans) 68%; Karen 4%, Shan 7%, Rakhine 3%. **Languages:** Burmese (official), Karen, Shan. **Religions:** Buddhist 85%; animist, Christian.

Geography: Area: 261,789 sq. mi., nearly as large as Texas. **Location:** Between S. and S.E. Asia, on Bay of Bengal. **Neighbors:** Bangladesh, India on W, China, Laos, Thailand on E. **Topography:** Mountains surround Myanmar on W, N, and E, and dense forests cover much of the nation. N-S rivers provide habitable valleys and communications, especially the Irrawaddy, navigable for 900 miles. The country has a tropical monsoon climate. **Capital:** Yangon. **Cities** (1983 est.): Yangon 2,458,712; Mandalay 458,000; Karbe ('73 cen.): 253,600; Moulmein 188,000.

Government: Type: Military. **Head of state and head of government:** Prime Min. Gen. Than Shwe; in office: Apr. 24, 1992. **Local divisions:** 7 states and 7 divisions. **Defense:** 3.0% of GDP (1989).

Economy: Industries: mining, textiles, footwear, petroleum, refining. **Chief crops:** Rice, sugarcane, peanuts, beans. **Minerals:** Oil, lead, silver, tin, tungsten, precious stones. **Crude oil reserves** (1985): 733 mln. bbls. **Other resources:** Rubber, teakwood. **Arable land:** 15%. **Livestock.** (1991): cattle: 9.3 mln.; pigs: 2.2 mln. **Fish catch** (1990): 743,000 metric tons. **Electricity prod.** (1991): 2.9 bln. kWh. **Labor force:** 66% agric.; 12% ind.

Finance: Monetary unit: Kyat (Mar. 1993: 6.19 = $1 US). **Gross domestic product** (1991): $22.2 bln. **Per capita GDP:** $530. **Imports** (1991): $1.1 bln.; partners: Jap. 50%, EC 20%. **Exports** (1991): $568 mln.; partners: SE Asian countries 30%; EC 12%. **Tourism** (1990): $5 mln. receipts. **National budget** (1991): $9.3 bln. **International reserves less gold** (Mar. 1993): $294 mln. **Gold:** 251,000 oz t. **Consumer prices** (change in 1992): 23.5%.

Transport: Railroads (1990): **Length:** 1,949 mi. **Motor vehicles:** in use (1989): 27,000 passenger cars, 42,000 comm. vehicles. **Civil aviation** (1988): 214 mln. passenger-km.; 21 airports with scheduled flights. **Chief ports:** Yangon, Bassein, Moulmein.

Communications: Television sets: 1 per 592 persons. **Radios:** 1 per 13 persons. **Telephones:** 1 per 501 persons. **Daily newspaper circ.** (1989): 14 per 1,000 pop.

Health: Life expectancy at birth (1992): 57 male; 61 female. **Births** (per 1,000 pop. 1992): 29. **Deaths** (per 1,000 pop. 1992): 10. **Natural increase:** 1.9%. **Hospital beds:** 1 per 1,602 persons. **Physicians:** 1 per 3,389 persons. **Infant mortality** (per 1,000 live births 1992): 68.

Education (1990): **Literacy:** 81%. **Years compulsory:** 4; **Attendance:** 84%.

Major International Organizations: UN (World Bank, IMF, GATT).

Embassy: 2300 S St. NW 20008; 332-9044.

The Burmese arrived from Tibet before the 9th century, displacing earlier cultures, and a Buddhist monarchy was established by the 11th. Burma was conquered by the Mongol dynasty of China in 1272, then ruled by Shans as a Chinese tributary, until the 16th century.

Britain subjugated Burma in 3 wars, 1824-84, and ruled the country as part of India until 1937, when it became self-governing. Independence outside the Commonwealth was achieved Jan. 4, 1948.

Gen. Ne Win dominated politics from 1962 to 1988, when he abdicated power, following waves of anti-government demonstrations. He led a Revolutionary Council which drove Indians from the civil service and Chinese from commerce. Socialization of the economy was advanced, isolation from foreign countries enforced.

In 1987 Burma, once the richest nation in SE Asia, was granted less developed country status by the UN. Following Ne Win's resignation, Sein Lwin and later Maung Maung, a civilian, took power but rioting and street violence continued. In Sept., Gen. Saw Maung, a close associate of Ne Win, seized power.

In 1989 the country's name was changed to Myanmar.

The first free, multiparty elections in 30 years took place May 27, 1990, with the main opposition party winning a decisive victory, but the military rulers refused to hand over power.

Namibia

Republic of Namibia

People: Population (1992 est.): 1,574,000. **Pop density:** 4 per sq. mi. **Urban** (1991): 33%. **Ethnic groups:** Ovambo 50%, Kavango 10%, Herero 7%, Damara 7%. **Languages:** Afrikaans, English, (official), several indigenous languages. **Religion:** Lutheran 50%, other Christian 30%.

Geography: Area: 317,818 sq. mi., slightly more than half the size of Alaska. **Location:** In S. Africa on the coast of the Atlantic Ocean. Angola on the N, Botswana on the E, and South Africa on the S. **Capital:** Windhoek. **Cities** (1990 est.): Windhoek, 114,000.

Government: Type: Republic. **Head of state:** Pres. Sam Nujoma; in office: Feb. 16, 1990. **Head of government:** Prime Min. Hage Geingob. **Local divisions:** 14 regions.

Economy: Mining accounts for over 40% of GDP. **Minerals:** Diamonds. **Fish catch** (1990): 289,000. **Electricity prod.** (1991): 1.2 mln. kWh.

Finance: Monetary unit: South African Rand. **Gross domestic product** (1991): $2.0 bln. **Per capital GDP:** $1,400. **Imports** (1989): $894 mln. **Exports** (1989): $1.0 bln. **National budget** (1992): $1.1 bln. expenditures.

Transport: Railroads: (1990): **Length:** 1,480 mi.

Communications: Television sets: 1 per 42 persons. **Radios:** 1 per 5.8 persons. **Telephones:** 1 per 17 persons.

Health: Life Expectancy at Birth (1992): 58 male; 63 female. **Births** (per 1,000 pop. 1992): 45. **Deaths** (per 1,000 pop 1992): 10. **Natural increase:** 3.5. **Hospital beds:** 1 per 166 persons. **Physicians:** 1 per 4,450 persons. **Infant mortality** (per 1,000 live births 1992): 66.

Education (1989): **Literacy:** 16% nonwhite.

Embassy: 1413 K St. NW 20005; 289-3871.

Namibia was declared a protectorate by Germany in 1890 and officially called South-West Africa. South Africa seized the territory from Germany in 1915 during World War I; the League of Nations gave South Africa a mandate over the territory in 1920. In 1966, the Marxist South-West Africa People's Organization (SWAPO) launched a guerrilla war for independence.

In 1968 the UN General Assembly gave the area the name Namibia.

In a 1977 referendum, white voters backed a plan for a multiracial interim government to lead to independence. SWAPO rejected the plan. Both S. Africa and Namibian rebels agreed to a UN plan for independence by the end of 1978. S. Africa rejected the plan, Sept. 20, 1978, and held elections for Namibia's constituent assembly, Dec., that were ignored by the major black opposition parties.

In 1982, So. Africa and SWAPO agreed in principle on a cease-fire and the holding of UN-supervised elections. So. Africa, however, insisted on the withdrawal of Cuban forces from Angola as a precondition to Namibian independence. On Jan. 18, 1983, South Africa dissolved the Namibian National Assembly and resumed direct control of the territory.

In 1988, A U.S.-mediated plan was agreed upon by So. Africa, Angola, and Cuba, which called for withdrawal of Cuban troops from Angola and black majority rule in Namibia.

Namibia became an independent nation March 21, 1990.

Walvis Bay, the principal deepwater port in the country, was turned over to South African administration in 1922. So. Africa said in 1978 it would discuss sovereignty only after Namibian independence. In Aug. 1993, So. Africa agreed to turn over control of the port to Namibia, with the transfer likely to occur in 1994.

Nauru

Republic of Nauru

Naoero

People: Population (1992): 9,460. **Pop density:** 1,182 per sq. mi. **Ethnic groups:** Nauruans 57%, Pacific Islanders 26%, Chinese 8%, European 8%. **Languages:** Nauruan (official). **Religions:** Predominately Christian.

Geography: Area: 8 sq. mi. **Location:** In Western Pacific O. just S of Equator. **Neighbors:** Nearest are Solomon Is. **Topography:** Mostly a plateau bearing high grade phosphate deposits, surrounded by a coral cliff and a sandy shore in concentric rings. **Capital:** Yaren.

Government: Type: Republic. **Head of state:** Pres. Bernard Dowiyogo; in office: Dec. 12, 1989. **Local divisions:** 14 districts.

Economy: Phosphate mining. **Electricity prod.** (1990): 48 mln. kWh.

Finance: Monetary unit: Australian dollar. **Gross national product** (1989): $60 mln.

Communications: Radios: 4,000 in use (1985). **Telephones in use** (1980): 1,500.

Health: Births (per 1,000 pop. 1992): 19. **Deaths** (per 1,000 pop. 1992): 5. **Natural increase:** 1.4%. **Infant mortality** (per 1,000 live births 1992): 41.

Education (1988): **Literacy:** 99%; compulsory ages 6-16.

The island was discovered in 1798 by the British but was formally annexed to the German Empire in 1886. After World War I, Nauru became a League of Nations mandate administered by Australia. During World War II the Japanese occupied the island and shipped 1,200 Nauruans to the fortress island of Truk as slave laborers.

In 1947 Nauru was made a UN trust territory, administered by Australia. Nauru became an independent republic Jan. 31, 1968.

Phosphate exports provide one of the world's highest per capita revenues for the Nauru people.

Nepal

Kingdom of Nepal

Nepal Adhirajya

People: Population (1992 est.): 20,086,000. **Age distrib.** (%): 0–14: 42.2; 15–59: 52.9; 60+: 4.9. **Pop. density:** 357 per sq. mi. **Urban** (1987): 8%. **Ethnic groups:** The many tribes are descendants of Indian, Tibetan, and Central Asian migrants. **Languages:** Nepali (official) (an Indic language), many others. **Religions:** Hindu (official) 90%, Buddhist 7%.

Geography: Area: 56,136 sq. mi., the size of North Carolina. **Location:** Astride the Himalaya Mts. **Neighbors:** China on N, India on S. **Topography:** The Himalayas stretch across the N, the hill country with its fertile valleys extends across the center, while the southern border region is part of the flat, subtropical Ganges Plain. **Capital:** Kathmandu. **Cities** (1987 est.): Kathmandu 422,000, Pokhara, Biratnagar, Birganj.

Government: Type: Parliamentary democracy. **Head of state:** King Birendra Bir Bikram Shah Dev; b. Dec. 28, 1945; in office: Jan. 31, 1972. **Head of government:** Prime Min. Giriga Prasad Koirala; in office: May 26, 1991. **Local divisions:** 14 zones. **Defense:** 2.0% of GDP (1992).

Economy: Industries: Sugar, jute mills, tourism. **Chief crops:** Jute, rice, grain. **Minerals:** Quartz. **Other resources:** Forests. **Arable land:** 17%. **Livestock** (1991): cattle: 6.3 mln. **Electricity prod.** (1990): 530 mln. kWh. **Labor force:** 93% agric.

Finance: Monetary unit: Rupee (Mar. 1993: 49 = $1 US). **Gross domestic product** (1991): $3.2 bln. **Per capita GDP:** $165. **Imports** (1991): $545 mln.; partners: India 47%, Jap. 25%. **Exports** (1991): $180 mln.; partners: India 68%. **Tourism** (1990): receipts: $57 mln. **National budget** (1991): $624 mln. **International reserves less gold** (Mar. 1993): $480 mln. **Gold:** 152,000 oz t. **Consumer prices** (change in 1992): 17.1%.

Transport: Civil aviation (1989): 408 mln. passenger-km.

Communications: Radios: 1 per 32 persons. **Telephones:** 1 per 415 persons.

Health: Life expectancy at birth (1992): 51 male; 51 female. **Births** (per 1,000 pop. 1992): 38. **Deaths** (per 1,000 pop. 1992): 14. **Natural increase:** 2.4%. **Hospital beds:** 1 per 3,960 persons. **Physicians:** 1 per 19,644 persons. **Infant mortality** (per 1,000 live births 1992): 90.

Education (1989): **Literacy:** 29%. **Years compulsory:** 3; Attendance: 79% primary, 22% secondary.

Major International Organizations: UN (IMF).

Embassy: 2131 Leroy Pl. NW 20008; 667-4550.

Nepal was originally a group of petty principalities, the inhabitants of one of which, the Gurkhas, became dominant about 1769. In 1951 King Tribhubana Bir Bikram, member of the Shah family, ended the system of rule by hereditary premiers of the Ranas family, who had kept the kings virtual prisoners, and established a cabinet system of government.

Virtually closed to the outside world for centuries, Nepal is now linked to India and Pakistan by roads and air service and to Tibet by road. Polygamy, child marriage, and the caste system were officially abolished in 1963.

In response to numerous pro-democracy protests, the government, which had banned all political parties since 1960, announced the legalization of political parties in 1990. Multi-party elections were held in 1991.

Netherlands

Kingdom of the Netherlands

Koninkrijk der Nederlanden

People: Population (1992 est.) 15,112,000. **Age distrib.** (%): 0–14: 18.8; 15–60: 64.2; 60+: 17.0. **Pop. density:** 958 per sq. mi. **Urban** (1990): 88.3%. **Ethnic groups:** Dutch 97%. **Languages:** Dutch. **Religions:** Roman Catholic 40%, Dutch Reformed 19.3%.

Geography: Area: 15,770 sq. mi., the size of Mass., Conn., and R.I. combined. **Location:** In NW Europe on North Sea. **Topography:** The land is flat, an average alt. of 37 ft. above sea level, with much land below sea level reclaimed and protected by some 1,500 miles of dikes. Since 1920 the government has been draining the IJsselmeer, formerly the Zuider Zee. **Capital:** Amsterdam. **Cities** (1990): Amsterdam 694,000; Rotterdam 576,100; Hague 441,000.

Government: Type: Parliamentary democracy under a constitutional monarch. **Head of state:** Queen Beatrix; b. Jan. 31, 1938; in office: Apr. 30, 1980. **Head of government:** Prime Min. Ruud Lubbers; in office: Nov. 4, 1982. **Seat of govt.:** The Hague. **Local divisions:** 12 provinces. **Defense:** 2.7% of GDP (1991).

Economy: Industries: Metals, machinery, chemicals, oil refinery, diamond cutting, electronics, tourism. **Chief crops:** Grains, potatoes, sugar beets, vegetables, fruits, flowers. **Minerals:** Natural gas, oil. **Crude oil reserves** (1987): 195 mln. bbls. **Arable land:** 26%. **Livestock** (1990): cattle: 4.9 mln.; pigs: 13.9 mln. **Fish catch** (1989): 421,000 metric tons. **Electricity prod.** (1991): 63.0 bln. kWh. **Crude steel prod.** (1991): 5.1 mln. metric tons. **Labor force:** 1% agric.; 30% ind., 44% services, 23% govt.

Finance: Monetary unit: Guilder (June 1993: 1.90 = $1 US). **Gross domestic product** (1991): $249 bln. **Per capita GDP:** $16,600. **Imports** (1992): $156 bln.; partners: Ger. 26%, Belg. 14%, U.S. 9%, U.K. 9%. **Exports** (1992): $160 bln.; partners: Ger. 26%, Belg. 14%, Fr. 10%, UK 9%. **Tourism** (1990): receipts: $3.6 bln. **National budget** (1991): $110 bln. expenditures. **International reserves less gold** (Mar. 1993): $27.2 bln. **Gold:** 31.09 mln. oz t. **Consumer prices** (change in 1992): 3.7%.

Transport: Railroads (1990): **Length:** 2,828 km. **Motor vehicles:** in use (1990): 5.5 mln. passenger cars, 555,000 comm. vehicles. **Civil aviation** (1990): 28.3 bln. passenger-km; 5 airports. **Chief ports:** Rotterdam, Amsterdam, IJmuiden.

Communications: Television sets: 1 per 3.2 persons. **Radios:** 1 per 1.2 persons. **Telephones:** 1 per 1.6 persons. **Daily newspaper circ.** (1987): 312 per 1,000 pop.

Health: Life expectancy at birth (1992): 75 male; 81 female. **Births** (per 1,000 pop. 1992): 13 **Deaths** (per 1,000 pop. 1992): 9. **Natural increase:** .4%. **Hospital beds:** 1 per 164 persons. **Physicians:** 1 per 414 persons. **Infant mortality** (per 1,000 live births 1992): 7

Education (1991): **Literacy:** 99%. **Years compulsory:** 10; attendance: 100%.

Major International Organizations: UN and all of its specialized agencies, NATO, EC, OECD.

Embassy: 4200 Linnean Ave. NW 20008; 244-5300.

Julius Caesar conquered the region in 55 BC, when it was inhabited by Celtic and Germanic tribes.

After the empire of Charlemagne fell apart, the Netherlands (Holland, Belgium, Flanders) split among counts, dukes and bishops, passed to Burgundy and thence to Charles V of Spain. His son, Philip II, tried to check the Dutch drive toward political freedom and Protestantism (1568-1573). William the Silent, prince of Orange, led a confederation of the northern provinces, called Estates, in the Union of Utrecht, 1579. The Estates retained individual sovereignty, but were represented jointly in the States-General, a body that had control of foreign affairs and defense. In 1581 they repudiated allegiance to Spain. The rise of the Dutch republic to naval, economic, and artistic eminence came in the 17th century.

The United Dutch Republic ended 1795 when the French formed the Batavian Republic. Napoleon made his brother Louis king of Holland, 1806; Louis abdicated 1810 when Napoleon annexed Holland. In 1813 the French were expelled. In 1815 the Congress of Vienna formed a kingdom of the Netherlands, including Belgium, under William I. In 1830, the Belgians seceded and formed a separate kingdom.

The constitution, promulgated 1814, and subsequently revised, assures a hereditary constitutional monarchy.

The Netherlands maintained its neutrality in World War I, but was invaded and brutally occupied by Germany, 1940-45.

In 1949, after several years of fighting, the Netherlands granted independence to Indonesia, where it had ruled since the 17th century. In 1963, West New Guinea was turned over to Indonesia.

The independence of former Dutch colonies has instigated mass emigrations to the Netherlands.

Though the Netherlands has been heavily industrialized, its productive small farms export large quantities of pork and dairy foods. Rotterdam, located along the principal mouth of the Rhine, handles the most cargo of any ocean port in the world. Canals, of which there over 3,400 miles, are important in transportation.

Netherlands Antilles

The **Netherlands Antilles,** constitutionally on a level of equality with the Netherlands homeland within the kingdom, consist of 2 groups of islands in the West Indies. **Curacao, Aruba,** and **Bonaire** are near the South American coast; **St. Eustatius, Saba,** and the southern part of **St. Maarten** are SE of Puerto Rico. Northern two-thirds of St. Maarten belong to French Guadeloupe; the French call the island St. Martin. Total area of the 2 groups is 385 sq. mi., including: Aruba 75, Bonaire 111, Curacao 171, St. Eustatius 11, Saba 5, St. Maarten (Dutch part) 13.

Aruba was separated from The Netherlands Antilles on Jan. 1, 1986; it is an autonomous member of The Netherlands, the same status as the Netherland Antilles.

Total pop. (est. 1992) was 184,000. Willemstad, on Curacao, is the capital. Principal industry is the refining of crude oil from Venezuela. Tourism is an important industry, as is shipbuilding.

New Zealand

People: Population: (1991 est.): 3,347,000. **Age distrib. (%):** 0–14: 23.1, 15–59: 61.9; 60+: 15.0 **Pop. density:** 32 per sq. mi. **Urban** (1991): 76%. **Ethnic groups:** European (mostly British) 87%, Polynesian (mostly Maori) 9%. **Languages:** English, Maori (both official). **Religions:** Anglican 22%, Presbyterian 16%, Roman Catholic 15%, others.

Geography: Area: 103,736 sq. mi., the size of Colorado. **Location:** In SW Pacific O. **Neighbors:** Nearest are Australia on W, Fiji, Tonga on N. **Topography:** Each of the 2 main islands (North and South Is.) is mainly hilly and mountainous. The east coasts consist of fertile plains, especially the broad Canterbury Plains on South Is. A volcanic plateau is in center of North Is. South Is. has glaciers and 15 peaks over 10,000 ft. **Capital:** Wellington. **Cities** (1991 est.): Auckland 315,000; Christchurch 292,000; Wellington 148,000; Manukau 224,000.

Government: Type: Parliamentary democracy. **Head of state:** Queen Elizabeth II, represented by Gov.-Gen. Dame Catherine Tizard. **Head of government:** Prime Min. Jim Bolger; b. 1935; in office: Oct. 27, 1990. **Local divisions:** 93 counties, 12 towns & districts. **Defense:** 2.0% of GDP (1992).

Economy: Industries: Food processing, textiles, machinery, fish, forest prods. **Chief crops:** Grains, fruits. **Minerals:** Oil, gas, iron, coal **Crude oil reserves** (1987): 182 mln. bbls. **Other resources:** Wool, timber. **Arable land:** 2%. **Livestock** (1991): cattle: 8.0 mln.; sheep: 55 mln. **Fish catch** (1989): 509,000 metric tons. **Electricity prod.** (1991): 28.0 bln. kWh. **Labor force:** 11% agric. & mining; 41% ind. and commerce, 47% services and gov.

Finance: Monetary unit: Dollar (June 1993: 1.85 = $1 US). **Gross domestic product** (1991): $46 bln. **Per capita GDP:** $14,000. **Imports** (1992): $9.2 bln.; partners: Austral. 22%, U.S. 16%, Jap. 20%. **Exports** (1992): $9.8 bln.; partners: UK 9%, U.S. 15%, Jap. 15%, Austral. 16%. **Tourism** (1990): receipts $900,000 mln. **National budget** (1991): $18.3 bln. **International reserves less gold** (Feb. 1993): $3.0 bln. **Gold:** 1,000 oz t. **Consumer prices** (change in 1992): 1.0%.

Transport: Railroads (1990): **Length:** 2,627 mi. **Motor vehicles:** in use (1990): 1.5 mln. passenger cars; 310,000 comm. vehicles. **Civil aviation:** (1990): 10.5 bln. passenger-km, 36 airports. **Chief ports:** Auckland, Wellington, Lyttleton, Tauranga.

Communications: Television sets: 1 per 3.1 persons. **Radios:** 1 per 1.1 persons. **Telephones:** 1 per 1.4 persons. **Daily newspaper circ.** (1989): 306 per 1,000 pop.

Health: Life expectancy at birth (1992): 72 male; 80 female. **Births** (per 1,000 pop. 1992): 15. **Deaths** (per 1,000 pop. 1992): 8. **Natural increase:** .8%. **Hospital beds:** 1 per 111 persons. **Physicians:** 1 per 359 persons. **Infant mortality** (per 1,000 live births 1992): 10.

Education (1991): **Literacy:** 99%. Compulsory ages 6-15; attendance: 100%.

Major International Organizations: UN (GATT, World Bank, IMF), Commonwealth of Nations, OECD.

Embassy: 37 Observatory Cir. NW 20008; 328-4800.

The Maoris, a Polynesian group from the eastern Pacific, reached New Zealand before and during the 14th century. The first European to sight New Zealand was Dutch navigator Abel Janszoon Tasman, but Maoris refused to allow him to land. British Capt. James Cook explored the coasts, 1769-1770.

British sovereignty was proclaimed in 1840, with organized settlement beginning in the same year. Representative institutions were granted in 1853. Maori Wars ended in 1870 with British victory. The colony became a dominion in 1907, and is an independent member of the Commonwealth.

In July 1985, the *Rainbow Warrior,* flagship of the Greenpeace organization, was bombed and sunk in Auckland harbour by French secret service agents.

A labor tradition in politics dates back to the 19th century. Private ownership is basic to the economy, but state ownership or regulation affects many industries. Transportation, broadcasting, mining, and forestry are largely state-owned.

The native Maoris number about 325,000. Four of 97 members of the House of Representatives are elected directly by the Maori people.

New Zealand comprises **North Island,** 44,035 sq. mi.; **South Island,** 58,304 sq. mi.; **Stewart Island,** 674 sq. mi.; **Chatham Islands,** 372 sq. mi.

In 1965, the **Cook Islands** (pop. 1986 est., 17,185; area 93 sq. mi.) became self-governing although New Zealand retains responsibility for defense and foreign affairs. **Niue** attained the same status in 1974; it lies 400 mi. to W (pop. 1987 est., 2,500; area 100 sq. mi.). **Tokelau Is.,** (pop. 1987 est., 1,600; area 4 sq. mi.) are 300 mi. N of Samoa.

Ross Dependency, administered by New Zealand since 1923, comprises 160,000 sq. mi. of Antarctic territory.

Nicaragua

Republic of Nicaragua

República de Nicaragua

People: Population (1992 est.): 3,878,000. **Age distrib. (%):** 0–14: 45.8; 15–59: 49.9; 60+: 4.3. **Pop. density:** 77 per sq. mi. **Urban** (1990): 60%. **Ethnic groups:** Mestizo 69%, Caucasian 17%, black 9%, Indian 5%. **Languages:** Spanish, (official). **Religion:** Roman Catholic 88%.

Geography: Area: 50,193 sq. mi., about the size of Iowa. **Location:** In Central America. **Neighbors:** Honduras on N, Costa Rica on S. **Topography:** Both Atlantic and Pacific coasts are over 200 mi. long. The Cordillera Mtns., with many volcanic peaks, runs NW-SE through the middle of the country. Between this and a volcanic range to the E lie Lakes Managua and Nicaragua. **Capital:** Managua. **Cities** (1986): Managua 1 mln.

Government: Type: Republic. **Head of Government:** Violeta Barrios de Chamorro; b. 1929; in office Apr. 25, 1990. **Local divisions:** 16 departments. **Defense:** 3.8% of GDP (1991).

Economy: Industries: Oil refining, food processing, chemicals, textiles. **Chief crops:** Bananas, cotton, fruit, yucca, coffee, sugar, corn, beans, cocoa, rice, sesame, tobacco, wheat. **Minerals:** Gold, silver, copper, tungsten. **Other resources:** Forests, shrimp. **Arable land:** 10%. **Livestock** (1991): cattle: 1.6 mln.;

pigs: 709,000. **Electricity prod.** (1991): 1.4 bln. kWh. **Labor force:** 44% agric.; 13% ind.; 43% services.

Finance: Monetary unit: Cordoba oro (May 1993: 5.00 = $1 US). **Gross domestic product** (1991): $1.7 bln. **Per capita GDP:** $425. **Imports** (1991): $738 mln.; partners: U.S. 25%, Latin Amer. 30%, EC 20%. **Exports** (1991): $342 mln.; partners: OECD 75%. **National budget** (1991): $499 mln. expenditures. **Consumer prices** (change in 1990): 11,000%.

Transport: Railroads (1991): **Length:** 186 mi. **Motor vehicles:** in use (1990): 31,000 passenger cars, 42,000 comm. vehicles. **Chief ports:** Corinto, Puerto Somoza, San Juan del Sur.

Communications: Television sets: 1 per 18 persons. **Radios:** 1 per 4.3 persons. **Telephones:** 1 per 82 persons. **Daily newspaper circ.** (1991): 28 per 1,000 pop.

Health: Life expectancy at birth (1992): 61 male; 66 female. **Births** (per 1,000 pop. 1992): 37. **Deaths** (per 1,000 pop. 1992): 8. **Natural increase:** 2.9%. **Hospital beds:** 1 per 761 persons. **Physicians:** 1 per 1,678 persons. **Infant mortality** (per 1,000 live births 1992): 57.

Education (1991): **Literacy:** 57%. **Years compulsory:** 11 years or 16 years old.

Major International Organizations: UN and all of its specialized agencies, OAS.

Embassy: 1627 New Hampshire Ave. NW 20009; 387-4371.

Nicaragua, inhabited by various Indian tribes, was conquered by Spain in 1552. After gaining independence from Spain, 1821, Nicaragua was united for a short period with Mexico, then with the United Provinces of Central America, finally becoming an independent republic, 1838.

U.S. Marines occupied the country at times in the early 20th century, the last time from 1926 to 1933.

Gen. Anastasio Somoza Debayle was elected president 1967. He resigned 1972, but was elected president again in 1974. Martial law was imposed in Dec. 1974, after officials were kidnapped by the Marxist Sandinista guerrillas. Violent opposition spread to nearly all classes in 1978; nationwide strikes called against the government touched off a state of civil war. Months of simmering civil war ended when Somoza fled, July 19, 1979.

Relations with the U.S. were strained due to Nicaragua's aid to leftist guerrillas in El Salvador and the U.S. backing anti-Sandinista contra guerrilla groups.

In 1983, the contras launched their first major offensive; the Sandinistas imposed rule by decree. In 1985, the U.S. House rejected Pres. Reagan's request for military aid to the contras.

The diversion of funds to the contras from the proceeds of a secret arms sale to Iran caused a major scandal in the U.S. The plan, masterminded by the administration's national security advisor and his deputy, took place at a time when military aid to the contras was forbidden by law.

In a stunning upset, Violeta Barrios de Chamorro defeat Ortega in national elections, Feb. 25, 1990.

Niger

Republic of Niger

République du Niger

People: Population (1992 est.): 8,052,000. **Age distrib.** (%): 0–14: 46.7; 15–59: 48.5; 60+: 4.8. **Pop. density:** 16 per sq. mi. **Urban** (1988): 21%. **Ethnic groups:** Hausa 56%, Djerma 22%, Fulani 8%, Tuareg 8%. **Languages:** French (official), Hausa, Fulani. **Religions:** Sunni Moslem 80%.

Geography: Area: 489,189 sq. mi., almost 3 times the size of California. **Location:** In the interior of N. Africa. **Neighbors:** Libya, Algeria on N, Mali, Burkina Faso on W, Benin, Nigeria on S, Chad on E. **Topography:** Mostly arid desert and mountains. A narrow savanna in the S and the Niger R. basin in the SW contain most of the population. **Capital:** Niamey. **Cities** (1987 est.): Niamey 350,000.

Government: Type: Republic. **Head of government:** Pres. Ali Seibou; in office: Dec. 20, 1989. Prime Min. Amadou Cheiffou; in office: Oct. 27, 1991. **Local divisions:** 7 departments. **Defense:** 0.8% of GDP (1989).

Economy: Chief crops: Peanuts, cotton. **Minerals:** Uranium, coal, iron. **Arable land:** 3%. **Livestock** (1991): cattle: 2.2 mln.; sheep: 3.5 mln.; goats: 4.8 mln. **Electricity prod.** (1991): 230 mln. kWh. **Labor force:** 90% agric.

Finance: Monetary unit: CFA franc (Mar. 1993: 273 = $1 US). **Gross domestic product** (1991): $2.4 bln. **Per capita GDP:** $300. **Imports** (1990): $439 mln.; partners: Fr. 32%. **Exports** (1990): $320 mln.; partners: Fr. 65%, Nig. 11%. **National budget** (1989): $452 mln. expenditures. **International reserves less gold** (Jan. 1993): $225 mln. **Gold:** 11,000 oz t. **Consumer prices** (change in 1991): −7.8%.

Transport: Motor vehicles: in use (1989): 16,000 passenger cars, 18,000 comm. vehicles.

Communications: Television sets: 1 per 321 persons. **Radios:** 1 per 19 persons. **Telephones:** 1 per 563 persons. **Daily newspaper cir.** (1991): 1 per 1,000 pop.

Health: Life expectancy at birth (1992): 42 male; 45 female. **Births** (per 1,000 pop. 1992): 58. **Deaths** (per 1,000 pop. 1992): 23. **Natural increase:** 3.5%. **Infant mortality** (per 1,000 live births 1992): 125.

Education (1991): **Literacy:** 28%. **Years compulsory:** 6; attendance: 15%.

Major International Organizations: UN (GATT, IMF, WHO, FAO), OAU.

Embassy: 2204 R St. NW 20008; 483-4224.

Niger was part of ancient and medieval African empires. European explorers reached the area in the late 18th century. The French colony of Niger was established 1900-22, after the defeat of Tuareg fighters, who had invaded the area from the N a century before. The country became independent Aug. 3, 1960. The next year it signed a bilateral agreement with France retaining close economic and cultural ties.

Nigeria

Federal Republic of Nigeria

People: Population (1991 cen.): 88,500,000. **Pop. density:** 248 per sq. mi. **Urban** (1990): 35%. **Ethnic groups:** Hausa 21%, Yoruba 20%, Ibo 17%, Fulani 9%, others. **Languages:** English (official), Hausa, Yoruba, Ibo. **Religions:** Moslem 50% (in N), Christian 40% (in S), others.

Geography: Area: 356,667 sq. mi., more than twice the size of California. **Location:** On the S coast of W. Africa. **Neighbors:** Benin on W, Niger on N, Chad, Cameroon on E. **Topography:** 4 E-W regions divide Nigeria: a coastal mangrove swamp 10-60 mi. wide, a tropical rain forest 50-100 mi. wide, a plateau of savanna and open woodland, and semidesert in the N. **Capital:** Abuja. **Cities:** (1992): Lagos 1,347,000; Ibadan 1,295,000.

Government: Type: In transition. **Head of state:** Pres. Ernest Shonekan; in office: Aug. 26, 1993. **Local divisions:** 30 states plus federal capital territory. **Defense:** 1.0% of GNP (1990).

Economy: Industries: Crude oil (95% of export), food processing, assembly of vehicles, textiles. **Chief crops:** Cocoa (main export crop), tobacco, palm products, peanuts, cotton, soybeans. **Minerals:** Oil, gas, coal, iron, limestone, columbium, tin. **Crude oil reserves** (1991): 17.4 bln. bbls. **Other resources:** Timber, rubber, hides. **Arable land:** 31%. **Livestock** (1991): cattle: 14.5 mln.; goats: 36 mln.; sheep: 24 mln. **Fish catch** (1989): 315,000 metric tons. **Electricity prod.** (1991): 11.2 bln. kWh. **Labor force:** 54% agric., 19% ind., comm. and serv.

Finance: Monetary unit: Naira (Feb. 1993: 24.86 = $1 US). **Gross domestic product** (1990): $28 bln. **Per capita GDP:** $230. **Imports** (1990): $9.5 bln.; partners: U.S., EC. **Exports** (1990): $13.0 bln.; partners: U.S., EC. **Tourism receipts** (1990): $21 mln. **National budget** (1992): $10.0 bln. expenditures. **International reserves less gold** (Jan. 1993): $966 mln. **Gold:** 687,000 oz t. **Consumer prices** (change in 1992): 53.9%.

Transport: Motor vehicles: in use (1990): 785,000 passenger cars, 625,000 comm. vehicles. **Civil aviation** (1991): 774 mln. passenger-km; 14 airports. **Chief ports:** Port Harcourt, Lagos, Warri, Calabar.

Communications: Television sets: 1 per 30 persons. **Radios:** 1 per 12 persons. **Telephones:** 1 per 240 persons. **Daily newspaper circ.** (1990): 12 per 1,000 pop.

Health: Life expectancy at birth (1992): 48 male; 50 female. **Births** (per 1,000 pop. 1992): 46. **Deaths** (per 1,000 pop. 1992): 17. **Natural increase:** 2.9%. **Hospital beds:** 1 per 1,142 persons. **Physicians:** 1 per 6,900 persons. **Infant mortality** (per 1,000 live births 1992): 110.

Education (1991): **Literacy:** 51%. **Primary school attendance:** 42%.

Major International Organizations: UN (GATT, IMO, WHO), OPEC, OAU, Commonwealth of Nations.

Embassy: 2201 M St. NW 20037; 822-1500.

Early cultures in Nigeria date back to at least 700 BC. From the 12th to the 14th centuries, more advanced cultures developed in the Yoruba area, at Ife, and in the north, where Moslem influence prevailed.

Portuguese and British slavers appeared from the 15th-16th centuries. Britain seized Lagos, 1861, during an anti-slave trade campaign, and gradually extended control inland until 1900. Nigeria became independent Oct. 1, 1960, and a republic Oct. 1, 1963.

On May 30, 1967, the Eastern Region seceded, proclaiming itself the Republic of Biafra, plunging the country into civil war. Casualties in the war were est. at over 1 million, including many "Biafrans" (mostly Ibos) who died of starvation despite international efforts to provide relief. The secessionists, after steadily losing ground, capitulated Jan. 12, 1970. Within a few years, the Ibos were reintegrated into national life.

Oil revenues have made possible a massive economic development program, largely using private enterprise, but agriculture has lagged.

After 13 years of military rule, the nation experienced a peaceful return to civilian government, Oct., 1979.

Military rule returned to Nigeria, Dec. 31, 1983 as a coup ousted the democratically elected government. The government had promised a return to civilian rule. However, the June 23, 1993, presidential election was voided by the incumbent president, Gen. Ibrahim Babangida, who rescinded his promise to surrender power to an elected civilian government. Babangida resigned and appointed a civilian to head an interim government Aug. 26.

Norway

Kingdom of Norway

Kongeriket Norge

People: Population (1992 est.): 4,294,000. **Age distrib.** (%): 0–14: 19.0; 15–59: 59.9; 60+: 21.1. **Pop. density:** 34 per sq. mi. **Urban** (1990): 75%. **Ethnic groups:** Germanic (Nordic, Alpine, Baltic), minority Lapps. **Languages:** Norwegian (official). **Religions:** Evangelical Lutheran 94%.

Geography: Area: 125,181 sq. mi., slightly larger than New Mexico. **Location:** Occupies the W part of Scandinavian peninsula in NW Europe (extends farther north than any European land). **Neighbors:** Sweden, Finland, Russia on E. **Topography:** A highly indented coast is lined with tens of thousands of islands. Mountains and plateaus cover most of the country, which is only 25% forested. **Capital:** Oslo. **Cities** (1991): Oslo 467,000; Bergen 215,000.

Government: Type: Hereditary constitutional monarchy. **Head of state:** King Harald V; b. Feb. 21, 1937; in office: Jan. 17, 1991. **Head of government:** Prime Min. Gro Harlem Brundtland; in office: Nov. 3, 1990. **Local divisions:** Oslo, Svalbard and 18 fylker (counties). **Defense:** 3.2% of GDP (1991).

Economy: Industries: Paper, shipbuilding, engineering, metals, chemicals, food processing oil, gas. **Chief crops:** Grains, potatoes, fruits. **Minerals:** Oil, copper, pyrites, nickel, iron, zinc, lead. **Crude oil reserves** (1987): 11.1 bln. bbls. **Other resources:** Timber. **Arable land:** 3%. **Livestock** (1991): sheep: 1.0 mln.; cattle: 967,000; pigs: 721,000. **Fish catch** (1991): 1.9 mln. metric tons. **Electricity prod.** (1991): 121 bln. kWh. **Labor force:** 7% agric.; 47% ind., banking, comm.; 18% services, 26% govt.

Finance: Monetary unit: Kroner (July 1993: 7.18 = $1 US). **Gross domestic product** (1991): $72.9 bln. **Per capita GDP:** $17,100. **Imports** (1992): $25.9 bln.; partners: EC 47%. **Exports** (1992): $35.1 bln.; partners: EC 65%. **Tourism** (1990): receipts: $1.5 bln. **National budget** (1991): $52 bln. expenditures. **International reserves less gold** (Mar. 1993): $11.9 bln. **Gold:** 1.18 mln. oz t. **Consumer prices** (change in 1992): 2.3%.

Transport: Railroads (1990): **Length:** 2,600 mi. **Motor vehicles:** in use (1991): 1.6 mln. passenger cars, 383,000 comm. vehicles. **Civil aviation:** (1990): 7.6 bln. passenger-km; 47 airports. **Chief ports:** Bergen, Stavanger, Oslo, Tonsberg.

Communications: Television sets: 1 per 2.9 persons. **Radios:** 1 per 1.3 persons. **Telephones:** 1 per 1.6 persons. **Daily newspaper circ.** (1991): 510 per 1,000 pop.

Health: Life expectancy at birth (1992): 74 male; 81 female. **Births** (per 1,000 pop. 1992): 14. **Deaths** (per 1,000 pop. 1992): 11. **Natural increase:** .3%. **Hospital beds:** 1 per 168 persons. **Physicians:** 1 per 309 persons. **Infant mortality** (per 1,000 live births 1992): 7.1.

Education (1991): **Literacy:** 99%. **Years Compulsory:** 9.

Major International Organizations: UN and all of its specialized agencies, NATO, OECD.

Embassy: 2720 34th St. NW 20008; 388-6000.

The first supreme ruler of Norway was Harald the Fairhaired who came to power in 872 AD. Between 800 and 1000, Norway's Vikings raided and occupied widely dispersed parts of Europe.

The country was united with Denmark 1381-1814, and with Sweden, 1814-1905. In 1905, the country became independent with Prince Charles of Denmark as king.

Norway remained neutral during World War I. Germany attacked Norway Apr. 9, 1940, and held it until liberation May 8, 1945. The country abandoned its neutrality after the war, and joined the NATO alliance.

Abundant hydroelectric resources provided the base for Norway's industrialization, producing one of the highest living standards in the world.

Norway's merchant marine is one of the world's largest.

Svalbard is a group of mountainous islands in the Arctic O., c. 23,957 sq. mi., pop. varying seasonally from 1,500 to 3,600. The largest, Spitsbergen (formerly called West Spitsbergen), 15,060 sq. mi., seat of governor, is about 370 mi. N of Norway. By a treaty signed in Paris, 1920, major European powers recognized the sovereignty of Norway, which incorporated it in 1925.

Oman

Sultanate of Oman

Saltanat 'Uman

People: Population (1992 est.): 1,587,000. **Pop. density:** 19 per sq. mi. **Urban** (1990): 10%. **Ethnic groups:** Omani Arab 74%, Pakistani 21%. **Languages:** Arabic (official). **Religions:** Ibadhi Moslem 75%, Sunni Moslem.

Geography: Area: 82,030 sq. mi., about the size of New Mexico. **Location:** On SE coast of Arabian peninsula. **Neighbors:** United Arab Emirates, Saudi Arabia, Yemen on W. **Topography:** Oman has a narrow coastal plain up to 10 mi. wide, a range of barren mountains reaching 9,900 ft., and a wide, stony, mostly waterless plateau, avg. alt. 1,000 ft. Also the tip of the Ruus-al-Jebal peninsula controls access to the Persian Gulf. **Capital:** Muscat. **Cities** (1990 est.): Muscat 85,000.

Government: Type: Absolute monarchy. **Head of state:** Sultan Qabus bin Said; b. Nov. 18, 1942; in office: July 23, 1970. **Defense:** 16% of GDP (1992).

Economy: Chief crops: Dates, fruits, vegetables, wheat, bananas. **Minerals:** Oil (95% of exports). **Crude oil reserves** (1987): 4.5 bln. bbls. **Fish catch** (1990): 110,000 metric tons. **Electricity prod.** (1991): 5.0 bln. kWh. **Labor force:** 60% agric. & fishing.

Finance: Monetary unit: Rial Omani (Mar. 1993: .38 = $1 US). **Gross domestic product** (1989): $7.7 bln. **Imports** (1990): $2.6 bln.; partners: Jap. 21%, UAE 17%, UK 14%. **Exports** (1990): $2.6 bln.; partners: Jap. 58%, Europe 30%. **National budget** (1990): $4.9 bln. revenues; $5.4 bln. expenditures. **International reserves less gold** (Mar. 1993): $1.6 bln. **Gold:** 289,000 oz t.

Transport: Motor vehicles: in use (1990): 96,000 passenger cars, 70,000 comm. vehicles. **Civil aviation** (1990): 1.6 bln. passenger-km. 6 airports. Chief ports: Matrah, Muscat.

Communications: Television sets: 1 per 1.4 persons. **Radios:** 1 per 1.6 persons. **Telephones:** 1 per 14 persons.

Health: Life expectancy at birth (1992): 65 male; 69 female. **Hospital beds:** 1 per 380 persons. **Physicians:** 1 per 1,071 persons. **Infant mortality** (per 1,000 live births 1992): 40.

Education (1989): **Literacy:** 20%. **Attendance:** 80% primary, 30% secondary.

Major International Organizations: UN (World Bank, IMF), Arab League.

Embassy: 2342 Massachusetts Ave. NW 20008; 387-1980.

A long history of rule by other lands, including Portugal in the 16th century, ended with the ouster of the Persians in 1744. By the early 19th century, Muscat and Oman was one of the most important countries in the region, controlling much of the Persian and Pakistan coasts, and ruling far-away Zanzibar, which was separated in 1861 under British mediation.

British influence was confirmed in a 1951 treaty, and Britain helped suppress an uprising by traditionally rebellious interior tribes against control by Muscat in the 1950s.

On July 23, 1970, Sultan Said bin Taimur was overthrown by his son who changed the nation's name to Sultanate of Oman.

Oil is the major source of income.

Oman opened its air bases to Western forces following the Iraqi invasion of Kuwait on Aug. 2, 1990.

Pakistan

Islamic Republic of Pakistan

Islam-i Jamhuriya-e Pakistan

People: Population (1992 est.): 121,664,000. **Pop. density:** 391 per sq. mi. **Urban** (1988): 32%. **Ethnic groups:** Punjabi 66%, Sindhi 13%, Pathan 8.5%, Urdu 7.6%, Baluchi 2.5%, others. **Languages:** Urdu, (official), Punjabi, Sindhi, Pushtu, Baluchi, Brahvi. **Religions:** Moslem 97%.

Geography: Area: 310,403 sq. mi., about the size of Texas. **Location:** In W part of South Asia. **Neighbors:** Iran on W, Afghanistan, China on N, India on E. **Topography:** The Indus R. rises in the Hindu Kush and Himalaya mtns. in the N (highest is K2, or Godwin Austen, 28,250 ft., 2d highest in world), then flows over 1,000 mi. through fertile valley and empties into Arabian Sea. Thar Desert, Eastern Plains flank Indus Valley. **Capital:** Islamabad. **Cities** (1992 est.): Karachi 7.0 mln.; Lahore 3.5 mln.; Faisalabad 2.0 mln.; Hyderabad 795,000; Rawalpindi 928,000.

Government: Type: Parliamentary democracy in a federal setting. **Head of state:** Pres. Ghulam Ishaq Khan; in office: Dec. 12, 1988. **Head of government:** Prime Min. Nawaz Sharif; in office: Nov. 6, 1990. **Local divisions:** Federal capital, 4 provinces, tribal areas. **Defense:** 6.4% of GDP (1992).

Economy: Industries: Textiles, food processing, chemicals, petroleum prods. **Chief crops:** Rice, wheat. **Minerals:** Natural gas, iron ore. **Crude oil reserves** (1987): 116 mln. bbls. **Other resources:** Wool. **Arable land:** 26%. **Livestock** (1990): cattle: 17.2 mln.; sheep: 28.3 mln.; goats: 34.2 mln. **Fish catch** (1990): 479,000 metric tons. **Electricity prod.** (1991): 35 bln. kWh. **Labor force:** 53% agric.; 13% ind; 33% services.

Finance: Monetary unit: Rupee (Aug. 1993: 29.75 = $1 US). **Gross domestic product** (1991): $45 bln. **Per capita GDP** (1991): $380. **Imports** (1991): $7.9 bln.; partners: EC 21%, Jap. 13%, U.S. 16%. **Exports** (1991): $6.0 bln.; partners: EC 31%, Jap. 10%, U.S. 10%. **Tourism** (1990): $156 mln. receipts. **National budget** (1992): $10.0 bln. expenditures. **International reserves less gold** (Mar. 1993): $797 mln. **Gold:** 2.0 mln. oz t. **Consumer prices** (change in 1992): 9.5%.

Transport: Railroads (1990): **Length:** 5,453 mi. **Motor vehicles:** in use (1989): 738,000 passenger cars, 171,000 comm. vehicles. **Civil aviation** (1990): 9.3 bln. passenger-km; 35 airports with scheduled flights. **Chief ports:** Karachi.

Communications: Television sets: 1 per 61 persons. **Radios:** 1 per 13 persons. **Telephones:** 1 per 131 persons. **Daily newspaper circ.** (1990): 9 per 1,000 pop.

Health: Life expectancy at birth (1992): 56 male; 57 female. **Births** (per 1,000 pop. 1992): 43 **Deaths** (per 1,000 pop. 1992): 14. **Natural increase:** 2.9%. **Hospital beds:** 1 per 1,706 persons. **Physicians:** 1 per 2,364 persons. **Infant mortality** (per 1,000 live births 1992): 105.

Education (1991): **Literacy:** 35%.

Major International Organizations: UN (GATT, ILO, IMF, WHO).

Embassy: 2315 Massachusetts Ave. NW 20008; 939-6200.

Present-day Pakistan shares the 5,000-year history of the India-Pakistan sub-continent. At present day Harappa and Mohenjo Daro, the Indus Valley Civilization, with large cities and elaborate irrigation systems, flourished c. 4,000-2,500 BC.

Aryan invaders from the NW conquered the region around 1,500 BC, forging a Hindu civilization that dominated Pakistan as well as India for 2,000 years.

Beginning with the Persians in the 6th century BC, and continuing with Alexander the Great and with the Sassanians, successive nations to the west ruled or influenced Pakistan, eventually separating the area from the Indian cultural sphere.

The first Arab invasion, 712 AD, introduced Islam. Under the Mogul empire (1526-1857), Moslems ruled most of India, yielding to British encroachment and resurgent Hindus.

After World War I the Moslems of British India began agitation for minority rights in elections. Mohammad Ali Jinnah (1876-1948) was the principal architect of Pakistan. A leader of the Moslem League from 1916, he worked for dominion status for India; from 1940 he advocated a separate Moslem state.

When the British withdrew Aug. 14, 1947, the Islamic majority areas of India acquired self-government as Pakistan, with dominion status in the Commonwealth. Pakistan was divided into 2 sections, West Pakistan and East Pakistan. The 2 areas were nearly 1,000 mi. apart on opposite sides of India.

Pakistan became a republic in 1956. Pakistan had a National Assembly (legislature) with equal membership from East and West Pakistan, and 2 Provincial Assemblies. In Oct. 1958, Gen. Mohammad Ayub Khan took power in a coup. He was elected president in 1960, reelected in 1965.

Ayub resigned Mar. 25, 1969, after several months of violent rioting and unrest, most of it in East Pakistan, which demanded autonomy. The government was turned over to Gen. Agha Mohammad Yahya Khan and martial law was declared.

The Awami League, which sought regional autonomy for East Pakistan, won a majority in Dec. 1970 elections to a National Assembly which was to write a new constitution. In March, 1971 Yahya postponed the Assembly. Rioting and strikes broke out in the East.

On Mar. 25, 1971, government troops launched attacks in the East. The Easterners, aided by India, proclaimed the independent nation of Bangladesh. In months of widespread fighting, countless thousands were killed. Some 10 million Easterners fled into India.

Full scale war between India and Pakistan had spread to both the East and West fronts by Dec. 3. Pakistan troops in the East surrendered Dec. 16; Pakistan agreed to a cease-fire in the West Dec. 17. On July 3, 1972, Pakistan and India signed a pact agreeing to withdraw troops from their borders and seek peaceful solutions to all problems.

Zulfikar Ali Bhutto, leader of the Pakistan People's Party, which had won the most West Pakistan votes in the Dec. 1970 elections, became president Dec. 20.

Bhutto was overthrown in a military coup July, 1977. Convicted of complicity in a 1974 political murder, Bhutto was executed Apr.4, 1979. Benazir Bhutto, his daughter, returned to Pakistan from exile in Europe in 1986. Her efforts to relaunch the Pakistan People's Party sparked violence and antigovernment riots.

Pres. Mohammad Zia ul-Haq was killed when his plane exploded in Aug. 1988. Following Nov. elections, Benazir Bhutto was named Prime Minister, the first woman leader of a Moslem nation. Her party was soundly defeated in the Oct. 1990 elections; there were charges of corruption against Bhutto.

Legislation was submitted in 1991 to adopt Islamic law in place of the current secular code.

Prime Min. Nawaz Sharif was ousted from office by Pres. Khan, Apr. 18, 1993; he was reinstated by Pakistan's Supreme Court on May 26.

Panama

Republic of Panama

República de Panamá

People: Population (1992 est.): 2,529,000. **Age distrib.** (%): 0–14: 35.5; 15–59: 57.6; 60+: 6.9. **Pop. density:** 84 per sq. mi. **Urban** (1990): 53%. **Ethnic groups:** Mestizo 70%, West Indian 14%, Caucasian 10%, Indian 6%. **Languages:** Spanish (official), English. **Religions:** Roman Catholic 93%, Protestant 6%.

Geography: Area: 29,762 sq. mi., slightly larger than West Virginia. **Location:** In Central America. **Neighbors:** Costa Rica on W., Colombia on E. **Topography:** 2 mountain ranges run the length of the isthmus. Tropical rain forests cover the Caribbean coast and eastern Panama. **Capital:** Panama. **Cities** (1990 est.): Panama City 411,000.

Government: Type: Constitutional democracy. **Head of state and head of government:** Pres. Guillermo Endara Galimany; in office: Dec. 20, 1989. **Local divisions:** 9 provinces, 1 territory. **Defense:** 1.5% of GDP (1990).

Economy: Industries: Oil refining, international banking. **Chief crops:** Bananas, pineapples, cocoa, corn, coconuts, sugar. **Minerals:** Copper. **Other resources:** Forests (mahogany), shrimp. **Arable land:** 6%. **Livestock** (1990): cattle: 1.5 mln.; pigs: 240,000. **Electricity prod.** (1991): 3.3 mln. kWh. **Labor force:** 26% agric., 20%, govt. & community services.

Finance: Monetary unit: Balboa (Apr. 1993: 1.00 = $1 US). **Gross domestic product** (1991): $5.2 bln. **Per capita GDP:** $1,150. **Imports** (1991): $1.5 bln.; partners: U.S. 37%. **Exports** (1991): $380 mln.; partners: U.S. 44%. **Tourism** (1990): $167 mln. receipts. **National budget** (1992): $1.7 mln. **International reserves less gold** (Jan. 1993): $553 mln. **Consumer prices** (change in 1992): 1.8%.

Transport: Motor vehicles: in use (1990): 186,000 passenger cars, 49,000 comm. vehicles. **Civil aviation** (1990): 195 mln. passenger-km; 8 airports with scheduled flights. **Chief ports:** Balboa, Cristobal.

Communications: Television sets: 1 per 12 persons. **Radios:** 1 per 2.5 persons. **Telephones:** 1 per 9.3 persons. **Daily newspaper circ.** (1990): 60 per 1,000 pop.

Health: Life expectancy at birth (1992): 73 male; 77 female. **Births** (per 1,000 pop. 1992): 26. **Deaths** (per 1,000 pop. 1992): 5. **Natural increase:** 2.1%. **Hospital beds:** 1 per 330 persons. **Physicians:** 1 per 880 persons. **Infant mortality** (per 1,000 live births 1992): 17.

Education (1991): **Literacy:** 87%. **Primary school attendance:** almost 100%.

Major International Organizations: UN (IMF, IMO, World Bank), OAS.

Embassy: 2862 McGill Terrace NW 20008; 483-1407.

The coast of Panama was sighted by Rodrigo de Bastidas, sailing with Columbus for Spain in 1501, and was visited by Columbus in 1502. Vasco Nunez de Balboa crossed the isthmus and "discovered" the Pacific O. Sept. 13, 1513. Spanish colonies were ravaged by Francis Drake, 1572-95, and Henry Morgan, 1668-71. Morgan destroyed the old city of Panama which had been founded in 1519. Freed from Spain, Panama joined Colombia in 1821.

Panama declared its independence from Colombia Nov. 3, 1903, with U.S. recognition. U.S. naval forces deterred action by Colombia. On Nov. 18, 1903, Panama granted use, occupation and control of the Canal Zone to the U.S. by treaty, ratified Feb. 26, 1904.

In 1978, a new treaty provided for a gradual takeover by Panama of the canal, and withdrawal of U.S. troops, to be completed by 1999. U.S. payments were substantially increased in the interim. The permanent neutrality of the canal was also guaranteed.

President Delvalle was ousted by the National Assembly, Feb. 26, 1988, after he tried to fire the head of the Panama Defense Forces, Gen. Manuel Antonio Noriega. Noreiga had been indicted by 2 U.S. federal grand juries on drug charges. A general strike followed. Despite U.S.-imposed economic sanctions Noriega remained in power. Voters went to the polls to elect a new president May 7, 1989. Noriega claimed victory but foreign observers said that the opposition had won overwhelmingly and that Noriega was trying to steal the election. The government voided the election May 10, charging foreign interference. There was an attempted coup against Noriega Oct. 3.

U.S. troops invaded Panama Dec. 20 following a series of incidents, including the killing of a U.S. Marine by Panamanian soldiers. The operation had as its chief objective the capture of Noriega, who was wanted in the U.S. on drug trafficking charges. Noriega took refuge in the Vatican diplomatic mission, but surrendered after 10 days to U.S. officials Jan. 3, 1990. He was convicted on 8 counts of racketeering and drug trafficking in a U.S. District Court in Miami, Fla., Apr. 9, 1992.

Papua New Guinea

People: Population (1992 est.): 4,006,000. **Age distrib.** (%): 0–14: 41.6; 15–59: 52.8; 60+: 5.6. **Pop. density:** 22 per sq. mi. **Urban** (1990): 15%. **Ethnic groups:** Papuans (in S and interior), Melanesian (N,E), pygmies, minorities of Chinese, Australians, Polynesians. **Languages:** English (official), Melanesian languages, Papuan languages. **Religions:** Protestant 63%, Roman Catholic 31%, local religions.

Geography: Area: 178,260 sq. mi., slightly larger than California. **Location:** Occupies eastern half of island of New Guinea. **Neighbors:** Indonesia (West Irian) on W, Australia on S. **Topography:** Thickly forested mtns. cover much of the center of the country, with lowlands along the coasts. Included are some of the nearby islands of Bismarck and Solomon groups, including Admiralty Is., New Ireland, New Britain, and Bougainville. **Capital:** Port Moresby. **Cities** (1991): Port Moresby 193,000; Lae 80,000.

Government: Type: Parliamentary democracy. **Head of state:** Queen Elizabeth II, represented by Gov. Gen. Wiwa Korowi; in office: Oct. 4, 1991. **Head of government:** Prime Min. Paias Wingti; in office: July 17, 1992. **Local divisions:** 20 provinces. **Defense:** approx. 1.5% of GDP (1989).

Economy: Chief crops: Coffee, coconuts, cocoa. **Minerals:** Gold, copper, silver. **Arable land:** 1%. **Livestock** (1990): pigs: 1.7 mln. **Electricity prod.** (1991): 1.5 bln. kWh. **Labor force:** 82% agric., 3% ind. and commerce, 8% services.

Finance: Monetary unit: Kina (Mar. 1993: 1.00 = $1.02 US). **Gross domestic product** (1991): $3.1 bln. **Per capita GDP:** $800. **Imports** (1992): $1.5 bln.; partners: Austral. 40%, Jap. 17%; U.S. 9%. **Exports** (1992): $1.8 bln.; partners: Jap. 26%, W. Ger. 36%, Austral. 8%. **National budget** (1992): $1.4 bln. **International reserves less gold** (Mar. 1993): $180 mln. **Gold:** 63,000 oz t. **Consumer prices** (change in 1992): 3.6%.

Transport: Motor vehicles: in use (1989): 17,000 passenger cars, 26,000 comm. vehicles. **Chief ports:** Port Moresby, Lae.

Communications: Television sets: 1 per 375 persons. **Radios:** 1 per 15 persons. **Telephones:** 1 per 48 persons. **Daily newspaper circ.** (1988): 8 per 1,000 pop.

Health: Life expectancy at birth (1992): 55 male; 56 female. **Births** (per 1,000 pop. 1992): 34. **Deaths** (per 1,000 pop. 1992): 11. **Natural increase:** 2.3%. **Hospital beds:** 1 per 222 persons. **Physicians:** 1 per 11,904 persons. **Infant mortality** (per 1,000 live births 1992): 55.

Education (1991): **Literacy:** 52%. **Attendance:** 65% primary school; 13% secondary school.

Major International Organizations: UN (GATT), Commonwealth of Nations.

Embassy: 1330 Connecticut Ave., NW 20036; 659-0856

Human remains have been found in the interior of New Guinea dating back at least 10,000 years and possibly much earlier. Successive waves of peoples probably entered the country from Asia through Indonesia. Europeans visited in the 15th century, but land claims did not begin until the 19th century, when the Dutch took control of the western half of the island.

The southern half of eastern New Guinea was first claimed by Britain in 1884, and transferred to Australia in 1905. The northern half was claimed by Germany in 1884, but captured in World War I by Australia, which was granted a League of Nations mandate and then a UN trusteeship over the area. The 2 territories were administered jointly after 1949, given self-government Dec. 1, 1973, and became independent Sept. 16, 1975.

The indigenous population consists of a huge number of tribes, many living in almost complete isolation with mutually unintelligible languages.

Paraguay

Republic of Paraguay

República del Paraguay

People: Population (1992 est.): 4,929,000. **Age distrib.** (%): 0–14: 41.0; 15–59: 52.0; 60+: 7.0. **Pop. density:** 31 per sq. mi. **Urban** (1990): 46%. **Ethnic groups:** Mestizo 95%, small Caucasian, Indian, black minorities. **Languages:** Spanish (official), Guarani. **Religions:** Roman Catholic (official) 97%.

Geography: Area: 157,047 sq. mi., the size of California. **Location:** One of the 2 landlocked countries of S. America. **Neighbors:** Bolivia on N, Argentina on S, Brazil on E. **Topography:** Paraguay R. bisects the country. To E are fertile plains, wooded slopes, grasslands. To W is the Chaco plain, with marshes and scrub trees. Extreme W is arid. **Capital:** Asunción. **Cities** (1990 est.): Asunción 607,000.

Government: Type: Republic. **Head of state:** Pres. Juan Carlos Wasmosy; in office: Aug. 15, 1993. **Local divisions:** 19 departments. **Defense:** 1.0% of GDP (1988).

Economy: Industries: Food processing, wood products, textiles, cement. **Chief crops:** Corn, cotton, beans, sugarcane. **Minerals:** Iron, manganese, limestone. **Other resources:** Forests. **Arable land:** 20%. **Livestock** (1991): cattle: 8.2 mln.; pigs:

2.4 mln. **Electricity prod.** (1991): 15.4 bln. kWh. **Labor force:** 44% agric., 34% ind. and commerce, 18% services.

Finance: Monetary unit: Guarani (Mar. 1993: 1,631 = $1 US). **Gross domestic product** (1991): $7.0 bln. **Per capita GDP:** $1,460. **Imports** (1991): $1.8 bln.; partners: Braz. 32%, EC 20%. **Exports** (1991): $642 mln.; partners: EC 37%, Braz. 25%. **Tourism** (1990): $113 mln. receipts. **National budget** (1991): $1.2 bln. expenditures. **International reserves less gold** (Mar. 1993): $561 mln. **Gold:** 35,000 oz t. **Consumer prices** (change in 1991): 27.3%.

Transport: Motor vehicles: in use (1990): 117,000 passenger cars, 5,000 comm. vehicles. **Civil aviation** (1990): 571 mln. passenger-km; 1 airport with scheduled flights. **Chief ports:** Asuncion.

Communications: Television sets: 1 per 12 persons. **Radios:** 1 per 5.4 persons. **Telephones:** 1 per 42 persons. **Daily newspaper circ.** (1990): 29 per 1,000 pop.

Health: Life expectancy at birth (1992): 71 male; 74 female. **Births** (per 1,000 pop. 1992): 33. **Deaths** (per 1,000 pop. 1992): 5. **Natural increase:** 2.8%. **Hospital beds:** 1 per 931 persons. **Physicians:** 1 per 1,008 persons. **Infant mortality** (per 1,000 live births 1992): 28.

Education (1991): **Literacy:** 90%. **Years compulsory:** 7. **Attendance:** 83%.

Major International Organizations: UN (IMF, WHO, ILO), OAS.

Embassy: 2400 Massachusetts Ave. NW 20008; 483-6960.

The Guarani Indians were settled farmers speaking a common language before the arrival of Europeans.

Visited by Sebastian Cabot in 1527 and settled as a Spanish possession in 1535, Paraguay gained its independence from Spain in 1811. It lost much of its territory to Brazil, Uruguay, and Argentina in the War of the Triple Alliance, 1865-1870. Large areas were won from Bolivia in the Chaco War, 1932-35.

Gen. Alfredo Stroessner, who ruled since 1954, was ousted in a military coup led by Gen. Andres Rodriguez on Feb. 3, 1989. Rodriguez was elected president May 1. Juan Carlos Wasmosy was elected the nation's first civilian head of state in 1993.

Peru

Republic of Peru

República del Peru

People: Population (1992 est.): 22,767,000. **Age distrib.** (%): 0–14: 37.2; 15–59: 56.8; 60+: 6.0. **Pop. density:** 45 per sq. mi. **Urban** (1992): 70%. **Ethnic groups:** Indians 45%, Mestizos 37%, Caucasians 15%, blacks, Asians. **Languages:** Spanish, Quechua (both official), Aymara. **Religions:** Roman Catholic 90%.

Geography: Area: 496,222 sq. mi., slightly larger than Alaska. **Location:** On the Pacific coast of S. America. **Neighbors:** Ecuador, Colombia on N, Brazil, Bolivia on E, Chile on S. **Topography:** An arid coastal strip, 10 to 100 mi. wide, supports much of the population thanks to widespread irrigation. The Andes cover 27% of land area. The uplands are well-watered, as are the eastern slopes reaching the Amazon basin, which covers half the country with its forests and jungles. **Capital:** Lima. **Cities** (1990 est.): Lima 5,826,000; Arequipa 634,000; Callao 589,000.

Government: Type: in transition. **Head of state:** Pres. Alberto Fujimori; b. July 28, 1938; in office: July 28, 1990. **Head of government:** Prime Min. Oscar de la Puente Raygada; in office: Apr. 6, 1992. **Local divisions:** 24 departments, 1 province. **Defense:** 2.4% of GDP (1991).

Economy: Industries: Fish meal, mineral processing, light industry, textiles. **Chief crops:** Cotton, sugar, coffee, corn. **Minerals:** Copper, lead, molybdenum, silver, zinc, iron, oil. **Crude oil reserves** (1987): 535 mln. bbls. **Other resources:** Wool, sardines. **Arable land:** 3%. **Livestock** (1991): cattle: 3.6 mln.; pigs: 2.3 mln.; sheep: 11.2 mln. **Fish catch** (1990): 6.1 mln. metric tons. **Electricity prod.** (1991): 15.8 bln. kWh. **Labor force:** 38% agric.; 17% ind. and mining; 45% govt. and other services.

Finance: Monetary unit: Nuevo Sol (July 1993: 2.01 = $1 US). **Gross domestic product** (1991): $20.6 bln. **Per capita GDP:** $920. **Imports** (1991): $3.5 bln.; partners: U.S. 32%, EC 17%. **Exports** (1991): $3.3 bln.; partners: U.S. 20%, EC 28%, Jap. 13%. **Tourism** (1990): $353 mln. receipts. **National budget** (1991): $1.8 bln. **International reserves less gold** (Mar. 1993): $2.9 bln. **Gold:** 1.8 mln. oz t. **Consumer prices** (change in 1992): 73.5%.

Transport: Railroads (1991): **Length:** 2,157 mi. **Motor vehicles:** in use (1990): 368,000 passenger cars, 237,000 comm. vehicles. **Civil aviation** (1990): 2.0 bln. passenger-km; 22 airports. **Chief ports:** Callao, Chimbate, Mollendo.

Communications: Television sets: 1 per 11 persons. **Radios:** 1 per 5.2 persons. **Telephones:** 1 per 28 persons. **Daily newspaper circ.** (1987): 57 per 1,000 pop.

Health: Life expectancy at birth (1992): 63 male; 67 female. **Births** (per 1,000 pop. 1992): 28. **Deaths** (per 1,000 pop. 1992): 8. **Natural increase:** 2.0%. **Hospital beds:** 1 per 625 persons. **Physicians:** 1 per 997 persons. **Infant mortality** (per 1,000 live births 1992): 59.

Education (1991): **Literacy:** 85%. **Years compulsory:** 10.

Major International Organizations: UN and all of its specialized agencies, OAS.

Embassy: 1700 Massachusetts Ave. NW 20036; 833-9860.

The powerful Inca empire had its seat at Cuzco in the Andes covering most of Peru, Bolivia, and Ecuador, as well as parts of Colombia, Chile, and Argentina. Building on the achievements of 800 years of Andean civilization, the Incas had a high level of skill in architecture, engineering, textiles, and social organization.

A civil war had weakened the empire when Francisco Pizarro, Spanish conquistador, began raiding Peru for its wealth, 1532. In 1533 he had the seized ruling Inca, Atahualpa, fill a room with gold as a ransom, then executed him and enslaved the natives.

Lima was the seat of Spanish viceroys until the Argentine liberator, Jose de San Martin, captured it in 1821; Spain was defeated by Simon Bolivar and Antonio J. de Sucre; recognized Peruvian independence, 1824.

On Oct. 3, 1968, a military coup ousted Pres. Fernando Belaunde Terry. In 1968-74, the military government put through sweeping agrarian changes, and nationalized oil, mining, fishmeal, and banking industries.

Food shortages, escalating foreign debt, and strikes led to another coup, Aug. 29, 1976, and to a slowdown of socialist programs.

After 12 years of military rule, Peru returned to democratic leadership under former Pres. Fernando Belaunde Terry, July 1980.

Pres. Fujimori dissolved the National Congress, suspended parts of the constitution, and instituted press censorship, Apr. 5, 1992.

Philippines

Republic of the Philippines

People: Population (1992 est.): 67,114,000. **Age distrib.** (%): 0–14: 39.0; 15–59: 56.2; 60+: 4.8. **Pop. density:** 579 per sq. mi. **Urban** (1991): 43%. **Ethnic groups:** Malays the large majority, Chinese, Americans, Spanish are minorities. **Languages:** Pilipino (based on Tagalog), English (both official), Cebuano, Bicol, Ilocano, Pampango, many others. **Religions:** Roman Catholics 83%, Protestants 9%, Moslems 5%.

Geography: Area: 115,831 sq. mi., slightly larger than Arizona. **Location:** An archipelago off the SE coast of Asia. **Neighbors:** Nearest are Malaysia, Indonesia on S, Taiwan on N. **Topography:** The country consists of some 7,100 islands stretching 1,100 mi. N-S. About 95% of area and population are on 11 largest islands, which are mountainous, except for the heavily indented coastlines and for the central plain on Luzon. **Capital:** Quezon City (Manila is de facto capital). **Cities** (1990 est.): Manila 1.8 mln.; Quezon City 1.5 mln.; Cebu 552,000.

Government: Type: Republic. **Head of state:** Pres. Fidel V. Ramos; b. 1928; in office: June 30, 1992. **Local divisions:** 72 provinces, 61 cities. **Defense:** 2.1% of GNP (1991).

Economy: Industries: Food processing, textiles, clothing, drugs, wood prods., appliances. **Chief crops:** Sugar, rice, corn, pineapple, coconut. **Minerals:** Cobalt, copper, gold, nickel, silver, iron, petroleum. **Other resources:** Forests (42% of area). **Arable land:** 26%. **Livestock** (1990): cattle: 1.4 mln.; pigs: 7.8 mln. **Fish catch** (1990): 2.0 mln. metric tons. **Electricity prod.** (1991): 31 bln. kWh. **Labor force:** 47% agric., 20% ind. and comm., 13% services.

Finance: Monetary unit: Peso (May 1993: 25.51 = $1 US). **Gross national product** (1991): $47 bln. **Per capita GNP:** $720. **Imports** (1991): $12.3 bln.; partners: U.S. 25%, Jap. 16%. **Exports** (1991): $8.7 bln.; partners: U.S. 35%, Jap. 17%,

EC 19%. **Tourism** (1990): $1.3 bln. receipts. **National budget** (1991): $9.3 bln. expenditures. **International reserves less gold** (Mar. 1993): $5.7 bln. **Gold:** 2.8 mln. oz t. **Consumer prices** (change in 1992): 8.9%.

Transport: Railroads (1991): **Length:** 658 mi. **Motor vehicles:** in use (1990): 454,000 passenger cars, 783,000 comm. vehicles. **Civil aviation** (1991): 9.3 bln. passenger-km; 31 airports with scheduled flights. **Chief ports:** Cebu, Manila, Iloilo, Davao.

Communications: Television sets: 1 per 8.8 persons. **Radios:** 1 per 16 persons. **Telephones:** 1 per 60 persons. **Daily newspaper circ.** (1988): 44 per 1,000 pop.

Health: Life expectancy at birth (1992): 62 male; 68 female. **Births** (per 1,000 pop. 1992): 29. **Deaths** (per 1,000 pop. 1992): 7. **Natural increase:** 2.2%. **Hospital beds:** 1 per 683 persons. **Physicians:** 1 per 1,062 persons. **Infant mortality** (per 1,000 live births 1992): 54.

Education (1989): **Literacy:** 88%. **Attendance:** 97% in elementary, 55% secondary.

Major International Organizations: UN (World Bank, IMF, GATT), ASEAN.

Embassy: 1617 Massachusetts Ave. NW 20036; 483-1414

The Malay peoples of the Philippine islands, whose ancestors probably migrated from Southeast Asia, were mostly hunters, fishers, and unsettled cultivators when first visited by Europeans.

The archipelago was visited by Magellan, 1521. The Spanish founded Manila, 1571. The islands, named for King Philip II of Spain, were ceded by Spain to the U.S. for $20 million, 1898, following the Spanish-American War. U.S. troops suppressed a guerrilla uprising in a brutal 6-year war, 1899-1905.

Japan attacked the Philippines Dec. 8, 1941 and occupied the islands during WW II.

On July 4, 1946, independence was proclaimed in accordance with an act passed by the U.S. Congress in 1934. A republic was established.

Riots by radical youth groups and terrorism by leftist guerrillas and outlaws, increased from 1970. On Sept. 21, 1972, President Marcos declared martial law. Ruling by decree, he ordered some land reform and stabilized prices. But opposition was suppressed, and a high population growth rate aggravated poverty and unemployment. Political corruption was widespread. On Jan. 17, 1973, Marcos proclaimed a new constitution with himself as president. His wife received wide powers in 1978 to supervise planning and development.

Government troops battled Moslem (Moro) secessionists, 1973-76, in southern Mindanao. Fighting resumed, 1977, after a Libyan-mediated agreement on autonomy was rejected by the region's mainly Christian voters.

Martial law was lifted Jan. 17, 1981. Marcos turned over legislative power to the National Assembly, released political prisoners, and said he would no longer rule by decree. He was re-elected to a new 6-year term as president.

The assassination of prominent opposition leader Benigno S. Aquino Jr, Aug. 21, 1983, sparked demonstrations calling for the resignation of Marcos.

A bitter presidential election campaign ended Feb. 7, 1986 as elections were held amid allegations of widespread fraud. On Feb. 16, Marcos was declared the victor over Corazon Aquino, widow of slain opposition leader Benigno Aquino. Aquino declared herself president and announced a nonviolent "active resistance" to overthrow the Marcos government.

On Feb. 22, 2 leading military allies of Marcos quit their posts to protest the rigged elections. Marcos, Feb. 24, declared a state of emergency as his military and religious support continued to erode. That same day U.S. President Ronald Reagan urged Marcos to resign. Marcos ended his 20-year tenure as president Feb. 26 as he fled the country. Aquino was recognized immediately as president by the U.S. and other nations.

In 1987, Aquino announced the start of land reforms. Candidates endorsed by Aquino won large majorities in legislative elections held in May, attesting to her popularity. She was plagued, however, by a weak economy, widespread poverty, communist insurgents, and lukewarm support from the military.

Rebel troops seized military bases, TV stations, and bombed the presidential palace, Dec. 1, 1989. Government forces defeated the attempted coup with the aid of air cover provided by U.S. F-4s.

The U.S. vacated the Subic Bay Naval Station at the end of 1992; the Philippine government served a notice of eviction following the collapse of talks on a gradual 3-year pull out.

The archipelago has a coastline of 10,850 mi. Manila Bay, with an area of 770 sq. mi., and a circumference of 120 mi., is the finest harbor in the Far East.

All natural resources of the Philippines belong to the state.

Poland

Republic of Poland

Rzeczpospolita Polska

People: Population (1992 est.): 38,385,000. **Age distrib.** (%): 0–14: 25.7; 15–59: 60.2; 60+: 14.1. **Pop. density:** 317 per sq. mi. **Urban** (1992): 62%. **Ethnic groups:** Polish 98%, Germans, Ukrainians, Belorussians. **Language:** Polish. **Religion:** Roman Catholic 94%.

Geography: Area: 120,727 sq. mi., slightly smaller than New Mexico. **Location:** On the Baltic Sea in E Central Europe. **Neighbors:** Germany on W, Czech Rep., Slovakia on S, Lithuania, Belarus, Ukraine on E. **Topography:** Mostly lowlands forming part of the Northern European Plain. The Carpathian Mts. along the southern border rise to 8,200 ft. **Capital:** Warsaw. **Cities** (1991 est.): Warsaw 1.6 mln., Lodz 851,000, Kracow 748,000, Wroclaw 631,000, Poznan 570,000.

Government: Type: Democratic state. **Head of state:** Pres. Lech Walesa; in office: Dec. 22, 1990. **Head of government:** Prime Min. Hanna Suchocka (prior to Sept. 1993 elections). **Local divisions:** 49 provinces.

Economy: Industries: Shipbuilding, chemicals, metals, autos, food processing. **Chief crops:** Grains, potatoes, sugar beets, tobacco, flax. **Minerals:** Coal, copper, zinc, silver, zinc, sulphur, natural gas. **Arable land:** 46%. **Livestock** (1991): cattle: 10.0 mln.; pigs: 19.4 mln. **Fish catch** (1990): 473,000 metric tons. **Electricity prod.** (1991): 136 bln. kWh. **Crude steel prod.** (1991): 10.4 mln. metric tons. **Labor force:** 27% agric.; 36% ind. & comm.; 21% services.

Finance: Monetary unit: Zloty (July 1993: 17,225 = $1 US). **Gross domestic product** (1991): $162.7 bln. **Per capita GDP:** $4,300. **Imports** (1991): $15.7 bln.; partners: CIS 18%, Ger. 15%, Czech. 5%. **Exports** (1991): $14.9 bln.; partners: CIS 25%, E. Ger. 14%, Czech. 6%. **National budget** (1991): $22.4 bln. expenditures. **Tourism** (1990): $266 mln. receipts. **International reserves less gold** (Mar. 1993): $3.5 bln. **Gold:** 473,000. **Consumer prices** (change in 1992): 43.0%.

Transport: Railroads (1991): **Length:** 25,848 km. **Motor vehicles:** in use (1991): 5.2 mln. passenger cars, 1.1 mln. comm. vehicles. **Civil aviation** (1991): 3.4 bln. passenger-km; 12 airports. **Chief ports:** Gdansk, Gdynia, Szczecin.

Communications: Television sets: 1 per 3.9 persons. **Radios:** 1 per 3.6 persons. **Telephones:** 1 per 7.5 persons. **Daily newspaper circ.** (1991): 217 per 1,000 pop.

Health: Life expectancy at birth (1992): 68 male; 76 female. **Births** (per 1,000 pop. 1992): 14. **Deaths** (per 1,000 pop. 1992): 9. **Natural increase:** .5%. **Hospital beds:** 1 per 154 persons. **Physicians:** 1 per 471 persons. **Infant mortality** (per 1,000 live births 1992): 14.

Education (1991): **Literacy:** 98%. **Years compulsory:** 8; attendance 97%.

Major International Organizations: UN (GATT, WHO).

Embassy: 2640 16th St. NW 20009; 234-3800.

Slavic tribes in the area were converted to Latin Christianity in the 10th century. Poland was a great power from the 14th to the 17th centuries. In 3 partitions (1772, 1793, 1795) it was apportioned among Prussia, Russia, and Austria. Overrun by the Austro-German armies in World War I, its independence, self-declared on Nov.11, 1918, was recognized by the Treaty of Versailles, June 28, 1919. Large territories to the east were taken in a war with Russia, 1921.

Germany and the USSR invaded Poland Sept. 1-27, 1939, and divided the country. During the war, some 6 million Polish citizens were killed by the Nazis, half of them Jews. With Germany's defeat, a Polish government-in-exile in London was recognized by the U.S., but the USSR pressed the claims of a rival group. The election of 1947 was completely dominated by the Communists.

In compensation for 69,860 sq. mi. ceded to the USSR, 1945, Poland received approx. 40,000 sq. mi. of German territory E of the Oder-Neisse line comprising Silesia, Pomerania, West Prussia, and part of East Prussia.

In 12 years of rule by Stalinists, large estates were abolished, industries nationalized, schools secularized, and Roman Catholic prelates jailed. Farm production fell off. Harsh working conditions caused a riot in Poznan, June 28-29, 1956.

A new Politburo, committed to development of a more independent Polish Communism, was named Oct. 1956, with Wladyslaw Gomulka as first secretary of the Communist Party. Collectivization of farms was ended and many collectives were abolished.

In Dec. 1970 workers in port cities rioted because of price rises and new incentive wage rules. On Dec. 20 Gomulka resigned as party leader; he was succeeded by Edward Gierek; the incentive rules were dropped, price rises were revoked.

A law promulgated Feb. 13, 1953, required government consent to high Roman Catholic church appointments. In 1956 Gomulka agreed to permit religious liberty and religious publications, provided the church kept out of politics. In 1961 religious studies in public schools were halted.

After 2 months of labor turmoil had crippled the country, the Polish government, Aug. 30, 1980, met the demands of striking workers at the Lenin Shipyard, Gdansk. Among the 21 concessions granted were the right to form independent trade unions and the right to strike — unprecedented political developments in the Soviet bloc. By 1981, 9.5 mln. workers had joined the independent trade union (Solidarity). Farmers won official recognition for their independent trade union in May. Solidarity leaders proposed, Dec. 12, a nationwide referendum on establishing a non-Communist government if the government failed to agree to a series of demands which included access to the mass media and free elections to local councils in the provinces.

Spurred by the fear of Soviet intervention, the government, Dec. 13, imposed martial law. Public gatherings, demonstrations, and strikes were banned and an internal and external blackout was imposed. Solidarity leaders called for a nationwide strike, but there were only scattered work stoppages. Lech Walesa and other Solidarity leaders were arrested. The U.S. imposed economic sanctions which were lifted when martial law was suspended Dec. 1982.

On Apr. 5, 1989, an accord was reached between the government and opposition factions on a broad range of political and economic reforms incl. free elections. In the first free elections in over 40 years, candidates endorsed by Solidarity swept the parliamentary elections, June 4. On Aug. 19, Tadeusz Mazowiecki became the first non-Communist to head an Eastern bloc nation, when he became prime minister. Lech Walesa became president, 1990.

A radical economic program designed to transform the economy into a free-market system drew protests from unions, farmers, and miners because it resulted in inflation and unemployment. In Sept. 1993 elections former Communists and other leftists won a majority of seats in the lower house of parliament.

Portugal

Republic of Portugal

República Portuguesa

People: Population (1992 est.): 10,448,000 (incl. Azores & Madeira Islands). **Age distrib.** (%): 0–14: 22.7; 15–59: 59.9; 60+: 17.4. **Pop. density:** 287 per sq. mi. **Urban** (1990): 34%. **Ethnic groups:** Homogeneous Mediterranean stock with small African minority. **Languages:** Portuguese. **Religions:** Roman Catholics 97%.

Geography: Area: 36,390 sq. mi., incl. the Azores and Madeira Islands, slightly smaller than Indiana. **Location:** At SW extreme of Europe. **Neighbors:** Spain on N, E. **Topography:** Portugal N of Tajus R, which bisects the country NE-SW, is mountainous, cool and rainy. To the S there are drier, rolling plains, and a warm climate. **Capital:** Lisbon. **Cities** (1987 est.): Lisbon 2 mln. (met.), Oporto, 1.5 mln. (met.).

Government: Type: Parliamentary democracy. **Head of state:** Pres. Mario Soares; b. Dec. 7, 1924; in office: Mar. 9, 1986. **Head of government:** Prime Min. Anibal Cavaco Silva; in office: Nov. 6, 1985. **Local divisions:** 18 districts, 2 autonomous regions, one dependency. **Defense:** 2.8% of GDP (1991).

Economy: Industries: Textiles, footwear, cork, chemicals, fish canning, wine, paper. **Chief crops:** Grains, potatoes, rice, grapes, olives, fruits. **Minerals:** Tungsten, uranium, copper, iron. **Other resources:** Forests (world leader in cork production). **Arable land:** 32%. **Livestock** (1991): sheep: 5.6 mln.; pigs: 2.6 mln; cattle: 1.3 mln. **Fish catch** (1990): 321,000 metric tons. **Electricity prod.** (1991): 16 bln. kWh. **Labor force:** 19% agric.; 34% ind. and comm.; 46% services and govt.

Finance: Monetary unit: Escudo (July 1993: 166 = $1 US). **Gross domestic product** (1991): $87 bln. **Per capita GDP:** $8,400. **Imports** (1992): $30.0 bln.; partners: Ger. 12%, UK 8%, Fr. 11%. **Exports** (1992): $18.2 bln.; partners: UK 15%, Ger. 13%, Fr. 13%. **Tourism** (1990): $3.5 bln. receipts. **National budget** (1991): $33.9 bln. expenditures. **International reserves less gold** (Mar. 1993): $19.4 bln. **Gold:** 16.0 mln. oz t. **Consumer prices** (change in 1992): 8.9%.

Transport: Railroads (1991): **Length:** 2,229 mi. **Motor vehicles:** in use (1990): 3.2 mln. passenger cars, 189,000 comm. vehicles. **Civil aviation** (1990): 6.8 bln. passenger-km; 13 airports. **Chief ports:** Lisbon, Setubal, Leixoes.

Communications: Television sets: 1 per 5.8 persons. **Radios:** 1 per 4.2 persons. **Telephones:** 1 per 3.6 persons. **Daily newspaper circ.** (1991): 50 per 1,000 pop.

Health: Life expectancy at birth (1992): 71 male; 78 female. **Births** (per 1,000 pop. 1992): 12. **Deaths** (per 1,000 pop. 1992): 10. **Natural increase:** .2%. **Hospital beds:** 1 per 230 persons. **Physicians:** 1 per 352 persons. **Infant mortality** (per 1,000 live births 1992): 10.

Education (1990): **Literacy:** 83%. **Years compulsory:** 6; attendance 60%.

Major International Organizations: UN (GATT, IMF, WHO), NATO, EC, OECD.

Embassy: 2125 Kalorama Rd. NW 20008; 328-8610.

Portugal, an independent state since the 12th century, was a kingdom until a revolution in 1910 drove out King Manoel II and a republic was proclaimed.

From 1932 a strong, repressive government was headed by Premier Antonio de Oliveira Salazar. Illness forced his retirement in Sept. 1968.

On Apr. 25, 1974, the government was seized by a military junta led by Gen. Antonio de Spinola, who was named president.

The new government reached agreements providing independence for Guinea-Bissau, Mozambique, Cape Verde Islands, Angola, and Sao Tome and Principe. Despite a 64% victory for democratic parties in April 1975, the Soviet-supported Communist party increased its influence. Banks, insurance companies, and other industries were nationalized.

Parliament approved, June 1, 1989, a package of reforms that did away with the socialist economy and created a "democratic" economy and the denationalization of industries.

Azores Islands, in the Atlantic, 740 mi. W. of Portugal, have an area of 868 sq. mi. and a pop. (1992) of 236,000. A 1951 agreement gave the U.S. rights to use defense facilities in the Azores. The **Madeira Islands,** 350 mi. off the NW coast of Africa, have an area of 307 sq. mi. and a pop. (1992) of 253,000. Both groups were offered partial autonomy in 1976.

Macau, area of 6 sq. mi., is an enclave, a peninsula and 2 small islands, at the mouth of the Canton R. in China. Portugal granted broad autonomy in 1976. In 1987, Portugal and China agreed that Macau would revert to China in 1999. Macao, like Hong Kong, was guaranteed 50 years of noninterference in its way of life and capitalist system. Pop. (1992 est.): 367,000.

Qatar

State of Qatar

Dawlet al-Qatar

People: Population (1992 est.): 484,000. **Pop. density:** 113 per sq. mi. **Ethnic groups:** Arab 40%, Pakistani 18%, Indian 10%, Iranian 14%, others. **Languages:** Arabic (official), English. **Religions:** Moslem 95%.

Geography: Area: 4,247 sq. mi., smaller than Connecticut and Rhode Island combined. **Location:** Occupies peninsula on W coast of Persian Gulf. **Neighbors:** Saudi Arabia on W, United Arab Emirates on S. **Topography:** Mostly a flat desert, with some limestone ridges, vegetation of any kind is scarce. **Capital:** Doha. **Cities** (1987 est.): Doha 250,000.

Government: Type: Traditional monarchy. **Head of state and head of government:** Emir & Prime Min. Khalifah ibn Hamad ath-Thani; b. 1932; in office: Feb. 22, 1972 (amir), 1970 (prime min.) **Defense:** 8.0% of GDP (1989).

Economy: Arable land: 2.9%. **Electricity prod.** (1991): 4.2 bln. kWh. **Labor force:** 10% agric., 70% ind., services and commerce.

Finance: Monetary unit: Riyal (Mar. 1993: 3.64 = $1.00 US). **Gross domestic product** (1990): $7.4 bln. **Per capita GDP:** $15,000. **Imports** (1990): $1.4 bln.; partners: Jap. 11%, UK 13%, U.S. 9%. **Exports** (1990): $3.2 bln.; partners: Jap. 61%. **National budget** (1991): $3.2 bln. expenditures.

Transport: Chief ports: Doha, Musayid.

Communications: Television sets: 1 per 2.5 persons. **Radios:** 1 per 2.5 persons. **Telephones:** 1 per 3.4 persons.

Health: Life expectancy at birth (1992): 69 male; 74 female. **Hospital beds:** 1 per 399 persons. **Physicians:** 1 per 568 persons. **Infant mortality** (per 1,000 live births 1992): 24.

Education (1991): **Literacy:** 76%. **Compulsory:** ages 6-16; attendance: 98%.

Major International Organizations: UN (FAO, GATT, IMF, World Bank), Arab League, OPEC.

Embassy: 600 New Hampshire Ave. NW 20037; 338-0111.

Qatar was under Bahrain's control until the Ottoman Turks took power, 1872 to 1915. In a treaty signed 1916, Qatar gave Great Britain responsibility for its defense and foreign relations. After Britain announced it would remove its military forces from the Persian Gulf area by the end of 1971, Qatar sought a federation with other British protected states in the area; this failed and Qatar declared itself independent, Sept. 1 1971.

Oil revenues give Qatar a per capita income among the highest in the world, but lack of skilled labor hampers development plans.

Romania

People: Population (1992 est.): 23,169,000. **Age distrib.** (%): 0–14: 24.7; 15–59: 60.9; 60+: 14.4. **Pop. density:** 252 per sq. mi. **Urban** (1992): 55%. **Ethnic groups:** Romanians 78%, Hungarians 11%. **Languages:** Romanian (official), Hungarian, German. **Religions:** Orthodox 80%, Roman Catholic 6%.

Geography: Area: 91,699 sq. mi., slightly smaller than Oregon. **Location:** In SE Europe on the Black Sea. **Neighbors:** Moldova on E, Ukraine on N, Hungary, Yugoslavia on W, Bulgaria on S. **Topography:** The Carpathian Mts. encase the north-central Transylvanian plateau. There are wide plains S and E of the mountains, through which flow the lower reaches of the rivers of the Danube system. **Capital:** Bucharest. **Cities** (1992 est.): Bucharest 2,064,000, Constanta 350,000, Iasi 342,000, Timisoara 333,000.

Government: Type: Republic. **Head of state:** Pres. Ion Iliescu; in office; Dec. 25, 1989. **Head of government:** Prime Min. Nicolae Vacaroiu; in office; Nov. 4, 1992. **Local divisions:** Bucharest and 40 counties. **Defense:** 4.3% of GNP (1985).

Economy: Industries: Steel, metals, machinery, oil products, chemicals, textiles, shoes, tourism. **Chief crops:** Grains, sunflower, vegetables, potatoes. **Minerals:** Oil, gas, coal. **Other resources:** Timber. **Arable land:** 45%. **Livestock** (1991): cattle: 6.2 mln.; pigs: 11.6 mln.; sheep: 15.4 mln. **Fish catch** (1990): 127,000 metric tons. **Electricity prod.** (1990): 64 bln. kWh. **Crude steel prod.** (1991): 7 mln. metric tons. **Labor force:** 28% agric.; 34% ind. & comm.

Finance: Monetary unit: Lei (Mar. 1993: 598 = $1 US). **Gross domestic product** (1991): $71.9 bln. **Per capita GDP:** $3,100. **Imports** (1991): $15.4 bln.; partners: CIS 50%. **Exports** (1991): $14.0 bln.; partners: CIS 30%. **Tourism** (1990): $106 mln. receipts. **National budget** (1991): $20 bln. expenditures.

Transport: Railroads (1991): **Length:** 6,887 mi. **Motor vehicles:** in use (1992): 1.3 mln. passenger cars; 332,000 comm. vehicles. **Civil aviation** (1991): 1.6 bln. passenger-km; 14 airports. **Chief ports:** Constanta, Galati, Braila.

Communications: Television sets: 1 per 6.0 persons. **Radios:** 1 per 7.3 persons. **Telephones:** 1 per 7.7 persons. **Daily newspaper circ.** (1991): 134 per 1,000 pop.

Health: Life expectancy at birth (1992): 68 male; 74 female. **Births** (per 1,000 pop. 1992): 14. **Deaths** (per 1,000 pop. 1992): 10. **Hospital beds:** 1 per 107 persons. **Physicians:** 1 per 472 persons. **Infant mortality** (per 1,000 live births 1992): 22.

Education (1991): **Literacy:** 96%. **Years compulsory:** 10; attendance 98%.

Major International Organizations: UN (World Bank, IMF, GATT).

Embassy: 1607 23d St. NW 20008; 232-4747.

Romania's earliest known people merged with invading Proto-Thracians, preceding by centuries the Dacians. The Dacian kingdom was occupied by Rome, 106 AD-271 AD; people and language were Romanized. The principalities of Wallachia and Moldavia, dominated by Turkey, were united in 1859, became Romania in 1861. In 1877 Romania proclaimed independence from Turkey, became an independent state by the Treaty of Berlin, 1878, a kingdom, 1881, under Carol I. In 1886 Romania became a constitutional monarchy with a bicameral legislature.

Romania helped Russia in its war with Turkey, 1877-78. After World War I it acquired Bessarabia, Bukovina, Transylvania, and Banat. In 1940 it ceded Bessarabia and Northern Bukovina to the USSR, part of southern Dobrudja to Bulgaria, and northern Transylvania to Hungary.

In 1941, Romanian premier Marshal Ion Antonescu led his country in support of Germany against the USSR. In 1944 Antonescu was overthrown by King Michael and Romania joined the Allies.

With occupation by Soviet troops the communist-headed National Democratic Front displaced the National Peasant party. A People's Republic was proclaimed, Dec. 30, 1947; Michael was forced to abdicate. Land owners were dispossessed; most banks, factories and transportation units were nationalized.

On Aug. 22, 1965, a new constitution proclaimed Romania a Socialist, rather than a People's Republic.

Internal policies were oppressive. Ethnic Hungarians protested cultural and job discrimination, which has led to strained relations with Hungary.

Romania became industrialized, but lagged in consumer goods and in personal freedoms. All industry was state owned, and state farms and cooperatives owned almost all the arable land.

On Dec. 16, 1989, security forces opened fire on demonstrators in Timisoara; hundreds were buried in mass graves. President Nicolae Ceausescu declared a state of emergency as protests spread to other cities. By Dec. 21, the protests had spread to Bucharest where security forces fired on protestors. Army units joined the rebellion, Dec. 22, and a group known as the "Council of National Salvation" announced that it had overthrown the government. Fierce fighting took place between the army, which backed the new government, and forces loyal to Ceausescu.

Ceausescu was captured, Dec. 23 and, following a trial in which he and his wife were found guilty of genocide, was executed Dec. 25. The U.S. and USSR quickly recognized the new government.

Russia

Russian Federation

(Figures prior to 1990 are for the former USSR)

People: Population (1992 est.): 149,527,000. **Age distrib.** (%): –14: 23.1; 15 –59: 61.5; 60+: 15.4. **Pop. density:** 22 per sq. mi. **Urban** (1991): 74%. **Ethnic groups:** Russians 82%, Tatar 3%. **Languages:** Russian (official), Ukrainian, Belorussian, Uzbek, Armenian, Azerbaijani, Georgian, many others. **Religions:** Russian Orthodox 25%, non-religious 60%.

Geography: Area: 6,592,800 sq. mi., over 76% of the total area of the former USSR and is the largest country in the world. **Location:** Stretches from E. Europe across N Asia to the Pacific O. **Neighbors:** Finland, Poland, Norway, Estonia, Belarus, Ukraine on W, Georgia, Azerbaijan, Kazakhstan, China, Mongolia, N. Korea on S. **Topography:** Russia contains every type of climate except the distinctly tropical, and has a varied topography.

The European portion is a low plain, grassy in S, wooded in N, with Ural Mtns. on the E, and Caucasus Mts. on the S. Urals stretch N-S for 2,500 mi. The Asiatic portion is also a vast plain, with mountains on the S and in the E; tundra covers extreme N, with forest belt below; plains, marshes are in W, desert in SW. **Capital:** Moscow. **Cities** (1991 est.): Moscow 8.8 mln.; St. Petersburg 4.4 mln.; Samara 1.2 mln.; Nizhniy Novgorod 1.4 mln.

Government: Type: Federation. **Head of state:** Pres. Boris Yeltsin; b. Feb. 1, 1931; in office: July 10, 1991. **Head of government:** Prime Min. Viktor Chernomyrdin; in office: Dec. 14, 1992. **Local divisions:** 20 autonomous republics, 49 oblasts, 6 krays. **Defense:** 8% of GNP (1991).

Economy: Industries: Steel, machinery, machine tools, vehicles, chemicals, cement, textiles, appliances, paper. **Chief crops:** Grain, cotton, sugar beets, potatoes, vegetables, sunflowers. **Minerals:** Manganese, mercury, potash, bauxite, cobalt, chromium, copper, coal, gold, lead, molybdenum, nickel, phosphates, silver, tin, tungsten, zinc, oil, potassium salts. **Other resources:** Forests. **Arable land:** 11%. **Livestock** (1990): cattle: 118 mln.; sheep: 142 mln.; pigs: 77 mln.; goats 142 mln. **Fish catch** (1989): 10.9 mln. metric tons. **Electricity prod.** (1991): 1,100 bln. kwh. **Crude steel prod.** (1988): 164 mln. metric tons. **Labor force:** 22% agric.; 29% industry, 26% services.

Finance: Monetary unit: Ruble. (Aug. 1993: 987 = $1 US). **Gross domestic product** (1988): $2.5 trl. **Imports** (1991): $43.5 bln.; partners: EC, CIS. **Exports** (1991): $58.7 bln.; partners: EC, CIS. **National budget** (1989): $310 bln. expenditures. **Tourism** (1988): receipts: $216 mln.

Transport: Motor vehicles: in use (1991): 8.9 mln. passenger cars. **Civil aviation** (1990): 153 bln. passenger-km; 58 airports with scheduled flights. **Chief ports:** St. Petersburg, Murmansk, Tver, Archangelsk.

Communications: Television sets: 1 per 3.2 persons. **Radios:** 1 per 1.5 persons. **Telephones:** 1 per 6.7 persons. **Daily newspaper circ.** (1990): 112 per 1,000 pop.

Health: Life expectancy at birth (1992): 63 male; 74 female. **Births** (per 1,000 pop. 1992): 15. **Deaths** (per 1,000 pop. 1992): 11. **Natural increase:** .4%. **Hospital beds:** 1 per 77 persons. **Physicians:** 1 per 221 persons. **Infant mortality** (per 1,000 live births 1992): 31.

Education (1993): **Literacy:** 99%. Most receive 11 years of schooling.

Major International Organizations: UN (ILO, IMF, UNESCO, WHO), CIS.

Embassy: 1125 16th St. NW 20036; 628-7551.

History. Slavic tribes began migrating into Russia from the W in the 5th century AD. The first Russian state, founded by Scandinavian chieftains, was established in the 9th century, centering in Novgorod and Kiev.

In the 13th century the Mongols overran the country. It recovered under the grand dukes and princes of Muscovy, or Moscow, and by 1480 freed itself from the Mongols. Ivan the Terrible was the first to be formally proclaimed Tsar (1547). Peter the Great (1682-1725), extended the domain and in 1721, founded the Russian Empire.

Western ideas and the beginnings of modernization spread through the huge Russian empire in the 19th and early 20th centuries. But political evolution failed to keep pace.

Military reverses in the 1905 war with Japan and in World War I led to the breakdown of the Tsarist regime. The 1917 Revolution began in March with a series of sporadic strikes for higher wages by factory workers. A provisional democratic government under Prince Georgi Lvov was established but was quickly followed in May by the second provisional government, led by Alexander Kerensky. The Kerensky government and the freely-elected Constituent Assembly were overthrown in a communist coup led by Vladimir Ilyich Lenin Nov. 7.

Soviet Union

Lenin's death Jan. 21, 1924, resulted in an internal power struggle from which Joseph Stalin eventually emerged the absolute ruler of Russia. Stalin secured his position at first by exiling opponents, but from the 1930s to 1953, he resorted to a series of "purge" trials, mass executions, and mass exiles to work camps. These measures resulted in millions of deaths, according to most estimates.

Germany and the Soviet Union signed a non-aggression pact Aug. 1939; Germany launched a massive invasion of the Soviet Union, June 1941. Notable heroic episode was the "900 days" siege of Leningrad, lasting to Jan. 1944, and causing a million deaths; the city was never taken. Russian winter counterthrusts, 1941 to '42 and 1942 to '43, stopped the German advance. Turning point was the failure of German troops to take and hold Stalingrad, Sept. 1942 to Feb. 1943. With British and U.S. Lend-Lease aid and sustaining great casualties, the Russians drove the German forces from eastern Europe and the Balkans in the next 2 years.

After Stalin died, Mar. 5, 1953, Nikita Khrushchev was elected first secretary of the Central Committee. In 1956 he condemned Stalin. "De-Stalinization" of the country on all levels was effected after Stalin's body was removed from the Lenin-Stalin tomb in Moscow.

Under Khrushchev the open antagonism of Poles and Hungarians toward domination by Moscow was brutally suppressed in 1956. He advocated peaceful co-existence with the capitalist countries, but continued arming the Soviet Union with nuclear weapons. He aided the Cuban revolution under Fidel Castro but withdrew Soviet missiles from Cuba during confrontation by U.S. Pres. Kennedy, Sept.-Oct. 1962.

Khrushchev was suddenly deposed, Oct. 1964, and replaced as party first secretary by Leonid I. Brezhnev.

In Aug. 1968 Russian, Polish, East German, Hungarian, and Bulgarian military forces invaded Czechoslovakia to put a curb on liberalization policies of the Czech government.

Massive Soviet military aid to North Vietnam in the late 1960s and early 1970s helped assure communist victories throughout Indo-China. Soviet arms aid and advisers were sent to several African countries in the 1970s, including Algeria, Angola, Somalia, and Ethiopia.

In 1979, Soviet forces entered Afghanistan to support that government against rebels. In 1988, the Soviets announced withdrawal of their troops, ending a futile 8-year war.

Mikhail Gorbachev was chosen Gen. Secy. of the Communist Party, Mar. 1985. He was the youngest member of the Politburo and signaled a change in Soviet leadership from those whose attitudes were shaped by Stalinism and World War II.

He held 4 summit meetings with U.S. Pres. Reagan. In 1987, in Washington, an INF treaty was signed.

In 1987, Gorbachev initiated a program of reforms, including expanded freedoms and the democratization of the political process, through openness (*glasnost*) and restructuring (*perestroika*). The reforms were opposed by some Eastern bloc countries and many old-line communists in the USSR. In 1989, the first Soviet Parliament was held since 1918.

Gorbachev faced economic problems as well as ethnic and nationalist unrest in the republics in 1990; the economy was in its worst state since WWII.

On Aug. 19, 1991, it was announced that the vice president had taken over the country due to Gorbachev's ilness. A state of emergency was imposed for 6 months with all power resting with the State Committee on the State of Emergency. The Russian republic's pres. Boris Yeltsin denounced the coup and called for a general strike. Some 50,000 demonstrated at the Russian parliament in support of Yeltsin. By Aug. 21, the coup had failed and Gorbachev was restored as pres. On Aug. 24, Gorbachev resigned as leader of the Communist Party and recommended that its central committee be disbanded. Several republics declared their independence including Russia, Ukraine, and Kazakhstan. On Aug. 29, the Soviet parliament voted to suspend all activities of the Communist Party.

On Sept. 2, Gorbachev declared that the nation was "on the brink of catastrophe," and proposed to transfer all central authority to himself, the leaders of 10 republics, and an appointed legislative council in order to form a new kind of Soviet Union.

The Soviet Union officially broke up Dec. 26, 1991, one day after Gorbachev resigned. The Soviet hammer and sickle flying over the Kremlin was lowered and replaced by the flag of Russia, ending the domination of the Communist Party over all areas of national life since 1917.

Russian Federation

In the first major step in radical economic reform, Russia eliminated state subsidies of most goods and services, Jan. 1992. The effect was to allow prices to soar far beyond the means of ordinary workers. Pres. Yeltsin met with Pres. Bush in Washington, D.C., June 16-17. The two leaders agreed to massive arms reductions. Yeltsin addressed a joint session of Congress and appealed for economic aid for the CIS.

Russia launched a drive to privatize thousands of large and medium-sized state-owned enterprises in 1993. Pres. Yeltsin narrowly survived an impeachment vote by the Congress of People's Deputies, Mar. 28. Yeltsin received strong support from voters in a countrywide referendum Apr. 25, but he continued to feud with a legislature dominated by conservatives and former Communists.

Rwanda

Republic of Rwanda

Republika y'u Rwanda

People: Population (1992 est.): 8,206,000. **Age distrib.** (%): 0–14: 48.7; 15–59: 47.1; 60+: 4.2. **Pop. density:** 806 per sq. mi. **Urban** (1991): 5%. **Ethnic groups:** Hutu 90%, Tutsi 9%, Twa (pygmies) 1%. **Languages:** French, Rwanda (both official). **Religions:** Christian 74%, traditional 25%, Moslem 1%.

Geography: Area: 10,169 sq. mi., the size of Maryland. **Location:** In E central Africa. **Neighbors:** Uganda on N, Zaire on W, Burundi on S, Tanzania on E. **Topography:** Grassy uplands and hills cover most of the country, with a chain of volcanoes in the NW. The source of the Nile R. has been located in the headwaters of the Kagera (Akagera) R., SW of Kigali. **Capital:** Kigali. **Cities** (1991 est.): Kigali 232,000.

Government: Type: Republic. **Head of state:** Pres. Juvenal Habyarimana; b. Mar. 8, 1937; in office: July 5, 1973. **Head of government:** Prime Min. Dismas Nsengiyaremye; in office: Apr. 2, 1992. **Local divisions:** 10 prefectures. **Defense:** 1.6% of GDP (1989).

Economy: Chief crops: Coffee, tea. **Minerals:** Tin, gold, wolframite. **Arable land:** 29%. **Electricity prod.** (1991): 130 mln. kWh. **Labor force:** 91% agric.

Finance: Monetary unit: Franc (Apr. 1993: 145 = $1 US). **Gross domestic product** (1990): $2.1 bln. **Per capita GDP:** $310. **Imports** (1990): $279.2 mln.; partners: Ken. 21%, Belg. 16%, Jap. 12%, W. Ger. 9%. **Exports** (1990): $111.7 mln.; partners: EC, Ugan. **National budget** (1989): $491 million expenditures. **International reserves less gold** (Mar. 1993): $64 mln. **Consumer prices** (change in 1992): 9.5%.

Transport: Motor vehicles: in use (1990): 8,000 passenger cars, 10,000 comm. vehicles.

Communications: Radios: 1 per 11 persons. **Telephones:** 1 per 497 persons.

Health: Life expectancy at birth (1992): 51 male; 55 female. **Births** (per 1,000 pop. 1992): 52. **Deaths** (per 1,000 pop. 1992): 15. **Natural increase:** 3.7%. **Hospital beds** (1984): 9,000. **Physicians** (1984): 177. **Infant mortality** (per 1,000 live births 1992): 108.

Education (1991): **Literacy:** 50%. **Years compulsory:** 8; **attendance:** 70%.

Major International Organizations: UN (GATT, IMF, WHO), OAU.

Embassy: 1714 New Hampshire Ave. NW 20009; 232-2882.

For centuries, the Tutsi (an extremely tall people) dominated the Hutus (90% of the population). A civil war broke out in 1959 and Tutsi power was ended. A referendum in 1961 abolished the monarchic system. Some 8,000 exiled Tutsi invaded Rwanda from Uganda, Sept. 1990. A new constitution was signed into effect in 1991 calling for multiparty politics, freedom of the press, and a limited presidential term. A peace accord between the government and the Tutsi rebels was signed in Aug. 1993.

Rwanda, which had been part of the Belgian UN trusteeship of Rwanda-Urundi, became independent July 1, 1962. The government was overthrown in a 1973 military coup. Rwanda is one of the most densely populated countries in Africa. All available arable land is being used, and is being subject to erosion.

Saint Kitts and Nevis

Federation of Saint Kitts & Nevis

People: Population (1992 est.): 40,293. **Pop. density:** 398 per sq. mi. **Ethnic groups:** black African 95%. **Language:** English. **Religion:** Protestant 76%.

Geography: Area: 101 sq. mi. in the northern part of the Leeward group of the Lesser Antilles in the eastern Caribbean Sea. **Capitol:** Basseterre. (1989): 15,000.

Government: Constitutional monarchy. **Head of state:** Queen Elizabeth represented by Sir Clement Arrindell. **Head of government:** Prime Minister Kennedy A. Simmonds; b. Apr. 12, 1936; in office: Sept. 19, 1983.

Economy: Sugar is the principal industry.

Finance: Monetary unit: E. Caribbean Dollar (Mar. 1993): 2.70 = $1 U.S. **Gross domestic product** (1990): $146 mln. **Tourism** (1990): $63 mln. receipts.

Communications: Telephones: 1 per 6 persons.

Health: Infant mortality (per 1,000 live births, 1992): 22.

Education: Literacy (1991): 98%.

St. Kitts (known by the natives as Liamuiga) and Nevis were reached (and named) by Columbus in 1493. They were settled by Britain in 1623, but ownership was disputed with France until 1713. They were part of the Leeward Islands Federation, 1871-1956, and the Federation of the W. Indies, 1958-62. The colony achieved self-government as an Associated State of the UK in 1967, and became fully independent Sept. 19, 1983.

Saint Lucia

People: Population (1992 est.): 151,000. **Age distrib.** (%): 0–20: 44.5; 21–64: 47.5; 65+: 8.0. **Pop. density:** 634 per sq. mi. **Ethnic groups:** Predominantly African descent. **Languages:** English (official), French patois. **Religions:** Roman Catholic 90%.

Geography: Area: 238 sq. mi., about one-fifth the size of Rhode Island. **Location:** In Eastern Caribbean, 2d largest of the Windward Is. **Neighbors:** Martinique to N, St. Vincent to SW. **Topography:** Mountainous, volcanic in origin; Soufriere, a volcanic crater, in the S. Wooded mountains run N-S to Mt. Gimie, 3,145 ft., with streams through fertile valleys. **Capital:** Castries. **City:** Castries (1989 est.): 55,000.

Government: Type: Parliamentary democracy. **Head of state:** Queen Elizabeth II, represented by Gov.-Gen. S.A. James; **Head of government:** Prime Min. John Compton; in office: May 3, 1982. **Local divisions:** 11 quarters

Economy: Industries: Agriculture, tourism, manufacturing. **Chief crops:** Bananas, coconuts, cocoa, citrus fruits. **Other resources:** Forests. **Arable land:** 8%. **Electricity prod.** (1991): 112 mln. kWh. **Labor force:** 36% agric., 20% ind. & commerce, 18% services.

Finance: Monetary unit: East Caribbean dollar (Mar. 1993: 2.70 = $1 US). **Gross domestic product** (1990): $295 mln. **Per capita GDP:** $1,930. **Imports** (1990): $270 mln.; partners: U.S. 36%, UK 12%, Trin./Tob. 11%. **Exports** (1990): $127 mln.; partners: U.S. 19%, UK 51%. **Tourism** (1990): receipts: $155 mln.

Transport: Motor vehicles: in use (1989): 7,000 passenger cars, 4,000 comm. vehicles. **Chief ports:** Castries, Vieux Fort.

Communications: Television sets: 1 per 6 persons. **Radios:** 1 per 1.5 persons. **Telephones:** 1 per 10 persons.

Health: Life expectancy at birth (1992): 70 male; 75 female. **Births** (per 1,000 pop. 1992): 26. **Deaths** (per 1,000 pop. 1992): 5. **Natural increase:** 2.1%. **Hospital beds:** 1 per 283 persons. **Physicians:** 1 per 2,521 persons. **Infant mortality** (per 1,000 live births 1992): 18.

Education: Literacy (1989): 78%; **Years compulsory:** ages 5-15; **Attendance:** 80%.

Major International Organizations: UN (IMF, ILO), CARICOM, OAS.

St. Lucia was ceded to Britain by France at the Treaty of Paris, 1814. Self government was granted with the West Indies Act, 1967. Independence was attained Feb. 22, 1979.

Saint Vincent and the Grenadines

People: Population (1992 est.): 114,000. **Pop. density:** 760 per sq. mi. **Ethnic groups:** Mainly of African descent. **Languages:** English. **Religions:** Methodists, Anglicans, Roman Catholics.

Geography: Area: 150 sq. mi., about twice the size of Washington, D.C. **Location:** In the eastern Caribbean, St. Vincent (133 sq. mi.) and the northern islets of the Grenadines form a part of the Windward chain. **Neighbors:** St. Lucia to N, Barbados to E, Grenada to S. **Topography:** St. Vincent is volcanic, with a ridge of thickly wooded mountains running its length. **Capital:** Kingstown. **Cities** (1991 est.): Kingstown 15,000.

Government: Type: Constitutional monarchy. **Head of state:** Queen Elizabeth II, represented by Gov.-Gen. David Jack; in office: Sept. 20 1989. **Head of government:** James Mitchell; in office: July 30, 1984.

Economy: Industries: Agriculture, tourism. **Chief crops:** Bananas (62% of exports), arrowroot, coconuts. **Arable land:** 50%. **Electricity prod.** (1991): 63 mln. kWh. **Labor force:** 30% agric.

Finance: Monetary unit: East Caribbean dollar (Mar. 1993: 2.70 = $1 US). **Gross domestic product** (1989): $146 mln. **Per capita GDP** (1989): $1,315. **Tourism** (1991): $53 mln. receipts. **National budget** (1990): $67 mln. expenditures.

Transport: Motor vehicles: in use (1991): 5,000 passenger cars, 2,800 comm. vehicles. **Chief port:** Kingstown.

Communications: Telephones: 1 per 6 persons.

Health: Life expectancy at birth (1992): 71 male; 74 female. **Births** (per 1,000 pop. 1992): 23. **Deaths** (per 1,000 pop. 1992): 5. **Natural increase:** 1.7%. **Infant mortality** (per 1,000 live births 1992): 19.

Education (1989): **Literacy:** 85%.

Columbus landed on St. Vincent on Jan. 22, 1498 (St. Vincent's Day). Britain and France both laid claim to the island in the 17th and 18th centuries; the Treaty of Versailles, 1783, finally ceded it to Britain. Associated State status was granted 1969; independence was attained Oct. 27, 1979.

The entire economic life of St. Vincent is dependent upon agriculture and tourism.

San Marino

Most Serene Republic of San Marino

Serenissima Repubblica di San Marino

People: Population (1992 est.): 23,000. **Age distrib.** (%): 0–14: 16.1; 15–59: 65.3; 60+: 16.1. **Pop. density:** 958 per sq. mi. **Urban** (1992): 90.5%. **Ethnic groups:** Sanmarinese 80%, Italian 18%. **Languages:** Italian. **Religion:** mostly Roman Catholic.

Geography: Area: 24 sq. mi. **Location:** in N central Italy near Adriatic coast. **Neighbors:** Completely surrounded by Italy. **Topography:** The country lies on the slopes of Mt. Titano. **Capital:** San Marino. **Cities** (1991 est.): San Marino 4,643.

Government: Type: Republic. **Head of state:** Two co-regents appt. every 6 months. **Local divisions:** 9 municipalities.

Economy: Industries: Postage stamps, tourism, woolen goods, paper, cement, ceramics. **Arable land:** 17%.

Finance: Monetary unit: Italian lira. **Gross domestic product** (1991): $400 mln. **Tourism** (1991): 3.1 mln. arrivals.

Communications: Television sets: 1 per 3.4 persons. **Radios:** 1 per 1.8 persons. **Telephones:** 1 per 1.6 persons.

Births (per 1,000 pop. 1992): 8. **Deaths** (per 1,000 pop. 1992): 7. **Natural increase:** 0.1%. **Infant mortality** (per 1,000 live births 1992): 8.

Education (1991): **Literacy:** 97%. **Years compulsory:** 8. **Attendance:** 93%.

Major International Organizations: UN.

San Marino claims to be the oldest state in Europe and to have been founded in the 4th century. A communist-led coalition ruled 1947-57; a similar coalition ruled 1978-86. It has had a treaty of friendship with Italy since 1862.

São Tomé and Príncipe

Democratic Republic of São Tomé and Príncipe

República Democrática de São Tomé e Príncipe

People: Population (1992 est.): 132,000. **Pop. density:** 354 per sq. mi. **Ethnic groups:** Portuguese-African mixture, African minority (Angola, Mozambique immigrants). **Languages:** Portuguese. **Religions:** Christian 80%.

Geography: Area: 372 sq. mi., slightly larger than New York City. **Location:** In the Gulf of Guinea about 125 miles off W Central Africa. **Neighbors:** Gabon, Equatorial Guinea on E. **Topography:** São Tomé and Príncipe islands, part of an extinct volcano chain, are both covered by lush forests and croplands. **Capital:** São Tomé. **Cities** (1988 est.): São Tomé 40,000.

Government: Type: Republic. **Head of state:** Pres. Miguel Trovoada; in office: Apr. 3, 1991. **Head of government:** Prime Min. Norberto Jose D'Alva Costa Alegre Daio; in office: May 16, 1992. **Local divisions:** 2 districts.

Economy: Chief crops: Cocoa (82% of exports), coconut products. **Arable land:** 38%. **Electricity prod.** (1991): 10 mln. kWh.

Finance: Monetary unit: Dobra (Jan. 1993: 240 = $1 US). **Gross domestic product** (1989): $46 mln. **Per capita GDP:** $384. **Imports** (1990): $21.3 mln.; partners: Port. 61%, Angola 13%. **Exports** (1990): $4.4 mln.; partners: Neth. 52%, Port. 33%, Ger. 8%.

Transport: Chief ports: São Tomé, Santo Antonio.

Communications: Radios: 1 per 3.9 persons.

Health: Births (per 1,000 pop. 1992): 38. **Deaths** (per 1,000 pop. 1992): 7. **Natural increase:** 3.0%. **Physicians:** 1 per 2,819 persons. **Infant mortality** (per 1,000 live births 1992): 58.

Education (1988): **Literacy:** 50%.

Major International Organizations: UN, OAU.

Embassy: 801 2d Ave., New York, NY 10017; 212-697-4211.

The islands were uninhabited when discovered in 1471 by the Portuguese, who brought the first settlers — convicts and exiled Jews. Sugar planting was replaced by the slave trade as the chief economic activity until coffee and cocoa were introduced in the 19th century.

Portugal agreed, 1974, to turn the colony over to the Gabon-based Movement for the Liberation of São Tomé and Principe, which proclaimed as first president its East German-trained leader Manuel Pinto da Costa. Independence came July 12, 1975. Democratic reforms were instituted in 1987. In 1991 Miguel Trovoada won the first free presidential election following the withdrawal of Pres. Manuel Pinto da Costa. Da Costa had ruled the country since independence.

Agriculture and fishing are the mainstays of the economy.

Saudi Arabia

Kingdom of Saudi Arabia

al-Mamlaka al-'Arabiya as-Sa'udiya

People: Population (1992 cen.): 16,900,000. **Pop. density:** 20 per sq. mi. **Urban** (1990): 78%. **Ethnic groups:** Arab tribes, immigrants from other Arab and Moslem countries. **Language:** Arabic. **Religion:** Moslem 99%.

Geography: Area: 839,996 sq. mi., one-third the size of the U.S. **Location:** Occupies most of Arabian Peninsula in Middle East. **Neighbors:** Kuwait, Iraq, Jordan on N, Yemen, Oman on S, United Arab Emirates, Qatar on E. **Topography:** The highlands on W, up to 9,000 ft., slope as an arid, barren desert to the Persian Gulf. **Capital:** Riyadh. **Cities** (1986 est.): Riyadh 1,380,000; Jidda 1,210,000; Mecca 463,000.

Government: Type: Monarchy with council of ministers. **Head of state and head of government:** King Fahd; b. 1922; in office: June 13, 1982. **Local divisions:** 14 emirates. **Defense:** 13% of GDP (1992).

Economy: Industries: Oil products. **Chief crops:** Dates, wheat, barley, fruit. **Minerals:** Oil, gas, gold, copper, iron. **Crude oil reserves** (1990): 255 bln. barrels. **Arable land:** 2%. **Livestock** (1991): sheep: 5.6 mln.; goats; 3.5 mln. **Electricity prod.** (1991): 60 bln. kWh. **Labor force:** 14% agric.; 11% ind.; 53% serv., comm., & govt.; 20% construction.

Finance: Monetary unit: Riyal (July 1993: 3.70 = $1 US). **Gross domestic product** (1991): $104 bln. **Per capita GDP:** $5,800. **Imports** (1990): $21.5 bln.; partners: US 15%, Jap. 12%, UK 14%. **Exports** (1990): $28.3 bln.; partners: U.S. 22%, Jap. 20%. **National budget** (1990): $38 bln. expenditures. **International reserves less gold** (Mar. 1992): $11.6 bln. **Gold:** 4.59 mln. oz t. **Consumer prices** (change in 1991): 4.1%.

Transport: Railroads (1989): **Length:** 555 mi. **Motor vehicles:** in use (1989): 2.2 mln. passenger cars, 2.0 mln. comm. vehicles. **Civil aviation** (1990): 16.0 bln.; passenger-km.; 25 airports. **Chief ports:** Jidda, Ad-Dammam, Ras Tannurah.

Communications: Television sets: 1 per 3.5 persons. **Radios:** 1 per 3.3 persons. **Telephones:** 1 per 13 persons. **Daily newspaper circ.** (1989): 49 per 1,000 pop.

Health: Life expectancy at birth (1991): 65 male; 68 female. **Births** (per 1,000 pop. 1991): 38. **Deaths** (per 1,000 pop. 1991): 7. **Natural increase:** 3.1%. **Hospital beds:** 1 per 406 persons. **Physicians:** 1 per 852 persons. **Infant mortality** (per 1,000 live births 1991): 69.

Education (1990): **Literacy:** 62%.

Major International Organizations: UN (IMF, WHO, FAO), Arab League, OPEC.

Embassy: 601 New Hampshire Ave. NW 20037; 342-3800.

Arabia was united for the first time by Mohammed, in the early 7th century. His successors conquered the entire Near East and North Africa, bringing Islam and the Arabic language. But Arabia itself soon returned to its former status.

Nejd, long an independent state and center of the Wahhabi sect, fell under Turkish rule in the 18th century, but in 1913 Ibn Saud, founder of the Saudi dynasty, overthrew the Turks and captured the Turkish province of Hasa; took the Hejaz in 1925 and by 1926, most of Asir. The discovery of oil in the 1930s transformed the new country.

Crown Prince Khalid was proclaimed king on Mar. 25, 1975, after the assassination of King Faisal. Fahd became king on June 13, 1982 following Khalid's death. There is no constitution and no parliament. The king exercises authority together with a Council of Ministers. The Islamic religious code is the law of the land. Alcohol and public entertainments are restricted, and women have an inferior legal status.

Saudi units fought against Israel in the 1948 and 1973 Arab-Israeli wars. Many billions of dollars of advanced arms have been purchased from Britain, France, and the U.S., including jet fighters, missiles, and, in 1981, 5 airborne warning and control system (AWACS) aircraft from the U.S., despite strong opposition from Israel. Beginning with the 1967 Arab-Israeli war, Saudi Arabia provided large annual financial gifts to Egypt; aid was later extended to Syria, Jordan, and Palestinian guerrilla groups, as well as to other Moslem countries.

Faisal played a leading role in the 1973-74 Arab oil embargo against the U.S. and other nations in an attempt to force them to adopt an anti-Israel policy. Saudi Arabia joined most other Arab states, 1979, in condemning Egypt's peace treaty with Israel.

In the 1980s, Saudi Arabia's moderate position on crude oil prices often prevailed at OPEC meetings.

The Hejaz contains the holy cities of Islam — Medina where the Mosque of the Prophet enshrines the tomb of Mohammed, who died in the city June 7, 632, and Mecca, his birthplace. More than 600,000 Moslems from 60 nations pilgrimage to Mecca annually.

Two Saudi oil tankers were attacked May 1984, as Iran and Iraq began air attacks against shipping in the Persian Gulf. On May 29, the U.S., citing grave concern over the growing escalation of the Iran-Iraq war in the Persian Gulf, authorized the sale of 400 Stinger antiaircraft missiles.

In 1987, Iranians making a pilgrimage to Mecca clashed with anti-Iranian pilgrims and Saudi police; over 400 were killed. Saudi Arabia broke diplomatic relations with Iran in 1988. Some 1,426 Moslem pilgrims died July 2, 1990 when a stampede occurred in a pedestrian tunnel leading to Mecca.

Following Iraq's attack on Kuwait, Aug. 2, 1990, Saudi Arabia accepted the Kuwait royal family and over 400,000 Kuwaiti refugees. King Fahd invited Western and Arab troops to deploy on its soil in support of Saudi defense forces. During the Persian Gulf war, Iraq fired a series of Scud missiles at Saudi Arabia; most were intercepted by U.S. Patriot missiles, although 28 U.S. soldiers were killed when a scud hit their barracks in Dhahran, Feb. 25. The nation's northern Gulf coastline suffered severe pollution as a result of Iraqi sabotage of the Kuwaiti oil fields.

Senegal

Republic of Senegal

République du Sénégal

People: Population (1992 est.): 8,205,000. **Age distrib.** (%): 0–14: 47.5; 15–59: 47.5; 60+: 5.0. **Pop. density:** 108 per sq. mi. **Urban** (1986): 30%. **Ethnic groups:** Wolof 36%, Serer 17%, Fulani 17%, Diola 9%, Toucouleur 9%, Mandingo 6%. **Languages:** French (official), Wolof, Serer, Peul, Tukulor, others. **Religions:** Moslem 92%, Christian 2%.

Geography: Area: 75,750 sq. mi., the size of South Dakota. **Location:** At western extreme of Africa. **Neighbors:** Mauritania on N, Mali on E, Guinea, Guinea-Bissau on S, Gambia surrounded on three sides. **Topography:** Low rolling plains cover most of Senegal, rising somewhat in the SE. Swamp and jungles are in SW. **Capital:** Dakar. **Cities** (1992): Dakar 1.7 mln.; Thies 201,000; Kaolack 179,000.

Government: Type: Republic. **Head of state:** Pres. Abdou Diouf; b. Sept. 7, 1935; in office: Jan. 1, 1981. **Head of government:** Habib Thiam; in office: Apr. 8, 1991. **Local divisions:** 10 regions. **Defense:** 2.0% of GDP (1989).

Economy: Industries: Food processing, fishing. **Chief crops:** Peanuts are chief export; millet, rice. **Minerals:** Phosphates. **Arable land:** 27%. **Livestock** (1991): cattle: 2.8 mln.; sheep: 4.0 mln.; goats: 1.2 mln. **Fish catch** (1989): 255,000 metric tons. **Electricity prod.** (1991): 758 mln. kWh. **Labor force:** 77% agric.

Finance: Monetary unit: CFA franc (Mar. 1993: 273 = $1 US). **Gross domestic product** (1990): $5.0 bln. **Per capita GDP:** $615. **Imports** (1990): $1.0 bln.; partners Fr. 37%, U.S. 6%. **Exports** (1990): $814 mln.; partners Fr. 25%, UK 6%. **Tourism** (1990): $152 mln. receipts. **National budget** (1989): $1.0 bln. expenditures. **International reserves less gold** (Jan. 1993): $12.4 mln. **Gold:** 29,000 oz t. **Consumer prices** (change in 1991): 1.8%.

Transport: Railroads (1992): **Length:** 562 mi. **Motor vehicles:** in use (1989): 90,000 passenger cars, 36,000 comm. vehicles. **Chief ports:** Dakar, Saint-Louis.

Communications: Television sets: 1 per 125 persons. **Radios:** 1 per 8.7 persons. **Telephones:** 1 per 150 persons. **Daily newspaper circ.** (1990): 7 per 1,000 pop.

Health: Life expectancy at birth (1992): 54 male, 57 female. **Births** (per 1,000 pop. 1992): 44. **Deaths** (per 1,000 pop. 1992): 13. **Natural increase:** 2.9%. **Hospital beds:** 1 per 1,134 persons. **Physicians:** 1 per 17,072 persons. **Infant mortality** (per 1,000 live births 1992): 80.

Education (1988): **Literacy:** 10%. **Attendance:** 48% primary, 11% secondary.

Major International Organizations: UN and all of its specialized agencies, OAU.

Embassy: 2112 Wyoming Ave. NW 20008; 234-0540.

Portuguese settlers arrived in the 15th century, but French control grew from the 17th century. The last independent Moslem state was subdued in 1893. Dakar became the capital of French West Africa.

Independence as part, along with the Sudanese Rep., of the Mali Federation, came June 20, 1960. Senegal withdrew Aug. 20. French political and economic influence is strong.

Senegal, Dec. 17, 1981, signed an agreement with The Gambia for confederation of the 2 countries under the name of Senegambia. The confederation began Feb. 1, 1982. The 2 nations retained their individual sovereignty but adopted joint defense and monetary policies. The confederation collapsed in 1989, although in 1991 the 2 nations signed a friendship and cooperation treaty.

In 1989, a border incident sparked ethnic violence against Senegalese in Mauritania and, in retaliation, against Mauritanians in Senegal.

Seychelles

Republic of Seychelles

People: Population (1992 est.): 68,000. **Age distrib.** (%): 0–14: 36.3; 15–64; 57.3; 65+: 6.4. **Pop. density:** 397 per sq. mi. **Urban** (1990): 60% **Ethnic groups:** Creoles (mixture of Asians, Africans, and French) predominate. **Languages:** English, French, (both official). **Religions:** Roman Catholic 90%.

Geography: Area: 171 sq. mi. **Location:** In the Indian O. 700 miles NE of Madagascar. **Neighbors:** Nearest are Madagascar on SW, Somalia on NW. **Topography:** A group of 86 islands, about half of them composed of coral, the other half granite, the latter predominantly mountainous. **Capital:** Victoria. **Cities** (1986): Victoria 23,000.

Government: Type: Single party republic. **Head of state:** Pres. France-Albert Rene, b. Nov. 16, 1935; in office: June 5, 1977. **Local divisions:** 23 districts. **Defense:** 6.0% of GDP (1990).

Economy: Industries: Food processing. **Chief crops:** Coconut products, cinnamon, vanilla, patchouli. **Electricity prod.** (1991): 80 mln. kWh. **Labor force:** 12% agric.; 19.4% tourism, comm.; 32% serv.; 40% govt.

Finance: Monetary unit: Rupee (Mar. 1993: 5.21 = $1 US). **Gross domestic product** (1991): $350 mln. **Per capita GDP:** $5,200. **Imports** (1991): $172 mln.; partners: UK 20%, So. Afr. 13%. **Exports** (1991): $48 mln.; partners: Pak. 38%; Jap. 26%. **National Budget** (1989): $168 mln. **Tourism** (1991): $97 mln. receipts. **International reserves less gold** (Mar. 1993): $26.5 mln. **Consumer prices** (change in 1992): 3.3%.

Transport: Motor vehicles: in use (1989): 4,000 passenger cars, 1,300 comm. vehicles. **Port:** Victoria.

Communications: Radios: 1 per 3 persons. **Telephones:** 1 per 5 persons. **Daily newspaper circ.** (1990): 47 per 1,000 pop.

Health: Life expectancy at birth (1992): 65 male; 75 female. **Births** (per 1,000 pop. 1992): 23. **Deaths** (per 1,000 pop. 1992): 7. **Natural increase:** 1.6%. **Hospital beds:** 1 per 171 persons. **Physicians:** 1 per 992 persons. **Infant mortality** (per 1,000 live births 1992): 15.

Education (1991): **Literacy:** 85%. **Years compulsory** 9; attendance 98%.

Major International Organizations: UN, OAU, Commonwealth of Nations.

The islands were occupied by France in 1768, and seized by Britain in 1794. Ruled as part of Mauritius from 1814, the Seychelles became a separate colony in 1903. The ruling party had opposed independence as impractical, but pressure from the OAU and the UN became irresistible, and independence was declared June 29, 1976. The first president was ousted in a coup a year later by a socialist leader.

A new constitution, announced Mar. 1979, turned the country into a one-party state.

Sierra Leone

Republic of Sierra Leone

People: Population (1992 est.): 4,456,000. **Age distrib.** (%): 0–14: 41.4; 15–59: 53.5; 60+: 5.1. **Pop. density:** 159 per sq. mi. **Urban** (1991): 33%. **Ethnic groups:** Temne 30%, Mende 29%, others. **Languages:** English (official), tribal languages. **Religions:** animist 30%, Moslem 30%, Christian 10%.

Geography: Area: 27,925 sq. mi., slightly smaller than South Carolina. **Location:** On W coast of W. Africa. **Neighbors:** Guinea on N, E, Liberia on S. **Topography:** The heavily-indented, 210-mi. coastline has mangrove swamps. Behind are wooded hills, rising to a plateau and mountains in the E. **Capital:** Freetown. **Cities** (1985 est.): Freetown 469,000; Bo, Kenema, Makeni.

Government: Type: Military. **Head of government:** Capt. Valentine E. M. Strasser; in office: May 7, 1992. **Local divisions:** 4 provinces.

Economy: Industries: Mining, tourism. **Chief crops:** Cocoa, coffee, palm kernels, rice, ginger. **Minerals:** Diamonds, bauxite. **Arable land:** 25%. **Fish catch** (1990): 52,000 metric tons. **Electricity prod.** (1991): 185 mln. kWh. **Labor force:** 75% agric.; 15% ind. & serv.

Finance: Monetary unit: Leone (Mar. 1993: 561 = $1.00 US). **Gross domestic product** (1991): $1.4 bln. **Per capita GDP:** $330. **Imports** (1992): $131 mln.; partners: UK 22%, Fr. 11%. **Exports** (1992): $145 mln.; partners: Neth. 31%; UK 15%, U.S. 9%. **National budget** (1991): $181 mln. expenditures. **International reserves less gold** (Mar. 1993): $23 mln. **Consumer prices** (change in 1992): 65.5%.

Transport: Motor Vehicles: in use (1989): 29,000 passenger cars, 10,000 comm. vehicles. **Chief ports:** Freetown, Bonthe.

Communications: Television sets: 1 per 170 persons. **Radios:** 1 per 4.2 persons. **Telephones:** 1 per 160 persons. **Daily newspaper circ.** (1991): 3 per 1,000 pop.

Health: Life expectancy at birth (1992): 43 male; 48 female. **Births** (per 1,000 pop. 1992): 46. **Deaths** (per 1,000 pop. 1992): 21. **Natural increase:** 2.5%. **Hospital beds:** 1 per 980 persons. **Physicians:** 1 per 13,150 persons. **Infant mortality** (per 1,000 live births 1992): 148.

Education (1991): **Literacy:** 21%.

Major International Organizations: UN (GATT, IMF, WHO), Commonwealth of Nations, OAU.

Embassy: 1701 19th St. NW 20009; 939-9261.

Freetown was founded in 1787 by the British government as a haven for freed slaves. Their descendants, known as Creoles, number more than 60,000.

Successive steps toward independence followed the 1951 constitution. Full independence arrived Apr. 27, 1961. Sierra Leone became a republic Apr. 19, 1971. A one-party state approved by referendum 1978, brought political stability, but the economy has been plagued by inflation, corruption, and dependence upon the International Monetary Fund and creditors.

Mutinous soldiers ousted Pres. Momoh Apr. 30, 1992.

Singapore

Republic of Singapore

People: Population (1992 est.): 2,792,000. **Age distrib.** (%): 0–14: 23.4; 15–59: 68.4; 60+: 8.2. **Pop. density:** 12,464 per sq. mi. **Ethnic groups:** Chinese 77%, Malays 15%, Indians 6%. **Languages:** Chinese, Malay, Tamil, English all official. **Religions:** Buddhism 29%, Taoism 13%, Moslem 16%, Christian 19%.

Geography: Area: 224 sq. mi., smaller than New York City. **Location:** Off tip of Malayan Peninsula in S.E. Asia. **Neighbors:** Nearest are Malaysia on N, Indonesia on S. **Topography:** Singapore is a flat, formerly swampy island. The nation includes 40 nearby islets. **Capital:** Singapore.

Government: Type: Republic. **Head of state:** Pres. Ong Teng Cheong; in office: Sept. 2, 1993. **Head of government:** Prime Min. Goh Chok Tong; b. May 20, 1941; in office: Nov. 28, 1990. **Defense:** 4% of GDP (1990).

Economy: Industries: Shipbuilding, oil refining, electronics, banking, textiles, food, rubber, lumber processing, tourism. **Arable land:** 11%. **Livestock** (1989): pigs: 321,000. **Electricity prod.** (1990): 14.4 bln. kWh. **Labor force:** 1% agric.; 58% ind. & comm.; 35% services.

Finance: Monetary unit: Dollar (May 1993: 1.64 = $1 US). **Gross domestic product** (1991): $38.3 bln. **Per capita GDP:** $13,900. **Imports** (1992): $72.1 bln.; partners: Jap. 18%, Malay. 13%, U.S. 17%, Sau. Ar. 9%. **Exports** (1992): $63.4 bln., partners: U.S. 20%, Malay. 16%, Jap. 11%, HK 6%. **Tourism** (1990): $4.3 bln. receipts. **National budget** (1991): $9.0 bln. expenditures. **Consumer prices** (change in 1992): 2.3%.

Transport: Motor vehicles: in use (1991): 300,000 passenger cars, 127,000 comm. vehicles. **Civil aviation:** (1991) 33.4 bln. passenger-km; 1 airport.

Communications: Television sets: 1 per 4.9 persons. **Radios:** 1 per 4.2 persons. **Telephones:** 1 per 2.1 persons. **Daily newspaper circ.** (1990): 289 per 1,000 pop.

Health: Life expectancy at birth (1992): 73 male; 78 female. **Births** (per 1,000 pop. 1992): 18. **Deaths** (per 1,000 pop. 1992): 5. **Natural increase:** 1.3%. **Hospital beds:** 1 per 272 persons. **Physicians:** 1 per 779 persons. **Infant mortality** (per 1,000 live births 1992): 6.

Education (1990): **Literacy:** 87%. **Years compulsory:** none; attendance 94%.

Major International Organizations: UN (GATT, IMF, WHO), ASEAN.

Embassy: 1824 R St. NW 20009; 667-7555.

Founded in 1819 by Sir Thomas Stamford Raffles, Singapore was a British colony until 1959 when it became autonomous within the Commonwealth. On Sept. 16, 1963, it joined with Malaya, Sarawak and Sabah to form the Federation of Malaysia.

Tensions between Malayans, dominant in the federation, and ethnic Chinese, dominant in Singapore, led to an agreement under which Singapore became a separate nation, Aug. 9, 1965.

Singapore is one of the world's largest ports. Standards in health, education, and housing are high. International banking has grown.

Slovakia

Slovensko

People: Population (1993 est.): 5,300,000. **Pop. density:** 279 per sq. mi. **Ethnic groups:** Slovak 87%, Hungarian 10%.

Geography: Area: 18,932 sq. mi. **Location:** In E central Europe. **Neighbors:** Poland on N., Hungary on S, Austria, Czech Rep. on W, Ukraine on E. **Topography:** mountains (Carpathians) in N, fertile Danube plane in S. **Capital:** Bratislava. **Cities** (1991 est.): Bratislava 440,000, Kosice 236,000.

Government: Type: Republic. **Head of state:** Pres. Michal Kovac; b. 1931; in office: Feb. 2, 1993. **Head of government:** Prime Min. Vladimir Meciar; in office: Jan. 1, 1993.

Economy: Industries: Iron and steel, glass, chemicals, cement. **Chief crops:** Wheat potatoes, rye, corn.

Finance: Monetary unit: new Koruna (Feb. 1993: 29.00 = $1 US).

Education (1993): **Literacy:** 99%.

Major International Organizations: UN.

Slovakia was originally settled by Illyrian, Celtic, and Germanic tribes and was incorporated into Great Moravia in the 9th century. It became part of Hungary in the 11th century. Overrun by Czech Hussites in the 15th century, it was restored to Hungarian rule in 1526. The Slovaks disassociated themselves from Hungary following World War I and joined the Czechs of Bohemia to form the Republic of Czechoslovakia, Oct. 28, 1918.

Germany invaded Czechoslovakia, 1939, and declared Slovakia an independent state. Slovakia rejoined Czechoslovakia in 1945.

Czechoslovakia split into 2 seperate states—the Czech Republic and Slovakia—on Jan. 1, 1993.

Slovenia

Republic of Slovenia

Republica of Slovenija

People: Population (1992 est.): 1,974,000. **Pop. density:** 252 per sq. mi. **Ethnic groups:** Slovenes 91%. **Language:** Slovenian, Serbo-Croatian. **Religions:** Mostly Roman Catholic.

Geography: Area: 7,819 sq. mi., slightly larger than New Jersey. **Location:** in SE Europe. **Neighbors:** Italy, Austria, Hungary, Croatia. **Topography:** mostly hilly; 42% of the land is forested. **Capital:** Ljubljana. **Cities** (1991): Ljubljana 323,000.

Government: Type: Republic. **Head of state:** Pres. Milan Kucan. **Head of government:** Janez Drnovsek; in office: May 14, 1992.

Economy: Industries: Steel, textiles. **Minerals:** Coal, mercury. **Chief crops:** Wheat, potatoes. **Livestock** (1991): cattle: 546,000; pigs: 576,000. **Electricity prod.** (1991): 12.2 bln. kWh.

Finance: Monetary unit: Tolar. **Gross domestic product** (1991): $21 bln. **Per capita GDP:** $10,700. **Imports** (1990): $4.6 bln. **Exports** (1990): $4.1 bln.

Transport: Motor vehicles: in use (1990): 581,000 passenger cars.

Communications: Television sets: 1 per 3.7 persons. **Telephones:** 1 per 3 persons. **Newspaper circ.** (1990): 112 per 1,000 pop.

Health: Life expectancy at birth (1992): 70 male; 78 female. **Hospital beds:** 1 per 143 persons. **Physicians:** 1 per 481 persons. **Infant mortality:** (per 1,000 live births 1991): 9.

Education: Literacy (1991): 90%.

Major International Organizations: UN.

The Slovenes settled in their current territory in the period from the 6th to the 8th centuries. They fell under German domination as early as the 9th century. Modern Slovenian political history began after 1848 when the Slovenes, who were divided among several Austrian provinces, began their struggle for political and national unification. With the establishment of Yugoslavia in 1918, this unification was largely achieved when the majority of the Slovenes entered the new state, which became the Kingdom of the Serbs, Croats, and Slovenes.

Slovenia declared independence June 25, 1991.

Solomon Islands

People: Population (1992 est.): 360,000. **Age distrib.** (%): 0–14: 49; 15–59: 45.5; 60+: 5.5. **Pop. density:** 33 per sq. mi. **Urban** (1986): 15%. **Ethnic groups:** Melanesian 93%, Polynesian 4%. **Languages:** English (official), Papuan, Melanesian, Polynesian languages. **Religions:** Anglican 34%, Roman Catholic 19%, Evangelical 24%, traditional religions.

Geography: Area: 10,640 sq. mi., slightly larger than Maryland. **Location:** Melanesian archipelago in the western Pacific O. **Neighbors:** Nearest is Papua New Guinea on W. **Topography:** 10 large volcanic and rugged islands and 4 groups of smaller ones. **Capital:** Honiara. **Cities:** (1988): Honiara 30,000.

Government: Type: Parliamentary democracy within the Commonwealth of Nations. **Head of state:** Queen Elizabeth II, represented by Gov.-Gen. George Lepping. **Head of government:** Prime Min. Solomon Mamaloni; in office: Mar. 28, 1989. **Local divisions:** 7 provinces and Honiara.

Economy: Industries: Fish canning. **Chief crops:** Coconuts, rice, bananas, yams. **Other resources:** Forests, marine shell. **Arable land:** 2%. **Fish catch** (1990): 25,000 metric tons. **Electricity prod.** (1991): 39 mln. kWh. **Labor force:** 32% agric., 32% services, 18% ind. & comm.

Finance: Monetary unit: Dollar (Mar. 1993: 3.16 = $1 US). **Gross domestic product** (1990): $200 mln. **Per capita GDP:** $600. **Imports** (1990): $92 mln.; partners: Austral. 31%, Jap. 14%, Sing. 18%. **Exports** (1990): $70 mln.; partners: Jap. 37%, UK 11%.

Communications: Radios: 1 per 4.6 persons. **Telephones:** 1 per 44 persons.

Health: Life expectancy at birth (1992): 67 male; 72 female. **Births:** (per 1,000 pop. 1992): 41. **Deaths** (per 1,000 pop. 1992): 5. **Natural increase:** 3.6%. **Infant mortality** (per 1,000 live births 1992): 30.

Education (1989): **Literacy:** 60%. **Primary school** 78%. **Secondary school:** 21%.

Major International Organizations: UN, Commonwealth of Nations.

The Solomon Islands were sighted in 1568 by an expedition from Peru. Britain established a protectorate in the 1890s over most of the group, inhabited by Melanesians. The islands saw major World War II battles. Self-government came Jan. 2, 1976, and independence was formally attained July 7, 1978.

Somalia

Somali Democratic Republic

Jamhuriyadda Dimugradiga Somaliya

People: Population (1992 est.): 7,235,000. **Pop. density:** 29 per sq. mi. **Urban** (1990): 36%. **Ethnic groups:** mainly Hamitic, others. **Languages:** Somali, Arabic (both official). **Religions:** Sunni Moslems 99%.

Geography: Area: 246,300 sq. mi., slightly smaller than Texas. **Location:** Occupies the eastern horn of Africa. **Neighbors:** Djibouti, Ethiopia, Kenya on W. **Topography:** The coastline extends for 1,700 mi. Hills cover the N; the center and S are flat. **Capital:** Mogadishu. **Cities** (1986 est.): Mogadishu 700,000.

Government: Type: In transition. **Local divisions:** 16 regions.

Economy: Chief crops: Incense, sugar, bananas, sorghum, corn, gum. **Minerals:** Iron, tin, gypsum, bauxite, uranium. **Arable land:** 2%. **Livestock** (1991): cattle: 4.9 mln.; goats: 20 mln.; sheep: 14 mln. **Fish catch** (1990): 18,000 metric tons. **Electricity prod.** (1991): 60 mln. kWh. **Labor force:** 82% agric.

Finance: Monetary unit: Shilling (Dec. 1992: 2,615 = $1 US). **Gross domestic product** (1989): $1.7 bln. **Per capita GDP** (1989): $170. **Imports** (1990): $249 mln.; partners: It. 29%, Fra. 18%. **Exports** (1990): $58 mln.; partners: It. 17%. **Consumer prices** (change in 1990): 102%.

Transport: Motor vehicles: in use (1990): 20,000 passenger cars, 12,000 comm. vehicles. **Chief ports:** Mogadishu, Berbera.

Communications: Radios: 1 per 20 persons.

Health: Life expectancy at birth (1992): 56 male; 56 female. **Births** (per 1,000 pop. 1992): 46. **Deaths** (per 1,000 pop. 1992): 13. **Natural increase:** 3.3%. **Hospital beds:** 1 per 1,053 persons. **Physicians:** 1 per 19,071 persons. **Infant mortality** (per 1,000 live births 1992): 116.

Education (1990): **Literacy:** 24%. 50% attend primary school, 7% attend secondary school.

Major International Organizations: UN, OAU, Arab League.

Embassy: 600 New Hampshire Ave. NW 20037; 342-1575.

The UN in 1949 approved eventual creation of Somalia as a sovereign state and in 1950 Italy took over the trusteeship held by Great Britain since World War II.

British Somaliland was formed in the 19th century in the NW. Britain gave it independence June 26, 1960; on July 1 it joined with the former Italian part to create the independent Somali Republic.

On Oct. 21, 1969, a Supreme Revolutionary Council seized power in a bloodless coup, named a Council of Secretaries of State, and abolished the Assembly. In May, 1970, several foreign companies were nationalized.

Somalia has laid claim to Ogaden, the huge eastern region of Ethiopia, peopled mostly by Somalis. Ethiopia battled Somali rebels in 1977. Some 11,000 Cuban troops with Soviet arms defeated Somali army troops and ethnic Somali rebels in Ethiopia, 1978. As many as 1.5 mln. refugees entered Somalia. Guerrilla fighting in Ogaden continued until 1988 when a peace agreement was reached with Ethiopia.

Twenty-one years of one-man rule ended in Jan. 1991 with the flight of Gen. Muhammad Siyad Barrah from the capital. Fighting between rival factions caused 40,000 casualties in 1991 and 1992, and by mid-1992 the civil war, drought, and banditry combined to produce a famine that threatened some 1.5 million people with starvation. In July 1992 the UN secretary general declared Somalia to be a country without a government. In Dec. 1992 the UN accepted a U.S. offer of troops to safeguard the delivery of food to the starving. The UN took control of the multinational relief effort from the U.S. May 4, 1993, and sponsored negotiations among rival factions aimed at establishing an interim government. U.S. and UN forces carried out attacks against the forces of and sought the capture of Gen. Mohammed Farah Aidid, the strongest Somali warlord, who opposed the UN role in Somalia.

South Africa

Republic of South Africa

Republiek van Suid-Afrika

People: Population (1992 est.): 41,688,000. **Age distrib.** (%): 0–14: 32.1; 15–59: 60.6; 60+: 7.3. **Pop. density:** 88 per sq. mi. **Urban** (1991): 60%. **Ethnic groups:** black 70%, white 16%, Coloured 8%, Asian 3%. **Religions:** Mainly Christian, Hindu, Moslem minorities. **Languages:** Afrikaans, English (both official), Nguni, Sotho languages.

Geography: Area: 472,359 sq. mi., about twice the size of Texas. **Location:** At the southern extreme of Africa. **Neighbors:** Namibia, Botswana, Zimbabwe on N, Mozambique, Swaziland on E; surrounds Lesotho. **Topography:** The large interior plateau reaches close to the country's 2,700-mi. coastline. There are few major rivers or lakes; rainfall is sparse in W, more plentiful in E. **Capitals:** Cape Town (legislative). Pretoria (administrative), and Bloemfontein (judicial). **Cities** (1990 met.): Durban 1 mln. Cape Town 1.9 mln. Johannesburg 1.7 mln. Pretoria 850,000.

Government: Type: Republic with tricameral parliament, with one chamber each for whites, Coloureds (people of mixed race), and Asians; no franchise or parliamentary representation for blacks. **Head of State:** State Pres. Frederik W. de Klerk; b. Mar. 18, 1936; in office: Sept. 20, 1989. **Local divisions:** 4 provinces, 10 "homelands" for black Africans. **Defense:** 3% of GDP (1992).

Economy: Industries: Steel, tires, motors, textiles, plastics. **Chief crops:** Corn, wool, dairy products, grain, tobacco, sugar, fruit, peanuts, grapes. **Minerals:** Gold (largest producer), chromium, antimony, coal, iron, manganese, nickel, phosphates, tin, uranium, gem diamonds, platinum, copper, vanadium. **Other resources:** Wool. **Arable land:** 12%. **Livestock** (1989): cattle: 11.8 mln.; sheep: 30.3 mln. **Fish catch** (1989): 878,000 metric tons. **Electricity prod.** (1991): 180 bln. kWh. **Crude steel prod.** (1991): 9.3 mln. metric tons. **Labor force:** 25% agric.; 32% ind. and commerce; 34% serv.; 7% mining.

Finance: Monetary unit: Rand (Aug. 1993: 3.38 = $1 US). **Gross domestic product** (1991): $104 bln. **Per capita GDP** $2,600. **Imports** (1992): $21.2 bln.; partners: Ger. 19%, U.S. 68%, UK. 12%. **Exports** (1992): $23.8 bln.; partners: U.S. 43%, Jap. 9%. **Tourism** (1990): $1.0 bln. receipts. **National budget** (1993): $35.0 bln. **International reserves less gold** (Mar. 1993): $1.5 bln. **Gold:** 5.6 mln. oz t. **Consumer prices** (change in 1992): 13.9%.

Transport: Railroads (1990): **Length:** 15,793 mi. **Motor vehicles:** in use (1990): 3.3 mln. passenger cars, 1.4 mln. comm. vehicles. **Civil aviation:** (1991): 8.3 bln. passenger-km: 41 airports. **Chief ports:** Durban, Cape Town, East London, Port Elizabeth.

Communications: Television sets: 1 per 11 persons. **Radios:** 1 per 3.0 persons. **Telephones:** 1 per 6.1 persons. **Daily newspaper circ.** (1990): 48 per 1,000 pop.

Health: Life expectancy at birth (1992): 62 Male; 67 Female. **Births** (per 1,000 pop. 1992): 35. **Deaths** (per 1,000 pop. 1992): 8. **Natural increase:** 2.7%. **Physicians:** 1 per 1,320 persons. **Infant mortality** (per 1,000 live births 1992) 51.

Education (1990): **Literacy:** 99% (whites), 69% (Asians), 62% (Coloureds), 50% (Africans).

Major International Organizations: UN (GATT).

Embassy: 3051 Massachusetts Ave. NW 20008; 232-4400.

Bushmen and Hottentots were the original inhabitants. Bantus, including Zulu, Xhosa, Swazi, and Sotho, had occupied the area from Transvaal to south of Transkei before the 17th century.

The Cape of Good Hope area was settled by Dutch, beginning in the 17th century. Britain seized the Cape in 1806. Many Dutch trekked north and founded 2 republics, the Transvaal and the Orange Free State. Diamonds were discovered, 1867, and gold, 1886. The Dutch (Boers) resented encroachments by the British and others; the Anglo-Boer War followed, 1899-1902. Britain won and, effective May 31, 1910, created the Union of South Africa, incorporating the British colonies of the Cape and Natal, the Transvaal and the Orange Free State. After a referendum, the Union became the Republic of South Africa, May 31, 1961, and withdrew from the Commonwealth.

With the election victory of Daniel Malan's National party in 1948, the policy of separate development of the races, or apartheid, already existing unofficially, became official. This called for separate development, separate residential areas, and ultimate political independence for the whites, Bantus, Asians, and Coloureds. In 1959 the government passed acts providing the eventual creation of several Bantu nations or Bantustans on 13% of the country's land area, though most black leaders opposed the plan.

Under apartheid, blacks were severely restricted to certain occupations, and paid far lower wages than whites for similar work. Only whites could vote or run for public office. There is an advisory Indian Council, partly elected, partly appointed. In 1969, a Coloured People's Representative Council was created.

At least 600 persons, mostly Bantus, were killed in 1976 riots protesting apartheid. Black protests continued through the 1980s as violence broke out in several black townships. A new constitution was approved by referendum, Nov. 1983, which extended the parliamentary franchise to the Coloured and Asian minorities. Laws banning interracial sex and marriage were repealed in 1985.

In 1963, the Transkei, an area in the SE, became the first of these partially self-governing territories or "Homelands." Transkei became independent on Oct. 26, 1976, Bophuthatswana on Dec. 6, 1977, and Venda on Sept. 13, 1979; none received international recognition.

In 1981, So. Africa launched military operations in Angola and Mozambique to combat terrorists groups; So. African troops attacked the South West African People's Organization (SWAPO) guerrillas in Angola, March, 1982. South Africa and Mozambique signed a non-aggression pact in 1984.

In 1986, Nobel Peace Prize winner Bishop Desmond Tutu called for Western nations to apply sanctions against So. Africa to force an end to apartheid. President Botha announced in Apr. the end to the nation's system of racial pass laws and offered blacks an advisory role in government.

On May 19, So. Africa attacked 3 neighboring countries—Zimbabwe, Botswana, Zambia—to strike at guerrilla strongholds of the African National Congress.

A nationwide state of emergency was declared June 12, giving almost unlimited power to the security forces. On Apr. 22, 1987, a 6-week-old walkout by railway workers erupted into violence after the dismissal of 16,000 strikers. As confrontation between blacks and government increased, there was widespread support in Western nations for a complete trade embargo on So. Africa.

Some 2 million South African black workers staged a massive strike, June 6-8, 1988, to protest the government's new labor laws and the banning of political activity by trade unions and antiapartheid groups. P.W. Botha, head of the government since 1978, resigned Aug. 14, 1989, and was replaced by Frederik W. de Klerk.

In 1990, the government lifted its bar on the African National Congress, the primary black group fighting to end white minority rule. On Feb. 11, black nationalist leader Nelson Mandela was freed after more than 27 years in prison. In Oct. the Separate Amenities Act was repealed, ending the legal basis of segregation in public places. In Feb. 1991 Pres. de Klerk announced plans to end all apartheid laws. In June the race registration law was repealed.

A band of marauders swept through the township of Boipatong, June 17, 1992, killing some 40 blacks and prompting the African National Congress to temporarily break off constitutional talks with the white-minority government. Violence involving rival black groups continued later in the year. Violence flared in several black townships following the assassination of Chris Hani, head of the South African Communist Party, Apr. 10, 1993. The nation's negotiating parties, June 3, settled upon Apr. 27, 1994, as the tentative date for South Africa's first elections, in which all races can vote, which would choose multiracial constituent assembly that would serve as an interim legislature and write a new constitution. Negotiators agreed, Sept. 7, on the creation of a multiracial transition committee to oversee government operations prior to the elections.

Bophuthatswana: Population (1992 est.): 2,056,000. **Area:** 16,988 sq. mi., 6 discontinuous geographic units. **Capital:** Mmabatho. **Head of state:** Pres. Kgosi Lucas Manyane Mangope, b. Dec. 27, 1923; in office: Dec. 6, 1977.

Ciskei: Population (1992 est.): 854,000. **Area:** 2,996 sq. mi. **Capitol:** Bisho. **Head of State:** Brig. Joshua Oupa Gqozo.

Transkei: Population (1992 est.): 3,301,000. **Area:** 16,855 sq. mi., 3 discontinuous geographic units. **Capital:** Umtata. **Head of government:** Gen. Bantu Holomisa; in office: Dec. 30, 1987.

Venda: Population (1992 est.): 567,000. **Area:** 2,771 sq. mi., 2 discontinuous geographic units. **Capital:** Thohoyandou. **Head of state:** Gabriel Ramushwana; in office: Apr. 5, 1990.

Spain

España

People: Population (1992 est.): 39,118,000 (incl. Balearic & Canary Islands). **Age distrib.** (%): 0–14: 18.4; 15–59: 62.2; 60+: 19.4. **Pop. density:** 200 per sq. mi. **Urban** (1990): 79%. **Ethnic groups:** Spanish (Castilian, Valencian, Andalusian, Asturian) 72.8%, Catalan 16.4%, Galician 8.2%, Basque 2.3%. **Languages:** Spanish (official), Catalan, Galician, Basque. **Religions:** Roman Catholic 90%.

Geography: Area: 194,896 sq. mi., the size of Arizona and Utah combined. **Location:** In SW Europe. **Neighbors:** Portugal on W. France on N. **Topography:** The interior is a high, arid plateau broken by mountain ranges and river valleys. The NW is heavily watered, the south has lowlands and a Mediterranean climate. **Capital:** Madrid. **Cities** (1991 est.): Madrid 2,909,000; Barcelona 1,623,000; Valencia 752,000; Seville 659,000.

Government: Type: Constitutional monarchy. **Head of state:** King Juan Carlos I de Borbon y Borbon, b. Jan. 5, 1938; in office: Nov. 22, 1975. **Head of government:** Prime Min. Felipe Gonzalez Marquez; in office: Dec. 2, 1982. **Local divisions:** 17 autonomous communities. **Defense:** 2.0% of GDP (1991).

Economy: Industries: Machinery, steel, textiles, shoes, autos, processed foods. **Chief crops:** Grains, olives, grapes, citrus fruits, vegetables, olives. **Minerals:** Lignite, uranium, lead, iron, copper, zinc, coal. **Other resources:** Forests (cork). **Arable land:** 31%. **Livestock** (1990): cattle: 4.9 mln.; pigs: 16.9 mln.; sheep: 23.7 mln. **Fish catch** (1989): 974,000 tons. **Electricity prod.** (1991): 157 bln. kWh. **Crude steel prod.** (1991): 12.7 mln. metric tons. **Labor force:** 16% agric.; 24% ind. and comm.; 52% serv.

Finance: Monetary unit: Peseta (July 1993: 133.29 = $1 US). **Gross domestic product** (1991): $487 bln. **Per capita GDP:** $12,400. **Imports** (1992): $99.7 bln.; partners: U.S. 8%, EC 57%. **Exports** (1992): $64.3 bln.; partners: EC 71%, U.S. 6%. **Tourism** (1990): $18.5 bln. receipts. **National budget** (1991): $115 bln. expenditures. **International reserves less gold** (Mar. 1993): $44.4 bln. **Gold:** 15.6 mln. oz t. **Consumer prices** (change in 1992): 5.8%.

Transport: Railroads (1991): **Length:** 12,563 km. **Motor vehicles:** in use (1990): 11.9 mln. passenger cars, 2.4 mln. comm. **Civil aviation:** (1990): 22.1 bln. passenger-km; 25 airports with scheduled flights. **Chief ports:** Barcelona, Bilbao, Valencia, Cartagena, Gijon.

Communications: Television sets: 1 per 2.6 persons. **Radios:** 1 per 3.4 persons. **Telephones:** 1 per 2.5 persons. **Daily newspaper circ.** (1991): 76 per 1,000 pop.

Health: Life expectancy at birth (1992): 75 male; 82 female. **Births** (per 1,000 pop. 1992): 11. **Deaths** (per 1,000 pop. 1992): 8. **Natural increase:** .3%. **Hospital beds:** 1 per 198 persons. **Physicians:** 1 per 275 persons. **Infant mortality** (per 1,000 live births 1992): 6.

Education (1991): **Literacy:** 97%. **School compulsory:** to age 16.

Major International Organizations: UN and all of its specialized agencies, NATO, OECD, EC.

Embassy: 2700 15th St. NW 20009; 265-0190.

Spain was settled by Iberians, Basques, and Celts, partly overrun by Carthaginians, conquered by Rome c.200 BC. The Visigoths, in power by the 5th century AD, adopted Christianity but by 711 AD lost to the Islamic invasion from Africa. Christian reconquest from the N led to a Spanish nationalism. In 1469 the kingdoms of Aragon and Castile were united by the marriage of Ferdinand II and Isabella I, and the last Moorish power was broken by the fall of the kingdom of Granada, 1492. Spain became a bulwark of Roman Catholicism.

Spain obtained a colonial empire with the discovery of America by Columbus, 1492, the conquest of Mexico by Cortes, and Peru by Pizarro. It also controlled the Netherlands and parts of Italy and Germany. Spain lost its American colonies in the early 19th century. It lost Cuba, the Philippines, and Puerto Rico during the Spanish-American War, 1898.

Primo de Rivera became dictator in 1923. King Alfonso XIII revoked the dictatorship, 1930, but was forced to leave the country 1931. A republic was proclaimed which disestablished the church, curtailed its privileges, and secularized education. A conservative reaction occurred 1933 but was followed by a Popular Front (1936-1939) composed of socialists, communists, republicans, and anarchists.

Army officers under Francisco Franco revolted against the government, 1936. In a destructive 3-year war, in which some one million died, Franco received massive help and troops from Italy and Germany, while the USSR, France, and Mexico supported the republic. War ended Mar. 28, 1939. Franco was named caudillo, leader of the nation. Spain was neutral in World War II but its relations with fascist countries caused its exclusion from the UN until 1955.

In July 1969, Franco and the Cortes designated Prince Juan Carlos as the future king and chief of state. After Franco's death, Nov. 20, 1975, Juan Carlos was sworn in as king. He presided over the formal dissolution of the institutions of the Franco regime. In free elections June 1977, moderates and democratic socialists emerged as the largest parties.

Catalonia and the Basque country were granted autonomy, Jan. 1980, following overwhelming approval in home-rule referendums. Basque extremists, however, have continued their campaign for independence.

The **Balearic Islands** in the western Mediterranean, 1,935 sq. mi., are a province of Spain; they include **Majorca** (Mallorca), with the capital, Palma; **Minorca, Cabrera, Ibiza** and **Formentera.** The **Canary Islands,** 2,807 sq. mi., in the Atlantic W of Morocco, form 2 provinces, including the islands of **Tenerife, Palma, Gomera, Hierro, Grand Canary, Fuerteventura,** and **Lanzarote** with Las Palmas and Santa Cruz thriving ports. **Ceuta** and **Melilla,** small enclaves on Morocco's Mediterranean coast, are part of Metropolitan Spain.

Spain has sought the return of Gibraltar, in British hands since 1704.

Sri Lanka

Democratic Socialist Republic of Sri Lanka

Sri Lanka Prajathanthrika Samajavadi Janarajaya

People: Population (1992 est.): 17,631,000. **Age distrib.** (%): 0–14: 35.3; 15–59: 58.1; 60+: 6.6. **Pop. density:** 695 per sq. mi. **Urban** (1991): 26%. **Ethnic groups:** Sinhalese 74%, Tamils 17%, Moors 7%. **Languages:** Sinhalese, and Tamil, (both official). **Religions:** Buddhist 69%, Hindu 15%, Christian 8%, Moslem 7%.

Geography: Area: 25,332 sq. mi. about the size of W. Va. **Location:** In Indian O. off SE coast of India. **Neighbors:** India on NW. **Topography:** The coastal area and the northern half are flat; the S-central area is hilly and mountainous. **Capital:** Colombo. **Cities** (1990): Colombo 615,000.

Government: Type: Republic. **Head of state:** Pres. Dingiri Banda Wijetungle; b. 1923; in office: May 7, 1993. **Head of government:** Prime Minister Ranil Wickremasinghe; in office: May 7, 1993. **Local divisions:** 9 provinces, 24 districts. **Defense:** 5% of GDP (1991).

Economy: Industries: Plywood, paper, milling, chemicals, textiles. **Chief crops:** Tea, coconuts, rice. **Minerals:** Graphite, limestone, gems, phosphate. **Other resources:** Forests, rubber. **Arable land:** 16%. **Livestock** (1991): cattle: 1.8 mln. **Fish catch** (1990): 165,000 metric tons. **Electricity prod.** (1991): 4.2 bln. kWh. **Labor force:** 46% agric.; 27% ind. and comm.; 26% serv.

Finance: Monetary unit: Rupee (Mar. 1993: 47 = $1 US). **Gross domestic product** (1991): $7.2 bln. **Per capita GDP:** $410. **Imports** (1991): $3.0 bln.; partners: Jap. 15%, UK 7%. **Exports** (1991): $2.3 bln.; partners: U.S. 22%, UK 7%. **Tourism** (1990): $125 mln. receipts. **National budget** (1992): $3.7 bln. expenditures. **International reserves less gold** (Mar. 1993): $1.0 bln. **Gold:** 160,000 oz t. **Consumer prices** (change in 1992): 11.4%.

Transport: Railroads (1990): **Length:** 1,453 km. **Motor vehicles:** in use (1990): 173,000 passenger cars, 146,000 comm. vehicles. **Civil aviation** (1991): 3.4 bln. passenger-km; 1 airport. **Chief ports:** Colombo, Trincomalee, Galle.

Communications: Television sets: 1 per 25 persons. **Radios:** 1 per 8 persons. **Telephones:** 1 per 102 persons.

Health: Life expectancy at birth (1992): 69 male; 74 female. **Births** (per 1,000 pop. 1992): 21. **Deaths** (per 1,000 pop. 1992): 6. **Natural increase:** 1.5%. **Hospital beds:** 1 per 356 persons. **Physicians:** 1 per 6,609 persons. **Infant mortality** (per 1,000 live births 1992): 21.

Education (1990): **Literacy:** 90%. **Years compulsory:** To age 12; attendance 98%.

Major International Organizations: UN (World Bank, IMF), Commonwealth of Nations.

Embassy: 2148 Wyoming Ave. NW 20008; 483-4025.

The island was known to the ancient world as Taprobane (Greek for copper-colored) and later as Serendip (from Arabic). Colonists from northern India subdued the indigenous Veddahs about 543 BC; their descendants, the Buddhist Sinhalese, still form most of the population. Hindu descendants of Tamil immigrants from southern India account for one-fifth of the population. Parts were occupied by the Portuguese in 1505 and by the Dutch in 1658. The British seized the island in 1796. As Ceylon it became an independent member of the Commonwealth in 1948. On May 22, 1972, Ceylon became the Republic of Sri Lanka.

Prime Min. W. R. D. Bandaranaike was assassinated Sept. 25, 1959. In new elections, the Freedom Party was victorious under Mrs. Sirimavo Bandaranaike, widow of the former prime minister.

After May 1970 elections, Mrs. Bandaranaike became prime minister again. In 1971 the nation suffered economic problems and terrorist activities by ultra-leftists, thousands of whom were executed. Massive land reform and nationalization of foreign-owned plantations was undertaken in the mid-1970s. Mrs. Bandaranaike was ousted in 1977 elections. A presidential form of government was installed in 1978 to restore stability.

Tension between the Sinhalese and Tamil separatists erupted into violence repeatedly in the 1980s. In 1987, hundreds died in an attack by Tamil rebels Apr. 17. Sri Lanka forces retaliated in June with attacks on the rebel-held Jaffna peninsula. Over 20,000 have died in the civil war, which continued into the 1990s. Pres. Ranasinghe Premadasa was assassinated May 1, 1993, by a Tamil rebel.

Sudan

Republic of the Sudan

Jamhuryat as-Sudan

People: Population (1992 est.): 28,305,000. **Pop. density:** 29 per sq. mi. **Urban** (1990): 22%. **Ethnic groups:** black 52%, Arab 39%, Beja 6%. **Languages:** Arabic (official), Dinka, Nubian, Nuer, Beja, others. **Religions:** Sunni Moslem 70%, animist 18%, Christians 5%.

Geography: Area: 966,757 sq. mi., the largest country in Africa, over one-fourth the size of the U.S. **Location:** At the E end of Sahara desert zone. **Neighbors:** Egypt on N, Libya, Chad, Central African Republic on W, Zaire, Uganda, Kenya on S, Ethiopia and Eritrea on E. **Topography:** The N consists of the Libyan Desert in the W, and the mountainous Nubia desert in E, with narrow Nile valley between. The center contains large, fertile, rainy areas with fields, pasture, and forest. The S has rich soil, heavy rain. **Capital:** Khartoum. **Cities** (1983 est.): Khartoum 476,000; Omdurman 526,000; North Khartoum 341,000; Port Sudan 206,000.

Government: Type: Military. **Head of government:** Prime Min. Gen. Omar Al-Bashir; in office: June 30, 1989. **Local divisions:** 9 states. **Defense:** 7% of GDP (1990).

Economy: Industries: Textiles, food processing. **Chief crops:** Gum arabic (principal world source), durra (sorghum), cotton (main export), sesame, peanuts, rice, coffee, sugar cane, wheat, dates. **Minerals:** Chrome, copper. **Other resources:** Mahogany. **Arable land:** 5%. **Livestock** (1991): cattle: 20 mln.; sheep: 15 mln.; goats: 15 mln. **Electricity prod.** (1991): 905 mln. kWh. **Labor force:** 78% agric.; 9% ind., comm.

Finance: Monetary unit: Dinar (Mar. 1993: 1.00 = $2.74 US). **Gross domestic product** (1991): $12.1 bln. **Per capita GDP:** $450. **Imports** (1991): $1.4 bln.; partners: EC 32%, U.S. 13%. **Exports** (1991): $325 mln.; partners: EC 46%. **National budget** (1991): $2.1 bln. expenditures. **International reserves less gold** (Mar. 1993): $3.7 mln. **Consumer prices** (change in 1992): 112.6%.

Transport: Railroads (1988): **Length:** 5,503 km. **Motor vehicles:** in use (1990): 116,000 passenger cars, 56,000 comm. vehicles. **Civil aviation:** (1991): 425 mln. passenger-km; 12 airports with scheduled flights. **Chief ports:** Port Sudan.

Communications: Television sets: 1 per 117 persons. **Radios:** 1 per 4.6 persons. **Telephones:** 1 per 338 persons. **Daily newspaper circ.** (1990): 21 per 1,000 pop.

Health: Life expectancy at birth (1992): 53 male; 54 female. **Births** (per 1,000 pop. 1992): 44. **Deaths** (per 1,000 pop. 1992): 14. **Natural increase:** 3.0%. **Hospital beds:** 1 per 1,110 persons. **Physicians** (1983): 2,169. **Infant mortality** (per 1,000 live births 1992): 85.

Education (1991): **Literacy:** 27%. **Years compulsory:** 9; attendance 50%.

Major International Organizations: UN (IMF, WHO, FAO), Arab League, OAU.

Northern Sudan, ancient Nubia, was settled by Egyptians in antiquity, and was converted to Coptic Christianity in the 6th century. Arab conquests brought Islam in the 15th century.

In the 1820s Egypt took over the Sudan, defeating the last of earlier empires, including the Fung. In the 1880s a revolution was led by Mohammed Ahmed who called himself the Mahdi (leader of the faithful) and his followers, the dervishes.

In 1898 an Anglo-Egyptian force crushed the Mahdi's successors. In 1951 the Egyptian Parliament abrogated its 1899 and 1936 treaties with Great Britain, and amended its constitution, to provide for a separate Sudanese constitution.

Sudan voted for complete independence as a parliamentary government effective Jan. 1, 1956.

In 1969, a Revolutionary Council took power, but a civilian premier and cabinet were appointed; the government announced it would create a socialist state. The northern 12 provinces are predominantly Arab-Moslem and have been dominant in the central government. The 3 southern provinces are black Christians and animists. A 1972 peace agreement gave the South regional autonomy. The 2 halves of the nation began a civil war in 1988. Some 50,000 government soldiers launched a massive offensive against the southern rebels in 1992.

Economic problems plagued the nation in the 1980s, aggravated by a huge influx of refugees from neighboring countries. After 16 years in power, Pres. Nimeiry was overthrown in a bloodless military coup, Apr. 6, 1985. The Sudan held its first democratic parliamentary elections in 18 years in 1986. The elected government was overthrown in a bloodless coup June 30, 1989.

Sudan agreed to allow large-scale UN relief efforts in 1991, as some 7 million people were threatened with famine. The UN suspended aid to southern Sudan in 1992 because of the fighting. In 1993, Amnesty International accused Sudan of practicing "ethnic cleansing" against the Nuba people of southern Sudan and of gross human rights violations in other war zones in the south.

Suriname

Republic of Suriname

People: Population (1992 est.): 410,000. **Pop. density:** 6 per sq. mi. **Ethnic groups** Hindustanis 37%, Creole 31%, Javanese 15%. **Languages:** Dutch (official), Sranantonga, English. **Religions:** Moslem 19%, Hindu 27%, Christian 47%.

Geography: Area: 63,037 sq. mi., slightly larger than Georgia. **Location:** On N shore of S. America. **Neighbors:** Guyana on W, Brazil on S, French Guiana on E. **Topography:** A flat Atlantic coast, where dikes permit agriculture. Inland is a forest belt; to the S, largely unexplored hills cover 75% of the country. **Capital:** Paramaribo. **Cities** (1989): Paramaribo 192,000.

Government: Type: Republic. **Head of state:** Pres. Roland Venetiaan; in office: Sept. 16, 1991. **Head of government:**

Prime Min. Jules Adjodhia; in office: Sept. 16, 1991. **Local divisions:** 10 districts.

Economy: Industries: Aluminum. **Chief crops:** Rice, sugar, fruits. **Minerals:** Bauxite. **Other resources:** Forests, shrimp. **Arable land:** 1%. **Electricity prod.** (1991): 2.0 bln. kWh. **Labor force:** 29% agric.; 15% ind. and commerce; 42% govt.

Finance: Monetary unit: Guilder (Mar. 1993: 1.78 = $1 US). **Gross domestic product** (1990): $472 mln. **Per capita GDP:** $3,400. **Imports** (1990): $370 mln.; partners: U.S. 37%, Neth. 15%, Trin./Tob. 9%. **Exports** (1990): $472 mln.; partners: Nor. 33%, U.S. 13%, Neth. 26%. **Tourism** (1990): receipts: $11 mln. **National budget** (1990): $716 mln. expenditures. **International reserves less gold** (Mar. 1993): $12.9 mln. **Gold:** 54,000 oz t.

Transport: Motor vehicles: in use (1990): 36,000 passenger cars, 14,000 comm. vehicles. **Chief ports:** Paramaribo, Nieuw-Nickerie.

Communications: Television sets: 1 per 10 persons. **Radios:** 1 per 1.6 persons. **Telephones:** 1 per 8 persons. **Daily newspaper circ.** (1991): 43 per 1,000 pop.

Health: Life expectancy at birth (1992): 66 male; 71 female. **Births** (per 1,000 pop. 1992): 27. **Deaths** (per 1,000 pop. 1992): 5. **Natural increase:** 2.1%. **Infant mortality** (per 1,000 live births 1992): 34.

Education (1989): Literacy: 65%; compulsory ages 6–12.

Major International Organizations: UN (WHO, ILO, FAO, World Bank, IMF), OAS.

Embassy: 2600 Virginia Ave. NW 20037; 338-6980.

The Netherlands acquired Suriname in 1667 from Britain, in exchange for New Netherlands (New York). The 1954 Dutch constitution raised the colony to a level of equality with the Netherlands and the Netherlands Antilles. In the 1970s the Dutch government pressured for Suriname independence, which came Nov. 25, 1975, despite objections from East Indians. Some 40% of the population (mostly East Indians) emigrated to the Netherlands in the months before independence.

The National Military Council took over control of the government, Feb. 1982. The government came under democratic leadership in 1988.

Swaziland

Kingdom of Swaziland

People: Population (1992 est.): 913,000. **Age distrib.** (%): 0–14: 47.3; 15–59: 47.4; 60+: 5.3. **Pop. density:** 136 per sq. mi. **Urban** (1990): 30%. **Ethnic groups:** Swazi 90%, Zulu 2.3%, European 2.1%, other African, non-African groups. **Languages:** Swazi, English, (both official). **Religions:** Christians 60%, indigenous beliefs 40%.

Geography: Area: 6,704 sq. mi., slightly smaller than New Jersey. **Location:** In southern Africa, near Indian O. coast. **Neighbors:** South Africa on N, W, S, Mozambique on E. **Topography:** The country descends from W-E in broad belts, becoming more arid in the lowveld region, then rising to a plateau in the E. **Capital:** Mbabane. **Cities** (1990 est.): Mbabane 46,000; Manzini 53,000.

Government: Type: Monarchy. **Head of state:** King Mswati 3d; as of: Apr. 25, 1986. **Head of government:** Prime Min. Obed Dlamini; in office: July 12, 1989. **Local divisions:** 4 districts, 2 municipalities, 40 regions.

Economy: Industries: Wood pulp. **Chief crops:** Sugar, corn, cotton, rice, pineapples, sugar, citrus fruits. **Minerals:** Asbestos, iron, coal. **Other resources:** Forests. **Arable land:** 8%. **Electricity prod.** (1991): 155 mln. kWh. **Labor force:** 53% agric.; 9% ind. and commerce; 9% serv.

Finance: Monetary unit: Lilangeni (Mar. 1993: 1.00 = $.31 US). **Gross domestic product** (1990): $563 mln. **Per capita GDP:** $752. **Imports** (1992): $746 mln.; partners: So. Afr., 92%. **Exports** (1990): $543 mln.; partners: So. Afr. 40%. **National budget** (1993): $360 mln. expenditures. **International reserves less gold** (Feb. 1993): $256 mln. **Consumer prices** (change in 1991): 12.1%.

Transport: Motor vehicles: in use (1991): 25,000 passenger cars, 28,000 comm. vehicles.

Communications: Radios: 1 per 6.3 persons. **Telephones:** 1 per 34 persons. **Daily newspaper circ.** (1990): 24 per 1,000 pop.

Health: Life expectancy at birth (1992): 52 male; 60 female. **Births** (per 1,000 pop. 1992): 44. **Deaths** (per 1,000 pop. 1992): 12. **Natural increase:** 3.2%. **Hospital beds** (1984): 1,608. **Physicians** (1984): 80. **Infant mortality rate** (per 1,000 live births 1992): 98.

Education (1990): **Literacy:** 65%. 82% attend primary school.

Major International Organizations: UN (IMF, WHO, FAO), OAU, Commonwealth of Nations.

Embassy: 3400 International Dr. NW 20008; 362-6683.

The royal house of Swaziland traces back 400 years, and is one of Africa's last ruling dynasties. The Swazis, a Bantu people, were driven to Swaziland from lands to the N by the Zulus in 1820. Their autonomy was later guaranteed by Britain and Transvaal, with Britain assuming control after 1903. Independence came Sept. 6, 1968. In 1973 the king repealed the constitution and assumed full powers.

Under the constitution political parties are forbidden; parliament's role in government is limited to debate and advice.

Sweden

Kingdom of Sweden

Konungariket Sverige

People: Population (1992 est.): 8,602,000. **Age distrib.** (%): 0–14: 17.9; 15–59: 59.0; 60+: 23.1. **Pop. density:** 49 per sq. mi. **Urban** (1985): 85%. **Ethnic groups:** Swedish 91%, Finnish 3%, Lapps, European immigrants. **Languages:** Swedish. **Religion:** Lutheran (official) 95%.

Geography: Area: 173,731 sq. mi., larger than California. **Location:** On Scandinavian Peninsula in N. Europe. **Neighbors:** Norway on W, Denmark on S (across Kattegat), Finland on E. **Topography:** Mountains along NW border cover 25% of Sweden, flat or rolling terrain covers the central and southern areas, which includes several large lakes. **Capital:** Stockholm. **Cities** (1992): Stockholm 679,000; Goteborg 433,000; Malmo 234,000.

Government: Type: Constitutional monarchy. **Head of state:** King Carl XVI Gustaf; b. Apr. 30, 1946; in office: Sept. 19, 1973. **Head of government:** Prime Min. Carl Bildt; b. July 15, 1949; in office: Oct. 3, 1991. **Local divisions:** 24 provinces. **Defense:** 3.9% of GDP (1991).

Economy: Industries: Steel, machinery, instruments, autos, shipbuilding, shipping, paper. **Chief crops:** Grains, potatoes, sugar beets. **Minerals:** Zinc, iron, lead, copper, gold, silver. **Other resources:** Forests (half the country); yield one fourth exports. **Arable land:** 7%. **Livestock** (1990): cattle: 1.7 mln.; pigs: 2.2 mln. **Fish catch** (1990): 240,000 metric tons. **Electricity prod.** (1991): 142 bln. kWh. **Crude steel prod.** (1991): 4.2 mln. metric tons. **Labor force:** 5% agric.; 24% manuf. & mining; 37% social services.

Finance: Monetary unit: Krona (July 1993: 7.97 = $1 US). **Gross domestic product** (1991): $147 bln. **Per capita GDP:** $17,200. **Imports** (1992): $49.7 bln.; partners: EC 56%. **Exports** (1992): $56.1 bln.; partners: EC 55%. **Tourism** (1990): $2.8 bln. receipts. **National budget** (1991): $78.7 bln. expenditures. **International reserves less gold** (Mar. 1993): $19.7 bln. **Gold:** 6.06 mln. oz t. **Consumer prices** (change in 1992): 2.3%.

Transport: Railroads (1990): **Length:** 6,960 mi. **Motor vehicles:** in use (1991): 3.6 mln. passenger cars, 324,000 comm. vehicles. **Civil aviation** (1990): 7.2 bln. passenger-km; 42 airports. **Chief ports:** Goteborg, Stockholm, Malmo.

Communications: Television sets: 1 per 2.4 persons. **Radios:** 1 per 1.2 persons. **Telephones:** 1 per 1.1 persons. **Daily newspaper circ.** (1990): 572 per 1,000 pop.

Health: Life expectancy at birth (1992): 75 male; 81 female. **Births** (per 1,000 pop. 1992): 13. **Deaths** (per 1,000 pop. 1992): 11. **Hospital beds:** 1 per 148 persons. **Physicians:** 1 per 320 persons. **Infant mortality** (per 1,000 live births (1992): 6.

Education (1991): **Literacy:** 99%. **Years compulsory:** 12; attendance 100%.

Major International Organizations: UN and all of its specialized agencies, EFTA, OECD.

Embassy: 600 New Hampshire Ave. NW 20037; 944-5600.

The Swedes have lived in present-day Sweden for at least 5,000 years, longer than nearly any other European people. Gothic tribes from Sweden played a major role in the disintegration of the Roman Empire. Other Swedes helped create the first Russian state in the 9th century.

The Swedes were Christianized from the 11th century, and a strong centralized monarchy developed. A parliament, the Riksdag, was first called in 1435, the earliest parliament on the European continent, with all classes of society represented.

Swedish independence from rule by Danish kings (dating from 1397) was secured by Gustavus I in a revolt, 1521-23; he built up the government and military and established the Lutheran Church. In the 17th century Sweden was a major European power, gaining most of the Baltic seacoast, but its international position subsequently declined.

The Napoleonic wars, in which Sweden acquired Norway (it became independent 1905), were the last in which Sweden participated. Armed neutrality was maintained in both world wars.

Over 4 decades of Social Democratic rule was ended in 1976 parliamentary elections but the party was returned to power in the 1982 elections. Although 90% of the economy is in private hands, the government holds a large interest in water power production and the railroads are operated by a public agency.

Carl Bildt, a non-Socialist, became prime minister Oct. 1991. His coalition government promised to turn the nation away from long-established economic and social programs.

Switzerland

Swiss Confederation

People: Population (1992 est.): 6,828,000. **Age distrib.** (%): 0–14: 17.0; 15–59: 63.7; 60+: 19.3. **Pop. density:** 428 per sq. mi. **Urban** (1991): 60%. **Ethnic groups:** Mixed European stock. **Languages:** German, French, Italian (all official). **Religions:** Roman Catholic 49%, Protestant 48%.

Geography: Area: 15,941 sq. mi., as large as Mass., Conn., and R.I., combined. **Location:** In the Alps Mts. in Central Europe. **Neighbors:** France on W, Italy on S, Austria on E, Germany on N. **Topography:** The Alps cover 60% of the land area, the Jura, near France, 10%. Running between, from NE to SW, are midlands, 30%. **Capital:** Bern. **Cities** (1991): Zurich 342,000; Basel 171,200; Geneva 161,000; Bern 135,000.

Government: Type: Federal republic. **Head of government:** Pres. Adolf Ogi; in office: Jan. 1, 1993. **Local divisions:** 20 full cantons, 6 half cantons. **Defense:** 2.2% of GDP (1990).

Economy: Industries: Machinery, machine tools, steel, instruments, watches, textiles, foodstuffs (cheese, chocolate), banking, tourism. **Chief crops:** Grains, potatoes, sugar beets, vegetables, tobacco. **Minerals:** Salt. **Other resources:** Hydro power potential. **Arable land:** 10%. **Livestock** (1991): cattle: 1.8 mln.; pigs: 1.9 mln. **Electricity prod.** (1991): 59 bln. kWh. **Crude steel prod.** (1988): 825,000 metric tons. **Labor force:** 39% ind. and commerce, 7% agric., 50% serv.

Finance: Monetary unit: Franc (July 1993: 1.49 = $1 US). **Gross domestic product** (1991): $147 bln. **Per capita GDP:** $21,700. **Imports** (1992): $61.7 bln.; partners: EC 71%. **Exports** (1992): $61.3 bln.; partners: EC 56%. **Tourism** (1990); receipts: $6.8 bln. **National budget** (1990): $23.8 bln. **International reserves less gold** (Mar. 1993): $31.3 bln. **Gold:** 83.28 mln. oz t. **Consumer prices** (change in 1992): 4.0%.

Transport: Railroads (1989): **Length:** 3,119 mi. **Motor vehicles:** in use (1990): 3.0 mln. passenger cars, 285,000 comm. vehicles. **Civil aviation:** (1991): 15.1 bln. passenger-km; 6 airports with scheduled flights.

Communications: Television sets: 1 per 2.9 persons. **Radios:** 1 per 2.6 persons. **Telephones:** 1 per 1.2 persons. **Daily newspaper circ.** (1990): 471 per 1,000 pop.

Health: Life expectancy at birth (1992): 76 male; 83 female. **Births** (per 1,000 pop. 1992): 12 **Deaths** (per 1,000 pop. 1992): 10 **Natural increase:** .2%. **Physicians:** 1 per 317 persons. **Infant mortality** (per 1,000 live births 1992): 5.

Education (1991): **Literacy:** 99%. **Years compulsory:** 9; attendance 100%.

Major International Organizations: Many UN specialized agencies (though not a member).

Embassy: 2900 Cathedral Ave. NW 20008; 745-7900.

Switzerland, the Roman province of Helvetia, is a federation of 23 cantons (20 full cantons and 6 half cantons), 3 of which in 1291 created a defensive league and later were joined by other districts. Voters in the French-speaking part of Canton Bern voted for self-government, 1978; Canton Jura was created Jan. 1, 1979.

In 1648 the Swiss Confederation obtained its independence from the Holy Roman Empire. The cantons were joined under a federal constitution in 1848, with large powers of local control retained by each canton.

Switzerland has maintained an armed neutrality since 1815, and has not been involved in a foreign war since 1515. It is the seat of many UN and other international agencies.

Switzerland is a leading world banking center; stability of the currency brings funds from many quarters. The nation's famed secret bank accounts were phased out in 1992.

Syria

Syrian Arab Republic

al-Jumhuriyah al-Arabiyah

People: Population (1992 est.): 13,730,000. **Age distrib.** (%): 0–14: 49.3; 15–59: 44.2; 60+: 6.5. **Pop. density:** 192 per sq. mi. **Urban** (1990): 50%. **Ethnic groups:** Arab 90%, Kurd, Armenian, others. **Languages:** Arabic (official), Kurdish, Armenian. **Religions:** Sunni Moslem 74%, other Moslem 16%, Christian 10%.

Geography: Area: 71,498 sq. mi., slightly larger than North Dakota. **Location:** At eastern end of Mediterranean Sea. **Neighbors:** Lebanon, Israel on W, Jordan on S, Iraq on E, Turkey on N. **Topography:** Syria has a short Mediterranean coastline, then stretches E and S with fertile lowlands and plains, alternating with mountains and large desert areas. **Capital:** Damascus. **Cities** (1992 est.): Damascus 1,451,000; Aleppo 1,445,000; Homs 518,000.

Government: Type: Republic (under military regime). **Head of state:** Pres. Hafez al-Assad; b. Mar. 1930; in office: Feb. 22, 1971. **Head of government:** Prime Min. Mahmoud Zuabi; in office: Nov. 1, 1987. **Local divisions:** Damascus and 13 provinces. **Defense:** 10.9% of GDP (1989).

Economy: Industries: Oil products, textiles, tobacco, glassware, brassware. **Chief crops:** Cotton, grain, olives, fruits, vegetables. **Minerals:** Oil, phosphate, gypsum. **Crude oil reserves** (1987): 1.4 bln. bbls. **Other resources:** Wool. **Arable land:** 28%. **Livestock** (1990): sheep: 13 mln., goats: 1 mln. **Electricity prod.** (1991): 8 bln. kWh. **Labor force:** 32% agric.; 29% ind. & comm.; 39% services.

Finance: Monetary unit: Pound (Mar. 1993: 11.22 = $1 US). **Gross domestic product** (1991): $30.0 bln. **Per capita GDP:** $2,300.1. **Imports** (1991): $2.7 bln.; partners: EC 42%. **Exports** (1991): $3.6 bln.; partners: E. Europe 42%, EC 31%. **Tourism** (1990): receipts: $244 mln. **National budget** (1991): $7.5 bln. expenditures. **Consumer prices** (change in 1991): 7.7%.

Transport: Railroads (1991): **Length:** 948 mi. **Motor vehicles:** in use (1990): 117,000 passenger cars, 138,000 comm. vehicles. **Civil aviation** (1989): 833 mln. passenger-km; 5 airports with scheduled flights. **Chief ports:** Latakia, Tartus.

Communications: Television sets: 1 per 17 persons. **Radios:** 1 per 4.1 persons. **Telephones:** 1 per 17 persons. **Daily newspaper circ.** (1990): 21 per 1,000 pop.

Health: Life expectancy at birth (1992): 65 male; 67 female. **Births** (per 1,000 pop. 1992): 44. **Deaths** (per 1,000 1992): 7. **Natural increase:** 3.7%. **Hospital beds:** 1 per 840 persons. **Physicians:** 1 per 1,347 persons. **Infant mortality** (per 1,000 live births 1992): 45.

Education (1990): **Literacy:** 64%. **Years compulsory:** 6; attendance: 94%.

Major International Organizations: UN (IMF, WHO, FAO), Arab League.

Embassy: 2215 Wyoming Ave. NW 20008; 232-6313.

Syria contains some of the most ancient remains of civilization. It was the center of the Seleucid empire, but later became absorbed in the Roman and Arab empires. Ottoman rule prevailed for 4 centuries, until the end of World War I.

The state of Syria was formed from former Turkish districts, made a separate entity by the Treaty of Sevres 1920 and divided into the states of Syria and Greater Lebanon. Both were administered under a French League of Nations mandate 1920-1941.

Syria was proclaimed a republic by the occupying French Sept. 16, 1941, and exercised full independence effective Apr. 17, 1946. Syria joined in the Arab invasion of Israel in 1948.

Syria joined with Egypt in Feb. 1958 in the United Arab Republic but seceded Sept. 30, 1961. The Socialist Baath party and military leaders seized power in Mar. 1963. The Baath, a pan-Arab organization, became the only legal party. The government has been dominated by members of the minority Alawite sect.

In the Arab-Israeli war of June 1967, Israel seized and occupied the Golan Heights area inside Syria, from which Israeli settlements had for years been shelled by Syria.

On Oct. 6, 1973, Syria joined Egypt in an attack on Israel. Arab oil states agreed in 1974 to give Syria $1 billion a year to aid anti-Israel moves. Some 30,000 Syrian troops entered Lebanon in 1976 to mediate in a civil war. They fought Palestinian guerrillas and, later, Christian militiamen. Syrian troops again battled Christian forces in Lebanon, Apr. 1981, ending a cease-fire that had been in place.

Following the June 6, 1982 Israeli invasion of Lebanon, Israeli planes destroyed 17 Syrian antiaircraft missile batteries in the Bekka Valley, June 9. Some 25 Syrian planes were downed during the engagement. Israel and Syria agreed to a cease fire June 11. In 1983, Syria backed the PLO rebels who ousted Yasir Arafat's forces from Tripoli.

Syria's role in promoting acts of international terrorism led to the breaking of diplomatic relations with Great Britain and the implementation of limited sanctions by the European Communities in 1986.

Syria condemned the Aug. 1990 Iraqi invasion on Kuwait and sent troops to help Allied Forces in the Gulf War.

In 1991, Syria accepted U.S. proposals for the terms of an Arab-Israeli peace conference.

Taiwan

Republic of China

Chung-hua Min-kuo

People: Population (1992 est.): 20,878,000. **Age distrib.** (%): 0–14: 27.1; 15–59: 63.2; 60+: 9.7. **Pop. density:** 1,503 per sq. mi. **Urban** (1990): 75%. **Ethnic groups:** Taiwanese 85%, Chinese 14%. Languages: Mandarin Chinese (official), Taiwan, Hakka dialects. **Religions:** Buddhism, Taoism, Confucianism prevail.

Geography: Area: 13,885 sq. mi., about the size of Connecticut & New Hampshire combined. **Location:** Off SE coast of China, between E. and S. China Seas. **Neighbors:** Nearest is China. **Topography:** A mountain range forms the backbone of the island; the eastern half is very steep and craggy, the western slope is flat, fertile, and well-cultivated. **Capital:** Taipei. **Cities** (1991): Taipei (met.) 2,716,000; Kaohsiung 1,398,000; Taichung 777,000; Tainan 685,000.

Government: Type: Democracy. **Head of state and Nationalist Party chmn.:** Pres. Lee Teng-hui; b. Jan. 15, 1923; in office: Jan. 13, 1988. **Head of government:** Prime Min. Lien Chan; in office: Feb. 10, 1993. **Local divisions:** 16 counties, 5 cities, Taipei & Kao-Hsiung. **Defense:** 4.6% of GNP (1991).

Economy: Industries: Textiles, clothing, electronics, processed foods, chemicals, plastics. **Chief crops:** Rice, bananas, pineapples, sugarcane, sweet potatoes, peanuts. **Minerals:** Coal, limestone, marble. **Crude oil reserves** (1987): 10 mln. bbls, **Arable land:** 25%. **Livestock** (1989): pigs: 6.9 mln. **Fish catch** (1989): 1.2 mln. metric tons. **Electricity prod.** (1991): 76 bln. kWh. **Crude steel prod.** (1991): 10.9 mln. metric tons. **Labor force:** 15% agric.; 53% ind. & comm.; 22% services.

Finance: Monetary unit: New Taiwan dollar (July 1993: 26.28 = $1 US). **Gross national product** (1991): $180.1 bln. **Per capita GNP:** $8,790. **Imports** (1992): $72 bln.; partners: U.S. 23%, Jap. 30%. **Exports** (1992): $81 bln.; partners: U.S. 39%, Jap. 13%, Hong Kong 8%. **Tourists** (1990): $1.7 bln. receipts. **National budget** (1991): $30.1 bln.

Transport: Motor vehicles: in use (1991): 2.6 mln. passenger cars, 653,000 commercial vehicles. **Civil Aviation** (1991): 29.0 bln. passenger-km; 12 airports. **Chief ports:** Kaohsiung, Keelung, Hualien, Taichung.

Communications: Television sets: 1 per 3.2 persons. **Radios:** 1 per 1.5 persons. **Telephones:** 1 per 3.0 persons. **Daily newspaper circ.** (1989): 202 per 1,000 pop.

Health: Life expectancy at birth (1992): 72 male; 78 female. **Births** (per 1,000 pop. 1992): 16. **Deaths** (per 1,000 pop. 1992): 5. **Natural increase:** 1.1%. **Physicians:** 1 per 910 persons. **Hospital beds:** 1 per 227 persons. **Infant mortality** (per 1,000 live births 1992): 6.

Education (1991): **Literacy:** 90%. **Years compulsory:** 9; attendance 99%.

Large-scale Chinese immigration began in the 17th century. The island came under mainland control after an interval of Dutch rule, 1620-62. Taiwan (also called Formosa) was ruled by Japan 1895-1945. Two million Kuomintang supporters fled to Taiwan in 1949. Both the Taipei and Peking governments consider Taiwan an integral part of China. Taiwan has rejected Pekings efforts at reunification, but unofficial dealings with the mainland have grown more flexible in the 1980s.

The U.S. upon its recognition of the People's Republic of China, Dec. 15, 1978, severed diplomatic ties with Taiwan. It maintains the unofficial American Institute in Taiwan, while Taiwan has established the Coordination Council for North American Affairs in Washington, D.C.

Land reform, government planning, U.S. aid and investment, and free universal education have brought huge advances in industry, agriculture, and mass living standards. In 1987, martial law was lifted after 38 years and in 1991, the 43-year period of emergency rule ended.

Taiwan has one of the world's strongest economies and is among the 10 leading capital exporters.

The Penghu (Pescadores), 50 sq. mi., pop. 120,000, lie between Taiwan and the mainland. **Quemoy** and **Matsu,** pop. (1990) 70,000 lie just off the mainland.

Tajikistan

Republic of Tajikistan

Respubliki i Tojikiston

People: Population (1992 est.): 5,680,000. **Pop. density:** 105 per sq. mi. **Urban** (1991): 32%. **Ethnic groups:** Tajik 62%, Uzbek 23%, Russian 8%. **Languages:** Tadzhik, Russian. **Religion:** Mostly Sunni Moslem.

Geography: Area: 54,019 sq. mi., slightly smaller than Wisconsin. **Neighbors:** Uzbekistan and Kyrgyzstan on N and W, China on E, Afghanistan on S and E. **Topography:** Mountainous region which contains the Pamirs, Trans Alai mountain system. **Capital:** Dushanbe.

Government: Type: Parliamentary republic. **Head of state:** Pres. Imomali Rakhmonov; in office: Nov. 20, 1992. **Head of government:** vacant.

Economy: Industries: Cement, knitwear, footwear. **Chief crops:** Barley, cotton, wheat, vegetables. **Minerals:** Coal, lead, zinc. **Livestock** (1990): cattle: 1.3 mln., sheep: 3.3 mln. **Electricity prod.** (1991): 17 bln. kWh.

Finance: Monetary Unit: Ruble. **Imports** (1990): 1.3 bln. **Exports** (1990): $706 mln.

Transportation: Railroads (1990): **Length:** 554 mi. **Civil aviation** (1990): 5.1 bln. passenger-km.; 1 airport.

Communications: Television sets: 1 per 6 persons. **Telephones:** 1 per 10 persons. **Newspaper circ.** (1990): 298 per 1,000 pop.

Health: Life expectancy at birth (1992): 64 male; 70 female. **Births** (per 1,000 pop. 1992): 40. **Deaths** (per 1,000 pop. 1992): 8. **Hospital beds:** 1 per 93 persons. **Physicians:** 1 per 362 persons. **Infant mortality** (per 1,000 live births 1992): 74.

Major International Organizations: UN, CIS.

There were settled societies in the region from about 3000 B.C. Throughout history, the region has undergone invasions by Iranians (Arabs who converted the population to Islam), Mongols, Uzbeks, Afghans, and Russians. In 1924, the Tadzhik ASSR was created within the Uzbek SSR. The Tadzhik SSR was proclaimed in 1929. Tajikistan declared independence Sept. 9, 1991. It became an independent state when the Soviet Union disbanded Dec. 26, 1991. The ruling Communist Party has retained power in Tajikistan. There were demonstrations by opposition forces—anti-communists and Islamic fundamentalists—in 1992.

Tanzania

United Republic of Tanzania

Jamhuri ya Mwungano wa Tanzania

People: Population (1992 est.) 27,791,000. **Pop. density:** 76 per sq. mi. **Urban** (1990): 32%. **Ethnic groups:** African. **Languages:** Swahili, English (both official), many others. **Religions:** Moslems 33%, Christians 33%, traditional beliefs 33%.

Geography: Area: 364,886 sq. mi., more than twice the size of California. **Location:** On coast of E. Africa. **Neighbors:** Kenya, Uganda on N, Rwanda, Burundi, Zaire on W, Zambia, Malawi, Mozambique on S. **Topography:** Hot, arid central plateau, surrounded by the lake region in the W, temperate highlands in N and S, the coastal plains. Mt. Kilimanjaro, 19,340 ft., is highest in Africa. **Capital:** Dar-es-Salaam. **Cities** (1992): Dar-es-Salaam 1.4 mln.

Government: Type: Republic. **Head of state:** Pres. Ali Hassan Mwinyi; b. May 8, 1925; in office: Nov. 5, 1985. **Head of government:** Prime Min. John Malecela; in office: Nov. 9, 1990. **Local divisions:** 25 regions. **Defense:** 3.9% of GDP (1992).

Economy: Industries: Food processing, clothing. **Chief crops:** Sisal, cotton, coffee, tea, tobacco. **Minerals:** Diamonds, gold, nickel. **Other resources:** Hides. **Arable land:** 6%. **Livestock** (1991): cattle: 14 mln.; goats: 8.8 mln.; sheep: 3.5 mln. **Fish catch** (1989): 340,000 metric tons. **Electricity prod.** (1991): 905 mln. kWh. **Labor force:** 90% agric., 10% ind., comm. & govt.

Finance: Monetary unit: Shilling (Mar. 1993: 350 = $1 US). **Gross domestic product** (1991): $6.9 bln. **Per capita GDP:** $260. **Imports** (1991): $1.5 bln.; partners: UK 14%, Jap. 12%, Ger. 10%. **Exports** (1991): $418 mln.; partners: Ger. 15%, UK 13%. **Tourism** (1990): $63 mln. receipts. **National budget** (1990): $631 mln. expenditures. **International reserves less gold** (Jan. 1993): $204 mln. **Consumer prices** (change in 1992): 21.1%.

Transport: Motor vehicles: in use (1990): 44,000 passenger cars; 52,000 comm. vehicles. **Civil aviation** (1991): $280 mln. passenger-km; 19 airports. **Chief ports:** Dar-es-Salaam, Mtwara, Tanga.

Communications: Radios: 1 per 6 persons. **Telephones:** 1 per 174 persons. **Daily newspaper circ.** (1989): 8 per 1,000 pop.

Health: Life expectancy at birth (1992): 50 male; 55 female. **Births** (per 1,000 pop. 1992): 50. **Deaths** (per 1,000 pop. 1992): 16. **Natural increase:** 3.4%. **Hospital beds** (1984): 22,800. **Physicians** (1984): 1,065. **Infant mortality** (per 1,000 live births 1992): 103.

Education (1987): **Literacy:** 85%. **Attendance:** 87% attend primary school.

Major International Organizations: UN and all of its specialized agencies, OAU, Commonwealth of Nations.

Embassy: 2139 R. St. NW 20008; 939-6125.

The Republic of Tanganyika in E. Africa and the island Republic of Zanzibar, off the coast of Tanganyika, joined into a single nation, the United Republic of Tanzania, Apr. 26, 1964. Zanzibar retains internal self-government.

Tanganyika. Arab colonization and slaving began in the 8th century AD; Portuguese sailors explored the coast by about 1500. Other Europeans followed.

In 1885 Germany established German East Africa of which Tanganyika formed the bulk. It became a League of Nations mandate and, after 1946, a UN trust territory, both under Britain. It became independent Dec. 9, 1961, and a republic within the Commonwealth a year later.

In 1967 the government set on a socialist course; it nationalized all banks and many industries. The government also ordered that Swahili, not English, be used in all official business.

Tanzanian forces drove Idi Amin from Uganda, Mar., 1979.

Zanzibar, the Isle of Cloves, lies 23 mi. off the coast of Tanganyika; its area is 621 sq. mi. The island of **Pemba,** 25 mi. to the NE, area 380 sq. mi., is included in the administration. The total population (1990 est.) is 375,000.

Chief industry is the production of cloves and clove oil of which Zanzibar and Pemba produce the bulk of the world's supply.

Zanzibar was for centuries the center for Arab slave-traders. Portugal ruled for 2 centuries until ousted by Arabs around 1700. Zanzibar became a British Protectorate in 1890; independence came Dec. 10, 1963. Revolutionary forces overthrew the Sultan Jan. 12, 1964. The new government ousted Western diplomats and newsmen, slaughtered thousands of Arabs, and nationalized farms. Union with Tanganyika followed, 1964. The ruling parties of Tanganyika and Zanzibar were united in 1977, as political tension eased.

Thailand

Kingdom of Thailand

Muang Thai or Prathet Thai

People: Population (1992 est.): 57,624,000. **Age distrib.** (%): 0–14: 45.0; 15–59: 49.0; 60+: 6.0. **Pop. density:** 290 per sq. mi. **Urban** (1990): 20%. **Ethnic groups:** Thai 75%, Chinese 14%, others 11%. **Languages:** Thai, (official), Chinese, Malay, regional dialects. **Religions:** Buddhist 95%, Moslem 4%.

Geography: Area: 198,456 sq. mi., about the size of Texas. **Location:** On Indochinese and Malayan Peninsulas in S.E. Asia. **Neighbors:** Myanmar on W. Laos on N, Cambodia on E, Malaysia on S. **Topography:** A plateau dominates the NE third of Thailand, dropping to the fertile alluvial valley of the Chao Phraya R. in the center. Forested mountains are in N, with narrow fertile valleys. The southern peninsula region is covered by rain forests. **Capital:** Bangkok. **Cities** (1991 est.): Bangkok (met.): 6.0 mln.

Government: Type: Constitutional monarchy. **Head of state:** King Bhumibol Adulyadej; b. Dec. 5, 1927; in office: June 9, 1946. **Head of government:** Prime Min. Chuan Leekpai; in office: Sept. 23, 1992. **Local divisions:** 72 provinces. **Defense:** 3.0% of GNP (1992).

Economy: Industries: Textiles, mining, wood prods., tourism. **Chief crops:** Rice (a major export), corn tapioca, sugarcane. **Minerals:** Antimony, tin (among largest producers), tungsten, iron, gas. **Other resources:** Forests (teak is exported), rubber. **Arable land:** 34%. **Livestock** (1991): cattle: 5.6 mln.; pigs: 4.9 mln. **Fish catch** (1989): 2.3 mln. metric tons. **Electricity prod.** (1991): 37.5 bln. kWh. **Labor force:** 59% agric.; 26% ind. & comm.; 10% serv.; 8% govt.

Finance: Monetary unit: Baht (Mar. 1993: 25.36 = $1 US). **Gross national product** (1991): $92.6 bln. **Per capita GNP:** $1,630. **Imports** (1991): $39.0 bln.; partners: Jap. 30%, U.S. 11%. **Exports** (1991): $27.5 bln.; partners: Jap. 17%, U.S. 22%. **Tourism** (1990): $4.3 mln. receipts. **National budget** (1992): $17.9 bln. **International reserves less gold** (Mar. 1993): $21.4 bln. **Gold:** 2.47 mln. oz t. **Consumer prices** (change in 1991): 5.7%.

Transport: Railroads (1990): **Length:** 2,399 mi. **Motor vehicles:** in use (1990): 655,000 passenger cars, 1.5 mln. comm. vehicles. **Civil aviation** (1991): 18.2 bln. passenger-km; 24 airports with scheduled flights. **Chief ports:** Bangkok, Sattahip.

Communication: Television sets: 1 per 17 persons. **Radios:** 1 per 5.7 persons. **Telephones:** 1 per 41 persons. **Daily newspaper circ.** (1989): 50 per 1,000 pop.

Health: Life expectancy at birth (1992): 67 male; 71 female. **Births** (per 1,000 pop. 1992): 20 **Deaths** (per 1,000 pop. 1992): 7. **Natural increase:** 1.3%. **Hospital beds:** 1 per 597 persons. **Physicians:** 1 per 4,227 persons. **Infant mortality** (per 1,000 live births 1992): 35.

Education (1991): **Literacy:** 89%. **Years compulsory:** 6; attendance 96%.

Major International Organizations: UN (GATT, World Bank).

Embassy: 2300 Kalorama Rd. NW 20008; 483-7200.

Thais began migrating from southern China in the 11th century. Thailand is the only country in SE Asia never taken over by a European power, thanks to King Mongkut and his son King Chulalongkorn who ruled from 1851 to 1910, modernized the country, and signed trade treaties with both Britain and France. A bloodless revolution in 1932 limited the monarchy.

Japan occupied the country in 1941.

The military took over the government in a bloody 1976 coup. Kriangsak Chomanan, prime minister resigned, Feb. 1980, under opposition over soaring inflation, oil price increases, labor unrest and growing crime. Chatichai Choonhavan was chosen prime minister in a democratic election, Aug. 1988. In Feb. 1991, the military ousted Choonhavan in a bloodless coup. Elections were held Sept. 1992; Chuan Leekpai was chosen prime minister.

Vietnamese troops had crossed the border and been repulsed by Thai forces in the 1980s.

Togo

Republic of Togo

République Togolaise

People: Population (1992 est.): 3,958,000. **Age distrib.** (%): 0–14: 45.3; 15–59: 49.7; 60+:5.0.**Pop. density:** 176 per sq. mi. **Urban** (1990): 25%. **Ethnic groups:** Ewe 35%, Mina 6%, Kabye 22%. **Languages:** French (official), Gur & Kwa languages. **Religions:** Traditional 50%, Christian 30%, Moslem 20%.

Geography: Area: 21,622 sq. mi., slightly smaller than West Virginia. **Location:** On S coast of W. Africa. **Neighbors:** Ghana on W, Burkina Faso on N, Benin on E. **Topography:** A range of hills running SW-NE splits Togo into 2 savanna plains regions. **Capital:** Lomé. **Cities** (1989 est.): Lomé 600,000.

Government: Type: in transition. **Head of state:** Pres. Gnassingbe Eyadema; b. Dec. 26, 1937; in office: Apr. 14, 1967. **Head of government:** Prime Min. Joseph Kokou Koffgoh. In office: Aug. 27, 1991. **Local divisions:** 21 prefectures.

Economy: Industries: Textiles, shoes. **Chief crops:** Coffee, cocoa, yams, manioc, millet, rice. **Minerals:** Phosphates. **Arable land:** 26%. **Electricity prod.** (1991): 209 mln. kWh. **Labor force:** 75% agric.; 20% industry.

Finance: Monetary unit: CFA franc (Mar. 1993: 273 = $1 US). **Gross domestic product** (1990): $1.5 bln. **Per capita GDP:** $400. **Imports** (1990): $502 mln.; partners: EC 61%. **Exports** (1990): $363 mln.; partners: EC 70%. **Tourism** (1990): $23 mln. receipts. **International reserves less gold** (Jan. 1993): $272 mln. **Gold:** 13,000 oz t. **Consumer prices** (change in 1991): 1.0%.

Transport: Railroads (1991): **Length:** 326 mi. **Motor vehicles:** in use (1990): 45,000 passenger cars. **Chief ports:** Lome.

Communications: Television sets: 1 per 156 persons. **Radios:** 1 per 5.0 persons. **Telephones:** 1 per 169 persons. **Daily newspaper circ.** (1991): 3 per 1,000 pop.

Health: Life expectancy at birth (1992): 54 male; 58 female. **Births** (per 1,000 pop. 1992): 48. **Deaths** (per 1,000 pop. 1992): 12. **Natural increase:** 3.6%. **Hospital beds:** 1 per 752 persons. **Physicians:** 1 per 12,992 persons. **Infant mortality** (per 1,000 live births 1992): 94.

Education (1990): **Literacy:** 45%.

Major International Organizations: UN (GATT, IMF), OAU.

Embassy: 2208 Massachusetts Ave. NW 20008; 234-4212.

The Ewe arrived in southern Togo several centuries ago. The country later became a major source of slaves. Germany took control in 1884. France and Britain administered Togoland as UN trusteeships. The French sector became the republic of Togo Apr. 27, 1960.

The population is divided between Bantus in the S and Hamitic tribes in the N. Togo has actively promoted regional integration, as a means of stimulating the economy.

Some 25,000 people fled Togo to the neighboring countries of Ghana and Benin as a result of civil unrest in 1993.

Tonga

Kingdom of Tonga

Pule 'anga Tonga

People: Population (1992 est.): 102,000. **Age distrib.** (%): 0–14: 44.4; 15–59; 50.5; 60+: 5.1. **Pop. density:** 377 per sq. mi. **Ethnic groups:** Tongans 98%, other Polynesian, European. **Languages:** Tongan, English (both official). **Religions:** Free Wesleyan 47%, Roman Catholics 14%, Free Church of Tonga 14%, Mormons 9%, Church of Tonga 9%.

Geography: Area: 270 sq. mi., smaller than New York City. **Location:** In western S. Pacific O. **Neighbors:** Nearest is Fiji, on W, New Zealand, on S. **Topography:** Tonga comprises 169 volcanic and coral islands, 45 inhabited. **Capital:** Nuku'alofa. **Cities** (1986): Nuku'alofa (met.) 29,000.

Government: Type: Constitutional monarchy. **Head of state:** King Taufa'ahau Tupou IV; b. July 4, 1918; in office: Dec. 16, 1965. **Head of government:** Prime Min. Baron Vaea; in office: Aug. 21, 1991. **Local divisions:** 3 main island groups.

Economy: Industries: Tourism. **Chief crops:** Coconut products, bananas are exported. **Other resources:** Fish. **Arable land:** 25%. **Electricity prod.** (1991): 8 mln. kWh. **Labor force:** 45% agric, 27% services.

Finance: Monetary unit: Pa'anga (Apr. 1993: 1.36 = $1 US). **Gross domestic product** (1990): $92 mln. **Imports** (1991): $59 mln.; partners: N Z 39%, Aust. 25%. **Exports** (1991): $13 mln.; partners: Aust. 29%, N Z 56%. **Tourism** (1991): $7.6 mln. receipts.

Transport: Motor vehicles: in use (1989): 1,400 passenger cars, 2,700 comm. vehicles. **Chief ports:** Nuku'alofa.

Communications: Radios: 1 per 1.2 persons. **Telephones:** 1 per 18 persons.

Health: Life expectancy at birth (1992): 65 male; 70 female. **Births** (per 1,000 pop. 1992): 27. **Deaths** (per 1,000 pop. 1992): 5. **Natural increase:** 2.2%. **Infant mortality** (per 1,000 live births 1992): 23.

Education (1988): **Literacy:** 99%. **Years compulsory:** 8. **Attendance:** 77%.

The islands were first visited by the Dutch in the early 17th century. A series of civil wars ended in 1845 with establishment of the Tupou dynasty. In 1900 Tonga became a British protectorate. On June 4, 1970, Tonga became independent and a member of the Commonwealth.

Trinidad and Tobago

Republic of Trinidad and Tobago

People: Population (1992 est.): 1,285,000. **Age distrib.** (%): 0–14: 32.9; 15–59: 58.7; 60+: 8.4. **Pop. density:** 648 per sq. mi. **Ethnic groups:** Africans 43%, East Indians 40%, mixed 14%. **Languages:** English (official). **Religions:** Roman Catholic 32%, Protestant 29%, Hindu 25%, Moslem 6%.

Geography: Area: 1,980 sq. mi., the size of Delaware. **Location:** Off eastern coast of Venezuela. **Neighbors:** Nearest is Venezuela on SW. **Topography:** Three low mountain ranges cross Trinidad E-W, with a well-watered plain between N and Central Ranges. Parts of E and W coasts are swamps. Tobago, 116 sq. mi., lies 20 mi. NE. **Capital:** Port-of-Spain. **Cities** (1990 met. est.): Port-of-Spain 300,000; San Fernando 50,000.

Government: Type: Parliamentary democracy. **Head of state:** Pres. Noor Hassanali; in office: Mar. 19, 1987. **Head of government:** Prime Min. Patrick Manning; in office: Dec. 17, 1991. **Local divisions:** 8 counties, 3 municipilities.

Economy: Industries: Oil products, rum, cement, tourism. **Chief crops:** Sugar, cocoa, coffee, citrus fruits, bananas. **Minerals:** Asphalt, oil, **Crude oil reserves** (1987): 567 mln. bbls. **Arable land:** 14%. **Electricity prod.** (1991): 3.4 bln. kWh. **Labor force:** 18% construction-utilities, 14% manuf., mining, commerce, 47% services.

Finance: Monetary unit: Dollar (Mar. 1993: 4.25 = $1 US). **Gross domestic product** (1990): $4.9 bln. **Per capita GDP:** $3,600. **Imports** (1991): $1.6 bln.; partners: U.S. 51%, UK 8%. **Exports** (1991): $1.9 bln.; partners: U.S. 53%. **Tourism** (1990): $122 mln. receipts. **National budget** (1991): $1.7 bln. expenditures. **International reserves less gold** (Mar. 1993): $172 mln. **Gold:** 54,000 oz t. **Consumer prices** (change in 1992): 6.5%.

Transport: Motor vehicles: in use (1989): 269,000 passenger cars, 68,000 comm. vehicles. **Civil aviation:** (1990): 2.7 bln. passenger-km; 2 airports. **Chief ports:** Port-of-Spain.

Communications: Television sets: 1 per 5 persons. **Radios:** 1 per 3.1 persons. **Telephones:** 1 per 5 persons. **Daily newspaper circ.** (1990): 140 per 1,000 pop.

Health: Life expectancy at birth (1992): 68 male; 73 female. **Births** (per 1,000 pop. 1992): 21. **Deaths** (per 1,000 pop. 1992): 6. **Natural increase:** 1.5%. **Hospital beds:** 1 per 318 persons. **Physicians:** 1 per 1,543 persons. **Infant mortality** (per 1,000 pop. 1992): 18.

Education (1988): **Literacy:** 97%. **Years compulsory:** 8.

Major International Organizations: UN (GATT, IMF, WHO), Commonwealth of Nations, OAS.

Embassy: 1708 Massachusetts Ave. NW 20036; 467-6490.

Columbus sighted Trinidad in 1498. A British possession since 1802, Trinidad and Tobago won independence Aug. 31, 1962. It became a republic in 1976. The People's National Movement party has held control of the government since 1956.

The nation is one of the most prosperous in the Caribbean. Oil production has increased with offshore finds. Middle Eastern oil is refined and exported, mostly to the U.S.

In July 1990, some 120 Moslem extremists captured the parliament building and TV station and took about 50 hostages including Prime Minister Arthur Robinson, who was beaten, shot in the legs, and tied to explosives. After a 6-day siege, the rebels surrendered.

Tunisia

Republic of Tunisia

al Jumhuriyah at-Tunisiyah

People: Population (1992 est.): 8,445,000. **Age distrib.** (%) 0–14: 39.0; 15–59: 54.2; 60+: 6.8. **Pop. density:** 133 per sq. mi. **Ethnic groups:** Arab 98%. **Languages:** Arabic (official), French. **Religions:** Moslem 99%.

Geography: Area: 63,170 sq. mi., about the size of Missouri. **Location:** On N coast of Africa. **Neighbors:** Algeria on W, Libya on E. **Topography:** The N is wooded and fertile. The central coastal plains are given to grazing and orchards. The S is arid, approaching Sahara Desert. **Capital:** Tunis. **Cities** (1984 est.): Tunis 1,000,000, Sfax 475,000.

Government: Type: Republic. **Head of state:** Pres. Gen. Zine al-Abidine Ben Ali; b. Sept 3, 1936; in office: Nov. 7, 1987. **Head of government:** Prime Min. Hamed Karoui; in office: Sept. 27, 1989. **Local divisions:** 23 governorates. **Defense:** 5.0% of GDP (1992).

Economy: Industries: Food processing, textiles, oil products, mining, construction materials. **Chief crops:** Grains, dates, olives, citrus fruits, figs, vegetables, grapes. **Minerals:** Phosphates, iron, oil, lead, zinc. **Crude oil reserves** (1987): 1.7 bln. bbls. **Arable land:** 20%. **Livestock** (1990): sheep: 5.0 mln.; goats: 1 mln. **Fish catch** (1990): 95,000 metric tons. **Electricity prod.** (1991): 4.2 bln. kWh. **Labor force:** 25% agric.; 34% industry; 40% serv.

Finance: Monetary unit: Dinar (Mar. 1993: 1.00 = $1 US). **Gross domestic product** (1991): $10.9 bln. **Per capita GDP:** $1,320. **Imports** (1992): $6.4 bln.; partners: EC 68%. **Exports** (1992): $4.0 bln.; partners: EC 73%. **Tourism** (1990): $953 mln. receipts. **National budget** (1992): $5.4 bln. expenditures. **International reserves less gold** (Mar. 1993): $730 mln. **Gold:** 215,000 oz t. **Consumer prices** (change in 1992): 5.4%.

Transport: Railroads (1990): **Length:** 1,343 mi. **Motor vehicles:** in use (1989): 321,000 passenger cars, 208,000 comm. vehicles; **Civil aviation:** (1991): 1.5 bln. passenger-km; 5 airports. **Chief ports:** Tunis, Sfax, Bizerte.

Communications: Television sets: 1 per 13 persons. **Radios:** 1 per 4.7 persons. **Telephones:** 1 per 24 persons. **Daily newspaper circ.** (1991): 28 per 1,000 pop.

Health: Life expectancy at birth (1992): 70 male; 74 female. **Births** (per 1,000 pop. 1992): 26. **Deaths** (per 1,000 pop. 1992): 5. **Natural increase:** 2.1%. **Hospital beds:** 1 per 506 persons. **Physicians:** 1 per 1,834 persons. **Infant mortality** (per 1,000 pop. live births 1992): 38.

Education (1990): **Literacy:** 62%. **Years compulsory:** 8; attendance 85%.

Major International Organizations: UN, Arab League, OAU.

Embassy: 1515 Massachusetts Ave. NW 20005; 862-1850.

Site of ancient Carthage and a former Barbary state under the suzerainty of Turkey, Tunisia became a protectorate of France under a treaty signed May 12, 1881. The nation became independent Mar. 20, 1956, and ended the monarchy the following year.

Tunisia has actively repressed Islamic fundamentalism.

Turkey

Republic of Turkey

Turkiye Cumhuriyeti

People: Population (1992 est.): 59,640,000. **Age distrib.** (%): 0–14: 38.5; 15–59: 54.9; 60+: 6.6. **Pop. density:** 197 per sq. mi. **Urban** (1990): 61%. **Ethnic groups:** Turks 80%, Kurds 17%. **Languages:** Turkish (official), Kurdish, Arabic. **Religions:** Moslem 98%.

Geography: Area: 301,381 sq. mi., twice the size of California. **Location:** Occupies Asia Minor, between Mediterranean and Black Seas. **Neighbors:** Bulgaria, Greece on W, Georgia, Armenia on N, Iran on E, Iraq, Syria on S. **Topography:** Central Turkey has wide plateaus, with hot, dry summers and cold winters. High mountains ring the interior on all but W, with more than 20 peaks over 10,000 ft. Rolling plains are in W; mild, fertile coastal plains are in S, W. **Capital:** Ankara. **Cities** (1990 est.): Istanbul 6,700,000; Ankara 2,553,000; Izmir 1,700,000; Adana 931,000.

Government: Type: Republic. **Head of state:** Pres. Suleyman Demirel; in office: May 16, 1993. **Head of government:** Prime Min. Tansu Ciller; in office: July 5, 1993. **Local divisions:** 73 provinces. **Defense:** 3.5% of GDP (1992).

Economy: Industries: Iron, steel, machinery, metal prods., cars, processed foods. **Chief crops:** Tobacco, cereals, cotton, barley, corn, fruits, potatoes, sugar beets. **Minerals:** Chromium, mercury, boron, copper, coal. **Crude oil reserves** (1987): 139 mln. bbls. **Other resources:** Wool, silk, forests. **Arable land:** 30%. **Livestock** (1991): cattle: 12.0 mln.; sheep: 31 mln. **Fish catch** (1989): 457,000 metric tons. **Electricity prod.** (1991): 44 bln. kWh. **Crude steel prod.** (1991): 9.2 mln. metric tons. **Labor force:** 56% agric.; 14% ind. and comm.; 29% serv.

Finance: Monetary unit: Lira (Aug. 1993: 11,366= $1 US). **Gross domestic product** (1991): $198 bln. **Per capita GDP:** $3,400. **Imports** (1991): $21.0 bln.; partners: EC 49%, U.S. 7%. **Exports** (1991): $13.5 bln.; partners: EC 49%. **Tourism** (1991): $2.5 bln. receipts. **National budget** (1992): $49.7 bln. expenditures. **International reserves less gold** (Feb. 1993): $6.4 bln. **Gold:** 4.0 mln. oz t. **Consumer prices** (change in 1992): 70.1%.

Transport: Railroads (1991): **Length:** 5,238 mi. **Motor vehicles:** in use (1990): 1.6 mln. passenger cars, 584,000 comm. vehicles. **Civil aviation** (1991): 4.2 bln. passenger-km; 12 airports with scheduled flights. **Chief ports:** Istanbul, Izmir, Mersin, Samsun.

Communications: Television sets: 1 per 5 persons. **Radios:** 1 per 7.8 persons. **Telephones:** 1 per 7 persons.

Health: Life expectancy at birth (1992): 68 male; 72 female. **Births** (per 1,000 pop. 1992): 28. **Deaths** (per 1,000 pop. 1992): 6. **Natural increase:** 2.2%. **Hospital beds:** 1 per 465 persons. **Physicians:** 1 per 1,108 persons. **Infant mortality** (per 1,000 live births 1992): 54.

Education (1990): **Literacy:** 81%. **Years compulsory:** 6; attendance 95%.

Major International Organizations: UN (GATT, WHO, IMF), NATO, OECD, EC.

Embassy: 1714 Massachusetts Ave. NW 20036.

Ancient inhabitants of Turkey were among the worlds first agriculturalists. Such civilizations as the Hittite, Phrygian, and Lydian flourished in Asiatic Turkey (Asia Minor), as did much of Greek civilization. After the fall of Rome in the 5th century, Constantinople was the capital of the Byzantine Empire for 1,000 years. It fell in 1453 to Ottoman Turks, who ruled a vast empire for over 400 years.

Just before World War I, Turkey, or the Ottoman Empire, ruled what is now Syria, Lebanon, Iraq, Jordan, Israel, Saudi Arabia, Yemen, and islands in the Aegean Sea.

Turkey joined Germany and Austria in World War I and its defeat resulted in loss of much territory and fall of the sultanate. A republic was declared Oct. 29, 1923. The Caliphate (spiritual leadership of Islam) was renounced 1924.

Long embroiled with Greece over Cyprus, off Turkey's south coast, Turkey invaded the island July 20, 1974, after Greek officers seized the Cypriot government as a step toward unification with Greece. Turkey sought a new government for Cyprus, with Greek Cypriot and Turkish Cypriot zones. In reaction to Turkey's moves, the U.S. cut off military aid in 1975. Turkey, in turn, suspended the use of most U.S. bases. Aid was restored in 1978. There was a military takeover, Sept. 12, 1980.

Religious and ethnic tensions and active left and right extremists have caused endemic violence. Martial law, imposed in 1978, was lifted in 1984. The military formally transferred power to an elected parliament in 1983.

Turkey was a member of the Allied forces which ousted Iraq from Kuwait, 1991. In the aftermath of the war, millions of Kurdish refugees fled to Turkey's border to escape Iraqi forces.

Kurdish militants raided Turkish diplomatic missions in some 25 Western European cities June 24, 1993. The militants were demanding an independent state for the Kurds.

Turkmenistan

Republic of Turkmenistan

People: Population (1992 est.): 3,838,000. **Pop. density:** 20 per sq. mi. **Urban** (1991): 46%. **Ethnic groups:** Turkmen 72%, Russian 9%, Uzbek 9%. **Languages:** Turkmen, Russian. **Religion:** Moslem 85%.

Geography: Area: 188,417 sq. mi., slightly larger than California. **Neighbors:** Uzbekistan, Kazakhstan on N, NE, Afghanistan and Iran on S. The Kara Kum desert occupies 80% of the area. **Capital:** Ashkhabad. **Cities** (1991): Ashkhabad 416,000.

Government: Type: Republic. **Head of state:** Pres. Saparmurad Niyazov. **Head of government:** Prime Min. Khan A. Akhmedov. **Local divisions:** 5 regions.

Economy: Industries: Mining, textiles. **Chief crops:** Grain, cotton, grapes. **Minerals:** Coal, sulfur, salt. **Livestock** (1990): sheep: 5.0 mln. **Electricity prod.** (1991): 14.9 bln. kWh.

Finance: Monetary unit: Ruble. **Imports** (1990): $970 mln. **Exports** (1990): $239 mln.

Transportation: Railroads: (1990): **Length:** 1,317 mi.

Communications: Telephones: 1 per 15 persons.

Health: Life expectancy at birth (1992): 59 male; 66 female. **Births** (per 1,000 pop. 1992): 36. **Deaths** (per 1,000 pop. 1992): 9. **Hospital beds:** 1 per 86 persons. **Physicians:** 1 per 274 persons. **Infant mortality** (1 per 1,000 live births 1992): 94.

Major International Organizations: UN, CIS.

The region has been inhabited by Turki tribes since the 10th century. It became part of Russian Turkistan 1881, and a constituent republic of the USSR 1925. Turkmenistan declared independence Oct. 27, 1991, and became an independent state when the Soviet Union disbanded Dec. 25, 1991.

Power rests mostly with the former Communist Party apparatus.

Tuvalu

People: Population (1992 est.): 9,494. **Pop. density:** 949 per sq. mi. **Ethnic group:** Polynesian. **Languages:** Tuvaluan, English. **Religions:** mainly Protestant.

Geography: Area: 10 sq. mi., less than one-half the size of Manhattan. **Location:** 9 islands forming a NW-SE chain 360 mi. long in the SW Pacific O. **Neighbors:** Nearest are Samoa on SE, Fiji on S. **Topography:** The islands are all low-lying atolls, nowhere rising more than 15 ft. above sea level, composed of coral reefs. **Capital:** Funafuti (pop. 1985): 2,800.

Government: Head of state: Queen Elizabeth II, represented by Gov.-Gen. Toaripi Lauti; in office: Oct. 1, 1990. **Head of government:** Prime Min. Bikenibeu Paeniu; in office: Oct. 16, 1989. **Local divisions:** 8 island councils on the permanently inhabited islands.

Economy: Industries: Copra. **Chief crops:** Coconuts. **Labor force:** Approx. 1,500 Tuvaluans work overseas in the Gilberts' phosphate industry, or as overseas seamen.

Finance: Monetary unit: Australian dollar.

Transport: Chief port: Funafuti.

Health: (including former Gilbert Is.) **Life expectancy at birth** (1992): 61 male; 64 female. **Births** (per 1,000 pop. 1992): 29. **Deaths** (per 1,000 pop. 1992): 10. **Natural increase:** 1.9%. **Infant mortality** (per 1,000 live births 1992): 33.

Education: Literacy (1990): 96%.

The Ellice Islands separated from the British Gilbert and Ellice Islands colony in 1975 and became independent Tuvalu, Oct. 1, 1978.

Uganda

Republic of Uganda

People: Population (1992 est.): 19,386,000. **Age distrib.** (%): 0–14: 48.5; 15–59: 47.3; 60+: 4.2. **Pop. density:** 207 per sq. mi. **Urban** (1991): 11%. **Ethnic groups:** Bantu, Nilotic, Nilo-Hamitic, Sudanic tribes. **Languages:** English (official), Luganda, Swahili. **Religions:** Christian 63%, Moslem 6%, traditional beliefs.

Geography: Area: 93,354 sq. mi., slightly smaller than Oregon. **Location:** In E. Central Africa. **Neighbors:** Sudan on N, Zaire on W, Rwanda, Tanzania on S, Kenya on E. **Topography:** Most of Uganda is a high plateau 3,000-6,000 ft. high, with high Ruwenzori range in W (Mt. Margherita 16,750 ft.), volcanoes in SW, NE is arid, W and SW rainy. Lakes Victoria, Edward, Albert form much of borders. **Capital:** Kampala. **Cities** (1991): Kampala 773,000.

Government: Type: Republic. **Head of state:** Pres. Yoweri Kaguta Museveni; b. 1944; in office: Jan. 29, 1986. **Head of government:** Prime Min. George Cosmas Adyebo; in office: Jan. 22, 1991. **Local divisions:** 10 provinces. **Defense:** 1.5% of GDP (1989).

Economy: Chief Crops: Coffee, cotton, tea, corn, bananas, sugar. **Minerals:** Copper, cobalt. **Arable land:** 23%. **Livestock** (1991): cattle: 5.2 mln.; goats: 3.3 mln.; sheep: 1.9 mln. **Fish catch** (1990): 245,000 metric tons. **Electricity prod.** (1991): 312 mln. kWh. **Labor force:** 90% agric.

Finance: Monetary unit: Shilling (Mar. 1993: 1,217 = $1 US). **Gross domestic product** (1991): $5.6 bln. **Per capita GDP:** $300. **Imports** (1991): $196 mln.; partners: Kenya 24%, U.K. 17%. **Exports** (1991): $200 mln.; partners: U.S. 14%, U.K. 12%, Neth. 15%. **National budget** (1989): $790 mln. expenditures. **International reserves less gold** (Jan. 1993): $59 mln. **Consumer prices** (change in 1992): 52.4%.

Transport: Motor vehicles: in use (1990): 35,000 passenger cars, 6,000 comm. vehicles.

Communications: Television sets: 1 per 191 persons. **Radios:** 1 per 5.1 persons. **Telephones:** 1 per 286 persons. **Daily newspaper circ.** (1990): 2 per 1,000 pop.

Health: Life expectancy at birth (1992): 50 male; 52 female. **Births** (per 1,000 pop. 1992): 51. **Deaths** (per 1,000 pop. 1992): 15. **Natural increase:** 3.6%. **Hospital beds:** 1 per 817 persons. **Physicians:** 1 per 20,000 persons. **Infant mortality** (per 1,000 live births 1992): 91.

Education (1989): **Literacy:** 52%. About 50% attend primary school.

Major International Organizations: UN (GATT, WHO, IMF), OAU, Commonwealth of Nations.

Embassy: 5909 16th St. NW 20011; 726-7100.

Britain obtained a protectorate over Uganda in 1894. The country became independent Oct. 9, 1962, and a republic within the Commonwealth a year later. In 1967, the traditional kingdoms, including the powerful Buganda state, were abolished and the central government strengthened.

Gen. Idi Amin seized power from Prime Min. Milton Obote in 1971. As many as 300,000 of his opponents were reported killed in subsequent years. Amin was named president for life in 1976.

In 1972 Amin expelled nearly all of Uganda's 45,000 Asians. In 1973 the U.S. withdrew all diplomatic personnel.

Amid worsening economic and domestic crises, Uganda's troops exchanged invasion attacks with long-standing foe Tanzania, 1978 to 1979. Tanzanian forces, coupled with Ugandan exiles and rebels, ended the dictatorial rule of Amin, Apr. 11, 1979.

Ukraine

Ukrayina

People: Population (1992 est.): 51,994,000. **Age distrib.** (%): 0-19: 24.8; 20-59: 62.1; 60+: 13.0. **Pop. density:** 223 per sq. mi. **Urban** (1991): 68%. **Official language:** Ukrainian. **Ethnic groups:** Ukrainian 73%, Russian 22%. **Religion:** Orthodox 76%, Ukrainian Catholic 13.5%, Moslem 8.2%.

Geography: Area: 233,100 sq. mi. **Location:** In SE Europe. **Neighbors:** Belarus on N, Russia on NE and E, Moldova and Romania on SW, Hungary, Slovakia, and Poland on W. **Topography:** Part of the E. European plain. Mountainous areas include the Carpathians in the SW and the Crimean chain in the S. Arable black soil constitutes a large part of the country. **Climate:** Average temperature range from 21F in Jan. to 66F in July. Annual precipitation averages 27.5 in. in the W. part of the country and less than 11 in. in the East. **Capital:** Kiev. **Cities** (1991 est.): Kiev 2,637,000; Kharkiv 1,622,000; Donetsk 1,121,000; Dnipropetrovsk 1,100,000; Odessa 1,104,000.

Government: Type: Constitutional republic. **Head of state:** Pres. Leonid M. Kravchuk; b. 1934; in office: December 5, 1991. **Local divisions:** 24 provinces (oblasts), 1 autonomous province.

Economy: Industries: Steel, chemicals, machinery, vehicles, cement. **Chief crops:** Grains, sugar beets, potatoes. **Minerals:** Iron, manganese, chromium, copper, coal, lead, gold, nickel, potassium salts. **Other resources:** Forests. **Arable land:** 56%. **Fish catch** (1990): 550,000 metric tons. **Electricity prod.**

(1990): 76.2 bln. kWh. **Crude steel prod.** (1990): 43.1 mln. metric tons. **Labor force:** 19% agric.; 41% ind. & comm.; 28% services.

Finance: Monetary unit: Karbovanet (May 1993: 3,000 = $1 US). **Gross national product** (1990): $47.6 bln. **Per capita income** (1987): $2,500. **Imports** (1990): $16.7 bln. **Exports** (1990): $13.5 bln. **National budget** (1990): $8 bln. expenditures.

Transport: Railway traffic (1990): 75.8 bln. passenger-km.; 484.1 bln. net ton-km. **Civil aviation** (1990): 16.1 bln. passenger-km., 20 airports. **Chief ports:** Odessa, Kherson, Zhdanov, Sevastopil, Berdiansk.

Communications: Television sets: 1 per 3 persons. **Radios:** 1 per 4 persons. **Daily newspaper circ.** (1990): 202 per 1,000 pop.

Health: Life expectancy at birth (1992): 65 male; 75 female. **Births** (per 1,000 pop. 1992): 14. **Deaths** (per 1,000 pop. 1992): 12. **Hospital beds:** 1 per 74 persons. **Physicians:** 1 per 229 persons. **Infant mortality** (per 1,000 live births 1992): 22.

Education (1990): **Literacy:** 99%.

Major International Organizations: UN, CIS.

The ancient ancestors of Ukrainians, the Trypilians, flourished along the Dnipro River, Ukraine's main artery, from 6000-1000 BC. The Slavic ancestors of the Ukrainians inhabited modern Ukrainian territory well before the first century AD.

The princes of Kyyiv established a strong state called Kyyivan Rus in the 9th century. A strong dynasty was established, with ties to virtually all major European royal families. St. Volodymyr the Great, ruler of Kyyivan Ukraine, accepted Christianity as the national faith in 988. At the crossroads of major European trade routes, Kyyivan Rus reached its zenith during the reign of Iaroslav the Wise (1019-1054). While directly absorbing most of the Asian invasion of Europe in the 13th century, the Ukrainian state slowly disintegrated and was divided mainly between Russia and Poland.

The Ukrainian Cossack State, founded in the late 16th century, waged numerous wars of liberation against the occupiers of Ukraine: Russia, Poland, and Turkey. By the late 18th century, Ukrainian independence was lost. Ukraine's neighbors once again divided its territory. At the turn of the last century, Ukraine was occupied by 2 colonial powers, Russia and Austria-Hungary.

An independent Ukrainian National Republic was proclaimed on January 22, 1918. In 1921, Ukraine's neighbors occupied and divided Ukrainian territory. In 1932-33, the Soviet government engineered a man-made famine in eastern Ukraine, resulting in the deaths of 7-10 million Ukrainians.

In March 1939, independent Carpatho-Ukraine was the first European state to wage war against Nazi-led aggression in the region. During WW2 the Ukrainian nationalist underground and its Ukrainian Insurgent Army (UPA) fought both Nazi German and Soviet forces. The restoration of Ukrainian independence was declared on June 30, 1941. Over 5 million Ukrainians lost their lives during the War. With the reoccupation of Ukraine by Soviet troops in 1944 came a renewed wave of mass arrests, executions, and deportations of Ukrainians.

The world's worst nuclear power plant disaster occurred in Chernobyl, Ukraine, in April 1986.

Ukrainian independence was restored in 1991 with the dissolution of the Soviet Union. In a landslide national referendum, over 90% of Ukraine's population voted for independence on Dec. 1, 1991.

Ukraine suffered economic hardships in 1993; inflation hit 170% in the first quarter, and the GDP fell 10 percent from the previous year.

United Arab Emirates

Ittihād al-Imarat al-Arabiyah

People: Population (1992 est.): 2,522,000. **Pop. density:** 78 per sq. mi. **Ethnic groups:** Arab, Iranian, Pakistani, Indian. **Languages:** Arabic (official), several others. **Religions:** Moslem 96%, Christian, Hindu.

Geography: Area: 32,000 sq. mi., the size of Maine. **Location:** On the S shore of the Persian Gulf. **Neighbors:** Qatar on N, Saudi Ar. on W, S, Oman on E. **Topography:** A barren, flat coastal plain gives way to uninhabited sand dunes on the S. Hajar Mtns. are on E. **Capital:** Abu Dhabi. **Cities** (1990 est.): Abu Dhabi 722,000; Dubavy 266,000.

Government: Type: Federation of emirates. **Head of state:** Pres. Zaid ibn Sultan an-Nahayan b. 1923; in office: Dec. 2, 1971. **Head of government:** Prime Min. Sheikh Maktum ibn Rashid al-Maktum; in office: Nov. 20, 1990. **Local divisions:** 7 autonomous emirates: Abu Dhabi, Ajman, Dubai, Fujaira, Ras al-Khaimah, Sharjah, Umm al-Qaiwain. **Defense:** 6.8% of GDP (1989).

Economy: Chief crops: Vegetables, dates, limes. **Minerals:** Oil. **Crude oil reserves** (1991): 66 bln. barrels. **Arable land:** 1%. **Electricity prod.** (1991): 17.0 bln. kWh. **Labor force:** 5% agric.; 85% ind. and commerce; 5% serv.; 5% gvt.

Finance: Monetary unit: Dirham (July 1993: 3.67 = $1 US). **Gross domestic product** (1989): $28.4 bln. **Per capita GDP:** $12,100. **Imports** (1992): $13.7 bln.; partners: Jap. 14%, UK 11%, Ger. 6%. **Exports** (1990): $21.3 bln.; partners: Jap. 36%. **International reserves less gold** (Feb. 1993): $5.5 bln. **Gold:** 797,000 oz t.

Transport: Motor Vehicles (1990): 302,000 passenger cars; 157,000 commercial vehicles. **Civil aviation** (1991): 3.8 bln. passenger-km., 4 airports with scheduled flights. **Chief ports:** Dubavy, Abu Dhabi.

Communications: Television sets: 1 per 12 persons. **Radios:** 1 per 4.7 persons. **Telephones:** 1 per 4.3 persons.

Health: Life expectancy at birth (1992): 70 male, 74 female. **Hospital beds:** 1 per 442 persons. **Physicians:** 1 per 1,057 persons. **Infant mortality** (per 1,000 live births 1992): 23%.

Education (1989): **Literacy:** 68%. **Years Compulsory:** ages 6-12.

Major International Organizations: UN (World Bank, IMF, ILO), Arab League, OPEC.

Embassy: 600 New Hampshire Ave. NW 20037; 338-6500.

The 7 "Trucial Sheikdoms" gave Britain control of defense and foreign relations in the 19th century. They merged to become an independent state Dec. 2, 1971.

The Abu Dhabi Petroleum Co. was fully nationalized in 1975. Oil revenues have given the UAE one of the highest per capita GDPs in the world. International banking has grown in recent years.

United Kingdom of Great Britain and Northern Ireland

People: Population (1992 est.): 57,797,800. **Age distrib.** (%): 0–14: 19.2; 15–59: 60.1; 60+: 20.7. **Pop. density:** 613 per sq. mi. **Urban** (1990): 90%. **Ethnic groups:** English 81.5%, Scottish 9.6%, Irish 2.4%, Welsh 1.9%, Ulster 1.8%; West Indian, Indian, Pakistani over 2%; others. **Languages:** English, Welsh spoken in western Wales. **Religions:** Church of England, Roman Catholic.

Geography: Area: 94,226 sq. mi., slightly smaller than Oregon. **Location:** Off the NW coast of Europe, across English Channel, Strait of Dover, and North Sea. **Neighbors:** Ireland to W, France to SE. **Topography:** England is mostly rolling land, rising to Uplands of southern Scotland; Lowlands are in center of Scotland, granite Highlands are in N. Coast is heavily indented, especially on W. British Isles have milder climate than N Europe, due to the Gulf Stream, and ample rainfall. Severn, 220 mi., and Thames, 215 mi., are longest rivers. **Capital:** London. **Cities** (1988 est.): London 6,735,000; Birmingham 993,000; Glasgow 703,000; Leeds 710,000; Sheffield 532,000; Liverpool 469,000; Manchester 445,000; Edinburgh 433,000; Bradford 463,000; Bristol 377,000.

Government: Type: Constitutional monarchy. **Head of state:** Queen Elizabeth II; b. Apr. 21, 1926; in office: Feb. 6, 1952. **Head of government:** Prime Min. John Major; b. Mar. 29, 1943; in office: Nov. 28, 1990. **Local divisions:** England and Wales: 47 non-metro counties, 7 metro counties, Greater London; Scotland: 9 regions, 3 island areas; N. Ireland: 26 districts. **Defense:** 4.3% of GDP (1991).

Economy: Industries: Steel, metals, vehicles, shipbuilding, banking, textiles, chemicals, electronics, aircraft, machinery, distilling. **Chief crops:** Grains, sugar beets, fruits, vegetables. **Minerals:** Coal, tin, oil, gas, limestone, iron, salt, clay. **Crude oil reserves** (1991): 4.0 bln. bbls. **Arable land:** 30%. **Livestock** (1991): cattle: 11.8 mln.; pigs: 7.3 mln.; sheep: 29.9 mln. **Fish catch** (1990): 803,000 metric tons. **Electricity prod.** (1991): 316 bln. kWh. **Crude steel prod.** (1991): 16.4 mln. metric tons. **Labor force:** 2% agric.; 26% manuf. & eng., 60% services.

Finance: Monetary unit: Pound (June 1992: .54 = $1 US). **Gross domestic product** (1991): $915 bln. **Per capita GDP:** $15,900. **Imports** (1992): $221 bln.; partners: EC 52%, U.S. 10%. **Exports** (1992): $190 bln.; partners: EC 53%, U.S. 13%. **Tourism** (1991): receipts: $18.8 bln. **National budget** (1992): $469 bln. expenditures. **International reserves less gold** (Mar. 1993): $38 bln. **Gold:** 19.0 mln. oz t. **Consumer prices** (change in 1992): 3.7%.

Transport: Railroads (1991): **Length:** 23,518 mi. **Motor vehicles:** in use (1991): 19.7 mln. passenger cars, 2.7 mln. comm. vehicles. **Civil aviation** (1990): 79.5 bln. passenger-km: 56 airports with scheduled flights. **Chief ports:** London, Liverpool, Glasgow, Southampton, Cardiff, Belfast.

Communications: Television sets: 1 per 3 persons. **Radios:** 1 per 1 person. **Telephones:** 1 per 1.9 persons. **Daily newspaper circ.** (1990): 388 per 1,000 pop.

Health: Life expectancy at birth: (1992): 73 male; 79 female. **Births:** (per 1,000 pop. 1992): 14. **Deaths:** (per 1,000 pop. 1992): 11. **Natural increase:** 0.3%. **Hospital beds:** 1 per 138 persons. **Physicians:** 1 per 611 persons. **Infant mortality:** (per 1,000 live births 1992): 8.

Education (1991): **Literacy:** 99%. **Years compulsory:** 12; attendance 99%.

Major International Organizations: UN all of and its specialized agencies, NATO, EC, OECD.

Embassy: 3100 Massachusetts Ave. NW 20008; 462-1340.

The United Kingdom of Great Britain and Northern Ireland comprises England, Wales, Scotland, and Northern Ireland.

Queen and Royal Family. The ruling sovereign is Elizabeth II of the House of Windsor, born Apr. 21, 1926, elder daughter of King George VI. She succeeded to the throne Feb. 6, 1952, and was crowned June 2, 1953. She was married Nov. 20, 1947, to Lt. Philip Mountbatten, born June 10, 1921, former Prince of Greece. He was created Duke of Edinburgh, Earl of Merioneth, and Baron Greenwich, and given the style H.R.H., Nov. 19, 1947; he was given the title Prince of the United Kingdom and Northern Ireland Feb. 22, 1957. Prince Charles Philip Arthur George, born Nov. 14, 1948, is the Prince of Wales and heir apparent. His son, William Philip Arthur Louis, born June 21, 1982, is second in line to the throne.

Parliament is the legislative governing body for the United Kingdom, with certain powers over dependent units. It consists of 2 houses: The **House of Lords** includes 763 hereditary and 314 life peers and peeresses, certain judges, 2 archbishops and 24 bishops of the Church of England. Total membership is over 1,000. The **House of Commons** has 650 members, who are elected by direct ballot and divided as follows: England 516; Wales 36; Scotland 71; Northern Ireland 12.

Resources and Industries. Great Britain's major occupations are manufacturing and trade. Metals and metal-using industries contribute more than 50% of the exports. Of about 60 million acres of land in England, Wales and Scotland, 46 million are farmed, of which 17 million are arable, the rest pastures.

Large oil and gas fields have been found in the North Sea. Commercial oil production began in 1975. There are large deposits of coal.

Britain imports all of its cotton, rubber, sulphur, about 80% of its wool, half of its food and iron ore, also certain amounts of paper, tobacco, chemicals. Manufactured goods made from these basic materials have been exported since the industrial age began. Main exports are machinery, chemicals, woolen and synthetic textiles, clothing, autos and trucks, iron and steel, locomotives, ships, jet aircraft, farm machinery, drugs, radio, TV, radar and navigation equipment, scientific instruments, arms, whisky.

Religion and Education. The Church of England is Protestant Episcopal. The queen is its temporal head, with rights of appointments to archbishoprics, bishoprics, and other offices. There are 2 provinces, Canterbury and York, each headed by an archbishop. The most famous church is Westminster Abbey (1050-1760), site of coronations, tombs of Elizabeth I, Mary of Scots, kings, poets, and of the Unknown Warrior.

The most celebrated British universities are Oxford and Cambridge, each dating to the 13th century. There are about 40 other universities.

History. Britain was part of the continent of Europe until about 6,000 BC, but migration of peoples across the English Channel continued long afterward. Celts arrived 2,500 to 3,000 years ago. Their language survives in Welsh, and Gaelic enclaves.

England was added to the Roman Empire in 43 AD. After the withdrawal of Roman legions in 410, waves of Jutes, Angles, and Saxons arrived from German lands. They contended with Danish raiders for control from the 8th through 11th centuries.

The last successful invasion was by French speaking Normans in 1066, who united the country with their dominions in France.

Opposition by nobles to royal authority forced King John to sign the Magna Carta in 1215, a guarantee of rights and the rule of law. In the ensuing decades, the foundations of the parliamentary system were laid.

English dynastic claims to large parts of France led to the Hundred Years War, 1338-1453, and the defeat of England. A long civil war, the War of the Roses, lasted 1455-85, and ended with the establishment of the powerful Tudor monarchy. A distinct English civilization flourished. The economy prospered over long periods of domestic peace unmatched in continental Europe. Religious independence was secured when the Church of England was separated from the authority of the Pope in 1534.

Under Queen Elizabeth I, England became a major naval power, leading to the founding of colonies in the new world and the expansion of trade with Europe and the Orient. Scotland was united with England when James VI of Scotland was crowned James I of England in 1603.

A struggle between Parliament and the Stuart kings led to a bloody civil war, 1642-49, and the establishment of a republic under the Puritan Oliver Cromwell. The monarchy was restored in 1660, but the "Glorious Revolution" of 1688 confirmed the sovereignty of Parliament: a Bill of Rights was granted 1689.

In the 18th century, parliamentary rule was strengthened. Technological and entrepreneurial innovations led to the Industrial Revolution. The 13 North American colonies were lost, but replaced by growing empires in Canada and India. Britain's role in the defeat of Napoleon, 1815, strengthened its position as the leading world power.

The extension of the franchise in 1832 and 1867, the formation of trade unions, and the development of universal public education were among the drastic social changes which accompanied the spread of industrialization and urbanization in the 19th century. Large parts of Africa and Asia were added to the empire during the reign of Queen Victoria, 1837-1901.

Though victorious in World War I, Britain suffered huge casualties and economic dislocation. Ireland became independent in 1921, and independence movements became active in India and other colonies.

The country suffered major bombing damage in World War II, but held out against Germany singlehandedly for a year after the fall of France in 1940.

Industrial growth continued in the postwar period, but Britain lost its leadership position to other powers. Labor governments passed socialist programs nationalizing some basic industries and expanding social security. The Thatcher government has however, tried to increase the role of private enterprise. In 1987, Margaret Thatcher became the first British leader in 160 years to be elected to a 3d consecutive term as prime minister. She resigned as prime minister in Nov. 1990.

The UK supported the UN resolutions against Iraq and sent military forces to the Persian Gulf war.

Wales

The Principality of Wales in western Britain has an area of 8,019 sq. mi. and a population (1991 cen.) of 2,798,000. Cardiff is the capital, pop. (1981 est.) 273,856.

England and Wales are administered as a unit. Less than 20% of the population of Wales speak both English and Welsh; about 32,000 speak Welsh solely. A 1979 referendum rejected, 4-1, the creation of an elected Welsh Assembly.

Early Anglo-Saxon invaders drove Celtic peoples into the mountains of Wales, terming them Waelise (Welsh, or foreign). There they developed a distinct nationality. Members of the ruling house of Gwynedd in the 13th century fought England but were crushed, 1283. Edward of Caernarvon, son of Edward I of England, was created Prince of Wales, 1301.

Scotland

Scotland, a kingdom now united with England and Wales in Great Britain, occupies the northern 37% of the main British island, and the Hebrides, Orkney, Shetland and smaller islands. Length, 275 mi., breadth approx. 150 mi., area, 30,405 sq. mi., population (1991 cen.) 4,957,000.

The Lowlands, a belt of land approximately 60 mi. wide from the Firth of Clyde to the Firth of Forth, divide the farming region of the Southern Uplands from the granite Highlands of the North, contain 75% of the population and most of the industry. The Highlands, famous for hunting and fishing, have been opened to industry by many hydroelectric power stations.

Edinburgh, pop. (1986 est.) 439,000, is the capital. Glasgow, pop. (1986 est.) 733,000, is Britain's greatest industrial center. It is a shipbuilding complex on the Clyde and an ocean port. Aberdeen, pop. (1986 est.) 215,000, NE of Edinburgh, is a major port, center of granite industry, fish processing, and North Sea oil exploitation. Dundee, pop. (1986 est.) 177,000, NE of Edinburgh, is an industrial and fish processing center. About 90,000 persons speak Gaelic as well as English.

History. Scotland was called Caledonia by the Romans who battled early Celtic tribes and occupied southern areas from the 1st to the 4th centuries. Missionaries from Britain introduced Christianity in the 4th century; St. Columba, an Irish monk, converted most of Scotland in the 6th century.

The Kingdom of Scotland was founded in 1018. William Wallace and Robert Bruce both defeated English armies 1297 and 1314, respectively.

In 1603 James VI of Scotland, son of Mary, Queen of Scots, succeeded to the throne of England as James I, and effected the Union of the Crowns. In 1707 Scotland received representation in the British Parliament, resulting from the union of former separate Parliaments. Its executive in the British cabinet is the Secretary of State for Scotland. The growing Scottish National Party urges independence. A 1979 referendum on the creation of an elected Scotland Assembly was defeated.

Memorials of Robert Burns, Sir Walter Scott, John Knox, Mary, Queen of Scots draw many tourists, as do the beauties of the Trossachs, Loch Katrine, Loch Lomond and abbey ruins.

Industries. Engineering products are the most important industry, with growing emphasis on office machinery, autos, electronics and other consumer goods. Oil has been discovered offshore in the North Sea, stimulating on-shore support industries.

Scotland produces fine woolens, worsteds, tweeds, silks, fine linens and jute. It is known for its special breeds of cattle and sheep. Fisheries have large hauls of herring, cod, whiting. Whisky is the biggest export.

The Hebrides are a group of c. 500 islands, 100 inhabited, off the W coast. The Inner Hebrides include **Skye, Mull,** and **Iona,** the last famous for the arrival of St. Columba, 563 AD. The Outer Hebrides include **Lewis** and **Harris.** Industries include sheep raising and weaving. The **Orkney Islands,** c. 90, are to the NE. The capital is Kirkwall, on Pomona Is. Fish curing, sheep raising and weaving are occupations. NE of the Orkneys are the 200 **Shetland Islands,** 24 inhabited, home of Shetland pony. The Orkneys and Shetlands have become centers for the North Sea oil industry.

Northern Ireland

Six of the 9 counties of Ulster, the NE corner of Ireland, constitute Northern Ireland, with the parliamentary boroughs of Belfast and Londonderry. Area 5,463 sq. mi., 1991 cen. pop. 1,570,000, capital and chief industrial center, Belfast, (1990 est.) 297,000.

Industries. Shipbuilding, including large tankers, has long been an important industry, centered in Belfast, the largest port. Linen manufacture is also important, along with apparel, rope, and twine. Growing diversification has added engineering products, synthetic fibers, and electronics. They are large numbers of cattle, hogs, and sheep, potatoes, poultry, and dairy foods are also produced.

Government. An act of the British Parliament, 1920, divided Northern from Southern Ireland, each with a parliament and government. When Ireland became a dominion, 1921, and later a republic, Northern Ireland chose to remain a part of the United Kingdom. It elects 12 members to the British House of Commons.

During 1968-69, large demonstrations were conducted by Roman Catholics who charged they were discriminated against in voting rights, housing, and employment. The Catholics, a minority comprising about a third of the population, demanded abolition of property qualifications for voting in local elections. Violence and terrorism intensified, involving branches of the Irish Republican Army (outlawed in the Irish Republic), Protestant groups, police, and British troops.

A succession of Northern Ireland prime ministers pressed reform programs but failed to satisfy extremists on both sides. Over 2,000 were killed in over 15 years of bombings and shootings through 1990, many in England itself. Britain suspended the Northern Ireland parliament Mar. 30, 1972, and imposed direct British rule. A coalition government was formed in 1973 when moderates won election to a new one-house Assembly. But a Protestant general strike overthrew the government in 1974 and direct rule was resumed.

The turmoil and agony of Northern Ireland was dramatized in 1981 by the deaths of 10 imprisoned Irish nationalist hunger strikers in Maze Prison near Belfast. The inmates had starved themselves to death in an attempt to achieve status as political prisoners, but the British government refused to yield to their demands. In 1985, the Hillsborough agreement gave the Rep. of Ireland a voice in the governing of Northern Ireland; the accord was strongly opposed by Ulster loyalists.

Education and Religion. Northern Ireland is 2/3 Protestant, 1/3 Roman Catholic. Education is compulsory through age 15.

Channel Islands

The Channel Islands, area 75 sq. mi., est. pop. 1986 145,000, off the NW coast of France, the only parts of the one-time Dukedom of Normandy belonging to England, are **Jersey, Guernsey** and the dependencies of Guernsey — **Alderney, Brechou, Great Sark, Little Sark, Herm, Jethou and Lihou.** Jersey and Guernsey have separate legal existences and lieutenant governors named by the Crown. The islands were the only British soil occupied by German troops in World War II.

Isle of Man

The Isle of Man, area 227 sq. mi., 1991 cen. pop. 69,788, is in the Irish Sea, 20 mi. from Scotland, 30 mi. from Cumberland. It is rich in lead and iron. The island has its own laws and a lieutenant governor appointed by the Crown. The Tynwald (legislature) consists of the Legislative Council, partly elected, and House of Keys, elected. Capital: Douglas. Farming, tourism, fishing (kippers, scallops) are chief occupations. Man is famous for the Manx tailless cat.

Gibraltar

Gibraltar, a dependency on the southern coast of Spain, guards the entrance to the Mediterranean. The Rock has been in British possession since 1704. The Rock is 2.75 mi. long, 3/4 of a mi. wide and 1,396 ft. in height; a narrow isthmus connects it with the mainland. Est. pop. 1992, 29,651.

In 1966 Spain called on Britain to give "substantial sovereignty" of Gibraltar to Spain and imposed a partial blockade. In 1967, residents voted for remaining under Britain. A new constitution, May 30, 1996, gave an elected House of Assembly more control in domestic affairs. A UN General Assembly resolution requested Britain to end Gibraltar's colonial status by Oct. 1, 1996. No settlement has been reached.

British West Indies

Swinging in a vast arc from the coast of Venezuela NE, then N and NW toward Puerto Rico are the Leeward Islands, forming a coral and volcanic barrier sheltering the Caribbean from the open Atlantic. Many of the islands are self-governing British possessions. Universal suffrage was instituted 1951-54; ministerial systems were set up 1956-1960.

The **Leeward Islands,** still associated with the UK are **Montserrat** (1987 pop. 11,600, area 32 sq. mi., capital Plymouth), the small **British Virgin Islands** (pop. 1991 cen.: 16,749), and **Anguilla** (pop. 1990 est.: 7,000), the most northerly of the Leeward Islands.

The three **Cayman Islands,** a dependency, lie S of Cuba, NW of Jamaica. Pop. 23,000 (1987), most of it on Grand Cayman. It is a free port; in the 1970s Grand Cayman became a tax-free refuge for foreign funds and branches of many Western banks were opened there. Total area 102 sq. mi., capital Georgetown.

The **Turks and Caicos Islands,** at the SE end of the Bahama Islands, are a separate possession. There are about 30 islands, only 6 inhabited (pop. 1990 cen.: 11,696; area 193 sq. mi.; capital Grand Turk). Salt, crayfish and conch shells are the main exports.

Bermuda

Bermuda is a British dependency governed by a royal governor and an assembly, dating from 1620, the oldest legislative body among British dependencies. Capital is Hamilton.

It is a group of 360 small islands of coral formation, 20 inhabited, comprising 20.6 sq. mi. in the western Atlantic, 580 mi. E of North Carolina. Pop., 1992 est., was 60,213 (about 61% of African descent). Density is high.

The U.S. has air and naval bases under long-term lease, and a NASA tracking facility.

Bermuda boasts many resort hotels. The government raises most revenue from import duties. Exports: petroleum products, medicine.

South Atlantic

Falkland Islands and Dependencies, a British dependency, lies 300 mi. E of the Strait of Magellan at the southern end of South America.

The Falklands or Islas Malvinas include about 200 islands, area 4,700 sq. mi., pop. (1991 cen.) 2,121. Sheep-grazing is the main industry; wool is the principal export. There are indications of large oil and gas deposits. The islands are also claimed by Argentina though 97% of inhabitants are of British origin. Argentina invaded the islands Apr. 2, 1982. The British responded by sending a task force to the area, landing their main force on the Falklands, May 21, and forcing an Argentine surrender at Port Stanley, June 14.

British Antarctic Territory, south of 60° S lat., was made a separate colony in 1962 and comprises mainly the **South Shetland Islands,** the **South Orkneys** and **Graham's Land.** A chain of meteorological stations is maintained.

St. Helena, an island 1,200 mi. off the W coast of Africa and 1,800 E of South America, has 47 sq. mi. and est. pop., 1985 of 5,400. Flax, lace and rope making are the chief industries. After Napoleon Bonaparte was defeated at Waterloo the Allies exiled him to St. Helena, where he lived from Oct. 16, 1815, to his death, May 5, 1821. Capital is Jamestown.

Tristan da Cunha is the principal of a group of islands of volcanic origin, total area 40 sq. mi., half way between the Cape of Good Hope and South America. A volcanic peak 6,760 ft. high erupted in 1961. The 262 inhabitants were removed to England, but most returned in 1963. The islands are dependencies of St. Helena.

Ascension is an island of volcanic origin, 34 sq. mi. in area, 700 mi. NW of St. Helena, through which it is administered. It is a communications relay center for Britain, and has a U.S. satellite tracking center. Est. pop., 1985, was 1,500, half of them communications workers. The island is noted for sea turtles.

Hong Kong

A Crown Colony at the mouth of the Canton R. in China, 90 mi. S of Canton. Its nucleus is Hong Kong Is., 35½ sq. mi., acquired from China 1841, on which is located Victoria, the capital. Opposite is Kowloon Peninsula, 3 sq. mi. and Stonecutters Is., ¼ sq. mi., added, 1860. An additional 355 sq. mi. known as the New Territories, a mainland area and islands, were leased from China, 1898, for 99 years. Britain and China, Dec. 19, 1984, signed an agreement under which Hong Kong would be allowed to keep its capitalist system for 50 years after 1997, the year that the 99-year lease will expire. Total area of the colony is 409 sq. mi., with a population, 1992 est., of 5.8 million including fewer than 20,000 British. From 1949 to 1962 Hong Kong absorbed more than a million refugees from China.

Hong Kong harbor was long an important British naval station and one of the world's great trans-shipment ports.

Principal industries are textiles and apparel; also tourism, $4.9 bln. expenditures (1991), shipbuilding, iron and steel, fishing, cement, and small manufactures.

Spinning mills, among the best in the world, and low wages compete with textiles elsewhere and have resulted in the protective measures in some countries. Hong Kong also has a booming electronics industry.

British Indian Ocean Territory

Formed Nov. 1965, embracing islands formerly dependencies of Mauritius or Seychelles: the Chagos Archipelago (including Diego Garcia), Aldabra, Farquhar and Des Roches. The latter 3 were transferred to Seychelles, which became independent in 1976. Area 22 sq mi. No civilian population remains.

Pacific Ocean

Pitcairn Island is in the Pacific, halfway between South America and Australia. The island was discovered in 1767 by Carteret but was not inhabited until 23 years later when the mutineers of the Bounty landed there. The area is 1.7 sq. mi. and 1991 pop. was 59. It is a British colony and is administered by a British Representative in New Zealand and a local Council. The uninhabited islands of **Henderson, Ducie** and **Oeno** are in the Pitcairn group.

United States of America

People: Population (1993 est.): 256,561,239 (incl. 50 states & Dist. of Columbia). **Age distrib.**(%): 0–14: 21.7; 15–59: 61.4; 60+: 16.9. **Pop. density:** 70 per sq. mi. **Urban** (1990): 76%.

Geography: 3,618,770 sq. mi. (incl. 50 states and D. of C.). Vast central plain, mountains in west, hills and low mountains in east.

Government: Federal republic, strong democratic tradition. **Head of state:** Bill Clinton; b. Aug. 19, 1946; in office: Jan. 20, 1993. **Administrative divisions:** 50 states and Dist. of Columbia. **Defense:** 5.7% of GNP (1991).

Economy: Minerals: Coal, copper, lead, molybdenum, phosphates, uranium, bauxite, gold, iron, mercury, nickel, potash, silver, tungsten, zinc. **Crude oil reserves** (1991): 26 bln. barrels. **Arable land:** 21%. **Livestock** (1991): cattle: 98 mln.; pigs: 54 mln.; sheep: 11.3 mln. **Fish catch** (1991): 4.3 mln. metric tons. **Electricity prod.** (1991): 2,822 bln. kWh. **Crude steel prod.** (1991): 79.2 mln. metric tons.

Finance: Gross domestic product (1991): 5.6 trl. **Per capita GDP:** $22,470. **Imports** (1992): $553 bln.; partners: Can. 17%, Jap. 20%, Mex. 6%. **Exports** (1992): $447 bln.; partners: Can. 22%, Jap. 12%, Mex. 6%, UK 5%. **Tourism** (1991): receipts $45.5 bln. **International reserves less gold** (Mar. 1993): $63.3 bln. **Gold:** 261.8 mln. oz t. **Consumer prices** (change in 1992): 3.0%.

Transport: Railroads (1990): **Length:** 144,000 mi. **Motor vehicles:** in use (1990): 143 mln. passenger cars, 45 mln. comm. vehicles. **Civil aviation** (1990): 751 bln. passenger-km; 834 airports with scheduled flights.

Communications: Television sets: 1 per 1.3 persons. **Radios:** 1 per 0.5 persons. **Telephones:** 1 per 1.9 persons. **Daily newspaper circ.** (1990): 255 per 1,000 pop.

Health: Life expectancy at birth (1992): 72 male; 79 female. **Births** (per 1,000 pop. 1992): 14. **Deaths** (per 1,000 pop. 1992): 9. **Natural increase:** .5%. **Hospital beds:** 1 per 198 persons. **Physicians:** 1 per 404 persons. **Infant mortality** (per 1,000 live births 1992): 10.

Major International Organizations: UN (GATT, IMF, WHO, FAO), OAS, NATO, OECD.

Education (1991): **Literacy:** 97%.

Uruguay

Republic of Uruguay

República del Uruguay

People: Population (1992 est.): 3,121,000. **Age distrib.** (%): 0–14: 26.9; 15–59: 57.7; 60+: 15.4. **Pop. density:** 45 per sq. mi. **Urban** (1990): 86.0%. **Ethnic groups:** Caucasians (Iberians, Italians) 89%, mestizos 10%, mulatto and black. **Languages:** Spanish. **Religions:** Roman Catholic 66%.

Geography: Area: 68,037 sq. mi., the size of Washington State. **Location:** In southern S. America, on the Atlantic O. **Neighbors:** Argentina on W, Brazil on N. **Topography:** Uruguay is composed of rolling, grassy plains and hills, well-watered by rivers flowing W to Uruguay R. **Capital:** Montevideo. **Cities** (1991 est.): Montevideo 1,400,000.

Government: Type: Republic. **Head of state:** Pres. Luis Alberto Lacalle; in office: Nov. 26, 1989. **Local divisions:** 19 departments. **Defense:** 1.4% of GDP (1989).

Economy: Industries: Meat-packing, textiles, wine, cement, oil products. **Chief crops:** Corn, wheat, citrus fruits, rice, oats, linseed. **Arable land:** 8%. **Livestock** (1990): cattle: 8.7 mln.; sheep: 25.2 mln. **Fish catch** (1990): 88,000 metric tons. **Electricity prod.** (1991): 5.6 bln. kWh. **Labor force** 13% agric.; 22% manuf.; 16% serv.; 20% govt., 17% comm.

Finance: Monetary unit: New Peso (May 1993: 3,621 = $1 US). **Gross domestic product** (1991): $9.1 bln. **Per capita GDP:** $2,935. **Imports** (1991): $1.3 bln.; partners: EC 27%, Braz. 24%, Arg. 14%, U.S. 8%. **Exports** (1991): $1.6 bln.; partners: Braz. 28%, U.S. 11%, EC 23%. **Tourism** (1990): $261 mln. receipts. **National budget** (1989): $1.5 bln. expeditures. **International reserves less gold** (Jan. 1993): $538 mln. **Gold:** 2.0 mln. oz t. **Consumer prices** (change in 1992): 68.5%

Transport: Railroads (1989): **Length:** 3,002 km. **Motor vehicles:** in use (1989): 190,000 passenger cars, 100,000 comm. vehicles. **Civil aviation** (1990): 471 mln. passenger-km; 7 airports. **Chief ports:** Montevideo.

Communications: Television sets: 1 per 4.8 persons. **Radios:** 1 per 1.0 persons. **Telephones:** 1 per 5.8 persons. **Daily newspaper circ.** (1989): 227 per 1,000 pop.

Health: Life expectancy at birth (1992): 69 male; 76 female. **Births** (per 1,000 pop. 1992): 17. **Deaths** (per 1,000 pop. 1992): 10. **Natural increase:** .7%. **Hospital beds:** 1 per 127 persons. **Physicians:** 1 per 341 persons. **Infant mortality** (per 1,000 live births 1992): 22.

Education (1990): **Literacy:** 96%.

Major International Organizations: UN (GATT, IMF, WHO), OAS.

Embassy: 1919 F St. NW 20006; 331-1313.

Spanish settlers did not begin replacing the indigenous Charrua Indians until 1624. Portuguese from Brazil arrived later, but Uruguay was attached to the Spanish Viceroyalty of Rio de la Plata in the 18th century. Rebels fought against Spain beginning in 1810. An independent republic was declared Aug. 25, 1825.

Socialist measures were adopted as far back as 1911. The state owns the power, telephone, railroad, cement, oil-refining and other industries.

Uruguay's standard of living was one of the highest in South America, and political and labor conditions among the freest. Economic stagnation, inflation, floods and drought, and a general strike in the late 1960s brought government attempts to strengthen the economy through devaluation of the peso and wage and price controls.

Terrorist activities led to Pres. Juan Maria Bordaberry agreeing to military control of his administration Feb. 1973. In June he abolished Congress and set up a Council of State in its place. Bordaberry was removed by the military in a 1976 coup. Civilian government was restored to the country in 1985.

Uzbekistan

Republic of Uzbekistan

Ozbekiston Republikasy

People: Population (1992 est.): 21,626,000. **Pop. density:** 125 per sq. mi. **Urban** (1991): 40%. **Ethnic groups:** Uzbek 70%, Russian 11%. **Religion:** Mostly Sunni Moslem.

Geography: Area: 172,700 sq. mi., slightly larger than California. **Neighbors:** Kazakhstan on N and W, Kyrgyzstan and Tajikistan on E, Afghanistan and Turkmenistan on S. **Topography:** mostly plains and desert. **Capital:** Tashkent.

Government: Type: Republic. **Head of state:** Pres. Islam A. Karimov. **Head of government:** Prime Min. Abdulkhashim Mutalov; in office: Jan. 8, 1992. **Local divisions:** 11 oblasts, 1 autonomous republic.

Economy: Industries: Steel, tractors, cars, textiles. **Chief crops:** Cotton, rice. **Minerals:** Coal, copper. **Livestock** (1990): cattle: 4.1 mln., sheep: 8.7 mln. **Electricity prod.** (1991): 54 bln. kWh. **Labor force:** 39% agric. & forestry; 39% ind. & comm.

Finance: Monetary unit: Ruble. **Imports** (1990): $3.5 bln. **Exports** (1990): $1.5 bln.

Transportation: Railroads: (1990): **Length:** 4,225 mi. **Civil aviation** (1990): 11.0 bln. passenger-km; 1 airport.

Communications: Television sets: 1 per 6 persons. **Telephones:** 1 per 15 persons.

Health: Life expectancy at birth (1992): 64 male; 70 female. **Births** (per 1,000 pop. 1992): 34. **Deaths** (per 1,000 pop. 1992): 7. **Hospital beds:** 1 per 82 persons. **Physicians:** 1 per 281 persons. **Infant mortality rate** (per 1,000 live births 1992): 65.

Major International Organizations: UN, CIS.

The region was overrun by the Mongols under Genghis Khan in 1220. In the 14th century, Uzbekistan became the center of a native empire—that of the Timurids. In later centuries Moslem feudal states emerged. Russian military conquest began in the 19th century.

The Uzbek SSR became a Soviet Union republic in 1925. Uzbekistan declared independence Aug. 29, 1991. It became an independent republic when the Soviet Union disbanded Dec. 26, 1991.

Vanuatu

Republic of Vanuatu

Ripablik Blong Vanuatu

People: Population (1992 est.): 174,000. **Pop. density:** 30 per sq. mi. **Ethnic groups:** Mainly Melanesian, some European, Polynesian, Micronesian. **Languages:** Bislama, French, and English all official. **Religions:** Presbyterian 40%, Anglican 14%, Roman Catholic 16%, animist 15%.

Geography: Area: 5,700 sq. mi., slightly larger than Connecticut. **Location:** SW Pacific, 1,200 mi. NE of Brisbane, Australia. **Topography:** dense forest with narrow coastal strips of cultivated land. **Capital:** Port-Vila. **Cities:** Vila (1990): 19,000.

Government: Type: Republic. **Head of state:** Pres. Fred Timakata; in office: Jan. 12, 1989. **Head of gov't:** Prime Min. Maxime Carlot Korman; in office: Dec. 16, 1991.

Economy: Industries: Fish-freezing, meat canneries, tourism. **Chief crops:** Copra (38% of export), cocoa, coffee. **Minerals:** Manganese. **Other resources:** Forests, cattle. **Fish catch** (1990): 3.3 metric tons.

Finance: Monetary unit: Vatu (Mar. 1993): 120 = $1 US). **Gross domestic product** (1990): $142 mln. **Imports** (1990): $60 mln.; partners: Aus. 36%, Fr. 8%, Japan 13%. **Exports** (1990): $15 mln.; partners: Neth. 34%, Jap. 17%, Fr. 27%.

Health: Life expectancy at birth (1992): 67 male, 72 female. **Infant mortality** (per 1,000 live births 1992): 30.

Education: Literacy (1990): 90%. Education not compulsory, but 85-90% of children of primary school age attend primary schools.

The Anglo-French condominium of the New Hebrides, administered jointly by France and Great Britain since 1906, became the independent Republic of Vanuatu on July 30, 1980.

Vatican City

The Holy See

People: Population (1992 est.): 802. **Ethnic groups:** Italians, Swiss. **Languages:** Italian, Latin.

Geography: Area: 108.7 acres. **Location:** In Rome, Italy. **Neighbors:** Completely surrounded by Italy.

Monetary unit: Lira.

Apostolic Nunciature in U.S.: 3339 Massachusetts Ave. NW 20008; 333-7121.

The popes for many centuries, with brief interruptions, held temporal sovereignty over mid-Italy (the so-called Papal States), comprising an area of some 16,000 sq. mi., with a population in the 19th century of more than 3 million. This territory was incorporated in the new Kingdom of Italy, the sovereignty of the pope being confined to the palaces of the Vatican and the Lateran in Rome and the villa of Castel Gandolfo, by an Italian law, May 13, 1871. This law also guaranteed to the pope and his successors a yearly indemnity of over $620,000. The allowance, however, remained unclaimed.

A Treaty of Conciliation, a concordat and a financial convention were signed Feb. 11, 1929, by Cardinal Gasparri and Premier Mussolini. The documents established the independent state of Vatican City, and gave the Catholic religion special status in Italy. The treaty (Lateran Agreement) was made part of the Constitution of Italy (Article 7) in 1947. Italy and the Vatican reached preliminary agreement in 1976 on revisions of the concordat, that would eliminate Roman Catholicism as the state religion and end required religious education in Italian schools.

Vatican City includes St. Peter's, the Vatican Palace and Museum covering over 13 acres, the Vatican gardens, and neighboring buildings between Viale Vaticano and the Church. Thirteen buildings in Rome, outside the boundaries, enjoy extraterritorial rights; these buildings house congregations or officers necessary for the administration of the Holy See.

The legal system is based on the code of canon law, the apostolic constitutions and the laws especially promulgated for the Vatican City by the pope. The Secretariat of State represents the Holy See in its diplomatic relations. By the Treaty of Conciliation the pope is pledged to a perpetual neutrality unless his mediation is specifically requested. This, however, does not prevent the defense of the Church whenever it is persecuted.

The present sovereign of the State of Vatican City is the Supreme Pontiff John Paul II, Karol Wojtyla, born in Wadowice, Poland, May 18, 1920, elected Oct. 16, 1978 (the first non-Italian to be elected Pope in 456 years).

The U.S. restored formal relations in 1984 after the U.S. Congress repealed an 1867 ban on diplomatic relations with the Vatican.

Venezuela

Republic of Venezuela

Republica de Venezuela

People: Population (1992 est.): 20,675,000. **Age distrib.** (%): 0–14: 38.3; 15–59: 56.0; 60+: 5.7. **Pop. density:** 58 per sq. mi. **Urban** (1990): 83%. **Ethnic groups:** Mestizo 69%, white (Spanish, Portuguese, Italian) 20%, black 9%, Indian 2%. **Languages:** Spanish (official). **Religions:** Roman Catholic 92%.

Geography: Area: 352,143 sq. mi., more than twice the size of California. **Location:** On the Caribbean coast of S. America. **Neighbors:** Colombia on W, Brazil on S, Guyana on E. **Topography:** Flat coastal plain and Orinoco Delta are bordered by Andes Mtns. and hills. Plains, called llanos, extend between mountains and Orinoco. Guyana Highlands and plains are S of Orinoco, which stretches 1,600 mi. and drains 80% of Venezuela. **Capital:** Caracas. **Cities** (1990 est.): Caracas 1,290,000; Maracaibo 1,206,000; Barquisimeto 723,000; Valencia 955,000.

Government: Type: Federal republic. **Head of state:** Pres. Ramon Jose Velaquez; in office: June 5, 1993. **Local divisions:** 21 states, territory, federal district, federal dependency. **Defense:** 4.3% of GDP (1991).

Economy: Industries: Steel, oil products, textiles, containers, paper. **Chief crops:** Coffee, rice, fruits, sugar. **Minerals:** Oil, iron (extensive reserves and production), gold. **Crude oil reserves** (1991): 60 bln. barrels. **Arable land:** 4%. **Livestock** (1990): cattle: 13.8 mln. **Fish catch** (1990): 327,000 metric tons. **Electricity prod.** (1991): 55.7 bln. kWh. **Crude steel prod.** (1991): 3.2 mln. metric tons. **Labor force:** 6% agric.; 35% ind.; 26% services.

Finance: Monetary unit: Bolivar (Apr. 1993: 84 = $1 US). **Gross domestic product** (1991): $52.3 bln. **Per capita GDP:** $2,590. **Imports** (1991): $10.2 bln.; partners: U.S. 44%. **Exports** (1991): $15.1 bln.; partners: U.S. 50%. **Tourism** (1990): $359 mln. receipts. **National budget** (1991): $13 bln. expenditures. **International reserves less gold** (Mar. 1993): $8.5 bln. **Gold:** 11.46 mln. oz t. **Consumer prices** (change in 1992): 31.4%.

Transport: Railroads (1990): **Length:** 226 mi. **Motor vehicles:** in use (1990): 1.6 mln. passenger cars, 459 mln. mm. vehicles. **Civil aviation** (1990): 4.0 mln. passenger-km; 32 airports with scheduled flights. **Chief ports:** Maracaibo, La Guaira, Puerto Cabello.

Communications: Television sets: 1 per 5.6 persons. **Radios:** 1 per 2.4 persons. **Telephones:** 1 per 11 persons. **Daily newspaper circ.** (1989): 111 per 1,000 pop.

Health: Life expectancy at birth (1992): 71 male; 78 female. **Births** (per 1,000 pop. 1992): 28. **Deaths** (per 1,000 pop. 1992): 4. **Natural increase:** 2.4%. **Hospital beds:** 1 per 370 persons. **Physicians:** 1 per 576 persons. **Infant mortality** (per 1,000 live births 1992): 23.

Education (1991): **Literacy:** 88%. **Years compulsory:** 8; attendance 82%.

Major International Organizations: UN (IMF, WHO, FAO), OAS, OPEC.

Embassy: 1099 30th St. NW 20007; 342-2214.

Columbus first set foot on the South American continent on the peninsula of Paria, Aug. 1498. Alonso de Ojeda, 1499, found Lake Maracaibo, called the land Venezuela, or Little Venice, because natives had houses on stilts. Venezuela was under Spanish domination until 1821. The republic was formed after secession from the Colombian Federation in 1830.

Military strongmen ruled Venezuela for most of the 20th century. They promoted the oil industry; some social reforms were implemented. Since 1959, the country has had democratically-elected governments.

Venezuela helped found the Organization of Petroleum Exporting Countries (OPEC). The government, Jan. 1, 1976, nationalized the oil industry with compensation. Oil accounts for much of total export earnings and the economy suffered a severe cash crisis in the 1980s as the result of falling oil revenues.

The government has attempted to reduce dependence on oil.

A coup attempt, led by mid-level military officers, was thwarted by loyalist troops Feb. 4, 1992. Pres. Perez announced a series of economic and political reforms Mar. 5.

A second coup attempt was thwarted in Nov. Perez was suspended from office and charged with misappropriating government funds, May 1993.

Vietnam

Socialist Republic of Vietnam

Cong Hoa Xa Hoi Chu Nghia Viet Nam

People: Population (1992 est.): 68,964,000. **Age distrib.** (%): 0–14: 40.8; 15–59: 53.6; 60+: 5.6 **Pop. density:** 541 per sq. mi. **Urban** (1989): 20%. **Ethnic groups:** Vietnamese 84%, Chinese 2%, remainder Muong, Thai, Meo, Khmer, Man, Cham. **Languages:** Vietnamese (official), Chinese. **Religions:** Buddhists, Confucians, and Taoists most numerous, Roman Catholics, animists, Muslims, Protestants.

Geography: Area: 127,330 sq. mi., the size of New Mexico. **Location:** On the E coast of the Indochinese Peninsula in SE Asia. **Neighbors:** China on N, Laos, Cambodia on W. **Topography:** Vietnam is long and narrow, with a 1,400-mi. coast. About 24% of country is readily arable, including the densely settled Red R. valley in the N, narrow coastal plains in center, and the wide, often marshy Mekong R. Delta in the S. The rest consists of semi-arid plateaus and barren mountains, with some stretches of tropical rain forest. **Capital:** Hanoi. **Cities** (1992): Ho Chi Minh City 4.0 mln.; Hanoi 2.0 mln.

Government: Type: Communist. **Head of state:** Pres. Lee Duc Anh; in office: Sept. 23, 1992. **Head of government:** Prime Min. Vo Van Kiet; in office: Aug. 8, 1991. **Local divisions:** 50 provinces, 3 municipalities. **Defense:** 19.4% of GNP (1986).

Economy: Industries: Food processing, textiles, cement, chemical fertilizers. **Chief crops:** Rice, rubber, fruits and vegetables, corn, manioc, sugarcane. **Minerals:** Phosphates, coal, iron, manganese, bauxite, apatite, chromate. **Other resources:** Forests. **Arable land:** 23%. **Livestock** (1991): cattle: 3.2 mln.; pigs: 12.5 mln. **Fish catch** (1990): 850,000 metric tons. **Electricity prod.** (1991): 9.2 bln. kWh. **Labor force:** 65% agric.; 35% ind. and service.

Finance: Monetary unit: Dong (Jan. 1993: 10,881 = $1 US). **Gross national product** (1991): $15.2 bln. **Per capita GNP:** $230. **Imports** (1991): $1.9 bln.; partners: CIS, Jap. **Exports** (1991): $1.8 bln.; partners: CIS. **National budget** (1990): $1.3 bln. expenditures.

Transport: Motor vehicles: in use (1976): 100,000 passenger cars, 200,000 comm. vehicles. **Civil Aviation** (1988): 10.3 bln. passenger km; 3 airports with scheduled flights. **Chief ports:** Ho Chi Minh City, Haiphong, Da Nang.

Communications: Television sets: 1 per 31 persons. **Radios:** 1 per 10 persons. **Telephones:** 1 per 544 persons. **Daily newspaper circ.** (1990): 38 per 1,000 pop.

Health: Life expectancy at birth (1992): 63 male; 67 female. **Births** (per 1,000 pop. 1992): 29. **Deaths** (per 1,000 pop. 1992): 8. **Natural increase:** 2.1%. **Hospital beds:** 1 per 292 persons. **Physicians:** 1 per 3,096 persons. **Infant mortality** (per 1,000 live births 1992): 48.

Education (1989): **Literacy:** 88%.

Major International Organizations: UN (IMF, WHO).

Vietnam's recorded history began in Tonkin before the Christian era. Settled by Viets from central China, Vietnam was held by China, 111 BC-939 AD, and was a vassal state during subsequent periods. Vietnam defeated the armies of Kublai Khan, 1288. Conquest by France began in 1858 and ended in 1884 with the protectorates of Tonkin and Annam in the N. and the colony of Cochin-China in the S.

In 1940 Vietnam was occupied by Japan; nationalist aims gathered force. A number of groups formed the Vietminh (Independence) League, headed by Ho Chi Minh, communist guerrilla leader. In Aug. 1945 the Vietminh forced out Bao Dai, former emperor of Annam, head of a Japan-sponsored regime. France, seeking to reestablish colonial control, battled communist and nationalist forces, 1946-1954, and was finally defeated at Dienbienphu, May 8, 1954. Meanwhile, on July 1, 1949, Bao Dai had formed a State of Vietnam, with himself as chief of state, with French approval. China backed Ho Chi Minh.

A cease-fire accord signed in Geneva July 21, 1954, divided Vietnam along the Ben Hai R. It provided for a buffer zone, withdrawal of French troops from the North and elections to determine the country's future. Under the agreement the communists gained control of territory north of the 17th parallel, with its capital at Hanoi and Ho Chi Minh as president. South Vietnam came to comprise the 39 southern provinces. Some 900,000 North Vietnamese fled to South Vietnam.

On Oct. 26, 1955, Ngo Dinh Diem, premier of the interim government of South Vietnam, proclaimed the Republic of Vietnam and became its first president.

The North, adopted a constitution Dec. 31, 1959, based on communist principles and calling for reunification of all Vietnam. North Vietnam sought to take over South Vietnam beginning in 1954. Fighting persisted from 1956, with the communist Vietcong, aided by North Vietnam, pressing war in the South. Northern aid to Vietcong guerrillas was intensified in 1959, and large-scale troop infiltration began in 1964, with Soviet and Chinese arms assistance. Large Northern forces were stationed in border areas of Laos and Cambodia.

A serious political conflict arose in the South in 1963 when Buddhists denounced authoritarianism and brutality. This paved the way for a military coup Nov. 1-2, 1963, which overthrew Diem. Several military coups followed.

In 1964, the U.S. began air strikes against North Vietnam. Beginning in 1965, the raids were stepped up and U.S. troops became combatants. U.S. troop strength in Vietnam, which reached a high of 543,400 in Apr. 1969, was ordered reduced by President Nixon in a series of withdrawals, beginning in June 1969. U.S. bombings were resumed in 1972-73.

A cease-fire agreement was signed in Paris Jan. 27, 1973 by the U.S., North and South Vietnam, and the Vietcong. It was never implemented.

North Vietnamese forces launched attacks against remaining government outposts in the Central Highlands in the first months of 1975. Government retreats turned into a rout, and the Saigon regime surrendered April 30. North Vietnam assumed control, and began transforming society along communist lines. All businesses and farms were collectivized.

The war's toll included — Combat deaths: U.S. 47,369; South Vietnam over 200,000; other allied forces 5,225. Civilian casualties were over a million. Displaced war refugees in South Vietnam totaled over 6.5 million.

The first National Assembly of both parts of the country met and the country was officially reunited July 2, 1976. The Northern capital, flag, anthem, emblem, and currency were applied to the new state. Nearly all major government posts went to officials of the former Northern government.

Heavy fighting with Cambodia took place, 1977-80, amid mutual charges of aggression and atrocities against civilians. Increasing numbers of Vietnamese civilians, ethnic Chinese, escaped the country, via the sea, or the overland route across Cambodia. Vietnam launched an offensive against Cambodian refugee strongholds along the Thai-Cambodian border in 1985; they also engaged Thai troops.

Relations with China soured as 140,000 ethnic Chinese left Vietnam charging discrimination; China cut off economic aid. Reacting to Vietnam's invasion of Cambodia, China attacked 4 Vietnamese border provinces, Feb., 1979, instigating heavy fighting.

Vietnam announced a package of reforms aimed at reducing central control of the economy in 1987, as many of the old revolutionary followers of Ho Chi Minh were removed from office.

Progress has been made with the U.S. over the repatriating of "Amerasians," the children fathered by U.S. servicemen.

Western Samoa

Independent State of Western Samoa

Malotuto'atasi o Samoa i Sisifo

People: Population (1992 est.): 190,000. **Age distrib.** (%): 0–14: 50.4; 15–59: 45.4; 60+: 4.3. **Pop. density:** 167 per sq. mi. **Urban** (1981): 21.2%. **Ethnic groups:** Samoan (Polynesian) 88%, Euronesian (mixed) 10%, European, other Pacific Islanders. **Languages:** Samoan, English both official. **Religions:** Protestant 70%, Roman Catholic 20%.

Geography: Area: 1,133 sq. mi., the size of Rhode Island. **Location:** In the S. Pacific O. **Neighbors:** Nearest are Fiji on W, Tonga on S. **Topography:** Main islands, Savai'i (670 sq. mi.) and Upolu (429 sq. mi.), both ruggedly mountainous, and small islands Manono and Apolima. **Capital:** Apia. **Cities** (1983 est.): Apia 35,000.

Government: Type: Constitutional monarchy. **Head of state:** Malietoa Tanumafili II; b. Jan. 4, 1913; in office: Jan. 1, 1962. **Head of government:** Prime Min. Toflau Eti Alesana; in office: Apr. 11, 1988. **Local divisions:** 11 districts.

Economy: Chief crops: Cocoa, copra, bananas. **Other resources:** Hardwoods, fish. **Arable land:** 43%. **Electricity prod.** (1991): 45 mln. kWh. **Labor force:** 67% agric.

Finance: Monetary unit: Tala (Mar. 1993: 1.00 = $.39 US). **Gross domestic product** (1990): $114 mln. **Per capita GDP** (1990): $690. **Imports** (1992): $113 mln.; partners: NZ 28% Austral. 20%, Jap. 13%, U.S. 5%. **Exports** (1992): $6.0 mln.; partners: EC 28%. **International reserves less gold** (Mar. 1993): $57 mln. **Consumer prices** (change in 1992): 8.5%.

Transport: Motor vehicles: in use (1990): 2,500 passenger cars, 3,000 comm. vehicles. **Chief ports:** Apia, Asau.

Communications: Radios: 1 per 2.3 persons. **Telephones:** 1 per 29 persons.

Health: Life expectancy at birth (1992): 65 male; 70 female. **Births** (per 1,000 pop. 1992): 34. **Deaths** (per 1,000 pop. 1992): 7. **Natural increase:** 2.8%. **Hospital beds:** 1 per 255 persons. **Physicians:** 1 per 3,584 persons. **Infant mortality** (per 1,000 live births 1992): 40.

Education (1989): **Literacy:** 90%. 95% attend elementary school.

Major International Organizations: UN (IMF, World Bank), Commonwealth of Nations.

Western Samoa was a German colony, 1899 to 1914, when New Zealand landed troops and took over. It became a New Zealand mandate under the League of Nations and, in 1945, a New Zealand UN Trusteeship.

An elected local government took office in Oct. 1959 and the country became fully independent Jan. 1, 1962.

Yemen

Republic of Yemen

al-Jumhūrīyah al-Yamanīyah

People: Population (1992 est.): 10,394,000. **Pop. density:** 51 per sq. mi. **Urban** (1991): 29%. **Ethnic groups:** Arabs, Indians, some Negroids. **Languages:** Arabic. **Religions:** Sunni Moslem 53%; Shute Moslem 46%.

Geography: Area: 203,796 sq. mi., slightly smaller than France. **Location:** On the southern coast of the Arabian Peninsula. **Neighbors:** Saudi Arabia on NE, Oman on the E. **Topography:** A sandy coastal strip leads to well-watered fertile mountains in interior. **Capital:** Sanaa. **Cities** (1986 est.): Sanaa 427,000; Aden 250,000.

Government: Type: Republic. **Head of state:** Pres. Ali Abdullah Saleh, b. 1942; in office: July 17, 1978. **Head of government:** Prime Min. Haydar Abu Bakr-al Attas; in office: May 22, 1990. **Local divisions:** 17 provinces. **Defense:** 20% of GDP (1990).

Economy: Industries: Food processing, mining, petroleum refining. **Chief crops:** Wheat, sorghum, fruits, coffee, cotton. **Minerals:** Salt. **Crude oil reserves** (1984): 600 mln. bbls. **Arable land:** 6%. **Livestock** (1990): goats: 3.1 mln.; sheep: 3.6 mln. **Fish catch** (1990): 89,000 metric tons. **Electricity prod.** (1990): 1 bln. kWh. **Labor force:** 64% agric.; 11% ind. and commerce; 25% serv.

Finance: Monetary unit: Rial (Jan. 1993: 16.50 = $1 US). **Gross domestic product** (1990): $5.3 bln. **Per capita GDP:** $545. **Imports** (1990): $2.1 bln.; partners: Saudi Ar. 20%, Fr. 8%, Jap. 16%. **Exports** (1990): $908 mln.; partners: S. Yemen 23%, Saudi Ar. 8%, Pak. 19%.

Transport: Motor vehicles in use (1990): 150,000 passenger cars, 220,000 commercial vehicles. **Civil aviation** (1990): 1.0 bln. passenger-km.; 12 airports with scheduled flights. **Chief ports:** Al-Hudaydah, Al-Mukha, Aden.

Communications: Television sets: 1 per 38 persons. **Radios:** 1 per 35 persons. **Telephones:** 1 per 157 persons.

Health: Life expectancy at birth (1992): 49 male; 51 female. **Births** (per 1,000 pop. 1992): 51. **Deaths** (per 1,000 pop. 1992): 16. **Natural increase:** 3.5%. **Hospital beds:** 1 per 995 persons.

Physicians: 1 per 5,531 persons. **Infant mortality** (per 1,000 live births 1992): 118.

Education (1990): **Literacy:** 38%. **Primary school attendance:** 59%.

Major International Organizations: UN (IMF, WHO), Arab League.

Embassy: 2600 Virginia Ave. NW 20037; 965-4760.

Yemen's territory once was part of the ancient kindgom of Sheba, or Saba, a prosperous link in trade between Africa and India. A Biblical reference speaks of its gold, spices and precious stones as gifts borne by the Queen of Sheba to King Solomon.

Yemen became independent in 1918, after years of Ottoman Turkish rule, but remained politically and economically backward. Imam Ahmed ruled 1948-1962. Army officers headed by Brig. Gen. Abdullah al-Salal declared the country to be the Yemen Arab Republic.

The Imam Ahmed's heir, the Imam Mohamad al-Badr, fled to the mountains where tribesmen joined royalist forces; internal warfare between them and the republican forces continued. About 150,000 people died in the fighting.

There was a bloodless coup Nov. 5, 1967. In April 1970 hostilities ended with an agreement between Yemen and Saudi Arabia.

On June 13, 1974, an army group, led by Col. Ibrahim al-Hamidi, seized the government. He was assassinated in 1977.

Meanwhile, South Yemen won independence from Britain in 1967, formed out of the British colony of Aden and the British protectorate of South Arabia. It became the Arab world's only Marxist state, taking the name People's Democratic Republic of Yemen in 1970 and signing a 20-year friendship treaty with the USSR in 1979 that allowed for the stationing of Soviet troops in the south.

More than 300,000 Yemenis fled from the south to the north after independence, contributing to 2 decades of hostility between the 2 states that flared into warfare twice in the 1970's.

An Arab League-sponsored agreement between North and South Yemen on unification of the 2 countries was signed Mar. 29, 1979. An agreement providing for widespread political and economic cooperation was signed in 1988.

The 2 countries were formally united on May 21, 1990.

Yugoslavia

Federal Republic of Yugoslavia

Federativna Republika Jugoslavija

(Data prior to 1992 include former republics Croatia, Slovenia, Bosnia and Herzegovina, and Macedonia)

People: Population (1992 est.): 10,337,000. **Age distrib.** (%): 0–14: 23.5; 15-59: 63.7; 60+: 12.8. **Pop. density:** 262 per sq. mi. **Urban** (1990): 50%. **Ethnic groups** (1992): Serbs 80%, Albanians 15%. **Languages:** Serbian (official), Macedonian, Hungarian, Albanian. **Religions:** Serbian Orthodox 80%, Roman Catholic, Moslem.

Geography: Area: 39,449 sq. mi. **Location:** On the Balkan Peninsula in SE Europe. Present-day Yugoslavia consists of the former republics of Serbia and Montenegro. **Neighbors:** Croatia, Bosnia and Herzegovina on W., Hungary on N, Romania, Bulgaria on E, Greece, Albania, Macedonia on S. **Capital:** Belgrade. **Cities** (1992 est.): Belgrade 1,553,000.

Government: Type: Republic. **Head of state:** Pres. Zoran Lilic; in office: June 1993. **Local divisions:** 2 republics. **Defense:** 4.6% of GDP (1991).

Economy: Industries: Steel, wood products. **Chief crops:** Corn, grains, tobacco, sugar beets. **Minerals:** Antimony, bauxite, lead, mercury, coal, iron, copper, chrome, zinc, salt. **Arable land:** 28%. **Livestock** (1991): cattle: 2.0 mln.; pigs: 4.5 mln.; sheep: 3.0 mln. **Fish catch:** (1990): 8,000 metric tons. **Electricity prod.** (1990): 83.4 bln. kWh. **Crude steel prod.** (1990): 3.6 mln. metric tons. **Labor force:** 22% agric.; 70% ind.

Finance: Monetary unit: Dinar (Feb. 1993: 225 = $1 US). **Gross national product** (1990): $120.1 bln. **Per capita GNP:** $5,040. **Imports** (1990): $19.1 bln.; partners: EC 54%, USSR 15%. **Exports** (1990): $14.6 bln.; partners: EC 54%, USSR 17%. **Tourism** (1990): $2.7 bln. receipts. **National budget** (1990): $6.4 bln. expenditures. **International reserves less gold** (Mar. 1993): $1.4 bln. **Gold:** 1.90 mln. oz t. **Consumer prices** (change in 1991): 117.4%.

Transport: Motor vehicles: in use (1990): 1.4 mln. passenger cars, 132,000 comm. vehicles. **Civil aviation** (1992): 7 airports.

Communications: Television sets: 1 per 3.6 persons. **Radios:** 1 per 6 persons. **Telephones:** 1 per 4.9 persons. **Daily newspaper circ.** (1990): 88 per 1,000 pop.

Health: Life expectancy at birth (1991): 70 male; 76 female. **Births** (per 1,000 pop. 1991): 14. **Deaths** (per 1,000 pop. 1991): 9. **Natural increase:** .5%. **Hospital beds:** 1 per 163 persons. **Physicians:** 1 per 490 persons. **Infant mortality** (per 1,000 live births 1991): 21.

Education (1991): **Literacy:** 90%. Almost all attend primary school.

Major International Organizations: UN (IMF, World Bank).

Embassy: 2410 California St. NW 20008; 462-6566.

Serbia, which had since 1389 been a vassal principality of Turkey, was established as an independent kingdom by the Treaty of Berlin, 1878. Montenegro, independent since 1389, also obtained international recognition in 1878. After the Balkan wars Serbia's boundaries were enlarged by the annexation of Old Serbia and Macedonia, 1913.

When the Austro-Hungarian empire collapsed after World War I, the Kingdom of the Serbs, Croats, and Slovenes was formed from the former provinces of Croatia, Dalmatia, Bosnia, Herzegovina, Slovenia, Voyvodina and the independent state of Montenegro. The name was later changed to Yugoslavia.

Nazi Germany invaded in 1941. Many Yugoslav partisan troops continued to operate. Among these were the Chetniks led by Draja Mikhailovich, who fought other partisans led by Josip Broz, known as Marshal Tito. Tito, backed by the USSR and Britain from 1943, was in control by the time the Germans had been driven from Yugoslavia in 1945. Mikhailovich was executed July 17, 1946, by the Tito regime.

A constituent assembly proclaimed Yugoslavia a republic Nov. 29, 1945. It became a federated republic Jan. 31, 1946, and Marshal Tito, a communist, became head of the government.

The Stalin policy of dictating to all communist nations was rejected by Tito. He accepted economic aid and military equipment from the U.S. and received aid in foreign trade also from France and Great Britain. Tito also supported the liberal government of Czechoslovakia in 1968 before the Soviet invasion.

A separatist movement among Croatians brought arrests and a change of leaders in the Croatian Republic in Jan. 1972. Violence by Croatian nationalists and fears of Soviet political intervention led to restrictions on political and intellectual dissent.

Beginning in 1965, reforms designed to decentralize the administration of economic development and to force industries to produce more efficiently in competition with foreign producers were introduced, and considerable trade with the West was developed.

Pres. Tito died May 4, 1980; with his death, the post as head of the Collective Presidency and also that as head of the League of Communists became a rotating system of succession among the members representing each republic.

On Jan. 22, 1990, a Communist Party conference renounced its constitutionally guaranteed leading role in society and called on parliament to enact "political pluralism, including a multiparty system."

Croatia and Slovenia formally declared independence June 25, 1991. In Croatia, fighting began between Croats and ethnic Serbs. Serbia sent arms and medical supplies to the Serb rebels in Croatia. In Aug., there were numerous clashes between Croatian forces and Yugoslavian army units and their Serb supporters.

The republics of Serbia and Montenegro proclaimed a new "Federal Republic of Yugoslavia" Apr. 17, 1992. Serbia was the main supplier of arms to the ethnic Serb fighters in Bosnia and Herzegovina. The UN imposed sweeping international sanctions on Yugoslavia as a means of ending the bloodshed in Bosnia, May 30. Some 100,000 protesters in Belgrade called for the ouster of Serbian President Milosevic, June 28. As the result of UN trade sanctions and the nation's continued printing of money to support Serb forces in the Bosnian and Croatian conflicts, inflation was over 200 percent and unemployment at 40 percent, Feb. 1993.

Kosovo: An area in southern Serbia (4,203 sq. mi.), with a population of about 2,000,000, mostly Albanians. The capital is Pristina. The Albanian majority has declared its independence, which Serbia has not recognized.

Vojvodina: An area in northern Serbia (3,304 sq. mi.), with a population of about 2,000,000, mostly Serbian. The capital is Novi Sad.

Zaire

Republic of Zaire

République du Zaïre

People: Population (1992 est.): 39,084,000. **Pop. density:** 43 per sq. mi. **Urban** (1988): 44.2%. **Ethnic groups:** Bantu tribes 80%, over 200 other tribes. **Languages:** French (official), Kongo, Luba, Mongo, Rwanda, others. **Religions:** Christian 70%, Moslem 10%.

Geography: Area: 905,563 sq. mi., one-fourth the size of the U.S. **Location:** In central Africa. **Neighbors:** Congo on W, Central African Republic, Sudan on N, Uganda, Rwanda, Burundi, Tanzania on E, Zambia, Angola on S. **Topography:** Zaire includes the bulk of the Zaire (Congo) R. Basin. The vast central region is a low-lying plateau covered by rain forest. Mountainous terraces in the W, savannas in the S and SE, grasslands toward the N, and the high Ruwenzori Mtns. on the E surround the central region. A short strip of territory borders the Atlantic O. The Zaire R. is 2,718 mi. long. **Capital:** Kinshasa. **Cities** (1991 est.): Kinshasa 3,741,000; Lubumbashi 709,000.

Government: Type: Republic with strong presidential authority (in transition). **Head of state:** Pres. Mobutu Sese Seko; b. Oct. 14, 1930; in office: Nov. 25, 1965. **Head of government:** Prime Min. Etienne Tshisekedi wa Mulumba; in office: Aug. 15, 1992. **Local divisions:** 10 regions, Kinshasa. **Defense:** 1% of GDP (1988).

Economy: Chief crops: Coffee, rice, sugar cane, bananas, plantains, manioc, mangoes, tea, cocoa, palm oil. **Minerals:** Cobalt (60% of world reserves), copper, cadmium, gold, silver, tin, germanium, zinc, iron, manganese, uranium, radium. **Crude oil reserves** (1987): 111 mln. bbls. **Other resources:** Forests, rubber, ivory. **Arable land:** 3%. **Livestock** (1991): cattle: 1.6 mln.; goats: 2.9 mln. **Fish catch** (1990): 162,000 metric tons. **Electricity prod.** (1991): 6.0 bln. kWh. **Labor force:** 75% agric.

Finance: Monetary unit: Zaire (Mar. 1993: 2,652 = $1 US). **Gross domestic product** (1990): $6.6 bln. **Per capita GDP:** $180. **Imports** (1991): $710 mln.; partners: Chi. 38%, Belg. 16%, Ger. 7%, Fra. 7%. **Exports** (1991): $828 mln.; partners: Belg.-Lux. 36%, U.S. 19%. **National budget** (1990): $1.1 bln. expenditures. **International reserves less gold** (Mar. 1993): $156 mln. **Gold:** 27,000 oz t. **Consumer prices** (change in 1992): 6,921.

Transport: Railroads (1989): **Length:** 3,193 mi. **Motor vehicles:** in use (1985): 24,000 passenger cars, 60,000 comm. vehicles. **Civil aviation** (1990): 487 mln. passenger-km; 26 airports with scheduled flights. **Chief ports:** Matadi, Boma.

Communications: Television sets: 1 per 1,707 persons. **Radios:** 1 per 9.7 persons. **Telephones:** 1 per 1,026 persons. **Daily newspaper circ.** (1988): 1 per 1,000 pop.

Health: Life expectancy at birth (1992): 52 male; 56 female. **Births** (per 1,000 pop. 1992): 45. **Deaths** (per 1,000 pop. 1992): 14. **Natural increase:** 3.1%. **Hospital beds:** 1 per 476 persons. **Physicians:** 1 per 23,193 persons. **Infant mortality** (per 1,000 live births 1992): 97.

Education (1990): **Literacy:** 72%.

Major International Organizations: UN and all of its specialized agencies, OAU.

Embassy: 1800 New Hampshire Ave. NW 20008; 234-7690.

The earliest inhabitants of Zaire may have been the pygmies, followed by Bantus from the E and Nilotic tribes from the N. The large Bantu Bakongo kingdom ruled much of Zaire and Angola when Portuguese explorers visited in the 15th century.

Leopold II, king of the Belgians, formed an international group to exploit the Congo in 1876. In 1877 Henry M. Stanley explored the Congo and in 1878 the king's group sent him back to organize the region and win over the native chiefs. The Conference of Berlin, 1884-85, organized the Congo Free State with Leopold as king and chief owner. Exploitation of native laborers on the rubber plantations caused international criticism and led to granting of a colonial charter, 1908.

Belgian and Congolese leaders agreed Jan. 27, 1960, that the Congo would become independent June 30. In the first general elections, May 31, the National Congolese movement of Patrice Lumumba won 35 of 137 seats in the National Assembly. He was appointed premier June 21, and formed a coalition cabinet.

Widespread violence caused Europeans and others to flee. The UN Security Council Aug. 9, 1960, called on Belgium to withdraw its troops and sent a UN contingent. President Kasavubu removed Lumumba as premier; he was murdered in 1961.

The last UN troops left the Congo June 30, 1964, and Moise Tshombe became president.

On Sept. 7, 1964, leftist rebels set up a "People's Republic" in Stanleyville. Tshombe hired foreign mercenaries and sought to rebuild the Congolese Army. In Nov. and Dec. 1964 rebels slew scores of white hostages and thousands of Congolese; Belgian paratroops, dropped from U.S. transport planes, rescued hundreds. By July 1965 the rebels had lost their effectiveness.

In 1965 Gen. Joseph D. Mobutu was named president. He later changed his name to Mobutu Sese Seko. The country changed its name to Republic of Zaire on Oct. 27, 1971; in 1972 Zairians with Christian names were ordered to change them to African names.

Serious economic difficulties, amid charges of corruption by government officials, plagued Zaire in the 1980s. In 1990, Pres. Mobutu announced an end to a 20-year ban on multiparty politics. In 1993, Prime Min. Etienne Tshisekedi wa Mulumba called for foreign military assistance in toppling Pres. Mobuto Sese Soto, who had held office for almost 28 years.

Zambia

Republic of Zambia

People: Population (1992 est.): 8,745,000. **Age distrib.** (%): 0–14: 48.2; 15–59: 47.8; 60+: 4.0. **Pop. density:** 30 per sq. mi. **Urban** (1990): 49%. **Ethnic groups:** Mostly Bantu tribes. **Languages:** English (official), Bantu dialects. **Religions:** Predominantly animist, Roman Catholic 21%, Protestant, Hindu, Moslem minorities.

Geography: Area: 290,586 sq. mi., larger than Texas. **Location:** In southern central Africa. **Neighbors:** Zaire on N, Tanzania, Malawi, Mozambique on E, Zimbabwe, Namibia on S, Angola on W. **Topography:** Zambia is mostly high plateau country covered with thick forests, and drained by several important rivers, including the Zambezi. **Capital:** Lusaka. **Cities** (1992): Lusaka 982,000; Kitwe 348,000; Ndola 376,000.

Government: Type: Republic. **Head of state:** Pres. Frederick Chiluba; b. 1943; in office: Nov. 2, 1991. **Local divisions:** 9 provinces. **Defense:** 6.8% of GDP (1985).

Economy: Chief crops: Corn, tobacco, peanuts, cotton, sugar. **Minerals:** Cobalt, copper, zinc, gold, lead, vanadium, manganese, coal. **Other resources:** Rubber, ivory. **Arable land:** 7%. **Livestock** (1990): cattle: 2.8 mln. **Fish catch** (1989): 68,000 metric tons. **Electricity prod.** (1991): 12 bln. kWh. **Labor force:** 60% agric.; 40% ind. and commerce.

Finance: Monetary unit: Kwacha (Mar. 1993: 1.00 = $.01 US). **Gross domestic product** (1991): $4.2 bln. **Per capita GDP:** $380. **Imports** (1991): $1.3 bln.; S. Af. 13%, Ger. 6%, U.S. 7%. **Exports** (1991): $1.1 bln.; partners: Jap. 4%, UK 3%, U.S. 10%, Ger. 9%. **National budget** (1991): $1.5 bln. expenditures. **International reserves less gold** (Jan. 1992): $184 mln. **Gold:** 15,000 oz t. **Consumer prices** (change in 1991): 92%.

Transport: Motor vehicles: in use (1982): 105,000 passenger cars, 97,000 comm. vehicles. **Civil aviation** (1991): 322 mln. passenger-km; 8 airports with scheduled flights.

Communications: Television sets: 1 per 44 persons. **Radios:** 1 per 14 persons. **Telephones:** 1 per 78 persons. **Daily newspaper circ.** (1989): 15 per 1,000 pop.

Health: Life expectancy at birth (1992): 55 male; 59 female. **Births** (per 1,000 pop. 1992): 48. **Deaths** (per 1,000 pop. 1992): 11. **Natural increase:** 3.7%. **Hospital beds:** 1 per 311 persons. **Physicians:** 1 per 8,437 persons. **Infant mortality** (per 1,000 live births 1992): 77.

Education (1991): **Literacy:** 54%. **Attendance:** less than 50% in grades 1–7.

Major International Organizations: UN (GATT, IMF, WHO), OAU, Commonwealth of Nations.

Embassy: 2419 Massachusetts Ave. NW 20008; 265-9717.

As Northern Rhodesia, the country was under the administration of the South Africa Company, 1889 until 1924, when the office of governor was established, and, subsequently, a legislature. The country became an independent republic within the Commonwealth Oct. 24, 1964.

After the white government of Rhodesia declared its independence from Britain Nov. 11, 1965, relations between Zambia and Rhodesia became strained.

As part of a program of government participation in major industries, a government corporation in 1970 took over 51% of the ownership of 2 foreign-owned copper mining companies. Privately-held land and other enterprises were nationalized in 1975, as were all newspapers. In the 1980s, decline in copper prices hurt the economy and severe drought caused famine.

Food riots erupted in June 1990, as the nation suffered its worst violence since independence.

Elections held Oct. 1991, resulted in an end to one-party rule.

Zimbabwe

Republic of Zimbabwe

People: Population (1992 est.): 11,033,000. **Age distrib.** (%): 0–14: 44.9; 15–59: 51.1; 60+: 4.0. **Pop. density:** 73 per sq. mi. **Urban** (1990): 25%. **Ethnic groups:** Shona 80%, Ndebele 19%. **Languages:** English (official), Shona, Sinde bele. **Religions:** Predominantly traditional tribal beliefs, Christian minority.

Geography: Area: 150,803 sq. mi., slightly larger than Montana. **Location:** In southern Africa. **Neighbors:** Zambia on N, Botswana on W, S. Africa on S, Mozambique on E. **Topography:** Zimbabwe is high plateau country, rising to mountains on eastern border, sloping down on the other borders. **Capital:** Harare. **Cities** (1988 est.): Harare 730,000; Bulawayo (met.) 415,000.

Government: Type: Parliamentary democracy. **Head of state:** Pres. Robert Mugabe; b. Feb. 21, 1924; in office: Jan. 1, 1988. **Local divisions:** 8 provinces. **Defense:** 6.0% of GDP (1991).

Economy: Industries: Clothing, chemicals, light industries. **Chief crops:** Tobacco, sugar, cotton, corn, wheat. **Minerals:** Chromium, gold, nickel, asbestos, copper, iron, coal. **Arable land:** 7%. **Livestock** (1991): cattle: 5.9 mln.; goats: 2.4 mln. **Electricity prod.** (1991): 7.5 bln. kWh. **Labor force:** 74% agric.; 16% serv.

Finance: Monetary unit: Dollar (Mar. 1993: 1.00 = $.15 US). **Gross domestic product** (1991): $7.1 bln. **Per capita GDP:** $660. **Imports** (1991): $1.6 bln. partners: EC 31%, So. Afr. 21%. **Exports** (1991): $1.8 bln.; partners: EC 40%. **National budget** (1991): $3.3 bln. expenditures. **Total reserves less gold** (Mar. 1992): $278 mln. **Consumer prices** (change in 1992): 46.3%.

Transport: Motor vehicles: in use (1990): 178,000 passenger cars, 82,000 comm. vehicles. **Civil aviation** (1989): 709 mln. passenger-km. 8 airports with scheduled flights.

Communications: Television sets: 1 per 70 persons. **Radios:** 1 per 18 persons. **Telephones:** 1 per 31 persons. **Daily newspaper circ.** (1990): 23 per 1,000 pop.

Health: Life expectancy at birth (1992): 60 male; 64 female. **Births** (per 1,000 pop. 1992): 41. **Deaths** (per 1,000 pop. 1992): 8. **Natural increase:** 3.3%. **Physicians:** 1 per 6,951 persons. **Infant mortality** (per 1,000 live births 1992): 59.

Education (1990): **Literacy:** 67%. **Attendance:** 90% primary, 15% secondary for Africans; higher for whites, Asians.

Major International Organizations: UN (IMF, World Bank), OAU, Commonwealth of Nations.

Embassy: 2852 McGill Terrace NW 20008; 332-7100.

Britain took over the area as Southern Rhodesia in 1923 from the British South Africa Co. (which, under Cecil Rhodes, had conquered the area by 1897) and granted internal self-government. Under a 1961 constitution, voting was restricted to maintain whites in power. On Nov. 11, 1965, Prime Min. Ian D. Smith announced his country's unilateral declaration of independence. Britain termed the act illegal, and demanded Zimbabwe (known as Rhodesia until 1980) broaden voting rights to provide for eventual rule by the majority Africans.

Urged by Britain, the UN imposed sanctions, including embargoes on oil shipments to Zimbabwe. Some oil and gasoline reached Zimbabwe, however, from South Africa and Mozambique, before the latter became independent in 1975. In May 1968, the UN Security Council ordered a trade embargo.

A new constitution came into effect, Mar. 2, 1970. The election law effectively prevented full black representation through income tax requirements.

Intermittent negotiations between the government and various black nationalist groups failed to prevent increasing skirmishes. An "internal settlement" signed Mar. 1978 in which Smith and 3 popular black leaders share control until transfer of power to the black majority was rejected by guerrilla leaders.

In the country's first universal-franchise election, Apr. 21, 1979, Bishop Abel Muzorewa's United African National Council gained a bare majority control of the black-dominated parliament. Britain, 1979, began efforts to normalize its relationship with Zimbabwe. A British cease-fire was accepted by all parties, Dec. 5th. Independence was finally achieved Apr. 18, 1980.

Pres. Mugabe declared Zimbabwe's drought a national disaster and appealed to foreign donors for food, money, and medicine, Mar. 6, 1992.

Area and Population of the World

Source: Bureau of the Census, U.S. Dept. of Commerce; prior to 1950, Rand McNally & Co.

			Population (est., thousands)							
Continent	Area (1,000 sq. mi.)	% of Earth	1650	1750	1850	1900	1950[1]	1980[1]	1991[1]	% World Total, 1991[1]
North America	9,400	16.2	5,000	5,000	39,000	106,000	166,000	252,000	279,000	5.1
South America	6,900	11.9	8,000	7,000	20,000	38,000	—	—	—	—
Latin America, Caribbean	—	—	—	—	—	—	166,000	364,000	458,000	8.4
Europe	3,800	6.6	100,000	140,000	265,000	400,000	392,000	484,000	502,000	9.2
Asia	17,400	30.1	335,000	476,000	754,000	932,000	1,368,000	2,494,000	3,046,000	56.2
Africa	11,700	20.2	100,000	95,000	95,000	118,000	281,000	594,000	817,000	15.0
Former USSR	—	—	—	—	—	—	180,000	266,000	293,000	5.4
Oceania, incl. Australia	3,300	5.7	2,000	2,000	2,000	6,000	12,000	23,000	27,000	0.4
Antarctica	5,400	9.3	Uninhabited							
World	**57,900**	—	**550,000**	**725,000**	**1,175,000**	**1,600,000**	**2,564,000**	**4,478,000**	**5,423,000**	—

(1) Figures do not add to total because of independent rounding.

Leading Countries in Population and Area in 1992

China has the highest population in the world, with 1.17 billion inhabitants, which is more than one-fifth of the world's population. India has almost 900 million people and is expected to reach 1 billion by the end of the decade. The United States has the third largest population, with over 250 million, followed by Indonesia, Brazil, and Russia. Russia is the largest country in area, with over 6.5 million square miles, followed by Canada, China, the United States, and Brazil.

Population of World's Largest Cities

Source: Bureau of the Census, U.S. Dept. of Commerce

The table below represents one attempt at comparing the world's largest cities. The cities are defined as population clusters of continuous built-up areas with a population density of a least 5,000 persons per square mile. The boundary of the city was determined by examining detailed maps of each city in conjunction with the most recent official population statistics. Exclaves of areas exceeding the minimum population density were added to the city if the intervening gap was less than one mile. To the extent practical, nonresidential areas such as parks, airports, industrial complexes, and water were excluded from the area reported for each city, thus making the population density reflective of the concentrations in the residential portions of the city. By using a consistent definition for the city, it is possible to make comparisons of the cities on the basis of total population, area, and population density.

The population of each city was projected based on projected country populations and the proportion of each city population to the total population of the country at the time of the last 2 censuses. Figures in the table below may differ from city population figures elsewhere in The World Almanac because of different methods of determining population.

City, Country	1991 (thousands)	2000 (thousands projected)	Area (sq. mi.)	Density 1991 (pop per sq. mi.)
Tokyo-Yokohama, Japan	27,245	29,971	1,089	25,019
Mexico City, Mexico	20,899	27,872	522	40,037
São Paulo, Brazil	18,701	25,354	451	41,466
Seoul, South Korea	16,792	21,976	342	49,101
New York, U.S.	14,625	14,648	1,274	11,480
Osaka-Kobe-Kyoto, Japan	13,872	14,287	495	28,025
Bombay, India	12,101	15,357	95	127,461
Calcutta, India	11,898	14,088	209	56,927
Rio de Janeiro, Brazil	11,688	14,169	260	44,952
Buenos Aires, Argentina	11,657	12,911	535	21,790
Moscow, Russia	10,446	11,121	379	27,562
Manila, Philippines	10,156	12,846	188	54,024
Los Angeles, U.S.	10,130	10,714	1,110	9,126
Cairo, Egypt	10,099	12,512	104	97,106
Jakarta, Indonesia	9,882	12,804	76	130,026
Teheran, Iran	9,779	14,251	112	87,312
London, U.K.	9,115	8,574	874	10,429
Delhi, India	8,778	11,849	138	63,612
Paris, France	8,720	8,803	432	20,185
Karachi, Pakistan	8,014	11,299	190	42,179
Lagos, Nigeria	7,998	12,528	56	142,821
Essen, Germany	7,452	7,239	704	10,585
Shanghai, China	6,936	7,540	78	88,924
Lima, Peru	6,815	9,241	120	56,794
Taipei, Taiwan	6,695	8,516	138	48,517
Istanbul, Turkey	6,678	8,875	165	40,476
Chicago, U.S.	6,529	6,568	762	8,568
Bangkok, Thailand	5,955	7,587	102	58,379
Bogotá, Colombia	5,913	7,935	79	74,851
Madras, India	5,896	7,384	115	51,270
Beijing, China	5,762	5,993	151	38,156
Hong Kong	5,693	5,956	23	247,501
Santiago, Chile	5,378	6,294	128	40,018
Pusan, South Korea	5,008	6,700	54	92,735
Tianjin, China	4,850	5,298	49	98,990
Bangalore, India	4,802	6,764	50	96,041
Nagoya, Japan	4,791	5,303	307	15,606
Milan, Italy	4,749	4,839	344	13,806
St. Petersburg, Russia	4,672	4,738	139	33,614
Madrid, Spain	4,513	5,104	66	68,385
Dhaka, Bangladesh	4,419	6,492	32	138,108
Lahore, Pakistan	4,376	5,864	57	76,779
Shenyang, China	4,289	4,684	39	109,974
Barcelona, Spain	4,227	4,834	87	48,584
Baghdad, Iraq	4,059	5,239	97	41,843
Manchester, U.K.	4,030	3,827	357	11,287
Philadelphia, U.S.	4,003	3,979	471	8,499
San Francisco, U.S.	3,986	4,214	428	9,315
Belo Horizonte, Brazil	3,812	5,125	79	48,249
Kinshasa, Zaire	3,747	5,646	57	65,732
Ho Chi Minh City, Vietnam	3,725	4,481	31	120,168
Ahmadabad, India	3,709	4,837	32	115,893
Hyderabad, India	3,673	4,765	88	41,741
Sydney, Australia	3,536	3,708	338	10,460
Athens, Greece	3,507	3,866	116	30,237
Miami, U.S.	3,471	3,894	448	7,748
Guadalajara, Mexico	3,370	4,451	78	43,205
Guangzhou, China	3,360	3,652	79	42,537
Surabaya, Indonesia	3,248	3,632	43	75,544
Caracas, Venezuela	3,217	3,435	54	59,582
Wuhan, China	3,200	3,495	65	49,225
Toronto, Canada	3,145	3,296	154	20,420
Porto Alegre, Brazil	3,114	4,109	231	13,479
Rome, Italy	3,033	3,129	69	43,949
Berlin, Germany	3,021	3,006	274	11,026
Naples, Italy	2,978	3,134	62	48,032
Casablanca, Morocco	2,973	3,795	35	84,953
Detroit, U.S.	2,969	2,735	468	6,343
Alexandria, Egypt	2,941	3,304	35	84,022
Monterrey, Mexico	2,939	3,974	77	38,169
Montreal, Canada	2,916	3,071	164	17,779
Melbourne, Australia	2,915	2,968	327	8,914
Ankara, Turkey	2,872	3,777	55	52,221
Yangon, Myanmar	2,864	3,332	47	60,927
Kiev, Ukraine	2,796	3,237	62	45,095
Dallas, U.S.	2,787	3,257	419	6,652
Singapore, Singapore	2,719	2,913	78	34,856
Taegu, South Korea	2,651	4,051	NA	NA
Harbin, China	2,643	2,887	30	88,110
Washington, U.S.	2,565	2,707	357	7,184
Poona, India	2,547	3,647	NA	NA
Boston, U.S.	2,476	2,485	303	8,172
Lisbon, Portugal	2,426	2,717	NA	NA
Tashkent, Uzbekistan	2,418	2,947	NA	NA
Chongqing, China	2,395	2,961	NA	NA
Chengdu, China	2,372	2,591	25	94,870
Vienna, Austria	2,344	2,647	NA	NA
Houston, U.S.	2,329	2,651	310	7,512
Budapest, Hungary	2,303	2,335	138	16,691
Salvador, Brazil	2,298	3,286	NA	NA

Population Projections, by Region and for Selected Countries: 2000 and 2020

Source: Bureau of the Census, U.S. Dept. of Commerce

(in thousands)

Region and Country	2000	2020
Sub-Saharan Africa[1]	736,325	1,279,014
Angola	11,424	19,153
Benin	6,509	11,901
Botswana	1,554	2,181
Burkina Faso	12,464	23,016
Burundi	7,731	13,725
Cameroon	14,453	23,487
Central African Republic	3,702	5,944
Chad	6,204	9,361
Congo	2,995	4,955
Côte d'Ivoire	18,144	33,581
Ethiopia[2]	69,374	123,584
Ghana	20,527	35,579
Guinea	9,232	14,419
Guinea-Bissau	1,265	1,926
Kenya	34,259	57,265
Liberia	3,674	6,534
Madagascar	16,185	29,183
Malawi	11,892	22,235
Mali	10,667	19,169
Mauritania	2,652	4,849
Mozambique	20,936	35,443
Namibia	2,081	3,925
Niger	11,056	20,606
Nigeria	160,751	273,197
Rwanda	11,047	21,948
Senegal	10,482	18,466
Sierra Leone	5,399	8,919

Region and Country	2000	2020
Somalia	9,409	17,190
South Africa	51,375	82,882
Sudan	35,870	59,307
Tanzania	36,489	68,772
Togo	5,248	9,900
Uganda	25,802	48,393
Zaire	50,043	89,164
Zambia	11,572	21,973
Zimbabwe	13,806	21,338
Near East and North Africa[1]	**327,119**	**506,134**
Algeria	32,024	46,007
Cyprus	768	889
Egypt	66,498	97,505
Iraq	27,205	50,943
Israel	5,321	6,850
Jordan	4,880	8,987
Kuwait	2,879	4,564
Lebanon	4,058	5,755
Libya	5,599	8,549
Morocco	31,392	43,324
Oman	2,099	4,163
Saudi Arabia	25,003	45,836
Syria	18,212	35,761
Tunisia	9,713	12,597
Turkey	70,368	96,514
United Arab Emirates	3,598	6,182
Yemen	13,603	25,907
Asia[1]	**3,528,307**	**4,500,233**
Afghanistan	24,935	39,915
Bangladesh	143,226	209,898
Cambodia	8,498	11,947
China	1,303,342	1,541,143
India	1,018,092	1,316,989
Indonesia	223,820	287,289
Iran	78,246	143,230
Japan	128,144	127,716
Korea, North	25,491	30,969
Korea, South	45,962	48,649
Laos	4,964	6,923
Malaysia	21,950	31,598
Mongolia	2,836	4,390
Nepal	24,340	37,488
Myanmar (Burma)	49,787	67,689
Pakistan	149,147	251,305
Philippines	77,734	101,387
Singapore	3,021	3,401
Sri Lanka	19,296	23,283
Taiwan	22,441	25,059
Thailand	63,832	76,108
Vietnam	79,801	102,948

(1) Includes countries not shown separately.
(2) Includes Eritrea.

Region and Country	2000	2020
Latin America and the Caribbean[1]	**537,168**	**704,930**
Argentina	36,036	43,462
Belize	301	451
Bolivia	8,721	12,435
Brazil	180,536	231,672
Chile	15,025	18,484
Colombia	39,745	51,443
Costa Rica	3,803	5,294
Cuba	11,613	12,795
Dominican Republic	8,676	11,439
Ecuador	12,997	18,029
El Salvador	6,471	8,811
Guatemala	11,315	15,632
Haiti	7,649	11,374
Honduras	6,243	9,064
Jamaica	2,762	3,533
Mexico	108,754	147,911
Nicaragua	4,729	7,013
Panama	2,937	3,908
Paraguay	6,023	8,812
Peru	26,435	35,055
Trinidad and Tobago	1,425	1,761
Uruguay	3,289	3,620
Venezuela	24,596	34,357
North America, Europe, and the former USSR[1]	**1,125,095**	**1,204,719**
Albania	3,824	4,677
Austria	7,762	7,488
Belgium	9,989	9,692
Bulgaria	9,004	9,071
Canada	29,301	33,128
Czechoslovakia (Former)	16,303	16,995
Denmark	5,147	4,980
Finland	5,075	5,024
France	58,548	60,149
Germany	81,532	81,883
Greece	10,166	9,902
Hungary	10,604	10,393
Ireland	3,509	3,837
Italy	58,592	56,068
Netherlands	15,642	15,698
Norway	4,411	4,497
Poland	38,889	41,698
Portugal	10,652	10,671
Romania	24,534	25,981
Spain	40,456	40,428
Sweden	8,761	8,645
Switzerland	7,018	6,843
USSR (Former)	311,637	355,092
United Kingdom	58,719	59,431
United States	268,266	294,364
Yugoslavia (Former)	25,112	26,349

Customs Exemptions and Advice to Travelers

Source: U.S. Customs Service

U.S. residents returning after a stay abroad of at least 48 hours are usually granted customs exemptions of $400 each. The duty-free articles must accompany the traveler at the time of his or her return, be for personal or household use, have been acquired as an incident of the trip, and be properly declared to Customs. Not more than one liter of alcoholic beverages may be included in the $400 exemption.

If a U.S. resident arrives directly or indirectly from the U.S. Virgin Islands, or a contiguous country that maintains a free zone or a free port, the purchase may be valued up to $800 fair retail value, but not more than $400 of the exemption may be applied to the value of articles acquired elsewhere than in such insular possessions, and 5 liters of alcoholic beverages may be included in the exemption, but not more than one liter of such beverages may have been acquired elsewhere than in the designated islands.

The exemption for alcoholic beverages is accorded only when the returning resident has attained 21 years of age at the time of arrival. One hundred cigars and 200 cigarettes may be included in either exemption. Cuban cigars may be included if obtained in Cuba and all articles acquired there do not exceed $100 in retail value.

The $400 or $800 exemption may be granted only if the exemption, or any part of it, has not been used within the preceding 30-day period and the stay abroad was for at least 48 hours. The 48-hour absence requirement does not apply to travelers returning from Mexico or the U.S. Virgin Islands.

Gifts costing no more than $50 fair retail value or $100 from American Samoa, Guam, or the Virgin Islands may be mailed duty-free.

Most items—including alcoholic beverages, cigars, cigarettes and perfume—made in designated Caribbean and Central American countries may enter the U.S. duty-free under the Caribbean Basin Economic Recovery Act. Countries currently designated for such duty-free treatment are: Aruba, Antigua and Barbuda, Bahamas, Barbados, Belize, British Virgin Islands, Costa Rica, Dominica, Dominican Republic, El Salvador, Grenada, Guatemala, Guyana, Honduras, Jamaica, Montserrat, Netherlands Antilles, Nicaragua, Panama, Saint Kitts and Nevis, Saint Lucia, Saint Vincent and the Grenadines, and Trinidad and Tobago. Exceptions are: most textiles (incl. clothing), footwear, handbags, luggage, flat goods, work gloves and leather wearing apparel, and certain watches and watch parts. Alcoholic beverages and perfumes remain subject to IRS tax.

The World's Refugees

(as of Dec. 31, 1992)

Source: *World Refugee Survey 1993,* U.S. Committee for Refugees, a nonprofit corp. The refugees in this table include only those who are in need of protection and/or assistance and do not include refugees who have resettled.

Country of Asylum	Mostly From	Number
Total Africa		**5,698,540**
Algeria	W. Sahara, Mali	165,000[1]
Angola	Zaire	9,000
Benin	Togo	4,300
Botswana	S. Africa, Angola	5,000
Burkina Faso	Mali	6,300
Burundi	Rwanda, Zaire	107,350[1]
Cameroon	Chad	1,500
Central African Rep.	Chad, Sudan	18,000
Congo	Chad, Angola	9,400
Côte d'Ivoire	Liberia	195,500
Djibouti	Ethiopia, Somalia	96,000
Egypt	Palestinians, Somalia	10,650
Ethiopia/Eritrea	Sudan, Somalia	416,000[1]
Gabon	various	200
Gambia, The	Senegal, Liberia	3,300
Ghana	Liberia, Togo	12,100
Guinea	Liberia, Sierra Leone	485,000[1]
Guinea-Bissau	Senegal	12,000
Kenya	Ethiopia, Sudan, Somalia	422,900[1]
Lesotho	South Africa	200
Liberia	Sierra Leone	100,000
Malawi	Mozambique	1,070,000
Mali	Mauritania	10,000
Mauritania	Mali	40,000
Morocco	various	800
Mozambique	various	250
Namibia	various	150
Niger	Chad	3,600
Nigeria	Chad, Liberia	2,900
Rwanda	Burundi	24,500
Senegal	Mauritania	55,100
Sierra Leone	Liberia	7,600
Somalia	Ethiopia/Eritrea	10,000[1]
S. Africa	Mozambique	250,000[1]
Sudan	Ethiopia/Eritrea, Chad	750,500[1]
Swaziland	South Africa, Mozambique	52,000
Tanzania	Burundi, Mozambique	257,800
Togo	various	350
Uganda	Sudan, Rwanda	179,600[1]
Zaire	Angola, Burundi, Sudan	442,400
Zambia	Angola, Mozambique, Zaire	155,700
Zimbabwe	Mozambique	265,000 1[1]
Total East Asia/Pacific		**398,600**
Australia	various	24,000
China	Myanmar	12,500[1]
Hong Kong	Vietnam	45,300
Indonesia	Vietnam, Cambodia	15,600
Japan	Vietnam	700
Korea	Vietnam	150
Malaysia	Vietnam, Myanmar	16,700
Papua New Guinea	Indonesia	3,800
Philippines	Vietnam	5,600
Singapore	Vietnam	100
Taiwan	Vietnam	150
Thailand	Myanmar, Laos, Cambodia	255,000
Vietnam	Cambodia	19,000
Total Europe & No. America		**3,423,600**
Armenia	Azerbaijan	300,000[1]
Austria	Former Yugoslavia	82,100
Azerbaijan	Armenia	246,000[1]
Belarus	various	3,700
Belgium	various	19,100
Bosnia and Herzegovina	Former Yugoslavia	70,000[1]
Canada	various	37,700
Croatia	Former Yugoslavia	420,000[1]
Czech Rep./Slovakia	Former Yugoslavia	2,200
Denmark	Former Yugoslavia	13,900
Finland	various	3,500
France	various	29,400
Germany	Former Yugoslavia	536,000
Greece	various	1,900
Hungary	Former Yugoslavia	40,000
Italy	Former Yugoslavia	19,100
Luxembourg	Former Yugoslavia	1,800
Macedonia	Former Yugoslavia	32,700[1]
Netherlands	various	24,600
Norway	various	5,700
Poland	Former Yugoslavia	1,500
Russia	various	460,000[1]
Slovenia	Former Yugoslavia	68,900[1]
Spain	various	12,700
Sweden	Former Yugoslavia	88,400
Switzerland	Former Yugoslavia	81,700
Turkey	Iraq, Former Yugoslavia	31,700
Ukraine	various	40,000[1]
United Kingdom	various	24,600
United States	various	103,700
Yugoslavia[2]	Former Yugoslavia	621,000[1]
Total Latin America/Caribbean		**107,700**
Belize	El Salvador, Guatemala	6,100
Brazil	various	200
Colombia	various	400
Costa Rica	El Salvador, Nicaragua	34,350
Cuba	Haiti	1,100
Ecuador	various	200
El Salvador	various	250
French Guiana	Suriname	1,600
Guatemala	El Salvador, Nicaragua	4,900
Honduras	various	150
Mexico	Guatemala, El Salvador	47,300
Nicaragua	El Salvador	5,850
Panama	various	850
Peru	Cuba	400
Uruguay	various	100
Venezuela	Cuba, Haiti	1,350
Total Middle East/South & Central Asia		**7,938,550**
Afghanistan	Tajikistan	52,000
Bangladesh	Myanmar	245,000
India	Bangladesh, Tibet, Sri Lanka	378,000[1]
Iran	Afghanistan, Iraq	2,781,800[1]
Iraq	Iran	64,000
Nepal	Tibet, Bhutan	89,400
Pakistan	Afghanistan	1,577,000
Saudi Arabia	Iraq	27,400
Yemen	Somalia	52,500
Palestinians		
Gaza Strip		560,200
Jordan		1,010,850[3]
Lebanon		322,900[3]
Syria		307,400[3]
West Bank		459,100
Total Refugees		**17,556,900**

(1) Significant variance among sources in number reported. (2) Incl. Serbia/Montenegro. (3) Incl. some non-Palestinians.

Principal Sources of Refugees

Afghanistan	4,286,000[1]
Palestinians	2,658,000
Mozambique	1,725,000[1]
Bosnia and Herzegovina	940,000
Somalia	864,800[1]
Ethiopia/Eritrea	834,800[1]
Liberia	599,200[1]
Angola	404,200
Croatia	350,000
Azerbaijan	350,000[1]
Myanmar	333,700[1]
Sudan	263,000
Armenia	202,000[1]
Rwanda	201,500[1]
Sierra Leone	200,000
Burundi	184,000
Sri Lanka	181,000
Western Sahara	165,000[1]
Cambodia	148,600

(1) Significant variance among sources in number reported.

U.S. Immigration Law

Source: Immigration and Naturalization Service, U.S. Dept. of Justice

The Immigration Act of 1990 became law when it was signed by President Bush on Nov. 29, 1990. Bush called the bill the "most comprehensive reform of U.S. immigration laws in 66 years." Most of its provisions amend the Immigration and Nationality Act which remains the basic law. The new law raised the total number of numerically limited immigrants entering the U.S. annually in FY 1992-94 to 700,000 (excluding refugees whose admission numbers are announced annually and some others not subject to limitation). The visas would be distributed as follows:

- 465,000 for family immigrants;
- 55,000 for the spouses and children of aliens legalized under IRCA;
- 140,000 for employment-based immigrants;
- 40,000 for nationals from "adversely affected" countries.

Beginning in FY 1995 the number drops to a minimum of 675,000. These visas would be distributed as follows:

- 480,000 for family immigrants;
- 140,000 for employment based immigrants;
- 55,000 for "diversity immigrants."

Family Immigrants

Fiscal year 1992-94: 465,000 minus the number of "immediate relatives" admitted the previous fiscal year, *plus* any numbers unused by the employment-based preference system. During this period, the number of family-sponsored visas cannot fall below 226,000 (10,000 visas higher than the current allocation). If visa availability dips below this new floor, the shortfall will be made up from the category below.

During this period, 55,000 additional visas will be made available to the spouses and children of aliens legalized under the Immigration Reform and Control Act (IRCA) of 1986.

Fiscal year 1995 and beyond: 480,000 minus the number of "immediate relatives" admitted during the previous fiscal year, plus any unused numbers under the employment-based preference system. That number may not drop below a floor of 226,000. If it does (*as it is certain to*), the "cap" simply gets pierced.

New Family Preference System

First preference—unmarried sons and daughters of U.S. citizens: 23,400 visas plus unused visas from the 4th preference.

Second preference—spouses and unmarried children of Lawful Permanent Residents (LPRs): 114,200 visas, plus any visas available above the floor of 226,000 family preference visas, plus any unused visas from the previous preference.

The category is subdivided as follows: A minimum of 77 percent of the visas allocated to the category goes to the spouses and minor children of LPRs; 75 percent of the visas are issued without regard to per country ceilings; these visas will be distributed in the order in which the petitions were filed; a maximum of 23 percent of the category visa allocation goes to the unmarried sons and daughters of LPRs. This group of visas will continue to be subject to per country ceilings.

Third preference—married sons and daughters of U.S. citizens; 23,400 visas plus unused visas from all earlier preferences.

Fourth preference—brothers and sisters of U.S. citizens: 65,000 plus unused visas from all earlier preferences.

Employment-Based Immigrants

A total of 140,000 plus, beginning in 1994, any unused numbers under the family-sponsored system. These visas would be distributed as follows:

First preference—Priority Workers—28.6 percent of the employment-based limit; 40,040 visas in 1992 plus visas unused by the fourth and fifth employment-based preferences "investors" and "special immigrants". The category is subdivided as follows: extraordinary ability, demonstrated by sustained national or international acclaim, in the sciences, arts, education, business, and athletics. No U.S. employer required;

Outstanding, internationally recognized and with at least 3 years of experience, professors and researchers seeking to enter in senior positions. U.S. employer required; executives and managers of multinationals—requires one year of prior service with the firm during the preceding 3 years. The terms are extensively defined. U.S. employer required.

Second preference—Professionals with advanced degrees and aliens of exceptional ability—28.6 percent of the employment-based limit; 40,040 visas in 1992 plus any unused "priority worker" visas. A U.S. employer and labor certification are required—although the Attorney General can waive both requirements. Members of the professions with advanced degrees or exceptional ability in the sciences, arts, or business. The possession of a degree, certificate, or license is not by itself considered sufficient evidence of exceptional ability.

Third preference—Skilled workers, professionals, and "Other" Workers—40,000 visas plus any visas unused by the 2 previous categories. Requires a U.S. employer and labor certification. Skilled workers must be in an occupation that requires at least 2 years training or experience. Professionals need a Bachelor's degree. "Other" workers refers to unskilled workers. Their numbers are limited to no more than 10,000 visas per year.

Fourth preference—Special immigrants—7.1 percent of the employment-based limit; 9,040 visas in 1992. This category includes ministers of religion and persons working for religious organizations for at least 2 years, foreign medical graduates, employees of the U.S. government abroad including certain employees of the U.S. mission in Hong Kong who file for admission as special immigrants before Jan. 1, 2002, retired employees of international organizations, etc.

Fifth preference—7.1 percent of the employment-based limit; 9,040 employment creation (investor) visas in 1992—7,000 for investors of $1 million in urban areas and 3,000 for investors of no less than $500,000 in rural or high-unemployment areas. The Attorney General may increase the required investment amount up to $3 million for high employment areas. Investment must create employment for at least 10 U.S. workers.

Labor Certification

A pilot program is created for FY 1992-94 giving Dept. of Labor the authority to identify up to 10 "shortage" or "surplus" occupations and make certifications for these occupations. If the occupation is in "shortage," automatic certification would be offered; if the occupation is in "surplus," the employer may still petition for the immigrant but will be required to demonstrate that he/she has undertaken extensive recruitment.

Student Visas

A 3-year program (FY 1992-94) allows foreign students to be employed off-campus for up to 20 hours per week during the school year, and without restrictions when school is out of session. The employment can only come after their first year of school but may be unrelated to their studies.

The employer must attest that he has recruited for U.S. workers for at least 60 days and that he offers both foreign and U.S. workers the actual wage level for the occupation at the place of employment or, if greater, the prevailing wage level for the occupation in the area of employment. If the Secretary of Labor finds the attestation to be a misrepresentation, the employer can be disqualified from employing a foreign student.

Major International Organizations

As of mid-1993

Association of Southeast Asian Nations (ASEAN), formed in 1967 to promote economic, social, and cultural cooperation and development among the non-communist states of the region. Members in 1993 are Brunei Darussalam, Indonesia, Malaysia, Philippines, Singapore, Thailand. Annual ministerial meetings set policy; a central Secretariat in Jakarta and specialized intergovernmental committees work in trade, transportation, communications, agriculture, science, finance, and culture.

Caribbean Community and Common Market (Caricom), established July 4, 1973. Its function is to further cooperation in economics, health, education, culture, science and technology, and tax administration, as well as the coordination of foreign policy. Members in 1993 are Antigua and Barbuda, Bahamas, Barbados, Belize, Dominica, Grenada, Guyana, Jamaica, Montserrat, Saint Kitts and Nevis, Saint Lucia, Saint Vincent and the Grenadines, Trinidad and Tobago.

Commonwealth of Independent States (CIS), created Dec. 1991 upon the disbanding of the Soviet Union. It is made up of 10 of the 15 former Soviet constituent republics. Members are Armenia, Belarus, Kazakhstan, Kyrgyzstan, Moldova, Russia, Tajikistan, Turkmenistan, Ukraine, and Uzbekistan. The commonwealth is not in itself a state, but an alliance of fully independent states. Commonwealth policy is set through coordinating bodies such as a Council of Heads of State and Council of Heads of Government. The capital of the commonwealth is Minsk, Belarus.

Commonwealth of Nations, originally called the British Commonwealth of Nations, an association of nations and dependencies loosely joined by a common interest based on having been parts of the old British Empire. The British monarch is the symbolic head of the Commonwealth.

There are 50 self-governing independent nations in the Commonwealth, plus various colonies and protectorates. As of 1993, the members were the United Kingdom of Great Britain and Northern Ireland and 15 other nations recognizing the British monarch, represented by a governor-general, as their head of state: Antigua and Barbuda, Australia, The Bahamas, Barbados, Belize, Canada, Grenada, Jamaica, New Zealand, Papua New Guinea, Saint Kitts and Nevis, Saint Lucia, Saint Vincent and the Grenadines, Solomon Islands, and Tuvalu (a special member); and 34 countries with their own heads of state: Bangladesh, Botswana, Brunei Darussalam, Cyprus, Dominica, The Gambia, Ghana, Guyana, India, Kenya, Kiribati, Lesotho, Malawi, Malaysia, The Maldives, Malta, Mauritius, Namibia, Nauru (a special member), Nigeria, Pakistan, Seychelles, Sierra Leone, Singapore, Sri Lanka, Swaziland, Tanzania, Tonga, Trinidad and Tobago, Uganda, Vanuatu, Western Samoa, Zambia, and Zimbabwe.

The Commonwealth facilitates consultation among member states through meetings of prime ministers and finance ministers, and through a permanent Secretariat. Members consult on economic, scientific, educational, financial, legal, and military matters, and try to coordinate policies.

European Community (EC)—officially, the European Communities—the collective designation of three organizations with common membership: the European Economic Community (Common Market), the European Coal and Steel Community, and the European Atomic Energy Community (Euratom). The 12 full members are: Belgium, Denmark, France, Germany, Greece, Ireland, Italy, Luxembourg, Netherlands, Portugal, Spain, United Kingdom. Some 60 nations in Africa, the Caribbean, and the Pacific are affiliated under the Lomé Convention.

A merger of the 3 communities' executives went into effect July 1, 1967, though the component organizations date back to 1951 and 1958. The Council of Ministers, the Commission of the European Communities, the European Parliament, and the European Court of Justice comprise the permanent structure. The EC aims to integrate the economies, coordinate social developments, and bring about political union of the democratic states of Europe. Effective Dec. 31, 1992, there are no restrictions on the movement of goods, services, capital, workers, and tourists within the community. There are also common agricultural, fisheries, and nuclear research policies.

Leaders of the 12 European Community nations met Dec. 9–11, 1991, in Maastricht, the Netherlands. Treaties on monetary union and political union and accompanying protocols agreed upon by the leaders:

- Committed the EC to launching a common currency for at least some nations by 1999. Britain and, later, Denmark were allowed to "opt out" of joining.
- Sought to establish common foreign policies for the 12 members.
- Laid the groundwork for a common defense policy under the Western European Union.
- Expanded the policy issues in which the EC would have a voice.
- Gave the EC a leading role in social policy. Britain was not included in this plan.
- Pledged increased aid for the community's four poorest nations—Ireland, Greece, Spain, and Portugal.
- Slightly increased the powers of the 518-member European Parliament.

The treaties require ratification by all 12 members before they can go into effect.

European Free Trade Association (EFTA), created May 3, 1960, to promote expansion of free trade. Current members are Austria, Finland, Iceland, Liechtenstein, Norway, Sweden, and Switzerland. By Dec. 31, 1966, tariffs and quotas between members nations had been eliminated. Members of the association entered into free trade agreements with the EC in 1972 and 1973. In 1992 the EFTA and EC concluded an agreement to create a single market—with free flow of goods, services, capital, and labor—encompassing the 19 nations of the two organizations.

Group of Seven (G-7), organization of seven major industrial democracies who meet periodically to discuss world economic and other issues. Established Sept. 22, 1985. Members are Canada, France, Germany, Italy, Japan, United Kingdom, and United States.

International Criminal Police Organization (Interpol), created June 13, 1956, to ensure and promote the widest possible mutual assistance between all police authorities within the limits of the law existing in the different countries and in the spirit of the Universal Declaration of Human Rights. There are 152 members in 1993.

League of Arab States (The Arab League), created Mar. 22, 1945. Members in 1993 are Algeria, Bahrain, Djibouti, Egypt, Iraq, Jordan, Kuwait, Lebanon, Libya, Mauritania, Morocco, Oman, The Palestine Liberation Org., Qatar, Saudi Arabia, Somalia, Sudan, Syria, Tunisia, United Arab Emirates, Yemen. The League promotes economic, social, political, and military cooperation and mediates disputes among the Arab states; it represents Arab states in certain international negotiations. The league's headquarters is in Cairo.

North Atlantic Treaty Organization (NATO), created by treaty (signed Apr. 4, 1949; in effect Aug. 24, 1949). Members in 1993 are Belgium, Canada, Denmark, France, Germany, Greece, Iceland, Italy, Luxembourg, Netherlands, Norway, Portugal, Spain, Turkey, United Kingdom, and United States. The members agreed to settle disputes by peaceful means; to develop their individual and collective capacity to resist armed attack; to regard an attack on one as an attack on all; and to take necessary action to repel an attack under Article 51 of the United Nations Charter.

The NATO structure consists of a Council and a Military Committee of 3 commands (Allied Command Europe, Allied Command Atlantic, Allied Command Channel) and the Canada-U.S. Regional Planning Group.

With the dissolution of the Soviet Union and end of the cold war in the early 1990's, NATO members sought to modify the organization's mission, putting greater stress on political action and creating a rapid deployment force to react to local crises. Former Warsaw Pact members were no longer considered adversaries, and Hungary gained associate membership in 1991.

Organization of African Unity (OAU), formed May 25, 1963, by 32 African countries (51 members in 1993) to promote peace and security as well as economic and social development. It holds annual conferences of heads of state. Headquarters is in Addis Ababa, Ethiopia.

Organization of American States (OAS), formed in Bogotá, Colombia, Apr. 30, 1948. Headquarters is in Washington, D.C. It has a Permanent Council, Inter-American Economic and Social Council, Inter-American Council for Education, Science, and Culture, Juridical Committee, and Commission on Human Rights. The Permanent Council can call meetings of foreign ministers to deal with urgent security matters. A General Assembly meets annually. A secretary general and assistant are elected for 5-year terms. There are 35 members, each with one vote in the various organizations: Antigua and Barbuda, Argentina, The Bahamas, Barbados, Belize, Bolivia, Brazil, Canada, Chile, Colombia, Costa Rica, Cuba, Dominica, Dominican Republic, Ecuador, El Salvador, Grenada, Guatemala, Guyana, Haiti, Honduras, Jamaica, Mexico, Nicaragua, Panama, Paraguay, Peru, Saint Kitts and Nevis, Saint Lucia, Saint Vincent and the Grenadines, Suriname, Trinidad and Tobago, United States, Uruguay, Venezuela. In 1962, the OAS excluded Cuba from OAS activities but not from membership.

Organization for Economic Cooperation and Development (OECD), established Sept. 30, 1961, to promote economic and social welfare in member countries, and to stimulate and harmonize efforts on behalf of developing nations. The OECD collects and disseminates economic and environmental information. Members in 1993 are: Australia, Austria, Belgium, Canada, Denmark, Finland, France, Germany, Greece, Iceland, Ireland, Italy, Japan, Luxembourg, Netherlands, New Zealand, Norway, Portugal, Spain, Sweden, Switzerland, Turkey, United Kingdom, United States. Headquarters is in Paris.

Organization of Petroleum Exporting Countries (OPEC), created Sept. 14, 1960. The group attempts to set world oil prices by controlling oil production. It is also involved in advancing members' interests in trade and development dealings with industrialized oil-consuming nations. Members in 1993 are Algeria, Gabon, Indonesia, Iran, Iraq, Kuwait, Libya, Nigeria, Qatar, Saudi Arabia, United Arab Emirates, Venezuela.

United Nations

The 48th regular session of United Nations General Assembly opened in September 1993.

UN headquarters is in New York, N.Y., between First Ave. and Roosevelt Drive and E. 42d St. and E. 48th St. The General Assembly Bldg., Secretariat, Conference and Library bldgs. are interconnected.

A European office at Geneva includes Secretariat and agency staff members. Other offices of UN bodies and related organizations with a staff of some 23,000 from some 150 countries are scattered throughout the world.

The UN has a post office originating its own stamps.

Proposals to establish an organization of nations for maintenance of world peace led to the United Nations Conference on International Organization at San Francisco, Apr. 25-June 26, 1945, where the charter of the United Nations was drawn up. It was signed June 26 by 50 nations, and by Poland, one of the original 51 UN members, on Oct. 15, 1945. The charter came into effect Oct. 24, 1945, upon ratification by the permanent members of the Security Council and a majority of other signatories.

Purposes: To maintain international peace and security; to develop friendly relations among nations; to achieve international cooperation in solving economic, social, cultural, and humanitarian problems and in promoting respect for human rights and fundamental freedoms; to be a center for harmonizing the actions of nations in attaining these common ends.

Visitors to the UN: Headquarters is open to the public every day of the year except Christmas and New Year's Day. Guided tours are given approximately every half hour from 9:15 a.m. to 4:45 p.m. daily. Groups of 15 or more persons should write to the Group Program Unit, Visitors' Service, Room GA-56, United Nations, New York, NY 10017, or telephone (212) 963-4440. Children under 5 are not permitted on tours.

Roster of the United Nations

The 184 members of the United Nations, with the years in which they became members; as of Sept. 1993

Member	Year	Member	Year	Member	Year	Member	Year
Afghanistan	1946	Cambodia	1955	Finland	1955	Korea, N.	1991
Albania	1955	Cameroon	1960	France	1945	Korea, S.	1991
Algeria	1962	Canada	1945	Gabon	1960	Kuwait	1963
Andorra	1993	Cape Verde	1975	Gambia, The	1965	Kyrgyzstan	1992
Angola	1976	Central Afr. Rep.	1960	Georgia	1992	Laos	1955
Antigua and Barbuda	1981	Chad	1960	Germany	1973	Latvia	1991
Argentina	1945	Chile	1945	Ghana	1957	Lebanon	1945
Armenia	1992	China[1]	1945	Greece	1945	Lesotho	1966
Australia	1945	Colombia	1945	Grenada	1974	Liberia	1945
Austria	1955	Comoros	1975	Guatemala	1945	Libya	1955
Azerbaijan	1992	Congo	1960	Guinea	1958	Liechtenstein	1990
Bahamas	1973	Costa Rica	1945	Guinea-Bissau	1974	Lithuania	1991
Bahrain	1971	Côte d'Ivoire	1960	Guyana	1966	Luxembourg	1945
Bangladesh	1974	Croatia	1992	Haiti	1945	Macedonia[5]	1993
Barbados	1966	Cuba	1945	Honduras	1945	Madagascar	1960
Belarus	1945	Cyprus	1960	Hungary	1955	Malawi	1964
Belgium	1945	Czech Rep.[2]	1993	Iceland	1946	Malaysia[6]	1957
Belize	1981	Denmark	1945	India	1945	Maldives	1965
Benin	1960	Djibouti	1977	Indonesia[4]	1950	Mali	1960
Bhutan	1971	Dominica	1978	Iran	1945	Malta	1964
Bolivia	1945	Dominican Rep.	1945	Iraq	1945	Marshall Islands	1991
Bosnia and Herzegovina	1992	Ecuador	1945	Ireland	1955	Mauritania	1961
Botswana	1966	Egypt[3]	1945	Israel	1949	Mauritius	1968
Brazil	1945	El Salvador	1945	Italy	1955	Mexico	1945
Brunei Darussalam	1984	Equatorial Guinea	1968	Jamaica	1962	Micronesia	1991
Bulgaria	1955	Eritrea	1993	Japan	1956	Moldova	1992
Burkina Faso	1960	Estonia	1991	Jordan	1955	Monaco	1993
Burundi	1962	Ethiopia	1945	Kazakhstan	1992	Mongolia	1961
		Fiji	1970	Kenya	1963	Morocco	1956

Member	Year	Member	Year	Member	Year	Member	Year
Mozambique	1975	Portugal	1955	Slovakia[2]	1993	Turkey	1945
Myanmar (Burma)	1948	Qatar	1971	Slovenia	1992	Turkmenistan	1992
Namibia	1990	Romania	1955	Solomon Islands	1978	Uganda	1962
Nepal	1955	Russia	1945	Somalia	1960	Ukraine	1945
Netherlands	1945	Rwanda	1962	South Africa[7]	1945	United Arab Emirates	1971
New Zealand	1945	Saint Kitts and Nevis	1983	Spain	1955	United Kingdom	1945
Nicaragua	1945	Saint Lucia	1979	Sri Lanka	1955	United States	1945
Niger	1960	Saint Vincent and the Grenadines	1980	Sudan	1956	Uruguay	1945
Nigeria	1960	Samoa (Western)	1976	Suriname	1975	Uzbekistan	1992
Norway	1945	San Marino	1992	Swaziland	1968	Vanuatu	1981
Oman	1971	São Tomé and Príncipe	1975	Sweden	1946	Venezuela	1945
Pakistan	1947	Saudi Arabia	1945	Syria[3]	1945	Vietnam	1977
Panama	1945	Senegal	1960	Tajikistan	1992	Yemen[9]	1947
Papua New Guinea	1975	Seychelles	1976	Tanzania[8]	1961	Yugoslavia[10]	1945
Paraguay	1945	Sierra Leone	1961	Thailand	1946	Zaire	1960
Peru	1945	Singapore[6]	1965	Togo	1960	Zambia	1964
Philippines	1945			Trinidad and Tobago	1962	Zimbabwe	1980
Poland	1945			Tunisia	1956		

(1) The General Assembly voted in 1971 to expel the Chinese government on Taiwan and admit the Beijing government in its place. (2) Czechoslovakia, which split into the separate nations of the Czech Republic and Slovakia on Jan. 1, 1993, was a UN member from 1945 to 1992. (3) Egypt and Syria were original members of the UN. In 1958, the United Arab Republic was established by a union of Egypt and Syria and continued as a single member of the UN. In 1961, Syria resumed its separate membership. (4) Indonesia withdrew from the UN in 1965 and rejoined in 1966. (5) Admitted under the provisional name of The Former Yugoslav Republic of Macedonia. (6) Malaya joined the UN in 1957. In 1963, its name was changed to Malaysia following the accession of Singapore, Sabah, and Sarawak. Singapore became an independent UN member in 1965. (7) The General Assembly rejected the credentials of the South African delegates in 1974 and suspended the country from the Assembly. (8) Tanganyika was a member of the United Nations from 1961 and Zanzibar was a member from 1963. Following the ratification in 1964 of Articles of Union between Tanganyika and Zanzibar, the United Republic of Tanganyika and Zanzibar continued as a single member of the United Nations, later changing its name to United Republic of Tanzania. (9) The Yemen Arab Republic was admitted in 1947; the People's Republic of Yemen, in 1967. The two nations merged in 1990. (10) The Socialist Federal Republic of Yugoslavia became a member in 1945. After four of its six republics (Bosnia and Herzegovina, Croatia, Macedonia, and Slovenia) declared independence in 1991-1992, the two remaining republics, Montenegro and Serbia, reconstituted themselves as the Federal Republic of Yugoslavia, which assumed Yugoslavia's UN seat Apr. 8, 1992. The General Assembly suspended Yugoslavia in September 1992 for violating UN resolutions relating to the civil wars in the former Yugoslav republics.

United Nations Secretaries General

Year	Secretary, Nation
1946	Trygve Lie, Norway
1953	Dag Hammarskjold, Sweden
1961	U Thant, Burma
1972	Kurt Waldheim, Austria
1982	Javier Perez de Cuellar, Peru
1992	Boutros Boutros-Ghali, Egypt

U.S. Representatives to the United Nations

The U.S. Representative to the United Nations is the Chief of the U.S. Mission to the United Nations in New York and holds the rank and status of Ambassador Extraordinary and Plenipotentiary.

Year	Representative
1946	Edward R. Stettinius Jr.
1946	Herschel V. Johnson (act.)
1947	Warren R. Austin
1953	Henry Cabot Lodge Jr.
1960	James J. Wadsworth
1961	Adlai E. Stevenson
1965	Arthur J. Goldberg
1968	George W. Ball
1968	James Russell Wiggins
1969	Charles W. Yost
1971	George Bush
1973	John A. Scali
1975	Daniel P. Moynihan
1976	William W. Scranton
1977	Andrew Young
1979	Donald McHenry
1981	Jeane J. Kirkpatrick
1985	Vernon A. Walters
1989	Thomas R. Pickering
1992	Edward J. Perkins
1993	Madeleine K. Albright

Organization of the United Nations

The text of the UN Charter may be obtained from the Office of Public Information, United Nations, New York, NY 10017.

General Assembly. The General Assembly is composed of representatives of all the member nations. Each nation is entitled to one vote.

The General Assembly meets in regular annual sessions and in special session when necessary. Special sessions are convoked by the Secretary General at the request of the Security Council or of a majority of the members of the UN.

On important questions a two-thirds majority of members present and voting is required; on other questions a simple majority is sufficient.

The General Assembly must approve the budget and apportion expenses among members. A member in arrears will have no vote if the amount of arrears equals or exceeds the amount of the contributions due for the preceding two full years.

Security Council. The Security Council consists of 15 members, 5 with permanent seats. The remaining 10 are elected for 2-year terms by the General Assembly; they are not eligible for immediate reelection.

Permanent members of the Council are: China, France, Russia, United Kingdom, United States.

Nonpermanent members are: Cape Verde, Hungary, Japan, Morocco, Venezuela (until Dec. 31, 1993); Brazil, Djibouti, New Zealand, Pakistan, Spain (until Dec. 31, 1994).

The Security Council has the primary responsibility within the UN for maintaining international peace and security. The Council may investigate any dispute that threatens international peace and security.

Any member of the UN at UN headquarters may participate in its discussions and a nation not a member of UN may appear if it is a party to a dispute.

Decisions on procedural questions are made by an affirmative vote of 9 members. On all other matters the affirmative vote of 9 members must include the concurring votes of all permanent members; it is this clause which gives rise to the so-called veto power of permanent members. A party to a dispute must refrain from voting.

The Security Council directs the various peacekeeping forces deployed throughout the world.

Economic and Social Council. The Economic and Social Council consists of 54 members elected by the General Assembly for 3-year terms of office. The council is responsible under the General Assembly for carrying out the functions of the United Nations with regard to international economic, social, cultural, educational, health, and related matters. The council usually meets twice a year.

Trusteeship Council. The administration of trust territories is under UN supervision. The only remaining trust territory is Palau, administered by the U.S.

Secretariat. The Secretary General is the chief administrative officer of the UN. He may bring to the attention of the Security Council any matter that threatens international peace. He reports to the General Assembly.

Budget: The General Assembly approved a total budget for 1992-93 of $2.36 billion.

International Court of Justice (World Court). The International Court of Justice is the principal judicial organ of the United Nations. All members are *ipso facto* parties to the statute of the Court. Other states may become parties to the Court's statute.

The jurisdiction of the Court comprises cases which the parties submit to it and matters especially provided for in the charter or in treaties. The Court gives advisory opinions and renders judgments. Its decisions are binding only between the parties concerned and in respect to a particular dispute. If any party to a case fails to heed a judgment, the other party may have recourse to the Security Council.

The 15 judges are elected for 9-year terms by the General Assembly and the Security Council. Retiring judges are eligible for reelection. The Court remains permanently in session, except during vacations. All questions are decided by majority. The Court sits in The Hague, Netherlands.

Selected Specialized and Related Agencies

These agencies are autonomous, with their own memberships and organs, which have a functional relationship or working agreement with the UN (headquarters.)

Food and Agriculture Organization (FAO), aims to increase production from farms, forests, and fisheries; improve food distribution and marketing, nutrition, and the living conditions of rural people. (Viale delle Terme di Caracalla, 00100 Rome, Italy.)

General Agreement on Tariffs and Trade (GATT), the only treaty setting rules for world trade, provides a forum for settling trade disputes and negotiating trade liberalization. (Centre William Rappard, 154 rue de Lausanne, 1211 Geneva 21, Switzerland.)

International Atomic Energy Agency (IAEA), aims to promote the safe, peaceful uses of atomic energy. (Vienna International Centre, PO Box 100, A-1400, Vienna, Austria.)

International Bank for Reconstruction and Development (IBRD) (World Bank), provides loans and technical assistance for economic development projects in developing member countries; encourages cofinancing for projects from other public and private sources. The **International Development Association (IDA),** an affiliate of the Bank, provides funds for development projects on concessionary terms to the poorer developing member countries. The **International Finance Corporation (IFC),** an affiliate of the Bank, promotes the growth of the private sector in developing member countries; encourages the development of local capital markets; stimulates the international flow of private capital. (1818 H St., NW, Washington, DC 20433.)

International Civil Aviation Organization (ICAO), promotes international civil aviation standards and regulations. (1000 Sherbrooke St. W., Montreal, Quebec, Canada H3A 2R2.)

International Fund for Agricultural Development (IFAD), aims to mobilize funds for agricultural and rural projects in developing countries. (107 Via del Serafico, Rome, Italy.)

International Labor Organization (ILO), aims to promote employment; improve labor conditions and living standards. (4 route de Morillons, CH-1211 Geneva 22, Switzerland.)

International Maritime Organization (IMO), aims to promote cooperation on technical matters affecting international shipping. (4 Albert Embankment, London SE1 7SR, England.)

International Monetary Fund (IMF), aims to promote international monetary cooperation and currency stabilization and expansion of international trade. (700 19th St., NW, Washington, DC 20431.)

International Telecommunication Union (ITU), establishes international regulations for radio, telegraph, telephone, and space radio-communications, allocates radio frequencies. (Place des Nations, 1211 Geneva 20, Switzerland.)

United Nations Children's Fund (UNICEF), provides aid and development assistance to programs for children and mothers in developing countries. (1 UN Plaza, New York, NY 10017.)

United Nations Development Fund For Women (INIFEM), aims to assist poor women in their economic roles in Africa, Asia, and Latin America. (304 E. 45th St., New York, NY 10017.)

United Nations Educational, Scientific, and Cultural Organization (UNESCO), aims to promote collaboration among nations through education, science, and culture. (7 Place de Fontenoy, 75352 Paris 07SP, France.)

United Nations High Commissioner for Refugees (UNHCR), provides essential assistance for refugees. (Place des Nations, 1211 Geneva 10, Switzerland.)

Universal Postal Union (UPU) aims to perfect postal services and promote international collaboration. (Weltpoststrasse 4, 3000 Berne, 15 Switzerland.)

World Health Org. (WHO) aims to aid the attainment of the highest possible level of health. (1211 Geneva 27, Switzerland.)

World Intellectual Property Organization (WIPO) seeks to protect, through international cooperation, literary, industrial, scientific, and artistic works. (34, Chemin des Colom Bettes, 1211 Geneva, Switzerland.)

World Meteorological Org. (WMO) aims to co-ordinate and improve world meteorological work. (Case Postale 5, CH-1211 Geneva 20, Switzerland.)

Geneva Conventions

As of mid-1992

The Geneva Conventions are 4 international treaties governing the protection of civilians in time of war, the treatment of prisoners of war, and the care of the wounded and sick in the armed forces. The first convention, covering the sick and wounded, was concluded in Geneva, Switzerland, in 1864; it was amended and expanded in 1906. A third convention, in 1929, covered prisoners of war. Outrage at the treatment of prisoners and civilians during World War II by some belligerents, notably Germany and Japan, prompted the conclusion, in August 1949, of 4 new conventions. Three of these restated and strengthened the previous conventions, and the fourth codified general principles of international law governing the treatment of civilians in wartime.

The 1949 convention for civilians provided for special safeguards for the wounded, children under 15, pregnant women, and the elderly. Discrimination was forbidden on racial, religious, national, or political grounds. Torture, collective punishment, reprisals, the unwarrented destruction of property, and the forced use of civilians for an occupier's armed forces were also prohibited.

Also included in the new 1949 treaties was a pledge to treat prisoners humanely, feed them adequately, and deliver relief supplies to them. They were not to be forced to disclose more than minimal information.

Most countries have formally accepted all or most of the humanitarian conventions as binding. A nation is not free to withdraw its ratification of the conventions during wartime. However, there is no permanent machinery in place to apprehend, try, or punish violators.

Ambassadors and Envoys

As of mid-1993

The address of U.S. embassies abroad is the appropriate foreign capital. The U.S. does not have diplomatic relations with the following countries: Liechtenstein, Maldives, Cambodia,[1] Taiwan,[2] Cuba,[3] Iran,[4] Libya,[5] Vietnam,[1] N. Korea, Iraq,[6] Somalia.[7] There are informal relations with Bhutan and Vanuatu.

Countries	Envoys from United States	Envoys to United States
Afghanistan	Vacancy	Abdul Ghafoor Jawshan, Chargé
Albania	William E. Ryerson, Amb.	Roland Bimo, Amb.
Algeria	Mary Ann Casey, Amb.	Vacancy
Angola	Vacancy	Vacancy
Antigua & Barbuda	Bryant J. Salter, Amb.	Patrick A. Lewis, Amb.
Argentina	Terence A. Todman, Amb.	Carlos Ortiz de Rosas, Amb.
Armenia	Thomas L. Price, Chargé	Alexandre Arzoumanian, Chargé
Australia	Marilyn A. Meyers, Chargé	Michael J. Cook, Amb.
Austria	James W. Swihart Jr., Chargé	Helmut Turk
Azerbaijan	Richard Miles, Amb.	D. N. Molla-Zade, Chargé
Bahamas	Lino Gutierrez, Chargé	Timothy B. Donaldson
Bahrain	David S. Robins, Chargé	Abdul Al-Khalifa, Amb.
Bangladesh	William B. Milam, Amb.	Abdul Ahsan, Amb.
Barbados	C. Philip Hughes, Amb.	Rudi V. Webster, Amb.
Belarus	David Swartz, Amb.	Serguei Martynov, Chargé
Belgium	Bruce S. Gelb, Amb.	Jean Cassiers, Amb.
Belize	Eugene L. Scassa, Amb.	James V. Hyde, Amb.
Benin	Ruth A. Davis, Amb.	Candide Pierre Ahouansou, Amb.
Bolivia	Charles R. Bowers, Amb.	Jose Crespo-Velasco, Amb.
Bosnia and Herzegovina	Victor Jackovich, Chargé	Vacancy
Botswana	David Passage, Amb.	Botsweletse K. Sebele, Amb.
Brazil	Richard H. Melton, Amb.	Rubens Ricupero, Amb.
Brunei	Donald B. Ensanet, Amb.	D.H. Mohammad Kassim, Amb.
Bulgaria	H. Kenneth Hill, Amb.	Ognian R. Pishev, Amb.
Burkina Faso	Edward P. Byrnn, Amb.	Thomas Kambou, Chargé
Burundi	Franklin P. Huddle Jr., Chargé	Julien Kavakure, Amb.
Cameroon	Tibor P. Nagy Jr., Chargé	Paul Pondi, Amb.
Canada	James J. Blanchard, Amb.	John G. D. de Chastelain, Amb.
Cape Verde	Joseph M. Segars, Amb.	Carlos Silva, Amb.
Central African Rep.	Robert E. Gribbon 3d, Amb.	Jean-Pierre Sobahong-Kombet, Amb.
Chad	William W. Bogosian, Amb.	E. Acheikh ibn Oumar, Amb.
Chile	Curtis W. Kamman, Amb.	Patricio Silva, Amb.
China	J. Stapleton Roy, Amb.	Zhu Qizhen, Amb.
Colombia	Morris D. Busby, Amb.	Jamie Garcia-Parra, Amb.
Comoros	Kenneth N. Peltier, Amb.	Amini Ali Moumin, Amb.
Congo	James D. Phillips, Amb.	Roger Issombo, Amb.
Costa Rica	Luis Guinot Jr., Amb.	Gonzalo Facio, Amb.
Côte d'Ivoire	Hume A. Horan, Amb.	Charles Gomis, Amb.
Croatia	Peter W. Galbraith, Amb.	Peter A. Sarcevic, Amb.
Cyprus	Robert E. Lamb, Amb.	Michael E. Sherifis, Amb.
Czech Rep.	Adrian A. Basora, Amb.	Michael Zantovsky, Amb.
Denmark	Richard B. Stone, Amb.	Peter P. Dyvig, Amb.
Djibouti	Charles Baquet 3d, Amb.	Roble Olhale, Amb.
Dominica	C. Philip Hughes, Amb.	Edward I. Watty, Amb.
Dominican Republic	Robert S. Pastorino, Amb.	Jose del Carmen Ariza, Amb.
Ecuador	James F. Mack, Chargé	Edgar Teran-Teran, Amb.
Egypt	Robert H. Pelletreau Jr., Amb.	Ahmed Maher El Sayed, Amb.
El Salvador	Alan H. Flanigan, Amb.	Miguel A. Salaverria, Amb.
Equatorial Guinea	John E. Bennett, Amb.	Damaso Obiang Ndong, Amb.
Estonia	Robert C. Frasure, Amb.	Ernst Jaakson, Amb.
Ethiopia	Marc Baas, Amb.	Berhane Gebre-Chirstos, Amb.
Fiji	Evelyn I.H. Teegen, Amb.	Pita Kewa Nacuva, Amb.
Finland	John H. Kelly, Amb.	Jukka Valtasaari, Amb.
France	Pamela C. Herriman, Amb.	Jacques Andreani, Amb.
Gabon	Joseph C. Wilson, Amb.	Guy M. Eboumi, Chargé
Gambia, The	Arlene Render, Amb.	Ousman A. Sallah, Amb.
Georgia	Kent N. Brown, Amb.	Vacancy
Germany	Richard C. Holbrooke, Amb.	Immo Stabreit, Amb.
Ghana	Kenneth L. Brown, Amb.	Joseph Abbey, Amb.
Greece	James A. Williams, Chargé	Christos Zacharakis, Amb.
Grenada	C. Annette T. Veler, Chargé	Denneth Modeste, Amb.
Guatemala	James F. Keane, Chargé	Magdalena Toriello, Chargé
Guinea	Dane F. Smith, Amb.	Elhadj B. Barry, Amb.
Guinea-Bissau	Rogert A. McGuire, Amb.	Alfredo Lopes Cabral, Amb.
Guyana	George F. Jones, Amb.	June Persaud, Chargé
Haiti	Charles E. Redman, Chargé	Jean Casimir, Amb.
Honduras	Cresencio S. Arcos, Amb.	R. E. Bendana-Valenzuela, Amb.
Hungary	Charles H. Thomas, Amb.	Pal Tar, Amb.
Iceland	Jon Gundersen, Chargé	Tomas Tomasson, Amb.
India	Kenneth C. Brill, Chargé	Siddhartha S. Ray, Amb.
Indonesia	Robert L. Barry, Amb.	Abdul Rachman Ramly, Amb.
Ireland	Thomas M. Tonkin, Chargé	Dermot A. Gallagher, Amb.
Israel	Vacancy	Zalman Shoval, Amb.
Italy	Daniel P. Serwer, Chargé	Boris Biancheri, Amb.
Jamaica	Shirley Chisholm	Richard L. Bernal, Amb.
Japan	Walter F. Mondale, Amb.	Takakazu Kuriyama, Amb.
Jordan	Roger G. Harrison, Amb.	Fayez A. Tarawneh, Amb.
Kazakhstan	William Courtney, Amb.	Alim S. Djambourchine, Amb.
Kenya	E. Michael Southwick, Chargé	Denis D. Afande, Amb.

Countries	Envoys from United States	Envoys to United States
Kiribati	Evelyn I.H. Teegen, Amb.	Vacancy
Korea, South	Raymond F. Burghardt Jr., Chargé	Hong-Choo Hyun, Amb.
Kuwait	Edward Gnehm, Amb.	Shaikh S. N. Al-Sabah, Amb.
Kyrgyzstan	Edward Hurwitz, Amb.	Roza Otumbayeva, Amb.
Laos	Charles B. Salmon Jr., Amb.	Hiem Phommachanh, Amb.
Latvia	Ints M. Silins, Amb.	Ojars E. Kalnins, Amb.
Lebanon	Ryan C. Crocker, Amb.	Simon M. Karam, Amb.
Lesotho	Karl Hoffman, Chargé	Teboho E. Kitleli, Amb.
Liberia	William P. Twaddell, Chargé	Konah Blackett, Chargé
Lithuania	Darryl N. Johnson, Amb.	Stasys Lozoraitis Jr., Amb.
Luxembourg	Edward M. Rowell, Amb.	Alphonse Berns, Amb.
Madagascar	Dennis P. Barrett, Amb.	Pierrot J. Rajaonarivelo, Amb.
Malawi	Michael T. F. Pistor, Amb.	Robert Mbaya, Amb.
Malaysia	John S. Wolf, Amb.	Dato Abdul Majid, Amb.
Maldives	Teresita C. Schaffer	Vacancy
Mali	Herbert D. Gelber, Amb.	Siragatou I. Cisse, Amb.
Malta	William A. Moffitt, Chargé	Borg Olivier de Puget, Amb.
Marshall Islands	David C. Fields, Amb.	Wilfred Kendall, Amb.
Mauritania	Gordon S. Brown, Amb.	Mohammed Fall Ainini, Amb.
Mauritius	David B. Dunn, Chargé	Chitmansing Jesseramsing, Amb.
Mexico	Jim Jones, Amb.	Jorge Montoya, Amb.
Micronesia	Aurelia E. Brazeal, Amb.	Jesse B. Marehalau, Amb.
Moldova	Mary C. Pendleton, Amb.	Vacancy
Mongolia	Donald C. Johnson, Amb.	Luvsandort Dawagiv, Amb.
Morocco	Joan M. Plaisted, Chargé	Mohamed Belkhayat, Amb.
Mozambique	Townsend B. Friedman Jr., Amb.	Hipolito Patricio, Amb.
Myanmar	Franklin P. Huddle Jr., Chargé	U Thaung, Amb.
Namibia	Howard J. Jeter, Chargé	Tuliameni Kalomoh, Amb.
Nauru	Marilyn A. Meyers, Chargé	Vacancy
Nepal	Julia Chang Bloch, Amb.	Yog Prasad Upadhyay, Amb.
Netherlands	Thomas H. Gewecke, Chargé	Johan H. Meesman, Amb.
New Zealand	David M. Walker, Chargé	Denis B.G. McLean, Amb.
Nicaragua	John Maisto, Amb.	Ernesto Palizio, Amb.
Niger	Jennifer C. Ward, Amb.	Adamou Seydou, Amb.
Nigeria	William L. Swing, Amb.	Zubair Kazaure, Amb.
Norway	William C. McCahill, Chargé	Kjeld Vibe, Amb.
Oman	David J. Dunford, Amb.	Awadh Bader Al-Shanfari, Amb.
Pakistan	John C. Monjo, Amb.	Syeda A. Hussain, Amb.
Panama	Deane R. Hinton, Amb.	Jaime F. Boyd, Amb.
Papua New Guinea	Robert W. Farrand, Amb.	Margaret Taylor, Amb.
Paraguay	Jon David Glassman, Amb.	Juan E. Aguirre, Amb.
Peru	Charles H. Brayshaw, Chargé	Ricardo V. Luna, Amb.
Philippines	Vacancy	Franklin M. Ebdalin, Amb.
Poland	Michael M. Hornblow, Chargé	Kazimierz Dziewanowski, Amb.
Portugal	Edward Ellis Briggs, Amb.	Francisco Knopfli, Amb.
Qatar	Kenneth W. Keith, Amb.	Ali Saad Al-Kharji, Amb.
Romania	John R. Davis Jr., Amb.	Aurel-Dragos Munteanu, Amb.
Russia	Thomas Pickering, Amb.	Vladimir P. Lukin
Rwanda	Robert A. Flaten, Amb.	Aloys Uwimana, Amb.
St. Kitts & Nevis	C. Philip Hughes, Amb.	Aubrey Hart, Chargé
St. Lucia	C. Philip Hughes, Amb.	Joseph E. Edmunds, Amb.
St. Vincent and The Grenadines	C. Philip Hughes, Amb.	Kingsley C.A. Layne, Amb.
Sao Tome and Principe	Joseph C. Wilson, Amb.	Vacancy
Saudi Arabia	C. David Welch, Chargé	Bandar Bin Sultan, Amb.
Senegal	Robert J. Kott, Chargé	Ibra Deguene Ka, Amb.
Seychelles	F. Stephen Malott, Chargé	Marc Marengo, Chargé
Sierra Leone	Lauralee M. Peters, Amb.	William Wright, Chargé
Singapore	John M. Huntsman, Amb.	S.R. Nathan, Amb.
Slovakia	Vacancy	Milan Erban, Chargé
Slovenia	Allan Wendt, Amb.	Ernest Petric, Amb.
Solomon Islands	Robert W. Farrand, Amb.	Vacancy
South Africa	Princeton N. Lyman, Amb.	Harry H. Schwarz, Amb.
Spain	David N. Greenlee, Chargé	Jaime de Ojeda, Amb.
Sri Lanka	Teresita C. Schaffer, Amb.	Anada W. P. Guruge, Amb.
Sudan	David K. Petterson, Amb.	Abdalla Ahmed Abdalla, Amb.
Suriname	John P. Leonard, Amb.	Willem A. Udenhout, Amb.
Swaziland	Stephen H. Rogers, Amb.	Absalom V. Mamba, Amb.
Sweden	Michael Klosson, Chargé	Carl Sihver Liljegren, Amb.
Switzerland	John Hall, Chargé	Edouard Brunner, Amb.
Syria	Christopher W. S. Ross, Amb.	Walid Al-Moualem, Amb.
Tajikistan	Stanley Escudero, Amb.	Vacancy
Tanzania	Peter Jon de Vos, Amb.	Charles M. Nyirabu, Amb.
Thailand	David F. Lambertson, Amb.	M. L. B. Kasemeri, Amb.
Togo	Harmon E. Kirby, Amb.	Edem F. Hegbe, Chargé
Tonga	Evelyn I.H. Teegen, Amb.	Sione Kite, Amb.
Trinidad and Tobago	Sally G. Cowal, Amb.	Corinne A. McKnight, Amb.
Tunisia	John T. McCarthy, Amb.	Ismail Khelil, Amb.
Turkey	Richard C. Barkley, Amb.	Nuzhet Kandemir, Amb.
Turkmenistan	Joseph S. Hulings 3d, Amb.	Vacancy
Tuvalu	Evelyn I.H. Teegen, Amb.	Vacancy
Uganda	Johnnie Carson, Amb.	Stephen K. Katenta-Apuli, Amb.
Ukraine	Roman Popadiuk, Amb.	Oleh H. Bilorus, Amb.
United Arab Emirates	William A. Rugh, Amb.	Mohammad ben Hussein Al-Shaali, Amb.
United Kingdom	William J. Crowe Jr., Amb.	Robin R. Renwick, Amb.
Uruguay	Thomas J. Dodd, Amb.	Eduardo MacGillycuddy
Uzbekistan	Henry L. Clarke, Amb.	Vacancy
Vatican	Cameron Hume, Chargé	Agostino Cacciavillan, Pro-Nuncio

Countries	Envoys from United States	Envoys to United States
Venezuela	Jeffrey Davidow, Amb.	Simon A. Consalvi, Amb.
Western Samoa	Eric D. Tunis, Chargé	Terry Toomata, Chargé
Yemen	Arthur H. Hughes, Amb.	Mohsin A. Alaini, Amb.
Yugoslavia	Robert Rackmales, Chargé	Ivan Zivkovic, Chargé
Zaire	John M. Yates, Chargé	Tatanee Manata, Amb.
Zambia	Gordon L. Streeb, Amb.	Dustin W. Kamana, Amb.
Zimbabwe	Edward G. Lanpher, Amb.	Mark Marongwe, Chargé

Special Missions

U.S. Mission to North Atlantic Treaty Organization, Brussels—Vacancy 4th
U.S. Mission to the European Communities, Brussels—Stuart E. Eizenstat
U.S. Mission to the United Nations, New York—Madeleine K. Albright, Amb.
U.S. Mission to the European Office of the UN, Geneva—Morris B. Abram, Amb.
U.S. Mission to the Organization for Economic Cooperation and Development, Paris—David L. Aaron
U.S. Mission to the Organization of American States, Washington—Luigi R. Einaudi, Amb.

(1) U.S. embassy closed in 1975. (2) U.S. severed relations in 1978; unofficial relations are maintained. (3) Relations severed in 1961; limited ties restored in 1977. (4) U.S. severed relations on Apr. 7, 1980. (5) Embassy closed on May 2, 1980. U.S. closed the Libyan mission on May 6, 1981. (6) Operations temporarily suspended. (7) Embassy evacuated Jan. 5, 1991.

Codes for International Direct Dial Calling From the U.S.

Station-to-station: 011+country code (below)+city code+local number.
Person-to-person (operator assisted, collect calls, credit card calls, and calls billed to another number): 01+country code (below)+city code+local number.

Country	Code
Algeria	213
American Samoa	684
Andorra	33
Anguilla	809*
Antigua	809*
Argentina	54
Aruba	297
Ascension Island	247
Australia	61
Austria	43
Bahamas	809*
Bahrain	973
Bangladesh	880
Barbados	809*
Belgium	32
Belize	501
Benin	229
Bermuda	809*
Bolivia	591
Botswana	267
Brazil	55
British Virgin Islands	809*
Brunei	673
Bulgaria	359
Burkina Faso	226
Cameroon	237
Canada	Use Area Codes
Cape Verde Islands	238
Cayman Islands	809*
Chile	56
China	86
Colombia	57
Congo	242
Costa Rica	506
Cote d'Ivoire	225
Cyprus	357
Czech. Rep.	42
Denmark	45
Djibouti	253
Dominica	809*
Dominican Republic	809*
Ecuador	593
Egypt	20
El Salvador	503
Ethiopia	251
Faeroe Islands	298
Fiji Islands	679
Finland	358
France	33
French Antilles	596
French Guiana	594
French Polynesia	689
Gabon	241
Gambia	220
Germany	49
Ghana	233
Gibraltar	350
Greece	30

Country	Code
Greenland	299
Grenada	809*
Guadeloupe	590
Guam	671
Guantanamo	53
Guatemala	502
Guinea	224
Guyana	592
Haiti	509
Honduras	504
Hong Kong	852
Hungary	36
Iceland	354
India	91
Indonesia	62
Iran	98
Iraq	964
Ireland	353
Israel	972
Italy	39
Jamaica	809*
Japan	81
Jordan	962
Kenya	254
Kiribati	686
Korea	82
Kuwait	965
Lebanon	961
Lesotho	266
Liberia	231
Libya	218
Liechtenstein	41
Luxembourg	352
Macao	853
Malawi	265
Malaysia	60
Maldives	960
Mali Republic	223
Malta	356
Marshall Islands	692
Mauritius	230
Mexico	52
Micronesia	691
Monaco	33
Montserrat	809*
Morocco	212
Namibia	264
Nauru	674
Nepal	977
Netherlands	31
Netherlands Antilles	599
Nevis	809*
New Caledonia	687
New Zealand	64
Nicaragua	505
Niger	227
Nigeria	234
Norway	47

Country	Code
Oman	968
Pakistan	92
Panama	507
Papua New Guinea	675
Paraguay	595
Peru	51
Philippines	63
Poland	48
Portugal	351
Qatar	974
Reunion Island	262
Romania	40
Russia (Moscow)	7
Rwanda	250
Saipan	670
San Marino	39
Saudi Arabia	966
Senegal	221
Seychelles Islands	248
Sierra Leone	232
Singapore	65
Slovakia	42
Solomon Island	677
South Africa	27
Spain	34
Sri Lanka	94
St. Kitts	809*
St. Lucia	809*
St. Pierre & Miquelon	508
St. Vincent	809*
Suriname	597
Swaziland	268
Sweden	46
Switzerland	41
Syria	963
Taiwan	886
Tanzania	255
Thailand	66
Togo	228
Tonga	676
Trinidad & Tobago	809*
Tunisia	216
Turkey	90
Turks & Caicos Islands	809*
Uganda	256
United Arab Emirates	971
United Kingdom	44
Uruguay	598
Vatican City	39
Venezuela	58
Western Samoa	685
Yemen Arab Republic	967
Yugoslavia	38
Zaire	243
Zambia	260
Zimbabwe	263

* Follow Domestic Dialing instructions: dial "1" + 809 + number you're calling.

U.S. Aid to Foreign Nations in 1992

Source: Bureau of Economic Analysis, U.S. Dept. of Commerce

Figures are in millions of dollars. (*Less than $500,000.) Data include military supplies and services furnished under the Foreign Assistance Act and direct Defense Department appropriations, and include credits extended to private entities.

Net grants and credits take into account all known returns to the U.S., including reverse grants, returns of grants, and payments of principal. Also included are contributions received from coalition partners for Persian Gulf operations. A minus sign (—) indicates that the total of the returns is greater than the total grants or credits. Nations with net grants or credits under $2 million are included with "Other and Unspecified." Other Assistance represents the transfer of U.S. farm products in exchange for foreign currencies, less the government's disbursements of such currencies as grants or credits or for purchases.

Amounts do not include investments in the following: Asian Development Bank, $86 mln.; Inter-American Development Bank, $128 mln.; International Development Assn., $835 mln.; International Bank for Reconstruction and Development, $94 mln.; African Development Fund, $131 mln.; International Finance Corp., $25 mln; European Bank for Reconstruction and Development, $99 mln.; Inter-American Investment Corporation, $12 mln.; African Development Bank, $9 mln.

	Total	Net grants	Net credits	Net other
Total	**14,784**	**14,614**	**170**	**(*)**
Western Europe	**131**	**484**	**−353**	**(*)**
Austria	−1	(*)	−1	—
Finland	−5	—	−5	—
France	−2	(*)	−1	—
Ireland	−6	—	−6	—
Norway	−15	—	−15	—
Portugal	158	223	−64	—
Spain	−123	1	−124	(*)
United Kingdom	−115	(*)	−115	—
Yugoslavia	−21	(*)	−21	—
Other & Unspecified	260	260	(*)	—
Eastern Europe	**577**	**479**	**100**	**−2**
Albania	29	29	—	—
Armenia	16	16	—	—
Belarus	22	(*)	22	—
Bulgaria	29	29	—	—
Czechoslovakia	46	46	—	—
Estonia	24	14	10	—
Hungary	38	38	—	—
Kazakhstan	2	2	—	—
Latvia	25	15	9	—
Lithuania	25	16	9	—
Moldova	9	(*)	9	—
Poland	112	115	—	−2
Romania	25	15	10	—
Russia	47	26	21	—
Tajikistan	10	(*)	10	—
Turkmenistan	5	5	—	—
Ukraine	8	8	—	—
Other & unspecified	106	106	—	—
Near East & South Asia	**7,241**	**7,467**	**−228**	**2**
Afghanistan	70	70	(*)	—
Bangladesh	136	165	−29	—
Cyprus	10	10	(*)	(*)
Egypt	2,539	2,494	37	7
Greece	388	55	334	−1
India	17	127	−110	(*)
Iraq	9	9	—	—
Israel	4,746	4,989	−243	—
Jordan	118	50	67	(*)
Kuwait	−2	−2	—	—
Lebanon	11	14	−3	(*)
Nepal	19	20	(*)	(*)
Oman	13	11	2	—
Pakistan	89	240	−148	−3
Saudi Arabia	−1,328	−1,328	—	—
Sri Lanka	53	49	4	−1
Turkey	231	372	−141	(*)
Yemen	14	14	(*)	—
Other & unspecified	109	109	—	—
East Asia & Pacific	**583**	**552**	**32**	**(*)**
Australia	−18	—	−18	—
Cambodia	54	54	(*)	—
China	31	—	31	—
Indonesia	81	72	9	(*)
Japan	−30	−30	—	—
Korea, South	−132	(*)	−133	—
Mongolia	2	2	—	—
New Zealand	−1	—	−1	—
Papua New Guinea	9	1	9	—
Philippines	503	383	120	(*)
Singapore	3	3	—	—
Taiwan	−7	—	−7	(*)
Thailand	43	21	22	—
Other & unspecified	46	45	1	—
Africa	**1,363**	**1,983**	**−620**	**−1**
Algeria	−13	(*)	−14	—
Angola	−30	5	−35	—
Benin	16	16	—	—
Botswana	8	10	−2	—
Burkina Faso	14	14	—	(*)
Burundi	16	16	—	—
Cameroon	34	28	6	—
Cape Verde	8	8	—	—
Central African Rep.	3	3	—	—
Chad	32	32	—	—
Comoros	2	2	—	—
Congo	4	1	3	—
Côte d'Ivoire	46	13	33	—
Djibouti	6	6	—	—
Ethiopia	62	68	−6	—
Gambia, The	11	11	—	—
Ghana	28	28	(*)	(*)
Guinea	16	15	(*)	1
Guinea Bissau	5	5	—	—
Kenya	75	53	22	—
Lesotho	14	14	—	—
Liberia	19	18	(*)	—
Madagascar	12	12	—	—
Malawi	38	38	—	—
Mali	31	31	—	(*)
Mauritania	2	2	—	—
Morocco	13	56	−43	(*)
Mozambique	61	61	1	—
Namibia	5	5	—	—
Niger	34	34	(*)	—
Nigeria	31	20	11	—
Rwanda	7	7	—	—
São Tomé and Príncipe	2	2	—	—
Senegal	37	37	(*)	—
Seychelles	5	5	—	—
Sierra Leone	14	5	8	—
Somalia	307	307	(*)	—
South Africa	44	44	—	—
Sudan	11	10	1	—
Swaziland	12	12	(*)	—
Tanzania	28	28	—	—
Togo	11	11	(*)	—
Tunisia	16	23	−7	(*)
Uganda	22	22	—	—
Zaire	33	33	(*)	3—
Zambia	76	106	−30	—
Zimbabwe	72	52	20	—
Other & Unspecified	98	100	−3	—
Western Hemisphere	**2,244**	**1,590**	**655**	**−1**
Argentina	90	6	83	—
Belize	10	8	2	—
Bolivia	174	171	3	—
Brazil	494	4	490	—
Canada	−38	—	−38	—
Chile	−56	7	−63	—
Colombia	−77	137	−214	—
Costa Rica	23	40	−17	—
Dominican Republic	3	23	−20	—
Ecuador	26	31	−6	—
El Salvador	288	272	17	—
Guatemala	105	95	9	(*)
Guyana	9	2	7	—
Haiti	40	40	1	−1
Honduras	126	126	1	(*)
Jamaica	83	50	33	—
Mexico	−172	16	−188	—
Nicaragua	205	155	50	—
Panama	193	185	8	—
Peru	607	84	524	—
Suriname	5	(*)	5	—
Trinidad and Tobago	−10	(*)	−10	—
Uruguay	−3	2	−4	—
Venezuela	−13	(*)	−3	—
Other & Unspecified	119	136	−16	—
Intl. orgs. & unspecified	**2,612**	**2,612**	**(*)**	**—**

SPORTS IN 1993

Summer Olympic Games Records

The modern Olympic Games, first held in Athens, Greece in 1896, were the result of efforts by Baron Pierre de Coubertin, a French educator, to promote interest in education and culture, also to foster better international understanding through the universal medium of youth's love of athletics.

His source of inspiration for the Olympic Games was the ancient Greek Olympic Games, most notable of the four Panhellenic celebrations. The games were combined patriotic, religious, and athletic festivals held every four years. The first such recorded festival was held in 776 B.C., the date from which the Greeks began to keep their calendar by "Olympiads," or four-year spans between the games.

The first Olympiad is said to have consisted merely of a 200-yard foot race near the small city of Olympia, but the games gained in scope and became demonstrations of national pride. Only Greek citizens — amateurs — were permitted to participate. Winners received laurel, wild olive, and palm wreaths and were accorded many special privileges. Under the Roman emperors, the games deteriorated into professional carnivals and circuses. Emperor Theodosius banned them in 394 A.D.

Baron de Coubertin enlisted 9 nations to send athletes to the first modern Olympics in 1896; now more than 100 nations compete. Winter Olympic Games were started in 1924.

Sites of Olympic Games

1896 Athens, Greece
1900 Paris, France
1904 St. Louis, U.S.
1906 Athens*, Greece
1908 London, England
1912 Stockholm, Sweden
1920 Antwerp, Belgium
1924 Paris, France
1928 Amsterdam, Netherlands
1932 Los Angeles, U.S.
1936 Berlin, Germany
1948 London, England
1952 Helsinki, Finland
1956 Melbourne, Australia
1960 Rome, Italy
1964 Tokyo, Japan
1968 Mexico City, Mexico
1972 Munich, W. Germany
1976 Montreal, Canada
1980 Moscow, USSR
1984 Los Angeles, U.S.
1988 Seoul, S. Korea
1992 Barcelona, Spain
1996 Atlanta, U.S.

* Games not recognized by International Olympic Committee. Games 6 (1916), 12 (1940), and 13 (1944) were not celebrated. The 1980 games were boycotted by 62 nations, including the U.S. The 1984 games were boycotted by the USSR and most eastern bloc nations. East and West Germany competed separately 1968-88. The 1992 Unified Team consisted of 12 former Soviet republics. The 1992 Independent Olympic Participants (I.O.C.) were athletes from Serbia, Montenegro, and Macedonia.

Olympic Games Champions, 1896—1992

(*Indicates Gold Medal-Winning Record)

Track and Field — Men

100-Meter Run

1896	Thomas Burke, United States	12s
1900	Francis W. Jarvis, United States	11.0s
1904	Archie Hahn, United States	11s
1908	Reginald Walker, South Africa	10.8s
1912	Ralph Craig, United States	10.8s
1920	Charles Paddock, United States	10.8s
1924	Harold Abrahams, Great Britain	10.6s
1928	Percy Williams, Canada	10.8s
1932	Eddie Tolan, United States	10.3s
1936	Jesse Owens, United States	10.3s
1948	Harrison Dillard, United States	10.3s
1952	Lindy Remigino, United States	10.4s
1956	Bobby Morrow, United States	10.5s
1960	Armin Hary, Germany	10.2s
1964	Bob Hayes, United States	10.0s
1968	Jim Hines, United States	9.95s
1972	Valery Borzov, USSR	10.14s
1976	Hasely Crawford, Trinidad	10.06s
1980	Allan Wells, Great Britain	10.25s
1984	Carl Lewis, United States	9.99s
1988	Carl Lewis, United States	9.92s*
1992	Linford Christie, Great Britain	9.96s

200-Meter Run

1900	Walter Tewksbury, United States	22.2s
1904	Archie Hahn, United States	21.6s
1908	Robert Kerr, Canada	22.6s
1912	Ralph Craig, United States	21.7s
1920	Allan Woodring, United States	22s
1924	Jackson Scholz, United States	21.6s
1928	Percy Williams, Canada	21.8s
1932	Eddie Tolan, United States	21.2s
1936	Jesse Owens, United States	20.7s
1948	Mel Patton, United States	21.1s
1952	Andrew Stanfield, United States	20.7s
1956	Bobby Morrow, United States	20.6s
1960	Livio Berruti, Italy	20.5s
1964	Henry Carr, United States	20.3s
1968	Tommie Smith, United States	19.83s
1972	Valeri Borzov, USSR	20.00s
1976	Donald Quarrie, Jamaica	20.23s
1980	Pietro Mennea, Italy	20.19s
1984	Carl Lewis, United States	19.80s
1988	Joe DeLoach, United States	19.75s*
1992	Mike Marsh, United States	20.01s

400-Meter Run

1896	Thomas Burke, United States	54.2s
1900	Maxey Long, United States	49.4s
1904	Harry Hillman, United States	49.2s
1908	Wyndham Halswelle, Great Britain, walkover	50s
1912	Charles Reidpath, United States	48.2s
1920	Bevil Rudd, South Africa	49.6s
1924	Eric Liddell, Great Britain	47.6s
1928	Ray Barbuti, United States	47.8s
1932	William Carr, United States	46.2s
1936	Archie Williams, United States	46.5s
1948	Arthur Wint, Jamaica	46.2s
1952	George Rhoden, Jamaica	45.9s
1956	Charles Jenkins, United States	46.7s
1960	Otis Davis, United States	44.9s
1964	Michael Larrabee, United States	45.1s
1968	Lee Evans, United States	43.8s
1972	Vincent Matthews, United States	44.66s
1976	Alberto Juantorena, Cuba	44.26s
1980	Viktor Markin, USSR	44.60s
1984	Alonzo Babers, United States	44.27s
1988	Steven Lewis, United States	43.87s
1992	Quincy Watts, United States	43.50s*

800-Meter Run

1896	Edwin Flack, Australia	2m. 11s
1900	Alfred Tysoe, Great Britain	2m. 1.2s
1904	James Lightbody, United States	1m. 56s
1908	Mel Sheppard, United States	1m. 52.8s
1912	James Meredith, United States	1m. 51.9s
1920	Albert Hill, Great Britain	1m. 53.4s
1924	Douglas Lowe, Great Britain	1m. 52.4s
1928	Douglas Lowe, Great Britain	1m. 51.8s
1932	Thomas Hampson, Great Britain	1m. 49.8s
1936	John Woodruff, United States	1m. 52.9s
1948	Mal Whitfield, United States	1m. 49.2s
1952	Mal Whitfield, United States	1m. 49.2s
1956	Thomas Courtney, United States	1m. 47.7s
1960	Peter Snell, New Zealand	1m. 46.3s
1964	Peter Snell, New Zealand	1m. 45.1s
1968	Ralph Doubell, Australia	1m. 44.3s

1972	Dave Wottle, United States	1m. 45.9s
1976	Alberto Juantorena, Cuba	1m. 43.50s
1980	Steve Ovett, Great Britain	1m. 45.40s
1984	Joaquim Cruz, Brazil	1m. 43.00s*
1988	Paul Ereng, Kenya	1m. 43.45s
1992	William Tanui, Kenya	1m. 43.66s

1,500-Meter Run

1896	Edwin Flack, Australia	4m. 33.2s
1900	Charles Bennett, Great Britain	4m. 6.2s
1904	James Lightbody, United States	4m. 5.4s
1908	Mel Sheppard, United States	4m. 3.4s
1912	Arnold Jackson, Great Britain	3m. 56.8s
1920	Albert Hill, Great Britain	4m. 1.8s
1924	Paavo Nurmi, Finland	3m. 53.6s
1928	Harry Larva, Finland	3m. 53.2s
1932	Luigi Beccali, Italy	3m. 51.2s
1936	Jack Lovelock, New Zealand	3m. 47.8s
1948	Henri Eriksson, Sweden	3m. 49.8s
1952	Joseph Barthel, Luxemburg	3m. 45.2s
1956	Ron Delany, Ireland	3m. 41.2s
1960	Herb Elliott, Australia	3m. 35.6s
1964	Peter Snell, New Zealand	3m. 38.1s
1968	Kipchoge Keino, Kenya	3m. 34.9s
1972	Pekka Vasala, Finland	3m. 36.3s
1976	John Walker, New Zealand	3m. 39.17s
1980	Sebastian Coe, Great Britain	3m. 38.4s
1984	Sebastian Coe, Great Britain	3m. 32.53s*
1988	Peter Rono, Kenya	3m. 35.96s
1992	Fermin Cacho Ruiz, Spain	3m. 40.12s

3,000-Meter Steeplechase

1920	Percy Hodge, Great Britain	10m. 0.4s
1924	Willie Ritola, Finland	9m. 33.6s
1928	Toivo Loukola, Finland	9m. 21.8s
1932	Volmari Iso-Hollo, Finland	10m. 33.4s
	(About 3,450 mtrs. extra lap by error)	
1936	Volmari Iso-Hollo, Finland	9m. 3.8s
1948	Thore Sjoestrand, Sweden	9m. 4.6s
1952	Horace Ashenfelter, United States	8m. 45.4s
1956	Chris Brasher, Great Britain	8m. 41.2s
1960	Zdzislaw Krzyszkowiak, Poland	8m. 34.2s
1964	Gaston Roelants, Belgium	8m. 30.8s
1968	Amos Biwott, Kenya	8m. 51s
1972	Kipchoge Keino, Kenya	8m. 23.6s
1976	Anders Garderud, Sweden	8m. 08.2s
1980	Bronislaw Malinowski, Poland	8m. 09.7s
1984	Julius Korir, Kenya	8m. 11.8s
1988	Julius Kariuki, Kenya	8m. 05.51s*
1992	Matthew Birir, Kenya	8m. 08.84s

5,000-Meter Run

1912	Hannes Kolehmainen, Finland	14m. 36.6s
1920	Joseph Guillemot, France	14m. 55.6s
1924	Paavo Nurmi, Finland	14m. 31.2s
1928	Willie Ritola, Finland	14m. 38s
1932	Lauri Lehtinen, Finland	14m. 30s
1936	Gunnar Hockert, Finland	14m. 22.2s
1948	Gaston Reiff, Belgium	14m. 17.6s
1952	Emil Zatopek, Czechoslovakia	14m. 6.6s
1956	Vladimir Kuts, USSR	13m. 39.6s
1960	Murray Halberg, New Zealand	13m. 43.4s
1964	Bob Schul, United States	13m. 48.8s
1968	Mohamed Gammoudi, Tunisia	14m. 05.0s
1972	Lasse Viren, Finland	13m. 26.4s
1976	Lasse Viren, Finland	13m. 24.76s
1980	Miruts Yifter, Ethiopia	13m. 21.0s
1984	Said Aouita, Morocco	13m. 05.59s*
1988	John Ngugi, Kenya	13m. 11.70s
1992	Dieter Baumann, Germany	13m. 12.52s

10,000-Meter Run

1912	Hannes Kolehmainen, Finland	31m. 20.8s
1920	Paavo Nurmi, Finland	31m. 45.8s
1924	Willie Ritola, Finland	30m. 23.2s
1928	Paavo Nurmi, Finland	30m. 18.8s
1932	Janusz Kusocinski, Poland	30m. 11.4s
1936	Ilmari Salminen, Finland	30m. 15.4s
1948	Emil Zatopek, Czechoslovakia	29m. 59.6s
1952	Emil Zatopek, Czechoslovakia	29m. 17.0s
1956	Vladimir Kuts, USSR	28m. 45.6s
1960	Pyotr Bolotnikov, USSR	28m. 32.2s
1964	Billy Mills, United States	28m. 24.4s
1968	Naftali Temu, Kenya	29m. 27.4s
1972	Lasse Viren, Finland	27m. 38.4s
1976	Lasse Viren, Finland	27m. 40.38s
1980	Miruts Yifter, Ethiopia	27m. 42.7s
1984	Alberto Cova, Italy	27m. 47.54s
1988	Brahim Boutaib, Morocco	27m. 21.46s*
1992	Khalid Skah, Morocco	27m. 46.70s

Marathon

1896	Spiridon Loues, Greece	2h. 58m. 50s
1900	Michel Theato, France	2h. 59m. 45s
1904	Thomas Hicks, United States	3h. 28m. 63s
1908	John J. Hayes, United States	2h. 55m. 18.4s
1912	Kenneth McArthur, South Africa	2h. 36m. 54.8s
1920	Hannes Kolehmainen, Finland	2h. 32m. 35.8s
1924	Albin Stenroos, Finland	2h. 41m. 22.6s
1928	A.B. El Ouafi, France	2h. 32m. 57s
1932	Juan Zabala, Argentina	2h. 31m. 36s
1936	Kijung Son, Japan (Korean)	2h. 29m. 19.2s
1948	Delfo Cabrera, Argentina	2h. 34m. 51.6s
1952	Emil Zatopek, Czechoslovakia	2h. 23m. 03.2s
1956	Alain Mimoun, France	2h. 25m.
1960	Abebe Bikila, Ethiopia	2h. 15m. 16.2s
1964	Abebe Bikila, Ethiopia	2h. 12m. 11.2s
1968	Mamo Wolde, Ethiopia	2h. 20m. 26.4s
1972	Frank Shorter, United States	2h. 12m. 19.8s
1976	Waldemar Cierpinski, E. Germany	2h. 09m. 55s
1980	Waldemar Cierpinski, E. Germany	2h. 11m. 03s
1984	Carlos Lopes, Portugal	2h. 09m. 21 s*
1988	Gelindo Bordin, Italy	2h. 10m. 32s
1992	Hwang Young-Cho, S. Korea	2h. 13m. 23s

20-Kilometer Walk

1956	Leonid Spirin, USSR	1h. 31m. 27.4s
1960	Vladimir Golubnichy, USSR	1h. 33m. 7.2s
1964	Kenneth Mathews, Great Britain	1h. 29m. 34.0s
1968	Vladimir Golubnichy, USSR	1h. 33m. 58.4s
1972	Peter Frenkel, E. Germany	1h. 26m. 42.4s
1976	Daniel Bautista, Mexico	1h. 24m. 40.6s
1980	Maurizio Damilano, Italy	1h. 23m. 35.5s
1984	Ernesto Canto, Mexico	1h. 23m. 13.0s
1988	Josef Pribilinec, Czech.	1h. 19m. 57.0s*
1992	Daniel Plaza Montero, Spain	1h. 21m. 45.0s

50-Kilometer Walk

1932	Thomas W. Green, Great Britain	4h. 50m. 10s
1936	Harold Whitlock, Great Britain	4h. 30m. 41.4s
1948	John Ljunggren, Sweden	4h. 41m. 52s
1952	Giuseppe Dordoni, Italy	4h. 28m. 07.8s
1956	Norman Read, New Zealand	4h. 30m. 42.8s
1960	Donald Thompson, Great Britain	4h. 25m. 30s
1964	Abdon Pamich, Italy	4h. 11m. 12.4s
1968	Christoph Hohne, E. Germany	4h. 20m. 13.6s
1972	Bern Kannenberg, W. Germany	3h. 56m. 11.6s
1980	Hartwig Gauter, E. Germany	3h. 49m. 24.0s
1984	Raul Gonzalez, Mexico	3h. 47m. 26.0s
1988	Vayachselav Ivanenko, USSR	3h. 38m. 29.0s*
1992	Andrei Perlov, Unified Team	3h 50m. 13.0s

110-Meter Hurdles

1896	Thomas Curtis, United States	17.6s
1900	Alvin Kraenzlein, United States	15.4s
1904	Frederick Schule, United States	16s
1908	Forrest Smithson, United States	15s
1912	Frederick Kelly, United States	15.1s
1920	Earl Thomson, Canada	14.8s
1924	Daniel Kinsey, United States	15s
1928	Sydney Atkinson, South Africa	14.8s
1932	George Saling, United States	14.6s
1936	Forrest Towns, United States	14.2s
1948	William Porter, United States	13.9
1952	Harrison Dillard, United States	13.7
1956	Lee Calhoun, United States	13.5
1960	Lee Calhoun, United States	13.8
1964	Hayes Jones, United States	13.6
1968	Willie Davenport, United States	13.3
1972	Rod Milburn, United States	13.24
1976	Guy Drut, France	13.30
1980	Thomas Munkelt, E. Germany	13. 39
1984	Roger Kingdom, United States	13.20
1988	Roger Kingdom, United States	12.98s
1992	Mark McCoy, Canada	13.12

400-Meter Hurdles

1900	J.W.B. Tewksbury, United States	57.6
1904	Harry Hillman, United States	53

1908	Charles Bacon, United States	55s
1920	Frank Loomis, United States	54s
1924	F. Morgan Taylor, United States	52.6s
1928	Lord Burghley, Great Britain	53.4s
1932	Robert Tisdall, Ireland	51.7s
1936	Glenn Hardin, United States	52.4s
1948	Roy Cochran, United States	51.1s
1952	Charles Moore, United States	50.8s
1956	Glenn Davis, United States	50.1s
1960	Glenn Davis, United States	49.3s
1964	Rex Cawley, United States	49.6s
1968	Dave Hemery, Great Britain	48.12s
1972	John Akii-Bua, Uganda	47.82s
1976	Edwin Moses, United States	47.64s
1980	Volker Beck, E. Germany	48.70s
1984	Edwin Moses, United States	47.75s
1988	Andre Phillips, United States	47.19s
1992	Kevin Young, United States	46.78s*

High Jump

1896	Ellery Clark, United States	5ft. 11 1-4 in.
1900	Irving Baxter, United States	6ft. 2 4-5 in.
1904	Samuel Jones, United States	5ft. 11 in.
1908	Harry Porter, United States	6ft. 3 in.
1912	Alma Richards, United States	6ft. 4 in.
1920	Richmond Landon, United States	6ft. 4 in.
1924	Harold Osborn, United States	6ft. 6 in.
1928	Robert W. King, United States	6ft. 4 1-2 in.
1932	Duncan McNaughton, Canada	6ft. 5 5-8 in.
1936	Cornelius Johnson, United States	6ft. 8 in.
1948	John L. Winter, Australia	6ft. 6 in.
1952	Walter Davis, United States	6ft. 8.32 in.
1956	Charles Dumas, United States	6ft. 11 1-2 in.
1960	Robert Shavlakadze, USSR	7ft. 1 in.
1964	Valery Brumel, USSR	7ft. 1 3-4 in.
1968	Dick Fosbury, United States	7ft. 4 1-4 in.
1972	Yuri Tarmak, USSR	7ft. 3 3-4 in.
1976	Jacek Wszola, Poland	7ft. 4 1-2 in.
1980	Gerd Wessig, E. Germany	7ft. 8 3-4 in.
1984	Dietmar Mogenburg, W. Germany	7ft. 8 1-2 in.
1988	Guennadi Avdeenko, USSR	7ft. 9 1-2 in.*
1992	Javier Sotomayor, Cuba	7ft. 8 in.

Long Jump

1896	Ellery Clark, United States	20ft. 10 in.
1900	Alvin Kraenzlein, United States	23ft. 6 3-4 in.
1904	Myer Prinstein, United States	24ft. 1 in.
1908	Frank Irons, United States	24ft. 6 1-2 in.
1912	Albert Gutterson, United States	24ft. 11 1-4 in.
1920	William Petterssen, Sweden	23ft. 5 1-2 in.
1924	DeHart Hubbard, United States	24ft. 5 in.
1928	Edward B. Hamm, United States	25ft. 4 1-2 in.
1932	Edward Gordon, United States	25ft. 3-4 in.
1936	Jesse Owens, United States	26ft. 5 1-2 in.
1948	William Steele, United States	25ft. 8 in.
1952	Jerome Biffle, United States	24ft. 10 in.
1956	Gregory Bell, United States	25ft. 8 1-4 in.
1960	Ralph Boston, United States	26ft. 7 3-4 in.
1964	Lynn Davies, Great Britain	26ft. 5 3-4 in.
1968	Bob Beamon, United States	29ft. 2 1-2 in.*
1972	Randy Williams, United States	27ft. 1-2 in.
1976	Arnie Robinson, United States	27ft. 4 1-2 in.
1980	Lutz Dombrowski, E. Germany	28ft. 1-4 in.
1984	Carl Lewis, United States	28ft. 1-4 in.
1988	Carl Lewis, United States	28ft. 7 1-4 in.
1992	Carl Lewis, United States	28ft. 5 1-2 in.

400-Meter Relay

1912	Great Britain	42.4s
1920	United States	42.2s
1924	United States	41s
1928	United States	41s
1932	United States	40s
1936	United States	39.8s
1948	United States	40.6s
1952	United States	40.1s
1956	United States	39.5s
1960	Germany (U.S. disqualified)	39.5s
1964	United States	39.0s
1968	United States	38.2s
1972	United States	38.19s
1976	United States	38.33s
1980	USSR	38.26s
1984	United States	37.83s
1988	USSR (U.S. disqualified)	38.19s
1992	United States	37.40s*

1,600-Meter Relay

1908	United States	3m. 29.4s
1912	United States	3m. 16.6s
1920	Great Britain	3m. 22.2s
1924	United States	3m. 16s
1928	United States	3m. 14.2s
1932	United States	3m. 8.2s
1936	Great Britain	3m. 9s
1948	United States	3m. 10.4s
1952	Jamaica	3m. 03.9s
1956	United States	3m. 04.8s
1960	United States	3m. 02.2s
1964	United States	3m. 00.7s
1968	United States	2m. 56.16s
1972	Kenya	2m. 59.8s
1976	United States	2m. 58.65s
1980	USSR	3m. 01.1s
1984	United States	2m. 57.91s
1988	United States	2m. 56.16s
1992	United States	2m. 55.74s*

Pole Vault

1896	William Hoyt, United States	10ft. 10 in.
1900	Irving Baxter, United States	10ft. 10 in.
1904	Charles Dvorak, United States	11ft. 5 3-4 in.
1908	A. C. Gilbert, United States Edward Cook Jr., United States	12ft. 2 in.
1912	Harry Babcock, United States	12ft. 11 1-2 in.
1920	Frank Foss, United States	13ft. 5 in.
1924	Lee Barnes, United States	12ft. 11 1-2 in.
1928	Sabin W. Carr, United States	13ft. 9 1-4 in.
1932	William Miller, United States	14ft. 1 3-4 in.
1936	Earle Meadows, United States	14ft. 3 1-4 in.
1948	Gulnn Smith, United States	14ft. 1 1-4 in.
1952	Robert Richards, United States	14ft. 11 in.
1956	Robert Richards, United States	14ft. 11 1-2 in.
1960	Don Bragg, United States	15ft. 5 in.
1964	Fred Hansen, United States	16ft. 8 3-4 in.
1968	Bob Seagren, United States	17ft. 8 1-2 in.
1972	Wolfgang Nordwig, E. Germany	18ft. 1-2 in.
1976	Tadeusz Slusarski, Poland	18ft. 1-2 in.
1980	Wladyslaw Kozakiewicz, Poland	18ft. 11 1-2 in.
1984	Pierre Quinon, France	18ft. 10 1-4 in.
1988	Sergei Bubka, USSR	19ft. 9 1-4 in.*
1992	Maksim Tarassov, Unified Team	19ft. 1-4 in.

Hammer Throw

1900	John Flanagan, United States	163ft. 1 in.
1904	John Flanagan, United States	168ft. 1 in.
1908	John Flanagan, United States	170ft. 4 1-4 in.
1912	Matt McGrath, United States	179ft. 7 1-8 in.
1920	Pat Ryan, United States	173ft. 5 5-8 in.
1924	Fred Tootell, United States	174ft. 10 1-8 in.
1928	Patrick O'Callaghan, Ireland	168ft. 7 1-2 in.
1932	Patrick O'Callaghan, Ireland	176ft. 11 1-8 in.
1936	Karl Hein, Germany	185ft. 4 in.
1948	Imre Nemeth, Hungary	183ft. 11 1-2 in.
1952	Jozsef Csermak, Hungary	197ft. 11 9-16 in.
1956	Harold Connolly, United States	207ft. 3 1-2 in.
1960	Vasily Rudenkov, USSR	220ft. 1 5-8 in.
1964	Romuald Klim, USSR	228ft. 9 1-2 in.
1968	Gyula Zsivotsky, Hungary	240ft. 8 in.
1972	Anatoli Bondarchuk, USSR	247ft. 8 in.
1976	Yuri Syedykh, USSR	254ft. 4 in.
1980	Yuri Syedykh, USSR	268ft. 4 1-2 in.
1984	Juha Tiainen, Finland	256ft. 2 in.
1988	Sergei Litinov, USSR	278ft. 2 1-2 in.*
1992	Andrey Abduvaliyev, Unified Team	270ft. 9 1-2 in.

Discus Throw

1896	Robert Garrett, United States	95ft. 7 1-2 in.
1900	Rudolf Bauer, Hungary	118ft. 3 in.
1904	Martin Sheridan, United States	128ft. 10 1-2 in.
1908	Martin Sheridan, United States	134ft. 2 in.
1912	Armas Taipale, Finland	148ft. 3 in.
	Both hands—Armas Taipale, Finland	271ft. 10 1-4 in.
1920	Elmer Niklander, Finland	146ft. 7 in.
1924	Clarence Houser, United States	151ft. 4 in.
1928	Clarence Houser, United States	155ft. 3 in.
1932	John Anderson, United States	162ft. 4 in.
1936	Ken Carpenter, United States	165ft. 7 in.
1948	Adolfo Consolini, Italy	173ft. 2 in.
1952	Sim Iness, United States	180ft. 6.85 in.
1956	Al Oerter, United States	184ft. 10 1-2 in.
1960	Al Oerter, United States	194ft. 2 in.
1964	Al Oerter, United States	200ft. 1 1-2 in.

1968	Al Oerter, United States	212ft. 6 1-2 in.
1972	Ludvik Danek, Czechoslovakia	211ft. 3 in.
1976	Mac Wilkins, United States	221ft. 5 4 in.
1980	Viktor Rashchupkin, USSR	218ft. 8 in.
1984	Rolf Dannenberg, W. Germany	218ft. 6 in.
1988	Jurgen Schult, E. Germany	225ft. 9 1-4 in.*
1992	Romas Ubartas, Lithuania	213ft. 7 3-4 in.

Triple Jump

1896	James Connolly, United States	44ft. 11 3-4 in.
1900	Myer Prinstein, United States	47ft. 5 3-4 in.
1904	Myer Prinstein, United States	47 ft.
1908	Timothy Ahearne, Great Britain, Ireland	48ft. 11 1-4 in.
1912	Gustaf Lindblom, Sweden	48ft. 5 1-4 in.
1920	Vilho Tuulos, Finland	47ft. 7 in.
1924	Anthony Winter, Australia	50ft. 11 1-4 in.
1928	Mikio Oda, Japan	49ft. 11 in
1932	Chuhei Nambu, Japan	51ft. 7 in.
1936	Naoto Tajima, Japan	52ft. 6 in.
1948	Arne Ahman, Sweden	50ft. 6 1-4 in.
1952	Adhemar da Silva, Brazil	53ft. 2 3-4 in.
1956	Adhemar da Silva, Brazil	53ft. 7 3-4 in.
1960	Jozef Schmidt, Poland	55ft. 2 in.
1964	Jozef Schmidt, Poland	55ft. 3 1-2 in.
1968	Viktor Saneev, USSR	57ft. 3-4 in.
1972	Viktor Saneev, USSR	56ft. 11 in.
1976	Viktor Saneev, USSR	56ft. 8 3-4 in.
1980	Jaak Uudmae, USSR	56ft. 11 1-4 in.
1984	Al Joyner, United States	56ft. 7 1-2 in.
1988	Hristo Markov, Bulgaria	57ft. 9 1-4 in.
1992	Mike Conley, United States	59ft. 7 1-2 in.*

16-lb. Shot Put

1896	Robert Garrett, United States	36ft. 9 3-4 in.
1900	Richard Sheldon, United States	46ft. 3 1-4 in.
1904	Ralph Rose, United States	48ft. 7 in.
1908	Ralph Rose, United States	46ft. 7 1-2 in.
1912	Pat McDonald, United States	50ft. 4 in.
	Both hands—Ralph Rose, United States	90ft. 5 1-2 in.
1920	Ville Porhola, Finland	48ft. 7 1-4 in.
1924	Clarence Houser, United States	49ft. 2 1-4 in.
1928	John Kuck, United States	52ft. 3-4 in.
1932	Leo Sexton, United States	52ft. 6 in.
1936	Hans Woellke, Germany	53ft. 1 3-4 in.
1948	Wilbur Thompson, United States	56ft. 2 in.
1952	Parry O'Brien, United States	57ft. 1-2 in.
1956	Parry O'Brien, United States	60ft. 11 1-4 in.
1960	William Nieder, United States	64ft. 6 3-4 in.
1964	Dallas Long, United States	66ft. 8 1-2 in.
1968	Randy Matson, United States	67ft. 4 3-4 in.
1972	Wladyslaw Komar, Poland	69ft. 6 in.
1976	Udo Beyer, E. Germany	69ft. 3-4 in.
1980	Vladimir Kiselyov, USSR	70ft. 1-2 in.
1984	Alessandro Andrei, Italy	69ft. 9 in.
1988	Ulf Timmermann, E. Germany	73ft. 8 3-4 in.*
1992	Michael Stulce, United States	71ft. 2 1-4 in.

Javelin

1908	Erik Lemming, Sweden	178ft. 7 1-2 in.
	Held in middle—Erik Lemming, Sweden	179ft. 10 1-2 in.
1912	Erik Lemming, Sweden	198ft. 11 1-4 in.
	Both hands, Julius Saaristo, Finland	358ft. 11 7-8 in.
1920	Jonni Myyra, Finland	215ft. 9 3-4 in.
1924	Jonni Myyra, Finland	206ft. 6 3-4 in.
1928	Eric Lundkvist, Sweden	218ft. 6 1-8 in.
1932	Matti Jarvinen, Finland	238ft. 6 in.
1936	Gerhard Stoeck, Germany	235ft. 8 5-16 in.
1948	Tapio Rautavaara, Finland	228ft. 10 1-2 in.
1952	Cy Young, United States	242ft. 0.79 in.
1956	Egil Danielson, Norway	281ft. 2 1-4 in.
1960	Viktor Tsibulenko, USSR	277ft. 8 3-8 in.
1964	Pauli Nevala, Finland	271ft. 2 1-2 in.
1968	Janis Lusis, USSR	295ft. 7 1-4 in.
1972	Klaus Wolfermann, W. Germany	296ft. 10 in.
1976	Miklos Nemeth, Hungary	310ft. 4 in.*
1980	Dainis Kula, USSR	299ft. 2 3-8 in.
1984	Arto Haerkoenen, Finland	284ft. 8 in.
1988	Tapio Korjus, Finland	276ft. 6 in.
1992	Jan Zelezny, Czech.	294ft. 2 in.

Decathlon

1912	Hugo Wieslander, Sweden	7,724.49 pts.(a)
1920	Helge Lovland, Norway	6,804.35 pts.
1924	Harold Osborn, United States	7,710.77 pts.
1928	Paavo Yrjola, Finland	8,053.29 pts.
1932	James Bausch, United States	8,462.23 pts.
1936	Glenn Morris, United States	7,900 pts.
1948	Robert Mathias, United States	7,139 pts.
1952	Robert Mathias, United States	7,887 pts.
1956	Milton Campbell, United States	7,937 pts.
1960	Rafer Johnson, United States	8,392 pts.
1964	Willi Holdorf, Germany	7,887 pts.(c)
1968	Bill Toomey, United States	8,193 pts.
1972	Nikolai Avilov, USSR	8,454 pts.
1976	Bruce Jenner, United States	8,617 pts.
1980	Daley Thompson, Great Britain	8,495 pts.
1984	Daley Thompson, Great Britain	8,798 pts.*(b)
1988	Christian Schenk, E. Germany	8,488 pts.
1992	Robert Zmelik, Czech.	8,611 pts.

(a) Jim Thorpe of the U.S. won the 1912 Decathlon with 8,413 pts. but was disqualified and had to return his medals because he had played professional baseball prior to the Olympic games. The medals were restored posthumously in 1982. (b) Scoring change effective Apr., 1985. (c) Former point systems used prior to 1964.

Track and Field—Women

100-Meter Run

1928	Elizabeth Robinson, United States	12.2s
1932	Stella Walsh, Poland	11.9s
1936	Helen Stephens, United States	11.5s
1948	Francina Blankers-Koen, Netherlands	11.9s
1952	Marjorie Jackson, Australia	11.5s
1956	Betty Cuthbert, Australia	11.5s
1960	Wilma Rudolph, United States	11.0s
1964	Wyomia Tyus, United States	11.4s
1968	Wyomia Tyus, United States	11.0s
1972	Renate Stecher, E. Germany	11.07s
1976	Annegret Richter, W. Germany	11.08s
1980	Lyudmila Kondratyeva, USSR	11.6s
1984	Evelyn Ashford, United States	10.97s
1988	Florence Griffith-Joyner, United States	10.54s*
1992	Gail Devers, United States	10.82s

200-Meter Run

1948	Francina Blankers-Koen, Netherlands	24.4s
1952	Marjorie Jackson, Australia	23.7s
1956	Betty Cuthbert, Australia	23.4s
1960	Wilma Rudolph, United States	24.0s
1964	Edith McGuire, United States	23.0s
1968	Irena Szewinska, Poland	22.5s
1972	Renate Stecher, E. Germany	22.40s
1976	Barbel Eckert, E. Germany	22.37s
1980	Barbel Wockel, E. Germany	22.03s
1984	Valerie Brisco-Hooks, United States	21.81s
1988	Florence Griffith-Joyner, United States	21.34s*
1992	Gwen Torrence, United States	21.81s

400-Meter Run

1964	Betty Cuthbert, Australia	52s
1968	Colette Besson, France	52s
1972	Monika Zehrt, E. Germany	51.08s
1976	Irena Szewinska, Poland	49.29s
1980	Marita Koch, E. Germany	48.88s
1984	Valerie Brisco-Hooks, United States	48.83s
1988	Olga Bryzgina, USSR	48.65s*
1992	Marie-Jose Perec, France	48.83s

800-Meter Run

1928	Lina Radke, Germany	2m. 16.8s
1960	Ludmila Shevtsova, USSR	2m. 4.3s
1964	Ann Packer, Great Britain	2m. 1.1s
1968	Madeline Manning, United States	2m. 0.9s
1972	Hildegard Falck, W. Germany	1m. 58.6s
1976	Tatyana Kazankina, USSR	1m. 54.94s
1980	Nadezhda Olizayrenko, USSR	1m. 53.5s*
1984	Doina Melinte, Romania	1m. 57.6s
1988	Sigrun Wodars, E. Germany	1m. 56.10s
1992	Ellen Van Langen, Netherlands	1m. 55.54s

1,500-Meter Run

1972	Lyudmila Bragina, USSR	4m. 01.4s
1976	Tatyana Kazankina, USSR	4m. 05.48s
1980	Tatyana Kazankina, USSR	3m. 56.6s
1984	Gabriella Dorio, Italy	4m. 03.25s
1988	Paula Ivan, Romania	3m. 53.96s*
1992	Hassiba Boulmerka, Algeria	3m. 55.30s

3,000-Meter Run

1984	Maricica Puica, Romania	8:35.96s
1988	Tatyana Samolenko, USSR	8:26.53s*
1992	Elena Romanova, Unified Team	8:46.04s

10,000-Meter Run

1988	Olga Boldarenko, USSR	31m. 44.69s
1992	Derartu Tulu, Ethiopia	31m. 06.02s*

400-Meter Relay

1928	Canada	48.4s
1932	United States	46.9s
1936	United States	46.9s
1948	Netherlands	47.5s
1952	United States	45.9s
1956	Australia	44.5s
1960	United States	44.5s
1964	Poland	43.6s
1968	United States	42.8s
1972	West Germany	42.81s
1976	East Germany	42.55s
1980	East Germany	41.60s*
1984	United States	41.65s
1988	United States	41.98s
1992	United States	42.11s

1,600-Meter Relay

1972	East Germany	3m. 23s
1976	East Germany	3m. 19.23s
1980	USSR	3m. 20.02s
1984	United States	3m. 18.29s
1988	USSR	3 m. 15.18s*
1992	Unified Team	3m. 20.20s

100-Meter Hurdles

1972	Annelie Ehrhardt, E. Germany	12.59s
1976	Johanna Schaller, E. Germany	12.77s
1980	Vera Komisova, USSR	12.56s
1984	Benita Brown-Fitzgerald, United States	12.84s
1988	Jordanka Donkova, Bulgaria	12.38s*
1992	Paraskevi Patoulidou, Greece	12.64s

400-Meter Hurdles

1984	Nawal el Moutawakii, Morocco	54.61s
1988	Debra Flintoff-King, Australia	53.17s*
1992	Sally Gunnell, Great Britain	53.23s

Heptathlon

1984	Glynis Nunn, Australia	6,390 pts.
1988	Jackie Joyner-Kersee, United States	7,215 pts.*
1992	Jackie Joyner-Kersee, United States	7,044 pts.

High Jump

1928	Ethel Catherwood, Canada	5ft. 2 1-2 in.
1932	Jean Shiley, United States	5ft. 5 1-4 in.
1936	Ibolya Csak, Hungary	5ft. 3 in.
1948	Alice Coachman, United States	5ft. 6 1-8 in.
1952	Esther Brand, South Africa	5ft. 5 3-4 in.
1956	Mildred L. McDaniel, United States	5ft. 9 1-4 in.
1960	Iolanda Balas, Romania	6ft. 3-4 in.
1964	Iolanda Balas, Romania	6ft. 2 3-4 in.
1968	Miloslava Reskova, Czechoslovakia	5ft. 11 1-2 in.
1972	Ulrike Meyfarth, W. Germany	6ft. 4 in.
1976	Rosemarie Ackermann, E. Germany	6ft. 3 3-4 in.
1980	Sara Simeoni, Italy	6ft. 5 1-2 in.
1984	Ulrike Meyfarth, W. Germany	6ft. 7 1-2 in.
1988	Louise Ritter, United States	6ft. 8 in.*
1992	Heike Henkel, Germany	6ft. 7 1-2 in.

Discus Throw

1928	Helena Konopacka, Poland	129ft. 11 3-4 in.
1932	Lillian Copeland, United States	133ft. 2 in.
1936	Gisela Mauermayer, Germany	156ft. 3 in.
1948	Micheline Ostermeyer, France	137ft. 6 1-2 in.
1952	Nina Romaschkova, USSR	168ft. 8 in.
1956	Olga Fikotova, Czechoslovakia	176ft. 1 in.
1960	Nina Ponomareva, USSR	180ft. 8 1-4 in.
1964	Tamara Press, USSR	187ft. 10 in.
1968	Lia Manoliu, Romania	191ft. 2 in.
1972	Faina Melnik, USSR	218ft. 7 in.
1976	Evelin Schlaak, E. Germany	226ft. 4 in.
1980	Evelin Jahl, E. Germany	229ft. 6 in.
1984	Ria Stalman, Netherlands	214ft. 5 in.
1988	Martina Hellmann, E. Germany	237ft. 2 1-4 in.*
1992	Maritza Marten Garcia, Cuba	222ft. 10 in.

Javelin Throw

1932	"Babe" Didrikson, United States	143ft. 4 in.
1936	Tilly Fleischer, Germany	148ft. 2 3-4 in.
1948	Herma Bauma, Austria	149ft. 6 in.
1952	Dana Zatopkova, Czechoslovakia	165ft. 7 in.
1956	Inese Jaunzeme, USSR	176ft. 8 in.
1960	Elvira Ozolina, USSR	183ft. 8 in.
1964	Mihaela Penes, Romania	198ft. 7 1-2 in.
1968	Angela Nemeth, Hungary	198ft. 1-2 in.
1972	Ruth Fuchs, E. Germany	209ft. 7 in.
1976	Ruth Fuchs, E. Germany	216ft. 4 in.
1980	Maria Colon, Cuba	224ft. 5 in.
1984	Tessa Sanderson, Great Britain	228ft. 2 in.
1988	Petra Felke, E. Germany	245ft.*
1992	Silke Renke, Germany	224ft. 2 1-2 in.

Shot Put (8lb., 13oz.)

1948	Micheline Ostermeyer, France	45ft. 1 1-2 in.
1952	Galina Zybina, USSR	50ft. 1 3-4 in.
1956	Tamara Tishkyevich, USSR	54ft. 5 in.
1960	Tamara Press, USSR	56ft. 10 in.
1964	Tamara Press, USSR	59ft. 6 1-4 in.
1968	Margitta Gummel, E. Germany	64ft. 4 in.
1972	Nadezhda Chizova, USSR	69ft.
1976	Ivanka Hristova, Bulgaria	69ft. 5 1-4 in.
1980	Ilona Slupianek, E. Germany	73ft. 6 1-4 in.*
1984	Claudia Losch, W. Germany	67ft. 2 1-4 in.
1988	Natalya Lisovskaya, USSR	72ft 11 1-2 in.
1992	Svetlana Kriveleva, Unified Team	69ft. 1 1-2in.

Long Jump

1948	Olga Gyarmati, Hungary	18ft. 8 1-4 in.
1952	Yvette Williams, New Zealand	20ft. 5 3-4 in.
1956	Elzbieta Krzeskinska, Poland	20ft. 9 3-4 in.
1960	Vyera Krepkina, USSR	20ft. 10 3-4 in.
1964	Mary Rand, Great Britain	22ft. 2 1-4 in.
1968	Viorica Viscopoleanu, Romania	22ft. 4 1-2 in.
1972	Heidemarie Rosendahl, W. Germany	22ft. 3 in.
1976	Angela Voigt, E. Germany	22ft. 3-4 in.
1980	Tatyana Kolpakova, USSR	23ft. 2 in.
1984	Anisoara Stanciu, Romania	22ft. 10 in.
1988	Jackie Joyner-Kersee, United States	24ft. 3 1-2 in.
1992	Heike Drechsler, Germany	23ft. 5 1-4 in.*

Marathon

1984	Joan Benoit, United States	2h. 24m. 52s*
1988	Rosa Mota, Portugal	2h. 25m. 40s
1992	Valentina Yegorova, Unified Team	2h. 32m. 41s

Swimming and Diving—Men

50-Meter Freestyle

1988	Matt Biondi, U.S.	22.14
1992	Alexandre Popov, Unified Team	21.91*

100-Meter Freestyle

1896	Alfred Hajos, Hungary	1:22.2
1904	Zoltan de Halmay, Hungary (100 yards)	1:02.8
1908	Charles Daniels, U.S.	1:05.6
1912	Duke P. Kahanamoku, U.S.	1:03.4
1920	Duke P. Kahanamoku, U.S.	1:01.4
1924	John Weissmuller, U.S.	59.0
1928	John Weissmuller, U.S.	58.6
1932	Yasuji Miyazaki, Japan	58.2
1936	Ferenc Csik, Hungary	57.6
1948	Wally Ris, U.S.	57.3
1952	Clark Scholes, U.S.	57.4
1956	Jon Henricks, Australia	55.4
1960	John Devitt, Australia	55.2
1964	Don Schollander, U.S.	53.4
1968	Mike Wenden, Australia	52.2
1972	Mark Spitz, U.S.	51.22
1976	Jim Montgomery, U.S.	49.99
1980	Jorg Woithe, E. Germany	50.40
1984	Rowdy Gaines, U.S.	49.80
1988	Matt Biondi, United States	48.63*
1992	Alexandre Popov, Unified Team	49.02

200-Meter Freestyle

1968	Mike Wenden, Australia	1:55.2
1972	Mark Spitz, U.S.	1:52.78
1976	Bruce Furniss, U.S.	1:50.29
1980	Sergei Kopliakov, USSR	1:49.81
1984	Michael Gross, W. Germany	1:47.44
1988	Duncan Armstrong, Australia	1:47.25
1992	Yevgeny Sadovyi, Unified Team	1:46.70*

400-Meter Freestyle

1904	C. M. Daniels, U.S. (440 yards)	6:16.2
1908	Henry Taylor, Great Britain	5:36.8
1912	George Hodgson, Canada	5:24.4
1920	Norman Ross, U.S.	5:26.8
1924	John Weissmuller, U.S.	5:04.2
1928	Albert Zorilla, Argentina	5:01.6
1932	Clarence Crabbe, U.S.	4:48.4
1936	Jack Medica, U.S.	4:44.5
1948	William Smith, U.S.	4:41.0
1952	Jean Boiteux, France	4:30.7
1956	Murray Rose, Australia	4:27.3
1960	Murray Rose, Australia	4:18.3
1964	Don Schollander, U.S.	4:12.2
1968	Mike Burton, U.S.	4:09.0
1972	Brad Cooper, Australia	4:00.27
1976	Brian Goodell, U.S.	3:51.93
1980	Vladimir Salnikov, USSR	3:51.31
1984	George DiCarlo, U.S.	3:51.23
1988	Ewe Dassler, E. Germany	3:46.95
1992	Yevgeny Sadovyi, Unified Team	3:45.00*

1,500-Meter Freestyle

1908	Henry Taylor, Great Britain	22:48.4
1912	George Hodgson, Canada	22:00.0
1920	Norman Ross, U.S.	22:23.2
1924	Andrew Charlton, Australia	20:06.6
1928	Arne Borg, Sweden	19:51.8
1932	Kusuo Kitamura, Japan	19:12.4
1936	Noboru Terada, Japan	19:13.7
1948	James McLane, U.S.	19:18.5
1952	Ford Konno, U.S.	18:30.3
1956	Murray Rose, Australia	17:58.9
1960	Jon Konrads, Australia	17:19.6
1964	Robert Windle, Australia	17:01.7
1968	Mike Burton, U.S.	16:38.9
1972	Mike Burton, U.S.	15:52.58
1976	Brian Goodell, U.S.	15:02.40
1980	Vladimir Salnikov, USSR	14:58.27
1984	Michael O'Brien, U.S.	15:05.20
1988	Vladimir Salnikov, USSR	15:00.40
1992	Kieren Perkins, Australia	14:43.48*

400-Meter Medley Relay

1960	United States	4:05.4
1964	United States	3:58.4
1968	United States	3:54.9
1972	United States	3:48.16
1976	United States	3:42.22
1980	Australia	3:45.70
1984	United States	3:39.30
1988	United States	3:36.93*
1992	United States	3:36.93*

400-Meter Freestyle Relay

1964	United States	3:31.2
1968	United States	3:31.7
1972	United States	3:26.42
1984	United States	3:19.03
1988	United States	3:16.53*
1992	United States	3:16.74

800-Meter Freestyle Relay

1908	Great Britain	10:55.6
1912	Australia	10:11.6
1920	United States	10:04.4
1924	United States	9:53.4
1928	United States	9:36.2
1932	Japan	8:58.4
1936	Japan	8:51.5
1948	United States	8:46.0
1952	United States	8:31.1
1956	Australia	8:23.6
1960	United States	8:10.2
1964	United States	7:52.1
1968	United States	7:52.33
1972	United States	7:35.78
1976	United States	7:23.22
1980	USSR	7:23.50
1984	United States	7:15.69
1988	United States	7:12.51
1992	Unified Team	7:11.95*

100-Meter Backstroke

1904	Walter Brack, Germany (100 yds.)	1:16.8
1908	Arno Bieberstein, Germany	1:24.6
1912	Harry Hebner, U.S.	1:21.2
1920	Warren Kealoha, U.S.	1:15.2
1924	Warren Kealoha, U.S.	1:13.2
1928	George Kojac, U.S.	1:08.2
1932	Masaji Kiyokawa, Japan	1:08.6
1936	Adolph Kiefer, U.S.	1:05.9
1948	Allen Stack, U.S.	1:06.4
1952	Yoshi Oyakawa, U.S.	1:05.4
1956	David Thiele, Australia	1:02.2
1960	David Thiele, Australia	1:01.9
1968	Roland Matthes, E. Germany	58.7
1972	Roland Matthes, E. Germany	56.58
1976	John Naber, U.S.	55.49
1980	Bengt Baron, Sweden	56.33
1984	Rick Carey, U.S.	55.79
1988	Daichi Suzuki, Japan	55.05
1992	Mark Tewksbury, Canada	53.98*

200-Meter Backstroke

1964	Jed Graef, U.S.	2:10.3
1968	Roland Matthes, E. Germany	2:09.6
1972	Roland Matthes, E. Germany	2:02.82
1976	John Naber, U.S.	1:59.19
1980	Sandor Wladar, Hungary	2:01.93
1984	Rick Carey, U.S.	2:00.23
1988	Igor Polianski, USSR	1:59.37
1992	Martin Lopez-Zubero, Spain	1:58.47*

100-Meter Breaststroke

1968	Don McKenzie, U.S.	1:07.7
1972	Nobutaka Taguchi, Japan	1:04.94
1976	John Hencken, U.S.	1:03.11
1980	Duncan Goodhew, Great Britain	1:03.44
1984	Steve Lundquist, U.S.	1:01.65
1988	Adrian Moorhouse, Great Britain	1:02.04
1992	Nelson Diebel, U.S.	1:01.50*

200-Meter Breaststroke

1908	Frederick Holman, Great Britain	3:09.2
1912	Walter Bathe, Germany	3:01.8
1920	Haken Malmroth, Sweden	3:04.4
1924	Robert Skelton, U.S.	2:56.6
1928	Yoshiyuki Tsuruta, Japan	2:48.8
1932	Yoshiyuki Tsuruta, Japan	2:45.4
1936	Tetsuo Hamuro, Japan	2:41.5
1948	Joseph Verdeur, U.S.	2:39.3
1952	John Davies, Australia	2:34.4
1956	Masura Furukawa, Japan	2:34.7
1960	William Mulliken, U.S.	2:37.4
1964	Ian O'Brien, Australia	2:27.8
1968	Felipe Munoz, Mexico	2:28.7
1972	John Hencken, U.S.	2:21.55
1976	David Wilkie, Great Britain	2:15.11
1980	Robertas Zhulpa, USSR	2:15.85
1984	Victor Davis, Canada	2:13.34
1988	Jozsef Szabo, Hungary	2:13.52
1992	Mike Barrowman, U.S.	2:10.16*

100-Meter Butterfly

1968	Doug Russell, U.S.	55.9
1972	Mark Spitz, U.S.	54.27
1976	Matt Vogel, U.S.	54.35
1980	Par Arvidsson, Sweden	54.92
1984	Michael Gross, W. Germany	53.08
1988	Anthony Nesty, Suriname	53.00*
1992	Pablo Morales, U.S.	53.32

200-Meter Butterfly

1956	William Yorzyk, U.S.	2:19.3
1960	Michael Troy, U.S.	2:12.8
1964	Kevin J. Berry, Australia	2:06.6
1968	Carl Robie, U.S.	2:08.7
1972	Mark Spitz, U.S.	2:00.70
1976	Mike Bruner, U.S.	1:59.23
1980	Sergei Fesenko, USSR	1:59.76
1984	Jon Sieben, Australia	1:57.04
1988	Michael Gross, W. Germany	1:56.94
1992	Mel Stewart, U.S.	1:56.26*

200-Meter Individual Medley

1968	Charles Hickcox, U.S.	2:12.0
1972	Gunnar Larsson, Sweden	2:07.17
1984	Alex Baumann, Canada	2:01.42
1988	Tamas Darnyi, Hungary	2:00.17*
1992	Tamas Darnyi, Hungary	2:00.76

400-Meter Individual Medley

1964	Dick Roth, U.S.	4:45.4
1968	Charles Hickcox, U.S.	4:48.4
1972	Gunnar Larsson, Sweden	4:31.98
1976	Rod Strachan, U.S.	4:23.68
1980	Aleksandr Sidorenko, USSR	4:22.89
1984	Alex Baumann, Canada	4:17.41
1988	Tamas Darnyi, Hungary	4:14.75
1992	Tamas Darnyi, Hungary	4:14.23*

Springboard Diving

		Points
1908	Albert Zurner, Germany	85.5
1912	Paul Guenther, Germany	79.23
1920	Louis Kuehn, U.S.	675.40
1924	Albert White, U.S.	97.46
1928	Pete Desjardins, U.S.	185.04
1932	Michael Galitzen, U.S.	161.38
1936	Richard Degener, U.S.	163.57
1948	Bruce Harlan, U.S.	163.64
1952	David Browning, U.S.	205.29
1956	Robert Clotworthy, U.S.	159.56
1960	Gary Tobian, U.S.	170.00
1964	Kenneth Sitzberger, U.S.	159.90
1968	Bernie Wrightson, U.S.	170.15
1972	Vladimir Vasin, USSR	594.09
1976	Phil Boggs, U.S.	619.52
1980	Aleksandr Portnov, USSR	905.02
1984	Greg Louganis, U.S.	754.41
1988	Greg Louganis, U.S.	730.80
1992	Mark Lenzi, U.S.	676.530

Platform Diving

		Points
1904	Dr. G.E. Sheldon, U.S.	12.75
1908	Hjalmar Johansson, Sweden	83.75
1912	Erik Adlerz, Sweden	73.94
1920	Clarence Pinkston, U.S.	100.67
1924	Albert White, U.S.	97.46
1928	Pete Desjardins, U.S.	98.74
1932	Harold Smith, U.S.	124.80
1936	Marshall Wayne, U.S.	113.58
1948	Sammy Lee, U.S.	130.05
1952	Sammy Lee, U.S.	156.28
1956	Joaquin Capilla, Mexico	152.44
1960	Robert Webster, U.S.	165.56
1964	Robert Webster, U.S.	148.58
1968	Klaus Dibiasi, Italy	164.18
1972	Klaus Dibiasi, Italy	504.12
1976	Klaus Dibiasi, Italy	600.51
1980	Falk Hoffmann, E. Germany	835.65
1984	Greg Louganis, U.S.	710.91
1988	Greg Louganis, U.S.	638.61
1992	Sun Shuwei, China	677.310

Swimming and Diving—Women

50-Meter Freestyle

1988	Kristin Otto, E. Germany	25.49
1992	Yang Wenyi, China	24.76*

100-Meter Freestyle

1912	Fanny Durack, Australia	1:22.2
1920	Ethelda Bleibtrey, U.S.	1:13.6
1924	Ethel Lackie, U.S.	1:12.4
1928	Albina Osipowich, U.S.	1:11.0
1932	Helene Madison, U.S.	1:06.8
1936	Hendrika Mastenbroek, Holland	1:05.9
1948	Greta Andersen, Denmark	1:06.3
1952	Katalin Szoke, Hungary	1:06.8
1956	Dawn Fraser, Australia	1:02.0
1960	Dawn Fraser, Australia	1:01.2
1964	Dawn Fraser, Australia	59.5
1968	Jan Henne, U.S.	1:00.0
1972	Sandra Neilson, U.S.	58.59
1976	Kornelia Ender, E. Germany	55.65
1980	Barbara Krause, E. Germany	54.79
1984	(tie) Carrie Steinseifer, U.S.	55.92
	Nancy Hogshead, U.S.	55.92
988	Kristin Otto, E. Germany	54.93
992	Zhuang Yong, China	54.64*

200-Meter Freestyle

1968	Debbie Meyer, U.S.	2:10.5
1972	Shane Gould, Australia	2:03.56
1976	Kornelia Ender, E. Germany	1:59.26
1980	Barbara Krause, E. Germany	1:58.33
1984	Mary Wayte, U.S.	1:59.23
1988	Heike Friedrich, E. Germany	1:57.65*
1992	Nicole Haislett, U.S.	1:57.90

400-Meter Freestyle

1924	Martha Norelius, U.S.	6:02.2
1928	Martha Norelius, U.S.	5:42.8
1932	Helene Madison, U.S.	5:28.5
1936	Hendrika Mastenbroek, Netherlands	5:26.4
1948	Ann Curtis, U.S.	5:17.8
1952	Valerie Gyenge, Hungary	5:12.1
1956	Lorraine Crapp, Australia	4:54.6
1960	Susan Chris von Saltza, U.S.	4:50.6
1964	Virginia Duenkel, U.S.	4:43.3
1968	Debbie Meyer, U.S.	4:31.8
1972	Shane Gould, Australia	4:19.44
1976	Petra Thuemer E. Germany	4:09.89
1980	Ines Diers, E. Germany	4:08.76
1984	Tiffany Cohen, U.S.	4:07.10
1988	Janet Evans, U.S.	4:03.85*
1992	Dagmar Hase, Germany	4:07.18

800-Meter Freestyle

1968	Debbie Meyer, U.S.	9:24.0
1972	Keena Rothhammer, U.S.	8:53.68
1976	Petra Thuemer, E. Germany	8:37.14
1980	Michelle Ford, Australia	8:28.90
1984	Tiffany Cohen, U.S.	8:24.95
1988	Janet Evans, U.S.	8:20.20*
1992	Janet Evans, U.S.	8:25.52

100-Meter Backstroke

1924	Sybil Bauer, U.S.	1:23.2
1928	Marie Braun, Netherlands	1:22.0
1932	Eleanor Holm, U.S.	1:19.4
1936	Dina Senff, Netherlands	1:18.9
1948	Karen Harup, Denmark	1:14.4
1952	Joan Harrison, South Africa	1:14.3
1956	Judy Grinham, Great Britain	1:12.9
1960	Lynn Burke, U.S.	1:09.3
1964	Cathy Ferguson, U.S.	1:07.7
1968	Kaye Hall, U.S.	1:06.2
1972	Melissa Belote, U.S.	1:05.78
1976	Ulrike Richter, E. Germany	1:01.83
1980	Rica Reinisch, E. Germany	1:00.86
1984	Theresa Andrews, U.S.	1:02.55
1988	Kristin Otto, E. Germany	1:00.89
1992	Krisztina Egerszegi, Hungary	1:00.68*

200-Meter Backstroke

1968	Pokey Watson, U.S.	2:24.8
1972	Melissa Belote, U.S.	2:19.19
1976	Ulrike Richter, E. Germany	2:13.43
1980	Rica Reinisch, E. Germany	2:11.77
1984	Jolanda De Rover, Netherlands	2:12.38
1988	Krisztina Egerszegi, Hungary	2:09.29
1992	Krisztina Egerszegi, Hungary	2:07.06*

100-Meter Breaststroke

1968	Djurdjica Bjedov, Yugoslavia	1:15.8
1972	Cathy Carr, U.S.	1:13.58
1976	Hannelore Anke, E. Germany	1:11:16
1980	Ute Geweniger, E. Germany	1:10.22
1984	Petra Van Staveren, Netherlands	1:09.88
1988	Tania Dangalakova, Bulgaria	1:07.95*
1992	Elena Roudkovskaia, Unified Team	1:08.00

200-Meter Breaststroke

1924	Lucy Morton, Great Britain	3:33.2
1928	Hilde Schrader, Germany	3:12.6
1932	Clare Dennis, Australia	3:06.3
1936	Hideko Maehata, Japan	3:03.6
1948	Nelly Van Vliet, Netherlands	2:57.2
1952	Eva Szekely, Hungary	2:51.7
1956	Ursula Happe, Germany	2:53.1
1960	Anita Lonsbrough, Great Britain	2:49.5
1964	Galina Prozumenschikova, USSR	2:46.4
1968	Sharon Wichman, U.S.	2:44.4
1972	Beverly Whitfield, Australia	2:41.71
1976	Marina Koshevaia, USSR	2:33.35
1980	Lina Kachushite, USSR	2:29.54
1984	Anne Ottenbrite, Canada	2:30.38
1988	Silke Hoerner, E. Germany	2:26.71
1992	Kyoko Iwasaki, Japan	2:26.65*

200-Meter Individual Medley

1968	Claudia Kolb, U.S.	2:24.7
1972	Shane Gould, Australia	2:23.07
1984	Tracy Caulkins, U.S.	2:12.64
1988	Daniela Hunger, E. Germany	2:12.59
1992	Lin Li, China	2:11.65*

400-Meter Individual Medley

1964	Donna de Varona, U.S.	5:18.7
1968	Claudia Kolb, U.S.	5:08.5
1972	Gail Neall, Australia	5:02.97
1976	Ulrike Tauber, E. Germany	4:42.77
1980	Petra Schneider, E. Germany	4:36.29*
1984	Tracy Caulkins, U.S.	4:39.24
1988	Janet Evans, U.S.	4:37.76
1992	Krisztina Egerszegi, Hungary	4:36.54

100-Meter Butterfly

1956	Shelley Mann, U.S.	1:11.0
1960	Carolyn Schuler, U.S.	1:09.5
1964	Sharon Stouder, U.S.	1:04.7
1968	Lynn McClements, Australia	1:05.5
1972	Mayumi Aoki, Japan	1:03.34
1976	Kornelia Ender, E. Germany	1:00.13
1980	Caren Metschuck, E. Germany	1:00.42
1984	Mary T. Meagher, U.S.	59.26
1988	Kristin Otto, E. Germany	59.00
1992	Qian Hong, China	58.62*

200-Meter Butterfly

1968	Ada Kok, Netherlands	2:24.7
1972	Karen Moe, U.S.	2:15.57
1976	Andrea Pollack, E. Germany	2:11.41
1980	Ines Geissler, E. Germany	2:10.44
1984	Mary T. Meagher, U.S.	2:06.90*
1988	Kathleen Nord, E. Germany	2:09.51
1992	Summer Sanders, U.S.	2:08.67

400-Meter Medley Relay

1960	United States	4:41.1
1960	United States	4:33.9
1968	United States	4:28.3
1972	United States	4:20.75
1976	East Germany	4:07.95
1980	East Germany	4:06.67
1984	United States	4:08.34
1988	E. Germany	4:03.74
1992	United States	4:02.54*

400-Meter Freestyle Relay

1912	Great Britain	5:52.8
1920	United States	5:11.6
1924	United States	4:58.8
1928	United States	4:47.6
1932	United States	4:38.0
1936	Netherlands	4:36.0
1948	United States	4:29.2
1952	Hungary	4:24.4
1956	Australia	4:17.1
1960	United States	4:08.9
1964	United States	4:03.8
1968	United States	4:02.5
1972	United States	3:55.19
1976	United States	3:44.82
1980	East Germany	3:42.71
1984	United States	3:43.43
1988	E. Germany	3:40.63
1992	United States	3:39.46*

Springboard Diving

		Points
1920	Aileen Riggin, U.S.	539.90
1924	Elizabeth Becker, U.S.	474.50
1928	Helen Meany, U.S.	78.62
1932	Georgia Coleman U.S.	87.52
1936	Marjorie Gestring, U.S.	89.27
1948	Victoria M. Draves, U.S.	108.74
1952	Patricia McCormick, U.S.	147.30
1956	Patricia McCormick, U.S.	142.36
1960	Ingrid Kramer, Germany	155.81
1964	Ingrid Engel-Kramer, Germany	145.00
1968	Sue Gossick, U.S.	150.77
1972	Micki King, U.S.	450.03
1976	Jenni Chandler, U.S.	506.19
1980	Irina Kalinina, USSR	725.91
1984	Sylvie Bernier, Canada	530.70
1988	Gao Min, China	580.23
1992	Gao Min, China	572.400

Platform Diving

		Points
1912	Greta Johansson, Sweden	39.90
1920	Stefani Fryland-Clausen, Denmark	34.60
1924	Caroline Smith, U.S.	33.20
1928	Elizabeth B. Pinkston, U.S.	31.60
1932	Dorothy Poynton, U.S.	40.26

1936	Dorothy Poynton Hill, U.S.	33.93
1948	Victoria M. Draves, U.S.	68.87
1952	Patricia McCormick, U.S.	79.37
1956	Patricia McCormick, U.S.	84.85
1960	Ingrid Kramer, Germany	91.28
1964	Lesley Bush, U.S.	99.80
1968	Milena Duchkova, Czech	109.59
1972	Ulrika Knape, Sweden	390.00
1976	Elena Vaytsekhouskaya, USSR	406.59
1980	Martina Jaschke, E. Germany	596.25
1984	Zhou Jihong, China	435.51
1988	Xu Yanmei, China	445.20
1992	Fu Mingxia, China	461.430

Boxing

Light Flyweight (106 lbs)

1968 Francisco Rodriguez, Venezuela
1972 Gyorgy Gedo, Hungary
1976 Jorge Hernandez, Cuba
1980 Shamil Sabyrov, USSR
1984 Paul Gonzalez, U.S.
1988 Ivailo Hristov, Bulgaria
1992 Rogelio Marcelo, Cuba

Flyweight (112 lbs)

1904 George Finnegan, U.S.
1920 William Di Gennara, U.S.
1924 Fidel LaBarba, U.S.
1928 Antal Kocsis, Hungary
1932 Istvan Enekes, Hungary
1936 Willi Kaiser, Germany
1948 Pascual Perez, Argentina
1952 Nathan Brooks, U.S.
1956 Terence Spinks, Great Britain
1960 Gyula Torok, Hungary
1964 Fernando Atzori, Italy
1968 Ricardo Delgado, Mexico
1972 Georgi Kostadinov, Bulgaria
1976 Leo Randolph, U.S.
1980 Peter Lessov, Bulgaria
1984 Steve McCrory, U.S.
1988 Kim Kwang Sun, S. Korea
1992 Su Choi Choi, N. Korea

Bantamweight (119 lbs)

1904 Oliver Kirk, U.S.
1908 A Henry Thomas, Great Britain
1920 Clarence Walker, South Africa
1924 William Smith, South Africa
1928 Vittorio Tamagnini, Italy
1932 Horace Gwynne, Canada
1936 Ulderico Sergo, Italy
1948 Tibor Csik, Hungary
1952 Pentti Hamalainen, Finland
1956 Wolfgang Behrendt, E. Germany
1960 Oleg Grigoryev, USSR
1964 Takao Sakurai, Japan
1968 Valery Sokolov, USSR
1972 Orlando Martinez, Cuba
1976 Yong-Jo Gu, N. Korea
1980 Juan Hernandez, Cuba
1984 Maurizio Stecca, Italy
1988 Kennedy McKinney, U.S.
1992 Joel Casamayor, Cuba

Featherweight (126 lbs)

1904 Oliver Kirk, U.S.
1908 Richard Gunn, Great Britain
1920 Paul Fritsch, France
1924 John Fields, U.S.
1928 Lambertus van Klaveren, Netherlands
1932 Carmelo Robledo, Argentina
1936 Oscar Casanovas, Argentina
1948 Ernesto Formenti, Italy
1952 Jan Zachara, Czech.
1956 Vladimir Safronov, USSR
1960 Francesco Musso, Italy
1964 Stanislav Stephashkin, USSR
1968 Antonin Roldan, Mexico
1972 Boris Kousnetsov, USSR
1976 Angel Herrera, Cuba
1980 Rudi Fink, E. Germany
1984 Meldrick Taylor, U.S.
1988 Giovanni Parisi, Italy
1992 Andreas Tews, Germany

Lightweight (132 lbs)

1904 Harry Spanger, U.S.
1908 Frederick Grace, Great Britain
1920 Samuel Mosberg, U.S.
1924 Hans Nielsen, Denmark
1928 Carlo Orlandi, Italy
1932 Lawrence Stevens, South Africa
1936 Imre Harangi, Hungary
1948 Gerald Dreyer, South Africa
1952 Aureliano Bolognesi, Italy
1956 Richard McTaggart, Great Britain
1960 Kazimierz Pazdzior, Poland
1964 Jozef Grudzien, Poland
1968 Ronald Harris, U.S.
1972 Jan Szczepanski, Poland
1976 Howard Davis, U.S.
1980 Angel Herrera, Cuba
1984 Pernell Whitaker, U.S.
1988 Andreas Zuelow, E. Germany
1992 Oscar De La Hoya, U.S.

Light Welterweight (140 lbs)

1952 Charles Adkins, U.S.
1956 Vladimir Yengibaryan, USSR
1960 Bohumil Nemecek, Czech.
1964 Jerzy Kulej, Poland
1968 Jerzy Kulej, Poland
1972 Ray Seales, U.S.
1976 Ray Leonard, U.S.
1980 Patrizio Oliva, Italy
1984 Jerry Page, U.S.
1988 Viatcheslav Janovski, USSR
1992 Hector Vinent, Cuba

Welterweight (147 lbs)

1904 Albert Young, U.S.
1920 Albert Schneider, Canada
1924 Jean Delarge, Belgium
1928 Edward Morgan, New Zealand
1932 Edward Flynn, U.S.
1936 Sten Suvio, Finland
1948 Julius Torma, Czech.
1952 Zygmunt Chychia, Poland
1956 Nicolae Linca, Romania
1960 Giovanni Benvenuti, Italy
1964 Marian Kasprzyk, Poland
1968 Manfred Wolke, E. Germany
1972 Emilio Correa, Cuba
1976 Jochen Bachfeld, E. Germany
1980 Andres Aldama, Cuba
1984 Mark Breland, U.S.
1988 Robert Wangila, Kenya
1992 Michael Carruth, Ireland

Light Middleweight (157 lbs)

1952 Laszlo Papp, Hungary
1956 Laszlo Papp, Hungary
1960 Wilbert McClure, U.S.
1964 Boris Lagutin, USSR
1968 Boris Lagutin, USSR
1972 Dieter Kottysch, W. Germany
1976 Jerzy Rybicki, Poland
1980 Armando Martinez, Cuba
1984 Frank Tate, U.S.
1988 Park Si Hun, S. Korea
1992 Juan Lemus, Cuba

Middleweight (165 lbs)

1904 Charles Mayer, U.S.
1908 John Douglas, Great Britain
1920 Harry Mallin, Great Britain
1924 Harry Mallin, Great Britain
1928 Piero Toscani, Italy
1932 Carmen Barth, U.S.
1936 Jean Despeaux, France
1948 Laszio Papp, Hungary
1952 Floyd Patterson, U.S.
1956 Gennady Schatkov, USSR
1960 Edward Crook, U.S.
1964 Valery Popenchenko, USSR
1968 Christopher Finnegan, Great Britain
1972 Vyacheslav Lemechev, USSR
1976 Michael Spinks, U.S.
1980 Jose Gomez, Cuba
1984 Joon-Sup Shin, S. Korea
1988 Henry Maske, E. Germany
1992 Ariel Hernandez, Cuba

Light Heavyweight (179 lbs)

1920 Edward Eagan, U.S.
1924 Harry Mitchell, Great Britain
1928 Victor Avendano, Argentina
1932 David Carstens, South Africa
1936 Roger Michelot, France
1948 George Hunter, South Africa
1952 Norvel Lee, U.S.
1956 James Boyd, U.S.
1960 Cassius Clay, U.S.
1964 Cosimo Pinto, Italy
1968 Dan Poznyak, USSR
1972 Mate Parlov, Yugoslavia
1976 Leon Spinks, U.S.
1980 Slobodan Kacar, Yugoslavia
1984 Anton Josipovic, Yugoslavia
1988 Andrew Maynard, U.S.
1992 Torsten May, Germany

Heavyweight (201 lbs)

1984 Henry Tillman, U.S.
1988 Ray Mercer, U.S.
1992 Felix Savon, Cuba

Super Heavyweight (Unlimited)
(known as heavyweight from 1904-1980)

1904 Samuel Berger, U.S.
1908 Albert Oldham, Great Britain
1920 Ronald Rawson, Great Britain
1924 Otto von Porat, Norway
1928 Arturo Rodriguez Jurado, Argentina
1932 Santiago Lovell, Argentina
1936 Herbert Runge, Germany
1948 Rafael Inglesias, Argentina
1952 H. Edward Sanders, U.S.
1956 T. Peter Rademacher, U.S.
1960 Franco De Piccoli, Italy
1964 Joe Frazier, U.S.
1968 George Foreman, U.S.
1972 Teofilo Stevenson, Cuba
1976 Teofilo Stevenson, Cuba
1980 Teofilo Stevenson, Cuba
1984 Tyrell Biggs, U.S.
1988 Lennox Lewis, Canada
1992 Roberto Balado, Cuba

25th Summer Olympics

Barcelona, Spain, July 25–Aug. 9, 1992

Over 14,000 athletes gathered in Barcelona, Spain in July and August for 16 days to compete in the Games of the XXV Olympiad. The athletes represented a record 172 nations, 11 more than had participated in any previous Olympics, and competed for medals in 257 events.

The 1992 games will be remembered mostly for the appearance of the Dream Team—the United States basketball team—featuring, for the first time, the stars of the National Basketball Association. As expected, the team crushed all its opponents on the way to a gold medal. Other notable events at the games were the victory in the long jump for Carl Lewis, his third consecutive gold medal in the event; the successful defense in the heptathlon by Jackie Joyner-Kersee; and the domination in men's gymnastics by Vitaly Shcherbo of the Unified Team. Perhaps the biggest surprise was the failure of world-record holder Sergei Bubka (Ukraine) to win a medal in the pole vault. Also notable was the appearance of South African athletes after missing 7 consecutive Olympiads.

The Unified Team made up of athletes of 12 republics of the former Soviet Union won the most gold medals, 45, and the most medals, 112. The United States finished second with 37 gold medals and 108 medals overall.

Final Medal Standings

Medals Standing

	Gold	Silver	Bronze	Total		Gold	Silver	Bronze	Total
Unified Team[1]	45	38	29	**112**	Ethiopia	1	0	2	**3**
United States	37	34	37	**108**	Latvia	0	2	1	**3**
Germany	33	21	28	**82**	Croatia	0	1	2	**3**
China	16	22	16	**54**	Belgium	0	1	2	**3**
Cuba	14	6	11	**31**	Iran	0	1	2	**3**
Hungary	11	12	7	**30**	I.O.P.[2]	0	1	2	**3**
South Korea	12	5	12	**29**	Greece	2	0	0	**2**
France	8	5	16	**29**	Ireland	1	1	0	**2**
Australia	7	9	11	**27**	Algeria	1	0	1	**2**
Spain	13	7	2	**22**	Estonia	1	0	1	**2**
Japan	3	8	11	**22**	Lithuania	1	0	1	**2**
Britain	5	3	12	**20**	Austria	0	2	0	**2**
Italy	6	5	8	**19**	Namibia	0	2	0	**2**
Poland	3	6	10	**19**	South Africa	0	2	0	**2**
Canada	6	5	7	**18**	Israel	0	1	1	**2**
Romania	4	6	8	**18**	Mongolia	0	0	2	**2**
Bulgaria	3	7	6	**16**	Slovenia	0	0	2	**2**
Netherlands	2	6	7	**15**	Switzerland	1	0	0	**1**
Sweden	1	7	4	**12**	Mexico	0	1	0	**1**
New Zealand	1	4	5	**10**	Peru	0	1	0	**1**
North Korea	4	0	5	**9**	Taiwan	0	1	0	**1**
Kenya	2	4	2	**8**	Argentina	0	0	1	**1**
Czechoslovakia	4	2	1	**7**	Bahamas	0	0	1	**1**
Norway	2	4	1	**7**	Colombia	0	0	1	**1**
Turkey	2	2	2	**6**	Ghana	0	0	1	**1**
Denmark	1	1	4	**6**	Malaysia	0	0	1	**1**
Indonesia	2	2	1	**5**	Pakistan	0	0	1	**1**
Finland	1	2	2	**5**	Philippines	0	0	1	**1**
Jamaica	0	3	1	**4**	Puerto Rico	0	0	1	**1**
Nigeria	0	3	1	**4**	Qatar	0	0	1	**1**
Brazil	2	1	0	**3**	Suriname	0	0	1	**1**
Morocco	1	1	1	**3**	Thailand	0	0	1	**1**

(1) Athletes from 12 former Soviet republics. (2) Independent Olympic Participants (athletes from Serbia, Montenegro, Macedonia).

Other Summer Olympics Gold Medalists in 1992

Archery

Men's 70-Meter Individual—Sebastien Flute, France.
Men's Team—Spain.
Women's 70-Meter Individual—Cho Youn Jeong, S. Korea.
Women's Team—S. Korea.

Badminton

Men's Singles—Alan Budi Kusuma, Indonesia.
Men's Doubles—Kim Moon Soo and Park Joo Bong, S. Korea.
Women's Singles—Susi Susanti, Indonesia.
Women's Doubles—Hwang Hye Young and Chung So-Young, S. Korea.

Baseball

G-Cuba; S-Taiwan; B-Japan.

Basketball

Men—G-U.S.; S-Croatia; B-Lithuania.
Women—G-Cuba; S-China; B-U.S.

Canoe/Kayak

Men

Single Kayak Slalom—Pierpaolo Ferrazzi, Italy.
Kayak 500M Singles—Mikko Yrjoe Kolehmainen, Finland.
Kayak 500M Doubles—Germany.
Kayak 1,000M Singles—Clint Robinson, Australia.
Kayak 1,000M Doubles—Germany.
Kayak 1,000M Fours—Germany.
Double Canoe Slalom—U.S.
Canoe Slalom—Lukas Pollert, Czechoslovakia.
Canoe 500M Singles—Nikolai Boukhalov, Bulgaria.
Canoe 500M Doubles—Unified Team.
Canoe 1,000M Singles—Nikolai Boukhalov, Bulgaria.
Canoe 1,000M Doubles—Germany.

Women

Kayak Slalom—Elisabeth Micheler, Germany.
Kayak 500M Singles—Birgit Schmidt, Germany.
Kayak 500M Doubles—Germany.
Kayak 500M Fours—Hungary.

Cycling

Men

Individual Road Race—Fabio Casartelli, Italy.
Sprint—Jens Fiedler, Germany.
Individual Points Race—Giovanni Lombardi, Italy.
4,000 Team Pursuit—Germany.
4K Individual Pursuit—Chris Boardman, Great Britain.
1 KM Time Trial—Jose Moreno, Spain.
Road Race—Germany.

Women

Sprint—Erika Salumae, Estonia.
Individual Pursuit—Petra Rossner, Germany.
Individual Road Race—Kathryn Watt, Australia.

Diving

Men's Platform—Sun Shuwei, China.
Men's Springboard—Mark Lenzi, U.S.
Women's Platform—Fu Mingxia, China.
Women's Springboard—Gao Min, China.

Equestrian

Ind. Three-Day Event—Matthew Ryan, Australia.
Team Three-Day Event—Australia.
Individual Dressage—Nicole Uphoff, Germany.
Team Dressage—Germany.
Individual Jumping—Ludger Beerbaum, Germany.
Team Jumping—Netherlands.

Fencing

Men

Individual Foil—Philippe Omnes, France.
Team Foil—Germany.
Individual Saber—Bence Szabo, Hungary.
Team Saber—Unified Team.
Individual Épée—Eric Srecki, France.
Team Épée—Germany.

Women

Individual Foil—Giovanna Trillini, Italy.
Team Foil—Italy.

Field Hockey

Men—G-Germany; S-Australia; B-Pakistan.
Women—G-Spain; S-Germany; B-Great Britain.

Gymnastics

Men

Floor Exercise—Li Xiaosahuang, China.
Horizontal Bar—Trent Dimas, U.S.
Parallel Bars—Vitaly Shcherbo, Unified Team.
Pommel Horse—(tie) Vitaly Shcherbo, Unified Team; Pae Gil Su, N. Korea.
Rings—Vitaly Shcherbo, Unified Team.
Vault—Vitaly Shcherbo, Unified Team.
Individual All-Around—Vitaly Shcherbo, Unified Team.
Team—Unified Team.

Women

Balance Beam—Tatiana Lisenko, Unified Team.
Floor Exercise—Lavinia Corina Milosovici, Romania.
Uneven Bars—Lu Li, China.
Vault—(tie) Henrietta Onodi, Hungary; Lavinia Corina Milosovici, Romania.
All - Around—Tatiana Gutsu, Unified Team.
Team Artistic—Unified Team.

Rhythmic Gymnastics

Alexandra Timoshenko, Unified Team.

Judo

Men

132 Pounds—Nazim Gousseinov, Unified Team.
143 Pounds—Rogerio Sampalo Cardoso, Brazil.
157 Pounds—Toshihiko Koga, Japan.
172 Pounds—Hidehiko Yoshida, Japan.
198 Pounds—Waldemar Legien, Poland.
209 Pounds—Antal Kovacs, Hungary.
Heavyweight—David Khakhaleichvili, Unified Team.

Women

106 Pounds—Cecile Nowak, France.
115 Pounds—Almudena Munoz Martinez, Spain.
123 Pounds—Miriam Blasco Soto, Spain.
134 Pounds—Catherine Fleury, France.
146 Pounds—Odalis Reve Jimenez, Cuba.
159 Pounds—Kim Mi Jung, S. Korea.
Over 159 Pounds—Zhuang Xiaoyan, China.

Modern Pentathlon

Individual—Arkadiusz Skrzypaszek, Poland.
Team—Poland.

Rowing

Men

Single Sculls—Thomas Lange, Germany.
Double Sculls—Australia.
Coxless Pairs—Great Britain.
Coxed Pairs—Great Britain.
Coxed Fours—Romania.
Coxless Fours—Australia.
Quadruple Sculls—Germany.
Coxed Eights—Canada.

Women

Single Sculls—Elisabeta Lipa, Romania.
Double Sculls—Germany.
Coxless Pairs—Canada.
Coxless Fours—Canada.
Quadruple Sculls—Germany.
Coxed Eights—Canada.

Shooting

Men

Running Game Target—Michael Jakosits, Germany.
Rapid Fire Pistol—Ralf Schumann, Germany.
Three-Position Rifle—Gratchia Petikiane, Unified Team.
Free Rifle—Lee Eun Chul, S. Korea.
Air Pistol—Wang Yifu, China.
Air Rifle—Iouri Fedkine, Unified Team.
Free Pistol—Konstantine Loukachik, Unified Team.

Women

Air Pistol—Marina Logvinenko, Unified Team.
Three-Position Rifle—Launi Meili, U.S.
Sport Pistol—Marina Logvinenko, Unified Team.
Air Rifle—Yeo Kab Soon, S. Korea.

Mixed

Trap—Petr Hrdlicka, Czechoslovakia.
Skeet—Zhang Shan, China.

Soccer

G-Spain; S-Poland; B-Ghana.

Synchronized Swimming

Solo—Kristen Babb-Sprague, U.S.
Duet—Karen Josephson and Sarah Josephson, U.S.

Table Tennis

Men's Singles—Jan Waldner, Sweden.
Men's Doubles—Lu Lin and Wang Tao, China.
Women's Singles—Deng Yaping, China.
Women's Doubles—Deng Yaping and Qiao Hong, China.

Team Handball

Men—G-Unified Team; S-Sweden; B-France.
Women—G-S. Korea; S-Norway; B-Unified Team.

Tennis

Men's Singles—Marc Rosset, Switzerland.
Men's Doubles—Boris Becker and Michael Stich, Germany.
Women's Singles—Jennifer Capriati, U.S.
Women's Doubles—Gigi Fernandez and Mary Joe Fernandez, U.S.

Volleyball

Men—G-Brazil; S-Netherlands; B-U.S.
Women—G-Cuba; S-Unified Team; B-U.S.

Water Polo

G-Italy; S-Spain; B-Unified Team.

Weight Lifting

115 Pounds—Ivan Ivanov, Bulgaria.
123 Pounds—Chun Byung Kwan, S. Korea.
132 Pounds—Naim Suleymanoglu, Turkey.
148 Pounds—Israel Militossian, Unified Team.
165 Pounds—Fedor Kassapu, Unified Team.
180 Pounds—Pyrros Dimas, Greece.
198 Pounds—Kakhi Kakhiachvili, Unified Team.
220 Pounds—Victor Tregoubov, Unified Team.
243 Pounds—Ronny Weller, Germany.
Over 243 Pounds—Aleksandr Kourlovitch, Unified Team.

Wrestling

Freestyle

106 Pounds—Kim Il, N. Korea.
115 Pounds—Li Hak Son, S. Korea.
126 Pounds—Alejandro Puerto Diaz, Cuba.
137 Pounds—John Smith, U.S.
150 Pounds—Arsen Fadzaev, Unified Team.
163 Pounds—Park Jang Soon, S. Korea.
182 Pounds—Kevin Jackson, U.S.
198 Pounds—Makharbek Khadartsev, Unified Team.
220 Pounds—Leri Khabelov, Unified Team.
286 Pounds—Bruce Baumgartner, U.S.

Greco-Roman

106 Pounds—Oleg Koutherenko, Unified Team.
115 Pounds—Jon Ronningen, Norway.
126 Pounds—An Han Bong, S. Korea.
137 Pounds—M. Akif Pirim, Turkey.
150 Pounds—Attila Repka, Hungary.
163 Pounds—Mnatsakan Iskandarian, Unified Team.
181 Pounds—Peter Farkas, Hungary.
198 Pounds—Maik Bullmann, Germany.
220 Pounds—Hector Milian Perez, Cuba.
286 Pounds—Aleksandr Karelin, Unified Team.

Yachting

Soling—Denmark.
Finn—Jose Van Der Ploeg, Spain.
Tornado—France.
Europe—Linda Anderson, Norway.
Flying Dutchman—Spain.
Star—U.S.
Men's Sailboard—Franck David, France.
Women's Sailboard—Barbara Kendall, New Zealand.
Men's 470—Spain.
Women's 470—Spain.

Olympic Information

Symbol: Five rings or circles, linked together to represent the sporting friendship of all peoples. The rings also symbolize 5 geographic areas—Europe, Asia, Africa, Australia, and America. Each ring is a different color—blue, yellow, black, green, and red.

Flag: The symbol of the 5 rings on a plain white background.

Motto: "Citius, Altius, Fortius." Latin meaning "faster, higher, braver," or the modern interpretation "swifter, higher, stronger." The motto was coined by Father Didon, a French educator, in 1895.

Creed: "The most important thing in the Olympic Games is not to win but to take part, just as the most important thing in life is not the triumph but the struggle. The essential thing is not to have conquered but to have fought well."

Oath: An athlete of the host country recites the following at the opening ceremony. "In the name of all competitors I promise that we will take part in these Olympic Games, respecting and abiding by the rules which govern them, in the true spirit of sportsmanship for the glory of sport and the honor of our teams." Both the oath and the creed were composed by Pierre de Coubertin, the founder of the modern Games.

Flame: Symbolizes the continuity between the ancient and modern Games. The modern version of the flame was adopted in 1936. The torch used to kindle the flame is first lit by the sun's rays at Olympia, Greece, and then carried to the site of the Games by relays of runners. Ships and planes are used when necessary.

Winter Olympic Games Champions, 1924-1992

Sites of Games

1924 Chamonix, France
1928 St. Moritz, Switzerland
1932 Lake Placid, N.Y.
1936 Garmisch-Partenkirchen, Germany
1948 St. Moritz, Switzerland
1952 Oslo, Norway
1956 Cortina d'Ampezzo, Italy
1960 Squaw Valley, Cal.
1964 Innsbruck, Austria
1968 Grenoble, France
1972 Sapporo, Japan
1976 Innsbruck, Austria
1980 Lake Placid, N.Y.
1984 Sarajevo, Yugoslavia
1988 Calgary, Alberta
1992 Albertville, France
1994 Lillehammer, Norway

In 1992, the Unified Team represented the former Soviet republics of Russia, Ukraine, Belarus, Kazakhstan, and Uzbekistan.

Bobsledding

4-Man Bob

	(Driver in parentheses)	Time
1924	Switzerland (Eduard Scherrer)	5:45.54
1928	United States (William Fiske) (5-man)	3:20.50
1932	United States (William Fiske)	7:53.68
1936	Switzerland (Pierre Musy)	5:19.85
1948	United States (Francis Tyler)	5:20.10
1952	Germany (Andreas Ostler)	5:07.84
1956	Switzerland (Franz Kapus)	5:10.44
1964	Canada (Victor Emery)	4:14.46
1968	Italy (Eugenio Monti) (2 races)	2:17.39
1972	Switzerland (Jean Wicki)	4:43.07
1976	E. Germany (Meinhard Nehmer)	3:40.43
1980	E. Germany (Meinhard Nehmer)	3:59.92
1984	E. Germany (Wolfgang Hoppe)	3:20.22
1988	Switzerland (Ekkehard Fasser)	3:47.51
1992	Austria (Ingo Appelt)	3:53.90

2-Man Bob

		Time
1932	United States (Hubert Stevens)	8:14.74
1936	United States (Ivan Brown)	5:29.29
1948	Switzerland (F. Endrich)	5:29.20
1952	Germany (Andreas Ostler)	5:24.54
1956	Italy (Dalla Costa)	5:30.14
1964	Great Britain (Anthony Nash)	4:21.90
1968	Italy (Eugenio Monti)	4:41.54
1972	W. Germany (Wolfgang Zimmerer)	4:57.07
1976	E. Germany (Meinhard Nehmer)	3:44.42
1980	Switzerland (Erich Schaerer)	4:09.36
1984	E.Germany (Wolfgang Hoppe)	3:25.56
1988	USSR (Janis Kipours)	3:54.19
1992	Switzerland (Gustav Weber)	4:03.26

Luge

Men's Singles	Time
1964 Thomas Keohler, Germany	3:26.77
1968 Manfred Schmid, Austria	2:52.48
1972 Wolfgang Scheidel, E. Germany	3:27.58
1976 Detlef Guenther, E. Germany	3:27.688
1980 Bernhard Glass, E. Germany	2:54.796
1984 Paul Hildgartner, Italy	3:04.258
1988 Jens Mueller, E. Germany	3:05.548
1992 Georg Hackl, Germany	3:02.363

Men's Pairs	Time
1964 Austria	1:41.62
1968 E. Germany	1:35.85
1972 Italy, E. Germany (tie)	1:28.35
1976 E. Germany	1:25.604
1980 E. Germany	1:19.331
1984 W. Germany	1:23.620
1988 E. Germany	1:31.940
1992 Germany	1:32.053

Women's Singles	Time
1964 Ortun Enderlein, Germany	3:24.67
1968 Erica Lechner, Italy	2:28.66
1972 Anna M. Muller, E. Germany	2:59.18
1976 Margit Schumann, E. Germany	2:50.621
1980 Vera Zozulya, USSR	2:36.537
1984 Steffi Martin, E. Germany	2:46.570
1988 Steffi Walter, E. Germany	3:03.973
1992 Doris Neuner, Austria	3:06.696

Biathlon

Men's 10 Kilometers	Time
1980 Frank Ullrich, E. Germany	32:10.69
1984 Eirik Kvalfoss, Norway	30:53.80
1988 Frank-Peter Roetsch, E. Germany	25:08.10
1992 Mark Kirchner, Germany	26:02.30

Men's 20 Kilometers	Time
1960 Klas Lestander,Sweden	1:33:21.6
1964 Vladimir Melanin, USSR	1:20:26.8
1968 Magnar Solberg, Norway	1:13:45.9
1972 Magnar Solberg, Norway	1:15:55.50
1976 Nikolai Kruglov, USSR	1:14:12.26
1980 Anatoly Aljabiev, USSR	1:08:16.31
1984 Peter Angerer, W. Germany	1:11:52.7
1988 Frank-Peter Roetsch, E. Germany	0:56:33.33
1992 Yevgeny Redkine, Unified Team	0:57:34.4

Men's 30-Kilometer Relay	Time
1968 USSR, Norway, Sweden	2:13:02.4
1972 USSR, Finland, E. Germany	1:51:44.92
1976 USSR, Finland, E. Germany	1:57:55.64
1980 USSR, E. Germany, W. Germany (30 km.)	1:34:03.27
1984 USSR, Norway, W. Germany	1:38:51.70
1988 USSR, W. Germany, Italy	1:22:30.00
1992 Germany, Unified Team, Sweden	1:24:43.50

Women's 7.5 Kilometers	Time
1992 Anfissa Restsova, Unified Team	24:29.20

Women's 22.5 Kilometer Relay	Time
1992 France, Germany, Unified Team	1:15:55.6

Women's 15 Kilometers	Time
1992 Antje Misersky, Germany	51:47.2

Figure Skating

Men's Singles

1908 Ulrich Salchow, Sweden
1920 Gillis Grafstrom, Sweden
1924 Gillis Grafstrom, Sweden
1928 Gillis Grafstrom, Sweden
1932 Karl Schaefer, Austria
1936 Karl Schaefer, Austria
1948 Richard Button, U.S.
1952 Richard Button, U.S.
1956 Hayes Alan Jenkins, U.S.
1960 David W. Jenkins, U.S.
1964 Manfred Schnelldorfer, Germany
1968 Wolfgang Schwartz, Austria
1972 Ondrej Nepela, Czechoslovakia
1976 John Curry, Great Britain
1980 Robin Cousins, Great Britain
1984 Scott Hamilton, U.S.
1988 Brian Boitano, U.S.
1992 Viktor Petrenko, Unified Team

Women's Singles

1908 Madge Syers, Great Britain
1920 Magda Julin-Mauroy, Sweden
1924 Herma von Szabo-Planck, Austria
1928 Sonja Henie, Norway
1932 Sonja Henie, Norway
1936 Sonja Henie, Norway
1948 Barbara Ann Scott, Canada
1952 Jeanette Altwegg, Great Britain
1956 Tenley Albright, U.S.
1960 Carol Heiss, U.S.
1964 Sjoukje Dijkstra, Netherlands
1968 Peggy Fleming, U.S.
1972 Beatrix Schuba, Austria
1976 Dorothy Hamill, U.S.
1980 Anett Poetzsch, E. Germany
1984 Katarina Witt, E. Germany
1988 Katarina Witt, E. Germany
1992 Kristi Yamaguchi, U.S.

Pairs

1908 Anna Hubler & Heinrich Burger, Germany
1920 Ludovika & Walter Jakobsson, Finland
1924 Helene Engelman & Alfred Berger, Austria
1928 Andree Joly & Pierre Brunet, France
1932 Andree Joly & Pierre Brunet, France
1936 Maxi Herber & Ernst Baier, Germany
1948 Micheline Lannoy & Pierre Baugniet, Belgium
1952 Ria and Paul Falk, Germany
1956 Elisabeth Schwartz & Kurt Oppelt, Austria
1960 Barbara Wagner & Robert Paul, Canada
1964 Ludmila Beloussova & Oleg Protopopov, USSR
1968 Ludmila Beloussova & Oleg Protopopov, USSR
1972 Irina Rodnina & Alexei Ulanov, USSR
1976 Irina Rodnina & Aleksandr Zaitzev, USSR
1980 Irina Rodnina & Aleksandr Zaitzev, USSR
1984 Elena Valova & Oleg Vassiliev, USSR
1988 Ekaterina Gordeeva & Sergei Grinkov, USSR
1992 Natalia Mishkutienok & Artur Dimitriev, Unified Team

Ice Dancing

1976 Ludmila Pakhomova & Aleksandr Gorschkov, USSR
1980 Natalya Linichuk & Gennadi Karponosov, USSR
1984 Jayne Torvill & Christopher Dean, Great Britain
1988 Natalia Bestemianova & Andrei Bukin, USSR
1992 Marina Klimova & Sergei Ponomarenko, Unified Team

Ice Hockey

1920 Canada, U.S., Czechoslovakia
1924 Canada, U.S., Great Britain
1928 Canada, Sweden, Switzerland
1932 Canada, U.S., Germany
1936 Great Britain, Canada, U.S.
1948 Canada, Czechoslovakia, Switzerland
1952 Canada, U.S., Sweden
1956 USSR, U.S., Canada
1960 U.S., Canada, USSR
1964 USSR, Sweden, Czechoslovakia
1968 USSR, Czechoslovakia, Canada
1972 USSR, U.S., Czechoslovakia,
1976 USSR, Czechoslovakia, W. Germany
1980 U.S., USSR, Sweden
1984 USSR, Czechoslovakia, Sweden
1988 USSR, Finland, Sweden
1992 Unified Team, Canada, Czechlosovakia

Alpine Skiing

Men's Downhill	Time
1948 Henri Oreiller, France	2:55.0
1952 Zeno Colo, Italy	2:30.8
1956 Anton Sailer, Austria	2:52.2
1960 Jean Vuarnet, France	2:06.0
1964 Egon Zimmermann, Austria	2:18.16
1968 Jean-Claude Killy, France	1:59.85
1972 Bernhard Russi, Switzerland	1:51.43
1976 Franz Klammer, Austria	1:45.73
1980 Leonhard Stock, Austria	1:45.50
1984 Bill Johnson, U.S.	1:45:59

1988	Pirmin Zurbriggen, Switzerland	1:59.63
1992	Patrick Ortlieb, Austria	1:50.37

Men's Super Giant Slalom

		Time
1988	Franck Piccard, France	1:39.66
1992	Kjetil-Andre Aamodt, Norway	1:13.04

Men's Giant Slalom

		Time
1952	Stein Eriksen, Norway	2:25.0
1956	Anton Sailer, Austria	3:00.1
1960	Roger Staub, Switzerland	1:48.3
1964	Francois Bonlieu, France	1:46.71
1968	Jean-Claude Killy, France	3:29.28
1972	Gustavo Thoeni, Italy	3:09.62
1976	Heini Hemmi, Switzerland	3:26.97
1980	Ingemar Stenmark, Sweden	2:40.74
1984	Max Julen, Switzerland	2:41.18
1988	Alberto Tomba, Italy	2:06:37
1992	Alberto Tomba, Italy	2:06.98

Men's Slalom

		Time
1948	Edi Reinalter, Switzerland	2:10.3
1952	Othmar Schneider, Austria	2:00.0
1956	Anton Sailer, Austria	194.7 pts.
1960	Ernst Hinterseer, Austria	2:08.9
1964	Josef Stiegler, Austria	2:11.13
1968	Jean-Claude Killy, France	1:39.73
1972	Francisco Fernandez Ochoa, Spain	1:49.27
1976	Piero Gros, Italy	2:03.29
1980	Ingemar Stenmark, Sweden	1:44.26
1984	Phil Mahre, U.S.	1:39.41
1988	Alberto Tomba, Italy	1:39.47
1992	Finn Christian Jagge, Norway	1:44.39

Men's Combined

		Points
1988	Hubert Strolz, Austria	36.55
1992	Josef Polig, Italy	14.58

Women's Downhill

		Time
1948	Hedi Schlunegger, Switzerland	2:28.3
1952	Trude Jochum-Beiser, Austria	1:47.1
1956	Madeleine Berthod, Switzerland	1:40.7
1960	Heidi Biebl, Germany	1:37.6
1964	Christl Haas, Austria	1:55.39
1968	Olga Pall, Austria	1:40.87
1972	Marie Therese Nadig, Switzerland	1:36.68
1976	Rosi Mittermaier, W. Germany	1:46.16
1980	Annemarie Proell Moser, Austria	1:37.52
1984	Michela Figini, Switzerland	1:13.36
1988	Marina Kiehl, W. Germany	1:25.86
1992	Kerrin Lee-Gartner, Canada	1:52.55

Women's Super Giant Slalom

		Time
1988	Sigrid Wolf, Austria	1:19.03
1992	Deborah Compagnoni, Italy	1:21.22

Women's Giant Slalom

		Time
1952	Andrea Mead Lawrence, U.S.	2:06.8
1956	Ossi Reichert, Germany	1:56.5
1960	Yvonne Ruegg, Switzerland	1:39.9
1964	Marielle Goitschel, France	1:52.24
1968	Nancy Greene, Canada	1:51.97
1972	Marie Therese Nadig, Switzerland	1:29.90
1976	Kathy Kreiner, Canada	1:29.13
1980	Hanni Wenzel, Liechtenstein (2 runs)	2:41.66
1984	Debbie Armstrong, U.S.	2:20.98
1988	Vreni Schneider, Switzerland	2:06.49
1992	Pernilla Wiberg, Sweden	2:12.74

Women's Slalom

		Time
1948	Gretchen Fraser, U.S.	1:57.2
1952	Andrea Mead Lawrence, U.S.	2:10.6
1956	Renee Colliard, Switzerland	112.3 pts.
1960	Anne Heggtveigt, Canada	1:49.6
1964	Christine Goitschel, France	1:29.86
1968	Marielle Goitschel, France	1:25.86
1972	Barbara Cochran, U.S.	1:31.24
1976	Rosi Mittermaier, W. Germany	1:30.54
1980	Hanni Wenzel, Liechtenstein	1:25.09
1984	Paoletta Magoni, Italy	1:36.47
1988	Vreni Schneider, Switzerland	1:36.69
1992	Petra Kronberger, Austria	1:32.68

Women's Combined

		Points
1988	Anita Wachter, Austria	29.25
1992	Petra Kronberger, Austria	2.55

Freestyle Skiing

Men's Moguls

		Points
1992	Edgar Grospiron, France	25.81

Women's Moguls

		Points
1992	Donna Weinbrecht, U.S.	23.69

Cross-Country Skiing

Men's 10 kilometers (6.2 miles)

		Time
1992	Vegard Ulvang, Norway	27:36.0

Men's 15 kilometers (9.3 miles)

		Time
1924	Thorleif Haug, Norway	1:14:31
1928	Johan Grottumsbraaten, Norway	1:37:01
1932	Sven Utterstrom, Sweden	1:23:07
1936	Erik-August Larsson, Sweden	1:14:38
1948	Martin Lundstrom, Sweden	1:13:50
1952	Hallgeir Brenden, Norway	1:01:34
1956	Hallgeir Brenden, Norway	49:39.0
1960	Haakon Brusveen, Norway	51:55.5
1964	Eero Maentyranta, Finland	50:54.1
1968	Harald Groenningen, Norway	47:54.2
1972	Sven-Ake Lundback, Sweden	45:28.24
1976	Nikolai Balukov, USSR	43:58.47
1980	Thomas Wassberg, Sweden	41:57.63
1984	Gunde Svan, Sweden	41:25.6
1988	Mikhail Deviatiarov, USSR	41:18.9
1992	Bjorn Dahlie, Norway	38:01.9

(Note: approx. 18-km. course 1924-1952)

30 kilometers (18.6 miles)

		Time
1956	Veikko Hakulinen, Finland	1:44:06.0
1960	Sixten Jernberg, Sweden	1:51:03.9
1964	Eero Maentyranta, Finland	1:30:50.7
1968	Franco Nones, Italy	1:35:39.2
1972	Vyacheslav Vedenine, USSR	1:36:31.15
1976	Sergei Saveliev, USSR	1:30:29.38
1980	Nikolai Zimyatov, USSR	1:27:02.80
1984	Nikolai Zimyatov, USSR	1:28:56.3
1988	Aleksei Prokourorov, USSR	1:24:26.3
1992	Vegard Ulvang, Norway	1:22:27.8

50 kilometers (31.2 miles)

		Time
1924	Thorleif Haug, Norway	3:44:32.0
1928	Per Erik Hedlund, Sweden	4:52:03.0
1932	Veli Saarinen, Finland	4:28:00.0
1936	Elis Wiklund, Sweden	3:30:11.0
1948	Nils Karlsson, Sweden	3:47:48.0
1952	Veikko Hakulinen, Finland	3:33:33.0
1956	Sixten Jernberg, Sweden	2:50:27.0
1960	Kalevi Hamalainen, Finland	2:59:06.3
1964	Sixten Jernberg, Sweden	2:43:52.6
1968	Ole Ellefsaeter, Norway	2:28:45.8
1972	Paal Tyldum, Norway	2:43:14.75
1976	Ivar Formo, Norway	2:37:30.05
1980	Nikolai Zimyatov, USSR	2:27:24.60
1984	Thomas Wassberg, Sweden	2:15:55.8
1988	Gunde Svan, Sweden	2:04:30.9
1992	Bjorn Dahlie, Norway	2:03:41.5

40-km. Relay

		Time
1936	Finland, Norway, Sweden	2:41:33.0
1948	Sweden, Finland, Norway	2:32:08.0
1952	Finland, Norway, Sweden	2:20:16.0
1956	USSR, Finland, Sweden	2:15:30.0
1960	Finland, Norway, USSR	2:18:45.6
1964	Sweden, Finland, USSR	2:18:34.6
1968	Norway, Sweden, Finland	2:08:33.5
1972	USSR, Norway, Switzerland	2:04:47.94
1976	Finland, Norway, USSR	2:07:59.72
1980	USSR, Norway, Finland	1:57:03.46
1984	Sweden, USSR, Finland	1:55:06.30
1988	Sweden, USSR, Czechoslovakia	1:43:58.60
1992	Norway, Italy, Finland	1:39:26.00

Combined Cross-Country & Jumping

		Points
1924	Thorleif Haug, Norway	453.800
1928	Johan Grottumsbraaten, Norway	427.800
1932	Johan Grottumsbraaten, Norway	446.000
1936	Oddbjorn Hagen, Norway	430.300
1948	Heikki Hasu, Finland	448.800
1952	Simon Slattvik, Norway	451.621
1956	Sverre Stenersen, Norway	455.000
1960	Georg Thoma, Germany	457.952
1964	Tormod Knutsen, Norway	469.280

1968	Franz Keller, W. Germany	449.040
1972	Ulrich Wehling, E. Germany	413.340
1976	Ulrich Wehling, E. Germany	423.390
1980	Ulrich Wehling, E. Germany	432.200
1984	Tom Sandberg, Norway	422.595
1988	Hippolyt Kempf, Switzerland	235.8
1992	Fabrice Guy, France	426.470

	Men's Team Ski Jumping (90 meters)	Points
1988	Finland, Yugoslavia, Norway	634.4
1992	Finland, Austria, Czechoslovakia	644.4

	Ski Jumping (90 meters)	Points
1924	Jacob Thams, Norway	227.5
1928	Alfred Andersen, Norway	230.5
1932	Birger Ruud, Norway	228.1
1936	Birger Ruud, Norway	232.0
1948	Petter Hugsted, Norway	228.1
1952	Arnfinn Bergmann, Norway	226.0
1956	Antti Hyvarinen, Finland	227.0
1960	Helmut Recknagel, Germany	227.2
1964	Toralf Engan, Norway	230.7
1968	Vladimir Beloussov, USSR	231.3
1972	Wojiech Fortuna, Poland	219.9
1976	Karl Schnabl, Austria	234.8
1980	Jouko Tormanen, Finland	271.0
1984	Matti Nykaenen, Finland	231.2
1988	Matti Nykaenen, Finland	224.0
1992	Ernst Vettori, Austria	222.8

	Ski Jumping (120 meters)	Points
1992	Toni Nicminen, Finland	239.5

	Men's Nordic Team Combined	Time
1988	W. Germany, Switzerland, Austria	1:20:46.0
1992	Japan, Norway, Austria	1:23:36.5

Women's Events

	5 kilometers (approx. 3.1 miles)	Time
1964	Claudia Boyarskikh, USSR	17:50.5
1968	Toini Gustafsson, Sweden	16:45.2
1972	Galina Koulacova, USSR	17:00.50
1976	Helena Takalo, Finland	15:48.69
1980	Raisa Smetanina, USSR	15:06.92
1984	Marja-Liisa Haemaelainen, Finland	17:04.0
1988	Marjo Matikainen, Finland	15:04.0
1992	Marjut Lukkarinen, Finland	14:13.8

	10 kilometers (6.2 miles)	Time
1952	Lydia Wideman, Finland	41:40.0
1956	Lyubov Kosyreva, USSR	38:11.0
1960	Maria Gusakova, USSR	39:46.6
1964	Claudia Boyarskikh, USSR	40:24.3
1968	Toini Gustafsson, Sweden	36:46.5
1972	Galina Koulacova, USSR	34:17.82
1976	Raisa Smetanina, USSR	30:13.41
1980	Barbara Petzold, E. Germany	30:31.54
1984	Marja-Liisa Haemaelainen, Finland	31:44.2
1988	Vida Ventsene, USSR	30:08.3
1992	Lyubov Yegorova, Unified Team	25:53.7

	15 kilometers (9.3 miles)	Time
1992	Lyubov Yegorova, Unified Team	42:20.8

	30 kilometers (18.6 miles)	Time
1992	Stefania Belmondo, Italy	1:22:30.1

	20-km. Relay	Time
1956	Finland, USSR, Sweden (15 km.)	1:09:01.0
1960	Sweden, USSR, Finland (15 km.)	1:04:21.4
1964	USSR, Sweden, Finland (15 km.)	59:20.2
1968	Norway, Sweden, USSR (15 km.)	57:30.0
1972	USSR, Finland, Norway (15 km.)	48:46.15
1976	USSR, Finland, E. Germany	1:07:49.75
1980	E. Germany, USSR, Norway	1:02:11.10
1984	Norway, Czechoslovakia, Finland	1:06:49.70
1988	USSR, Norway, Finland	59:51.1
1992	United Team, Norway, Italy	59:34.8

Speed Skating

	Men's 500 meters	Time
1924	Charles Jewtraw, U.S.	0:44.0
1928	Thunberg, Finland & Evensen, Norway (tie)	0:43.4
1932	John A. Shea, U.S.	0:43.4
1936	Ivar Ballangrud, Norway	0:43.4
1948	Finn Helgesen, Norway	0:43.1
1952	Kenneth Henry, U.S.	0:43.2
1956	Evgeniy Grishin, USSR	0:40.2
1960	Evgeniy Grishin, USSR	0:40.2
1964	Terry McDermott, U.S.	0:40.1
1968	Erhard Keller, W. Germany	0:40.3
1972	Erhard Keller, W. Germany	0:39.44
1976	Evgeny Kulikov, USSR	0:39.17
1980	Eric Heiden, U.S.	0:38.03
1984	Sergei Fokichev, USSR	0:38.19
1988	Uwe-Jens Mey, E. Germany	0:36.45
1992	Uwe-Jens Mey, Germany	0:37.14

	Men's 1,000 meters	Time
1976	Peter Mueller, U.S.	1:19.32
1980	Eric Heiden, U.S.	1:15.18
1984	Gaetan Boucher, Canada	1:15.80
1988	Nikolai Guiliaev, USSR	1:13.03
1992	Olaf Zinke, Germany	1:14.85

	Men's 1,500 meters	Time
1924	Clas Thunberg, Finland	2:20.8
1928	Clas Thunberg, Finland	2:21.1
1932	John A. Shea, U.S.	2:57.5
1936	Charles Mathiesen, Norway	2:19.2
1948	Sverre Farstad, Norway	2:17.6
1952	Hjalmar Andersen, Norway	2:20.4
1956	Grishin, & Mikhailov, both USSR (tie)	2:08.6
1960	Aas, Norway & Grishin, USSR (tie)	2:10.4
1964	Ants Anston, USSR	2:10.3
1968	Cornetis Verkerk, Netherlands	2:03.4
1972	Ard Schenk, Netherlands	2:02.96
1976	Jan Egil Storholt, Norway	1:59.38
1980	Eric Heiden, U.S.	1:55.44
1984	Gaetan Boucher, Canada	1:58.36
1988	Andre Hoffmann, E. Germany	1:52.06
1992	Johann Koss, Norway	1:54.81

	Men's 5,000 meters	Time
1924	Clas Thunberg, Finland	8:39.0
1928	Ivar Ballangrud, Norway	8:50.5
1932	Irving Jaffee, U.S.	9:40.8
1936	Ivar Ballangrud, Norway	8:19.6
1948	Reidar Liaklev, Norway	8:29.4
1952	Hjalmar Andersen, Norway	8:10.6
1956	Boris Shilkov, USSR	7:48.7
1960	Viktor Kosichkin, USSR	7:51.3
1964	Knut Johannesen, Norway	7:38.4
1968	F. Anton Maier, Norway	7:22.4
1972	Ard Schenk, Netherlands	7:23.61
1976	Sten Stensen, Norway	7:24.48
1980	Eric Heiden, U.S.	7:02.29
1984	Sven Tomas Gustafson, Sweden	7:12.28
1988	Tomas Gustafson, Sweden	6:44.63
1992	Geir Karlstad, Norway	6:59.97

	Men's 10,000 meters	Time
1924	Julius Skutnabb, Finland	18:04.8
1928	Event not held, thawing of ice	
1932	Irving Jaffee, U.S.	19:13.6
1936	Ivar Ballangrud, Norway	17:24.3
1948	Ake Seyffarth, Sweden	17:26.3
1952	Hjalmar Andersen, Norway	16:45.8
1956	Sigvard Ericsson, Sweden	16:35.9
1960	Knut Johannesen, Norway	15:46.6
1964	Jonny Nilsson, Sweden	15:50.1
1968	Jonny Hoeglin, Sweden	15:23.6
1972	Ard Schenk, Netherlands	15:01.35
1976	Piet Kleine, Netherlands	14:50.59
1980	Eric Heiden, U.S.	14:28.13
1984	Igor Malkov, USSR	14:39.90
1988	Tomas Gustafson, Sweden	13:48.20
1992	Bart Veldkamp, Netherlands	14:12.12

	Women's 500 meters	Time
1960	Helga Haase, Germany	0:45.9
1964	Lydia Skoblikova, USSR	0:45.0
1968	Ludmila Titova, USSR	0:46.1
1972	Anne Henning, U.S.	0:43.33
1976	Sheila Young, U.S.	0:42.76
1980	Karin Enke, E. Germany	0:41.78
1984	Christa Rothenburger, E. Germany	0:41.02
1988	Bonnie Blair, U.S.	0:39.10
1992	Bonnie Blair, U.S.	0:40.33

	Women's 1,000 meters	Time
1960	Klara Guseva, USSR	1:34.1
1964	Lydia Skoblikova, USSR	1:33.2
1968	Carolina Geijssen, Netherlands	1:32.6
1972	Monika Pflug, W. Germany	1:31.40
1976	Tatiana Averina, USSR	1:28.43

1980	Natalya Petruseva, USSR	1:24.10
1984	Karin Enke, E. Germany	1:21.61
1988	Christa Rothenburger, E. Germany	1:17.65
1992	Bonnie Blair, U.S.	1:21.90

Women's 1,500 meters		Time
1960	Lydia Skoblikova, USSR	2:52.2
1964	Lydia Skoblikova, USSR	2:22.6
1968	Kaija Mustonen, Finland	2:22.4
1972	Dianne Holum, U.S.	2:20.85
1976	Galina Stepanskaya, USSR	2:16.58
1980	Anne Borckink, Netherlands	2:10.95
1984	Karin Enke, E. Germany	2:03.42
1988	Yvonne van Gennip, Netherlands	2:00.68
1992	Jacqueline Boerner, Germany	2:05.87

Women's 3,000 meters		Time
1960	Lydia Skoblikova, USSR	5:14.3
1964	Lydia Skoblikova, USSR	5:14.9
1968	Johanna Schut, Netherlands	4:56.2
1972	Christina Baas-Kaiser, Netherlands	4:52.14
1976	Tatiana Averina, USSR	4:45.19
1980	Bjoerg Eva Jensen, Norway	4:32.13
1984	Andrea Schoene, E. Germany	4:24.79
1988	Yvonne van Gennip, Netherlands	4:11.94
1992	Gunda Niemann, Germany	4:19.90

Women's 5,000 meters		Time
1988	Yvonne van Gennip, Netherlands	7:14:13
1992	Gunda Niemann, Germany	7:31.57

Short Track Speed Skating

Men's 1,000 meters		Time
1992	Kim Ki-Hoon, S. Korea	1:30.76

Men's 5,000-meter relay		Time
1992	S. Korea, Canada, Japan	7:14.02

Women's 500 meters		Time
1992	Cathy Turner, U.S.	47:04

Women's 3,000-meter relay		Time
1992	Canada, U.S., Unified Team	4:36.62

Winter Olympic Games in 1992

Albertville, France, Feb. 8-23, 1992

The 16th Olympics winter games in Albertville, France featured a record 2,174 athletes from 63 countries competing for medals. Germany, whose athletes won a games-high 26 medals, competed as a single team for the first time since 1964. The Unified Team, made up of some former Soviet republics, finished second with 23 medals.

Medal Winners

	Gold	Silver	Bronze	Total
Germany	10	10	6	26
Unified Team	9	6	8	23
Austria	6	7	8	21
Norway	9	6	5	20
Italy	4	6	4	14
United States	5	4	2	11
France	3	5	1	9
Canada	2	3	2	7
Finland	3	1	3	7
Japan	1	2	4	7
Netherlands	1	1	2	4
South Korea	2	1	1	4
Sweden	1	0	3	4
China	0	3	0	3
Czechoslovakia	0	0	3	3
Switzerland	1	0	2	3
Luxembourg	0	2	0	2
New Zealand	0	1	0	1
North Korea	0	0	1	1
Spain	0	0	1	1

HOCKEY

National Hockey League, 1992-1993

Final Standings

Wales Conference

Adams Division

	W	L	T	GF	GA	PTS
Boston	51	26	7	332	268	109
Quebec	47	27	10	351	300	104
Montreal	48	30	6	326	280	102
Buffalo	38	36	10	335	297	86
Hartford	26	52	6	284	369	58
Ottawa	10	70	4	202	395	24

Patrick Division

	W	L	T	GF	GA	PTS
Pittsburgh	56	21	7	367	268	119
Washington	43	34	7	325	286	93
N.Y. Islanders	40	37	7	335	297	87
New Jersey	40	37	7	308	299	87
Philadelphia	36	37	11	319	319	83
N.Y. Rangers	34	39	11	304	308	79

Campbell Conference

Norris Division

	W	L	T	GF	GA	PTS
Chicago	47	25	12	279	230	106
Detroit	47	28	9	369	280	103
Toronto	44	29	11	288	241	99
St. Louis	37	36	11	282	278	85
Minnesota	36	38	10	272	293	82
Tampa Bay	23	54	7	245	332	53

Smythe Division

	W	L	T	GF	GA	PTS
Vancouver	46	29	9	346	278	101
Calgary	43	30	11	322	282	97
Los Angeles	39	35	10	338	340	88
Winnipeg	40	37	7	322	320	87
Edmonton	26	50	8	242	337	60
San Jose	11	71	2	218	414	24

Montreal Wins Stanley Cup Championship

The Montreal Canadiens won the 1993 Stanley Cup by defeating the Los Angeles Kings in five games. It was the 24th Stanley Cup championship for the Canadiens. Montreal goalie Patrick Roy won the Conn Smythe Trophy as the most valuable player in the playoffs.

Stanley Cup Playoff Results

Wales Conference

Buffalo defeated Boston 4-0
Pittsburgh defeated New Jersey 4-1
N.Y. Islanders defeated Washington 4-2
Montreal defeated Quebec 4-2
Montreal defeated Buffalo 4-0
N.Y. Islanders defeated Pittsburgh 4-3
Montreal defeated N.Y. Islanders 4-1

Campbell Conference

St. Louis defeated Chicago 4-0
Vancouver defeated Winnipeg 4-2
Los Angeles defeated Calgary 4-2
Toronto defeated Detroit 4-3
Los Angeles defeated Vancouver 4-2
Toronto defeated St. Louis 4-3
Los Angeles defeated Toronto 4-3

Finals

Montreal defeated Los Angeles 4-1

Stanley Cup Champions Since 1927

Year	Champion	Coach	Final opponent
1927	Ottawa	Dave Gill	Boston
1928	N.Y. Rangers	Lester Patrick	Montreal
1929	Boston	Cy Denneny	N.Y. Rangers
1930	Montreal	Cecil Hart	Boston
1931	Montreal	Cecil Hart	Chicago
1932	Toronto	Dick Irvin	N.Y. Rangers
1933	N.Y. Rangers	Lester Patrick	Toronto
1934	Chicago	Tommy Gorman	Detroit
1935	Montreal Maroons	Tommy Gorman	Toronto
1936	Detroit	Jack Adams	Toronto
1937	Detroit	Jack Adams	N.Y. Rangers
1938	Chicago	Bill Stewart	Toronto
1939	Boston	Art Ross	Toronto
1940	N.Y. Rangers	Frank Boucher	Toronto
1941	Boston	Cooney Weiland	Detroit
1942	Toronto	Hap Day	Detroit
1943	Detroit	Jack Adams	Boston
1944	Montreal	Dick Irvin	Chicago
1945	Toronto	Hap Day	Detroit
1946	Montreal	Dick Irvin	Boston
1947	Toronto	Hap Day	Montreal
1948	Toronto	Hap Day	Detroit
1949	Toronto	Hap Day	Detroit
1950	Detroit	Tommy Ivan	N.Y. Rangers
1951	Toronto	Joe Primeau	Montreal
1952	Detroit	Tommy Ivan	Montreal
1953	Montreal	Dick Irvin	Boston
1954	Detroit	Tommy Ivan	Montreal
1955	Detroit	Jimmy Skinner	Montreal
1956	Montreal	Toe Blake	Detroit
1957	Montreal	Toe Blake	Boston
1958	Montreal	Toe Blake	Boston
1959	Montreal	Toe Blake	Toronto
1960	Montreal	Toe Blake	Toronto
1961	Chicago	Rudy Pilous	Detroit
1962	Toronto	Punch Imlach	Chicago
1963	Toronto	Punch Imlach	Detroit
1964	Toronto	Punch Imlach	Detroit
1965	Montreal	Toe Blake	Chicago
1966	Montreal	Toe Blake	Detroit
1967	Toronto	Punch Imlach	Montreal
1968	Montreal	Toe Blake	St. Louis
1969	Montreal	Claude Ruel	St. Louis
1970	Boston	Harry Sinden	St. Louis
1971	Montreal	Al MacNeil	Chicago
1972	Boston	Tom Johnson	N.Y. Rangers
1973	Montreal	Scotty Bowman	Chicago
1974	Philadelphia	Fred Shero	Boston
1975	Philadelphia	Fred Shero	Buffalo
1976	Montreal	Scotty Bowman	Philadelphia
1977	Montreal	Scotty Bowman	Boston
1978	Montreal	Scotty Bowman	Boston
1979	Montreal	Scotty Bowman	N.Y. Rangers
1980	N.Y. Islanders	Al Arbour	Philadelphia
1981	N.Y. Islanders	Al Arbour	Minnesota
1982	N.Y. Islanders	Al Arbour	Vancouver
1983	N.Y. Islanders	Al Arbour	Edmonton
1984	Edmonton	Glen Sather	N.Y. Islanders
1985	Edmonton	Glen Sather	Philadelphia
1986	Montreal	Jean Perron	Calgary
1987	Edmonton	Glen Sather	Philadelphia
1988	Edmonton	Glen Sather	Boston
1989	Calgary	Terry Crisp	Montreal
1990	Edmonton	John Muckler	Boston
1991	Pittsburgh	Bob Johnson	Minnesota
1992	Pittsburgh	Scotty Bowman	Chicago
1993	Montreal	Jacques Demers	Los Angeles

Individual Leaders

Points

Mario Lemieux, Pittsburgh, 160; Pat Lafontaine, Buffalo, 148; Adam Oates, Boston, 142; Steve Yzerman, Detroit, 137; Teemu Selanne, Winnipeg, 132; Pierre Turgeon, N.Y. Islanders, 132.

Goals

Alexander Mogilny, Buffalo, 76; Teemu Selanne, Winnipeg, 76; Mario Lemieux, Pittsburgh, 69; Luc Robitaille, Los Angeles, 63; Pavel Bure, Vancouver, 60.

Assists

Adam Oates, Boston, 97; Doug Gilmour, Toronto, 95; Pat Lafontaine, Buffalo, 95; Mario Lemieux, Pittsburgh, 91; Craig Janney, St. Louis, 82.

Power-play goals

Dave Andreychuk, Buff.-Tor., 32; Brett Hull, St. Louis, 29; Alexander Mogilny, Buffalo, 27; Kevin Stevens, Pittsburgh, 26.

Shorthanded goals

Pavel Bure, Vancouver, 7; Steve Yzerman, Detroit, 7; Mario Lemieux, Pittsburgh, 6; Scott Young, Quebec, 6.

Shooting percentage

(minimum 80 shots)

Craig Simpson, Edmonton, 26.4; Petr Nedved, Vancouver, 25.5; Dimitri Khristich, Washington, 24.4; Mario Lemieux, Pittsburgh, 24.1; Luc Robitaille, Los Angeles, 23.8.

Plus/Minus

Mario Lemieux, Pittsburgh, 55; Larry Murphy, Pittsburgh, 45; Ray Bourque, Boston, 38; Ulf Samuelsson, Pittsburgh, 36; Lyle Odelein, Montreal, 35; Pavel Bure, Vancouver, 35.

GOALTENDING LEADERS

(minimum 25 games)

Goals against average

Felix Potvin, Toronto, 2.50; Ed Belfour, Chicago, 2.59; Tom Barrasso, Pittsburgh, 3.01; Curtis Joseph, St. Louis, 3.02; Kay Whitmore, Vancouver, 3.10.

Wins

Tom Barrasso, Pittsburgh, 43; Ed Belfour, Chicago, 41; Andy Moog, Boston, 37; Tim Cheveldae, Detroit, 34; Bob Essensa, Winnipeg, 33.

Save percentage

Curtis Joseph, St. Louis, .911; Felix Potvin, Toronto, .910; Ed Belfour, Chicago; .906; Tom Barrasso, Pittsburgh, .901; John Vanbiesbrouck, N.Y. Rangers, .900.

Shutouts

Ed Belfour, Chicago, 7; Tommy Soderstrom, Philadelphia, 5; John Vanbiesbrouck, N.Y. Rangers, 4; Tom Barrasso, Pittsburgh, 4; Tim Cheveldae, Detroit, 4.

Individual Scoring

(40 or more games played)

Boston Bruins

	GP	G	A	Pts	+/–	PIM
Adam Oates	84	45	97	142	15	32
Joe Juneau	84	32	70	102	23	33
Ray Bourque	78	19	63	82	38	40
Dmitri Kvartalnov	73	30	42	72	9	16
Stephen Leach	79	26	25	51	6–	126
Dave Poulin	84	16	33	49	29	62
Vladimir Ruzicka	60	19	22	41	6–	38
Dave Reid	65	20	16	36	12	10
Ted Donato	82	15	20	35	2	61
Don Sweeney	84	7	27	34	34	68
Glen Wesley	64	8	25	33	2–	47
Stephen Heinze	73	18	13	31	20	24
David Shaw	77	10	14	24	10	108
Gord Murphy	49	5	12	17	13–	62
Gordie Roberts	65	5	12	17	23	105
C.J. Young	43	7	7	14	6–	32
Darin Kimble	55	7	3	10	4	177
Brent Hughes	62	5	4	9	4–	191
Andy Moog	55	0	1	1	0	14

Coach—Brian Sutter

Buffalo Sabres

	GP	G	A	Pts	+/–	PIM
Pat Lafontaine	84	53	95	148	11	63
Alexander Mogilny	77	76	51	127	7	40
Dale Hawerchuk	81	16	80	96	17–	52
Doug Bodger	81	9	45	54	14	87
Bob Sweeney	80	21	26	47	2	118
Randy Wood	82	18	25	43	6	77
Yuri Khmylev	68	20	19	39	6	28
Wayne Presley	79	15	17	32	5	96
Richard Smehlik	80	4	27	31	9	59
Brad May	82	13	13	26	3	242
Petr Svoboda	40	2	24	26	3	59
Ken Sutton	63	8	14	22	3–	30
Dave Hannan	55	5	15	20	8	43
Donald Audette	44	12	7	19	8–	51
Bob Errey	62	9	9	18	0	80
Grant Ledyard	50	2	14	16	2–	45
Gord Donnelly	60	3	8	11	5	221
Bob Corkum	68	6	4	10	3–	38
Rob Ray	68	3	2	5	3–	211
Grant Fuhr	58	0	0	0	0–	10

Coach—John Muckler

Calgary Flames

	GP	G	A	Pts	+/–	PIM
Theoren Fleury	83	34	66	100	14	88
Robert Reichel	80	40	48	88	25	54
Gary Suter	81	23	58	81	1–	112
Gary Roberts	58	38	41	79	32	172
Joe Nieuwendyk	79	38	37	75	9	52
Sergei Makarov	71	18	39	57	0	40
Al MacInnis	50	11	43	54	15	61
Joel Otto	75	19	33	52	2	150
Paul Ranheim	83	21	22	43	4–	26
Greg Paslawski	73	18	24	42	3	12
Ronnie Stern	70	10	15	25	4	207
Brent Ashton	58	10	13	23	11	52
Chris Lindberg	62	9	12	21	3–	18
Roger Johansson	77	4	16	20	13	62
Trent Yawney	63	1	16	17	9	67
Frank Musil	80	6	10	16	28	131
Craig Berube	77	4	8	12	6–	209
Kevin Dahl	61	2	9	11	9	56
Chris Dahlquist	74	3	7	10	0	66
Mike Vernon	64	0	2	2	0	42

Coach—Dave King

Chicago Blackhawks

	GP	G	A	Pts	+/–	PIM
Jeremy Roenick	84	50	57	107	15	86
Chris Chelios	84	15	58	73	14	282
Steve Larmer	84	35	35	70	23	48
Steve Smith	78	10	47	57	12	214
Brent Sutter	65	20	34	54	10	67
Christian Ruuttu	84	17	37	54	14	134
Michel Goulet	63	23	21	44	10	41
Dirk Graham	84	20	17	37	0	141
Stephane Matteau	79	15	18	33	6	98
Greg Gilbert	77	13	19	32	5	57
Jocelyn Lemieux	81	10	21	31	5	111
Brian Noonan	63	16	14	30	3	82
Bryan Marchment	78	5	15	20	15	313
Frantisek Kucera	71	5	14	19	7	59
Dave Christian	60	4	14	18	6	12
Troy Murray	51	4	7	11	15–	59
Craig Muni	81	0	11	11	14–	75
Cam Russell	67	2	4	6	5	151
Ed Belfour	71	0	3	3	0	28
Stu Grimson	78	1	1	2	2	193

Coach—Darryl Sutter

Detroit Red Wings

	GP	G	A	Pts	+/–	PIM
Steve Yzerman	84	58	79	137	33	44
Dino Ciccarelli	82	41	56	97	12	81
Sergei Fedorov	73	34	53	87	33	72
Paul Coffey	80	12	75	87	16	77
Ray Sheppard	70	32	34	66	7	29
Paul Ysebaert	80	34	28	62	19	42
Steve Chiasson	79	12	50	62	14	155
Dallas Drake	72	18	26	44	15	93
Bob Probert	80	14	29	43	9–	292
Nicklas Lidstrom	84	7	34	41	7	28
Yves Racine	80	9	31	40	10	80
Shawn Burr	80	10	25	35	18	74
Mark Howe	60	3	31	34	22	22
Keith Primeau	73	15	17	32	6–	152
Sheldon Kennedy	68	19	11	30	1–	46
Gerard Gallant	67	10	20	30	20	188
Vlad. Konstantinov	82	5	17	22	22	137
Mike Sillinger	51	4	17	21	0	16
Jim Hiller	61	8	12	20	7	109
Steve Konroyd	65	3	12	15	15–	67
Brad McCrimmon	60	1	14	15	21	71
Tim Cheveldae	67	0	4	4	0	4

Coach—Bryan Murray

Edmonton Oilers

	GP	G	A	Pts	+/–	PIM
Petr Klima	68	32	16	48	15–	100
Doug Weight	78	17	31	48	2	65
Shayne Corson	80	16	31	47	19–	209
Craig Simpson	60	24	22	46	14–	36
Dave Manson	83	15	30	45	28–	210
Todd Elik	60	14	27	41	4–	56
Zdeno Ciger	64	13	23	36	13–	8
Brian Benning	55	10	24	34	1–	152
Scott Mellanby	69	15	17	32	4–	147
Kelly Buchberger	83	12	18	30	27–	133
Craig MacTavish	82	10	20	30	16–	110
Igor Kravchuk	55	10	17	27	3	32
Martin Gelinas	65	11	12	23	3	30
Kevin Todd	55	9	14	23	9–	26
Shjon Podein	40	13	6	19	2–	25
Geoff Smith	78	4	14	18	11–	30
Brian Glynn	64	4	12	16	13–	60
Luke Richardson	82	3	10	13	18–	142
Louie Debrusk	51	8	2	10	16–	205
Mike Hudson	41	1	7	8	7–	46
Bill Ranford	67	0	3	3	0	10

Coach—Ted Green

Hartford Whalers

	GP	G	A	Pts	+/–	PIM
Geoff Sanderson	82	46	43	89	21–	28
Andrew Cassels	84	21	64	85	11–	62
Pat Verbeek	84	39	43	82	7–	197
Zarley Zalapski	83	14	51	65	34–	94
Terry Yake	66	22	31	53	3	46
Patrick Poulin	81	20	31	51	19–	37
Eric Weinrich	79	7	29	36	11–	76
Michael Nylander	59	11	22	33	7–	36
Mark Janssens	76	12	17	29	15–	237
Nick Kypreos	75	17	10	27	5–	325
Robert Kron	45	14	13	27	5	18
Yvon Corriveau	57	8	12	20	20–	14
Adam Burt	65	6	14	20	11–	116
Robert Petrovicky	42	3	6	9	10–	45
Jim McKenzie	64	3	6	9	10–	202
Doug Houda	60	2	6	8	19–	167
Randy Ladouceur	62	2	4	6	18–	109

	GP	G	A	Pts	+/–	PIM
Allen Pedersen	59	1	4	5	0	60
Sean Burke	50	0	2	2	0	25

Coach—Paul Holmgren

Los Angeles Kings

	GP	G	A	Pts	+/–	PIM
Luc Robitaille	84	63	62	125	18	100
Jari Kurri	82	27	60	87	19	38
Tony Granato	81	37	45	82	1–	171
Jimmy Carson	86	37	36	73	2–	32
Mike Donnelly	84	29	40	69	17	45
Wayne Gretzky	45	16	49	65	6	6
Rob Blake	76	16	43	59	18	152
Alexei Zhitnik	78	12	36	48	3–	80
Marty McSorley	81	15	26	41	1	399
Corey Millen	42	23	16	39	16	42
Darryl Sydor	80	6	23	29	2–	63
Charlie Huddy	82	2	25	27	16	64
Lonnie Loach	53	10	13	23	3	27
Pat Conacher	81	9	8	17	16–	20
Dave Taylor	48	6	9	15	1	49
Mark Hardy	55	1	13	14	2–	89
Warren Rychel	70	6	7	13	15–	314
Kelly Hrudey	50	0	4	4	0	10

Coach—Barry Melrose

Minnesota North Stars

	GP	G	A	Pts	+/–	PIM
Mike Modano	82	33	60	93	7–	83
Russ Courtnall	84	36	43	79	1	49
Dave Gagner	84	33	43	76	13–	141
Ulf Dahlen	83	35	39	74	20–	6
Mark Tinordi	69	15	27	42	1–	157
Mike McPhee	84	18	22	40	2–	44
Mike Craig	70	15	23	38	11–	106
Tommy Sjodin	77	7	29	36	25–	30
Neal Broten	82	12	21	33	7	22
Gaetan Duchesne	84	16	13	29	6	32
Trent Klatt	47	4	19	23	2	38
Jim Johnson	79	3	20	23	9	105
Brent Gilchrist	68	10	11	21	12–	49
Shane Churla	73	5	16	21	8–	286
Derian Hatcher	67	4	15	19	27–	178
Stewart Gavin	63	10	8	18	4–	59
Bobby Smith	45	5	7	12	9–	10
Craig Ludwig	78	1	10	11	1	153
Richard Matvichuk	53	2	3	5	8–	26
Mark Osiecki	43	1	4	5	20–	19
Jon Casey	60	0	3	3	0	28
Brad Berry	63	0	3	3	2	109

Coach—Bob Gainey

Montreal Canadiens

	GP	G	A	Pts	+/–	PIM
Vincent Damphousse	84	39	58	97	5	98
Kirk Muller	80	37	57	94	8	77
Brian Bellows	82	40	48	88	4	44
Stephan Lebeau	71	31	49	80	23	20
Mike Keane	77	15	45	60	29	95
Denis Savard	63	16	34	50	1	90
Gilbert Dionne	75	20	28	48	5	63
Eric Desjardins	82	13	32	45	20	98
John Leclair	72	19	25	44	11	33
Matt Schneider	60	13	31	44	8	91
Gary Leeman	50	15	17	32	14	24
Patrice Brisebois	70	10	21	31	6	79
Kevin Haller	73	11	14	25	7	117
Benoit Brunet	47	10	15	25	13	19
J. J. Daigneault	66	8	10	18	25	57
Rob Ramage	74	5	13	18	24–	146
Guy Carbonneau	61	4	13	17	9–	20
Lyle Odelein	83	2	14	16	35	205
Todd Ewen	75	5	9	14	6	193
Ed Ronan	53	5	7	12	6	20
Mario Roberge	50	4	4	8	2	142
Patrick Roy	62	0	2	2	0	16

Coach—Jacques Demers

New Jersey Devils

	GP	G	A	Pts	+/–	PIM
Claude Lemieux	77	30	51	81	3	155
Alexander Semak	82	37	42	79	24	70
Stephane Richer	78	38	35	73	1–	44
Valeri Zelepukin	78	23	41	64	19	70
Bernie Nicholls	69	13	47	60	13–	80
Scott Stevens	81	12	45	57	14	120
Bruce Driver	83	14	40	54	10–	66
John Maclean	80	24	24	48	6	102
Peter Stastny	62	17	23	40	5–	22
Scott Niedermayer	80	11	29	40	8	47
Bobby Holik	61	20	19	39	6–	76
Bill Guerin	65	14	20	34	14	63
Viacheslav Fetisov	76	4	23	27	7	158
Randy McKay	73	11	11	22	0	206
Scott Pellerin	45	10	11	21	1–	41
Tom Chorske	50	7	12	19	1–	25
Alexei Kasatonov	64	3	14	17	4	57
Dave Barr	62	6	8	14	1	61
Ken Daneyko	84	2	11	13	4	236
Craig Billington	42	0	1	1	0	8
Chris Terreri	48	0	0	0	0	6

Coach—Herb Brooks

New York Islanders

	GP	G	A	Pts	+/–	PIM
Pierre Turgeon	83	58	74	132	1–	26
Steve Thomas	79	37	50	87	3	111
Derek King	77	38	38	76	3–	47
Benoit Hogue	70	33	42	75	13	108
Patrick Flatley	80	13	47	60	4	63
Vladimir Malakhov	64	14	38	52	14	59
Jeff Norton	66	12	38	50	3–	45
Uwe Krupp	80	9	29	38	7	67
Tom Kurvers	52	8	30	38	8	38
Brian Mullen	81	18	14	32	5	28
Brad Dalgarno	57	15	17	32	17	62
Marty McInnis	56	10	20	30	7	24
Ray Ferraro	46	14	13	27	0	40
Tom Fitzgerald	77	9	18	27	2–	34
Travis Green	61	7	18	25	4	43
Scott Lachance	75	7	17	24	1–	67
Dave Volek	56	8	13	21	1–	34
Darius Kasparaitis	79	4	17	21	15	166
Claude Loiselle	41	5	3	8	5–	90
Mick Vukota	74	2	5	7	3	216
Richard Pilon	44	1	3	4	4–	164
Glenn Healy	47	0	2	2	0	2

Coach—Al Arbour

New York Rangers

	GP	G	A	Pts	+/–	PIM
Mark Messier	75	25	66	91	6–	72
Tony Amonte	83	33	43	76	0	49
Mike Gartner	84	45	23	68	4–	59
Adam Graves	84	36	29	65	4–	148
Sergei Nemchinov	81	23	31	54	15	34
Darren Turcotte	71	25	28	53	3–	40
Ed Olczyk	71	21	28	49	2–	52
Esa Tikkanen	81	16	24	40	24–	94
Alexei Kovalev	65	20	18	38	10–	79
Sergei Zubov	49	8	23	31	1–	4
James Patrick	60	5	21	26	1	61
Phil Bourque	55	6	14	20	9–	39
Jeff Beukeboom	82	2	17	19	9	153
Jan Erixon	45	5	11	16	11	10
Kevin Lowe	49	3	12	15	2–	58
Paul Broten	60	5	9	14	6–	48
Jay Wells	53	1	9	10	2–	107
Joe Cirella	55	3	6	9	1	85
Joey Kocur	65	3	6	9	9–	131
Mike Hartman	61	4	4	8	7–	160
John McIntyre	60	3	5	8	14–	84
John Vanbiesbrouck	48	0	1	1	0	18

Coach—Roger Neilson; Ron Smith

Ottawa Senators

	GP	G	A	Pts	+/–	PIM
Norm Maciver	80	17	46	63	46–	84
Jamie Baker	76	19	29	48	20–	54
Sylvain Turgeon	72	25	18	43	29–	104
Bob Kudelski	63	24	17	41	25–	30
Brad Shaw	81	7	34	41	47–	34
Jody Hull	69	13	21	34	24–	14
Mark Lamb	71	7	19	26	40–	64
Mike Peluso	81	15	10	25	35–	318
Mark Freer	63	10	14	24	35–	39
Neil Brady	55	7	17	24	25–	57
Andrew McBain	59	7	16	23	37–	43
Laurie Boschman	70	9	7	16	26–	101
Darren Rumble	69	3	13	16	24–	61
David Archibald	44	9	6	15	16–	32
Doug Smail	51	4	10	14	34–	51
Tomas Jelinek	49	7	6	13	21–	52

Chris Luongo	76	3	9	12	47–	68
Rob Murphy	44	3	7	10	23–	30
Darcy Loewen	79	4	5	9	26–	145
Ken Hammond	62	4	4	8	42–	104
Brad Marsh	59	0	3	3	29–	30
Peter Sidorkiewicz	64	0	0	0	0	8

Coach—Rick Bowness

Philadelphia Flyers

	GP	G	A	Pts	+/–	PIM
Mark Recchi	84	53	70	123	1	95
Rod Brind'Amour	81	37	49	86	8–	89
Eric Lindros	61	41	34	75	28	147
Kevin Dineen	83	35	28	63	14	201
Garry Galley	83	13	49	62	18	115
Brent Fedyk	74	21	38	59	14	48
Per-Erik Eklund	55	11	38	49	12	16
Greg Hawgood	69	11	35	46	8–	74
Josef Beranek	66	15	18	33	8–	78
Dimitri Yushkevich	82	5	27	32	12	71
Keith Acton	83	8	15	23	10–	51
Doug Evans	65	8	13	21	9–	70
Andrei Lomakin	51	8	12	20	15	34
Terry Carkner	83	3	16	19	18	150
Ric Nattress	44	7	10	17	1	29
V. Butsayev	52	2	14	16	3	61
Ryan McGill	72	3	10	13	9	238
Tommy Soderstrom	44	0	2	2	0	4
Dave Brown	70	0	2	2	5–	78

Coach—Bill Dineen

Pittsburgh Penguins

	GP	G	A	Pts	+/–	PIM
Mario Lemieux	60	69	91	160	55	38
Kevin Stevens	72	55	56	111	17	177
Rick Tocchet	80	48	61	109	28	252
Ron Francis	84	24	76	100	6	68
Jaromir Jagr	81	34	60	94	30	61
Larry Murphy	83	22	63	85	45	73
Joe Mullen	72	33	37	70	19	14
Shawn McEachern	84	28	33	61	21	46
Ulf Samuelsson	77	3	26	29	36	249
Dave Tippett	74	6	19	25	5	56
Troy Loney	82	5	16	21	1	99
Jim Paek	77	3	15	18	13	64
Paul Stanton	77	4	12	16	7	97
Martin Straka	42	3	13	16	2	29
Peter Taglianetti	72	2	12	14	12	184
Mike Needham	56	8	5	13	1–	14
Mike Stapleton	78	4	9	13	8–	10
Mike Ramsey	45	3	10	13	17	28
Jeff Daniels	58	5	4	9	5–	14
Kjell Samuelsson	63	3	6	9	25	106
Tom Barrasso	63	0	8	8	0	24
Grant Jennings	58	0	5	5	6	65

Coach—Scotty Bowman

Quebec Nordiques

	GP	G	A	Pts	+/–	PIM
Mats Sundin	80	47	67	114	21	96
Joe Sakic	78	48	57	105	3–	40
Steve Duchesne	82	20	62	82	15	57
Mike Ricci	77	27	51	78	8	123
Owen Nolan	73	36	41	77	1–	185
Andrei Kovalenko	81	27	41	68	13	57
Scott Young	82	30	30	60	5	20
Martin Rucinsky	77	18	30	48	16	51
Claude LaPointe	74	10	26	36	5	98
Curtis Leschyshyn	82	9	23	32	25	61
Mike Hough	77	8	22	30	11–	69
Alexei Gusarov	79	8	22	30	18	57
Gino Cavallini	67	9	15	24	10	34
Kerry Huffman	52	4	18	22	0	54
Adam Foote	81	4	12	16	6	168
Scott Pearson	41	13	1	14	3	95
Steven Finn	80	5	9	14	3–	160
Bill Lindsay	44	4	9	13	0	16
Ron Hextall	54	0	2	2	0	56

Coach—Pierre Page

St. Louis Blues

	GP	G	A	Pts	+/–	PIM
Craig Janney	84	24	82	106	4–	12
Brett Hull	80	54	47	101	27–	41
Brendan Shanahan	71	51	43	94	10	174
Jeff Brown	71	25	53	78	6–	58
Nelson Emerson	82	22	51	73	2	62
Kevin Miller	82	24	25	49	2	100
Doug Crossman	59	10	28	38	7–	28
Rich Sutter	84	13	14	27	4–	100
Ron Sutter	59	12	15	27	11–	99
Igor Korolev	74	4	23	27	1–	20
Bob Bassen	53	9	10	19	0	63
Ron Wilson	78	8	11	19	8–	44
Garth Butcher	84	5	10	15	0	211
Rick Zombo	71	0	15	15	2–	78
Dave Lowry	58	5	8	13	18–	101
Philippe Bozon	54	6	6	12	3–	55
Stephane Quintal	75	1	10	11	6–	100
Basil McRae	47	3	6	9	16–	169
Bret Hedican	42	0	8	8	2–	30
Kelly Chase	49	2	5	7	9–	204
Murray Baron	53	2	2	4	5–	59
Curt Giles	48	0	4	4	2	40
Curtis Joseph	68	0	2	2	0	8

Coach—Bob Plager; Bob Berry

San Jose Sharks

	GP	G	A	Pts	+/–	PIM
Kelly Kisio	78	26	52	78	15–	90
Johan Garpenlov	79	22	44	66	26–	56
Rob Gaudreau	59	23	20	43	18–	18
Dean Evason	84	12	19	31	35–	132
Pat Falloon	41	14	14	28	25–	12
Jeff Odgers	66	12	15	27	26–	253
Tom Pederson	44	7	13	20	16–	31
Doug Wilson	42	3	17	20	28–	40
Mark Pederson	41	10	7	17	22–	28
John Carter	55	7	9	16	25–	81
Doug Zmolek	84	5	10	15	50–	229
Mike Sullivan	81	6	8	14	42–	30
David Williams	40	1	11	12	27–	49
Jay More	73	5	6	11	35–	179
David Maley	56	2	7	9	28–	155
Peter Ahola	50	3	5	8	10–	36
Neil Wilkinson	59	1	7	8	50–	96
Rob Zettler	80	0	7	7	50–	150
Robin Bawa	42	5	0	5	25–	47

Coach—George Kingston

Tampa Bay Lightning

	GP	G	A	Pts	+/–	PIM
Brian Bradley	80	42	44	86	24–	92
John Tucker	78	17	39	56	12–	69
Chris Kontos	66	27	24	51	7–	12
Rob Zamuner	84	15	28	43	25–	74
Adam Creighton	83	19	20	39	19–	110
Shawn Chambers	55	10	29	39	21–	36
Bob Beers	64	12	24	36	25–	70
Marc Bureau	63	10	21	31	12–	111
Mikael Andersson	77	16	11	27	14–	14
Danton Cole	67	12	15	27	2–	23
Rob DiMaio	54	9	15	24	0	62
Roman Hamrlik	67	6	15	21	21–	71
Steve Maltais	63	7	13	20	20–	35
Marc Bergevin	78	2	12	14	16–	66
Joe Reekie	42	2	11	13	2	69
Steve Kasper	68	4	7	11	17–	20
Randy Gilhen	44	3	4	7	14–	14
Pat Jablonski	43	0	2	2	0	7

Coach—Terry Crisp

Toronto Maple Leafs

	GP	G	A	Pts	+/–	PIM
Doug Gilmour	83	32	95	127	32	100
Dave Andreychuk	83	54	45	99	4	56
Nikolai Borschevsky	78	34	40	74	33	28
Glenn Anderson	76	22	43	65	19	117
John Cullen	66	18	32	50	23–	111
Todd Gill	69	11	32	43	4	66
Dave Ellett	70	6	34	40	19	46
Mike Krushelnyski	84	19	20	39	3	62
Wendel Clark	66	17	22	39	2	193
Rob Pearson	78	23	14	37	2–	211
Peter Zezel	70	12	23	35	0	24
Dimitri Mironov	59	7	24	31	1–	40
Mark Osborne	76	12	14	26	7–	89
Bill Berg	80	13	11	24	3	103
Drake Berehowsky	41	4	15	19	1	61
Jamie Macoun	77	4	15	19	3	55
Dave McIlwain	66	14	4	18	18–	30
Mike Foligno	55	13	5	18	2	84
Bob Rouse	82	3	11	14	7	130

Sylvain LeFebvre	81	2	12	14	8	90
Ken Baumgartner	63	1	0	1	11–	155
Felix Potvin	48	0	1	1	0	4

Coach—Pat Burns

Vancouver Canucks

	GP	G	A	Pts	+/–	PIM
Pavel Bure	83	60	50	110	35	69
Cliff Ronning	79	29	56	85	19	30
Geoff Courtnall	84	31	46	77	27	167
Murray Craven	77	25	52	77	1–	32
Trevor Linden	84	33	39	72	19	64
Petr Nedved	84	38	33	71	20	96
Greg Adams	53	25	31	56	31	14
Dixon Ward	70	22	30	52	34	82
Anatoli Semenov	75	12	37	49	16	32
Jyrki Lumme	74	8	36	44	30	55
Sergio Momesso	84	18	20	38	11	200
Jim Sandlak	59	10	18	28	2	122
Adrien Plavsic	57	6	21	27	28	53
Jiri Slegr	41	4	22	26	16	109
Doug Lidster	71	6	19	25	9	36
Gerald Diduck	80	6	14	20	32	171
Dave Babych	43	3	16	19	6	44
Gino Odjick	75	4	13	17	3	370
Dana Murzyn	79	5	11	16	34	196
Garry Valk	48	6	7	13	6	77
Tim Hunter	74	5	7	12	3–	193
Robert Dirk	69	4	8	12	25	150
Kirk McLean	54	0	1	1	0	16

Coach—Pat Quinn

Washington Capitals

	GP	G	A	Pts	+/–	PIM
Peter Bondra	83	37	48	85	8	70
Mike Ridley	84	26	56	82	5	44
Kevin Hatcher	83	34	45	79	7–	114
Dale Hunter	84	20	59	79	3	198
Michal Pivonka	69	21	53	74	14	66
Dimitri Khristich	64	31	36	67	29	28
Al Iafrate	81	25	41	66	15	169
Pat Elynuik	80	22	35	57	3	66
Sylvain Cote	77	21	29	50	28	34
Kelly Miller	84	18	27	45	2–	32
Calle Johansson	77	7	38	45	3	56
Bob Carpenter	68	11	17	28	16–	65
Keith Jones	71	12	14	26	18	124
Todd Krygier	77	11	12	23	13–	60
Paul MacDermid	72	9	8	17	13–	80
Paul Cavallini	82	6	11	17	6	56
Alan May	83	6	10	16	1	268
Shawn Anderson	60	2	6	8	2–	18
Don Beaupre	58	0	1	1	0	20

Coach—Terry Murray

Winnipeg Jets

	GP	G	A	Pts	+/–	PIM
Teemu Selanne	84	76	56	132	8	45
Phil Housley	80	18	79	97	14–	52
Alexei Zhamnov	68	25	47	72	7	58
Thomas Steen	80	22	50	72	8–	75
Darrin Shannon	84	20	40	60	4–	91
Fredrik Olausson	68	16	41	57	4–	22
Keith Tkachuk	83	28	23	51	13–	201
Evgeny Davydov	79	28	21	49	2–	66
Teppo Numminen	66	7	30	37	4	33
Luciano Borsato	67	15	20	35	1–	38
Mike Eagles	84	8	18	26	1–	131
Sergei Bautin	71	5	18	23	2–	96
John Druce	50	6	14	20	4–	37
Kris King	78	8	11	19	4	203
Bryan Erickson	41	4	12	16	2	14
Igor Ulanov	56	2	14	16	6	124
Tie Domi	61	5	10	15	1	344
Mike Lalor	64	1	8	9	10–	76
Dean Kennedy	78	1	7	8	3–	105
Bob Essensa	67	0	5	5	0	2

Coach—John Paddock

Ross Trophy (Leading Scorer)

1927 Bill Cook, N.Y. Rangers
1928 Howie Morenz, Montreal
1929 Ace Bailey, Toronto
1930 Cooney Weiland, Boston
1931 Howie Morenz, Montreal
1932 Harvey Jackson, Toronto
1933 Bill Cook, N.Y. Rangers
1934 Charlie Conacher, Toronto
1935 Charlie Conacher, Toronto
1936 Dave Schriner, N.Y. Americans
1937 Dave Schriner, N.Y. Americans
1938 Gordie Drillon, Toronto
1939 Toe Blake, Montreal
1940 Milt Schmidt, Boston
1941 Bill Cowley, Boston
1942 Bryan Hextall, N.Y. Rangers
1943 Doug Bentley, Chicago
1944 Herbie Cain, Boston
1945 Elmer Lach, Montreal
1946 Max Bentley, Chicago
1947 Max Bentley, Chicago
1948 Elmer Lach, Montreal
1949 Roy Conacher, Chicago
1950 Ted Lindsay, Detroit
1951 Gordie Howe, Detroit
1952 Gordie Howe, Detroit
1953 Gordie Howe, Detroit
1954 Gordie Howe, Detroit
1955 Bernie Geoffrion, Montreal
1956 Jean Beliveau, Montreal
1957 Gordie Howe, Detroit
1958 Dickie Moore, Montreal
1959 Dickie Moore, Montreal
1960 Bobby Hull, Chicago
1961 Bernie Geoffrion, Montreal
1962 Bobby Hull, Chicago
1963 Gordie Howe, Detroit
1964 Stan Mikita, Chicago
1965 Stan Mikita, Chicago
1966 Bobby Hull, Chicago
1967 Stan Mikita, Chicago
1968 Stan Mikita, Chicago
1969 Phil Esposito, Boston
1970 Bobby Orr, Boston
1971 Phil Esposito, Boston
1972 Phil Esposito, Boston
1973 Phil Esposito, Boston
1974 Phil Esposito, Boston
1975 Bobby Orr, Boston
1976 Guy Lafleur, Montreal
1977 Guy Lafleur, Montreal
1978 Guy Lafleur, Montreal
1979 Bryan Trottier, N.Y. Islanders
1980 Marcel Dionne, Los Angeles
1981 Wayne Gretzky, Edmonton
1982 Wayne Gretzky, Edmonton
1983 Wayne Gretzky, Edmonton
1984 Wayne Gretzky, Edmonton
1985 Wayne Gretzky, Edmonton
1986 Wayne Gretzky, Edmonton
1987 Wayne Gretzky, Edmonton
1988 Mario Lemieux, Pittsburgh
1989 Mario Lemieux, Pittsburgh
1990 Wayne Gretzky, Los Angeles
1991 Wayne Gretzky, Los Angeles
1992 Mario Lemieux, Pittsburgh
1993 Mario Lemieux, Pittsburgh

James Norris Memorial Trophy (Outstanding Defenseman)

1954 Red Kelly, Detroit
1955 Doug Harvey, Montreal
1956 Doug Harvey, Montreal
1957 Doug Harvey, Montreal
1958 Doug Harvey, Montreal
1959 Tom Johnson, Montreal
1960 Doug Harvey, Montreal
1961 Doug Harvey, Montreal
1962 Doug Harvey, N.Y. Rangers
1963 Pierre Pilote, Chicago
1964 Pierre Pilote, Chicago
1965 Pierre Pilote, Chicago
1966 Jacques Laperriere, Montreal
1967 Harry Howell, N.Y. Rangers
1968 Bobby Orr, Boston
1969 Bobby Orr, Boston
1970 Bobby Orr, Boston
1971 Bobby Orr, Boston
1972 Bobby Orr, Boston
1973 Bobby Orr, Boston
1974 Bobby Orr, Boston
1975 Bobby Orr, Boston
1976 Denis Potvin, N.Y. Islanders
1977 Larry Robinson, Montreal
1978 Denis Potvin, N.Y. Islanders
1979 Denis Potvin, N.Y. Islanders
1980 Larry Robinson, Montreal
1981 Randy Carlyle, Pittsburgh
1982 Doug Wilson, Chicago
1983 Rod Langway, Washington
1984 Rod Langway, Washington
1985 Paul Coffey, Edmonton
1986 Paul Coffey, Edmonton
1987 Ray Bourque, Boston
1988 Ray Bourque, Boston
1989 Chris Chelios, Montreal
1990 Ray Bourque, Boston
1991 Ray Bourque, Boston
1992 Brian Leetch, N.Y. Rangers
1993 Chris Chelios, Chicago

*Vezina Trophy (Leading Goalie)

1927	George Hainsworth, Montreal
1928	George Hainsworth, Montreal
1929	George Hainsworth, Montreal
1930	Tiny Thompson, Boston
1931	Roy Worters, N.Y. Americans
1932	Charlie Gardiner, Chicago
1933	Tiny Thompson, Boston
1934	Charlie Gardiner, Chicago
1935	Lorne Chabot, Chicago
1936	Tiny Thompson, Boston
1937	Normie Smith, Detroit
1938	Tiny Thompson, Boston
1939	Frank Brimsek, Boston
1940	Dave Kerr, N.Y. Rangers
1941	Turk Broda, Toronto
1942	Frank Brimsek, Boston
1943	Johnny Mowers, Detroit
1944	Bill Durnan, Montreal
1945	Bill Durnan, Montreal
1946	Bill Durnan, Montreal
1947	Bill Durnan, Montreal
1948	Turk Broda, Toronto
1949	Bill Durnan, Montreal
1950	Bill Durnan, Montreal
1951	Al Rollins, Toronto
1952	Terry Sawchuk, Detroit
1953	Terry Sawchuk, Detroit
1954	Harry Lumley, Toronto
1955	Terry Sawchuk, Detroit
1956	Jacques Plante, Montreal
1957	Jacques Plante, Montreal
1958	Jacques Plante, Montreal
1959	Jacques Plante, Montreal
1960	Jacques Plante, Montreal
1961	John Bower, Toronto
1962	Jacques Plante, Montreal
1963	Glenn Hall, Chicago
1964	Charlie Hodge, Montreal
1965	Sawchuk, Bower, Toronto
1966	Worsley, Hodge, Montreal
1967	Hall, DeJordy, Chicago
1968	Worsley, Vachon, Montreal
1969	Hall, Plante, St. Louis
1970	Tony Esposito, Chicago
1971	Giacomin, Villemure, N.Y. Rangers
1972	Esposito, Smith, Chicago
1973	Ken Dryden, Montreal
1974	Bernie Parent, Philadelphia; Tony Esposito, Chicago
1975	Bernie Parent, Philadelphia
1976	Ken Dryden, Montreal
1977	Dryden, Larocque, Montreal
1978	Dryden, Larocque, Montreal
1979	Dryden, Larocque, Montreal
1980	Sauve, Edwards, Buffalo
1981	Sevigny, Larocque, Herron, Montreal
1982	Bill Smith, N.Y. Islanders
1983	Pete Peeters, Boston
1984	Tom Barrasso, Buffalo
1985	Pelle Lindbergh, Philadelphia
1986	John Vanbiesbrouck, N.Y. Rangers
1987	Ron Hextall, Philadelphia
1988	Grant Fuhr, Edmonton
1989	Patrick Roy, Montreal
1990	Patrick Roy, Montreal
1991	Ed Belfour, Chicago
1992	Patrick Roy, Montreal
1993	Ed Belfour, Chicago

* Awarded to goalie who played a minimum 25 games for the team which allowed the fewest goals; since 1982, awarded to outstanding goalie.

Calder Memorial Trophy (Rookie of the Year)

1933	Carl Voss, Detroit
1934	Russ Blinco, Montreal Maroons
1935	Dave Schriner, N.Y. Americans
1936	Mike Karakas, Chicago
1937	Syl Apps, Toronto
1938	Cully Dahlstrom, Chicago
1939	Frank Brimsek, Boston
1940	Kilby Macdonald, N.Y. Rangers
1941	John Quilty, Montreal
1942	Grant Warwick, N.Y. Rangers
1943	Gaye Stewart, Toronto
1944	Gus Bodnar, Toronto
1945	Frank McCool, Toronto
1946	Edgar Laprade, N.Y. Rangers
1947	Howie Meeker, Toronto
1948	Jim McFadden, Detroit
1949	Pentti Lund, N.Y. Rangers
1950	Jack Gelineau, Boston
1951	Terry Sawchuk, Detroit
1952	Bernie Geoffrion, Montreal
1953	Gump Worsley, N.Y. Rangers
1954	Camille Henry, N.Y. Rangers
1955	Ed Litzenberger, Chicago
1956	Glenn Hall, Detroit
1957	Larry Regan, Boston
1958	Frank Mahovlich, Toronto
1959	Ralph Backstrom, Montreal
1960	Bill Hay, Chicago
1961	Dave Keon, Toronto
1962	Bobby Rousseau, Montreal
1963	Kent Douglas, Toronto
1964	Jacques Laperriere, Montreal
1965	Roger Crozier, Detroit
1966	Brit Selby, Toronto
1967	Bobby Orr, Boston
1968	Derek Sanderson, Boston
1969	Danny Grant, Minnesota
1970	Tony Esposito, Chicago
1971	Gilbert Perreault, Buffalo
1972	Ken Dryden, Montreal
1973	Steve Vickers, N.Y. Rangers
1974	Denis Potvin, N.Y. Islanders
1975	Eric Vail, Atlanta
1976	Bryan Trottier, N.Y. Islanders
1977	Willi Plett, Atlanta
1978	Mike Bossy, N.Y. Islanders
1979	Bobby Smith, Minnesota
1980	Ray Bourque, Boston
1981	Peter Stastny, Quebec
1982	Dale Hawerchuk, Winnipeg
1983	Steve Larmer, Chicago
1984	Tom Barrasso, Buffalo
1985	Mario Lemieux, Pittsburgh
1986	Gary Suter, Calgary
1987	Luc Robitaille, Los Angeles
1988	Joe Nieuwendyk, Calgary
1989	Brian Leetch, N.Y. Rangers
1990	Sergei Makarov, Calgary
1991	Ed Belfour, Chicago
1992	Pavel Bure, Vancouver
1993	Teemu Selanne, Winnipeg

Lady Byng Memorial Trophy (Most Gentlemanly Player)

1925	Frank Nighbor, Ottawa
1926	Frank Nighbor, Ottawa
1927	Billy Burch, N.Y. Americans
1928	Frank Boucher, N.Y. Rangers
1929	Frank Boucher, N.Y. Rangers
1930	Frank Boucher, N.Y. Rangers
1931	Frank Boucher, N.Y. Rangers
1932	Joe Primeau, Toronto
1933	Frank Boucher, N.Y. Rangers
1934	Frank Boucher, N.Y. Rangers
1935	Frank Boucher, N.Y. Rangers
1936	Doc Romnes, Chicago
1937	Marty Barry, Detroit
1938	Gordie Drillon, Toronto
1939	Clint Smith, N.Y. Rangers
1940	Bobby Bauer, Boston
1941	Bobby Bauer, Boston
1942	Syl Apps, Toronto
1943	Max Bentley, Chicago
1944	Clint Smith, Chicago
1945	Bill Mosienko, Chicago
1946	Toe Blake, Montreal
1947	Bobby Bauer, Boston
1948	Buddy O'Connor, N.Y. Rangers
1949	Bill Quackenbush, Detroit
1950	Edgar Laprade, N.Y. Rangers
1951	Red Kelly, Detroit
1952	Sid Smith, Toronto
1953	Red Kelly, Detroit
1954	Red Kelly, Detroit
1955	Sid Smith, Toronto
1956	Earl Reibel, Detroit
1957	Andy Hebenton, N.Y. Rangers
1958	Camille Henry, N.Y. Rangers
1959	Alex Delvecchio, Detroit
1960	Don McKenney, Boston
1961	Red Kelly, Toronto
1962	Dave Keon, Toronto
1963	Dave Keon, Toronto
1964	Ken Wharram, Chicago
1965	Bobby Hull, Chicago
1966	Alex Delvecchio, Detroit
1967	Stan Mikita, Chicago
1968	Stan Mikita, Chicago
1969	Alex Delvecchio, Detroit
1970	Phil Goyette, St. Louis
1971	John Bucyk, Boston
1972	Jean Ratelle, N.Y. Rangers
1973	Gil Perreault, Buffalo
1974	John Bucyk, Boston
1975	Marcel Dionne, Detroit
1976	Jean Ratelle, N.Y. R.-Boston
1977	Marcel Dionne, Los Angeles
1978	Butch Goring, Los Angeles
1979	Bob MacMillan, Atlanta
1980	Wayne Gretzky, Edmonton
1981	Rick Kehoe, Pittsburgh
1982	Rick Middleton, Boston
1983	Mike Bossy, N.Y. Islanders
1984	Mike Bossy, N.Y. Islanders
1985	Jari Kurri, Edmonton
1986	Mike Bossy, N.Y. Islanders
1987	Joe Mullen, Calgary
1988	Mats Naslund, Montreal
1989	Joe Mullen, Calgary
1990	Brett Hull, St. Louis
1991	Wayne Gretzky, Los Angeles
1992	Wayne Gretzky, Los Angeles
1993	Pierre Turgeon, N.Y. Islanders

Frank J. Selke Trophy (Best Defensive Forward)

1978	Bob Gainey, Montreal
1979	Bob Gainey, Montreal
1980	Bob Gainey, Montreal
1981	Bob Gainey, Montreal
1982	Steve Kasper, Boston
1983	Bobby Clarke, Philadelphia
1984	Doug Jarvis, Washington
1985	Craig Ramsay, Buffalo
1986	Troy Murray, Chicago
1987	Dave Poulin, Philadelphia
1988	Guy Carbonneau, Montreal
1989	Guy Carbonneau, Montreal
1990	Rick Meagher, St. Louis
1991	Dirk Graham, Chicago
1992	Guy Carbonneau, Montreal
1993	Doug Gilmour, Toronto

Hart Memorial Trophy (MVP)

1927 Herb Gardiner, Montreal
1928 Howie Morenz, Montreal
1929 Roy Worters, N.Y. Americans
1930 Nels Stewart, Montreal Maroons
1931 Howie Morenz, Montreal
1932 Howie Morenz, Montreal
1933 Eddie Shore, Boston
1934 Aurel Joliat, Montreal
1935 Eddie Shore, Boston
1936 Eddie Shore, Boston
1937 Babe Siebert, Montreal
1938 Eddie Shore, Boston
1939 Toe Blake, Montreal
1940 Ebbie Goodfellow, Detroit
1941 Bill Cowley, Boston
1942 Tom Anderson, N.Y. Americans
1943 Bill Cowley, Boston
1944 Babe Pratt, Toronto
1945 Elmer Lach, Montreal
1946 Max Bentley, Chicago
1947 Maurice Richard, Montreal
1948 Buddy O'Connor, N.Y. Rangers
1949 Sid Abel, Detroit
1950 Chuck Rayner, N.Y. Rangers
1951 Milt Schmidt, Boston
1952 Gordie Howe, Detroit
1953 Gordie Howe, Detroit
1954 Al Rollins, Chicago
1955 Ted Kennedy, Toronto
1956 Jean Beliveau, Montreal
1957 Gordie Howe, Detroit
1958 Gordie Howe, Detroit
1959 Andy Bathgate, N.Y. Rangers
1960 Gordie Howe, Detroit
1961 Bernie Geoffrion, Montreal
1962 Jacques Plante, Montreal
1963 Gordie Howe, Detroit
1964 Jean Beliveau, Montreal
1965 Bobby Hull, Chicago
1966 Bobby Hull, Chicago
1967 Stan Mikita, Chicago
1968 Stan Mikita, Chicago
1969 Phil Esposito, Boston
1970 Bobby Orr, Boston
1971 Bobby Orr, Boston
1972 Bobby Orr, Boston
1973 Bobby Clarke, Philadelphia
1974 Phil Esposito, Boston
1975 Bobby Clarke, Philadelphia
1976 Bobby Clarke, Philadelphia
1977 Guy Lafleur, Montreal
1978 Guy Lafleur, Montreal
1979 Bryan Trottier, N.Y. Islanders
1980 Wayne Gretzky, Edmonton
1981 Wayne Gretzky, Edmonton
1982 Wayne Gretzky, Edmonton
1983 Wayne Gretzky, Edmonton
1984 Wayne Gretzky, Edmonton
1985 Wayne Gretzky, Edmonton
1986 Wayne Gretzky, Edmonton
1987 Wayne Gretzky, Edmonton
1988 Mario Lemieux, Pittsburgh
1989 Wayne Gretzky, Los Angeles
1990 Mark Messier, Edmonton
1991 Brett Hull, St. Louis
1992 Mark Messier, N.Y. Rangers
1993 Mario Lemieux, Pittsburgh

Conn Smythe Trophy (MVP in Playoffs)

1965 Jean Beliveau, Montreal
1966 Roger Crozier, Detroit
1967 Dave Keon, Toronto
1968 Glenn Hall, St. Louis
1969 Serge Savard, Montreal
1970 Bobby Orr, Boston
1971 Ken Dryden, Montreal
1972 Bobby Orr, Boston
1973 Yvan Cournoyer, Montreal
1974 Bernie Parent, Philadelphia
1975 Bernie Parent, Philadelphia
1976 Reg Leach, Philadelphia
1977 Guy Lafleur, Montreal
1978 Larry Robinson, Montreal
1979 Bob Gainey, Montreal
1980 Bryan Trottier, N.Y. Islanders
1981 Butch Goring, N.Y. Islanders
1982 Mike Bossy, N.Y. Islanders
1983 Billy Smith, N.Y. Islanders
1984 Mark Messier, Edmonton
1985 Wayne Gretzky, Edmonton
1986 Patrick Roy, Montreal
1987 Ron Hextall, Philadelphia
1988 Wayne Gretzky, Edmonton
1989 Al MacInnis, Calgary
1990 Bill Ranford, Edmonton
1991 Mario Lemieux, Pittsburgh
1992 Mario Lemieux, Pittsburgh
1993 Patrick Roy, Montreal

Most NHL Goals in a Season

Player	Team	Season	Goals
Wayne Gretzky	Edmonton	1981-82	92
Wayne Gretzky	Edmonton	1983-84	87
Brett Hull	St. Louis	1990-91	86
Mario Lemieux	Pittsburgh	1988-89	85
Phil Esposito	Boston	1970-71	76
Alexander Mogilny	Buffalo	1992-93	76
Teemu Selanne	Winnipeg	1992-93	76
Wayne Gretzky	Edmonton	1984-85	73
Brett Hull	St. Louis	1989-90	72
Wayne Gretzky	Edmonton	1982-83	71
Jari Kurri	Edmonton	1984-85	71
Mario Lemieux	Pittsburgh	1987-88	70
Bernie Nicholls	Los Angeles	1988-89	70
Bret Hull	St. Louis	1991-92	70
Mike Bossy	N.Y. Islanders	1978-79	69
Mario Lemieux	Pittsburgh	1992-93	69
Phil Esposito	Boston	1973-74	68
Mike Bossy	N.Y. Islanders	1980-81	68
Jari Kurri	Edmonton	1985-86	68
Phil Esposito	Boston	1971-72	66
Lanny McDonald	Calgary	1982-83	66
Steve Yzerman	Detroit	1988-89	65
Mike Bossy	N.Y. Islanders	1981-82	64
Luc Robitaille	Los Angeles	1992-93	63
Wayne Gretzky	Edmonton	1986-87	62
Steve Yzerman	Detroit	1989-90	62
Mike Bossy	N.Y. Islanders	1985-86	61
Phil Esposito	Boston	1974-75	61
Reggie Leach	Philadelphia	1975-76	61
Mike Bossy	N.Y. Islanders	1982-83	60
Guy Lafleur	Montreal	1977-78	60
Steve Shutt	Montreal	1976-77	60
Dennis Maruk	Washington	1981-82	60
Pavel Bure	Vancouver	1992-93	60

NCAA Hockey Champions

1948 Michigan
1949 Boston College
1950 Colorado College
1951 Michigan
1952 Michigan
1953 Michigan
1954 RPI
1955 Michigan
1956 Michigan
1957 Colorado College
1958 Denver
1959 North Dakota
1960 Denver
1961 Denver
1962 Michigan Tech
1963 North Dakota
1964 Michigan
1965 Michigan Tech
1966 Michigan State
1967 Cornell
1968 Denver
1969 Denver
1970 Cornell
1971 Boston Univ.
1972 Boston Univ.
1973 Wisconsin
1974 Minnesota
1975 Michigan Tech
1976 Minnesota
1977 Wisconsin
1978 Boston Univ.
1979 Minnesota
1980 North Dakota
1981 Wisconsin
1982 North Dakota
1983 Wisconsin
1984 Bowling Green
1985 RPI
1986 Michigan State
1987 North Dakota
1988 Lake Superior St.
1989 Harvard
1990 Wisconsin
1991 N. Michigan
1992 Lake Superior St.
1993 Maine

THOROUGHBRED RACING

Triple Crown Winners

Since 1920, colts have carried 126 lbs. in triple crown events; fillies 121 lbs.

(Kentucky Derby, Preakness, and Belmont Stakes)

Year	Horse	Jockey	Trainer
1919	Sir Barton	J. Loftus	H. G. Bedwell
1930	Gallant Fox	E. Sande	J. Fitzsimmons
1935	Omaha	W. Sanders	J. Fitzsimmons
1937	War Admiral	C. Kurtsinger	G. Conway
1941	Whirlaway	E. Arcaro	B.A. Jones
1943	Count Fleet	J. Longden	G.D. Cameron
1946	Assault	W. Mehrtens	M. Hirsch
1948	Citation	E. Arcaro	H.A. Jones
1973	Secretariat	R. Turcotte	L. Laurin
1977	Seattle Slew	J. Cruguet	W.H. Turner Jr.
1978	Affirmed	S. Cauthen	L.S. Barrera

Kentucky Derby

Churchill Downs, Louisville, Ky.; inaugurated 1875; distance 1-1/4 miles; 1-1/2 miles until 1896. 3-year olds.
Best time: 1:59.2, Secretariat, 1973

Year	Winner	Jockey
1875	Aristides	O. Lewis
1876	Vagrant	R. Swim
1877	Baden Baden	W. Walker
1878	Day Star	J. Carter
1879	Lord Murphy	C. Schauer
1880	Fonso	G. Lewis
1881	Hindoo	J. McLaughlin
1882	Apollo	B. Hurd
1883	Leonatus	W. Donohue
1884	Buchanan	I. Murphy
1885	Joe Cotton	E. Henderson
1886	Ben Ali	P. Duffy
1887	Montrose	I. Lewis
1888	Macbeth II	G. Covington
1889	Spokane	T. Kiley
1890	Riley	I. Murphy
1891	Kingman	I. Murphy
1892	Azra	A. Clayton
1893	Lookout	E. Kunze
1894	Chant	F. Goodale
1895	Halma	J. Perkins
1896	Ben Brush	W. Simms
1897	Typhoon II	F. Garner
1898	Plaudit	W. Simms
1899	Manuel	F. Taral
1900	Lieut. Gibson	J. Boland
1901	His Eminence	J. Winkfield
1902	Alan-a-Dale	J. Winkfield
1903	Judge Himes	H. Booker
1904	Elwood	F. Prior
1905	Agile	J. Martin
1906	Sir Huon	R. Troxler
1907	Pink Star	A. Minder
1908	Stone Street	A. Pickens
1909	Wintergreen	V. Powers
1910	Donau	F. Herbert
1911	Meridian	G. Archibald
1912	Worth	C.H. Shilling
1913	Donerail	R. Goose
1914	Old Rosebud	J. McCabe
1915	Regret*	J. Notter
1916	George Smith	J. Loftus
1917	Omar Khayyam	C. Borel
1918	Exterminator	W. Knapp
1919	Sir Barton	J. Loftus
1920	Paul Jones	T. Rice
1921	Behave Yourself	C. Thompson
1922	Morvich	A. Johnson
1923	Zev	E. Sande
1924	Black Gold	J. D. Mooney
1925	Flying Ebony	E. Sande
1926	Bubbling Over	A. Johnson
1927	Whiskery	L. McAtee
1928	Reigh Count	C. Lang
1929	Clyde Van Dusen	L. McAtee
1930	Gallant Fox	E. Sande
1931	Twenty Grand	C. Kurtsinger
1932	Burgoo King	E. James
1933	Brokers Tip	D. Meade
1934	Cavalcade	M. Garner
1935	Omaha	W. Saunders
1936	Bold Venture	I. Hanford
1937	War Admiral	C. Kurtsinger
1938	Lawrin	E. Arcaro
1939	Johnstown	J. Stout
1940	Gallahadion	C. Bierman
1941	Whirlaway	E. Arcaro
1942	Shut Out	W. D. Wright
1943	Count Fleet	J. Longden
1944	Pensive	C. McCreary
1945	Hoop, Jr.	E. Arcaro
1946	Assault	W. Mehrtens
1947	Jet Pilot	E. Guerin
1948	Citation	E. Arcaro
1949	Ponder	S. Brooks
1950	Middleground	W. Boland
1951	Count Turf	C. McCreary
1952	Hill Gail	E. Arcaro
1953	Dark Star	H. Moreno
1954	Determine	R. York
1955	Swaps	W. Shoemaker
1956	Needles	D. Erb
1957	Iron Liege	W. Hartack
1958	Tim Tam	I. Valenzuela
1959	Tomy Lee	W. Shoemaker
1960	Venetian Way	W. Hartack
1961	Carry Back	J. Sellers
1962	Decidedly	W. Hartack
1963	Chateaugay	B. Baeza
1964	Northern Dancer	W. Hartack
1965	Lucky Debonair	W. Shoemaker
1966	Kauai King	D. Brumfield
1967	Proud Clarion	R. Ussery
1968	Dancer's Image (a)	R. Ussery
1969	Majestic Prince	W. Hartack
1970	Dust Commander	M. Manganello
1971	Canonero II	G. Avila
1972	Riva Ridge	R. Turcotte
1973	Secretariat	R. Turcotte
1974	Cannonade	A. Cordero
1975	Foolish Pleasure	J. Vasquez
1976	Bold Forbes	A. Cordero
1977	Seattle Slew	J. Cruguet
1978	Affirmed	S. Cauthen
1979	Spectacular Bid	R. Franklin
1980	Genuine Risk*	J. Vasquez
1981	Pleasant Colony	J. Velasquez
1982	Gato del Sol	E. Delahoussaye
1983	Sunny's Halo	E. Delahoussaye
1984	Swale	L. Pincay
1985	Spend a Buck	A. Cordero
1986	Ferdinand	W. Shoemaker
1987	Alysheba	C. McCarron
1988	Winning Colors*	G. Stevens
1989	Sunday Silence	P. Valenzuela
1990	Unbridled	C. Perret
1991	Strike The Gold	C. Antley
1992	Lil E. Tee	P. Day
1993	Sea Hero	J. Bailey

(a) Dancer's Image was disqualified from purse money after tests disclosed that he had run with a pain-killing drug, phenylbutazone, in his system. All wagers were paid on Dancer's Image. Forward Pass was awarded first place money.

The Kentucky Derby has been won five times by two jockeys, Eddie Arcaro, 1938, 1941, 1945, 1948, and 1952; and Bill Hartack, 1957, 1960, 1962, 1964, and 1969; four times by Willie Shoemaker, 1955, 1959, 1965, and 1986; and three times by each of three jockeys, Isaac Murphy, 1884, 1890, and 1891; Earle Sande, 1923, 1925, and 1930, and Angel Cordero in 1974, 1976, and 1985. * Regret, Genuine Risk, and Winning Colors are the only fillies to win the Derby.

Preakness

Pimlico, Baltimore, Md.; inaugurated 1873; 1-3/16 miles. 3 yr. olds. Best time: 1:53.2, Tank's Prospect, 1985

Year	Winner	Jockey
1873	Survivor	G. Barbee
1874	Culpepper	M. Donohue
1875	Tom Ochiltree	L. Hughes
1876	Shirley	G. Barbee
1877	Cloverbrook	C. Holloway
1878	Duke of Magenta	C. Holloway
1879	Harold	L. Hughes
1880	Grenada	L. Hughes
1881	Saunterer	W. Costello
1882	Vanguard	W. Costello
1883	Jacobus	G. Barbee
1884	Knight of Ellerslie	S. H. Fisher
1885	Tecumseh	J. McLaughlin
1886	The Bard	S. H. Fisher
1887	Dunboyne	W. Donohue
1888	Refund	F. Littlefield
1889	Buddhist	G. Anderson
1890	Montague	W. Martin
1894	Assignee	F. Taral
1895	Belmar	F. Taral
1896	Margrave	H. Griffin
1897	Paul Kauvar	C. Thorpe
1898	Sly Fox	W. Simms
1899	Half Time	R. Clawson
1900	Hindus	H. Spencer
1901	The Parader	F. Landry
1902	Old England	L. Jackson
1903	Flocarline	W. Gannon
1904	Bryn Mawr	E. Hildebrand
1905	Cairngorm	W. Davis
1906	Whimsical	W. Miller
1907	Don Enrique	G. Mountain
1908	Royal Tourist	E. Dugan
1909	Effendi	W. Doyle
1910	Layminster	R. Estep
1911	Watervale	E. Dugan
1912	Colonel Holloway	C. Turner
1913	Buskin	J. Butwell
1914	Holiday	A. Schuttinger
1915	Rhine Maiden	D. Hoffman
1916	Damrosch	L. McAtee
1917	Kalitan	E. Haynes

Year	Winner	Jockey
1918	War Cloud	J. Loftus
	Jack Hare Jr.	C. Peak
1919	Sir Barton	J. Loftus
1920	Man o' War	C. Kummer
1921	Broomspun	F. Coltiletti
1922	Pillory	L. Morris
1923	Vigil	B. Marinelli
1924	Nellie Morse	J. Merimee
1925	Coventry	C. Kummer
1926	Display	J. Malben
1927	Bostonian	A. Abel
1928	Victorian	R. Workman
1929	Dr. Freeland	L. Schaefer
1930	Gallant Fox	E. Sande
1931	Mate	G. Ellis
1932	Burgoo King	E. James
1933	Head Play	C. Kurtsinger
1934	High Quest	R. Jones
1935	Omaha	W. Saunders
1936	Bold Venture	G. Woolf
1937	War Admiral	C. Kurtsinger
1938	Dauber	M. Peters
1939	Challedon	G. Seabo
1940	Bimelech	F.A. Smith
1941	Whirlaway	E. Arcaro
1942	Alsab	B. James
1943	Count Fleet	J. Longden
1944	Pensive	C. McCreary
1945	Polynesian	W.D. Wright
1946	Assault	W. Mehrtens
1947	Faultless	D. Dodson
1948	Citation	E. Arcaro
1949	Capot	T. Atkinson
1950	Hill Prince	E. Arcaro
1951	Bold	E. Arcaro
1952	Blue Man	C. McCreary
1953	Native Dancer	E. Guerin
1954	Hasty Road	J. Adams
1955	Nashua	E. Arcaro
1956	Fabius	W. Hartack
1957	Bold Ruler	E. Arcaro
1958	Tim Tam	I. Valenzuela
1959	Royal Orbit	W. Harmatz
1960	Bally Ache	R. Ussery
1961	Carry Back	J. Sellers
1962	Greek Money	J.L. Rotz
1963	Candy Spots	W. Shoemaker
1964	Northern Dancer	W. Hartack
1965	Tom Rolfe	R. Turcotte
1966	Kauai King	D. Brumfield
1967	Damascus	W. Shoemaker
1968	Forward Pass	I. Valenzuela
1969	Majestic Prince	W. Hartack
1970	Personality	E. Belmonte
1971	Canonero II	G. Avila
1972	Bee Bee Bee	E. Nelson
1973	Secretariat	R. Turcotte
1974	Little Current	M. Rivera
1975	Master Derby	D. McHargue
1976	Elocutionist	J. Lively
1977	Seattle Slew	J. Cruguet
1978	Affirmed	S. Cauthen
1979	Spectacular Bid	R. Franklin
1980	Codex	A. Cordero
1981	Pleasant Colony	J. Velasquez
1982	Aloma's Ruler	J. Kaenel
1983	Deputed Testamony	D. Miller
1984	Gate Dancer	A. Cordero
1985	Tank's Prospect	P. Day
1986	Snow Chief	A. Solis
1987	Alysheba	C. McCarron
1988	Risen Star	E. Delahoussaye
1989	Sunday Silence	P. Valenzuela
1990	Summer Squall	P. Day
1991	Hansel	J. Bailey
1992	Pine Bluff	C. McCarren
1993	Prairie Bayou	M. Smith

Belmont Stakes

Elmont, N.Y.; inaugurated 1867; 1-1/2 miles. 3 year olds. Fastest time: 2:24, Secretariat, 1973

Year	Winner	Jockey
1867	Ruthless	J. Gilpatrick
1868	General Duke	R. Swim
1869	Fenian	C. Miller
1870	Kingfisher	W. Dick
1871	Harry Bassett	W. Miller
1872	Joe Daniels	J. Rowe
1873	Springbok	J. Rowe
1874	Saxon	G. Barbee
1875	Calvin	R. Swim
1876	Algerine	W. Donohue
1877	Cloverbrook	C. Holloway
1878	Duke of Magenta	L. Hughes
1879	Spendthrift	S. Evans
1880	Grenada	L. Hughes
1881	Saunterer	T. Costello
1882	Forester	J. McLaughlin
1883	George Kinney	J. McLaughlin
1884	Panique	J. McLaughlin
1885	Tyrant	P. Duffy
1886	Inspector B.	J. McLaughlin
1887	Hanover	J. McLaughlin
1888	Sir Dixon	J. McLaughlin
1889	Eric	W. Hayward
1890	Burlington	S. Barnes
1891	Foxford	E. Garrison
1892	Patron	W. Hayward
1893	Comanche	W. Simms
1894	Henry of Navarre	W. Simms
1895	Belmar	F. Taral
1896	Hastings	H. Griffin
1897	Scottish Chieftain	J. Scherrer
1898	Bowling Brook	F. Littlefield
1899	Jean Bereaud	R.R. Clawson
1900	Ildrim	N. Turner
1901	Commando	H. Spencer
1902	Masterman	J. Bullman
1903	Africander	J. Bullman
1904	Delhi	G. Odom
1905	Tanya	E. Hildebrand
1906	Burgomaster	L. Lyne
1907	Peter Pan	G. Mountain
1908	Colin	J. Notter
1909	Joe Madden	E. Dugan
1910	Sweep	J. Butwell
1913	Prince Eugene	R. Troxler
1914	Luke McLuke	M. Buxton
1915	The Finn	G. Byrne
1916	Friar Rock	E. Haynes
1917	Hourless	J. Butwell
1918	Johren	F. Robinson
1919	Sir Barton	J. Loftus
1920	Man o' War	C. Kummer
1921	Grey Lag	E. Sande
1922	Pillory	C.H. Miller
1923	Zev	E. Sande
1924	Mad Play	E. Sande
1925	American Flag	A. Johnson
1926	Crusader	A. Johnson
1927	Chance Shot	E. Sande
1928	Vito	C. Kummer
1929	Blue Larkspur	M. Garner
1930	Gallant Fox	E. Sande
1931	Twenty Grand	C. Kurtsinger
1932	Faireno	T. Malley
1933	Hurryoff	M. Garner
1934	Peace Chance	W.D. Wright
1935	Omaha	W. Saunders
1936	Granville	J. Stout
1937	War Admiral	C. Kurtsinger
1938	Pasteurized	J. Stout
1939	Johnstown	J. Stout
1940	Bimelech	F.A. Smith
1941	Whirlaway	E. Arcaro
1942	Shut Out	E. Arcaro
1943	Count Fleet	J. Longden
1944	Bounding Home	G.L. Smith
1945	Pavot	E. Arcaro
1946	Assault	W. Mehrtens
1947	Phalanx	R. Donoso
1948	Citation	E. Arcaro
1949	Capot	T. Atkinson
1950	Middleground	W. Boland
1951	Counterpoint	D. Gorman
1952	One Count	E. Arcaro
1953	Native Dancer	E. Guerin
1954	High Gun	E. Guerin
1955	Nashua	E. Arcaro
1956	Needles	D. Erb
1957	Gallant Man	W. Shoemaker
1958	Cavan	P. Anderson
1959	Sword Dancer	W. Shoemaker
1960	Celtic Ash	W. Hartack
1961	Sherluck	B. Baeza
1962	Jaipur	W. Shoemaker
1963	Chateaugay	B. Baeza
1964	Quadrangle	M. Ycaza
1965	Hail to All	J. Sellers
1966	Amberoid	W. Boland
1967	Damascus	W. Shoemaker
1968	Stage Door Johnny	H. Gustines
1969	Arts and Letters	B. Baeza
1970	High Echelon	J.L. Rotz
1971	Pass Catcher	W. Blum
1972	Riva Ridge	R. Turcotte
1973	Secretariat	R. Turcotte
1974	Little Current	M. Rivera
1975	Avatar	W. Shoemaker
1976	Bold Forbes	A. Cordero
1977	Seattle Slew	J. Cruguet
1978	Affirmed	S. Cauthen
1979	Coastal	R. Hernandez
1980	Temperence Hill	E. Maple
1981	Summing	G. Martens
1982	Conquistador Cielo	L. Pincay
1983	Caveat	L. Pincay
1984	Swale	L. Pincay
1985	Creme Fraiche	E. Maple
1986	Danzig Connection	C. McCarron
1987	Bet Twice	C. Perret
1988	Risen Star	E. Delahoussaye
1989	Easy Goer	P. Day
1990	Go and Go	M. Kinane
1991	Hansel	J. Bailey
1992	A.P. Indy	E. Delahoussaye
1993	Colonial Affair	J. Krone

Annual Leading Jockey—Money Won

Year	Jockey	Dollars
1957	Bill Hartack	3,060,501
1958	Willie Shoemaker	2,961,693
1959	Willie Shoemaker	2,843,133
1960	Willie Shoemaker	2,123,961
1961	Willie Shoemaker	2,690,819
1962	Willie Shoemaker	2,916,844
1963	Willie Shoemaker	2,526,925
1964	Willie Shoemaker	2,649,553
1965	Braulio Baeza	2,582,702
1966	Braulio Baeza	2,951,022
1967	Braulio Baeza	3,088,888
1968	Braulio Baeza	2,835,108
1969	Jorge Velasquez	2,542,315
1970	Laffit Pincay Jr.	2,626,526
1971	Laffit Pincay Jr.	3,784,377
1972	Laffit Pincay Jr.	3,225,827
1973	Laffit Pincay Jr.	4,093,492
1974	Laffit Pincay Jr.	4,251,060
1975	Braulio Baeza	3,695,198
1976	Angel Cordero Jr.	4,709,500
1977	Steve Cauthen	6,151,750
1978	Darrel McHargue	6,029,885
1979	Laffit Pincay Jr.	8,193,535
1980	Chris McCarron	7,663,300
1981	Chris McCarron	8,397,604
1982	Angel Cordero Jr.	9,483,590
1983	Angel Cordero Jr.	10,116,697
1984	Chris McCarron	12,045,813
1985	Laffit Pincay Jr.	13,353,299
1986	Jose Santos	11,329,297
1987	Jose Santos	12,375,433
1988	Jose Santos	14,877,298
1989	Jose Santos	13,838,389
1990	Gary Stevens	13,881,198
1991	Chris McCarron	14,441,083
1992	Kent Desormeaux	14,193,006

Breeders' Cup

The Breeders' Cup was inaugurated in 1984 and consists of seven races at one track on one day late in the year to determine thoroughbred racing's champion contenders.

Juvenile

Distances: one mile 1984-85, 87; $1\frac{1}{16}$ miles 1986 and since 1988

Year	Winner	Jockey
1984	Chief's Crown	Don MacBeth
1985	Tasso	Laffit Pincay Jr.
1986	Capote	Laffit Pincay Jr.
1987	Success Express	Jose Santos
1988	Is It True	Laffit Pincay Jr.
1989	Rhythm	Craig Perret
1990	Fly So Free	Jose Santos
1991	Arazi	Pat Valenzuela
1992	Gilded Time	Chris McCarron

Juvenile Fillies

Distances: one mile 1984-85, 87; $1\frac{1}{16}$ miles 1986 and since 1988

Year	Winner	Jockey
1984	*Outstandingly	Walter Guerra
1985	Twilight Ridge	Jorge Velasquez
1986	Brave Raj	Pat Valenzuela
1987	Epitome	Pat Day
1988	Open Mind	Angel Cordero Jr.
1989	Go for Wand	Randy Romero
1990	Meadow Star	Jose Santos
1991	Pleasant Stage	Eddie Delahoussaye
1992	Eliza	Pat Valenzuela

*By disqualification.

Sprint

Distance: six furlongs

Year	Winner	Jockey
1984	Eillo	Craig Perret
1985	Precisionist	Chris McCarron
1986	Smile	Jacinto Vasquez
1987	Very Subtle	Pat Valenzuela
1988	Gulch	Angel Cordero Jr.
1989	Dancing Spree	Angel Cordero Jr.
1990	Safely Kept	Craig Perret
1991	Sheikh Albadou	Pat Eddery
1992	Thirty Slews	Eddie Delahoussaye

Mile

Year	Winner	Jockey
1984	Royal Heroine	Fernando Toro
1985	Cozzene	Walter Guerra
1986	Last Tycoon	Yves St.-Martin
1987	Miesque	Freddie Head
1988	Miesque	Freddie Head
1989	Steinlen	Jose Santos
1990	Royal Academy	Lester Piggott
1991	Opening Verse	Pat Valenzuela
1992	Lure	Mike Smith

Distaff

Distances: $1\frac{1}{4}$ miles 1984-87; $1\frac{1}{8}$ miles since 1988

Year	Winner	Jockey
1984	Princess Rooney	Eddie Delahoussaye
1985	Life's Magic	Angel Cordero Jr.
1986	Lady's Secret	Pat Day
1987	Sacahuista	Randy Romero
1988	Personal Ensign	Randy Romero
1989	Bayakoa	Laffit Pincay Jr.
1990	Bayakoa	Laffit Pincay Jr.
1991	Dance Smartly	Pat Day
1992	Paseana	Chris McCarron

Turf

Distance: $1\frac{1}{2}$ miles

Year	Winner	Jockey
1984	Lashkari	Yves St.-Martin
1985	Pebbles	Pat Eddery
1986	Manila	Jose Santos
1987	Theatrical	Pat Day
1988	Great Communicator	Ray Sibille
1989	Prized	Eddie Delahoussaye
1990	In The Wings	Gary Stevens
1991	Miss Alleged	Eric Legrix
1992	Fraise	Pat Valenzuela

Classic

Distance: $1\frac{1}{4}$ miles

Year	Winner	Jockey
1984	Wild Again	Pat Day
1985	Proud Truth	Jorge Velasquez
1986	Skywalker	Laffit Pincay Jr.
1987	Ferdinand	Bill Shoemaker
1988	Alysheba	Chris McCarron
1989	Sunday Silence	Chris McCarron
1990	Unbridled	Pat Day
1991	Black Tie Affair	Jerry Bailey
1992	A.P. Indy	Eddie Delahoussaye

Eclipse Awards

The Eclipse Awards, honoring the Horse of the Year and other champions of the sport, began in 1971, and are sponsored by the *Daily Racing Form,* the Thoroughbred Racing Associations and the National Turf Writers Assn. Prior to 1971, the DRF (1936-70) and the TRA (1950-70) issued separate selections for horse of the year.

Eclipse Awards in 1992

Horse of the Year—A.P. Indy
2-year-old colt—Gilded Time
2-year-old filly—Eliza
3-year-old colt—A.P. Indy
3-year-old filly—Saratoga Dew
Colt, horse, or gelding (4-year-olds & up)—Pleasant Tap
Filly or mare (4-year-olds & up)—Paseana
Male turf horse—Sky Classic
Turf filly or mare—Flawlessly
Sprinter—Rubiano
Steeplechase horse—Lonesome Glory
Trainer—Ron McNally
Jockey—Kent Desormeaux
Apprentice jockey—Mickey Walls
Breeder—William S. Farish 3d

Horse of the Year

Year	Horse	Year	Horse	Year	Horse	Year	Horse
1936	Granville	1952	One Count (DRF)	1965	Roman Brother (DRF)	1978	Affirmed
1937	War Admiral		Native Dancer (TRA)		Moccasin (TRA)	1979	Affirmed
1938	Seabiscuit	1953	Tom Fool	1966	Buckpasser	1980	Spectacular Bid
1939	Challedon	1954	Native Dancer	1967	Damascus	1981	John Henry
1940	Challedon	1955	Nashua	1968	Dr. Fager	1982	Conquistador Cielo
1941	Whirlaway	1956	Swaps	1969	Arts and Letters	1983	All Along
1942	Whirlaway	1957	Bold Ruler (DRF)	1970	Fort Marcy (DRF)	1984	John Henry
1943	Count Fleet		Dedicate (TRA)		Personality (TRA)	1985	Spend A Buck
1944	Twilight Tear	1958	Round Table	1971	Ack Ack	1986	Lady's Secret
1945	Busher	1959	Sword Dancer	1972	Secretariat	1987	Ferdinand
1946	Assault	1960	Kelso	1973	Secretariat	1988	Alysheba
1947	Armed	1961	Kelso	1974	Forego	1989	Sunday Silence
1948	Citation	1962	Kelso	1975	Forego	1990	Criminal Type
1949	Capot	1963	Kelso	1976	Forego	1991	Black Tie Affair
1950	Hill Prince	1964	Kelso	1977	Seattle Slew	1992	A.P. Indy
1951	Counterpoint						

NATIONAL BASKETBALL ASSOCIATION

Final Standings, 1992-1993 Season

Eastern Conference

Atlantic Division

	W	L	Pct	GB
New York	60	22	.732	—
Boston	48	34	.585	12
New Jersey	43	39	.524	17
Orlando	41	41	.500	19
Miami	36	46	.439	24
Philadelphia	26	56	.317	34
Washington	22	60	.268	38

Central Division

	W	L	Pct	GB
Chicago	57	25	.695	—
Cleveland	54	28	.659	3
Charlotte	44	38	.537	13
Atlanta	43	39	.524	14
Indiana	41	41	.500	16
Detroit	40	42	.488	17
Milwaukee	28	54	.341	29

Western Conference

Midwest Division

	W	L	Pct	GB
Houston	55	27	.671	—
San Antonio	49	33	.598	6
Utah	47	35	.573	8
Denver	36	46	.439	19
Minnesota	19	63	.232	36
Dallas	11	71	.134	44

Pacific Division

	W	L	Pct	GB
Phoenix	62	20	.756	—
Seattle	55	27	.671	7
Portland	51	31	.622	11
L.A. Clippers	41	41	.500	21
L.A. Lakers	39	43	.476	23
Golden State	34	48	.415	28
Sacramento	25	57	.305	37

NBA Regular Season Individual Highs in 1992-1993

Most minutes played, season — 3,323: Larry Johnson, Charlotte.

Most points, game — 64: Michael Jordan, Chicago vs. Orlando, Jan. 16 (OT).

Most field goals made, game — 27: Michael Jordan, Chicago vs. Orlando, Jan. 16 (OT).

Most field goal attempts, game — 49: Michael Jordan, Chicago vs. Orlando, Jan. 16 (OT).

Most 3-point field goals made, game — 10: Brian Shaw, Miami vs. Milwaukee, April 8.

Most 3-point field goal attempts, game — 19: Dennis Scott, Orlando vs. Milwaukee, April 13.

Most free throws made, game — 23: Dominique Wilkins, Atlanta vs. Chicago, Dec. 8.

Most rebounds, game — 34: Rony Seikaly, Miami vs. Washington, March 3.

Most offensive rebounds, season — 367: Dennis Rodman, Detroit.

Most defensive rebounds, season — 789: Patrick Ewing, New York.

Most assists, game — 23: Mookie Blaylock, Atlanta vs. Utah, March 6.

Most personal fouls, season — 332: Stanley Roberts, L.A. Clippers.

Most games disqualified, season — 15: Stanley Roberts, L.A. Clippers.

Bulls Win Third Straight Championship by Beating Phoenix Suns in Six Games

The Chicago Bulls won their third consecutive National Basketball Association championship by defeating the Phoenix Suns 4 games to 2. It was the first time a team had won more than two straight titles since the Boston Celtics ran off eight in a row, 1959-1966. Michael Jordan was chosen the most valuable player in the finals for the third consecutive year.

Chicago Bulls

	FG M-A	FT M-A	Reb	Ast	Avg
Jordan	101-199	34-39	15-51	38	41.0
Pippen	54-123	19-35	16-55	46	21.2
Armstrong	32-63	7-7	2-11	30	13.5
Grant	28-53	11-19	25-62	14	11.2
Paxson	13-21	0-0	4-9	5	5.8
S. Williams	13-32	2-7	12-38	10	4.7
Cartwright	12-30	2-4	7-19	10	4.3
Tucker	7-10	0-0	1-2	4	2.8
King	3-11	7-8	3-8	3	2.2
Walker	0-0	0-1	0-0	1	0.0
McCray	0-0	0-0	0-1	0	0.0
Perdue	0-2	0-0	1-3	0	0.0
Totals	**263-544**	**82-130**	**86-321**	**161**	**106.7**

Phoenix Suns

	FG M-A	FT M-A	Reb	Ast	Avg
Barkley	60-126	42-56	22-78	33	27.3
K. Johnson	40-95	23-25	2-18	39	17.2
Majerle	35-79	16-20	12-49	22	17.2
Dumas	44-77	7-9	15-26	6	15.8
Ainge	19-40	7-9	7-18	15	8.8
Chambers	14-39	12-15	5-18	3	6.7
West	13-21	8-15	12-26	4	5.7
Miller	12-27	6-8	10-25	8	5.0
F. Johnson	7-17	4-4	1-2	5	3.6
Mustaf	0-0	0-0	0-0	0	0.0
Totals	**244-521**	**125-161**	**86-260**	**135**	**106.7**

1993 NBA Playoff Results

Eastern Division

New York defeated Indiana 3 games to 1
Chicago defeated Atlanta 3 games to 0
Charlotte defeated Boston 3 games to 1
Cleveland defeated New Jersey 3 games to 2
Chicago defeated Cleveland 4 games to 0
New York defeated Charlotte 4 games to 1
Chicago defeated New York 4 games to 2

Western Division

Phoenix defeated L.A. Lakers 3 games to 2
San Antonio defeated Portland 3 games to 1
Houston defeated L.A. Clippers 3 games to 2
Seattle defeated Utah 3 games to 2
Phoenix defeated San Antonio 4 games to 2
Seattle defeated Houston 4 games to 3
Phoenix defeated Seattle 4 games to 3

Championship

Chicago defeated Phoenix 4 games to 2

MVP in Playoffs

1969	Jerry West, Los Angeles
1970	Willis Reed, New York
1971	Lew Alcindor, Milwaukee
1972	Wilt Chamberlain, Los Angeles
1973	Willis Reed, New York
1974	John Havlicek, Boston
1975	Rick Barry, Golden State
1976	Jo Jo White, Boston
1977	Bill Walton, Portland
1978	Wes Unseld, Washington
1979	Dennis Johnson, Seattle
1980	Magic Johnson, Los Angeles
1981	Cedric Maxwell, Boston
1982	Magic Johnson, Los Angeles
1983	Moses Malone, Philadelphia
1984	Larry Bird, Boston
1985	Kareem Abdul-Jabbar, L.A. Lakers
1986	Larry Bird, Boston
1987	Magic Johnson, L.A. Lakers
1988	James Worthy, L.A. Lakers
1989	Joe Dumars, Detroit
1990	Isiah Thomas, Detroit
1991	Michael Jordan, Chicago
1992	Michael Jordan, Chicago
1993	Michael Jordan, Chicago

NBA Scoring Leaders

Year	Scoring champion	Pts	Avg
1947	Joe Fulks, Philadelphia	1,389	23.2
1948	Max Zaslofsky, Chicago	1,007	21.0
1949	George Mikan, Minneapolis	1,698	28.3
1950	George Mikan, Minneapolis	1,865	27.4
1951	George Mikan, Minneapolis	1,932	28.4
1952	Paul Arizin, Philadelphia	1,674	25.4
1953	Neil Johnston, Philadelphia	1,564	22.3
1954	Neil Johnston, Philadelphia	1,759	24.4
1955	Neil Johnston, Philadelphia	1,631	22.7
1956	Bob Pettit, St. Louis	1,849	25.7
1957	Paul Arizin, Philadelphia	1,817	25.6
1958	George Yardley, Detroit	2,001	27.8
1959	Bob Pettit, St. Louis	2,105	29.2
1960	Wilt Chamberlain, Philadelphia	2,707	37.9
1961	Wilt Chamberlain, Philadelphia	3,033	38.4
1962	Wilt Chamberlain, Philadelphia	4,029	50.4
1963	Wilt Chamberlain, San Francisco	3,586	44.8
1964	Wilt Chamberlain, San Francisco	2,948	36.5
1965	Wilt Chamberlain, San Fran., Phila.	2,534	34.7
1966	Wilt Chamberlain, Philadelphia	2,649	33.5
1967	Rick Barry, San Francisco	2,775	35.6
1968	Dave Bing, Detroit	2,142	27.1
1969	Elvin Hayes, San Diego	2,327	28.4
1970	Jerry West, Los Angeles	2,309	31.2
1971	Lew Alcindor, Milwaukee	2,596	31.7
1972	Kareem Abdul-Jabbar (Alcindor), Milwaukee	2,822	34.8
1973	Nate Archibald, Kansas City-Omaha	2,719	34.0
1974	Bob McAdoo, Buffalo	2,261	30.6
1975	Bob McAdoo, Buffalo	2,831	34.5
1976	Bob McAdoo, Buffalo	2,427	31.1
1977	Pete Maravich, New Orleans	2,273	31.1
1978	George Gervin, San Antonio	2,232	27.2
1979	George Gervin, San Antonio	2,365	29.6
1980	George Gervin, San Antonio	2,585	33.1
1981	Adrian Dantley, Utah	2,452	30.7
1982	George Gervin, San Antonio	2,551	32.3
1983	Alex English, Denver	2,326	28.4
1984	Adrian Dantley, Utah	2,418	30.6
1985	Bernard King, New York	1,809	32.9
1986	Dominique Wilkins, Atlanta	2,366	30.3
1987	Michael Jordan, Chicago	3,041	37.1
1988	Michael Jordan, Chicago	2,868	35.0
1989	Michael Jordan, Chicago	2,633	32.5
1990	Michael Jordan, Chicago	2,753	33.6
1991	Michael Jordan, Chicago	2,580	31.5
1992	Michael Jordan, Chicago	2,404	30.1
1993	Michael Jordan, Chicago	2,541	32.6

NBA Most Valuable Player

1956	Bob Pettit, St. Louis
1957	Bob Cousy, Boston
1958	Bill Russell, Boston
1959	Bob Pettit, St. Louis
1960	Wilt Chamberlain, Philadelphia
1961	Bill Russell, Boston
1962	Bill Russell, Boston
1963	Bill Russell, Boston
1964	Oscar Robertson, Cincinnati
1965	Bill Russell, Boston
1966	Wilt Chamberlain, Philadelphia
1967	Wilt Chamberlain, Philadelphia
1968	Wilt Chamberlain, Philadelphia
1969	Wes Unseld, Baltimore
1970	Willis Reed, New York
1971	Lew Alcindor, Milwaukee
1972	Kareem Abdul-Jabbar (Alcindor), Milwaukee
1973	Dave Cowens, Boston
1974	Kareem Abdul-Jabbar, Milwaukee
1975	Bob McAdoo, Buffalo
1976	Kareem Abdul-Jabbar, Los Angeles
1977	Kareem Abdul-Jabbar, Los Angeles
1978	Bill Walton, Portland
1979	Moses Malone, Houston
1980	Kareem Abdul-Jabbar, Los Angeles
1981	Julius Erving, Philadelphia
1982	Moses Malone, Houston
1983	Moses Malone, Philadelphia
1984	Larry Bird, Boston
1985	Larry Bird, Boston
1986	Larry Bird, Boston
1987	Magic Johnson, L.A. Lakers
1988	Michael Jordan, Chicago
1989	Magic Johnson, L.A. Lakers
1990	Magic Johnson, L.A. Lakers
1991	Michael Jordan, Chicago
1992	Michael Jordan, Chicago
1993	Charles Barkley, Phoenix

NBA Champions 1947-1993

	Regular season		Playoffs		
Year	Eastern Conference	Western Conference	Winner	Coach	Runner-up
1947	Washington	Chicago	Philadelphia	Ed Gottlieb	Chicago
1948	Philadelphia	St. Louis	Baltimore	Buddy Jeannette	Philadelphia
1949	Washington	Rochester	Minneapolis	John Kundla	Washington
1950	Syracuse	Minneapolis	Minneapolis	John Kundla	Syracuse
1951	Philadelphia	Minneapolis	Rochester	Lester Harrison	New York
1952	Syracuse	Rochester	Minneapolis	John Kundla	New York
1953	New York	Minneapolis	Minneapolis	John Kundla	New York
1954	New York	Minneapolis	Minneapolis	John Kundla	Syracuse
1955	Syracuse	Ft. Wayne	Syracuse	Al Cervi	Ft. Wayne
1956	Philadelphia	Ft. Wayne	Philadelphia	George Senesky	Ft. Wayne
1957	Boston	St. Louis	Boston	Red Auerbach	St. Louis
1958	Boston	St. Louis	St. Louis	Alex Hannum	Boston
1959	Boston	St. Louis	Boston	Red Auerbach	Minneapolis
1960	Boston	St. Louis	Boston	Red Auerbach	St. Louis
1961	Boston	St. Louis	Boston	Red Auerbach	St. Louis
1962	Boston	Los Angeles	Boston	Red Auerbach	Los Angeles
1963	Boston	Los Angeles	Boston	Red Auerbach	Los Angeles
1964	Boston	San Francisco	Boston	Red Auerbach	San Francisco
1965	Boston	Los Angeles	Boston	Red Auerbach	Los Angeles
1966	Philadelphia	Los Angeles	Boston	Red Auerbach	Los Angeles
1967	Philadelphia	San Francisco	Philadelphia	Alex Hannum	San Francisco
1968	Philadelphia	St. Louis	Boston	Bill Russell	Los Angeles
1969	Baltimore	Los Angeles	Boston	Bill Russell	Los Angeles
1970	New York	Atlanta	New York	Red Holzman	Los Angeles

	Atlantic	Central	Midwest	Pacific	Winner	Coach	Runner-up
1971	New York	Baltimore	Milwaukee	Los Angeles	Milwaukee	Larry Costello	Baltimore
1972	Boston	Baltimore	Milwaukee	Los Angeles	Los Angeles	Bill Sharman	New York
1973	Boston	Baltimore	Milwaukee	Los Angeles	New York	Red Holzman	Los Angeles
1974	Boston	Capital	Milwaukee	Los Angeles	Boston	Tom Heinsohn	Milwaukee
1975	Boston	Washington	Chicago	Golden State	Golden State	Al Attles	Washington
1976	Boston	Cleveland	Milwaukee	Golden State	Boston	Tom Heinsohn	Phoenix
1977	Philadelphia	Houston	Denver	Los Angeles	Portland	Jack Ramsay	Philadelphia
1978	Philadelphia	San Antonio	Denver	Portland	Washington	Dick Motta	Seattle
1979	Washington	San Antonio	Kansas City	Seattle	Seattle	Len Wilkens	Washington
1980	Boston	Atlanta	Milwaukee	Los Angeles	Los Angeles	Paul Westhead	Philadelphia
1981	Boston	Milwaukee	San Antonio	Phoenix	Boston	Bill Fitch	Houston
1982	Boston	Milwaukee	San Antonio	Los Angeles	Los Angeles	Pat Riley	Philadelphia
1983	Philadelphia	Milwaukee	San Antonio	Los Angeles	Philadelphia	Billy Cunningham	Los Angeles
1984	Boston	Milwaukee	Utah	Los Angeles	Boston	K.C. Jones	Los Angeles
1985	Boston	Milwaukee	Denver	L.A. Lakers	L.A. Lakers	Pat Riley	Boston
1986	Boston	Milwaukee	Houston	L.A. Lakers	Boston	K.C. Jones	Houston
1987	Boston	Atlanta	Dallas	L.A. Lakers	L.A. Lakers	Pat Riley	Boston
1988	Boston	Detroit	Denver	L.A. Lakers	L.A. Lakers	Pat Riley	Detroit
1989	New York	Detroit	Utah	L.A. Lakers	Detroit	Chuck Daly	L.A. Lakers
1990	Philadelphia	Detroit	San Antonio	L.A. Lakers	Detroit	Chuck Daly	Portland
1991	Boston	Chicago	San Antonio	Portland	Chicago	Phil Jackson	L.A. Lakers
1992	Boston	Chicago	Utah	Portland	Chicago	Phil Jackson	Portland
1993	New York	Chicago	Houston	Phoenix	Chicago	Phil Jackson	Phoenix

NBA Coach of the Year, 1963-1993

1963 Harry Gallatin, St. Louis Hawks
1964 Alex Hannum, San Francisco Warriors
1965 Red Auerbach, Boston Celtics
1966 Dolph Schayes, Philadelphia 76ers
1967 Johnny Kerr, Chicago Bulls
1968 Richie Guerin, St. Louis Hawks
1969 Gene Shue, Baltimore Bullets
1970 Red Holzman, New York Knicks
1971 Dick Motta, Chicago Bulls
1972 Bill Sharman, Los Angeles Lakers
1973 Tom Heinsohn, Boston Celtics
1974 Ray Scott, Detroit Pistons
1975 Phil Johnson, Kansas City-Omaha Kings
1976 Bill Fitch, Cleveland Cavaliers
1977 Tom Nissalke, Houston Rockets
1978 Hubie Brown, Atlanta Hawks
1979 Cotton Fitzsimmons, Kansas City Kings
1980 Bill Fitch, Boston Celtics
1981 Jack McKinney, Indiana Pacers
1982 Gene Shue, Washington Bullets
1983 Don Nelson, Milwaukee Bucks
1984 Frank Layden, Utah Jazz
1985 Don Nelson, Milwaukee Bucks
1986 Mike Fratello, Atlanta Hawks
1987 Mike Schuler, Portland Trail Blazers
1988 Doug Moe, Denver Nuggets
1989 Cotton Fitzsimmons, Phoenix Suns
1990 Pat Riley, Los Angeles Lakers
1991 Don Chaney, Houston Rockets
1992 Don Nelson, Golden State Warriors
1993 Pat Riley, New York Knicks

NBA All-League Team in 1993

First team	Position	Second team
Karl Malone, Utah	Forward	Dominique Wilkins, Atlanta
Charles Barkley, Phoenix	Forward	Larry Johnson, Charlotte
Hakeem Olajuwon, Houston	Center	Patrick Ewing, New York
Mark Price, Cleveland	Guard	Joe Dumars, Detroit
Michael Jordan, Chicago	Guard	John Stockton, Utah

NBA Statistical Leaders, 1992-1993

Scoring
(70 Games or 1,400 Pts.)

	G	FG	Pts	Avg
Jordan, Chicago	78	992	2541	32.6
Wilkins, Atlanta	71	741	2121	29.9
K. Malone, Utah	82	797	2217	27.0
Olajuwon, Houston	82	848	2140	26.1
Barkley, Phoenix	76	716	1944	25.6
Ewing, New York	81	779	1959	24.2
Dumars, Detroit	77	677	1809	23.5
O'Neal, Orlando	81	733	1893	23.4
Robinson, San Antonio	82	676	1916	23.4
Manning, L.A. Clippers	79	702	1800	22.8
Petrovic, New Jersey	70	587	1564	22.3
Johnson, Charlotte	82	728	1810	22.1
Hardaway, Golden St.	66	522	1419	21.5
Miller, Indiana	82	571	1736	21.2
Mourning, Charlotte	78	572	1639	21.0
Lewis, Boston	80	663	1666	20.8
Coleman, New Jersey	76	564	1572	20.7
Hawkins, Philadelphia	81	551	1643	20.3
Daugherty, Cleveland	71	520	1432	20.2
Anderson, Orlando	79	594	1574	19.9

Rebounds Per Game
(70 Games or 800 Rebounds)

	G	Def	Tot	Avg
Rodman, Detroit	62	765	1132	18.3
O'Neal, Orlando	81	780	1122	13.9
Mutombo, Denver	82	726	1070	13.0
Olajuwon, Houston	82	785	1068	13.0
Willis, Atlanta	80	693	1028	12.9
Barkley, Phoenix	76	691	928	12.2
Ewing, New York	81	789	980	12.1
Seikaly, Miami	72	587	846	11.8
Robinson, San Antonio	82	727	956	11.7
Coleman, New Jersey	76	605	852	11.2
K. Malone, Utah	82	692	919	11.2

Field Goal Percentage
(300 Field Goals)

	FG	FGA	Pct
Ceballos, Phoenix	381	662	.576
Daugherty, Cleveland	520	911	.571
Davis, Indiana	304	535	.568
O'Neal, Orlando	733	1304	.562
Thorpe, Houston	385	690	.558
K. Malone, Utah	797	1443	.552
Nance, Cleveland	533	971	.549
Brickowski, Milwaukee	456	836	.545
Stewart, Washington	306	564	.543
Carr, San Antonio	379	705	.538

Free Throw Percentage
(125 Free Throws Made)

	FT	FTA	Pct
Price, Cleveland	289	305	.948
Jackson, Denver	217	232	.935
Johnson, Seattle	234	257	.911
Williams, Minnesota	419	462	.907
Skiles, Orlando	289	324	.892
Pierce, Seattle	313	352	.889
Miller, Indiana	427	485	.880
Smith, Houston	195	222	.878
Petrovic, New Jersey	315	362	.870
Lewis, Boston	326	376	.867

3-Point Field Goal Percentage
(50 3-Point Field Goals)

	FG	FGA	Pct
Armstrong, Chicago	63	139	.453
Mullin, Golden St.	60	133	.451
Petrovic, New Jersey	75	167	.449
Smith, Houston	96	219	.438
Les, Sacramento	66	154	.429
Price, Cleveland	122	293	.416
Porter, Portland	143	345	.414
Ainge, Phoenix	150	372	.403
Scott, Orlando	108	268	.403
Smith, Miami	53	132	.402

Assists
(70 Games or 400 Assists)

	G	Ast	Avg
Stockton, Utah	82	987	12.0
Hardaway, Golden St.	66	699	10.6
Skiles, Orlando	78	735	9.4
M. Jackson, L.A. Clippers	82	724	8.8
Bogues, Charlotte	81	711	8.8
Williams, Minnesota	76	661	8.7
Thomas, Detroit	79	671	8.5
Blaylock, Atlanta	80	671	8.4
Anderson, New Jersey	55	449	8.2
Price, Cleveland	75	602	8.0

Steals
(70 Games or 125 Steals)

	G	Stl	Avg
Jordan, Chicago	78	221	2.83
Blaylock, Atlanta	80	203	2.54
Stockton, Utah	82	199	2.43
McMillan, Seattle	73	173	2.37
Robertson, Mil.-Det.	69	155	2.25
Harper, L.A. Clippers	80	177	2.21
Murdock, Milwaukee	79	174	2.20
Williams, Minnesota	76	165	2.17
Payton, Seattle	82	177	2.16
Pippen, Chicago	81	173	2.14

Blocked Shots
(70 Games or 100 Blocked Shots)

	G	Blk	Avg
Olajuwon, Houston	82	342	4.17
O'Neal, Orlando	81	286	3.53
Mutombo, Denver	82	287	3.50
Mourning, Charlotte	78	271	3.47
Robinson, San Antonio	82	264	3.22
Nance, Cleveland	77	198	2.57
Ellison, Washington	49	108	2.20
Bol, Philadelphia	58	119	2.05
Robinson, Portland	82	163	1.99
Ewing, New York	81	161	1.99

NBA Rookie of the Year

Year	Player
1953	Don Meineke, Ft. Wayne
1954	Ray Felix, Baltimore
1955	Bob Pettit, Milwaukee
1956	Maurice Stokes, Rochester
1957	Tom Heinsohn, Boston
1958	Woody Sauldsberry, Philadelphia
1959	Elgin Baylor, Minneapolis
1960	Wilt Chamberlain, Philadelphia
1961	Oscar Robertson, Cincinnati
1962	Walt Bellamy, Chicago
1963	Terry Dischinger, Chicago
1964	Jerry Lucas, Cincinnati
1965	Willis Reed, New York
1966	Rick Barry, San Francisco
1967	Dave Bing, Detroit
1968	Earl Monroe, Baltimore
1969	Wes Unseld, Baltimore
1970	Lew Alcindor, Milwaukee
1971	Dave Cowens, Boston; Geoff Petrie, Portland (tie)
1972	Sidney Wicks, Portland
1973	Bob McAdoo, Buffalo
1974	Ernie DiGregorio, Buffalo
1975	Keith Wilkes, Golden State
1976	Alvan Adams, Phoenix
1977	Adrian Dantley, Buffalo
1978	Walter Davis, Phoenix
1979	Phil Ford, Kansas City
1980	Larry Bird, Boston
1981	Darrell Griffith, Utah
1982	Buck Williams, New Jersey
1983	Terry Cummings, San Diego
1984	Ralph Sampson, Houston
1985	Michael Jordan, Chicago
1986	Patrick Ewing, New York
1987	Chuck Person, Indiana
1988	Mark Jackson, New York
1989	Mitch Richmond, Golden State
1990	David Robinson, San Antonio
1991	Derrick Coleman, New Jersey
1992	Larry Johnson, Charlotte
1993	Shaquille O'Neal, Orlando

Individual Statistics, 1992-1993

(Over 600 Minutes Played)

Atlanta Hawks

	Min	FG%	FT%	Reb	Ast	Pts	Avg
Wilkins	2647	.468	.828	482	227	2121	29.9
Willis	2878	.506	.653	1028	165	1435	17.9
Augmon	2112	.501	.739	287	170	1021	14.0
Blaylock	2820	.429	.728	280	671	1069	13.4
Ferrell	1736	.470	.779	191	132	839	10.2
Graham	1508	.457	.733	190	164	650	8.1
Mays	787	.417	.659	53	72	341	7.0
Keefe	1549	.500	.700	432	80	542	6.6
Henson	719	.390	.850	55	155	213	4.0
Koncak	1975	.464	.480	427	140	275	3.5

Coach—Bob Weiss

Boston Celtics

	Min	FG%	FT%	Reb	Ast	Pts	Avg
Lewis	3144	.470	.867	347	298	1666	20.8
McDaniel	2215	.495	.793	489	163	1111	13.5
Gamble	2541	.507	.826	246	226	1093	13.3
Parish	2146	.535	.689	740	61	994	12.6
Brown	2254	.468	.793	246	461	874	10.9
McHale	1656	.459	.841	358	73	762	10.7
Douglas	1932	.498	.560	162	508	618	7.8
Abdelnaby	1311	.518	.759	337	27	578	7.7
Fox	1082	.484	.802	159	113	453	6.4
Kleine	1129	.404	.707	346	39	257	3.3

Coach—Chris Ford

Charlotte Hornets

	Min	FG%	FT%	Reb	Ast	Pts	Avg
Johnson	3323	.526	.767	864	353	1810	22.1
Mourning	2644	.511	.781	805	76	1639	21.0
Gill	2430	.449	.772	340	268	1167	16.9
Curry	2094	.452	.866	286	180	1227	15.3
Newman	1471	.522	.808	143	117	764	11.9
Bogues	2833	.453	.833	298	711	808	10.0
Gattison	1475	.529	.604	353	68	508	6.8
Wingate	1471	.536	.738	174	183	440	6.1
Bennett	857	.423	.732	63	136	276	3.7

Coach—Allan Bristow

Chicago Bulls

	Min	FG%	FT%	Reb	Ast	Pts	Avg
Jordan	3067	.495	.837	522	428	2541	32.6
Pippen	3123	.473	.663	621	507	1510	18.6
Grant	2745	.508	.619	729	201	1017	13.2
Armstrong	2492	.499	.861	149	330	1009	12.3
S. Williams	1369	.466	.714	451	68	422	5.9
Cartwright	1253	.411	.735	233	83	354	5.6
King	1059	.471	.705	207	71	408	5.4
Tucker	909	.485	.818	71	82	356	5.2
Perdue	998	.557	.604	287	74	341	4.7
Paxson	1030	.451	.850	48	136	246	4.2
McCray	1019	.451	.692	158	81	222	3.5

Coach—Phil Jackson

Cleveland Cavaliers

	Min	FG%	FT%	Reb	Ast	Pts	Avg
Daugherty	2691	.571	.795	726	312	1432	20.2
Price	2380	.484	.948	201	602	1365	18.2
Nance	2753	.549	.818	668	223	1268	16.5
Ehlo	2559	.490	.717	403	254	949	11.6
Wilkins	2079	.453	.840	214	183	890	11.1
Williams	2055	.470	.716	415	152	738	11.0
Brandon	1622	.478	.825	179	302	725	8.8
Sanders	1189	.497	.756	170	75	454	8.6
Ferry	1461	.479	.876	279	137	573	7.5

Coach—Lenny Wilkins

Dallas Mavericks

	Min	FG%	FT%	Reb	Ast	Pts	Avg
Harper	2108	.419	.756	123	334	1126	18.2
Jackson	938	.395	.739	122	131	457	16.3
Rooks	2087	.493	.602	536	95	970	13.5
Davis	2462	.455	.594	701	68	955	12.7
Smith	1524	.434	.757	328	104	634	10.4
White	1433	.435	.750	370	49	618	9.7
Legler	635	.436	.803	59	46	289	8.8
Iuzzolino	1769	.462	.765	140	328	610	8.7
Bond	1578	.402	.772	196	122	590	8.0
Cambridge	885	.484	.687	167	58	370	7.0
Howard	1295	.442	.766	212	67	439	6.5
Hodge	1267	.403	.683	294	75	393	5.0
Wiley	995	.378	.654	91	181	263	4.5

Coach—Richie Adubato; Garfield Heard

Denver Nuggets

	Min	FG%	FT%	Reb	Ast	Pts	Avg
Jackson	2710	.450	.935	225	344	1553	19.2
Williams	2722	.458	.804	428	295	1341	17.0
Ellis	2749	.504	.748	744	151	1205	14.7
Mutombo	3029	.510	.681	1070	147	1131	13.8
Pack	1579	.470	.768	160	335	810	10.5
Stith	865	.446	.832	124	49	347	8.9
Liberty	1585	.406	.654	335	105	628	8.1
Macon	1141	.415	.700	103	126	358	7.5
Lichti	752	.449	.794	102	52	331	6.9
Plummer	737	.465	.726	173	40	281	4.7
Hammonds	713	.475	.613	127	24	248	4.6
Hastings	670	.509	.727	137	34	156	2.1

Coach—Dan Issel

Detroit Pistons

	Min	FG%	FT%	Reb	Ast	Pts	Avg
Dumars	3094	.466	.864	148	308	1809	23.5
Thomas	2922	.418	.737	232	671	1391	17.6
Mills	2183	.461	.791	472	111	1199	14.8
Woolridge	1477	.479	.673	176	112	655	13.1
Aguirre	1056	.443	.767	152	105	503	9.9
Robertson	2006	.458	.656	269	263	618	9.0
Laimbeer	1933	.509	.894	419	127	687	8.7
Rodman	2410	.427	.534	1132	102	468	7.5
Polynice	1299	.490	.465	418	29	486	7.3
Glass	848	.419	.641	142	77	316	5.3
Young	836	.413	.875	47	119	188	2.9

Coach—Ron Rothstein

Golden State Warriors

	Min	FG%	FT%	Reb	Ast	Pts	Avg
Mullin	1902	.510	.810	232	166	1191	25.9
Hardaway	2609	.447	.744	263	699	1419	21.5
Marciulionis	836	.543	.761	97	105	521	17.4
Owens	1201	.501	.639	264	144	612	16.5
Sprewell	2741	.464	.746	271	295	1182	15.4
Alexander	1753	.516	.685	420	93	809	11.2
Gatling	1248	.539	.725	320	40	648	9.3
Grayer	1025	.467	.669	157	70	423	8.8
Hill	2070	.508	.624	754	68	640	8.6
Buechler	1287	.437	.747	195	94	437	6.2
Houston	1274	.446	.665	315	69	421	5.3

Coach—Don Nelson

Houston Rockets

	Min	FG%	FT%	Reb	Ast	Pts	Avg
Olajuwon	3242	.529	.779	1068	291	2140	26.1
Maxwell	2251	.407	.719	221	297	982	13.8
Smith	2422	.520	.878	160	446	1065	13.0
Thorpe	2357	.558	.598	589	181	923	12.8
Horry	2330	.474	.715	392	191	801	10.1
Herrara	1800	.541	.710	454	61	605	7.5
Bullard	1356	.431	.784	222	110	575	7.3
Floyd	867	.407	.794	86	132	345	6.6
Brooks	1516	.475	.830	99	243	519	6.3
Garland	1004	.443	.910	108	138	391	5.9

Coach—Rudy Tomjanovich

Indiana Pacers

	Min	FG%	FT%	Reb	Ast	Pts	Avg
Miller	2954	.479	.880	258	262	1736	21.2
Schrempf	3098	.476	.804	780	493	1567	19.1
Smits	2072	.486	.732	432	121	1155	14.3
Richardson	2396	.479	.742	267	573	769	10.4
Fleming	1503	.505	.726	169	224	710	9.5
Davis	2264	.568	.529	723	69	727	8.9
McCloud	1500	.411	.735	205	192	565	7.2
Mitchell	1402	.445	.811	248	76	584	7.2
Williams	844	.532	.706	228	38	348	6.1
Sealy	672	.426	.689	112	47	330	5.7
Thompson	730	.488	.744	178	34	237	3.8

Coach—Bob Hill

Los Angeles Clippers

	Min	FG%	FT%	Reb	Ast	Pts	Avg
Manning	2761	.509	.802	520	207	1800	22.8
Harper	2970	.451	.769	425	360	1443	18.0

	Min	FG%	FT%	Reb	Ast	Pts	Avg
Norman	2477	.511	.595	571	165	1137	15.0
M. Jackson	3117	.486	.803	388	724	1181	14.4
Roberts	1816	.527	.488	478	59	870	11.3
Vaught	1653	.508	.748	492	54	743	9.4
Williams	1638	.430	.543	316	142	492	6.6
Grant	1624	.441	.743	139	353	486	6.6

Coach—Larry Brown

Los Angeles Lakers

	Min	FG%	FT%	Reb	Ast	Pts	Avg
Threatt	2893	.508	.823	273	564	1235	15.1
Worthy	2359	.447	.810	247	278	1221	14.9
Perkins	1589	.459	.829	379	128	673	13.7
Scott	1677	.449	.848	134	157	792	13.7
Green	2819	.537	.739	711	116	1051	12.8
Divac	2525	.485	.680	720	232	1050	12.8
Peeler	1656	.468	.786	179	166	802	10.4
Campbell	1551	.458	.637	332	48	606	7.7
Edwards	617	.452	.712	100	41	328	6.3
Smith	752	.484	.756	87	63	330	6.0
Benjamin	754	.491	.663	209	22	335	5.7
Cooper	645	.392	.714	50	150	156	2.4

Coach—Randy Pfund

Miami Heat

	Min	FG%	FT%	Reb	Ast	Pts	Avg
Rice	3082	.440	.820	424	180	1554	19.0
Seikaly	2456	.480	.735	846	100	1232	17.1
Smith	1610	.451	.787	197	267	766	16.0
Long	2728	.469	.765	568	182	1061	14.0
Edwards	1134	.468	.844	121	120	556	13.9
Coles	2232	.464	.805	166	373	855	10.6
Miner	1383	.475	.762	147	73	750	10.3
Salley	1422	.502	.799	313	83	423	8.3
Shaw	1603	.393	.782	257	235	498	7.3
Askins	935	.413	.725	198	31	227	3.3

Coach—Kevin Loughery

Milwaukee Bucks

	Min	FG%	FT%	Reb	Ast	Pts	Avg
Brickowski	2075	.545	.728	405	196	1115	16.9
Edwards	2729	.512	.790	382	214	1382	16.9
Murdock	2437	.468	.780	284	603	1138	14.4
Day	1931	.432	.717	291	117	983	13.8
Woolridge	1555	.482	.678	185	115	698	12.0
Avent	2285	.433	.651	512	91	806	9.8
Lohaus	1766	.461	.723	276	127	724	9.1
Robertson	1065	.479	.629	137	156	339	8.7
Roberts	1488	.528	.799	237	118	599	7.6
Mayberry	1503	.456	.574	118	273	424	5.2
Schayes	1124	.399	.818	249	78	322	4.6

Coach—Mike Dunleavy

Minnesota Timberwolves

	Min	FG%	FT%	Reb	Ast	Pts	Avg
West	3104	.517	.841	247	235	1543	19.3
Laettner	2823	.474	.835	708	223	1472	18.2
Person	2985	.433	.649	433	343	1309	16.8
Williams	2661	.446	.907	273	661	1151	15.1
Bailey	1276	.455	.838	215	61	525	7.5
McCann	1536	.488	.625	282	68	495	6.3
Longley	1045	.455	.716	240	51	319	5.8
Smith	1266	.433	.792	96	196	347	4.3
Spencer	1296	.465	.654	324	17	293	4.1
Blanks	642	.433	.625	68	72	161	2.6

Coach—Jimmy Rodgers; Sidney Lowe

New Jersey Nets

	Min	FG%	FT%	Reb	Ast	Pts	Avg
Petrovic	2660	.518	.870	190	247	1564	22.3
Coleman	2759	.460	.808	852	276	1572	20.7
Anderson	2010	.435	.776	226	449	927	16.9
Morris	2302	.481	.794	454	106	1086	14.1
Bowie	2092	.450	.779	556	127	717	9.1
Robinson	1585	.423	.574	159	323	672	8.4
Addison	1164	.443	.814	132	53	428	6.3
Brown	1186	.483	.724	232	51	391	5.1
Mahorn	1077	.472	.800	279	33	291	3.9
Dudley	1398	.353	.518	513	16	245	3.5

Coach—Chuck Daly

New York Knickerbockers

	Min	FG%	FT%	Reb	Ast	Pts	Avg
Ewing	3003	.503	.719	980	151	1959	24.2
Starks	2477	.428	.795	204	404	1397	17.5
Smith	2172	.469	.782	432	142	1003	12.4
Mason	2482	.502	.682	640	170	831	10.3
Blackman	1434	.443	.789	102	157	580	9.7
Rivers	1886	.437	.821	192	405	604	7.8
Campbell	1062	.490	.678	155	62	449	7.7
Oakley	2230	.508	.722	708	126	565	6.9
Anthony	1699	.415	.673	170	398	459	6.6
Davis	815	.438	.796	56	83	269	5.4

Coach—Pat Riley

Orlando Magic

	Min	FG%	FT%	Reb	Ast	Pts	Avg
O'Neal	3071	.562	.592	1122	152	1893	23.4
Anderson	2920	.449	.741	477	265	1574	19.9
Scott	1759	.431	.786	186	136	858	15.9
Skiles	3086	.467	.892	290	735	1201	15.4
Royal	1636	.496	.815	295	80	706	9.2
Tolbert	1838	.498	.726	412	91	583	8.1
Bowie	1761	.471	.798	194	175	618	8.0
Turner	1479	.529	.800	252	107	528	7.0
Green	626	.439	.625	34	116	235	4.5
Kite	640	.452	.542	193	10	89	1.4

Coach—Matt Guokas

Philadelphia 76ers

	Min	FG%	FT%	Reb	Ast	Pts	Avg
Hawkins	2977	.470	.860	346	317	1643	20.3
Hornacek	2860	.470	.865	342	548	1511	19.1
Weatherspoon	2654	.469	.713	589	147	1280	15.6
Gilliam	1742	.464	.843	472	116	992	12.4
Perry	2104	.468	.710	409	126	731	9.0
Dawkins	1598	.437	.796	136	339	655	8.9
Anderson	1263	.414	.809	184	93	561	8.1
Lang	1861	.425	.763	436	79	386	5.3
Grant	996	.350	.645	67	206	194	2.7
Bol	855	.409	.632	193	18	126	2.2

Coach—Doug Moe; Fred Carter

Phoenix Suns

	Min	FG%	FT%	Reb	Ast	Pts	Avg
Barkley	2859	.520	.765	928	385	1944	25.6
Majerle	3199	.464	.778	383	311	1388	16.9
K. Johnson	1643	.499	.819	104	384	791	16.1
Dumas	1320	.524	.707	223	60	757	15.8
Ceballos	1607	.576	.725	408	77	949	12.8
Chambers	1723	.447	.837	345	101	892	12.2
Ainge	2163	.462	.848	214	260	947	11.8
Knight	888	.391	.779	64	145	315	6.1
Miller	1069	.475	.710	275	118	313	5.6
West	1558	.614	.518	458	29	436	5.3
F. Johnson	1122	.436	.776	113	186	332	4.3

Coach—Paul Westphal

Portland Trail Blazers

	Min	FG%	FT%	Reb	Ast	Pts	Avg
Drexler	1671	.429	.839	309	278	976	19.9
Robinson	2575	.473	.690	542	182	1570	19.1
Porter	2883	.454	.843	316	419	1476	18.2
Strickland	2474	.485	.717	337	559	1069	13.7
Kersey	1719	.438	.634	406	121	686	10.6
Duckworth	1762	.438	.730	387	70	729	9.9
Elie	1757	.458	.855	216	177	708	8.6
Williams	2498	.511	.645	690	75	678	8.3
Bryant	1396	.503	.703	324	41	476	6.0

Coach—Rick Adelman

Sacramento Kings

	Min	FG%	FT%	Reb	Ast	Pts	Avg
Richmond	1728	.474	.845	154	221	987	21.9
Simmons	2502	.444	.819	495	312	1235	17.9
Williams	1673	.435	.742	265	178	1001	17.0
Tisdale	2283	.509	.758	500	108	1263	16.6
Webb	2335	.433	.851	193	481	1000	14.5
Bonner	1764	.461	.593	455	96	601	8.6
Higgins	1425	.412	.861	193	119	571	8.3
Causwell	1211	.545	.624	303	35	453	8.2
Brown	1726	.463	.732	212	196	567	7.6
Chilcutt	834	.485	.696	194	64	362	6.1
Les	881	.425	.840	89	169	328	4.5
Rambis	822	.519	.662	227	53	177	2.5

Coach—Garry St. Jean

San Antonio Spurs

	Min	FG%	FT%	Reb	Ast	Pts	Avg
Robinson	3211	.501	.732	956	301	1916	23.4
Elliott	2604	.491	.795	322	265	1207	17.2
Ellis	2731	.499	.797	312	107	1366	16.7

	Min	FG%	FT%	Reb	Ast	Pts	Avg
Carr	1947	.538	.777	388	97	932	13.1
Reid	1887	.476	.764	456	80	780	9.4
Daniels	1573	.443	.727	216	148	701	9.1
Johnson	2030	.502	.791	146	561	656	8.7
Del Negro	1526	.507	.863	163	291	543	7.4
Smith	833	.437	.409	268	28	85	1.3

Coach—Jerry Tarkanian; John Lucas

Seattle SuperSonics

	Min	FG%	FT%	Reb	Ast	Pts	Avg
Pierce	2218	.489	.889	192	220	1403	18.2
Kemp	2582	.492	.712	833	155	1388	17.8
Johnson	1869	.467	.911	272	135	1177	14.4
Payton	2548	.494	.770	281	399	1110	13.5
McKey	2439	.496	.741	327	197	1034	13.4
Perkins	2351	.477	.820	524	156	1036	13.1
Barros	1243	.451	.831	107	151	541	7.8
McMillan	1977	.464	.709	306	384	546	7.5
Cage	2156	.526	.469	659	69	499	6.1
Askew	1129	.492	.705	161	122	411	5.6

Coach—George Karl

Utah Jazz

	Min	FG%	FT%	Reb	Ast	Pts	Avg
K. Malone	3099	.552	.740	919	308	2217	27.0
J. Malone	2558	.494	.852	173	128	1429	18.1
Stockton	2863	.486	.798	237	987	1239	15.1
Corbin	2555	.503	.826	519	173	950	11.6
Humphries	2034	.436	.777	143	317	690	8.8
Benoit	1712	.436	.750	392	43	664	8.1
Krystkowiak	1362	.466	.796	279	68	513	7.2
Brown	1551	.430	.689	391	64	465	5.7
Eaton	1104	.546	.700	264	17	177	2.8

Coach—Jerry Sloan

Washington Bullets

	Min	FG%	FT%	Reb	Ast	Pts	Avg
Grant	2667	.487	.727	412	205	1339	18.6
Ellison	1701	.521	.702	433	117	852	17.4
Adams	2499	.439	.856	240	526	1035	14.8
Gugliotta	2795	.426	.644	781	306	1187	14.7
Chapman	1300	.477	.810	88	116	749	12.5
Stewart	1823	.543	.727	383	146	796	9.8
Smith	1546	.458	.859	106	186	639	9.3
Overton	990	.471	.728	106	157	366	8.1
MacLean	674	.435	.811	122	39	407	6.6
Johnson	1287	.479	.730	195	89	478	6.5
Price	859	.358	.794	103	154	262	3.9

Coach—Wes Unseld

Michael Jordan's Career Scoring Statistics With the Chicago Bulls

	Regular Season					Playoffs				
Year	G	FG%	FT%	PTS	PPG	G	FG%	FT%	PTS	PPG
84-85	82	.515	.845	2,313	28.2	4	.436	.828	117	29.3
85-86	18	.457	.840	408	22.7	3	.505	.872	131	43.7
86-87	82	.482	.857	3,041	37.1	3	.417	.897	107	35.7
87-88	82	.535	.841	2,868	35.0	10	.530	.869	363	36.3
88-89	81	.538	.850	2,633	32.5	17	.510	.799	591	34.8
89-90	82	.526	.848	2,753	33.6	16	.514	.836	587	36.7
90-91	82	.539	.851	2,580	31.5	17	.524	.845	529	31.1
91-92	80	.519	.832	2,404	30.1	22	.499	.857	759	34.5
92-93	78	.495	.837	2,541	32.6	19	.475	.805	666	35.1
Totals	**667**	**.516**	**.846**	**21,541**	**32.3**	**111**	**.501**	**.834**	**3,820**	**34.7**

1993 NBA Player Draft, First Round Picks

Orlando—Chris Webber,* Michigan
Philadelphia—Shawn Bradley, Brigham Young
Golden State—Anfernee Hardaway,* Memphis St.
Dallas—Jamal Mashbrun, Kentucky
Minnesota—J.R. Rider, UNLV
Washington—Calbert Cheaney, Indiana
Sacramento—Bobby Hurley, Duke
Milwaukee—Vin Baker, Hartford
Denver—Rodney Rogers, Wake Forest
Detroit—Lindsey Hunter, Jackson St.
Detroit—Allan Houston, Tennessee
L.A. Lakers—George Lynch, North Carolina
L.A. Clippers—Terry Dehere, Seton Hall
Indiana—Scott Haskin, Oregon St.
Atlanta—Doug Edwards, Florida St.
New Jersey—Rex Walters, Kansas
Charlotte—Greg Graham, Indiana
Utah—Luther Wright, Seton Hall
Boston—Acie Earl, Iowa
Charlotte—Scott Burrell, Connecticut
Portland—James Robinson, Alabama
Cleveland—Chris Mills, Arizona
Seattle—Ervin Johnson, New Orleans
Houston—Sam Cassell, Florida St.
Chicago—Corie Blount, Cincinnati
Orlando—Geert Hammink, LSU
Phoenix—Malcolm Mackey, Georgia Tech

* Webber traded to Golden State for Hardaway and future draft choices.

Number One First Round NBA Draft Picks, 1966-1993

Year	Team	Player, college
1966	New York	Cazzie Russell, Michigan
1967	Detroit	Jimmy Walker, Providence
1968	Houston	Elvin Hayes, Houston
1969	Milwaukee	Lew Alcindor[1], UCLA
1970	Detroit	Bob Lanier, St. Bonaventure
1971	Cleveland	Austin Carr, Notre Dame
1972	Portland	LaRue Martin, Loyola-Chicago
1973	Philadelphia	Doug Collins, Illinois St.
1974	Portland	Bill Walton, UCLA
1975	Atlanta	David Thompson[2], N.C. State
1976	Houston	John Lucas, Maryland
1977	Milwaukee	Kent Benson, Indiana
1978	Portland	Mychal Thompson, Minnesota
1979	L.A. Lakers	Magic Johnson, Michigan St.
1980	Golden State	Joe Barry Carroll, Purdue
1981	Dallas	Mark Aguirre, DePaul
1982	L.A. Lakers	James Worthy, N. Carolina
1983	Houston	Ralph Sampson, Virginia
1984	Houston	Akeem Olajuwon, Houston
1985	New York	Patrick Ewing, Georgetown
1986	Cleveland	Brad Daugherty, N. Carolina
1987	San Antonio	David Robinson, Navy
1988	L.A. Clippers	Danny Manning, Kansas
1989	Sacramento	Pervis Ellison, Louisville
1990	New Jersey	Derrick Coleman, Syracuse
1991	Charlotte	Larry Johnson, UNLV
1992	Orlando	Shaquille O'Neal, LSU
1993	Orlando	Chris Webber[3], Michigan

(1) Later Kareem Abdul-Jabbar. (2) Signed with Denver of the ABA. (3) Traded to Golden State.

NBA All-Defensive Team in 1993

First team	Position	Second team
Dennis Rodman, Detroit	Forward	Larry Nance, Cleveland
Scottie Pippen, Chicago	Forward	Horace Grant, Chicago
Hakeem Olajuwon, Houston	Center	David Robinson, San Antonio
Michael Jordan, Chicago	Guard	Dan Majerle, Phoenix
Joe Dumars, Detroit	Guard	John Starks, New York

All-Time NBA Statistical Leaders

(At the start of the 1992-93 season. *Includes 1992-93 season)

Scoring Average
(400 games or 10,000 Points Minimum)

	G	Pts.	Avg
*Michael Jordan	667	21,541	32.2
Wilt Chamberlain	1,045	31,419	30.1
Elgin Baylor	846	23,149	27.4
Jerry West	932	25,192	27.0
*Dominique Wilkins	833	22,096	26.5
Bob Pettit	792	20,880	26.4
George Gervin	791	20,708	26.2
*Karl Malone	652	16,987	26.0
Oscar Robertson	1,040	26,710	25.7
Kareem Abdul-Jabbar	1,560	38,387	24.6

Field Goal Percentage
(2,000 FGM Minimum)

	FGA	FGM	Pct.
Artis Gilmore	9,570	5,732	.599
James Donaldson	5,109	2,941	.576
Charles Barkley	7,596	4,403	.580
Steve Johnson	4,965	2,841	.572
Darryl Dawkins	6,060	3,468	.572
Jeff Ruland	3,685	2,080	.564
Kevin McHale	11,051	6,209	.562
Kareem Abdul-Jabbar	28,307	15,837	.559
Buck Williams	8,583	4,752	.554
Bobby Jones	6,199	3,412	.550

Free Throw Percentage
(1,200 FTM Minimum)

	FTA	FTM	Pct.
Rick Barry	4,243	3,818	.900
Calvin Murphy	3,864	3,445	.892
Larry Bird	4,126	3,647	.884
Bill Sharman	3,357	3,143	.884
Chris Mullen	1,928	1,695	.879
Kiki Vandeweghe	2,562	3,102	.871
Mike Newlin	3,456	3,005	.870
Jeff Malone	2,231	1,939	.869
John Long	2,051	1,765	.861

Points

	Pts.
Kareem Abdul-Jabbar	38,387
Wilt Chamberlain	31,419
Elvin Hayes	27,313
*Moses Malone	27,066
Oscar Robertson	26,710
John Havlicek	26,395
Alex English	25,643
Jerry West	25,192
Adrian Dantley	23,177

Games Played

Kareem Abdul-Jabbar	1,560
*Robert Parish	1,339
Elvin Hayes	1,303
John Havlicek	1,270
*Moses Malone	1,257
Paul Silas	1,254
Alex English	1,193
Hal Greer	1,122
Dennis Johnson	1,100

Assists

Magic Johnson	9,921
Oscar Robertson	9,887
*Isiah Thomas	8,662
*John Stockton	8,352
*Maurice Cheeks	7,392
Len Wilkens	7,211
Bob Cousy	6,955
Guy Rodgers	6,917
Nate Archibald	6,476

Field Goals Made

Kareem Abdul-Jabbar	15,837
Wilt Chamberlain	12,681
Elvin Hayes	10,976
Alex English	10,659
John Havlicek	10,513
Oscar Robertson	9,508
*Moses Malone	9,320
Jerry West	9,016
Elgin Baylor	8,693

Rebounds

Wilt Chamberlain	23,924
Bill Russell	21,620
Kareem Addul-Jabbar	17,440
Elvin Hayes	16,279
*Moses Malone	15,940
Nate Thurmond	14,464
Walt Bellamy	14,241
Wes Unseld	13,769
Jerry Lucas	12,942

Individuals in the Basketball Hall of Fame

Springfield, Mass.

Players
Archibald, Nate
Arizin, Paul
Barlow, Thomas
Barry, Rick
Baylor, Elgin
Beckman, John
Bellamy, Walt
Belov, Sergei
Bing, Dave
Borgmann, Bennie
Bradley, Bill
Brennan, Joseph
Cervi, Al
Chamberlain, Wilt
Cooper, Charles
Cousy, Bob
Cowens, Dave
Cunningham, Billy
Davies, Bob
DeBernardi, Forrest
DeBusschere, Dave
Dehnert, Dutch
Endacott, Paul
Erving, Julius
Foster, Bud
Frazier, Walt
Friedman, Max
Fulks, Joe
Gale, Lauren
Gallatin, Harry
Gates, Pop
Gola, Tom
Greer, Hal
Gruenig, Ace
Hagan, Cliff
Hanson, Victor
Harris, Luisa
Havlicek, John
Hawkins, Connie
Hayes, Elvin
Heinsohn, Tom
Holman, Nat
Houbregs, Bob
Hyatt, Chuck
Issel, Dan
Johnson, William
Johnston, Neil
Jones, K.C.
Jones, Sam
Krause, Moose
Kurland, Bob
Lanier, Bob
Lapchick, Joe
Lovellette, Clyde
Lucas, Jerry
Luisetti, Hank
Macauley, Ed
Maravich, Pete
Martin, Slater
McCracken, Branch
McCracken, Jack
McDermott, Bobby
McGuire, Dick
Meyers, Ann
Mikan, George
Monroe, Earl
Murphy, Calvin
Murphy, Stretch
Page, Pat
Pettit, Bob
Phillip, Andy
Pollard, Jim
Ramsey, Frank
Reed, Willis
Robertson, Oscar
Roosma, John S.
Russell, Honey
Russell, Bill
Schayes, Adolph
Schmidt, Ernest
Schommer, John
Sedran, Barney
Semyonova, Ulyona
Sharman, Bill
Steinmetz, Christian
Thompson, Cat
Thurmond, Nate
Twyman, Jack
Unseld, Wes
Vandivier, Fuzzy
Wachter, Edward
Walton, Bill
Wanzer, Bobby
West, Jerry
White, Nera
Wilkins, Lenny
Wooden, John

Coaches
Auerbach, Red
Barry, Sam
Blood, Ernest
Cann, Howard
Carlson, Dr. H. C.
Carnesecca, Lou
Carnevale, Ben
Case, Everett
Dean, Everett
Diddle, Edgar
Drake, Bruce
Gaines, Clarence
Gardner, Jack
Gill, Slats
Hickey, Edgar
Hobson, Howard
Holzman, Red
Iba, Hank
Julian, Alvin
Keaney, Frank
Keogan, George
Knight, Bob
Lambert, Ward
Litwack, Harry
Loeffler, Kenneth
Lonborg, Dutch
McCutchan, Arad
McGuire, Al
McGuire, Frank
McLendon, John
Meyer, Ray
Meanwell, Dr. W.E.
Miller, Ralph
Newell, Pete
Ramsay, Jack
Rupp, Adolph
Sachs, Leonard
Shelton, Everett
Smith, Dean
Taylor, Fred
Teague, Bertha
Wade, Margaret
Watts, Stan
Wooden, John
Woolpert, Phil

Referees
Enright, James
Hepburn, George
Hoyt, George
Kennedy, Matthew
Leith, Lloyd
Mihalik, Red
Nucatola, John
Quigley, Ernest
Shirley, J. Dallas
Tobey, David
Walsh, David

Contributors
Abbott, Sendra B.
Allen, Phog
Bee, Clair
Brown, Walter
Bunn, John
Douglas, Bob
Duer, Al O.
Fagan, Cliff
Fisher, Harry
Fleisher, Larry
Gottlieb, Edward
Gulick, Dr. L. H.
Harrison, Lester
Hepp, Dr. Ferenc
Hickox, Edward
Hinkle, Tony
Irish, Ned
Jones, R. W.
Kennedy, Walter
Liston, Emil
Mokray, Bill
Morgan, Ralph
Morgenweck, Frank
Naismith, Dr. James
O'Brien, John
O'Brien, Larry
Olsen, Harold
Podoloff, Maurice
Porter, H. V.
Reis, William
Ripley, Elmer
St. John, Lynn
Saperstein, Abe
Schabinger, Arthur
Stagg, Amos Alonzo
Steitz, Edward
Taylor, Chuck
Tower, Oswald
Trester, Arthur
Wells, Clifford
Wilke, Lou

Skiing

World Cup Alpine Champions

Men

1967	Jean Claude Killy, France
1968	Jean Claude Killy, France
1969	Karl Schranz, Austria
1970	Karl Schranz, Austria
1971	Gustavo Thoeni, Italy
1972	Gustavo Thoeni, Italy
1973	Gustavo Thoeni, Italy
1974	Piero Gros, Italy
1975	Gustavo Thoeni, Italy
1976	Ingemar Stenmark, Sweden
1977	Ingemar Stenmark, Sweden
1978	Ingemar Stenmark, Sweden
1979	Peter Luescher, Switzerland
1980	Andreas Wenzel, Liechtenstein
1981	Phil Mahre, U.S.
1982	Phil Mahre, U.S.
1983	Phil Mahre, U.S.
1984	Pirmin Zurbriggen, Switzerland
1985	Marc Girardelli, Luxembourg
1986	Marc Girardelli, Luxembourg
1987	Pirmin Zurbriggen, Switzerland
1988	Pirmin Zurbriggen, Switzerland
1989	Marc Girardelli, Luxembourg
1990	Pirmin Zurbriggen, Switzerland
1991	Marc Girardelli, Luxembourg
1992	Paul Accola, Switzerland
1993	Marc Girardelli, Luxembourg

Women

1967	Nancy Greene, Canada
1968	Nancy Greene, Canada
1969	Gertrud Gabl, Austria
1970	Michele Jacot, France
1971	Annemarie Proell, Austria
1972	Annemarie Proell, Austria
1973	Annemarie Proell, Austria
1974	Annemarie Proell, Austria
1975	Annemarie Proell, Austria
1976	Rose Mittermaier, W. Germany
1977	Lise-Marie Morerod, Switzerland
1978	Hanni Wenzel, Liechtenstein
1979	Annemarie Proell Moser, Austria
1980	Hanni Wenzel, Liechtenstein
1981	Marie-Theres Nadig, Switzerland
1982	Erika Hess, Switzerland
1983	Tamara McKinney, U.S.
1984	Erika Hess, Switzerland
1985	Michela Figini, Switzerland
1986	Maria Walliser, Switzerland
1987	Maria Walliser, Switzerland
1988	Michela Figini, Switzerland
1989	Vreni Schneider, Switzerland
1990	Petra Kronberger, Austria
1991	Petra Kronberger, Austria
1992	Petra Kronberger, Austria
1993	Anita Wachter, Austria

Curling Champions

Source: U.S. Curling News

World Champions

Year	Country, skip
1979	Norway, Kristian Soerum
1980	Canada, Rich Folk
1981	Switzerland, Jurg Tanner
1982	Canada, Al Hackner
1983	Canada, Ed Werenich
1984	Norway, Eigil Ramsfjell
1985	Canada, Al Hackner
1986	Canada, Ed Luckowich
1987	Canada, Russ Howard
1988	Norway, Eigil Ramsfjell
1989	Canada, Pat Ryan
1990	Canada, Ed Werenich
1991	Scotland, David Smith
1992	Switzerland, Marcus Eggler
1993	Canada, Russ Howard

U.S. Men's Champions

Year	State, skip
1979	Minnesota, Scott Baird
1980	Minnesota, Paul Pustover
1981	Wisconsin, Somerville-Nichols
1982	Wisconsin, Steve Brown
1983	Colorado, Don Cooper
1984	Minnesota, Bruce Roberts
1985	Illinois, Tim Wright
1986	Wisconsin, Steve Brown
1987	Washington, Jim Vukich
1988	Washington, Doug Jones
1989	Washington, Jim Vukich
1990	Washington, Doug Jones
1991	Wisconsin, Steve Brown
1992	Washington, Doug Jones
1993	Minnesota, Scott Baird

U.S. Women's Champions

Year	State, skip
1982	Illinois, Ruth Schwenker
1983	Washington, Nancy Langley
1984	Minnesota, Amy Hatten
1985	Alaska, Bev Birklid
1986	Minnesota, Gerri Tilden
1987	Washington, Sharon Good
1988	Washington, Nancy Langey
1989	North Dakota, Jan Lagasse
1990	Colorado, Bev Behnke
1991	Texas, Maymar Gemmell
1992	Wisconsin, Lisa Schoeneberg
1993	Colorado, Bev Behnke

Westminster Kennel Club

Year	Best-in-show	Breed	Owner
1984	Ch. Seaward's Blackbeard	Newfoundland	Elinor Ayers
1985	Ch. Braeburn's Close Encounter	Scottish terrier	Sonnie Novick
1986	Ch. Marjetta National Acclaim	Pointer	Mrs. Alan Robson & Michael Zollo
1987	Ch. Covy Tucker Hill's Manhattan	German shepherd	Shirley Braunstein & Jane Firestone
1988	Ch. Great Elms Prince Charming II	Pomeranian	Skip Piazza & Olga Baker
1989	Ch. Royal Tudor's Wild As The Wind	Doberman	Sue & Art Kemp, Richard & Carolyn Vida, Beth Wilhite
1990	Ch. Wendessa Crown Prince	Pekingese	Ed Jenner
1991	Ch. Whisperwind on a Carousel	Poodle	Joan & Frederick Hartsock
1992	Ch. Registry's Lonesome Dove	Fox terrier	Marion & Sam Lawrence
1993	Ch. Salilyn's Condor	English springer spaniel	Donna & Roger Herzig

Iditarod Trail Sled Dog Race in 1993

Jeff King won the 1993 Iditarod Trail Sled Dog Race on March 17, 1993, in a record time of 10 days 15 hours and 38 minutes. By winning the 1,159-mile race from Anchorage to Nome, King received $50,000 in prize money and a pickup truck valued at about $25,000. DeeDee Jonrowe finished second and Rick Mackey finished third.

IGFA Freshwater & Saltwater All-Tackle World Records

Source: International Game Fish Association. Records confirmed to May 1993

Saltwater Fish

Species	Weight	Where caught	Date	Angler
Albacore	88 lbs. 2 oz.	Pt. Mogan, Canary Islands	Nov. 19, 1977	Siegfried Dickemann
Amberjack, greater	155 lbs. 10 oz.	Bermuda	June 24, 1981	Joseph Dawson
Barracuda, great	85 lbs.	Christmas Island	Apr. 11, 1992	John Helfrich
Barracuda, Mexican	21 lbs.	Costa Rica	Mar. 27, 1987	E. Greg Kent
Barracuda, Pacific	6 lbs. 3 oz.	Pt. Loma, San Diego, Cal.	Apr. 4, 1992	James Seibert
Bass, barred sand	13 lbs. 3 oz.	Huntington Beach, Cal.	Aug. 29, 1988	Robert Halal
Bass, black sea	9 lbs. 8 oz.	Virginia Beach, Va.	Jan. 9, 1987	Joe Mizelle Jr.
		Virginia Beach, Va.	Dec. 22, 1990	Jack Stallings, Jr.
Bass, giant sea	563 lbs. 8 oz.	Anacaba Island, Cal.	Aug. 20, 1968	James D. McAdam Jr.
Bass, striped	78 lbs. 8 oz.	Atlantic City, N.J.	Sept. 21, 1982	Albert McReynolds
Bass, white	6 lbs. 3 oz.	L. Orange, Va.	July 31, 1989	Ronald Sprouse
Bluefish	31 lbs. 12 oz.	Hatteras Inlet, N.C.	Jan. 30, 1972	James M. Hussey
Bonefish	19 lbs.	Zululand, S. Africa	May 26, 1962	Brian W. Batchelor
Bonito, Atlantic	18 lbs. 14 oz.	Fayal I., Azores	July 8, 1953	D. G. Higgs
Bonito, Pacific	14 lbs. 12 oz.	San Benitos Is., Mexico	Oct. 12, 1980	Jerome Rilling
Cabezon	23 lbs.	Juan De Fuca Strait, Wash.	Aug. 4, 1990	Wesley Hunter
Cobia	135 lbs. 9 oz.	Shark Bay, Australia	July 9, 1985	Peter W. Goulding
Cod, Atlantic	98 lbs. 12 oz.	Isle of Shoals, N.H.	June 8, 1969	Alphonse Bielevich
Cod, Pacific	30 lbs.	Andrew Bay, Alaska	June 7, 1984	Donald Vaughn
Conger	110 lbs. 8 oz.	Plymouth, England	Aug. 20, 1991	Hans Clausen
Dolphin	87 lbs.	Papagallo Gulf, Costa Rica	Sept. 25, 1976	Manual Salazar
Drum, black	113 lbs. 1 oz.	Lewes, Del.	Sept. 15, 1975	Gerald Townsend
Drum, red	94 lbs. 2 oz.	Avon, N.C.	Nov. 7, 1984	David Deuel
Eel, American	8 lbs. 8 oz.	Brewster, Mass.	May 17, 1992	Gerald LaPierre
Eel, marbled	36 lbs. 1 oz.	Hazelmere Dam, S. Africa	June 10, 1984	Ferdie van Nooten
Flounder, southern	20 lbs. 9 oz.	Nassau Sound, Fla.	Dec. 23, 1983	Larenza Mungin
Flounder, summer	22 lbs. 7 oz.	Montauk, N.Y.	Sept. 15, 1975	Charles Nappi
Grouper, Warsaw	436 lbs. 12 oz.	Gulf of Mexico, Destin, Fla.	Dec. 22, 1985	Steve Haeusler
Halibut, Atlantic	255 lbs. 4 oz.	Gloucester, Mass.	July 28, 1989	Sonny Manley
Halibut, California	53 lbs. 4 oz.	Santa Rosa Is., Cal.	July 7, 1988	Russell Harmon
Halibut, Pacific	368 lbs.	Gustavus, Alaska	July 5, 1991	Celia Deuitt
Jack, crevalle	54 lbs. 7 oz.	Pt. Michel, Gabon	Jan. 15, 1982	Thomas Gibson Jr.
Jack, horse-eye	24 lbs. 8 oz.	Miami, Fla.	Dec. 20, 1982	Tito Schnau
Jack, Pacific crevalle	26 lbs. 12 oz.	Golfito, Costa Rica	Aug. 2, 1992	Jerome Matthews
Jewfish	680 lbs.	Fernandina Beach, Fla.	May 20, 1961	Lynn Joyner
Kawakawa	29 lbs.	Clarion Is., Mexico	Dec. 17, 1986	Ronald Nakamura
Lingcod	69 lbs.	Langara Is., B.C.	June 16, 1992	Murray Romer
Mackerel, cero	17 lbs. 2 oz.	Islamorada, Fla.	Apr. 5, 1986	G. Michael Mills
Mackerel, king	90 lbs.	Key West, Fla.	Feb. 16, 1976	Norton Thomton
Mackerel, Spanish	13 lbs.	Ocracoke Inlet, N.C.	Nov. 4, 1987	Robert Cranton
Marlin, Atlantic blue	1,402 lbs. 2 oz.	Vitoria, Brazil	Feb. 29, 1992	Paulo Amorim
Marlin, black	1,560 lbs.	Cabo Blanco, Peru	Aug. 4, 1953	A. C. Glassell Jr.
Marlin, Pacific blue	1,376 lbs.	Kaaiwa Pt., Hawaii	May 31, 1982	J.W. deBeaubien
Marlin, striped	494 lbs.	Tutukaka, New Zealand	Jan. 16, 1986	Bill Boniface
Marlin, white	181 lbs. 14 oz.	Vitoria, Brazil	Dec. 8, 1979	Evandro Luiz Caser
Permit	51 lbs. 8 oz.	Lake Worth, Fla.	Apr. 28, 1978	William M. Kenney
Pollack	27 lbs. 6 oz.	Devon, England	Jan. 16, 1986	Robert Milkins
Pollock	46 lbs. 10 oz.	Perkins Cove, Me.	Oct. 24, 1990	Linda Paul
Pompano, African	50 lbs. 8 oz.	Daytona Beach, Fla.	Apr. 21, 1990	Tom Sargent
Roosterfish	114 lbs.	La Paz, Mexico	June 1, 1960	Abe Sackheim
Runner, blue	8 lbs. 4 oz.	Bimini, Bahamas	Sept. 9, 1990	Brent Rowland
Runner, rainbow	37 lbs. 9 oz.	Clarion Is., Mexico	Nov. 21, 1991	Tom Pfleger
Sailfish, Atlantic	135 lbs. 5 oz.	Lagos, Nigeria	Nov. 10, 1991	Ron King
Sailfish, Pacific	221 lbs.	Santa Cruz Is., Ecuador	Feb. 12, 1947	C. W. Stewart
Seabass, white	83 lbs. 12 oz.	San Felipe, Mexico	Mar. 31, 1953	L.C. Baumgardner
Seatrout, spotted	16 lbs.	Mason's Beach, Va.	May 28, 1977	William Katko
Shark, bigeye thresher	802 lbs.	Tutukaka, New Zealand	Feb. 8, 1981	Dianne North
Shark, blue	437 lbs.	Catherine Bay, N.S.W. Australia	Oct. 2, 1976	Peter Hyde
Shark, great hammerhead	991 lbs.	Sarasota, Fla.	May 30, 1982	Allen Ogle
Shark, Greenland	1,708 lbs. 9 oz.	Trondheim, Norway	Oct. 18, 1987	Terje Nordtvedt
Shark, man-eater or white	2,664 lbs.	Ceduna, Australia	Apr. 21, 1959	Alfred Dean
Shark, porbeagle	465 lbs.	Cornwall, England	July 23, 1976	Jorge Potier
Shark, shortfin mako	1,115 lbs.	Black R., Mauritius	Nov. 16, 1988	Patrick Guillanton
Shark, tiger	1,780 lbs.	Cherry Grove, S.C.	June 14, 1964	Walter Maxwell
Skipjack, black	26 lbs.	Baja, Mexico	Oct. 23, 1991	Clifford Hamishi
Snapper, cubera	121 lbs. 8 oz.	Cameron, La.	July 5, 1982	Mike Hebert
Snook	53 lbs. 10 oz.	Costa Rica	Oct. 18, 1978	Gilbert Ponzi
Spearfish, Mediterranean	90 lbs. 13 oz.	Madeira Island, Portugal	June 2, 1980	Joseph Larkin
Swordfish	1,182 lbs.	Iquique, Chile	May 7, 1953	L. Marron
Tarpon	283 lbs. 4 oz.	Sierra Leone	Apr. 16, 1991	Yvon Sebag
Tautog	24 lbs.	Wachapreagee, Va.	Aug. 25, 1987	Gregory Bell
Tope	72 lbs. 12 oz.	Parengarenga Harbor, New Zealand	Dec. 19, 1986	Melanie Feldman
Trevally, bigeye	15 lbs. 8 oz.	Waianae, Hawaii	Mar. 6, 1992	Darryl Bailey
Trevally, giant	145 lbs. 8 oz.	Makena, Hawaii	Mar. 28, 1991	Russell Mori
Tuna, Atlantic bigeye	375 lbs. 8 oz.	Ocean City, Md.	Aug. 26, 1977	Cecil Browne
Tuna, blackfin	42 lbs.	Bermuda	June 2, 1978	Alan J. Card
		Bermuda	July 18, 1989	Gilbert Pearman
Tuna, bluefin	1,496 lbs.	Aulds Cove, Nova Scotia	Oct. 26, 1979	Ken Fraser
Tuna, longtail	79 lbs. 2 oz.	Montague Is., N.S.W., Australia	Apr. 12, 1982	Tim Simpson
Tuna, Pacific bigeye	435 lbs.	Cabo Blanco, Peru	Apr. 17, 1957	Dr. Russel Lee

Species	Weight	Where caught	Date	Angler
Tuna, skipjack	41 lbs. 14 oz.	Mauritius	Nov. 12, 1985	Edmund Heinzen
Tuna, southern bluefin	348 lbs. 5 oz.	Whakatane, New Zealand	Jan. 16, 1981	Rex Wood
Tuna, yellowfin	388 lbs. 12 oz.	San Benedicto Island, Mexico	Apr. 1, 1977	Curt Wiesenhutter
Tunny, little	35 lbs. 2 oz.	Cap de Garde, Algeria	Dec. 14, 1988	Jean Yves Chatard
Wahoo	155 lbs. 8 oz.	Bahamas	Apr. 3, 1990	William Bourne
Weakfish	19 lbs. 2 oz.	Jones Beach Inlet, N.Y.	Oct. 11, 1984	Dennis Rooney
		Delaware Bay, Delaware	May 20, 1989	William Thomas
Yellowtail, California	79 lbs. 4 oz.	Alijos Rocks, Mexico	July 2, 1991	Robert Walker
Yellowtail, southern	114 lbs. 10 oz.	Tauranga, New Zealand	Feb. 5, 1984	Mike Godfrey

Freshwater Fish

Barramundi	63 lbs. 2 oz.	Normah R., Australia	Apr. 28, 1991	Scott Barnsley
Bass, largemouth	22 lbs. 4 oz.	Montgomery Lake, Ga.	June 2, 1932	George W. Perry
Bass, peacock	26 lbs. 8 oz.	Matevini R., Colombia	Jan. 26, 1982	Rod Neubert
Bass, redeye	8 lbs. 3 oz.	Flint River, Ga.	Oct. 23, 1977	David A. Hubbard
Bass, rock	3 lbs.	York River, Ont.	Aug. 1, 1974	Peter Gulgin
Bass, smallmouth	11 lbs. 15 oz.	Dale Hollow Lake, Ky.	July 9, 1955	David L. Hayes
Bass, Suwannee	3 lbs. 14 oz.	Suwannee River, Fla.	Mar. 2, 1985	Ronnie Everett
Bass, white	6 lbs. 13 oz.	L. Orange, Va.	July 31, 1989	Ronald Sprouse
Bass, whiterock	24 lbs. 3 oz.	Leesville L., Va.	May 12, 1989	David Lambert
Bass, yellow	2 lbs. 4 oz.	Lake Monroe, Ind.	Mar. 27, 1977	Donald L. Stalker
Bluegill	4 lbs. 12 oz.	Ketona Lake, Ala.	Apr. 9, 1950	T.S. Hudson
Bowfin	21 lbs. 8 oz.	Florence, S.C.	Jan. 29, 1980	Robert Harmon
Buffalo, bigmouth	70 lbs. 5 oz.	Bastrop, La.	Apr. 21, 1980	Delbert Sisk
Buffalo, black	55 lbs. 8 oz.	Cherokee L., Tenn.	May 3, 1984	Edward McLain
Buffalo, smallmouth	68 lbs. 8 oz.	L. Hamilton, Ark.	May 16, 1984	Jerry Dolezal
Bullhead, brown	5 lbs. 8 oz.	Veal Pond, Ga.	May 22, 1975	Jimmy Andrews
Bullhead, yellow	4 lbs. 4 oz.	Mormon Lake, Ariz.	May 11, 1984	Emily Williams
Burbot	18 lbs. 4 oz.	Pickford, Mich.	Jan. 31, 1980	Thomas Courtemanche
Carp	75 lbs. 11 oz.	Lac de St. Cassien, France	May 21, 1987	Leo van der Gugten
Catfish, blue	109 lbs. 4 oz.	Cooper R., S.C.	Mar. 14, 1991	George Lijewski
Catfish, channel	58 lbs.	Santee-Cooper Res., S.C.	July 7, 1964	W.B. Whaley
Catfish, flathead	91 lbs. 4 oz.	L. Lewisville, Tex.	Mar. 28, 1982	Mike Rogers
Catfish, white	18 lbs. 14 oz.	Withlacoochee R., Fla.	Sept. 21, 1991	Jim Miller
Char, Arctic	32 lbs. 9 oz.	Tree River, Canada	July 30, 1981	Jeffrey Ward
Crappie, white	5 lbs. 3 oz.	Enid Dam, Miss.	July 31, 1957	Fred L. Bright
Dolly Varden	16 lbs. 12 oz.	Mashutuk R., Alaska	July 21, 1991	Gary King Jr.
Dorado	51 lbs. 5 oz.	Corrientes, Argentina	Sept. 27, 1984	Armando Giudice
Drum, freshwater	54 lbs. 8 oz.	Nickajack Lake, Tenn.	Apr. 20, 1972	Benny E. Hull
Gar, alligator	279 lbs.	Rio Grande River, Tex.	Dec. 2, 1951	Bill Valverde
Gar, Florida	21 lbs. 3 oz.	Boca Raton, Fla.	June 3, 1981	Jeff Sabol
Gar, longnose	50 lbs. 5 oz.	Trinity River, Tex.	July 30, 1954	Townsend Miller
Gar, shortnose	5 lbs.	Sally Jones L., Oklahoma	Apr. 26, 1985	Buddy Croslin
Gar, spotted	8 lbs. 12 oz.	Tennessee R., Ala.	Aug. 26, 1987	Winston Baker
Grayling, Arctic	5 lbs. 15 oz.	Katseyedie River, N.W.T.	Aug. 16, 1967	Jeanne P. Branson
Inconnu	53 lbs.	Pah R., Alaska	Aug. 20, 1986	Lawrence Hudnall
Kokanee	9 lbs. 6 oz.	Okanagan Lake, Vernon, B.C.	June 18, 1988	Norm Kuhn
Muskellunge	65 lbs.	Blackstone Harbor, Ont.	Oct. 16, 1988	Kenneth O'Brien
Muskellunge, tiger	51 lbs. 3 oz.	Lac Vieux-Desert, Wis., Mich.	July 16, 1919	John Knobla
Perch, Nile	191 lbs. 8 oz.	L. Victoria, Kenya	Sept. 5, 1991	Andy Davison
Perch, white	4 lbs. 12 oz.	Messalonskee Lake, Me.	June 4, 1949	Mrs. Earl Small
Perch, yellow	4 lbs. 3 oz.	Bordentown, N.J.	May, 1865	Dr. C.C. Abbot
Pickerel, chain	9 lbs. 6 oz.	Homerville, Ga.	Feb. 17, 1961	Baxley McQuaig Jr.
Pike, northern	55 lbs. 1 oz.	Lake of Grefeern, W. Germany	Oct. 16, 1986	Lothar Louis
Redhorse, greater	9 lbs. 3 oz.	Salmon R., Pulaski, N.Y.	May 11, 1985	Jason Wilson
Redhorse, silver	11 lbs. 7 oz.	Plum Creek, Wis.	May 29, 1985	Neal Long
Salmon, Atlantic	79 lbs. 2 oz.	Tana River, Norway	1928	Henrik Henriksen
Salmon, chinook	97 lbs. 4 oz.	Kenai R., Alas.	May 17, 1985	Les Anderson
Salmon, chum	32 lbs.	Behm Canal, Alas.	June 7, 1985	Fredrick Thynes
Salmon, coho	33 lbs. 4 oz.	Salmon R., Pulaski, N.Y.	Sept. 27, 1989	Jerry Lifton
Salmon, pink	13 lbs. 1 oz.	St. Mary's R., Ontario	Sept. 23, 1992	Ray Higaki
Salmon, sockeye	15 lbs. 3 oz.	Kenai R., Alaska	Aug. 9, 1987	Stan Roach
Sauger	8 lbs. 12 oz.	Lake Sakakawea, N.D.	Oct. 6, 1971	Mike Fischer
Shad, American	11 lbs. 4 oz.	Connecticut R., Mass.	May 19, 1986	Bob Thibodo
Sturgeon, white	468 lbs.	Benicia, Cal.	July 9, 1983	Joey Pallotta 3d
Sunfish, green	2 lbs. 2 oz.	Stockton Lake, Mo.	June 18, 1971	Paul M. Dilley
Sunfish, redbreast	1 lb. 12 oz.	Suwannee R., Fla.	May 29, 1984	Alvin Buchanan
Sunfish, redear	4 lbs. 13 oz.	Marianna, Fla.	Mar. 13, 1986	Joey Floyd
Tigerfish, giant	97 lbs.	Zaire R., Kinshasa, Zaire	July 9, 1988	Raymond Houtmans
Tilapia	6 lbs.	L. Okeechobee, Fla.	June 24, 1989	Joseph M. Tucker
Trout, Apache	5 lb. 3 oz.	Apache Res., Ariz.	May 29, 1991	John Baldwin
Trout, brook	14 lbs. 8 oz.	Nipigon River, Ont.	July 1916	Dr. W.J. Cook
Trout, brown	40 lbs. 4 oz.	Little Red R., Ark.	May 9, 1992	Howard Collins
Trout, bull	32 lbs.	L. Pend Oreille, Ida.	Oct. 27, 1949	N.L. Higgins
Trout, cutthroat	41 lbs.	Pyramid Lake, Nev.	Dec. 1925	J. Skimmerhorn
Trout, golden	11 lbs.	Cook's Lake, Wyo.	Aug. 5, 1948	Charles S. Reed
Trout, lake	66 lbs. 8 oz.	Great Bear Lake, N.W.T.	July 19, 1991	Rodney Harback
Trout, rainbow	42 lbs. 2 oz.	Bell Island, Alas.	June 22, 1970	David Robert White
Trout, tiger	20 lbs. 13 oz.	Lake Michigan, Wis.	Aug. 12, 1978	Pete Friedland
Walleye	25 lbs.	Old Hickory Lake, Tenn.	Aug. 1, 1960	Mabry Harper
Warmouth	2 lbs. 7 oz.	Yellow R., Holt, Fla.	Oct. 19, 1985	Tony D. Dempsey
Whitefish, lake	14 lbs. 6 oz.	Meaford, Ont.	May 21, 1984	Dennis Laycock
Whitefish, mountain	5 lbs. 6 oz.	Rioh R., Sask.	June 15, 1988	John Bell
Whitefish, river	11 lbs. 2 oz.	Nymoua, Sweden	Dec. 9, 1984	Jorgen Larsson
Whitefish, round	6 lbs.	Putahow R., Manitoba	June 14, 1984	Allen Ristori
Zander	22 lbs. 2 oz.	Trosa, Sweden	June 12, 1986	Harry Lee Tennison

COLLEGE BASKETBALL

Final Division I Conference Standing, 1992–1993

Atlantic Coast

Team	Conference W	Conference L	Overall Record W	Overall Record L
North Carolina	14	2	34	4
Florida St.	12	4	25	10
Duke	10	6	24	8
Wake Forest	10	6	21	9
Virginia	9	7	21	10
Georgia Tech	8	8	19	11
Clemson	5	11	17	13
Maryland	2	14	12	16
North Carolina St.	2	14	8	19

Tournament Champion—Georgia Tech.

Atlantic 10

Team	Conference W	Conference L	Overall Record W	Overall Record L
Massachusetts	11	3	24	7
George Washington	8	6	21	9
Rhode Island	8	6	19	11
St. Joseph's (Pa.)	8	6	18	11
Temple	8	6	20	13
West Virginia	7	7	17	12
Rutgers	6	8	13	15
St. Bonaventure	0	14	10	17

Tournament Champion—Massachusetts.

Big East

Team	Conference W	Conference L	Overall Record W	Overall Record L
Seton Hall	14	4	28	7
St. John's (N.Y.)	12	6	19	11
Syracuse	10	8	20	9
Pittsburgh	9	9	17	11
Providence	9	9	20	13
Boston College	9	9	18	13
Connecticut	9	9	15	13
Georgetown	8	10	20	13
Miami (Fla.)	7	11	10	17
Villanova	3	15	8	19

Tournament Champion—Seton Hall.

Big Eight

Team	Conference W	Conference L	Overall Record W	Overall Record L
Kansas	11	3	29	7
Oklahoma St.	8	6	20	9
Iowa St.	8	6	20	11
Nebraska	8	6	20	11
Kansas St.	7	7	19	11
Oklahoma	7	7	20	12
Missouri	5	9	19	14
Colorado	2	12	10	17

Tournament Champion—Missouri.

Big Sky

Team	Conference W	Conference L	Overall Record W	Overall Record L
Idaho	11	3	24	8
Boise St.	10	4	21	8
Weber St.	10	4	20	8
Montana	8	6	17	11
Idaho St.	5	9	10	18
Montana St.	5	9	9	18
Northern Arizona	4	10	10	16
E. Washington	3	11	6	20

Tournament Champion—Boise St.

Big South

Team	Conference W	Conference L	Overall Record W	Overall Record L
Towson St.	14	2	18	9
Coastal Carolina	12	4	22	10
Campbell	10	6	12	15
Liberty	9	7	16	14
Radford	8	8	15	16
Md.-Baltimore County	7	9	12	16
Winthrop	5	11	14	16
Charleston So.	5	11	9	18
N.C.-Asheville	2	14	4	23

Tournament Champion—Coastal Carolina.

Big Ten

Team	Conference W	Conference L	Overall Record W	Overall Record L
Indiana	17	1	31	4
Michigan	15	3	31	5
Iowa	11	7	23	9
Illinois	11	7	19	13
Minnesota	9	9	22	10
Purdue	9	9	18	10
Ohio St.	8	10	15	13
Michigan St.	7	11	15	13
Wisconsin	7	11	14	14
Northwestern	3	15	8	19
Penn St.	2	16	7	20

Big West

Team	Conference W	Conference L	Overall Record W	Overall Record L
New Mexico St.	15	3	26	8
UNLV	13	5	21	8
Pacific	12	6	16	11
Long Beach St.	11	7	22	10
UC Santa Barbara	10	8	18	11
Cal St. Fullerton	10	8	15	12
Utah St.	7	11	10	17
Nevada	4	14	9	17
San Jose St.	4	14	7	19
UC Irvine	4	14	6	21

Tournament Champion—Long Beach St.

Colonial Athletic

Team	Conference W	Conference L	Overall Record W	Overall Record L
Old Dominion	11	3	21	8
James Madison	11	3	21	9
Richmond	10	4	15	12
N.C.-Wilmington	6	8	17	11
William & Mary	6	8	14	13
American	6	8	11	17
East Carolina	4	10	13	17
George Mason	2	12	7	21

Tournament Champion—East Carolina.

Great Midwest

Team	Conference W	Conference L	Overall Record W	Overall Record L
Cincinnati	8	2	27	5
Memphis St.	7	3	20	12
Marquette	6	4	20	8
Ala.-Birmingham	5	5	21	14
DePaul	3	7	16	15
St. Louis	1	9	12	17

Tournament Champion—Cincinnati.

Ivy League

Team	Conference W	Conference L	Overall Record W	Overall Record L
Pennsylvania	14	0	22	5
Cornell	10	4	16	10
Columbia	9	5	16	10
Princeton	7	7	15	11
Yale	6	8	10	16
Dartmouth	5	9	11	15
Harvard	3	11	6	20
Brown	2	12	7	19

Metropolitan

Team	Conference W	Conference L	Overall Record W	Overall Record L
Louisville	11	1	22	9
Tulane	9	3	22	9
Va. Commonwealth	7	5	20	10
N.C.-Charlotte	6	6	15	13
Southern Mississippi	6	6	10	17
South Florida	2	10	8	19
Virginia Tech	1	11	10	18

Tournament Champion—Louisville.

Metro Atlantic Athletic

Team	Conference W	Conference L	Overall Record W	Overall Record L
Manhattan	12	2	23	7
Niagara	11	3	23	7
Iona	9	5	16	11
Siena	8	6	16	13
Fairfield	7	7	14	13
Canisius	5	9	10	18
St. Peter's	3	11	9	18
Loyola (Md.)	1	13	2	25

Tournament Champion—Manhattan.

Mid-American

Team	Conference W	Conference L	Overall Record W	Overall Record L
Ball St.	14	4	26	8
Miami (Ohio)	14	4	22	9
Western Michigan	12	6	17	12
Ohio	11	7	14	13
Toledo	9	9	12	16
Eastern Michigan	8	10	13	17
Bowling Green	8	10	11	16
Kent	7	11	10	17
Central Michigan	4	14	8	18
Akron	3	15	8	18

Tournament Champion—Ball St.

Mid-Continent

Team	Conference W	Conference L	Overall Record W	Overall Record L
Cleveland St.	15	1	22	6
Wright St.	10	6	20	10
Northern Illinois	10	6	15	12
Illinois-Chicago	9	7	17	15
Wisconsin Green Bay	0	7	13	14
Valparaiso	7	9	12	16
Eastern Illinois	7	9	10	17
Western Illinois	4	12	7	20
Youngstown St.	1	15	3	23

Tournament Champion—Wright St.

Mid-Eastern Athletic

Team	Conference W	Conference L	Overall Record W	Overall Record L
Coppin St.	16	0	22	8
South Carolina St.	9	7	16	13
North Carolina A&T	9	7	14	13
Morgan St.	9	7	9	17
Florida A&M	8	8	10	18
Md.-East Shore	7	9	12	15
Delaware St.	6	10	13	16
Howard	6	10	10	18
Bethune-Cookman	2	14	3	24

Tournament Champion—Coppin St.

Midwestern Collegiate

Team	Conference W	Conference L	Overall Record W	Overall Record L
Xavier (Ohio)	12	2	24	6
Evansville	12	2	23	7
La Salle	9	5	14	13
Detroit Mercy	7	7	15	12
Duquesne	5	9	13	15
Butler	5	9	11	17
Loyola (Ill.)	3	11	7	20
Dayton	3	11	4	26

Tournament Champion—Evansville.

Missouri Valley

Team	Conference W	Conference L	Overall Record W	Overall Record L
Illinois St.	13	5	19	10
Southern Illinois	12	6	23	10
Southwest Missouri St.	11	7	20	11
Tulsa	10	8	15	14
Drake	9	9	14	14
Northern Iowa	8	10	12	15
Bradley	7	11	11	16
Indiana St.	7	11	11	17
Wichita St.	7	11	10	17
Creighton	6	12	8	18

Tournament Champion—S. Illinois.

North Atlantic

Team	Conference W	Conference L	Overall Record W	Overall Record L
Drexel	12	2	22	7
Northeastern	12	2	20	8
Delaware	10	4	22	8
Hartford	7	7	14	14
Maine	4	10	10	17
Vermont	4	10	10	17
New Hampshire	4	10	6	21
Boston Univ.	3	11	6	21

Tournament Champion—Drexel.

Northeast

Team	Conference W	Conference L	Overall Record W	Overall Record L
Rider	14	4	19	11
Wagner	12	6	18	12
Marist	10	8	14	16
Mt. St. Mary's (Md.)	10	8	13	15
FDU-Teaneck	8	10	11	17
St. Francis (N.Y.)	8	10	9	18
LIU-Brooklyn	7	11	11	17
Monmouth (N.J.)	7	11	11	17
Robert Morris	7	11	9	18
St. Francis (Pa.)	7	11	9	18

Tournament Champion—Rider.

Ohio Valley

Team	Conference W	Conference L	Overall Record W	Overall Record L
Tennessee St.	13	3	19	10
Murray St.	11	5	18	12
Eastern Kentucky	11	5	15	12
Southeast Mo. St.	9	7	16	11
Tennessee Tech	9	7	15	13
Morehead St.	6	10	6	21
Middle Tenn. St.	5	11	10	16
Tenn.-Martin	4	12	7	19
Austin Peay	4	12	7	20

Tournament Champion—Tennessee St.

Pacific-10

	Conference W	Conference L	Overall Record W	Overall Record L
Arizona	17	1	24	4
California	12	6	21	9
UCLA	11	7	22	11
Arizona St.	11	7	18	10
USC	9	9	18	12
Washington St.	9	9	15	12
Oregon St.	9	9	13	14
Washington	7	11	13	14
Oregon	3	15	10	20
Stanford	2	16	7	23

Patriot

	Conference W	Conference L	Overall Record W	Overall Record L
Bucknell	13	1	23	6
Holy Cross	12	2	23	7
Colgate	9	5	18	10
Fordham	9	5	15	16
Navy	5	9	8	19
Lafayette	4	10	7	20
Army	2	12	4	22
Lehigh	2	12	4	23

Tournament Champion—Holy Cross.

Southeastern

Eastern Division	Conference W	Conference L	Overall Record W	Overall Record L
Vanderbilt	14	2	28	6
Kentucky	13	3	30	4
Florida	9	7	16	12
Georgia	8	8	15	14
South Carolina	5	11	9	18
Tennessee	4	12	13	17
Western Division				
Arkansas	10	6	22	9
Louisiana St.	9	7	22	11
Auburn	8	8	15	12
Alabama	7	9	16	13
Mississippi St.	5	11	13	16
Mississippi	4	12	10	18

Tournament Champion—Kentucky.

Southern

	Conference W	Conference L	Overall Record W	Overall Record L
Tenn.-Chattanooga	16	2	26	7
Ga. Southern	12	6	19	9
East Tenn. St.	12	6	19	10
Marshall	11	7	16	11
Davidson	10	8	14	14
Appalachian St.	8	10	13	15
Furman	8	10	11	17
Citadel	8	10	10	17
Va. Military	3	15	5	22
Western Carolina	2	16	6	21

Tournament Champion—Tenn.-Chattanooga.

Southland

	Conference W	Conference L	Overall Record W	Overall Record L
Northeast La.	17	1	26	5
Nicholls St.	11	7	14	12
Texas-Arlington	10	8	16	12
Texas-San Antonio	10	8	15	14
Southwest Tex. St.	9	9	14	13
McNeese St.	9	9	12	16
Stephen F. Austin	8	10	12	14
Northwestern La.	7	11	13	13
North Texas	5	13	5	21
Sam Houston St.	4	14	6	19

Tournament Champion—Northeast La.

Southwest

	Conference W	Conference L	Overall Record W	Overall Record L
SMU	12	2	20	8
Rice	11	3	18	10
Houston	9	5	21	9
Baylor	7	7	16	11
Texas Tech	6	8	18	12
Texas A&M	5	9	10	17
Texas	4	10	11	17
Texas Christian	2	12	6	22

Tournament Champion—Texas Tech.

Southwestern Athletic

	Conference W	Conference L	Overall Record W	Overall Record L
Jackson St.	13	1	25	9
Southern-B.R.	9	5	21	10
Alabama St.	9	5	14	13
Texas Southern	8	6	12	15
Mississippi Valley	7	7	13	15
Grambling	5	9	13	14
Alcorn St.	5	9	7	20
Prairie View	0	14	1	26

Tournament Champion—Southern-B.R.

Sun Belt

	Conference W	Conference L	Overall Record W	Overall Record L
New Orleans	18	0	26	4
Western Kentucky	14	4	26	6
Arkansas St.	11	7	16	12
Southwestern La.	11	7	17	13
Arkansas-Little Rock	10	8	15	12
Lamar	9	9	15	12
South Ala.	9	9	15	13
Louisiana Tech	3	15	7	21
Jacksonville	3	15	5	22
Texas-Pan American	2	16	2	20

Tournament Champion—Western Ky.

Trans America Athletic

	Conference W	Conference L	Overall Record W	Overall Record L
Florida International	9	3	20	10
Samford	7	5	17	10
Mercer	7	5	13	14
Stetson	6	6	13	14
Georgia St.	5	7	13	14
Southeastern La.	4	8	12	15
Centenary	4	8	9	18

West Coast

	Conference W	Conference L	Overall Record W	Overall Record L
Pepperdine	11	3	23	8
Gonzaga	10	4	19	9
Santa Clara	9	5	19	12
San Francisco	8	6	19	12
San Diego	7	7	13	14
St. Mary's (Cal.)	6	8	11	16
Portland	3	11	9	18
Loyola (Cal.)	2	12	7	20

Tournament Champion—Santa Clara.

Western Athletic

	Conference W	Conference L	Overall Record W	Overall Record L
Utah	15	3	24	7
Brigham Young	15	3	25	9
New Mexico	13	5	24	7
UTEP	10	8	21	13
Colorado St.	9	9	17	12
Fresno St.	8	10	13	15
Wyoming	7	11	13	15
Hawaii	7	11	12	16
Air Force	3	15	9	19
San Diego St.	3	15	8	21

Tournament Champion—New Mexico.

Independents

	W	L
Wis.-Milwaukee	23	4
Charleston	19	8
Mo.-Kansas City	15	12
Southern Utah St.	14	13
Northeastern Ill.	11	16
Cal St. Northridge	10	17
Central Florida	10	17
N.C.-Greensboro	10	17
Hofstra	9	18
Notre Dame	9	18
Central Conn. St.	8	19
Buffalo	5	22
Chicago St.	4	23
Cal St. Sacramento	3	24

Major College Basketball Tournaments

The National Invitation Tournament (NIT), first played in 1938, is the nation's oldest basketball tournament. The National Collegiate Athletic Association's (NCAA) national championship tournament was first played a year later. Selections for both tournaments are made in March, with the NCAA selecting first from among the top Division I teams.

National Invitation Tournament Champions

Year	Champion	Year	Champion	Year	Champion	Year	Champion
1938	Temple	1952	LaSalle	1966	Brigham Young	1980	Virginia
1939	Long Island Univ.	1953	Seton Hall	1967	Southern Illinois	1981	Tulsa
1940	Colorado	1954	Holy Cross	1968	Dayton	1982	Bradley
1941	Long Island Univ.	1955	Duquesne	1969	Temple	1983	Fresno State
1942	West Virginia	1956	Louisville	1970	Marquette	1984	Michigan
1943	St. John's	1957	Bradley	1971	North Carolina	1985	UCLA
1944	St. John's	1958	Xavier (Ohio)	1972	Maryland	1986	Ohio State
1945	De Paul	1959	St. John's	1973	Virginia Tech	1987	Southern Mississippi
1946	Kentucky	1960	Bradley	1974	Purdue	1988	Connecticut
1947	Utah	1961	Providence	1975	Princeton	1989	St. John's
1948	St. Louis	1962	Dayton	1976	Kentucky	1990	Vanderbilt
1949	San Francisco	1963	Providence	1977	St. Bonaventure	1991	Stanford
1950	CCNY	1964	Bradley	1978	Texas	1992	Virginia
1951	Brigham Young	1965	St. John's	1979	Indiana	1993	Minnesota

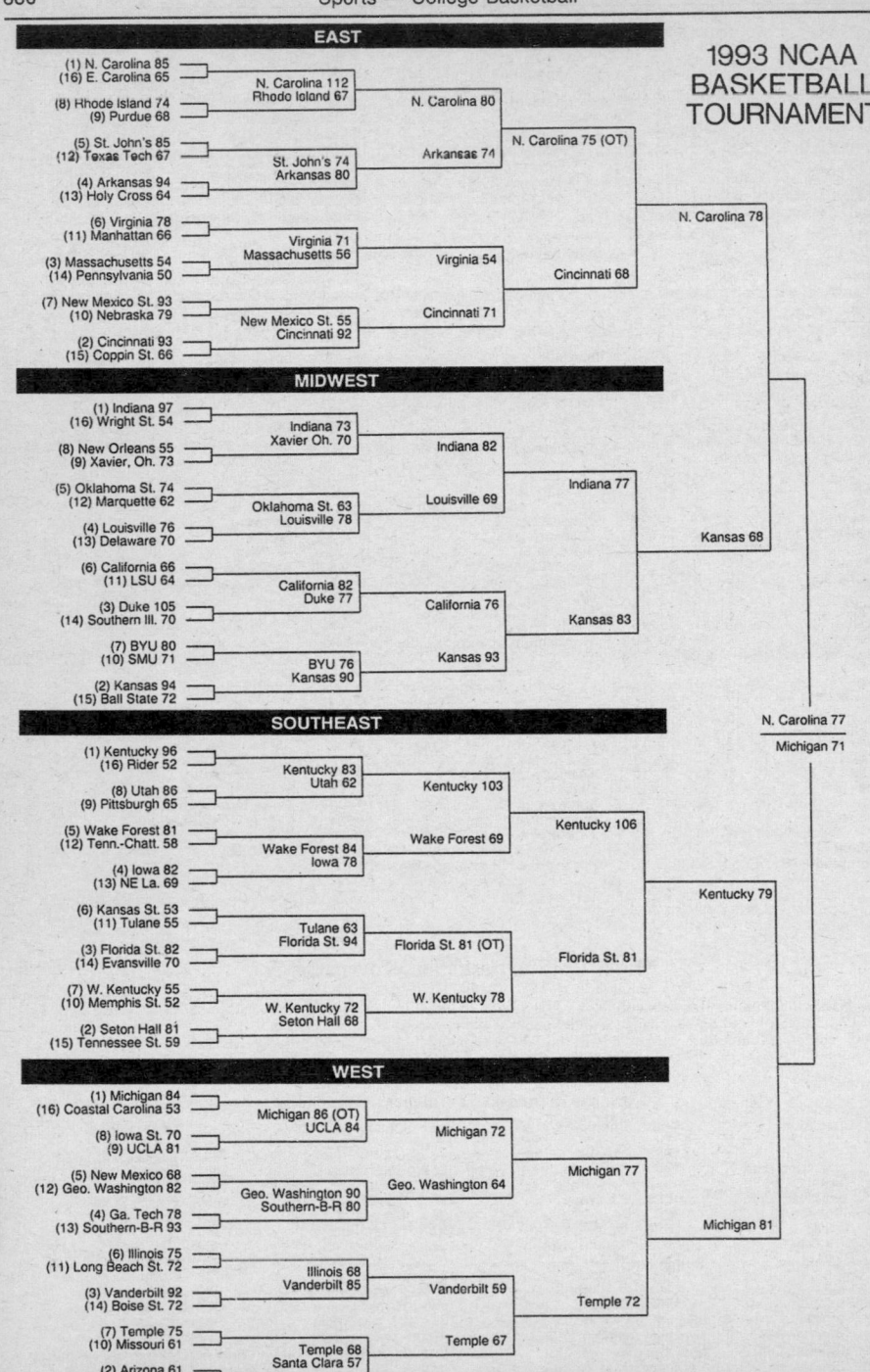

1993 NCAA BASKETBALL TOURNAMENT

EAST

(1) N. Carolina 85
(16) E. Carolina 65

(8) Rhode Island 74
(9) Purdue 68

(5) St. John's 85
(12) Texas Tech 67

(4) Arkansas 94
(13) Holy Cross 64

(6) Virginia 78
(11) Manhattan 66

(3) Massachusetts 54
(14) Pennsylvania 50

(7) New Mexico St. 93
(10) Nebraska 79

(2) Cincinnati 93
(15) Coppin St. 66

N. Carolina 112
Rhode Island 67

St. John's 74
Arkansas 80

Virginia 71
Massachusetts 56

New Mexico St. 55
Cincinnati 92

N. Carolina 80
Arkansas 74

Virginia 54
Cincinnati 71

N. Carolina 75 (OT)
Cincinnati 68

MIDWEST

(1) Indiana 97
(16) Wright St. 54

(8) New Orleans 55
(9) Xavier, Oh. 73

(5) Oklahoma St. 74
(12) Marquette 62

(4) Louisville 76
(13) Delaware 70

(6) California 66
(11) LSU 64

(3) Duke 105
(14) Southern Ill. 70

(7) BYU 80
(10) SMU 71

(2) Kansas 94
(15) Ball State 72

Indiana 73
Xavier Oh. 70

Oklahoma St. 63
Louisville 78

California 82
Duke 77

BYU 76
Kansas 90

Indiana 82
Louisville 69

California 76
Kansas 93

Indiana 77
Kansas 83

SOUTHEAST

(1) Kentucky 96
(16) Rider 52

(8) Utah 86
(9) Pittsburgh 65

(5) Wake Forest 81
(12) Tenn.-Chatt. 58

(4) Iowa 82
(13) NE La. 69

(6) Kansas St. 53
(11) Tulane 55

(3) Florida St. 82
(14) Evansville 70

(7) W. Kentucky 55
(10) Memphis St. 52

(2) Seton Hall 81
(15) Tennessee St. 59

Kentucky 83
Utah 62

Wake Forest 84
Iowa 78

Tulane 63
Florida St. 94

W. Kentucky 72
Seton Hall 68

Kentucky 103
Wake Forest 69

Florida St. 81 (OT)
W. Kentucky 78

Kentucky 106
Florida St. 81

WEST

(1) Michigan 84
(16) Coastal Carolina 53

(8) Iowa St. 70
(9) UCLA 81

(5) New Mexico 68
(12) Geo. Washington 82

(4) Ga. Tech 78
(13) Southern-B-R 93

(6) Illinois 75
(11) Long Beach St. 72

(3) Vanderbilt 92
(14) Boise St. 72

(7) Temple 75
(10) Missouri 61

(2) Arizona 61
(15) Santa Clara 64

Michigan 86 (OT)
UCLA 84

Geo. Washington 90
Southern-B-R 80

Illinois 68
Vanderbilt 85

Temple 68
Santa Clara 57

Michigan 72
Geo. Washington 64

Vanderbilt 59
Temple 67

Michigan 77
Temple 72

Semifinals

N. Carolina 78
Kansas 68

Kentucky 79
Michigan 81

Final

N. Carolina 77
Michigan 71

NCAA Division I Champions

Year	Champion	Coach	Final opponent	Score	Outstanding player	Site
1939	Oregon	Howard Hobson	Ohio St.	46-33	None	Evanston, Ill.
1940	Indiana	Branch McCracken	Kansas	60-42	Marvin Huffman, Indiana	Kansas City, Mo.
1941	Wisconsin	Harold Foster	Washington St.	39-34	John Kotz, Wisconsin	Kansas City, Mo.
1942	Stanford	Everett Dean	Dartmouth	53-38	Howard Dallmar, Stanford	Kansas City, Mo.
1943	Wyoming	Everett Shelton	Georgetown	46-34	Ken Sailors, Wyoming	New York, N.Y.
1944	Utah	Vadal Peterson	Dartmouth	42-40(1)	Arnold Ferrin, Utah	New York, N.Y.
1945	Oklahoma St.(2)	Henry Iba	NYU	49-45	Bob Kurland, Oklahoma St.	New York, N.Y.
1946	Oklahoma St.(2)	Henry Iba	N. Carolina	43-40	Bob Kurland, Oklahoma St.	New York, N.Y.
1947	Holy Cross	Alvin Julian	Oklahoma	58-47	George Kaftan, Holy Cross	New York, N.Y.
1948	Kentucky	Adolph Rupp	Baylor	58-42	Alex Groza, Kentucky	New York, N.Y.
1949	Kentucky	Adolph Rupp	Oklahoma St.	46-36	Alex Groza, Kentucky	Seattle, Wash.
1950	CCNY	Nat Holman	Bradley	71-68	Irwin Dambrot, CCNY	New York, N.Y.
1951	Kentucky	Adolph Rupp	Kansas St.	68-58	None	Minneapolis, Minn.
1952	Kansas	Forrest Allen	St. John's	80-63	Clyde Lovellette, Kansas	Seattle, Wash.
1953	Indiana	Branch McCracken	Kansas	69-68	B.H. Born, Kansas	Kansas City, Mo.
1954	La Salle	Kenneth Loeffler	Bradley	92-76	Tom Gola, La Salle	Kansas City, Mo.
1955	San Francisco	Phil Woolpert	LaSalle	77-63	Bill Russell, San Francisco	Kansas City, Mo.
1956	San Francisco	Phil Woolpert	Iowa	83-71	Hal Lear, Temple	Evanston, Ill.
1957	N. Carolina	Frank McGuire	Kansas	54-53(1)	Wilt Chamberlain, Kansas	Kansas City, Mo.
1958	Kentucky	Adolph Rupp	Seattle	84-72	Elgin Baylor, Seattle	Louisville, Ky.
1959	California	Pete Newell	W. Virginia	71-70	Jerry West, W. Virginia	Louisville, Ky.
1960	Ohio St.	Fred Taylor	California	75-55	Jerry Lucas, Ohio St.	San Francisco, Cal.
1961	Cincinnati	Edwin Jucker	Ohio St.	70-65(1)	Jerry Lucas, Ohio St.	Kansas City, Mo.
1962	Cincinnati	Edwin Jucker	Ohio St.	71-59	Paul Hogue, Cincinnati	Louisville, Ky.
1963	Loyola (Ill.)	George Ireland	Cincinnati	60-58(1)	Art Heyman, Duke	Louisville, Ky.
1964	UCLA	John Wooden	Duke	98-83	Walt Hazzard, UCLA	Kansas City, Mo.
1965	UCLA	John Wooden	Michigan	91-80	Bill Bradley, Princeton	Portland, Ore.
1966	Texas-El Paso(3)	Don Haskins	Kentucky	72-65	Jerry Chambers, Utah	College Park, Md.
1967	UCLA	John Wooden	Dayton	79-64	Lew Alcindor, UCLA	Louisville, Ky.
1968	UCLA	John Wooden	N. Carolina	78-55	Lew Alcindor, UCLA	Los Angeles, Cal.
1969	UCLA	John Wooden	Purdue	92-72	Lew Alcindor, UCLA	Louisville, Ky.
1970	UCLA	John Wooden	Jacksonville	80-69	Sidney Wicks, UCLA	College Park, Md.
1971	UCLA	John Wooden	Villanova*	68-62	Howard Porter, Villanova*	Houston, Tex.
1972	UCLA	John Wooden	Florida St.	81-76	Bill Walton, UCLA	Los Angeles, Cal.
1973	UCLA	John Wooden	Memphis St.	87-66	Bill Walton, UCLA	St. Louis, Mo.
1974	N. Carolina St.	Norm Sloan	Marquette	76-64	David Thompson, N.C. St.	Greensboro, N.C.
1975	UCLA	John Wooden	Kentucky	92-85	Richard Washington, UCLA	San Diego, Cal.
1976	Indiana	Bob Knight	Michigan	86-68	Kent Benson, Indiana	Philadelphia, Pa.
1977	Marquette	Al McGuire	N. Carolina	67-59	Butch Lee, Marquette	Atlanta, Ga.
1978	Kentucky	Joe Hall	Duke	94-88	Jack Givens, Kentucky	St. Louis, Mo.
1979	Michigan St.	Jud Heathcote	Indiana St.	75-64	Magic Johnson, Michigan St.	Salt Lake City, Ut.
1980	Louisville	Denny Crum	UCLA*	59-54	Darrell Griffith, Louisville	Indianapolis, Ind.
1981	Indiana	Bob Knight	N. Carolina	63-50	Isiah Thomas, Indiana	Philadelphia, Pa.
1982	N. Carolina	Dean Smith	Georgetown	63-62	James Worthy, N. Carolina	New Orleans, La.
1983	N. Carolina St.	Jim Valvano	Houston	54-52	Hakeem Olajuwon, Houston	Albuquerque, N.M.
1984	Georgetown	John Thompson	Houston	84-75	Patrick Ewing, Georgetown	Seattle, Wash.
1985	Villanova	Rollie Massimino	Georgetown	66-64	Ed Pinckney, Villanova	Lexington, Ky.
1986	Louisville	Denny Crum	Duke	72-69	Pervis Ellison, Louisville	Dallas, Tex.
1987	Indiana	Bob Knight	Syracuse	74-73	Keith Smart, Indiana	New Orleans, La.
1988	Kansas	Larry Brown	Oklahoma	83-79	Danny Manning, Kansas	Kansas City, Mo.
1989	Michigan	Steve Fisher	Seton Hall	80-79(1)	Glen Rice, Michigan	Seattle, Wash.
1990	UNLV	Jerry Tarkanian	Duke	103-73	Anderson Hunt, UNLV	Denver, Col.
1991	Duke	Mike Krzyzewski	Kansas	72-65	Christian Laettner, Duke	Indianapolis, Ind.
1992	Duke	Mike Krzyzewski	Michigan	71-51	Bobby Hurley, Duke	Minneapolis, Minn.
1993	N. Carolina	Dean Smith	Michigan	77-71	Donald Williams, N. Carolina	New Orleans, La.

* Declared ineligible subsequent to the tournament. (1) Overtime. (2) Known as Oklahoma A&M at that time. (3) Known as Texas Western at that time.

John R. Wooden Award

Awarded annually to the nation's outstanding college basketball player by the United States Basketball Writers Assn.

1977	Marques Johnson, UCLA
1978	Phil Ford, North Carolina
1979	Larry Bird, Indiana State
1980	Darrell Griffith, Louisville
1981	Danny Ainge, Brigham Young
1982	Ralph Sampson, Virginia
1983	Ralph Sampson, Virginia
1984	Michael Jordan, North Carolina
1985	Chris Mullin, St. John's
1986	Walter Berry, St. John's
1987	David Robinson, Navy
1988	Danny Manning, Kansas
1989	Sean Elliott, Arizona
1990	Lionel Simmons, La Salle
1991	Larry Johnson, UNLV
1992	Christian Laettner, Duke
1993	Calbert Cheaney, Indiana

NCAA Division I Women's Champions

Year	Champion	Coach	Final opponent
1982	Louisiana Tech	Sonja Hogg	Cheyney
1983	USC	Linda Sharp	Louisiana Tech
1984	USC	Linda Sharp	Tennessee
1985	Old Dominion	Marianne Stanley	Georgia
1986	Texas	Jody Conradt	USC
1987	Tennessee	Pat Summitt	Louisiana Tech
1988	Louisiana Tech	Leon Barmore	Auburn
1989	Tennessee	Pat Summitt	Auburn
1990	Stanford	Tara VanDerveer	Auburn
1991	Tennessee	Pat Summitt	Virginia
1992	Stanford	Tara VanDerveer	W. Kentucky
1993	Texas Tech	Marsha Sharp	Ohio St.

Selected Division I Basketball Coaches in 1993

College	Coach	College	Coach	College	Coach
Akron	Coleman Crawford	Iowa	Tom Davis	Rutgers	Bob Wenzel
Alabama	David Hobbs	Iowa St.	Johnny Orr	St. Bonaventure	Jim Baron
Ala-Birmingham	Gene Barton	James Madison	Lefty Driesell	St. John's (N.Y.)	Brian Mahoney
American	Chris Knoche	Kansas	Roy Williams	St. Joseph's (Pa.)	John Griffin
Arizona	Lute Olson	Kansas St.	Dana Altman	St. Louis	Charlie Spoonhour
Arizona St.	Bill Frieder	Kent	Dave Grube	St. Mary's (Cal.)	Ernie Kent
Arkansas	Nolan Richardson	Kentucky	Rick Pitino	San Diego	Hank Egan
Army	Dino Gaudio	Long Beach St.	Seth Greenberg	San Diego St.	Tony Fuller
Auburn	Tommy Joe Eagles	LSU	Dale Brown	San Francisco	Jim Brovelli
Austin Peay	Dave Loos	Louisville	Denny Crum	San Jose St.	Stan Morrison
Ball St.	Dick Hunsaker	Loyola (Cal.)	John Olive	Santa Clara	Dick Dewey
Baylor	Darrel Johnson	Loyola (Ill.)	Will Rey	Seton Hall	P. J. Carlesimo
Boise St.	Bobby Dye	Marquette	Kevin O'Neill	S. Carolina	Eddie Folger
Boston Coll.	Jim O'Brien	Maryland	Gary Williams	S. Florida	Bobby Paschal
Bowling Green	Jim Larrange	Massachusetts	John Calipari	SE Mo. St.	Ron Shumate
Bradley	Jim Molinari	Memphis St.	Larry Finch	USC	George Raveling
BYU	Roger Reid	Miami (Fla.)	Leonard Hamilton	So. Illinois	Rick Herrin
Brown	Frank Dobbs	Miami (Oh.)	Joby Wright	SMU	John Shumate
Butler	Barry Collier	Michigan	Steve Fisher	So. Mississippi	M. K. Turk
California	Todd Bozeman	Michigan St.	Jud Heathcote	SW Mo. St.	Mark Bernsen
Cal. St. Fullerton	Brad Holland	Middle Tenn. St.	David Farrar	Stanford	Mike Montgomery
UC Irvine	Rod Baker	Minnesota	Clem Haskins	Syracuse	Jim Boeheim
UC Santa Barbara	Jerry Pimm	Mississippi	Rob Evans	Temple	John Chaney
Central Mich.	Keith Dambrot	Mississippi St.	Richard Williams	Tennessee	Wade Houston
Cincinnati	Bob Huggins	Missouri	Norm Stewart	Tennessee St.	Frankie Allen
Clemson	Cliff Ellis	Montana	Blaine Taylor	Tennessee Tech	Frank Harrell
Cleveland St.	Mike Boyd	Montana St.	Mick Durham	Tennessee-Chatt.	Mark McCarthy
Colorado	Joe Harrington	Morehead St.	Dick Fick	Tennessee-Martin	Calvin C. Luther
Colorado St.	Stew Morrill	Murray St.	Scott Edgar	Texas	Tom Penders
Columbia	Jack Rohan	Nebraska	Danny Nee	Texas A&M	Tony Barone
Connecticut	Jim Calhoun	Nevada-Reno	Len Stevens	Tex. Christian	Moe Iba
Cornell	Al Walker	UNLV	Rollie Massimino	Tex.-Arlington	Mark Nixon
Creighton	Rick Johnson	New Mexico	Dave Bliss	UTEP	Don Haskins
Dartmouth	Dave Faucher	New Mexico St.	Neil McCarthy	Toledo	Larry Gipson
Dayton	Jim O'Brien	North Carolina	Dean Smith	Tulane	Perry Clark
DePaul	Joey Meyer	N.C. A&T	Don Corbett	Tulsa	Tubby Smith
Detroit Mercy	Ricky Byrdsong	N.C. State	Les Robinson	UCLA	Jim Harrick
Drake	Rudy Washington	N.C.-Charlotte	Jeff Mullins	Utah	Rick Mejerus
Duke	Mike Trzyzewski	N.C.-Wilmington	Kevin Eastman	Utah St.	Kohn Smith
E. Carolina	Eddie Payne	N. Arizona	Harold Merritt	Valparaiso	Homer Drew
E. Illinois	Rick Samuels	N. Illinois	Brian Hammel	Vanderbilt	Jan van Breda Kolff
E. Kentucky	Mike Calhoun	N. Iowa	Eldon Miller	Villanova	Steve Lappas
E. Michigan	Ben Braun	Northwestern	Ricky Byrdsong	Virginia	Jeff Jones
E. Washington	John Wade	Notre Dame	John MacLeod	Va. Commonwealth	Sonny Smith
Evansville	Jim Crews	Ohio	Larry Hunter	Va. Tech	Bill Foster
Florida	Lon Kruger	Ohio St.	Randy Ayers	Wake Forest	Dave Odem
Florida St.	Pat Kennedy	Oklahoma	Billy Tubbs	Washington	Lynn Nance
Fresno St.	Gary Colson	Oklahoma St.	Eddie Sutton	Washington St.	Kelvin Sampson
George Mason	Paul Westhead	Old Dominion	Oliver Purnell	Weber St.	Ron Abegglen
Geo. Washington	Mike Jarvis	Oregon	Jerry Green	W. Virginia	Gale Catlett
Georgetown	John Thompson	Oregon St.	Jim Anderson	W. Illinois	Jim Kerwin
Georgia	Hugh Durham	Pacific (Cal.)	Bob Thomason	W. Kentucky	Ralph Willard
Georgia Tech	Bobby Cremins	Pennsylvania	Fran Dunphy	W. Michigan	Bob Donewald
Gonzaga	Dan Fitzgerald	Penn St.	Bruce Parkhill	Wichita St.	Scott Thompson
Harvard	Frank Sullivan	Pepperdine	Tom Asbury	William & Mary	Chuck Swenson
Hawaii	Riley Wallace	Pittsburgh	Paul Evans	Wisconsin	Stu Jackson
Houston	Pat Foster	Portland	Larry Steele	Wis.-Green Bay	Dick Bennett
Idaho	Larry Eustachy	Princeton	Pete Carril	Wright St.	Tom Moore
Idaho St.	Herb Williams	Providence	Rick Barnes	Wyoming	Benny Dees
Illinois	Lou Henson	Purdue	Gene Keady	Xavier (Oh.)	Pete Gillen
Illinois St.	Bob Bender	Rhode Island	Al Skinner	Yale	Dick Kuchen
Illinois-Chi.	Bob Hallberg	Rice	Willis Wilson		
Indiana	Bob Knight	Richmond	Dick Tarrant		
Indiana St.	Tates Locke				

Most Coaching Victories in the NCAA Tournament Through 1993

Coach, school, years	Wins	Tournaments
Dean Smith, North Carolina, 1967-93	55	23
John Wooden, UCLA, 1950-75	47	16
Bob Knight, Indiana, 1973-93	38	17
Jerry Tarkanian, Long Beach State and UNLV, 1970-91	37	16
Denny Crum, Louisville, 1972-93	35	17
Mike Krzyzewski, Duke, 1984-93	34	10
Adolph Rupp, Kentucky, 1942-72	30	20
John Thompson, Georgetown, 1975-92	28	16
Guy Lewis, Houston, 1961-84	26	14
Joe Hall, Kentucky, 1973-85	20	10
Rollie Massimino, Villanova, 1978-91	20	11
Al McGuire, Marquette, 1968-77	20	9

NCAA Division I Basketball Statistical Trends

Averages and percentages are for both teams, per game.

Year	Games	FG Made	FG Att.	Pct.	FT Made	FT Att.	Pct.	PF	Pts.
1948	3945	40.6	138.7	29.3	25.3	42.2	59.8	36.9	106.5
1950	3659	43.2	136.8	31.6	28.7	46.5	61.8	39.0	115.1
1952	4009	47.5	140.6*	33.7	31.6	50.5	62.6	44.9*	126.6
1953	3754	48.0	138.1	34.7	42.1	65.8*	64.0	42.5	138.1
1955	3829	51.1	138.6	36.9	43.1*	64.7	66.5	37.9	145.3
1958	4153	51.6	134.2	38.4	33.6	50.5	66.4	36.4	136.8
1960	4295	52.6	132.3	39.8	34.7	51.5	67.4	36.7	139.9
1963	4180	53.2	127.6	41.7	32.6	47.8	68.2	36.4	139.0
1965	4520	58.3	135.4	43.1	34.7	50.3	69.0	38.5	151.4
1971	5232	60.2	135.6	44.4	35.0	51.3	68.1	38.5	155.4*
1973	5582	62.3*	139.2	44.8	26.2	38.3	68.4	38.4	150.9
1975	6147	62.9	136.7	46.0	27.4	39.7	69.0	40.3	153.1
1979	7131	59.2	124.1	47.7	29.5	42.2	69.7*	41.1	147.9
1983	7957	54.3	114.0	47.7	29.0	42.3	68.5	39.7	138.7
1985	8269	54.5	113.9	47.9*	29.3	42.5	68.9	39.3	138.3
1986	8360	54.7	114.6	47.7	29.4	42.5	69.1	39.1	138.7
1987	8580	54.4	117.3	46.6	29.7	43.0	69.1	39.3	145.5
1988	8587	54.8	116.6	47.0	30.2	43.8	68.9	39.4	147.8
1989	8677	55.7	118.5	47.0	31.1	45.0	69.1	40.2	151.4
1990	8646	54.7	118.9	46.0	31.1	45.1	68.9	39.6	149.8
1991	8720	55.6	121.3	45.8	31.7	46.3	68.5	39.2	152.9
1992	8803*	53.0	116.6	45.5	31.6	46.4	68.1	40.0	147.6

*All-time high.

HARNESS RACING

Harness Horse of the Year

(Chosen by the U.S. Trotting Assn. and the U.S. Harness Writers Assn.)

1951	Pronto Don	1962	Su Mac Lad	1973	Sir Dalrae	1983	Cam Fella
1952	Good Time	1963	Speedy Scot	1974	Delmonica Hanover	1984	Fancy Crown
1953	Hi Lo's Forbes	1964	Bret Hanover	1975	Savior	1985	Nihilator
1954	Stenographer	1965	Bret Hanover	1976	Keystone Ore	1986	Forrest Skipper
1955	Scott Frost	1966	Bret Hanover	1977	Green Speed	1987	Mack Lobell
1956	Scott Frost	1967	Nevele Pride	1978	Abercrombie	1988	Mack Lobell
1957	Torpid	1968	Nevele Pride	1979	Niatross	1989	Matt's Scooter
1958	Emily's Pride	1969	Nevele Pride	1980	Niatross	1990	Beach Towel
1959	Bye Bye Byrd	1970	Fresh Yankee	1981	Fan Hanover	1991	Precious Bunny
1960	Adios Butler	1971	Albatross	1982	Cam Fella	1992	Artsplace
1961	Adios Butler	1972	Albatross				

The Hambletonian (3-year-old trotters)

Year	Winner	Driver	Year	Winner	Driver
1965	Egyptian Candor	Del Cameron	1980	Burgomeister	Bill Haughton
1966	Kerry Way	Frank Ervin	1981	Shiaway St. Pat	Ray Remmen
1967	Speedy Streak	Del Cameron	1982	Speed Bowl	Tommy Haughton
1968	Nevele Pride	Stanley Dancer	1983	Duenna	Stanley Dancer
1969	Lindy's Pride	Howard Beissinger	1984	Historic Freight	Ben Webster
1970	Timothy T	John Simpson Sr.	1985	Prakas	Bill O'Donnell
1971	Speedy Crown	Howard Beissinger	1986	Nuclear Kosmos	Ulf Thoresen
1972	Super Bowl	Stanley Dancer	1987	Mack Lobell	John Campbell
1973	Flirth	Ralph Baldwin	1988	Armbro Goal	John Campbell
1974	Christopher T	Bill Haughton	1989	Park Avenue Joe	Ron Waples
1975	Bonefish	Stanley Dancer	1990	Harmonious	John Campbell
1976	Steve Lobell	Bill Haughton	1991	Giant Victory	Jack Moiseyev
1977	Green Speed	Bill Haughton	1992	Alf Palema	Mickey McNicholl
1978	Speedy Somolli	Howard Beissinger	1993	American Winner	Ron Pierce
1979	Legend Hanover	George Sholty			

BOWLING

Professional Bowlers Association

Hall of Fame

Performance

Bill Allen
Glenn Allison
Earl Anthony
Barry Asher
Ray Bluth
Roy Buckley
Nelson Burton Jr.
Don Carter
Pat Colwell
Steve Cook
Dave Davis
Gary Dickinson
Mike Durbin
Buzz Fazio
Skee Foremsky
Jim Godman
Johnny Guenther
Billy Hardwick
Tommy Hudson
Don Johnson
Joe Joseph
Larry Laub
Don McCune
Mike McGrath
George Pappas
Johnny Petraglia
Dick Ritger
Mark Roth
Jim St. John
Carmen Salvino
Bob Strampe
Harry Smith
Dave Soutar
Jim Stefanich
Wayne Webb
Dick Weber
Billy Welu
Wayne Zahn

Meritorious service

Joe Antenora
John Archibald
Eddie Elias
Frank Esposito
Dick Evans
Raymond Firestone
E.A. "Bud" Fisher
Lou Frantz
Harry Golden
Ted Hoffman Jr.
John Jowdy
Joe Kelley
Steve Nagy
Chuck Pezzano
Jack Reichert
Joe Richards
Chris Schenkel
Lorraine Stilzlein
Al Thompson

Tournament of Champions

Year	Winner	Year	Winner	Year	Winner	Year	Winner
1965	Billy Hardwick	1973	Jim Godman	1981	Steve Cook	1989	Del Ballard Jr.
1966	Wayne Zahn	1974	Earl Anthony	1982	Mike Durbin	1990	Dave Ferraro
1967	Jim Stefanich	1975	Dave Davis	1983	Joe Berardi	1991	David Ozio
1968	Dave Davis	1976	Marshall Holman	1984	Mike Durbin	1992	Marc McDowell
1969	Jim Godman	1977	Mike Berlin	1985	Mark Williams	1993	George Branham 3d
1970	Don Johnson	1978	Earl Anthony	1986	Marshall Holman		
1971	Johnny Petraglia	1979	George Pappas	1987	Pete Weber		
1972	Mike Durbin	1980	Wayne Webb	1988	Mark Williams		

PBA Leading Money Winners

Total winnings are from PBA, ABC Masters, and BPAA All-Star tournaments only, and do not include numerous other tournaments or earnings from special television shows and matches.

Year	Bowler	Amount	Year	Bowler	Amount	Year	Bowler	Amount
1962	Don Carter	$49,972	1973	Don McCune	$69,000	1984	Mark Roth	$158,712
1963	Dick Weber	46,333	1974	Earl Anthony	99,585	1985	Mike Aulby	201,200
1964	Bob Strampe	33,592	1975	Earl Anthony	107,585	1986	Walter Ray Williams Jr.	145,550
1965	Dick Weber	47,674	1976	Earl Anthony	110,833	1987	Pete Weber	175,491
1966	Wayne Zahn	54,720	1977	Mark Roth	105,583	1988	Brian Voss	225,485
1967	Dave Davis	54,165	1978	Mark Roth	134,500	1989	Mike Aulby	298,237
1968	Jim Stefanich	67,377	1979	Mark Roth	124,517	1990	Amieto Monacelli	204,775
1969	Billy Hardwick	64,160	1980	Wayne Webb	116,700	1991	David Ozio	225,585
1970	Mike McGrath	52,049	1981	Earl Anthony	164,735	1992	Marc McDowell	174,215
1971	Johnny Petraglia	85,065	1982	Earl Anthony	134,760			
1972	Don Johnson	56,648	1983	Earl Anthony	135,605			

Leading PBA Averages by Year

Year	Bowler	Average	Year	Bowler	Average	Year	Bowler	Average
1962	Don Carter	212.844	1973	Earl Anthony	215.799	1984	Marshall Holman	213.911
1963	Billy Hardwick	210.346	1974	Earl Anthony	219.394	1985	Mark Baker	213.718
1964	Ray Bluth	210.512	1975	Earl Anthony	219.060	1986	John Gant	214.378
1965	Dick Weber	211.895	1976	Mark Roth	215.970	1987	Marshall Holman	216.801
1966	Wayne Zahn	208.663	1977	Mark Roth	218.174	1988	Mark Roth	218.036
1967	Wayne Zahn	212.342	1978	Mark Roth	219.834	1989	Pete Weber	215.432
1968	Jim Stefanich	211.895	1979	Mark Roth	221.662	1990	Amieto Monacelli	218.158
1969	Bill Hardwick	212.957	1980	Earl Anthony	218.535	1991	Norm Duke	218.208
1970	Nelson Burton Jr.	214.908	1981	Mark Roth	216.699	1992	Dave Ferraro	219.702
1971	Don Johnson	213.977	1982	Marshall Holman	212.844			
1972	Don Johnson	215.290	1983	Earl Anthony	216.645			

American Bowling Congress Masters Tournament Champions

Year	Winner
1980	Neil Burton, St. Louis, Mo.
1981	Randy Lightfoot, St. Charles, Mo.
1982	Joe Berardi, Brooklyn, N.Y.
1983	Mike Lastowski, Havre de Grace, Md.
1984	Earl Anthony, Dublin, Cal.
1985	Steve Wunderlich, St. Louis, Mo.
1986	Mark Fahy, Chicago, Ill.
1987	Rick Steelsmith, Wichita, Kan.
1988	Del Ballard Jr., Richardson, Tex.
1989	Mike Aulby, Indianapolis, Ind.
1990	Chris Warren, Dallas, Tex.
1991	Doug Kent, Canandaigua, N.Y.
1992	Ken Johnson, N. Richmond Hills, Tex.
1993	Norm Duke, Oklahoma City, Okla.

Most Sanctioned 300 Games

Bowler	Games
Bob Learn Jr., Erie, Pa.	43
Mike Whalin, Cincinnati, Oh.	41
Jim Johnson Jr., Wilmington, Del.	38
Ron Woolet, Louisville, Ky.	33
John Wilcox Jr., Shavertown, Pa.	32
Elvin Mesger, Sullivan, Mo.	27
Ralph Burley Jr., Dayton, Oh.	26
Steve Gehringer, Reading, Pa.	26
Alan Hulsizer, Reading, Pa.	25
Tony Torrice, Wolcott, Conn.	24
Jerry Kessler, Dayton, Oh.	23
Teata Semiz, Fairfield, N.J.	23
Don Anthony, Columbus, Oh.	22
Mitch Jabczenski, Detroit, Mich.	22
Jerome Penxa, Detroit, Mich.	22
Steve Carson, Oklahoma City, Okla.	21
Dave Heller, Highland Falls, N.Y.	21
Mark Stibora, Cleveland, Oh.	21
Jeff Jensen, Wichita, Kan.	20
Dave Soutar, Kansas City, Mo.	20
Joe Vito Buenrostro, San Antonio, Tex.	19
Paul Cannon, Binghamton, N.Y.	19
Randy Choat, Granite City, Ill.	19
Steve Wilson, Ft. Lauderdale, Fla.	19
Jim Doherty, Oklahoma City, Okla.	18
Frank May Jr., Reading, Pa.	18
Dick Weber, St. Louis, Mo.	18

Women's International Bowling Congress

Champions in 1993

Queens Tournament—Jan Schmidt, Rochelle, Ill.

Singles Event—(tie) Karen Collura, Toronto, Ont., and Kari Murph, Dayton, Oh.

All Events—Anne Marie Duggan, Edmond, Okla.

Doubles Event—Gloria Collura and Karen Collura, Toronto, Ont.

Team—Strike Zone Pro Shop, Rolling, Ill.

Most Sanctioned 300 Games

Jeanne Maiden-Naccarato, Tacoma, Wash. 20
Vicki Fischel, Wheat Ridge, Col. 15
Aleta Sill, Dearborn, Mich. 14
Tish Johnson, Panorama City, Cal. 13
Leanne Barrette, Youkon, Okla. 12
Betty Morris, Stockton, Cal. 12
Donna Adamek, Apple Valley, Cal. 11
Cindy Coburn-Carroll, Tonawanda, N.Y. 10
Robin Romeo, Van Nuys, Cal. 9
Cheryl Daniels, Detroit, Mich. 9

Figure Skating Champions

U.S. Champions			World Champions	
Men	**Women**	**Year**	**Men**	**Women**
Dick Button	Tenley Albright	1952	Dick Button, U.S.	Jacqueline du Bief, France
Hayes Jenkins	Tenley Albright	1953	Hayes Jenkins, U.S.	Tenley Albright, U.S.
Hayes Jenkins	Tenley Albright	1954	Hayes Jenkins, U.S.	Gundi Busch, W. Germany
Hayes Jenkins	Tenley Albright	1955	Hayes Jenkins, U.S.	Tenley Albright, U.S.
Hayes Jenkins	Tenley Albright	1956	Hayes Jenkins, U.S.	Carol Heiss, U.S.
Dave Jenkins	Carol Heiss	1957	Dave Jenkins, U.S.	Carol Heiss, U.S.
Dave Jenkins	Carol Heiss	1958	Dave Jenkins, U.S.	Carol Heiss, U.S.
Dave Jenkins	Carol Heiss	1959	Dave Jenkins, U.S.	Carol Heiss, U.S.
Dave Jenkins	Carol Heiss	1960	Alain Giletti, France	Carol Heiss, U.S.
Bradley Lord	Laurence Owen	1961	none	none
Monty Hoyt	Barbara Roles Pursley	1962	Don Jackson, Canada	Sjoukje Dijkstra, Neth.
Tommy Litz	Lorraine Hanlon	1963	Don McPherson, Canada	Sjoukje Dijkstra, Neth.
Scott Allen	Peggy Fleming	1964	Manfred Schnelldorfer, W. Germany	Sjoukje Dijkstra, Neth.
Gary Visconti	Peggy Fleming	1965	Alain Calmat, France	Petra Burka, Canada
Scott Allen	Peggy Fleming	1966	Emmerich Danzer, Austria	Peggy Fleming, U.S.
Gary Visconti	Peggy Fleming	1967	Emmerich Danzer, Austria	Peggy Fleming, U.S.
Tim Wood	Peggy Fleming	1968	Emmerich Danzer, Austria	Peggy Fleming, U.S.
Tim Wood	Janet Lynn	1969	Tim Wood, U.S.	Gabriele Seyfert, E. Germany
Tim Wood	Janet Lynn	1970	Tim Wood, U.S.	Gabriele Seyfert, E. Germany
John Misha Petkevich	Janet Lynn	1971	Ondrej Nepela, Czech.	Beatrix Schuba, Austria
Ken Shelley	Janet Lynn	1972	Ondrej Nepela, Czech.	Beatrix Schuba, Austria
Gordon McKellen Jr.	Janet Lynn	1973	Ondrej Nepela, Czech.	Karen Magnussen, Canada
Gordon McKellen Jr.	Dorothy Hamill	1974	Jan Hoffmann, E. Germany	Christine Errath, E. Germany
Gordon McKellen Jr.	Dorothy Hamill	1975	Sergei Volkov, USSR	Dianne de Leeuw, Neth.-U.S.
Terry Kubicka	Dorothy Hamill	1976	John Curry, Gt. Britain	Dorothy Hamill, U.S.
Charles Tickner	Linda Fratianne	1977	Vladimir Kovalev, USSR	Linda Fratianne, U.S.
Charles Tickner	Linda Fratianne	1978	Charles Tickner, U.S.	Anett Potzsch, E. Germany
Charles Tickner	Linda Fratianne	1979	Vladimir Kovalev, USSR	Linda Fratianne, U.S.
Charles Tickner	Linda Fratianne	1980	Jan Hoffmann, E. Germany	Anett Potzsch, E. Germany
Scott Hamilton	Elaine Zayak	1981	Scott Hamilton, U.S.	Denise Biellmann, Switzerland
Scott Hamilton	Rosalynn Sumners	1982	Scott Hamilton, U.S.	Elaine Zayak, U.S.
Scott Hamilton	Rosalynn Sumners	1983	Scott Hamilton, U.S.	Rosalynn Sumners, U.S.
Scott Hamilton	Rosalynn Sumners	1984	Scott Hamilton, U.S.	Katarina Witt, E. Germany
Brian Boitano	Tiffany Chin	1985	Aleksandr Fadeev, USSR	Katarina Witt, E. Germany
Brian Boitano	Debi Thomas	1986	Brian Boitano, U.S.	Debi Thomas, U.S.
Brian Boitano	Jill Trenary	1987	Brian Orser, Canada	Katarina Witt, E. Germany
Brian Boitano	Debi Thomas	1988	Brian Boitano, U.S.	Katarina Witt, E. Germany
Christopher Bowman	Jill Trenary	1989	Kurt Browning, Canada	Midori Ito, Japan
Todd Eldredge	Jill Trenary	1990	Kurt Browning, Canada	Jill Trenary, U.S.
Todd Eldredge	Tonya Harding	1991	Kurt Browning, Canada	Kristi Yamaguchi, U.S.
Christopher Bowman	Kristi Yamaguchi	1992	Viktor Petrenko, Ukraine	Kristi Yamaguchi, U.S.
Scott Davis	Nancy Kerrigan	1993	Kurt Browning, Canada	Oksana Baiul, Ukraine

James E. Sullivan Memorial Trophy Winners

The James E. Sullivan Memorial Trophy, named after the former president of the AAU and inaugurated in 1930, is awarded annually by the AAU to the athlete who "by his or her performance, example and influence as an amateur, has done the most during the year to advance the cause of sportsmanship."

Year	Winner	Sport
1930	Bobby Jones	Golf
1931	Barney Berlinger	Track
1932	Jim Bausch	Track
1933	Glenn Cunningham	Track
1934	Bill Bonthron	Track
1935	Lawson Little	Golf
1936	Glenn Morris	Track
1937	Don Budge	Tennis
1938	Don Lash	Track
1939	Joe Burk	Rowing
1940	Greg Rice	Track
1941	Leslie MacMitchell	Track
1942	Cornelius Warmerdam	Track
1943	Gilbert Dodds	Track
1944	Ann Curtis	Swimming
1945	Doc Blanchard	Football
1946	Arnold Tucker	Football
1947	John Kelly Jr.	Rowing
1948	Robert Mathias	Track
1949	Dick Button	Skating
1950	Fred Wilt	Track
1951	Rev. Robert Richards	Track
1952	Horace Ashenfelter	Track
1953	Dr. Sammy Lee	Diving
1954	Mal Whitfield	Track
1955	Harrison Dillard	Track
1956	Patricia McCormick	Diving
1957	Bobby Joe Morrow	Track
1958	Glenn Davis	Track
1959	Parry O'Brien	Track
1960	Rafer Johnson	Track
1961	Wilma Rudolph Ward	Track
1962	James Beatty	Track
1963	John Pennel	Track
1964	Don Schollander	Swimming
1965	Bill Bradley	Basketball
1966	Jim Ryun	Track
1967	Randy Matson	Track
1968	Debbie Meyer	Swimming
1969	Bill Toomey	Track
1970	John Kinsella	Swimming
1971	Mark Spitz	Swimming
1972	Frank Shorter	Track
1973	Bill Walton	Basketball
1974	Rick Wohlhutter	Track
1975	Tim Shaw	Swimming
1976	Bruce Jenner	Track
1977	John Naber	Swimming
1978	Tracy Caulkins	Swimming
1979	Kurt Thomas	Gymnastics
1980	Eric Heiden	Speed Skating
1981	Carl Lewis	Track
1982	Mary Decker	Track
1983	Edwin Moses	Track
1984	Greg Louganis	Diving
1985	Joan Benoit Samuelson	Marathon
1986	Jackie Joyner-Kersee	Track
1987	Jim Abbott	Baseball
1988	Florence Griffith Joyner	Track
1989	Janet Evans	Swimming
1990	John Smith	Wrestling
1991	Mike Powell	Track
1992	Bonnie Blair	Speed Skating

Professional Sports Directory

Major League Baseball

Commissioner's Office
350 Park Ave.
New York, NY 10022

National League

National League Office
350 Park Ave.
New York, NY 10022

Atlanta Braves
PO Box 4064
Atlanta, GA 30302

Chicago Cubs
Wrigley Field
Chicago, IL 60613

Cincinnati Reds
100 Riverfront Stadium
Cincinnati, OH 45202

Colorado Rockies
1700 Broadway
Denver, CO 80290

Florida Marlins
100 NE 3d Ave.
Ft. Lauderdale, FL 33301

Houston Astros
PO Box 288
Houston, TX 77001

Los Angeles Dodgers
Dodger Stadium
Los Angeles, CA 90012

Montreal Expos
PO Box 500, Station M
Montreal, Que. H1V 3P2

New York Mets
Shea Stadium
Flushing, NY 11368

Philadelphia Phillies
PO Box 7575
Philadelphia, PA 19101

Pittsburgh Pirates
Three Rivers Stadium
Pittsburgh, PA 15212

St. Louis Cardinals
Busch Stadium
St. Louis, MO 63102

San Diego Padres
PO Box 2000
San Diego, CA 92112

San Francisco Giants
Candlestick Park
San Francisco, CA 94124

American League

American League Office
350 Park Ave.
New York, NY 10022

Baltimore Orioles
333 W. Camden St.
Baltimore, MD 21202

Boston Red Sox
24 Yawkey Way
Boston, MA 02215

California Angels
Anaheim Stadium
Anaheim, CA 92803

Chicago White Sox
333 W. 35th St.
Chicago, IL 60616

Cleveland Indians
Cleveland Stadium
Cleveland, OH 44114

Detroit Tigers
Tiger Stadium
Detroit, MI 48216

Kansas City Royals
P.O. Box 419969
Kansas City, MO 64141

Milwaukee Brewers
Milwaukee County Stadium
Milwaukee, WI 53214

Minnesota Twins
501 Chicago Ave. South
Minneapolis, MN 55415

New York Yankees
Yankee Stadium
Bronx, NY 10451

Oakland A's
Oakland Coliseum
Oakland, CA 94621

Seattle Mariners
P.O. Box 4100
Seattle, WA 98104

Texas Rangers
PO Box 90111
Arlington, TX 76004

Toronto Blue Jays
300 Bremner Blvd.
Toronto, Ont. M5V 3B3

National Basketball Association

League Office
645 5th Ave.
New York, NY 10022

Atlanta Hawks
1 CNN Center
Atlanta, GA 30303

Boston Celtics
151 Merrimac St.
Boston, MA 02114

Charlotte Hornets
Hive Drive
Charlotte, NC 28217

Chicago Bulls
980 North Michigan Ave.
Chicago, IL 60611

Cleveland Cavaliers
2923 Statesboro Rd.
Richfield, OH 44286

Dallas Mavericks
777 Sports St.
Dallas, TX 75207

Denver Nuggets
1635 Clay St.
Denver, CO 80204

Detroit Pistons
2 Championship Dr.
Auburn Hills, MI 48326

Golden State Warriors
Oakland Coliseum
Oakland, CA 94621

Houston Rockets
The Summit
Houston, TX 77277

Indiana Pacers
300 E. Market St.
Indianapolis, IN 46204

Los Angeles Clippers
3939 S. Figueroa
Los Angeles, CA 90037

Los Angeles Lakers
Great Western Forum
Inglewood, CA 90306

Miami Heat
Miami Arena
Miami, FL 33136

Milwaukee Bucks
1001 N. 4th St.
Milwaukee, WI 53203

Minnesota Timberwolves
600 First Ave. N.
Minneapolis, MN 55403

New Jersey Nets
Meadowlands Arena
E. Rutherford, NJ 07073

New York Knickerbockers
4 Pennsylvania Plaza
New York, NY 10001

Orlando Magic
1 Magic Place
Orlando, FL 32801

Philadelphia 76ers
Veterans Stadium
Philadelphia, PA 19148

Phoenix Suns
P.O. Box 1369
Phoenix, AZ 85001

Portland Trail Blazers
700 NE Multnomah St.
Portland, OR 97232

Sacramento Kings
One Sports Pkwy.
Sacramento, CA 95834

San Antonio Spurs
600 E. Market St.
San Antonio, TX 78205

Seattle SuperSonics
190 Queen Ann Ave. N.
Seattle, WA 98109

Utah Jazz
5 Delta Center
Salt Lake City, UT 84101

Washington Bullets
1 Harry S. Truman Dr.
Landover, MD 20785

National Hockey League

League Headquarters
Sun Life Bldg.
Montreal, Quebec H3B 2W2

Mighty Ducks of Anaheim
500 Buena Vista St.
Burbank, CA 91521

Boston Bruins
150 Causeway St.
Boston, MA 02114

Buffalo Sabres
Memorial Auditorium
Buffalo, NY 14202

Calgary Flames
P.O. Box 1540
Calgary, Alta. T2P 3B9

Chicago Blackhawks
1800 W. Madison St.
Chicago, IL 60612

Detroit Red Wings
600 Civic Center Drive
Detroit, MI 48226

Edmonton Oilers
Northlands Coliseum
Edmonton, Alta. T5B 4M9

Florida Panthers
200 S. Andrews Ave.
Ft. Lauderdale, FL 33301

Hartford Whalers
242 Trumbull St.
Hartford, CT 06103

Los Angeles Kings
3900 W. Manchester Blvd.
Inglewood, CA 90306

Minnesota North Stars
7901 Cedar Ave. S.
Bloomington, MN 55425

Montreal Canadiens
2313 St. Catherine St., West
Montreal, Quebec H3H 1N2

New Jersey Devils
Meadowlands Arena
E. Rutherford, NJ 07073

New York Islanders
Nassau Coliseum
Uniondale, NY 11553

New York Rangers
4 Pennsylvania Plaza
New York, NY 10121

Ottawa Senators
301 Moodie Dr.
Ottawa, Ont. K2H 9C4

Philadelphia Flyers
Pattison Place
Philadelphia, PA 19148

Pittsburgh Penguins
Civic Arena
Pittsburgh, PA 15219

Quebec Nordiques
2205 Ave. du Colisee
Quebec, Que. G1L 4W7

St. Louis Blues
5700 Oakland Ave.
St. Louis, MO 63110

San Jose Sharks
10 Almaden Blvd.
San Jose, CA 95113

Tampa Bay Lightning
501 E. Kennedy Blvd.
Tampa, FL 33602

Toronto Maple Leafs
60 Carlton St.
Toronto, Ont. M5B 1L1

Vancouver Canucks
100 North Renfrew St.
Vancouver, B.C. V5K 3N7

Washington Capitals
Capital Centre
Landover, MD 20785

Winnipeg Jets
15-1430 Maroons Road
Winnipeg, Man. R3G 0L5

National Football League

League Office
410 Park Avenue
New York, NY 10022

Atlanta Falcons
2745 Burnett Road
Suwanee, GA 30174

Buffalo Bills
1 Bills Drive
Orchard Park, NY 14127

Chicago Bears
250 N. Washington Rd.
Lake Forest, IL 60045

Cincinnati Bengals
200 Riverfront Stadium
Cincinnati, OH 45202

Cleveland Browns
80 1st Ave.
Berea, OH 44017

Dallas Cowboys
One Cowboys Pkwy.
Irving, TX 75063

Denver Broncos
13655 E. Dove Valley Pkwy.
Englewood, CO 80112

Detroit Lions
1200 Featherstone Rd.
Pontiac, MI 48342

Green Bay Packers
PO Box 10628
Green Bay, Wi 54307

Houston Oilers
6910 Fannin St.
Houston, TX 77030

Indianapolis Colts
P.O. Box 53500
Indianapolis, IN 46253

Kansas City Chiefs
1 Arrowhead Drive
Kansas City, MO 64129

Los Angeles Raiders
332 Center St.
El Segundo, CA 90245

Los Angeles Rams
2327 W. Lincoln Ave.
Anaheim, CA 92801

Miami Dolphins
2269 NW 199 St.
Miami, FL 33056

Minnesota Vikings
9520 Viking Dr.
Eden Prairie, MN 55344

New England Patriots
Foxboro Stadium
Foxboro, MA 02035

New Orleans Saints
6928 Saints Dr.
Metairie, LA 70003

New York Giants
Giants Stadium
E. Rutherford, NJ 07073

New York Jets
1000 Fulton Ave.
Hempstead, NY 11550

Philadelphia Eagles
Veterans Stadium
Philadelphia, PA 19148

Phoenix Cardinals
PO Box 888
Phoenix, AZ 85001

Pittsburgh Steelers
Three Rivers Stadium
Pittsburgh, PA 15212

San Diego Chargers
P.O. Box 609609
San Diego, CA 92160

San Francisco 49ers
4949 Centennial Blvd.
Santa Clara, CA 95054

Seattle Seahawks
11220 NE 53d St.
Kirkland, WA 98033

Tampa Bay Buccaneers
1 Buccaneer Place
Tampa, FL 33607

Washington Redskins
21300 Redskin Park Dr.
Ashburn, VA 22011

Other Sports Organizations

Amateur Athletic Union
3400 W. 86th St.
Indianapolis, IN 46268

Amateur Softball Assn.
2801 NE 50th St.
Oklahoma City, OK 73111

American Horse Show Assn.
220 E. 42d St.
New York, NY 10017

American Kennel Club
51 Madison Ave.
New York, NY 10010

American Water Ski Assn.
799 Overlook Dr. SE
Winter Haven, FL 33884

Canadian Football League
CFL Bldg.
Toronto, Ont. M4R 1A3

Indy-Car
390 Enterprise Court
Bloomfield, MI 48302

Intl. Game Fish Assn.
1301 E. Atlantic Blvd.
Pompano Beach, FL 33060

LPGA
2570 Volusra Ave.
Daytona Beach, FL 32114

Little League Baseball
PO Box 3485
S. Williamsport, PA 17701

National Archery Assn.
One Olympic Plaza
Colorado Springs, CO 80909

NASCAR
PO Box 2875
Daytona Beach, FL 32120

NCAA
6201 College Blvd.
Overland Park, KS 66211

National Rifle Assn.
1600 Rhode Island Ave. NW
Washington, DC 20036

Pro Bowlers Assn.
1720 Merriman Rd.
Akron, OH 44334

Pro Rodeo Cowboys Assn.
101 Pro Rodeo Dr.
Colorado Springs, CO 80919

Special Olympics
1350 New York Ave. NW
Washington, DC 20005

Thoroughbred Racing Assns.
420 Fair Hill Dr.
Elkton, MD 21921

USA Track & Field
P.O. Box 120
Indianapolis, IN 46206

U.S. Auto Club
4910 W. 16th St.
Speedway, IN 46224

U.S. Figure Skating Assn.
20 1st St.
Colorado Springs, CO 80906

U.S. Olympic Committee
1750 E. Boulder St.
Colorado Springs, CO 80909

U.S. Skiing Assn.
1500 Kearns
Park City, UT 84060

U.S. Tennis Assn.
1212 Ave. of the Americas
New York, NY 10036

U.S. Trotting Assn.
750 Michigan Ave.
Columbus, OH 43215

NCAA Wrestling Champions

Year	Champion	Year	Champion	Year	Champion	Year	Champion	Year	Champion
1964	Oklahoma State	1970	Iowa State	1976	Iowa	1982	Iowa	1988	Arizona State
1965	Iowa State	1971	Oklahoma State	1977	Iowa State	1983	Iowa	1989	Oklahoma State
1966	Oklahoma State	1972	Iowa State	1978	Iowa	1984	Iowa	1990	Oklahoma State
1967	Michigan State	1973	Iowa State	1979	Iowa	1985	Iowa	1991	Iowa
1968	Oklahoma State	1974	Oklahoma	1980	Iowa	1986	Iowa	1992	Iowa
1969	Iowa State	1975	Iowa	1981	Iowa	1987	Iowa State	1993	Iowa

World Swimming Records

As of Aug. 1993

Men's Records

Freestyle

Distance	Time	Holder	Country	Where made	Date
50 Meters	**0:21.81**	Tom Jager	U.S.	Nashville, Tenn.	Mar. 24, 1990
100 Meters	**0:48.42**	Matt Biondi	U.S.	Austin, Tex.	Aug. 10, 1988
200 Meters	**1:46.69**	Giorgio Lamberti	Italy	Bonn	Aug. 15, 1989
400 Meters	**3:45.00**	Evgeny Sadovyi	Unified Team	Barcelona	July 29, 1992
800 Meters	**7:47.85**	Kieren Perkins	Australia	Edmonton	Aug. 25, 1991
1,500 Meters	**14:43.48**	Kieren Perkins	Australia	Barcelona	July 31, 1992

Breaststroke

Distance	Time	Holder	Country	Where made	Date
100 Meters	**1:01.29**	Norbert Rosza	Hungary	Athens	Aug. 20, 1991
200 Meters	**2:10.16**	Mike Barrowman	U.S.	Barcelona	July 29, 1992

Butterfly

Distance	Time	Holder	Country	Where made	Date
100 Meters	**0:52.84**	Pablo Morales	U.S.	Orlando, Fla.	June 23, 1986
200 Meters	**1:55.69**	Melvin Stewart	U.S.	Perth, Australia	Jan. 12, 1991

Backstroke

Distance	Time	Holder	Country	Where made	Date
100 Meters	**0:53.86**	Jeff Rouse	U.S.	Barcelona	July 29, 1992
200 Meters	**1:56.57**	Martin Lopez-Zubero	Spain	Tuscaloosa, Ala.	Nov. 23, 1991

Individual Medley

Distance	Time	Holder	Country	Where made	Date
200 Meters	**1:56.62**	Jani Sievinen	Finland	Paris	Feb. 6, 1993
400 Meters	**4:12.36**	Tamas Darnyi	Hungary	Perth, Australia	Jan. 8, 1991

Freestyle Relays

Distance	Time	Holder	Country	Where made	Date
400 M. (4×100)	**3:16.53**	(Jacobs, Dalbey, Jager, Biondi)	U.S.	Seoul	Sept. 23, 1988
800 M. (4×200)	**7:11.95**	(Lepikov, Pychnenko, Taianovitch, Sadovyi)	Unified Team	Barcelona	July 27, 1992

Medley Relays

Distance	Time	Holder	Country	Where made	Date
400 M. (4×100)	**3:36.93**	(Berkoff, Schroeder, Jacobs, Biondi)	U.S.	Seoul	Sept. 25, 1988
		(Rouse, Diebel, Morales, Olsen)	U.S.	Barcelona	July 31, 1992

Women's Records

Freestyle

Distance	Time	Holder	Country	Where made	Date
50 Meters	**0:24.79**	Yang Wenyi	China	Barcelona	Aug. 31, 1992
100 Meters	**0:54.48**	Jenny Thompson	U.S.	Indianapolis	Mar. 1, 1992
200 Meters	**1:57.55**	Heike Friedrich	E. Germany	Berlin	June 18, 1986
400 Meters	**4:03.85**	Janet Evans	U.S.	Seoul	Sept. 22, 1988
800 Meters	**8:16.22**	Janet Evans	U.S.	Tokyo	Aug. 20, 1989
1,500 Meters	**15:52.10**	Janet Evans	U.S.	Orlando, Fla.	Mar. 26, 1988

Breaststroke

Distance	Time	Holder	Country	Where made	Date
100 Meters	**1:07.91**	Silke Hoerner	E. Germany	Strasbourg, France	Aug. 21, 1987
200 Meters	**2:25.35**	Anita Nall	U.S.	Indianapolis	Mar. 2, 1992

Butterfly

Distance	Time	Holder	Country	Where made	Date
100 Meters	**0:57.93**	Mary T. Meagher	U.S.	Brown Deer, Wis.	Aug. 16, 1981
200 Meters	**2:05.96**	Mary T. Meagher	U.S.	Brown Deer, Wis.	Aug. 13, 1981

Backstroke

Distance	Time	Holder	Country	Where made	Date
100 Meters	**1:00.31**	Krisztina Egerszegi	Hungary	Athens	Aug. 22, 1991
200 Meters	**2:06.62**	Krisztina Egerszegi	Hungary	Athens	Aug. 25, 1991

Individual Medley

Distance	Time	Holder	Country	Where made	Date
200 Meters	**2:11.65**	Lin Li	China	Barcelona	July 30, 1992
400 Meters	**4:36.10**	Petra Schneider	E. Germany	Ecuador	Aug. 1, 1982

Freestyle Relays

Distance	Time	Holder	Country	Where made	Date
400 M. (4×100)	**3:39.46**	(Haislett, Torres, Martino, Thompson)	U.S.	Barcelona	July 28, 1992

Medley Relays

Distance	Time	Holder	Country	Where made	Date
400 M. (4×100)	**4:02.54**	(Loveless, Nall, Ahmann-Leighton, Thompson)	U.S.	Barcelona	July 30, 1992

COLLEGE FOOTBALL

Annual Results of Major Bowl Games

(Note: Dates indicate the year that the game was played.)

Rose Bowl, Pasadena

1902 Michigan 49, Stanford 0
1916 Wash. State 14, Brown 0
1917 Oregon 14, Pennsylvania 0
1918-19 Service teams
1920 Harvard 7, Oregon 6
1921 California 28, Ohio State 0
1922 Wash. & Jeff. 0, California 0
1923 So. California 14, Penn State 3
1924 Navy 14, Washington 14
1925 Notre Dame 27, Stanford 10
1926 Alabama 20, Washington 19
1927 Alabama 7, Stanford 7
1928 Stanford 7, Pittsburgh 6
1929 Georgia Tech 8, California 7
1930 So. California 47, Pittsburgh 14
1931 Alabama 24, Wash. State 0
1932 So. California 21, Tulane 12
1933 So. California 35, Pittsburgh 0
1934 Columbia 7, Stanford 0
1935 Alabama 29, Stanford 13
1936 Stanford 7, So. Methodist 0
1937 Pittsburgh 21, Washington 0
1938 California 13, Alabama 0
1939 So. California 7, Duke 3
1940 So. California 14, Tennessee 0
1941 Stanford 21, Nebraska 13
*1942 Oregon St. 20, Duke 16
1943 Georgia 9, UCLA 0
1944 So. California 29, Washington 0
1945 So. California 25, Tennessee 0
1946 Alabama 34, So. California 14
1947 Illinois 45, UCLA 14
1948 Michigan 49, So. California 0
1949 Northwestern 20, California 14
1950 Ohio State 17, California 14
1951 Michigan 14, California 6
1952 Illinois 40, Stanford 7
1953 So. California 7, Wisconsin 0
1954 Mich. State 28, UCLA 20
1955 Ohio State 20, So. California 7
1956 Mich. State 17, UCLA 14
1957 Iowa 35, Oregon St. 19
1958 Ohio State 10, Oregon 7
1959 Iowa 38, California 12
1960 Washington 44, Wisconsin 8
1961 Washington 17, Minnesota 7
1962 Minnesota 21, UCLA 3
1963 So. California 42, Wisconsin 37
1964 Illinois 17, Washington 7
1965 Michigan 34, Oregon St. 7
1966 UCLA 14, Mich. State 12
1967 Purdue 14, So. California 13
1968 Southern Cal. 14, Indiana 3
1969 Ohio State 27, Southern Cal 16
1970 Southern Cal 10, Michigan 3
1971 Stanford 27, Ohio State 17
1972 Stanford 13, Michigan 12
1973 So. California 42, Ohio State 17
1974 Ohio State 42, So. California 21
1975 So. California 18, Ohio State 17
1976 UCLA 23, Ohio State 10
1977 So. California 14, Michigan 6
1978 Washington 27, Michigan 20
1979 So. California 17, Michigan 10
1980 So. California 17, Ohio State 16
1981 Michigan 23, Washington 6
1982 Washington 28, Iowa 0
1983 UCLA 24, Michigan 14
1984 UCLA 45, Illinois 9
1985 So. California 20, Ohio State 17
1986 UCLA 45, Iowa 28
1987 Arizona St. 22, Michigan 15
1988 Mich. State 20, Southern Cal. 17
1989 Michigan 22, Southern Cal. 14
1990 Southern Cal. 17, Michigan 10
1991 Washington 46, Iowa 34
1992 Washington 34, Michigan 14
1993 Michigan 38, Washington 31
*Played at Durham, N.C.

Orange Bowl, Miami

1935 Bucknell 26, Miami (Fla.) 0
1936 Catholic U. 20, Mississippi 19
1937 Duquesne 13, Miss. State 12
1938 Auburn 6, Mich. State 0
1939 Tennessee 17, Oklahoma 0
1940 Georgia Tech 21, Missouri 7
1941 Miss. State 14, Georgetown 7
1942 Georgia 40, TCU 26
1943 Alabama 37, Boston Col. 21
1944 LSU 19, Texas A&M 14
1945 Tulsa 26, Georgia Tech 12
1946 Miami (Fla.) 13, Holy Cross 6
1947 Rice 8, Tennessee 0
1948 Georgia Tech 20, Kansas 14
1949 Texas 41, Georgia 28
1950 Santa Clara 21, Kentucky 13
1951 Clemson 15, Miami (Fla.) 14
1952 Georgia Tech 17, Baylor 14
1953 Alabama 61, Syracuse 6
1954 Oklahoma 7, Maryland 0
1955 Duke 34, Nebraska 7
1956 Oklahoma 20, Maryland 6
1957 Colorado 27, Clemson 21
1958 Oklahoma 48, Duke 21
1959 Oklahoma 21, Syracuse 6
1960 Georgia 14, Missouri 0
1961 Missouri 21, Navy 14
1962 LSU 25, Colorado 7
1963 Alabama 17, Oklahoma 0
1964 Nebraska 13, Auburn 7
1965 Texas 21, Alabama 17
1966 Alabama 39, Nebraska 28
1967 Florida 27, Georgia Tech 12
1968 Oklahoma 26, Tennessee 24
1969 Penn State 15, Kansas 14
1970 Penn State 10, Missouri 3
1971 Nebraska 17, Louisiana St. 12
1972 Nebraska 38, Alabama 6
1973 Nebraska 40, Notre Dame 6
1974 Penn State 16, Louisiana St. 9
1975 Notre Dame 13, Alabama 11
1976 Oklahoma 14, Michigan 6
1977 Ohio State 27, Colorado 10
1978 Arkansas 31, Oklahoma 6
1979 Oklahoma 31, Nebraska 24
1980 Oklahoma 24, Florida St. 7
1981 Oklahoma 18, Florida St. 17
1982 Clemson 22, Nebraska 15
1983 Nebraska 21, Louisiana St. 20
1984 Miami (Fla.) 31, Nebraska 30
1985 Washington 28, Oklahoma 17
1986 Oklahoma 25, Penn State 10
1987 Oklahoma 42, Arkansas 8
1988 Miami (Fla.) 20, Oklahoma 14
1989 Miami (Fla.) 23, Nebraska 3
1990 Notre Dame 21, Colorado 6
1991 Colorado 10, Notre Dame 9
1992 Miami (Fla.) 22, Nebraska 0
1993 Florida St. 27, Nebraska 14

Sugar Bowl, New Orleans

1935 Tulane 20, Temple 14
1936 TCU 3, LSU 2
1937 Santa Clara 21, LSU 14
1938 Santa Clara 6, LSU 0
1939 TCU 15, Carnegie Tech 7
1940 Texas A&M 14, Tulane 13
1941 Boston Col. 19, Tennessee 13
1942 Fordham 2, Missouri 0
1943 Tennessee 14, Tulsa 7
1944 Georgia Tech 20, Tulsa 18
1945 Duke 29, Alabama 26
1946 Oklahoma A&M 33, St. Mary's 13
1947 Georgia 20, No. Carolina 10
1948 Texas 27, Alabama 7
1949 Oklahoma 14, No. Carolina 6
1950 Oklahoma 35, LSU 0
1951 Kentucky 13, Oklahoma 7
1952 Maryland 28, Tennessee 13
1953 Georgia Tech. 24, Mississippi 7
1954 Georgia Tech 42, West Virginia 19
1955 Navy 21, Mississippi 0
1956 Georgia Tech 7, Pittsburgh 0
1957 Baylor 13, Tennessee 7
1958 Mississippi 39, Texas 7
1959 LSU 7, Clemson 0
1960 Mississippi 21, LSU 0
1961 Mississippi 14, Rice 6
1962 Alabama 10, Arkansas 3
1963 Mississippi 17, Arkansas 13
1964 Alabama 12, Mississippi 7
1965 LSU 13, Syracuse 10
1966 Missouri 20, Florida 18
1967 Alabama 34, Nebraska 7
1968 LSU 20, Wyoming 13
1969 Arkansas 16, Georgia 2
1970 Mississippi 27, Arkansas 22
1971 Tennessee 34, Air Force 13
1972 Oklahoma 40, Auburn 22
*1972 (Dec.) Okla. 14, Penn State 0
1973 Notre Dame 24, Alabama 23
1974 Nebraska 13, Florida 10
1975 Alabama 13, Penn State 6
1977 (Jan.) Pittsburgh 27, Georgia 3
1978 Alabama 35, Ohio State 6
1979 Alabama 14, Penn State 7
1980 Alabama 24, Arkansas 9
1981 Georgia 17, Notre Dame 10
1982 Pittsburgh 24, Georgia 20
1983 Penn State 27, Georgia 23
1984 Auburn 9, Michigan 7
1985 Nebraska 28, Louisiana St. 10
1986 Tennessee 35, Miami (Fla.) 7
1987 Nebraska 30, Louisiana St. 15
1988 Syracuse 16, Auburn 16
1989 Florida St. 13, Auburn 7
1990 Miami 33, Alabama 25
1991 Tennessee 23, Virginia 22
1992 Notre Dame 39, Florida 28
1993 Alabama 34, Miami (Fla.) 13
* Penn St. awarded game by forfeit

Fiesta Bowl, Tempe

1971 Arizona St. 45, Florida St. 38
1972 Arizona St. 49, Missouri 35
1973 Arizona St. 28, Pittsburgh 7
1974 Okla. St. 16, Brigham Young 6
1975 Arizona St. 17, Nebraska 14
1976 Oklahoma 41, Wyoming 7
1977 Penn St. 42, Arizona St. 30
1978 UCLA 10, Arkansas 10
1979 Pittsburgh 16, Arizona 10
1980 Penn St. 31, Ohio St. 19
1982 (Jan.) Penn St. 26, USC 10
1983 Arizona St. 32, Oklahoma 21
1984 Ohio State 28, Pittsburgh 23
1985 UCLA 39, Miami 37
1986 Michigan 27, Nebraska 23
1987 Penn St. 14, Miami (Fla.) 10
1988 Florida St. 31, Nebraska 28
1989 Notre Dame 34, W. Virginia 21
1990 Florida St. 41, Nebraska 17
1991 Louisville 34, Alabama 7
1992 Penn St. 42, Tennessee 17
1993 Syracuse 26, Colorado 22

Hall of Fame Bowl, Tampa

1986 (Dec.) Boston Coll. 27, Georgia 24
1988 (Jan.) Michigan 28, Alabama 24
1989 Syracuse 23, LSU 10
1990 Auburn 31, Ohio St. 14
1991 Clemson 30, Illinois 0
1992 Syracuse 24, Ohio St. 17
1993 Tennessee 38, Boston College 23

Cotton Bowl, Dallas

1937 TCU 16, Marquette 6
1938 Rice 28, Colorado 14
1939 St. Mary's 20, Texas Tech 13
1940 Clemson 6, Boston Col. 3
1941 Texas A&M 13, Fordham 12
1942 Alabama 29, Texas A&M 21
1943 Texas 14, Georgia Tech 7
1944 Randolph Field 7, Texas 7
1945 Oklahoma A&M 34, TCU 0
1946 Texas 40, Missouri 27
1947 Arkansas 0, LSU 0
1948 So. Methodist 13, Penn State 13
1949 So. Methodist 21, Oregon 13
1950 Rice 27, No. Carolina 13
1951 Tennessee 20, Texas 14
1952 Kentucky 20, TCU 7
1953 Texas 16, Tennessee 0
1954 Rice 28, Alabama 6
1955 Georgia Tech 14, Arkansas 6
1956 Mississippi 14, TCU 13
1957 TCU 28, Syracuse 27
1958 Navy 20, Rice 7
1959 TCU 0, Air Force 0
1960 Syracuse 23, Texas 14
1961 Duke 7, Arkansas 6
1962 Texas 12, Mississippi 7
1963 LSU 13, Texas 0
1964 Texas 28, Navy 6
1965 Arkansas 10, Nebraska 7
1966 LSU 14, Arkansas 7
1967 Georgia 24, So. Methodist 9
1968 Texas A&M 20, Alabama 16
1969 Texas 36, Tennessee 13
1970 Texas 21, Notre Dame 17
1971 Notre Dame 24, Texas 11
1972 Penn State 30, Texas 6
1973 Texas 17, Alabama 13
1974 Nebraska 19, Texas 3
1975 Penn State 41, Baylor 20
1976 Arkansas 31, Georgia 10
1977 Houston 30, Maryland 21
1978 Notre Dame 38, Texas 10
1979 Notre Dame 35, Houston 34
1980 Houston 17, Nebraska 14
1981 Alabama 30, Baylor 2
1982 Texas 14, Alabama 12
1983 SMU 7, Pittsburgh 3
1984 Georgia 10, Texas 9
1985 Boston Coll. 45, Houston 28
1986 Texas A&M 36, Auburn 16
1987 Ohio St. 28, Texas A&M 12
1988 Texas A&M 35, Notre Dame 10
1989 UCLA 17, Arkansas 3
1990 Tennessee 31, Arkansas 27
1991 Miami (Fla.) 46, Texas 3
1992 Florida St. 10, Texas A&M 2
1993 Notre Dame 28, Texas A&M 3

John Hancock Bowl, El Paso (Sun Bowl until 1989)

1936 Hardin Simmons 14, New Mex. St. 14
1937 Hardin-Simmons 34, Texas Mines 6
1938 West Virginia 7, Texas Tech 6
1939 Utah 26, New Mexico 0
1940 Catholic U. 0, Arizona St. 0
1941 Western Reserve 26, Arizona St. 13
1942 Tulsa 6, Texas Tech 0
1943 2d Air Force 13, Hardin-Simmons 7
1944 Southwestern (Tex.) 7, New Mexico 0
1945 Southwestern (Tex.) 35, U. of Mex. 0
1946 New Mexico 34, Denver 24
1947 Cincinnati 18, Virginia Tech 6
1948 Miami (O.) 13, Texas Tech 12
1949 West Virginia 21, Texas Mines 12
1950 Texas Western 33, Georgetown 20
1951 West Texas St. 14, Cincinnati 13
1952 Texas Tech 25, Col. Pacific 14
1953 Col. Pacific 26, Miss. Southern 7
1954 Texas Western 37, Miss. Southern 14
1955 Texas Western 47, Florida St. 20
1956 Wyoming 21, Texas Tech 14
1957 Geo. Washington 13, Tex. Western 0
1958 Louisville 34, Drake 20
1959 Wyoming 14, Hardin-Simmons 6
1960 New Mexico St. 28, No. Texas St. 8
1961 New Mexico St. 20, Utah State 13
1962 Villanova 17, Wichita 9
1963 West Texas St. 15, Ohio U. 14
1964 Oregon 21, So. Methodist 14
1965 Georgia 7, Texas Tech 0
1966 Texas Western 13, TCU 12
1967 Wyoming 28, Florida St. 20
1968 UTex El Paso 14, Mississippi 7
1969 Auburn 34, Arizona 10
1969 (Dec.) Nebraska 45, Georgia 6
1970 Georgia Tech. 17, Texas Tech. 9
1971 LSU 33, Iowa State 15
1972 North Carolina 32, Texas Tech 28
1973 Missouri 34, Auburn 17
1974 Mississippi St. 26, No. Carolina 24
1975 Pittsburgh 33, Kansas 19
1977 (Jan.) Texas A&M 37, Florida 14
1977 (Dec.) Stanford 24, Louisiana St. 14
1978 Texas 42, Maryland 0
1979 Washington 14, Texas 7
1980 Nebraska 31, Mississippi St. 17
1981 Oklahoma 40, Houston 14
1982 North Carolina 26, Texas 10
1983 Alabama 28, SMU 7
1984 Maryland 28, Tennessee 27
1985 Georgia 13, Arizona 13
1986 Alabama 28, Washington 6
1987 Oklahoma St. 35, West Virginia 33
1988 Alabama 29, Army 28
1989 Pittsburgh 31, Texas A&M 28
1990 Michigan St. 17, USC 16
1991 UCLA 6, Illinois 3
1992 Baylor 20, Arizona 15

Gator Bowl, Jacksonville

1946 Wake Forest 26, So. Carolina 14
1947 Oklahoma 34, N.C. State 13
1948 Maryland 20, Georgia 20
1949 Clemson 24, Missouri 23
1950 Maryland 20, Missouri 7
1951 Wyoming 20, Wash. & Lee 7
1952 Miami (Fla.) 14, Clemson 0
1953 Florida 14, Tulsa 13
1954 Texas Tech 35, Auburn 13
1955 Auburn 33, Baylor 13
1956 Vanderbilt 25, Auburn 13
1957 Georgia Tech 21, Pittsburgh 14
1958 Tennessee 3, Texas A&M 0
1959 Mississippi 7, Florida 3
1960 Arkansas 14, Georgia Tech 7
1961 Florida 13, Baylor 12
1962 Penn State 30, Georgia Tech 15
1963 Florida 17, Penn State 7
1964 No. Carolina 35, Air Force 0
1965 Florida St. 36, Oklahoma 19
1966 Georgia Tech 31, Texas Tech 21
1967 Tennessee 18, Syracuse 12
1968 Penn State 17, Florida St. 17
1969 Missouri 35, Alabama 10
1969 (Dec.) Florida 14, Tenn. 13
1971 (Jan.) Auburn 35, Mississippi 28
1972 Georgia 7, N. Carolina 3
1973 Auburn 24, Colorado 3
1973 (Dec.) Tex. Tech. 28, Tenn. 19
1974 Auburn 27, Texas 3
1975 Maryland 13, Florida 0
1976 Notre Dame 20, Penn State 9
1977 Pittsburgh 34, Clemson 3
1978 Clemson 17, Ohio State 15
1979 No. Carolina 17, Michigan 15
1980 Pittsburgh 37, So. Carolina 9
1981 No. Carolina 31, Arkansas 27
1982 Florida St. 31, West Va. 12
1983 Florida 14, Iowa 6
1984 Oklahoma St. 21, So. Carolina 14
1985 Florida St. 34, Oklahoma St. 23
1986 Clemson 27, Stanford 21
1987 LSU 30, So. Carolina 13
1989 (Jan.) Georgia 34, Michigan St. 27
1989 (Dec.) Clemson 27, W. Va. 7
1991 (Jan.) Michigan 35, Mississippi 3
1991 (Dec.) Oklahoma 48, Virginia 14
1992 Florida 27, N.C. State 10

Liberty Bowl, Memphis

1959 Penn State 7, Alabama 0
1960 Penn State 41, Oregon 12
1961 Syracuse 15, Miami 14
1962 Oregon State 6, Villanova 0
1963 Miss. State 16, N.C. State 12
1964 Utah 32, West Virginia 6
1965 Mississippi 13, Auburn 7
1966 Miami (Fla.) 14, Va. Tech 7
1967 N.C. State 14, Georgia 7
1968 Mississippi 34, Va. Tech 17
1969 Colorado 47, Alabama 33
1970 Tulane 17, Colorado 3
1971 Tennessee 14, Arkansas 13
1972 Georgia Tech 31, Iowa State 30
1973 No. Carolina St. 31, Kansas 18
1974 Tennessee 7, Maryland 3
1975 USC 20, Texas A&M 0
1976 Alabama 36, UCLA 6
1977 Nebraska 21, N. Carolina 17
1978 Missouri 20, Louisiana St. 15
1979 Penn St. 9, Tulane 6
1980 Purdue 28, Missouri 25
1981 Ohio State 31, Navy 28
1982 Alabama 21, Illinois 15
1983 Notre Dame 19, Boston Coll. 18
1984 Auburn 21, Arkansas 15
1985 Baylor 21, Louisiana St. 7
1986 Tennessee 21, Minnesota 14
1987 Georgia 20, Arkansas 17
1988 Indiana 34, S. Carolina 10
1989 Mississippi 42, Air Force 29
1990 Air Force 23, Ohio State 11
1991 Air Force 38, Mississippi St. 15
1992 Mississippi 13, Air Force 0

Freedom Bowl, Anaheim

1984 Iowa 55, Texas 17
1985 Washington 20, Colorado 17
1986 UCLA 31, Brigham Young 10
1987 Arizona St. 33, Air Force 28
1988 Brigham Young 20, Colorado 17
1989 Washington 34, Florida 7
1990 Colorado St. 32, Oregon 31
1991 Tulsa 28, San Diego St. 17
1992 Fresno St. 24, USC 7

Copper Bowl, Tucson

1989 Arizona 17, N.C. St. 10
1990 California 17, Wyoming 15
1991 Indiana 24, Baylor 0
1992 Washington St. 31, Utah 28

Independence Bowl, Shreveport

1976 McNeese St. 20, Tulsa 16
1977 Louisiana Tech 24, Louisiville 14
1978 E. Carolina 35, La. Tech 13
1979 Syracuse 31, McNeese St. 7
1980 So. Miss. 16, McNeese St. 14
1981 Texas A&M 33, Oklahoma St. 16
1982 Wisconsin 14, Kansas St. 3
1983 Air Force 9, Mississippi 3
1984 Air Force 23, Virginia Tech 7
1985 Minnesota 20, Clemson 13
1986 Mississippi 20, Texas Tech 17
1987 Washington 24, Tulane 12
1988 S. Mississippi 38, UTEP 18
1989 Oregon 27, Tulsa 24
1990 Louisiana Tech 34, Maryland 34
1991 Georgia 24, Arkansas 15
1992 Wake Forest 39, Oregon 35

Citrus Bowl, Orlando

1947 Catawba 31, Maryville 6
1948 Catawba 7, Marshall 0
1949 Murray State 21, Sul Ross St. 21
1950 St. Vincent 7, Emory & Henry 6
1951 Morris Harvey 35, Emory & Henry 14
1952 Stetson 35, Arkansas St. 20
1953 East Texas St. 33, Tenn. Tech 0
1954 East Texas St. 7, Arkansas St. 7
1955 Neb.-Omaha 7, Eastern Kentucky 6
1956 Juniata 6, Missouri Valley 6
1957 West Texas St. 20, So. Miss. 13
1958 East Texas St. 10, So. Miss. 9
1958 (Dec.) East Texas St. 26, Missouri Valley 7
1960 (Jan.) Middle Tenn. 21, Presbyterian 12
1960 (Dec.) Citadel 27, Tenn. Tech 0
1961 Lamar 21, Middle Tennessee 14
1962 Houston 49, Miami (O.) 21
1963 Western Ky. 27, Coast Guard 0
1964 E. Carolina 14, Massachusetts 13
1965 East Carolina 31, Maine 0
1966 Morgan State 14, West Chester 6
1967 Tenn.-Martin 25, West Chester 8
1968 Richmond 49, Ohio U. 42
1969 Toledo 56, Davidson 33
1970 Toledo 40, William & Mary 12
1971 Toledo 28, Richmond 3
1972 Tampa 21, Kent State 18
1973 Miami (O.) 16, Florida 7
1974 Miami (O.) 21, Georgia 10
1975 Miami (O.) 20, South Carolina 7
1976 Okla. St. 49, Brigham Young 21
1977 Florida St. 40, Texas Tech 17
1978 N.C. State 30, Pittsburgh 17
1979 LSU 34, Wake Forest 10
1980 Florida 35, Maryland 20
1981 Missouri 19, Southern Miss. 17
1982 Auburn 33, Boston College 26
1983 Tennessee 30, Maryland 23
1984 Georgia 17, Florida St. 17
1985 Ohio St. 10, Brigham Young 7
1987 (Jan.) Auburn 16, USC 7
1988 Clemson 35, Penn St. 10
1989 Clemson 13, Oklahoma 6
1990 Illinois 31, Virginia 21
1991 Georgia Tech 45, Nebraska 21
1992 California 37, Clemson 13
1993 Georgia 21, Ohio St. 14

Peach Bowl, Atlanta

1968 LSU 31, Florida St. 27
1969 West Virginia 14, S. Carolina 3
1970 Arizona St. 48, N. Carolina 26
1971 Mississippi 41, Georgia Tech. 18
1972 N. Carolina St. 49, W. Va. 13
1973 Georgia 17, Maryland 16
1974 Vanderbilt 6, Texas Tech. 6
1975 W. Virginia 13, No. Carolina St. 10
1976 Kentucky 21, North Carolina 0
1977 N. Carolina St. 24, Iowa St. 14
1978 Purdue 41, Georgia Tech. 21
1979 Baylor 24, Clemson 18
1981 (Jan.) Miami (Fla.) 20, Virginia Tech. 10
1981 (Dec.) West Virginia 26, Florida 6
1982 Iowa 28, Tennessee 22
1983 Florida St. 28, North Carolina 3
1984 Virginia 27, Purdue 22
1985 Army 31, Illinois 29
1986 Va. Tech 25, N.C. State 24
1988 (Jan.) Tennessee 28, Indiana 22
1988 (Dec.) N.C. State 28, Iowa 23
1989 Syracuse 19, Georgia 18
1990 Auburn 27, Indiana 23
1992 (Jan.) E. Carolina 37, N.C. State 34
1993 North Carolina 21, Mississippi St. 17

Holiday Bowl, San Diego

1978 Navy 23, Brigham Young 16
1979 Indiana 38, Brigham Young 37
1980 Brigham Young 46, SMU 45
1981 Brigham Young 38, Wash. St. 36
1982 Ohio State 47, Brigham Young 17
1983 Brigham Young 21, Missouri 17
1984 Brigham Young 24, Michigan 17
1985 Arkansas 18, Arizona St. 17
1986 Iowa 39, San Diego St. 38
1987 Iowa 20, Wyoming 19
1988 Oklahoma St. 62, Wyoming 14
1989 Penn St. 50, Brigham Young 39
1990 Texas A&M 65, Brigham Young 14
1991 Iowa 13, Brigham Young 13
1992 Hawaii 27, Illinois 17

Aloha Bowl, Honolulu

1982 Washington 21, Maryland 20
1983 Penn State 13, Washington 10
1984 SMU 27, Notre Dame 20
1985 Alabama 24, USC 3
1986 Arizona 30, North Carolina 21
1987 UCLA 20, Florida 16
1988 Washington St. 24, Houston 22
1989 Michigan St. 33, Hawaii 13
1990 Syracuse 28, Arizona 0
1991 Georgia Tech 18, Stanford 17
1992 Kansas 23, Brigham Young 20

Blockbuster Bowl, Miami

1990 Florida St. 24, Penn St. 17
1991 Alabama 30, Colorado 25
1993 (Jan.) Stanford 24, Penn St. 3

Las Vegas Bowl, Las Vegas

1992 Bowling Green 35, Nevada 34

Outland Award

Honoring the outstanding interior lineman selected by the Football Writers' Association of America.

1946 George Connor, Notre Dame, T
1947 Joe Steffy, Army, G
1948 Bill Fischer, Notre Dame, G
1949 Ed Bagdon, Michigan St., G
1950 Bob Gain, Kentucky, T
1951 Jim Weatherall, Oklahoma, T
1952 Dick Modzelewski, Maryland, T
1953 J. D. Roberts, Oklahoma, G
1954 Bill Brooks, Arkansas, G
1955 Calvin Jones, Iowa, G
1956 Jim Parker, Ohio State, G
1957 Alex Karras, Iowa, T
1958 Zeke Smith, Auburn, G
1959 Mike McGee, Duke, T
1960 Tom Brown, Minnesota, G
1961 Merlin Olsen, Utah State, T
1962 Bobby Bell, Minnesota, T
1963 Scott Appleton, Texas, T
1964 Steve Delong, Tennessee, T
1965 Tommy Nobis, Texas, G
1966 Loyd Phillips, Arkansas, T
1967 Ron Yary, Southern Cal, T
1968 Bill Stanfill, Georgia, T
1969 Mike Reid, Penn State, DT
1970 Jim Stillwagon, Ohio State, LB
1971 Larry Jacobson, Nebraska, DT
1972 Rich Glover, Nebraska, MG
1973 John Hicks, Ohio State, G
1974 Randy White, Maryland, DE
1975 Lee Roy Selmon, Oklahoma, DT
1976 Ross Browner, Notre Dame, DE
1977 Brad Shearer, Texas, DT
1978 Greg Roberts, Oklahoma, G
1979 Jim Ritcher, No. Carolina St., C
1980 Mark May, Pittsburgh, OT
1981 Dave Rimington, Nebraska, C
1982 Dave Rimington, Nebraska, C
1983 Dean Steinkuhler, Nebraska, G
1984 Bruce Smith, Virginia Tech, DT
1985 Mike Ruth, Boston College, DT
1986 Jason Buck, BYU, DT
1987 Chad Hennings, Air Force, DT
1988 Tracy Rocker, Auburn, DT
1989 Mohammed Elewonibi, BYU, G
1990 Russell Maryland, Miami (Fla.), DT
1991 Steve Emtman, Washington, DL
1992 Will Shields, Nebraska, G

Selected College Division I Football Teams

Team	Nickname	Team colors	Conference	Coach	1992 record (W-L-T)
Air Force	Falcons	Blue & silver	Western Athletic	Fisher De Berry	7-5-0
Akron	Zips	Blue & gold	Mid-American	Gerry Faust	7-3-1
Alabama	Crimson Tide	Crimson & white	Southeastern	Gene Stallings	13-0-0
Arizona	Wildcats	Red & blue	Pacific Ten	Dick Tomey	6-5-1
Arizona State	Sun Devils	Maroon & gold	Pacific Ten	Bruce Snyder	6-5-0
Arkansas	Razorbacks	Cardinal & white	Southeastern	Danny Ford	3-7-1
Arkansas State	Indians	Scarlet & black	Big West	John Bobo	2-9-0
Army	Cadets	Black, gold, gray	Independent	Bob Sutton	5-6-0
Auburn	Tigers	Orange & blue	Southeastern	Terry Bowden	5-5-1
Ball State	Cardinals	Cardinal & white	Mid-American	Paul Schudel	5-6-0
Baylor	Bears	Green & gold	Southwest	Chuck Reedy	7-5-0
Boston College	Eagles	Maroon & gold	Big East	Tom Coughlin	8-3-1
Boston Univ.	Terriers	Scarlet & white	Yankee	Dan Allen	3-8-1
Bowling Green	Falcons	Orange & brown	Mid-American	Gary Blackney	10-2-0
Brigham Young	Cougars	Royal blue & white	Western Athletic	LaVell Edwards	8-5-0
Brown	Bears	Brown, cardinal, white	Ivy	Mickey Kwiatowski	0-10-0
California	Golden Bears	Blue & gold	Pacific Ten	Keith Gilbertson	4-7-0
Central Michigan	Chippewas	Maroon & gold	Mid-American	Herb Deromedi	5-6-0
Cincinnati	Bearcats	Red & black	Independent	Tim Murphy	3-8-0
Citadel	Bulldogs	Blue & white	Southern	Charles Taaffe	11-2-0
Clemson	Tigers	Purple & orange	Atlantic Coast	Ken Hatfield	5-6-0
Colgate	Red Raiders	Maroon	Patriot	Mike Foley	4-7-0
Colorado State	Rams	Green & gold	Western Athletic	Sonny Lubick	5-7-0
Colorado	Buffaloes	Silver, gold & black	Big Eight	Bill McCartney	9-2-1
Cornell	Big Red	Carnelian & white	Ivy	Jim Hofher	7-3-0
Dartmouth	Big Green	Dartmouth green & white	Ivy	John Lyons	8-2-0
Delaware	Fightin' Blue Hens	Blue & gold	Yankee	Harold Raymond	11-3-0
Delaware State	Hornets	Red & blue	Mid-Eastern	William Collick	6-5-0
Duke	Blue Devils	Royal blue & white	Atlantic Coast	Barry Wilson	2-9-0
East Carolina	Pirates	Purple & gold	Independent	Steve Logan	5-6-0
East Tennessee St.	Buccaneers	Blue & gold	Southern	Mike Cavan	5-6-0
Eastern Illinois	Panthers	Blue & gray	Gateway	Bob Spoo	5-6-0
Eastern Kentucky	Colonels	Maroon & white	Ohio Valley	Roy Kidd	9-3-0
Eastern Michigan	Eagles	Green & white	Mid-American	Ron Cooper	1-10-0
Eastern Washington	Eagles	Red & white	Big Sky	Dick Zornes	7-4-0
Florida	Gators	Orange & blue	Southeastern	Steve Spurrier	9-4-0
Florida A&M	Rattlers	Orange & green	Mid-Eastern	Ken Riley	7-5-0
Florida State	Seminoles	Garnet & gold	Atlantic Coast	Bobby Bowden	11-1-0
Fresno State	Bulldogs	Cardinal & blue	Western Athletic	Jim Sweeney	9-4-0
Furman	Paladins	Purple & white	Southern	Jimmy Satterfield	6-5-0
Georgia	Bulldogs	Red & black	Southeastern	Ray Goff	10-2-0
Georgia Southern	Eagles	Blue & white	Southern	Tim Stowers	7-4-0
Georgia Tech	Yellow Jackets	Old gold & white	Atlantic Coast	Bill Lewis	5-6-0
Grambling	Tigers	Black & gold	Southwestern	Eddie Robinson	10-2-0
Harvard	Crimson	Crimson	Ivy	Joe Restic	3-7-0
Hawaii	Rainbow Warriors	Green & white	Western Athletic	Bob Wagner	11-2-0
Holy Cross	Crusaders	Royal purple	Patriot	Peter Vaas	6-5-0
Houston	Cougars	Scarlet & white	Southwest	Kim Helton	4-7-0
Howard	Bison	Blue & white	Mid-Eastern	Steve Wilson	7-4-0
Idaho	Vandals	Silver & gold	Big Sky	John L. Smith	9-3-0
Idaho State	Bengals	Orange & black	Big Sky	Brian McNeely	3-8-0
Illinois	Fighting Illini	Orange & blue	Big Ten	Lou Tepper	6-5-1
Illinois State	Redbirds	Red & white	Gateway	Jim Heacock	5-6-0
Indiana	Hoosiers	Cream & crimson	Big Ten	Bill Mallory	5-6-0
Indiana State	Sycamores	Blue & white	Gateway	Dennis Raetz	4-7-0
Iowa	Hawkeyes	Old gold & black	Big Ten	Hayden Fry	5-7-0
Iowa State	Cyclones	Cardinal & gold	Big Eight	Jim Walden	4-7-0
Jackson State	Tigers	Blue & white	Southwestern	James Carson	7-4-0
James Madison	Dukes	Purple & gold	Yankee	Rip Scherer	4-7-0
Kansas	Jayhawks	Crimson & blue	Big Eight	Glen Mason	8-4-0
Kansas State	Wildcats	Purple & white	Big Eight	Bill Snyder	5-6-0
Kent	Golden Flashes	Blue & gold	Mid-American	Pete Cordelli	2-9-0
Kentucky	Wildcats	Blue & white	Southeastern	Bill Curry	4-7-0
Lafayette	Leopards	Maroon & white	Patriot	Bill Russo	8-3-0
Lehigh	Engineers	Brown & white	Patriot	Hank Small	3-8-0
Liberty	Flames	Red, white, blue	Independent	Sam Rutigliano	7-4-0
Louisiana State	Fighting Tigers	Purple & gold	Southeastern	Curley Hallman	2-9-0
Louisiana Tech	Bulldogs	Red & blue	Big West	Joe Raymond Peace	5-6-0
Louisville	Cardinals	Red, black, white	Independent	Howard Schnellenberger	5-6-0
Maine	Black Bears	Blue & white	Yankee	Jack Cosgrove	6-5-0
Marshall	Thundering Herd	Green & white	Southern	Jim Donnan	11-4-0
Maryland	Terps	Red, white, black & gold	Atlantic Coast	Mark Duffner	3-8-0
Massachusetts	Minutemen	Maroon & white	Yankee	Mike Hodges	7-3-0
McNeese State	Cowboys	Blue & gold	Southland	Bobby Keasler	9-4-0
Memphis State	Tigers	Blue & gray	Independent	Chuck Stobart	6-5-0
Miami (Fla.)	Hurricanes	Orange, green, white	Big East	Dennis Erickson	11-1-0
Miami (Ohio)	Redskins	Red & white	Mid-American	Randy Walker	6-4-1
Michigan	Wolverines	Maize & blue	Big Ten	Gary Moeller	9-0-3
Michigan State	Spartans	Green & white	Big Ten	George Perles	5-6-0
Middle Tennessee St.	Blue Raiders	Blue & white	Ohio Valley	Boots Donnelly	10-3-0
Minnesota	Golden Gophers	Maroon & gold	Big Ten	Jim Wacker	2-9-0

Team	Nickname	Team colors	Conference	Coach	1992 record (W-L-T)
Mississippi	Rebels	Red & blue	Southeastern	Billy Brewer	9-3-0
Mississippi State	Bulldogs	Maroon & white	Southeastern	Jackie Sherrill	7-5-0
Miss. Valley	Delta Devils	Green & white	Southwestern	Larry Dorsey	4-5-0
Missouri	Tigers	Old gold & black	Big Eight	Bob Stull	3-8-0
Montana	Grizzlies	Copper, silver, gold	Big Sky	Don Read	6-5-0
Montana State	Bobcats	Blue & gold	Big Sky	Cliff Hyself	4-7-0
Morehead State	Eagles	Blue & gold	Ohio Valley	Cole Proctor	3-8-0
Morgan State	Bears	Blue & orange	Mid-Eastern	Ricky Diggs	2-8-0
Murray State	Racers	Blue & gold	Ohio Valley	Houston Nutt	2-9-0
Navy	Midshipmen	Navy blue & gold	Independent	George Chaump	1-10-0
Nebraska	Cornhuskers	Scarlet & cream	Big Eight	Tom Osborne	9-3-0
Nevada-Las Vegas	Rebels	Scarlet & gray	Big West	Jim Strong	6-5-0
Nevada-Reno	Wolf Pack	Silver & blue	Big West	Jeff Horton	7-5-0
New Hampshire	Wildcats	Blue & white	Yankee	Bill Bowes	5-5-1
New Mexico	Lobos	Cherry & silver	Western Athletic	Dennis Franchione	3-8-0
New Mexico State	Aggies	Crimson & white	Big West	Jim Hess	6-5-0
Nicholls St.	Colonels	Red & grey	Southland	Rick Rhoades	1-9-1
North Carolina	Tar Heels	Blue & white	Atlantic Coast	Mack Brown	9-3-0
North Carolina A & T	Aggies	Blue & gold	Mid-Eastern	Bill Hayes	9-3-0
North Carolina State	Wolfpack	Red & white	Atlantic Coast	Dick Sheridan	9-3-1
North Texas	Mean Green, Eagles	Green & white	Southland	Dennis Parker	4-7-0
Northeast Louisiana	Indians	Maroon & gold	Southland	Dave Roberts	10-3-0
Northeastern	Huskies	Red & black	Yankee	Barry Gallup	5-5-1
Northern Arizona	Lumberjacks	Blue & gold	Big Sky	Steve Axman	4-7-0
Northern Illinois	Huskies	Cardinal & black	Big West	Charlie Sadler	5-6-0
Northern Iowa	Panthers	Purple & old gold	Gateway	Terry Allen	12-2-0
Northwestern	Wildcats	Purple & white	Big Ten	Gary Barnett	3-8-0
Northwestern State	Demons	Purple & white	Southland	Sam Goodwin	7-4-0
Notre Dame	Fighting Irish	Gold & blue	Independent	Lou Holtz	10-1-1
Ohio State	Buckeyes	Scarlet & gray	Big Ten	John Cooper	8-3-1
Ohio Univ	Bobcats	Green & white	Mid-American	Tom Lichtenberg	1-10-0
Oklahoma	Sooners	Crimson & cream	Big Eight	Gary Gibbs	5-4-2
Oklahoma State	Cowboys	Orange & black	Big Eight	Pat Jones	4-6-1
Oregon	Ducks	Green & yellow	Pacific Ten	Rich Brooks	6-6-0
Oregon State	Beavers	Orange & black	Pacific Ten	Jerry Pettibone	1-9-1
Pacific	Tigers	Orange & black	Big West	Chuck Shelton	3-8-0
Penn State	Nittany Lions	Blue & white	Big Ten	Joe Paterno	7-5-0
Pennsylvania	Red & Blue, Quakers	Red & blue	Ivy	Al Bagnoli	7-3-0
Pittsburgh	Panthers	Gold & blue	Big East	Johnny Majors	3-9-0
Princeton	Tigers	Orange & black	Ivy	Steve Tosches	8-2-0
Purdue	Boilermakers	Old gold & black	Big Ten	Jim Colletto	4-7-0
Rhode Island	Rams	Blue & white	Yankee	Floyd Keith	1-10-0
Rice	Owls	Blue & gray	Southwest	Fred Goldsmith	6-5-0
Richmond	Spiders	Red & blue	Yankee	Jim Marshall	7-4-0
Rutgers	Scarlet Knights	Scarlet	Big East	Doug Graber	7-4-0
Sam Houston State	Bearkats	Orange & white	Southland	Ron Randleman	6-3-2
Samford	Bulldogs	Crimson & blue	Independent	Chan Galley	9-3-0
San Diego State	Aztecs	Scarlet & black	Western Athletic	Al Luginbill	5-5-1
San Jose State	Spartans	Gold & white	Big West	John Ralston	7-4-0
South Carolina	Fighting Gamecocks	Garnet & black	Southeastern	Sparky Woods	5-6-0
South Carolina State	Bulldogs	Garnet & blue	Mid-Eastern	Willie Jeffries	7-4-0
SE Missouri St.	Indians	Red & black	Ohio Valley	John Mumford	2-9-0
Southern-Baton Rouge	Jaguars	Blue & gold	Southwestern	Pete Richardson	5-6-0
Southern California	Trojans	Cardinal & gold	Pacific Ten	John Robinson	6-5-1
Southern Illinois	Salukis	Maroon & white	Gateway	Bob Smith	4-7-0
Southern Methodist	Mustangs	Red & blue	Southwest	Tom Rossley	5-6-0
Southern Mississippi	Golden Eagles	Black & gold	Independent	Jeff Bower	7-4-0
SW Missouri St	Bears	Maroon & white	Gateway	Jesse Branch	6-5-0
SW Texas St.	Bobcats	Maroon & gold	Southland	Jim Bob Helduser	5-5-1
Southwestern La.	Ragin' Cajuns	Vermillion & white	Big West	Nelson Stokley	2-9-0
Stanford	Cardinal	Cardinal & white	Pacific Ten	Bill Walsh	10-3-0
Stephen F. Austin St.	Lumberjacks	Purple & white	Southland	John Pearce	3-8-0
Syracuse	Orangemen	Orange	Big East	Paul Pasqualoni	10-2-0
Temple	Owls	Cherry & white	Big East	Ron Dickerson	1-10-0
Tennessee	Volunteers	Orange & white	Southeastern	Philip Fulmer	9-3-0
Tenn.-Chattanooga	Moccasins	Navy blue & gold	Southern	Tommy West	2-9-0
Tenn.-Martin	Pacers	Orange, white, blue	Ohio Valley	Don McLeary	3-8-0
Tennessee State	Tigers	Blue & white	Ohio Valley	Bill Davis	5-6-0
Tennessee Tech	Golden Eagles	Purple & gold	Ohio Valley	Jim Ragland	5-6-0
Texas	Longhorns	Orange & white	Southwest	John Mackovic	6-5-0
Texas A & M	Aggies	Maroon & white	Southwest	R.C. Slocum	12-1-0
Texas Christian	Horned Frogs	Purple & white	Southwest	Pat Sullivan	2-8-1
Texas Southern	Tigers	Maroon & gray	Southwestern	Walter Highsmith	5-6-0
Texas Tech	Red Raiders	Scarlet & black	Southwest	Spike Dykes	5-6-0
Toledo	Rockets	Blue & gold	Mid-American	Gary Pinkel	8-3-0
Towson St.	Tigers	Gold & white	Independent	Gordy Combs	5-5-0
Tulane	Green Wave	Olive green & sky blue	Independent	Buddy Teevens	2-9-0
Tulsa	Golden Hurricane	Blue & gold	Independent	Dave Rader	4-7-0
UCLA	Bruins	Blue & gold	Pacific Ten	Terry Donahue	6-5-0
Utah	Utes	Crimson & white	Western Athletic	Ron McBride	6-6-0
Utah State	Aggies	Navy blue & white	Big West	Charlie Weatherbie	5-6-0
UTEP	Miners	Orange, blue, white	Western Athletic	David Lee	1-10-0
Vanderbilt	Commodores	Black & gold	Southeastern	Gerry DiNardo	4-7-0
Villanova	Wildcats	Blue & white	Yankee	Andy Talley	9-3-0
Virginia	Cavaliers	Orange & blue	Atlantic Coast	George Welsh	7-4-0

Team	Nickname	Team colors	Conference	Coach	1992 record (W-L-T)
VMI	Keydets	Red, white & yellow	Southern	Jim Shuck	3-8-0
Virginia Tech	Gobblers, Hokies	Orange & maroon	Big East	Frank Beamer	2-8-1
Wake Forest	Demon Deacons	Old gold & black	Atlantic Coast	Jim Caldwell	8-4-0
Washington	Huskies	Purple & gold	Pacific Ten	Jim Lambright	9-3-0
Washington State	Cougars	Crimson & gray	Pacific Ten	Mike Price	9-3-0
Weber State	Wildcats	Purple & white	Big Sky	Dave Arslanian	6-5-0
West Virginia	Mountaineers	Old gold & blue	Big East	Don Nehlen	5-4-2
Western Carolina	Catamounts	Purple & gold	Southern	Steve Hodgin	7-4-0
Western Illinois	Leathernecks	Purple & gold	Gateway	Randy Ball	7-4-0
Western Kentucky	Hilltoppers	Red & white	Independent	Jack Harbaugh	4-6-0
Western Michigan	Broncos	Brown & gold	Mid-American	Al Molde	7-3-1
William & Mary	Tribe	Green, gold & silver	Yankee	Jimmye Laycock	9-2-0
Wisconsin	Badgers	Cardinal & white	Big Ten	Barry Alvarez	5-6-0
Wyoming	Cowboys	Brown & yellow	Western Athletic	Joe Tiller	5-7-0
Yale	Bulldogs, Elis	Yale blue & white	Ivy	Carmen Cozza	4-6-0
Youngstown St.	Penguins	Scarlet & white	Independent	Jim Tressel	11-3-1

Heisman Trophy Winners

Awarded annually to the nation's outstanding college football player.

1935 Jay Berwanger, Chicago, HB
1936 Larry Kelley, Yale, E
1937 Clinton Frank, Yale, HB
1938 David O'Brien, Tex. Christian, QB
1939 Nile Kinnick, Iowa, HB
1940 Tom Harmon, Michigan, HB
1941 Bruce Smith, Minnesota, HB
1942 Frank Sinkwich, Georgia, HB
1943 Angelo Bertelli, Notre Dame, QB
1944 Leslie Horvath, Ohio State, QB
1945 Felix Blanchard, Army, FB
1946 Glenn Davis, Army, HB
1947 John Lujack, Notre Dame, QB
1948 Doak Walker, SMU, HB
1949 Leon Hart, Notre Dame, E
1950 Vic Janowicz, Ohio State, HB
1951 Richard Kazmaier, Princeton, HB
1952 Billy Vessels, Oklahoma, HB
1953 John Lattner, Notre Dame, HB
1954 Alan Ameche, Wisconsin, FB
1955 Howard Cassady, Ohio St., HB
1956 Paul Hornung, Notre Dame, QB
1957 John Crow, Texas A & M, HB
1958 Pete Dawkins, Army, HB
1959 Billy Cannon, La. State, HB
1960 Joe Bellino, Navy, HB
1961 Ernest Davis, Syracuse, HB
1962 Terry Baker, Oregon State, QB
1963 Roger Staubach, Navy, QB
1964 John Huarte, Notre Dame, QB
1965 Mike Garrett, USC, HB
1966 Steve Spurrier, Florida, QB
1967 Gary Beban, UCLA, QB
1968 O. J. Simpson, USC, RB
1969 Steve Owens, Oklahoma, RB
1970 Jim Plunkett, Stanford, QB
1971 Pat Sullivan, Auburn, QB
1972 Johnny Rodgers, Nebraska, RB-R
1973 John Cappelletti, Penn State, RB
1974 Archie Griffin, Ohio State, RB
1975 Archie Griffin, Ohio State, RB
1976 Tony Dorsett, Pittsburgh, RB
1977 Earl Campbell, Texas, RB
1978 Billy Sims, Oklahoma, RB
1979 Charles White, USC, RB
1980 George Rogers, So. Carolina, RB
1981 Marcus Allen, USC, RB
1982 Herschel Walker, Georgia, RB
1983 Mike Rozier, Nebraska, RB
1984 Doug Flutie, Boston College, QB
1985 Bo Jackson, Auburn, RB
1986 Vinny Testaverde, Miami, QB
1987 Tim Brown, Notre Dame, WR
1988 Barry Sanders, Oklahoma St., RB
1989 Andre Ware, Houston, QB
1990 Ty Detmer, BYU, QB
1991 Desmond Howard, Michigan, WR
1992 Gino Torretta, Miami, QB

All-Time Division I-A Percentage Leaders

(Classified as Division I-A for the last 10 years; record includes bowl games; ties computed as half won and half lost)

	Years	Won	Lost	Tied	Pct.	Bowl Games W	L	T
Notre Dame	104	712	210	41	.761	11	6	0
Michigan	113	731	238	36	.745	11	13	0
Alabama	98	682	234	43	.734	25	17	3
Oklahoma	98	650	237	52	.720	19	10	1
Texas	100	682	268	31	.711	16	16	2
USC	100	622	249	52	.702	22	13	0
Ohio St.	103	649	264	52	.699	12	13	0
Penn St.	106	664	289	41	.689	17	10	2
Nebraska	103	662	289	40	.688	14	17	0
Tennessee	96	627	274	52	.685	18	15	0
Central Michigan	92	475	249	36	.649	3	1	0
Washington	103	555	306	49	.637	12	8	1
Army	103	582	322	50	.636	2	1	0
Miami (Ohio)	104	542	301	42	.636	5	2	0
Louisiana St.	99	568	319	46	.633	11	16	1
Georgia	99	584	327	53	.633	15	13	3
Arizona St.	80	438	250	24	.632	9	5	1
Florida St.	46	304	175	16	.630	13	7	2
Auburn	100	547	335	46	.614	12	9	2
Colorado	103	549	345	35	.610	5	12	0
Michigan St.	96	515	322	43	.610	5	5	0
Miami (Fla.)	66	402	257	19	.607	10	9	0
Bowling Green	74	383	240	50	.606	2	3	0
Minnesota	109	551	352	43	.605	2	3	0
UCLA	74	429	276	37	.603	10	7	1

All-Time Division I-A Coaching Victories (Incl. Bowl Games)

Paul "Bear" Bryant	323
Amos Alonzo Stagg	314
Glenn "Pop" Warner	313
Joe Paterno	247
Woody Hayes	238
Bo Schembechler	234
Bobby Bowden	227
Jess Neely	207
Warren Woodson	203
Eddie Anderson	201
Vince Dooley	201
Dana Bible	198
Dan McGugin	197
Fielding Yost	196
Tom Osborne	195
Howard Jones	194
Hayden Fry	194
LaVell Edwards	191
John Vaught	190
John Heisman	185
Darrell Royal	184
Lou Holtz	182
Carl Snavely	180
Gil Dobie	180
Jerry Claiborne	179
Ben Schwartzwalder	178
Jim Sweeney	178

Eddie Robinson of Grambling State Univ. holds the record for most college football victories with 381 at the start of the 1993 season.

National College Football Champions

The unofficial national champion as selected each year by the AP poll of writers and the USA Today-CNN (until 1992 the UPI) poll of coaches. When the polls disagree both teams are listed. The AP poll originated in 1936 and the UPI poll in 1950.

1936 Minnesota
1937 Pittsburgh
1938 Texas Christian
1939 Texas A&M
1940 Minnesota
1941 Minnesota
1942 Ohio State
1943 Notre Dame
1944 Army
1945 Army
1946 Notre Dame
1947 Notre Dame
1948 Michigan
1949 Notre Dame
1950 Oklahoma
1951 Tennessee
1952 Michigan State
1953 Maryland
1954 Ohio State, UCLA
1955 Oklahoma
1956 Oklahoma
1957 Auburn, Ohio State
1958 Louisiana State
1959 Syracuse
1960 Minnesota
1961 Alabama
1962 Southern Cal.
1963 Texas
1964 Alabama
1965 Alabama, Mich. State
1966 Notre Dame
1967 Southern Cal.
1968 Ohio State
1969 Texas
1970 Nebraska, Texas
1971 Nebraska
1972 Southern Cal.
1973 Notre Dame, Alabama
1974 Oklahoma, So. Cal.
1975 Oklahoma
1976 Pittsburgh
1977 Notre Dame
1978 Alabama, So. Cal.
1979 Alabama
1980 Georgia
1981 Clemson
1982 Penn State
1983 Miami (Fla.)
1984 Brigham Young
1985 Oklahoma
1986 Penn State
1987 Miami (Fla.)
1988 Notre Dame
1989 Miami (Fla.)
1990 Colorado, Georgia Tech
1991 Miami (Fla.), Washington
1992 Alabama

College Football Coach of the Year

(Selected by the American Football Coaches Assn. & the Football Writers Assn. of America)

Year	AFCA
1935	Lynn Waldorf, Northwestern
1936	Dick Harlow, Harvard
1937	Edward Mylin, Lafayette
1938	Bill Kern, Carnegie Tech
1939	Eddie Anderson, Iowa
1940	Clark Shaughnessy, Stanford
1941	Frank Leahy, Notre Dame
1942	Bill Alexander, Georgia Tech
1943	Amos Alonzo Stagg, Pacific
1944	Carroll Widdoes, Ohio St.
1945	Bo McMillin, Indiana
1946	Earl "Red" Blaik, Army
1947	Fritz Crisler, Michigan
1948	Bennie Oosterbaan, Michigan
1949	Bud Wilkinson, Oklahoma
1950	Charlie Caldwell, Princeton
1951	Chuck Taylor, Stanford
1952	Biggie Munn, Michigan St.
1953	Jim Tatum, Maryland
1954	Henry "Red" Sanders, UCLA
1955	Duffy Daugherty, Michigan St.
1956	Bowden Wyatt, Tennessee

Year	FWAA	AFCA
1957	Woody Hayes, Ohio St.	Woody Hayes, Ohio St.
1958	Paul Dietzel, LSU	Paul Dietzel, LSU
1959	Ben Schwartzwalder, Syracuse	Ben Schwartzwalder, Syracuse
1960	Murray Warmath, Minnesota	Murray Warmath, Minnesota
1961	Darrell Royal, Texas	Paul "Bear" Bryant, Alabama
1962	John McKay, USC	John McKay, USC
1963	Darrell Royal, Texas	Darrell Royal, Texas
1964	Ara Parseghian, Notre Dame	Frank Broyles, Arkansas; Ara Paraseghian, Notre Dame
1965	Duffy Daugherty, Michigan St.	Tommy Prothro, UCLA
1966	Tom Cahill, Army	Tom Cahill, Army
1967	John Pont, Indiana	John Pont, Indiana
1968	Woody Hayes, Ohio St.	Joe Paterno, Penn St.
1969	Bo Schembechler, Michigan	Bo Schembechler, Michigan
1970	Alex Agase, Northwestern	Charles McClendon, LSU; Darrell Royal, Texas
1971	Bob Devaney, Nebraska	Paul "Bear" Bryant, Alabama
1972	John McKay, USC	John McKay, USC
1973	Johnny Majors, Pittsburgh	Paul "Bear" Bryant, Alabama
1974	Grant Teaff, Baylor	Grant Teaff, Baylor
1975	Woody Hayes, Ohio St.	Frank Kush, Arizona St.
1976	Johnny Majors, Pittsburgh	Johnny Majors, Pittsburgh
1977	Lou Holtz, Arkansas	Don James, Washington
1978	Joe Paterno, Penn St.	Joe Paterno, Penn St.
1979	Earle Bruce, Ohio St.	Earle Bruce, Ohio St.
1980	Vince Dooley, Georgia	Vince Dooley, Georgia
1981	Danny Ford, Clemson	Danny Ford, Clemson
1982	Joe Paterno, Penn St.	Joe Paterno, Penn St.
1983	Howard Schnellenberger, Miami (Fla.)	Ken Hatfield, Air Force
1984	LaVell Edwards, Brigham Young	LaVell Edwards, Brigham Young
1985	Fisher De Berry, Air Force	Fisher De Berry, Air Force
1986	Joe Paterno, Penn St.	Joe Paterno, Penn St.
1987	Dick MacPherson, Syracuse	Dick MacPherson, Syracuse
1988	Lou Holtz, Notre Dame	Don Nehlen, W. Virginia
1989	Bill McCartney, Colorado	Bill McCartney, Colorado
1990	Bobby Ross, Georgia Tech	Bobby Ross, Georgia Tech
1991	Don James, Washington	Don James, Washington
1992	Gene Stallings, Alabama	Gene Stallings, Alabama

Longest Division I-A Winning Streaks

(Includes Bowl Games)

Wins	Team	Years	Ended by	Score
47	Oklahoma	1953-57	Notre Dame	7-0
39	Washington	1908-14	Oregon State	0-0
37	Yale	1890-93	Princeton	6-0
37	Yale	1887-89	Princeton	10-0
35	Toledo	1969-71	Tampa	21-0
34	Pennsylvania	1894-96	Lafayette	6-4
31	Oklahoma	1948-50	Kentucky	13-7
31	Pittsburgh	1914-18	Cleveland Naval Reserve	10-9
31	Pennsylvania	1896-98	Harvard	10-0
30	Texas	1968-70	Notre Dame	24-11
29	Michigan	1901-03	Minnesota	6-6
29	Miami (Fla.)	1990-93	Alabama	34-13
28	Alabama	1978-80	Mississippi State	6-3
28	Oklahoma	1973-75	Kansas	23-3
28	Michigan State	1950-53	Purdue	6-0
27	Nebraska	1901-04	Colorado	6-0
26	Cornell	1921-24	Williams	14-7
26	Michigan	1903-05	Chicago	2-0
25	Michigan	1946-49	Army	21-7
25	Army	1944-46	Notre Dame	0-0
25	Southern Cal	1931-33	Oregon State	0-0
25	Brigham Young	1983-85	UCLA	27-24

College Football Conference Champions

	Atlantic Coast		Ivy		Big Eight		Big Ten
1979	No. Carolina St.	1979	Yale	1979	Oklahoma	1979	Ohio State
1980	North Carolina	1980	Yale	1980	Oklahoma	1980	Michigan
1981	Clemson	1981	Yale, Dartmouth	1981	Nebraska	1981	Iowa, Ohio State
1982	Clemson	1982	Harvard, Dartmouth, Penn	1982	Nebraska	1982	Michigan
1983	Maryland	1983	Harvard, Penn	1983	Nebraska	1983	Illinois
1984	Maryland	1984	Penn	1984	Nebraska, Oklahoma	1984	Ohio State
1985	Maryland	1985	Penn	1985	Oklahoma	1985	Iowa
1986	Clemson	1986	Penn	1986	Oklahoma	1986	Michigan, Ohio State
1987	Clemson	1987	Harvard	1987	Oklahoma	1987	Michigan St.
1988	Clemson	1988	Penn, Cornell	1988	Nebraska	1988	Michigan
1989	Virginia, Duke	1989	Yale, Princeton	1989	Colorado	1989	Michigan
1990	Georgia Tech	1990	Dartmouth	1990	Colorado	1990	Iowa, Illinois, Michigan, Michigan St.
1991	Clemson	1991	Dartmouth	1991	Nebraska, Colorado	1991	Michigan
1992	Florida St.	1992	Dartmouth, Princeton	1992	Nebraska	1992	Michigan

	Mid-America		Southern		Southeastern		Southwest
1979	Central Michigan	1979	Tenn.-Chattanooga	1979	Alabama	1979	Houston, Arkansas
1980	Central Michigan	1980	Furman	1980	Georgia	1980	Baylor
1981	Toledo	1981	Furman	1981	Georgia, Alabama	1981	SMU
1982	Bowling Green	1982	Furman	1982	Georgia	1982	SMU
1983	Northern Illinois	1983	Furman	1983	Auburn	1983	Texas
1984	Toledo	1984	Tenn.-Chattanooga	1984	Florida (title vacated)	1984	SMU, Houston
1985	Bowling Green	1985	Furman	1985	Tennessee	1985	Texas A&M
1986	Miami	1986	Appalachian St.	1986	LSU	1986	Texas A&M
1987	E. Michigan	1987	Appalachian St.	1987	Auburn	1987	Texas A&M
1988	W. Michigan	1988	Marshall, Furman	1988	Auburn, LSU	1988	Arkansas
1989	Ball State	1989	Furman	1989	Alabama, Tennessee, Auburn	1989	Arkansas
1990	Central Michigan	1990	Furman	1990	Tennessee	1990	Texas
1991	Bowling Green	1991	Appalachian St.	1991	Florida	1991	Texas A&M
1992	Bowling Green	1992	Citadel	1992	Alabama	1992	Texas A&M

	Pacific Ten		Western Athletic		Big West
1979	USC	1979	Brigham Young	1979	San Jose St.
1980	Washington	1980	Brigham Young	1980	Long Beach State
1981	Washington	1981	Brigham Young	1981	San Jose State
1982	UCLA	1982	Brigham Young	1982	Fresno State
1983	UCLA	1983	Brigham Young	1983	Cal State-Fullerton
1984	USC	1984	Brigham Young	1984	Nevada-Las Vegas
1985	UCLA	1985	Brigham Young, Air Force	1985	Fresno State
1986	Arizona State	1986	San Diego State	1986	San Jose State
1987	UCLA, USC	1987	Wyoming	1987	San Jose State
1988	USC	1988	Wyoming	1988	Fresno State
1989	USC	1989	Brigham Young	1989	Fresno State
1990	Washington	1990	Brigham Young	1990	San Jose State
1991	Washington	1991	Brigham Young	1991	San Jose St., Fresno St.
1992	Washington, Stanford	1992	Hawaii, Brigham Young	1992	Nevada-Reno

Canadian Football League

Grey Cup Championship Game

1956	Edmonton Eskimos 50, Montreal Alouettes 27	1975	Edmonton Eskimos 9, Montreal Alouettes 8
1957	Hamilton Tiger-Cats 32, Winnipeg Blue Bombers 7	1976	Ottawa Rough Riders 23, Saskatchewan Roughriders 20
1958	Winnipeg Blue Bombers 35, Hamilton Tiger-Cats 28	1977	Montreal Alouettes 41, Edmonton Eskimos 6
1959	Winnipeg Blue Bombers 21, Hamilton Tiger-Cats 7	1978	Edmonton Eskimos 20, Montreal Alouettes 13
1960	Ottawa Rough Riders 16, Edmonton Eskimos 6	1979	Edmonton Eskimos 17, Montreal Alouettes 9
1961	Winnipeg Blue Bombers 21, Hamilton Tiger-Cats 14	1980	Edmonton Eskimos 48, Hamilton Tiger-Cats 10
1962	Winnipeg Blue Bombers 28, Hamilton Tiger-Cats 27	1981	Edmonton Eskimos 26, Ottawa Rough Riders 23
1963	Hamilton Tiger-Cats 21, British Columbia Lions 10	1982	Edmonton Eskimos 32, Toronto Argonauts 16
1964	British Columbia Lions 34, Hamilton Tiger-Cats 24	1983	Toronto Argonauts 18, B.C. Lions 17
1965	Hamilton Tiger-Cats 22, Winnipeg Blue Bombers 16	1984	Winnipeg Blue Bombers 47, Hamilton Tiger-Cats 17
1966	Saskatchewan Roughriders 29, Ottawa Rough Riders 14	1985	B.C. Lions 37, Hamilton Tiger-Cats 24
1967	Hamilton Tiger-Cats 24, Saskatchewan Roughriders 1	1986	Hamilton Tiger-Cats 39, Edmonton Eskimos 15
1968	Ottawa Rough Riders 24, Calgary Stampeders 21	1987	Edmonton Eskimos 38, Toronto Argonauts 36
1969	Ottawa Rough Riders 29, Saskatchewan Roughriders 11	1988	Winnipeg Blue Bombers 22, B.C. Lions 21
1970	Montreal Alouettes 23, Calgary Stampeders 10	1989	Saskatchewan Roughriders 43, Hamilton Tiger-Cats 40
1971	Calgary Stampeders 14, Toronto Argonauts 11	1990	Winnipeg Blue Bombers 50, Edmonton Eskimos 11
1972	Hamilton Tiger-Cats 13, Saskatchewan Roughriders 10	1991	Toronto Argonauts 36, Calgary Stampeders 21
1973	Ottawa Rough Riders 22, Edmonton Eskimos 18	1992	Calgary Stampeders 24, Winnipeg Blue Bombers 10
1974	Montreal Alouettes 20, Edmonton Eskimos 7		

CFL Teams, Divisions

(at start of 1993 season)

Western Division
British Columbia Lions
Calgary Stampeders
Edmonton Eskimos
Sacramento Gold Miners
Saskatchewan Roughriders

Eastern Division
Hamilton Tiger-Cats
Ottawa Rough Riders
Toronto Argonauts
Winnipeg Blue Bombers

NATIONAL FOOTBALL LEAGUE

Final 1992 Standings

National Conference

Eastern Division

	W	L	T	Pct	Pts	Opp
Dallas	13	3	0	.813	409	243
Philadelphia	11	5	0	.688	354	245
Washington	9	7	0	.563	300	255
N.Y. Giants	6	10	0	.375	306	367
Phoenix	4	12	0	.250	243	332

Central Division

	W	L	T	Pct	Pts	Opp
Minnesota	11	5	0	.688	374	249
Green Bay	9	7	0	.563	276	296
Tampa Bay	5	11	0	.313	267	365
Chicago	5	11	0	.313	295	361
Detroit	5	11	0	.313	273	332

Western Division

	W	L	T	Pct	Pts	Opp
San Francisco	14	2	0	.875	431	236
New Orleans	12	4	0	.750	330	202
Atlanta	6	10	0	.375	327	414
L.A. Rams	6	10	0	.375	313	383

American Conference

Eastern Division

	W	L	T	Pct	Pts	Opp
Miami	11	5	0	.688	340	281
Buffalo	11	5	0	.688	381	283
Indianapolis	9	7	0	.563	216	302
N.Y. Jets	4	12	0	.250	220	315
New England	2	14	0	.125	205	363

Central Division

	W	L	T	Pct	Pts	Opp
Pittsburgh	11	5	0	.688	299	225
Houston	10	6	0	.625	352	258
Cleveland	7	9	0	.438	272	275
Cincinnati	5	11	0	.313	274	364

Western Division

	W	L	T	Pct	Pts	Opp
San Diego	11	5	0	.688	335	241
Kansas City	10	6	0	.625	348	282
Denver	8	8	0	.500	262	329
L.A. Raiders	7	9	0	.438	249	281
Seattle	2	14	0	.125	140	312

NFC Playoffs—Washington 24, Minnesota 7; Philadelphia 36, New Orleans 20; Dallas 34, Philadelphia 10; San Francisco 20, Washington 13; Dallas 30, San Francisco 20.
AFC Playoffs—San Diego 17, Kansas City 0; Buffalo 41, Houston 38; Miami 31, San Diego 0; Buffalo 24, Pittsburgh 3; Buffalo 29, Miami 10.

National Football League Champions

Year	East Winner (W-L-T)	West Winner (W-L-T)	Playoff
1933	New York Giants (11-3-0)	Chicago Bears (10-2-1)	Chicago Bears 23, New York 21
1934	New York Giants (8-5-0)	Chicago Bears (13-0-0)	New York 30, Chicago Bears 13
1935	New York Giants (9-3-0)	Detroit Lions (7-3-2)	Detroit 26, New York 7
1936	Boston Redskins (7-5-0)	Green Bay Packers (10-1-1)	Green Bay 21, Boston 6
1937	Washington Redskins (8-3-0)	Chicago Bears (9-1-1)	Washington 28, Chicago Bears 21
1938	New York Giants (8-2-1)	Green Bay Packers (8-3-0)	New York 23, Green Bay 17
1939	New York Giants (9-1-1)	Green Bay Packers (9-2-0)	Green Bay 27, New York 0
1940	Washington Redskins (9-2-0)	Chicago Bears (8-3-0)	Chicago Bears 73, Washington 0
1941	New York Giants (8-3-0)	Chicago Bears (10-1-1)(a)	Chicago Bears 37, New York 9
1942	Wash. Redskins (10-1-1)	Chicago Bears (11-0-0)	Washington 14, Chicago Bears 6
1943	Wash. Redskins (6-3-1)(a)	Chicago Bears (8-1-1)	Chicago Bears, 41, Washington 21
1944	New York Giants (8-1-1)	Green Bay Packers (8-2-0)	Green Bay 14, New York 7
1945	Wash. Redskins (8-2-0)	Cleveland Rams (9-1-0)	Cleveland 15, Washington 14
1946	New York Giants (7-3-1)	Chicago Bears (8-2-1)	Chicago Bears 24, New York 14
1947	Philadelphia Eagles (8-4-0)(a)	Chicago Cardinals (9-3-0)	Chicago Cardinals 28, Philadelphia 21
1948	Philadelphia Eagles (9-2-1)	Chicago Cardinals (11-1-0)	Philadelphia 7, Chicago Cardinals 0
1949	Philadelphia Eagles (11-1-0)	Los Angeles Rams (8-2-2)	Philadelphia 14, Los Angeles 0
1950	Cleveland Browns (10-2-0)(a)	Los Angeles Rams (9-3-0)(a)	Cleveland 30, Los Angeles 28
1951	Cleveland Browns (11-1-0)	Los Angeles Rams (8-4-0)	Los Angeles 24, Cleveland 17
1952	Cleveland Browns (8-4-0)	Detroit Lions (9-3-0)(a)	Detroit 17, Cleveland 7
1953	Cleveland Browns (11-1-0)	Detroit Lions (10-2-0)	Detroit 17, Cleveland 16
1954	Cleveland Browns (9-3-0)	Detroit Lions (9-2-1)	Cleveland 56, Detroit 10
1955	Cleveland Browns (9-2-1)	Los Angeles Rams (8-3-1)	Cleveland 38, Los Angeles 14
1956	New York Giants (8-3-1)	Chicago Bears (9-2-1)	New York 47, Chicago Bears 7
1957	Cleveland Browns (9-2-1)	Detroit Lions (8-4-0)(a)	Detroit 59, Cleveland 14
1958	New York Giants (9-3-0)(a)	Baltimore Colts (9-3-0)	Baltimore 23, New York 17(b)
1959	New York Giants (10-2-0)	Baltimore Colts (9-3-0)	Baltimore 31, New York 16
1960	Philadelphia Eagles (10-2-0)	Green Bay Packers (8-4-0)	Philadelphia 17, Green Bay 13
1961	New York Giants (10-3-1)	Green Bay Packers (11-3-0)	Green Bay 37, New York 0
1962	New York Giants (12-2-0)	Green Bay Packers (13-1-0)	Green Bay 16, New York 7
1963	New York Giants (11-3-0)	Chicago Bears (11-1-2)	Chicago 14, New York 10
1964	Cleveland Browns (10-3-1)	Baltimore Colts (12-2-0)	Cleveland 27, Baltimore 0
1965	Cleveland Browns (11-3-0)	Green Bay Packers (10-3-1)(a)	Green Bay 23, Cleveland 12
1966	Dallas Cowboys (10-3-1)	Green Bay Packers (12-2-0)	Green Bay 34, Dallas 27

(a) Won divisional playoff. (b) Won at 8:15 sudden death overtime period.

Year	Conference	Division	Winner (W-L-T)	Playoff
1967	East	Century	Cleveland (9-5-0)	Dallas 52, Cleveland 14
		Capitol	Dallas (9-5-0)	
	West	Central	Green Bay (9-4-1)	Green Bay 28, Los Angeles 7
		Coastal	Los Angeles (11-1-2)(a)	Green Bay 21, Dallas 17
1968	East	Century	Cleveland (10-4-0)	Cleveland 31, Dallas 20
		Capitol	Dallas (12-2-0)	
	West	Central	Minnesota (8-6-0)	Baltimore 24, Minnesota 14
		Coastal	Baltimore (13-1-0)	Baltimore 34, Cleveland 0

(continued)

Year	Conference	Division	Winner (W-L-T)	Playoff
1969	East	Century	Cleveland (10-3-1)	Cleveland 38, Dallas 14
		Capitol	Dallas (11-2-1)	
	West	Central	Minnesota (12-2-0)	Minnesota 23, Los Angeles 20
		Coastal	Los Angeles (11-3-0)	Minnesota 27, Cleveland 7
1970	American	Eastern	Baltimore (11-2-1)	Baltimore 17, Cincinnati 0
		Central	Cincinnati (8-6-0)	Oakland 21, Miami 14
		Western	Oakland (8-4-2)	Baltimore 27, Oakland 17
	National	Eastern	Dallas (10-4-0)	Dallas 5, Detroit 0
		Central	Minnesota (12-2-0)	San Francisco 17, Minnesota 14
		Western	San Francisco (10-3-1)	Dallas 17, San Francisco 10
1971	American	Eastern	Miami (10-3-1)	Miami 27, Kansas City 24
		Central	Cleveland (9-5-0)	Baltimore 20, Cleveland 3
		Western	Kansas City (10-3-1)	Miami 21, Baltimore 0
	National	Eastern	Dallas (11-3-0)	Dallas 20, Minnesota 12
		Central	Minnesota (11-3-0)	San Francisco 24, Washington 20
		Western	San Francisco (9-5-0)	Dallas 14, San Francisco 3
1972	American	Eastern	Miami (14-0-0)	Miami 20, Cleveland 14
		Central	Pittsburgh (11-3-0)	Pittsburgh 13, Oakland 7
		Western	Oakland (10-3-1)	Miami 21, Pittsburgh 17
	National	Eastern	Washington (11-3-0)	Washington 16, Green Bay 3
		Central	Green Bay (10-4-0)	Dallas 30, San Francisco 28
		Western	San Francisco (8-5-1)	Washington 26, Dallas 3
1973	American	Eastern	Miami (12-2-0)	Miami 34, Cincinnati 16
		Central	Cincinnati (10-4-0)	Oakland 33, Pittsburgh 14
		Western	Oakland (9-4-1)	Miami 27, Oakland 10
	National	Eastern	Dallas (10-4-0)	Dallas 27, Los Angeles 16
		Central	Minnesota (12-2-0)	Minnesota 27, Washington 20
		Western	Los Angeles (12-2-0)	Minnesota 27, Dallas 10
1974	American	Eastern	Miami (11-3-0)	Oakland 28, Miami 26
		Central	Pittsburgh (10-3-1)	Pittsburgh 32, Buffalo 14
		Western	Oakland (12-2-0)	Pittsburgh 24, Oakland 13
	National	Eastern	St. Louis (10-4-0)	Minnesota 30, St. Louis 14
		Central	Minnesota (10-4-0)	Los Angeles 19, Washington 10
		Western	Los Angeles (10-4-0)	Minnesota 14, Los Angeles 10
1975	American	Eastern	Baltimore (10-4-0)	Pittsburgh 28, Baltimore 10
		Central	Pittsburgh (12-2-0)	Oakland 31, Cincinnati 28
		Western	Oakland (11-3-0)	Pittsburgh 16, Oakland 10
	National	Eastern	St. Louis (11-3-0)	Dallas 17, Minnesota 14
		Central	Minnesota (12-2-0)	Los Angeles 35, St. Louis 23
		Western	Los Angeles (12-2-0)	Dallas 37, Los Angeles 7
1976	American	Eastern	Baltimore (11-3-0)	Pittsburgh 40, Baltimore 14
		Central	Pittsburgh (10-4-0)	Oakland 24, New England 21
		Western	Oakland (13-1-0)	Oakland 24, Pittsburgh 7
	National	Eastern	Dallas (11-3-0)	Minnesota 35, Washington 20
		Central	Minnesota (11-2-1)	Los Angeles 14, Dallas 12
		Western	Los Angeles (10-3-1)	Minnesota 24, Los Angeles 13
1977	American	Eastern	Baltimore (10-4-0)	Oakland 37, Baltimore 31
		Central	Pittsburgh (9-5-0)	Denver 34, Pittsburgh 21
		Western	Denver (12-2-0)	Dallas 37, Chicago 7
	National	Eastern	Dallas (12-2-0)	Minnesota 14, Los Angeles 7
		Central	Minnesota (9-5-0)	Denver 20, Oakland 17
		Western	Los Angeles (10-4-0)	Dallas 23, Minnesota 6
1978	American	Eastern	New England (11-5-0)	Pittsburgh 33, Denver 10
		Central	Pittsburgh (14-2-0)	Houston 31, New England 14
		Western	Denver (10-6-0)	Pittsburgh 34, Houston 5
	National	Eastern	Dallas (12-4-0)	Dallas 27, Atlanta 20
		Central	Minnesota (8-7-1)	Los Angeles 34, Minnesota 10
		Western	Los Angeles (12-4-0)	Dallas 28, Los Angeles 0
1979	American	Eastern	Miami (10-6-0)	Houston 17, San Diego 14
		Central	Pittsburgh (12-4-0)	Pittsburgh 34, Miami 14
		Western	San Diego (12-4-0)	Pittsburgh 27, Houston 13
	National	Eastern	Dallas (11-5-0)	Tampa Bay 24, Philadelphia 17
		Central	Tampa Bay (10-6-0)	Los Angeles 21, Dallas 19
		Western	Los Angeles (9-7-0)	Los Angeles 9, Tampa Bay 0
1980	American	Eastern	Buffalo (11-5-0)	San Diego 20, Buffalo 14
		Central	Cleveland (11-5-0)	Oakland 14, Cleveland 12
		Western	San Diego (11-5-0)	Oakland 34, San Diego 27
	National	Eastern	Philadelphia (12-4-0)	Philadelphia 31, Minnesota 16
		Central	Minnesota (9-7-0)	Dallas 30, Atlanta 27
		Western	Atlanta (12-4-0)	Philadelphia 20, Dallas 7
1981	American	Eastern	Miami (11-4-1)	San Diego 41, Miami 38
		Central	Cincinnati (12-4-0)	Cincinnati 28, Buffalo 21
		Western	San Diego (10-6-0)	Cincinnati 27, San Diego 7
	National	Eastern	Dallas (12-4-0)	Dallas 38, Tampa Bay 0
		Central	Tampa Bay (9-7-0)	San Francisco 38, N.Y. Giants 24
		Western	San Francisco (13-3-0)	San Francisco 28, Dallas 27
1982	American		L.A. Raiders (8-1-0)	
	National		Washington (8-1-0)	Strike-shortened season

AFC playoffs—Miami 28, New England 13; L.A. Raiders 27, Cleveland 10; N.Y. Jets 44, Cincinnati 17; San Diego 31, Pittsburgh 28; N.Y. Jets 17, L.A. Raiders 14; Miami 34, San Diego 13; Miami 14, N.Y. Jets 0. **NFC playoffs**—Washington 31, Detroit 7; Green Bay 41, St. Louis 16; Dallas 30, Tampa Bay 17; Minnesota 30, Atlanta 24; Washington 21, Minnesota 7; Dallas 37, Green Bay 26; Washington 31, Dallas 17.

Year	Conference	Division	Winner (W-L-T)	Playoff
1983	American	Eastern	Miami (12-4-0)	Seattle 27, Miami 20
		Central	Pittsburgh (10-6-0)	L.A. Raiders 38, Pittsburgh 10
		Western	L.A. Raiders (12-4-0)	L.A. Raiders 30, Seattle 14
	National	Eastern	Washington (14-2-0)	Washington 51, L.A. Rams 7

Year	Conference	Division	Winner (W-L-T)	Playoff
		Central	Detroit (9-7-0)	San Francisco 24, Detroit 23
		Western	San Francisico (10-6-0)	Washington 24, San Francisco 21
1984	American	Eastern	Miami (14-2-0)	Miami 31, Seattle 10
		Central	Pittsburgh (9-7-0)	Pittsburgh 24, Denver 17
		Western	Denver (13-3-0)	Miami 45, Pittsburgh 28
	National	Eastern	Washington (11-5-0)	Chicago 23, Washington 19
		Central	Chicago (10-6-0)	San Francisco 21, N.Y. Giants 10
		Western	San Francisco (15-1-0)	San Francisco 23, Chicago 0
1985	American	Eastern	Miami (12-4-0)	New England 27, L.A. Raiders 20
		Central	Cleveland (8-8-0)	Miami 24, Cleveland 21
		Western	L.A. Raiders (12-4-0)	New England 31, Miami 14
	National	Eastern	Dallas (10-6-0)	Chicago 21, N.Y. Giants 0
		Central	Chicago (15-1-0)	L.A. Rams 20, Dallas 0
		Western	L.A. Rams (11-5-0)	Chicago 24, L.A. Rams 0
1986	American	Eastern	New England (11-5-0)	Denver 22, New England 17
		Central	Cleveland (12-4-0)	Cleveland 23, N.Y. Jets 20
		Western	Denver (11-5-0)	Denver 23, Cleveland 20
	National	Eastern	N.Y. Giants (14-2-0)	N.Y. Giants 49, San Francisco 3
		Central	Chicago (14-2-0)	Washington 27, Chicago 13
		Western	San Francisco (10-5-1)	N.Y. Giants 17, Washington 0
1987	American	Eastern	Indianapolis (9-6-0)	Cleveland 38, Indianapolis 21
		Central	Cleveland (10-5-0)	Denver 34, Houston 10
		Western	Denver (10-4-1)	Denver 38, Cleveland 33
	National	Eastern	Washington (11-4-0)	Washington 21, Chicago 17
		Central	Chicago (11-4-0)	Minnesota 36, San Francisco 24
		Western	San Francisco (13-2-0)	Washington 17, Minnesota 10
1988	American	Eastern	Buffalo (12-4-0)	Buffalo 17, Houston 10
		Central	Cincinnati (12-4-0)	Cincinnati 21, Seattle 13
		Western	Seattle (9-7-0)	Cincinnati 21, Buffalo 10
	National	Eastern	Philadelphia (10-6-0)	Chicago 20, Philadelphia 12
		Central	Chicago (12-4-0)	San Francisco 34, Minnesota 9
		Western	San Francisco (10-6-0)	San Francisco 28, Chicago 3
1989	American	Eastern	Buffalo (9-7-0)	Cleveland 34, Buffalo 30
		Central	Cleveland (9-6-1)	Denver 24, Pittsburgh 23
		Western	Denver (11-5-0)	Denver 37, Cleveland 21
	National	Eastern	N.Y. Giants (12-4-0)	San Francisco 41, Minnesota 13
		Central	Minnesota (10-6-0)	L.A. Rams 19, N.Y. Giants 13
		Western	San Francisco (14-2-0)	San Francisco 30, L.A. Rams 3
1990	American	Eastern	Buffalo (13-3-0)	L.A. Raiders 20, Cincinnati 10
		Central	Cincinnati (9-7-0)	Buffalo 44, Miami 34
		Western	L.A. Raiders (12-4-0)	Buffalo 51, L.A. Raiders 3
	National	Eastern	N.Y. Giants (13-3-0)	San Francisco 28, Washington 10
		Central	Chicago (11-5-0)	N.Y. Giants 31, Chicago 3
		Western	San Francisco (14-2-0)	N.Y. Giants 15, San Francisco 13
1991	American	Eastern	Buffalo (13-3-0)	Denver 26, Houston 24
		Central	Houston (11-5-0)	Buffalo 37, Kansas City 14
		Western	Denver (12-4-0)	Buffalo 10, Denver 7
	National	Eastern	Washington (14-2-0)	Washington 24, Atlanta 7
		Central	Detroit (12-4-0)	Detroit 38, Dallas 6
		Western	New Orleans (11-5-0)	Washington 41, Detroit 10
1992	American	Eastern	Miami (11-5-0)	Miami 31, San Diego 0
		Central	Pittsburgh (11-5-0)	Buffalo 24, Pittsburgh 3
		Western	San Diego (11-5-0)	Buffalo 29, Miami 10
	National	Eastern	Dallas (13-3-0)	Dallas 34, Philadelphia 10
		Central	Minnesota (11-5-0)	San Francisco 20, Washington 13
		Western	San Francisco (14-2-0)	Dallas 30, San Francisco 20

NFL Head Coaches at Start of 1993 Season

AFC

Buffalo—Marv Levy
Cincinnati—David Shula
Cleveland—Bill Belichick
Denver—Wade Phillips
Houston—Jack Pardee
Indianapolis—Ted Marchibroda
Kansas City—Marty Schottenheimer
L.A. Raiders—Art Shell
Miami—Don Shula
New England—Bill Parcells
N.Y. Jets—Bruce Coslet
Pittsburgh—Bill Cowher
San Diego—Bobby Ross
Seattle—Tom Flores

NFC

Atlanta—Jerry Glanville
Chicago—Dave Wannstedt
Dallas—Jimmy Johnson
Detroit—Wayne Fontes
Green Bay—Mike Holmgren
L.A. Rams—Chuck Knox
Minnesota—Dennis Green
New Orleans—Jim Mora
N.Y. Giants—Dan Reeves
Philadelphia—Rich Kotite
Phoenix—Joe Bugel
San Francisco—George Seifert
Tampa Bay—Sam Wyche
Washington—Joe Gibbs

George Halas Trophy Winners

The George Halas Trophy is awarded annually to the outstanding defensive player in the NFL as chosen by a panel of sports experts.

1966	Larry Wilson, St. Louis
1967	Deacon Jones, Los Angeles
1968	Deacon Jones, Los Angeles
1969	Dick Butkus, Chicago
1970	Dick Butkus, Chicago
1971	Carl Eller, Minnesota
1972	Joe Greene, Pittsburgh
1973	Alan Page, Minnesota
1974	Joe Greene, Pittsburgh
1975	Curley Culp, Houston
1976	Jerry Sherk, Cleveland
1977	Harvey Martin, Dallas
1978	Randy Gradishar, Denver
1979	Lee Roy Selmon, Tampa Bay
1980	Lester Hayes, Oakland
1981	Joe Klecko, N.Y. Jets
1982	Mark Gastineau, N.Y. Jets
1983	Jack Lambert, Pittsburgh
1984	Mike Haynes, L.A. Raiders
1985	Howie Long, L.A. Raiders
	Andre Tippett, New England
1986	Lawrence Taylor, N.Y. Giants
1987	Reggie White, Philadelphia
1988	Mike Singletary, Chicago
1989	Tim Harris, Green Bay
1990	Bruce Smith, Buffalo
1991	Pat Swilling, New Orleans
1992	Junior Seau, San Diego

Cowboys Defeat Bills in Super Bowl

The Dallas Cowboys dominated throughout the game and defeated the Buffalo Bills 52-17 to win Super Bowl XXVII on January 31, 1993. It was the third Super Bowl victory for the Cowboys, who were champions in 1972 and 1978. Troy Aikman, quarterback for the Cowboys, was chosen the game's most valuable player.

Score by Quarters

Buffalo	7	3	7	0	—17
Dallas	14	14	3	21	—52

Scoring

Buffalo—Thomas 2 yd. run (Christie kick)
Dallas—Novacek 23 yd. pass from Aikman (Elliott kick)
Dallas—J. Jones 2 yd. fumble return (Elliott kick)
Buffalo—Christie 21 yd. field goal
Dallas—Irvin 19 yd. pass from Aikman (Elliott kick)
Dallas—Irvin 18 yd. pass from Aikman (Elliott kick)
Dallas—Elliott 20 yd. field goal
Buffalo—Beebe 40 yd. pass from Reich (Christie kick)
Dallas—Harper 45 yd. pass from Aikman (Elliott kick)
Dallas—E. Smith 10 yd. run (Elliott kick)
Dallas—Norton 9 yd. fumble return (Elliott kick)

Individual Statistics

Rushing — Buffalo, K. Davis 15-86, Thomas 11-19, Gardner 1-3, Reich 2-0. Dallas, E. Smith 22-108, Aikman 3-28, Gainer 2-1, Johnston 1-0, Beuerlein 1-0.

Passing — Buffalo, Kelly 4-7-2-82, Reich 18-31-2-194. Dallas, Aikman 22-30-0-273.

Receiving — Buffalo, Reed 8-152, Thomas 4-10, K. Davis 3-16, Beebe 2-50, Tasker 2-30, Metzelaars 2-12, McKeller 1-6. Dallas, Novacek 7-72, Irvin 6-114, E. Smith 6-27, Johnston 2-15, Harper 1-45.

Team Statistics

	Buffalo	Dallas
First downs	22	20
Total net yards	362	408
Rushing yards	108	137
Passing yards	254	271
Completed-Attempted	22-38	22-30
Yards per pass	6.0	8.7
Punts-average	3-45	4-33
Total return yards	90	149
Penalties-yards	4-30	8-53
Fumbles-lost	8-5	4-2
Time of possession	28:48	31:12

Super Bowl

Year	Winner	Loser	Winning coach	Site
1967	Green Bay Packers, 35	Kansas City Chiefs, 10	Vince Lombardi	Los Angeles Coliseum
1968	Green Bay Packers, 33	Oakland Raiders, 14	Vince Lombardi	Orange Bowl, Miami
1969	New York Jets, 16	Baltimore Colts, 7	Weeb Ewbank	Orange Bowl, Miami
1970	Kansas City Chiefs, 23	Minnesota Vikings, 7	Hank Stram	Tulane Stadium, New Orleans
1971	Baltimore Colts, 16	Dallas Cowboys, 13	Don McCafferty	Orange Bowl, Miami
1972	Dallas Cowboys, 24	Miami Dolphins, 3	Tom Landry	Tulane Stadium, New Orleans
1973	Miami Dolphins, 14	Washington Redskins, 7	Don Shula	Los Angeles Coliseum
1974	Miami Dolphins, 24	Minnesota Vikings, 7	Don Shula	Rice Stadium, Houston
1975	Pittsburgh Steelers, 16	Minnesota Vikings, 6	Chuck Noll	Tulane Stadium, New Orleans
1976	Pittsburgh Steelers, 21	Dallas Cowboys, 17	Chuck Noll	Orange Bowl, Miami
1977	Oakland Raiders, 32	Minnesota Vikings, 14	John Madden	Rose Bowl, Pasadena
1978	Dallas Cowboys, 27	Denver Broncos, 10	Tom Landry	Superdome, New Orleans
1979	Pittsburgh Steelers, 35	Dallas Cowboys, 31	Chuck Noll	Orange Bowl, Miami
1980	Pittsburgh Steelers, 31	Los Angeles Rams, 19	Chuck Noll	Rose Bowl, Pasadena
1981	Oakland Raiders, 27	Philadelphia Eagles, 10	Tom Flores	Superdome, New Orleans
1982	San Francisco 49ers, 26	Cincinnati Bengals, 21	Bill Walsh	Silverdome, Pontiac, Mich.
1983	Washington Redskins, 27	Miami Dolphins, 17	Joe Gibbs	Rose Bowl, Pasadena
1984	Los Angeles Raiders, 38	Washington Redskins, 9	Tom Flores	Tampa Stadium
1985	San Francisco 49ers, 38	Miami Dolphins, 16	Bill Walsh	Stanford Stadium, Palo Alto, Cal.
1986	Chicago Bears, 46	New England Patriots, 10	Mike Ditka	Superdome, New Orleans
1987	New York Giants, 39	Denver Broncos, 20	Bill Parcells	Rose Bowl, Pasadena
1988	Washington Redskins, 42	Denver Broncos, 10	Joe Gibbs	San Diego Stadium
1989	San Francisco 49ers, 20	Cincinnati Bengals, 16	Bill Walsh	Joe Robbie Stadium, Miami
1990	San Francisco 49ers, 55	Denver Broncos, 10	George Seifert	Superdome, New Orleans
1991	New York Giants, 20	Buffalo Bills, 19	Bill Parcells	Tampa Stadium
1992	Washington Redskins, 37	Buffalo Bills, 24	Joe Gibbs	Metrodome, Minneapolis
1993	Dallas Cowboys, 52	Buffalo Bills, 17	Jimmy Johnson	Rose Bowl, Pasadena

Super Bowl MVPs

1967 Bart Starr, Green Bay
1968 Bart Starr, Green Bay
1969 Joe Namath, N.Y. Jets
1970 Len Dawson, Kansas City
1971 Chuck Howley, Dallas
1972 Roger Staubach, Dallas
1973 Jake Scott, Miami
1974 Larry Csonka, Miami
1975 Franco Harris, Pittsburgh
1976 Lynn Swann, Pittsburgh
1977 Fred Biletnikoff, Oakland
1978 Randy White, Harvey Martin, Dallas
1979 Terry Bradshaw, Pittsburgh
1980 Terry Bradshaw, Pittsburgh
1981 Jim Plunkett, Oakland
1982 Joe Montana, San Francisco
1983 John Riggins, Washington
1984 Marcus Allen, L.A. Raiders
1985 Joe Montana, San Francisco
1986 Richard Dent, Chicago
1987 Phil Simms, N.Y. Giants
1988 Doug Williams, Washington
1989 Jerry Rice, San Francisco
1990 Joe Montana, San Francisco
1991 Ottis Anderson, N.Y. Giants
1992 Mark Rypien, Washington
1993 Troy Aikman, Dallas

American Football League

Year	Eastern Division	Western Division	Playoff
1960	Houston Oilers (10-4-0)	L. A. Chargers (10-4-0)	Houston 24, Los Angeles 16
1961	Houston Oilers (10-3-1)	San Diego Chargers (12-2-0)	Houston 10, San Diego 3
1962	Houston Oilers (11-3-0)	Dallas Texans (11-3-0)	Dallas 20, Houston 17(b)
1963	Boston Patriots (8-6-1)(a)	San Diego Chargers (11-3-0)	San Diego 51, Boston 10
1964	Buffalo Bills (12-2-0)	San Diego Chargers (8-5-1)	Buffalo 20, San Diego 7
1965	Buffalo Bills (10-3-1)	San Diego Chargers (9-2-3)	Buffalo 23, San Diego 0
1966	Buffalo Bills (9-4-1)	Kansas City Chiefs (11-2-1)	Kansas City 31, Buffalo 7
1967	Houston Oilers (9-4-1)	Oakland Raiders (13-1-0)	Oakland 40, Houston 7
1968	New York Jets (11-3-0)	Oakland Raiders (12-2-0)(a)	New York 27, Oakland 23
1969	New York Jets (10-4-0)	Oakland Raiders (12-1-1)	Kansas City 17, Oakland 7(c)

(a) won divisional playoff (b) won at 2:45 of second overtime. (c) Kansas City defeated Jets to make playoffs.

National Football Conference Leaders

(National Football League, 1960-69)

Passing

Player, team	Atts	Com	YG	TD	Year
Milt Plum, Cleveland	250	151	2,297	21	**1960**
Milt Plum, Cleveland	302	177	2,416	18	**1961**
Bart Starr, Green Bay	285	178	2,438	12	**1962**
Y.A. Tittle, N.Y. Giants	367	221	3,145	36	**1963**
Bart Starr, Green Bay	272	163	2,144	15	**1964**
Rudy Bukich, Chicago	312	176	2,641	20	**1965**
Bart Starr, Green Bay	251	156	2,257	14	**1966**
Sonny Jurgensen, Washington	508	288	3,747	31	**1967**
Earl Morrall, Baltimore	317	182	2,909	26	**1968**
Sonny Jurgensen, Washington	442	274	3,102	22	**1969**
John Brodie, San Francisco	378	223	2,941	24	**1970**
Roger Staubach, Dallas	211	126	1,882	15	**1971**
Norm Snead, N.Y. Giants	325	196	2,307	17	**1972**
Roger Staubach, Dallas	286	179	2,428	23	**1973**
Sonny Jurgensen, Washington	167	107	1,185	11	**1974**
Fran Tarkenton, Minnesota	425	273	2,294	25	**1975**
James Harris, Los Angeles	158	91	1,460	8	**1976**
Roger Staubach, Dallas	361	210	2,620	18	**1977**
Roger Staubach, Dallas	413	231	3,190	25	**1978**
Roger Staubach, Dallas	461	267	3,586	27	**1979**
Ron Jaworski, Philadelphia	451	257	3,529	27	**1980**
Joe Montana, San Francisco	488	311	3,565	19	**1981**
Joe Thiesmann, Washington	252	161	2,033	13	**1982**
Steve Bartkowski, Atlanta	423	274	3,167	22	**1983**
Joe Montana, San Francisco	432	279	3,630	28	**1984**
Joe Montana, San Francisco	494	303	3,653	27	**1985**
Tommy Kramer, Minnesota	372	208	3,000	24	**1986**
Joe Montana, San Francisco	398	266	3,054	31	**1987**
Wade Wilson, Minnesota	332	204	2,746	15	**1988**
Joe Montana, San Francisco	386	271	3,521	26	**1989**
Phil Simms, N.Y. Giants	311	184	2,284	15	**1990**
Steve Young, San Francisco	279	180	2,517	17	**1991**
Steve Young, San Francisco	402	268	3,465	25	**1992**

Pass-Receiving

Player, team	Ct	YG	TD
Raymond Berry, Baltimore	74	1,298	10
Jim Phillips, L.A. Rams	78	1,092	5
Bobby Mitchell, Washington	72	1,384	11
Bobby Joe Conrad, St. Louis	73	967	10
Johnny Morris, Chicago	93	1,200	10
Dave Parks, San Francisco	80	1,344	12
Charley Taylor, Washington	72	1,119	12
Charley Taylor, Washington	70	990	9
Clifton McNeil, San Francisco	71	994	7
Dan Abramowicz, New Orleans	73	1,015	7
Dick Gordon, Chicago	71	1,026	13
Bob Tucker, Giants	59	791	4
Harold Jackson, Philadelphia	62	1,048	4
Harold Carmichael, Philadelphia	67	1,116	9
Charles Young, Philadelphia	63	696	3
Chuck Foreman, Minnesota	73	691	9
Drew Pearson, Dallas	58	806	6
Ahmad Rashad, Minnesota	51	681	2
Rickey Young, Minnesota	88	704	5
Ahmad Rashad, Minnesota	80	1,156	9
Earl Cooper, San Francisco	83	567	4
Dwight Clark, San Francisco	85	1,105	4
Dwight Clark, San Francisco	60	913	5
Roy Green, St. Louis	78	1,227	14
Charlie Brown, Washington	78	1,225	8
Earnest Gray, N.Y. Giants	78	1,139	5
Art Monk, Washington	106	1,372	7
Roger Craig, San Francisco	92	1,016	6
Jerry Rice, San Francisco	86	1,570	15
J.T. Smith, St. Louis	91	1,117	8
Henry Ellard, L.A. Rams	86	1,414	10
Sterling Sharpe, Green Bay	90	1,423	12
Jerry Rice, San Francisco	100	1,502	13
Michael Irvin, Dallas	93	1,523	8
Sterling Sharpe, Green Bay	108	1,461	13

Scoring

Player, team	TD	PAT	FG	Pts	Year
Paul Hornung, Green Bay	15	41	15	176	**1960**
Paul Hornung, Green Bay	10	41	15	146	**1961**
Jim Taylor, Green Bay	19	0	0	114	**1962**
Don Chandler, N.Y. Giants	0	52	18	106	**1963**
Lenny Moore, Baltimore	20	0	0	120	**1964**
Gale Sayers, Chicago	22	0	0	132	**1965**
Bruce Gossett, L.A. Rams	0	29	28	113	**1966**
Jim Bakken, St. Louis	0	36	27	117	**1967**
Leroy Kelly, Cleveland	20	0	0	120	**1968**
Fred Cox, Minnesota	0	43	26	121	**1969**
Fred Cox, Minnesota	0	35	30	125	**1970**
Curt Knight, Washington	0	27	29	114	**1971**
Chester Marcol, Green Bay	0	29	33	128	**1972**
David Ray, Los Angeles	0	40	30	130	**1973**
Chester Marcol, Green Bay	0	19	25	94	**1974**
Chuck Foreman, Minnesota	22	0	0	132	**1975**
Mark Moseley, Washington	0	31	22	97	**1976**
Walter Payton, Chicago	16	0	0	96	**1977**
Frank Corrall, Los Angeles	0	31	29	118	**1978**
Mark Moseley, Washington	0	39	25	114	**1979**
Ed Murray, Detroit	0	35	27	116	**1980**
Ed Murray, Detroit	0	46	25	121	**1981**
Wendell Tyler, L.A. Rams	13	0	0	78	**1982**
Mark Moseley, Washington	0	62	33	161	**1983**
Ray Wersching, San Francisco	0	56	25	131	**1984**
Kevin Butler, Chicago	0	51	31	144	**1985**
Kevin Butler, Chicago	0	36	28	120	**1986**
Jerry Rice, San Francisco	23	0	0	138	**1987**
Mike Cofer, San Francisco	0	40	27	121	**1988**
Mike Cofer, San Francisco	0	49	29	136	**1989**
Chip Lohmiller, Washington	0	41	30	131	**1990**
Chip Lohmiller, Washington	0	56	31	149	**1991**
Morten Andersen, New Orleans	0	33	29	120	**1992**

Rushing

Player, team	Yds	Atts	TD
Jim Brown, Cleveland	1,257	215	9
Jim Brown, Cleveland	1,408	305	8
Jim Taylor, Green Bay	1,474	272	19
Jim Brown, Cleveland	1,863	291	12
Jim Brown, Cleveland	1,446	280	7
Jim Brown, Cleveland	1,544	289	17
Gale Sayers, Chicago	1,231	229	8
Leroy Kelly, Cleveland	1,205	235	11
Leroy Kelly, Cleveland	1,239	248	16
Gale Sayers, Chicago	1,032	236	8
Larry Brown, Washington	1,125	237	5
John Brockington, Green Bay	1,105	216	4
Larry Brown, Washington	1,216	285	8
John Brockington, Green Bay	1,144	265	3
Lawrence McCutcheon, Los Angeles	1,109	236	3
Jim Otis, St. Louis	1,076	269	5
Walter Payton, Chicago	1,390	311	13
Walter Payton, Chicago	1,852	339	14
Walter Payton, Chicago	1,395	333	11
Walter Payton, Chicago	1,610	369	14
Walter Payton, Chicago	1,460	317	15
George Rogers, New Orleans	1,674	378	13
Tony Dorsett, Dallas	745	177	5
Eric Dickerson, L.A. Rams	1,808	390	18
Eric Dickerson, L.A. Rams	2,105	379	14
Gerald Riggs, Atlanta	1,719	397	10
Eric Dickerson, L.A. Rams	1,821	404	11
Charles White, L.A. Rams	1,374	324	11
Herschel Walker, Dallas	1,514	361	5
Barry Sanders, Detroit	1,470	280	14
Barry Sanders, Detroit	1,304	255	13
Emmitt Smith, Dallas	1,563	365	12
Emmitt Smith, Dallas	1,713	373	18

American Football Conference Leaders

(American Football League, 1960-1969)

Passing / Pass-Receiving

Player, team	Atts	Com	YG	TD	Year	Player, team	Ct	YG	TD
Jack Kemp, Los Angeles	406	211	3,018	20	**1960**	Lionel Taylor, Denver	92	1,235	12
George Blanda, Houston	362	187	3,330	36	**1961**	Lionel Taylor, Denver	100	1,176	4
Len Dawson, Dallas	310	189	2,759	29	**1962**	Lionel Taylor, Denver	77	908	4
Tobin Rote, Kansas City	286	170	2,510	20	**1963**	Lionel Taylor, Denver	78	1,101	10
Len Dawson, Kansas City	354	199	2,879	30	**1964**	Charley Hennigan, Houston	101	1,546	8
John Hadl, San Diego	348	174	2,798	20	**1965**	Lionel Taylor, Denver	85	1,131	6
Len Dawson, Kansas City	284	159	2,527	26	**1966**	Lance Alworth, San Diego	73	1,383	13
Daryle Lamonica, Oakland	425	220	3,228	30	**1967**	George Sauer, N.Y. Jets	75	1,189	6
Len Dawson, Kansas City	224	131	2,109	17	**1968**	Lance Alworth, San Diego	68	1,312	10
Greg Cook, Cincinnati	197	106	1,854	15	**1969**	Lance Alworth, San Diego	64	1,003	4
Daryle Lamonica, Oakland	356	179	2,516	22	**1970**	Marlin Briscoe, Buffalo	57	1,036	8
Bob Griese, Miami	263	145	2,089	19	**1971**	Fred Biletnikoff, Oakland	61	929	9
Earl Morrall, Miami	150	83	1,360	11	**1972**	Fred Biletnikoff, Oakland	58	802	7
Ken Stabler, Oakland	260	163	1,997	14	**1973**	Fred Willis, Houston	57	371	1
Ken Anderson, Cincinnati	328	213	2,667	18	**1974**	Lydell Mitchell, Baltimore	72	544	2
Ken Anderson, Cincinnati	377	228	3,169	21	**1975**	Reggie Rucker, Cleveland	60	770	3
						Lydell Mitchell, Baltimore	60	554	4
Ken Stabler, Oakland	291	194	2,737	27	**1976**	MacArthur Lane, Kansas City	66	686	1
Bob Griese, Miami	307	180	2,252	22	**1977**	Lydell Mitchell, Baltimore	71	620	4
Terry Bradshaw, Pittsburgh	368	207	2,915	28	**1978**	Steve Largent, Seattle	71	1,168	8
Dan Fouts, San Diego	530	332	4,082	24	**1979**	Joe Washington, Baltimore	82	750	3
Brian Sipe, Cleveland	554	337	4,132	30	**1980**	Kellen Winslow, San Diego	89	1,290	9
Ken Anderson, Cincinnati	479	300	3,754	29	**1981**	Kellen Winslow, San Diego	88	1,075	10
Ken Anderson, Cincinnati	309	218	2,495	12	**1982**	Kellen Winslow, San Diego	54	721	6
Dan Marino, Miami	296	173	2,210	20	**1983**	Todd Christensen, L.A. Raiders	92	1,247	12
Dan Marino, Miami	564	362	5,084	48	**1984**	Ozzie Newsome, Cleveland	89	1,001	5
Ken O'Brien, N.Y. Jets	488	297	3,888	25	**1985**	Lionel James, San Diego	86	1,027	6
Dan Marino, Miami	623	378	4,746	44	**1986**	Todd Christensen, L.A. Raiders	95	1,153	8
Bernie Kosar, Cleveland	389	241	3,033	22	**1987**	Al Toon, N.Y. Jets	68	976	5
Boomer Esiason, Cincinnati	388	223	3,572	28	**1988**	Al Toon, N.Y. Jets	93	1,067	5
Boomer Esiason, Cincinnati	455	258	3,525	28	**1989**	Andre Reed, Buffalo	88	1,312	9
Jim Kelly, Buffalo	346	219	2,829	24	**1990**	Haywood Jeffires, Houston	74	1,048	8
						Drew Hill, Houston	74	1,019	5
Jim Kelly, Buffalo	474	304	3,844	33	**1991**	Haywood Jeffires, Houston	100	1,181	7
Warren Moon, Houston	346	224	2,521	18	**1992**	Haywood Jeffires, Houston	90	913	9

Scoring / Rushing

Player, team	TD	PAT	FG	Pts	Year	Player, team	Yds	Atts	TD
Gene Mingo, Denver	6	33	18	123	**1960**	Abner Haynes, Dallas	875	156	9
Gino Cappelletti, Boston	8	48	17	147	**1961**	Billy Cannon, Houston	948	200	6
Gene Mingo, Denver	4	32	27	137	**1962**	Cookie Gilchrest, Buffalo	1,096	214	13
Gino Cappelletti, Boston	2	35	22	113	**1963**	Clem Daniels, Oakland	1,099	215	3
Gino Cappelletti, Boston	7	36	25	155	**1964**	Cookie Gilchrest, Buffalo	981	230	6
Gino Cappelletti, Boston	9	27	17	132	**1965**	Paul Lowe, San Diego	1,121	222	7
Gino Cappelletti, Boston	6	35	16	119	**1966**	Jim Nance, Boston	1,458	299	11
George Blanda, Oakland	0	56	20	116	**1967**	Jim Nance, Boston	1,216	269	7
Jim Turner, N.Y. Jets	0	43	34	145	**1968**	Paul Robinson, Cincinnati	1,023	238	8
Jim Turner, N.Y. Jets	0	33	32	129	**1969**	Dick Post, San Diego	873	182	6
Jan Stenerud, Kansas City	0	26	30	116	**1970**	Floyd Little, Denver	901	209	3
Garo Yepremian, Miami	0	33	28	117	**1971**	Floyd Little, Denver	1,133	284	6
Bobby Howfield, N.Y. Jets	0	40	27	121	**1972**	O.J. Simpson, Buffalo	1,251	292	6
Roy Gerela, Pittsburgh	0	36	29	123	**1973**	O.J. Simpson, Buffalo	2,003	332	12
Roy Gerela, Pittsburgh	0	33	20	93	**1974**	Otis Armstrong, Denver	1,407	263	9
O.J. Simpson, Buffalo	23	0	0	138	**1975**	O.J. Simpson, Buffalo	1,817	329	16
Toni Linhart, Baltimore	0	49	20	109	**1976**	O.J. Simpson, Buffalo	1,503	290	8
Errol Mann, Oakland	0	39	20	99	**1977**	Mark van Eeghen, Oakland	1,273	324	7
Pat Leahy, N.Y. Jets	0	41	22	107	**1978**	Earl Campbell, Houston	1,450	302	13
John Smith, New England	0	46	23	115	**1979**	Earl Campbell, Houston	1,697	368	19
John Smith, New England	0	51	26	129	**1980**	Earl Campbell, Houston	1,934	373	13
Jim Breech, Cincinnati	0	49	22	115	**1981**	Earl Campbell, Houston	1,376	361	10
Marcus Allen, L.A. Raiders	14	0	0	84	**1982**	Freeman McNeil, N.Y. Jets	786	151	6
Gary Anderson, Pittsburgh	0	38	27	119	**1983**	Curt Warner, Seattle	1,446	335	13
Gary Anderson, Pittsburgh	0	45	24	117	**1984**	Earnest Jackson, San Diego	1,179	296	8
Gary Anderson, Pittsburgh	0	40	33	139	**1985**	Marcus Allen, L.A. Raiders	1,759	380	11
Tony Franklin, New England	0	44	32	140	**1986**	Curt Warner, Seattle	1,481	319	13
Jim Breech, Cincinnati	0	25	24	97	**1987**	Eric Dickerson, L.A. Rams, Indianapolis	1,288*	283	6
Scott Norwood, Buffalo	0	33	32	129	**1988**	Eric Dickerson, Indianapolis	1,659	388	14
David Treadwell, Denver	0	39	27	120	**1989**	Christian Okoye, Kansas City	1,480	370	12
Nick Lowery, Kansas City	0	37	34	139	**1990**	Thurman Thomas, Buffalo	1,297	271	11
Pete Stoyanovich, Miami	0	28	31	121	**1991**	Thurman Thomas, Buffalo	1,407	288	7
Pete Stoyanovich, Miami	0	34	30	124	**1992**	Barry Foster, Pittsburgh	1,690	390	11

* 1,011 AFC yards led conference.

1992 NFL Individual Leaders

National Football Conference

Passing

	Att	Comp	Pct comp	Yds	Avg gain	TD	Pct TD	Int	Rating points
Young, Steve, San Francisco	402	268	66.7	3465	8.62	25	6.2	7	107.0
Miller, Chris, Atlanta	253	152	60.1	1739	6.87	15	5.9	6	90.7
Aikman, Troy, Dallas	473	302	63.8	3445	7.28	23	4.9	14	89.5
Cunningham, Randall, Philadelphia	384	233	60.7	2775	7.23	19	4.9	11	87.3
Favre, Brett, Green Bay	471	302	64.1	3227	6.85	18	3.8	13	85.3
Hebert, Bobby, New Orleans	422	249	59.0	3287	7.79	19	4.5	16	82.9
Everett, Jim, L.A. Rams	475	281	59.2	3323	7.00	22	4.6	18	80.2
Chandler, Chris, Phoenix	413	245	59.3	2832	6.86	15	3.6	15	77.1
Harbaugh, Jim, Chicago	358	202	56.4	2486	6.94	13	3.6	12	76.2
Testaverde, Vinny, Tampa Bay	358	206	57.5	2554	7.13	14	3.9	16	74.2
Gannon, Rich, Minnesota	279	159	57.0	1905	6.83	12	4.3	13	72.9
Rypien, Mark, Washington	479	269	56.2	3282	6.85	13	2.7	17	71.7

Rushing

	Att	Yds	Avg	TD
Smith, Emmitt, Dallas	373	1713	4.6	18
Sanders, Barry, Detroit	312	1352	4.3	9
Allen, Terry, Minnesota	266	1201	4.5	13
Cobb, Reggie, Tampa Bay	310	1171	3.8	9
Hampton, Rodney, N.Y. Giants	257	1141	4.4	14
Gary, Cleveland, L.A. Rams	279	1125	4.0	7
Walker, Herschel, Philadelphia	267	1070	4.0	8
Watters, Ricky, San Francisco	206	1013	4.9	9
Byner, Earnest, Washington	262	998	3.8	6
Johnson, Johnny, Phoenix	178	734	4.1	6

Pass Receiving

	No	Yds	Avg	TD
Sharpe, Sterling, Green Bay	108	1461	13.5	13
Rison, Andre, Atlanta	93	1119	12.0	11
Rice, Jerry, San Francisco	84	1201	14.3	10
Irvin, Michael, Dallas	78	1396	17.9	7
Pritchard, Mike, Atlanta	77	827	10.7	5
Perriman, Brett, Detroit	69	810	11.7	4
Martin, Eric, New Orleans	68	1041	15.3	5
Novacek, Jay, Dallas	68	630	9.3	6
Barnett, Fred, Philadelphia	67	1083	16.2	6
Clark, Gary, Washington	64	912	14.3	5

Scoring-Touchdowns

	TD	Rush	Pass	Pts
Smith, Emmitt, Dallas	19	18	1	114
Allen, Terry, Minnesota	15	13	2	90
Hampton, Rodney, N.Y. Giants	14	14	0	84
Sharpe, Sterling, Green Bay	13	0	13	78

Scoring-Kicking

	PAT	FG	Pts
Andersen, Morten, New Orleans	33/34	29/34	120
Lohmiller, Chip, Washington	30/30	30/40	120
Elliott, Lin, Dallas	47/48	24/35	119
Cofer, Mike, San Francisco	53/54	18/27	107
Reveiz, Fuad, Minnesota	45/45	19/25	102

Interceptions

	No	Yds	Long	TD
McMillian, Audray, Minnesota	8	157	51	2
Woolford, Donnell, Chicago	7	67	32	0
Edwards, Brad, Washington	6	157	53	1
Cook, Toi, New Orleans	6	90	48	1
Massey, Robert, Phoenix	5	147	46	3
Scott, Todd, Minnesota	5	79	35	1
Glenn, Vencie, Minnesota	5	65	39	0
Griffin, Don, San Francisco	5	4	2	0

Kickoff Returns

	No	Yds	Avg	TD
Sanders, Deion, Atlanta	40	1067	26.7	2
Bailey, Johnny, Phoenix	28	690	24.6	0
Gray, Mel, Detroit	42	1006	24.0	1
Meggett, Dave, N.Y. Giants	20	455	22.8	1
Lewis, Darren, Chicago	23	511	22.2	1

Punt Returns

	No	Yds	Avg	TD
Bailey, Johnny, Phoenix	20	263	13.2	0
Martin, Kelvin, Dallas	42	532	12.7	2
Sikahema, Vai, Philadelphia	40	503	12.6	1
Parker, Anthony, Minnesota	33	336	10.2	0
Buckley, Terrell, Green Bay	21	211	10.0	1

Punters

	No	Yds	Long	Avg
Newsome, Harry, Minnesota	72	3243	84	45.0
Barnhardt, Tommy, New Orleans	67	2947	62	44.0
Arnold, Jim, Detroit	65	2846	71	43.8
Landeta, Sean, N.Y. Giants	53	2317	71	43.7
Saxon, Mike, Dallas	61	2620	58	43.0

Sacks

	No
Simmons, Clyde, Philadelphia	19.0
Harris, Tim, San Francisco	17.0
Martin, Wayne, New Orleans	15.5
Doleman, Chris, Minnesota	14.5
White, Reggie, Philadelphia	14.0

American Football Conference

Passing

	Att	Comp	Pct comp	Yds	Avg gain	TD	Pct TD	Int	Rating points
Moon, Warren, Houston	346	224	64.7	2521	7.29	18	5.2	12	89.3
Marino, Dan, Miami	554	330	59.6	4116	7.43	24	4.3	16	85.1
O'Donnell, Neil, Pittsburgh	313	185	59.1	2283	7.29	13	4.2	9	83.6
Kelly, Jim, Buffalo	462	269	58.2	3457	7.48	23	5.0	19	81.2
Carlson, Cody, Houston	227	149	65.6	1710	7.53	9	4.0	11	81.2
Krieg, Dave, Kansas City	413	230	55.7	3115	7.54	15	3.6	12	79.9
Humphries, Stan, San Diego	454	263	57.9	3356	7.39	16	3.5	18	76.4
Elway, John, Denver	316	174	55.1	2242	7.09	10	3.2	17	65.7
Schroeder, Jay, L.A. Raiders	253	123	48.6	1476	5.83	11	4.3	11	63.3
George, Jeff, Indianapolis	306	167	54.6	1963	6.42	7	2.3	15	61.5
Esiason, Boomer, Cincinnati	278	144	51.8	1407	5.06	11	4.0	15	57.0
Nagle, Browning, N.Y. Jets	387	192	49.6	2280	5.89	7	1.8	17	55.7
Gelbaugh, Stan, Seattle	255	121	47.5	1307	5.13	6	2.4	11	52.9

Rushing

	Att	Yds	Avg	TD
Foster, Barry, Pittsburgh	390	1690	4.3	11
Thomas, Thurman, Buffalo	312	1487	4.8	9
White, Lorenzo, Houston	265	1226	4.6	7
Green, Harold, Cincinnati	265	1170	4.4	2
Warren, Chris, Seattle	223	1017	4.6	3
Higgs, Mark, Miami	256	915	3.6	7
Butts, Marion, San Diego	218	809	3.7	4
Dickerson, Eric, L.A. Raiders	187	729	3.9	2
Baxter, Brad, N.Y. Jets	152	698	4.6	6
Green, Gaston, Denver	161	648	4.0	2

Pass Receiving

	No	Yds	Avg	TD
Jeffires, Haywood, Houston	90	913	10.1	9
Duncan, Curtis, Houston	82	954	11.6	1
Harmon, Ronnie, San Diego	79	914	11.6	1
Williams, John L., Seattle	74	556	7.5	2
Miller, Anthony, San Diego	72	1060	14.7	7
Givins, Earnest, Houston	67	787	11.7	10
Reed, Andre, Buffalo	65	913	14.0	3
Langhorne, Reggie, Indianapolis	65	811	12.5	1
Thomas, Thurman, Buffalo	58	626	10.8	3
Burkett, Chris, N.Y. Jets	57	724	12.7	1
White, Lorenzo, Houston	57	641	11.2	1

Scoring-Touchdowns

	TD	Rush	Pass	Pts
Thomas, Thurman, Buffalo	12	9	3	72
Foster, Barry, Pittsburgh	11	11	0	66
Givins, Earnest, Houston	10	0	10	60
Culver, Rodney, Indianapolis	9	7	2	54
Jeffires, Haywood, Houston	9	0	9	54

Scoring-Kicking

	PAT	FG	Pts
Stoyanovich, Pete, Miami	34/36	30/37	124
Christie, Steve, Buffalo	43/44	24/30	115
Anderson, Gary, Pittsburgh	29/31	28/36	113
Carney, John, San Diego	35/35	26/32	113
Lowery, Nick, Kansas City	39/39	22/24	105

Interceptions

	No	Yds	Long	TD
Jones, Henry, Buffalo	8	263	82	2
Robinson, Eugene, Seattle	7	126	49	0
Carter, Dale, Kansas City	7	65	36	1
Kelso, Mark, Buffalo	7	21	13	0

Kickoff Returns

	No	Yds	Avg	TD
Vaughn, Jon, New England	20	564	28.2	1
Baldwin, Randy, Cleveland	30	675	22.5	0
Montgomery, Alton, Denver	21	466	22.2	0
Verdin, Clarence, Indianapolis	39	815	20.9	0
Ball, Eric, Cincinnati	20	411	20.6	0

Punt Returns

	No	Yds	Avg	TD
Woodson, Rod, Pittsburgh	32	364	11.4	1
Verdin, Clarence, Indianapolis	24	268	11.2	2
Marshall, Arthur, Denver	33	349	10.6	0
Carter, Dale, Kansas City	38	398	10.5	2
Brown, Tim, L.A. Raiders	37	383	10.4	0

Punters

	No	Yds	Long	Avg
Montgomery, Greg, Houston	53	2487	66	46.9
Stark, Rohn, Indianapolis	83	3716	64	44.8
Tuten, Rick, Seattle	108	4760	65	44.1
Barker, Bryan, Kansas City	75	3245	65	43.3
Royals, Mark, Pittsburgh	73	3119	58	42.7

Sacks

	No
O'Neal, Leslie, San Diego	17.0
Fletcher, Simon, Denver	16.0
Smith, Neil, Kansas City	14.5
Thomas, Derrick, Kansas City	14.5
Cox, Bryan, Miami	14.0
Kennedy, Cortez, Seattle	14.0
Smith, Bruce, Buffalo	14.0

Jim Thorpe Trophy Winners

The Jim Thorpe Trophy goes to the most valuable player as chosen by the NFL Players Association.

1955 Harlon Hill, Chicago Bears
1956 Frank Gifford, N.Y. Giants
1957 John Unitas, Baltimore Colts
1958 Jim Brown, Cleveland Browns
1959 Charley Conerly, N.Y. Giants
1960 Norm Van Brocklin, Philadelphia Eagles
1961 Y.A. Tittle, N.Y. Giants
1962 Jim Taylor, Green Bay Packers
1963 Jim Brown, Cleveland Browns; Y.A. Tittle, N.Y. Giants
1964 Lenny Moore, Baltimore Colts
1965 Jim Brown, Cleveland Browns
1966 Bart Starr, Green Bay Packers
1967 John Unitas, Baltimore Colts
1968 Earl Morrall, Baltimore Colts
1969 Roman Gabriel, Los Angeles Rams
1970 John Brodie, San Francisco 49ers
1971 Bob Griese, Miami Dolphins
1972 Larry Brown, Washington Redskins
1973 O.J. Simpson, Buffalo Bills
1974 Ken Stabler, Oakland Raiders
1975 Fran Tarkenton, Minnesota Vikings
1976 Bert Jones, Baltimore Colts
1977 Walter Payton, Chicago Bears
1978 Earl Campbell, Houston Oilers
1979 Earl Campbell, Houston Oilers
1980 Earl Campbell, Houston Oilers
1981 Ken Anderson, Cincinnati Bengals
1982 Dan Fouts, San Diego Chargers
1983 Joe Theismann, Washington Redskins
1984 Dan Marino, Miami Dolphins
1985 Walter Payton, Chicago Bears
1986 Phil Simms, N.Y. Giants
1987 Jerry Rice, San Francisco
1988 Roger Craig, San Francisco
1989 Joe Montana, San Francisco
1990 Warren Moon, Houston
1991 Thurman Thomas, Buffalo
1992 Steve Young, San Francisco

NFL Stadiums

Name, location (built)	Capacity
Anaheim Stadium, Anaheim, Cal. (1966)	69,007
Arrowhead Stadium, Kansas City, Mo. (1972)	78,067
Astrodome, Houston, Tex. (1965)	60,502
Candlestick Park, San Francisco, Cal. (1960)	66,455
Cleveland Stadium (1931)	80,098
Foxboro Stadium, Mass. (1971)	60,794
Georgia Dome, Atlanta (1992)	71,594
Giants Stadium, E. Rutherford, N.J. (1976)	76,891
Hoosier Dome, Indianapolis, Ind. (1984)	60,127
Robert F. Kennedy Stadium, Wash., D.C. (1961)	55,683
Kingdome, Seattle, Wash. (1976)	64,984
Lambeau Field, Green Bay, Wis. (1957)	59,543
Los Angeles Memorial Coliseum (1923)	92,488
Louisiana Superdome, New Orleans (1975)	69,065
Metrodome, Minneapolis (1982)	63,000
Mile High Stadium, Denver, Col. (1948)	76,273
Milwaukee County Stadium (1953)	56,051
Pontiac Silverdome, Mich. (1975)	80,500
Rich Stadium, Buffalo, N.Y. (1973)	80,290
Riverfront Stadium, Cincinnati, Oh. (1970)	60,389
Joe Robbie Stadium, Miami, Fla. (1987)	73,000
San Diego Jack Murphy Stadium (1967)	60,835
Soldier Field, Chicago, Ill. (1924)	66,949
Sun Devil Stadium, Tempe, Ariz. (1958)	72,608
Tampa Stadium, Tampa, Fla. (1967)	74,314
Texas Stadium, Irving, Tex. (1971)	65,024
Three Rivers Stadium, Pittsburgh, Pa. (1970)	60,750
Veterans Stadium, Philadelphia, Pa. (1971)	65,356

THE BULLS "THREEPEAT"

AP/WIDE WORLD PHOTOS

Michael Jordan—who soon after announced his retirement—leads the Chicago Bulls to their third straight NBA title.

Sports Highlights

FOCUS ON SPORTS

Most Valuable Player Troy Aikman of the Dallas Cowboys, during their Super Bowl win over the Buffalo Bills.

Eric Montross helps North Carolina defeat Michigan for the NCAA college basketball championship.

Goaltender Patrick Roy, the playoffs MVP, in action, as the Montreal Canadiens win the NHL finals.

Australian Greg Norman raises his arms in triumph after winning the British Open golf tournament.

AP/WIDE WORLD PHOTOS

AP (ARD VIA CNN)(SH)

Tennis star Monica Seles after being stabbed at courtside in a Hamburg, Germany, tournament April 30.

FOCUS ON SPORTS

Over 80,000 fans—and a host of souvenir sellers—pack Mile High Stadium in Denver for the first home opener, April 9, of the Colorado Rockies.

FOCUS ON SPORTS

PEOPLE IN THE NEWS

AP/WIDE WORLD PHOTOS

Rock veteran Eric Clapton with the six Grammy Awards he received in Los Angeles February 24.

Connie Chung joins Dan Rather as co-anchor of the CBS Evening News *on June 1.*

AP/WIDE WORLD PHOTOS

BRIAN SMALE/ONYX

Author John Grisham, who at one point had four books on the best-seller lists (left). Below: Louis V. Gerstner is named, March 26, as the new chairman of troubled corporate giant IBM.

RICK MAIMAN/SYGMA

AP/WIDE WORLD PHOTOS

Kim Campbell, selected in June as Canada's first female prime minister.

AP/WIDE WORLD PHOTOS

Dr. Jack Kevorkian, proponent and practitioner of doctor-assisted suicides, leaves a Michigan court.

AP/WIDE WORLD PHOTOS

Maintaining his presence on the talk-show circuit, Ross Perot chats with Tonight Show *host Jay Leno.*

ON STAGE AND SCREEN

The T. rex in action in Jurassic Park, *a summer blockbuster directed by Steven Spielberg.*

WIDE WORLD PHOTOS

REUTERS/BETTMANN

Reclusive pop star Michael Jackson grants a rare interview February 10 to talk-show host Oprah Winfrey.

Russian-born ballet great Rudolf Nureyev, who died of AIDS January 6.

Clint Eastwood in Unforgiven, *which won four Oscars (below). A scene from* Angels in America: Millennium Approaches, *a Pulitzer Prize-winning play dramatizing the AIDS crisis (right).*

JOAN MARCUS/BONEAU BRYAN BROWN

EDDIE ADAMS/SYGMA

Comedian David Letterman announces his move from NBC to CBS (below).

AP/WIDE WORLD PHOTOS

May 20: curtain call for the final episode of the long-running NBC comedy Cheers.

ROYAL FAMILIES

Charles and Diana in a rare post-separation appearance together May 30 (below). Tourists line up August 7 for the first public tours of Buckingham Palace (right).

TIM GRAHAM/SYGMA

REUTERS/BETTMANN

AP/WIDE WORLD PHOTOS

Japanese Crown Prince Naruhito and new Crown Princess Masako following their June wedding.

Number One NFL Draft Choices, 1936-1993

Year	Team	Player, Pos., College	Year	Team	Player, Pos., College
1936	Philadelphia	Jay Berwanger, HB, Chicago	1966	Atlanta	Tommy Nobis, LB, Texas
1937	Philadelphia	Sam Francis, FB, Nebraska	1967	Baltimore	Bubba Smith, DT, Michigan St.
1938	Cleve.Rams	Corbett Davis, FB, Indiana	1968	Minnesota	Ron Yary, T, USC
1939	Chi.Cards	Ki Aldrich, C, TCU	1969	Buffalo	O.J. Simpson, RB, USC
1940	Chi.Cards	George Cafego, HB, Tennessee	1970	Pittsburgh	Terry Bradshaw, QB, La.Tech
1941	Chi.Bears	Tom Harmon, HB, Michigan	1971	New England	Jim Plunkett, QB, Stanford
1942	Pittsburgh	Bill Dudley, HB, Virginia	1972	Buffalo	Walt Patulski, DE, Notre Dame
1943	Detroit	Frank Sinkwich, HB, Georgia	1973	Houston	John Matuszak, DE, Tampa
1944	Boston Yanks	Angelo Bertelli, QB, Notre Dame	1974	Dallas	Ed "Too Tall" Jones, Tenn.St.
1945	Chi.Cards	Charley Trippi, HB, Georgia	1975	Atlanta	Steve Bartkowski, QB, Cal.
1946	Boston Yanks	Frank Dancewicz, QB, Notre Dame	1976	Tampa Bay	Lee Roy Selmon, DE, Oklahoma
1947	Chi.Bears	Bob Fenimore, HB, Okla. A&M	1977	Tampa Bay	Ricky Bell, RB, USC
1948	Washington	Harry Gilmer, QB, Alabama	1978	Houston	Earl Campbell, RB, Texas
1949	Philadelphia	Chuck Bednarik, C, Penn	1979	Buffalo	Tom Cousineau, LB, Ohio St.
1950	Detroit	Leon Hart, E, Notre Dame	1980	Detroit	Billy Sims, RB, Oklahoma
1951	N.Y. Giants	Kyle Rote, HB, SMU	1981	New Orleans	George Rogers, RB, S.Carolina
1952	L.A. Rams	Bill Wade, QB, Vanderbilt	1982	New England	Kenneth Sims, DT, Texas
1953	San Francisco	Harry Babcock, E, Georgia	1983	Baltimore	John Elway, QB, Stanford
954	Cleveland	Bobby Garrett, QB, Stanford	1984	New England	Irving Fryar, WR, Nebraska
955	Baltimore	George Shaw, QB, Oregon	1985	Buffalo	Bruce Smith, DE, Va.Tech
956	Pittsburgh	Gary Glick, DB, Col. A&M	1986	Tampa Bay	Bo Jackson, RB, Auburn
957	Green Bay	Paul Hornung, QB, Notre Dame	1987	Tampa Bay	Vinny Testaverde, QB, Miami, (Fla.)
958	Chi.Cards	King Hill, QB, Rice	1988	Atlanta	Aundray Bruce, LB, Auburn
959	Green Bay	Randy Duncan, QB, Iowa	1989	Dallas	Troy Aikman, QB, UCLA
960	L.A. Rams	Billy Cannon, HB, LSU	1990	Indianapolis	Jeff George, QB, Illinois
961	Minnesota	Tommy Mason, HB, Tulane	1991	Dallas	Russell Maryland, DL, Miami
962	Washington	Ernie Davis, HB, Syracuse	1992	Indianapolis	Steve Emtman, DL, Washington
963	L.A. Rams	Terry Baker, QB, Oregon St.	1993	New England	Drew Bledsoe, QB, Washington St.
964	San Francisco	Dave Parks, E, Texas Tech			
965	N.Y. Giants	Tucker Frederickson, HB, Auburn			

First-Round Selections in the 1993 NFL Draft

Team	Player	Pos.	College	Team	Player	Pos.	College
1—New England	Drew Bledsoe*	QB	Washington St.	16—Indianapolis	Sean Dawkins*	WR	California
2—Seattle	Rick Mirer	QB	Notre Dame	17—Washington	Tom Carter*	DB	Notre Dame
3—Phoenix	Garrison Hearst*	RB	Georgia	18—Phoenix	Ernest Dye	OT	S. Carolina
4—N.Y. Jets	Marvin Jones*	LB	Florida St.	19—Philadelphia	Lester Holmes	OT	Jackson St.
5—Cincinnati	John Copeland	DT	Alabama	20—New Orleans	Irv Smith	TE	Notre Dame
6—Tampa Bay	Eric Curry	DE	Alabama	21—Minnesota	Robert Smith*	RB	Ohio St.
7—Chicago	Curtis Conway*	WR	USC	22—San Diego	Darrien Gordon	DB	Stanford
8—New Orleans	Willie Roaf	OT	La. Tech	23—Pittsburgh	Deon Figures	DB	Colorado
9—Atlanta	Lincoln Kennedy	OT	Washington	24—Philadelphia	Leonard Renfroe*	DE	Colorado
0—L.A. Rams	Jerome Bettis*	RB	Notre Dame	25—Miami	O.J. McDuffie	WR	Penn St.
1—Denver	Dan Williams	DE	Toledo	26—San Francisco	Dana Stubblefield	DE	Kansas
2—L.A. Raiders	Patrick Bates*	DB	Texas A&M	27—San Francisco	Todd Kelly	DE	Tennessee
3—Houston	Brad Hopkins	OG	Illinois	28—Buffalo	Thomas Smith	DB	N. Carolina
4—Cleveland	Steve Everitt	C	Michigan	29—Green Bay	George Teague	DB	Alabama
5—Green Bay	Wayne Simmons	LB	Clemson				

* Under classmen who chose to enter the NFL draft.

Pro Football Hall of Fame, Canton, Ohio

erb Adderley
ance Alworth
oug Atkins
orris (Red) Badgro
am Barney
iff Battles
ammy Baugh
huck Bednarik
ert Bell
obby Bell
aymond Berry
harles Bidwell
ed Biletnikoff
eorge Blanda
el Blount
erry Bradshaw
n Brown
aul Brown
oosevelt Brown
illie Brown
ack Buchanan
ck Butkus
rl Campbell
ny Canadeo
e Carr
y Chamberlin
ck Christiansen
tch Clark
eorge Connor
n Conzelman
rry Csonka
Davis
llie Davis
n Dawson

Mike Ditka
Art Donovan
Paddy Driscoll
Bill Dudley
Turk Edwards
Weeb Ewbank
Tom Fears
Ray Flaherty
Len Ford
Dr. Daniel Fortmann
Dan Fouts
Frank Gatski
Bill George
Frank Gifford
Sid Gillman
Otto Graham
Red Grange
Joe Greene
Forrest Gregg
Bob Griese
Lou Groza
Joe Guyon
George Halas
Jack Ham
John Hannah
Franco Harris
Ed Healey
Mel Hein
Ted Hendricks
Pete Henry
Arnold Herber
Bill Hewitt
Clarke Hinkle
Elroy (Crazy Legs) Hirsch

Paul Hornung
Ken Houston
Cal Hubbard
Sam Huff
Lamar Hunt
Don Hutson
John Henry Johnson
Deacon Jones
Stan Jones
Sonny Jurgensen
Walt Kiesling
Frank (Bruiser) Kinard
Curly Lambeau
Jack Lambert
Tom Landry
Dick (Night Train) Lane
Jim Langer
Willie Lanier
Yale Lary
Dante Lavelli
Bobby Layne
Tuffy Leemans
Bob Lilly
Larry Little
Vince Lombardi
Sid Luckman
Link Lyman
John Mackey
Tim Mara
Gino Marchetti
George Marshall
Ollie Matson
Don Maynard
George McAfee

Mike McCormack
Hugh McElhenny
John (Blood) McNally
Mike Michalske
Wayne Millner
Bobby Mitchell
Ron Mix
Lenny Moore
Marion Motley
George Musso
Bronko Nagurski
Joe Namath
Greasy Neale
Ernie Nevers
Ray Nitschke
Chuck Noll
Leo Nomellini
Merlin Olsen
Jim Otto
Steve Owen
Alan Page
Clarence (Ace) Parker
Jim Parker
Walter Payton
Joe Perry
Pete Pihos
Hugh (Shorty) Ray
Dan Reeves
John Riggins
Jim Ringo
Andy Robustelli
Art Rooney
Pete Rozelle
Bob St. Clair

Gale Sayers
Joe Schmidt
Tex Schramm
Art Shell
O.J. Simpson
Bart Starr
Roger Staubach
Ernie Stautner
Jan Stenerud
Ken Strong
Joe Stydahar
Fran Tarkenton
Charlie Taylor
Jim Taylor
Jim Thorpe
Y.A. Tittle
George Trafton
Charlie Trippi
Emlen Tunnell
Clyde (Bulldog) Turner
Johnny Unitas
Gene Upshaw
Norm Van Brocklin
Steve Van Buren
Doak Walker
Bill Walsh
Paul Warfield
Bob Waterfield
Arnie Weinmeister
Bill Willis
Larry Wilson
Alex Wojciechowicz
Willie Wood

All-Time NFL Coaching Victories

(at start of 1993 season)

Coach	Years	Teams	Regular Season W	L	T	Pct	Career W	L	T	Pct
George Halas	40	Bears	319	148	31	.672	325	151	31	.672
Don Shula	30	Colts, Dolphins	300	136	6	.685	318	151	6	.676
Tom Landry	29	Cowboys	250	162	6	.605	270	178	6	.601
Curly Lambeau	33	Packers, Cardinals, Redskins	226	132	22	.623	229	134	22	.623
Chuck Noll	23	Steelers	193	148	1	.566	209	156	1	.572
Chuck Knox	20	Rams, Bills, Seahawks	177	124	1	.588	184	135	1	.577
Paul Brown	21	Browns, Bengals	166	100	6	.621	170	108	6	.609
Bud Grant	18	Vikings	158	96	5	.620	168	108	5	.607
Steve Owen	23	Giants	151	100	17	.595	153	108	17	.582
Joe Gibbs	12	Redskins	124	60	0	.674	140	65	0	.683
Hank Stram	17	Chiefs, Saints	131	97	10	.571	136	100	10	.573
Weeb Ewbank	20	Colts, Jets	130	129	7	.502	134	130	7	.507
Sid Gillman	18	Rams, Chargers, Oilers	122	99	7	.550	123	104	7	.541
George Allen	12	Rams, Redskins	116	47	5	.705	118	54	5	.681
Dan Reeves	12	Broncos	110	73	1	.601	117	79	1	.596
Don Coryell	14	Cardinals, Chargers	111	83	1	.572	114	89	1	.561
John Madden	10	Raiders	103	32	7	.750	112	39	7	.731
Mike Ditka	11	Bears	106	62	0	.631	112	68	0	.622
Buddy Parker	15	Cardinals, Lions, Steelers	104	75	9	.577	107	76	9	.581
Marv Levy	12	Chiefs, Bills	98	77	0	.560	106	82	0	.564

All-Time Professional Football Records

NFL and AFL

(at start of 1993 season)

Leading Lifetime Rushers

Player	League	Yrs	Att	Yards	Avg
Walter Payton	NFL	13	3,838	16,726	4.4
Eric Dickerson	NFL	10	2,970	13,168	4.4
Tony Dorsett	NFL	12	2,936	12,739	4.3
Jim Brown	NFL	9	2,359	12,312	5.2
Franco Harris	NFL	13	2,949	12,120	4.1
John Riggins	NFL	14	2,916	11,352	3.9
O.J. Simpson	AFL-NFL	11	2,404	11,236	4.7
Ottis Anderson	NFL	14	2,562	10,273	4.0
Earl Campbell	NFL	8	2,187	9,407	4.3
Jim Taylor	NFL	10	1,941	8,597	4.4
Marcus Allen	NFL	11	2,090	8,545	4.[illegible]
Joe Perry	NFL	14	1,737	8,378	4.[illegible]
Gerald Riggs	NFL	10	1,989	8,188	4.[illegible]
Larry Csonka	AFL-NFL	11	1,891	8,081	4.[illegible]
Freeman McNeil	NFL	12	1,798	8,074	4.[illegible]
Roger Craig	NFL	10	1,953	8,070	4.[illegible]
James Brooks	NFL	12	1,685	7,962	4.[illegible]
Mike Pruitt	NFL	11	1,844	7,378	4.[illegible]
Leroy Kelly	NFL	10	1,727	7,274	4.[illegible]

Most Yards Gained, Season — 2,105, Eric Dickerson, Los Angeles Rams, 1984.
Most Yards Gained, Game — 275, Walter Payton, Chicago Bears vs. Minnesota Vikings, Nov. 20, 1977.
Most Touchdowns Rushing, Career — 110, Walter Payton, Chicago Bears, 1975-1987.
Most Touchdowns Rushing, Season — 24, John Riggins, Washington Redskins, 1983.
Most Touchdowns Rushing, Game — 6, Ernie Nevers, Chicago Cardinals vs. Chicago Bears, Nov. 8, 1929.
Most Rushing Attempts, Game — 45, Jamie Morris, Washington Redskins vs. Cincinnati Bengals, Dec. 17, 1988.
Longest run from Scrimmage — 99 yds., Tony Dorsett, Dallas vs. Minnesota, Jan. 3, 1983 (scored touchdown).

Leading Lifetime Passers

(Minimum 1,500 attempts)

Player	League	Yrs	Att	Comp	Yds	Pts*
Joe Montana	NFL	13	4,600	2,929	35,124	93.5
Steve Young	NFL	8	1,506	908	11,877	90.4
Dan Marino	NFL	10	5,284	3,128	39,502	87.8
Jim Kelly	NFL	7	3,024	1,824	23,031	86.9
Mark Rypien	NFL	5	1,888	1,078	14,414	84.3
Roger Staubach	NFL	11	2,958	1,685	22,700	83.4
Neil Lomax	NFL	8	3,153	1,817	22,771	82.7
Sonny Jurgensen	NFL	18	4,262	2,433	32,224	82.6
Len Dawson	NFL-AFL	19	3,741	2,136	28,711	82.6
Dave Krieg	NFL	13	3,989	2,326	29,247	82.1
Ken Anderson	NFL	16	4,475	2,654	32,838	81.[illegible]
Boomer Esiason	NFL	9	3,378	1,897	25,671	81.[illegible]
Bernie Kosar	NFL	8	3,012	1,174	21,097	81.[illegible]
Danny White	NFL	13	2,950	1,761	21,959	81.[illegible]
Ken O'Brien	NFL	9	3,465	2,039	34,386	81.[illegible]
Warren Moon	NFL	9	4,026	2,329	30,200	81.[illegible]
Bart Starr	NFL	16	3,149	1,808	24,718	80[illegible]
Fran Tarkenton	NFL	18	6,467	3,686	47,003	80.[illegible]
Dan Fouts	NFL	15	5,604	3,294	43,040	80[illegible]

* Rating points based on performances in the following categories: Percentage of completions, percentage of touchdown passes, percentag[illegible] of interceptions, and average gain per pass attempt.

Most Yards Gained, Season — 5,084, Dan Marino, Miami Dolphins, 1984.
Most Yards Gained, Game — 554, Norm Van Brocklin, Los Angeles Rams vs. New York Yankees, Sept. 18, 1951 (27 completions [illegible] 41 attempts).
Most Touchdowns Passing, Career — 342, Fran Tarkenton, Minnesota Vikings, 1961-66; N.Y. Giants, 1967-71; Vikings, 1972-78.
Most Touchdowns Passing, Season — 48, Dan Marino, Miami Dolphins, 1984.
Most Touchdowns Passing, Game — 7, Sid Luckman, Chicago Bears vs. New York Giants, Nov. 14, 1943; Adrian Burk, Philade[illegible]phia Eagles vs. Washington Redskins, Oct. 17, 1954; George Blanda, Houston Oilers vs. New York Titans, Nov. 19, 1961; Y.A. T[illegible]tle, New York Giants vs. Washington Redskins, Oct. 28, 1962; Joe Kapp, Minnesota Vikings vs. Baltimore Colts, Sept. 28, 1969.
Most Passes Completed, Season — 404, Warren Moon, Houston Oilers, 1991.
Most Passes Completed, Game — 42, Richard Todd, N.Y. Jets vs. San Francisco 49ers, Sept. 21, 1980.

Leading Lifetime Receivers

Player	League	Yrs	No	Yds	Avg
Art Monk	NFL	13	847	11,628	13.7
Steve Largent	NFL	14	819	13,089	16.0
Charlie Joiner	NFL	18	750	12,146	16.2
James Lofton	NFL	15	750	13,821	18.4
Ozzie Newsome	NFL	13	662	7,980	12.1
Charley Taylor	NFL	13	649	9,110	14.0
Don Maynard	AFL-NFL	15	633	11,834	18.7
Raymond Berry	NFL	13	631	9,275	14.7
Jerry Rice	NFL	8	610	10,273	16.8
Drew Hill	NFL	13	600	9,447	15.7
Harold Carmichael	NFL	14	590	8,985	15.2
Fred Biletnikoff	AFL-NFL	14	589	8,974	15.2
Harold Jackson	NFL	16	579	10,372	17.9
Lionel Taylor	AFL	10	567	7,195	12.7
Wes Chandler	NFL	11	559	8,966	16.0
Stanley Morgan	NFL	14	557	10,716	19.2
Roy Green	NFL	14	559	8,965	16.0
Mark Clayton	NFL	10	550	8,643	15.7
Roger Craig	NFL	10	547	4,742	8.7
J.T. Smith	NFL	13	544	6,974	12.8

Most Yards Gained, Season — 1,746, Charley Hennigan, Houston Oilers, 1961.
Most Yards Gained, Game — 336, Flipper Anderson, L.A. Rams vs. New Orleans, Nov. 26, 1989.
Most Pass Receptions, Season — 108, Sterling Sharpe, Green Bay Packers, 1992.
Most Pass Receptions, Game — 18, Tom Fears, Los Angeles Rams vs. Green Bay Packers, Dec. 3, 1950 (189 yards).
Most Touchdown Passes, Season — 22, Jerry Rice, San Francisco 49ers, 1987.
Most Touchdown Passes, Game — 5, Bob Shaw, Chicago Cardinals vs. Baltimore Colts, Oct. 2, 1950; Kellen Winslow, San Diego vs. Oakland, Nov. 22, 1981; Jerry Rice, San Francisco vs. Atlanta, Oct. 14, 1990.

Leading Lifetime Scorers

Player	League	Yrs	TD	PAT	FG	Total
George Blanda	NFL-AFL	26	9	943	335	2,002
Jan Stenerud	AFL-NFL	19	0	580	373	1,699
Pat Leahy	NFL	18	0	558	304	1,470
Jim Turner	AFL-NFL	16	1	521	304	1,439
Mark Moseley	NFL	16	0	482	300	1,382
Jim Bakken	NFL	17	0	534	282	1,380
Nick Lowery	NFL	14	0	449	306	1,367
Fred Cox	NFL	15	0	519	282	1,365
Lou Groza	NFL	17	1	641	234	1,349
Jim Breech	NFL	14	0	517	243	1,246
Chris Bahr	NFL	14	0	490	241	1,213
Matt Bahr	NFL	14	0	431	237	1,142
Gino Cappelletti	AFL	11	42	350	176	1,130
Gary Anderson	NFL	11	0	356	258	1,130
Ray Wersching	NFL	15	0	456	222	1,122
Eddie Murray	NFL	12	0	381	244	1,113
Don Cockroft	NFL	13	0	432	216	1,080
Garo Yepremian	AFL-NFL	14	0	444	210	1,074
Morten Anderson	NFL	11	0	347	246	1,085
Bruce Gossett	NFL	11	0	374	219	1,031
Sam Baker	NFL	15	2	428	179	977

Most Points, Season — 176, Paul Hornung, Green Bay Packers, 1960 (15 TD's, 41 PAT's, 15 FG's).
Most Points, Game — 40, Ernie Nevers, Chicago Cardinals vs. Chicago Bears, Nov. 28, 1929 (6 TD's, 4 PAT's).
Most Touchdowns, Season — 24, John Riggins, Washington Redskins, 1984 (24 rushing).
Most Touchdowns, Game — 6, Ernie Nevers, Chicago Cardinals vs. Chicago Bears, Nov. 28, 1929 (6 rushing); Dub Jones, Cleveland Browns vs. Chicago Bears, Nov. 25, 1951 (4 rushing, 2 pass receptions); Gale Sayers, Chicago Bears vs. San Francisco 49ers, Dec. 12, 1965 (4 rushing, 1 pass reception, 1 punt return).
Most Points After Touchdown, Season — 66, Uwe von Schamann, Miami Dolphins, 1984.
Most Consecutive Points After Touchdown — 234, Tommy Davis, San Francisco 49ers, 1959-1969.
Most Field Goals, Game — 7, Jim Bakken, St. Louis Cardinals vs. Pittsburgh Steelers, Sept. 24, 1967; Rich Karlis, Minn. Vikings vs. L.A. Rams, Nov. 5, 1989.
Longest Field Goal — 63 yds., Tom Dempsey, New Orleans Saints vs. Detroit Lions, Nov. 8, 1970.

Bert Bell Memorial Trophy Winners

The Bert Bell Memorial Trophy, named after the former NFL commissioner, is awarded annually to the outstanding NFL rookie.

1964	Charlie Taylor, Washington, WR
1965	Gale Sayers, Chicago, RB
1966	Tommy Nobis, Atlanta, LB
1967	Mel Farr, Detroit, RB
1968	Earl McCullouch, Detroit, WR
1969	Calvin Hill, Dallas, RB
1970	Raymond Chester, Oakland, TE
1971	AFC: Jim Plunkett, New England, QB NFC: John Brockington, Green Bay, RB
1972	AFC: Franco Harris, Pittsburgh, RB NFC: Willie Buchanon, Green Bay, DB
1973	AFC: Boobie Clark, Cincinnati, RB NFC: Chuck Foreman, Minnesota, RB
1974	Don Woods, San Diego, RB
1975	AFC: Robert Brazile, Houston, LB NFC: Steve Bartkowski, Atlanta, QB
1976	AFC: Mike Haynes, New England, CB NFC: Sammy White, Minnesota, WR
1977	Tony Dorsett, Dallas, RB
1978	Earl Campbell, Houston, RB
1979	Ottis Anderson, St. Louis, RB
1980	Billy Sims, Detroit, RB
1981	Lawrence Taylor, N.Y. Giants, LB
1982	Marcus Allen, L.A. Raiders, RB
1983	Eric Dickerson, L.A. Rams, RB
1984	Louis Lipps, Pittsburgh, WR
1985	Eddie Brown, Cincinnati, WR
1986	Rueben Mayes, New Orleans, RB
1987	Bo Jackson, L.A. Raiders, RB
1988	John Stephens, New England, RB
1989	Barry Sanders, Detroit, RB
1990	Eric Green, Pittsburgh, TE
1991	Mike Croel, Denver, LB
1992	Dale Carter, Kansas City, CB

Boston Marathon in 1993

Cosmos N'Deti of Kenya won the 1993 Boston Marathon with a time of 2 hours 9 minutes 33 seconds. Kim Jae-Yong of South Korea finished second. Olga Markova of Russia was the first woman to cross the finish line.

GOLF

United States Open Winners

Year	Winner
1903	Willie Anderson
1904	Willie Anderson
1905	Willie Anderson
1906	Alex Smith
1907	Alex Ross
1908	Fred McLeod
1909	George Sargent
1910	Alex Smith
1911	John McDermott
1912	John McDermott
1913	Francis Ouimet*
1914	Walter Hagen
1915	Jerome Travers*
1916	Chick Evans*
1917-18	(Not played)
1919	Walter Hagen
1920	Edward Ray
1921	Jim Barnes
1922	Gene Sarazen
1923	Bobby Jones*
1924	Cyril Walker
1925	Willie MacFarlane
1926	Bobby Jones*
1927	Tommy Armour
1928	John Farrell
1929	Bobby Jones*
1930	Bobby Jones*
1931	Wm. Burke
1932	Gene Sarazen
1933	John Goodman*
1934	Olin Dutra
1935	Sam Parks Jr.
1936	Tony Manero
1937	Ralph Guldahl
1938	Ralph Guldahl
1939	Byron Nelson
1940	Lawson Little
1941	Craig Wood
1942-45	(Not played)
1946	Lloyd Mangrum
1947	L. Worsham
1948	Ben Hogan
1949	Cary Middlecoff
1950	Ben Hogan
1951	Ben Hogan
1952	Julius Boros
1953	Ben Hogan
1954	Ed Furgol
1955	Jack Fleck
1956	Cary Middlecoff
1957	Dick Mayer
1958	Tommy Bolt
1959	Billy Casper
1960	Arnold Palmer
1961	Gene Littler
1962	Jack Nicklaus
1963	Julius Boros
1964	Ken Venturi
1965	Gary Player
1966	Billy Casper
1967	Jack Nicklaus
1968	Lee Trevino
1969	Orville Moody
1970	Tony Jacklin
1971	Lee Trevino
1972	Jack Nicklaus
1973	Johnny Miller
1974	Hale Irwin
1975	Lou Graham
1976	Jerry Pate
1977	Hubert Green
1978	Andy North
1979	Hale Irwin
1980	Jack Nicklaus
1981	David Graham
1982	Tom Watson
1983	Larry Nelson
1984	Fuzzy Zoeller
1985	Andy North
1986	Ray Floyd
1987	Scott Simpson
1988	Curtis Strange
1989	Curtis Strange
1990	Hale Irwin
1991	Payne Stewart
1992	Tom Kite
1993	Lee Janzen

* Amateur

Professional Golfer's Association Championship Winners

Year	Winner
1922	Gene Sarazen
1923	Gene Sarazen
1924	Walter Hagen
1925	Walter Hagen
1926	Walter Hagen
1927	Walter Hagen
1928	Leo Diegel
1929	Leo Diegel
1930	Tommy Armour
1931	Tom Creavy
1932	Olin Dutra
1933	Gene Sarazen
1934	Paul Runyan
1935	Johnny Revolta
1936	Denny Shute
1937	Denny Shute
1938	Paul Runyan
1939	Henry Picard
1940	Byron Nelson
1941	Victor Ghezzi
1942	Sam Snead
1944	Bob Hamilton
1945	Byron Nelson
1946	Ben Hogan
1947	Jim Ferrier
1948	Ben Hogan
1949	Sam Snead
1950	Chandler Harper
1951	Sam Snead
1952	James Turnesa
1953	Walter Burkemo
1954	Melvin Harbert
1955	Doug Ford
1956	Jack Burke
1957	Lionel Hebert
1958	Dow Finsterwald
1959	Bob Rosburg
1960	Jay Hebert
1961	Jerry Barber
1962	Gary Player
1963	Jack Nicklaus
1964	Bob Nichols
1965	Dave Marr
1966	Al Geiberger
1967	Don January
1968	Julius Boros
1969	Ray Floyd
1970	Dave Stockton
1971	Jack Nicklaus
1972	Gary Player
1973	Jack Nicklaus
1974	Lee Trevino
1975	Jack Nicklaus
1976	Dave Stockton
1977	Lanny Wadkins
1978	John Mahaffey
1979	David Graham
1980	Jack Nicklaus
1981	Larry Nelson
1982	Ray Floyd
1983	Hal Sutton
1984	Lee Trevino
1985	Hubert Green
1986	Bob Tway
1987	Larry Nelson
1988	Jeff Sluman
1989	Payne Stewart
1990	Wayne Grady
1991	John Daly
1992	Nick Price
1993	Paul Azinger

Masters Golf Tournament Winners

Year	Winner
1934	Horton Smith
1935	Gene Sarazen
1936	Horton Smith
1937	Byron Nelson
1938	Henry Picard
1939	Ralph Guldahl
1940	Jimmy Demaret
1941	Craig Wood
1942	Byron Nelson
1943-1945	(Not played)
1946	Herman Keiser
1947	Jimmy Demaret
1948	Claude Harmon
1949	Sam Snead
1950	Jimmy Demaret
1951	Ben Hogan
1952	Sam Snead
1953	Ben Hogan
1954	Sam Snead
1955	Cary Middlecoff
1956	Jack Burke
1957	Doug Ford
1958	Arnold Palmer
1959	Art Wall Jr.
1960	Arnold Palmer
1961	Gary Player
1962	Arnold Palmer
1963	Jack Nicklaus
1964	Arnold Palmer
1965	Jack Nicklaus
1966	Jack Nicklaus
1967	Gay Brewer Jr.
1968	Bob Goalby
1969	George Archer
1970	Billy Casper
1971	Charles Coody
1972	Jack Nicklaus
1973	Tommy Aaron
1974	Gary Player
1975	Jack Nicklaus
1976	Ray Floyd
1977	Tom Watson
1978	Gary Player
1979	Fuzzy Zoeller
1980	Severiano Ballesteros
1981	Tom Watson
1982	Craig Stadler
1983	Severiano Ballesteros
1984	Ben Crenshaw
1985	Bernhard Langer
1986	Jack Nicklaus
1987	Larry Mize
1988	Sandy Lyle
1989	Nick Faldo
1990	Nick Faldo
1991	Ian Woosnam
1992	Fred Couples
1993	Bernhard Langer

British Open Winners

Year	Winner
1931	Tommy Armour
1932	Gene Sarazen
1933	Denny Shute
1934	Henry Cotton
1935	Alf Perry
1936	Alf Padgham
1937	T.H. Cotton
1938	R.A. Whitcombe
1939	Richard Burton
1940-45	(Not played)
1946	Sam Snead
1947	Fred Daly
1948	Henry Cotton
1949	Bobby Locke
1950	Bobby Locke
1951	Max Faulkner
1952	Bobby Locke
1953	Ben Hogan
1954	Peter Thomson
1955	Peter Thomson
1956	Peter Thomson
1957	Bobby Locke
1958	Peter Thomson
1959	Gary Player
1960	Kel Nagle
1961	Arnold Palmer
1962	Arnold Palmer
1963	Bob Charles
1964	Tony Lema
1965	Peter Thomson
1966	Jack Nicklaus
1967	Roberto de Vicenzo
1968	Gary Player
1969	Tony Jacklin
1970	Jack Nicklaus
1971	Lee Trevino
1972	Lee Trevino
1973	Tom Weiskopf
1974	Gary Player
1975	Tom Watson
1976	Johnny Miller
1977	Tom Watson
1978	Jack Nicklaus
1979	Seve Ballesteros
1980	Tom Watson
1981	Bill Rogers
1982	Tom Watson
1983	Tom Watson
1984	Seve Ballesteros
1985	Sandy Lyle
1986	Greg Norman
1987	Nick Faldo
1988	Seve Ballesteros
1989	Mark Calcavecchia
1990	Nick Faldo
1991	Ian Baker-Finch
1992	Nick Faldo
1993	Greg Norman

Professional Golf Tournaments in 1993

Men

Date	Event	Winner	Score	Prize
Jan. 10	Tournament of Champions, Carlsbad, Cal.	Davis Love 3d	272	$144,000
Jan. 17	Hawaiian Open, Honolulu	Howard Twitty	269	216,000
Jan. 24	Northern Telecom Open, Tucson, Ariz.	Larry Mize	271	198,000
Jan. 31	Phoenix Open, Ariz.	Lee Janzen	273	180,000
Feb. 7	A.T.&T. National Pro-Am, Pebble Beach, Cal.	Bret Ogle	276	225,000
Feb. 14	Bob Hope Classic, La Quinta, Cal.	Tom Kite	325	198,000
Feb. 21	Buick Invitational, La Jolla, Cal.	Phil Mickelson	278	180,000
Feb. 28	Los Angeles Open	Tom Kite	206	180,000
Mar. 8	Doral Open, Miami, Fla.	Greg Norman	265	252,000
Mar. 14	Honda Classic, Ft. Lauderdale, Fla.	Fred Couples	207	198,000
Mar. 21	Nestle Invitational, Orlando, Fla.	Ben Crenshaw	280	180,000
Mar. 27	Tournament Players Championship, Ponte Vedra, Fla.	Nick Price	270	450,000
Apr. 11	Masters Tournament, Augusta, Ga.	David Frost	266	180,000
Apr. 18	Heritage Classic, Hilton Head, S.C.	David Edwards	269	180,000
Apr. 25	Greater Greensboro Open, N.C.	Rocco Mediate	*281	270,000
May 9	Atlanta Classic, Marietta, Ga.	Nolan Henke	271	216,000
May 16	Byron Nelson Classic, Irving, Tex.	Scott Simpson	270	216,000
May 23	Kemper Open, Potomac, Md.	Grant Waite	275	234,000
June 6	Memorial Tournament, Dublin, Oh.	Paul Azinger	274	252,000
June 13	Buick Classic, Harrison, N.Y.	Vijay Singh	*280	180,000
June 20	U.S. Open, Springfield, N.J.	Lee Janzen	272	290,000
June 27	Greater Hartford Open, Cromwell, Conn.	Nick Price	271	180,000
July 4	Western Open, Lemont, Ill.	Nick Price	269	216,000
July 11	Anheuser-Busch Classic, Williamsburg, Va.	Jim Gallagher	269	198,000
July 25	New England Classic, Sutton, Mass.	Paul Azinger	268	180,000
Aug. 1	St. Jude Classic, Memphis, Tenn.	Nick Price	266	198,000
Aug. 8	Buick Open, Grand Blanc, Mich.	Larry Mize	272	180,000
Aug. 15	PGA Championship, St. Louis	Paul Azinger	*272	280,000
Aug. 22	The International, Castle Rock, Col.	Phil Mickelson	45 pts.	234,000
Aug. 29	World Series of Golf, Akron, Oh.	Fulton Allem	270	252,000
Sept. 5	Greater Milwaukee Open	Billy Mayfair	*270	180,000
Sept. 12	Canadian Open, Oakville, Ont.	David Frost	279	180,000
Sept. 19	Hardee's Classic, Coal Valley, Ill.	David Frost	259	180,000
Sept. 26	B.C. Open, Endicott, N.Y.	Blaine McCallister	271	144,000

Women

Date	Event	Winner	Score	Prize
Feb. 21	Hawaiian Open, Honolulu	Lisa Walters	210	$67,000
Mar. 2	Sprint Classic, Tallahassee, Fla.	Kristi Albers	279	180,000
Mar. 14	Ping Championship, Tucson, Ariz.	Meg Mallon	272	60,000
Mar. 21	Standard Register Classic, Phoenix, Ariz.	Patty Sheehan	275	105,000
Mar. 27	Dinah Shore Invitational, Rancho Mirage, Cal.	Helen Alfredsson	284	105,000
May 9	Sara Lee Classic, Nashville, Tenn.	Meg Mallon	*205	78,000
May 16	McDonald's Championship, Wilmington, Del.	Laura Davies	277	135,000
May 30	Corning Classic, Corning, N.Y.	Kelly Robbins	277	75,000
June 6	Oldsmobile Classic, E. Lansing, Mich.	Jane Geddes	277	82,000
June 13	Mazda Championship, Bethesda, Md.	Patty Sheehan	275	150,000
June 20	Rochester International, Pittsford, N.Y.	Tammy Green	276	75,000
June 27	ShopRite Classic, Somers Pt., N.J.	Shelley Hamlin	204	67,000
July 4	Jamie Farr Toledo Classic, Oh.	Brandie Burton	201	67,000
July 11	Warren Classic, Warren, Oh.	Nancy Lopez	203	75,000
July 18	Big Apple Classic, New Rochelle, N.Y.	Hiromi Kobayashi	278	90,000
July 25	U.S. Women's Open, Carmel, Ind.	Lauri Merten	280	144,000
Aug. 1	Ping-Welch Championship, Canton, Mass.	Missie Berteotti	276	67,000
Aug. 8	McCall's Classic, Vt.	Dana Lofland-Dormann	275	75,000
Aug. 16	Chicago Sun-Times Challenge, Naperville, Ill.	Cindy Schreyer	272	71,000
Aug. 23	Minnesota Classic, Brooklyn Park, Minn.	Hiromi Kobayashi	205	67,000
Sept. 5	Rail Charity Classic, Springfield, Ill.	Helen Dobson	*203	75,000
Sept. 12	Ping Championship, Portland, Ore.	Donna Andrews	208	67,000
Sept. 19	Safeco Classic, Kent, Wash.	Brandie Burton	274	67,000
Sept. 26	Inamori Classic, San Diego, Cal.	Kris Monaghan	275	63,000

* Won playoff.

U.S. Women's Open Golf Champions

Year	Winner	Year	Winner	Year	Winner	Year	Winner
1948	"Babe" Zaharias	1960	Betsy Rawls	1972	Susie Maxwell Berning	1983	Jan Stephenson
1949	Louise Suggs	1961	Mickey Wright	1973	Susie Maxwell Berning	1984	Hollis Stacy
1950	"Babe" Zaharias	1962	Murle Lindstrom	1974	Sandra Haynie	1985	Kathy Baker
1951	Betsy Rawls	1963	Mary Mills	1975	Sandra Palmer	1986	Jane Geddes
1952	Louise Suggs	1964	Mickey Wright	1976	JoAnne Carner	1987	Laura Davies
1953	Betsy Rawls	1965	Carol Mann	1977	Hollis Stacy	1988	Liselotte Neumann
1954	"Babe" Zaharias	1966	Sandra Spuzich	1978	Hollis Stacy	1989	Betsy King
1955	Fay Crocker	1967	Catherine Lacoste*	1979	Jerilyn Britz	1990	Betsy King
1956	Mrs. K. Cornelius	1968	Susie Maxwell Berning	1980	Amy Alcott	1991	Meg Mallon
1957	Betsy Rawls	1969	Donna Caponi	1981	Pat Bradley	1992	Patty Sheehan
1958	Mickey Wright	1970	Donna Caponi	1982	Janet Alex	1993	Lauri Merten
1959	Mickey Wright	1971	JoAnne Carner				

* Amateur

PGA Leading Money Winners

Year	Player	Dollars	Year	Player	Dollars	Year	Player	Dollars
1946	Ben Hogan	$42,556	1962	Arnold Palmer	$81,448	1978	Tom Watson	$362,429
1947	Jimmy Demaret	27,006	1963	Arnold Palmer	128,230	1979	Tom Watson	462,636
1948	Ben Hogan	36,812	1964	Jack Nicklaus	113,284	1980	Tom Watson	530,808
1949	Sam Snead	31,593	1965	Jack Nicklaus	140,752	1981	Tom Kite	375,699
1950	Sam Snead	35,758	1966	Billy Casper	121,944	1982	Craig Stadler	446,462
1951	Lloyd Mangrum	26,088	1967	Jack Nicklaus	188,988	1983	Hal Sutton	426,668
1952	Julius Boros	37,032	1968	Billy Casper	205,168	1984	Tom Watson	476,260
1953	Lew Worsham	34,002	1969	Frank Beard	175,223	1985	Curtis Strange	542,321
1954	Bob Toski	65,819	1970	Lee Trevino	157,037	1986	Greg Norman	653,296
1955	Julius Boros	65,121	1971	Jack Nicklaus	244,490	1987	Curtis Strange	925,941
1956	Ted Kroll	72,835	1972	Jack Nicklaus	320,542	1988	Curtis Strange	1,147,644
1957	Dick Mayer	65,835	1973	Jack Nicklaus	308,362	1989	Tom Kite	1,395,278
1958	Arnold Palmer	42,407	1974	Johnny Miller	353,201	1990	Greg Norman	1,165,477
1959	Art Wall Jr.	53,167	1975	Jack Nicklaus	323,149	1991	Corey Pavin	979,430
1960	Arnold Palmer	75,262	1976	Jack Nicklaus	266,438	1992	Fred Couples	1,344,188
1961	Gary Player	64,540	1977	Tom Watson	310,653			

LPGA Leading Money Winners

Year	Player	Dollars	Year	Player	Dollars	Year	Player	Dollars
1954	Patty Berg	$16,011	1967	Kathy Whitworth	$32,937	1980	Beth Daniel	$231,000
1955	Patty Berg	16,492	1968	Kathy Whitworth	48,379	1981	Beth Daniel	206,977
1956	Marlene Hagge	20,235	1969	Carol Mann	49,152	1982	JoAnne Carner	310,399
1957	Patty Berg	16,272	1970	Kathy Whitworth	30,235	1983	JoAnne Carner	291,404
1958	Beverly Hanson	12,629	1971	Kathy Whitworth	41,181	1984	Betsy King	266,771
1959	Betsy Rawls	26,774	1972	Kathy Whitworth	65,063	1985	Nancy Lopez	416,472
1960	Louise Suggs	16,892	1973	Kathy Whitworth	82,854	1986	Pat Bradley	492,021
1961	Mickey Wright	22,236	1974	JoAnne Carner	87,094	1987	Ayako Okamoto	466,034
1962	Mickey Wright	21,641	1975	Sandra Palmer	94,805	1988	Sherri Turner	347,255
1963	Mickey Wright	31,269	1976	Judy Rankin	150,734	1989	Betsy King	654,132
1964	Mickey Wright	29,800	1977	Judy Rankin	122,890	1990	Beth Daniel	863,578
1965	Kathy Whitworth	28,658	1978	Nancy Lopez	189,813	1991	Pat Bradley	763,118
1966	Kathy Whitworth	33,517	1979	Nancy Lopez	215,987	1992	Dottie Mochrie	693,335

Rifle and Pistol Individual Championships in 1993

Source: National Rifle Association

National Outdoor Rifle and Pistol Championships

Pistol—Steve Reiter, Daly City, Cal., 2660-123X.
Civilian Pistol—Richard Rodriquez, Stafford, Va., 2647-125X.
Woman Pistol—Delores J. Williams, Summersville, W.Va., 2567-63X.
Smallbore Rifle Prone—Carolyn D. Millard-Sparks, Atlanta, Ga., 6370-442X.
Smallbore Rifle NRA 3-Position—James Meredith, Columbus, Ga., 2267-82X.
Civilian Smallbore Rifle NRA 3-Position—Kenneth M. Benyo, New Tripoli, Pa., 2254-82X.
Woman Smallbore Rifle NRA 3-Position—Kristin Ann Peterson, Ft. Benning, Ga., 2178-69X.
High Power Rifle—G. David Tubb, Canandian, Tex., 2383-110X.
Woman High Power Rifle—Nancy H. Tompkins-Gallagher, Prescott, Ariz., 2368-105X.

National Indoor Rifle and Pistol Championships

Smallbore Rifle 4-Position—Karen E. Monez, Colorado Springs, Col., 800.
Smallbore Rifle NRA 3-Position—Glenn Dubis, Ft. Benning, Ga., 1190.
Woman Smallbore Rifle NRA 3-Position—Tammie Deangelis, Colorado Springs, Col., 1176.
Smallbore Rifle International—Michael E. Anti, Columbus, Ga., 1185.
Woman Smallbore Rifle International—Kristin Ann Peterson, Columbus, Ga., 1174.
Air Rifle—Ann Pfiffner, Dubuque, Ia., 593.
Conventional Pistol—Gregory J. Derr, Marshfield, Mass., 888.
Woman Conventional Pistol—Kathy S. Chatterton, Millburn, N.J., 864.
International Free Pistol—Donald Carl, Ft. Benning, Ga., 547.
Woman International Free Pistol—Dorothea Martin, Detroit, Mich., 473.
International Standard Pistol—Christopher Alvarez, Woodinville, Wash., 572.
Woman International Standard Pistol—Kathie Woolard, Point Richmond, Cal., 534.
Air Pistol—James Henderson, Ft. Benning, Ga., 574.
Woman Air Pistol—Rhonda Barush, Columbus, Ga., 559.

NRA Bianchi Cup National Action Pistol Championships

Action Pistol—Bruce Piatt, Montvale, N.J., 1920-170X.
Woman Action Pistol—Judith Woolley, Plains, Mont., 1898-148X.
Junior Action Pistol—Chad Dietrich, Bismarck, N.D., 1908-154X.

American Power Boat Assn. Gold Cup Champions

Year	Boat	Driver	Year	Boat	Driver
1975	Pay 'N Pak	George Henley	1984	Atlas Van Lines	Chip Hanauer
1976	Miss U.S.	Tom D'Eath	1985	Miller American	Chip Hanauer
1977	Atlas Van Lines	Bill Muncey	1986	Miller American	Chip Hanauer
1978	Atlas Van Lines	Bill Muncey	1987	Miller American	Chip Hanauer
1979	Atlas Van Lines	Bill Muncey	1988	Miller American	Chip Hanauer
1980	Miss Budweiser	Dean Chenoweth	1989	Miss Budweiser	Tom D'Eath
1981	Miss Budweiser	Dean Chenoweth	1990	Miss Budweiser	Tom D'Eath
1982	Atlas Van Lines	Chip Hanauer	1991	Winston Eagle	Mark Tate
1983	Atlas Van Lines	Chip Hanauer	1992	Miss Budweiser	Chip Hanauer
			1993	Miss Budweiser	Chip Hanauer

Notable Sports Personalities

Henry Aaron, b. 1934: Milwaukee-Atlanta outfielder hit record 755 home runs; led NL 4 times.
Kareem Abdul-Jabbar, b. 1947: Milwaukee, L.A. Lakers center; MVP 6 times; leading scorer twice; playoff MVP, 1971, 1985; all-time leading NBA scorer.
Grover Cleveland Alexander, (1887-1950): pitcher won 374 NL games; pitched 16 shutouts, 1916.
Muhammad Ali, b. 1942: 3-time heavyweight champion.
Ken Anderson, b. 1949: Cinn. Bengals quarterback led AFC in passing 4 times.
Mario Andretti, b. 1940; won Indy 500, 1969; Grand Prix champ, 1978.
Eddie Arcaro, b. 1916: jockey rode 4,779 winners including the Kentucky Derby 5 times; the Preakness and Belmont Stakes 6 times each.
Henry Armstrong, (1912-1988): boxer held feather-, welter-, light-weight titles simultaneously, 1937-38.
Arthur Ashe, (1943-1993): U.S. singles champ, 1968, Wimbledon champ, 1975.
Red Auerbach, b. 1917: coached Boston Celtics to 9 NBA championships.
Ernie Banks, b. 1931: Chicago Cubs slugger hit 512 NL homers: twice MVP.
Roger Bannister, b. 1929: Briton ran first sub 4-minute mile, May 6, 1954.
Rick Barry, b. 1944: NBA scoring leader, 1967; ABA, 1969.
Sammy Baugh, b. 1914: Washington Redskins quarterback held numerous records upon retirement after 16 pro seasons.
Elgin Baylor, b. 1934: L.A. Lakers forward; 1st team all-star 10 times.
Boris Becker, b. 1967: German tennis star; won U.S. Open 1989; Wimbledon champ 3 times.
Jean Beliveau, b. 1931: Montreal Canadiens center scored 507 goals; twice MVP.
Johnny Bench, b. 1947: Cincinnati Reds catcher; MVP twice; led league in home runs twice, RBIs 3 times.
Patty Berg, b. 1918: won over 80 golf tournaments: AP Woman Athlete-of-the-Year 3 times.
Yogi Berra, b. 1925: N.Y. Yankees catcher; MVP 3 times; played in 14 World Series.
Raymond Berry, b. 1933: Baltimore Colts receiver caught 631 passes.
Matt Biondi, b. 1965: swimmer won 5 gold medals at 1988 Olympics.
Larry Bird, b. 1956: Boston Celtics forward; chosen MVP 1984-86, playoff MVP, 1984, 1986.
George Blanda, b. 1927: quarterback, kicker; 26 years as active player, scoring record 2,002 points.
Wade Boggs, b. 1958: AL batting champ, 1983, 1985-88.
Bjorn Borg, b. 1956: led Swedon to first Davis Cup, 1975; Wimbledon champion, 5 times.
Mike Bossy, b.1957; N.Y. Islanders right wing scored over 50 goals 8 times.
Ray Bourque, b. 1960: Boston Bruins defenseman won Norris Trophy 4 times.
Terry Bradshaw, b. 1948; Pittsburgh Steelers quarterback led team to 4 Super Bowl titles.
George Brett, b. 1953: Kansas City Royals infielder led AL in batting, 1976, 1980, 1990; MVP, 1980.
Lou Brock, b. 1939: St. Louis Cardinals outfielder stole record 118 bases, 1974; led NL 8 times.
Jimmy Brown, b. 1936: Cleveland Browns fullback ran for 12,312 career yards; MVP 3 times.
Paul Brown, (1908-1991), football owner, coach; led Cleveland Browns to 3 NFL championships.
Paul "Bear" Bryant, (1913-1983), college football coach with 323 victories.
Sergei Bubka, b. 1963: Ukrainian pole vaulter; first to clear 20 feet both indoors and outdoors.
Maria Bueno, b. 1939: U.S. singles champ 4 times; Wimbledon champ 3 times.
Dick Butkus, b. 1942: Chicago Bears linebacker twice chosen best NFL defensive player.
Dick Button, b. 1929: figure skater won 1948, 1952 Olympic gold medals; world titlist, 1948-52.
Walter Camp, (1859-1925): Yale football player, coach, athletic director; established many rules; promoted All-America designations.
Roy Campanella, (1921-1993): Brooklyn Dodgers catcher; MVP 3 times.
Earl Campbell, b. 1955: NFL running back; NFL MVP 1978-1980.
Rod Carew, b. 1945: AL infielder won 7 batting titles; MVP, 1977.
Steve Carlton, b. 1944: NL pitcher won 20 games 5 times, Cy Young award 4 times.
Billy Casper, b. 1931: PGA Player-of-the-Year 3 times; U.S. Open champ twice.
Wilt Chamberlain, b. 1936: center was NBA leading scorer 7 times; MVP 4 times.
Bobby Clarke, b. 1949: Philadelphia Flyers center led team to 2 Stanley Cup championships: MVP 3 times.
Roger Clemens, b. 1962: Boston Red Sox pitcher; AL MVP 1986; Cy Young Award 1986, 1987, 1991.
Roberto Clemente, (1934-1972): Pittsburgh Pirates outfielder won 4 batting titles; MVP, 1966.
Ty Cobb, (1886-1961): Detroit Tigers outfielder had record .367 lifetime batting average, 12 batting titles.
Sebastian Coe, b. 1956: Briton won Olympic 1,500-meter run, 1980, 1984.
Nadia Comaneci, b. 1961: Romanian gymnast won 3 gold medals, achieved 7 perfect scores, 1976 Olympics.
Maureen Connolly, (1934-1969): won tennis "grand slam," 1953; AP Woman-Athlete-of-the-Year 3 times.
Jimmy Connors, b. 1952: U.S. singles champ 5 times; Wimbledon champ twice.
James J. Corbett, (1866-1933): heavyweight champion, 1892-97; credited with being the first "scientific" boxer.
Angel Cordero, b. 1942: leading money winner, 1976, 1982-83; rode 3 Kentucky Derby winners.
Margaret Smith Court, b. 1942: Australian won U.S. singles championship 5 times; Wimbledon champ 3 times.
Bob Cousy, b. 1928: Boston Celtics guard led team to 6 NBA championships: MVP, 1957.
Andre Dawson, b. 1954: slugger led NL in home runs, MVP, 1987.
Dizzy Dean, (1911-1974): colorful pitcher for St. Louis Cardinals "Gashouse Gang" in the 30s; MVP, 1934.
Jack Dempsey, (1895-1983); heavyweight champion, 1919-26.
Eric Dickerson, b. 1960: running back ran for NFL record 2,105 yds., 1984; led NFC 3 times, AFC twice.
Joe DiMaggio, b. 1914: N.Y. Yankees outfielder hit safely in record 56 consecutive games, 1941; MVP 3 times.
Leo Durocher, (1906-1991); manager won 3 NL pennants.
Stefan Edberg, b. 1966; U.S. singles champ 1991, 1992; Wimbledon champ 1988, 1990.
Gertrude Ederle, b. 1906: first woman to swim English Channel, broke existing men's record, 1926.
Julius Erving, b. 1950: MVP and leading scorer in ABA 3 times; NBA MVP, 1981.
Phil Esposito, b. 1942: NHL scoring leader 5 times.
Chris Evert, b. 1954: U.S. singles champ 6 times, Wimbledon champ 3 times.
Patrick Ewing, b. 1962: center led Georgetown Univ. to 1984 NCAA championship.
Ray Ewry, (1873-1937): track and field star won 8 gold medals, 1900, 1904, and 1908 Olympics.
Nick Faldo, 1957: British golfer won Masters, 1989-90; British Open 3 times.
Juan Fangio, b. 1911: World Grand Prix champion 5 times.
Bob Feller, b. 1918: Cleveland Indians pitcher won 266 games; pitched 3 no-hitters, 12 one-hitters.
Peggy Fleming, b. 1948: world figure skating champion, 1966-68; gold medalist 1968 Olympics.
Whitey Ford, b. 1928: N.Y. Yankees pitcher won record 10 World Series games.
Dick Fosbury, b. 1947: high jumper won 1968 Olympic gold medal; developed the "Fosbury Flop."
Jimmie Foxx, (1907-1967): Red Sox, Athletics slugger; MVP 3 times; triple crown, 1933.
A.J. Foyt, b. 1935: won Indy 500 4 times; U.S. Auto Club champ 7 times.
Joe Frazier, b. 1944: heavyweight champion, 1970-73.
Lou Gehrig, (1903-1941): N.Y. Yankees 1st baseman played record 2,130 consecutive games; MVP, 1936.
George Gervin, b. 1952: leading NBA scorer, 1978-80, 1982.
Althea Gibson, b. 1927: twice U.S. and Wimbledon singles champ.
Bob Gibson, b. 1935: St. Louis Cardinals pitcher won Cy Young award twice; struck out 3,117 batters.
Frank Gifford, b. 1930: N.Y. Giants back; MVP, 1956.
Dwight Gooden, b. 1964: N.Y. Mets pitcher was NL Rookie of Year, 1984; Cy Young award, 1985.
Steffi Graf, b. 1969: German won tennis "grand slam," 1988; U.S. champ 1988, 1989, 1993; Wimbledon champ 5 times.
Otto Graham, b. 1921: Cleveland Browns quarterback; all-pro 44 times.
Red Grange, (1903-1991): All-America at Univ. of Illinois 1923-25; played for Chicago Bears, 1925-35.
Joe Greene, b. 1946: Pittsburgh Steelers lineman; twice NFL outstanding defensive player.

Wayne Gretzky, b. 1961: Edmonton Oilers center scored record 92 goals, 212 pts., 1982; MVP, 1980-87, 1989.
Florence Griffith Joyner, b. 1959: sprinter won 3 gold medals at 1988 Olympics.
Lefty Grove, (1900-1975): pitcher won 300 AL games; 20-game winner 8 times.
Tony Gwynn, b. 1960: NL batting champ, 1984, 1987-1989.
Walter Hagen, (1892-1969): won PGA championship 5 times. British Open 4 times.
George Halas, (1895-1983); founder-coach of Chicago Bears; won 5 NFL championships.
Bill Hartack, b. 1932: jockey rode 5 Kentucky Derby winners.
John Havlicek, b. 1940: Boston Celtics forward scored over 26,000 NBA points.
Rickey Henderson, b. 1958; AL outfielder stole record 130 bases, 1982, record lifetime steals; AL MVP, 1990.
Sonja Henie, (1912-1969): world champion figure skater, 1927-36; Olympic gold medalist, 1928, 1932, 1936.
Ben Hogan, b. 1912: won 4 U.S. Open championships, 2 PGA, 2 Masters.
Rogers Hornsby, (1896-1963): NL 2d baseman batted record .424 in 1924; twice won triple crown; batting leader, 1920-25.
Paul Hornung, b. 1935: Green Bay Packers runner-placekicker scored record 176 points, 1960.
Gordie Howe, b. 1928: hockey forward; NHL MVP 6 times.
Carl Hubbell, (1903-1988): N.Y. Giants pitcher; 20-game winner 5 consecutive years, 1933-37.
Bobby Hull, b. 1939: NHL all-star 10 times.
Brett Hull, b. 1964; St. Louis Blues forward led NHL in goals, 1990-92; MVP 1991.
Catfish Hunter, b. 1946: pitched perfect game, 1968; 20-game winner 5 times.
Don Hutson, b. 1913: Green Bay Packers receiver caught 99 NFL touchdown passes.
Reggie Jackson, b. 1946: slugger led AL in home runs 4 times; MVP, 1973; hit 5 World Series home runs, 1977.
Jack Johnson, (1878-1946): heavyweight champion, 1910-15.
Magic Johnson, b. 1959: NBA MVP 1987, 1989, 1990. Playoff MVP 1980, 1982, 1987.
Walter Johnson, (1887-1946): Washington Senators pitcher won 413 games.
Bobby Jones, (1902-1971); won "grand slam of golf" 1930; U.S. Amateur champ 5 times, U.S. Open champ 4 times.
Deacon Jones, b. 1938: L.A. Rams lineman; twice NFL outstanding defensive player.
Michael Jordan, b. 1963: NBA leading scorer, 1987-93; MVP, 1988, 1991, 1992; Playoff MVP, 1991, 1992, 1993.
Jackie Joyner-Kersee, b. 1962; Olympic gold medalist in heptathlon, 1988, 1992.
Sonny Jurgensen, b. 1934: quarterback named all-pro 5 times.
Duke Kahanamoku, (1890-1968): swimmer won 1912, 1920 Olympic gold medals in 100-meter freestyle.
Harmon Killebrew, b. 1936: Minnesota Twins slugger led AL in home runs 6 times.
Jean Claude Killy, b. 1943: French skier won 3 1968 Olympic gold medals.
Ralph Kiner, b. 1922: Pittsburgh Pirates slugger led NL in home runs 7 consecutive years, 1946-52.
Billie Jean King, b. 1943: U.S. singles champ 4 times; Wimbledon champ 6 times.
Bob Knight, b. 1940: Indiana U. basketball coach lead team to NCAA championships, 1976, 1981, 1987.
Olga Korbut, b. 1955: Soviet gymnast won 3 1972 Olympic gold medals.
Sandy Koufax, b. 1935: Dodgers pitcher won Cy Young award 3 times; lowest ERA in NL, 1962-66; pitched 4 no-hitters, one a perfect game.
Guy Lafleur, b. 1951: forward led NHL in scoring 3 times; MVP, 1977, 1978.
Tom Landry, b. 1924: Dallas Cowboys head coach 1960-88.
Rod Laver, b. 1938: Australian won tennis "grand slam," 1962, 1969; Wimbledon champ 4 times.
Mario Lemieux, b. 1965: NHL leading scorer, 1988-89, 1992-93; MVP, 1988, 1993; Playoff MVP, 1991, 1992.
Ivan Lendl, b. 1960: U.S. singles champ, 1985-87.
Sugar Ray Leonard, b. 1956: former world welterweight champ.
Carl Lewis, b. 1961: track and field star won 8 Olympic gold medals in sprinting and the long jump.
Vince Lombardi, (1913-1970): Green Bay Packers coach led, team to 5 NFL championships and 2 Super Bowl victories.
Joe Louis, (1914-1981): heavyweight champion, 1937-49.
Sid Luckman, b. 1916: Chicago Bears quarterback led team to 4 NFL championships; MVP, 1943.
Connie Mack, (1862-1956): Philadelphia Athletics manager, 1901-50; won 9 pennants, 5 championships.
Bill Madlock, b. 1951: NL batting leader 4 times.
Moses Malone, b. 1955: NBA center was MVP 1979, 1982, 1983.
Mickey Mantle, b. 1931: N.Y. Yankees outfielder; triple crown, 1956; 18 World Series home runs.
Pete Maravich (1948-1988): guard scored NCAA record 44.2 ppg during collegiate career; led NBA in scoring, 1977.
Rocky Marciano, (1923-1969): heavyweight champion, 1952-56; retired undefeated.
Dan Marino, b. 1961: Miami Dolphins quarterback passed for NFL record 5,084 yds, 1984.
Roger Maris, (1934-1985): N.Y. Yankees outfielder hit record 61 home runs, 1961; MVP, 1960 and 1961.
Eddie Mathews, b. 1931: Milwaukee-Atlanta 3d baseman hit 512 career home runs.
Christy Mathewson, (1880-1925): N.Y. Giants pitcher won 373 games.
Bob Mathias, b. 1930: decathlon gold medalist, 1948, 1952.
Don Mattingly, b. 1961: N.Y. Yankees 1st baseman won 1984 AL batting title; MVP, 1985.
Willie Mays, b. 1931: N.Y.-S.F. Giants center fielder hit 660 home runs; twice MVP.
Willie McCovey, b. 1938: S.F. Giants slugger hit 521 home runs; led NL 3 times.
John McEnroe, b. 1959: U.S. singles champ, 1979-81, 1984; Wimbledon champ, 1981, 1983-84.
John McGraw, (1873-1934): N.Y. Giants manager led team to 10 pennants, 3 championships.
Mark Messier, center chosen NHL MVP, 1990; Conn Smythe Trophy, 1984.
George Mikan, b. 1924: Minn. Lakers center considered the best basketball player of the first half of the century.
Stan Mikita, b. 1940: Chicago Black Hawks center led NHL in scoring 4 times; MVP twice.
Joe Montana, b. 1956: QB was Super Bowl MVP, 1982, 1985, 1990.
Archie Moore, b. 1913: world light-heavyweight champion, 1952-62.
Howie Morenz, (1902-1937): Montreal Canadiens forward considered the best hockey player of the first half of the century.
Joe Morgan, b. 1943: National League MVP, 1975, 1976.
Thurman Munson, (1947-1979): N.Y. Yankees catcher; MVP, 1976.
Dale Murphy, b. 1956: outfielder chosen NL MVP 1982, 1983.
Stan Musial, b. 1920: St. Louis Cardinals star won 7 NL batting titles; MVP 3 times.
Bronko Nagurski, (1908-1990): Chicago Bears fullback and tackle; gained over 4,000 yds. rushing.
Joe Namath, b. 1943: quarterback led N.Y. Jets to 1969 Super Bowl title.
Martina Navratilova, b. 1956: Wimbledon champ 8 times, U.S. champ 1983-1984; 1986-87.
Byron Nelson, b. 1912: won 11 consecutive golf tournaments in 1945; twice Masters and PGA titlist.
Ernie Nevers, (1903-1976): Stanford star selected the best college fullback to play between 1919-1969.
John Newcombe, b. 1943: Australian twice U.S. singles champ; Wimbledon titlist 3 times.
Jack Nicklaus, b. 1940: PGA Player-of-the-Year, 1967, 1972; leading money winner 8 times; won Masters 6 times.
Chuck Noll, b. 1931: coach led Pittsburgh Steelers to 4 Super Bowl titles.
Paavo Nurmi, (1897-1973): Finnish distance runner won 6 Olympic gold medals, 1920, 1924, 1928.
Al Oerter, b. 1936: discus thrower won gold medal at 4 consecutive Olympics, 1956-68.
Bobby Orr, b. 1948: Boston Bruins defenseman; Norris Trophy 8 times; led NHL in scoring twice, assists 5 times.
Mel Ott, (1909-1958): N.Y. Giants outfielder hit 511 home runs; led NL 6 times.
Jesse Owens, (1913-1980): track and field star won 4 1936 Olympic gold medals.
Satchel Paige, (1906-1982): pitcher starred in Negro leagues, 1924-48; entered major leagues at age 42.
Arnold Palmer, b. 1929: golf's first $1 million winner; won 4 Masters, 2 British Opens.
Jim Palmer, b. 1945: Baltimore Orioles pitcher; Cy Young award 3 times; 20-game winner 7 times.
Floyd Patterson, b. 1935: twice heavyweight champion.
Walter Payton, b. 1954: Chicago Bears running back has most rushing yards in NFL history; leading NFC rusher, 1976-80.
Pele, b. 1940: Brazilian soccer star scored 1,281 goals during 22-year career.
Bob Pettit, b. 1932: first NBA player to score 20,000 points; twice NBA scoring leader.
Richard Petty, b. 1937: NASCAR national champ 7 times; 7-times Daytona 500 winner.
Laffit Pincay Jr., b. 1946: leading money-winning jockey, 1970-74, 1979.
Jacques Plante, (1929-1986): goalie, 7 Vezina trophies; first goalie to wear a mask in a game.

Kirby Puckett, b. 1961: Minn. Twins outfielder won AL Batting Title, 1989; led Al in hits, 1987-89, 1992.
Willis Reed, b. 1942: N.Y. Knicks center; MVP, 1970; playoff MVP, 1970, 1973.
Jerry Rice, b. 1962: S.F. 49ers receiver chosen 1989 Super Bowl MVP.
Jim Rice, b. 1953: Boston Red Sox outfielder led AL in home runs, 1977-78, 1983; MVP 1978.
Maurice Richard, b. 1921: Montreal Canadiens forward scored 544 regular season goals, 82 playoff goals.
Branch Rickey, (1881-1965): executive instrumental in breaking baseball's color barrier, 1947; initiated farm system, 1919.
Pat Riley, b. 1945: coached L.A. Lakers to 4 NBA championships.
Cal Ripken Jr., b. 1961: Baltimore Orioles shortstop; AL MVP 1983, 1991.
Oscar Robertson, b. 1938: guard averaged career 25.7 points per game; record 9,887 career assists; MVP, 1964.
Brooks Robinson, b. 1937: Baltimore Orioles 3d baseman played in 4 World Series; MVP, 1964.
Frank Robinson, b. 1935: slugger MVP in both NL and AL; triple crown winner, 1966; first black manager in majors.
Jackie Robinson, (1919-1972): broke baseball's color barrier with Brooklyn Dodgers, 1947; MVP, 1949.
Larry Robinson, b. 1951: NHL defenseman won Norris trophy, 1977, 1980.
Sugar Ray Robinson, (1920-1989): middleweight champion 5 times, welterweight champion.
Knute Rockne, (1888-1931): Notre Dame football coach, 1918-31; revolutionized game by stressing forward pass.
Pete Rose, b. 1941: won 3 NL batting titles; hit safely in 44 consecutive games, 1978; has most major league hits.
Wilma Rudolph, b. 1940: sprinter won 3 1960 Olympic gold medals.
Bill Russell, b. 1934: Boston Celtics center led team to 11 NBA titles; MVP 5 times; first black coach of major pro sports team.
Babe Ruth, (1895-1948): N.Y. Yankees outfielder hit 60 home runs, 1927; 714 lifetime; led AL 11 times.
Johnny Rutherford, b. 1938: auto racer won Indy 500 3 times.
Nolan Ryan, b. 1947: pitcher struck out record 383 batters, 1973; record 5,714 career; pitched record 7 no-hitters; won 324 ML games.
Bret Saberhagen, b. 1964: Pitcher won AL Cy Young award, 1985, 1989; WS MVP, 1985.
Gene Sarazen, b. 1902: won PGA championship 3 times, U.S. Open twice; developer of sand wedge.
Gale Sayers, b. 1943: Chicago Bears back twice led NFC in rushing.
Mike Schmidt, b. 1949: Phillies 3d baseman led NL in home runs, 1974-76, 1980-81, 1983-84, 1986; NL MVP, 1980, 1981, 1986.
Tom Seaver, b. 1944: pitcher won NL Cy Young award 3 times, won 311 major league games.
Monica Seles, b. 1973; U.S. Open champ 1991, 1992.
Bill Shoemaker, b. 1931: jockey rode 3 Kentucky Derby and 5 Belmont Stakes winners; leading career money winner.
Eddie Shore, (1902-1985): Boston Bruins defenseman; MVP 4 times, first-team all-star 7 times.
Al Simmons, (1902-1956): AL outfielder had lifetime .334 batting average.
O.J. Simpson, b. 1947: running back rushed for 2,003 yds., 1973; AFC leading rusher 4 times.
George Sisler, (1893-1973): St. Louis Browns 1st baseman had record 257 hits, 1920; batted .340 lifetime.
Billy Smith, b. 1950: N.Y. Islanders goalie led team to 4 Stanley Cup championships.
Sam Snead, b. 1912: PGA and Masters champ 3 times each.
Warren Spahn, b. 1921: pitcher won 363 NL games; 20-game winner 13 times; Cy Young award, 1957.
Tris Speaker, (1885-1958): AL outfielder batted .344 over 22 seasons; hit record 793 career doubles.
Mark Spitz, b. 1950: swimmer won 7 1972 Olympic gold medals.
Amos Alonzo Stagg, (1862-1965): coached Univ. of Chicago football team for 41 years, including 5 undefeated seasons; introduced huddle, man-in-motion, and end-around play.
Bart Starr, b. 1934: Green Bay Packers quarterback led team to 5 NFL titles and 2 Super Bowl victories.
Roger Staubach, b. 1942: Dallas Cowboys quarterback; leading NFC passer 5 times.
Casey Stengel, (1890-1975): managed Yankees to 10 pennants, 7 championships, 1949-60.
Jackie Stewart, b. 1939: Scot auto racer retired with 27 Grand Prix victories.
John L. Sullivan, (1858-1918): last bareknuckle heavyweight champion, 1882-1892.
Fran Tarkenton, b. 1940: quarterback holds career passing records for touchdowns, completions, yardage.
Lawrence Taylor, b. 1959; linebacker led N.Y. Giants to 2 Super Bowl titles; played in 10 Pro Bowls.
Gustavo Thoeni, b. 1951: Italian 4-time world alpine ski champ.
Jim Thorpe, (1888-1953): football All-America, 1911, 1912; won pentathlon and decathlon, 1912 Olympics.
Bill Tilden, (1893-1953): U.S. singles champ 7 times; played on 11 Davis Cup teams.
Y.A. Tittle, b. 1926: N.Y. Giants quarterback; MVP, 1961, 1963.
Lee Trevino, b. 1939: won the U.S. and British Open championships twice.
Bryan Trottier, b. 1956: center played on 6 Stanley Cup championship teams.
Wyomia Tyus, b. 1945: sprinter won 1964, 1968 Olympic 100-meter dash.
Johnny Unitas, b. 1933: Baltimore Colts quarterback passed for over 40,000 yds.; MVP, 1957, 1967.
Al Unser, b. 1939: Indy 500 winner, 4 times.
Bobby Unser, b. 1934: Indy 500 winner 3 times.
Norm Van Brocklin, (1926-1983); quarterback passed for game record 554 yds., 1951; MVP, 1960.
Honus Wagner, (1874-1955): Pittsburgh Pirates shortstop won 8 NL batting titles.
Tom Watson, b. 1949: golfer won British Open 5 times.
Johnny Weissmuller, (1903-1984); swimmer won 52 national championships, 5 Olympic gold medals; set 67 world records.
Jerry West, b. 1938: L.A. Lakers guard had career average 27 points per game; first team all-star 10 times.
Kathy Whitworth, b. 1939: women's golf leading money winner 8 times: first woman to earn over $300,000.
Ted Williams, b. 1918: Boston Red Sox outfielder won 6 batting titles; last major leaguer to hit over .400: .406 in 1941; .344 lifetime batting average.
Katarina Witt, b. 1965: German figure skater; won Olympic gold medal, 1984, 1988.
John Wooden, b. 1910: coached UCLA basketball team to 10 national championships.
Mickey Wright, b. 1935: won LPGA championship 4 times, Vare Trophy 5 times; twice AP Woman-Athlete-of-the-Year.
Carl Yastrzemski, b. 1939: Boston Red Sox slugger won 3 batting titles, triple crown, 1967.
Cy Young, (1867-1955): pitcher won record 511 major league games.
Babe Didrikson Zaharias, (1914-1956): track star won 2 1932 Olympic gold medals; won numerous golf tournaments.

Tour de France in 1993

On July 25, Miguel Indurain of Spain won the Tour de France, the world's most prestigious bicycle race, for the third consecutive year. His margin of victory in the 80th Tour de France was 4 minutes 59 seconds, and he completed the 21-day, 2,312-mile race in a total time of 95 hours, 57 minutes, 9 seconds. Tony Rominger of Switzerland finished second.

World Gymnastics Championships in 1993

Vitali Scherbo of Belarus won the men's all-around title at the World Gymnastics Championship in Birmingham, England. Scherbo also won the vault and parallel bars titles. Shannon Miller of Edmond, Okla., won the women's all-around title.

TRACK AND FIELD

World Track and Field Records

As of Sept. 1993

*Indicates pending record; some new records await confirmation. The International Amateur Atheletic Federation, the world body of track and field, recognizes only records in metric distances except for the mile.

Men's Records

Running

Event	Record	Holder	Country	Date	Where made
100 meters	**9.86 s.**	Carl Lewis	U.S.	Aug. 25, 1991	Tokyo
200 meters	**19.72 s.**	Pietro Mennea	Italy	Sept. 12, 1979	Mexico City
400 meters	**43.29 s.**	Butch Reynolds	U.S.	Aug. 16, 1988	Zurich
800 meters	**1 m., 41.73 s.**	Sebastian Coe	Gr. Britain	June 10, 1981	Florence, Italy
1,000 meters	**2 m., 12.18 s.**	Sebastian Coe	Gr. Britain	July 11, 1981	Oslo
1,500 meters	**3 m., 28.86 s.**	Noureddine Morceli	Algeria	Sept. 6, 1992	Rieti, Italy
1 mile	***3 m., 44.39 s.**	Noureddine Morceli	Algeria	Sept. 5, 1993	Rieti, Italy
2,000 meters	**4 m., 50.81 s.**	Said Aouita	Morocco	July 16, 1987	Paris
3,000 meters	**7 m., 28.96 s.**	Moses Kiptanui	Kenya	Aug. 16, 1992	Cologne
5,000 meters	**12 m., 58.39 s.**	Said Aouita	Morocco	July 22, 1987	Rome
10,000 meters	***26 m., 58.38 s.**	Yobes Ondieki	Kenya	July 10, 1993	Oslo
20,000 meters	**56 m., 55.6 s.**	Arturo Barrios	Mexico	May 30, 1991	France
25,000 meters	**1 hr., 13 m., 55.8 s.**	Toshihiko Seko	Japan	Mar. 22, 1981	New Zealand
3,000 meter stpl	**8 m., 02.08 s.**	Moses Kiptanui	Kenya	Aug. 19, 1992	Zurich
Marathon	**2 hr., 6 m., 50 s.**	Belayneh Densimo	Ethiopia	Apr. 17, 1988	Rotterdam

Hurdles

Event	Record	Holder	Country	Date	Where made
110 meters	***12.91 s.**	Colin Jackson	U.K.	Aug. 20, 1993	Stuttgart
400 meters	**46.78 s.**	Kevin Young	U.S.	Aug. 6, 1992	Barcelona

Relay Races

Event	Record	Holder	Country	Date	Where made
400 mtrs.	**37.40 s.**	(Marsh, Burrell, Mitchell, Lewis)	U.S.	Aug. 8, 1992	Barcelona
		(Drummond, Cason, Mitchell, Burrell)	U.S.	Aug. 22, 1993	Sheffield, Eng.
800 mtrs. (4×200)	**1m., 19.11 s.**	(Marsh, Burrell, Heard Lewis)	U.S.	Apr. 25, 1992	Philadelphia
1,600 mtrs. (4×400)	***2 m., 54.29 s.**	(Valmon, Watts, Johnson, Reynolds)	U.S.	Aug. 22, 1993	Sheffield, Eng.
3,200 mtrs. (4×800)	**7 m., 03.89 s.**	(Elliott, Cook, Cram, Coe)	Gr. Britain	Aug. 30, 1982	London

Field Events

Event	Record	Holder	Country	Date	Where made
High jump	***8 ft., ½ in.**	Javier Sotomayor	Cuba	July 27, 1993	Salamanca, Spain
Long jump	**29 ft., 4½ in.**	Mike Powell	U.S.	Aug. 30, 1992	Tokyo
Triple jump	**58 ft., 11½ in.**	Willie Banks	U.S.	June 16, 1985	Indianapolis
Pole vault	**20 ft., 1½ in.**	Sergei Bubka	Ukraine	Sept. 19, 1992	Tokyo
16 lb. shot put	**75 ft., 10¼ in.**	Randy Barnes	U.S.	May 20, 1990	Los Angeles
Discus	**243 ft.**	Juergen Schult	E. Germany	June 6, 1986	E. Germany
Javelin	***313 ft., 10 in.**	Jan Zelezny	Czech Rep.	Aug. 29, 1993	Sheffield, Eng.
16 lb. hammer	**284 ft., 7 in.**	Yuri Sedykh	USSR	Aug. 30, 1986	Stuttgart
Decathlon	**8,891 pts.**	Dave O'Brien	U.S.	Sept. 4-5, 1992	Talence, France

Women's Records

Running

Event	Record	Holder	Country	Date	Where made
100 meters	**10.49 s.**	Florence Griffith Joyner	U.S.	July 16, 1988	Indianapolis
200 meters	**21.34 s.**	Florence Griffith Joyner	U.S.	Sept. 29, 1988	Seoul
400 meters	**47.60 s.**	Marita Koch	E. Germany	Oct. 6, 1985	Canberra
800 meters	**1 m., 53.28 s.**	Jarmila Kratochvilova	Czech.	July 26, 1983	Munich
1,000 meters	**2 m., 30.60 s.**	Tatyana Providokhina	USSR	Aug. 20, 1978	USSR
1,500 meters	***3 m., 50.56 s.**	Qu Yunxia	China	Sept. 11, 1993	Beijing
1 mile	**4 m., 15.61 s.**	Paula Ivan	Romania	July 10, 1989	Nice
2,000 meters	**5 m., 28.69 s.**	Maricica Puica	Romania	July 11, 1986	London
3,000 meters	***8 m., 06.11 s.**	Wang Junxia	China	Sept. 13, 1993	Beijing
5,000 meters	**14 m., 37.33 s.**	Ingrid Kristiansen	Norway	Aug. 5, 1986	Stockholm
10,000 meters	***29 m., 31.78 s.**	Wang Junxia	China	Sept. 8, 1993	Beijing
Marathon	**2 h., 21 m., 06 s.**	Ingrid Kristiansen	Norway	Apr. 21, 1985	London

Hurdles

Event	Record	Holder	Country	Date	Where made
100 meters	**12.21 s.**	Yordanka Donkova	Bulgaria	Aug. 21, 1988	Bulgaria
400 meters	***52.74 s.**	Sally Gunnell	U.K.	Aug. 19, 1993	Sheffield, Eng.

Field Events

Event	Record	Holder	Country	Date	Where made
High jump	**6 ft., 10¼ in.**	Stefka Kostadinova	Bulgaria	Aug. 30, 1987	Rome
Shot put	**74 ft., 3 in.**	Natalya Lisouskaya	USSR	June 7, 1987	Moscow
Long jump	**24 ft., 8¼ in.**	Galina Chistyakova	USSR	June 11, 1988	Leningrad
Triple Jump	***49 ft., 6¼ in.**	Ana Biryukova	Russia	Aug. 21, 1993	Sheffield, Eng.
Discus	**252 ft.**	Gabriele Reinsch	E. Germany	July 9, 1988	E. Germany
Javelin	**262 ft., 5 in.**	Petra Felke	E. Germany	Sept. 9, 1988	Potsdam
Heptathlon	**7,291 pts.**	Jackie Joyner-Kersee	U.S.	Sept. 23-24, 1988	Seoul

Relay Races

400 mtrs. (4×100)	**41.37 s.**	National team	E. Germany	Oct. 6, 1985	Canberra
800 mtrs. (4×200)	**1 m., 28.15 s.**	National team	E. Germany	Aug. 9, 1980	E. Germany
1,600 mtrs. (4×400)	**3 m., 15.18 s.**	National team	USSR	Oct. 1, 1988	Seoul
3,200 mtrs. (4×800)	**7 m., 50.17 s.**	National team	USSR	Aug. 5, 1984	Moscow

World Track and Field Indoor Records

As of Sept. 1993

The International Amateur Athletic Federation began recognizing world indoor track and field records as official on January 1, 1987. Prior to that, there were only unofficial world indoor bests. World indoor bests set prior to January 1, 1987, are subject to approval as world records providing they meet the prescribed IAAF world records criteria, including drug testing. To be accepted as a world indoor record, a performance must meet the same criteria as a world record outdoors except that a track performance can not be set on an indoor track larger than 200 meters. *Record pending.

Men

Event	Record	Holder	Country	Date	Where made
50 meters	**5.61**	Manfred Kokot	E. Germany	Feb. 4, 1973	E. Berlin
60 meters	**6.41**	Andre Cason	U.S.	Feb. 14, 1992	Madrid
200 meters	**20.36**	Bruno Marie-Rose	France	Feb. 22, 1987	Lievin, France
400 meters	**45.02**	Danny Everett	U.S.	Feb. 2, 1992	Germany
800 meters	**1:44.84**	Paul Ereng	Kenya	Mar. 4, 1989	Budapest
1,000 meters	**2:15.26**	Noureddine Morceli	Algeria	Feb. 22, 1992	Birmingham, England
1,500 meters	**3:34.16**	Noureddine Morceli	Algeria	Feb. 28, 1991	Seville, Spain
1 Mile	**3:49.78**	Eamonn Coghlan	Ireland	Feb. 27, 1983	E. Rutherford, N.J.
3,000 meters	**7:37.31**	Moses Kiptanui	Kenya	Feb. 20, 1992	Seville, Spain
5,000 meters	**13:20.40**	Suleiman Nyambui	Tanzania	Feb. 6, 1981	New York
50-meter hurdles	**6.25**	Mark McKoy	Canada	Jan. 27, 1985	Rosemont, Ill.
60-meter hurdles	**7.36**	Greg Foster	U.S.	Jan. 16, 1987	Los Angeles
High Jump	**7 ft. 11½ in.**	Javier Sotomayor	Cuba	Mar. 4, 1989	Budapest
Pole Vault	***20 ft. 2 in.**	Sergei Bubka	Ukraine	Feb. 21, 1993	Ukraine
Long Jump	**28 ft. 10¼ in.**	Carl Lewis	U.S.	Feb. 27, 1984	New York
Triple Jump	**58 ft. 3¼ in.**	Mike Conley	U.S.	Feb. 27, 1987	New York
Shot Put	**74 ft. 4¼ in.**	Randy Barnes	U.S.	Jan. 20, 1989	Los Angeles

Women

50 meters	***6.00**	Irina Privalova	Russia	Feb. 2, 1993	Moscow
60 meters	***6.95**	Gail Devers	U.S.	Mar. 12, 1993	Toronto
200 meters	**21.87**	Merlene Ottey	Jamaica	Feb. 13, 1993	Lievin, France
400 meters	**49.59**	Jarmila Kratochvilova	Czechoslovakia	Mar. 7, 1982	Milan
800 meters	**1:56.40**	Christine Wachtel	E. Germany	Feb. 13, 1988	Vienna
1,000 meters	**2:34.67**	Lilia Nurutdinova	Russia	Feb. 7, 1992	Moscow
1,500 meters	**4:00.27**	Doina Melinte	Romania	Feb. 9, 1990	E. Rutherford, N.J.
1 Mile	**4:17.13**	Doina Melinte	Romania	Feb. 9, 1990	E. Rutherford, N.J.
3,000 meters	**8:33.82**	Elly Van Hulst	Netherlands	Feb. 8, 1986	England
5,000 meters	**15:03.17**	Liz McColgan	Scotland	Feb. 22, 1992	Birmingham, England
50-meter hurdles	**6:58**	Cornelia Oschkenat	E. Germany	Feb. 20, 1988	Berlin
60-meter hurdles	***7.63**	Lyudmila Narozhilenko	Russia	Mar. 4, 1993	Seville, Spain
High Jump	**6 ft. 9½ in.**	Heike Henkel	Germany	Feb. 8, 1992	Germany
Long Jump	**24 ft. 2¼ in.**	Heike Dreschler	E. Germany	Feb. 13, 1988	Vienna
Triple Jump	**47 ft. 4½ in.**	Inessa Kravets	USSR	Mar. 9, 1991	Seville, Spain
Shot Put	**73 ft. 10 in.**	Helena Fibingerova	Czechoslovakia	Feb. 19, 1977	Czech.

World Track & Field Championships in 1993

Stuttgart, Germany, Aug. 14-22, 1993

Men

100 Meters —Linford Christie, Gt. Britain. **Time—0:09.87.**
200 Meters—Frank Fredericks, Namibia. **Time—0:19.85.**
400 Meters—Michael Johnson, U.S. **Time—0:43.65.**
800 Meters—Paul Ruto, Kenya. **Time—1:44.71.**
1,500 Meters—Noureddine Morceli, Algeria. **Time—3:34.24.**
3,000-Meter Steeplechase—Moses Kiptanui, Kenya. **Time — 8:06.36.**
5,000 Meters—Ismael Kirui, Kenya. **Time—13:02.75.**
10,000 Meters—Haile Gebresilasie, Ethiopia. **Time—27:46.02.**
Marathon—Mark Plaatjes, U.S. **Time—2:13.57.**
400-Meter Relay—U.S. **Time—0:37.48.**
1,600-Meter Relay—U.S. **Time—2:54.29.**
110-Meter Hurdles—Colin Jackson, Gt. Britain. **Time—0:12.91.**
400-Meter Hurdles—Kevin Young, U.S. **Time—0:47.18.**
High Jump—Javier Sotomayor, Cuba. **7 Ft. 10½ in.**
Pole Vault—Sergei Bubka, Ukraine. **19 Ft. 8¼ in.**
Long Jump—Mike Powell, U.S. **28 Ft. 2¼ in.**
Triple Jump—Mike Conley, U.S. **58 Ft. 7¼ in.**
Shot Put—Werner Guenthor, Switzerland. **72 Ft. 1 in.**
Discus—Lars Riedel, Germany. **222 Ft. 2 in.**
Javelin—Jan Zelezny, Czech Rep. **282 Ft. 1 in.**
Decathlon—Dan O'Brien, U.S. **8,817 Pts.**

Women

100 Meters—Gail Devers, U.S. **Time—0:10.82.**
200 Meters—Merlene Ottey, Jamaica. **Time—0:21.98.**
400 Meters—Jearl Miles, U.S. **Time—0:49.82.**
800 Meters—Maria Mutola, Mozambique. **Time—1:55.43.**
1,500 Meters—Dong Liu, China. **Time—4:00.50.**
3,000 Meters—Yunxia Qu, China. **Time—8:28.71.**
400-Meter Relay—Russia. **Time—0:41.49.**
1,600-Meter Relay—U.S. **Time—3:16.71.**
100-Meter Hurdles—Gail Devers, U.S. **Time—0:12.46.**
400-Meter Hurdles—Sally Gunnell, Gt. Britain. **Time—0:52.74.**
High Jump—Ioamnet Quintero, Cuba. **6 Ft. 6¼ in.**
Long Jump—Heike Drechsler, Germany. **23 Ft. 4 in.**
Triple Jump—Ana Biryukova, Russia. **49 Ft. 6¼ in.**
Shot Put—Zhihong Huang, China. **67 Ft. 6 in.**
Discus—Olga Burova, Russia. **221 Ft. 1 in.**
Javelin—Trine Hattestad, Norway. **227 Ft.**
Heptathlon—Jackie Joyner-Kersee, U.S. **6,837 Pts.**

TENNIS

U.S. Open Champions

Men's Singles

Year	Champion	Final opponent
1910	William Larned	T. C. Bundy
1911	William Larned	Maurice McLoughlin
1912	Maurice McLoughlin	Wallace Johnson
1913	Maurice McLoughlin	Richard Williams
1914	Richard Williams	Maurice McLoughlin
1915	William Johnston	Maurice McLoughlin
1916	Richard Williams	William Johnston
1917	R. L. Murray	N. W. Niles
1918	R. L. Murray	Bill Tilden
1919	William Johnston	Bill Tilden
1920	Bill Tilden	William Johnston
1921	Bill Tilden	Wallace Johnson
1922	Bill Tilden	William Johnston
1923	Bill Tilden	William Johnston
1924	Bill Tilden	William Johnston
1925	Bill Tilden	William Johnston
1926	Rene Lacoste	Jean Borotra
1927	Rene Lacoste	Bill Tilden
1928	Henri Cochet	Francis Hunter
1929	Bill Tilden	Francis Hunter
1930	John Doeg	Francis Shields
1931	H. Ellsworth Vines	George Lott
1932	H. Ellsworth Vines	Henri Cochet
1933	Fred Perry	John Crawford
1934	Fred Perry	Wilmer Allison
1935	Wilmer Allison	Sidney Wood
1936	Fred Perry	Don Budge
1937	Don Budge	Baron G. von Cramm
1938	Don Budge	C. Gene Mako
1939	Robert Riggs	S. Welby Van Horn
1940	Don McNeill	Robert Riggs
1941	Robert Riggs	F. L. Kovacs
1942	F. R. Schroeder Jr.	Frank Parker
1943	Joseph Hunt	Jack Kramer
1944	Frank Parker	William Talbert
1945	Frank Parker	William Talbert
1946	Jack Kramer	Thomas Brown Jr.
1947	Jack Kramer	Frank Parker
1948	Pancho Gonzales	Eric Sturgess
1949	Pancho Gonzales	F. R. Schroeder Jr.
1950	Arthur Larsen	Herbert Flam
1951	Frank Sedgman	E. Victor Seixas Jr.
1952	Frank Sedgman	Gardnar Mulloy
1953	Tony Trabert	E. Victor Seixas Jr.
1954	E. Victor Seixas Jr.	Rex Hartwig
1955	Tony Trabert	Ken Rosewall
1956	Ken Rosewall	Lewis Hoad
1957	Malcolm Anderson	Ashley Cooper
1958	Ashley Cooper	Malcolm Anderson
1959	Neale A. Fraser	Alejandro Olmedo
1960	Neale A. Fraser	Rod Laver
1961	Roy Emerson	Rod Laver
1962	Rod Laver	Roy Emerson
1963	Rafael Osuna	F. A. Froehling 3d
1964	Roy Emerson	Fred Stolle
1965	Manuel Santana	Cliff Drysdale
1966	Fred Stolle	John Newcombe
1967	John Newcombe	Clark Graebner
1968	Arthur Ashe	Tom Okker
1969	Rod Laver	Tony Roche
1970	Ken Rosewall	Tony Roche
1971	Stan Smith	Jan Kodes
1972	Ilie Nastase	Arthur Ashe
1973	John Newcombe	Jan Kodes
1974	Jimmy Connors	Ken Rosewall
1975	Manuel Orantes	Jimmy Connors
1976	Jimmy Connors	Bjorn Borg
1977	Guillermo Vilas	Jimmy Connors
1978	Jimmy Connors	Bjorn Borg
1979	John McEnroe	Vitas Gerulaitis
1980	John McEnroe	Bjorn Borg
1981	John McEnroe	Bjorn Borg
1982	Jimmy Connors	Ivan Lendl
1983	Jimmy Connors	Ivan Lendl
1984	John McEnroe	Ivan Lendl
1985	Ivan Lendl	John McEnroe
1986	Ivan Lendl	Miloslav Mecir
1987	Ivan Lendl	Mats Wilander
1988	Mats Wilander	Ivan Lendl
1989	Boris Becker	Ivan Lendl
1990	Pete Sampras	Andre Agassi
1991	Stefan Edberg	Jim Courier
1992	Stefan Edberg	Pete Sampras
1993	Pete Sampras	Cedric Pioline

Women's Singles

Year	Champion	Final opponent
1926	Molla B. Mallory	Elizabeth Ryan
1927	Helen Wills	Betty Nuthall
1928	Helen Wills	Helen Jacobs
1929	Helen Wills	M. Watson
1930	Betty Nuthall	L. A. Harper
1931	Helen Wills Moody	E. B. Whittingstall
1932	Helen Jacobs	Carolin A. Babcock
1933	Helen Jacobs	Helen Wills Moody
1934	Helen Jacobs	Sarah H. Palfrey
1935	Helen Jacobs	Sarah P. Fabyan
1936	Alice Marble	Helen Jacobs
1937	Anita Lizana	Jadwiga Jedrzejowska
1938	Alice Marble	Nancye Wynne
1939	Alice Marble	Helen Jacobs
1940	Alice Marble	Helen Jacobs
1941	Sarah Palfrey Cooke	Pauline Betz
1942	Pauline Betz	Louise Brough
1943	Pauline Betz	Louise Brough
1944	Pauline Betz	Margaret Osborne
1945	Sarah P. Cooke	Pauline Betz
1946	Pauline Betz	Doris Hart
1947	Louise Brough	Margaret Osborne
1948	Margaret Osborne duPont	Louise Brough
1949	Margaret Osborne duPont	Doris Hart
1950	Margaret Osborne duPont	Doris Hart
1951	Maureen Connolly	Shirley Fry
1952	Maureen Connolly	Doris Hart
1953	Maureen Connolly	Doris Hart
1954	Doris Hart	Louise Brough
1955	Doris Hart	Patricia Ward
1956	Shirley Fry	Althea Gibson
1957	Althea Gibson	Louise Brough
1958	Althea Gibson	Darlene Hard
1959	Maria Bueno	Christine Truman
1960	Darlene Hard	Maria Bueno
1961	Darlene Hard	Ann Haydon
1962	Margaret Smith	Darlene Hard
1963	Maria Bueno	Margaret Smith
1964	Maria Bueno	Carole Graebner
1965	Margaret Smith	Billie Jean Moffitt
1966	Maria Bueno	Nancy Richey
1967	Billie Jean King	Ann Haydon Jones
1968	Virginia Wade	Billie Jean King
1969	Margaret Court	Nancy Richey
1970	Margaret Court	Rosemary Casals
1971	Billie Jean King	Rosemary Casals
1972	Billie Jean King	Kerry Melville
1973	Margaret Court	Evonne Goolagong
1974	Billie Jean King	Evonne Goolagong
1975	Chris Evert	Evonne Goolagong
1976	Chris Evert	Evonne Goolagong
1977	Chris Evert	Wendy Turnbull
1978	Chris Evert	Pam Shriver
1979	Tracy Austin	Chris Evert Lloyd
1980	Chris Evert Lloyd	Hana Mandlikova
1981	Tracy Austin	Martina Navratilova
1982	Chris Evert Lloyd	Hana Mandlikova
1983	Martina Navratilova	Chris Evert Lloyd
1984	Martina Navratilova	Chris Evert Lloyd
1985	Hana Mandlikova	Martina Navratilova
1986	Martina Navratilova	Helena Sukova
1987	Martina Navratilova	Steffi Graf
1988	Steffi Graf	Gabriela Sabatini
1989	Steffi Graf	Martina Navratilova
1990	Gabriela Sabatini	Steffi Graf
1991	Monica Seles	Martina Navratilova
1992	Monica Seles	Arantxa Sanchez Vicario
1993	Steffi Graf	Helena Sukova

All-England Champions, Wimbledon

Men's Singles

Year	Champion	Final opponent	Year	Champion	Final opponent
1933	Jack Crawford	Ellsworth Vines	1966	Manuel Santana	Dennis Ralston
1934	Fred Perry	Jack Crawford	1967	John Newcombe	Wilhelm Bungert
1935	Fred Perry	Gottfried von Cramm	1968	Rod Laver	Tony Roche
1936	Fred Perry	Gottfried von Cramm	1969	Rod Laver	John Newcombe
1937	Donald Budge	Gottfried von Cramm	1970	John Newcombe	Ken Rosewall
1938	Donald Budge	Wilfred Austin	1971	John Newcombe	Stan Smith
1939	Bobby Riggs	Elwood Cooke	1972	Stan Smith	Ilie Nastase
1940-45	not held		1973	Jan Kodes	Alex Metreveli
1946	Yvon Petra	Geoff E. Brown	1974	Jimmy Connors	Ken Rosewall
1947	Jack Kramer	Tom P. Brown	1975	Arthur Ashe	Jimmy Connors
1948	Bob Falkenburg	John Bromwich	1976	Bjorn Borg	Ilie Nastase
1949	Ted Schroeder	Jaroslav Drobny	1977	Bjorn Borg	Jimmy Connors
1950	Budge Patty	Frank Sedgman	1978	Bjorn Borg	Jimmy Connors
1951	Dick Savitt	Ken McGregor	1979	Bjorn Borg	Roscoe Tanner
1952	Frank Sedgman	Jaroslav Drobny	1980	Bjorn Borg	John McEnroe
1953	Vic Seixas	Kurt Nielsen	1981	John McEnroe	Bjorn Borg
1954	Jaroslav Drobny	Ken Rosewall	1982	Jimmy Connors	John McEnroe
1955	Tony Trabert	Kurt Nielsen	1983	John McEnroe	Chris Lewis
1956	Lew Hoad	Ken Rosewall	1984	John McEnroe	Jimmy Connors
1957	Lew Hoad	Ashley Cooper	1985	Boris Becker	Kevin Curren
1958	Ashley Cooper	Neale Fraser	1986	Boris Becker	Ivan Lendl
1959	Alex Olmedo	Rod Laver	1987	Pat Cash	Ivan Lendl
1960	Neale Fraser	Rod Laver	1988	Stefan Edberg	Boris Becker
1961	Rod Laver	Chuck McKinley	1989	Boris Becker	Stefan Edberg
1962	Rod Laver	Martin Mulligan	1990	Stefan Edberg	Boris Becker
1963	Chuck McKinley	Fred Stolle	1991	Michael Stich	Boris Becker
1964	Roy Emerson	Fred Stolle	1992	Andre Agassi	Goran Ivanisevic
1965	Roy Emerson	Fred Stolle	1993	Pete Sampras	Jim Courier

Women's Singles

Year	Champion	Year	Champion	Year	Champion	Year	Champion
1946	Pauline Betz	1958	Althea Gibson	1970	Margaret Smith Court	1982	Martina Navratilova
1947	Margaret Osborne	1959	Maria Bueno	1971	Evonne Goolagong	1983	Martina Navratilova
1948	Louise Brough	1960	Maria Bueno	1972	Billie Jean King	1984	Martina Navratilova
1949	Louise Brough	1961	Angela Mortimer	1973	Billie Jean King	1985	Martina Navratilova
1950	Louise Brough	1962	Karen Hantze-Susman	1974	Chris Evert	1986	Martina Navratilova
1951	Doris Hart	1963	Margaret Smith	1975	Billie Jean King	1987	Martina Navratilova
1952	Maureen Connolly	1964	Maria Bueno	1976	Chris Evert	1988	Steffi Graf
1953	Maureen Connolly	1965	Margaret Smith	1977	Virginia Wade	1989	Steffi Graf
1954	Maureen Connolly	1966	Billie Jean King	1978	Martina Navratilova	1990	Martina Navratilova
1955	Louise Brough	1967	Billie Jean King	1979	Martina Navratilova	1991	Steffi Graf
1956	Shirley Fry	1968	Billie Jean King	1980	Evonne Goolagong	1992	Steffi Graf
1957	Althea Gibson	1969	Ann Haydon-Jones	1981	Chris Evert Lloyd	1993	Steffi Graf

Davis Cup Challenge Round

Year	Result	Year	Result	Year	Result
1900	United States 5, British Isles 0	1932	France 3, United States 2	1965	Australia 4, Spain 1
1901	(not played)	1933	Great Britain 3, France 2	1966	Australia 4, India 1
1902	United States 3, British Isles 2	1934	Great Britain 4, United States 1	1967	Australia 4, Spain 1
1903	British Isles 4, United States 1	1935	Great Britain 5, United States 0	1968	United States 4, Australia 1
1904	British Isles 5, Belgium 0	1936	Great Britain 3, Australia 2	1969	United States 5, Romania 0
1905	British Isles 5, United States 0	1937	United States 4, Great Britain 1	1970	United States 5, W. Germany 0
1906	British Isles 5, United States 0	1938	United States 3, Australia 2	1971	United States 3, Romania 2
1907	Australia 3, British Isles 2	1939	Australia 3, United States 2	1972	United States 3, Romania 2
1908	Australasia 3, United States 2	1940-45	(not played)	1973	Australia 5, United States 0
1909	Australasia 5, United States 0	1946	United States 5, Australia 0	1974	South Africa (default by India)
1910	(not played)	1947	United States 4, Australia 1	1975	Sweden 3, Czech. 2
1911	Australasia 5, United States 0	1948	United States 5, Australia 0	1976	Italy 4, Chile 1
1912	British Isles 3, Australasia 2	1949	United States 4, Australia 1	1977	Australia 3, Italy 1
1913	United States 3, British Isles 2	1950	Australia 4, United States 1	1978	United States 4, Great Britain 1
1914	Australasia 3, United States 2	1951	Australia 3, United States 2	1979	United States 5, Italy 0
1915-18	(not played)	1952	Australia 4, United States 1	1980	Czechoslovakia 4, Italy 1
1919	Australasia 4, British Isles 1	1953	Australia 3, United States 2	1981	United States 3, Argentina 1
1920	United States 5, Australasia 0	1954	United States 3, Australia 2	1982	United States 3, France, 0
1921	United States 5, Japan 0	1955	Australia 5, United States 0	1983	Australia 3, Sweden 1
1922	United States 4, Australasia 1	1956	Australia 5, United States 0	1984	Sweden 3, United States 0
1923	United States 4, Australasia 1	1957	Australia 3, United States 2	1985	Sweden 3, W. Germany 2
1924	United States 5, Australasia 0	1958	United States 3, Australia 2	1986	Australia 3, Sweden 2
1925	United States 5, France 0	1959	Australia 3, United States 2	1987	Sweden 5, India 0
1926	United States 4, France 1	1960	Australia 4, Italy 1	1988	W. Germany 4, Sweden 1
1927	France 3, United States 2	1961	Australia 5, Italy 0	1989	W. Germany 3, Sweden 2
1928	France 4, United States 1	1962	Australia 5, Mexico 0	1990	United States 3, Australia 2
1929	France 3, United States 2	1963	United States 3, Australia 2	1991	France 3, United States 1
1930	France 4, United States 1	1964	Australia 3, United States 2	1992	United States 3, Switzerland 1
1931	France 3, Great Britain 2				

French Open Champions

Year	Men	Women
1969	Rod Laver	Margaret Smith Court
1970	Jan Kodes	Margaret Smith Court
1971	Jan Kodes	Evonne Goolagong
1972	Andres Gimeno	Billie Jean King
1973	Ilie Nastase	Margaret Smith Court
1974	Bjorn Borg	Chris Evert
1975	Bjorn Borg	Chris Evert
1976	Adriano Panatta	Sue Barker
1977	Guillermo Vilas	Mima Jausovec
1978	Bjorn Borg	Virginia Ruzici
1979	Bjorn Borg	Chris Evert Lloyd
1980	Bjorn Borg	Chris Evert Lloyd
1981	Bjorn Borg	Hana Mandlikova
1982	Mats Wilander	Martina Navratilova
1983	Yannick Noah	Chris Evert Lloyd
1984	Ivan Lendl	Martina Navratilova
1985	Mats Wilander	Chris Evert Lloyd
1986	Ivan Lendl	Chris Evert Lloyd
1987	Ivan Lendl	Steffi Graf
1988	Mats Wilander	Steffi Graf
1989	Michael Chang	Arantxa Sanchez
1990	Andres Gomez	Monica Seles
1991	Jim Courier	Monica Seles
1992	Jim Courier	Monica Seles
1993	Sergi Bruguera	Steffi Graf

Australian Open Champions

Year*	Men	Women
1969	Rod Laver	Margaret Smith Court
1970	Arthur Ashe	Margaret Smith Court
1971	Ken Rosewall	Margaret Smith Court
1972	Ken Rosewall	Virginia Wade
1973	John Newcombe	Margaret Smith Court
1974	Jimmy Connors	Evonne Goolagong
1975	John Newcombe	Evonne Goolagong
1976	Mark Edmondson	Evonne Goolagong
1977	Roscoe Tanner	Kerry Reid
	Vitas Gerulaitis	Evonne Goolagong
1978	Guillermo Vilas	Chris O'Neill
1979	Guillermo Vilas	Barbara Jordan
1980	Brian Teacher	Hana Mandlikova
1981	Johan Kriek	Martina Navratilova
1982	Johan Kriek	Chris Evert Lloyd
1983	Mats Wilander	Martina Navratilova
1984	Mats Wilander	Chris Evert Lloyd
1985	Stefan Edberg	Martina Navratilova
1986	Not held	Not held
1987	Stefan Edberg	Hana Mandlikova
1988	Mats Wilander	Steffi Graf
1989	Ivan Lendl	Steffi Graf
1990	Ivan Lendl	Steffi Graf
1991	Boris Becker	Monica Seles
1992	Jim Courier	Monica Seles
1993	Jim Courier	Monica Seles

* Two tournaments were held in 1977 (Jan. & Dec.). Tournament moved back to Jan. in 1987, so no championship was decided in 1986.

AUTO RACING

Indianapolis 500 Winners

Year	Winner, Car	MPH
1911	Ray Harroun, Marmon Wasp	74.59
1912	Joe Dawson, National	78.72
1913	Jules Goux, Peugeot	75.933
1914	Rene Thomas, Delage	82.47
1915	Ralph DePalma, Mercedes	89.84
1916	Dario Resta, Peugeot	84.00
1917-18	race not held	
1919	Howdy Wilcox, Peugeot	88.05
1920	Gaston Chevrolet, Monroe	88.16
1921	Tommy Milton, Frontenac	89.62
1922	Jimmy Murphy, Murphy Special	94.48
1923	Tommy Milton, H.C.S.	90.95
1924	L.L. Corum-Joe Boyer, Duesenberg	98.23
1925	Pete DePaolo, Duesenberg	101.13
1926	Frank Lockhart, Miller	95.904
1927	George Souders, Duesenberg	97.545
1928	Louis Meyer, Miller	99.482
1929	Ray Keech, Simplex	97.585
1930	Billy Arnold, Miller-Hartz	100.448
1931	Louis Schneider, Bowes Seal Fast	96.629
1932	Fred Frame, Miller-Hartz	104.144
1933	Louis Meyer, Tydol	104.162
1934	Bill Cummings, Boyle Products	104.863
1935	Kelly Petillo, Gilmore Speedway	106.240
1936	Louis Meyer, Ring Free	109.069
1937	Wilbur Shaw, Shaw-Gilmore	113.580
1938	Floyd Roberts, Burd Piston Ring	117.200
1939	Wilbur Shaw, Boyle	115.035
1940	Wilbur Shaw, Boyle	114.277
1941	Floyd Davis-Mauri Rose, Knock-Out-Hose Clip	115.117
1942-45	race not held	
1946	George Robson, Thorne Engineering	114.820
1947	Mauri Rose, Blue Crown Special	116.338
1948	Mauri Rose, Blue Crown Special	119.814
1949	Bill Holland, Blue Crown Special	121.327
1950	Johnny Parsons, Wynn Kurtis Kraft	124.002
1951	Lee Wallard, Belanger	126.224
1952	Troy Ruttman, Agajanian	128.922
1953	Bill Vukovich, Fuel Injection	128.740
1954	Bill Vukovich, Fuel Injection	130.840

Year	Winner, Car	MPH
1955	Bob Sweikert, John Zink Special	128.209
1956	Pat Flaherty, John Zink Special	128.490
1957	Sam Hanks, Belond Exhaust	135.601
1958	Jimmy Bryan, Belond A.P.	133.791
1959	Rodger Ward, Leader Card Special	135.857
1960	Jim Rathmann, Ken Paul Special	138.767
1961	A.J. Foyt, Bowes Seal Fast	139.130
1962	Rodger Ward, Leader Card Special	140.293
1963	Parnelli Jones, Agajanian Special	143.137
1964	A.J. Foyt, Sheraton-Thompson Special	147.350
1965	Jim Clark, Lotus-Ford	150.686
1966	Graham Hill, American Red Ball	144.317
1967	A.J. Foyt, Sheraton-Thompson Special	151.207
1968	Bobby Unser, Rislone Special	152.882
1969	Mario Andretti, STP Oil Treatment Special	156.867
1970	Al Unser, Johnny Lightning Special	155.749
1971	Al Unser, Johnny Lightning Special	157.735
1972	Mark Donohue, Sunoco McLaren	162.962
1973	Gordon Johncock, STP Double Oil Filter	159.036
1974	Johnny Rutherford, McLaren	158.589
1975	Bobby Unser, Jorgenson Eagle	149.213
1976	Johnny Rutherford, Hygain McLaren	148.725
1977	A.J. Foyt, Gilmore Coyote-Ford	161.331
1978	Al Unser, Lola Cosworth	161.363
1979	Rick Mears, Penske-Cosworth	158.899
1980	Johnny Rutherford, Chaparral-Cosworth	142.862
1981	Bobby Unser, Penske-Cosworth	139.085
1982	Gordon Johncock, Wildcat-Cosworth	162.026
1983	Tom Sneva, March-Cosworth	162.117
1984	Rick Mears, March-Cosworth	163.621
1985	Danny Sullivan, March-Cosworth	152.982
1986	Bobby Rahal, March-Cosworth	170.722
1987	Al Unser, March-Cosworth	162.175
1988	Rick Mears, Penske-Chevy V8	144.809
1989	Emerson Fittipaldi, Penske PC 18-Chevy	167.581
1990	Arie Luyendyk, Lola-Chevy	185.984
1991	Rick Mears, Penske-Chevy	176.457
1992	Al Unser Jr., Galmer-Chevy A	134.477
1993	Emerson Fittipaldi, Penske-Chevy C	157.207

The race was less than 500 miles in the following years: 1916 (300 mi.), 1926 (400 mi.), 1950 (345 mi.), 1973 (332.5 mi.), 1975 (435 mi.), 1976 (255 mi.). Race record—185.984 MPH, Arie Luyendyk, 1990.

Notable One-Mile Speed Records

Date	Driver	Car	MPH
1/26/06	Marriott	Stanley (Steam)	127.659
3/16/10	Oldfield	Benz	131.724
4/23/11	Burman	Benz	141.732
2/12/19	DePalma	Packard	149.875
4/27/20	Milton	Dusenberg	155.046
4/28/26	Parry-Thomas	Thomas Spl.	170.624
3/29/27	Seagrave	Sunbeam	203.790
4/22/28	Keech	White Triplex	207.552
3/11/29	Seagrave	Irving-Napier	231.446
2/ 5/31	Campbell	Napier-Campbell	246.086
2/24/32	Campbell	Napier-Campbell	253.96
2/22/33	Campbell	Napier-Campbell	272.109
9/ 3/35	Campbell	Bluebird Special	301.13
11/19/37	Eyston	Thunderbolt 1	311.42
9/16/38	Eyston	Thunderbolt 1	357.5
8/23/39	Cobb	Railton	368.9
9/16/47	Cobb	Railton-Mobil	394.2
8/ 5/63	Breedlove	Spirit of America	407.45
10/27/64	Arfons	Green Monster	536.71
11/15/65	Breedlove	Spirit of America	600.601
10/23/70	Gabelich	Blue Flame	622.407
10/9/79	Barrett	Budweiser Rocket	638.637*
10/4/83	Noble	Thrust 2	633.6

*not recognized as official by sanctioning bodies.

IndyCar Champions

(U.S. Auto Club Champions prior to 1979; Cart Champions, 1979-93)

Year	Driver
1960	A. J. Foyt
1961	A. J. Foyt
1962	Rodger Ward
1963	A. J. Foyt
1964	A. J. Foyt
1965	Mario Andretti
1966	Mario Andretti
1967	A. J. Foyt
1968	Bobby Unser
1969	Mario Andretti
1970	Al Unser
1971	Joe Leonard
1972	Joe Leonard
1973	Roger McCluskey
1974	Bobby Unser
1975	A. J. Foyt
1976	Gordon Johncock
1977	Tom Sneva
1978	Tom Sneva
1979	Rick Mears
1980	Johnny Rutherford
1981	Rick Mears
1982	Rick Mears
1983	Al Unser
1984	Mario Andretti
1985	Al Unser
1986	Bobby Rahal
1987	Bobby Rahal
1988	Danny Sullivan
1989	Emerson Fittipaldi
1990	Al Unser Jr.
1991	Michael Andretti
1992	Bobby Rahal
1993	Nigel Mansell

Le Mans 24-Hour Race in 1993

Christophe Bouchut and Eric Helary of France and Geoff Brabham of Australia drove their Peugeot 905 to victory in the 1993 Le Mans 24-hour race. They traveled the 2,779 miles at an average of 133.34 mph.

World Grand Prix Champions

Year	Driver
1951	Jan Fangio, Argentina
1952	Alberto Ascari, Italy
1953	Alberto Ascari, Italy
1954	Juan Fangio, Argentina
1955	Juan Fangio, Argentina
1956	Juan Fangio, Argentina
1957	Juan Fangio, Argentina
1958	Mike Hawthorne, England
1959	Jack Brabham, Australia
1960	Jack Brabham, Australia
1961	Phil Hill, United States
1962	Graham Hill, England
1963	Jim Clark, Scotland
1964	John Surtees, England
1965	Jim Clark, Scotland
1966	Jack Brabham, Australia
1967	Denis Hulme, New Zealand
1968	Graham Hill, England
1969	Jackie Stewart, Scotland
1970	Jochen Rindt, Austria
1971	Jackie Stewart, Scotland
1972	Emerson Fittipaldi, Brazil
1973	Jackie Stewart, Scotland
1974	Emerson Fittipaldi, Brazil
1975	Niki Lauda, Austria
1976	James Hunt, England
1977	Niki Lauda, Austria
1978	Mario Andretti, U.S.
1979	Jody Scheckter, So. Africa
1980	Alan Jones, Australia
1981	Nelson Piquet, Brazil
1982	Keke Rosberg, Finland
1983	Nelson Piquet, Brazil
1984	Niki Lauda, Austria
1985	Alain Prost, France
1986	Alain Prost, France
1987	Nelson Piquet, Brazil
1988	Ayrton Senna, Brazil
1989	Alain Prost, France
1990	Ayrton Senna, Brazil
1991	Ayrton Senna, Brazil
1992	Nigel Mansell, Britain

Grand Prix for Formula 1 Cars in 1993

Grand Prix	Winner, car
Belgian	Damon Hill, Williams-Renault
Brazilian	Ayrton Senna, McLaren-Ford
British	Alain Prost, Williams-Renault
Canadian	Alain Prost, Williams-Renault
European	Ayrton Senna, McLaren-Ford
French	Alain Prost, Williams-Renault
German	Alain Prost, Williams-Renault
Hungarian	Damon Hill, Williams-Renault
Italian	Damon Hill, Williams-Renault
Monaco	Ayrton Senna, McLaren-Honda
San Marino	Alain Prost, Williams-Renault
South Africa	Alain Prost, Williams-Renault
Spanish	Alain Prost, Williams-Renault

Winston Cup Champions (NASCAR)

Year	Driver
1949	Red Byron
1950	Bill Rexford
1951	Herb Thomas
1952	Tim Flock
1953	Herb Thomas
1954	Lee Petty
1955	Tim Flock
1956	Buck Baker
1957	Buck Baker
1958	Lee Petty
1959	Lee Petty
1960	Rex White
1961	Ned Jarrett
1962	Joe Weatherly
1963	Joe Weatherly
1964	Richard Petty
1965	Ned Jarrett
1966	David Pearson
1967	Richard Petty
1968	David Pearson
1969	David Pearson
1970	Bobby Isaac
1971	Richard Petty
1972	Richard Petty
1973	Benny Parsons
1974	Richard Petty
1975	Richard Petty
1976	Cale Yarborough
1977	Cale Yarborough
1978	Cale Yarborough
1979	Richard Petty
1980	Dale Earnhardt
1981	Darrell Waltrip
1982	Darrell Waltrip
1983	Bobby Allison
1984	Terry Labonte
1985	Darrell Waltrip
1986	Dale Earnhardt
1987	Dale Earnhardt
1988	Bill Elliott
1989	Rusty Wallace
1990	Dale Earnhardt
1991	Dale Earnhardt
1992	Alan Kulwicki

Daytona 500 Winners

Year	Driver, car	Avg. MPH	Year	Driver, car	Avg. MPH
1959	Lee Petty, Oldsmobile	135.521	1977	Cale Yarborough, Chevrolet	153.218
1960	Junior Johnson, Chevrolet	124.740	1978	Bobby Allison, Ford	159.730
1961	Marvin Panch, Pontiac	149.601	1979	Richard Petty, Oldsmobile	143.977
1962	Fireball Roberts, Pontiac	152.529	1980	Buddy Baker, Oldsmobile	177.602
1963	Tiny Lund, Ford	151.566	1981	Richard Petty, Buick	169.651
1964	Richard Petty, Plymouth	154.334	1982	Bobby Allison, Buick	153.991
1965	Fred Lorenzen, Ford (a)	141.539	1983	Cale Yarborough, Pontiac	155.979
1966	Richard Petty, Plymouth (b)	160.627	1984	Cale Yarborough, Chevrolet	150.994
1967	Mario Andretti, Ford	146.926	1985	Bill Elliott, Ford	172.265
1968	Cale Yarborough, Mercury	143.251	1986	Geoff Bodine, Chevrolet	148.124
1969	Lee Roy Yarborough, Ford	160.875	1987	Bill Elliott, Ford	176.263
1970	Pete Hamilton, Plymouth	149.601	1988	Bobby Allison, Buick	137.531
1971	Richard Petty, Plymouth	144.456	1989	Darrell Waltrip, Chevrolet	148.466
1972	A. J. Foyt, Mercury	161.550	1990	Derrike Cope, Chevrolet	165.761
1973	Richard Petty, Dodge	157.205	1991	Ernie Irvin, Chevrolet	148.148
1974	Richard Petty, Dodge (c)	140.894	1992	Davey Allison, Ford	160.256
1975	Benny Parsons, Chevrolet	153.649	1993	Dale Jarrett, Chevrolet	154.972
1976	David Pearson, Mercury	152.181			

(a) 322.5 miles. (b) 495 miles. (c) 450 miles.

NASCAR Racing in 1993

Winston Cup Races

Date	Race, site	Winner	Car
Feb. 14	Daytona 500, Daytona Beach, Fla.	Dale Jarrett	Chevrolet
Feb. 28	Goodwrench 500, Rockingham, N.C.	Rusty Wallace	Pontiac
Mar. 8	Pontiac Excitement 400, Richmond, Va.	Davey Allison	Ford
Mar. 20	Motorcraft 500, Hampton, Ga.	Morgan Shepherd	Ford
Mar. 28	Transouth 500, Darlington, S.C.	Dale Earnhardt	Chevrolet
Apr. 4	Food City 500, Bristol, Tenn.	Rusty Wallace	Pontiac
Apr. 18	First Union 400, N. Wilkesboro, N.C.	Rusty Wallace	Pontiac
Apr. 25	Hanes 500, Martinsville, Va.	Rusty Wallace	Pontiac
May 2	Winston 500, Talladega, Ala.	Ernie Irvan	Chevrolet
May 30	Coca Cola 600, Concord, N.C.	Dale Earnhardt	Chevrolet
June 6	Budweiser 500, Dover, Del.	Dale Earnhardt	Chevrolet
June 13	Champion Spark Plug 500, Pocono, Pa.	Kyle Petty	Pontiac
June 20	Miller Genuine Draft 400, Brooklyn, Mich.	Ricky Rudd	Chevrolet
July 3	Pepsi 400, Daytona Beach, Fla.	Dale Earnhardt	Chevrolet
July 18	Miller Genuine Draft 500, Pocono, Pa.	Dale Earnhardt	Chevrolet
July 25	Die-Hard 500, Talladega, Ala.	Dale Earnhardt	Chevrolet
Aug. 8	Budweiser at The Glen, Watkins Glen, N.Y.	Mark Martin	Ford
Aug. 15	Champion Spark Plug 400, Brooklyn, Mich.	Mark Martin	Ford
Aug. 27	Bud 500, Bristol, Tenn.	Mark Martin	Ford
Sept. 5	Southern 500, Darlington, S.C.	Mark Martin	Ford
Sept. 11	Miller Genuine Draft 400, Richmond, Va.	Rusty Wallace	Pontiac
Sept. 19	Spitfire Spark Plug 500, Dover, Del.	Rusty Wallace	Pontiac
Sept. 26	Goody's 500, Martinsville, Va.	Ernie Irvan	Ford

LACROSSE

Lacrosse Champions in 1993

U.S. Club Lacrosse Association Championship—Baltimore, Md., June 19: Mount Washington 18, Brine L.C. 16.

NCAA Division I Championship—College Park, Md., May 31: Syracuse 13, North Carolina 12.

NCAA Division II Championship—Brookville, N.Y., May 15: Adelphi 11, C. W. Post 7.

NCAA Division III Championship—College Park, Md., May 30: Hobart 16, Ohio Wesleyan 10.

USILA Division I All-Star Game—Baltimore, Md., June 18: North 28, South 16.

USILA Division III All-Star Game—Baltimore, Md., June 18: South 16, North 12.

National Junior College Championship—Corning, N.Y., May 9: Herkimer (N.Y.) C.C. 17, Essex (Md.) C.C. 11.

NCAA Women's Division I Championship—College Park, Md., May 16: Virginia 8, Princeton 6 (Double O.T.).

NCAA Women's Division III Championship—College Park, Md., May 16: Trenton State 10, William Smith 9.

USILA Division I All America Team

Attack: Brian Piccola, Johns Hopkins; Mark Millon, Massachusetts; Matt Riter, Syracuse.

Midfield: Andy Towers, Brown; Dom Fin, Syracuse; Ryan Wade, North Carolina; Roy Colsey, Syracuse.

Defense: David Morrow, Princeton; Alex Martin, North Carolina; Greg Paradine, North Carolina.

Goal: Scott Bacigalupo, Princeton.

Coach of the Year: John Danowski, Hofstra.

Note: 4 midfielders selected for the 3 midfield positions

NCAA Division I Champions

Year	Champion	Year	Champion	Year	Champion	Year	Champion
1972	Virginia	1978	Johns Hopkins	1984	Johns Hopkins	1989	Syracuse
1973	Maryland	1979	Johns Hopkins	1985	Johns Hopkins	1990	Syracuse
1974	Johns Hopkins	1980	Johns Hopkins	1986	North Carolina	1991	North Carolina
1975	Maryland	1981	North Carolina	1987	Johns Hopkins	1992	Princeton
1976	Cornell	1982	North Carolina	1988	Syracuse	1993	Syracuse
1977	Cornell	1983	Syracuse				

BOXING

Champions by Classes

There are numerous governing bodies in boxing including the World Boxing Council, the World Boxing Assn., the International Boxing Federation, the United States Boxing Assn., the North American Boxing Federation, and the European Boxing Union. Other organizations are recognized by TV networks and the print media. All the governing bodies have their own champions and assorted boxing divisions. The following are the recognized champions, as of mid-1993, in the principal divisions of the World Boxing Association, the World Boxing Council, and the International Boxing Federation.

Class, Weight limit	WBA	WBC	IBF
Heavyweight	Riddick Bowe, U.S.	Lennox Lewis, U.K.	Riddick Bowe, U.S.
Cruiserweight (195 lbs.)	Bobby Cruz, U.S.	Anaclet Wamba, France	Al Cole, U.S.
Light Heavyweight (175 lbs.)	Virgil Hill, U.S.	Jeff Harding, Australia	Henry Maske, Germany
Super Middleweight (168 lbs.)	Michael Nunn, U.S.	Nigel Benn, U.K.	Chris Eubank, U.K.
Middleweight (160 lbs.)	Reggie Johnson, U.S.	Gerald McClellan, U.S.	Roy Jones, U.S.
Jr. Middleweight (154 lbs.)	Julio Cesar Vasquez, Argentina	Terry Norris, U.S.	Gianfranco Rosi, Italy
Welterweight (147 lbs.)	Crisanto Espana, N. Ireland	Pernell Whitaker, U.S.	Felix Trinidad, Puerto Rico
Jr. Welterweight (140 lbs.)	Juan Coggi, Argentina	Julio Cesar Chavez, Mexico	Charles Murray, U.S.
Lightweight (135 lbs.)	Dingaan Thobela, S. Africa	Miguel Angel Gonzalez, Mexico	Freddie Pendleton, U.S.
Jr. Lightweight (130 lbs.)	Genaro Hernandez, U.S.	Azumah Nelson, Ghana	John-John Molina, Puerto Rico
Featherweight (126 lbs.)	Yung Kyun Park, S. Korea	Goyo Vargas, Mexico	Tom Johnson, U.S.
Jr. Featherweight (122 lbs.)	Wilfredo Vasquez, Puerto Rico	Tracy Patterson, U.S.	Kennedy McKinney, U.S.
Bantamweight (118 lbs.)	Eliecer Julio, Colombia	Jung Il Byun, S. Korea	Orlando Canizales, U.S.
Flyweight (112 lbs.)	David Griman, Venezuela	Yuri Arbachakov, Japan	Phichit Sithbang Prachan, Thailand
Jr. Flyweight (108 lbs.)	Myung Woo Yuh, S. Korea	Michael Carbajal, U.S.	Michael Carbajal, U.S.

Ring Champions by Years

*Abandoned title

Heavyweights

1882-1892	John L. Sullivan (a)
1892-1897	James J. Corbett (b)
1897-1899	Robert Fitzsimmons
1899-1905	James J. Jeffries (c)
1905-1906	Marvin Hart
1906-1908	Tommy Burns
1908-1915	Jack Johnson
1915-1919	Jess Willard
1919-1926	Jack Dempsey
1926-1928	Gene Tunney*
1928-1930	vacant
1930-1932	Max Schmeling
1932-1933	Jack Sharkey
1933-1934	Primo Carnera
1934-1935	Max Baer
1935-1937	James J. Braddock
1937-1949	Joe Louis*
1949-1951	Ezzard Charles
1951-1952	Joe Walcott
1952-1956	Rocky Marciano*
1956-1959	Floyd Patterson
1959-1960	Ingemar Johansson
1960-1962	Floyd Patterson
1962-1964	Sonny Liston
1964-1967	Cassius Clay* (Muhammad Ali) (d)
1970-1973	Joe Frazier
1973-1974	George Foreman
1974-1978	Muhammad Ali
1978-1979	Leon Spinks (e), Muhammad Ali*
1978	Ken Norton (WBC), Larry Holmes (WBC) (f)
1979	John Tate (WBA)
1980	Mike Weaver (WBA)
1982	Michael Dokes (WBA)
1983	Gerrie Coetzee (WBA)
1984	Tim Witherspoon (WBC); Pinklon Thomas (WBC); Greg Page (WBA)
1985	Tony Tubbs (WBA); Michael Spinks (IBF)
1986	Tim Witherspoon (WBA); Trevor Berbick (WBC); Mike Tyson (WBC); James (Bonecrusher) Smith (WBA).
1987	Mike Tyson (WBA, 1988—IBF).
1990	James "Buster" Douglas (WBA, WBC, IBF)
1990	Evander Holyfield (WBA, WBC, IBF)
1992	Riddick Bowe (WBA, IBF, WBC); Lennox Lewis (WBC) (g)

(a) London Prize Ring (bare knuckle champion).
(b) First Marquis of Queensberry champion.
(c) Jeffries abandoned the title (1905) and designated Marvin Hart and Jack Root as logical contenders. Hart defeated Root in 12 rounds (1905) and in turn was defeated by Tommy Burns (1906) who laid claim to the title. Jack Johnson defeated Burns (1908) and was recognized as champion. He clinched the title by defeating Jeffries in an attempted comeback (1910).
(d) Title declared vacant by the WBA and other groups in 1967 after Clay's refusal to fulfill his military obligation. Joe Frazier was recognized as champion by 6 states, Mexico, and So. America. Jimmy Ellis was declared champion by the WBA. Frazier KOd Ellis, Feb. 16, 1970.
(e) After Spinks defeated Ali, the WBC recognized Ken Norton as champion. Norton subsequently lost his title to Larry Holmes.
(f) Holmes was stripped of his WBC title in 1984. He was the IBF champion when he lost to Michael Spinks.
(g) Lewis was named WBC champion when Bowe refused to fight him.

Light Heavyweights

1903	Jack Root, George Gardner
1903-1905	Bob Fitzsimmons
1905-1912	Philadelphia Jack O'Brien*
1912-1916	Jack Dillon
1916-1920	Battling Levinsky
1920-1922	George Carpentier
1922-1923	Battling Siki
1923-1925	Mike McTigue
1925-1926	Paul Berlenbach
1926-1927	Jack Delaney*
1927-1929	Tommy Loughran*
1930-1934	Maxey Rosenbloom
1934-1935	Bob Olin
1935-1939	John Henry Lewis*
1939	Melio Bettina
1939-1941	Billy Conn*
1941	Anton Christoforidis (won NBA title)
1941-1948	Gus Lesnevich, Freddie Mills
1948-1950	Freddie Mills
1950-1952	Joey Maxim
1952-1960	Archie Moore
1961-1962	vacant
1962-1963	Harold Johnson
1963-1965	Willie Pastrano
1965-1966	Jose Torres
1966-1968	Dick Tiger
1968-1974	Bob Foster*, John Conteh (WBA)
1975-1977	John Conteh (WBC), Miguel Cuello (WBC), Victor Galindez (WBA)
1978	Mike Rossman (WBA), Mate Parlov (WBC), Marvin Johnson (WBC)
1979	Matthew Saad Muhammad (WBC), Victor Galindez (WBA), Marvin Johnson (WBA)
1980	Eddie Mustafa Muhammad (WBA)
1981	Michael Spinks (WBA), Dwight Braxton (WBC)
1983-1985	Michael Spinks*
1985	J. B. Williamson (WBC)
1986	Marvin Johnson (WBA); Dennis Andries (WBC)
1987	Thomas Hearns (WBC); Leslie Stewart (WBA); Virgil Hill (WBA); Don Lalonde (WBC)
1988	Ray Leonard* (WBC)
1989	Jeff Harding (WBC)
1990	Dennis Andries (WBC)

1991	Thomas Hearns (WBA); Jeff Harding (WBC)
1992	Iran Barkley* (WBA); Virgil Hill (WBA)

Middleweights

1884-1891	Jack "Nonpareil" Dempsey
1891-1897	Bob Fitzsimmons*
1897-1907	Tommy Ryan*
1907-1908	Stanley Ketchel, Billy Papke
1908-1910	Stanley Ketchel
1911-1913	vacant
1913	Frank Klaus, George Chip
1914-1917	Al McCoy
1917-1920	Mike O'Dowd
1920-1923	Johnny Wilson
1923-1926	Harry Greb
1926-1931	Tiger Flowers, Mickey Walker
1931-1932	Gorilla Jones (NBA)
1932-1937	Marcel Thil
1938	Al Hostak (NBA), Solly Krieger (NBA)
1939-1940	Al Hostak (NBA)
1941-1947	Tony Zale
1947-1948	Rocky Graziano
1948	Tony Zale, Marcel Cerdan
1949-1951	Jake LaMotta
1951	Ray Robinson, Randy Turpin, Ray Robinson*
1953-1955	Carl (Bobo) Olson
1955-1957	Ray Robinson
1957	Gene Fullmer, Ray Robinson, Carmen Basilio
1958	Ray Robinson
1959	Gene Fullmer (NBA); Ray Robinson (N.Y.)
1960	Gene Fullmer (NBA); Paul Pender (New York and Mass.)
1961	Gene Fullmer (NBA); Terry Downes (New York, Mass., Europe)
1962	Gene Fullmer, Dick Tiger (NBA), Paul Pender (New York and Mass.)*
1963	Dick Tiger (universal).
1963-1965	Joey Giardello
1965-1966	Dick Tiger
1966-1967	Emile Griffith
1967	Nino Benvenuti
1967-1968	Emile Griffith
1968-1970	Nino Benvenuti
1970-1977	Carlos Monzon*
1977-1978	Rodrigo Valdez
1978-1979	Hugo Corro
1979-1980	Vito Antuofermo
1980	Alan Minter, Marvin Hagler
1987	Ray Leonard* (WBC); Thomas Hearns (WBC); Sumbu Kalambay (WBA).
1988	Iran Barkley (WBC)
1989	Mike McCallum (WBA); Roberto Duran (WBC)
1991	Julian Jackson (WBC)
1992	Reggie Johnson (WBA)
1993	Gerald McClellan (WBC)

Welterweights

1892-1894	Mysterious Billy Smith
1894-1896	Tommy Ryan
1896	Kid McCoy*
1900	Rube Ferns, Matty Matthews
1901	Rube Ferns
1901-1904	Joe Walcott
1904-1906	Dixie Kid, Joe Walcott, Honey Mellody
1907-1911	Mike Sullivan
1911-1915	vacant
1915-1919	Ted Lewis
1919-1922	Jack Britton
1922-1926	Mickey Walker
1926	Pete Latzo
1927-1929	Joe Dundee
1929	Jackie Fields
1930	Jack Thompson, Tommy Freeman
1931	Freeman, Thompson, Lou Brouillard
1932	Jackie Fields
1933	Young Corbett, Jimmy McLarnin
1934	Barney Ross, Jimmy McLarnin
1935-1938	Barney Ross
1938-1940	Henry Armstrong
1940-1941	Fritzie Zivic
1941-1946	Fred Cochrane
1946-1946	Marty Servo*; Ray Robinson (a)
1946-1950	Ray Robinson*
1951	Johnny Bratton (NBA)
1951-1954	Kid Gavilan
1954-1955	Johnny Saxton
1955	Tony De Marco, Carmen Basilio
1956	Carmen Basilio, Johnny Saxton, Basilio
1957	Carmen Basilio*
1958-1960	Virgil Akins, Don Jordan
1960	Benny Paret
1961	Emile Griffith, Benny Paret
1962	Emile Griffith
1963	Luis Rodriguez, Emile Griffith
1964-1966	Emile Griffith*
1966-1969	Curtis Cokes
1969-1970	Jose Napoles, Billy Backus
1971-1975	Jose Napoles
1975-1976	John Stracey (WBC), Angel Espada (WBA)
1976-1979	Carlos Palomino (WBC), Jose Cuevas (WBA)
1979	Wilfredo Benitez (WBC), Sugar Ray Leonard (WBC)
1980	Roberto Duran (WBC), Thomas Hearns (WBA), Sugar Ray Leonard (WBC)
1981-1982	Sugar Ray Leonard*
1983	Donald Curry (WBA); Milton McCrory (WBC)
1985	Donald Curry
1986	Lloyd Honeyghan (WBC)
1987	Mark Breland (WBA); Marlon Starling (WBA); Jorge Vaca (WBC).
1988	Tomas Molinares (WBA); Lloyd Honeyghan (WBC).
1989	Marlon Starling (WBC); Mark Breland (WBA)
1990	Maurice Blocker (WBC); Aaron Davis (WBA)
1991	Meldrick Taylor (WBA); Simon Brown (WBC); Buddy McGirt (WBC)
1992	Crisanto Espana (WBA)
1993	Pernell Whitaker (WBC)

(a) Robinson gained the title by defeating Tommy Bell in an elimination agreed to by the NY Commission and the NBA. Both claimed Robinson waived his title when he won the middleweight crown from LaMotta in 1951.

Lightweights

1896-1899	Kid Lavigne
1899-1902	Frank Erne
1902-1908	Joe Gans
1908-1910	Battling Nelson
1910-1912	Ad Wolgast
1912-1914	Willie Ritchie
1914-1917	Freddie Welsh
1917-1925	Benny Leonard*
1925	Jimmy Goodrich, Rocky Kansas
1926-1930	Sammy Mandell
1930	Al Singer, Tony Canzoneri
1930-1933	Tony Canzoneri
1933-1935	Barney Ross*
1935-1936	Tony Canzoneri
1936-1938	Lou Ambers
1938	Henry Armstrong
1939	Lou Ambers
1940	Lew Jenkins
1941-1943	Sammy Angott
1944	S. Angott (NBA), J. Zurita (NBA)
1945-1951	Ike Williams (NBA: later universal)
1951-1952	James Carter
1952	Lauro Salas, James Carter
1953-1954	James Carter
1954	Paddy De Marco; James Carter
1955	James Carter; Bud Smith
1956	Bud Smith, Joe Brown
1956-1962	Joe Brown
1962-1965	Carlos Ortiz
1965	Ismael Laguna
1965-1968	Carlos Ortiz
1968-1969	Teo Cruz
1969-1970	Mando Ramos
1970	Ismael Laguna, Ken Buchanan (WBA)
1971	Mando Ramos (WBC), Pedro Carrasco (WBC)
1972-1979	Roberto Duran* (WBA)
1972	Pedro Carrasco, Mando Ramos, Chango Carmona, Rodolfo Gonzalez (all WBC)
1974-1976	Guts Ishimatsu (WBC)
1976-1977	Esteban De Jesus (WBC)
1979	Jim Watt (WBC), Ernesto Espana (WBA)
1980	Hilmer Kenty (WBA)
1981	Alexis Arguello (WBC), Sean O'Grady (WBA), Arturo Frias (WBA)
1982-1984	Ray Mancini (WBA)
1983	Edwin Rosario (WBC)
1984	Livingstone Bramble (WBA); Jose Luis Ramirez (WBC)
1985	Hector (Macho) Camacho (WBC)
1986	Edwin Rosario (WBA); Jose Luis Ramirez (WBC).
1987	Julio Cesar Chavez (WBA).

1989	Edwin Rosario (WBA); Pernell Whitaker (WBC).
1990	Juan Nazario (WBA); Pernell Whitaker (WBA)
1992	Joey Gamache (WBA)
1992	Tony Lopez (WBA); Miguel Angel Gonzalez (WBC)
1993	Dingaan Thobela (WBA)

Featherweights

1892-1900	George Dixon (disputed)
1900-1901	Terry McGovern, Young Corbett*
1901-1912	Abe Attell
1912-1923	Johnny Kilbane
1923	Eugene Criqui, Johnny Dundee
1923-1925	Johnny Dundee*
1925-1927	Kid Kaplan*
1927-1928	Benny Bass, Tony Canzoneri
1928-1929	Andre Routis
1929-1932	Battling Battalino*
1932-1934	Tommy Paul (NBA)
1933-1936	Freddie Miller
1936-1937	Petey Sarron
1937-1938	Henry Armstrong*
1938-1940	Joey Archibald (b)
1940-41	Harry Jeffra
1942-1948	Willie Pep
1948-1949	Sandy Saddler
1949-1950	Willie Pep
1950-1957	Sandy Saddler*
1957-1959	Hogan (Kid) Bassey
1959-1963	Davey Moore
1963-1964	Sugar Ramos
1964-1967	Vicente Saldivar*
1968-1971	Paul Rojas (WBA), Sho Saijo (WBA)
1971	Antonio Gomez (WBA), Kuniaki Shibada (WBC)
1972	Ernesto Marcel* (WBA), Clemente Sanchez* (WBC), Jose Legra (WBC)
1973	Eder Jofre (WBC)
1974	Ruben Olivares (WBA), Alexis Arguello (WBA), Bobby Chacon (WBC)
1975	Ruben Olivares (WBC), David Kotey (WBC)
1976	Danny Lopez (WBC)
1977	Rafael Ortega (WBA)
1978	Cecilio Lastra (WBA), Eusebio Pedrosa (WBA)
1980	Salvador Sanchez (WBC)
1982	Juan LaPorte (WBC)
1984	Wilfredo Gomez (WBC); Azumah Nelson (WBC)
1985	Barry McGuigan (WBA)
1986	Steve Cruz (WBA)
1987	Antonio Esparragoza (WBA)
1988	Jeff Fenech (WBC)
1990	Marcos Villasana (WBC)
1991	Park Yung Kyun (WBA)
1991	Paul Hodkinson (WBC)
1993	Goyo Vargas (WBC)

(b) After Petey Scalzo knocked out Archibald in an overweight match and was refused a title bout, the NBA named Scalzo champion. The NBA title succession: Scalzo, 1938-1941; Richard Lemos, 1941; Jackie Wilson, 1941-1943; Jackie Callura, 1943; Phil Terranova, 1943-1944; Sal Bartolo, 1944-1946.

History of Heavyweight Championship Bouts

*Title Changed Hands

1889—July 8—John L. Sullivan def. Jake Kilrain, 75, Richburg, Miss. Last championship bare knuckles bout.

***1892**—Sept. 7—James J. Corbett def. John L. Sullivan, 21, New Orleans. Big gloves used for first time.

1894—Jan. 25—James J. Corbett KOd Charley Mitchell, 3, Jacksonville, Fla.

***1897**—Bob Fitzsimmons def. James J. Corbett, 14, Carson City, Nev.

***1899**—June 9—James J. Jeffries def. Bob Fitzsimmons, 11, Coney Island, N.Y.

1899—Nov. 3—James J. Jeffries def. Tom Sharkey, 25, Coney Island, N.Y.

1900—May 11—James J. Jeffries KOd James J. Corbett, 23, Coney Island, N.Y.

1901—Nov. 15—James J. Jeffries KOd Gus Ruhlin, 5, San Francisco.

1902—July 25—James J. Jeffries KOd Bob Fitzsimmons, 8, San Francisco.

1903—Aug. 14—James J. Jeffries KOd James J. Corbett, 10, San Francisco.

1904—Aug. 26—James J. Jeffries KOd Jack Monroe, 2, San Francisco.

***1905**—James J. Jeffries retired, July 3—Marvin Hart KOd Jack Root, 12, Reno. Jeffries refereed and presented the title to the victor. Jack O'Brien also claimed the title.

***1906**—Feb. 23—Tommy Burns def. Marvin Hart, 20, Los Angeles.

1906—Nov. 28—Philadelphia Jack O'Brien and Tommy Burns, 20, draw, Los Angeles.

1907—May 8—Tommy Burns def. Jack O'Brien, 20, Los Angeles.

1907—July 4—Tommy Burns KOd Bill Squires, 1, Colma, Cal.

1907—Dec. 2—Tommy Burns KOd Gunner Moir, 10, London.

1908—Feb. 10—Tommy Burns KOd Jack Palmer, 4, London.

1908—March 17—Tommy Burns KOd Jem Roche, 1, Dublin.

1908—April 18—Tommy Burns KOd Jewey Smith, 5, Paris.

1908—June 13—Tommy Burns KOd Bill Squires, 8, Paris.

1908—Aug. 24—Tommy Burns KOd Bill Squires, 13, Sydney, New South Wales.

1908—Sept. 2—Tommy Burns KOd Bill Lang, 2, Melbourne, Australia.

***1908**—Dec. 26—Jack Johnson KOd Tommy Burns, 14, Sydney, Australia. Police halted contest.

1909—May 19—Jack Johnson and Jack O'Brien, 6, draw, Philadelphia.

1909—June 30—Jack Johnson and Tony Ross, 6, draw, Pittsburgh.

1909—Sept. 9—Jack Johnson and Al Kaufman, 10, draw, San Francisco.

1909—Oct. 16—Jack Johnson KOd Stanley Ketchel, 12, Colma, Cal.

1910—July 4—Jack Johnson KOd Jim Jeffries, 15, Reno, Nev. Jeffries came back from retirement.

1912—July 4—Jack Johnson def. Jim Flynn, 9, Las Vegas, N.M. Contest stopped by police.

1913—Nov. 28—Jack Johnson KOd Andre Spaul, 2, Paris.

1913—Dec. 9—Jack Johnson and Jim Johnson, 10, draw, Paris. Bout called a draw when Jack Johnson declared he had broken his arm.

1914—June 27—Jack Johnson def. Frank Moran, 20, Paris.

***1915**—April 5—Jess Willard KOd Jack Johnson, 26, Havana. Cuba.

1916—March 25—Jess Willard and Frank Moran, 10, draw, New York.

***1919**—July 4—Jack Dempsey KOd Jess Willard, Toledo, Oh. Willard failed to answer bell for 4th round.

1920—Sept. 6—Jack Dempsey KOd Billy Miske, 3, Benton Harbor, Mich.

1920—Dec. 14—Jack Dempsey KOd Bill Brennan, 12, New York.

1921—July 2—Jack Dempsey KOd George Carpentier, 4, Boyle's Thirty Acres, Jersey City, N.J. Carpentier had held the so-called white heavyweight title since July 16, 1914, in a series established in 1913, after Jack Johnson's exile in Europe late in 1912.

1923—July 4—Jack Dempsey def. Tom Gibbons, 15, Shelby, Mont.

1923—Sept. 14—Jack Dempsey KOd Luis Firpo, 2, New York.

***1926**—Sept. 23—Gene Tunney def. Jack Dempsey, 10, Philadelphia.

1927—Sept. 22—Gene Tunney def. Jack Dempsey, 10, Chicago.

1928—July 26—Gene Tunney KOd Tom Heeney, 11, New York; soon afterward he announced his retirement.

***1930**—June 12—Max Schmeling def. Jack Sharkey, 4, New York. Sharkey fouled Schmeling in a bout which was generally considered to have resulted in the election of a successor to Gene Tunney, New York.

1931—July 3—Max Schmeling KOd Young Stribling, 15, Cleveland.

***1932**—June 21—Jack Sharkey def. Max Schmeling, 15, New York.

***1933**—June 29—Primo Carnera KOd Jack Sharkey, 6, New York.

1933—Oct. 22—Primo Carnera def. Paulino Uzcudun, 15, Rome.

1934—March 1—Primo Carnera def. Tommy Loughran, 15, Miami.

***1934**—June 14—Max Baer KOd Primo Carnera, 11, New York.

***1935**—June 13—James J. Braddock def. Max Baer, 15, New York.

***1937**—June 22—Joe Louis KOd James J. Braddock, 8, Chicago.

1937—Aug. 30—Joe Louis def. Tommy Farr, 15, New York.

1938—Feb. 23—Joe Louis KOd Nathan Mann, 3, New York.
1938—April 1—Joe Louis KOd Harry Thomas, 5, Chicago.
1938—June 22—Joe Louis KOd Max Schmeling, 1, New York.
1939—Jan. 25—Joe Louis KOd John H. Lewis, 1, New York.
1939—April 17—Joe Louis KOd Jack Roper, 1, Los Angeles.
1939—June 28—Joe Louis KOd Tony Galento, 4, New York.
1939—Sept. 20—Joe Louis KOd Bob Pastor, 11, Detroit.
1940—February 9—Joe Louis def. Arturo Godoy, 15, New York.
1940—March 29—Joe Louis KOd Johnny Paycheck, 2, New York.
1940—June 20—Joe Louis KOd Arturo Godoy, 8, New York.
1940—Dec. 16—Joe Louis KOd Al McCoy, 6, Boston.
1941—Jan. 31—Joe Louis KOd Red Burman, 5, New York.
1941—Feb. 17—Joe Louis KOd Gus Dorzaio, 2, Philadelphia.
1941—March 21—Joe Louis KOd Abe Simon, 13, Detroit.
1941—April 8—Joe Louis KOd Tony Musto, 9, St. Louis.
1941—May 23—Joe Louis def. Buddy Baer, 7, Washington, D.C., on a disqualification.
1941—June 18—Joe Louis KOd Billy Conn, 13, New York.
1941—Sept. 29—Joe Louis KOd Lou Nova, 6, New York.
1942—Jan. 9—Joe Louis KOd Buddy Baer, 1, New York.
1942—March 27—Joe Louis KOd Abe Simon, 6, New York.
1946—June 19—Joe Louis KOd Billy Conn, 8, New York.
1946—Sept. 18—Joe Louis KOd Tami Mauriello, 1, New York.
1947—Dec. 5—Joe Louis def. Joe Walcott, 15, New York.
1948—June 25—Joe Louis KOd Joe Walcott, 11, New York.
***1949**—June 22—Following Joe Louis' retirement Ezzard Charles def. Joe Walcott, 15, Chicago, NBA recognition only.
1949—Aug. 10—Ezzard Charles KOd Gus Lesnevich, 7, New York.
1949—Oct. 14—Ezzard Charles KOd Pat Valentino, 8, San Francisco; clinched American title.
1950—Aug. 15—Ezzard Charles KOd Freddy Beshore, 14, Buffalo.
1950—Sept. 27—Ezzard Charles def. Joe Louis in latter's attempted comeback, 15, New York; universal recognition.
1950—Dec. 5—Ezzard Charles KOd Nick Barone, 11, Cincinnati.
1951—Jan. 12—Ezzard Charles KOd Lee Oma, 10, New York.
1951—March 7—Ezzard Charles def. Joe Walcott, 15, Detroit.
1951—May 30—Ezzard Charles def. Joey Maxim, light heavyweight champion, 15, Chicago.
***1951**—July 18—Joe Walcott KOd Ezzard Charles, 7, Pittsburgh.
1952—June 5—Joe Walcott def. Ezzard Charles, 15, Philadelphia.
***1952**—Sept. 23—Rocky Marciano KOd Joe Walcott, 13, Philadelphia.
1953—May 15—Rocky Marciano KOd Joe Walcott, 1, Chicago.
1953—Sept. 24—Rocky Marciano KOd Roland LaStarza, 11, New York.
1954—June 17—Rocky Marciano def. Ezzard Charles, 15, New York.
1954—Sept. 17—Rocky Marciano KOd Ezzard Charles, 8, New York.
1955—May 16—Rocky Marciano KOd Don Cockell, 9, San Francisco.
1955—Sept. 21—Rocky Marciano KOd Archie Moore, 9, New York. Marciano retired undefeated, Apr. 27, 1956.
***1956**—Nov. 30—Floyd Patterson KOd Archie Moore, 5, Chicago.
1957—July 29—Floyd Patterson KOd Hurricane Jackson, 10, New York.
1957—Aug. 22—Floyd Patterson KOd Pete Rademacher, 6, Seattle.
1958—Aug. 18—Floyd Patterson KOd Roy Harris, 12, Los Angeles.
1959—May 1—Floyd Patterson KOd Brian London, 11, Indianapolis.
***1959**—June 26—Ingemar Johansson KOd Floyd Patterson, 3, New York.
***1960**—June 20—Floyd Patterson KOd Ingemar Johansson, 5, New York. First heavyweight in boxing history to regain title.
1961—Mar. 13—Floyd Patterson KOd Ingemar Johansson, 6, Miami Beach.
1961—Dec. 4—Floyd Patterson KOd Tom McNeeley, 4, Toronto.
***1962**—Sept. 25—Sonny Liston KOd Floyd Patterson, 1, Chicago.
1963—July 22—Sonny Liston KOd Floyd Patterson, 1, Las Vegas.
***1964**—Feb. 25—Cassius Clay KOd Sonny Liston, 7, Miami Beach.
1965—May 25—Cassius Clay KOd Sonny Liston, 1, Lewiston, Maine.
1965—Nov. 11—Cassius Clay KOd Floyd Patterson, 12, Las Vegas.
1966—Mar. 29—Cassius Clay def. George Chuvalo, 15, Toronto.
1966—May 21—Cassius Clay KOd Henry Cooper, 6, London.
1966—Aug. 6—Cassius Clay KOd Brian London, 3, London.
1966—Sept. 10—Cassius Clay KOd Karl Mildenberger, 12, Frankfurt, Germany.
1966—Nov. 14—Cassius Clay KOd Cleveland Williams, 3, Houston.
1967—Feb. 6—Cassius Clay def. Ernie Terrell, 15, Houston.
1967—Mar. 22—Cassius Clay KOd Zora Folley, 7, New York. Clay was stripped of his title by the WBA and others for refusing military service.
***1970**—Feb. 16—Joe Frazier KOd Jimmy Ellis, 5, New York.
1970—Nov. 18—Joe Frazier KOd Bob Foster, 2, Detroit.
1971—Mar. 8—Joe Frazier def. Cassius Clay (Muhammad Ali), 15, New York.
1972—Jan. 15—Joe Frazier KOd Terry Daniels, 4, New Orleans.
1972—May 25—Joe Frazier KOd Ron Stander, 5, Omaha.
***1973**—Jan. 22—George Foreman KOd Joe Frazier, 2, Kingston, Jamaica.
1973—Sept. 1—George Foreman KOd Joe Roman, 1, Tokyo.
1974—Mar. 3—George Foreman KOd Ken Norton, 2, Caracas.
***1974**—Oct. 30—Muhammad Ali KOd George Foreman, 8, Zaire.
1975—Mar. 24—Muhammad Ali KOd Chuck Wepner, 15, Cleveland.
1975—May 16—Muhammad Ali KOd Ron Lyle, 11, Las Vegas.
1975—June 30—Muhammad Ali def. Joe Bugner, 15, Malaysia.
1975—Oct. 1—Muhammad Ali KOd Joe Frazier, 14, Manila.
1976—Feb. 20—Muhammad Ali KOd Jean-Pierre Coopman, 5, San Juan.
1976—Apr. 30—Muhammad Ali def. Jimmy Young, 15, Landover, Md.
1976—May 25—Muhammad Ali KOd Richard Dunn, 5, Munich.
1976—Sept. 28—Muhammad Ali def. Ken Norton, 15, New York.
1977—May 16—Muhammad Ali def. Alfredo Evangelista, 15, Landover, Md.
1977—Sept. 29—Muhammad Ali def. Earnie Shavers, 15, New York.
***1978**—Feb. 15—Leon Spinks def. Muhammad Ali, 15, Las Vegas.
***1978**—Sept. 15—Muhammad Ali def. Leon Spinks, 15, New Orleans. Ali retired in 1979.

(Bouts when title changed hands only)

***1978**—June 9—(WBC) Larry Holmes def. Ken Norton, 15, Las Vegas.
***1980**—Mar. 31—(WBA) Mike Weaver KOd John Tate, 15, Knoxville.
***1982**—Dec. 10—(WBA) Michael Dokes KOd Mike Weaver, 1, Las Vegas.
***1983**—Sept. 23—(WBA) Gerrie Coetzee KOd Michael Dokes, 10, Richfield, Oh.
***1984**—Mar. 10—(WBC) Tim Witherspoon def. Greg Page, 12, Las Vegas, Nev.
***1984**—Aug. 31—(WBC) Pinklon Thomas def. Tim Witherspoon, 12, Las Vegas, Nev.
***1984**—Dec. 2—(WBA) Greg Page KOd Gerrie Coetzee, 8 Sun City, Bophuthatswana
***1985**—Apr. 29—(WBA) Tony Tubbs def. Greg Page, 15, Buffalo, N.Y.
***1985**—Sept. 21—(IBF) Michael Spinks def. Larry Holmes 15, Las Vegas, Nev.
***1986**—Jan. 17—(WBA) Tim Witherspoon def. Tony Tubbs 15, Atlanta, Ga.
***1986**—Mar. 23—(WBC) Trevor Berbick def. Pinklon Thomas 12, Miami, Fla.
***1986**—Nov. 22—(WBC) Mike Tyson KOd Trevor Berbick, 2 Las Vegas.
***1986**—Dec. 12—(WBA) James (Bonecrusher) Smith KOd Tim Witherspoon, 1, New York.
***1987**—Mar. 7—(WBA) Mike Tyson def. James (Bonecrusher) Smith, 12, Las Vegas.
***1988**—June 27—(IBF) Mike Tyson KOd Michael Spinks, 1 Atlantic City.
***1990**—Feb. 11—(WBA, WBC, IBF) James "Buster" Douglas KOd Mike Tyson, 10, Tokyo.
***1990**—Oct. 25—(WBA, WBC, IBF) Evander Holyfield KOd James "Buster" Douglas, 3, Las Vegas.
***1992**—Nov. 13—(WBA, WBC, IBF) Riddick Bowe def. Evander Holyfield, 12, Las Vegas.

Pro Rodeo Championship Standings in 1992

Event	Winner	Money won
All Around	Ty Murray, Stephenville, Tex.	$225,992
Saddle Bronc	Robert Etbauer, Ree Heights, S.D.	184,675
Bareback	Wayne Herman, Dickinson, N.D.	122,949
Bull Riding	Cody Custer, Wickenburg, Ariz.	149,814
Calf Roping	Joe Beaver, Huntsville, Tex.	124,525
Steer Wrestling	Mark Roy, Dalemead, Alta.	$112,103
Steer Roping	Guy Allen, Vinita, Okla.	44,729
Women's Barrel Racing	Charmayne Rodman, Galt, Cal.	110,868

Pro Rodeo Cowboy All Around Champions

Year	Winner	Money won
1972	Phil Lyne, George West, Tex.	$60,852
1973	Larry Mahan, Dallas, Tex.	64,447
1974	Tom Ferguson, Miami, Okla.	66,929
1975	Leo Camarillo, Oakdale, Cal.	50,300
	Tom Ferguson, Miami, Okla.	50,300
1976	Tom Ferguson, Miami, Okla.	87,908
1977	Tom Ferguson, Miami, Okla.	76,730
1978	Tom Ferguson, Miami, Okla.	103,734
1979	Tom Ferguson, Miami, Okla.	96,272
1980	Paul Tierney, Rapid City, S.D.	105,568
1981	Jimmie Cooper, Monument, N.M.	105,862
1982	Chris Lybbert, Coyote, Cal.	$123,709
1983	Roy Cooper, Durant, Okla.	153,391
1984	Dee Pickett, Caldwell, Ida.	122,618
1985	Lewis Feild, Elk Ridge, Ut.	130,347
1986	Lewis Feild, Elk Ridge, Ut.	166,042
1987	Lewis Feild, Elk Ridge, Ut.	144,335
1988	Dave Appleton, Arlington, Tex.	121,546
1989	Ty Murray, Odessa, Tex.	134,806
1990	Ty Murray, Stephenville, Tex.	213,772
1991	Ty Murray, Stephenville, Tex.	244,230
1992	Ty Murray, Stephenville, Tex.	225,992

The America's Cup

In the 1992 America's Cup match the United States yacht *America* [3] defeated the Italian yacht *Il Moro di Venezia* 4-1 in the waters off San Diego, Cal. *America* [3] was skippered by Bill Koch. The next America's Cup competition is scheduled for 1995 in San Diego.

Competition for the America's Cup grew out of the first contest to establish a world yachting championship, one of the carnival features of the London Exposition of 1851. The race, open to all classes of yachts from all over the world, covered a 60-mile course around the Isle of Wight; the prize was a cup worth about $500, donated by the Royal Yacht Squadron of England, known as the "America's Cup" because it was first won by the United States yacht *America.*

Winners of the America's Cup

1851	America
1870	Magic defeated Cambria, England, (1-0)
1871	Columbia (first three races) and Sappho (last two races) defeated Livonia, England, (4-1)
1876	Madeline defeated Countess of Dufferin, Canada, (2-0)
1881	Mischief defeated Atalanta, Canada, (2-0)
1885	Puritan defeated Genesta, England, (2-0)
1886	Mayflower defeated Galatea, England, (2-0)
1887	Volunteer defeated Thistle, Scotland, (2-0)
1893	Vigilant defeated Valkyrie II, England, (3-0)
1895	Defender defeated Valkyrie III, England, (3-0)
1899	Columbia defeated Shamrock, England, (3-0)
1901	Columbia defeated Shamrock II, England, (3-0)
1903	Reliance defeated Shamrock III, England, (3-0)
1920	Resolute defeated Shamrock IV, England, (3-2)
1930	Enterprise defeated Shamrock V, England, (4-0)
1934	Rainbow defeated Endeavour, England, (4-2)
1937	Ranger defeated Endeavour II, England, (4-0)
1958	Columbia defeated Sceptre, England, (4-0)
1962	Weatherly defeated Gretel, Australia, (4-1)
1964	Constellation defeated Sovereign, England, (4-0)
1967	Intrepid defeated Dame Pattie, Australia, (4-0)
1970	Intrepid defeated Gretel II, Australia, (4-1)
1974	Courageous defeated Southern Cross, Australia, (4-0)
1977	Courageous defeated Australia, Australia, (4-0)
1980	Freedom defeated Australia, Australia, (4-1)
1983	Australia II, Australia defeated Liberty, (4-3)
1987	Stars & Stripes defeated Kookaburra III, Australia, (4-0)
1988	Stars & Stripes defeated New Zealand, New Zealand, (2-0)
1992	America[3] defeated Il Moro di Venezia, Italy, (4-1)

The World Cup

The World Cup, emblematic of international soccer supremacy, was won by West Germany on July 8, 1990, with a 1-0 victory over defending champion Argentina on a penalty shot in the 84th minute. It was the lowest-scoring final in the 60 years of World Cup play. It was the 3d World Cup title for West Germany, equaling Brazil and Italy. In 1994 the U.S. will host the tournament for the first time. Winners and sites of previous World Cup play follow:

Year	Winner	Final opponent	Site
1930	Uruguay	Argentina	Uruguay
1934	Italy	Czechoslovakia	Italy
1938	Italy	Hungary	France
1950	Uruguay	Brazil	Brazil
1954	W. Germany	Hungary	Switzerland
1958	Brazil	Sweden	Sweden
1962	Brazil	Czechoslovakia	Chile
1966	England	W. Germany	England
1970	Brazil	Italy	Mexico
1974	W. Germany	Netherlands	W. Germany
1978	Argentina	Netherlands	Argentina
1982	Italy	W. Germany	Spain
1986	Argentina	W. Germany	Mexico
1990	W. Germany	Argentina	Italy

BASEBALL
Major League Pennant Winners, 1901–1993

National League

Year	Winner	Won	Lost	Pct	Manager
1901	Pittsburgh	90	49	.647	Clarke
1902	Pittsburgh	103	36	.741	Clarke
1903	Pittsburgh	91	49	.650	Clarke
1904	New York	106	47	.693	McGraw
1905	New York	105	48	.686	McGraw
1906	Chicago	116	36	.763	Chance
1907	Chicago	107	45	.704	Chance
1908	Chicago	99	55	.643	Chance
1909	Pittsburgh	110	42	.724	Clarke
1910	Chicago	104	50	.675	Chance
1911	New York	99	54	.647	McGraw
1912	New York	103	48	.682	McGraw
1913	New York	101	51	.664	McGraw
1914	Boston	94	59	.614	Stallings
1915	Philadelphia	90	62	.592	Moran
1916	Brooklyn	94	60	.610	Robinson
1917	New York	98	56	.636	McGraw
1918	Chicago	84	45	.651	Mitchell
1919	Cincinnati	96	44	.686	Moran
1920	Brooklyn	93	60	.604	Robinson
1921	New York	94	56	.614	McGraw
1922	New York	93	61	.604	McGraw
1923	New York	95	58	.621	McGraw
1924	New York	93	60	.608	McGraw
1925	Pittsburgh	95	58	.621	McKechnie
1926	St. Louis	89	65	.578	Hornsby
1927	Pittsburgh	94	60	.610	Bush
1928	St. Louis	95	59	.617	McKechnie
1929	Chicago	98	54	.645	McCarthy
1930	St. Louis	92	62	.597	Street
1931	St. Louis	101	53	.656	Street
1932	Chicago	90	64	.584	Grimm
1933	New York	91	61	.599	Terry
1934	St. Louis	95	58	.621	Frisch
1935	Chicago	100	54	.649	Grimm
1936	New York	91	62	.597	Terry
1937	New York	95	57	.625	Terry
1938	Chicago	89	63	.586	Hartnett
1939	Cincinnati	97	57	.630	McKechnie
1940	Cincinnati	100	53	.654	McKechnie
1941	Brooklyn	100	54	.649	Durocher
1942	St. Louis	106	48	.688	Southworth
1943	St. Louis	105	49	.682	Southworth
1944	St. Louis	105	49	.682	Southworth
1945	Chicago	98	56	.636	Grimm
1946	St. Louis	98	58	.628	Dyer
1947	Brooklyn	94	60	.610	Shotton
1948	Boston	91	62	.595	Southworth
1949	Brooklyn	97	57	.630	Shotton
1950	Philadelphia	91	63	.591	Sawyer
1951	New York	98	59	.624	Durocher
1952	Brooklyn	96	57	.627	Dressen
1953	Brooklyn	105	49	.682	Dressen
1954	New York	97	57	.630	Durocher
1955	Brooklyn	98	55	.641	Alston
1956	Brooklyn	93	61	.604	Alston
1957	Milwaukee	95	59	.617	Haney
1958	Milwaukee	92	62	.597	Haney
1959	Los Angeles	88	68	.564	Alston
1960	Pittsburgh	95	59	.617	Murtaugh
1961	Cincinnati	93	61	.604	Hutchinson
1962	San Francisco	103	62	.624	Dark
1963	Los Angeles	99	63	.611	Alston
1964	St. Louis	93	69	.574	Keane
1965	Los Angeles	97	65	.599	Alston
1966	Los Angeles	95	67	.586	Alston
1967	St. Louis	101	60	.627	Schoendienst
1968	St. Louis	97	65	.599	Schoendienst

American League

Year	Winner	Won	Lost	Pct	Manager
1901	Chicago	83	53	.610	Griffith
1902	Philadelphia	83	53	.610	Mack
1903	Boston	91	47	.659	Collins
1904	Boston	95	59	.617	Collins
1905	Philadelphia	92	56	.622	Mack
1906	Chicago	93	58	.616	Jones
1907	Detroit	92	58	.613	Jennings
1908	Detroit	90	63	.588	Jennings
1909	Detroit	98	54	.645	Jennings
1910	Philadelphia	102	48	.680	Mack
1911	Philadelphia	101	50	.669	Mack
1912	Boston	105	47	.691	Stahl
1913	Philadelphia	96	57	.627	Mack
1914	Philadelphia	99	53	.651	Mack
1915	Boston	101	50	.669	Carrigan
1916	Boston	91	63	.591	Carrigan
1917	Chicago	100	54	.649	Rowland
1918	Boston	75	51	.595	Barrow
1919	Chicago	88	52	.629	Gleason
1920	Cleveland	98	56	.636	Speaker
1921	New York	98	55	.641	Huggins
1922	New York	94	60	.610	Huggins
1923	New York	98	54	.645	Huggins
1924	Washington	92	62	.597	Harris
1925	Washington	96	55	.636	Harris
1926	New York	91	63	.591	Huggins
1927	New York	110	44	.714	Huggins
1928	New York	101	53	.656	Huggins
1929	Philadelphia	104	46	.693	Mack
1930	Philadelphia	102	52	.662	Mack
1931	Philadelphia	107	45	.704	Mack
1932	New York	107	47	.695	McCarthy
1933	Washington	99	53	.651	Cronin
1934	Detroit	101	53	.656	Cochrane
1935	Detroit	93	58	.616	Cochrane
1936	New York	102	51	.667	McCarthy
1937	New York	102	52	.662	McCarthy
1938	New York	99	53	.651	McCarthy
1939	New York	106	45	.702	McCarthy
1940	Detroit	90	64	.584	Baker
1941	New York	101	53	.656	McCarthy
1942	New York	103	51	.669	McCarthy
1943	New York	98	56	.636	McCarthy
1944	St. Louis	89	65	.578	Sewell
1945	Detroit	88	65	.575	O'Neill
1946	Boston	104	50	.675	Cronin
1947	New York	97	57	.630	Harris
1948	Cleveland	97	58	.626	Boudreau
1949	New York	97	57	.630	Stengel
1950	New York	98	56	.636	Stengel
1951	New York	98	56	.636	Stengel
1952	New York	95	59	.617	Stengel
1953	New York	99	52	.656	Stengel
1954	Cleveland	111	43	.721	Lopez
1955	New York	96	58	.623	Stengel
1956	New York	97	57	.630	Stengel
1957	New York	98	56	.636	Stengel
1958	New York	92	62	.597	Stengel
1959	Chicago	94	60	.610	Lopez
1960	New York	97	57	.630	Stengel
1961	New York	109	53	.673	Houk
1962	New York	96	66	.593	Houk
1963	New York	104	57	.646	Houk
1964	New York	99	63	.611	Berra
1965	Minnesota	102	60	.630	Mele
1966	Baltimore	97	63	.606	Bauer
1967	Boston	92	70	.568	Williams
1968	Detroit	103	59	.636	Smith

National League

Year	East Winner	W	L	Pct	Manager	West Winner	W	L	Pct	Manager	Playoff winner
1969	N.Y. Mets	100	62	.617	Hodges	Atlanta	93	69	.574	Harris	New York
1970	Pittsburgh	89	73	.549	Murtaugh	Cincinnati	102	60	.630	Anderson	Cincinnati
1971	Pittsburgh	97	65	.599	Murtaugh	San Francisco	90	72	.556	Fox	Pittsburgh
1972	Pittsburgh	96	59	.619	Virdon	Cincinnati	95	59	.617	Anderson	Cincinnati
1973	N.Y. Mets	82	79	.509	Berra	Cincinnati	99	63	.611	Anderson	New York
1974	Pittsburgh	88	74	.543	Murtaugh	Los Angeles	102	60	.630	Alston	Los Angeles
1975	Pittsburgh	92	69	.571	Murtaugh	Cincinnati	108	54	.667	Anderson	Cincinnati
1976	Philadelphia	101	61	.623	Ozark	Cincinnati	102	60	.630	Anderson	Cincinnati

	East					West					
Year	Winner	W	L	Pct	Manager	Winner	W	L	Pct	Manager	Playoff winner
1977	Philadelphia .	101	61	.623	Ozark	Los Angeles . . .	98	64	.605	Lasorda	Los Angeles
1978	Philadelphia .	90	72	.556	Ozark	Los Angeles . . .	95	67	.586	Lasorda	Los Angeles
1979	Pittsburgh. . .	98	64	.605	Tanner	Cincinnati.	90	71	.559	McNamara	Pittsburgh
1980	Philadelphia .	91	71	.562	Green	Houston.	93	70	.571	Virdon	Philadelphia
1981(a)	Philadelphia .	34	21	.618	Green	Los Angeles . . .	36	21	.632	Lasorda	(c)
1981(b)	Montreal . . .	30	23	.566	Williams, Fanning	Houston.	33	20	.623	Virdon	Los Angeles
1982	St. Louis . . .	92	70	.568	Herzog	Atlanta	89	73	.549	Torre	St. Louis
1983	Philadelphia .	90	72	.556	Corrales, Owens	Los Angeles . . .	91	71	.562	Lasorda	Philadelphia
1984	Chicago. . . .	96	65	.596	Frey	San Diego	92	70	.568	Williams	San Diego
1985	St. Louis . . .	101	61	.623	Herzog	Los Angeles . . .	95	67	.586	Lasorda	St. Louis
1986	N.Y. Mets. . .	108	54	.667	Johnson	Houston.	96	66	.593	Lanier	New York
1987	St. Louis . . .	95	67	.586	Herzog	San Francisco . .	90	72	.556	Craig	St. Louis
1988	N.Y. Mets. . .	100	60	.625	Johnson	Los Angeles . . .	94	67	.584	Lasorda	Los Angeles
1989	Chicago. . . .	93	69	.571	Zimmer	San Francisco . .	92	70	.568	Craig	San Francisco
1990	Pittsburgh. . .	95	67	.586	Leyland	Cincinnati.	91	71	.562	Piniella	Cincinnati
1991	Pittsburgh. . .	98	64	.605	Leyland	Atlanta	94	68	.580	Cox	Atlanta
1992	Pittsburgh. . .	96	66	.593	Leyland	Atlanta	98	64	.605	Cox	Atlanta
1993	Philadelphia .	97	65	.599	Fregosi	Atlanta	104	58	.642	Cox	Philadelphia

American League

	East					West					
Year	Winner	W	L	Pct	Manager	Winner	W	L	Pct	Manager	Playoff winner
1969	Baltimore . . .	109	53	.673	Weaver	Minnesota	97	65	.599	Martin	Baltimore
1970	Baltimore . . .	108	54	.667	Weaver	Minnesota	98	64	.605	Rigney	Baltimore
1971	Baltimore . . .	101	57	.639	Weaver	Oakland	101	60	.627	Williams	Baltimore
1972	Detroit	86	70	.551	Martin	Oakland	93	62	.600	Williams	Oakland
1973	Baltimore . . .	97	65	.599	Weaver	Oakland	94	68	.580	Williams	Oakland
1974	Baltimore . . .	91	71	.562	Weaver	Oakland	90	72	.556	Dark	Oakland
1975	Boston.	95	65	.594	Johnson	Oakland	98	64	.605	Dark	Boston
1976	New York . . .	97	62	.610	Martin	Kansas City	90	72	.556	Herzog	New York
1977	New York . . .	100	62	.617	Martin	Kansas City	102	60	.630	Herzog	New York
1978	New York . . .	100	63	.613	Martin, Lemon	Kansas City	92	70	.568	Herzog	New York
1979	Baltimore . . .	102	57	.642	Weaver	California.	88	74	.543	Fregosi	Baltimore
1980	New York . . .	103	59	.636	Howser	Kansas City	97	65	.599	Frey	Kansas City
1981(a)	New York . . .	34	22	.607	Michael	Oakland	37	23	.617	Martin	(d)
1981(b)	Milwaukee . .	31	22	.585	Rodgers	Kansas City	30	23	.566	Frey, Howser	New York
1982	Milwaukee . .	95	67	.586	Rodgers, Kuenn	California.	93	69	.574	Mauch	Milwaukee
1983	Baltimore . . .	98	64	.605	Altobelli	Chicago	99	63	.611	LaRussa	Baltimore
1984	Detroit	104	58	.642	Anderson	Kansas City	84	78	.519	Howser	Detroit
1985	Toronto	99	62	.615	Cox	Kansas City	91	71	.562	Howser	Kansas City
1986	Boston.	95	66	.590	McNamara	California.	92	70	.568	Mauch	Boston
1987	Detroit	98	64	.605	Anderson	Minnesota	85	77	.525	Kelly	Minnesota
1988	Boston.	89	73	.549	McNamara, Morgan	Oakland	104	58	.642	LaRussa	Oakland
1989	Toronto	89	73	.549	Williams, Gaston	Oakland	99	63	.611	LaRussa	Oakland
1990	Boston.	88	74	.543	Morgan	Oakland	103	59	.636	LaRussa	Oakland
1991	Toronto	91	71	.562	Gaston	Minnesota	95	67	.586	Kelly	Minnesota
1992	Toronto	96	66	.593	Gaston	Oakland	96	66	.593	LaRussa	Toronto
1993	Toronto	95	67	.586	Gaston	Chicago	94	68	.580	Lamont	Toronto

(a) First half; (b) Second half; (c) Montreal and L.A. won the divisional playoffs; (d) N.Y. and Oakland won the divisional playoffs.

The Sporting News Gold Glove Awards in 1992

National League

Mark Grace, Chicago, first base
Jose Lind, Pittsburgh, second base
Terry Pendleton, Atlanta, third base
Ozzie Smith, St. Louis, shortstop
Larry Walker, Montreal, outfield
Andy Van Slyke, Pittsburgh, outfield
Barry Bonds, Pittsburgh, outfield
Tom Pagnozzi, St. Louis, catcher
Greg Maddux, Chicago, pitcher

American League

Don Mattingly, New York, first base
Roberto Alomar, Toronto, second base
Robin Ventura, Chicago, third base
Cal Ripken Jr., Baltimore, shortstop
Devon White, Toronto, outfield
Kirby Puckett, Minnesota, outfield
Ken Griffey Jr., Seattle, outfield
Ivan Rodriguez, Texas, catcher
Mark Langston, California, pitcher

The following are the players at each position who have won the most Gold Gloves since the award was instituted in 1957.

First base:	Keith Hernandez . . .	11
	George Scott.	8
Second base:	Ryne Sandberg . . .	9
	Bill Mazeroski . . .	8
	Frank White	8
Third base:	Brooks Robinson. . .	16
	Mike Schmidt.	10
Shortstop:	Ozzie Smith	13
	Luis Aparicio	9
Outfield:	Roberto Clemente . .	12
	Willie Mays	12
	Al Kaline	10
	Paul Blair	8
	Dwight Evans.	8
	Garry Maddox	8
Catcher:	Johnny Bench	10
	Bob Boone	7
Pitcher:	Jim Kaat	16
	Bob Gibson.	9

Home Run Leaders

National League

Year	Player, Club	HR
1901	Sam Crawford, Cincinnati	16
1902	Thomas Leach, Pittsburgh	6
1903	James Sheckard, Brooklyn	9
1904	Harry Lumley, Brooklyn	9
1905	Fred Odwell, Cincinnati	9
1906	Timothy Jordan, Brooklyn	12
1907	David Brain, Boston	10
1908	Timothy Jordan, Brooklyn	12
1909	Red Murray, New York	7
1910	Fred Beck, Bos., Frank Schulte, Chi.	10
1911	Frank Schulte, Chicago	21
1912	Henry Zimmerman, Chicago	14
1913	Gavvy Cravath, Philadelphia	19
1914	Gavvy Cravath, Philadelphia	19
1915	Gavvy Cravath, Philadelphia	24
1916	Dave Robertson, N.Y., Fred (Cy) Williams, Chi.	12
1917	Dave Robertson, N.Y., Gavvy Cravath, Phil.	12
1918	Gavvy Cravath, Philadelphia	8
1919	Gavvy Cravath, Philadelphia	12
1920	Cy Williams, Philadelphia	15
1921	George Kelly, New York	23
1922	Rogers Hornsby, St. Louis	42
1923	Cy Williams, Philadelphia	41
1924	Jacques Fournier, Brooklyn	27
1925	Rogers Hornsby, St. Louis	39
1926	Hack Wilson, Chicago	21
1927	Hack Wilson, Chicago; Cy Williams, Philadelphia	30
1928	Hack Wilson, Chicago; Jim Bottomley, St. Louis	31
1929	Chuck Klein, Philadelphia	43
1930	Hack Wilson, Chicago	56
1931	Chuck Klein, Philadelphia	31
1932	Chuck Klein, Philadelphia, Mel Ott, New York	38
1933	Chuck Klein, Philadelphia	28
1934	Rip Collins, St. Louis; Mel Ott, New York	35
1935	Walter Berger, Boston	34
1936	Mel Ott, New York	33
1937	Mel Ott, New York; Joe Medwick, St. Louis	31
1938	Mel Ott, New York	36
1939	John Mize, St. Louis	28
1940	John Mize, St. Louis	43
1941	Dolph Camilli, Brooklyn	34
1942	Mel Ott, New York	30
1943	Bill Nicholson, Chicago	29
1944	Bill Nicholson, Chicago	33
1945	Tommy Holmes, Boston	28
1946	Ralph Kiner, Pittsburgh	23
1947	Ralph Kiner, Pittsburgh; John Mize, New York	51
1948	Ralph Kiner, Pittsburgh; John Mize, New York	40
1949	Ralph Kiner, Pittsburgh	54
1950	Ralph Kiner, Pittsburgh	47
1951	Ralph Kiner, Pittsburgh	42
1952	Ralph Kiner, Pittsburgh; Hank Sauer, Chicago	37
1953	Ed Mathews, Milwaukee	47
1954	Ted Kluszewski, Cincinnati	49
1955	Willie Mays, New York	51
1956	Duke Snider, Brooklyn	43
1957	Hank Aaron, Milwaukee	44
1958	Ernie Banks, Chicago	47
1959	Ed Mathews, Milwaukee	46
1960	Ernie Banks, Chicago	41
1961	Orlando Cepeda, San Francisco	46
1962	Willie Mays, San Francisco	49
1963	Hank Aaron, Milwaukee, Willie McCovey, S.F.	44
1964	Willie Mays, San Francisco	47
1965	Willie Mays, San Francisco	52
1966	Hank Aaron, Atlanta	44
1967	Hank Aaron, Atlanta	39
1968	Willie McCovey, San Francisco	36
1969	Willie McCovey, San Francisco	45
1970	Johnny Bench, Cincinnati	45
1971	Willie Stargell, Pittsburgh	48
1972	Johnny Bench, Cincinnati	40
1973	Willie Stargell, Pittsburgh	44
1974	Mike Schmidt, Philadelphia	36
1975	Mike Schmidt, Philadelphia	38
1976	Mike Schmidt, Philadelphia	38
1977	George Foster, Cincinnati	52
1978	George Foster, Cincinnati	40
1979	Dave Kingman, Chicago	48
1980	Mike Schmidt, Philadelphia	48
1981	Mike Schmidt, Philadelphia	31
1982	Dave Kingman, New York	37

American League

Year	Player, Club	HR
1901	Napoleon Lajoie, Philadelphia	14
1902	Socks Seybold, Philadelphia	16
1903	Buck Freeman, Boston	13
1904	Harry Davis, Philadelphia	10
1905	Harry Davis, Philadelphia	8
1906	Harry Davis, Philadelphia	12
1907	Harry Davis, Philadelphia	8
1908	Sam Crawford, Detroit	7
1909	Ty Cobb, Detroit	9
1910	Jake Stahl, Boston	10
1911	J. Franklin Baker, Philadelphia	11
1912	J. Franklin Baker, Philadelphia, Tris Speaker, Boston	10
1913	J. Franklin, Baker, Philadelphia	12
1914	J. Franklin, Baker, Philadelphia	9
1915	Robert Roth, Chicago-Cleveland	7
1916	Wally Pipp, New York	12
1917	Wally Pipp, New York	9
1918	Babe Ruth, Bos., Tilly Walker, Phil.	11
1919	Babe Ruth, Boston	29
1920	Babe Ruth, New York	54
1921	Babe Ruth, New York	59
1922	Ken Williams, St. Louis	39
1923	Babe Ruth, New York	41
1924	Babe Ruth, New York	46
1925	Bob Meusel, New York	33
1926	Babe Ruth, New York	47
1927	Babe Ruth, New York	60
1928	Babe Ruth, New York	54
1929	Babe Ruth, New York	46
1930	Babe Ruth, New York	49
1931	Babe Ruth, Lou Gehrig, New York	46
1932	Jimmie Foxx, Philadelphia	58
1933	Jimmie Foxx, Philadelphia	48
1934	Lou Gehrig, New York	49
1935	Jimmie Foxx, Philadelphia, Hank Greenberg, Detroit	36
1936	Lou Gehrig, New York	49
1937	Joe DiMaggio, New York	46
1938	Hank Greenberg, Detroit	58
1939	Jimmie Foxx, Boston	35
1940	Hank Greenberg, Detroit	41
1941	Ted Williams, Boston	37
1942	Ted Williams, Boston	36
1943	Rudy York, Detroit	34
1944	Nick Etten, New York	22
1945	Vern Stephens, St. Louis	24
1946	Hank Greenberg, Detroit	44
1947	Ted Williams, Boston	32
1948	Joe DiMaggio, New York	39
1949	Ted Williams, Boston	43
1950	Al Rosen, Cleveland	37
1951	Gus Zernial, Chicago-Philadelphia	33
1952	Larry Doby, Cleveland	32
1953	Al Rosen, Cleveland	43
1954	Larry Doby, Cleveland	32
1955	Mickey Mantle, New York	37
1956	Mickey Mantle, New York	52
1957	Roy Sievers, Washington	42
1958	Mickey Mantle, New York	42
1959	Rocky Colavito, Cleve., Harmon Killebrew, Wash.	42
1960	Mickey Mantle, New York	40
1961	Roger Maris, New York	61
1962	Harmon Killebrew, Minnesota	48
1963	Harmon Killebrew, Minnesota	45
1964	Harmon Killebrew, Minnesota	49
1965	Tony Conigliaro, Boston	32
1966	Frank Robinson, Baltimore	49
1967	Carl Yastrzemski, Boston, Harmon Killebrew, Minn.	44
1968	Frank Howard, Washington	44
1969	Harmon Killebrew, Minnesota	49
1970	Frank Howard, Washington	44
1971	Bill Melton, Chicago	33
1972	Dick Allen, Chicago	37
1973	Reggie Jackson, Oakland	32
1974	Dick Allen, Chicago	32
1975	George Scott, Milwaukee; Reggie Jackson, Oakland	36
1976	Graig Nettles, New York	32
1977	Jim Rice, Boston	39
1978	Jim Rice, Boston	46
1979	Gorman Thomas, Milwaukee	45
1980	Reggie Jackson, New York; Ben Oglivie, Milwaukee	41
1981	Bobby Grich, California; Tony Armas, Oakland; Dwight Evans, Boston; Eddie Murray, Baltimore	22
1982	Gorman Thomas, Milwaukee; Reggie Jackson, Cal.	39

Year	Player, Club	HR
1983	Mike Schmidt, Philadelphia	40
1984	Mike Schmidt, Phil.; Dale Murphy, Atlanta	36
1985	Dale Murphy, Atlanta	37
1986	Mike Schmidt, Philadelphia	37
1987	Andre Dawson, Chicago	49
1988	Darryl Strawberry, New York	39
1989	Kevin Mitchell, San Francisco	47
1990	Ryne Sandberg, Chicago	40
1991	Howard Johnson, New York	38
1992	Fred McGriff, San Diego	35
1993	Barry Bonds, San Francisco	46

Year	Player, Club	HR
1983	Jim Rice, Boston	39
1984	Tony Armas, Boston	43
1985	Darrell Evans, Detroit	40
1986	Jesse Barfield, Toronto	40
1987	Mark McGwire, Oakland	49
1988	Jose Canseco, Oakland	42
1989	Fred McGriff, Toronto	36
1990	Cecil Fielder, Detroit	51
1991	Cecil Fielder, Detroit; Jose Canseco, Oakland	44
1992	Juan Gonzalez, Texas	43
1993	Juan Gonzalez, Texas	46

Runs Batted In Leaders

National League

Year	Player, Club	RBI
1907	Honus Wagner, Pittsburgh	91
1908	Honus Wager, Pittsburgh	106
1909	Honus Wager, Pittsburgh	102
1910	Sherwood Magee, Philadelphia	116
1911	Frank Schulte, Chicago	121
1912	Henry Zimmerman, Chicago	98
1913	Gavvy Cravath, Philadelphia	118
1914	Sherwood Magee, Philadelphia	101
1915	Gavvy Cravath, Philadelphia	118
1916	Hal Chase, Cincinnati	94
1917	Henry Zimmerman, New York	100
1918	Frederick Merkle, Chicago	71
1919	Hi Myers, Boston	72
1920	George Kelly, N.Y., Rogers Hornsby, St. Louis	94
1921	Rogers Hornsby, St. Louis	126
1922	Rogers Hornsby, St. Louis	152
1923	Emil Meusel, New York	125
1924	George Kelly, New York	136
1925	Rogers Hornsby, St. Louis	143
1926	Jim Bottomley, St. Louis	120
1927	Paul Waner, Pittsburgh	131
1928	Jim Bottomley, St. Louis	136
1929	Hack Wilson, Chicago	159
1930	Hack Wilson, Chicago	190
1931	Chuck Klein, Philadelphia	121
1932	Don Hurst, Philadelphia	143
1933	Chuck Klein, Philadelphia	120
1934	Mel Ott, New York	135
1935	Walter Berger, Boston	130
1936	Joe Medwick, St. Louis	138
1937	Joe Medwick, St. Louis	154
1938	Joe Medwick, St. Louis	122
1939	Frank McCormick, Cincinnati	128
1940	John Mize, St. Louis	137
1941	Adolph Camilli, Brooklyn	120
1942	John Mize, New York	110
1943	Bill Nicholson, Chicago	128
1944	Bill Nicholson, Chicago	122
1945	Dixie Walker, Brooklyn	124
1946	Enos Slaughter, St. Louis	130
1947	John Mize, New York	138
1948	Stan Musial, St. Louis	131
1949	Ralph Kiner, Pittsburgh	127
1950	Del Ennis, Philadelphia	126
1951	Monte Irvin, New York	121
1952	Hank Sauer, Chicago	121
1953	Roy Campanella, Brooklyn	142
1954	Ted Kluszewski, Cincinnati	141
1955	Duke Snider, Brooklyn	136
1956	Stan Musial, St. Louis	109
1957	Hank Aaron, Milwaukee	132
1958	Ernie Banks, Chicago	129
1959	Ernie Banks, Chicago	143
1960	Hank Aaron, Milwaukee	126
1961	Orlando Cepeda, San Francisco	142
1962	Tommy Davis, Los Angeles	153
1963	Hank Aaron, Milwaukee	130
1964	Ken Boyer, St. Louis	119
1965	Deron Johnson, Cincinnati	130
1966	Hank Aaron, Atlanta	127
1967	Orlando Cepeda, St. Louis	111
1968	Willie McCovey, San Francisco	105
1969	Willie McCovey, San Francisco	126
1970	Johnny Bench, Cincinnati	148
1971	Joe Torre, St. Louis	137
1972	Johnny Bench, Cincinnati	125
1973	Willie Stargell, Pittsburgh	119
1974	Johnny Bench, Cincinnati	129
1975	Greg Luzinski, Philadelphia	120

American League

Year	Player, Club	RBI
1907	Ty Cobb, Detroit	116
1908	Ty Cobb, Detroit	101
1909	Ty Cobb, Detroit	115
1910	Sam Crawford, Detroit	115
1911	Ty Cobb, Detroit	144
1912	J. Franklin Baker, Philadelphia	133
1913	J. Franklin Baker, Philadelphia	126
1914	Sam Crawford, Detroit	112
1915	Sam Crawford, Detroit	116
1916	Wally Pipp, New York	99
1917	Robert Veach, Detroit	115
1918	George Burns, Phila., Robert Veach, Detroit	74
1919	Babe Ruth, Boston	112
1920	Babe Ruth, New York	137
1921	Babe Ruth, New York	171
1922	Ken Williams, St. Louis	155
1923	Babe Ruth, New York	131
1924	Goose Goslin, Washington	129
1925	Bob Meusel, New York	138
1926	Babe Ruth, New York	145
1927	Lou Gehrig, New York	175
1928	Babe Ruth, N.Y., Lou Gehrig, N.Y.	142
1929	Al Simmons, Philadelphia	157
1930	Lou Gehrig, New York	174
1931	Lou Gehrig, New York	184
1932	Jimmie Foxx, Philadelphia	169
1933	Jimmie Foxx, Philadelphia	163
1934	Lou Gehrig, New York	165
1935	Hank Greenberg, Detroit	170
1936	Hal Trosky, Cleveland	162
1937	Hank Greenberg, Detroit	183
1938	Jimmie Foxx, Boston	175
1939	Ted Williams, Boston	145
1940	Hank Greenberg, Detroit	150
1941	Joe DiMaggio, New York	125
1942	Ted Williams, Boston	137
1943	Rudy York, Detroit	118
1944	Vern Stephens, St. Louis	109
1945	Nick Etten, New York	111
1946	Hank Greenberg, Detroit	127
1947	Ted Williams, Boston	114
1948	Joe DiMaggio, New York	155
1949	Ted Williams, Bos., Vern Stephens, Bos.	159
1950	Walt Dropo, Bos., Vern Stephens, Bos.	144
1951	Gus Zernial, Chicago-Philadelphia	129
1952	Al Rosen, Cleveland	105
1953	Al Rosen, Cleveland	145
1954	Larry Doby, Cleveland	126
1955	Ray Boone, Detroit, Jackie Jensen, Boston	116
1956	Mickey Mantle, New York	130
1957	Roy Sievers, Washington	114
1958	Jackie Jensen, Boston	122
1959	Jackie Jensen, Boston	112
1960	Roger Maris, New York	112
1961	Roger Maris, New York	142
1962	Harmon Killebrew, Minnesota	126
1963	Dick Stuart, Boston	118
1964	Brooks Robinson, Baltimore	118
1965	Rocky Colavito, Cleveland	108
1966	Frank Robinson, Baltimore	122
1967	Carl Yastrzemski, Boston	121
1968	Ken Harrelson, Boston	109
1969	Harmon Killebrew, Minnesota	140
1970	Frank Howard, Washington	126
1971	Harmon Killebrew, Minnesota	119
1972	Dick Allen, Chicago	113
1973	Reggie Jackson, Oakland	117
1974	Jeff Burroughs, Texas	118
1975	George Scott, Milwaukee	109

Year	Player, Club	RBI
1976	George Foster, Cincinnati	121
1977	George Foster, Cincinnati	149
1978	George Foster, Cincinnati	120
1979	Dave Winfield, San Diego	118
1980	Mike Schmidt, Philadelphia	121
1981	Mike Schmidt, Philadelphia	91
1982	Dale Murphy, Atlanta; Al Oliver, Montreal	109
1983	Dale Murphy, Atlanta	121
1984	Mike Schmidt, Phil.; Gary Carter, Montreal	106
1985	Dave Parker, Cincinnati	125
1986	Mike Schmidt, Philadelphia	119
1987	Andre Dawson, Chicago	137
1988	Will Clark, San Francisco	109
1989	Kevin Mitchell, San Francisco	125
1990	Matt Williams, San Francisco	122
1991	Howard Johnson, New York	117
1992	Darren Daulton, Philadelphia	109
1993	Barry Bonds, San Francisco	123

Year	Player, Club	RBI
1976	Lee May, Baltimore	109
1977	Larry Hisle, Minnesota	119
1978	Jim Rice, Boston	139
1979	Don Baylor, California	139
1980	Cecil Cooper, Milwaukee	122
1981	Eddie Murray, Baltimore	78
1982	Hal McRae, Kansas City	133
1983	Cecil Cooper, Milwaukee; Jim Rice, Boston	126
1984	Tony Armas, Boston	123
1985	Don Mattingly, New York	145
1986	Joe Carter, Cleveland	121
1987	George Bell, Toronto	134
1988	Jose Canseco, Oakland	124
1989	Ruben Sierra, Texas	119
1990	Cecil Fielder, Detroit	132
1991	Cecil Fielder, Detroit	133
1992	Cecil Fielder, Detroit	124
1993	Albert Belle, Cleveland	129

Batting Champions

National League

Year	Player	Club	Pct.
1901	Jesse C. Burkett	St. Louis	.382
1902	Clarence Beaumont	Pittsburgh	.357
1903	Honus Wagner	Pittsburgh	.355
1904	Honus Wagner	Pittsburgh	.349
1905	James Seymour	Cincinnati	.377
1906	Honus Wagner	Pittsburgh	.339
1907	Honus Wagner	Pittsburgh	.350
1908	Honus Wagner	Pittsburgh	.354
1909	Honus Wagner	Pittsburgh	.339
1910	Sherwood Magee	Philadelphia	.331
1911	Honus Wagner	Pittsburgh	.334
1912	Henry Zimmerman	Chicago	.372
1913	Jacob Daubert	Brooklyn	.350
1914	Jacob Daubert	Brooklyn	.329
1915	Larry Doyle	New York	.320
1916	Hal Chase	Cincinnati	.339
1917	Edd Roush	Cleveland	.341
1918	Zach Wheat	Brooklyn	.335
1919	Edd Roush	Cincinnati	.321
1920	Rogers Hornsby	St. Louis	.370
1921	Rogers Hornsby	St. Louis	.397
1922	Rogers Hornsby	St. Louis	.401
1923	Rogers Hornsby	St. Louis	.384
1924	Rogers Hornsby	St. Louis	.424
1925	Rogers Hornsby	St. Louis	.403
1926	Eugene Hargrave	Cincinnati	.353
1927	Paul Waner	Pittsburgh	.380
1928	Rogers Hornsby	Boston	.387
1929	Lefty O'Doul	Philadelphia	.398
1930	Bill Terry	New York	.401
1931	Chick Hafey	St. Louis	.349
1932	Lefty O'Doul	Brooklyn	.368
1933	Chuck Klein	Philadelphia	.368
1934	Paul Waner	Pittsburgh	.362
1935	Arky Vaughan	Pittsburgh	.385
1936	Paul Waner	Pittsburgh	.373
1937	Joe Medwick	St. Louis	.374
1938	Ernie Lombardi	Cincinnati	.342
1939	John Mize	St. Louis	.349
1940	Debs Garms	Pittsburgh	.355
1941	Pete Reiser	Brooklyn	.343
1942	Ernie Lombardi	Boston	.330
1943	Stan Musial	St. Louis	.357
1944	Dixie Walker	Brooklyn	.357
1945	Phil Cavarretta	Chicago	.355
1946	Stan Musial	St. Louis	.365
1947	Harry Walker	Philadelphia	.363
1948	Stan Musial	St. Louis	.376
1949	Jackie Robinson	Brooklyn	.342
1950	Stan Musial	St. Louis	.346
1951	Stan Musial	St. Louis	.355
1952	Stan Musial	St. Louis	.336
1953	Carl Furillo	Brooklyn	.344
1954	Willie Mays	New York	.345
1955	Richie Ashburn	Philadelphia	.338
1956	Hank Aaron	Milwaukee	.328
1957	Stan Musial	St. Louis	.351
1958	Richie Ashburn	Philadelphia	.350
1959	Hank Aaron	Milwaukee	.355
1960	Dick Groat	Pittsburgh	.325
1961	Roberto Clemente	Pittsburgh	.351
1962	Tommy Davis	Los Angeles	.346
1963	Tommy Davis	Los Angeles	.326
1964	Roberto Clemente	Pittsburgh	.339

American League

Year	Player	Club	Pct.
1901	Napoleon Lajoie	Philadelphia	.422
1902	Ed Delahanty	Washington	.376
1902	Napoleon Lajoie	Cleveland	.355
1904	Napoleon Lajoie	Cleveland	.381
1905	Elmer Flick	Cleveland	.308
1906	George Stone	St. Louis	.358
1907	Ty Cobb	Detroit	.350
1908	Ty Cobb	Detroit	.324
1909	Ty Cobb	Detroit	.377
1910	Ty Cobb	Detroit	.385
1911	Ty Cobb	Detroit	.420
1912	Ty Cobb	Detroit	.410
1913	Ty Cobb	Detroit	.390
1914	Ty Cobb	Detroit	.368
1915	Ty Cobb	Detroit	.369
1916	Tris Speaker	Cleveland	.386
1917	Ty Cobb	Detroit	.383
1918	Ty Cobb	Detroit	.382
1919	Ty Cobb	Detroit	.384
1920	George Sisler	St. Louis	.407
1921	Harry Heilmann	Detroit	.394
1922	George Sisler	St. Louis	.420
1923	Harry Heilmann	Detroit	.403
1924	Babe Ruth	New York	.378
1925	Harry Heilmann	Detroit	.393
1926	Henry Manush	Detroit	.378
1927	Harry Heilmann	Detroit	.398
1928	Goose Goslin	Washington	.379
1929	Lew Fonseca	Cleveland	.369
1930	Al Simmons	Philadelphia	.381
1931	Al Simmons	Philadelphia	.390
1932	Dale Alexander	Detroit-Boston	.367
1933	Jimmie Foxx	Philadelphia	.356
1934	Lou Gehrig	New York	.363
1935	Buddy Myer	Washington	.349
1936	Luke Appling	Chicago	.388
1937	Charlie Gehringer	Detroit	.371
1938	Jimmie Foxx	Boston	.349
1939	Joe DiMaggio	New York	.381
1940	Joe DiMaggio	New York	.352
1941	Ted Williams	Boston	.406
1942	Ted Williams	Boston	.356
1943	Luke Appling	Chicago	.328
1944	Lou Boudreau	Cleveland	.327
1945	George Stirnweiss	New York	.309
1946	Mickey Vernon	Washington	.353
1947	Ted Williams	Boston	.343
1948	Ted Williams	Boston	.369
1949	George Kell	Detroit	.343
1950	Billy Goodman	Boston	.354
1951	Ferris Fain	Philadelphia	.344
1952	Ferris Fain	Philadelphia	.327
1953	Mickey Vernon	Washington	.337
1954	Roberto Avila	Cleveland	.341
1955	Al Kaline	Detroit	.340
1956	Mickey Mantle	New York	.353
1957	Ted Williams	Boston	.388
1958	Ted Williams	Boston	.328
1959	Harvey Kuenn	Detroit	.353
1960	Pete Runnels	Boston	.320
1961	Norm Cash	Detroit	.361
1962	Pete Runnels	Boston	.326
1963	Carl Yastrzemski	Boston	.321
1964	Tony Oliva	Minnesota	.323

Year	Player	Club	Pct.
1965	Roberto Clemente	Pittsburgh	.329
1966	Matty Alou	Pittsburgh	.342
1967	Roberto Clemente	Pittsburgh	.357
1968	Pete Rose	Cincinnati	.335
1969	Pete Rose	Cincinnati	.348
1970	Rico Carty	Atlanta	.366
1971	Joe Torre	St. Louis	.363
1972	Billy Williams	Chicago	.333
1973	Pete Rose	Cincinnati	.338
1974	Ralph Garr	Atlanta	.353
1975	Bill Madlock	Chicago	.354
1976	Bill Madlock	Chicago	.339
1977	Dave Parker	Pittsburgh	.338
1978	Dave Parker	Pittsburgh	.334
1979	Keith Hernandez	St. Louis	.344
1980	Bill Buckner	Chicago	.324
1981	Bill Madlock	Pittsburgh	.341
1982	Al Oliver	Montreal	.331
1983	Bill Madlock	Pittsburgh	.323
1984	Tony Gwynn	San Diego	.351
1985	Willie McGee	St. Louis	.353
1986	Tim Raines	Montreal	.334
1987	Tony Gwynn	San Diego	.369
1988	Tony Gwynn	San Diego	.313
1989	Tony Gwynn	San Diego	.336
1990	Willie McGee	St. Louis	.335
1991	Terry Pendleton	Atlanta	.319
1992	Gary Sheffield	San Diego	.330
1993	Andres Galarraga	Colorado	.370

Year	Player	Club	Pct.
1965	Tony Oliva	Minnesota	.321
1966	Frank Robinson	Baltimore	.316
1967	Carl Yastrzemski	Boston	.326
1968	Carl Yastrzemski	Boston	.301
1969	Rod Carew	Minnesota	.332
1970	Alex Johnson	California	.328
1971	Tony Oliva	Minnesota	.337
1972	Rod Carew	Minnesota	.318
1973	Rod Carew	Minnesota	.350
1974	Rod Carew	Minnesota	.364
1975	Rod Carew	Minnesota	.359
1976	George Brett	Kansas City	.333
1977	Rod Carew	Minnesota	.388
1978	Rod Carew	Minnesota	.333
1979	Fred Lynn	Boston	.333
1980	George Brett	Kansas City	.390
1981	Carney Lansford	Boston	.336
1982	Willie Wilson	Kansas City	.332
1983	Wade Boggs	Boston	.361
1984	Don Mattingly	New York	.343
1985	Wade Boggs	Boston	.368
1986	Wade Boggs	Boston	.357
1987	Wade Boggs	Boston	.363
1988	Wade Boggs	Boston	.366
1989	Kirby Puckett	Minnesota	.339
1990	George Brett	Kansas City	.329
1991	Julio Franco	Texas	.342
1992	Edgar Martinez	Seattle	.343
1993	John Olerud	Toronto	.363

Cy Young Award Winners

Year	Player, club
1956	Don Newcombe, Dodgers
1957	Warren Spahn, Braves
1958	Bob Turley, Yankees
1959	Early Wynn, White Sox
1960	Vernon Law, Pirates
1961	Whitey Ford, Yankees
1962	Don Drysdale, Dodgers
1963	Sandy Koufax, Dodgers
1964	Dean Chance, Angels
1965	Sandy Koufax, Dodgers
1966	Sandy Koufax, Dodgers
1967	(NL) Mike McCormick, Giants
	(AL) Jim Lonborg, Red Sox
1968	(NL) Bob Gibson, Cardinals
	(AL) Dennis McLain, Tigers
1969	(NL) Tom Seaver, Mets
	(AL) (tie) Dennis McLain, Tigers
	Mike Cuellar, Orioles
1970	(NL) Bob Gibson, Cardinals
	(AL) Jim Perry, Twins
1971	(NL) Ferguson Jenkins, Cubs
	(AL) Vida Blue, A's
1972	(NL) Steve Carlton, Phillies
	(AL) Gaylord Perry, Indians
1973	(NL) Tom Seaver, Mets
	(AL) Jim Palmer, Orioles
1974	(NL) Mike Marshall, Dodgers
	(AL) Jim (Catfish) Hunter, A's
1975	(NL) Tom Seaver, Mets
	(AL) Jim Palmer, Orioles
1976	(NL) Randy Jones, Padres
	(AL) Jim Palmer, Orioles
1977	(NL) Steve Carlton, Phillies
	(AL) Sparky Lyle, Yankees
1978	(NL) Gaylord Perry, Padres
	(AL) Ron Guidry, Yankees
1979	(NL) Bruce Sutter, Cubs
	(AL) Mike Flanagan, Orioles
1980	(NL) Steve Carlton, Phillies
	(AL) Steve Stone, Orioles
1981	(NL) Fernando Valenzuela, Dodgers
	(AL) Rollie Fingers, Brewers
1982	(NL) Steve Carlton, Phillies
	(AL) Pete Vuckovich, Brewers
1983	(NL) John Denny, Phillies
	(AL) LaMarr Hoyt, White Sox
1984	(NL) Rick Sutcliffe, Cubs
	(AL) Willie Hernandez, Tigers
1985	(NL) Dwight Gooden, Mets
	(AL) Bret Saberhagen, Royals
1986	(NL) Mike Scott, Astros
	(AL) Roger Clemens, Red Sox
1987	(NL) Steve Bedrosian, Phillies
	(AL) Roger Clemens, Red Sox
1988	(NL) Orel Hershiser, Dodgers
	(AL) Frank Viola, Twins
1989	(NL) Mark Davis, Padres
	(AL) Bret Saberhagen, Royals
1990	(NL) Doug Drabek, Pirates
	(AL) Bob Welch, A's
1991	(NL) Tom Glavine, Braves
	(AL) Roger Clemens, Red Sox
1992	(NL) Greg Maddux, Cubs
	(AL) Dennis Eckersley, A's

Pitchers with 300 Major League Wins

Cy Young	511	Warren Spahn	363	Steve Carlton	329	Nolan Ryan	324	Mickey Welch	311		
Walter Johnson	416	Pud Galvin	361	Eddie Plank	327	Phil Niekro	318	Old Hoss Radbourn	308		
Christy Mathewson	373	Kid Nichols	360	John Clarkson	326	Gaylord Perry	314	Lefty Grove	300		
Grover Alexander	373	Tim Keefe	344	Don Sutton	324	Tom Seaver	311	Early Wynn	300		

Division Realignment in 1994

The National and American leagues are expected to switch from a two-division to a three-division alignment for the 1994 season. Postseason play will have an additional playoff series. Four teams in each league will make the playoffs—the three division winners and the non-division winner with the best record (the wild card team). The new format was not official as of Oct. 1993.

National League

East	Central	West
Atlanta	Chicago	Colorado
Florida	Cincinnati	Los Angeles
Montreal	Houston	San Diego
New York	Pittsburgh	San Francisco
Philadelphia	St. Louis	

American League

East	Central	West
Baltimore	Chicago	California
Boston	Cleveland	Oakland
Detroit	Kansas City	Seattle
New York	Milwaukee	Texas
Toronto	Minnesota	

Most Valuable Player

Baseball Writers' Association

National League

Year	Player, team
1931	Frank Frisch, St. Louis
1932	Charles Klein, Philadelphia
1933	Carl Hubbell, New York
1934	Dizzy Dean, St. Louis
1935	Gabby Hartnett, Chicago
1936	Carl Hubbell, New York
1937	Joe Medwick, St. Louis
1938	Ernie Lombardi, Cincinnati
1939	Bucky Walters, Cincinnati
1940	Frank McCormick, Cincinnati
1941	Dolph Camilli, Brooklyn
1942	Mort Cooper, St. Louis
1943	Stan Musial, St. Louis
1944	Martin Marion, St. Louis
1945	Phil Cavarretta, Chicago
1946	Stan Musial, St. Louis
1947	Bob Elliott, Boston
1948	Stan Musial, St. Louis
1949	Jackie Robinson, Brooklyn
1950	Jim Konstanty, Philadelphia
1951	Roy Campanella, Brooklyn
1952	Hank Sauer, Chicago
1953	Roy Campanella, Brooklyn
1954	Willie Mays, New York
1955	Roy Campanella, Brooklyn
1956	Don Newcombe, Brooklyn
1957	Henry Aaron, Milwaukee
1958	Ernie Banks, Chicago
1959	Ernie Banks, Chicago
1960	Dick Groat, Pittsburgh
1961	Frank Robinson, Cincinnati
1962	Maury Wills, Los Angeles
1963	Sandy Koufax, Los Angeles
1964	Ken Boyer, St. Louis
1965	Willie Mays, San Francisco
1966	Roberto Clemente, Pittsburgh
1967	Orlando Cepeda, St. Louis
1968	Bob Gibson, St. Louis
1969	Willie McCovey, San Francisco
1970	Johnny Bench, Cincinnati
1971	Joe Torre, St. Louis
1972	Johnny Bench, Cincinnati
1973	Pete Rose, Cincinnati
1974	Steve Garvey, Los Angeles
1975	Joe Morgan, Cincinnati
1976	Joe Morgan, Cincinnati
1977	George Foster, Cincinnati
1978	Dave Parker, Pittsburgh
1979	(tie) Willie Stargell, Pittsburgh Keith Hernandez, St. Louis
1980	Mike Schmidt, Philadelphia
1981	Mike Schmidt, Philadelphia
1982	Dale Murphy, Atlanta
1983	Dale Murphy, Atlanta
1984	Ryne Sandberg, Chicago
1985	Willie McGee, St. Louis
1986	Mike Schmidt, Philadelphia
1987	Andre Dawson, Chicago
1988	Kirk Gibson, Los Angeles
1989	Kevin Mitchell, San Francisco
1990	Barry Bonds, Pittsburgh
1991	Terry Pendleton, Atlanta
1992	Barry Bonds, Pittsburgh

American League

Year	Player, team
1931	Lefty Grove, Philadelphia
1932	Jimmie Foxx, Philadelphia
1933	Jimmie Foxx, Philadelphia
1934	Mickey Cochrane, Detroit
1935	Hank Greenberg, Detroit
1936	Lou Gehrig, New York
1937	Charley Gehringer, Detroit
1938	Jimmie Foxx, Boston
1939	Joe DiMaggio, New York
1940	Hank Greenberg, Detroit
1941	Joe DiMaggio, New York
1942	Joe Gordon, New York
1943	Spurgeon Chandler, New York
1944	Hal Newhouser, Detroit
1945	Hal Newhouser, Detroit
1946	Ted Williams, Boston
1947	Joe DiMaggio, New York
1948	Lou Boudreau, Cleveland
1949	Ted Williams, Boston
1950	Phil Rizzuto, New York
1951	Yogi Berra, New York
1952	Bobby Shantz, Philadelphia
1953	Al Rosen, Cleveland
1954	Yogi Berra, New York
1955	Yogi Berra, New York
1956	Mickey Mantle, New York
1957	Mickey Mantle, New York
1958	Jackie Jensen, Boston
1959	Nellie Fox, Chicago
1960	Roger Maris, New York
1961	Roger Maris, New York
1962	Mickey Mantle, New York
1963	Elston Howard, New York
1964	Brooks Robinson, Baltimore
1965	Zoilo Versalles, Minnesota
1966	Frank Robinson, Baltimore
1967	Carl Yastrzemski, Boston
1968	Denny McLain, Detroit
1969	Harmon Killebrew, Minnesota
1970	John (Boog) Powell, Baltimore
1971	Vida Blue, Oakland
1972	Dick Allen, Chicago
1973	Reggie Jackson, Oakland
1974	Jeff Burroughs, Texas
1975	Fred Lynn, Boston
1976	Thurman Munson, New York
1977	Rod Carew, Minnesota
1978	Jim Rice, Boston
1979	Don Baylor, California
1980	George Brett, Kansas City
1981	Rollie Fingers, Milwaukee
1982	Robin Yount, Milwaukee
1983	Cal Ripken Jr., Baltimore
1984	Willie Hernandez, Detroit
1985	Don Mattingly, New York
1986	Roger Clemens, Boston
1987	George Bell, Toronto
1988	Jose Canseco, Oakland
1989	Robin Yount, Milwaukee
1990	Rickey Henderson
1991	Cal Ripken Jr., Baltimore
1992	Dennis Eckersley, Oakland

Rookie of the Year

Baseball Writers' Association

1947—Combined selection—Jackie Robinson, Brooklyn, 1b

1948—Combined selection—Alvin Dark, Boston, N.L. ss

National League

Year	Player, team
1949	Don Newcombe, Brooklyn, p
1950	Sam Jethroe, Boston, of
1951	Willie Mays, New York, of
1952	Joe Black, Brooklyn, p
1953	Jim Gilliam, Brooklyn, 2b
1954	Wally Moon, St. Louis, of
1955	Bill Virdon, St. Louis, of
1956	Frank Robinson, Cincinnati, of
1957	Jack Sanford, Philadelphia, p
1958	Orlando Cepeda, S.F., 1b
1959	Willie McCovey, S.F., 1b
1960	Frank Howard, Los Angeles, of
1961	Billy Williams, Chicago, of
1962	Ken Hubbs, Chicago, 2b
1963	Pete Rose, Cincinnati, 2b
1964	Richie Allen, Philadelphia, 3b
1965	Jim Lefebvre, Los Angeles, 2b
1966	Tommy Helms, Cincinnati, 2b
1967	Tom Seaver, New York, p
1968	Johnny Bench, Cincinnati c
1969	Ted Sizemore, Los Angeles, 2b
1970	Carl Morton, Montreal, p
1971	Earl Williams, Atlanta, c
1972	Jon Matlack, New York, p
1973	Gary Matthews, S.F., of
1974	Bake McBride, St. Louis, of
1975	John Montefusco, S.F., p
1976	(tie) Butch Metzger, San Diego, p Pat Zachry, Cincinnati, p
1977	Andre Dawson, Montreal, of
1978	Bob Horner, Atlanta, 3b
1979	Rick Sutcliffe, Los Angeles, p
1980	Steve Howe, Los Angeles, p
1981	Fernando Valenzuela, Los Angeles, p
1982	Steve Sax, Los Angeles, 2b
1983	Darryl Strawberry, New York, of
1984	Dwight Gooden, New York, p
1985	Vince Coleman, St. Louis, of
1986	Todd Worrell, St. Louis, p
1987	Benito Santiago, San Diego, c
1988	Chris Sabo, Cincinnati, 3b
1989	Jerome Walton, Chicago, of
1990	Dave Justice, Atlanta, 1b
1991	Jeff Bagwell, Houston, 1b
1992	Eric Karros, Los Angeles, 1b

American League

Year	Player, team
1949	Roy Sievers, St. Louis, of
1950	Walt Dropo, Boston, 1b
1951	Gil McDougald, New York, 3b
1952	Harry Byrd, Philadelphia, p
1953	Harvey Kuenn, Detroit, ss
1954	Bob Grim, New York, p
1955	Herb Score, Cleveland, p
1956	Luis Aparicio, Chicago, ss
1957	Tony Kubek, New York, if-of
1958	Albie Pearson, Washington, of
1959	Bob Allison, Washington, of
1960	Ron Hansen, Baltimore, ss
1961	Don Schwall, Boston, p
1962	Tom Tresh, New York, if-of
1963	Gary Peters, Chicago, p
1964	Tony Oliva, Minnesota, of
1965	Curt Blefary, Baltimore, of
1966	Tommie Agee, Chicago, of
1967	Rod Carew, Minnesota, 2b
1968	Stan Bahnsen, New York, p
1969	Lou Piniella, Kansas City, of
1970	Thurman Munson, New York, c
1971	Chris Chambliss, Cleveland, 1b
1972	Carlton Fisk, Boston, c
1973	Al Bumbry, Baltimore, of
1974	Mike Hargrove, Texas, 1b
1975	Fred Lynn, Boston, of
1976	Mark Fidrych, Detroit, p
1977	Eddie Murray, Baltimore, dh
1978	Lou Whitaker, Detroit, 2b
1979	(tie) John Castino, Minnesota, 3b Alfredo Griffin, Toronto, ss
1980	Joe Charboneau, Cleveland, of
1981	Dave Righetti, New York, p
1982	Cal Ripken Jr., Baltimore, ss
1983	Ron Kittle, Chicago, of
1984	Alvin Davis, Seattle, 1b
1985	Ozzie Guillen, Chicago, ss
1986	Jose Canseco, Oakland, of
1987	Mark McGwire, Oakland, 1b
1988	Walt Weiss, Oakland, ss
1989	Gregg Olson, Baltimore, p
1990	Sandy Alomar Jr., Cleveland, c
1991	Chuck Knoblauch, Minnesota, 2b
1992	Pat Listach, Milwaukee, ss

National League Records, 1993

Final standings

Eastern Division

	W	L	Pct.	GB	Home	vs. RHP	Grass	Night
Philadelphia	97	65	.599	—	52-29	61-46	30-19	72-45
Montreal	94	68	.580	3	55-26	65-47	24-25	72-40
St. Louis	87	75	.537	10	49-32	62-57	27-23	56-56
Chicago	84	78	.519	13	43-38	66-52	66-58	43-31
Pittsburgh	75	87	.463	22	40-41	55-59	26-24	54-65
Florida	64	98	.395	33	35-46	43-75	54-70	49-78
New York	59	103	.364	38	28-53	48-70	47-77	38-65

Western Division

	W	L	Pct.	GB	Home	vs. RHP	Grass	Night
Atlanta	104	58	.642	—	51-30	75-43	82-43	77-43
San Francisco	103	59	.636	1	50-31	71-38	78-47	49-33
Houston	85	77	.525	19	44-37	58-48	27-24	56-53
Los Angeles	81	81	.500	23	41-40	60-59	64-61	60-57
Cincinnati	73	89	.451	31	41-40	56-66	20-30	52-63
Colorado	67	95	.414	37	39-42	54-75	53-72	41-63
San Diego	61	101	.377	43	34-47	38-74	50-75	42-69

National League Championship Series

Philadelphia 4, Atlanta 3 (10 innings)
Atlanta 14, Philadelphia 3
Atlanta 9, Philadelphia 4
Philadelphia 2, Atlanta 1
Philadelphia 4, Atlanta 3 (10 innings)
Philadelphia 6, Atlanta 3

Team Batting

	Avg.	AB	R	H	HR	RBI
San Francisco	**.276**	5557	808	1534	168	759
Philadelphia	**.274**	5685	877	1555	156	811
Colorado	**.273**	5517	758	1507	142	704
St. Louis	**.272**	5551	758	1508	118	724
Chicago	**.270**	5627	738	1521	161	706
Pittsburgh	**.267**	5549	707	1482	110	664
Houston	**.267**	5464	716	1459	138	656
Cincinnati	**.264**	5517	722	1457	137	669
Atlanta	**.262**	5515	767	1444	169	712
Los Angeles	**.261**	5588	675	1458	130	639
Montreal	**.257**	5493	732	1410	122	682
San Diego	**.252**	5503	679	1386	153	633
New York	**.248**	5448	672	1350	158	632
Florida	**.248**	5475	581	1356	94	542

Team Pitching

	ERA	IP	H	BB	SO	SV
Atlanta	**3.14**	1455	1297	480	1036	46
Houston	**3.49**	1441⅓	1363	476	1056	42
Los Angeles	**3.50**	1472⅔	1406	567	1043	36
Montreal	**3.55**	1456⅔	1369	521	934	61
San Francisco	**3.61**	1456⅔	1385	442	982	50
Philadelphia	**3.95**	1472⅔	1419	573	1117	46
New York	**4.05**	1438	1483	434	867	22
St. Louis	**4.09**	1453	1553	383	775	54
Florida	**4.13**	1440⅓	1437	598	945	48
Chicago	**4.18**	1449⅔	1514	470	905	56
San Diego	**4.23**	1437⅔	1470	558	957	32
Cincinnati	**4.51**	1434	1510	508	996	37
Pittsburgh	**4.77**	1445⅔	1557	485	832	34
Colorado	**5.41**	1431⅓	1664	609	913	35

Individual Batting (at least 175 at-bats); Individual Pitching (at least 75 innings or 10 saves)

Atlanta Braves

Batting	Avg	AB	R	H	HR	RBI
Blauser	**.305**	597	110	182	15	73
McGriff	**.291**	557	111	162	37	101
Sanders	**.276**	272	42	75	6	28
Gant	**.274**	606	113	166	36	117
Pendleton	**.272**	633	81	172	17	84
Justice	**.270**	585	90	158	40	120
Nixon	**.269**	461	77	124	1	24
Bream	**.260**	277	33	72	9	35
Lemke	**.252**	493	52	124	7	49
Berryhill	**.245**	335	24	82	8	43
Olson	**.225**	262	23	59	4	24

Pitching	W	L	ERA	IP	H	BB	SO
McMichael	2	3	**2.06**	91.2	68	29	89
Maddux	20	10	**2.36**	267.0	228	52	197
Avery	18	6	**2.94**	223.1	216	43	125
Glavine	22	6	**3.20**	239.1	236	90	120
Smoltz	15	11	**3.62**	243.2	208	100	208
Smith	4	8	**4.37**	90.2	92	36	53

Manager—Bobby Cox

Chicago Cubs

Batting	Avg	AB	R	H	HR	RBI
Grace	**.325**	594	86	193	14	98
Sandberg	**.309**	456	67	141	9	45
Wilkins	**.303**	446	78	135	30	73
Smith	**.300**	310	51	93	11	35
May	**.295**	465	62	137	10	77
Vizcaino	**.287**	551	74	158	4	54
Sanchez	**.282**	344	35	97	0	28
Buechele	**.272**	460	53	125	15	65
Sosa	**.261**	598	92	156	33	93
Wilson	**.258**	221	29	57	1	11
Roberson	**.189**	180	23	34	9	27

Pitching	W	L	ERA	IP	H	BB	SO
Bautista	10	3	**2.82**	111.2	105	27	63
Myers	2	4	**3.11**	75.1	65	26	86
Hibbard	15	11	**3.96**	191.0	209	47	82
Morgan	10	15	**4.03**	207.2	206	74	111
Guzman	12	10	**4.34**	191.0	188	74	163
Scanlan	4	5	**4.54**	75.1	79	28	44
Castillo	5	8	**4.84**	141.1	162	39	84
Harkey	10	10	**5.26**	157.1	187	43	67

Manager—Jim LeFebvre

Cincinnati Reds

Batting	Avg	AB	R	H	HR	RBI
Mitchell	**.341**	323	56	110	19	64
Kelly	**.319**	320	44	102	9	35
Morris	**.317**	379	48	120	7	49
Larkin	**.315**	384	57	121	8	51
Sanders	**.274**	496	90	136	20	83
Milligan	**.274**	234	30	64	6	29
Brumfield	**.268**	272	40	73	6	23
Sabo	**.259**	552	86	143	21	82
Branson	**.241**	381	40	92	3	22
Roberts	**.240**	292	46	70	1	18
Oliver	**.239**	482	40	115	14	75
Samuel	**.230**	261	31	60	4	26

Pitching	W	L	ERA	IP	H	BB	SO
Rijo	14	9	**2.48**	257.1	218	62	227
Belcher	9	6	**4.47**	137.0	134	47	101
Luebbers	2	5	**4.54**	77.1	74	38	38
Browning	7	7	**4.74**	114.0	159	20	53
Pugh	10	15	**5.26**	164.1	200	59	94
Ayala	7	10	**5.60**	98.0	106	45	65
Smiley	3	9	**5.62**	105.2	117	31	60
Roper	2	5	**5.63**	80.0	92	36	54

Manager—Tony Perez; Dave Johnson

Colorado Rockies

Batting	Avg	AB	R	H	HR	RBI
Galarraga	**.370**	470	71	174	22	98
Bichette	**.310**	538	93	167	21	89
Hayes	**.305**	573	89	175	25	98
Girardi	**.290**	310	35	90	3	31
Benavides	**.286**	213	20	61	3	26
Clark	**.282**	478	65	135	13	67
Sheaffer	**.278**	216	26	60	4	32
Jones	**.273**	209	29	57	6	31
E. Young	**.269**	490	82	132	3	42
Boston	**.261**	291	46	76	14	40
Cole	**.256**	348	50	89	0	24
Castilla	**.255**	337	36	86	9	30
Mejia	**.231**	229	31	53	5	20

Pitching	W	L	ERA	IP	H	BB	SO
Ruffin	6	5	**3.87**	139.2	145	69	126
Reynoso	12	11	**4.00**	189.0	206	63	117
Holmes	3	3	**4.05**	66.2	56	20	60
Reed	9	5	**4.48**	84.1	80	30	51
Harris	11	17	**4.59**	225.1	239	69	123
Blair	6	10	**4.75**	146.0	184	42	84
Bottenfield	5	10	**5.07**	159.2	179	71	63
Nied	5	9	**5.17**	87.0	99	42	46

Manager—Don Baylor

Florida Marlins

Batting	Avg	AB	R	H	HR	RBI
Sheffield	**.294**	494	67	145	20	73
Conine	**.292**	595	75	174	12	79
Magadan	**.286**	227	22	65	4	29
Barberie	**.277**	375	45	104	5	33
Arias	**.269**	249	27	67	2	20
Carr	**.267**	551	75	147	4	41
Weiss	**.266**	500	50	133	1	39
Destrade	**.255**	569	61	145	20	87
Renteria	**.255**	263	27	67	2	30
Felix	**.238**	214	25	51	7	22
Santiago	**.230**	469	49	108	13	50
Whitmore	**.204**	250	24	51	4	19

Pitching	W	L	ERA	IP	H	BB	SO
Harvey	1	5	**1.70**	69.0	45	13	73
Lewis	6	3	**3.26**	77.1	68	43	65
Aquino	6	8	**3.42**	110.2	115	40	67
Rodriguez	2	4	**3.79**	76.0	73	33	43
Rapp	4	6	**4.02**	94.0	101	39	57
Hough	9	16	**4.27**	204.1	202	71	126
Bowen	8	12	**4.42**	156.2	156	87	98
Armstrong	9	17	**4.49**	196.1	210	78	118
Hammond	11	12	**4.66**	191.0	207	66	108

Manager—Rene Lachemann

Houston Astros

Batting	Avg	AB	R	H	HR	RBI
Bagwell	**.320**	535	76	171	20	88
Gonzalez	**.300**	540	82	162	15	72
Biggio	**.287**	610	98	175	21	64
Bass	**.284**	229	31	65	3	37
Cedeno	**.283**	505	69	143	11	56
Finley	**.266**	545	69	145	8	44
Caminiti	**.262**	543	75	142	13	75
Donnels	**.257**	179	18	46	2	24
Taubensee	**.250**	288	26	72	9	42
Anthony	**.249**	486	70	121	15	66
Servais	**.244**	258	24	63	11	32

Pitching	W	L	ERA	IP	H	BB	SO
Hernandez	4	5	**2.61**	96.2	75	28	101
Portugal	18	4	**2.77**	208.0	194	77	131
Harnisch	16	9	**2.98**	217.2	171	79	185
Kile	15	8	**3.51**	171.2	152	69	141
Drabek	9	18	**3.79**	237.2	242	60	157
Swindell	12	13	**4.16**	190.1	215	40	124
D. Jones	4	10	**4.54**	85.1	102	21	66
Williams	4	4	**4.83**	82.0	76	38	56

Manager—Art Howe

Los Angeles Dodgers

Batting	Avg	AB	R	H	HR	RBI
Piazza	**.318**	547	81	174	35	112
Butler	**.298**	607	80	181	1	42
Reed	**.276**	445	48	123	2	31
Offerman	**.269**	590	77	159	1	62
Snyder	**.266**	516	61	137	11	56
Karros	**.247**	619	74	153	23	80
Davis	**.234**	376	57	88	14	53
Wallach	**.222**	477	42	106	12	62
Rodriguez	**.222**	176	20	39	8	23

Pitching	W	L	ERA	IP	H	BB	SO
Gott	4	8	**2.32**	77.2	71	17	67
P. Martinez	10	5	**2.61**	107.0	76	57	119
Candiotti	8	10	**3.12**	213.2	192	71	155
R. Martinez	10	12	**3.44**	211.2	202	104	127
Astacio	14	9	**3.57**	186.1	165	68	122
Hershiser	12	14	**3.59**	215.2	201	72	141
Ke. Gross	13	13	**4.14**	202.1	224	74	150

Manager—Tommy Lasorda

Montreal Expos

Batting	Avg	AB	R	H	HR	RBI
Grissom	**.298**	630	104	188	19	95
DeShields	**.295**	481	75	142	2	29
Lansing	**.287**	491	64	141	3	45
Alou	**.286**	482	70	138	18	85
Frazier	**.286**	189	27	54	1	16
Walker	**.265**	490	85	130	22	86
Berry	**.261**	299	50	78	14	49
Fletcher	**.255**	396	33	101	9	60
Cordero	**.248**	475	56	118	10	58
Vanderwal	**.233**	215	34	50	5	30
Bolick	**.211**	213	25	45	4	24

Pitching	W	L	ERA	IP	H	BB	SO
Wetteland	9	3	**1.37**	85.1	58	28	113
Fassero	12	5	**2.29**	149.2	119	54	140
Rueter	8	0	**2.73**	85.2	85	18	31
Rojas	5	8	**2.95**	88.1	80	30	48
Hill	9	7	**3.23**	183.2	163	74	90
Martinez	15	9	**3.85**	224.2	211	64	138
Nabholz	9	8	**4.09**	116.2	100	63	74
Shaw	2	7	**4.14**	95.2	91	32	50
Barnes	2	6	**4.41**	100.0	105	48	60
Henry	3	9	**6.12**	103.0	135	28	47

Manager—Felipe Alou

New York Mets

Batting	Avg	AB	R	H	HR	RBI
Murray	.285	610	77	174	27	100
Orsulak	.284	409	59	116	8	35
Coleman	.279	373	64	104	2	25
Gallagher	.274	201	34	55	6	28
Kent	.270	496	65	134	21	80
Bonilla	.265	502	81	133	34	87
O'Brien	.255	188	15	48	4	23
Thompson	.250	288	34	72	11	26
Bogar	.244	205	19	50	3	25
Burnitz	.243	263	49	64	13	38
Johnson	.238	235	32	56	7	26
Hundley	.228	417	40	95	11	53
Walker	.225	213	18	48	5	19

Pitching	W	L	ERA	IP	H	BB	SO
S. Fernandez	5	6	2.93	119.2	82	36	81
Saberhagen	7	7	3.29	139.1	131	17	93
Gooden	12	15	3.45	208.2	188	61	149
Maddux	3	8	3.60	75.0	67	27	57
Young	1	16	3.77	100.1	103	42	62
Hillman	2	9	3.97	145.0	173	24	60
Innis	2	3	4.11	76.2	81	38	36
Tanana	7	15	4.48	183.0	198	48	104
Telgheder	6	2	4.76	75.2	82	21	35
Franco	4	3	5.20	36.1	46	19	29
Schourek	5	12	5.96	128.1	168	45	72

Manager—Jeff Torborg; Dallas Green

Philadelphia Phillies

Batting	Avg	AB	R	H	HR	RBI
Stocker	.324	259	46	84	2	31
Eisenreich	.318	362	51	115	7	54
Kruk	.316	535	100	169	14	85
Dykstra	.305	637	143	194	19	66
Duncan	.282	496	68	140	11	73
Chamberlain	.282	284	34	80	12	45
Incaviglia	.274	368	60	101	24	89
Hollins	.273	543	104	148	18	93
Thompson	.262	340	42	89	4	44
Daulton	.257	510	90	131	24	105
Morandini	.247	425	57	105	3	33

Pitching	W	L	ERA	IP	H	BB	SO
West	6	4	2.92	86.1	60	51	87
Mulholland	12	9	3.25	191.0	177	40	116
Williams	3	7	3.34	62.0	56	44	60
Greene	16	4	3.42	200.0	175	62	167
Jackson	12	11	3.77	210.1	214	80	120
Schilling	16	7	4.02	235.1	234	57	186
Mason	5	12	4.06	99.2	90	34	71
Rivera	13	9	5.02	163.0	175	85	123

Manager—Jim Fregosi

Pittsburgh Pirates

Batting	Avg	AB	R	H	HR	RBI
Merced	.313	447	68	140	8	70
Bell	.310	604	102	187	9	51
Van Slyke	.310	323	42	100	8	50
Slaught	.300	377	34	113	10	55
King	.295	611	82	180	9	98
L. Smith	.286	199	35	57	6	24
Martin	.281	480	85	135	18	64
Clark	.271	277	43	75	11	46
Garcia	.269	546	77	147	12	47
Foley	.253	194	18	49	3	22
Young	.236	449	38	106	6	47
McClendon	.221	181	21	40	2	19
Prince	.196	179	14	35	2	24

Pitching	W	L	ERA	IP	H	BB	SO
Belinda	3	1	3.61	42.1	35	11	30
Cooke	10	10	3.89	210.2	207	59	132
Minor	8	6	4.10	94.1	94	26	84
Wagner	8	8	4.27	141.1	143	42	114
Z. Smith	3	7	4.55	83.0	97	22	32
Tomlin	4	8	4.85	98.1	109	15	44
Neagle	3	5	5.31	81.1	82	37	73
Wakefield	6	11	5.61	128.1	145	75	59
Walk	13	14	5.68	187.0	214	70	80

Manager—Jim Leyland

St. Louis Cardinals

Batting	Avg	AB	R	H	HR	RBI
Jefferies	.342	544	89	186	16	83
Jordan	.309	223	33	69	10	44
Gilkey	.305	557	99	170	16	70
O. Smith	.288	545	75	157	1	53
Alicea	.279	362	50	101	3	46
Zeile	.277	571	82	158	17	103
Pappas	.276	228	25	63	1	28
Pagnozzi	.258	330	31	85	7	41
Pena	.256	254	34	65	5	30
Whiten	.253	562	81	142	25	99
Lankford	.238	407	64	97	7	45

Pitching	W	L	ERA	IP	H	BB	SO
Osborne	10	7	3.76	155.2	153	47	83
Arocha	11	8	3.78	188.0	197	31	96
Tewksbury	17	10	3.83	213.2	258	20	97
Olivares	5	3	4.17	118.2	134	54	63
Cormier	7	6	4.33	145.1	163	27	75
L. Smith	2	4	4.50	50.0	49	9	49
Watson	6	7	4.60	86.0	90	28	49
Magrane	8	10	4.97	116.0	127	37	38

Manager—Joe Torre

San Diego Padres

Batting	Avg	AB	R	H	HR	RBI
Gwynn	.358	489	70	175	7	59
Clark	.313	240	33	75	9	33
Gardner	.262	404	53	106	1	24
Bell	.262	542	73	142	21	72
Bean	.260	177	19	46	5	32
Gutierrez	.251	438	76	110	5	26
Teufel	.250	200	26	50	7	31
Cianfrocco	.243	296	30	72	12	48
Plantier	.240	462	67	111	34	100
Shipley	.235	230	25	54	4	22
Higgins	.221	181	17	40	0	13

Pitching	W	L	ERA	IP	H	BB	SO
Ge. Harris	6	6	3.03	59.1	57	37	39
Benes	15	15	3.78	230.2	200	86	179
Whitehurst	4	7	3.83	105.2	109	30	57
Hoffman	4	6	3.90	90.0	80	39	79
Brocail	4	13	4.56	128.1	143	42	70
Worrell	2	7	4.92	100.2	104	43	52
Ashby	3	10	6.80	123.0	168	56	77

Manager—Jim Riggleman

San Francisco Giants

Batting	Avg	AB	R	H	HR	RBI
Bonds	.336	539	129	181	46	123
Thompson	.312	494	85	154	19	65
McGee	.301	475	53	143	4	46
Williams	.294	579	105	170	38	110
Benzinger	.288	177	25	51	6	26
Clark	.283	491	82	139	14	73
Clayton	.282	549	54	155	6	70
Manwaring	.275	432	48	119	5	49
Lewis	.253	522	84	132	2	48
Martinez	.241	241	28	58	5	27

Pitching	W	L	ERA	IP	H	BB	SO
Beck	3	1	2.16	79.1	57	13	86
Rogers	2	2	2.68	80.2	71	28	62
Swift	21	8	2.82	232.2	195	55	157
Jackson	6	6	3.03	77.1	58	24	70
Black	8	2	3.56	93.2	89	33	45
Wilson	7	5	3.60	110.0	110	40	57
Burkett	22	7	3.65	231.2	224	40	145
Burba	10	3	4.25	95.1	95	37	88
Hickerson	7	5	4.26	120.1	137	39	69
Brantley	5	6	4.28	113.2	112	46	76

Manager—Dusty Baker

American League Records, 1993

Final standings

Eastern Division

	W	L	Pct.	GB	Home	vs. RHP	Grass	Night
Toronto	95	67	.586	—	48-33	72-40	39-24	57-51
New York	88	74	.543	7	50-31	55-50	77-61	54-56
Baltimore	85	77	.525	10	48-33	61-55	75-63	63-53
Detroit	85	77	.525	10	44-37	59-59	72-65	53-50
Boston	80	82	.494	15	43-38	58-61	67-70	50-56
Cleveland	76	86	.469	19	46-35	55-62	69-69	52-54
Milwaukee	69	93	.426	26	38-43	45-61	58-79	44-58

Western Division

	W	L	Pct.	GB	Home	vs. RHP	Grass	Night
Chicago	94	68	.580	—	45-36	68-44	77-61	68-47
Texas	86	76	.531	8	50-31	70-56	76-61	65-60
Kansas City	84	78	.519	10	43-38	62-56	31-31	57-55
Seattle	82	80	.506	12	46-35	51-58	26-36	61-56
California	71	91	.438	23	44-37	54-68	63-72	52-63
Minnesota	71	91	.438	23	36-45	53-69	28-34	47-61
Oakland	68	94	.420	26	38-43	48-66	52-84	45-48

American League Championship Series

Toronto 7, Chicago 3
Toronto 3, Chicago 1
Chicago 6, Toronto 1
Chicago 7, Toronto 4
Toronto 5, Chicago 3
Toronto 6, Chicago 3

Team Batting

	Avg.	AB	R	H	HR	RBI
New York	**.279**	5615	821	1568	178	793
Toronto	**.279**	5579	847	1556	159	796
Cleveland	**.275**	5619	790	1547	141	747
Detroit	**.275**	5620	899	1546	178	853
Texas	**.267**	5510	835	1472	181	780
Baltimore	**.267**	5508	786	1470	157	744
Chicago	**.265**	5483	776	1454	162	731
Minnesota	**.264**	5601	693	1480	121	642
Boston	**.264**	5496	686	1451	114	644
Kansas City	**.263**	5522	675	1455	125	641
Seattle	**.260**	5494	734	1429	161	681
California	**.260**	5391	684	1399	114	644
Milwaukee	**.258**	5525	733	1426	125	688
Oakland	**.254**	5543	715	1408	158	679

Team Pitching

	ERA	IP	H	BB	SO	Sv
Chicago	**3.70**	1454	1398	566	974	48
Boston	**3.77**	1452⅓	1379	552	997	44
Kansas City	**4.04**	1445⅓	1379	571	985	48
Seattle	**4.20**	1453⅔	1421	605	1083	41
Toronto	**4.21**	1441⅓	1441	620	1023	50
Texas	**4.28**	1438⅓	1476	562	957	45
Baltimore	**4.31**	1442⅔	1427	579	900	42
California	**4.34**	1430⅓	1482	550	843	41
New York	**4.35**	1438⅓	1467	552	899	38
Milwaukee	**4.45**	1447	1511	522	810	29
Cleveland	**4.58**	1445⅔	1591	591	888	45
Detroit	**4.65**	1436⅔	1547	542	828	36
Minnesota	**4.71**	1444⅓	1591	514	901	44
Oakland	**4.90**	1452⅓	1551	680	864	42

Individual Batting (at least 175 at-bats); Individual Pitching (at least 75 innings or 10 saves)

Baltimore Orioles

Batting	Avg	AB	R	H	HR	RBI
Baines	**.313**	416	64	130	20	78
Hoiles	**.310**	419	80	130	29	82
Pagliarulo	**.303**	370	55	112	9	44
Hulett	**.300**	260	40	78	2	23
McLemore	**.284**	581	81	165	4	72
Segui	**.273**	450	54	123	10	60
Anderson	**.263**	560	87	147	13	66
Ripkin	**.257**	641	87	165	24	90
Reynolds	**.252**	485	64	122	4	47
Devereaux	**.250**	527	72	132	14	75
Gomez	**.197**	244	30	48	10	25

Pitching	W	L	ERA	IP	H	BB	SO
Olson	0	2	**1.60**	45.0	37	18	44
Mills	5	4	**3.23**	100.1	80	51	68
McDonald	13	14	**3.39**	220.1	185	86	171
Moyer	12	9	**3.43**	152.0	154	38	90
Frohwirth	6	7	**3.83**	96.1	91	44	50
Mussina	14	6	**4.46**	167.2	163	44	117
Williamson	7	5	**4.91**	88.0	106	25	45
Valenzuela	8	10	**4.94**	178.2	179	79	78
Sutcliffe	10	10	**5.75**	166.0	212	74	80
Rhodes	5	6	**6.51**	85.2	91	49	49

Manager—John Oates

Boston Red Sox

Batting	Avg	AB	R	H	HR	RBI
Greenwell	**.315**	540	77	170	13	72
Vaughn	**.297**	539	86	160	29	101
Hatcher	**.287**	508	71	146	9	57
Fletcher	**.285**	480	81	137	5	45
Cooper	**.279**	526	67	147	9	63
Valentin	**.278**	468	50	130	11	66
Dawson	**.273**	461	44	126	13	67
Quintana	**.244**	303	31	74	1	19
Zupcic	**.241**	286	40	69	2	26
Melvin	**.222**	176	13	39	3	23
Deer	**.210**	466	66	98	21	55
Pena	**.181**	304	20	55	4	19

Pitching	W	L	ERA	IP	H	BB	SO
Russell	1	4	**2.70**	46.2	39	14	45
Sele	7	2	**2.74**	111.2	100	48	93
Viola	11	8	**3.14**	183.2	180	72	91
Darwin	15	11	**3.26**	229.1	196	49	130
Harris	6	7	**3.77**	112.1	95	60	103
Quantrill	6	12	**3.91**	138.0	151	44	66
Clemens	11	14	**4.46**	191.2	175	67	160
Dopson	7	11	**4.97**	155.2	170	59	89

Manager—Butch Hobson

California Angels

Batting	Avg	AB	R	H	HR	RBI
Easley	.313	230	33	72	2	22
Javier	.291	237	33	69	3	28
Curtis	.285	583	94	166	6	59
Salmon	.283	515	93	146	31	95
Polonia	.271	576	75	156	1	32
Myers	.255	290	27	74	7	40
R. Gonzales	.251	335	34	84	2	31
Lovullo	.251	367	42	92	6	30
Perez	.250	180	16	45	4	30
Davis	.243	573	74	139	27	112
Snow	.241	419	60	101	16	57
DiSarcina	.238	416	44	99	3	45

Pitching	W	L	ERA	IP	H	BB	SO
Grahe	4	1	2.86	56.2	54	25	31
Frey	2	3	2.98	48.1	41	26	22
Finley	16	14	3.15	251.1	243	82	187
Langston	16	11	3.20	256.1	220	85	196
Leftwich	4	6	3.79	80.2	81	27	31
Sanderson	7	11	4.46	135.1	153	27	66
Farrell	3	12	7.35	90.2	110	44	45

Manager—Buck Rodgers

Chicago White Sox

Batting	Avg	AB	R	H	HR	RBI
homas	.317	549	106	174	41	128
ohnson	.311	540	75	168	0	47
Raines	.306	415	75	127	16	54
Guillen	.280	457	44	128	4	50
Burks	.275	499	75	137	17	74
Cora	.268	579	95	155	2	51
Ventura	.262	554	85	145	22	94
ackson	.232	284	32	66	16	45
Karkovice	.228	403	60	92	20	54
Grebeck	.226	190	25	43	1	12
Bell	.217	410	36	89	13	64
Calderon	.209	239	26	50	1	22
Pasqua	.205	176	22	36	5	20

Pitching	W	L	ERA	IP	H	BB	SO
Hernandez	3	4	2.29	78.2	66	20	71
Alvarez	15	8	2.95	207.2	168	122	155
Fernandez	18	9	3.13	247.1	221	67	169
McDowell	22	10	3.37	256.2	261	69	158
Bere	12	5	3.47	142.2	109	81	129
McCaskill	4	8	5.23	113.2	144	36	65

Manager—Gene Lamont

Cleveland Indians

Batting	Avg	AB	R	H	HR	RBI
ofton	.325	569	116	185	1	42
Baerga	.321	624	105	200	21	114
Treadway	.303	221	25	67	2	27
Belle	.290	594	93	172	38	129
Espinoza	.278	263	34	73	4	27
Alomar	.270	215	24	58	6	32
irby	.269	458	71	123	6	60
Fermin	.263	480	48	126	2	45
orrento	.257	463	75	119	18	65
efferson	.249	366	35	91	10	34
Martinez	.244	262	26	64	5	31
oward	.236	178	26	42	3	23
Ortiz	.221	249	19	55	0	20

Pitching	W	L	ERA	IP	H	BB	SO
lliquist	4	4	2.25	64.0	64	19	40
iPoto	4	4	2.40	56.1	57	30	41
lunk	4	5	2.79	71.0	61	30	77
Hernandez	6	5	3.14	77.1	75	27	44
Kramer	7	3	4.02	121.0	126	59	71
Clark	7	5	4.28	109.1	119	25	57
Mesa	10	12	4.92	208.2	232	62	118
Mutis	3	6	5.78	81.0	93	33	29

Manager—Mike Hargrove

Detroit Tigers

Batting	Avg	AB	R	H	HR	RBI
Trammell	.329	401	72	132	12	60
Phillips	.313	566	113	177	7	57
Fryman	.300	607	98	182	22	97
Livingstone	.293	304	39	89	2	39
Whitaker	.290	383	72	111	9	67
Kreuter	.286	374	59	107	15	51
Fielder	.267	573	80	153	30	117
Gladden	.267	356	52	95	13	56
Gibson	.261	403	62	105	13	62
Tettleton	.245	522	79	128	32	110
Cuyler	.213	249	46	53	0	19

Pitching	W	L	ERA	IP	H	BB	SO
Henneman	5	3	2.64	71.2	69	32	58
Krueger	6	4	3.40	82.0	90	30	60
Boever	6	3	3.61	102.1	101	44	63
Wells	11	9	4.19	187.0	183	42	139
Doherty	14	11	4.44	184.2	205	48	63
Bolton	6	6	4.47	102.2	113	45	66
Leiter	6	6	4.73	106.2	111	44	70
S. Davis	2	8	5.05	98.0	93	48	73
Moore	13	9	5.22	213.2	227	89	89
Gullickson	13	9	5.37	159.1	186	44	70

Manager—Sparky Anderson

Kansas City Royals

Batting	Avg	AB	R	H	HR	RBI
Gwynn	.300	287	36	86	1	25
Joyner	.292	497	83	145	15	65
McRae	.282	627	78	177	12	69
Gagne	.280	540	66	151	10	57
Macfarlane	.273	388	55	106	20	67
Brett	.266	560	69	149	19	75
Mayne	.254	205	22	52	2	22
Jose	.253	499	64	126	6	43
Lind	.248	431	33	107	0	37
McReynolds	.245	351	44	86	11	42
Gaetti	.245	331	40	81	14	50
Hiatt	.218	238	30	52	7	36

Pitching	W	L	ERA	IP	H	BB	SO
Montgomery	7	5	2.27	87.1	65	23	66
Appier	18	8	2.56	238.2	183	81	186
Cone	11	14	3.33	254.0	205	114	191
Gordon	12	6	3.58	155.2	125	77	143
Pichardo	7	8	4.04	165.0	183	53	70
Gubicza	5	8	4.66	104.1	128	43	80
Haney	9	9	6.02	124.0	141	53	65
Gardner	4	6	6.19	91.2	92	36	54

Manager—Hal McRae

Milwaukee Brewers

Batting	Avg	AB	R	H	HR	RBI
Hamilton	.310	520	74	161	9	48
Surhoff	.274	552	66	151	7	79
Thon	.269	245	23	66	1	33
Seitzer	.269	417	45	112	11	57
Vaughn	.267	569	97	152	30	97
Jaha	.264	515	78	136	19	70
Yount	.258	454	62	117	8	51
Nilsson	.257	296	35	76	7	40
Reimer	.249	437	53	109	13	60
Listach	.244	356	50	87	3	30
Spiers	.238	340	43	81	2	36
Bell	.234	286	42	67	5	29
Brunansky	.183	224	20	41	6	29

Pitching	W	L	ERA	IP	H	BB	SO
Miranda	4	5	3.30	120.0	100	52	88
Eldred	16	16	4.01	258.0	232	91	180
Wegman	4	14	4.48	120.2	135	34	50
Bones	11	11	4.86	203.2	222	63	63
Navarro	11	12	5.33	214.1	254	73	114

Manager—Phil Garner

Minnesota Twins

Batting	Avg	AB	R	H	HR	RBI
Hale	.333	186	25	62	3	27
Harper	.304	530	52	161	12	73
Puckett	.296	622	89	184	22	89
Knoblauch	.277	602	82	167	2	41
Mack	.276	503	66	139	10	61
Winfield	.271	547	72	148	21	76
Reboulet	.258	240	33	62	1	15
Meares	.251	346	33	87	0	33
Hrbek	.242	392	60	95	25	83
Munoz	.233	326	34	76	13	38
McCarty	.214	350	36	75	2	21

Pitching	W	L	ERA	IP	H	BB	SO
Aguilera	4	3	3.11	72.1	60	14	59
Hartley	1	2	4.00	81.0	86	36	57
Banks	11	12	4.04	171.1	186	78	138
Deshaies	11	13	4.41	167.1	159	51	80
Tapani	12	15	4.43	225.2	243	57	150
Trombley	6	6	4.88	114.1	131	41	85
Erickson	8	19	5.19	218.2	266	71	116
Guardado	3	8	6.18	94.2	123	36	46

Manager—Tom Kelly

Seattle Mariners

Batting	Avg	AB	R	H	HR	RBI
Griffey	.309	582	113	180	45	109
Amaral	.290	373	53	108	1	44
Blowers	.280	379	55	106	15	57
Buhner	.272	563	91	153	27	98
T. Martinez	.265	408	48	108	17	60
Magadan	.259	228	27	59	1	21
Valle	.258	423	48	109	13	63
O'Brien	.257	210	30	54	7	27
Vizquel	.255	560	68	143	2	31
Boone	.251	271	31	68	12	38
Sasser	.218	188	18	41	1	21
Felder	.211	342	31	72	1	20

Pitching	W	L	ERA	IP	H	BB	SO
Charlton	1	3	2.34	34.2	22	17	48
Johnson	19	8	3.24	255.1	185	99	308
Bosio	9	9	3.45	164.1	138	59	119
Hanson	11	12	3.47	215.0	215	60	163
Fleming	12	5	4.36	167.1	189	67	75
Leary	11	9	5.05	169.1	202	58	68

Manager—Lou Piniella

New York Yankees

Batting	Avg	AB	R	H	HR	RBI
James	.332	343	62	114	7	36
O'Neill	.311	498	71	155	20	75
Leyritz	.309	259	43	80	14	53
Stanley	.305	423	70	129	26	84
Boggs	.302	560	83	169	2	59
Velarde	.301	226	28	68	7	24
Mattingly	.291	530	78	154	17	86
Gallego	.283	403	63	114	10	54
Kelly	.273	406	49	111	7	51
B. Williams	.268	567	67	152	12	68
Tartabull	.250	513	87	128	31	102
Nokes	.249	217	25	54	10	35
Owen	.234	334	41	78	2	20

Pitching	W	L	ERA	IP	H	BB	SO
Key	18	6	3.00	236.2	219	43	173
Kamieniecki	10	7	4.08	154.1	163	59	72
Farr	2	2	4.21	47.0	44	28	39
Abbott	11	14	4.37	214.0	221	73	95
Wickman	14	4	4.63	140.0	156	69	70
Monteleone	7	4	4.94	85.2	85	35	50
Perez	6	14	5.19	163.0	173	64	148

Manager—Buck Showalter

Texas Rangers

Batting	Avg	AB	R	H	HR	RBI
Gonzalez	.310	536	105	166	46	118
Palmeiro	.295	597	124	176	37	105
Hulse	.290	407	71	118	1	29
Franco	.289	532	85	154	14	84
Redus	.288	222	28	64	6	3
Diaz	.273	205	24	56	2	2
Rodriguez	.273	473	56	129	10	6
Strange	.256	484	58	124	7	6
Canseco	.255	231	30	59	10	4
Palmer	.245	519	88	127	33	9
Lee	.220	205	31	45	1	1

Pitching	W	L	ERA	IP	H	BB	SO
Henke	5	5	2.91	74.1	55	27	7
Pavlik	12	6	3.41	166.1	151	80	13
Brown	15	12	3.59	233.0	228	74	14
Rogers	16	10	4.10	208.1	210	71	14
Leibrandt	9	10	4.55	150.1	169	45	8
Bohanon	4	4	4.76	92.2	107	46	4
Lefferts	3	9	6.05	83.1	102	28	5

Manager—Kevin Kennedy

Oakland Athletics

Batting	Avg	AB	R	H	HR	RBI
Neel	.290	427	59	124	19	63
Gates	.290	535	64	155	7	69
Steinbach	.285	389	47	111	10	43
Aldrete	.267	255	40	68	10	33
Hemond	.256	215	31	55	6	26
Browne	.250	260	27	65	2	19
Bordick	.249	546	60	136	3	48
Brosius	.249	213	26	53	6	25
Sierra	.233	630	77	147	22	101
D. Henderson	.220	382	37	84	20	53
Paquette	.219	393	35	86	12	46
Blankenship	.190	252	43	48	2	23

Pitching	W	L	ERA	IP	H	BB	SO
Nunez	3	6	3.81	75.2	89	29	58
Eckersley	2	4	4.16	67.0	67	13	80
Witt	14	13	4.21	220.0	226	91	131
Van Poppel	6	6	5.04	84.0	76	62	47
Darling	5	9	5.16	178.0	198	72	95
Welch	9	11	5.29	166.2	208	56	63
Downs	5	10	5.64	119.2	135	60	66

Manager—Tony LaRussa

Toronto Blue Jays

Batting	Avg	AB	R	H	HR	RBI
Olerud	.363	551	109	200	24	10
Molitar	.332	636	121	211	22	11
Alomar	.326	589	109	192	17	9
Fernandez	.306	353	45	108	4	5
Henderson	.289	481	114	139	21	5
White	.273	598	116	163	15	5
Sprague	.260	546	50	142	12	7
Borders	.254	488	38	124	9	5
Carter	.254	603	92	153	33	12
Coles	.253	194	26	49	4	2
Jackson	.216	176	15	38	5	1

Pitching	W	L	ERA	IP	H	BB	SO
D. Ward	2	3	2.13	71.2	49	25	9
Cox	7	6	3.12	83.2	73	29	8
Hentgen	19	9	3.87	216.1	215	74	12
Guzman	14	3	3.99	221.0	211	110	19
Leiter	9	6	4.11	105.0	93	56	6
Stewart	12	8	4.44	162.0	146	72	9
Stottlemyre	11	12	4.84	176.2	204	69	9
Morris	7	12	6.19	152.2	189	65	10

Manager—Cito Gaston

National Baseball Hall of Fame and Museum, Cooperstown, N.Y.

aron, Hank
lexander, Grover Cleveland
lston, Walt
nson, Cap
paricio, Luis
ppling, Luke
verill, Earl
aker, Home Run
ancroft, Dave
anks, Ernie
arlick, Al
arrow, Edward G.
eckley, Jake
ell, Cool Papa
ench, Johnny
ender, Chief
erra, Yogi
ottomley, Jim
oudreau, Lou
resnahan, Roger
rock, Lou
routhers, Dan
rown, Mordecai (Three Finger)
ulkeley, Morgan C.
urkett, Jesse C.
ampanella, Roy
arew, Rod
arey, Max
artwright, Alexander
hadwick, Henry
hance, Frank
handler, Happy
harleston, Oscar
hesbro, John
larke, Fred
larkson, John
lemente, Roberto
obb, Ty
ochrane, Mickey
ollins, Eddie
ollins, James
ombs, Earle
omiskey, Charles A.
onlan, Jocko
Connolly, Thomas H.
Connor, Roger
Coveleski, Stan
Crawford, Sam
Cronin, Joe
Cummings, Candy
Cuyler, Kiki
Dandridge, Ray
Dean, Dizzy
Delahanty, Ed
Dickey, Bill
DiHigo, Martin
DiMaggio, Joe
Doerr, Bobby
Drysdale, Don
Duffy, Hugh
Evans, Billy
Evers, John
Ewing, Buck
Faber, Urban
Feller, Bob
Ferrell, Rick
Fingers, Rollie
Flick, Elmer H.
Ford, Whitey
Foster, Andrew
Foxx, Jimmie
Frick, Ford
Frisch, Frank
Galvin, Pud
Gehrig, Lou
Gehringer, Charles
Gibson, Bob
Gibson, Josh
Giles, Warren
Gomez, Lefty
Goslin, Goose
Greenberg, Hank
Griffith, Clark
Grimes, Burleigh
Grove, Lefty
Hafey, Chick
Haines, Jesee
Hamilton, Bill
Harridge, Will
Harris, Bucky
Hartnett, Gabby
Heilmann, Harry
Herman, Billy
Hooper, Harry
Hornsby, Rogers
Hoyt, Waite
Hubbard, Cal
Hubbell, Carl
Huggins, Miller
Hunter, Catfish
Irvin, Monte
Jackson, Reggie
Jackson, Travis
Jenkins, Ferguson
Jennings, Hugh
Johnson, Byron
Johnson, William (Judy)
Johnson, Walter
Joss, Addie
Kaline, Al
Keefe, Timothy
Keeler, William
Kell, George
Kelley, Joe
Kelly, George
Kelly, King
Killebrew, Harmon
Kiner, Ralph
Klein, Chuck
Klem, Bill
Koufax, Sandy
Lajoie, Napoleon
Landis, Kenesaw M.
Lazzeri, Tony
Lemon, Bob
Leonard, Buck
Lindstrom, Fred
Lloyd, Pop
Lombardi, Ernie
Lopez, Al
Lyons, Ted
Mack, Connie
MacPhail, Larry
Mantle, Mickey
Manush, Henry
Maranville, Rabbit
Marichal, Juan
Marquard, Rube
Mathews, Eddie
Mathewson, Christy
Mays, Willie
McCarthy, Joe
McCarthy, Thomas
McCovey, Willie
McGinnity, Joe
McGowan, Bill
McGraw, John
McKechnie, Bill
Medwick, Joe
Mize, Johnny
Morgan, Joe
Musial, Stan
Newhouser, Hal
Nichols, Kid
O'Rourke, James
Ott, Mel
Paige, Satchel
Palmer, Jim
Pennock, Herb
Perry, Gaylord
Plank, Ed
Radbourn, Charlie
Reese, Pee Wee
Rice, Sam
Rickey, Branch
Rixey, Eppa
Roberts, Robin
Robinson, Brooks
Robinson, Frank
Robinson, Jackie
Robinson, Wilbert
Roush, Edd
Ruffing, Red
Rusie, Amos
Ruth, Babe
Schalk, Ray
Schoendienst, Red
Seaver, Tom
Sewell, Joe
Simmons, Al
Sisler, George
Slaughter, Enos
Snider, Duke
Spahn, Warren
Spalding, Albert
Speaker, Tris
Stargell, Willie
Stengel, Casey
Terry, Bill
Thompson, Sam
Tinker, Joe
Traynor, Pie
Vance, Dazzy
Vaughan, Arky
Veeck, Bill
Waddell, Rube
Wagner, Honus
Wallace, Roderick
Walsh, Ed
Waner, Lloyd
Waner, Paul
Ward, John
Weiss, George
Welch, Mickey
Wheat, Zach
Wilhelm, Hoyt
Williams, Billy
Williams, Ted
Wilson, Hack
Wright, George
Wright, Harry
Wynn, Early
Yastrzemski, Carl
Yawkey, Tom
Young, Cy
Youngs, Ross

Hall of Famers Chosen in First Year of Eligibility

962	Jackie Robinson, Bob Feller
966	Ted Williams
969	Stan Musial
972	Sandy Koufax
973	Warren Spahn
1974	Mickey Mantle
1977	Ernie Banks
1979	Willie Mays
1980	Al Kaline
1981	Bob Gibson
1982	Hank Aaron, Frank Robinson
1983	Brooks Robinson
1985	Lou Brock
1986	Willie McCovey
1988	Willie Stargell
1989	Johnny Bench, Carl Yastrzemski
1990	Jim Palmer, Joe Morgan
1992	Tom Seaver
1993	Reggie Jackson

All-Star Baseball Games, 1933-1993

ear	Winner	Score	Location
933	American	4-2	Chicago
934	American	9-7	New York
935	American	4-1	Cleveland
936	National	4-3	Boston
937	American	8-3	Washington
938	National	4-1	Cincinnati
939	American	3-1	New York
940	National	4-0	St. Louis
941	American	7-5	Detroit
942	American	3-1	New York
43*	American	5-3	Philadelphia
44*	National	7-1	Pittsburgh
45	(not played)		
46	American	12-0	Boston
47	American	2-1	Chicago
48	American	5-2	St. Louis
49	American	11-7	New York
50	National (1)	4-3	Chicago
51	National	8-3	Detroit
52	National	3-2	Philadelphia
53	National	5-1	Cincinnati
54	American	11-9	Cleveland
55	National (2)	6-5	Milwaukee
56	National	7-3	Washington
57	American	6-5	St. Louis
58	American	4-3	Baltimore
59	National	5-4	Pittsburgh
59	American	5-3	Los Angeles
60	National	5-3	Kansas City
60	National	6-0	New York
61	National (3)	5-4	San Francisco
61	Called-rain	1-1	Boston
62	National (3)	3-1	Washington
1962	American	9-4	Chicago
1963	National	5-3	Cleveland
1964	National	7-4	New York
1965	National	6-5	Minnesota
1966	National (3)	2-1	St. Louis
1967	National (4)	2-1	Anaheim
1968*	National	1-0	Houston
1969	National	9-3	Washington
1970*	National (2)	5-4	Cincinnati
1971*	American	6-4	Detroit
1972*	National	4-3	Atlanta
1973*	National	7-1	Kansas City
1974*	National	7-2	Pittsburgh
1975*	National	6-3	Milwaukee
1976*	National	7-1	Philadelphia
1977*	National	7-5	New York
1978*	National	7-3	San Diego
1979*	National	7-6	Seattle
1980*	National	4-2	Los Angeles
1981*	National	5-4	Cleveland
1982*	National	4-1	Montreal
1983*	American	13-3	Chicago
1984*	National	3-1	San Francisco
1985*	National	6-1	Minneapolis
1986*	American	3-2	Houston
1987*	National (5)	2-0	Oakland
1988*	American	2-1	Cincinnati
1989*	American	5-3	Anaheim
1990*	American	2-0	Chicago
1991*	American	4-2	Toronto
1992*	American	13-6	San Diego
1993*	American	9-3	Baltimore

(1) 14 innings, (2) 12 innings, (3) 10 innings, (4) 15 innings; (5) 13 innings. * Night game.

Major League Leaders in 1993

American League

Batting

Olerud, Toronto, .363; Molitor, Toronto, .332; Alomar, Toronto, .326; Lofton, Cleveland, .325; Baerga, Cleveland, .321.

Runs

Palmeiro, Texas, 124; Molitor, Toronto, 121; Lofton, Cleveland, 116; White, Toronto, 116; Henderson, Toronto, 114.

Runs Batted In

Belle, Cleveland, 129; Thomas, Chicago, 128; Carter, Toronto, 121; Gonzalez, Texas, 118; Fielder, Detroit, 117.

Hits

Molitor, Toronto, 211; Baerga, Cleveland, 200; Olerud, Toronto, 200; Alomar, Toronto, 192; Lofton, Cleveland, 185.

Doubles

Olerud, Toronto, 54; White, Toronto, 42; Valentin, Boston, 40; Palmeiro, Texas, 40; Puckett, Minnesota, 39.

Triples

L. Johnson, Chicago, 14; Cora, Chicago, 13; Hulse, Texas, 10; McRae, Kansas City, 9; Fernandez, Toronto, 9.

Home Runs

Gonzalez, Texas, 46; Griffey Jr, Seattle, 45; Thomas, Chicago, 41; Belle, Cleveland, 38; Palmeiro, Texas, 37.

Stolen Bases

Lofton, Cleveland, 70; Alomar, Toronto, 55; Polonia, California, 55; Henderson, Toronto, 53; Curtis, California, 48.

Pitching (17 Decisions)

Guzman, Toronto, 14-3, .824, 3.99; Wickman, New York, 14-4, .778, 4.63; Key, New York, 18-6, .750, 3.00; Bere, Chicago, 12-5, .706, 3.47; Fleming, Seattle, 12-5, .706, 4.36.

Strikeouts

R. Johnson, Seattle, 308; Langston, California, 196; Guzman, Toronto, 194; Cone, Kansas City, 191; Finley, California, 187.

Saves

Montgomery, Kansas City, 45; Ward, Toronto, 45; Henke, Texas, 40; Hernandez, Chicago, 38; Eckersley, Oakland, 36.

National League

Batting

Galarraga, Colorado, .370; Gwynn, San Diego, .358; Jefferies St. Louis, .342; Bonds, San Francisco, .336; Grace, Chicago .325.

Runs

Dykstra, Philadelphia, 143; Bonds, San Francisco, 129; Gant Atlanta, 113; McGriff, Atlanta, 111; Blauser, Atlanta, 110.

Runs Batted In

Bonds, San Francisco, 123; Justice, Atlanta, 120; Gant, Atlanta, 117; Piazza, Los Angeles, 112; Williams, San Francisco 110.

Hits

Dykstra, Philadelphia, 193; Grace, Chicago, 193; Grissom Montreal, 188; Bell, Pittsburgh, 187; Jefferies, St. Louis, 186.

Doubles

Hayes, Colorado, 45; Dykstra, Philadelphia, 44; Bichette, Colorado, 43; Biggio, Houston, 41; Gwynn, San Diego, 41.

Triples

Finley, Houston, 13; Butler, Los Angeles, 10; Morandini, Philadelphia, 9; Bell, Pittsburgh, 9; Young, Colorado, 8; Martin, Pittsburgh, 8; Coleman, New York, 8.

Home Runs

Bonds, San Francisco, 46; Justice, Atlanta, 40; Williams, Sa Francisco, 38; McGriff, Atlanta, 37; Gant, Atlanta, 36.

Stolen Bases

Carr, Florida, 58; Grissom, Montreal, 53; Nixon, Atlanta, 47 Lewis, San Francisco, 46; Jefferies, St. Louis, 46.

Pitching (17 Decisions)

Portugal, Houston, 18-4, .818, 2.77; Greene, Philadelphia 16-4, .800, 3.42; Glavine, Atlanta, 22-6, .786, 3.20; Burkett, Sa Francisco, 22-7, .759, 3.65; Avery, Atlanta, 18-6, .750, 2.94.

Strikeouts

Rijo, Cincinnati, 227; Smoltz, Atlanta, 208; Maddux, Atlanta 197; Schilling, Philadelphia, 186; Harnisch, Houston, 185.

Saves

Myers, Chicago, 53; Beck, San Francisco, 48; Harvey, Florida 45; Wettleland, Montreal, 43; Williams, Philadelphia, 43; Smith St. Louis, 43.

Earned-Run Average Leaders

National League

Year	Player, club	G	IP	ERA
1972	Steve Carlton, Philadelphia. . .	41	346	**1.98**
1973	Tom Seaver, New York	36	290	**2.07**
1974	Buzz Capra, Atlanta.	39	217	**2.28**
1975	Randy Jones, San Diego	37	285	**2.24**
1976	John Denny, St. Louis.	30	207	**2.52**
1977	John Candelaria, Pittsburgh . .	33	231	**2.34**
1978	Craig Swan, New York	29	207	**2.43**
1979	J. R. Richard, Houston	38	292	**2.71**
1980	Don Sutton, Los Angeles	32	212	**2.21**
1981	Nolan Ryan, Houston	21	149	**1.69**
1982	Steve Rogers, Montreal.	35	277	**2.40**
1983	Atlee Hammaker, San Fran. . .	23	172	**2.25**
1984	Alejandro Pena, Los Angeles .	28	199	**2.48**
1985	Dwight Gooden, New York . . .	35	276	**1.53**
1986	Mike Scott, Houston.	37	275	**2.22**
1987	Nolan Ryan, Houston	34	211	**2.76**
1988	Joe Magrane, St. Louis	24	165	**2.18**
1989	Scott Garrelts, San Francisco .	30	193	**2.28**
1990	Danny Darwin, Houston.	48	162	**2.21**
1991	Dennis Martinez, Montreal . . .	31	222	**2.39**
1992	Bill Swift, San Francisco	30	164	**2.08**
1993	Greg Maddux, Atlanta.	36	267	**2.36**

American League

Year	Player, club	G	IP	ERA
1972	Luis Tiant, Boston.	43	179	**1.9**
1973	Jim Palmer, Baltimore	38	296	**2.4**
1974	Catfish Hunter, Oakland	41	318	**2.4**
1975	Jim Palmer, Baltimore	39	323	**2.0**
1976	Mark Fidrych, Detroit	31	250	**2.3**
1977	Frank Tanana, California.	31	241	**2.5**
1978	Ron Guidry, New York	35	274	**1.7**
1979	Ron Guidry, New York	33	236	**2.7**
1980	Rudy May, New York.	41	175	**2.4**
1981	Steve McCatty, Oakland.	22	186	**2.3**
1982	Rick Sutcliffe, Cleveland	34	216	**2.9**
1983	Rick Honeycutt, Texas	25	174	**2.4**
1984	Mike Boddicker, Baltimore	34	261	**2.7**
1985	Dave Stieb, Toronto	36	265	**2.4**
1986	Roger Clemens, Boston	33	254	**2.4**
1987	Jimmy Key, Toronto	36	261	**2.7**
1988	Allan Anderson, Minnesota . . .	30	202	**2.4**
1989	Bret Saberhagen, Kansas City .	36	262	**2.1**
1990	Roger Clemens, Boston	31	228	**1.9**
1991	Roger Clemens, Boston	35	271	**2.6**
1992	Roger Clemens, Boston	32	246	**2.4**
1993	Kevin Appier, Kansas City	34	238	**2.5**

ERA is computed by multiplying earned runs allowed by 9, then dividing by innings pitched.

Nolan Ryan's No-Hit Games

May 15, 1973: California (AL), at Kansas City, 3-0.
July 15, 1973: California (AL), at Detroit, 6-0.
Sept. 28, 1974: California (AL), vs. Minnesota, 4-0.
June 1, 1975: California (AL), vs. Baltimore, 1-0.
Sept. 26, 1981: Houston (NL), vs. Los Angeles, 5-0.
June 11, 1990: Texas (AL), at Oakland, 5-0.
May 1, 1991: Texas (AL), vs. Toronto, 3-0.

All-Time Major League Leaders

(Includes 1993 season)

Games		At Bats		Runs Batted In		Stolen Bases (since 1898)	
ete Rose	3562	Pete Rose	14,043	Hank Aaron	2297	Rickey Henderson	1095
arl Yastrzemski	3308	Hank Aaron	12,364	Babe Ruth	2204	Lou Brock	938
ank Aaron	3298	Carl Yastrzemski	11,988	Lou Gehrig	1990	Ty Cobb	892
y Cobb	3033	Ty Cobb	11,429	Ty Cobb	1961	Tim Raines	751
tan Musial	3026	Robin Yount	11,008	Stan Musial	1951	Eddie Collins	742
Villie Mays	2992	Stan Musial	10,972	Jimmie Foxx	1922	Max Carey	738
usty Staub	2951	Willie Mays	10,881	Willie Mays	1903	Honus Wagner	703
rooks Robinson	2896	Brooks Robinson	10,654	Mel Ott	1860	Joe Morgan	689
obin Yount	2856	Dave Winfield	10,594	Carl Yastrzemski	1844	Willie Wilson	667
ave Winfield	2850	Honus Wagner	10,427	Ted Williams	1839	Bert Campaneris	649

Runs		Hits		Strikeouts		Shutouts	
y Cobb	2245	Pete Rose	4256	Nolan Ryan	5714	Walter Johnson	110
ank Aaron	2174	Ty Cobb	4191	Steve Carlton	4136	Grover C. Alexander	90
abe Ruth	2174	Hank Aaron	3771	Bert Blyleven	3701	Christy Mathewson	83
ete Rose	2165	Stan Musial	3630	Tom Seaver	3640	Cy Young	77
'illie Mays	2062	Tris Speaker	3515	Don Sutton	3574	Eddie Plank	69
tan Musial	1949	Honus Wagner	3430	Gaylord Perry	3534	Warren Spahn	63
ou Gehrig	1888	Carl Yastrzemski	3419	Walter Johnson	3508	Mordecai Brown	63
is Speaker	1881	Eddie Collins	3309	Phil Niekro	3340	Tom Seaver	61
el Ott	1859	Willie Mays	3283	Ferguson Jenkins	3192	Nolan Ryan	61
ank Robinson	1829	Nap Lajoie	3252	Bob Gibson	3117	Bert Blyleven	60

All-Time Home Run Leaders

layer	HR	Player	HR	Player	HR	Player	HR
ank Aaron	755	Ted Williams	521	Carl Yastrzemski	452	Graig Nettles	390
abe Ruth	714	Willie McCovey	521	Dave Kingman	442	Johnny Bench	389
'illie Mays	660	Ed Mathews	512	Eddie Murray	441	Dwight Evans	385
'ank Robinson	586	Ernie Banks	512	Billy Williams	426	Frank Howard	382
armon Killebrew	573	Mel Ott	511	Darrell Evans	414	Jim Rice	382
eggie Jackson	563	Lou Gehrig	493	Andre Dawson	412	Orlando Cepeda	379
ike Schmidt	548	Stan Musial	475	Duke Snider	407	Tony Perez	379
ickey Mantle	536	Willie Stargell	475	Al Kaline	399		
mmy Foxx	534	Dave Winfield	453	Dale Murphy	398		

Players With 3,000 Major League Hits

In 1993, Dave Winfield of the Minnesota Twins became the 19th player to record 3,000 major league hits.

ayer	Hits	Player	Hits	Player	Hits
ete Rose	4,256	Eddie Collins	3,309	Rod Carew	3,053
Cobb	4,191	Willie Mays	3,283	Lou Brock	3,023
ank Aaron	3,771	Nap Lajoie	3,252	Dave Winfield	3,014
an Musial	3,630	George Brett	3,154	Al Kaline	3,007
is Speaker	3,515	Paul Waner	3,152	Roberto Clemente	3,000
onus Wagner	3,430	Robin Yount	3,142		
arl Yastrzemski	3,419	Cap Anson	3,081		

Baseball Stadiums

National League

eam	Stadium (built)	Surface	Home run distances (ft.) LF	Center	RF	Seating capacity
lanta Braves	Atlanta-Fulton County Stadium (1965)	Grass	330	402	330	52,003
icago Cubs	Wrigley Field (1914)	Grass	355	400	353	38,710
ncinnati Reds	Riverfront Stadium (1970)	Artificial	330	404	330	52,952
olorado Rockies	Mile High Stadium (1948)	Artificial	335	423	370	76,100
orida Marlins	Joe Robbie Stadium (1987)	Grass	335	410	345	48,000
ouston Astros	Astrodome (1965)	Artificial	325	400	325	54,816
s Angeles Dodgers	Dodger Stadium (1962)	Grass	330	395	330	56,000
ontreal Expos	Olympic Stadium (1976)	Artificial	325	404	325	43,739
w York Mets	Shea Stadium (1964)	Grass	338	410	338	55,601
iladelphia Phillies	Veterans Stadium (1971)	Artificial	330	408	330	62,382
tsburgh Pirates	Three Rivers Stadium (1970)	Artificial	335	400	335	58,727
Louis Cardinals	Busch Stadium (1966)	Artificial	330	402	330	56,227
n Diego Padres	Jack Murphy Stadium (1967)	Grass	327	405	327	59,022
n Francisco Giants	Candlestick Park (1960)	Grass	335	400	330	62,000

American League

ltimore Orioles	Camden Yards (1992)	Grass	333	400	318	48,041
ston Red Sox	Fenway Park (1912)	Grass	315	390	302	34,142
lifornia Angels	Anaheim Stadium (1966)	Grass	333	404	333	64,593
icago White Sox	Comiskey Park (1991)	Grass	347	400	347	44,702
eveland Indians	Cleveland Stadium (1931)	Grass	320	404	320	74,483
troit Tigers	Tiger Stadium (1912)	Grass	340	440	325	52,416
nsas City Royals	Kauffman Stadium (1973)	Artificial	330	410	330	40,625
ilwaukee Brewers	Milwaukee County Stadium (1953)	Grass	315	402	315	53,192
nnesota Twins	Hubert H. Humphrey Metrodome (1982)	Artificial	343	408	327	55,883
w York Yankees	Yankee Stadium (1923)	Grass	318	408	314	57,545
kland A's	Oakland Alameda County Coliseum (1968)	Grass	330	400	330	47,313
attle Mariners	Kingdome (1976)	Artificial	331	405	312	59,702
xas Rangers	Arlington Stadium (1972)	Grass	330	400	330	43,521
ronto Blue Jays	Sky-Dome (1989)	Artificial	328	400	328	50,516

1993 World Series

Joe Carter hit a three-run home run in the bottom of the ninth of game 6, Oct. 23, to give the Toronto Blue Jays a come-from-behind 8-6 victory over the Philadelphia Phillies and their second consecutive World Series triumph, 4 games to 2. I was the first time in 15 years that a team had won back-to-back championships. The Blue Jays' designated hitter, Paul Molitor, who had 2 doubles, 2 triples, 2 homers, and 8 RBIs in the 6 games, was named the Series' most valuable player.

First Game

Philadelphia	ab	r	h	bi	Toronto	ab	r	h	bi
Dykstra, cf	4	1	1	0	Henderson, lf	3	1	1	0
Duncan, 2b	5	2	3	0	White, cf	4	3	2	2
Kruk, 1b	4	2	3	2	Alomar, 2b	4	0	1	2
Hollins, 3b	4	0	0	0	Carter, rf	3	1	1	1
Daulton, c	4	0	1	1	Olerud, 1b	3	2	2	1
Eisenreich, rf	5	0	1	1	Molitor, dh	4	0	1	1
Jordan, dh	5	0	1	0	Fernandez, ss	3	0	0	1
Thompson, lf	3	0	0	0	Sprague, 3b	4	0	1	0
Incaviglia, ph-lf	1	0	0	0	Borders, c	4	1	1	0
Stocker, ss	3	0	1	0	**Totals**	**32**	**8**	**10**	**8**
Totals	**38**	**5**	**11**	**4**					

Philadelphia	2	0	1	0	1	0	0	0	1—5
Toronto	0	2	1	0	1	1	3	0	x—8

	ip	h	r	er	bb	so
Philadelphia						
Schilling L, 0-1	6⅓	8	7	6	2	3
West	0	2	1	1	0	0
Andersen	⅔	0	0	0	1	1
Mason	1	0	0	0	0	1
Toronto						
Guzman	5	5	4	4	4	6
Leiter W, 1-0	2⅔	4	0	0	1	2
Ward S, 1	1⅓	2	1	0	0	3

E - Thompson (1), Alomar (1), Carter (1), Sprague (1). LOB - Philadelphia 11, Toronto 4. 2B - White (1), Alomar (1). 3B - Duncan (1). HR - White (1), Olerud (1). RBI - Kruk 2 (2), Daulton (1), Eisenreich (1), White 2 (2), Alomar 2 (2), Carter (1), Olerud (1), Molitor (1), Fernandez (1). SB - Dykstra (1), Duncan (1), Alomar (1). SF - Carter.

How runs were scored—Two in Phillies first: Dykstra walked and stole second. Kruk singled scoring Dykstra. Hollins walked. Daulton singled scoring Kruk.

Two in Blue Jays second: Carter and Olerud singled. Molitor singled scoring Carter. Fernandez grounded out scoring Olerud.

One in Phillies third: Duncan singled and stole second. Kruk singled scoring Duncan.

One in Blue Jays third: White reached third on an error. Carter hit a sacrifice fly scoring White.

One in Phillies fifth: Duncan tripled and scored on a wild pitch.

One in Blue Jays fifth: White hit a home run.

One in Blue Jays sixth: Olerud hit a home run.

Three in Blue Jays seventh: Borders and Henderson singled. White doubled scoring Borders. Alomar doubled scoring Henderson and White.

One in Phillies ninth: Kruk singled and went to second on an error. Eisenreich singled scoring Kruk.

Second Game

Philadelphia	ab	r	h	bi	Toronto	ab	r	h	bi
Dykstra, cf	4	2	2	1	Henderson, lf	3	0	0	0
Duncan, 2b	4	1	1	0	White, cf	4	0	1	0
Kruk, 1b	5	1	2	1	Molitor, dh	3	2	2	0
Hollins, 3b	4	1	2	1	Carter, rf	4	1	1	2
Batiste, 3b	0	0	0	0	Olerud, 1b	3	0	0	1
Daulton, c	5	0	1	0	Alomar, 2b	3	1	1	0
Eisenreich, rf	4	1	1	3	Fernandez, ss	3	0	2	1
Incaviglia, lf	4	0	1	0	Sprague, 3b	4	0	0	0
Thompson, pr-lf	0	0	0	0	Griffin, pr	0	0	0	0
Jordan, dh	4	0	1	0	Borders, c	4	0	1	0
Stocker, ss	3	0	1	0	**Totals**	**31**	**4**	**8**	**4**
Totals	**37**	**6**	**12**	**6**					

Philadelphia	0	0	5	0	0	0	1	0	0—6
Toronto	0	0	0	2	0	1	0	1	0—4

	ip	h	r	er	bb	so
Philadelphia						
Mulholland W, 1-0	5⅔	7	3	3	2	4
Mason H, 1	1⅔	1	1	1	0	2
Williams S, 1	1⅔	0	0	0	2	0
Toronto						
Stewart L, 0-1	6	6	5	5	4	6
Castillo	1	3	1	1	0	0
Eichhorn	⅓	1	0	0	1	0
Timlin	1⅔	2	0	0	0	2

LOB - Philadelphia 9, Toronto 5. 2B - White (2), Molitor (1) Fernandez (1). HR - Carter (1), Dykstra (1), Eisenreich (1). RBI Dykstra (1), Kruk (3), Hollins (1), Eisenreich 3 (4), Carter 2 (3) Olerud (2), Fernandez (2). SB - Molitor (1), Alomar (2). SF Olerud.

How runs were scored—Five in Phillies third: Dykstra and Duncan walked. Kruk singled scoring Dykstra. Hollins singled scoring Duncan. Eisenreich hit a home run scoring Kruk and Hollins.

Two in Blue Jays fourth: Molitor singled. Carter hit a home run scoring Molitor.

One in Blue Jays sixth: Alomar singled. Fernandez doubled scoring Alomar.

One in Phillies seventh: Dykstra hit a home run.

One in Blue Jays eighth: Molitor doubled and stole third Olerud hit a sacrifice fly scoring Molitor.

Third Game

Toronto	ab	r	h	bi	Philadelphia	ab	r	h	b
Henderson, lf	4	2	2	0	Dykstra, cf	5	0	1	
White, cf	4	2	1	1	Duncan, 2b	5	0	2	
Molitor, 1b	4	3	3	3	Kruk, 1b	3	1	2	
Carter, rf	4	1	1	1	Hollins, 3b	3	0	0	
Alomar, 2b	5	2	4	2	Daulton, c	3	0	0	
Fernandez, ss	3	0	2	2	Eisenreich, rf	4	0	1	
Sprague, 3b	4	0	0	1	Incaviglia, lf	3	0	0	
Borders, c	4	0	0	0	Thigpen, p	0	0	0	
Hentgen, p	3	0	0	0	Morandini, ph	0	0	0	
Cox, p	1	0	0	0	Andersen, p	0	0	0	
Ward, p	0	0	0	0	Stocker, ss	4	0	1	
Totals	**36**	**10**	**13**	**10**	Jackson, p	1	0	0	
					Chamberlain, ph	1	0	0	
					Rivera, p	0	0	0	
					Thompson, lf	2	2	2	
					Totals	**34**	**3**	**9**	

Toronto	3	0	1	0	0	1	3	0	2—1
Philadelphia	0	0	0	0	0	1	1	0	1—

	ip	h	r	er	bb	so
Toronto						
Hentgen W, 1-0	6	5	1	1	3	6
Cox	2	3	1	1	2	2
Ward	1	1	1	1	0	2
Philadelphia						
Jackson L, 0-1	5	6	4	4	1	1
Rivera	1⅓	4	4	4	2	3
Thigpen	1⅔	0	0	0	1	0
Andersen	1	3	2	2	0	0

E - Carter (2). LOB - Toronto 7, Philadelphia 9. 2B Henderson (1), Kruk (1). 3B - White (1), Molitor (1), Alomar (1 HR - Thompson (1), Molitor (1). RBI - White (3), Molitor 3 (4 Carter (4), Alomar 2 (4), Fernandez 2 (4), Sprague (1), Dunca (1), Eisenreich (5), Thompson (1). SB - Alomar 2 (4). SF Carter, Fernandez, Sprague.

How runs were scored—Three in Blue Jays first: Henderso singled. White walked. Molitor tripled scoring Henderson ar White. Carter hit a sacrifice fly scoring Molitor.

One in Blue Jays third: Molitor hit a home run.

One in Blue Jays sixth: Alomar singled and stole second ar third. Fernandez hit a sacrifice fly scoring Alomar.

One in Phillies sixth: Kruk and Daulton walked. Eisenreich singled scoring Kruk.

Three in Blue Jays seventh: Henderson doubled. White triple scoring Henderson. Molitor walked. Alomar singled scorir White and moving Molitor to third. Sprague hit a sacrifice scoring Molitor.

One in Phillies seventh: Thompson and Dykstra singled. Du can singled scoring Thompson.

Two in Blue Jays ninth: Molitor singled. Carter hit into a for play. Alomar tripled scoring Carter. Fernandez singled scori Alomar.

One in Phillies ninth: Thompson hit a home run.

Fourth Game

oronto	ab	r	h	bi	Philadelphia	ab	r	h	bi
enderson, lf	5	2	2	2	Dykstra, cf	5	4	3	4
/hite, cf	5	2	3	4	Duncan, 2b	6	1	3	1
lomar, 2b	6	1	2	1	Kruk, 1b	5	0	0	0
arter, rf	6	2	3	0	Hollins, 3b	4	3	2	0
lerud, 1b	4	2	1	0	Daulton, c	3	2	1	3
lolitor, 3b	4	2	2	2	Eisenreich, rf	4	2	1	1
riffin, 3b	0	0	0	0	Thompson, lf	5	1	3	5
ernandez, ss	6	2	3	5	Stocker, ss	4	0	0	0
orders, c	4	1	1	1	Greene, p	1	1	1	0
tottlemyre, p	0	0	0	0	Mason, p	1	0	0	0
utler, ph	1	1	0	0	Jordan, ph	1	0	0	0
eiter, p	1	0	1	0	West, p	0	0	0	0
astillo, p	1	0	0	0	Chamberlain, ph	1	0	0	0
prague, ph	1	0	0	0	Andersen, p	0	0	0	0
mlin, p	0	0	0	0	Williams, p	0	0	0	0
'ard, p	0	0	0	0	Morandini, ph	1	0	0	0
otals	44	15	18	15	Thigpen, p	0	0	0	0
					Totals	41	14	14	14

oronto	3	0	4	0	0	2	0	6	0—15
hiladelphia	4	2	0	1	5	1	1	0	0—14

	ip	h	r	er	bb	so
oronto						
tottlemyre	2	3	6	6	4	1
eiter	2⅔	8	6	6	0	1
astillo W, 1-0	2⅓	3	2	2	3	1
mlin	⅔	0	0	0	0	2
'ard S, 2	1⅓	0	0	0	0	2
hiladelphia						
reene	2⅓	7	7	7	4	1
ason	2⅔	2	0	0	1	2
'est	1	3	2	2	0	0
ndersen	1⅓	2	3	3	1	2
'illiams L, 0-1	⅔	3	3	3	1	1
nigpen	1	1	0	0	0	0

LOB - Toronto 10, Philadelphia 8. 2B - Henderson (2), White), Molitor (2), Carter (1), Leiter (1), Dykstra (1), Hollins (1), nompson (1). 3B - White (2), Thompson (1). HR - Dykstra 2 (3), aulton (1). RBI - Henderson 2 (2), White 4 (7), Alomar (5), Molir 2 (6), Fernandez 5 (9), Borders (1), Dykstra 4 (5), Duncan), Daulton 3 (4), Eisenreich (6), Thompson 5 (6). SB - Hendern (1), White (1), Dykstra (2), Duncan (2).

How runs were scored—Three in Blue Jays first: Henderson oubled. White walked. Carter singled. Molitor walked scoring enderson. Fernandez singled scoring White and Carter.

Four in Phillies first: Dykstra walked and stole second. Hollins id Daulton walked. Eisenreich walked scoring Dykstra. Thompn tripled scoring Hollins, Daulton and Eisenreich.

Two in Phillies second: Greene singled. Dykstra hit a home run oring Greene.

Four in Blue Jays third: Olerud walked. Molitor singled. Ferındez singled scoring Olerud. Borders singled scoring Molitor. utler reached on a fielder's choice. Henderson walked. White ngled scoring Fernandez and Butler.

One in Phillies fourth: Dykstra doubled. Duncan singled scor- Dykstra.

Five in Phillies fifth: Hollins singled. Daulton hit a home run oring Hollins. Eisenreich singled. Thompson doubled scoring senreich. Dykstra hit a home run scoring Thompson.

Two in Blue Jays sixth: White doubled. Alomar singled scoring hite. Olerud singled. Molitor hit by pitch. Fernandez bounced it scoring Alomar.

One in Phillies sixth: Hollins doubled. Thompson singled scor- Hollins.

One in Phillies seventh: Duncan singled. Kruk and Hollins alked. Daulton hit by pitch scoring Duncan.

Six in Blue Jays eighth: Carter singled. Olerud walked. Molitor ubled scoring Carter. Fernandez singled scoring Olerud. Borrs walked. Henderson singled scoring Molitor and Fernandez. hite tripled scoring Borders and Henderson.

World Series Records—The 29 runs scored in game 4 repsented the highest total ever in a World Series game, breaking 57-year-old record set in game 2 of the 1936 "Subway" Ses. In that game, the New York Yankees decisively defeated e Giants, at that time also of New York, by a score of 18-4. ame 4 was also the longest World Series game ever, lasting 4 urs and 14 minutes.

Fifth Game

ronto	ab	r	h	bi	Philadelphia	ab	r	h	bi
enderson, lf	3	0	0	0	Dykstra, cf	2	1	0	0
nite, cf	3	0	0	0	Duncan, 2b	4	0	0	0
Alomar, 2b	3	0	1	0	Kruk, 1b	3	0	1	1
Carter, rf	4	0	0	0	Hollins, 3b	3	0	1	0
Olerud, 1b	4	0	0	0	Batiste, 3b	0	0	0	0
Molitor, 3b	4	0	1	0	Daulton, c	4	1	1	0
Fernandez, ss	3	0	0	0	Eisenreich, rf	4	0	0	0
Borders, c	3	0	2	0	Thompson, lf	3	0	0	0
Canate, pr	0	0	0	0	Stocker, ss	2	0	1	1
Knorr, c	0	0	0	0	Schilling, p	2	0	1	0
Guzman, p	2	0	0	0	**Totals**	27	2	5	2
Butler, ph	1	0	1	0					
Cox, p	0	0	0	0					
Totals	30	0	5	0					

Toronto	0	0	0	0	0	0	0	0	0—0
Philadelphia	1	1	0	0	0	0	0	0	0—2

	ip	h	r	er	bb	so
Toronto						
Guzman L, 0-1	7	5	2	1	4	6
Cox	1	0	0	0	2	3
Philadelphia						
Schilling W, 1-1	9	5	0	0	3	6

E - Borders (1), Duncan (1). LOB - Toronto 6, Philadelphia 8. 2B - Daulton (1), Stocker (1). RBI - Kruk (4), Stocker (1). SB - Dykstra (3). CS - Alomar (2). S - Schilling.

How runs were scored—One in Phillies first: Dykstra walked. Dykstra stole second and advanced to third on catcher Borders' throwing error. Kruk grounded out scoring Dykstra.

One in Phillies second: Daulton doubled. Eisenreich grounded out moving Daulton to third. Stocker doubled scoring Daulton.

Sixth Game

Philadelphia	ab	r	h	bi	Toronto	ab	r	h	bi
Dykstra, cf	3	1	1	3	Henderson, lf	4	1	0	0
Duncan, dh	5	1	1	0	White, cf	4	1	0	0
Kruk, 1b	3	0	0	0	Molitor, dh	5	3	3	2
Hollins, 3b	5	1	1	1	Carter, rf	4	1	1	4
Batiste, 3b	0	0	0	0	Olerud, 1b	3	1	1	0
Daulton, c	4	1	1	0	Griffin, pr-3b	0	0	0	0
Eisenreich, rf	5	0	2	1	Alomar, 2b	4	1	3	1
Thompson, lf	3	0	0	0	Fernandez, ss	3	0	0	0
Incaviglia, ph-lf	0	0	0	1	Sprague, 3b-1b	2	0	0	1
Stocker, ss	3	1	0	0	Borders, c	4	0	2	0
Morandini, 2b	4	1	1	0	**Totals**	33	8	10	8
Totals	35	6	7	6					

Philadelphia	0	0	0	1	0	0	5	0	0—6
Toronto	3	0	0	1	1	0	0	0	3—8

	ip	h	r	er	bb	so
Philadelphia						
Mulholland	5	7	5	5	1	1
Mason	2⅓	1	0	0	0	2
West	0	0	0	0	1	0
Andersen	⅔	0	0	0	1	0
Williams L, 0-2	⅓	2	3	3	1	0
Toronto						
Stewart	6	4	4	4	4	2
Cox	⅓	3	2	2	1	1
Leiter	1⅔	0	0	0	1	2
Ward W, 1-0	1	0	0	0	0	0

E - Alomar (2), Sprague (2). LOB - Philadelphia 9, Toronto 7. 2B - Daulton (2), Olerud (1), Alomar (2). 3B - Molitor (2). HR - Molitor (2), Carter (2), Dykstra (4). RBI - Dykstra 3 (8), Hollins (2), Eisenreich (7), Incaviglia (1), Molitor 2 (8), Carter 4 (8), Alomar (6), Sprague (2). SB - Dykstra (4), Duncan (3). SF - Incaviglia, Carter, Sprague.

How runs were scored—Three in Blue Jays first: White walked. Molitor tripled scoring White. Carter hit a sacrifice fly scoring Molitor. Olerud doubled. Alomar singled scoring Olerud.

One in Phillies fourth: Daulton doubled. Eisenreich singled scoring Daulton.

One in Blue Jays fourth: Alomar doubled. Fernandez grounded out moving Alomar to third. Sprague hit a sacrifice fly scoring Alomar.

One in Blue Jays fifth: Molitor hit a home run.

Five in Phillies seventh: Stocker walked. Morandini singled moving Stocker to third. Dykstra hit a home run scoring Stocker and Morandini. Duncan singled and stole second. Hollins singled scoring Duncan. Daulton walked. Eisenreich singled to load the bases. Incaviglia hit a sacrifice fly scoring Hollins.

Three in Blue Jays ninth: Henderson walked. Molitor singled. Carter hit a home run scoring Henderson and Molitor.

1993 World Series Composite Box Score

Philadelphia Phillies Batting

	g	ab	r	h	2b	3b	hr	rbi	so	bb	avg	po	a	e	pct
Tommy Greene p	1	1	1	1	0	0	0	0	0	0	1.000	0	0	0	—
Curt Schilling p	2	2	0	1	0	0	0	0	1	0	.500	0	3	0	1.000
Lenny Dykstra cf	6	23	9	8	1	0	4	8	4	7	.348	19	1	0	1.000
John Kruk 1b	6	23	4	8	1	0	0	4	7	7	.348	42	3	0	1.000
Mariano Duncan 2b-dh	6	29	5	10	0	1	0	2	7	1	.345	10	17	1	.964
Milt Thompson lf-pr	6	16	3	5	1	1	1	6	2	1	.313	10	0	1	.909
Dave Hollins 3b	6	23	5	6	1	0	0	2	5	6	.261	9	9	0	1.000
Jim Eisenreich rf	6	26	3	6	0	0	1	7	4	2	.231	18	0	0	1.000
Darren Daulton c	6	23	4	5	2	0	1	4	5	4	.217	31	4	0	1.000
Kevin Stocker ss	6	19	1	4	1	0	0	1	5	5	.211	8	13	0	1.000
Ricky Jordan dh-ph	3	10	0	2	0	0	0	0	2	0	.200	0	0	0	—
Mickey Morandini ph-2b	3	5	1	1	0	0	0	0	2	1	.200	2	0	0	1.000
Pete Incaviglia ph-lf	4	8	0	1	0	0	0	1	4	0	.125	7	0	0	1.000
Wes Chamberlain ph	2	2	0	0	0	0	0	0	1	0	.000	0	0	0	—
Danny Jackson p	1	1	0	0	0	0	0	0	1	0	.000	0	0	0	—
Roger Mason p	4	1	0	0	0	0	0	0	0	0	.000	0	0	0	—
Larry Andersen p	4	0	0	0	0	0	0	0	0	0	—	0	0	0	—
Kim Batiste 3b	2	0	0	0	0	0	0	0	0	0	—	0	1	0	1.000
Terry Mulholland p	2	0	0	0	0	0	0	0	0	0	—	1	1	0	1.000
Ben Rivera p	1	0	0	0	0	0	0	0	0	0	—	1	0	0	—
Bobby Thigpen p	2	0	0	0	0	0	0	0	0	0	—	0	1	0	1.000
David West p	3	0	0	0	0	0	0	0	0	0	—	0	0	0	—
Mitch Williams p	3	0	0	0	0	0	0	0	0	0	—	0	1	0	1.000
Totals	**6**	**212**	**36**	**58**	**7**	**2**	**7**	**35**	**50**	**34**	**.274**	**157**	**54**	**2**	**.991**

Toronto Blue Jays Batting

	g	ab	r	h	2b	3b	hr	rbi	so	bb	avg	po	a	e	pct
Al Leiter p	3	1	0	1	1	0	0	0	0	0	1.000	0	0	0	—
Paul Molitor dh-1b-3b	6	24	10	12	2	2	2	8	0	3	.500	7	3	0	1.000
Rob Butler ph	2	2	1	1	0	0	0	0	0	0	.500	0	0	0	—
Roberto Alomar 2b	6	25	5	12	2	1	0	6	3	2	.480	10	21	2	.939
Tony Fernandez ss	6	21	2	7	1	0	0	9	3	3	.333	11	8	0	1.000
Pat Borders c	6	23	2	7	0	0	0	1	1	2	.304	50	2	1	.981
Devon White cf	6	24	8	7	3	2	1	7	7	4	.292	16	0	0	1.000
Joe Carter rf	6	25	6	7	1	0	2	8	4	0	.280	12	0	2	.857
John Olerud 1b	5	17	5	4	1	0	1	2	1	4	.235	36	0	0	1.00
Rickey Henderson lf	6	22	6	5	2	0	0	2	2	5	.227	8	0	0	1.00
Ed Sprague 3b-ph-1b	5	15	0	1	0	0	0	2	6	1	.067	4	9	2	.867
Pat Hentgen p	1	3	0	0	0	0	0	0	1	0	.000	0	0	0	—
Juan Guzman p	2	2	0	0	0	0	0	0	1	0	.000	0	1	0	1.00
Tony Castillo p	2	1	0	0	0	0	0	0	1	0	.000	0	0	0	—
Danny Cox p	3	1	0	0	0	0	0	0	0	0	.000	1	0	0	1.000
Alfredo Griffin pr-3b	3	0	0	0	0	0	0	0	0	0	—	0	0	0	—
Willie Canate pr	1	0	0	0	0	0	0	0	0	0	—	0	0	0	—
Mark Eichhorn p	1	0	0	0	0	0	0	0	0	0	—	0	0	0	—
Randy Knorr c	1	0	0	0	0	0	0	0	0	0	—	3	0	0	1.00
Dave Stewart p	2	0	0	0	0	0	0	0	0	0	—	1	1	0	1.00
Todd Stottlemyre p	1	0	0	0	0	0	0	0	0	1	—	0	0	0	—
Mike Timlin p	2	0	0	0	0	0	0	0	0	0	—	0	0	0	—
Duane Ward p	4	0	0	0	0	0	0	0	0	0	—	0	0	0	—
Totals	**6**	**206**	**45**	**64**	**13**	**5**	**6**	**45**	**30**	**25**	**.311**	**159**	**45**	**7**	**.96**

Philadelphia Phillies Pitching

	g	cg	ip	h	r	bb	so	hb	wp	w	l	sv	pct	er	er
Bobby Thigpen	2	0	2 2/3	1	0	1	0	1	0	0	0	0	—	0	0.0
Roger Mason	4	0	7 2/3	4	1	1	7	0	0	0	0	0	—	1	1.1
Curt Schilling	2	1	15 1/3	13	7	5	9	0	0	1	1	0	.500	6	3.5
Terry Mulholland	2	0	10 2/3	14	8	3	5	0	0	1	0	0	1.000	8	6.7
Danny Jackson	1	0	5	6	4	1	1	0	0	0	1	0	.000	4	7.2
Larry Andersen	4	0	3 2/3	5	5	3	3	1	0	0	0	0	—	5	12.2
Mitch Williams	3	0	2 2/3	5	6	4	1	0	0	0	2	1	.000	6	20.2
Tommy Greene	1	0	2 1/3	7	7	4	1	0	0	0	0	0	—	7	27.0
Ben Rivera	1	0	1 1/3	4	4	2	3	0	0	0	0	0	—	4	27.0
David West	3	0	1	5	3	1	0	1	0	0	0	0	—	3	27.0
Totals	**6**	**1**	**52 1/3**	**64**	**45**	**25**	**30**	**3**	**0**	**2**	**4**	**1**	**.333**	**44**	**7.5**

Toronto Blue Jays Pitching

	g	cg	ip	h	r	bb	so	hb	wp	w	l	sv	pct	er	er
Mike Timlin	2	0	2 1/3	2	0	0	4	0	0	0	0	0	—	0	0.0
Mark Eichhorn	1	0	1/3	1	0	1	0	0	0	0	0	0	—	0	0.0
Pat Hentgen	1	0	6	5	1	3	6	0	0	1	0	0	1.000	1	1.5
Duane Ward	4	0	4 2/3	3	2	0	7	0	0	1	0	2	1.000	1	1.9
Juan Guzman	2	0	12	10	6	8	12	0	1	0	1	0	.000	5	3.7
Dave Stewart	2	0	12	10	9	8	8	0	1	0	1	0	.000	9	6.7
Al Leiter	3	0	7	12	6	2	5	0	0	1	0	0	1.000	6	7.7
Tony Castillo	2	0	3 1/3	6	3	3	1	1	0	1	0	0	1.000	3	8.1
Danny Cox	3	0	3 1/3	6	3	5	6	0	0	0	0	0	—	3	8.1
Todd Stottlemyre	1	0	2	3	6	4	1	0	0	0	0	0	—	6	27.0
Totals	**6**	**0**	**53**	**58**	**36**	**34**	**50**	**1**	**2**	**4**	**2**	**2**	**.667**	**34**	**5.7**

Score By Innings

Philadelphia	7	3	6	2	6	2	8	0	2	—	3
Toronto	9	2	6	3	2	5	6	7	5	—	4

World Series Results, 1903-1993

1903 Boston AL 5, Pittsburgh NL 3
1904 No series
1905 New York NL 4, Philadelphia AL 1
1906 Chicago AL 4, Chicago NL 2
1907 Chicago NL 4, Detroit AL 0, 1 tie
1908 Chicago NL 4, Detroit AL 1
1909 Pittsburgh NL 4, Detroit AL 3
1910 Philadelphia AL 4, Chicago NL 1
1911 Philadelphia AL 4, New York NL 2
1912 Boston AL 4, New York NL 3, 1 tie
1913 Philadelphia AL 4, New York NL 1
1914 Boston NL 4, Philadelphia AL 0
1915 Boston AL 4, Philadelphia NL 1
1916 Boston AL 4, Brooklyn NL 1
1917 Chicago AL 4, New York NL 2
1918 Boston AL 4, Chicago NL 2
1919 Cincinnati NL 5, Chicago AL 3
1920 Cleveland AL 5, Brooklyn NL 2
1921 New York NL 5, New York AL 3
1922 New York NL 4, New York AL 0, 1 tie
1923 New York AL 4, New York NL 2
1924 Washington AL 4, New York NL 3
1925 Pittsburgh NL 4, Washington AL 3
1926 St. Louis NL 4, New York AL 3
1927 New York AL 4, Pittsburgh NL 0
1928 New York AL 4, St. Louis NL 0
1929 Philadelphia AL 4, Chicago NL 1
1930 Philadelphia AL 4, St. Louis NL 2
1931 St. Louis NL 4, Philadelphia AL 3
1932 New York AL 4, Chicago NL 0
1933 New York NL 4, Washington AL 1
1934 St. Louis NL 4, Detroit AL 3
1935 Detroit AL 4, Chicago NL 2
1936 New York AL 4, New York NL 2
1937 New York AL 4, New York NL 1
1938 New York AL 4, Chicago NL 0
1939 New York AL 4, Cincinnati NL 0
1940 Cincinnati NL 4, Detroit AL 3
1941 New York AL 4, Brooklyn NL 1
1942 St. Louis NL 4, New York AL 1
1943 New York AL 4, St. Louis NL 1
1944 St. Louis NL 4, St. Louis AL 2
1945 Detroit AL 4, Chicago NL 3
1946 St. Louis NL 4, Boston AL 3
1947 New York AL 4, Brooklyn NL 3
1948 Cleveland AL 4, Boston NL 2
1949 New York AL 4, Brooklyn NL 1
1950 New York AL 4, Philadelphia NL 0
1951 New York AL 4, New York NL 2
1952 New York AL 4, Brooklyn NL 3
1953 New York AL 4, Brooklyn NL 2
1954 New York NL 4, Cleveland AL 0
1955 Brooklyn NL 4, New York AL 3
1956 New York AL 4, Brooklyn NL 3
1957 Milwaukee NL 4, New York AL 3
1958 New York AL 4, Milwaukee NL 3
1959 Los Angeles NL 4, Chicago AL 2
1960 Pittsburgh NL 4, New York AL 3
1961 New York AL 4, Cincinnati NL 1
1962 New York AL 4, San Francisco NL 3
1963 Los Angeles NL 4, New York AL 0
1964 St. Louis NL 4, New York AL 3
1965 Los Angeles NL 4, Minnesota AL 3
1966 Baltimore AL 4, Los Angeles NL 0
1967 St. Louis NL 4, Boston AL 3
1968 Detroit AL 4, St. Louis NL 3
1969 New York NL 4, Baltimore AL 1
1970 Baltimore AL 4, Cincinnati NL 1
1971 Pittsburgh NL 4, Baltimore AL 3
1972 Oakland AL 4, Cincinnati NL 3
1973 Oakland AL 4, New York NL 3
1974 Oakland AL 4, Los Angeles NL 1
1975 Cincinnati NL 4, Boston AL 3
1976 Cincinnati NL 4, New York AL 0
1977 New York AL 4, Los Angeles NL 2
1978 New York AL 4, Los Angeles NL 2
1979 Pittsburgh NL 4, Baltimore AL 3
1980 Philadelphia NL 4, Kansas City AL 2
1981 Los Angeles NL 4, New York AL 2
1982 St. Louis NL 4, Milwaukee AL 3
1983 Baltimore AL 4, Philadelphia NL 1
1984 Detroit AL 4, San Diego NL 1
1985 Kansas City AL 4, St. Louis NL 3
1986 New York NL 4, Boston AL 3
1987 Minnesota AL 4, St. Louis NL 3
1988 Los Angeles NL 4, Oakland AL 1
1989 Oakland AL 4, San Francisco NL 0
1990 Cincinnati NL 4, Oakland AL 0
1991 Minnesota AL 4, Atlanta NL 3
1992 Toronto AL 4, Atlanta NL 2
1993 Toronto AL 4, Philadelphia NL 2

Chess

Source: U.S. Chess Federation

Chess dates back to antiquity, its exact origin unknown. The best players of their time, regarded by later generations as world champions, were Francois Philidor, Alexandre Deschappelles, Louis de la Bourdonnais, all France; Howard Staunton, England; Adolph Anderssen, Germany and Paul Morphy, U.S. In 1866 Wilhelm Steinitz defeated Adolph Anderssen and claimed the world champion title. Official world champions since the title was first used follow:

1866-1894 Wilhelm Steinitz, Austria
1894-1921 Emanuel Lasker, Germany
1921-1927 Jose R. Capablanca, Cuba
1927-1935 Alexander A. Alekhine, France
1935-1937 Max Euwe, Netherlands
1937-1946 Alexander A. Alekhine, France
1948-1957 Mikhail Botvinnik, USSR
1957-1958 Vassily Smyslov, USSR
1958-1959 Mikhail Botvinnik, USSR
1960-1961 Mikhail Tal, USSR
1961-1963 Mikhail Botvinnik, USSR
1963-1969 Tigran Petrosian, USSR
1969-1972 Boris Spassky, USSR
1972-1975 Bobby Fischer, U.S. (a)
1975-1985 Anatoly Karpov, USSR
1985 Gary Kasparov, USSR/Russia (b)

(a) Defaulted championship after refusal to accept International Chess Federation rules for a championship match, April 1975. (b) Kasparov broke with the International Chess Federation (FIDE), Feb. 26, 1993. FIDE stripped Kasparov of his title Mar. 23. Kasparov defeated Nigel Short of Great Britain in a world championship match played Sept.-Oct. 1993 under the auspices of a new organization the two had founded, the Professional Chess Association. FIDE held a championship match between Anatoly Karpov (Russia) and Jan Timman (the Netherlands).

Ten Most Dramatic Sports Events, Nov. 1992—Oct. 1993

—John Paxson sank a 3-point shot with 3.9 seconds left in the game to give the Chicago Bulls a 99-98 victory over the Phoenix Suns, June 20, and their third consecutive National Basketball Association championship. The Bulls defeated the Suns 4 games to 2.

—The University of Alabama defeated the top-ranked University of Miami in the Sugar Bowl, 34-13, on New Year's Day. The victory broke a 29-game winning streak for Miami and propelled the Crimson Tide into the top spot in the national polls for collegiate champion.

—North Carolina won the NCAA basketball championship, April 5, by defeating Michigan, 77-71. Chris Webber of Michigan called an illegal time-out with 11 seconds left in the game and his team trailing by 2 points, giving the Tar Heels 2 technical foul shots and the ball, which sealed the victory.

—Noureddine Morceli of Algeria broke the world record in the mile, Sept. 5, with a time of 3 minutes 44.39 seconds at a meet in Rieti, Italy. Morceli took nearly 2 seconds off the old record, set by Steve Cram in 1985.

—Mark Whiten of the St. Louis Cardinals hit 4 home runs in a game against the Cincinnati Reds, Sept. 7. He became the 12th major leaguer to hit 4 homers in a game. He also tied the major league record of 12 RBI's in a game, set in 1924.

—In the biggest comeback in NFL history, the Buffalo Bills overcame a 35-3 deficit to beat the Houston Oilers, 41-38, in overtime, Jan. 3, in the first round of the National Football League playoffs. The Bills were eventually defeated in the Super Bowl, Jan. 31, by the Dallas Cowboys, 52-17.

—Welterweights Julio Cesar Chavez and Pernell Whitaker fought to a 12-round draw in San Antonio, Texas, Sept. 10, in a bout billed as a fight to decide who was the world's best boxer "pound for pound." The result was widely criticized, as Whitaker was perceived by most to have won easily.

—With a 4-1 victory on June 9, the Montreal Canadiens won their 24th National Hockey League Stanley Cup championship, defeating the Los Angeles Kings, 4 games to 1. It was the first Stanley Cup title for the Canadiens since 1986.

—Monica Seles, the No. 1-ranked women's tennis player, was seriously injured when she was stabbed in the back by a spectator during a tournament in Hamburg, Germany, April 30. The attacker was apparently a fanatical fan of Seles' rival, Steffi Graf of Germany. Seles, who required lengthy rehabilitation and was unable to play for months, lost her No. 1 ranking to Graf June 3.

—A dramatic ninth-inning home run by Joe Carter in game 6, Oct. 23, gave the Toronto Blue Jays an 8-6 win and their second straight World Series victory, 4 games to 2 over the Philadelphia Phillies. Three days earlier a 6-run eighth inning in game 4 had given the Blue Jays a come-from-behind 15-14 victory in the highest scoring (29 runs) and longest (4 hours, 14 minutes) game in World Series history.

VITAL STATISTICS

Births, Deaths, Marriages, and Divorces, First Quarter 1993

Source: National Center for Health Statistics, U.S. Dept. of Health and Human Services

Births

According to provisional statistics for the first quarter of 1993, there were 991,000 births, a slight decrease from the number reported for the same 3-month period in 1992 (998,000). The birthrate declined by 1 percent, from 15.8 per 1,000 population in the first quarter of 1992 to 15.7 in the first quarter of 1993.

During the 12 months ending with March 1993, there were an estimated 4,078,000 live births, 1 percent less than reported for the comparable period ending a year earlier (4,126,000). The birthrate was 15.9 per 1,000 population, 2 percent below the rate for the 12 months ending with March 1992 (16.3).

Marriages

The total number of marriages for the first quarter of 1993 was 412,000, a decrease of 3 percent from the number for the comparable period in 1992 (423,000). The marriage rate was 6.6 per 1,000 population, a decrease of 1 percent from the first quarter of 1992.

During the 12 months ending with March 1993, an estimated 2,351,000 couples married, a decrease of 1 percent from the previous 12-month period. The 12-month marriage rate was 9.2, down 2 percent from the rate for the 12 months ending with March 1992.

Divorces

A total of 292,000 couples divorced during the first quarter of 1993, a 3 percent decrease compared to the first quarter of 1992 (300,000). The divorce rate was 4.6 per 1,000 population, a decrease of 4 percent from the first quarter of 1992 (4.8).

During the 12 months ending with March 1993, an estimated 1,206,000 couples divorced, up slightly from 1,203,000 during the 12 months ending March 1992, and the rate declined from 4.8 to 4.7 per 1,000 population.

Deaths

According to provisional statistics, there were 600,000 deaths during the first quarter of 1993, 2 percent more than for the first quarter of 1992 (587,000). The death rate was 9.5 per 1,000 population, 2 percent higher than the Jan.-March 1992 rate. Among the deaths for the first quarter of 1993 were 8,700 deaths at ages under 1 year, yielding an infant mortality rate of 8.7 per 1,000 live births, 6 percent lower than the rate of 9.3 for the first quarter of 1992.

The death rate for the 12 months ending with March 1993 (8.6 deaths per 1,000 population) was the same as the rate for the comparable 12-month period a year earlier. The infant mortality rate for this 12-month-period was 8.3 per 1,000 live births, 6 percent lower than the rate of 8.8 for the 12 months ending with March 1992.

Provisional Statistics
12 months ending with March

	Number		Rate*	
	1993	1992	1993	1992
Live births	4,078,000	4,126,000	15.9	16.3
Deaths	2,190,000	2,186,000	8.6	8.6
Natural increase.	1,888,000	1,940,000	7.3	7.7
Marriages	2,351,000	2,384,000	9.2	9.4
Divorces	1,206,000	1,203,000	4.7	4.8
Infant deaths. . .	33,700	36,300	8.3	8.8

* Per 1,000 population. **Note:** Figures include revisions.

Annual Report for the Year 1992 (Provisional Statistics)

Source: National Center for Health Statistics, U.S. Dept. of Health and Human Services

Highlights

Provisional data for 1992 show that both the birthrate and the death rate per 1,000 population were lower than the comparable rates for the previous year. Between 1991 and 1992 a decrease was also observed for the infant mortality rate per 1,000 live births. The marriage rate per 1,000 population decreased in comparison with the rate for 1991. Only the divorce rate increased from 1991 to 1992.

Births

An estimated 4,084,000 babies were born in the United States in 1992, a decline of 1 percent from the 4,111,000 births in 1991. The birthrate of 16.0 per 1,000 population was 2 percent lower than the rate of 16.3 for the preceding year. The fertility rate (the number of live births per 1,000 women aged 15-44 years) for 1992 was 69.2, 1 percent lower than the rate for 1991 (69.6).

Deaths

The provisional count of deaths during 1992 was 2,177,000, about 1 percent more than in the previous year (2,165,000). The death rate of 853.3 deaths per 100,000 population was 1 percent lower than the rate of 858.5 for 1991. About 34,400 of these deaths were to infants under 1 year of age. The infant mortality rate was 848.7 per 1,000 live births, 5 percent lower than the rate of 892.8 for 1991.

Natural Increase

As a result of natural increase, the excess of births over deaths, an estimated 1,907,000 persons were added to the population in 1992. This rate was 7.5, per 1,000 population, 3 percent lower than the rate of 7.7 for 1991. The decline in the rate of natural increase continues to be due to a larger decrease in the birthrate than in the death rate.

Marriages

An estimated 2,362,000 marriages were performed in 1992, slightly lower than the number in 1991 (2,371,000). The marriage rate was 1 percent lower in 1992 (9.3) than in 1991 (9.4).

Divorces

The number of divorces granted in 1992 (1,215,000) was 2 percent higher than in 1991 (1,187,000). Although the number was an all-time high, the divorce rate in 1992 (4.8 per 1,000 population) was 9 percent lower than the peak rate of 1981 (5.3) but slightly higher than the rate of 4.7 from 1988 to 1991.

Births and Deaths in the U.S.

Source: National Center for Health Statistics, U.S. Dept. of Health and Human Services

Refers only to events occurring within the U.S. Excludes fetal deaths. Rates per 1,000 population enumerated as of April 1 for 1960, and 1970; estimated as of July 1 for all other years. Beginning 1970 excludes births and deaths occurring to nonresidents of the U.S.

	Births		Deaths	
Year	Total number	Rate	Total number	Rate
1960.	4,257,850	23.7	1,711,982	9.5
1970.	3,731,386	18.4	1,921,031	9.5
1980.	3,612,258	15.9	1,986,000	8.7
1990.	4,179,000	16.7	2,162,000	8.6
1991.	4,111,000	16.3	2,165,000	8.6
1992.	4,084,000	16.0	2,177,000	8.5

Births and Deaths by States and Regions, 1991-1992

Source: National Center for Health Statistics, U.S. Dept. of Health and Human Services

Area	Live births				Deaths			
	1991		1992		1991		1992	
	Number	Rate	Number	Rate	Number	Rate	Number	Rate
New England	**189,547**	**14.4**	**189,276**	**14.3**	**112,411**	**8.5**	**116,218**	**8.8**
Maine	16,581	13.4	15,623	12.7	10,952	8.9	10,900	8.8
New Hampshire	16,060	14.5	15,719	14.1	8,513	7.7	8,555	7.7
Vermont	7,712	13.6	7,625	13.4	4,541	8.0	4,732	8.3
Massachusetts	86,321	14.4	88,185	14.7	51,366	8.6	54,292	9.1
Rhode Island	14,591	14.5	14,789	14.7	9,294	9.2	9,444	9.4
Connecticut	48,282	14.7	47,335	14.4	27,745	8.4	28,295	8.6
Middle Atlantic	**578,773**	**15.3**	**570,697**	**15.1**	**360,314**	**9.5**	**359,395**	**9.5**
New York	292,400	16.2	285,568	15.8	166,795	9.2	164,869	9.1
New Jersey	117,789	15.2	119,923	15.4	69,983	9.0	71,201	9.1
Pennsylvania	168,584	14.1	165,206	13.8	123,536	10.3	123,325	10.3
East North Central	**662,427**	**15.6**	**654,228**	**15.3**	**379,282**	**8.9**	**372,449**	**8.7**
Ohio	158,638	14.5	169,067	15.3	99,104	9.1	99,601	9.0
Indiana	84,707	15.1	83,832	14.8	51,780	9.2	50,144	8.9
Illinois	193,987	16.8	192,483	16.5	104,677	9.1	101,590	8.7
Michigan	153,359	16.3	138,968	14.7	79,972	8.5	79,307	8.4
Wisconsin	71,736	14.5	69,878	14.0	43,749	8.8	41,807	8.3
West North Central	**262,368**	**14.7**	**259,737**	**14.5**	**164,055**	**9.2**	**162,094**	**9.0**
Minnesota	67,020	15.1	65,477	14.6	35,270	8.0	34,909	7.8
Iowa	36,011	12.9	38,120	13.6	25,906	9.3	27,002	9.6
Missouri	77,991	15.1	75,437	14.5	53,461	10.4	50,447	9.7
North Dakota	9,071	14.3	8,935	14.0	5,648	8.9	5,797	9.1
South Dakota	11,042	15.7	11,281	15.9	6,594	9.4	6,927	9.7
Nebraska	23,933	15.0	23,003	14.3	14,665	9.2	14,852	9.2
Kansas	37,300	14.9	37,484	14.9	22,511	9.0	22,160	8.8
South Atlantic	**689,068**	**15.5**	**680,220**	**15.1**	**396,655**	**8.9**	**403,745**	**9.0**
Delaware	11,175	16.4	10,902	15.8	5,880	8.6	5,937	8.6
Maryland	84,452	17.4	76,173	15.5	37,982	7.8	37,806	7.7
District of Columbia	9,971	16.8	10,052	17.1	6,961	11.7	6,578	11.2
Virginia	96,610	15.4	97,600	15.3	49,151	7.8	49,541	7.8
West Virginia	22,195	12.3	22,123	12.2	19,801	11.0	20,107	11.1
North Carolina	102,442	15.2	103,047	15.1	58,909	8.7	59,478	8.7
South Carolina	57,742	16.2	56,635	15.7	29,983	8.4	30,609	8.5
Georgia	110,024	16.6	111,397	16.5	52,708	8.0	53,288	7.9
Florida	194,457	14.7	192,291	14.3	135,280	10.2	140,401	10.4
East South Central	**232,052**	**15.1**	**234,462**	**15.1**	**144,284**	**9.4**	**147,410**	**9.5**
Kentucky	54,913	14.8	53,906	14.4	35,281	9.5	35,341	9.4
Tennessee	73,104	14.8	74,048	14.7	45,351	9.2	47,149	9.4
Alabama	60,513	14.8	63,021	15.2	38,027	9.3	39,630	9.6
Mississippi	43,522	16.8	43,487	16.6	25,625	9.9	25,290	9.7
West South Central	**482,024**	**17.8**	**479,421**	**17.4**	**221,795**	**8.2**	**224,221**	**8.1**
Arkansas	34,588	14.6	34,967	14.6	24,230	10.2	25,202	10.5
Louisiana	74,562	17.5	71,743	16.7	38,290	9.0	37,446	8.7
Oklahoma	47,312	14.9	47,850	14.9	30,349	9.6	30,626	9.5
Texas	325,562	18.8	324,861	18.4	128,926	7.4	130,947	7.4
Mountain	**243,405**	**17.3**	**245,352**	**17.1**	**99,248**	**7.1**	**103,301**	**7.2**
Montana	11,544	14.3	11,551	14.0	7,071	8.7	7,151	8.7
Idaho	17,233	16.6	17,475	16.4	7,789	7.5	8,063	7.6
Wyoming	6,801	14.8	6,823	14.6	3,167	6.9	3,333	7.2
Colorado	53,968	16.0	54,586	15.7	22,334	6.6	22,528	6.5
New Mexico	28,160	18.2	28,463	18.0	11,116	7.2	11,561	7.3
Arizona	67,656	18.1	66,698	17.4	29,329	7.8	30,659	8.0
Utah	35,070	19.8	37,411	20.6	9,199	5.2	9,904	5.5
Nevada	22,973	17.9	22,345	16.8	9,243	7.2	10,102	7.6
Pacific	**759,966**	**19.0**	**753,550**	**18.5**	**290,482**	**7.3**	**287,474**	**7.1**
Washington	75,734	15.1	79,300	15.4	37,682	7.5	37,272	7.3
Oregon	42,807	14.6	41,606	14.0	25,205	8.6	25,862	8.7
California	610,166	20.1	601,028	19.5	218,735	7.2	215,206	7.0
Alaska	11,245	19.7	11,706	19.9	2,145	3.8	2,225	3.8
Hawaii	20,014	17.6	19,910	17.2	6,715	5.9	6,909	6.0

Notes: Data are provisional estimates, reported by state of residence. Figures include revisions, and so may differ from those previously published. Rates for births and deaths are per 1,000 population. Rates for deaths in 1991 have been recomputed based on revised population estimates.

Deaths Under 1 Year and Infant Mortality Rates, for 10 Selected Causes, 1991-92

Source: National Center for Health Statistics, U.S. Dept. of Health and Human Services

Age and cause of death	1991 Number	1991 Rate	1992 Number	1992 Rate
Total, under 1 year	**36,500**	**892.8**	**34,400**	**848.7**
Under 28 days	22,640	554.2	21,860	538.6
28 days to 11 months	13,830	338.6	12,570	309.7
Certain gastrointestinal diseases	320	7.8	340	8.3
Pneumonia and influenza	610	14.9	720	17.6
Congenital anomalies	7,600	186.0	7,500	183.6
Disorders relating to short gestation and unspecified low birthweight	4,500	110.2	3,790	92.8

Age and cause of death	1991 Number	1991 Rate	1992 Number	1992 Rate
Birth trauma	160	3.9	170	4.2
Intrauterine hypoxia and birth asphyxia	730	17.9	720	17.6
Respiratory distress syndrome	2,300	56.3	2,380	58.3
Other conditions originating in the prenatal period	8,730	213.7	8,550	209.3
Sudden infant death syndrome	5,170	126.6	4,660	114.1
All other causes	6,340	155.2	5,610	137.4

Notes: Data are provisional, estimated from a 10 percent sample of deaths. Rates are on an annual basis per 100,000 live births. Due to rounding of estimates, figures may not add to totals.

Infant Mortality Rates, by Race and Sex, 1960-1990[1]

Source: National Center for Health Statistics, U.S. Dept. of Health and Human Services

Year	All races: Both sexes	All races: Male	All races: Female	White: Both sexes	White: Male	White: Female	Black: Both sexes	Black: Male	Black: Female
1960	26.0	29.3	22.6	22.9	26.0	19.6	44.3	49.1	39.4
1970	20.0	22.4	17.5	17.8	20.0	15.4	32.6	36.2	29.0
1980	12.6	13.9	11.2	11.0	12.3	9.6	21.4	23.3	19.4
1981	11.9	13.1	10.7	10.5	11.7	9.2	20.0	21.7	18.3
1982	11.5	12.8	10.2	10.1	11.2	8.9	19.6	21.5	17.7
1983	11.2	12.3	10.0	9.7	10.8	8.6	19.2	21.1	17.2
1984	10.8	11.9	9.6	9.4	10.5	8.3	18.4	19.8	16.9
1985	10.6	11.9	9.3	9.3	10.6	8.0	18.2	19.9	16.5
1986	10.4	11.5	9.1	8.9	10.0	7.8	18.0	20.0	16.0
1987	10.1	11.2	8.9	8.6	9.6	7.6	17.9	19.6	16.0
1988	10.0	11.0	8.9	8.5	9.5	7.4	17.6	19.0	16.1
1989	9.8	10.8	8.8	8.1	9.0	7.1	18.6	20.0	17.2
1990	9.2	10.3	8.1	7.6	8.5	6.6	18.0	19.6	16.2

(1) Final data.

The 10 Leading Causes of Death, 1992[1]

Source: National Center for Health Statistics, U.S. Dept. of Health and Human Services

Rank	Cause of death	Number	Death rate[2]	Percent of total deaths
	All causes	2,177,000	853.3	100.0
1.	Heart Disease	720,480	282.5	33.1
2.	Cancer	521,090	204.3	23.9
3.	Stroke	143,640	56.3	6.6
4.	Chronic obstructive lung diseases and allied conditions	91,440	35.8	4.2
5.	Accidents and adverse effects	86,310	33.8	4.0
	Motor vehicle accidents	41,710	16.4	1.9
	All other accidents and adverse effects	44,600	17.5	2.0
6.	Pneumonia and influenza	76,120	29.8	3.5
7.	Diabetes mellitus	50,180	19.7	2.3
8.	Human immunodeficiency virus (HIV) infection[3]	33,590	13.2	1.5
9.	Suicide	29,760	11.7	1.4
10.	Homicide and legal intervention	26,570	10.4	1.2

(1) Data are provisional, estimated from a 10 percent sample of deaths. Figures may not add to totals due to rounding. Rates have been recomputed based on revised population estimates. (2) Per 100,000 population. (3) HIV is the virus that causes AIDS.

Suicides by Age, Race, and Sex, 1992

Source: National Center for Health Statistics, U.S. Dept. of Health and Human Services

	All ages	1-14 yrs.	15-24 yrs.	25-34 yrs.	35-44 yrs.	45-54 yrs.	55-64 yrs.	65-74 yrs.	75-84 yrs.	85 yrs. & over	Age not stated
All races, both sexes	29,760	310	4,650	6,030	5,740	3,970	3,040	2,620	2,780	600	10
Male	24,260	220	3,970	4,980	4,650	2,970	2,390	2,120	2,430	520	10
Female	5,500	90	690	1,050	1,090	1,000	650	500	350	80	—
White, both sexes	26,980	290	3,950	5,220	5,230	3,670	2,870	2,530	2,670	550	—
Male	22,050	210	3,360	4,360	4,280	2,710	2,260	2,050	2,350	470	—
Female	4,930	80	580	860	960	960	600	490	320	80	—
Black, both sexes	2,000	10	500	630	320	220	160	30	80	40	10
Male	1,670	10	460	500	260	190	110	30	60	40	10
Female	330	—	40	140	60	30	40	—	20	—	—

Note: Data are provisional, estimated from a 10 percent sample of deaths. Due to rounding of estimates, figures may not add to totals.

Ownership of Life Insurance in the U.S. and Assets of U.S. Life Insurance Companies

Source: American Council of Life Insurance

(millions of dollars)

Year	Purchases of life insurance: Ordinary	Purchases: Group	Purchases: Industrial	Purchases: Total	Insurance in force: Ordinary	In force: Group	In force: Industrial	In force: Credit	In force: Total	Assets
1940	6,689	691	3,350	10,730	79,346	14,938	20,866	380	115,530	30,802
1950	17,326	6,068	5,402	28,796	149,116	47,793	33,415	3,844	234,168	64,020
1960	52,883	14,645	6,880	74,408	341,881	175,903	39,563	29,101	586,448	119,576
1965	83,485	51,385*	7,296	142,166*	499,638	308,078	39,818	53,020	900,554	158,884
1970	122,820	63,690*	6,612	193,122*	734,730	551,357	38,644	77,392	1,402,123	207,254
1975	188,003	95,190*	6,729	289,922*	1,083,421	904,695	39,423	112,032	2,139,571	289,304
1980	385,575	183,418	3,609	572,602	1,760,474	1,579,355	35,994	165,215	3,541,038	479,210
1985	910,944	319,503	722	1,231,169	3,247,289	2,561,595	28,250	215,973	6,053,107	825,901
1986	933,592	374,741*	418	1,308,751*	3,658,203	2,801,049	27,168	233,859	6,720,279	937,551
1987	986,660	365,529	324	1,352,513	4,139,071	3,043,782	26,668	242,977	7,452,498	1,044,459
1988	995,686	410,848	320	1,406,854	4,511,608	3,232,080	25,456	251,015	8,020,159	1,166,870
1989	1,020,719	420,707	252	1,441,678	4,939,964	3,469,498	24,446	260,107	8,694,015	1,299,756
1990	1,069,660	459,271	220	1,529,151	5,366,982	3,753,506	24,071	248,038	9,392,597	1,408,402
1991	1,041,508	573,953*	198	1,615,659*	5,677,777	4,057,606	22,475	228,478	9,986,336	1,551,201
1992	1,048,135	440,143	222	1,488,500	5,941,810	4,240,919	20,973	202,090	10,405,792	1,664,531

* Includes Servicemen's Group Life Insurance $27.8 billion in 1965, $17.1 billion in 1970, $1.7 billion in 1975, $51.0 billion in 1986, and $166.7 billion in 1991, as well as $10.8 billion of Federal Employees' Group Life Insurance in 1986.

Marriage and Divorce in the U.S. in 1992

Source: Bureau of the Census, U.S. Dept. of Commerce; Dec. 1992.

• Although 90 percent of current young adult Americans expect to marry at some time, this figure is lower than the historical 95 percent marriage rate for Americans.

• Among young adult Americans, about 90 percent of white women expect to marry at some time, but fewer than 75 percent of black women expect to do so.

• Women are marrying later. In 1990 the proportion of women 20 to 24 years old who had married for the first time was 38 percent, a drop of 25 percentage points from the 1975 rate of 63 percent.

• There are different divorce patterns for women under 30, those between 30 and 44, and those between 45 and 54. Women in the 30 to 44 age group are expected to end up with the highest divorce rates, (an estimated 40 to 42 percent). Women under 30 are expected to have divorce rates of 38 to 39 percent, and women 45 to 54 are expected to have divorce rates of about 30 to 36 percent. The same general pattern holds true across racial and ethnic groups.

• The younger the woman at her first marriage, the greater the likelihood she will divorce.

• Women who complete 16 years of school are the least likely of all ever-married women to be divorced from their first husbands.

• Mothers who conceive or bear a child before their first marriage have a greater likelihood of divorce than mothers whose children are all conceived after marriage.

• The median duration of first marriages that end in divorce is about 6.3 years. However, women in their late 20s and early 30s, the prime ages for divorce, spend a median of 3.4 and 4.9 years, respectively, in their first marriages before divorcing.

• The median duration between a first divorce and remarriage is 2.5 years. Three-quarters of remarriages occur within 5 years of divorce.

• Twenty-one percent of all households containing a married couple and children include at least one stepchild under 18 years of age. This figure compares with about 16 percent of such households in 1980.

Parenthood in the U.S. in 1992

Source: Bureau of the Census, U.S. Dept. of Commerce

• Increasing proportions of never-married mothers were being found in all regions and most socioeconomic groups across the country in 1992. About 24 percent of single women age 18 to 44 had borne a child (as of June 1992), compared with 15 percent a decade earlier. The proportion of single mothers more than doubled among women with one or more years of college (4.4 percent in 1982; 11.3 percent in 1992) and nearly doubled among women with a high school diploma (17.2 percent in 1982; 32.5 percent in 1992). The proportion of single mothers among women who did not complete high school was also higher in 1992 (48.4 percent) than in 1982 (35.2 percent).

• Out-of-wedlock childbearing increased among all racial and ethnic groups between 1982 and 1992. About two-thirds (67 percent) of births to black women in 1992 were out of wedlock, compared to 27 percent for Hispanic women and 17 percent for white women. Comparable figures in 1982 were 49 percent, 16 percent, and 10 percent, respectively.

• The proportion of dual-employed married couples with children increased between 1976 and 1992. Of the wives 15 to 44 years old in 1992 (30 million), 47 percent were in families with children where both spouses were employed (14 percentage points higher than the figure for 1976). The traditional family, where only the husband worked while the wife remained at home with the children, declined from 43 to 24 percent; there were 7 million such families in 1992.

• Rates of home ownership were significantly higher in 1992 among dual-employed married couples with children (78 percent) than among childless couples (66 percent).

• The majority of women with infants were in the labor force. Among women 18 to 44 years old who had a child in the 12-month period ending in June 1992, 54 percent were in the labor force, compared with 44 percent in June 1982. Women 18 to 44 years old with a graduate or professional degree had a labor force participation rate (72 percent) more than double that of women who had less than four years of high school (31 percent).

• In 1992, about 65 percent of teenage (15 to 19 years old) births were out of wedlock. Ninety-four percent of black American teenage births were out of wedlock, compared to 60 percent of Hispanic and 56 percent of white teenage births.

• Women in their thirties had the largest increases in fertility rates during the 1980s and early 1990s. For women 30 to 34 years old in 1992, the fertility rate was 76.1 births per 1,000 women, up from 60.0 in 1980. And for women 35 to 39 in 1992, the fertility rate was 38 births per 1,000 women, up from 26.9 in 1980.

• In 1992, women 30 to 34 and 35 to 39 years old were nearing completion of their childbearing years with levels of childlessness at 26 and 19 percent, respectively. Each of these rates was 4 percentage points higher than in 1982.

• The average number of lifetime births expected for women 18 to 34 years old in June 1992 was 2,098 per 1,000 women, slightly lower than the 1976 average of 2,160.

Sixty-Five Plus in the U.S.

Source: Bureau of the Census, U.S. Dept. of Commerce

America is an aging society. In colonial times, half the population was under age 16; in 1990, fewer than 1 in 4 Americans were under age 16 and half were 33 or older; by 2050, at least half could be 39 or older.

The 1990 census counted 31.1 million Americans age 65 or older, 12.5 percent of the total population. Among the elderly, 18 million were age 65 to 74, 10 million were age 75 to 84, and 3 million were 85 or older.

The elderly population increased by 22 percent over the decade of the 1980s. Undramatic growth of the older population from 1990 to 2010 is projected. From 2010 to 2030, however, the Bureau of Census predicts, the elderly population will grow 76 percent while the population under age 65 increases 6.5 percent.

The United States had 6.9 million persons age 80 or older in 1990, and that population could grow to more than 29 million by 2050. One in 35 Americans were 80 or older in 1990; by 2050, at least 1 in 13 could be 80 or older.

• Centenarians, those who had reached the age of 100 years or older, numbered 35,808 in 1990. The centenarian population more than doubled during the 1980s. This population group is 80 percent white and 79 percent female.

• Nine states had more than 1 million elderly in 1990. California had the largest number of persons age 65 or older (3.1 million). Florida had the largest proportion of elderly (18 percent).

• From 1980 to 1990, America's oldest old population (85 years and over) increased almost 38 percent. Eight states had more than 100,000 persons age 85 or older in 1990.

• There is increasing racial diversity within the elderly population. In 1990, 1 in 10 elderly persons were nonwhite. That could increase to about 2 in 10 by the middle of the next century. Additionally, the Census Bureau expects a greater proportion of the elderly will be persons of Hispanic origin (who may be of any race).

U.S. Population 65 Years and Over, 1990

Source: Bureau of the Census, U.S. Dept. of Commerce

Race and sex	Total 65 years and over	65 to 69 years	70 to 74 years	Total 75 years and over	75 to 7[illegible] years
All Races					
Total	31,078,895	10,065,835	7,979,660	13,033,400	6,102,92[illegible]
Male	12,492,766	4,507,539	3,399,275	4,585,952	2,388,89[illegible]
Female	18,586,129	5,558,296	4,580,385	8,447,448	3,714,03[illegible]
Males per 100 females	67.2	81.1	74.2	54.3	64.[illegible]
White					
Total	28,020,562	8,983,978	7,191,013	11,845,571	5,518,34[illegible]
Male	11,284,407	4,047,535	3,079,801	4,157,071	2,165,06[illegible]
Female	16,736,155	4,936,443	4,111,212	7,688,500	3,353,28[illegible]
Males per 100 females	67.4	82.0	74.9	54.1	64.[illegible]
Black					
Total	2,492,221	859,694	638,077	994,450	483,53[illegible]
Male	956,936	360,653	252,967	343,316	178,69[illegible]
Female	1,535,285	499,041	385,110	651,134	304,84[illegible]
Males per 100 females	62.3	72.3	65.7	52.7	58.[illegible]
American Indian, Eskimo, and Aleut					
Total	116,153	43,374	29,831	42,948	21,52[illegible]
Male	48,874	19,658	12,759	16,457	8,55[illegible]
Female	67,279	23,716	17,072	26,491	12,97[illegible]
Males per 100 females	72.6	82.9	74.7	62.1	65.[illegible]
Asian and Pacific Islander					
Total	449,959	178,789	120,739	150,431	79,53[illegible]
Male	202,549	79,693	53,748	69,108	36,58[illegible]
Female	247,410	99,096	66,991	81,323	42,94[illegible]
Males per 100 females	81.9	80.4	80.2	85.0	85.[illegible]
Hispanic Origin[1]					
Total	1,146,223	431,000	284,085	431,138	211,43[illegible]
Male	474,830	192,949	118,696	163,185	82,36[illegible]
Female	671,393	238,051	165,389	267,953	129,06[illegible]
Males per 100 females	70.7	81.1	71.8	60.9	63.[illegible]

(1) People of Hispanic origin may be of any race.

U.S. Population 80 Years and Over, 1990

Source: Bureau of the Census, U.S. Dept. of Commerce

Race and sex	Total 80 years and over	80 to 84 years	Total 85 years and over	85 to 89 years	90 to 94 years	95 to 99 years	Tot[illegible] 100 year[illegible] and ov[illegible]
All Races							
Total	6,930,471	3,909,046	3,021,425	2,034,661	747,979	202,977	35,80[illegible]
Male	2,197,057	1,355,830	841,227	605,936	184,048	43,544	7,69[illegible]
Female	4,733,414	2,553,216	2,180,198	1,428,725	563,931	159,433	28,10[illegible]
Males per 100 females	46.4	53.1	38.6	42.4	32.6	27.3	27[illegible]
White							
Total	6,327,230	3,566,268	2,760,962	1,858,176	689,928	183,505	29,35[illegible]
Male	1,992,010	1,232,184	759,826	547,832	167,568	38,559	5,86[illegible]
Female	4,335,220	2,334,084	2,001,136	1,310,344	522,360	144,946	23,48[illegible]
Males per 100 females	45.9	52.8	38.0	41.8	32.1	26.6	25[illegible]
Black							
Total	510,915	288,283	222,632	150,294	49,599	17,049	5,69[illegible]
Male	164,621	98,351	66,270	46,949	13,485	4,277	1,55[illegible]
Female	346,294	189,932	156,362	103,345	36,114	12,772	4,13[illegible]
Males per 100 females	47.5	51.8	42.4	45.4	37.3	33.5	37[illegible]
American Indian, Eskimo, and Aleut							
Total	21,426	12,236	9,190	6,287	1,982	659	2[illegible]
Male	7,905	4,641	3,264	2,265	680	222	[illegible]
Female	13,521	7,595	5,926	4,022	1,302	437	1[illegible]
Males per 100 females	58.5	61.1	55.1	56.3	52.2	50.8	58[illegible]
Asian and Pacific Islander							
Total	70,900	42,259	28,641	19,904	6,470	1,764	5[illegible]
Male	32,521	20,654	11,867	8,890	2,315	486	1[illegible]
Female	38,379	21,605	16,774	11,014	4,155	1,278	3[illegible]
Males per 100 females	84.7	95.6	70.7	80.7	55.7	38.0	53[illegible]
Hispanic Origin[1]							
Total	219,706	128,302	91,404	64,945	19,257	5,616	1,5[illegible]
Male	80,821	48,430	32,391	23,695	6,405	1,726	5[illegible]
Female	138,885	79,872	59,013	41,250	12,852	3,890	1,0[illegible]
Males per 100 females	58.2	60.6	54.9	57.4	49.8	44.4	55[illegible]

(1) People of Hispanic orgin may be of any race.

Countries With More Than 1 Million Octogenarians in 1991

Source: Bureau of the Census, U.S. Dept. of Commerce; in thousands

Country	Population 80 and over	Country	Populati[illegible] 80 and ov[illegible]
China	9,173	France	2,170
United States	7,310	United Kingdom	2,130
India	3,578	Italy	1,853
Japan	3,089	Spain	1,164
Germany	3,081		

Percent Change of U.S. Population 65 and Over, 1980-1990

Source: Bureau of the Census, U.S. Dept. of Commerce

egion, division, and state	Percent change 1980 to 1990
nited States	22.3
ortheast	15.2
New England	16.4
Middle Atlantic	14.8
idwest	15.8
East North Central	17.9
West North Central	11.4
outh	26.3
South Atlantic	33.6
East South Central	16.5
West South Central	20.1
est	34.3
Mountain	43.6
Pacific	31.3
ew England	16.4
Maine	15.9
Vermont	13.7
New Hampshire	21.4
Massachusetts	12.8
Rhode Island	18.6
Connecticut	22.2
iddle Atlantic	14.8
New York	9.4
New Jersey	20.0
Pennsylvania	19.5
ast North Central	17.9
Ohio	20.3
Indiana	18.9
Illinois	13.8
Michigan	21.5
Wisconsin	15.4
est North Central	11.4
Minnesota	14.0
Iowa	9.9
Missouri	10.7
North Dakota	13.2
South Dakota	12.4
Nebraska	8.5
Kansas	11.9
South Atlantic	33.6
Delaware	36.4
Maryland	30.8
District of Columbia	4.8
Virginia	31.5
West Virginia	13.0
North Carolina	33.3
South Carolina	38.1
Georgia	26.6
Florida	40.4
East South Central	16.5
Kentucky	13.9
Tennessee	19.6
Alabama	18.9
Mississippi	11.0
West South Central	20.1
Arkansas	12.0
Louisiana	16.0
Oklahoma	12.8
Texas	25.2
Mountain	43.6
Montana	25.9
Idaho	29.4
Wyoming	27.0
Colorado	33.2
New Mexico	40.7
Arizona	55.8
Utah	37.3
Nevada	94.1
Pacific	31.3
Washington	33.3
Oregon	29.0
California	29.9
Alaska	93.7
Hawaii	64.2

Countries With More Than 2 Million Elderly Persons in 1991

Source: Bureau of the Census, U.S. Dept. of Commerce; in thousands

ountry	Population 65 and over
hina	67,967
dia	32,780
nited States	32,045
apan	15,253
ermany	12,010
nited Kingdom	9,025
aly	8,665
ance	8,074
razil	6,680
Indonesia	5,962
Spain	5,378
Pakistan	4,734
Poland	3,851
Mexico	3,522
Bangladesh	3,492
Vietnam	3,196
Canada	3,140
Argentina	3,012
Turkey	2,789
Nigeria	2,676
Romania	2,489
Philippines	2,380
Thailand	2,350
Yugoslavia	2,328
South Korea	2,135
Egypt	2,077
Iran	2,052

Countries Projected to Have More Than 2 Million Elderly Persons in 2020

Source: Bureau of the Census, U.S. Dept. of Commerce; in thousands

ountry	Population 65 and over
hina	179,561
dia	88,495
nited States	53,627
apan	33,421
donesia	22,183
azil	18,800
ermany	18,396
aly	13,078
ance	12,119
nited Kingdom	12,108
exico	10,857
akistan	9,678
geria	9,152
angladesh	9,057
pain	8,162
irkey	7,990
hailand	7,828
Poland	7,243
Vietnam	6,707
Philippines	6,646
South Korea	6,550
Canada	6,404
Egypt	5,680
Iran	5,235
Yugoslavia	4,933
Argentina	4,862
Romania	4,588
Colombia	4,464
South Africa	4,084
Australia	3,956
Ethiopia	3,920
Taiwan	3,500
Netherlands	3,461
Burma (Myanmar)	3,425
Czechoslovakia	3,149
Morocco	2,972
Venezuela	2,912
Saudi Arabia	2,867
North Korea	2,734
Zaire	2,643
Peru	2,580
Sri Lanka	2,527
Algeria	2,450
Greece	2,237
Hungary	2,186
Malaysia	2,139
Chile	2,133
Belgium	2,071
Portugal	2,053

Living Arrangements of the Elderly, 1980 and 1990

Source: Bureau of the Census, U.S. Dept. of Commerce; in thousands; noninstitutional population.

Living arrangement and age	1980 Number Total	1980 Number Men	1980 Number Women	1980 Percent distribution Total	1980 Percent distribution Men	1980 Percent distribution Women	1990 Number Total	1990 Number Men	1990 Number Women	1990 Percent distribution Total	1990 Percent distribution Men	1990 Percent distribution Women
65 years and over	**24,157**	**9,889**	**14,268**	**100.0**	**100.0**	**100.0**	**29,566**	**12,334**	**17,232**	**100.0**	**100.0**	**100.**
Living:												
Alone	7,067	1,447	5,620	29.3	14.6	39.4	9,176	1,942	7,233	31.0	15.7	42.
With spouse	12,781	7,441	5,340	52.9	75.2	37.4	16,003	9,158	6,845	54.1	74.3	39.
With other relatives	3,892	832	3,060	16.1	8.4	21.4	3,734	953	2,782	12.6	7.7	16.
With nonrelatives only[1]	417	169	248	1.7	1.7	1.7	653	281	372	2.2	2.3	2.
65 to 74 years	**15,302**	**6,621**	**8,681**	**100.0**	**100.0**	**100.0**	**17,979**	**8,013**	**9,966**	**100.0**	**100.0**	**100.**
Living:												
Alone	3,750	797	2,953	24.5	12.0	34.0	4,350	1,042	3,309	24.2	13.0	33.
With spouse	9,436	5,285	4,151	61.7	79.8	47.8	11,353	6,265	5,089	63.1	78.2	51.
With other relatives	1,890	436	1,454	12.4	6.6	16.7	1,931	528	1,401	10.7	6.6	14.
With nonrelatives only[1]	226	103	123	1.5	1.6	1.4	345	178	167	1.9	2.2	1.
75 to 84 years	**7,172**	**2,708**	**4,464**	**100.0**	**100.0**	**100.0**	**9,354**	**3,562**	**5,792**	**100.0**	**100.0**	**100.**
Living:												
Alone	2,664	505	2,159	37.1	18.6	48.4	3,774	688	3,086	40.3	19.3	53.
With spouse	2,977	1,882	1,095	41.5	69.5	24.5	4,145	2,537	1,607	44.3	71.2	27.
With other relatives	1,394	271	1,123	19.4	10.0	25.2	1,237	264	974	13.2	7.4	16.
With nonrelatives only[1]	137	50	87	1.9	1.8	1.9	198	73	125	2.1	2.0	2.
85 years and over	**1,683**	**560**	**1,123**	**100.0**	**100.0**	**100.0**	**2,233**	**758**	**1,475**	**100.0**	**100.0**	**100.**
Living:												
Alone	653	145	508	38.8	25.9	45.2	1,051	213	838	47.1	28.1	56.
With spouse	368	274	94	21.9	48.9	8.4	505	356	150	22.6	47.0	10.
With other relatives	608	125	483	36.1	22.3	43.0	567	160	406	25.4	21.1	27.
With nonrelatives only[1]	54	16	38	3.2	2.9	3.4	110	29	81	4.9	3.8	5.

(1) 1980 data include a small number of persons in unrelated subfamilies.

Persons Living Alone, 1970-1991

Source: Bureau of the Census, U.S. Dept. of Commerce

Sex and Age	Number of Persons (1,000) 1970	1980	1990	1991	Percent Distribution 1970	1980	1990	199
Both sexes	**10,851**	**18,296**	**22,999**	**23,590**	**100**	**100**	**100**	**10**
15 to 24 years old[1]	558	1,726	1,210	1,140	5	9	5	
25 to 34 years old	1,604[2]	4,729[2]	3,972	4,116	15[2]	26[2]	17	1
35 to 44 years old	(2)	(2)	3,138	3,402	(2)	(2)	14	1
45 to 64 years old	3,622	4,514	5,502	5,550	33	25	24	2
65 to 74 years old	2,815	3,851	4,350	4,494	26	21	19	1
75 years old and over	2,258	3,477	4,825	4,887	21	19	21	2
Male	**3,532**	**6,966**	**9,049**	**9,450**	**33**	**38**	**39**	**4**
15 to 24 years old[1]	274	947	674	622	3	5	3	
25 to 34 years old	933[2]	2,920[2]	2,395	2,491	9[2]	16[2]	10	1
35 to 44 years old	(2)	(2)	1,836	2,008	(2)	(2)	8	
45 to 64 years old	1,152	1,613	2,203	2,319	11	9	10	1
65 to 74 years old	611	775	1,042	1,096	6	4	5	
75 years old and over	563	711	901	914	5	4	4	
Female	**7,319**	**11,330**	**13,950**	**14,141**	**68**	**62**	**61**	**6**
15 to 24 years old[1]	282	779	538	518	3	4	2	
25 to 34 years old	671[2]	1,809[2]	1,578	1,626	6[2]	10[2]	7	
35 to 44 years old	(2)	(2)	1,303	1,394	(2)	(2)	6	
45 to 64 years old	2,470	2,901	3,300	3,232	23	16	14	1
65 to 74 years old	2,204	3,076	3,309	3,397	20	17	14	1
75 years old and over	1,693	2,766	3,924	3,973	16	15	17	1

(1) 1970, persons 14 to 24 years old. (2) Data for persons 35 to 44 years old included with persons 25 to 34 years old.

Female Family Householders With No Spouse Present, 1980-1991

Source: Bureau of the Census, U.S. Dept. of Commerce; as of March; persons 15 years old and over.

Characteristic	Unit	White 1980	White 1990	White 1991	Black 1980	Black 1990	Black 1991	Hispanic Origin[1] 1980	Hispanic Origin[1] 1990	Hispanic Origin[1] 1991
Female family householder	1,000	**6,052**	**7,306**	**7,512**	**2,495**	**3,275**	**3,430**	**610**	**1,116**	**1,1**
Percent of all families	Percent	12	13	13	40	44	46	20	23	[illegible]
Median age	Years	43.7	42.5	41.9	37.4	37.6	38.5	37.0	38.8	39
Marital status:										
Single (never married)	Percent	11	15	17	27	39	41	23	27	[illegible]
Married, spouse absent	Percent	17	16	18	29	21	19	32	29	[illegible]
Separated	Percent	14	14	14	27	19	16	29	23	[illegible]
Other	Percent	3	3	4	2	2	3	4	6	
Widowed	Percent	33	26	24	22	17	17	15	16	[illegible]
Divorced	Percent	40	43	42	22	23	23	30	29	[illegible]
Presence of children under 18:										
No own children	Percent	41	43	42	28	32	33	25	33	[illegible]
With own children	Percent	59	58	58	72	68	67	75	67	[illegible]
1 child	Percent	28	30	30	26	30	28	28	25	[illegible]
2 children	Percent	20	19	19	23	22	21	23	22	[illegible]
3 children	Percent	7	7	7	11	9	11	15	13	
4 or more children	Percent	3	2	2	11	7	7	9	6	
Children per family	Number	1.03	0.95	0.95	1.51	1.26	1.27	1.56	1.37	1.

(1) Person of Hispanic origin may be of any race.

Living Arrangements of Children, 1970-1991

Source: Bureau of the Census, U.S. Dept. of Commerce; as of March; excludes persons under 18 yrs. who maintained households or family groups.

ace, Hispanic Origin and Year	Number (1,000)	Both parents	Percent Living With— Mother only: Total	Divorced	Married spouse absent	Single[1]	Wid-owed	Father only	Neither parent
White									
970	58,790	90	8	3	3	Z	2	1	2
980	52,242	83	14	7	4	1	2	2	2
990	51,390	79	16	8	4	3	1	3	2
991	51,918	79	17	8	5	3	1	3	2
Black									
970	9,422	59	30	5	16	4	4	2	10
980	9,375	42	44	11	16	13	4	2	12
990	10,018	38	51	10	12	27	2	4	8
991	10,209	36	54	10	11	31	2	4	7
Hispanic[2]									
970	4,006[3]	78	NA	NA	NA	NA	NA	NA	NA
980	5,459	75	20	6	8	4	2	2	4
990	7,174	67	27	7	10	8	2	3	3
991	7,462	66	27	7	10	9	2	3	4

A=Not available. Z=Less than .5 percent. (1) Never married. (2) Hispanic persons may be of any race. (3) All persons under 18 ears old.

Living Arrangements of Young Adults, 1960-1990

Source: Bureau of the Census, U.S. Dept. of Commerce; in thousands

Living arrangement	1960	1970	1980	1990	Percent distribution 1960	1970	1980	1990
dults 18-24 Years, Total	**14,718**	**22,357**	**29,122**	**25,310**	**100.0**	**100.0**	**100.0**	**100.0**
Male.	**6,842**	**10,398**	**14,278**	**12,450**	**100.0**	**100.0**	**100.0**	**100.0**
hild of householder[1]	3,583	5,641	7,755	7,232	52.4	54.3	54.3	58.1
amily householder or spouse	2,160	3,119	3,041	1,838	31.6	30.0	21.3	14.8
onfamily householder.	182	563	1,581	1,228	2.7	5.4	11.1	9.9
ther.	917	1,075	1,902	2,152	13.4	10.3	13.3	17.3
Female	**7,876**	**11,959**	**14,844**	**12,860**	**100.0**	**100.0**	**100.0**	**100.0**
hild of householder[1]	2,750	4,941	6,336	6,135	34.9	41.3	42.7	47.7
amily householder or spouse	4,026	5,351	5,367	3,793	51.1	44.7	36.2	29.5
onfamily householder.	172	503	1,195	1,024	2.2	4.2	8.1	8.0
ther.	928	1,164	1,946	1,908	11.8	9.7	13.1	14.8
dults 25-34 Years, Total	**22,483**	**24,556**	**36,796**	**43,240**	**100.0**	**100.0**	**100.0**	**100.0**
Male.	**10,896**	**11,929**	**18,107**	**21,462**	**100.0**	**100.0**	**100.0**	**100.0**
hild of householder	1,185	1,129	1,894	3,213	10.9	9.5	10.5	15.0
amily householder or spouse	8,557	9,455	12,024	11,998	78.5	79.3	66.4	55.9
onfamily householder.	398	775	2,765	3,467	3.7	6.5	15.3	16.2
ther.	756	570	1,424	2,784	6.9	4.8	7.9	13.0
Female	**11,587**	**12,637**	**18,689**	**21,779**	**100.0**	**100.0**	**100.0**	**100.0**
hild of householder	853	829	1,300	1,774	7.4	6.6	7.0	8.1
amily householder or spouse	9,981	10,877	14,591	15,966	86.1	86.1	78.1	73.3
onfamily householder.	244	440	1,646	2,151	2.1	3.5	8.8	9.9
ther.	509	491	1,153	1,888	4.4	3.9	6.2	8.7

) Child of householder includes unmarried college students living in dormitories.

One-Parent Family Groups in 1970, 1980, and 1991

Source: Bureau of the Census, U.S. Dept. of Commerce; in thousands

	1970 Number	Percent	1980 Number	Percent	1991 Number	Percent	Average annual change 1970-80	1980-91
/hite								
ne-parent family groups .	2,638	100.0	4,664	100.0	6,550	100.0	5.7	3.1
Maintained by mother . .	2,330	88.3	4,122	88.4	5,482	83.7	5.7	2.6
Never married	73	2.8	379	8.1	1,271	19.4	16.5	11.0
Spouse absent	796	30.2	1,033	22.1	1,301	19.9	2.6	2.1
Separated	477	18.1	840	18.0	1,062	16.2	5.7	2.1
Divorced	930	35.3	2,201	47.2	2,565	39.2	8.6	1.4
Widowed	531	20.1	511	11.0	345	5.3	−0.4	−3.6
Maintained by father . . .	307	11.6	542	11.6	1,068	16.3	5.7	6.2
Never married	18	0.7	32	0.7	255	3.9	(B)	(B)
Spouse absent[1]	196	7.4	141	3.0	223	3.4	−3.3	4.2
Divorced	(NA)	(NA)	288	6.2	531	8.1	(NA)	5.6
Widowed	93	3.5	82	1.8	59	0.9	−1.3	−3.0
lack								
ne-parent family groups .	1,148	100.0	2,114	100.0	3,240	100.0	6.1	3.9
Maintained by mother . .	1,063	92.6	1,984	93.9	3,000	92.6	6.2	3.8
Never married	173	15.1	665	31.5	1,755	54.2	13.5	8.8
Spouse absent	570	49.7	667	31.6	567	17.5	1.6	−1.5
Separated	479	41.7	616	29.1	472	14.6	2.5	−2.4
Divorced	172	15.0	477	22.6	551	17.0	10.2	1.3
Widowed	148	12.9	174	8.2	128	4.0	1.6	−2.8
Maintained by father . . .	85	7.4	129	6.1	239	7.4	4.2	5.6
Never married	4	0.3	30	1.4	99	3.1	(B)	(B)
Spouse absent[1]	50	4.4	37	1.8	50	1.5	(B)	(B)
Divorced	(NA)	(NA)	43	2.0	79	2.4	(NA)	(B)
Widowed	30	2.6	19	0.9	11	0.3	(B)	(B)

A = Not available. B = Base less than 75,000. (1) Data for 1970 include divorced fathers. **Note:** Family groups comprise family ouseholds, related subfamilies, and unrelated subfamilies.

Principal Types of Accidental Deaths, 1970-1992

Source: National Safety Council

Year	Motor vehicle	Falls	Poison (solid, liquid)	Drowning	Fires, Burns	Injestion of Food, Object	Firearms	Poison (gases)
1970	54,633	16,926	3,679	7,860	6,718	2,753	2,406	1,620
1975	45,853	14,896	4,694	8,000	6,071	3,106	2,380	1,577
1980	53,172	13,294	3,089	7,257	5,822	3,249	1,955	1,242
1985	45,901	12,001	4,091	5,316	4,938	3,551	1,649	1,079
1990	46,300	12,400	5,700	5,200	4,300	3,200	1,400	800
1991	43,500	12,200	5,600	4,600	4,200	2,900	1,400	800
1992	40,300	12,400	5,200	4,300	4,000	2,700	1,400	700
				Death rates per 100,000 population				
1970	26.8	8.3	1.8	3.9	3.3	1.4	1.2	0.8
1975	21.3	6.9	2.2	3.7	2.8	1.4	1.1	0.7
1980	23.4	5.9	1.4	3.2	2.6	1.4	0.9	0.5
1985	19.2	5.0	1.7	2.2	2.1	1.5	0.7	0.5
1990	18.8	5.0	2.3	2.1	1.7	1.3	0.6	0.3
1991	17.2	4.8	2.2	1.8	1.7	1.1	0.6	0.3
1992	15.8	4.9	2.0	1.7	1.6	1.1	0.5	0.3

Note: There were 12,000 other accidental deaths in 1992; the most frequently occurring types were medical complications, machinery, air transport, water transport, mechanical suffocation, and excessive cold.

Motor Vehicle Accidents, 1992

Source: National Safety Council

Motor vehicle deaths decreased 7 percent from 1991 to 1992, while mileage increased 3 percent, the number of vehicles increased 1 percent, and the population increased 1 percent. Almost 2 out of 3 deaths in 1992 occurred in places classified as rural. In urban areas, more than one-fourth of the victims were pedestrians; in rural areas, the victims were mostly occupants of motor vehicles. More than one-half of all deaths occurred in night accidents. About 48 percent of all traffic fatalities in 1992 involved an intoxicated or alcohol-impaired driver or nonoccupant. Of these 19,899 alc hol-related traffic fatalities, an estimated 15,944 occurred i accidents in which a driver or nonoccupant was intoxicate and the remainder involved a driver or nonoccupant wh had been drinking but was not legally intoxicated. Alcoh was also a factor in about 19 percent of serious injury acc dents and 6 percent of property damage accidents. The est mated cost of all alcohol-related motor vehicle accidents i 1992 was about $32.7 billion.

	Death Total	% Change from 1991	Death Rate[1]
All motor vehicle accidents	**40,300**	**−7**	**15.8**
Urban	14,400	−6	
Rural	25,900	−8	
Collision between motor vehicles	**17,400**	**−6**	**6.8**
Urban	6,300	−9	
Rural	11,100	−5	
Collision with fixed object	**10,900**	**−9**	**4.3**
Urban	3,000	−12	
Rural	7,900	−8	
Pedestrian accidents	**6,500**	**−3**	**2.5**
Urban	4,100	+5	
Rural	2,400	−14	

	Death Total	% Change from 1991	Death Rate
Noncollision accidents	**4,200**	**−9**	**1.6**
Urban	500	0	
Rural	3,700	−10	
Collision with pedalcycle	**700**	**−22**	**0.3**
Urban	400	−33	
Rural	300	0	
Collision with railroad train	**500**	**−17**	**0.2**
Urban	100	0	
Rural	400	−20	
Other collision (animal, animal-drawn vehicles, street cars)	**100**	**0**	**(2)**

(1) Deaths per 100,000 population. (2) Death rate was less than 0.05.

Improper Driving Reported in Accidents, 1992

Source: National Safety Council; in percent

Kind of Improper Driving	Fatal Accidents Total	Fatal Urban	Fatal Rural	Injury Accidents Total	Injury Urban	Injury Rural	All Accidents Total	All Urban	All Rural
Total	100.0%	100.0%	100.0%	100.0%	100.0%	100.0%	100.0%	100.0%	100.0%
Improper driving	**55.5**	**52.3**	**57.3**	**68.6**	**69.7**	**63.5**	**67.2**	**67.0**	**68.5**
Speed too fast or unsafe	16.5	15.9	17.2	13.2	19.5	11.7	11.7	10.8	16.0
Right of way	12.5	14.0	10.6	24.1	27.8	14.5	20.8	22.2	15.1
Failed to yield	7.8	8.2	7.2	17.0	19.0	11.7	15.7	16.4	12.3
Passed stop sign	2.6	2.8	2.4	2.2	2.4	1.6	1.6	1.7	1.5
Disregarded signal	2.2	3.0	1.0	4.9	6.4	1.2	3.6	4.1	1.2
Drove left of center	7.5	5.7	9.8	2.2	1.8	3.8	1.9	1.4	3.9
Improper overtaking	1.0	0.9	1.2	0.9	0.8	1.5	1.3	1.2	1.9
Made improper turn	2.5	2.0	3.2	3.1	3.1	3.5	4.2	4.1	4.8
Followed too closely	0.6	0.7	0.5	6.9	7.4	3.4	7.2	8.0	3.8
Other improper driving	13.8	13.2	14.6	18.1	19.4	21.3	20.1	19.4	23.0
No improper driving stated . . .	**45.5**	**47.7**	**42.7**	**31.4**	**30.3**	**36.5**	**32.8**	**33.0**	**31.5**

Notes: Based on reports from 14 state traffic authorities. When a driver was under the influence of alcohol or drugs, the accident w considered a result of the driver's physical condition—not a driving error. For this reason, accidents in which the driver was reported be under the influence are classified under "no improper driving."

Deaths Involving Firearms

Source: National Safety Council

	All Ages	Under 5	5-14	15-24	25-44	45-64	65-74	75 & Over
			1990 Firearm Deaths by Age					
Total Firearm Deaths[1]	**36,866**	**103**	**681**	**9,463**	**15,340**	**6,255**	**2,596**	**2,428**
ale	31,458	63	516	8,382	12,880	5,175	2,232	2,210
emale	5,408	40	165	1,081	2,460	1,080	364	218
Accidents	**1,416**	**34**	**202**	**500**	**442**	**149**	**50**	**39**
ale	1,255	24	180	457	385	131	42	36
emale	161	10	22	43	57	18	8	3
Suicide	**18,885**	**0**	**144**	**3,165**	**6,818**	**4,356**	**2,245**	**2,157**
ale	16,285	0	106	2,778	5,721	3,671	1,976	2,033
emale	2,600	0	38	387	1,097	685	269	124
Homicide	**16,218**	**69**	**321**	**5,679**	**7,951**	**1,703**	**282**	**213**
ale	13,629	39	218	5,046	6,672	1,334	197	123
emale	2,589	30	103	633	1,279	369	85	90
Undetermined[2]	**347**	**0**	**14**	**119**	**129**	**47**	**19**	**19**
ale	289	0	12	101	102	39	17	18
emale	58	0	2	18	27	8	2	1

1) Excludes firearm deaths by legal intervention. These deaths totaled 318 in 1990. (2) Undetermined means the intentionality of the eath (accident, suicide, homicide) cannot be determined.

andguns. Handguns are involved in the majority of firearm deaths and injuries in the U.S. According to the Center to Prevent Hand-un Violence, there are an estimated 24,000 handgun-related deaths in America every year. Handguns account for about one-third of ll firearms, but account for two-thirds of all firearm-related deaths. In 1989, about 75 percent of firearm homicides were by handguns, ccording to the FBI. Comparable police data are not available for suicides, but local studies suggest that about two-thirds of firearm uicides are due to handguns. For children 10-14 years of age, handguns account for 73 percent of firearm homicides and 70 per cent f firearm suicides. Of all children ages 16 and under, half of those injured in a handgun accident were shot in their own home.

Home Accident Deaths, 1950-1992

Source: National Safety Council

Year	Total	Falls	Poison (solid, liquid)	Fires burns[2]	Suffo., ingesting object	Fire-arms	Suffo., mech-anical	Poison (gases)	All Other[4]
950	29,000	14,800	1,300	5,000	(1)	950	1,600	1,250	4,100
960	28,000	12,300	1,350	6,350	1,850	1,200	1,500	900	2,550
970	27,000	3,000	5,600	1,800	1,100*	1,100	1,400	3,300	—
980	22,800	7,100	2,500	4,800	2,000	1,100	500	700	4,100[3]
990	21,500	6,500	4,700	3,300	2,000	800	800	400	2,400
991	20,500	6,100	4,400	3,500	1,800	800	600	500	2,200
992	19,500	6,200	4,100	3,200	1,700	500	700	400	2,700

Data for this year and subsequent years not comparable with previous years due to classification changes. (1) Included in ll Other. (2) Includes deaths resulting from conflagration, regardless of nature of injury. (3) Includes about 1,000 excessive eaths due to summer heat wave. (4) Includes drowning in swimming pools and bathtubs.

Worldwide Airline Fatalities

Source: National Safety Council

ear	Aircraft Accidents[1]	Passenger Deaths	Death Rate[2]	Year	Aircraft Accidents[1]	Passenger Deaths	Death Rate[2]
980	22	814	0.14	1987	24	890	0.10
981	21	362	0.06	1988	25	699	0.08
982	26	764	0.13	1989	27	817	0.08
983	20	809	0.13	1990	22	440	0.04
984	16	223	0.03	1991	25	510	0.05
985	22	1,066	0.15	1992[3]	25	990	0.09
986	17	331	0.04				

) Involving a passenger fatality. (2) Passenger deaths per 100 million passenger miles. (3) Preliminary.

U.S. Civil Aviation Accidents

Source: National Safety Council

1992	Accidents Total	Accidents Fatal	Deaths[1]	Accident Rates Per 100,000 Aircraft-Hours Total	Fatal	Accident Rates Per million Aircraft-Miles Total	Fatal
Large airlines	19	4	33	0.155	0.033	0.0038	0.0008
Commuter airlines	23	7	21	1.055	0.321	0.056	0.017
On-demand air taxis	74	24	66	3.32	1.08	—	—
General aviation	1,956	408	812	7.19	1.50	—	—

(1) Includes passengers, crew members, and others.

Occupational Injuries for Industries with 100,000 or More Injury Cases, 1990 and 1991

Source: Bureau of Labor Statistics, U.S. Dept. of Labor; total cases in thousands

Industry	Total cases 1990	Total cases 1991	Incidence rate[1] 1990	Incidence rate[1] 1991
ating and drinking places	353.6	310.0	8.4	7.4
ospitals	282.4	308.9	10.0	10.8
rocery stores	246.4	238.4	12.1	11.7
rucking and courier services, except air	203.8	200.6	14.1	14.4
Nursing and personal care facilities	168.2	174.1	15.4	15.0
Department stores	165.4	154.8	11.1	11.0
Motor vehicles and equipment manufacturing	148.5	139.2	18.9	18.6
Hotels and motels	126.0	118.9	10.4	10.2

) Per 100,000 full-time workers.

Crime in the U.S., 1973-1992

Source: 1992 *Uniform Crime Reports*, FBI

Population[1]	Crime Index total[2]	Violent crime[3]	Property crime[3]	Murder and non-negligent man-slaughter	Forcible rape	Robbery	Burglary	Larceny theft
				Number of offenses				
Population by year								
1973-209,851,000. . .	8,718,000	875,910	7,842,200	19,640	51,400	384,220	2,565,500	4,347,90
1974-211,392,000. . .	10,253,400	974,720	9,278,700	20,710	55,400	442,400	3,039,200	5,262,50
1975-213,124,000. . .	11,292,400	1,039,710	10,252,700	20,510	56,090	470,500	3,265,300	5,977,70
1976-214,659,000. . .	11,349,700	1,004,210	10,345,500	18,780	57,080	427,810	3,108,700	6,270,80
1977-216,332,000. . .	10,984,500	1,029,580	9,955,000	19,120	63,500	412,610	3,071,500	5,905,70
1978-218,059,000. . .	11,209,000	1,085,550	10,123,400	19,560	67,610	426,930	3,128,300	5,991,00
1979-220,099,000. . .	12,249,500	1,208,030	11,041,500	21,460	76,390	480,700	3,327,700	6,601,00
1980-225,349,264. . .	13,408,300	1,344,520	12,063,700	23,040	82,990	565,040	3,795,200	7,136,90
1981-229,146,000. . .	13,423,800	1,361,820	12,061,900	22,520	82,500	592,910	3,779,700	7,194,40
1982-231,534,000. . .	12,974,400	1,322,390	11,652,000	21,010	78,770	553,130	3,447,100	7,142,50
1983-233,981,000. . .	12,108,600	1,258,090	10,850,500	19,310	78,920	506,570	3,129,900	6,712,80
1984-236,158,000. . .	11,881,800	1,273,280	10,608,500	18,690	84,230	485,010	2,984,400	6,591,90
1985-238,740,000. . .	12,431,400	1,328,800	11,102,600	18,980	88,670	497,870	3,073,300	6,926,40
1986-241,077,000. . .	13,211,900	1,489,170	11,722,700	20,610	91,460	542,780	3,241,400	7,257,20
1987-243,400,000. . .	13,508,700	1,484,000	12,024,700	20,100	91,110	517,700	3,236,200	7,499,90
1988-245,807,000. . .	13,923,100	1,566,220	12,356,900	20,680	92,490	542,970	3,218,100	7,705,90
1989-248,239,000. . .	14,251,400	1,646,040	12,605,400	21,500	94,500	578,330	3,168,200	7,872,40
1990-248,709,873. . .	14,475,600	1,820,130	12,655,500	23,440	102,560	639,270	3,073,900	7,945,70
1991-252,177,000. . .	14,872,900	1,911,770	12,961,100	24,700	106,590	687,730	3,157,200	8,142,20
1992-255,082,000. . .	14,438,200	1,932,270	12,505,900	23,760	109,060	672,480	2,979,900	7,915,20
Percent change: number of offenses								
1992/1991.	−2.9	+1.1	−3.5	−3.8	+2.3	−2.2	−5.6	−2
1992/1988.	+3.7	+23.4	+1.2	+14.9	+17.9	+23.9	−7.4	+2
1992/1983.	+19.2	+53.6	+15.3	+23.0	+38.2	+32.8	−4.8	+17
				Rate per 100,000 inhabitants				
Year								
1973	4,154.4	417.4	3,737.0	9.4	24.5	183.1	1,222.5	2,071
1974	4,850.4	461.1	4,389.3	9.8	26.2	209.3	1,437.7	2,489
1975	5,298.5	487.8	4,810.7	9.6	26.3	220.8	1,532.1	2,804
1976	5,287.3	467.8	4,819.5	8.8	26.6	199.3	1,448.2	2,921
1977	5,077.6	475.9	4,601.7	8.8	29.4	190.7	1,419.8	2,729
1978	5,140.3	497.8	4,642.5	9.0	31.0	195.8	1,434.6	2,747
1979	5,565.5	548.9	5,016.6	9.7	34.7	218.4	1,511.9	2,999
1980	5,950.0	596.6	5,353.3	10.2	36.8	251.1	1,684.1	3,167
1981	5,858.2	594.3	5,263.9	9.8	36.0	258.7	1,649.5	3,139
1982	5,603.6	571.1	5,032.5	9.1	34.0	238.9	1,488.8	3,084
1983	5,175.0	537.7	4,637.4	8.3	33.7	216.5	1,337.7	2,868
1984	5,031.3	539.2	4,492.1	7.9	35.7	205.4	1,263.7	2,791
1985	5,207.1	556.6	4,650.5	7.9	37.1	208.5	1,287.3	2,901
1986	5,480.4	617.7	4,862.6	8.6	37.9	225.1	1,344.6	3,010
1987	5,550.0	609.7	4,940.3	8.3	37.4	212.7	1,329.6	3,081
1988	5,664.2	637.2	5,027.1	8.4	37.6	220.9	1,309.2	3,134
1989	5,741.0	663.1	5,077.9	8.7	38.1	233.0	1,276.3	3,171
1990	5,820.3	731.8	5,088.5	9.4	41.2	257.0	1,235.9	3,194
1991	5,897.8	758.1	5,139.7	9.8	42.3	272.7	1,252.0	3,228
1992	5,660.2	757.5	4,902.7	9.3	42.8	263.6	1,168.2	3,103
Percent change: rate per 100,000 inhabitants								
1992/1991.	−4.0	−.1	−4.6	−5.1	+1.2	−3.3	−6.7	−3
1992/1988.	−.1	+18.9	−2.5	+10.7	+13.8	+19.3	−10.8	−1
1992/1983.	+9.4	+40.9	+5.7	+12.0	+27.0	+21.8	−12.7	+8

(1) Populations are Bureau of the Census provisional estimates as of July 1, except 1980 and 1990, which are the decennial cens counts. (2) Because of rounding, the offenses may not add to totals. (3) Violent crimes are murder, forcible rape, robbery, and aggr vated assault. Property crimes are burglary, larceny-theft, and motor vehicle theft. Data are not included for the property crime of a son. **Note:** All rates were calculated on the offenses before rounding.

Law Enforcement Officers

Source: 1992 *Uniform Crime Reports*, FBI

The U.S. law enforcement community employed an average of 2.3 full-time officers for every 1,000 inhabitants as of October 31, 1992. Considering full-time civilians, the overall law enforcement employee rate was 3.1 per 1,000 inhabitants according to 13,032 city, county, and state police agencies. These agencies collectively offered law enforcement service to a population of over 241 million, employing 544,309 officers and 204,521 civilians.

The law enforcement employee average for all cities nationwide was 2.8 per 1,000 inhabitants. City law enforcement employee averages ranged from 3.4 per 1,000 inhabitants in those with populations of less than 10,000 to 3.6 for those with populations of 250,000 or more. Rural and suburban counties averaged full-time law enforcement employee rates of 3.9 and 3.6 per 1,000 population, respectively.

Regionally, the highest law enforcement employee ra was in the South, with 3.2, and lowest in the West, 2.4.

Nationally, males comprised 91 percent of all sworn er ployees. Ninety-three percent of the officers in rural counti and 91 percent of those in cities were males, while in subu ban counties males accounted for 89 percent.

Civilians made up 27 percent of the total U.S. law e forcement employee force. They represented 22 percent the police employees in cities, 34 percent of those in rur counties, and 36 percent in suburban counties.

Sixty-one law enforcement officers were feloniously sla in the line of duty in 1992, 10 fewer than in 1991. Anoth 66 officers were killed due to accidents occurring while pe forming official duties.

Prison Situation Among the States, 1992

Source: *Prisoners in 1992*, Bureau of Justice Statistics, U.S. Dept. of Justice; year-end 1992.

States with e Largest 92 Prison opulations	Number of Inmates	10 States with the Highest Incarceration Rates, 1992*	Prisoners per 100,000 Residents	10 States with the Largest % Increases in Prison Population: 1991-92	% Increase	1987-92*	% Increase
alifornia	109,496	Louisiana	478	Texas	18.4%	New Hampshire	105.0%
ew York	61,736	South Carolina	477	West Virgina	16.2	Rhoda Island	94.3
exas	61,178	Oklahoma	463	New Hampshire	15.9	Colorado	87.1
orida	48,302	Nevada	461	Idaho	15.5	Idaho	72.5
ichigan	39,019	Arizona	415	Wisconsin	15.4	Vermont	66.9
hio	38,378	Michigan	414	Vermont	13.3	California	63.5
nois	31,640	Alabama	404	Oklahoma	11.1	Michigan	63.4
eorgia	25,290	Maryland	380	Minnesota	10.1	Washington	62.4
ennsylvania	24,974	Delaware	371	Nevada	9.9	Kentucky	61.0
ew Jersey	22,653	Georgia	366	Massachusetts	9.8	Massachusetts	60.5

ote: The District of Columbia as a wholly urban jurisdiction is excluded. * Prisoners with sentences of more than 1 year.

State and Federal Prison Population; Death Penalty

Source: Prison population: Bureau of Justice Statistics, U.S. Dept. of Justice, Dec. 31, 1992; Death penalty: NAACP Legal Defense and Education Fund; Bureau of Justice Statistics; "Executions" and "Death penalty" as of Dec. 31, 1992; "Under sentence of death" as of April, 1992.

The number of prisoners under the jurisdiction of federal or state correctional authorities at year-end 1992 reached a record gh of 883,593. The states and the District of Columbia added 50,809 prisoners; the federal system, 8,651. The increase for 92 brought total growth in the prison population since 1980 to 553,772—an increase of about 168% in the 12-year period. he 1992 growth rate of 7.2 percent was greater than the percentage increase recorded during 1991 (6.6 percent), and the umber of new prisoners added during 1992 was 8,451 more than the number added during the preceding year (51,009). The 92 increase translated into a nationwide need for approximately 1,143 prison bedspaces per week, compared to the 981 prin bedspaces per week needed in 1991. In 1980, about 1 of every 15 court-committed entries to state prison was an offender nvicted of a drug offense. In 1990, drug offenses accounted for about 1 in 3 new commitments to state prisons. During the me period, the percentage of prison admissions entering as violators of probation or parole conditions also increased—from out 17% to about 30%.

	Sentenced to more than 1 yr.: Final 1991	Advance 1992	% change 1991-92	Death penalty: Under sentence of death	Executions	Death penalty
otal	**789,349**	**846,695**	**7.3%**	**2,600**	**31**	**—**
Federal institutions	**56,696**	**65,706**	**15.9**	**6**	**1**	**Yes**
State institutions	**732,653**	**780,989**	**6.6**	**2,594**	**30**	**36**
ortheast	**127,450**	**133,372**	**4.7**	**152**	**0**	**—**
Connecticut	8,585	8,794	2.4	4	0	Yes
Maine	1,558	1,488	−4.5	0	0	No
Massachusetts	8,561	9,382	9.6	0	0	No
New Hampshire	1,533	1,777	15.9	0	0	Yes
New Jersey	23,483	22,653	−3.5	8	0	Yes
New York	57,862	61,736	6.7	0	0	No
Pennsylvania	23,386	24,966	6.8	140	0	Yes
Rhode Island	1,749	1,709	−2.3	0	0	No
Vermont	733	867	18.3	0	0	No
idwest	**155,573**	**166,042**	**6.7**	**395**	**1**	**—**
Illinois	29,115	31,640	8.7	145	0	Yes
Indiana	12,865	13,012	1.1	52	0	Yes
Iowa	4,145	4,518	9.0	0	0	No
Kansas	5,903	6,028	2.1	0	0	No
Michigan	36,423	39,019	7.1	0	0	No
Minnesota	3,472	3,822	10.1	0	0	No
Missouri	15,897	16,198	1.9	82	1	Yes
Nebraska	2,375	2,492	4.9	12	0	Yes
North Dakota	441	415	−5.9	0	0	No
Ohio	35,744	38,378	7.4	104	0	Yes
South Dakota	1,374	1,487	8.2	0	0	Yes
Wisconsin	7,819	9,033	15.5	0	0	No
outh	**292,542**	**315,280**	**7.8**	**1,488**	**25**	**—**
Alabama	16,400	16,938	3.3	115	2	Yes
Arkansas	7,722	8,129	5.3	35	2	Yes
Delaware	2,430	2,665	9.7	6	1	Yes
District of Columbia	7,106	7,528	5.9	0	0	No
Florida	46,533	48,302	3.8	315	2	Yes
Georgia	22,910	24,848	8.5	110	0	Yes
Kentucky	9,799	10,364	5.8	29	0	Yes
Louisiana	20,003	20,603	3.0	40	0	Yes
Maryland	17,824	18,808	5.5	14	0	Yes
Mississippi	8,682	8,877	2.3	52	0	Yes
North Carolina	18,272	20,024	9.6	105	1	Yes
Oklahoma	13,340	14,821	11.1	125	1	Yes
South Carolina	17,208	17,612	2.4	46	0	Yes
Tennessee	11,474	11,849	3.3	100	0	Yes
Texas	51,677	61,178	18.4	349	12	Yes
Virginia	19,660	20,989	6.8	47	4	Yes
West Virginia	1,502	1,745	16.2	0	0	No

(continued)

	Sentenced to more than 1 yr. Final 1991	Advance 1992	% change 1991-92	Death penalty Under sentence of death	Executions	Death penalty
West	**157,088**	**166,295**	**5.9**	**559**	**4**	**—**
Alaska	1,840	1,944	5.7	0	0	No
Arizona	14,843	15,850	6.8	101	1	Yes
California	98,515	105,467	7.1	328	1	Yes
Colorado	8,392	8,997	7.2	3	0	Yes
Hawaii	1,766	1,922	8.8	0	0	No
Idaho	2,143	2,475	15.5	21	0	Yes
Montana	1,478	1,553	5.1	8	0	Yes
Nevada	5,503	6,049	9.9	60	0	Yes
New Mexico	3,016	3,154	4.6	1	0	Yes
Oregon	6,732	5,216	—*	16	0	Yes
Utah	2,605	2,687	3.2	12	1	Yes
Washington	9,156	9,959	8.8	9	0	Yes
Wyoming	1,099	1,022	−7.0	0	1	Yes

Note: Prisoner counts for 1991 may differ from those reported previously. Counts for 1992 are subject to revision. *Before 1992, Ore gon reported all prisoners as having sentences of more than 1 year.

Total Estimated Arrests,[1] 1992

Source: 1992 *Uniform Crime Reports*, FBI

Total[2]	**14,075,100**
Murder and nonnegligent manslaughter	22,510
Forcible rape	39,100
Robbery	173,310
Aggravated assault	507,210
Burglary	424,000
Larceny-theft	1,504,500
Motor vehicle theft	197,600
Arson	19,900
Violent crimes[3]	**742,130**
Property crime[4]	**2,146,000**
Crime Index total[5]	**2,888,200**
Other assaults	1,074,700
Forgery and counterfeiting	105,400
Fraud	424,200
Embezzlement	13,700
Stolen property: buying, receiving, possessing	161,500
Vandalism	323,10
Weapons: carrying, possessing, etc.	239,30
Prostitution and commercialized vice	96,20
Sex offenses (except forcible rape and prostitution)	108,40
Drug abuse violations	1,066,40
Gambling	17,10
Offenses against family and children	109,20
Driving under the influence	1,624,50
Liquor laws	541,70
Drunkenness	832,30
Disorderly conduct	753,10
Vagrancy	34,30
All other offenses	3,389,50
Suspicion (not included in totals)	18,40
Curfew and loitering law violations	91,10
Runaways	181,30

(1) Arrest totals are based on all reporting agencies and estimates for unreported areas. (2) Because of rounding, figures may not ac to totals. (3) Violent crimes are murder, forcible rape, robbery, and aggravated assault. (4) Property crimes are burglary, larceny-thef motor vehicle theft, and arson. (5) Includes arson.

Crime, by Type of Area, 1992

Source: 1992 *Uniform Crime Reports*, FBI

Area	Population[1]	Crime Index total	Violent crime[2]	Property crime[3]	Murder	Forcible rape	Robbery	Aggravated assault	Burglary	Larceny-theft	Motor vehicle theft
United States											
Total	**255,082,000**	**14,438,191**	**1,932,274**	**12,505,917**	**23,760**	**109,062**	**672,478**	**1,126,974**	**2,979,884**	**7,915,199**	**1,610,8**
Rate per 100,000 inhabitants		5,660.2	757.5	4,902.7	9.3	42.8	263.6	441.8	1,168.2	3,103.0	631
Metropolitan Statistical Area	**201,843,745**										
Area actually reporting[4]	97.0%	12,425,059	1,736,064	10,688,995	20,712	91,248	647,785	976,319	2,503,818	6,675,499	1,509,6
Estimated totals	100.0%	12,660,331	1,758,505	10,901,826	20,943	93,114	652,364	992,084	2,553,535	6,818,473	1,529,8
Rate per 100,000 inhabitants		6,272.3	871.2	5,401.1	10.4	46.1	323.2	491.5	1,265.1	3,378.1	757
Cities outside metropolitan areas	**21,254,000**										
Area actually reporting[4]	90.0%	1,012,709	91,616	921,093	997	7,080	13,274	70,265	191,215	688,686	41,1
Estimated totals	100.0%	1,129,982	103,346	1,026,636	1,147	7,912	14,904	79,383	215,062	765,446	46,1
Rate per 100,000 inhabitants		5,316.6	486.2	4,830.3	5.4	37.2	70.1	373.5	1,011.9	3,601.4	217
Rural Counties	**31,983,255**										
Area actually reporting[4]	86.1%	571,898	60,336	511,562	1,408	7,141	4,472	47,315	186,528	294,309	30,7
Estimated totals	100.0%	647,878	70,423	577,455	1,670	8,036	5,210	55,507	211,287	331,280	34,8
Rate per 100,000 inhabitants		2,025.7	220.2	1,805.5	5.2	25.1	16.3	173.6	660.6	1,035.8	109

(1) Populations are Bureau of the Census provisional estimates as of July 1, 1992, and are subject to change. (2) Violent crimes a murder, forcible rape, robbery, and aggravated assault. (3) Property crimes are burglary, larceny-theft, and motor vehicle theft. Da are not included for the property crime of arson. (4) The percentage representing area actually reporting will not coincide with the ra between reported and estimated crime totals, since these data represent the sum of the calculations for individual states, which ha varying populations, portions reporting, and crime rates.

Murder Weapons and Circumstances, 1988-1992

Source: 1992 *Uniform Crime Reports*, FBI

	1988	1990	1992
otal Murders[1]	**17,971**	**20,273**	**22,540**
Weapon or Method Used			
rearms	10,895	13,035	15,377
Handguns	8,147	10,099	12,489
Rifles	753	746	698
Shotguns	1,105	1,245	1,104
Other guns	15	25	42
Type not known	875	920	1,044
nives or cutting instruments	3,457	3,526	3,265
unt objects (clubs, hammers, etc.)	1,126	1,085	1,029
ersonal weapons (hands, fists, feet, etc.)[2]	1,105	1,119	1,121
oison	15	11	13
xplosives	34	13	19
re	255	288	203
arcotics	36	29	23
owning	38	36	27
trangulation	331	312	313
sphyxiation	73	96	114
ther weapons or weapon not known	606	723	1,036
Circumstances			
elony	3,417	4,209	4,887
Rape	144	152	137
Robbery	1,497	1,871	2,254
Burglary	210	202	206
Larceny-theft	16	28	41
Motor Vehicle theft	30	55	65
Arson	184	152	148
Prostitution and commercialized vice	16	27	32
Other sex offenses	61	50	34
Narcotic drug laws	1,003	1,367	1,291
Gambling	26	11	20
Other—not specified	230	294	659
Suspected felony	225	148	280
Other than felony	9,604	10,889	11,152
Romatic triangle	310	407	335
Child killed by babysitter	23	34	36
Brawl due to alcohol	418	533	426
Brawl due to narcotics	197	242	249
Argument over money or property	483	514	481
Other arguments	5,410	6,044	6,027
Gangland killings	45	104	137
Juvenile gang killings	327	679	809
Institutional killings	24	16	18
Sniper attack	56	41	33
Other—not specified	2,311	2,275	2,601
Unknown	4,725	5,027	6,221

) Total number of murder victims for whom supplemental homicide information was received. (2) Includes murders in which victim as pushed.

U.S. Fires, 1991

Source: National Fire Protection Assn.

ires

- Public fire departments responded to 2,041,500 fires in 1991, a 1.1 percent increase from 1990.
- There were 640,500 structure fires in 1991, a 2.6 percent increase from 1990.
- 75 percent of all structure fires, or 478,000 fires, occurred in residential properties.
- There were 428,500 vehicle fires in 1991, virtually no change from 1990.
- The number of fires in outside properties increased by 1.5 percent, to 972,500 fires.
- The South and the Northeast—with 9.6 fires per 1,000 population—had the highest fire incidence rate in the nation.

ivilian deaths

- The number of civilian fire deaths decreased significantly in 1991—by 14.1 percent to 4,465.
- About 78 percent of all fire deaths occurred in homes.
- There were 3,500 home fire deaths in 1991, a drop of 13.6 percent from 1990.
- The North Central region had the highest regional death rate, with 22.7 civilian deaths per million population, followed closely by the South, with 21.4 deaths per million.

ivilian injuries

- There were 29,375 civilian fire injuries in 1991, a 2.7 percent increase from the year before. This estimate is low because of underreporting of civilian injuries to the fire service.
- 21,850 civilian injuries, or 74.4 percent, occurred in residential properties; 11.6 percent, or 3,125 injuries, occurred in nonresidential structure fires.
- The Northeast had the highest civilian injury rate, with 148.3 civilian injuries per million population.

Property damage

- Property damage resulting from fires in 1991 jumped by 21.1 percent, to an estimated $9.467 billion. The increase was due almost entirely to the Oakland, California, fire, which resulted in an estimated $1.5 billion loss.
- Structure fires account for 88 percent of all property damage, or $8.320 billion.
- 67 percent of all structure property loss occurred in residential properties. The cost totaled $5.552 billion.
- The West had the highest property loss rate in the nation: $57.2 per person, which reflects the loss resulting from the Oakland fire.

Incendiary and suspicious fires

- 15.3 percent of all structure fires, or an estimated 98,000 fires, were deliberately set or suspected of having been deliberately set. This represents a slight increase from 1990.
- Incendiary or suspicious structure fires resulted in the deaths of 490 people in 1991, a 35.4 percent decrease from the year before. These fires cost $1.531 billion in property damage. This represents 18.4 percent of all structure property loss, an increase of 9.8 percent from 1990.
- Vehicle fires of incendiary or suspicious origin decreased by 3.9 percent, to 49,000. They cost $182 million in property damage, up 9.0 percent from the previous year.

Physicians by Age, Sex, and Specialty

Source: American Medical Assn., Jan. 1, 1992

	Total Physicians*		Under 35 yrs.		35–44 yrs.		45–54 yrs.		55–64 yrs.	
	Male	Female	Male	Female	Male	Female	Male	Female	Male	Female
ll Specialties	**534,543**	**118,519**	**93,287**	**40,431**	**153,921**	**44,336**	**110,790**	**18,026**	**80,288**	**7,224**
Aerospace Medicine	650	41	103	15	208	20	151	4	122	2
Allergy & Immunology	2,889	552	198	96	868	248	813	123	600	48
Anesthesiology	22,978	5,170	5,379	1,408	8,044	1,958	4,757	1,144	3,288	460
Cardiovascular Disease	15,563	915	1,923	210	6,288	469	4,024	160	2,179	48
Child Psychiatry	2,981	1,637	269	245	999	688	889	397	577	204
Colon/Rectal Surgery	840	29	47	7	304	18	235	3	135	1
Dermatology	6,006	1,906	745	716	1,838	805	1,777	265	1,020	88
Diagnostic Radiology	14,354	2,899	3,628	1,165	5,389	1,296	3,690	336	1,217	78
Emergency Medicine	13,111	2,359	2,543	788	6,378	1,133	2,716	331	978	77
Family Practice	41,261	9,708	8,556	4,104	16,661	4,135	6,828	971	5,377	314

(continued)

	Total Physicians* Male	Total Physicians* Female	Under 35 yrs. Male	Under 35 yrs. Female	35–44 yrs. Male	35–44 yrs. Female	45–54 yrs. Male	45–54 yrs. Female	55–64 yrs. Male	55–64 yrs. Fema
Forensic Pathology	325	98	15	8	100	46	83	26	83	1
Gastroenterology	7,438	508	1,040	136	3,242	287	2,052	72	784	
General Practice	18,391	2,328	367	111	1,998	625	3,170	721	5,297	45
General Preventive Med.	877	299	102	75	254	130	213	48	160	2
General Surgery	36,380	2,831	9,737	1,623	8,694	940	7,656	179	6,147	5
Internal Medicine	67,138	18,701	22,286	9,573	21,321	6,531	10,279	1,770	7,579	55
Neurological Surgery	4,355	146	785	53	1,196	73	1,139	16	834	
Neurology	8,110	1,632	1,273	464	3,238	784	2,141	250	1,078	10
Nuclear Medicine	1,156	216	91	41	349	96	358	58	271	1
Obstetrics/Gynecology	23,497	8,090	3,802	3,607	6,914	3,028	6,099	1,013	4,566	30
Occupational Medicine	2,465	322	107	35	539	148	424	61	659	4
Ophthalmology	14,691	1,742	2,245	643	4,322	742	4,049	219	2,670	8
Orthopedic Surgery	20,126	514	4,056	228	6,192	225	5,305	40	3,241	
Otolaryngology	7,882	491	1,425	206	2,209	226	2,228	35	1,388	1
Pathology-Anat./Clin.	12,849	4,156	1,722	1,069	3,590	1,646	3,243	934	2,966	33
Pediatric Cardiology	829	211	116	59	302	68	219	46	143	2
Pediatrics	23,842	16,573	5,191	6,761	7,415	5,824	5,410	2,625	3,649	88
Physical Med./Rehab.	3,124	1,345	857	398	1,030	494	580	272	397	13
Plastic Surgery	4,354	334	352	59	1,532	183	1,456	64	754	2
Psychiatry	27,377	9,028	3,315	2,360	7,092	3,243	7,003	1,832	5,887	96
Public Health	1,505	479	41	24	316	136	350	92	350	10
Pulmonary Diseases	5,777	560	746	146	2,757	272	1,491	82	507	3
Radiation Oncology	2,447	566	501	157	776	237	679	130	344	3
Radiology	7,064	784	231	90	962	268	2,387	261	2,312	11
Thoracic Surgery	2,090	30	150	7	514	17	571	5	543	
Urological Surgery	9,290	162	1,341	70	2,490	73	2,796	14	1,812	
Other	6,304	991	364	111	1,618	372	1,345	216	1,483	15
Unspecified	6,024	2,085	3,680	1,373	1,168	484	446	139	327	5

* Includes physicians 65 and over, those living in U.S. possessions, those "Inactive," "Not Classified," and "Address Unknown."

Patients Receiving Home Health Care or Hospice Care, 1992

Source: National Center for Health Statistics, U.S. Dept. of Health and Human Services

Patient characteristic	Total	Percent distribution	Home health care Total	Home health care Percent distribution	Hospice care Total	Hospice care Percent distributio
All patients	**1,284,200**	**100.0**	**1,237,100**	**100.0**	**47,200**	**100.0**
Age						
Under 45 years	140,700	11.0	137,800	11.1	3,000	6.3
45-54 years	49,900	3.9	47,800	3.9	2,100	4.5
55-64 years	115,900	9.0	111,100	9.0	4,900	10.3
65 years and over	965,700	75.2	929,500	75.1	36,200	76.7
65-69 years	136,100	10.6	129,400	10.5	6,700	14.3
70-74 years	176,900	13.8	170,600	13.8	6,200	13.2
75-79 years	212,100	16.5	203,700	16.5	8,300	17.7
80-84 years	220,800	17.2	211,700	17.1	9,100	19.3
85 years and over	219,900	17.1	214,100	17.3	5,800	12.3
Unknown	12,000	0.9	10,900	0.9	—	—
Sex						
Male	432,600	33.7	411,300	33.2	21,300	45.1
Female	851,600	66.3	825,800	66.8	25,900	54.9
Race						
White	879,700	68.5	840,500	67.9	39,200	83.2
Black	169,200	13.2	165,600	13.4	3,600	7.6
Other or unknown	235,300	18.3	231,000	18.7	4,300	9.2

Note: Figures may not add to totals because of rounding.

Persons Receiving Care in Nursing Homes, 1980 and 1990

Source: Bureau of the Census, U.S. Dept. of Commerce

Age	1980 Number	1980 Percent	1990 Number	1990 Percent	Percent change, 1980 to 1990	1990 Male	1990 Fema
Total	**1,426,371**	**100.0**	**1,772,032**	**100.0**	**24.2**	**493,609**	**1,278,42**
Under 35 years	29,418	2.1	19,362	1.1	−34.2	11,880	7,48
35 to 44 years	20,764	1.5	27,303	1.5	31.5	16,178	11,12
45 to 54 years	42,857	3.0	40,903	2.3	−4.6	21,662	19,24
55 to 64 years	100,374	7.0	93,701	5.3	−6.6	46,844	46,85
65 to 74 years	238,962	16.8	244,676	13.8	2.4	97,873	146,80
75 to 79 years	219,571	15.4	245,972	13.9	12.0	75,542	170,43
80 to 84 years	286,679	20.1	361,330	20.4	26.0	88,362	272,9
85 to 89 years	276,251	19.4	378,612	21.4	37.1	135,268	603,5
90 to 94 years	158,807	11.1	247,648	14.0	55.9	(NA)	(N
95 years and over	52,688	3.7	112,525	6.4	113.6	(NA)	(N
Under 25 years	12,902	0.9	4,231	0.2	−67.2	2,399	1,83
Under 55 years	93,039	6.5	87,568	4.9	−5.9	49,720	37,84
Under 65 years	193,413	13.6	181,269	10.2	−6.3	96,564	84,7
65 years and over	1,232,958	86.4	1,590,763	89.8	29.0	397,045	1,193,7
85 years and over	487,746	34.2	738,785	41.7	51.5	135,268	603,5

(NA)—Not available; included in previous age group. **NOTE:** In the 1990 decennial census, "Nursing homes" include skilled-nursi facilities, intermediate-care facilities, long-term care rooms in wards or buildings on the grounds of hospitals, or long-term care roor nursing wings in congregate housing facilities. Also included are nursing, convalescent, and rest homes, such as soldiers', sailors', v erans', and fraternal or religious homes for the aged, with or without nursing care.

AIDS Deaths and New AIDS Cases in the U.S., 1985-1992

Source: *Health United States 1992.* National Center for Health Statistics, U.S. Dept. of Health and Human Services

	All years[1]	1985	1986	1987	1988	1989	1990	1991	1992
OTAL DEATHS	**166,211**	**6,681**	**11,535**	**15,451**	**19,656**	**26,151**	**28,053**	**30,579**	**22,660**
IEW AIDS CASES									
All races	**244,939**	**8,210**	**13,147**	**21,088**	**30,719**	**33,595**	**41,653**	**43,701**	**45,472**
Male									
All males, 13 years and over	**214,981**	**7,555**	**12,002**	**19,082**	**27,108**	**29,625**	**36,378**	**37,656**	**38,789**
Vhite, not Hispanic	124,778	4,798	7,527	12,332	16,060	17,509	20,935	20,686	20,740
Black, not Hispanic	59,083	1,712	2,760	4,321	7,159	8,055	10,292	11,105	12,031
Hispanic	28,809	987	1,608	2,242	3,648	3,729	4,749	5,431	5,498
American Indian[2]	374	7	19	24	33	57	68	68	94
Asian or Pacific Islander[3]	1,435	48	78	130	163	213	254	252	276
3-19 years	635	31	44	68	85	89	100	99	95
0-29 years	39,959	1,470	2,490	3,798	5,464	5,719	6,845	6,478	6,292
0-39 years	99,956	3,620	5,654	8,868	12,612	13,904	16,844	17,414	17,795
0-49 years	51,837	1,663	2,576	4,290	6,112	6,823	8,914	9,642	10,317
0-59 years	16,367	605	917	1,471	1,995	2,241	2,657	2,904	3,059
0 years and over	6,227	166	321	587	840	849	1,018	1,119	1,231
Female									
All females, 13 years and over	**25,928**	**526**	**962**	**1,684**	**3,040**	**3,374**	**4,552**	**5,378**	**5,940**
Vhite, not Hispanic	6,924	143	268	545	853	949	1,228	1,362	1,457
Black, not Hispanic	14,538	286	523	896	1,655	1,896	2,543	3,101	3,391
Hispanic	4,207	93	160	229	500	493	741	862	1,026
American Indian[2]	61	3	2	3	5	9	10	12	16
Asian or Pacific Islander[3]	141	1	8	11	22	17	19	25	36
3-19 years	259	4	12	11	23	29	63	53	57
0-29 years	6,454	175	275	482	771	889	1,106	1,222	1,359
0-39 years	12,128	236	446	749	1,506	1,620	2,100	2,540	2,730
0-49 years	4,398	46	127	229	412	506	787	1,001	1,240
0-59 years	1,468	26	47	91	151	172	277	342	344
0 years and over	1,221	39	55	122	177	158	219	220	210
Children									
All children, under 13 years	**4,030**	**129**	**183**	**322**	**571**	**596**	**723**	**667**	**743**
Vhite, not Hispanic	871	27	42	85	150	111	162	145	128
Black, not Hispanic	2,308	83	105	162	304	342	385	403	468
Hispanic	811	19	35	72	112	136	168	112	138
American Indian[2]	13	—	—	2	—	2	4	2	3
Asian or Pacific Islander[3]	19	—	1	1	4	3	4	4	2
Under 1 year	1,601	54	78	141	193	239	284	248	305
-12 years	2,429	75	105	181	378	357	439	419	438

1) Includes cases and deaths prior to 1985. (2) Includes Aleut and Eskimo. (3) Includes Chinese, Japanese, Filipino, Hawaiian and art Hawaiian, and other Asian or Pacific Islander. **Notes:** The AIDS case definition was changed in Sept. 1987 to allow for the pre-umptive diagnosis of AIDS-associated diseases and conditions and to expand the spectrum of human immunodeficiency virus-associ-ted diseases reportable as AIDS. Excludes residents of U.S. territories. Data are updated periodically because of reporting delays. ata for all years have been updated through Dec. 31, 1992.

New AIDS Cases in the U.S., 1985-1992, by Transmission Category

Source: *Health United States 1992.* National Center for Health Statistics, U.S. Dept. of Health and Human Services

Sex and transmission category	All years[1]	1985	1986	1987	1988	1989	1990	1991	1992
ale	214,981	7,555	12,002	19,082	27,108	29,625	36,378	37,656	38,789
len who have sex with men	141,137	5,429	8,542	13,550	17,860	19,688	23,890	23,872	23,653
jecting drug use	39,865	1,111	1,767	2,708	5,296	5,441	6,992	7,664	7,879
len who have sex with men and injecting drug use	15,244	592	989	1,551	2,037	2,189	2,389	2,454	2,355
emophilia/coagulation disorder	1,958	73	118	202	293	279	328	303	310
orn in Caribbean/African countries	2,075	109	160	187	262	236	304	325	283
eterosexual contact[2]	3,942	28	65	161	326	504	721	881	1,243
Sex with injecting drug user	2,413	25	44	114	228	369	462	521	639
ransfusion[3]	2,952	111	193	399	488	438	467	424	387
ndetermined[4]	7,808	102	168	324	546	850	1,287	1,733	2,679
emale	25,928	526	962	1,684	3,040	3,374	4,552	5,378	5,940
jecting drug use	12,925	284	477	840	1,630	1,771	2,260	2,683	2,701
emophilia/coagulation disorder	43	1	4	4	4	6	9	8	3
orn in Caribbean/African countries	885	31	56	74	108	130	111	167	170
eterosexual contact[2]	8,236	116	276	486	861	1,003	1,499	1,826	2,092
Sex with injecting drug user	5,374	82	193	330	634	694	1,019	1,160	1,207
ransfusion[3]	1,848	60	105	217	322	284	324	239	263
ndetermined[4]	1,991	34	44	63	115	180	349	455	711

) Includes cases prior to 1985. (2) Includes persons who have had heterosexual contact with a person with human immunodefi-ency virus (HIV) infection or at risk of HIV infection. (3) Receipt of blood transfusion, blood components, or tissue. (4) Includes per-ons for whom risk information is incomplete, men reported only to have had heterosexual contact with prostitutes, and interviewed ersons for whom no specific risk is identified. **Notes:** The AIDS case definition was changed in Sept. 1987 to allow for the presump-ve diagnosis of AIDS-associated diseases and conditions and to expand the spectrum of HIV-associated diseases reportable as IDS. Excludes residents of U.S. territories. Data are updated periodically because of reporting delays. Data for all years have been odated through Dec. 31, 1992.

Health Services: Estimated Annual Revenue, 1990-1991

Source: Bureau of the Census, U.S. Dept. of Commerce

Kind of business	Revenue (millions of dollars) 1990	1991	Percent change 1990-1991
Health services	$521,700	$571,392	9.5
Offices and clinics of MDs	128,763	138,048	7.2
Offices and clinics of dentists	29,202	30,488	4.4
Offices and clinics of osteopaths	2,513	2,599	3.5
Offices and clinics of other health practitioners	14,802	15,628	5.6
Offices and clinics of chiropractors	4,828	4,986	3.3
Offices and clinics of optometrists	4,275	4,430	3.6
Offices and clinics of podiatrists	1,689	1,826	8.1
Nursing and personal care facilities	35,749	39,319	10.0
Skilled nursing care facilities	29,168	31,866	9.3
Intermediate care facilities	4,382	4,910	12.0
Nursing and personal care facilities	2,198	2,543	15.7
Hospitals	276,273	305,971	10.8
General medical and surgical hospitals	247,923	275,106	11.0
Psychiatric hospitals	14,639	15,368	5.0
Specialty hospitals, except psychiatric	13,711	15,496	13.0
Medical and dental laboratories	9,872	10,528	6.6
Medical laboratories	8,209	8,849	7.8
Dental laboratories	1,663	1,678	0.9
Home health care services	9,429	11,240	19.2
Miscellaneous health and allied services	15,098	17,572	16.4
Kidney dialysis centers	1,545	1,824	18.0
Specialty outpatient facilities	8,276	9,715	17.4

Health Insurance Coverage, 1990

Source: Bureau of the Census, U.S. Dept. of Commerce

(monthly average, first through fourth quarters)

	Quarter 1	Quarter 2	Quarter 3	Quarter 4
All persons	246,194	246,818	247,492	248,195
% Covered by Private or Gvt. Health Insurance				
Total	86.4	87.0	87.2	87.1
Age				
Less than 16 years	85.4	86.0	86.4	86.2
16 to 24 years	78.2	78.7	78.7	78.1
25 to 34 years	81.3	82.8	83.1	83.0
35 to 44 years	86.9	87.4	88.1	87.9
45 to 54 years	88.3	88.6	88.5	88.6
55 to 64 years	89.9	89.9	89.9	89.5
65 years and over	99.6	99.7	99.7	99.7
Race and Hispanic Origin				
White	87.3	87.8	88.1	88.0
Black	81.4	82.2	82.2	82.0
Hispanic origin[1]	68.7	70.2	71.2	71.8
Covered by Private Health Insurance				
Total	75.6	76.3	76.5	76.1
Age				
Less than 16 years	70.8	71.2	71.1	70.7
16 to 24 years	69.8	70.1	70.6	70.0
25 to 34 years	73.4	74.8	75.0	74.9
35 to 44 years	81.4	82.1	82.9	82.7
45 to 54 years	83.2	83.8	83.9	83.8
55 to 64 years	80.8	80.9	80.8	80.2
65 years and over	77.1	78.4	77.8	77.4
Race and Hispanic Origin				
White	79.0	79.7	79.9	79.5
Black	56.0	56.9	56.2	55.9
Hispanic origin[1]	50.4	52.3	52.9	53.0
Covered by Private Health Insurance Related to Employment of Self or Other Family Member				
Total	61.1	61.6	61.4	61.3
Age				
Less than 16 years	59.6	59.5	59.1	59.0
16 to 24 years	54.8	54.3	54.0	53.4
25 to 34 years	66.3	67.6	67.3	67.1
35 to 44 years	74.1	75.0	75.7	75.3
45 to 54 years	72.9	73.7	73.4	73.5
55 to 64 years	65.0	65.4	64.8	64.7
65 years and over	34.2	34.6	34.6	35.1
Race and Hispanic Origin				
White	63.6	64.1	64.1	64.0
Black	47.0	46.9	46.4	46.2
Hispanic origin[1]	42.8	43.8	44.1	44.8
% Covered by Medicaid				
Total	7.5	7.8	7.9	8.1
Age				
Less than 16 years	13.8	14.5	14.9	15.5
16 to 24 years	7.4	7.8	7.7	8.0
25 to 34 years	6.2	6.6	6.6	6.8
35 to 44 years	3.7	3.6	3.7	3.8
45 to 54 years	3.2	3.3	3.2	3.4
55 to 64 years	4.6	4.6	4.9	5.1
65 years and over	7.6	7.5	7.6	7.4
Race and Hispanic Origin				
White	5.2	5.4	5.4	5.7
Black	21.7	22.6	22.8	23.0
Hispanic origin[1]	15.8	15.9	16.4	16.9

(1) Persons of Hispanic origin may be of any race.

Selected Health Services: Estimated Sources of Revenue, 1991

Source: Bureau of the Census, U.S. Dept. of Commerce; in millions of dollars

Source of revenue	Health practitioners: Revenue	Percent of total revenue	Offices and clinics of MDs: Revenue	Percent of total revenue	Offices and clinics of dentists: Revenue	Percent of total revenue	Nursing and personal care: Revenue	Percent of total revenue
Total	$186,763	100.0	$138,048	100.0	$30,488	100.0	$39,319	100.0
Medicare	33,439	17.9	31,159	22.6	184	0.6	3,218	8.2
Medicaid	8,778	4.7	7,580	5.5	610	2.0	20,799	52.9
Other government	3,955	2.1	3,298	2.4	213	0.7	835	2.1
Private insurance	80,134	42.9	58,094	42.1	14,520	47.6	1,762	4.5
Patient	49,428	26.5	28,655	20.7	14,623	48.0	10,643	27.1
Other	11,028	5.9	9,262	6.7	338	1.1	2,061	5.2

U.S. Health Expenditures, 1960-1991

Source: Health Care Financing Administration, Office of the Actuary; data from Office of National Health Statistics; in billions of dollars.

Type of expenditure	1960	1970	1980	1985	1986	1987	1988	1989	1990	1991
National health expenditures	**$27.1**	**$74.4**	**$250.1**	**$422.6**	**$454.8**	**$494.1**	**$546.0**	**$604.3**	**$675.0**	**$751.8**
Health services & supplies	**25.4**	**69.1**	**238.9**	**407.2**	**438.9**	**476.9**	**526.2**	**583.6**	**652.4**	**728.6**
Personal health care	23.9	64.9	219.4	369.7	400.8	439.3	482.8	530.9	591.5	660.2
Hospital care	9.3	27.9	102.4	168.3	179.8	194.2	212.0	232.4	258.1	288.6
Physician services	5.3	13.6	41.9	74.0	82.1	93.0	105.1	116.1	128.8	142.0
Dental services	2.0	4.7	14.4	23.3	24.7	27.1	29.4	31.6	34.1	37.1
Other professional services	0.6	1.5	8.7	16.6	18.6	21.1	23.8	27.1	30.7	35.8
Home health care	0.0	0.1	1.3	3.8	4.0	4.1	4.5	5.6	7.6	9.8
Drugs & other medical nondurables	4.2	8.8	21.6	36.2	39.7	43.2	46.3	50.5	55.6	60.7
Vision products & other medical durables	0.8	2.0	4.6	7.1	8.1	9.1	10.1	10.4	11.7	12.4
Nursing home care	1.0	4.9	20.0	34.1	36.7	39.7	42.8	47.5	53.3	59.9
Other personal health care	0.7	1.4	4.6	6.4	7.1	7.8	8.7	9.8	11.5	14.0
Program administration & net cost of private health insurance	1.2	2.8	12.2	25.2	24.6	23.0	26.9	33.8	38.9	43.9
Government public health activities	0.4	1.4	7.2	12.3	13.5	14.6	16.6	18.9	22.0	24.5
Research & construction	**1.7**	**5.3**	**11.3**	**15.4**	**16.0**	**17.3**	**19.8**	**20.7**	**22.7**	**23.1**
Research[1]	0.7	2.0	5.4	7.8	8.5	9.0	10.3	11.0	11.9	12.6
Construction	1.0	3.4	5.8	7.6	7.4	8.2	9.5	9.7	10.8	10.6
	Average annual % change from previous year shown									
National health expenditures	—	**10.6**	**12.9**	**11.1**	**7.6**	**8.6**	**10.5**	**10.7**	**11.7**	**11.4**
Health services & supplies	—	**10.5**	**13.2**	**11.3**	**7.8**	**8.6**	**10.3**	**10.9**	**11.8**	**11.7**
Personal health care	—	10.5	13.0	11.0	8.4	9.6	9.9	10.0	11.4	11.6
Hospital care	—	11.7	13.9	10.4	6.8	8.0	9.2	9.6	11.1	11.8
Physician services	—	9.9	11.9	12.1	10.9	13.3	13.1	10.4	11.0	10.2
Dental services	—	9.1	11.9	10.1	6.4	9.6	8.5	7.5	7.7	8.8
Other professional services	—	9.6	19.1	13.8	12.0	13.6	12.4	13.8	13.5	16.7
Home health care	—	14.5	25.2	23.3	3.6	3.4	9.9	24.4	34.4	29.0
Drugs & other medical nondurables	—	7.6	9.4	10.8	9.9	8.6	7.2	9.1	10.3	9.0
Vision products & other medical durables	—	9.6	8.5	9.4	13.0	12.3	11.8	2.8	12.6	5.4
Nursing home care	—	17.4	15.2	11.3	7.6	8.0	7.8	11.1	12.3	12.4
Other personal health care	—	7.1	12.8	6.9	11.1	10.0	12.1	11.8	17.4	21.9
Program administration & net cost of private health insurance	—	9.0	16.0	15.5	−2.5	−6.6	16.8	25.7	15.3	12.7
Government public health activities	—	13.9	18.0	11.3	9.6	8.3	13.5	14.3	16.0	11.6
Research & construction	—	**12.1**	**7.8**	**6.4**	**3.7**	**8.2**	**14.9**	**4.2**	**9.6**	**2.1**
Research[1]	—	10.9	10.8	7.4	9.5	5.7	14.5	6.2	8.0	6.1
Construction	—	12.8	5.6	5.4	−2.4	11.1	15.3	1.9	11.5	−2.2

(1) Research and development expenditures of drug companies and other manufacturers and providers of medical equipment and supplies are excluded from "research expenditures," but included in the expenditure class in which the product falls. **Note:** Numbers may not add to totals because of rounding.

The 25 Drugs Most Frequently Prescribed in Physicians' Offices, 1990

Source: National Center for Health Statistics, U.S. Dept. of Health and Human Services; in thousands

Rank	Name of drug and principal generic substance[1]	Number of times prescribed	Therapeutic use
1.	Amoxicillin	17,891	Antibiotic
2.	Amoxil (amoxicillin)	13,448	Antibiotic
3.	Ceclor (cefaclor)	8,910	Antibiotic
4.	Lasix (furosemide)	8,868	Diuretic, antihypertensive
5.	Prednisone	7,830	Steroid replacement therapy, anti-inflammatory agent
6.	Naprosyn (naproxen)	7,585	Nonsteroidal anti-inflammatory agent
7.	Seldane (terfenadine)	7,251	Antihistaminic
8.	Motrin (ibuprofen)	6,988	Nonsteroidal anti-inflammatory agent
9.	Zantac (ranitidine)	6,501	Duodenal or gastric ulcer
10.	Premarin (estrogens)	6,327	Estrogen replacement therapy
11.	Lanoxin (digoxin)	6,275	Cardiotonic/digitalis
12.	Vasotec (enalapril)	5,991	Antihypertensive
13.	Aspirin or A.S.A.	5,896	Analgesic, anti-inflammatory, antipyretic
14.	Proventil (albuterol)	5,614	Bronchodilator
15.	Dyazide (triamterene, hydrochlorothiazide)	5,584	Diuretic, antihypertensive
16.	Diphtheria tetanus toxoids pertussis	5,176	Immunization
17.	Voltaren (diclofenac sodium)	5,160	Nonsteroidal anti-inflammatory agent
18.	Tylenol (acetaminophen)	5,144	Analgesic
19.	Synthroid (levothyroxine)	5,137	Thyroid hormone therapy
20.	Xanax (alprazolam)	5,089	Anxiety disorders
21.	Cardizem (diltiazem)	4,979	Cardiotonic/calcium channel blocking agent
22.	Capoten (captopril)	4,785	Antihypertensive
23.	Prozac (fluoxetine)	4,785	Antidepressant
24.	Calan (verapamil)	4,755	Cardiotonic/calcium channel blocking agent
25.	Ventolin (albuterol)	4,666	Bronchodilator

(1) The trade or generic name used by the physician on the prescription or other medical records. The use of trade names is for identification only and does not imply endorsement by the Public Health Service or the U.S. Department of Health and Human Services. Because of its nonspecific nature, the entry "Allergy relief or shots," with 4,184,000 mentions, is omitted.

Years of Life Expected at Birth

Source: National Center for Health Statistics

Year	All Races Total	All Races Male	All Races Female	White Total	White Male	White Female	Black and Other Total	Black and Other Male	Black and Other Female
1920*	54.1	53.6	54.6	54.9	54.4	55.6	45.3	45.5	45.2
1930	59.7	58.1	61.6	61.4	59.7	63.5	48.1	47.3	49.2
1940	62.9	60.8	65.2	64.2	62.1	66.6	53.1	51.5	54.9
1950	68.2	65.6	71.1	69.1	66.5	72.2	60.8	59.1	62.9
1960	69.7	66.6	73.1	70.6	67.4	74.1	63.6	61.1	66.3
1965	70.2	66.8	73.7	71.0	67.6	74.7	64.1	61.1	67.4
1970	70.8	67.1	74.7	71.7	68.0	75.6	65.3	61.3	69.4
1971	71.1	67.4	75.0	72.0	68.3	75.8	65.6	61.6	69.8
1972	71.2	67.4	75.1	72.0	68.3	75.9	65.7	61.5	70.1
1973	71.4	67.6	75.3	72.2	68.5	76.1	66.1	62.0	70.3
1974	72.0	68.2	75.9	72.8	69.0	76.7	67.1	62.9	71.3
1975	72.6	68.8	76.6	73.4	69.5	77.3	68.0	63.7	72.4
1976	72.9	69.1	76.8	73.6	69.9	77.5	68.4	64.2	72.7
1977	73.3	69.5	77.2	74.0	70.2	77.9	68.9	64.7	73.2
1978	73.5	69.6	77.3	74.1	70.4	78.0	68.1	63.7	72.4
1979	73.9	70.0	77.8	74.6	70.8	78.4	69.8	65.4	74.1
1980	73.7	70.0	77.5	74.4	70.7	78.1	69.5	65.3	73.6
1981	74.2	70.4	77.8	74.8	71.1	78.4	70.3	66.2[r]	74.4
1982	74.5	70.9	78.1	75.1	71.5	78.7	70.9[r]	66.8	74.9[r]
1983	74.6	71.0	78.1	75.2	71.7	78.7	70.9[r]	67.0[r]	74.7[r]
1984	74.7	71.2	78.2	75.3	71.8	78.7	71.1[r]	67.2[r]	74.9[r]
1985	74.7	71.2	78.2	75.3	71.9	78.7	67.0[r]	64.8[r]	69.3[r]
1986	74.8	71.3	78.3	75.4	72.0	78.8	70.9[r]	66.8[r]	74.9[r]
1987	75.0	71.5	78.4	75.6	72.2	78.9	66.9[r]	65.0[r]	69.1[r]
1988	74.9	71.5	78.3	75.6	72.3	78.9	70.8[r]	66.7[r]	74.8[r]
1989	75.1	71.7	78.5	75.9	72.5	79.2	70.9[r]	66.7[r]	74.9[r]
1990	75.4	71.8	78.8	76.1	72.9	79.4	71.2[r]	67.0[r]	75.2[r]
1992[p]	75.7	72.3	79.0	76.5	73.2	79.7	71.8	67.8	75.6

p= preliminary. r= revised. * Data prior to 1940 for death-registration states only.

Average Height and Weight for Children

Source: *Physicians Handbook*, 1990

Boys Age Years	Height ft	Height in	cm	Weight lb	Weight kg	Girls Age Years	Height ft	Height in	cm	Weight lb	Weight kg
(Birth)	1	8	50.8	7½	3.4	(Birth)	1	8	50.8	7½	3.4
½	2	2	66.0	17	7.7	½	2	2	66.0	16	7.2
1	2	5	73.6	21	9.5	1	2	5	73.6	20	9.1
2	2	9	83.8	26	11.8	2	2	9	83.8	25	11.3
3	3	0	91.4	31	14.0	3	3	0	91.4	30	13.6
4	3	3	99.0	34	15.4	4	3	3	99.0	33	15.0
5	3	6	106.6	39	17.7	5	3	5	104.1	38	17.2
6	3	9	114.2	46	20.9	6	3	8	111.7	45	20.4
7	3	11	119.3	51	23.1	7	3	11	119.3	49	22.2
8	4	2	127.0	57	25.9	8	4	2	127.0	56	25.4
9	4	4	132.0	63	28.6	9	4	4	132.0	62	28.1
10	4	6	137.1	69	31.3	10	4	6	137.1	69	31.3
11	4	8	142.2	77	34.9	11	4	8	142.2	77	34.9
12	4	10	147.3	83	37.7	12	4	10	147.3	86	39.0
13	5	0	152.4	92	41.7	13	5	0	152.4	98	45.5
14	5	2	157.5	107	48.5	14	5	2	157.5	107	48.5

This table gives a general picture of American children at specific ages. When used as a standard, the individual variation in children's growth should not be overlooked. In most cases the height-weight relationship is probably a more valid index of weight status than a weight-for-age assessment.

Average Weight of Americans by Height and Age

Source: Society of Actuaries

The figures represent weights in ordinary indoor clothing and shoes, and heights with shoes.

Men Height	20-24	25-29	30-39	40-49	50-59	60-69
5'2"	130	134	138	140	141	140
5'3"	136	140	143	144	145	144
5'4"	139	143	147	149	150	149
5'5"	143	147	151	154	155	153
5'6"	148	152	156	158	159	158
5'7"	153	156	160	163	164	163
5'8"	157	161	165	167	168	167
5'9"	163	166	170	172	173	172
5'10"	167	171	174	176	177	176
5'11"	171	175	179	181	182	181
6'0"	176	181	184	186	187	186
6'1"	182	186	190	192	193	191
6'2"	187	191	195	197	198	196
6'3"	193	197	201	203	204	200
6'4"	198	202	206	208	209	207

Women Height	20-24	25-29	30-39	40-49	50-59	60-69
4'10"	105	110	113	118	121	123
4'11"	110	112	115	121	125	127
5'0"	112	114	118	123	127	130
5'1"	116	119	121	127	131	133
5'2"	120	121	124	129	133	136
5'3"	124	125	128	133	137	140
5'4"	127	128	131	136	141	143
5'5"	130	132	134	139	144	147
5'6"	133	134	137	143	147	150
5'7"	137	138	141	147	152	155
5'8"	141	142	145	150	156	158
5'9"	146	148	150	155	159	161
5'10"	149	150	153	158	162	163
5'11"	155	156	159	162	166	167
6'0"	157	159	164	168	171	172

OBITUARIES

Deaths, Oct. 26, 1992-Oct. 15, 1993

A

Abe, Kobo, 68; Japanese novelist and poet; Tokyo, Jan. 22.
Acuff, Roy, 89; singer and fiddler, star of the Grand Ole Opry for over 50 years; Nashville, Nov. 23.
Adams, Diana, 66; a leading ballerina of the 1950s and 1960s; San Andreas, Cal., Jan. 10.
Adler, Stella, 91; acting teacher, was a leading exponent of "Method" acting; Los Angeles, Dec. 21.
Albert, Stephen J., 51; composer of symphonic music, won the 1985 Pulitzer Prize; Truro, Mass., Dec. 27.
Albertson, Joseph A., 86; founder of supermarket chain; Boise, Jan. 20.
Allison, Davey, 32; stock-car driver; Birmingham, Ala., July 13.
Ames, Leon, 91; film and TV actor best-known for his roles as a kind, affectionate father ("Meet Me in St. Louis"); Laguna Beach, Cal., Oct. 12.
Anderson, Marian, 96; contralto who shattered racial barriers; Portland, Ore., Apr. 8.
Andre the Giant, 46; professional wrestler; Paris, reported Jan. 30.
Andrews, Dana, 83; actor, starred in films in the 1940s and 1950s; Los Alamitos, Cal., Dec. 17.
Ashe, Arthur, 49; tennis player, won the 1968 U.S. Open; New York, Feb. 6.

B

Baudouin, 62; king of Belgium for 42 years; Motril, Spain, July 31.
Boulding, Kenneth, 83; British-born economist, philosopher, and poet; Boulder, Col., Mar. 19.
Boyle, Kay, 90; novelist and short-story writer; Mill Valley, Cal., Dec. 27.
Brian, David, 82; actor, appeared in films and TV in the 1940s and 1950s; Sherman Oaks, Cal., July 15.
Bridges, James, 57; film writer and director; Los Angeles, June 6.
Brusati, Franco, 66; Italian film director, "Bread and Chocolate"; Rome, Feb. 28.
Buell, Marjorie, 88; creator of the Little Lulu cartoon character; Elyria, Oh., May 30.
Burdett, Winston, 79; radio and TV correspondent for CBS News; Rome, May 19.
Burr, Raymond, 76; actor, starred in the "Perry Mason" and "Ironside" TV series; Dry Creek Valley, Cal., Sept. 12.
Bush, Dorothy Walker, 91; mother of Pres. George Bush; Greenwich, Conn., Nov. 19.
Butts, Alfred M., 93; inventor of the Scrabble board game; Rhinebeck, N.Y., Apr. 4.

C

Cahn, Sammy, 79; lyricist, collaborated with Jule Styne, Jimmy Van Heusen for numerous hit songs, "All the Way", "High Hopes"; Los Angeles, Jan. 15.
Campanella, Roy, 71; Hall of Fame catcher for the Brooklyn Dodgers; Woodland Hills, Cal., June 26.
Cantinflas, 81; Mexican comic actor, "Around the World in 80 Days"; Mexico City, Apr. 20.
Charteris, Leslie, 85; mystery writer, created Simon Templar, a hero known as "The Saint"; Windsor, England, Apr. 15.
Chavez, Cesar, 66; labor leader, founded the United Farm Workers of America; San Luis, Ariz., Apr. 23.
Coles, Charles "Honi", 81; tap dancer known for elegance and speed; New York, Nov. 12.
Conn, Billy, 75; boxer famed for 1941 heavyweight title bout against Joe Louis; Pittsburgh, May 29.
Connally, John B., 76; Texas governor shot in the Kennedy assassination, Treasury secretary in the Nixon administration; Houston, June 15.
Connors, Chuck, 71; actor, starred in "The Rifleman" TV series, 1958-1963; Los Angeles, Nov. 10.
Crews, Tim, 31; pitcher for the Cleveland Indians; Little Lake Nellie, Fla., Mar. 22.
Crichton, Robert, 68; author of best-sellers "The Imposter", "The Secret of Santa Vittoria"; New Rochelle, N.Y., Mar. 23.
Crosby, Bob, 80; swing-era bandleader; Torrey Pines, Cal., Mar. 9.
Culliford, Pierre, 64; creator of the "Smurf" cartoon characters; Brussels, Belgium, Dec. 24.
Cunningham, Harry, 85; developer of Kmart, pioneered discount mass-merchandising; North Palm Beach, Fla., Nov. 11.
Cusack, Cyril, 82; Irish actor in theater and films; London, Oct. 7.

D

De Mille, Agnes, 88; noted choreographer of ballets ("Rodeo," "Fall River Legend") and musicals ("Oklahoma," "Carousel") on American themes; New York, Oct. 7.
DeRita, Curly Joe, 83; last surviving member of the Three Stooges comedy team; Woodland Hills, Cal., July 3.
De Vries, Peter, 83; writer, best known as a contributor to *The New Yorker* magazine; Norwalk, Conn., Sept. 28.
Diebenkorn, Richard, 71; artist, was a leading American painter of the postwar era; Berkeley, Cal., Mar. 30.
Doolittle, James, 96; aviation pioneer, Air Force general who led daylight air raid on Tokyo 4 months after Pearl Harbor attack; Pebble Beach, Cal., Sept. 27.
Dopsie, Rockin', 61; leading player of zydeco music; Opelousas, La., Aug. 26.
Dorsey, Thomas A., 93; pianist known as the father of gospel music; Chicago, Jan. 23.
Drysdale, Don, 56; Hall of Fame pitcher for the L.A. Dodgers, sportscaster; Montreal, July 3.
Dubcek, Alexander, 70; Czechoslovak leader whose attempt at liberalization was crushed by Warsaw Pact troops in 1968; Prague, Nov. 7.

E

Eckstine, Billy, 78; singer and bandleader popular in the 1940s and 1950s; Pittsburgh, Mar. 8.

F

Falco, Louis, 50; Modern dance choreographer; New York, Mar. 26.
Ford, Constance, 69; actress, appeared on the "Another World" daytime serial for 25 years; New York, Feb. 26.

G

Gallo, Julio, 83; winery owner; nr. Tracy, Cal., May 2.
Gardenia, Vincent, 71; character actor in theater, films, and TV; Philadelphia, Dec. 9.
Gehringer, Charlie, 89; Hall of Fame 2d baseman for the Detroit Tigers, had a .320 career batting average; Bloomfield Hills, Mich., Jan. 21.
Gesell, Gerhard, 82; federal judge who presided over high-profile cases in the Watergate scandal; Washington, D.C., Feb. 19.
Gillespie, Dizzy, 75; trumpet player and a founding father of modern jazz; Englewood, N.J., Jan. 6.
Gish, Lillian, 99; actress, was a major star of silent films; New York, Feb. 27.
Gleason, Thomas, 92; labor leader, headed the international Longshoremen's Assn., 1963-1987; New York, Dec. 24.
Golding, William, 81; author, "Lord of the Flies"; won 1983 Nobel Prize for literature; Perranarworthal, England, June 19.
Goodson, Mark, 77; game show creator, "What's My Line?", "The Price Is Right"; New York, Dec. 18.
Gould, Jack, 79; TV and radio critic for the *New York Times*, 1944-1972; Concord, Cal., May 24.
Granger, Stewart, 80; leading man in swashbuckler films in the 1950s; Santa Monica, Cal., Aug. 16.
Grey, Nan, 75; leading lady in Hollywood films in the 1930s; San Diego, July 25.
Gwynne, Fred, 66; actor, best known as Herman Munster in the 1960s TV series "The Munsters"; Taneytown, Md., July 2.

H

Hale, Clara "Mother", 87; founder of Hale House, nurtured hundreds of abandoned and orphaned babies in New York City; New York, Dec. 18.
Hamlin, Vincent, 93; cartoonist, created the Alley Oop cartoon strip; Spring Hill, Fla., June 14.
Hamner, Granville, 66; major league shortstop for 17 seasons; Philadelphia, Sept. 12.
Harken, Dwight, 83; pioneering heart surgeon; Washington, D.C., Aug. 25.
Hayes, Helen, 92; actress, starred in the theater for some 65 years and, from 1931, in films; Nyack, N.Y., Mar. 17.
Hearst, William Randolph, Jr., 85; editor in chief of the Hearst newspaper empire; New York, May 14.
Henry, Paul, 51; U.S. representative from Michigan since 1985; Grand Rapids, Mich., July 31.
Hepburn, Audrey, 63; actress, starred in numerous films in the 1950s and 1960s, "Roman Holiday," "Breakfast at Tiffany's"; Tolochenaz, Switzerland, Jan. 20.
Hersey, John, 78; journalist and novelist; Key West, Fla., Mar. 24.
Hibbert, Eleanor, 80s; author of some 200 novels, mostly as Victoria Holt or Jean Plaidy; at sea, Jan. 18.
Holley, Robert W., 71; biologist, won the 1968 Nobel Prize for physiology or medicine; Los Gatos, Cal., Feb. 11.
Holloway, Sterling, 87; actor, was the voice of "Winnie-the-Pooh" in several animated films; Los Angeles, Nov. 22.
Howe, Irving, 72; literary and social critic, editor; New York, May 5.
Hunt, James, 45; British race car driver, won 1976 Formula One world championship; London, June 15.

I

Iba, Henry, 88; basketball coach, won 767 games, mostly with Oklahoma St.; won 2 national championships, 3 Olympic gold medals; Stillwater, Okla., Jan. 15.

J

Janeway, Eliot, 80; political economist and author; New York, Feb. 8.

Jordan, James, 57; father of NBA star Michael Jordan; Fayetteville, N.C., July 23.

Jordan, Richard, 56; actor, director, and writer; Los Angeles, Aug. 30.

K

Kanin, Michael, 83; screenwriter, producer, and director; Los Angeles, Mar. 12.

Kauffman, Ewing M., 76; owner of the Kansas City Royals baseball team; Mission Hills, Kan., Aug. 1.

Keeler, Ruby, 82; tap-dancing star of musicals in the 1930s; Palm Springs, Cal., Feb. 28.

Kemeny, John, 66, computer pioneer and educator; Lebanon, N.H., Dec. 26.

King, Albert, 69; blues guitarist and singer; Memphis, Dec. 21.

Kirchner, Claude, 77; pioneer in children's TV, ringmaster of Tarrytown Circus in the 1950s and 1960s; Hawthorne, N.Y., Mar. 8.

Kirsten, Dorothy, 82; lyric soprano, sang at the Metropolitan Opera for over 30 years; Los Angeles, Nov. 18.

Knebel, Fletcher, 81; coauthor of best-selling novel "Seven Days in May"; Honolulu, Feb. 26.

Kulwicki, Alan, 38; auto racer, won the 1992 NASCAR championship; nr. Bristol, Tenn., Apr. 1.

Kurtzman, Harvey, 68; cartoonist, created *Mad* magazine; Mt. Vernon, N.Y., Feb. 21.

Kusch, Polykarp, 82; Nobel Prize winner in physics in 1955; Dallas, Mar. 20.

L

Lamborghini, Ferruccio, 76; founder of Italian sports car company; Perugia, Italy, Feb. 20.

Lee, Brandon, 27; actor, starred in martial arts films; Wilmington, N.C., Mar. 31.

Lee, Pinky, 85; vaudeville comic, hosted children's TV shows in the 1950s; Mission Viejo, Cal., Apr. 3.

Lewis, Reggie, 27; basketball player for the Boston Celtics; Waltham, Mass., July 27.

Lewis, Reginald F., 50; financier, acquired Beatrice Cos. for $1 billion in 1987; New York, Jan. 19.

M

MacMillan, Kenneth, 62; choreographer, headed the Royal Ballet in Britain, 1970-1977; London, Oct. 29.

Maglie, Sal, 75; pitcher for the N.Y. Giants in the 1950s; Niagara Falls, N.Y., Dec. 28.

Maleska, Eugene T., 77; crossword puzzle editor of the *New York Times* since 1978; Daytona Beach, Fla., Aug. 3.

Mankiewicz, Joseph L., 83; film writer, director, and producer; won 4 Oscars; Mt. Kisco, N.Y., Feb. 5.

Marshall, Thurgood, 84; associate justice of the U.S. Supreme Court, 1967-1991; as a civil rights lawyer, won landmark 1954 "Brown vs. Board of Education" decision to desegregate public schools; Bethesda, Md., Jan. 24.

Maynard, Robert C., 56; journalist who was the first black owner and editor of a major daily U.S. newspaper; Oakland, Cal., Aug. 17.

McCluskey, Roger, 63; race car driver, was U.S.A.C. national champion 5 times; Indianapolis, Ind., Aug. 29.

McFarland, Spanky, 64; child star of the "Our Gang" and "Little Rascals" films; Grapeville, Tex., June 30.

Mickelson, George S., 52; governor of South Dakota; nr. Dubuque, Ia., Apr. 19.

Milstein, Nathan, 88; Russian-born violin virtuoso; London, Dec. 21.

Mize, Johnny, 80; baseball Hall of Famer, won 4 NL home run titles; Demorest, Ga., June 2.

Montoya, Carlos, 89; flamenco guitarist; Wainscott, N.Y., Mar. 3.

Morgan, Edward P., 82; radio and TV journalist; McLean, Va., Jan. 27.

Mosconi, Willie, 80; world pocket billiards champion 13 times from 1941 through 1956; Haddon Heights, N.J., Sept. 16.

Most, Johnny, 69; radio voice of the Boston Celtics for almost 40 years; Cape Cod, Mass., Jan. 3.

N

Nixon, "Pat", 81; wife of former President Richard Nixon; Park Ridge, N.J., June 22.

Nureyev, Rudolf, 54; dancer who was a leading ballet star of the 20th century; Paris, Jan. 6.

O

O'Connell, Helen, 73; big-band singer of the 1940s; San Diego, Cal., Sept. 9.

Olin, Steve, 27; pitcher for the Cleveland Indians; Little Lake Nellie, Fla., Mar. 22.

Oort, Jan H., 92; Dutch astronomer; Leiden, the Netherlands, Nov. 5.

Ozal, Turgut, 66; president and former premier of Turkey; Ankara, Turkey, Apr. 17.

P

Parish, Mitchell, 92; lyricist, "Star Dust," "Deep Purple"; New York, Mar. 31.

Pennel, John, 53; pole vaulter, was the first to clear 17 feet; Santa Monica, Cal., Sept. 26.

Petrovic, Drazen, 28; basketball player for the N.J. Nets; Germany, June 7.

Philbrick, Herbert, 78; FBI spy whose book "I Led Three Lives" inspired a 1950s TV series; North Hampton, N.H., Aug. 16.

Pollard, Jim, 70; basketball Hall of Famer, played on 5 NBA championship teams; Stockton, Cal., Jan. 22.

Pulitzer, Joseph, Jr., 80; chairman of the Pulitzer Publishing Co.; St. Louis, May 26.

R

Ra, Sun, 79; jazz pianist and bandleader; Birmingham, Ala., May 30.

Reid, Kate, 62; actress who appeared in films, TV, and the theater for some 40 years; Stratford, Ont., Mar. 27.

Ridgway, Matthew B., 98; Army general who led U.S. forces in Normandy and UN troops in Korea; Fox Chapel, Pa., July 27.

Riegels, Roy, 84; football player famed for running 69 yards in the wrong direction at the 1929 Rose Bowl game; Woodland, Cal., Mar. 26.

Roach, Hal, 100; writer, producer, and director who was a leading pioneer in film comedy; Los Angeles, Nov. 2.

Ross, Steven J., 65; entrepreneur who built and ran Time Warner Inc.; Los Angeles, Dec. 20.

S

Sabin, Albert, 86; pioneering researcher on viruses and viral diseases; developed oral polio vaccine; Washington, D.C., Mar. 3.

St. Aubin, Helen, 69; baseball player whose career inspired the film "A League of Their Own"; Los Angeles, Cal., Dec. 8.

Salant, Richard S., 78; head of CBS News in the 1960s and 1970s; Bridgeport, Conn., Feb. 16.

Salisbury, Harrison E., 84; Pulitzer Prize-winning foreign correspondent and *New York Times* editor; author of 29 books; Providence, R.I., July 5.

Schwartzwalder, Ben, 83; football coach at Syracuse University, 1949-1973; St. Petersburg, Fla., Apr. 28.

Sharaff, Irene, 83; costume designer who won 5 Oscars and a Tony award; New York, Aug. 16.

Sharkey, Ray, 40; film and TV actor; New York, June 11.

Shawn, William, 85; editor of *The New Yorker* magazine, 1952-1987; New York, Dec. 8.

Sheaffer, Louis, 80; biographer of Eugene O'Neill who won the 1974 Pulitzer Prize; New York, Aug. 7.

Shirley, Anne, 75; actress, starred in films in the 1930s and 1940s; Los Angeles, July 4.

Simon, Norton, 86; industrialist and art collector; Los Angeles, June 2.

Slayton, Donald "Deke", 69; one of the original 7 U.S. astronauts; League City, Tex., June 13.

Smith, Alexis, 72; stage and screen actress; Los Angeles, June 9.

Stegner, Wallace, 84; novelist and short story writer, won 1972 Pulitzer Prize, "Angle of Repose"; Santa Fe, N.M., Apr. 13.

Sulzberger, C. L., 80; foreign correspondent and foreign affairs columnist for the *New York Times* for nearly 40 years; Paris, Sept. 20.

Swift, Kay, 95; songwriter, "Can't We Be Friends," "Fine and Dandy"; Southington, Conn., Jan. 28.

T

Tajo, Italo, 77; Italian operatic bass noted for comic roles; Cincinnati, Ohio, Mar. 29.

Todd, Ann, 84; British stage and film actress, "The Seventh Veil"; London, May 6.

Trace, Al, 92; bandleader and songwriter, "Mairzy Doats"; Sun City West, Ariz., Aug. 31

Troyanos, Tatiana, 54; mezzo-soprano; New York, Aug. 21.

Twitty, Conway, 59; country and western singer, had over 50 No. 1 songs on the country charts; Springfield, Mo., June 5.

V

Valvano, Jim, 47; basketball coach and TV commentator, led North Carolina State to the 1983 national championship; Durham, N.C., Apr. 28.

Varsi, Diane, 54; actress, starred in films in the 1950s; Los Angeles, Nov. 19.

Villechaize, Herve, 50; actor, best known as Tattoo in the "Fantasy Island" TV series; Los Angeles, Sept. 4.

W

Waymer, David, 34; NFL defensive back; Mooresville, N.C., Apr. 30.

Westall, Robert ,63; author of children's books; Cheshire, England, Apr. 15.

White, F. Clifton, 74; political strategist, served 4 Republican presidents; Greenwich, Conn., Jan. 9.

Whitney, C. V. 93; prominent figure in horse racing and the arts; Saratoga Springs, N.Y., Dec. 13.

Wood, Walter A., 85; explorer, participated in over 100 mountaineering treks on 4 continents; West Palm Beach, Fla., May 18.

Offbeat News Stories of 1993

Hot Streak — Soccer fans in the Bolivian village of Ixiamas were so excited with their team's 3-1 victory against Uruguay in a World Cup qualifying game that they didn't notice their homes were on fire. By the time the fire was spotted, it had spread to 40 homes. The fire began when firecrackers thrown by fans landed on the thatched roofs of homes.

Body Shop — The Los Angeles County Coroner's Office has gone into business. The office opened a shop called Skeletons in the Closet that offers such items as a toe tag like the ones attached to bodies, a tote bag with a skeleton figure (called Sherlock Bones) wearing a trench coat, and a beach towel with a chalk body outline. The profits help pay for a program to educate youths on the dangers of drunken driving.

Goldberg Variations: A Boy Named Beerhall — It is against the law in Germany to name a child after Whoopi Goldberg. Parents are forbidden by law from choosing names that blur gender or otherwise "endanger the well-being of the child." Whoopi was rejected by authorities as being too suggestive of the phrase "making whoopee." Other proscribed names included Bierstübl (beerhall) and Störenfried (disturber of the peace).

Dog Gone — A dog was suspended from baseball for the 1993 season. Baseball's Executive Council, which had suspended Cincinnati Reds owner Marge Schott for the 1993 season for using racial slurs, shortly afterward suspended her dog, Schottzie 02, from the field of Riverfront Stadium. The dog's suspension was welcomed by Reds players because the dog interfered with workouts at the ballpark and frequently soiled the artificial turf.

Are You A Marxist? — About 20 first-term House members were asked, "Do you approve of what we're doing to stop what's going on in Freedonia?" or "Do you approve of what we're doing to stop ethnic cleansing in Freedonia?" Replies included "take action" and "it's a different situation than the Middle East." None of the 20 House freshmen recognized the fictitious nation of Freedonia from the 1933 Marx Brothers movie *Duck Soup*. The joker was *Spy* magazine, whose national editor, Jamie Malanowski, characterized the responses as "completely understandable." "In campaigning," he said of the new lawmakers, "they are asked a lot of dumb questions, and they are all used to supplying answers."

Too Late — The Italian cabinet quickly abolished a regulation making people still responsible for the $50 annual health tax in the year in which they had died. Health Minister Maria Pia Garavaglia, who had issued the regulation, conceded that there was no way to enforce it.

Hang 'Em High School — Outlaw Tiburcio Vasquez was the hands-down winner in a local contest to name a new high school in Agua Dulce, Cal., winning out over the likes of John Wayne and Magic Johnson. Vasquez, whose reputation for cattle rustling and stagecoach robbing earned him the title Scourge of California, was hanged for murder in 1875.

Isn't This A Rerun? — The cable television company that serves Columbia, S.C., aimed a camera full-time at an aquarium to occupy a vacant channel while awaiting the start-up of the Science-Fiction Channel. When the Science-Fiction Channel replaced the "fish channel," complaints were so numerous that the cable company was forced to find another channel for the aquarium, which it ran 14 hours a day.

Turning On — A suspected drug dealer in Charles City, Va., tried to elude sheriff's deputies by slipping into the woods, but he was caught because he was wearing the wrong sneakers. He was wearing L.A. Gear's Light Gear sneakers, which feature battery-operated lights that flash when the heel hits the ground. "Every time he took a step, we knew exactly where he was," said a member of the sheriff's department.

Miscellaneous Facts

—What has been the greatest upset in sports? In a survey of visitors by the Las Vegas Hilton, the most commonly picked event was the U.S. hockey team's defeat of the Soviet team at the 1980 Winter Olympics. Buster Douglas's 1990 knockout of heavyweight champion Mike Tyson was ranked second, and the N.Y. Jets' defeat of the Baltimore Colts in the 1969 Super Bowl ranked third.

—Psychiatric disorders affect 15 percent of American adults in any six-month period, according to the National Institute of Mental Health Advisory Council. The Council also reported that 12 percent of youths under 18 have mental, behavioral, or developmental disorders and that 10.9 percent of the U.S. population seeks mental health treatment annually.

—A survey by the National Opinion Research Center at the Univ. of Chicago found that nine of every ten Americans believe in God and that 78 percent believe in a life after death. Seven of every ten Americans believe in miracles, and four of ten report contact with the dead. About four of every ten attend church at least two or three times a month.

—There are laws against drunken driving and none against drunken walking, yet more than a third of the 5,546 pedestrians killed by cars in the U.S. in 1992 were drunk, according to the National Highway Traffic Safety Administration. The blood-alcohol level of 36 percent of pedestrians over age 14 who were killed by motor vehicles was high enough for them to be cited for drunken driving had they been behind the wheel.

—Have you been wondering whatever happened to the baseball hit by Mookie Wilson of the N.Y. Mets that rolled between Bill Buckner's legs in Game 6 of the 1986 World Series with the Boston Red Sox? In 1992 the ball was purchased at auction by actor Charlie Sheen for $85,000. At that same auction, a jersey used by Tom Seaver in 1969, the year the Mets won their first World Series, sold for $50,000, and Ty Cobb's full Detroit Tigers uniform from 1924 sold for $160,000.

—It cost the U.S. Census Bureau $2.51 billion to conduct the 1990 census. The Bureau counted 248.7 million people, at a cost of some $10 a person.

—Ludwig van Beethoven is the Elvis of classical music lovers, according to a listeners poll conducted by radio station WQXR-FM in New York City. Five of his works placed in the top ten, with his Ninth Symphony voted the most popular. His other works in the top ten were Symphonies no. 5, 6, and 7, and his Piano Concerto no. 5 (*Emperor*). Other works in the top ten were Bach's *Brandenburg Concerti*, Handel's *Messiah*, Dvorak's *New World Symphony*, Vivaldi's *The Four Seasons*, and Mozart's *Eine Kleine Nachtmusik*.

—The risk of a heart attack on Monday is as much as 50 percent greater than on any other day, according to findings by German researchers presented at an American Heart Association meeting.

QUICK REFERENCE INDEX

For complete Index, see pp. 3-30